2017 Higher Education Directory®

Published by

Higher Education Publications, Inc.

Edited by

Mary Pat Rodenhouse

Editor Emerita

Jeanne M. Burke

Reston, Virginia

2017

2017 Edition

Higher Education Publications, Inc.
1801 Robert Fulton Drive, Suite 350
Reston, VA 20191-5495
(888) 349-7715
(571) 313-0478
FAX (571) 313-0526
Email: info@hepinc.com
Internet address: www.hepinc.com

Carnegie classification codes with permission from The Carnegie Foundation for the Advancement of Teaching.

Internet addresses (URL's) were originally drawn from lists maintained by Washington and Lee University and the University of North Carolina-Chapel Hill and through the annual survey sent out by Higher Education Publications, Inc.

Printed in the United States of America

ISBN-10: 0-914927-77-9; ISBN-13: 978-0-914927-77-8
ISSN 0736-0797
Library of Congress Catalogue Card Number: 83-641119
Library of Congress Cataloging-in Publication Data

HEP. . . Higher Education Directory®
Reston, VA; Higher Education Publications.
V.: 28cm
Annual
Began with issue for 1983.

A directory of accredited postsecondary, degree-granting institutions in the U.S., its possessions and territories accredited by regional, national, professional and specialized agencies recognized as accrediting bodies by the U.S. Secretary of Education and the Council for Higher Education Accreditation (CHEA) which honors recognition provided by the former Council on Postsecondary Accreditation (COPA)/Commission on Recognition of Postsecondary Accreditation (CORPA)
Description based on 2016.
Cover title: 2017 Higher Education Directory®
Spine title: 2017 Higher Education Directory® Thirty-fifth Edition

ISSN 0736-0797 = The Higher Education Directory®.

1. Education, Higher—United States—Directories.
2. Recognized accrediting agencies and associations—United States—Directories.
3. Acronyms, explanatory notes and symbols—United States—Directories.
4. Institution changes (additions, deletions, mergers and name changes)—United States—Directories.
5. Administrative officers, titles and title codes—United States—Directories.
6. United States Department of Education offices, statewide agencies for higher education and educational associations (and consortia)—United States—Directories.
7. Religious affiliation by denomination.
8. Carnegie classification codes.
9. Statistics.
10. Universities and colleges—United States—Directories.
11. College administrators alphabetical listing, phone numbers—United States—Directories.
12. Regional, national, professional and specialized accreditation alphabetical listing—United States—Directories.
13. Institutional FICE & Unit ID Number listing—United States—Directories.
14. Institutional alphabetical listing—United States—Directories.

I. Higher Education Publications, Inc.
II. Title: Higher Education Directory®.

L901.E34 378.73-dc19 83-641119 AACR 2 MARC-S

Table of Contents

Acknowledgments

Thirty-four years ago, Higher Education Publications, Inc. was formed to produce a directory to succeed the Department of Education's *Education Directory: Colleges and Universities*.

When we undertook the *Higher Education Directory* project, we worked toward three main goals: To publish accurate data, to make the directory more usable, and to have the directory ready for distribution much earlier in the academic year.

We continue to meet these objectives and more, while keeping the changing landscape of reference publishing in mind. In 2014, we modified our definition of branch campuses to conform to the definition used by the United States Department of Education (34 CFR §600.2). As a result, we added or reclassified over 1,400 institutional listings. Due to space limitations in the printed directory, we list limited information on these additional branch campuses, but more detailed information is available online with HED-Connect.

Our thanks to the thousands of people who have supplied us the necessary data contained in the directory. Over this past year we have had a response/update rate of 99.5% from main campuses—truly outstanding! We are most appreciative of the many subscribers who have supported us in our efforts to bring you the most accurate and current information available. And, a special thanks to all of you who suggest improvements to our directory.

We continue to work on a tight schedule starting in mid-June to distribution in November—especially when you consider the complexity and increase in the size of the database.

The accuracy and completeness of the contents of the 2017 edition was assured by a group of editors, updating and proofing specialists including Mary Pat Rodenhouse, Jodi Mondragon, Emmy Brown, Jackie Hafner, Doris Jean, Ebony Neal and Fred Hafner. Barbara Herrman handled our typesetting. Mark Schreiber managed the HED-Connect update system and the database.

You may be familiar with our new Website, but if you have not yet visited it, I encourage you to go to www.hepinc.com. The site features the latest news on higher education, accreditations and administrative changes along with many helpful resources. Also, please visit our new LinkedIn and Facebook pages. We feel that our increased Internet and social media presence will help us to continue to meet the goals we established for ourselves thirty-four years ago—to provide you with the most authoritative, timely and accurate information on the higher education community.

Frederick F. Hafner
Publisher

Reston, Virginia

Foreword

The 2017 edition of the *Higher Education Directory®* contains listings of accredited, degree-granting institutions of postsecondary education in the United States and its territories.

Criteria for Listing in this Directory

To be listed in this Directory, an institution must meet the following guidelines:

(1) They are degree-granting (legally authorized to offer and are offering a program of college-level studies leading toward a degree[1]);
(2) They have submitted the information required for listing; and
(3) They meet one of the following criteria for listing:
   A. The institution is accredited at the college level by an accrediting agency that is recognized by the U.S. Secretary of Education;
   B. The institution holds pre-accredited status with an accrediting agency recognized by the U.S. Secretary of Education whose recognition includes the pre-accreditation status;
   C. The institution is accredited at the college level by an accrediting agency recognized by the Council for Higher Education Accreditation (CHEA).

"College level" means a postsecondary associate, baccalaureate, post-baccalaureate, or rabbinical education program.

Verification of Accreditations

Verification of each accreditation for all institutions was done by comparing the accreditation against the current Directory (and updated lists) for each respective regional, national, professional and specialized association or agency, along with telephone calls to numerous accrediting associations whenever there was a question of accuracy. Over 22,000 accreditations were verified through September 2016.

The reader is reminded that many institutions have programs which may not be recognized by a professional or specialized association, but are considered fine programs. The institutions may or may not have sought such recognition.

General Organization of the Directory

Our approach to the organization of the material is to make the desired information readable and easy to find. There are four indexes which are cross-referenced to the main institutional listing.

A. Prologue
   1. Accrediting agencies with addresses. Regional accrediting commissions are listed alphabetically while national, professional and specialized bodies are listed alphabetically under headings showing their specialties.
   2. Acronyms used in the Directory for accrediting bodies are listed alphabetically.
   3. Explanatory notes and symbols.
   4. U.S. postal abbreviations of states.
   5. Institution changes.
   6. Administrative officers' description and job codes.
   7. U.S. Department of Education offices.
   8. Statewide agencies of higher education.
   9. Higher education associations.
   10. Consortia of institutions of higher education.
   11. Association name index.
   12. Religious affiliation by denomination.
   13. Carnegie classification codes.
   14. Statistical data.

B. College and university listings by state with institutional characteristics and administrative officers.
   1. Institution Name. If an * appears before the institution's name, it is a part of a system. A line between institutions separates two systems.
   2. Alpha Code. The first institution listed on a page is coded (A), the second (B), etc. The Administrators' index is also coded to enable the reader to locate the desired institution quickly.
   3. Address.
   4. County.
   5. FICE Identification. This was the Federal Interagency Commission on Education number originally assigned by the Department of Education. We continue to use the term FICE. However, the Department of Education in their Office of Student Financial Assistance uses OPEID, Office of Postsecondary Education Identification. OPEID consists of the first six digits of the FICE plus two more digits indicating branch campuses. Numbers beginning with 66 are for accredited institutions for which we cannot locate a FICE or OPEID number. These are identification numbers only.
   6. Telephone Number.
   7. Unit ID Number. A unique number developed by the National Center for Education Statistics (NCES) for the Education Department's IPEDS Reports.
   8. Carnegie Classification Code. (see page **xlix**)
   9. Main FAX Number.
   10. School Calendar.
   11. URL (Universal Resource Locator).
   12. Date Established.
   13. Annual Tuition & Fees for 2015-16 school year.
   14. Fall 2014 Enrollment. Head count (not FTE) in degree programs as reported on the latest IPEDS survey.
   15. Type of Student Body.
   16. Affiliation or Control.
   17. IRS Status.
   18. Highest Degree Offered.
   19. Accreditation (see page **vi**). **N.B. Institutional accreditation is in bold face.**
   20. Administrative and academic officers with job classification code (see page **xxviii** for descriptions).
   21. Non-system branch campuses. The names of these campuses are in italic type and their listings are shortened. Non-system branch campuses are listed if they are identified by the parent institutions' accrediting organization as a branch campus.

C. Index of administrators is an alphabetical listing of all the administrators with their most direct phone number and E-mail address. The page and reference letter indicate the page on which the administrator's institution listing begins.

D. Index of regional, national, professional and specialized accreditation alphabetically by state. This index standardizes and simplifies reviewing of the 140 accrediting classifications.

E. FICE number index. Numeric listing of FICE number and school.

F. Alphabetic index of institutions.

---

[1]The *Higher Education Directory®* lists degree-granting institutions approved by regional, national, professional or specialized accrediting agencies.

Accrediting Agencies

The following regional, national, professional and specialized accrediting agencies are recognized by the U.S. Secretary of Education or the Council for Higher Education Accreditation (CHEA). The U.S. Department of Education (USDE) dates specified are the date of initial listing as a U.S. Department of Education recognized agency, the date of the U.S. Secretary's most recent grant of renewed recognition based on the last full review of the agency by the National Advisory Committee on Institutional Quality and Integrity, and the date of the agency's next scheduled review for renewal of recognition.[1] The Council for Higher Education (CHEA) date reflects initial or continued recognition by CHEA.

Regional Accrediting Bodies

Delaware, District of Columbia, Maryland, New Jersey, New York, Pennsylvania, Puerto Rico, Virgin Islands

Middle States Commission on Higher Education M
USDE: 1952/2012/2017 CHEA: 2013
3624 Market Street, Second Floor West
Philadelphia, PA 19104
(267) 284-5000 Fax (215) 662-5501
Elizabeth H. Sibolski, President
E-mail: info@msche.org
URL: www.msche.org

Connecticut, Maine, Massachusetts, New Hampshire, Rhode Island, Vermont

Commission on Institutions of Higher Education
New England Association of Schools and Colleges EH
USDE: 1952/2015/2017 CHEA: 2013
3 Burlington Woods Drive, Suite 100
Burlington, MA 01803-4514
(781) 425-7700 Fax (781) 425-1001
Barbara E. Brittingham, President
E-mail: cihe@neasc.org
URL: http://cihe.neasc.org

Arizona, Arkansas, Colorado, Illinois, Indiana, Iowa, Kansas, Michigan, Minnesota, Missouri, Nebraska, New Mexico, North Dakota, Ohio, Oklahoma, South Dakota, West Virginia, Wisconsin, Wyoming

Higher Learning Commission NH
USDE: 1952/2015/2017 CHEA: 2015
230 South LaSalle Street, Suite 7-500
Chicago, IL 60604-1411
(800) 621-7440 Fax (312) 263-7462
Barbara Gelman-Danley, President
E-mail: info@hlcommission.org
URL: www.hlcommission.org

Alaska, Idaho, Montana, Nevada, Oregon, Utah, Washington

Northwest Commission on Colleges and Universities NW
USDE: 1952/2015/2016
8060 165th Avenue, NE, Suite 100
Redmond, WA 98052
(425) 558-4224 Fax (425) 376-0596
Sandra E. Elman, President
E-mail: selman@nwccu.org
URL: www.nwccu.org

Alabama, Florida, Georgia, Kentucky, Louisiana, Mississippi, North Carolina, South Carolina, Tennessee, Texas, Virginia

Commission on Colleges
Southern Association of Colleges and Schools SC
USDE: 1952/2014/2017 CHEA: 2015
1866 Southern Lane
Decatur, GA 30033-4097
(404) 679-4500 Fax (404) 679-4558
Belle S. Wheelan, President
E-mail: questions@sacscoc.org
URL: www.sacscoc.org

California, Hawaii, American Samoa, Guam, Commonwealth of the Northern Marianas, Federated States of Micronesia, Republic of the Marshall Islands, Republic of Palau

Accrediting Commission for Senior Colleges and Universities
Western Association of Schools and Colleges WC
USDE: 1952/2012/2017 CHEA: 2014
985 Atlantic Avenue, Suite 100
Alameda, CA 94501
(510) 748-9001 Fax (510) 748-9797
Mary Ellen Petrisko, President
E-mail: wasc@wascsenior.org
URL: www.wascsenior.org

Accrediting Commission for Community and Junior Colleges
Western Association of Schools and Colleges WJ
USDE: 1952/2015/2017 CHEA: 2003
10 Commercial Boulevard, Suite 204
Novato, CA 94949
(415) 506-0234 Fax (415) 506-0238
Barbara A. Beno, President
E-mail: accjc@accjc.org
URL: www.accjc.org

[1]U.S. Department of Education, Nationally Recognized Accrediting Agencies, www2.ed.gov/admins/finaid/accred/accreditation.html.

National, Professional and Specialized Accrediting Bodies

Acupuncture

Accreditation Commission for Acupuncture and Oriental Medicine (ACAOM)
USDE: 1988/2013/2016
8941 Aztec Drive
Eden Praire, MN 55347
(952) 212-2434 Fax (952) 657-7068
Mark S. McKenzie, Executive Director
E-mail: info@acaom.org
URL: www.acaom.org

First-professional master's degree, professional master's level certificate and diploma programs and professional post-graduate doctoral programs in acupuncture and Oriental medicine, and free-standing institutions that offer such programs **ACUP**

Allied Health

Accrediting Bureau of Health Education Schools (ABHES)
USDE: 1969/2011/2016
7777 Leesburg Pike, Suite 314N
Falls Church, VA 22043
(703) 917-9503 Fax (703) 917-4109
Florence Tate, Executive Director
E-mail: info@abhes.org
URL: www.abhes.org

Institutions specializing in allied health education **ABHES**
Specialized programs for
Medical assistant **MAAB**
Medical laboratory technician **MLTAB**
Surgical technologist **SURTEC**

Commission on Accreditation of Allied Health Education Programs (CAAHEP)
CHEA: 2011
25400 US Hwy 19 N., Suite 158
Clearwater, FL 33756
(727) 210-2350 Fax (727) 210-2354
Kathleen Megivern, Executive Director
E-mail: mail@caahep.org
URL: www.caahep.org

The Commission on Accreditation of Allied Health Education Programs (CAAHEP) is recognized as an accrediting agency for accreditation of education for the allied health occupations. In carrying out its accreditation activities, CAAHEP cooperates with the Committees on Accreditation sponsored by various allied health and medical specialty organizations. CAAHEP is the coordinating agency for accreditation of education for the following allied health occupations:
Anesthesiologist assistant **AA**
Blood bank technology **BBT**
Cardiovascular technologist **CVT**
Cytotechnologist **CYTO**
Diagnostic medical sonographer **DMS**
Emergency medical technician-paramedic **EMT**
Exercise science **EXSC**
Kinesiotherapy **KIN**
Medical assistant **MAC**
Medical illustrator **MIL**
Neurodiagnostic technologist **NDT**
Orthotist/prosthetist **OPE**
Perfusionist **PERF**
Polysomnographic technologist **POLYT**
Recreation therapist **CARTE**
Surgical assistant **SURGA**
Surgical technologist **SURGT**

Anesthesiologist Assistant

Commission on Accreditation of Allied Health Education Programs (see listing under Allied Health)
Accreditation Review Committee for the Anesthesiologist Assistant
N84 W33137 Becker Lane
Merton, WI 53066
(612) 836-3311
Jennifer Anderson Warwick, Executive Director
E-mail: jennifer@arc-aa.org
URL: www.caahep.org/arc-aa

Post-baccalaureate programs for anesthesiologist assistant **AA**

Art

Commission on Accreditation
National Association of Schools of Art and Design (NASAD)
USDE: 1966/2014/2017
11250 Roger Bacon Drive, Suite 21
Reston, VA 20190
(703) 437-0700 Fax (703) 437-6312
Karen P. Moynahan, Executive Director
E-mail: info@arts-accredit.org
URL: www.arts-accredit.org

Institutions and departments within institutions offering degree and non-degree granting programs in art/design and art/design-related programs **ART**

Athletic Training

Commission on Accreditation of Athletic Training Education (CAATE)
CHEA: 2014
6850 Austin Center Boulevard, Suite 100
Austin, TX 78731-3184
(512) 733-9700
Micki Cuppett, Executive Director
E-mail: micki@caate.net
URL: www.caate.net

Programs for athletic training **CAATE**

Audiology

Accreditation Commission for Audiology Education
CHEA: 2012
11480 Commerce Park Drive, Suite 220
Reston, VA 20191
(202) 986-9500 Fax (202) 986-9550
Doris Gordon, Executive Director
E-mail: info@acaeaccred.org
URL: www.acaeaccred.org

Programs leading to the Doctor of Audiology degree **ACAE**

Council on Academic Accreditation in Audiology and Speech Language Pathology
American Speech-Language-Hearing Association (ASHA)
USDE: 1967/2015/2020 CHEA: 2014
2200 Research Boulevard
Rockville, MD 20850-3289
(301) 296-5700 Fax (301) 296-8580
Patrima L. Tice, Director of Accreditation
E-mail: accreditation@asha.org
URL: www.asha.org

Doctoral degree programs in audiology **AUD**

Aviation

Aviation Accreditation Board International
CHEA: 2013
3410 Skyway Drive
Auburn, AL 36830
(334) 844-2431 Fax (334) 844-2432
Gary J. Northam, President
E-mail: bayenva@auburn.edu
URL: www.aabi.aero

Non-engineering programs for aviation **AAB**

Bible College Education

Commission on Accreditation
Association for Biblical Higher Education (ABHE)
USDE: 1952/2014/2017 CHEA: 2011
5850 T. G. Lee Boulevard, Suite 130
Orlando, FL 32822
(407) 207-0808 Fax (407) 207-0840
Ron Kroll, Director
E-mail: info@abhe.org
URL: www.abhe.org

Bible colleges and programs offering undergraduate and graduate programs **BI**

Blood Bank Technology

Commission on Accreditation of Allied Health Education Programs (see listing under Allied Health)
American Association of Blood Banks (AABB) Committee on Accreditation of Specialists in Blood Bank Technology Schools
8101 Glenbrook Road
Bethesda, MD 20814-2749
(301) 907-6977 Fax (301) 907-6895
Anne Chenoweth, Senior Deputy Director
Accreditation and Quality Department
E-mail: aabb@aabb.org
URL: www.aabb.org

Programs for blood bank technologist **BBT**

Business

AACSB International-The Association to Advance Collegiate Schools of Business
CHEA: 2002
777 South Harbour Island Boulevard, Suite 750
Tampa, FL 33602
(813) 769-6500 Fax (813) 769-6559
Robert Reid, Executive Vice President and Chief Accreditation Officer
E-mail: accreditation@aacsb.edu
URL: www.aacsb.edu

Programs for:
Business administration education **BUS**
Accounting **BUSA**

Accrediting Council for Independent Colleges and Schools (ACICS)
USDE: 1956/2013/2016 CHEA: 2012
750 First Street NE, Suite 980
Washington, DC 20002-4223
(202) 336-6780 Fax (202) 842-2593
Roger Williams, Interim President
E-mail: info@acics.org
URL: www.acics.org

Institutions offering certificates/diplomas, associate, baccalaureate and master's degree programs to educate students for professional, technical, or occupational careers **ACICS**

Accreditation Council for Business Schools and Programs (ACBSP)
CHEA: 2011
11520 West 119th Street
Overland Park, KS 66213
(913) 339-9356 Fax (913) 339-6226
Jeffrey Alderman, President/CEO
E-mail: info@acbsp.org
URL: www.acbsp.org

Business administration, management, accounting and related business fields **ACBSP**

International Assembly for Collegiate Business Education
CHEA: 2011
11374 Strang Line Rd
Lenexa, KS 66215
(913) 631-3009 Fax (913) 631-9154

Dennis N. Gash, President
E-mail: iacbe@iacbe.org
URL: www.iacbe.org

Undergraduate and graduate level business programs in institutions that grant bachelor's and/or graduate degrees **IACBE**

Cardiovascular Technology

Commission on Accreditation of Allied Health Education Programs (see listing under Allied Health)
Joint Review Committee on Education in Cardiovascular Technology (JRC-CVT)
1449 Hill Street
Whitinsville, MA 01588-1032
(978) 456-5594 Fax (727) 210-2354
Jackie Long-Goding, Executive Director
E-mail: office@jrccvt.org
URL: www.jrccvt.org

Programs for cardiovascular technology **CVT**

Chiropractic

The Council on Chiropractic Education (CCE)
USDE: 1974/2013/2016 CHEA: 2015
8049 North 85th Way
Scottsdale, AZ 85258-4321
(480) 443-8877 Fax (480) 483-7333
Craig S. Little, President
E-mail: cce@cce-usa.org
URL: www.cce-usa.org

Programs leading to and institutions offering the Doctorate of Chiropractic (D.C.) degree **CHIRO**

Christian Studies Education

Accreditation Commission
Transnational Association of Christian Colleges and Schools (TRACS)
USDE: 1991/2013/2016 CHEA: 2011
15935 Forest Road
Forest, VA 24551
(434) 525-9539 Fax (434) 525-9538
Timothy Eaton, Interim President
E-mail: info@tracs.org
URL: www.tracs.org

Christian liberal arts institutions which offer certificates/diplomas and associate, baccalaureate and graduate degrees **TRACS**

Clinical Laboratory Sciences

National Accrediting Agency for Clinical Laboratory Sciences (NAACLS)
CHEA: 2013
5600 North River Road, Suite 720
Rosemont, IL 60018
(773) 714-8880 Fax (773) 714-8886
Dianne M. Cearlock, Chief Executive Officer
E-mail: info@naacls.org
URL: www.naacls.org

Programs for:
- clinical assistant **CA**
- cytogenetic technologist **CGTECH**
- diagnostic molecular scientist **DMOLS**
- histologic technician/technologist **HT**
- medical laboratory technician **MLTAD**
- medical technologist/laboratory scientist **MT**
- pathologists' assistant **PA**
- phlebotomy **PHLEB**

Clinical Pastoral Education

Accreditation Commission
Association for Clinical Pastoral Education, Inc. (ACPEI)
USDE: 1969/2013/2017
One West Court Square, Suite 325
Decatur, GA 30030
(404) 320-1472 Fax (404) 320-0849
Trace Haythorn, Executive Director
E-mail: acpe@acpe.edu
URL: www.acpe.edu

Basic, advanced and supervisory clinical pastoral education programs **PAST**

Construction Education

American Council for Construction Education (ACCE)
CHEA: 2011
825 West Bitters Road, Suite 103
San Antonio, TX 78216
(210) 495-6161 Fax (210) 495-6168
Michael Holland, President
E-mail: mholland@acce-hq.org
URL: www.acce-hq.org

Associate and baccalaureate degree programs **CONST**

Continuing Education

Accrediting Council for Continuing Education and Training (ACCET)
USDE: 1978/2013/2018
1722 N Street NW
Washington, DC 20036
(202) 955-1113 Fax (202) 955-1118
William V. Larkin, Executive Director
E-mail: info@accet.org
URL: www.accet.org

Institutions offering noncollegiate continuing education and institutions offering occupational associate degree programs **CNCE**

Cosmetology

National Accrediting Commission of Career Arts and Sciences (NACCAS)
USDE: 1970/2015/2020
4401 Ford Avenue, Suite 1300
Alexandria, VA 22302-1432
(703) 600-7600 Fax (703) 379-2200
Anthony Mirando, Executive Director
E-mail: info@naccas.org
URL: www.naccas.org

Postsecondary schools and departments of cosmetology arts and sciences and massage therapy **COSME**

Counseling and Related Educational Programs

Council for Accreditation of Counseling and Related Educational Programs (CACREP)
CHEA: 2015
1001 North Fairfax Street, Suite 510
Alexandria, VA 22314
(703) 535-5990 Fax (703) 739-6209
Carol L. Bobby, President and CEO
E-mail: cacrep@cacrep.org
URL: www.cacrep.org

Master's degree programs in addiction counseling, career counseling, marriage, couple and family counseling, mental health counseling, school counseling, student affairs and college counseling and doctorate degree programs in counselor education and supervision **CACREP**

Culinary Arts

Accrediting Commission
American Culinary Federation
CHEA: 2004
180 Center Place Way
St. Augustine, FL 32095
(904) 824-4468 Fax (904) 940-0741
Heidi Cramb, Executive Director
E-mail: acf@acfchefs.net
URL: www.acfchefs.org

Programs in culinary arts which award certificates, diplomas or associate degrees and bachelor degree programs in culinary management **ACFEI**

Cytotechnology

Commission on Accreditation of Allied Health Education Programs (see listing under Allied Health)
Cytotechnology Programs Review Committee
American Society of Cytopathology
100 West 10th Street, Suite 605
Wilmington, DE 19801
(302) 543-6583 Fax (302) 543-6597
Elizabeth Jenkins, Executive Director
E-mail: asc@cytopathology.org
URL: www.cytopathology.org

Programs for the cytotechnologist **CYTO**

Dance

Commission on Accreditation
National Association of Schools of Dance (NASD)
USDE: 1983/2015/2019
11250 Roger Bacon Drive, Suite 21
Reston, VA 20190
(703) 437-0700 Fax (703) 437-6312
Karen P. Moynahan, Executive Director
E-mail: info@arts-accredit.org
URL: www.arts-accredit.org

Institutions and departments within institutions offering degree and non-degree-granting programs in dance and dance-related disciplines **DANCE**

Dental and Dental Auxiliary Programs

Commission on Dental Accreditation
American Dental Association (ADA)
USDE: 1952/2013/2017
211 East Chicago Avenue, Suite 1900
Chicago, IL 60611
(800) 621-8099 Fax (312) 440-2915
Sherin Tooks, Director
E-mail: tookss@ada.org
URL: www.ada.org

Programs leading to:
- D.D.S. or D.M.D. degree, advanced general dentistry and specialty programs **DENT**
- Dental hygiene **DH**
- Dental assisting **DA**
- Dental laboratory technology **DT**

Diagnostic Medical Sonography

Commission on Accreditation of Allied Health Education Programs (see listing under Allied Health)
Joint Review Committee on Education in Diagnostic Medical Sonography
6021 University Boulevard, Suite 500
Ellicot City, MD 21043-6090
(443) 973-3251 Fax (866) 738-3444
Gerry Magat, Interim Executive Director
E-mail: mail@jrcdms.org
URL: www.jrcdms.org

Programs for the diagnostic medical sonographer **DMS**

Dietetics

Accreditation Council for Education in Nutrition and Dietetics
Academy of Nutrition and Dietetics
USDE: 1974/2012/2017
120 South Riverside Plaza, Suite 2000

Chicago, IL 60606-6995
(312) 899-0040 Fax (312) 899-4817
Mary B. Gregoire, Executive Director
E-mail: acend@eatright.org
URL: www.eatright.acend.org

Coordinated programs in dietetics **DIETC**
Didactic programs **DIETD**
Post-baccalaureate internships **DIETI**
Dietetic technician programs **DIETT**

Distance Education and Training

Distance Education Accrediting Commission
USDE: 1959/2012/2017 CHEA: 2013
1101 17th Street NW, Suite 808
Washington, DC 20036
(202) 234-5100 Fax (202) 332-1386
Leah K. Matthews, Executive Director
E-mail: info@deac.org
URL: www.deac.org

Distance education institutions including associate, baccalaureate, master's, and doctoral degree-granting programs primarily through the distance learning method **DEAC** (formerly DETC)

Emergency Medical Services

Commission on Accreditation for Allied Health Programs (see listing under Allied Health)
Committee on Accreditation of Educational Programs for the Emergency Medical Services Professions
8301 Lakeview Parkway, Suite 111-312
Rowlett, TX 75088
(214) 703-8445 Fax (214) 703-8992
George Hatch, Executive Director
E-mail: george@coaemsp.org
URL: www.coaemsp.org

Programs for the emergency medical technician-paramedic **EMT**

Engineering

ABET, Inc.
CHEA: 2015
415 North Charles Street
Baltimore, MD 21201
(410) 347-7700 Fax (410) 625-2238
Michael Milligan, Executive Director
E-mail: accreditation@abet.org
URL: www.abet.org

Baccalaureate programs in computer science **CS**
Basic (baccalaureate) and advanced (master's) level programs in engineering **ENG**
Applied science programs at the associate, baccalaureate and master's level **ENGR**
Associate and baccalaureate degree programs in engineering technology **ENGT**

English Language

Commission on English Language Program Accreditation (CEA)
USDE: 2003/2013/2016
1001 North Fairfax Drive, Suite 630
Alexandria, VA 22314
(703) 665-3400 Fax (703) 519-2071
Mary Reeves, Executive Director
E-mail: info@cea-accredit.org
URL: www.cea-accredit.org

English language programs **CEA**

Exercise Sciences

Commission on Accreditation of Allied Health Education Programs (see listing under Allied Health)
Committee on Accreditation for the Exercise Sciences
401 West Michigan Street
Indianapolis, IN 46202
(317) 637-9200 Fax (317) 634-7817
Traci Sue Rush, Executive Director
E-mail: trush@acsm.org
URL: www.coaes.org

Programs for exercise science and related departments **EXSC**

Family and Consumer Sciences

Council for Accreditation
American Association of Family and Consumer Sciences (AAFCS)
CHEA: 2014
400 North Columbus Street, Suite 202
Alexandria, VA 22314
(703) 706-4600 Fax (703) 706-4663
Carolyn W. Jackson, Executive Director
E-mail: accreditation@aafcs.org
URL: www.aafcs.org

Baccalaureate programs in family and consumer sciences **AAFCS**

Fire and Emergency

International Fire Service Accreditation Congress
CHEA: 2011
1812 West Tyler Avenue
Oklahoma State University
Stillwater, OK 74078
(405) 744-8303 Fax (405) 744-8802
Clayton Moorman, Director IFSAC Administration
E-mail: admin@ifsac.org
URL: www.ifsac.org

Undergraduate fire and emergency related programs **IFSAC**

Forensic Science

Forensic Science Educational Program Accreditation Commission
American Academy of Forensic Sciences (AAFS)
CHEA: 2012
410 North 21st Street
Colorado Springs, CO 80904
(719) 636-1100 Fax (719) 636-1993
Nancy J. Jackson, Director of Development and Accreditation
Email: njackson@aafs.org
URL: www.aafs.org

Bachelor or master's degree programs in forensic science **FEPAC**

Funeral Service Education

Committee on Accreditation
American Board of Funeral Service Education (ABFSE)
USDE: 1972/2015/2017 CHEA: 2012
992 Mantua Pike, Suite 108
Woodbury Heights, NJ 08097
(816) 233-3747 Fax (856) 579-7354
Robert C. Smith III, Executive Director
E-mail: exdir@abfse.org
URL: www.abfse.org

Institutions and programs awarding diplomas, associate and bachelor's degrees in funeral service or mortuary science **FUSER**

Health Informatics and Information Management

Commission on Accreditation for Health Informatics and Information Management Education (CAHIIM)
CHEA: 2012
233 North Michigan Avenue, 21st Floor
Chicago, IL 60601-5800
(312) 233-1100 Fax (312) 233-1948
Claire Dixon-Lee, Executive Director
Email: info@cahiim.org
URL: www.cahiim.org

Associate and baccalaureate degree programs in health information management and master's degree programs in health informatics and health information management **CAHIIM**

Healthcare Management

Commission on Accreditation of Healthcare Management Education (CAHME)
CHEA: 2014
6110 Executive Boulevard, Suite 614
Rockville, MD 20852
(301) 298-1820 Fax (301) 298-1830
Anthony Stanowski, President and CEO
E-mail: info@cahme.org
URL: www.cahme.org

Graduate programs in healthcare management **HSA**

Human Services

Council for Standards in Human Services Education (CSHSE)
CHEA: 2014
3337 Duke Street
Alexandria, VA 22314
(571) 257-3959
Elaine Green, President
E-mail: info@cshse.org
URL: www.cshse.org

Human services educational programs **CSHSE**

Industrial Technology

The Association of Technology, Management, and Applied Engineering
CHEA: 2013
275 North York Street, Suite 401
Elmhurst, IL 60126
(630) 433-4514 Fax (630) 563-9181
Kelly Schild, Director of Accreditation
E-mail: kelly@atmae.org
URL: www.atmae.org

Technology, applied technology, engineering technology and technology-related programs at the associate, baccalaureate and master's degree level **NAIT**

Interior Design

Council for Interior Design Accreditation (CIDA)
CHEA: 2013
206 Grandville Avenue, Suite 350
Grand Rapids, MI 49503
(616) 458-0400 Fax (616) 458-0460
Holly Mattson, Executive Director
E-mail: info@accredit-id.org
URL: www.accredit-id.org

First professional degree level programs (master's and baccalaureate degrees) **CIDA**

Jewish Studies

Association of Institutions of Jewish Studies (AIJS)
USDE: 2015/2020
500 West Kennedy Bouevard
Lakewood, NJ 08701
(732) 363-7330 Fax (732) 415-8198
Alex Lowinger, CEO
E-mail: info@theaijs.com
URL: theaijs.com

Postsecondary institutions of Jewish studies **AIJS**

Journalism and Mass Communications

Accrediting Committee
Accrediting Council on Education in Journalism and Mass Communications (ACEJMC)
CHEA: 2014
University of Kansas School of Journalism
Stauffer-Flint Hall
1435 Jayhawk Boulevard
Lawrence, KS 66045-7575
(785) 864-3973 Fax (785) 864-5225
Susanne Shaw, Executive Director
E-mail: sshaw@ku.edu
URL: www2.ku.edu/~acejmc

Units within institutions offering professional baccalaureate and master's degree programs in journalism and mass communications **JOUR**

Kinesiotherapy

Commission on Accreditation of Allied Health Education Programs (see listing under Allied Health)
Committee on Accreditation of Education Programs for Kinesiotherapy
118 College Drive #5142
Hattiesburg, MS 39406-0002
(601) 266-5371 Fax (601) 266-4445
Jerry W. Purvis, Coord COPSKT
E-mail: jerry.purvis@usm.edu
URL: www.akta.org

Kinesiotherapy programs **KIN**

Landscape Architecture

Landscape Architectural Accreditation Board
American Society of Landscape Architects (ASLA)
CHEA: 2015
636 Eye Street, NW
Washington, DC 20001-3736
(202) 898-2444 Fax (202) 898-1185
Kristopher Pritchard, Accreditation Manager
E-mail: info@asla.org
URL: www.asla.org

Baccalaureate and master's programs leading to the first professional degree **LSAR**

Law

Council of the Section of Legal Education and Admissions to the Bar
American Bar Association (ABA)
USDE: 1952/2013/2016
321 North Clark Street, 21st Fl
Chicago, IL 60654-7598
(312) 988-6738 Fax (312) 988-5681
Barry A. Currier, Managing Director of Accreditation and Legal Education
E-mail: legaled@americanbar.org
URL: www.americanbar.org/groups/legal_education.html

Programs in legal education; professional schools of law **LAW**

Librarianship

Committee on Accreditation
American Library Association (ALA)
CHEA: 2012
50 East Huron Street
Chicago, IL 60611-2795
(312) 280-2432 Fax (312) 280-2433
Karen O'Brien, Director of Accreditation
E-mail: accred@ala.org
URL: www.ala.org/accreditation

Master's programs in library and information studies **LIB**

Marriage and Family Therapy

Commission on Accreditation for Marriage and Family Therapy Education
American Association for Marriage and Family Therapy (AAMFT)
CHEA: 2014
112 South Alfred Street
Alexandria, VA 22314-3061
(703) 838-9808 Fax (703) 838-9805
Tanya A. Tamarkin, Director of Accreditation
E-mail: coa@aamft.org
URL: www.aamft.org

Clinical training programs at the master's, doctorate and post-graduate levels **MFCD**

Massage Therapy

Commission on Massage Therapy Accreditation
USDE: 2002/2015/2020
5335 Wisconsin Avenue NW, Suite 440
Washington, DC 20015
(202) 888-6790 Fax (202) 888-6787
Kate Zulaski, Executive Director
E-mail: info@comta.org
URL: www.comta.org

Institutions that award postsecondary certificates, diplomas, and associate degrees in the practice of massage therapy, bodywork, aesthetics/esthetics and skin care **COMTA**

Medical Assistant Education

(see listing under Allied Health)
Accrediting Bureau of Health Education Schools (ABHES)

Medical assistant programs **MAAB**

Commission on Accreditation of Allied Health Education Programs (see listing under Allied Health)
Medical Assisting Education Review Board
20 North Wacker Drive, Suite 1575
Chicago, IL 60606-2963
(312) 899-1500 Fax (312) 899-1259
Sarah R. Marino, Executive Director
E-mail: maerb@maerb.org
URL: www.maerb.org

One and two year medical assistant programs **MAC**

Medical Illustrator Education

Commission on Accreditation of Allied Health Education Programs (see listing under Allied Health)
Accreditation Review Committee for the Medical Illustrator
Saint Luke's Hospital Instructional Resources
32531 Meadowlark Way
Pepper Pike, OH 44124
(216) 595-9363
Kathy Jung, Chair, ARC-MI
E-mail: kijung@aol.com
URL: www.ami.org

Programs for medical illustrator **MIL**

Medical Laboratory Technician Education

(see listing under Allied Health)
Accrediting Bureau of Health Education Schools (ABHES)

Schools and programs for the medical laboratory technician **MLTAB**

(see listing under Clinical Laboratory Sciences)
National Accrediting Agency for Clinical Laboratory Sciences (NAACLS)

Programs for medical laboratory technician **MLTAD**

Medical Technology

(see listing under Clinical Laboratory Sciences)
National Accrediting Agency for Clinical Laboratory Sciences (NAACLS)

Programs for medical technologist/laboratory scientist **MT**

Medicine

Liaison Committee on Medical Education (LCME) of the Council on Medical Education of the American Medical Association and the Association of American Medical Colleges
USDE: 1952/2014/2017
The LCME is administered in odd-numbered years, beginning each July 1, by:
Council on Medical Education of the American Medical Association (AMA)
330 North Wabash Avenue
Chicago, IL 60611
(312) 464-4690 Fax (312) 464-5830
Barbara Barzansky, LCME Co-Secretary
E-mail: barbara.barzansky@ama-assn.org
URL: www.ama-assn.org

The LCME is administered in even-numbered years, beginning each July 1, by:
Association of American Medical Colleges (AAMC)
655 K Street NW, Suite 100
Washington, DC 20001-2399
(202) 828-0400 Fax (202) 828-1125
Veronica Catanese, LCME Co-Secretary
E-mail: vcatanese@aamc.org
URL: www.aamc.org

Programs leading to the M.D. degree **MED**

Midwifery Education

Midwifery Education Accreditation Council (MEAC)
USDE: 2001/2015/2017
850 Mt. Pleasant Avenue
Ann Arbor, MI 48103
(360) 466-2080 Fax (480) 907-2936
Tracy Vilella Gartenmann, Executive Director
E-mail: info@meacschools.org
URL: www.meacschools.org

Accreditation of direct-entry midwifery educational institutions and programs conferring degrees and certificates **MEAC**

Montessori Teacher Education

Montessori Accreditation Council for Teacher Education (MACTE)
USDE: 1995/2015/2017
420 Park Street
Charlottesville, VA 22902
(434) 202-7793 Fax (888) 525-8838
Rebecca Pelton, Executive Director
E-mail: info@macte.org
URL: www.macte.org

Montessori teacher-education programs and institutions **MACTE**

Music

Commission on Accreditation
National Association of Schools of Music (NASM)
USDE: 1952/2015/2019
11250 Roger Bacon Drive, Suite 21
Reston, VA 20190
(703) 437-0700 Fax (703) 437-6312
Karen P. Moynahan, Executive Director

E-mail: info@arts-accredit.org
URL: www.arts-accredit.org

Institutions and departments within institutions offering degree and non-degree-granting programs in music and music-related disciplines **MUS**

Naturopathic Medical Education

Council on Naturopathic Medical Education (CNME)
USDE: 2003/2015/2020
PO Box 178
Great Barrington, MA 01230
(413) 528-8877 Fax (413) 528-8880
Daniel Seitz, Executive Director
E-mail: council@cnme.org
URL: www.cnme.org

Graduate-level, four-year naturopathic medical education programs **NATUR**

Neurodiagnostic Technology

Commission on Accreditation of Allied Health Education Programs (see listing under Allied Health)
Committee on Accreditation for Education in Neurodiagnostic Technology
1449 Hill Street
Whitinsville, MA 01588
(978) 338-6300 Fax (978) 832-2638
Jackie Long-Goding, Executive Director
E-mail: office@coa-ndt.org
URL: http://coa-ndt.org

Programs for the electroneurodiagnostic technologist **NDT**

Nuclear Medicine Technology

Joint Review Committee on Educational Programs in Nuclear Medicine Technology
CHEA: 2013
2000 West Danforth Road, Suite 130, #203
Edmund, OK 73003
(405) 285-0546 Fax (405) 285-0579
Jan M. Winn, Executive Director
E-mail: mail@jrcnmt.org
URL: www.jrcnmt.org

Programs for the nuclear medicine technologist **NMT**

Nurse Anesthetists

Council on Accreditation of Nurse Anesthesia Educational Programs
USDE: 1955/2015/2018 CHEA: 2014
222 South Prospect Avenue, Suite 304
Park Ridge, IL 60068-4001
(847) 655-1160 Fax (847) 692-7137
Francis Gerbasi, Executive Director
E-mail: accreditation@coa.us.com
URL: home.coa.us.com

Nurse anesthesia educational institutions and programs at the post-master's certificate, master's and doctoral degree levels **ANEST**

Nurse-Midwifery

Accreditation Commission for Midwifery Education
USDE: 1982/2014/2017
8403 Colesville Road, Suite 1550
Silver Spring, MD 20910
(240) 485-1800 Fax (240) 485-1818
Heather Maurer, Executive Director
E-mail: hmaurer@acnm.org
URL: www.midwife.org/accreditation

Pre-certification, basic certificate and master's degree nurse-midwifery educational programs **MIDWF**

Nursing

Commission on Collegiate Nursing Education (CCNE)
USDE: 2000/2014/2017
One Dupont Circle NW, Suite 530
Washington, DC 20036-1120
(202) 887-6791 Fax (202) 887-8476
Jennifer Butlin, Executive Director
E-mail: info@aacn.nche.edu
URL: www.aacn.nche.edu/ccne-accreditation

Baccalaureate and higher degree nursing education **NURSE**

Accreditation Commission for Education in Nursing
USDE: 1952/2015/2017 CHEA: 2011
3343 Peachtree Road NE, Suite 850
Atlanta, GA 30326
(404) 975-5000 Fax (404) 975-5020
Marsal P. Stoll, CEO
E-mail: info@acenursing.org
URL: www.acenursing.org

Programs in:
- Practical nursing (certificate) **PNUR**
- Diploma nurse education **DNUR**
- Associate degree **ADNUR**
- Baccalaureate and higher degree nurse education **NUR**

Occupational Education

Council on Occupational Education (COE)
USDE: 1969/2013/2016
7840 Roswell Road, Bldg 300, Suite 325
Atlanta, GA 30350
(770) 396-3898 Fax (770) 396-3790
Gary Puckett, Executive Director
E-mail: info@council.org
URL: www.council.org

Occupational/vocational institutions that grant certificates or diplomas and the applied associate degree in specific career and technical education **COE**

Occupational Therapy

Accreditation Council for Occupational Therapy Education
American Occupational Therapy Association
USDE: 1952/2012/2017 CHEA: 2013
4720 Montgomery Lane, Suite 200
Bethesda, MD 20814-3449
(301) 652-6611 Fax (301) 652-7711
Heather Stagliano, Director of Accreditation
E-mail: accred@aota.org
URL: www.aota.org

Occupational therapy programs **OT**
Occupational therapy assistant programs **OTA**

Opticianry

Commission on Opticianry Accreditation
CHEA: 2010
PO Box 592
Canton, NY 13617
(703) 468-0566
Debra White, Director of Accreditation
E-mail: director@COAccreditation.com
URL: www.coaccreditation.com

Two-year opticianry degree programs **OPD**
One year programs for opthalmic laboratory technician **OPLT**

Optometry

Accreditation Council on Optometric Education
American Optometric Association (AOA)
USDE: 1952/2015/2017 CHEA: 2012
243 North Lindbergh Boulevard
St. Louis, MO 63141
(314) 991-4100 Fax (314) 991-4101
Joyce L. Urbeck, Administrative Director
E-mail: accredit@aoa.org
URL: www.theacoe.org

Programs in:
- First professional **OPT**
- Optometric residency **OPTR**
- Optometric technology **OPTT**

Orthotic and Prosthetic Education

Commission on Accreditation of Allied Health Education Programs (see listing under Allied Health)
National Commission on Orthotic and Prosthetic Education (NCOPE)
330 John Carlyle Street, Suite 200
Alexandria, VA 22314
(703) 836-7114 Fax (703) 836-0838
Robin C. Seabrook, Executive Director
E-mail: info@ncope.org
URL: www.ncope.org

Programs for orthotic and prosthetic education **OPE**

Osteopathic Medicine

Commission on Osteopathic College Accreditation
American Osteopathic Association
USDE: 1952/2011/2016
Department of Education
142 East Ontario Street
Chicago, IL 60611-2864
(312) 202-8048 Fax (312) 202-8200
Alissa Craft, Secretary, COCA
E-mail: predoc@osteopathic.org
URL: www.aoacoca.org

Programs leading to and institutions offering the D.O. (Doctor of Osteopathy/Osteopathic Medicine) degree **OSTEO**

Perfusion

Commission on Accreditation of Allied Health Education Programs (see listing under Allied Health)
Accreditation Committee - Perfusion Education
6663 South Sycamore Street
Littleton, CO 80120
(303) 794-6283 Fax (206) 350-1651
Theresa Sisneros, Executive Director
E-mail: office@ac-pe.org
URL: www.ac-pe.org

Programs for the perfusionist **PERF**

Pharmacy

Accreditation Council for Pharmacy Education (ACPE)
USDE: 1952/2014/2017 CHEA: 2014
135 South LaSalle Street, Suite 4100
Chicago, IL 60603
(312) 664-3575 Fax (312) 664-4652
Peter H. Vlasses, Executive Director
E-mail: csinfo@acpe-accredit.org
URL: www.acpe-accredit.org

Professional degree programs in pharmacy **PHAR**

Physical Therapy

Commission on Accreditation in Physical Therapy Education
American Physical Therapy Association (APTA)
USDE: 1977/2014/2017 CHEA: 2012

Trans Potomac Plaza
1111 North Fairfax Street
Alexandria, VA 22314
(703) 706-3245 Fax (703) 684-7343
Sandra Wise, Senior Director
E-mail: accreditation@apta.org
URL: www.capteonline.org

Professional programs for the physical therapist **PTA**
Programs for the physical therapist assistant **PTAA**

Physician Assistant

Accreditation Review Commission on Education for the Physician Assistant (ARC-PA)
CHEA: 2015
12000 Findley Road, Suite 150
John's Creek, GA 30097
(770) 476-1224 Fax (770) 476-1738
Sharon Luke, Executive Director
E-mail: arc-pa@arc-pa.org
URL: www.arc-pa.org

Programs for the physician assistant **ARCPA**

Planning (City and Regional)

Planning Accreditation Board
CHEA: 2013
2334 West Lawrence Avenue, Suite 209
Chicago, IL 60625
(773) 334-7200
Shonagh Merits, Executive Director
E-mail: smerits@planningaccreditationboard.org
URL: www.planningaccreditationboard.org

Bachelor and master's level programs in planning **PLNG**

Podiatry

Council on Podiatric Medical Education
American Podiatric Medical Association (APMA)
USDE: 1952/2013/2016 CHEA: 2015
9312 Old Georgetown Road
Bethesda, MD 20814-1621
(301) 581-9200 Fax (301) 571-4903
Alan R. Tinkleman, Director
E-mail: artinkleman@apma.org
URL: www.cpme.org

Colleges and programs of podiatric medicine, including first professional and doctorate degree programs **POD**

Polysomnographic Technology

Commission on Accreditation of Allied Health Education Programs (see listing under Allied Health)
Committee on Accreditation for Polysomnographic Technologist Education
1711 Frank Avenue
New Bern, NC 28560
(252) 626-3238
Karen Monarchy Rowe, Executive Director
E-mail: office@coapsg.org
URL: www.coapsg.org

Programs for polysomnographic technology **POLYT**

Psychology

Psychological Clinical Science Accreditation System (PCSAS)
CHEA: 2012
1800 Massachusetts Avenue NW, Suite 402
Washington, DC 20036-1218
(301) 455-8046
Alan G. Kraut, Executive Director
Email: akraut@pcsas.org
URL: www.pcsas.org

Psychological clinical science doctoral training programs **PCSAS**

Commission on Accreditation
American Psychological Association (APA)
USDE: 1970/2013/2016 CHEA: 2013
750 First Street NE
Washington, DC 20002-4242
(202) 336-5979 Fax (202) 336-5978
Jacqueline Remondet Wall, Director Program Consultation and Accreditation
E-mail: apaaccred@apa.org
URL: www.apa.org

Doctoral programs in:
- Clinical psychology **CLPSY**
- Counseling psychology **COPSY**
- Combined professional-scientific psychology **PSPSY**
- School psychology **SCPSY**
- Pre-doctoral internship program in health service psychology **IPSY**
- Post-doctoral residency in health service psychology **PDPSY**

Public Affairs and Administration

Commission on Peer Review and Accreditation
Network of Schools of Public Policy, Affairs and Administration (NASPAA)
CHEA: 2014
1029 Vermont Avenue, NW, Suite 1100
Washington, DC 20005
(202) 628-8965 Fax (202) 626-4978
Crystal Calarusse, Chief Accreditation Officer
E-mail: copra@naspaa.org
URL: www.naspaa.org

Master's degree programs in public affairs, public policy and administration **SPAA**

Public Health

Council on Education for Public Health (CEPH)
USDE: 1974/2013/2018
1010 Wayne Avenue, Suite 220
Silver Spring, MD 20910-5600
(202) 789-1050 Fax (202) 789-1895
Laura Rasar King, Executive Director
E-mail: lking@ceph.org
URL: www.ceph.org

Baccalaureate and graduate level programs in schools of public health and public health programs outside of schools of public health **PH**

Rabbinical and Talmudic Education

Accreditation Commission
Association of Advanced Rabbinical and Talmudic Schools (AARTS)
USDE: 1974/2015/2017 CHEA: 2011
11 Broadway, Suite 405
New York, NY 10004
(212) 363-1991 Fax (212) 533-5335
Bernard Fryshman, Interim Executive Director
E-mail: office@aarts-schools.org

Advanced rabbinical and Talmudic schools **RABN**

Radiologic Technology

Joint Review Committee on Education in Radiologic Technology
USDE: 1957/2013/2016 CHEA: 2014
20 North Wacker Drive, Suite 2850
Chicago, IL 60606-3182
(312) 704-5300 Fax (312) 704-5304
Leslie F. Winter, Chief Executive Officer
E-mail: mail@jrcert.org
URL: www.jrcert.org

Programs for:
- Magnetic resonance **RADMAG**
- Medical dosimetry **RADDOS**
- Radiographer **RAD**
- Radiation therapist technologist **RTT**

Recreation, Park and Leisure Studies

Council on Accreditation of Parks, Recreation, Tourism and Related Professions
National Recreation and Park Association
CHEA: 2014
22377 Belmont Ridge Road
Ashburn, VA 20148-4501
(703) 858-2141 Fax (703) 858-0794
Jennifer Stromberg, Awards and Accreditation Manager
E-mail: coaprt@nrpa.org
URL: www.nrpa.org

Baccalaureate degree programs in recreation, park resources and leisure studies **NRPA**

Recreation Therapy

Commission on Accreditation of Allied Health Education Programs (see listing under Allied Health)
Committee on Accreditation of Recreational Therapy Education (CARTE)
CIRS Indiana University
Dept of Park and Tourism Studies
Bloomington, IN 47405-7109
(812) 855-3482
Bryan McCormick
E-mail: bmccormi@indiana.edu
URL: www.atra-online.com/education

Recreational therapy education programs **CARTE**

Rehabilitation Education

Commission on Standards and Accreditation
Council on Rehabilitation Education (CORE)
CHEA: 2012
1699 Woodfield Road, Suite 300
Schaumburg, IL 60173
(847) 944-1345 Fax (847) 944-1346
Frank Lane, CEO
E-mail: flane@core-rehab.org
URL: www.core-rehab.org

Rehabilitation counselor education programs at the master's level and rehabilitation services at the bachelor's level **CORE**

Respiratory Care

Commission on Accreditation for Respiratory Care (CoARC)
CHEA: 2012
1248 Harwood Road
Bedford, TX 76021-4244
(817) 283-2835 Fax (817) 354-8519
Thomas Smalling, Executive Director
Email: tom@coarc.com
URL: www.coarc.com

Degree programs in respiratory care **COARC**
Certificate programs in polysomnography **COARCP**

Social Work

Commission on Accreditation
Council on Social Work Education (CSWE)
CHEA: 2014
1701 Duke Street, Suite 200
Alexandria, VA 22314-3457
(703) 683-8080 Fax (703) 683-8099
Jo Ann Regan, Vice President of Education

E-mail: info@cswe.org
URL: www.cswe.org

Master's and baccalaureate degree programs **SW**

Speech-Language Pathology

Council on Academic Accreditation in Audiology and Speech Language Pathology
American Speech-Language-Hearing Association (ASHA)
USDE: 1967/2015/2017 CHEA: 2014
2200 Research Boulevard
Rockville, MD 20850-3289
(301) 296-5700 Fax (301) 296-8580
Patrima L. Tice, Director of Accreditation
E-mail: accreditation@asha.org
URL: www.asha.org

Master's in speech-language pathology **SP**

Surgical Assisting and Technology

(see listing under Allied Health)
Accrediting Bureau of Health Education Schools (ABHES)

Surgical technologist programs **SURTEC**

Commission on Accreditation of Allied Health Education Programs (see listing under Allied Health)
Accreditation Review Council on Education in Surgical Technology and Surgical Assisting
6 West Dry Creek Circle, Suite 110
Littleton, CO 80120
(303) 694-9262 Fax (303) 741-3655
Keith Orloff, Executive Director
E-mail: info@arcstsa.org
URL: www.arcstsa.org

Programs for the surgical technologist **SURGT**
Programs for the surgical assistant **SURGA**

Teacher Education

Council for the Accreditation of Educator Preparation*
CHEA: 2014
1140 19th Street NW, Suite 400
Washington, DC 20036
(202) 223-0077 Fax (202) 296-6620
Christopher Koch, President
Email: caep@caepnet.org
URL: caepnet.org

Educator preparation programs **CAEP**

*On July 1 2013, the National Council for Accreditation of Teacher Education (NCATE) and the Teacher Education Accreditation Council (TEAC) consolidated, making the Council for the Accreditation of Educator Preparation (CAEP) the new, sole specialized accreditor for educator preparation. Under the consolidation, NCATE and TEAC are subsidiaries of CAEP, maintaining their recognition by the U.S. Department of Education and the Council for Higher Education Accreditation for the purpose of maintaining the accreditation of educator preparation providers until such time as said providers come up for accreditation under CAEP.

National Council for Accreditation of Teacher Education (NCATE)
USDE: 1952/2006/2014 CHEA: 2013

Baccalaureate and graduate programs for the preparation of teachers and other professional personnel for elementary and secondary schools **TED**

Accreditation Committee
Teacher Education Accreditation Council (TEAC)
USDE: 2003/2005/2014 CHEA: 2012

Professional teacher education programs in institutions offering baccalaureate and graduate degrees for the preparation of K-12 teachers **TEAC**

Theatre

Commission on Accreditation
National Association of Schools of Theatre (NAST)
USDE: 1982/2015/2019
11250 Roger Bacon Drive, Suite 21
Reston, VA 20190
(703) 437-0700 Fax (703) 437-6312
Karen P. Moynahan, Executive Director
E-mail: info@arts-accredit.org
URL: www.arts-accredit.org

Institutions and departments within institutions offering degree granting and non-degree-granting programs in theatre and theatre-related disciplines **THEA**

Theology

Commission on Accrediting of the Association of Theological Schools (ATS)
USDE: 1952/2013/2016 CHEA: 2012
10 Summit Park Drive
Pittsburgh, PA 15275-1103
(412) 788-6505 Fax (412) 788-6510
Daniel O. Aleshire, Executive Director
E-mail: ats@ats.edu
URL: www.ats.edu

Freestanding schools, as well as schools or programs affiliated with larger institutions, offering graduate professional education for ministry and graduate study of theology **THEOL**

Trade and Technical Education

Accrediting Commission of Career Schools and Colleges (ACCSC)
USDE: 1967/2011/2016
2101 Wilson Boulevard, Suite 302
Arlington, VA 22201
(703) 247-4212 Fax (703) 247-4533
Michale McComis, Executive Director
E-mail: info@accsc.org
URL: www.accsc.org

Private, postsecondary degree-granting and non-degree-granting institutions that are predominantly organized to educate students for trade, occupational or technical careers **ACCSC**

Veterinary Medicine

Council on Education
American Veterinary Medical Association (AVMA)
USDE: 1952/2012/2016 CHEA: 2012
1931 North Meacham Road, Suite 100
Schaumburg, IL 60173
(800) 248-2862 Fax (847) 285-5732
Karen Martens Brandt, Director Education and Research
E-mail: avmainfo@avma.org
URL: www.avma.org

Colleges of veterinary medicine offering programs leading to a D.V.M./D.M.V. professional degree **VET**

Other

New York State Board of Regents Commission of Education
USDE: 1952/2012/2017
State Education Department
The University of the State of New York
89 Washington Avenue, Room 1106B
Albany, NY 12234
(518) 474-5844 Fax (518) 473-4909
Mary Ellen Elia, Commissioner of Education
E-mail: commissioner@nysed.edu
URL: www.nysed.gov

Degree-granting institutions of higher education in New York that designate the agency as their sole or primary nationally recognized accrediting agency for purposes of establishing eligibility to participate in Higher Education Act programs **NY**

Accrediting Agencies Recognized for their Pre-accreditation Categories[1]

Under the terms of the Higher Education Act and other Federal legislation providing funding assistance to postsecondary education, an institution or program is eligible to apply for participation in certain Federal programs if, in addition to meeting other statutory requirements, it is accredited by a nationally recognized accrediting agency—or if it is an institution with respect to which the U.S. Secretary of Education has determined that there is satisfactory assurance the institution or program will meet the accreditation standards of such agency or association within a reasonable time. An institution or program may establish satisfactory assurance of accreditation by acquiring pre-accreditation status with a nationally recognized accrediting agency which has been recognized by the U.S. Secretary of Education for the award of such status. According to the Criteria for Nationally Recognized Accrediting Agencies, if an accrediting agency has developed a pre-accreditation status, it must demonstrate that it applies criteria and follows procedures that are appropriately related to those used to award accreditation status. The criteria for recognition also requires an agency's standards for pre-accreditation to permit an institution or program to hold pre-accreditation no more than five years.

The following is a list of accrediting agencies recognized by the U.S. Secretary of Education for their pre-accreditation categories and the categories which are recognized.

Regional Institution Accrediting Bodies

Middle States Commission on Higher Education:
Candidate for Accreditation

New England Association of Schools and Colleges:
Commission on Institutions of Higher Education: *Candidate for Accreditation*

Higher Learning Commission: *Candidate for Accreditation*

Northwest Commission on Colleges and Universities:
Candidate for Accreditation

Southern Association of Colleges and Schools
Commission on Colleges: *Candidate for Accreditation*

Western Association of Schools and Colleges
Accrediting Commission for Community and Junior Colleges: *Candidate for Accreditation*

Western Association of Schools and Colleges
Accrediting Commission for Senior Colleges and Universities: *Candidate for Accreditation*

National, Institutional and Specialized Accrediting Bodies

Academy of Nutrition and Dietetics
Accreditation Council for Education in Nutrition and Dietetics: *Pre-accreditation*

Accreditation Commission for Acupuncture and Oriental Medicine: *Pre-accreditation, Candidate for Accreditation*

Accreditation Commission for Midwifery Education: *Pre-accreditation*

Accreditation Council for Pharmacy Education: *Candidate, Pre-candidate*

American Optometric Association
Accreditation Council on Optometric Education: *Preliminary Approval* (for professional degree programs); *Candidacy Pending* (for optometric residency programs in Veterans Administration facilities)

American Osteopathic Association
Commission on Osteopathic College Accreditation: *Provisional Accreditation*

American Physical Therapy Association
Commission on Accreditation in Physical Therapy Education: *Candidate for Accreditation*

American Podiatric Medical Association
Council on Podiatric Medical Education: *Candidate for Accreditation*

American Speech-Language-Hearing Association
Council on Academic Accreditation: *Candidate for Accreditation*

American Veterinary Medical Association
Council on Education: *Reasonable Assurance of Accreditation*

Association for Biblical Higher Education
Commission on Accreditation: *Candidate for Accreditation*

Association of Advanced Rabbinical and Talmudic Schools
Accreditation Commission: *Correspondent, Candidate for Accreditation*

Commission on Accrediting of the Association of Theological Schools: *Candidate for Accredited Membership*

Council on Education for Public Health: *Pre-accreditation*

Council on Naturopathic Medical Education: *Pre-accreditation*

Council on Occupational Education: *Candidate for Accreditation*

Midwifery Education Accreditation Council: *Pre-accreditation*

Teacher Education Accreditation Council Accreditation Committee: *Pre-accreditation*

Transnational Association of Christian Colleges and Schools
Accreditation Commission: *Candidate for Accreditation*

[1]U.S. Department of Education, Nationally Recognized Accrediting Agencies and Associations, www2.ed.gov/admins/finaid/accred/accreditation_pg8.html.

Abbreviations, Explanatory Notes and Symbols

Abbreviations

Listed below are the abbreviations used in this Directory for the recognized regional accrediting commissions and the recognized national, professional and specialized accrediting bodies. Addresses for these associations can be found under our listing of Accrediting Agencies beginning on page viii.

The recognized regional accrediting commissions are indicated throughout this Directory by the following abbreviations:

EH New England Association of Schools and Colleges, Commission on Institutions of Higher Education

M Middle States Commission on Higher Education

NH Higher Learning Commission, North Central Association

NW Northwest Commission on Colleges and Universities

SC Southern Association of Colleges and Schools, Commission on Colleges

WC Western Association of Schools and Colleges, Accrediting Commission for Senior Colleges and Universities

WJ Western Association of Schools and Colleges, Accrediting Commission for Community and Junior Colleges

National, professional and specialized accrediting agencies and associations are listed below. Wherever possible, degree levels are shown by the following symbols: (C) diploma/certificate; (A) associate; (B) baccalaureate; (M) master's; (S) beyond master's but less than doctorate; (FP) first professional; (D) doctorate.

AA Commission on Accreditation of Allied Health Education Programs: anesthesiologist assistant (M)

AAB Aviation Accreditation Board International: aviation (A,B,M)

AAFCS American Association of Family and Consumer Sciences: family and consumer sciences (B)

ABHES Accrediting Bureau of Health Education Schools: allied health (C,A,B)

ACAE Accreditation Commission for Audiology Education: audiology (D)

ACBSP Accreditation Council for Business Schools and Programs: business administration, management, accounting and related business fields (A,B,M,D)

ACCSC Accrediting Commission of Career Schools and Colleges: occupational, trade and technical education (C,A,B,M)

ACFEI American Culinary Federation, Inc.: culinary arts and culinary management (C,A,B)

ACICS Accrediting Council for Independent Colleges and Schools: business and business-related programs (C,A,B,M)

ACUP Accreditation Commission for Acupuncture and Oriental Medicine: acupuncture (C,M,D)

ADNUR Accreditation Commission for Education in Nursing: nursing (A)

AIJS Association of Institutions of Jewish Studies: Jewish studies (C, A,B)

ANEST Council on Accreditation of Nurse Anesthesia Educational Programs: nurse anesthesia (C,M,D)

ARCPA Accreditation Review Commission on Education for the Physician Assistant: physician assisting programs (C,A,B,M)

ART National Association of Schools of Art and Design: art and design (C,A,B,M,D)

AUD American Speech-Language-Hearing Association: audiology (D)

BBT Commission on Accreditation of Allied Health Education Programs: blood bank technology (C,M)

BI Association for Biblical Higher Education: bible college education (C,A,B,M,FP,D)

BUS AACSB-The Association to Advance Collegiate Schools of Business: business and management (B,M,D)

BUSA AACSB-The Association to Advance Collegiate Schools of Business: accounting (B,M,D)

CA National Accrediting Agency for Clinical Laboratory Sciences: clinical assistant (C)

CAATE Commission on Accreditation of Athletic Training Education: athletic training (B,M)

CACREP Council for Accreditation of Counseling & Related Education programs: addiction counseling, career counseling, marriage, couple and family counseling, mental health counseling, school counseling, student affairs and college counseling (M) and counselor education and supervision (D)

CAEP Council for the Accreditation of Educator Preparation: teacher education (B,M,D)

CAHIIM Commission on Accreditation for Health Informatics and Information Management Education: health information management and health informatics (A,B,M)

CARTE Commission on Accreditation of Recreational Therapy Education: recreational therapy (B,M)

CEA Commission on English Language Program Accreditation: english language (C)

CGTECH National Accrediting Agency for Clinical Laboratory Sciences: cytogenetic technologist (B)

CHIRO Council on Chiropractic Education: chiropractic education (FP,D)

CIDA Council for Interior Design Accreditation: interior design (B,M)

CLPSY American Psychological Association: clinical psychology (D)

CNCE Accrediting Council for Continuing Education and Training: continuing education (C,A)

COARC Commission on Accreditation for Respiratory Care: respiratory care (A,B,M)

COARCP Commission on Accreditation for Respiratory Care: polysomnography (C)

COE Council on Occupational Education: occupational, trade, and technical education (C,A)

COMTA Commission on Massage Therapy Accreditation: massage therapy, bodywork, aesthetics/esthetics and skin care (C,A)

CONST American Council for Construction Education: construction education (A,B)

COPSY American Psychological Association: counseling psychology (D)

CORE Council on Rehabilitation Education: rehabilitation counseling and rehabilitation services (B,M)

COSME National Accrediting Commission of Career Arts and Sciences: cosmetology and massage therapy (C)

CS ABET, Inc.: computer science (B)

CSHSE Council for Standards in Human Services Education: human services (A,B,M)

CVT Commission on Accreditation of Allied Health Education Programs: cardiovascular technology (C,A,B)

CYTO Commission on Accreditation of Allied Health Education Programs: cytotechnology (C,B,M)

DA American Dental Association: dental assisting (C,A)

DANCE National Association of Schools of Dance: dance (C,A,B,M,D)

DEAC Distance Education and Accrediting Commission: home study schools (A,B,M,D)

DENT American Dental Association: dentistry (FP,D)

DH American Dental Association: dental hygiene (C,A,B,M)

DIETC Academy of Nutrition and Dietetics: coordinated dietetics programs (B,M)

DIETD Academy of Nutrition and Dietetics: didactic dietetics programs (B,M)

DIETI Academy of Nutrition and Dietetics: dietetic post-baccalaureate internships

DIETT Academy of Nutrition and Dietetics: dietetic technician (A)

DMOLS National Accrediting Agency for Clinical Laboratory Sciences: diagnostic molecular scientist (C,B,M)

DMS Commission on Accreditation of Allied Health Education Programs: diagnostic medical sonography (C,A,B,M)

DNUR Accreditation Commission for Education in Nursing: nursing (C)

DT American Dental Association: dental laboratory technology (C,A)

EMT Commission on Accreditation of Allied Health Education Programs: emergency medical technician-paramedic (C,A,B)

ENG ABET, Inc.: engineering (B,M)

ENGR ABET, Inc.: applied science (A,B,M)

ENGT ABET, Inc.: engineering technology (A,B)

EXSC Commission on Accreditation of Allied Health Education Programs: exercise science (C,B,M)

FEPAC American Academy of Forensic Sciences: forensic science (B,M)

FUSER American Board of Funeral Service Education: funeral service education (C,A,B)

HSA Commission on Accreditation of Healthcare Management Education: healthcare management (B,M)

HT National Accrediting Agency for Clinical Laboratory Sciences: histologic technology (C,A,B)

IACBE International Assembly for Collegiate Business Education: business programs in institutions that grant bachelor/graduate degrees (A,B,M,D)

IFSAC International Fire Service Accreditation Congress Degree Assembly: fire and emergency related degree (A,B)

IPSY American Psychological Association: pre-doctoral internships in health service psychology

JOUR Accrediting Council on Education for Journalism and Mass Communications: journalism and mass communications (B,M)

KIN Commission on Accreditation of Allied Health Education Programs: kinesiotherapy (B)

LAW American Bar Association: law (FP,D)

LIB American Library Association: librarianship (M)

LSAR American Society for Landscape Architects: landscape architecture (B,M)

MAAB Accrediting Bureau of Health Education Schools: medical assisting (C,A)

MAC Commission on Accreditation of Allied Health Education Programs: medical assisting (C,A)

MACTE Montessori Accreditation Council for Teacher Education: Montessori teacher education (C)

MEAC Midwifery Education Accreditation Council: midwifery education (C,A,B,M,D)

MED Liaison Committee on Medical Education: medicine (FP,D)

MFCD American Association for Marriage and Family Therapy: marriage and family therapy (M,D)

MIDWF Accreditation Commission for Midwifery Education: nurse midwifery (C,M,D)

MIL Commission on Accreditation of Allied Health Education Programs: medical illustrator (M)

MLTAB Accrediting Bureau of Health Education Schools: medical laboratory technician (C,A)

MLTAD National Accrediting Agency for Clinical Laboratory Sciences: medical laboratory technician (C,A)

MT National Accrediting Agency for Clinical Laboratory Sciences: medical technology/laboratory scientist (C,B)

MUS National Association of Schools of Music: music (C,A,B,M,D)

NAIT The Association of Technology, Management, and Applied Engineering: technology, applied technology, engineering technology and technology-related programs (A,B,M)

NATUR Council on Naturopathic Medical Education: naturopathic medical education (FP,D)

NDT Commission on Accreditation of Allied Health Education Programs: neurodiagnostic technology (C,A)

NMT Joint Review Committee on Educational Programs in Nuclear Medicine Technology: nuclear medicine technology (C,A,B)

NRPA National Recreation and Park Association: recreation, park resources, and leisure studies (B)

NUR Accreditation Commission for Education in Nursing: nursing (B, M,D)

NURSE Commission on Collegiate Nursing Education: nursing (B,M,D)

NY New York State Board of Regents:
Degree-granting institutions of higher education in New York that designate the agency as their sole or primary nationally recognized accrediting agency for purposes of establishing elibility to participate in Higher Education Act programs

OPD Commission on Opticianry Accreditation: opticianry (A)

OPE Commission on Accreditation of Allied Health Education Programs: orthotics and prosthetics (C,B,M)

OPLT Commission on Opticianry Accreditation: opthalmic laboratory technician (C)

OPT American Optometric Association: optometry (FP,D)

OPTR American Optometric Association: optometric residency programs

OPTT American Optometric Association: optometric technician (C,A)

OSTEO American Osteopathic Association, Office of Osteopathic Education: osteopathic medicine (FP,D)

OT American Occupational Therapy Association: occupational therapy (M,D)

OTA American Occupational Therapy Association: occupational therapy assistant (C,A)

PA National Accrediting Agency for Clinical Laboratory Sciences: pathologist's assistant (C,M)

PAST Association for Clinical Pastoral Education: clinical pastoral education

PCSAS Psychological Clinical Science Accreditation System: psychological clinical science (D)

PDPSY American Psychological Association: post-doctorate residency in health service psychology

PERF Commission on Accreditation of Allied Health Education Programs: perfusionist (C,B,M)

PH Council on Education for Public Health: public health (B,M,D)

PHAR Accreditation Council for Pharmaceutical Education: pharmacy (FP,D)

PHLEB National Accrediting Agency for Clinical Laboratory Sciences: phlebotomist (C)

PLNG Planning Accreditation Board: certified planning (B,M)

PNUR Accreditation Commission for Education in Nursing: practical nursing (C)

POD American Podiatric Medical Association: podiatry (FP,D)

POLYT Commission on Accreditation of Allied Health Education Programs: polysomnographic technologist education (C,A)

PSPSY American Psychological Association: combined professional-scientific psychology (D)

PTA American Physical Therapy Association: physical therapy (M,D)

PTAA American Physical Therapy Association: physical therapy assistant (A)

RABN Association of Advanced Rabbinical and Talmudic Schools: rabbinical and Talmudic education (B,M,D)

RAD Joint Review Committee on Education in Radiologic Technology: radiography (C,A,B)

RADDOS Joint Review Committee on Education in Radiologic Technology: medical dosimetry (C,B,M)

RADMAG Joint Review Committee on Education in Radiologic Technology: magnetic resonance (C,B)

RTT Joint Review Committee on Education in Radiologic Technology: radiation therapist/technologist (C,A,B)

SCPSY American Psychological Association: school psychology (D)

SP American Speech-Language-Hearing Association: speech-language pathology (M)

SPAA Network of Schools of Public Policy, Affairs and Administration: public affairs and administration (M)

SURGA Commission on Accreditation of Allied Health Education Programs: surgical assistant (C,A)

SURGT Commission on Accreditation of Allied Health Education Programs: surgical technology (C,A)

SURTEC Accrediting Bureau of Health Education Schools: surgical technologist (C,A)

SW Council on Social Work Education: social work (B,M)

TEAC Teacher Education Accreditation Council: teacher education (B, M,D)

TED National Council for Accreditation of Teacher Education: teacher education (B,M,D)

THEA National Association of Schools of Theatre: theatre (C,A,B,M,D)

THEOL Association of Theological Schools: theology (M,FP,D)

TRACS Transnational Association of Christian Colleges and Schools: christian studies education (C,A,B,M,D)

VET American Veterinary Medical Association: veterinary medicine (FP,D)

Explanatory Notes and Symbols

Associate degree: includes junior colleges, community colleges, technical institutes, and schools offering at least a two-year program of college-level studies, either leading to an associate degree wholly or principally creditable toward a baccalaureate degree.

Baccalaureate: includes those institutions offering programs of studies leading to the customary bachelor of arts or bachelor of science degrees.

First professional degree: includes those institutions that offer the academic requirements for selected professions based on programs that require at least two academic years of previous college work for entrance and a total of at least six years of college work for completion.

Master's: includes those institutions offering the customary first graduate degree, master of arts or master of science degree in the liberal arts and sciences or the next degree in the same field after the first professional degree.

Beyond master's but less than doctorate: includes those institutions offering "postgraduate pre-doctoral degrees".

Graduate non-degree granting: includes institutions offering work beyond the bachelor's level but not conferring degrees. In some instances the degrees are conferred by cooperating institutions.

Doctorate: includes those institutions offering a Ph.D. or its equivalent in any field.

Postdoctoral research only: includes institutions operating solely for the purpose of research at the postdoctoral level.

First Talmudic degree: undergraduate degree granted by accredited Rabbinical schools. The schools in New York "using this designation do not imply that the 'First Talmudic Degree' is equivalent to any secular academic degree recognized by the Board of Regents".*

Second Talmudic degree: graduate degree granted by accredited Rabbinical schools. The schools in New York "using this designation do not imply that the 'Second Talmudic Degree' is equivalent to any secular academic degree recognized by the Board of Regents".*

---

*The University of the State of New York, The State Education Department, Albany, New York, letter August 17, 1983.

Symbols

* The institution is part of a system.

Used preceding any of the acronyms for the accrediting agencies the following symbols indicate that:

The accrediting agency has stated publicly that the institution or program is preliminary or provisionally accredited, accredited with some reservations, or approved on probation.

@ The institution or program has attained a pre-accredited status.

& The institution is covered under the regional accreditation of the parent institution.

U.S. Postal Abbreviation of States and Territories

Alabama .... AL
Alaska .... AK
American Samoa .... AS
Arizona .... AZ
Arkansas .... AR
California .... CA
Colorado .... CO
Connecticut .... CT
Delaware .... DE
District of Columbia .... DC
Florida .... FL
Georgia .... GA
Guam .... GU
Hawaii .... HI
Idaho .... ID
Illinois IL
Indiana .... IN
Iowa .... IA
Kansas .... KS
Kentucky .... KY
Louisiana .... LA
Maine .... ME
Maryland .... MD
Marshall Islands .... MH
Massachusetts .... MA
Michigan .... MI
Micronesia .... FM
Minnesota .... MN
Mississippi .... MS
Missouri .... MO
Montana .... MT
Nebraska .... NE
Nevada .... NV
New Hampshire .... NH
New Jersey .... NJ
New Mexico .... NM
New York .... NY
North Carolina .... NC
North Dakota .... ND
Northern Marianas .... MP
Ohio .... OH
Oklahoma .... OK
Oregon .... OR
Palau .... PW
Pennsylvania .... PA
Puerto Rico .... PR
Rhode Island .... RI
South Carolina .... SC
South Dakota .... SD
Tennessee .... TN
Texas .... TX
Utah .... UT
Vermont .... VT
Virgin Islands VI
Virginia .... VA
Washington .... WA
West Virginia .... WV
Wisconsin .... WI
Wyoming .... WY

Institution Changes

Institutions and Offices Added

Alabama

	FICE/ID Number
Edward Via College of Osteopathic Medicine-Auburn Campus	770965

California

	FICE/ID Number
American Medical Sciences Center	041597
California Institute of Advanced Management	042506
California Institute of Arts & Technology	667289
Chamberlain College of Nursing-Sacramento	770978
Golden State University	667261
Hussian College-Relativity Campus California	770969
Merit University	667293
META Business School	667286
Nobel University	667274
Sacramento Ultrasound Institute	667264
Saint Katherine College	667263
San Diego Global Knowledge University	667294
San Joaquin Valley College-Antelope Valley	770968
Spartan College of Aeronautics and Technology	025964
Union University of California	667269
West Coast Baptist College	667268

District of Columbia

	FICE/ID Number
Inter-American Defense College	667275

Florida

	FICE/ID Number
Azure College	770981
Cambridge Institute of Allied Health & Technology-Altamonte Springs	038425
Express Training Services	667276
Florida College of Health Science	667265
Florida Polytechnic University	667279
Hope College of Arts & Sciences	042517
Larkin Health Sciences Institute	667288
Medical Career Institute	667266
Medical Prep Institute	667267
Premiere International College	667295
Sullivan and Cogliano Training Centers	040393
Suncoast College of Health	667296
UAC School of Global Management	667277

Georgia

	FICE/ID Number
Gwinnett College-Sandy Springs	034183

Illinois

	FICE/ID Number
Midwestern Career College	041390
Realtor University	667270
SAE Institute Chicago	770970

Indiana

	FICE/ID Number
MJS College School of Nursing	667272

Maryland

	FICE/ID Number
Women's Institute of Torah Seminary	667271

Michigan

	FICE/ID Number
MIAT College of Technology	770972
Western Michigan University Homer Stryker MD School of Medicine	667287

Nevada

	FICE/ID Number
Touro University Nevada	770966
Wongu University of Oriental Medicine	667262

New Jersey

	FICE/ID Number
Bais Medrash Mayan Hatorah	667280
Bard High School Early College Newark	770980
Yeshiva Bais Aharon	667291
Yeshiva Chemdas Hatorah	667281
Yeshiva Gedolah Keren Hatorah	667282
Yeshiva Gedolah Tiferes Boruch	667283

New York

	FICE/ID Number
Elyon College	667290
Yeshiva Ohr Naftoli	667284

North Carolina

	FICE/ID Number
Chamberlain College of Nursing-Charlotte	770979
ECPI University-Charlotte	770951
ECPI University-Greensboro	770952
ECPI University-Raleigh	770953

Oklahoma

	FICE/ID Number
Platt College	770971

Oregon

	FICE/ID Number
Process Work Institute	667297

Puerto Rico

	FICE/ID Number
Monteclaro Escuela de Hoteleria y Artes Culinarias	034143
Universidad Ana G. Mendez	667292

South Carolina

	FICE/ID Number
ECPI University-Charleston	770955
ECPI University-Columbia	770956
ECPI University-Greenville	770954
The Art Institute of Charleston	770976

Tennessee

	FICE/ID Number
Merician Institute of Surgical Assisting	041650
The Art Institute of Tennessee-Nashville	770975

Texas

	FICE/ID Number
Ana G. Mendez University System-Dallas	770947
Cardiotech Ultrasound School	041385
Carrington College - Mesquite	770967
Fortis College	034244
Interactive College of Technology	023313
Northeast Lakeview College	667278
Pima Medical Institute-El Paso	770962

Institution Changes

	FICE/ID Number
Texas Southmost College	003643
The Art Institute of Austin	770973
The Art Institute of San Antonio	770974
The College of Health Care Professions-McAllen	770963
The College of Health Care Professions-San Antonio	770964

Virginia

American College of Commerce and Technology	667273
Culinary Institute of Virginia	770960
ECPI University-Northern Virginia	770957
ECPI University-Richmond/Innsbrook	770961
ECPI University-Richmond/Moorefield	770958
ECPI University-Roanoke	770959
Faith Bible College	667285
The Art Institute of Virginia Beach	770977

Washington

Washington State University-Spokane	770948
Washington State University-Tri Cities	770949
Washington State University-Vancouver	770950

West Virginia

Valley College - Martinsburg Campus	026094
Valley College - Princeton Campus	030842

Institutions and Offices Dropped

Alabama

Fortis College-Montgomery (Atlanta Highway) *(No longer degree granting)*	770511
ITT Technical Institute *(Closed)*	666165
ITT Technical Institute *(Closed)*	666530
ITT Technical Institute *(Closed)*	666695

Arizona

American Indian College of the Assemblies of God *(Accreditation withdrawn by NH)*	021999
Aventis College *(Closed)*	667225
ITT Technical Institute *(Closed)*	020652
ITT Technical Institute *(Closed)*	023611
ITT Technical Institute *(Closed)*	666696
ITT Technical Institute *(Closed)*	667190

Arkansas

ITT Technical Institute *(Closed)*	666531

California

	FICE/ID Number
Ashdown College of Health Sciences *(Closed)*	041789
Brooks Institute *(Closed)*	001123
Charter College-Canyon Country *(Closed)*	032783
Charter College-Lancaster Campus *(Closed)*	770846
ITT Technical Institute *(Closed)*	021209
ITT Technical Institute *(Closed)*	023218
ITT Technical Institute *(Closed)*	023219
ITT Technical Institute *(Closed)*	030704
ITT Technical Institute *(Closed)*	666144
ITT Technical Institute *(Closed)*	666533
ITT Technical Institute *(Closed)*	666534
ITT Technical Institute *(Closed)*	666697
ITT Technical Institute *(Closed)*	667192
ITT Technical Institute *(Closed)*	667193
ITT Technical Institute *(Closed)*	667194
ITT Technical Institute *(Closed)*	667195
Sage College *(Closed)*	666304
Stanton University *(No longer recognized by ACUP)*	667053
The National Hispanic University *(Closed)*	025184
Westwood College-Anaheim *(Closed)*	666047
Westwood College-Inland Empire *(Closed)*	666104
Westwood College-Los Angeles Campus *(Closed)*	030727
Westwood College-South Bay *(Closed)*	011626

Colorado

Everest College *(Closed)*	666412
ITT Technical Institute *(Closed)*	667189
ITT Technical Institute *(Closed)*	770636
Jones International University *(Closed)*	035343
Redstone College-Denver East *(Closed)*	770611
Westwood College *(Closed)*	667029
Westwood College-Denver North *(Closed)*	007548
Westwood College-Denver South *(Closed)*	666512
Westwood College-Online *(Closed)*	770673

District of Columbia

Graduate School USA *(No longer degree granting)*	667121

	FICE/ID Number
Medtech College *(Closed)*	666591
Radians College *(Closed)*	667005

Florida

Dade Medical College *(Closed)*	038323
Dade Medical College-Hollywood *(Closed)*	770522
Dade Medical College-Homestead *(Closed)*	770523
Dade Medical College-Jacksonville *(Closed)*	770524
Dade Medical College-Miami *(Closed)*	770525
Dade Medical College-West Palm Beach *(Closed)*	770526
Everest University-Jacksonville Campus *(Closed)*	666994
Everest University-Lakeland Campus *(Closed)*	666415
Everest University-North Orlando Campus *(Closed)*	001499
Fortis Institute *(Closed)*	770541
Fortis Institute *(Closed)*	770542
Fortis Institute-Fort Lauderdale *(Closed)*	666269
Institute of Technical Arts *(Closed)*	036183
ITT Technical Institute *(Closed)*	022865
ITT Technical Institute *(Closed)*	030876
ITT Technical Institute *(Closed)*	666026
ITT Technical Institute *(Closed)*	666163
ITT Technical Institute *(Closed)*	666537
ITT Technical Institute *(Closed)*	666669
ITT Technical Institute *(Closed)*	770638
ITT Technical Institute *(Closed)*	770641
Lincoln Tech Fern Park Orlando Campus *(Closed)*	033903
Mattia College *(Closed)*	033484
Remington College-Tampa Campus *(Closed)*	007586
Sanford-Brown Institute *(Closed)*	667031
Southeastern College *(Closed)*	035533
Southeastern College *(Closed)*	770568
Southeastern College *(Closed)*	770569
University of Southernmost Florida *(Closed)*	025982
University of Southernmost Florida-Coral Gables Campus *(Closed)*	770614

	FICE/ID Number

Georgia

ITT Technical Institute *(Closed)*	666325
ITT Technical Institute *(Closed)*	666378
ITT Technical Institute *(Closed)*	666595
ITT Technical Institute *(Closed)*	770655
Medtech College *(Closed)*	770536
Sanford-Brown College *(Closed)*	021160
Westwood College-Atlanta Midtown *(Closed)*	666421
Westwood College-Atlanta Northlake *(Closed)*	666597

Idaho

ITT Technical Institute *(Closed)*	004553

Illinois

ITT Technical Institute *(Closed)*	666118
ITT Technical Institute *(Closed)*	666538
ITT Technical Institute *(Closed)*	666539
ITT Technical Institute *(Closed)*	770649
Westwood College-Chicago Loop *(Closed)*	666424
Westwood College-DuPage *(Closed)*	030792
Westwood College-O'Hare Airport *(Closed)*	023139
Westwood College-River Oaks *(Closed)*	666440

Indiana

American National University *(Closed)*	770696
Brown Mackie College-Michigan City *(Closed)*	666426
ITT Technical Institute *(Closed)*	007327
ITT Technical Institute *(Closed)*	007329
ITT Technical Institute *(Closed)*	008329
ITT Technical Institute *(Closed)*	666700
ITT Technical Institute *(Closed)*	770650
ITT Technical Institute *(Closed)*	770651
MedTech College *(Closed)*	007362
MedTech College *(Closed)*	666677
MedTech College *(Closed)*	666678

Institution Changes

FICE/ID Number

Iowa

AIB College of Business 003963
(Closed)

ITT Technical Institute 666596
(Closed)

University of Phoenix Des Moines Campus 770203
(Closed)

Kansas

ITT Technical Institute 666168
(Closed)

ITT Technical Institute 770652
(Closed)

Wright Career College 025909
(Closed)

Wright Career College 770721
(Closed)

Kentucky

ITT Technical Institute 666158
(Closed)

ITT Technical Institute 666540
(Closed)

Louisville Bible College 041418
(Voluntary withdrawal from BI)

MedTech College-Lexington 770722
(Closed)

St. Catharine College 001983
(Closed)

Louisiana

Blue Cliff College 034225
(No longer degree granting)

Blue Cliff College 034226
(No longer degree granting)

ITT Technical Institute 666031
(Closed)

ITT Technical Institute 666164
(Closed)

Maryland

ITT Technical Institute 666377
(Closed)

ITT Technical Institute 770644
(Closed)

Massachusetts

ITT Technical Institute 666119
(Closed)

ITT Technical Institute 666541
(Closed)

Michigan

Cleary University-Livingston Campus 770263
(No longer listed as branch campus by HLC)

Davenport University Battle Creek 770264
(Closed)

Davenport University Kalamazoo 770267
(Closed)

ITT Technical Institute 010627
(Closed)

ITT Technical Institute 666146
(Closed)

FICE/ID Number

ITT Technical Institute 666323
(Closed)

ITT Technical Institute 666542
(Closed)

ITT Technical Institute 770645
(Closed)

ITT Technical Institute 770647
(Closed)

Manthano Christian College 667140
(Voluntary withdrawal from TRACS)

Michigan Jewish Institute 032843
(Voluntary withdrawal from ACICS)

Robert B. Miller College 040943
(Closed)

Minnesota

ITT Technical Institute 666319
(Closed)

ITT Technical Institute 770653
(Closed)

Minnesota School of Business 770720
(Closed)

Mississippi

ITT Technical Institute 666701
(Closed)

Missouri

Everest College 022506
(Closed)

ITT Technical Institute 007557
(Closed)

ITT Technical Institute 666033
(Closed)

ITT Technical Institute 666380
(Closed)

ITT Technical Institute 666702
(Closed)

Missouri Tech 023040
(Closed)

National American University-Weldon Spring 770405
(Closed)

Nebraska

ITT Technical Institute 666543
(Closed)

Wright Career College 770739
(Closed)

Nevada

ITT Technical Institute 666544
(Closed)

ITT Technical Institute 770658
(Closed)

New Hampshire

Mount Washington College 004729
(Closed)

New Jersey

ITT Technical Institute 770657
(Closed)

	FICE/ID Number
Mesivta Keser Torah *(Voluntary withdrawal from AARTS)*	041803
Rowan University at Camden *(No longer listed as branch campus by MSACS)*	770132
Saint Peter's University Englewood Cliffs Campus *(No longer listed as branch campus by MSACS)*	770133
Union County College Scotch Plains *(No longer listed as branch campus by MSACS)*	770136
University of Northern New Jersey *(Closed)*	667216

New Mexico

ITT Technical Institute *(Closed)*	666545
Southwest Acupuncture College-Albuquerque *(Closed)*	666666

New York

Business Informatics Center, Inc. *(No longer accredited by ACCSC)*	025729
Dowling College *(Accreditation withdrawn)*	002667
Globe Institute of Technology *(Closed)*	025408
ITT Technical Institute *(Closed)*	666137
ITT Technical Institute *(Closed)*	666138
ITT Technical Institute *(Closed)*	666609
Professional Business College *(Closed)*	023065
Rabbinical College Ch'san Sofer *(Voluntary withdrawal from AARTS)*	003977

North Carolina

Carolina Graduate School of Divinity *(Closed)*	039395
ITT Technical Institute *(Closed)*	666161
ITT Technical Institute *(Closed)*	666703
ITT Technical Institute *(Closed)*	666704
ITT Technical Institute *(Closed)*	666705
ITT Technical Institute *(Closed)*	770656

North Dakota

Rasmussen College - Bismarck *(Closed)*	666301

Ohio

ITT Technical Institute *(Closed)*	009088
ITT Technical Institute *(Closed)*	009837
ITT Technical Institute *(Closed)*	666160
ITT Technical Institute *(Closed)*	666318
ITT Technical Institute *(Closed)*	666379
ITT Technical Institute *(Closed)*	666546

	FICE/ID Number
ITT Technical Institute *(Closed)*	666547
ITT Technical Institute *(Closed)*	666706
ITT Technical Institute *(Closed)*	770659
ITT Technical Institute *(Closed)*	770660

Oklahoma

ITT Technical Institute *(Closed)*	666147
ITT Technical Institute *(Closed)*	666159
University of Phoenix Oklahoma City Campus *(Closed)*	770221
Wright Career College *(Closed)*	770762
Wright Career College *(Closed)*	770763

Oregon

Everest College *(Closed)*	009079
ITT Technical Institute *(Closed)*	011852
ITT Technical Institute *(Closed)*	770637
National American University-Tigard *(Closed)*	770410

Pennsylvania

Cambria-Rowe Business College *(Closed)*	004889
Cambria-Rowe Business College *(Closed)*	666476
DuBois Business College *(Closed)*	004893
DuBois Business College *(Closed)*	666479
DuBois Business College *(Closed)*	666480
Everest Institute *(Closed)*	007091
ITT Technical Institute *(Closed)*	666150
ITT Technical Institute *(Closed)*	666482
ITT Technical Institute *(Closed)*	666483
ITT Technical Institute *(Closed)*	666548
ITT Technical Institute *(Closed)*	667161
ITT Technical Institute *(Closed)*	667162
Moravian Theological Seminary *(No longer listed as branch campus by MSACS)*	770163
Prism Career Institute-Upper Darby Campus *(Closed)*	023013

South Carolina

ITT Technical Institute *(Closed)*	666162
ITT Technical Institute *(Closed)*	666549

Institution Changes

	FICE/ID Number
ITT Technical Institute *(Closed)*	770661
ITT Technical Institute *(Closed)*	770662

South Dakota

Colorado Technical University *(Closed)*	666731
Kilian Community College *(Closed)*	021446

Tennessee

ITT Technical Institute *(Closed)*	023598
ITT Technical Institute *(Closed)*	030734
ITT Technical Institute *(Closed)*	666550
ITT Technical Institute *(Closed)*	666708
ITT Technical Institute *(Closed)*	770663

Texas

Everest College *(Closed)*	666254
International Business College *(Voluntary withdrawal from ACICS)*	009082
International Business College-East Campus *(Voluntary withdrawal from ACICS)*	770622
ITT Technical Institute *(Closed)*	023286
ITT Technical Institute *(Closed)*	023287
ITT Technical Institute *(Closed)*	030714
ITT Technical Institute *(Closed)*	666327
ITT Technical Institute *(Closed)*	666551
ITT Technical Institute *(Closed)*	666552
ITT Technical Institute *(Closed)*	666554
ITT Technical Institute *(Closed)*	770633
ITT Technical Institute *(Closed)*	770635
Sanford-Brown College *(Closed)*	026150
University of Phoenix McAllen Campus *(Closed)*	770230

Utah

Broadview University *(Closed)*	770810
Broadview University *(Closed)*	770811
ITT Technical Institute *(Closed)*	023610

Vermont

Burlington College *(Closed)*	012183

Virginia

	FICE/ID Number
Everest College *(Closed)*	009267
ITT Technical Institute *(Closed)*	666040
ITT Technical Institute *(Closed)*	666321
ITT Technical Institute *(Closed)*	666324
ITT Technical Institute *(Closed)*	666555
ITT Technical Institute *(Closed)*	770664
Medtech College *(Closed)*	025889
Skyline College *(Closed)*	030927
Westwood College-Annandale *(Closed)*	666599
Westwood College-Arlington Ballston *(Closed)*	666660

Washington

Charter College *(No longer degree granting)*	770821
Charter College-Lynnwood *(Closed)*	770624
DeVry University - Federal Way Campus *(Closed)*	666224
Everest College *(Closed)*	023001
Everest College *(No longer ACICS acceredited/closed)*	666737
Everest College *(No longer degree granting)*	770793
Everest College *(No longer degree granting)*	770794
Interface College *(Closed)*	023265
ITT Technical Institute *(Closed)*	008443
ITT Technical Institute *(Closed)*	030718
ITT Technical Institute *(Closed)*	666326
Northwest Institute of Literary Arts *(Closed)*	041889
Trinity Lutheran College *(Closed)*	021067

West Virginia

ITT Technical Institute *(Closed)*	666709

Wisconsin

Brensten Education *(Closed)*	041379
Globe University-Green Bay *(Closed)*	770802
Globe University-Middleton *(Closed)*	770805
ITT Technical Institute *(Closed)*	666317
ITT Technical Institute *(Closed)*	770666
National-Louis University Milwaukee/Beloit Campus *(Closed)*	770088

Merged Institutions

FICE/ID Number

Georgia

Georgia Perimeter College *into* 001562
Georgia State University 001574

Louisiana

Louisiana State University Paul M. Hebert Law Center *into* 667028
Louisiana State University and Agricultural and Mechanical College 002010

Massachusetts

School of the Museum of Fine Arts, Boston *into* 004667
Tufts University 002219

The Boston Conservatory *into* 002129
Berklee College of Music 002126

Michigan

Davenport University Saginaw *into* 770271
Davenport University Midland 770270

Nebraska

Nebraska Christian College *into* 012976
Hope International University 001252

New York

Rabbi Isaac Elchanan Theological Seminary *into* 033104
Yeshiva University 002903

Union Graduate College *into* 038813
Clarkson University 002699

North Carolina

South College-Asheville *into* 010264
South College 004938

Texas

Texas State Technical College Harlingen *into* 009225
Texas State Technical College Waco 003634

Texas State Technical College Marshall *into* 033965
Texas State Technical College Waco 003634

Texas State Technical College System *into* 009642
Texas State Technical College Waco 003634

Texas State Technical College West Texas *into* 009932
Texas State Technical College Waco 003634

Name Changes

FICE/ID Number

Arizona

from: Carrington College - Phoenix 021006
to: Carrington College - Phoenix North

from: Carrington College - Westside 666248
to: Carrington College - Phoenix East

Arkansas

from: National Park Community College 012105
to: National Park College

from: University of Arkansas Community College at Hope 005732
to: University of Arkansas at Hope-Texarkana

California

from: Angeles College-Garden Grove 770518
to: Angeles College-City of Industry

from: California State University Maritime Academy 001134
to: CSU Maritime Academy

from: Fashion Institute of Design and Merchandising-San Diego 666005
to: FIDM/Fashion Institute of Design & Merchandising-San Diego

from: Fashion Institute of Design and Merchandising-San Francisco 013041
to: FIDM/Fashion Institute of Design and Merchandising-San Francisco

from: Golden Gate Baptist Theological Seminary 001204
to: Gateway Seminary

from: Kaplan College 020917
to: Brightwood College

from: Kaplan College 023063
to: Brightwood College

from: Kaplan College 023519
to: Brightwood College

from: Kaplan College 025391
to: Brightwood College

from: Kaplan College 025490
to: Brightwood College

from: Kaplan College 666291
to: Brightwood College

from: Kaplan College 770558
to: Brightwood College

from: Kaplan College 770559
to: Brightwood College

from: Kaplan College 770560
to: Brightwood College

from: Palmer College of Chiropractic, West Campus 021849
to: Palmer College of Chiropractic, San Jose Campus

from: Phillips Graduate Institute 022372
to: Phillips Graduate University

from: Santa Barbara Business College 009989
to: SBBCollege Ventura

from: Santa Barbara Business College 025779
to: SBBCollege Bakersfield

from: Santa Barbara Business College 025780
to: SBBCollege Santa Maria

from: Santa Barbara Business College 666099
to: SBBCollege Santa Barbara

from: Santa Barbara Business College 666582
to: SBBCollege Rancho Mirage

from: Santa Barbara Business College-Online 770628
to: SBBCollege Online

from: Shepherd University School of Theology 667056
to: Shepherd University

Colorado

from: Institute of Business and Medical Careers 770631
to: IBMC College

Florida

from: Allied Health Institute 041359
to: Orion College

Institution Changes

	FICE/ID Number
from: Cambridge Institute of Allied Health & Technology *to:* Cambridge College	040834
from: Institute of Healthcare Professions *to:* International College of Health Sciences	667238
from: Management Resources College *to:* Miami Regional University	041284
from: Palmer College of Chiropractic, Florida Campus *to:* Palmer College of Chiropractic, Port Orange Campus	666330
from: Remington College of Nursing *to:* ECPI University College of Nursing	770566
from: San Ignacio College *to:* San Ignacio University	667130

Georgia

from: Medtech College *to:* Gwinnett College-Marietta	038044

Hawaii

from: University of Hawaii System Office *to:* University of Hawaii System	007885

Illinois

from: Southern Illinois University *to:* Southern Illinois University System	008237
from: University of Illinois Chicago College of Medicine at Rockford *to:* University of Illinois College of Medicine at Rockford	770183
from: University of Illinois University Administration *to:* University of Illinois System	008001

Indiana

from: Kaplan College *to:* Brightwood College	022018
from: Kaplan College *to:* Brightwood College	770575
from: Purdue University Calumet *to:* Purdue University Northwest	001827

Kansas

from: Kansas State University-Salina, College of Technology and Aviation *to:* Kansas State University Polytechnic, College of Technology and Aviation	004611
from: Seward County Community College/Area Technical School *to:* Seward County Community College	008228

Louisiana

from: Career Technical College *to:* McCann School of Business and Technology	026068
from: Our Lady of Holy Cross College *to:* University of Holy Cross	002023

Maryland

from: TESST College of Technology *to:* Brightwood College	007491
from: TESST College of Technology *to:* Brightwood College	010410
from: TESST College of Technology *to:* Brightwood College	020836

Michigan

	FICE/ID Number
from: Kendall College of Art & Design *to:* Kendall College of Art & Design of Ferris State University	770273

Minnesota

from: William Mitchell College of Law *to:* Mitchell Hamline School of Law	002391

Missouri

from: Calvary Bible College and Theological Seminary *to:* Calvary University	002450

Nebraska

from: Doane College *to:* Doane University	002544

Nevada

from: Kaplan College *to:* Brightwood College	030432

New Jersey

from: Felician College *to:* Felician University	002610
from: Rutgers School of Health Related Professions *to:* Rutgers School of Health Professions	020668
from: Thomas Edison State College *to:* Thomas Edison State University	021922

New York

from: Mandl School *to:* Mandl School - The College of Allied Health	007401
from: State University of New York College of Agriculture and Technology at Morri *to:* Morrisville State College	002859

North Carolina

from: Kaplan College *to:* Brightwood College	770543
from: Laurel University *to:* John Wesley University	002935

North Dakota

from: Ft. Berthold Community College *to:* Nueta Hidatsa Sahnish College	025537
from: Trinity Bible College *to:* Trinity Bible College & Graduate School	012059

Ohio

from: Kaplan College *to:* Brightwood College	020520

Oklahoma

from: Hillsdale Free Will Baptist College *to:* Randall University	010266

Oregon

from: National College of Natural Medicine *to:* National University of Natural Medicine	025340

FICE/ID Number

from: National College of Technical Instruction-College of Emergency Services — 667128
to: College of Emergency Services

Pennsylvania

from: Cabrini College — 003241
to: Cabrini University

from: Kaplan Career Institute — 004910
to: Brightwood Career Institute

from: Kaplan Career Institute — 022898
to: Brightwood Career Institute

from: Kaplan Career Institute - ICM Campus — 007436
to: Brightwood Career Institute

from: Kaplan Career Institute/Broomall Campus — 007781
to: Brightwood Career Institute - Broomall Campus

from: Metropolitan Career Center Computer Technology Institute — 031091
to: The Workforce Institute's City College

from: Venango College of Clarion University — 003319
to: Clarion University Venango College

from: Williamson Free School of Mechanical Trades — 041238
to: Williamson College of the Trades

Tennessee

from: Daymar Institute — 004934
to: Daymar College

from: Daymar Institute — 666392
to: Daymar College

from: Daymar Institute — 666492
to: Daymar College

from: Kaplan College — 023262
to: Brightwood College

from: Vatterot Career College — 770592
to: Vatterott Career College

Texas

from: Chamberlain College of Nursing-Houston — 770500
to: Chamberlain College of Nursing-Houston Campus

from: Chamberlain College of Nursing-Pearland Campus — 770934
to: Chamberlain College of Nursing-Pearland

from: Fortis Institute — 770937
to: Fortis College

from: Kaplan College — 009466
to: Brightwood College

from: Kaplan College — 025919
to: Brightwood College

from: Kaplan College — 031158
to: Brightwood College

from: Kaplan College — 032723
to: Brightwood College

from: Kaplan College — 770544
to: Brightwood College

from: Kaplan College — 770545
to: Brightwood College

from: Kaplan College — 770546
to: Brightwood College

from: Kaplan College — 770547
to: Virginia College

from: Kaplan College — 770595
to: Brightwood College

from: Kaplan College — 770596
to: Brightwood College

from: Kaplan College — 770597
to: Brightwood College

from: Kaplan College — 770598
to: Brightwood College

FICE/ID Number

from: School of Automotive Machinists — 030323
to: School of Automotive Machinists & Technology

from: South Texas College of Law/Houston — 004977
to: Houston College of Law

from: Texas School of Business — 023122
to: Brightwood College

from: Texas School of Business-Friendswood — 667051
to: Brightwood College-Friendswood

from: University of Texas - Pan American — 003599
to: The University of Texas Rio Grande Valley

Vermont

from: Castleton State College — 003683
to: Castleton University

from: SIT — 008860
to: School for International Training (SIT)

Virginia

from: Career Training Solutions — 036543
to: Eastern Virginia Career College

from: Riverside School of Health Careers — 021400
to: Riverside College of Health Careers

Washington

from: Green River Community College — 003780
to: Green River College

from: Yakima Valley Community College — 003805
to: Yakima Valley College

Codes and Descriptions of Administrative Officers

(01) **Chief Executive Officer (President/Chancellor)** - Directs all affairs and operations of a higher education institution.

(02) **Chief Executive Officer Within a System (President/Chancellor)** - Directs all affairs and operations of a campus or an institution which is part of a university-wide system.

(03) **Executive Vice President** - Responsible for all or most functions and operations of an institution under the direction of the Chief Executive Officer.

(04) **Administrative Assistant to the President** - Senior administrative assistant to the Chief Executive Officer.

(05) **Chief Academic Officer** - Directs the academic program of the institution. Typically includes academic planning, teaching, research, extensions and coordination of interdepartmental affairs. May include Provost.

(06) **Registrar** - Responsible for student registration, scheduling of classes, examinations and classroom facilities, student records and related matters.

(07) **Director of Admissions** - Responsible for the recruitment, selection and admission of students.

(08) **Chief Library Officer** - Directs the activities of all institutional libraries.

(09) **Director of Institutional Research** - Conducts research and studies on the institution including design of studies, data collection, analysis and reporting.

(10) **Chief Financial/Business Officer** - Directs business and financial affairs including accounting, purchasing, investments, auxiliary enterprises and related business matters.

(11) **Chief of Operations/Administration** - Responsible for administrative functions that are generally non-academic and non-financial.

(12) **Director of Branch Campus** - Official who is in charge of a branch campus.

(13) **Chief Information Technology Officer (CIO)** - Responsible for oversight of IT infrastructure and support, computation and communication infrastructure and services, and administrative information systems across the institution.

(14) **Associate Information Technology Officer** - Assists and reports to the Chief Information Officer.

(15) **Chief Human Resources Officer** - Administers the institution's personnel policies and programs for staff or faculty and staff.

(16) **Associate Human Resources Officer** - Assists and reports to the Chief Human Resources Officer.

(17) **Chief of Health Care Professions** - Senior administrator of academic health care programs, hospitals, clinic or affiliated healthcare programs.

(18) **Chief Facilities/Physical Plant Officer** - Responsible for the construction, rehabilitation and maintenance of buildings and grounds.

(19) **Director of Security/Safety** - Manages campus police. Responsible for security programs, training, traffic and parking regulations.

(20) **Associate Academic Officer** - Responsible for many of the functions and operations under the direction of the Chief Academic Officer.

(21) **Associate Business Officer** - Assists and reports to the Chief Business Officer. May include Controller.

(22) **Director of Affirmative Action/Equal Opportunity** - Responsible for the institution's program relating to affirmative action and equal opportunity.

(23) **Director of Health Services** - Directs the operation of clinics, medical staff and other programs which provide institutional health services.

(24) **Director of Educational Media** - Responsible for audio-visual services and multimedia learning devices.

(25) **Chief Contract and Grants Administrator** - Conducts administrative activities in connection with contracts and grants.

(26) **Chief Public Relations/Marketing/Communications Officer** - Directs public relations program. May include alumni relations, publication, marketing and development.

(27) **Associate Public Relations/Marketing/Communications Officer** - Assists and reports to the Chief Public Relations/Marketing/Communications Officer.

(28) **Director of Diversity** - Responsible for the institution's diversity programs.

(29) **Director of Alumni Relations** - Coordinates alumni activities between the institution and the alumni.

(30) **Chief Development/Advancement Officer** - Organizes and directs programs connected with the fund raising activities of the institution. May include Advancement.

(31) **Chief Community Relations Officer** - Directs the educational (usually non-credit), cultural and recreational services to the community.

(32) **Chief Student Affairs/Student Life Officer** - Responsible for the direction of student life programs including counseling and testing, housing, placement, student union, relationships with student organizations and related functions.

(33) **Dean of Men** - Directs student life activities solely concerned with male students.

(34) **Dean of Women** - Directs student life activities solely concerned with female students.

(35) **Associate Student Affairs/Student Life Officer** - Assists Chief Student Life Officer in the non-academic student life activities.

(36) **Director of Student Placement** - Directs the operation of the student placement office to provide career counseling and job placement services to undergraduates, graduates and alumni.

(37) **Director of Student Financial Aid** - Directs the administration of all forms of student aid.

(38) **Director of Student Counseling** - Directs non-academic counseling and testing for students including referral to outside agencies.

(39) **Director of Student Housing** - Manages student housing operations.

(40) **Director of Bookstore** - Responsible for the operation of the bookstore including purchasing, advertising, sales, employment, inventory and related functions.

(41) **Athletic Director** - Manages intramural and intercollegiate programs including employment, scheduling, promotion, maintenance and related functions.

(42) **Chaplain/Director Campus Ministry** - Plans, directs the pastoral ministry and religious activities.

(43) **Director of Legal Services (General Counsel)** - Salaried staff person responsible for advising on legal rights, obligations and related matters.

(44) **Director of Annual or Planned Giving** - Operates the annual giving from all supporters of the institutions.

(45) **Chief Institutional Planning Officer** - Directs the long-range planning and the allocation of the institution's resources.

(46) **Chief Research Officer** - Initiates and directs research in using the facilities and personnel in new areas of academic and scientific exploration.

Dean or Director. Serves as the principal administrator for the institutional program indicated:

(47) **Agriculture**
(48) **Architecture**
(49) **Art and Sciences**
(50) **Business**
(51) **Continuing Education**
(52) **Dentistry**
(53) **Education**
(54) **Engineering**
(55) **Evening Division**
(56) **Extension**
(57) **Fine Arts**
(58) **Graduate Programs**
(59) **Home Economics**
(60) **Journalism/Communications**
(61) **Law**
(62) **Library Services**
(63) **Medicine**
(64) **Music**
(65) **Natural Resources**
(66) **Nursing**
(67) **Pharmacy**
(68) **Physical Education**
(69) **Public Health**
(70) **Social Work**
(71) **Special Session**
(72) **Technology**
(73) **Theology**
(74) **Veterinary Medicine**
(75) **Vocational/Occupational Education**
(76) **Allied Health Sciences**
(77) **Computer Science**
(78) **Cooperative Education**
(79) **Humanities**
(80) **Government/Public Affairs**
(81) **Mathematics/Sciences**
(82) **Political Science/International Affairs**
(83) **Social and Behavioral Sciences**
(87) **Summer School/Session**
(89) **Freshmen Studies**
(92) **Honors Program**
(93) **Minority Students**
(94) **Women's Studies**
(97) **General Studies**
(106) **Online Education/E-learning**
(107) **Professional Studies**

(84) **Director of Enrollment Management** - Plans, develops, and implements strategies to sustain enrollment. Supervises administration of all admissions and financial aid operations.

(85) **Director of Foreign Students** - Directs student life activities solely concerned with foreign students.

(86) **Director of Government Relations** - Coordinates institution's relations with local, state, and federal government.

(90) **Director of Academic Computing** - Responsible for operation and coordination of the institution's various academic computer facilities and labs.

(91) **Director of Administrative Computing** - Responsible for operation of the institution's administrative computing facility.

(96) **Director of Purchasing** - Coordinates purchasing of goods and services.

(100) **Chief of Staff** - Senior non-secretarial staff assistant to the President/Chancellor. Manages administration and operations of The Office of the President.

(101) **Secretary of the Institution/Board of Governors** - Responsible for liaison between the Board and the institution. Maintains governance and official Board records.

(102) **Director of Foundation/Corporate Relations** - Directs institution's efforts in the area of soliciting grants and gifts from foundations and corporations.

(103) **Director of Workforce Development** - Directs the institution's efforts in course development and instruction for students and the community in skills necessary to gain employment.

(104) **Director of Study Abroad** - Coordinates and advises students and faculty on academic studies conducted internationally.

(105) **Director of Web Services** - Directs the development, operations and content of the institution's web sites.

(108) **Director of Institutional Assessment** - Facilitates and directs institution-wide assessment activities for academic programs and non-academic departments.

(109) **Chief Auxiliary Services Officer** - Responsible for management and operations of college support services including food service, bookstore, vending, student union, and printing.

(88) Use this code for those titles that do not fit the above positions.

(00) **President/Chancellor Emeritus, Chairman of the Board**

United States Department of Education Offices

Dr. John B. King Jr. (A)
Secretary of Education
United States Department of Education
400 Maryland Avenue, SW
Washington, DC 20202
(202) 401-3000
FAX: (202) 260-7867
URL: www.ed.gov

Mr. Ted Mitchell (B)
Under Secretary of Education
United States Department of Education
400 Maryland Avenue, SW
Room 7E307
Washington, DC 20202
(202) 401-0264
URL: www.ed.gov/ous/

Lynn Mahaffie (C)
Assistant Secretary
Office of Postsecondary Education
United States Department of Education
400 Maryland Avenue, SW
Room 6C107
Washington, DC 20202
(202) 453-7862
URL: www2.ed.gov/about/offices/list/ope/index.html

Jennifer Hong Ed.D. (D)
Executive Director
National Advisory Committee on Institutional Quality & Integrity
Office of Postsecondary Education
United States Department of Education
400 Maryland Avenue, SW
Room 6W250
Washington, DC 20202
(202) 453-7805
E-MAIL: jennifer.hong@ed.gov
URL: www.ed.gov/about/bdscomm/list/naciqi.html

Herman Bounds Jr., Ed.S. (E)
Director
Accreditation Group
Office of Postsecondary Education
U.S. Department of Education
400 Maryland Avenue, SW
Room 6W243
Washington, DC 20202
(202) 453-7615
E-MAIL: herman.bounds@ed.gov
URL: www2.ed.gov/admins/finaid/accred/index.html

Dr. Peggy G. Carr (F)
Acting Commissioner
National Center for Education Statistics
550 12th Street, SW
Room 4067
Washington, DC 20202
(202) 245-6168
URL: www.nces.ed.gov

Jennifer Hong Ed.D. (G)
Executive Director
National Committee on Foreign Medical Education
and Accreditation (NCFMEA)
Office of Postsecondary Education
United States Department of Education
400 Maryland Avenue, SW
Room 6W250
Washington, DC 20202
(202) 453-7805
E-MAIL: jennifer.hong@ed.gov
URL: www2.ed.gov/about/bdscomm/list/ncfmea.html

Statewide Agencies of Higher Education

ALABAMA

Alabama Commission on Higher Education (H)
PO Box 302000
Montgomery, AL 36130-2000
(334) 242-1998
FAX: (334) 242-0268
Dr. Gregory G. Fitch
Executive Director
E-MAIL: gregory.fitch@ache.alabama.gov
URL: www.ache.alabama.gov

Alabama Community College System (I)
PO Box 302130
Montgomery, AL 36130-2130
(334) 293-4524
FAX: (334) 293-4526
Mark A. Heinrich Ph.D.
Chancellor
E-MAIL: mark.heinrich@accs.edu
URL: www.accs.edu

ALASKA

Alaska Commission on Postsecondary Education (J)
PO Box 110505
Juneau, AK 99811-0505
(907) 465-6740
FAX: (907) 465-3293
Ms. Stephanie Butler
Interim Executive Director
E-MAIL: ACPE.execdirector@alaska.gov
URL: www.acpe.alaska.gov

ARIZONA

Arizona Board of Regents (K)
2020 North Central Avenue
Suite 230
Phoenix, AZ 85004-4593
(602) 229-2500
FAX: (602) 229-2555
Eileen Klein
President
E-MAIL: eileen.klein@azregents.edu
URL: www.azregents.edu

Arizona Commission for Postsecondary Education (L)
2020 North Central Avenue
Suite 650
Phoenix, AZ 85004-4503
(602) 258-2435
FAX: (602) 258-2483
Dr. April L. Osborn
Executive Director
E-MAIL: acpe@azhighered.gov
URL: highered.az.gov

ARKANSAS

Arkansas Department of Higher Education (M)
423 Main Street
Suite 400
Little Rock, AR 72201
(501) 371-2030
FAX: (501) 371-2003
Dr. Maria Markham
Director of Higher Education
E-MAIL: maria.markham@adhe.edu
URL: www.adhe.edu

CALIFORNIA

California Community Colleges Chancellor's Office (N)
1102 Q Street
Suite 4550
Sacramento, CA 95811
(916) 322-4005
FAX: (916) 322-4783
Mr. Erik E. Skinner
Interim Chancellor
E-MAIL: eskinner@cccco.edu
URL: www.cccco.edu

COLORADO

Colorado Department of Higher Education (O)
1560 Broadway
Suite 1600
Denver, CO 80202
(303) 862-3001
FAX: (303) 996-1329
Lt.Gov. Donna Lynne
Acting Executive Director
E-MAIL: donnalynne.executivedirector@dhe.state.co.us
URL: highered.colorado.gov

Colorado Community College System (P)
9101 East Lowry Boulevard
Denver, CO 80230-6011
(303) 595-1552
FAX: (303) 620-4043
Dr. Nancy J. McCallin
President
E-MAIL: president@cccs.edu
URL: www.cccs.edu

CONNECTICUT

Board of Regents for Higher Education (Q)
Connecticut State Colleges & Universities
39 Woodland Street
Hartford, CT 06105
(860) 723-0011
FAX: (860) 723-0009
Mark Ojakian
President
E-MAIL: ojakianm@ct.edu
URL: www.ct.edu

Office of Higher Education (R)
61 Woodland Street
Hartford, CT 06105-2326
(860) 947-1801
FAX: (860) 947-1309
Mr. Keith M. Norton
Acting Executive Director
E-MAIL: knorton@ctohe.org
URL: www.ctohe.org

DELAWARE

Delaware Department of Education Higher Education Office (S)
Townsend Building
401 Federal Street
Suite 2
Dover, DE 19901
(302) 735-4120
FAX: (302) 739-5894
Shana Payne
Director
E-MAIL: dheo@doe.k12.de.us
URL: www.doe.k12.de.us

Delaware Technical Community College (T)
PO Box 897
Dover, DE 19903
(302) 857-1667
FAX: (302) 857-1647
Dr. Mark T. Brainard
President
E-MAIL: brainard@dtcc.edu
URL: www.dtcc.edu

DISTRICT OF COLUMBIA

Office of the State Superintendent of Education Government of the District of Columbia (U)
810 First Street, NE
3rd Floor
Washington, DC 20002
(202) 741-0471
FAX: (202) 727-2019
Antoinette S. Mitchell
Asst Superintendent, Postsecondary & Career Educ
E-MAIL: antoinette.mitchell@dc.gov
URL: www.osse.dc.gov

District of Columbia Higher Education Licensure Commission (V)
810 First Street, NE
2nd Floor
Washington, DC 20002
(202) 481-3951
FAX: (202) 741-0229
Ms. Angela Lee
Executive Director
E-MAIL: osse.elcmail@dc.gov
URL: osse.dc.gov/service/education-licensure-commission-elc

FLORIDA

Board of Governors State University System of Florida (W)
325 West Gaines Street
Suite 1614
Tallahassee, FL 32399-0400
(850) 245-0466
FAX: (850) 245-9685
Mr. Marshall M. Criser III
Chancellor
E-MAIL: chancellor@flbog.edu
URL: www.flbog.edu

Florida Department of Education Division of Florida Colleges (X)
325 West Gaines Street
Suite 1544 Turlington Building
Tallahassee, FL 32399
(850) 245-0407
FAX: (850) 245-9525
Ms. Madeline M. Pumariega
Chancellor
E-MAIL: chancellorfcs@fldoe.org
URL: www.fldoe.org/schools/higher-ed/fl-college-system/

GEORGIA

Board of Regents of the University System of Georgia (Y)
270 Washington Street, SW
Atlanta, GA 30334
(404) 962-3000
FAX: (404) 962-3013
Mr. Henry Huckaby
Chancellor
E-MAIL: chancellor@usg.edu
URL: www.usg.edu

University System of Georgia (Z)
270 Washington Street, SW
Atlanta, GA 30334
(404) 962-3000
FAX: (404) 962-3013
Mr. Henry M. Huckaby
Chancellor
E-MAIL: chancellor@usg.edu
URL: www.usg.edu

HAWAII

University of Hawaii Board of Regents (a)
2444 Dole Street
Bachman Hall, Room 209
Honolulu, HI 96822
(808) 956-8213
FAX: (808) 956-5156
Ms. Jan Sullivan
Chair
E-MAIL: bor@hawaii.edu
URL: www.hawaii.edu/offices/bor/

Statewide Agencies of Higher Education

IDAHO

Idaho State Board of Education (A)
PO Box 83720
Boise, ID 83720-0037
(208) 334-2270
FAX: (208) 334-2632
Mr. Matt Freeman
Executive Director
E-MAIL: matt.freeman@osbe.idaho.gov
URL: www.boardofed.idaho.gov

ILLINOIS

Illinois Board of Higher Education (B)
1 N. Old State Capitol Plaza
Suite 333
Springfield, IL 62701-1377
(217) 782-2551
FAX: (217) 782-8548
Dr. James L. Applegate
Executive Director
E-MAIL: applegate@ibhe.org
URL: www.ibhe.org

Illinois Community College Board (C)
401 East Capitol Avenue
Springfield, IL 62701-1874
(217) 785-0123
FAX: (217) 785-7495
Dr. Karen Hunter Anderson
Executive Director
E-MAIL: karen.h.anderson@illinois.gov
URL: www.iccb.org

INDIANA

Indiana Commission for Higher Education (D)
101 West Ohio Street
Suite 300
Indianapolis, IN 46204
(317) 464-4400
FAX: (317) 464-4410
Mrs. Teresa Lubbers
Commissioner for Higher Education
E-MAIL: tlubbers@che.in.gov
URL: www.che.in.gov

IOWA

Board of Regents, State of Iowa (E)
11260 Aurora Avenue
Urbandale, IA 50322
(515) 281-3934
FAX: (515) 281-6420
Mr. Robert Donley
Executive Director and CEO
E-MAIL: bdonley@iastate.edu
URL: www.regents.iowa.gov

Iowa College Student Aid Commission (F)
430 East Grand Avenue
3rd Floor
Des Moines, IA 50309
(515) 725-3410
FAX: (515) 725-3401
Ms. Karen Misjak
Executive Director
E-MAIL: karen.misjak@iowa.gov
URL: www.iowacollegeaid.gov

Iowa Department of Education Division of Community Colleges and Workforce Preparation (G)
400 East 14th Street
Grimes State Office Building
Des Moines, IA 50319-0146
(515) 281-8260
FAX: (515) 242-5988
Jeremy Varner
Administrator
E-MAIL: jeremy.varner@iowa.gov
URL: www.educateiowa.gov

KANSAS

Kansas Board of Regents (H)
1000 SW Jackson
Suite 520
Topeka, KS 66612-1368
(785) 296-3421
FAX: (785) 296-0983
Dr. Blake Flanders
President and CEO
E-MAIL: bflanders@ksbor.org
URL: www.kansasregents.org

Kansas Legislative Research Department (I)
Room 68 West, State Capitol Building
300 SW 10th Avenue
Topeka, KS 66612-1504
(785) 296-3181
FAX: (785) 296-3824
Mr. Raney L. Gilliland
Director
E-MAIL: kslegres@klrd.ks.gov
URL: www.kslegresearch.org

KENTUCKY

Kentucky Council on Postsecondary Education (J)
1024 Capital Center Drive
Suite 320
Frankfort, KY 40601
(502) 573-1555
FAX: (502) 573-1535
Mr. Robert L. King
President
E-MAIL: mary.allison@ky.gov
URL: cpe.ky.gov

Kentucky Community & Technical College System (K)
300 North Main Street
Versailles, KY 40383
(859) 256-3132
FAX: (859) 256-3116
Dr. Jay K. Box
President
E-MAIL: president@kctcs.edu
URL: www.kctcs.edu

LOUISIANA

Louisiana Board of Regents (L)
PO Box 3677
Baton Rouge, LA 70821-3677
(225) 342-4253
FAX: (225) 342-9318
Dr. Joseph C. Rallo
Commissioner of Higher Education
E-MAIL: joseph.rallo@la.gov
URL: www.regents.la.gov

Louisiana Department of Education (M)
PO Box 94064
Baton Rouge, LA 70804-9064
(225) 342-3607
FAX: (225) 342-7316
Mr. John White
State Superintendent of Education
E-MAIL: louisianabelieves@la.gov
URL: www.louisianabelieves.com

MAINE

Maine Department of Education Office of Higher Education (N)
23 State House Station
Augusta, ME 04333-0023
(207) 624-6600
FAX: (207) 624-6700
Mr. William Beardsley
Deputy Commissioner
E-MAIL: commish.doe@maine.gov
URL: www.maine.gov/doe/

MARYLAND

Maryland Higher Education Commission (O)
6 North Liberty Street, 10th Floor
Baltimore, MD 21201
(410) 767-3301
FAX: (410) 332-0270
James D. Fielder Jr., Ph.D.
Secretary of Higher Education
E-MAIL: james.fielder@maryland.gov
URL: www.mhec.maryland.gov

MASSACHUSETTS

Massachusetts Department of Higher Education (P)
One Ashburton Place
Room 1401
Boston, MA 02108
(617) 994-6901
FAX: (617) 727-6656
Mr. Carlos Santiago
Commissioner
E-MAIL: commissioner@bhe.mass.edu
URL: www.mass.edu

MICHIGAN

Department of Licensing and Regulatory Affairs Corporations, Securities & Commercial Licensing Bureau Licensing Division (Q)
PO Box 30714
Lansing, MI 48909-8214
(517) 241-1017
FAX: (517) 373-3085
Mr. Michael Beamish
Director
E-MAIL: beamishm@michigan.gov
URL: www.michigan.gov/pss

Workforce Development Agency, State of Michigan Division of Education and Career Success (R)
201 North Washington Square
Victor Building, 3rd Floor
Lansing, MI 48913
(517) 335-5858
FAX: (517) 241-8217
Mr. Sean Lively
Division Director
URL: www.michigan.gov/adulteducation

MINNESOTA

Minnesota Office of Higher Education (S)
1450 Energy Park Drive
Suite 350
St. Paul, MN 55108-5227
(651) 642-0567
FAX: (651) 642-0597
Mr. Larry Pogemiller
Commissioner
E-MAIL: info.ohe@state.mn.us
URL: www.ohe.state.mn.us

Minnesota State Colleges and Universities (T)
30 7th Street East
Suite 350
St. Paul, MN 55101-7804
(651) 201-1696
FAX: (651) 297-7465
Dr. Steven J. Rosenstone
Chancellor
E-MAIL: steven.rosenstone@so.mnscu.edu
URL: www.mnscu.edu

MISSISSIPPI

Mississippi Board of Trustees of State Institutions of Higher Learning (U)
3825 Ridgewood Road
Jackson, MS 39211
(601) 432-6198
FAX: (601) 432-6972
Dr. Glenn F. Boyce
Commissioner of Higher Education
E-MAIL: gboyce@ihl.state.ms.us
URL: www.mississippi.edu

Mississippi Community College Board (V)
3825 Ridgewood Drive
Jackson, MS 39211
(601) 432-6684
FAX: (601) 432-6480
Dr. Andrea Mayfield Ph.D.
Executive Director
E-MAIL: info@mccb.edu
URL: www.mccb.edu

MISSOURI

Coordinating Board for Higher Education Missouri Department of Higher Education (W)
PO Box 1469
Jefferson City, MO 65102-1469
(573) 751-2361
FAX: (573) 751-6635
Commissioner of Higher Education
URL: www.dhe.mo.gov/cbhe/

MONTANA

Office of the Commissioner of Higher Education (X)
PO Box 203201
Helena, MT 59620-3201
(406) 444-0374
FAX: (406) 444-1469
Mr. Clayton Christian
Commissioner
E-MAIL: cchristian@montana.edu
URL: www.mus.edu/che

NEBRASKA

Coordinating Commission for Postsecondary Education (Y)
PO Box 95005
Lincoln, NE 68509-5005
(402) 471-2847
FAX: (402) 471-2886
Dr. Michael Baumgartner
Executive Director
E-MAIL: mike.baumgartner@nebraska.gov
URL: ccpe.nebraska.gov

NEVADA

Nevada System of Higher Education (Z)
4300 S. Maryland Parkway
Las Vegas, NV 89119
(702) 889-8426
FAX: (702) 889-8492
Mr. John White
Chancellor
E-MAIL: chancellor@nevada.edu
URL: www.nevada.edu

Nevada System of Higher Education (a)
2601 Enterprise Road
Reno, NV 89512
(775) 784-4901
FAX: (775) 784-1127
Mr. John White
Chancellor
E-MAIL: chancellor@nevada.edu
URL: www.nevada.edu

NEW HAMPSHIRE

New Hampshire Department of Education Division of Higher Education Higher Education Commission (b)
101 Pleasant Street
Concord, NH 03301
(603) 271-0256
FAX: (603) 271-1953
Dr. Edward R. MacKay
Director
E-MAIL: patricia.edes@doe.nh.gov
URL: www.education.nh.gov/highered

Community College System of New Hampshire (c)
26 College Drive
Concord, NH 03301
(603) 230-3501
FAX: (603) 271-2725
Dr. Ross Gittell
Chancellor
E-MAIL: rgittell@ccsnh.edu
URL: www.ccsnh.edu

NEW JERSEY

State of New Jersey Office of the Secretary of Higher Education (d)
20 West State Street, 4th Floor
PO Box 542
Trenton, NJ 08625-0542
(609) 292-4310
FAX: (609) 292-7225
Rochelle Hendricks
Secretary of Higher Education
E-MAIL: njhe@njhe.state.nj.us
URL: www.state.nj.us/highereducation

NEW MEXICO

New Mexico Higher Education Department (e)
2044 Galisteo Street
Santa Fe, NM 87505
(505) 476-8404
FAX: (505) 476-8454
Dr. Barbara Damron
Cabinet Secretary
E-MAIL: exec.admin@state.nm.us
URL: www.hed.state.nm.us

NEW YORK

New York State Education Department (f)
89 Washington Avenue
Education Building, Room 111
Albany, NY 12234
(518) 474-5844
FAX: (518) 473-4909
MaryEllen Elia
Commissioner
E-MAIL: commissioner@nysed.gov

Community Colleges and the Education Pipeline (A)
The State University of New York
SUNY Plaza, 353 Broadway, Room T7
Albany, NY 12246
(518) 320-1276
FAX: (518) 320-1570
Johanna Duncan-Poitier
Senior Vice Chancellor
E-MAIL: johanna.duncan-poitier@suny.edu
URL: www.suny.edu/powerofsuny/educationpipeline/

New York State Education Department Office of Higher Education (B)
Education Building Annex
Room 977
Albany, NY 12234
(518) 486-3633
FAX: (518) 486-2254
Mr. John D'Agati
Deputy Commissioner
E-MAIL: john.dagati@nysed.gov
URL: www.highered.nysed.gov

NORTH CAROLINA

The University of North Carolina (C)
910 Raleigh Road
Chapel Hill, NC 27514
(919) 962-9000
FAX: (919) 843-9695
Dr. Margaret Spellings
President
E-MAIL: president@northcarolina.edu
URL: www.northcarolina.edu

North Carolina Community College System (D)
200 West Jones Street
Raleigh, NC 27603
(919) 807-6950
FAX: (919) 807-7166
Dr. James C. Williamson
President
E-MAIL: williamsonj@nccommunitycolleges.edu
URL: www.nccommunitycolleges.edu

NORTH DAKOTA

North Dakota State Board of Higher Education (E)
600 East Boulevard Avenue
State Capitol
10th Floor, Dept. 215
Bismarck, ND 58505-0230
(701) 328-2960
FAX: (701) 328-2961
Ms. Kathleen Neset
Board Chair
E-MAIL: k.neset@ndus.edu
URL: www.ndus.edu/board

OHIO

Ohio Department of Higher Education (F)
25 South Front Street
Columbus, OH 43215
(614) 466-6000
FAX: (614) 466-5866
Mr. John Carey
Chancellor
E-MAIL: chancellor@regents.state.oh.us
URL: www.regents.ohio.gov

OKLAHOMA

Oklahoma State Regents for Higher Education (G)
655 Research Parkway
Suite 200
Oklahoma City, OK 73104
(405) 225-9100
FAX: (405) 225-9235
Dr. Glen D. Johnson
Chancellor
E-MAIL: gjohnson@osrhe.edu
URL: www.okhighered.org

OREGON

Higher Education Coordinating Commission (H)
775 Court Street NE
Salem, OR 97301
(503) 378-5690
FAX: (503) 947-2435
Ben Cannon
Executive Director
E-MAIL: info.HECC@state.or.us
URL: www.oregon.gov/HigherEd

Oregon Office of Community Colleges and Workforce Development (I)
255 Capitol Street, NE
Salem, OR 97310
(503) 947-2414
Mr. Patrick Crane
Director
E-MAIL: patrick.crane@state.or.us
URL: www.oregon.gov/ccwd

PENNSYLVANIA

Pennsylvania Department of Education Postsecondary and Higher Education Institutions (J)
333 Market Street
12th Floor
Harrisburg, PA 17126-0333
(717) 772-3737
FAX: (717) 772-3622
Dr. Wil Del Pilar
Actg Deputy Secretary, Postsecondary & Higher Educ
E-MAIL: widelpilar@pa.gov
URL: www.education.pa.gov

Pennsylvania Department of Education Liaison to Postsecondary and Higher Education Institutions (K)
333 Market Street
12th Floor
Harrisburg, PA 17126-0333
(717) 783-8228
FAX: (717) 772-3622
Ms. Patricia Landis
Division Chief - Higher and Career Education
E-MAIL: plandis@pa.gov
URL: www.education.pa.gov

RHODE ISLAND

Rhode Island Council on Postsecondary Education (L)
560 Jefferson Boulevard
Warwick, RI 02886
(401) 736-1100
Mr. Jim Purcell
Commissioner of Postsecondary Education
URL: www.ribghe.org

Community College of Rhode Island (M)
400 East Avenue
Warwick, RI 02886
(401) 825-2188
FAX: (401) 825-2166
Dr. Meghan Hughes
President
E-MAIL: president@ccri.edu
URL: www.ccri.edu

SOUTH CAROLINA

South Carolina Commission on Higher Education (N)
1122 Lady Street
Suite 300
Columbia, SC 29201
(803) 737-2275
FAX: (803) 737-2297
Mr. Gary S. Glenn
Interim Executive Director
E-MAIL: gglenn@che.sc.gov
URL: www.che.sc.gov

South Carolina State Board for Technical and Comprehensive Education (O)
111 Executive Center Drive
Columbia, SC 29210
(803) 896-5320
FAX: (803) 896-5281
Dr. Susan Winsor
Interim System President
URL: www.sctechsystem.edu

SOUTH DAKOTA

South Dakota Board of Regents (P)
306 East Capitol Avenue
Suite 200
Pierre, SD 57501
(605) 773-3455
FAX: (605) 773-5320
Dr. Michael G. Rush
Executive Director and Chief Executive Officer
E-MAIL: mike.rush@sdbor.edu
URL: www.sdbor.edu

South Dakota Department of Education (Q)
Office of the Secretary
800 Governors Drive
Pierre, SD 57501-2291
(605) 773-5669
FAX: (605) 773-6139
Dr. Melody Schopp
Secretary
E-MAIL: melody.schopp@state.sd.us
URL: www.doe.sd.gov

TENNESSEE

Tennessee Higher Education Commission (R)
404 James Robertson Parkway
Suite 1900
Nashville, TN 37243
(615) 741-3605
FAX: (615) 741-6230
Mr. Mike Krause
Executive Director
URL: www.tn.gov/thec/

Tennessee Board of Regents (S)
1415 Murfreesboro Pike
Suite 350
Nashville, TN 37217
(615) 366-4448
FAX: (615) 366-3903
Dr. Tristan Denley
Vice Chancellor for Academics
E-MAIL: tristan.denley@tbr.edu
URL: www.tbr.edu

University of Tennessee Board of Trustees (T)
719 Andy Holt Tower
Knoxville, TN 37996-0170
(865) 974-3245
FAX: (865) 974-3074
Ms. Catherine S. Mizell
General Counsel and Secretary
E-MAIL: cmizell@tennessee.edu
URL: trustees.tennessee.edu

TEXAS

Texas Higher Education Coordinating Board (U)
PO Box 12788
Austin, TX 78711
(512) 427-6101
FAX: (512) 427-6127
Dr. Raymund A. Paredes
Commissioner of Higher Education
E-MAIL: raymund.paredes@thecb.state.tx.us
URL: www.thecb.state.tx.us

Texas Higher Education Coordinating Board Division of College Readiness and Success (V)
PO Box 12788
Austin, TX 78711-2788
(512) 427-6247
FAX: (512) 427-6444
Jerel Booker J.D
Assistant Commissioner
E-MAIL: jerel.booker@thecb.state.tx.us
URL: www.thecb.state.tx.us

UTAH

Utah System of Higher Education State Board of Regents (W)
60 South 400 West
Salt Lake City, UT 84101-1284
(801) 321-7101
FAX: (801) 321-7156
David L. Buhler
Commissioner of Higher Education
E-MAIL: dbuhler@ushe.edu
URL: higheredutah.org

VERMONT

Vermont Agency of Education (X)
219 North Main Street
Suite 402
Barre, VT 05641
(802) 479-1043
Mr. Brad James
Education Finance Manager
E-MAIL: brad.james@vermont.gov
URL: www.education.vermont.gov

VIRGINIA

State Council of Higher Education for Virginia (Y)
101 North 14th Street
James Monroe Building
10th Floor
Richmond, VA 23219
(804) 225-2600
FAX: (804) 225-2604
Mr. Peter Blake
Director
E-MAIL: peterblake@schev.edu
URL: www.schev.edu

Virginia Community College System (Z)
300 Arboretum Place
Suite 200
Richmond, VA 23236
(804) 819-4903
FAX: (804) 819-4760
Dr. Glenn DuBois
Chancellor
E-MAIL: gdubois@vccs.edu
URL: www.vccs.edu

WASHINGTON

Washington Student Achievement Council (a)
917 Lakeridge Way, SW
PO Box 43430
Olympia, WA 98504-3430
(360) 753-7872
FAX: (360) 753-7808
Dr. Rachelle Sharpe Ph.D.
Acting Executive Director
E-MAIL: info@wsac.wa.gov
URL: www.wsac.wa.gov

Washington State Board for Community and Technical Colleges (b)
PO Box 42495
Olympia, WA 98504-2495
(360) 704-4355
FAX: (360) 704-4415
Mr. Marty Brown
Executive Director
E-MAIL: mbrown@sbctc.edu
URL: www.sbctc.edu

WEST VIRGINIA

West Virginia Higher Education Policy Commission (c)
1018 Kanawha Boulevard, East
Suite 700
Charleston, WV 25301-2800
(304) 558-0699
FAX: (304) 558-1011
Dr. Paul L. Hill
Chancellor
E-MAIL: paul.hill@hepc.wvnet.edu
URL: www.wvhepc.edu

WISCONSIN

State of Wisconsin Higher Educational Aids Board (d)
PO Box 7885
Madison, WI 53707-7885
(608) 267-2206
FAX: (608) 267-2808
Mr. John Reinemann
Executive Secretary
E-MAIL: heabmail@wi.gov
URL: heab.wi.gov

Wisconsin Technical College System (e)
PO Box 7874
Madison, WI 53707-7874
(608) 267-9066
FAX: (608) 266-1285
Dr. Morna K. Foy
President
E-MAIL: president@wtcsystem.edu
URL: www.wtcsystem.edu

WYOMING

Wyoming Community College Commission **(A)**
2300 Capitol Avenue
5th Floor, Suite B
Cheyenne, WY 82002
(307) 777-7763
FAX: (307) 777-6567
Dr. Jim Rose
Executive Director
E-MAIL: jim.rose@wyo.gov
URL: communitycolleges.wy.edu

AMERICAN SAMOA

Board of Higher Education (American Samoa) American Samoa Community College **(B)**
PO Box 2609
Pago Pago, AS 96799
(684) 699-9155
FAX: (684) 699-6259
E-MAIL: info@amsamoa.edu
URL: www.amsamoa.edu

FEDERATED STATES OF MICRONESIA

Board of Regents College of Micronesia-FSM **(C)**
PO Box 159
Kolonia Pohnpei, FM 96941
(691) 320-2480
FAX: (691) 320-2479
E-MAIL: national@comfsm.fm
URL: www.comfsm.fm

PUERTO RICO

Puerto Rico Council on Education **(D)**
PO Box 19900
San Juan, PR 00910-1900
(787) 641-7100, ext. 2045
FAX: (787) 641-2573
Mr. David Baez-Davila
Interim Executive Director
E-MAIL: dbaez@ce.pr.gov
URL: www.ce.pr.gov

Higher Education Associations

AACSB International-The Association to Advance Collegiate Schools of Business (A)
777 South Harbour Island Boulevard
Suite 750
Tampa, FL 33602-5730
(813) 769-6500
FAX: (813) 769-6559
Mr. Thomas R. Robinson
President and Chief Executive Officer
E-MAIL: mediarelations@aacsb.edu
URL: www.aacsb.edu

AASA, The School Superintendents Association (B)
1615 Duke Street
Alexandria, VA 22314
(703) 528-0700
FAX: (703) 841-1543
Dr. Daniel A. Domenech
Executive Director
E-MAIL: ddomenech@aasa.org
URL: www.aasa.org

AAUW (C)
1310 L Street, NW
Suite 1000
Washington, DC 20005
(202) 785-7700
FAX: (202) 872-1425
Linda D. Hallman CAE
Chief Executive Officer
E-MAIL: connect@aauw.org
URL: www.aauw.org

ABET (D)
415 North Charles Street
Baltimore, MD 21201
(410) 347-7700
FAX: (443) 552-3644
Michael K. J. Milligan Ph.D., PE
Executive Director and CEO
E-MAIL: info@abet.org
URL: www.abet.org

Academy of Legal Studies in Business (E)
University of Florida
College of Business Administration
PO Box 117165
Gainesville, FL 32611-7165
(352) 392-0136
Mr. Robert E. Thomas
Interim Secretary-Treasurer
E-MAIL: rethomas@ufl.edu
URL: www.alsb.org

Academy of Nutrition and Dietetics Accreditation Council for Education in Nutrition and Dietetics (ACEND) (F)
120 South Riverside Plaza
Suite 2000
Chicago, IL 60606-6995
(312) 899-0040, ext. 5400
FAX: (312) 899-4817
Dr. Mary B. Gregoire
Executive Director
E-MAIL: acend@eatright.org
URL: www.eatright.org/acend

Accreditation Commission for Acupuncture and Oriental Medicine (ACAOM) (G)
8941 Aztec Drive
Eden Prairie, MN 55347
(952) 212-2434
FAX: (952) 657-7068
Mr. Mark McKenzie
Executive Director
E-MAIL: mark.mckenzie@acaom.org
URL: www.acaom.org

Accreditation Commission for Education in Nursing (ACEN) (H)
3343 Peachtree Road, NE
Suite 850
Atlanta, GA 30326
(404) 975-5000
FAX: (404) 975-5020
Dr. Marsal Stoll
CEO
E-MAIL: mstoll@acenursing.org
URL: www.acenursing.org

Accreditation Commission for Midwifery Education (ACME) (I)
8403 Colesville Road
Suite 1550
Silver Spring, MD 20910
(240) 485-1803
FAX: (240) 485-1818
Heather L. Maurer MA
Executive Director
E-MAIL: hmaurer@acnm.org
URL: www.midwife.org/Accreditation

Accreditation Committee - Perfusion Education (J)
6663 South Sycamore Street
Littleton, CO 80120
(303) 794-6283
Ms. Theresa Sisneros
Executive Director
E-MAIL: office@ac-pe.org
URL: www.ac-pe.org

Accreditation Council for Business Schools and Programs (K)
11520 West 119th Street
Overland Park, KS 66213
(913) 339-9356
FAX: (913) 339-6226
Mr. Jeffrey Alderman
President & CEO
E-MAIL: info@acbsp.org
URL: www.acbsp.org

Accreditation Council for Pharmacy Education (L)
135 South LaSalle Street
Suite 4100
Chicago, IL 60603
(312) 664-3575
FAX: (312) 664-4652
Peter H. Vlasses, PharmD BCPS
Executive Director
E-MAIL: pvlasses@acpe-accredit.org
URL: www.acpe-accredit.org

Accreditation Review Commission on Education for the Physician Assistant (ARC-PA) (M)
12000 Findley Road
Suite 150
John's Creek, GA 30097
(770) 476-1224
FAX: (770) 476-1738
Ms. Sharon Luke
Executive Director
E-MAIL: executivedirector@arc-pa.org
URL: www.arc-pa.org

Accreditation Review Committee for the Anesthesiologist Assistant (N)
N84 W33137 Becker Lane
Oconomowoc, WI 53066
(612) 836-3311
Ms. Jennifer Anderson Warwick
Executive Director
E-MAIL: arc-aa@arc-aa.org
URL: www.caahep.org/arc-aa

Accreditation Review Committee for the Medical Illustrator (O)
32531 Meadowlark Way
Pepper Pike, OH 44124
(216) 595-9363
Kathleen Jung
ARC-MI Chair
E-MAIL: kijung@aol.com
URL: www.caahep.org/arc-mi

Accreditation Review Council on Education in Surgical Technology and Surgical Assisting (P)
6 West Dry Creek Circle
Suite 110
Littleton, CO 80120
(303) 694-9262
FAX: (303) 741-3655
Mr. Keith Orloff
Executive Director
E-MAIL: info@arcstsa.org
URL: www.arcstsa.org

Accrediting Bureau of Health Education Schools (Q)
7777 Leesburg Pike
Suite 314 N
Falls Church, VA 22043
(703) 917-9503
FAX: (703) 917-4109
Florence Tate
Executive Director
E-MAIL: info@abhes.org
URL: www.abhes.org

Accrediting Commission for Community and Junior Colleges Western Association of Schools and Colleges (R)
10 Commercial Boulevard
Suite 204
Novato, CA 94949
(415) 506-0234
FAX: (415) 506-0238
Dr. Barbara A. Beno
President
E-MAIL: accjc@accjc.org
URL: www.accjc.org

Accrediting Commission of Career Schools and Colleges (S)
2101 Wilson Boulevard
Suite 302
Arlington, VA 22201
(703) 247-4212
FAX: (703) 247-4533
Dr. Michale McComis
Executive Director
E-MAIL: mccomis@accsc.org
URL: www.accsc.org

Accrediting Council for Continuing Education & Training (ACCET) (T)
1722 N Street, NW
Washington, DC 20036
(202) 955-1113
FAX: (202) 955-1118
Mr. Bill Larkin
Executive Director
E-MAIL: info@accet.org
URL: www.accet.org

Accrediting Council for Independent Colleges and Schools (U)
750 First Street, NE
Suite 980
Washington, DC 20002-4223
(202) 336-6780
FAX: (202) 842-2593
Mr. Roger J. Williams
Interim CEO & President
E-MAIL: rwilliams@acics.org
URL: www.acics.org

Accrediting Council on Education in Journalism and Mass Communications (V)
University of Kansas, School of Journalism
1435 Jayhawk Boulevard
Stauffer-Flint Hall
Lawrence, KS 66045-7515
(785) 864-3986
FAX: (785) 864-5225
Prof. Susanne Shaw
Executive Director
E-MAIL: sshaw@ku.edu
URL: www2.ku.edu/~acejmc

ACT, Inc (W)
500 ACT Drive
Box 168
Iowa City, IA 52243-0168
(319) 337-1079
FAX: (319) 337-1059
Mr. Marten Roorda
CEO
E-MAIL: sandy.sermousek@act.org
URL: www.act.org

ACUTA: the Association for College and University Technology Advancement (X)
152 West Zandale Drive
Suite 200
Lexington, KY 40503
(859) 278-3338
FAX: (859) 278-3268
Ms. Corinne Hoch
CEO
E-MAIL: choch@acuta.org
URL: www.acuta.org

American Academy for Liberal Education (AALE) (Y)
1200 G Street NW
Suite 883
Washington, DC 20005
(202) 434-8971
Diane Auer Jones
President
E-MAIL: aaleinfo@aale.org
URL: www.aale.org

American Anthropological Association (Z)
2300 Clarendon Boulevard
Suite 1301
Arlington, VA 22201
(703) 528-1902
FAX: (703) 528-3546
Mr. Edward Liebow
Executive Director
E-MAIL: eliebow@aaanet.org
URL: www.aaanet.org

American Association for Adult and Continuing Education (AAACE) (a)
1827 Powers Ferry Road
Building 14, Suite 100
Atlanta, GA 30339
(678) 271-4319
FAX: (404) 393-9506
Dr. Margaret Eggleston
President
E-MAIL: office@aaace.org
URL: www.aaace.org

American Association for Employment in Education (b)
PO Box 173
Slippery Rock, PA 16057
(614) 485-1111
FAX: (360) 244-7802
Ms. Deb Snyder
Executive Director
E-MAIL: execdir@aaee.org
URL: www.aaee.org

American Association for Marriage and Family Therapy Commission on Accreditation for Marriage and Family Therapy Education (c)
112 South Alfred Street
Alexandria, VA 22314-3061
(703) 253-0517
FAX: (703) 253-0508
Ms. Tanya A. Tamarkin
Director of Education
E-MAIL: coa@aamft.org
URL: www.aamft.org

American Association for Vocational Instructional Materials (d)
220 Smithonia Road
Winterville, GA 30683
(706) 742-5355
FAX: (706) 742-7005
Mr. Gary Farmer
Manager
E-MAIL: sales@aavim.com
URL: www.aavim.com

American Association for Women in Community Colleges (AAWCC) (e)
PO Box 3098
Gaithersburg, MD 20855
Dr. Beverly Walker-Griffea
President
E-MAIL: info@aawccnatl.org
URL: www.aawccnatl.org

American Association of Blood Banks Committee on Accreditation of Specialist in Blood Banking Technology Schools (f)
8101 Glenbrook Road
Bethesda, MD 20814-2749
(301) 215-6586
FAX: (301) 657-0957
Anne Chenoweth
Senior Director Accreditation and Quality
E-MAIL: accreditation@aabb.org
URL: www.aabb.org

American Association of Colleges for Teacher Education (g)
1307 New York Avenue, NW
Suite 300
Washington, DC 20005-4701
(202) 293-2450
FAX: (202) 457-8095
Dr. Sharon P. Robinson
President & Chief Executive Officer
E-MAIL: smonroe@aacte.org
URL: www.aacte.org

American Association of Colleges of Nursing (A)
1 Dupont Circle, NW
Suite 530
Washington, DC 20036-1120
(202) 463-6930
FAX: (202) 785-8320
Dr. Deborah Trautman
President & Chief Executive Officer
E-MAIL: dtrautman@aacn.nche.edu
URL: www.aacn.nche.edu

American Association of Colleges of Osteopathic Medicine (B)
5550 Friendship Boulevard
Suite 310
Chevy Chase, MD 20815-7231
(301) 968-4142
FAX: (301) 968-4101
Stephen C. Shannon DO, MPH
President and CEO
E-MAIL: president@aacom.org
URL: www.aacom.org

American Association of Collegiate Registrars and Admissions Officers (AACRAO) (C)
1 Dupont Circle, NW
Suite 520
Washington, DC 20036-1135
(202) 293-9161
FAX: (202) 872-8857
Mr. Michael Reilly
Executive Director
E-MAIL: reillym@aacrao.org
URL: www.aacrao.org

American Association of Community Colleges (D)
1 Dupont Circle, NW
Suite 410
Washington, DC 20036
(202) 728-0200, ext. 235
FAX: (202) 452-1461
Dr. Walter G. Bumphus
President/CEO
E-MAIL: wbumphus@aacc.nche.edu
URL: www.aacc.nche.edu

American Association of Family and Consumer Sciences (AAFCS) (E)
400 North Columbus Street
Suite 202
Alexandria, VA 22314
(703) 706-4600
FAX: (703) 706-4663
Ms. Carolyn W. Jackson
Chief Executive Officer
E-MAIL: accreditation@aafcs.org
URL: www.aafcs.org

American Association of Medical Assistants (F)
20 North Wacker Drive
Suite 1575
Chicago, IL 60606
(312) 899-1500
FAX: (312) 899-1259
Mr. Donald A. Balasa J.D., MBA
Executive Director
E-MAIL: dbalasa@aama-ntl.org
URL: www.aama-ntl.org

American Association of Physics Teachers (G)
One Physics Ellipse
College Park, MD 20740-3845
(301) 209-3311
FAX: (301) 209-0845
Dr. Beth A. Cunningham
Executive Officer
E-MAIL: eo@aapt.org
URL: www.aapt.org

American Association of Presidents of Independent Colleges and Universities (H)
PO Box 7070
Provo, UT 84602-7070
(801) 422-2235
FAX: (801) 422-0265
Mr. Steven M. Sandberg
Executive Director
E-MAIL: aapicu@byu.edu
URL: www.aapicu.org

American Association of State Colleges and Universities (I)
1307 New York Avenue, NW
5th Floor
Washington, DC 20005-4701
(202) 293-7070
FAX: (202) 296-5819
Dr. Muriel A. Howard
President
E-MAIL: howardm@aascu.org
URL: www.aascu.org

American Association of Teachers of Slavic and East European Languages (J)
University of Southern California
3501 Trousdale Parkway
THH 255L
Los Angeles, CA 90089-4353
(213) 740-2734
FAX: (213) 740-8550
Dr. Elizabeth Durst
Executive Director
E-MAIL: aatseel@usc.edu
URL: www.aatseel.org

American Association of University Professors (K)
1133 19th Street, NW
Suite 200
Washington, DC 20036
(202) 737-5900
FAX: (202) 737-5526
Dr. Julie Schmid
Executive Director
E-MAIL: aaup@aaup.org
URL: www.aaup.org

American Bar Association Section of Legal Education and Admissions to the Bar (L)
321 North Clark Street
21st Floor
Chicago, IL 60654
(312) 988-6746
FAX: (312) 988-5681
Mr. Barry A. Currier
Managing Director Accreditation & Legal Education
E-MAIL: legaled@americanbar.org
URL: www.americanbar.org/groups/legal_education

American Board of Funeral Service Education Committee on Accreditation (M)
992 Mantua Pike
Suite 108
Woodbury Heights, NJ 08097
(816) 233-3747
Robert C. Smith III
Executive Director
E-MAIL: exdir@abfse.org
URL: www.abfse.org

American Catholic Philosophical Association (N)
University of St. Thomas
3800 Montrose Boulevard
Houston, TX 77006
(713) 942-5062
FAX: (713) 942-3464
Dr. Mirela Oliva
National Secretary
E-MAIL: acpa@stthom.edu
URL: www.acpaweb.org

American Chemical Society Committee on Professional Training (O)
1155 Sixteenth Street, NW
Washington, DC 20036
(202) 872-4589
FAX: (202) 872-6066
Ms. Cathy A. Nelson
Assistant Director
E-MAIL: cpt@acs.org
URL: www.acs.org/cpt

American College of Microbiology Committee on Postgraduate Educational Programs (P)
1752 N Street, NW
Washington, DC 20036-2804
(202) 942-9225
FAX: (202) 942-9353
Ms. Peggy McNult
Director
E-MAIL: clinmicro@asmusa.org
URL: www.asm.org/index.php/about-cpep

American College of Nurse-Midwives (Q)
8403 Colesville Road
Suite 1550
Silver Spring, MD 20910
(240) 485-1800
FAX: (240) 485-1818
Ms. Wendy Scott CAE
Interim Executive Director
E-MAIL: info@acnm.org
URL: www.midwife.org

American College Personnel Association (ACPA) (R)
1 Dupont Circle, NW
Suite 300
Washington, DC 20036-1188
(202) 835-2272
FAX: (202) 827-0601
Dr. Cindi Love
Executive Director
E-MAIL: info@acpa.nche.edu
URL: www.myacpa.org

American Collegiate Retailing Association (S)
Texas State University
School of Family and Consumer Sciences
601 University Drive
San Marcos, TX 78666
(512) 245-2155
Dr. Rodney C. Runyan
Director
E-MAIL: rcr56@txstate.edu
URL: www.acraretail.org

American Conference of Academic Deans (ACAD) (T)
1818 R Street, NW
Washington, DC 20009
(202) 884-7419
FAX: (202) 265-9532
Ms. Laura A. Rzepka
Executive Director
E-MAIL: info@acad.org
URL: www.acad.org

American Council for Construction Education (U)
825 W. Bitters Road
Suite 103
San Antonio, TX 78216
(210) 495-6161
FAX: (210) 495-6168
Mr. Michael Holland
President
E-MAIL: acce@acce-hq.org
URL: www.acce-hq.org

American Council of Trustees and Alumni (V)
1730 M Street, NW
Suite 600
Washington, DC 20036-4511
(202) 467-6787
FAX: (202) 467-6784
Mr. Michael Poliakoff
President
E-MAIL: info@goacta.org
URL: www.goacta.org

American Council on Education (W)
1 Dupont Circle, NW
Washington, DC 20036
(202) 939-9300
FAX: (202) 833-4760
Molly Corbett Broad
President
E-MAIL: president@acenet.edu
URL: www.acenet.edu

American Council on Education Center for Education Attainment and Innovation (X)
1 Dupont Circle, NW
Suite 250
Washington, DC 20036
(202) 939-9306
FAX: (202) 833-3005
Dr. Deborah Seymour
Chief Academic Innovation Officer
E-MAIL: dseymour@acenet.edu
URL: www.acenet.edu

American Counseling Association (Y)
6101 Stevenson Avenue
Alexandria, VA 22304
(800) 347-6647, ext. 231
FAX: (800) 473-2329
Mr. Richard Yep CAE, FASAE
Chief Executive Officer
E-MAIL: ryep@counseling.org
URL: www.counseling.org

American Culinary Federation Education Foundation Accrediting Commission (Z)
180 Center Place Way
St. Augustine, FL 32095
(904) 824-4468
FAX: (904) 940-0741
Ms. Lori Weber
Director of Education & Programs
E-MAIL: lweber@acfchefs.net
URL: www.acfchefs.org

American Educational Research Association (a)
1430 K Street, NW
Suite 1200
Washington, DC 20005
(202) 238-3200
FAX: (202) 238-3250
Dr. Felice J. Levine
Executive Director
E-MAIL: flevine@aera.net
URL: www.aera.net

American Forensic Association (b)
Box 256
River Falls, WI 54022-0256
(800) 228-5424
FAX: (715) 425-9533
Dr. James W. Pratt
Executive Secretary
E-MAIL: amforensicassoc@aol.com
URL: www.americanforensics.org

American Institute of Architecture Students (c)
1735 New York Avenue, NW
Washington, DC 20006-5209
(202) 808-0075
Sarah Wahlgren Assoc. AIA
2016-2017 AIAS President
E-MAIL: mailbox@aias.org
URL: www.aias.org

American Library Association Office for Accreditation (d)
50 East Huron Street
Chicago, IL 60611-2729
(312) 280-2432
FAX: (312) 280-2433
Karen O'Brien
Director, Office for Accreditation
E-MAIL: accred@ala.org
URL: www.ala.org/accreditation

American Mathematical Association of Two Year Colleges (e)
Southwest Tennessee Community College
5983 Macon Cove
Memphis, TN 38134
(901) 333-5643
FAX: (901) 333-5651
Wanda Garner
Executive Director
E-MAIL: amatyc@amatyc.org
URL: www.amatyc.org

American Occupational Therapy Association (f)
4720 Montgomery Lane
Suite 200
Bethesda, MD 20814-3449
(301) 652-6611 Ext. 2914
FAX: (240) 762-5140
Dr. Heather Stagliano
Director of Accreditation
E-MAIL: accred@aota.org
URL: www.aota.org

American Optometric Association Accreditation Council on Optometric Education (g)
243 North Lindbergh Boulevard
Floor 1
St. Louis, MO 63141
(314) 991-4100
FAX: (314) 991-4101
Ms. Joyce L. Urbeck
Director
E-MAIL: jlurbeck@aoa.org
URL: www.theacoe.org

American Osteopathic Association (h)
Commission on Osteopathic College Accreditation
142 East Ontario Street
Chicago, IL 60611-2864
(312) 202-8124
Dr. Alissa Craft DO, MBA
Secretary
E-MAIL: predoc@osteopathic.org
URL: www.aoacoca.org

American Physical Therapy Association (A)
1111 North Fairfax Street
Alexandria, VA 22314
(703) 706-3253
Mr. Justin Moore
Chief Executive Officer
E-MAIL: dorisellmore@apta.org
URL: www.apta.org

American Political Science Association (B)
1527 New Hampshire Avenue, NW
Washington, DC 20036
(202) 483-2512
FAX: (202) 483-2657
Dr. Steven Rathgeb Smith
Executive Director
E-MAIL: apsa@apsanet.org
URL: www.apsanet.org

American Psychological Association Office of Program Consultation & Accreditation (C)
750 First Street, NE
Washington, DC 20002-4242
(202) 572-3037
Dr. Jacqueline Remondet Wall
Director
E-MAIL: apaaccred@apa.org
URL: www.apa.org/ed/accreditation/

American Real Estate and Urban Economics Association (D)
PO Box 3061110
Tallahassee, FL 32306-1110
(850) 644-7898
FAX: (850) 644-4077
Ms. Liz Laffitte
Executive Director
E-MAIL: elaffitte@fsu.edu
URL: www.areuea.org

American Society for Engineering Education (E)
1818 N Street, NW
Suite 600
Washington, DC 20036
(202) 331-3545
FAX: (202) 265-8504
Dr. Norman L. Fortenberry
Executive Director
E-MAIL: n.fortenberry@asee.org
URL: www.asee.org

American Society for Microbiology (F)
1752 N Street, NW
Washington, DC 20036
(202) 942-9264
FAX: (202) 942-9329
Ms. Amy L. Chang
Director, Education Department
E-MAIL: education@asmusa.org
URL: www.asm.org

American Society of Cytopathology Cytotechnology Programs Review Committee (CPRC) (G)
100 West 10th Street
Suite 605
Wilmington, DE 19801
(302) 543-6583
FAX: (302) 543-6597
Deborah M. Sheldon
Cytology Education Coordinator
E-MAIL: asc@cytopathology.org
URL: www.cytopathology.org

American Society of Landscape Architects Landscape Architectural Accreditation Board (H)
636 Eye Street, NW
Washington, DC 20001-3736
(202) 216-2359
FAX: (202) 898-1185
Mr. Kristopher Pritchard
Accred & Education Programs Manager
E-MAIL: kpritchard@asla.org
URL: www.asla.org

American Speech-Language-Hearing Association (I)
2200 Research Boulevard
Rockville, MD 20850
(301) 296-5700
Dr. Arlene A. Pietrantan
Chief Executive Officer
E-MAIL: accreditation@asha.org
URL: www.asha.org

American Student Government Association (J)
412 NW 16th Avenue
Gainesville, FL 32601-4203
(352) 373-6907
FAX: (352) 373-8120
Mr. W. H. Oxendine Jr.
Executive Director
E-MAIL: info@asgaonline.com
URL: www.asgahome.com

American Veterinary Medical Association (K)
1931 North Meacham Road
Suite 100
Schaumburg, IL 60173
(800) 248-2862
FAX: (847) 285-5732
Dr. Karen Martens Brandt
Director Education and Research
E-MAIL: kbrandt@avma.org
URL: www.avma.org

APPA (L)
1643 Prince Street
Alexandria, VA 22314
(703) 684-1446
FAX: (703) 549-2772
E. Lander Medlin
Executive Vice President
E-MAIL: lander@appa.org
URL: www.appa.org

Association for Asian Studies (M)
825 Victors Way
Suite 310
Ann Arbor, MI 48108
(734) 665-2490
FAX: (734) 665-3801
Mr. Michael Paschal
Executive Director
E-MAIL: mpaschal@asian-studies.org
URL: www.asian-studies.org

Association for Biblical Higher Education Commission on Accreditation (N)
5850 T.G. Lee Boulevard
Suite 130
Orlando, FL 32822
(407) 207-0808
FAX: (407) 207-0840
Dr. Ronald C. Kroll
Director, Commission on Accreditation
E-MAIL: coa@abhe.org
URL: www.abhe.org

Association for Business Communication (O)
355 Shanks Hall (0112)
181 Turner Street, NW
Blacksburg, VA 24061
(540) 231-8460
FAX: (540) 231-1452
Dr. James Dubinsky
Executive Director
E-MAIL: exec_director@businesscommunication.org
URL: www.businesscommunication.org

Association for Business Simulation and Experiential Learning (P)
University of South Carolina Aiken
School of Business Administration
471 University Parkway
Aiken, SC 29801
(803) 641-3340
Dr. Mick Fekula
VP/Executive Director
E-MAIL: mickf@usca.edu
URL: www.absel.org

The Association for Canadian Studies in the United States (ACSUS) (Q)
732 Clemens Hall
University of Buffalo - SUNY
Buffalo, NY 14260
(716) 645-0829
FAX: (716) 645-5976
Mr. Munroe Eagles
President
E-MAIL: info@acsus.org
URL: www.acsus.org

Association for Clinical Pastoral Education, Inc. (R)
One West Court Square
Suite 325
Decatur, GA 30030
(404) 320-1472
FAX: (404) 320-0849
RevDr. Trace Haythorn
Executive Director
E-MAIL: acpe@acpe.edu
URL: www.acpe.edu

Association for Collaborative Leadership (ACL) (S)
c/o NELLCO
80 New Scotland Avenue
Albany, NY 12208
(518) 772-3921
FAX: (518) 694-3027
E-MAIL: admin@national-acl.org
URL: www.national-acl.org

Association for Continuing Higher Education (T)
University of Oklahoma
OCCE Administration Building, Room 129C
1700 Asp Avenue
Norman, OK 73072-6400
(800) 807-2243
FAX: (405) 325-4888
Ynez Henningsen
Executive Secretary
E-MAIL: yhenningsen@acheinc.org
URL: www.acheinc.org

Association for Education in Journalism and Mass Communication (U)
234 Outlet Pointe Boulevard
Suite A
Columbia, SC 29210-5667
(803) 798-0271
FAX: (803) 772-3509
Ms. Jennifer H. McGill
Executive Director
E-MAIL: aejmchq@aol.com
URL: www.aejmc.org

Association for General and Liberal Studies (V)
428 5th Street
Columbus IN 47201
(812) 376-7468
Ms. Joyce Lucke
Executive Director
E-MAIL: execdir@agls.org
URL: www.agls.org

Association for Information Systems (W)
PO Box 2712
Atlanta, GA 30301-2712
(404) 413-7445
Mr. Jody McGinnis
Associate Executive Director
E-MAIL: ed@aisnet.org
URL: aisnet.org

Association for Institutional Research (X)
1983 Centre Pointe Boulevard #101
Tallahassee, FL 32308
(850) 385 4155
FAX: (850) 385-5180
Mr. Jason Lewis
Interim Executive Director & CFO
E-MAIL: jlewis@airweb.org
URL: www.airweb.org

Association for Library and Information Science Education (ALISE) (Y)
2150 N. 107th Street
Suite 205
Seattle, WA 98133
(206) 209-5267
FAX: (206) 367-8777
Mr. Andrew Estep
Executive Director
E-MAIL: office@alise.org
URL: www.alise.org

Association for Prevention Teaching and Research (Z)
1001 Connecticut Avenue, NW
Suite 610
Washington, DC 20036
(202) 463-0550
FAX: (202) 463-0555
Ms. Allison L. Lewis
Executive Director
E-MAIL: info@aptrweb.org
URL: www.aptrweb.org

Association for the Study of Higher Education (ASHE) (a)
UNLV
4505 South Maryland Parkway
Box 453068
Las Vegas, NV 89154-3068
(702) 895-2737
FAX: (702) 895-4269
Dr. Kimberly Nehls
Executive Director
E-MAIL: ASHE@unlv.edu
URL: www.ashe.ws

Association for Theatre in Higher Education (ATHE) (b)
9700 W. Bryn Mawr Avenue
Suite 210
Rosemont, IL 60028
(847) 447-1701
FAX: (847) 447-1150
Mr. Eric Ewald
Executive Director
E-MAIL: erice@athe.org
URL: www.athe.org

Association of Advanced Rabbinical and Talmudic Schools Accreditation Commission (c)
11 Broadway
Suite 405
New York, NY 10004
(212) 363-1991
FAX: (212) 533-5335
Dr. Bernard Fryshman
Interim Executive Director

Association of American Colleges & Universities (d)
1818 R Street, NW
Washington, DC 20009
(202) 387-3760
Dr. Lynn Pasquerella
President
E-MAIL: info@aacu.org
URL: www.aacu.org

Association of American Law Schools (e)
1614 20th Street, NW
Washington, DC 20009-1001
(202) 296-1526
FAX: (202) 296-8869
Ms. Judith Areen
Executive Director
E-MAIL: aals@aals.org
URL: www.aals.org

Association of American Medical Colleges (f)
655 K Street, NW
Suite 100
Washington, DC 20001-2399
(202) 828-0460
FAX (202) 481-7801
Dr. Darrell G. Kirch
President/CEO
E-MAIL: aamcpresident@aamc.org
URL: www.aamc.org

Association of American Universities (g)
1200 New York Avenue, NW
Suite 550
Washington, DC 20005
(202) 408-7500
FAX: (202) 408-8184
Dr. Mary Sue Coleman
President
E-MAIL: leah.norton@aau.edu
URL: www.aau.edu

Association of American University Presses (h)
28 West 36th Street
Suite 602
New York, NY 10018
(212) 989-1010
Peter M. Berkery Jr.
Executive Director
E-MAIL: info@aaupnet.org
URL: www.aaupnet.org

Association of Catholic Colleges and Universities (i)
1 Dupont Circle, NW
Suite 650
Washington, DC 20036
(202) 457-0650
FAX: (202) 728-0977
Michael Galligan-Stierle Ph.D.
President/CEO
E-MAIL: accu@accunet.org
URL: www.accunet.org

Association of College and University Housing Officers-International (A)
1445 Summit Street
Columbus, OH 43201-2105
(614) 292-0099
FAX: (614) 292-3205
Ms. Mary DeNiro
Executive Director
E-MAIL: office@acuho-i.org
URL: www.acuho-i.org

Association of College and University Religious Affairs (B)
University of Puget Sound
1500 N. Warner
CMB #1082
Tacoma, WA 98416
(253) 879-2751
Mr. David P. Wright
President
E-MAIL: dwright@pugetsound.edu
URL: www.acura-online.org

Association of College Unions International (C)
One City Centre
Suite 200
120 West Seventh Street
Bloomington, IN 47404-3925
(812) 245-2284
FAX: (812) 245-6710
Mr. John Taylor
Chief Executive Officer
E-MAIL: acui@acui.org
URL: www.acui.org

Association of Collegiate Conference and Events Directors-International (D)
2900 South College Avenue
Suite 3B
Fort Collins, CO 80525
(970) 449-4960, ext. 300
FAX: (970) 449-4965
Ms. Karen Nedbal
Executive Director
E-MAIL: karen@acced-i.org
URL: www.acced-i.org

Association of Collegiate Schools of Architecture (E)
1735 New York Avenue, NW
3rd Floor
Washington, DC 20006
(202) 785-2324
FAX: (202) 628-0448
Michael Monti Ph.D.
Executive Director
E-MAIL: mmonti@acsa-arch.org
URL: www.acsa-arch.org

Association of Collegiate Schools of Planning (F)
c/o Donna Dodd, Association Manager
6311 Mallard Trace Drive
Tallahassee, FL 32312
(850) 385-2054
FAX: (850) 385-2084
Dr. Lois Takahashi
President
E-MAIL: ddodd@acsp.org
URL: www.acsp.org

Association of Community College Trustees (G)
1101 17th Street NW
Suite 300
Washington, DC 20036
(202) 775-4667
FAX: (202) 223-1297
Mr. J. Noah Brown
President and CEO
E-MAIL: nbrown@acct.org
URL: www.acct.org

Association of Departments of English (H)
85 Broad Street
Suite 500
New York, NY 10004-2434
(646) 576-5130
Dr. David Laurence
Director
E-MAIL: dlaurence@mla.org
URL: ade.mla.org

Association of Departments of Foreign Languages (I)
85 Broad Street
Suite 500
New York, NY 10004-2434
(646) 576-5140
FAX: (646) 458-0033
Dr. Dennis Looney
Director
E-MAIL: adfl@mla.org
URL: www.adfl.org

Association of Governing Boards of Universities and Colleges (J)
1133 20th Street, NW
Suite 300
Washington, DC 20036
(202) 296-8400
FAX: (202) 223-7053
Mr. Richard Legon
President
E-MAIL: rlegon@agb.org
URL: www.agb.org

Association of Graduate Liberal Studies Programs (K)
c/o Duke University
Box 90095
Durham, NC 27708-0095
(919) 684-1987
FAX: (919) 681-8905
Ms. Marialana Weitzel
Administrative Manager
E-MAIL: info@aglsp.org
URL: www.aglsp.org

Association of International Education Administrators (L)
Campus Box 90404
Duke University
Durham, NC 27708-0404
(919) 668-1928
FAX: (919) 684-8749
Dr. Darla K. Deardorff
Executive Director
E-MAIL: aiea@duke.edu
URL: www.aieaworld.org

Association of Jesuit Colleges and Universities (M)
1 Dupont Circle, NW
Suite 405
Washington, DC 20036
(202) 862-9893
FAX: (202) 862-8523
Rev. Michael J. Sheeran S.J.
President
E-MAIL: msheeran@ajcunet.edu
URL: www.ajcunet.edu

Association of Military Colleges and Schools of the United States (N)
12332 Washington Brice Road
Fairfax, VA 22033
(703) 272-8406
Ray Rottman
Executive Director
E-MAIL: amcsus1@gmail.com
URL: www.amcsus.org

Association of Performing Arts Presenters (O)
1211 Connecticut Avenue, NW
Suite 200
Washington, DC 20036
(202) 833-2787
FAX: (202) 833-1543
Ms. Margaret Stevens
Director, Executive Affairs
E-MAIL: info@artspresenters.org
URL: www.apap365.org

Association of Practical Theology (P)
Fordham University
441 East Fordham Road
Keating Hall 303H
Bronx, NY 10458
(718) 817-5965
FAX: (718) 817-3352
Prof. Thomas M. Beaudoin
President
E-MAIL: tbeaudoin@fordham.edu
URL: www.practicaltheology.org

Association of Presbyterian Colleges and Universities (Q)
c/o Agnes Scott College
Box 1102
141 E. College Avenue
Decatur, GA 30030
(470) 443-1948
Mr. Jeff Arnold
Executive Director
E-MAIL: jeff.arnold@presbyteriancolleges.org
URL: www.presbyteriancolleges.org

Association of Public and Land-Grant Universities (R)
1307 New York Avenue, NW
Suite 400
Washington, DC 20005-4722
(202) 478-6040
FAX: (202) 478-6046
M. Peter McPherson
President
E-MAIL: pmcpherson@aplu.org
URL: www.aplu.org

Association of Research Libraries (S)
21 Dupont Circle, NW
Suite 800
Washington, DC 20036
(202) 296-2296
FAX: (202) 872-0884
Dr. Elliott Shore
Executive Director
E-MAIL: elliott@arl.org
URL: www.arl.org

Association of Schools of Allied Health Professions (T)
122 C Street, NW
Suite 650
Washington, DC 20001-2151
(202) 237-6481
FAX: (202) 237-6485
Mr. John Colbert
Executive Director
E-MAIL: john@asahp.org
URL: www.asahp.org

Association of Specialized and Professional Accreditors (U)
3304 North Broadway Street
#214
Chicago, IL 60657
(773) 857-7900
Mr. Joseph Vibert
Executive Director
E-MAIL: aspa@aspa-usa.org
URL: www.aspa-usa.org

Association of Teacher Educators (V)
PO Box 793
Manassas, VA 20113
(703) 659-1708
FAX: (703) 595-4792
Dr. David Ritchey
Executive Director
E-MAIL: dritchey@ate1.org
URL: www.ate1.org

The Association of Technology, Management, and Applied Engineering (ATMAE) (W)
275 N. York Street
Suite 401
Elmhurst, IL 60126
(630) 433-4514
FAX: (630) 563-9181
Mr. John Hausoul
Executive Director
E-MAIL: john@atmae.org
URL: www.atmae.org

Association of Theological Schools in the United States and Canada The Commission on Accrediting (X)
10 Summit Park Drive
Pittsburgh, PA 15275-1110
(412) 788-6505
FAX: (412) 788-6510
Dr. Daniel O. Aleshire
Executive Director
E-MAIL: ats@ats.edu
URL: www.ats.edu

Association of University Programs in Health Administration (Y)
2000 14th Street North
Suite 780
Arlington, VA 22201-2543
(703) 894-0940
FAX: (703) 894-0941
Gerald L. Glandon Ph.D.
President & CEO
E-MAIL: gglandon@aupha.org
URL: www.aupha.org

Association of University Research Parks (Z)
6262 North Swan Road
Suite 125
Tucson, AZ 85718
(520) 529-2521
FAX: (520) 529-2499
CEO
E-MAIL: info@aurp.net
URL: www.aurp.net

Aviation Accreditation Board International (a)
3410 Skyway Drive
Auburn, AL 36830
(334) 844-2431
FAX: (334) 844-2432
Mr. Gary J. Northam
President
E-MAIL: bayenva@auburn.edu
URL: www.aabi.aero

Big Ten Academic Alliance (b)
1819 South Neil Street
Suite D
Champaign, IL 61820
(217) 333-8475
FAX: (217) 244-7127
Ms. Barbara McFadden Allen
Executive Director
E-MAIL: info@btaa.org
URL: www.btaa.org

Broadcast Education Association (c)
1771 N Street, NW
Washington, DC 20036-2891
(202) 602-0584
FAX: (202) 609-9940
Ms. Heather Birks
Executive Director
E-MAIL: heather@beaweb.org
URL: www.beaweb.org

Career Education Colleges & Universities (d)
1101 Connecticut Avenue, NW
Suite 900
Washington, DC 20036
(202) 336-6700
FAX: (202) 336-6828
Mr. Steve Gunderson
President and CEO
E-MAIL: president@career.org
URL: www.career.org

The Carnegie Foundation for the Advancement of Teaching (e)
51 Vista Lane
Stanford, CA 94305
(650) 566-5100
FAX: (650) 326-0278
Dr. Anthony S. Bryk
President
URL: www.carnegiefoundation.org

Center for Women Policy Studies (f)
4620 North Park Avenue
Suite 302W
Chevy Chase, MD 20815
(202) 872-1770
Leslie R. Wolfe
President
E-MAIL: lwolfe@centerwomenpolicy.org
URL: www.centerwomenpolicy.org

CETE (Center on Education and Training for Employment) (g)
The Ohio State University
1900 Kenny Road
Columbus, OH 43210-1016
(614) 292-9072
FAX: (614) 292-3742
Mr. Robert A. Mahlman
Director
E-MAIL: mahlman.1@osu.edu
URL: www.cete.org

College and University Professional Association for Human Resources (CUPA-HR) (A)
1811 Commons Point Drive
Knoxville, TN 37932-1989
(877) 287-2474
FAX: (865) 637-7674
Mr. Andy Brantley
President & Chief Executive Officer
E-MAIL: memberservice@cupahr.org
URL: www.cupahr.org

College Art Association (B)
50 Broadway
Floor 21
New York, NY 10004
(212) 691-1051
FAX: (212) 627-2381
Mr. Hunter O'Hanian
Executive Director
E-MAIL: nyoffice@collegeart.org
URL: www.collegeart.org

The College Board (C)
250 Vesey Street
New York, NY 10281
(212) 713-8000
David Coleman
President and CEO
E-MAIL: asacco@collegeboard.org
URL: www.collegeboard.org

College English Association (D)
Borough of Manhattan Community College
Dept. of Academic Literacy and Linguistics
199 Chambers Street, N499L
New York, NY 10007
(212) 220-1406
Dr. Juliet Emanuel
Executive Director
E-MAIL: cea.english@gmail.com
URL: cea-web.org

College Media Association (E)
355 Lexington Avenue
15th Floor
New York, NY 10017
(212) 297-2195
Meredith Taylor
Executive Director
E-MAIL: mltaylor@kellencompany.com
URL: www.collegemedia.org

Columbia Scholastic Press Association (F)
Columbia University
90 Morningside Drive
Suite B01
New York, NY 10027
(212) 854-9400
FAX: (212) 854-9401
Mr. Edmund J. Sullivan
Executive Director
E-MAIL: cspa@columbia.edu
URL: www.columbia.edu/cu/cspa

Commission on Accreditation for Health Informatics and Information Management Education (CAHIIM) (G)
233 North Michigan Avenue
21st Floor
Chicago, IL 60601-5800
(312) 233-1100
FAX: (312) 233-1948
Dr. Claire Dixon-Lee
Executive Director
E-MAIL: info@cahiim.org
URL: www.cahiim.org

Commission on Accreditation of Allied Health Education Programs (H)
25400 US Hwy 19 N
Suite 158
Clearwater, FL 33763
(727) 210-2350
FAX: (727) 210-2354
Dr. Kathleen Megivern J.D.
Executive Director
E-MAIL: megivern@caahep.org
URL: www.caahep.org

Commission on Accreditation of Healthcare Management Education (CAHME) (I)
6110 Executive Boulevard
Suite 614
Rockville, MD 20852
(301) 298-1820
Mr. Anthony Stanowski
President & CEO
E-MAIL: astanowski@cahme.org
URL: www.cahme.org

Commission on Collegiate Nursing Education (CCNE) (J)
One Dupont Circle, NW
Suite 530
Washington, DC 20036-1120
(202) 887-6791
FAX: (202) 887-8476
Dr. Jennifer Butlin
Executive Director
E-MAIL: jbutlin@aacn.nche.edu
URL: www.aacn.nche.edu/ccne-accreditation

Commission on Dental Accreditation (K)
211 East Chicago Avenue
Suite 1900
Chicago, IL 60611
(312) 440-4653
FAX: (312) 587-5107
Dr. Sherin Tooks
Director
E-MAIL: tookss@ada.org
URL: www.ada.org/coda

Commission on English Language Program Accreditation (CEA) (L)
1001 North Fairfax Street
Suite 630
Alexandria, VA 22314
(703) 665-3400, x101
Dr. Mary Reeves
Executive Director
E-MAIL: mhreeves@cea-accredit.org
URL: www.cea-accredit.org

The Commission on Independent Colleges and Universities (CICU) in New York (M)
17 Elk Street
Albany, NY 12207
(518) 436-4781
FAX: (518) 436-0417
Ms. Laura L. Anglin
President
E-MAIL: info@cicu.org
URL: www.cicu.org

Commission on Massage Therapy Accreditation (N)
5335 Wisconsin Avenue, NW
Suite 440
Washington, DC 20015
(202) 888-6790
FAX: (202) 888-6787
Ms. Kate Ivane Henri Zulaski
Executive Director
E-MAIL: kzulaski@comta.org
URL: www.comta.org

Commission on Opticianry Accreditation (O)
PO Box 592
Canton, NY 13617
(703) 468-0566
Mrs. Debra White
Director of Accreditation
E-MAIL: director@coaccreditation.com
URL: www.coaccreditation.com

Committee on Accreditation for Education in Neurodiagnostic Technology (P)
1449 Hill Street
Whitinsville, MA 01588
(978) 338-6300
FAX: (978) 832-2638
Dr. Jackie Long-Goding RRT-NPS
Executive Director
E-MAIL: office@coa-ndt.org
URL: www.coa-ndt.org

Committee on Accreditation for Polysomnographic Technologist Education (Q)
1711 Frank Avenue
New Bern, NC 28560
(252) 626-3238
Ms. Karen Monarchy Rowe
Executive Director
E-MAIL: office@coapsg.org
URL: www.coapsg.org

Committee on Accreditation for the Exercise Sciences (R)
401 West Michigan Street
Indianapolis, IN 46202
(317) 637-9200
FAX: (317) 634-7817
E-MAIL: trush@acsm.org
URL: www.coaes.org

Committee on Accreditation of Education Programs for Kinesiotherapy (S)
University of Southern Mississippi
118 College Drive
#5142
Hattiesburg, MS 39406-0002
(601) 266-5371
FAX: (601) 266-4445
Jerry W. Purvis
E-MAIL: jerry.purvis@usm.edu
URL: www.akta.org

Committee on Accreditation of Educational Programs for the Emergency Medical Services Professions (T)
8301 Lakeview Parkway
Suite 111-312
Rowlett, TX 75088
(214) 703-8445, ext. 112
FAX: (214) 703-8992
Dr. George W. Hatch Jr.
Executive Director
E-MAIL: george@coaemsp.org
URL: www.coaemsp.org

Conference on College Composition and Communication (U)
1111 West Kenyon Road
Urbana, IL 61801-1096
(877) 369-6283
FAX: (217) 328-0977
Dr. Jessie L. Moore
Secretary
E-MAIL: cccc@ncte.org
URL: www.ncte.org/cccc

Council for Accreditation of Counseling and Related Educational Programs (CACREP) (V)
1001 North Fairfax Street
Suite 510
Alexandria, VA 22314
(703) 535-5990
FAX: (703) 739-6209
Dr. Carol L. Bobby
President and CEO
E-MAIL: cacrep@cacrep.org
URL: www.cacrep.org

Council for Adult and Experiential Learning (W)
55 East Monroe Street
Suite 2710
Chicago, IL 60603
(312) 499-2600
FAX: (312) 499-2601
Ms. Pamela Tate
President & CEO
E-MAIL: ptate@cael.org
URL: www.cael.org

Council for Advancement and Support of Education (X)
1307 New York Avenue, NW
Suite 1000
Washington, DC 20005-4701
(202) 328-2273
FAX: (202) 387-4973
Ms. Sue Cunningham
President
E-MAIL: president@case.org
URL: www.case.org

Council for Agricultural Science and Technology (CAST) (Y)
4420 West Lincoln Way
Ames, IA 50014-3447
(515) 292-2125
FAX: (515) 292-4512
Mr. Kent G. Schescke
Executive Vice President
E-MAIL: cast@cast-science.org
URL: www.cast-science.org

Council for Aid to Education (Z)
215 Lexington Avenue
New York, NY 10016-6023
(212) 661-5800, x308
FAX: (212) 661-9766
Dr. Roger Benjamin
President & CEO
E-MAIL: roger@cae.org
URL: www.cae.org

Council for Christian Colleges & Universities (a)
321 8th Street, NE
Washington, DC 20002-6107
(202) 546-8713
FAX: (202) 546-8913
Shirley V. Hoogstra J.D.
President
E-MAIL: council@cccu.org
URL: www.cccu.org

Council for Economic Education (b)
122 East 42nd Street
Suite 2600
New York, NY 10168
(212) 730-7007 or (800) 338-1192
FAX: (212) 730-1793
Ms. Nan Morrison
President and CEO
E-MAIL: njmorrison@councilforeconed.org
URL: www.councilforeconed.org

Council for Higher Education Accreditation (c)
1 Dupont Circle, NW
Suite 510
Washington, DC 20036-1135
(202) 955-6126
FAX: (202) 955-6129
Dr. Judith Eaton
President
E-MAIL: chea@chea.org
URL: www.chea.org

Council for Interior Design Accreditation (CIDA) (formerly FIDER) (d)
206 Grandville Avenue
Suite 350
Grand Rapids, MI 49503
(616) 458-0400
FAX: (616) 458-0460
Ms. Holly Mattson
Executive Director
E-MAIL: info@accredit-id.org
URL: www.accredit-id.org

Council for Research in Music Education (e)
University of Illinois at Urbana-Champaign
1114 West Nevada
Urbana, IL 61801
(217) 244-6310
Dr. Janet R. Barrett
Editor
E-MAIL: crme@illinois.edu
URL: bcrme.press.illinois.edu

Council for the Accreditation of Educator Preparation (f)
1140 19th Street, NW
Suite 400
Washington, DC 20036
(202) 223-0077
Mr. Christopher Koch
President
E-MAIL: caep@caepnet.org
URL: www.caepnet.org

Council for the Advancement of Standards in Higher Education (g)
PO Box 1369
Fort Collins, CO 80522
(202) 862-1400
FAX: (202) 296-3286
Dr. Marybeth Drechsler Sharp
Executive Director
E-MAIL: executive_director@cas.edu
URL: www.cas.edu

Council of Colleges of Acupuncture and Oriental Medicine (CCAOM) (h)
PO Box 65120
Baltimore, MD 21209
(410) 464-6041
FAX: (410) 464-6042
Mr. David M. Sale J.D., LL.M
Executive Director
E-MAIL: executivedirector@ccaom.comcastbiz.net
URL: www.ccaom.org

Council of Colleges of Arts and Sciences (i)
c/o The College of William and Mary
PO Box 8795
Williamsburg, VA 23187-8795
(757) 221-1784
FAX: (757) 221-1776
Amber Elaine Cox MSW
Executive Director
E-MAIL: ccas@wm.edu
URL: www.ccas.net

Council of Graduate Schools (A)
1 Dupont Circle, NW
Suite 230
Washington, DC 20036-1146
(202) 223-3791
FAX: (202) 296-9194
Dr. Suzanne Ortega
President
E-MAIL: president@cgs.nche.edu
URL: www.cgsnet.org

Council of Independent Colleges (B)
1 Dupont Circle, NW
Suite 320
Washington, DC 20036-1142
(202) 466-7230
FAX: (202) 466-7238
Dr. Richard Ekman
President
E-MAIL: cic@cic.nche.edu
URL: www.cic.edu

The Council of Writing Program Administrators (C)
University of Delaware
Department of English
212 Memorial Hall
Newark, DE 19716
(302) 831-2361
Mr. Michael McCamley
Secretary
E-MAIL: mccamley@udel.edu
URL: www.wpacouncil.org

Council on Accreditation of Nurse Anesthesia Educational Programs (COA) (D)
222 South Prospect Avenue
Park Ridge, IL 60068-4001
(847) 655-1154
FAX: (847) 692-7137
Francis Gerbasi CRNA,Ph.D.
Executive Director/Chief Executive Officer
E-MAIL: fgerbasi@coa.us.com
URL: www.home.coa.us.com

Council on Chiropractic Education (E)
8049 North 85th Way
Scottsdale, AZ 85258-4321
(480) 443-8877
FAX: (480) 483-7333
Craig S. Little D.C., M.Ed
President
E-MAIL: cce@cce-usa.org
URL: www.cce-usa.org

Council on Education for Public Health (F)
1010 Wayne Avenue
Suite 220
Silver Spring, MD 20910-5660
(202) 789-1050
FAX: (202) 789-1895
Ms. Laura Rasar King
Executive Director
E-MAIL: lking@ceph.org
URL: www.ceph.org

Council on Governmental Relations (G)
1200 New York Avenue, NW
Suite 460
Washington, DC 20005
(202) 289-6655
FAX: (202) 289-6698
Mr. Anthony DeCrappeo
President
E-MAIL: tdecrappeo@cogr.edu
URL: www.cogr.edu

Council on Higher Education Solutions for Adults (H)
104 Johnson Street
Marshall, TX 75670
(903) 472-2762
FAX: (903) 935-3890
Dr. Tracy Andrus
President/CEO
E-MAIL: tandrus@chesa1.com
URL: www.chesa1.com

Council on Law in Higher Education (I)
9386 Via Classico West
Wellington, FL 33411
(561) 792-4440
FAX: (561) 792-4441
Mr. Daren Bakst
President
E-MAIL: info@clhe.org
URL: www.clhe.org

Council on Naturopathic Medical Education (J)
PO Box 178
Great Barrington, MA 01230
(413) 528-8877
Dr. Daniel Seitz J.D., Ed.D
Executive Director
E-MAIL: danseitz@cnme.org
URL: www.cnme.org

Council on Occupational Education (K)
7840 Roswell Road
Building 300, Suite 325
Atlanta, GA 30350
(800) 917-2081
FAX: (770) 396-3790
Dr. Gary Puckett
President/Executive Director
E-MAIL: puckettg@council.org
URL: www.council.org

Council on Podiatric Medical Education (L)
9312 Old Georgetown Road
Bethesda, MD 20814
(301) 581-9200
FAX: (301) 571-4903
Mr. Alan R. Tinkleman
Director
E-MAIL: artinkleman@apma.org
URL: www.cpme.org

Council on Rehabilitation Education (CORE) (M)
1699 E. Woodfield Road
Suite 300
Schaumburg, IL 60173
(847) 944-1345
FAX: (847) 944-1346
Dr. Frank Lane
Chief Executive Officer
E-MAIL: flane@core-rehab.org
URL: www.core-rehab.org

Council on Social Work Education (N)
1701 Duke Street
Suite 200
Alexandria, VA 22314-3457
(703) 519-2048
FAX: (703) 683-8099
Dr. Jo Ann Regan
VP of Education
E-MAIL: jregan@cswe.org
URL: www.cswe.org

Council on Undergraduate Research (O)
734 15th Street, NW
Suite 550
Washington, DC 20005
(202) 783-4810
FAX: (202) 783-4811
Dr. Elizabeth L. Ambos
Executive Officer
E-MAIL: eambos@cur.org
URL: www.cur.org

CSAB, Inc. (P)
417 Terrace Way
Towson, MD 21204-3725
(410) 339-5456
Ms. Liz Glazer
Executive Director
E-MAIL: lglazer@csab.org
URL: www.csab.org

Cultural Vistas (Q)
440 Park Avenue South
2nd Floor
New York, NY 10016
(212) 497-3500
FAX: (212) 497-3535
Mr. Robert Fenstermacher
President & CEO
E-MAIL: info@culturalvistas.org
URL: www.culturalvistas.org

Decision Sciences Institute (R)
University of Houston
C.T. Bauer College of Business
4750 Calhoun Road
Houston, TX 77204-6021
(713) 743-4815
FAX: (713) 743-8984
M. Johnny Rungtusanathan
Interim Executive Director
E-MAIL: info@decisionsciences.org
URL: www.decisionsciences.org

Direct Marketing Association, Inc. (S)
1333 Broadway
Suite 301
New York, NY 10018
(212) 768-7277
FAX: (212) 302-6714
Mr. Thomas J. Benton
CEO
E-MAIL: dmaeducationinfo@the-dma.org
URL: www.thedma.org

Distance Education Accrediting Commission (T)
1101 17th Street, NW
Suite 808
Washington, DC 20036
(202) 234-5100
FAX: (202) 332-1386
Dr. Leah K. Matthews
Executive Director
E-MAIL: info@deac.org
URL: www.deac.org

Education Commission of the States (U)
700 Broadway
Suite 810
Denver, CO 80203-3442
(303) 299-3600
FAX: (303) 296-8332
Mr. Jeremy Anderson
President
E-MAIL: janderson@ecs.org
URL: www.ecs.org

Education Development Center, Inc. (V)
43 Foundry Avenue
Waltham, MA 02453-8313
(617) 969-7100
FAX: (617) 969-5979
Mr. David Offensend
President and CEO
E-MAIL: contact@edc.org
URL: www.edc.org

EDUCAUSE (W)
1150 18th Street, NW
Suite 900
Washington, DC 20036-3816
(202) 872-4200
FAX: (202) 872-4318
John O'Brien Ph.D.
President and CEO
E-MAIL: jobrien@educause.edu
URL: www.educause.edu

FHI 360 (X)
359 Blackwell Street
Suite 200
Durham, NC 27701
(202) 884-8000
FAX: (202) 884-8400
Dr. Patrick C. Fine
Chief Executive Officer
URL: www.fhi360.org

Financial Management Association International (Y)
University of South Florida
College of Business Administration
4202 East Fowler Avenue, BSN 3416
Tampa, FL 33620-9951
(813) 974-2084
FAX: (813) 974-3318
Ms. Michelle Lui
Executive Director
E-MAIL: fma@coba.usf.edu
URL: www.fma.org

Friends Association for Higher Education (Z)
1501 Cherry Street
Philadelphia, PA 19102
(215) 241-7116
FAX: (215) 241-7078
Ms. Kimberley Haas
Recording Clerk
E-MAIL: fahe@quaker.org
URL: www.quakerfahe.com

The George Washington University HEATH Resource Center at the National Youth Transitions Center Graduate School of Education & Human Development (a)
2134 G Street, NW
Suite 308
Washington, DC 20052-0001
E-MAIL: askheath@gwu.edu
URL: www.heath.gwu.edu

The Gerontological Society of America (b)
1220 L Street, NW
Suite 901
Washington, DC 20005-4001
(202) 587-2821
FAX: (202) 587-2850
Mr. James Appleby
Executive Director and CEO
E-MAIL: geron@geron.org
URL: www.geron.org

Graduate Record Examinations Board (c)
Educational Testing Service
Mail Stop 57L
660 Rosedale Road
Princeton, NJ 08541
(609) 683-2014
FAX: (609) 683-2040
Dr. David G. Payne
Vice President & COO of Global Education Division
E-MAIL: dpayne@ets.org
URL: www.ets.org/highered

H. Wiley Hitchcock Institute for Studies in American Music (d)
Brooklyn College, CUNY
2900 Bedford Avenue
Brooklyn, NY 11210-2889
(718) 951-5655
FAX: (718) 951-4502
Dr. Jeffrey J. Taylor
Director
E-MAIL: isam@brooklyn.cuny.edu
URL: www.hisam.org

Higher Education Resource Services (HERS) (e)
University of Denver
1901 East Asbury Avenue
Denver, CO 80208
(303) 871-6866
FAX: (303) 871-6766
Dr. Judith White
President/Executive Director
E-MAIL: judith.white@du.edu
URL: www.hersnet.org

Higher Learning Commission (f)
230 South LaSalle Street
Suite 7-500
Chicago, IL 60604-1411
(312) 263-0456 / (800) 621-7440
FAX: (312) 263-7462
Dr. Barbara Gellman-Danley
President
E-MAIL: info@hlcommission.org
URL: hlcommission.org

Hispanic Association of Colleges and Universities (g)
8415 Datapoint Drive
Suite 400
San Antonio, TX 78229
(210) 692-3805
FAX: (210) 692-0823
Dr. Antonio R. Flores
President and CEO
E-MAIL: hacu@hacu.net
URL: www.hacu.net

IACLEA (International Association of Campus Law Enforcement Administrators) (h)
342 N. Main Street
West Hartford, CT 06117-2507
(860) 586-7517
FAX: (860) 586-7550
Ms. Sue Riseling
Executive Director
E-MAIL: sriseling@iaclea.org
URL: www.iaclea.org

The Institute for Higher Education Policy (i)
1825 K Street, NW
Suite 720
Washington, DC 20006
(202) 861-8223
FAX: (202) 861-9307
Michelle A. Cooper Ph.D.
President
E-MAIL: institute@ihep.org
URL: www.ihep.org

Institute of International Education (A)
809 United Nations Plaza
New York, NY 10017-3580
(212) 883-8200
Fax: (212) 984-5496
E-mail: info@iie.org
URL: www.iie.org

Institute of International Education Council for International Exchange of Scholars (B)
1400 K Street, NW
Suite 700
Washington, DC 20005
(202) 686-4000
Fax: (202) 686-4029
Maria de los Angeles Crummet
Executive Director
E-mail: scholars@iie.org
URL: www.cies.org

Intercollegiate Broadcasting System, Inc. (C)
367 Windsor Highway
New Windsor, NY 12553-7900
(845) 565-0003
Mr. Fritz Kass
Director-Operations
E-mail: ibshq@aol.com
URL: www.collegeradio.tv

International Assembly for Collegiate Business Education (D)
11374 Strang Line Road
Lenexa, KS 66215
(913) 631-3009
Fax: (913) 631-9154
Mr. Dennis N. Gash
President
E-mail: iacbe@iacbe.org
URL: www.iacbe.org

International Association of Baptist Colleges and Universities (E)
Samford University
800 Lakeshore Drive
Birmingham, AL 35229
(205) 726-2036
Mrs. Ashley Hill
Executive Secretary
E-mail: ashleyhill@baptistschools.org
URL: www.baptistschools.org

International Communication Association (F)
1500 21st Street, NW
Washington, DC 20036
(202) 955-1444
Fax: (202) 955-1448
Ms. Laura Sawyer
Executive Director
E-mail: lsawyer@icahdq.org
URL: www.icahdq.org

International Council on Education for Teaching (G)
5201 University Boulevard
Sue and Radcliffe Killam Library 429A
Laredo, TX 78041
(847) 947-5881
Fax: (847) 947-5881
James O'Meara
President
E-mail: president@icet4u.org
URL: www.icet4u.org

International Fire Service Accreditation Congress (H)
1812 W. Tyler Avenue
Stillwater, OK 74078
(405) 744-8303
Fax: (405) 744-8802
Mr. Clayton Moorman
Director
E-mail: admin@ifsac.org
URL: ifsac.org

Joint Review Committee on Education in Cardiovascular Technology (JRC-CVT) (I)
1449 Hill Street
Whitinsville, MA 01588-1032
(978) 456-5594
Fax: (727) 210-2354
Ms. Jackie Long-Goding
Executive Director
E-mail: office@jrccvt.org
URL: www.jrccvt.org

Joint Review Committee on Education in Diagnostic Medical Sonography (J)
6021 University Boulevard
Suite 500
Ellicott City, MD 21043-6090
(443) 973-3251
Fax: (866) 738-3444
Mr. Gerry Magat
Accreditation Specialist
E-mail: mail@jrcdms.org
URL: www.jrcdms.org

Joint Review Committee on Education in Radiologic Technology (K)
20 North Wacker Drive
Suite 2850
Chicago, IL 60606-3182
(312) 704-5300
Fax: (312) 704-5304
Leslie F. Winter
Chief Executive Officer
E-mail: lwinter@jrcert.org
URL: www.jrcert.org

Joint Review Committee on Educational Programs in Nuclear Medicine Technology (L)
2000 West Danforth Road
Suite 130, #203
Edmond, OK 73003
(405) 285-0546
Fax: (405) 285-0579
Ms. Jan M. Winn
Executive Director
E-mail: mail@jrcnmt.org
URL: www.jrcnmt.org

Journalism Association of Community Colleges (M)
c/o CNPA Services, Inc.
2701 K Street
Sacramento, CA 95816-5131
(916) 288-6021
Fax: (916) 288-6002
Mr. Joe Wirt
Administrator
E-mail: joe@cnpa.com
URL: jacconline.org

LASPAU: Academic and Professional Programs for the Americas (N)
25 Mount Auburn Street
Suite 203
Cambridge, MA 02138-6095
(617) 495-5255
Fax: (617) 495-8990
Ms. Angelica Natera
Executive Director
E-mail: angelica_natera@harvard.edu
URL: www.laspau.harvard.edu

Law School Admission Council (O)
662 Penn Street
Newtown, PA 18940
(215) 968-1001
Fax: (215) 968-1119
President
E-mail: lsacinfo@lsac.org
URL: www.lsac.org

Liaison Committee on Medical Education (LCME) American Medical Association (P)
330 North Wabash
Suite 39300
Chicago, IL 60611-5885
(312) 464-4933
Barbara Barzansky Ph.D.,MHPE
LCME Co-Secretary
E-mail: barbara.barzansky@ama-assn.org
URL: www.lcme.org

Linguistic Society of America (Q)
522 21st Street, NW
Suite 120
Washington, DC 20006-5012
(202) 835-1714
Fax: (202) 835-1717
Ms. Alyson Reed
Executive Director
E-mail: lsa@lsadc.org
URL: www.linguisticsociety.org

Literacy Research Association, Inc. (R)
222 South Westmonte Drive
#101
Altamonte Springs, FL 32714
(407) 774-7880
Fax: (407) 774-6440
Lynn Hupp
Executive Director
E-mail: lhupp@kmgnet.com
URL: www.LiteracyResearchAssociation.org

Lutheran Educational Conference of North America (S)
PMB #377
2601 South Minnesota Avenue
Suite 105
Sioux Falls, SD 57105-4750
(605) 271-9894
Fax: (605) 271-9895
Ms. Wendy Hoyne
Director of Business Operations
E-mail: hoyne@lutherancolleges.org
URL: www.lutherancolleges.org

Marketing EDGE (T)
1333 Broadway
Suite 301
New York, NY 10018
(212) 768-7277
Fax: (212) 790-1561
Terri L. Bartlett
President
E-mail: admin@marketingedge.org
URL: www.marketingedge.org

Medical Assisting Education Review Board (U)
20 N. Wacker Drive
Suite 1575
Chicago, IL 60606-2963
(800) 228-2262
Fax: (312) 899-1259
Mr. Jim Hardman
Assistant Director of Accreditation
E-mail: jhardman@maerb.org
URL: www.maerb.org

Middle States Commission on Higher Education (V)
3624 Market Street
Second Floor West
Philadelphia, PA 19104-2680
(267) 284-5025
Fax: (215) 662-5501
Dr. Elizabeth H. Sibolski
President
E-mail: info@msche.org
URL: www.msche.org

Midwest Association of Colleges and Employers (W)
3601 East Joppa Road
Baltimore, MD 21234
(410) 931-8100
Fax: (410) 931-8111
Ms. Renee Theragood
Executive Director
E-mail: admin@mwace.org
URL: www.mwace.org

Midwestern Higher Education Compact (MHEC) (X)
105 Fifth Avenue South
Suite 450
Minneapolis, MN 55401
(612) 677-2777
Fax: (612) 767-3353
Mr. Larry A. Isaak
President
E-mail: mhec@mhec.org
URL: www.mhec.org

Midwifery Education Accreditation Council (MEAC) (Y)
850 Mt. Pleasant Avenue
Ann Arbor, MI 48103
(360) 466-2080, ext. 4
Ms. Tracy Gartermann
Executive Director
E-mail: info@meacschools.org
URL: www.meacschools.org

Modern Language Association (Z)
85 Broad Street
Suite 500
New York, NY 10004-2434
(646) 576-5000
Fax: (646) 458-0030
Dr. Rosemary G. Feal
Executive Director
E-mail: execdirector@mla.org
URL: www.mla.org

Montessori Accreditation Council for Teacher Education (MACTE) (a)
420 Park Street
Charlottesville, VA 22902
(434) 202-7793
Fax: (888) 525-8838
Dr. Rebecca Pelton
President
E-mail: rebecca@macte.org
URL: www.macte.org

NACAS (b)
3 Boar's Head Lane
Suite B
Charlottesville, VA 22903-4610
(434) 245-8425
Fax: (434) 245-8453
CEO
E-mail: info@nacas.org
URL: www.nacas.org

NASPA-Student Affairs Administrators in Higher Education (c)
111 K Street, NE
10th Floor
Washington, DC 20002-4409
(202) 265-7500
Fax: (202) 898-5737
Dr. Kevin Kruger
President
E-mail: office@naspa.org
URL: www.naspa.org

National Academic Advising Association (d)
2323 Anderson Avenue
Suite 225
Manhattan, KS 66502-2912
(785) 532-5717
Fax: (785) 532-7732
Dr. Charlie L. Nutt
Executive Director
E-mail: nacada@ksu.edu
URL: www.nacada.ksu.edu

The National Academy of Education (e)
500 5th Street, NW
Washington, DC 20001
(202) 334-2340
Fax: (202) 334-2350
Mr. Gregory White
Executive Director
E-mail: info@naeducation.org
URL: www.naeducation.org

National Academy of Kinesiology (f)
PO Box 5076
Champaign, IL 61825-5076
(217) 403-7545
Fax: (217) 351-1549
Ms. Kim Scott
Business Manager
E-mail: nak@hkusa.com
URL: www.nationalacademyofkinesiology.org

National Accreditation Council for Blind and Low Vision Services (g)
PO Box 15368
Chattanooga, TN 37415
(423) 875-2033
Mr. William A. Robinson III
Executive Director
E-mail: bill@nacblvs.org
URL: www.nacblvs.org

National Accrediting Agency for Clinical Laboratory Sciences (h)
5600 North River Road
Suite 720
Rosemont, IL 60018
(773) 714-8880
Fax: (773) 714-8886
Dr. Dianne M. Cearlock Ph.D.
CEO
E-mail: dcearlock@naacls.org
URL: www.naacls.org

National Accrediting Commission of Career Arts & Sciences (i)
4401 Ford Avenue
Suite 1300
Alexandria, VA 22302-1432
(703) 600-7600
Fax: (703) 379-2200
Tony Mirando M.S., D.C.
Executive Director
E-mail: amirando@naccas.org
URL: www.naccas.org

Higher Education Associations

National Association for College Admission Counseling (A)
1050 North Highland Street
Suite 400
Arlington, VA 22201
(703) 836-2222
FAX: (703) 836-8015
Ms. Joyce E. Smith
Chief Executive Officer
E-MAIL: jsmith@nacacnet.org
URL: www.nacacnet.org

National Association for Equal Opportunity in Higher Education (B)
1800 K Street, NW
Suite 900
Washington, DC 20006-2202
(202) 552-3300
FAX: (202) 552-3330
Lezli Baskerville Esquire
President & CEO
E-MAIL: lbaskerville@nafeo.org
URL: www.nafeonation.org

National Association for Ethnic Studies (C)
Virginia Commonwealth University
Founders Hall, Third Floor
827 W. Franklin Street
PO Box 842542
Richmond, VA 23284
(804) 828-8051
E-MAIL: naes@ethnicstudies.org
URL: www.ethnicstudies.org

National Association for Legal Support of Alternative Schools (D)
18520 N.W. 67th Avenue #188
Miami, FL 33015
(800) 456-7784
FAX: (954) 538-8041
Mrs. Chan Trinh
Institutional Representative
E-MAIL: educate@nalsas.org
URL: www.nalsas.org

National Association for Practical Nurse Education and Service, Inc. (E)
2071 N. Bechtle Avenue
PMB 307
Springfield, OH 45504
(703) 933-1003
FAX: (703) 940-4089
Ann Bauer LPN
President
E-MAIL: president@napnes.org
URL: www.napnes.org

National Association of Agricultural Educators (F)
300 Garrigus Building
University of Kentucky
Lexington, KY 40546-0215
(859) 257-2224
FAX: (859) 323-3919
Dr. Wm. Jay Jackman
Executive Director
E-MAIL: jjackman.naae@uky.edu
URL: www.naae.org

National Association of College and University Attorneys (G)
1 Dupont Circle, NW
Suite 620
Washington, DC 20036
(202) 833-8390
FAX: (202) 296-8379
Ms. Kathleen Curry Santora Esq.
President & Chief Executive Officer
E-MAIL: ksantora@nacua.org
URL: www.nacua.org

National Association of College and University Business Officers (H)
1110 Vermont Avenue, NW
Suite 800
Washington, DC 20005
(202) 861-2500
FAX: (202) 861-2583
Mr. John D. Walda
President & Chief Executive Officer
E-MAIL: john.walda@nacubo.org
URL: www.nacubo.org

The National Association of College & University Food Services (I)
2525 Jolly Road
Suite 280
Okemos, MI 48864-3680
(517) 332-2494
FAX: (517) 332-8144
Gretchen M. Couraud CAE, CFRE
Executive Director
E-MAIL: gcouraud@nacufs.org
URL: www.nacufs.org

National Association of College Stores (J)
500 East Lorain Street
Oberlin, OH 44074-1294
(440) 775-7777
FAX: (440) 775-4769
Mr. Robert A. Walton
Chief Executive Officer
E-MAIL: info@nacs.org
URL: www.nacs.org

National Association of College Wind and Percussion Instructors (K)
Department of Music
University of Montevallo
Davis Hall, Station 6670
Montevallo, AL 35115
Dr. Lori Ardovino
President
E-MAIL: ardovinl@montevallo.edu
URL: www.nacwpi.org

National Association of Colleges and Employers (L)
62 Highland Avenue
Bethlehem, PA 18017-9481
(610) 868-1421
FAX: (610) 868-0208
Dr. Marilyn Mackes
Executive Director
E-MAIL: mmackes@naceweb.org
URL: www.naceweb.org

National Association of Educational Procurement (M)
8840 Stanford Boulevard
Suite 2000
Columbia, MD 21045
(443) 543-5540
FAX: (443) 219-9687
Mrs. Doreen Murner
CEO
E-MAIL: dmurner@naepnet.org
URL: www.naepnet.org

National Association of Independent Colleges and Universities (N)
1025 Connecticut Avenue, NW
Suite 700
Washington, DC 20036-5405
(202) 785-8866
FAX: (202) 835-0003
Dr. David L. Warren
President
E-MAIL: geninfo@naicu.edu
URL: www.naicu.edu

National Association of Schools of Art and Design (O)
11250 Roger Bacon Drive
Suite 21
Reston, VA 20190
(703) 437-0700
FAX: (703) 437-6312
Karen P. Moynahan
Executive Director
E-MAIL: info@arts-accredit.org
URL: www.arts-accredit.org

National Association of Schools of Dance (P)
11250 Roger Bacon Drive
Suite 21
Reston, VA 20190
(703) 437-0700
FAX: (703) 437-6312
Karen P. Moynahan
Executive Director
E-MAIL: info@arts-accredit.org
URL: www.arts-accredit.org

National Association of Schools of Music (Q)
11250 Roger Bacon Drive
Suite 21
Reston, VA 20190
(703) 437-0700
FAX: (703) 437-6312
Karen P. Moynahan
Executive Director
E-MAIL: info@arts-accredit.org
URL: www.arts-accredit.org

National Association of Schools of Theatre (R)
11250 Roger Bacon Drive
Suite 21
Reston, VA 20190
(703) 437-0700
FAX: (703) 437-6312
Karen P. Moynahan
Executive Director
E-MAIL: info@arts-accredit.org
URL: www.arts-accredit.org

National Association of State Directors of Teacher Education and Certification (S)
1629 K Street, NW
Suite 300
Washington, DC 20006
(202) 204-2208
FAX: (202) 204-2210
Dr. Phillip S. Rogers
Executive Director
E-MAIL: philrogers@nasdtec.com
URL: www.nasdtec.net

National Association of Student Financial Aid Administrators (T)
1101 Connecticut Avenue, NW
Suite 1100
Washington, DC 20036-4303
(202) 785-0453
FAX: (202) 785-1487
Mr. Justin Draeger
President
E-MAIL: info@nasfaa.org
URL: www.nasfaa.org

National Association of System Heads (U)
3300 Metzerott Road
Adelphi, MD 20783
(301) 445-2780
Rebecca Martin
Executive Director
E-MAIL: rebecca@nash-dc.org
URL: www.nashonline.org

National Catholic Educational Association (V)
1005 North Glebe Road
Suite 525
Arlington, VA 22201-5792
(800) 711-6232
FAX: (703) 243-0025
Dr. Thomas W. Burnford
President/CEO
E-MAIL: president@ncea.org
URL: www.ncea.org

National Coalition for Campus Childrens Centers (W)
P.O. Box 6899
Folsom, CA 95763-6899
(916) 790-8261
FAX: (916) 790-8261
Ms. Tonya Palla
Executive Director
E-MAIL: info@campuschildren.org
URL: www.campuschildren.org

National Collegiate Athletic Association (X)
PO Box 6222
Indianapolis, IN 46206-6222
(317) 917-6222
FAX: (317) 917-6888
Mr. Todd Petr
Managing Director of Research
E-MAIL: tpetr@ncaa.org
URL: www.ncaa.org

National Commission on Orthotic and Prosthetic Education (NCOPE) (Y)
330 John Carlyle Street
Suite 200
Alexandria, VA 22314
(703) 836-7114 x 225
FAX: (703) 836-0838
Ms. Robin Seabrook
Executive Director
E-MAIL: rseabrook@ncope.org
URL: www.ncope.org

National Communication Association (Z)
1765 N Street, NW
Washington, DC 20036
(202) 464-4622
FAX: (202) 464-4600
Nancy Kidd Ph.D.
Executive Director
E-MAIL: nkidd@natcom.org
URL: www.natcom.org

National Council for Continuing Education and Training (a)
PO Box 2916
Columbus, OH 43216-2916
(888) 771-0179
FAX: (877) 835-5798
Jennifer Starkey
Executive Director
E-MAIL: nccetdirector@nccet.org
URL: www.nccet.org

National Council of Instructional Administrators (NCIA) Dept of Educational Administration (b)
141 Teachers College Hall
PO Box 880360
University of Nebraska - Lincoln
Lincoln, NE 68588-0360
(402) 472-8958
FAX: (402) 472-4300
Katherine Wesley
Executive Director
E-MAIL: ncia@unl.edu
URL: ncia.unl.edu

National Council of University Research Administrators (c)
1015 18th Street, NW
Suite 901
Washington, DC 20036
(202) 466-3894
FAX: (202) 223-5573
Mrs. Kathleen M. Larmett
Executive Director
E-MAIL: info@ncura.edu
URL: www.ncura.edu

National Education Association (d)
1201 16th Street, NW
Suite 810
Washington, DC 20036
(202) 833-4000
FAX: (202) 822-7974
Mr. John C. Stocks
Executive Director
E-MAIL: lmallard@nea.org
URL: www.nea.org/he

National Forensic Association (e)
Illinois State University
School of Communication
Campus Box 4480
Normal, IL 61790-4480
(309) 438-8447
FAX: (309) 438-3048
Prof. Megan Koch
National Secretary-Treasurer
E-MAIL: mkoch@ilstu.edu
URL: www.nationalforensics.org

National Institute for Learning Outcomes Assessment (f)
University of Illinois at Urbana-Champaign
360 Education Building
Champaign, IL 61820
(217) 244-2155
FAX: (217) 244-3647
E-MAIL: njankow2@illinois.edu
URL: www.learningoutcomeassessment.org

National League for Nursing (g)
The Watergate Building, 8th Floor
2600 Virginia Avenue, NW
Washington, DC 20037
(800) 669-1656
Dr. Beverly Malone
Chief Executive Officer
E-MAIL: oceo@nln.org
URL: www.nln.org

National Recreation and Park Association Council on Accreditation for Parks, Recreation, Tourism and Related Professions (COAPRT) (A)
22377 Belmont Ridge Road
Ashburn, VA 20148-4501
(703) 858-2141
FAX: (703) 858-0794
Ms. Brenda Beales
Awards and Accreditation Manager
E-MAIL: coaprt@nrpa.org
URL: www.nrpa.org

National Rural Education Association (B)
Purdue University
Beering Hall of Liberal Arts & Education
100 North University Street
West Lafayette, IN 47907
(765) 494-0086
FAX: (765) 496-1228
Dr. John Hill
Executive Director
E-MAIL: jehill@purdue.edu
URL: www.nrea.net

National Society for Experiential Education (C)
c/o Talley Management Group, Inc.
19 Mantua Road
Mt. Royal, NJ 08061
(856) 423-3427
FAX: (856) 423-3420
Haley Brust
Executive Director
E-MAIL: nsee@talley.com
URL: www.nsee.org

National Writing Project (D)
2105 Bancroft Way
#1042
University of California
Berkeley, CA 94720-1042
(510) 642-0963
FAX: (510) 642-4545
Elyse Eidman-Aadahl
Executive Director
E-MAIL: nwp@nwp.org
URL: www.nwp.org

Network of Schools of Public Policy, Affairs, and Administration (E)
1029 Vermont Avenue, NW
Suite 1100
Washington, DC 20005
(202) 628-8965
FAX: (202) 626-4978
Laurel McFarland
Executive Director
E-MAIL: naspaa@naspaa.org
URL: www.naspaa.org

New England Association of Schools and Colleges, Inc. Commission on Institutions of Higher Education (F)
3 Burlington Woods Drive
Suite 100
Burlington, MA 01803-4514
(781) 425-7747
FAX: (781) 425-1001
Dr. Barbara E. Brittingham
President of the Commission
E-MAIL: cihe@neasc.org
URL: cihe.neasc.org

New England Board of Higher Education (G)
45 Temple Place
Boston, MA 02111
(617) 357-9620, ext. 128
FAX: (617) 338-1577
Dr. Michael K. Thomas
President and CEO
E-MAIL: mthomas@nebhe.org
URL: www.nebhe.org

North American Association of Summer Sessions (H)
342 N. Main Street
Suite 301
West Hartford, CT 06117
(860) 586-7530
Mr. Jeffrey D. Melin
Executive Director
E-MAIL: jmelin@naass.org
URL: www.naass.org

Northwest Commission on Colleges and Universities (I)
8060 165th Avenue, NE
Suite 100
Redmond, WA 98052
(425) 558-4224
FAX: (425) 376-0596
Dr. Sandra E. Elman
President
E-MAIL: selman@nwccu.org
URL: www.nwccu.org

Planning Accreditation Board (J)
2334 W. Lawrence Avenue
Suite 209
Chicago, IL 60625
(773) 334-7200
Ms. Shonagh Merits
Executive Director
E-MAIL: smerits@planningaccreditationboard.org
URL: www.planningaccreditationboard.org

Quality Education for Minorities (QEM) Network (K)
1818 N Street, NW
Suite 350
Washington, DC 20036
(202) 659-1818
FAX: (202) 659-5408
Ivory Toldson
President
E-MAIL: itoldson@qem.org
URL: qemnetwork.qem.org

Society for College and University Planning (L)
1330 Eisenhower Place
Ann Arbor, MI 48108
(734) 669-3270
FAX: (734) 661-0157
Mike Moss CAE
President
E-MAIL: info@scup.org
URL: www.scup.org

Society for Slovene Studies (M)
381 Cathance Road
Topsham, ME 04086
Ms. Kristina Helena Reardon
Secretary
E-MAIL: kristina.reardon@gmail.com
URL: www.slovenestudies.com

Society for Values in Higher Education (N)
c/o Western Kentucky University
1906 College Heights Boulevard
#8020
Bowling Green, KY 42101
(270) 745-2907
FAX: (270) 745-5347
Dr. Eric Bain-Selbo
Executive Director
E-MAIL: society@svhe.org
URL: www.svhe.org

Society of American Foresters (O)
10100 Laureate Way
Bethesda, MD 20814-2198
(866) 897-8720
FAX: (301) 897-3690
Mr. Matt Menashes
Chief Executive Officer
E-MAIL: membership@safnet.org
URL: www.eforester.org

Society of Professors of Education (P)
University of West Georgia
Department of L & I
1600 Maple Street
Carrollton, GA 30118-5160
(678) 839-6132
FAX: (678) 839-6097
Dr. Robert C. Morris
Secretary-Treasurer
E-MAIL: rmorris@westga.edu

Southeastern Universities Research Association (Q)
1201 New York Avenue, NW
Suite 430
Washington, DC 20005
(202) 408-7872
FAX: (202) 408-8250
Dr. Jerry Draayer
President & CEO
E-MAIL: draayer@sura.org
URL: www.sura.org

Southern Association for College Student Affairs (R)
Armstrong State University
11935 Abercorn Street
Savannah, GA 31419
(912) 344-2510
Dr. Joe Buck
Executive Director
E-MAIL: joe.buck@armstrong.edu
URL: www.sacsa.org

Southern Association of Colleges and Schools Commission on Colleges (S)
1866 Southern Lane
Decatur, GA 30033-4097
(404) 679-4500
FAX: (404) 994-6592
Dr. Belle S. Wheelan
President
E-MAIL: bwheelan@sacscoc.org
URL: www.sacscoc.org

Southern States Communication Association (T)
College of Charleston
Office of the Dean
School of Humanities and Social Sciences
2 Green Way
Charleston, SC 29424
(843) 953-0760
FAX: (843) 953-0756
Mr. Jerry L. Hale
Executive Director
E-MAIL: director@ssca.net
URL: www.ssca.net

State Higher Education Executive Officers (U)
3035 Center Green Drive
Suite 100
Boulder, CO 80301-2205
(303) 541-1600
FAX: (303) 541-1639
Mr. George Pernsteiner
President
E-MAIL: george@sheeo.org
URL: www.sheeo.org

Tennessee Independent Colleges and Universities Association (V)
1031 17th Avenue South
Nashville, TN 37212
(615) 242-6400
FAX: (615) 242-8033
Dr. Claude O. Pressnell Jr.
President
E-MAIL: pressnell@ticua.org
URL: www.ticua.org

Transnational Association of Christian Colleges and Schools (TRACS) (W)
15935 Forest Road
Forest, VA 24551
(434) 525-9539
Dr. Timothy Eaton
Interim President
E-MAIL: info@tracs.org
URL: www.tracs.org

The Tuition Exchange, Inc. (X)
3 Bethesda Metro Center
Suite 700
Bethesda, MD 20814
(301) 941-1827
FAX: (301) 657-9776
Mr. Robert D. Shorb
Executive Director/CEO
E-MAIL: rshorb@tuitionexchange.org
URL: www.tuitionexchange.org

UNCF (Y)
1805 7th Street NW
Washington, DC 20001
(202) 810-0200
FAX: (202) 234-0222
Dr. Michael Lomax
President & CEO
URL: www.uncf.org

University Aviation Association (Z)
2415 Moore's Mill Road
Suite 265-216
Auburn, AL 36830-6444
(334) 528-0300
Ms. Dawn Vinson
Executive Director
E-MAIL: uaamail@uaa.aero
URL: www.uaa.aero

University Film and Video Association (a)
UNLV Department of Film
4505 Maryland Parkway
Box 455015
Las Vegas, NV 89154-5015
(702) 235-7297
Mr. Francisco Menendez
President
E-MAIL: ufvahome@gmail.com
URL: www.ufva.org

University Photographers' Association of America (b)
Moraine Valley Community College
9000 W. College Parkway
Palos Hills, IL 60465
(708) 974-5495
Mr. Glenn Carpenter
UPAA President
E-MAIL: carpenter@morainevalley.edu
URL: www.upaa.org

University Professional & Continuing Education Association (UPCEA) (c)
One Dupont Circle, NW
Suite 615
Washington, DC 20036
(202) 659-3130
FAX: (202) 785-0374
Dr. Robert Hansen
CEO
E-MAIL: rhansen@upcea.edu
URL: www.upcea.edu

Urban Affairs Association (d)
c/o Urban Studies Program
University of Wisconsin-Milwaukee
PO Box 413
Milwaukee, WI 53201-0413
(414) 229-3025
Dr. Margaret Wilder
UAA Executive Director
E-MAIL: info@uaamail.org
URL: www.urbanaffairsassociation.org

WASC Senior College and University Commission (e)
985 Atlantic Avenue
Suite 100
Alameda, CA 94501
(510) 748-9001
FAX: (510) 748-9797
Mary Ellen Petrisko
President
URL: www.wascsenior.org

Western Interstate Commission for Higher Education (f)
3035 Center Green Drive
Suite 200
Boulder, CO 80301-2204
(303) 541-0201
FAX: (303) 541-0245
Mr. Joseph A. Garcia
President
E-MAIL: jgarcia@wiche.edu
URL: www.wiche.edu

Consortia of Institutions of Higher Education

Alabama Association of Independent Colleges and Universities (A)
5950 Carmichael Place
Suite 213
Montgomery, AL 36117
(334) 356-2220
FAX: (334) 356-2202
Paul M. Hankins
President
E-MAIL: hankinsp@knology.net
URL: www.aaicu.net

Arkansas' Independent Colleges and Universities (B)
One Riverfront Place
Suite 610
North Little Rock, AR 72114
(501) 378-0843
FAX: (501) 374-1523
Dr. Rex M. Horne
President
E-MAIL: rhorne@arkindcolleges.org
URL: www.arkindcolleges.org

Associated Colleges of Central Kansas (C)
210 South Main Street
McPherson, KS 67460
(620) 241-5150
FAX: (620) 241-5153
Ms. Beverly Schottler
Program Director
E-MAIL: bev@mail.acck.edu
URL: www.acck.edu

Associated Colleges of the Midwest (D)
11 East Adams Street
Suite 800
Chicago, IL 60603
(312) 263-5000
FAX: (312) 263-5879
Dr. Christopher Welna
President
E-MAIL: acm@acm.edu
URL: www.acm.edu

Association of Independent California Colleges and Universities (E)
1121 L Street
Suite 802
Sacramento, CA 95814
(916) 446-7626
FAX: (916) 446-7948
Ms. Kristen F. Soares
President
E-MAIL: aiccu@aiccu.edu
URL: www.aiccu.edu

Association of Independent Colleges and Universities in Massachusetts (F)
11 Beacon Street
Suite 1224
Boston, MA 02108-3093
(617) 742-5147
FAX: (617) 742-3089
Mr. Richard Doherty
President
E-MAIL: richard.doherty@aicum.org
URL: www.aicum.org

Association of Independent Colleges and Universities in New Jersey (G)
797 Springfield Avenue
Summit, NJ 07901-1107
(908) 277-3738
FAX: (908) 277-0851
Mr. John B. Wilson
President and CEO
E-MAIL: jbwilson@njcolleges.org
URL: www.njcolleges.org

Association of Independent Colleges and Universities of Nebraska (H)
635 South 14th Street
Suite 310
Lincoln, NE 68508
(402) 434-2818
FAX: (402) 434-2825
Mr. Thomas O'Neill
President
E-MAIL: tiponeill2@aol.com
URL: aicunebraska.org

Association of Independent Colleges and Universities of Ohio (I)
41 South High Street
Suite 1690
Columbus, OH 43215
(614) 228-2196
FAX: (614) 228-8406
Mr. C. Todd Jones
President & General Counsel
E-MAIL: tjones@aicuo.edu
URL: www.aicuo.edu

Association of Independent Colleges and Universities of Pennsylvania (J)
101 North Front Street
Harrisburg, PA 17101-1405
(717) 232-8649
FAX: (717) 233-8574
Dr. Don L. Francis
President
E-MAIL: francis@aicup.org
URL: www.aicup.org

Association of Independent Colleges and Universities of Rhode Island (K)
50 Park Row West
Suite 100
Providence, RI 02903
(401) 272-8270
Mr. Daniel Egan
President
E-MAIL: degan@aicuri.org
URL: www.aicuri.org

Association of Independent Colleges of Art & Design (L)
236 Hope Street
Providence, RI 02906
(401) 270-5991
FAX: (401) 270-5993
Ms. Deborah Obalil
President & Executive Director
E-MAIL: deborah@aicad.org
URL: www.aicad.org

Association of Independent Kentucky Colleges and Universities (M)
484 Chenault Road
Frankfort, KY 40601
(502) 695-5007
FAX: (502) 695-5057
Dr. Gary S. Cox
President
E-MAIL: gary.cox@aikcu.org
URL: www.aikcu.org

Association of Vermont Independent Colleges (N)
PO Box 254
Montpelier, VT 05601
(802) 828-8826
Susan Stitely
President
E-MAIL: sstitely@vermont-icolleges.org
URL: www.vermont-icolleges.org

Atlanta Regional Council for Higher Education (O)
133 Peachtree Street, NE
Suite 4925
Atlanta, GA 30303-2923
(404) 651-2668
FAX: (404) 880-9816
Ms. Tracey Johnson
Sr. Program Coordinator
E-MAIL: tjohnson@atlantahighered.org
URL: www.atlantahighered.org

Boston Theological Institute (P)
PO Box 391395
Cambridge, MA 02139
(617) 527-4880
FAX: (617) 527-1073
Dr. Ann McClenahan
Executive Director
E-MAIL: mcclenahan@bostontheological.org
URL: www.bostontheological.org

Central Pennsylvania Consortium (Q)
c/o Franklin & Marshall College
PO Box 3003
Lancaster, PA 17604-3003
(717) 291-4282
FAX: (717) 358-4455
Ms. Kathryn Missildine
Executive Assistant
E-MAIL: kathy.missildine@fandm.edu
URL: www.centralpennsylvaniaconsortium.org

CHESLA (R)
10 Columbus Boulevard
Hartford, CT 06106-1978
(860) 761-8453
Ms. Jeanette W. Weldon
Executive Director
E-MAIL: jweldon@chesla.org
URL: www.chesla.org

Christian College Consortium (S)
255 Grapevine Road
Wenham, MA 01984-1813
(978) 867-4802
FAX: (978) 867-4650
Dr. Stan D. Gaede
President
E-MAIL: president@gordon.edu
URL: www.ccconsortium.org

Community College Futures Assembly (T)
University of Florida, College of Education
Box 117040
229 Norman Hall
Gainesville, FL 32611-7044
(352) 273-4293
Dr. Dale F. Campbell
Director
E-MAIL: futures@coe.ufl.edu
URL: www.education.ufl.edu/futures/

The Consortium for Graduate Study in Management (U)
229 Chesterfield Business Parkway
Chesterfield, MO 63005
(636) 681-5487
FAX: (636) 681-5497
Mr. Peter J. Aranda III
Executive Director and CEO
E-MAIL: recruiting@cgsm.org
URL: www.cgsm.org

Consortium of College & University Media Centers (V)
Indiana University
306 N. Union Street
Bloomington, IN 47405-3888
(812) 855-6049
Aileen Scales
Executive Director
E-MAIL: ccumc@ccumc.org
URL: www.ccumc.org

Consortium of Universities of the Washington Metropolitan Area (W)
1100 H Street, NW
Suite 500
Washington, DC 20005
(202) 331-8080
FAX: (202) 331-7925
Dr. John Cavanaugh
President & CEO
E-MAIL: jcavanaugh@consortium.org
URL: www.consortium.org

Consortium on Financing Higher Education (X)
1 Main Street
Suite 1210
Cambridge, MA 02142
(617) 253-5030
FAX: (617) 258-8280
Dr. Kristine E. Dillon
President
E-MAIL: kedillon@mit.edu
URL: www.cofhe.org

Cooperating Raleigh Colleges (Y)
Meredith College
3800 Hillsborough Street
Raleigh, NC 27607-5298
(919) 760-8538
Ms. Jenny Spiker
Director
E-MAIL: crc@meredith.edu
URL: www.crcraleighcolleges.org

Council of Independent Colleges in Virginia (Z)
PO Box 1005
Bedford, VA 24523
(540) 586-0606
FAX: (540) 586-2630
Mr. Robert B. Lambeth Jr.
President
E-MAIL: lambeth@cicv.org
URL: www.cicv.org

Council of North Central Two Year Colleges (a)
200 South 14th Street
Parsons, KS 67357
(620) 820-1223
FAX: (620) 421-0921
Dr. George Knox
Executive Director
E-MAIL: meganf@labette.edu
URL: www.labette.edu/cnctyc

Council of Presidents (b)
410 Eleventh Avenue, SE
Suite 101
Olympia, WA 98501
(360) 292-4100
FAX: (360) 292-4110
Mr. Paul Francis
Executive Director
E-MAIL: pfrancis@cop.wsu.edu
URL: www.councilofpresidents.org

Federation of Independent Illinois Colleges and Universities (c)
1123 South Second Street
Springfield, IL 62704
(217) 789-1400
FAX: (217) 789-6259
Mr. David W. Tretter
President
E-MAIL: davetretter@federationedu.org
URL: www.federationedu.org

Five Colleges, Incorporated (d)
97 Spring Street
Amherst, MA 01002
(413) 542-4009
FAX: (413) 542-4029
Dr. Neal B. Abraham
Executive Director
E-MAIL: nabraham@fivecolleges.edu
URL: www.fivecolleges.edu

Georgia Independent College Association (e)
600 West Peachtree Street, NW
Suite 1710
Atlanta, GA 30308
(404) 233-5433
FAX: (404) 233-6309
Dr. Susanna Baxter
President
E-MAIL: sbaxter@georgiacolleges.org
URL: www.georgiacolleges.org

Graduate Theological Foundation Oxford/Rome/Indiana Consortia (f)
Dodge House
415 Lincoln Way East
Mishawaka, IN 46544-2213
(800) 423-5983
FAX: (574) 255-7520
Bethany Morgan MBA
Registrar
E-MAIL: information@gtfeducation.org
URL: www.gtfeducation.org

Great Lakes Colleges Association (g)
535 West William
Suite 301
Ann Arbor, MI 48103
(734) 661-2350
FAX: (734) 661-2349
Dr. Richard A. Detweiler
President
E-MAIL: detweiler@glca.org
URL: www.glca.org

Greater Cincinnati Consortium of Colleges and Universities (h)
Northern Kentucky University
241 Campbell Hall
Highland Heights, KY 41099
(859) 392-2428
Ms. Janet Piccirillo
Executive Director
E-MAIL: gcccu@nku.edu
URL: www.gcccu.org

Hartford Consortium for Higher Education (i)
31 Pratt Street
5th Floor
Hartford, CT 06103
(860) 702-3800
FAX: (860) 241-1130
Dr. Martin Estey
Executive Director
E-MAIL: mestey@metrohartford.com
URL: www.hartfordconsortium.org

Higher Education Consortium for Urban Affairs, Inc. (HECUA) (A)
2233 University Avenue West
Suite 210
St. Paul, MN 55114
(651) 287-3300
FAX: (651) 659-9421
Dr. Jenny Keyser
Executive Director
E-MAIL: hecua@hecua.org
URL: www.hecua.org

Higher Education Consortium of Metropolitan St. Louis (B)
8420 Delmar Boulevard
Suite 504
St. Louis, MO 63124-2180
(314) 991-2700
FAX: (314) 991-2874
Mr. Thomas George
Chair
E-MAIL: purchasing@heccstl.com
URL: www.heccstl.com

Higher Education Data Sharing (HEDS) Consortium (C)
Wabash College
410 West Wabash Avenue
Crawfordsville, IN 47933
(765) 361-6331
Charles Blaich
Director
E-MAIL: charles.blaich@gmail.com
URL: www.hedsconsortium.org

Independent Colleges and Universities of Missouri (D)
PO Box 1865
Jefferson City, MO 65102-1865
(573) 635-9160
FAX: (573) 635-6258
Mr. William A. Gamble
Executive Director
E-MAIL: bill@molobby.com
URL: www.icum.org

Independent Colleges and Universities of Texas, Inc. (E)
400 West 15th Street
Suite 850
Austin, TX 78701
(512) 472-9522
FAX: (512) 472-2371
Ray Martinez III
President
E-MAIL: lois.hollis@icut.org
URL: www.icut.org

Independent Colleges of Indiana (F)
30 S. Meridian Street
Suite 800
Indianapolis, IN 46204
(317) 236-6090
FAX: (317) 236-6086
Dr. Richard L. Ludwick
President and CEO
E-MAIL: smartchoice@icindiana.org
URL: www.icindiana.org

Independent Colleges of Washington (G)
600 Stewart Street
Suite 600
Seattle, WA 98101
(206) 623-4494
Ms. Violet A. Boyer
President & CEO
E-MAIL: info@icwashington.org
URL: www.icwashington.org

Inter-University Consortium for Political and Social Research (H)
The University of Michigan
Institute for Social Research
PO Box 1248
Ann Arbor, MI 48106-1248
(734) 615-8400
FAX: (734) 647-8200
Dr. Margaret Levenstein
Director
E-MAIL: maggiel@umich.edu
URL: www.icpsr.umich.edu

Inter-University Council of Ohio (IUC) (I)
10 West Broad Street
Suite 450
Columbus, OH 43215
(614) 464-1266
FAX: (614) 464-9281
Ms. Cindy McQuade
Vice President of Operations
E-MAIL: mcquade.2@osu.edu
URL: www.iuc-ohio.org

Iowa Association of Community College Trustees (J)
855 East Court Avenue
Des Moines, IA 50309
(515) 282-4692
FAX: (515) 282-3743
M. J. Dolan J.D.
Executive Director
E-MAIL: mjdolan@iacct.com
URL: www.iacct.com

Iowa Association of Independent Colleges and Universities (K)
505 Fifth Avenue
Suite 1030
Des Moines, IA 50309-2315
(515) 282-3175
FAX: (515) 282-8177
Mr. Gary W. Steinke
President
E-MAIL: president@iaicu.org
URL: www.iowaprivatecolleges.org

Kansas Independent College Association (L)
700 South Kansas Avenue
Suite 622
Topeka, KS 66603
(785) 235-9877
FAX: (785) 235-1437
Mr. Matthew E. Lindsey
President
E-MAIL: matt@kscolleges.org
URL: www.kscolleges.org

Lehigh Valley Association of Independent Colleges (M)
1309 Main Street
Bethlehem, PA 18018
(610) 625-7888
Diane Dimitroff
Executive Director
E-MAIL: dimitroffd@lvaic.org
URL: www.lvaic.org

Louisiana Association of Independent Colleges and Universities (N)
320 Third Street
Suite 104
Baton Rouge, LA 70801
(225) 389-9885
FAX: (225) 389-0149
Ms. Mary Ann Coleman
President
E-MAIL: maryann@laicu.org
URL: www.laicu.org

Maryland Independent College and University Association (O)
140 South Street
Annapolis, MD 21401
(410) 269-0306
FAX: (410) 269-5905
Ms. Tina M. Bjarekull
President
E-MAIL: tbjarekull@micua.org
URL: www.micua.org

Massachusetts Education & Career Opportunities Inc (P)
484 Main Street
Suite 500
Worcester, MA 01608
(508) 754-6829
FAX: (508) 797-0069
Ms. Pamela Boisvert
CEO
E-MAIL: pboisvert@massedco.org
URL: www.massedco.org

Michigan Independent Colleges & Universities (Q)
One Michigan Avenue
Suite 950
Lansing, MI 48933
(517) 372-9160
FAX: (517) 372-9165
Robert LeFevre
E-MAIL: rlefevre@micolleges.org
URL: www.micolleges.org

Minnesota Private College Council, Inc. (R)
445 Minnesota Street
Suite 500
St. Paul, MN 55101-2903
(651) 228-9061
FAX: (651) 228-0379
E-MAIL: colleges@mnprivatecolleges.org
URL: www.mnprivatecolleges.org

Mississippi Association of Independent Colleges and Universities (S)
PO Box 2933
Ridgeland, MS 39158-2933
(601) 957-2052
FAX: (601) 977-0233
Dr. E. Harold Fisher
Executive Director
E-MAIL: ehfisher@bellsouth.net

National Student Exchange (T)
4656 West Jefferson
Suite 140
Fort Wayne, IN 46804
(260) 436-2634
FAX: (260) 436-5676
Ms. Bette Worley
President
E-MAIL: bworley@nse2.org
URL: www.nse.org

New England Faculty Development Consortium (U)
Mount Ida College
777 Dedham Street
Newton, MA 02459
(617) 928-7396
Dakin Burdick Ph.D.
President
E-MAIL: dburdick@mountida.edu
URL: www.nefdc.org

New Hampshire College & University Council (V)
3 Barrell Court
Suite 100
Concord, NH 03301-8543
(603) 225-4199
FAX: (603) 225-8108
Thomas F. Horgan
President and CEO
E-MAIL: horgan@nhcuc.org
URL: www.nhcuc.org

New Jersey Association of State Colleges and Universities (W)
150 West State Street
Trenton, NJ 08608
(609) 989-1100
Dr. Michael W. Klein
CEO
E-MAIL: crpipher@njascu.org
URL: www.njascu.org

New Jersey Council of County Colleges (X)
330 West State Street
Trenton, NJ 08618
(609) 392-3434
FAX: (609) 392-8158
Dr. Lawrence A. Nespoli
President
E-MAIL: info@njccc.org
URL: www.njccc.org

New Orleans Educational Telecommunications Consortium, Inc. (Y)
2045 Lakeshore Drive
Suite 401
New Orleans, LA 70122
(504) 524-0350
E-MAIL: noetc@noetc.org
URL: www.noetc.com

North Carolina Independent Colleges and Universities (Z)
530 North Blount Street
Raleigh, NC 27604
(919) 832-5817
FAX: (919) 833-0794
Dr. A. Hope Williams
President
E-MAIL: williams@ncicu.org
URL: www.ncicu.org

North Dakota Independent College Fund (a)
University of Mary
7500 University Drive
Bismarck, ND 58504
(701) 355-8222
FAX: (701) 255-7687
Mr. Neal Kalberer
Executive Director
E-MAIL: kalberer@umary.edu

Northeast Consortium of Colleges and Universities in Massachusetts (NECCUM) (b)
c/o Office of the President
Salem State University
352 Lafayette Street
Salem, MA 01970
(978) 542-6134
FAX: (978) 542-6126
Katie Sadowski
E-MAIL: ksadowski@salemstate.edu
URL: www.salemstate.edu/students/27600.php

Northeast Ohio Council on Higher Education (c)
1501 Euclid Avenue
Suite 423
Cleveland, OH 44115
(216) 420-9200
Ms. Holly J. Harris Bane
President
E-MAIL: hharrisbane@noche.org
URL: www.noche.org

Oak Ridge Associated Universities (d)
MC-100-22
PO Box 117
Oak Ridge, TN 37831-0117
(865) 576-3300
FAX: (865) 576-3816
Mr. Harry A. Page
President and CEO
E-MAIL: andy.page@orau.org
URL: www.orau.org

Oklahoma Independent Colleges and Universities (e)
PO Box 57148
Oklahoma City, OK 73157-7148
(405) 371-1780
Lesa Smaligo
Executive Director
E-MAIL: lesa@oicu.org
URL: www.oicu.org

Oregon Alliance of Independent Colleges & Universities (f)
1211 SW Fifth Avenue
Suite 1900
Portland, OR 97204
(503) 796-2852
Mr. Ron Saxton
President
E-MAIL: info@oaicu.org
URL: www.oaicu.org

Pennsylvania Association of Colleges and Universities (g)
950 Walnut Bottom Road
Suite 15-214
Carlisle, PA 17015
(800) 687-9010
FAX: (717) 240-0673
URL: www.pacu.org

Pennsylvania's State System of Higher Education Foundation, Inc. (h)
2986 North Second Street
Harrisburg, PA 17110
(717) 720-4056
FAX: (717) 720-7082
Ms. Jennifer S. Hartman
President/CEO
E-MAIL: jhartman@thepafoundation.org
URL: www.thepafoundation.org

Pittsburgh Council on Higher Education (i)
201 Wood Street
Pittsburgh, PA 15222
(412) 657-8105
Ms. Karina Chavez
Executive Director
E-MAIL: kchavez@pointpark.edu
URL: www.pchepa.org

Quad-Cities Graduate Study Center (j)
WIU - QC Campus
3300 River Drive
Moline, IL 61265
(309) 762-9481
Shirley Moore
Administrative Assistant
E-MAIL: qc@gradcenter.org
URL: www.gradcenter.org

Consortia of Institutions of Higher Education

South Carolina Independent Colleges & Universities, Inc. (A)
PO Box 12007
Columbia, SC 29211
(803) 799-7122
FAX: (803) 254-7504
Mr. Michael G. LeFever
President & CEO
E-MAIL: mike@scicu.org
URL: www.scicu.org

South Metropolitan Higher Education Consortium (B)
202 S. Halsted Street
ATOC-144
Chicago Heights, IL 60411
(708) 709-2942
Ms. Genevieve F. Boesen
Executive Director
E-MAIL: gboesen@prairiestate.edu
URL: www.southmetroed.org

Southern Regional Education Board (C)
592 Tenth Street, NW
Atlanta, GA 30318-5776
(404) 875-9211
FAX: (404) 872-1477
Dr. David S. Spence
President
E-MAIL: dave.spence@sreb.org
URL: www.sreb.org

Southwestern Ohio Council for Higher Education (SOCHE) (D)
3155 Research Boulevard
Suite 204
Dayton, OH 45420-4015
(937) 258-8890
FAX: (937) 258-8899
Dr. Sean Creighton
President
E-MAIL: soche@soche.org
URL: www.soche.org

Texas International Education Consortium (E)
1103 West 24th Street
Austin, TX 78705
(512) 477-9283, ext. 114
FAX: (512) 322-0592
Dr. Ronald Aqua
President & CEO
E-MAIL: ron.aqua@tiec.org
URL: www.tiec.org

Tuition Plan Consortium/Private College 529 Plan (F)
7425 Forsyth Boulevard
St. Louis, MO 63105
(314) 727-0900
FAX: (314) 727-0930
Ms. Nancy Farmer
President
E-MAIL: nancy@pc529.com
URL: www.privatecollege529.com

University City Science Center (G)
3711 Market Street
8th Floor
Philadelphia, PA 19104
(215) 966-6000
FAX: (215) 966-6002
Dr. Stephen Tang
President & CEO
E-MAIL: info@sciencecenter.org
URL: www.sciencecenter.org

The Virginia College Fund (H)
4900 Augusta Avenue
Suite 101
Richmond, VA 23230
(804) 355-3271
FAX: (804) 359-5765
Mr. James K. Dill
President
E-MAIL: jkdill@thevcf.org
URL: www.thevcf.org

Virginia Tidewater Consortium for Higher Education (I)
4900 Powhatan Avenue
Norfolk, VA 23508-1836
(757) 683-3183
FAX: (757) 683-4515
Dr. Lawrence G. Dotolo
President
E-MAIL: lgdotolo@aol.com
URL: www.vtc.odu.edu

Washington Theological Consortium (J)
415 Michigan Avenue, NE
Suite 105
Washington, DC 20017
(202) 832-2675
FAX: (202) 526-0818
Dr. Larry Golemon
Executive Director
E-MAIL: wtc@washtheocon.org
URL: washtheocon.org

West Virginia Independent Colleges & Universities, Inc. (K)
c/o Suttle & Stainaker
1411 Virginia Street East
Suite 100
Charleston, WV 25301
(304) 433-2604
FAX: (304) 345-5526
Jessica Carter JD MBA
Executive Director
E-MAIL: jessicacarter@wvicu.org
URL: www.wvicu.org

Wisconsin Association of Independent Colleges and Universities (L)
122 West Washington Avenue
Suite 700
Madison, WI 53703-2723
(608) 256-7761
FAX: (608) 256-7065
Dr. Rolf Wegenke
President
E-MAIL: mail@waicu.org
URL: www.waicu.org

The Work Colleges Consortium (M)
CPO 2163
Berea, KY 40404
(859) 985-3154
Ms. Robin Taffler
Executive Director
E-MAIL: robin@workcolleges.org
URL: www.workcolleges.org

NAME INDEX

US Department of Education Offices, Statewide Agencies of Higher Education, Higher Education Associations, Consortia of Institutions of Higher Education

A

B

C

D

E

F

G

H

I

J

K

L

M

N

O

P

R

S

T

U

V

W

Y

Institutions By Religious Affiliation

African Methodist Episcopal
Allen University ... SC
Edward Waters College ... FL
Paul Quinn College ... TX
Payne Theological Seminary ... OH
Shorter College ... AR
Wilberforce University ... OH

African Methodist Episcopal Zion Church
Clinton College ... SC
Hood Theological Seminary ... NC
Livingstone College ... NC

Alabama Baptist State Convention
Judson College ... AL

American Baptist
Alderson Broaddus University ... WV
American Baptist Seminary of the West .. CA
Bacone College ... OK
Eastern University ... PA
Franklin College of Indiana ... IN
Judson University ... IL
Linfield College ... OR
Northern Seminary ... IL
Ottawa University ... KS
Palmer Theological Seminary of Eastern University ... PA
University of Sioux Falls ... SD

Assemblies Of God Church
Assemblies of God Theological Seminary MO
Bethel College ... VA
Evangel University ... MO
Global University ... MO
Native American Bible College ... NC
North Central University ... MN
Northpoint Bible College ... MA
Northwest University ... WA
Southeastern University ... FL
Southwestern Assemblies of God University ... TX
Trinity Bible College & Graduate School . ND
University of Valley Forge ... PA
Vanguard University of Southern California ... CA

Baptist
American Baptist College ... TN
Arkansas Baptist College ... AR
Arlington Baptist College ... TX
Baptist Bible College ... MO
Baptist Missionary Association Theological Seminary ... TX
Baptist University of the Americas ... TX
Baylor University ... TX
Bethel University ... MN
Bluefield College ... VA
Boston Baptist College ... MA
Brewton-Parker College ... GA
Campbell University ... NC
Campbellsville University ... KY
Cedarville University ... OH
Central Baptist College ... AR
Central Baptist Theological Seminary ... KS
Central Baptist Theological Seminary of Minneapolis ... MN
Chowan University ... NC
Dallas Baptist University ... TX
Gardner-Webb University ... NC
Georgetown College ... KY
Hardin-Simmons University ... TX
Howard Payne University ... TX
Huntsville Bible College ... AL
International Baptist College and Seminary ... AZ
Jacksonville College ... TX
Maple Springs Baptist Bible College & Seminary ... MD
Missouri Baptist University ... MO
Morris College ... SC
Oakland City University ... IN
Selma University ... AL
Shaw University ... NC
Shorter University ... GA
Simmons College of Kentucky ... KY
Southeastern Baptist College ... MS
Summit University of Pennsylvania ... PA
The Crown College of the Bible ... TN
The John Leland Center for Theological Studies ... VA
Trinity Baptist College ... FL
Truett McConnell College ... GA
University of the Cumberlands ... KY
Virginia Baptist College ... VA
Virginia Beach Theological Seminary ... VA
Virginia Union University ... VA
Washington University of Virginia ... VA
West Coast Baptist College ... CA

Brethren Church
Ashland University ... OH

Christian Church (Disciples Of Christ)
Barton College ... NC
Bethany College ... WV
Chapman University ... CA
Christian Theological Seminary ... IN
Columbia College ... MO
Culver-Stockton College ... MO
Eureka College ... IL
Jarvis Christian College ... TX
Lexington Theological Seminary ... KY
Lynchburg College ... VA
Midway University ... KY
Northwest Christian University ... OR
Phillips Theological Seminary ... OK
Texas Christian University ... TX
Transylvania University ... KY
William Woods University ... MO

Christian Churches And Churches of Christ
Belmont University ... TN
Boise Bible College ... ID
Central Christian College of the Bible ... MO
Cincinnati Christian University ... OH
Crossroads College ... MN
Dallas Christian College ... TX
Great Lakes Christian College ... MI
Johnson University ... TN
Kentucky Christian University ... KY
Lincoln Christian University ... IL
Manhattan Christian College ... KS
Point University ... GA

Christian Methodist Episcopal
Lane College ... TN
Miles College ... AL
Texas College ... TX

Christian Reformed Church
Calvin College ... MI
Calvin Theological Seminary ... MI
Dordt College ... IA

Church Of Christ
Pepperdine University ... CA

Church Of God
Anderson University ... IN
Lee University ... TN
Mid-America Christian University ... OK
Pentecostal Theological Seminary ... TN
The University of Findlay ... OH
Universidad Teologica Del Caribe ... PR
Warner Pacific College ... OR
Warner University ... FL

Church of New Jerusalem
Bryn Athyn College of the New Church ... PA

Church Of The Brethren
Bethany Theological Seminary ... IN
Bridgewater College ... VA
Elizabethtown College ... PA
Manchester University ... IN
McPherson College ... KS

Church Of The Nazarene
Eastern Nazarene College ... MA
MidAmerica Nazarene University ... KS
Mount Vernon Nazarene University ... OH
Nazarene Bible College ... CO
Nazarene Theological Seminary ... MO
Northwest Nazarene University ... ID
Olivet Nazarene University ... IL
Point Loma Nazarene University ... CA
Southern Nazarene University ... OK
Trevecca Nazarene University ... TN

Churches Of Christ
Abilene Christian University ... TX
Amridge University ... AL
Crowley's Ridge College ... AR
Faulkner University ... AL
Freed-Hardeman University ... TN
Harding University Main Campus ... AR
Heritage Christian University ... AL
Lipscomb University ... TN
Lubbock Christian University ... TX
Mid-Atlantic Christian University ... NC
Ohio Valley University ... WV
Southwestern Christian College ... TX
York College ... NE

Cumberland Presbyterian
Bethel University ... TN
Memphis Theological Seminary ... TN

Evangelical Congregational Church
Evangelical Theological Seminary ... PA

Evangelical Covenant Church Of America
North Park University ... IL

Evangelical Free Church Of America
Trinity International University ... IL

Evangelical Lutheran Church In America
Augsburg College ... MN
Augustana College ... IL
Augustana University ... SD
Bethany College ... KS
California Lutheran University ... CA
Capital University ... OH
Carthage College ... WI
Concordia College ... MN
Finlandia University ... MI
Gettysburg College ... PA
Grand View University ... IA
Gustavus Adolphus College ... MN
Lenoir-Rhyne University ... NC
Luther College ... IA
Luther Seminary ... MN
Lutheran School of Theology at Chicago ... IL
Lutheran Theological Seminary at Gettysburg ... PA
Lutheran Theological Seminary at Philadelphia ... PA
Midland University ... NE
Muhlenberg College ... PA
Newberry College ... SC
Pacific Lutheran University ... WA
Roanoke College ... VA
St. Olaf College ... MN
Susquehanna University ... PA
Texas Lutheran University ... TX
Thiel College ... PA
Trinity Lutheran Seminary ... OH
Wartburg College ... IA
Wartburg Theological Seminary ... IA
Wittenberg University ... OH

Evangelical Lutheran Synod
Bethany Lutheran College ... MN

Fellowship Of Grace Brethren Churches
Grace College and Seminary ... IN

Free Methodist
Central Christian College of Kansas ... KS
Greenville College ... IL
Seattle Pacific University ... WA
Spring Arbor University ... MI

Free Will Baptist
California Christian College ... CA
Randall University ... OK
Welch College ... TN

Friends
Earlham College and Earlham School of Religion ... IN
George Fox University ... OR
Guilford College ... NC
Malone University ... OH
William Penn University ... IA
Wilmington College ... OH

Greek Orthodox
Hellenic College-Holy Cross Greek Orthodox School of Theology ... MA

Interdenominational
Bethany Global University ... MN
Christian Witness Theological Seminary . CA
Denver Seminary ... CO
Evangelical Seminary of Puerto Rico ... PR
Faith Evangelical College & Seminary ... WA
God's Bible School and College ... OH
Inste Bible College ... IA
Interdenominational Theological Center .. GA
Legacy Christian University ... AL
Messiah College ... PA
Oak Hills Christian College ... MN
Palm Beach Atlantic University ... FL
Phoenix Seminary ... AZ
Rocky Mountain College ... MT
South Florida Bible College ... FL
Union Bible College ... IN
Wesley Biblical Seminary ... MS

Jewish
Academy for Jewish Religion ... CA
Hebrew Union College-Jewish Institute of Religion ... NY
New York Medical College ... NY
Reconstructionist Rabbinical College ... PA
Women's Institute of Torah Seminary ... MD

Latter-day Saints
Brigham Young University ... UT
Brigham Young University Hawaii ... HI
Brigham Young University-Idaho ... ID
LDS Business College ... UT

Lutheran
Valparaiso University ... IN

Lutheran Church - Missouri Synod
Concordia College ... NY
Concordia College Alabama ... AL
Concordia Seminary ... MO
Concordia Theological Seminary ... IN
Concordia University ... CA
Concordia University ... NE
Concordia University ... OR
Concordia University Ann Arbor ... MI
Concordia University Chicago ... IL
Concordia University Texas ... TX
Concordia University Wisconsin ... WI
Concordia University, St. Paul ... MN

Mennonite Brethren Church
Fresno Pacific University ... CA
Tabor College ... KS

Mennonite Church
Anabaptist Mennonite Biblical Seminary .. IN
Bethel College ... KS
Bluffton University ... OH
Eastern Mennonite University ... VA
Goshen College ... IN
Hesston College ... KS
Rosedale Bible College ... OH

Missionary Church
Bethel College ... IN

Moravian Church
Moravian College ... PA
Salem College ... NC

Multiple Protestant Denominations
Huston-Tillotson University ... TX
LeMoyne-Owen College ... TN
Paine College ... GA

Non-denominational
Carolina College of Biblical Studies ... NC
Cedar Crest College ... PA
China Evangelical Seminary North America ... CA
Faith Theological Seminary ... MD
Grove City College ... PA
Heartland Christian College ... MO
Midwest University ... MO
Montreat College ... NC
North American University ... TX
Pacific Bible College ... OR
Providence Christian College ... CA
University of Fort Lauderdale ... FL
Williamson College ... TN

North American Baptist
Sioux Falls Seminary ... SD

Original Free Will Baptist Church
University of Mount Olive ... NC

Other Protestant
Beulah Heights University ... GA
Grace College of Divinity ... NC
Ohio Christian University ... OH
Saint Louis Christian College ... MO

Urshan Graduate School of Theology ..... MO

Pentecostal Church of God
Messenger College .... TX
Universidad Pentecostal Mizpa .... PR

Pentecostal Holiness Church
Emmanuel College .... GA
Southwestern Christian University .... OK

Pentecostal/Charismatic Non-Denominational
Christian Life College IL

Presbyterian
Sterling College .... KS
Whitworth University .... WA

Presbyterian Church (U.S.A.)
Agnes Scott College .... GA
Austin College .... TX
Austin Presbyterian Theological Seminary .... TX
Belhaven University .... MS
Blackburn College IL
Bloomfield College .... NJ
Buena Vista University .... IA
Carroll University .... WI
Columbia Theological Seminary .... GA
Davidson College .... NC
Davis & Elkins College .... WV
Eckerd College .... FL
Hampden-Sydney College .... VA
Hanover College .... IN
Hastings College .... NE
King University .... TN
Lees-McRae College .... NC
Louisville Presbyterian Theological Seminary .... KY
Lyon College .... AR
Macalester College .... MN
Mary Baldwin College .... VA
Maryville College .... TN
McCormick Theological Seminary IL
Millikin University IL
Missouri Valley College .... MO
Monmouth College IL
Muskingum University .... OH
Pittsburgh Theological Seminary .... PA
Presbyterian College .... SC
Princeton Theological Seminary .... NJ
Queens University of Charlotte .... NC
Rhodes College .... TN
San Francisco Theological Seminary ...... CA
Schreiner University .... TX
Stillman College .... AL
Tusculum College .... TN
Union Presbyterian Seminary .... VA
University of Dubuque .... IA
University of Jamestown .... ND
University of Pikeville .... KY
University of the Ozarks .... AR
Warren Wilson College .... NC
Waynesburg University .... PA
Westminster College .... PA
William Peace University .... NC
Wilson College .... PA

Presbyterian Church In America
Covenant College .... GA
Covenant Theological Seminary .... MO
Grace Mission University .... CA
Presbyterian Theological Seminary in America .... CA
Reformed University .... GA

Protestant Episcopal
Bexley Seabury IL
Church Divinity School of the Pacific .... CA
Episcopal Divinity School .... MA
General Theological Seminary .... NY
Nashotah House .... WI
Protestant Episcopal Theological Seminary in Virginia .... VA
Saint Augustine's University .... NC
Seminary of the Southwest .... TX
Sewanee: The University of the South .... TN
Trinity Episcopal School for Ministry .... PA
Voorhees College .... SC

Reformed Church In America
Central College .... IA
Hope College .... MI
New Brunswick Theological Seminary ..... NJ
Northwestern College .... IA
Western Theological Seminary .... MI

Reformed Episcopal Church
Reformed Episcopal Seminary .... PA

Reformed Presbyterian Church
Evangelia University .... CA
Geneva College .... PA
Reformed Presbyterian Theological Seminary .... PA

Roman Catholic
Alvernia University .... PA
Ancilla College .... IN
Anna Maria College .... MA
Aquinas College .... MI
Aquinas College .... TN
Aquinas Institute of Theology .... MO
Assumption College .... MA
Assumption College for Sisters .... NJ
Athenaeum of Ohio .... OH
Augustine Institute .... CO
Ave Maria School of Law .... FL
Avila University .... MO
Barry University .... FL
Belmont Abbey College .... NC
Benedictine College .... KS
Benedictine University IL
Boston College .... MA
Brescia University .... KY
Briar Cliff University .... IA
Cabrini University .... PA
Caldwell University .... NJ
Calumet College of Saint Joseph .... IN
Canisius College .... NY
Cardinal Stritch University .... WI
Carlow University .... PA
Carroll College .... MT
Catholic Theological Union IL
Chestnut Hill College .... PA
Christ the King Seminary .... NY
Christendom College .... VA
Christian Brothers University .... TN
Clarke University .... IA
College of Our Lady of the Elms .... MA
College of Saint Benedict .... MN
College of Saint Elizabeth .... NJ
College of Saint Mary .... NE
College of St. Joseph .... VT
College of the Holy Cross .... MA
Conception Seminary College .... MO
Creighton University .... NE
DePaul University IL
DeSales University .... PA
Divine Word College .... IA
Dominican School of Philosophy and Theology .... CA
Dominican University IL
Donnelly College .... KS
Duquesne University .... PA
Edgewood College .... WI
Emmanuel College .... MA
Fairfield University .... CT
Felician University .... NJ
Fontbonne University .... MO
Franciscan University of Steubenville ..... OH
Gannon University .... PA
Georgetown University .... DC
Georgian Court University .... NJ
Gonzaga University .... WA
Gwynedd Mercy University .... PA
Holy Apostles College and Seminary ...... CT
Holy Cross College .... IN
Holy Family University .... PA
Immaculata University .... PA
John Carroll University .... OH
Kenrick-Glennon Seminary, Kenrick School of Theology .... MO
King's College .... PA
La Roche College .... PA
La Salle University .... PA
Laboure College .... MA
Lewis University IL
Loras College .... IA
Lourdes University .... OH
Loyola Marymount University .... CA
Loyola University Chicago IL
Loyola University Maryland .... MD
Loyola University New Orleans .... LA
Madonna University .... MI
Marian University .... IN
Marian University .... WI
Marquette University .... WI
Marygrove College .... MI
Marymount California University .... CA
Marymount University .... VA
Marywood University .... PA
Mercy College of Health Sciences .... IA
Mercy College of Ohio .... OH
Mercyhurst University .... PA
Merrimack College .... MA
Misericordia University .... PA
Mount Angel Seminary .... OR
Mount Carmel College of Nursing .... OH
Mount Marty College .... SD
Mount Mary University .... WI
Mount Mercy University .... IA
Mount Saint Mary's University .... CA
Mount St. Joseph University .... OH
Mount St. Mary's University .... MD
Neumann University .... PA
Newman University .... KS
Northeast Catholic College .... NH
Notre Dame College .... OH
Notre Dame of Maryland University .... MD
Notre Dame Seminary, Graduate School of Theology .... LA
Oblate School of Theology .... TX
Ohio Dominican University .... OH
Our Lady of the Lake College .... LA
Our Lady of the Lake University .... TX
Pontifical College Josephinum .... OH
Pontifical Faculty of the Immaculate Conception at the Dominican House of Studies .... DC
Pontifical John Paul II Institute for Studies on Marriage and Family .... DC
Pope St. John XXIII National Seminary ... MA
Presentation College .... SD
Providence College .... RI
Quincy University IL
Regis University .... CO
Rivier University .... NH
Rockhurst University .... MO
Rosemont College .... PA
Sacred Heart Major Seminary .... MI
Sacred Heart Seminary and School of Theology .... WI
Saint Anselm College .... NH
Saint Anthony College of Nursing IL
Saint Bernard's School of Theology & Ministry .... NY
Saint Charles Borromeo Seminary .... PA
Saint Francis Medical Center College of Nursing IL
Saint Francis University .... PA
Saint Gregory the Great Seminary .... NE
Saint John's Seminary .... CA
Saint John's Seminary .... MA
Saint John's University .... MN
Saint Joseph Seminary College .... LA
Saint Joseph's College .... IN
Saint Joseph's College of Maine .... ME
Saint Joseph's Seminary .... NY
Saint Joseph's University .... PA
Saint Leo University .... FL
Saint Louis University .... MO
Saint Martin's University .... WA
Saint Mary Seminary and Graduate School of Theology .... OH
Saint Mary's College .... IN
Saint Mary's College of California .... CA
Saint Mary's Seminary and University ..... MD
Saint Mary's University of Minnesota ...... MN
Saint Mary-of-the-Woods College .... IN
Saint Meinrad School of Theology .... IN
Saint Michael's College .... VT
Saint Norbert College .... WI
Saint Patrick's Seminary & University ..... CA
Saint Peter's University .... NJ
Saint Vincent College .... PA
Saint Vincent Seminary .... PA
Saint Xavier University IL
Salve Regina University .... RI
Seattle University .... WA
Seton Hall University .... NJ
Seton Hill University .... PA
Siena Heights University .... MI
Silver Lake College of the Holy Family .... WI
Spring Hill College .... AL
SS. Cyril and Methodius Seminary .... MI
St. Ambrose University .... IA
St. Bonaventure University .... NY
St. Catherine University .... MN
St. Gregory's University .... OK
St. John Vianney College Seminary .... FL
St. John Vianney Theological Seminary .. CO
St. John's University .... NY
St. Mary's University .... TX
St. Thomas University .... FL
St. Vincent De Paul Regional Seminary .. FL
Stonehill College .... MA
The Catholic University of America .... DC
The College of Saint Scholastica .... MN
The Pontifical Catholic University of Puerto Rico .... PR
The University of Scranton .... PA
Thomas More College .... KY
Trinity Washington University .... DC
Universidad Central de Bayamon .... PR
University of Dallas .... TX
University of Dayton .... OH
University of Detroit Mercy .... MI
University of Great Falls .... MT
University of Holy Cross .... LA
University of Mary .... ND
University of Notre Dame .... IN
University of Saint Francis .... IN
University of Saint Joseph .... CT
University of Saint Mary .... KS
University of Saint Mary of the Lake-Mundelein Seminary IL
University of Saint Thomas .... MN
University of San Diego .... CA
University of San Francisco .... CA
University of St. Francis IL
University of St. Thomas .... TX
University of the Incarnate Word .... TX
University of the Sacred Heart .... PR
Ursuline College .... OH
Villanova University .... PA
Viterbo University .... WI
Walsh University .... OH
Wheeling Jesuit University .... WV
Wyoming Catholic College .... WY
Xavier University .... OH
Xavier University of Louisiana .... LA

Russian Orthodox
Holy Trinity Orthodox Seminary .... NY

Seventh-day Adventist
Adventist University of Health Sciences .. FL
Andrews University .... MI
Kettering College .... OH
La Sierra University .... CA
Loma Linda University .... CA
Oakwood University .... AL
Pacific Union College .... CA
Southern Adventist University .... TN
Southwestern Adventist University .... TX
Union College .... NE
Universidad Adventista de las Antillas ..... PR
Walla Walla University .... WA
Washington Adventist University .... MD

Southern Baptist
B.H. Carroll Theological Institute .... TX
Blue Mountain College .... MS
California Baptist University .... CA
Carson-Newman University .... TN
Charleston Southern University .... SC
Clear Creek Baptist Bible College .... KY
East Texas Baptist University .... TX
Gateway Seminary .... CA
Hannibal-LaGrange University .... MO
Houston Baptist University .... TX
Louisiana College .... LA
Midwestern Baptist Theological Seminary MO
Mississippi College .... MS
New Orleans Baptist Theological Seminary .... LA
North Greenville University .... SC
Oklahoma Baptist University .... OK
Ouachita Baptist University .... AR
Samford University .... AL
Southeastern Baptist Theological Seminary .... NC
Southwest Baptist University .... MO
Southwestern Baptist Theological Seminary .... TX
The Baptist College of Florida .... FL
The Southern Baptist Theological Seminary .... KY
Union University .... TN
University of Mary Hardin-Baylor .... TX
University of Mobile .... AL
Wayland Baptist University .... TX
William Carey University .... MS
Williams Baptist College .... AR
Wingate University .... NC

The Christian And Missionary Alliance
Crown College .... MN
Nyack College .... NY
Simpson University .... CA
Toccoa Falls College .... GA

Unification Church
Unification Theological Seminary .... NY

Unitarian Universalist
Meadville Lombard Theological School IL
Starr King School for the Ministry .... CA

United Brethren Church
Huntington University .... IN

United Church Of Christ
Catawba College .... NC
Chicago Theological Seminary IL
Doane University .... NE
Eden Theological Seminary .... MO
Elmhurst College IL
Heidelberg University .... OH
Lakeland College .... WI
Lancaster Theological Seminary .... PA

Northland College ..... WI
Piedmont College ..... GA
The Defiance College ..... OH
Tougaloo College ..... MS
United Theological Seminary of the Twin Cities ..... MN

United Methodist

Adrian College ..... MI
Albion College ..... MI
Albright College ..... PA
Allegheny College ..... PA
American University ..... DC
Andrew College ..... GA
Baker University ..... KS
Baldwin Wallace University ..... OH
Bennett College ..... NC
Bethune Cookman University ..... FL
Birmingham-Southern College ..... AL
Brevard College ..... NC
Centenary College of Louisiana ..... LA
Central Methodist University ..... MO
Claflin University ..... SC
Claremont School of Theology ..... CA
Clark Atlanta University ..... GA
Columbia College ..... SC
Cornell College ..... IA
Dakota Wesleyan University ..... SD
DePauw University ..... IN
Dillard University ..... LA
Emory & Henry College ..... VA
Emory University ..... GA
Ferrum College ..... VA
Florida Southern College ..... FL
Garrett-Evangelical Theological Seminary IL
Greensboro College ..... NC
Hamline University ..... MN
Hendrix College ..... AR
High Point University ..... NC
Hiwassee College ..... TN
Huntingdon College ..... AL
Iliff School of Theology ..... CO
Iowa Wesleyan University ..... IA
Kansas Wesleyan University ..... KS
Kentucky Wesleyan College ..... KY
LaGrange College ..... GA
Lebanon Valley College ..... PA
Lindsey Wilson College ..... KY
Louisburg College ..... NC
Lycoming College ..... PA
MacMurray College IL
Martin Methodist College ..... TN
McKendree University IL
McMurry University ..... TX
Methodist Theological School in Ohio ..... OH
Methodist University ..... NC
Millsaps College ..... MS
Morningside College ..... IA
Nebraska Wesleyan University ..... NE
North Carolina Wesleyan College ..... NC
North Central College IL
Ohio Northern University ..... OH
Ohio Wesleyan University ..... OH
Oklahoma City University ..... OK
Otterbein University ..... OH
Pfeiffer University ..... NC
Philander Smith College ..... AR
Randolph College ..... VA
Randolph-Macon College ..... VA
Reinhardt University ..... GA
Rust College ..... MS
Saint Paul School of Theology ..... KS
Shenandoah University ..... VA
Simpson College ..... IA
Southern Methodist University ..... TX
Southwestern College ..... KS
Southwestern University ..... TX
Spartanburg Methodist College ..... SC
Tennessee Wesleyan College ..... TN
Texas Wesleyan University ..... TX
Union College ..... KY
United Theological Seminary ..... OH
University of Evansville ..... IN
University of Indianapolis ..... IN
University of Mount Union ..... OH
Virginia Wesleyan College ..... VA
Wesley College ..... DE
Wesley Theological Seminary ..... DC
Wesleyan College ..... GA
West Virginia Wesleyan College ..... WV
Wiley College ..... TX
Wofford College ..... SC
Young Harris College ..... GA

Wesleyan Church

Allegheny Wesleyan College ..... OH
Houghton College ..... NY
Indiana Wesleyan University ..... IN
Oklahoma Wesleyan University ..... OK
Southern Wesleyan University ..... SC

Wisconsin Evangelical Lutheran Synod

Martin Luther College ..... MN

Carnegie Classification Code Definitions*

This year, the Higher Education Directory lists the updated 2015 Carnegie Classifications. Due to space limitation, the *Higher Education Directory®* only lists the basic classification—which was substantially revised in 2015. These new codes are listed below:

Associate's Colleges: Institutions at which the highest level degree awarded is an associate's degree. The institutions are sorted into nine categories based on the intersection of two factors: disciplinary focus (transfer, career & technical or mixed) and dominant student type (traditional, nontraditional or mixed). Excludes Special Focus Institutions and Tribal Colleges.

Assoc/HT-High Trad: Associate's Colleges: High Transfer-High Traditional

Assoc/HT-Mix Trad/Non: Associate's Colleges: High Transfer-Mixed Traditional/Nontraditional

Assoc/HT-High Non: Associate's Colleges: High Transfer-High Nontraditional

Assoc/MT-VT-High Trad: Associate's Colleges: Mixed Transfer/Vocational & Technical-High Traditional

Assoc/MT-VT-Mix Trad/Non: Associate's Colleges: Mixed Transfer/Vocational & Technical-Mixed Traditional/Nontraditional

Assoc/MT-VT-High Non: Associate's Colleges: Mixed Transfer/Vocational & Technical-High Nontraditional

Assoc/HVT-High Trad: Associate's Colleges: High Vocational & Technical-High Traditional

Assoc/HVT-Mix Trad/Non: Associate's Colleges: High Vocational & Technical-Mixed Traditional/Nontraditional

Assoc/HVT-High Non: Associate's Colleges: High Vocational & Technical-High Nontraditional

Baccalaureate/Associate's Colleges. Includes four-year colleges (by virtue of having at least one baccalaureate degree program) that conferred more than 50 percent of degrees at the associate's level. Excludes Special Focus Institutions, Tribal Colleges, and institutions that have sufficient masterÖs or doctoral degrees to fall into those categories.

Bac/Assoc-Assoc Dom: Baccalaureate/Associate's Colleges: Associate's Dominant

Bac/Assoc-Mixed: Baccalaureate/Associate's Colleges: Mixed Baccalaureate/Associate's

Baccalaureate Colleges. Includes institutions where baccalaureate or higher degrees represent at least 50 percent of all degrees but where fewer than 50 master's degrees or 20 doctoral degrees were awarded during the update year. (Some institutions above the master's degree threshold are also included; see Methodology) Excludes Special Focus Institutions and Tribal Colleges.

Bac-A&S: Baccalaureate Colleges: Arts & Sciences Focus

Bac-Diverse: Baccalaureate Colleges: Diverse Fields

Master's Colleges and Universities. Generally includes institutions that awarded at least 50 master's degrees and fewer than 20 doctoral degrees during the update year (with occasional exceptions; see Methodology). Excludes Special Focus Institutions and Tribal Colleges.

Masters/L: Master's Colleges & Universities: Larger Programs

Masters/M: Master's Colleges & Universities: Medium Programs

Masters/S: Master's Colleges & Universities: Small Programs

Doctoral Universities. Includes institutions that awarded at least 20 research/scholarship doctoral degrees during the update year (this does not include professional practice doctoral-level degrees, such as the JD, MD, PharmD, DPT, etc.). Excludes Special Focus Institutions and Tribal Colleges.

DU-Highest: Doctoral Universities: Highest Research Activity

DU-Higher: Doctoral Universities: Higher Research Activity

DU-Mod: Doctoral Universities: Moderate Research Activity

Special Focus Institutions, Two-year. Institutions where a high concentration of degrees is in a single field or set of related fields. Excludes Tribal Colleges.

Spec 2-yr-Health: Special Focus Two-Year: Health Professions

Spec 2-yr-Tech: Special Focus Two-Year: Technical Professions

Spec 2-yr-A&S: Special Focus Two-Year: Arts & Design

Spec 2-yr-Other: Special Focus Two-Year: Other Fields

Special Focus Institutions, Four-year. Institutions where a high concentration of degrees is in a single field or set of related fields. Excludes Tribal Colleges.

Spec-4-yr-Faith: Special Focus Four-Year: Faith-Related Institutions

Spec-4-yr-Med: Special Focus Four-Year: Medical Schools & Centers

Spec-4-yr-Other Health: Special Focus Four-Year: Other Health Professions Schools

Spec-4-yr-Eng: Special Focus Four-Year: Engineering Schools

Spec-4-yr-Other Tech: Special Focus Four-Year: Other Technology-Related Schools

Spec-4-yr-Bus: Special Focus Four-Year: Business & Management Schools

Spec-4-yr-Arts: Special Focus Four-Year: Arts, Music & Design Schools

Spec-4-yr-Law: Special Focus Four-Year: Law Schools

Spec-4-yr-Other: Special Focus Four-Year: Other Special Focus Institutions

Tribal Colleges. Colleges and universities that are members of the American Indian Higher Education Consortium, as identified in IPEDS Institutional Characteristics.

Tribal: Tribal Colleges

*All data provided by Carnegie Classification of Institutions of Higher Education by Indiana University Center for Postsecondary Research. For more detailed information on the revised Carnegie Codes, please visit http://carnegieclassifications.iu.edu/. Basic Classification methodology can be found at http://carnegieclassifications.iu.edu/methodology/basic.php.

Statistics

Institutions of Higher Education by Control, Level and State

STATE	TWO YEAR		FOUR YEAR		TOTAL		SYSTEM	GRAND
	PRIVATE	PUBLIC	PRIVATE	PUBLIC	PRIVATE	PUBLIC	OFFICE	TOTAL
AL	2	26	23	15	25	41	2	68
AK	2	1	3	3	5	4	1	10
AZ	9	19	26	4	35	23	1	59
AR	2	22	12	11	14	33	2	49
CA	51	104	242	48	293	152	28	473
CO	19	13	27	16	46	29	2	77
CT	0	12	20	7	20	19	1	40
DE	1	0	4	3	5	3	0	8
DC	0	0	14	3	14	3	0	17
FL	43	3	75	39	118	42	1	161
GA	9	24	38	29	47	53	1	101
HI	2	6	7	4	9	10	2	21
ID	0	4	5	4	5	8	0	13
IL	17	47	95	12	112	59	6	177
IN	6	1	46	14	52	15	2	69
IA	1	18	39	3	40	21	3	64
KS	3	25	25	9	28	34	0	62
KY	1	16	33	8	34	24	1	59
LA	8	18	14	16	22	34	4	60
ME	3	7	11	8	14	15	2	31
MD	4	16	22	16	26	32	1	59
MA	3	16	81	14	84	30	2	116
MI	4	23	43	21	47	44	1	92
MN	3	30	48	11	51	41	3	95
MS	0	15	10	9	10	24	0	34
MO	12	17	61	13	73	30	3	106
MT	6	5	6	6	12	11	1	24
NE	6	7	17	7	23	14	2	39
NV	4	1	3	6	7	7	1	15
NH	1	7	11	4	12	11	2	25
NJ	4	19	35	13	39	32	1	72
NM	0	13	9	8	9	21	0	30
NY	30	36	189	44	219	80	5	304
NC	2	59	51	16	53	75	2	130
ND	1	4	7	7	8	11	1	20
OH	24	24	74	17	98	41	1	140
OK	5	12	16	15	21	27	0	48
OR	5	16	27	8	32	24	0	56
PA	51	16	115	20	166	36	1	203
RI	0	1	8	3	8	4	0	12
SC	2	19	23	14	25	33	0	58
SD	0	5	10	6	10	11	1	22
TN	10	13	52	10	62	23	2	87
TX	25	62	76	47	101	109	8	218
UT	2	3	13	7	15	10	1	26
VT	0	1	16	5	16	6	1	23
VA	17	24	59	17	76	41	1	118
WA	2	22	23	17	25	39	2	66
WV	9	8	12	11	21	19	2	42
WI	2	16	32	14	34	30	2	66
WY	1	7	1	1	2	8	0	10
AS	0	0	0	1	0	1	0	1
GU	0	1	1	1	1	2	0	3
MH	0	1	0	0	0	1	0	1
MP	0	0	0	1	0	1	0	1
PR	8	0	41	14	49	14	3	66
FM	0	1	0	0	0	1	0	1
PW	0	1	0	0	0	1	0	1
VI	0	0	0	1	0	1	0	1
Total	**422**	**887**	**1951**	**681**	**2373**	**1568**	**109**	**4050**

Figures do not include 1,222 additional branch campuses.

50 Largest Universities by Fall 2014 Enrollment

Institution	Enrollment
1. Liberty University	81459
2. Grand Canyon University	62304
3. Texas A & M University	61642
4. University of Central Florida	60767
5. The Ohio State University Main Campus	58322
6. Western Governors University	57821
7. American Public University System	57539
8. Walden University	52188
9. Kaplan University	52018
10. University of Texas at Austin	51313
11. Ashford University	51237
12. University of Minnesota-Twin Cities	51147
13. Arizona State University	50320
14. Michigan State University	50081
15. Florida International University	49610
16. University of Florida	49459
17. New York University	49274
18. Rutgers the State University of New Jersey New Brunswick Campus	48378
19. University of Maryland University College	47906
20. Penn State University Park	47040
21. University of Illinois at Urbana-Champaign	45140
22. University of Washington	44784
23. University of Michigan-Ann Arbor	43625
24. Southern New Hampshire University	43274
25. University of Wisconsin-Madison	42598
26. University of Southern California	42453
27. University of Arizona	42236
28. University of South Florida	41938
29. University of California-Los Angeles	41845
30. Florida State University	41226
31. University of Houston	40914
32. California State University-Northridge	40131
33. Purdue University Main Campus	39752
34. The University of Texas at Arlington	39740
35. Ohio University (all campuses)	39201
36. California State University-Fullerton	38128
37. University of Maryland College Park	37610
38. University of California-Berkeley	37565
39. Temple University	37485
40. California State University-Long Beach	36809
41. Texas State University	36739
42. Brigham Young University-Idaho	36624
43. University of North Texas	36486
44. The University of Alabama	36047
45. University of Missouri - Columbia	35425
46. University of Cincinnati Main Campus	35313
47. University of Georgia	35197
48. Texas Tech University	35158
49. Capella University	35061
50. University of California-Davis	34508

Institutions by Control and Tuition Range

Tuition	Public*	Private	Total
0 - 1,000	90	752	842
1,001 - 2,000	158	2	160
2,001 - 4,000	483	24	507
4,001 - 6,000	345	58	403
6,001 - 8,000	233	62	295
8,001 - 10,000	129	81	210
Over 10,000	130	1394	1524
Total	**1568**	**2373**	**3941**

* Figures for Public Institutions are In-State Tuitions

Universities, Colleges and Schools

by State*

*Includes the District of Columbia and, separately, U.S. Service Schools, American Samoa, Federated States of Micronesia, Guam, Marshall Islands, Northern Marianas, Palau, Puerto Rico, and Virgin Islands.

ALABAMA

Alabama Agricultural and Mechanical University (A)

4900 Meridian Street, Normal AL 35762-1357

County: Madison FICE Identification: 001002
Unit ID: 100654
Telephone: (256) 372-5230 Carnegie Class: Masters/L
FAX Number: (256) 372-5244 Calendar System: Semester
URL: www.aamu.edu
Established: 1875 Annual Undergrad Tuition & Fees (In-State): $9,366
Enrollment: 5,333 Coed
Affiliation or Control: State IRS Status: 501(c)3
Highest Offering: Doctorate
Accreditation: SC, AAFCS, CORE, CS, DIETD, ENG, ENGT, PLNG, SP, SW, TED

01 President Dr. Andrew HUGINE, JR.
03 Executive VP/COO Dr. Kevin A. ROLLE
05 Provost/VP Academic Affairs Dr. Daniel K. WIMS
10 Vice Pres of Business & Finance Mr. Clayton GIBSON
26 Int VP Mktg/Comm/Advancement Mr. Archie TUCKER
32 Interim VP Student Affairs Dr. Gary CROSBY
46 Interim VP Inst Rsrch/Spons Pgms Dr. James WALKE
21 AVP Budget & Planning Mr. Gregory JACKSON
84 AVP of Enrollment Management Ms. Venita KING
13 Chief Information Officer Dr. Kimberly MARSHALL
21 AVP Finance/Comptroller Mr. Norman JONES
15 Director Human Resources Ms. Cassandra TARVER-ROSS
18 Int Director Facilities Services Mr. Brian SHIPP
06 Registrar Ms. Brenda K. WILLIAMS
30 Int Director of Development Ms. Reba JASMIN
41 Director of Athletics Mr. Bryan HICKS
35 Director of Student Activities Ms. Diann ANDERSON
37 Director of Financial Aid Mr. Darryl JACKSON
88 Director of Emergency Management Vacant
23 Dir Student Health & Counseling Dr. Michael JOHNSON
36 Dir Career Development Services Ms. Yvette CLAYTON
09 Dir Institutional Research Dr. James WALKE
88 Director Marketing & PR Mr. Jerome SAINTJONES
39 Dir of Residential Housing Mr. Kenneth MADDOX
19 Chief of Police Vacant
08 Dean Learn Resources Center Dr. Annie PAYTON
96 Director of Purchasing Mr. Jeffrey ROBINSON
58 Dean Graduate School/AVP Acad Affs Dr. Colmore CHRISTIAN
47 Dean Col Agricultural/Life/Nat Sci Dr. Lloyd WALKER
53 Dean College of Education Dr. Curtis MARTIN
54 Dean College of Engineering Dr. Chance GLENN
50 Int Dean Col of Business/Pub Affs Dr. Del SMITH
49 Interim Dean University College Dr. Juarine STEWART
04 Administrative Asst to President Ms. Michele WESSON
102 Dir Foundation/Corporate Relations Mr. Allen VITAL
103 Dir Workforce/Career Development Mrs. Velma TRIBUE
29 Director Alumni Relations Mrs. Sandra STUBBS
43 Dir Legal Services/General Counsel Mrs. Angela DEBRO
45 Chief Institutional Planning Mr. Archie TUCKER

Alabama College of Osteopathic Medicine (B)

445 Health Sciences Boulevard, Dothan AL 36303

County: Houston Identification: 667138
Telephone: (334) 699-2266 Carnegie Class: Not Classified
FAX Number: N/A Calendar System: Semester
URL: www.acomedu.org
Established: 2011 Annual Graduate Tuition & Fees: N/A
Enrollment: N/A Coed
Affiliation or Control: Independent Non-Profit IRS Status: 501(c)3
Highest Offering: First Professional Degree; No Undergraduates
Accreditation: @OSTEO

01 President Rick SUTTON
05 Dean/Senior Vice President Craig J. LENZ
32 Assoc Dean Student Services Philip REYNOLDS

Alabama Southern Community College (C)

PO Box 2000, Monroeville AL 36461-2000

County: Monroe FICE Identification: 001034
Unit ID: 101949
Telephone: (251) 575-3156 Carnegie Class: Assoc/MT-VT-High Trad
FAX Number: (251) 575-5356 Calendar System: Semester
URL: www.ascc.edu
Established: 1965 Annual Undergrad Tuition & Fees (In-State): $4,320
Enrollment: 1,398 Coed
Affiliation or Control: State IRS Status: 501(c)3
Highest Offering: Associate Degree
Accreditation: SC, ADNUR

01 Interim President Mr. Roger CHANDLER
05 Dean of Instruction Mrs. Linda GRANT
32 Dean of Students Dr. Melissa HAAB
08 Director of Library Services Ms. Alisha LINAM
06 Registrar Ms. Jana HORTON
37 Director of Financial Aid Ms. Amy ROWELL
26 Director of Public Information Mrs. Lindsay HUTCHERSON
18 Director of Maintenance Mr. Tom REED
41 Athletic Director Mr. Daniel HEAD
15 Human Resources Associate Mrs. Kristi SMITH

Alabama State University (D)

915 S Jackson Street, Montgomery AL 36101-0271

County: Montgomery FICE Identification: 001005
Unit ID: 100724
Telephone: (334) 229-4200 Carnegie Class: Masters/M
FAX Number: (334) 834-6861 Calendar System: Semester
URL: www.alasu.edu
Established: 1867 Annual Undergrad Tuition & Fees (In-State): $8,720
Enrollment: 5,519 Coed
Affiliation or Control: State IRS Status: 501(c)3
Highest Offering: Doctorate
Accreditation: SC, ACBSP, ART, CACREP, CAHIIM, CORE, MUS, OPE, OT, PTA, SW, TED, THEA

01 President Dr. Gwendolyn E. BOYD
05 Provost/Vice Pres Academic Affs Dr. Leon C. WILSON
100 Chief of Staff Mr. Bernard HOUSTON
10 Vice President Business & Finance Ms. Wanda SMITH
13 Vice President Technology Services Ms. Diane ALEXANDER
30 Vice Pres Institutional Advancement Ms. Zillah FLUKER
15 Director Human Resources Mrs. Willie DIXON
04 Administrative Asst to President Mrs. Kathy GRANT
32 Vice Pres Student Affairs Dr. Davida HAYWOOD
84 Assistant Vice Pres Enrollment Mgmt Dr. Ronald BROWN
20 Assoc Provost Academic Affairs Dr. Karyn GUNN
45 Assoc Prov Institutional Effectiv Dr. Legand BURGE
35 Asst Vice Pres Student Affairs Vacant
21 Int Comt/Asst VP Business & Finance Mrs. Alondrea J. FRITCHETT
20 Assistant VP Academic Advisement Vacant
108 Dir Acad Planning & Evaluation Dr. Christine C. THOMAS
09 Director Institutional Research Dr. Yiyun JIE
88 Dir Quality Enhancement Plng Dr. Denise VAUGHN
08 Dean Libraries/Learning Resource Dr. Janice FRANKLIN
07 Director Admissions/Recruitment Dr. William SMITH
37 Financial Aid Director Mr. Marcus BYRD
36 Dir Placement Svcs/Cooperative Educ Mr. Jeremy HODGE
50 Dean College Business Admin Dr. LaQuita BOOTH
89 Dean University College Dr. Evelyn HODGE
53 Dean College of Education Dr. Doris SCREWS
64 Dean Visual & Performing Arts Dr. Tommie T. STEWART
58 Dean Graduate Studies Dr. William PERSON
81 Dean College of Sci Math & Tech Dr. Kennedy WEKESA
49 Dean Liberal Arts/Social Sci Dr. Anthony T. ADAMS
76 Dean College Health Sciences Vacant
51 Director Continuing Education Mr. Olan L. WESLEY
29 Director Alumni Relations Mr. Cromwell HANDY
23 Director Student Health Services Ms. Gwendolyn MANN
19 Chief of Campus Police Mr. James GRAYBOYS
38 Dir Counseling & Development Svcs Vacant
39 Dir Housing/Residential Life Mr. Gourdine WADE
41 Director of Athletics Mr. Melvin HINES
25 Director Grants Sponsored Pgms Mrs. Tamara LEE
96 Director of Purchasing Ms. Arlene THOMPSON
101 Board Liaison Vacant
106 Dir Online Education/E-learning Dr. William PERSON
43 General Counsel Mr. Kenneth THOMAS
06 Registrar Ms. Marie MCNEAR
26 Chief Public Relations/Marketing Mr. Kenneth MULLINAX

Amridge University (E)

1200 Taylor Road, Montgomery AL 36117-3553

County: Montgomery FICE Identification: 025034
Unit ID: 100690
Telephone: (800) 351-4040 Carnegie Class: Masters/S
FAX Number: (334) 387-3878 Calendar System: Semester
URL: www.amridgeuniversity.edu
Established: 1967 Annual Undergrad Tuition & Fees: $6,900
Enrollment: 625 Coed
Affiliation or Control: Churches Of Christ IRS Status: 501(c)3
Highest Offering: Doctorate
Accreditation: SC

01 President Dr. Michael C. TURNER
05 Academic Vice President/Dean Dr. Lee TAYLOR
32 VP of Student Affairs Mrs. Laina T. COSTANZA
06 Registrar Mrs. Elaine P. TARENCE
08 Director of Library Ms. Kay S. NEWMAN
10 Chief Business Officer Mrs. B. P. TURNER
21 Chief Accountant Dr. Anita L. CROSBY
37 Financial Aid Director Ms. Starr FAIN
42 Director of Church Relations Mr. Curtis SAMPLEY
88 Director of World Missions Mr. Demar ELAM
29 Director of Alumni Relations Vacant
13 System Admin Network Operations Mr. Jack TEMPLE
18 Chief Facilities/Physical Plant Mr. Robert SHIRLEY
24 Coordinator of Network Opers Mr. Thomas PATTERSON
38 Director of Student Counseling Vacant
26 Chief Public Relations Officer Mrs. Laina COSTANZA
73 Dean of School of Theology Dr. Rodney CLOUD
50 Dean of Col of Business & Ldrshp Dr. Kenyetta MCCURTY
97 Dean of College of General Studies Dr. Roger SHEPHERD
88 Dean of Sch of Human Svcs Dr. Jerry MARTIN
15 Director Personnel Services Vacant
08 Head Librarian Mr. Terence SHERIDAN
84 Enrollment Management Coordinator Mr. Brooks HOUSLEY

Athens State University (F)

300 N Beaty Street, Athens AL 35611-1902

County: Limestone FICE Identification: 001008
Unit ID: 100812
Telephone: (256) 233-8100 Carnegie Class: Bac-Diverse
FAX Number: (256) 216-3324 Calendar System: Semester
URL: www.athens.edu
Established: 1822 Annual Undergrad Tuition & Fees (In-State): N/A
Enrollment: 3,128 Coed
Affiliation or Control: State IRS Status: 501(c)3
Highest Offering: Master's
Accreditation: SC, ACBSP, CS, TED

01 President Dr. Robert K. GLENN
05 Provost & VP for Academic Affs Dr. Joseph DELAP
20 Associate VP for Academic Affairs Ms. Belinda KRIGEL
20 Asst VP for Academic Affairs Dr. Jackie SMITH
32 Vice Pres for Enroll & Student Supp Ms. Sarah MCABEE
35 Asst VP for Enrollment & Stdnt Svcs Ms. Crystal CREEKMORE
10 Vice President Financial Affairs Mr. Mike MCCOY
21 Associate Business Officer Vacant
26 Vice Pres for University Advance Dr. Keith FERGUSON
08 Director of Libraries Vacant
50 Dean College of Business Dr. Kimberly LAFEVOR
53 Dean College of Education Dr. Patricia SIMS
49 Dean College of Arts & Sciences Dr. Ronald FRITZE
36 Dir of Career Services Ms. Saralyn MITCHELL
37 Dir of Student Financial Services Ms. Mary CHAMBLISS
06 Registrar Ms. Teresa SUIT
07 Director of Admissions & Records Ms. Necedah HENDERSON
35 Director of Student Activities Mr. Terry STEPP
29 Director of Alumni Affairs/Ann Giv Ms. Trish DI LULLO
30 Director of Development Vacant
88 Director of Printing & Public Rels Mr. Guy MCCLURE
09 Director of Institutional Research Ms. Sylvia CORREA
18 Director of Physical Plant Mr. Jerry BRADFORD
15 Director of Human Resources Ms. Suzanne SIMS
51 Director of Ctr for Lifelong Lrng Vacant
88 Director of Student Success Ctr Mr. Derrek SMITH
04 Administrative Asst to President Mrs. Carol E. RACHAL
101 Secretary of the Institution/Board Mrs. Jackie GOOCH
13 Chief Info Technology Officer (CIO) Ms. Belinda KRIGEL
19 Chief of Security/Safety Mr. Jerry CRABTREE

Auburn University (G)

Auburn AL 36849

County: Lee FICE Identification: 001009
Unit ID: 100858
Telephone: (334) 844-4000 Carnegie Class: DU-Higher
FAX Number: N/A Calendar System: Semester
URL: www.auburn.edu
Established: 1856 Annual Undergrad Tuition & Fees (In-State): $10,424
Enrollment: 25,912 Coed
Affiliation or Control: State IRS Status: 501(c)3
Highest Offering: Doctorate
Accreditation: SC, AAB, ART, AUD, BUS, BUSA, CACREP, CIDA, CLPSY, CONST, COPSY, CORE, CS, DIETD, ENG, JOUR, LSAR, MFCD, MUS, NURSE, PHAR, SP, SPAA, SW, TED, THEA, VET

01 President Dr. Jay GOGUE
03 Executive Vice President Dr. Donald L. LARGE, JR.
05 Provost/VP Academic Affairs Dr. Timothy R. BOOSINGER
29 VP Alumni Affairs Ms. Gretchen R. VANVALKENBURG
10 VP Business & Finance & CFO Ms. Kelli D. SHOMAKER
30 VP Development Ms. Jane DIFOLCO PARKER
32 VP & Assoc Provost Student Affairs Dr. Bobby R. WOODARD
46 VP Research & Economic Development Dr. John M. MASON
101 Secretary to Board of Trustees Mr. C. Grant DAVIS, JR.
43 General Counsel Mr. Lee F. ARMSTRONG
13 Chief Information Officer Mr. James O'CONNOR
84 Dean of Enrollment Services Dr. Charles W. ALDERMAN
56 Dir AL Cooperative Extension Syst Dr. Gary D. LEMME
41 Director of Athletics Mr. John O. JACOBS, JR.
86 Exec Director Governmental Affairs Ms. Sherri FULFORD
11 Director Public Affairs Mr. Brian C. KEETER
88 Assoc VP Int Audit/Compl & Privcy Mr. M. Kevin ROBINSON
88 Exec Director Risk Mgmt & Safety Ms. Christine L. EICK
26 Director Univ Communications Mr. Mike CLARDY, JR.
88 Univ Ombudsperson Mr. Kevin COONROD
20 Associate Provost & Professor Dr. Emmett WINN
28 Assoc Prov & VP Inclu & Diversity Vacant
46 Assoc VP & Assoc Provost Research Dr. Zhanjiang LIU
20 Assoc Provost Undergrad Studies Dr. Constance C. RELIHAN
25 Assistant VP Research Ms. Martha M. TAYLOR
35 Assistant VP Student Affairs Ms. Lady D. COX
56 VP University Outreach Dr. Royrickers COOK
92 Asst Provost & Dir Honors College Dr. Melissa J. BAUMANN
85 Asst Provost Intl Programs Dr. Andrew R. GILLESPIE
28 Asst Provost Women's Initiatives Dr. Donna L. SOLLIE
109 Associate VP Auxiliary Services Mr. Robert C. RITENBAUGH, III
18 Associate VP Facilities Mr. Daniel P. KING
15 Associate VP Human Resources Ms. Karla S. MCCORMICK
21 Controller Ms. Amy K. DOUGLAS
96 Exec Dir Procurement/Payment Svcs Ms. Melissa M. MORRIS
37 Exec Dir Student Financial Svcs Mr. Michael C. REYNOLDS
22 Director Affirmative Action/EEO Ms. Kelley G. TAYLOR
108 Director Academic Assessment Dr. Megan R. GOOD
09 Director Institutional Research Dr. James A. CLARK
88 Director University Writing Dr. Margaret J. MARSHALL
88 Director Teaching & Learning Center Dr. Diane E. BOYD
88 Director JCS Museum of Art Dr. Marilyn LAUFER
39 Director Residence Life Dr. Virginia A. KOCH
36 Director Student Career Services Mrs. Nancy M. BERNARD
38 Director Student Counseling Svcs Dr. Doug HANKES
14 Director IT Mr. Bliss BAILEY
40 Director University Bookstore Ms. Catherine LEE

06 University Registrar ..... Ms. Laura Ann FOREST
47 Dean Agriculture & Dir AAES ..... Dr. Paul M. PATTERSON
48 Dean Architecture/Design/Construct ..... Dr. Vini NATHAN
50 Dean Business ..... Dr. Bill HARDGRAVE
53 Dean Education ..... Dr. Betty Lou WHITFORD
54 Dean Engineering ..... Dr. Christopher B. ROBERTS
65 Dean Forestry/Wildlife Sci ..... Dr. Janaki R. ALAVALAPATI
59 Dean Human Sciences ..... Dr. June M. HENTON
49 Dean Liberal Arts ..... Dr. Joseph AISTRUP
66 Dean Nursing ..... Dr. Gregg NEWSCHWANDER
67 Dean Pharmacy ..... Dr. R. Lee EVANS, JR.
81 Dean Sciences & Mathematics ..... Dr. Nicholas J. GIORDANO
74 Dean Veterinary Medicine ..... Dr. Calvin M. JOHNSON
58 Dean Graduate School ..... Dr. George FLOWERS
08 Dean University Libraries ..... Dr. Bonnie MACEWAN
04 Administrative Asst to President ..... Ms. Jolene M. PATTERSON

Auburn University at Montgomery (A)

PO Box 244023, Montgomery AL 36124-4023
County: Montgomery FICE Identification: 008310
Unit ID: 100830
Telephone: (334) 244-3000 Carnegie Class: Masters/L
FAX Number: (334) 244-3762 Calendar System: Semester
URL: www.aum.edu
Established: 1967 Annual Undergrad Tuition & Fees (In-State): $9,350
Enrollment: 5,057 Coed
Affiliation or Control: State IRS Status: 501(c)3
Highest Offering: Doctorate
Accreditation: SC, BUS, BUSA, CACREP, MT, NURSE, SPAA, TED

01 Chancellor ..... Dr. John G. VERES, III
05 Provost ..... Dr. Joe M. KING
30 Vice Chancellor Advancement ..... Ms. Carolyn GOLDEN
88 Vice Chanc Outreach/Strat Init ..... Dr. Katherine JACKSON
32 Vice Chancellor of Student Affairs ..... Ms. Janice LYN
58 Assoc Provost Research/Grad Studies ..... Dr. Matthew RAGLAND
20 Assoc Provost Undergraduate Studies ..... Dr. Joy CLARK
09 Asst Provost IE & Accreditation ..... Dr. Cara Mia BRASWELL
41 Athletic Director ..... Mr. Jim HERLIHY
85 Director of Global Initiatives ..... Mr. Gokhan ALKANAT
21 Chief Accounting Officer/Controller ..... Ms. Kim DECKER
15 Chief Human Resources Officer ..... Ms. Jeanine BODDIE-LAVAN
18 Sodexo ..... Mr. Ken CORNELIUS
08 Dean of Library ..... Mr. Phil JOHNSON
07 Director of Admissions/Recruiting ..... Mr. Rahmel COWEN
37 Sr Director of Financial Aid ..... Mr. Anthony RICHEY
109 Chief Campus Services Officer ..... Mr. Daryl MORRIS
39 Dir Housing & Residence Life ..... Mr. Iyisha HAMPTON
13 Chief Information Officer ..... Mr. Tobias MENSE
35 Associate Dean of Student Affairs ..... Dr. Chaundra THOMPSON
19 Director of Police Operations ..... Ms. Brenda MITCHELL
06 Registrar ..... Ms. Holly BENSON
36 Director Career Development ..... Mr. Bradley ROBBINS
40 Director of Bookstore ..... Mr. Jeffrey P. VINZANT
26 Exec Dir Strategic Comm & Marketing ..... Ms. Marla VICKERS
25 Director of Sponsored Programs ..... Ms. Fariba S. DERAVI
85 Coord Intl Student Admissions ..... Ms. Krystin BRYMER
49 Dean of College of Arts & Sciences ..... Dr. Michael BURGER
50 Dean of College of Business ..... Dr. Wanda Rhea INGRAM
53 Dean of College of Education ..... Dr. Sheila AUSTIN
66 Int Dean of Nursing ..... Dr. Jean LEUNER
51 Exec Dir of Continuing Education ..... Ms. Kathy GUNTER
38 Director Student Counseling ..... Ms. Jennifer BRADLEY
96 Dir of Procurement & Payment Svcs ..... Ms. Lori NIELSEN
04 Executive Admin Assoc to Chancellor ..... Ms. Chanell DAVIS
106 Dir Online Education/E-learning ..... Ms. Carolyn RAWL

Bevill State Community College (B)

1411 Indiana Avenue, Jasper AL 35501
County: Walker FICE Identification: 005733
Unit ID: 102429
Telephone: (205) 387-0511 Carnegie Class: Assoc/HVT-Mix Trad/Non
FAX Number: (205) 387-5192 Calendar System: Semester
URL: www.bscc.edu
Established: 1965 Annual Undergrad Tuition & Fees (In-State): $4,350
Enrollment: 3,609 Coed
Affiliation or Control: State IRS Status: 501(c)3
Highest Offering: Associate Degree
Accreditation: SC, ADNUR, EMT, PNUR, SURGT

01 President ..... Dr. Larry A. FERGUSON
05 Dean of Instruction ..... Dr. Leslie CUMMINGS
32 Dean of Students ..... Dr. Kim ENNIS
26 Director of Public Relations ..... Dr. Chris FRANKLIN
10 Director of Accounting & Finance ..... Ms. Carolyn MORGAN
35 Asst Dean of Students ..... Ms. Melissa STOWE
15 Director of Personnel Services ..... Ms. Mary KINARD
18 Director of Facilities & Security ..... Mr. Randy STULTS

Birmingham-Southern College (C)

900 Arkadelphia Road, Birmingham AL 35254-0001
County: Jefferson FICE Identification: 001012
Unit ID: 100937
Telephone: (205) 226-4600 Carnegie Class: Bac-A&S
FAX Number: (205) 226-4627 Calendar System: 4/1/4
URL: www.bsc.edu
Established: 1856 Annual Undergrad Tuition & Fees: $33,128
Enrollment: 1,185 Coed
Affiliation or Control: United Methodist IRS Status: 501(c)3
Highest Offering: Baccalaureate
Accreditation: SC, MUS, TED

01 President ..... Ms. Linda F. GOLDSMITH
05 Sr VP and Provost ..... Dr. Michelle BEHR
10 Sr VP of Finance/CFO ..... Mr. Eli PHILLIPS
11 VP Admin/Community Relations ..... Mr. Lane ESTES
30 Sr VP Advancement ..... Mr. Joe DEAN
26 Director of Communications ..... Ms. Hannah WOLFSON
13 VP Information Technology ..... Mr. Anthony HAMBEY
32 VP Student Development ..... Dr. David EBERHARDT
84 VP Admission and Financial Planning ..... Ms. Sara NEWHOUSE
88 Asst to the President Emeriti ..... Mrs. Terri HICKS
20 VP/Assoc Provost Academic Affairs ..... Dr. Susan HAGEN
20 Assistant Provost Academic Affairs ..... Ms. Martha STEVENSON
06 Registrar ..... Mr. Keith KARRIKER
42 Chaplain ..... Rev. Julie HOLLY
29 Director Alumni Affairs/Stewardship ..... Vacant
23 Assoc Director of Health Services ..... Ms. Yvette SPENCER
04 Asst to the President ..... Mrs. Tammie DODD
08 Director of the Library ..... Vacant
18 Director of Facilities & Events ..... Ms. Anne CURRY
37 Director of Financial Planning ..... Mr. Brian QUISENBERRY
15 Assoc VP/Director Human Resources ..... Ms. Susan KINNEY
27 Director of Church Relations ..... Ms. Laura SISSON
88 Director of New Media ..... Mr. Mike HAMILTON
38 Director of Counseling/Health Svcs ..... Ms. Sara HOOVER
41 Athletic Director ..... Ms. Kyndall WATERS
19 Chief of Campus Police ..... Mr. Randy YOUNGBLOOD
36 Director of Career Services ..... Mr. Michael LEBEAU
30 Director Advancement Services ..... Mr. Jeff SHERRELL
28 Director of Multi-Cultural Affairs ..... Ms. Erica BROWN
108 VP Planning and Effectiveness ..... Dr. Noreen GAUBATZ
68 Dir Physical Fitness & Recreation ..... Mr. Mike ROBINSON
88 Director of Leadership Studies ..... Mr. Kent ANDERSEN
88 Director of Service Learning ..... Ms. Kristin HARPER
88 Assoc Dir of International Programs ..... Ms. Anne LEDVINA
88 Manager of Printing Services ..... Mr. Jerome DAVIS
40 Bookstore Manager ..... Mr. William ALEXANDER
96 Purchasing Manager ..... Mr. Tim WILDING
102 Director of Development ..... Ms. Jennifer SHOLUND
44 Director Development/Annual Giving ..... Mr. Bobby WATSON

Bishop State Community College (D)

351 N Broad Street, Mobile AL 36603-5898
County: Mobile FICE Identification: 001030
Unit ID: 102030
Telephone: (251) 405-7000 Carnegie Class: Assoc/HVT-Mix Trad/Non
FAX Number: N/A Calendar System: Semester
URL: www.bishop.edu
Established: 1965 Annual Undergrad Tuition & Fees (In-State): $4,320
Enrollment: 3,320 Coed
Affiliation or Control: State IRS Status: 501(c)3
Highest Offering: Associate Degree
Accreditation: SC, ACBSP, ADNUR, CAHIIM, FUSER, PNUR, PTAA

01 Acting President ..... Dr. Reginald SYKES
11 Interim Vice President of Opers ..... Mrs. Ann CLANTON
05 Dean of Instructional Services ..... Dr. Latitia MCCANE
12 Director of Carver Campus ..... Vacant
12 Dir Baker-Gaines Central Campus ..... Mrs. Madeline STOKES
72 Dean of Tech Educ/Workforce Dev ..... Mr. Karl HENRY
32 Dean of Students ..... Dr. Terry HAZZARD
10 Dean of Business/Finance ..... Mrs. Bonita ALLEN
06 Registrar ..... Mr. Philip URBANEK
15 Director of Human Resources ..... Ms. Marquita LYONS
18 Director of Physical Plant ..... Mr. Lorenzo GRAYSON
26 Director of Public Relations ..... Ms. Harietta EATON
45 Director of Inst Effectiveness ..... Mr. Roderick MCSWAIN
37 Mgr Student Fin Aid/Veterans Svcs ..... Dr. Samuel CHUKS

Brown Mackie College - Birmingham (E)

105 Vulcan Road, Birmingham AL 35209
Telephone: (205) 909-1500 Identification: 770625
Accreditation: &NH, OTA, SURTEC

† Regional accreditation is carried under the parent institution in Salina, KS.

Calhoun Community College (F)

PO Box 2216, Decatur AL 35609-2216
County: Limestone FICE Identification: 001013
Unit ID: 101514
Telephone: (256) 306-2500 Carnegie Class: Assoc/MT-VT-Mix Trad/Non
FAX Number: (256) 306-2877 Calendar System: Semester
URL: www.calhoun.edu
Established: 1963 Annual Undergrad Tuition & Fees (In-State): $4,320
Enrollment: 10,802 Coed
Affiliation or Control: State IRS Status: 501(c)3
Highest Offering: Associate Degree
Accreditation: SC, ADNUR, DA, EMT, MLTAD, PNUR, PTAA, SURGT

01 President ..... Dr. James S. KLAUBER
05 Acting VP Instruct/Student Success ..... Dr. Stephen CALATRELLO
32 Dean of Student Affairs ..... Dr. Patricia WILSON
10 Vice Pres for Finance & Admin Svcs ..... Mr. James B. HELMS
07 Actg Dir Admiss/Records/Registrar ..... Ms. Alanna THOMPSON
08 Director of Library Services ..... Mr. James LOYD
13 Director Information Systems ..... Mr. Nathan TYLER
30 Actg Dean Institutional Advancement ..... Ms. Janet KINCHERLOW-MARTIN
12 Dean Research Park Campus ..... Mr. Mark BRANNON
55 Coordinator of Evening Program ..... Dr. Vinetta WESLEY
26 Director of Public Relations ..... Ms. Janet KINCHERLOW-MARTIN
18 Director of Physical Plant ..... Mr. Bruce CAUSEY
09 Dean Planning/Research & Grants ..... Dr. Debra HENDERSHOT
103 Acting Director Workforce Solutions ..... Mr. Vincent VINCENT
84 Act Dir of Recruit/Retent & Success ..... Mrs. Kelli MORRIS
76 Dean Health Sciences ..... Mr. Bret MCGILL
81 Int Dean Math/Natural Sciences ..... Mr. Rodney ALFORD
79 Dean Humanities & Social Sciences ..... Dr. Donna ESTILL
15 Director Human Resources & Payroll ..... Mrs. Kim GAINES
19 Director Public Safety ..... Mr. Kevin DAVENPORT
36 Graduation & Job Placement Spec ..... Mrs. Kelli MORRIS
37 Director Student Financial Aid ..... Mrs. Janett SPENCER
04 Secretary to President ..... Ms. Belinda NOE
41 Athletic Director ..... Dr. Nancy KEENUM

Central Alabama Community College (G)

1675 Cherokee Road, Alexander City AL 35010
County: Tallapoosa FICE Identification: 001007
Unit ID: 100760
Telephone: (256) 234-6346 Carnegie Class: Assoc/HT-High Trad
FAX Number: (256) 234-0384 Calendar System: Semester
URL: www.cacc.edu
Established: 1963 Annual Undergrad Tuition & Fees (In-State): $4,320
Enrollment: 1,726 Coed
Affiliation or Control: State IRS Status: 501(c)3
Highest Offering: Associate Degree
Accreditation: SC, ADNUR

01 President ..... Dr. Susan BURROW
10 Executive Vice President/CFO ..... Vacant
05 Dean of Instruction ..... Ms. Barbara Anne SPEARS
32 Dean of Students ..... Dr. Sherri TAYLOR
35 Associate Dean of Student Services ..... Ms. Glenda BLAND
09 Assoc Dean of Inst Effect/Compl ..... Ms. Helen GALLAGHER
76 Associate Dean of Health Science ..... Dr. Melanie BOLTON
08 Librarian ..... Ms. Denita OLIVER
06 Records Manager ..... Ms. Marian MARTIN
26 Public Relations Officer ..... Mr. Brett PRITCHARD
37 Director Student Financial Aid ..... Ms. Cindy ENTREKIN
04 Executive Asst to President ..... Mr. Mark MCGHEE

Chattahoochee Valley Community College (H)

2602 College Drive, Phenix City AL 36869-7960
County: Russell FICE Identification: 012182
Unit ID: 101028
Telephone: (334) 291-4900 Carnegie Class: Assoc/HT-High Trad
FAX Number: (334) 291-4944 Calendar System: Semester
URL: www.cv.edu
Established: 1973 Annual Undergrad Tuition & Fees (In-State): $4,380
Enrollment: 1,805 Coed
Affiliation or Control: State IRS Status: 501(c)3
Highest Offering: Associate Degree
Accreditation: SC, ADNUR, PNUR

01 Interim President ..... Mr. Mark ELLARD
05 Vice President/Dean of the College ..... Dr. David HODGE
32 Dean of Student Services ..... Vacant
103 Assoc Dean of Workforce Development . Dr. Shirley ARMSTRONG
50 Chair of Business & Social Sciences ..... Dr. Bob DANSBY
81 Chair of Science ..... Ms. Susan MCCOLLUM
57 Chair of Humanities ..... Mr. Andy SCALES
76 Chair of Health Sciences ..... Ms. Resa LORD
81 Chair of Mathematics ..... Ms. Mary JOHNSON
88 Program Dir Public Safety Academy ..... Mr. Kenneth HARRISON
77 Chair Computer & Information Tech ..... Ms. Debra PLOTTS
08 Director Learning Resources Center ..... Ms. Rachel COTNEY
37 Director of Financial Aid ..... Mrs. Joan WATERS
18 Director Facilities & Maintenance ..... Mr. Johann WELLS
30 Dean of Advancement/Inst Effect ..... Dr. Joree JONES
41 Director of Athletics ..... Mr. Adam THOMAS
38 Dir Counseling/Advising & Testing ..... Vacant
13 Director of Information Systems ..... Mr. Jody NOLES
88 Director of Student Development ..... Mrs. Vickie WILLIAMS
51 Director of Adult Education ..... Ms. Laodecea SEAY
15 Director of Human Resources ..... Ms. Debbie BOONE
44 Director of Development ..... Ms. Karen KELLY
10 Business Manager ..... Ms. Christer SANKS
55 Evening Coordinator ..... Mr. Reggie GORDY
07 Director of Admissions/Registrar ..... Ms. Sanquita ALEXANDER
04 Administrative Asst to President ..... Ms. Connie ARMSTRONG
19 Security/Safety ..... Mr. Keith MANUEL
26 Marketing & Media Coordinator . Ms. Kelly WILLIAMS-SOWERS

Columbia Southern University (I)

21982 University Lane, Orange Beach AL 36561-3845
County: Baldwin FICE Identification: 041215
Unit ID: 450933
Telephone: (251) 981-3771 Carnegie Class: Masters/L
FAX Number: (251) 981-3815 Calendar System: Other
URL: www.columbiasouthern.edu
Established: 1993 Annual Undergrad Tuition & Fees: $5,175
Enrollment: 21,359 Coed
Affiliation or Control: Proprietary IRS Status: Proprietary
Highest Offering: Master's

Accreditation: DEAC

01 President .... Mr. Robert G. MAYES, JR.
03 Executive Vice President .... Ms. Chantell COOLEY
05 Provost/CAO .... Dr. Jeffrey BARKSDALE
09 VP of IE and Accreditation .... Dr. Anna WAGGENER
26 VP of University Relations .... Mr. Billy HAYES
13 Vice Pres Information Technology .... Mr. Scott OSWALD
10 Chief Financial Officer .... Mr. Pat TROUP
26 Chief Marketing Officer .... Mr. Eric MCHANEY
88 VP Business Development/Mil Init .... Mr. Rick COOPER
15 VP of Human Resources .... Ms. Sue BUTTS
49 Asst Provost Col Arts & Sciences .... Dr. John WEIDERT
32 Vice Provost Student Affairs .... Mr. Scott ROUNDS
20 Asst Prov/Dean of Faculty Services .... Dr. Elwin JONES
108 Asst Prov Inst Effect/Accreditation .... Ms. Khalilah BURTON
07 Int Director of Admissions .... Mr. Andrew SCHNEIDER
24 Dean of Instructional Design .... Dr. John HOPE
29 Dir Student & Alumni Engagement .... Ms. Amanda MANJONE
40 Director of Bookstore Operations .... Mr. David BARNES
09 Dir of Inst Research/Assessment .... Ms. Cherea SCHELLHASE
06 Registrar .... Ms. Rachel FARRIS
37 Director of Financial Aid .... Ms. Tammy COMALANDER
88 Director of Quality Assurance .... Ms. Mona MCPHERSON
08 Director of Learning Resources .... Ms. Marsha HINNEN
88 Director of State Authorization .... Ms. Alexis BANKS

Concordia College Alabama (A)

1712 Broad Street, Selma AL 36701

County: Dallas — FICE Identification: 010554
Unit ID: 101073
Telephone: (334) 874-5700 — Carnegie Class: Bac-Diverse
FAX Number: (334) 874-5755 — Calendar System: Semester
URL: www.ccal.edu
Established: 1922 — Annual Undergrad Tuition & Fees: $10,320
Enrollment: 546 — Coed
Affiliation or Control: Lutheran Church - Missouri Synod — IRS Status: 501(c)3
Highest Offering: Baccalaureate
Accreditation: SC

01 Int President/Chief Exec Officer .... Mr. Dexter JACKSON
05 Vice Pres Academic Affairs .... Dr. Cheryl WASHINGTON
10 Exec VP/Chief Fin Ofcr/Int COO .... Mr. Dexter JACKSON
32 VP of Student Services .... Dr. Donald JEFFERSON
30 VP Institutional Advancement .... Mr. Daniel JENKINS
37 Director Financial Aid .... Mrs. Tharsteen BRIDGES
09 Dir Effectiveness/Research/Plng .... Ms. Betty HUBBARD
64 Band Director .... Mr. Steven JOHNSON
08 Library Director .... Mr. J. Scott WHITING
06 Registrar .... Mrs. Chinester GRAYSON
29 Director Alumni Affairs/Development .... Mrs. Minnie MCMILLAN
26 Director Public Relations .... Ms. Abigail CAMPBELL
36 Dir Student Placement/Counseling .... Ms. Sadie JARETT
15 Director of Human Respources .... Vacant
13 IT Director .... Mr. Wayne GREEN
41 Director of Athletics .... Mr. Frankie PEOPLES
35 Director Student Activities .... Mr. Coley C. CHESTNUT, SR.
85 Director of International Students .... Mr. Katiso ALEMU
42 Church Relations Director .... Mr. James PINDRAS
21 Controller .... Mr. Aron EZAZ
07 Asst Director of Enrollment .... Ms. Theresa BROWN
84 Director Enrollment Management .... Ms. Meseret ALEMU

*Education Corporation of America (B)

3660 Grandview Parkway Suite 300,
Birmingham AL 35243

County: Jefferson — Identification: 666006
Telephone: (205) 329-7900 — Carnegie Class: N/A
FAX Number: (205) 329-7906
URL: www.ecacolleges.com

01 President/Chief Executive Officer .... Mr. Stuart C. REED
43 Exec VP/Chf Compl Ofcr/Gen Counsel .... Mr. Roger L. SWARTZWELDER
26 Exec VP/Chief Marketing Officer .... Mr. Charles S. TRIERWEILER
10 Exec VP/Chief Financial Officer .... Mr. Christopher BOEHM
15 EVP/Chief Human Resources Officer .... Ms. Paula FREY
05 Exec VP Chief Academic Officer .... Dr. John WOODS
13 Exec VP Chief Information Officer .... Mr. Mark MULLISON
21 SVP Finance .... Mr. Ryan BREWER
37 SVP Student Finance .... Ms. Kathy CHEATHAM
27 SVP of Marketing .... Mr. Jason MANN
84 SVP of Student Enrollment .... Mr. Mike MILLER
20 SVP Academic Operations .... Ms. Rita CHUBICK
20 SVP Academic Compliance Curriculum .... Ms. Judy E. LIMA
88 SVP Associate General Counsel .... Mr. Benjamin J. DEGWECK
88 Group President .... Mr. John SCHUMAN
88 Group President Emerging Brands .... Mr. Geoffrey BAIRD
88 Group President .... Mr. Dominick FEDELE

*Virginia College (C)

488 Palisades Boulevard, Birmingham AL 35209

County: Jefferson — FICE Identification: 030106
Unit ID: 420307
Telephone: (205) 802-1200 — Carnegie Class: Bac/Assoc-Mixed
FAX Number: (205) 271-8225 — Calendar System: Quarter
URL: www.vc.edu
Established: 1993 — Annual Undergrad Tuition & Fees: $13,932
Enrollment: 2,818 — Coed
Affiliation or Control: Proprietary — IRS Status: Proprietary
Highest Offering: Master's
Accreditation: ACICS, ACFEI, CIDA, COARC, DMS, MAAB, SURGT

02 Campus President .... Mr. Dale TURNER
07 Vice President of Enrollment .... Mr. Kenneth MACON
05 Academic Dean .... Mr. Keven W. ROBINSON

*Virginia College (D)

2021 Drake Avenue SW, Huntsville AL 35801

Telephone: (256) 533-7387 — Identification: 666400
Accreditation: ACICS, MAAB

*Virginia College (E)

3725 Airport Boulevard, Suite 165, Mobile AL 36608

Telephone: (251) 343-7227 — Identification: 666069
Accreditation: ACICS, ACFEI, MAAB, SURGT

*Virginia College (F)

6200 Atlanta Highway, Montgomery AL 36117-2802

Telephone: (334) 277-3390 — Identification: 666408
Accreditation: ACICS, MAAB

Edward Via College of Osteopathic Medicine-Auburn Campus (G)

910 S. Donahue Drive, Auburn AL 36832

Telephone: (334) 442-4000 — Identification: 770965
Accreditation: &OSTEO

† Regional accreditation is carried under the parent institution in Blacksburg, VA

Enterprise State Community College (H)

PO Box 1300, Enterprise AL 36331-1300

County: Coffee — FICE Identification: 001015
Unit ID: 101143
Telephone: (334) 347-2623 — Carnegie Class: Assoc/HVT-Mix Trad/Non
FAX Number: (334) 393-6223 — Calendar System: Semester
URL: www.escc.edu
Established: 1963 — Annual Undergrad Tuition & Fees (In-State): $4,320
Enrollment: 2,011 — Coed
Affiliation or Control: State — IRS Status: 501(c)3
Highest Offering: Associate Degree
Accreditation: SC

01 Interim President .... Dr. Vicky OHLSON
05 Dean of Instruction .... Ms. Leslie REEDER
32 Dean of Students .... Dr. Olivier CHARLES
10 Dean Administration & Finance ... Ms. Alonzetta LANDRUM-SIMS
35 Associate Dean of Students .... Mr. Kevin AMMONS
26 Dir Marketing & Media Relations .... Mr. Brandon PIERCE
37 Director Student Financial Aid ... Dr. Henry L. QUISENBERRY, JR.
55 Director Evening Division .... Mr. Carl HOLBROOK
04 Administrative Asst to President .... Ms. Jennifer ADAMS
07 Director of Admissions .... Mr. Joey HOLLEY
08 Head Librarian .... Ms. Linda STEPHENS
09 Director of Institutional Research .... Mr. Andrew DAVIS
102 Dir Foundation/Corporate Relations .... Ms. Chelye STUMP
103 Dir Workforce/Career Development .... Ms. Ann KELLEY
13 Chief Info Technology Officer (CIO) .... Mr. Jason TRULL
15 Director Personnel Services .... Ms. Jessica HERBSTER
18 Chief Facilities/Physical Plant .... Mr. Michael HELMS
38 Director Student Counseling .... Dr. Felicia FORD

Faulkner University (I)

5345 Atlanta Highway, Montgomery AL 36109-3398

County: Montgomery — FICE Identification: 001003
Unit ID: 101189
Telephone: (334) 272-5820 — Carnegie Class: Masters/S
FAX Number: (334) 386-7107 — Calendar System: Semester
URL: www.faulkner.edu
Established: 1942 — Annual Undergrad Tuition & Fees: $19,280
Enrollment: 3,335 — Coed
Affiliation or Control: Churches Of Christ — IRS Status: 501(c)3
Highest Offering: Doctorate
Accreditation: SC, LAW, TED, @THEOL

01 President .... Dr. Michael D. WILLIAMS
00 Chancellor .... Dr. Billy D. HILYER
05 Vice President Academic Affairs .... Dr. Dave RAMPERSAD
10 Vice President Financial Services .... Mrs. Wilma D. PHILLIPS
32 Vice President Student Services .... Dr. Jean-Noel THOMPSON
84 Vice President Enrollment Mgmt .... Mr. Keith MOCK
30 Vice President Advancement .... Dr. John TYSON
43 General Counsel .... Dr. Gerald JONES
61 Dean Jones School of Law .... Mr. Charles NELSON
49 Dean College Arts & Sciences .... Dr. Dave RAMPERSAD
50 Dean College Business/Exec Educ .... Dr. Dave KHADANGA
73 Dean College of Biblical Studies .... Dr. Scott GLEAVES
53 Dean College of Education .... Vacant
20 Associate VP Academic Affairs .... Dr. Jendia GRISSETT
21 Associate Vice President of Finance .... Mr. Jamie HORN
44 Assoc Vice President Development .... Mr. Billy CAMP
88 Assoc Vice Pres Exec & Prof Enroll .... Mr. Mark HUNT
15 Asst VP Human Resources/Diversity .... Mrs. Renee DAVIS
88 Assoc Dean Academics Jones Law .... Mr. Charles CAMPBELL
06 Registrar .... Mr. Don REYNOLDS
37 Director Student Financial Aid .... Mr. Buddy JACKSON
12 Director Mobile Center .... Mrs. Diane NEWELL
12 Director Birmingham Center .... Mrs. Karen BRUCE
12 Director Huntsville Center .... Mr. Douglas CURE
41 Athletic Director .... Mr. Hal WYNN
08 Director of Libraries .... Mrs. Barbara KELLY
88 Director Quality Enhancement Plan .... Dr. Cindy WALKER
104 Director of Study Abroad .... Dr. Ed HICKS
26 Director of University Marketing .... Mr. Patrick GREGORY
07 Director of Admissions .... Mr. Neil SCOTT
88 Director Student Success .... Mrs. Michelle OTWELL
29 Director of Alumni Relations .... Mr. Adam DONALDSON
92 Director of Honors Program .... Mr. Andrew JACOBS
36 Director Career Services .... Mrs. Marie OTTINGER
38 Counselor .... Mrs. Michelle BOND
04 Exec Assistant to the President .... Mrs. Darlene GREGORY
19 Director Security/Safety .... Mr. Anthony DEAN
39 Director Student Housing .... Mrs. Keri ALFORD

Fortis College (J)

7033 Airport Blvd, Mobile AL 36608

County: Mobile — FICE Identification: 023410
Unit ID: 371052
Telephone: (251) 344-1203 — Carnegie Class: Spec 2-yr-Health
FAX Number: (251) 344-1299 — Calendar System: Other
URL: www.fortiscollege.edu
Established: 1978 — Annual Undergrad Tuition & Fees: $14,194
Enrollment: 352 — Coed
Affiliation or Control: Proprietary — IRS Status: Proprietary
Highest Offering: Associate Degree
Accreditation: ABHES

01 Campus President .... Joseph DALTO
05 Chief Academic Officer .... Dr. Christine GRAHAM
06 Registrar .... Katherine MCKINTYRE
07 Director of Admissions .... Aquila TORIAN
19 Director Security/Safety .... Darren DAIGLE
32 Chief Student Affairs/Student Life .... Nakita GABLE
36 Director Student Placement .... Laura PINION
37 Director Student Financial Aid .... Felicia WILLIAMS
10 Business Office .... Shantreese YOUNG

Fortis College-Montgomery (Eastdale Circle) (K)

3470 Eastdale Circle, Montgomery AL 36117

Telephone: (334) 244-1827 — Identification: 770512
Accreditation: ABHES

Fortis Institute (L)

100 London Parkway Suite 150, Birmingham AL 35211

Telephone: (205) 940-7800 — Identification: 666683
Accreditation: ACICS, DH

† Branch campus of Fortis Institute, Erie, PA.

Gadsden State Community College (M)

1001 George Wallace Dr, PO Box 227,
Gadsden AL 35902-0227

County: Etowah — FICE Identification: 001017
Unit ID: 101240
Telephone: (256) 549-8200 — Carnegie Class: Assoc/HVT-Mix Trad/Non
FAX Number: (256) 549-8288 — Calendar System: Semester
URL: www.gadsdenstate.edu
Established: 1925 — Annual Undergrad Tuition & Fees (In-State): $3,216
Enrollment: 5,289 — Coed
Affiliation or Control: State — IRS Status: 501(c)3
Highest Offering: Associate Degree
Accreditation: SC, ADNUR, COMTA, EMT, MLTAD, PNUR, RAD

01 President .... Dr. Martha G. LAVENDER
10 Dean Financial/Administrative Svcs .... Dr. James R. PRUCNAL
84 Dean Enrollment & Retention .... Dr. Teresa C. RHEA
72 Dean Tech Educ/Workforce Develop .... Mr. Tim GREEN
76 Dean Health Sciences .... Dr. Deborah CURRY
05 Dean of Academic Programs/Services . Dr. Leslie WORTHINGTON
30 Assoc Dean Instl Advance/Cmty Svcs .... Ms. Pam JOHNSON
51 Assoc Dean Instruct Svcs/Adult Educ .. Dr. Karen BLYTHE-SMITH
26 Director Public Relations/Marketing .... Ms. Jackie EDMONDSON
19 Director Physical Plant .... Mr. Stewart DAVIS
21 Director of Financial Services .... Ms. Jacqueline CLARK
43 Director of Legal Affairs/Title IX .... Ms. Michele BRADFORD
15 Director Human Resources .... Ms. Kim S. COBB
41 Athletic Director .... Mr. Mike CANCILLA
38 Assoc Dean Stdnt Svcs & Counse Svcs ... Dr. Cheryl C. VICKERS
37 Director of Financial Aid .... Ms. Kelly D'EATH
06 Registrar .... Mrs. Jennie P. DOBSON
13 Chief Information Officer .... Mr. Tim SMITH

George C. Wallace Community College - Dothan (N)

1141 Wallace Drive, Dothan AL 36303-9234

County: Dale — FICE Identification: 001018
Unit ID: 101286
Telephone: (334) 983-3521 — Carnegie Class: Assoc/HVT-High Trad
FAX Number: (334) 983-6066 — Calendar System: Semester
URL: www.wallace.edu

Established: 1947 Annual Undergrad Tuition & Fees (In-State): $4,260
Enrollment: 4,854 Coed
Affiliation or Control: State IRS Status: 501(c)3
Highest Offering: Associate Degree
Accreditation: SC, ADNUR, COARC, EMT, MAC, PNUR, PTAA, RAD

01 President Dr. Linda C. YOUNG
32 Dean of Student Affs/Sparks Campus Ms. Jacqueline B. SCREWS
05 Dean of Instructional Affairs Mr. Tony HOLLAND
10 Dean of Business Affairs Mr. Lynn BELL
07 Director Enroll Svcs/Registrar Mr. Keith SAULSBERRY
08 Dir Learning Resources Ctrs System Mr. A. P. HOFFMAN
37 Director of Financial Aid Ms. Erma PERRY
13 AS-400 Program/System Admin Mr. Anthony HARDY
15 Director of Human Resources Ms. Brooke STRICKLAND
09 Dir Institutional Effectiveness Ms. Mandy LANIER
40 Bookstore Manager Mr. Jeremy JAMES
21 Director of Accounting & Finance Ms. Kay GAMBLE
26 Dir Public Relations & Marketing Ms. Barbara THOMPSON
30 Dean Institutional Svcs/Com Dev Dr. Ashli WILKINS
41 Athletic Director Mr. Mackey SASSER

George Corley Wallace State Community College - Selma (A)

PO Box 2530, 3000 Earl Goodwin Pkwy, Selma AL 36702-2530
County: Dallas FICE Identification: 005699
Unit ID: 101301
Telephone: (334) 876-9227 Carnegie Class: Assoc/HVT-High Non
FAX Number: (334) 876-9250 Calendar System: Semester
URL: www.wccs.edu
Established: 1963 Annual Undergrad Tuition & Fees (In-State): $4,020
Enrollment: 1,663 Coed
Affiliation or Control: State IRS Status: 501(c)3
Highest Offering: Associate Degree
Accreditation: SC, ACBSP, ADNUR, PNUR

01 President Dr. James M. MITCHELL
05 Acting Dean of Instruction Mrs. Donitha GRIFFIN
20 Instructional Administrator Mr. Raji GOURDINE
10 Dean of Business & Finance Mrs. Jacqueline SMITH
32 Dean of Students/Exec to President Mrs. Donitha GRIFFIN
08 Librarian Ms. Minnie CARSTARPHEN
66 Int Assoc Degree Nursing Coord Dr. Tracey SHANNON
37 Financial Aid Director Ms. Anessa KIDD
38 Counselor College Division Mr. Lonzy CLIFTON
09 Director of Institutional Research Mrs. Earlene LARKIN
26 Coord College Rels/Instl Research Vacant
19 Director Security/Safety Mr. Charles DYSART
41 Athletic Director Mr. Marcus HANNAH
18 Chief Facilities/Physical Plant Vacant
28 Director of Diversity Vacant
40 Bookstore Manager Ms. Marie JONES
15 Human Resource Coordinator Mrs. Heather DRAKE

Heritage Christian University (B)

PO Box HCU, Florence AL 35630-0050
County: Lauderdale FICE Identification: 021997
Unit ID: 101453
Telephone: (256) 766-6610 Carnegie Class: Spec-4-yr-Faith
FAX Number: N/A Calendar System: Semester
URL: www.hcu.edu
Established: 1971 Annual Undergrad Tuition & Fees: $9,792
Enrollment: 93 Coed
Affiliation or Control: Churches Of Christ IRS Status: 501(c)3
Highest Offering: Master's
Accreditation: BI

01 President Mr. Dennis H. JONES
05 Vice President of Academic Affairs Dr. Bill BAGENTS
10 VP Business/Finance/Operations Mr. Freddie P. MOON
30 Vice President of Advancement Mr. Philip GOAD
32 Dean of Students Mr. Brad MCKINNON
33 Dean of Men Dr. Ed GALLAGHER
34 Dean of Women Dr. Rosemary SNODGRASS
58 Director of Graduate Studies Dr. Jeremy BARRIER
06 Registrar Mrs. Alana MARKS
08 Librarian Miss Jamie S. COX
42 Director of Christian Service Mr. Brad MCKINNON
84 Dir Enrollment Svcs/Stdnt Fin Aid Mr. Jim COLLINS
04 Administrative Asst to President Ms. Brittany MCGUIRE
106 Dir Online Education/E-learning Mr. Travis HARMON
108 Director of Institutional Effective Mr. Michael JACKSON
13 Web Communications and Tech Manager Mr. Justin CONNOLLY

Herzing University (C)

280 W Valley Avenue, Birmingham AL 35209-4816
Telephone: (205) 916-2800 FICE Identification: 010193
Accreditation: &NH, EMT

† Regional accreditation is carried under the parent institution in Madison, WI.

Huntingdon College (D)

1500 East Fairview Avenue, Montgomery AL 36106-2148
County: Montgomery FICE Identification: 001019
Unit ID: 101435
Telephone: (334) 833-4497 Carnegie Class: Bac-Diverse
FAX Number: (334) 833-4347 Calendar System: Semester
URL: www.huntingdon.edu
Established: 1854 Annual Undergrad Tuition & Fees: $25,050
Enrollment: 1,160 Coed
Affiliation or Control: United Methodist IRS Status: 501(c)3
Highest Offering: Baccalaureate
Accreditation: SC, MUS

01 President Rev. J. Cameron WEST
10 Treasurer & SVP for IE/Plng & Admin Mr. Jay A. DORMAN
30 SVP Inst Dev & Alumni Relations Mr. Anthony J. LEIGH
05 Provost & Dean of College Dr. Chadwick L. EGGLESTON
84 VP for Enrollment Management Ms. Laura H. DUNCAN
32 VP for Student Life Dr. Frank R. PARSONS, JR.
09 VP Academic Svcs & Inst Research Dr. Sidney J. STUBBS
26 Assoc VP Communication & Marketing Ms. Suellen S. OFE
20 Associate Provost Dr. Frank W. BUCKNER, JR.
50 Dean School of Bus & Prof Studies Dr. Samir R. MOUSSALLI
53 Dean School Teacher Educ/Sport Sci Dr. Lisa OLENIK-DORMAN
81 Dean School Natural Sciences & Math Dr. Erastus C. DUDLEY
79 Dean School of Arts & Humanities Dr. Lynn DISBROW
35 Dean of Students Ms. Francis H. TAYLOR
06 Registrar Ms. Adrienne S. GAINES
55 Director Evening Studies Program Mr. Vinson BRADLEY
35 Director of Student Activities Ms. Sallie FORRESTER
88 Dir Staton Ctr for Lrng Enrichment Ms. Maryann M. BECK
04 Exec Asst to President/Corp Secy Ms. Sandra B. KELSER
88 Dir of Student Financial Services Ms. Belinda G. DUETT
13 Dir of Institutional Technology Mr. Frank O. GRIER
18 Director of Facilities and Grounds Mr. T. Michael DUNN
37 Dir of Student Financial Aid Ms. Brittany DAVIS
36 Dir of Center for Career & Vocation Ms. Sherry Leigh LACEY
08 Director Houghton Memorial Library Mr. Eric A. KIDWELL
41 Director of Athletics Mr. Michael W. TURK
23 Director of Student Health Services Ms. Camilla IRVIN
38 Director of Counseling Services Ms. Kelley REHM
21 Comptroller Ms. Jo-Ann M. HOLSTON
19 Chief of Security Mr. Michael S. WARD
42 Chaplain Rev. Woods B. LISENBY
40 Manager Follett Bookstore Ms. Sharon HENDERSON

Huntsville Bible College (E)

906 Oakwood Avenue NW, Huntsville AL 35811-1632
County: Madison FICE Identification: 038943
Unit ID: 449348
Telephone: (256) 469-7536 Carnegie Class: Spec-4-yr-Faith
FAX Number: (256) 469-7549 Calendar System: Semester
URL: www.hbc1.edu
Established: 1986 Annual Undergrad Tuition & Fees: $4,320
Enrollment: 138 Coed
Affiliation or Control: Baptist IRS Status: 501(c)3
Highest Offering: Master's
Accreditation: BI

01 President Dr. John L. CLAY
05 Dean of Academics/Instruction Rev. David L. FAYLOR
07 Admissions Officer Ms. Jessica COPELAND
10 Chief Financial Officer Ms. Jacqueline ROBINSON
30 Advancement Officer Ms. Eloise MCNEALEY

J.F. Drake State Community and Technical College (F)

3421 Meridian Street N, Huntsville AL 35811-1584
County: Madison FICE Identification: 005260
Unit ID: 101462
Telephone: (256) 539-8161 Carnegie Class: Assoc/HVT-High Non
FAX Number: (256) 539-6439 Calendar System: Semester
URL: www.drakestate.edu
Established: 1961 Annual Undergrad Tuition & Fees (In-State): $4,290
Enrollment: 1,062 Coed
Affiliation or Control: State IRS Status: 501(c)3
Highest Offering: Associate Degree
Accreditation: SC

01 Interim President Dr. Kemba K. CHAMBERS
05 Dean of Instruction Mrs. Joyce L. RENTZ
10 Dean of Fiscal Affairs Vacant
103 Dean of Workforce Development Dr. Mary J. CAYLOR
45 Dean of Planning & Research Dev Vacant
15 Human Resource Specialist Mrs. Katie CHANCE
13 Director Computer Services Vacant
08 Director of Library Services Ms. Carla CLIFT
07 Director of Admissions/Registrar Mr. Cedric ARRINGTON
37 Director Student Financial Aid Ms. Jennifer O'LINGER
26 Director of Public Relations Mrs. Amelia DAWKINS-FALTER
36 College Counselor Ms. Denise GAYMON
09 Dean of Institutional Effectiveness Dr. Alice RAYMOND
32 Dean of Student Support Services Dr. Nicole BARNETT
51 Interim Director of Adult Educ Ms. Deione CRUTCHER
18 Dean of Operations Mr. Bruce BULLUCK
84 Enrolllment Services Manager Ms. Tiffany GREEN

J.F. Ingram State Technical College (G)

PO Box 220350, Deatsville AL 36022-0350
County: Elmore FICE Identification: 030025
Unit ID: 101471
Telephone: (334) 285-5177 Carnegie Class: Assoc/HVT-Mix Trad/Non
FAX Number: (334) 285-5328 Calendar System: Semester
URL: www.istc.edu
Established: 1965 Annual Undergrad Tuition & Fees (In-State): $4,824
Enrollment: 473 Coed
Affiliation or Control: State IRS Status: 501(c)3
Highest Offering: Associate Degree
Accreditation: COE

01 President Dr. Hank DASINGER
45 Dean of Strategic Planning and Eval Mr. Bill GRISWOLD
11 Dean of Administration Dr. Brannon LENTZ
05 Dean of Instruction Mr. Bill GRISWOLD
32 Dean Students/Support Services Mrs. Rosie EDWARDS
15 Human Resources Coordinator Ms. Erica PORTIS-TURNER
35 Student Services Director Mrs. Tawanna THORNTON
04 Administrative Asst to President Mrs. Julie VARNER
08 Head Librarian Mrs. Mary ROOTES

Jacksonville State University (H)

700 Pelham Road N, Jacksonville AL 36265-1602
County: Calhoun FICE Identification: 001020
Unit ID: 101480
Telephone: (256) 782-5781 Carnegie Class: Masters/L
FAX Number: (256) 782-5291 Calendar System: Semester
URL: www.jsu.edu
Established: 1883 Annual Undergrad Tuition & Fees (In-State): $7,500
Enrollment: 8,659 Coed
Affiliation or Control: State IRS Status: 501(c)3
Highest Offering: Doctorate
Accreditation: SC, AAFCS, ART, BUS, CACREP, CS, DIETD, JOUR, MUS, NAIT, NURSE, SPAA, SW, TED, THEA

01 President Dr. John M. BEEHLER
05 Provost/VP Academic Affairs Dr. Rebecca O. TURNER
10 VP Finance & Administration Dr. Ashok ROY
30 VP University Advancement Dr. Charles R. LEWIS
13 Chief Information Officer Mr. Vinson HOUSTON
32 VP Student Affairs Dr. Tim KING
84 VP Enrollment Management Ms. Cherise PETERS
20 Vice Provost Dr. Joe WALSH
08 Dean of Library Services Mr. John-Bauer GRAHAM
49 Dean School Arts & Humanities Dr. James E. WADE
66 Dean/School Health Prof/Wellness Dr. Christie SHELTON
53 Dean School of Education Dr. John HAMMETT
50 Dean School of Business & Industry Dr. William FIELDING
83 Dean School Human Svc/Soc Science Vacant
81 Dean School of Science Vacant
21 University Controller Mr. Kevin MCFRY
07 Director of Enrollment Management Mr. Andy GREEN
109 Executive Director Auxiliary Svcs Mr. Joe WHITMORE
44 Director University Development Mr. Earl WARREN
39 Acting Dir Housing/Residence Life Ms. Rochelle SMITH
88 Dir International House Ms. Chandni KHADKA
29 Director of Alumni Relations Ms. Kaci OGLE
15 Chief Human Resources Officer Dr. Heidi LOUISY
37 Acting Dir Student Financial Svcs Ms. Stephanie MILLER
54 Dir Dept of Applied Engineering Mr. Terry MARBUT
41 Director Athletics Mr. Greg SEITZ
09 Chief Research & Planning Officer Dr. Alicia SIMMONS
06 Registrar Ms. Emily WHITE
18 Dir Capital Planning/Facilities Mr. David THOMPSON
36 Director Career Placement Services Ms. Rebecca E. TURNER
38 Dir Counseling/Disability Sppt Svcs Ms. Julie NIX
32 Director Student Life Mr. Terry CASEY
96 Dir of Procurement/Fixed Assets Ms. Pamela L. FINDLEY
26 Chief Marketing Officer Mr. Tim GARNER
100 Spec Asst to Pres/Dir Univ Rel Dr. Don KILLINGSWORTH
19 Director Security/Safety Mr. Shawn GIDDY
22 Dir Diversity/EEO/Title IX Mr. Jai INGRAHAM
43 Legal Counsel Mr. Sam MONK

James H. Faulkner State Community College (I)

1900 Highway 31 S, Bay Minette AL 36507-2698
County: Baldwin FICE Identification: 001060
Unit ID: 101161
Telephone: (251) 580-2100 Carnegie Class: Assoc/HT-High Trad
FAX Number: (251) 580-2253 Calendar System: Semester
URL: www.faulknerstate.edu
Established: 1965 Annual Undergrad Tuition & Fees (In-State): $4,320
Enrollment: 4,481 Coed
Affiliation or Control: State IRS Status: 501(c)3
Highest Offering: Associate Degree
Accreditation: SC, ACFEI, ADNUR, DA, EMT, PNUR, SURGT

01 President Dr. Gary L. BRANCH
32 VP of Inst Adv & Student Dev Dr. Brenda J. KENNEDY
05 Dean of Instruction Ms. Melinda BYRD-MURPHY
35 Dean of Student Services Mr. Michael NIKOLAKIS
86 Dean of Federal Programs Mrs. Lena DEXTER
11 Dean Administrative Services Mr. Jim FITZ-GERALD
103 Dean of Workforce Development Ms. Patty HUGHSTON
26 Director College Relations Vacant
06 Registrar Ms. Beth BRYARS
08 Dir Learning Resource Ms. Rheena ELMORE
37 Financial Aid Director Dr. Jim THEEUWES
88 Director High School Relations Ms. Carmelita MIKKELSEN
18 Director of Buildings & Ground Mr. Jim FITZ-GERALD
19 Chief of Police Mr. Chris JOHNSON
15 Director Human Resources Mrs. Laura BURKS
39 Dir of Housing and Special Events Ms. Linda CALDWELL
66 Director Nursing & Allied Health Ms. Jean GRAHAM
07 Admissions Officer Ms. Theresa MCCLELLAND

Jefferson Davis Community College (A)

PO Box 958, Brewton AL 36427-0958
County: Escambia FICE Identification: 001021
Unit ID: 101499
Telephone: (251) 867-4832 Carnegie Class: Assoc/MT-VT-High Trad
FAX Number: (251) 867-7399 Calendar System: Semester
URL: www.jdcc.edu
Established: 1965 Annual Undergrad Tuition & Fees (In-State): $4,028
Enrollment: 1,086 Coed
Affiliation or Control: State IRS Status: 501(c)3
Highest Offering: Associate Degree
Accreditation: SC, ADNUR

01 Interim President .... Dr. William BLOW
05 Dean of Instruction .... Vacant
10 Dean of Business Affairs .... Dr. Donald KELLY
32 Dean of Student Affairs .... Mr. David JONES
20 Associate Dean of Instruction .... Vacant
15 Director of Human Resources .... Ms. Denise STEWART
06 Registrar .... Ms. Robin SESSIONS
13 Director of MIS .... Mr. Anthony HARDY
26 Director Mktg & Community Relations .... Vacant
08 Librarian .... Mr. Jeffrey FAUST
37 Financial Aid Director .... Ms. Vanessa M. KYLES
09 Dir Institutional Research/Testing .... Mr. Anthony HARDY
18 Chief Facilities/Physical Plant .... Mr. Richard LYNN
35 Dir Stdnt Support Svcs/Development .... Ms. Kina BURKETT
84 Dir of Stdnt Recruitment/Enrollment .... Mr. Lee BARRENTINE

Jefferson State Community College (B)

2601 Carson Road, Birmingham AL 35215-3098
County: Jefferson FICE Identification: 001022
Unit ID: 101505
Telephone: (205) 853-1200 Carnegie Class: Assoc/MT-VT-Mix Trad/Non
FAX Number: (205) 853-8505 Calendar System: Semester
URL: www.jeffersonstate.edu
Established: 1963 Annual Undergrad Tuition & Fees (In-State): $4,380
Enrollment: 8,516 Coed
Affiliation or Control: State IRS Status: 501(c)3
Highest Offering: Associate Degree
Accreditation: SC, ACBSP, ACFEI, ADNUR, CONST, EMT, FUSER, MLTAD, PTAA, RAD

01 Interim President .... Mr. Keith A. BROWN
05 Dean of Instruction .... Ms. Danielle COBURN
75 Dean Career & Technical Education .... Ms. Norma G. BELL
30 Dean Campus Development/Campus Svcs .... Mr. Keith A. BROWN
10 Director Financial Services .... Ms. Mary WATSON
32 Director of Student Services .... Dr. Linda J. HOOTON
97 Assoc Dean Transf Gen Stds Shelby .... Ms. Liesl W. HARRIS
97 Assoc Dean Transf Gen Stds Jeffrsn .... Dr. Aliakbar R. YAZDI
106 Associate Dean Distance Education .... Mr. Alan B. DAVIS
51 Director College/Cmty/Corp Educ .... Ms. Kay C. POTTER
13 Chief Information Officer .... Mr. Nader ZANDI
37 Director Financial Aid .... Ms. Theresa MAYS
84 Dean of Enrollment Services .... Dr. Phillip M. HOBBS
18 Director Maintenance .... Mr. Bill MIXON
08 Director of Learning Resources .... Ms. Barbara GOSS
36 Director Career/Job Resource Center .... Dr. Tamara PAYNE
07 Director Admissions and Retention .... Dr. Lillian OWENS
15 Director Human Resources .... Mr. Shain WILSON
26 Director Media Relations .... Mr. David BOBO
96 Purchasing Coordinator .... Ms. Ann CIMALORE
19 Director Safety & Security .... Mr. Mark BAILEY
09 Assoc Dean Inst Effectiveness .... Ms. Amanda E. KIN
04 Administrative Asst to President .... Ms. Janie STARNES
25 Chief Contracts/Grants Admin .... Ms. Kelli CREAMER
86 Director Government Relations .... Mr. Guin ROBINSON

Judson College (C)

302 Bibb Street, Marion AL 36756-2504
County: Perry FICE Identification: 001023
Unit ID: 101541
Telephone: (334) 683-5100 Carnegie Class: Bac-A&S
FAX Number: (334) 683-5147 Calendar System: Semester
URL: www.judson.edu
Established: 1838 Annual Undergrad Tuition & Fees: $16,868
Enrollment: 378 Female
Affiliation or Control: Alabama Baptist State Convention
IRS Status: 501(c)3
Highest Offering: Baccalaureate
Accreditation: SC, MUS, SW

01 President .... Dr. David E. POTTS
05 Sr Vice Pres & Academic Dean .... Dr. Scott W. BULLARD
32 Sr VP & Dean of Students .... Ms. Susan JONES
84 Exec Dir for Enrollment Services .... Mrs. Layne HOGGLE
30 VP Institutional Advancement .... Dr. Terry SMITH MORGAN
06 Registrar .... Ms. Susanna BARKLEY
106 Dir Online Education/E-learning .... Dr. Kathy CHEN
13 Chief Info Technology Officer (CIO) .... Mrs. Traci L. FOSTER
36 Director Student Placement .... Mrs. Kendel GILCHREST
37 Director Student Financial Aid .... Ms. Melina VERITY
26 Marketing/Web Communications Spec .... Ms. Mary A. TAYLOR

Lawson State Community College (D)

3060 Wilson Road, SW, Birmingham AL 35221-1798
County: Jefferson FICE Identification: 001059
Unit ID: 101569
Telephone: (205) 925-2515 Carnegie Class: Assoc/MT-VT-Mix Trad/Non
FAX Number: (205) 925-8526 Calendar System: Semester
URL: www.lawsonstate.edu
Established: 1949 Annual Undergrad Tuition & Fees (In-State): $4,320
Enrollment: 3,090 Coed
Affiliation or Control: State IRS Status: 501(c)3
Highest Offering: Associate Degree
Accreditation: SC, ACBSP, ADNUR, DA, PNUR

01 President .... Dr. Perry W. WARD
05 Vice Pres Instructional Services .... Dr. Bruce CRAWFORD
11 Vice President of Administration .... Mrs. Sharon CREWS
32 Interim Dean of Students .... Mr. Darren ALLEN
09 Coordinator of Data Management .... Mrs. Jamie GLASS
10 Dir Fin Services/Risk Assessment .... Dr. Craig D. LAWRENCE
20 Academic Dean .... Dr. Sherri DAVIS
21 Director of Accounting .... Ms. Monique SILAS
50 Assoc Dean Bus/Information Tech .... Dr. Alice MILTON
49 Assoc Dean Lib Arts/Coll Trans Pgms .... Dr. Karl PRUITT
76 Assoc Dean of Health Occupations .... Dr. Shelia MARABLE
75 Assoc Dean Career Tech Programs .... Mr. Donald SLEDGE
84 Asst Dean of Admissions/Records .... Mr. Darren ALLEN
07 Director of Admissions .... Dr. Jeff SHELLEY
08 Librarian .... Ms. Sandra HENDERSON
37 Director Student Financial Aid .... Ms. Cassandra HOLLINS
15 Director of Personnel Services .... Mrs. Janice MCGEE
26 Chief Public Relations Officer .... Mrs. Geri ALBRIGHT
18 Chief Facilities/Physical Plant .... Mr. Chad YANCY
19 Director Safety/Security .... Mr. James BLANTON
13 Dir Computing and Information Mgmt .... Mr. James MANKOWICH
40 Director Bookstore .... Dr. Craig LAWRENCE
41 Athletic Director .... Mr. Carlton RICE
06 Registrar .... Ms. Lori CHISEM
39 Director Student Housing .... Mr. Robert SMITH
38 Coordinator Student Counseling .... Dr. Renee HERNDON
106 Dir Online Education/E-learning .... Dr. Keisha JAMES
25 Chief Contracts/Grants Admin .... Dr. Myrtes D. GREEN

Legacy Christian University (E)

6806 Whitesburg Drive, Huntsville AL 35802
County: Madison Identification: 667251
Telephone: (256) 924-0511 Carnegie Class: Not Classified
FAX Number: N/A Calendar System: Semester
URL: www.legacyu.net
Established: 1981 Annual Undergrad Tuition & Fees: N/A
Enrollment: N/A Coed
Affiliation or Control: Interdenominational IRS Status: 501(c)3
Highest Offering: Master's
Accreditation: @BI

01 President .... Dr. Lee BARNETT
05 Provost/VP for Academic Affairs .... Dr. Bobby BURT
11 Vice Pres Operations .... Mr. Charles GARRETT
10 Chief Financial Officer .... Ms. Vicki HEREFORD
32 Dean of Students .... Mr. Chris KENNEDY
42 Campus Pastor .... Rev. Tim PAYNE
108 Dir of Institutional Effectiveness .... Ms. L.A BREANDAU
30 Director of Develop & Alumni Rels .... Mr. Charles GARRETT
84 Dean of Enrollment Mgmt & Registrar .... Mrs. Trish BROWN

Lurleen B. Wallace Community College (F)

PO Drawer 1418, 1000 Dannelly Blvd, Andalusia AL 36420-1224
County: Covington FICE Identification: 008988
Unit ID: 101602
Telephone: (334) 222-6591 Carnegie Class: Assoc/HVT-High Trad
FAX Number: (334) 881-2300 Calendar System: Semester
URL: www.lbwcc.edu
Established: 1969 Annual Undergrad Tuition & Fees (In-State): $4,320
Enrollment: 1,599 Coed
Affiliation or Control: State IRS Status: 501(c)3
Highest Offering: Associate Degree
Accreditation: SC, ADNUR, DMS, EMT

01 President .... Dr. Herbert H. RIEDEL
05 Dean of Instruction .... Ms. Peggy LINTON
32 Dean of Student Affairs .... Mr. Jason JESSIE
10 Director of Finance/Comptroller .... Ms. Lynne DAYTON
21 Director of Business Services .... Ms. Debra MOODY
12 Vice Pres/Greenville Campus Dir .... Dr. James D. KRUDOP
103 Assoc Dean Adult Educ/Workforce Dev .... Mr. Jimmy HUTTO
13 Assoc Dean Instr/Info Technology .... Mr. Greg APLIN
15 Director of Human Resources .... Ms. Paige JOSEY
09 Dir Inst Effectiveness & Quality .... Dr. Shannon LEVITZKE
18 Dir College Facilities/Maintenance .... Mr. Tim JONES
07 Director Admissions & Records .... Ms. Jan RILEY
41 Athletic Director .... Mr. Steve HELMS
08 Director of Learning Resources .... Mr. Hugh CARTER
88 Director Student Support Services .... Dr. Patricia POWELL
88 Dir Upward Bound/Andalusia Camp Dir .... Mr. Bridges ANDERSON
37 Director of Financial Aid .... Mrs. Donna BASS
26 Public Info Officer/Dir Mktg & Dev .... Ms. Renee LEMAIRE

Marion Military Institute (G)

1101 Washington Street, Marion AL 36756-3213
County: Perry FICE Identification: 001026
Unit ID: 101648
Telephone: (800) 664-1842 Carnegie Class: Assoc/HT-High Trad
FAX Number: (334) 683-2380 Calendar System: Semester
URL: www.marionmilitary.edu
Established: 1842 Annual Undergrad Tuition & Fees (In-State): $8,778
Enrollment: 439 Coed
Affiliation or Control: State IRS Status: 501(c)3
Highest Offering: Associate Degree
Accreditation: SC

01 President .... Col. David J. MOLLAHAN
03 Executive Vice President/CAO .... Dr. Susan G. STEVENSON
10 VP for Finance & Business Affs .... Mr. Brian HARRISON
05 Chief Instructional Officer .... LTC. Timothy ULLMANN
32 VP for Student Affairs & Commandant .... Dr. Kevin C. DOPF
30 VP for Institutional Advancement .... Mrs. Suzanne MCKEE
103 Dir Career/Leadership Initiatives .... Vacant
41 Director of Athletics .... Dr. Michelle IVEY
07 Director of Admissions .... Mrs. Brittany CRAWFORD
29 Director of Alumni and Comm Affairs .... Mrs. O'Neal HOLMES
88 ROTC Professor of Military Science .... Maj. Gregory WALL
09 Director of Institutional Research .... Mrs. Donna LEEMON
06 Registrar .... 1Lt. Caleb LOGAN
38 Director of Guidance .... Ms. Brenda A. COOK
37 Director of Financial Aid .... Ms. Jacqueline WILSON
08 Library Director .... Vacant
18 Director of Facilities .... SCPO. Robert D. SUMLIN
17 Director of Health Services .... Mrs. Rene SUMLIN

Miles College (H)

5500 Myron Massey Boulevard, Fairfield AL 35064-2621
County: Jefferson FICE Identification: 001028
Unit ID: 101675
Telephone: (205) 929-1000 Carnegie Class: Bac-Diverse
FAX Number: (205) 929-1453 Calendar System: Semester
URL: www.miles.edu
Established: 1898 Annual Undergrad Tuition & Fees: $11,604
Enrollment: 1,782 Coed
Affiliation or Control: Christian Methodist Episcopal IRS Status: 501(c)3
Highest Offering: Baccalaureate
Accreditation: SC, ACBSP, SW, TED

01 President .... Dr. George T. FRENCH, JR.
05 Dean & VP Academic Affairs .... Dr. Emmanuel CHEKWA
10 Sr VP Finance/Business Admin .... Ms. Diana KNIGHTON
29 VP Alumni Affairs/Security .... Mr. Charles CROCKROM, SR.
42 VP/Dean Student Engagement/Chapel .... Rev. Larry BATIE
100 Special Asst/Chief of Staff .... Mr. Kenneth COACHMAN
07 Director Admissions & Recruitment .... Mr. Christopher ROBERTSON
08 Director Library .... Dr. Geraldine BELL
32 Director Student Activities .... Ms. Diane BROWN
20 Associate Dean .... Dr. Joyce DUGAN-WOOD
09 Director Strategic Initiatives .... Dr. Ba-Shen T. WELCH
37 Director Financial Aid .... Mr. Percy LANIER
18 Director Physical Plant .... Mr. Thomas BROWN
38 Dir Counseling/Advising/Testing .... Ms. Keisha LEWIS
15 Director Human Resources .... Ms. Verlanda TATE
13 Manager of Data Processing .... Ms. Jackie HUDSON

Northeast Alabama Community College (I)

PO Box 159, 138 Alabama Highway 35, Rainsville AL 35986-0159
County: DeKalb/Jackson FICE Identification: 001031
Unit ID: 101897
Telephone: (256) 638-4418 Carnegie Class: Assoc/HVT-High Trad
FAX Number: (256) 638-3052 Calendar System: Semester
URL: www.nacc.edu
Established: 1963 Annual Undergrad Tuition & Fees (In-State): $4,320
Enrollment: 2,708 Coed
Affiliation or Control: State IRS Status: 501(c)3
Highest Offering: Associate Degree
Accreditation: SC, ADNUR, EMT, PNUR

01 President .... Dr. J. David CAMPBELL
05 Vice Pres/Dean of Instruction .... Dr. Joseph D. BURKE
56 Director Extended Day/Distance Educ .... Mr. Chad GORHAM
32 Dean of Student Services .... Ms. Sherie GRACE
11 Dean of Admin Services .... Mr. Larry D. GUFFEY
37 Director of Financial Aid .... Mr. Nixon WILLMON
103 Dir Workforce Devel/Skills Training .... Mr. Mike KENNAMER
26 Director of Promotions & Marketing .... Mrs. Debra A. BARRENTINE
45 Dir Inst Planning & Assessment .... Mr. Brad FRICKS
18 Chief Facilities/Physical Plant .... Mr. Kent JONES
06 Registrar/Chief Bus Ofcr/Dir Purchg .... Mr. Larry D. GUFFEY
30 Development Director .... Ms. Heather RICE
19 Director of Police/Security .... Mr. Norman SMITH
04 Administrative Asst to President .... Ms. Brenda STRINGER
08 Dir Learning Resource Ctr/Library .... Mrs. Julia EVERETT
15 Human Resources Director .... Mrs. Lynde MANN
29 Event Planning/Alumni Relations .... Ms. Chasley BELLOMY
13 Director of Educational Technology .... Ms. Patricia COMBS

Northwest - Shoals Community College (A)

800 George Wallace Boulevard,
Muscle Shoals AL 35661-3205
County: Colbert FICE Identification: 005697
Unit ID: 101736
Telephone: (256) 331-5200 Carnegie Class: Assoc/HVT-High Trad
FAX Number: (256) 331-5222 Calendar System: Semester
URL: www.nwscc.edu
Established: 1963 Annual Undergrad Tuition & Fees (In-State): $4,291
Enrollment: 3,891 Coed
Affiliation or Control: State IRS Status: 501(c)3
Highest Offering: Associate Degree
Accreditation: SC, ADNUR, EMT

01 President ... Dr. Humphrey LEE
05 Vice President of Instruction ... Dr. Glenda COLAGROSS
10 Chief Fiscal Officer ... Mr. Paul MERRILL
09 Assoc Dean Inst Effect/Dist Ed/Dev ... Mr. John MCINTOSH
20 Assoc Dean Instructional Programs ... Dr. Timmy JAMES
30 Director of Foundation/Advancement ... Vacant
37 Director of Financial Aid ... Ms. Shauna JAMES
07 Asst Dean Recruit/Adm/FA ... Mr. Tom CARTER
15 Human Resources Coordinator ... Ms. Tia STONE
29 Director of Alumni Relations ... Vacant
36 Director/Counselor ETS/YSP ... Vacant
13 Director of Management Info Systems ... Mr. Alan MITCHELL
19 Director of Safety and Security ... Mr. Doug HARGETT
06 Registrar ... Ms. Tracy WALDROP
07 Coordinator Admissions ... Vacant
103 Assoc Dean of Workforce Develop ... Ms. Rose JONES
21 Comptroller ... Ms. Janet JONES
88 Director of Adult Education ... Mr. Donnie SWEENEY
88 Dir College and Career Readiness ... Mr. Ed CARTER
88 Coordinator/Advisor RTW ... Ms. Tara BRANSCOME
04 Administrative Asst to President ... Ms. Teresa K. HARRISON
18 Chief Facilities/Physical Plant ... Mr. Joe HACKWORTH
26 Chief Public Relations/Marketing ... Mr. Trent RANDOLPH

Oakwood University (B)

7000 Adventist Boulevard, NW, Huntsville AL 35896-0003
County: Madison FICE Identification: 001033
Unit ID: 101912
Telephone: (256) 726-7000 Carnegie Class: Bac-Diverse
FAX Number: (256) 726-8335 Calendar System: Semester
URL: www.oakwood.edu
Established: 1896 Annual Undergrad Tuition & Fees: $16,720
Enrollment: 1,939 Coed
Affiliation or Control: Seventh-day Adventist IRS Status: 501(c)3
Highest Offering: Master's
Accreditation: SC, ACBSP, DIETD, DIETI, NUR, SW, TED

01 President ... Dr. Leslie POLLARD
03 Provost & Sr Vice President ... Vacant
05 Vice Pres Academic Affairs ... Dr. Karen BENN-MARSHALL
10 Vice President Financial Affairs ... Ms. Sabrina COTTON
32 Vice President Student Services ... Mr. David KNIGHT
30 Executive Director Advancement/Dev ... Ms. Kisha NORRIS
20 Asst VP Academic Affairs ... Dr. Finbar BENJAMIN
21 Asst VP Financial Affs/Controller ... Mrs. Gail CALDWELL
35 Asst Vice Pres Student Services ... Ms. Adrienne MATTHEWS
15 Exec Dir of Employee Srvs/Human Res ... Dr. LaVerne BARNETT
25 Contracts ... Mrs. Evangeline RIVERS LANG
26 Director Public Relations ... Vacant
07 Director Enrollment Management ... Mr. Malcolm TAYLOR
37 Director Financial Aid ... Mrs. Lynda BARTHOLOMEW
06 Registrar ... Mr. John HILL
39 Residence Life Coordinator-Men ... Mr. Woodrow VAUGHN
88 Resident Life Coordinator-Women ... Ms. Linda ANDERSON
08 Director Library Services ... Mrs. Paulette JOHNSON
09 Director Inst Effectiveness ... Vacant
18 Director Physical Plant ... Mr. Ian ROBINSON
19 Director Security ... Mr. Melvin HARRIS
29 Director Alumni Relations ... Vacant
38 Dir Counseling & Health Services ... Ms. Wanda MISORI
51 Dir Adult & Continuing Education ... Mrs. Ellengold GOODRIDGE
42 Chaplain ... Dr. Howard WEEMS
46 Dir Research & Faculty Dev ... Dr. Prudence L. POLLARD
88 Dean for Student Success ... Mrs. Helen FISCHLE
50 Chair Business & Info Systems ... Vacant
53 Chair Education ... Dr. James MBYIRUKIRA
76 Chair Allied Health ... Dr. Earl HENRY
60 Chair English & Foreign Languages ... Dr. Benson PRIGG
64 Chair Music ... Dr. Jason FERDINAND
65 Chair Biological Sciences ... Dr. Juliett BAILEY PENROD
65 Chair Chemistry ... Dr. Kenneth LAI HING
66 Chair Nursing ... Dr. Arlene JOHNSON
68 Chair Health & Exercise Sciences ... Dr. Andrew YOUNG
70 Chair Social Work ... Dr. Octavio RAMIREZ
73 Chair Religion & Theology ... Dr. Dedrick BLUE
81 Chair Math & Computer Science ... Dr. Lisa JAMES
82 Chair History ... Dr. Samuel LONDON
83 Chair Psychology ... Dr. Martin HODNETT
60 Chair Communication ... Dr. Rennae ELLIOTT
96 Director Purchasing ... Vacant
13 Chief Info Technology Officer (CIO) ... Mr. Kirk NUGENT

Reid State Technical College (C)

PO Box 588, 100 Hwy 83, Evergreen AL 36401-0588
County: Conecuh FICE Identification: 005692
Unit ID: 101994
Telephone: (251) 578-1313 Carnegie Class: Assoc/HVT-Mix Trad/Non
FAX Number: (251) 578-5355 Calendar System: Semester
URL: www.rstc.edu
Established: 1966 Annual Undergrad Tuition & Fees (In-State): $4,380
Enrollment: 549 Coed
Affiliation or Control: State IRS Status: 501(c)3
Highest Offering: Associate Degree
Accreditation: COE

01 Acting President/Business Manager ... Mr. David J. RHODES
05 Dean Students/Instructional Svcs ... Dr. Tangela PURIFOY
103 Assoc Dean Workforce Development ... Dr. Alesia K. STUART
09 Asst Dean for Institutional Effect ... Ms. Coretta BOYKIN
37 Director Financial Aid ... Ms. Christy GOODWIN
15 Director of Human Resources ... Ms. Brenda JACKSON
07 Asst Dir Admissions & Records ... Ms. Theresa RYLAND
10 Office Administration ... Ms. Lois ROBINSON
06 Registrar ... Ms. Vickie NICHOLSON
38 Director of Counseling/ADA Coord ... Ms. Monica ROBINSON

Remington College, Mobile Campus (D)

828 Downtowner Loop W, Mobile AL 36609-5404
County: Mobile FICE Identification: 026055
Unit ID: 366535
Telephone: (251) 343-8200 Carnegie Class: Spec 2-yr-Tech
FAX Number: (251) 343-0577 Calendar System: Quarter
URL: www.remingtoncollege.edu
Established: 1986 Annual Undergrad Tuition & Fees: $14,566
Enrollment: 518 Coed
Affiliation or Control: Independent Non-Profit IRS Status: 501(c)3
Highest Offering: Associate Degree
Accreditation: ACCSC

01 President ... Mr. Michael SELTZER
06 Registrar ... Mr. Donald SCHERMERHORN

Samford University (E)

800 Lakeshore Drive, Birmingham AL 35229-0001
County: Jefferson FICE Identification: 001036
Unit ID: 102049
Telephone: (205) 726-2011 Carnegie Class: Masters/L
FAX Number: (205) 726-2171 Calendar System: 4/1/4
URL: www.samford.edu
Established: 1841 Annual Undergrad Tuition & Fees: $28,370
Enrollment: 4,933 Coed
Affiliation or Control: Southern Baptist IRS Status: 501(c)3
Highest Offering: Doctorate
Accreditation: SC, ANEST, BUS, #CAATE, CIDA, #COARC, DIETD, @DIETI, LAW, MUS, NURSE, PHAR, @PTA, @SP, @SW, TED, THEA, THEOL

01 President ... Dr. T. Andrew WESTMORELAND
03 Provost ... Dr. Michael HARDIN
32 Vice President for Student Affairs ... Dr. Phil KIMREY
30 Vice President of Advancement ... Mr. W. Randall PITTMAN
10 Exec VP Business/Financial Affairs ... Mr. Harry B. BROCK, III
31 Chief Marketing Officer ... Dr. Betsy B. HOLLOWAY
45 Chief Strategy Officer ... Mr. Colin M. COYNE
04 Assistant to the President ... Dr. Michael D. MORGAN
21 Controller ... Mr. Mike DARWIN
13 Chief Information Officer ... Mr. Doug RIGNEY
43 General Counsel ... Mr. W. Clark WATSON
11 Associate Provost Administration ... Dr. Nancy BIGGIO
108 Asst Provost Assess & Accreditation ... Dr. Katrina H. MINTZ
05 Associate Provost Academics ... Dr. Chris METRESS
41 Athletic Director ... Mr. Martin NEWTON
88 Director of Ethics & Leadership ... Mr. Drayton NABERS, JR.
88 Director of Donor Relations ... Mrs. Judi F. AUCOIN
29 Director of Alumni Programs ... Ms. Molly MCGUIRE
88 Director Parent Programs ... Ms. Susan DOYLE
21 Director of Business Services ... Mr. Mike MCCORMACK
88 Director of Capital Planning & Imp ... Mr. David T. WHITT
88 Dir Event Management ... Ms. Allison TOLAR
18 Director of Facilities Management ... Mr. Mark FULLER
37 Dir of Student Financial Services ... Mr. Lane M. SMITH
15 Director of Human Resources ... Mr. Fred R. ROGAN
09 Dir Institutional Effectiveness ... Mrs. Karen G. HAMBY
43 Assoc VP Business Affairs/Invest ... Ms. Lisa IMBRAGULIO
08 Dean of University Library ... Dr. Kimmetha D. HERNDON
30 Exec Dir of Advancement ... Mr. Douglas WILSON
19 Dir Public Safety & Emergency Mgmt ... Mr. Wayne PITTMAN
39 Asst VP Residential & Univ Services ... Ms. Lauren M. TAYLOR
88 Director of Risk Mmgt & Insurance ... Mr. James A. CLEMENT
10 Dir of Budget & Financial Planning ... Mr. Matt DEFORE
102 Director Development/Auxiliary ... Ms. Sharon SMITH
07 Dean of Admissions ... Mr. Jason BLACK
42 Asst VP for Spiritual Life ... Dr. Matthew S. KERLIN
35 Asst VP for Student Services ... Mr. Garry L. ATKINS
35 Asst VP for Student Life ... Mrs. Renie MOSS
26 Exec Dir University Communication ... Mr. Philip POOLE
88 Director of University Fellows ... Mr. Bryan M. JOHNSON
53 Dean Education/Professional Studies ... Dr. Jean A. BOX
49 Dean Howard College Arts/Sciences ... Dr. David W. CHAPMAN
17 Vice Provost College Health Science ... Dr. Nena F. SANDERS
76 Dean of Health Professions ... Dr. Alan JUNG
69 Dean of Public Health ... Dr. Keith ELDER
67 Dean School of Pharmacy ... Dr. Michael A. CROUCH
73 Dean Beeson School of Divinity ... Dr. Timothy F. GEORGE
50 Dean Brock School of Business ... Dr. J. Howard FINCH
61 Dean Cumberland School of Law ... Mr. Henry C. STRICKLAND
57 Dean School of the Arts ... Dr. Joseph HOPKINS
06 Registrar ... Mr. John FLYNN
44 Director of Annual Giving ... Ms. Kimberly CRIPPS
44 Director Gift and Estate Planning ... Mr. Stan DAVIS
28 Dir Diversity & Intercultural Educ ... Dr. Denise GREGORY
104 Director of International Education ... Dr. Angela FERGUSON

Selma University (F)

1501 Lapsley Street, Selma AL 36701-5232
County: Dallas FICE Identification: 001037
Unit ID: 102058
Telephone: (334) 872-2533 Carnegie Class: Spec-4-yr-Faith
FAX Number: (334) 872-7746 Calendar System: Semester
URL: www.selmauniversity.edu
Established: 1878 Annual Undergrad Tuition & Fees: $6,705
Enrollment: 558 Coed
Affiliation or Control: Baptist IRS Status: 501(c)3
Highest Offering: Master's
Accreditation: BI

01 President ... Dr. Alvin A. CLEVELAND, SR.
05 Vice President Academic Affairs ... Dr. Rosa ASHMON
32 Vice Pres Student Affairs ... Rev. Frankie HUTCHINS
06 Registrar ... Mr. Terrence JACKSON
37 Director of Financial Aid ... Ms. Yolanda GORDON
07 Director of Admissions ... Mrs. Tammy MAUL
10 Chief Financial/Business Officer ... Mrs. Robin THOMAS

Shelton State Community College (G)

9500 Old Greensboro Road, Tuscaloosa AL 35405-8522
County: Tuscaloosa FICE Identification: 005691
Unit ID: 102067
Telephone: (205) 391-2211 Carnegie Class: Assoc/HVT-Mix Trad/Non
FAX Number: (205) 391-2426 Calendar System: Semester
URL: www.sheltonstate.edu
Established: 1953 Annual Undergrad Tuition & Fees (In-State): $3,933
Enrollment: 4,978 Coed
Affiliation or Control: State IRS Status: 501(c)3
Highest Offering: Associate Degree
Accreditation: SC, ADNUR, COARC, PNUR

01 Interim President ... Dr. Cynthia ANTHONY
05 Associate Dean of Academic Services ... Mr. Lee AMMONS
10 Comptroller Business Services ... Mrs. Ann BRACKNELL
32 Dean of Student Services ... Mrs. Amanda HARBISON
13 Dean Technology/Inst Research ... Dr. Michelle JARRELL
12 Dean Fredd Campus/Title III ... Mr. Ronald RANGE
88 Assoc Dean for Corporate Programs ... Mr. Jason MOORE
30 Assoc Dean of Advancement ... Mr. Byron ABSTON
76 Allied Health Assistant Dean ... Ms. Gladys HILL
37 Director of Financial Aid ... Ms. Rhonda SMITH
88 Executive Asst to the President ... Ms. Channing H. MARLOWE
07 Director of Admissions/Registrar ... Mrs. Fannie BATES-REESE
08 Director Library Services ... Mr. Glen JOHNSON
103 Dean of Instruction & Workforce Dev ... Ms. Joye JONES
88 Director Adult Education ... Mr. Phillip JOHNSON
38 Director of Student Support ... Ms. Holly ELLIOTT
15 Dean of Human Resources ... Mrs. Patricia WILSON
88 Dean of Technical Services ... Mr. Steve FAIR
109 Dean of Auxiliary Services ... Dr. Thomas TAYLOR
04 Administrative Asst to President ... Mrs. Betty PRUITT
09 Director of Institutional Research ... Mr. Louis SHEDD
106 Instructional Tech and eLearning ... Mr. John ALEXANDER
106 Instructional Tech and eLearning ... Ms. Molly BOOTH
18 Chief of Facilities ... Mr. Tim HINTON
26 Asst Dir of Media Communication ... Ms. Lisa WALDROP
105 Assoc Dean of Info/Tech Services ... Mr. Claude LAKE

Snead State Community College (H)

PO Box 734, Boaz AL 35957-0734
County: Marshall FICE Identification: 001038
Unit ID: 102076
Telephone: (256) 593-5120 Carnegie Class: Assoc/HT-High Trad
FAX Number: (256) 593-7180 Calendar System: Semester
URL: www.snead.edu
Established: 1898 Annual Undergrad Tuition & Fees (In-State): $4,380
Enrollment: 2,258 Coed
Affiliation or Control: State IRS Status: Exempt
Highest Offering: Associate Degree
Accreditation: SC, ADNUR

01 President ... Dr. Robert EXLEY
32 Vice President for Student Services ... Mr. Jason CANNON
10 Chief Financial Officer ... Mr. Mark RICHARD
09 Dean for IE/IR ... Dr. Jason WATTS
13 Chief IT Officer ... Mr. Randy MALTBIE
26 Director of Marketing/PR ... Ms. Shelley SMITH
88 Coordinator of Testing/Secondary Ed ... Ms. Tonya SHIELDS
05 Vice President for Academic Affairs ... Dr. Annette CEDERHOLM
20 Associate Dean for Online Learning ... Vacant
81 Science Division Director ... Ms. Deborah RHODEN
79 English/Languages Division Director ... Dr. Cynthia DENHAM
83 Soc Sci/Human Svcs/PS Div Director ... Dr. Karen WATTS
81 Mathematics Division Director ... Mr. Blake LEETH
50 Business Division Director ... Mr. Vann SCOTT
72 Technology/Computer Sci Div Dir ... Mr. Greg RANDALL
57 Humanites/Fine Arts Div Director ... Dr. Jonathan WATTS
103 Director Workforce Development ... Ms. Teresa WALKER
76 Director Health Sciences ... Ms. Amy LANGLEY

41 Athletic Director .... Mr. Mark RICHARD
08 Head Librarian .... Mr. John MILLER
15 Director of Human Resources .... Ms. Amanda GUNNELS
18 Director of Physical Plant .... Mr. Steve WILLIAMS
07 Director of Admissions/Recruitment .... Ms. Ina SMITH
19 Director Security/Safety .... Mr. Paul GORE
29 Director Alumni Relations .... Ms. Shelley SMITH
30 Development Coordinator .... Ms. Kelli CONLEY
37 Financial Aid Coordinator .... Ms. Amanda CHILDRESS
04 Administrative Asst to President .... Ms. Kelli CONLEY

South University (A)

5355 Vaughn Road, Montgomery AL 36116-1120
Telephone: (334) 395-8800 FICE Identification: 004463
Accreditation: &SC, ACBSP, MAC, NURSE, PTAA

† Regional accreditation is carried under the parent institution in Savannah, GA.

Southeastern Bible College (B)

2545 Valleydale Road, Birmingham AL 35244-2083
County: Shelby FICE Identification: 022704
Unit ID: 102261
Telephone: (205) 970-9200 Carnegie Class: Spec-4-yr-Faith
FAX Number: (205) 970-9207 Calendar System: Semester
URL: www.sebc.edu
Established: 1935 Annual Undergrad Tuition & Fees: $12,600
Enrollment: 173 Coed
Affiliation or Control: Independent Non-Profit IRS Status: 501(c)3
Highest Offering: Baccalaureate
Accreditation: BI

01 President .... Dr. Alexander GRANADOS
05 Provost .... Dr. Vicki WOLFE
32 Dean of Students .... Ms. Kristie HARRICK
49 Chair Dept of Arts & Sciences .... Dr. Dwain WALDREP
53 Chair Dept of Education .... Dr. Lynn GANNETT-MALICK
73 Chair Dept of Biblical Studies .... Dr. Jason SNYDER
10 Business Manager .... Mrs. Carme PHILLIPS
04 Admin Asst to the President .... Mrs. Anita SCROGGINS
06 Dir of Inst Effect & Registrar .... Mr. Joel WOLFE
30 Director of Advancement .... Dr. Orrett BAILEY
08 Director of Library Services .... Mr. Paul ROBERTS
37 Director of Financial Aid .... Mrs. Joanne BELIN
55 Dir of ACHIEVE Adult Educ .... Dr. Steven CLECKLER

Southern Union State Community College (C)

PO Box 1000, Wadley AL 36276-1000
County: Randolph FICE Identification: 001040
Unit ID: 251260
Telephone: (256) 395-2211 Carnegie Class: Assoc/HT-High Trad
FAX Number: (256) 395-2215 Calendar System: Semester
URL: www.suscc.edu
Established: 1922 Annual Undergrad Tuition & Fees (In-State): $3,752
Enrollment: 4,727 Coed
Affiliation or Control: State IRS Status: 501(c)3
Highest Offering: Associate Degree
Accreditation: SC, ADNUR, EMT, RAD, SURGT

01 Interim President .... Dr. Glenda COLAGROSS
05 Dean of Academics .... Dr. Linda NORTH
32 Dean of Students .... Ms. Tiffany SANDERS
20 Assoc Dean of Instruction .... Mr. Steve SPRATLIN
72 Dean of Technical Educ/Wrkfce Dev .... Dr. Darin BALDWIN
35 Dean Student Development .... Mr. Gary BRANCH
41 Athletic Director .... Mr. Ron RADFORD
06 Registrar .... Ms. Catherine STRINGFELLOW
10 Business Manager .... Mr. Ben JORDAN

Spring Hill College (D)

4000 Dauphin Street, Mobile AL 36608-1791
County: Mobile FICE Identification: 001041
Unit ID: 102234
Telephone: (251) 380-4000 Carnegie Class: Bac-A&S
FAX Number: (251) 460-2182 Calendar System: Semester
URL: www.shc.edu
Established: 1830 Annual Undergrad Tuition & Fees: $34,092
Enrollment: 1,376 Coed
Affiliation or Control: Roman Catholic IRS Status: 501(c)3
Highest Offering: Master's
Accreditation: #SC, NURSE

01 President .... Dr. Christopher PUTO
05 Provost/Vice Pres Academic Affairs .... Dr. George E. SIMS
10 Vice President Finance/Accounting .... Ms. Rhonda SHIRAZI
30 Vice Pres Alumni Relations/Devel .... Ms. Beverly BYL
32 Vice Pres Student Affairs .... Ms. Rosalie CARPENTER
84 Vice Pres Enrollment Svcs .... Mr. Robert STEWART
13 Chief Information Officer .... Dr. Margaret MASSEY
20 Associate Provost .... Ms. Jennifer GOOD
35 Associate Dean of Students .... Mr. Peter RIVERA
21 Controller .... Ms. Marianne WILKINS
37 Director of Financial Aid .... Ms. Tara JONES
06 Registrar .... Ms. Linnea BATTLES
88 Director Student Advising Services .... Ms. Ashley DUNKLIN
29 Director of Alumni Programs .... Mrs. Mindy HOVELL
15 Director of Personnel .... Ms. Patricia A. DAVIS
19 Director of Public Safety/Security .... Mr. Todd WARREN
23 Director of Health Services .... Mrs. Melissa MELTON
42 Director of Campus Ministry .... Ms. Maureen BERGAN
41 Director Athletics & Recreation .... Mr. James HALL
31 Dir Foley Community Service Center .... Vacant
26 Dir Communications/Instl Mktng .... Mrs. Donna HEROUX
27 Communications Officer .... Ms. Natasha MOORE
36 Director of Career Services .... Mr. Jeremy MOORE
40 Bookstore Manager .... Mr. Blaike PATTERSON
38 Director of Counseling Services .... Dr. Chelsea GREER

Stillman College (E)

3601 Stillman Boulevard, POB 1430,
Tuscaloosa AL 35403-1430
County: Tuscaloosa FICE Identification: 001044
Unit ID: 102270
Telephone: (205) 349-4240 Carnegie Class: Bac-A&S
FAX Number: (205) 366-8996 Calendar System: Semester
URL: www.stillman.edu
Established: 1876 Annual Undergrad Tuition & Fees: $10,418
Enrollment: 1,056 Coed
Affiliation or Control: Presbyterian Church (U.S.A.) IRS Status: 501(c)3
Highest Offering: Baccalaureate
Accreditation: SC, IACBE, MUS, TED

01 President .... Dr. Peter MILLET
05 Provost/VP Academic Affairs .... Vacant
10 Int Vice President Fiscal Affairs .... Ms. Delphine HARRIS
84 Vice President Retention .... Dr. Charlotte CARTER
30 VP Institutional Advancement .... Mr. Anthony HOLLOMAN
32 Vice President for Students Affairs .... Dr. Sharon WHITTAKER-DAVIS
31 Vice Pres External Affairs .... Dr. Eddie B. THOMAS
44 Associate VP for Development .... Mr. Adrian L. SCOTT
26 Assoc Vice President/Marketing & PR .... Mrs. Daryka REEVES
21 Asst Vice Pres/Business Manager .... Vacant
29 Assoc Vice Pres Alumni Affairs .... Mr. Adrian SCOTT
18 Int Plant Operations Director .... Mr. Edward WARD
53 Dean of Professional Educ/Asst VP .... Dr. Linda BRADFORD
49 Dean of Arts & Sciences/Asst VP .... Dr. Mary Jane KROTZER
08 Dean of Library .... Mr. Robert HEATH
09 Director of Institutional Research .... Ms. Cynthia LEATHERWOOD
06 Registrar .... Mrs. Barbara SMITH
37 Director of Financial Aid .... Mrs. Jacqueline MORRIS
38 Dir Student Development/Health Svcs .... Ms. Jacqueline CURRIE
13 Director of Info Technology .... Mr. Dominic MURUAKO
07 Director of Admissions .... Mr. Joseph TINSLEY
19 Chief of Campus Police .... Mr. James TAGGART
41 Interim Athletic Director .... Ms. Cassandra MOORER
15 Director Human Resources .... Ms. Lakeya GOINS
42 College Chaplain .... Dr. Mark MCCORMICK

Talladega College (F)

627 W. Battle Street, Talladega AL 35160-2354
County: Talladega FICE Identification: 001046
Unit ID: 102298
Telephone: (256) 761-6100 Carnegie Class: Bac-Diverse
FAX Number: (256) 761-9206 Calendar System: Semester
URL: www.talladega.edu
Established: 1867 Annual Undergrad Tuition & Fees: $12,510
Enrollment: 879 Coed
Affiliation or Control: Independent Non-Profit IRS Status: 501(c)3
Highest Offering: Baccalaureate
Accreditation: SC, SW

01 President .... Dr. Billy C. HAWKINS
05 Int Provost/VP for Academic Affairs .... Dr. Lisa LONG
10 Vice Pres Finance & Administration .... Dr. Gerald WILLIAMS
32 Int Vice President Student Affairs .... Mr. Anthony M. JONES, JR.
30 Vice Pres Institutional Advancement .... Ms. Kimberly ALEXANDER
18 Director Facilities Management .... Mr. Gary LAWSON
37 Director Financial Aid .... Vacant
07 Int Director of Admissions .... Ms. Kelia AREMU
09 Int Director Institutional Research .... Dr. Syed RAZA
35 Dean/Director of Student Activities .... Mr. Anthony M. JONES, JR.
41 Athletic Director .... Mr. Wilberto RAMOS
08 Librarian .... Dr. Joseph MCDONALD
13 Director Information Technology .... Mr. LaRita BREWSTER
36 Director of Career Placement .... Ms. Delores TRAYLOR
19 Chief Campus Police .... Mr. Kevin GILLILAN
50 Dean Div Administration & Business .... Ms. Charmaine BALFOUR
79 Dean Div Humanities/Fine Arts .... Dr. Isaac BRUNSON
81 Dean Div of Natural Sci/Math .... Dr. Charlie STINSON
83 Dean Div EWJ Social Sciences/Educ .... Dr. Susan VICKERSTAFF
51 Dean of Adult Degree Programs .... Vacant
21 Controller .... Mr. Bruce SMITH
23 Health Services on Campus .... Mrs. Valarie ALFRED
25 Title III Coor/Grants Administrator .... Ms. Peggy ROXBURY
29 Director Alumni Relations .... Ms. Kimberly ALEXANDER
06 Registrar .... Vacant
38 Director Student Counseling .... Ms. Delores TRAYLOR
04 Exec Admin Asst to President .... Ms. Teresa EMBRY
104 Director Study Abroad .... Mr. John VERBURG
22 Dir Affirmative Action/EEO .... Mrs. Brenda RHODEN
15 Human Resources Manager .... Mrs. Brenda RHODEN
26 Director of Public Relations .... Ms. Kimberly ALEXANDER

Trenholm State Technical College (G)

PO Box 10048, Montgomery AL 36108
County: Montgomery FICE Identification: 005734
Unit ID: 102313
Telephone: (334) 420-4200 Carnegie Class: Assoc/HVT-Mix Trad/Non
FAX Number: (334) 420-4206 Calendar System: Semester
URL: www.trenholmstate.edu
Established: 1963 Annual Undergrad Tuition & Fees (In-State): $4,074
Enrollment: 1,338 Coed
Affiliation or Control: State IRS Status: 501(c)3
Highest Offering: Associate Degree
Accreditation: SC, ACFEI, DA, DMS, EMT, MAC, PNUR, RAD

01 President .... Mr. Sam MUNNERLYN
10 Dean of Finance/Admin Svcs .... Ms. Cathy WRIGHT
05 Dean of Instruction .... Mr. Lee AMMONS
30 Dean of Development .... Dr. Suresh C. KAUSHIK
32 Dean of Students .... Dr. Greg HUDSON
103 Dean of Workforce Development .... Mr. Wilford HOLT
13 Assoc Dean of IT .... Mr. Charles HARRIS
09 Director of Institutional Research .... Dr. Mimi JOHNSON
18 Director Physical Plant .... Mr. Robert ALLEN
37 Director Student Financial Aid .... Ms. Betty EDWARDS
07 Director of Admissions/Registrar .... Mrs. Tennie S. MCBRYDE
26 Public Information Officer .... Vacant
15 Director of Human Resources .... Ms. Pam ROLLINS
51 Dir Title II/Marketing/Cont Educ .... Ms. Arlinda KNIGHT
36 Coordinator Job Placement .... Ms. Maria RICHARDSON
04 Administrative Asst to President .... Ms. Angela W. CONE
08 Head Librarian .... Mr. Paul BLACKMON

Troy University (H)

University Avenue, Troy AL 36082-0001
County: Pike FICE Identification: 001047
Unit ID: 102368
Telephone: (334) 670-3100 Carnegie Class: Masters/L
FAX Number: (334) 670-3774 Calendar System: Semester
URL: www.troy.edu
Established: 1887 Annual Undergrad Tuition & Fees (In-State): $7,924
Enrollment: 19,041 Coed
Affiliation or Control: State IRS Status: 501(c)3
Highest Offering: Doctorate
Accreditation: SC, ACBSP, ADNUR, CAATE, CACREP, CORE, ENGR, MUS, NUR, SPAA, SW, TED

01 Chancellor .... Dr. Jack HAWKINS, JR.
05 Sr Vice Chanc for Academic Affairs .... Dr. Earl INGRAM
32 Sr Vice Chanc Student Svcs/Admin .... Dr. John R. DEW
30 Sr Vice Chanc Advance/External Affs .... Gen. Walter GIVHAN
10 Sr VC for Finance & Business Affs .... Dr. James BOOKOUT
15 Vice Chancellor/Dir Human Resources .... Dr. Ray WHITE
12 Assoc VC for Troy Online .... Dr. Glynn CAVIN
12 Vice Chancellor Troy Dothan .... Dr. Don JEFFREY
12 Vice Chancellor Troy Phenix City .... Dr. David WHITE
35 Assoc Dean of Student Svcs Dothan .... Ms. Sandra HENRY
49 Asst Dean Col Arts/Sci Troy Dothan .... Dr. Robert SAUNDERS
20 Asst Dean of Academics .... Dr. Carmen LEWIS
53 Interim Assoc Dean Col of Education .Dr. Dionne ROSSER-MIMS
12 Vice Chanc Troy Montgomery .... Mr. Lance TATUM
49 Asst Dean Arts/Sci Troy Montgomery .... Dr. Sig HARDEN
53 Assoc Dean Col Educ Troy Montgomery .... Dr. Pamela ARRINGTON
30 Assoc Vice Chanc for Development .... Dr. Jean LALIBERTE
37 Assoc Vice Chanc for Financial Aid .... Ms. Carol BALLARD
20 Associate Provost for Academics .... Dr. Lee VARDAMAN
26 Assoc VC for Mktg/Communication .... Ms. Donna SCHUBERT
06 Registrar .... Ms. Vickie MILES
84 Assoc VC for Enrollment Management .... Mr. Buddy STARLING
08 Dean Library Services .... Dr. Chris SHAFFER
13 Chief Technology Officer .... Mr. Greg PRICE
27 Director University Relations .... Mr. Matthew CLOWER
29 Director Alumni Affairs .... Ms. Faith W. WARD
36 Coordinator Career Services .... Ms. Lauren COLE
18 Director Facilities/Physical Plant .... Mr. Mark SALMON
60 Director of Journalism .... Dr. Jefferson SPURLOCK
04 Exec Assistant to the Chancellor .... Mr. Tom DAVIS
38 Director Student Counseling .... Ms. Teresa P. RODGERS
07 Director of Graduate Admissions .... Ms. Jessica KIMBRO
88 Dir Not for Profit/Assoc Controller .... Ms. Lauri DORRILL
106 eTROY Dir Educational Technology .... Mr. Ronnie CREEL
86 Director of Governmental Relations .... Mr. Marcus PARAMORE
44 Director of Annual Giving .... Ms. Bronda DENISON
25 Director Sponsored Programs .... Ms. Judy FULMER
62 Dir of Library Svcs Troy Dothan .... Mr. Chris SHAFFER
62 Dir of Library Svcs Troy Montgomery .... Mr. Kent SNOWDEN
20 Dean Undergrad Pgms/Assoc Provost .... Dr. Hal FULMER
35 Dean of Student Svcs Troy Campus .... Mr. Herbert REEVES
49 Dean Arts & Sciences .... Dr. Steven TAYLOR
49 Assoc Dean Col Arts/Sci .... Dr. Bill GRANTHAM
50 Dean Business .... Dr. Judson EDWARDS
53 Interim Dean Education .... Dr. Lance TATUM
58 Interim Dean Graduate Programs .... Dr. Robin BYNUM
76 Int Dean Health/Human Services .... Dr. Denise GREEN
57 Dean Communication/Fine Arts .... Dr. Larry BLOCHER
35 Assoc Dean Student Svcs Troy Mont .... Dr. James SMITH
09 Director of Institutional Research .... Ms. Kimberly B. JONES
39 Director Student Housing .... Mr. Herbert REEVES
41 Athletic Director .... Mr. Jeremy MCCLAIN
104 Director Study Abroad .... Ms. Maria FRIGGE
105 Director Web Services .... Mr. John LESTER
108 Director Institutional Assessment .... Ms. Wendy BROYLES
19 Police Chief .... Mr. John MCCALL

Tuskegee University (A)

1200 W. Montgomery Road, Tuskegee Inst. AL 36088
County: Macon FICE Identification: 001050
Unit ID: 102377
Telephone: (334) 727-8011 Carnegie Class: Masters/S
FAX Number: (334) 727-5276 Calendar System: Semester
URL: www.tuskegee.edu
Established: 1881 Annual Undergrad Tuition & Fees: $20,015
Enrollment: 3,103 Coed
Affiliation or Control: Independent Non-Profit IRS Status: 501(c)3
Highest Offering: Doctorate
Accreditation: SC, BUS, CS, #DIETD, ENG, MT, NUR, OT, SW, TED, #VET

Code	Title	Name
01	President	Dr. Brian L. JOHNSON
05	Provost/VP Academic Affairs	Dr. Cesar D. FERMIN
10	Vice President Finance/CFO	Mr. Glenn DICKERSON
30	Vice Pres Dev & Advancement	Mr. Robert BLAKELY
46	Vice Pres Research/Sponsored Pgms	Dr. Shaik JEELANI
18	Int VP Capital Proj/Facility Svcs	Mr. Marcus DEAN
84	VP Student Affairs/Enrollment Mgmt	Ms. Regina BURDEN
26	Sr Dir Comm/Public Rels/Mktg	Mr. Jeremy R. ALPHORD
101	Exec Asst to Pres/Secy to the Board	Mrs. Verna S. LITTLE
100	Chief of Staff	Mr. Edward BROWN
13	Chief Information Officer	Ms. Jenell SARGENT
45	Asst VP & Dir Budget & Planning	Ms. Belinda HOGUE
20	Assoc Provost & Director Intl Pgms	Dr. Eloise CARTER
47	Vice Provost/Dean of CAENS	Dr. Walter A. HILL
49	Dean School of Education	Dr. Carlton E. MORRIS
50	Int Dean Col Business/Info Sci	Dr. Charlotte P. MORRIS
54	Dean College of Engineering	Dr. Heshmat AGLAN
74	Int Dean Sch Nursing/Allied Health	Dr. Doris HOLEMAN
32	Dean of Students	Ms. Bomani SPELLS
42	Dean of the Chapel	Dr. Gregory S. GRAY
08	Director of Library Services	Mrs. Juanita ROBERTS
29	Alumni Affairs Director	Vacant
86	Director Federal Relations	Mrs. Willa HALL SMITH
51	Int Assoc Prov Cont Educ/Extension	Dr. Ntam BAHARANYI
36	Assoc Dir Career Devel/Placement	Ms. Sarah STRINGER
21	Bursar	Ms. Barbara CHISHOLM
37	Director of Financial Aid	Mr. Advergus D. JAMES, JR.
15	Director Human Resources	Dr. Shantay BOLTON
18	Project Mgr Sodexho/Physical Plant	Mr. Tony WARD
91	Director of Applications Support	Mr. James E. COOPER
06	Registrar	Mr. Edrice LEFTWICH
38	Director Student Counseling	Dr. Joyce RHODEN
09	Coordinator Institutional Research	Dr. Courtney L. GRIFFIN
96	Director of Purchasing	Vacant

United States Sports Academy (B)

One Academy Drive, Daphne AL 36526-7055
County: Baldwin FICE Identification: 021706
Unit ID: 102395
Telephone: (251) 626-3303 Carnegie Class: Spec-4-yr-Other
FAX Number: (251) 621-2527 Calendar System: Semester
URL: www.ussa.edu
Established: 1972 Annual Undergrad Tuition & Fees: N/A
Enrollment: 339 Coed
Affiliation or Control: Independent Non-Profit IRS Status: 501(c)3
Highest Offering: Doctorate
Accreditation: SC

Code	Title	Name
01	President & CEO	Dr. Thomas J. ROSANDICH
00	President Emeritus	Dr. Thomas P. ROSANDICH
05	Dean of Academic Affairs	Dr. Stephen L. BUTLER
10	Dean of Admin & Finance	Ms. Holly H. MCLELLAN
88	Director of Sports Management	Dr. Brandon SPRADLEY
32	Director of Student Services	Vacant
26	Communications Assistant	Ms. Leigha BOLTON
06	Registrar	Ms. Sara LEE
08	Director of Library/Archivist	Ms. Marcie BOUTWELL
37	Director of Financial Aid	Vacant
18	Building and Grounds	Mr. Bob KLINE

*University of Alabama System Office (C)

500 University Boulevard East, Tuscaloosa AL 35401
County: Tuscaloosa FICE Identification: 008004
Unit ID: 100733
Telephone: (205) 348-5861 Carnegie Class: N/A
FAX Number: (205) 348-9788
URL: www.uasystem.ua.edu

Code	Title	Name
01	Chancellor	Mr. Ray HAYES
101	Sec Board & Exec Asst to Chanc	Vacant
05	Vice Chanc Academic/Student Affairs	Dr. Charles R. NASH
10	Vice Chanc Finance/Administration	Dr. Dana KEITH
26	Vice Chanc Communications/Cmty Rels	Mrs. Kellee C. REINHART
86	Vice Chanc/Economic Development	Mr. Jo BONNER
43	General Counsel	Mr. R. Cooper SHATTUCK
21	General Auditor	Ms. Sabrina B. HEARN

*The University of Alabama (D)

Tuscaloosa AL 35487-0100
County: Tuscaloosa FICE Identification: 001051
Unit ID: 100751
Telephone: (205) 348-6010 Carnegie Class: DU-Higher
FAX Number: (205) 348-9046 Calendar System: Semester
URL: www.ua.edu
Established: 1831 Annual Undergrad Tuition & Fees (In-State): $10,170
Enrollment: 36,047 Coed
Affiliation or Control: State IRS Status: 501(c)3
Highest Offering: Doctorate
Accreditation: SC, ART, BUS, BUSA, CAATE, CACREP, CEA, CIDA, CLPSY, CORE, CS, DANCE, DIETC, DIETD, ENG, JOUR, LAW, LIB, MUS, NURSE, SP, SW, TED, THEA

Code	Title	Name
02	President	Dr. Stuart R. BELL
05	Interim Provost	Dr. Kevin WHITAKER
10	Vice Pres for Financial Affairs	Dr. Lynda GILBERT
30	Vice Pres for Advancement	Mr. Robert "Bob" PIERCE
46	Vice President for Research	Dr. Carl PINKERT
32	Vice Pres for Student Affairs	Dr. David L. GRADY
31	Vice Pres for Community Affairs	Dr. Samory T. PRUITT
26	Vice President Communications	Ms. Linda BONNIN
13	Vice Provost/Chief Information Ofcr	Dr. John MCGOWAN
18	Assistant VP University Facilities	COL. Duane LAMB
18	Ast VP Univ Facilities/Construction	Mr. Tim LEOPARD
19	Assoc VP Public Safety	Mr. Ronnie ROBERTSON
20	Assoc Provost Academic Affairs	Ms. Lisa RHINEY
20	Assoc Provost Academic Affairs	Dr. Patty SOBECKY
11	Assoc Provost for Administration	Dr. Jennifer GREER
15	Assoc VP Human Resources	Ms. Nancy H. WHITTAKER
21	Assoc Vice President for Finance	Ms. Julie SHELTON
21	Assoc Vice Pres Financial Affairs	Vacant
27	Asst VP Communications	Vacant
29	Director of Alumni Affairs	Mr. Calvin BROWN
85	Assoc Provost Internatl Educ	Dr. Teresa WISE
06	University Registrar	Dr. Kenneth H. FOSHEE
09	Director Inst Research/Assessment	Dr. Lorne KUFFEL
36	Exec Director of Career Center	Ms. Melinda KING
07	Dir of Undergraduate Admissions	Ms. Mary K. SPIEGEL
22	Dir & University Compliance Officer	Ms. Gwendolyn D. HOOD
37	Director of Student Financial Aid	Ms. Helen ALLEN
84	Director Enrollment Management	Mr. Landon WAID
39	Director Dept of Housing/Res Cmty	Mr. Matthew KERCH
40	Director of University Supply Store	Ms. Teresa SHREVE
41	Athletic Director	Mr. Bill BATTLE
43	Chief University Counsel	Mr. Mike SPEARING
08	Dean of University Libraries	Dr. Donald GILSTRAP
49	Dean of Arts & Sciences	Dr. Robert F. OLIN
50	Dean College of C&BA	Dr. Kay M. PALAN
51	Dean Col of Cont Studies	Dr. Craig EDELBROCK
53	Dean College of Education	Dr. Peter HLEBOWITSH
54	Dean College of Engineering	Dr. Charles L. KARR
58	Dean Graduate School/Asst Acad VP	Dr. David A. FRANCKO
59	Dean Human Environmental Sciences	Dr. Milla BOSCHUNG
60	Dean Col of Communication/Info Sci	Dr. Mark NELSON
61	Dean School of Law	Dr. Mark E. BRANDON
62	Int Dir Sch of Library/Info Studies	Dr. Ann E. PRENTICE
38	Manager Stdnt Support Svcs-Trio Pgm	Ms. Wendy L. COGBURN
96	Asc Purchasing Mgr Genl Procurement	Ms. Pollye HARDY
96	Purchasing Manager	Mr. Lane COX
76	Dean Cmty Health Sciences	Dr. Rick STREIFFER
66	Dean Capstone College of Nursing	Dr. Suzanne S. PREVOST
70	Dean School of Social Work	Dr. Vikki VANDIVER
92	Dean of Honors College	Dr. Shane SHARPE
94	Dir Women & Gender Resource Ctr	Ms. Lamea SHAABAN-MAGANA

*University of Alabama at Birmingham (E)

1720 2nd Avenue South, Birmingham AL 35294-0001
County: Jefferson FICE Identification: 001052
Unit ID: 100663
Telephone: (205) 934-4011 Carnegie Class: DU-Highest
FAX Number: N/A Calendar System: Semester
URL: www.uab.edu
Established: 1969 Annual Undergrad Tuition & Fees (In-State): $7,766
Enrollment: 18,698 Coed
Affiliation or Control: State IRS Status: 501(c)3
Highest Offering: Doctorate
Accreditation: SC, ANEST, ARCPA, ART, BUS, BUSA, CACREP, CEA, CLPSY, CS, DENT, DIETI, ENG, FEPAC, HSA, IPSY, MED, MT, MUS, NMT, NURSE, OPT, OPTR, OT, PAST, PH, PTA, SPAA, SW, TED, THEA

Code	Title	Name
02	President	Dr. Ray L. WATTS
05	Provost	Dr. Linda C. LUCAS
10	Vice Pres Financial Affairs/Admin	Mr. G. Allen BOLTON
17	CEO UAB Health System	Dr. Will FERNIANY
30	Interim VP Development	Mr. Thomas I. BRANNAN
13	Vice Pres Info Technology/CIO	Dr. Curtis A. CARVER, JR.
28	Vice Pres for Equity and Diversity	Dr. Paulette P. DILWORTH
46	Vice Pres for Research/Economic Dev	Dr. Richard B. MARCHASE
63	Sr VP/Dean School of Medicine	Dr. Selwyn M. VICKERS
20	Sr VP Student/Faculty Success	Dr. Suzanne E. AUSTIN
32	Vice Pres Student Affairs	Dr. John R. JONES, III
43	University Counsel	Mr. W. John DANIEL
49	Dean College of Arts & Sciences	Dr. Robert PALAZZO
50	Dean School of Business	Dr. Eric JACK
52	Dean School of Dentistry	Dr. Michael S. REDDY
53	Dean School of Education	Dr. Deborah L. VOLTZ
54	Dean School of Engineering	Dr. Iwan ALEXANDER
76	Dean School of Health Professions	Dr. Harold P. JONES
66	Dean School of Nursing	Dr. Doreen C. HARPER
88	Dean School of Optometry	Dr. Kelly NICHOLS
69	Dean School of Public Health	Dr. Max MICHAEL, III
58	Dean Graduate School	Dr. Lori L. MCMAHON
18	Assoc Vice President Facilities	Mr. Robert E. MCMAINS, III
109	Assoc VP Business/Auxiliary Svcs	Mr. Christopher CLIFFORD
29	Int AssocVP Alumni/Annual Giving	Dr. Jennifer R. BRELAND
44	Asst Vice Pres Development	Ms. Rebecca J. GORDON
26	Assoc VP Public Relations & Mktg	Ms. Anne BUCKLEY
84	Assoc Provost Enrollment Management	Dr. Bradley BARNES
21	Interim Assoc VP Financial Affairs	Ms. Stephanie B. MULLINS
08	Dean of Libraries	Mr. John M. MEADOR
08	Director Lister Hill Library	Mr. Scott PLUTCHAK
41	Athletic Director	Mr. Mark T. INGRAM
15	Chief Human Resources Officer	Ms. Alesia M. JONES
09	Exec Dir Inst Effect & Analysis	Mr. Jon CORLISS
19	Assistant VP & Chief of Police	Mr. Anthony B. PURCELL
07	Director Undergraduate Admissions	Mr. Tyler M. PETERSON
37	Director of Financial Aid	Ms. Helen M. MCINTYRE
06	University Registrar	Ms. Tina DENEEN
39	Director Student Housing	Mr. Marc BOOKER
36	Interim Exec Dir Career Services	Ms. Melissa L. WHATLEY
38	Asst VP Student Dev/Health & Well	Mr. Jacob BAGGOTT
04	Executive Asst to President	Ms. Jane K. LUCAS
106	Int Dir E-Learning & Prof Studies	Dr. Elizabeth A. FISHER
96	Director of Purchasing	Ms. Belinda MITCHELL

*University of Alabama in Huntsville (F)

301 Sparkman Drive, Huntsville AL 35899-1911
County: Madison FICE Identification: 001055
Unit ID: 100706
Telephone: (256) 824-1000 Carnegie Class: DU-Higher
FAX Number: (256) 824-6073 Calendar System: Semester
URL: www.uah.edu
Established: 1950 Annual Undergrad Tuition & Fees (In-State): $9,128
Enrollment: 7,348 Coed
Affiliation or Control: State IRS Status: 501(c)3
Highest Offering: Doctorate
Accreditation: SC, ART, BUS, CS, ENG, MUS, NURSE, TED

Code	Title	Name
02	President	Dr. Robert A. ALTENKIRCH
05	Provost & Exec VP Academic Affairs	Dr. Christine CURTIS
10	Sr VP Finance & Administration	Mr. Ray PINNER
41	Director Intercollegiate Athletics	Dr. William E. BROPHY, JR.
43	University Counsel	Mr. John CATES
46	VP Research & Econ Dev	Dr. Ray VAUGHN
30	VP University Advancement	Mr. Robert LYON
28	VP Diversity	Ms. Delois SMITH
32	VP of Student Affairs	Dr. Kristi MOTTER
100	Chief of Staff/Dir Community Rels	Mr. Ray GARNER
30	Asst VP for Development	Vacant
35	Assoc VP for Student Affairs	Mr. John MAXON
46	Assoc VP Research	Dr. Thomas M. KOSHUT
46	Associate VP for Research	Dr. Robert LINDQUIST
35	Interim Dean of Students	Mr. TJ BRECCIAROLI
11	Assoc VP Finance & Business Svcs	Mr. Robert LEONARD
13	Interim CIO	Mr. Malcolm RICE
18	Assoc VP Facilities & Operations	Mr. Mark COWHERD
20	Assoc Provost UG Studies/Inst Effec	Dr. Brent M. WREN
21	Associate VP Budgets & Fin Planning	Mr. Chih LOO
26	Assoc VP of Marketing and Comm	Mr. Joel C. LONERGAN
15	Assoc VP Human Resources	Ms. Laurel LONG
09	Director Institutional Research	Dr. Suzanne SIMPSON
88	Director Internal Audit	Ms. Tharanee M. RAVINDRAN
85	Dir International Engagement	Dr. David BERKOWITZ
36	Dir Student Success Center	Dr. Brent WREN
25	Director Sponsored Programs	Ms. Gloria GREENE
88	Director Institute for Science Educ	Dr. James A. MILLER
08	Director Library	Dr. David P. MOORE
79	Dean Arts/Humanities/Soc Science	Dr. Mitch BERBRIER
81	Dean College of Science	Dr. Sundar CHRISTOPHER
50	Dean College Business Admin	Dr. Jason GREENE
51	Dean Prof & Cont Studies	Dr. Karen CLANTON
54	Dean College of Engineering	Dr. Shankar MAHALINGAM
58	Dean Graduate Studies	Dr. David BERKOWITZ
66	Dean College of Nursing	Dr. Marsha ADAMS
53	Dean Education	Dr. Beth QUICK
88	Dir of Cybersecurity Research & Edu	Mr. Tommy MORRIS
40	Bookstore Manager	Ms. Amber YOUNG
37	Director Financial Aid	Mr. Patrick JAMES
38	Dir Counseling & Disability	Ms. Rebecca MATTER
23	Dir Faculty & Staff Clinic	Ms. Louise O'KEEFE
19	Director Public Safety	Mr. Michael R. SNELLGROVE
06	Registrar	Ms. Janet WALLER
07	Director Admissions	Ms. Peggy MASTERS
29	Director Alumni Relations	Ms. Rachel V. OSBY
88	Director Advancement Services	Ms. Marcie T. EPPLING
23	Director Student Health Services	Ms. Kathleen S. RHODES
88	Director ITSC	Dr. Sara J. GRAVES
88	Dir Small Business Develop Center	Mr. Foster PERRY
102	Asst Dir Corp & Foundation Gifts	Ms. Katie S. THURSTON
96	Director of Procurement	Mr. Terence HALEY
88	Director Library Computer Systems	Mr. Jack DROST
90	Manager Academic Technology	Mr. John THYGERSON
88	Director Research Institute	Dr. Steven MESSERVY
88	Director CMSA	Dr. Sara GRAVES
88	Director SMAP Center	Dr. Gary MADDUX
88	Director Rotocraft Center	Mr. Dave ARTERBURN
88	Director Ctr for Applied Optics	Dr. Robert LINDQUIST
88	Dir Ctr Mgmt & Econ Research	Mr. Nic LOYD
88	Director Propulsion Research Center	Dr. Robert FREDERICK
88	Dir Center Space Plsm & Aeron Res	Dr. Gary ZANK
88	Director Earth Systems Science Ctr	Dr. John R. CHRISTY
88	Dir University Ctr & Charger Union	Mr. William M. HALL
91	Director Enterprise Apps & IAM	Mr. Malcolm RICE
104	Director Global Studies Program	Dr. David JOHNSON
92	Dean of the Honors College	Dr. William WILKERSON

University of Mobile (A)

5735 College Parkway, Mobile AL 36613-2842
County: Mobile FICE Identification: 001029
Unit ID: 101693
Telephone: (251) 675-5990 Carnegie Class: Bac-Diverse
FAX Number: (251) 675-6293 Calendar System: Semester
URL: www.umobile.edu
Established: 1961 Annual Undergrad Tuition & Fees: $20,470
Enrollment: 1,600 Coed
Affiliation or Control: Southern Baptist IRS Status: 501(c)3
Highest Offering: Master's
Accreditation: SC, ACBSP, #CAATE, MUS, NURSE

01 President ....Dr. Timothy SMITH
05 Vice Pres for Academic Affairs ....Dr. Chris MCCAGHREN
10 Vice President for Business Affairs ....Mr. Lindsey BONEY
30 Vice Pres for Development ....Mr. Kevin WILBURN
84 VP Enrollment/Student Life ....Mrs. Kim LEOUSIS
11 VP for Operations ....Mr. Kris NELSON
21 Associate VP for Business Affairs ....Ms. Carol CAMP
84 Assoc VP Enroll/Dir Financial Aid ....Ms. Marie BATSON
09 Dir of Institutional Effectiveness ....Mrs. Debra H. CHANCEY
26 Executive Director of Marketing ....Ms. Lesa MOORE
41 Athletic Director ....Mr. Joe NILAND
07 Director of Enrollment Services ....Mrs. Charity WITTNER
08 Director of Library Services ....Mr. Jeffrey D. CALAMETTI
27 Director of Media Relations ....Mrs. Kathy L. DEAN
50 Dean School of Business ....Dr. Jane FINLEY
49 Dean College of Arts & Sciences ....Dr. Lonnie BURNETT
53 Dean School of Education ....Dr. Joyce WOODBURN
66 Dean School of Nursing ....Dr. Jan WOOD
64 Dean School of Music ....Dr. Al MILLER
88 Dean Sch of Worship Leadership ....Dr. Al MILLER
73 Dean School of Christian Ministries ....Dr. Doug WILSON
44 Director Annual Giving ....Mrs. Tonya GOLLETTE
102 Dev Officer for Corp/Govt Relations ....Mr. Claude BUMPERS
90 Director Academic Computing Lab ....Mr. Mitch DAVIS
32 Dir of Campus Life/Dean of Student ....Mr. Neal LEDBETTER
15 Director of Human Resources ....Mrs. Diane BLACK
13 Director of Information Technology ....Mr. Buck NORRED
18 Director of Campus Operations ....Mrs. Vicki BURGIN
38 Director Student Retention ....Mrs. Shirley SUTTERFIELD
88 VP for Project Development ....Dr. Roger BRELAND
06 Registrar ....Mr. Stuart MOORE
106 Director Adult/Online Programs ....Mr. Danny CHANCEY
29 Director of Alumni ....Mr. David CAGLE
36 Director Career Services ....Mrs. Brenda DAVIS
88 Director Faculty Support and QEP ....Dr. Pamela B. MILLER

University of Montevallo (B)

Station 6001, Montevallo AL 35115-6001
County: Shelby FICE Identification: 001004
Unit ID: 101709
Telephone: (205) 665-6000 Carnegie Class: Masters/M
FAX Number: (205) 665-6003 Calendar System: Semester
URL: www.montevallo.edu
Established: 1896 Annual Undergrad Tuition & Fees (In-State): $11,410
Enrollment: 3,070 Coed
Affiliation or Control: State IRS Status: 501(c)3
Highest Offering: Beyond Master's But Less Than Doctorate
Accreditation: SC, AAFCS, ART, BUS, CACREP, DIETC, MUS, SP, SW, TED

01 President ....Dr. John W. STEWART, III
05 Provost and VP Academic Affairs ....Dr. Suzanne OZMENT
32 Dean of Students ....Dr. Tammi DAHLE
30 VP for Enrollment Management ....Dr. Rick BARTH
10 VP Business Affairs ....Vacant
18 Director Physical Plant ....Mr. Billy HUGHES
35 Director Student Life ....Ms. Jenny BELL
06 Registrar ....Mr. Daniel STRICKLAND
08 Director Libraries ....Vacant
07 Director Admissions ....Mr. Greg EMBRY
13 Chief Information Officer ....Mr. Craig GRAY
37 Dir of Student Financial Services ....Mr. Robert WALKER
38 Director Counseling Services ....Mr. Joshua MILLER
19 Chief of Police ....Mr. Chadd ADAMS
39 Dir Housing & Residence Life ....Mr. John DENSON
41 Director Athletics ....Mr. Mark RICHARD
15 Director of HR and Risk Management ....Ms. Barbara FORREST
51 Dir of Regional Inservice Center ....Mr. Dwight JINRIGHT
58 Dir Graduate Admissions & Records ....Mr. Kevin THORNTHWAITE
49 Dean College Arts & Sciences ....Dr. Mary Beth ARMSTRONG
50 Dean College of Business ....Dr. Stephen CRAFT
53 Dean College of Education ....Dr. Anna E. MCEWAN
57 Dean College of Fine Arts ....Dr. Steven PETERS
09 Director of Institutional Research ....Ms. Kris MASCETTI

University of North Alabama (C)

One Harrison Plaza, Florence AL 35632-0001
County: Lauderdale FICE Identification: 001016
Unit ID: 101879
Telephone: (256) 765-4100 Carnegie Class: Masters/L
FAX Number: (256) 765-4644 Calendar System: Semester
URL: www.una.edu
Established: 1830 Annual Undergrad Tuition & Fees (In-State): $7,774
Enrollment: 6,841 Coed
Affiliation or Control: State IRS Status: 501(c)3
Highest Offering: Beyond Master's But Less Than Doctorate
Accreditation: SC, ACBSP, ART, BUS, CACREP, CIDA, CS, ENGR, JOUR, MUS, NURSE, SW, TED

01 President ....Dr. Kenneth KITTS
05 Vice Pres Acad Affairs & Provost ....Dr. John THORNELL
88 Senior Vice Provost Intl Affairs ....Dr. Chunsheng ZHANG
10 VP Business/Financial Affs ....Mr. Clinton P. CARTER
32 Vice President Student Affairs ....Mr. David P. SHIELDS, JR.
30 Vice President Advancement ....Dr. Deborah L. SHAW
84 Assoc VP Enrollment Management ....Mr. Ron PATTERSON
44 Assoc VP Advancement Services ....Dr. Judy T. JACKSON
49 Dean College of Arts & Sciences ....Dr. Carmen L. BURKHALTER
50 Dean College of Business ....Dr. Gregory A. CARNES
53 Dean Col Education/Human Sciences ....Dr. Donna F. LEFORT
66 Dean College of Nursing ....Dr. Vicki G. PIERCE
31 Director University Events ....Mr. Bret JENNINGS
41 Director of Athletics ....Mr. Mark LINDER
43 University Attorney ....Ms. Amber FITE-MORGAN
21 Controller ....Mr. Evan THORNTON
37 Director Student Financial Svcs ....Ms. Shauna JAMES
15 Asst VP for Human Resources ....Ms. Catherine D. WHITE
26 Dir Univ Communications ....Mr. Bryan RACHAL
18 Asst VP for Facilities ....Mr. Michael B. GAUTNEY
19 Chief of University Police ....Mr. Kevin L. GILLILAN
23 Director University Health Services ....Ms. Teresa U. DAWSON
35 Dir Judicial Affairs/Stdnt Aff Plng ....Dr. Kimberly GREENWAY
07 Int Director of Admissions ....Ms. Julie Y. TAYLOR
09 Dir Inst Rsrch/Plng & Assessment ....Dr. Andrew L. LUNA
29 Director Alumni Relations ....Ms. Carol S. LYLES
96 Asst VP Business Services ....Ms. Cindy H. CONLON
28 Dir Diversity/Institutional Equity ....Ms. Joan J. WILLIAMS
36 Dir Career Planning & Development ....Ms. Melissa T. MEDLIN
06 Registrar ....Ms. Cassie N. MORGAN
38 Director University Advising ....Dr. Amy CREWS
40 Manager University Bookstore ....Mr. Griffin HITE
08 Dean Library/Educ Tech Svcs ....Dr. Melvin D. DAVIS
13 Chief Info Technology Officer (CIO) ....Mr. Stephen PUTMAN

University of Phoenix Birmingham Campus (D)

100 Corporate Parkway, Suite 250,
Birmingham AL 35242-2982
Telephone: (205) 747-1001 Identification: 770187
Accreditation: &NH, ACBSP

† No longer accepting campus-based students.

University of South Alabama (E)

307 University Boulevard, N, Mobile AL 36688-0002
County: Mobile FICE Identification: 001057
Unit ID: 102094
Telephone: (251) 460-6101 Carnegie Class: DU-Higher
FAX Number: (251) 461-1537 Calendar System: Semester
URL: www.southalabama.edu
Established: 1963 Annual Undergrad Tuition & Fees (In-State): $7,332
Enrollment: 15,805 Coed
Affiliation or Control: State IRS Status: 501(c)3
Highest Offering: Doctorate
Accreditation: SC, ARCPA, AUD, BUS, BUSA, CACREP, COARC, CS, EMT, ENG, MED, MUS, NURSE, OT, PSPSY, PTA, RAD, RTT, SP, SW, TED

01 President ....Dr. Tony G. WALDROP
03 Executive Vice President ....Dr. John SMITH
05 Provost & Sr VP Academic Affairs ....Dr. G. David JOHNSON
23 Vice Pres Med Affairs/Dean COM ....Dr. John MARYMONT
10 VP Financial Affairs & Admin ....Mr. Scott WELDON
30 Vice Pres Developmental/Alumni Rels ....Dr. Joseph F. BUSTA
46 VP for Research & Economic Devel ....Dr. Lynne CHRONISTER
43 Sr University Attorney ....Ms. Jean TUCKER
58 Int Assc VP Acad Affs/Dean Grad Sch ....Dr. Julio TURRENS
84 Dir Enrollment Services ....Mr. Christopher LYNCH
13 Exec Director of Information Tech ....Mr. Chris CANNON
20 Assoc Vice Pres Academic Affairs ....Dr. Charles GUEST
15 Asst Vice President Human Resources ....Ms. Pamela HENDERSON
17 Dean College of Medicine ....Dr. Samuel J. STRADA
86 Exec Dir Government Relations ....Mr. William J. FULFORD
32 VP Stdnt Affairs/Dean of Stdnt ....Dr. Michael MITCHELL
88 Dir Student Acad Success/Retention ....Dr. Nicole T. CARR
88 Director of Assessment ....Ms. Cecelia MARTIN
26 Exec Dir Marketing/Communication ....Mr. Michael HASKINS
41 Director of Athletics ....Dr. Joel ERDMANN
07 Director of Admissions ....Ms. Norma J. TANNER
85 Director Intl Student Services ....Ms. Brenda HINSON
07 Director New Student Recruitment ....Mr. Christopher LYNCH
09 Dir Inst Research/Plng & Analysis ....Dr. Gordon E. MILLS, JR.
06 Registrar ....Ms. Kelly OSTERBIND
29 Director Alumni Relations ....Ms. Karen EDWARDS
19 Chief of Police ....Mr. Zeke AULL, JR.
37 Director of Financial Aid ....Ms. Emily JOHNSTON
36 Director Career Services ....Ms. Bevley W. GREEN
12 Director USA Baldwin County ....Ms. Cynthia WILSON
18 Director Facilities Management ....Mr. Randy MOON
38 Dir Student Counseling/Test ....Dr. Robert HANKS
28 Director Multicultural Student Affs ....Dr. Carl G. CUNNINGHAM
96 Purchasing Agent ....Mr. Robert M. BROWN
54 Dean College of Engineering ....Dr. John STEADMAN
51 Int Dean Continuing Educ/Spec Pgms ....Dr. Charles GUEST
49 Dean of Arts and Sciences ....Dr. Andrzej WIERZBICKI
08 Dean of University Libraries ....Dr. Richard J. WOOD
50 Dean Mitchell College of Business ....Dr. Carl C. MOORE
53 Dean of Education ....Dr. Richard L. HAYES
66 Dean of College of Nursing ....Dr. Debra C. DAVIS
76 Dean of Allied Health Professions ....Dr. Richard TALBOTT
77 Dean Computer & Information Science ....Dr. Alec YASINSAC
39 Director Student Housing ....Dr. Mary Christine VINET

The University of West Alabama (F)

205 N Washington Street, Livingston AL 35470-2099
County: Sumter FICE Identification: 001024
Unit ID: 101587
Telephone: (205) 652-3400 Carnegie Class: Masters/L
FAX Number: (205) 652-3718 Calendar System: Semester
URL: www.uwa.edu
Established: 1835 Annual Undergrad Tuition & Fees (In-State): $8,734
Enrollment: 3,989 Coed
Affiliation or Control: State IRS Status: 501(c)3
Highest Offering: Beyond Master's But Less Than Doctorate
Accreditation: SC, ACBSP, ADNUR, #CAATE, TED

01 President ....Dr. Ken TUCKER
05 Provost ....Dr. Tim EDWARDS
10 Vice President Financial Affairs ....Mr. T. Raiford NOLAND
44 Vice Pres Institutional Advancement ....Mr. Chris THOMASON
32 Vice President for Student Affairs ....Mr. Richard HESTER
49 Interim Dean of Liberal Arts ....Dr. Mark DAVIS
50 Dean of Business & Technology ....Dr. Wayne BEDFORD
53 Dean College of Education ....Dr. Jan MILLER
81 Dean of Natural Science/Math ....Dr. John MCCALL
58 Dean of Graduate Studies ....Dr. B.J KIMBROUGH
51 Dean Continuing Education ....Dr. Tina N. JONES
106 Dean Online Programs ....Dr. Jan MILLER
66 Chairperson of Nursing ....Mrs. Lynn LASHLEY
08 Director of Library ....Dr. Neil SNIDER
09 Dir Institutional Effectiveness ....Mrs. Angel JOWERS
41 Athletic Director ....Mr. Stan WILLIAMSON
35 Director of Student Life ....Mr. Byron THETFORD
06 Registrar ....Mrs. Susan SPARKMAN
37 Director Student Financial Aid ....Mr. Don RAINER
13 Director Information Systems ....Mr. Michael PRATT
18 Director of Physical Plant ....Mr. Bobby TRUELOVE
109 Director of Auxiliary Services ....Mr. Lee WALKER
36 Director Career Services/Placement ....Ms. Tammy S. WHITE
29 Director Alumni Relations ....Ms. Danielle BUCKALEW
38 Director Student Success Center ....Dr. Vicki P. SPRUIELL
86 Director Government Relations ....Mr. Tom TARTT
07 Dir of Undergraduate Recruiting ....Dr. Blake BEDSOLE
96 Director of Purchasing ....Mr. Lawson C. EDMONDS
89 Director Freshmen Studies ....Dr. James GENTSCH
92 Director Honors Program ....Dr. Lesa SHAUL
15 Director Personnel Services ....Mrs. Brenda KILLOUGH
30 Director of Development ....Mr. Chris THOMASON
20 Associate Academic Officer ....Mrs. Angel JOWERS
26 Chief Public Relations Officer ....Ms. Betsy COMPTON
19 Director of Security/Safety ....Mr. Jeff MANUEL
103 Director Economic Development ....Mrs. Allison BRANTLEY
105 Director of Web Services ....Mrs. Christi GEORGE
101 Secretary Board of Trustees ....Mrs. Katie BEARD
28 Director of Diversity ....Dr. Tim EDWARDS
85 Int Director of Foreign Students ....Dr. Mark DAVIS

Wallace State Community College - Hanceville (G)

PO Box 2000, 801 Main Street, NW,
Hanceville AL 35077-2000
County: Cullman FICE Identification: 007871
Unit ID: 101295
Telephone: (256) 352-8000 Carnegie Class: Assoc/HVT-High Trad
FAX Number: (256) 352-8228 Calendar System: Semester
URL: www.wallacestate.edu
Established: 1966 Annual Undergrad Tuition & Fees (In-State): $4,320
Enrollment: 5,343 Coed
Affiliation or Control: State IRS Status: 501(c)3
Highest Offering: Associate Degree
Accreditation: SC, ACBSF, ACFEI, ADNUR, CAHIIM, COARC, DA, DH, DMS, EMT, MAC, MLTAD, OTA, PNUR, POLYT, PTAA, RAD

01 President ....Dr. Vicki HAWSEY KAROLEWICS
03 Executive Vice President ....Dr. Tomesa SMITH
10 Dean of Finance & Admin Svcs ....Jason MORGAN
05 Dean of Academic Affairs ....Beth BOWNES JOHNSON
20 Dean of Applied Technologies ....Jimmy HODGES
26 Dean of Institutional Outreach ....Melinda EDWARDS
76 Dean of Health Sciences ....Lisa GERMAN
84 Asst Dean Enrollment Management ....Jennifer HILL
109 Auxiliary Director ....Mark BOLIN
08 Head Librarian ....Lisa HULLETT
07 Director Admissions ....Vacant
37 Director of Financial Aid ....Becky GRAVES
53 Extended Day Program Director ....Wayne MANORD
15 Director of Human Resources ....Alyce FLANAGAN
30 Director of Advancement ....Suzanne HARBIN
13 Director of Physical Plant ....Billy ROSE
27 Director of Communication/Marketing ....Kristen HOLMES
06 Registrar ....Jennifer TWITTY

ALASKA

Alaska Bible College (H)

248 East Elmwood Avenue, Palmer AK 99645
County: Matanuska-Susitna FICE Identification: 008843
Unit ID: 102580
Telephone: (907) 745-3201 Carnegie Class: Spec-4-yr-Faith

FAX Number: (907) 745-3210 Calendar System: Semester
URL: www.akbible.edu
Established: 1966 Annual Undergrad Tuition & Fees: $9,300
Enrollment: 46 Coed
Affiliation or Control: Independent Non-Profit IRS Status: 501(c)3
Highest Offering: Baccalaureate
Accreditation: BI

01 President Mr. David LEY
05 Vice Pres Academic Affairs Mr. John FERCH
32 Vice Pres Student Development Mr. Jonathan GARLAND
11 Vice Pres Business Admin Mr. Chris GATES
06 Registrar Mr. Ben OLSON
08 Library Director Ms. Noel MAXWELL
07 Director of Admissions Ms. Becky OLSON
37 Director Financial Aid Ms. Sandy ANDERSON

Alaska Career College (A)

1415 E. Tudor Road, Anchorage AK 99507-1033
County: Anchorage FICE Identification: 025410
Unit ID: 103501
Telephone: (907) 563-7575 Carnegie Class: Spec 2-yr-Other
FAX Number: (907) 563-8330 Calendar System: Other
URL: www.alaskacareercollege.edu
Established: 1985 Annual Undergrad Tuition & Fees: N/A
Enrollment: 479 Coed
Affiliation or Control: Proprietary IRS Status: Proprietary
Highest Offering: Associate Degree
Accreditation: ACCSC

01 Director Ms. Linda STURE

Alaska Pacific University (B)

4101 University Drive, Anchorage AK 99508-4672
County: Anchorage FICE Identification: 001061
Unit ID: 102669
Telephone: (907) 561-1266 Carnegie Class: Masters/S
FAX Number: (907) 562-4276 Calendar System: Semester
URL: www.alaskapacific.edu
Established: 1957 Annual Undergrad Tuition & Fees: $19,610
Enrollment: 579 Coed
Affiliation or Control: Independent Non-Profit IRS Status: 501(c)3
Highest Offering: Doctorate
Accreditation: NW, IACBE, TED

01 President Dr. Don BANTZ
04 Assistant to the President Ms. Debbie ROLL
05 Provost Ms. Tracy STEWART
10 Chief Financial Officer Ms. Deborah JOHNSTON
32 Dean of Students Mr. Ben HAHN
06 Registrar Ms. Michelle WHEELER
07 Asst Director of Admissions Mr. Brian MCDERMOTT
37 Director of Financial Aid Mr. Scott GRAVES
18 Director Facilities Management Ms. Kathy MINCKS
13 Director Information Technology Mr. Dave WILGA
30 Chief Development Officer Vacant
42 Chaplain Vacant
15 Director Human Resources Ms. Kathleen WYRICK
40 Campus Store Manager Ms. Lydia HARVEY
29 Alumni Relations Coordinator Vacant
19 Director Security/Safety Mr. Tyler EGGEN
38 Dir of Career/Counseling & Disabil Vacant
39 Director Student Housing Ms. Manda HILL

Charter College (C)

2221 E Northern Lights Blvd, #120,
Anchorage AK 99508-4157
County: Anchorage FICE Identification: 025769
Unit ID: 102845
Telephone: (907) 277-1000 Carnegie Class: Bac/Assoc-Mixed
FAX Number: (907) 274-3342 Calendar System: Quarter
URL: www.chartercollege.edu
Established: 1985 Annual Undergrad Tuition & Fees: $20,137
Enrollment: 3,267 Coed
Affiliation or Control: Proprietary IRS Status: Proprietary
Highest Offering: Master's
Accreditation: ACICS, ADNUR

01 President Ms. Brenda YOUNG
36 Director of Career Services Ms. Wendy NOVAK
07 Director of Admission Ms. Callie EASTMAN
32 Director of Student Success Ms. Kayla TAYLOR

Ilisagvik College (D)

PO Box 749, Barrow AK 99723
County: North Slope Borough FICE Identification: 034613
Unit ID: 434584
Telephone: (907) 852-3333 Carnegie Class: Tribal
FAX Number: (907) 852-3003 Calendar System: Semester
URL: www.ilisagvik.edu
Established: 1996 Annual Undergrad Tuition & Fees: $3,340
Enrollment: 243 Coed
Affiliation or Control: Independent Non-Profit IRS Status: 501(c)3
Highest Offering: Associate Degree
Accreditation: NW

01 President Ms. Pearl K. BROWER
06 Registrar Mrs. Meghan GALLIGAN
05 Chief Academic Officer Mrs. Birgit MEANY
15 Director Human Resources Mrs. Linda STANFORD
18 Chief Facilities/Physical Plant Mr. Tom CARAWAY
26 Chief Public Relations Officer Mr. John BERGMAN
32 Dean of Students Ms. Amanda SIALOFI
37 Director Student Financial Aid Mrs. Nancy GRANT
04 Administrative Asst to President Mr. Malcolm X. NOBLE

*University of Alaska System (E)

910 Yukon Drive, Suite 202, Fairbanks AK 99775-5000
County: Fairbanks FICE Identification: 008005
Unit ID: 103529
Telephone: (907) 450-8000 Carnegie Class: N/A
FAX Number: (907) 450-8012
URL: www.alaska.edu

01 President Mr. James R. JOHNSEN
26 Vice President for Univ Relations Ms. Michelle RIZK
05 VP for Academic Affairs & Research Dr. Daniel WHITE
10 Int Vice Pres Finance & Admin/CFO Dr. Myron DOSCH
102 VP Univ Rels/Pres UA Foundation Ms. Carla BEAM
46 Chief Strategy/Planning/Budget Ofcr Ms. Michelle RIZK
09 AVP Institutional Rsrch & Analysis Ms. Gwendolyn GRUENIG
84 Assoc VC Student/Enrollment Svcs Mr. Saichi OBA
86 AVP Public Affairs/Federal Rels Mr. Robbie GRAHAM
43 General Counsel Mr. Michael HOSTINA
15 Chief HR Officer Mr. Erik SEASTEDT
13 Chief Information Technology Ofcr Mr. Karl KOWALSKI
06 Registrar & Director of Admissions Ms. Libby EDDY
16 Director Labor & Employee Relations Ms. Rhonda OOMS
88 Chief Risk Officer Ms. Nancy SPINK

*University of Alaska Anchorage (F)

3211 Providence Drive, Anchorage AK 99508-8000
County: Anchorage FICE Identification: 011462
Unit ID: 102553
Telephone: (907) 786-1800 Carnegie Class: Masters/L
FAX Number: (907) 786-4888 Calendar System: Semester
URL: www.uaa.alaska.edu
Established: 1954 Annual Undergrad Tuition & Fees (In-State): $5,545
Enrollment: 17,151 Coed
Affiliation or Control: State IRS Status: 501(c)3
Highest Offering: Doctorate
Accreditation: NW, ACFEI, ADNUR, ART, BUS, CLPSY, CONST, CS, CSHSE, DA, DH, DIETD, DIETI, EMT, ENG, ENGR, JOUR, MAC, MT, MUS, NUR, PH, PTAA, SW, TED

02 Chancellor Gen. Tom CASE
05 Provost & Exec VC Academic Affairs Dr. Sam GINGERICH
11 Vice Chancellor Administrative Svcs Dr. William SPINDLE
09 Sr Vice Provost Inst Effectiveness Ms. Renee M. CARTER-CHAPMAN
84 Assoc Vice Chanc Enrollment Svcs Mr. Eric R. PEDERSEN
30 Vice Chancellor Univ Advancement Ms. Megan OLSON
32 Vice Chancellor Student Affairs Dr. Bruce SCHULTZ
26 Asst Vice Chanc Univ Relations Ms. Kristin DESMITH
13 CIO/Associate Vice Chancellor Mr. Pat SHIER
09 Assoc Vice Provost Inst Research Dr. Erin HOLMES
18 Assoc Vice Chanc Facilities Mr. Christopher TURLETES
96 Assoc Vice Chanc Financial Services Ms. Sandi CULVER
29 Asst Vice Chanc Alumni Relations Ms. Rachel MORSE
88 AVC Student Access/Advis/Transition Dr. Lacy KARPILO
88 Int Exec Dir Acad/Multicul Success Ms. Theresa LYONS
35 Dean of Students Dr. Dewain LEE
37 Dir Student Financial Assistance Ms. Sonya STEIN
85 Director Multicultural Center Mr. Andre THORN
35 Director Student Life & Leadership Ms. Annie ROUTE
07 Interim Director of Admissions Ms. Cathy EWING
41 Director Athletics Mr. Keith HACKETT
06 University Registrar Ms. Lora VOLDEN
36 Director Career Services Center Ms. Diane KOZAK
15 Director Human Resources Mr. Ron KAMAHELE
08 Dean Consortium Library Mr. Stephen J. ROLLINS
63 Director Biomedical Program Dr. Jane SHELBY
88 Director Native Student Services Mr. William TEMPLETON
38 Director Student Health/Counseling Ms. Georgia DEKEYSER
50 Dean Col Business/Public Policy Dr. Rashmi PRASAD
51 Dean Community/Tech College Dr. Bonnie K. NYGARD
76 Dean College of Health Mr. William HOGAN
54 Interim Dean College of Engineering Dr. T. Bart QUIMBY
49 Dean College Arts & Sciences Dr. John STALVEY
53 Dean College of Education Dr. Paul DEPUTY
92 Interim Dean Honors College Dr. John MOURACADE
27 Senior Public Relations Specialist Ms. Jessica HAMLIN
106 Director Academic Innov E-learning Dr. Dave DANNENBERG
20 Vice Provost Undergrad Acad Affairs Dr. Susan KALINA
58 Vice Prov Research & Grad School Dr. Helena WISNIEWSKI
39 Director Univ Housing Dining & Conf Mr. David WEAVER
44 Annual Giving Director Mr. Jim SMITH

*University of Alaska Fairbanks (G)

505 South Chandlar Drive, Fairbanks AK 99775
County: Fairbanks North Star Borough FICE Identification: 001063
Unit ID: 102614
Telephone: (907) 474-7500 Carnegie Class: DU-Higher
FAX Number: (907) 474-5379 Calendar System: Semester
URL: www.uaf.edu
Established: 1917 Annual Undergrad Tuition & Fees (In-State): $5,674
Enrollment: 8,620 Coed
Affiliation or Control: State IRS Status: 501(c)3
Highest Offering: Doctorate
Accreditation: NW, BUS, BUSA, CLPSY, CS, DH, EMT, ENG, MAC, MUS, SW, TED

02 Interim Chancellor Mr. Dana L. THOMAS
05 Provost Dr. Susan M. HENRICHS
11 Vice Chancellor Administrative Svcs Ms. Kari BURRELL
18 Assoc Vice Chancellor Facilities Mr. Scott BELL
32 VC University & Student Advancement Dr. Mike SFRAGA
45 Vice Chancellor Research Mr. Larry HINZMAN
10 Interim AVC for Financial Services Mrs. Julie QUEEN
84 Assoc VC for Enrollment Mgmt Mr. Eric PEDERSEN
30 Director of Development Ms. Emily DRYGAS
58 Interim Dean Graduate School Dr. Michael CASTELLINI
81 Dean Col of Natural Science/Math Dr. Paul LAYER
35 Assoc Vice Chanc for Student Life Mr. Alexis KNABE
31 VC Rural/Cmty & Native Educ Mr. Evon PETER
12 Dean UAF Comm & Tech College Ms. Michele STALDER
47 Interim Dean/Director SNRAS/AFES Dr. Stephen SPARROW
88 Dean Sch Fisheries & Ocean Sciences Mr. Bradley MORAN
50 Dean School of Management Dr. Mark HERRMANN
54 Dean Col of Engineering & Mines Dr. Doug GOERING
88 Dir Intl Arctic Research Center Dr. Hajo EICKEN
88 Dir Institute of Arctic Biology Dr. Brian M. BARNES
54 Int Dir Inst Northern Engineering Dr. William SCHNABEL
15 Director Human Resources Mr. Brad LOBLAND
19 Chief of Police Mr. Stephen GOETZ
37 Director Financial Aid Ms. Deanna L. DIERINGER
41 Director Athletics Dr. Gary GRAY
39 Director Residence Life Ms. Laura L. MCCOLLOUGH
56 Vice Provost for Extension/Outreach Mr. Fred SCHLUTT
109 Director of Aux/Recharge/Cntrct Ops Vacant
85 Director International Programs Ms. Donna ANGER
88 Fire Chief Mr. Doug SCHRAGE
88 Dir Institute of Marine Science Dr. Terry WHITLEDGE
49 Dean College of Liberal Arts Mr. Todd SHERMAN
53 Dean School of Education Dr. Steve ATWATER
12 Director Bristol Bay Campus Dr. Deborah MCLEAN
12 Director Chukchi Campus Mr. Pete PINNEY
12 Director Interior Aleutians Campus Ms. Teisha SIMMONS
12 Director Kuskokwim Campus Ms. Mary C. PETE
12 Director Northwest Campus Mr. Robert METCALF
28 Interim Dir Diversity & EO Mr. Kevin CALDERARA
23 Director Health and Counseling Dr. B.J ALDRICH
29 Exec Director Alumni Association Ms. Kate RIPLEY
06 Registrar Mr. Mike EARNEST
88 Director Geophysical Institute Mr. Robert MCCOY
21 Director Business Operations Ms. Amanda WALL
36 Director Career Services Ms. Patti PICHA
38 Director Academic Advising Center Ms. Linda M. HAPSMITH
92 Director Honors Program Ms. Marsha SOUSA
94 Coordinator Women's Studies Dr. Sine ANAHITA
09 Dir Planning/Analysis/Inst Research Mr. Ian OLSON
26 Director University Relations Ms. Michelle RENFREW
08 Interim Dean of Libraries Ms. Suzan HAHN
88 Interim Dir UA Museum of the North Dr. Aldona JONAITIS
13 Chief Info Technology Officer Mr. Karl KOWALSKI
22 Director for Disability Services Ms. Mary MATTHEWS
96 Dir of Procurement & Contract Svcs Mr. John HEBARD
88 Director Wood Center Student Union Vacant
97 Vice Provost/Dean Gen Studies Dr. Alex FITTS

*University of Alaska Southeast (H)

11120 Glacier Highway, Juneau AK 99801-8681
County: Juneau FICE Identification: 001065
Unit ID: 102632
Telephone: (907) 796-6000 Carnegie Class: Masters/M
FAX Number: N/A Calendar System: Semester
URL: www.uas.alaska.edu
Established: 1956 Annual Undergrad Tuition & Fees (In-State): $6,132
Enrollment: 2,989 Coed
Affiliation or Control: State IRS Status: 501(c)3
Highest Offering: Master's
Accreditation: NW, CAHIIM, TED

02 Chancellor Dr. Richard CAULFIELD
05 Provost & Executive Dean SCE Dr. Karen CAREY
75 Exec Dean Sch of Career Educ Mr. Pete TRAXLER
46 Vice Provost for Research Dr. Karen SCHMITT
11 Vice Chanc Admin Svcs & Dir IT Mr. Michael CIRI
12 Sitka Campus Director Dr. Paula MARTIN
12 Ketchikan Campus Director Dr. Priscilla SCHULTE
49 Dean of Arts & Sciences Dr. Karen SCHMITT
88 Dean of School of Management Ms. Vickie WILLIAMS
53 Dean Education & Graduate Studies Dr. Deborah LO
37 Acting Financial Aid Director Mr. Eric RAMAEKERS
26 Public Relations Ms. Keni CAMPBELL
06 Registrar Ms. Barbara HEGEL
84 VC Enrollment Mgmt & Stdnt Affs Mr. Joseph NELSON
09 Institutional Effectiveness Manager Mr. Brad EWING
10 Director Business Services Mr. Tom DIENST
15 Director Personnel Services Dr. Gail CHENEY
18 Director Facilities Services Mr. Keith GERKEN
08 Director Library Services Ms. Elise TOMLINSON
13 Director Information/Technology Mr. Michael CIRI
30 Dir Development/Alumni Relations Ms. Lynne JOHNSON
29 Alumni Relations/Annual Fund Mgr Ms. Jessy POSTY
21 Chief Budget Officer Ms. Roxy J. FELKL
88 Director Learning Center Ms. Hildegard SELLNER
32 Title IX Coordinator/HR Training Ms. Lori KLEIN
39 Director of Campus Life Mr. Eric SCOTT
88 Director of PITAAS Ms. Ronalda CADIENTE-BROWN
88 Director of AK Coastal Rainforest Ms. Allison BIDLACK

*Prince William Sound Community College (A)

PO Box 97, Valdez AK 99686-0097
County: Valdez-Cordova-Glennallen Identification: 666659
Unit ID: 103361
Telephone: (907) 834-1600 Carnegie Class: Not Classified
FAX Number: (907) 834-1611 Calendar System: Semester
URL: www.pwscc.edu
Established: 1978 Annual Undergrad Tuition & Fees (In-State): N/A
Enrollment: N/A Coed
Affiliation or Control: State IRS Status: 501(c)3
Highest Offering: Associate Degree
Accreditation: NW

02 President .... Mr. J. Daniel O'CONNOR
05 Director of Academic Affairs .... Vacant
10 Director Administrative Services .... Mr. Steve SHIELL
32 Director Student Affairs .... Ms. Ana HINKLE
30 Inst Development/Advancement Ofcr .... Mr. Ryan BELNAP
26 Chief Public Relations Officer .... Ms. Wendy GOLDSTEIN
38 Director Student Counseling .... Vacant
88 Director of Training .... Mr. BJ WILLIAMS
06 Records/Registration Coordinator .... Ms. Shannon FOSTER

ARIZONA

Acacia University (B)

7665 South Research Drive, Tempe AZ 85284-1812
County: Maricopa Identification: 667017
Telephone: (480) 428-6034 Carnegie Class: Not Classified
FAX Number: (480) 428-6033 Calendar System: Other
URL: www.acacia.edu
Established: 2003 Annual Undergrad Tuition & Fees: N/A
Enrollment: N/A Coed
Affiliation or Control: Proprietary IRS Status: Proprietary
Highest Offering: Master's
Accreditation: DEAC

01 President .... Mr. Tim MOMAN
05 Provost/Executive Vice President .... Dr. Marilynn D. HENLEY
26 CIO .... Mr. Michael TURICO

Argosy University, Phoenix (C)

2233 W Dunlap Avenue, Phoenix AZ 85021
Telephone: (602) 216-2600 Identification: 666790
Accreditation: &WC, ACBSP, CACREP, CLPSY

† Regional accreditation is carried under the parent institution in Orange, CA.

Arizona Christian University (D)

2625 E Cactus Road, Phoenix AZ 85032-7042
County: Maricopa FICE Identification: 007113
Unit ID: 105899
Telephone: (602) 489-5300 Carnegie Class: Bac-Diverse
FAX Number: (602) 404-2159 Calendar System: Semester
URL: www.arizonachristian.edu
Established: 1960 Annual Undergrad Tuition & Fees: $23,110
Enrollment: 737 Coed
Affiliation or Control: Independent Non-Profit IRS Status: 501(c)3
Highest Offering: Baccalaureate
Accreditation: NH

01 President .... Mr. Len MUNSIL
03 Interim Provost .... Dr. Gary DAMORE
10 Chief Financial Officer .... Mr. Timothy FISCHER
84 VP for Enrollment .... Mr. Pete HAMSTRA
107 VP Profess/Adult & Online Studies .... Dr. Karl STERNER
21 Controller .... Mr. Rick SHARPE
09 Director of Institutional Research .... Ms. Theresa MILTON
06 Registrar & Asst Dir of Enroll Mgmt .... Mr. Lambert CRUZ
37 Director Financial Aid .... Ms. Joyce HATCH
13 Director of Information Technology .... Mr. Robert TERRY
08 Librarian .... Mr. Robert OLIVERIO
19 Director of Campus Security .... Mr. John HOEBEE
18 Director of Facilities .... Mr. David HOOK
41 Athletic Director .... Mr. Jeff RUTTER
39 Residence Director .... Ms. Wendy CLYDE
15 Human Resources Coordinator .... Ms. Nancy STOCKING
04 Executive Assistant to President .... Mrs. Amanda RISINGER

Arizona College (E)

4425 W Olive Avenue, Suite 300, Glendale AZ 85302-3851
County: Maricopa FICE Identification: 031150
Unit ID: 421708
Telephone: (602) 222-9300 Carnegie Class: Spec 2-yr-Health
FAX Number: (602) 200-8726 Calendar System: Other
URL: www.arizonacollege.edu
Established: 1991 Annual Undergrad Tuition & Fees: $15,110
Enrollment: 630 Coed
Affiliation or Control: Proprietary IRS Status: Proprietary
Highest Offering: Associate Degree
Accreditation: ABHES

01 President .... Mr. Nick MANSOUR

Arizona College-Mesa (F)

163 N. Dobson Road, Mesa AZ 85201
Telephone: (480) 265-3600 Identification: 770514
Accreditation: ABHES

Arizona School of Acupuncture and Oriental Medicine (G)

2856 E Fort Lowell Rd., Tucson AZ 85716
County: Pima FICE Identification: 036955
Unit ID: 446039
Telephone: (520) 795-0787 Carnegie Class: Spec-4-yr-Other Health
FAX Number: (877) 222-4606 Calendar System: Quarter
URL: www.asaom.edu
Established: 1996 Annual Graduate Tuition & Fees: N/A
Enrollment: 40 Coed
Affiliation or Control: Proprietary IRS Status: Proprietary
Highest Offering: Master's; No Undergraduates
Accreditation: #ACUP

01 CEO/Owner .... Mr. Jonathan HU
05 Academic Dean .... Dr. Julian CHANG
37 Financial Aid Advisor .... Ms. Susan WAGNER
07 Admissions Director .... Mr. Tim DUNN

Arizona State University (H)

300 E. University Drive, Tempe AZ 85281
County: Maricopa FICE Identification: 001081
Unit ID: 104151
Telephone: (855) 278-5080 Carnegie Class: DU-Highest
FAX Number: N/A Calendar System: Semester
URL: www.asu.edu
Established: 1885 Annual Undergrad Tuition & Fees (In-State): $10,158
Enrollment: 50,320 Coed
Affiliation or Control: State IRS Status: 501(c)3
Highest Offering: Doctorate
Accreditation: NH, AAB, ART, AUD, BUS, BUSA, CACREP, CIDA, CLPSY, CONST, COPSY, CS, DIETD, DIETI, ENG, ENGT, IPSY, JOUR, LAW, LSAR, MT, MUS, NRPA, NURSE, PCSAS, PLNG, SCPSY, SP, SPAA, SW

01 President .... Dr. Michael M. CROW
05 Exec VP & University Provost .... Dr. Mark S. SEARLE
10 Exec Vice President/Treasurer & CFO .... Dr. Morgan R. OLSEN
03 Sr Vice Pres/Sec of the University .... Dr. Christine K. WILKINSON
102 CEO ASU Foundation .... Mr. Rick SHANGRAW
43 Sr Vice President & General Counsel .... Mr. José A. CÁRDENAS
32 Sr VP Educ Outreach & Student Svcs .... Dr. James A. RUND
41 Vice President for Athletics .... Mr. Ray ANDERSON
13 Chief Information Officer .... Mr. Gordon D. WISHON
15 VP & Chief Human Resources Ofc .... Mr. Kevin J. SALCIDO
100 Sr VP Univ Affairs/Chief of Staff .... Mr. Jim O'BRIEN
106 Exec Vice Provost/Dean EdPlus .... Dr. Philip R. REGIER
49 VP/Dean of Liberal Arts & Sciences .... Dr. Patrick KENNEY
84 Vice Provost Enrollment Management .... Mr. Kent HOPKINS
50 Dean WP Carey School of Business .... Dr. Amy HILLMAN
54 Dean Fulton School of Engineering .... Dr. Kyle SQUIRES
53 Dean Mary Lou Fulton Teachers Col .... Dr. Mari E. KOERNER
92 Dean of Barrett Honors College .... Dr. Mark JACOBS
12 Dean New College of Int Arts & Sci .... Dr. Marlene TROMP
57 Dean Herberger Inst for Design/Arts .... Dr. Steven J. TEPPER
60 Dean Cronkite Sch Journal/Mass Comm .... Mr. Christopher CALLAHAN
61 Dean College of Law .... Mr. Douglas SYLVESTER
66 Dean College of Nursing & Health In .... Dr. Teri PIPE
47 Dean School of Sustainability .... Dr. Christopher G. BOONE
20 Vice Provost Undergrad Education .... Dr. Frederick C. COREY
76 Exec VP/Dean Health Solutions .... Dr. Keith D. LINDOR
88 Dean College of Public Svc & Comm .... Mr. Jonathan KOPPELL
07 Exec Director of Admissions .... Vacant
08 University Librarian .... Dr. James O'DONNELL
107 CEO/DirGen Thunderbird Sch Glbl Mgt .... Dr. Allen MORRISON
97 Dean Col Letters & Sci/Univ College .... Mr. Duane ROEN

Arizona Summit Law School (I)

One North Central Avenue, 14th Flr, Phoenix AZ 85004
County: Maricopa FICE Identification: 041314
Unit ID: 450942
Telephone: (602) 682-6800 Carnegie Class: Spec-4-yr-Law
FAX Number: (602) 682-6999 Calendar System: Semester
URL: www.azsummitlaw.edu
Established: 2005 Annual Graduate Tuition & Fees: N/A
Enrollment: 752 Coed
Affiliation or Control: Proprietary IRS Status: Proprietary
Highest Offering: First Professional Degree; No Undergraduates
Accreditation: LAW

01 Dean .... Ms. Shirley L. MAYS
05 Vice Dean of Academic Operations .... Mr. Joe PEREZ
13 Vice Pres Technology .... Mr. Ken SCHOBLOHER
10 Senior Director Finance/Fin Aid .... Ms. Gail SAUERS
06 Dir Acad Svcs & Registration .... Mr. Tim DOWNING
07 Assoc Dean of Admissions .... Mr. Rick JOHNSON

Arizona Western College (J)

2020 Avenue 8E, Yuma AZ 85365
County: Yuma FICE Identification: 001071
Unit ID: 104160
Telephone: (928) 317-6000 Carnegie Class: Assoc/MT-VT-Mix Trad/Non
FAX Number: (928) 344-7730 Calendar System: Semester
URL: www.azwestern.edu
Established: 1963 Annual Undergrad Tuition & Fees (In-District): $2,540
Enrollment: 7,702 Coed
Affiliation or Control: State/Local IRS Status: Exempt
Highest Offering: Associate Degree
Accreditation: NH, ADNUR, RAD

01 President .... Dr. Daniel P. CORR
10 Vice Pres Finance/Administration .... Mrs. Carole T. COLEMAN
26 Dean Public Relations & Marketing .... Mrs. Lori STOFFT
09 Dean Instl Effect/Research/Grants .... Dr. Mary SCHAAL
05 Vice President Learning Services .... Dr. Linda ELLIOTT-NELSON
51 Assoc Dean of Continuing Educ .... Mrs. Maria E. AGUIRRE
07 Vice President for Student Services .... Mr. Bryan E. DOAK
75 Int Dean of Career & Tech Educ .... Mrs. Maria AGUIRRE
30 Director Institutional Advancement .... Mrs. Renee L. SMITH
06 Director of Admissions/Registrar .... Mrs. Nicole D. HARRAL
21 Dir Financial Services/Controller .... Mrs. Diana G. DOUCETTE
15 Chief Human Resources Officer .... Ms. Kari HEILMAN
96 Dir Purchasing & Auxiliary Services .... Ms. Margaret HAYES
18 Director of District Operations .... Mr. Steve ECKERT
13 Director of Computer Info Services .... Mrs. Adele EDWARDS
14 Director of Tech Support Services .... Ms. Brenda WARNOCK
08 Director of Library Services .... Ms. Angie CREEL
41 Director of Athletics .... Mr. Jerry SMITH
19 Chief of Police .... Mr. John EDMUNDSON
32 Dean for Campus Life .... Ms. Mary Kay HARTON
12 Associate Dean La Paz County Svcs .... Ms. Kathy OCAMPO
12 Assoc Dean for South Yuma County .... Mr. Everardo MARTINEZ
37 Interim Director of Financial Aid .... Ms. Ana ENGLISH
85 Director of International Program .... Mr. Ken KUNTZELMAN
106 Associate Dean for Distance Educ .... Mrs. Jana MOORE
88 Director of Testing Services .... Mrs. Leticia MARTINEZ
105 Webmaster II .... Mr. Damien BATES
04 Executive Assistant to President .... Mrs. Rachel CALDWELL
36 Director Career/Advisement Services .... Mr. James R. HUTCHISON

The Art Institute of Phoenix (K)

2233 W Dunlap Avenue, Phoenix AZ 85021-2859
County: Maricopa FICE Identification: 040513
Unit ID: 428444
Telephone: (602) 331-7500 Carnegie Class: Spec-4-yr-Arts
FAX Number: (602) 331-5301 Calendar System: Quarter
URL: www.artinstitutes.edu/phoenix
Established: 1995 Annual Undergrad Tuition & Fees: $17,412
Enrollment: 1,009 Coed
Affiliation or Control: Proprietary IRS Status: Proprietary
Highest Offering: Baccalaureate
Accreditation: #ACICS, ACFEI, CIDA

01 President .... Mr. Chad WILLIAMS
05 Dean of Academic Affairs .... Mr. Gil MEJIA
07 Senior Director of Admissions .... Ms. Breean FULP
32 Dean of Student Affairs .... Ms. Tanisha FRASIER
36 Director of Career Services .... Ms. Jennifer BOHNSACK
15 Human Resources Generalist .... Mr. Daniel ALLEN
13 Technology Support Supervisor .... Mr. Nate YOUNG
37 Director of Student Financial Svcs .... Ms. Abigail GARCIA
06 Registrar .... Mr. Joseph SALINAS

The Art Institute of Tucson (L)

5099 East Grant Road, Suite 100, Tucson AZ 85712-2733
Telephone: (520) 318-2700 FICE Identification: 037405
Accreditation: #ACICS

† In teach-out mode.

Benedictine University at Mesa (M)

51 E Main Street, Suite 105, Mesa AZ 85201
Telephone: (602) 888-5000 Identification: 770068
Accreditation: &NH

† Regional accreditation is carried under the parent institution in Lisle, IL

Brighton College (N)

8777 E. Via de Ventura, Scottsdale AZ 85258
County: Maricopa Identification: 666710
Telephone: (602) 212-0501 Carnegie Class: Not Classified
FAX Number: (602) 212-0502 Calendar System: Other
URL: www.brightoncollege.edu
Established: 1961 Annual Undergrad Tuition & Fees: N/A
Enrollment: N/A Coed
Affiliation or Control: Proprietary IRS Status: Proprietary
Highest Offering: Associate Degree
Accreditation: DEAC

01 President .... Paul ZAGNONI
03 Executive Vice President .... Sam FERNENDEZ
26 Vice President Marketing Operations .... Chris CARAWAY
84 Vice Pres Enrollment Management .... Robert BLAKELY
10 Dir of Financial Operations .... Patricia MCCOY
32 Director of Student Management .... Kayla HOBBIEBRUNKEN

Brookline College (O)

2445 West Dunlap Avenue, Suite 100, Phoenix AZ 85021
County: Maricopa FICE Identification: 022188
Unit ID: 104090
Telephone: (602) 242-6265 Carnegie Class: Bac-Diverse

FAX Number: (602) 973-2572 Calendar System: Other
URL: www.brooklinecollege.edu
Established: 1979 Annual Undergrad Tuition & Fees: N/A
Enrollment: 1,468 Coed
Affiliation or Control: Proprietary IRS Status: Proprietary
Highest Offering: Baccalaureate
Accreditation: ACICS, MLTAD, NUR, NURSE, PTAA

01 Campus Director .... Ms. Valentina CREWSE

Brookline College (A)
1140 South Priest Drive, Tempe AZ 85281
Telephone: (480) 545-8755 Identification: 666403
Accreditation: ACICS, SURTEC

† Branch campus of Brookline College, Phoenix, AZ.

Brookline College (B)
5441 E 22nd Street, Suite 125, Tucson AZ 85711-5444
Telephone: (520) 748-9799 Identification: 666402
Accreditation: ACICS

† Branch campus of Brookline College, Phoeniz, AZ.

Brown Mackie College-Phoenix (C)
13430 North Black Canyon Highway, Phoenix AZ 85029
Telephone: (602) 337-3044 Identification: 666782
Accreditation: ACICS, OTA, SURTEC

† Branch Campus of The Art Institute of Phoenix, Phoenix, AZ.

Brown Mackie College-Tucson (D)
4585 E Speedway Boulevard, Tucson AZ 85712-5300
Telephone: (520) 319-3300 FICE Identification: 009451
Accreditation: ACICS, OTA, SURTEC

Bryan University (E)
350 West Washington Street, Ste 100, Tempe AZ 85281
Telephone: (602) 384-2555 Identification: 770627
Accreditation: ACICS

† Branch campus of Bryan University, Springfield, MO.

Carrington College - Mesa (F)
1001 W Southern Avenue, Suite 130, Mesa AZ 85210
Telephone: (480) 212-1600 FICE Identification: 023352
Accreditation: &WJ, DH, MAAB, PTAA

† Regional accreditation is carried under the parent institution in Sacramento, CA.

Carrington College - Phoenix East (G)
2149 W Dunlap Avenue, Phoenix AZ 85021-2982
Telephone: (602) 216-7700 Identification: 666248
Accreditation: &WJ, COARC

† Regional accreditation is carried under the parent institution in Sacramento, CA.

Carrington College - Phoenix North (H)
8503 N 27th Avenue, Phoenix AZ 85051-4063
Telephone: (602) 393-5900 FICE Identification: 021006
Accreditation: &WJ, ADNUR, MAAB

† Regional accreditation is carried under the parent institution in Sacramento, CA.

Carrington College - Tucson (I)
201 N. Bonita Ave., Ste. 101, Tucson AZ 85745
Telephone: (520) 888-5885 FICE Identification: 030898
Accreditation: &WJ, MAAB

† Regional accreditation is carried under the parent institution in Sacramento, CA.

Central Arizona College (J)
8470 N Overfield Road, Coolidge AZ 85128-9779
County: Pinal FICE Identification: 007283
Unit ID: 104346
Telephone: (520) 494-5444 Carnegie Class: Assoc/MT-VT-High Non
FAX Number: (520) 494-5008 Calendar System: Semester
URL: www.centralaz.edu
Established: 1962 Annual Undergrad Tuition & Fees (In-District): $2,460
Enrollment: 5,937 Coed
Affiliation or Control: Local IRS Status: 501(c)3
Highest Offering: Associate Degree
Accreditation: NH, ADNUR, CAHIIM, DIETT, EMT, IFSAC, MAC, RAD

01 President .... Dr. Jacquelyn ELLIOTT
05 VP Academic Affairs .... Dr. Mary K. GILLILAND
05 Interim VP Student Services .... Ms. Jennifer CARDENAS
107 Academic Dean .... Dr. Janice PRATT
49 Academic Dean .... Ms. Terri ACKLAND
10 Vice President Business Affairs .... Mr. Chris WODKA
15 Executive Director Human Resources .... Ms. Brandi CLARK
08 Director Library Services .... Ms. Adriana SAAVEDRA
37 Director of Financial Aid .... Ms. Elisa JUAREZ
41 Athletic Director .... Mr. Chuck SCHNOOR
39 Director of Residence Life .... Ms. Rosemary RAMIREZ
18 Exec Director of Facilities .... Mr. Ernesto VALENZUELA
96 Director of Purchasing .... Mr. Mark SALAZ
06 Registrar .... Ms. Veronica DURAN
07 Director of Admissions/Recruitment .... Mr. Luis SANCHEZ
21 Exec Dir Accounting Svc/Comptroller .... Ms. Luisa OTT
30 Chief Development/Advancement .... Ms. Margaret DOOLEY
35 Asst Dean Student Life .... Mr. Tramaine RAUSAW
04 Exec Asst to President & Gov Board . Ms. Mary Lou HERNANDEZ
13 Chief Info Technology Officer (CIO) .... Ms. Candice ROSS
19 Chief of Police .... Mr. James MATHENEY
26 Exec Dir PR & Marketing .... Ms. Angela ASKEY

Chamberlain College of Nursing-Phoenix Campus (K)
2149 West Dunlap Avenue, Phoenix AZ 85021
Telephone: (602) 331-2720 Identification: 770502
Accreditation: &NH, NURSE

† Regional accreditation is carried under the parent institution in Addison, IL

Cochise College (L)
4190 West Highway 80, Douglas AZ 85607-6190
County: Cochise FICE Identification: 001072
Unit ID: 104425
Telephone: (800) 966-7943 Carnegie Class: Assoc/HVT-High Non
FAX Number: (520) 417-4006 Calendar System: Semester
URL: www.cochise.edu
Established: 1964 Annual Undergrad Tuition & Fees (In-District): $1,848
Enrollment: N/A Coed
Affiliation or Control: State/Local IRS Status: 170(c)1
Highest Offering: Associate Degree
Accreditation: NH, #COARC

01 Chief Executive Officer (President) .... Dr. James D. ROTTWEILER
04 Administrative Asst to President .... Ms. Loretta MOUNTJOY
05 VP for Instruction/Provost .... Dr. Verlyn FICK
10 VP Administration .... Mr. LaMont SCHIERS
15 VP Human Resources .... Dr. Wendy DAVIS
13 VP Information Technology .... Mr. Carlos CARTAGENA
102 Exec Dir Foundation & Ext Affairs .... Ms. Denise HOYOS
18 Exec Dir Fac Mgt Planning .... Mr. Frank DYKSTRA
07 Registrar/Director of Admissions .... Ms. Debra QUICK
06 Assistant Registrar .... Ms. Heather AUGENSTEIN
49 Dean Liberal Arts .... Mr. Chuck HOYACK
81 Dean Math and Science .... Dr. Beth KRUEGER
76 Dean Nursing/Allied Health .... Ms. Jennifer LAKOSIL
50 Dean Business and Technology .... Dr. Clyne NAMUO
56 Dean Extended Learning .... Mr. George SELF
32 Dean Student Services/Athl Director .... Dr. James HALL
09 Dean Institutional Effectiveness .... Ms. Sandy BRYAN
35 Asst Dean Student Services .... Mr. Mark BOGGIE
08 Director Library Services .... Dr. John WALSH
96 Procurement Services Manager .... Ms. Lupita MORALES
39 Director Student Housing .... Ms. Marisol ARENIVAS
88 Director Occ Health Safety .... Mr. Randy DENNEY
37 Director Student Financial Aid .... Ms. Karen EMMER
38 Director Counseling and Advising .... Ms. Nanette ROMO
88 Dir TRIO Student Support Services .... Ms. Gabriela AMAVIZCA
22 Director Disability Support Service .... Ms. Carla BOYD
26 Director Marketing & Communication .... Ms. Robyn MARTIN
88 Director Continuous Improvement .... Ms. Karen DALE
66 Director Nursing .... Ms. Polly GOSA
88 Acting Director Aviation Programs .... Mr. Kevin AUSTIN
88 Director Adult Education .... Ms. Susan MORSS
88 Director Small Business Dev Center .... Mr. Mark SCHMITT
51 Director Ctr for Lifelong Learning .... Ms. Sharon GILMAN
12 Director Fort Huachuca .... Mr. John SOMERS
12 Director Willcox Center .... Ms. Barbara RICHARDSON
12 Director Santa Cruz Center .... Mr. Gabriel GALINDO
12 Director Benson Center .... Ms. Barbara RICHARDSON
106 Director Virtual Campus .... Ms. Tasneem ASHRAF
88 Assistant Director Virtual Campus .... Mr. Adam WOODROW

Cochise College (M)
901 N. Colombo Ave., Sierra Vista AZ 85635-2317
Telephone: (800) 966-7943 Identification: 770004
Accreditation: &NH, ADNUR, EMT

† Regional accreditation is carried under the parent institution in Douglas, AZ

Coconino Community College (N)
2800 S Lone Tree Road, Flagstaff AZ 86005
County: Coconino FICE Identification: 031004
Unit ID: 404426
Telephone: (928) 527-1222 Carnegie Class: Assoc/HT-High Non
FAX Number: (928) 226-4105 Calendar System: Semester
URL: www.coconino.edu
Established: 1991 Annual Undergrad Tuition & Fees (In-State): $2,970
Enrollment: 3,607 Coed
Affiliation or Control: State IRS Status: 501(c)3
Highest Offering: Associate Degree
Accreditation: NH

01 President .... Dr. Colleen A. SMITH
05 Interim VP for Academic Affairs .... Dr. Dudley GARDNER
10 VP for Business & Administration .... Ms. Jami VAN ESS
32 Dean of Student Services .... Ms. Veronica HIPOLITO
12 Page Campus Director .... Mr. Jim HUNTER
49 Interim Dean of Art and Sciences .... Mr. Jeff JONES
49 Interim Dean of Arts and Sciences .... Ms. Colleen CARSCALLEN
15 Int Director for Human Resources .... Ms. Allison ECKERT
09 Dir Institutional Research/Assess .... Mr. Michael MERICA
37 Director for Financial Aid .... Mr. Robert VOYTEK
06 Registrar/Dir Enrollment Services .... Ms. Kimmi GRULKE
75 Dean of Career & Tech Education .... Dr. Monica BAKER
18 Director Facilities .... Mr. Mark EASTON
13 Chief Technical Officer .... Mr. Andrew LAWLOR
96 Director Purchasing/Auxiliary Svcs .... Ms. Mary TALENTINO
21 Dean of Finance .... Ms. Siri MULLANEY
30 Exec Dir Institutional Advancement .... Mr. Scott TALBOOM
04 Exec Assistant to the President .... Ms. April SANDOVAL

Coconino County Community College Flagstaff Fourth Street Campus (O)
3000 N Fourth Street, Flagstaff AZ 86004
Telephone: (928) 526-7600 Identification: 770005
Accreditation: &NH

† Regional accreditation is carried under the parent institution in Flagstaff, AZ

Coconino County Community College Page/ Lake Powell Campus (P)
475 S Lake Powell Blvd., PO Box 728,
Page AZ 86040-0728
Telephone: (928) 645-3987 Identification: 770006
Accreditation: &NH

† Regional accreditation is carried under the parent institution in Flagstaff, AZ

CollegeAmerica-Flagstaff (Q)
399 S. Malpais, 2nd Floor, Flagstaff AZ 86001
County: Coconino FICE Identification: 031203
Unit ID: 103945
Telephone: (928) 213-6060 Carnegie Class: Spec-4-yr-Other Health
FAX Number: (928) 526-3468 Calendar System: Other
URL: www.collegeamerica.edu
Established: 2001 Annual Undergrad Tuition & Fees: $16,968
Enrollment: 176 Coed
Affiliation or Control: Independent Non-Profit IRS Status: 501(c)3
Highest Offering: Baccalaureate
Accreditation: ACCSC

01 Executive Director .... Dr. Kathy A. TURNER
07 Director of Admissions .... Doreen EVANS

CollegeAmerica-Phoenix (R)
9801 N. Metro Parkway East, Phoenix AZ 85051
Telephone: (602) 589-9860 Identification: 666017
Accreditation: ACCSC

† Branch campus of CollegeAmerica-Flagstaff, Flagstaff, AZ

DeVry University - Phoenix Campus (S)
2149 W Dunlap Avenue, Phoenix AZ 85021-2995
Telephone: (602) 749-7301 FICE Identification: 008322
Accreditation: &NH, ENGT, MT

† Regional accreditation is carried under the parent institution in Downers Grove, IL.

Diné College (T)
One Circle Drive, Tsaile AZ 86556-9998
County: Apache FICE Identification: 008246
Unit ID: 105297
Telephone: (928) 724-6671 Carnegie Class: Tribal
FAX Number: (928) 724-3327 Calendar System: Semester
URL: www.dinecollege.edu
Established: 1968 Annual Undergrad Tuition & Fees (In-District): $725
Enrollment: 1,488 Coed
Affiliation or Control: Local IRS Status: 501(c)3
Highest Offering: Baccalaureate
Accreditation: NH

01 Interim President .... Dr. Martin AHUMADA
10 Vice President for Finance .... Ms. Cheryl THOMPSON
32 Int Vice Pres of Student Success .... Mr. Abe BITOK
05 Vice President of Academics .... Mr. Martin AHUMADA
30 Director of Development .... Mr. Cameron DAINES
06 Registrar .... Ms. Louise LITZIN
20 Dean .... Vacant
37 Director Student Financial Aid .... Mr. Formon THOMPSON
15 Dir Department of Human Resources .... Mrs. Perphelia FOWLER
18 Supt Maintenance Operations .... Mr. Delbert PAQUIN
21 Controller .... Vacant
26 Public Relations Director .... Mr. Ed MCCOMBS
46 Dir Inst Grants/Sponsored Projects .... Ms. Amanda MCNEIL

Dunlap-Stone University (A)

19820 North 7th Street, Suite 100, Phoenix AZ 85024

County: Maricopa — Identification: 666315
Telephone: (602) 648-5750 — Carnegie Class: Not Classified
FAX Number: (602) 648-5755 — Calendar System: Other
URL: www.dunlap-stone.edu
Established: 1995 — Annual Undergrad Tuition & Fees: N/A
Enrollment: N/A — Coed
Affiliation or Control: Proprietary — IRS Status: Proprietary
Highest Offering: Master's
Accreditation: DEAC

01 President .... Dr. Donald N. BURTON
05 Chief Academic Officer .... Mrs. Caulyne BARRON

Eastern Arizona College (B)

615 N Stadium Avenue, Thatcher AZ 85552-0769

County: Graham — FICE Identification: 001073
Unit ID: 104577
Telephone: (928) 428-8233 — Carnegie Class: Assoc/HVT-Mix Trad/Non
FAX Number: (928) 428-2578 — Calendar System: Semester
URL: www.eac.edu
Established: 1888 — Annual Undergrad Tuition & Fees (In-District): $2,080
Enrollment: 6,379 — Coed
Affiliation or Control: State/Local — IRS Status: 501(c)3
Highest Offering: Associate Degree
Accreditation: NH, ADNUR

01 President .... Mr. Mark BRYCE
03 Executive Vice President .... Mr. Brent MCEUEN
10 Chief Business Officer .... Mr. Timothy CURTIS
05 Provost .... Mrs. Jeanne BRYCE
20 Dean of Instruction .... Mr. Michael CROCKETT
20 Dean of Instruction .... Dr. Phil MCBRIDE
20 Dean of Curriculum and Instruction .... Dr. Janice LAWHORN
32 Dean of Students .... Dr. Gary SORENSEN
06 Associate Dean/Registrar .... Dr. Randall SKINNER
38 Assistant Dean of Counseling .... Ms. Sharon ALLEN
12 Director of Discovery Park Campus .... Mr. Paul ANGER
21 Director Fiscal Control/Controller .... Mr. Heston WELKER
37 Director of Financial Aid .... Mr. William OSBORN
13 Director of Information Resources .... Mr. Thomas THOMPSON
09 Director of Institutional Research .... Mr. Glen SNIDER
08 Director of Library Services .... Mrs. Karen JAGGERS
26 Dir of Marketing & Public Relations .... Mr. Todd HAYNIE
18 Director of Physical Resources .... Mr. Dan WELKER
102 Executive Director EAC Foundation .... Mr. David UDALL
35 Director of Student Life .... Mr. Danny BATTRAW
41 Athletic Director .... Mr. James BAGNALL
15 Assoc Director Admin Support EEO Co .... Ms. Lauri AVILA
04 Exec Asst to the President and DGB .... Mrs. Laurie PENNINGTON

Eastern Arizona College Gila Pueblo Campus (C)

8274 Six Shooter Canyon PO Box 2656, Globe AZ 85502

Telephone: (928) 425-8481 — Identification: 770008
Accreditation: &NH

† Regional accreditation is carried under the parent institution in Thatcher, AZ

Eastern Arizona College Payson Campus (D)

201 N Mud Springs Rd., PO Box 359, Payson AZ 85547

Telephone: (928) 468-8039 — Identification: 770009
Accreditation: &NH

† Regional accreditation is carried under the parent institution in Thatcher, AZ

Embry-Riddle Aeronautical University-Prescott (E)

3700 Willow Creek Road, Prescott AZ 86301-3270

Telephone: (800) 888-3728 — FICE Identification: 021047
Accreditation: &SC, AAB, ENG

† Regional accreditation is carried under the parent institution in Daytona Beach, FL.

Fortis College, Phoenix (F)

555 N 18th Street, Suite 110, Phoenix AZ 85006

Telephone: (602) 254-3099 — Identification: 666761
Accreditation: ACCSC, DH

† Branch campus of Fortis College, Centerville, OH. Tuition varies by degree program.

Frank Lloyd Wright School of Architecture (G)

PO Box 4430, Scottsdale AZ 85261-4430

County: Maricopa — FICE Identification: 025332
Unit ID: 104665
Telephone: (480) 860-2700 — Carnegie Class: Spec-4-yr-Arts
FAX Number: N/A — Calendar System: Other
URL: www.taliesin.edu
Established: 1932 — Annual Undergrad Tuition & Fees: N/A
Enrollment: 8 — Coed
Affiliation or Control: Independent Non-Profit — IRS Status: 501(c)3
Highest Offering: Master's
Accreditation: NH

01 Head of School and Dean .... Mr. Aaron BETSKEY
05 Director of Academic Affairs .... Dr. Chris LASCH
08 Director of Libraries .... Ms. Elizabeth AL-HAZZAM DAWASARI
07 Dir Admissions/Student Services .... Mr. Gerasimos (Jerry) KAVALIERATOS
10 COO and Vice President Finance .... Ms. Lisa MURPHY
30 Director of Development .... Mr. Jason DONOFRIO

Golf Academy of America (H)

2031 N. Arizona Ave Suite 2, Chandler AZ 85225

Telephone: (800) 342-7342 — Identification: 666023
Accreditation: ACICS

† Branch campus of Virginia College, Birmingham, AL.

Grand Canyon University (I)

3300 W Camelback Road, Phoenix AZ 85017-3030

County: Maricopa — FICE Identification: 001074
Unit ID: 104717
Telephone: (602) 639-7500 — Carnegie Class: DU-Mod
FAX Number: N/A — Calendar System: Semester
URL: www.gcu.edu
Established: 1949 — Annual Undergrad Tuition & Fees: $17,050
Enrollment: 62,304 — Coed
Affiliation or Control: Proprietary — IRS Status: Proprietary
Highest Offering: Doctorate
Accreditation: NH, ACBSP, CAATE, NURSE

01 President/Chief Executive Officer .... Mr. Brian MUELLER
10 Chief Financial Officer .... Mr. Dan BACHUS
11 Chief Operations Officer .... Mr. Stan MEYER
05 Provost .... Dr. Hank RADDA
20 Sr VP Academic Affs/Univ Registrar .... Dr. Jennifer LECH
108 Vice Pres Inst Effectiveness .... Dr. Antoinette FARMER
41 Vice President of Athletics .... Mr. Mike VAUGHT
32 VP Student Svcs/Dean of Students .... Pastor Tim GRIFFIN
50 Dean Ken Blanchard Col Business .... Dr. Randy GIBB
53 Dean College of Education .... Dr. Kimberly LAPRADE
66 Dean College Nursing/Hlth Care Prof .... Dr. Melanie LOGUE
49 Dean College Sci/Engineering/Tech .... Dr. K. Mark WOODEN
58 Dean College Doctoral Studies .... Dr. Michael BERGER
57 Dean of Fine Arts and Production .... Mr. Claude PENSIS
73 Dean College of Theology .... Dr. Jason HILES
79 Dean College Human/Social Science .... Dr. Sherman ELLIOTT

Han University of Traditional Medicine (J)

2856 E. Fort Lowell Road, Tucson AZ 85716

County: Pima — FICE Identification: 041193
Telephone: (520) 322-6330 — Carnegie Class: Not Classified
FAX Number: (520) 322-5661 — Calendar System: Quarter
URL: www.hanuniversity.edu
Established: 2000 — Annual Undergrad Tuition & Fees: N/A
Enrollment: N/A — Coed
Affiliation or Control: Proprietary — IRS Status: Proprietary
Highest Offering: Master's
Accreditation: ACUP

01 President .... Mr. Alex HOLLAND
05 Academic Dean .... Ms. Rebecca SOBIN
07 Admissions Director .... Mrs. Jamie SZYBALA
06 Registrar .... Mr. Alex HOLLAND

Harrison Middleton University (K)

1105 East Broadway Road, Tempe AZ 85282-1505

County: Maricopa — Identification: 666169
Telephone: (877) 248-6724 — Carnegie Class: Not Classified
FAX Number: (800) 762-1622 — Calendar System: Other
URL: www.hmu.edu
Established: 1998 — Annual Undergrad Tuition & Fees: N/A
Enrollment: N/A — Coed
Affiliation or Control: Proprietary — IRS Status: Proprietary
Highest Offering: Doctorate
Accreditation: DEAC

01 President .... Mr. David CURD
05 Vice Pres/Director of Education .... Mr. Michael CURD
51 VP/Dir of Continuing Education .... Ms. Rebecca FISHER
06 Registrar/Director of Accreditation .... Ms. Lauren GUTHRIE

International Baptist College and Seminary (L)

2211 W Germann Road, Chandler AZ 85286

County: Maricopa — FICE Identification: 033473
Unit ID: 436614
Telephone: (480) 245-7903 — Carnegie Class: Spec-4-yr-Faith
FAX Number: (480) 245-7909 — Calendar System: 4/1/4
URL: www.ibcs.edu
Established: 1980 — Annual Undergrad Tuition & Fees: $10,500
Enrollment: 69 — Coed
Affiliation or Control: Baptist — IRS Status: 501(c)3
Highest Offering: Doctorate
Accreditation: TRACS

00 Chancellor .... Dr. Jerry C. TETREAU
01 President .... Rev. Kenneth M. ENDEAN
32 Dean of Students .... Mr. Jeffrey G. CAUPP
05 Chief Academic Officer .... Dr. Wayne A. BLEY
10 Chief Financial Officer .... Mr. Matt EBERLE
84 Director of Enrollment .... Mrs. Lauren BRADY
09 Director of Inst Effectiveness .... Mrs. Lauren BRADY
20 Graduate Academic Officer .... Dr. David SHUMATE
88 Teaching Site Liaison .... Dr. Keith HUHTA
08 Media Center Director .... Mr. Lee WILL
34 Dean of Women .... Mrs. Marcia L. GAMMON
06 Registrar .... Mrs. Rebecca M. STERTZBACH
37 Financial Aid Administrator .... Mrs. Jane L. BUSHEY
04 Administrative Asst to President .... Mrs. Rebecca M. STERTZBACH
30 Chief Development/Advancement .... Dr. Jerry C. TETREAU

Le Cordon Bleu College of Culinary Arts in Scottsdale (M)

8100 E Camelback Road, Ste 1001, Scottsdale AZ 85251-3940

County: Maricopa — FICE Identification: 026167
Unit ID: 262332
Telephone: (480) 990-3773 — Carnegie Class: Spec-4-yr-Other
FAX Number: (480) 990-0351 — Calendar System: Other
URL: www.chefs.edu/scottsdale
Established: 1986 — Annual Undergrad Tuition & Fees: $11,377
Enrollment: 1,567 — Coed
Affiliation or Control: Proprietary — IRS Status: Proprietary
Highest Offering: Baccalaureate
Accreditation: ACCSC, ACFEI, ACICS

01 President .... Mr. Craig BARTHOLOMEW
37 Vice Pres/Director of Financial Aid .... Ms. Saundra ASCHENDRENER
11 Director Administration .... Mr. Jason KIMMELL
36 Director Career Services .... Ms. Kathleen DOELLER
06 Registrar .... Ms. Polly GIBSON

† In teach-out mode through September 2017.

*Maricopa County Community College District Office (N)

2411 W 14th Street, Tempe AZ 85281-6941

County: Maricopa — FICE Identification: 001075
Unit ID: 105136
Telephone: (480) 731-8000 — Carnegie Class: N/A
FAX Number: (480) 731-8850
URL: www.maricopa.edu

01 Chancellor .... Dr. Maria HARPER-MARINICK
05 Int Exec Vice Chancellor/Provost .... Dr. Paul DALE
102 President/CEO Foundation .... Ms. Christina SCHULTZ
10 Vice Chanc Business Services .... Ms. Debra THOMPSON
15 Vice Chancellor Human Resources .... Ms. LaCoya SHELTON-JOHNSON
13 Chief Information Officer .... Mr. Ed KELTY
21 Assoc Vice Chanc Business Services .... Ms. Gaye MURPHY
103 Dir Center Workforce Development .... Dr. Randy KIMMENS
30 Exec Director Resource Development .... Ms. Mary O'CONNOR
09 Assoc VC Inst Strategy/Rsrch/Effect .... Vacant
18 Assoc Vice Chanc Cap Plng/Spec Proj .... Mr. Arlen SOLOCHEK

*Chandler-Gilbert Community College (O)

2626 E Pecos Road, Chandler AZ 85225-2499

County: Maricopa — FICE Identification: 030722
Unit ID: 364025
Telephone: (480) 732-7000 — Carnegie Class: Assoc/HT-Mix Trad/Non
FAX Number: (480) 732-7090 — Calendar System: Semester
URL: www.cgc.maricopa.edu
Established: 1992 — Annual Undergrad Tuition & Fees (In-District): $2,046
Enrollment: 14,500 — Coed
Affiliation or Control: State/Local — IRS Status: 501(c)3
Highest Offering: Associate Degree
Accreditation: NH, ADNUR, DIETT

02 President .... Dr. William GUERRIERO
04 Administrative Asst to President .... Ms. Susan D. AROZ
05 Vice President Academic Affairs .... Dr. Sylvia ORR
32 Vice President Student Affairs .... Dr. William H. CRAWFORD, III
11 Vice Pres Administrative Services .... Mr. Bradley S. KENDREX
49 Dean of Arts and Sciences .... Mr. Chris SCHNICK
31 Dean of Community Affairs .... Dr. Cindy BARNES
75 Dean of Career & Technical Educ .... Ms. Maria A. REYES
32 Dean of Student Affairs .... Mr. Daniel HERBST
10 Assoc Dean for Business Operations .... Ms. Bernadette LA MAZZA
07 Dir Admissions/Registr & Records .... Ms. Linda SHAW
13 Vice President of IT & Media Svcs .... Dr. Charles NWANKWO
09 Dir Research/Planning/Development .... Ms. Theresa WONG
36 Dir Career/Education Planning Svcs .... Vacant
85 Director International Educ Program .... Ms. Anna A. JIMENEZ
32 Director College Student Services .... Ms. Dawn GRUICHICH
18 Director Col Facilities Plng & Dev .... Mr. Charles POURE
35 Director Student Life & Leadership .... Mr. Mike GREENE
41 Director Athletics .... Mr. Ed YEAGER
19 Public Safety Commander .... Mr. Robert EVERETT

37 Director Financial Aid .... Mr. Timothy WOLSEY
26 Director Marketing/Public Relations .... Vacant
88 Director Learning Center .... Ms. Eva R. FALLETTA
88 Director Early Outreach Programs .... Ms. Laura MATYAS
88 Director Instr Tech & Course Prod .... Ms. Juliane M. ROYBAL
66 Director Nursing & Health Sciences .... Mr. Gregory TRONE
14 Director Computer Labs/Instr Svcs .... Ms. Joni M. BRUMMER
21 Manager College Cashier Services .... Ms. Julie WRIGHT
15 Senior Manager Human Resources .... Ms. Bernadette LA MAZZA

*Estrella Mountain Community College (A)

3000 N Dysart Road, Avondale AZ 85392
County: Maricopa FICE Identification: 031563
Unit ID: 384333
Telephone: (623) 935-8000 Carnegie Class: Assoc/HT-Mix Trad/Non
FAX Number: (623) 935-8008 Calendar System: Semester
URL: www.estrellamountain.edu
Established: 1990 Annual Undergrad Tuition & Fees (In-District): $2,046
Enrollment: 9,164 Coed
Affiliation or Control: State/Local IRS Status: 501(c)3
Highest Offering: Associate Degree
Accreditation: NH, ADNUR

02 President .... Dr. Ernest LARA
11 Vice President Admin Services .... Ms. Sue TAVAKOLI
32 Vice President Student Affairs .... Dr. Patricia CARDENAS-ADAME
05 Vice President of Learning .... Dr. Clay GOODMAN
20 Dean of Academic Affairs .... Dr. Kathleen IUDICELLO
20 Dean of Academic Affairs .... Dr. Sylvia ORR
35 Dean of Student Services .... Ms. Laura DULGAR
09 Dean Planning/Rsrch/Effectiveness .... Dr. Rene G. WILLEKENS
08 Division Chair Information Resource .... Ms. Nikol PRICE
18 Director Facilities Planning/Devel .... Mr. Randy L. NAUGHTON
13 Director Information Technology .... Mr. Chad GALLIGAN
07 Director of Enrollment Services .... Mr. Frank AMPARO
10 Mgr College Fiscal/Budget Services .... Ms. Leda JOHNSON
102 Dir Corp Foundation Rels/Dev Ops .... Mr. Jonathan ROBLES
37 Director Student Financial Aid .... Ms. Rosanna SHORT
21 Manager College Budget .... Ms. Maggie CASTILLO

*Gateway Community College (B)

108 N 40th Street, Phoenix AZ 85034-1795
County: Maricopa FICE Identification: 008303
Unit ID: 105145
Telephone: (602) 286-8000 Carnegie Class: Assoc/HVT-High Non
FAX Number: (602) 286-8072 Calendar System: Semester
URL: www.gatewaycc.edu/
Established: 1968 Annual Undergrad Tuition & Fees (In-District): $2,046
Enrollment: 5,950 Coed
Affiliation or Control: State/Local IRS Status: 501(c)3
Highest Offering: Associate Degree
Accreditation: NH, ADNUR, COARC, DMS, NDT, NMT, POLYT, PTAA, RAD, RTT, SURGT

02 President .... Dr. Steven GONZALEZ
05 Vice President Academic Affairs .... Dr. Maria WISE
32 Vice President Student Affairs .... Dr. Maria WISE
11 Vice President Administrative Svcs .... Mr. Tony ASTI
07 Director Enrollment Services .... Ms. Kristie FOK
09 Dir Research Planning & Development .... Ms. Cathy HERNANDEZ
88 College Budget Analyst .... Ms. Janet BOSE
10 Manager College Fiscal Services .... Ms. Cecilia SOTO
18 Chief Facilities/Physical Plant .... Vacant
26 Director Marketing/Public Relations .... Ms. Christine LAMBRAKIS
30 Director Inst Advance & Entrep Pgm .... Vacant
37 Director Student Financial Aid .... Ms. Suzanne RINGLE
84 Coordinator Enrollment Services .... Ms. Kelly MCPHEE
15 Manager College Employee Services .... Ms. Chantal LUGO
06 Registrar .... Ms. Kristie FOK

*Glendale Community College (C)

6000 W Olive Avenue, Glendale AZ 85302-3006
County: Maricopa FICE Identification: 001076
Unit ID: 104708
Telephone: (623) 845-3000 Carnegie Class: Assoc/HT-Mix Trad/Non
FAX Number: (623) 845-3329 Calendar System: Semester
URL: www.gccaz.edu
Established: 1965 Annual Undergrad Tuition & Fees (In-District): $2,046
Enrollment: 20,506 Coed
Affiliation or Control: State/Local IRS Status: 170(c)1
Highest Offering: Associate Degree
Accreditation: NH, ADNUR, EMT

02 Interim President .... Dr. Teresa LEYBA RUIZ
05 Acting VP Academic Affairs .... Mr. Eric LESHINSKIE
11 Int VP Admin Services & CIO .... Ms. Augustine ERPELDING
20 Dean of Academic Affairs .... Dr. Fernando CAMOU
20 Dean of Academic Affairs .... Mr. Scott SCHULZ
20 Dean of Academic Affairs .... Mr. Charles JEFFERY
84 Dean Enrollment Services .... Ms. Mary D. BLACKWELL
32 Interim Dean Student Life .... Ms. Laura DODRILL
12 Dean GCC North .... Vacant
37 Director Financial Aid .... Ms. Jennifer KESTER
18 Director Facilities .... Mr. Al GONZALES
10 Director College Business Services .... Ms. Kim GOLIS
26 Dir Sales Mktg & Public Rels .... Ms. Tressa JUMPS
45 Dean of Strat/Plng & Accountability .... Dr. Alka ARORA SINGH
15 Manager College Employee Svcs .... Ms. June S. FESSENDEN
30 Director of Development .... Ms. Frances MATEO
38 Dept Chair Counseling .... Ms. Marjane MATON
08 Dept Chair Librarian .... Mr. Frank TORRES
19 Director College Safety .... Ms. Debra PALOK
04 Admin Assistant I to College Pres .... Ms. Esmeralda M. ACOSTA

*Mesa Community College (D)

1833 W Southern Avenue, Mesa AZ 85202-4866
County: Maricopa FICE Identification: 001077
Unit ID: 105154
Telephone: (480) 461-7000 Carnegie Class: Assoc/HT-Mix Trad/Non
FAX Number: (480) 461-7805 Calendar System: Semester
URL: www.mesacc.edu/
Established: 1965 Annual Undergrad Tuition & Fees (In-District): $2,046
Enrollment: 22,711 Coed
Affiliation or Control: State/Local IRS Status: 501(c)3
Highest Offering: Associate Degree
Accreditation: NH, ADNUR, DH, FUSER

02 Interim President .... Mr. Sasan POUREETEZADI
05 Interim Vice Pres Academic Affairs .... Dr. Rodney HOLMES
32 Vice Pres Student Affairs .... Dr. Sonya PEARSON
10 Vice Pres Admin Services .... Mr. Jeff DARBUT
13 Interim VP Information Technology .... Mr. Andrew GIDDINGS
09 Dean of Inst Planning & Analysis .... Mr. Matthew ASHCRAFT
35 Interim Dean of Student Affairs .... Ms. Vivian MIRANDA
20 Dean Instruction .... Dr. Jeffrey ANDELORA
20 Dean Instruction .... Ms. Carol ACHS
12 Vice Provost MCC Red Mountain .... Dr. Nora REYES
06 Registrar .... Dr. Carmen NEWLAND
26 Director of Institutional Advance .... Ms. Sonia FILAN
30 Director of Development .... Mr. Jared LANGKILDE
37 Dir Fin Aid/Scholarships .... Ms. Patricia PEPPIN
38 Dept Chair Counseling .... Dr. Karen HARDIN
19 Director Security/Safety .... Mr. Steve LIEBER
25 Chief Contracts/Grants Admin .... Mr. Kenichi MARUYAMA
29 Director Alumni Relations .... Ms. Marcy SNITZER
41 Athletic Director .... Mr. John MULHERN
18 Interim Director Facilities .... Mr. Steve AZEVEDO
04 Administrative Asst to President .... Ms. Kacie TAKATA

*Paradise Valley Community College (E)

18401 N 32nd Street, Phoenix AZ 85032-1210
County: Maricopa FICE Identification: 026236
Unit ID: 364016
Telephone: (602) 787-6500 Carnegie Class: Assoc/HT-High Non
FAX Number: (602) 787-6625 Calendar System: Semester
URL: www.paradisevalley.edu
Established: 1985 Annual Undergrad Tuition & Fees (In-District): $2,046
Enrollment: 8,909 Coed
Affiliation or Control: State/Local IRS Status: 501(c)3
Highest Offering: Associate Degree
Accreditation: NH, ADNUR, DIETT, EMT

02 President .... Dr. Paul DALE
05 Vice President of Academic Affairs .... Dr. Mary Lou MOSLEY
11 VP Administrative Services .... Mr. Herman GONZALEZ
32 Vice President of Student Affairs .... Ms. Veronica GARCIA
20 Dean of Academic Affairs .... Dr. Denise DIGIANFILIPPO
35 Dean of Students .... Dr. Shirley GREEN
13 Dean of Information Technology .... Vacant
84 Dean Admin Affs/Enrollment Services .... Ms. Sandy MCDILL
15 Director Personnel Services .... Ms. Lori LINDSETH
18 Chief Facilities/Physical Plant .... Mr. Robert METEVIER
37 Director Student Financial Aid .... Ms. Katharine JOHNSON
38 Director Student Counseling .... Dr. James RUBIN
06 Registrar .... Ms. Angela ACUNA
36 Director Student Placement .... Ms. Norma CHANDLER
26 Dir of Marketing/Public Relations .... Ms. Candace OEHLER
09 Dir Institutional Research/Effect .... Mr. John SNELLING
19 Director Security/Safety .... Mr. Scott MEEK
41 Athletic Director .... Ms. Christina HUNDLEY
30 Dir Development/Community Relations .... Vacant

*Phoenix College (F)

1202 W Thomas Road, Phoenix AZ 85013-4234
County: Maricopa FICE Identification: 001078
Unit ID: 105428
Telephone: (602) 285-7800 Carnegie Class: Assoc/HT-Mix Trad/Non
FAX Number: (602) 285-7700 Calendar System: Semester
URL: www.pc.maricopa.edu
Established: 1920 Annual Undergrad Tuition & Fees (In-District): $2,046
Enrollment: 12,107 Coed
Affiliation or Control: State/Local IRS Status: 501(c)3
Highest Offering: Associate Degree
Accreditation: NH, ADNUR, CAHIIM, DA, DH, EMT, HT, MLTAD

02 Interim President .... Ms. Christina HAINES
05 VP of Academic Affairs .... Dr. Casandra KAKAR
11 VP Administrative Services .... Mr. Paul DEROSE
32 Vice Pres of Student Affairs .... Dr. Meredith WARNER
35 Dean of Student Affairs .... Dr. Heather KRUSE
20 Dean of Academic Affairs .... Mr. Wilbert NELSON
88 Dean of Industry & Public Service .... Dr. Sharon HALFORD
13 Dean of Technology .... Dr. Mark KOAN
08 Department Chair Library .... Ms. Linda SOLAND
38 Department Chair Counseling .... Ms. Nancy NAVARRETE
06 Dir Admissions/Registration/Records .... Ms. Brenda STARCK
07 Director of Enrollment Services .... Vacant
41 Athletic Director .... Ms. Samantha EZELL
37 Director Financial Aid .... Ms. Cynthia RAMOS
88 Int Director Student Leadership .... Ms. Diana MARTINEZ
84 Director Advisement Enrollment .... Ms. Felicia RAMIREZ-PEREZ
09 Dir Instl Plng/Rsrch/Effectiveness .... Ms. Jan BINDER
19 Director of College Safety .... Mr. Doug SPARKS
30 Director Institutional Advancement .... Ms. Michelle KLINGER
18 Director of Facilities .... Mr. Douglas MCCARTHY
10 Manager Business Services .... Ms. Angela GENNA
15 Supv College Employee Services .... Ms. Martha ANDERSON
29 Coord Alumni/Community Relations .... Ms. Deborah SPOTTS
04 Assistant to the President .... Ms. Renee HOLGUIN

*Rio Salado College (G)

2323 W 14th Street, Tempe AZ 85281-6950
County: Maricopa FICE Identification: 021775
Unit ID: 105668
Telephone: (480) 517-8000 Carnegie Class: Assoc/HVT-High Non
FAX Number: (480) 377-4719 Calendar System: Semester
URL: www.riosalado.edu
Established: 1978 Annual Undergrad Tuition & Fees (In-District): $2,046
Enrollment: 20,215 Coed
Affiliation or Control: State/Local IRS Status: 501(c)3
Highest Offering: Associate Degree
Accreditation: NH, DA, DH

02 President .... Dr. Chris BUSTAMANTE
05 Vice President Academic Affairs .... Ms. Kate SMITH
10 Vice Pres Business & Employee Svcs .... Mr. Todd SIMMONS
32 Vice President Student Affairs .... Dr. LeRodrick TERRY
13 Vice President Information Services .... Mr. David O'SHEA
20 Dean of Instruction .... Mr. Rick KEMP
20 Dean Instructional Tech & Support .... Ms. Dana REID
20 Dean of Instruction .... Dr. Shannon MCCARTY
20 Dean of Instruction .... Mr. Corey PRUITT
88 Assoc Dean Instruction and Support .... Ms. Earnestine HARRISON
86 Assoc Dean Institutional Integrity .... Ms. Janelle ELIAS
88 Assoc Dean Instruction & Community .... Ms. Barbara KHALSA
88 Assoc Dean Adult Basic Education .... Mr. Blair LIDDICOAT
88 Assoc Dean Community Development .... Mr. Greg PEREIRA
84 Dean of Enrollment Management .... Mr. Kevin BILDER
07 Dean of Enrollment Services .... Ms. Rachelle CLARKE
88 Assoc Dean Judicial Affairs .... Ms. Ruby MILLER
37 Associate Dean of Financial Aid .... Ms. Nanci REGEHR
09 Assoc Dean Institutional Research .... Mr. Dustin MARONEY
18 Director of Facilities .... Mr. Ernest ADKINS
19 Public Safety Lieutenant .... Mr. Juan FLOWERS
21 Interim Assoc Dean Business Service .... Mr. Anthony DISCALA
15 Dean Admin and Employee Services .... Dr. Sharon KOBERNA
16 Senior Manager Employee Services .... Ms. Anna FLORES
16 Senior Manager Employee Services .... Ms. Maria BELLINO
08 Library Faculty Chair .... Ms. Hazel DAVIS

*Scottsdale Community College (H)

9000 E Chaparral, Scottsdale AZ 85256-2626
County: Maricopa FICE Identification: 008304
Unit ID: 105747
Telephone: (480) 423-6000 Carnegie Class: Assoc/HT-High Non
FAX Number: (480) 423-6200 Calendar System: Semester
URL: www.scottsdalecc.edu
Established: 1970 Annual Undergrad Tuition & Fees (In-District): $2,046
Enrollment: 9,863 Coed
Affiliation or Control: State/Local IRS Status: 501(c)3
Highest Offering: Associate Degree
Accreditation: NH, ACFEI, ADNUR

02 President .... Dr. Jan L. GEHLER
32 Vice Pres Student Affairs .... Dr. Donna YOUNG
05 Vice Pres Academic Affairs .... Dr. Stephanie FUJII
11 Vice Pres Administrative Services .... Ms. Colleen O'NEILL
13 Dir ITS/College CTO .... Mr. Vargha MOHEBBI
20 Dean of Instruction .... Dr. Tom TROLLEN
32 Dean of Student Affairs .... Ms. Larissa TRAIN
84 Dean of Student Enrollment .... Ms. Gia TAYLOR
07 Director of Admissions .... Ms. Laura KRUEGER
09 Director of Institutional Research .... Dr. Laurie COHEN
30 Exec Dir Instl Advance/Cmty Eng .... Ms. Nancy NEFF
08 Director of Library Services .... Ms. Danielle CARLOCK
37 Director Financial Aid/Placement .... Ms. Stacie BECK
18 Director Buildings/Grounds .... Mr. Samuel J. VAN CLEAVE
19 Director of College Safety .... Mr. Les STRICKLAND
41 Athletic Director .... Mr. Michael MCNALLY
38 Director Student Advisement .... Mr. Michael CORNELIUS

*South Mountain Community College (I)

7050 S 24th Street, Phoenix AZ 85042-5806
County: Maricopa FICE Identification: 021466
Unit ID: 105792
Telephone: (602) 243-8000 Carnegie Class: Assoc/HT-Mix Trad/Non
FAX Number: (602) 243-8329 Calendar System: Semester
URL: www.southmountaincc.edu
Established: 1979 Annual Undergrad Tuition & Fees (In-District): $2,046
Enrollment: 4,287 Coed
Affiliation or Control: State/Local IRS Status: 501(c)3
Highest Offering: Associate Degree

Accreditation: NH, MACTE

02 President .... Dr. Shari L. OLSON
05 Vice Pres Academic Affairs .... Vacant
11 Vice Pres Administrative Svcs .... Dr. Janet ORTEGA
32 Vice Pres Student Affairs .... Dr. Osaro IGHODARO
09 Dean Research/Plng & Development .... Ms. Damita KALOOSTIAN
20 Dean Academic Affairs .... Ms Matilda CHAVEZ
84 Dean Enrollment Services .... Mr. Guy GOODMAN
37 Director Financial Aid .... Ms. Inez MORENO-WEINERT
07 Director of Admission & Records .... Ms. Jean WATERMOLEN
10 Director College Business Services .... Mr. John MOLL
18 Director of Facilities .... Mr. Robert HOLMES
26 Director Marketing/Public Relations .... Ms. Jennifer GRENTZ
21 Manager Fiscal Services .... Ms. Jeanette CERNETIC
15 Coordinator Human Resources .... Ms. Judy BELSHER
07 Coordinator Advisement/Recruitment .... Ms. Christine NEILL
36 Coordinator Job Placement .... Ms. Suzanne HIPPS

* Chandler-Gilbert Community College-Williams Campus (A)

7360 E Tahoe Avenue, Mesa AZ 85212-0908
Telephone: (480) 988-8000　Identification: 770178
Accreditation: &NH

† Regional accreditation is carried under the parent institution in Chandler, AZ

* Glendale Community College North (B)

5727 W Happy Valley Road, Phoenix AZ 85310
Telephone: (623) 845-4000　Identification: 770179
Accreditation: &NH

† Regional accreditation is carried under the parent institution in Glendale, AZ

* Mesa Community College at Red Mountain (C)

7110 East McKellips Road, Mesa AZ 85207
Telephone: (480) 654-7200　Identification: 770180
Accreditation: &NH

† Regional accreditation is carried under the parent institution in Mesa, AZ

Midwestern University (D)

19555 N 59th Avenue, Glendale AZ 85308
Telephone: (623) 572-3215　Identification: 666001
Accreditation: &NH, ANEST, ARCPA, CLPSY, DENT, OPT, CSTEO, OT, PERF, PHAR, POD, PTA, @SP, @VET

† Regional accreditation is carried under the parent institution in Downers Grove, IL.

Mohave Community College (E)

1971 E. Jagerson Avenue, Kingman AZ 86409-1238
County: Mohave　FICE Identification: 011864
Unit ID: 105206
Telephone: (928) 757-0879　Carnegie Class: Assoc/MT-VT-High Non
FAX Number: (928) 757-0836　Calendar System: Semester
URL: www.mohave.edu
Established: 1971　Annual Undergrad Tuition & Fees (In-District): $2,112
Enrollment: 4,744　Coed
Affiliation or Control: State/Local　IRS Status: 501(c)3
Highest Offering: Associate Degree
Accreditation: NH, ADNUR, DH, EMT, PTAA, RAD, SURGT

01 President .... Dr. Michael KEARNS
03 Executive Vice President .... Dr. Diana STITHEM
05 Dean of Instruction .... Dr. Paula NORBY
32 Dean of Student Services .... Ms. Ana MASTERSON
10 Dean of Business Services .... Ms. Sonni MARBURY
30 Assoc Dean College Advancement .... Mr. Dan LARA
13 Chief Information Officer .... Mr. Mark VANPELT
26 Chief Public Relations Officer .... Vacant
12 Campus Dean Bullhead City .... Mr. Shawn BRISTLE
12 Campus Dean Lake Havasu .... Ms. Jann WOODS
12 Campus Dean Neal Kingman .... Dr. Fred GILBERT
12 Campus Dean North Mohave .... Ms. Carolyn HAMBLIN
21 Bursar .... Vacant
37 Financial Aid Director .... Ms. Shannon SHEAFF
09 Dir of Institutional Research .... Mr. Bob FAUBERT
15 Director Personnel Services .... Ms. Jenny DIXON
84 Enrollment Services Manager .... Ms. Sharon HANKS
06 Registrar .... Mr. Brian ZOLL

National Paralegal College (F)

717 East Maryland Avenue, Phoenix AZ 85014-1561
County: Maricopa　FICE Identification: 041574
Unit ID: 461023
Telephone: (800) 371-6105　Carnegie Class: Spec-4-yr-Other
FAX Number: (866) 347-2744　Calendar System: Other
URL: nationalparalegal.edu
Established: 2003　Annual Undergrad Tuition & Fees: $7,395
Enrollment: 1,116　Coed
Affiliation or Control: Proprietary　IRS Status: Proprietary
Highest Offering: Master's
Accreditation: DEAC

01 President .... Avi KATZ
05 Dean/Director .... Stephen HAAS
88 Technical Director .... David COHEN
07 Director of Admissions .... Danielle ECKMAN
37 Director Student Financial Aid .... Lisa PIMBER

Northcentral University (G)

10000 E University Drive, Prescott Valley AZ 86314-2336
County: Yavapai　FICE Identification: 038133
Unit ID: 444130
Telephone: (928) 541-7777　Carnegie Class: DU-Mod
FAX Number: (928) 541-7817　Calendar System: Other
URL: www.ncu.edu
Established: 1996　Annual Undergrad Tuition & Fees: N/A
Enrollment: 11,160　Coed
Affiliation or Control: Proprietary　IRS Status: Proprietary
Highest Offering: Doctorate
Accreditation: NH, ACBSP, MFCD, TEAC

01 President .... Dr. George A. BURNETT
05 Provost/Chief Academic Officer .... Dr. David HARPOOL
20 Sr Vice Pres Academic Affairs .... Dr. John LA NEAR
10 Chief Financial Officer .... Ms. Karen WHITNEY
13 Chief Information Officer .... Mr. Patrick PENDLETON
26 Chief Marketing Officer .... Mr. Russel NATOCE
100 Chief of Staff .... Mr. Eric STODDARD
43 General Counsel/Chief Compliance .... Mr David HARPOOL
04 Director Office of the President .... Vacant
50 Dean School of Business & Tech Mgmt .... Dr. Peter BEMSKI
53 Dean School of Education .... Dr. Rebecca WARDLOW
83 Dean School of Psychology .... Dr. Robert HALSSMANN
83 Dean Sch of Social/Behavioral Sci .... Dr. James BILLINGS
97 Chair of General Education .... Ms. Melinda LYONS
21 Controller .... Ms. Shannyn STERN
06 Registrar .... Ms. Barbara HICKS
37 Dir of Learner Financial Services .... Ms. Valerie STEINBOCK
08 Director of Library Services .... Mr. Ed SALAZAR
50 Director of Strategic Business Know .... Vacant
84 Enrollment Manager .... Mr. Bob HANKS

Northern Arizona University (H)

South San Francisco Street, Flagstaff AZ 86011-0001
County: Coconino　FICE Identification: 001082
Unit ID: 105330
Telephone: (928) 523-9011　Carnegie Class: DU-Higher
FAX Number: (928) 523-1848　Calendar System: Semester
URL: www.nau.edu
Established: 1899　Annual Undergrad Tuition & Fees (In-State): $10,358
Enrollment: 27,705　Coed
Affiliation or Control: State　IRS Status: 501(c)3
Highest Offering: Doctorate
Accreditation: NH, ACBSP, ARCPA, BUS, CAATE, CACREP, CIDA, CONST, CS, DH, ENG, MUS, NRPA, NURSE, OT, PTA, SP, SW, TED

01 President .... Dr. Rita CHENG
03 Executive VP and Chief of Staff .... Ms. Joanne KEENE
05 Provost .... Dr. James COLEMAN
30 VP Development and Alumni Engmnt .... Dr. Betsy MENNELL
84 VP Enrollment Mgmt/Student Affs .... Ms. Sheila Jane KUHN
09 VP Planning/Budget/Inst Research .... Mr. Bjorn FLUGSTAD
10 VP Finance and Administration .... Dr Jennus L BURTON
46 Vice President Research .... Dr. William GRABE
56 Interim VP Extended Campuses .... Dr. Astrid KLOCKE
86 VP Govt Affairs/Business Ptnr .... Ms. Christy FARLEY
41 VP Intercollegiate Athletics .... Ms. Lisa CAMPOS
88 VP of Native American Initiatives .... Dr. Chad HAMILL
43 General Counsel .... Ms. Michelle PARKER
88 Vice Provost Academic Personnel .... Dr. Daniel KAIN
13 Chief Information Officer .... Dr Steven BURRELL
32 Associate VP Student Affairs .... Ms. Erin GRISHAM
28 Chief Diversity Officer .... Dr. Carmen PHELPS
12 Assoc VP/Campus Executive Officer .... Dr. Michael SABATH
15 Associate VP Human Resources .... Ms. Diane VERKEST
18 Assoc VP Facility Services .... Mr. John MORRIS
21 Associate VP Financial Services .... Ms. Wency SWARTZ
20 Vice Provost Academic Affairs .... Dr. Pauline ENTIN
85 Interim Vice Provost Intl Educ .... Mr. Daniel PALM
108 Assoc VP Inst Effectiveness .... Ms. Laura JONES
29 Interim Assoc VP Dev & Alum Engmt .... Ms. Bonnie O'DONNELL
08 Dean/University Librarian .... Ms. Cynthia A. CHILDREY
53 Dean College of Education .... Dr. Ramona MELLOTT
54 Dean College Eng/Forestry/Nat Sci .... Dr. Paul JAGODZINSKI
50 Dean WA Franke College of Business .... Dr. Craig VAN SLYKE
49 Interim Dean Col of Arts & Letters .... Dr. Jean BOREEN
83 Dean Col Social/Behavioral Sciences .... Dr. Karen L. PUGLIESI
17 Exec Dean Col of Health/Human Svcs .... Dr. Debera THOMAS
06 University Registrar .... Ms. Pamela L. ANASTASSIOU
19 Director University Police .... Mr. Gregory T. FOWLER
22 Assistant VP Equity and Access .... Ms. Priscilla L. MILLS
23 Exec Dir Campus Health Svcs .... Ms. Julie RYAN
39 Exec Dir Housing/Residence Life .... Mr. Rich PAYNE
36 Dir Gateway Student Success Center .... Ms. Monica BAI
07 Director of Admissions .... Ms. Anika OLSEN
26 Chief Mktg & Comm Officer .... Ms. Carla ANDREWS-O'HARA
35 Dean of Students .... Ms. Cynthia ANDERSON
38 Dir Counseling & Testing Center .... Ms. Carol O'SABEN
96 Director of Procurement .... Ms. Becky E. MCGAUGH
04 Assistant to the President .... Ms. Isa RUEDA
102 Chief Foundation Officer .... Ms. Cheryl HEITZ
104 Director Study Abroad .... Dr. Eric DESCHAMPS
25 Assistant VP Grant & Contracts .... Vacant
37 Director Student Financial Aid .... Ms. Nydia NITTMANN
27 Exec Dir of University Marketing .... Ms. Eva PUTZOVA
40 Bookstore Manager .... Ms. Diana WHITE
16 Director Human Resource Programs .... Ms. Cynthia A. CHILCOAT
64 Director School of Music .... Mr. Todd SULLIVAN
92 Director Honors Program .... Dr. George GUMERMAN
94 Director Women and Gender Studies .... Ms. Sheila NAIR
58 Dean Graduate College .... Dr. Maribeth WATWOOD
106 Director E-Learning Center .... Mr. Don CARTER
14 IT Support Svcs Director .... Mr. Ricky ROBERTS
31 Dir Community Relations .... Ms. Shannon SHOOTS
88 Exec Dir Academic Advising .... Ms. Terri HAYES

Northern Arizona University Yuma Branch Campus (I)

2020 S Avenue 8E, Yuma AZ 85365
Telephone: (928) 317-6400　Identification: 770011
Accreditation: &NH

† Regional accreditation is carried under the parent institution in Flagstaff, AZ

Northland Pioneer College (J)

PO Box 610, Holbrook AZ 86025-0610
County: Navajo　FICE Identification: 011862
Unit ID: 105349
Telephone: (928) 524-7311　Carnegie Class: Not Classified
FAX Number: (928) 524-7312　Calendar System: Semester
URL: www.npc.edu
Established: 1973　Annual Undergrad Tuition & Fees (In-State): N/A
Enrollment: N/A　Coed
Affiliation or Control: State　IRS Status: 501(c)3
Highest Offering: Associate Degree
Accreditation: NH, ADNUR, EMT

01 President .... Dr. Jeanne SWARTHOUT
05 Vice Pres Learning/Student Services .... Mr. Mark H. VEST
11 Vice Pres Administrative Services .... Ms. Maderia ELLISON
13 Director of Information Services .... Mr. Phillip WAY
32 Director of Student Services .... Mr. Josh ROGERS
04 Assistant to the President .... Mr. John Paul HEMPSEY
10 Director of Financial Services .... Ms. Maderia ELLISON
21 Controller .... Ms. Amber HILL
15 Director of Human Resources .... Mr. William FEE
37 Director of Financial Aid .... Ms. Beaulah BOB-PENNYPACKER
88 Director of Developmental Services .... Mr. Rickey JACKSON
103 Dean of Career/Technical Education .... Ms. Peggy BELKNAP
49 Dean of Arts & Sciences .... Dr. Eric HENDERSON
66 Dean of Nursing and Allied Health .... Ms. Peg ERDMAN
18 Director of Facilities and Vehicles .... Mr. David HUISH
26 Dir of Marketing/Public Relations .... Ms. Ann HESS
09 Director of Institutional Effective .... Vacant
14 Network and Systems Administrator .... Vacant
88 Director Small Business Development .... Ms. Tracy MANCUSO
08 Head Librarian .... Mr. Stan PIROG
19 Director of Public Safety .... Mr. Stuart BISHOP
84 Director of Enrollment Services .... Mr. Jeremy RAISOR

Northland Pioneer College Little Colorado Campus (K)

1400 E. Third Street, Winslow AZ 86047
Telephone: (928) 289-6511　Identification: 770015
Accreditation: &NH

† Regional accreditation is carried under the parent institution in Holbrook, AZ

Northland Pioneer College Painted Desert Campus (L)

2251 E Navajo Boulevard, Holbrook AZ 86025
Telephone: (928) 524-7311　Identification: 770012
Accreditation: &NH

† Regional accreditation is carried under the parent institution in Holbrook, AZ

Northland Pioneer College Silver Creek Campus (M)

1611 S Main Street, Snowflake AZ 85937
Telephone: (928) 536-6211　Identification: 770014
Accreditation: &NH

† Regional accreditation is carried under the parent institution in Holbrook, AZ

Northland Pioneer College White Mountain Campus (N)

1001 W Deuce of Clubs, Show Low AZ 85901
Telephone: (928) 532-6111　Identification: 770013
Accreditation: &NH

† Regional accreditation is carried under the parent institution in Holbrook, AZ

Ottawa University Arizona (A)
9414 North 25th Avenue, Phoenix AZ 85021
Telephone: (602) 371-1188 Identification: 666066
Accreditation: &NH

† Regional accreditation is carried under the parent institution in Ottawa, KS.

The Paralegal Institute at Brighton College (B)
8777 E. Via de Ventura, Suite 300, Scottsdale AZ 85258
County: Maricopa FICE Identification: 030737
Unit ID: 105385
Telephone: (602) 212-0501 Carnegie Class: Not Classified
FAX Number: (602) 212-0502 Calendar System: Other
URL: www.theparalegalinstitute.edu
Established: 1974 Annual Undergrad Tuition & Fees: N/A
Enrollment: N/A Coed
Affiliation or Control: Proprietary IRS Status: Proprietary
Highest Offering: Associate Degree
Accreditation: DEAC

01 President .... Paul ZAGNONI
03 Vice President .... Sam FERNANDEZ
26 Vice President Marketing .... Chris CARAWAY
10 Director Financial Operations .... Keith RICHMOND
32 Director of Student Management .... Kayla HOBBIEBRUNKEN

Penn Foster College (C)
14300 N Northsight Blvd, Suite 125,
Scottsdale AZ 85260-3673
County: Maricopa FICE Identification: 004049
Unit ID: 211486
Telephone: (480) 947-6644 Carnegie Class: Not Classified
FAX Number: (480) 951-6030 Calendar System: Other
URL: www.pennfostercollege.edu
Established: 1974 Annual Undergrad Tuition & Fees: N/A
Enrollment: N/A Coed
Affiliation or Control: Proprietary IRS Status: Proprietary
Highest Offering: Baccalaureate
Accreditation: DEAC, MAAB

01 Chief Executive Officer .... Mr. Frank BRITT
05 Chief Certification/Licensing Ofcr .... Ms. Connie DEMPSEY
10 Chief Financial Officer .... Mr. Thomas BLESSO
26 Vice Pres Marketing .... Ms. Kate MOSTELLER
07 Vice Pres Admissions .... Mr. Pat GAFFEY
06 Registrar .... Ms. Stephanie SCHROEDER

Phoenix Institute of Herbal Medicine and Acupuncture (D)
301 E Bethany Home Road, Ste A-100,
Phoenix AZ 85012-1275
County: Maricopa FICE Identification: 036175
Unit ID: 447698
Telephone: (602) 274-1885 Carnegie Class: Spec-4-yr-Other Health
FAX Number: (602) 274-1895 Calendar System: Semester
URL: www.pihma.edu
Established: 1996 Annual Graduate Tuition & Fees: N/A
Enrollment: 132 Coed
Affiliation or Control: Proprietary IRS Status: Proprietary
Highest Offering: Master's; No Undergraduates
Accreditation: ACUP

01 President .... Ms. Catherine NIEMIEC
05 Dean for Academic Affairs .... Mr. David MYRICK
07 Admissions .... Ms. Yvette MORAN
06 Registrar .... Ms. Judy DRAYER

Phoenix Seminary (E)
4222 E Thomas Road, Suite 400, Phoenix AZ 85018-7607
County: Maricopa FICE Identification: 034784
Unit ID: 381459
Telephone: (602) 850-8000 Carnegie Class: Spec-4-yr-Faith
FAX Number: (602) 850-8080 Calendar System: Semester
URL: www.phoenixseminary.edu
Established: 1988 Annual Graduate Tuition & Fees: N/A
Enrollment: 178 Coed
Affiliation or Control: Interdenominational IRS Status: 501(c)3
Highest Offering: Doctorate; No Undergraduates
Accreditation: NH, THEOL

01 President .... Dr. Darryl L. DELHOUSAYE
05 Executive Vice President/Provost .... Dr. W. Bingham HUNTER
32 Vice President Student Development .... Dr. Chip MOODY
20 Dir Acad Services/Admiss/Assess .... Ms. Roma ROYER
06 Registrar .... Mrs. Merry STENSON
84 Director of Enrollment .... Mr. Jonathan GRIFFIN
08 Director of Library Services .... Mr. Doug OLBERT
10 Director of Finance .... Mr. Dave HESTON
37 Financial Aid Officer .... Ms. Julia FRIEDNER
26 Director of Communications .... Mr. Don BALTZER

Pima Community College (F)
4905 East Broadway Boulevard, Tucson AZ 85709-1005
County: Pima FICE Identification: 007266
Unit ID: 105525
Telephone: (520) 206-4500 Carnegie Class: Assoc/HT-Mix Trad/Non
FAX Number: (520) 206-4535 Calendar System: Semester
URL: www.pima.edu
Established: 1966 Annual Undergrad Tuition & Fees (In-District): $1,974
Enrollment: 28,070 Coed
Affiliation or Control: State/Local IRS Status: 501(c)3
Highest Offering: Associate Degree
Accreditation: NH, ADNUR, COARC, DA, DH, DT, EMT, MAC, MLTAD, RAD, SURGT

01 Chancellor .... Mr. Lee D. LAMBERT
05 Actg Provost/Chief Academic Ofcr .... Dr. Dolores DURAN-CERDA
10 Exec Vice Chanc for Finance/Admin .... Dr. David BEA
15 Vice Chanc for Human Resources .... Mr. Daniel BERRYMAN
30 Vice Chancellor External Relations .... Ms. Lisa BROSKY
18 Vice Chancellor Facilities .... Mr. Bill WARD
12 President Northwest Campus .... Dr. David DORE
12 President East Campus .... Dr. Lorraine MORALES
12 President Downtown Campus .... Dr. David DORE
12 President Community Campus .... Dr. Lorraine MORALES
12 President West Campus .... Dr. Morgan PHILLIPS
12 President Desert Vista Campus .... Dr. Morgan PHILLIPS
43 College General Counsel .... Mr. Jeffrey SILVYN
13 Asst Vice Chanc Information Tech .... Dr. Raj MURTHY
88 Asst Vice Chanc Accreditation .... Dr. Bruce MOSES
09 AVC Planning & Inst Research .... Dr. Nicola RICHMOND
84 AVC Enrollment Mgmt/Stdnt Affairs .... Dr. Karrie MITCHELL
26 Exec Dir Media & Govt Rels .... Ms. Elizabeth HOWELL
102 Interim Exec Director Foundation .... Ms. Rachel SCHAMING
19 Actg Exec Dir Dept of Public Safety .... Ms. Michelle NIEUWENHUIS
103 VP Workforce Development .... Dr. Ian ROARK
76 Dean of Allied Health Programs .... Mr. James CRAIG
41 Dean of Athletics .... Mr. Edgar SOTO
37 Director of Financial Aid . Ms. Norma NAVARRO-CASTELLANOS
07 Director & Registrar .... Ms. Yolanda ESPINOZA
96 Director of Purchasing .... Mr. Mark DWORSCHAK

Pima Community College Community Campus (G)
401 North Bonita Avenue, Tucson AZ 85709
Telephone: (520) 206-3933 Identification: 770016
Accreditation: &NH

† Regional accreditation is carried under the parent institution in Tucson, AZ

Pima Community College Desert Vista Campus (H)
5901 South Calle Santa Cruz, Tucson AZ 85709
Telephone: (520) 206-5000 Identification: 770017
Accreditation: &NH

† Regional accreditation is carried under the parent institution in Tucson, AZ

Pima Community College Downtown Campus (I)
1255 North Stone Avenue, Tucson AZ 85709-3000
Telephone: (520) 206-7171 Identification: 770018
Accreditation: &NH

† Regional accreditation is carried under the parent institution in Tucson, AZ

Pima Community College East Campus (J)
8181 East Arrington Road, Tucson AZ 85709-4000
Telephone: (520) 206-7000 Identification: 770019
Accreditation: &NH

† Regional accreditation is carried under the parent institution in Tucson, AZ

Pima Community College Northwest Campus (K)
7600 North Shannon Road, Tucson AZ 85709-7200
Telephone: (520) 206-2200 Identification: 770020
Accreditation: &NH

† Regional accreditation is carried under the parent institution in Tucson, AZ

Pima Community College West Campus (L)
2202 West Alklam Road, Tucson AZ 85709-0001
Telephone: (520) 206-6600 Identification: 770021
Accreditation: &NH

† Regional accreditation is carried under the parent institution in Tucson, AZ

Pima Medical Institute-East Valley (M)
2160 S Power Road, Mesa AZ 85209
Telephone: (480) 898-9898 Identification: 770515
Accreditation: ABHES

Pima Medical Institute-Mesa (N)
957 S Dobson Road, Mesa AZ 85202-2903
Telephone: (480) 644-0267 FICE Identification: 011570
Accreditation: ABHES, COARC, OTA, PTAA, RAD

Pima Medical Institute-Tucson (O)
3350 E Grant Road, Suite 200, Tucson AZ 85716-2932
County: Pima FICE Identification: 022171
Unit ID: 105534
Telephone: (520) 326-1600 Carnegie Class: Spec-4-yr-Other Health
FAX Number: (520) 326-4125 Calendar System: Other
URL: www.pmi.edu
Established: 1972 Annual Undergrad Tuition & Fees: N/A
Enrollment: 1,948 Coed
Affiliation or Control: Proprietary IRS Status: Proprietary
Highest Offering: Baccalaureate
Accreditation: ABHES, COARC, OTA, PTAA, RAD

01 Director .... Mr. Dale BERG

Prescott College (P)
220 Grove Avenue, Prescott AZ 86301-2912
County: Yavapai FICE Identification: 020653
Unit ID: 105589
Telephone: (928) 350-2100 Carnegie Class: Masters/S
FAX Number: (928) 776-5137 Calendar System: Semester
URL: www.prescott.edu
Established: 1966 Annual Undergrad Tuition & Fees: $27,503
Enrollment: 848 Coed
Affiliation or Control: Independent Non-Profit IRS Status: 501(c)3
Highest Offering: Doctorate
Accreditation: NH

01 President .... Mr. John FLICKER
05 Executive Vice President & Provost .... Dr. Paul BURKHARDT
10 Chief Financial Officer .... Ms. Andrea JAECKEL
30 Chief Advancement Officer .... Ms. Ashley MAINS
32 Chief Student Affairs Officer .... Ms. Kristine PREZIOSI
84 Dean of Enrollment Management .... Ms. Jerri BROWN
06 Registrar .... Ms. Bobbie DAVIDSON
88 Assoc Dean Enrollment Management ..Ms. Mary Frances CAUSEY
04 Executive Assistant .... Ms. Cathy CHURCH
07 Director of Admissions .... Mr. David WHITE
09 Director of Institutional Research .... Mr. Thomas PERCONTI
15 Chief Human Resources Officer .... Ms. Lavinia NOWOSIELSKI
35 Associate Student Affairs Officer .... Ms. Megan LETCHWORTH
18 Director of Facilities .... Mr. Greg LAZZELL
08 Director of Library .... Mr. Richard LEWIS
13 Dir Information Technology Services .... Mr. Eric WARTHAN
29 Director of Alumni Relations .... Ms. Marie SMITH
20 Academic Operations Coordinator .... Ms. Karyn FINNELL

The Refrigeration School (Q)
4210 E Washington Street, Phoenix AZ 85034-1816
County: Maricopa FICE Identification: 011689
Unit ID: 105659
Telephone: (602) 275-7133 Carnegie Class: Spec 2-yr-Tech
FAX Number: (602) 267-4805 Calendar System: Other
URL: www.refrigerationschool.com
Established: 1965 Annual Undergrad Tuition & Fees: N/A
Enrollment: 695 Coed
Affiliation or Control: Proprietary IRS Status: Proprietary
Highest Offering: Associate Degree
Accreditation: ACCSC

01 Campus President .... Mr. Stephen M. MALUTICH
37 Director of Financial Aid .... Ms. Melanie ZUVERINK
07 Director of Admissions .... Mr. John PALUMBO
05 Director of Education .... Mr. Greg HARRIS
10 Director of Accounting .... Mr. David FULFORD
06 Registrar .... Ms. Tara BOURLOTOS

Sessions College for Professional Design (R)
51 W. Third Street, Suite E-301, Tempe AZ 85281
County: Maricopa FICE Identification: 042176
Unit ID: 475839
Telephone: (480) 212-1704 Carnegie Class: Spec 2-yr-A&S
FAX Number: (480) 212-1705 Calendar System: Semester
URL: www.sessions.edu
Established: 1997 Annual Undergrad Tuition & Fees: $8,000
Enrollment: 99 Coed
Affiliation or Control: Proprietary IRS Status: Proprietary
Highest Offering: Associate Degree
Accreditation: DEAC

00 CEO .... Ms. Doris GRANATOWSKI
01 President .... Mr. Gordon DRUMMOND
03 Executive Vice President .... Mr. Louis J. SCHILT
11 Chief Operating Officer .... Mr. Robert TIMM
10 Chief Financial Officer/Bursar .... Ms. Carole Anne BAILO
32 Dir Student Services/Acad Pgms .... Mr. Tyler DRAKE

Sonoran Desert Institute (A)

8767 E. Via de Ventura, Suite 126,
Scottsdale AZ 85258-3376

County: Maricopa — Identification: 667057
Telephone: (480) 314-2102 — Carnegie Class: Not Classified
FAX Number: (480) 314-2138 — Calendar System: Semester
URL: www.sdi.edu
Established: 2000 — Annual Undergrad Tuition & Fees: N/A
Enrollment: N/A — Coed
Affiliation or Control: Proprietary — IRS Status: Proprietary
Highest Offering: Associate Degree
Accreditation: DEAC

- 01 President ... Paul L. ZAGNONI

Southwest College of Naturopathic Medicine & Health Sciences (B)

2140 E Broadway Road, Tempe AZ 85282-1751

County: Maricopa — FICE Identification: 031070
Unit ID: 420246
Telephone: (480) 858-9100 — Carnegie Class: Spec-4-yr-Other Health
FAX Number: (480) 858-9116 — Calendar System: Quarter
URL: www.scnm.edu
Established: 1993 — Annual Graduate Tuition & Fees: N/A
Enrollment: 402 — Coed
Affiliation or Control: Independent Non-Profit — IRS Status: 501(c)3
Highest Offering: First Professional Degree; No Undergraduates
Accreditation: NH, NATUR

- 01 President/Chief Executive Officer ... Paul A. MITTMAN
- 05 Chief Academic Officer ... Margot L. GREGORY
- 10 Vice Pres Finance & Administration ... Dawn RECTOR
- 32 Vice President Student Affairs ... Melissa WINQUIST
- 13 Chief IT Officer ... Mark LIERLEY

Southwest Institute of Healing Arts (C)

1100 E Apache Boulevard, Tempe AZ 85281-5822

County: Maricopa — FICE Identification: 035933
Unit ID: 442879
Telephone: (480) 994-9244 — Carnegie Class: Spec 2-yr-Health
FAX Number: (480) 994-3228 — Calendar System: Other
URL: www.swiha.edu
Established: 1992 — Annual Undergrad Tuition & Fees: N/A
Enrollment: 986 — Coed
Affiliation or Control: Proprietary — IRS Status: Proprietary
Highest Offering: Associate Degree
Accreditation: CNCE

- 01 President/Owner ... Mrs. K. C. MILLER
- 05 Exec Director of Online Education ... Mr. David DYE
- 10 Dir Finance & Human Res/Controller ... Ms. Salisha TAMANDL
- 32 Director Online Student Services ... Ms. Bernadett BILACH
- 07 Sr Admissions Advisor ... Ms. Janell ERICKSON
- 37 Director of Financial Aid ... Ms. Alicia STEUBER
- 06 Registrar ... Ms. Frannie WALSH
- 35 Student Services Support Manager ... Ms. Angelica VALENZUELA

Southwest University of Visual Arts (D)

2525 N Country Club Road, Tucson AZ 85716-2505

County: Pima — FICE Identification: 024915
Unit ID: 104188
Telephone: (520) 325-0123 — Carnegie Class: Spec-4-yr-Arts
FAX Number: (520) 325-5535 — Calendar System: Semester
URL: www.suva.edu
Established: 1983 — Annual Undergrad Tuition & Fees: $23,069
Enrollment: 172 — Coed
Affiliation or Control: Proprietary — IRS Status: Proprietary
Highest Offering: Master's
Accreditation: NH, CIDA

- 01 President ... Mrs. Sharmon WOODS
- 84 Director of Enrollment Management ... Mr. Rob MAIRS
- 32 Director of Student Services ... Mr. Rob MAIRS
- 07 Asst Director of Enrollment Mgmt ... Ms. Joanne PILS
- 06 Registrar ... Mrs. Keila DUARTE

Tohono O'odham Community College (E)

PO Box 3129, Sells AZ 85634-3129

County: Pima — FICE Identification: 037844
Unit ID: 442781
Telephone: (520) 383-8401 — Carnegie Class: Tribal
FAX Number: (520) 383-0029 — Calendar System: Semester
URL: www.tocc.edu
Established: 1998 — Annual Undergrad Tuition & Fees: $1,604
Enrollment: 225 — Coed
Affiliation or Control: Tribal Control — IRS Status: 501(c)3
Highest Offering: Associate Degree
Accreditation: NH

- 01 President ... Dr. Paul ROBERTSON
- 05 Vice President for Education ... Ms. Juana Clare JOSE
- 10 Vice Pres Admin Services/Finance ... Ms. Karla VOLPI
- 32 Vice Pres of Student Services ... Ms. Sylvia HENDRICKS
- 46 Vice Pres Inst Research/Development ... Ms. Jane LATANE
- 75 Acad Chair Occupational Pgms ... Mr. George MIGUEL
- 97 Acad Chair for General Education ... Dr. Maria MONTES-HELU
- 07 Director of Admissions/Records ... Mr. Leslie LUNA
- 08 College Librarian ... Ms. Elaine CUBBINS
- 37 Director of Financial Aid ... Mr. Al RIVERA
- 88 Director Project NATIVE ... Ms. Camille MARTINEZ-YADEN
- 88 Director Project NATIVE ... Dr. Sandra LUCAS
- 30 Director of Fundraising ... Ms. Andrea AHMED
- 15 Human Resources Director ... Ms. Stacy OWSLEY
- 25 Sponsored Projects Manager ... Mr. Antonio BENAVIDEZ

Tohono O'odham Community College West Campus (F)

PO Box 3129, Sells AZ 85634-3129

Telephone: (520) 383-8401 — Identification: 770022
Accreditation: &NH

† Regional accreditation is carried under the parent institution in Sells, AZ

Universal Technical Institute (G)

10695 W Pierce Street, Avondale AZ 85323-7946

County: Maricopa — FICE Identification: 008221
Unit ID: 106041
Telephone: (623) 245-4600 — Carnegie Class: Spec 2-yr-Tech
FAX Number: (623) 245-4601 — Calendar System: Other
URL: www.uti.edu
Established: 1965 — Annual Undergrad Tuition & Fees: N/A
Enrollment: 2,340 — Coed
Affiliation or Control: Proprietary — IRS Status: Proprietary
Highest Offering: Associate Degree
Accreditation: ACCSC

- 01 Campus President ... Mr. Michael ROMANO
- 05 Director of Education ... Mr. Patrick BENNETT
- 32 Director of Student Services ... Ms. Lindsay KINGSLEY
- 10 Director of Campus Accounting ... Mrs. Gayle PARSONS
- 07 Admissions Director ... Mr. Adam HELLER
- 36 Director of Graduate Employment ... Ms. Cheryl RADKE
- 37 Director of Financial Aid ... Ms. Terri MEIXSEL-CORDERO
- 18 Maintenance Director ... Mr. George MICKENS

University of Advancing Technology (H)

2625 W Baseline Road, Tempe AZ 85283-1056

County: Maricopa — FICE Identification: 025590
Unit ID: 363934
Telephone: (602) 383-8228 — Carnegie Class: Spec-4-yr-Other Tech
FAX Number: (602) 383-8250 — Calendar System: Other
URL: www.uat.edu
Established: 1983 — Annual Undergrad Tuition & Fees: $23,750
Enrollment: 819 — Coed
Affiliation or Control: Proprietary — IRS Status: Proprietary
Highest Offering: Master's
Accreditation: NH

- 01 President ... Mr. Jason PISTILLO
- 05 Provost and Dean ... Mr. Dave BOLMAN
- 100 Chief of Staff ... Ms. Valerie CIMAROSSA
- 07 Director of Admissions ... Ms. Megan BENSON
- 10 Senior Controller ... Ms. Erika GARNEY

University of Arizona (I)

1401 E University Blvd, Tucson AZ 85721-0001

County: Pima — FICE Identification: 001083
Unit ID: 104179
Telephone: (520) 621-2211 — Carnegie Class: DU-Highest
FAX Number: (520) 621-9323 — Calendar System: Semester
URL: www.arizona.edu
Established: 1885 — Annual Undergrad Tuition & Fees (In-State): $11,403
Enrollment: 42,236 — Coed
Affiliation or Control: State — IRS Status: 501(c)3
Highest Offering: Doctorate
Accreditation: NH, ANEST, ART, AUD, BUS, BUSA, CACREP, CEA, CLPSY, CORE, CS, DANCE, DIETD, ENG, ENGR, IPSY, JOUR, LAW, LIB, LSAR, MED, MUS, NURSE, PCSAS, PERF, PH, PHAR, PLNG, SCPSY, SP, SPAA, THEA

- 01 President ... Dr. Ann WEAVER HART
- 05 Sr VP for Acad Affairs & Provost ... Dr. Andrew C. COMRIE
- 10 Sr VP and CFO/Business Affairs ... Mr. Gregg GOLDMAN
- 26 Sr VP University Relations ... Dr. Teresa THOMPSON
- 17 Sr VP Health Sciences ... Dr. Joe GARCIA
- 32 Sr VP Student Affairs & Enroll Mgmt ... Dr. Melissa VITO
- 46 Sr VP for Research ... Dr. Kimberly A. ESPY
- 41 VP and Director Athletics ... Mr. Gregory K. BYRNE
- 88 VP Strategic Planning & Analysis ... Dr. Barbara BRYSON
- 43 VP Legal Affs/General Counsel ... Dr. Laura T. JOHNSON
- 88 VP Global Initiatives ... Dr. Michael A. PROCTOR
- 49 VP Innovation & Strategy ... Dr. Joaquin RUIZ
- 21 VP Business Affairs ... Mr. Robert R. SMITH
- 29 VP Alumni Relations ... Ms. Melinda W. BURKE
- 15 VP Institutional Effectiveness & HR ... Dr. Allison M. VAILLANCOURT
- 88 VP Digital Learning/Student Engmnt ... Mr. Vincent J. DEL CASINO
- 88 VP Tech Launch AZ ... Dr. David N. ALLEN
- 27 VP Communications ... Mr. Chris W. SIGURDSON
- 07 VP/Std Aff/Enr Mgmt/Dean Adm ... Dr. Kasandra K. URQUIDEZ
- 88 Vice Provost Faculty Affairs ... Dr. Thomas P. MILLER
- 47 V Provost/Dean Agri/Life Sci ... Dr. Shane C. BURGESS
- 20 Sr Vice Provost Academic Affairs ... Dr. Gail D. BURD
- 86 Sr Assoc VP Legis & Comm Relations ... Mr. Timothy S. BEE
- 88 Sr Assoc VP Health Sciences ... Mr. Mike JONEN
- 88 Sr Assoc to the Pres/Secretary Univ ... Dr. Jon DUDAS
- 88 Assoc VP External Relations-Phoenix ... Ms. Judith A. BERNAS
- 88 Assoc VP Research ... Ms. Caroline M. GARCIA
- 88 Assoc VP for Research ... Dr. Jennifer K. BARTON
- 88 Assoc VP Health Sci-Interprof Educ ... Dr. Sally J. REEL
- 88 Assoc VP Precision Health Sciences ... Mr. Kenneth RAMOS
- 88 Assoc VP Clinical Affairs ... Mr. Steven GOLDSCHMID
- 88 Assoc VP Institutional Analysis ... Mr. James S. FLORIAN
- 88 Assoc VP Tech Parks Arizona ... Mr. Bruce A. WRIGHT
- 88 Assoc VP Marketing/Brand Mgmt ... Mr. Michael A. PROUDFOOT
- 88 Assoc VP & Chief Health Sci Develop ... Ms. Jennifer L. FLORES
- 108 Assoc Vice Provost Instruc/Assess ... Dr. Debra J. TOMANEK
- 88 Assoc VP Federal Relations ... Mr. Shay D. STAUTZ
- 88 Assoc VP Population Health Sciences ... Ms. Elizabeth CALHOUN
- 88 Assoc VP Research ... Mr. Neal R. ARMSTRONG
- 88 Interim Assoc VP Financial Services ... Mr. Duc D. MA
- 13 Int CIO/Exec Dir UITS/Dean of Lib ... Ms. Karen A. WILLIAMS
- 88 Sr Asst VP Finance Administration ... Ms. Marilyn TAYLOR
- 35 Asst VP Student Affs/Enroll Mgmt ... Mr. Joel S. HAUFF
- 09 Asst Provost Inst Research ... Dr. Angela Y. BALDASARE
- 18 Asst VP Plng/Design & Construction ... Mr. Peter DOURLEIN
- 88 Asst VP Tribal Relations ... Ms. Karen F. BEGAY
- 88 Asst VP Program Innovation ... Dr. Randy M. BURD
- 37 Asst VP Community Relations ... Ms. Tannya R. GAXIOLA GAXIOLA
- 88 Asst VP Health Sciences/Pub Affairs ... Mr. George D. HUMPHREY
- 88 Asst VP Budget ... Ms. Kathryn E. WHISMAN
- 88 Asst VP Admin Systems Integration ... Mr. Barry T. BRUMMUND
- 88 Asst VP Hemispheric Programs ... Mr. Francisco J. MARMOLEJO
- 18 Asst VP Facilities Management ... Mr. Christopher M. KOPACH
- 19 Asst VP Risk Management/Safety ... Mr. Steven C. HOLLAND
- 88 Asst VP Finance & Administration ... Ms. Karen L. TUMLINSON
- 88 Asst VP Divisional Inititatives ... Ms. Jennifer M. PICKARD
- 06 Asst VP Registrar/Enrollment Mgmt ... Dr. Elizabeth A. ACREE
- 88 Asst VP Govt Affairs ... Mr. Ethan R. ORR
- 83 Dean Social/Behav Science ... Dr. John P. JONES
- 88 Asst VP Dean of Students ... Ms. Kendal H. WASHINGTON WHITE
- 92 Dean Honors College ... Dr. Patricia MACCORQUODALE
- 48 Dean Col Arch & Landscape Arch ... Dr. Janice A. CERVELLI
- 53 Dean Education ... Dr. Ronald W. MARX
- 58 Dean Graduate College ... Dr. Andrew H. CARNIE
- 61 Dean James E Rogers College of Law ... Dr. Marc L. MILLER
- 66 Dean College of Nursing ... Dr. Joan L. SHAVER
- 12 Dean UA South ... Dr. James W. SHOCKEY
- 79 Dean College of Humanities ... Dr. Mary E. WILDNER-BASSETT
- 57 Dean Fine Arts ... Dr. Jory L. HANCOCK
- 54 Dean College of Engineering ... Dr. Jeffrey B. GOLDBERG
- 50 Dean Eller College of Management ... Dr. Jeffrey W. SCHATZBERG
- 69 Dean Public Health ... Dr. Iman A. HAKIM
- 63 Interim Dean College of Medicine ... Dr. Charles B. CAIRNS
- 63 Dean College of Med-Phoenix Campus ... Dr. Stuart D. FLYNN
- 81 Dean College of Optical Sciences ... Dr. Thomas L. KOCH
- 67 Dean Pharmacy ... Dr. J. L. BOOTMAN
- 22 Dir Office of Institutional Equity ... Ms. Mary E. TUCKER
- 36 Exec Director Career Services ... Ms. Eileen M. MCGARRY
- 40 Exec Director Univ of AZ Bookstores ... Ms. Debby L. SHIVELY
- 88 Exec Director Campus Health ... Mr. Harry MCDERMOTT
- 88 Exec Dir Analytics & Inst Research ... Mr. Henry A. CHILDERS
- 96 Dir Procurement & Contract Services ... Mr. Edward D. NASSER
- 25 Director Sponsored Proj/Services ... Ms. Sherry L. ESHAM
- 85 Director International Admissions ... Dr. Rachel A. BEECH

University of Arizona Phoenix Biomedical Campus (J)

550 E Van Buren Street, Phoenix AZ 85004

Telephone: (602) 827-2001 — Identification: 770023
Accreditation: &NH, #MED, PHAR

† Regional accreditation is carried under the parent institution in Tucson, AZ

University of Arizona South (K)

1140 N Colombo Avenue, Sierra Vista AZ 85635

Telephone: (520) 458-8278 — Identification: 770024
Accreditation: &NH

† Regional accreditation is carried under the parent institution in Tucson, AZ

University of Phoenix (L)

1625 W. Fountainhead Parkway, Tempe AZ 85282

County: Maricopa — FICE Identification: 020988
Unit ID: 484613
Telephone: (480) 557-2000 — Carnegie Class: Not Classified
FAX Number: N/A — Calendar System: Other
URL: www.phoenix.edu
Established: 1976 — Annual Undergrad Tuition & Fees: $10,554
Enrollment: 195,059 — Coed
Affiliation or Control: Proprietary — IRS Status: Proprietary
Highest Offering: Doctorate
Accreditation: NH, ACBSP, CACREP, NURSE

01 President University of Phoenix ....Mr. Timothy SLOTTOW
04 Assistant to the President ....Ms. Cindy WHIPPO
05 Provost ....Dr. Meredith CURLEY
03 Chief Operating Officer ....Mr. Raghu KRISHNAIAH
88 Vice Provost Inst Tech & Learning ....Dr. Becky LODEWYCK
09 Vice Provost Inst Effectiveness ....Dr. Kathleen SCHNIER
20 Associate Provost ....Dr. Len KELPSH
53 Exec Dean College of Education ....Dr. Andy DROTOS
50 Exec Dean School of Business ....Ms. Ruth VELORIA
88 Exec Dean Sch of Advanced Studies ....Dr. Hinrich EYLERS
88 Exec Dean Col of Security & CJ ....Mr. Spider MARKS
76 Exec Dean Col of Health Prof ....Ms. Doris SAVRON
72 Exec Dean Info Systems/Technology ....Mr. Dennis BONILLA
79 Exec Dean Col of Humanities & Sci ....Dr. Constance ST. GERMAIN
83 Exec Dean Col of Social Sciences ... Dr. Constance ST. GERMAIN
10 Chief Financial Officer ....Mr. Byron JONES
15 Chief Human Resources ....Ms. Cheryl NAUMANN
88 SVP Academic Operations ....Dr. Russ PADEN
37 SVP Student Administrative Services .... Mr. Jeff SONNENBERG
88 SVP Campus Services ....Mr. Matt JOHNSTON
84 SVP Enrollment Services ....Vacant
88 VP Financial Services ....Mr. Bronson LEDBETTER
06 Registrar ....Ms. Audra MCQUARIE

University of Phoenix Southern Arizona Campus (A)

300 S Craycroft Road, Tucson AZ 85711-4574
Telephone: (520) 881-6512 Identification: 770236
Accreditation: &NH, ACBSP

† Regional accreditation is carried under the parent institution in Tempe, AZ

West Coast Ultrasound Institute (B)

4250 E Camelback Road, #K158, Phoenix AZ 85018
Telephone: (602) 954-3834 Identification: 770550
Accreditation: ACCSC

† Branch campus of West Coast Ultrasound Institute, Beverly Hills, CA

Western International University (C)

1601 W. Fountainhead Parkway, Tempe AZ 85282
County: Maricopa FICE Identification: 021715
Unit ID: 106102
Telephone: (602) 943-2311 Carnegie Class: Spec-4-yr-Bus
FAX Number: (602) 371-8637 Calendar System: Other
URL: www.west.edu
Established: 1978 Annual Undergrad Tuition & Fees: $6,000
Enrollment: 1,374 Coed
Affiliation or Control: Proprietary IRS Status: Proprietary
Highest Offering: Master's
Accreditation: NH

01 President ....Ms. Tracy LORENZ
05 Provost ....Dr. Christopher DAVIS
11 Sr VP University Operations ....Mr. Kris MCCALL
13 SVP Product &Technology ....Ms. Stephanie LEACH
10 CFO ....Ms. Heidi PHIPPS
26 VP of Marketing ....Mr. Chris HEWITT
15 Human Resource Director ....Mr. Daniel BERARD
109 Senior Dir of University Services ....Ms. Hue HASLIM
88 VP Operations/Business Intelligence ....Mr. Ken COSTELLO
06 Sr Dir Student Admin Svcs/Registrar ....Ms. Beth CARLISLE

Yavapai College (D)

1100 E Sheldon Street, Prescott AZ 86301-3297
County: Yavapai FICE Identification: 001079
Unit ID: 106148
Telephone: (928) 445-7300 Carnegie Class: Assoc/MT-VT-Mix Trad/Non
FAX Number: (928) 776-2109 Calendar System: Semester
URL: www.yc.edu
Established: 1966 Annual Undergrad Tuition & Fees (In-District): $2,064
Enrollment: 7,842 Coed
Affiliation or Control: Local IRS Status: 501(c)3
Highest Offering: Associate Degree
Accreditation: NH, ADNUR, EMT, IFSAC, RAD

01 President ....Dr. Penelope WILLS
05 VP Instruction/Stdnt Dev ....Dr. Ron LISS
10 Vice Pres Finance/Admin Svcs ....Dr. Clint EWELL
30 VP College Development/Foundation ....Mr. Steve WALKER
20 Dean for Comp Tech & Instr Support ....Ms. Stacey HILTON
12 Exec Dean Verde Valley Campus ....Dr. James PEREY
75 Dean Career Technical Education ....Mr. John MORGAN
66 Dean Sci/Health/Public Safety ....Mr. Scott FARNSWORTH
79 Dean Arts & Humanities ....Dr. Craig RALSTON
32 Dean for Student Development ....Ms. Tania SHELDAHL
26 Director of Marketing/Public Info ....Mr. Kim KAPIN
37 Assoc Dean Stdnt Dev & Dir Fin Aid ....Vacant
09 Dir Inst Effectiveness & Research ....Mr. Tom HUGHES
15 Director for Human Resources ....Dr. Monica BELKNAP
19 Chief of Police ....Mr. Jerald MONAHAN
21 Dir of Business Svcs & Controller ....Mr. Frank D'ANGELO
07 Recruitment Officer ....Vacant
18 Director for Facilities ....Mr. David LAURENCE
13 Chief Information Officer ....Mr. Patrick BURNS
06 Registrar ....Ms. Sheila JARRELL
96 Director of Purchasing ....Mr. Ryan BOUWHUIS

Yavapai College Verde Valley Campus (E)

601 Black Hills Drive, Clarkdale AZ 86324
Telephone: (928) 634-7501 Identification: 770029
Accreditation: &NH

† Regional accreditation is carried under the parent institution in Prescott, AZ

ARKANSAS

Arkansas Baptist College (F)

1621 Martin Luther King Drive, Little Rock AR 72202-6099
County: Pulaski FICE Identification: 001087
Unit ID: 106306
Telephone: (501) 370-4000 Carnegie Class: Bac/Assoc-Mixed
FAX Number: (501) 372-7992 Calendar System: Semester
URL: www.arkansasbaptist.edu
Established: 1884 Annual Undergrad Tuition & Fees: $8,760
Enrollment: 899 Coed
Affiliation or Control: Baptist IRS Status: 501(c)3
Highest Offering: Baccalaureate
Accreditation: NH

01 President ....Dr. Joseph JONES
04 President's Executive Assistant ....Ms. Patsy BIGGS
10 Director of Business Office ....Ms. Charlotte COMER
100 Chief of Staff ....Mrs. LaCresha NEWTON
05 VP of Academic Affairs ....Dr. Joyce O. JENKINS
09 Director of Institutional Research ....Dr. Jerelyn L. DUNCAN
103 Dir of Adult Ed & Workforce Dev ....Vacant
07 Director of Admissions/Recruitment ....Mr. Willie HICKS
84 Dean of Enrollment Management ....Dr. Yvette WIMBERLY
88 Ombudsman ....Dr. Vicki WILLIAMS
37 Director of Financial Aid ....Mr. Phillip RODGERS
08 Director of Library/Media Services ....Dr. Wille HARDIN
26 Dir College Relations/Marketing ....Mrs. Linda GILLAM WEIR
32 Dean of Students ....Mr. Brian MILLER
19 Chief of Campus Safety ....Mr. Curtis JOHNSON
18 Director Facilities/Maintenance ....Mr. Larry THOMPSON
06 Registrar ....Dr. Jerelyn DUNCAN

Arkansas Northeastern College (G)

2501 S Division Street, Blytheville AR 72315-5111
County: Mississippi FICE Identification: 012860
Unit ID: 107327
Telephone: (870) 762-1020 Carnegie Class: Assoc/HVT-Mix Trad/Non
FAX Number: (870) 763-3704 Calendar System: Semester
URL: www.anc.edu
Established: 1974 Annual Undergrad Tuition & Fees (In-District): $2,150
Enrollment: 1,425 Coed
Affiliation or Control: State/Local IRS Status: 501(c)3
Highest Offering: Associate Degree
Accreditation: NH, DA, EMT

01 President ....Dr. James SHEMWELL
05 Executive Vice President/CAO ....Mrs. June WALTERS
10 Vice President for Adminstration ....Mr. Don RAY
88 Vice Pres for College Readiness ....Mrs. Sherri BENNETT
13 Vice President Student Affairs/IT ....Mr. James W. MCCLAIN
26 Assoc VP for Dev/College Relations ....Ms. Rachel GIFFORD
09 Dean Efectiveness/Assess/Planning ....Mrs. Robin SINGLETON
20 Associate Vice Pres/Asst CAO ....Mrs. Deborah PARKER
88 Assoc VP for Economic Development ....Mr. Gene BENNETT
21 Assoc Vice President for Finance ....Ms. Pacey BOWENS
66 Dean Nursing/Allied Hlth/PE/Rec ....Mrs. Brenda HOLIFIELD
49 Dean for Arts and Sciences ....Mrs. Deanita HICKS
32 Director for Student Services ....Mrs. Courtney FISHER
31 Community Education Specialist ....Ms. Mary Ann GARREN
08 Director of College Library/AV ....Vacant
36 Director ACE Advising Center ....Dr. Bridget SHEMWELL
37 Director Financial Aid ....Mrs. Melinda WALKER
72 Associate Dean MITS ....Mrs. Ruby MEADOR
21 Controller ....Mrs. Melissa ANDREW
15 Human Resources & ADA Coordinator ....Mrs. Tabatha HAMPTON
90 Director Academic Tech Services ....Mr. James ODOM
18 Director Physical Plant and Grounds ....Mr. Scott CREECY
88 Director Talent Search/Educ Opp Ctr ....Mrs. Tonya HARRIS
88 Director Student Support Services ....Ms. Lisa MCGHEE
04 Assistant to Board/President ....Mrs. Jody HIPWELL
06 Registrar ....Mrs. Rosemary LOWE
27 Information/Marketing Specialist ....Ms. Sheiron BEARDON

*Arkansas State University System (H)

501 Woodlane Drive, Suite 600, Little Rock AR 72201
County: Pulaski Identification: 666187
Telephone: (501) 660-1000 Carnegie Class: N/A
FAX Number: (501) 660-1010
URL: www.asusystem.edu

01 President ....Dr. Charles L. WELCH
04 Exec Assistant to the President ....Ms. Pam KAIL
10 Executive Vice President ....Ms. Julie BATES
86 Vice Pres Governmental Relations ....Mr. Shane BROADWAY
45 Vice Pres Strategic Comm/Econ Dev ....Mr. Jeff HANKINS
102 President ASU System Foundation ....Mr. Philip JACKSON
43 Legal Counsel ....Ms. Lucinda MCDANIEL
88 Internal Auditor ....Ms. Jo LUNBECK

*Arkansas State University-Beebe (I)

PO Box 1000, Beebe AR 72012-1000
County: White FICE Identification: 001091
Unit ID: 106449
Telephone: (501) 882-3600 Carnegie Class: Assoc/MT-VT-High Non
FAX Number: (501) 882-8970 Calendar System: Semester
URL: www.asub.edu
Established: 1927 Annual Undergrad Tuition & Fees (In-State): $3,480
Enrollment: 4,140 Coed
Affiliation or Control: State IRS Status: 501(c)3
Highest Offering: Associate Degree
Accreditation: NH, EMT, MLTAD, NAIT

02 Chancellor ....Dr. Karla FISHER
100 Executive Assistant to Chancellor ....Mr. Joe BERRY
12 Vice Chancellor ASU-Heber Springs ....Dr. James C. BOYETT
12 Vice Chancellor of ASU-Searcy ....Mr. Barry FARRIS
05 Vice Chancellor Academic Affairs ....Dr. Theodore J. KALTHOFF
32 Vice Chancellor Student Services ....Dr. Deborah A. GARRETT
10 Vice Chanc Finance & Administration ....Mr. Jerry H. CARLISLE
30 Vice Chanc Inst Advancement ....Dr. Keith PINCHBACK
26 Director of Marketing/PR ....Ms. Nancy MEADOR
06 Registrar ....Ms. Amy J. MAHAN
08 Head Librarian ....Ms. Tracy D. SMITH
15 Director of Human Resources ....Ms. Susan A. COLLIE
19 Chief of Police ....Mr. James J. MARTIN
18 Director of Physical Plant ....Mr. Jerry L. THOMPSON
37 Director Student Financial Aid ....Ms. Louise DRIVER
09 Director of Institutional Research ... Ms. Bonnie SMYTH-MCGAHA
13 Chief Information Technology Office ....Mr. Chris LEE
21 Business Manager ....Ms. Charlette MOORE
21 Controller ....Ms. Sharon A. BEEN
84 Director of Enrollment Management ....Mr. David M. MAYES
38 Dir Student Success and Retention ....Mr. Roger MOORE
36 College/Career Links Mgr ....Ms. Kristine PENIX
39 Director of Student Life ....Vacant
24 Director of Learning Center ....Ms. Rebecca E. WOLF
72 Director Advanced Tech/Allied Hlth ....Dr. Keith MCCLANAHAN
106 Director of Distance Learning ....Ms. Rhonda DURHAM
96 Dir Administrative Support Services ....Ms. Robin LANCASTER
12 Dir ASU-Beebe Degree Ctr at LRAFB . Ms. Nancy A. SHEFFLETTE
07 Director of Admissions ....Ms. Robin A. HAYES
35 Coordinator of Campus Life ....Mr. Andy ISOM
105 Website Coordinator ....Mr. Rikky L. FREE

*Arkansas State University-Jonesboro (J)

PO Box 600, State University AR 72467
County: Craighead FICE Identification: 001090
Unit ID: 106458
Telephone: (870) 972-2100 Carnegie Class: Masters/L
FAX Number: (870) 972-3465 Calendar System: Semester
URL: www.astate.edu
Established: 1909 Annual Undergrad Tuition & Fees (In-State): $8,050
Enrollment: 13,144 Coed
Affiliation or Control: State IRS Status: 501(c)3
Highest Offering: Doctorate
Accreditation: NH, ADNUR, ANEST, ART, BUS, #CAATE, CEA, CORE, DIETC, DMS, ENG, JOUR, MLTAD, MT, MUS, NUR, OTA, PTA, PTAA, RAD, RADMAG, RTT, SP, SPAA, SW, TED, THEA

02 Interim Chancellor ....Dr. Doug WHITLOCK
100 Chief of Staff ....Ms. Shawnie CARRIER
05 Provost & VC Acad Affair & Research ....Dr. Lynita COOKSEY
10 VC Finance & Administration ....Dr. Len T. FREY
32 Vice Chancellor Student Affairs ....Dr. William R. STRIPLING
30 Vice Chancellor Univ Advancement ....Dr. Jason PENRY
28 Asst Vice Chancellor Diversity ....Dr. Maurice GIPSON
41 Director of Athletics ....Mr. Terry MOHAJIR
20 Assoc Vice Chanc Academic Svcs ....Dr. Gina HOGUE
21 Assoc Vice Chancellor Finance ....Dr. Russ HANNAH
21 Asst Vice Chanc Budget ....Ms. Donna MCMILLIN
15 Asst VC Human Resources ....Ms. Lori WINN
35 Assoc Vice Chanc Student Affairs ....Dr. Lonnie R. WILLIAMS
46 Vice Provost Resrch & Grad Studies ....Dr. Andrew SUSTICH
35 Asst Vice Chanc Student Affairs ....Dr. Craig JOHNSON
13 Asst Vice Chanc/CIO ....Mr. Henry TORRES
18 Asst Vice Chancellor Facilities ....Mr. Al STOVERINK
37 Dir of Financial Aid & Scholarship ....Mr. Terry FINNEY
09 Dir Inst Research/Plng/Assessment ....Dr. Kathryn C. JONES
06 Dir Admissions/Records/Registration ....Ms. Tracy FINCH
07 Admissions/Records/Registration ......Mr. Christopher BOOTHMAN
39 Director of Residence Life ....Mr. Patrick DIXON
88 Director of Leadership Center ....Ms. Martha SPACK
19 Chief University Police ....Mr. Randy MARTIN
22 Director of Disability Services ....Dr. Jenifer RICE-MASON
36 Director Career Services ....Vacant
38 Director Counseling Center ....Dr. Phil HESTAND
23 Director Student Health Center ....Ms. Victoria WILLIAMS
29 Exec Dir Alumni Relations ....Ms. Beth SMITH
26 Exec Dir Mktg & Communications ....Dr. Bill SMITH
27 Director of Media Relations/Comm ....Ms. Gina BOWMAN
88 Director Pub & Creative Services ....Mr. Mark REEVES
96 Dir Procurement & Travel Svcs ....Ms. Carol BARNHILL
04 Admin Assistant to the Chancellor ....Ms. Julie WYATT
62 Dir Library ....Mr. Jeff BAILEY
47 Dean College Agri/Technology ....Dr. Timothy BURCHAM
81 Dean College Sciences & Math ....Dr. John PRATTE
50 Dean College of Business ....Dr. Shane HUNT
53 Dean Col of Educ & Behavioral Sci ....Dr. Gina HOGUE

60 Dean Humanities/Soc Sci/Media/Comm .... Dr. Brad RAWLINS
66 Dean College of Nursing Health Prof .... Dr. Susan N. HANRAHAN
88 Dean University College .... Dr. Jill SIMONS
57 Dean Fine Arts .... Dr. Donald BOWYER
92 Director of The Honors College .... Ms. Rebecca OLIVER
54 Interim Dean College of Engineering .... Dr. Paul MIXON

*Arkansas State University-Mid-South (A)

2000 W Broadway, West Memphis AR 72301-3829
County: Crittenden FICE Identification: 023482
Unit ID: 107318
Telephone: (870) 733-6722 Carnegie Class: Assoc/HVT-High Non
FAX Number: (870) 733-6799 Calendar System: Semester
URL: www.asumidsouth.edu
Established: 1992 Annual Undergrad Tuition & Fees (In-District): $2,554
Enrollment: 1,895 Coed
Affiliation or Control: State/Local IRS Status: 501(c)3
Highest Offering: Associate Degree
Accreditation: NH, #COARC

02 Chancellor .... Dr. Debra WEST
05 Sr Vice Chanc Learning/Instruction .... Dr. Cliff JONES
10 Vice Chanc Finance & Administration ..... Mrs. Susan MARSHALL
30 Vice Chanc Inst Advancement .... Ms. Diane HAMPTON
32 Vice Chanc Student Affairs .... Mr. Jeremy REECE
103 AVC Workforce Education .... Mr. Pete SELDEN
21 AVC Finance .... Ms. Karyn WEAVER
20 AVC Learning/Instruction .... Ms. Roshell COLEMAN
37 Director of Financial Aid .... Ms. Carol CARTER-PRIEST
08 Director of Library/Media Center .... Ms. Rene JONES
06 Registrar .... Ms. Leslie ANDERSON
15 Director of Human Resources .... Ms. Jackie LEECH
18 Director Facilities/Physical Plant .... Mr. Randy WEBB
84 AVC Enrollment Management .... Mr. John EASLEY
35 AVC Student Success .... Dr. Derek MOORE
13 Dir of Information Systems Tech .... Mr. Phillip MARSHALL
09 AVC Institutional Research .... Dr. Callie DUNAVIN
108 Dir of Institutional Effectiveness .... Ms. Michelle MCMILLEN
88 Dir of Learning Success Center .... Ms. Erin SCHLAUCH
04 Administrative Asst to Chancellor .... Ms. Deborah WEBB
19 Director Public Safety .... Mr. Ross PROCTOR
25 Chief Contracts/Grants Admin .... Ms. Sherri REID
41 Athletic Director .... Mr. Chris PARKER
44 Director of Development .... Ms. Elizabeth WILLIAMS
90 Instructional Tech Coordinator .... Ms. Melissa POWERS
96 Business Manager .... Ms. Wendy CRAWFORD

*Arkansas State University-Mountain Home (B)

1600 S College Street, Mountain Home AR 72653-5326
County: Baxter Identification: 666311
Unit ID: 420538
Telephone: (870) 508-6100 Carnegie Class: Assoc/MT-VT-High Non
FAX Number: (870) 508-6287 Calendar System: Semester
URL: www.asumh.edu
Established: 1995 Annual Undergrad Tuition & Fees (In-District): $2,736
Enrollment: 1,393 Coed
Affiliation or Control: State/Local IRS Status: 501(c)3
Highest Offering: Associate Degree
Accreditation: NH, EMT, FUSER

02 Chancellor .... Dr. Robin MYERS
05 Vice Chanc Academic Affairs .... Dr. Martin EGGENSPERGER
10 Vice Chanc Administrative Affairs .... Ms. Laura YARBROUGH
32 Vice Chancellor for Student Affairs .... Mrs. Rosalyn BLAGG
30 Vice Chancellor Development .... Vacant
88 Assoc VC Special Projects .... Mrs. Karen S. HOPPER
06 Registrar .... Vacant
18 Chief Facilities/Physical Plant .... Mr. Nickey L. ROBBINS
26 Director Comm & Inst Advancement .... Mrs. Christy C. KEIRN
35 Director Student Affairs .... Mr. Mason CAMPBELL
37 Director Student Financial Aid .... Mr. Clay BERRY
08 Director of Library .... Ms. Tina BRADLEY
09 Dir of Inst Research/Effectiveness .... Mr. David CULLIPHER

*Arkansas State University-Newport (C)

7648 Victory Boulevard, Newport AR 72112-8912
County: Jackson Identification: 666153
Unit ID: 440402
Telephone: (870) 512-7800 Carnegie Class: Assoc/HVT-High Non
FAX Number: (870) 512-7807 Calendar System: Semester
URL: www.asun.edu
Established: 1991 Annual Undergrad Tuition & Fees (In-State): $2,616
Enrollment: 2,477 Coed
Affiliation or Control: State IRS Status: Exempt
Highest Offering: Associate Degree
Accreditation: NH, SURGT

02 Chancellor .... Dr. Sandra MASSEY
04 Assistant to the Chancellor .... Ms. Laura KING
05 Vice Chancellor Academic Affairs .... Dr. Holly AYERS
10 Vice Chancellor Fiscal Affairs .... Mr. Adam ADAIR
32 Vice Chancellor Student Affairs .... Dr. Ashley BUCHMAN
103 Vice Chancellor Econ/Workforce Dev .... Mr. Charley APPLEBY
45 Vice Chanc Strategic Initiatives .... Mr. Jeff BOOKOUT
30 Dean Institutional Advancement .... Mr. Ike WHEELER
09 Dean of Institutional Effectiveness .... Dr. Allen MOONEYHAN
72 Dean for Applied Science .... Mr. Robert SUMMERS
97 Dean for General Education .... Mr. Joeseph CAMPBELL
84 Dean of Enrollment Services .... Ms. Candace GROSS
13 Director of IT Services .... Ms. Tamya STALLINGS
15 Director Human Resources .... Ms. Sara LONG
18 Director of Physical Plant .... Mr. David WINSTON
21 Controller .... Ms. Melissa WATSON
25 Dir Budget/Grants Management .... Ms. Monika PHILLIPS
37 Director Financial Aid .... Ms. Bonnie BURGOYNE
35 Dean of Students .... Ms. Kimberly LONG
08 Librarian .... Ms. Jennifer BALLARD
20 Director Academic Support Center .... Ms. Christy MANN
19 Public Safety Officer .... Mr. Jeff GRIZZLE
96 Director of Procurement .... Ms. Lee WEBB
66 Director of Nursing/Allied Health .... Ms. Crystal GILLIHAN
36 Director of Career Pathways .... Ms. Penny LOGAN
75 Adult Education Coordinator .... Ms. Martha TAUSSIG

*Arkansas State University-Heber Springs (D)

101 River Crest Drive, Heber Springs AR 72543
Telephone: (501) 362-1100 Identification: 770001
Accreditation: &NH

† Regional accreditation is carried under the parent institution in Beebe, AR

*Arkansas State University-Searcy (E)

1800 East Moncroe Avenue, Searcy AR 72143
Telephone: (501) 207-6200 Identification: 770002
Accreditation: &NH

† Regional accreditation is carried under the parent institution in Beebe, AR

Arkansas Tech University (F)

1509 North Boulder Avenue, Russellville AR 72801-2222
County: Pope FICE Identification: 001089
Unit ID: 106467
Telephone: (479) 968-0389 Carnegie Class: Masters/L
FAX Number: (479) 964-0522 Calendar System: Semester
URL: www.atu.edu
Established: 1909 Annual Undergrad Tuition & Fees (In-State): $6,192
Enrollment: 12,002 Coed
Affiliation or Control: State IRS Status: 501(c)3
Highest Offering: Doctorate
Accreditation: NH, BUS, CAHIIM, CORE, CS, EMT, ENG, JMC, MUS, NRPA, NUR, PTAA, TED

01 President .... Dr. Robin E. BOWEN
10 Vice Pres Administration/Finance .... Ms. Bernadette HINKLE
05 Vice Pres Academic Affairs .... Dr. Mohamed ABDELRAHMAN
32 VP Student Services/Univ Rels .... Ms. Susie S. NICHOLSON
30 Vice President Advancement .... Mr. Michael V. HUTCHISON
12 Chancellor Ozark Campus .... Mr. Bruce SIKES
20 Assoc Vice Pres Academic Affairs .... Dr. David UNDERWOOD
43 Associate VP & Counsel to President .Mr. Thomas PENNINGTON
88 Assoc VP University Initiatives .... Dr. Rick MASSENGALE
20 Assistant VP for Academic Affairs .... Dr. Hanna NORTON
84 Assistant VP Enrollment Management ... Ms. Shauna H. DONNELL
35 Chief Student Officer Ozark Campus .... Mr. Richard HARRIS
05 Chief Academic Officer Ozark Campus ...... Dr. Michael MURDERS
10 Chief Fiscal Officer Ozark Campus .... Ms. Sandra CHEFFER
100 Chief of Staff .... Dr. Jeff MOTT
06 Registrar .... Ms. Tammy WEAVER
88 Controller .... Ms. Donna RANKIN
08 Librarian .... Mr. Brent ETZEL
09 Director of Institutional Research .... Mr. Wyatt WATSON
13 Director Information Systems .... Mr. Ken WESTER
37 Director of Student Accounts .... Ms. Angela CROW
15 Interim Dir Human Resources .... Ms. Brooke SOUTHARD
37 Director Student Financial Aid .... Ms. Shirley M. GOINES
29 Director Alumni Relations .... Mr. Kelly DAVIS
85 Director of International Students .... Mr. Yasushi ONODERA
18 Director of Physical Plant Services .... Mr. Brian LASEY
96 Director of Purchasing .... Ms. Jessica HOLLOWAY
92 Director of Honors Program .... Dr. Jan JENKINS
22 Director of Affirmative Action .... Ms. Jennifer FLEMING
108 Dir Assessment/Inst Effectiveness .... Dr. Christine AUSTIN
58 Dean of Graduate College .... Dr. Mary GUNTER
53 Dean of College of Education .... Dr. Mary GUNTER
49 Dean College of Arts & Humanities .... Dr. Jeffrey WOODS
50 Dean of College of Business .... Dr. Edward BASHAW
77 Dn Col Engineering & Applied Sci .... Dr. Douglas BARLOW
81 Dean College of Natural & Health Sc .... Dr. Jeff ROBERTSON
102 Dir Foundation/Corporate Relations .... Ms. Debra FITHEN
105 Director Web Strategies/Operations .... Mr. Michael STOKER
19 Director Public Safety .... Mr. Josh MCMILLIAN
26 Director of University Relations .... Mr. Sam STRASNER
28 Assoc Dean Diversity & Inclusion .... Dr. MarTeze HAMMONDS
36 Director of Career Services .... Mr. Brandon WRIGHT
38 Assoc Dean Student Student Wellness .... Ms. Kristy DAVIS
39 Associate Dean Residence Life .... Mr. Aaron HOGAN
41 Athletic Director .... Mr. Steve MULLINS

Arkansas Tech University-Ozark Campus (G)

1700 Helberg Lane, Ozark AR 72949
Telephone: (866) 225-2884 Identification: 770003
Accreditation: &NH, CVT, EMT, MAC, OTA

† Regional accreditation is carried under the parent institution in Russellville, AR

Black River Technical College (H)

PO Box 468/1410 Hwy 304 East,
Pocahontas AR 72455-0468
County: Randolph FICE Identification: 020522
Unit ID: 106625
Telephone: (870) 248-4000 Carnegie Class: Assoc/MT-VT-Mix Trad/Non
FAX Number: (870) 248-4100 Calendar System: Semester
URL: www.blackrivertech.org
Established: 1991 Annual Undergrad Tuition & Fees (In-State): $2,832
Enrollment: 1,963 Coed
Affiliation or Control: State IRS Status: 501(c)3
Highest Offering: Associate Degree
Accreditation: NH, #COARC, DIETT, EMT

01 President .... Dr. Eric TURNER
05 Vice President General Education .... Dr. Roger JOHNSON
72 Vice President Technical Education .... Mrs. Angela CALDWELL
32 Vice President of Student Affairs .... Mrs. Martha NELSON
30 VP of Institutional Advancement .... Mrs. Karen LIEBHABER
10 Vice President for Finance .... Mrs. Rhonda STONE
37 Director of Financial Aid .... Mrs. Brandi CHESTER
06 Registrar .... Mrs. Kimberly BIGGER
04 Administrative Asst to President .... Mrs. Vickie FRENCH
08 Head Librarian .... Mrs. Anne SIMPSON
106 Dir Online Education/E-learning .... Mrs. Regina MOORE
15 Director Personnel Services .... Mrs. Julie EDINGTON
19 Director Security/Safety .... Mr. Tony SAYLORS
26 Chief Public Relations/Marketing .... Ms. Ann SAVAGE
96 Director of Purchasing .... Mr. Michael SMITH
13 Chief Info Technology Officer (CIO) .... Mr. Michael GREENE
18 Chief Facilities/Physical Plant .... Mr. Trent INGRAM
09 Director of Institutional Research .... Mr. Daniel PARKER
07 Director of Admissions .... Mrs. Angie FRENCH

Bryan University (I)

3704 West Walnut Street, Rogers AR 72756-1825
Telephone: (479) 899-6644 Identification: 666252
Accreditation: ACICS

† Branch campus of Bryan University, Springfield, MO.

Central Baptist College (J)

1501 College Avenue, Conway AR 72034-6470
County: Faulkner FICE Identification: 001093
Unit ID: 106713
Telephone: (501) 329-6872 Carnegie Class: Bac-Diverse
FAX Number: (501) 329-2941 Calendar System: Semester
URL: www.cbc.edu
Established: 1952 Annual Undergrad Tuition & Fees: $14,400
Enrollment: 858 Coed
Affiliation or Control: Baptist IRS Status: 501(c)3
Highest Offering: Baccalaureate
Accreditation: NH

01 President .... Mr. Terry KIMBROW
04 Admin Asst to President .... Mrs. Peggy PILLOW
05 VP for Academic Affairs .... Dr. Gary MCALLISTER
10 VP for Finance .... Mr. Paul CHERRY
30 VP for Advancement .... Mrs. Sancy FAULK
84 VP for Enrollment Mgmt .... Mr. Ryan JOHNSON
32 Assoc VP for Student Services .... Mrs. Rachel STEELE
06 Registrar .... Mrs. Stacy JORDAN
07 Director of Admissions .... Mr. Jason POOLE
19 Dean of Students/Campus Security .... Mr. Chris MITCHELL
08 Library Director .... Mrs. Rachel WHITTINGHAM
26 Director of Public Relations .... Mrs. Deanna OTT
37 Director of Financial Aid .... Mrs. Tonya HAMMONTREE
88 Director of Special Events .... Ms. Jessica FAULKNER
09 Dir of Institutional Effectiveness .... Mr. Steve ELDER
41 Athletic Director .... Mr. Lyle MIDDLETON
39 Director of Student Housing .... Mr. Michael MAYO
15 Director of Human Resources .... Ms. Pam TEAGUE
29 Alumni & Communications Officer .... Ms. Meagan LOWRY
88 Director of Military Relations .... Mr. Steven HALL
108 Director Institutional Assessment .... Mr. Dwain EAST
18 Director of Physical Plant .... Mr. Jerry CLIFTON
105 Director of Online Studies .... Mr. Chad LINN

College of the Ouachitas (K)

One College Circle, Malvern AR 72104-0816
County: Hot Spring FICE Identification: 009976
Unit ID: 107521
Telephone: (501) 337-5000 Carnegie Class: Assoc/HVT-High Non
FAX Number: (501) 337-9382 Calendar System: Semester
URL: www.coto.edu
Established: 1991 Annual Undergrad Tuition & Fees (In-State): $3,620
Enrollment: 1,444 Coed
Affiliation or Control: State IRS Status: 501(c)3
Highest Offering: Associate Degree
Accreditation: NH

01 President .... Dr. Steve ROOK
04 Administrative Asst to President .... Mrs. Jill HOULIHAN
05 Vice President of Instruction .... Mr. Pat SIMMS
32 Vice President Student Affairs .... Dr. Kim ARMSTRONG
10 Vice Pres Admin & Operations .... Mr. David SEE
30 Exec Dir College Advancement .... Ms. Amber CHILDERS
103 Exec Dir Planning & Assessment .... Ms. Carla CRUTCHFIELD

20 Dean of Learning ... Ms. Tricia BAAR
76 Dean of Health Sciences ... Ms. Melinda SANDERS
88 Director Adult Education ... Mrs. Brenda KEISLER
08 Director Learning Resources ... Ms. Mary Ann HARPER
75 Director Career & Technical Studies ... Mr. Mike DINGLER
92 Director Honors College ... Mrs. Tricia BAAR
60 Director Concurrent Enrollment ... Mrs. Terri COLANANNI
37 Director of Financial Aid ... Ms. Vickie YOUNG
36 Director Career Pathways ... Ms. Johnnie MITCHELL
88 Dir TRIO Student Support Services ... Ms. Vergina SMITH
35 Interim Director Student Success ... Ms. Janet HUNT
06 Director of Admissions/Registrar ... Ms. Keesha JOHNSON
21 Controller ... Ms. Anita MARTGIN
15 Human Resources ... Mrs. Kori CLAYTON
16 Interim Director IT ... Mr. Kee KRATZ

Crowley's Ridge College (A)

100 College Drive, Paragould AR 72450-9775
County: Greene FICE Identification: 001095
Unit ID: 106810
Telephone: (870) 236-6901 Carnegie Class: Bac/Assoc-Mixed
FAX Number: (870) 236-7748 Calendar System: Semester
URL: www.crc.edu
Established: 1964 Annual Undergrad Tuition & Fees: $11,900
Enrollment: 224 Coed
Affiliation or Control: Churches Of Christ IRS Status: 501(c)3
Highest Offering: Baccalaureate
Accreditation: NH

01 President ... Mr. Ken HOPPE
05 Vice President for Academic Affairs ... Dr. Rob WILLIAMS
32 Vice President for Student Affairs ... Mr. Art SMITH
30 Vice President for Advancement ... Mr. Richard JOHNSON
06 Registrar ... Mr. Paul MCFADDEN
37 Director Student Financial Services ... Mr. David W. GOFF
26 Director Public Information ... Mrs. Andrea JOHNSON
07 Director Admissions ... Mr. Chris HUGHES
41 Athletic Director/Campus Minister ... Mr. Paul MCFADDEN
08 Director Learning Center ... Mr. Mark WARNICK
10 Business Office Manager ... Mrs. Sonia JOHNSON
13 Director of Information Services ... Mr. Larry JOHNSON

East Arkansas Community College (B)

1700 Newcastle Road, Forrest City AR 72335-2204
County: Saint Francis FICE Identification: 012260
Unit ID: 106883
Telephone: (870) 633-4480 Carnegie Class: Assoc/HT-High Non
FAX Number: (870) 633-7222 Calendar System: Semester
URL: www.eacc.edu
Established: 1974 Annual Undergrad Tuition & Fees (In-District): $2,790
Enrollment: 1,268 Coed
Affiliation or Control: State/Local IRS Status: 501(c)3
Highest Offering: Associate Degree
Accreditation: NH, ADNUR, EMT

01 President ... Dr. Coy F. GRACE
05 Vice President Academic Affairs ... Dr. Janie BAILEY
10 Vice President Business Affairs ... Mr. Richard STIPE
32 Vice President Student Affairs ... Mrs. Catherine T. COLEMAN
37 Director Student Financial Aid ... Vacant
88 Assoc VP for Applied Sciences ... Mrs. Joanne LAWSON
88 AVP for Community/Business Outreach ... Mrs. Tiffany BILLINGSLEY
97 Assoc VP for General Studies ... Dr. Cathie CLINE
08 Director Library Services ... Mrs. Paige LAWS
84 Director Enrollment Management ... Mrs. Sharon COLLIER
26 Director of Public Relations/Mktg ... Mrs. Lindsay MIDKIFF
15 Director of Human Resources ... Mrs. Yvonne RUCKER-FRANKLIN
18 Director Physical Plant ... Mr. Glenn FORD
35 Assoc VP for Student Affairs ... Mrs. Michelle WILSON
96 Purchasing Specialist ... Mrs. Susan GUEST
88 Title III Project Manager ... Mr. Christopher A. HEIGLE
51 Director of Continuing Education ... Mrs. Kara DOSS

Ecclesia College (C)

9653 Nations Drive, Springdale AR 72762-8159
County: Benton FICE Identification: 038553
Unit ID: 446233
Telephone: (479) 248-7236 Carnegie Class: Spec-4-yr-Faith
FAX Number: (479) 248-1455 Calendar System: Semester
URL: www.ecollege.edu
Established: 1975 Annual Undergrad Tuition & Fees: $15,140
Enrollment: 164 Coed
Affiliation or Control: Independent Non-Profit IRS Status: 501(c)3
Highest Offering: Master's
Accreditation: BI

01 President ... Mr. Oren PARIS, III
05 Academic Dean ... Dr. Robert HEADRICK
10 Business Office Manager ... Ms. Shannon NEWMAN
32 Dean of Students ... Mr. Jesse E. WADKINS
30 Director of Financial Development ... Mr. Mike NOVAK
26 Director of Communications ... Ms. Angie P. SNYDER
37 Director Student Financial Aid ... Mr. Tommy STRINGFELLOW
41 Athletic Director ... Mr. Dean SKINNER
06 Registrar ... Mrs. Donna BROWN
08 Head Librarian ... Mrs. Joanne CAMPBELL
103 Director Work/Learning/Service Pgms ... Mr. Jesse E. WADKINS
07 Director of Admissions ... Mr. Chad HOWARD
04 Administrative Asst to President ... Mrs. Elizabeth NEWLUN
18 Chief Facilities/Physical Plant ... Mr. Dennis HAGGARD
106 Director Distance Education ... Vacant
39 Director Student Housing ... Ms. Kathrynn FINK

Harding University Main Campus (D)

915 E. Market Avenue, Searcy AR 72149-5615
County: White FICE Identification: 001097
Unit ID: 107044
Telephone: (501) 279-4000 Carnegie Class: Masters/L
FAX Number: (501) 279-4600 Calendar System: Semester
URL: www.harding.edu
Established: 1924 Annual Undergrad Tuition & Fees: $17,805
Enrollment: 6,059 Coed
Affiliation or Control: Churches Of Christ IRS Status: 501(c)3
Highest Offering: Doctorate
Accreditation: NH, ACBSP, ARCPA, #CAATE, CACREP, CIDA, DIETD, ENG, MUS, NUR, PHAR, PTA, SP, SW, TED

01 President ... Dr. Bruce D. MCLARTY
03 Executive Vice President ... Dr. David COLLINS
05 Provost ... Dr. Marty SPEARS
88 Senior Vice President ... Dr. James W. CARR
10 Vice President Finance ... Dr. Mel SANSOM
30 Vice President Advancement ... Dr. Bryan BURKS
42 Vice President of Church Relations ... Dr. Dan WILLIAMS
13 VP Information Systems & Technology ... Mr. Keith CRONK
41 Athletic Director ... Mr. Greg HARNDEN
29 VP of Alumni Relations ... Mrs. Liz HOWELL
20 Assistant Provost for Accreditation .. Dr. Julie HIXSON-WALLACE
88 Dean College of Bible & Ministry ... Dr. Monte COX
92 Dean of Honors College ... Dr. Mike JAMES
50 Dean College of Business ... Dr. Al FRAZIER
53 Dean College of Education ... Dr. Donny LEE
66 Dean College of Nursing ... Dr. Susan KEHL
79 Dean College of Arts & Humanities ... Dr. Warren CASEY
81 Dean College of Sciences ... Dr. Travis THOMPSON
76 Dean College of Allied Health ... Dr. Beckie WEAVER
88 Dean of International Programs ... Dr. Jeffrey HOPPER
84 Asst VP Enrollment Management ... Mr. Glenn DILLARD
21 Asst VP Finance ... Mrs. Tammy HALL
32 Asst VP Student Life/Dean Students ... Mr. Zach NEAL
88 Asst VP of IS&T ... Mr. Mike CHALENBURG
06 Registrar ... Mr. Tod MARTIN
38 Director of Counseling ... Dr. Lew MOORE
19 Director Security/Safety ... Mr. Craig RUSSELL
26 VP of Communication ... Mrs. Jana RUCKER
37 Director Student Financial Aid ... Dr. Jonathan ROBERTS
58 Director of Graduate Studies ... Vacant
08 Librarian ... Mrs. Jean WALDROP
18 Chief Facilities/Physical Plant ... Mr. Danny DERAMUS
15 Director Personnel Services ... Mr. David ROSS
36 Director Student Placement ... Mr. Butch GARDNER
09 Director of Institutional Research ... Mr. Dustin HOWELL
96 Purchasing Coordinator ... Mrs. Shelly MATHEWS
35 Assistant Dean of Students ... Mr. Brandon TITTLE
35 Assistant Dean of Students ... Mrs. Kara ABSTON
35 Assistant Dean of Students ... Mrs. Ranan HESTER
35 Assistant Dean of Students ... Mr. Chad JOICE
28 Director of Diversity ... Mrs. Tiffany BYERS
39 Director Student Housing ... Mrs. Kathy ALLEN
07 Director of Admissions ... Mr. Glenn DILLARD

Henderson State University (E)

1100 Henderson Street, Arkadelphia AR 71999-0001
County: Clark FICE Identification: 001098
Unit ID: 107071
Telephone: (870) 230-5000 Carnegie Class: Masters/M
FAX Number: (870) 230-5144 Calendar System: Semester
URL: www.hsu.edu
Established: 1890 Annual Undergrad Tuition & Fees (In-State): $8,100
Enrollment: 3,627 Coed
Affiliation or Control: State IRS Status: 501(c)3
Highest Offering: Beyond Master's But Less Than Doctorate
Accreditation: NH, BUS, #CAATE, CACREP, DIETD, MUS, NURSE, TED

01 President ... Dr. Glendell JONES
05 Provost/VPAA ... Dr. Steve ADKISON
10 Vice Pres Finance & Administration ... Mr. Brett POWELL
32 VP Student Services/External Affair ... Dr. Lewis A. SHEPHERD, JR.
30 VP Advancement/Exec Dir Found ... Ms. Jennifer BOYETT
43 General Counsel ... Ms. Elaine KNEEBONE
35 Asst VP/Dean of Students ... Mr. Chad FIELDING
39 Asst VP/Director of Residence Life ... Vacant
13 Director Computer/Communication Svc ... Vacant
29 Director of Development & Alumni ... Ms. Carrie ROBERSON
41 Director Athletics ... Mr. Shawn JONES
26 Exec Director of Marketing/Comm ... Ms. Tonya OAKS SMITH
49 Dean Ellis Col Arts/Sciences ... Dr. John HARDEE
50 Dean of School of Business ... Dr. Marc MILLER
53 Dean Teachers College Henderson ... Dr. Judy HARRISON
58 Dean of Graduate School ... Dr. Kenneth TAYLOR
06 Registrar ... Mr. Tom GATTIN
08 Director Huie Library ... Ms. Lea Ann ALEXANDER
15 Director of Human Resources ... Ms. Kathy TAYLOR
19 Director of University Police ... Mr. Jonathan CAMPBELL
38 Dir Student Health/Counseling Ctr ... Ms. Deborah COLLINS
07 Director Univ Relations/Admissions ... Ms. Vikita B. HARDWRICK
37 Director of Financial Aid ... Vacant
92 Director of Honors College ... Dr. David T. THOMSON
88 Director of Student Research ... Dr. David BATEMAN
96 Director of Purchasing ... Mr. Tim JONES
24 Dir Multi Media Learning Center ... Ms. Jennifer HOLBROOK
85 Director International Students ... Dr. Drew SMITH

Hendrix College (F)

1600 Washington Avenue, Conway AR 72032-3080
County: Faulkner FICE Identification: 001099
Unit ID: 107080
Telephone: (501) 329-6811 Carnegie Class: Bac-A&S
FAX Number: (501) 450-1200 Calendar System: Semester
URL: www.hendrix.edu
Established: 1876 Annual Undergrad Tuition & Fees: $40,870
Enrollment: 1,358 Coed
Affiliation or Control: United Methodist IRS Status: 501(c)3
Highest Offering: Master's
Accreditation: NH, MUS, TED

01 President ... Dr. William M. TSUTSUI
04 Executive Assistant to President ... Ms. Donna PLEMMONS
88 VP for Strategic Initiatives/Chief ... Ms. Courtney Lee CORWIN
30 Sr Exec Vice Pres/Dean Inst Advance ... Mr. W. Ellis ARNOLD, III
05 Provost ... Dr. Terri BONEBRIGHT
26 Vice Pres Marketing Communications ... Ms. Helen PLOTKIN
10 Executive Vice President and CFO ... Mr. Tom SIEBENMORGEN
84 Vice Pres for Enrollment ... Ms. Karen R. FOUST
15 Vice Pres for Human Resources ... Ms. Vicki LYNN
18 VP Operations/Facilities ... Mr. Skip HARTSELL
32 Exec VP Student Affs/Dean of Stdnts ... Mr. Jim WILTGEN, JR.
27 Assoc VP Marketing Communications ... Mr. Rob O'CONNOR
06 Registrar ... Ms. Brenda ADAMS
08 Director of Libraries ... Ms. Britt Anne MURPHY
13 VP Technology/Chief Info Officer ... Mr. Sam NICHOLS
29 Director Alumni Relations ... Ms. Pamela OWEN
37 Director of Financial Aid ... Ms. Kristina BURFORD
40 Bookstore Manager ... Ms. Dee Dee ALLEN
79 Area Head/Humanities ... Dr. Alex VERNON
81 Area Head/Natural Sciences ... Dr. Matt MORAN
83 Area Head/Social Sciences ... Dr. Leslie TEMPLETON
42 Interim Chaplain ... Rev. J.J WHITNEY
07 Director of Admission ... Mr. Fred BAKER
20 Associate Academic Officer ... Dr. David SUTHERLAND
21 Associate Business Officer ... Mr. Shawn MATHIS
36 Assistant Director Career Services ... Ms. Jamie FOTIOO
38 Director Student Counseling ... Ms. Mary Anne SIEBERT
09 Director of Institutional Research ... Mr. Randy PETERSON
28 Director of Diversity ... Dr. Dionne JACKSON

Jefferson Regional Medical Center School of Nursing (G)

1600 W. 40th Avenue, Pine Bluff AR 71603
County: Jefferson FICE Identification: 023308
Telephone: (870) 541-7850 Carnegie Class: Not Classified
FAX Number: (870) 541-7807 Calendar System: Semester
URL: www.jrmc.org
Established: 1981 Annual Undergrad Tuition & Fees: N/A
Enrollment: N/A Coed
Affiliation or Control: Independent Non-Profit IRS Status: 501(c)3
Highest Offering: Associate Degree
Accreditation: ABHES, PAST

01 Director ... Ms. Kathy PIERCE
06 Registrar ... Ms. Lucy MULLIGAN

John Brown University (H)

2000 W University Street, Siloam Springs AR 72761-2121
County: Benton FICE Identification: 001100
Unit ID: 107141
Telephone: (479) 524-9500 Carnegie Class: Masters/M
FAX Number: (479) 524-7278 Calendar System: Semester
URL: www.jbu.edu
Established: 1919 Annual Undergrad Tuition & Fees: $24,468
Enrollment: 2,850 Coed
Affiliation or Control: Independent Non-Profit IRS Status: 501(c)3
Highest Offering: Master's
Accreditation: NH, ACBSP, CONST, ENG, TED

01 President ... Dr. Charles POLLARD
10 Vice Pres Finance & Administration ... Dr. Kim HADLEY
84 Vice Pres Enrollment Management ... Mr. Donald W. CRANDALL
30 Vice Pres of University Advancement ... Dr. Jim KRALL
32 Vice Pres for Student Development ... Dr. Stephen T. BEERS
05 VP Academic Affairs/Dean of Faculty ... Dr. Ed ERICSON, III
88 Dean Degree Completion Program ... Dr. Stacey DUKE
42 Campus Pastor/Assoc Dean of Stdnts ... Dr. Rod REED
06 Registrar ... Dr. Rebecca LAMBERT
21 Controller ... Mr. Tom PERRY
13 Chief Information Systems Ofcr ... Mr. Paul NAST
18 Director of Facilities Services ... Mr. Steve BRANKLE
44 Director of Planned Giving ... Mr. Eric GREENHAW
08 Director of Library ... Mr. Brent SWEARINGEN
85 Director International Programs ... Mr. Bill STEVENSON
29 Director of Alumni/Parent Relations ... Vacant
37 Assoc Director of Financial Aid ... Mr. David BURNEY
07 Director of Admissions ... Mr. Kent SHAFFER
41 Athletic Director ... Ms. Robyn DAUGHERTY
38 Director of Counseling ... Dr. Tim DINGER
04 Administrative Asst to President ... Ms. Kory J. DALE

Lyon College (A)

PO Box 2317, Batesville AR 72503-2317
County: Independence FICE Identification: 001088
Unit ID: 106342
Telephone: (870) 307-7000 Carnegie Class: Bac-A&S
FAX Number: (870) 307-7001 Calendar System: Semester
URL: www.lyon.edu
Established: 1872 Annual Undergrad Tuition & Fees: $25,280
Enrollment: 712 Coed
Affiliation or Control: Presbyterian Church (U.S.A.) IRS Status: 501(c)3
Highest Offering: Baccalaureate
Accreditation: NH, TED

01 President .... Dr. Donald V. WEATHERMAN
05 Provost .... Dr. Philip CAVALIER
10 Vice President Business & Finance .... Mr. John D. JONES
11 Vice Pres for Administration .... Mr. Joshau MANNING
32 Vice President Student Life .... Dr. Patrick MULICK
30 VP Institutional Advancement .... Mrs. Ann TURNEY
07 Director of Admissions .... Mr. Donald R. TAYLOR
08 Director Library .... Vacant
26 Dir of Marketing and Communications .... Mr. Eric BORK
29 Executive Dir of Advancement .... Mrs. Gina GARRETT
15 Director of Administration and HR .... Mrs. Clarinda L. FOOTE
37 Director of Financial Assistance .... Mr. Tommy TUCKER
36 Director Career Development .... Mrs. Annettee CASTLEBERRY
13 Director Information Services .... Mr. Josh KEMP
41 Director of Athletics .... Mr. Kevin JENKINS
42 Chaplain .... Rev. Ray MCCALLA
53 Int Director of Teacher Education .... Ms. Kim CROSBY
38 Director Student Counseling .... Ms. Diane ELLIS
18 Director Security .... Mr. Donald HUTCHINS
40 Director Bookstore .... Mrs. Donna GLASCOCK
08 Head Librarian .... Ms. Kathy WHITTENTON
23 Director of Health Services .... Mrs. LuAnn BAKER
18 Chief Facilities/Physical Plant .... Vacant
20 Associate Academic Officer .... Dr. Anthony GRAFTON
06 Registrar .... Mrs. Tami HALL

National Park College (B)

101 College Drive,
Hot Springs National Park AR 71913-9174
County: Garland FICE Identification: 012105
Unit ID: 106980
Telephone: (501) 760-4222 Carnegie Class: Assoc/HT-Mix Trad/Non
FAX Number: (501) 760-4100 Calendar System: Semester
URL: www.np.edu
Established: 1973 Annual Undergrad Tuition & Fees (In-District): $3,200
Enrollment: 3,001 Coed
Affiliation or Control: State/Local IRS Status: 501(c)3
Highest Offering: Associate Degree
Accreditation: NH, ADNUR, CAHIIM, #COARC, EMT, MLTAD, RAD

01 President .... Dr. John HOGAN
05 Vice Pres Academic Affairs .... Dr. Wade DERDEN
10 Vice Pres Finance & Admin .... Mr. Steve TRUSTY
32 Vice Pres Student Affairs .... Dr. Jerry THOMAS
26 Vice Pres External Relations .... Mr. Jeff WEAVER
103 Vice Pres Workforce Initiatives .... Ms. Kelli ALBRECHT
21 Assoc Vice Pres Business & Tech .... Mr. David HUGHES
15 Assoc Vice Pres Human Resources .... Ms. Janet BREWER
35 Dean of Students .... Mr. John TUCKER
07 Dean of Enrollment Services .... Mr. Jason HUDNELL
08 Director of Library Services .... Ms. Sara SEAMAN
37 Director of Financial Aid .... Ms. Lisa HOPPER
30 Director of Development .... Ms. Sara BROWN
06 Registrar .... Ms. Ana HUNT
100 Chief of Staff .... Ms. Darla THURBER
13 Chief Info Technology Officer (CIO) .... Mr. Blake BUTLER

North Arkansas College (C)

1515 Pioneer Drive, Harrison AR 72601-5599
County: Boone FICE Identification: 012261
Unit ID: 107460
Telephone: (870) 743-3000 Carnegie Class: Assoc/MT-VT-High Trad
FAX Number: (870) 391-3250 Calendar System: Semester
URL: www.northark.edu
Established: 1974 Annual Undergrad Tuition & Fees (In-District): $2,040
Enrollment: 1,976 Coed
Affiliation or Control: State/Local IRS Status: 501(c)3
Highest Offering: Associate Degree
Accreditation: NH, ACBSP, ADNUR, EMT, MLTAD, RAD, SURGT

01 President .... Dr. Randy ESTERS
05 Exec Vice President of Learning .... Vacant
10 Vice Pres Finance & Administration .... Mr. Donald SUGG
30 Vice Pres Institutional Advancement .... Dr. Rodney ARNOLD
04 Executive Assistant to President .... Mrs. Trish VILLINES
49 Dean Arts & Science/Business & IT .... Dr. Laura BERRY
66 Dean Nursing/Allied Hlth/Tech Pgms .... Mrs. Cindy MAYO
31 Dean of Outreach .... Mrs. Nell BONDS
08 Interim Director of Libraries .... Mrs. Michelle PALMER
44 Dir Institutional Effectiveness .... Mrs. Katherine VAUGHN
32 Interim VP of Student Success .... Mrs. Tavonda BROWN
41 Athletic Director .... Mrs. Stacie KLOTT
15 Director Human Resources .... Mrs. Kris GREENING
18 Chief Facilities/Physical Plant .... Mr. Kevin SOMERS
96 Director of Purchasing .... Mrs. Shari HOLT
37 Director Student Financial Aid .... Mrs. Jennifer HADDOCK
06 Registrar .... Mrs. Charla JENNINGS
07 Director of Admissions .... Mr. Randy SCAGGS
26 Director of Public Relations .... Mrs. Micki SOMERS
90 Director Academic Computing .... Mr. Rick WILLIAMS
91 Director Administrative Computing .... Mr. Glenn COLMAN
31 Director of Community Education .... Mrs. Amy BELL

NorthWest Arkansas Community College (D)

1 College Drive, Bentonville AR 72712-5091
County: Benton FICE Identification: 030633
Unit ID: 367459
Telephone: (479) 636-9222 Carnegie Class: Assoc/HT-Mix Trad/Non
FAX Number: (479) 619-4335 Calendar System: Semester
URL: www.nwacc.edu
Established: 1989 Annual Undergrad Tuition & Fees (In-District): $3,208
Enrollment: 8,098 Coed
Affiliation or Control: State/Local IRS Status: 501(c)3
Highest Offering: Associate Degree
Accreditation: NH, ACBSP, ACFEI, CAHIIM, COARC, EMT, IFSAC, PTAA

01 President .... Dr. Evelyn E. JORGENSON
10 VP of Finance & Administration .... Ms. Debi BUCKLEY
05 Vice Pres for Learning .... Dr. Ricky TOMPKINS
32 VP of Student Services .... Dr. Todd KITCHEN
36 VP of Career & Workforce Education .... Mr. Tim CORNELIUS
103 Dean of Workforce Development .... Mr. Keith PETERSON
13 AVP IT/Chief Information Officer .... Mr. Jason DEGN
88 Dir Retail & Supplier Education .... Ms. Teresa WARREN
11 Executive Director of Operations .... Mr. Jack THOMPSON
51 Dean of Adult Education .... Mr. Ben ALDAMA
35 Dean of Students .... Mr. Dale MONTGOMERY
06 Dean of Learner Success & Registrar .... Ms. Brooke HOLT
30 Executive Director of Development .... Dr. Meredith BRUNEN
84 Exec Dir High School Relations .... Dr. Diana JOHNSON
26 Exec Director of Public Relations .... Mr. Steven HINDS
86 Exec Dir Community/Government Rels .... Mr. Jim HALL
21 Assistant Controller .... Mr. John HIXSON
21 Dir Budget/Fin Analysis/Reporting .... Ms. Gulizar BAGGSON
15 Exec Director of Human Resources .... Ms. Wendi CADLE
106 Director of Distance Learning .... Dr. Kate BURKES
50 Exec Dir of Business Development .... Ms. Teresa WHITMIRE
88 Coordinator of Building Sciences .... Mr. Mike DEWBERRY
88 Director of Learning Resources .... Ms. Gwen DOBBS
25 Exec Dir Effectiveness & Grants .... Dr. Lisa ANDERSON
88 Associate Dean Student Success .... Ms. Tay Sha CARTER
07 Director of Admissions/Advising .... Mr. Zach PHARR
37 Director Student Financial Aid .... Ms. Michelle CORDELL
88 Director Academic Success Center .... Mr. Eric VEST
28 Ethics & Compliance Officer .Ms. Teresa TAYLOR WILLIAMSON
109 Dir Food Services/Event Management .... Ms. Diane BOSS
09 Institutional Research Manager .... Ms. Kim PURDY
18 Director of Physical Plant .... Mr. Jim NELSON
88 Coordinator Culinary & Hospitality .... Ms. Dade HAMM
77 Dean for Bus Computer Information .... Dr. Christine DAVIS
76 Dean of Health Professions .... Vacant
04 Administrative Asst to President .... Ms. Lindsey WHITE
19 Exec Director Policy/Risk & Comp .... Mr. Ethan BECKCOM
44 Planned Giving Officer .... Ms. Jean ANDERSON

Ouachita Baptist University (E)

410 Ouachita Street, Arkadelphia AR 71998-0001
County: Clark FICE Identification: 001102
Unit ID: 107512
Telephone: (870) 245-5000 Carnegie Class: Bac-A&S
FAX Number: (870) 245-5500 Calendar System: Semester
URL: www.obu.edu
Established: 1886 Annual Undergrad Tuition & Fees: $24,120
Enrollment: 1,501 Coed
Affiliation or Control: Southern Baptist IRS Status: 501(c)3
Highest Offering: Baccalaureate
Accreditation: NH, BUS, DIETD, MUS, TED

01 President .... Dr. Ben R. SELLS
44 Vice Pres Institutional Advancement .... Dr. Keldon HENLEY
05 Vice President Academic Affairs .... Dr. Stan POOLE
10 Chief Financial Officer .... Mr. Jason TOLBERT
32 Vice Pres for Student Development .... Dr. Wesley KLUCK
30 Vice President for Development .... Mrs. Terry G. PEEPLES
26 Vice Pres for Communications .... Mr. Trennis HENDERSON
04 Asst to President/Administration .... Mr. Philip W. HARDIN
07 Director of Admissions Counseling .... Mrs. Lori MOTL
09 Director of Institutional Research .... Mr. Phil HARDIN
15 Director of Human Resources .... Mrs. Sherri PHELPS
18 Chief Facilities/Physical Plant .... Mr. John HARDMAN
29 Director of Alumni Relations .... Mr. Jon MERRYMAN
35 Dean of Students .... Dr. Scott HAYNES
20 Assoc Vice Pres Academic Affairs .... Dr. Doug REED
36 Director of Career Services .... Mrs. Rachel JONES
38 University Counselor .... Mr. Dan JARBOE
08 Librarian .... Dr. Ray GRANADE
06 Registrar/Director of Admissions .... Mrs. Susan ATKINSON
37 Director Student Financial Svcs .... Mrs. Susan HURST
96 Director of Purchasing .... Mrs. Heather MOORE
92 Director Honors Program .... Dr. Barbara PEMBERTON
13 Asst to Pres for Info Tech Svcs .... Mr. Bill PHELPS
39 Director of Housing .... Ms. Stacey PERRY
41 Athletic Director .... Mr. David SHARP
43 General Counsel .... Mr. Bryan MCKINNEY
21 Director of Financial Services .... Mr. Jason TOLBERT
40 Bookstore Manager .... Ms. Beverly DICKERSON
57 Dean of School of Fine Arts .... Dr. Gary GERBER
50 Dean of the School of Business .... Mr. Bryan MCKINNEY
53 Dean Sch of Interdisciplinary Stds .... Dr. Stan POOLE
73 Dean School of Christian Studies .... Dr. Danny HAYS
53 Interim Dean School of Education .... Dr. Jeff ROOT
79 Dean School of Humanities .... Dr. Jeff ROOT
81 Dean School of Natural Sciences .... Dr. Tim KNIGHT
83 Dean School of Social Sciences .... Dr. Randall WIGHT

Ozarka College (F)

PO Box 10, Melbourne AR 72556-0010
County: Izard FICE Identification: 020870
Unit ID: 107549
Telephone: (870) 368-7371 Carnegie Class: Assoc/MT-VT-Mix Trad/Non
FAX Number: (870) 368-2091 Calendar System: Semester
URL: www.ozarka.edu
Established: 1991 Annual Undergrad Tuition & Fees (In-State): $2,776
Enrollment: 1,326 Coed
Affiliation or Control: State IRS Status: 501(c)3
Highest Offering: Associate Degree
Accreditation: NH

01 President .... Dr. Richard L. DAWE
05 Executive Vice Pres & Provost .... Dr. Keith MCCLANAHAN
10 Vice President of Finance .... Ms. Tina WHEELIS
11 Vice President of Administration .... Mr. Jason LAWRENCE
32 Vice President of Student Services .... Mr. Josh WILSON
45 Assoc Vice President of Planning/IR .... Ms. Deltha SHELL
13 Chief Information Officer .... Mr. Scott PINKSTON
04 Executive Asst to the President .... Ms. Tess WEATHERFORD
30 Director of College Advancement .... Ms. Suellen DAVIDSON
29 Development Officer/Dir Alumni Rels .... Vacant
37 Director of Financial Aid .... Ms. Laura LAWRENCE
07 Director of Admissions .... Vacant
06 Registrar .... Mrs. Zeda WILKERSON
26 Dir Public Relations/Marketing .... Ms. Manda JACKSON
21 Business Manager .... Ms. Amber RUSH

Philander Smith College (G)

900 W. Daisy L. Gatson Bates Drive,
Little Rock AR 72202-3799
County: Pulaski FICE Identification: 001103
Unit ID: 107600
Telephone: (501) 375-9845 Carnegie Class: Bac-A&S
FAX Number: (501) 370-5277 Calendar System: Semester
URL: www.philander.edu
Established: 1877 Annual Undergrad Tuition & Fees: $12,564
Enrollment: 567 Coed
Affiliation or Control: United Methodist IRS Status: 501(c)3
Highest Offering: Baccalaureate
Accreditation: NH, ACBSP, SW, TED

01 President .... Dr. Roderick L. SMOTHERS, SR.
04 Admin Assistant to the President .... Mrs. Raveen JOB
05 VP of Academic Affairs .... Dr. Hazel ERVIN
10 Vice President for Fiscal Affairs .... Mr. Terry WALLACE
32 Interim VP of Student Affairs .... Mr. David LEWIS
30 Interim VP Inst Advancement .... Mrs. Sercia COLE
108 VP of Institutional Effectiveness .... Dr. Annie WILLIAMS
20 Assoc VP Academic Affairs .... Dr. Zollie STEPHENSON
100 Executive VP to President .... Dr. Darnell WILLIAMS
06 Registrar .... Ms. Bertha OWENS
21 Controller .... Ms. LaTonya HAYES
42 Chaplain/Dean of Religious Life .... Rev. Ronnie MILLER-YOW
35 Dean of Students/Residential Life .... Mr. Kevin HAMILTON
15 Exec Director of Human Resources .... Mr. Christopher NEWTON
37 Director of Financial Aid .... Ms. Kisa HINTON
18 Director of Physical Plant .... Mr. Robert YOUNG
26 Director Marketing/Public Relations .... Mrs. Jenelle PRIMM
88 Executive Director of WISE-P3 .... Mr. Glenn SARGEANT
07 Director of Admissions/Enroll Mgmt .... Mr. Maurice OSBORNE
08 Director of the Library .... Ms. Teresa OJEZUA
84 Interim VP of Enrollment Management .... Mr. David LEWIS
29 Director of Alumni Relations .... Ms. Yvonne ALEXANDER
41 Interim Athletic Director .... Mr. Brandon GREENWOOD
13 Director Computer Information Sys .... Mr. Brian CLAY
09 Director of Institutional Research .... Vacant
19 Chief of Security .... Ms. Jennifer LUSK
51 Dir of Continuing Education (PSMI) .... Mr. Bruce JAMES
88 Kendall Mission Center Director .... Dr. Cynthia BURROUGHS
40 Bookstore Manager .... Mr. Alvin HARRIS
17 Campus Nurse .... Ms. Martie SAVAGE
88 Dean of Campus Culture .... Mr. Ronnie MILLER-YOW
49 Div Chair Natural/Physical Sciences .... Dr. Samar SWAID
50 Div Chair of Business/Economics .... Dr. Kathryn DAVIS
53 Division Chair of Education .... Dr. Lloyd HERVEY
70 Director of Social Work .... Dr. Daniel EGBE
79 Div Chair Humanities .... Dr. Lia STEELE-MARCELL
83 Div Chair Social Sciences .... Dr. Daniel EGBE
38 Director Student Counseling .... Mrs. LaTisha JACKSON
39 Director Student Housing .... Mr. Waylon METOYER

Pulaski Technical College (H)

3000 W Scenic Drive, North Little Rock AR 72118-3399
County: Pulaski FICE Identification: 020753
Unit ID: 107664
Telephone: (501) 812-2200 Carnegie Class: Assoc/MT-VT-High Trad
FAX Number: (501) 771-2844 Calendar System: Semester
URL: www.pulaskitech.edu
Established: 1991 Annual Undergrad Tuition & Fees (In-State): $4,332

Enrollment: 9,241 Coed
Affiliation or Control: State IRS Status: 501(c)3
Highest Offering: Associate Degree
Accreditation: NH, ACFEI, COARC, DA, OTA

01 President ... Dr. Margaret ELLIBEE
05 Executive Vice President/Provost ... Mr. Michael DELONG
20 Vice President for Learning ... Vacant
32 Vice President for Student Services ... Ms. Kelly OWENS
10 Vice President for Finance ... Vacant
30 VP for Economic Development ... Mr. Bentley WALLACE
20 Associate Vice President/Learning ... Dr. Pam CICIRELLO
44 Chief Development Officer ... Ms. Shannon BOSHEARS
84 Dean Enrollment Svcs ... Mr. Zachary PERRINE
07 Director of Admissions ... Mr. Ronald HUDSON
08 Library Director ... Ms. Wendy DAVIS
18 Director of Physical Plant ... Mr. David KROAMER
09 Assoc VP for Institutional Research ... Ms. Jasmine RAY
21 Assoc Vice President for Finance ... Ms. Stacey HOGUE
96 Director of Purchasing ... Ms. Carlas SMITH
13 Assoc VP for Information Services ... Mr. David GLOVER
15 Assoc VP of Human Resources ... Ms. Sherry YOUNG
04 Assistant to the President ... Ms. Tena CARRIGAN
37 Director of Financial Aid ... Ms. Lavonne JUHL
26 Assoc VP Public Relations/Marketing ... Mr. Tim JONES
72 Dean Technical Education Division ... Mr. Dick BURCHETT
81 Dean Mathematics/Nat Social Scis ... Mr. Ben RAINS
50 Dean Business/IT Division ... Mr. Mike MCMILLAN
57 Dean Fine Arts & Humanities ... Mr. Joey COLE
06 Registrar ... Ms. Catherine DIVITO
76 Dean Allied Health/Human Services ... Ms. Jeanne WILLIAMS

Remington College-Little Rock (A)

10600 Colonel Glenn Road, Suite 100,
Little Rock AR 72204
Telephone: (501) 312-0007 Identification: 666286
Accreditation: ACCSC

† Branch campus of Remington College, Dallas, TX.

Rich Mountain Community College (B)

1100 College Drive, Mena AR 71953-2500
County: Polk FICE Identification: 021111
Unit ID: 107743
Telephone: (479) 394-7622 Carnegie Class: Assoc/MT-VT-High Non
FAX Number: (479) 394-7295 Calendar System: Semester
URL: www.rmcc.edu
Established: 1983 Annual Undergrad Tuition & Fees (In-District): $2,448
Enrollment: 1,005 Coed
Affiliation or Control: State/Local IRS Status: 501(c)3
Highest Offering: Associate Degree
Accreditation: NH

01 President ... Dr. Phillip WILSON
05 Vice Pres Academic Affairs ... Dr. Krystal THRAILKILL
32 Vice Pres Student Affairs/Registrar ... Mr. Chad FIELDS
10 VP Administration/CFO ... Mr. Morris BOYDSTUN
13 Chief Information Officer ... Mr. J. Mark BARTON
08 Director Library Services ... Ms. Brenda MINER
37 Financial Aid Director ... Ms. Mary STANDERFER
30 Director of Development ... Ms. Tammy YOUNG
18 Director of Physical Plant ... Mr. Dennis HILL
53 Director of Adult Basic Education ... Ms. Terry FRANCIS
15 Director of Human Resources ... Ms. Amy LUDWIG
07 Director of Admissions ... Ms. Wendy MCDANIEL
21 Controller ... Ms. Patricia HALL
26 Chief Public Relations Officer ... Ms. Tammy YOUNG
40 Bookstore Manager ... Mr. Jason WOOD
09 Coordinator Institutional Research ... Ms. Tammy ODOM
21 Fiscal Project Coordinator ... Ms. Amy LUDWIG

Shorter College (C)

604 Locust Street, North Little Rock AR 72114
County: Pulaski FICE Identification: 001105
Unit ID: 107840
Telephone: (501) 374-6305 Carnegie Class: Assoc/HT-Mix Trad/Non
FAX Number: (501) 374-9333 Calendar System: Semester
URL: www.shortercollege.edu
Established: 1886 Annual Undergrad Tuition & Fees: $4,904
Enrollment: 403 Coed
Affiliation or Control: African Methodist Episcopal IRS Status: 501(c)3
Highest Offering: Associate Degree
Accreditation: TRACS

01 President ... Dr. O. Jerome GREEN
05 Dean of Academic Affairs ... Dr. Jean MANNING
32 Student Services Coordinator ... Mrs. Mary WILLIAMS
10 Director of Fiscal Affairs ... Mr. Richard DENNY

South Arkansas Community College (D)

300 S West Avenue, PO Box 7010,
El Dorado AR 71731-7010
County: Union FICE Identification: 020746
Unit ID: 107974
Telephone: (870) 862-8131 Carnegie Class: Assoc/HVT-Mix Trad/Non
FAX Number: (870) 864-7190 Calendar System: Semester
URL: www.southark.edu
Established: 1992 Annual Undergrad Tuition & Fees (In-State): $2,402
Enrollment: 1,693 Coed
Affiliation or Control: State IRS Status: 501(c)3
Highest Offering: Associate Degree
Accreditation: NH, COARC, EMT, MLTAD, OTA, PHLEB, PTAA, RAD, SURGT

01 President ... Dr. Barbara JONES
05 VP of Academic Learning ... Dr. Mickey BEST
32 Vice Pres for Student Services ... Dr. Jim BULLOCK
11 VP for Fianance & Administration ... Mr. Carey TUCKER
13 Chief Information Officer ... Dr. Tim KIRK
26 Public Information Officer ... Mr. Heath WALDROP
84 Dean of Enrollment Services ... Mr. Dean INMAN
08 Director Library Media Center ... Mr. Philip SHACKELFORD
31 Dean Workforce & Continuing Educ ... Ms. Sherry HOWARD
37 Director of Financial Aid ... Ms. Veronda TATUM
04 Executive Asst to the President ... Ms. Susan JORDAN
15 Interim Human Resources Director ... Ms. Marla BENSON
18 Director of Physical Plant ... Mr. Justin SMALL
30 Dir of Foundation/External Funding ... Ms. Cynthia REYNA
09 CIEAO ... Dr. Stephanie TULLY-DARTEZ
96 Director of Purchasing ... Ms. Ann SOUTHALL
07 Student Recruitment ... Ms. Kara LOWERY
49 Dean of Liberal Arts ... Dr. James YATES
76 Dean Health/Natural Sciences ... Ms. Caroline HAMMOND

Southeast Arkansas College (E)

1900 Hazel Street, Pine Bluff AR 71603-3900
County: Jefferson FICE Identification: 005707
Unit ID: 107637
Telephone: (870) 543-5900 Carnegie Class: Assoc/HVT-High Trad
FAX Number: (870) 850-8636 Calendar System: Semester
URL: www.seark.edu
Established: 1991 Annual Undergrad Tuition & Fees (In-State): $3,070
Enrollment: 1,432 Coed
Affiliation or Control: State IRS Status: 501(c)3
Highest Offering: Associate Degree
Accreditation: NH, ADNUR, COARC, EMT, PHLEB, RAD, SURGT

01 President ... Dr. Stephen HILTERBRAN
05 Vice President Academic Affairs ... Dr. Kaleybra MOREHEAD
32 Vice President Student Affairs ... Mr. Scott KUTTENKULER
10 Vice President Financial Affairs ... Ms. Debbie WALLACE
21 Controller ... Mr. Steve BALLARD
13 Director of Technology Services ... Ms. JoAnn DUPRA
06 Registrar/Director of Admissions ... Ms. Lozanne CALHOUN
15 Director of Human Resources ... Ms. Kristi CAMPBELL
18 Chief Facilities/Physical Plant ... Mr. Joel BARBAREE
37 Director Student Financial Aid ... Ms. Donna COX
04 Administrative Asst to President ... Ms. Karen BOGARD
08 Head Librarian ... Ms. Kim WILLIAMS
103 Dir Workforce/Career Development ... Ms. Wanda LINDSAY
105 Webmaster ... Mr. Terry CLAUSEN
53 Dean or Director Education ... Dr. Mark SHANLEY
96 Director of Purchasing ... Ms. Alice WEATHERLY

Southern Arkansas University (F)

100 E University Street, Magnolia AR 71753-5000
County: Columbia FICE Identification: 001107
Unit ID: 107983
Telephone: (870) 235-4000 Carnegie Class: Masters/M
FAX Number: (870) 235-5005 Calendar System: Semester
URL: www.saumag.edu
Established: 1909 Annual Undergrad Tuition & Fees (In-State): $7,961
Enrollment: 3,546 Coed
Affiliation or Control: State IRS Status: 501(c)3
Highest Offering: Master's
Accreditation: NH, BUS, #CAATE, MUS, NUR, SW, TED

01 President ... Dr. Trey BERRY
05 Provost/Vice Pres Academic Affairs ... Dr. David LANOUE
11 VP Administration/General Counsel ... Mr. Roger W. GILES
32 Vice President Student Affairs ... Dr. Donna Y. ALLEN
18 Vice President of Facilities ... Mr. C. Jasper LEWIS
10 Vice President for Finance ... Ms. Shawana REED
30 Asst Vice President for Development ... Mr. Josh KEE
49 Dean Col Liberal/Perform Arts ... Dr. Helmut LANGERBEIN
50 Dean College of Business ... Dr. Lisa C. TOMS
53 Dean College of Education ... Dr. Zaidy MOHDZAIN
72 Dean College of Sci & Technology ... Dr. Scott MCKAY
58 Dean School of Graduate Studies ... Dr. Kim K. BLOSS
06 Registrar ... Mrs. Sandra WALKER
84 Dean Enrollment Services ... Ms. Sarah E. JENNINGS
35 Associate Deans of Students ... Mr. Carey BAKER
08 Director of Library ... Mr. Del G. DUKE
13 Director Info Technology Services ... Mr. Mike A. ARGO
38 Director Counsel/Testing Center ... Ms. Paula WASHINGTON-WOODS
35 Dean of Students ... Ms. Sandra E. MARTIN
29 Director of Alumni Affairs ... Ms. Ceil L. BRIDGES
44 Director of Development ... Ms. Jeanie BISMARK
37 Director of Financial Aid ... Ms. Marcela C. MCRAE-BRUNSON
51 Director of Continuing Education ... Ms. Caroline WALLER
41 Director of Athletics ... Mr. Steve BROWNING
88 Director Student Support Services ... Ms. Eunice E. WALKER
36 Director of Placement Services ... Vacant
26 Asst Dean Integrated Marketing ... Mr. Aaron J. STREET
28 Assoc Dean Multicultural Affairs ... Mr. Cledis D. STUART
21 Coordinator of Fringe Benefits ... Mr. Alan DAVIS
27 Assoc Dir Communications Center ... Ms. Vicki BUTLER
04 Administrative Asst to President ... Ms. LaTricia DAVIS
09 Director of Institutional Research ... Ms. Smitty H. WOOD

Southern Arkansas University Tech (G)

Post Office Box 3499, Camden AR 71711
County: Calhoun FICE Identification: 007738
Unit ID: 107992
Telephone: (870) 574-4500 Carnegie Class: Assoc/MT-VT-High Non
FAX Number: (870) 574-4520 Calendar System: Semester
URL: www.sautech.edu
Established: 1967 Annual Undergrad Tuition & Fees (In-State): $4,677
Enrollment: 1,559 Coed
Affiliation or Control: State IRS Status: 501(c)3
Highest Offering: Associate Degree
Accreditation: NH

00 Chancellor Emeritus ... Mr. Corbet J. LAMKIN
01 Chancellor ... Vacant
10 VC for Finance & Administration ... Mrs. Gaye MANNING
05 Vice Chancellor for Academics ... Mr. Robert GUNNELS
32 VC for Student Services ... Mr. David MCLEANE
13 VC for Info/Planning & Tech Sys ... Dr. Valerie WILSON
26 Director of Communications ... Mrs. Kim COKER
09 Director of Research ... Mr. Lee SANDERS
84 Director of Enrollment Services ... Mrs. Jenny SANDERS
103 Director of Career Pathways ... Ms. LaTonya REED
88 Director of Career Academy ... Mrs. Juanita MITCHELL
88 Director of AETA ... Mr. Randy HARPER
88 Director of AFTA ... Mrs. Rachel NIX
14 Director of ITS ... Mrs. Laura JOHNSON
37 Director of Financial Aid ... Ms. Jennifer WILLIAMS
18 Director of Physical Plant ... Mr. Mike LARKINS
35 Director of Student Life ... Mr. Courtney HAYGOOD
06 Registrar ... Mr. Wayne BANKS
08 Director of LRC ... Ms. Allison MALONE
04 Assistant to the Chancellor ... Vacant
15 Human Resources Director ... Mrs. Olivia CLACK
21 Controller ... Mr. Dale TOMMEY
39 Residential Advisor ... Mrs. LaDonna FUSILIER
96 Buyer ... Mrs. Angela FRY
51 Director of Adult Education ... Mrs. Barbara HAMILTON
19 Director Security/Safety ... Mr. Jud MITCHELL
103 Director of Workforce & Cmty Educ ... Mrs. Ophelia LINDSEY

*University of Arkansas System Office (H)

2404 N University Avenue, Little Rock AR 72207-3608
County: Pulaski FICE Identification: 008008
Unit ID: 108056
Telephone: (501) 686-2500 Carnegie Class: N/A
FAX Number: (501) 686-2507
URL: www.uasys.edu

01 President ... Dr. Donald R. BOBBITT
04 Assistant to the President ... Ms. Angela HUDSON
05 Vice President Academic Affairs ... Dr. Michael K. MOORE
10 Vice President for Finance & CFO ... Ms. Barbara GOSWICK
11 Vice President for Administration ... Ms. Ann KEMP
26 Vice President University Relations ... Ms. Melissa RUST
47 Vice President Agriculture ... Dr. Mark J. COCHRAN
43 General Counsel ... Mr. Fred H. HARRISON
88 Director Internal Audit ... Mr. Jacob W. FLOURNOY
21 Assoc Vice President for Finance ... Ms. Rita FLEMING
27 Director of Communications ... Mr. Nate HINKEL

*University of Arkansas Main Campus (I)

Fayetteville AR 72701-1201
County: Washington FICE Identification: 001108
Unit ID: 106397
Telephone: (479) 575-2000 Carnegie Class: DU-Highest
FAX Number: (479) 575-2361 Calendar System: Semester
URL: www.uark.edu
Established: 1871 Annual Undergrad Tuition & Fees (In-State): $8,522
Enrollment: 26,237 Coed
Affiliation or Control: State IRS Status: 501(c)3
Highest Offering: Doctorate
Accreditation: NH, AAFCS, BUS, BUSA, CAATE, CACREP, CIDA, CLPSY, CORE, CS, DIETD, ENG, #JOUR, LAW, LSAR, MUS, NURSE, SP, SW, TED

02 Chancellor ... Dr. Joseph E. STEINMETZ
04 Executive Asst to the Chancellor ... Ms. Sally Ann ADAMS
05 Provost & Vice Chanc Academic Affs ... Dr. Ashok SAXENA
10 Interim Vice Chanc Finance & Admin ... Mr. Tim O'DONNELL
30 Vice Chanc University Advancement ... Mr. Chris WYRICK
86 Vice Chanc Governmental Relations ... Mr. Randy MASSANELLI
09 Vice Provost Planning/Dir Inst Res ... Dr. Kathy M. VAN LANINGHAM
46 Vice Provost Research/Econ Dev ... Dr. James M. RANKIN
28 Vice Chanc Diversity & Community ... Mr. Charles ROBINSON
84 Vice Prov Enrol Mgt/Dean Admissions ... Dr. Suzanne MCCRAY
26 Assoc Vice Chanc Univ Relations ... Ms. Laura JACOBS
15 Assoc Vice Chanc Human Resources ... Ms. Barbara A. ABERCROMBIE
18 Assoc Vice Chanc Facilities Mgmt ... Mr. Mike JOHNSON
21 Assoc Vice Chanc Business Affairs ... Ms. Colleen M. BRINEY
32 Dean of Students ... Ms. Melissa HARDWOOD-ROM
08 Dean of Libraries ... Ms. Carolyn H. ALLEN
49 Dean of Arts & Sciences ... Dr. Todd G. SHIELDS
50 Dean Sam Walton College of Business ... Dr. Eli JONES

47 Dean of Agriculture .... Dr. Michael E. VAYDA
53 Dean Education/Health Professions .... Dr. Tom SMITH
48 Dean of Architecture .... Mr. Peter MACKEITH
51 Interim Dean of Graduate School .... Dr. Kim NEEDY
54 Dean of Engineering .... Dr. John ENGLISH
92 Dean Honors College .... Dr. Lynda COON
61 Dean of the Law School .... Ms. Stacy LEEDS
29 Assoc Vice Chanc for Alumni .... Ms. Brandy A. COX
22 Director of Equal Opportunity .... Ms. Danielle L. WOOD
37 Exec Director Financial Aid .... Ms. Wendy D. STOUFFER
38 Dir of Counseling/Psych Services .... Dr. Jonathan C. PERRY
25 Director Research & Sponsored Pgms .... Ms. Rosemary H. RUFF
19 Director University Police .... Mr. Steve GAHAGANS
36 Dir of Career Development Center .... Ms. Angela S. WILLIAMS
13 Assoc VC for Info Technology .... Dr. Dennis BREWER
06 Registrar .... Mr. Dave DAWSON
96 Director of Purchasing .... Ms. Linda FAST
58 Director Graduate & Intl Admissions .... Ms. Lynn MOSESSO

*University of Arkansas at Fort Smith (A)

PO Box 3649, Fort Smith AR 72913-3649
County: Sebastian FICE Identification: 001110
Unit ID: 108092
Telephone: (479) 788-7000 Carnegie Class: Bac-Diverse
FAX Number: (479) 788-7003 Calendar System: Semester
URL: www.uafs.edu
Established: 1928 Annual Undergrad Tuition & Fees (In-District): $5,062
Enrollment: 6,830 Coed
Affiliation or Control: State/Local IRS Status: 501(c)3
Highest Offering: Master's
Accreditation: NH, BUS, DH, DMS, MUS, NAIT, NUR, RAD, SURGT, TED

02 Chancellor .... Dr. Paul B. BERAN
05 Provost/Vice Chanc Academic Affairs .... Dr. Georgia HALE
30 Vice Chancellor Univ Advancement .... Dr. Mary LACKIE
10 Vice Chanc Finance & Administration .... Mr. Brad SHERIFF
32 Vice Chancellor Student Affairs .... Dr. Lee KREHBIEL
58 Assoc Provost/Dir of Grad Studies .... Dr. Margaret TANNER
31 Assoc VC Campus/Cmty Events .... Mr. Stacey JONES
86 Assoc VC Govt & Univ Relations .... Dr. Elizabeth UNDERWOOD
20 Asst to Provost/Dir Dev Educ .... Ms. Diana ROWDEN
20 Asst to Provost .... Ms. Penny PENDLETON
100 Chief of Staff & Assoc Vice Chanc .... Mr. Edward SERNA
76 Dean College of Health Sciences .... Dr. Carolyn MOSLEY
50 Dean College of Business .... Dr. Ashok SUBRAMANIAN
72 Dean Col Applied Science/Tech .... Dr. Ken WARDEN
72 Dean Col Sci/Tech/Engineering/Math .... Dr. Ron DARBEAU
60 Dean Col of Comm/Lang/Arts & Soc .... Dr. Paul HANKINS
15 Dir Human Resources/EEO Officer .... Ms. Bev MCCLENDON
12 Dir Western Arkansas Tech Ctr .... Dr. Darrell C. RINK
88 Dir of Student Professional Dev Ctr .... Mr. Ron ORICK
45 Dir Institutional Effectiveness .... Dr. Fnu MIHIR
88 Director of Instructional Support .... Dr. Tara MISHRA
08 Director of Library Services .... Mr. Robert FRIZZELL
39 Director of Student Housing .... Ms. Beth EPPINGER
37 Director of Financial Aid .... Mr. David SEWARD
07 Dean of Admissions .... Mr. Steve ERVIN
88 Director of Advisement .... Ms. Julie MOSLEY
06 Registrar .... Mr. Wayne WOMACK
88 Exec Dir of International Relations .... Mr. Nicolas PATTILLO
26 Dir Creative Mktg/Comm .... Ms. Laura WATTLES
41 Director of Athletics .... Vacant
96 Director of Procurement Services .... Ms. Rhonda CATON
27 Director of Public Information .... Mr. John POST
18 Director of Plant Operations .... Mr. Bill PIERCE
103 Dir CBPD/Family Enterprise Ctr .... Mr. Dave ROBERTSON
88 Asst Dir Engineering .... Mr. Terry MEADOWS
19 Dir Chief of University Police .... Mr. Ray OTTMAN
29 Director of Alumni Affairs .... Mr. Rick GOINS
44 Director of Planned Giving .... Ms. Anne THOMAS
36 Asst Director Career Services .... Mr. Jeff ADAMS
53 Executive Director Education .... Dr. Glenda EZELL

*University of Arkansas at Little Rock (B)

2801 S University Avenue, Little Rock AR 72204-1099
County: Pulaski FICE Identification: 001101
Unit ID: 106245
Telephone: (501) 569-3000 Carnegie Class: DU-Mod
FAX Number: (501) 569-8915 Calendar System: Semester
URL: www.ualr.edu
Established: 1927 Annual Undergrad Tuition & Fees (In-State): $7,624
Enrollment: 11,645 Coed
Affiliation or Control: State IRS Status: 501(c)3
Highest Offering: Doctorate
Accreditation: NH, ADNUR, ART, BUS, CONST, CORE, CS, DENT, ENG, ENGT, LAW, MUS, NUR, SPAA, SW, TED, THEA

02 Chancellor .... Dr. Joel E. ANDERSON
05 Executive Vice Chancellor & Provost .... Dr. Zulma R. TORO
32 Vice Provost for Student Affairs .... Dr. Randall B. PATTERSON
10 Vice Chanc Finance & Administration .. Mr. Steve J. MCCLELLAN
30 Vice Chancellor Advancement .... Mr. Christian O'NEAL
13 Associate Vice Chancellor & CIO .... Mr. John M. RATHJE
84 Vice Chanc Enrollment Management .... Dr. Dean R. KAHLER
06 Int Registrar .... Ms. Malissa MATHIS
15 Director of Human Resources .... Dr. Ignatius C. AZEBEOKHAI
26 Associate VC of Communications Mktg ... Ms. Judy G. WILLIAMS
09 Director Inst Research .... Dr. William C. DECKER
37 Director Financial Aid .... Ms. Carlia C. SMITH
29 Vice Chancellor for Alumni and Dev .... Ms. Andrea ANGEL
07 Director of Admissions .... Ms. Kathryn YOUNG
88 Assoc Prov for UALR Collect and Arc .... Dr. Deborah J. BALDWIN
19 Director of Public Safety .... Ms. Regina W. CARTER
25 Int Chief Contracts/Grants Admin .... Ms. Tammie L. CASH
41 Athletic Director .... Mr. Chasse S. CONQUE

*University of Arkansas for Medical Sciences (C)

4301 W Markham, Little Rock AR 72205-7199
County: Pulaski FICE Identification: 001109
Unit ID: 106263
Telephone: (501) 686-7000 Carnegie Class: Spec-4-yr-Med
FAX Number: (501) 686-5905 Calendar System: Semester
URL: www.uams.edu
Established: 1879 Annual Undergrad Tuition & Fees (In-State): N/A
Enrollment: 2,890 Coed
Affiliation or Control: State IRS Status: 501(c)3
Highest Offering: Doctorate
Accreditation: NH, #ARCPA, AUD, CAHIIM, COARC, CYTO, DH, DIETI, DMS, EMT, HSA, IPSY, MED, MT, NMT, NURSE, PH, PHAR, @PTA, RAD, SP, SURGT

02 Chancellor .... Dr. Daniel RAHN
05 Provost and CAO .... Dr. Stephanie F. GARDNER
10 Vice Chancellor Finance & CEO .... Mr. Bill BOWES
26 Vice Chancellor Communications .... Ms. Leslie W. TAYLOR
30 Vice Chancellor Development .... Mr. Lance E. BURCHETT
11 Vice Chancellor Campus Operations .... Mr. Mark A. KENNEDAY
28 Vice Chancellor for Diversity .... Dr. Billy R. THOMAS
08 Assoc Provost Library/Stdnt Svcs .... Dr. Jan HART
13 Chief Information Officer .... Ms. Rhonda JORDEN
15 Assoc Vice Chancellor for HR .... Mr. Jeff A. FISINGER
20 Assoc Provost Teaching Lrng Support .... Dr. Steve E. BOONE
07 Assoc Provost Enroll Svcs Admin .... Ms. Elizabeth BARD
37 Director Financial Services .... Ms. Gloria KEMP
63 Dean College of Medicine .... Dr. Pope H. MOSELEY
76 Dean College of Health Professions .... Dr. Douglas L. MURPHY
66 Interim Dean College of Nursing .... Dr. Jean MCSWEENEY
67 Dean College of Pharmacy .... Dr. Keith M. OLSEN
58 Dean of the Graduate School .... Dr. Robert E. MCGEHEE, JR.
88 Dean College of Public Health .... Dr. James M. RACZYNSKI
06 Chief Registrar .... Mr. Clinton D. EVERHART
39 Dir Campus Life/Stdnt Support Svcs .... Ms. Cheri D. GOFORTH

† Tuition figure is for Medical School. Other school's tuitions vary widely.

*University of Arkansas at Monticello (D)

346 University Drive, Monticello AR 71656-3596
County: Drew FICE Identification: 001085
Unit ID: 106485
Telephone: (870) 367-1020 Carnegie Class: Bac/Assoc-Mixed
FAX Number: (870) 460-1321 Calendar System: Semester
URL: www.uamont.edu
Established: 1909 Annual Undergrad Tuition & Fees (In-State): $6,446
Enrollment: 3,854 Coed
Affiliation or Control: State IRS Status: 501(c)3
Highest Offering: Master's
Accreditation: NH, EMT, MUS, NUR, SW, TED

02 Chancellor .... Dr. Karla HUGHES
100 Chief of Staff .... Ms. Lisa SHEMWELL
05 Interim VC for Acad Affairs .... Dr. Peggy DOSS
10 VC for Finance & Administration .... Mr. Jay JONES
30 Interim VC Advancement/Univ Rels .... Mr. Jay JONES
32 VC for Student Affairs .... Mr. Jay HUGHES
12 VC for UAM College of Tech-Crossett .... Ms. Linda RUSHING
12 VC for UAM College of Tech-McGehee .... Mr. Bob WARE
21 Assoc VC for Finance and Admin .... Ms. Debbie GASAWAY
06 Registrar .... Ms. Carol DOLBERRY
07 Director of Admissions .... Vacant
84 Exec Dir of Enrollment Mgmt .... Ms. Tawana GREENE
41 Director of Athletics .... Mr. Chris RATCLIFF
35 Dean of Students .... Vacant
13 Director Information Technology .... Ms. Anissa ROSS
08 Director of Library .... Mr. Daniel BOICE
26 Director of Media Services .... Mr. Jim L. BREWER
37 Director of Financial Aid .... Ms. Susan BREWER
09 Director of Institutional Research .... Ms. Lisa CATER
04 Assistant to the Chancellor .... Ms. Christy PACE
18 Director of Physical Plant .... Mr. Chester ASHCRAFT
38 Dir Counseling/Testing Services .... Ms. Laura HUGHES
96 Director of Purchasing .... Ms. Gay PACE
29 Director of Alumni Affairs .... Ms. Lisa Jo ROSS
86 Director Government Relations .... Vacant
19 Director of Public Safety .... Mr. John KIDWELL

*University of Arkansas at Pine Bluff (E)

1200 N University Drive, Pine Bluff AR 71601-2799
County: Jefferson FICE Identification: 001086
Unit ID: 106412
Telephone: (870) 575-8000 Carnegie Class: Bac-Diverse
FAX Number: (870) 543-8009 Calendar System: Semester
URL: www.uapb.edu
Established: 1873 Annual Undergrad Tuition & Fees (In-State): $6,538
Enrollment: 2,513 Coed
Affiliation or Control: State IRS Status: 501(c)3
Highest Offering: Doctorate
Accreditation: NH, AAFCS, ACBSP, ART, MUS, NAIT, SW, TED

02 Chancellor .... Dr. Laurence B. ALEXANDER
05 Vice Chanc Academic Affairs .... Dr. Jacquelyn MCCRAY
10 Vice Chanc Finance & Admin .... Dr. Carla M. MARTIN
32 Vice Chancellor Student Affairs .... Mr. Elbert BENNETT
45 Vice Chanc Research/Innovation .... Dr. Mary E. BENJAMIN
100 Chief of Staff .... Mrs. Janet BROILES
41 Athletics Director .... Mr. Lonza HARDY
15 Director of Human Resources .... Mrs. Gladys BENFORD
13 Director of Technical Services .... Mrs. Willette TOTTEN
09 Director of Institutional Research .... Mrs. Margaret TAYLOR
06 Registrar .... Mrs. Erica FULTON
29 Director of Alumni Affairs .... Mr. John KUYKENDALL
08 Head Librarian .... Mr. Edward FONTENETTE
103 Dir Workforce/Career Development .... Mrs. Shirley CHERRY
108 Director Institutional Assessment .... Dr. Steve LOCHMANN
37 Director Student Financial Aid .... Mrs. Janice KEARNEY
22 Dir Affirmative Action/EEO .... Ms. Karen BAKER

*Cossatot Community College of the University of Arkansas (F)

183 College Drive, De Queen AR 71832
County: Sevier FICE Identification: 022209
Unit ID: 106795
Telephone: (870) 584-4471 Carnegie Class: Assoc/HVT-Mix Trad/Non
FAX Number: N/A Calendar System: Semester
URL: www.cccua.edu
Established: 1991 Annual Undergrad Tuition & Fees (In-District): $2,670
Enrollment: 1,611 Coed
Affiliation or Control: State/Local IRS Status: 501(c)3
Highest Offering: Associate Degree
Accreditation: NH, ACBSP, OTA

02 Chancellor .... Dr. Steve COLE
05 Vice Chancellor of Academics .... Dr. Maria PARKER
45 VC of Planning and Facilities .... Mr. Mike KINKADE
10 Vice Chancellor Business/Finance .... Mrs. Charlotte JOHNSON
32 Director of Student Services .... Mr. Justin WHITE
37 Director Student Financial Aid .... Mrs. Denise HAMMOND
30 Director Institutional Advancement .... Ms. Alisha LEWIS
06 Registrar/Institutional Reporting .... Mrs. Brenda MORRIS
103 Dir of Public Svc/Workforce Dev .... Mrs. Tammy COLEMAN
12 Director of Ashdown Campus .... Mr. Barrett REED
15 Director of Human Resources .... Ms. Kelly PLUNK
13 Director of Technology .... Mr. Tony HARGROVE
44 Coordinator of Development .... Mr. Dustin ROBERTS

*Phillips Community College of the University of Arkansas (G)

PO Box 785, Helena AR 72342-0785
County: Phillips FICE Identification: 001104
Unit ID: 107619
Telephone: (870) 338-6474 Carnegie Class: Assoc/MT-VT-High Non
FAX Number: (870) 338-7542 Calendar System: Semester
URL: www.pccua.edu
Established: 1965 Annual Undergrad Tuition & Fees (In-District): $2,593
Enrollment: 1,796 Coed
Affiliation or Control: State/Local IRS Status: 501(c)3
Highest Offering: Associate Degree
Accreditation: NH, ACBSP, ADNUR, MLTAD, PHLEB

02 Chancellor .... Dr. G. Keith PINCHBACK
05 Vice Chancellor for Instruction .... Dr. Deborah KING
10 Vice Chanc Finance & Administration .... Mr. Stan SULLIVANT
32 Vice Chanc Student Svcs/Registrar .... Mr. Scott POST
30 Vice Chanc Col Advancement/Res Dev .... Mrs. Rhonda ST. COLUMBIA
12 Vice Chancellor Stuttgart Campus .... Mrs. Kim KIRBY
12 Vice Chancellor DeWitt Campus .... Mrs. Carolyn TURNER

*University of Arkansas Community College at Batesville (H)

2005 White Drive, PO Box 3350,
Batesville AR 72503-3350
County: Independence FICE Identification: 020735
Unit ID: 106999
Telephone: (870) 612-2000 Carnegie Class: Assoc/MT-VT-High Trad
FAX Number: (870) 793-4988 Calendar System: Semester
URL: www.uaccb.edu
Established: 1975 Annual Undergrad Tuition & Fees (In-District): $2,262
Enrollment: 1,315 Coed
Affiliation or Control: State/Local IRS Status: 501(c)3
Highest Offering: Associate Degree
Accreditation: NH, ADNUR, EMT

02 Chancellor .... Ms. Deborah J. FRAZIER
04 Assistant to the Chancellor .... Ms. Hannah KELLER
05 Vice Chancellor for Academics .... Dr. Brian SHONK
32 Vice Chanc Student Affairs .... Mr. Greg THORNBURG
10 Vice Chancellor Finance and Admin .... Mr. Gayle COOPER
09 VC Research/Planning/Assessment .... Dr. Anne AUSTIN
49 Chair Div of Arts & Humanities .... Ms. Susan TRIPP
50 Chair Div Business/Tech/Public Svc .... Dr. Tamara GRIFFIN
76 Chair Div Nursing/Allied Health .... Ms. Marietta CANDLER
81 Chair Div of Math and Science .... Mr. Douglas MUSE

103 Dir of Workforce Development .... Mr. Zachery HARBER
09 Dir of Institutional Research .... Ms. Beth BRUCE
07 Director of Admissions .... Ms. Amy FOREE
13 Director Information Services .... Mr. Steve COLLINS
06 Dir Student Information/Registrar .... Ms. Shelly MOSER
37 Director of Financial Aid .... Ms. Kristen CROSS
30 Director of Development .... Ms. Tina PAUL
18 Director of Maintenance .... Mr. Heath WOOLDRIDGE
36 Director Student Development .... Ms. Louise HUGHES
38 Career/Disabilities Coordinator .... Ms. Becky WARREN
08 Director Library .... Mr. Jay STRICKLAND
21 Controller .... Ms. Waynna DOCKINS
15 Personnel Officer .... Ms. Alexa SMITH
96 Purchasing Agent .... Ms. Peggy JACKSON
40 Bookstore Manager .... Ms. Luanne BARBER

*University of Arkansas at Hope-Texarkana (A)

PO Box 140, 2500 S Main Street, Hope AR 71802-0140
County: Hempstead FICE Identification: 005732
Unit ID: 107725
Telephone: (870) 777-5722 Carnegie Class: Assoc/HVT-Mix Trad/Non
FAX Number: (870) 777-5957 Calendar System: Semester
URL: www.uacch.edu
Established: 1991 Annual Undergrad Tuition & Fees (In-State): $2,460
Enrollment: 1,360 Coed
Affiliation or Control: State IRS Status: 501(c)3
Highest Offering: Associate Degree
Accreditation: NH, EMT, FUSER

02 Chancellor .... Mr. Chris THOMASON
05 Vice Chancellor for Academics .... Ms. Laura CLARK
32 Vice Chancellor Student Services .... Mr. Brian BERRY
10 Vice Chancellor for Finance .... Dr. Belinda AARON
08 Librarian .... Ms. Marielle MCFARLAND
51 Director of Cont Educ/Ind Relations .... Mr. Shaun CLARK
30 Dir of Institutional Advancement .... Ms. Jill BOBO
24 Director of Telecommunications .... Mr. Dave PHILLIPS
15 Human Resources Officer .... Ms. Kathryn HOPKINS
06 Registrar .... Ms. Diana SYATA
12 Texarkana Campus Director .... Ms. Jolane COOK

*University of Arkansas Community College at Morrilton (B)

1537 University Boulevard, Morrilton AR 72110-9601
County: Conway FICE Identification: 005245
Unit ID: 107585
Telephone: (501) 354-2465 Carnegie Class: Assoc/MT-VT-High Trad
FAX Number: (501) 977-2044 Calendar System: Semester
URL: www.uaccm.edu
Established: 1961 Annual Undergrad Tuition & Fees (In-State): $2,852
Enrollment: 1,995 Coed
Affiliation or Control: State IRS Status: 501(c)3
Highest Offering: Associate Degree
Accreditation: NH

02 Chancellor .... Dr. Larry D. DAVIS
05 Vice Chancellor Academic Services .... Ms. Diana ARN
10 Vice Chancellor for Finance .... Ms. Lisa WILLENBERG
11 Vice Chancellor for Administration .... Dr. Linda M. BIRKNER
32 Vice Chancellor Student Services .... Mr. Darren JONES
09 Director of Institutional Research .... Ms. Beth HAWKINS
08 Librarian .... Ms. Rebecka VIRDEN
06 Registrar .... Ms. Linda HOLLAND
37 Financial Aid Director .... Mrs. Teresa Y. CASH
26 Dir Marketing & Public Relations .... Ms. Mary CLARK
13 Chief Information Officer .... Mr. Richard O. GROWNS
18 Director of the Physical Plant .... Mr. C. Allen HOLLOWAY
07 Director of Admissions .... Ms. Rachel MULLINS
103 Coord Workforce Develop/Cmty Educ .... Ms. Vicki SHADELL
15 Director Personnel Services .... Ms. Judy SANDERS
30 Chief Development .... Ms. Morgan ZIMMERMAN
38 Director Student Counseling .... Ms. Staci DUVALL
96 Director of Purchasing .... Ms. Anna HALBROOK

*Phillips Community College of the University of Arkansas-DeWitt (C)

1210 Rice Belt Avenue, DeWitt AR 72042
Telephone: (870) 946-3506 Identification: 770174
Accreditation: &NH

† Regional accreditation is carried under the parent institution in Helena, AR

*Phillips Community College of the University of Arkansas-Stuttgart (D)

2807 Hwy 165 South, Stuttgart AR 72160-2408
Telephone: (870) 673-4201 Identification: 770175
Accreditation: &NH

† Regional accreditation is carried under the parent institution in Helena, AR

*University of Arkansas at Monticello College of Technology-Crossett (E)

1326 Highway 52 W, Crossett AR 71635
Telephone: (870) 364-6414 Identification: 770176
Accreditation: &NH

† Regional accreditation is carried under the parent institution in Monticello, AR

*University of Arkansas at Monticello College of Technology-McGehee (F)

PO Box 747, McGehee AR 71654
Telephone: (870) 222-5360 Identification: 770177
Accreditation: &NH

† Regional accreditation is carried under the parent institution in Monticello, AR

University of Central Arkansas (G)

201 Donaghey Avenue, Conway AR 72035-0001
County: Faulkner FICE Identification: 001092
Unit ID: 106704
Telephone: (501) 450-5000 Carnegie Class: Masters/L
FAX Number: (501) 450-5003 Calendar System: Semester
URL: uca.edu
Established: 1907 Annual Undergrad Tuition & Fees (In-State): $7,889
Enrollment: 11,698 Coed
Affiliation or Control: State IRS Status: 501(c)3
Highest Offering: Doctorate
Accreditation: NH, ART, BUS, CAATE, CIDA, COPSY, CS, DIETD, DIETI, MUS, NURSE, OT, PTA, SCPSY, SP, TED, THEA

01 President .... Mr. Tom COURTWAY
05 Provost/Exec VP Academic Affairs .... Dr. Steve RUNGE
10 VP Finance/Administration .... Ms. Diane D. NEWTON
32 VP Student Services/Inst Diversity .... Mr. Ronnie D. WILLIAMS
43 General Counsel .... Mr. Warren READNOUR
30 VP for UCA Advancement .... Dr. Taylor K. GOBER
41 Athletics Director .... Dr. Brad TEAGUE
15 Assoc Vice Pres for Human Resources .... Dr. Graham GILLIS
85 AVP International Engagement .... Ms. Jane Ann WILLIAMS
21 Assoc Provost Finance & Admin .... Ms. Laura YOUNG
20 Assoc Provost/Academic Services .... Dr. Jonathan A. GLENN
20 Assoc Provost/Instructional Support .... Dr. Kurt BONIECKI
26 Assoc VP Comm/PR/Marketing .... Ms. Christina MADSEN
100 Chief of Staff .... Mr. Kelley ERSTINE
21 Controller .... Mr. Jeremy BRUNER
58 Dean of Graduate School .... Dr. Joan B. SIMON
50 Dean of Col Business Admin .... Dr. Michael HARGIS
53 Dean of College of Education .... Dr. Victoria GROVES-SCOTT
76 Dean Col Health/Applied Science .... Dr. Jimmy ISHEE
49 Dean of Liberal Arts .... Dr. Maurice A. LEE
81 Dean Col Natural Sci/Math .... Dr. Steve ADDISON
57 Dean Fine Arts & Communication .... Mr. Terry WRIGHT
35 Dean of Students .... Dr. Gary A. ROBERTS
92 Dean of Honors College .... Dr. Richard I. SCOTT
07 Director Admissions .... Ms. Courtney MULLEN
08 Library Director .... Mr. Robert D. COVINGTON
06 Registrar .... Ms. Becky D. RASNICK
09 Dir Institutional Research .... Ms. Amber L. HALL
13 Chief Technology Officer .... Dr. Chris DAVIS
37 Director Student Financial Aid .... Ms. Cheryl C. LYONS
36 Dir Career Svcs/Cooperative Educ .... Dr. Kathy RICE-CLAYBORN
19 Chief University Police .... Mr. Larry K. JAMES
38 Director Counseling Center .... Dr. Susan SOBEL
39 Asst VP for Housing & Contract Svcs .... Mr. Rick L. MCCOLLUM
29 Director of Alumni Services .... Mr. Jesse THILL
21 Director Internal Audits .... Ms. Pamela L. MASSEY
18 Director Physical Plant .... Mr. Larry D. LAWRENCE
24 Director Creative Services .... Mr. Richard R. HANCOCK
96 Director of Purchasing .... Ms. Cassandra MCCUIEN-SMITH
21 Director Student Accounts .... Mr. Chad HEARNE

University of Phoenix Little Rock Campus (H)

10800 Financial Ctr Pkwy, Suite 125,
Little Rock AR 72211-3552
Telephone: (501) 225-9337 Identification: 770188
Accreditation: &NH, ACBSP

† No longer accepting campus-based students.

University of the Ozarks (I)

415 College Avenue, Clarksville AR 72830-2880
County: Johnson FICE Identification: 001094
Unit ID: 107558
Telephone: (479) 979-1000 Carnegie Class: Bac-Diverse
FAX Number: (479) 979-1355 Calendar System: Semester
URL: www.ozarks.edu
Established: 1834 Annual Undergrad Tuition & Fees: $24,440
Enrollment: 587 Coed
Affiliation or Control: Presbyterian Church (U.S.A.) IRS Status: 501(c)3
Highest Offering: Baccalaureate
Accreditation: NH, IACBE, TED

01 President .... Mr. Richard L. DUNSWORTH
05 Provost .... Mr. Travis FEEZELL
10 VP for Finance & Administration .... Mr. Jeff SCACCIA
07 Assistant Director of Admission .... Mr. Joseph HUGHES
07 Dean of Admissions & Financial Aid .... Ms. Jana D. HART
42 Chaplain .... Rev. Jeremy WILHEMI
06 Registrar .... Ms. Wilma K. HARRIS
08 Librarian .... Mr. Stuart P. STELZER
36 Director of Career Services .... Ms. Ruth WALTON
29 Director Alumni Affairs .... Mr. Brett WOOD
41 Athletic Director .... Mr. Jimmy CLARK
26 Dir University/Public Relations .... Mr. Larry A. ISCH
30 VP of Advancement .... Ms. Lori A. MCBEE
88 Director Jones Learning Center .... Ms. Julia H. FROST
09 Director of Institutional Research .... Vacant
89 Director of Freshmen Studies .... Vacant
13 Director of Information Technology .... Ms. Vickie ALSTON
32 Dean of Students .... Mr. Steven WEAVER
81 Dean Div of Mathematics & Sciences .... Mr. Stacy KEY
53 Dean Div Business/Comm/Education .... Dr. Brett STONE
79 Dean Div Fine Arts/Human/Soc Sci .... Dr. Steve OATIS
105 Director Web Services .... Ms. Cara FLINN
15 Human Resources Manager .... Ms. Karen SCHLUTERMAN
19 Director Security/Safety .... Mr. Cyrus SMITH
21 Controller .... Mr. Albert LEDING

Williams Baptist College (J)

60 W. Fulbright Avenue, Walnut Ridge AR 72476
County: Lawrence FICE Identification: 001106
Unit ID: 107877
Telephone: (870) 886-6741 Carnegie Class: Bac-Diverse
FAX Number: (870) 886-3924 Calendar System: Semester
URL: www.wbcoll.edu
Established: 1941 Annual Undergrad Tuition & Fees: $16,430
Enrollment: 560 Coed
Affiliation or Control: Southern Baptist IRS Status: 501(c)3
Highest Offering: Baccalaureate
Accreditation: NH, TED

01 President .... Dr. Tom O. JONES
05 Vice Pres Academic Affairs .... Dr. Brad BAINE
10 Vice President for Business Affairs .... Mr. W. Dale LEATHERMAN
30 Vice Pres Institutional Advancement .... Dr. Brett COOPER
84 VP for Enrollment Mgmt/Student Svcs . Dr. Jeremy D. DUTSCHKE
32 Dean of Students .... Ms. Amber N. GRADY
06 Registrar .... Mrs. Tonya D. BOLTON
04 Administrative Asst to President .... Mrs. Jo C. PHILLIPS
08 Director Library Services .... Mrs. Pamela MERIDITH
37 Director Student Financial Aid .... Mrs. Barbara J. TURNER
38 Director of Counseling .... Ms. Aneita COOPER
42 Campus Minister .... Mr. Hayes HOWELL
18 Director Physical Plant .... Mr. Tony CONLEY
44 Dir of Annual Giving & Alumni Rels .... Mr. Aaron ANDREWS
13 Director Information Technologies .... Mr. Blake MCGINNIS
41 Athletic Director .... Mr. Jeff RIDER
106 Dean of Adult Education .... Dr. Eric TURNER
85 Director of International Programs .... Mr. Adam ADAMS
07 Director of Admissions .... Mr. Andrew WATSON

CALIFORNIA

Abraham Lincoln University (K)

3530 Wilshire Blvd, Ste 1430, Los Angeles CA 90010
County: Los Angeles Identification: 667049
Unit ID: 480444
Telephone: (213) 252-5100 Carnegie Class: Not Classified
FAX Number: (213) 252-5112 Calendar System: Other
URL: www.alu.edu
Established: 1996 Annual Undergrad Tuition & Fees: N/A
Enrollment: N/A Coed
Affiliation or Control: Proprietary IRS Status: Proprietary
Highest Offering: First Professional Degree
Accreditation: DEAC

01 President & CEO/Dean School of Law .... Mr. Hyung PARK
61 CIO & Dir of School of Law .... Ms. Jessica PARK
11 Director of Univ Programs .... Dr. Susan LOMELI
13 Technology Coordinator .... Mr. Daniel JUNG
06 Registrar .... Ms. Elizabeth GOMEZ
14 Software Engineer .... Mr. Tae KIM
07 Director of Admissions .... Mr. Richard LINGLE
10 Chief Financial Officer .... Mr. Joshua SUNG
37 Director Student Financial Aid .... Ms. Lisa INGOLDSBY

Academy for Jewish Religion (L)

574 Hilgard Avenue, Los Angeles CA 90024-3234
County: Los Angeles FICE Identification: 041555
Unit ID: 457271
Telephone: (310) 824-1586 Carnegie Class: Spec-4-yr-Faith
FAX Number: (310) 824-1614 Calendar System: Trimester
URL: www.ajrca.org
Established: 2001 Annual Graduate Tuition & Fees: N/A
Enrollment: 65 Coed
Affiliation or Control: Jewish IRS Status: 501(c)3
Highest Offering: Master's; No Undergraduates
Accreditation: WC

01 Interim President .... Rabbi Laura OWENS
73 Int VP/Dean of Rabbinical School .... Rabbi Rochelle ROBINS
05 Provost .... Dr. Tamar FRANKIEL
10 Chief Financial Officer .... Dr. Alvin MARTIN
11 Director Administration .... Ms. Lauren GOLDNER
06 Registrar/Operations Manager .... Ms. Reesa ROTMAN
07 Director of Admissions/Recruitment .... Ms. Robin FEDERMAN
26 Chief Public Relations Officer .... Vacant
36 Director of Internships/Placement .... Rabbi Faith TESSLER

88 Dean of Cantorial School .... Cantor Hazzan Nathan LAM
88 Associate Dean of Cantorial School .... Cantor Perryne ANKER

Academy of Art University (A)

79 New Montgomery Street,
San Francisco CA 94105-3410
County: San Francisco FICE Identification: 007531
Unit ID: 108232
Telephone: (415) 274-2200 Carnegie Class: Spec-4-yr-Arts
FAX Number: (415) 274-8665 Calendar System: Semester
URL: www.academyart.edu
Established: 1929 Annual Undergrad Tuition & Fees: $20,340
Enrollment: 15,212 Coed
Affiliation or Control: Proprietary IRS Status: Proprietary
Highest Offering: Master's
Accreditation: WC, ART, #CIDA

01 President .... Dr. Elisa STEPHENS

Academy of Chinese Culture and Health Sciences (B)

1600 Broadway Street, Suite 200, Oakland CA 94612
County: Alameda FICE Identification: 032883
Unit ID: 108269
Telephone: (510) 763-7787 Carnegie Class: Spec-4-yr-Other Health
FAX Number: (510) 834-8646 Calendar System: Other
URL: www.acchs.edu
Established: 1982 Annual Undergrad Tuition & Fees: N/A
Enrollment: 146 Coed
Affiliation or Control: Independent Non-Profit IRS Status: 501(c)3
Highest Offering: Master's; No Lower Division
Accreditation: ACUP

01 President .... Dr. Jun WANG
03 Vice President .... Mr. Phillip TOU
11 Dean of Administration .... Ms. Jane ZHANG

Academy of Couture Art (C)

8484 Wilshire Boulevard, Suite 730,
Beverly Hills CA 90211-3235
County: Los Angeles FICE Identification: 041855
Unit ID: 475635
Telephone: (310) 360-8888 Carnegie Class: Spec-4-yr-Arts
FAX Number: (310) 857-6974 Calendar System: Quarter
URL: www.academyofcoutureart.edu
Established: 2005 Annual Undergrad Tuition & Fees: $22,338
Enrollment: 22 Coed
Affiliation or Control: Proprietary IRS Status: Proprietary
Highest Offering: Baccalaureate
Accreditation: ACICS

01 CEO .... Sonia ETE
05 Chief Academic Officer .... Sarey TORRES
11 Chief Operating Officer .... Thierry ETE
07 Director of Admissions .... Jennifer PARK ZERBEL

Acupuncture and Integrative Medicine College-Berkeley (D)

2550 Shattuck Avenue, Berkeley CA 94704-2724
County: Alameda FICE Identification: 033274
Unit ID: 384306
Telephone: (510) 666-8248 Carnegie Class: Spec-4-yr-Other Health
FAX Number: (510) 666-0111 Calendar System: Trimester
URL: www.aimc.edu
Established: 1990 Annual Undergrad Tuition & Fees: N/A
Enrollment: 138 Coed
Affiliation or Control: Independent Non-Profit IRS Status: 501(c)3
Highest Offering: Master's; No Lower Division
Accreditation: ACUP

01 President .... Mr. Yasuo TANAKA
05 Academic Dean .... Ms. Megan HAUNGS
88 Clinic Dean .... Mr. Mike MORGAN
07 Director of Admissions .... Ms. Julie SCHEFF
06 Registrar .... Mr. Brian LIESKE
20 Student Advisor .... Mr. Peter BLACKMAN
08 Head Librarian .... Ms. Patricia WARD
37 Director Student Financial Aid .... Ms. Victoria LABRADOR

Advanced College (E)

13180 Paramount Boulevard, South Gate CA 90280-7956
County: Los Angeles FICE Identification: 037863
Unit ID: 444343
Telephone: (562) 408-6969 Carnegie Class: Spec 2-yr-Health
FAX Number: (562) 408-0471 Calendar System: Other
URL: www.advancedcollege.edu
Established: 1999 Annual Undergrad Tuition & Fees: N/A
Enrollment: 125 Coed
Affiliation or Control: Proprietary IRS Status: Proprietary
Highest Offering: Associate Degree
Accreditation: COE

01 President .... Dr. Lida MANSOURIAN
66 Director Vocational Nursing .... Dr. Minnie L. DOUGLAS
11 Director of Operations .... Dr. Mehdi KARIMPOUR

Advanced Computing Institute (F)

3470 Wilshire Blvd #1100, Los Angeles CA 90010
County: Los Angeles Identification: 667142
Unit ID: 481234
Telephone: (213) 383-8999 Carnegie Class: Spec 2-yr-Tech
FAX Number: (213) 383-5765 Calendar System: Semester
URL: www.advancedcomputinginstitute.com
Established: 1992 Annual Undergrad Tuition & Fees: N/A
Enrollment: 354 Coed
Affiliation or Control: Proprietary IRS Status: Proprietary
Highest Offering: Associate Degree
Accreditation: COE

01 School Director/CEO .... Mr. Daniel MAINCA
05 Vice Pres Academic Affairs .... Dr. Michael RAHNI

Advanced Training Associates (G)

1810 Gillespie Way, Suite 104, El Cajon CA 92020-1234
County: San Diego FICE Identification: 035324
Unit ID: 444361
Telephone: (619) 596-2766 Carnegie Class: Spec 2-yr-Tech
FAX Number: (619) 596-4526 Calendar System: Other
URL: www.advancedtraining.edu
Established: 2000 Annual Undergrad Tuition & Fees: N/A
Enrollment: 85 Coed
Affiliation or Control: Proprietary IRS Status: Proprietary
Highest Offering: Associate Degree
Accreditation: COE

01 President/CEO .... Henry MARENTES
11 Senior Director of Operations .... Valerie PHILLIPS
06 Registrar .... Jo WARREN
07 Director of Admissions .... Steven HOWARD
19 Director Security/Safety .... Nick FLEETWOOD
53 Director of Education .... James R. KYLE

Alhambra Medical University (H)

55 S. Raymond Avenue, Alhambra CA 91801
County: Los Angeles Identification: 667052
Telephone: (626) 289-7719 Carnegie Class: Not Classified
FAX Number: (626) 289-8641 Calendar System: Quarter
URL: www.amuedu.com
Established: 2005 Annual Graduate Tuition & Fees: N/A
Enrollment: N/A Coed
Affiliation or Control: Proprietary IRS Status: Proprietary
Highest Offering: Master's; No Undergraduates
Accreditation: ACUP

01 President .... Dr. Jonathan WU
05 Academic Dean .... Jerome JIANG
23 Director of University Clinic .... Yue LU
07 Director of Admissions .... Qing MA
06 Registrar .... Alan LIU
08 Librarian .... Dr. Luke CHEN

Allan Hancock College (I)

800 S College Drive, Santa Maria CA 93454-6399
County: Santa Barbara FICE Identification: 001111
Unit ID: 108807
Telephone: (805) 922-6966 Carnegie Class: Assoc/HT-Mix Trad/Non
FAX Number: (805) 347-9896 Calendar System: Semester
URL: www.hancockcollege.edu
Established: 1920 Annual Undergrad Tuition & Fees (In-District): $1,346
Enrollment: 11,047 Coed
Affiliation or Control: State/Local IRS Status: 501(c)3
Highest Offering: Associate Degree
Accreditation: WJ

01 Superintendent/President .... Dr. Kevin G. WALTHERS
10 Assoc Supt/VP Finance/Admin .... Dr. Michael R. BLACK
05 Assoc Supt/VP Academic Affairs .... Dr. George A. RAILEY
32 VP Student Services .... Ms. Nohemy ORNELAS
11 Vice Pres Operations .... Mr. Felix HERNANDEZ
108 Vice Pres Inst Effectiveness .... Dr. Paul MURPHY
15 Director Human Resources .... Ms. Kelly UNDERWOOD
35 Dean Student Services .... Mr. Rob PARISI
38 Dean Counseling & Matriculation .... Ms. Yvonne TENIENTE
20 Dean Academic Affairs .... Ms. Nancy MEDDINGS
20 Dean Academic Affairs .... Dr. Sofia RAMIREZ-GELPI
20 Dean Academic Affairs .... Ms. Margaret LAU
56 Dean The Extended Campus .... Mr. Rick RANTZ
41 Assoc Dean Kines/Rec/Athletics .... Ms. Kim ENSING
30 Exec Director College Advancement .... Ms. Susan HOUGHTON
88 Artistic Director PCPA .... Mr. Mark BOOHER
13 Director Information Technology .... Ms. Carol MOORE
21 Director Business Services .... Ms. Jessica BLAZER
07 Director Admissions & Records .... Ms. Marian QUAID-MALTAGLIATI
37 Director Student Financial Aid .... Mr. Robert PARISI
26 Int Dir Public Affairs/Publications .... Mr. Andrew MASUDA
78 Dir Cooperative Work Experience .... Ms. Emily SMITH
88 Director EOPS & Special Outreach .... Mr. Will BRUCE
18 Director Plant .... Mr. Rex VANDENBERG
19 Int Dir Public Safety/Chf of Police .... Mr. Chris MARTAREZ
88 Director Cal-SOAP .... Ms. Diana PEREZ
88 Director College Achievement Now .... Ms. Petra GOMEZ
25 Director Institutional Grants .... Dr. Suzanne VALERY
88 Counselor/Coordinator MESA .... Ms. Christine REED
88 Managing Director PCPA .... Ms. Jennifer SCHWARTZ

* Alliant International University President's Office (J)

One Beach Street, Suite 100,
San Francisco CA 94133-1221
County: San Francisco Identification: 666132
Unit ID: 110431
Telephone: (415) 955-2100 Carnegie Class: N/A
FAX Number: (414) 955-2062
URL: www.alliant.edu

01 Interim President .... Mr. Andy VAUGHN
05 Provost/Vice Pres Academic Affairs .... Dr. Tracy HELLER
32 VP Student Services .... Dr. Mary OLING-SISAY
07 Vice President for Admissions .... Ms. Amy KWIATKOWSKI
10 Vice Pres Finance/Int CFO .... Ms. Diane ERDEI
06 Registrar .... Mr. Paul WELCH
15 Chief Human Resources Officer .... Dr. Michael RUSSELL
13 Chief Information Officer .... Ms. Sue WIERENGA

* Alliant International University-San Diego (K)

10455 Pomerado Road, San Diego CA 92131-1799
County: San Diego FICE Identification: 011117
Unit ID: 110468
Telephone: (858) 635-4772 Carnegie Class: DU-Mod
FAX Number: (858) 693-8562 Calendar System: Semester
URL: www.alliant.edu
Established: 1952 Annual Undergrad Tuition & Fees: $16,800
Enrollment: 3,957 Coed
Affiliation or Control: Independent Non-Profit IRS Status: 501(c)3
Highest Offering: Doctorate
Accreditation: WC, CLPSY, MFCD

02 Asst VP Student Life/Alumni Rels .... Ms. Kathy MCINTOSH
05 Provost/Vice Pres Academic Affairs .... Dr. Tracy HELLER

* *Alliant International University-Fresno* (L)

5130 E Clinton Way, Fresno CA 93727-2014
Telephone: (559) 456-2777 FICE Identification: 001158
Accreditation: &WC, CLPSY, MFCD

† Regional accreditation is carried under the parent institution in San Diego, CA

* *Alliant International University-Irvine* (M)

2855 Michelle Drive, Suite 300, Irvine CA 92606
Telephone: (949) 812-7440 Identification: 666157
Accreditation: &WC, MFCD

† Regional accreditation is carried under the parent institution in San Diego, CA

* *Alliant International University-Los Angeles* (N)

1000 S Fremont Avenue, Unit 5,
Alhambra CA 91803-1360
Telephone: (626) 284-2777 FICE Identification: 010013
Accreditation: &WC, CLPSY, MFCD

† Regional accreditation is carried under the parent institution in San Diego, CA

* *Alliant International University-San Francisco* (O)

One Beach Street, San Francisco CA 94133-1221
Telephone: (415) 955-2100 FICE Identification: 011881
Accreditation: &WC, CLPSY, IPSY, MFCD

† Regional accreditation is carried under the parent institution in San Diego, CA

Allied American University (P)

22952 Alcalde Drive, Laguna Hills CA 92653-1337
County: Orange FICE Identification: 041893
Unit ID: 460729
Telephone: (888) 384-0849 Carnegie Class: Bac/Assoc-Mixed
FAX Number: (949) 707-2978 Calendar System: Other
URL: www.allied.edu
Established: 2008 Annual Undergrad Tuition & Fees: N/A
Enrollment: 2,244 Coed
Affiliation or Control: Proprietary IRS Status: Proprietary
Highest Offering: Baccalaureate
Accreditation: DEAC

01 President .... Bill LUTON
05 Provost .... Dr. Chelsea HANSEN
20 Chief Innovation/Outcomes Officer .... Eric SHARKEY
11 Chief Operating Officer .... Christopher BISHOP
06 Registrar .... Abby DOLAN
84 Chief Enrollment Mgmt Officer .... Lindsay OGLESBY
09 Institutional Research Officer .... Sasha HEARD

100 Chief of Staff ... Frank VAZQUEZ

† Accredited through Dec 2016 until teach out plan is complete.

AMDA College and Conservatory of the Performing Arts (A)

6305 Yucca Street, Los Angeles CA 90028
County: Los Angeles Identification: 666721
Telephone: (323) 469-3300 Carnegie Class: Not Classified
FAX Number: (323) 469-1448 Calendar System: Semester
URL: www.amda.edu
Established: 1964 Annual Undergrad Tuition & Fees: N/A
Enrollment: N/A Coed
Affiliation or Control: Independent Non-Profit IRS Status: 501(c)3
Highest Offering: Baccalaureate
Accreditation: THEA

01 President/Artistic Director ... David MARTIN
05 Executive Director/Vice President ... Jan RUGGAR MARTIN
07 Natl Dir of Admissions/Career Svcs ... Karen JACKSON
37 Associate Director of Financial Aid ... Jillian DOYLE
26 Associate Marketing Manager ... Jenny YU

American Academy of Dramatic Arts, Los Angeles Campus (B)

1336 N La Brea Avenue, Hollywood CA 90028-7504
Telephone: (323) 464-2777 FICE Identification: 021069
Accreditation: &M, THEA

† Regional accreditation is carried under the parent institution in New York, NY.

American Baptist Seminary of the West (C)

2606 Dwight Way, Berkeley CA 94704-3097
County: Alameda FICE Identification: 001120
Unit ID: 108861
Telephone: (510) 841-1905 Carnegie Class: Spec-4-yr-Faith
FAX Number: (510) 841-2446 Calendar System: Semester
URL: www.absw.edu
Established: 1871 Annual Graduate Tuition & Fees: N/A
Enrollment: 53 Coed
Affiliation or Control: American Baptist IRS Status: 501(c)3
Highest Offering: Doctorate; No Undergraduates
Accreditation: THEOL

01 Interim President ... Dr. Nick CARTER
03 Vice President ... Rev. Michelle M. HOLMES
05 Academic Dean ... Dr. LeAnn SNOW FLESHER
10 Chief Financial Officer ... Rev. Michelle M. HOLMES
06 Registrar ... Dr. Valerie MILES-TRIBBLE
07 Director of Admissions ... Rev. Tripp HUDGINS
32 Director of Student Services ... Dr. Valerie MILES-TRIBBLE
04 Administrative Asst to President ... Rev. Carolyn E. MATTHEWS

American Career College-Los Angeles (D)

4021 Rosewood Avenue, Los Angeles CA 90004
County: Los Angeles FICE Identification: 022418
Unit ID: 109040
Telephone: (323) 668-7555 Carnegie Class: Spec 2-yr-Health
FAX Number: (322) 953-3654 Calendar System: Other
URL: www.americancareercollege.edu
Established: 1978 Annual Undergrad Tuition & Fees: N/A
Enrollment: 1,613 Coed
Affiliation or Control: Proprietary IRS Status: Proprietary
Highest Offering: Associate Degree
Accreditation: ABHES, SURTEC

01 Director ... Mr. Chris TUREN

American Career College-Ontario (E)

3130 East Sedona Court, Ontario CA 91764
County: San Bernardino FICE Identification: 039713
Unit ID: 447768
Telephone: (909) 218-3253 Carnegie Class: Spec 2-yr-Health
FAX Number: (909) 218-3340 Calendar System: Other
URL: www.americancareercollege.edu
Established: 2006 Annual Undergrad Tuition & Fees: N/A
Enrollment: 1,483 Coed
Affiliation or Control: Proprietary IRS Status: Proprietary
Highest Offering: Associate Degree
Accreditation: ABHES, COARC, SURTEC

01 Campus President ... Mr. Scott WARDALL

American Career College-Orange County (F)

1200 North Magnolia Avenue, Anaheim CA 92801-2607
Telephone: (714) 952-9066 Identification: 667073
Accreditation: ABHES, CAHIIM, COARC, OTA, PTAA, SURTEC

American Conservatory Theater (G)

30 Grant Avenue, 6th floor, San Francisco CA 94108-5800
County: San Francisco FICE Identification: 020992
Unit ID: 109086
Telephone: (415) 439-2350 Carnegie Class: Spec-4-yr-Arts
FAX Number: (415) 834-3210 Calendar System: Semester
URL: www.act-sf.org
Established: 1969 Annual Graduate Tuition & Fees: $26,951
Enrollment: 48 Coed
Affiliation or Control: Independent Non-Profit IRS Status: 501(c)3
Highest Offering: Master's; No Undergraduates
Accreditation: WC

01 Conservatory Director ... Melissa SMITH
88 Artistic Director ... Carey PERLOFF
05 Director of Academic Affairs ... Jack SHARRAR
10 Finance Director ... Jason SEIFER
30 Director Development ... Amber Jo MANUEL
37 Director of Financial Aid ... Jerry LOPEZ
26 Marketing Manager ... Christine MILLER

American Evangelical University (H)

1818 S. Western Avenue #409, Los Angeles CA 90006
County: Los Angeles Identification: 667090
Telephone: (323) 643-0301 Carnegie Class: Not Classified
FAX Number: (323) 643-0302 Calendar System: Semester
URL: www.aeu.edu
Established: 2001 Annual Undergrad Tuition & Fees: N/A
Enrollment: N/A Coed
Affiliation or Control: Independent Non-Profit IRS Status: 501(c)3
Highest Offering: Doctorate
Accreditation: BI

01 President ... Dr. Jongkil RYU
05 Academic Dean ... Dr. Mark SUKKIL YOON
32 Dean of Student Affairs ... Rev. Timothy LEE
10 CFO ... Rev. Kim ZION
30 Chief Development Officer ... Dr. Yo Han PYEON
08 Director of Library ... Dr. Duk YOUNG WON

American Film Institute Conservatory (I)

2021 N Western Avenue, Los Angeles CA 90027-1657
County: Los Angeles FICE Identification: 022220
Unit ID: 108870
Telephone: (323) 856-7600 Carnegie Class: Spec-4-yr-Arts
FAX Number: (323) 467-4578 Calendar System: Semester
URL: www.afi.com
Established: 1969 Annual Graduate Tuition & Fees: N/A
Enrollment: 324 Coed
Affiliation or Control: Independent Non-Profit IRS Status: 501(c)3
Highest Offering: Master's; No Undergraduates
Accreditation: WC, ART

01 Director American Film Institute ... Mr. Bob GAZZALE
11 Chief Operating Officer ... Ms. Nancy HARRIS
30 Chief Advancement Officer ... Mr. Tom WEST
05 Exec Vice Dean of Conservatory ... Mr. Joe PETRICCA
20 Vice Dean for Production/Post Prod ... Vacant
20 Dean of Academic Affairs ... Mr. David CHASE
20 Dean of Conservatory ... Ms. Jan SCHUETTE
32 Director Fellow Affairs ... Vacant
57 Artistic Director ... Mr. James L. BROOKS
06 Registrar ... Ms. Carmela CHANEY
15 Director Human Resources ... Ms. Roschoune FRANKLIN
37 Financial Aid Director ... Ms. Trina RODLER
08 Librarian ... Mr. Robert VAUGHN
13 Director Information Technology ... Mr. Scott BLY

American Graduate University (J)

733 N Dodsworth Avenue, Covina CA 91724-2408
County: Los Angeles Identification: 666982
Unit ID: 109095
Telephone: (626) 966-4576 Carnegie Class: Not Classified
FAX Number: (626) 915-1709 Calendar System: Other
URL: www.agu.edu
Established: 1969 Annual Graduate Tuition & Fees: N/A
Enrollment: N/A Coed
Affiliation or Control: Proprietary IRS Status: Proprietary
Highest Offering: Master's; No Undergraduates
Accreditation: DEAC

01 President ... Mr. Paul R. MCDONALD
05 Director Academic Affairs ... Mr. Paul R. MCDONALD
11 Dir of Administration/Admissios ... Ms. Laurie MEJIA
32 Director of Student Services ... Ms. Rachel RUIZ
06 Registrar ... Ms. Debbie MCDONALD
26 Director of Marketing ... Ms. Barbara YOUNG

American Jewish University (K)

15600 Mulholland Drive, Los Angeles CA 90077-1599
County: Los Angeles FICE Identification: 002741
Unit ID: 116846
Telephone: (310) 476-9777 Carnegie Class: Bac-A&S
FAX Number: (310) 471-1278 Calendar System: Semester
URL: www.aju.edu
Established: 1947 Annual Undergrad Tuition & Fees: $30,236
Enrollment: 204 Coed
Affiliation or Control: Independent Non-Profit IRS Status: 501(c)3
Highest Offering: Master's
Accreditation: WC

01 President ... Dr. Robert WEXLER

American Medical Sciences Center (L)

225 West Broadway, Ste 115, Glendale CA 91204
FICE Identification: 041597
Unit ID: 461263
Telephone: (818) 240-6900 Carnegie Class: Not Classified
FAX Number: (818) 240-6902 Calendar System: Semester
URL: www.amscedu.com
Established: Annual Undergrad Tuition & Fees: N/A
Enrollment: 84 Coed
Affiliation or Control: Proprietary IRS Status: Proprietary
Highest Offering: Associate Degree
Accreditation: ABHES

01 President ... Vardan KARAGEZIAN

American University of Armenia (M)

1000 Broadway, Suite 280, Oakland CA 94607
County: Alameda Identification: 666013
Telephone: (510) 925-4282 Carnegie Class: Not Classified
FAX Number: (510) 925-4283 Calendar System: Semester
URL: www.aua.am
Established: 1991 Annual Undergrad Tuition & Fees: N/A
Enrollment: N/A Coed
Affiliation or Control: Independent Non-Profit IRS Status: 501(c)3
Highest Offering: Master's
Accreditation: WC

01 President ... Dr. Armen DER KIUREGHIAN
05 Provost ... Dr. Randall RHODES
11 Vice President Operations ... Ashot GHAZARYAN
10 Vice President of Finance ... Gevorg GOYUNYAN
30 VP Development/External Relations ... Lorraine ALEXANDER
06 Associate Registrar ... Chaghig ARZROUNI-CHAHINIAN
26 Public Relations Coordinator ... Diana MANUKYAN
07 Dir Admissions/Recruit/Intl Stdnts ... Arina ZOHRABIAN
09 Institutional Research Manager ... Anush BEZHANYAN
08 Head Librarian ... Satenik AVAKIAN
101 Secretary of the Institution/Board ... Caren MEGHREBLIAN
15 Director Personnel Services ... Arina BEKCHIAN
29 Director Alumni Relations ... Narine PETROSYAN
50 Dean of Business and Economics ... Eric VAN GENDEREN
69 Dean of Public Health ... Varduhi PETROSYAN

American University of Health Sciences (N)

1600 E Hill St Building #1, Signal Hill CA 90755
County: Los Angeles FICE Identification: 032253
Unit ID: 433004
Telephone: (562) 988-2278 Carnegie Class: Spec-4-yr-Other Health
FAX Number: (562) 988-1791 Calendar System: Quarter
URL: www.auhs.edu
Established: 1994 Annual Undergrad Tuition & Fees: $23,223
Enrollment: 282 Coed
Affiliation or Control: Proprietary IRS Status: Proprietary
Highest Offering: Master's
Accreditation: ACICS, NURSE

01 Interim President ... Dr. Kim DANG
11 Chief Operating Officer ... Dr. Gregory A. JOHNSON

Anaheim University (O)

1240 S State College Blvd, Ste 110,
Anaheim CA 92806-5152
County: Orange Identification: 666651
Telephone: (714) 772-3330 Carnegie Class: Not Classified
FAX Number: (714) 772-3331 Calendar System: Other
URL: www.anaheim.edu
Established: 1996 Annual Graduate Tuition & Fees: N/A
Enrollment: N/A Coed
Affiliation or Control: Proprietary IRS Status: Proprietary
Highest Offering: Doctorate; No Undergraduates
Accreditation: DEAC

01 President ... Dr. Andrew E. HONEYCUTT
32 Vice Pres Student/Alumni Affs ... Dr. William HARTLEY
11 Administrative Director ... Ms. Kate STRAUSS

Angeles College (P)

3440 Wilshire Boulevard, Suite 310,
Los Angeles CA 90010
County: Los Angeles FICE Identification: 041604
Unit ID: 457299
Telephone: (213) 487-2211 Carnegie Class: Spec-4-yr-Other Health
FAX Number: (213) 487-2299 Calendar System: Semester
URL: www.angelescollege.edu
Established: 2004 Annual Undergrad Tuition & Fees: N/A
Enrollment: 94 Coed
Affiliation or Control: Proprietary IRS Status: Proprietary
Highest Offering: Baccalaureate

Accreditation: ABHES

01 CEO/School Director .... Ms. Teresa KRAUSE

Angeles College-City of Industry **(A)**

17595 Almahurst Street, Suite 101-3,
City of Industry CA 91748
Telephone: (626) 965-5566 Identification: 770518
Accreditation: ABHES

Antelope Valley College (B)

3041 W Avenue K, Lancaster CA 93536-5426
County: Los Angeles FICE Identification: 001113
Unit ID: 109350
Telephone: (661) 722-6300 Carnegie Class: Assoc/HT-High Trad
FAX Number: (661) 722-6333 Calendar System: Semester
URL: www.avc.edu
Established: 1929 Annual Undergrad Tuition & Fees (In-District): $1,104
Enrollment: 14,578 Coed
Affiliation or Control: State/Local IRS Status: 501(c)3
Highest Offering: Baccalaureate
Accreditation: WJ, COARC, RAD

01 President/Superintendent .... Mr. Edward T. KNUDSON
05 VP Academic Affairs .... Dr. Bonnie SUDERMAN
32 VP Student Services .... Dr. Erin E. VINES
15 Vice President Human Resources .... Mr. Mark BRYANT
84 Dean Enrollment Services .... Ms. LaDonna TRIMBLE
35 Dean of Student Services .... Dr. Jill ZIMMERMAN
22 Director Disabled Students .... Dr. Louis LUCERO
26 Exec Director Marketing/Public Info .... Ms. Elizabeth DIACHUN
18 Director Facilities Services .... Mr. Doug JENSEN
13 Director Information Technology .... Mr. Rick SHAW
30 Dir Inst Advancement & Foundation .... Ms. Dianne KNIPPEL
09 Director Inst Research & Planning .... Dr. Meeta GOEL
37 Director Financial Aid .... Ms. Nichelle WILLIAMS
68 Dean PE/Athlet/Visual and Perf Arts .... Mr. Newton CHELETTE
79 Dean Language Arts/Academic Dev .... Dr. Charlotte FORTE-PARNELL
83 Dean Soc & Beh Sci/Bus/Comp Stds .... Dr. Tom O'NEIL
38 Dean Counseling & Matriculation .... Mr. Gary ROGGENSTEIN
76 Dean Health Sciences/Tech Educ .... Dr. Karen COWELL
81 Dean of Math/Science & Engineering .... Dr. Les UHAZY

Antioch University Los Angeles **(C)**

400 Corporate Pointe, Culver City CA 90230
Telephone: (310) 578-1080 Identification: 666236
Accreditation: &NH

† Regional accreditation is carried under the parent institution in Yellow Springs, OH.

Antioch University Santa Barbara **(D)**

602 Anacapa Street, Santa Barbara CA 93101
Telephone: (805) 962-8179 Identification: 666231
Accreditation: &NH

† Regional accreditation is carried under the parent institution in Yellow Springs, OH.

Apollos University (E)

17011 Beach Boulevard, Ste 900,
Huntington Beach CA 92647
County: Orange Identification: 667096
Telephone: (714) 841-6252 Carnegie Class: Not Classified
FAX Number: (866) 287-1938 Calendar System: Quarter
URL: www.apollos-university.edu
Established: 2005 Annual Undergrad Tuition & Fees: N/A
Enrollment: N/A Coed
Affiliation or Control: Proprietary IRS Status: Proprietary
Highest Offering: Doctorate
Accreditation: DEAC

00 CEO .... Dr. Paul EIDSON
01 President/CAO .... Dr. Scott EIDSON
05 Executive Vice President/Provost .... Dr. Robin WESTERIK

APT College (F)

1939 Palomar Oaks Way, Suite A,
Carlsbad CA 92011-1311
County: San Diego Identification: 666245
Telephone: (800) 431-8488 Carnegie Class: Not Classified
FAX Number: (888) 431-8588 Calendar System: Quarter
URL: www.aptc.edu
Established: 1993 Annual Undergrad Tuition & Fees: N/A
Enrollment: N/A Coed
Affiliation or Control: Proprietary IRS Status: Proprietary
Highest Offering: Associate Degree
Accreditation: DEAC

01 President/Chief Executive Officer .... Mr. Anthony MORENO
05 Director of Academics .... Dr. Gabriella MAIELLO
06 Registrar/Academic Comp Manager .... Ms. Julie B. LOVE
10 Dir of Accounting & Administration .... Ms. Cheryl DODDS

Argosy University, Inland Empire **(G)**

3401 Centre Lake Drive, Suite 200, Ontario CA 91761
Telephone: (909) 472-0800 Identification: 666007
Accreditation: &WC, ACBSP

† Regional accreditation is carried under the parent institution in Orange, CA.

Argosy University, Los Angeles **(H)**

5230 Pacific Concourse Drive, Los Angeles CA 90045
Telephone: (310) 531-9700 Identification: 666011
Accreditation: &WC, ACBSP

† Regional accreditation is carried under the parent institution in Orange, CA.

Argosy University, Orange County (I)

601 South Lewis Street, Orange CA 92868
County: Orange FICE Identification: 021799
Unit ID: 436438
Telephone: (714) 620-3700 Carnegie Class: DU-Mod
FAX Number: (714) 620-3802 Calendar System: Semester
URL: www.argosy.edu/orangecounty
Established: 1999 Annual Undergrad Tuition & Fees: $13,560
Enrollment: 606 Coed
Affiliation or Control: Proprietary IRS Status: Proprietary
Highest Offering: Doctorate
Accreditation: WC, ACBSP, CLPSY, #TED

01 University President .... Dr. Cynthia BAUM
12 Campus President .... Dan RICHINS
05 Vice President of Acadmic Affairs .... Diana SIGANOFF
32 Director of Student Services .... Christy MCAFEE
06 Registrar .... Yee LIAU

† Main Campus and HQ moved from Chicago, IL to Orange, CA

Argosy University, San Diego **(J)**

1615 Murray Canyon Rd, Suite 100,
San Diego CA 92108-4423
Telephone: (619) 321-3000 Identification: 666034
Accreditation: &WC ACBSP

† Regional accreditation is carried under the parent institution in Orange, CA.

Argosy University, San Francisco Bay Area **(K)**

1005 Atlantic Avenue, Alameda CA 94501-1148
Telephone: (510) 217-4700 Identification: 666081
Accreditation: &WC ACBSP, CLPSY

† Regional accreditation is carried under the parent institution in Orange, CA.

Art Center College of Design (L)

1700 Lida Street, Pasadena CA 91103-1999
County: Los Angeles FICE Identification: 001116
Unit ID: 109651
Telephone: (626) 396-2200 Carnegie Class: Spec-4-yr-Arts
FAX Number: N/A Calendar System: Semester
URL: www.artcenter.edu
Established: 1930 Annual Undergrad Tuition & Fees: $39,230
Enrollment: 2,045 Coed
Affiliation or Control: Independent Non-Profit IRS Status: 501(c)3
Highest Offering: Master's
Accreditation: WC, ART

01 President .... Dr. Lorne M. BUCHMAN
10 Sr VP/Chief Financial Officer .... Mr. Rich HALUSCHAK
05 Provost .... Mr. Fred FEHLAU
30 Sr Vice Pres Development .... Ms. Emily LASKIN
07 Sr VP Admissions/Enrollment Mgmt .... Ms. Kit BARON
88 VP Exhibitions .... Mr. Steve NOWLIN
13 VP Information Technology .... Ms. Theresa ZIX
26 VP Marketing & Communication .... Mr. Jered GOLD
15 Vice Pres Human Resources .... Ms. Lisa M. SANCHEZ
32 Associate Provost Student Affairs .... Mr. Ray QUIROLGICO
08 College Librarian & Managing Dir .... Mr. Mario ASCENCIO
21 Controller .... Ms. Diane WITTENBERG
37 Managing Director Financial Aid .... Ms. Victoria AMEZCUA
29 Director of Alumni Affairs .... Ms. Kristine BOWNE
06 Director of Enrollment & Registrar .... Mr. William GARTRELL
09 Director of Institutional Research .... Ms. Esmeralda NAVA
19 Dir Environmental Health & Safety .... Vacant
102 Sr Dir Foundation/Govt Relations .... Mr. Darryl MORI
36 Director of Career Development .... Ms. Denise GIANOUSSOPOULOS
18 Director of Facilities .... Mr. Jess RIVAS
96 Director of Purchasing .... Ms. Monica MATSUO

The Art Institute of California, A College of Argosy University - Hollywood **(M)**

5250 Lankershim Boulevard, North Hollywood CA 91601
Telephone: (213) 251-3636 FICE Identification: 031254
Accreditation: &WC, CIDA

† Regional accreditation is carried under the parent institution, Argosy University in Orange, CA.

The Art Institute of California, A College of Argosy University - Inland Empire **(N)**

674 East Brier Drive, San Bernardino CA 92408-2800
Telephone: (909) 915-2100 FICE Identification: 016471
Accreditation: &WC

† Regional accreditation is carried under the parent institution, Argosy University in Orange, CA.

The Art Institute of California, A College of Argosy University - Los Angeles **(O)**

2900 31st Street, Santa Monica CA 90405-3035
Telephone: (310) 752-4700 Identification: 666045
Accreditation: &WC, ACFEI CIDA

† In teach-out plan. Regional accreditation is carried under the parent institution, Argosy University in Orange, CA.

The Art Institute of California, A College of Argosy University - Orange County **(P)**

3601 W Sunflower Avenue, Santa Ana CA 92704-7931
Telephone: (714) 830-0200 Identification: 666182
Accreditation: &WC, ACFEI CIDA

† Regional accreditation is carried under the parent institution, Argosy University in Orange, CA.

The Art Institute of California, A College of Argosy University - Sacramento **(Q)**

2850 Gateway Oaks Drive, Suite 100,
Sacramento CA 95833-4348
Telephone: (916) 830-6320 Identification: 666619
Accreditation: &WC

† Regional accreditation is carried under the parent institution, Argosy University in Orange, CA

The Art Institute of California, A College of Argosy University - San Diego **(R)**

7650 Mission Valley Road, San Diego CA 92108-4423
Telephone: (858) 598-1200 FICE Identification: 023276
Accreditation: &WC, ACFEI, CIDA

† Regional accreditation is carried under the parent institution, Argosy University in Orange, CA.

The Art Institute of California - San Francisco, a campus of Argosy University **(S)**

10 United Nations Plaza, San Francisco CA 94102-4928
Telephone: (888) 493-3261 FICE Identification: 007236
Accreditation: &WC

† Regional accreditation is carried under the parent institution, Argosy University in Orange, CA.

The Art Institute of California, A College of Argosy University - Sunnyvale **(T)**

1120 Kifer Road, Sunnyvale CA 94086-5303
Telephone: (408) 962-6400 Identification: 666620
Accreditation: &WC

† In teach-out mode. Regional accreditation is carried under the parent institution, Argosy University in Orange, CA. Campus is in teach-out plan.

Asher College (U)

1215 Howe Street, Suite 101, Sacramento CA 95825
County: Sacramento FICE Identification: 040573
Unit ID: 447777
Telephone: (916) 649-9600 Carnegie Class: Spec 2-yr-Tech
FAX Number: N/A Calendar System: Other
URL: www.asher.edu
Established: 1998 Annual Undergrad Tuition & Fees: N/A
Enrollment: 716 Coed
Affiliation or Control: Proprietary IRS Status: Proprietary
Highest Offering: Associate Degree
Accreditation: CNCE

01 President .... David VICE

Ashford University (V)

8620 Spectrum Center Blvd, San Diego CA 92123
County: San Diego FICE Identification: 001881
Unit ID: 154022
Telephone: (866) 974-5700 Carnegie Class: Masters/L
FAX Number: (866) 685-4091 Calendar System: Semester
URL: www.ashford.edu
Established: 1918 Annual Undergrad Tuition & Fees: $10,720
Enrollment: 51,237 Coed
Affiliation or Control: Proprietary IRS Status: Proprietary
Highest Offering: Master's
Accreditation: WC, IACBE

01 University President/CEO .... Mr. Craig SWENSON
05 VP Academic Affairs .... Dr. Mihaela TANASESCU
10 Chief Finance Officer .... Mr. Jim SMITH
11 Sr VP University Svcs & Strat Plng .... Ms. Sheri JONES
88 VP University Services & Policy .... Mr. Mike ROBINSON
06 VP University Registrar .... Mr. Kirk MORRISON
32 VP Student Services .... Ms. Shelley SCHAFFER
35 AVP Student Affairs .... Ms. Poppy FITCH
37 Dir Financial Aid & Policy .... Ms. Stephanie STEWART
49 Dean Division of General Education .... Dr. Justin HARRISON
50 Dean Forbes School of Business .... Mr. Bob DAUGHERTY
53 Dean College of Education .... Dr. Tony FARRELL

Azusa Pacific University (A)

901 E Alosta Avenue, Azusa CA 91702-7000
County: Los Angeles FICE Identification: 001117
Unit ID: 109785
Telephone: (626) 969-3434 Carnegie Class: DU-Mod
FAX Number: (626) 969-7180 Calendar System: Semester
URL: www.apu.edu
Established: 1899 Annual Undergrad Tuition & Fees: $34,754
Enrollment: 9,972 Coed
Affiliation or Control: Independent Non-Profit IRS Status: 501(c)3
Highest Offering: Doctorate
Accreditation: WC, ART, CAATE, CLPSY, IACBE, MUS, NURSE, PTA, SW, TED, THEOL

01 President .... Dr. Jon R. WALLACE
05 Provost .... Dr. Mark STANTON
26 Exec Vice Pres External Affairs .... Mr. David E. BIXBY
12 Chancellor University College .... Dr. John C. REYNOLDS
32 Senior Vice Pres for Student Life .... Dr. Terry FRANSON
10 Vice President Business Affairs/CFO .... Mr. Bob L. JOHANSEN
43 Senior Vice President/Gen Counsel .... Dr. Mark DICKERSON
13 Vice President/CIO .... Dr. Don DAVIS
84 VP Grad/Nontrdtnl Enroll/Stdnt Svc .... Dr. Heather PETRIDIS
84 VP for Enrollment Management .... Mr. David DUFAULT-HUNTER
58 Vice Provost Graduate Programs .... Dr. Diane GUIDO
20 Vice Provost Undergraduate Programs .... Dr. Vicky BOWDEN
35 AVP Student Life/Chief Judicial Ofc .... Mr. Willie HAMLETT
88 Assoc VP University Services .... Mr. Roger HODSDON
27 VP University Relations .... Dr. David PECK
49 Dean College Liberal Arts/Sci .... Dr. Jennifer WALSH
83 Dean School Behav/Applied Sciences .... Dr. Robert WELSH
50 Dean School of Business Mgmt .... Dr. Robert ROLLER
53 Dean School of Education .... Dr. Anita HENCK
73 Int Dean Haggard Sch of Theology .... Dr. Robert DUKE
64 Dean College of Music and the Arts .... Dr. Stephen JOHNSON
66 Dean School of Nursing .... Dr. Aja LESH
92 Dean Honors College .... Dr. David WEEKS
35 Assoc Dean Students/Dir Student Act .... Mrs. Shino SIMONS
15 Exec Director Human Resources .... Mr. John BAUGUS
30 VP University Advancement .... Mr. Corbin HOORNBEEK
21 Executive Director Finance .... Vacant
42 Campus Pastor .... Dr. Woody MOORWOOD
37 Dir Graduate Student Financial Svcs .... Mrs. Michelle JOHNSON
06 Registrar-Graduate .... Mrs. Norma MOCABEE
06 Associate Registrar-Undergraduate .... Ms. Mona MIKHAIL
29 Director Alumni Relations .... Vacant
09 Director Acad Info Mgmt Analysis .... Vacant
41 Director Athletics .... Mr. Gary PINE
38 Director Counseling Center .... Dr. Bill FIALA
37 AVP for UG Academic Financial Svcs .... Mr. Todd ROSS
18 Associate VP Facilities Management .... Mr. Thomas HUNT
07 Director Undergraduate Admissions .... Mrs. Kimberly WIEDEFELD
36 Director Career Services .... Ms. Lynn PEARSON
28 Exec Dir Diversity Planning/Assess .... Mr. Richard MARTINEZ
96 Purchasing Manager .... Mrs. Jo Ann BENGEL

Barstow Community College District (B)

2700 Barstow Road, Barstow CA 92311-6699
County: San Bernardino FICE Identification: 001119
Unit ID: 109907
Telephone: (760) 252-2411 Carnegie Class: Assoc/HT-High Non
FAX Number: (760) 252-1875 Calendar System: Semester
URL: www.barstow.edu
Established: 1959 Annual Undergrad Tuition & Fees (In-District): $1,104
Enrollment: 1,859 Coed
Affiliation or Control: State/Local IRS Status: 170(c)1
Highest Offering: Associate Degree
Accreditation: WJ

01 Superintendent/President .... Dr. Deborah DITHOMAS
04 Exec Assistant to the President .... Ms. Michelle HENDERSON
10 Vice President Admin Services .... Mr. George WALTERS
05 Vice President Academic Affairs .... Mr. Stephen B. EATON
32 Vice President Student Services .... Dr. Khushnur Z. DADABHOY
15 Assoc Vice President of HR .... Mr. Clint DOUGHERTY
22 Dean Student Success & Equity .... Ms. Tonia TERESH
106 Dean DE & Learning Support Svc .... Mr. Richard BOTENGAN
49 Dean of Instruction .... Ms. Penny SHREVE
103 Dean Workforce & Econ Dev .... Ms. Sandi THOMAS
09 Dir Research Dev & Planning .... Ms. Lisa HOLMES
26 Dir of Public Rels/Comm & Marketing .... Mr. Chris CLARKE
18 Director Maintenance & Operations .... Mr. Richard HERNANDEZ
21 Director Fiscal Services .... Ms. Shawna L. ROBBINS
84 Director Enrollment Services .... Ms. Heather MINEHART
88 Civic Center & Event Manager .... Vacant
41 Assoc Dean of Students & Athletics .... Vacant
35 Director Student Life & Dev .... Ms. Joann GARCIA
88 Director CTE Grants .... Mr. James LEE
88 Director Military Programs .... Mr. Jerry PETERS
88 Director Special Pgms & Svcs .... Vacant
21 Budget Analyst .... Ms. Maureen DAVIS

Bergin University of Canine Studies (C)

5860 Labath Avenue, Rohnert Park CA 94928
County: Sonoma FICE Identification: 041763
Unit ID: 461643
Telephone: (707) 545-3647 Carnegie Class: Bac/Assoc-Mixed
FAX Number: (707) 545-0800 Calendar System: Semester
URL: www.berginu.edu
Established: 1991 Annual Undergrad Tuition & Fees: N/A
Enrollment: 65 Coed
Affiliation or Control: Independent Non-Profit IRS Status: 501(c)3
Highest Offering: Master's
Accreditation: ACICS

01 President .... Dr. Bonita M. BERGIN
05 Chief Academic Officer .... Dr. Bonita BERGIN
06 Registrar .... Denise GREGERSEN
07 Director of Admissions .... Connie VAN GUILDER

Bethesda University of California (D)

730 N Euclid Street, Anaheim CA 92801-4115
County: Orange FICE Identification: 032663
Unit ID: 110060
Telephone: (714) 517-1945 Carnegie Class: Spec-4-yr-Faith
FAX Number: (714) 683-1440 Calendar System: Semester
URL: www.buc.edu
Established: 1976 Annual Undergrad Tuition & Fees: $9,120
Enrollment: 331 Coed
Affiliation or Control: Independent Non-Profit IRS Status: 501(c)3
Highest Offering: Doctorate
Accreditation: BI, TRACS

01 President .... Dr. Daniel CHUNG
10 Vice President/Chief Financial Ofcr .... Dr. Esther CHO
05 Chief Academic Officer .... Dr. Sin Ho KIM
32 Dean of Student Affairs .... Dr. Hyoin KIM
08 Librarian .... Ms. Ho Kyung WOO
07 Admissions Director .... Ms. Helen CHUN
37 Financial Aid Officer .... Ms. Patricia MEDINA

Biola University (E)

13800 Biola Avenue, La Mirada CA 90639-0001
County: Los Angeles FICE Identification: 001122
Unit ID: 110097
Telephone: (562) 903-6000 Carnegie Class: DU-Mod
FAX Number: (562) 903-4748 Calendar System: 4/1/4
URL: www.biola.edu
Established: 1908 Annual Undergrad Tuition & Fees: $34,498
Enrollment: 6,358 Coed
Affiliation or Control: Independent Non-Profit IRS Status: 501(c)3
Highest Offering: Doctorate
Accreditation: WC, ACBSP, ART, CLPSY, IPSY, MUS, NURSE, @SP, THEOL

01 President .... Dr. Barry H. COREY
05 Provost/Sr Vice President .... Dr. Deborah TAYLOR
10 Vice Pres Business/Financial Affs .... Mr. Michael PIERCE
30 Vice President Advancement .... Dr. Adam MORRIS
11 Vice President University Services .... Mr. Gregory R. BALSANO
84 Vice Pres Enrollment Management .... Mr. Greg VAUGHAN
26 VP Univ Communications & Marketing .... Mr. Lee WILHITE
20 Vice Provost/Academic Admin .... Dr. Patricia PIKE
28 Vice Prov Incl/Cross Cultural Eng .... Dr. Pamela CHRISTIAN
07 Assoc VP University Admissions .... Mr. Andre STEPHENS
73 Dean Talbot School Theology .... Dr. Clinton E. ARNOLD
83 Dean Rosemead School Psychology .... Dr. Clark D. CAMPBELL
88 Dean Cook Sch Intercultural Studies .... Dr. Bulus GALADIMA
53 Dean School of Education .... Dr. June HETZEL
50 Dean Crowell School of Business .... Dr. Gary LINDBALD
81 Dean of Science and Health .... Dr. Walt STANGL
57 Dean of Fine Arts and Communication .... Dr. Douglas TARPLEY
08 Dean of the Library .... Dr. Gregg GEARY
42 Dean of Spiritual Development .... Dr. Todd PICKETT
32 Dean of Students .... Mr. Danny PASCHALL
06 Dean Academic Records/Inst Research .... Mr. Ken GILSON
79 Assoc Dean of Humanities/Soc Sci .... Ms. Jamie CAMPBELL
57 Assoc Dean Fine Arts & Comm .... Mr. Jonathan PULS
15 Sr Director Human Resources .... Mr. Ronald G. MOORADIAN
45 Sr Dir Financial Plng/Operations .... Ms. Sandie WEAVER
29 Sr Dir Alumni & Parent Relations .... Dr. Richard BEE
37 Sr Director Financial Aid .... Mr. Geoff MARSH
21 Director Financial Mgmt/Reporting .... Mr. David KOONTZ
19 Chief Campus Safety .... Mr. John O. OJEISEKHOBA
90 Sr Director Information Technology .... Mr. Steven R. EARLE
36 Director Career Dev & Success .... Vacant
41 Athletics Director .... Dr. Bethany MILLER
40 Manager Bookstore .... Ms. Melissa CASTELLANO
18 Sr Director Facilities Management .... Mr. Brian PHILLIPS
38 Director Counseling Center .... Dr. Melanie TAYLOR
96 Purchasing Manager .... Mrs. Breanna KLETT
13 Chief Education Technology Officer .... Mrs. Susan ISHII
07 Sr Director Graduate Admissions .... Vacant
106 Dir Digital Learning and Pgm Devel .... Dr. Ron G. HANNAFORD
108 Director of University Assessment .... Dr. Rebecca HONG
43 University Legal Counsel .... Mr. Jerry MACKEY

Brandman University (F)

16355 Laguna Canyon Road, Irvine CA 92618
County: Orange FICE Identification: 041618
Unit ID: 262086
Telephone: (949) 753-4774 Carnegie Class: Masters/L
FAX Number: (714) 753-7875 Calendar System: Other
URL: www.brandman.edu
Established: 1958 Annual Undergrad Tuition & Fees: $12,240
Enrollment: 7,795 Coed
Affiliation or Control: Independent Non-Profit IRS Status: 501(c)3
Highest Offering: Doctorate
Accreditation: TED, WC, NURSE, SW

01 Chancellor .... Dr. Gary BRAHM
12 Campus Director .... Mr. Jan HARTZ
05 Associate Dean School of Education .... Ms. Patricia CLARK-WHITE
07 Director of Admissions .... Ms. Leticia TORRES

† A member of the Chapman University System.

Brightwood College (G)

1914 Wible Road, Bakersfield CA 93304
Telephone: (661) 836-6300 Identification: 666291
Accreditation: ACICS

† Branch campus of Brightwood College, Sacramento, CA.

Brightwood College (H)

555 Broadway, Suite 144, Chula Vista CA 91910-5342
Telephone: (619) 498-4100 Identification: 770560
Accreditation: ACICS

Brightwood College (I)

44 Shaw Avenue, Clovis CA 93612
Telephone: (559) 325-5100 Identification: 770559
Accreditation: ACICS

Brightwood College (J)

6180 Laurel Canyon Blvd., Ste 101,
North Hollywood CA 91606
County: Los Angeles FICE Identification: 025391
Unit ID: 118967
Telephone: (818) 763-2563 Carnegie Class: Not Classified
FAX Number: (818) 763-1623 Calendar System: Other
URL: www.brightwood.edu
Established: 1982 Annual Undergrad Tuition & Fees: N/A
Enrollment: 789 Coed
Affiliation or Control: Proprietary IRS Status: Proprietary
Highest Offering: Associate Degree
Accreditation: ACICS, RAD

01 Campus President .... Mr. Josh LEVENSON

Brightwood College (K)

2475 E Tahquitz Canyon Way, Palm Springs CA 92262
Telephone: (760) 778-3540 Identification: 770558
Accreditation: ACICS

Brightwood College (L)

4330 Watt Avenue, Suite 400,
Sacramento CA 95821-7000
County: Sacramento FICE Identification: 023519
Unit ID: 118259
Telephone: (916) 649-8168 Carnegie Class: Spec 2-yr-Other
FAX Number: (916) 649-8344 Calendar System: Quarter
URL: www.brightwood.edu
Established: 1982 Annual Undergrad Tuition & Fees: N/A
Enrollment: 429 Coed
Affiliation or Control: Proprietary IRS Status: Proprietary
Highest Offering: Associate Degree
Accreditation: ACICS

01 Executive Director .... Scott KING
05 Director of Education .... Jeff GRAVES
37 Director of Student Financial Aid .... Ryan SMITH
07 Director of Admissions .... Zach FELDHEGE
36 Director of Career Services .... Julie MUIR

Brightwood College (M)

5172 Kiernan Court, Salida CA 95368
County: Stanislaus FICE Identification: 023063
Unit ID: 366960
Telephone: (209) 543-7000 Carnegie Class: Spec 2-yr-Health
FAX Number: (209) 543-1755 Calendar System: Other
URL: www.brightwood.edu
Established: 1986 Annual Undergrad Tuition & Fees: N/A
Enrollment: 429 Coed
Affiliation or Control: Proprietary IRS Status: Proprietary
Highest Offering: Associate Degree
Accreditation: ACICS, COARC

01 Campus President .... Mr. Bill JONES

Brightwood College (A)

9055 Balboa Avenue, San Diego CA 92123-1509

County: San Diego | FICE Identification: 020917
Unit ID: 118277
Telephone: (858) 279-4500 | Carnegie Class: Spec 2-yr-Health
FAX Number: (858) 279-4885 | Calendar System: Other
URL: www.brightwood.edu
Established: 1976 | Annual Undergrad Tuition & Fees: N/A
Enrollment: 1,297 | Coed
Affiliation or Control: Proprietary | IRS Status: Proprietary
Highest Offering: Associate Degree
Accreditation: ACICS, CAHIIM, MAAB

01 Campus President ... Mr. David MOVSESIAN
05 Director of Education ... Ms. Tammy ESQUIVEL
07 Director of Admissions ... Ms. Serica ERVIN

Brightwood College (B)

2022 University Drive, Vista CA 92083-7736

County: San Diego | FICE Identification: 025490
Unit ID: 118236
Telephone: (760) 630-1555 | Carnegie Class: Spec 2-yr-Other
FAX Number: (760) 630-1656 | Calendar System: Other
URL: www.brightwood.edu
Established: 1976 | Annual Undergrad Tuition & Fees: N/A
Enrollment: 812 | Coed
Affiliation or Control: Proprietary | IRS Status: Proprietary
Highest Offering: Associate Degree
Accreditation: ACICS

01 Executive Director ... Ms. Laura PITTS
05 Director of Education ... Mr. Destry LIEVANOS
07 Director of Admissions ... Ms. Renee CODNER
36 Director of Career Services ... Ms. Sipel TAHA
37 Director of Financial Aid ... Ms. Peetee MALLORY
66 Dean of Nursing ... Ms. Beth BUNYI

Bristol University (C)

2390 E Orangewood Avenue, Suite 485,
Anaheim CA 92806

County: Orange | FICE Identification: 033083
Unit ID: 397270
Telephone: (714) 542-8086 | Carnegie Class: Spec-4-yr-Bus
FAX Number: (714) 245-2425 | Calendar System: Semester
URL: www.bristoluniversity.edu
Established: 1991 | Annual Undergrad Tuition & Fees: N/A
Enrollment: 62 | Coed
Affiliation or Control: Proprietary | IRS Status: Proprietary
Highest Offering: Master's
Accreditation: ACICS

01 President ... Dr. Fathiah E. INSERTO
03 Vice President Compliance ... Ms. Lourdes CRUZ
37 Financial Aid Dir/Human Resources ... Ms. Lourdes CRUZ
06 Registrar ... Ms. Gina BORELLI

The Broad Center for the Management of School Systems (D)

2121 Avenue of the Stars, Ste 3000,
Los Angeles CA 90067

County: Los Angeles | Identification: 667228
Telephone: (310) 954-5080 | Carnegie Class: Not Classified
FAX Number: N/A | Calendar System: Other
URL: www.broadcenter.org
Established: | Annual Graduate Tuition & Fees: N/A
Enrollment: N/A | Coed
Affiliation or Control: Independent Non-Profit | IRS Status: 501(c)3
Highest Offering: Master's; No Undergraduates
Accreditation: WC

01 Executive Director ... Becca BRACY KNIGHT
13 Asst Director Information Systems ... Eulogio GALLO
26 Senior Director Communications ... Stephanie GERMERAAD

Bryan University (E)

3580 Wilshire Boulevard, Suite 400,
Los Angeles CA 90010

County: Los Angeles | FICE Identification: 007164
Unit ID: 110219
Telephone: (213) 484-8850 | Carnegie Class: Bac/Assoc-Assoc Dom
FAX Number: (213) 483-3936 | Calendar System: Semester
URL: www.bryancollege.edu
Established: 1940 | Annual Undergrad Tuition & Fees: $11,945
Enrollment: 1,358 | Coed
Affiliation or Control: Proprietary | IRS Status: Proprietary
Highest Offering: Master's
Accreditation: ACICS

01 President ... Mr. John KOLACINSKI

Butte College (F)

3536 Butte Campus Drive, Oroville CA 95965-8399

County: Butte | FICE Identification: 008073
Unit ID: 110246
Telephone: (530) 895-2511 | Carnegie Class: Assoc/MT-VT-High Trad
FAX Number: (530) 895-2345 | Calendar System: Semester
URL: www.butte.edu
Established: 1966 | Annual Undergrad Tuition & Fees (In-District): $1,364
Enrollment: 12,161 | Coed
Affiliation or Control: State/Local | IRS Status: 501(c)3
Highest Offering: Associate Degree
Accreditation: WJ, COARC, EMT

01 Superintendent/President ... Dr. Samia YAQUB
05 Int Vice Pres Student Learning ... Mr. Matthews JACKSON
10 VP Administrative Service/CBO ... Mr. Andrew SULESKI
45 Vice President Planning/Research ... Mr. Lester JAURON
32 Vice President Student Services ... Mr. Allen RENVILLE
20 Dean Student Learning ... Ms. Suzanne GRIPENSTRAW
20 Dean Student Learning ... Ms. Kam BULL
20 Dean Student Learning ... Ms. Donna WEAVER
20 Dean Student Learning ... Ms. Denise ADAMS
20 Int Dean Student Learning ... Dr. Cheryl BABLER
37 Director Financial Aid/Vet Svcs ... Ms. Tammera SHINAR
15 Director Human Resources ... Ms. Kelly BARRON
18 Dir Facilities Planning/Management ... Mr. Ken ALBRIGHT
09 Director of Institutional Research ... Dr. Bada ADAM
07 Director Admissions/Records ... Ms. Monica BOYES
103 Exec Dir Econ Workforce Development ... Ms. Linda ZORN
30 Director Institutional Advancement ... Ms. Lisa DELABY
41 Director Athletics/Kinesiology ... Mr. Craig RIGSBEE
13 Chief Technology Officer ... Mr. Tom ONWILER
08 Director of Library Services ... Dr. Cheryl BABLER
21 Director Business Services ... Mr. Trevor STEWART
38 Coordinator of Counseling ... Ms. Debbie REYNOLDS

Cabrillo College (G)

6500 Soquel Drive, Aptos CA 95003-3194

County: Santa Cruz | FICE Identification: 001124
Unit ID: 110334
Telephone: (831) 479-6100 | Carnegie Class: Assoc/MT-VT-High Trad
FAX Number: (831) 479-6425 | Calendar System: Semester
URL: www.cabrillo.edu
Established: 1959 | Annual Undergrad Tuition & Fees (In-District): $1,358
Enrollment: 13,594 | Coed
Affiliation or Control: State/Local | IRS Status: 501(c)3
Highest Offering: Associate Degree
Accreditation: WJ, DH, MAC, RAD

01 Superintendent/President ... Dr. Laurel JONES
05 Asst Supt/Vice Pres Instruction ... Dr. Kathleen WELCH
32 Asst Supt/Vice Pres Student Svcs ... Mr. Dennis BAILEY-FOUGNIER
10 Asst Supt/VP Administrative Svcs ... Ms. Victoria LEWIS
35 Dean Student Services ... Ms. Michelle DONOHUE
13 Director Information Technology ... Ms. Spring ANDREWS
08 Library Director ... Mr. Georg ROMERO
26 Director Marketing & Communications ... Ms. Kristin FABOS
15 Asst Director Human Resources ... Ms. Diane GOODY
21 Director Business Services ... Mr. Graciano MENDOZA
07 Director of Admissions/Records ... Mr. Kip NEAD
09 Dir Planning/Research/Knowledge Sys ... Mr. Terrence WILLETT
18 Dir Facilities Planning/Plant Ops ... Mr. Joe NUGENT
40 Bookstore Manager ... Ms. Linda CULLENS
102 Exec Dir Cabrillo Col Foundation ... Ms. Melinda SILVERSTEIN
37 Director Financial Aid ... Ms. Tootie TZIMBAL
38 Dn Stdnt Counseling/Educ Spprt Svcs ... Ms. Margery REGALADO RODRIGUEZ
96 Dir Purchasing/Contracts/Risk Mgmt ... Mr. Michael ROBINS
04 Administrative Asst to President ... Vacant

California Baptist University (H)

8432 Magnolia Avenue, Riverside CA 92504-3297

County: Riverside | FICE Identification: 001125
Unit ID: 110361
Telephone: (951) 689-5771 | Carnegie Class: Masters/L
FAX Number: (951) 351-1808 | Calendar System: Semester
URL: www.calbaptist.edu
Established: 1950 | Annual Undergrad Tuition & Fees: $30,384
Enrollment: 7,957 | Coed
Affiliation or Control: Southern Baptist | IRS Status: 501(c)3
Highest Offering: Doctorate
Accreditation: WC, ACBSP, #ARCPA, CAATE, CONST, ENG, MUS, NURSE, @SP

01 President ... Dr. Ronald L. ELLIS
04 Admin Asst to the President ... Ms. Julie MOULTON
10 VP for Finance & Administration ... Mr. Mark HOWE
15 Director of Human Resources ... Ms. Julie FRESQUEZ
18 Director Facilities/Planning Svcs ... Mr. Steve SMITH
21 Director of Financial Services ... Mr. Calvin SPARKMAN
21 Director of Accounting ... Ms. Jackie STILWELL
37 Director of Financial Aid ... Mr. Joshua MOREY
40 Director of University Campus Store ... Ms. Carol BRACEY
26 VP for Marketing & Communication ... Dr. Mark A. WYATT
88 Director of Conferences & Events ... Mr. Corey/lon POLK
27 Director of Marketing ... Mr. Jeremy ZIMMERMAN
27 Director of Communications ... Mr. Isaiah AGUIRRE
105 Sr Web Services Manager ... Mr. Waylon BAUMGARDNER
32 VP Enrollment & Student Services ... Mr. Kent DACUS
35 Dean of Students ... Mr. Anthony LAMMONS
07 Dean of Admissions ... Mr. Allen JOHNSON
41 Director of Athletics ... Dr. Micah PARKER
42 Dean Spiritual Life/Campus Minister ... Mr. John MONTGOMERY
19 Director of Public Safety ... Mr. Jim WALTERS
39 Director of Residence Life ... Mr. Daron HUBBERT
36 Sr Director Career Services ... Mr. Mike BISHOP
30 Assoc VP University Advancement ... Mr. Michael MEYER
44 Director Annual Giving/Stewardship ... Mr. Brian BUNNELL
102 Grants Administrator ... Mr. Sam LIVELY
29 Director Alumni & Parent Relations ... Ms. Gail RONVEAUX
88 VP for Global Initiatives ... Dr. Larry LINAMEN
07 Dir of International Admissions ... Vacant
85 Dean of International Programs ... Mr. Bryan DAVIS
106 VP for Online & Prof Studies ... Dr. David POOLE
13 Assoc VP of Technology ... Dr. Tran HONG
106 Assoc VP Academics Online/Prof Stds ... Dr. Dirk DAVIS
43 VP and General Counsel ... Mr. Adam BURTON
05 VP of Academic Affairs/Provost ... Dr. Charles SANDS
88 Assoc Provost/Administration ... Dr. Tracy WARD
20 Assoc Provost/Faculty Dev ... Dr. Dawn Ellen JACOBS
108 Assoc Provost/Accred & Assessment ... Dr. Elizabeth MORRIS
06 University Registrar ... Ms. Shawnn KONING
08 Director of Library ... Dr. Steve EMERSON
90 Dir of Instructional Technology ... Mr. Keith CASTILLO
20 Dean of Academic Services ... Dr. Jeffrey BARNES
09 Director of Institutional Research ... Ms. Vicki CLEVELAND
48 Dean College of Architecture ... Mr. Mark A. ROBERSON
49 Dean College of Arts & Sciences ... Dr. Gayne ANACKER
50 Dean School of Business ... Vacant
53 Dean School of Education ... Dr. John SHOUP
54 Dean College of Engineering ... Dr. Anthony DONALDSON
64 Dean School of Music ... Vacant
66 Dean School of Nursing ... Dr. Geneva OAKS
73 Dean School of Christian Ministries ... Dr. Chris MORGAN
83 Dean School Behavioral Sciences ... Dr. Jacqueline GUSTAFSON
76 Dean College of Health Science ... Dr. David PEARSON

California Christian College (I)

5364 E. Belmont Ave, Fresno CA 93727

County: Fresno | FICE Identification: 008844
Unit ID: 110918
Telephone: (559) 251-4215 | Carnegie Class: Spec-4-yr-Faith
FAX Number: (559) 335-2329 | Calendar System: Semester
URL: www.calchristiancollege.edu
Established: 1955 | Annual Undergrad Tuition & Fees: $8,750
Enrollment: 20 | Coed
Affiliation or Control: Free Will Baptist | IRS Status: 501(c)3
Highest Offering: Baccalaureate
Accreditation: TRACS

01 President ... Mr. Wendell L. WALLEY
05 VP of Academic Affairs ... Dr. Timothy M. POWELL
06 Registrar ... Mrs. Makenzie ZUERCHER
10 Chief Business Officer ... Mrs. Anna-Jean WALLEY
09 Dir Institutional Effectiveness ... Ms. Ingrid VOSS
08 Head Librarian ... Mrs. Nancy SINGH
37 Coordinator Financial Aid ... Ms. Melinda SCROGGINS
07 Director of Admissions ... Mr. Trent WALLEY
39 Director Student Housing ... Ms. Jennifer WALLEY

California Coast University (J)

925 N. Spurgeon Street, Santa Ana CA 92701-3515

County: Orange | FICE Identification: 041276
Unit ID: 110936
Telephone: (714) 547-9625 | Carnegie Class: Not Classified
FAX Number: (714) 547-5777 | Calendar System: Other
URL: www.calcoast.edu
Established: 1973 | Annual Undergrad Tuition & Fees: N/A
Enrollment: N/A | Coed
Affiliation or Control: Proprietary | IRS Status: Proprietary
Highest Offering: Doctorate
Accreditation: DEAC

01 President ... Dr. Thomas M. NEAL
03 Executive Vice President ... Ms. Shelly MARQUARDT
32 Vice President of Student Affairs ... Dr. Murl TUCKER
05 Director of Academic Affairs ... Mr. Douglas PETRIKAT
06 Registrar ... Ms. Angela CENINA

California College of the Arts (K)

1111 Eighth Street, San Francisco CA 94107-2247

County: San Francisco | FICE Identification: 001127
Unit ID: 110370
Telephone: (415) 703-9500 | Carnegie Class: Spec-4-yr-Arts
FAX Number: (510) 655-5541 | Calendar System: Semester
URL: www.cca.edu
Established: 1907 | Annual Undergrad Tuition & Fees: $43,708
Enrollment: 1,938 | Coed
Affiliation or Control: Independent Non-Profit | IRS Status: 501(c)3
Highest Offering: Master's
Accreditation: WC, ART, #CIDA

01 President ... Mr. Stephen BEAL
05 Provost ... Ms. Tammy Rae CARLAND
10 Sr VP Finance & Administration ... Mrs. Laura HAZLETT
30 Sr Vice President of Advancement ... Ms. Susan AVILA
11 Vice President of Operations ... Ms. Jennifer STEIN
84 Sr Vice Pres of Enrollment Mgmt ... Ms. Sheri MCKENZIE
26 Vice Pres Marketing/Comm Strategy ... Ms. Becky RUDEN
32 Vice President Student Affairs ... Mr. George SEDANO
15 Assoc Vice Pres Human Resources ... Ms. Leslie GRAY
21 Assoc Vice Pres Financial Services ... Mr. Ken TANZER
20 Associate Provost ... Dr. Thomas O. HAAKENSON

36 Director Career Development ....Dr. Diana CHAVEZ
06 Registrar ....Mr. Jerry ALLEN
37 Director Financial Aid ....Mr. Dewayne BARNES
29 Dir of Alumni/Parent Engagement ....Ms. Jessica AREVALO-HILLEN
13 Chief Information Officer ....Ms. Mara HANCOCK
07 Director Undergrad Admissions ....Mr. Arnold ICASIANO
38 Director Student Counseling ....Dr. Tara RECH
45 Director Research and Planning ....Mr. David MECKEL
18 Chief Facilities/Physical Plant ....Mr. Noah BARTLETT
07 Director Graduate Admissions ....Mr. Noel DAHL
09 Director of Institutional Research ....Vacant
96 Manager of Purchasing ....Ms. Jackie CRADDOCK

California College San Diego (A)

6602 Convoy Court Suite 100, San Diego CA 92111
County: San Diego FICE Identification: 021108
Unit ID: 485263
Telephone: (619) 680-4430 Carnegie Class: Not Classified
FAX Number: (619) 295-5985 Calendar System: Other
URL: www.cc-sd.edu
Established: 1978 Annual Undergrad Tuition & Fees: $16,968
Enrollment: 912 Coed
Affiliation or Control: Independent Non-Profit IRS Status: 501(c)3
Highest Offering: Baccalaureate
Accreditation: ACCSC, COARC

01 Executive Director ....Dr. Ken WEBB
03 Executive Vice President ....Mr. Eric JUHLIN
05 Chief Academic Officer ....Dr. Jason KART
06 Registrar ....Ms. Lashanna BOYKIN
07 Director of Admissions ....Mr. Baris YUCELT
08 Head Librarian ....Ms. Patricia BERMEL
36 Director Student Placement ....Mr. Bill KILBY

California College San Diego (B)

277 Rancheros Drive, Suite 200, San Marcos CA 92069
Telephone: (619) 680-4430 Identification: 770551
Accreditation: ACCSC, COARC

California Health Sciences University (C)

120 N. Clovis Ave, Clovis CA 93612
County: Fresno Identification: 667218
Telephone: (559) 325-3600 Carnegie Class: Not Classified
FAX Number: (559) 473-1487 Calendar System: Semester
URL: www.chsu.org
Established: 2012 Annual Graduate Tuition & Fees: N/A
Enrollment: N/A Coed
Affiliation or Control: Proprietary IRS Status: Proprietary
Highest Offering: Doctorate; No Undergraduates
Accreditation: @PHAR

01 President ....Florence DUNN
04 Administrative Asst to President ....Kathleen HAEBERLE
05 Sr VP Academic Affairs/Provost ....Wendy DUNCAN
100 Chief of Staff ....McKenna WALKER
09 Dir Inst Effectiveness & Research ....Julie MARTY-PEARSON
11 VP Operations ....Jimmy DUNN
10 Controller ....Aron FLORES
13 Exec Dir of Info Technology ....John BRIAR
32 VP of Student Affairs ....Carolyn HARRIS
06 Registrar ....Kevin HOOVER
07 Director of Admissions ....Leslie WILLIAMS
26 VP Marketing/Communications ....Richele KLEISER
30 Dir of Development and Comm ....Sherrie BAKKE
20 Asst Dean of Education ....Will OFSTAD
88 Assoc Dean Professional Devel ....Patty HAVARD
08 Librarian ....Anna YANG

California Institute of Advanced Management (D)

9550 Flair Dr, Ste #201, El Monte CA 91731
FICE Identification: 042506
Unit ID: 487649
Telephone: (626) 350-1500 Carnegie Class: Not Classified
FAX Number: (626) 350-1515 Calendar System: Other
URL: www.ciam.edu
Established: Annual Graduate Tuition & Fees: N/A
Enrollment: N/A Coed
Affiliation or Control: Independent Non-Profit IRS Status: 501(c)3
Highest Offering: Master's; No Undergraduates
Accreditation: ACICS

01 President ....Jennie TA
00 President Emeritus ....Dr. William A. COHEN
05 Vice Pres/Chief Academic Officer ....Dr. Eric MCLAUGHLIN

California Institute of the Arts (E)

24700 McBean Parkway, Valencia CA 91355-2397
County: Los Angeles FICE Identification: 001132
Unit ID: 111081
Telephone: (661) 255-1050 Carnegie Class: Spec-4-yr-Arts
FAX Number: (661) 254-8352 Calendar System: Semester
URL: www.calarts.edu
Established: 1961 Annual Undergrad Tuition & Fees: $43,986
Enrollment: 1,471 Coed
Affiliation or Control: Independent Non-Profit IRS Status: 501(c)3
Highest Offering: Doctorate
Accreditation: WC, ART, DANCE

01 President ....Dr. Steven D. LAVINE
05 Provost ....Dr. Jeannene PRZYBLYSKI
10 Vice Pres/Chief Financial Officer ....Donald MATTHEWSON
11 Vice President/Operations & COO ....Michael CARTER
30 Vice Pres/Advancement ....Elizabeth ROBISON
21 Assoc Vice President and Controller ....Karla TALAVERA
15 Assoc Vice Pres Human Resources ....Charmagne SHEARRILL
18 Assoc Vice Pres Facilities ....Jesse SMITH
88 Asst VP Special Projects ....Patricia GONZALEZ
09 Assoc Provost Academic Affairs ....Brian HARLAN
28 Institute Diversity Officer ....Eva GRAHAM
20 Assistant Provost Academic Affairs ....Bree HOWARD
08 Dean Div of Library & Info Resource ....Vacant
32 Dean of Students ....Travis GREENE
57 Dean School of Art ....Thomas LAWSON
64 Dean Herb Alpert School of Music ....David ROSENBOOM
88 Dean School of Critical Studies ....Amanda BEECH
88 Dean Sharon D Lund School of Dance ....Vacant
88 Dean School Film & Video ....Leighton PIERCE
88 Dean School of Theater ....Travis PRESTON
06 Registrar ....Anna JABLONSKI
07 Executive Director of Admissions ....Molly RYAN
37 Director of Financial Aid ....Robin BAILEY-CHEN
29 Director Alumni & Parent Engagement ....Rageshwar GOLDBERG
88 Artistic Director Community Arts ....Glenna AVILA
88 Director Community Arts Partnership ....Nadine RAMBEAU
39 Asst Director of Residence Life ....Alexandra LEWIN
87 Director of Summer Session ....Hilary DARLING
19 Campus Safety Supervisor ....Mark FARLEY
88 Director of Leadership Gifts ....Sally BICKERTON
88 Director of Institute Partnerships ....Claudia BLOOM
44 Director of Development/Major Gift ....Aaron CAMPBELL
23 Director Health Services ....Audrey HAMPTON
88 Director Advancement Services ....Korey JANSE
88 Director Prospect Strategy ....Natalie LARMON
13 Director Information Technology ....Sean MURPHY
102 Director Corp/Foundation/Govt ....Sarah NELSON
44 Director Development/Indiv Giving ....Aiza KEESEY
88 Director Special Events ....Lindsey SCHIFF-ABRAMS
36 Director Career Services ....Rita SOLTANIAN
18 Director Facilities Management ....John THOMAS
04 Sr Administrative Asst to President ....Judy MCGINNIS
104 Asst Dir Intl Students & Programs ....Anessa ESCOBAR
105 Director Web Communications ....Christine ZIEMBA
88 Director of Creative Services ....Stuart SMITH
26 Senior Director of Communications ....Stears DEBBIE
88 Director of Project Development ....Lisa BARR
88 Director Academic Contracts/Budget ....Trish PATRYLA

California Institute of Arts & Technology (F)

2820 Camino Del Rio South, Ste 100, San Diego CA 92108
County: San Diego Identification: 667289
Telephone: (858) 225-4301 Carnegie Class: Not Classified
FAX Number: N/A Calendar System: Other
URL: www.calarttech.edu
Established: 2008 Annual Undergrad Tuition & Fees: N/A
Enrollment: N/A Coed
Affiliation or Control: Proprietary IRS Status: Proprietary
Highest Offering: Associate Degree
Accreditation: CNCE

01 President ....Jamie DOYLE
11 Director of Operations ....Claire LEE
10 Controller ....Richard GORMLY
06 Registrar ....Ed BRANCHEAU
07 Director of Admissions ....Frank GANAN

California Institute of Integral Studies (G)

1453 Mission Street, 4th Floor, San Francisco CA 94103-2557
County: San Francisco FICE Identification: 012154
Unit ID: 110316
Telephone: (415) 575-6100 Carnegie Class: DU-Mod
FAX Number: (415) 575-1264 Calendar System: Semester
URL: www.ciis.edu
Established: 1968 Annual Undergrad Tuition & Fees: N/A
Enrollment: 1,251 Coed
Affiliation or Control: Independent Non-Profit IRS Status: 501(c)3
Highest Offering: Doctorate
Accreditation: WC, ACUP

01 President ....Mr. Joseph L. SUBBIONDO
05 Academic Vice President ....Dr. Judie WEXLER
10 Controller/VP of Finance ....Mr. David BLOHM
30 Vice President of Development ....Ms. Dorotea REYNA
88 VP China Projects/Exec Dir ACTCM ....Mr. Lixin HUANG
32 Dean of Students ....Ms. Yunny YIP
29 Dean of Alumni/Dir of Travel Pgms ....Dr. Richard BUGGS
20 Dean Academic Plng/Administration ....Mr. Chip B. GOLDSTEIN
15 Director of Human Resources ....Ms. S. Michelle COLEMAN
07 Director of Admissions ....Ms. Ellen DURST
13 Director Information Technology ....Ms. Janet CRAGIN
08 Library Director ....Mr. Noah LOWENSTEIN
06 Registrar ....Mr. Dan GURLER
26 Director of Communications ....Mr. Jim David MARTIN
37 Int Director of Financial Aid ....Mr. Michael SZKOTAK
51 Dir Public Programs/ Performances ....Ms. Britta CONROY-RANDALL
18 Director Facilities & Operations ....Mr. Frank TALAMANTEZ
40 Bookstore Manager ....Mr. Steven SWANSON
85 International Student Advisor ....Ms. Jody O'CONNOR

California Institute of Technology (H)

1200 E California Boulevard, Pasadena CA 91125-0001
County: Los Angeles FICE Identification: 001131
Unit ID: 110404
Telephone: (626) 395-6811 Carnegie Class: DU-Highest
FAX Number: (626) 795-1547 Calendar System: Trimester
URL: www.caltech.edu
Established: 1891 Annual Undergrad Tuition & Fees: $45,390
Enrollment: 2,209 Coed
Affiliation or Control: Independent Non-Profit IRS Status: 501(c)3
Highest Offering: Doctorate
Accreditation: WC, ENG

01 President ....Dr. Thomas F. ROSENBAUM
04 Secretary to the BOT/Exec Asst ....Mrs. Mary L. WEBSTER
05 Provost ....Dr. Edward M. STOLPER
88 Vice President/Director JPL ....Dr. Michael WATKINS
10 VP of Admin/Business/Finance ....Ms. Margo STEURBAUT
21 AVP for Finance & Treasurer ....Ms. Sharon E. PATTERSON
30 Vice Pres Devel/Institute Relations ....Mr. Brian K. LEE
88 VP for Strategy Implementation ....Dr. Diana JERGOVIC
32 Vice President Student Affairs ....Dr. Joseph E. SHEPHERD
43 General Counsel ....Ms. Victoria D. STRATMAN
20 Vice Provost ....Dr. Cindy A. WEINSTEIN
20 Vice Provost ....Dr. Kaushik BHATTACHARYA
15 Assoc Vice Pres Human Resources ....Ms. Julia M. MCCALLIN
44 Assoc Vice President Development ....Ms. Valerie A. OTTEN
88 AVP for Campaigns ....Ms. Diane M. BINNEY
44 Asst VP Engagement & Annual Program ....Ms. Theresa A. DAVIS
86 Director Government Relations ....Mr. Hall P. DAILY
35 Senior Director Student Activities ....Mr. Tom N. MANNION
26 Chief Strat Communications Officer ....Ms. Farnaz KHADEM
81 Chair Biology & Biological Engr Div ....Dr. Stephen L. MAYO
81 Chair Chemistry & Chemical Engr Div .Dr. Jacqueline K. BARTON
54 Chair Engr & Applied Science Div ....Dr. Guruswami RAVICHANDRAN
65 Chair Geology/Planet Science Div ....Dr. John P. GROTZINGER
79 Chair Humanities/Social Science Div ....Dr. Jean-Laurent ROSENTHAL
81 Chair Physics/Math/Astro Division ....Dr. Fiona HARRISON
06 Registrar ....Mrs. Mary N. MORLEY
07 Exec Director of Admissions ....Mr. Jarrid WHITNEY
08 University Librarian ....Ms. Kristin ANTELMAN
13 Chief Information Officer ....Mr. Rich E. FAGEN
18 Assoc Vice Pres for Facilities ....Mr. James W. COWELL, JR.
18 Sr Director Facilities Management ....Mr. William R. TAYLOR
19 Chief of Campus Security & Parking ....Mr. Gregg HENDERSON
16 Exec Director of Human Resources ....Ms. Tara KRUCKEBERG
23 Director Health Services ....Dr. Stuart C. MILLER
25 Director Sponsored Research ....Dr. Richard P. SELIGMAN
29 Executive Director Alumni Assoc ....Ms. Alexandra C. TOBEK
37 Director Financial Aid ....Mr. Don CREWELL
36 Director Career Development ....Ms. Lauren B. STOLPER
40 Manager Bookstore ....Ms. Karyn SEIXAS
41 Dir Athletics & Physical Education ....Ms. Betsy MITCHELL
58 Dean of Graduate Studies ....Dr. Doug C. REES
35 Dean of Students ....Dr. Kevin M. GILMARTIN
85 Assoc Dir International Student Pgm ....Ms. Laura FLOWER KIM
96 Dir Purchasing & Payment Services ....Ms. Tina LOWENTHAL
101 Secretary of the Board ....Ms. Mary L. WEBSTER
102 Director Foundation Relations ....Ms. Marjorie A. BEALE
104 Dir Fellowshp Advising/Study Abroad ....Ms. Lauren B. STOLPER
38 Acting Director Counseling Center ....Ms. Jennifer HOWES
09 Dir of Inst Rsrch & Educ Assessment ....Mr. Ray A. GONZALES

California Intercontinental University (I)

17310 Red Hill Ave, Ste 200, Irvine CA 91765-3954
County: Orange Identification: 666670
Unit ID: 455451
Telephone: (866) 687-2258 Carnegie Class: Not Classified
FAX Number: (909) 804-5151 Calendar System: Semester
URL: www.caluniversity.edu
Established: 2003 Annual Undergrad Tuition & Fees: N/A
Enrollment: N/A Coed
Affiliation or Control: Proprietary IRS Status: Proprietary
Highest Offering: Doctorate
Accreditation: DEAC

00 Executive Chairman ....Dr. Finian TAN
01 Chief Executive Officer ....Dr. Leslie GARGIULO
58 Dean of Graduate Studies ....Dr. Steve HESS
05 Chief Academic Officer ....Dr. Bonny NICKLE
10 Director of Finance ....Mr. Bryan KELLY
06 Registrar ....Mr. Mark WILLS
37 Director Student Financial Aid ....Mr. Richard MADRIGAL

California International Business University (A)

520 West Ash Street, Ste. 300, San Diego CA 92101
County: San Diego Identification: 666711
Telephone: (619) 702-9400 Carnegie Class: Not Classified
FAX Number: (619) 702-9476 Calendar System: Quarter
URL: www.cibu.edu
Established: 1994 Annual Undergrad Tuition & Fees: N/A
Enrollment: N/A Coed
Affiliation or Control: Independent Non-Profit IRS Status: 501(c)3
Highest Offering: Master's
Accreditation: ACICS

01 President .... Dr. Anya ESKILDSEN
58 Director Doctoral Program .... Dr. Tem BUGARIN
32 Dean Student Affairs/Special Pgms .... Mr. Brian HAWKINS
30 Dir Inst Development/Compliance .... Dr. Marcus BENNIEFIELD
37 Financial Aid Director .... Mr. Mike MARTIN
11 Administrative Officer .... Ms. Amy CULLEY

California Jazz Conservatory (B)

2087 Addison Street, Berkeley CA 94704
County: Alameda Identification: 667217
Telephone: (510) 845-5373 Carnegie Class: Not Classified
FAX Number: (510) 841-5373 Calendar System: Semester
URL: www.cjc.edu
Established: 2009 Annual Undergrad Tuition & Fees: N/A
Enrollment: N/A Coed
Affiliation or Control: Independent Non-Profit IRS Status: 501(c)3
Highest Offering: Baccalaureate
Accreditation: MUS

01 President and Dean of Instruction .... Susan MUSCARELLA
11 Director of Operations .... Dean MUENCH

California Lutheran University (C)

60 W Olsen Road, Thousand Oaks CA 91360-2787
County: Ventura FICE Identification: 001133
Unit ID: 110413
Telephone: (805) 492-2411 Carnegie Class: Masters/L
FAX Number: (805) 493-3513 Calendar System: Semester
URL: www.callutheran.edu
Established: 1959 Annual Undergrad Tuition & Fees: $38,430
Enrollment: 4,160 Coed
Affiliation or Control: Evangelical Lutheran Church In America
IRS Status: 501(c)3
Highest Offering: Doctorate
Accreditation: WC, CLPSY, TED, THEOL

01 President .... Dr. Christopher KIMBALL
05 Provost/Vice Pres Academic Affairs .... Dr. Leanne NEILSON
30 Vice Pres University Advancement .... Mr. Stephen WHEATLY
10 Vice Pres Admin/Finance/Treasurer .... Ms. Karen DAVIS
32 Vice Pres Stdnt Life/Dean of Stdnts .... Ms. Melinda ROPER
84 VP Enrollment Mgmt & Marketing .... Dr. Matthew WARD
13 Chief Information Officer .... Mr. Zareh MARSELIAN
18 Assoc Vice Pres Facilities .... Mr. Ryan VAN OMMEREN
26 Assoc VP University Relations .... Ms. Lynda FULFORD
49 Dean College Arts & Sciences .... Dr. Joan GRIFFIN
53 Dean of School of Education .... Dr. Michael HILLIS
50 Dean of School of Management .... Dr. Gerhard APFELTHALER
83 Dean Grad School of Psychology .... Dr. Rick HOLIGROCKI
15 Asst VP for Human Resources .... Ms. Patricia PARHAM
06 Assoc Prov Academic Svcs/Registrar .... Ms. Maria KOHNKE
42 University Pastor .... Rev. Scott MAXWELL-DOHERTY
42 Vice President Mission and Identity .... Rev. Melissa MAXWELL-DOHERTY
44 Director Major Planned Giving .... Mr. Richard HOLMES, IV
41 Director Athletics .... Mr. Daniel KUNTZ
107 Director Professionals .... Dr. Lisa BUONO
36 Director of Career Services .... Ms. Cindy LEWIS
85 Sr Dir Multicultural/Intl Std Svc .... Dr. Juanita HALL
21 Dir of Budget/Management Analysis .... Ms. Barbara REX
29 Dir Alumni and Family Relations .... Ms. Rachel RONNING LINDGREN
38 Director Counseling Services .... Dr. Alan GOODWIN
19 Director Security/Safety .... Mr. David HILKE
07 Director of Undergrad Admissions .... Mr. Michael ELGARICO
09 Director of Institutional Research .... Dr. Rodney REYNOLDS
37 Director of Financial Aid .... Mr. Jerry MCKEEN

California Miramar University (D)

3550 Camino Del Rio N. Suite 208, San Diego CA 92108
County: San Diego Identification: 666713
Unit ID: 480781
Telephone: (858) 653-3000 Carnegie Class: Spec-4-yr-Bus
FAX Number: (858) 653-6786 Calendar System: Other
URL: www.calmu.edu
Established: 2005 Annual Undergrad Tuition & Fees: $8,240
Enrollment: 324 Coed
Affiliation or Control: Proprietary IRS Status: Proprietary
Highest Offering: Doctorate
Accreditation: ACICS

01 Dean .... Kim LOBERA
07 International Admissions Director .... Carol KULIS
06 Registrar .... Brooke NELSON

California National University for Advanced Studies (E)

18520 Hawthorne Blvd 1st Floor, Torrance CA 90504
County: Los Angeles Identification: 666786
Telephone: (800) 782-2422 Carnegie Class: Not Classified
FAX Number: (310) 370-7072 Calendar System: Trimester
URL: www.cnuas.edu
Established: 1993 Annual Undergrad Tuition & Fees: N/A
Enrollment: N/A Coed
Affiliation or Control: Proprietary IRS Status: Proprietary
Highest Offering: Master's
Accreditation: DEAC

01 President .... Mr. Carlton G. BRYANT
32 Vice Pres Student Affs/Registrar .... Ms. Stephanie M. SMITH
07 Admissions .... Ms. Cynthia SPEED
05 Director of Instruction .... Dr. Carol BACKER
50 Assoc Dean Business Administration .... Dr. Philip CHONG
54 Associate CNU Col of Engineering .... Dr. Robert RYAN
13 MIS Director .... Mr. Charles NG
06 Registrar .... Ms. Stephanie M. SMITH

California Northstate University College of Pharmacy (F)

9700 West Taron Dr, Elk Grove CA 95757
County: Sacramento Identification: 667020
Telephone: (916) 686-7400 Carnegie Class: Not Classified
FAX Number: (916) 686-8143 Calendar System: Semester
URL: pharmacy.cnsu.edu
Established: 2008 Annual Undergrad Tuition & Fees: N/A
Enrollment: N/A Coed
Affiliation or Control: Independent Non-Profit IRS Status: 501(c)3
Highest Offering: Doctorate
Accreditation: WC, #MED, PHAR

01 President .... Dr. Alvin CHEUNG
03 Vice President .... Mr. Norman FONG
108 VP of Inst Effect/Assessment .... Ms. Karen MCCLENDON
43 Legal Counsel .... Mr. Paul WAGSTAFFE
05 Dean .... Dr. Hieu TRAN
32 Assoc Dean Student Affs/Admissions .... Ms. Cyndi PORTER-FRASER
10 Financial Controller .... Ms. Shoua XIONG
08 Director of Library Resources .... Mr. Scott MINOR
06 Registrar .... Ms. Melissa DEAN

California Southern University (G)

930 Roosevelt, Irvine CA 92620
County: Orange Identification: 666770
Telephone: (714) 882-7800 Carnegie Class: Not Classified
FAX Number: (714) 480-0834 Calendar System: Semester
URL: www.calsouthern.edu
Established: 1978 Annual Undergrad Tuition & Fees: N/A
Enrollment: N/A Coed
Affiliation or Control: Independent Non-Profit IRS Status: 501(c)3
Highest Offering: Doctorate
Accreditation: WC

01 President .... Dr. Caroll RYAN

*The California State University System Office (H)

401 Golden Shore, Long Beach CA 90802-4210
County: Los Angeles FICE Identification: 001136
Unit ID: 110501
Telephone: (562) 951-4000 Carnegie Class: N/A
FAX Number: (562) 951-4986
URL: www.calstate.edu

01 Chancellor .... Dr. Timothy P. WHITE
05 Exec Vice Chanc Acad/Stdnt Affairs .... Dr. Loren J. BLANCHARD
10 Executive Vice Chancellor & CFO .... Mr. Steve RELYEA
15 Int Vice Chanc Human Resources .... Mr. Andrew JONES
30 Vice Chanc Univ Rels/Advancement .... Mr. Garrett P. ASHLEY
43 Exec Vice Chanc/General Counsel .... Mr. Framroze M. VIRJEE
21 Vice Chancellor/Chief Audit Officer .... Mr. Larry MANDEL
100 Chief of Staff .... Dr. Lars WALTON

*California Polytechnic State University-San Luis Obispo (I)

1 Grand Avenue, San Luis Obispo CA 93407-9000
County: San Luis Obispo FICE Identification: 001143
Unit ID: 110422
Telephone: (805) 756-1111 Carnegie Class: Masters/L
FAX Number: (805) 756-5400 Calendar System: Quarter
URL: www.calpoly.edu
Established: 1901 Annual Undergrad Tuition & Fees (In-State): $9,001
Enrollment: 20,186 Coed
Affiliation or Control: State IRS Status: 501(c)3
Highest Offering: Master's
Accreditation: WC, ART, BUS, CONST, CS, DIETD, DIETI, ENG, LSAR, MUS, NAIT, NRPA, PLNG

02 President .... Dr. Jeffrey D. ARMSTRONG
100 AVP & Chief of Staff .... Ms. Jessica DARIN
05 Provost .... Dr. Kathleen ENZ FINKEN
32 Vice President Student Affairs .... Dr. Keith HUMPHREY
30 Vice Pres Univ Advance/CEO Found .... Vacant
10 Senior Vice Pres Admin & Finance .... Ms. Cynthia VILLA
20 Senior Vice Provost Academic Pgms .... Dr. Mary E. PEDERSEN
20 Vice Provost Intl/Grad & Ext Educ .... Dr. Brian TIETJE
41 Athletic Director .... Mr. Don OBERHELMAN
13 Int CIO/Cybrsec Ctr Dir .... Mr. Bill BRITTON
88 Exec Dir CalPoly Corporation .... Ms. Lorlie LEETHAM
46 Int VP Research & Economic Dev .... Mr. Bradford ANDERSON
21 Associate Vice Pres Admin & Finance .... Mr. Victor BARNCART
44 Assoc Vice Pres Advancement Ops .... Mr. Grant TREXLER
44 Assoc VP Development .... Vacant
26 Exec Director Univ Communications .... Mr. Chris MURPHY
18 Associate Vice Pres Facilities Mgmt .... Ms. Juanita HOLLER
39 Exec Dir Univ Housing & Assoc VP/SA .... Vacant
15 Assoc Vice Prov Academic Personnel .... Dr. Al LIDDICOAT
88 Assoc Vice Prov Systems & Resources .... Ms. Kimi M. IKEDA
84 Assoc Vice Prov Mktg & Enrollment .... Mr. James L. MARAVIGLIA
88 Director Center Teach Learn & Tech .... Mr. Patrick O'SULLIVAN
29 Int Asst Vice Pres Alumni Relations .... Ms. Ellen COHUNE
19 University Police Department .... Chief George HUGHES
06 University Registrar .... Mr. Cem SUNATA
28 Interim Director Diversity & Incl .... Dr. Jean DECOSTA
22 Director Employment Equity/Title IX .... Mr. Brian GNANDT
45 Dir Facil Planning/Capital Projects .... Mr. Joel NEEL
23 Exec Dir Health & Well Being .... Dr. David HARRIS
38 Director of Counseling Services .... Dr. Geneva ABIKO
35 ASI Executive Director .... Ms. Marcy MALONEY
24 Technology Strategist .... Mr. Ryan MATTESON
40 Interim Dir University Bookstore .... Ms. Lynnette HELD
35 Dean of Students .... Dr. Kathleen PERLMUTTER
46 Dean of Research .... Dr. Dean WENDT
102 Industry Outreach/Applied Research .... Mr. Jim DUNNING
47 Dean Agriculture/Food & Env Sci .... Dr. Andrew THULIN
48 Dean Architect/Environmental Design .... Ms. Christine THEODOROPOULOS
50 Dean College of Business .... Dr. Scott DAWSON
54 Dean College of Engineering .... Dr. Debra LARSON
49 Dean College of Liberal Arts .... Dr. Douglas EPPERSON
81 Dean Science & Mathematics .... Dr. Philip S. BAILEY, JR.
53 Dean School of Education .... Dr. J. Kevin TAYLOR
16 Executive Director Human Resources .... Ms. Beth E. GALLAGHER
96 Dir Contract & Procurement Svcs .... Mr. Dru ZACHMEYER
37 Director Financial Aid .... Ms. Lois M. KELLY
36 Director Career Services .... Ms. Eileen C. BUECHER
09 Director Institutional Research .... Mr. Mauricio SAAVEDRA
104 Director of International Center .... Ms. Caroline MOORE
92 Director Honors Program .... Dr. Gregg FIEGEL
04 Administrative Asst to President .... Ms. Diane HAUPT
07 Director Admissions Operations .... Mr. Terrance HARRIS
08 Dean of Library Services .... Ms. Anna GOLD
25 Director Grants Development .... Ms. Amy VELASCO
43 Dir Legal Services/General Counsel .... Ms. Dawn S. THEODORA
91 Director Administrative Computing .... Ms. Sharon ANDERSON
86 Director Government Relations .... Mr. Justin WELLNER

*California State Polytechnic University-Pomona (J)

3801 W Temple Avenue, Pomona CA 91768-2557
County: Los Angeles FICE Identification: 001144
Unit ID: 110529
Telephone: (909) 869-7659 Carnegie Class: Masters/L
FAX Number: (909) 869-4535 Calendar System: Quarter
URL: www.cpp.edu
Established: 1938 Annual Undergrad Tuition & Fees (In-State): $7,016
Enrollment: 23,966 Coed
Affiliation or Control: State IRS Status: 501(c)3
Highest Offering: Master's
Accreditation: WC, ART, BUS, CEA, CIDA, CS, DIETD, DIETI, ENG, ENGT, LSAR, MUS, PLNG, SFAA

02 President .... Dr. Soraya M. COLEY
05 Provost/VP Academic Affairs .... Dr. Sylvia A. ALVA
32 Vice Pres Student Affairs .... Dr. Lea M. JARNAGIN
10 VP Administrative Affairs/CFO .... Ms. Danielle MANNING
30 AIC University Advancement .... Ms. Theresa MENDOZA
102 Exec Dir Cal Poly Pomona Found Inc .... Mr. G. Paul STOREY
20 Assoc Provost Academic Affairs .... Vacant
18 Assoc VP Facilities Planning & Mgmt .... Dr. Walter MARQUEZ
35 Acting Assoc VP & Dean of Students .... Dr. Byron E. HOWLETT
84 Assoc VP Enroll Management & Svcs .... Ms. Kathleen A. STREET
88 Exec Asst to the Provost .... Ms. Marissa M. MARTINEZ
46 AVP Research/Innovation/Econ Dev .... Dr. Sadiq SHAH
20 AVP Acad Planning & Faculty Affairs .... Dr. Shanthi A. SRINIVAS
26 Assoc Vice Pres for Univ Relations .... Vacant
21 Assoc VP Finance/Admin Svcs .... Mr. Darwin LABORDO
35 Assoc VP Student Services .... Dr. Kevin T. COLANER
35 AVP Student Affairs Administration .... Ms. Christi R. CHISLER
13 Vice President & CIO .... Mr. John W. MCGUTHRY
15 AVP for Human Resources .... Ms. Sharon L. REITER
100 Chief of Staff .... Mr. Gary A. HAMILTON
04 Exec Assistant to the President .... Ms. Paulette M. BLUMBERG
47 Dean College of Agriculture .... Dr. Mary HOLZ-CLAUSE
49 Dean Col Letters/Arts/Soc Sci .... Dr. Sharon HILLES
50 Interim Dean Col of Business Admin .... Dr. Erik ROLLAND
54 Int Dean College of Engineering .... Dr. Cordelia ONTIVEROS
48 Dean Col Environmental Design .... Mr. Michael WOO
88 Dean Collins College of Hosp Mgmt .... Dr. Lea R. DOPSON
81 Dean College of Science .... Dr. Alison BASKI
53 Interim Dean Col Educ/Integrat Stds .... Dr. Nancy HURLBUT

44 Assoc VP for Development Vacant
08 Dean University Library Dr. Ray WANG
41 Director of Athletics Mr. Brian R. SWANSON
86 Dir of Government/External Affairs Ms. Julie LAPPIN
19 Chief of Police Mr. Dario ROBINSON
09 Exec Dir Inst Rsrch & Acad Resource Ms. Lisa M. ROTUNNI
37 Dir Financial Aid & Scholarships Ms. Diana Y. MINOR
06 Registrar/Academic Records Svcs Ms. Maria L. MARTINEZ
96 Director of Procurement Ms. Kathleen A. PRUNTY
07 Exec Dir Admissions & Outreach Ms. Deborah L. BRANDON

*California State University-Bakersfield (A)

9001 Stockdale Highway, Bakersfield CA 93311-1022
County: Kern FICE Identification: 007993
Unit ID: 110486
Telephone: (661) 654-2011 Carnegie Class: Masters/L
FAX Number: (661) 654-3194 Calendar System: Quarter
URL: www.csub.edu
Established: 1965 Annual Undergrad Tuition & Fees (In-State): $6,811
Enrollment: 8,720 Coed
Affiliation or Control: State IRS Status: 501(c)3
Highest Offering: Doctorate
Accreditation: WC, BUS, NURSE, SPAA, SW, TED

02 President Dr. Horace MITCHELL
100 Executive Asst to the President Ms. Evelyn YOUNG
04 Admin Asst to the President Ms. Tina GIBLIN
05 Provost/Vice Pres Academic Affairs Dr. Jenny ZORN
10 Vice Pres Business/Admin Services Mr. Thom DAVIS
32 Vice President Student Affairs Dr. Thomas WALLACE
44 Int VP University Advancement Dr. Victor MARTIN
20 VP Faculty Affairs Dr. David SCHECTER
84 Assoc VP for Enrollment Management Dr. Jacqueline MIMMS
20 Assoc VP for Academic Programs Dr. Vernon HARPER
15 AVP Human Res/Administrative Svcs Ms. Kellie GARCIA
88 Int AVP Information Tech Services Mr. Kallya SHENOY
88 Spec Asst to Provost Academic Aff Vacant
21 Asst Vice Pres Fiscal Services Mr. Douglas WADE
13 Asst Vice Pres Info Technology Svcs Mr. Kallya SHENOY
18 Asst VP Facilities Management/Dev Mr. Pat JACOBS
09 Asst VP Inst Rsrch/Planning/Assess Dr. Kris KRISNAN
25 Assoc Vice Pres Grants/Resources Dr. Imeh EBONG
35 Assoc VP Student Success Dr. Vikash LAKHANI
12 Int Dean Antelope Valley Center Dr. Randy SCHULTZ
50 Int Dean Business/Public Admin Dr. John STARK
53 Int Dean Social Sciences/Education Dr. Steve BACON
79 Int Dean Arts & Humanities Dr. Llora GUBKIN
81 Int Dean Natural Sciences/Math/Eng Dr. Kathleen MADDEN
56 Dean Extended University Dr. Mark NOVAK
58 Dir of Academic Operation & Support Dr. John DIRKSE
08 Dean University Library Dr. Curt ASHER
06 Registrar Ms. Lisa ZUZARTE
88 Director Academic Advising Vacant
91 Dir Admn Computing Svcs/CMS Pgm Dir Mr. Kallya SHENOY
07 Director Admissions & Records Mr. Ben PERLADO
29 Director Alumni Relations Ms. Sarah HENDRICK
41 Director Athletics Mr. Kenneth (Ziggy) SIEGFRIED
36 Dir for Cmty Engagement/Career Edu Dr. Markel QUARLES
88 Director Children's Center Ms. Gladys GARCIA
96 Dir Contract Services/Procurement Mr. Michael CHAVEZ
38 Admin Supervisor Counseling Center Dr. Janet MILLAR
106 Director E-Learning Services Vacant
37 Int Director Financial Aid Mr. Chad MORRIS
92 Int Director CSUB Honors Program Dr. Jacquelyn KEGLEY
39 Director Housing & Residential Life Ms. Crystal BECKS
88 Director Safety & Risk Management Mr. Tim RIDLEY
22 Dir Svcs Students w/Disabilities Ms. Janice CLAUSEN
17 Director Student Health Services Dr. Oscar RICO
30 Director of Development Dr. Victor MARTIN
88 Director Outreach Services Mr. Darius RIGGINS
19 Chief University Police Chief Marty WILLIAMSON
109 Director of Food Services Mr. Matt MORRIS
18 Manager Facilities Operations Mr. Tom VELASQUEZ
40 Bookstore Manager Ms. Lori FULLER
26 Public Affairs/Communications Coord Ms. Elizabeth FERGON
28 Asst to the President for EIC Ms. Claudia CATOTA

*California State University Channel Islands (B)

One University Drive, Camarillo CA 93012-8599
County: Ventura FICE Identification: 039803
Unit ID: 441937
Telephone: (805) 437-8400 Carnegie Class: Masters/S
FAX Number: (805) 437-8414 Calendar System: Semester
URL: www.csuci.edu
Established: 2002 Annual Undergrad Tuition & Fees (In-District): $6,547
Enrollment: 5,879 Coed
Affiliation or Control: State/Local IRS Status: 501(c)3
Highest Offering: Master's
Accreditation: WC, NURSE

02 President Dr. Erika D. BECK
05 Interim Provost/VP Academic Affairs Dr. Daniel W. WAKELEE
10 VP Business & Financial Affairs Ms. Ysabel TRINIDAD
32 VP Student Affairs Dr. Wm. Gregory SAWYER
13 VP Technology & Communication Dr. Michael BERMAN
30 VP University Advancement Ms. Nichole IPACH
100 Chief of Staff Dr. Genevieve EVANS TAYLOR
20 Associate Provost Vacant
20 Assistant Provost Dr. Elizabeth HARTUNG
56 Associate VP & Dean Extended Univ Dr. Gary BERG
49 Dean of Arts & Sciences Dr. James H. MERIWETHER
50 Dean of MVS School of Bus & Econ Dr. William CORDEIRO
84 Associate VP Enrollment Management Vacant
53 Interim Dean of School of Education Dr. Merilyn BUCHANAN
46 Senior Research Officer Dr. Jason MILLER
08 Dean of University Library Ms. Amy WALLACE
35 Associate VP & Dean of Students Vacant
88 Associate VP Wellness & Athletics Mr. Ed LEBIODA
21 Associate VP Financial Services Ms. Missy JARNAGIN
15 Associate VP HR Programs Ms. Anna PAVIN
88 Dir Special Projects & Operations Ms. Melissa REMOTTI
09 Dir Instl Rsrch/Plng/Effectivness Dr. Michael BOURGEOIS
86 Sr Dir Community & Govt Relations Ms. Celina ZACARIAS
88 Title IX & Inclusion Officer Ms. Brittany GRICE
30 Dir Advancement Operations Mr. Christopher ABE
44 Dir Major Gifts Mr. Carrick DEHART
29 Dir Development/Alumni Relations Ms. Tania GARCIA
44 Director Planned & Major Gifts Ms. Grace G. ROBINSON
44 Dir Annual Giving & Special Gifts Ms. Eva C. GOMEZ
19 Dir Public Safety & Chief of Police Mr. John REID
88 Interim Dir Conferences & Events Mr. Ray PORRAS
39 AVP Housing/Rsdntl Edu & ASI Ms. Cindy DERRICO
06 Assoc Dir Records & Registration Vacant
07 Dir of Admissions & Records Ms. Ginger REYES
108 Assoc VP for SA/Dean of Students Ms. Toni DEBONI
104 Dir Intl Prgms/AD Ctr Intl Affairs Ms. Mayumi KOWTA
26 Dir Communication & Marketing Ms. Nancy GILL
37 Dir Financial Aid & Scholarships Ms. Sunshine GARCIA
88 Dir Special Projects for F&A Ms. Caroline DOLL
96 Dir Procurement & Contract Services Vacant
04 Presidential Aide Ms. Alanna TREJO

*California State University-Chico (C)

400 W First Street, Chico CA 95929-0001
County: Butte FICE Identification: 001146
Unit ID: 110538
Telephone: (530) 898-6116 Carnegie Class: Masters/L
FAX Number: (530) 898-6824 Calendar System: Semester
URL: www.csuchico.edu
Established: 1887 Annual Undergrad Tuition & Fees (In-State): $7,022
Enrollment: 17,287 Coed
Affiliation or Control: State IRS Status: 501(c)3
Highest Offering: Master's
Accreditation: WC, ART, BUS, CONST, CS, DIETD, DIETI, ENG, JOUR, MUS, NAIT, NRPA, NURSE, SP, SPAA, SW, TED, THEA

02 President Dr. Gayle E. HUTCHINSON
100 Interim Chief of Staff Dr. Russell S. MILLS
05 Interim Provost Dr. Michael G. WARD
10 Vice Pres Business & Finance/CFO Ms. Lorraine B. HOFFMAN
32 Vice President Student Affairs Mr. Drew CALANDRELLA
30 Vice Pres University Advancement Mr. Ahmad BOURA
45 Vice Prov Planning/Res Allocation Vacant
46 Interim Assoc Vice Pres Research Dr. Kevin M. KELLEY
84 Assoc Vice Pres Enroll Management Ms. Barbara FORTIN
13 Vice Prov Information Resources/CIO Mr. Michael SCHILLING
21 Assoc VP Financial Svcs/Univ Budget Ms. Stacie CORONA
15 Asst Vice Pres Staff HR Ms. Sheryl WOODWARD
16 Acting Assoc Vice Pres Fac Affairs Ms. Sarah BLAKESLEE
47 Interim Dean College of Agriculture Dr. David DALEY
51 Dean Continuing Education Ms. Debra E. BARGER
72 Dean Col Engr/Comp Sci/Const Mgmt Dr. Ricardo JACQUEZ
83 Dean Col Behavior & Social Sci Dr. Eddie VELA
50 Dean College of Business Dr. Judith HENNESSEY
79 Dean College Humanities/Fine Arts Dr. Robert M. KNIGHT
81 Dean College Natural Sciences Dr. David M. HASSENZAHL
60 Dean Coll Communication & Educ Dr. Angela TRETHEWEY
20 Dean Undergraduate Education Dr. William M. LOKER
58 Interim Dean Graduate Studies Dr. Sharon A. BARRIOS
08 Dean Library Dr. Patrick A. NEWELL
26 Director Public Affairs Mr. Joe WILLS
29 Asst Vice Pres Alumni Relations Ms. Susan M. ANDERSON
09 Director Institutional Research Vacant
06 Registrar Ms. Jean H. IRVING
07 Director of Admissions Mr. Adam STOLTZ
36 Director Career Center Ms. Megan ODOM
37 Director Financial Aid/Scholarships Mr. Dan REED
18 Dir Facilities Management Svcs Mr. Kevin DOYLE
96 Director of Procurement Ms. Sara RUMIANO
92 Director Univ Honors Program Mr. John MAHONEY
35 Interim Dir Student Judic Affairs Ms. Sandy PARSONS-ELLIS
28 Director of Diversity and Inclusion Mr. Tray ROBINSON
04 Executive Asst to President Ms. Kathleen A. HASSIG
104 Interim Director International Educ Dr. Joel A. ZIMBELMAN
19 Chief of Police Mr. John J. FEENEY
25 Exec Director Research Foundation Ms. Katy THOMA
109 Exec Director Associated Students Mr. David BUCKLEY
23 Medical Chief of Staff Dr. Deborah C. STEWART
38 Assoc Director Counseling Dr. Juni BANERJEE-STEVENS
39 Director University Housing Vacant
41 Athletic Director Ms. Anita S. BARKER
53 Director School of Education Dr. Deborah SUMMERS

*California State University-Dominguez Hills (D)

1000 E Victoria Street, Carson CA 90747-0005
County: Los Angeles FICE Identification: 001141
Unit ID: 110547
Telephone: (310) 243-3696 Carnegie Class: Masters/L
FAX Number: N/A Calendar System: Semester
URL: www.csudh.edu
Established: 1960 Annual Undergrad Tuition & Fees (In-State): $6,213
Enrollment: 14,687 Coed
Affiliation or Control: State IRS Status: 501(c)3
Highest Offering: Master's
Accreditation: WC, CS, MT, MUS, NURSE, OPE, OT, SPAA, SW, TED, THEA

02 President Dr. Willie J. HAGAN
05 Interim Provost/VP Academic Affairs Dr. Rodrick HAY
10 Interim VP Administration/Finance Ms. Naomi GOODWIN
32 Vice President Student Affairs Dr. William FRANKLIN
30 VP Univ Advancement Ms. Carrie E. STEWART
11 Assoc VP Administration/Finance Mr. Stephen MASTRO
44 Assoc Vice President Development Mr. Jeff POLTORAK
13 VP/Chief Information Officer Mr. Chris MANRIQUEZ
35 Int AVP Student Life/Dean of Stdnts Dr. David BRAVERMAN
37 Director of Financial Aid Ms. Delores LEE
84 Assoc VP Enrollment Mgmt Ms. Brandy MCLELLAND
09 Assoc Director Institutional Rsrch Mr. Pete VAN HAMERSVELD

*California State University-East Bay (E)

25800 Carlos Bee Boulevard, Hayward CA 94542-3001
County: Alameda FICE Identification: 001138
Unit ID: 110574
Telephone: (510) 885-3000 Carnegie Class: Masters/L
FAX Number: N/A Calendar System: Quarter
URL: www.csueastbay.edu
Established: 1957 Annual Undergrad Tuition & Fees (In-State): $6,564
Enrollment: 14,823 Coed
Affiliation or Control: State IRS Status: 501(c)3
Highest Offering: Doctorate
Accreditation: WC, BUS, ENG, MUS, NURSE, SP, SW

02 President Dr. Leroy M. MORISHITA
05 Provost/VP Academic Affairs Dr. Edward INCH
10 Interim Vice Pres Admin & Finance Ms. Debbie CHAW
30 Vice President Univ Advancement Ms. Tanya HAUCK
32 Vice President Student Affs Dr. Julie WONG
28 University Diversity Officer Dr. Dianne RUSH WOODS
100 Chief of Staff Mr. Derek AITKEN
49 Dean Col of Ltrs/Arts/Soc Sci Dr. Kathleen ROUNTREE
50 Dean Col of Business/Economics Dr. Jagdish AGRAWAL
53 Dean Col of Educ/Allied Studies Dr. Carolyn NELSON
81 Dean College of Science Dr. Jason SINGLEY
08 Dean of Libraries Dr. John WENZLER
13 Interim CIO Ms. Phoebe KWAN
06 Registrar Ms. Angela SCHNEIDER

*California State University-Fresno (F)

5200 N. Barton Avenue, Fresno CA 93740-8027
County: Fresno FICE Identification: 001147
Unit ID: 110556
Telephone: (559) 278-4240 Carnegie Class: DU-Mod
FAX Number: (559) 278-4715 Calendar System: Semester
URL: www.csufresno.edu
Established: 1911 Annual Undergrad Tuition & Fees (In-State): $6,311
Enrollment: 23,179 Coed
Affiliation or Control: State IRS Status: 501(c)3
Highest Offering: Doctorate
Accreditation: WC, BUS, CAATE, CACREP, CIDA, CONST, CORE, DIETD, DIETI, ENG, MUS, NRPA, NURSE, PH, PTA, SP, SPAA, SW, TED, THEA

02 President Dr. Joseph I. CASTRO
05 Provost/Vice Pres Academic Affs Dr. Lynnette ZELEZNY
10 VP Administration/Asc VP Auxiliary Dr. Deborah ADISHIAN-ASTONE
30 Vice Pres University Advancement Ms. Paula CASTADIO
32 Vice Pres Student Affs/Enroll Mgmt Dr. Frank LAMAS
100 Chief of Staff Ms. Diana RALLS
15 Assoc VP Academic Personnel Dr. Michael CALDWELL
26 Assoc VP University Communications Ms. Shirley ARMBRUSTER
20 Vice Provost Academic Affairs Dr. Dennis L. NEF
45 Assoc Vice President Research Dr. Thomas H. MCCLANAHAN
44 Assoc Vice Pres Univ Development Vacant
21 Int Chief Fin Ofcr/Asc VP Fin Svcs Mr. Clinton MOFFITT
18 Associate Vice President Facilities Mr. Robert BOYD
84 Assoc Vice Pres Enrollment Services Mr. Bernie VINOVRSKI
51 Int Dean/AVP Continuing/Global Ed Dr. Scott MOORE
47 Dean Agricultural Science/Tech Dr. Sandra WHITE
79 Dean of Arts & Humanities Dr. Saul JIMENEZ-SANDOVAL
50 Dean Craig School of Business Dr. Robert HARPER
53 Dean of Kremen School of Education Dr. Paul BEARE
54 Dean of Engineering Dr. Ramakrishna NUNNA
76 Dean of Health/Human Services Dr. Jody HIRONAKA-JUTEAU
83 Int Dean of Social Sciences Dr. Michelle DENBESTE
81 Int Dean of Science & Mathematics Dr. Robert G. DUNDAS
08 Dean of Library Services Mr. Peter MCDONALD
58 Dean of Graduate Studies Dr. Sandra WITTE
23 Dir Univ Health/Psyc Svcs Oper Ms. Maria MADRIGAL-SHAFFER
19 Director of Public Safety Mr. David HUERTA
41 Director of Athletics Mr. Jim BARTKO
16 Director of Human Resources Ms. Janice PARTEN
13 Chief Information Officer Mr. Orlando LEON
09 Dir of Inst Research/Assessment Dr. Angel SANCHEZ
37 Director of Financial Aid Mr. Bernie OGDEN
27 Director of Publications Mr. Bruce WHITWORTH
29 Executive Director Alumni Relations Ms. Jacquelyn GLASENER

36 Director of Career Services ... Ms. Rita BOCCHINFUSO-COHEN
39 Director Univ Courtyard (Housing) ... Ms. Erin BOELE
96 Dir Procurement & Support Services ... Mr. Brian COTHAM
07 Director of Admissions & Records ... Ms. Tina BEDDALL
35 Director of Student Involvement ... Ms. Melissa GINOTTI
40 Bookstore Manager ... Mr. Curt PARKINSON

*California State University-Fullerton (A)

PO Box 34080, 800 N State Col Blvd,
Fullerton CA 92831-3547

County: Orange
FICE Identification: 001137
Unit ID: 110565
Telephone: (657) 278-2011
Carnegie Class: DU-Mod
FAX Number: (657) 278-2649
Calendar System: Semester
URL: www.fullerton.edu
Established: 1957
Annual Undergrad Tuition & Fees (In-State): $6,437
Enrollment: 38,128
Coed
Affiliation or Control: State
IRS Status: 501(c)3
Highest Offering: Doctorate
Accreditation: WC, ANEST, ART, BUS, BUSA, CAATE, CACREP, CS, CSHSE, DANCE, ENG, IPSY, JOUR, MIDWF, MUS, NURSE, PH, SP, SPAA, SW, TED, THEA

02 President ... Dr. Mildred GARCIA
100 Chief of Staff ... Ms. Ann CAMP
05 Int Provost & VP Academic Affairs ... Dr. Anil PURI
10 VP Admin & Finance/CFO ... Mr. Danny C. KIM
32 Vice President of Student Affairs ... Dr. Berenecea J. EANES
30 VP University Advancement ... Mr. Greg SAKS
13 VP Info Tech/Chief Info Ofcr ... Mr. Amir DABIRIAN
15 Int VP of HR/Diversity & Inclusion ... Ms. Gail BROOKS
102 Executive Director/CFO Foundation ... Ms. Tara GARCIA
44 Assoc VP University Advancement ... Mrs. Michele CESCA
58 AVP Academic Programs ... Dr. Peter NWOSU
26 Assoc VP Strategic Communications ... Mr. Jeffrey COOK
20 Deputy Provost & AVP Acad Affs ... Dr. Shari MCMAHAN
88 AVP Research/Creative/Technology ... Dr. Patrick PELLICANE
88 AVP South County Ops & Initiatives ... Dr. Marteza RAHMATIAN
21 Associate VP of Financial Services ... Vacant
86 Assc VP Public Affs/Government Rels ... Mr. Owen HOLMES
44 Assoc VP Advancement ... Ms. Theresa DAVIS
45 Dir Budget Planning & Admin ... Ms. Laleh GRAYLEE
35 Int AVP Student Affairs ... Mr. Darren BUSH
11 Chief of Operations ... Vacant
18 Int AVP Facilities Planning/Mgmt ... Mr. Willem VAN DER POL
84 Asst Vice Pres Enrollment Services ... Ms. Nancy DORITY
09 Int Dir Inst Res/Analytical Stds ... Dr. Sunny MOON
16 AVP Human Res/Diversity & Inclusion ... Vacant
14 Asst VP for Information Technology ... Mr. Rommel HIDALGO
29 Exec Director Alumni Relations ... Ms. Dianna L. FISHER
88 Exec Dir/CEO Auxiliary Svcs Corp ... Mr. Frank MUMFORD
06 University Registrar ... Ms. Melissa WHATLEY
08 Interim University Librarian ... Dr. Scott HEWITT
07 Director of Admissions ... Ms. Jessica WAGONER
36 Director Career Center ... Mr. Jim CASE
40 Director Titan Shops ... Ms. Kimberly BALL
23 Director Health Center ... Ms. Kathy SPOFFORD
19 Chief University Police ... Mr. Dennis DEMAIO
28 Director Diversity/Equity Programs ... Vacant
37 Director Financial Aid ... Ms. Cecilia SCHOUWE
41 Director of Athletics ... Mr. James DONOVAN
96 Director of Contracts & Procurement ... Mr. Don GREEN
35 Dean of Students ... Dr. Tonantzin OSEGUERA
88 Dir Intl Admissions & Outreach ... Mr. Joseph SAÑOSA
85 Dir Intl Students & Scholars ... Ms. Christine PIRCHER-BARNES
88 Director Women's Center/Re-Entry ... Ms. Mary BECERRA
88 Dir Educational Partnerships ... Ms. Melba CASTRO
39 Director Housing ... Mr. Larry MARTIN
88 Int Dir Univ Outreach/New Stdnt Pgm ... Ms. Deanna MERINO
88 Dir Athletic Academic Services ... Ms. Meredith BASIL
88 Dir Center for Internship/Com Eng ... Ms. Dawn MACY
88 Dir Student Academic Services ... Dr. Rochelle WOODS
88 Dir Veteran Student Services ... Mr. Lui AMADOR
38 Dir Counseling/Psychological Svcs ... Dr. Leticia GUTIERREZ-LOPEZ
14 Int AVP IT/Infrastructure Services ... Mr. Berhanu TADESSE
90 AVP IT/Academic Technology Svcs ... Dr. Kenneth KASS
51 Int Dean Extend Educ/AVP Intl Pgm . Dr. Kari KNUTSON-MILLER
79 Dean Humanities/Social Sciences ... Dr. Sheryl FONTAINE
81 Int Dean Natural Sciences & Math ... Dr. David BOWMAN
50 Dean Mihaylo Col Business/Economics ... Dr. Anil PURI
83 Int Dean Health/Human Development ... Dr. Jessie JONES
57 Dean College of the Arts ... Mr. Dale MERRILL
53 Dean College of Education ... Dr. Claire CAVALLARO
54 Dean Col Engineering & Computer Sci ... Dr. Raman UNNIKRISHNAN
60 Int Dean College of Communications ... Dr. Irene MATZ
12 Dean Irvine Campus ... Dr. Susan COOPER

*California State University-Long Beach (B)

1250 Bellflower Boulevard, Long Beach CA 90840

County: Los Angeles
FICE Identification: 001139
Unit ID: 110583
Telephone: (562) 985-4111
Carnegie Class: Masters/L
FAX Number: (562) 985-5419
Calendar System: Semester
URL: www.csulb.edu
Established: 1949
Annual Undergrad Tuition & Fees (In-State): $6,452
Enrollment: 36,809
Coed
Affiliation or Control: State
IRS Status: 501(c)3
Highest Offering: Doctorate
Accreditation: WC, AAFCS, ART, BUS, CAATE, CEA, CONST, CS, DANCE, DIETD, DIETI, ENG, HSA, IPSY, JOUR, MUS, NRPA, NURSE, PH, PTA, SP, SPAA, SW, TED, THEA

02 President ... Dr. Jane C. CONOLEY
05 Provost/Sr Vice Pres Academic Affs ... Dr. Brian JERSKY
11 Vice Pres Administration/Finance ... Ms. Mary E. STEPHENS
32 Vice President Student Affairs ... Dr. Carmen TILLERY TAYLOR
30 Vice Pres University Rels/Devel ... Ms. Andrea TAYLOR
100 Chief of Staff ... Dr. Karen NAKAI
10 Assoc VP Financial Management ... Ms. Sharon TAYLOR
20 Assoc VP Undergraduate Studies ... Dr. Nele HEMPEL-LAMER
35 Assoc Vice Pres Student Affairs ... Dr. Mary Ann TAKEMOTO
82 Assoc VP Intl Education ... Dr. Jeet JOSHEE
18 Assoc VP Phys Plng/Facilities Mgt ... Mr. David SALAZAR
20 Vice Provost/Dean Graduate Studies ... Dr. Cecile LINDSAY
46 Assoc Vice Pres University Research ... Dr. Simon KIM
15 Assoc VP Human Resource Mgmt ... Mr. Scott APEL
91 Assoc VP Academic Technology ... Dr. Shawna DARK
29 Assoc VP Alumni and Univ Relations ... Ms. Janice HATANAKA
09 Director Institutional Research ... Dr. Mahmoud ALBAWANEH
84 Interim AVP Enrollment Services ... Ms. Donna GREEN
13 Assoc VP Information Technology ... Ms. Janet FOSTER
76 Dean College Health/Human Svcs ... Dr. Monica LOUNSBERY
50 Dean College of Business Admin ... Dr. Michael SOLT
53 Dean College of Education ... Dr. Marquita GRENOT-SCHEYER
54 Dean College of Engineering ... Dr. Forouzan GOLSHANI
57 Dean College of the Arts ... Ms. Cyrus PARKER-JEANNETTE
81 Dean College Natural Science/Math ... Dr. Laura KINGSFORD
49 Dean College of Liberal Arts ... Dr. David WALLACE
51 Dean Col Continuing & Profess Educ ... Dr. Jeet JOSHEE
08 Dean Library/Learning Resources ... Mr. Roman KOCHAN
06 Dir of Registration/Records/Evals ... Ms. Donna GREEN
39 Interim Dir Housing & Res Life ... Ms. Claudia PLAZA
16 Director Staff Human Resources ... Ms. Nancy TORRES
41 Interim Director Athletics ... Ms. Cindy MASNER
07 Interim Director of Admissions ... Ms. Janice MILLER
36 Director Career Development Ctr ... Mr. Marcel PEREZ
23 Director Health Services ... Dr. Mary Ann TAKEMOTO
19 Chief University Police ... Mr. Fernando SOLORZANO
38 Director Counseling/Psych Services ... Dr. Brad COMPLIMENT
37 Director Financial Aid ... Mr. Nicolas VALDIVIA
25 Director Foundation Grants/Contract ... Ms. Sandra SHEREMAN
102 Chief Op Ofcr/Rsrch Foundation ... Dr. Brian NOWLIN
28 Director of Equity & Diversity ... Ms. Larisa HAMADA
96 Director Procurement & Contracts ... Ms. Malia KINIMAKA
109 General Manager/49'er Shops ... Mr. Donald PENROD
104 Director Education Abroad ... Ms. Sharon OLSON
44 Dir Leadership Annual Giving ... Vacant
86 AVP Legislative & External Rels ... Ms. Terri CARBAUGH
88 Assoc VP Budget & Univ Svcs ... Mr. Ted KADOWAKI
88 Asst VP Administrative Services ... Ms. Mishelle LAWS
88 Assoc VP Faculty Affairs ... Dr. Mark WILEY
04 Administrative Asst to President ... Ms. Coleen FOLLOWELL
106 AVP Academic Technology Services ... Ms. Shawna DARK
108 Director Institutional Assessment ... Dr. Sharlene SAYEGH
22 Dir Affirmative Action/EEO ... Ms. Larisa HAMADA
26 Assoc VP Univ Rels & Communications ... Mr. Andy HOANG
90 VP/Chief Information Officer ... Dr. Min YAO

*California State University-Los Angeles (C)

5151 State University Drive, Los Angeles CA 90032-8530

County: Los Angeles
FICE Identification: 001140
Unit ID: 110592
Telephone: (323) 343-3000
Carnegie Class: Masters/L
FAX Number: (323) 343-2670
Calendar System: Quarter
URL: www.calstatela.edu
Established: 1947
Annual Undergrad Tuition & Fees (In-State): $6,355
Enrollment: 24,488
Coed
Affiliation or Control: State
IRS Status: 501(c)3
Highest Offering: Doctorate
Accreditation: WC, ART, BUS, CACREP, CORE, CS, DIETC, DIETD, ENG, MUS, NAIT, NURSE, SP, SPAA, SW, TED

02 President ... Dr. William A. COVINO
11 Exec VP and Chief Operating Officer ... Dr. Jose A. GOMEZ
05 Provost/Vice Pres Academic Affs ... Dr. Lynn MAHONEY
10 VP Administration & CFO ... Ms. Lisa M. CHAVEZ
32 Vice President Student Life ... Dr. Nancy WADA-MCKEE
13 AVP for Information Technology ... Ms. Tosha PHAM
44 Vice Pres University Advancement ... Dr. Janet S. DIAL
84 Vice Provost for Enrollment Svcs ... Mr. Tom ENDERS
21 Assoc VP Admin & Finance/Budget ... Ms. Mae SANTOS
35 Dean of Students ... Dr. Jennifer MILLER
30 Assoc VP University Advancement ... Dr. Mario PEREZ
20 Int AVP Research/Academic Personnel ... Dr. Scott R. BOWMAN
29 Exec Director Alumni Relations ... Ms. Maria UBAGO
26 Exec Dir Comm/Public Affairs ... Mr. Robert LOPEZ
41 Exec Dir Intercollegiate Athletics ... Mr. Daryl J. GROSS
83 Dean Natural & Social Sciences ... Dr. Pamela SCOTT-JOHNSON
08 Dean of the University Library ... Mr. Carlos RODRIGUEZ
06 University Registrar ... Mr. Christopher COBB
58 Dean Graduate Studies ... Dr. Karin A. ELLIOTT BROWN
09 Director Institutional Research ... Dr. Mark PAVELCHAK
36 Director Career Placement & Plng ... Mr. Christopher LENZ
37 Director Student Financial Services ... Ms. Tamie NGUYEN
23 Director Health Center ... Dr. Monica JAZZABI
39 Director Housing Svc/Residence Life ... Ms. Rebecca PALMER
22 Director Equal Opportunity Pgm ... Ms. Becky HOPKINS
18 AVP Fac/Plng/Design & Construct ... Mr. Warren JACOBS
19 Chief of Police ... Mr. Rick WALL
15 AVP Human Resources Management ... Ms. Susie VARELA
85 Director Intl Programs & Services ... Ms. Amy WANG
43 University Counsel ... Mr. Victor I. KING
07 Director Admissions & Recruitment ... Mr. Vince LOPEZ
96 Director Procurement & Contracts ... Mr. Thomas JOHNSON
09 Asst Dir Institutional Research ... Ms. Michelle DUNBAR
28 Dir Equity/Diversity/Inclusion ... Ms. Mariel MULET
40 Manager Bookstore ... Mr. Todd MURPHY
88 Assoc Dean Undergrad Studies ... Dr. Margaret GARCIA
49 Int Dean Arts & Letters ... Dr. Rennie SCHOEPFLIN
54 Dean Engr/Computer Science/Tech ... Dr. Emily ALLEN
107 Dean Col of Profess/Global Studies ... Dr. Eric A. BULLARD
76 Dean Health & Human Services ... Dr. Ronald VOGEL
53 Dean Charter Col of Education ... Dr. Cheryl L. NEY
50 Dean Business & Economics ... Dr. James A. GOODRICH
97 Dean Undergraduate Studies ... Dr. Michelle HAWLEY
92 Director Honors College ... Dr. Trinh PHAM

† Grants Joint Doctoral degree in cooperation with the University of California-Los Angeles.

*CSU Maritime Academy (D)

200 Maritime Academy Drive, Vallejo CA 94590-0644

County: Solano
FICE Identification: 001134
Unit ID: 111188
Telephone: (707) 654-1000
Carnegie Class: Bac-Diverse
FAX Number: (707) 654-1001
Calendar System: Semester
URL: www.csum.edu
Established: 1929
Annual Undergrad Tuition & Fees (In-State): $6,558
Enrollment: 1,047
Coed
Affiliation or Control: State
IRS Status: 501(c)3
Highest Offering: Master's
Accreditation: WC, ENG, ENGT, IACBE

02 President ... RADM. Thomas A. CROPPER, USMS
05 Provost/VP Academic Affairs ... Dr. Susan OPP
10 VP of Administration/Finance ... Mr. Franz LOZANO
32 VP of Student Affairs ... Mr. Steve KRETA
30 VP of University Advancement ... Mr. Robert ARP
15 Assistant VP of Human Resources ... Dr. Ingrid WILLIAMS
13 Chief Information Officer ... Mr. Daman GREWAL
100 Director of University Affairs ... Mr. Brigham TIMPSON
88 Master of Training Ship ... Capt. Harry BOLTON
20 Academic Dean ... Capt. Samuel PECOTA
44 Senior Development Officer ... Ms. Melissa COHEA
06 Registrar ... Ms. Peg SOLVESON
08 Dean of Library ... Ms. Michele VAN HOECK
07 Director of Admissions ... Mr. Marc MCGEE
37 Director of Financial Aid ... Ms. Priscilla MUHA
109 Exec Director Auxiliary Services ... Ms. Diane RAWICZ
88 Director of SEAS ... Ms. Vineeta DHILLON
35 Dean of Students ... Mr. James DALSKE
18 Director Facilities Planning ... Mr. Isidro FARIAS
19 Chief of Police Services ... Chief Donny GORDON
21 Budget Officer ... Mr. Andrew SOM
41 Director of Athletics ... Mr. Marv CHRISTOPHER
26 Director of Public Relations ... Mr. Robert KING
40 Bookstore Manager ... Mr. Andre JIMENEZ
96 Director of Purchasing ... Ms. Lorrie DINEEN-THACKERAY
04 Confidential Asst to President ... Mrs. Lisa RAQUEL
09 Director of Institutional Research ... Mr. Gary MOSER
29 Director of Alumni Relations ... Mr. Eric COOPER

*California State University-Monterey Bay (E)

100 Campus Center, Seaside CA 93955-8000

County: Monterey
FICE Identification: 032603
Unit ID: 409698
Telephone: (831) 582-3000
Carnegie Class: Masters/M
FAX Number: (831) 582-3783
Calendar System: Semester
URL: www.csumb.edu
Established: 1994
Annual Undergrad Tuition & Fees (In-State): $6,119
Enrollment: 6,631
Coed
Affiliation or Control: State
IRS Status: 501(c)3
Highest Offering: Master's
Accreditation: WC, SW

02 President ... Dr. Eduardo M. OCHOA
05 Provost ... Dr. Bonnie IRWIN
10 Vice Pres Admin & Finance/CFO ... Mr. Kevin SAUNDERS
30 Vice Pres University Development ... Ms. Barbara ZAPPAS
32 VP Student Affairs & Enroll Service ... Dr. Ronnie HIGGS
26 Assoc VP for University Affairs ... Mr. Andre LEWIS
35 Dean of Student Life ... Dr. Christine ERICKSON
21 Assoc Vice President for Finance ... Mr. John FITZGIBBON
28 Assoc VP Inclusive Excellence ... Dr. Patti HIRAMOTO
108 AVP Institutional Effect/Acad Plng ... Dr. Fran HORVATH
06 Registrar ... Ms. Sheila HERNANDEZ
22 Director Employee Rels/EEO & ADA ... Ms. Tamberly PETROVICH
37 Director Financial Aid ... Ms. Angeles FUENTES
15 Assoc VP for Human Resources ... Ms. Natalie KING
19 Chief of Police ... Chief Earl LAWSON
18 AVP Facilities Services & Operation ... Mr. Mario FORTE
07 Dir for Admissions & Recruitment ... Mr. David LINNEVERS
29 Director Alumni Relations ... Ms. Annie WARR
41 Athletic Director ... Mr. Kirby GARRY
96 Director of Purchasing ... Mr. Art EVJEN

*California State University-Northridge (A)

18111 Nordhoff Street, Northridge CA 91330-0001
County: Los Angeles FICE Identification: 001153
Unit ID: 110608
Telephone: (818) 677-1200 Carnegie Class: Masters/L
FAX Number: N/A Calendar System: Semester
URL: www.csun.edu
Established: 1958 Annual Undergrad Tuition & Fees (In-State): $6,569
Enrollment: 40,131 Coed
Affiliation or Control: State IRS Status: 501(c)3
Highest Offering: Doctorate
Accreditation: WC, AAFCS, ART, BUS, CAATE, CACREP, CIDA, CONST, CS, DIETD, DIETI, ENG, IPSY, JOUR, MUS, NRPA, NURSE, PH, PTA, RAD, SP, SW, TED, THEA

02 President .... Dr. Dianne F. HARRISON
05 Provost/Vice Pres Academic Affairs .... Dr. Yi LI
10 Vice President Admin/Finance .... Mr. Colin DONAHUE
32 VP Student Affairs/Dean of Students .... Dr. William WATKINS
30 Vice Pres University Advancement .... Dr. Robert GUNSALUS
13 Vice President IT/CIO .... Ms. Hilary BAKER
88 Exec Director University Corp .... Mr. Rick EVANS
20 Vice Provost Academic Affairs .... Dr. Michael NEUBAUER
100 Chief of Staff .... Ms. Jill SMITH
18 Assoc VP Facilities Dev/Operations .... Mr. Ken ROSENTHAL
58 Assoc VP Grad Studies/Intl Pgms .... Dr. Crist KHACHIKIAN
21 Associate VP Financial Services .... Ms. Deborah WALLACE
15 Assoc VP of Human Resources .... Ms. Kristina DE LA VEGA
29 Asst Vice Pres Alumni Relations .... Vacant
26 Assoc VP of Mktg/Comm .... Mr. Jeffrey NOBLITT
20 Assoc VP of Undergraduate Studies .... Dr. Elizabeth T. ADAMS
91 Assoc VP of Academic Resources .... Ms. Diane S. STEPHENS
07 Director of Admissions and Records .... Ms. Patty R. LORD
08 Dean University Library .... Dr. Mark STOVER
51 Dean College of Extended Learning .... Dr. Joyce A. FEUCHT-HAVIAR
79 Dean College of Humanities .... Dr. Elizabeth A. SAY
50 Dean College Business/Economics .... Dr. Kenneth R. LORD
53 Dean College of Education .... Dr. Michael E. SPAGNA
57 Int Dean College Arts/Media/Comm .... Mr. Dan HOSKEN
83 Dean Col Social/Behavioral Sci .... Dr. Stella Z. THEODOULOU
76 Dean Col Health/Human Development .... Dr. Farrell WEBB
81 Dean College Science & Math .... Dr. Jerry STINNER
54 Dean College Engr/Computer Science .... Dr. S. K. RAMESH
09 Interm Dir Institutional Research .... Dr. Janet S. OH
37 Director Financial Aid/Scholarships .... Mrs. Lili C. VIDAL
38 Director Univ Counseling Services .... Dr. Mark STEVENS
36 Director Career Center .... Ms. Ann N. MOREY
25 Dir Research/Sponsored Projects .... Mr. Scott L. PEREZ
18 Senior Dir Physical Plant Mgmt .... Mr. Jason WANG
19 Director of Police Services .... Ms. Anne P. GLAVIN
28 Director of Equity and Diversity .... Ms. Susan HUA
86 Dir Government/Community Relations .... Ms. Francesca VEGA
23 Director Student Health Center .... Dr. Linda REID-CHASSIAKOS
39 Dir Student Housing/Conf Services .... Mr. Timothy J. TREVAN
40 Director Matador Bookstore .... Ms. Amy C. BERGER
41 Director of Athletics .... Dr. Brandon MARTIN
88 Director Student Involvement & Dev .... Mr. Patrick BAILEY
92 Dir General Education Honors Pgm .... Dr. Beth A. WIGHTMAN
96 Manager Purchasing .... Ms. Deborah FLUGUM
84 Director Enrollment Management .... Dr. William WATKINS
06 Registrar .... Mr. Todd WOLFE
28 Chief Diversity Officer .... Dr. Raji RHYS

*California State University-Sacramento (B)

6000 J Street, Sacramento CA 95819-2694
County: Sacramento FICE Identification: 001150
Unit ID: 110617
Telephone: (916) 278-6011 Carnegie Class: Masters/L
FAX Number: (916) 278-6664 Calendar System: Semester
URL: www.csus.edu
Established: 1947 Annual Undergrad Tuition & Fees (In-State): $6,872
Enrollment: 29,349 Coed
Affiliation or Control: State IRS Status: 501(c)3
Highest Offering: Doctorate
Accreditation: WC, ART, BUS, CAATE, CIDA, CONST, CORE, CS, DIETD, DIETI, EMT, ENG, MUS, NRPA, NURSE, PTA, SP, SW, THEA

02 President .... Dr. Robert S. NELSEN
05 Interim Provost/VP Acad Affairs .... Dr. Ming-Tung (Mike) LEE
10 Interim Chief Financial Officer .... Ms. Stacy HAYANO
11 Interim VP of Administration .... Dr. Ali IZADIAN
30 Vice Pres University Advancement .... Mr. Vince SALES
32 VP Student Affairs .... Dr. Edward MILLS
13 VP & Chief Information Officer .... Dr. Larry GILBERT
15 Vice President for Human Resources .... Dr. Christine D. LOVELY
26 Vice Pres Public Affairs/Advocacy .... Dr. Phil GARCIA
46 Assoc VP Research Affairs .... Mr. David EARWICKER
20 Interim Vice Provost .... Dr. Stephen PEREZ
18 Assoc Vice Pres Facilities Mgmt .... Dr. Ali IZADIAN
27 Assoc VP University Communications .... Ms. Jeannie WONG
35 AVP Student Engagement & Support .... Dr. Beth LESEN
21 Interim Assoc VP Financial Svcs .... Ms. Gina CURRY
43 University Counsel .... Ms. Jill PETERSON
09 Director Institutional Research .... Dr. Jing WANG
07 Interim Dir Outreach & Admissions .... Dr. Jeff WESTON
08 Library Dean .... Ms. Amy KAUTZMAN
29 Assoc VP Alumni Relations .... Ms. Jennifer BARBER
19 Chief of Police .... Mr. Mark IWASA
39 Dir Housing and Residential Life .... Mr. Michael SPEROS
41 Interim Director Intercol Athletics .... Dr. Bill MACRISS
37 Director Financial Aid .... Ms. Anita KERMES
22 Director of Equal Opportunity .... Mr. William BISHOP
40 Bookstore Director .... Ms. Pam PARSONS
100 Chief of Staff .... Ms. Lisa CARDOZA
06 University Registrar .... Mr. Dennis GEYER
85 AVP Intl Pgm/Global Engagement .... Dr. Paul HOFMANN
23 Dir Student Health Ctr & Psych Svcs .... Dr. Joy STEWART-JAMES
96 Mgr Procurement/Contract Services .... Mr. John GUION
49 Dean College of Arts & Letters .... Vacant
50 Dean Col of Business Admin .... Dr. Pierre BALTHAZARD
53 Admin-In-Charge College of Educ .... Dr. Caroline TURNER
54 Dean College of Engr/Computer Sci .... Dr. Lorenzo SMITH
76 Dean College of Health/Human Svcs .... Dr. Fred BALDINI
81 Dean College of Natural Sci/Math .... Dr. Jill TRAINER
51 Dean College Continuing Education .... Dr. Helen WUSSOW
83 Dean College Soc Sci/Interdisc Stds .... Dr. Orn BODVARSSON
58 Dean Graduate Studies .... Dr. Chevelle NEWSOME

*California State University-San Bernardino (C)

5500 University Parkway, San Bernardino CA 92407-2393
County: San Bernardino FICE Identification: 001142
Unit ID: 110510
Telephone: (909) 537-5000 Carnegie Class: Masters/L
FAX Number: N/A Calendar System: Quarter
URL: www.csusb.edu
Established: 1960 Annual Undergrad Tuition & Fees (In-State): $6,577
Enrollment: 18,952 Coed
Affiliation or Control: State IRS Status: 501(c)3
Highest Offering: Doctorate
Accreditation: WC, ART, BUS, CORE, CS, DIETD, ENG, MUS, NURSE, SPAA, SW, TED, THEA

02 President .... Dr. Tomas MORALES
05 Provost/VP Academic Affairs .... Dr. Shari MCMAHAN
10 Vice Pres Administration/Finance .... Dr. Doug FREER
32 Vice Pres Student Affairs .... Dr. Brian L. HAYNES
30 Vice Pres University Advancement .... Dr. Ronald FREMONT
13 Vice Pres ITS/CIO .... Dr. Samuel SUDHAKAR
28 Co-Chief Diversity Officer .... Mr. Cesar PORTILLO
28 Co-Chief Diversity Officer .... Dr. Jacqueline HUGHES
88 Director Executive Affairs .... Ms. Pamela LANGFORD
20 Int Assoc Provost Acad Programs .... Dr. Rong CHEN
88 Interim Assoc Provost Research .... Dr. Cynthia CRAWFORD
16 Assoc Provost Academic Personnel .... Dr. Jacqueline HUGHES
20 Assoc VP & Dean Undergrad Studies .... Vacant
21 Assoc VP Finance .... Mr. M. Monir AHMED
15 Assoc VP Human Resources .... Mr. Cesar PORTILLO
84 Assoc VP Enrollment Mgmt .... Ms. Olivia ROSAS
35 Assoc VP and Dean of Students .... Dr. Alysson M. SATTERLUND
88 Assoc VP ITS .... Mr. Gerard AU
88 Assoc VP Development .... Vacant
26 Assoc VP Strategic Communications .... Mr. Bob TENCZAR
09 AVP Inst Effectiveness & Dir IR .... Dr. Muriel LOPEZ-WAGNER
88 Director Title IX & Gender Equity .... Ms. Cristina MARTIN
36 Interim Director Career Center .... Ms. Sarai MALDONADO
06 Director/University Registrar .... Ms. Grace KING
07 Director Admissions .... Vacant
23 Interim Dir Health & Counseling Ctr .... Dr. Diana MCELROY
08 University Librarian .... Mr. Cesar CABALLERO
37 Director Financial Aid .... Ms. Roseanna RUIZ
39 Director Housing & Residential Life .... Dr. John YAUN
45 Director Plng Design/Construction .... Mr. Hamid U. AZHAND
18 Director Facilities Management .... Ms. Jennifer SORENSON
41 Interim Director Athletics .... Mr. Morgan WALKER
29 Director Alumni Affairs .... Ms. Doreen HATCHER
96 Interim Director Purchasing .... Ms. Linda GUTTERUD
40 Director Bookstore .... Mr. David WATTS
94 Director Gender & Sexuality Studies .... Dr. Todd JENNINGS
92 Director University Honors Program .... Dr. David MARSHALL
56 Dean Col of Extended Learning .... Dr. Tatiana KARMANOVA
49 Dean College of Arts & Letters .... Dr. Terry BALLMAN
81 Dean Col Natural Sciences .... Dr. Kirsten FLEMING
83 Dean Col Social/Behavioral Sciences .... Dr. Rafik MOHAMED
53 Dean College of Education .... Dr. Jay FIENE
50 Dean College of Business .... Dr. Lawrence D. ROSE
58 Dean Graduate Studies .... Vacant
12 Dean CSUSB Palm Desert .... Dr. Sharon BROWN-WELTY
100 Chief of Staff .... Ms. Tracy L. WISE
102 Sr Dir Foundation/Corp Rels .... Ms. Kimberly SHINER
44 Director Annual Giving .... Ms. Terri CARLOS

*California State University-San Marcos (D)

333 S Twin Oaks Valley Road,
San Marcos CA 92096-0001
County: San Diego FICE Identification: 030113
Unit ID: 366711
Telephone: (760) 750-4000 Carnegie Class: Masters/M
FAX Number: (760) 750-4030 Calendar System: Semester
URL: www.csusm.edu
Established: 1989 Annual Undergrad Tuition & Fees (In-State): $7,269
Enrollment: 12,154 Coed
Affiliation or Control: State IRS Status: 501(c)3
Highest Offering: Doctorate
Accreditation: WC, NURSE, SP, SW

02 President .... Dr. Karen S. HAYNES
04 Presidential Aide .... Ms. Viviana GARCIA
10 Vice President Finance/Admin Svcs .... Dr. Linda HAWK
05 Vice President Academic Affairs .... Dr. Graham OBEREM
32 Vice President of Student Affairs .... Dr. Lorena CHECA
30 Vice Pres University Advancement .... Mr. Neal HOSS
20 Assoc Vice Pres Academic Affairs .... Dr. Regina EISENBACH
88 Assoc VP Planning/Acad Resources .... Dr. Kamel HADDAD
84 Assoc Vice Pres Enrollment Mgmt .... Mr. Scott HAGG
15 Assoc VP Human Resource/Equal Oppty .... Mr. Travis GREGORY
49 Dean Col Hum Arts/Behav & Soc Sci .... Dr. Adam SHAPIRO
50 Dean Col Business Administration .... Dr. Jim HAMERLY
53 Dean Col Educ/Health & Human Svcs .... Dr. Janet POWELL
08 Dean of Library Services .... Dr. Jennifer FABBI
81 Dean Col of Science & Mathematics .... Dr. Katherine KANTARDJIEFF
56 Dean of Extended Studies .... Mr. Michael SCHRODER
72 Dean Instructional/Info Technology .... Mr. Kevin MORNINGSTAR
06 Registrar .... Mr. Thomas SWANGER
07 Dir of Admissions & Recruitment .... Ms. Carol MCALLISTER
100 Chief of Staff/Dir Inst Plng & Anal .... Mr. Matthew CEPPI
21 Associate Business Officer .... Mrs. Mary HINCHMAN
29 Director Alumni/Parent Relations .... Ms. Lori BROCKETT
96 Director Procurement/Support Svcs .... Ms. Bella NEWBERG
38 Director Undergraduate Advising .... Mr. Andres FAVELA

† Grants Joint Doctoral degree in cooperation with the University of California-San Diego.

*California State University-Stanislaus (E)

1 University Circle, Turlock CA 95382-0299
County: Stanislaus FICE Identification: 001157
Unit ID: 110495
Telephone: (209) 667-3122 Carnegie Class: Masters/L
FAX Number: N/A Calendar System: Semester
URL: www.csustan.edu
Established: 1957 Annual Undergrad Tuition & Fees (In-State): $6,704
Enrollment: 9,045 Coed
Affiliation or Control: State IRS Status: 170(c)1
Highest Offering: Doctorate
Accreditation: WC, ART, BUS, MUS, NURSE, SPAA, SW, THEA

02 President .... Dr. Ellen JUNN
05 Provost/VP Academic Affairs .... Dr. James T. STRONG
10 VP Business/Finance/CFO .... Mr. Douglas DAWES
84 VP Enrollment/Student Affairs .... Dr. Suzanne M. ESPINOZA
30 VP University Advancement .... Ms. Shirley M. POK
15 VP Faculty Affairs/HR .... Mr. Dennis W. SHIMEK
32 AVP Student Services .... Dr. J. Martyn GUNN
100 Exec Assistant to the President .... Ms. Carrie M. RASMUSSEN
79 Dean College Arts/Humanities & SS .... Dr. James A. TUEDIO
50 Int Dean College of Business Admin .... Dr. David LINDSAY
53 Dean College of Education .... Dr. Oddmund R. MYHRE
81 Int Dean College of Science .... Dr. Mark A. GROBNER
08 Dean Library Services .... Mr. Ron RODRIGUEZ
106 Interim Dean Stockton Center .... Dr. Ashour BADAL
51 Dean Extended Education .... Dr. Helene CAUDILL
20 Int AVP Academic Planning/Analysis .... Dr. Marjorie A. JAASMA
41 Director Athletics .... Mr. Michael MATOSO
35 AVP Student Affairs/Dean of Student .... Mr. Ronald J. NOBLE
21 Assoc VP Financial Services .... Ms. Julie K. BENEVEDES
13 Int Assoc VP Information Technology .... Mr. Stan TREVENA
18 Assoc VP Facilities Services .... Ms. Melody MAFFEI
26 AVP Communications & Public Affairs .... Mr. Tim LYNCH
44 Assoc VP University Advancement .... Ms. Michele LAHTI
19 Chief of Police .... Mr. Andy ROY
22 Campus Compliance Officer .... Ms. Julie A. JOHNSON
06 Registrar .... Ms. Lisa M. BERNARDO

*Humboldt State University (F)

1 Harpst Street, Arcata CA 95521-8222
County: Humboldt FICE Identification: 001149
Unit ID: 115755
Telephone: (707) 826-3011 Carnegie Class: Masters/M
FAX Number: (707) 826-5555 Calendar System: Semester
URL: www.humboldt.edu
Established: 1913 Annual Undergrad Tuition & Fees (In-State): $7,195
Enrollment: 8,485 Coed
Affiliation or Control: State IRS Status: 501(c)3
Highest Offering: Master's
Accreditation: WC, ART, ENG, IACBE, MUS, SW

02 President .... Dr. Lisa ROSSBACHER
100 Chief of Staff .... Ms. Denice HELWIG
05 Provost .... Dr. Alex ENYEDI
20 Vice Prov Acad Pgms/Undergrad Stds .... Dr. Jena BURGES
32 VP Student Affairs & Enroll Mgmt .... Dr. Peg BLAKE
10 Vice Pres Admin & Finance .... Ms. Joyce LOPES
30 Vice President of Advancement .... Mr. Craig WRUCK
15 Sr AVP Faculty Affairs and HR .... Dr. Colleen MULLERY
88 Executive Director Philanthropy .... Ms. Kimberley PITTMAN-SCHULZ
106 Assoc VP eLearning & Ext Educ .... Dr. Alex HWU
26 Assoc VP for Mktg & Communications .... Mr. Frank WHITLATCH
18 Assoc Vice President Facilities .... Ms. Traci FERDOLAGE
88 Assoc Vice President of Retention .... Ms. Radha WEBLEY
88 Director University Budget Office .... Ms. Amber BLAKESLEE
88 Director of Academic Resources .... Mr. Volga KOVAL
06 Registrar .... Mr. Clint REBIK

Code	Title	Name
07	Director of Admissions	Vacant
08	Dean of Library	Dr. Cyril OBERLANDER
44	Director of Annual Giving	Mr. Travis WILLIAMS
19	Chief of University Police	Chief Donn PETERSON
41	Athletic Director	Mr. Dan COLLEN
39	Director of Housing	Mr. Stephen ST. ONGE
13	Chief Information Officer	Ms. Anna KIRCHER
36	Director Career Devel Center	Ms. Kathy THORNHILL
28	Director Diversity & Inclusion	Vacant
46	Dean of Research & Sponsored Prgms	Mr. Steve KARP
104	Study Abroad Advisor	Ms. Penelope SHAW
35	Dean Student Affairs	Ms. Randi DARNALL BURKE
37	Director Student Financial Aid	Ms. Peggy METZGER
09	Dir Institutional Research & Plng	Dr. Lisa CASTELLINO
96	Director of Contracts & Procurement	Mr. Michael BURGHART
90	Director ITS User Support	Ms. Jeanne WIELGUS
14	Director ITS Enterprise Data	Ms. Bethany RIZZARDI
23	Dir Health/Counseling/Psych Svcs	Dr. Brian MISTLER
38	Director Counseling & Psy Svc	Dr. Jennifer SANFORD
56	Dean of eLearning & Ext Education	Mr. Carl F. HANSEN
79	Dean Col Arts/Humanities/Soc Sci	Vacant
107	Dean College Professional Studies	Dr. John LEE
81	Dean Col Natural Resources/Science	Dr. Richard BOONE
21	Director Financial Services	Mr. Brian MITCHELL
06	Registrar eLearning & Ext Educ	Mr. Christian GUILLEN
105	Web Manager	Mr. Matt HODGSON
29	Alumni Relations Outreach	Ms. Stephanie LANE
04	Administrative Asst to President	Ms. Mary HACKETT

*San Diego State University (A)

5500 Campanile Drive, San Diego CA 92182-8000

County: San Diego FICE Identification: 001151

Unit ID: 122409

Telephone: (619) 594-5200 Carnegie Class: DU-Higher

FAX Number: (619) 594-8894 Calendar System: Semester

URL: www.sdsu.edu

Established: 1897 Annual Undergrad Tuition & Fees (In-State): $6,976

Enrollment: 33,483 Coed

Affiliation or Control: State IRS Status: 501(c)3

Highest Offering: Doctorate

Accreditation: WC, ART, AUD, BUS, BUSA, CAATE, #CIDA, CLPSY, CORE, CS, DIETD, ENG, HSA, JOUR, MFCD, MIDWF, NURSE, PH, PTA, SP, SPAA, SW, TED, THEA

Code	Title	Name
02	President	Dr. Elliot HIRSHMAN
05	Provost and Senior Vice President	Dr. Chukuka S. ENWEMEKA
10	Vice President/CFO Business Affairs	Mr. Tom MCCARRON
32	Vice President for Student Affairs	Mr. Eric RIVERA
30	VP University Relations/Development	Ms. Mary Ruth CARLETON
46	VP for Research & Graduate Dean	Dr. Stephen WELTER
20	Assoc Vice Pres Academic Affairs	Dr. Radmila PRISLIN
88	Assoc VP Real Estate Planning & Dev	Mr. Robert SCHULZ
88	Assoc Vice Pres Faculty Affairs	Dr. Joanna BROOKS
21	Assoc VP for Financial Operations	Dr. Agnes WONG NICKERSON
15	Associate VP Administration	Ms. Jessica RENTTO
85	Asst Vice President Intl Programs	Dr. Alan R. SWEEDLER
26	Chief Communications Officer	Mr. Greg BLOCK
35	Assoc VP for Student Affairs	Mr. Tony CHUNG
35	Assoc VP for Student Affairs	Dr. Vitaliano FIGUEROA
35	Assoc VP for Student Affairs	Dr. Antionette MARBRAY
35	Assoc VP for Student Affairs	Ms. Christy SAMARKOS
88	Assoc VP Special Projects	Mr. James S. HERRICK
100	Chief of Staff President's Office	Ms. Megan COLLINS
23	Dir Student Health Services	Dr. Gregg LICHTENSTEIN
84	Assoc VP Enrollment Management	Dr. Sandra COOK
38	Director Counseling/Psych Services	Dr. Jennifer RIKARD
08	Dean Library/Information Access	Dr. Gale ETSCHMAIER
44	Associate VP for Development	Ms. Leslie SCHIBSTED
45	Acting Executive Dir Rsrch Found	Ms. Michele GOETZ
51	Dean College of Extended Studies	Dr. Joe SHAPIRO
58	Assoc Dean Graduate & Rsrch Affairs	Dr. Edmund BALSDON
49	Assoc VP AA/Student Achievement	Dr. Norah SHULTZ
79	Dean of College Arts & Letters	Dr. Norma BOUCHARD
81	Dean of College of Sciences	Dr. Stanley MALOY
54	Dean of College of Engineering	Dr. Monte MEHRABADI
50	Int Dean College of Business Admin	Dr. Joe BELCH
76	Interim Dean Col Health/Human Svcs	Dr. Larry VERITY
53	Dean of College of Education	Dr. Joseph JOHNSON
12	Interim Dean Imperial Valley Campus	Dr. Gregorio PONCE
57	Dean Professional Studies/Fine Arts	Dr. Joyce M. GATTAS
84	Assoc Director Enrollment Services	Ms. Sandra TEMORES-VALDEZ
88	Interim Director of Emergency Svcs	Mr. Josh MAYS
28	Chief Diversity Officer	Dr. Aaron I. BRUCE
06	Registrar	Ms. Rayanne WILLIAMS
07	Director of Admissions	Ms. Sabrina CORTELL
36	Executive Director Career Services	Dr. James TARBOX
39	Director Office of Housing Admin	Dr. Eric HANSEN
40	CEO Aztec Shops	Mrs. Donna TUSACK
41	Director Intercollegiate Athletics	Mr. Jim STERK
85	Dir International Student Center	Mr. Noah HANSEN
88	Director Environ Health & Safety	Mr. Terry GEE
13	Assoc Vice President & CIO	Mr. Christopher XANTHOS
09	Dir Analytic Studies/Inst Research	Ms. Jeanne STRONACH
31	Community Relations Manager	Ms. Nicole BORUNDA
96	Mgr Contract/Procurement Mgmt	Vacant
21	University Controller	Mr. Chris BRONSDON
18	Director of Facilities Services	Mr. John FERRIS
88	Director of Communications	Vacant
22	Dir Educational Opportunity Program	Dr. Emilio ULLOA
37	Dir Financial Aid & Scholarships	Ms. Rose PASENELLI
88	Ombudsman	Ms. Marit EESSESEN
39	Assoc Dir of Residential Education	Ms. Kara BAUER
88	Director Student Disability Svcs	Dr. Pamela STARR
88	Sr Director Enterprise Tech Svcs	Mr. Rick NORNHOLM

*San Francisco State University (B)

1600 Holloway Avenue, San Francisco CA 94132-1740

County: San Francisco FICE Identification: 001154

Unit ID: 122597

Telephone: (415) 338-1111 Carnegie Class: DU-Mod

FAX Number: (415) 338-2514 Calendar System: Semester

URL: www.sfsu.edu

Established: 1899 Annual Undergrad Tuition & Fees (In-State): $6,476

Enrollment: 29,465 Coed

Affiliation or Control: State IRS Status: 501(c)3

Highest Offering: Doctorate

Accreditation: WC, AAFCS, ART, BUS, CACREP, CORE, DIETD, DIETI, ENG, JOUR, MT, MUS, NRPA, NURSE, PH, PTA, SP, SPAA, SW, THEA

Code	Title	Name
02	President	Dr. Leslie E. WONG
05	Provost & VP Academic Affairs	Dr. Sue V. ROSSER
30	Vice Pres University Advancement	Mr. Robert J. NAVA
10	VP & CFO Administration and Finance	Mr. Ronald S. CORTEZ
32	VP Student Affairs/Enroll Mgmt	Dr. Luoluo HONG
43	University Counsel	Mr. Daniel OJEDA
20	Assoc VP Academic Resources	Dr. Alan JUNG
46	Assoc VP Research Sponsored Pgms	Mr. Michael SCOTT
20	Assoc VP Academic Affairs Operation	Dr. Brian BEATTY
85	Assoc VP International Education	Dr. Yenbo WU
45	Assoc VP Capital Plan Design Const	Mr. Simon Y. LAM
13	Interim AVP Info Tech Services	Mr. Nish MALIK
84	Senior AVP Enrollment Management	Dr. Jo VOLKERT
18	Sr Assoc VP Physical Plng & Develop	Mr. Thomas LOLLINI
21	Assoc VP Fiscal Affairs	Ms. Maureen PASAG
15	Sr Assoc VP Human Resources	Ms. Ann M. SHERMAN
35	Assoc VP Student Affairs	Mr. Gene CHELBERG
88	Int AVP Univ Property Management	Ms. Jeny VALDEZ
100	Chief of Staff	Ms. Alison SANDERS
50	Dean College Business	Ms. Linda OUBRE
53	Dean College Education	Dr. Judith MUNTER
88	Dean College Ethnic Studies	Dr. Kenneth P. MONTEIRO
51	Interim AVP/Dean of CELIA	Dr. Guido KRICKX
69	Int Dean Col Health & Soc Science	Dr. Alvin ALVAREZ
79	Int Dean Col Lib & Creative Arts	Dr. Andrew HARRIS
81	Dean College Science & Engineering	Dr. Keith BOWMAN
88	Dean Faculty Affairs & Prof Dev	Dr. Sacha BUNGE
58	Dean Graduate Studies	Dr. Ann HALLUM
88	Dean Undergraduate Studies	Dr. Jennifer SUMMIT
102	SF State President Foundation	Mr. Robert J. NAVA
08	University Librarian	Ms. Deborah C. MASTERS
24	Director Academic Technology	Dr. Maggie BEERS
85	Director International Programs	Ms. Hildy HEATH
30	Associate Vice Pres Development	Ms. Anne HARRIS
86	Director Government & Community Rel	Ms. Noriko SHINZATO
26	AVP University Communications	Ms. Monique BEELER
88	Risk Manager	Mr. Michael BEATTY
39	Director Resident Life	Mr. David ROURKE
37	Director Student Financial Aid	Ms. Barbara HUBLER
88	Director Student Outreach Services	Ms. Reeshema THORNTON
07	Interim Dir Undergrad Admissions	Mr. Edward CARRIGAN
21	Director Univ Budget Planning	Mr. Jay ORENDORFF
06	Registrar	Ms. Renee MONTE
41	Director Athletics	Mr. Charles GUTHRIE
38	Director Counseling & Psych Svcs	Dr. Derethia DUVAL
22	Director Disability Pgms/Res Ctr	Ms. Nicole BOHN
22	Dir Education Opportunity Program	Mr. Oscar M. GARDEA
19	Int Chief Police/Dir Public Safety	Chief Reginald PARSON
23	Medical Dir Student Health Svcs	Dr. Alastair SMITH
35	Interim Dean of Students	Dr. Mary Ann BEGLEY
96	Director Procurement Department	Mr. Stephen C. SMITH
29	Director Alumni Relations	Mr. Doug HUPKE
88	Budget Officer	Vacant
36	Dir Student Involvement	Vacant
44	Chief of Operations Advancement	Ms. Venesia THOMPSON
88	Dir Internal Audit/Audit & Adv Svcs	Ms. Helen STORRS
36	Interim Director Career Center	Ms. Mariko HINGSTON
88	Exec Dir Budget Adm & Oper	Mr. Jay ORENDORFF
88	Dir Environmental Health & Safety	Mr. Marc MAJEWSKI
109	Int AVP Facilities & Service Enter	Mr. Frank FASANO

† Grants additional Doctoral degrees in cooperation with the UC-Berkeley and UC-San Francisco.

*San Jose State University (C)

One Washington Square, San Jose CA 95192-0001

County: Santa Clara FICE Identification: 001155

Unit ID: 122755

Telephone: (408) 924-1000 Carnegie Class: Masters/L

FAX Number: (408) 924-1018 Calendar System: Semester

URL: www.sjsu.edu

Established: 1857 Annual Undergrad Tuition & Fees (In-State): $7,378

Enrollment: 32,713 Coed

Affiliation or Control: State IRS Status: 501(c)3

Highest Offering: Doctorate

Accreditation: WC, ART, BUS, CAATE, CEA, CS, DANCE, DIETD, DIETI, ENG, IPSY, #JOUR, LIB, MT, MUS, NAIT, NRPA, NURSE, OT, PH, PLNG, SP, SPAA, SW, TED, THEA

Code	Title	Name
02	President	Dr. Mary PAPAZIAN
05	Provost/Vice Pres Acad Affairs	Dr. Andrew FEINSTEIN
10	Vice Pres Administration & Finance	Mr. Charles FAAS
32	Vice President Student Affairs	Mr. Reginald BLAYLOCK
30	VP University Advancement	Mr. Paul LANNING
13	Deputy CIO	Ms. Terry VAHEY
45	Vice Provost Academic Budgets/Plng	Ms. Marna GENES
100	Chief of Staff	Ms. Stacy GLEIXNER
20	Associate Vice Pres Faculty Affairs	Dr. Elna GREEN
20	Assoc VP Research	Dr. Pamela STACKS
20	Assoc VP Grad/Undergrad Studies	Dr. Thalia ANAGNOS
21	Assoc VP Finance	Ms. Josee LAROCHELLE
18	Assoc VP for Facilities/Operations	Vacant
15	Associate VP Human Resources	Ms. Beth PUGLIESE
26	Assoc VP Public Affairs	Mr. Barry SHILLER
29	Assoc VP Devel/Exec Dir Alumni Rels	Mr. Brian BATES
51	Assoc VP/Dean Intl/Extended Stds	Dr. Ruth HUARD
84	Int Assoc VP Enroll/Academic Svcs	Ms. Sharon WILLEY
08	Dean of the University Library	Dr. Tracy ELLIOTT
28	Dir Equal Opportunity & Emp Rel	Ms. Julie PAISANT
27	AVP Marketing Communications	Mr. Barry SHILLER
06	Registrar	Ms. Marian SOFISH
41	Director Intercollegiate Athletics	Mr. Gene BLEYMAIER
96	Director Procurement Services	Vacant
40	Director Spartan Bookstore	Mr. Ryland METZINGER
19	Chief of Police	Mr. Peter DECENA
36	Interim Director Career Center	Ms. Susan ROCKWELL
38	Director Counseling Services	Ms. Ellen LIN
37	Director Fin Aid/Schlarship Ofc	Ms. Coleetta MCELROY
39	Dir University Housing Svcs	Mr. Victor CULATTA
23	Dir Student Health Center	Dr. Roger ELROD
49	Dean College of Applied Sci & Art	Dr. Mary SCHUTTEN
50	Interim Dean College of Business	Dr. Marlene TURNER
53	Dean College of Education	Dr. Elaine CHIN
54	Interim Dean College of Engineering	Dr. Ping HSU
79	Dean College of Humanities/Arts	Dr. Lisa VOLLENDORF
81	Dean College of Science	Dr. J. Michael PARRISH
83	Dean College Social Sciences	Dr. Walt JACOBS
04	Administrative Asst to President	Ms. Zaynna TELLO

*Sonoma State University (D)

1801 E Cotati Avenue, Rohnert Park CA 94928-3609

County: Sonoma FICE Identification: 001156

Unit ID: 123572

Telephone: (707) 664-2880 Carnegie Class: Masters/L

FAX Number: (707) 664-2505 Calendar System: Semester

URL: www.sonoma.edu

Established: 1960 Annual Undergrad Tuition & Fees (In-State): $7,330

Enrollment: 9,290 Coed

Affiliation or Control: State IRS Status: 501(c)3

Highest Offering: Master's

Accreditation: WC, ART, BUS, CACREP, MUS, NUR

Code	Title	Name
02	President	Dr. Ruben ARMINANA
05	Provost & Vice Pres Academic Affs	Dr. Andrew ROGERSON
10	Vice Pres Administration & Finance	Mr. Laurence FURUKAWA-SCHLERETH
26	Vice President University Affairs	Mr. Dan CONDRON
30	Vice President Development	Vacant
32	VP of Student Affairs	Mr. Matthew LOPEZ-PHILLIPS
20	Assoc VP for Faculty Affairs	Dr. Deborah ROBERTS
09	Sr Dir Records/Report & Analytics	Mr. Sean JOHNSON
13	Assoc VP CIO/Information Technology	Mr. Jason WENRICK
08	Dean of Library	Ms. Karen SCHNEIDER
79	Dean School of Arts & Humanities	Dr. Thaine STEARNS
50	Dean Sch of Business/Economic	Dr. William SILVER
53	Dean School of Education	Dr. Carlos AYALA
81	Dean School Science & Tech	Dr. Lynn STAUFFER
83	Dean of Social Sciences	Dr. John D. WINGARD
56	Dean School of Extended Education	Dr. Robert EYLER
38	Dir of Counseling/Psych Services	Dr. Laura WILLIAMS
37	Director of Financial Aid	Mrs. Susan GUTIERREZ
18	Assoc VP Facilities Services/CPDC	Mr. Christopher DINNO
27	Assoc VP for Communications & Mktg	Ms. Susan KASHACK
41	Director Athletics	Mr. William J. FUSCO
19	Chief Police Services	Mr. Nathan JOHNSON
2?	Director Seawolf Services	Ms. Elizabeth O'BRIEN
88	Assoc VP Entrepreneurial Srvcs	Mr. Neil MARKLEY
06	Registrar	Ms. Lisa NOTO
07	Director of Admissions	Ms. Natalie KALOGIANNIS
84	Director of Enrollment Management	Mr. Gustavo FLORES
29	Dir Alumni Relations/Annual Giving	Ms. Laurie OGG
28	Mg Dir Employee Rel/Comp Svcs	Ms. Joyce SUZUKI
15	Sr Director Human Resources	Ms. Tammy KENBER
96	Managing Dir for Purchasing	Ms. Jenifer BARNETT

California University of Management and Sciences (E)

721 North Euclid Street, Anaheim CA 92801

County: Orange FICE Identification: 041331

Unit ID: 460075

Telephone: (714) 533-3946 Carnegie Class: Not Classified

FAX Number: (714) 533-7778 Calendar System: Quarter

URL: www.calums.edu

Established: 1998 Annual Undergrad Tuition & Fees: $9,570

Enrollment: 592 Coed

Affiliation or Control: Independent Non-Profit IRS Status: 501(c)3

Highest Offering: Master's

Accreditation: ACICS

Code	Title	Name
01	President	David PARK
03	Vice President	Jason SHIN
10	Director of Finance	Chang J. KIM

05 Academic Dean .... Silviu VELOVICI
20 Associate Academic Dean .... Sasha SAFARZADEH
11 Director of Administration .... Jeffrey BEASCA
07 Director of Admissions .... Lisa LEE
84 Enrollment Director .... Andrew PRESS
32 Director of Student Services .... Monica SHOWRANK
08 Librarian .... Karine PARRY
90 IT Administrator .... Donghyun SUNG
06 Registrar .... Hongjun AHN
85 International Student Advisor .... Tyler COPE
101 Board Secretary .... Jong S. YOON
26 Director of Marketing .... Hyun Chul KIM
37 Financial Aid Officer .... Jeff BEASCA

California Western School of Law (A)

225 Cedar Street, San Diego CA 92101-3046
County: San Diego FICE Identification: 013103
Unit ID: 111391
Telephone: (619) 239-0391 Carnegie Class: Spec-4-yr-Law
FAX Number: (619) 525-7092 Calendar System: Trimester
URL: www.cwsl.edu
Established: 1924 Annual Graduate Tuition & Fees: N/A
Enrollment: 781 Coed
Affiliation or Control: Independent Non-Profit IRS Status: 501(c)3
Highest Offering: First Professional Degree; No Undergraduates
Accreditation: LAW

01 President & Dean .... Dean Neils SCHAUMANN
05 Vice Dean Academic Affairs .... Prof. Barbara J. COX
46 Associate Dean Research & Fac Devel .... Prof. Joanna SAX
88 Assoc Dean of Exper Learning .... Prof. Linda MORTON
32 Associate Dean of Student Life .... Ms. Wendy BASHANT
32 Asst Dean Students/Diversity Svcs .... Ms. Susan GARRETT FINSTER
36 Assistant Dean Career Services .... Ms. Courtney MIKLUSAK
88 Asst Dean Mission Development .... Mr. James M. COOPER
37 Exec Director Financial Aid .... Mr. William KAHLER
13 Exec Director Computer Services .... Vacant
18 Exec Dir Facilities Management .... Ms. Jolie L. CARTIER
88 Ex Dir Inst for Criminal Def Advoc .... Prof. Justin P. BROOKS
88 Dir Inst of Health Law Studies .... Prof. Susan A. CHANNICK
08 Assoc Dean Law Library/Info Res .... Prof. Philip T. GRAGG
10 Chief Financial Officer .... Ms. Pamela A. DUFFY
07 Assistant Dean Admissions .... Mr. Christopher E. BAIDOO
06 Registrar .... Ms. Sandra E. MOREAU
88 Director MCL/LLM Program .... Prof. Lisa BLACK
26 Director Marketing Communications .... Mr. Joshua NUNN
29 Director Alumni Relations .... Ms. Lori BOYLE
15 VP Human Resources .... Ms. Rikklyn S. UEDA
28 Director Diversity .... Ms. Marion E. CLOETE
21 Director Business Office .... Ms. Ruth GOULDING
04 Administrative Asst to President .... Ms. Marilyn L. JORDAN
43 Dir Legal Services/General Counsel .... Ms. Lisa JORDAN
44 Director Annual or Planned Giving .... Vacant
30 Director of Development .... Mr. Brian DALY

Cambridge Junior College (B)

990-A Klamath Lane, Yuba City CA 95993-8978
County: Sutter FICE Identification: 038743
Unit ID: 446093
Telephone: (530) 674-9199 Carnegie Class: Spec 2-yr-Other
FAX Number: (530) 671-7319 Calendar System: Other
URL: www.cambridge.edu
Established: 2010 Annual Undergrad Tuition & Fees: N/A
Enrollment: 159 Coed
Affiliation or Control: Proprietary IRS Status: Proprietary
Highest Offering: Associate Degree
Accreditation: ACICS

01 Director .... Ms. Sandy FOWLER

Carnegie Mellon University Silicon Valley Campus (C)

NASA Research Pk, Bld 23 MS 23-11,
Moffett Field CA 94035
Telephone: (650) 335-2810 Identification: 770149
Accreditation: &M

† Regional accreditation is carried under the parent institution in Pittsburgh, PA

*Carrington College - Administrative Office (D)

7801 Folsom Boulevard, Suite 210,
Sacramento CA 95826-2620
County: Sacramento Identification: 666086
Telephone: (916) 388-2800 Carnegie Class: N/A
FAX Number: (916) 381-1609
URL: www.carrington.edu

01 President Carrington Colleges .... Dr. Donna LORAINE
05 Provost VP Academic Affairs .... Dr. Danika BOWEN
11 Senior Director Operations .... Mr. Jim MURPHY
11 Senior Director Operations .... Mr. Craig JACOB
11 Senior Director Operations .... Mr. David KAYE
07 Vice President Enrollment Services .... Mr. Mitch CHARLES
32 Sr Dir Student Services .... Dr. Scott SAND
10 VP Finance .... Ms. Beth ROGERS
13 VP IT .... Mr. David MCMURTRY

*Carrington College - Sacramento (E)

8909 Folsom Boulevard, Sacramento CA 95826-3203
County: Sacramento FICE Identification: 009748
Unit ID: 125532
Telephone: (916) 361-1660 Carnegie Class: Spec 2-yr-Health
FAX Number: (916) 361-6666 Calendar System: Other
URL: www.carrington.edu
Established: 1983 Annual Undergrad Tuition & Fees: N/A
Enrollment: 1,385 Coed
Affiliation or Control: Proprietary IRS Status: Proprietary
Highest Offering: Associate Degree
Accreditation: WJ, DH, MAC

02 Executive Director .... Ms. Sue SMITH
06 Registrar .... Ms. Ryanne GREEN-QUARLES
07 Director Enrollment Services .... Ms. Carmen DARDAR
05 Dean of Academic Affairs .... Mr. John ROTH
36 Director Career Services .... Ms. Louella DIETRICH
88 Mgr Academic Success Ctr .... Ms. Becky CARDWELL

**Carrington College - Citrus Heights* (F)

7301 Greenback Lane, Suite A,
Citrus Heights CA 95621-5591
Telephone: (916) 722-8200 Identification: 667042
Accreditation: &WJ, MAC, SURGT

† Regional accreditation is carried under the parent institution in Sacramento, CA.

**Carrington College - Pleasant Hill* (G)

380 Civic Drive, Suite 300, Pleasant Hill CA 94523-1984
Telephone: (925) 609-6650 Identification: 666043
Accreditation: &WJ, COARC, MAC, PTAA

† Regional accreditation is carried under the parent institution in Sacramento, CA.

**Carrington College - Pomona* (H)

901 Corporate Center Drive, #300, Pomona CA 91768
Telephone: (909) 868-5800 Identification: 770506
Accreditation: &WJ, MAC

† Regional accreditation is carried under the parent institution in Sacramento, CA.

**Carrington College - San Jose* (I)

5883 Rue Ferrari, Ste. 125, San Jose CA 95138
Telephone: (408) 960-0162 Identification: 666042
Accreditation: &WJ, DH, MAC, SURGT

† Regional accreditation is carried under the parent institution in Sacramento, CA.

**Carrington College - San Leandro* (J)

15555 E 14th Street, Suite 500,
San Leandro CA 94578-1977
Telephone: (510) 276-3888 Identification: 666751
Accreditation: &WJ, MAC

† Regional accreditation is carried under the parent institution in Sacramento, CA.

**Carrington College - Stockton* (K)

1313 W Robinhood Drive, Suite B,
Stockton CA 95207-5509
Telephone: (209) 956-1240 Identification: 666140
Accreditation: &WJ, MAC

† Regional accreditation is carried under the parent institution in Sacramento, CA.

Casa Loma College-Anaheim (L)

421 N. Brookhurst Street #100, Anaheim CA 92801-2666
Telephone: (818) 785-2726 Identification: 770519
Accreditation: ABHES

Casa Loma College-Van Nuys (M)

6725 Kester Avenue, Van Nuys CA 91405
County: Los Angeles FICE Identification: 006731
Unit ID: 111638
Telephone: (818) 785-2726 Carnegie Class: Spec 2-yr-Health
FAX Number: (818) 785-2191 Calendar System: Other
URL: www.casalomacollege.edu
Established: 1966 Annual Undergrad Tuition & Fees: N/A
Enrollment: 446 Coed
Affiliation or Control: Independent Non-Profit IRS Status: 501(c)3
Highest Offering: Associate Degree
Accreditation: ABHES, #PTAA

01 Campus Director/Controller .... Ms. Veronica PANTOJA
05 Dean of Education .... Dr. Stephanie SHELBURNE
66 Director of Nursing .... Ms. Stephanie AYO-AKINYEMI
06 Registrar .... Ms. Vicki KIM
07 Director of Admissions .... Ms. Deanna BERNAL
86 Director of Compliance .... Vacant
37 Director Student Financial Aid .... Vacant
08 Head Librarian .... Vacant
106 Dir Online Education/E-learning .... Ms. Stephanie SHELBURNE
13 Chief Info Technology Officer .... Mr. Cyrill REISER
18 Chief Facilities/Physical Plant .... Ms. Veronica PANTOJA
36 Director Student Placement .... Ms. Desiree TERCERO

CBD College (N)

3699 Wilshire Boulevard, 4th Floor,
Los Angeles CA 90010
County: Los Angeles FICE Identification: 032503
Unit ID: 439367
Telephone: (213) 427-2200 Carnegie Class: Not Classified
FAX Number: (213) 427-9278 Calendar System: Other
URL: www.cbd.edu
Established: 1982 Annual Undergrad Tuition & Fees: N/A
Enrollment: 411 Coed
Affiliation or Control: Independent Non-Profit IRS Status: 501(c)3
Highest Offering: Associate Degree
Accreditation: ABHES, DMS, OTA, PTAA, SURTEC

01 President .... Mr. Alan HESHEL

Cedars-Sinai Medical Center Graduate Program in Biomedical Sciences and Translational Medicine (O)

8700 Beverly Boulevard, Los Angeles CA 90048
County: Los Angeles Identification: 667071
Telephone: (310) 423-8294 Carnegie Class: Not Classified
FAX Number: N/A Calendar System: Trimester
URL: www.cedars-sinai.edu
Established: 1902 Annual Graduate Tuition & Fees: N/A
Enrollment: N/A Coed
Affiliation or Control: Independent Non-Profit IRS Status: 501(c)3
Highest Offering: Doctorate; No Undergraduates
Accreditation: WC

01 President/CEO .... Mr. Thomas PRISELAC
05 Exec Vice Pres Academic Affairs .... Dr. Shlomo MELMED

Cerritos College (P)

11110 Alondra Boulevard, Norwalk CA 90650-6298
County: Los Angeles FICE Identification: 001161
Unit ID: 111887
Telephone: (562) 860-2451 Carnegie Class: Assoc/MT-VT-High Trad
FAX Number: (562) 467-5005 Calendar System: Semester
URL: www.cerritos.edu
Established: 1955 Annual Undergrad Tuition & Fees (In-District): $1,346
Enrollment: 21,774 Coed
Affiliation or Control: State/Local IRS Status: 501(c)3
Highest Offering: Associate Degree
Accreditation: WJ, ADNUR, DA, DH, PTAA

01 President .... Dr. Jose L. FIERRO
05 Actg Vice President Academic Affs . Mr. Edmund (Rick) MIRANDA
10 Actg Vice President Business Svcs .... Mr. Noorali DELAWALLA
32 Vice President Student Services .... Dr. Stephen JOHNSON
15 Int Vice President Human Resources .... Mr. Harry JOEL
20 Dean of Academic Affairs .... Mr. Edmund (Rick) MIRANDA
07 Dean of Admissions/Records & Svcs .... Ms. Stephanie MURGUIA
38 Dean of Counseling Services .... Dr. Renee DELONG
86 Dir College/Govt Rels & Pub Affs .... Ms. Miya WALKER
22 Dean Disabled Student Pgms & Svcs .... Dr. Lucinda ABORN
88 Dean of Student Support Services .... Ms. Kim WESTBY
50 Instr Dean Business/Humanities/SS .... Ms. Rachel MASON
57 Instr Dean Fine Arts/Communications .... Dr. Gary PRITCHARD
76 Instr Dean Health Occupations .... Ms. Sandra MARKS
83 Dean Academic Success .... Ms. Shawna BASKETTE
49 Instr Dean Liberal Arts .... Mr. David FABISH
68 Instr Dean Health/PE/Dance/Athletic .... Dr. Daniel SMITH
54 Instr Dean Science/Engineering/Math .... Ms. Connie BOARDMAN
73 Instr Dean Technology .... Dr. Yannick REAL
13 Director Information Technology .... Mr. Patrick O'DONNELL
21 Director of Fiscal Services .... Mr. Noorali DELAWALLA
35 Dean of Student Services .... Dr. Gilbert J. CONTRERAS
36 Dir of Career/Assessment Services .... Ms. Theresa LOPEZ
18 Director Physical Plant & Const Svc .... Mr. David C. MOORE
102 Executive Director Foundation .... Mr. Steven RICHARDSON
88 Director Community Advancement .... Ms. Bellegran GOMEZ
96 Dir Purchasing/Contract Admin .... Mr. Mark LOGAN
16 Director Human Resources/Risk Mgmt .... Dr. Adriana FLORES-CHURCH
105 Web Administrator .... Mr. Ty BOWMAN
19 Chief of Campus Police .... Mr. Thomas GALLIVAN
28 Assoc Dn Adult Educ/Diversity Pgms .... Ms. Graciela VASQUEZ
31 Director Community Education .... Dr. Patricia ROBBINS SMITH
88 Director Child Development Center .... Ms. Debra WARD
88 Operations Manager .... Mr. Thomas RICHEY
88 Payroll Manager .... Ms. Deanna HART
88 Budget Manager .... Mr. Conrad SELORIO
14 Manager Information Technology .... Mr. Javier BANUELOS

23 Assoc Dean Student Health Wellness .... Dr. Hillary MENNELLA
88 Director of Student Program Svcs .... Ms. Norma RODRIGUEZ
09 Dir Inst Effec Research & Planning .... Dr. Kristi BLACKBURN
88 Director Adv Trans Tech Projects .... Ms. Jannet MALIG
22 Dir Diver/Compliance/Title IX Coord .... Ms. Valencia RAPHAEL
88 EOPS Assistant Director .... Ms. Yvette TAFOYA
19 Dir Educational Partnerships .... Ms. Sue PARSONS
88 Accounting Manager .... Ms. Kathy BURGOS
88 Facilities Manager .... Mr. Shannon KAVENEY

*Chabot-Las Positas Community College District (A)

7600 Dublin Blvd., 3rd Flr., Dublin CA 94568
County: Alameda Identification: 666925
Telephone: (925) 485-5208 Carnegie Class: N/A
FAX Number: (925) 485-5256
URL: www.clpccd.org

01 Chancellor .... Dr. Jannett N. JACKSON
10 Vice Chanc Business Svcs .... Mr. Lorenzo LEGASPI
05 Vice Chanc Educational Svcs .... Ms. Krista JOHNS
15 Vice Chanc Human Resource Svcs .... Mr. Wyman FONG

*Chabot College (B)

25555 Hesperian Boulevard, Hayward CA 94545-2400
County: Alameda FICE Identification: 001162
Unit ID: 111920
Telephone: (510) 723-6600 Carnegie Class: Assoc/HT-High Trad
FAX Number: (510) 782-9315 Calendar System: Semester
URL: www.chabotcollege.edu
Established: 1961 Annual Undergrad Tuition & Fees (In-District): $1,138
Enrollment: 13,047 Coed
Affiliation or Control: State/Local IRS Status: 501(c)3
Highest Offering: Associate Degree
Accreditation: WJ, DH, #MAC

02 President .... Dr. Susan S. SPERLING
05 VP Academic Services .... Ms. Stacy THOMPSON
32 Vice President Student Services .... Dr. Matthew KRITSCHER
11 Vice Pres Administrative Services .... Dr. Carla WALTER
04 Exec Asst to the College President .... Ms. Kirti REDDY
08 Librarian .... Ms. Kim MORRISON
38 Dean Counseling/Guidance .... Dr. Matt KRITSCHER
41 Dean Health/PE/Athletics .... Mr. Jeff DROUIN
07 Dir Admissions & Records/Registrar .... Mrs. Paulette LINO
37 Director of Financial Aid .... Ms. Kathryn LINZMEYER
19 Director Safety & Security .... Sgt. Bobbie KOLLER
09 Director of Institutional Research .... Dr. Carolyn ARNOLD
15 Director Human Resources .... Dr. Wyman FONG
18 Chief Facilities/Physical Plant .... Mr. Tim NELSON
30 Exec Dir Devel/Foundation .... Dr. Maria OCHOA
35 Dir Student Life/Student Services .... Mr. Arnold PAGLIO
96 Manager Purchasing/Warehouse Svcs .... Ms. Victoria LAMICA

*Las Positas College (C)

3000 Campus Hill Drive, Livermore CA 94551-7623
County: Alameda FICE Identification: 030357
Unit ID: 366401
Telephone: (925) 424-1000 Carnegie Class: Assoc/HT-High Trad
FAX Number: (925) 443-0742 Calendar System: Semester
URL: www.laspositascollege.edu
Established: 1975 Annual Undergrad Tuition & Fees (In-District): $1,138
Enrollment: 8,835 Coed
Affiliation or Control: State/Local IRS Status: 501(c)3
Highest Offering: Associate Degree
Accreditation: WJ

02 President .... Dr. Barry A. RUSSELL
05 Vice President Academic Svcs .... Roanna BENNIE
32 Vice President Student Svcs .... Vacant
11 Vice Pres Administrative Services .... Ms. Diane BRADY
04 Exec Assistant to the President .... Ms. Kelly ABAD
35 Dean of Student Services .... Ms. Barbara MORRISSEY
49 Dean Arts & Humanities .... Dr. Donald MILLER
81 Dean Math/Science/Eng/Public Safety .... Vacant
50 Dean Bus/Health/Athletics/Work Exp .... Vacant
77 Dn Computing/Applied Tech/Soc Svcs .... Mr. Don CARLSON
07 Dean of Admissions/Records .... Ms. Sylvia RODRIGUEZ
45 Director of Research & Planning .... Mr. Rajinder SAMRA
37 Financial Aid/Veterans Assistance .... Ms. Andi SCHREIBMAN
19 Campus Safety Supervisor .... Mr. Sean PRATHER
08 Head Librarian .... Dr. Tina INZERILLA
102 Executive Director LPC Foundation .... Mr Kenneth COOPER
41 Athletic Director .... Vacant
10 Associate Business Officer .... Ms. Natasha LANG
18 Project Planner/Manager Facilities .... Vacant
06 Registrar .... Ms. Sylvia RODRIGUEZ
88 Project Manager CTE .... Ms. Vicki SHIPMAN
88 Director Child Development Center .... Ms. Corinna CALICA

Chaffey College (D)

5885 Haven Avenue, Rancho Cucamonga CA 91737-3002
County: San Bernardino FICE Identification: 001163
Unit ID: 111939
Telephone: (909) 652-6000 Carnegie Class: Assoc/HT-High Trad
FAX Number: (909) 652-6006 Calendar System: Semester
URL: www.chaffey.edu
Established: 1883 Annual Undergrad Tuition & Fees (In-District): $1,153
Enrollment: 19,557 Coed
Affiliation or Control: State/Local IRS Status: 501(c)3
Highest Offering: Associate Degree
Accreditation: WJ, ADNUR, DA, RAD

01 Superintendent/President .... Dr. Henry D. SHANNON
11 Vice Pres Administrative Affairs .... Ms. Melanie SIDDIQI
10 Assoc Supt Bus Svcs/Econ Dev .... Ms. Lisa BAILEY
05 Assoc Supt Instruction/Inst Effect .... Meridith RANDALL
09 Dean Inst Research/Research Dev .... Mr. Jim FILLPOT
29 Director Alumni Relations .... Ms. Janeth RODRIGUEZ
85 Int Director International Students .... Ms. Saba KAZMI
32 Dean Student Life .... Mr. Christopher BRUNELLE
07 Admin Admissions/Records .... Ms. Kathy LUCERO
21 Exec Director Business Services .... Ms. Kim ERICKSON
88 Director Technical Services .... Mr. Michael FINK
88 Director Childrens Center .... Ms. Birgit MONKS
23 Director Student Health Services .... Ms. Katherine PEEK
37 Director Financial Aid .... Ms. Patricia BOPKO
109 Director Auxiliary Services .... Vacant
26 Director Marketing/Public Relations .... Ms. Alisha ROSAS
21 Exec Dir Budgeting & Fiscal Svc .... Ms. Anita UNDERCOFFER
88 Director Museum Gallery .... Ms. Rebecca TRAWICK
18 Manager Facilities Development .... Ms. Sarah RILEY
12 Dean Chino Campus .... Dr. Teresa HULL
88 Dean Visual Performing Arts .... Dr. Jason CHEVALIER
50 Dean Bus & Applied Tech .... Ms. Joy HAERENS
81 Dean Mathematics & Science .... Mr. Theodore YOUNGLOVE
83 Dean Social & Behav Sci & PE .... Dr. Lorene SCHWARTZ
88 Dean Language Arts & Health Science .... Mr. Anthony DISALVO
38 Dean Counseling & Matriculation .... Ms. Amy NEVAREZ
12 Int Dean Fontana Campus .... Dr. Yolanda FRIDAY
08 Dean Instruc Support/Library Svcs .... Ms. Laura HOPE
04 Exec Assistant Supt/Pres Office .... Ms. Kathy NAPOLI
88 Dean Discipline/Grievance .... Mr. Len CROW
41 Interim Director Athletics .... Mr. Jeff KLEIN
86 Manager Government Relations .... Ms. Lorena CORONA
15 Director Human Resources .... Ms. Susan HARDIE
102 Executive Director Foundation .... Ms. Lisa NASHUA

Chamberlain College of Nursing-Sacramento (E)

10971 Sun Center Drive, Rancho Cordova CA 95670
Telephone: (916) 330-3410 Identification: 770978
Accreditation: &NH, NURSE

† Regional accreditation is carried under the parent institution in Addison, IL

Chapman University (F)

One University Drive, Orange CA 92866-1099
County: Orange FICE Identification: 001164
Unit ID: 111948
Telephone: (714) 997-6815 Carnegie Class: Masters/L
FAX Number: (714) 997-6713 Calendar System: 4/1/4
URL: www.chapman.edu
Established: 1861 Annual Undergrad Tuition & Fees: $47,260
Enrollment: 8,132 Coed
Affiliation or Control: Christian Church (Disciples Of Christ)
IRS Status: 501(c)3
Highest Offering: Doctorate
Accreditation: WC, BUS, CAATE, DANCE, LAW, MFCD, MUS, @PHAR, PTA, #SP, TEAC, THEA

01 President .... Dr. Daniele C. STRUPPA
05 Interim Chancellor .... Dr. Glenn PFEIFFER
03 Executive Vice President & COO .... Mr. Harold W. HEWITT, JR.
30 Exec VP University Advancement .... Ms. Sheryl BOURGEOIS
32 Vice Chancellor & Dean of Students .... Dr. Jerry PRICE
84 Vice Chancellor/Dean Enrollment Mgt .... Mr. Michael PELLY
20 Int Vice Chanc for Academic Admin .... Dr. Kenneth E. MURPHY
09 Vice Chan Inst Eff & Fac Affairs .... Mr. Joseph SLOWENSKY
49 Dean Wilkinson Col Hum/Soc Sci .... Dr. Patrick FUERY
61 Dean School of Law .... Dr. Tom CAMPBELL
50 Dean School Business/Economics .... Mr. Reginald GILYARD
67 Dean School of Pharmacy .... Dr. Ronald JORDAN
53 Dean College of Educational Studies .... Dr. Margaret GROGAN
88 Dean College of Film & Media Arts .... Mr. Robert BASSETT
88 Dean College of Performing Arts .... Dr. Guilic ONGARO
81 Dean Col of Science/Tech .... Dr. Jeneen HILL
88 Dean/Artistic Dir Center for Arts .... Dr. William HALL
88 Director Ctr for Global Education .... Dr. James COYLE
97 Vice Chancellor Undergrad Education .... Dr. Nina LENOIR
45 Vice President Campus Planning .... Mr. Kris OLSEN
15 Vice President of Human Resources .... Ms. Becky CAMPOS
43 Assoc Vice Pres of Legal Affairs .... Ms. Janine DUMONTELLE
10 Assoc Vice President & Controller .... Mr. Behzad BINESH
07 Dir UG Admission .... Ms. Marcela MEJIA MARTINEZ
88 Assistant Chancellor .... Ms. Iris GERBASI
18 Assoc VP Facilities .... Mr. Rick TURNER
26 Director Public Relations .... Ms. Mary PLATT
08 Dean of Library .... Ms. Charlene BALDWIN
29 Asst VP Strategic Engagement/Dev .... Ms. Delite TRAVIS
13 Chief Information Officer .... Ms. Helen NORRIS
09 Director of Institutional Research .... Dr. Marisol ARREDONDO
06 Registrar .... Ms. Jan MCCUEN
46 Director Sponsored Research .... Ms. Yolanda UZZELL
37 Director Financial Aid .... Mr. Jack MILLIS
85 Director Intl Student Services .... Ms. Susan SAMS
19 Chief of Public Safety .... Mr. Randy BURBA
39 Assoc Dean/Director Residence Life .... Ms. Deborah MILLER
41 Athletic Director .... Mr. Terry BOESEL
42 Dean of the Chapel .... Dr. Gail STEARNS

04 Associate to the President .... Ms. Ann CAMERON
88 Exec Assistant to the Chancellor .... Ms. Christina ZERMENO
23 Director Student Health Services .... Ms. Jacqueline DEATS
35 Director of Student Engagement .... Mr. Chris HUTCHISON
36 Asst Dir Career Education .... Ms. Sally JAFARI
38 Assoc Dean/Dir Student Psych Couns .... Ms. Jeannie WALKER
96 Purchasing Coordinator .... Ms. Wendy SEIRUP
04 Assistant to the President .... Ms. Dorothy FAROL
58 Vice Chancellor for Graduate Educ .... Dr. Richard REDDING
102 Dir Corporate/Foundation Relations .... Mr. Mike STRINGER
44 Dir Legacy Planning .... Mr. David MOORE
90 Dir Academic Tech/Digital Media .... Dr. Mary LITCH
105 Webmaster .... Ms. Mandy THOMAS

Charles R. Drew University of Medicine & Science (G)

1731 E 120th Street, Los Angeles CA 90059-3025
County: Los Angeles FICE Identification: 010365
Unit ID: 111966
Telephone: (323) 563-4800 Carnegie Class: Spec-4-yr-Other Health
FAX Number: (323) 563-5987 Calendar System: Semester
URL: www.cdrewu.edu
Established: 1966 Annual Undergrad Tuition & Fees: N/A
Enrollment: 481 Coed
Affiliation or Control: Independent Non-Profit IRS Status: 501(c)3
Highest Offering: Master's
Accreditation: WC, #ARCPA, NURSE, PH, RAD

01 President & CEO .... Dr. David M. CARLISLE
05 EVP Academic Affairs/Provost .... Dr. Steve O. MICHAEL
100 Chief of Staff .... Ms. Jackie BROWN
45 VP Research & Health Affairs .... Dr. Jadutt VADGAMA
30 VP for Strategic Advancement .... Ms. Angela L. MINNIEFIELD
15 Chief Human Resources Officer .... Vacant
10 VP Finance/Chief Business Officer .... Mr. Carl MCLANEY
63 Dean College of Medicine .... Dr. Deborah PROTHROW-STITH
66 Interim Dean School of Nursing .... Dr. Margaret AVILA
76 Dean College of Science & Health .... Dr. Hector BALCAZAR
20 Asst Provost Faculty Affairs .... Dr. William SHAY
32 Dean Student Affairs .... Dr. Jinny OH
58 Director GME .... Dr. Sandra GONZALEZ
20 Sr Assoc Dean Academic Affairs .... Dr. Ronald A. EDELSTEIN
09 Director Inst Research & Effectiv ...... Mr. Richard W. LINDSTROM
37 Interim Chief Financial Officer .... Mr. John GERAGHTY
08 Director Health Sciences Library ...... Ms. Darlene PARKER-KELLY
06 Assistant Registrar .... Ms. Raquel MUNOZ
07 Director of Admissions .... Mr. Amin MAGHSOODI

Charter College-Oxnard (H)

2000 Outlet Center Drive, Suite 150, Oxnard CA 93036
Telephone: (805) 973-1240 Identification: 666675
Accreditation: ACICS

† Branch campus of Charter College, Anchorage, AK.

Chicago School of Professional Psychology Los Angeles Campus (I)

617 West 7th Street, Los Angeles CA 90017
County: Los Angeles FICE Identification: 021553
Unit ID: 455664
Telephone: (213) 615-2700 Carnegie Class: Spec-4-yr-Other Health
FAX Number: (213) 615-7274 Calendar System: Semester
URL: www.thechicagoschool.edu
Established: 2008 Annual Graduate Tuition & Fees: N/A
Enrollment: 1,877 Coed
Affiliation or Control: Independent Non-Profit IRS Status: 501(c)3
Highest Offering: Doctorate; No Undergraduates
Accreditation: WC

01 President .... Dr. Michele NEALON-WOODS
05 Provost/Chief Academic Officer .... Vacant
10 Chief Financial Officer .... Mr. Raul PETRIS
32 Vice Pres Student Affairs .... Ms. Jennifer STRIPE PORTILLO
15 Vice Pres Human Resources .... Dr. David IWANE
106 Dean Online Programs .... Vacant
07 Assoc Vice Pres Admissions .... Ms. Katie CURRAN
30 Chief Development Officer .... Vacant
26 National Director of Communications .... Ms. Elinor GILBERT
04 Administrative Asst to President .... Ms. Jamie INGRAM
06 Registrar .... Ms. Connie KUANG
08 Head Librarian .... Mr. Oliver CUTSHAW
100 Chief of Staff .... Ms. Shari MIKOS
101 Secretary of the Institution/Board .... Ms. Patti TYRA
19 Director Security/Safety .... Mr. Rene LARA
29 Director Alumni Relations .... Ms. Karen WILSON
37 Director Student Financial Aid .... Ms. Steph RODRIGUEZ
38 Director Student Counseling .... Ms. Christina MARRERO

Chicago School of Professional Psychology-Irvine Campus (J)

4199 Campus Drive, Irvine CA 92612
Telephone: (949) 769-7700 Identification: 770492
Accreditation: &WC

† Regional accreditation is carried under the parent institution in Los Angeles, CA

China Evangelical Seminary North America (A)

1520 W. Cameron Avenue Ste 275,
West Covina CA 91790
County: Los Angeles — Identification: 667256
Telephone: (626) 917-9482 — Carnegie Class: Not Classified
FAX Number: (626) 851-1371 — Calendar System: Semester
URL: www.cesna.edu
Established: 2007 — Annual Graduate Tuition & Fees: N/A
Enrollment: N/A — Coed
Affiliation or Control: Non-denominational — IRS Status: 501(c)3
Highest Offering: Doctorate; No Undergraduates
Accreditation: THEOL

01 President .... Katheryn LEUNG
05 Academic Dean .... Gee LOWE

Christian Witness Theological Seminary (B)

1975 Concourse Drive, San Jose CA 95131
County: Santa Clara — Identification: 667255
Telephone: (408) 433-2280 — Carnegie Class: Not Classified
FAX Number: (408) 433-9855 — Calendar System: Other
URL: www.cwts.edu
Established: 1978 — Annual Graduate Tuition & Fees: N/A
Enrollment: N/A — Coed
Affiliation or Control: Interdenominational — IRS Status: 501(c)3
Highest Offering: Doctorate; No Undergraduates
Accreditation: @THEOL

01 President .... Rev. Jeffrey LU
05 Dean .... Lvshao CHANG
07 Director of Admissions .... Dr. Cai Ming MOU

Church Divinity School of the Pacific (C)

2451 Ridge Road, Berkeley CA 94709-1217
County: Alameda — FICE Identification: 001165
Unit ID: 112127
Telephone: (510) 204-0700 — Carnegie Class: Spec-4-yr-Faith
FAX Number: (510) 644-0712 — Calendar System: Semester
URL: www.cdsp.edu
Established: 1893 — Annual Graduate Tuition & Fees: N/A
Enrollment: 64 — Coed
Affiliation or Control: Protestant Episcopal — IRS Status: 501(c)3
Highest Offering: Doctorate; No Undergraduates
Accreditation: THEOL

01 President & Dean .... Dr. W. Mark RICHARDSON
05 Dean Academic Affairs .... Dr. Ruth MEYERS
10 Director of Operations & Personnel .... Mr. Bob RYBICKI
30 Int Dir Institutional Advancement .... Ms. Barbara KIMPORT
32 Dean of Students .... Rev. L. Ann HALLISEY
06 Registrar .... Ms. Elly RHEE
07 Director of Recruitment/Admissions .... Rev. Andrew HYBL
88 Program Manager .... Ms. Alissa FENCSIK
37 Director of Financial Aid .... Ms. Elly RHEE
04 Administrative Asst to President .... Ms. Elsbeth WETHERILL
29 Director Alumni Relations .... Ms. Laurel JOHNSTON

Citrus College (D)

1000 W Foothill Boulevard, Glendora CA 91741-1899
County: Los Angeles — FICE Identification: 001166
Unit ID: 112172
Telephone: (626) 963-0323 — Carnegie Class: Assoc/HT-High Trad
FAX Number: (626) 914-8618 — Calendar System: Semester
URL: www.citruscollege.edu
Established: 1915 — Annual Undergrad Tuition & Fees (In-District): $1,174
Enrollment: 12,780 — Coed
Affiliation or Control: State/Local — IRS Status: 501(c)3
Highest Offering: Associate Degree
Accreditation: WJ, DA

01 Superintendent/President .... Dr. Geraldine M. PERRI
05 Vice President Academic Affairs .... Dr. Arvid SPOR
32 Vice President Student Services .... Dr. Martha MCDONALD
10 Vice Pres Finance/Admin Services .... Ms. Claudette E. DAIN
07 Dean Admissions & Records .... Dr. Gerald SEQUEIRA
51 Dean Career/Technical/Continuing Ed .... Dr. James LANCASTER
38 Dean of Counseling .... Dr. Lucinda OVER
15 Director Human Resources .... Dr. Robert L. SAMMIS
102 Director Foundation .... Ms. Christina M. GARCIA
35 Dean of Students .... Dr. Maryann TOLANO-LEVEQUE
18 Director Facilities & Construction .... Mr. Fred DIAMOND
09 Director of Institutional Research .... Dr. Lan HAO
06 Registrar .... Ms. Kristina HANNON
37 Director Financial Aid .... Ms. Carol THOMAS
96 Director of Purchasing .... Mr. Robert IVERSON
21 Director of Fiscal Services .... Ms. Rosalinda BUCHWALD
26 Director of Communication .... Vacant
28 Staff Diversity Officer .... Mrs. Brenda FINK
13 Chief Information Services Officer .... Ms. Linda WELZ
19 Campus Security Supervisor .... Mr. Benjamin MACIAS
83 Dean Social/Behavioral Sciences/DE .... Dr. Dana HESTER
41 Dean of Kinesiology & Athletics .... Ms. Jody WISE
79 Dean Lang Arts & Enrollment Mgmt .... Dr. Samuel LEE
65 Dean Library/Natural & Physical Sci .... Dr. Eric RABITOY
57 Dean of Fine & Performing Arts .... Mr. Robert SLACK
81 Dean Math/Business/Health Sciences .... Mr. James MCCLAIN
88 Director EOPS CARE CalWORKS .... Ms. Sarah GONZALES-TAPIA
88 Project Director RACE to STEM .... Ms. Marianne SMITH
101 Secretary of the Institution/Board .... Ms. Christine A. LINK

City College of San Francisco (E)

33 Gough Street, San Francisco CA 94103-1292
County: San Francisco — FICE Identification: 001167
Unit ID: 112190
Telephone: (415) 239-3000 — Carnegie Class: Assoc/MT-VT-Mix Trad/Non
FAX Number: (415) 239-3919 — Calendar System: Semester
URL: www.ccsf.edu
Established: 1935 — Annual Undergrad Tuition & Fees (In-District): $1,598
Enrollment: 23,610 — Coed
Affiliation or Control: State/Local — IRS Status: 501(c)3
Highest Offering: Associate Degree
Accreditation: WJ, ACFEI, CAHIIM, DA, EMT, MAC, RAD, RTT

01 Chancellor .... Ms. Susan E. LAMB
10 Vice Chanc Finance/Administration .... Dr. Mark ZACOVIC
05 Vice Chancellor Academic Affairs .... Dr. Anna DAVIES
46 Dean of Institutional Effectiveness .... Dr. Pam MERY
12 Dean Civic Center Campus .... Mr. Carl JEW
12 Dean Southeast Campus .... Mr. Torrance BYNUM
12 Dean Mission Campus .... Mr. Jorge BELL
12 Dean Downtown/Business School .... Dr. Geisce LY
26 Dir of Communications/Marketing .... Vacant
32 Vice President Student Development .... Mr. Samuel SANTOS
37 Dean Financial Aid & Scholarships .... Ms. Elizabeth CORIA
07 Dean Admissions & Records .... Ms. Marylou LEYBA-FRANK
20 Assoc Vice Chanc of Instruction .... Mr. Tom BOEGEL
103 Assoc Vice Chanc Workforce Dev .... Ms. Theresa ROWLAND
15 Assoc Vice Chanc Human Resources .... Ms. Clara STARR
38 Dean/Dir Counseling/Student Support .... Vacant
108 Assoc Dean Matriculation/Assessment .... Ms. Margaret SANCHEZ
85 Dean Chinatown/Intl Educ/ESL .... Dr. Minh-Hoa TA
88 Dean School of Visual & Performing .... Vacant
83 Int Dean Behavioral/Social Sci .... Ms. Jill YEE
81 Dean Science/Math/Technology/Engr .... Mr. David YEE
68 Dean J Adams Campus/Sch Hlth Educ .... Mr. Terry HALL
30 Assoc Vice Chanc Institutional Dev .... Ms. Kristin CHARLES
13 Director Information Services .... Mr. Doug RE
16 Director Employee Relations .... Mr. Mickey BRANCA
18 Int Director Buildings/Grounds .... Mr. Theodore ARANAS
14 Chief Technology Officer .... Mr. Jay FIELD
96 Director of Purchasing .... Ms. Kathy HENNIG
19 Chief of Police/Public Safety .... Mr. Andre BARNES
88 ADA Compliance Officer .... Dr. Leilani BATTISTE
21 Assoc Vice Chanc/CFO .... Mr. David MARTIN
25 Int Dean Grants & Resource Dev .... Ms. Ilona MCGRIFF
06 Assoc Dean Admission & Records .... Ms. Monika LIU
88 Dean Faculty Support Svcs .... Dr. Minh-Hoa TA
23 Director Student Health .... Dr. Elizabeth PERELLI
101 Liaison to the Board of Trustees .... Ms. Linda SHAW
41 Athletic Director .... Mr. Harold BROWN
43 Dir Legal Services/General Counsel .... Mr. Steve BRUCKMAN
100 Exec Director to Chancellor .... Mr. Jeff HAMILTON

City of Hope (F)

1500 East Duarte Road, Duarte CA 91010-3000
County: Los Angeles — FICE Identification: 035924
Unit ID: 441238
Telephone: (626) 256-4673 — Carnegie Class: Spec-4-yr-Med
FAX Number: (626) 301-8105 — Calendar System: Semester
URL: www.cityofhope.org
Established: 1994 — Annual Graduate Tuition & Fees: N/A
Enrollment: 89 — Coed
Affiliation or Control: Independent Non-Profit — IRS Status: 501(c)3
Highest Offering: Doctorate; No Undergraduates
Accreditation: WC

01 President/CEO .... Robert STONE
05 Provost/Chief Scientific Officer .... Dr. Steven T. ROSEN
58 Dean of Graduate School .... Dr. John J. ROSSI
06 Registrar .... Queenie DU
07 Director of Admissions .... Stephanie PATTERSON
08 Head Librarian .... Andrea LYNCH

Claremont Lincoln University (G)

250 West First Street Ste 330, Claremont CA 91711
County: Los Angeles — Identification: 667215
Telephone: (909) 667-4400 — Carnegie Class: Not Classified
FAX Number: (909) 399-3443 — Calendar System: Quarter
URL: claremontlincoln.edu
Established: 2011 — Annual Graduate Tuition & Fees: N/A
Enrollment: N/A — Coed
Affiliation or Control: Independent Non-Profit — IRS Status: 501(c)3
Highest Offering: Master's; No Undergraduates
Accreditation: WC

01 President .... Dr. Eileen ARANDA
03 Exec Vice President .... Dr. Laura BURGIS
13 Sr Vice Pres & Chief Info Officer .... Mr. Jay SAMPLE
10 Chief Financial Officer .... Ms. Linda RABITOY
07 Director of Admission & Recruitment .... Ms. Natalie DYMCHENKO
32 Director of Student Services .... Ms. Heather CASE PRYOR
04 Administrative Asst to President .... Ms. Judy MORAVITZ

105 Director Web Services .... Mr. Jon PIEHL
15 Director Personnel Services .... Ms. Nancy BARNES
30 Chief Development/Advancement .... Mr. Kerry NEAL
37 Director Student Financial Aid .... Ms. Deb BARKER-GARCIA

*Claremont University Consortium (H)

101 South Mills Avenue, Claremont CA 91711-5053
County: Los Angeles — Identification: 666003
Telephone: (909) 621-8026 — Carnegie Class: N/A
FAX Number: (909) 621-8517
URL: www.cuc.claremont.edu

01 Chief Executive Officer .... Mr. Stig LANESSKOG
10 Vice Pres for Bus Admin/Treasurer .... Ms. Lori HUSEIN
32 Vice President of Student Affairs .... Dr. Denise HAYES
26 Director of Communications .... Ms. Kim LANE
19 Director Campus Safety .... Mr. Stan SKIPWORTH
101 Sec to Brd of Overseers/Asst to CEO .... Dr. Bonnie CLEMENS
08 Dean Library .... Dr. Kevin MULROY
15 Director Human Resources .... Ms. Stephanie DORNES

*Claremont Graduate University (I)

150 E 10th Street, Claremont CA 91711-5909
County: Los Angeles — FICE Identification: 001169
Unit ID: 112251
Telephone: (909) 621-8000 — Carnegie Class: DU-Higher
FAX Number: (909) 621-8390 — Calendar System: Semester
URL: www.cgu.edu
Established: 1925 — Annual Graduate Tuition & Fees: N/A
Enrollment: 2,160 — Coed
Affiliation or Control: Independent Non-Profit — IRS Status: 501(c)3
Highest Offering: Doctorate; No Undergraduates
Accreditation: WC, BUS, PH

02 President .... Mr. Robert W. SCHULT
04 Exec Asst to the President .... Ms. Donna STANDLEA
05 Exec Vice President and Provost .... Dr. Jacob ADAMS
10 VP for Finance and Admin/Treasurer .... Ms. Leslie NEGRITTO
30 Vice President for Advancement .... Mr. Ernie ISEMINGER
84 Vice Pres Enroll/Student Services .... Dr. Patricia EASTON
46 Vice Provost/Research .... Dr. Dean GERSTEIN
108 Director Institutional Effectivenes .... Ms. Alana OLSCHWANG
15 Assoc VP for Human Resources .... Ms. Brenda LESWICK
47 Botany Center .... Dr. Lucinda MCDADE
50 Drucker-Ito Grad School of Mgt .... Mr. Thomas HORAN
83 Behavioral & Organizational Sci .... Dr. Stewart DONALDSON
69 Community & Global Health .... Dr. Stewart DONALDSON
53 Educational Studies .... Dr. Allen OMOTO
77 Center for Information Science .... Dr. Thomas HORAN
81 Institute for Math Sciences .... Dr. Ali NADIM
82 Politics & Economics .... Dr. Stewart DONALDSON
73 Arts and Humanities .... Dr. Tammi SCHNEIDER
09 Institutional Research Officer .... Ms. Jeannette GURROLA
44 Senior Director of Development .... Mr. Eric EWING
44 Director of Development .... Ms. Teresa WILMOTT
21 Assoc VP Finance/Admin .... Mr. Jim IRWIN
29 Director of Alumni Engagement .... Mr. Jason BARQUERO
26 Ex Dir Mktg & Communications .... Ms. Andrea GUTIERREZ
06 Dir of Records/Enrollment Mgmt .... Ms. Lindsay STADLER
37 Director Student Financial Aid .... Ms. Beverly GREEN
85 International Student Coordinator .... Vacant
07 Assoc Director of Admissions .... Ms. Edlyn DELANO
32 Assoc Dean of Student Services .... Ms. Lisa FLORES GRIFFITH
18 Director of Facilities .... Mr. Edward BRATHWAITE
39 Housing Manager .... Mr. Chris BASS
13 Asst VP/Tech & Info Systems .... Mr. Manoj CHITRE
91 Director of Enterprise Infras .... Mr. Robert FORD
101 Secretary to the Board .... Ms. Louise WEBBER

*Claremont McKenna College (J)

500 E 9th Street, Claremont CA 91711-6400
County: Los Angeles — FICE Identification: 001170
Unit ID: 112260
Telephone: (909) 621-8000 — Carnegie Class: Bac-A&S
FAX Number: (909) 621-8790 — Calendar System: Semester
URL: www.claremontmckenna.edu
Established: 1946 — Annual Undergrad Tuition & Fees: $49,045
Enrollment: 1,324 — Coed
Affiliation or Control: Independent Non-Profit — IRS Status: 501(c)3
Highest Offering: Master's
Accreditation: WC

02 President and CEO .... Hiram E. CHODOSH
05 VP Academic Affs/Dean Faculty .... Peter UVIN
30 Vice President for Development .... Carroll STEVENS
10 Vice Pres Business Admin/Treasurer .... Robin J. ASPINALL
11 VP for Planning and Administration .... Matthew G. BIBBENS
32 VP Student Affs/Admissions/Fin Aid .... Jefferson HUANG
21 VP and Chief Investment Officer .... James J. FLOYD
29 Vice President for Alumni Relations .... Evan RUTTER
35 Dean of Students .... Sharon BASSO
07 AVP & Dean Admission/Financial Aid .... Georgette DEVERES
26 Assoc VP Public Affs/Communications .... Max BENAVIDEZ
13 Assoc VP/Chief Technology Officer .... Cynthia HUMES
36 Assoc Dean/Dir Career Services .... Diana SEDER
06 Registrar/Dir Institutional Rsrch .... Elizabeth MORGAN
15 Director of Human Resources .... Andrea GALE
104 Director of Off-Campus Study .... Kristen MALLORY
41 Athletic Director .... Michael SUTTON
04 Special Assistant to the President .... Cheryl M. AGUILAR

*Claremont School of Theology (A)

1325 N College Avenue, Claremont CA 91711-3199
County: Los Angeles FICE Identification: 001288
Unit ID: 124283
Telephone: (909) 447-2500 Carnegie Class: Spec-4-yr-Faith
FAX Number: (909) 626-7062 Calendar System: Semester
URL: www.cst.edu
Established: 1885 Annual Graduate Tuition & Fees: N/A
Enrollment: 285 Coed
Affiliation or Control: United Methodist IRS Status: 501(c)3
Highest Offering: Doctorate; No Undergraduates
Accreditation: WC, THEOL

02 President .... Dr. Jeffrey KUAN
04 Exec Assistant to the President .... Ms. Maria Lise IANNUZZI
10 Vice Pres for Business Affairs/CFO .... Mr. Gamward QUAN
05 Vice Pres Academic Affairs & Dean .... Dr. Sheryl KUJAWA-HOLBROOK
20 Associate Dean/Vice President .... Rev. Belva Brown JORDAN
08 Dean of Library & Info Services .... Dr. Tom PHILLIPS
18 Director of Facilities .... Mr. Charles BRYANT
32 Assoc Dean Student & Community Life .... Ms. Lea APPLETON
30 VP Advancement & Communications .... Ms. Wendy LEE
26 Director of Communications .... Mr. Nathaniel KATZ
29 Director of Alumni/ae Relations .... Ms. Noemi ORTEGA
21 Controller .... Mr. Haroon AHMED
07 Sr Dir Admissions/Enrollment Svcs .... Mr. Murad DUBBINI
37 Director Student Financial Services .... Ms. Brenda NIEVES
06 Registrar .... Ms. Jennie ALLEN
42 Director of Field Education .... RevDr. Karen DALTON
22 Affirmative Action Officer .... Ms. Christine WHANG

*Keck Graduate Institute (B)

535 Watson Drive, Claremont CA 91711-4817
County: Los Angeles FICE Identification: 038533
Unit ID: 440031
Telephone: (909) 607-7855 Carnegie Class: Masters/S
FAX Number: (909) 607-8086 Calendar System: Semester
URL: www.kgi.edu
Established: 1997 Annual Graduate Tuition & Fees: N/A
Enrollment: 310 Coed
Affiliation or Control: Independent Non-Profit IRS Status: 501(c)3
Highest Offering: Doctorate; No Undergraduates
Accreditation: WC, @PHAR

02 President .... Dr. Sheldon M. SCHUSTER
101 Assoc VP/Sec to Board of Trustees .... Elizabeth WRIGHT
10 Vice Pres for Finance & Operations .... Michael JONES
06 Registrar .... Melissa S. BROWN
84 Dean of Stdnt Engagement/Enrol Svcs .... Sofia TORO
07 Director of Admissions .... Marcia PARKER

CNI College (C)

702 West Town and Country Road, Orange CA 92868
County: Orange FICE Identification: 032423
Unit ID: 433013
Telephone: (714) 437-9697 Carnegie Class: Not Classified
FAX Number: (714) 437-9356 Calendar System: Other
URL: www.cnicollege.edu
Established: 1994 Annual Undergrad Tuition & Fees: N/A
Enrollment: 651 Coed
Affiliation or Control: Proprietary IRS Status: Proprietary
Highest Offering: Baccalaureate
Accreditation: ABHES, SURTEC

01 President .... Mr. James BUFFINGTON

*Coast Community College District Administration Offices (D)

1370 Adams Avenue, Costa Mesa CA 92626-5429
County: Orange FICE Identification: 008711
Unit ID: 112376
Telephone: (714) 438-4600 Carnegie Class: N/A
FAX Number: (714) 438-4882
URL: www.cccd.edu

01 Chancellor .... Dr. John WEISPFENNING
10 Vice Chancellor Finance & Adm Svcs .... Dr. Andrew DUNN
05 Vice Chanc Educ Svcs & Technology .... Dr. Andreea SERBAN
15 Vice Chanc Human Resources .... Dr. Cindy VYSKOCIL
26 Dir Public Affairs/Mktg/Govt .... Ms. Letitia CLARK
96 Director of Purchasing .... Mr. John ERIKSEN

*Coastline Community College (E)

11460 Warner Avenue, Fountain Valley CA 92708-2597
County: Orange FICE Identification: 020635
Unit ID: 112385
Telephone: (714) 546-7600 Carnegie Class: Assoc/HT-High Non
FAX Number: (714) 241-6277 Calendar System: Semester
URL: www.coastline.edu
Established: 1976 Annual Undergrad Tuition & Fees (In-District): $1,136
Enrollment: 11,313 Coed
Affiliation or Control: State/Local IRS Status: 501(c)3
Highest Offering: Associate Degree
Accreditation: WJ

02 President .... Dr. Loretta P. ADRIAN
05 Vice Pres of Instruction .... Mr. Vince RODRIGUEZ
10 VP of Administrative Services .... Ms. Christine NGUYEN
32 Vice Pres Student Services .... Mr. Ross MIYASHIRO
84 Dean of Enrollment Services .... Ms. Lois WILKERSON
46 Admin Dean Instr Systems Devel .... Vacant
38 Dean Counseling/Matriculation .... Mr. Bruce KEELER
106 Assoc Dean of Distance Learning .... Mr. Bob NASH
12 Dean of Instruction Newport Beach .... Vacant
12 Dean Instruct Tech Ed Garden Grove .... Ms. Nancy JONES
79 Dean Instruction Hum/Basic Skills .... Ms. Dana EMERSON
88 Dean Military Pgms/Contract Educ .... Ms. Joycelyn GROOT
26 Director Public Relations/Marketing .... Ms. Nhadira JOHNSON
07 Director of Admissions/Records .... Ms. Jennifer MCDONALD
37 Director of Financial Aid .... Mr. Steve WOODYARD
18 Director Maintenance & Operations .... Mr. David CANT
21 Director Business Services .... Ms. Helen ROTHGEB
102 Exec Director College Foundation .... Ms. Mariam KHOSRAVANI
40 Director Bookstore .... Mr. Mathew IRBY
09 Director Research/Planning/Develop .... Dr. Jorge R. SANCHEZ
38 Mgr Contract Education Program Dev .... Mr. Peter MAHARAJ
24 Director of Electronic Media .... Ms. Judy GARVEY
15 Director of Personnel Services .... Vacant
88 Director of EBUS program .... Ms. Laurie MELBY
13 Exec Dean eLearning Research/IT .... Mr. Dan JONES
103 Int Dir Workforce & Economic Dev .... Ms. Sallie SALINAS
35 Director Student Life .... Mr. Nathan BRAIS

*Golden West College (F)

15744 Golden West Street,
Huntington Beach CA 92647-2748
County: Orange FICE Identification: 001206
Unit ID: 115126
Telephone: (714) 892-7711 Carnegie Class: Assoc/HT-High Trad
FAX Number: (714) 895-8243 Calendar System: Semester
URL: www.gwc.info
Established: 1966 Annual Undergrad Tuition & Fees (In-District): $1,176
Enrollment: 12,394 Coed
Affiliation or Control: State/Local IRS Status: Exempt
Highest Offering: Associate Degree
Accreditation: WJ, ADNUR

02 President .... Mr. Wes BRYAN
05 VP Instruction & Student Learning .... Mr. Omid POURZANJANI
32 Vice Pres Student Life & Admin Supp .... Ms. Janet M. HOULIHAN
38 Dean Counseling & Social Sciences .... Ms. Robyn BRAMMER
72 Dean Business & CTE .... Dr. David GATEWOOD
81 Dean Math & Science .... Mr. Jeff COURCHAINE
49 Dean Arts & Letters .... Dr. David C. HUDSON
66 Associate Dean School of Nursing .... Ms. Beverley BROWNELL
23 Assoc Dean/Dir Student Health Svcs .... Mr. Robin BACHMANN
09 Admin Dir Research/Plan/Inst Effect .... Dr. Kay NGUYEN
88 Dean Criminal Justice .... Mr. Ron LOWENBERG
35 Dean Student Life .... Ms. Carla MARTINEZ
84 Dean Enrollment Management .... Dr. Claudia LEE-SADDUL
88 Dean Learning Resource .... Dr. Alex MIRANDA
15 Director Human Resources .... Ms. Danielle FEINBUCH
10 Director Fiscal Services .... Mr. Paul WISNER
102 Director Foundation/Community Rels .... Mr. Bruce BERMAN
88 Coord Scholarships & Spec Events .... Ms. Valerie A. VENEGAS
07 Director of Admissions .... Ms. Jennifer L. ORTBERG
37 Director of Financial Aid .... Ms. Adrienne BURTON
18 Director Maintenance & Operations .... Mr. Joseph B. DOWLING
68 Dean Health PE & Athleics .... Mr. Albert GASPARIAN
04 Executive Asst to President .... Ms. Christina OJA
19 Dir Public Safety/Emerg Prep .... Mr. Jon ARNOLD

*Orange Coast College (G)

2701 Fairview Road, POB 5005,
Costa Mesa CA 92628-5005
County: Orange FICE Identification: 001250
Unit ID: 120342
Telephone: (714) 432-0202 Carnegie Class: Assoc/HT-High Trad
FAX Number: (714) 432-5609 Calendar System: Semester
URL: www.orangecoastcollege.edu
Established: 1947 Annual Undergrad Tuition & Fees (In-District): $1,184
Enrollment: 21,775 Coed
Affiliation or Control: State/Local IRS Status: 501(c)3
Highest Offering: Associate Degree
Accreditation: WJ, ACFEI, CEA, COARC, CVT, DA, DIETT, DMS, NDT, POLYT, RAD

02 President .... Dr. Dennis HARKINS
05 Vice President Instruction .... Mr. Kevin M. BALLINGER
32 Vice President Student Services .... Dr. Madjid NIROUMAND
10 Director of Fiscal Services .... Ms. Rachel KUBIK
11 Vice Pres Administrative Services .... Dr. Richard PAGEL
84 Dean Enrollment Services .... Mr. Madjid NIROUMAND
38 Dean of Counseling .... Dr. Hue PHAM
35 Director Student Life .... Mr. Michael MORVICE
26 Director Marketing & PR .... Mr. Juan GUTIERREZ
30 Exec Dir Institutional Advancement .... Mr. Douglas BENNETT
09 Admin Dir Research/Planning/IE .... Ms. Sheri STERNER
07 Director Admiss/Records/Enroll Tech .... Mr. Efren GALVAN
15 Interim Director HR & Staff Develop .... Ms. Denise LEAT
06 Manager Enrollment Services .... Mr. James K. WEST
18 Director M & O .... Mr. Mark GOODE
37 Director Financial Aid .... Ms. Tanisha BRADFIELD
13 Director Information Technology .... Ms. Rupa SARAN
23 Associate Dean Health Services .... Ms. Sylvia WORDEN
88 Director Child Care Center .... Ms. Sue BIERLICH
41 Dean Kinesiology & Athletics .... Dr. Michael SUTLIFF
88 Dean Consumer Health & Sciences .... Dr. Jane MCLAUGHLIN
68 Dean of Kinesiology & Athletics .... Dr. Michael SUTLIFF
72 Dean of Technology .... Dr. Daniel SHRADER
50 Dean of Business & Computer Science .... Dr. Ronald JOHNSON
83 Dean of Social & Behavioral Science .... Dr. Kevin HENSON
88 Dean of Literature & Languages .... Dr. Michael MANDELKERN
81 Dean of Math & Sciences .... Dr. Tara GIBLIN
57 Dean of Visual & Performing Arts .... Ms. Larissa NAZARENKO
25 Director CTE/Grants .... Ms. Lisa KNUPPEL
19 Director Security/Safety .... Mr. John FARMER
40 Manager Bookstore .... Mr. Todd MURPHY
85 Director International Center .... Mr. Nathan JENSEN
88 Dean Student Success & Student Serv .... Mr. Stephen TAMANAHA
96 Director Fiscal Services .... Ms. Rachel KUBIK

Cogswell Polytechnical College (H)

191 Baypointe Parkway, San Jose CA 95134-1697
County: Santa Clara FICE Identification: 001177
Unit ID: 112394
Telephone: (408) 498-5100 Carnegie Class: Bac-Diverse
FAX Number: (408) 877-7373 Calendar System: Semester
URL: www.cogswell.edu
Established: 1887 Annual Undergrad Tuition & Fees: $16,640
Enrollment: 611 Coed
Affiliation or Control: Proprietary IRS Status: Proprietary
Highest Offering: Baccalaureate
Accreditation: WC

01 Acting CEO .... Mr. Kenneth BANKS
05 Dean of the College .... Mr. Jerome SOLOMON
10 Chief Financial Officer .... Mr. Kenneth BANKS
26 VP of Marketing .... Mr. Brian ROUCH
06 Registrar .... Mr. David NORIEGA
08 Librarian & Resource Manager .... Ms. Lauren MIKLOVIC
07 Director of Admissions .... Mr. Aaron KARK
04 Executive Assistant to President .... Ms. Barbara GURNARI
09 Executive Director of IR and QA .... Ms. Milla ZLATANOV
13 VP of Information Technology .... Dr. Andrey FEDIN
32 Dean of Students .... Ms. Brittany BOGLE
36 Director of Career Services .... Mr. Nando GAPASIN
37 Financial Aid Manager .... Ms. Yariela PEREZ-GONZALEZ
88 Director of Compliance .... Ms. Nikki LOVE

The Colburn School (I)

200 S Grand Avenue, Los Angeles CA 90012-3007
County: Los Angeles Identification: 666233
Telephone: (213) 621-2200 Carnegie Class: Not Classified
FAX Number: (213) 621-2110 Calendar System: Semester
URL: www.colburnschool.edu
Established: 2003 Annual Undergrad Tuition & Fees: N/A
Enrollment: N/A Coed
Affiliation or Control: Independent Non-Profit IRS Status: 501(c)3
Highest Offering: Master's
Accreditation: MUS

01 President & CEO .... Mr. Sel KARDAN
05 Provost .... Dr. Adrian DALY
30 Sr VP Advancement/External Affairs .... Mr. Ed HORNER
26 Vice President Communications .... Dr. Mark A. BERRY
10 Chief Financial Officer .... Mr. Seth WEINTRAUB

† Full room, board, and tuition are provided to accepted students through the school's endowment.

Coleman University (J)

8888 Balboa Avenue, San Diego CA 92123-1506
County: San Diego FICE Identification: 007296
Unit ID: 112446
Telephone: (858) 499-0202 Carnegie Class: Spec-4-yr-Other Tech
FAX Number: (858) 499-0233 Calendar System: Other
URL: www.coleman.edu
Established: 1963 Annual Undergrad Tuition & Fees: $20,725
Enrollment: 796 Coed
Affiliation or Control: Independent Non-Profit IRS Status: 501(c)3
Highest Offering: Master's
Accreditation: @WC, ACICS

01 President/CEO .... Mr. Norbert J. KUBILUS
05 VP Academics .... Mr. Jason ABEL
07 Director Admissions .... Vacant
32 Director Student Services .... Vacant
10 Chief Financial Officer .... Mr. Ron D. KLINGENSMITH
13 Chief Technology Officer .... Mr. Jason T. ABEL
09 VP Institutional Effectiveness .... Mr. Bruce F. GILDEN
15 Director Human Resource .... Ms. Maria HAMZAVI
06 Registrar .... Mr. Alex WISSMAN
37 Director Financial Aid .... Mr. Axel N. HERNANDEZ
36 Director Career Services .... Mr. Bob SWEIGART
21 Comptroller .... Ms. Laura SALES
08 Librarian .... Mr. Manuel A. BERNAD
29 Alumni Relations Coordinator .... Ms. Julia V. KATAWAZI
14 Network Administrator .... Mr. Brian J. MORGAN
105 Web Master .... Mr. Chris J. CAREY
30 Chief Development Officer .... Mr. Rod P. WEISS
18 Facilities Manager .... Mr. Terry S. GLYNN
84 VP Enrollment Management .... Ms. Brandi LANDRUM

College of the Canyons (A)

26455 Rockwell Canyon Road,
Santa Clarita CA 91355-1899
County: Los Angeles FICE Identification: 008903
Unit ID: 111461
Telephone: (661) 259-7800 Carnegie Class: Assoc/HT-High Non
FAX Number: (661) 259-8302 Calendar System: Semester
URL: www.canyons.edu
Established: 1967 Annual Undergrad Tuition & Fees (In-District): $1,154
Enrollment: 17,148 Coed
Affiliation or Control: State/Local IRS Status: 501(c)3
Highest Offering: Associate Degree
Accreditation: WJ, ADNUR

01 Chancellor SCCCD & President COC ...Dr. Dianne G. VAN HOOK
03 Deputy Chancellor ....Dr. Barry GRIBBONS
05 Asst Supt/Vice Pres Instruction ....Dr. Jerry BUCKLEY
10 Asst Supt/VP Business Services ....Ms. Sharlene COLEAL
15 Asst Supt/Vice Pres Human Resources ....Dr. Diane FIERO
18 Asst Supt/VP Facil Plan Op/Const ....Mr. Jim SCHRAGE
32 Asst Superintendent/VP Student Svcs ....Dr. Michael WILDING
26 VP Public Info/Advoc/Ext Relations ....Mr. Eric HARNISH
13 Vice President Technology ....Dr. James TEMPLE
12 VP Canyon Country Campus and Grants ....Dr. Ryan THEULE
20 VP Academic Affairs ....Ms. Audrey GREEN
21 Assoc VP Business Services ....Ms. Cynthia GRANDGEORGE
57 Dean School of Visual and Perf Arts ....Dr. Carmen DOMINGUEZ
88 Dean Educ Tech/Lrng Resrc/Dist Educ ....Mr. James GLAPA-GROSSKLAG
35 Dean Student Services ....Mr. Mike JOSLIN
72 Dean School of Applied Tech ....Mr. Ronald MCFARLAND
46 Dean Inst Research/Plng/Inst Effect ....Dr. Daylene MEUSCHKE
88 Dean Instr Support & Student Succ ....Ms. Denee PESCARMONA
84 Dean Enrollment Services ....Ms. Deborah RIO
36 Act Dean Campus Ops CCC/Career Svs ....Mr. Anthony MICHAELIDES
56 Dean Canyons Extension ....Ms. Diane STEWART
81 Dean School of Math/Sci & Health ....Mr. Omar TORRES
50 Dean School of Business ....JD. Russell WALDON
41 Division Dean PE/Athletics ....Mr. Len MOHNEY
88 Act Asst Dean Inter/Job Dev/Cr Ctr ....Ms. Gina BOGNA
88 Interim Dean Ctr Civic Engagement ....Dr. Patricia ROBINSON
88 Dean Economic Development ....Vacant
102 COO COC Foundation/Int Dir UC ....Ms. Cathy RITZ
30 Chief Devel Officer COC Foundation ....Mr. Murray WOOD
88 Deputy Sector Navigator Health ....Mr. John CORDOVA
88 Deputy Sector Navigator ICT/DM ....Ms. Paula HODGE
88 Deputy Sector Navigator Adv Manuf ....Mr. Michael BASTINE
103 Director WorkSource Center ....Ms. Keri AAVER
88 Director Student Business Office ....Ms. Kathleen BENZ
37 Director Financial Aid ....Mr. Tom BILBRUCK
88 Director Professional Development ....Ms. Leslie CARR
19 Director Campus Safety ....Ms. Tammy CASTOR
88 Director Fiscal Services ....Ms. Balbir CHANDI
85 Director International Students Pgm ....Dr. Jia-Yi CHENG-LEVINE
16 Director Human Resources ....Ms. Christina CHUNG
88 Dir Student Dev & Campus Activity ....Ms. Kelly DAPP
88 Dir Central Energy Syst/Reg Comp ....Mr. Carl EBAUGH
44 Director Development ....Ms. Michele EDMONSON
91 Director Mgmt Info Systems ....Mr. Mark GARCIA
96 Director Contracts Proc & Risk Mgmt ....Ms. April GRAHAM
88 Director Small Bus Devel Ctr ....Ms. Catherine GROOMS
14 Director Information Technology ....Mr. Mike GUNTHER
88 Director Technology Services ....Mr. Hsiawen HULL
88 Director Art Gallery ....Mr. Larry HURST
88 Dirr Volunteer & Stdnt Employment ....Mr. Yasser ISSA
88 Director Facilities Projects ....Mr. William KARRAT
23 Director Student Health & Wellness ....Ms. Mary MANUEL
88 Director Employee Training Inst ....Mr. John MILBURN
88 Director Public Relations & Sports ....Mr. Jesse MUNOZ
88 Director Infant/Toddler Programs ....Ms. Wendy RUIZ
07 Dir Admissions/Records/Online Svcs ....Dr. Jasmine RUYS
88 Director Grant & Categ Accounting ....Ms. Carolyn SHAW
88 Dir Outreach & School Relations ....Ms. Kari SOFFA
88 Director Payroll Services ....Ms. Mimi SPANKROY
88 Director Reentry & Vet Affairs ....Mr. Renard THOMAS
27 Dir Advertising/Social Media ....Ms. Wendy TRUJILLO
75 Director Career and Technical Educ ....Mr. Thomas VESSELLA
88 Director Distance & Acc Learning ....Mr. Brian WESTON
88 Director Civic Center ....Mr. Robin WILLIAMS
25 Director Grants Development ....Ms. Theresa ZUZEVICH
22 Director Diversity/EEO & Title IX ....Vacant
04 Special Assistant to the Chancellor ....Ms. Claudia DUNN-MARTINTEZ

College of the Desert (B)

43-500 Monterey Avenue, Palm Desert CA 92260-9399
County: Riverside FICE Identification: 001182
Unit ID: 113573
Telephone: (760) 346-8041 Carnegie Class: Assoc/HT-High Trad
FAX Number: (760) 341-8678 Calendar System: Semester
URL: www.collegeofthedesert.edu
Established: 1958 Annual Undergrad Tuition & Fees (In-District): $1,336
Enrollment: 9,719 Coed
Affiliation or Control: State/Local IRS Status: 501(c)3
Highest Offering: Associate Degree
Accreditation: WJ

01 Superintendent/President ....Dr. Joel L. KINNAMON
05 Vice President Student Learning ....Dr. Pamela RALSTON
20 Vice President Student Success ....Dr. Annebelle NERY
10 Vice President Admin Services ....Ms. Lisa HOWELL
15 Vice Pres Human Resources ....Dr. Mary Anne GULARTE
30 Exec Dir Institutional Advancement ....Ms. Pam HUNTER
09 Exec Dean Inst Effectiveness ....Vacant
102 Exec Dir of Foundation ....Mr. Jim HUMMER
13 Exec Dir Educational Technology ....Ms. Sherilyn WILLIS
18 Director of Maintenance/Operations ....Mr. Brandon TOEPFER
29 Exec Director Alumni Relations ....Ms. Cindy STILLMAN
37 Director Financial Aid ....Ms. Kristen MILLIGAN
21 Director of Fiscal Services ....Mr. John RAMONT
06 Registrar/Director of Admissions ....Mr. Curt LUTTRELL

College of Marin (C)

835 College Avenue, Kentfield CA 94904-2590
County: Marin FICE Identification: 001178
Unit ID: 118347
Telephone: (415) 457-8811 Carnegie Class: Assoc/HT-Mix Trad/Non
FAX Number: (415) 456-6017 Calendar System: Semester
URL: www.marin.edu
Established: 1926 Annual Undergrad Tuition & Fees (In-District): $1,488
Enrollment: 5,500 Coed
Affiliation or Control: State/Local IRS Status: 501(c)3
Highest Offering: Associate Degree
Accreditation: WJ, DA

01 Superintendent/President ....Dr. David W. COON
05 Senior VP Student Svcs & Learning ....Mr. Jonathan ELDRIDGE
20 Asst VP Instructional Support ....Ms. Cari TORRES
10 Vice President Finance & Oper ....Mr. Greg NELSON
15 Exec Dir Human Res/Labor Relations ....Ms. Kristina A. COMBS
84 Dean Enrollment Services ....Vacant
32 Dean Student Success ....Mr. Derek LEVY
49 Dean Arts & Humanities ....Dr. David SNYDER
103 Dean Career & Tech Education ....Ms. Elizabeth PRATT
81 Dean Math/Sciences ....Dr. Carol HERNANDEZ
21 Director Fiscal Services ....Ms. Peggy ISOZAKI
09 Exec Dir Plng/Research/Inst Plng ....Dr. Christina LEIMER
37 Asst Dean Enroll/Financial Aid ....Ms. Robin DARCANGELO
18 Dir Facil Planning & M&O ....Ms. Heidi RANK
13 CIO & Director of IT ....Mr. Patrick EKOUE-TOTOU
35 Dir Student Activities/Advocacy ....Ms. Sadika SULAIMAN HARA
19 Chief of Police/Director of Safety ....Mr. John ADAMS
68 Dir Kinesiology/Athletics ....Mr. Ryan BYRNE
76 Dean Health Sciences ....Dr. Marshall ALAMEIDA
31 Dir Cmty/Lifelong/Intl Education ....Ms. Carol HILDEBRAND
30 Exec Director of Development ....Dr. Linda FRANK
08 Director of Library Services ....Vacant
04 Exec Asst to Pres/Board ....Ms. Kathy JOYNER

College of the Redwoods Community College District (D)

7351 Tompkins Hill Road, Eureka CA 95501-9300
County: Humboldt FICE Identification: 001185
Unit ID: 121707
Telephone: (707) 476-4100 Carnegie Class: Assoc/HT-High Non
FAX Number: (707) 476-4400 Calendar System: Semester
URL: www.redwoods.edu
Established: 1964 Annual Undergrad Tuition & Fees (In-District): $1,142
Enrollment: 4,965 Coed
Affiliation or Control: State/Local IRS Status: 501(c)3
Highest Offering: Associate Degree
Accreditation: WJ, DA, EMT, NAIT

01 Interim President/Superintendent ....Mr. Keith SNOW-FLAMER
05 Vice President Instruction ....Mr. Keith SNOW-FLAMER
04 Exec Assistant to the President ....Ms. Kimberly SWEET
10 VP Administrative Services ....Mr. Lee LINDSEY
32 VP Student Development ....Dr. Keith SNOW-FLAMER
20 Int VP Instruction/Student Dev ....Dr. Angelina HILL
31 Exec Dir Cmty/Economic Development ....Ms. Ahn FIELDING
15 Director Human Resources/EEO ....Ms. Wendy BATES
12 Director Del Norte Center ....Mr. Rory JOHNSON
12 Manager Mendocino Coast Center ....Ms. Kathrine WYLIE
68 Dean PE/Athletics/Health Occup ....Mr. Joseph HASH
37 Director Financial Aid ....Ms. Lynn THIESEN
88 Dir Special Pgms/Academic Support ....Ms. Cheryl TUCKER
22 Director Disabled Student Pgm Svcs ....Ms. Patricia BLAIR
18 Director Maintenance & Operations ....Mr. Garry PATRICK
26 Public Information Officer ....Mr. Paul DEMARK
08 Dir Learning Resource Ctr/Library ....Ms. Ruth MOON
07 Manager Admissions/Records ....Ms. Rianne CONNOR
19 Lead Public Safety Officer ....Mr. George KAPITAN
88 Director Administration of Justice ....Mr. Ron WATERS

College of the Sequoias (E)

915 S Mooney Boulevard, Visalia CA 93277-2234
County: Tulare FICE Identification: 001186
Unit ID: 123217
Telephone: (559) 730-3700 Carnegie Class: Assoc/MT-VT-High Trad
FAX Number: (559) 730-3894 Calendar System: Semester
URL: www.cos.edu
Established: 1925 Annual Undergrad Tuition & Fees (In-District): $1,388
Enrollment: 10,647 Coed
Affiliation or Control: State/Local IRS Status: 501(c)3
Highest Offering: Associate Degree
Accreditation: WJ, PTAA

01 Superintendent/President ....Mr. Stan A. CARRIZOSA
05 Vice President Academic Services ....Dr. Jennifer VEGA-LA SERNA
11 Vice President Administrative Svcs ....Ms. Christine STATTON
10 Dir Budgets & Categorical Accts ....Ms. Leangela MILLER-HERNANDEZ
32 Vice President Student Services ....Mr. Brent CALVIN
37 Dean Student Svcs/Financial Aid ....Ms. Jessica FIGALLO
88 Provost Tulare Center ....Dr. Louann WALDNER
88 Provost Hanford Center ....Dr. Kristin ROBINSON
81 Dean Science/Math/Eng ....Dr. Robert URTECHO
76 Dean Allied Health/Phys Education ....Ms. Cindy DELAIN
49 Dean Arts & Letters ....Vacant
15 Dean Human Resources/Legal Affairs ....Mr. John BRATSCH
18 Dean Facilities ....Mr. Byron WOODS
102 Director Foundation ....Mr. Tim FOSTER
66 Dir Nursing/Allied Health ....Ms. Belen KERSTEN
08 Dir Library/Instructional Tech ....Ms. Mary-Catherine OXFORD
09 Director of Research ....Dr. Mehmet OZTURK
06 Registrar/Record Technician ....Ms. Velia RODRIGUEZ
41 Associate Dean/Athletic Director ....Mr. Brent DAVIS
19 Chief District Police ....Vacant
40 Bookstore Manager ....Ms. Dorianna MENDIETTA
23 Coord Health Center ....Ms. Patricia ALVAREZ
35 Dir Student Activities/Affairs ....Ms. Debbie DOUGLASS
103 Dean CTE/Voc Ed ....Mr. Thad RUSSELL
88 Coord Welcome/Transfer Center ....Ms. Catherine MCGUIRE
26 Coord Mktg/Public Info ....Ms. Kristen FOSTER
04 Executive Asst to President ....Ms. Meghan TIERCE
13 Dean Info Technology ....Mr. Tim HOLLABAUGH

College of the Siskiyous (F)

800 College Avenue, Weed CA 96094-2899
County: Siskiyou FICE Identification: 001187
Unit ID: 123484
Telephone: (530) 938-5555 Carnegie Class: Assoc/MT-VT-High Non
FAX Number: (530) 938-5506 Calendar System: Semester
URL: www.siskiyous.edu
Established: 1957 Annual Undergrad Tuition & Fees (In-District): $1,154
Enrollment: 2,060 Coed
Affiliation or Control: State/Local IRS Status: 501(c)3
Highest Offering: Associate Degree
Accreditation: WJ

01 Superintendent/President ....Mr. Scotty THOMASON
04 Exec Assistant II President & Board ....Ms. Sheila GRIMES
10 Vice President Administrative Svcs ....Ms. Nancy FUNK
05 Vice President Instruction ....Dr. Todd SCOTT
32 Vice President Student Services ....Ms. Melissa GREEN
35 Director Student Life ....Mr. Doug HAUGEN
09 Director Research & Evaluation ....Mr. Bart SCOTT
41 Assoc Dean Instruction/Dir Athletic ....Mr. Dennis ROBERTS
20 Dean Student Learning ....Dr. Gregory SOUTH
103 Dean Career & Technical Education ....Dr. Robert TAYLOR
07 Director Enrollment Services ....Ms. Meghan WITHERELL
15 Assoc Vice Pres Human Resources ....Ms. Theresa RICHMOND
37 Director Financial Aid ....Ms. Janette HARRIS
18 Director MOT ....Mr. Eric RULOFSON
30 Dir of Institutional Advancement ....Vacant
28 Director of Diversity ....Ms. Theresa RICHMOND

Columbia College Hollywood (G)

18618 Oxnard Street, Tarzana CA 91356-1411
County: Los Angeles FICE Identification: 021102
Unit ID: 112570
Telephone: (800) 785-0585 Carnegie Class: Spec-4-yr-Arts
FAX Number: (818) 345-9053 Calendar System: Quarter
URL: www.columbiacollege.edu
Established: 1952 Annual Undergrad Tuition & Fees: $21,105
Enrollment: 308 Coed
Affiliation or Control: Independent Non-Profit IRS Status: 501(c)3
Highest Offering: Baccalaureate
Accreditation: WC

01 President/CEO ....Mr. Bill SMITH
05 Vice Pres Academic Affairs ....Mr. Lex SANDERSON
101 Board Secretary ....Mr. Theodore O'KARMA
22 Sr Compliance/Accreditation Manager ....Mr. Jan HASTINGS
10 Sr Director of Finance/Comptroller ....Mr. Richard CROWE
32 Dean of Student Services ....Dr. Yolanda DAWSON
13 Director of IT and Production Svcs ....Mr. Ronald REEVES
07 Director of Admissions ....Ms. Carmen MUNOZ
37 Financial Aid Manager ....Mr. James BURGESS
36 Student Placement ....Ms. Kate MCARDLE
06 Registrar ....Ms. LaVona THOMAS

Community Christian College (H)

1849 N. Wabash, Redlands CA 92374
County: San Bernardino FICE Identification: 038744
Unit ID: 446163
Telephone: (909) 794-1084 Carnegie Class: Assoc/HT-High Trad
FAX Number: (909) 794-1093 Calendar System: Quarter
URL: www.communitychristiancollege.com
Established: 1995 Annual Undergrad Tuition & Fees: $6,485
Enrollment: 104 Coed
Affiliation or Control: Independent Non-Profit IRS Status: 501(c)3
Highest Offering: Associate Degree
Accreditation: #TRACS

01 President ....Mr. Josh TURNSKY

05 Chief Academic Officer .... Dr. Steve AVALOS
07 Admissions Advisor .... Mr. David ZAMORA

Concord Law School of Kaplan University (A)

10866 Wilshire Blvd, Suite 1200,
Los Angeles CA 90024-4356
Telephone: (310) 689-3200 FICE Identification: 041259
Accreditation: &NH

† Regional accreditation is carried under the parent institution in Davenport, IA.

Concorde Career College (B)

12951 Euclid Street, Suite 101,
Garden Grove CA 92840-1451
County: Orange FICE Identification: 008071
Unit ID: 123679
Telephone: (714) 703-1900 Carnegie Class: Spec 2-yr-Health
FAX Number: (714) 530-8421 Calendar System: Semester
URL: www.concorde.edu
Established: 1960 Annual Undergrad Tuition & Fees: N/A
Enrollment: 974 Coed
Affiliation or Control: Proprietary IRS Status: Proprietary
Highest Offering: Associate Degree
Accreditation: ACCSC, COARC, DH, PTAA

01 Campus President .... Mr. Nicholas EWELL

Concorde Career College (C)

12412 Victory Boulevard, North Hollywood CA 91606-3134
County: Los Angeles FICE Identification: 007607
Unit ID: 124937
Telephone: (818) 766-8151 Carnegie Class: Spec 2-yr-Health
FAX Number: (818) 766-1587 Calendar System: Quarter
URL: www.concorde.edu
Established: 1955 Annual Undergrad Tuition & Fees: N/A
Enrollment: 620 Coed
Affiliation or Control: Proprietary IRS Status: Proprietary
Highest Offering: Associate Degree
Accreditation: ACCSC, COARC, PTAA, SURGT

01 Campus President .... Carmen BOWEN
05 Academic Dean .... Weyland MORSE
07 Director of Admissions .... Allan GUECO
37 Director Student Financial Aid .... Cynthia STEIN

Concorde Career College (D)

201 E Airport Drive, San Bernadino CA 92408
County: San Bernardino FICE Identification: 008537
Unit ID: 124706
Telephone: (909) 884-8891 Carnegie Class: Spec 2-yr-Health
FAX Number: (909) 884-1831 Calendar System: Semester
URL: www.concorde.edu
Established: 1970 Annual Undergrad Tuition & Fees: N/A
Enrollment: 668 Coed
Affiliation or Control: Proprietary IRS Status: Proprietary
Highest Offering: Associate Degree
Accreditation: ACCSC, COARC, DH, NDT, SURGT

01 Campus President .... Ken GUERRERO

Concorde Career College (E)

4393 Imperial Avenue, Suite 100,
San Diego CA 92113-1962
County: San Diego FICE Identification: 007930
Unit ID: 120661
Telephone: (619) 688-0800 Carnegie Class: Spec 2-yr-Health
FAX Number: (619) 220-4177 Calendar System: Other
URL: www.concorde.edu
Established: 1966 Annual Undergrad Tuition & Fees: N/A
Enrollment: 967 Coed
Affiliation or Control: Proprietary IRS Status: Proprietary
Highest Offering: Associate Degree
Accreditation: ACCSC, COARC, DH, PTAA, SURGT

01 Campus President .... Ms. Rachel SASSEL

Concordia University (F)

1530 Concordia W, Irvine CA 92612-3299
County: Orange FICE Identification: 020705
Unit ID: 112075
Telephone: (949) 854-8002 Carnegie Class: Masters/L
FAX Number: (949) 214-3520 Calendar System: Semester
URL: www.cui.edu
Established: 1972 Annual Undergrad Tuition & Fees: $31,590
Enrollment: 4,311 Coed
Affiliation or Control: Lutheran Church - Missouri Synod
IRS Status: 501(c)3
Highest Offering: Doctorate
Accreditation: WC, CAATE, IACBE, NURSE

01 President .... Dr. Kurt J. KRUEGER
05 Exec Vice Pres Acad Affairs/Provost .... Dr. Peter SENKBEIL
32 Exec VP Student & Enroll Services .... Dr. Gary R. MCDANIEL
30 Exec VP Advancement .... Mr. Timothy J. JAEGER
10 Exec VP/Chief Finance Officer .... Mr. Kevin TILDEN
84 Assoc Provost/VP Enrollment Mgmt .... Dr. Doug GROVE
49 Dean School of Arts and Sciences .... Dr. Timothy PREUSS
50 EVP Ext Rels/Dean Sch of Business .. Mr. Stephen CHRISTENSEN
50 Dean of Business Administration .... Mr. George WRIGHT
107 Dean School of Professional Studies .... Dr. Timothy C. PETERS
53 Dean School of Education .... Dr. Deborah MERCIER
73 Dean Christ College .... Dr. Steven P. MUELLER
06 Dean of Academic Records/Registrar .... Ms. Wanda BURCH
09 Director of Institutional Research .... Mrs. Deborah LEE
35 Dean of Students .... Dr. Gilbert FUGITT
07 Director of Undergrad Admissions .... Mr. Doug WIBLE
07 Director of Graduate Admissions .... Mrs. Rina CAMPBELL
37 Director of Financial Aid .... Ms. Lori MCDONALD
21 Bursar .... Mr. Edgar LOPEZ
43 AVP & General Counsel .... Mr. Ronald VAN BLARCOM
15 Director of Human Resources .... Mrs. Penny MOCK
08 Director of Library Services .... Prof. Carolina BARTON
41 Athletic Director .... Mr. Mo ROBERSON
39 Director Residence Life .... Ms. Brianna SPRINGER
19 Director Security/Safety .... Mr. Steven RODRIGUEZ
29 Exec Director of Alumni Relations .... Mr. Michael BERGLER
24 Director Educational Media .... Prof. John RANDALL
36 Director of Career Services .... Mrs. Victoria JAFFEE
44 Director Major Gift Planning .... Mr. Dennis COX
85 Exec Director Global Programs .... Dr. Dan WAITE
13 Director of IT Services .... Mr. Chris HARRIS
28 Director of Inclusion/Diversity .... Dr. Terilyn JACKSON

*Contra Costa Community College District Office (G)

500 Court Street, Martinez CA 94553-1278
County: Contra Costa FICE Identification: 001189
Unit ID: 112817
Telephone: (925) 229-1000 Carnegie Class: N/A
FAX Number: (925) 370-2019
URL: www.4cd.edu

01 Chancellor .... Dr. Helen BENJAMIN
05 Exec VC Education & Technology .... Vacant
11 Exec VC Administrative Services .... Mr. Eugene C. HUFF
18 Chief Facilities Planner .... Mr. Ray PYLE
10 Assoc Vice Chanc/CFO .... Mr. Johah NICHOLAS

*Contra Costa College (H)

2600 Mission Bell Drive, San Pablo CA 94806-3195
County: Contra Costa FICE Identification: 001190
Unit ID: 112826
Telephone: (510) 235-7800 Carnegie Class: Assoc/HT-High Non
FAX Number: (510) 236-6768 Calendar System: Semester
URL: www.contracosta.edu
Established: 1948 Annual Undergrad Tuition & Fees (In-District): $1,298
Enrollment: 6,697 Coed
Affiliation or Control: State/Local IRS Status: 501(c)3
Highest Offering: Associate Degree
Accreditation: WJ

02 President .... Ms. Majdeh MEHDIZADEH
03 Vice President .... Ms. Tammeil GILKERSON
05 Senior Dean of Instruction .... Dr. Donna FLOYD
32 Dean of Student Services .... Ms. Vicki FERGUSON
103 Dir Econ & Workforce Development .... Ms. Kelly SCHELIN
07 Director Admissions & Records .... Ms. Catherine FROST
10 Director Business Services .... Ms. Mariles MAGALONG
09 Director of Institutional Research .... Vacant
37 Financial Aid Supervisor .... Ms. Monica RODRIGUEZ
18 Manager Buildings & Grounds .... Mr. Bruce KING
04 Senior Exec Asst to the President .... Mr. Michael L. PETERSON
30 Development Officer .... Ms. Sara MARCELLINO
41 Athletic Director .... Mr. John WADE

*Diablo Valley College (I)

321 Golf Club Road, Pleasant Hill CA 94523-1544
County: Contra Costa FICE Identification: 001191
Unit ID: 113634
Telephone: (925) 685-1230 Carnegie Class: Assoc/HT-Mix Trad/Non
FAX Number: (925) 685-1551 Calendar System: Semester
URL: www.dvc.edu
Established: 1949 Annual Undergrad Tuition & Fees (In-District): $1,298
Enrollment: 20,089 Coed
Affiliation or Control: State/Local IRS Status: 501(c)3
Highest Offering: Associate Degree
Accreditation: WJ, ACFEI, DA, DH

02 Interim President .... Mr. Ted WIEDEN
05 Vice President Instruction .... Ms. Rachel WESTLAKE
32 Vice President Student Services .... Dr. Newin ORANTE
10 Vice Pres Business & Admin Svcs .... Mr. John NAHLEN
20 Senior Dean of Curriculum & Instr .... Ms. Kimberely SCHENK
84 Dean Outreach/Enroll Mgt/
Matric .... Ms. Elizabeth HAUSCARRIAGUE
12 Dean San Ramon Campus .... Mr. Mike HOLZCLAW
41 Dean of PE/Athl/Dance/Athletic Dir .... Ms. Christine WORSLEY
62 Dean Library/Ed Tech & Learn Sup .... Mr. Rick ROBISON
26 Dir of Marketing & Communications .... Ms. Chriseanne KNOX
57 Interim Dean Applied & Fine Arts .... Ms. Toni FANNIN
54 Dean Physical Sci/Engr/Bio Sci .... Dr. Patricia YOUNG
83 Dean English & Social Science .... Mr. Obed VAZQUEZ
50 Int Dean Business Ed/Math/Comp
Sci .... Ms. Despina PRAPAVESSI
06 Registrar .... Ms. Stephanie ALVES
35 Dean Student Support Services .... Ms. Emily STONE

*Los Medanos College (J)

2700 E Leland Road, Pittsburg CA 94565-5197
County: Contra Costa FICE Identification: 010340
Unit ID: 117894
Telephone: (925) 439-2181 Carnegie Class: Assoc/MT-VT-High Trad
FAX Number: (925) 427-1599 Calendar System: Semester
URL: www.losmedanos.edu
Established: 1973 Annual Undergrad Tuition & Fees (In-District): $1,298
Enrollment: 8,695 Coed
Affiliation or Control: State/Local IRS Status: 501(c)3
Highest Offering: Associate Degree
Accreditation: WJ

02 President .... Mr. Bob KRATOCHVIL
04 Senior Executive Assistant .... Ms. Jennifer ADAMS
05 VP Instruction & Student Services .... Dr. Kevin HORAN
10 Director of Business Services .... Ms. Aderonke OLATUNJI
45 Sr Dean Plng & Inst Effectiveness .... Vacant
32 Sr Dean Stdnt Svcs & Brentwood Ctr .... Ms. Gail NEWMAN
35 Dean of Student Success .... Mr. David BELMAN
102 Senior Foundation Director .... Ms. Ruth GOODIN
07 Director of Admissions/Records .... Ms. Robin ARMOUR
37 Financial Aid Supervisor .... Ms. Jennifer MA
88 Dir Student Success/Support Pgms .... Ms. Carla ROSAS
108 Int Outreach/Assessment Svcs Mgr .... Mr. Jorge CEA
40 Bookstore Manager .... Mr. Robert ESTRADA
36 Director Transfer/Career Services .... Ms. Kristin CONNOR
88 Director Early Childhood Lab School .... Ms. Kathryn NIELSEN
26 Director Marketing & Media Design .... Ms. Barbara CELLA
13 Technology Systems Manager .... Mr. Mike BECKER
18 Buildings & Grounds Manager .... Mr. Russ HOLT
88 Custodial Manager .... Mr. Barry EDWARDS
88 Office of Instruction Supervisor .... Ms. Eileen VALENZUELA
19 Police Services .... Lt. Ryan HUDDLESTON
81 Dean of Math & Sciences .... Dr. A'kilah MOORE
75 Dean of Career Tech Educ/Social Sci .... Ms. Natalie HANNUM
79 Dean of Liberal Arts .... Ms. Nancy YBARRA
38 Dean Counseling & Student Support .... Mr. Jeffrey BENFORD

Copper Mountain College (K)

6162 Rotary Way, Box 1398, Joshua Tree CA 92252-6102
County: San Bernardino FICE Identification: 035424
Unit ID: 395362
Telephone: (760) 366-3791 Carnegie Class: Assoc/HT-High Trad
FAX Number: (760) 366-5255 Calendar System: Semester
URL: www.cmccd.edu
Established: 1999 Annual Undergrad Tuition & Fees (In-District): $1,108
Enrollment: 1,652 Coed
Affiliation or Control: State/Local IRS Status: 170(c)1
Highest Offering: Associate Degree
Accreditation: WJ

01 Superintendent/President .... Mr. Jeff CUMMINGS
05 VP of Academic and Student Success .... Dr. David NORTON
12 Dean of Instruction .... Mr. Zachary GINDER
32 Assoc Dean of Student Success & Eq .... Mr. Trevor WALKER
15 Chief Human Resources Officer .... Ms. Andrea RIESGO
18 Director of Facilities & Operations .... Mr. Jerry PHIPPS
102 Executive Director of Foundation .... Ms. Sandy SMITH
10 Chief Business Officer .... Ms. Meredith PLUMMER
35 Associate Dean of Student Services .... Mr. Brian HEINEMANN
45 Dir of Institutional Effectiveness .... Mr. Jacob KEVARI
76 Dir Hlth Science-Registered Nursing .... Ms. Christi BLAUWKAMP
13 Director of Information Systems .... Mr. Steve KEMP
26 Public Relations & Event Specialist .... Ms. Jolie ALPIN
04 Executive Asst to the President .... Ms. Karen COGHILL

Cuesta College (L)

PO Box 8106, San Luis Obispo CA 93403-8106
County: San Luis Obispo FICE Identification: 001192
Unit ID: 113193
Telephone: (805) 546-3100 Carnegie Class: Assoc/HT-Mix Trad/Non
FAX Number: (805) 546-3904 Calendar System: Semester
URL: www.cuesta.edu
Established: 1963 Annual Undergrad Tuition & Fees (In-District): $1,234
Enrollment: 9,221 Coed
Affiliation or Control: State/Local IRS Status: 501(c)3
Highest Offering: Associate Degree
Accreditation: WJ, EMT

01 Superintendent/President .... Dr. Gilbert H. STORK
05 VP/Asst Supt Academic Affairs .... Dr. Deborah WULFF
10 VP/Asst Supt Administrative Svcs .... Mr. Dan TROY
32 VP/Asst Supt Student Svcs Col Ctrs ... Ms. Sandee MCLAUGHLIN
12 Dean North Co Campus/S Co Ctr .... Dr. Maria ESCOBEDO
35 Dean of Student Services .... Ms. Catherine RIEDSTRA
30 Exec Dir Foundation/Inst Adv .... Ms. Shannon HILL
08 Director Library/Lrng Resources/DE .... Mr. Mark STENGEL
35 Coordinator Student Life/Leadership .... Dr. Anthony GUTIERREZ
13 Exec Director Info Sys and Tech .... Mr. Keith STEARNS
66 Director of Nursing .... Ms. Marcia SCOTT
15 Vice Pres Human Resource/Labor Rels . Ms. Melissa RICHERSON
19 Director of Public Safety .... Mr. Joseph ARTEAGA
40 Director of Bookstore .... Ms. Trudy BELL

41 Director of Athletics ... Mr. Robert MARIUCCI
18 Dir Maintenance/Operations/Grounds ... Mr. Terry REECE
38 Director Counseling Services ... Mr. Candelario MUNOZ
103 Dir Workforce Econ Devel Cmty Pgm ... Dr. Matthew GREEN
23 Coordinator of Health Services ... Ms. Joan DUFFY
81 Dean Acad Affs Sciences & Math ... Dr. Jason CURTIS
79 Dean Ac Aff Arts/Humanities/Soc Sci ... Vacant
103 Dean Ac Aff Workforce Econ Dev ... Dr. John CASCAMO
07 Director of Admissions & Records ... Ms. Kristin PIMENTEL
09 Director of Institutional Research ... Dr. Ryan CARTNAL
21 Director Fiscal Services ... Mr. Chris GREEN
102 Director Foundation Programs ... Ms. Karen TACKET

The Culinary Institute of America at Greystone (A)

2555 Main Street, Saint Helena CA 94574-9504
Telephone: (707) 967-1100 Identification: 666260
Accreditation: &M

† Regional accreditation is carried under the parent institution in Hyde Park, NY.

Deep Springs College (B)

HC 72 Box 45001, Via Dyer, NV 89010-9803
County: Inyo FICE Identification: 001194
Unit ID: 113528
Telephone: (760) 872-2000 Carnegie Class: Not Classified
FAX Number: (760) 874-7077 Calendar System: Other
URL: www.deepsprings.edu
Established: 1917 Annual Undergrad Tuition & Fees: $0
Enrollment: N/A Male
Affiliation or Control: Independent Non-Profit IRS Status: 501(c)3
Highest Offering: Associate Degree
Accreditation: WJ

01 President ... Mr. David NEIDORF
05 Academic Dean ... Ms. Amity WILCZEK
88 Ranch Manager ... Ms. Janice HUNTER
10 Director of Operations ... Mr. Padraic MACLEISH
30 Development Officer ... Mr. David WELLE
06 Registrar/Librarian ... Ms. Gwen VON KLAN
21 Office Manager ... Ms. Niki FRISHMAN
88 Chef/BH Manager ... Mr. Marc MORA
88 Farm Manager/Maintenance ... Mr. Noah BEYELER

Dell'Arte International School of Physical Theatre (C)

P.O. Box 816, 131 H Street, Blue Lake CA 95525
County: Humboldt FICE Identification: 030256
Unit ID: 113537
Telephone: (707) 668-5663 Carnegie Class: Spec-4-yr-Arts
FAX Number: (707) 668-5665 Calendar System: Other
URL: www.dellarte.com
Established: 1975 Annual Graduate Tuition & Fees: $13,350
Enrollment: 42 Coed
Affiliation or Control: Independent Non-Profit IRS Status: 501(c)3
Highest Offering: Master's; No Undergraduates
Accreditation: THEA

01 Executive Director ... Ms. Fran BEATTY
05 Producing Artistic Director ... Mr. Michael FIELDS
10 Chief Financial Officer ... Ms. Stephanie WITZEL
30 Development/Community Coordinator ... Ms. Claire REYNOLDS
06 School Administrator/Registrar ... Ms. Sarah PETERS
07 Director of Admissions ... Mr. Matt CHAPMAN

Design Institute of San Diego (D)

8555 Commerce Avenue, San Diego CA 92121-2685
County: San Diego FICE Identification: 022980
Unit ID: 113582
Telephone: (858) 566-1200 Carnegie Class: Spec-4-yr-Arts
FAX Number: (858) 566-2711 Calendar System: Semester
URL: www.disd.edu
Established: 1977 Annual Undergrad Tuition & Fees: $20,410
Enrollment: 171 Coed
Affiliation or Control: Proprietary IRS Status: Proprietary
Highest Offering: Baccalaureate
Accreditation: ACICS, CIDA

01 President ... Mr. Arthur ROSENSTEIN
11 Campus Director/CEO ... Ms. Margot DOUCETTE
05 Program Director ... Ms. Natalia WORDEN
07 Admissions ... Ms. Liz BARRY
37 Director Financial Aid ... Ms. Jackie GLORIA
32 Director of Student Services ... Ms. Tena MOIOLA
08 Librarian ... Ms. Lisa SCHATTMAN
06 Registrar ... Ms. Tracy GULINO
07 Outreach & Admissions ... Mr. Christopher PFEIL
36 Director Student Placement ... Mr. Richard HESS

DeVry University - Pomona Campus (E)

901 Corporate Center Drive, Pomona CA 91768-2642
Telephone: (909) 622-8866 FICE Identification: 023329
Accreditation: &NH, CAHIIM, ENGT

† Regional accreditation is carried under the parent institution in Downers Grove, IL.

Dominican School of Philosophy and Theology (F)

2301 Vine Street, Berkeley CA 94708-1816
County: Alameda FICE Identification: 001296
Unit ID: 113704
Telephone: (510) 849-2030 Carnegie Class: Spec-4-yr-Faith
FAX Number: (510) 849-1372 Calendar System: Semester
URL: www.dspt.edu
Established: 1932 Annual Undergrad Tuition & Fees: N/A
Enrollment: 80 Coed
Affiliation or Control: Roman Catholic IRS Status: 501(c)3
Highest Offering: Master's
Accreditation: WC, THEOL

01 President ... Rev. Michael SWEENEY
05 Academic Dean ... Rev. Christopher M. RENZ
10 COO/CFO ... Mr. Ian BROOKS
07 Director of Admissions ... Ms. Jamie D. MARTOS
06 Registrar ... Sr. Francis Marie SEALE
105 Director of Communications ... Ms. Heidi MCKENNA
30 Director of Development ... Mr. Manuel NIKEL-ZUEGER

Dominican University of California (G)

50 Acacia Avenue, San Rafael CA 94901-2298
County: Marin FICE Identification: 001196
Unit ID: 113698
Telephone: (415) 457-4440 Carnegie Class: Masters/M
FAX Number: (415) 485-3205 Calendar System: Semester
URL: www.dominican.edu
Established: 1890 Annual Undergrad Tuition & Fees: $42,550
Enrollment: 2,001 Coed
Affiliation or Control: Independent Non-Profit IRS Status: 501(c)3
Highest Offering: Master's
Accreditation: WC, ART, NURSE, OT

01 President ... Dr. Mary B. MARCY
05 Vice President Academic Affairs ... Dr. Nicola PITCHFORD
10 Vice President Business & Finance ... Ms. Tammi JACKSON
32 Dean of Students ... Dr. Paul RACCANELLO
84 Vice President Enrollment Mgmt ... Vacant
20 Associate VP Academic Affairs ... Dr. Mojgan BEHMAND
26 Director Marketing ... Ms. Nancy BULETTE
27 Director Comm & Media Relations ... Ms. Sarah GARDNER
04 Exec Assistant to the President ... Mrs. Sarita PURECE
100 Dir Board Relations/Special Events ... Ms. Jackie GENTILE
79 Dean Sch Arts/Humanities/Soc Sci ... Dr. Laura STIVERS
76 Dean Sch Health/Natural Sci ... Dr. Ching-Hua WANG
53 Dean Sch Educ/Counsel Psych ... Dr. Robin GAYLE
50 Dean Barowsky Sch Business ... Dr. Sam BELDONA
18 Exec Dir Facilities/Physical Plant ... Mr. Jacques CHARTON
08 University Librarian ... Mr. Gary GORKA
09 Director Institutional Research ... Mr. Christopher ANTONS
37 Director Financial Aid ... Ms. Shanon LITTLE
07 Director Undergrad Admissions ... Vacant
06 AVP Academic Services & Registrar ... Ms. Marianne STICKEL
29 Director Alumni Relations ... Ms. Katherine KUNZ
15 Director Human Resources ... Ms. Wendy LEE
36 Director Career Services ... Ms. Vanessa IOANNIDES
28 Dean Diversity and Equity ... Dr. Suresh APPAVOO
92 Director Honors Program ... Vacant
38 Director Counseling Center ... Dr. Charles BILLINGS
85 Director Global Education ... Dr. Kati BELL
30 VP Advancement/Alumni Engagement ... Vacant
41 Athletic Director ... Ms. Amy HENKELMAN
45 Sr Advisor Strategy & Planning ... Dr. Hanna RODRIGUEZ-FARRAR
102 Director Foundation ... Ms. Cyndi WEINGARD
108 Director of Assessment ... Dr. Matthew BRONSON

Dongguk University (H)

440 Shatto Place, Los Angeles CA 90020-1704
County: Los Angeles FICE Identification: 031095
Unit ID: 122117
Telephone: (213) 487-0110 Carnegie Class: Spec-4-yr-Other Health
FAX Number: (213) 487-0527 Calendar System: Quarter
URL: www.dula.edu
Established: 1979 Annual Undergrad Tuition & Fees: N/A
Enrollment: 171 Coed
Affiliation or Control: Independent Non-Profit IRS Status: 501(c)3
Highest Offering: Master's; No Lower Division
Accreditation: ACUP

01 President ... Dr. Seung Deok LEE
05 Dean of Academic Affairs ... Vacant
10 Director Administrative Affairs ... Mr. Albert KIM
37 Financial Aid Officer ... Ms. Barbara CORZO
06 Registrar ... Mr. Hoon SEO
17 Clinic Director ... Ms. Doris JOHNSON
18 Director of Facilities ... Mr. Arturo AGUIRRE
21 Office Manager ... Ms. Min PARK
85 International Student Advisor ... Mr. Phillip YEW

East San Gabriel Valley Regional Occupational Program and Technical Center (I)

1501 W. Del Norte Street, West Covina CA 91790
County: Los Angeles FICE Identification: 031166
Unit ID: 413802
Telephone: (626) 472-5121 Carnegie Class: Assoc/HVT-High Non
FAX Number: (626) 472-5125 Calendar System: Semester
URL: www.esgvrop.org
Established: Annual Undergrad Tuition & Fees (In-District): N/A
Enrollment: 581 Coed
Affiliation or Control: State/Local IRS Status: 501(c)3
Highest Offering: Associate Degree
Accreditation: COE, MAC

01 Superintendent ... Dr. Laurel ADLER
10 Chief Financial Officer ... Ms. Josephine QUACH

El Camino College (J)

16007 Crenshaw Boulevard, Torrance CA 90506-0002
County: Los Angeles FICE Identification: 001197
Unit ID: 113980
Telephone: (310) 660-3670 Carnegie Class: Assoc/HT-High Trad
FAX Number: (310) 660-7798 Calendar System: Semester
URL: www.elcamino.edu
Established: 1947 Annual Undergrad Tuition & Fees (In-District): $1,142
Enrollment: 24,207 Coed
Affiliation or Control: State/Local IRS Status: 501(c)3
Highest Offering: Associate Degree
Accreditation: WJ, COARC, RAD

01 President ... Dr. Dena P. MALONEY
05 Vice President Academic Affairs ... Dr. Jean SHANKWEILER
11 Vice Pres Administrative Services ... Dr. Jo Ann HIGDON
32 Vice Pres Student/Community Advance ... Dr. Jeanie NISHIME
15 Vice Pres of Human Resources ... Ms. Linda BEAM
30 Dean Community Advancement ... Mr. Jose ANAYA
45 Director Research Planning ... Ms. Irene GRAFF
72 Dean Industry & Technology ... Dr. Stephanie RODRIGUEZ
81 Dean Math ... Ms. Jacquelyn SIMS
50 Dean of Business ... Dr. Virginia RAPP
83 Dean Behavioral & Social Science ... Dr. Gloria MIRANDA
68 Dean Health/Exer/Science/Sport ... Mr. Rory NATIVIDAD
57 Dean Fine Arts ... Dr. Connie FITZSIMONS
76 Dean Natural Sciences ... Dr. Amy GRANT
79 Dean Humanities ... Mr. Tom LEW
38 Dean Counseling Matriculation Svcs ... Dr. Dipte PALEL
88 Dean of Student Support Services ... Mr. William GARCIA
13 Chief Technology Officer ... Dr. Art LEIBLE
31 Director of Community Relations ... Ms. Ann GARTEN
66 Director of Nursing ... Dr. Wanda MORRIS
07 Dir Admissions/Records/Registrar ... Mr. Bill MULROONEY
10 Chief Business Officer ... Dr. Jo Ann HIGDON
26 Chief Public Relations Officer ... Ms. Ann M. GARTEN
102 Executive Director Foundation ... Ms. Andrea SALA
96 Director of Purchasing ... Mr. Rocky BONURA
40 Director of Bookstore ... Ms. Julie BOURLIER
19 Chief of Campus Police ... Mr. Michael TREVIS
18 Director of Facilities Plng/Svcs ... Mr. Tom BROWN
35 Director of Student Affairs ... Dr. Gregory TOYA
37 Director Student Financial Aid ... Ms. Melissa GUESS
06 Registrar ... Mr. Bill MULROONEY
29 Director Alumni Relations ... Ms. Andrea SALA
09 Director Institutional Research ... Ms. Irene GRAFF
28 Director of Diversity ... Ms. Jayne ISHIKAWA
21 Business Manager ... Ms. Janice ELY
25 Resource Devel/Grants Coordinator ... Ms. Andrea SALA
04 Executive Asst to President ... Ms. Cynthia CONSTANTINO

El Camino College Compton Center (K)

1111 E Artesia Boulevard, Compton CA 90221-5393
Telephone: (310) 900-1600 FICE Identification: 001188
Accreditation: &WJ

† Regional accreditation is carried under the parent institution in Torrance, CA.

Emperor's College of Traditional Oriental Medicine (L)

1807-B Wilshire Boulevard, Santa Monica CA 90403-5678
County: Los Angeles FICE Identification: 026090
Unit ID: 114114
Telephone: (310) 453-8300 Carnegie Class: Spec-4-yr-Other Health
FAX Number: (310) 829-3838 Calendar System: Quarter
URL: www.emperors.edu
Established: 1983 Annual Undergrad Tuition & Fees: N/A
Enrollment: 222 Coed
Affiliation or Control: Proprietary IRS Status: Proprietary
Highest Offering: Doctorate
Accreditation: ACUP

01 Chief Executive Officer/President ... Yun KIM
05 Academic Dean ... Jacques MORAMARCO
07 Admissions Director ... Nicole WETHERINGTON
37 Financial Aid Officer ... Farida LUGEMBE
11 COO/Administrator ... George PARK
58 Associate Dean Doctoral Programs ... Chris RUTH

Empire College (M)

3035 Cleveland Avenue, Santa Rosa CA 95403-2100
County: Sonoma FICE Identification: 009032
Unit ID: 114123
Telephone: (707) 546-4000 Carnegie Class: Assoc/HVT-High Trad
FAX Number: (707) 546-4058 Calendar System: Other
URL: www.empcol.edu

Established: 1961 Annual Undergrad Tuition & Fees: N/A
Enrollment: 417 Coed
Affiliation or Control: Proprietary IRS Status: Proprietary
Highest Offering: Master's
Accreditation: ACICS

01 President ... Mr. Roy HURD
26 Vice Pres Marketing/Administration ... Mrs. Sherie HURD
05 Director of Education ... Mr. Mark KALAGORGEVICH
61 Dean Law School ... Mr. Michael MULLINS
07 Director of Admissions ... Ms Dahnja STRAUB
37 Director Student Financial Aid ... Mrs. Mary O'BRIEN
11 Administrative Services Manager ... Ms. Karina NUNO
10 Director of Accounting ... Mr. David YARBROUGH
06 Registrar ... Ms. Debbie BENEDETTI
15 Director Human Resources ... Mr. David YARBROUGH
36 Co-Advisor Career Placement ... Ms. Tammy SAMS
36 Co-Advisor Career Placement ... Ms. Jennifer SEDNA
40 Bookstore Manager ... Ms. Georgie MICALLEF
38 Student Success Advisor ... Ms. Nora SONGSTER

Epic Bible College & Graduate School (A)

4330 Auburn Boulevard, Sacramento CA 95841
County: Sacramento FICE Identification: 034033
Unit ID: 124487
Telephone: (916) 348-4689 Carnegie Class: Spec-4-yr-Faith
FAX Number: (916) 468-0866 Calendar System: Trimester
URL: www.EPIC.edu
Established: 1974 Annual Undergrad Tuition & Fees: $9,689
Enrollment: 231 Coed
Affiliation or Control: Independent Non-Profit IRS Status: 501(c)3
Highest Offering: Master's
Accreditation: TRACS

01 President ... Dr. Ronald W. HARDEN
05 Vice President of Academics ... Dr. Greg L. HARTLEY
88 Director MA in Ethical Leadership ... Dr. Ed FUNK
88 Director MA In Biblical Studies ... Dr. Gene MAYNARD
108 Director of Assessment ... Ms. Rosemarie HOWELL
08 Director Learning Resource ... Rev. Dale SOLBERG
10 Chief Financial Officer ... Mr. C. Steven CHANEY
37 Director of Financial Services ... Mr. David PINESCHI
06 Director of Records ... Ms. Kathy CLARKE
106 Director of Online Program ... Rev. John GALLEGOS
26 Director of Marketing ... Rev. Daniel HARDEN

Eternity Bible College (B)

2136 Winifred Street, Simi Valley CA 93063
County: Ventura Identification: 667045
Telephone: (805) 581-1233 Carnegie Class: Not Classified
FAX Number: (805) 581-1245 Calendar System: Semester
URL: www.eternitybiblecollege.com
Established: 2004 Annual Undergrad Tuition & Fees: N/A
Enrollment: N/A Coed
Affiliation or Control: Independent Non-Profit IRS Status: 501(c)3
Highest Offering: Baccalaureate
Accreditation: BI

01 President ... Spencer MACCUISH
05 Academic Dean ... Joshua WALKER
07 Director of Admissions ... Mary Beth DRAGOUN
06 Registrar/Finance Manager ... Ryan MCGLADDERY
32 Dir Student Life/Exec Asst ... Nicole MCGLADDERY

Evangelia University (C)

2660 West Woodland Drive, Suite 200,
Anaheim CA 92801-2650
County: Orange Identification: 666640
Telephone: (714) 527-0691 Carnegie Class: Not Classified
FAX Number: (714) 527-0693 Calendar System: Other
URL: www.evangelia.edu
Established: 1999 Annual Undergrad Tuition & Fees: N/A
Enrollment: N/A Coed
Affiliation or Control: Reformed Presbyterian Church IRS Status: 501(c)3
Highest Offering: Doctorate
Accreditation: TRACS

01 President ... Dr. David H. SHIN
05 Dean of Academic Affairs ... Dr. Soo Young LEE
11 Dean Admin/Chief Operating Officer ... Ki Won HAN
32 Dean of Student Affairs ... Ki Won HAN
06 Registrar/Foreign Student Advisor ... Charley LEE
57 Chair Masters of Arts Program ... Cha Hi WON
106 Director of Distance Education ... Soohae KANG

Ex'pression College (D)

6601 Shellmound Street, Emeryville CA 94608-1021
County: Alameda FICE Identification: 039733
Unit ID: 447458
Telephone: (510) 654-2934 Carnegie Class: Spec-4-yr-Arts
FAX Number: (510) 658-3414 Calendar System: Quarter
URL: www.expression.edu
Established: 1999 Annual Undergrad Tuition & Fees: $23,747
Enrollment: 445 Coed
Affiliation or Control: Proprietary IRS Status: Proprietary
Highest Offering: Baccalaureate
Accreditation: ACCSC

01 Campus Director ... Mr. Elmo FRAZER
05 Director of Education ... Mr. Adam RUCH

Ex'pression College - San Jose (E)

1751 Fox Drive, San Jose CA 95131
Telephone: (408) 620-3300 Identification: 770552
Accreditation: ACCSC

Fashion Institute of Design and Merchandising-Orange County (F)

17590 Gillette Avenue, Irvine CA 92614-5610
Telephone: (888) 974-3436 Identification: 666004
Accreditation: &WC, ART

† Regional accreditation is carried under the parent institution in Los Angeles, CA.

Feather River College (G)

570 Golden Eagle Avenue, Quincy CA 95971-9124
County: Plumas FICE Identification: 008597
Unit ID: 114433
Telephone: (530) 283-0202 Carnegie Class: Assoc/HT-High Non
FAX Number: (530) 283-3757 Calendar System: Semester
URL: www.frc.edu
Established: 1968 Annual Undergrad Tuition & Fees (In-District): $1,461
Enrollment: 1,715 Coed
Affiliation or Control: State/Local IRS Status: 501(c)3
Highest Offering: Baccalaureate
Accreditation: WJ

01 Superintendent/President ... Dr. Kevin TRUTNA
10 Chief Financial Officer ... Mr. Jim SCOUBES
05 Chief Instructional Officer ... Dr. Derek LERCH
32 Chief Student Services Officer ... Dr. Karen PIERSON
15 Director Human Resources/EEO ... Mr. David BURRIS
18 Director of Facilities/CTO ... Mr. Nick BOYD
06 Registrar/Dir of Admissions ... Ms. Leslie MIKESELL
37 Director Student Financial Aid ... Mr. Andre VAN DER VELDEN
96 Purchasing Agent ... Ms. Tamara CLINE
04 Administrative Asst to President ... Ms. Cynthia HALL
09 Director of Institutional Research ... Dr. Agnes KOOS

FIDM/Fashion Institute of Design & Merchandising-San Diego (H)

350 10th Avenue, 3rd Floor, San Diego CA 92101
Telephone: (619) 235-2049 Identification: 666005
Accreditation: &WC, ART

† Regional accreditation is carried under the parent institution in Los Angeles, CA.

FIDM/Fashion Institute of Design and Merchandising-San Francisco (I)

55 Stockton Street, San Francisco CA 94108-5829
Telephone: (415) 675-5200 FICE Identification: 013041
Accreditation: &WC, ART

† Regional accreditation is carried under the parent institution in Los Angeles, CA.

FIDM/Fashion Institute of Design and Merchandising-Los Angeles (J)

919 S Grand Avenue, Los Angeles CA 90015-1421
County: Los Angeles FICE Identification: 011112
Unit ID: 114354
Telephone: (213) 624-1200 Carnegie Class: Spec-4-yr-Arts
FAX Number: (213) 624-9354 Calendar System: Quarter
URL: www.fidm.edu
Established: 1969 Annual Undergrad Tuition & Fees: $29,930
Enrollment: 3,142 Coed
Affiliation or Control: Proprietary IRS Status: Proprietary
Highest Offering: Baccalaureate
Accreditation: WC, ART

01 President ... Ms. Tonian HOHBERG
10 Vice President Finance ... Ms. Annie JOHNSON
46 Vice President Planning ... Ms. Vivien LOWY
05 Vice President Education ... Ms. Barbara BUNDY
108 Dean of Accreditation ... Ms. Lisa SCHOENING
08 Director Library ... Ms. Kathy BAILON
06 Registrar ... Mr. Michael GILBERT
37 Director Financial Aid ... Mr. Chris JENNINGS
26 Director Public Rels/Publicity ... Ms. Shirley WILSON
09 Dir Institutional Effectiveness ... Dr. Andrea E. HELEKAR
38 Personal Counselor ... Ms. Jessica CATTANI
96 Director College Services ... Ms. Darlene LATINVILLE
07 Exec Director of Admissions ... Ms. Susan ARONSON
13 Chief Info Technology Officer (CIO) ... Ms. Suzanna GRUESER
15 Human Resources Manager ... Ms. Julie Ann OTTESON
04 Executive Asst to President ... Ms. Megan NOWAK
104 Director International Affairs ... Ms. Sarah REPETTO
105 Director Web Mktg Ops/Publications ... Mr. Michael KAMINSKI
18 Director of FIDM Facilities ... Mr. John (Buddy) BOLOGNONE
19 Director of Security ... Mr. Todd J. ANDERSON

22 Title IX Coordinator ... Ms. Katherine SLAUTA
29 Director Alumni Relations ... Mr. Bill CLIATT
32 Director of Student Activities ... Ms. Caitlin MADDEN
36 Executive Director Industry Relati ... Ms. Sharon RYAN
39 Housing Administrator ... Ms. Sonialina ERWIN
53 Dean of Education ... Ms. Sheryl RABINOVICH
86 Director Government Relations ... Ms. Norine FULLER
90 Director Academic Computing ... Mr. Dave MELONE

Fielding Graduate University (K)

2020 De La Vina Street, Santa Barbara CA 93105-3538
County: Santa Barbara FICE Identification: 020961
Unit ID: 114549
Telephone: (800) 340-1099 Carnegie Class: DU-Mod
FAX Number: (805) 687-9793 Calendar System: Trimester
URL: www.fielding.edu
Established: 1974 Annual Graduate Tuition & Fees: N/A
Enrollment: 1,201 Coed
Affiliation or Control: Independent Non-Profit IRS Status: 501(c)3
Highest Offering: Doctorate; No Undergraduates
Accreditation: WC, CLPSY

01 President ... Dr. Katrina ROGERS
101 Exec Asst to President & Provost ... Ms. Maisee THAO
05 Provost & Senior Vice President ... Dr. Gerald PORTER
09 VP Strategic Initiative/Research ... Mr. Orlando TAYLOR
10 VP and Chief Financial Officer ... Ms. Lisa LEWIS
30 VP Univ Advancement & Development ... Mr. David EDELMAN
45 VP Institutional Planning & Effect ... Dr. Monique L. SNOWDEN
15 Director Human Resources ... Ms. Amy RAMOS
06 Registrar/Dir Enrollment Services ... Ms. Bridget BRADY

Five Branches University, Graduate School of Traditional Chinese Medicine (L)

1885 Lundy Avenue, Suite 108, San Jose CA 95131
County: Santa Clara Identification: 667008
Telephone: (408) 260-0208 Carnegie Class: Not Classified
FAX Number: (408) 261-3166 Calendar System: Semester
URL: www.fivebranches.edu
Established: 2005 Annual Undergrad Tuition & Fees: N/A
Enrollment: N/A Coed
Affiliation or Control: Proprietary IRS Status: Proprietary
Highest Offering: Doctorate; No Lower Division
Accreditation: ACUP

01 President/CEO ... Ron ZAIDMAN
05 VP Academic Affairs ... Joanna ZHAO
06 Registrar ... Gina HUANG
88 Director of Doctoral Program ... Fei-Ing TZENG
10 Chief Financial Officer ... Liana CHEN
88 Associate Director Doctoral ... Nan WANG
88 Associate Director Doctoral ... E-Sing HONG
88 Director of Chinese Masters of TCM ... Jasmine HUANG
88 Director of Korean Masters of TCM ... Heerei PARK
56 Director of Extension Program ... Sumedha GOH
88 Clinic Manager ... Yi-Chia LEE

Five Branches University, Graduate School of Traditional Chinese Medicine (M)

200 7th Avenue, Santa Cruz CA 95062-4669
County: Santa Cruz FICE Identification: 031313
Unit ID: 114585
Telephone: (831) 476-9424 Carnegie Class: Spec-4-yr-Other Health
FAX Number: (831) 476-8928 Calendar System: Semester
URL: www.fivebranches.edu
Established: 1984 Annual Undergrad Tuition & Fees: N/A
Enrollment: 371 Coed
Affiliation or Control: Proprietary IRS Status: Proprietary
Highest Offering: Master's; No Lower Division
Accreditation: ACUP

01 President & CEO ... Ron ZAIDMAN
05 Vice President of Academic Affairs ... Joanna ZHAO
11 Director of Operations ... Gina HUANG
10 Chief Accounting Officer ... Liana CHEN
26 Dir of Marketing & Public Relations ... Ali POLK
08 Librarian ... Jim EMDY
17 Clinic Quality Control Director ... Sally LEWIS
06 Registrar ... Ling ZHANG
07 Admissions Director ... Eleonor MENDELSON
37 Director Student Financial Aid ... Mecca MATILDA
32 Director of Student Services ... Ana LOBATO
56 Director of Extension Programs ... Sumheda GOH
88 Student Accounts Manager ... Kayoko YAMAMOTO

*Foothill-De Anza Community College District System Office (N)

12345 El Monte Road, Los Altos Hills CA 94022-4597
County: Santa Clara FICE Identification: 009020
Unit ID: 114831
Telephone: (650) 949-6100 Carnegie Class: N/A
FAX Number: (650) 941-5289
URL: www.fhda.edu

01 Chancellor ... Dr. Judy C. MINER
10 Vice Chancellor Business Services ... Mr. Kevin MCELROY
15 Vice Chancellor Human Resources ... Ms. Dorene NOVOTNY
13 Vice Chancellor Technology ... Mr. Joseph MOREAU
18 Exec Dir Facilities/Operations ... Mr. Steve KITCHEN

*De Anza College (A)

21250 Stevens Creek Boulevard,
Cupertino CA 95014-5793
County: Santa Clara FICE Identification: 004480
Unit ID: 113333
Telephone: (408) 864-5678 Carnegie Class: Assoc/HT-Mix Trad/Non
FAX Number: (408) 864-8238 Calendar System: Quarter
URL: www.deanza.edu
Established: 1967 Annual Undergrad Tuition & Fees (In-District): $1,542
Enrollment: 23,104 Coed
Affiliation or Control: State/Local IRS Status: 501(c)3
Highest Offering: Associate Degree
Accreditation: WJ, MLTAD

02 President ... Dr. Brian MURPHY
05 Vice Pres of Instruction ... Ms. Christina ESPINOSA-PIEB
32 Vice Pres of Student Services ... Dr. Stacey A. COOK
10 VP Finance/College Operations ... Ms. Susan CHEU
20 Assoc Vice Pres Instruction ... Vacant
35 Dean Student Development/EOPS ... Ms. Michele LEBLEU BURNS
38 Dean Counseling & Matriculation ... Dr. Sheila WHITE-DANIELS
07 Dean Admissions & Records ... Ms. Tamika WARD
37 Director Student Financial Aid ... Ms. Lisa MANDY
15 Director Personnel Services ... Mr. Bret WATSON
18 Assoc Vice Pres College Operations ... Ms. Donna JONES-DULIN
26 AVP Communications & External Rel ... Ms. Marisa SPATAFORE
102 Exec Director Foundation ... Ms. Tess CHANDLER
28 Director of Diversity ... Dr. Veronica NEAL
96 Director of Purchasing ... Ms. Pam GREY
36 Director Student Placement ... Dr. Stephen FLETCHER
09 Institutional Research Specialist ... Dr. Mallory NEWELL
06 Supervisor Admissions and Records ... Mr. Barry JOHNSON
04 Administrative Asst to President ... Ms. Tina WOO
08 Head Librarian ... Mr. Tom DOLEN
13 Chief Info Technology Officer (CIO) ... Mr. Joe MOREAU
41 Athletic Director ... Mr. Kulwant SINGH
50 Dean Business/Comp Sys/Applied Tech ... Mr. Moaty FAYEK
86 Director Government Relations ... Dr. Jerry ROSENBERG

*Foothill College (B)

12345 El Monte Road, Los Altos Hills CA 94022-4599
County: Santa Clara FICE Identification: 001199
Unit ID: 114716
Telephone: (650) 949-7777 Carnegie Class: Assoc/HT-High Non
FAX Number: (650) 949-7375 Calendar System: Quarter
URL: www.foothill.edu
Established: 1957 Annual Undergrad Tuition & Fees (In-District): $1,551
Enrollment: 15,030 Coed
Affiliation or Control: State/Local IRS Status: 501(c)3
Highest Offering: Baccalaureate
Accreditation: WJ, COARC, DA, DH, DMS, EMT, RAD

02 President ... Ms. Thuy NGUYEN
04 Executive Asst to the President ... Mr. Justin SCHULTZ
45 VP Finance & Admin Services ... Ms. Bernata SLATER
05 VP Instruction & Inst Research ... Dr. Kimberlee MESSINA
32 VP Student Services ... Dr. Denise SWETT
20 Associate VP Instruction ... Dr. Andrew LAMANQUE
35 Associate VP Student Services ... Ms. Laureen BALDUCCI
35 Dean Student Affairs & Activities ... Mr. Thom SHEPARD
85 Dean International Education ... Ms. Vinita BALI
38 Dean Counseling & Special Programs ... Ms. Lan TRUONG
12 Dean Sunnyvale Center ... Ms. Dawn GIRADELLI
88 Dean Disb Student Svcs & Vet Pgms ... Ms. Teresa ONG
35 Dir Student Activities & Affairs ... Ms. Daphne SMALL
40 Director Bookstore ... Mr. Romeo PAULE
84 Dean Enrollment Services ... Ms. Nazy GALOYAN
37 Director Financial Aid ... Mr. Kevin HARRAL
26 Dir Marketing & Public Relations ... Ms. Andrea HANSTEIN
23 Director Health Services ... Vacant
76 Dean Biology & Health Sciences ... Dr. Nanette SOLVASON
50 Dean Business & Social Sciences ... Mr. Kurt HUEG
106 Dean Foothill Online Learning ... Dr. Judy BAKER
57 Dean Fine Arts & Communications ... Mr. Simon PENNINGTON
88 Dean Language Arts & LRC ... Mr. Paul STARER
81 Dean Phys Sci/Math & Engr ... Vacant
09 College Researcher ... Dr. Elaine KUO
41 Athletic Director ... Mr. Mike TEIJEIRO

Franciscan School of Theology (C)

4050 Mission Avenue, Oceanside CA 92057
County: San Diego FICE Identification: 011792
Unit ID: 114734
Telephone: (760) 547-1800 Carnegie Class: Spec-4-yr-Faith
FAX Number: (760) 547-1806 Calendar System: Semester
URL: www.fst.edu
Established: 1968 Annual Graduate Tuition & Fees: N/A
Enrollment: 32 Coed
Affiliation or Control: Independent Non-Profit IRS Status: 501(c)3
Highest Offering: Master's; No Undergraduates
Accreditation: WC, THEOL

01 President and Rector ... Fr. Michael HIGGINS, TOR
05 Vice President for Academic Affairs ... Fr. Garrett GALVIN, OFM
06 Registrar ... Ms. Jackie GAMBLE
07 Co-Director of Recruitment ... Vacant
07 Co-Director of Recruitment ... Ms. Gabriela HEINTSCHEL
30 Executive Director of Development ... Ms. Randi QUAID
10 Chief Financial Officer ... Ms. Kimberly RENNA

Fremont College (D)

18000 Studebaker Road, 9th Floor, Cerritos CA 90703
County: Los Angeles FICE Identification: 030399
Unit ID: 372073
Telephone: (562) 809-5100 Carnegie Class: Bac/Assoc-Assoc Dom
FAX Number: (562) 809-7100 Calendar System: Other
URL: www.fremont.edu
Established: 1985 Annual Undergrad Tuition & Fees: N/A
Enrollment: 387 Coed
Affiliation or Control: Proprietary IRS Status: Proprietary
Highest Offering: Baccalaureate
Accreditation: ACCSC

01 Chancellor/CEO ... Dr. Sabrina KAY
05 Chief Academic Officer ... Jonathan DAITCH
11 Director of Operations ... Tony WONG
36 Director of Student Placement ... Vanessa ORTEGA
37 Director of Financial Aid ... Joanne BRENNAN

Fremont College (E)

3440 Wilshire Blvd, 10th Floor, Los Angeles CA 90010
Telephone: (213) 355-7777 Identification: 770553
Accreditation: ACCSC

Fresno Pacific University (F)

1717 S Chestnut Avenue, Fresno CA 93702-4798
County: Fresno FICE Identification: 001253
Unit ID: 114813
Telephone: (559) 453-2000 Carnegie Class: Masters/L
FAX Number: (559) 453-2007 Calendar System: Semester
URL: www.fresno.edu
Established: 1944 Annual Undergrad Tuition & Fees: $27,954
Enrollment: 3,458 Coed
Affiliation or Control: Mennonite Brethren Church IRS Status: 501(c)3
Highest Offering: Master's
Accreditation: WC, NURSE, THEOL

01 President ... Dr. Richard KRIEGBAUM
05 Interim Provost/Senior VP ... Dr. Dale SIMMONS
10 Vice President Finance ... Mr. Robert LIPPERT
26 Vice Pres Integrated Marketing ... Mrs. Diana BATES MOCK
11 Vice Pres of Operations ... Vacant
84 Vice Pres Enrollment Mgmt ... Mr. Jon ENDICOTT
30 VP for Advancement/Univ Relations ... Mr. Mark ISAAC
50 Interim Dean School of Business ... Dr. Susan COX
79 Dean Sch of Human/Rel/Soc Sci ... Dr. Ron HERMS
53 Dean School of Education ... Dr. Gary GRAMENZ
78 Dean School of Natural Sciences ... Dr. Karen CIANCI
42 Dean of Spiritual Formation ... Rev. Angulus WILSON
32 Dean of Student Life ... Dr. Randy WORDEN
06 Registrar ... Mr. Michael ALLEN
08 Director of Library ... Mr. Kevin ENNS-REMPEL
36 Director of Career Resource Center ... Ms. Alicia ANDRADE
15 Human Resources Director ... Vacant
27 Publications Director ... Mr. Wayne STEFFEN
29 Director Alumni Development ... Ms. Ali SENA
37 Interim Director of Financial Aid ... Ms. Stacie BENEDICT
41 Athletic Director ... Mr. Aaron HENDERSON
19 Chief of Campus Safety ... Mr. Javier CAMPOS
26 Chief Public Relations Officer ... Mr. Wayne STEFFENS
104 Dir International Pgms/Svcs Ofc ... Mr. Arnie PRIEB
07 Director of Admissions ... Mrs. Krista BROOKS
18 Facilities Manager ... Mr. Gary METCALF
04 Executive Asst to President ... Ms. Gwenevera E. BURKS
88 Seminary President ... Dr. Terry BRENSINGER
102 Dir Foundation/Corporate Relations ... Mr. Mark DEFFENBACHER
44 Director Major Gifts ... Mrs. Karin CHAO-BUSHOVEN
21 Controller ... Mr. Orren WANG
09 Director of Institutional Research ... Ms. Maribel VIVEROS
28 Director of Diversity ... Dr. Karen CROZIER
108 Assoc Prov Inst Effectiveness ... Dr. Cindy CARTER
13 Exec Director ITS ... Mr. Dave RICHERT

Fuller Theological Seminary (G)

135 N Oakland, Pasadena CA 91182-1780
County: Los Angeles FICE Identification: 001200
Unit ID: 114840
Telephone: (626) 584-5200 Carnegie Class: Spec-4-yr-Faith
FAX Number: (626) 795-8767 Calendar System: Quarter
URL: www.fuller.edu
Established: 1947 Annual Graduate Tuition & Fees: N/A
Enrollment: 2,550 Coed
Affiliation or Control: Independent Non-Profit IRS Status: 501(c)3
Highest Offering: Doctorate; No Undergraduates
Accreditation: WC, CLPSY, THEOL

01 President ... Dr. Mark A. LABBERTON
05 Provost ... Dr. Joel B. GREEN
100 Chief of Staff/Strategy ... Mr. Bill CLARK
10 Chief Financial Officer ... Mr. Lenny MOON
30 Vice President Development ... Mr. Jon YASUDA
26 Vice President Comm/Mktg & Admiss ... Mrs. Irene NELLER
88 Vice President Vocation & Formation ... Dr. Tod BOLSINGER
73 Dean School of Theology ... Dr. Joel B. GREEN
88 Dean School of Psychology ... Dr. Mari CLEMENTS
88 Dean School Intercultural Studies ... Dr. Scott W. SUNQUIST
32 Dean of Students ... Dr. Steve YAMAGUCHI
71 Dean of the Chapel and Spirit Form ... Dr. Laura HARBERT
13 Assoc Provost Information Svc/CIO ... Dr. Kevin OSBORN
108 Assoc Prov Accreditation & Educ Eff ... Dr. Mignon R. JACOBS
88 Assoc Dean Doctor of Ministry Pgm ... Dr. Kurt FREDRICKSON
06 Registrar ... Mr. David E. KIEFER
15 Exec Director of HR & Org Dev ... Ms. Bernadette (BJ) BARBER
35 Assistant Dean of Students ... Mr. Sam BANG
07 Exec Dir Admiss & Stdnt Fin Svcs ... Mr. Steve SMITH
39 Director of Housing Services ... Ms. Inge-Lise TITHERADGE
04 Assistant to President ... Mr. Len TANG
18 Facilities Director ... Mr. Nathan MERRITT
109 Director of Auxiliary Services ... Mrs. Jeanne HANDOJO
43 General Counsel ... Ms. Rita K. ROWLAND
85 Dir Student Affs/International Svcs ... Mr. Sam BANG
37 Director Student Financial Services ... Mr. David RICHARDS
106 Dir Online Education/E-learning ... Mr. Tommy LISTER

Gateway Seminary (H)

3210 E. Guasti RD, Ontario CA 91761-8642
County: San Bernadino FICE Identification: 001204
Unit ID: 115047
Telephone: (909) 687-1800 Carnegie Class: Not Classified
FAX Number: N/A Calendar System: Semester
URL: www.gs.edu
Established: 1944 Annual Graduate Tuition & Fees: N/A
Enrollment: N/A Coed
Affiliation or Control: Southern Baptist IRS Status: 501(c)3
Highest Offering: Doctorate; No Undergraduates
Accreditation: WC, THEOL

00 President Emeritus ... Dr. William O. CREWS
01 President/Chairman of the Faculty ... Dr. Jeff IORG
30 Vice Pres Institutional Advancement ... Dr. Jeff JONES
10 Vice Pres Strategic Services/CFO ... Mr. Gary GROAT
05 Vice President Academic Affairs ... Dr. D. Michael MARTIN
84 VP Enrollment/Student Svcs/Dn Stdts ... Dr. Adam GROZA
21 Controller ... Mr. Harry WEAVER
06 Registrar ... Ms. Jennifer PEACH
08 Director of Library Services ... Dr. Bob PHILLIPS
12 Director PNW Campus ... Dr. Mark BRADLEY
12 Director Arizona Campus ... Dr. Dallas BIVINS
12 Director Rocky Mountain Campus ... Dr. Steve VETETO
13 Director Information Technology ... Mr. Steve POLCYN
15 Director Personnel Services ... Vacant
18 Chief Facilities/Physical Plant ... Mr. Robert DVORAK
44 Director of Development ... Mr. Jay BADRY
84 Director Enrollment Management ... Ms. Max STABENOW
32 Director of Student Life ... Mr. Shane TANIGAWA

Gavilan College (I)

5055 Santa Teresa Boulevard, Gilroy CA 95020-9599
County: Santa Clara FICE Identification: 001202
Unit ID: 114938
Telephone: (408) 848-4800 Carnegie Class: Assoc/HT-High Non
FAX Number: (408) 848-4801 Calendar System: Semester
URL: www.gavilan.edu
Established: 1919 Annual Undergrad Tuition & Fees (In-District): $1,246
Enrollment: 5,531 Coed
Affiliation or Control: State/Local IRS Status: 501(c)3
Highest Offering: Associate Degree
Accreditation: WJ

01 Superintendent/President ... Dr. Kathleen A. ROSE
05 Vice Pres Instructional Svcs ... Dr. Kathleen A. ROSE
11 Vice Pres Administrative Services ... Mr. Fred HARRIS
32 Vice President Student Services ... Ms. Kathleen MOBERG
06 Director of Admissions and Records ... Ms. Candice WHITNEY
08 Head Librarian ... Dr. Douglas ACHTERMAN
37 Director Student Financial Aid ... Vacant
09 Director of Institutional Research ... Dr. Peter WRUCK
15 Director Human Resources ... Mr. Eric RAMONES
18 Director of Facilities and Maint ... Mr. Jeff GOPP
13 Dir Computing & Information Mgmt ... Ms. Mimi ARVIZU
26 Director Public Information ... Ms. Jan CHARGIN
23 Student Health Nurse ... Ms. Alice DUFRESNE-REYES
41 Dean of Kinesiology and Athletics ... Mr. Ron HANNON
40 Manager Bookstore ... Ms. Alexis BOLIN
49 Dean Liberal Art and Sciences ... Ms. Fran LOZANO
72 Dean Career Technical Education ... Ms. Sherrean CARR
07 Director of Admissions ... Ms. Candice WHITNEY
10 Chief Business Officer ... Ms. Wade ELLIS
96 Purchasing Specialist ... Ms. Connie CAMPOS

Glendale Career College (J)

240 N. Brand Blvd, Lower Level, Glendale CA 91203
County: Los Angeles FICE Identification: 023385
Unit ID: 115010
Telephone: (818) 243-1131 Carnegie Class: Not Classified
FAX Number: (818) 243-6028 Calendar System: Semester
URL: www.glendalecareer.com
Established: 1946 Annual Undergrad Tuition & Fees: N/A
Enrollment: 346 Coed
Affiliation or Control: Proprietary IRS Status: Proprietary
Highest Offering: Associate Degree

Accreditation: ABHES, SURGT, SURTEC

01 Campus Director .... Mr. Vivek SHARMA

Glendale Community College (A)

1500 N Verdugo Road, Glendale CA 91208-2894
County: Los Angeles FICE Identification: 001203
Unit ID: 115001
Telephone: (818) 240-1000 Carnegie Class: Assoc/MT-VT-High Trad
FAX Number: (818) 549-9436 Calendar System: Semester
URL: www.glendale.edu
Established: 1927 Annual Undergrad Tuition & Fees (In-District): $1,175
Enrollment: 15,112 Coed
Affiliation or Control: State/Local IRS Status: 501(c)3
Highest Offering: Associate Degree
Accreditation: WJ

01 Superintendent/President .... Dr. David VIAR
11 Exec Vice Pres Administrative Svcs .... Mr. Ron NAKASONE
05 Vice Pres Instructional Services .... Mr. Michael RITTERBROWN
32 Vice President Student Services .... Dr. Ricardo PEREZ
51 Admn Dn Workforce Dev Cont/Cmty Ed .... Mr. Alfred RAMIREZ
15 Assoc VP Human Resources .... Ms. Teyanna WILLIAMS
45 Dean Research/Planning/Grants .... Dr. Edward KARPP
07 Director Admissions & Records .... Ms. Michelle MORA
20 Int Dean Instructional Services .... Mr. Peter STATHIS
103 Dean Workforce Development .... Ms. Jan SWINTON
32 Dean Student Affairs .... Dr. Paul SCHLOSSMAN
35 Dean of Student Services .... Dr. Robert HILL
37 Assoc Dean Stdnt Financial Aid Svcs .... Vacant
10 Director Business Services .... Ms. Susan COURTEY
102 Exec Director College Foundation .... Ms. Lisa BROOKS

Golden Gate University (B)

536 Mission Street, San Francisco CA 94105-2968
County: San Francisco FICE Identification: 001205
Unit ID: 115083
Telephone: (415) 442-7000 Carnegie Class: Masters/L
FAX Number: (415) 495-2671 Calendar System: Trimester
URL: www.ggu.edu
Established: 1901 Annual Undergrad Tuition & Fees: $14,640
Enrollment: 2,909 Coed
Affiliation or Control: Independent Non-Profit IRS Status: 501(c)3
Highest Offering: Doctorate
Accreditation: WC, LAW

01 President .... Dr. David J. FIKE
05 VP of Academic Affairs .... Ms. Barbara H. KARLIN
10 VP of Business Affairs & CFO .... Mr. Robert D. HITE
30 VP of University Advancement .... Ms. Tasia NEEVE
15 VP Human Resources/EEO .... Ms. Terri SHULTIS
61 Dean School of Law .... Ms. Rachel VAN CLEAVE
50 Dean Ageno School of Business .... Dr. Paul FOUTS
88 Dean School Taxation & Accounting .... Mr. Fred SROKA
49 Dean Undergraduate Programs .... Dr. Nate HINERMAN
100 Executive Director Ofc of President .... Dr. John FYFE
106 Director E-Learning .... Mr. Doug GEIER
32 Dean of Students & Student Affairs .... Ms. Kayla KRUPNICK
08 Director University Library .... Mr. James KRUSLING
08 Associate Dean Law Library .... Mr. Michael DAW
84 Director Enrollment Services .... Mr. Louis D. RICCARDI, JR.
06 University Registrar .... Ms. Amy BARRON CHUNG
27 Chief Information Officer .... Vacant
26 Director Marketing & Communications .... Ms. Sandra HENAO
88 Director PLUS Program .... Dr. Karen MCROBIE
09 Dir Planning/Resources/Analysis .... Dr. Mercy LIM
18 Director Business Svcs/Facilities .... Mr. Mike KOPERSKI
21 Controller .... Mr. Altaf RAJAN
37 Director Student Financial Aid .... Ms. Kathi KELLEY
38 Clinical Director/Counseling Svcs .... Ms. Michael Anne CONLEY
108 Director Institutional Assessment .... Ms. Lisa KRAMER

Golden State University (C)

9047 E. Florence Ave #L, Downey CA 90240
County: Los Angeles Identification: 667261
Telephone: (562) 622-3368 Carnegie Class: Not Classified
FAX Number: N/A Calendar System: Quarter
URL: www.goldenstateuniv.us
Established: Annual Graduate Tuition & Fees: N/A
Enrollment: N/A Coed
Affiliation or Control: Proprietary IRS Status: Proprietary
Highest Offering: Master's; No Undergraduates
Accreditation: @ACUP

01 President & Dean of Academics .... Sunny S. KIM
20 Assoc Dean of Academics .... Fataneh ZARGAR
07 Dean of Admiss & Student Affairs .... Howard SUNGJI KIM

Golf Academy of America (D)

1950 Camino Vida Roble, Suite 125, Carlsbad CA 92008
Telephone: (800) 342-7342 FICE Identification: 015609
Accreditation: ACICS

† Branch campus of Virginia College, Birmingham, AL.

Grace Communion Seminary (E)

2011 E. Financial Way, PO Box 5005, Glendora CA 91740-0730
County: Los Angeles Identification: 667115
Telephone: (626) 650-2306 Carnegie Class: Not Classified
FAX Number: (626) 650-2307 Calendar System: Semester
URL: www.gcs.edu
Established: 2008 Annual Graduate Tuition & Fees: N/A
Enrollment: N/A Coed
Affiliation or Control: Independent Non-Profit IRS Status: 501(c)3
Highest Offering: Master's; No Undergraduates
Accreditation: DEAC

01 President/CEO .... Dr. Gary DEDDO
05 Dean of Faculty .... Dr. Michael MORRISON
06 Registrar .... Ms. Susan WILLIAMS
10 CFO/Liaison Officer .... Dr. Russell DUKE

Grace Mission University (F)

1645 West Valencia Drive, Fullerton CA 92833-3860
County: Orange Identification: 666642
Unit ID: 481058
Telephone: (714) 525-0088 Carnegie Class: Spec-4-yr-Faith
FAX Number: (714) 525-0089 Calendar System: Semester
URL: www.gm.edu
Established: 1995 Annual Undergrad Tuition & Fees: $2,690
Enrollment: 88 Coed
Affiliation or Control: Presbyterian Church In America IRS Status: 501(c)3
Highest Offering: Doctorate
Accreditation: BI, @THEOL, TRACS

01 President .... Kwangsin KIM
03 Executive Vice President & CEO .... Dr. Kyunam CHOI
05 Academic Dean .... Dr. Hyun Wan KIM
10 Chief Financial Officer .... Mr. David Chang S. LEE
32 Dean of Students .... Mr. Dong Hyun HUH
11 Dir Administration/Financial Aid .... Mr. James KOO
06 Registrar .... Ms. Jung Mo YOOK
08 Librarian .... Ms. Eun Ja SUH

Graduate Theological Union (G)

2400 Ridge Road, Berkeley CA 94709-1212
County: Alameda FICE Identification: 001207
Unit ID: 115214
Telephone: (510) 649-2400 Carnegie Class: Spec-4-yr-Faith
FAX Number: (510) 649-1417 Calendar System: Semester
URL: www.gtu.edu
Established: 1962 Annual Graduate Tuition & Fees: N/A
Enrollment: 237 Coed
Affiliation or Control: Independent Non-Profit IRS Status: 501(c)3
Highest Offering: Doctorate; No Undergraduates
Accreditation: WC, THEOL

01 President .... Dr. Riess POTTERVELD
05 Int Dean/Vice Pres Academic Affairs .... Dr. Judith A. BERLING
10 Vice Pres Administration/Finance .... Mr. Steven G. ARGYRIS
30 Vice President for Advancement .... Mr. Alan KELCHNER
32 VP Student Affairs/Dean Students .... Dr. Kathleen KOOK
07 Director of Admissions .... Dr. Andrea SHEAFFER
08 Interim Library Director .... Mr. Clay-Edward DIXON
06 Consortial Registrar .... Mr. John SEAL
13 Chief Information Officer .... Mr. Jeffrey DIGREORIO
18 Building & Grounds Engineer .... Mr. Curtis OSBORNE
15 Director Human Resources .... Ms. Deborah WALKER
37 Asst Director of Financial Aid .... Ms. Michelle SIMON
04 Executive Assistant to President .... Ms. Teresa JOYE

*Grossmont-Cuyamaca Community College District (H)

8800 Grossmont College Drive, El Cajon CA 92020-1799
County: San Diego FICE Identification: 007006
Unit ID: 115287
Telephone: (619) 644-7010 Carnegie Class: N/A
FAX Number: (619) 644-7936
URL: www.gcccd.edu

01 Chancellor .... Dr. Cindy MILES
10 Vice Chanc Business Services .... Vacant
15 Vice Chanc Human Resources .... Mr. Tim CORCORAN

*Cuyamaca College (I)

900 Rancho San Diego Parkway, El Cajon CA 92019-4304
County: San Diego FICE Identification: 021113
Unit ID: 113218
Telephone: (619) 660-4000 Carnegie Class: Assoc/HT-Mix Trad/Non
FAX Number: (619) 660-4399 Calendar System: Semester
URL: www.cuyamaca.edu
Established: 1978 Annual Undergrad Tuition & Fees (In-District): $1,388
Enrollment: 8,644 Coed
Affiliation or Control: State/Local IRS Status: 501(c)3
Highest Offering: Associate Degree
Accreditation: WJ

02 President .... Dr. Julianna BARNES
05 Interim Vice President Instruction .... Mr. Pat SETZER
32 Vice Pres Student Services .... Dr. Scott THAYER
11 Vice Pres Admin Services .... Ms. Sahar ABUSHABAN
81 Dean of Math/Sci/Engineering .... Dr. Scott HERRIN
79 Int Dean of Arts/Human/Social Sci .... Dr. Peter UTGAARD
72 Dean of Career Technical Education .... Dr. Kate ALDER
08 Dean Learning/Technology Resources .... Ms. Kerry KILBER REBMAN
88 Acting Assistant Dean EOPS .... Ms. Nanyamka HILL
41 Assoc Dean Athletics .... Mr. Ryan SHUMAKER
35 Assoc Dean Student Affairs .... Dr. Lauren VAKNIN
38 Interim Dean Counseling Services .... Ms. Nicole JONES
37 Director of Financial Aid .... Mr. Ray REYES
07 Int Director Admissions & Records .... Ms. Sheryl ASHLEY
18 Facilities Director .... Mr. Bruce FARNHAM
04 Executive Asst to President .... Ms. Valeri WILSON

*Grossmont College (J)

8800 Grossmont College Drive, El Cajon CA 92020-1799
County: San Diego FICE Identification: 001208
Unit ID: 115296
Telephone: (619) 644-7000 Carnegie Class: Assoc/HT-High Trad
FAX Number: (619) 644-7922 Calendar System: Semester
URL: www.grossmont.edu
Established: 1961 Annual Undergrad Tuition & Fees (In-District): $1,388
Enrollment: 18,040 Coed
Affiliation or Control: State/Local IRS Status: 501(c)3
Highest Offering: Associate Degree
Accreditation: WJ, ADNUR, CEA, COARC, CVT, OTA

02 President .... Dr. Nabil ABU-GHAZALEH
05 Vice Pres of Academic Affairs .... Dr. Katrina VANDERWOUDE
32 Int Sr Dean CPIE/Student Services .... Dr. Aaron STARCK
38 Dean Counseling Svcs .... Ms. Martha CLAVELLE
72 Dean Career & Technical Workforce .... Mr. Javier AYALA
81 Dean Math/Natural Sci/Phys Educ .... Dr. Mike REESE
60 Int Dean Arts/Languages/Comm .... Ms. Susan SCHWARZ
79 Dean English/Social & Behav Sci .... Mr. Agustin ALBARRAN
08 Int Dean of Learning Resources .... Dr. Taylor RUHL
35 Associate Dean Student Affairs .... Ms. Victoria KERBA MILLER
09 Director of Institutional Research .... Mr. Christopher TARMAN
10 Chief Business Officer .... Vacant
15 Director Personnel Services .... Vacant
18 Chief Facilities/Physical Plant .... Mr. Ken EMMONS
26 Chief Public Relations Officer .... Vacant
36 Director Student Placement .... Ms. Nancy DAVIS
37 Director Student Financial Aid .... Mr. Michael COPENHAVER
96 Director of Purchasing .... Ms. Linda BERTOLUCCI

Gurnick Academy of Medical Arts (K)

2121 S. El Camino Real Bldg C200, San Mateo CA 94403
County: San Mateo FICE Identification: 041698
Unit ID: 459213
Telephone: (650) 685-6616 Carnegie Class: Not Classified
FAX Number: (650) 685-6640 Calendar System: Other
URL: www.gurnick.edu
Established: 2004 Annual Undergrad Tuition & Fees: N/A
Enrollment: 873 Coed
Affiliation or Control: Proprietary IRS Status: Proprietary
Highest Offering: Associate Degree
Accreditation: ABHES, PTAA, RAD

01 CEO .... Konstantin GOURJI
12 Campus Director .... Debra FERRARI
11 Chief Operating Officer .... Burke MALIN
05 Chief Academic Officer .... Larisa REVZINA

Hartnell College (L)

411 Central Avenue, Salinas CA 93901-1697
County: Monterey FICE Identification: 001209
Unit ID: 115393
Telephone: (831) 755-6700 Carnegie Class: Assoc/HT-High Trad
FAX Number: (831) 755-6751 Calendar System: Semester
URL: www.hartnell.edu
Established: 1920 Annual Undergrad Tuition & Fees (In-District): $1,420
Enrollment: 9,800 Coed
Affiliation or Control: State/Local IRS Status: 501(c)3
Highest Offering: Associate Degree
Accreditation: WJ, #COARC

01 Superintendent/President .... Dr. Willard LEWALLEN
32 VP Student Affairs .... Dr. Romero JALOMO
10 VP Administrative Services .... Mr. Marty PARSONS
13 VP Information & Tech Systems .... Mr. David PHILLIPS
05 VP Academic Affairs .... Ms. Lori KILDAL
30 VP Advancement/Development .... Ms. Jackie CRUZ
15 Assoc VP Human Resources/EEO .... Ms. Terri PYER
21 Controller .... Vacant
18 Director of Facilities .... Mr. Joseph REYES
20 Dean Academic Aff Programs/Support .... Ms. Kathy MENDELSOHN
81 Dean Academic Afts Math/Science .... Ms. Shannon BLISS
35 Director of Student Life .... Mr. Augustine NEVAREZ
26 Director of Communications .... Ms. Esmeralda OWENS
88 Dir of Student Affairs EOPS/DSPS .... Mr. Paul CASEY
66 Dean Academic Affairs/Nursing .... Ms. Debra KACZMAR
72 Dean Academic Afts Adv Tech .... Dr. Zahi ATALLAH
83 Dean Acad Affs Soc/Fine Lang Arts .... Dr. Celine PINET
88 Dean South County Educ Programs .... Ms. Renata FUNKE
04 Senior Executive Assistant .... Ms. Lucille SERRANO
35 Dean of Student Affairs .... Ms. Mary DOMINGUEZ

09 Director of Institutional Research .... Dr. Brian LOFMAN
101 Secretary of the Institution/Board .... Ms. Lucille SERRANO
35 Dean of Student Affairs .... Dr. Mark SANCHEZ
41 Director Athletics .... Mr. Daniel TERESA
45 Dean Inst Planning and Effective .... Dr. Brian LOFMAN

Harvey Mudd College (A)

301 Platt Boulevard, Claremont CA 91711-5990
County: Los Angeles FICE Identification: 001171
Unit ID: 115409
Telephone: (909) 621-8000 Carnegie Class: Bac-A&S
FAX Number: (909) 621-8360 Calendar System: Semester
URL: www.hmc.edu
Established: 1955 Annual Undergrad Tuition & Fees: $50,649
Enrollment: 804 Coed
Affiliation or Control: Independent Non-Profit IRS Status: 501(c)3
Highest Offering: Baccalaureate
Accreditation: WC, ENG

01 President .... Dr. Maria M. KLAWE
30 Vice President Advancement .... Mr. Daniel MACALUSO
10 Vice President Admin/Fin/Treasurer .... Mr. Andrew R. DORANTES
05 VP Acad Affairs/Dean of the Faculty .... Dr. Jeffrey GROVES
07 Vice Pres Admissions/Financial Aid .... Ms. Thyra BRIGGS
32 VP Student Affairs/Dean of Students .... Dr. Jon JACOBSEN
13 VP/CIO .... Mr. Joseph VAUGHAN
09 Asst VP Institutional Research .... Vacant
15 AVP of Human Resources .... Ms. Cynthia A. BECKWITH
18 AVP Facilities/Physical Plant .... Ms. Theresa LAUER
28 Assoc Dean Institutional Diversity .... Ms. Sumun (Sumi) PENDAKUR
06 Registrar .... Mr. Mark ASHLEY
26 Director of College Relations .... Ms. Stephanie GRAHAM
29 Director of Alumni Relations .... Ms. Jennifer GREEN
37 Director of Student Financial Aid .... Ms. Gilma LOPEZ
101 Director of Pres Ofc/Secy to Board .... Ms. Karen ANGEMI
100 Chief of Staff .... Ms. Karen ANGEMI

Henley-Putnam University (B)

2107 N. First Street, Suite 210, San Jose CA 95131
County: Santa Clara Identification: 666120
Telephone: (408) 453-9900 Carnegie Class: Not Classified
FAX Number: (775) 255-2741 Calendar System: Quarter
URL: www.henley-putnam.edu
Established: 2001 Annual Undergrad Tuition & Fees: N/A
Enrollment: N/A Coed
Affiliation or Control: Proprietary IRS Status: Proprietary
Highest Offering: Doctorate
Accreditation: DEAC

01 President .... Jim P. KILLIN
05 Chief Academic Officer .... Dr. Amy DIMAIO
88 Provost of Co-Curricular Activites .... Amanda MORROW-JENSEN
10 Director of Finance .... Ray ASAD
07 Director of Admissions .... Nancy REGGIO

Herguan University (C)

595 Lawrence Expressway, Sunnyvale CA 94085
County: Santa Clara Identification: 667236
Telephone: (408) 481-9988 Carnegie Class: Not Classified
FAX Number: (408) 749-1111 Calendar System: Semester
URL: www.herguanuniversity.edu
Established: 2005 Annual Graduate Tuition & Fees: N/A
Enrollment: N/A Coed
Affiliation or Control: Proprietary IRS Status: Proprietary
Highest Offering: Master's; No Undergraduates
Accreditation: ACICS

01 President .... Dr. D. Kandy SIMMONS
07 Director of Admissions .... Sharon ZHOU

High Tech High Graduate School of Education (D)

2861 Womble Road, San Diego CA 92106-6025
County: San Diego Identification: 667118
Telephone: (619) 398-4902 Carnegie Class: Not Classified
FAX Number: (619) 758-1960 Calendar System: Other
URL: gse.hightechhigh.org
Established: 2007 Annual Graduate Tuition & Fees: N/A
Enrollment: N/A Coed
Affiliation or Control: Independent Non-Profit IRS Status: 501(c)3
Highest Offering: Master's; No Undergraduates
Accreditation: @WC

01 President .... Larry ROSENSTOCK
05 Acting Academic Dean .... Ben DALEY
11 Chief Admin Officer/General Counsel .... Maria HEREDIA
12 Director of Clinical Sites .... Ben DALEY
32 Director Student Affairs .... Hayley MURUGESAN

Holy Names University (E)

3500 Mountain Boulevard, Oakland CA 94619-1699
County: Alameda FICE Identification: 001183
Unit ID: 115728
Telephone: (510) 436-1000 Carnegie Class: Masters/M
FAX Number: (510) 436-1199 Calendar System: Semester
URL: www.hnu.edu
Established: 1868 Annual Undergrad Tuition & Fees: $35,666
Enrollment: 1,191 Coed
Affiliation or Control: Independent Non-Profit IRS Status: 501(c)3
Highest Offering: Master's
Accreditation: WC, NURSE

01 Interim President .... Dr. Jeanie WATSON
05 Vice President for Academic Affairs .... Dr. Lizbeth J. MARTIN
10 Vice President for Finance/Admin .... Mr. Michael GROENER
32 Vice President for Student Affairs .... Mr. Michael S. MILLER
30 Interim VP University Advance .... Ms. Theresa NELSON
84 VP Strategic Enroll Mgmt .... Mr. Alan LIEBRECHT
06 Registrar .... Ms. Margo LANDY
08 Director of Library Services .... Ms. Nicole GREENLAND
37 Dir Student Financial Assistance .... Ms. Tam LEE-OPERARIO
31 Director Campus Services .... Mr. Luis GUERRA
42 Co-Director of Campus Ministry ...... Ms. Jenny GIRARD-MALLEY
42 Co-Director of Campus Ministry .... Fr. Sal RAGUSA
41 Director of Athletics .... Ms. Debbie SNELL
26 Director Marketing/Communications .... Ms. Lesley SIMS
29 Director of Alumni Relations .... Ms. Frances WILLIAMS
13 Director Information Technology .... Mr. Jay CASTILLO
15 Director Human Resources .... Ms. Patricia BARTON
04 Executive Asst to President .... Ms. Vicki TOM
09 Director of Institutional Research .... Mr. Francisco HERRERA
18 Chief Facilities/Physical Plant .... Mr. Luis GUERRA

Hope International University (F)

2500 E Nutwood Avenue, Fullerton CA 92831-3104
County: Orange FICE Identification: 001252
Unit ID: 120537
Telephone: (714) 879-3901 Carnegie Class: Masters/M
FAX Number: (714) 681-7451 Calendar System: 4/1/4
URL: www.hiu.edu
Established: 1928 Annual Undergrad Tuition & Fees: $28,550
Enrollment: 1,329 Coed
Affiliation or Control: Independent Non-Profit IRS Status: 501(c)3
Highest Offering: Master's
Accreditation: WC, BI, MFCD

01 President .... Dr. John L. DERRY
04 Exec Asst to the President .... Mrs. Sharon L. CARTER
05 Vice President for Academic Affairs .... Dr. Paul H. ALEXANDER
49 Dean College of Arts and Sciences .... Dr. Steve EDGINGTON
50 Dean College of Business & Mgmt ...... Dr. LaSharnda BECKWITH
53 Dean College of Education .... Dr. Douglas S. DOMENE
88 Dean College of Ministry & Bib Stds .... Dr. Joe GRANA
83 Dean College of Psych & Counseling .... Dr. Laura L. STEELE
09 Assc VP for Education Effectiveness .... Dr. Tamsen MURRAY
08 Librarian .... Mrs. Robin HARTMAN
06 Registrar .... Mr. Ron ARCHER
10 Vice President for Business/Finance .... Mr. Frank SCOTTI
37 Director Student Financial Services ...... Mrs. Shannon O'SHIELDS
15 Director of Human Resources .... Mrs. Wende HOLTZEN
13 Director of Information Systems .... Mr. Mike CARTER
18 Director of Campus Facilities .... Mr. Steve MULLINS
30 Vice Pres Institutional Advancement .... Mr. Michael MULRYAN
26 Chief Public Relations Officer .... Mr. Michael MULRYAN
32 Vice President for Student Affairs .... Dr. Mark COMEAUX
36 Dean of Students .... Mr. Reid W. MCCORMICK
41 Athletic Director .... Mr. John G. TUREK
42 Chaplain/Director Campus Ministry .... Mr. Bryan A. SANDS
85 Director of International Students .... Mrs. Judy E. KIM
38 Director Student Counseling .... Dr. Laura L. STEELE
36 Dir Student Career Services .... Mrs. Kirsten M. MCCORMICK
84 Vice Pres for Enrollment Management .... Mrs. Teresa L. SMITH
07 Director Undergraduate Admissions .. Mrs. Dionne K. GUTIERREZ
106 Dir Learning Technology .... Ms. Micah N. ALSTON

Horizon University (G)

5331 Mt Alifan Drive, San Diego CA 92111
County: San Diego FICE Identification: 041405
Unit ID: 457226
Telephone: (858) 695-8587 Carnegie Class: Spec-4-yr-Faith
FAX Number: (858) 695-9527 Calendar System: Semester
URL: www.horizonuniversity.edu
Established: 1993 Annual Undergrad Tuition & Fees: $9,150
Enrollment: 34 Coed
Affiliation or Control: Independent Non-Profit IRS Status: 501(c)3
Highest Offering: Baccalaureate
Accreditation: BI

01 President .... Mr. Bill GOODRICH
05 Academic Dean & Exec Vice President ...... Mr. Dave KOSOBUCKI
11 Dean of Administration .... Ms. Becky KIRSININKAS
10 Chief Financial Officer .... Ms. Debbie MARSHALL
32 Dean of Students .... Mr. Tracy GRAY

Humphreys College (H)

6650 Inglewood Street, Stockton CA 95207-3896
County: San Joaquin FICE Identification: 001212
Unit ID: 115773
Telephone: (209) 478-0800 Carnegie Class: Bac-Diverse
FAX Number: (209) 478-8721 Calendar System: Quarter
URL: www.humphreys.edu
Established: 1896 Annual Undergrad Tuition & Fees: $13,212
Enrollment: 809 Coed
Affiliation or Control: Independent Non-Profit IRS Status: 501(c)3
Highest Offering: First Professional Degree
Accreditation: WC

01 President .... Dr. Robert G. HUMPHREYS, JR.
05 Dn Instruction/Dir Arts & Sciences .... Ms. Cynthia BECERRA
11 Dean Administration/Ofc Admin Pgm .... Ms. Wilma OKAMOTO-VAUGHN
09 Dean of Institutional Research .... Dr. Jess BONDS
61 Dean Law School .... Mr. Patrick L. PIGGOTT
20 Associate Dean of Instruction .... Dr. Lisa KOOREN
06 Registrar .... Ms. Maria GARCIA-MILLER
07 Director of Admissions .... Ms. Santa E. LOPEZ
26 Chief Public Relations Officer .... Vacant
08 Head Librarian .... Dr. Stanislav PERKNER
88 Director Court Reporting Program .... Mrs. Kay REINDL
10 Chief Business Officer .... Ms. Carol KRAMLICH
37 Director Student Financial Aid .... Ms. Rita FRANCO
13 Director of Information Services .... Mr. Fred WHITE

Hussian College-Relativity Campus California (I)

1201 West 5th St., Ste F10, Los Angeles CA 90017
Telephone: (800) 762-1993 Identification: 770969
Accreditation: ACCSC

† Branch campus of Hussian School of Art, Philadelphia, PA

Imperial Valley College (J)

380 E Aten Road, Imperial CA 92251-0158
County: Imperial FICE Identification: 001214
Unit ID: 115861
Telephone: (760) 352-8320 Carnegie Class: Assoc/HT-High Trad
FAX Number: (760) 355-2663 Calendar System: Semester
URL: www.imperial.edu
Established: 1922 Annual Undergrad Tuition & Fees (In-District): $1,365
Enrollment: 8,135 Coed
Affiliation or Control: Local IRS Status: 501(c)3
Highest Offering: Associate Degree
Accreditation: WJ, EMT

01 Superintendent/President .... Dr. Victor JAIME
05 Vice President Academic Services .... Dr. Nicholas AKINKUOYE
32 Vice Pres Student Services .... Dr. Martha GARCIA
10 VP Administrative Services .... Mr. John LAU
15 Int Chief Human Resources Officer .... Mr. John LAU
103 Dean Economic & Worforce Develop .... Mr. Efrain SILVA
76 Dean of Health & Public Safety .... Mrs. Tina AGUIRRE
49 Dean Arts/Letters/Learning Svc .... Mr. David ZIELINSKI
38 Dean of Counseling .... Vacant
35 Dean Student Affs/Enrollment Svcs .... Vacant
07 Director of Admissions and Records .... Ms. Gloria CARMONA
37 Director of Financial Aid .... Ms. Lisa SEALS
09 Dir Institutional Research .... Mr. Jose CARRILLO
59 Dir Child/Family/Consumer Sciences .... Ms. Rebecca GREEN
26 Chief Public Relations Officer .... Mr. Bill GAY
13 Chief Technology Officer .... Mr. Jeff ENZ
81 Dean of Math and Sciences .... Vacant
96 Director of Purchasing .... Mrs. Betty KAKIUCHI

Institute of Technology (K)

564 West Herndon Avenue, Clovis CA 93612
County: Fresno FICE Identification: 030675
Unit ID: 431141
Telephone: (559) 297-4500 Carnegie Class: Assoc/HVT-High Non
FAX Number: (559) 297-5822 Calendar System: Semester
URL: www.iot.edu
Established: Annual Undergrad Tuition & Fees: N/A
Enrollment: 1,509 Coed
Affiliation or Control: Proprietary IRS Status: Proprietary
Highest Offering: Associate Degree
Accreditation: ACCSC, ACFEI

01 President .... Timothy VOGELEY

Institute of Technology (L)

5601 Stoddard Road, Modesto CA 95356
Telephone: (209) 572-7800 Identification: 770554
Accreditation: ACCSC, ACFEI

Institute of Technology (M)

1755 Hilltop Drive, Redding CA 96002
Telephone: (530) 224-1000 Identification: 770555
Accreditation: ACCSC

Intercoast College (N)

3745 W. Chapman Avenue, Orange CA 92868
County: Orange FICE Identification: 025594
Unit ID: 366289
Telephone: (714) 712-7900 Carnegie Class: Spec 2-yr-Health
FAX Number: (714) 937-1983 Calendar System: Other
URL: www.intercoast.edu
Established: 1985 Annual Undergrad Tuition & Fees: N/A
Enrollment: 357 Coed
Affiliation or Control: Proprietary IRS Status: Proprietary
Highest Offering: Associate Degree
Accreditation: CNCE

01 President .... Geeta A. BROWN

Interior Designers Institute (A)

1061 Camelback Road, Newport Beach CA 92660-3228
County: Orange FICE Identification: 025203
Unit ID: 116226
Telephone: (949) 675-4451 Carnegie Class: Spec-4-yr-Arts
FAX Number: (949) 759-0667 Calendar System: Quarter
URL: www.idi.edu
Established: 1984 Annual Undergrad Tuition & Fees: $18,050
Enrollment: 210 Coed
Affiliation or Control: Proprietary IRS Status: Proprietary
Highest Offering: Master's
Accreditation: ACCSC, CIDA

01 Executive Director .... Ms. Judy DEATON
37 Financial Aid Director .... Ms. Shanen FOYE

International Professional School of Bodywork (B)

9025 Balboa Avenue, Suite 130, San Diego CA 92123
County: San Diego FICE Identification: 041347
Unit ID: 454740
Telephone: (858) 505-1100 Carnegie Class: Spec 2-yr-Health
FAX Number: (858) 565-4118 Calendar System: Quarter
URL: www.ipsb.edu
Established: 1977 Annual Undergrad Tuition & Fees: $7,544
Enrollment: 169 Coed
Affiliation or Control: Proprietary IRS Status: Proprietary
Highest Offering: Associate Degree
Accreditation: #COMTA

01 Chief Executive Officer (President) .... Vacant
05 Chief Academic Officer .... Shari GRAYSON
06 Registrar .... Abigail ALVAREZ
10 Chief Business Officer .... Cindy NAUTA

International Reformed University and Seminary (C)

125 S. Vermont Avenue, Los Angeles CA 90004
County: Los Angeles Identification: 667132
Telephone: (213) 381-0081 Carnegie Class: Not Classified
FAX Number: (213) 381-0010 Calendar System: Semester
URL: www.irus.edu
Established: 1977 Annual Undergrad Tuition & Fees: N/A
Enrollment: N/A Coed
Affiliation or Control: Independent Non-Profit IRS Status: 501(c)3
Highest Offering: Doctorate
Accreditation: BI

01 President .... Dr. Hun Sung PARK
05 Academic Dean .... Dr. Kwang Hoon LEE
32 Dean of Students .... Dr. Young Chung JIN
10 Business Manager .... Dr. Joha OH
108 Director for Assessment & Planning .... Dr. Yumee RAH
88 Accreditation Liaison .... Dr. Grace KOOK
08 Librarian .... Ms. Hannah LEE
88 Secretary .... Ms. Sunkyung KIM

International Technological University (D)

2711 N. First Street, San Jose CA 95134
County: Santa Clara Identification: 667070
Unit ID: 443128
Telephone: (888) 488-4968 Carnegie Class: Masters/L
FAX Number: (408) 331-1026 Calendar System: Trimester
URL: www.itu.edu
Established: 1994 Annual Graduate Tuition & Fees: N/A
Enrollment: 1,866 Coed
Affiliation or Control: Independent Non-Profit IRS Status: 501(c)3
Highest Offering: Doctorate; No Undergraduates
Accreditation: WC

01 President and CEO .... Dr. Gregory O'BRIEN
05 Provost .... Dr. Barry RYAN
10 CFO .... Edward LAM
06 Registrar .... Nancy Jo BLACK
08 Head Librarian .... Marion HAYES
101 Board Liaison .... Angie LO
26 Dir Marketing/Comm/Admissions .... Charles AMITH

International Theological Seminary (E)

3215-3225 Tyler Avenue, El Monte CA 91731-3355
County: Los Angeles Identification: 666360
Unit ID: 396985
Telephone: (626) 448-0023 Carnegie Class: Not Classified
FAX Number: (626) 350-6343 Calendar System: Quarter
URL: www.itsla.edu
Established: 1982 Annual Undergrad Tuition & Fees: N/A
Enrollment: N/A Coed
Affiliation or Control: Independent Non-Profit IRS Status: 501(c)3
Highest Offering: Doctorate
Accreditation: THEOL

01 President .... Dr. James S. LEE
05 Vice President for Academics .... Dr. Jaretha Joy PALMER
11 Vice President for Administration .... Ms. Monica KAO
32 Acting Dean of Students .... Dr. Premkumar DHARMARAJ
06 Registrar .... Mrs. Zenda Gay P. EUSEBIO
07 Director of Admissions .... Mr. Paul YANG

John F. Kennedy University (F)

100 Ellinwood Way, Pleasant Hill CA 94523-4817
County: Contra Costa FICE Identification: 004484
Unit ID: 116712
Telephone: (925) 969-3300 Carnegie Class: Masters/M
FAX Number: (925) 969-3399 Calendar System: Quarter
URL: www.jfku.edu
Established: 1964 Annual Undergrad Tuition & Fees: N/A
Enrollment: 1,230 Coed
Affiliation or Control: Independent Non-Profit IRS Status: 501(c)3
Highest Offering: Doctorate
Accreditation: WC, CLPSY, IACBE

01 President .... Ms. Debra BEAN

John Paul the Great Catholic University (G)

220 West Grand Avenue, Escondido CA 92025
County: San Diego FICE Identification: 041937
Unit ID: 462354
Telephone: (858) 653-6740 Carnegie Class: Bac-Diverse
FAX Number: (858) 653-3791 Calendar System: Quarter
URL: www.jpcatholic.com
Established: 2003 Annual Undergrad Tuition & Fees: $24,900
Enrollment: 284 Coed
Affiliation or Control: Independent Non-Profit IRS Status: 501(c)3
Highest Offering: Master's
Accreditation: WC

01 President .... Dr. Derry CONNOLLY
05 Chief Academic Officer .... Dr. Michael BARBER
10 VP for Finance .... Vlad BOLSAKOV
11 VP for Administration .... Lidy CONNOLLY
07 VP of Admissions .... Martin HAROLD
13 VP for Technology & Real Estate .... Kevin MEZIERE
32 Dean of Students .... Julia CARRANO
37 Director of Financial Aid .... Lisa WILLIAMS
06 Registrar .... Nick HEYE
42 Director Campus Ministry .... Fr Luke HEINTSCHEL
09 Director Institutional Research .... Clare OVEN
39 Director Student Life .... Joe CROSS

Kaiser Permanente School of Allied Health Sciences (H)

938 Marina Way South, Richmond CA 94804
County: Contra Costa Identification: 667152
Telephone: (510) 231-5000 Carnegie Class: Not Classified
FAX Number: (510) 231-5001 Calendar System: Quarter
URL: www.kpsahs.org
Established: 1989 Annual Undergrad Tuition & Fees: N/A
Enrollment: N/A Coed
Affiliation or Control: Proprietary IRS Status: Proprietary
Highest Offering: Baccalaureate
Accreditation: WC, DMS, NMT, RAD

01 Medical Director .... Dr. C. Daryl JONES
05 Dean of Academic Affairs .... Dr. Van MUSE
10 Assoc Director of Finance/CFO .... Pamela FRESSLEY
11 Regional School Administrator/CEO .... James FITZGIBBONS
09 Dir Assessment/Inst Research .... Mr. Bert CHRISTENSEN

*Kern Community College District (I)

2100 Chester Avenue, Bakersfield CA 93301-4099
County: Kern FICE Identification: 006994
Unit ID: 436313
Telephone: (661) 336-5100 Carnegie Class: N/A
FAX Number: (661) 336-5134
URL: www.kccd.edu

01 Chancellor .... Ms. Sandra V. SERRANO
05 Vice Chanc Educational Services .... Vacant
11 Vice Chanc Operations Management .... Mr. Sean P. JAMES
15 Vice Chanc Human Resources .... Mr. Abe ALI
30 Assoc Vice Chanc Govt/External Rels .... Ms. Michelle BRESSO
10 Chief Financial Officer .... Mr. Tom J. BURKE
13 Asst Dir Information Technology .... Mr. Eddie D. ALVARADO
43 General Counsel .... Mr. Christopher HINE

*Bakersfield College (J)

1801 Panorama Drive, Bakersfield CA 93305-1299
County: Kern FICE Identification: 001118
Unit ID: 109819
Telephone: (661) 395-4011 Carnegie Class: Assoc/MT-VT-High Trad
FAX Number: (661) 395-4241 Calendar System: Semester
URL: www.bakersfieldcollege.edu
Established: 1913 Annual Undergrad Tuition & Fees (In-District): $1,326
Enrollment: 18,698 Coed
Affiliation or Control: State/Local IRS Status: 501(c)3
Highest Offering: Baccalaureate
Accreditation: WJ, EMT, RAD

02 President .... Dr. Sonya CHRISTIAN
05 Exec VP Instruction .... Ms. Nan GOMEZ-HEITZEBERG
10 VP Finance & Administrative Svcs .... Dr. Anthony CULPEPPER
32 Vice Pres Student Affairs .... Dr. Zavareh DADABHOY
72 Dean Learning Resources/Info Tech .... Dr. Todd COSTON
30 Director Foundation & Development .... Mr. Tom GELDER
18 Dir Facilities/Maintenance/Ops .... Mr. Bill POTTER
12 Director Delano Center .... Mr. Rich MCCROW
37 Assistant Financial Aid Director .... Ms. Jennifer ACHAN
07 Director Enrollment Services .... Mrs. Suzanne A. VAUGHN
26 Dir Marketing & Public Relations .... Mrs. Amber CHIANG
04 Admin Assistant to the President .... Ms. Jennifer MARDEN
13 Director Information Technology .... Mr. Todd COSTON
20 Dean of Instruction .... Ms. Kate PLUTA
66 Dean of Instruction .... Ms. Cindy COLLIER
41 Director of Athletics .... Ms. Sandi TAYLOR
20 Dean of Instruction .... Ms. Liz ROZELL
20 Dean of Instruction .... Dr. Emmanuel MOURTZANOS

*Cerro Coso Community College (K)

College Heights Boulevard, Ridgecrest CA 93555-7777
County: Kern FICE Identification: 010111
Unit ID: 111896
Telephone: (760) 384-6100 Carnegie Class: Assoc/MT-VT-High Non
FAX Number: (760) 375-4776 Calendar System: Semester
URL: www.cerrocoso.edu
Established: 1973 Annual Undergrad Tuition & Fees (In-District): $1,290
Enrollment: 4,731 Coed
Affiliation or Control: State/Local IRS Status: 501(c)3
Highest Offering: Associate Degree
Accreditation: WJ

02 President .... Ms. A. Jill BOARD
05 Vice President Academic Affairs .... Dr. Corey MARVIN
32 Vice President of Student Services .... Ms. Heather OSTASH
10 Vice Pres Finance/Admin Services .... Ms. Gale LEBSOCK
12 Dir Eastern Sierra College Center .... Ms. Deanna CAMPBELL
12 Dir of East Kern/Kern River Valley .... Ms. Lisa STEPHENS
75 Dean Career Technical Education .... Mr. Michael KANE
38 Dir of Counseling Svcs/SSSP .... Ms. Christine SMALL
07 Dir Admiss/Records/VA/Fin Aid .... Ms. Jennifer SAN NICOLAS
21 Accounting Manager .... Ms. Lisa COUCH
15 Human Resources Manager .... Ms. Resa HESS
88 Program Mgr Child Development Ctr .... Ms. Jessica KRALL
26 Mgr Public Rel/Marketing & Dev .... Ms. Natalie DORRELL
13 Director Information Technology .... Mr. Michael CAMPBELL
35 Dir Student Programs & Outreach .... Ms. Pam CAMPBELL
106 Director Distance Education .... Ms. Rebecca PANG
04 Administrative Asst to President .... Ms. Jennifer CURTIS
41 Athletic Director .... Mr. Kristopher DICKSON
88 Director of Access Programs .... Ms. Paula SUOREZ

*Porterville College (L)

100 E College Avenue, Porterville CA 93257-6058
County: Tulare FICE Identification: 001268
Unit ID: 121363
Telephone: (559) 791-2200 Carnegie Class: Assoc/HT-High Trad
FAX Number: (559) 784-4779 Calendar System: Semester
URL: www.portervillecollege.edu
Established: 1927 Annual Undergrad Tuition & Fees (In-District): $1,322
Enrollment: 3,791 Coed
Affiliation or Control: State/Local IRS Status: 501(c)3
Highest Offering: Associate Degree
Accreditation: WJ

02 President .... Dr. Rosa F. CARLSON
05 Vice President Instruction .... Mr. Bill HENRY
32 Vice President Student Services .... Mr. Valentin GARCIA
10 Vice Pres Finance & Admin Services .... Dr. Arlitha WILLIAMS-HARMON
04 Administrative Asst to President .... Ms. Carol BROWN
20 Dean Instruction .... Ms. Sheri JONES
23 Assoc Dean Health Careers .... Ms. Kim BEHRENS
18 Maintenance & Operations Manager .... Mr. John WORD
84 Director Enrollment Management .... Ms. Erin CRUZ
15 Human Resources Manager .... Ms. Andreia CUEVAS
37 Assistant Director Financial Aid .... Ms. Tiffany HAYNES
09 Institutional Researcher .... Mr. Michael CARLEY
13 Director Information Technology .... Mr. Jay NAVARRETTE
35 Director Student Services .... Ms. Diane THOMPSON
21 Accounting Manager .... Ms. Sonia HUCKABAY
88 Program Manager Child Dev Center .... Ms. Karen BALL
08 Interim Director Library .... Ms. Lorie BARKER
26 Pub Relations/Mktng/Outreach Mgr .... Vacant
105 Web Content Editor .... Vacant
41 Athletic Director .... Mr. Joseph CASCIO

Kingston University (M)

12100 Imperial Hwy, Ste 101, Norwalk CA 90650
County: Los Angeles Identification: 667237
Telephone: (562) 868-6488 Carnegie Class: Not Classified
FAX Number: (562) 868-6378 Calendar System: Other
URL: www.kingstonuniversity.edu
Established: 2002 Annual Undergrad Tuition & Fees: N/A
Enrollment: N/A Coed
Affiliation or Control: Proprietary IRS Status: Proprietary
Highest Offering: Master's
Accreditation: ACICS

01 President .... Stephen ATCHLEY
05 Dean of Academics .... Gilbert SANCHEZ
11 Administrator .... Rosalia HSIEH

La Sierra University (A)

4500 Riverwalk Parkway, Riverside CA 92515-8247
County: Riverside FICE Identification: 001215
Unit ID: 117627
Telephone: (951) 785-2000 Carnegie Class: Masters/S
FAX Number: (951) 785-2901 Calendar System: Quarter
URL: www.lasierra.edu
Established: 1922 Annual Undergrad Tuition & Fees: $30,471
Enrollment: 2,510 Coed
Affiliation or Control: Seventh-day Adventist IRS Status: 501(c)3
Highest Offering: Doctorate
Accreditation: WC, MUS, SW, THEOL

01 President .... Dr. Randal R. WISBEY
05 Provost .... Dr. Joy FEHR
10 Vice President for Finance .... Mr. David GERIGUIS
32 Vice President for Student Life .... Ms. Yamilet BAZAN
30 Vice Pres Advancement/Univ Rels .... Mr. Norman YERGEN
84 Vice Pres Enrollment Services .... Mr. David R. LOFTHOUSE
26 VP Communication/Integrated Mktg .... Dr. Marilyn THOMSEN
21 Associate Vice President Finance .... Ms. Pamela CHRISPENS
20 Interim Associate Provost .... Ms. Cindy PARKHURST
49 Dean College Arts/Sciences .... Dr. April SUMMITT
50 Dean School of Business .... Dr. John THOMAS
53 Dean School of Education .... Dr. Ginger KETTING-WELLER
73 Dean School of Divinity .... Dr. Bailey GILLIESPIE
35 Dean of Students .... Ms. Marjorie ROBINSON
27 Exec Director University Relations .... Mr. Larry BECKER
55 Director Adult Evening Program .... Ms. Nancy DITTEMORE
29 Director Alumni Relations .... Ms. Julie NARDUCCI
15 Director Human Resources .... Ms. Dell Jean VAN FOSSEN
08 Director Library .... Ms. Kitty SIMMONS
37 Director Student Financial Services .... Ms. Esther KINZER
42 Director Campus Ministries .... Mr. Samuel E. LEONOR, JR.
13 Director Information Technology .... Mr. Geoff INGRAM
09 Director of Institutional Research .... Mr. Guru UPPALA
18 Director Physical Plant .... Mr. Al VALDEZ
38 Director Counseling Center .... Ms. Debra WRIGHT
92 Director Honors Program .... Dr. Douglas R. CLARK
07 Director of Admissions/Registrar .... Mr. Issmael NZAMUTUNA
36 Director Career Services .... Mr. Natan VIGNA
41 Athletic Director .... Mr. Javier KRUMM

LACM, Los Angeles College of Music (B)

300 South Fair Oaks Avenue, Pasadena CA 91105
County: Los Angeles FICE Identification: 038684
Unit ID: 446385
Telephone: (626) 568-8850 Carnegie Class: Spec-4-yr-Arts
FAX Number: (626) 568-8854 Calendar System: Quarter
URL: www.lacm.edu
Established: 1996 Annual Undergrad Tuition & Fees: $24,004
Enrollment: 147 Coed
Affiliation or Control: Proprietary IRS Status: Proprietary
Highest Offering: Associate Degree
Accreditation: MUS

01 President .... Tom AYLESBURY
05 EVP Academic Operations .... Mike PACKER
06 Registrar .... Jorge OJEDA
32 Dean of Students & Faculty .... Dave POZZI
37 Director of Financial Aid .... Mary OLMOS

Laguna College of Art & Design (C)

2222 Laguna Canyon Road,
Laguna Beach CA 92651-1136
County: Orange FICE Identification: 023305
Unit ID: 117168
Telephone: (949) 376-6000 Carnegie Class: Spec-4-yr-Arts
FAX Number: (949) 376-6009 Calendar System: Semester
URL: www.lcad.edu
Established: 1961 Annual Undergrad Tuition & Fees: $28,100
Enrollment: 566 Coed
Affiliation or Control: Independent Non-Profit IRS Status: 501(c)3
Highest Offering: Master's
Accreditation: WC, ART

01 President .... Dr. Jonathan BURKE
05 Vice President Academic Affairs .... Dr. Helene GARRISON
30 Vice Pres of Development .... Mr. Kevin CARTWRIGHT
07 Dean of Admissions .... Mr. Christopher BROWN
10 Chief Financial Officer .... Mr. Jim GODEK
06 Registrar .... Ms. Laura PATRICK
08 Library Director .... Ms. Jennifer WORMSER
04 Assistant to the President .... Ms. Jeni RICHARDS
37 Director Financial Aid .... Mr. Christopher BROWN
09 Director of Institutional Research .... Ms. Laura PATRICK
15 Human Resource Manager .... Ms. Caroline CARLSON
13 Chief Info Technology Officer (CIO) .... Mr. Matt MORTON
18 Chief Facilities/Physical Plant .... Mr. John EERTWEGH
26 Communications Manager .... Mr. Mike STICE
32 Chief Student Affairs/Student Life .... Mr. Doug DAVEE

Lake Tahoe Community College (D)

1 College Drive, South Lake Tahoe CA 96150-4524
County: El Dorado FICE Identification: 012907
Unit ID: 117195
Telephone: (530) 541-4660 Carnegie Class: Assoc/HT-High Non
FAX Number: (530) 541-7852 Calendar System: Quarter
URL: www.ltcc.edu
Established: 1975 Annual Undergrad Tuition & Fees (In-District): $1,224
Enrollment: 2,419 Coed
Affiliation or Control: State/Local IRS Status: 501(c)3
Highest Offering: Associate Degree
Accreditation: WJ

01 Superintendent/President .... Dr. Kindred MURILLO
04 Executive Assistant to President .... Ms. Lisa SHAFER
05 Interim VP Academic Affairs .... Dr. Michelle RISDON
10 Vice Pres Administrative Svcs .... Mr. Jeff DEFRANCO
20 Dean of Instruction & CTE .... Dr. Virginia BERRY
32 Executive Dean of Student Success .... Ms. Sue GOCHIS
20 Dean of Instruction .... Ms. Michelle SOWER
08 Director of Library .... Ms. Lisa FOLEY
13 Director Tech & Education Svcs .... Mr. Dave BURBA
84 Director Enrollment Services .... Ms. Alysa BORELLI
21 Director of Fiscal Services .... Ms. Andrea SALAZAR
15 Director of Human Resources .... Ms. Shelley HANSEN
18 Director of Facilities .... Mr. Randy JOSLIN
88 Int Dir Child Development Center .... Ms. Shawna SARVER
37 Director Financial Aid .... Ms. Julie CATHIE
09 Director of Institutional Research .... Mr. Jeremy BROWN
26 Public Information Officer .... Ms. Diane LEWIS
102 Foundation Director .... Ms. Nancy HARRISON
40 Bookstore Manager .... Mr. Trevor OSTENDORF
96 Purchasing Agent .... Ms. Heather CADE

Lassen Community College (E)

PO Box 3000, 478-200 Highway 139,
Susanville CA 96130-3000
County: Lassen FICE Identification: 001217
Unit ID: 117274
Telephone: (530) 257-6181 Carnegie Class: Assoc/HT-High Non
FAX Number: (530) 251-8872 Calendar System: Semester
URL: www.lassencollege.edu
Established: 1925 Annual Undergrad Tuition & Fees (In-District): $1,127
Enrollment: 2,557 Coed
Affiliation or Control: State/Local IRS Status: 501(c)3
Highest Offering: Associate Degree
Accreditation: WJ

01 District Superintendent/President .... Dr. Marlon R. HALL
04 Assistant to President .... Ms. Julie L. JOHNSTON
05 Exec Vice Pres of Academic Services ... Dr. Terri A. ARMSTRONG
11 Vice Pres Administrative Services .... Mr. Dave CLAUSEN
32 Dean of Student Services .... Mr. Patrick WALTON
08 Librarian .... Dr. John TAYLOR
09 Assoc Dean Inst Effectiveness/Rsrch .... Mr. Brian MURPHY
37 Director Financial Aid .... Mr. Matt LEVINE
35 Director Student Life .... Mr. Francis BEAUJON
41 Athletic Director .... Dr. Terri A. ARMSTRONG
18 Chief Facilities/Physical Plant .... Mr. Gregory COLLINS
15 Director Human Resources .... Ms. Vickie RAMSEY
13 Director of Information Technology .... Mr. David CORLEY

Laurus College (F)

81 Higuera Street, Ste 110, San Luis Obispo CA 93401
County: San Luis Obispo FICE Identification: 041414
Unit ID: 454786
Telephone: (805) 267-1690 Carnegie Class: Not Classified
FAX Number: (805) 352-1307 Calendar System: Quarter
URL: www.lauruscollege.com
Established: 2006 Annual Undergrad Tuition & Fees: N/A
Enrollment: 897 Coed
Affiliation or Control: Proprietary IRS Status: Proprietary
Highest Offering: Associate Degree
Accreditation: ACICS

00 President/CEO .... Dr. David AHN
01 School Chancellor .... Mr. Jeff REDMOND
32 Vice Pres Student Programs .... Ms. Cecilia MORTELA

Le Cordon Bleu College of Culinary Arts (G)

350 Rhode Island Street, San Francisco CA 94103
County: San Francisco FICE Identification: 022202
Unit ID: 111009
Telephone: (888) 897-3222 Carnegie Class: Spec 2-yr-A&S
FAX Number: (415) 771-2194 Calendar System: Other
URL: www.chefs.edu/san-francisco
Established: 1977 Annual Undergrad Tuition & Fees: $14,787
Enrollment: 442 Coed
Affiliation or Control: Proprietary IRS Status: Proprietary
Highest Offering: Associate Degree
Accreditation: ACCSC, ACICS, ACFEI

01 President .... Mr. Marvin SABIBO

† In teach-out mode through September 2017.

Le Cordon Bleu College of Culinary Arts in Los Angeles (H)

530 East Colorado Boulevard, Pasadena CA 91101
County: Los Angeles FICE Identification: 032103
Unit ID: 423980
Telephone: (626) 229-1300 Carnegie Class: Spec 2-yr-A&S
FAX Number: (626) 204-3907 Calendar System: Quarter
URL: www.chefs.edu/los-angeles
Established: 1994 Annual Undergrad Tuition & Fees: $13,975
Enrollment: 1,792 Coed
Affiliation or Control: Proprietary IRS Status: Proprietary
Highest Offering: Associate Degree
Accreditation: ACICS, ACFEI

01 President .... Mr. Michael GIACOMINI

† In teach-out mode through September 2017.

Learnet Academy (I)

3251 W. 6th Street, 2nd Floor, Los Angeles CA 90020
County: Los Angeles Identification: 667223
Telephone: (213) 387-4242 Carnegie Class: Not Classified
FAX Number: (213) 387-5365 Calendar System: Other
URL: www.learnet.edu
Established: 1993 Annual Undergrad Tuition & Fees: N/A
Enrollment: N/A Coed
Affiliation or Control: Proprietary IRS Status: Proprietary
Highest Offering: Associate Degree
Accreditation: ACICS

01 Executive Director .... Ms. Tia SHIN

Life Chiropractic College West (J)

25001 Industrial Boulevard, Hayward CA 94545-2801
County: Alameda FICE Identification: 022285
Unit ID: 117520
Telephone: (510) 780-4500 Carnegie Class: Spec-4-yr-Other Health
FAX Number: (510) 780-4525 Calendar System: Quarter
URL: www.lifewest.edu
Established: 1976 Annual Undergrad Tuition & Fees: N/A
Enrollment: 499 Coed
Affiliation or Control: Independent Non-Profit IRS Status: 501(c)3
Highest Offering: First Professional Degree; No Lower Division
Accreditation: CHIRO

01 President .... Dr. Brian KELLY
03 Executive Vice President .... Dr. Anatole BOGATSKI
05 Vice President of Academic Affairs .... Dr. Scott DONALDSON
17 Vice President of the Health Center .... Dr. Tim GAY
09 Director of Institutional Research .... Dr. Dale JOHNSON
71 Director of Special Projects .... Dr. George CASEY
10 Director of Finance .... Mr. Victor MADAMBA
07 Dean of Admissions .... Dr. Mary LUCUS-FLANNERY
108 Dir of Assessment & Educ Effectiv .... Dr. Kristen GATES
46 Director of Research .... Dr. Monica SMITH
30 Director Institutional Advancement .... Dr. Mark ZIEGLER
51 Director of Continuing Education .... Dr. Laurie ISENBERG
26 Chief Communications Officer .... Vacant
24 Director of Educational Technology .... Mr. Garet MARLING
08 Director Learning Resource Center .... Ms. Annette OSENGA
76 Chair Clinical Education .... Dr. Tamara MACINTYRE
29 Ambassador of Alumni Relations .... Dr. James HAWKINS
37 Director Financial Aid .... Ms. Brenda JOHNSON
06 Registrar .... Ms. Michelle MONTOYA
18 Manager Campus Enhancement .... Mr. Manuel GUTIERREZ
15 Manager Human Resources .... Ms. Joanne GAPUZ
32 Director of Student Life .... Mrs. Jackie BIRON
105 Webmaster .... Mr. Steve SARMIENTO
38 Academic Counselor .... Ms. Lori PINO
40 Bookstore Manager .... Mr. Michael BALDWIN
04 Executive Assistant to President .... Mr. Michael HURSCHMANN
41 Athletic Director .... Mr. Adriann FERRIS
84 Director Enrollment .... Mr. Marc MARTIN

Life Pacific College (K)

1100 W. Covina Boulevard, San Dimas CA 91773-3298
County: Los Angeles FICE Identification: 022706
Unit ID: 117104
Telephone: (909) 599-5433 Carnegie Class: Spec-4-yr-Faith
FAX Number: (909) 599-6690 Calendar System: Semester
URL: www.lifepacific.edu
Established: 1923 Annual Undergrad Tuition & Fees: $13,320
Enrollment: 584 Coed
Affiliation or Control: Other IRS Status: 501(c)3
Highest Offering: Master's
Accreditation: WC, BI

01 President .... Dr. Jim J. ADAMS
04 Exec Assistant to the President .... Mrs. Karli ALBANESE
05 Vice President Academic Affairs .... Dr. Michael SALMEIER
84 Vice President Enrollment Mgt .... Rev. Angie RICHEY
32 Director Student Development .... Mr. Joshua ARNOLD
10 CFO .... Mr. Todd ESKES
08 Librarian .... Mr. Gary MERRIMAN
06 Registrar .... Mr. Bruce PRIMROSE
18 Director of Facilities .... Mr. Rick MEYER
37 Director of Financial Aid .... Mrs. Luci PEREZ

09 Dean Institutional Effectiveness .... Mr. Brian TOMHAVE
15 Human Resources Director .... Ms. Heidi BONADIE
39 Director Residence Life .... Mr. George BOSTANIC
41 Athletic Director .... Mr. Tim COOK

Lincoln University (A)

401 15th Street, Oakland CA 94612-2801
County: Alameda FICE Identification: 006975
Unit ID: 117557
Telephone: (510) 628-8010 Carnegie Class: Spec-4-yr-Bus
FAX Number: (510) 628-8012 Calendar System: Semester
URL: www.lincolnuca.edu
Established: 1919 Annual Undergrad Tuition & Fees: $10,215
Enrollment: 603 Coed
Affiliation or Control: Independent Non-Profit IRS Status: 501(c)3
Highest Offering: Master's
Accreditation: ACICS

01 President/Rector .... Dr. Mikhail BRODSKY
05 Dean of Faculty .... Dr. Michael GUERRA
32 Dean of Students .... Mr. William HESS
07 Director of Admissions & Records .... Ms. Peggy AU
58 Director of Graduate Programs .... Dr. Marshall J. BURAK
08 Head Librarian .... Ms. Nicole Y. MARSH
35 Director of Student Services .... Ms. Effie TORNETTA
13 Director Computer Laboratory .... Mr. Shakil SHRESTHA
37 Chief Financial Aid Director .... Mr. James PETERSON
06 Registrar .... Ms. Maggie HUA
10 Controller .... Ms. Sherry LIANG
20 Assistant Dean of Academic Affairs .... Ms. Mariya ORSHANSKY

Logos Evangelical Seminary (B)

9358 Telstar Avenue, El Monte CA 91731-2816
County: Los Angeles FICE Identification: 039454
Unit ID: 397553
Telephone: (626) 571-5110 Carnegie Class: Not Classified
FAX Number: (626) 571-5119 Calendar System: Semester
URL: www.logos-seminary.edu
Established: 1989 Annual Graduate Tuition & Fees: N/A
Enrollment: N/A Coed
Affiliation or Control: Other IRS Status: 501(c)3
Highest Offering: Doctorate; No Undergraduates
Accreditation: WC, THEOL

01 President .... Dr. Kuo-Liang LIN
05 Academic Dean .... Dr. Ekron CHEN
30 Director of Advancement .... Mr. Steven WU
32 Dean of Students .... Dr. James HWANG
04 Executive Asst to President .... Ms. Kathleen LIN
08 Head Librarian .... Mr. Sheng-Chung CHANG
09 Institutional Research Specialist .... Ms. Teresa KAO
13 Chief Info Technology Officer (CIO) .... Mr. Alex HUNG

Loma Linda University (C)

Loma Linda CA 92350-0001
County: San Bernardino FICE Identification: 001218
Unit ID: 117636
Telephone: (909) 558-1000 Carnegie Class: Spec-4-yr-Med
FAX Number: (909) 558-0242 Calendar System: Quarter
URL: www.llu.edu
Established: 1905 Annual Undergrad Tuition & Fees: N/A
Enrollment: 4,600 Coed
Affiliation or Control: Seventh-day Adventist IRS Status: 501(c)3
Highest Offering: Doctorate
Accreditation: WC, ANEST, ARCPA, CAHIIM, CLPSY, COARC, CVT, CYTO, DENT, DH, DIETC, DMS, IPSY, MED, MFCD, MT, NURSE, OPE, OT, PAST, PH, PHAR, PTA, PTAA, RAD, RADDOS, RTT, SP, SW

01 President .... Dr. Richard H. HART
05 Provost .... Dr. Ronald L. CARTER
10 Sr Vice President Financial Affairs .... Mr. Rodney NEAL
30 Sr Vice President Advancement .... Mrs. Rachelle BUSSELL
13 Vice President Information Systems .... Dr. David P. HARRIS
84 VP Enrollment Mgmt/Student Services .... Dr. Rick E. WILLIAMS
63 Dean of Medicine .... Dr. H. Roger HADLEY
52 Dean of Dentistry .... Dr. Ronald DAILEY
69 Dean of Public Health .... Dr. Helen Hopp MARSHAK
66 Dean of Nursing .... Dr. Elizabeth (Becky) BOSSERT
76 Dean of Allied Health Professions .... Dr. Craig R. JACKSON
67 Dean School of Pharmacy .... Dr. Marilyn HERRMANN
83 Dean School of Behavioral Health .... Dr. Beverly J. BUCKLES
73 Dean of School of Religion .... Dr. Jon PAULIEN
58 Dean Faculty of Graduate Studies .... Dr. Anthony J. ZUCCARELLI
06 Director of Records .... Ms. Erin SEHEULT
08 Director of University Libraries .... Ms. Carlene DRAKE
38 Director of Counseling .... Dr. William G. MURDOCH
43 General Legal Counsel .... Mr. Kent A. HANSEN
33 Dean of Men .... Mr. John NAFIE
34 Dean of Women .... Ms. Lynette BATES
37 Director Student Financial Aid .... Ms. Verdell SCHAEFER
09 Dir Educational Effectiveness .... Dr. Marilyn EGGERS
15 Exec Director Human Services .... Ms. Charlene WILSON
18 Director Campus Engineering .... Mr. Randy STEVENS
96 Director of Purchasing .... Mr. Tim HICKMAN
40 Campus Bookstore Manager .... Ms. Michelle GURA
42 Campus Chaplain .... Pastor Terry SWENSON

Long Beach City College (D)

4901 E Carson Street, Long Beach CA 90808-1780
County: Los Angeles FICE Identification: 001219
Unit ID: 117645
Telephone: (562) 938-4111 Carnegie Class: Assoc/HVT-High Trad
FAX Number: (562) 938-4118 Calendar System: Other
URL: www.lbcc.edu
Established: 1927 Annual Undergrad Tuition & Fees (In-District): $1,182
Enrollment: 24,403 Coed
Affiliation or Control: State/Local IRS Status: 501(c)3
Highest Offering: Associate Degree
Accreditation: WJ, ADNUR

01 Superintendent-President .... Mr. Eloy OAKLEY
45 Exec Vice Pres Econ & Resource Dev .... Ms. Lou Anne BYNUM
05 Vice Pres Academic Affairs .... Dr. Terri LONG
10 Vice Pres Administrative Services .... Ms. Ann-Marie GABEL
15 Vice President Human Resources .... Ms. Rose DELGAUDIO
32 Vice Pres Student Support Services .... Dr. Greg PETERSON
16 Assoc VP Human Resources .... Vacant
13 Chief Information Systems Officer .... Ms. Sylvia LYNCH
07 Director Admissions/Records .... Ms. Lillian JUSTICE
20 Dean Academic Services .... Ms. Michelle GRIMES-HILLMAN
38 Dean Counseling/Stdnt Supp Svcs .... Ms. Nohel CORRAL
83 Dean Social Sciences & Arts .... Mrs. Dina HUMBLE
79 Dean of Language Arts .... Dr. Lee DOUGLAS
35 Interim Dean Student Affairs .... Ms. Alicia KRUIZENGA
76 Dean School Health & Science .... Mr. Paul CREASON
09 Assoc Dean Inst Effectiveness .... Dr. Eva BAGG
26 Dir Communications/College Adv .... Mr. John POPE
102 Exec Director Foundation .... Mrs. Elizabeth MCCANN
96 Director Business Support Services .... Mrs. Margie PADRON
18 Director of Facilities/Maint/Oper .... Mr. Tim WOOTTON
21 Director Fiscal Services & Payroll .... Mr. John THOMPSON
37 Dep Dir Enrollment Svcs/Fin Aid .... Mr. Juan MENJIVAR

Los Angeles Academy of Figurative Art (E)

16926 Saticoy Street, Van Nuys CA 91406
County: Los Angeles Identification: 667231
Telephone: (818) 708-9232 Carnegie Class: Not Classified
FAX Number: (818) 474-8679 Calendar System: Quarter
URL: www.laafa.org
Established: 2002 Annual Undergrad Tuition & Fees: N/A
Enrollment: N/A Coed
Affiliation or Control: Independent Non-Profit IRS Status: 501(c)3
Highest Offering: Baccalaureate
Accreditation: ART

01 President .... Maryam STORM

*Los Angeles Community College District Office (F)

770 Wilshire Boulevard, Los Angeles CA 90017
County: Los Angeles FICE Identification: 001221
Unit ID: 117681
Telephone: (213) 891-2000 Carnegie Class: N/A
FAX Number: N/A
URL: www.laccd.edu

01 Chancellor .... Dr. Francisco C. RODRIGUEZ
05 VC Educ Pgms/Inst Effective .... Dr. Ryan M. CORNNER
43 Interim General Counsel .... Dr. Kevin D. JETER
10 VC Finance and Resource Development .... Dr. Robert E. MILLER
103 Vice Chanc Econ Workforce Devel .... Vacant
15 VC Human Resources .... Dr. Albert J. ROMAN
18 Chief Facilities Executive .... James D O'REILLY
20 Deputy Chancellor .... Dr. Adriana D. BARRERA

*East Los Angeles College (G)

1301 Avenida Cesar Chavez, Monterey Park CA 91754-6001
County: Los Angeles FICE Identification: 022260
Unit ID: 113856
Telephone: (323) 265-8650 Carnegie Class: Assoc/HT-High Trad
FAX Number: (323) 265-8763 Calendar System: Semester
URL: www.elac.edu
Established: 1945 Annual Undergrad Tuition & Fees (In-District): $1,220
Enrollment: 36,012 Coed
Affiliation or Control: State/Local IRS Status: 501(c)3
Highest Offering: Associate Degree
Accreditation: WJ, CAHIIM, COARC

02 President .... Mr. Marvin MARTINEZ
05 VP Academic Affairs .... Dr. Richard MOYER
103 VP Workforce Educ/Academic Affairs .... Ms. Laura M RAMIREZ
32 VP Student Services/Special Pgms .... Ms. Julie BENAVIDES
10 VP Administrative Services .... Dr. Ann TOMLINSON
75 Dean Acad Affs/Career & Tech Educ .... Mr. Laureano FLORES
49 Dean Academic Affairs/Liberal Arts .... Ms. Carol KOZERACKI
49 Dean Academic Affairs Liberal Arts .... Ms. Kerrin MCMAHAN
49 Dean Academic Affairs Liberal Arts .... Ms. Vi LY
07 Dean Admissions & Records .... Mr. Jeremy F. ALLRED
12 Dean Academic Affairs Southgate Ctr .... Mr. Alfonso RIOS
30 Dean Resource & Inst Development .... Vacant
09 Dean Institutional Effectiveness .... Dr. Ryan CORNNER
51 Dean Continuing Education .... Ms. Adrienne A MULLEN
35 Dean Student Services .... Vacant
88 Dean EOP&S/CARE .... Ms. Danelle FALLERT
88 Dean CFES .... Ms. Angelica TOLEDO
25 Assoc Dean Resource Development .... Mr. Paul DE LA CERDA
25 Assistant Dean Grants Management .... Ms. Martha ERMIAS
26 Chief Public Relations Officer .... Vacant
22 Affirmative Action Officer .... Ms. Maria E. YEPES
37 Director Financial Aid .... Ms. Lindy FONG
40 Director Student Store .... Ms. Joyce GARCIA
41 Athletic Director (Men/Women) .... Mr. Allen J. CONE
28 Director of Diversity .... Ms. Maria Elena YEPES
88 Child Development Director .... Ms. Marcia CAGIGAS
38 Department Chair Counseling .... Mr. Daniel ORNELAS
21 College Fiscal Administrator .... Ms. Erlinda N. DEOCAMPO
08 Library Coordinator .... Ms. Choonhee L. RHIM
85 Foreign Student Advisement .... Ms. Nancy C. WONG
88 Director Vincent Price Art Museum .... Vacant

*Los Angeles City College (H)

855 N Vermont Avenue, Los Angeles CA 90029-9990
County: Los Angeles FICE Identification: 001223
Unit ID: 117788
Telephone: (323) 953-4000 Carnegie Class: Assoc/MT-VT-High Non
FAX Number: (323) 953-4013 Calendar System: Semester
URL: www.lacitycollege.edu
Established: 1929 Annual Undergrad Tuition & Fees (In-District): $1,220
Enrollment: 18,756 Coed
Affiliation or Control: Local IRS Status: 501(c)3
Highest Offering: Associate Degree
Accreditation: WJ, #DIETT, DT, RAD

02 President .... Mrs. Renee D. MARTINEZ
05 Vice President Academic Affairs .... Dr. Dan WALDEN
10 Vice President Administrative Svcs .... Dr. John AL-AMIN
32 Vice President of Student Services .... Dr. Regina SMITH
21 Asst Vice Pres Administrative Svcs .... Mr. Anil JAIN
20 Dean of Academic Affairs .... Dr. Thelma DAY
20 Dean of Academic Affairs .... Ms. Allison JONES
20 Dean of Academic Affairs .... Mr. Robert KLIER
103 Dean Workforce Development .... Dr. A. Alex DAVIS
09 Dean of Institutional Effectiveness .... Dr. Anna BADALYAN
84 Dean of Enrollment Services .... Vacant
35 Dean Student Svcs Special Programs .... Dr. Randy ANDERSON
35 Dean of EOPS .... Ms. Jeannette MAGEE
37 Dean Financial Aid .... Dr. Jeremy VILLAR
35 Dean Office of Student Life .... Mr. Alen ANDRIASSIAN
40 Bookstore Manager .... Ms. Christi O'CONNOR
85 Director International Students .... Vacant
15 Human Resources Manager .... Vacant
66 Nursing Department Chair .... Ms. Christiana BASKARAN
38 Counseling Chairperson .... Mr. Boris LOPEZ
18 Facilities Director .... Mr. Bob GARCIA

*Los Angeles Harbor College (I)

1111 Figueroa Place, Wilmington CA 90744-2397
County: Los Angeles FICE Identification: 001224
Unit ID: 117690
Telephone: (310) 233-4000 Carnegie Class: Assoc/HT-High Trad
FAX Number: (310) 233-4223 Calendar System: Semester
URL: www.lahc.edu
Established: 1949 Annual Undergrad Tuition & Fees (In-District): $1,220
Enrollment: 10,145 Coed
Affiliation or Control: State/Local IRS Status: 501(c)3
Highest Offering: Associate Degree
Accreditation: WJ, ADNUR

02 President .... Dr. Otto LEE
04 Executive Assistant to President .... Ms. Danielle JACK
05 Vice Pres Academic Affairs .... Dr. Bobbi VILLALOBOS
10 Vice Pres Administrative Services .... Mr. Robert E. SUPPELSA
32 Vice Pres Student Services .... Mr. Luis DORADO
21 Assoc Vice Pres Administrative Svcs .... Mr. Nestor TAN
09 Dean of Institutional Effectiveness .... Dr. Edward PAI
20 Dean of Academic Affairs .... Vacant
07 Dean Enrollment/Eve Ops .... Mr. Corey RODGERS
35 Dean of Student Services .... Ms. Mercedes YANEZ
20 Dean of Academic Affairs .... Dr. Stephanie ATKINSON-ALSTON
88 Assoc Dean EWD .... Ms. Priscilla LOPEZ
103 Dean of Economic/Workforce Devel .... Ms. Sandra SANCHEZ
88 Assistant Dean Title V .... Mr. Andrew SANCHEZ
83 Div Chair Behavioral/Social Sci .... Mr. Bradley J. YOUNG
50 Division Chairperson Business .... Mr. Stanley C. SANDELL
60 Div Chairperson Communications .... Ms. Ann WARREN
57 Div Chair Humanities/Fine Arts .... Mr. Juan BAEZ
81 Div Chairperson Math/Phys Science .... Ms. Farah SADDIGH
76 Div Chairperson Health Sciences .... Mrs. Lynn YAMAKAWA
68 Div Chairperson Physical Education .... Mr. Nabeel M. BARAKAT
88 Div Chrp Sci & Fam/Consum Stds .... Mrs. Joyce E. PARKER
08 Division Chairperson Library .... Mr. Jonathan LEE
38 Division Chairperson Counseling .... Ms. Joy FISHER
41 Athletic Director .... Mr. Nabeel BARAKAT
37 Director Student Financial Aid .... Ms. Peggy LOEWY-WELLISCH
18 Facilities Manager .... Mr. William C. ENGLERT
13 Manager Information Technology .... Mr. Ivan CLARKE
31 Community Services Manager .... Ms. Carla R. MUSSA-MULDOON
85 Foreign Student Advisor .... Vacant

*Los Angeles Mission College (J)

13356 Eldridge Avenue, Sylmar CA 91342-3244
County: Los Angeles FICE Identification: 012550
Unit ID: 117867

Telephone: (818) 364-7600 Carnegie Class: Assoc/HT-High Trad
FAX Number: (818) 364-7826 Calendar System: Semester
URL: www.lamission.edu
Established: 1975 Annual Undergrad Tuition & Fees (In-District): $1,220
Enrollment: 10,191 Coed
Affiliation or Control: State/Local IRS Status: 501(c)3
Highest Offering: Associate Degree
Accreditation: WJ

02 President .... Dr. Monte E. PEREZ
05 Vice President Academic Affairs .... Mr. Michael K. ALLEN
11 Vice President Administrative Svcs .... Mr. Daniel G. VILLANUEVA
32 Vice President of Student Services .... Dr. Christopher VILLA
20 Dean of Academic Affairs .... Ms. Darlene MONTES
35 Dean of Student Services .... Ms. Ludi VILLEGAS-VIDAL
88 Dean of CTE .... Ms. Marla ULIANA
35 Dean of Student Services .... Mr. Carlos R. GONZALEZ
09 Dean of Institutional Effectiveness .... Dr. Sarah L. MASTER
20 Dean of Academic Affairs .... Ms. Madelline HERNANDEZ
20 Dean DSP & S .... Dr. Larry RESENDEZ
26 Chief Public Relations Officer .... Mr. Alejandro GUZMAN
88 Director Child Development Center .... Ms. Diane STEIN
41 Athletic Director .... Mr. Steve RUYS
08 Head Librarian .... Ms. Donna AYERS
38 Counseling Chairperson .... Ms. Park MICHONG
37 Financial Aid Manager .... Mr. Dennis J. SCHROEDER
31 Community Services Manager .... Mr. Dennis SOLARES
18 Facilities/Physical Plant Manager .... Mr. Walter J. BORTMAN
88 EOP & S/Care Director .... Ms. Ludi VILLEGAS-VIDAL
04 Administrative Asst to President .... Mrs. Oliva AYALA
10 Chief Business Officer .... Mr. Jerry HUANG
102 Dir Foundation/Corporate Relations .... Mr. Albert ALVAREZ
15 Personnel Services Assistant .... Mr. Pio CASTILLO
07 Director of Admissions/Records .... Ms. Rosalie TORRES
36 Director Student Placement .... Ms. Wendy RIVERA
84 Director Enrollment Management .... Mr. Michael ALLEN
96 Director of Purchasing .... Ms. Isabel RUIZ-MORENO

*Los Angeles Pierce College (A)

6201 Winnetka Avenue, Woodland Hills CA 91371-0001
County: Los Angeles FICE Identification: 001226
Unit ID: 117706
Telephone: (818) 710-4100 Carnegie Class: Assoc/HT-High Trad
FAX Number: (818) 710-4300 Calendar System: Semester
URL: www.piercecollege.edu
Established: 1947 Annual Undergrad Tuition & Fees (In-District): $1,220
Enrollment: 21,034 Coed
Affiliation or Control: State/Local IRS Status: 501(c)3
Highest Offering: Associate Degree
Accreditation: WJ

02 President .... Dr. Kathleen F. BURKE
05 Vice President Academic Affairs .... Ms. Sheri BERGER
11 Vice President Administrative Svcs .... Mr. Rolf SCHLEICHER
32 Vice President Student Services .... Dr. Earic DIXON-PETERS
10 Assoc Vice President Admin Services .... Mr. Bruce ROSKY
10 Assoc Vice President Admin Services .... Mr. Larry KRAUS
08 Chairman Library Services .... Ms. Paula PAGGI
38 Chair Student Counseling .... Mr. Rudy DOMPE
20 Dean of Academic Affairs .... Dr. Donna-Mae VILLANUEVA
20 Dean of Academic Affairs .... Ms. Mary Anne GAVARRA-OH
20 Dean of Academic Affairs .... Ms. Susan RHI-KLEINERT
20 Dean of Academic Affairs .... Mr. Jose Luis FERNANDEZ
07 Dean Admissions/Records .... Mr. William MARMOLEJO
37 Director of Financial Aid .... Ms. Anafe ROBINSON
09 Dean Institutional Effectiveness .... Mr. Oleg BESPALOV
26 Public Information Officer .... Ms. Doreen CLAY
31 Director Community Services .... Ms. Cindy CHANG
102 Director of Foundation .... Vacant
18 Director of College Facilities .... Mr. Paul NIEMAN
41 Athletic Director .... Mr. Bob LOFRANO
106 Dir Online Education/E-learning .... Ms. Wendy BASS KEER
35 Dean Student Services .... Dr. Kalynda WEBBER MCLEAN
35 Associate Dean Student Services .... Ms. Stephanie SCHLATTER
06 Registrar .... Ms. Lorena LOPEZ
35 Dean Student Services .... Mr. Juan Carlos ASTORGA

*Los Angeles Southwest College (B)

1600 W Imperial Highway, Los Angeles CA 90047-4899
County: Los Angeles FICE Identification: 007047
Unit ID: 117715
Telephone: (323) 241-5225 Carnegie Class: Assoc/HT-High Non
FAX Number: (323) 241-5220 Calendar System: Semester
URL: www.lasc.edu
Established: 1967 Annual Undergrad Tuition & Fees (In-District): $1,220
Enrollment: 6,937 Coed
Affiliation or Control: State/Local IRS Status: 501(c)3
Highest Offering: Associate Degree
Accreditation: WJ

02 Interim President .... Dr. Denise NOLDON
05 Vice President Academic Affairs .... Dr. Lawrence BRADFORD
32 Vice President Student Services .... Dr. Harold IRVIN
10 Vice President Admin Services .... Mr. Daniel B. HALL
46 Dean Resource Development .... Vacant
30 Dean Institutional Advancement .... Mr. Jose Alfred GALLEGOS
103 Dean Career/Technical Education .... Mr. Rick HODGE
20 Dean Academic Affairs .... Dr. Tangelia ALFRED
20 Dean Academic Affairs .... Dr. Allison MOORE
38 Chairperson Counseling .... Mr. Reggie MORRIS
08 Chairperson Library .... Mrs. Tim REAM
06 Registrar .... Ms. Kimberly CARPENTER
18 Director of Facilities .... Mr. Al MAH
37 Prov Manager Student Financial Aid .... Ms. Muniece BRUTON
35 Dean Student Services .... Vacant
26 Chief Public Relations Officer .... Mr. Ben DEMERS

*Los Angeles Trade-Technical College (C)

400 W Washington Boulevard,
Los Angeles CA 90015-4108
County: Los Angeles FICE Identification: 001227
Unit ID: 117724
Telephone: (213) 763-7000 Carnegie Class: Assoc/HVT-Mix Trad/Non
FAX Number: (213) 763-5393 Calendar System: Semester
URL: www.lattc.edu
Established: 1925 Annual Undergrad Tuition & Fees (In-District): $1,220
Enrollment: 14,688 Coed
Affiliation or Control: State/Local IRS Status: 501(c)3
Highest Offering: Associate Degree
Accreditation: WJ, ACFEI

02 President .... Mr. Larry FRANK
11 VP Administrative Services .... Dr. Mary GALLAGHER
05 VP Academic Affs & Workforce Devel .... Ms. Leticia BARAJAS
32 Vice President Student Services .... Dr. Kaneesha TARRANT
21 Assoc Vice Pres Administrative Svcs .... Mr. William GASPER
20 Dean Academic Affairs & Workforce .... Mr. Vincent JACKSON
20 Dean Academic Affairs & Workforce .... Ms. Cynthia MORLEY-MOWER
20 Dean Academic Affairs & Workforce ..... Mr. Benjamin GOLDSTEIN
20 Dean Academic Affairs & Workforce .... Ms. Nicole ALBO-LOPEZ
37 Supervisor Financial Aid .... Ms. Ruth BLEDSOE
09 Dean Inst Effectiveness .... Vacant
35 Dean Student Services .... Ms. Dorothy SMITH
35 Dean Student Services .... Dr. Henan JOOF
18 Chief Facilities/Physical Plant .... Mr. Bill SMITH
06 Sr Supervisor Admission & Records .... Ms. Carolyn WALKER
10 Chief Business Officer .... Ms. Mary GALLAGHER
38 Chair Student Counseling .... Mr. Tom DAWKINS
96 Director of Purchasing .... Vacant
102 Director Foundation/Corporate Rels .... Vacant
26 Public Relations Manager .... Mr. David YSAIS
13 Mgr College Information System .... Mr. Sang BAIK

*Los Angeles Valley College (D)

5800 Fulton Avenue, Valley Glen CA 91401-4096
County: Los Angeles FICE Identification: 001228
Unit ID: 117733
Telephone: (818) 947-2600 Carnegie Class: Assoc/HT-Mix Trad/Non
FAX Number: N/A Calendar System: Semester
URL: www.lavc.edu
Established: 1949 Annual Undergrad Tuition & Fees (In-District): $1,220
Enrollment: 18,641 Coed
Affiliation or Control: State/Local IRS Status: 501(c)3
Highest Offering: Associate Degree
Accreditation: WJ, ADNUR, COARC

02 President .... Ms. Erika A. ENDRIJONAS
05 Vice President Academic Affairs .... Ms. Karen DAAR
10 Vice Pres Administrative Services .... Mr. Mike C. LEE
32 Vice Pres Student Services .... Mr. Florentino MANZANO
11 Assoc Vice Pres Administrative Svcs .... Ms. Sarah SONG
45 Financial Anaylst .... Ms. Violet AMRIKHAS
20 Dean Academic Affairs .... Dr. Laurie NALEPA
20 Dean of Academic Affairs .... Dr. Deborah A. DICESARE
20 Dean of Academic Affairs .... Mr. Matthew JORDAN
08 Chairperson of Library Service .... Ms. Dora E. ESTEN
37 Financial Aid Manager .... Mr. Vernon D. BRIDGES
09 Dean Research & Planning .... Ms. Michelle R. FOWLES
35 Dean of Student Life .... Dr. Elizabeth NEGRETE
88 Dean of Special Programs .... Dr. Sherri RODRIGUEZ
88 Associate Dean DSPS .... Mr. David M. GREEN
35 Assoc Dean of Student Services .... Ms. Annie G. REED
102 Director Foundation/Alumni Rels .... Mr. Raul V. CASTILLO
26 Public Relations Manager .... Ms. Jennifer C. BORUCKI
18 Director of College Facilities .... Mr. Tom LOPEZ
40 College Store Manager .... Ms. Mary JOHN
13 Manager College Info Svcs .... Ms. Hanh TRAN
31 Community Services Manager .... Mr. Michael B. ATKIN
38 Director Student Counseling .... Ms. Lynn BROWER
41 Athletic Director .... Mr. Jim FENWICK
06 Registrar .... Ms. Ashley DUNN
88 Dean Student Success & Support Svcs .... Mr. Marco DE LA GARZA

*West Los Angeles College (E)

9000 Overland Avenue, Culver City CA 90230-5002
County: Los Angeles FICE Identification: 008596
Unit ID: 125471
Telephone: (310) 287-4200 Carnegie Class: Assoc/MT-VT-Mix Trad/Non
FAX Number: (310) 841-0396 Calendar System: Semester
URL: www.wlac.edu
Established: 1969 Annual Undergrad Tuition & Fees (In-District): $1,220
Enrollment: 10,641 Coed
Affiliation or Control: State/Local IRS Status: 501(c)3
Highest Offering: Baccalaureate
Accreditation: WJ, DH

02 Interim President .... Mr. Robert SPRAGUE
11 Vice President Administrative Svcs .... Ms. Iris INGRAM
05 Acting VP Academic Affairs .... Ms. Aracely AGUIAR
32 Interim VP Student Services .... Mr. Michael GOLTERMANN
84 Acting Dean Student Svcs Enrollment .... Mr. Glenn SCHENK
97 Dean General Education/Transfer .... Dr. Walter JONES
20 Dean Advance Program Development .... Mr. Mark PRACHER
75 Acting Dean Career/Technology Edu .... Dr. Celena ALCALA
35 Dean of Student Support Services .... Dr. Shalamon DUKE
09 Dean of Research and Planning .... Ms. Rebecca TILLBERG
56 Dean Distance Learning/Inst Tech .... Mr. Eric ICHON
20 Dean of Academic Affairs .... Ms. Kathy S. WALTON
11 Associate Dean Contract Education .... Mr. Barry SLOAN
35 Acting Dean Student Services .... Ms. Maria MANCIA
88 Academic Senate President .... Dr. Adrienne FOSTER
10 Chief Financial Administrator .... Ms. Rasel MENENDEZ
102 Development Specialist Foundation .... Vacant
26 Dir Advtg/Marketing/Public Rels .... Ms. Michelle LONG-COFFEE
41 Athletic Director .... Mr. Ricardo HOOPER
18 Facilities Manager .... Mr. William SMITH
19 Sheriff/Deputy .... Mr. Leander DAVIS
37 Financial Aid Manager .... Vacant
40 College Enterprise Manager .... Mr. Larry PACKHAM
88 Operations Manager .... Mr. Bruce HICKS
22 Compliance Officer .... Vacant

Los Angeles County College of Nursing and Allied Health (F)

1237 N Mission Road, Los Angeles CA 90033-1083
County: Los Angeles FICE Identification: 006165
Unit ID: 117803
Telephone: (323) 226-4911 Carnegie Class: Spec 2-yr-Health
FAX Number: (323) 226-6343 Calendar System: Semester
URL: dhs.lacounty.gov/wps/portal/dhs/conah/
Established: 1895 Annual Undergrad Tuition & Fees (In-District): N/A
Enrollment: 204 Coed
Affiliation or Control: Local IRS Status: 501(c)3
Highest Offering: Associate Degree
Accreditation: WJ

01 Interim Provost .... Ms. Barbara COLLIER
05 Dean of Nursing Programs .... Ms. Barbara COLLIER
32 Dean Administrative/Student Svcs .... Ms. Maria C. CABALLERO
53 Dean Education/Consulting Services .... Ms. Tammy BLASS
37 Director of Financial Aid .... Ms. Doris DEHART

Los Angeles Film School (G)

6363 Sunset Boulevard, Hollywood CA 90028
County: Los Angeles FICE Identification: 040373
Unit ID: 436429
Telephone: (323) 860-0789 Carnegie Class: Bac/Assoc-Assoc Dom
FAX Number: (323) 646-0770 Calendar System: Other
URL: www.lafilm.edu
Established: 1999 Annual Undergrad Tuition & Fees: N/A
Enrollment: 2,284 Coed
Affiliation or Control: Proprietary IRS Status: Proprietary
Highest Offering: Baccalaureate
Accreditation: ACCSC

01 President/CEO .... Ms. Diana DERYCZ-KESSLER

Los Angeles ORT College (H)

6435 Wilshire Boulevard, Los Angeles CA 90048
County: Los Angeles FICE Identification: 025703
Unit ID: 368780
Telephone: (323) 966-5444 Carnegie Class: Assoc/HVT-Mix Trad/Non
FAX Number: (323) 966-5455 Calendar System: Other
URL: www.laort.edu
Established: 1985 Annual Undergrad Tuition & Fees: N/A
Enrollment: 306 Coed
Affiliation or Control: Independent Non-Profit IRS Status: 501(c)3
Highest Offering: Associate Degree
Accreditation: CNCE

01 Director .... Mr. Joseph NEMAN

Los Angeles Pacific College (I)

3325 Wilshire Boulevard, Ste 550, Los Angeles CA 90010
County: Los Angeles Identification: 667143
Telephone: (213) 384-2318 Carnegie Class: Not Classified
FAX Number: (213) 384-0419 Calendar System: Semester
URL: www.lapacific.net
Established: 1989 Annual Undergrad Tuition & Fees: N/A
Enrollment: N/A Coed
Affiliation or Control: Proprietary IRS Status: Proprietary
Highest Offering: Associate Degree
Accreditation: COE, CEA

01 President .... Ms. Mary YOON

*Los Rios Community College District Office (J)

1919 Spanos Court, Sacramento CA 95825-3981
County: Sacramento FICE Identification: 001231
Unit ID: 117900
Telephone: (916) 568-3021 Carnegie Class: N/A
FAX Number: (916) 568-3023
URL: www.losrios.edu

01 Chancellor .... Dr. Brian KING
04 Chancellor's Executive Assistant .... Ms. Jennifer DELUCCHI
10 Vice Chancellor Finance/Admin .... Ms. Theresa MATISTA
05 Deputy Chancellor .... Dr. Susan L. LORIMER
30 Vice Chanc Resource Development .... Vacant
26 Assoc Vice Chanc Comm/Media Rels .... Mr. Mitchel BENSON
18 Assoc Vice Chanc Facilities Mgmt .... Mr. Pablo MANZO
15 Assoc Vice Chanc Human Resources .... Mr. Ryan COX
13 Assoc Vice Chanc Information Tech .... Mr. Douglas MELINE
20 Assoc Vice Chanc Instruction .... Mr. Jamey NYE
32 Assoc Vice Chanc Student Services .... Dr. Victoria ROSARIO
43 General Counsel .... Mr. J.P SHERRY
37 Director Financial Aid .... Mr. Roy BECKHORN
96 Director General Services .... Mr. Jon AASTED
09 Director Institutional Research .... Ms. Betty GLYER-CULVER

*American River College (A)

4700 College Oak Drive, Sacramento CA 95841-4286
County: Sacramento FICE Identification: 001232
Unit ID: 109208
Telephone: (916) 484-8011 Carnegie Class: Assoc/HT-High Trad
FAX Number: (916) 484-8674 Calendar System: Semester
URL: www.arc.losrios.edu
Established: 1955 Annual Undergrad Tuition & Fees (In-District): $1,104
Enrollment: 29,133 Coed
Affiliation or Control: State/Local IRS Status: 501(c)3
Highest Offering: Associate Degree
Accreditation: WJ, COARC, EMT, FUSER

02 President .... Dr. Thomas G. GREENE
10 Vice President Admin Services .... Ms. Kuldeep KAUR
05 Vice President Instruction .... Vacant
32 Vice President Student Services .... Dr. Robin NEAL
20 Assoc VP Instruction .... Dr. Lisa LAWRENSON
62 Assoc VP Instruction/Lrng Res .... Dr. Tammy MONTGOMERY
32 Assoc VP Student Services .... Ms. Christine THOMAS
103 Assoc VP Workforce Development .... Mr. Jerome COUNTEE
57 Dean Fine & Applied Arts .... Dr. Kale BRADEN
07 Interim Dean Enrollment Services .... Mr. Parrish GEARY
83 Dean Behavioral & Social Science .... Mr. Carlos REYES
38 Dean Counseling & Student Svcs .... Dr. Jeff STEPHENSON
88 Dean English .... Mr. Doug HERNDON
79 Dean Humanities .... Ms. Kate JAQUES
68 Interim Dean Kinesiology/Athletics .... Dr. Derrick BOOTH
81 Dean Mathematics .... Dr. Roger DAVIDSON
56 Dean McClellan Center .... Mr. Steve SEGURA
35 Dean Student Services .... Ms. Kolleen OSTGAARD
09 Dean Planning/Research/Technology .... Dr. Adam KARP
66 Dean Health & Education .... Dr. Steven BOYD
81 Dean Science/Engineering .... Dr. Rina ROY
56 Dean Natomas Center .... Mr. Frank KOBAYASHI
35 Dean Student Development .... Mr. Manuel PEREZ
50 Dean Business/Computer Science .... Vacant
75 Dean Technical Education .... Dr. Trish CALDWELL
04 Administrative Asst to President .... Ms. Sue MCCOY
11 Director Administrative Services .... Mr. Dan MCKECHNIE
30 Director College Advancement .... Ms. Kirsten DUBRAY
26 Public Information Officer .... Mr. Scott CROW
28 Dean Equity & Educ Pathways .... Vacant
37 Financial Aid Supervisor .... Mr. Chad FUNK
88 Dean DE/Virtual Ed Center .... Vacant

*Cosumnes River College (B)

8401 Center Parkway, Sacramento CA 95823-5799
County: Sacramento FICE Identification: 007536
Unit ID: 113096
Telephone: (916) 691-7344 Carnegie Class: Assoc/MT-VT-High Trad
FAX Number: (916) 691-7375 Calendar System: Semester
URL: www.crc.losrios.edu
Established: 1970 Annual Undergrad Tuition & Fees (In-District): $1,104
Enrollment: 14,467 Coed
Affiliation or Control: State/Local IRS Status: 501(c)3
Highest Offering: Associate Degree
Accreditation: WJ, CAHIIM, MAC

02 President .... Dr. Edward C. BUSH
05 VP Instruction & Student Learning .... Mr. Whitney YAMAMURA
11 VP Admin Svcs & Student Support .... Mr. Cory WATHEN
32 VP Student Svcs/Enrollment Mgmt .... Dr. Kimberly MCDANIEL
84 Dean Student Svcs/Enrollment .... Vacant
20 Assoc VP Instruction/Student Lrng .... Mr. Torence POWELL
08 Dean Learning Res/College Tech .... Mr. Stephen MCGLOUGHLIN
38 Dean Counseling & Student Services .... Dr. Shannon DICKSON
50 Dean Business & Family Science .... Dr. Brian BEDFORD
79 Dean Humanities & Social Science .... Vacant
41 Dean Kinesiology & Athletics .... Vacant
81 Dean Science/Math/Engineering .... Dr. Kathryn SORENSEN
72 Dean Careers & Technology .... Dr. Kimberly HARRELL
60 Dean Comm/Visual/Performing Arts .... Dr. Colette HARRIS-MATHEWS
45 Int Dean of Col Planning & Research .... Dr. Alex CASARENO
06 Registrar/Admissions & Records .... Mr. Richard ANDREWS
18 Chief Facilities/Physical Plant .... Mr. Augustine CHAVEZ
26 Public Information Officer .... Ms. Kristie WEST
30 Chief Development/Advancement .... Mr. Peter BOSTIC

*Folsom Lake College (C)

10 College Parkway, Folsom CA 95630-6798
County: Sacramento FICE Identification: 038713
Unit ID: 444219
Telephone: (916) 608-6500 Carnegie Class: Assoc/HT-High Trad
FAX Number: (916) 608-6584 Calendar System: Semester
URL: www.flc.losrios.edu
Established: 2004 Annual Undergrad Tuition & Fees (In-District): $1,104
Enrollment: 7,942 Coed
Affiliation or Control: State/Local IRS Status: 501(c)3
Highest Offering: Associate Degree
Accreditation: WJ, MLTAD

02 President .... Dr. Rachel ROSENTHAL
11 Vice President Administration .... Kathleen KIRKLIN
05 Vice President Instruction .... Dr. Monica PACTOL
32 Int Vice President Student Services .... Kate JAQUES
20 Dean of Instruction/RCC .... Brian ROBINSON
35 Dean Student Success .... Melanie DIXON
20 Dean of Instruction & Technology .... Gary HARTLEY
20 Dean of Instruction/EDC .... Dale VAN DAM
20 Dean of Instruction/OIR & VAPA .... David WILLIAMS
09 Dean Planning & Research .... Molly SENECAL
35 Dean of Student Services .... Bernard GIBSON
88 Executive Director VAPAC .... David PIER
30 Director College Advancement .... Sally HOWARD
07 Admissions & Records Supervisor .... Christine WURZER
40 College Store Manager .... Rob MULLIGAN
10 Business Services Supervisor .... Joany HARMAN
88 Director of Administrative Services .... Melissa WILLIAMS
12 Educational Center Supervisor .... Adrienne ANDREWS
37 Financial Aid Supervisor .... Ali PADASH
26 Comm & Public Information Officer .... Kristy HART
04 Assistant to the President .... Sondra LEE

*Sacramento City College (D)

3835 Freeport Boulevard, Sacramento CA 95822-1386
County: Sacramento FICE Identification: 001233
Unit ID: 122180
Telephone: (916) 558-2111 Carnegie Class: Assoc/HT-High Trad
FAX Number: (916) 558-2449 Calendar System: Semester
URL: www.scc.losrios.edu
Established: 1916 Annual Undergrad Tuition & Fees (In-State): $1,104
Enrollment: 23,317 Coed
Affiliation or Control: State Related IRS Status: 501(c)3
Highest Offering: Associate Degree
Accreditation: WJ, DA, DH, OTA, PTAA

02 Interim President .... Mr. Michael POINDEXTER
05 Vice Pres Instructional Institution .... Mr. Don PALM
10 Vice Pres Administrative Services .... Mr. Laduan SMEDLEY
32 Interim Vice Pres Student Svcs .... Dr. Debra LUFF
20 Associate Vice Pres Instruction .... Ms. Gabriel MEEHAN
20 Associate Vice Pres Instruction .... Ms. Julia A. JOLLY
84 AVP Enrollment/Student Services .... Vacant
13 Dean Information Technology .... Dr. Elaine ADER
37 Dean Financial Aid/Student Svcs .... Ms. Christine HERNANDEZ
46 Dean Planning/Research/Development .... Dr. Marybeth BUECHNER
08 Dean Learning Resources .... Mr. Kevin FLASH
36 Dean Counseling/Student Success .... Mr. Andre COLEMAN
88 Dean Student Equity/Success .... Ms. Molly SPRINGER
40 Director College Store .... Mr. Randy CLEM
66 Director Nursing .... Ms. Carel MOUNTAIN
18 Director College Operations .... Ms. Margaret LEDNICKY
30 Interim Dir College Advancement .... Mr. Dan MCCARTY
26 Public Information Officer .... Mr. Rick BREWER
76 Dean Science & Allied Health .... Mr. James COLLINS
50 Dean Business .... Dr. Deborah SAKS
79 Dean Humanities/Fine Arts .... Mr. Chris IWATA
88 Dean Languages/Literature .... Dr. Albert GARCIA
72 Dean Advanced Technology .... Ms. Donnetta WEBB
41 Dean PE/Health/Athletics .... Mr. Mitchell L. CAMPBELL
81 Dean Statistics/Math/Engineering .... Dr. Daniel STYER
83 Int Dean Behavorial/Social Science .... Dr. Carl SJOVOLD
56 Interim Dean Davis Center .... Mr. Frank MALARET
56 Dean West Sacramento Ctr .... Mr. Art PIMENTEL
06 Records & Admissions Officer .... Ms Kim GOFF
04 Administrative Asst to President .... Ms. Pamela MORRISON
88 Director HSI-SAGE .... Dr. Lorena RUEDAS

Loyola Marymount University (E)

1 LMU Drive, Los Angeles CA 90045-2659
County: Los Angeles FICE Identification: 011649
Unit ID: 117946
Telephone: (310) 338-2700 Carnegie Class: Masters/L
FAX Number: N/A Calendar System: Semester
URL: www.lmu.edu
Established: 1911 Annual Undergrad Tuition & Fees: $42,795
Enrollment: 9,515 Coed
Affiliation or Control: Roman Catholic IRS Status: 501(c)3
Highest Offering: Doctorate
Accreditation: WC, ART, BUS, DANCE, ENG, LAW, MUS TED, THEA, THEOL

01 President .... Dr. Timothy L SNYDER
00 Chancellor .... Rev. Patrick J. CAHALAN, SJ
05 Exec Vice President & Provost .... Dr Joseph B HELLIGE
42 VP for Mission & Ministry .... Rev. Robert V CARO, SJ
20 Vice Provost for Academic Affairs .... Dr. Michael J. O'SULLIVAN
84 Vice Provost Enrollment Management .... Dr. Maureen WEATHERALL
10 Sr Vice Pres/Chief Financial Ofcr .... Mr. Tom C. FLEMING
30 Sr Vice Pres University Relations .... Mr. Dennis SLON
32 Sr Vice Pres for Student Affairs .... Dr. Elena M. BOVE
11 Sr Vice Pres for Administration .... Ms. Lynne B. SCARBORO
13 VP for Information Technology Svcs .... Mr. Patrick FRONTIERA
15 VP for Human Resources .... Ms. Rebecca CHANDLER
18 VP for Facilities Management .... Mr. Timothy HAWORTH
28 Vice Pres for Intercultural Affairs .... Dr. Abbie ROBINSON-ARMSTRONG
46 Assoc Provost Inst Effectiveness .... Dr. Margaret KASIMATIS
36 Assoc Provost Career & Professional .... Mr. Branden GRIMMETT
88 Assoc Provost for Faculty Affairs .... Dr. Deena GONZALEZ
88 Assoc Provost Rsrch Advance & Comp .... Dr. John CARFORA
109 Assoc VP Auxiliary Mgmt & Business .... Mr. Raymond DENNIS
100 Chief of Staff .... Dr. Joseph LABRIE
08 Dean of University Library .... Ms. Kristine BRANCOLINI
06 University Registrar .... Ms. Kathy REED
61 Dean Loyola Law School/Sr VP .... Mr. Michael WATERSTONE
49 Dean College Liberal Arts .... Dr. Robbin D. CRABTREE
53 Dean Sch of Educ/Dean Graduate Educ .... Dr. Shane P. MARTIN
50 Dean College of Business Admin .... Dr. Dennis DRAPER
57 Dean Communication & Fine Arts .... Dr. Bryant ALEXANDER
54 Dean College of Science & Engineer .... Dr. Tina CHOE
88 Dean School of Film/Television .... Mr. Stephen G. UJLAKI
44 Ex Dir Dev Plnd Gvng/Princpal Gifts .... Ms. Joanie POHAS
07 Director of Admissions .... Mr. Matthew X. FISSINGER
37 Director of Financial Aid .... Ms. Darlene WILSON
41 Athletic Director .... Dr. William HUSAK
27 Assistant Director of Marketing .... Mr. Benjamin ALKALY
09 Interim Dir Institutional Research .... Ms. Christine CHAVEZ
108 Director of Assessment .... Dr. Laura MASSA
26 Exec Dir Communications & Marketing .... Mr. John KIRALLA
29 Executive Director of Alumni Rels .... Ms. Lisa FARLAND
23 Director of Student Health Services .... Ms. Katherine ARCE
104 Interim Director Study Abroad .... Mr. Adrian DOYLE
25 Dir Research & Sponsored Projects .... Dr. Joseph MCNICHOLAS
90 Director of Academic Technology .... Ms. Crista COPP
04 Executive Asst to President .... Ms. Debbie CAVANAGH
88 Administrative Specialist .... Ms. Rosa CALDERON
102 Exec Dir Corp/Foundation Relations .... Mr. David A. TILLIPMAN
19 Chief of Public Safety .... Mr. Hampton CANTRELL
22 EEO Officer and Title IX Coord .... Ms. Sara TRIVEDI
39 Director Student Housing .... Mr. Steven NYGAARD
43 General Counsel .... Mr. Harold A. BRIDGES

Marshall B. Ketchum University (F)

2575 Yorba Linda Boulevard, Fullerton CA 92831-1699
County: Orange FICE Identification: 001230
Unit ID: 123943
Telephone: (714) 870-7226 Carnegie Class: Spec-4-yr-Other Health
FAX Number: (714) 879-9834 Calendar System: Quarter
URL: www.ketchum.edu
Established: 1904 Annual Graduate Tuition & Fees: N/A
Enrollment: 427 Coed
Affiliation or Control: Independent Non-Profit IRS Status: 501(c)3
Highest Offering: Doctorate; No Undergraduates
Accreditation: WC, #ARCPA, OPT, OPTR, @PHAR

01 President .... Dr. Kevin L. ALEXANDER
30 Vice Pres University Advancement .... Mr. Paul A. STOVER
100 Vice President and Chief of Staff .... Dr. Julie A. SCHORNACK
32 Vice President for Student Affairs .... Dr. Carmen N. BARNHARDT
15 Vice Pres Human Resources .... Ms. Gail S. DEUTSCH
10 Controller .... Ms. Andrea DUBOIS
46 Associate Dean for Research .... Dr. Jerry PAUGH
18 Director Campus Operations .... Mr. Gregory SMITH
51 Director Continuing Education .... Ms. Susan J. ATKINSON
13 Director of Information Technology .... Mr. Gary W. GRAY
84 Sr Dir Enroll Mgmt & Financial Aid .... Ms. Tami A. SATO
37 Director Financial Aid .... Ms. Barbara BREFFLE
07 Asst Dean for Optometry Admissions .... Dr. Jane Ann MUNROE
29 Dir Development/Alumni Affairs .... Ms. Erika BERNAL
08 Director of Library Services .... Ms. Donnajean MATTHEWS
23 Dir Special Clinic Programs .... Ms. Michele WHITECAVAGE
26 Dir Marketing/Communications .... Mrs. Katie SANTOS-COY
40 Manager Campus Store .... Ms. Debra WOODS
88 Dean for Optometry .... Dr. Stanley WOO
67 Dean for Pharmacy .... Dr. Edward FISHER
76 Dean for Health Sciences .... Ms. Judy ORTIZ
108 Dir Institutional Effectiveness .... Dr. Ajoy KOOMER

Marymount California University (G)

30800 Palos Verdes Drive E,
Rancho Palos Verdes CA 90275-6299
County: Los Angeles FICE Identification: 010474
Unit ID: 118541
Telephone: (310) 377-5501 Carnegie Class: Bac-Diverse
FAX Number: (310) 377-6223 Calendar System: Semester
URL: www.marymountcalifornia.edu
Established: 1932 Annual Undergrad Tuition & Fees: $34,680
Enrollment: 1,108 Coed
Affiliation or Control: Roman Catholic IRS Status: 501(c)3
Highest Offering: Master's
Accreditation: WC

01 President .... Dr. Lucas LAMADRID
03 Executive Vice President .... Dr. Ariane SCHAUER
10 Vice Pres Finance/Administration .... Mr. James REEVES
05 Provost/Dean of Faculty .... Dr. Ariane SCHAUER
30 Dean Institutional Development .... Ms. Kristi BIEBER
84 Vice President Enrollment Mgmt .... Mr. Roger JONES
32 Dean of Students .... Mr. Ryan ALCANTARA
20 Associate Academic Officer .... Ms. Susie MARTIN
08 Librarian .... Mr. Gary MEDINA
37 Director Student Financial Aid .... Mr. Pedro LADINO

15 Director Personnel Services .... Ms. Karen THORDARSON
18 Chief Facilities/Physical Plant .... Mr. Richard SCHULT
26 Chief Public Relations Officer .... Ms. Kelly CURTIS
29 Director Alumni Relations .... Ms. Kelly CURTIS
36 Director Student Placement .... Dr. Virginia WADE
38 Director Student Counseling .... Dr. Brad HESS
96 Director of Purchasing .... Ms. Denise FESSENBECKER
06 Registrar .... Ms. Paula AVERY
35 Dir Student Life & Engagement .... Ms. Kelly KRUSEE
09 Director of Institutional Research .... Mr. Michael SEMENOFF
21 Associate Business Officer .... Ms. Kathleen RUIZ
04 Administrative Asst to President .... Ms. Kimberly RAMSEY
19 Director Security/Safety .... Mr. Michael MACMENAMIE
39 Director Student Housing .... Ms. Laura DORFMAN
41 Athletic Director .... Mr. Gary WHITE
104 Director Study Abroad .... Dr. David DRAPER
105 Director Web Services .... Mr. Maury HILLSTROM
13 Chief Info Technology Officer (CIO) .... Mr. Monte SCHMEISER
101 Secretary of the Institution/Board .... Ms. Kimberly RAMSAY

The Master's College and Seminary (A)

21726 Placerita Canyon Road,
Santa Clarita CA 91321-1200
County: Los Angeles — FICE Identification: 001220
Unit ID: 117751
Telephone: (661) 259-3540 — Carnegie Class: Masters/S
FAX Number: N/A — Calendar System: Semester
URL: www.masters.edu
Established: 1927 — Annual Undergrad Tuition & Fees: $30,920
Enrollment: 1,572 — Coed
Affiliation or Control: Independent Non-Profit — IRS Status: 501(c)3
Highest Offering: Doctorate
Accreditation: WC, MUS

01 President .... Dr. John MACARTHUR
03 Exec Vice President .... Dr. Lee DUNCAN
05 Vice President Academic Affairs .... Dr. John STEAD
32 Dean of Student Life .... Mr. Joe KELLER
58 Vice President Graduate School .... Mr. Rich GREGORY
11 Vice President of Operations .... Vacant
30 Director of Development .... Mr. Luke CHERRY
46 Vice Pres Institutional Research .... Dr. John HUGHES
10 Chief Financial Officer .... Mr. Jason HARTUNG
18 Chief of Operations .... Mr. Jason HARTUNG
06 Registrar .... Mr. Don GILMORE
08 Director Library Services .... Mr. John STONE
20 Associate Dean of Students .... Mr. David HULET
84 Director Enrollment .... Ms. Hollie JACKSON
41 Athletic Director .... Mr. Steve WALDECK
37 Director Financial Aid .... Mr. Gary EDWARDS
35 Director Campus Activities .... Vacant
29 Director Alumni Affairs .... Ms. Shayna ANDERSON
09 Director of Institutional Research .... Mr. John M. WALTER
36 Director Student Placement .... Miss Hollie ROBB
85 International Students Advisor .... Miss Lisa LAGEORGE
04 Administrative Asst to President .... Ms. Sharon STAATS
13 Chief Info Technology Officer (CIO) .... Mr. Nate PRINCE
15 Director Personnel Services .... Mr. Kent HANEY
19 Director Security/Safety .... Mr. Chris POWELL

† The Master's Seminary is located at 13248 Roscoe Boulevard, Sun Valley, CA 91352.

Mayfield College (B)

35-325 Date Palm Drive, Suite 101,
Cathedral City CA 92234
County: Riverside — FICE Identification: 041156
Unit ID: 454698
Telephone: (760) 328-5554 — Carnegie Class: Spec 2-yr-Tech
FAX Number: (760) 328-5357 — Calendar System: Semester
URL: mayfieldcollege.org
Established: 1997 — Annual Undergrad Tuition & Fees: $12,648
Enrollment: 509 — Coed
Affiliation or Control: Proprietary — IRS Status: Proprietary
Highest Offering: Associate Degree
Accreditation: COE

01 Campus President .... Kevin HA

Mendocino College (C)

1000 Hensley Creek Road, Ukiah CA 95482-7821
County: Mendocino — FICE Identification: 011672
Unit ID: 118684
Telephone: (707) 468-3000 — Carnegie Class: Assoc/HT-High Non
FAX Number: (707) 468-3120 — Calendar System: Semester
URL: www.mendocino.edu
Established: 1973 — Annual Undergrad Tuition & Fees (In-District): $1,422
Enrollment: 3,769 — Coed
Affiliation or Control: State/Local — IRS Status: 501(c)3
Highest Offering: Associate Degree
Accreditation: WJ

01 Superintendent/President .... Mr. Arturo REYES
05 VP of Education & Student Services .... Ms. Virginia GULEFF
10 Vice Pres Administrative Services .... Ms. Eileen CICHOCKI
08 Head Librarian .... Mr. John KOETZNER
20 Dean of Instruction .... Ms. Rebecca MONTES
20 Dean of Centers .... Ms. Debra POLAK
75 Dean Applied Academics .... Mr. Dennis ASELTYNE
15 Director Human Resources .... Ms. Sabrina MEYER
18 Director of Facilities .... Mr. MacAdam LOJOWSKY
26 Director Communications & Cmty Rels .... Ms. Jessica SILVA
41 Director of Athletics .... Mr. Matthew GORDON
21 Director Fiscal Services .... Mr. Joe ATHERTON
13 Director Information Technology .... Ms. Karen CHRISTOPHERSON
09 Director of Institutional Research .... Ms. Minerva FLORES
07 Director Admissions/Registrar .... Ms. Anastasia SIMPSON-LOGG
37 Director of Financial Aid .... Mr. Ulises VELASCO
04 Administrative Asst to President .... Ms. Mary LAMB
12 Director of Lake Center .... Ms. Valerie JENSEN
102 Dir Foundation/Corporate Relations .... Ms. Katie FAIRBAIRN
88 MESA/Stem Success Director .... Ms. Amanda XU

Menlo College (D)

1000 El Camino Real, Atherton CA 94027-4301
County: San Mateo — FICE Identification: 001236
Unit ID: 118693
Telephone: (800) 556-3656 — Carnegie Class: Spec-4-yr-Bus
FAX Number: (650) 543-4085 — Calendar System: Semester
URL: www.menlo.edu
Established: 1927 — Annual Undergrad Tuition & Fees: $38,750
Enrollment: 794 — Coed
Affiliation or Control: Independent Non-Profit — IRS Status: 501(c)3
Highest Offering: Baccalaureate
Accreditation: WC, BUS

01 President .... Dr. Richard A. MORAN
05 Provost .... Dr. Terri GIVENS
03 Executive Vice President .... Mr. Steven WEINER
10 Dir Finance & Business Affairs .... Mr. Tim CHIOCHIOS
30 Chief Advancement Officer .... Ms. Joanne FERCHLAND-PARELLA
20 Dean for Academic/Prof Success .... Ms. Angela SCHMIEDE
84 Dean of Enrollment Management .... Ms. Priscila DESOUZA
08 Dean Library Services .... Ms. Linda SMITH
32 Dean of Student Affairs .... Dr. Lisa WEBB
108 Assoc Director IR & Assessment .... Ms. Ivana IZVONAR
15 Director of Human Resources .... Mr. Jay NAIDU
18 Director Facilities & Operations .... Mr. Robert TALBOTT
41 Director of Athletics .... Mr. Keith SPATARO
36 Internship Program Director .... Mr. Zach OSBORNE
26 Director of Communications .... Ms. Darcy BLAKE
06 Registrar .... Ms. Cristine RABAGO

Merced College (E)

3600 M Street, Merced CA 95348-2898
County: Merced — FICE Identification: 001237
Unit ID: 118718
Telephone: (209) 384-6000 — Carnegie Class: Assoc/MT-VT-High Trad
FAX Number: (209) 384-6043 — Calendar System: Semester
URL: www.mccd.edu
Established: 1962 — Annual Undergrad Tuition & Fees (In-District): $1,141
Enrollment: 10,214 — Coed
Affiliation or Control: State/Local — IRS Status: 501(c)3
Highest Offering: Associate Degree
Accreditation: WJ, DMS, RAD

01 Interim President .... Dr. Susan WALSH
04 Executive Assistant to President .... Mrs. Stacey MARTINEZ
05 Vice President Instruction .... Dr. Brian ELLISON
32 Vice President Student Services .... Mr. Chris VITELLI
12 Dean Los Banos Campus .... Dr. Brenda LATHAM
81 Dean Instructional Services .... Dr. Douglas KAIN
71 Interim Dean Instructional Services .... Vince PIRO
47 Dean Instructional Services .... Mr. Jim ANDERSEN
50 Dean Instructional Services .... Dr. Bobby ANDERSON
83 Dean Instructional Services .... Mr. John ALBANO
103 Dean Instructional Services .... Mrs. Shelly CONNER
35 Dean of Student Services .... Ms. Angela TOS
88 Dean of Student Equity & Success .... Mr. Michael MCCANDLESS
26 Chief Public Relations Officer .... Mr. Robin SHEPARD
06 Registrar & Dir Financial Aid .... Mrs. Sharon ALLRED
15 Director of Human Resources .... Ms. Tracie GREEN

Merit University (F)

3699 Wilshire Blvd., Ste 970, Los Angeles CA 90010
County: Los Angeles — Identification: 667293
Telephone: (213) 325-2760 — Carnegie Class: Not Classified
FAX Number: (213) 325-2761 — Calendar System: Quarter
URL: www.meritu.edu
Established: — Annual Graduate Tuition & Fees: N/A
Enrollment: N/A — Coed
Affiliation or Control: Proprietary — IRS Status: Proprietary
Highest Offering: Master's; No Undergraduates
Accreditation: ACICS

META Business School (G)

100 Bayview Circle, Newport Beach CA 92660
County: Orange — Identification: 667286
Telephone: (949) 872-2224 — Carnegie Class: Not Classified
FAX Number: (949) 872-2229 — Calendar System: Other
URL: www.metabusinessschool.edu
Established: 2010 — Annual Graduate Tuition & Fees: N/A
Enrollment: N/A — Coed
Affiliation or Control: Proprietary — IRS Status: Proprietary
Highest Offering: Master's; No Undergraduates
Accreditation: DEAC

05 Provost .... Dr. H. Clarissa CHAIY

Methodist Theological Seminary in America (H)

1800 N. Western Ave, Los Angeles CA 90027
County: Los Angeles — Identification: 667133
Telephone: (213) 386-0080 — Carnegie Class: Not Classified
FAX Number: (213) 386-5229 — Calendar System: Semester
URL: www.mtsamerica.org
Established: 1880 — Annual Undergrad Tuition & Fees: N/A
Enrollment: N/A — Coed
Affiliation or Control: Independent Non-Profit — IRS Status: 501(c)3
Highest Offering: Master's
Accreditation: @BI

01 Chancellor .... Dr. Eisung CHAE
05 Dean .... Dr. Sung Do KANG

Middlebury Institute of International Studies at Monterey (I)

460 Pierce Street, Monterey CA 93940-2691
Telephone: (831) 647-4100 — FICE Identification: 001241
Accreditation: &EH, BUS, CEA

† Regional accrediation is carried under parent institution Middlebury College, VT.

Mills College (J)

5000 MacArthur Boulevard, Oakland CA 94613-1301
County: Alameda — FICE Identification: 001238
Unit ID: 118888
Telephone: (510) 430-2255 — Carnegie Class: Masters/L
FAX Number: (510) 430-2256 — Calendar System: Semester
URL: www.mills.edu
Established: 1852 — Annual Undergrad Tuition & Fees: $44,258
Enrollment: 1,542 — Female
Affiliation or Control: Independent Non-Profit — IRS Status: 501(c)3
Highest Offering: Doctorate
Accreditation: WC

01 President .... Ms. Elizabeth L. HILLMAN
05 Interim Provost & Dean of Faculty .... Dr. Sharon WASHINGTON
10 VP Finance & Administration .... Ms. Maria CAMMARATA
26 VP Communications/Chief of Staff .... Ms. Renee JADUSHLEVER
30 VP for Inst Advancement .... Mr. Jeffrey JACKANICZ
20 Associate Provost .... Dr. Chinyere OPARAH
15 Chief HR Officer & Career Svcs Dir .... Mr. Vince RYAN
84 VP for Enrollment Management .... Ms. Kathy BAUGHER
32 VP Student Life/Dean of Students .... Dr. Chicora MARTIN
07 Director of Undergraduate Admission .... Vacant
09 Dir Acad Assess/Inst Research/Plng .... Dr. Alice B. KNUDSEN
101 Secretary of Board of Trustees .... Ms. Carrie HALL
06 Registrar .... Ms. Karen SIVERSON
18 Associate VP for Operations .... Ms. Linda ZITZNER
38 Assoc Dean/Dir Counsel/Psych Svcs .... Vacant
41 Director of Athletics .... Ms. Themy ADACHI

MiraCosta College (K)

One Barnard Drive, Oceanside CA 92056-3899
County: San Diego — FICE Identification: 001239
Unit ID: 118912
Telephone: (760) 757-2121 — Carnegie Class: Assoc/HT-High Trad
FAX Number: (760) 795-6609 — Calendar System: Semester
URL: www.miracosta.edu
Established: 1934 — Annual Undergrad Tuition & Fees (In-District): $1,152
Enrollment: 14,687 — Coed
Affiliation or Control: State/Local — IRS Status: 501(c)3
Highest Offering: Baccalaureate
Accreditation: WJ, SURGT

01 Superintendent/President .... Dr. Sunita COOKE
04 Exec Assistant to Supt/President .... Ms. Evelyn CROGAN
04 Exec Assistant to Supt/President .... Ms. Jeanne SWANSON
05 Vice President Instructional Svcs .... Dr. Mary BENARD
32 Vice President Student Svcs .... Dr. Alketa WOJCIK
10 Vice President Business/Admin Svcs .... Mr. Charles NG
12 Dean San Elijo Campus-Letters/Comm .... Ms. Dana SMITH
20 Dean Academic Information Svcs .... Dr. Mario VALENTE
38 Dean Counseling/Student Devel .... Dr. Wendy STEWART
07 Int Dean Admissions/Student Support .... Mr. Freddy RAMIREZ
88 Associate Dean San Elijo Campus .... Ms. Cynthia RICE-CARROLL
51 Dean Community Education .... Dr. Nikki SCHAPER
49 Dean Arts/Intl Languages .... Mr. Jonathan FOHRMAN
81 Dean Math/Sciences .... Mr. Mike FINO
75 Dean Career/Technical Education .... Dr. Al TACCONE
88 Director Small Business Dev Ctr .... Mr. Sudershan SHAUNAK
31 Director Community Services .... Ms. Linda KUROKAWA
06 Interim Registrar .... Ms. Jane SPARKS
09 Dean Institutional Research .... Dr. Chris HILL
26 Director Marketing/Communications .... Ms. Cheryl BROOM
102 Director Foundation/Fund Devel .... Ms. Linda FOGERSON
18 Director Facilities .... Mr. Tom MACIAS
37 Interim Director Financial Aid .... Mr. John BENEFIELD
88 Director Risk Management .... Mr. Joseph MAZZA
88 Director Cashiering Services .... Ms. Jo FERRIS
15 Director Human Resources .... Ms. Sheri WRIGHT

36 Director Career Center ... Ms. Donna DAVIS
88 Director Transfer Center ... Ms. Lise FLOCKEN
96 Director Purchasing/Material Mgmt ... Ms. Susan ASATO
88 Director Retention Services ... Dr. Edward POEHLERT
21 Director Fiscal Services ... Ms. Katie WHITE
19 Director Campus Police ... Chief Robert NORCROSS
106 Director Online Education ... Dr. James JULIUS

Monterey Peninsula College (A)

980 Fremont Street, Monterey CA 93940-4799
County: Monterey FICE Identification: 001242
Unit ID: 119067
Telephone: (831) 646-4000 Carnegie Class: Assoc/HT-High Non
FAX Number: (831) 655-2627 Calendar System: Semester
URL: www.mpc.edu
Established: 1947 Annual Undergrad Tuition & Fees (In-District): $1,174
Enrollment: 7,727 Coed
Affiliation or Control: State/Local IRS Status: 501(c)3
Highest Offering: Associate Degree
Accreditation: WJ, ADNUR

01 Superintendent/President ... Dr. Walter TRIBLEY
05 Vice President of Academic Affairs ... Ms. Kiran KAMATH
11 Vice Pres Administrative Services ... Dr. Steven L. CROW
32 Vice President of Student Services ... Dr. Kim MCGINNIS
20 Dean of Instruction ... Ms. Laura FRANKLIN
20 Dean of Instruction ... Dr. Jon KNOLLE
45 Dean of Instructional Planning ... Mr. Michael GILMARTIN
15 Associate Dean of Human Resources ... Ms. Susan KITAGAWA
35 Dean of Student Services ... Mr. Larry WALKER
09 Director of Institutional Research ... Dr. Rosaleen RYAN
06 Director of Admissions & Records ... Ms. Nicole DUNNE
08 Librarian ... Vacant
37 Student Financial Services Director ... Mr. Francisco TOSTADO
41 Athletic Director ... Mr. Lyndon SCHUTZLER
18 Facilities Operations Supervisor ... Mr. Pete OLSEN
96 Purchasing Agent ... Ms. Mary WEBER
19 Director of Security ... Vacant

Mount Saint Mary's University (B)

12001 Chalon Road, Los Angeles CA 90049-1599
County: Los Angeles FICE Identification: 001243
Unit ID: 119173
Telephone: (310) 954-4000 Carnegie Class: Masters/M
FAX Number: (310) 954-4379 Calendar System: Semester
URL: www.msmu.edu
Established: 1925 Annual Undergrad Tuition & Fees: $35,944
Enrollment: 3,292 Female
Affiliation or Control: Roman Catholic IRS Status: 501(c)3
Highest Offering: Doctorate
Accreditation: WC, NURSE, PTA

01 President ... Dr. Ann MCELANEY-JOHNSON
05 Provost ... Dr. Robert J. PERRINS
30 Vice Pres Institutional Advancement ... Dr. Stephanie CUBBA
10 Vice Pres Administration & Finance ... Mr. Chris MCALARY
13 VP Info Support Svcs ... Mr. Larry SMITH
32 Vice President Student Affairs ... Dr. Jane LINGUA
84 VP Enrollment Management ... Mr. Brian O'ROURKE
20 Assistant Provost ... Dr. Michele STARKEY
09 Asst VP Inst Planning & Research ... Dr. Heather BROWN
35 Asst VP Student Affairs ... Ms. Bernadette ROBERT
58 Graduate Dean ... Dr. Linda MOODY
55 Dean of Weekend College ... Ms. Suzanne WILLIAMS
88 Asst VP Enrollment Management ... Mr. Dean KILGOUR
06 Registrar ... Ms. Rocio DELEON
26 Director of Public Relations ... Ms. Debbie REAM
15 Director of Human Resources ... Ms. Dana LOPEZ
18 Director of Facilities Mgmt ... Mr. Rick TORKELSON
37 Director of Student Financing ... Ms. La Royce HOUSLEY
08 Interim Director of MSMU Libraries ... Dr. Ruth JACKSON
28 Director of Diversity ... Dr. Pam HALDEMAN
29 Director Alumni Relations ... Ms. Elizabeth ROBLES JIMENEZ
38 Director Student Counseling ... Dr. Susan SALEM
07 Assoc Director of Admissions ... Ms. Renee ROUZAN-KAY
36 Director Career Services ... Ms. Marlene SIMON
04 Administrative Asst to President ... Ms. Lucille VILLEGAS
19 Director Security/Safety ... Mr. Michael MCFATRIDGE
39 Director Residence Life ... Ms. Jessica CUEVAS
44 Director Individual Giving ... Ms. Maria SOLANO
104 Study Away Coordinator ... Ms. Jaime WOOD
105 Director Web Services ... Mr. Salvador RODRIGUEZ
106 Dir Online Education/E-learning ... Ms. Lisa DAWLEY

Mt. San Antonio College (C)

1100 N Grand, Walnut CA 91789-1399
County: Los Angeles FICE Identification: 001245
Unit ID: 119164
Telephone: (909) 594-5611 Carnegie Class: Assoc/MT-VT-High Trad
FAX Number: (909) 598-2303 Calendar System: Semester
URL: www.mtsac.edu
Established: 1946 Annual Undergrad Tuition & Fees (In-District): $1,348
Enrollment: 29,045 Coed
Affiliation or Control: State/Local IRS Status: 501(c)3
Highest Offering: Associate Degree
Accreditation: WJ, COARC, EMT, HT, RAD

01 President/CEO ... Dr. William T. SCROGGINS
05 Vice President Instruction ... Dr. Irene M. MALMGREN
10 Vice President Administrative Svcs ... Mr. Michael D. GREGORYK
32 Vice President Student Services ... Dr. Audrey YAMAGATA-NOJI
15 Vice President Human Resources ... Mr. Ibrahim ALI
20 Assoc Vice Pres Instruction ... Dr. Joumana MCGOWAN
35 Dean Student Services ... Ms. Carolyn KEYS
08 Dean Library/Learning Resources ... Ms. Meghan CHEN
38 Dean Counseling ... Mr. Tom MAUCH
13 Chief Technology Officer/Info Tech ... Mr. Victor BELINSKI
84 Dean Enrollment Management ... Dr. George BRADSHAW
21 Assoc Vice Pres Fiscal Services ... Ms. Rosa ROYCE
102 Executive Director of Foundation ... Mr. Bill LAMBERT
37 Director Financial Aid ... Ms. Chau DAO
88 Int Director Risk Management ... Ms. Duetta LANGEVIN
46 Director Grants ... Ms. Adrienne PRICE
26 Director Marketing/Communications ... Ms. Uyen MAI
09 Dir Research & Inst Effectiveness ... Ms. Barbara MCNEICE-STALLARD
18 Director Facilities Planning & Mgmt ... Mr. Gary NELLESEN
35 Director Student Life ... Ms. Andrea SIMA
36 Director Career & Transfer Services ... Vacant
96 Purchasing Manager ... Ms. Teresa PATTERSON
50 Dean Business ... Ms. Jennifer GALBRAITH
68 Dean Kinesiology/Athletics/Dance ... Mr. Joe JENNUM
79 Dean Humanities & Social Science ... Mr. Jim JENKINS
72 Dean Tech/Health Science ... Ms. Jemma BLAKE-JUDD
65 Assoc Dean Natural Sciences ... Mr. Matthew JUDD
57 Dean Arts ... Dr. Susan LONG
51 Dean School of Continuing Education ... Dr. Madelyn ARBALLO
04 Exec Asst to President & BOT ... Ms. Carol NELSON

Mt. San Jacinto College (D)

1499 N State Street, San Jacinto CA 92583-2399
County: Riverside FICE Identification: 001246
Unit ID: 119216
Telephone: (951) 487-6752 Carnegie Class: Assoc/HT-High Trad
FAX Number: (951) 654-9712 Calendar System: Semester
URL: www.msjc.edu
Established: 1962 Annual Undergrad Tuition & Fees (In-District): $1,386
Enrollment: 14,580 Coed
Affiliation or Control: State/Local IRS Status: 501(c)3
Highest Offering: Associate Degree
Accreditation: WJ, DMS

01 Superintendent/President ... Dr. Roger W. SCHULTZ
100 Director President's Office ... Ms. Kathy S. DONNELL
05 Vice Pres of Instruction ... Dr. Rudolph BESIKOF
32 Vice President Student Services ... Dr. William K. VINCENT
10 Vice President Business Svcs ... Ms. Becky ELAM
15 Int Vice Pres of Human Resources ... Dr. Jack MIYAMOTO
88 Executive Dean Inst Effect ... Mr. Brandon MOORE
19 Chief of Police ... Vacant
20 Dean of Academic Programs ... Dr. Jeremy BROWN
20 Dean of Academic Programs - SJC ... Dr. Carlos TOVARES
103 Dean Career Education ... Ms. Joyce JOHNSON
72 Dean Instruct Acad Success/Tech ... Mr. Micah ORLOFF
21 Dean of Business Services ... Ms. Julie VENABLE
13 Dean of Information Tech ... Mr. Brian ORLAUSKI
35 Dean Student Support Svcs ... Mr. Tom SPILLMAN
38 Dean Student Services ... Ms. Susan LOOMIS
41 Dean of Athletics ... Mr. Patrick SPRINGER
45 Dean Institutional Planning ... Ms. Rebecca TEAGUE
26 Public Information Officer ... Ms. Karin MARRIOTT
16 Int Assoc Dean of Human Resources ... Ms. Jeannine STOKES
37 Assoc Dean Financial Aid ... Ms. Dolores SMITH
66 Assoc Dean of Nursing/Allied Health ... Vacant
18 Director Maint & Operations ... Mr. Brian TWITTY
09 Director of Research ... Mr. Nikilos 'Nik' MESARIS
96 Assoc Dean Purchasing ... Vacant

Mt. Sierra College (E)

800 Royal Oaks Drive, Suite 101,
Monrovia CA 91016-3414
County: Los Angeles FICE Identification: 031287
Unit ID: 398130
Telephone: (626) 873-2100 Carnegie Class: Bac-Diverse
FAX Number: (626) 359-5528 Calendar System: Quarter
URL: www.mtsierra.edu
Established: 1991 Annual Undergrad Tuition & Fees: $15,588
Enrollment: 467 Coed
Affiliation or Control: Proprietary IRS Status: Proprietary
Highest Offering: Baccalaureate
Accreditation: ACCSC

01 President ... Mr. Jie (George) ZHAO
10 Chief Financial Officer ... Mr. John DAVIS
05 Chief Academic Officer ... Dr. Jon FERSAVICH
07 Manager of Admissions ... Ms. Isabel MONROY
37 Director Student Financial Aid ... Ms. Lida CASTILLO

MTI College (F)

5221 Madison Avenue, Sacramento CA 95841-3037
County: Sacramento FICE Identification: 012912
Unit ID: 118198
Telephone: (916) 339-1500 Carnegie Class: Assoc/HVT-High Non
FAX Number: (916) 339-0305 Calendar System: Quarter
URL: www.mticollege.edu
Established: 1965 Annual Undergrad Tuition & Fees: N/A
Enrollment: 1,020 Coed
Affiliation or Control: Proprietary IRS Status: Proprietary
Highest Offering: Associate Degree
Accreditation: WJ

01 President ... Mr. John A. ZIMMERMAN
10 Vice Pres/Chief Financial Officer ... Mr. David W. ALLEN
12 Campus Director ... Mr. Malcolm CARLING SMITH
11 Director of Operations ... Mr. Michael ZIMMERMAN

Musicians Institute (G)

6752 Hollywood Boulevard, Hollywood CA 90028
County: Los Angeles FICE Identification: 021618
Unit ID: 119270
Telephone: (323) 462-1384 Carnegie Class: Spec-4-yr-Arts
FAX Number: (323) 462-1575 Calendar System: Quarter
URL: www.mi.edu
Established: 1977 Annual Undergrad Tuition & Fees: $24,030
Enrollment: 1,142 Coed
Affiliation or Control: Proprietary IRS Status: Proprietary
Highest Offering: Baccalaureate
Accreditation: MUS

01 President ... Mr. Donny GRUENDLER
05 VP Academic Affairs ... Mr. Donny GRUENDLER
108 Dean Compliance and Assessment ... Mr. Tom ENGFER

Napa Valley College (H)

2277 Napa-Vallejo Highway, Napa CA 94558-6236
County: Napa FICE Identification: 001247
Unit ID: 119331
Telephone: (707) 256-7000 Carnegie Class: Assoc/HT-High Trad
FAX Number: (707) 253-3015 Calendar System: Semester
URL: www.napavalley.edu
Established: 1942 Annual Undergrad Tuition & Fees (In-District): $1,142
Enrollment: 6,348 Coed
Affiliation or Control: State/Local IRS Status: 501(c)3
Highest Offering: Associate Degree
Accreditation: WJ, COARC, EMT

01 Superintendent/President ... Dr. Ronald D. KRAFT
05 Int Vice President Instruction ... Mr. Erik SHEARER
10 Vice Pres Administrative Services ... Mr. Robert PARKER
32 Vice President Student Services ... Mr. Oscar DE HARO
38 Dean Counseling Svcs/Stdnt Success ... Mr. Howard WILLIS
20 Dean of Instruction ... Vacant
08 Dean Library/Learning Resource Ctr ... Ms. Rebecca SCOTT
37 Dean Fin Aid/EOPS/Pre-Col TRIO Pgms ... Ms. Patricia MORGAN
103 Dean Workforce Career/Devel ... Mr. Charles MONAHAN
13 Dean Institutional Technology ... Mr. Robert BUTLER
12 Assoc Dean Upper Valley Campus ... Ms. Mechele MANNO
07 Assoc Dean Admissions/Records ... Ms. Jessica ERICKSON
15 Exec Director Human Resources ... Ms. Charo ALBARRAN
26 Chief Public Relations Officer ... Ms. Lissa GIBBS
18 Dir Camp Plng/Constr/Risk Mgmt Svcs . Mr. Matt CHRISTENSEN
102 Exec Director NVC Foundation ... Ms. Lissa GIBBS
19 Director College Police ... Mr. Kenneth L. ARNOLD
09 Director Institutional Research ... Dr. Robyn WORNALL
84 Enrollment Management ... Dr. Terry GUIGNI
88 Counselor/Coord Trans Center ... Mr. Jose HURTADO
36 Counselor/Coordinator WA III ... Vacant

National Career College (I)

14355 Roscoe Boulevard, Panorama City CA 91402
County: Los Angeles FICE Identification: 041460
Unit ID: 455868
Telephone: (818) 988-2300 Carnegie Class: Not Classified
FAX Number: (818) 988-6944 Calendar System: Semester
URL: www.nccusa.edu
Established: 2005 Annual Undergrad Tuition & Fees: N/A
Enrollment: 147 Coed
Affiliation or Control: Proprietary IRS Status: Proprietary
Highest Offering: Associate Degree
Accreditation: ABHES

01 President ... Gayane KHANOYAN
37 Director Student Financial Aid ... Anna TOVMASYAN

National Polytechnic College (J)

6630 Telegraph Rd., Ste 200, Commerce CA 90040
County: Los Angeles FICE Identification: 039104
Unit ID: 447759
Telephone: (323) 728-9636 Carnegie Class: Not Classified
FAX Number: (323) 728-0952 Calendar System: Semester
URL: www.npcollege.edu
Established: 1996 Annual Undergrad Tuition & Fees: N/A
Enrollment: 198 Coed
Affiliation or Control: Proprietary IRS Status: Proprietary
Highest Offering: Associate Degree
Accreditation: ACCSC, CEA

01 CEO and President ... Dariush (David) MADDAHI

National Test Pilot School (K)

PO Box 658, Mojave CA 93502-0658
County: Kern Identification: 667009
Telephone: (661) 824-2977 Carnegie Class: Not Classified
FAX Number: (661) 824-2943 Calendar System: Semester
URL: www.ntps.edu
Established: 1981 Annual Graduate Tuition & Fees: N/A
Enrollment: N/A Coed

Affiliation or Control: Independent Non-Profit IRS Status: 501(c)3
Highest Offering: Master's; No Undergraduates
Accreditation: ENG

01 President/CEO .... Dr. Al L. PETERSON
05 CAO/Head of Training .... Mr. Gregory V. LEWIS
11 Chief Operations Officer .... Mr. James BROWN
54 Director NFTI .... Dr. Lester A. INGHAM
13 Chief of Systems Academics .... Mr. Chris MC ELROY
88 Chief of FW P&FQ Academics .... Dr. Gabriele DI FRANCESCO
88 Chief of RW P&FQ Academics .... Mr. Ilan ARUSH
88 Chief FW Test Pilot Instructor .... Mr. Ed SOLSKI
88 Chief RW Test Pilot Instructor .... Mr. Nigel SPEEDY
06 Registrar .... Ms. Sindy STANTON
10 Business Manager .... Ms. Lynda MATOS

National University (A)

11255 N Torrey Pines Road, La Jolla CA 92037-1011
County: San Diego FICE Identification: 011460
Unit ID: 119605
Telephone: (858) 642-8000 Carnegie Class: Masters/L
FAX Number: (858) 642-8714 Calendar System: Other
URL: www.nu.edu
Established: 1971 Annual Undergrad Tuition & Fees: $12,744
Enrollment: 17,608 Coed
Affiliation or Control: Independent Non-Profit IRS Status: 501(c)3
Highest Offering: Master's
Accreditation: WC, ANEST, CS, IACBE, NURSE, PH, RTT, TED

00 Chancellor .... Dr. Michael R. CUNNINGHAM
01 University President .... Dr. David ANDREWS
03 Executive Vice President .... Ms. Nancy ROHLAND-HEINRICH
05 Provost .... Dr. Gangaram SINGH
10 Vice Chancellor Business & Admin .... Mr. Randy C. FRISCH
20 Interim Associate Provost .... Dr. Jo BIRDSELL
32 Vice President for Student Services .... Dr. Joseph ZAVALA
13 Vice Chancellor of Info Technology .... Mr. Christopher KRUG
07 Vice Chancellor of Marketing .... Vacant
30 VP Alumni Relations & Outreach .... Mr. Chris GRAHAM
84 VP Enrollment Mgmt & Regional Ops .... Dr. Brandon JOUGANATOS
12 AVP Regional Oper LAX Region .... Dr. Mahvash YADEGAR
15 AVP Human Resources .... Ms. Jane SAWYER
88 AVP Military and VA Programs .... Mr. Vernon TAYLOR
50 Interim Dean School of Bus & Mgmt .... Dr. Lena RODRIGUEZ
53 Dean Sanford College of Education .... Dr. Judy MANTLE
54 Dean School Engineering & Computing .... Dr. John CICERO
49 Dean College of Letters & Sciences .... Dr. Carol RICHARDSON
76 Dean Health and Human Services .... Dr. Gloria J. MCNEAL
107 Dean School of Professional Studies .... Dr. Daniel DONALDSON
06 Registrar .... Ms. Veronica GARCIA
08 Director Library Services .... Ms. Anne-Marie SECORD
37 Director Financial Aid .... Ms. Valerie RYAN
18 Director of Facilities .... Mr. Martin GALLARDO
88 Director of Credentials .... Mr. Brad DAMON
19 Director Security .... Mr. Jack DAVIDSON

New York Film Academy, Los Angeles (B)

3300 Riverside Drive, Burbank CA 91505
County: Burbank FICE Identification: 041188
Unit ID: 461148
Telephone: (818) 333-3558 Carnegie Class: Not Classified
FAX Number: (818) 333-3557 Calendar System: Semester
URL: www.nyfa.edu
Established: 2006 Annual Undergrad Tuition & Fees: $28,000
Enrollment: 1,907 Coed
Affiliation or Control: Proprietary IRS Status: Proprietary
Highest Offering: Master's
Accreditation: ART

01 Director .... Mr. Dan MACKLER
05 Dean of College .... Mr. Sonny CALDERON
32 Dean of Students .... Mr. Michael SANDOVAL
06 Registrar .... Mr. Vince VOSKANIAN
07 Director of Admissions .... Mrs. Amy ELLENBERGER
08 Head Librarian .... Mr. Josh MOORMON
39 Director Student Housing .... Mr. Brennan DILLION

NewSchool of Architecture and Design (C)

1249 F Street, San Diego CA 92101-6634
County: San Diego FICE Identification: 030439
Unit ID: 119775
Telephone: (619) 684-8800 Carnegie Class: Spec-4-yr-Arts
FAX Number: (619) 684-8880 Calendar System: Quarter
URL: www.newschoolarch.edu
Established: 1980 Annual Undergrad Tuition & Fees: $26,463
Enrollment: 498 Coed
Affiliation or Control: Proprietary IRS Status: Proprietary
Highest Offering: Master's
Accreditation: WC

01 President .... Mr. Marvin MALECHA
05 Chief Academic Officer .... Ms. Fionna SCOTT
32 Exec Director Student Affairs .... Dr. Sheila SULLIVAN
88 Director Design .... Dr. Elena PACENTI
58 Graduate Architecture Program Chair .... Mr. Kurt HUNKER
48 Undergrad Architecture Pgm Chair .... Mr. Len ZEGARSKI
88 Construction Management Pgm Chair .... Mr. George WELCH
97 General Education Program Chair .... Mr. Bruce MATTHES
09 Director of Institutional Research .... Ms. Tiffany RODRIGUEZ
10 Finance Manager .... Ms. Julie CODINA
06 Registrar .... Mr. Allen MUTCHLER
84 Director of Enrollment .... Vacant
37 Director of Financial Aid .... Mr. Bryan CHARBONNEAU
36 Director of Career/Alumni Services .... Ms. Lisa GANEM
15 Director of Human Resources .... Ms. Marcy MADIX
26 Director of Marketing .... Ms. Heli FRAZIER
07 Admissions Manager .... Ms. La'Shea ENGLISH
21 Business Office Manager .... Ms. Terre CORTEZ-FARAH
32 Student Life Manager .... Ms. Ashley WAGNER
08 Librarian .... Ms. Lucy CAMPBELL
88 Faculty Coordinator .... Mr. Robin BRISEBOIS
27 Public Relations Manager .... Ms. Anna CEARLEY
35 Student Success Manager .... Ms. Virginia PHILLIPS
13 IT Specialist .... Mr. Joe SOSA
88 Materials Lab Manager .... Mr. Erik LUHTALA

Nine Star University of Health Sciences (D)

441 De Guigne Drive #201, Sunnyvale CA 94085
County: Santa Clara Identification: 667207
Telephone: (408) 532-5567 Carnegie Class: Not Classified
FAX Number: (408) 733-3610 Calendar System: Trimester
URL: www.nsuhs.org
Established: Annual Graduate Tuition & Fees: N/A
Enrollment: N/A Coed
Affiliation or Control: Independent Non-Profit IRS Status: 501(c)3
Highest Offering: Master's; No Undergraduates
Accreditation: @ACUP

01 President .... Philip YANG

Nobel University (E)

505 Shatto Place #300, Los Angeles CA 90020
County: Los Angeles Identification: 667274
Telephone: (213) 382-1136 Carnegie Class: Not Classified
FAX Number: (213) 382-1187 Calendar System: Semester
URL: nobeluniversity.edu
Established: 2000 Annual Undergrad Tuition & Fees: N/A
Enrollment: N/A Coed
Affiliation or Control: Proprietary IRS Status: Proprietary
Highest Offering: Master's
Accreditation: ACICS

01 President .... Chong S. KIM

*North Orange County Community College District (F)

1830 W Romneya Drive, Anaheim CA 92801-1819
County: Orange FICE Identification: 009742
Unit ID: 120023
Telephone: (714) 808-4500 Carnegie Class: N/A
FAX Number: (714) 808-4791
URL: www.nocccd.edu

01 Chancellor .... Dr. Cheryl A. MARSHALL
10 Vice Chanc Finance/Facilities .... Mr. Fred WILLIAMS
15 Vice Chancellor Human Resources .... Ms. Irma RAMOS
05 Vice Chanc Educational Svcs/Tech .... Dr. W. Cherry LI-BUGG
26 Vice Chanc Public/Govt Affairs .... Ms. Kai STEARNS MOORE
04 Exec Admin Aide to Chancellor .... Ms. Alba RECINOS
22 Dist Director Equity & Diversity .... Mr. Arturo OCAMPO

*Cypress College (G)

9200 Valley View, Cypress CA 90630-5897
County: Orange FICE Identification: 001193
Unit ID: 113236
Telephone: (714) 484-7000 Carnegie Class: Assoc/MT-VT-High Trad
FAX Number: (714) 527-8238 Calendar System: Semester
URL: www.cypresscollege.edu
Established: 1966 Annual Undergrad Tuition & Fees (In-District): $1,138
Enrollment: 15,816 Coed
Affiliation or Control: State/Local IRS Status: 501(c)3
Highest Offering: Baccalaureate
Accreditation: WJ, ADNUR, CAHIIM, DA, DH, DMS, FUSER, RAD

02 President .... Dr. Robert G. SIMPSON
05 Exec VP Educ Pgms/Student Svcs .... Dr. Santanu BANDYOPADHYAY
10 Vice Pres Admin/Business Svcs .... Ms. Karen CANT
08 Dean Library/Learning Resource Ctr .... Dr. Treisa CASSENS
88 Dean Language Arts .... Mr. Eldon YOUNG
07 Dean Counseling/Admiss & Records .... Dr. Paul DE DIOS
06 Registrar .... Mr. David BOOZE
26 Director Campus Communications .... Mr. Marc POSNER
102 Exec Dir Foundation/Community Rels .... Mr. Raul ALVAREZ
32 Dean Student Support Services .... Dr. Richard RAMS
22 Director Disabled Student Services .... Ms. Celeste PHELPS
90 Manager Systems Technology Svcs .... Mr. Michael KAVANAUGH
37 Director Financial Aid .... Mr. Chinh PHAM
09 Dir Institutional Research/Planning .... Mr. Philip DYKSTRA
18 Director Physical Plant/Facilities .... Mr. Albert MIRANDA
19 Director Campus Safety .... Dr. Shirley SMITH
04 Executive Assistant to President .... Ms. Ty VOLCY
68 Dean Physical Education .... Dr. Richard RAMS
57 Interim Dean Fine Arts .... Dr. Katy REALISTA
50 Interim Dean Business/CIS .... Dr. Steve DONLEY
83 Dean Social Sciences .... Ms. Nina DEMARKEY
53 Dean Science Engineering & Math .... Dr. Richard FEE
76 Dean Health Sciences .... Dr. John SCIACCA
75 Dean Career Technical Education .... Dr. Steve DONLEY
88 Spec Proj Director Student Equity .... Ms. Ashley GRIFFITH
88 Manager SSSP .... Mr. Tom TO
21 Bursar .... Ms. Dao DO
22 Director EOPS .... Dr. Elaine LIPIZ GONZALEZ
88 Project Manager Campus Cap Proj .... Ms. Susan RITTEL

*Fullerton College (H)

321 E Chapman Avenue, Fullerton CA 92832-2095
County: Orange FICE Identification: 001201
Unit ID: 114859
Telephone: (714) 992-7000 Carnegie Class: Assoc/HT-High Trad
FAX Number: (714) 992-9930 Calendar System: Semester
URL: www.fullcoll.edu
Established: 1913 Annual Undergrad Tuition & Fees (In-District): $1,138
Enrollment: 25,051 Coed
Affiliation or Control: State/Local IRS Status: 501(c)3
Highest Offering: Associate Degree
Accreditation: WJ

02 Interim President .... Dr. Greg SCHULZ
05 Vice President Instruction .... Dr. Jose Ramon NUNEZ
32 Vice Pres Student Services .... Dr. Gilbert CONTRERAS
11 Vice Pres Administrative Svcs .... Vacant
50 Dean Business & CIS .... Dr. Doug BENOIT
57 Interim Dean Fine Arts .... Mr. John TEBAY
79 Dean Humanities .... Mr. Dan WILLOUGHBY
81 Dean Math/Computer Science .... Mr. Mark GREENHALGH
82 Dean Natural Sciences .... Dr. Richard HARTMANN
68 Dean Physical Education .... Dr. David GROSSMAN
83 Dean Social Sciences .... Dr. Kathy BENOIT
72 Dean Technology & Engr .... Mr. Kenneth STARKMAN
37 Director of Financial Aid .... Mr. Greg RYAN
23 Director Health Services .... Dr. Vanessa MILLER
18 Dir Facilities/Physical Plant .... Mr. Larry LARA
40 Director of Bookstore .... Mr. Nick KARVIA
35 Director Student Affairs .... Ms. Naomi ABESAMIS
06 Registrar .... Ms. Rena MARTINEZ STLUKA
19 Director Campus Safety .... Mr. Steve SELBY
38 Dean Counseling/Student Development .... Ms. Lisa CAMPBELL
08 Dean Library (LLR & ISPS) .... Ms. Dani WILSON
07 Dean Admissions & Records .... Mr. Albert ABUTIN
90 Academic Computing Technologies .... Mr. Co HO
09 Director Inst Research & Planning .... Mr. Carlos AYON
88 Director Transfer Center .... Ms. Cecilia ARRIAZA
26 Director Campus Communications .... Ms. Lisa MCPHERON
04 Exec Assistant to the President .... Ms. Melinda TAYLOR
88 Dean Student Support Services .... Dr. Derek VERGARA

Northwestern Polytechnic University (I)

47671 Westinghouse Drive, Fremont CA 94539-7474
County: Alameda Identification: 666759
Unit ID: 120166
Telephone: (510) 592-9688 Carnegie Class: Not Classified
FAX Number: (510) 657-8975 Calendar System: Trimester
URL: www.npu.edu
Established: 1984 Annual Undergrad Tuition & Fees: N/A
Enrollment: N/A Coed
Affiliation or Control: Independent Non-Profit IRS Status: 501(c)3
Highest Offering: Master's
Accreditation: ACICS

01 President .... Mr. Peter HSIEH
03 Executive Vice President .... Mr. Paul CHOI
43 Legal Counsel & Director of HR .... Mr. Gerald WONG

† ACICS scope of recognition as approved by US Dept of Education and CHEA includes diploma programs and degree programs through the Master's degree. However, NPU offers an ACICS accredited Doctorate of Computer Science and a Doctorate of Business.

Notre Dame de Namur University (J)

1500 Ralston Avenue, Belmont CA 94002-1908
County: San Mateo FICE Identification: 001179
Unit ID: 120184
Telephone: (650) 508-3500 Carnegie Class: Masters/L
FAX Number: (000) 000-0000 Calendar System: Semester
URL: www.ndnu.edu
Established: 1851 Annual Undergrad Tuition & Fees: $32,608
Enrollment: 1,982 Coed
Affiliation or Control: Independent Non-Profit IRS Status: 501(c)3
Highest Offering: Master's
Accreditation: WC, ACBSP

01 President .... Dr. Judith M. GREIG
05 Interim Provost .... Dr. John LEMMON
10 Vice Pres Finance & Administration .... Mr. Henry ROTH
32 Dean of Students .... Mr. Marsh-Allen SMITH
84 Vice President of Enrollment Mgmt .... Mr. Jason MURRAY
30 Vice Pres for Advancement .... Mr. Dino HERNANDEZ
04 Exec Assistant to the President .... Ms. Alison LYON

49 Dean Arts & Sciences ... Dr. John LEMMON
50 Dean Business & Management ... Dr. Craig BREWER
53 Dean Education/Psychology ... Dr. Caryl HODGES
06 Registrar ... Mr. J. T BROWN
36 Director Career Development ... Ms. Carrie MCKNIGHT
37 Director Financial Aid ... Mr. Charles WALZ
38 Director Student Counseling ... Ms. Karin SPONHOLZ
41 Athletic Director ... Mr. Josh DOODY
42 Director Spirituality ... Ms. Amy JOBIN
19 Director of Public Safety ... Mr. William PALMINI, JR.
29 Director Events/Alumni Relations ... Ms. Elizabeth VALENTE
26 Exec Dir Marketing/Communication ... Ms. Karen SCHORNSTEIN
15 Executive Director Human Resources ... Ms. Mary HAESLOOP
08 Director Library Services ... Ms. Mary WEGMANN
13 Director Office of Information Tech ... Mr. Merle MASON
18 Director Facilities ... Mr. Ryan MARTINI
20 Associate Provost ... Mr. Greg WHITE
21 Controller ... Ms. Emiko YAMADA
35 Int Dir Student Life & Leadership ... Ms. Gillian WALLACE
09 Director of Institutional Research ... Mr. John HOFMANN
102 Dir Foundation/Corporate Relations ... Mr. Reginald DUHE

Occidental College (A)

1600 Campus Road, Los Angeles CA 90041-3314
County: Los Angeles — FICE Identification: 001249
Unit ID: 120254
Telephone: (323) 259-2500 — Carnegie Class: Bac-A&S
FAX Number: (323) 259-2958 — Calendar System: Semester
URL: www.oxy.edu
Established: 1887 — Annual Undergrad Tuition & Fees: $49,248
Enrollment: 2,040 — Coed
Affiliation or Control: Independent Non-Profit — IRS Status: 501(c)3
Highest Offering: Master's
Accreditation: WC

01 President ... Dr. Jonathan VEITCH
05 Int Vice Pres Academic Affairs ... Dr. Kerry THOMPSON
10 Vice Pres for Finance & Planning ... Mr. Amos HIMMELSTEIN
84 Vice Pres of Enrollment ... Mr. Vincent CUSEO
30 Vice Pres Inst Advancement ... Mr. Charlie CARDILLO
32 Acting Dean of Students ... Dr. Erica O'NEAL HOWARD
43 General Counsel ... Ms. Leora FRIEDMAN
41 Assoc Vice Pres/Dir Athletics ... Ms. Jaime HOFFMAN
18 Assoc VP for Facilities Management ... Mr. Thomas POLANSKY
29 Int Ast VP Alumni/Parent Engagement ... Ms. Suzy LACROIX
26 AVP Marketing/Communications ... Mr. Marty SHARKEY
13 Chief Info Officer/AVP for ITS ... Mr. James UHRICH
04 Int Exec Assistant to President ... Ms. Connie SANCHEZ
06 Registrar ... Mr. Victor T. EGITTO
08 Librarian ... Vacant
37 Director of Financial Aid ... Ms. Maureen MCRAE
36 Director Career Development Center ... Ms. Valerie SAVIOR
15 Director of Human Resources ... Ms. Danita MAXWELL
27 Director of Communications ... Mr. Jim TRANQUADA
09 Director of Institutional Research ... Ms. Teresa KALDOR
44 Director Advancement Services ... Ms. Sarah RAMAGE
39 Assoc Dean Students/Dir Res Life ... Mr. Tim CHANG
19 Chief of Campus Safety ... Mr. Victor CLAY

Ohlone College (B)

43600 Mission Boulevard, Fremont CA 94539-0390
County: Alameda — FICE Identification: 004481
Unit ID: 120290
Telephone: (510) 659-6000 — Carnegie Class: Assoc/HT-Mix Trad/Non
FAX Number: N/A — Calendar System: Semester
URL: www.ohlone.edu
Established: 1966 — Annual Undergrad Tuition & Fees (In-District): $1,162
Enrollment: 11,318 — Coed
Affiliation or Control: State/Local — IRS Status: 501(c)3
Highest Offering: Associate Degree
Accreditation: WJ, ADNUR, COARC, PTAA

01 President/Superintendent ... Dr. Gari BROWNING
05 Vice President Academic Affairs ... Dr. Leta STAGNARO
10 Vice Pres Administrative Services ... Ms. Susan YEAGER
32 Vice President Student Services ... Dr. Ron TRAVENICK
13 Assoc Vice Pres Information Tech ... Dr. Chris DELA ROSA
15 Assoc Vice Pres Human Resources ... Ms. Shairon ZINGSHEIM
08 Dean Learning Resource/Instruc Tech ... Ms. Lesley BUEHLER
38 Dean Counseling ... Dr. Susan GUTKIND
09 Dean Institutional Research ... Mr. Michael BOWMAN
57 Dean Arts and Social Science ... Mr. Walter BIRKEDAHL
76 Dean Health Sciences & Env Studies ... Dr. Gale CARLI
83 Dean Language & Communication ... Mr. Mark LIEU
81 Int Dean Science/Engineering/Math ... Dr. Bob BRADSHAW
88 Associate Dean Deaf Studies ... Ms. Darline GUNSAULS
102 Executive Director Foundation ... Mr. Paul IANNACCONE
35 Director EOPS/Student Services ... Ms. Debra TRIGG
21 Director Business Services ... Mr. Farhad SABIT
30 Director College Advancement ... Ms. Patrice BIRKEDAHL
19 Chief Safety & Security ... Mr. John WORLEY
18 Director of Facilities ... Mr. David ORIAS
37 Director Financial Aid ... Ms. Deborah GRIFFIN
96 Director of Purchasing ... Mr. Alex LEBEDEFF
104 Director International Programs ... Mr. Bill SHARAR
84 Director Enrollment Mgmt ... Ms. Kimberly ROBBIE
04 Administrative Asst to President ... Ms. Shelby FOSTER
07 Dean Enrollment Services ... Ms. Laura WEAVER
41 Dean Kinesiology & Athletics ... Mr. Chris WARDEN

Oikos University (C)

7850 Edgewater Drive, Oakland CA 94621
County: Alameda — Identification: 667212
Telephone: (510) 639-7879 — Carnegie Class: Not Classified
FAX Number: (510) 639-7810 — Calendar System: Semester
URL: www.oikosuniversity.edu
Established: 2004 — Annual Undergrad Tuition & Fees: N/A
Enrollment: N/A — Coed
Affiliation or Control: Independent Non-Profit — IRS Status: 501(c)3
Highest Offering: Doctorate
Accreditation: TRACS

01 President ... Dr. Jongin KIM

Olivet University (D)

1025 Howard Street, San Francisco CA 94103
County: San Francisco — Identification: 666176
Telephone: (415) 371-0002 — Carnegie Class: Not Classified
FAX Number: (415) 371-0003 — Calendar System: Quarter
URL: www.olivetuniversity.edu
Established: 1992 — Annual Undergrad Tuition & Fees: N/A
Enrollment: N/A — Coed
Affiliation or Control: Independent Non-Profit — IRS Status: 501(c)3
Highest Offering: Doctorate
Accreditation: BI

01 University President ... Dr. Tracy DAVIS
03 Vice President ... Mr. Nathanael TRAN
05 Academic Dean ... Dr. Christy TRAN
10 Chief Financial Officer ... Mr. Barnabas JUNG
11 Chief Operating Officer ... Dr. Walker TZENG

Otis College of Art and Design (E)

9045 Lincoln Boulevard, Los Angeles CA 90045-3550
County: Los Angeles — FICE Identification: 001251
Unit ID: 120403
Telephone: (310) 665-6800 — Carnegie Class: Spec-4-yr-Arts
FAX Number: (310) 665-6805 — Calendar System: Semester
URL: www.otis.edu
Established: 1918 — Annual Undergrad Tuition & Fees: $42,314
Enrollment: 1,146 — Coed
Affiliation or Control: Independent Non-Profit — IRS Status: 501(c)3
Highest Offering: Master's
Accreditation: WC, ART

01 President ... Dr. Bruce FERGUSON
05 Provost ... Mr. Randall LAVENDER
10 VP of Admin & Financial Services ... Mr. William SCHAEFFER
32 VP Student Success ... Dr. Laura KIRALLA
30 VP Institutional Advancement ... Ms. Susan POLLACK
15 Vice Pres Human Resources/Devel ... Ms. Jane MIYASHIRO
20 Assoc Provost Academic Admin ... Ms. Kim RUSSO
35 Dean of Students ... Dr. Laura KIRALLA
51 Dean of Continuing Ed/Pre-Col Pgms ... Ms. Amy GANTMAN
07 Dean of Admissions & Financial Aid ... Mr. Matthew GALLAGHER
06 Registrar ... Ms. Anna MANZANO
08 Director of Library & Instruc Tech ... Ms. Sue MABERRY
37 Director of Financial Aid ... Ms. Jessika VASQUEZ
36 Director Career Services ... Ms. Donna Lee ODA
13 Chief Information Officer ... Mr. Ankush MAHINDRA
18 Chief Facilities/Operation Officer ... Mr. Claude NICA
26 VP of Communications and Marketing ... Vacant
29 Director Alumni Relations ... Vacant
21 Controller ... Ms. Christine SANCHEZ
88 Director Tech Support Services ... Mr. Andrew ARMSTRONG
102 Director of Board & Donor Relations ... Ms. Kathy LAKE
88 Director of Strategic Partnerships ... Ms. Christine LEAHEY
04 Administrative Asst to President ... Ms. Mahtem SHIFERRAW
09 Director of Inst Research & Effecti ... Ms. Rosa BELERIQUE
104 Director International Education ... Mr. Darren GROSCH
108 Assoc Provost for Assess & Accred ... Ms. Debra BALLARD
19 Chief Safety and Security Officer ... Mr. Rick GONZALEZ
28 Asst Dean of Stdnt Affs/TitleIX ... Dr. Carol BRANCH
38 Director Student Health & Wellness ... Dr. Julie SPENCER
39 Director Housing & Res Life ... Ms. Morgan BROWN
90 Sr Director of End-User Computing ... Mr. Felipe GUTIERREZ
96 Director of Purchasing ... Ms. Barbara TECLE

Pacific College (F)

3160 Redhill Avenue, Costa Mesa CA 92626-3402
County: Orange — FICE Identification: 032993
Unit ID: 422695
Telephone: (800) 867-2243 — Carnegie Class: Spec-4-yr-Other Health
FAX Number: (714) 662-1702 — Calendar System: Semester
URL: www.pacific-college.edu
Established: 1993 — Annual Undergrad Tuition & Fees: N/A
Enrollment: 274 — Coed
Affiliation or Control: Proprietary — IRS Status: Proprietary
Highest Offering: Baccalaureate
Accreditation: WC, ACCSC, NURSE

01 President ... Mr. William L. NELSON
03 Vice President ... Ms. Donna WOO
05 Director of Education ... Mr. Brian CHILSTRON

Pacific College of Oriental Medicine (G)

7445 Mission Valley Road, #105,
San Diego CA 92108-4408
County: San Diego — FICE Identification: 030277
Unit ID: 378576
Telephone: (619) 574-6909 — Carnegie Class: Spec-4-yr-Other Health
FAX Number: (619) 574-6641 — Calendar System: Trimester
URL: www.pacificcollege.edu
Established: 1986 — Annual Undergrad Tuition & Fees: $8,912
Enrollment: 459 — Coed
Affiliation or Control: Proprietary — IRS Status: Proprietary
Highest Offering: Doctorate
Accreditation: WC, ACUP

01 President ... Mr. Jack MILLER
05 Vice Pres of Academic Affairs ... Ms. Stacy GOMES
10 Chief Operating Officer ... Mr. Malcolm YOUNGREN
37 Vice Pres of Financial Aid ... Ms. Beatrice SMITH
26 Vice President Marketing ... Ms. Gail VOGT
12 Campus Director NY Campus ... Mr. Malcolm YOUNGREN
12 Campus Director CH Campus ... Mr. Edward LAMADRID
07 Director Admissions ... Mr. Reza GARAJEEAGHI
06 Registrar ... Mr. Nayeli CORONA
20 Academic Dean ... Ms. Teri POWERS
23 Director of Clinical Services ... Mr. Greg LANE
08 Head Librarian ... Ms. Naomi BROERING
13 Information Technology Director ... Mr. Greg RUSSO
88 Office Manager ... Ms. Cindy FLOYD
40 Bookstore Manager ... Ms. Patti HINES
21 Bursar ... Ms. Patti HINES
27 Pacific Symposium & Events Coord ... Ms. Tiffany MCCORT

Pacific Oaks College (H)

55 Eureka Street, Pasadena CA 91103
County: Los Angeles — FICE Identification: 001255
Unit ID: 120768
Telephone: (626) 529-8500 — Carnegie Class: Spec-4-yr-Other
FAX Number: N/A — Calendar System: Semester
URL: www.pacificoaks.edu
Established: 1945 — Annual Undergrad Tuition & Fees: N/A
Enrollment: 1,176 — Coed
Affiliation or Control: Independent Non-Profit — IRS Status: 501(c)3
Highest Offering: Master's
Accreditation: WC

01 President ... Dr. Patricia A. BREEN
05 Dean Academic Affairs ... Mr. Terry RATCLIFF
11 Chief Operating Officer ... Ms. Melanie SAUER
32 Assoc Vice Pres Student Services ... Mr. Frank FRIAS
88 Exec Director Children's School ... Ms. Pam MCCOMAS
15 Director of Human Resources ... Ms. Carolyn MATHIS
10 Director of Finance ... Ms. Yug Fon CHIQUITO
08 Campus Librarian ... Ms. Kelsey VUKIC
35 Dir Ctr Stdnt Achievmt/Res/Enrich ... Ms. Pat MEDA
07 Senior Director Admissions ... Mr. Ron RUBALCABA
13 IT Director ... Mr. Carlos BONILLA
04 Dir Pres Office & Board Affairs ... Ms. Amy SEYERLE
88 Dir Northern CA Instructional Site ... Dr. Marian BROWNING
88 Assoc Dean School of CFP ... Dr. Bree DAVIS
88 Assoc Dean School of HD ... Dr. Donald GRANT
30 Director Advancement ... Ms. Debbie CORDANO
26 Director Communications/Marketing ... Mr. Larry RENICK

Pacific School of Religion (I)

1798 Scenic Avenue, Berkeley CA 94709-1323
County: Alameda — FICE Identification: 001256
Unit ID: 120795
Telephone: (510) 849-8200 — Carnegie Class: Spec-4-yr-Faith
FAX Number: (510) 845-8948 — Calendar System: Semester
URL: www.psr.edu
Established: 1866 — Annual Graduate Tuition & Fees: N/A
Enrollment: 175 — Coed
Affiliation or Control: Independent Non-Profit — IRS Status: 501(c)3
Highest Offering: Doctorate; No Undergraduates
Accreditation: WC, THEOL

01 President ... Rev. David VASQUEZ-LEVY
05 Dean/VP Academic Affairs ... Dr. Mary Donovan TURNER
10 Chief Business Officer ... Mr. Patrick O'LEARY
30 Chief Advancement Officer ... Ms. Wanda SCOTT
06 Asst Dean Academic Pgms/Registrar ... Ms. Delphine HWANG
07 Admissions/Financial Aid Officer ... Mr. Ruben CORTEZ
15 Personnel Director ... Ms. Deborah WALKER
04 Executive Asst to President ... Ms. Jen GALL
26 Marketing/Communications Manager ... Ms. Erin BURNS

Pacific States University (J)

3424 Wilshire Boulevard, 12th Floor,
Los Angeles CA 90010
County: Los Angeles — FICE Identification: 031633
Unit ID: 120838
Telephone: (323) 731-2383 — Carnegie Class: Spec-4-yr-Bus
FAX Number: (323) 731-7276 — Calendar System: Quarter
URL: www.psuca.edu
Established: 1928 — Annual Undergrad Tuition & Fees: $16,005
Enrollment: 172 — Coed
Affiliation or Control: Independent Non-Profit — IRS Status: 501(c)3

Highest Offering: Master's
Accreditation: ACICS

01 President ... Mr. Hee Young AHN
88 Asst Dean General Affairs ... Miss Rosy LIM
32 Associate Dean Student Affairs ... Mr. Moonsik KIM
26 Asst Dean Public Rels/Intl Affs ... Ms. Sarah MIN
13 Dir General & Technology Services ... Mr. Kuang Kai LU
88 Director ESL Program ... Ms. Maria CASTANEDA
08 University Librarian ... Vacant
06 Registrar ... Ms. Zolzaya ENKHBAYAR

Pacific Union College (A)

One Angwin Avenue, Angwin CA 94508-9797
County: Napa FICE Identification: 001258
Unit ID: 120865
Telephone: (707) 965-6311 Carnegie Class: Bac-A&S
FAX Number: (707) 965-6390 Calendar System: Quarter
URL: www.puc.edu
Established: 1882 Annual Undergrad Tuition & Fees: $29,064
Enrollment: 1,644 Coed
Affiliation or Control: Seventh-day Adventist IRS Status: 501(c)3
Highest Offering: Master's
Accreditation: WC, ADNUR, IACBE, MUS, NUR, SW

01 President ... Dr. Heather J. KNIGHT
05 Academic Dean/Vice Pres Admin ... Dr. Nancy LECOURT
10 VP Financial Administration/CFO ... Dr. Dave LAWRENCE
88 Vice President for Asset Management ... Dr. John COLLINS
32 Vice President Student Services ... Dr. Lisa BISSELL PAULSON
30 Vice President Advancement ... Mr. Walter COLLINS
84 Vice Pres Enrollment Mgt/Pub Rels ... Ms. Jennifer TYNER
33 Dean of Men ... Mr. James I. BOYD, JR.
34 Dean of Women ... Miss Janice R. WOOD
08 Director Library Services ... Mr. Adu WORKU
37 Director Student Financial Services ... Ms. Laurie WHEELER
13 Director Information Technology ... Mrs. Maria VANCE
06 Director Registration & Records ... Mrs. Marlo WATERS
15 Director Human Resources ... Ms. Iris CHUAH
21 Director Budgets & Fiscal Services ... Mrs. Joy L. HIRDLER
38 Director Counseling Center ... Mr. Michael JEFFERSON
18 Chief Facilities/Facil Management ... Mr. Dale WITHERS
20 Associate Academic Officer ... Mr. Edwin MOORE
07 Admissions Counselor ... Ms. Jordan THORNBURGH
09 Director of Institutional Research ... Mr. Serhii KALYNOVSKYI

Pacifica Graduate Institute (B)

249 Lambert Road, Carpinteria CA 93013-3019
County: Carpinteria FICE Identification: 031268
Unit ID: 115746
Telephone: (805) 969-3626 Carnegie Class: Spec-4-yr-Other Health
FAX Number: (805) 565-1932 Calendar System: Quarter
URL: www.pacifica.edu
Established: 1974 Annual Graduate Tuition & Fees: N/A
Enrollment: 970 Coed
Affiliation or Control: Proprietary IRS Status: Proprietary
Highest Offering: Doctorate; No Undergraduates
Accreditation: WC

01 Chancellor/Chief Executive Officer ... Dr. Stephen AIZENSTAT
05 Vice President/Provost ... Dr. Joseph CAMBRAY
10 Chief Financial Ofcr/VP Bus Svcs ... Mr. David HENKEL
43 General Counsel ... Mr. Frank MICHAELSON
37 Director of Financial Aid ... Ms. Tracie TEAGUE
06 Registrar ... Ms. Francine MATAS
30 Dir of Institutional Advancement ... Mr. Erik DAVIS
15 Director of Human Resources ... Ms. Cynthia BATASTINI
39 Director of Guest Services ... Mr. Jeffrey ABRAHAM
29 Director of Alumni Relations ... Ms. Dianne TRAVIS-TEAGUE

Palmer College of Chiropractic, San Jose Campus (C)

90 E Tasman Drive, San Jose CA 95134-1617
Telephone: (408) 944-6000 FICE Identification: 021849
Accreditation: &NH, &CHIRO

† Regional accreditation is carried under the parent institution in Davenport, IA.

Palo Alto University (D)

1791 Arastradero Road, Palo Alto CA 94304
County: San Mateo FICE Identification: 021383
Unit ID: 120698
Telephone: (800) 818-6136 Carnegie Class: Spec-4-yr-Other Health
FAX Number: (650) 433-3888 Calendar System: Quarter
URL: www.paloaltou.edu
Established: 1975 Annual Undergrad Tuition & Fees: N/A
Enrollment: 1,081 Coed
Affiliation or Control: Independent Non-Profit IRS Status: 501(c)3
Highest Offering: Doctorate
Accreditation: WC, CLPSY

01 President ... Dr. Maureen O'CONNOR
05 Provost/Academic Vice President ... Dr. William FROMING
32 Vice President Student Services ... Ms. Elizabeth HILT
31 Vice President for Community Devel ... Ms. Helen TING
88 Vice President for Prof Development ... Dr. Luli EMMONS
10 Vice Pres Business Affairs/CFO ... Ms. June KLEIN
20 Dean of Academic Admin/Oper ... Dr. James BRECKENRIDGE
17 Dir of Clinical Training-PhD Pgm ... Dr. Rowena GOMEZ
17 Dir of Clinical Training-PsyD Pgm ... Dr. Shelly HOWELL
23 Director of Clinic ... Dr. Sandy MACIAS
06 Registrar ... Ms. Nora MARQUEZ
37 Director Financial Aid ... Ms. Jessica AYRES
42 Chaplain/Ombudsman ... Rev. Byron BLAND
08 University Librarian/Dir Acad Tech ... Mr. Scott HINES
30 Director of Advancement ... Ms. Elizabeth SHAUGHNESSY
07 Director of Admissions ... Ms. Eirian WILLIAMS
13 Chief Information Officer ... Mr. David LEAVITT
29 Director of Alumni Relations ... Ms. Kemper MITCHELL
09 Institutional Research Admin ... Ms. Kristen GUY

Palo Verde College (E)

One College Drive, Blythe CA 92225-9561
County: Riverside FICE Identification: 001259
Unit ID: 120953
Telephone: (760) 921-5500 Carnegie Class: Assoc/MT-VT-Mix Trad/Non
FAX Number: (760) 921-5590 Calendar System: Semester
URL: www.paloverde.edu
Established: 1947 Annual Undergrad Tuition & Fees (In-District): $1,288
Enrollment: 3,446 Coed
Affiliation or Control: State/Local IRS Status: 501(c)3
Highest Offering: Associate Degree
Accreditation: WJ

01 Superintendent/President ... Dr. Donald WALLACE
05 Vice Pres Instructional/Stdnt Svcs ... Dr. Sean HANCOCK
04 Executive Asst to Supt/President ... Ms. Denise HUNT
66 Assoc Dean Nursing & Allied Health ... Ms. Virginia ARMSTRONG
08 Librarian ... Ms. June TURNER
07 Director of Admissions and Records ... Ms. Shelley HAMILTON
88 Site Supervsr Child Dev/Teacher Ctr ... Ms. Maria KEHL
09 Director of Institutional Research ... Mr. Adam HOUSTON
18 Facilities & Operations Director ... Mr. Shad LEE
13 Director of Information Technology ... Mr. Eric EGAN
26 Outreach & Events Coordinator ... Ms. Staci LEE
15 Chief Human Resources Officer/EEO ... Ms. Cecilia GARCIA
10 Vice Pres of Administrative Svcs ... Ms. Russi EGAN
20 Instructional Service Manager ... Ms. Denise TAYLOR
37 Director Student Financial Aid ... Ms. Diana MENDEZ
101 Exec Asst to Supt/President/Board ... Ms. Carrie MULLION

Palomar College (F)

1140 W Mission Road, San Marcos CA 92069-1487
County: San Diego FICE Identification: 001260
Unit ID: 120971
Telephone: (760) 744-1150 Carnegie Class: Assoc/HT-High Trad
FAX Number: (760) 744-8123 Calendar System: Semester
URL: www.palomar.edu
Established: 1946 Annual Undergrad Tuition & Fees (In-District): $1,338
Enrollment: 24,914 Coed
Affiliation or Control: State/Local IRS Status: 501(c)3
Highest Offering: Associate Degree
Accreditation: WJ, ADNUR, DA, EMT

01 Superintendent/President ... Dr. Joi Lin BLAKE
05 Int Asst Supt/Vice Pres Instruction ... Mr. Daniel SOURBEER
32 Asst Supt/VP Student Services ... Mr. Adrian GONZALES
10 Asst Supt/VP Finance/Admin Svcs ... Mr. Ron PEREZ
15 Int Asst Supt/VP Human Resources ... Mr. Michael POPIELSKI
04 Exec Assistant to the President ... Ms. Cheryl ASHOUR
79 Dean Languages & Literature ... Ms. Shayla SIVERT
81 Dean Math/Natural & Health Sciences ... Mr. Dan SOURBEER
38 Dean Counseling Services ... Mr. Brian STOCKERT
75 Int Dean Career/Tech/Extended Educ ... Mr. Paul KELLY
50 Dean Arts/Media/Bus & Computer Sci ... Vacant
83 Dean Social/Behavioral Sciences ... Mr. Jack HAHN
13 Director Info Systems & Services ... Vacant
84 Director Enrollment Svcs/Admissions ... Mr. Kendyl MAGNUSON
09 Sr Director Institutional Research ... Ms. Michelle BARTON
18 Director of Facilities ... Mr. Chris MILLER
35 Director Student Affairs ... Ms. Sherry TITUS
37 Director Student Financial Aid ... Vacant
26 Dir Comm/Marketing/Public Affairs ... Ms. Laura GROPEN
102 Executive Director for Foundation ... Mr. Richard TALMO
19 Chief of Police ... Mr. Mark DIMAGGIO
23 Director Health Services ... Ms. Judy HARRIS
41 Director Athletics ... Mr. Scott CATHCART

Pardee RAND Graduate School of Policy Studies (G)

1776 Main Street, Santa Monica CA 90407-2138
County: Los Angeles FICE Identification: 010441
Unit ID: 121628
Telephone: (310) 393-0411 Carnegie Class: Spec-4-yr-Other
FAX Number: (310) 451-6978 Calendar System: Quarter
URL: www.prgs.edu
Established: 1970 Annual Graduate Tuition & Fees: N/A
Enrollment: 102 Coed
Affiliation or Control: Independent Non-Profit IRS Status: 501(c)3
Highest Offering: Doctorate; No Undergraduates
Accreditation: WC

01 Dean ... Dr. Susan MARQUIS
05 Associate Dean ... Ms. Rachel SWANGER
06 Registrar ... Ms. Mary PARKER
10 Financial Aid/Budget Administrator ... Ms. Maggie CLAY

Pasadena City College (H)

1570 E Colorado Boulevard, Pasadena CA 91106-2041
County: Los Angeles FICE Identification: 001261
Unit ID: 121044
Telephone: (626) 585-7123 Carnegie Class: Assoc/HT-High Trad
FAX Number: (626) 585-7910 Calendar System: Semester
URL: www.pasadena.edu
Established: 1924 Annual Undergrad Tuition & Fees (In-District): $1,152
Enrollment: 26,611 Coed
Affiliation or Control: State/Local IRS Status: 501(c)3
Highest Offering: Associate Degree
Accreditation: #WJ, DA, DH, DT, MAC, RAD

01 Superintendent/President ... Dr. Rajen VURDIEN
05 Senior VP Academic & Student Affs ... Dr. Robert H. BELL
10 Senior VP Business & College Svcs ... Dr. Robert B. MILLER
32 Vice President Student Services ... Dr. Cynthia OLIVO
21 Exec Dir Business & College Svcs ... Mr. Joseph W. SIMONESCHI
15 Exec Dir Human Resources ... Ms. Terri HAMPTON
43 General Counsel ... Ms. Gail S. COOPER
09 Dir Inst Planning/Research ... Ms. Crystal KOLLROSS
31 Director Extension ... Ms. Elaine CHAPMAN
38 Int Assoc Dean Counseling ... Mr. Armando DURAN
88 Assistant Dean Special Services ... Dr. Kent YAMAUCHI
07 Dean Admissions/Records ... Ms. Susan BRICKER
37 Director Financial Aid ... Mr. Manuel CERDA
13 Director Technical Svcs ... Mr. Matthew KIAMAN
26 Public Relations ... Mr. Gilbert RIVERA
18 Exec Dir Facilities/Physical Plant ... Mr. Rueben SMITH
04 Administrative Asst to President ... Ms. Mary THOMPSON
19 Acting Director Security/Safety ... Mr. Steven MATCHAN
35 Dean Student Life ... Ms. Rebecca COBB
96 Director of Purchasing ... Mr. George CHIDIAC

Patten University (I)

2433 Coolidge Avenue, Oakland CA 94601-2699
County: Alameda FICE Identification: 004490
Unit ID: 121071
Telephone: (510) 535-9394 Carnegie Class: Not Classified
FAX Number: (510) 534-8696 Calendar System: Semester
URL: www.patten.edu
Established: 1944 Annual Undergrad Tuition & Fees: N/A
Enrollment: N/A Coed
Affiliation or Control: Proprietary IRS Status: Proprietary
Highest Offering: Master's
Accreditation: WC

01 President ... Dr. Thomas STEWART
05 Vice Pres Academic Affairs ... Dr. Marc PORTER
10 VP Finance/Administration ... Mr. Eric WAGENSONNER
106 Dean of Online Learning ... Dr. Tana MONACO
06 Registrar ... Mr. Aaron HIATT
85 Director of International Students ... Ms. Sharon BARTA
13 Director Information Technology ... Mr. Dennis CLARK
08 Director of Learning Commons ... Ms. Lisa HUBBELL
37 Director of Financial Operations ... Ms. La'Vetta JOSEPH
100 Chief of Staff ... Ms. Stacy CHIANG
19 Manager of Operations and Security ... Mrs. Patricia RUELAS

Pepperdine University (J)

24255 Pacific Coast Highway, Malibu CA 90263-0001
County: Los Angeles FICE Identification: 010149
Unit ID: 121150
Telephone: (310) 506-4000 Carnegie Class: DU-Mod
FAX Number: (310) 506-4861 Calendar System: Semester
URL: www.pepperdine.edu
Established: 1937 Annual Undergrad Tuition & Fees: $48,342
Enrollment: 7,417 Coed
Affiliation or Control: Church Of Christ IRS Status: 501(c)3
Highest Offering: Doctorate
Accreditation: WC, BUS, CLPSY, DIETD, LAW, MUS

01 President ... Dr. Andrew K. BENTON
100 Chief of Staff ... Ms. Marnie D. MITZE
03 Executive Vice President ... Mr. Gary A. HANSON
04 Exec Assistant to the President ... Mrs. Cynthia PAVELL
05 Provost ... Dr. Rick MARRS
00 Chancellor ... Dr. Michael ADAMS
30 Sr VP Advancement & Public Affairs ... Mr. Keith HINKLE
10 Senior Vice President Investments ... Mr. Jeff PIPPIN
43 General Counsel ... Mr. Marc P. GOODMAN
11 Vice President Administration ... Mr. Phil E. PHILLIPS
10 Chief Business Officer ... Mrs. Edna POWELL
13 Chief Information Officer ... Mr. Jonathan SEE
26 Chief Marketing Officer ... Mr. Rick GIBSON
10 VP and Chief Financial Officer ... Mr. Paul B. LASITER
21 Assoc VP Campus Ops/Business Svcs ... Mr. Alex PANG
06 Assoc VP & University Registrar ... Mr. Hung V. LE
104 Dean of International Programs ... Dr. Charles F. HALL
84 Dean of Admission/Enrollment Mgmt ... Dr. Kristy COLLINS
32 Dean of Student Affairs ... Dr. Mark DAVIS
08 Dean of Libraries ... Mr. Mark S. ROOSA
61 Dean of the School of Law ... Dr. Deanell TACHA
50 Dean of GSBM ... Dr. David M. SMITH
53 Dean of Graduate School Educ/Psych ... Dr. Helen E. WILLIAMS
49 Dean of Seaver College ... Dr. Michael E. FELTNER
80 Dean of School of Public Policy ... Mr. Pete PETERSON
42 University Chaplain ... Ms. Sara BARTON
46 Vice Provost for Research and Strat ... Dr. Lee KATS

108 Asst Provost Inst Effectiveness .... Dr. Lisa BORTMAN
29 Exec Director for Alumni Affairs .... Mr. Bob CLARK
15 Chief Human Resources Officer .... Mrs. Lauren COSENTINO
10 University Controller .... Mr. Brian THOMASON
10 Assistant Controller .... Mr. David BRANT
88 Director of Ministry Outreach .... Mr. Michael COPE
46 Director Research & Sponsored Pgm .... Mrs. Alexandra ROOSA
39 Assoc Dean of Students/Housing .... Mr. Jon MATHIS
88 Managing Dir Center for the Arts .... Ms. Rebecca CARSON
88 Director of Special Programs .... Ms. Kanet THOMAS
85 Sr Assoc Dir Intl Student Services .... Ms. Brooke CUTLER
27 Assoc VP IM Communications .... Mr. Matthew MIDURA
23 Director of Student Health Services .... Ms. Nancy SAFINICK
36 Assoc Dean of Students/Career Ctr .... Mr. Brad D. DUDLEY
41 Director of Athletics .... Dr. Steven POTTS
19 Assoc VP & Dir of Public Safety .... Mr. Lance BRIDGESMITH
18 Director Facilities Services .... Ms. Carly MISCHKE
86 Assoc VP Govt & Regulatory Affairs .... Ms. Rhiannon BAILARD
37 Director of Financial Assistance .... Mrs. Janet LOCKHART
38 Assoc VP & Dir Student Counseling .... Dr. Connie HORTON
09 Director of Institutional Research .... Ms. Lily PANG
44 Exec Dir Estate and Gift Planning .... Mr. Curt PORTZEL
22 Director Disability Services .... Ms. Sandra HARRISON
88 Director of Auditing Services .... Ms. Norma IADEVAIA

*Peralta Community Colleges District Office (A)

333 E Eighth Street, Oakland CA 94606-2889
County: Alameda FICE Identification: 001265
Unit ID: 121178
Telephone: (510) 466-7200 Carnegie Class: N/A
FAX Number: (510) 835-4078
URL: www.peralta.edu

01 Chancellor .... Dr. Jowel C. LAGUERRE
13 Assoc VC Information Technology .... Mr. Calvin MADLOCK
26 Exec Dir Public Info/Commun & Media .... Vacant

*Berkeley City College (B)

2050 Center Street, Berkeley CA 94704-1183
County: Alameda FICE Identification: 022427
Unit ID: 125170
Telephone: (510) 981-2800 Carnegie Class: Assoc/HT-High Non
FAX Number: (510) 841-7333 Calendar System: Semester
URL: www.berkeleycitycollege.edu
Established: 1974 Annual Undergrad Tuition & Fees (In-District): $1,156
Enrollment: 6,321 Coed
Affiliation or Control: State/Local IRS Status: 501(c)3
Highest Offering: Associate Degree
Accreditation: WJ

02 President .... Ms. Rowena M. TOMANENG
05 Vice President Instruction .... Ms. Tram VO-KUMAMOTO
32 Int Vice President Student Services .... Dr. Josefina BALTODANO
49 Dean Business Science MMART & AT .... Mr. Francisco GAMEZ
83 Dean Liberal Arts & Social Science .... Ms. Lisa R. COOK
88 Dean Student Support Services .... Ms. Brenda JOHNSON
10 Director Business Services & Admin ...... Ms. Shirley SLAUGHTER
51 Dir Program Adult College Education .... Vacant
35 Director of Campus and Student Life .... Mr. Andre SINGLETON
27 Public Information Officer .... Ms. Shirley FOGARINO
06 Registrar .... Ms. Adela ESQUIVEL-SWINSON
07 Director of Admissions .... Ms. Adela ESQUIVEL-SWINSON
09 Director of Institutional Research .... Dr. Mike ORKIN
15 Director Personnel Services .... Ms. Trudy LARGENT
18 Chief Facilities/Physical Plant .... Dr. Sadiq IKHARO
21 Associate Business Officer .... Mr. John PANG
26 Chief Public Relations Officer .... Mr. Jeffrey HEYMAN
28 Director of Diversity .... Ms. Trudy LARGENT
29 Interim Director Alumni Relations .... Ms. Kaia BURKETT
04 Executive Assistant to President .... Ms. Cynthia REESE
36 Director Student Placement .... Ms. Gail PENDLETON
37 Director Student Financial Aid .... Ms. Loan NGUYEN
38 Director Student Counseling .... Ms. Allene YOUNG
38 Director Student Counseling .... Ms. Susan TRUONG
96 Director of Purchasing .... Mr. John PANG

*College of Alameda (C)

555 Ralph Appezzato Memorial Pkwy,
Alameda CA 94501-2109
County: Alameda FICE Identification: 006720
Unit ID: 108667
Telephone: (510) 522-7221 Carnegie Class: Assoc/HT-High Non
FAX Number: (510) 337-0619 Calendar System: Semester
URL: www.alameda.peralta.edu
Established: 1968 Annual Undergrad Tuition & Fees (In-District): $1,156
Enrollment: 5,712 Coed
Affiliation or Control: State/Local IRS Status: 501(c)3
Highest Offering: Associate Degree
Accreditation: #WJ, DA

02 President .... Dr. Frances L. WHITE
05 Vice President of Instruction .... Mr. Tim KARAS
32 Vice President of Student Svcs .... Ms. Tina VASCONCELLOS
88 Dean Special Programs .... Ms. Toni COOK
26 Chief Public Relations Officer .... Vacant
84 Dean Enrollment Services .... Dr. Amy LEE
88 Dean Pathways/Stdnt Success .... Mr. Myron JORDAN
103 Dean Workforce Development .... Ms. Lilia CELHAY
10 Business & Administrative Svcs
Mgr .... Ms. Mary Beth BENVENUTTI

*Laney College (D)

900 Fallon Street, Oakland CA 94607-4893
County: Alameda FICE Identification: 001266
Unit ID: 117247
Telephone: (510) 834-5740 Carnegie Class: Assoc/MT-VT-High Non
FAX Number: (510) 464-3528 Calendar System: Semester
URL: www.laney.edu
Established: 1953 Annual Undergrad Tuition & Fees (In-District): $1,156
Enrollment: 10,548 Coed
Affiliation or Control: State/Local IRS Status: 501(c)3
Highest Offering: Associate Degree
Accreditation: WJ

02 Interim President .... Dr. Patricia STANLEY
05 Vice President of Instruction .... Mr. Zhanjing (John) YU
32 Vice President of Student Services .... Vacant
10 Director Business Services/Admin Services .... Ms. Phyllis CARTER
49 Div Dean Liberal Arts .... Dr. Chuen CHAN
81 Div Dean Mathematics and Science .... Ms. Denise RICHARDSON
75 Div Dean Career & Technical Educ .... Mr. Peter CRABTREE
23 Director Peralta Wellness Center .... Ms. Indra THADANI
84 Div Dean Enrollment Services .... Dr. Milcred LEWIS
79 Div Dean Humanities/Social Science .... Dr. Julianne KIRGIS
88 Div Dean Student Services .... Mr. Kevin WADE
04 Executive Assistant to President .... Ms. Maisha JAMESON
37 Financial Aid Supervisor .... Mr. Joseph KOROMA
41 Director Athletics .... Mr. John BEAM
88 Director Gateway to College Pgm .... Mr. Shawn TAYLOR
08 Head Librarian .... Ms. Evelyn LORD
35 Dir Student Activities/Campus Life .... Mr. Gary ALBURY

*Merritt College (E)

12500 Campus Drive, Oakland CA 94619-3196
County: Alameda FICE Identification: 001267
Unit ID: 118772
Telephone: (510) 531-4911 Carnegie Class: Assoc/HVT-High Non
FAX Number: (510) 436-2405 Calendar System: Semester
URL: www.merritt.edu
Established: 1953 Annual Undergrad Tuition & Fees (In-District): $1,156
Enrollment: 5,989 Coed
Affiliation or Control: State/Local IRS Status: 501(c)3
Highest Offering: Associate Degree
Accreditation: #WJ, DIETT, RAD

00 Chancellor .... Dr. Jowel LAGUERRE
02 Interim President .... Dr. Marie-Elaine BURNS
05 Vice President of Instruction .... Dr. Jeffrey LAMB
32 Vice President of Student Services .... Dr. Arnulfo CEDILLO
96 Vice Chancellor of General Services .... Dr. Sadiq IKHARO
15 Vice Chancellor for Human Resources .... Ms. Trudy LARGENT
20 Vice Chancellor Educational Services .... Dr. Michael ORKIN
13 Assoc VC of Information Technology .... Mr. Calvin MADLOCK
26 Exec Dir Marketing/Public Rels/Comm .... Mr. Jeffrey HEYMAN
08 Head Librarian .... Mr. Timothy HACKETT
06 Registrar .... Ms. Susana DE LA TORRE
10 Director of Business/Admin Services ..... Dr. Dativa DEL ROSARIO
35 Dir Student Activities/Campus Life .... Dr. Herbert KITCHEN
09 Director of Institutional Research .... Mr. Nathan FELLEGRIN
101 Board Clerk .... Ms. Brenda MARTINEZ
102 Interim Exec Dir Foundation .... Ms. Kaia BURKETT
18 Facilities Dir/Physical Plant .... Mr. Brian ADAIR
37 Director Student Financial Aid .... Mr. Dave NGUYEN

Phillips Graduate University (F)

19900 Plummer Street, Chatsworth CA 91311
County: Los Angeles FICE Identification: 022372
Unit ID: 110307
Telephone: (818) 386-5600 Carnegie Class: Spec-4-yr-Other Health
FAX Number: (818) 386-5636 Calendar System: Semester
URL: www.pgu.edu
Established: 1971 Annual Graduate Tuition & Fees: N/A
Enrollment: 222 Coed
Affiliation or Control: Independent Non-Profit IRS Status: 501(c)3
Highest Offering: Doctorate; No Undergraduates
Accreditation: WC

01 President .... Dr. Greg GORMAN
10 VP Finance & Business Affairs - CFO .... Ms. Tanya PONTEP
05 Vice President Academic Affairs .... Dr. Ellie KAUCHER
32 Dean of Students .... Dr. Theresa WRAY
07 Director of Admissions & Enrollment .... Mr. Matt KVETON
08 Director Library .... Ms. Caroline CISNEROS
06 Director of Registrar Services .... Mrs. Marylu ISSAEVITCH
108 Director Institutional Assessment .... Ms. Leslie WASSON
29 Director Alumni Relations .... Ms. Elida MACHUCA

Pima Medical Institute-Chula Vista (G)

780 Bay Boulevard, Suite 101,
Chula Vista CA 91910-5261
Telephone: (619) 425-3200 Identification: 666272
Accreditation: ABHES, COARC, RAD

† Branch campus of Pima Medical Institute, Tucson, AZ.

Pitzer College (H)

1050 N Mills Avenue, Claremont CA 91711-6110
County: Los Angeles FICE Identification: 001172
Unit ID: 121257
Telephone: (909) 621-8129 Carnegie Class: Bac-A&S
FAX Number: (909) 621-8770 Calendar System: Semester
URL: www.pitzer.edu
Established: 1963 Annual Undergrad Tuition & Fees: $48,670
Enrollment: 1,076 Coed
Affiliation or Control: Independent Non-Profit IRS Status: 501(c)3
Highest Offering: Baccalaureate
Accreditation: WC

01 Interim President .... Dr. Thomas POON
05 Vice Pres Acad Affs/Dean of Faculty .... Dr. Muriel POSTON
10 Treasurer/Vice Pres Administration .... Mr. Yuet LEE
30 Vice Pres College Advancement .... Dr. Adrian STEVENS
07 VP Admissions/Financial Aid .... Ms. Yvonne BERUMEN
32 Vice Pres Student Affairs .... Mr. Brian CARLISLE
26 VP Marketing/Public Relations .... Mr. Mark BAILEY
44 Assistant Vice Pres of Development .... Mrs. Pam JONES
20 Associate Dean of Faculty .... Ms. Kathleen PURVIS-ROBERTS
88 Assistant Dean of Faculty .... Mrs. Barbara JUNISBAI
06 Registrar .... Ms. Eva PETERS
37 Director Financial Aid .... Ms. Robin THOMPSON
09 Director of Institutional Research .... Mr. Marco Antonio CRUZ
15 Director Human Resources .... Ms. Marni BOBICH
18 Director Facilities .... Mr. Larry BURIK
21 Associate Treasurer .... Ms. Lori YOSHINO
36 Director Career Services .... Mr. Brad THARPE
29 Director Alumni Relations .... Ms. Nancy TRESER-OSGOOD
38 Director Student Counseling .... Dr. Rebecca KORNBLUH
04 Administrative Asst to President .... Ms. Melanie LACY

Platt College (I)

1000 S Fremont Avenue, Bldg A10 S,
Alhambra CA 91803-8845
County: Los Angeles FICE Identification: 030627
Unit ID: 260789
Telephone: (626) 300-5444 Carnegie Class: Spec-4-yr-Other Health
FAX Number: (626) 457-8295 Calendar System: Other
URL: www.plattcollege.edu
Established: 1987 Annual Undergrad Tuition & Fees: $15,196
Enrollment: 661 Coed
Affiliation or Control: Proprietary IRS Status: Proprietary
Highest Offering: Baccalaureate
Accreditation: ACCSC, #COARC, DMS

01 President .... Mr. Mike GIACOMINI

Platt College (J)

3700 Inland Empire Blvd, Ste 400, Ontario CA 91764-4906
Telephone: (909) 941-9410 Identification: 666056
Accreditation: ACCSC, #COARC

† Branch campus of Platt College, Alhambra, CA.

Platt College (K)

6465 Sycamore Canyon Boulevard, Riverside CA 95207
Telephone: (951) 572-4300 Identification: 770561
Accreditation: ACCSC

Platt College (L)

6250 El Cajon Boulevard, San Diego CA 92115-3919
County: San Diego FICE Identification: 023043
Unit ID: 121275
Telephone: (619) 265-0107 Carnegie Class: Spec-4-yr-Arts
FAX Number: (619) 265-8655 Calendar System: Semester
URL: www.platt.edu
Established: 1930 Annual Undergrad Tuition & Fees: $23,250
Enrollment: 316 Coed
Affiliation or Control: Proprietary IRS Status: Proprietary
Highest Offering: Baccalaureate
Accreditation: ACCSC

00 Chairman .... Mr. Robert D. LEIKER
01 President .... Mrs. Meg LEIKER
03 Vice President .... Mr. Alfred MEDRO

Point Loma Nazarene University (M)

3900 Lomaland Drive, San Diego CA 92106-2899
County: San Diego FICE Identification: 001262
Unit ID: 121309
Telephone: (619) 849-2200 Carnegie Class: Masters/L
FAX Number: (619) 849-2579 Calendar System: Semester
URL: www.pointloma.edu
Established: 1902 Annual Undergrad Tuition & Fees: $32,400
Enrollment: 3,374 Coed
Affiliation or Control: Church Of The Nazarene IRS Status: 501(c)3
Highest Offering: Beyond Master's But Less Than Doctorate
Accreditation: WC, ACBSP, CAATE, DIETD, EMT, MUS, NURSE, SW, TED

01 President .... Dr. Bob BROWER
03 Executive Vice President .... Dr. Joe WATKINS
05 Provost/Chief Academic Officer .... Dr. Kerry FULCHER
10 VP Finance/Administrative Svcs .... Mr. George LATTER
32 Vice Pres for Student Development .... Dr. Caye SMITH
88 Vice Pres Spiritual Development .... Dr. Mary PAUL
15 Assoc VP for Human Resources .... Mr. Jeffrey HERMAN
37 Assoc Vice President for Finance .... Mrs. Cindy CHAPPELL

35 Assc VP Stdnt Dev/Chf Diversity Ofc ... Dr. Jeffrey CARR
21 Assoc VP for Budget/Accounting ... Ms. Janet CAPRARIO
84 Assoc VP Enrollment ... Dr. Scott SHOEMAKER
20 Vice Prov Academic Administration ... Dr. Mark PITTS
108 Vice Prov Accred & IE ... Dr. Karen LEE
35 Dean of Students ... Dr. Jeff BOLSTER
13 Chief Information Officer ... Mr. Corey FLING
09 Dir Inst Effectiveness & Assessment ... Mr. Brent GOODMAN
12 Director of Wesleyan Center ... Dr. Mark MANN
18 Director of Campus Facilities ... Mr. Bruce KUNKEL
36 Executive Dir Strengths & Vocation ... Ms. Rebecca SMITH
88 Exec Dir of Enrollment Mgmt ... Ms. Jeanne COCHRAN
86 Dir Public Affairs ... Ms. Jill MONROE
88 Director Center Pastoral Leadship ... Dr. John CALHOUN
42 Ld Con for Mission Res & Pst Rel ... Dr. Ron BENEFIEL
88 Director of Community Ministries ... Ms. Dana HOJSACK
88 Director of Worship Arts ... Mr. George WILLIAMSON
49 Dean College of Arts & Sciences ... Dr. Jim DAICHENDT
83 Dean College of Social Sciences ... Dr. Holly IRWIN
07 Director Undergraduate Admissions ... Ms. Shannon HUTCHISON-CARAVEO
08 Director of Ryan Library ... Dr. Frank QUINN
56 Dean Extended Learning ... Dr. Dave PHILLIPS
06 Dir Records/Institutional Research ... Ms. Cheryl GAUGHAN
26 Director Marketing/Creative Svcs ... Ms. Michele CORBETT
88 Assoc Dean Stdnt Success/Wellness ... Dr. Kim BOGAN
19 Director of Public Safety ... Mr. Mark GALBRAITH
29 Exec Director of Alumni Relations ... Ms. Sheryl SMEE
40 Bookstore Manager ... Ms. Katelyn MERRILL
85 Dir Multicultural/Intl Stdnt Svcs ... Mr. Sam KWAPONG
41 Athletic Director ... Mr. Ethan HAMILTON
88 Director of Nicholson Commons ... Mr. Milton KARAHADIAN
94 Dir Stevenson Ctr for Women's Stds ... Dr. Linda BEAIL
104 Director Study Abroad ... Ms. Sandy SOOHOO-REFAEI
88 Dir of Programs & Operations ... Mr. Nick WOLF
04 Exec Asst to President ... Ms. Myra FISHER
106 Dir Online Education/E-learning ... Dr. Dave PHILLIPS
39 Asst Dir Student Housing ... Ms. Molly PETERSEN
30 Exec Dir Advancement Operations ... Ms. Christina GARDNER
50 Dean of Business ... Mr. Dan BOTHE
53 Dean of Education ... Ms. Deb ERICKSON
101 Secretary of the Institution/Board ... Dr. Joe WATKINS
28 Chief Diversity Officer ... Dr. Jeffrey CARR

Pomona College (A)

550 N College Avenue, #206, Claremont CA 91711-6301
County: Los Angeles — FICE Identification: 001173
Unit ID: 121345
Telephone: (909) 621-8000 — Carnegie Class: Bac-A&S
FAX Number: (909) 621-8403 — Calendar System: Semester
URL: www.pomona.edu
Established: 1887 — Annual Undergrad Tuition & Fees: $47,620
Enrollment: 1,650 — Coed
Affiliation or Control: Independent Non-Profit — IRS Status: 501(c)3
Highest Offering: Baccalaureate
Accreditation: WC

01 President ... Dr. David W. OXTOBY
05 Vice President/Dean of College ... Dr. Audrey BILGER
13 Vice President Information ... Mr. William MORSE
10 Vice President/Treasurer ... Dr. Karen SISSON
30 VP for Institutional Advancement ... Ms. Pamela BESNARD
32 Vice President/Dean of Students ... Mrs. Miriam FELDBLUM
07 VP of Admissions & Financial Aid ... Mr. Seth ALLEN
26 VP & Chief Communications Ofcr ... Ms. Marylou FERRY
04 Special Assistant to President ... Dr. Teresa SHAW
06 Registrar ... Ms. Margaret ADORNO
27 Director Public Relations ... Mr. Mark WOOD
29 Assistant VP Alumni & Parent Engage ... Mr. Craig ARTEAGA-JOHNSON
37 Director Financial Aid ... Vacant
36 Director Career Development ... Ms. Mary RAYMOND
15 Director Human Resources ... Ms. Brenda RUSHFORTH
41 Director Physical Education ... Ms. Lesley IRVINE
44 Director Annual Giving ... Mr. Michael SPICER
21 Assoc Treasurer/Controller ... Ms. Mary Lou WOODS
09 Director of Institutional Research ... Dr. Jennifer RACHFORD
18 Chief Facilities/Physical Plant ... Mr. Robert ROBINSON

Presbyterian Theological Seminary in America (B)

15605 Carmenita Rd., Santa Fe Springs CA 90670
County: Los Angeles — FICE Identification: 041228
Telephone: (562) 926-1023 — Carnegie Class: Not Classified
FAX Number: (562) 926-1025 — Calendar System: Semester
URL: www.ptsa.edu
Established: 1977 — Annual Undergrad Tuition & Fees: N/A
Enrollment: N/A — Coed
Affiliation or Control: Presbyterian Church In America — IRS Status: 501(c)3
Highest Offering: First Professional Degree
Accreditation: BI

01 President ... Dr. Sang Meyng LEE
05 Dean of Academic Affairs ... Rev. Kyungmo KOO
11 Dean of Administration ... Vacant
32 Dean of Students/Student Ministry ... Rev. Choong Gi PARK
85 Dean/Dir of Intl Students/Fin Aid ... Mrs. Karen CHOI
08 Librarian ... Ms. Youngsook CHOI
10 Managing Treasurer ... Mrs. Mihyun PARK
06 Registrar ... Mrs. Michelle YOON
106 Dir Online Education/E-learning ... Mr. Woo Joong KANG
13 IT Director ... Mr. Eliot LEE

Presidio Graduate School (C)

36 Lincoln Boulevard, Suite 120, San Francisco CA 94129
County: San Francisco — Identification: 667150
Telephone: (415) 561-6555 — Carnegie Class: Not Classified
FAX Number: (415) 561-6483 — Calendar System: Semester
URL: www.presidio.edu
Established: 2003 — Annual Graduate Tuition & Fees: N/A
Enrollment: N/A — Coed
Affiliation or Control: Independent Non-Profit — IRS Status: 501(c)3
Highest Offering: Master's; No Undergraduates
Accreditation: WC

01 President ... Mark SCHULMAN
05 Dean Academic Pgms/Student Svcs ... Dr. Steven CRANE
106 Dean of Online Programs ... Ryan CABINTE
10 Chief Financial Officer ... Santhi PERUMAL
32 Assoc Dir Student/Career Devel ... Dawn MOKUAU
07 Director of Admissions ... Kari DORTH

Professional Golfers Career College (D)

26109 Ynez Road, Temecula CA 92591-6013
County: Riverside — FICE Identification: 033673
Unit ID: 437750
Telephone: (951) 719-2994 — Carnegie Class: Spec 2-yr-Other
FAX Number: (951) 719-1643 — Calendar System: Semester
URL: www.golfcollege.edu
Established: 1990 — Annual Undergrad Tuition & Fees: $15,000
Enrollment: 248 — Coed
Affiliation or Control: Proprietary — IRS Status: Proprietary
Highest Offering: Associate Degree
Accreditation: ACICS

01 President ... Dr. Tim SOMERVILLE

Providence Christian College (E)

1539 E. Howard Street, Pasadena CA 91104
County: Los Angeles — FICE Identification: 041539
Unit ID: 455770
Telephone: (866) 323-0233 — Carnegie Class: Bac-A&S
FAX Number: (626) 696-4040 — Calendar System: Semester
URL: www.providencecc.edu
Established: 2002 — Annual Undergrad Tuition & Fees: $27,173
Enrollment: 91 — Coed
Affiliation or Control: Non-denominational — IRS Status: 501(c)3
Highest Offering: Baccalaureate
Accreditation: WC

01 President ... Dr. Jim BELCHER
05 Interim Chief Academic Officer ... Ann HAMILTON
10 VP Finance & Operations ... Dawn DIRKSEN
30 VP Advancement ... Michael KILEDJIAN
06 Registrar ... Patty TSAI
84 Director of Enrollment Management ... Larissa KAMPS
32 Director of Student Life ... Mark RIPPETOE
04 Administrative Asst to President ... Ruby BLEEKER

*Rancho Santiago Community College District (F)

2323 N. Broadway, Santa Ana CA 92706-1640
County: Orange — FICE Identification: 006991
Unit ID: 438665
Telephone: (714) 480-7300 — Carnegie Class: N/A
FAX Number: (714) 796-3915
URL: www.rsccd.edu

01 Chancellor ... Dr. Raul RODRIGUEZ
10 Vice Chanc Business & Fiscal Svcs ... Mr. Peter HARDASH
05 Vice Chanc Educational Svcs ... Mr. Enrique PEREZ
15 Vice Chanc Human Resources ... Ms. Judy CHITLIK
19 Interim Chief of Security ... Mr. Manny PACHECO
04 Exec Asst to the Chancellor ... Ms. Debra GERARD

*Santa Ana College (G)

1530 W 17th Street, Santa Ana CA 92706-3398
County: Orange — FICE Identification: 001284
Unit ID: 121619
Telephone: (714) 564-6000 — Carnegie Class: Assoc/HT-Mix Trad/Non
FAX Number: (714) 564-6379 — Calendar System: Semester
URL: www.sac.edu
Established: 1915 — Annual Undergrad Tuition & Fees (In-District): $1,142
Enrollment: 29,590 — Coed
Affiliation or Control: State/Local — IRS Status: 501(c)3
Highest Offering: Baccalaureate
Accreditation: WJ, ADNUR, OTA

02 President ... Dr. Linda D. ROSE
05 Vice President Academic Affairs ... Carlos LOPEZ
32 Vice President Student Services ... Dr. Sara LUNDQUIST
10 Vice Chanc Bus Ops/Fiscal Svcs ... Mr. Peter HARDASH
51 Vice President Continuing Educ ... James KENNEDY
35 Dean Student Affairs ... Dr. Lilia TANAKEYOWMA
11 Vice Pres Administrative Svcs ... Dr. Michael COLLINS
07 Dean Enrollment Services ... Mark LIANG
06 Registrar ... Chris TRUONG
50 Interim Dean Business Division ... Madeline GRANT
35 Assoc Dean Student Development ... Rosio BECERRA
38 Dean Counseling ... Dr. Micki BRYANT
37 Director of Financial Aid ... Robert MANSON
41 Dean KinesiologyAthletics ... Vacant
57 Dean Fine & Performing Arts ... Eve KIKAWA
30 Exec Director College Advancement ... Christina ROMERO
18 Facilities Manager ... Mark WHEELER
79 Dean Humanities & Social Siences ... Shelly JAFFRAY
81 Dean Science/Math/Hlth Sci ... Michelle PRIEST
103 Dean Career Educ/Workforce Develop ... Bart HOFFMAN
56 Associate Dean EOPS ... Christine LEON
88 Associate Dean DSPS ... Veronica OFORLEA
04 Assistant to the President ... Kennethia J. VEGA
26 Dir of Public Affs/Communications ... Judy IANNACCONE
09 Director of College Research ... Janice LOVE

*Santiago Canyon College (H)

8045 E Chapman Avenue, Orange CA 92869-4512
County: Orange — FICE Identification: 036957
Unit ID: 399212
Telephone: (714) 628-4900 — Carnegie Class: Assoc/HT-Mix Trad/Non
FAX Number: (714) 628-4723 — Calendar System: Semester
URL: www.sccollege.edu
Established: 1997 — Annual Undergrad Tuition & Fees (In-District): $1,142
Enrollment: 11,202 — Coed
Affiliation or Control: State/Local — IRS Status: 501(c)3
Highest Offering: Associate Degree
Accreditation: WJ

02 Interim President ... Dr. John HERNANDEZ
04 Assistant to the President ... Ms. Lynn MANZANO
32 Int Vice President Student Services ... Ms. Ruth BABESHOFF
05 Vice President Academic Affairs ... Vacant
51 Vice President Continuing Educ ... Mr. Jose VARGAS
11 Vice Pres Administrative Services ... Ms. Arleen SATELE
38 Interim Dean Counseling ... Dr. Jennifer COTO
41 Dean Math and Sciences ... Mr. Martin STRINGER
79 Dean Arts/Humanities/Social Science ... Ms. Marilyn FLORES
36 Dean Business/Career Tech Educ ... Mr. Von LAWSON
108 Dean Institutional Effectiveness ... Mr. Aaron VOELCKER
20 Dean Instruction/Student Services ... Ms. Lori FASBINDER
37 Dean Enrollment and Support Svcs ... Mr. Syed RIZVI
20 Dean Instruction/Student Svcs ... Vacant
35 Interim Dean Student Affairs ... Ms. Loretta JORDAN
20 Assoc Dean Bus/Career Tech Educ ... Ms. Kari IRWIN
07 Asst Dean of Admissions & Records ... Mr. Tuyen NGUYEN
37 Asst Dean Fin Aid/Scholarships ... Mr. Steven SALCIDO
18 Physical Plant Manager ... Vacant

Rio Hondo College (I)

3600 Workman Mill Road, Whittier CA 90601-1699
County: Los Angeles — FICE Identification: 001269
Unit ID: 121886
Telephone: (562) 692-0921 — Carnegie Class: Assoc/MT-VT-Mix Trad/Non
FAX Number: (562) 699-7386 — Calendar System: Semester
URL: www.riohondo.edu
Established: 1960 — Annual Undergrad Tuition & Fees (In-District): $1,360
Enrollment: 16,263 — Coed
Affiliation or Control: State/Local — IRS Status: 501(c)3
Highest Offering: Baccalaureate
Accreditation: WJ

01 Superintendent/President ... Ms. Teresa DREYFUSS
05 Int Vice President Academic Svcs ... Dr. JoAnna DOWNEY-SCHILLING
10 Vice President Finance/Business ... Ms. Myeshia ARMSTRONG
32 Int Vice President Student Services ... Mr. Henry GEE
86 Dir Govt & Community Relations ... Mr. Russell CASTANEDA-CALLEROS
15 Int Director Human Resources ... Mr. Loy NASHUA
26 Dir Marketing & Communications ... Ms. Ruthie RETANA
35 Dir Student Life & Leadership ... Ms. Shaina PHILLIPS
06 Dir Admin & Records/Registrar ... Ms. Leigh UNGER
38 Dean Counseling & Student Succes ... Dr. Mike MUNOZ
102 Exec Director RHC Foundation ... Mr. Howard KUMMERMAN
37 Director Financial Aid & Veteran's ... Ms. Yvonne GUTIERREZ-SANDOVAL
18 Director Facilities Services ... Vacant
96 Director of Purchasing ... Mr. Felix G. SARAO
04 Admin Assistant to President ... Ms. Sandy SANDELLO
09 Dean Institutional Research & Plng ... Mr. Howard KUMMERMAN
88 Dean Educational Centers ... Ms. Yolanda EMERSON

*Riverside Community College District (J)

3801 Market Street, Riverside CA 92501
County: Riverside — Identification: 667039
Telephone: (951) 222-8000 — Carnegie Class: N/A
FAX Number: (951) 682-5339
URL: www.rccd.edu

01 Chancellor ... Dr. Michael L. BURKE
05 VC Educ Svcs/Wrkforce Dev/Plng ... Vacant
10 VC Business & Financial Svcs ... Mr. Aaron BROWN
15 VC Div & Human Resources ... Dr. Terri HAMPTON

100 Chief of Staff & Facilities Devel .... Ms. Chris CARLSON
12 President Moreno Valley College .... Dr. Sandra MAYO
12 Int President Norco College .... Dr. Irving HENDRICK
12 President Riverside City Col .... Dr. Wolde-Ab ISAAC

*Moreno Valley College (A)

16130 Lasselle Street, Moreno Valley CA 92551
County: Riverside FICE Identification: 041735
Unit ID: 460394
Telephone: (951) 571-6100 Carnegie Class: Assoc/MT-VT-Mix Trad/Non
FAX Number: N/A Calendar System: Semester
URL: www.mvc.edu
Established: 2010 Annual Undergrad Tuition & Fees (In-District): $1,416
Enrollment: 8,731 Coed
Affiliation or Control: State/Local IRS Status: 501(c)3
Highest Offering: Associate Degree
Accreditation: WJ, DA, DH, EMT

02 Interim President .... Dr. Irving HENDRICK
05 Vice Pres Academic Affairs .... Dr. Robin STEINBECK
10 Vice Pres Business Services .... Dr. Nathaniel JONES
32 Vice Pres of Student Services .... Mr. Dyrell FOSTER
20 Dean of Instruction .... Mr. David VAKIL
06 Director Enrollment Services .... Ms. Jamie CLIFTON
37 Director Student Financial Services .... Ms. Linda PRATT
18 Director Facilities .... Mr. Jose RECINOS

*Norco College (B)

2001 Third Street, Norco CA 92860
County: Riverside FICE Identification: 041761
Unit ID: 460464
Telephone: (951) 372-7000 Carnegie Class: Assoc/HT-Mix Trad/Non
FAX Number: N/A Calendar System: Semester
URL: www.norcocollege.edu
Established: 2010 Annual Undergrad Tuition & Fees (In-District): $1,416
Enrollment: 9,304 Coed
Affiliation or Control: State/Local IRS Status: 501(c)3
Highest Offering: Associate Degree
Accreditation: WJ

02 Interim President .... Dr. Monica GREEN
05 Vice President Academic Affairs .... Dr. Diane DIECKMEYER
32 Int Vice Pres Student Services .... Dr. Koji UESUGI
04 Executive Asst to President .... Ms. Denise TERRAZAS
07 Dean Admissions & Records .... Mr. Mark DEASIS
09 Dean Institutional Effectiveness .... Dr. Greg AYCOCK
11 Vice President Business Services .... Ms. Beth GOMEZ
13 Dean Technology/Learning Resources .... Mr. Damon NANCE
18 Director Facilities .... Mr. Steve MONSANTO
25 Assistant Dean Grants .... Dr. Gustavo OCEGUERA
37 Director Student Financial Services .... Ms. Maria GONZALEZ
20 Dean Instruction .... Dr. Carol FARRAR
75 Dean Instruction/CTE .... Dr. Kevin FLEMING
35 Dean Student Services .... Vacant

*Riverside City College (C)

4800 Magnolia Avenue, Riverside CA 92506
County: Riverside FICE Identification: 001270
Unit ID: 121901
Telephone: (951) 222-8000 Carnegie Class: Assoc/MT-VT-Mix Trad/Non
FAX Number: (951) 222-8036 Calendar System: Semester
URL: www.rcc.edu
Established: 1916 Annual Undergrad Tuition & Fees (In-District): $1,426
Enrollment: 18,547 Coed
Affiliation or Control: State/Local IRS Status: 501(c)3
Highest Offering: Associate Degree
Accreditation: WJ, ADNUR, #ARCPA

02 President .... Dr. Wolde-Ab ISAAC
05 Acting Vice Pres Academic Affairs .... Ms. Virginia MCKEE-LEONE
10 Vice Pres Business Services .... Ms. Mazie L. BREWINGTON
103 VP Workforce & Resource Development .... Vacant
32 Int Vice President Student Services .... Ms. Cecilia ALVARADO
20 Dean of Instruction .... Vacant
66 Dean School of Nursing .... Dr. Sandy BAKER
08 Dean Instruction Library/Lrng Res ..... Dr. Fabienne CHAUDERLOT
57 Dean of Instr Fine & Perform Arts .... Dr. Scott BAUER
75 Dean of Career/Tech Educ .... Ms. Patricia AVILA
88 Assoc Dean Academic Support .... Ms. Debbie WHITAKER
84 Dean Enrollment Services .... Ms. Dawn VALENCIA
35 Int Dean Student Services .... Mr. Gregory FERRER
41 Interim Director Athletics .... Mr. James WOOLDRIDGE
23 Director Health Services .... Ms. Deborah CLOAN
19 Sergeant Safety & Police .... Mr. Robert KLEVENO

Rudolf Steiner College (D)

9200 Fair Oaks Boulevard, Fair Oaks CA 95628
County: Sacramento Identification: 667088
Telephone: (916) 961-8727 Carnegie Class: Not Classified
FAX Number: (877) 782-1884 Calendar System: Other
URL: www.rudolfsteinercollege.edu
Established: 1976 Annual Graduate Tuition & Fees: N/A
Enrollment: N/A Coed
Affiliation or Control: Independent Non-Profit IRS Status: 501(c)3
Highest Offering: Master's; No Undergraduates
Accreditation: @WC

01 Director .... Mr. Edmund KNIGHTON

Sacramento Ultrasound Institute (E)

2233 Watt Avenue #150, Sacramento CA 95825
County: Sacramento Identification: 667264
Telephone: (916) 434-7666 Carnegie Class: Not Classified
FAX Number: (916) 481-4032 Calendar System: Other
URL: www.sui.edu
Established: 2002 Annual Undergrad Tuition & Fees: N/A
Enrollment: N/A Coed
Affiliation or Control: Proprietary IRS Status: Proprietary
Highest Offering: Associate Degree
Accreditation: ABHES

01 CEO/President .... Mrs. Sima DERMISHYAN
07 Admissions Director .... Araida STEPANYAN

Sage College (F)

12125 Day Street, Building L,
Moreno Valley CA 92557-6720
County: Riverside FICE Identification: 030695
Unit ID: 410520
Telephone: (951) 781-2727 Carnegie Class: Spec 2-yr-Other
FAX Number: (951) 781-0570 Calendar System: Semester
URL: www.sagecollege.edu
Established: 1973 Annual Undergrad Tuition & Fees: $12,460
Enrollment: 407 Coed
Affiliation or Control: Proprietary IRS Status: Proprietary
Highest Offering: Associate Degree
Accreditation: ACICS

01 Executive Director .... Ms. Lauren SOMMA
03 Assistant Director .... Ms. Sharon GOUPIL

Saint John's Seminary (G)

5012 Seminary Road, Camarillo CA 93012-2500
County: Ventura FICE Identification: 001299
Unit ID: 123855
Telephone: (805) 482-2755 Carnegie Class: Spec-4-yr-Faith
FAX Number: (805) 482-3470 Calendar System: Semester
URL: www.stjohnsem.edu
Established: 1939 Annual Graduate Tuition & Fees: N/A
Enrollment: 104 Male
Affiliation or Control: Roman Catholic IRS Status: 501(c)3
Highest Offering: Master's; No Undergraduates
Accreditation: WC, THEOL

01 Rector .... Msgr Marc V. TRUDEAU
05 Academic Dean .... Dr. Anthony LILLES
07 Director of Admissions .... Dr. Anthony LILLES
06 Registrar .... Mr. Kevin GODFREY
04 Administrative Asst to President .... Ms. Maria GAETA
10 Director of Finance .... Ms. Jackie ROTTER
15 Director Personnel Services .... Ms. Mary B SSINGER
18 Chief Facilities/Physical Plant .... Mr. Greg JULIUS
30 Chief Development/Advancement .... Ms. Julia SCALISE
32 Chief Student Affairs/Student Life .... Fr. Timothy KLOSTERMAN
96 Director of Purchasing .... Ms. Julie ALLYN

Saint Katherine College (H)

1637 Capalina Road, San Marcos CA 92069
County: San Diego Identification: 667263
Telephone: (760) 471-1316 Carnegie Class: Not Classified
FAX Number: (760) 704-1314 Calendar System: Semester
URL: www.stkath.org
Established: Annual Undergrad Tuition & Fees: N/A
Enrollment: N/A Coed
Affiliation or Control: Independent Non-Profit IRS Status: 501(c)3
Highest Offering: Baccalaureate
Accreditation: WC

01 President & Founder .... Dr. Frank PAPATHEOFANIS
05 Provost & VP Academic Affairs .... Margaret BAILEY
10 CFO .... Ryan WEST
09 Dir of Inst Research/Effectiveness .... Christos KORGAN
07 Dean of Admissions/Registrar .... Marina KARAVOKIRIS
32 Dean of Students .... Bre WILLIAMS

Saint Mary's College of California (I)

1928 Saint Mary's Road, Moraga CA 94556-2744
County: Contra Costa FICE Identification: 001302
Unit ID: 123554
Telephone: (925) 631-4000 Carnegie Class: Masters/L
FAX Number: (925) 376-8497 Calendar System: 4/1/4
URL: www.stmarys-ca.edu
Established: 1863 Annual Undergrad Tuition & Fees: $42,930
Enrollment: 4,112 Coed
Affiliation or Control: Roman Catholic IRS Status: 501(c)3
Highest Offering: Doctorate
Accreditation: WC, BUS, MACTE

01 President .... Dr. James A. DONAHUE
05 Provost/Vice President Acad Affairs .... Dr. Bethami DOBKIN
32 Vice Provost Student Affairs .... Dr. Jane CAMARILLO
20 Vice Provost Undergrad Academics .... Dr. Richard M. CARP
10 Vice President for Finance/CFO .... Mr. Peter MICHELL
30 Vice President for Advancement .... Ms. Lisa MOORE
26 Asst VP College Communication .... Vacant
88 Vice President for Mission .... Dr. Carole SWAIN
84 Vice Provost Enrollment Services .... Mr. Hernan BUCHELI
107 Vice Prov Graduate/Professnl Stds .... Dr. Christopher SINDT
43 General Counsel .... Mr. Larry NUTI
53 Dean School of Education .... Dr. Christopher SINDT
50 Dean School Econ & Business Admin .... Dr. Zhan LI
81 Dean School of Science .... Dr. Roy WENSLEY
49 Dean School Liberal Arts .... Dr. Sheila HUGHES
35 Dean of Students .... Dr. Evette CASTILLO CLARK
08 Dean Academic Resources .... Ms. Patricia KREITZ
42 Director Mission & Ministry .... Ms. Karin MCCLELLAND
07 Dean of Admissions .... Mr. Michael MCKEON
15 Director Human Resources .... Mr. Eduardo SALAZ
58 Interim Assoc Dean Graduate Pgms .... Dr. Yung Jae LEE
06 Registrar .... Ms. Julia ODOM
20 Assistant Dean of Students .... Mr. Jim SCIUTO
37 Interim Director of Financial Aid .... Ms. Linda JUDGE
88 Director of Kinesiology .... Dr. Stephen MILLER
57 Director MFA in Creative Writing .... Ms. Brenda HILLMAN
29 Sr Director Alumni Engagement .... Ms. Courtney LOHMANN
14 Deputy CTO .... Mr. Lance HOURANY
13 Chief Technology Officer .... Mr. Peter GRECO
19 Director of Public Safety .... Mr. Adan TEJADA
38 Director of Counseling Center .... Ms. Dai L. TO
41 Dir of Athletic & Recreation Sports .... Mr. Mark C. ORR
88 Director Saint Mary's Art Museum .... Ms. Carrie BREWSTER
71 Director of January Term Program .... Dr. Sue FALLIS
18 Exec Director of Physical Plant .... Mr. Joseph KEHOE
102 Director of Foundation & Corp Rels .... Ms. Elizabeth GALLAGHER
30 Director of Development .... Mr. Daniel G. LEWIS
36 Interim Dir of Career Devel Center .... Ms. Jennifer BILLECI
23 Medical Director Health & Wellness .... Dr. Ali REZAPOUR
27 Int Director College Communications .... Mr. Michael MCALPIN
86 Director Community & Govt Relations .... Mr. Tim FARLEY
94 Director Women's Resource Ctr .... Ms. Sharon SOBOTTA
88 Director of CILSA .... Dr. Jennifer PIGZA
88 Associate Director of CILSA .... Vacant
21 Director of Finance/Controller .... Ms. Jeanne DEMATTEO
104 Director Ctr International Programs . Ms. M. Susan MILLER-REID
109 Director of Food Services .... Mr. Matt CARROLL
88 Director Conference Services .... Vacant
92 Dir Student Engagement & Academic ...... Ms. Tracy PASCUA DEA
28 Dir of Delphine Intercultural Ctr .... Vacant
09 Director of Institutional Research .... Mr. Gregg THOMSON
88 Dir New Student/Family Programs .... Ms. Jennifer HERZOG
96 Purchasing/Buyer .... Ms. Janie KLEIN
39 Director Student Housing .... Mr. Marcus WEEMES

Saint Patrick's Seminary & University (J)

320 Middlefield Road, Menlo Park CA 94025-3596
County: San Mateo FICE Identification: 010074
Unit ID: 122250
Telephone: (650) 325-5621 Carnegie Class: Not Classified
FAX Number: (650) 322-0997 Calendar System: Semester
URL: www.stpatricksseminary.org
Established: 1894 Annual Undergrad Tuition & Fees: N/A
Enrollment: N/A Male
Affiliation or Control: Roman Catholic IRS Status: 501(c)3
Highest Offering: Master's
Accreditation: WC, THEOL

01 President/Rector .... Rev. Gladstone H. STEVENS
05 Vice Rector/Academic Dean .... Rev. Anthony POGORELC
33 Dean Men/Interim Director Liturgy .... Rev. Daniel DONOHOO
26 Vice President for External Affairs .... Rev. James MYERS
10 Vice President Operations .... Mr. Marc COLELLI
42 Dean of Spiritual Life .... Rev. Vincent BUI
08 Library Director .... Mr. David KRIEGH
06 Registrar .... Mr. Manvinder SHAHI

The Salvation Army College for Officer Training at Crestmont (K)

30840 Hawthorne Boulevard,
Rancho Palos Verdes CA 90275-5301
County: Los Angeles FICE Identification: 036954
Unit ID: 122269
Telephone: (310) 377-0481 Carnegie Class: Not Classified
FAX Number: (310) 541-1697 Calendar System: Quarter
URL: www.crestmont.edu
Established: 1878 Annual Undergrad Tuition & Fees: N/A
Enrollment: N/A Coed
Affiliation or Control: Other IRS Status: 501(c)3
Highest Offering: Associate Degree
Accreditation: WJ

01 Training Principal .... Major Brian SAUNDERS
03 Assistant Training Principal .... Major Robert BIRKS
05 Director of Curriculum .... Major Brian JONES
10 Director of Business Administration .... Capt. Kelly NOLAN
32 Director of Campus Services .... Major Stacy BIRKS
04 Exec Secretary to Trng Principal .... Ms. Celeste SKINNER

Samuel Merritt University (L)

3100 Telegraph Avenue, Oakland CA 94609
County: Alameda FICE Identification: 007012
Unit ID: 122296
Telephone: (510) 869-6511 Carnegie Class: Spec-4-yr-Other Health
FAX Number: (510) 869-6525 Calendar System: Semester

URL: www.samuelmerritt.edu
Established: 1909 Annual Undergrad Tuition & Fees: N/A
Enrollment: 1,580 Coed
Affiliation or Control: Independent Non-Profit IRS Status: 501(c)3
Highest Offering: Doctorate
Accreditation: WC, ANEST, ARCPA, NURSE, OT, POD, PTA

01 President .... Dr. Sharon C. DIAZ
05 Academic Vice President/Provost .... Dr. Scot FOSTER
10 Vice Pres Finance/Admin/CFO .... Mr. Gregory GINGRAS
84 Vice President Enrollment Services .... Vacant
20 Assistant Academic Vice President .... Dr. Celeste VILLANUEVA
20 Asst Academic Vice President .... Dr. Michael NEGRETE
32 Asst Vice President Student Affairs .... Mr. Craig ELLIOTT
21 Asst VP Finance & Admin/Controller .... Vacant
04 Assistant to the President .... Ms. Margrette PETERSON
66 Dean & Professor of Nursing .... Dr. Audrey BERMAN
63 Dean Podiatric Medicine .... Dr. John VENSON
88 Chair Dept Physical Therapy .... Dr. Nicole CHRISTENSEN
88 Chair Dept Occupational Therapy .... Dr. Kate HAYNER
66 Chair ABSN .... Dr. Nancy HAUGEN
66 Chairperson Undergraduate Nursing .... Dr. Margaret EARLY
07 Dean Admission .... Mr. Timothy CRANFORD
15 Exec Director Human Resources .... Ms. Elaine LEMAY
45 Exec Dir Planning/Business Dev .... Ms. Cynthia ULMAN
26 Exec Dir Communications/Ext Rels .... Ms. Stephanie BANGERT
30 Exec Dir of Development/Alumni Affs .... Ms. Susan VALENCIA
09 Director Institutional Research .... Ms. Nandini DASGUPTA
06 Registrar .... Ms. Anne SCHER
08 Library Director .... Ms. Hai-Thom SOTA
37 Director Financial Aid .... Ms. Tanya GRIGGS
88 Dir Family Nurse Practitioner Pgm .... Ms. Suzanne AUGUST-SCHWARTZ
29 Director of Alumni Relations .... Ms. Carla ROSS
18 Director Facilities Management .... Ms. Lillian HARVIN
88 Director Physician Assistant Pgm .... Dr. Michael DEROSA
12 Site Manager Sacramento .... Ms. Rene ENGELHART
12 Site Manager San Mateo .... Dr. Mileva LEWIS SAULO
13 Dir of Information Technology Svcs .... Mr. Blair SIMMONS
28 Chief Diversity Officer .... Ms. Shirley STRONG

*San Bernardino Community College District (A)

114 S. Del Rosa Drive, San Bernardino CA 92401
County: San Bernardino Identification: 667040
Telephone: (909) 382-4091 Carnegie Class: N/A
FAX Number: (909) 382-0153
URL: www.sbccd.edu

01 Chancellor .... Bruce BARON
10 Vice Chanc Business/Fiscal Services .... Jose TORRES
15 Vice Chanc Human Resources .... Dr. Lisa NORMAN

*Crafton Hills College (B)

11711 Sand Canyon Road, Yucaipa CA 92399-1799
County: San Bernardino FICE Identification: 009272
Unit ID: 113111
Telephone: (909) 794-2161 Carnegie Class: Assoc/MT-VT-High Trad
FAX Number: (909) 794-0423 Calendar System: Semester
URL: www.craftonhills.edu
Established: 1972 Annual Undergrad Tuition & Fees (In-District): $1,142
Enrollment: 5,932 Coed
Affiliation or Control: State/Local IRS Status: 501(c)3
Highest Offering: Associate Degree
Accreditation: WJ, COARC, EMT

02 President .... Dr. Wei ZHOU
05 Vice President of Instruction .... Dr. Bryan REECE
11 Vice President Administrative Svcs .... Mr. Mike STRONG
32 Vice President Student Services .... Dr. Rebeccah WARREN-MARLATT
88 Dean Stdnt Svcs/Stdnt Development .... Mr. Joe CABRALES
49 Dean of Arts & Sciences .... Mr. Mark SNOWHITE
81 Dean Math/English/Reading/Inst Supp .... Ms. Sherrie LOEWEN
36 Dean Career Educ & Human Devel .... Ms. June Y. YAMAMOTO
38 Dean Student Services/Counseling .... Ms. Kirsten S. COLVEY
09 Dean Instl Effect/Research/Planning .... Dr. Keith WURTZ
30 Director Resource Development .... Ms. Michelle RIGGS
40 Director Bookstore .... Ms. Gloriann CHAVEZ
88 Director EOPS/CARE .... Dr. Rejoice CHAVIRA
37 Director Financial Aid .... Mr. John W. MUSKAVITCH
35 Director Student Life .... Dr. Ericka PADDOCK
18 Director Facilities .... Mr. Larry COOK
13 Director Technology Services .... Mr. Wayne BOGH
26 Director Marketing/Public Relations .... Ms. Donna HOFFMANN
08 Librarian .... Vacant
06 Admissions and Records Coordinator .... Mr. Larry K. AYCOCK
04 Administrative Asst to President .... Mrs. Cyndie ST. JEAN

*San Bernardino Valley College (C)

701 S Mt. Vernon Avenue,
San Bernardino CA 92410-2798
County: San Bernardino FICE Identification: 001272
Unit ID: 123527
Telephone: (909) 384-4400 Carnegie Class: Assoc/MT-VT-High Trad
FAX Number: N/A Calendar System: Semester
URL: www.valleycollege.edu
Established: 1926 Annual Undergrad Tuition & Fees (In-District): $1,238
Enrollment: 12,965 Coed
Affiliation or Control: State/Local IRS Status: 501(c)3
Highest Offering: Associate Degree
Accreditation: WJ, ADNUR

02 President .... Ms. Diana RODRIGUEZ
05 Interim Vice President Instruction .... Mr. Henry HUA
11 VP Administrative Services .... Mr. Scott STARK
32 VP Student Services .... Dr. Ricky SHABAZZ
72 Dean AT/TRANS/CULA .... Mr. Albert MANIAOL
79 Dean Arts & Humanities .... Dr. Kay WEISS
38 Dean Counseling/Matriculation .... Mr. Marco COTA
50 Interim Dean Math/Bus/Computer Tech .... Ms. Odette SALVAGGIO
09 Dean Research/Planning/Inst Effect .... Dr. James SMITH
81 Dean Sciences .... Dr. Susan BANGASSER
83 Dean SS/Human Development & PE .... Dr. Wallace JOHNSON
07 Director Admissions/Records .... Ms. April DALE-CARTER
40 Director Bookstores .... Ms. Gloriann CHAVEZ
88 Director Child Development Ctr .... Mr. Mark MERJIL
31 Dir Dev Community Relations .... Ms. Karen CHILDERS
88 Director EOP&S/CARE .... Ms. Carmen RODRIGUEZ
37 Director Financial Aid .... Ms. Amber GALLAGHER
25 Dir Grant Development/Management .... Vacant
08 Dir Library/Learning Support Svcs .... Mr. Ron HASTINGS
26 Director Marketing/PR .... Mr. Paul BRATULIN
35 Director Student Life .... Mr. Raymond CARLOS
13 Director Technology Services .... Mr. Rick HRDLICKA
88 Mgr Cafeteria & Snack Bar .... Mr. Erik MORDEN
103 Mgr CalWORKS/Workforce Dev .... Ms. Shalita TILLMAN
88 Project Dir HSI STEM PASS GO .... Mr. Marc DONNHAUSER
66 Assoc Dean & Nursing Director .... Ms. Carol WELLS
68 Director Athletics .... Mr. Dave RUBIO
88 Director Police Academies .... Mr. Jeff KLUG
18 Dir Facilities M&O .... Mr. Robert JENKINS
89 Dir First Year Experience .... Mr. Johnny CONLEY
88 Director DSP&S .... Mr. Marty MILLIGAN
88 AEBG Administrator .... Ms. Emma DIAZ

San Diego Christian College (D)

200 Riverview Parkway, Santee CA 92071
County: San Diego FICE Identification: 012031
Unit ID: 112084
Telephone: (619) 201-8700 Carnegie Class: Bac-Diverse
FAX Number: (619) 201-8749 Calendar System: Semester
URL: www.sdcc.edu
Established: 1970 Annual Undergrad Tuition & Fees: $28,470
Enrollment: 966 Coed
Affiliation or Control: Independent Non-Profit IRS Status: 501(c)3
Highest Offering: Master's
Accreditation: WC

01 President .... Dr. Paul E. AGUE
04 Exec Assistant to the President .... Mrs. Kelly BUCHANAN
10 VP for Finance .... Mr. Steve CHANEY
05 VP for Academic Affairs .... Dr. Jon DEPRIEST
32 VP for Student Services .... Dr. Jon DEPRIEST
35 Director of Student Life .... Mr. Pete GOODMAN
06 Registrar .... Mrs. Tammy DALLY
37 Director of Financial Aid .... Mr. Daniel REED
07 Director of Admissions .... Ms. Christine ROBERTS
42 Director of Spiritual Life .... Mr. Steve JENKINS
30 Director of Advancement .... Mr. Chad CUNNINGHAM
30 VP for Advancement & Administration .... Mr. Robert JENSEN
15 VP for Human Resources .... Mr. Robert JENSEN
08 Director of Library Services .... Ms. Ruth MARTIN
29 Manager of Alumni/Donor Relations .... Ms. Stephanie EDWARDS
09 Dean of Assessment and Planning .... Mrs. Lundie CARSTENSEN
41 Athletic Director .... Vacant
23 Director of Health Services .... Mrs. Malia JENKINS
28 Director of Diversity .... Mr. Carl CALDERSON
18 Operations Manager .... Mr. Dan HANSEN
36 Director Student Placement .... Vacant

*San Diego Community College District Administrative Offices (E)

3375 Camino Del Rio South, San Diego CA 92108-3883
County: San Diego FICE Identification: 008895
Unit ID: 122339
Telephone: (619) 388-6500 Carnegie Class: N/A
FAX Number: (619) 388-6913
URL: www.sdccd.edu

01 Chancellor .... Dr. Constance M. CARROLL
10 Exec Vice Chanc Business Tech Svcs .... Dr. Bonnie Ann DOWD
32 Vice Chancellor Student Services .... Dr. Lynn C. NEAULT
15 Vice Chancellor Human Resources .... Mr. Will SURBROOK
18 Vice Chanc Facilities Management .... Mr. Christopher MANIS
05 Vice Chanc Instructional Svcs .... Dr. Stephanie BULGER
26 Director Comm & Public Relations .... Mr. Jack BERESFORD
43 Director Legal Services & EEO .... Ms. Mary ROGERS
04 Exec Assistant to the Chancellor .... Ms. Margaret LAMB
13 Chief Info Technology Officer (CIO) .... Mr. Kent KEYSER
19 Chief of Police .... Mr. Raymond AGUIRRE

*San Diego City College (F)

1313 Park Boulevard, San Diego CA 92101-4787
County: San Diego FICE Identification: 001273
Unit ID: 122320
Telephone: (619) 388-3400 Carnegie Class: Not Classified
FAX Number: (619) 388-3063 Calendar System: Semester
URL: www.sdcity.edu
Established: 1914 Annual Undergrad Tuition & Fees (In-District): N/A
Enrollment: N/A Coed
Affiliation or Control: State/Local IRS Status: 501(c)3
Highest Offering: Associate Degree
Accreditation: WJ, ADNUR

02 President .... Ms. Denise WHISENHUNT
04 Administrative Asst to President .... Ms. Erin FLANAGAN
11 Vice President of Admin Services .... Ms. Seher AWAN
05 Vice President Instruction .... Ms. Renee KILMER
68 Dean Health/Exercise Sci/Athletics .... Mr. Randy BARNES
83 Dean Behav & Soc Sci/Consumer Stds .... Ms. Lori ERRECA
08 Dean Information/Learning Tech .... Mr. Robbi EWELL
79 Dean School of Arts/Humanities .... Ms. Trudy GERALD
50 Dean Sch Business/Info Tech .... Ms. Rose LAMURAGLIA
88 Actg Dean Student Dev/Matriculation .... Ms. Bernice LORENZO
32 Dean of Student Affairs .... Mr. Marciano PEREZ
54 Dean Engr & Tech/Math/Sci/Nurs .... Dr. Minou SPRADLEY
88 Actg Dean of Student Equity .... Ms. Jeanie TYLER
22 Affirmative Action Officer .... Mr. Edwin HIEL
40 Bookstore Supervisor .... Ms. DeeDee PORTER
26 Public Information Officer .... Ms. Heidi BUNKOWSKE
88 PgmMgr Disabled Student Services .... Ms. Brianne KENNEDY
37 Financial Aid Supervisor .... Mr. Gregory SANCHEZ
88 Director EOPS .... Ms. Beverly WARREN
56 Director Off-Campus Programs .... Ms. Jeanie TYLER
92 Director Honors Program .... Dr. Kelly MAYHEW
18 Chief Facilities/Physical Plant .... Mr. Derrall CHANDLER
07 Admissions & Records Supervisor .... Ms. Megan SOTO
88 Campus Researcher .... Ms. Sarah COLLIER

*San Diego Mesa College (G)

7250 Mesa College Drive, San Diego CA 92111-4998
County: San Diego FICE Identification: 001275
Unit ID: 122375
Telephone: (619) 388-2721 Carnegie Class: Assoc/HT-High Trad
FAX Number: (619) 388-2929 Calendar System: Semester
URL: www.sdmesa.edu
Established: 1962 Annual Undergrad Tuition & Fees (In-District): $1,142
Enrollment: 24,159 Coed
Affiliation or Control: State/Local IRS Status: 501(c)3
Highest Offering: Associate Degree
Accreditation: WJ, CAHIIM, DA, PTAA, RAD

02 President .... Dr. Pamela T. LUSTER
05 Vice President Instruction .... Dr. Tim MCGRATH
32 Vice Pres Student Services .... Dr. Ashanti HANDS
11 Vice Pres Administrative Services .... Ms. Rachelle AGATHA
88 Dean Student Development .... Ms. Susan TOPHAM
79 Dean Arts & Languages .... Ms. Leslie SHIMAZAKI
76 Dean Health Sciences/Public Svc .... Ms. Margie FRITCH
81 Dean School Math/Natural Sciences .... Dr. Saeid EIDGAHY
50 Dean Sch Business Technology .... Dr. Danene BROWN
62 Dean Lrng Res/Educational Tech .... Vacant
68 Dean PE/Health Educ/Athletics Dir .... Mr. Dave EVANS
79 Dean of Humanities .... Mr. Andrew J. MACNEILL
83 Dean Social/Behav Sci/Mult Stds .... Dr. Charles ZAPPIA
35 Dean Student Affairs .... Ms. Ashanti HANDS
09 Dean Institutional Effectiveness .... Dr. Madeleine HINKES
26 Public Information Officer .... Ms. Lina HEIL
37 Financial Aid Officer .... Ms. Gilda MALDONADO
07 Student Svcs Supervisor Admission .... Ms. Ivonne ALVAREZ
04 Exec Asst to the President .... Ms. Sara Beth CAIN

*San Diego Miramar College (H)

10440 Black Mountain Road, San Diego CA 92126-2999
County: San Diego FICE Identification: 011820
Unit ID: 122384
Telephone: (619) 388-7800 Carnegie Class: Assoc/MT-VT-Mix Trad/Non
FAX Number: (619) 388-7901 Calendar System: Semester
URL: www.sdmiramar.edu
Established: 1969 Annual Undergrad Tuition & Fees (In-District): $1,142
Enrollment: 11,876 Coed
Affiliation or Control: State/Local IRS Status: 501(c)3
Highest Offering: Associate Degree
Accreditation: WJ, MLTAD

02 President .... Dr. Patricia HSIEH
05 Int Vice President Instruction .... Dr. Paulette HOPKINS
32 Vice President Student Services .... Mr. Gerald RAMSEY
10 Vice President Admin Services .... Mr. Brett BELL
49 Dean of Liberal Arts .... Dr. Lou ASCIONE
50 Dean Business/Tech/Workforce Init .... Ms. Lynne ORNELAS
81 Actg Dean Math and Science .... Dr. Fred GARCES
88 Dean of Public Safety .... Mr. George BEITEY
81 Int Chair Physical Sciences .... Dr. Rebecca BOWERS-GENTRY
26 Information Officer .... Mr. Stephen QUIS
37 Financial Aid Officer .... Mr. Vincent NGO
18 Chief Facilities/Physical Plant .... Mr. Dane LINDSAY
88 Chair Child Development .... Ms. Dawn DIMARZO
35 Dean of Student Affairs .... Ms. Adela JACOBSON
08 Chair Library Sciences .... Ms. Mary HART
07 Admissions & Records Officer .... Ms. Dana STACK
61 Chair Administration of Justice .... Mr. Jordan OMENS
50 Chair Business .... Mr. Darrel HARRISON
72 Chair Fire Science .... Ms. Mary KJARTANSON
79 Chair Arts & Humanities .... Mr. Mark HERTICA
81 Chair Mathematics .... Mr. Francois BEREAUD
83 Chair Social & Behavioral Sciences .... Mr. Daniel IGOU
88 Chair Aeronautical & Aviation .... Mr. Larry PINK
88 Associate Dean ATTE Center Director .... Mr. Greg NEWHOUSE
88 Co-Chair Automotive & Diesel Tech .... Mr. Dan WILLKIE
88 Co-Chair Automotive & Diesel Tech .... Mr. Joseph YOUNG

38 Chair Counseling .... Mr. Rick CASSAR
88 Actg Chair Biological Sciences .... Mr. Dan TRUBOVITZ
68 Chair Exercise Science/Hlth & Nutr .... Mr. Nick GEHLER
60 Chair Engl/Comm/Foreign Language .... Dr. Carmen JAY
108 Dean PRIE/Library & Technology .... Dr. Daniel MIRAMONTEZ
04 Executive Assistant to President .... Ms. Briele WARREN

San Diego Global Knowledge University (A)

1095 K Street Suite B, San Diego CA 92101
County: San Diego Identification: 667294
Telephone: (619) 934-0797 Carnegie Class: Not Classified
FAX Number: N/A Calendar System: Semester
URL: www.sdgku.com
Established: Annual Undergrad Tuition & Fees: N/A
Enrollment: N/A Coed
Affiliation or Control: Proprietary IRS Status: Proprietary
Highest Offering: Master's
Accreditation: ACICS

01 President .... Dr. Miguel A. CARDENAS

San Francisco Art Institute (B)

800 Chestnut Street, San Francisco CA 94133-2206
County: San Francisco FICE Identification: 003948
Unit ID: 122454
Telephone: (415) 771-7020 Carnegie Class: Spec-4-yr-Arts
FAX Number: (415) 749-4590 Calendar System: Semester
URL: www.sfai.edu
Established: 1871 Annual Undergrad Tuition & Fees: $41,272
Enrollment: 699 Coed
Affiliation or Control: Independent Non-Profit IRS Status: 501(c)3
Highest Offering: Master's
Accreditation: WC, ART

00 Chair of the Board .... Christopher TELLIS
01 Interim President .... Rachel SCHREIBER
05 Interim Dean and VP Acad Affairs .... Jennifer RISSLER
31 VP Exhibitions and Public Programs .... Hesse MCGRAW
10 Chief Operating Officer .... Espi SANJANA
30 VP Development & Alumni Relations .... Maureen KEEFE
84 VP Enrollment and Student Affairs .... Mark CAMPBELL
26 Dir of Marketing & Communications .... Daryl CARR
06 Registrar .... Delphine HWANG
07 Director of Grad Admissions .... Nicole CRESCENZI
07 Director of Undergrad Admiss .... Colleen MULVEY
08 Head Librarian .... Lauren MACDONALD
09 Inst Research & Acad Planning Assoc .... Jose DE LOS REYES
11 Director of Operations .... Heather HICKMAN HOLLAND
13 Director of Technology .... Jeremy HOBBS
15 Director of Human Resources .... Heather GRONIGER
18 Assistant Director of Facilities .... John SEDEN
20 Assoc Dean of Academic Affairs .... Vacant
21 Controller .... Adrian TRUJILLO
24 Technical Director .... Benjamin ASHLOCK
25 Director of Academic Administration .... Jen SIKORA
29 Alumni Relations Coordinator .... Clea MASSIANI
32 Dean of Students .... Vacant
35 Assistant Dean of Students .... Galen CRAWFORD
37 Director of Financial Aid .... Annita ALLDREDGE
38 Director of Counseling Services .... Deb SCHNEIDER
39 Resident Director .... Jake HOGG
44 Institutional Giving .... Elisa ISAACSON
88 Director of Public Education .... Barbara GARBER
57 Chair of BFA Programs .... Paul KLEIN
57 Chair of BA Programs .... Nicole ARCHER
58 Chair of MFA Programs .... Tony LABAT
58 Chair of MA Programs .... Claire DAIGLE
58 Director of Graduate Administration .... Zeina BARAKEH
85 Global Programs Advisor/PDSO .... Jill TOLFA
88 Director of Academic Advising .... Kent RODRIGUEZ SEGURA
88 Director of Admissions Operations .... Jeremy SIMMONS
88 Director of BFA Studios .... Sherry KNUTSON
88 Director of City Studio .... JD BELTRAN
90 Academic Computing Manager .... Vacant
91 Director of Information Technology .... Andrew SIMAS
100 Chief of Staff .... Anne SHULOCK
101 Exec Assistant President and Board .... Jan-Marie BANNON
36 Career & Prof Practices Coordinator .... Eliza DENNIS

San Francisco Conservatory of Music (C)

50 Oak Street, San Francisco CA 94102-6011
County: San Francisco FICE Identification: 001278
Unit ID: 122506
Telephone: (415) 864-7326 Carnegie Class: Spec-4-yr-Arts
FAX Number: (415) 503-6299 Calendar System: Semester
URL: www.sfcm.edu
Established: 1917 Annual Undergrad Tuition & Fees: $42,210
Enrollment: 389 Coed
Affiliation or Control: Independent Non-Profit IRS Status: 501(c)3
Highest Offering: Beyond Master's But Less Than Doctorate
Accreditation: WC

01 President .... David STULL
05 Provost and Dean .... Kate SHEERAN
10 Vice Pres Finance & Administration .... Kathryn WITTENMYER
30 Vice Pres of Advancement .... Stacy CULLISON
45 Vice Pres of Strategic Initiatives .... Susan MCCONKEY
20 Asst Dean Acad Affairs .... Jonas WRIGHT
32 Associate Dean of Student Life .... Jason SMITH
64 Asc Dean for New Media & Music Tech .... MaryClare ERZYTWA
15 Human Resources Manager .... Michael PATTERSON
07 Director of Admission .... Melissa COCCO-MITTEN
37 Director of Financial Aid .... Doris HOWARD
56 Director Preparatory/Extension .... Joan GORDON
26 Director of Communications .... Margot FREY
09 Director of IR and Registrar .... Rebecca SORELL
08 Head Librarian .... Kevin MCLAUGHLIN
31 Performance Outreach Manager .... Elisabeth LOWRY
18 Chief Facilities Engineer .... David MITCHELL
04 Executive Assistant to President .... Jennifer SEAMAN
20 Assistant to the Dean .... Carissa IBERT

San Francisco Theological Seminary (D)

105 Seminary Road, San Anselmo CA 94960-2997
County: Marin FICE Identification: 001279
Unit ID: 122603
Telephone: (415) 451-2800 Carnegie Class: Spec-4-yr-Faith
FAX Number: (415) 451-2852 Calendar System: Semester
URL: www.sfts.edu
Established: 1871 Annual Graduate Tuition & Fees: N/A
Enrollment: 155 Coed
Affiliation or Control: Presbyterian Church (U.S.A.) IRS Status: 501(c)3
Highest Offering: Doctorate; No Undergraduates
Accreditation: WC, PAST, THEOL

01 President .... Dr. James L. MCDONALD
05 Dean Seminary/VP Academic Affs .... Dr. Jana CHILDERS
30 Vice Pres Advancement .... Dr. Larry SECREST
84 Vice Pres Enrollment Management .... Dr. David BEHRS
10 Vice Pres Finance/Operations .... Mr. Mike CAIRNS
32 Assoc Dean Student Svcs/Chaplain .... Rev. Scott CLARK
75 Assoc Dean for Vocations .... Rev. Elizabeth MCCORD
29 Dir Alumni/Church Relations .... Vacant
04 Exec Administrator to President .... Ms. Anne LUESING
06 Registrar .... Ms. Susan LAWLOR
21 Controller .... Mr. Robbin MCCULLOUGH
18 Director of Facilities .... Mr. Gary MILLER
91 Director of IT .... Mr. Larry PICKARD
35 Dir Student Services/Intl Programs .... Ms. Stephanie LAMONACA
15 Dir Human Resources .... Ms. Kathleen WATERS
44 Director of Annual Giving .... Mr. James SHARPE
26 Director of Communications .... Ms. Rachel HOWARD

San Joaquin College of Law (E)

901 Fifth Street, Clovis CA 93612-1312
County: Fresno FICE Identification: 025000
Unit ID: 122649
Telephone: (559) 323-2100 Carnegie Class: Spec-4-yr-Law
FAX Number: (559) 323-5566 Calendar System: Semester
URL: www.sjcl.edu
Established: 1969 Annual Graduate Tuition & Fees: N/A
Enrollment: 175 Coed
Affiliation or Control: Independent Non-Profit IRS Status: 501(c)3
Highest Offering: Doctorate; No Undergraduates
Accreditation: WC

01 Dean .... Janice L. PEARSON
05 Dean Academic Affairs .... Justin ATKINSON
18 Facilities Manager .... Richard RODRIGUEZ
10 Chief Financial Officer .... Jill A. RANDLES
32 Director of Student Services .... Joyce K. MORODOMI
37 Financial Aid Administrator .... Jeannie M. LEWIS
08 Library Director .... Alicia DIAZ WREST
26 Public Relations Director .... Missy M. CARTIER
15 Chief of Personnel .... Beth PITCOCK
30 Chief Development .... Janice L. PEARSON
84 Director Enrollment Management .... Diane M. STEEL
61 Law Program Coordinator .... Pat A. SMITH

San Joaquin Delta College (F)

5151 Pacific Avenue, Stockton CA 95207-6370
County: San Joaquin FICE Identification: 001280
Unit ID: 122658
Telephone: (209) 954-5151 Carnegie Class: Assoc/HT-High Trad
FAX Number: (209) 954-7001 Calendar System: Semester
URL: www.deltacollege.edu
Established: 1935 Annual Undergrad Tuition & Fees (In-District): $1,104
Enrollment: 18,572 Coed
Affiliation or Control: State/Local IRS Status: 501(c)3
Highest Offering: Associate Degree
Accreditation: WJ, ADNUR

01 Superintendent/President .... Dr. Kathleen HART
05 Asst Supt/VP of Instruction .... Dr. Matt WETSTEIN
32 Asst Supt/VP of Student Svc .... Dr. Lisa COOPER
10 Vice Pres of Administrative Svcs .... Vacant
15 Vice Pres of Human Resources .... Ms. Dianna GONZALES
13 Vice Pres of Operations .... Mr. Gerardo CALDERON
38 Dean Counseling & Special Svcs .... Mrs. Delecia NUNNALLY
09 Dean Plng Research/Regional Educ .... Dr. Ginger HOLDEN
103 Dean Workforce/Economic Development .... Mr. Salvador VARGAS
108 Dean Student Learning & Assessment .... Dr Charles JENNINGS
08 Div Dean Library/Learning Res/Lang .... Mr. Joe GONZALES
12 Associate Dean of Tracy Center .... Dr. Jessie GARZA-RODERICK
26 Director of Marketing/Stdnt Outrch .... Vacant
21 Controller .... Vacant
18 Director Facilities Management .... Vacant
07 Director of Admissions & Records .... Ms. Amy COURTRIGHT
37 Director of Financial Aid/Vet Svcs .... Ms. Tina LENT
96 Director of Purchasing .... Ms. Maria BERNARDINO
06 Registrar .... Ms. Karen SEA

San Joaquin Valley College, Inc. - Visalia (G)

8344 West Mineral King Avenue, Visalia CA 93291-9283
County: Tulare FICE Identification: 021207
Unit ID: 122685
Telephone: (559) 651-2500 Carnegie Class: Assoc/HVT-High Non
FAX Number: (559) 651-0574 Calendar System: Other
URL: www.sjvc.edu/campuses/central-california/visalia
Established: 1977 Annual Undergrad Tuition & Fees: N/A
Enrollment: 5,219 Coed
Affiliation or Control: Proprietary IRS Status: Proprietary
Highest Offering: Associate Degree
Accreditation: WJ, COARC, DH

01 President/Chief Executive Officer .... Mr. Michael PERRY
05 Campus Director .... Mr. Ben ALMAGUER
11 Vice President of Administration .... Ms. Wendy MENDES
88 Chief Administrative Officer .... Mr. Joseph HOLT
10 Chief Financial Officer .... Mr. Russ LEBO
37 VP Student Financial Services .... Mr. Kevin ROBINSON
96 Director of Purchasing .... Mr. Ralph ORTIZ

San Joaquin Valley College-Antelope Valley (H)

42135 10th Street West, Ste 147, Lancaster CA 93534
Telephone: (661) 974-8282 Identification: 770968
Accreditation: &WJ

† Regional accreditation is carried under the parent institution in Visalia, CA.

San Joaquin Valley College-Bakersfield (I)

201 New Stine Road, Bakersfield CA 93309-2668
Telephone: (661) 834-0126 FICE Identification: 023135
Accreditation: &WJ, COARC, SURGT

† Regional accreditation is carried under the parent institution in Visalia, CA.

San Joaquin Valley College-Fresno (J)

295 East Sierra Avenue, Fresno CA 93710-3616
Telephone: (559) 448-8282 Identification: 666008
Accreditation: &WJ, SURGT

† Regional accreditation is carried under the parent institution in Visalia, CA.

San Joaquin Valley College-Fresno Aviation Campus (K)

4985 East Andersen Avenue, Fresno CA 93727
Telephone: (559) 453-0123 Identification: 666009
Accreditation: &WJ

† Regional accreditation is carried under the parent institution in Visalia, CA.

San Joaquin Valley College-Hanford (L)

215 West 7th Street, Hanford CA 93230-4523
Telephone: (559) 584-8840 Identification: 770508
Accreditation: &WJ

† Regional accreditation is carried under the parent institution in Visalia, CA.

San Joaquin Valley College-Modesto (M)

5380 Pirrone Road, Salida CA 95368-9090
Telephone: (209) 543-8800 Identification: 666128
Accreditation: &WJ

† Regional accreditation is carried under the parent institution in Visalia, CA.

San Joaquin Valley College-Ontario (N)

4580 Ontario Mills Parkway, Ontario CA 91764
Telephone: (909) 948-7582 Identification: 666096
Accreditation: &WJ, COARC

† Regional accreditation is carried under the parent institution in Visalia, CA.

San Joaquin Valley College-Rancho Cordova (O)

11050 Olson Drive, Suite 210,
Rancho Cordova CA 95670-5600
Telephone: (916) 638-7582 Identification: 666133
Accreditation: &WJ, COARC

† Regional accreditation is carried under the parent institution in Visalia, CA.

San Joaquin Valley College-Temecula (A)

27270 Madison Avenue, Suite 305, Temecula CA 92590
Telephone: (951) 296-6015 Identification: 770507
Accreditation: &WJ, #COARC

† Regional accreditation is carried under the parent institution in Visalia, CA

San Joaquin Valley College-Victor Valley (Hesperia) (B)

9331 Mariposa Road, Hesperia CA 92344-8000
Telephone: (760) 948-1947 Identification: 667044
Accreditation: &WJ

† Regional accreditation is carried under the parent institution in Visalia, CA.

*San Jose/Evergreen Community College District (C)

4750 San Felipe Road, San Jose CA 95135-1599
County: Santa Clara FICE Identification: 029042
Unit ID: 122737
Telephone: (408) 274-6700 Carnegie Class: N/A
FAX Number: (408) 531-8722
URL: www.sjeccd.edu

01	Chancellor	Dr. Deborah BUDD
11	Vice Chanc Administrative Services	Mr. Douglas SMITH
15	Vice Chanc Human Resources	Ms. Kim L. GARCIA
13	Vice Chanc Information Tech Svcs	Dr. Ben SEABERRY
103	Interim Exec Dir of Workforce Inst	Mr. William WATSON
09	Int VC Inst Effect/Student Success	Ms. Tamela HAWLEY
86	Exec Dir Government/External Affs	Ms. Rosalie LEDESMA
18	Dir Facilities/Bond Program Mgmt	Mr. Owen LETCHER
07	Director Admiss/Records San Jose	Ms. Teresa PAIZ
10	Director of Fiscal Services	Mr. Peter FITZSIMMONS
26	Dir of Communications/Community Rel	Mr. Sam HO

*Evergreen Valley College (D)

3095 Yerba Buena Road, San Jose CA 95135-1598
County: Santa Clara FICE Identification: 012452
Unit ID: 114266
Telephone: (408) 274-7900 Carnegie Class: Assoc/HT-High Trad
FAX Number: (408) 238-3179 Calendar System: Semester
URL: www.evc.edu
Established: 1975 Annual Undergrad Tuition & Fees (In-District): $1,338
Enrollment: 9,133 Coed
Affiliation or Control: State/Local IRS Status: 501(c)3
Highest Offering: Associate Degree
Accreditation: WJ, ADNUR

02	President	Mr. Henry C. YONG
05	VP Academic Affairs	Mr. Keith AYTCH
32	Vice Pres Student Services	Ms. Irma ARCHULETA
10	VP Administrarive Services	Vacant
50	Dean Business & Workforce	Dr. Lena TRAN
66	Dean Nursing & Allied Health	Dr. Antoinette HERRERA
62	Dean Library/Lrng Res	Dr. Merryl KRAVITZ
81	Dean Math/Science/Engineering	Mr. Michael HIGHERS
83	Dean Soc Sci/PE/Arts/Humanities	Mr. Mark GONZALES
84	Dean Enrollment Services	Mr. Octavio CRUZ
79	Dean Language Arts	Dr. Merryl KRAVITZ
38	Int Dean Student Success/Counseling	Ms. Angelina DUARTE
35	Assoc Dean Student Life & EOPS	Dr. Victor GARZA, JR.
37	Director Financial Aid	Ms. Alma TANON
88	Director Student Life	Ms. Raniyah JOHNSON
88	Director CalWorks/WIN	Ms. Elizabeth TYRRELL
21	Director Business Services	Ms. Lauren MCKEE
13	Supervisor Campus Tech Svcs	Mr. Eugenio CANOY

*San Jose City College (E)

2100 Moorpark Avenue, San Jose CA 95128-2799
County: Santa Clara FICE Identification: 001282
Unit ID: 122746
Telephone: (408) 298-2181 Carnegie Class: Assoc/HVT-High Trad
FAX Number: (408) 298-1935 Calendar System: Semester
URL: www.sjcc.edu
Established: 1921 Annual Undergrad Tuition & Fees (In-District): $1,338
Enrollment: 9,072 Coed
Affiliation or Control: State/Local IRS Status: 501(c)3
Highest Offering: Associate Degree
Accreditation: WJ, DA

02	President	Dr. Byron BRELAND
05	Vice President Academic Affairs	Mr. Duncan GRAHAM
11	Vice President Administrative Svcs	Mr. Jorge ESCOBAR
32	Vice President Student Affairs	Mr. Roland MONTEMAYOR
88	Vice Pres Special Services	Ms. Marilyn BRODIE
84	Dean of Enrollment Services	Mr. Takeo KUBO
92	Director Honors Program	Mr. Sean ABEL
41	Director of Athletics & Kinesiology	Mr. Lamel HARRIS
04	Assistant to the President	Ms. Judy WESSLER
50	Dean Business/Workforce Development	Ms. Ingrid THOMPSON
79	Dean Humanities/Social Science	Mr. Sean ABEL
38	Int Dean Counseling/Matriculation	Dr. Eliazer AYALA-AUSTIN
88	Dean Language Arts	Dr. Keiko KIMURA
81	Dean Mathematics/Sciences Division	Vacant

*San Mateo County Community College District Office (F)

3401 CSM Drive, San Mateo CA 94402-3651
County: San Mateo FICE Identification: 004697
Unit ID: 122782
Telephone: (650) 574-6500 Carnegie Class: N/A
FAX Number: (650) 574-6566
URL: www.smccd.edu

01	Chancellor	Mr. Ron D. GALATOLO
03	Executive Vice Chancellor	Ms. Kathy BLACKWOOD
15	Vice Chanc Employee Rels/Human Res	Mr. Eugene WHITLOCK
05	Vice Chanc Educational Svcs/Plng	Dr. Jing LUAN
18	Vice Chanc Facil Plng/Maint/Oper	Mr. Jose NUNEZ
109	Vice Chanc Auxiliary Services	Mr. Tom BAUER
10	Chief Financial Officer	Mr. Raymond CHOW
13	Chief Technology Officer	Mr. Frank M. VASKELIS

*Cañada College (G)

4200 Farm Hill Boulevard, Redwood City CA 94061-1099
County: San Mateo FICE Identification: 006973
Unit ID: 111434
Telephone: (650) 306-3100 Carnegie Class: Assoc/MT-VT-High Non
FAX Number: (650) 306-3457 Calendar System: Semester
URL: www.canadacollege.edu
Established: 1968 Annual Undergrad Tuition & Fees (In-District): $1,344
Enrollment: 6,498 Coed
Affiliation or Control: State/Local IRS Status: 501(c)3
Highest Offering: Associate Degree
Accreditation: WJ, RAD

02	President	Dr. Jamillah MOORE
05	Vice President of Instruction	Mr. Gregory ANDERSON
32	Vice President of Student Services	Ms. Kim LOPEZ
11	Vice Pres Administrative Services	Ms. Michelle MARQUEZ
10	Chief Business Officer	Ms. Victoria NUNES
38	Dean Counseling Services	Ms. Kim LOPEZ
06	Registrar	Ms. Ruth MILLER
26	Director of Marketing	Vacant
45	Dean Plng/Research/Student Success	Ms. Chialin HSIEH
37	Director Financial Aid Services	Ms. Margie CARRINGTON
18	Interim Facilities Manager	Ms. Karen PINKHAM
103	Dean Business/Design & Workforce	Ms. Linda HAYES
79	Dean of Humanities & Social Science	Mr. David JOHNSON
81	Dean Science & Technology	Dr. Janet STRINGER
41	Dean Athletics/Kinesiology	Ms. Anniqua RANA

*College of San Mateo (H)

1700 W Hillsdale Boulevard, San Mateo CA 94402-3795
County: San Mateo FICE Identification: 001181
Unit ID: 122791
Telephone: (650) 574-6161 Carnegie Class: Assoc/HT-Mix Trad/Non
FAX Number: (650) 574-6680 Calendar System: Semester
URL: www.collegeofsanmateo.edu
Established: 1922 Annual Undergrad Tuition & Fees (In-District): $1,324
Enrollment: 8,935 Coed
Affiliation or Control: State/Local IRS Status: 501(c)3
Highest Offering: Associate Degree
Accreditation: WJ, DA

02	President	Mr. Michael CLAIRE
05	Vice President Instruction	Dr. Sandra Stefani COMERFORD
10	Vice Pres Administrative Services	Ms. Jan ROECKS
32	Vice President Student Services	Ms. Jennifer HUGHES
07	Dean Admissions & Records	Dr. Henry VILLAREAL
38	Dean Counsel/Advis/Matriculation	Ms. Krystal ROMERO
09	Dean Plng/Rsrch/Inst Effectiveness	Dr. John J. SEWART
35	Dean Student Services/Counseling	Ms. Marsha RAMEZANE
79	Dean Language Arts Division	Dr. James CARRANZA
68	Dean Kinesiology/Athletics Division	Mr. Andreas WOLF
81	Dean Math/Science Division	Dr. Charlene FRONTIERA
83	Dean Creative Arts/Social Sci Div	Dr. Laura DEMSETZ
50	Dean Business & Technology Division	Ms. Kathleen ROSS
06	Registrar	Ms. Niruba SRINIVASAN
37	Director Financial Aid Services	Ms. Claudia I. MENJIVAR
30	Dir College Development & Marketing	Ms. Beverly MADDEN
26	Dir Marketing/Comm/Public Relations	Ms. Cherie COLIN
18	Facilities Manager	Ms. Michelle RUDOVSKY

*Skyline College (I)

3300 College Drive, San Bruno CA 94066-1698
County: San Mateo FICE Identification: 007713
Unit ID: 123509
Telephone: (650) 738-4100 Carnegie Class: Assoc/MT-VT-High Non
FAX Number: (650) 738-4338 Calendar System: Semester
URL: www.skylinecollege.edu
Established: 1969 Annual Undergrad Tuition & Fees (In-District): $1,447
Enrollment: 9,820 Coed
Affiliation or Control: State/Local IRS Status: 501(c)3
Highest Offering: Baccalaureate
Accreditation: WJ, ACBSP, COARC, SURGT

02	President	Dr. Regina STANBACK STROUD
05	Vice President Instruction	Dr. Sarah F. PERKINS
32	Vice President Student Services	Dr. Angelica GARCIA
84	Dean Enrollment Svcs/Financial Aid	Mr. William MINNICH
09	Dean Plng/Rsrch/Inst Effective	Mr. Aaron D. MCVEAN
10	Vice President Business Service	Ms. Eloisa M. BRIONES
83	Dean Social Science/Creative Arts	Ms. Donna J. BESTOCK
50	Dean Business/Ed/Prof Pgm	Ms. Christine ROUMBANIS
60	Dean Language Arts/Learning Res	Ms. Mary GUTIERREZ
68	Dean Kinesiology/Athletics/Dance	Mr. Joseph MORELLO, JR.
81	Dean Science/Math/Technology	Mr. Raymond HERNANDEZ
38	Dean Counsel/Advis/Matric	Dr. Luis ESCOBAR
103	Director SparkPoint at Skyline Col	Dr. Chad THOMPSON
26	Director Marketing/Comm/PR	Ms. Cherie COLIN
08	Director Learning Commons	Dr. Pearl LY
103	Director Workforce Development	Dr. Rajesh LATHIGARA
85	Dean Global Learning Programs	Dr. Tammy ROBINSON
88	Dean Acad Support & Learning Tech	Vacant
06	Registrar	Ms. Susan LORENZO
04	Administrative Asst to President	Ms. Theresa TENTES
104	Director Study Abroad	Mr. Zaid GHORI
18	Facilities Manager	Mr. John DOCTOR
19	Chief Public Safety Officer	Mr. Jim VANGELE
37	Director Student Financial Aid	Ms. Regina MORRISON

Sanford Burnham Prebys Medical Discovery Institute (J)

10901 North Torrey Pines Road, La Jolla CA 92037
County: San Diego Identification: 667069
Unit ID: 481535
Telephone: (858) 646-3100 Carnegie Class: Spec-4-yr-Other Health
FAX Number: (858) 646-3199 Calendar System: Quarter
URL: www.shpdiscovery.org
Established: 2005 Annual Graduate Tuition & Fees: N/A
Enrollment: N/A Coed
Affiliation or Control: Independent Non-Profit IRS Status: 501(c)3
Highest Offering: Doctorate; No Undergraduates
Accreditation: WC

01	President	Dr. Kristiina VUORI
10	Chief Financial Officer	Dr. Gary CHESSUM
05	Dean	Dr. Guy SALVESEN
15	Vice Pres Human Res/Org Effect	Mr. John SCHIERER
26	Vice Pres for Communications	Ms. Deborah ROBISON
30	Vice President Inst Advancement	Mr. Philip GRAHAM

The Santa Barbara and Ventura Colleges of Law (K)

4475 Market Street, Ventura CA 93003
County: Ventura Identification: 667229
Unit ID: 125037
Telephone: (805) 765-9300 Carnegie Class: Spec-4-yr-Law
FAX Number: (805) 658-0529 Calendar System: Semester
URL: www.collegesoflaw.edu
Established: 1969 Annual Graduate Tuition & Fees: N/A
Enrollment: 93 Coed
Affiliation or Control: Independent Non-Profit IRS Status: 501(c)3
Highest Offering: Doctorate; No Undergraduates
Accreditation: WC

01	Executive Director	Dr. Matthew NEHMER
05	Dean	Ms. Jackie GARDINA
13	Director of Information Management	Ms. Diane MCREYNOLDS
07	Director of Admissions	Mr. Shawn TAYLOR
06	Asst Dean & Registrar	Ms. Barbara DOYLE
32	Student Services Coordinator	Ms. Jennifer MACKIE
18	Facilities Manager	Mr. Pete LOPEZ

SBBCollege Bakersfield (L)

5300 California Ave, Bakersfield CA 93309-2139
County: Kern FICE Identification: 025779
Unit ID: 122834
Telephone: (661) 835-1100 Carnegie Class: Bac/Assoc-Mixed
FAX Number: (661) 835-0242 Calendar System: Semester
URL: www.sbbcollege.edu
Established: 1982 Annual Undergrad Tuition & Fees: $14,949
Enrollment: 562 Coed
Affiliation or Control: Proprietary IRS Status: Proprietary
Highest Offering: Baccalaureate
Accreditation: ACICS

01	President	Matthew JOHNSTON
26	Marketing Coordinator	Monica RAYMOND

SBBCollege Rancho Mirage (M)

34275 Monterey Ave, Rancho Mirage CA 92270
Telephone: (760) 341-7602 Identification: 666582
Accreditation: ACICS

SBBCollege Santa Barbara (N)

506 Chapala Street, Santa Barbara CA 93101-3412
Telephone: (805) 967-9677 Identification: 666099
Accreditation: ACICS

† Branch campus of Santa Barbara Business College, Ventura, CA.

SBBCollege Santa Maria (A)

303 E Plaza Drive, Santa Maria CA 93454
County: Santa Barbara FICE Identification: 025780
Unit ID: 122852
Telephone: (805) 922-8256 Carnegie Class: Bac/Assoc-Assoc Dom
FAX Number: (805) 346-1857 Calendar System: Semester
URL: www.sbbcollege.edu
Established: 1980 Annual Undergrad Tuition & Fees: $15,203
Enrollment: 204 Coed
Affiliation or Control: Proprietary IRS Status: Proprietary
Highest Offering: Baccalaureate
Accreditation: ACICS

01 President .... Matthew JOHNSTON
26 Marketing Coordinator .... Monica RAYMOND

SBBCollege Ventura (B)

4839 Market Street, Ventura CA 93003
County: Ventura FICE Identification: 009989
Unit ID: 433420
Telephone: (805) 339-2999 Carnegie Class: Bac/Assoc-Mixed
FAX Number: (805) 339-2994 Calendar System: Other
URL: www.sbbcollege.edu
Established: 2003 Annual Undergrad Tuition & Fees: $13,708
Enrollment: 420 Coed
Affiliation or Control: Proprietary IRS Status: Proprietary
Highest Offering: Baccalaureate
Accreditation: ACICS

01 President .... Matthew JOHNSTON
26 Marketing Coordinator .... Monica RAYMOND

SBBCollege Online (C)

5777 Olivas Park Drive, Suite A, Ventura CA 93003
Telephone: (877) 305-7222 Identification: 770628
Accreditation: ACICS

Santa Barbara City College (D)

721 Cliff Drive, Santa Barbara CA 93109-2394
County: Santa Barbara FICE Identification: 001285
Unit ID: 122889
Telephone: (805) 965-0581 Carnegie Class: Assoc/HT-High Trad
FAX Number: (805) 963-7222 Calendar System: Semester
URL: www.sbcc.edu
Established: 1909 Annual Undergrad Tuition & Fees (In-District): $1,374
Enrollment: 17,927 Coed
Affiliation or Control: State/Local IRS Status: 501(c)3
Highest Offering: Associate Degree
Accreditation: WJ, ADNUR, CAHIIM, DMS, RAD

01 Superintendent/President .... Dr. Anthony E. BEEBE
03 Executive Vice Pres .... Dr. Jack FRIEDLANDER
05 Exec Vice Pres Educ Pgms .... Dr. Paul JARRELL
10 Vice President Business Services .... Mr. Joseph SULLIVAN
15 Vice Pres Human Resources .... Ms. Patricia ENGLISH
13 Vice President Info Technology .... Dr. Paul BISHOP
72 Dean Educational Programs .... Dr. Ben PARTEE
76 Dean Educational Programs .... Dr. Alan PRICE
81 Dean Educational Programs .... Ms. Marilynn SPAVENTA
57 Dean Educational Programs .... Dr. Alice PEREZ
53 Dean Educational Programs .... Ms. Melissa MORENO
72 Dean Educational Programs .... Mr. Kenley NEUFELD
07 Associate Dean Admissions .... Mr. Christopher JOHNSON
08 Librarian .... Ms. Elizabeth BOWMAN
102 Exec Dir Foundation for SBCC .... Mr. Geoff GREEN
09 Sr Director Institutional Research .... Mr. Robert ELSE
26 Communications Director .... Ms. Luz REYES-MARTIN
37 Director of Student Financial Aid .... Mr. Saul QUIROZ
18 Sr Dir of Facilities & Operations .... Ms. Julie HENDRICKS
85 Director International Students .... Ms. Carola SMITH
06 Director of Records .... Mr. Michael MEDEL
96 Manager of Purchasing .... Mr. Robert MORALES
04 Administrative Asst to President .... Ms. Angie ESQUEDA
19 Director Security/Safety .... Mr. Erik FRICKE
41 Athletic Director .... Vacant
84 Coordinator for Enrollment Services .... Ms. Vanessa PELTON

Santa Clara University (E)

500 El Camino Real, Santa Clara CA 95053-0001
County: Santa Clara FICE Identification: 001326
Unit ID: 122931
Telephone: (408) 554-4000 Carnegie Class: Masters/L
FAX Number: (408) 554-2700 Calendar System: Quarter
URL: www.scu.edu
Established: 1851 Annual Undergrad Tuition & Fees: $45,300
Enrollment: 9,015 Coed
Affiliation or Control: Independent Non-Profit IRS Status: 501(c)3
Highest Offering: Doctorate
Accreditation: WC, BUS, BUSA, CS, ENG, LAW, THEOL

01 President .... Rev. Michael E. ENGH, SJ
05 Provost .... Dr. Dennis JACOBS
10 Int Vice President Finance/Admin .... Mr. Chris SHAY
43 General Counsel .... Mr. John OTTOBONI
26 Vice President University Relations .... Mr. James LYONS
100 Chief of Staff to the President .... Ms. Molly MC DONALD
49 Dean of Arts & Sciences .... Dr. Debbie TAHMASSEBI
50 Dean of Business .... Ms. Caryn BECK-DUDLEY
53 Dean Educ & Counseling Psych .... Dr. Sabrina ZIRKEL
54 Dean of Engineering .... Dr. Godfrey MUNGAL
61 Dean of Law .... Ms. Lisa KLOPPENBERG
73 Dean Jesuit School of Theology .... Rev. Kevin O'BRIEN, SJ
88 Dean Academic Support Services .... Ms. Kathryn PALMIERI
88 Presidential Prof Global Outreach .... Dr. Don C. DODSON
20 Sr Vice Provost Academic Affairs .... Dr. Diane E. JONTE-PACE
32 Vice Provost and Dean Student Life .... Ms. Jeanne ROSENBERGER
84 Vice President for Enrollment Mgmt .... Mr. Mike B. SEXTON
45 Vice Prov Inst Effectiveness .... Dr. Ed RYAN
13 CIO/Vice Provost Info Services .... Dr. Robert OWEN
20 Assoc Vice Prov Undergrad Studies .... Dr. Philip R. KESTEN
20 Assoc Provost Undergraduate Studies .... Mr. Jim BENNETT
88 Sr Assoc Provost Rsrch Faculty Affs .... Dr. Amy M. SHACHTER
88 Assoc Vice Provost Faculty Devel .... Dr. Eileen R. ELROD
07 Dean Undergraduate Admission .... Ms. Eva BLANCO MASIAS
37 Dean University Financial Aid Svcs .... Ms. Nan MERZ
27 Assoc Vice President Mktg/Comm .... Vacant
21 Assoc Vice President Finance .... Mr. Harry M. FONG
15 Asst Vice President Human Resources .... Mr. Charlie AMBELANG
30 Assoc Vice President Development .... Mr. Mike J. WALLACE
109 Asst Vice Pres Auxiliary Services .... Ms. Jane BARRANTES
35 Assoc Dean for Student Life .... Mr. Matthew DUNCAN
06 University Registrar .... Ms. Monica L. AUGUSTIN
29 Asst Vice President Alumni Rels .... Ms. Kathy KALE
41 Director Athletics and Recreation .... Dr. Renee BAUMGARTNER
08 University Librarian .... Ms. Jennifer NUTEFALL
90 Director Academic Technology .... Ms. Nancy CUTLER
36 Director Career Center .... Ms. Elspeth ROSSETTI
09 Director Institutional Research .... Ms. Barbara A. STEWART
25 Director Sponsored Projects .... Ms. Mary-Ellen FORTINI
38 Director Health & Counseling Svcs .... Dr. Jill ROVARIS
85 Assoc Provost International Pgm .... Ms. Susan POPKO
21 University Director Budget .... Ms. Robin REYNOLDS
88 Chief Investment Officer .... Mr. John E. KERRIGAN
21 Controller .... Ms. Ramona SAUTER
18 Director of Facilities .... Mr. Jeffrey R. CHARLES
96 Director University Support Service .... Mr. Ed MERRYMAN
19 Director Campus Safety Services .... Mr. Philip BELTRAN
40 General Manager Bookstore .... Ms. Deborah KENDALL
42 Director of Campus Ministry .... Ms. Lulu SANTANA
22 EEO & Title IX Coordinator .... Ms. Belinda GUTHRIE
88 Director de Saisset Museum .... Ms. Rebecca M. SCHAPP
88 Exec Dir Ignatian Ctr Jesuit Educ .... Rev. Dorian LLYWELYN, SJ
88 Exec Dir Miller Ctr Soc Entrepren .... Dr. Thane KREINER
88 Exec Dir Markkula Ctr Applied Ethic .... Mr. Kirk O. HANSON
30 Assoc Vice President Development .... Ms. Nancy T. CALDERON
28 Assoc Provost Diversity & Inclusion .... Mr. Aldo BILLINGSLEA
44 Assoc Vice President Advance Svcs .... Ms. Caroline CHANG
92 Director University Honors Program .... Dr. Leilani M. MILLER
94 Director Womens & Gender Studies .... Dr. Linda GARBER
93 Director Ethnic Studies .... Dr. Anna C. SAMPAIO

Santa Monica College (F)

1900 Pico Boulevard, Santa Monica CA 90405-1628
County: Los Angeles FICE Identification: 001286
Unit ID: 122977
Telephone: (310) 434-4000 Carnegie Class: Assoc/HT-High Trad
FAX Number: (310) 434-4386 Calendar System: Semester
URL: www.smc.edu
Established: 1929 Annual Undergrad Tuition & Fees (In-District): $1,136
Enrollment: 30,158 Coed
Affiliation or Control: State/Local IRS Status: 501(c)3
Highest Offering: Associate Degree
Accreditation: WJ, ADNUR

01 Superintendent/President .... Dr. Kathryn E. JEFFERY
03 Executive Vice President .... Mr. Jeff SHIMIZU
10 Vice President Business/Admin .... Mr. Robert G. SOMOTO
15 Vice President Human Resources .... Ms. Marcia WADE
05 Vice President Academic Affairs .... Dr. Georgia LORENZ
84 Vice Pres Enrollment Development .... Dr. Teresita RODRIGUEZ
32 Vice President Student Affairs .... Mr. Michael TUITASI
20 Dean Academic Affairs .... Ms. Erica LEBLANC
16 Dean Human Resources .... Ms. Sherri LEE-LEWIS
08 Dean Learning Resources .... Dr. Fabienne CHAUDERLOT
85 Dean International Education .... Ms. Kelley BRAYTON
56 Dean Noncredit/External Programs .... Ms. Dione CARTER
38 Dean Counseling/Retention .... Ms. Brenda BENSON
13 Dean Information Technology .... Vacant
88 Interim Dean Education Enterprise .... Mr. Mitch HESKEL
43 Campus Counsel .... Mr. Robert MYERS
106 Assoc Dean Online Svcs & Support .... Ms. Julie YARRISH
51 Assoc Dean Emeritus College .... Ms. Gina RUNKLE
35 Dean Students .... Ms. Deyna HEARN
17 Associate Dean of Health Sciences .... Dr. Ida DANZEY
26 Public Information Officer .... Ms. Grace SMITH
31 Dean Community & Academic Relations .... Ms. Kiersten ELLIOTT
86 Sr Director Government Relations .... Mr. Don GIRARD
37 Assoc Dean Financial Aid/Scholarshp .... Mr. Steve MYROW
18 Chief Dir Facilities Management .... Mr. Bruce WYBAN
21 Budget Manager .... Ms. Veronica DIAZ
09 Dean Institutional Research .... Ms. Hannah LAWLER
104 Assoc Dean International Education .... Ms. Denise KINSELLA
41 Asst Director Athletics .... Mr. Reggie ELLIS
102 Associate Dean Grants .... Ms. Laurel MCQUAY-FENINGER
88 Director of Classified Personnel .... Ms. Carol LONG
88 Director Network Services .... Mr. Bob DAMMER
25 Director of Contracts .... Mr. Charlie YEN
96 Director of Purchasing .... Ms. Cynthia MOORE
19 Dean Camp Security Stdnt Hlth/Safe .... Dr. Albert VASQUEZ
04 Admin Asst to the President .... Ms. Letty KILIAN
14 Director Management Info Systems .... Mr. Lee JOHNSTON
24 Mgr Media & Reprographic Services .... Mr. Albert DESALLES
40 Bookstore Manager .... Mr. David DEVER
103 Dean Workforce Development .... Dr. Patricia RAMOS
101 Coordinator Board of Trustees .... Ms. Lisa ROSE
88 Interim Assoc Dean Student Life .... Ms. Nancy GRASS-HEMMERT
88 Director Radio Station (KCRW) .... Ms. Jennifer FERRO
88 Director Facilities Programming .... Ms. Linda SULLIVAN
88 Dean Student Success Initiatives .... Dr. Roberto GONZALEZ
88 Dir Sustainability Coordination .... Mr. Ferris KAWAR
75 Dir Career & Contract Education .... Ms. Michelle KING
88 Assoc Dir Dual Enroll/Instr Svcs .... Ms. Maral HYELER
88 Dir Supplemental Instruct/Tutoring .... Dr. Tony PRESTBY
88 Director STEM Initiatives .... Ms. Melanie BOCANEGRA
88 Acting Dir Small Business Dev Ctr .... Ms. Sasha KING
88 Assoc Dean Instruct/Stdnt Pgm .... Mr. Frank DAWSON
29 Dir Student and Alumni Rels .... Ms. Deirdre WEAVER
88 Special Assistant to the President .... Ms. Katharine MULLER

Santa Rosa Junior College (G)

1501 Mendocino Avenue, Santa Rosa CA 95401-4395
County: Sonoma FICE Identification: 001287
Unit ID: 123013
Telephone: (707) 527-4011 Carnegie Class: Assoc/MT-VT-High Trad
FAX Number: (707) 527-4816 Calendar System: Semester
URL: www.santarosa.edu
Established: 1918 Annual Undergrad Tuition & Fees (In-District): $1,318
Enrollment: 23,144 Coed
Affiliation or Control: State/Local IRS Status: 501(c)3
Highest Offering: Associate Degree
Accreditation: WJ, DA, DH, DIETT, EMT, RAD

01 Superintendent/President .... Dr. Frank CHONG
12 Vice President Petaluma Campus .... Dr. Jane SALDANA-TALLEY
05 VP Acad Affs/Asst Superintendent .... Dr. Mary Kay RUDOLPH
10 Vice President Business Services .... Mr. Doug ROBERTS
32 VP Student Svcs/Asst Superintendent .... Mr. Ricardo NAVARRETTE
15 VP Human Resources .... Ms. Karen FURUKAWA
88 Director Capital Projects .... Mr. Leigh SATA
04 Executive Assistant to CEO/BOT .... Ms. Erin MAGEE
75 Dean Career/Tech Ed/Economic Dev .... Mr. Jerry MILLER
18 Interim Dean Facility Planning/Ops .... Mr. Paul BIELEN
88 Dean Curriculum/Education Support .... Dr. Abraham FARKAS
49 Dean Liberal Arts & Sciences .... Dr. Kris ABRAHAMSON
08 Dean Learning Res/Educ Tech .... Ms. Alicia VIRTUE
38 Interim Dean Counseling/Support Svc .... Mr. Martin LEE
88 Dean Public Safety .... Ms. April CHAPMAN
81 Dean Sci/Tech/Engr/Math .... Mr. Victor TAM
17 Dean Health Sciences .... Ms. Deborah CHIGAZOLA
50 Dean Business/Professional Studies .... Mr. Joshua ADAMS
79 Dean Arts & Humanities .... Ms. Anna SZABADOS
88 Dean Language Arts/Acad Foundation .... Mr. Robert HOLCOMB
41 Dean Kinesiology/Dance/Athletic Dir .... Mr. Matthew MARKOVITCH
22 Dean Disabled Students Pgm & Svcs .... Ms. Patie WEGMAN
72 Dean Instruction & Enrollment Svcs .... Ms. Catherine WILLIAMS
35 Dean Student Services Petaluma .... Ms. Vanessa SHANNON
88 Dean Child Dev & Teacher Education .... Ms. Yolanda GARCIA
88 Dean Student Success & Retention .... Ms. Li COLLIER
47 Dean Agriculture/Natural Resources .... Mr. Ganesan SRINIVASAN
19 Chief of Police .... Mr. Lorenzo DUENAS
13 Director Information Technology .... Mr. Scott CONRAD
103 Director Workforce Development .... Ms. Eve NIGHSWONGER
21 Director of Fiscal Services .... Ms. Kate JOLLEY
37 Director Student Financial Services .... Ms. Jana COX
18 Director Facilities Operations .... Vacant
23 Director Student Health Services .... Ms. Susan QUINN
09 Director Institutional Research .... Dr. KC GREANEY
35 Dir Student Afts/New Student Pgm .... Mr. Robert ETHINGTON
96 Director Purchasing & Graphics .... Ms. Laura RIVERA
40 Director Bookstore .... Mr. Anthony MARTINEZ
102 Executive Director Foundation .... Ms. Kate MCCLINTOCK
66 Interim Director Nursing Program .... Ms. Anna VALDEZ
06 Dean Acad Records/Intl Admissions .... Ms. Freyja PEREIRA
07 Director Admissions/Enrollment Svcs .... Ms. Vayta SMITH
31 Director Community Education .... Mr. Jeffrey RHOADES
16 Director Human Resources .... Ms. Sarah HOPKINS
26 Director Public Relations
Manager .... Ms. Ellen MAREMONT-SILVER
90 Manager Instructional Computing .... Mr. Michael ROTH
24 Manager Media Services Petaluma .... Mr. Matt PEARSON

Saybrook University (H)

475 14th Street, Oakland CA 94612
County: Alameda FICE Identification: 021206
Unit ID: 123095
Telephone: (510) 593-2900 Carnegie Class: Spec-4-yr-Other Health
FAX Number: (510) 455-7046 Calendar System: Semester
URL: www.saybrook.edu
Established: 1971 Annual Graduate Tuition & Fees: N/A
Enrollment: 567 Coed
Affiliation or Control: Independent Non-Profit IRS Status: 501(c)3
Highest Offering: Doctorate; No Undergraduates
Accreditation: WC

01 President .... Dr. Nathan LONG
05 VP Academics/Student Affs (CAO) .... Dr. Carol R. HUMPHREYS
06 Registrar .... Mr. Thomas CHAMPION
08 Director of Library Services .... Ms. Lorelette KNOWLES
04 Executive Assistant .... Ms. LaTanya O. HICKS

07 Senior Director of Admissions ....Ms. Wendy OVEREND
15 Director Business Operations ....Ms. Connie SHULMAN
13 IT Manager ....Mr. Alex SALTZBERG
32 Director of Student Affairs ....Ms. Julia SONDEJ

Scripps College (A)

1030 Columbia, Claremont CA 91711-3948
County: Los Angeles FICE Identification: 001174
Unit ID: 123165
Telephone: (909) 621-8000 Carnegie Class: Bac-A&S
FAX Number: (909) 621-8323 Calendar System: Semester
URL: www.scrippscollege.edu
Established: 1926 Annual Undergrad Tuition & Fees: $49,152
Enrollment: 988 Female
Affiliation or Control: Independent Non-Profit IRS Status: 501(c)3
Highest Offering: Baccalaureate
Accreditation: WC

01 President ....Dr. Amy MARCUS-NEWHALL
05 Vice Pres/Dean of the Faculty ....Ms. Julia E. LISS
30 VP for Institutional Advancement ....Mr. Michael ARCHIBALD
10 VP for Business Affairs/Treasurer ....Mr. Dean CALVO
32 Vice President of Student Affairs ....Ms. Charlotte JOHNSON
07 Vice President for Enrollment ....Ms. Victoria ROMERO
26 VP for Communications & Marketing ....Ms. Binti HARVEY
29 Asst VP Alumnae & Parent Engagement ....Ms. Nikki KHURANA
101 VP/Secretary of Board of Trustees ....Ms. Denise NELSON NASH
04 Executive Asst to the President ....Ms. Christine COSTANZA
20 Associate Dean of Faculty ....Dr. Gretchen EDWALDS-GILBERT
15 Director of Human Resources ....Ms. Jennifer L. BERKLAS
09 Dir of Assessment/Inst Research ....Ms. Junelyn PEEPLES
08 Librarian ....Ms. Judy B. HARVEY-SAHAK
06 Registrar ....Ms. Kelly HOGENCAMP
37 Associate Director of Financial Aid ....Ms. Lindsay MORALES
36 Director of Career Planning ....Ms. Vicki P. KLOPSCH
13 Director of Information Technology ....Mr. Jeff SESSLER
18 Director of Facilities ....Mr. Josh REEDER
104 Director of Off-Campus Study ....Ms. Neva BARKER

The Scripps Research Institute (B)

10550 N Torrey Pines Road, TPC19,
La Jolla CA 92037-1000
County: San Diego FICE Identification: 033213
Unit ID: 435338
Telephone: (858) 784-8469 Carnegie Class: Not Classified
FAX Number: (858) 784-2802 Calendar System: Quarter
URL: www.scripps.edu
Established: 1989 Annual Graduate Tuition & Fees: N/A
Enrollment: N/A Coed
Affiliation or Control: Independent Non-Profit IRS Status: 501(c)3
Highest Offering: Doctorate; No Undergraduates
Accreditation: WC

01 President ....Dr. Steve A. KAY
43 Exec Vice Pres/General Counsel ....Mr. Douglas A. BINGHAM
05 VP Acad Affs/Dean Graduate Studies ....Dr. James R. WILLIAMSON
11 Chief Operating Officer ....Mr. Richard A. KING

Shasta Bible College and Graduate School (C)

2951 Goodwater Avenue, Redding CA 96002-1544
County: Shasta FICE Identification: 023593
Unit ID: 123280
Telephone: (530) 221-4275 Carnegie Class: Spec-4-yr-Faith
FAX Number: (530) 221-6929 Calendar System: Semester
URL: www.shasta.edu
Established: 1972 Annual Undergrad Tuition & Fees: $12,060
Enrollment: 51 Coed
Affiliation or Control: Independent Non-Profit IRS Status: 501(c)3
Highest Offering: Master's
Accreditation: TRACS

01 President ....Dr. David R. NICHOLAS
04 Exec Assistant to the President ....Mrs. Barbara WELLOCK
05 Academic Dean ....Dr. Stephen G. BROWN
07 Dean of Admissions & Records ....Mr. George A. GUNN
18 Coordinator Grounds & Maintenance ....Mr. Gary KELLOGG
06 Registrar ....Mrs. Faith MCCARTHY
10 Director of Finance/Controller ....Mr. Eric BROWN
37 Director of Financial Aid ....Ms. Linda ILES
56 Director External Studies ....Mrs. Faith MCCARTHY
08 Head Librarian ....Mrs. Virginia M. WILLIAMS
39 Director Student Housing ....Mrs. Donna R. NICHOLAS

Shasta College (D)

PO Box 496006, 11555 Old Oregon Tr,
Redding CA 96049-6006
County: Shasta FICE Identification: 001289
Unit ID: 123299
Telephone: (530) 242-7500 Carnegie Class: Assoc/HT-Mix Trad/Non
FAX Number: (530) 225-4990 Calendar System: Semester
URL: www.shastacollege.edu
Established: 1950 Annual Undergrad Tuition & Fees (In-District): $1,183
Enrollment: 8,342 Coed
Affiliation or Control: State/Local IRS Status: Exempt
Highest Offering: Baccalaureate
Accreditation: WJ, DH

01 Superintendent/President ....Dr. Joe WYSE
04 Asst to Superintendent/President ....Ms. Andree BLANCHIER
102 Executive Director SC Foundation ....Mr. Scott THOMPSON
05 VP Instruction ....Vacant
10 VP Administrative Services ....Mr. Morris RODRIGUE
32 VP of Student Services ....Dr. Kevin O'RORKE
15 Assoc VP of Human Resources ....Ms. Laura CYPHERS BENSON
13 Director of Information Technology ....Mr. James CRANDALL
21 Comptroller ....Ms. Jill AULT
84 Dean Enrollment Services ....Mr. Timothy JOHNSTON
57 Dean Arts/Communication/Soc Science ....Vacant
50 Dean Business/Ag/Ind/Tech/Safety ....Mr. Michael SLOAN
50 Dean EWD ....Ms. Eva JIMENEZ
76 Dean Health Sciences ....Ms. Kathy ROYCE
81 Dean Science/Language Arts/Math ....Dr. Frank NIGRO
56 Assoc Dean Extended Education ....Mr. Andy FIELDS
62 Dean Library Services/Educ Tech ....Mr. William BREITBACH
68 Dean Phys Education and Athletics ....Mr. Mike MARI
35 Assoc Dean Student Services ....Ms. Sandra HAMILTON SLANE
28 Assoc Dean Access and Equity ....Dr. Sharon BRISOLARA
88 Dean Found Skills/Inst Effectivenes ....Dr. Kate MAHAR
19 Director of Campus Safety ....Mr. Lonnie SEAY
37 Director Financial Aid/Veteran Svcs ....Ms. Becky MCCALL
109 Director Food Services ....Ms. Denise AXTELL
25 Director Grant Development ....Ms. Amy WEBB
18 Director Physical Plant ....Mr. George ESTRADA
06 Chief Records Technician ....Ms. Sheree WHALEY
88 Supervisor HazMat Compliance Pgm ....Vacant
39 Interim Director Residence Life ....Mr. Nick WEBB

Shepherd University (E)

3200 N San Fernando Rd, Los Angeles CA 90065
County: Los Angeles Identification: 667056
Telephone: (323) 550-8888 Carnegie Class: Not Classified
FAX Number: (323) 550-1313 Calendar System: Semester
URL: shepherduniversity.edu
Established: 1999 Annual Undergrad Tuition & Fees: N/A
Enrollment: N/A Coed
Affiliation or Control: Independent Non-Profit IRS Status: 501(c)3
Highest Offering: Doctorate
Accreditation: @WC, ACICS, NURSE, THEOL

05 Vice Pres & Academic Dean ....Shalom Y. KIM

Sierra College (F)

5000 Rocklin Road, Rocklin CA 95677-3397
County: Placer FICE Identification: 001290
Unit ID: 123341
Telephone: (916) 624-3333 Carnegie Class: Assoc/HT-High Trad
FAX Number: N/A Calendar System: Semester
URL: www.sierracollege.edu
Established: 1914 Annual Undergrad Tuition & Fees (In-District): $1,142
Enrollment: 18,565 Coed
Affiliation or Control: State/Local IRS Status: 501(c)3
Highest Offering: Associate Degree
Accreditation: WJ

01 Superintendent/President ....Mr. William H. DUNCAN
05 Supt/Vice President Instruction ....Dr. Debra SUTPHEN
10 Vice Pres Administrative Services ....Mr. Chris YATOOMA
32 Vice Pres Student Services ....Ms. Mandy DAVIES
04 Exec Assistant Presidents Office ....Ms. Jeannette BISCHOFF
08 Dean Library/Learning Resource Ctr ....Ms. Sabrina PAPE
50 Assoc Dean Business & Technology ....Ms. Darlene JACKSON
81 Dean Science & Mathematics ....Vacant
49 Dean Liberal Arts ....Dr. Rebecca BOCCHICCHIO
68 Dean Phys Educ/Athletics Director ....Mr. Lucas MOOSMAN
09 Dean Planning/Research/Res Devel ....Mr. Erik COOPER
66 Dean Nursing ....Ms. Nancy SCHWAB
21 Director of Finance ....Ms. Linda FISHER
15 Director Human Resources ....Mr. Cameron ABBOTT
18 Dir of Facilities & Construction ....Ms. Laura DOTY
88 Director Economic Development ....Vacant
37 Manager Financial Aid ....Dr. Linda WILLIAMS
31 Community Education Pgm Manager ....Ms. Jill ALCORN
22 EEO Program Manager ....Mr. Cameron ABBOTT
26 Manager Marketing/Public Relations ....Ms. Sue MICHAELS
39 Residence Life Supervisor ....Vacant
07 Manager of Admissions & Records ....Ms. Gail MODDER

Silicon Valley University (G)

2010 Fortune Drive, San Jose CA 95131
County: Santa Clara FICE Identification: 038103
Unit ID: 444848
Telephone: (408) 435-8989 Carnegie Class: Not Classified
FAX Number: (408) 955-0887 Calendar System: Trimester
URL: www.svuca.edu
Established: 1997 Annual Undergrad Tuition & Fees: N/A
Enrollment: N/A Coed
Affiliation or Control: Independent Non-Profit IRS Status: 501(c)3
Highest Offering: Master's
Accreditation: ACICS

01 President ....Mr. Jerry SHIAO
05 Associate Academic Dean ....Mr. Simon AU
06 Registrar ....Mr. Kevin CHENG

Simpson University (H)

2211 College View Drive, Redding CA 96003-8606
County: Shasta FICE Identification: 001291
Unit ID: 123457
Telephone: (530) 224-5600 Carnegie Class: Masters/S
FAX Number: (530) 226-4860 Calendar System: Semester
URL: www.simpsonu.edu
Established: 1921 Annual Undergrad Tuition & Fees: $25,200
Enrollment: 1,267 Coed
Affiliation or Control: The Christian And Missionary Alliance
IRS Status: 501(c)3
Highest Offering: Master's
Accreditation: WC

01 President ....Dr. Robin K. DUMMER
03 Executive Vice President ....Mr. Bradley E. WILLIAMS
05 Provost ....Dr. Gayle COPELAND
10 Chief Financial Officer ....Ms. Natalie E. MCKENZIE
30 Interim Director of Development ....Mr. Roger JANIS
32 Associate VP Student Development ....Dr. Michael LOOMIS
84 Senior Director of Enrollment Mgmt ....Mr. Dustin LOWE
07 Director of Undergrad Admissions ....Ms. Molly MCKEEVER
18 Director of Facilities ....Mr. Merlin D. WEBER
04 Exec Assistant to the President ....Mrs. Regina ERICKSON
08 Dir Lib Svcs/Ast Prof Librarianship ....Vacant
06 Registrar ....Mr. Harold E. LUND
88 Assoc Registrar for Records/Advis ....Ms. Cassandra A. HEATH
13 Director of IT ....Mr. Michael SUMPTION
41 Director of Athletics ....Mr. Thomas GALBRAITH
35 Director of Residence Life ....Mr. Mark ENDRASKE
38 Director of Wellness Center ....Ms. Beverly G. KLAIBER
09 Dir Institutional Research/ALO ....Ms. Jennifer FOX
21 Director of Accounting ....Ms. Karen CAPFER
41 Bookstore Manager ....Vacant
15 Director of Human Resources/TitleIX ....Mrs. Kori D. OECHSLI
109 Director of Auxiliary Services ....Mr. Paul R. DAVIS
26 Director of Marketing ....Mr. Mark U. WOOD
42 Campus Pastor ....Mr. Kevin M. BENNIE
73 Dean AW Tozer Seminary ....Dr. Patrick A. BLEWETT
53 Dean School of Education ....Dr. Craig COOK
37 Director Student Financial Services ....Mrs. Melissa A. HUDSON
66 Dean School of Nursing ....Mrs. Kristie STEPHENS
107 Dean of Adult & Graduate Prof Stds ....Dr. Addie R. JACKSON
88 Director of Academic Success Center ....Mr. Louis E. BURKWHAT
35 Director of Student Engagement ....Ms. Isis MARTIN
19 Campus Safety Operations Coord ....Mr. Dennis SMITH

Sofia University (formerly Institute of Transpersonal Psychology) (I)

1069 E Meadow Circle, Palo Alto CA 94303-4231
County: Santa Clara FICE Identification: 022676
Unit ID: 110778
Telephone: (650) 493-4430 Carnegie Class: Spec-4-yr-Other Health
FAX Number: (650) 493-6835 Calendar System: Quarter
URL: www.sofia.edu
Established: 1975 Annual Undergrad Tuition & Fees: N/A
Enrollment: 314 Coed
Affiliation or Control: Proprietary IRS Status: Proprietary
Highest Offering: Doctorate
Accreditation: WC

01 President & CEO ....Dr. Qiaoyun (Liz) LI
05 Dean of Faculty ....Dr. Barbara HECKER
10 Accounting Manager ....Ms. Linyan LIU
04 Admissions and Marketing Manager ....Ms. Kimberly Anne YARBROUGH
32 Dean Student Services ....Ms. Rosalie COOK
15 Human Resources Manager ....Ms. Aida SMAILAGIC
37 Director Student Financial Aid ....Ms. Josephine MELTON
18 Facilities Manager ....Mr. Henry WU

Soka University of America (J)

1 University Drive, Aliso Viejo CA 92656-8081
County: Orange FICE Identification: 038144
Unit ID: 399911
Telephone: (949) 480-4000 Carnegie Class: Bac-A&S
FAX Number: (949) 480-4001 Calendar System: Semester
URL: www.soka.edu
Established: 2001 Annual Undergrad Tuition & Fees: $30,642
Enrollment: 417 Coed
Affiliation or Control: Independent Non-Profit IRS Status: 501(c)3
Highest Offering: Master's
Accreditation: WC

01 President/Professor of Economics ....Dr. Daniel Y. HABUKI
04 Exec Asst to the President ....Mr. Hiro SAKAI
05 Provost/Vice Pres Academic Affairs ....Dr. Edward M. FEASEL
10 Vice President Finance & Admin/CFO ....Mr. Archibald E. ASAWA
09 VP Inst Rsch/Dean of Graduate Sch ....Dr. Tomoko TAKAHASHI
20 Dean of Faculty/CAO ....Dr. Edward M. FEASEL
84 Dean of Enrollment Services ....Mr. Andrew WOOLSEY
32 Dean of Students ....Dr. Hyon J. MOON
19 Director Safety/Security/Events ....Mr. Clifford D. MOSHER
31 Director of Community Relations ....Ms. Wendy WETZEL HARDER
41 Director of Athletics & Recreation ....Mr. Mike MOORE
35 Director of Student Services ....Mr. Brian DURICK
39 Dir Stdnt Activities/Resident Life ....Ms. Michelle HOBBY-MEARS
30 Director of Philanthropy ....Ms. Linda KENNEDY

13 Director Information Technology .... Mr. John MIN
44 Dir of International Development .... Ms. Toshiko SATO
15 Director of Human Resources .... Ms. Katherine KING
104 Dir Study Abroad & Intl Internships .... Mr. Alex H. OKUDA
06 Registrar .... Ms. Nancy YOSHIMURA
18 Chief of Operations .... Mr. Tom HARKENRIDER
84 Mgr Student Recruitment Programs .... Ms. Marilyn GOVE
08 Director of Library .... Mr. Hiroko TONONO

Solano Community College (A)

4000 Suisun Valley Road, Fairfield CA 94534-3197
County: Solano FICE Identification: 001292
Unit ID: 123563
Telephone: (707) 864-7000 Carnegie Class: Assoc/HT-Mix Trad/Non
FAX Number: (707) 864-0361 Calendar System: Semester
URL: www.solano.edu
Established: 1945 Annual Undergrad Tuition & Fees (In-District): $1,416
Enrollment: 9,824 Coed
Affiliation or Control: State/Local IRS Status: 501(c)3
Highest Offering: Associate Degree
Accreditation: **WJ**

01 Superintendent/President .... Dr. Celia ESPOSITO-NOY
05 VP Academic Affairs .... Ms. Leslie MINOR
10 Vice President Finance & Admin .... Mr. Yulian LIGIOSO
13 Interim Chief Technology Officer .... Mr. James (Kimo) CALILAN
32 Vice President Student Services .... Dr. Gregory BROWN
38 Dean Counseling/Special Services .... Ms. Jocelyn MOUTON
37 Int Director Financial Aid .... Ms. Maureen MASON-MUYCO
09 Dean Research and Planning .... Mr. Peter CAMMISH
21 Director of Fiscal Services .... Mr. Patrick KILLINGSWORTH
07 Associate Dean Admissions/Records .... Vacant
84 Director Enrollment Management .... Vacant
15 Human Resources Manager .... Ms. Rachel ANCHETA
18 Director Facilities .... Mr. James BUCHANAN
35 Director Student Life .... Ms. Rischa SLADE
06 Registrar .... Vacant
14 Director Technology Services .... Vacant
88 Director Children's Programs .... Ms. Christie SPECK
103 Assoc Dean Workforce Development .... Ms. Kelly PENWELL
57 Director Theater Operations .... Vacant
26 Outreach/Public Relations Manager .... Ms. Shemila JOHNSON
96 Purchasing Tech/Buyer .... Ms. Laura SCOTT
36 Career & Job Placement Coordinator .... Ms. Patricia YOUNG
49 Dean School of Liberal Arts .... Mr. Neil GLINES
83 Dean Sch of Social/Behav Science .... Dr. Sandy LAMBA
81 Dean School Math/Science .... Vacant
76 Dn Sch Career Tech Ed/Bus/Vcvl/TAFB .... Mrs. Maire MORINEC
12 Center Dean Vallejo .... Dr. Shirley LEWIS
100 Chief of Staff .... Dr. Yashica CRAWFORD
76 Dean Health Sciences .... Dr. Robert GABRIEL
41 Director of Athletics .... Mr. Erik VISSER

South Baylo University (B)

1126 N Brookhurst Street, Anaheim CA 92801-1702
County: Orange FICE Identification: 025973
Unit ID: 123633
Telephone: (714) 533-1495 Carnegie Class: Spec-4-yr-Other Health
FAX Number: (714) 533-6040 Calendar System: Quarter
URL: www.southbaylo.edu
Established: 1977 Annual Undergrad Tuition & Fees: N/A
Enrollment: 682 Coed
Affiliation or Control: Independent Non-Profit IRS Status: 501(c)3
Highest Offering: Doctorate
Accreditation: **ACUP**

01 President .... Dr. Jason SHIN
05 Academic Dean .... Dr. Pia MELEN
07 Director of Admission .... Dr. Young Jin AHN
06 Registrar .... Ms. Christina PARK
10 Director of Finance .... Ms. Michelle JANG
15 Operations/Personnel Director .... Dr. Yolanda JAINI
36 Program Student Advisor .... Dr. Henry CHOI
08 Director of Libraries .... Dr. Edwin FOLLICK
13 Dir Computer Information System .... Mr. James KIM
88 Director of Clinics .... Dr. Hyo Jeong KANG
37 Financial Aid Officer .... Ms. Mimi PARK
32 Stdnt/Alumni/English LG Coordinator .... Ms. Jillian FISHBACK
85 International Student Advisor .... Ms. Seon KIM
88 Doctoral Clerkship Coordinator .... Dr. Sheng LI
88 Doctoral Program Director .... Dr. Wayne CHENG
88 Master Program Director .... Dr. Hanjik KIM
18 Chief Facilities/Physical Plant .... Mr. Yong Hee PARK
38 CCE Coordinator .... Dr. Seongok KIM

South Baylo University (C)

2727 West 6th Street, Los Angeles CA 90057
Telephone: (213) 738-0712 Identification: 770911
Accreditation: **ACUP**

South Coast College (D)

2011 W Chapman Avenue, Orange CA 92868-2609
County: Orange FICE Identification: 022774
Unit ID: 123642
Telephone: (714) 867-5009 Carnegie Class: Spec 2-yr-Other
FAX Number: (714) 867-5026 Calendar System: Quarter
URL: www.southcoastcollege.com
Established: 1961 Annual Undergrad Tuition & Fees: N/A
Enrollment: 342 Coed
Affiliation or Control: Proprietary IRS Status: Proprietary
Highest Offering: Associate Degree
Accreditation: **ACICS**

01 President .... Ms. Jean GONZALEZ
03 Vice President .... Ms. Lonnie SKELTON
10 Dean Finance & Operations .... Ms. Jila ANDELIBI
11 Director of Operations .... Mr. Kevin MAGNER
37 Director of Financial Aid .... Mr. Michael LY
06 Registrar .... Ms. Yoshiko IZUMI

*South Orange County Community College District (E)

28000 Marguerite Parkway, Mission Viejo CA 92692-3697
County: Orange FICE Identification: 033433
Unit ID: 432144
Telephone: (949) 582-4850 Carnegie Class: N/A
FAX Number: (949) 364-2726
URL: www.socccd.edu

01 Chancellor .... Mr. Gary POERTNER
05 Vice Chanc Technology/Learning Svcs .... Dr. Robert S. BRAMUCCI
15 Vice Chancellor Human Resources .... Dr. David P. BUGAY
10 Vice Chancellor Business Services .... Ms. Debra FITZSIMONS
26 Dir Public Affairs/Government Rels .... Ms. Tere FLUEGEMAN
84 Dean Enroll Svcs Irvine Valley Col .... Ms. Arleen ELSEROAD
84 Int Dean Enroll Svcs Saddleback Col .... Mr. Christian ALVARADO

*Irvine Valley College (F)

5500 Irvine Center Drive, Irvine CA 92618-4399
County: Orange FICE Identification: 025395
Unit ID: 116439
Telephone: (949) 451-5100 Carnegie Class: Assoc/HT-High Trad
FAX Number: (949) 451-5270 Calendar System: Semester
URL: www.ivc.edu
Established: 1979 Annual Undergrad Tuition & Fees (In-District): $1,326
Enrollment: 13,157 Coed
Affiliation or Control: State/Local IRS Status: 501(c)3
Highest Offering: Associate Degree
Accreditation: **WJ**

02 President .... Dr. Glenn R. ROQUEMORE
05 Vice President Instruction .... Dr. Stephen C. JUSTICE
32 Vice President Student Services .... Dr. Linda FONTANILLA
10 Vice President Admin Services .... Mr. Davit KHACHATRYAN
45 Asst VP Institutional Effectivenes .... Dr. Christopher MCDONALD
26 Exec Director Market/Comm/Broadcast .... Ms. Diane G. OAKS
102 Exec Director College Foundation .... Ms. Elissa ORANSKY
20 Dean Instruction/EWD .... Dr. Corine DOUGHTY
38 Dean Counseling Services .... Dr. Elizabeth CIPRES
49 Dean Liberal Arts .... Dr. Karima FELDHUS
81 Dean Math/Sciences and Engr .... Dr. Lianna ZHAO
50 Dean Business Sciences Online/Ex Ed .... Dr. Cathleen GREINER
76 Dean Kinesiology/Health/Athletics .... Mr. Keith SHACKLEFORD
57 Dean The Arts .... Mr. Joseph POSHEK
83 Dean Social & Behavioral Sciences .... Ms. Traci FAHIMI
84 Dean of Enrollment Services .... Ms. Arleen ELSEROAD
37 Asst Dean Financial Aid/Student Sup .... Mr. Ken LIRA
18 Director IVC Facilities .... Mr. Jeffrey HURLBUT
09 Dir Research/Planning/Accreditation .... Dr. Craig HAYWARD
19 Chief of Police .... Mr. Will GLEN
35 Director Student Life .... Ms. Anissa HEARD
13 Director Technology Services .... Mr. Bruce HAGAN
88 Director Child Development Center .... Ms. Becky THOMAS
06 Registrar/Admissions/Records .... Mr. Ruben GUZMAN

*Saddleback College (G)

28000 Marguerite Parkway, Mission Viejo CA 92692-3635
County: Orange FICE Identification: 008918
Unit ID: 122205
Telephone: (949) 582-4500 Carnegie Class: Assoc/HT-Mix Trad/Non
FAX Number: (949) 347-0438 Calendar System: Semester
URL: www.saddleback.edu
Established: 1968 Annual Undergrad Tuition & Fees (In-District): $1,326
Enrollment: 20,007 Coed
Affiliation or Control: State/Local IRS Status: 501(c)3
Highest Offering: Associate Degree
Accreditation: **WJ, ADNUR, CAHIIM, EMT**

02 President .... Dr. Tod A. BURNETT
05 Vice President of Instruction .... Dr. Kathy WERLE
10 VP College Administrative Services .... Ms. Carol HILTON
32 Vice President of Student Services .... Dr. Juan AVALOS
04 Manager Office of the President .... Ms. Sophie MILLER-GILLILAND
45 Director Planning/Research/Grants .... Ms. Jennifer KLEIN
06 Registrar .... Ms. Joyce SEMANIK
84 Int Dean of Enrollment Services .... Mr. Christian ALVARADO
19 Chief Of Police .... Mr. Pat HIGA
26 Director Public Information .... Ms. Jennie MCCUE
88 Director Outreach and Recruitment .... Dr. Lesley HUMPHREY
102 Director College Foundation .... Dr. Donald RICKNER
35 Int Director Student Development .... Ms. Erlynne BALLO
31 Dean Cmty Educ/EI & K-12 Partnershp .... Dr. Estella CASTILLO-GARRISON
88 Director of Emeritus Institute .... Mr. Dan PREDOEHL
44 Director Annual/Planned Giving .... Ms. Erin MCHENRY
66 Director of Nursing .... Ms. Diane PESTOLESI
15 Director Human Resources .... Ms. Teddi LORCH
18 Dir Facilities/Maint/Operation .... Mr. John OZUROVICH
23 Director Student Health Center .... Dr. Jeanne HARRIS-CALDWELL
13 Director Technology Services .... Dr. Anthony MACIEL
37 Director Financial Assistance .... Mr. Christian ALVARADO
96 Director of Purchasing .... Ms. Brandye D'LENA
85 Intl Student Program Specialist .... Ms. Sonja ARNAK
92 Honors Program .... Ms. Alannah ROSENBERG
38 Dean Counseling Svcs/Special Pgms .... Ms. Penny SKAFF
57 Dean Fine Arts .... Mr. Bart MCHENRY
50 Dean Bus/Science/Economic/Workforce .... Dr. John JARAMILLO
76 Dean Hlth Sci/Human Svcs & Emeritus .... Dr. Donna RANE-SZOSTAK
81 Dean Math/Science & Engineering .... Dr. Akira NITTA
79 Dean Liberal Arts/Learning Res .... Dr. Kevin O'CONNOR
106 Dean Online Education/Learning Res .... Dr. Marina AMINY
72 Dean Advance Tech Appl Science .... Dr. Anthony TENG
68 Dean Kinesiology/Athletic Director .... Mr. Tony LIPOLD
83 Dean Social & Behavioral Sciences .... Dr. Cadence WYNTER
88 Director Learning Assistance .... Dr. Christina HINKLE
71 Dean Transfer/Career/Special Pgms .... Dr. Georgina GUY
103 Dir Economic/Workforce Development .... Mr. Israel DOMINGUEZ
25 Director Fiscal Contract Services .... Dr. Roxanne METZ

Southern California Institute of Architecture (H)

960 E 3rd Street, Los Angeles CA 90013-1822
County: Los Angeles FICE Identification: 020758
Unit ID: 123952
Telephone: (213) 613-2200 Carnegie Class: Spec-4-yr-Arts
FAX Number: (213) 613-2260 Calendar System: Semester
URL: www.sciarc.edu
Established: 1972 Annual Undergrad Tuition & Fees: $43,334
Enrollment: 523 Coed
Affiliation or Control: Independent Non-Profit IRS Status: 501(c)3
Highest Offering: Master's
Accreditation: **WC**

01 Director .... Mr. Herman DIAZ ALONSO
04 Director's Assistant .... Ms. Jessica WHEELER
05 Vice Director/Chief Academic Ofcr .... Mr. John ENRIGHT
11 Chief Operating Officer .... Mr. Jamie BENNETT
13 Chief Information Officer .... Mr. Vic JABRASSIAN
30 Assoc Director Development .... Ms. Maria ROBINSON GLOVER
58 Graduate Program Chair .... Ms. Elena MANFERDINI
88 Undergraduate Program Chair .... Mr. Tom WISCOMBE
20 Academic Affairs Manager .... Mr. Paul HOLLIDAY
20 Admin/Academic Affairs Assistant .... Ms. Nicole FISHER
10 Finance Director .... Mr. Christopher BANKS
07 Admissions Director .... Ms. Sandy FRIGO
37 Financial Aid Manager .... Mr. Pierre FLOOD
08 Library Manager .... Mr. Kevin MCMAHON
88 Wood & Metal Shop Manager .... Mr. Rodney ROJAS
88 Wood & Metal Shopmaster .... Mr. Katsumi MOROI
20 Academic Counselor .... Mr. Peter DUNG
06 Registrar/International Advisor .... Ms. Lisa RUSSO
18 Facilities Manager .... Mr. Andrew WERNER

Southern California Institute of Technology (I)

525 North Muller Street, Anaheim CA 92801-5454
County: Orange FICE Identification: 031136
Unit ID: 399869
Telephone: (714) 300-0300 Carnegie Class: Spec-4-yr-Eng
FAX Number: (714) 300-0311 Calendar System: Quarter
URL: www.scitech.edu
Established: 1987 Annual Undergrad Tuition & Fees: $17,235
Enrollment: 526 Coed
Affiliation or Control: Proprietary IRS Status: Proprietary
Highest Offering: Baccalaureate
Accreditation: **ACCSC**

01 President .... Dr. Parviz SHAMS
03 Vice President .... Mrs. Nazila SHAMS
05 Dean of Education .... Mr. Saravana RAMAN
13 MIS .... Mr. Arian SHAMS

Southern California Seminary (J)

2075 E Madison Avenue, El Cajon CA 92019-1108
County: San Diego FICE Identification: 033323
Unit ID: 117575
Telephone: (619) 201-8999 Carnegie Class: Spec-4-yr-Faith
FAX Number: (619) 201-8975 Calendar System: Trimester
URL: www.socalsem.edu
Established: 1946 Annual Undergrad Tuition & Fees: $14,244
Enrollment: 201 Coed
Affiliation or Control: Independent Non-Profit IRS Status: 501(c)3
Highest Offering: Doctorate
Accreditation: **TRACS**

00 Chancellor .... Dr. David JEREMIAH
01 President .... Dr. Gary F. COOMBS
05 CAO/Vice President Academics .... Dr. Gino PASQUARIELLO
32 Director of Student Services .... Mrs. Jillian HINES
83 Dean Grad Sch Behavioral Science .... Dr. Elizabeth ELENWO
73 Dean of Biblical Studies/Theology .... Mr. James I. FAZIO
06 Registrar .... Mrs. Cheryl OBST
37 Director of Financial Aid .... Mrs. Yuli MARTINEZ
08 Library Director .... Miss Jennifer EWING

07 Director of Admissions .... Mr. Bill GEORGE
06 Dean of Online Learning .... Dr. Joseph R. MILLER

Southern California University of Health Sciences (A)

16200 E Amber Valley Drive, Whittier CA 90604-4051
County: Los Angeles FICE Identification: 001229
Unit ID: 117672
Telephone: (562) 947-8755 Carnegie Class: Spec-4-yr-Other Health
FAX Number: (562) 947-5724 Calendar System: Trimester
URL: www.scuhs.edu
Established: 1911 Annual Undergrad Tuition & Fees: $8,779
Enrollment: 876 Coed
Affiliation or Control: Independent Non-Profit IRS Status: 501(c)3
Highest Offering: First Professional Degree
Accreditation: WC, ACUP, #ARCPA, CHIRO

01 President .... Dr. John SCARINGE
05 Vice Pres Academic Affairs .... Dr. Sheryl BERMAN
100 Chief of Staff/VP Govt Relations .... Dr. J. Todd KNUDSEN
32 VP Enroll Mgmt/Student Affairs .... Mrs. Debra MITCHELL BENAVENTE
10 VP Admin & Finance/CFO .... Mr. Thomas K. ARENDT
17 VP SCU Health Sys/Chief Clin Off .... Dr. Melissa KIMURA
20 CSIH Dean .... Dr. Heidi CROCKER
06 Registrar .... Mrs. Debra MITCHELL BENAVENTE
84 Dir Enrollment Svcs/Financial Aid .... Ms. Kate MCCUNE
04 Exec Asst to President/BOR .... Mrs. Regina TORRES-ELLIS
20 AVPAA Teaching/Learning/Leadership .... Dr. Noni THREINEN
07 Director of Admissions .... Vacant
88 Dean of Chiropractic .... Dr. Jonathon EGAN
88 Int Dean College of Eastern Med .... Dr. Bob DAMONE
13 Interim Chief Information Officer .... Mr. Chuck SWEET
21 Executive Director of Accounting .... Mrs. Kelly GALLO
10 Director of Auxiliary Services .... Mr. Joseph EGGLESTON
09 Dean OSIE .... Dr. Heather VANVOLKINBURG
32 Exec Director of Student Affairs .... Dr. Steven R. JAFFE
26 Executive Director of Marketing .... Mr. Luke PHILLIPS
08 Exec Dir of Seabury Learning Center .... Ms. Kathleen E. SMITH
96 Accounts Payable/Purchasing Coord .... Mrs. Catherine MCBRIDE
37 Asst Financial Aid Director .... Ms. Nida LABAO
88 Human Resources .... Ms. Cindy SCHEIBEL
06 AVP Student Affairs/Enroll Mgt .... Mr. Jeff CORRAL
88 Director of Physical Plant .... Mr. Bob HARRISON
88 Assistant Controller .... Mrs. Lupe YABUR

Southern California University School of Oriental Medicine & Acupuncture (B)

3460 Wilshire Boulevard, Suite 500,
Los Angeles CA 90010
County: Los Angeles FICE Identification: 041720
Unit ID: 459222
Telephone: (213) 413-9500 Carnegie Class: Spec-4-yr-Other Health
FAX Number: (213) 413-5400 Calendar System: Quarter
URL: www.scusoma.edu
Established: 2000 Annual Undergrad Tuition & Fees: N/A
Enrollment: 119 Coed
Affiliation or Control: Proprietary IRS Status: Proprietary
Highest Offering: Master's
Accreditation: ACUP

01 President .... Ms. Judy OH
05 Academic Dean .... Dr. Katherine H S. CHO
06 Registrar/Student Services .... Ms. Seolah JUNG
37 Director of Financial Aid .... Mr. Roberto QUINONES
07 Director of Admissions .... Mr. Dave PARK

Southern States University (C)

1601 Dove Street, Suite 105, Newport Beach CA 92660
Telephone: (949) 833-8868 Identification: 770629
Accreditation: ACICS

Southern States University (D)

123 Camino de la Reina Ste 100 East,
San Diego CA 92108
County: San Diego Identification: 667108
Telephone: (619) 298-1829 Carnegie Class: Not Classified
FAX Number: (619) 704-0175 Calendar System: Quarter
URL: www.ssu.edu
Established: 1985 Annual Undergrad Tuition & Fees: N/A
Enrollment: N/A Coed
Affiliation or Control: Proprietary IRS Status: Proprietary
Highest Offering: Master's
Accreditation: ACICS

01 Chancellor .... John D. TUCKER
05 Vice Chanc Academic Affairs/CAO .... Dr. Claudia ARAIZA
06 Univ Registrar/Compliance Officer .... Luke MARTIN
07 Dean Admissions/Academic Advising .... William AMOKE
08 University Librarian .... Jason ROGERS
11 Administrative Director .... Denise MASTRO

Southwestern College (E)

900 Otay Lakes Road, Chula Vista CA 91910-7299
County: San Diego FICE Identification: 001294
Unit ID: 123800
Telephone: (619) 421-6700 Carnegie Class: Assoc/HT-High Trad
FAX Number: (619) 482-6413 Calendar System: Semester
URL: www.swccd.edu
Established: 1961 Annual Undergrad Tuition & Fees (In-District): $1,336
Enrollment: 19,000 Coed
Affiliation or Control: State/Local IRS Status: 501(c)3
Highest Offering: Associate Degree
Accreditation: WJ, ADNUR, DH, EMT, MLTAD, SURGT

01 Interim Superintendent/President .... Mr. Robert DEEGAN
05 Vice President Academic Affairs .... Ms. Kathy TYNER
10 VP Business & Financial Affairs .... Mr. Tim FLOOD
32 Vice President Student Affairs .... Dr. Angelica SUAREZ
15 Interim VP Employee Services .... Mr. Karl SPARKS
12 Dn High Ed Ctr Otay Mesa/San Ysidro .... Ms. Silvia CORNEJO
12 Dean HEC Natl City/Crown Cove .... Ms. Christine PERRI
79 Dean Language & Literature .... Dr. Joel LEVINE
81 Dean Math/Science Engineering .... Dr. Michael ODU
30 Dean Inst Effect/Dir of Foundation .... Ms. Linda GILSTRAP
51 Dean Inst Support Svcs/Cont Educ .... Ms. Mia C. MCCLELLAN
38 Dean Couns/Student Support Pgms .... Dr. Jonathan KING
68 Dean Wellness/Ex Sci/Athletics .... Mr. James SPILLERS
50 Dean Business & Technology .... Dr. Mink STAVENGA
26 Chief Comm Cmty & Govt Rels Officer .... Ms. Lillian LEOPOLD
16 Director Human Resources .... Mr. Marvin CASTILLO
88 Director Payroll Services .... Ms. Janet TAYLOR
09 Dir Inst Rsrch Grants & Planning .... Ms. Linda HENSLEY
88 Dir Center Ops San Ysidro .... Ms. Cynthia K. NAGURA
88 Director Crown Cove Aq Ctr .... Ms. Patrice MILKOVICH
37 Director Financial Aid .... Ms. Patti LARKIN
07 Director Admissions/Records .... Mr. Nicholas MONTEZ
96 Dir Procurement/Cntrl Svc/Risk Mgt .... Ms. Priya JEROME
35 Dean Student Services .... Dr. Malia FLOOD
52 Director Dental Hygiene Program .... Ms. Vickie KIMBROUGH-WALLS
66 Director Nursing & Health Occup .... Ms. Cathy MCJANNET
88 Director EOPS .... Mr. Omar ORIHUELA
21 Director of Finance .... Mr. Wayne YANDA
88 Director Child Development Center .... Ms. Patricia BARTOW
04 Exec Asst to Supt & President .... Ms. Mary GANIO
19 Campus Police Chief .... Mr. Michael CASH
13 Chief Info Technology Officer (CIO) .... Mr. Daniel BORGES
60 Int Dean Arts & Comm .... Mr. William KINNEY
28 Director Equity/Inclusion/Diversi .... Dr. Guadalupe CORONA
102 Director Foundation .... Ms. Zaneta ENCARNACION
88 Director Title V .... Mr. Carlos FIGARI
88 Director Student Development .... Mr. Brett ROBERTSON
18 Director Facilities/Operations .... Ms. Charlotte ZOLEZZI

Southwestern Law School (F)

3050 Wilshire Boulevard, Los Angeles CA 90010-1106
County: Los Angeles FICE Identification: 001295
Unit ID: 123970
Telephone: (213) 738-6700 Carnegie Class: Spec-4-yr-Law
FAX Number: (213) 383-1688 Calendar System: Semester
URL: www.swlaw.edu
Established: 1911 Annual Graduate Tuition & Fees: N/A
Enrollment: 1,106 Coed
Affiliation or Control: Independent Non-Profit IRS Status: 501(c)3
Highest Offering: Master's; No Undergraduates
Accreditation: LAW

01 Dean/Chief Executive Officer .... Ms. Susan WESTERBERG PRAGER
10 Chief Financial Officer .... Mr. Paul KALUSH
04 Corporate Secretary .... Ms. Janis K. YOKOYAMA
03 Vice Dean .... Mr. Christopher CAMERON
32 Dean of Students & Div Aff .... Ms. Nydia DUENEZ
20 Sr Assoc Dean for Academic Admin .... Ms. Doreen E. HEYER
30 Assoc Dean for Institutional Advanc .... Ms. Debra L. LEATHERS
07 Asst Dean of Admissions .... Ms. Lisa L. GEAR
35 Assoc Dean of Student Affairs .... Dr. Robert MENA
37 Interim Director of Financial Aid .... Ms. Lina BORJORQUEZ
11 Assoc Dean Administrative Services .... Ms. Marcie CANAL
13 Chief Information Systems Officer .... Ms. Bo SUZOW
26 Assoc Dean for Public Affairs .... Ms. Leslie STEINBERG

Spartan College of Aeronautics and Technology (G)

8911 Aviation Blvd, Inglewood CA 90301
County: Los Angeles FICE Identification: 025964
Unit ID: 413680
Telephone: (310) 879-0554 Carnegie Class: Not Classified
FAX Number: N/A Calendar System: Other
URL: www.spartan.edu
Established: 2014 Annual Undergrad Tuition & Fees: N/A
Enrollment: 414 Coed
Affiliation or Control: Proprietary IRS Status: Proprietary
Highest Offering: Associate Degree
Accreditation: COE

01 President .... Dennis MANZO

Stanbridge College (H)

2041 Business Center Dr., Suite 107, Irvine CA 92612
County: Orange FICE Identification: 038893
Unit ID: 446561
Telephone: (949) 794-9090 Carnegie Class: Spec-4-yr-Other Health
FAX Number: (949) 794-9098 Calendar System: Other
URL: www.stanbridge.edu
Established: 1996 Annual Undergrad Tuition & Fees: N/A
Enrollment: 1,133 Coed
Affiliation or Control: Proprietary IRS Status: Proprietary
Highest Offering: Master's
Accreditation: ACCSC, NURSE, OT, OTA, PTAA

01 Chief Executive Officer .... Yasith WEERASURIYA
10 Chief Financial Officer .... Nazi MASOUM
37 Director of Financial Aid .... Brian SILVANO
07 Director of Admissions .... Edward RIEPMA
05 VP of Instruction .... Dr. Everett PROCTER
66 Director of Nursing .... Kim MARTIN
66 RN-BSN & MSN Program Director .... Dr. Judith MCLEOD
75 Director of Occupational Therapy .... Satch PURCELL
75 MSOT Program Director .... Dr. Janis DAVIS
88 Director of Physical Therapy .... Elizabeth PEYTON
106 Asst Director of Online Programs .... Jered MADRID
20 Dean of Instruction .... Tim POWERS
32 Dean of Students .... Susan DUNN
36 Director of Career Services .... Vacant
105 VP of Internet and Media Technology .... Monir BOKTOR
74 Asst Program Director ASVT .... Emma CUSACK
74 Asst Program Director ASVT .... Karen HARTMAN
06 Registrar .... Stephanie ISNALI
08 Librarian .... Kate ARAS
29 Alumni & Community Service Coord .... Nataly MCBRIDE

Stanford University (I)

450 Serra Mall, Stanford CA 94305-2004
County: Santa Clara FICE Identification: 001305
Unit ID: 243744
Telephone: (650) 723-2300 Carnegie Class: DU-Highest
FAX Number: (650) 725-6847 Calendar System: Quarter
URL: www.stanford.edu
Established: 1885 Annual Undergrad Tuition & Fees: $46,320
Enrollment: 16,963 Coed
Affiliation or Control: Independent Non-Profit IRS Status: 501(c)3
Highest Offering: Doctorate
Accreditation: WC, ARCPA, BUS, ENG, IPSY, LAW, MED, PDPSY

01 President .... Mr. Marc TESSIER-LAVIGNE
43 Vice President & General Counsel .... Ms. Debra L. ZUMWALT
05 Provost .... Dr. John W. ETCHEMENDY
30 Vice President for Development .... Mr. Martin SHELL
10 Vice President Business Affairs/CFO .... Mr. Randy LIVINGSTON
26 Vice President for Public Affairs .... Mr. David F. DEMAREST
29 President of Alumni Associaton .... Mr. Howard E. WOLF
46 Vice Provost/Dean of Research .... Dr. Ann ARVIN
20 Vice Provost for Academic Affairs .... Dr. Stephanie KALFAYAN
88 Vice Provost Faculty Development .... Ms. Karen COOK
20 Vice Provost Undergrad Education .... Mr. Harry J. ELAM
18 Vice Provost for Land & Buildings .... Mr. Robert C. REIDY
109 Vice Provost Budget & Auxiliaries .... Mr. Timothy R. WARNER
32 Vice Provost Student Affairs .... Mr. Gregory E. BOARDMAN
04 Sr Assistant to the President .... Mr. Jeffrey H. WACHTEL
63 Dean School of Medicine .... Dr. Lloyd MINOR
50 Dean Graduate School Business .... Dr. Garth SALONER
65 Dean School of Earth Sciences .... Dr. Pamela A. MATSON
53 Dean School of Education .... Dr. Deborah STIPEK
54 Dean School of Engineering .... Dr. Persis DRELL
49 Dean School Humanities & Sciences .... Mr. Richard P. SALLER
61 Dean School of Law .... Ms. M. Elizabeth MAGILL
87 Dean Summer Session/Cont Stds .... Dr. Charles L. JUNKERMAN
42 Dean for Religious Life .... Rev. Jane SHAW
88 Director Hoover Institution .... Dr. John RAISIAN
88 Director Stanford Lin Accelerator .... Mr. Chi-Chang KAO
13 Executive Director IT Services .... Mr. Bill CLEBSCH
08 University Librarian .... Mr. Michael A. KELLER
41 Athletic Director .... Mr. Bernard MUIR
07 Director of Admission .... Ms. Colleen LIM
88 CEO Stanford Management Company .... Mr. John POWERS
15 Director of Compensation .... Ms. Linda S. LEE
21 Director of Business Development .... Ms. Susan L. WEINSTEIN
06 Registrar .... Mr. Thomas BLACK
36 Director Career Development Center .... Mr. Farouk DEY
09 Dir Inst Research/Assessment .... Ms. Kathleen DETTMAN
37 Director of Student Financial Aid .... Ms. Karen S. COOPER
27 Director Stanford News Service .... Mr. Dan STOBER
19 Director Public Safety .... Ms. Laura L. WILSON
96 Chief Procurement Officer .... Mr. Ben MORENO
35 Director of Student Activities .... Ms. Nanci HOWE
38 Director Student Counseling .... Dr. Ronald ALBURCHER
101 Secretary of the Board of Trustees .... Mr. Phil TAUBMAN
102 Dir Foundation/Corporate Relations .... Ms. Kathy VEIT
104 Director Study Abroad .... Ms. Irene KENNEDY
105 Director Web Services .... Mr. Scott STOCKER
39 Director Student Housing .... Mr. Roger WHITNEY

Starr King School for the Ministry (J)

2441 Le Conte Avenue, Berkeley CA 94709-1299
County: Alameda FICE Identification: 004080
Unit ID: 123916
Telephone: (510) 845-6232 Carnegie Class: Spec-4-yr-Faith
FAX Number: (510) 845-6273 Calendar System: Semester
URL: www.sksm.edu
Established: 1904 Annual Graduate Tuition & Fees: N/A
Enrollment: 89 Coed
Affiliation or Control: Unitarian Universalist IRS Status: 501(c)3
Highest Offering: Master's; No Undergraduates
Accreditation: THEOL

01 President .... Rev. Rosemary Bray MCNATT
30 Vice President Advancement .... Ms. Jessica CLOUD
20 Dean of the Faculty .... Dr. Gabriella LETTINI
06 Registrar .... Ms. Katrina CROSWELL
07 Director of Admissions/Recruitment .... Mr. Jeremiah KALENDAE
10 VP for Finance & Admin .... Ms. Jane KOLMODIN
106 Director Online Education .... Dr. Hugo CORDOVA QUERO
26 Communications Officer .... Mr. Matt VIOLET

*State Center Community College District (A)

1525 E Weldon Avenue, Fresno CA 93704-6398

County: Fresno FICE Identification: 001306
Unit ID: 123925
Telephone: (559) 226-0720 Carnegie Class: N/A
FAX Number: (559) 499-6008
URL: www.scccd.edu

01 Chancellor .... Dr. Paul PARNELL
10 Vice Chancellor Finance & Admin .... Mr. Edwin ENG
05 Int VC Educ Svcs/Inst Effectiveness .... Dr. Barbara HIOCO
15 Int Vice Chanc Human Resources .... Annette LORIA
11 Assc Vice Chanc Business/Operations . Ms. Christine MIKTARIAN
07 AVC Enroll Mgmt/Admiss & Records/IS .... Mr. Pedro AVILA
16 Director Human Resources .... Ms. Samerah CAMPBELL
26 Exec Dir Pub/Legislative Rels .... Ms. Lucy RUIZ
102 Executive Director Foundation .... Mr. Rico GUERRERO
25 Int Dir Grants/External Funding .... Ms. Marilyn BEHRINGER
96 Director of Purchasing .... Mr. Randy VOGT
21 Director of Finance .... Mr. William SCHOFIELD
13 Director of Information Systems .... Mr. Scott OLDS
88 Director of Classified Personnel .... Ms. Elba GOMEZ
18 Director Maintenance/Operations .... Mr. Leroy BIBB
43 General Counsel .... Mr. Gregory TAYLOR
19 Int Chief of Police .... Chief Richard GAINES
32 Int Chief Student Affs/Student Life .... Mr. Rojelio VASQUEZ

*Clovis Community College (B)

10309 N. Willow Avenue, Fresno CA 93730

County: Fresno Identification: 667125
Telephone: (559) 325-5200 Carnegie Class: Not Classified
FAX Number: (559) 499-6065 Calendar System: Semester
URL: www.cloviscollege.edu
Established: 2007 Annual Undergrad Tuition & Fees (In-District): N/A
Enrollment: N/A Coed
Affiliation or Control: State/Local IRS Status: 501(c)3
Highest Offering: Associate Degree
Accreditation: WJ

02 President .... Dr. Lori BENNETT
05 VP Instruction & Student Services .... Ms. Kelly FOWLER
10 VP Administrative Services .... Ms. Lorrie HOPPER
79 Dean of Instruction .... Mr. Lee BROWN
75 Dean of Instruction CTE .... Dr. Linda THOMAS
32 Dean of Student Services .... Mr. Ryen HIRATA
13 Director of Technology .... Mr. Gary SAKAGUCHI
26 Director of Marketing .... Ms. Stephanie BABB
88 Dir Student Success/Equity/Outrch .... Ms. Gurdeep HEBERT
09 Director of Institutional Research .... Mr. James ATKINSON
12 Director of Herndon Campus .... Mr. Charles FRANCIS
41 Athletic Director .... Ms. Susan YATES
37 Financial Aid Manager .... Ms. Candy CANNON
07 Admissions & Records Manager .... Vacant
04 Secretary to the President .... Ms. Linda LITTLE

*Fresno City College (C)

1101 E University Avenue, Fresno CA 93741-0002

County: Fresno FICE Identification: 001307
Unit ID: 114789
Telephone: (559) 442-4600 Carnegie Class: Assoc/MT-VT-High Trad
FAX Number: (559) 499-6045 Calendar System: Semester
URL: www.fresnocitycollege.edu
Established: 1910 Annual Undergrad Tuition & Fees (In-District): $1,194
Enrollment: 22,307 Coed
Affiliation or Control: State/Local IRS Status: 501(c)3
Highest Offering: Associate Degree
Accreditation: WJ, CAHIIM, COARC, DH, EMT, RAD

02 President .... Dr. Carole GOLDSMITH
05 Int Vice President of Instruction .... Mr. Don LOPEZ
32 Int VP of Student Services .... Mr. Rojelio VASQUEZ
10 Vice Pres Administrative Services .... Ms. Cheryl SULLIVAN
07 District Dean Admissions & Records .... Ms. Mirna DUARTE
08 Dean Student Success/Learning .... Ms. Renee CRAIG-MARIUS
50 Int Dean Business Division .... Ms. Lydia ANDERSON
57 Dean Fine Perform Commun Arts .... Mr. Neil VANDERPOOL
79 Dean Humanities Division .... Dr. Jennifer JOHNSON
54 Dean Math/Science/Engineering Div .... Ms. Shirley MCMANUS
83 Dean Social Sciences Division .... Dr. Margaret E. MERICLE
76 Dean Health Sciences Division .... Ms. Lorraine SMITH
72 Dean Applied Technology Division .... Vacant
38 Dean Counseling-Guidance .... Ms. Monica CUEVAS
35 Int Dean of Student Services .... Mr. Sean HENDERSON
103 Dean Workforce Development & CTC .... Dr. Tim WOODS
75 Int Director FCC Training Institute .... Mr. Rob WEIL
22 Dir Disabled Student Pgms & Svcs .... Dr. Janice EMERZIAN
09 Director Institutional Research .... Dr. Lijuan ZHAI
88 Director Police Academy .... Mr. Gary FIEF
35 Int Director of Student Activities .... Mr. Ernie MARTINEZ

26 Director Marketing/Communications .... Ms. Cris M. BREMER
37 Director Financial Aid .... Ms. Kira TIPPINS
27 Public Information Officer .... Ms. Kathleen BONILLA
41 Athletic Director .... Mr. Eric SWAIN
38 Dir Distance Education/Inst Tech .... Ms. Jodie STEELEY
72 Interim Director of Technology .... Mr. Harry ZAHLIS
36 Dir College Relations & Outreach .... Ms. Emilee SLATER
66 Director of Nursing .... Ms. Stephanie R. ROBINSON
88 Acting Director CalWORKs Program .... Ms. Mary Beth MOSSETTE
06 Director Admissions & Records .... Ms. Robin TORRES
88 Director TRIO Programs .... Mr. Perry ANGLE
88 Director EOPS/CARE .... Mr. Thomas GAXIOLA

*Reedley College (D)

995 N Reed Avenue, Reedley CA 93654-2099

County: Fresno FICE Identification: 001308
Unit ID: 117052
Telephone: (559) 638-0300 Carnegie Class: Assoc/MT-VT-High Trad
FAX Number: N/A Calendar System: Semester
URL: www.reedleycollege.edu
Established: 1926 Annual Undergrad Tuition & Fees (In-District): $1,194
Enrollment: 14,633 Coed
Affiliation or Control: State/Local IRS Status: 501(c)3
Highest Offering: Associate Degree
Accreditation: WJ

02 President .... Dr. Sandra CALDWELL
05 Vice President of Instruction .... Mr. Jan DEKKER
11 Vice Pres Administrative Svcs .... Ms. Donna BERRY
32 Vice Pres of Student Services .... Dr. Claudia HABIB
12 Vice Pres Madera/Oakhurst Centers .... Dr. John FITZER
20 Dean of Instruction/Agri/Nat Res .... Mr. David CLARK
79 Dean of Instruction/Humanities .... Dr. G. Todd DAVIS
81 Dean Instruct/Math/Sci/Tech/PE/Hlth .... Ms. Marie BYRD-HARRIS
88 Dean Instruct/Madera/Oakhurst Ctrs .... Dr. Ganesan SRINIVASAN
35 Dean of Student Services .... Ms. Leticia CANALES
26 Public Information Officer .... Mr. George VILLAGRANA
22 Dir Disabled Student Programs/Svcs .... Dr. Janice EMERZIAN
22 Director EOPS .... Mr. Mario GONZALES
13 Director of Technology .... Mr. Gary SAKAGUCHI
37 Financial Aid Manager .... Ms. Chris CORTES
07 Admissions & Records Mgr/Registrar .... Ms. Veronica JURY
08 Librarian .... Ms. Shivon HESS

SUM Bible College and Theological Seminary (E)

735 105th Avenue, Oakland CA 94603-3603

County: Alameda FICE Identification: 037524
Unit ID: 447953
Telephone: (510) 567-6174 Carnegie Class: Spec-4-yr-Faith
FAX Number: (510) 568-1024 Calendar System: Trimester
URL: www.sum.edu
Established: 1999 Annual Undergrad Tuition & Fees: $10,144
Enrollment: 536 Coed
Affiliation or Control: Independent Non-Profit IRS Status: 501(c)3
Highest Offering: Master's
Accreditation: BI

01 President/Chancellor .... Rev. George NEAU
11 Vice President Operations .... Dr. Essie COOK
05 Chief Academic Officer .... Dr. Bruce COATS
10 Vice President Finance .... Mr. Robert HORNICK
26 Vice Pres Marketing/Enrollment .... Mr. Mike SAVAGE
42 Dean of Student Ministry .... Rev. Rondale TERRY
08 Director of the Library .... Ms. Catherine DIETERLY
32 Dean of Student Life .... Mr. Raymond HUDSON
20 Assistant Academic Dean .... Mr. Joey Alan LE
06 Registrar/Institutional Research .... Ms. Lauren WALDROFF
37 Financial Aid Director .... Mrs. Rose STADLER
07 Director of Admissions .... Ms. Rachel HUDSON
88 US Cohort Director .... Rev. Dave WALLACE
21 Business Administrator .... Mr. Don DIETERLY

† Affiliated with School of Urban Missions-New Orleans, Gretna, LA.

Taft College (F)

29 Cougar Court, Taft CA 93268-2329

County: Kern FICE Identification: 001309
Unit ID: 124113
Telephone: (661) 763-7700 Carnegie Class: Assoc/HT-High Non
FAX Number: (661) 763-7703 Calendar System: Semester
URL: www.taftcollege.edu
Established: 1922 Annual Undergrad Tuition & Fees (In-District): $1,134
Enrollment: 5,217 Coed
Affiliation or Control: State/Local IRS Status: 501(c)3
Highest Offering: Associate Degree
Accreditation: WJ, DH

01 Superintendent/President .... Dr. Debra DANIELS
10 Exec Vice Pres/Administrative Svcs .... Mr. Brock MCMURRAY
05 Vice President of Instruction .... Mr. Mark WILLIAMS
32 Vice Pres of Student Services .... Vacant
04 Assistant to the President .... Ms. Sarah CRISS
30 Director Foundation & Development .... Ms. Sheri HORN BUNK
13 Director Information Services .... Mr. Adrian AGUNDEZ
20 Dean of Instruction/Grants .... Ms. Agnes JOSE-EGUARAS
08 Research and Instruction Librarian .... Ms. Terri SMITH
46 Coord Inst Research/Assessment/Plng .... Dr. Eric BERUBE
41 Director Athletics .... Ms. Kance BANDY

15 Asst VP of Human Resources .... Dr. Robert METEAU
21 Director of Fiscal Services .... Mr. Jim NICHOLAS
07 Director of Admissions & Records .... Ms. Amber ANDERSON
18 Supervisor Maintenance/Operations .... Mr. Michael CAPELA
37 Director Student Financial Aid .... Ms. Barbara AMERIO
88 Dean of Student Success .... Ms. Primavera ARVIZU

Taft Law School (G)

3700 South Susan Street, Office 200,
Santa Ana CA 92704-6954

County: Orange Identification: 666398
Telephone: (714) 850-4800 Carnegie Class: Not Classified
FAX Number: (714) 708-2082 Calendar System: Other
URL: www.taftu.edu
Established: 1976 Annual Undergrad Tuition & Fees: N/A
Enrollment: N/A Coed
Affiliation or Control: Proprietary IRS Status: Proprietary
Highest Offering: Doctorate
Accreditation: DEAC

01 Chancellor .... Mr. David L. BOYD
05 Dean .... Mr. Robert K. STROUSE
86 VP of Governmental Relations .... Ms. Joan L. SLAVIN
20 Associate Dean .... Ms. Melody JOLLY
37 Director of Financial Aid .... Ms. Tina M. SAXON

Teachers College of San Joaquin (H)

2857 Transworld Dr, Stockton CA 95206

County: San Joaquin Identification: 667087
Telephone: (209) 468-4926 Carnegie Class: Not Classified
FAX Number: (209) 468-9124 Calendar System: Semester
URL: teacherscollegesj.edu
Established: 2009 Annual Graduate Tuition & Fees: N/A
Enrollment: N/A Coed
Affiliation or Control: State IRS Status: 501(c)3
Highest Offering: Master's; No Undergraduates
Accreditation: WC

01 President .... Dr. Diane CARNAHAN
06 Registrar/Admissions .... Ms. Lisa NEUGEBAUER
58 Director Graduate Studies .... Dr. Sylvia TURNER
04 Administrative Asst to President .... Ms. Victoria L. DE PRATER
10 Chief Business Officer .... Mr. Jim THOMAS
07 Director of Admissions .... Ms. Michele BADOVINAC
09 Director of Institutional Research .... Dr. Sylvia TURNER

Theatre of Arts (I)

1536 N Highland Avenue, Hollywood CA 90028

County: Los Angeles Identification: 667098
Telephone: (323) 463-2500 Carnegie Class: Not Classified
FAX Number: (323) 463-2500 Calendar System: Trimester
URL: www.toa.edu
Established: 1927 Annual Undergrad Tuition & Fees: N/A
Enrollment: N/A Coed
Affiliation or Control: Proprietary IRS Status: Proprietary
Highest Offering: Associate Degree
Accreditation: THEA

00 President .... Amir KORANGY
01 Executive Director .... Jason WEISS
84 Manager Enrollment Services .... Michael JURY
11 Chief of Administration .... Elizabeth INIGUEZ

Thomas Aquinas College (J)

10,000 Ojai Road, Santa Paula CA 93060-9621

County: Ventura FICE Identification: 023580
Unit ID: 124292
Telephone: (805) 525-4417 Carnegie Class: Bac-A&S
FAX Number: (805) 525-9342 Calendar System: Semester
URL: www.thomasaquinas.edu
Established: 1971 Annual Undergrad Tuition & Fees: $24,500
Enrollment: 378 Coed
Affiliation or Control: Independent Non-Profit IRS Status: 501(c)3
Highest Offering: Baccalaureate
Accreditation: WC

01 President .... Dr. Michael F. MCLEAN
04 Secretary to the President .... Miss Sarah J. KAISER
26 Asst to Pres/Dir College Relations .... Mrs. Anne S. FORSYTH
30 Vice President for Development .... Dr. Paul J. O'REILLY
43 General Counsel .... Mr. John Q. MASTELLER
10 Vice President for Admn & Finance .... Mr. Peter L. DELUCA
05 Academic Dean .... Dr. Brian KELLY
30 Director of Development .... Mr. Robert A. BAGDAZIAN
44 Director of Gift Planning .... Mr. Thomas J. SUSANKA
44 Director of the Annual Fund .... Mr. Paul LAZENBY
07 Director of Admissions .... Mr. Jonathan P. DALY
21 Supervisor Business/Finance .... Mr. Michael COLLINS
37 Director of Financial Aid .... Mr. Gregory J. BECHER
32 Asst Dean for Student Affairs .... Dr. Christopher DECAEN
06 Registrar/Dir of Student Placement .... Mr. Mark KRETSCHMER
08 Librarian .... Ms. Richena CURPHEY
42 Chaplain .... Fr. Paul RAFTERY, OP
27 Communications Manager .... Mr. Christopher WEINKOPF
13 Development Database Manager .... Mr. Aaron DUNKEL
102 Dir Foundation/Corporate Relations .... Mrs. Sharon REISER

Thomas Jefferson School of Law (A)

1155 Island Avenue, San Diego CA 92101

County: San Diego FICE Identification: 010854
Unit ID: 126049
Telephone: (619) 297-9700 Carnegie Class: Spec-4-yr-Law
FAX Number: (619) 961-4370 Calendar System: Semester
URL: www.tjsl.edu
Established: 1969 Annual Graduate Tuition & Fees: N/A
Enrollment: 849 Coed
Affiliation or Control: Independent Non-Profit IRS Status: 501(c)3
Highest Offering: Doctorate; No Undergraduates
Accreditation: @WC, LAW

01 President and Dean ... Dean Thomas F. GUERNSEY
05 Vice Dean & Assoc Dean Acad Affairs ... Dean Linda KELLER
43 Vice President and General Counsel ... Karin K. SHERR
04 Exec Asst to the President/Dean ... Jan DAUSS
10 VP and Chief Financial Officer ... Nancy VU
30 VP for Institutional Advancement ... Beth SAVAGE
29 Director of Dev & Alumni Relations ... Vacant
26 Dir of Marketing and Communications ... Edgar HOPIDA
32 Assistant Dean for Student Affairs ... Lisa FERREIRA
88 Asst Dean for Prog Devel & Dist Ed ... Jason FISKE
84 Asst Dean of Enrollment Mgmnt ... Michelle SLAUGHTER ALLISON
88 Asst Dir Recruitment and Outreach ... Leah STRALEY
08 Library Director ... Leigh INMAN
36 Director of Career Services ... Jeffrey CHINN
20 Director of Academic Administration ... Kayla MARTINEZ
37 Director of Financial Assistance ... Marc BERMAN
06 Registrar ... Carrie KAZYAKA
21 Financial Operations Specialist ... Anh PHAN
88 Externship Director/Pro Bono ... Judybeth TROPP
15 Director of Human Resources ... Lisa CHIGOS
13 Director of IT ... Gil SUSANA
18 Director of Facilities ... Dennis SABLE

Touro College Los Angeles (B)

1317 N Crescent Heights Blvd,
West Hollywood CA 90046-4506

County: Los Angeles Identification: 770944
Unit ID: 459727
Telephone: (323) 822-9700 Carnegie Class: Not Classified
FAX Number: (310) 654-2086 Calendar System: Semester
URL: www.touro.edu/losangeles/
Established: 2005 Annual Undergrad Tuition & Fees: N/A
Enrollment: 541 Coed
Affiliation or Control: Independent Non-Profit IRS Status: 501(c)3
Highest Offering: Baccalaureate
Accreditation: WC

01 CEO ... Dr. Yoram NEUMANN
03 Provost ... Dr. Edith NEUMANN
05 Dean ... Dr. Michael D. HAMLIN
07 Director of Admissions ... Ms. Leah MIZRAHI
09 Dir Inst Research/Assessment ... Dr. Aaron BROWNSTEIN
10 Chief Business Officer/Bursar ... Mr. Kamran MANUEL
06 Registrar & Fin Aid Coordinator ... Ms. Rivka WEINBERG

† Branch campus of Touro University Worldwide, Los Alamitos, CA.

Touro University California (C)

1310 Club Drive, Vallejo CA 94592

County: Solano FICE Identification: 041426
Unit ID: 459736
Telephone: (707) 638-5200 Carnegie Class: Spec-4-yr-Med
FAX Number: (707) 638-5255 Calendar System: Trimester
URL: www.tu.edu
Established: 1997 Annual Undergrad Tuition & Fees: N/A
Enrollment: 1,378 Coed
Affiliation or Control: Independent Non-Profit IRS Status: 501(c)3
Highest Offering: Doctorate
Accreditation: WC, ARCPA, OSTEO, PH, PHAR

01 President & CEO Univ System ... Dr. Alan KADISH
03 Sr Provost/CEO Touro Western Div ... Hon. Shelley BERKLEY
05 Provost & COO ... Dr. Marilyn HOPKINS
32 Dean of Students ... Dr. Lisa WAITS
35 Associate Dean of Students ... Dr. James BINKERD
07 Director of Admissions ... Mr. Steven DAVIS
09 Dir of Institutional Effectiveness ... Dr. Meiling TANG
10 Dir of Fiscal Affairs & Accounting ... Ms. Jonalee ADRIANO
15 Director Human Resources ... Ms. Kathy LOWE
11 Associate VP of Administration ... Mr. Jay RITCHIE
08 Director University Library ... Ms. Tamara TRUJILLO
63 Dean College of Osteopathic Med ... Dr. Michael CLEARFIELD
67 Dean College of Pharmacy ... Dr. Rae MATSUMOTO
53 Dean Col of Education & Health Sci ... Dr. Jim O'CONNOR
13 Director of Information Technology ... Ms. Julia WELCH
26 Director University Communication ... Ms. Andrea GARCIA
37 Director of Student Financial Aid ... Ms. Lynne MOSELEY
35 Director of Student Activities ... Rabbi Elchonon TENENBAUM
23 Director of Student Health Center ... Ms. Laura SCHWARTZ

Touro University Worldwide (D)

10601 Calle Lee Ste 179, Los Alamitos CA 90720

County: Orange FICE Identification: 041425
Unit ID: 459727
Telephone: (818) 575-6800 Carnegie Class: Masters/S
FAX Number: (818) 707-0316 Calendar System: Semester
URL: www.tuw.edu
Established: 2005 Annual Undergrad Tuition & Fees: $14,600
Enrollment: N/A Coed
Affiliation or Control: Independent Non-Profit IRS Status: 501(c)3
Highest Offering: Doctorate
Accreditation: WC

01 CEO ... Dr. Yoram NEUMANN
05 Provost & Chief Academic Officer ... Dr. Edith NEUMANN
10 CFO ... Mr. Jayson CAPUNO

Trident University International (E)

5757 Plaza Drive, Suite 100, Cypress CA 90630

County: Orange FICE Identification: 041279
Unit ID: 450979
Telephone: (714) 816-0366 Carnegie Class: DU-Mod
FAX Number: (714) 816-0367 Calendar System: Semester
URL: www.trident.edu
Established: 1998 Annual Undergrad Tuition & Fees: $9,000
Enrollment: 6,197 Coed
Affiliation or Control: Proprietary IRS Status: Proprietary
Highest Offering: Doctorate
Accreditation: WC

01 President/CEO ... Mr. Travis J. ALLEN
10 Chief Financial Officer ... Mr. David BARRETT
05 Interim Provost ... Dr. Afshin AFROOKHTEH
13 Exec Vice President/CIO ... Mr. Vahid SHARIAT
86 SVP/Chief Compliance Officer ... Dr. Afshin AFROOKHTEH
20 Dean of University Studies and Ext ... Dr. Scott AMUNDSEN
50 Dean GJ Col Business/Info Systems ... Dr. Simcha POLLARD
04 Executive Assistant ... Ms. Patricia PARKS
15 Director Human Resources ... Ms. Melissa ROTHMEYER
06 Registrar ... Mr. Mark MCKELLIP
37 Student Finance Manager ... Ms. Brittney DRAKE
09 Director of Institutional Research ... Dr. Heidi SATO
08 Librarian ... Ms. Leslie ANDERSEN
21 Director of Financial Operation ... Mr. Scott PAK
76 Dean Educ/Health Sciences ... Dr. Mickey SHACHAR
07 Vice President of Admissions ... Ms. Elizabeth HARRIS
18 Facilities Manager ... Mr. Fred WILSON
101 Board of Trustees Secretary ... Mr. Brian VAN KLOMPENBERG
108 Interim Assessment Director ... Dr. Belarmina RICHARDS

Trinity Law School (F)

2200 N Grand Avenue, Santa Ana CA 92705

Telephone: (714) 836-7500 Identification: 770098
Accreditation: &NH

† Regional accreditation is carried under the parent institution in Deerfield, IL

Union University of California (G)

14200 Goldenwest Street, Westminster CA 92683

County: Orange Identification: 667269
Telephone: (714) 903-2762 Carnegie Class: Not Classified
FAX Number: N/A Calendar System: Semester
URL: www.uuc.edu
Established: 1986 Annual Graduate Tuition & Fees: N/A
Enrollment: N/A Coed
Affiliation or Control: Independent Non-Profit IRS Status: 501(c)3
Highest Offering: Master's; No Undergraduates
Accreditation: DEAC

01 President ... Dr. Delmar SEWALL

United Education Institute (H)

6055 Pacific Boulevard, Huntington Park CA 90255

County: Los Angeles FICE Identification: 025593
Unit ID: 124681
Telephone: (323) 319-9500 Carnegie Class: Spec 2-yr-Other
FAX Number: (949) 788-2505 Calendar System: Other
URL: www.uei.edu
Established: 1986 Annual Undergrad Tuition & Fees: N/A
Enrollment: 3,564 Coed
Affiliation or Control: Proprietary IRS Status: Proprietary
Highest Offering: Associate Degree
Accreditation: CNCE

01 Executive Area President ... Mr. J.C RIVAS

United States University (I)

7675 Mission Valley Road, San Diego CA 92108

County: San Diego FICE Identification: 040053
Unit ID: 447050
Telephone: (629) 876-4250 Carnegie Class: Bac-Diverse
FAX Number: N/A Calendar System: Semester
URL: www.usuniversity.edu
Established: 1997 Annual Undergrad Tuition & Fees: $9,440
Enrollment: 451 Coed
Affiliation or Control: Proprietary IRS Status: Proprietary
Highest Offering: Master's
Accreditation: WC, NURSE

01 President and CEO ... Dr. Steven A. STARGARDTER
05 Provost/Chief Academic Officer ... Vacant
07 VP of Enroll Mgmt/Stdnt Svcs/Mktg ... Marianne B. FINGADO
10 Chief Financial Officer ... Will TITERA
88 Director of International Affairs ... Vacant
106 Associate Provost Online Learning ... Dr. Elizabeth ARCHER
09 Asst Provost Research & Assessment ... Nga PHAN
53 Dean College of Education ... Dr. Roberta MASO-FLEISHMAN
49 Dean College of Arts & Sciences ... Dr. Rosalinda MILLA
50 Dean College of Business ... Vacant
66 Dean College of Nursing ... Dr. Renee MCLEOD
06 Registrar ... Jennifer STROBEL
29 Director Alumni Relations ... Joe LEDESMA
37 Director Student Financial Aid ... Natalie ROBINSON

Unitek College (J)

4670 Auto Mall Parkway, Fremont CA 94538

County: Alameda FICE Identification: 041697
Unit ID: 459204
Telephone: (888) 775-1514 Carnegie Class: Spec-4-yr-Other Health
FAX Number: (510) 249-9125 Calendar System: Other
URL: www.unitekcollege.edu
Established: 1992 Annual Undergrad Tuition & Fees: $24,265
Enrollment: 1,017 Coed
Affiliation or Control: Proprietary IRS Status: Proprietary
Highest Offering: Baccalaureate
Accreditation: ACCSC, NURSE

01 School President ... Mr. Navraj BAWA

University of Antelope Valley (K)

44055 Sierra Hwy, Lancaster CA 93534

County: Los Angeles FICE Identification: 034275
Unit ID: 442930
Telephone: (661) 726-1911 Carnegie Class: Bac/Assoc-Mixed
FAX Number: (661) 726-5158 Calendar System: Other
URL: www.uav.edu
Established: Annual Undergrad Tuition & Fees: N/A
Enrollment: 772 Coed
Affiliation or Control: Proprietary IRS Status: Proprietary
Highest Offering: Master's
Accreditation: WC, ACICS, EMT

01 President ... Mr. Marco JOHNSON
03 Vice President/CEO ... Ms. Sandra JOHNSON
05 Assoc Dean of Academic Affairs ... Ms. Chonnea HARRIS
10 Chief Financial Officer ... Ms. Sandy SARGE
32 Dean of Student Affairs ... Mr. Ronald FELTS
37 Financial Aid Director ... Ms. Araceli JIMENEZ
09 Dir Institutional Effectiveness ... Ms. Crystal STEPHENS
13 Director Information Technology ... Mr. Noel SANCHEZ
36 Director Career Services ... Ms. Karyn FRAHM
107 Director of Admissions ... Ms. Mirna TURCIOS

*University of California Office of the President (L)

1111 Franklin Street, Oakland CA 94607-5200

County: Alameda FICE Identification: 001311
Unit ID: 124557
Telephone: (510) 987-0700 Carnegie Class: N/A
FAX Number: (510) 987-0328
URL: www.ucop.edu

01 President ... Janet NAPOLITANO
05 Provost/EVP Academic Affairs ... Aimee DORR
10 EVP/Chief Financial Officer ... Nathan E. BROSTROM
11 EVP/Chief Operating Officer ... Rachael NAVA
17 Exec Vice Pres UC Health ... John D. STOBO
26 Sr Vice Pres External Relations ... Julie HENDERSON
86 SVP Government Relations ... Nelson PEACOCK
108 Sr Vice Pres Compliance/Audit ... Sheryl S. VACCA
47 VP Agriculture/Natural Resources ... Barbara H. ALLEN-DIAZ
45 VP Budget & Capital Resources ... Patrick J. LENZ
44 Vice President of Investments ... Jagdeep S. BACHHER
09 Vice Pres Inst Rsrch/Acad Planning ... Pamela BROWN
88 VP Office of National Laboratories ... Kimberly S. BUDIL
15 Vice Pres Human Resources ... Dwaine B. DUCKETT
43 General Counsel/VP Legal Affairs ... Charles F. ROBINSON
32 Vice President Student Affairs ... Judy K. SAKAKI
46 Interim VP Innovation Alliance Svcs ... William TUCKER
13 CIO Information Technology Svcs ... Tom ANDRIOLA
20 Vice Provost Education Partnerships ... Yvette GULLATT
20 Vice Provost Academic Personnel ... Susan CARLSON
21 Assoc VP Budget Analysis & Planning ... Debora OBLEY

*University of California-Berkeley (M)

Berkeley CA 94720-0001

County: Alameda FICE Identification: 001312
Unit ID: 110635
Telephone: (510) 642-6000 Carnegie Class: DU-Highest
FAX Number: (510) 643-5499 Calendar System: Semester
URL: www.berkeley.edu
Established: 1868 Annual Undergrad Tuition & Fees (In-State): $13,431
Enrollment: 37,565 Coed
Affiliation or Control: State IRS Status: 501(c)3
Highest Offering: Doctorate
Accreditation: WC, BUS, CLPSY, CS, DIETD, ENG, IPSY, JOUR, LAW, LSAR, OPT, OPTR, PCSAS, PH, PLNG, SCPSY, SW

Code	Title	Name
02	Chancellor	Nicholas B. DIRKS
05	Int Exec Vice Chancellor/Provost	Carol CHRIST
11	Interim Vice Chanc Admin & Finance	Scott BIDDY
32	Vice Chancellor Student Affairs	Harry LE GRANDE
26	Vice Chanc University Relations	Scott BIDDY
18	Vice Chancellor Real Estate	Bob LALANNE
22	Vice Chanc Equity & Inclusion	Na'ilah NASIR
100	Assoc Chancellor/Chief of Staff	Phyllis HOFFMAN
25	Asst VC Research Admin & Compliance	Patrick SCHLESINGER
13	Asst Vice Chanc Info Technology	Lyle NEVELS
10	Assoc Vice Chancellor/CFO	Rosemarie RAE
84	Assc Vice Chanc Admiss & Enrollment	Anne DE LUCA
43	Chief Campus Counsel	Christopher M. PATTI
27	Assoc Vice Chanc Public Affairs	Claire HOLMES
21	Asst Vice Chanc Finance/Controller	Delphine REGALIA
07	Asst VC & Dir Undergrad Admissions	Amy JARICH
35	Assc Vice Chanc/Dean of Students	Joseph D. GREENWELL
37	Asst VC & Dir Fin Aid & Scholarship	Rachelle FELDMAN
08	University Librarian	Thomas C. LEONARD
06	Associate Registrar	Johanna METZGAR
38	Dir Counseling & Psychological Svcs	Jeff PRINCE
36	Director Career Center	Thomas C. DEVLIN
87	Dean Sum Sess/Study Abr/Life Lrng	Richard RUSSO
41	Int Director of Athletics	Michael WILLIAMS
58	Dean of the Graduate Division	Fiona M. DOYLE
61	Interim Dean of Law	Melissa MURRAY
88	Dean of Optometry	John FLANAGAN
54	Dean School of Engineering	S. Shankar SASTRY
88	Dean of Environmental Design	Jennifer WOLCH
65	Dean of Natural Resources	J. Keith GILLESS
50	Dean of Haas School of Business	Richard K. LYONS
70	Dean of Social Welfare	Jeffrey EDELSON
88	Dean School of Information	AnnaLee SAXENIAN
69	Dean of Public Health	Stefano BERTOZZI
53	Dean of Education	Prudence CARTER
60	Dean of Journalism	Ed WASSERMAN
88	Dean of Chemistry	Douglas S. CLARK
80	Dean Graduate School/Public Policy	Henry E. BRADY
79	Dean of Arts and Humanities	Anthony CASCARDI
88	Int Dean of Biological Sciences	Michael R. BOTCHAN
81	Dean Mathematical/Physical Sciences	Frances HELLMAN
83	Dean of Social Sciences	Carla HESSE
97	Dean of the Undergrad Division	Bob JACOBSON
56	Dean of University Extension	Diana WU

*University of California-Davis (A)

One Shields Avenue, Davis CA 95616-5270

County: Yolo FICE Identification: 001313
Unit ID: 110644
Telephone: (530) 752-1011 Carnegie Class: DU-Highest
FAX Number: N/A Calendar System: Quarter
URL: www.ucdavis.edu
Established: 1905 Annual Undergrad Tuition & Fees (In-State): $13,951
Enrollment: 34,508 Coed
Affiliation or Control: State IRS Status: 501(c)3
Highest Offering: Doctorate
Accreditation: WC, ARCPA, BUS, CS, DIETD, DIETI, ENG, IPSY, LAW, LSAR, MED, MT, NURSE, PAST, PH, VET

Code	Title	Name
02	Interim Chancellor	Dr. Ralph J. HEXTER
05	Int Provost & Exec Vice Chancellor	Dr. Ken BURTIS
100	Associate Chancellor	Mr. Karl M. ENGELBACH
26	Int Strategic Communication Leader	Ms. Dana TOPOUSIS
46	Interim Vice Chancellor Research	Dr. Cameron S. CARTER
30	Vice Chanc Dev/Alumni Relations	Dr. Shaun B. KEISTER
32	Vice Chancellor Student Affairs	Dr. Adela I. DE LATORRE
10	Int Lead Finance/Operation & Admin	Ms. Kelly RATLIFF
63	VC Human Health Sci/Dean Sch of Med	Dr. Julie FREISCHLAG
17	CEO UCD Medical Center	Ms. Ann M. RICE
66	Assoc VC/Dean Sch of Nursing	Dr. Heather M. YOUNG
22	Assoc Exec VC Campus Cmty Relations	Mr. Rahim REED
21	Sr Assoc VC Finance & Resource	Ms. Kelly RATLIFF
88	Exec Assoc VC Research	Dr. Cindy M. KIEL
88	Assoc VC Research	Dr. Paul DODD
88	Assoc VC Research	Dr. Dushyant PATHAK
15	Acting Chief Human Resources	Ms. Brenda REBMAN
88	Assoc VC Accounting/Financial Svcs	Mr. J. Michael ALLRED
88	Assoc VC Development	Mr. Jason L. WOHLMAN
88	Assoc VC Development	Mr. Paul PROKOP
88	Assoc VC Development Health Sci	Ms. Chong U. PORTER
39	Assoc VC Student Affairs	Ms. Emily GALINDO
84	Assoc VC Student Affairs	Mr. John CAMPBELL
35	Assoc VC Student Affairs	Dr. Milton LANG
07	Assoc VC Admissions & Enrollment	Mr. Walter A. ROBINSON
88	Assoc VC Safety Services	Ms. Jill PARKER
88	Assoc VC Design & Construct	Mr. Clayton HALLIDAY
86	Asst Chanc Govt & Comm Relations	Ms. Marjorie M. DICKINSON
88	Asst Exec VC Chanc/Provost Ofc	Mr. Karl MOHR
45	Asst VC Campus Planning	Mr. Robert B. SEGAR
88	Acting Asst VC Environ Stewardship	Mr. Robert B. SEGAR
18	Asst VC Facilities Management	Mr. Allen TOLLEFSON
88	Asst VC Capital Plng & Real Estate	Mr. Grant ROCKWELL
44	Asst VC Planned Giving	Mr. Brian CASEY
102	Asst VC Foundation & Corp Giving	Ms. Shelley MADDEX
88	Asst VC Student Affairs	Ms. Emily PRIETO-TSEREGOUNIS
29	AVC/Exec Director Alumni Relations	Mr. Richard R. ENGEL
13	CIO & VP Info/Educ Tech	Ms. Viji MURALI
88	VP & Dean Undergraduate Educ	Dr. Carolyn THOMAS
58	VP Grad Education/Dean Grad Studies	Dr. Prasant MOHAPATRA
20	Vice Provost Academic Affairs	Dr. Maureen L. STANTON
104	VP & Assoc Chanc Global Affairs	Dr. Joanna REGULSKA
88	Assoc Vice Provost Global Affairs	Dr. Ermias KEBREAB
88	Assoc Vice Provost Global Affairs	Dr. Fadi FATHALLAH
47	Dean Agricultural/Environ Sci	Dr. Helene DILLARD
88	Dean Biological Sciences	Dr. Mark WINEY
54	Dean Engineering	Dr. Jennifer SINCLAIR CURTIS
83	Int Dean Social Sciences	Dr. Li ZHANG
81	Int Dean Math & Physical Sciences	Dr. Alexandra NAVROTSKY
79	Int Dean Humanities/Arts & Culture	Dr. Susan B. KAISER
61	Dean School of Law	Dr. Kevin R. JOHNSON
50	Dean Grad School of Management	Dr. H. Rao UNNAVA
74	Dean Veterinary Medicine	Dr. Michael D. LAIRMORE
53	Interim Dean School of Education	Dr. Paul D. HASTINGS
56	Dean University Extension	Dr. Paul M. MCNEIL
88	Exec Director Mondavi Center	Dr. Don F. ROTH
23	Director Student Health Services	Dr. Thomas FERGUSON
37	Director Financial Aid	Ms. Deborah G. AGEE
38	Director Student Health Counseling	Dr. Sarah HAHN
36	Director Internship & Career Center	Ms. Marcie KIRK-HOLLAND
40	Director UC Davis Stores	Mr. Jason LORGAN
41	Dir Intercollegiate Athletics	Mr. Kevin BLUE
88	Director Internal Audit Services	Mr. Jeremiah J. MAHER
88	Director World Food Center	Dr. Jan HOPMANS
19	Interim Chief of Police	Chief Jennifer GARCIA
43	Chief Campus Counsel	Mr. Jacob A. APPELSMITH
06	Registrar	Dr. Elias S. LOPEZ
08	University Librarian	Ms. MacKenzie SMITH

*University of California-Hastings College of the Law (B)

200 McAllister Street, San Francisco CA 94102-4978

County: San Francisco FICE Identification: 003947
Unit ID: 110398
Telephone: (415) 565-4600 Carnegie Class: Spec-4-yr-Law
FAX Number: (415) 565-4865 Calendar System: Semester
URL: www.uchastings.edu
Established: 1878 Annual Graduate Tuition & Fees: N/A
Enrollment: 1,003 Coed
Affiliation or Control: State IRS Status: 501(c)3
Highest Offering: First Professional Degree; No Undergraduates
Accreditation: WC, LAW

Code	Title	Name
02	Chancellor and Dean	Mr. David L. FAIGMAN
05	Provost & Academic Dean	Ms. Elizabeth L. HILLMAN
43	General Counsel	Ms. Elise TRAYNUM
10	Chief Financial Officer	Mr. David SEWARD
20	Associate Academic Dean	Ms. Heather M. FIELD
19	Acting Chief Public Safety	Mr. Scott HALLAHAN
06	Registrar	Ms. Gina BARNETT
07	Director of Admissions	Mr. Bryan ZERBE
32	Director Student Services	Ms. Rupa BHANDARI
13	Chief Information Officer	Mr. Jake HORNSBY
36	Asst Dean Career & Profess Devel	Ms. Sari ZIMMERMAN
26	Dir Communications/Public Affairs	Mr. Alex A G. SHAPIRO
22	Director LEOP	Ms. Jan JEMISON
23	Student Health Manager/Admin Nurse	Ms. Laurie BROOKNER
21	Controller	Ms. Deborah TRAN
37	Director Financial Aid	Mr. Victor HO
18	Property Manager	Ms. Pansy MAR
96	Director of Purchasing	Mr. Darryl SWEET
30	Chief Development Officer	Mr. Eric DUMBLETON
108	Director of Accreditation & Assess	Ms. Andrea BING
84	Sr Assistant Dean of Enrollment Mgm	Ms. June SAKAMOTO

*University of California-Irvine (C)

Campus Drive, Irvine CA 92697-0001

County: Orange FICE Identification: 001314
Unit ID: 110653
Telephone: (949) 824-5011 Carnegie Class: DU-Highest
FAX Number: N/A Calendar System: Quarter
URL: www.uci.edu
Established: 1965 Annual Undergrad Tuition & Fees (In-State): $13,252
Enrollment: 30,051 Coed
Affiliation or Control: State IRS Status: 501(c)3
Highest Offering: Doctorate
Accreditation: WC, BUS, CEA, CS, ENG, IPSY, LAW, MED, MT, NURSE, PH, PLNG

Code	Title	Name
02	Chancellor	Howard A. GILLMAN
05	Provost & Exec Vice Chancellor	Enrique J. LAVERNIA
10	Vice Chanc Admin/Business Services	Wendell C. BRASE
46	Vice Chancellor for Research	Pramod KHARGONEKAR
32	Vice Chanc Student Affairs	Thomas A. PARHAM
30	Interim Vice Chanc Univ Advancement	Brian T. HERVEY
45	Vice Chanc Planning & Budget	Meredith MICHAELS
20	Vice Provost for Academic Planning	Judith STEPAN-NORRIS
15	Vice Provost for Academic Personnel	Diane K. O'DOWD
88	Vice Provost for AED&Inclusion	Douglas M. HAYNES
100	Associate Chancellor/Chief of Staff	Michael R. ARIAS
20	Associate Exec Vice Chancellor	Jeff LEFKOFF
22	Assoc Chancellor ED & Inclusion	Kirsten K. QUANBECK
15	Assoc Chancellor & Chief HR Exec	Ramona AGRELA
29	Asst Vice Chanc Alumni Relations	Barney ELLIS-PERRY
35	Assoc Vice Chancellor Stdnt Affairs	Daniel J. DOOROS
35	Asst Vice Chanc/Dean of Students	Rameen A. TALESH
84	Asst Vice Chanc Enrollment Services	Brent W. YUNEK
06	University Registrar	Elizabeth C. BENNETT
43	Chief Campus Counsel	Diane F. GEOCARIS
51	Dean Continuing Educ/Summer Session	Gary W. MATKIN
08	University Librarian	Lorelei A. TANJI
36	Director Career Center	Suzanne C. HELBIG
37	Director Financial Aid	Rebecca SANCHEZ
41	Director Intercollegiate Athletics	Michael A. IZZI
09	Asst Vice Chanc Inst Research	Ryan M. CHERLAND
20	Dean Undergrad Education & VP	Michael DENNIN
58	Dean Graduate Division & VP	Frances M. LESLIE
23	Vice Chancellor of Health Affairs	Howard FEDEROFF
49	Dean Arts	Stephen BARKER
50	Dean Paul Merage School of Business	Eric SPANGENBERG
53	Dean School of Education	Richard ARUM
81	Dean Biological Sciences	Frank LAFERLA
54	Dean School of Engineering	Gregory WASHINGTON
79	Dean Humanities	Georges VAN DEN ABBEELE
77	Dean Bren Sch of Info & Comp Sci	Hal S. STERN
61	Dean of Law School	Erwin CHEMERINSKY
63	Interim Dean School of Medicine	Michael STAMOS
81	Dean Physical Sciences	Kenneth C. JANDA
83	Dean Social Ecology	Nancy GUERRA
83	Dean School of Social Sciences	William M. MAURER
88	Chair Academic Senate	Alan TERRICCIANO
21	Assoc Vice Chanc Admin/Business Svc	Richard COULON
13	CIO and Assoc Vice Chancellor IT	Dana F. ROODE
26	Assoc Chanc Communications	Ria M. CARLSON
07	Director of Admissions	Patricia MORALES

*University of California-Los Angeles (D)

405 Hilgard Avenue, Los Angeles CA 90095-1405

County: Los Angeles FICE Identification: 001315
Unit ID: 110662
Telephone: (310) 825-4321 Carnegie Class: DU-Highest
FAX Number: N/A Calendar System: Quarter
URL: www.ucla.edu
Established: 1919 Annual Undergrad Tuition & Fees (In-State): $12,763
Enrollment: 41,845 Coed
Affiliation or Control: State IRS Status: 501(c)3
Highest Offering: Doctorate
Accreditation: WC, BJS, CLPSY, CS, CYTO, DENT, DIETI, EMT, ENG, ENGR, HSA, IPSY, LAW, LIB, MED, NURSE, PAST, PCSAS, PH, PLNG, RAD, SW, THEA

Code	Title	Name
02	Chancellor	Gene D. BLOCK
05	Exec Vice Chancellor and Provost	Scott WAUGH
11	Administrative Vice Chancellor	Michael J. BECK
10	Vice Chancellor/CFO	Steven A. OLSEN
15	Vice Chancellor Academic Personnel	Carole E. GOLDBERG
28	VChanc Equity Diversity & Inclusion	Jerry KANG
26	Vice Chancellor External Affairs	Rhea TURTELTAUB
23	Vice Chancellor Health Sciences	John MAZZIOTTA
43	Interim Vice Chanc Legal Affairs	Amy BLUM
46	Interim Vice Chanc Research	Ann R. KARAGOZIAN
32	Vice Chancellor Student Affairs	Janina MONTERO
58	Vice Provost & Dean Graduate Educ	Robin L. GARRELL
88	Vice Provost & Dean Undergrad Educ	Patricia A. TURNER
13	Vice Provost Information Technology	James DAVIS
82	V Provost Intl Stdnt/Global Engmt	C. Cindy FAN
88	V Provost New Collaborative Initiat	Kathryn Ann ATCHISON
17	President UCLA Health	Johnese Maria SPISSO
79	Dean Division of Humanities	David SCHABERG
81	Dean Division of Life Sciences	Victoria SORK
81	Dean Division of Physical Sciences	Joseph RUDNICK
83	Dean Division of Social Sciences	Alessandro DURANTI
52	Dean School of Dentistry	No Hee PARK
48	Interim Dean Sch of the Arts & Arch	David ROUSSÈVE
53	Dean Grad Sch Educ & Info Studies	Marcelo M. SUAREZ-OROZCO
54	Dean Sch of Eng & App Sci	Jayathi Y. MURTHY
61	Dean School of Law	Jennifer L. MNOOKIN
50	Dean Grad Sch of Mgmt	Judy D. OLIAN
63	Interim Dean Sch of Med	Kelsey C. MARTIN
64	Interim Dean Sch of Music	Judith L. SMITH
66	Interim Dean School of Nursing	Linda SARNA
80	Interim Dean Sch Pub Affrs	Lois TAKAHASHI
69	Dean Sch of Pub Health	Jody HEYMANN
88	Dean School of Theater Film & TV	Teri SCHWARTZ
51	Dean Continuing Ed and Extension	Wayne SMUTZ
21	Assoc VC Academic Planning & Budget	Jeff ROTH
29	Assoc VC Alumni Affairs/Advancemnt	Julie SINA
16	Assoc VC Campus Human Resources	Lubbe LEVIN
21	Assoc Vice Chancellor/Controller	Allison BAIRD-JAMES
30	Assoc VC Development	Kathryn CARRICO
30	Assoc VC Development	Laura Lavado PARKER
84	Assoc VC Enrollment Management	Youlonda COPELAND-MORGAN
91	Assoc VC Info Technology Services	Andrew WISSMILLER
35	Assoc VC Student Affairs Admin	Monroe GORDEN
27	Assoc VC UCLA Comm/Public Outreach	Kathryn KRANHOLD
20	Assistant Provost	Maryann J. GRAY
20	Assistant Provost	Margaret LEAL-SOTELO
18	Asst VC Facilities Management	Kelly J. SCHMADER
86	Asst VC Govt/Community Relations	Keith S. PARKER
39	Asst VC Housing & Hospitality Svcs	Peter ANGELIS
25	Asst VC Research/Compliance	Ann M. POLLACK
04	Executive Asst to the Chancellor	Dawn SCHERER
88	Executive Director ASUCLA	Robert WILLIAMS
09	Executive Director Inst Research	Vacant
88	Executive Director Volunteer Center	Vacant
96	Director Campus Purchasing & Payabl	William S. PROPST
36	Director Career Center	Wesley E. THORNE, II
85	Director Ctr for Intl Students	Shideh HANASSAB
22	Director Faculty Diversity	Vacant
37	Director Financial Aid Office	Ronald W. JOHNSON
41	Director Intercollegiate Athletics	Daniel G. GUERRERO
90	Director Res Comp & Acad Tech Svcs	William LABATE

38 Interim Exec Dir Couns & Psych Svcs .... Nicole GREEN
07 Director Undergraduate Admission .... Gary A. CLARK
06 Registrar .... Frank Y. WADA
08 University Librarian .... Virginia STEEL
19 Chief of Police .... James HERREN

*University of California-Merced (A)

5200 North Lake Road, Merced CA 95343
County: Merced FICE Identification: 041271
Unit ID: 445188
Telephone: (209) 228-4400 Carnegie Class: DU-Higher
FAX Number: (209) 228-4424 Calendar System: Semester
URL: www.ucmerced.edu
Established: 2005 Annual Undergrad Tuition & Fees (In-District): $13,208
Enrollment: 6,268 Coed
Affiliation or Control: State/Local IRS Status: 501(c)3
Highest Offering: Doctorate
Accreditation: WC, ENG

02 Chancellor .... Dr. Dorothy LELAND
88 Assoc Chancellor & Senior Advisor .... Luanna PUTNEY
05 Provost & Exec Vice Chancellor ....Dr. Tom PETERSON
11 Vice Chancellor Admin Svcs .... Michael REESE
30 Vice Chancellor Develop/Alumni Rels .... Kyle D. HOFFMAN
32 Int Vice Chancellor Student Affairs ....Dr. Charles NIES
10 Vice Chancellor Budget/Planning .... Daniel FEITELBERG
46 Vice Chancellor Research ....Dr. Samuel TRAINA
84 Assoc Vice Chanc Enrollment Mgmt ....Jill ORCUTT
26 Asst Vice Chanc Univ Communications .... Patti W. WAID
58 Vice Provost/Dean of Graduate Educ .... Marjorie ZATZ
20 Vice Provost UG Education ....Elizabeth WHITT
86 Exec Director of Govt Relations .... Cori LUCERO
100 Asst Chancellor & Chief of Staff ....Vacant
04 Exec Assistant to the Chancellor ....Kim GARNER
13 Chief Information Officer ....Ann KOVALCHICK
65 Dean Natural Sciences ....Dr. Juan MEZA
79 Dean School of SSHA ....Dr. Mark S. ALDENDERFER
54 Dean Engineering ....Dr. Mark MATSUMOTO
07 Director of Admissions ....Encarnacion RUIZ
06 University Registrar ....Dr. Laurie HERBRAND
37 Director of Financial Aid ....Diana RALLS
41 Director of Campus Athletics & Rec ....David DUNHAM
23 Assoc Vice Chanc Health & Wellness ....Dr. Fuji COLLINS
85 Director of International Programs .... Rebecca SWEELEY
08 University Librarian ....Haipeng LI
39 Director of Housing and Residence ....Martin REED
43 Campus Counsel .... Elisabeth GUNTHER
100 Associate Chancellor/Chief of Staff .... Ed KLOTZBIER
19 Chief of Police .... Albert VASQUEZ
15 Asst Vice Chanc Human Resource ....Brian POWELL

*University of California-Riverside (B)

900 University Avenue, Riverside CA 92521
County: Riverside FICE Identification: 001316
Unit ID: 110671
Telephone: (951) 827-1012 Carnegie Class: DU-Highest
FAX Number: (951) 827-3800 Calendar System: Quarter
URL: www.ucr.edu
Established: 1954 Annual Undergrad Tuition & Fees (In-State): $13,527
Enrollment: 21,498 Coed
Affiliation or Control: State IRS Status: 501(c)3
Highest Offering: Doctorate
Accreditation: WC, BUS, CS, ENG, IPSY, #MED, SCPSY

02 Chancellor ....Dr. Kim A. WILCOX
100 Associate Chancellor ....Ms. Cynthia R. GIORGIO
05 Exec Vice Chancellor/Provost ....Dr. Paul D'ANIERI
45 Vice Chanc Planning & Budget .... Ms. Maria ANGUIANO
32 Vice Chancellor Student Affairs ....Mr. James W. SANDOVAL
10 Vice Chanc Business & Admin Svcs .... Mr. Ron T. COLEY
26 Vice Chanc University Advancement ...... Mr. Peter A. HAYASHIDA
46 Vice Chancellor Research ....Dr. Michael J. PAZZANI
17 VC Hlth Affs/Dean School of Med .... Dr. Deborah DEAS
20 Vice Provost Academic Personnel .... Dr. Ameae WALKER
18 Assoc Vice Chanc Facil Plant Admin .... Mr. Robert SLATER
84 Assoc Vice Chanc Enrollment ....Ms. LaRae LUNDGREN
30 Int Assoc Vice Chanc Development .... Mr. Hieu NGUYEN
09 Asst Vice Chanc Strat Acad Rsrch An .... Mr. Charles GREER
28 Asst Vice Chanc Affirm Action .... Ms. Gladys BROWN
58 Dean Graduate Division .... Dr. Joseph CHILDERS
50 Dean School of Business Admin ....Dr. Yungzeng WANG
53 Dean Grad School of Educ ....Dr. Thomas SMITH
54 Dean Bourns College of Engineering ....Dr. Reza ABBASCHIAN
79 Dean College of Humanities Arts SS ....Dr. Milagros PENA
81 Dean Col of Nat and Agr Sciences ....Dr. Kathryn UHRICH
06 Registrar .... Ms. Bracken J. DAILEY
80 Dean School of Public Policy ....Dr. Anil DEOLALIKAR
36 Director Career Center ....Mr. Sean GILL
37 Director Financial Aid ....Mr. Jose A. AGUILAR
38 Director Counseling Center ....Ms. Elizabeth MONDRAGON
07 Director of Admissions ....Ms. Emily D. ENGELSCHALL
96 Director Material Management .... Mr. Russ LEWIS
08 Head Librarian ....Mr. Steve MANDEVILLE-GAMBLE

*University of California-San Diego (C)

9500 Gilman Drive, La Jolla CA 92093-0014
County: San Diego FICE Identification: 001317
Unit ID: 110680
Telephone: (858) 534-2230 Carnegie Class: DU-Highest
FAX Number: (858) 534-6523 Calendar System: Quarter
URL: www.ucsd.edu
Established: 1960 Annual Undergrad Tuition & Fees (In-State): $13,530
Enrollment: 30,709 Coed
Affiliation or Control: State IRS Status: 501(c)3
Highest Offering: Doctorate
Accreditation: WC, AUD, BUS, CEA, CLPSY, DIETI, DMS, ENG, IPSY, MED, MT, PDPSY, PHAR

02 Chancellor ....Dr. Pradeep K. KHOSLA
05 Interim EVC Academic Affairs .... Dr. Peter COWHEY
10 VC and Chief Financial Officer ....Mr. Pierre-Yves OUILLET
32 VC Student Affairs ....Dr. Juan GONZALEZ
11 Vice Chanc Resource Mgmt/Planning .... Mr. Gary C. MATTHEWS
65 Vice Chancellor Marine Sciences .... Dr. Margaret LEINEN
63 VC Health Science/Dean Sch Med ....Dr. David A. BRENNER
46 Vice Chancellor Research ....Dr. Sandra BROWN
28 VC for Equity Diversity & Inclusion ....Dr. Becky R. PETITT
30 Vice Chancellor Advancement ....Vacant
100 Associate Chancellor/Chief of Staff .... Ms. Clare M. KRISTOFCO
88 Chief Ethics and Compliance Officer ....Ms. Judith BRUNER
56 Assoc VC Public Pgms/Dean Univ Ext ...... Dr. Mary L. WALSHOK
43 Chief Campus Counsel ....Mr. Daniel W. PARK
13 Chief Information Officer ....Mr. Vince KELLEN
21 AVC Business Fin Svcs/Controller ....Ms. Cheryl ROSS
08 University Librarian ....Mr. Brian E C. SCHOTTLAENDER
88 Director Policy Admin ....Ms. Paula J. JOHNSON, CRM
23 Exec Dir Student Health/Wellness ....Ms. Karen J. CALFAS
26 University Communications .... Ms. Clare M. KRISTOFCO
20 Sr Assoc VC Academic Planning .... Dr. William S. HODGKISS
20 AVC Academic Affairs .... Dr. Barbara SAWREY
35 Assoc Vice Chanc Student Affairs ....Vacant
15 Int Asst VC Human Resources .... Ms. Catherine M. LEDFORD
88 Associate Vice Chancellor Research .... Dr. Miroslav KRSTIC
88 AVC Innovation & Commercialization .... Mr. Paul W. ROBEN
84 Assoc Vice Chanc Enrollment Mgmt ....Ms. Adele C. BRUMFIELD
06 University Registrar ....Vacant
23 CEO UCSD Medical Center .... Mr. Paul VIVIANO
29 Assistant Vice Chancellor ....Vacant
96 Assoc Controller/Chief Procurement ....Mr. Ted JOHNSON
54 Dean Jacobs Sch of Engineering ....Dr. Albert P. PISANO
49 Dean Arts & Humanities .... Dr. Cristina DELLA COLETTA
81 Dean Div of Biological Sciences .... Dr. William MCGINNIS
83 Dean of Social Sciences .... Dr. Carol A. PADDEN
88 Dean Rady School of Management .... Mr. Robert S. SULLIVAN
81 Interim Dean Physical Science ....Dr. Jeff REMMEL
82 Dean Global Policy and Strategy ....Dr. Gordon HANSON
58 Dean Graduate Studies ....Dr. Kim E. BARRETT
12 Provost John Muir College .... Dr. John C. MOORE
12 Prov Thurgood Marshall Coll .... Dr. Leslie CARVER
12 Provost Earl Warren College .... Dr. Emily ROXWORTHY
12 Provost Revelle College ....Dr. Paul K. YU
12 Provost Eleanor Roosevelt College ....Dr. Ivan EVANS
12 Provost Sixth College ....Dr. Daniel J. DONOGHUE
38 Director Stdt Psych/Counseling Svcs ....Dr. Reina JUAREZ
18 AVC EH&S and Facilities Management ....Mr. Garry L. MAC PHERSON
41 Athletic Director ....Mr. Earl W. EDWARDS
19 Police Chief Community Safety .... Mr. David S. ROSE

*University of California-San Francisco (D)

513 Parnassus Avenue, Box 0402,
San Francisco CA 94143
County: San Francisco FICE Identification: 001319
Unit ID: 110699
Telephone: (415) 476-9000 Carnegie Class: Spec-4-yr-Med
FAX Number: (415) 476-9634 Calendar System: Quarter
URL: www.ucsf.edu
Established: 1864 Annual Graduate Tuition & Fees: N/A
Enrollment: 3,170 Coed
Affiliation or Control: State IRS Status: 501(c)3
Highest Offering: Doctorate; No Undergraduates
Accreditation: WC, DENT, DIETI, IPSY, MED, MIDWF, NURSE, PAST, PHAR, PTA

02 Chancellor ....Dr. Samuel HAWGOOD
03 Executive Vice Chancellor & Provost ....Dr. Daniel H. LOWENSTEIN
100 Associate Chancellor .... Dr. Theresa O'BRIEN
10 VC and Chief Financial Officer ....Ms. Teresa COSTANTINIDIS
05 Vice Provost Academic Affairs ....Dr. Brian ALLDREDGE
63 Dean School of Medicine/VC Med Affs .... Dr. Talmadge E. KING, JR.
20 Vice Chanc Student Academic Affairs .... Dr. Elizabeth WATKINS
30 Vice Chanc Univ Develop & Alum Rels ....Mr. John FORD
88 VC Science Policy & Strategy .... Dr. Keith YAMAMOTO
26 VC Strat Communications & Univ Rels .... Ms. Barbara FRENCH
13 Assoc VC & Chief Info Officer - ITS ....Mr. Joseph BENGFORT
28 VC Diversity & Outreach ....Dr. Renee NAVARRO
32 Assoc VC Campus Life Services .... Ms. Clare SHINNERL
15 Assoc VC Human Resources .... Mr. David ODATO
18 Assoc VC Cap Pgms/Campus Architect ....Mr. Michael BADE
20 Vice Dean Academic Affairs ....Dr. Elena FUENTES-AFFLICK
37 Interim Dir Student Financial Svcs .... Mr. Ronald JAMES
43 Chief Campus Counsel ....Ms. Greta SCHNETZLER
08 University Librarian/AVC ....Vacant
19 Chief of Police ....Mr. Michael DENSON
22 Director Affirmative Action .... Ms. Cristina PEREZ
66 Dean School of Nursing .... Dr. David VLAHOV
52 Dean School of Dentistry ....Dr. John FEATHERSTONE
67 Dean School of Pharmacy ....Dr. B. Joseph GUGLIELMO
35 Exec Director Student Life ....Dr. Carol TAKAO
39 Exec Director Campus Life Svcs .... Dr. Gary FORMAN
96 Assoc VC/Chief Procurement Officer ....Mr. James HINE
06 Registrar/Asst VC Student Info ....Mr. Douglas CARLSON
88 Associate Registrar ....Ms. Jina SHAMIM
36 Exec Dir Career/Prof Development .... Mr. William LINDSTAEDT
23 Exec Dir Student Health Services ....Ms. Susan ROSEN
09 Director Institutional Research ....Dr. Ning WANG

*University of California-Santa Barbara (E)

552 University Road, Santa Barbara CA 93106-0001
County: Santa Barbara FICE Identification: 001320
Unit ID: 110705
Telephone: (805) 893-8000 Carnegie Class: DU-Highest
FAX Number: N/A Calendar System: Quarter
URL: www.ucsb.edu
Established: 1909 Annual Undergrad Tuition & Fees (In-State): $13,968
Enrollment: 23,051 Coed
Affiliation or Control: State IRS Status: 501(c)3
Highest Offering: Doctorate
Accreditation: WC, CS, DANCE, ENG, IPSY, PSPSY

02 Chancellor ....Dr. Henry T. YANG
04 Exec Assistant to the Chancellor .... Ms. Diane O'BRIEN
05 Executive Vice Chancellor ....Dr. David B. MARSHALL
10 Dir/Controller Business & Fin Svc .... Mr. Jim R. CORKILL
46 Interim Vice Chancellor Research ....Dr. Joe INCANDELA
11 Vice Chancellor Admin Services ....Mr. Marc FISHER
32 Vice Chancellor Student Affairs .... Ms. Margaret KLAWUNN
21 Finance & Resource Mgmt ....Mr. Todd G. LEE
45 Asst Chancellor Budget & Planning ....Mr. Chuck HAINES
15 Assoc Vice Chanc Acad Personnel ....Dr. Alison BUTLER
28 AVC Diversity/Equity/Acad Policy .....Dr. Maria HERRERA-SOBEK
20 AVC Academic Programs ....Vacant
30 Assoc Vice Chancellor Development ....Ms. Beverly COLGATE
26 AVC Public Affairs & Communications ....Vacant
84 Asst Vice Chanc Enrollment Svcs ....Ms. Mary JACOB
88 Assoc Dean Student Acad Support Svc ....Ms. Lupe GARCIA
29 Asst Vice Chanc Alumni Affairs .... Mr. George THURLOW, III
88 Dean College Creative Studies ....Dr. Bruce H. TIFFNEY
54 Dean College of Engineering ....Dr. Rod ALFERNESS
58 Dean Graduate Division .... Dr. Carol GENETTI
53 Co-Dean Gevirtz Grad Sch Educ ....Dr. Mary B. BRENNER
53 Co-Dean Gevirtz Grad Sch Educ ....Dr. Michael FURLONG
65 Dean Bren School of Env Sci & Mgmt ....Dr. Steven D. GAINES
56 Dean UC Santa Barbara Extension .... Dr. Michael T. BROWN
35 Dean of Student Life ....Ms. Katya ARMISTEAD
79 Interim Dean Humanities/Fine Arts ....Dr. John MAJEWSKI
81 Dean Math/Life & Physical Sciences .... Dr. Pierre WILTZIUS
87 Acting Director Summer Sessions ....Mr. James FORD
83 Dean Social Sciences ....Dr. Melvin L. OLIVER
85 Dir International Students/Scholars .... Dr. Simran SINGH
06 Registrar ....Ms. Leesa BECK
16 Acting Director Human Resources .... Ms. Cynthia SENERIZ
37 Director Financial Aid ....Dr. Michael MILLER
88 Director Audit & Advisory Service ....Mr. Robert TARSIA
07 Director Admissions ....Ms. Lisa PRZEKOP
09 Director Institutional Research ....Dr. Steven C. VELASCO
23 Exec Director Student Health Svcs .... Dr. Mary FERRIS
39 AVC Housing/Dining & Aux Enterpris ....Mr. Wilfred E. BROWN
40 Director of UCSB Bookstore .... Mr. Mark BEISECKER
19 Chief of Police ....Mr. Dustin OLSON
41 Director Intercollegiate Athletics ....Mr. John MCCUTCHEON
86 Dir Governmental Relations .... Ms. Kirsten DESHLER
21 Director Finance/Administration .... Mr. Eric J. SONQUIST
08 University Librarian ....Ms. Denise STEPHENS
89 Director Orientation Programs .... Ms. Tricia RASCON
88 Acting Director Capital Development .... Mr. Mark NOCCIOLO
46 Director Campus Planning & Design .... Ms. Alissa HUMMER
31 Director Arts & Lectures ....Ms. Celesta BILLECI
22 Director Disabled Students Pgm ....Mr. Gary R. WHITE
104 Dir Campus Education Abroad Program ....Dr. Juan E. CAMPO
88 Acting Dir Env Health & Safety .... Mr. Ali AGHAYAN
88 Director MultiCultural Center ....Ms. Zaveeni KHAN-MARCUS
38 Dir Counseling & Psychological Svcs .... Dr. Jeanne STANFORD
94 Director Women's Center ....Ms. Kim EQUINOA
88 Campus Ombuds ....Ms. Caroline ADAMS
88 Exec Dir Instructional Devel .... Mr. George H. MICHAELS
36 Director Career Services ....Mr. Ignacio GALLARDO
13 Chief Information Officer ....Mr. Matthew HALL
43 UCSB Legal Counsel ....Ms. Nancy G. HAMILL
22 Equal Op/Sexual Harassment/Title IX .... Mr. Ricardo ALCAINO
18 Director Design & Construction .... Mr. Jack WOLEVER
88 Director Univ Center/Events Center ....Mr. Gary LAWRENCE
68 Interim Director of Recreation .... Ms. Cathy CZULEGER
92 Honors Program Analyst ....Ms. Summer HOWATT-NAB

*University of California-Santa Cruz (F)

1156 High Street, Santa Cruz CA 95064-1077
County: Santa Cruz FICE Identification: 001321
Unit ID: 110714
Telephone: (831) 459-0111 Carnegie Class: DU-Highest
FAX Number: (831) 459-0146 Calendar System: Quarter
URL: www.ucsc.edu
Established: 1965 Annual Undergrad Tuition & Fees (In-State): $13,461
Enrollment: 17,866 Coed
Affiliation or Control: State IRS Status: 501(c)3
Highest Offering: Doctorate
Accreditation: WC, ENG, IPSY

02 Chancellor ... Dr. George R. BLUMENTHAL
05 Campus Provost/Exec Vice Chancellor ... Dr. Alison GALLOWAY
10 Vice Chanc Business/Admin Services ... Dr. Sarah LATHAM
45 Vice Chancellor Planning/Budget ... Dr. Peggy DELANEY
46 Vice Chancellor Research ... Dr. Scott BRANDT
30 Vice Chanc of University Relations ... Dr. Keith BRANT
13 Vice Chanc Information Technology ... Dr. Mary DOYLE
20 Vice Prov/Dean Undergrad Educ ... Dr. Richard HUGHEY
20 Vice Provost Academic Affairs ... Dr. Herbert LEE
84 Assoc VC Enrollment Mgmt ... Ms. Michelle WHITTINGHAM
16 Asst VC Academic Personnel ... Dr. Pamela PETERSON
18 Assoc VC & Campus Architect ... Mr. John BARNES
15 Assoc VC Staff Human Resources ... Mr. Steve STEIN
32 AVC Campus Life/Dn of Students ... Ms. Alma SIFUENTES
08 University Librarian ... Ms. Elizabeth COWELL
79 Dean of Humanities ... Dr. Tyler STOVALL
81 Dean Physical & Biological Sci ... Dr. Paul KOCH
49 Interim Dean of the Arts ... Dr. William LADUSAW
83 Dean of Social Sciences ... Dr. Sheldon KAMIENIECKI
54 Dean of Engineering ... Dr. Joseph KONOPELSKI
58 Vice Prov/Dean of Graduate Studies ... Dr. Tyrus MILLER
65 Director Institute Marine Sciences ... Dr. Gary B. GRIGGS
81 Director Institute Particle Physics ... Dr. Steven RITZ
88 Director UCO/Lick Observatory ... Dr. Claire MAX
12 Provost Stevenson College ... Dr. Alice YANG
12 Provost Cowell College ... Dr. Faye CROSBY
12 Provost Crown College ... Dr. Manel CAMPS
12 Provost Merrill College ... Dr. Elizabeth ABRAMS
12 Provost Porter College ... Dr. Sean KEILEN
12 Provost Kresge College ... Dr. Ben LEEDS CARSON
12 Provost College Eight ... Dr. Ronnie LIPSCHUTZ
12 Provost College Nine ... Dr. Flora LU
12 Provost College Ten ... Dr. Regina LANGHOUT
06 Registrar ... Mr. Tchad SANGER
09 Director Institutional Research ... Dr. Julian L. FERNALD
37 Director Financial Aid/Operations ... Mr. Patrick REGISTER
22 Staff Dir EEO/Affirmative Action ... Mr. Ashish SAHNI
29 Director of Alumni Relations ... Ms. Shayna KENT
26 Dir Marketing/Communications ... Ms. Lisa NIELSEN
86 Director Government Relations ... Ms. Donna M. BLITZER
38 Director Student Counseling ... Dr. Gary DUNN
07 Director of Admissions ... Mr. Michael MCCAWLEY
41 Athletic Director ... Mr. Cliff DOCHTERMAN
108 Asst Director for Assessment ... Dr. Anna SHER
102 Dir Foundation/Corporate Relations ... Ms. Lynne STOOPS

University of East-West Medicine (A)

595 Lawrence Expressway, Sunnyvale CA 94085

County: Santa Clara — FICE Identification: 039953
Unit ID: 447801
Telephone: (408) 733-1878 — Carnegie Class: Spec-4-yr-Other Health
FAX Number: (408) 636-7705 — Calendar System: Trimester
URL: www.uewm.edu
Established: 1997 — Annual Undergrad Tuition & Fees: N/A
Enrollment: 234 — Coed
Affiliation or Control: Proprietary — IRS Status: Proprietary
Highest Offering: Master's
Accreditation: ACUP

01 President ... Dr. Ying Qiu WANG
32 VP Student/Academic Affairs ... Dr. Doreen SIMMONS

† Granted candidacy at the Doctorate level.

University of La Verne (B)

1950 Third Street, La Verne CA 91750-4443

County: Los Angeles — FICE Identification: 001216
Unit ID: 117140
Telephone: (909) 593-3511 — Carnegie Class: DU-Mod
FAX Number: (909) 593-0965 — Calendar System: Semester
URL: www.laverne.edu
Established: 1891 — Annual Undergrad Tuition & Fees: $38,560
Enrollment: 8,517 — Coed
Affiliation or Control: Independent Non-Profit — IRS Status: 501(c)3
Highest Offering: Doctorate
Accreditation: WC, CAATE, CLPSY, LAW, SPAA, TED

01 President ... Dr. Devorah A. LIEBERMAN
05 Provost & Vice President ... Dr. Jonathan REED
88 Special Assistant to Provost ... Dr. Mark GOOR
10 Chief Financial Officer ... Mr. Avedis (Avo) KECHICHIAN
30 Vice President Univ Advancement ... Ms. Myra GARCIA
84 Vice Pres Strategic Enroll & Comm ... Dr. Homa SHABAHANG
50 Dean College Business/Public Mgmt ... Dr. Ibrahim (Abe) HELOU
53 Dean College Educ/Org Ldrship ... Dr. Kimberly WHITE-SMITH
61 Dean College of Law ... Mr. Gilbert HOLMES
32 Dean Student Affairs ... Dr. Loretta RAHMANI
12 Dean Regional & Online Programs ... Dr. David SMITH
07 Dean of Admissions ... Mr. Chris KRZAK
88 Assoc VP Academic Sppt/Retent Svcs ... Ms. Adeline CARDENAS-CLAGUE
21 Associate Vice President of Finance . Ms. Lori K. GORDIEN CASE
15 Chief Human Resources Officer ... Ms. Jody L. BOMBA
18 Vice President of Facilities/ Tech ... Dr. Clive K. HOUSTON-BROWN
35 Associate Dean Student Affairs ... Mrs. Ruby S. MONTANO-CORDOVA
88 Asst Dean Grad Acad Supp/Ret Svcs ... Ms. Jo Nell BAKER
84 Assoc VP & Chief Marketing Officer ... Mr. Fred A. CHYR
85 Director International Student Svcs ... Dr. Jeffrey NONEMAKER
18 Sr Dir Physical Plant Ops & Svcs ... Mr. Robert D. BEEBE
11 Director Admin & Operation ... Mr. Jason NEAL
26 Director of Public Relations ... Vacant
29 Sr Dir Advancement Oper & Services ... Ms. Bianca ROMERO
38 Dir Counseling & Psych Services ... Dr. Elleni R. KOULOS
88 Director Student Accounts ... Ms. Xochitl E. MARTINEZ
104 Study Abroad Advisor ... Dr. Alfred CLARK
96 Director Purchasing & Procurement ... Mrs. Deborah S. DEACY
28 Director Multicultural Affairs ... Dr. Daniel L. LOERA
23 Dir Health Svcs/Svcs for Stds-Disab ... Ms. Cynthia K. DENNE
39 Assoc Dean of Stdnts/Dir Stdnt Hous ... Mr. Juan REGALADO
36 Asst Dean Student Career Support ... Ms. Mindy BAGGISH
88 Dir Center for Adv/Teaching & Lrng ... Dr. Sammy ELZARKA
88 Director Graduate Success Center ... Dr. Linda DE LONG
41 Athletic Director ... Ms. Julie KLINE
06 Registrar ... Ms. Marilyn S. DAVIES
08 University Librarian ... Dr. Vinaya L. TRIPURANENI
28 Chief Diversity Officer ... D. Beatriz GONZALEZ
09 Director of Institutional Research ... Dr. Leeshawn MOORE
42 Chaplain/Dir of Campus Ministry ... Dr. Zandra L. WAGONER
88 Director of La Verne Experience ... Dr. Kathleen WEAVER
90 Sr Dir Admission Oper/Tech Svcs ... Mrs. Loreto D'MONTE
88 Director High Desert ... Ms. Jul ROBERTS
88 Director Inland Empire ... Mr. Allen STOUT
88 Director Kern County ... D. Nora DOMINGUEZ
88 Director Orange County ... Dr. Todd ECKEL
88 Director Point Mugu NAWC ... Mr. Jamie DEMPSEY
88 Sr Ex Dir San Fernando Valley ... Dr. Nelly KAZMAN
88 Director Vandenberg AFB ... Ms. Kitt VINCENT
88 Director Ventura County ... Mr. Kevin LAACK
88 Director International Admission ... Mr. Adam WU
20 Vice Provost ... Dr. Beatriz GONZALEZ
88 Director of Civic Engagement ... Ms. Marisol MORALES
04 Executive Asst to President ... Ms. Shannon HIGGINS

University of the Pacific (C)

3601 Pacific Avenue, Stockton CA 95211-0197

County: San Joaquin — FICE Identification: 001329
Unit ID: 120883
Telephone: (209) 946-2011 — Carnegie Class: DU-Mod
FAX Number: (209) 946-2845 — Calendar System: Semester
URL: www.pacific.edu
Established: 1851 — Annual Undergrad Tuition & Fees: $42,934
Enrollment: 6,304 — Coed
Affiliation or Control: Independent Non-Profit — IRS Status: 501(c)3
Highest Offering: Doctorate
Accreditation: WC, ART, @AUD, BUS, CAATE, CS, DENT, DH, ENG, IPSY, LAW, MUS, PHAR, PTA, SP, TED

01 President ... Pamela A. EIBECK
05 Provost ... Maria G. PALLAVICINI
10 Vice President Business & Finance ... Ken MULLEN
32 Vice President Student Life ... Patrick DAY
30 VP Development & Alumni Relations ... G. Burnham 'Burnie' ATTERBURY
101 VP & Secretary to Board of Regents ... Mary Lou LACKEY
13 VP Technology/CIO ... Art SPRECHER
21 Associate VP Business/Finance ... Ron ELLISON
84 Vice Provost for Enrollment Svcs ... J. Michael THOMPSON
88 Vice Provost for Distrib Learning ... Vernon SMITH
26 Interim Assoc VP Communications ... Stacy MCAFEE
51 Asst Provost Ctr Prof & Cont Educ ... Barbara L. SHAW
86 AVP External Relations ... Stacy MCAFEE
45 Assoc VP Planning ... Linda BUCKLEY
49 Dean College of the Pacific ... Rena FRADEN
50 Dean Eberhardt School Business ... Lewis GALE
52 Int Dean Dugoni School of Dentistry ... Nader NADERSHAHI
53 Int Dean Benerd School of Education ... Linda WEBSTER
54 Dean Sch of Eng/Comp Science ... Steven HOWELL
61 Dean McGeorge School of Law ... Jay MOOTZ
64 Interim Dean Conservatory of Music ... Daniel EBBERS
67 Dean Long Sch Pharm/Hlth Sciences ... Phillip R. OPPENHEIMER
36 Assoc VP for Career Development ... Tom VECCHIONE
08 Dean of the Library ... Vacant
58 Dean Research/Graduate Studies ... Bhaskara JASTI
25 Sponsored Pgms Administrator ... Vacant
29 Exec Dir of Alumni Relations ... Kelli PAGE
37 Director of Financial Aid ... Lynn FOX
07 Director of Admissions ... Jermaine CRUZ
06 Registrar ... Vacant
09 Director Institutional Research ... Mike ROGERS
35 Director Student Activities ... Vacant
96 Director of Purchasing ... Fonda MARR
92 Director Honors Program ... Balint SZATARAY
93 Director Multicultural Affairs ... Ines RUIZ-HUSTON
94 Director Gender Studies ... Traci ROBERTS-CAMPS
38 Director of Counseling Services ... Stacie TURKS
39 Director of Housing ... Torry BROUILLARD-BRUCE
41 Director of Athletics ... Ted LELAND
42 University Chaplain ... Joel LOHR
15 Asst VP Human Resources ... Greg WALTERS
40 Director of Bookstore ... Nicole CASTILLO
19 Director of Public Safety ... Michael BELCHER
18 Director of Physical Plant ... Scott HEATON
82 Director Sch International Studies ... William HERRIN
102 AVP Foundation/Corporate Relations ... Scott BIEDERMANN
44 AVP Development ... Bill JOHNSON
100 Chief of Staff ... Bett SCHUMACHER
104 Dir International Programs Services ... Ryan GRIFFITH
43 Dir Legal Services/General Counsel ... Kevin MILLS

University of the People (D)

225 S. Lake Ave, Ste300, Pasadena CA 91101

County: Los Angeles — Identification: 667160
Telephone: (626) 264-8880 — Carnegie Class: Not Classified
FAX Number: N/A — Calendar System: Other
URL: www.uopeople.edu
Established: 2009 — Annual Undergrad Tuition & Fees: N/A
Enrollment: N/A — Coed
Affiliation or Control: Independent Non-Profit — IRS Status: 501(c)3
Highest Offering: Master's
Accreditation: DEAC

01 President & Founder ... Mr. Shai RESHEF
05 Provost ... Dr. David HARRIS COHEN
45 VP for Strategy & Planning ... Mr. Yoav VENTURA
13 Vice President of Technology ... Ms. Hadass ADMON
10 Chief Financial Officer ... Mr. Paul AFFUSO
20 Vice Provost ... Dr. Roxie SMITH

University of Philosophical Research (E)

3910 Los Feliz Boulevard, Los Angeles CA 90027

County: Los Angeles — Identification: 666373
Telephone: (323) 663-2167 — Carnegie Class: Not Classified
FAX Number: (323) 663-9443 — Calendar System: Quarter
URL: www.uprs.edu
Established: 1998 — Annual Undergrad Tuition & Fees: N/A
Enrollment: N/A — Coed
Affiliation or Control: Independent Non-Profit — IRS Status: 501(c)3
Highest Offering: Master's
Accreditation: DEAC

01 President/Chief Executive Officer ... Dr. Obadiah HARRIS
05 Dean of Academic Affairs ... Dr. Debashish BANERJI
06 Registrar ... Mr. John CHASE
10 Chief Financial Officer ... Mr. Gregory WILLIS

University of Phoenix Bay Area Campus (F)

3590 N First Street, San Jose CA 95134-1805

Telephone: (800) 266-2107 — Identification: 770193
Accreditation: &NH, ACBSP

† Regional accreditation is carried under the parent institution in Tempe, AZ

University of Phoenix Central Valley Campus (G)

45 River Park Place West, Fresno CA 93720-1552

Telephone: (800) 266-2107 — Identification: 770190
Accreditation: &NH, ACBSP

† Regional accreditation is carried under the parent institution in Tempe, AZ

University of Phoenix Sacramento Valley Campus (H)

2860 Gateway Oaks Drive, Sacramento CA 95833-4334

Telephone: (800) 266-2107 — Identification: 770191
Accreditation: &NH, ACBSP

† Regional accreditation is carried under the parent institution in Tempe, AZ

University of Phoenix San Diego Campus (I)

9645 Granite Ridge Dr, Suite 200,
San Diego CA 92123-2658

Telephone: (800) 473-4346 — Identification: 770192
Accreditation: &NH, ACBSP

† Regional accreditation is carried under the parent institution in Tempe, AZ

University of Phoenix Southern California Campus (J)

3090 Bristol Street, Suite 400, Costa Mesa CA 92626

Telephone: (800) 888-1968 — Identification: 770189
Accreditation: &NH, ACBSP

† Regional accreditation is carried under the parent institution in Tempe, AZ

University of Redlands (K)

PO Box 3080, Redlands CA 92373-0999

County: San Bernardino — FICE Identification: 001322
Unit ID: 121691
Telephone: (909) 793-2121 — Carnegie Class: Masters/L
FAX Number: (909) 793-2029 — Calendar System: Semester
URL: www.redlands.edu
Established: 1907 — Annual Undergrad Tuition & Fees: $44,900
Enrollment: 5,333 — Coed
Affiliation or Control: Independent Non-Profit — IRS Status: 501(c)3
Highest Offering: Doctorate
Accreditation: WC, MUS, SP

01 President Dr. Ralph W. KUNCL
05 Provost/Chief Academic Officer Dr. Kathy OGREN
10 Vice Pres Finance/Administration Mr. Cory NOMURA
32 Vice President/Dean Student Life Ms. Charlotte G. BURGESS
84 Vice President for Enrollment Mr. Kevin M. DYERLY
30 Vice Pres for Advancement Ms. Anita WEST
26 Chief Communications Officer Ms. Wendy SHATTUCK
43 General Counsel Mr. Brent G. GERATY
100 Chief of Staff Ms. Michelle ROGERS
53 Dean School of Education Dr. Andrew WALL
50 Int Dean School of Business Dr. Keith ROBERTS
49 Dean Arts & Sciences Dr. Kendrick BROWN
64 Dean School of Music Dr. Andrew GLENDENING
44 Assoc Vice Pres Development Mr. Ray WATTS
21 Director Financial Ops & Controller Ms. Patricia M. CAUDLE
28 Asc Dean Campus Diversity/Inclusion Ms. Leela MADHAVA RAU
42 Chaplain Rev. John T. WALSH
06 Registrar Ms. Maria JOHNSON
104 Director Study Abroad Mr. Leo ROWLAND
37 Director of Financial Aid Ms. Emily HARRIS
90 Director Academic Computing Mr. Shariq AHMED
81 Director Center of Sciences & Math Dr. Barbara M. MURRAY
88 Director of Environmental Programs Dr. Lamont C. HEMPEL
08 Director of Library Services Ms. Gabriela SONNTAG
15 Director of Human Resources Vacant
22 EEO & Employee Relations Manager Vacant
09 Asst Provost Institutional Research Dr. Yan XIE
19 Chief of Public Safety Mr. Jeffrey TALBOTT
18 Director of Facilities Management Mr. Roger CELLINI
29 Director of Alumni Relations Ms. Shelli STOCKTON
20 Asst Dean of Academic/Student Life Ms. Amy WILMS
38 Director Student Counseling Ctr Dr. Lorraine YOUNG
41 Director of Athletics Mr. Jeffrey MARTINEZ
96 Office Services Manager Ms. Sandi TAYLOR
36 Director Student Employment Ms. Kathryn WOOD
07 Director of Admissions Ms. Belinda SANDOVAL-ZAZUETA
13 Exec Dir Information Tech Svcs Mr. Steve GARCIA
04 Executive Assistant to President Ms. Lauri GRIER
102 Director Foundation & Corp Rels Mr. Jerry YU
108 Director Assessment Ms. Sheila LLOYD
39 Director of Student Housing Ms. Cassandra MORTON

University of St. Augustine for Health Sciences (A)

700 Windy Point Drive, San Marcos CA 92069
County: San Diego FICE Identification: 031713
Unit ID: 367954
Telephone: (706) 591-3012 Carnegie Class: Spec-4-yr-Other Health
FAX Number: (706) 591-3068 Calendar System: Trimester
URL: www.usa.edu
Established: 1979 Annual Graduate Tuition & Fees: N/A
Enrollment: 1,913 Coed
Affiliation or Control: Proprietary IRS Status: Proprietary
Highest Offering: Doctorate; No Undergraduates
Accreditation: WC, OT, PTA

00 Interim CEO Dr. Susan SAXTON
01 President/Chief Academic Officer Dr. Wanda NITSCH
05 Vice President Academic Operations Dr. Cindy MATHENA
32 Vice Pres Student Administration Dr. Jeremy WELLS
10 Executive Director of Finance Ms. Jennifer BRIAR
75 Dir Inst of Occupational Therapy Dr. Karen HOWELL
75 Program Dir Occupational Therapy-CA Dr. Judith OLSON
88 Chair Institute of Physical Therapy Dr. Ellen LOWE
88 Dir Physical Therapy Program-FL Dr. Jeffrey ROT
88 Program Dir Physical Therapy-TX Dr. Manuel A. DOMENECH
88 Dir Trans Doctor Physical Therapy Dr. Jodi LIPHART
75 Chair Inst Physical Therapy Dr. Anne HULL
88 Director of DHSc/EdD Programs Dr. Betine A. MALHOTRA
06 Registrar Ms. Diane RONDINELLI
07 Director of Admissions Ms. Adrianne JONES
51 Director Continuing Prof Education Ms. Lori HANKINS
15 Director Human Resources Ms. Nicola MARTIN

University of San Diego (B)

5998 Alcala Park, San Diego CA 92110-2492
County: San Diego FICE Identification: 010395
Unit ID: 122436
Telephone: (619) 260-4600 Carnegie Class: DU-Mod
FAX Number: (619) 260-6833 Calendar System: 4/1/4
URL: www.sandiego.edu
Established: 1949 Annual Undergrad Tuition & Fees: $44,586
Enrollment: 8,349 Coed
Affiliation or Control: Roman Catholic IRS Status: 501(c)3
Highest Offering: Doctorate
Accreditation: WC, BUS, BUSA, CACREP, CEA, ENG, IPSY, LAW, MFCD, NURSE, TED

01 President Dr. James T. HARRIS
04 Special Assistant to the President Ms. Elaine ATENCIO
05 Vice President & Provost Dr. Andrew T. ALLEN
10 VP Finance/Chief Financial Officer Ms. Terry KALFAYAN
42 Vice President Mission & Ministry Msgr. Daniel J. DILLABOUGH
32 Vice President Student Affairs Ms. Carmen M. VAZQUEZ
30 Vice President Univ Relations Dr. Timothy L. O'MALLEY
41 Vice President for Athletics Mr. Ky L. SNYDER
49 Dean College of Arts & Sciences Dr. Noelle NORTON
50 Dean School of Business Admin Dr. Jaime A. GOMEZ
54 Dean Shiley-Marcos School of Engr Dr. Chell ROBERTS
61 Dean School of Law Mr. Stephen C. FERRUOLO
53 Dean Sch Leadership/Educ Sciences Dr. Nicholas LADANY
66 Dean School Nursing/Health Science Dr. Sally B. HARDIN
88 Dean School of Peace Studies Dr. Patricia MARQUEZ
51 Dean Prof & Continuing Education Dr. Jason LEMON
08 Dean University Library Dr. Theresa BYRD
43 General Counsel Ms. Kelly C. DOUGLAS
20 Vice Provost Dr. Thomas R. HERRINTON
13 Vice Provost & Chief Info Officer Mr. Christopher W. WESSELLS
06 University Registrar Ms. Elizabeth SILVA
20 Associate Provost Academic Planning Dr. Carole HUSTON
28 Assoc Provost for Incl & Diversity Dr. Esteban DEL RIO
20 Assoc Provost International Affairs Dr. Denise DIMON
21 Assoc Vice Pres & Controller Ms. Katy ROIG
84 Asst VP Enrollment Management Mr. Stephen F. PULTZ
15 AVP & Chief Human Resources Officer Ms. Karen BRIGGS
18 Asst VP Facilities Management Ms. Melissa PLASKONOS
26 Asst Vice Pres Univ Communications Mr. Peter MARLOW
26 Asst Vice Pres Media Communications Ms. Pamela GRAY PAYTON
19 Asst Vice President Public Safety Mr. Larry E. BARNETT
35 Asst VP & Dean of Students Dr. Donald R. GODWIN
109 Asst VP Auxiliary Services Mr. Andre MALLIE
07 Director of Admissions Ms. Minh-Ha HOANG
09 Dir Inst Research & Planning Dr. Paula S. KRIST
90 Sr Director Academic Tech Services Ms. Shahra MESHKATY
91 Senior Director EASS Mr. Avi BADWAL
102 Sr Director Foundation Relations Ms. Annette KETNER
86 Sr Dir Community/Govt Relations Mr. Thomas R. CLEARY
44 Senior Director Planned Giving Mr. John A. PHILLIPS
29 Senior Director Alumni Relations Mr. Charles BASS
44 Director Annual Giving Mr. Philip GARLAND
36 Director Career Services Ms. Robin DARMON
38 Director Counseling Center Dr. Stephen D. SPRINKLE
37 Director Financial Aid Services Ms. Judith LEWIS LOGUE
92 Director Honors Program Dr. James O. GUMP
39 Director Housing Vacant
85 Dir International Students/Scholars Ms. Chia-Yen LIN
104 Dir International Studies Abroad Dr. Kira A. ESPIRITU
93 Director Multicultural Center Dr. Mayte PEREZ-FRANCO
27 Director News Bureau Ms. Elizabeth HARMAN
96 Director Procurement Services Ms. Dawn L. ANDERSON
25 Director Sponsored Programs Ms. Traci MERRILL
23 Director Student Health Center Ms. Pamela J. SIKES
106 Dir Online Education/E-learning Ms. Roxanne MORRISON
22 Dir Affirmative Action/EEO Dr. Nicole SCHUESSLER

University of San Francisco (C)

2130 Fulton Street, San Francisco CA 94117-1080
County: San Francisco FICE Identification: 001325
Unit ID: 122612
Telephone: (415) 422-5555 Carnegie Class: DU-Mod
FAX Number: (415) 422-2303 Calendar System: 4/1/4
URL: www.usfca.edu
Established: 1855 Annual Undergrad Tuition & Fees: $42,634
Enrollment: 10,689 Coed
Affiliation or Control: Roman Catholic IRS Status: 501(c)3
Highest Offering: Doctorate
Accreditation: WC, BUS, IPSY, LAW, NURSE, PH, SPAA

01 President Rev. Paul J. FITZGERALD, SJ
00 Chancellor Rev. Stephen A. PRIVETT, SJ
05 Provost & Vice Pres Acad Affairs Dr. Donald HELLER
10 Vice President Business & Finance Mr. Charles E. CROSS
26 Vice Pres Marketing Communications Ms. Ellen RYDER
82 Vice Pres International Relations Dr. Stanley D. NEL
30 Vice President Development Mr. Peter J. WILCH
43 General Counsel Ms. Donna J. DAVIS
13 Vice President IT & CIO Mr. Opinder BAWA
20 Senior Vice Provost Acad Affairs Dr. Shirley MCGUIRE
32 Interim Vice Provost Student Life Ms. Julie J. ORIO
28 Vice Prov Diversity & Community Dr. Mary J. WARDELL-GHIRARDUZZI
45 Vice Prov Inst Budget/Plan/Effect Dr. Jeff HAMRICK
84 Vice Provost Strategic Enroll Mgmt Vacant
12 Vice Prov Branch Campus Vacant
61 Dean of the School of Law Mr. John D. TRASVINA
49 Dean College Arts & Sciences Dr. Marcelo F. CAMPERI
08 Dean of University Library Dr. Tyrone H. CANNON
53 Dean School of Education Dr. Kevin K. KUMASHIRO
66 Dean School of Nursing & Health Pgm Dr. Margaret W. BAKER
50 Dean School of Management Dr. Elizabeth B. DAVIS
18 Assoc Vice Pres Facilities Mgmt Mr. Michael LONDON
88 Assoc Vice Pres Finance & Treasury Ms. Stacy LEWIS
15 Assoc Vice Pres Human Resources Ms. Martha A. PEUGH-WADE
21 Assoc Vice Pres Account & Bus Svcs Mr. Frank M. WASILEWSKI
88 Rector of Jesuit Community Rev. John KOEPLIN, SJ
42 Director University Ministry Ms. Julia A. DOWD
07 Assoc Vice Prov Strategic Enrol Mgt Ms. Kathryn NAPPER
88 Asst Vice Prov Digital Strat/Online Mr. John DEVOY
37 Senior Assoc Dean Acad/Dir Fin Aid Ms. Susan L. MURPHY
04 Exec Asst to President/Sec BOT Ms. Jaci E. NEESAM
27 Assoc VP Public Affairs/Media Rels Mr. Gary MCDONALD
88 Assoc Vice Prov Acad Affs/Historian Dr. Alan L. ZIAJKA
88 Assoc Vice Prov Planning and Budget Mr. Michael J. HARRINGTON
30 Sr Assoc VP Development Mr. Preston S. WALTON
06 Assoc Dean University Registrar Mr. Robert L. BROMFIELD
91 Assoc VP & SR Dir Application Svcs Mr. Way LEON
96 Dir Purchasing & Ancillary Svc Ms. Janet L. TEYMOURTASH
38 Senior Dir Counseling & Psych Svcs Dr. Barbara J. THOMAS
36 Senior Director Career Svcs Mr. Alex HOCHMAN
19 Senior Director of Public Safety Dr. Daniel L. LAWSON
88 Assoc Dean Grad/Branch/Summ Admiss Mr. Michael HUGHES
88 Asst Vice Prov Integ Enrol Data Mgt Mr. Shawn HICKS
104 Director Ctr for Global Education Ms. Sharon F. LI
88 Dir Undergrad Admissions & Recruit Ms. April CRABTREE
85 Director Intl Student/Scholar Svcs Ms. Laura CHANEY
41 Director of Athletics Mr. Scott A. SIDWELL
102 Assoc Vice Pres Found/Corp Rel Ms. Marly A. NORRIS
29 Assoc VP Alumni & Donor Engagement Ms. Leslie THEODORE
44 Asst VP Annual Giving & Develop Svc Ms. Jessica JORDAN
29 Director University Inititives Mr. Bill CARTWRIGHT
16 Dir Employment & Employee Relations Ms. Diane L. NELSON
09 Director Institutional Research Mr. Theodore M. LYDON, JR.
39 Dir Student Housing/Resident Educ Vacant
24 Dir Ctr Learning Instruct & Tech Dr. John BANSAVICH
105 Sr Director Web Communications Ms. Marlene K. TOM
108 Dir Educ Effective/Assessment Ms. Deborah PANTER
25 Director Contracts/Grants Admin Vacant

University of Southern California (D)

University Park, Los Angeles CA 90089-0012
County: Los Angeles FICE Identification: 001328
Unit ID: 123961
Telephone: (213) 740-2311 Carnegie Class: DU-Highest
FAX Number: (213) 740-8502 Calendar System: Semester
URL: www.usc.edu
Established: 1880 Annual Undergrad Tuition & Fees: $50,277
Enrollment: 42,453 Coed
Affiliation or Control: Independent Non-Profit IRS Status: 501(c)3
Highest Offering: Doctorate
Accreditation: WC, ANEST, ARCPA, BUS, BUSA, CLPSY, CS, DENT, DH, @DIETC, DIETI, ENG, HSA, IPSY, JOUR, LAW, LSAR, MED, OT, PCSAS, PDPSY, PH, PHAR, PLNG, PTA, SPAA, SW, TED

01 President Dr. C. L. M. NIKIAS
05 Provost and Sr VP Academic Affairs Dr. Michael QUICK
11 Sr VP Administration Mr. Todd R. DICKEY
10 Sr VP Finance & CFO Mr. James STATEN
26 Sr VP University Relations Mr. Thomas SAYLES
30 Sr VP University Advancement Mr. Albert R. CHECCIO
23 Sr VP & CEO for USC Health Mr. Thomas E. JACKIEWICZ
88 Chief Investment Officer Ms. Lisa MAZZOCCO
43 Senior VP Admin and General Counsel Ms. Carol MAUCH AMIR
32 VP for Student Affairs Dr. Ainsley CARRY
07 VP Admissions and Planning Dr. L. Katharine HARRINGTON
46 VP for Research Dr. Randolph W. HALL
88 VP for Athletic Compliance Mr. David M. ROBERTS
88 VP Capital Construction/Facilities Mr. Lloyd SILBERSTEIN
88 VP for Health Sciences Development Mr. Dave CARRERA
27 VP Public Relations & Marketing Ms. Brenda K. MACEO
41 Athletic Director Mr. Lynn SWAN
100 Chief of Staff/Director of Protocol Mr. Dennis CORNELL
60 Dean Annenberg School Communication Dr. Ernest J. WILSON, III
48 Dean School of Architecture Mr. Qingyun MA
50 Dean Marshall School of Business Mr. James G. ELLIS
88 Dean School of Cinematic Arts Dr. Elizabeth M. DALEY
66 Dean Kaufman School of Dance Dr. Robert A. CUTIETTA
52 Dean Ostrow School of Dentistry Dr. Avishai SADAN
53 Dean Rossier School of Education Dr. Karen S. GALLAGHER
54 Dean Viterbi School of Engineering Dr. Yannis C. YORTSOS
57 Dean Roski School of Fine Arts Dr. Erica MUHL
88 Dean Davis School of Gerontology Dr. Pinchas COHEN
61 Dean Gould School of Law Dr. Andrew GUZMAN
63 Dean Keck School of Medicine Dr. Rohit VARMA
64 Dean Thornton School of Music Dr. Robert A. CUTIETTA
67 Dean School of Pharmacy Dr. Glenn STIMMEL
70 Dean School of Social Work Dr. Marilyn L. FLYNN
88 Dean School of Dramatic Arts Mr. David BRIDEL
88 Dean Price School of Public Policy Dr. Jack H. KNOTT
49 Dean Dornsife Col Ltrs Arts & Sci Dr. Amber MILLER
42 Dean Religious Life Dr. Varun SONI
06 Registrar Dr. Frank CHANG
08 Dean University Libraries Ms. Catherine QUINLAN
07 Dean of Admission Mr. Timothy BRUNOLD
37 Dean of Financial Aid Mr. Thomas MCWHORTER
88 Assoc Sr VP Admin Operations Mr. David W. WRIGHT
29 Assoc Sr VP and Campaign Director Mr. Sam M. LOPEZ
28 Exec Dir of Equity/Diversity Ms. Gretchen DAHLINGER MEANS
38 Dir Counseling & Psychological Svcs Dr. Ilene ROSENSTEIN
88 Vice Provost and Senior Advisor Dr. Martin L. LEVINE
20 Vice Prov for Graduate Programs Dr. Sarah PRATT
20 Vice Prov for Undergraduate Program Dr. Andrea HODGE
13 Chief Information Officer Dr. Douglas SHOOK
88 Vice Prov Academic Ops Dr. Mark TODD
88 Exec Dir USC Stevens Ctr for Innov Ms. Jennifer DYER
88 VP of Global Initiatives Dr. Anthony BAILEY
20 Vice Prov for Acad/Faculty Affairs Dr. Elizabeth GRADDY

University of the West (E)

1409 Walnut Grove Avenue, Rosemead CA 91770-3709
County: Los Angeles FICE Identification: 036963
Unit ID: 449870
Telephone: (626) 571-8811 Carnegie Class: Bac-Diverse
FAX Number: (626) 571-1413 Calendar System: Semester
URL: www.uwest.edu
Established: 1991 Annual Undergrad Tuition & Fees: $10,656
Enrollment: 368 Coed
Affiliation or Control: Independent Non-Profit IRS Status: 501(c)3

Highest Offering: Doctorate
Accreditation: WC

01 President .... Dr. Stephen MORGAN
05 Chief Academic Officer .... Dr. Peter M. ROJCEWICZ
32 Dean of Student Affairs .... Ms. Vanessa KARAM
84 Dean of Enrollment .... Dr. Maria AYON
10 Chief Financial Officer .... Dr. Bill CHEN
08 Director of Library .... Ms. Ling Ling KUO
06 Registrar .... Ms. Jeanette ANDERSON
35 Student Life Coordinator .... Mr. Eddie ESCALANTE
73 Chair of Religious Studies .... Dr. Jane IWAMURA
50 Chair of Business Admin .... Dr. Victor KANE
97 Chair of General Education .... Dr. Janice GORE
83 Chair of Psychology .... Dr. Hiroshi SASASKI
88 Chair of English/ESL .... Mr. Michael GROSSO

Valley College of Medical Careers (A)

8399 Topanga Canyon Blvd Ste 200, West Hills CA 91304
County: Los Angeles FICE Identification: 041145
Unit ID: 449445
Telephone: (818) 883-9002 Carnegie Class: Not Classified
FAX Number: (818) 883-9003 Calendar System: Semester
URL: www.vcmc.edu
Established: Annual Undergrad Tuition & Fees: N/A
Enrollment: 94 Coed
Affiliation or Control: Proprietary IRS Status: Proprietary
Highest Offering: Associate Degree
Accreditation: ABHES, SURTEC

01 Campus Director .... Mr. Ronny SUSSMAN

Vanguard University of Southern California (B)

55 Fair Drive, Costa Mesa CA 92626-6597
County: Orange FICE Identification: 001293
Unit ID: 123651
Telephone: (714) 556-3610 Carnegie Class: Masters/S
FAX Number: (714) 957-9317 Calendar System: Semester
URL: www.vanguard.edu
Established: 1920 Annual Undergrad Tuition & Fees: $30,050
Enrollment: 2,255 Coed
Affiliation or Control: Assemblies Of God Church IRS Status: 501(c)3
Highest Offering: Master's
Accreditation: WC, MUS, NURSE, THEA

01 President .... Dr. Michael J. BEALS
100 Exec Assistant to the President .... Ms. Shree CARTER
04 Exec Secretary to the President .... Ms. Alexis SCHNOOR
05 Provost/Vice President Acad Affairs .... Dr. Doretha O'QUINN
20 Assoc Provost/Dean Col Arts & Sci .... Dr. Michael D. WILSON
58 Interim Dean Professional Studies .... Mr. Dejon DAVIS
73 Director for Graduate Religion .... Dr. Richard ISRAEL
53 Director for Graduate Education .... Dr. Jerry TERNES
83 Director for Graduate Psychology .... Dr. Jerre WHITE
06 Registrar .... Ms. Judy HAMILTON
104 Director Global Outreach/Educ .... Ms. Kayli HILLEBRAND
09 Assoc Dir of Institutional Research .... Mr. John KIM
08 Head Librarian .... Ms. Pamela CRENSHAW
41 Athletic Director .... Mr. Rhett SOLIDAY
10 Chief Financial Officer .... Mr. Jeremy MOSER
21 Controller .... Ms. Jill ROBINSON
21 Asst Dir of Accounting Operations .... Ms. Krystal GOWENS
96 Asst Dir of Fiscal Management .... Ms. Katy MCINTOSH
19 Director of Campus Safety Services .... Mr. Paul TURGEON
13 Chief Information Officer .... Mr. Derek DENSBERGER
15 Director of Human Resources .... Mr. Joe BAFFA
18 Director of Facility Operations .... Mr. Dan TORO
40 Bookstore Manager .... Ms. Stephanie BUNT
101 Board Professional .... Ms. Shree CARTER
42 University Campus Pastor .... Rev. Jonathan ALLBAUGH
32 Vice President of Student Life .... Dr. Tim YOUNG
39 Student Housing Coordinator .... Ms. Nicole GIVENROD
24 Director of Learning Skills .... Ms. Barbi ROUSE
38 Director of Counseling Services .... Dr. Doug HUTCHINSON
36 Career Planning Coordinator .... Ms. Kimberly GREENE
28 Chief Diversity Officer .... Dr. April HARRIS
84 VP for Enrollment Management .... Ms. Kim JOHNSON
07 Director of Undergrad Admissions .... Vacant
07 Dir of Grad/Prof Studies Admissions .... Mr. Matthew NIXON
37 Director of Student Financial Aid .... Vacant
30 VP University Advancement .... Mr. Justin MCINTEE
44 Director of Annual Fund .... Mr. Brent THEOLBALD
29 Director of Alumni Relations .... Mr. Joel GACKLE
26 Chief Communications Officer .... Ms. Linsey CARBONE
86 Director of Veteran/Government Rels .... Mr. Brent THEOBALD
102 Director of External Relations .... Mr. David VAZQUEZ
108 Director Institutional Assessment .... Ms. Ludmilla PRASLOVA

*Ventura County Community College District (C)

255 W Stanley Avenue, Suite 150,
Ventura CA 93001-1348
County: Ventura FICE Identification: 006863
Unit ID: 125019
Telephone: (805) 652-5500 Carnegie Class: N/A
FAX Number: N/A
URL: www.vcccd.edu

01 Chancellor .... Dr. Bernard LUSKIN
05 Vice Chancellor Educ Services .... Mr. Rick POST
10 Vice Chanc Business Svcs/Fin Mgmt .... Mr. David EL FATTAL
15 Vice Chanc of Human Resources .... Mr. Michael SHANAHAN
13 Assoc Vice Chanc of IT .... Mr. Dave FUHRMANN

*Moorpark College (D)

7075 Campus Road, Moorpark CA 93021-1695
County: Ventura FICE Identification: 007115
Unit ID: 119137
Telephone: (805) 378-1400 Carnegie Class: Assoc/HT-High Trad
FAX Number: (805) 378-1499 Calendar System: Semester
URL: www.moorparkcollege.edu
Established: 1967 Annual Undergrad Tuition & Fees (In-State): $1,388
Enrollment: 13,880 Coed
Affiliation or Control: State IRS Status: 501(c)3
Highest Offering: Associate Degree
Accreditation: WJ, ADNUR, RAD

02 President .... Mr. Luis P. SANCHEZ
05 Exec Vice Pres Student Learning .... Vacant
10 Vice President Business Services .... Ms. Silvia BARAJAS
04 Executive Assistant to President .... Ms. Linda RESENDIZ
18 Director Maintainence/Operations .... Mr. John SINUTKO
109 College Business Services Manager .... Ms. Darlene MELBY
06 Registrar .... Mr. David ANTER
37 Student Financial Aid Officer .... Ms. Kim KORINKE

*Oxnard College (E)

4000 S Rose Avenue, Oxnard CA 93033-6699
County: Ventura FICE Identification: 012842
Unit ID: 120421
Telephone: (805) 678-5800 Carnegie Class: Assoc/MT-VT-High Trad
FAX Number: (805) 986-5806 Calendar System: Semester
URL: www.oxnardcollege.edu
Established: 1975 Annual Undergrad Tuition & Fees (In-District): $1,388
Enrollment: 7,148 Coed
Affiliation or Control: State/Local IRS Status: 501(c)3
Highest Offering: Associate Degree
Accreditation: WJ, DH, IFSAC

02 President .... Dr. Cynthia AZARI
05 VP Acad Affairs/Student Learning .... Kenneth SHERWOOD
10 Vice President of Business Services .... Dr. Michael BUSH
32 Vice Pres Student Development .... Dr. Oscar COBIAN
79 Dean Liberal Studies .... Mr. Art SANDFORD
88 Dean Career & Technical Education .... Dr. Christina TAFOYA
81 Dean Math Science/Health .... Dr. Carolyn INOUYE
09 Dean Institutional Effectiveness .... Dr. Cynthia HERRERA
18 Director Maintenance/Operations .... Mr. Bob SUBE
41 Director of Athletics .... Mr. Jonas CRAWFORD
06 Registrar .... Mr. Joel DIAZ
88 Director STEM .... Dr. Eliseo GONZALEZ
37 Financial Aid Officer .... Ms. Linda FAASUA
40 Bookstore Manager .... Mr. Christopher RENBARGER

*Ventura College (F)

4667 Telegraph Road, Ventura CA 93003-3899
County: Ventura FICE Identification: 001334
Unit ID: 125028
Telephone: (805) 289-6000 Carnegie Class: Assoc/HT-High Trad
FAX Number: (805) 289-6466 Calendar System: Semester
URL: www.venturacollege.edu
Established: 1925 Annual Undergrad Tuition & Fees (In-District): $1,388
Enrollment: 12,928 Coed
Affiliation or Control: State/Local IRS Status: 501(c)3
Highest Offering: Associate Degree
Accreditation: WJ, ADNUR, EMT

02 President .... Dr. Greg GILLESPIE
05 VP Academic Affs/Student Learning .... Dr. Kim HOFFMANS
32 Vice Pres Student Affairs .... Dr. Damien A. PENA
10 Vice Pres Business/Admin Services .... Mr. David KEEBLER
04 Exec Assistant to the President .... Ms. Laura BROWER
75 Dean Career & Tech Education .... Dr. Kathleen SCHRADER
88 Dean Institutional Effectiveness .... Mr. Phillip BRIGGS
81 Dean Sciences .... Mr. Dan KUMPF
60 Dean Comm/Kinesiology/Athl/OS Pgm .... Mr. Tim HARRISON
83 Dean Dist Ed/Prof Dev/Soc Sci/Hum .... Ms. Gwen HUDDLESTON
103 Dean Workforce/Economic Development .... Dr. Kathleen SCHRADER
81 Dean Math/Learning Resources .... Ms. Lynn WRIGHT
32 Dean Student Services .... Ms. Victoria LUGO
35 Asst Dean Student Services/Support .... Ms. Karen ENGELSEN
102 Executive Director Foundation .... Mr. Norbert N. TAN
06 Registrar .... Vacant
18 Director Maintenance/Operations .... Mr. Jay MOORE
35 Coordinator Student Activities .... Mr. Rick TREVINO
37 Financial Aid Officer .... Ms. Alma RODRIGUEZ
09 Institutional Research .... Mr. Michael CALLAHAN
85 International Students .... Ms. Rosie STUTTS
84 Enrollment Management .... Ms. Connie BAKER
23 Director Student Health Center .... Ms. Mary JONES
19 Campus Police .... Sgt. Mike PALLOTO

Veritas Evangelical Seminary (G)

3000 W. MacArthur Boulevard, Santa Ana CA 92704
County: Orange Identification: 667103
Telephone: (714) 966-8500 Carnegie Class: Not Classified
FAX Number: (714) 966-8500 Calendar System: Semester
URL: www.ves.edu
Established: 2008 Annual Graduate Tuition & Fees: N/A
Enrollment: N/A Coed
Affiliation or Control: Independent Non-Profit IRS Status: 501(c)3
Highest Offering: Master's; No Undergraduates
Accreditation: TRACS

00 Chancellor .... Norman L. GEISLER
01 President .... Joseph M. HOLDEN
06 Registrar/Dir of Admissions .... Vanessa ACOSTA
05 Chief Academic Officer .... Joel L. WINGO
08 Head Librarian .... Joe MCELROY
10 Chief Business Officer .... Deborah DELARGY
88 Director External Studies .... Scott MATSCHERZ
09 Dir Inst Effectiveness/Assessment .... Frank CORREA
32 Director Student Services .... Deborah DELARGY

Victor Valley College (H)

18422 Bear Valley Road, Victorville CA 92395-5850
County: San Bernardino FICE Identification: 001335
Unit ID: 125091
Telephone: (760) 245-4271 Carnegie Class: Assoc/HT-High Trad
FAX Number: (760) 245-9019 Calendar System: Semester
URL: www.vvc.edu
Established: 1961 Annual Undergrad Tuition & Fees (In-District): $1,114
Enrollment: 11,557 Coed
Affiliation or Control: State/Local IRS Status: 501(c)3
Highest Offering: Associate Degree
Accreditation: WJ, COARC, EMT

01 Superintendent/President .... Dr. Roger W. WAGNER
05 Exec VP Instruction/Stdnt Svcs .... Dr. Peter MAPHUMULO
10 Vice President Admin Services .... Ms. Tracey RICHARDSON
15 Director Human Resources .... Ms. Trinda BEST
76 Dean Health Science & Public Safety .... Mr. Ronald GRAHAM
20 Dean Academic Programs .... Vacant
79 Dean Acad Pgms Humanities/Soc Sci .... Dr. Patricia ELLERSON
21 Director Fiscal Services .... Ms. Karen HARDY
07 Director of Admissions .... Mrs. Greta MOON
26 Director Public Info/Marketing .... Mr. Robert SEWELL
41 Director Athletics/Athletic Trainer .... Mrs. Jaye TASHIMA
18 Exec Dir Facilities/Operations .... Mr. Stephen R. GARCIA
37 Director Financial Aid .... Mr. Jason JUDKINS
13 Director MIS .... Vacant
109 Director Auxiliary Services/ASB Adv .... Ms. Deanna MURPHY
32 Dean Student Services .... Mr. Arthur LOPEZ
18 Director Facilities Construction .... Vacant
19 Chief Campus Police .... Mr. Leonard KNIGHT
13 Chief Information Officer .... Mr. Kevin LEAHY
88 Director Child Development Center .... Mrs. Kelley JOHNSON
88 Dir Extended Optnty Pgms/Svcs/CARE .... Mr. Carl SMITH
09 Exec Dean Inst Effectiveness .... Ms. Virginia MORAN

West Coast Baptist College (I)

4010 E. Lancaster Blvd, Lancaster CA 93535
County: Los Angeles Identification: 667268
Telephone: (661) 946-2274 Carnegie Class: Not Classified
FAX Number: (661) 946-4510 Calendar System: Semester
URL: www.wcbc.edu
Established: 1995 Annual Undergrad Tuition & Fees: N/A
Enrollment: N/A Coed
Affiliation or Control: Baptist IRS Status: 501(c)3
Highest Offering: Master's
Accreditation: @TRACS

01 Founder & President .... Dr. Paul CHAPPELL

West Coast Ultrasound Institute (J)

291 S. La Cienega Blvd, Ste 500, Beverly Hills CA 90211
County: Los Angeles FICE Identification: 036393
Unit ID: 441229
Telephone: (310) 289-5123 Carnegie Class: Spec 2-yr-Health
FAX Number: (310) 289-5136 Calendar System: Quarter
URL: www.wcui.edu
Established: 1998 Annual Undergrad Tuition & Fees: $26,500
Enrollment: 800 Coed
Affiliation or Control: Proprietary IRS Status: Proprietary
Highest Offering: Associate Degree
Accreditation: ACCSC

01 Campus Director .... Ms. Myra CHASON

West Coast Ultrasound Institute (K)

3700 E. Inland Empire Blvd, Ste 235, Ontario CA 91764
Telephone: (310) 280-5123 Identification: 770942
Accreditation: ACCSC

† Main campus is West Coast Ultrasound Institute in Los Angeles, CA.

West Coast University (L)

1477 South Manchester Avenue, Anaheim CA 92802
Telephone: (949) 783-4841 Identification: 770480
Accreditation: &WC, DH

† Regional accreditation is carried under the parent institution in North Hollywood, CA

West Coast University (A)

12215 Victory Boulevard, North Hollywood CA 91606-3206
County: Los Angeles FICE Identification: 036983
Unit ID: 443331
Telephone: (818) 299-5500 Carnegie Class: Spec-4-yr-Other Health
FAX Number: (818) 299-5545 Calendar System: Semester
URL: www.westcoastuniversity.edu
Established: 1909 Annual Undergrad Tuition & Fees: $33,675
Enrollment: 1,659 Coed
Affiliation or Control: Proprietary IRS Status: Proprietary
Highest Offering: Doctorate
Accreditation: WC, NURSE, OT, @PHAR, @PTA

01 President .... Dr. William C. CLOHAN
03 Executive Director .... Mr. Tim GRAMLING
05 Provost .... Dr. Jeb EGBERT
66 Dean of Nursing Los Angeles Campus . Dr. Rosanne SILBERLING
20 Academic Dean .... Dr. Miriam KAHAN
76 Founding Dean Occupational Therapy .... Dr. Nicolaas VAN DEN HEEVER
67 Associate Dean School of Pharmacy .... Dr. Reza TAHERI
07 Director of Admissions .... Ms. Julie CHIN
37 Director of Financial Aid .... Ms. Tracy CABUCO
75 Founding Dean of Physical Therapy .... Dr. Stan HARTGRAVES
81 Chair Science Department .... Dr. Evan PEPPER
32 Director of Student Affairs .... Mr. Anthony STEIN
08 Librarian .... Mr. Greg ULLMAN
06 Registrar .... Ms. Felicia LOCKHART
09 Director of Institutional Research .... Mr. Mahmoud ALBAWANEH

West Coast University (B)

2855 E Guasti Road, Ontario CA 91761
Telephone: (909) 467-6100 Identification: 770484
Accreditation: &WC

† Regional accreditation is carried under the parent institution in North Hollywood, CA

*West Hills Community College District (C)

9900 Cody Street, Coalinga CA 93210
County: Fresno Identification: 667041
Telephone: (559) 934-2180 Carnegie Class: N/A
FAX Number: (559) 934-2810
URL: www.westhillscollege.com

01 Chancellor .... Dr. Frank P. GORNICK
10 Deputy Chancellor .... Mr. Ken STOPPENBRINK
05 VC Educ Svcs/Workforce Development .... Dr. Stuart VAN HORN
90 Assoc VC Enr Mgmt & Inst Eff .... Ms. Rita GROGAN
13 Assoc VC Educ Svcs/Info Technology . Ms. Michelle KOZLOWSKI
21 Assoc VC of Business Services .... Ms. Tammy WEATHERMAN
46 Assoc VC of Connected Learning .... Dr. Kelly COOPER
15 Director of Human Resources .... Ms. Becky CAZARES
102 Exec Director WHCC Foundation .... Ms. Frances SQUIRE
26 Dir of Marketing/Comm/Public Info .... Ms. Amber MYRICK
25 Director of Grants .... Ms. Anita WRIGHT
66 District Director of Health Careers .... Ms. Kathryn DEFEDE
88 Dir of Child Development Centers .... Ms. Conne CLEVELAND
103 Dir of Special Grant Programs .... Mr. David CASTILLO
04 Executive Assistant to Chancellor .... Ms. Donna ISAAC

*West Hills College Coalinga (D)

300 Cherry Lane, Coalinga CA 93210-1399
County: Fresno FICE Identification: 001176
Unit ID: 125462
Telephone: (559) 934-2000 Carnegie Class: Assoc/MT-VT-Mix Trad/Non
FAX Number: N/A Calendar System: Semester
URL: www.westhillscollege.com/coalinga
Established: 1932 Annual Undergrad Tuition & Fees (In-District): $1,380
Enrollment: 2,650 Coed
Affiliation or Control: State/Local IRS Status: 501(c)3
Highest Offering: Associate Degree
Accreditation: WJ

02 President .... Dr. Carole GOLDSMITH
05 Vice President of Educ Services .... Vacant
32 Vice Pres of Student Services .... Ms. Sandy MCGLOTHLIN
35 Assoc Dean of Student Services .... Mr. Mark GRITTON
20 Assoc Dean of Educational Services .... Mr. Robert PIMENTEL
47 Director of Farm of the Future .... Mr. Clint COWDEN
85 Dir of International Student Svcs .... Mr. Daniel TAMAYO
88 Director of Title IV Projects .... Ms. Raquel RODRIGUEZ
88 Director of North District Center .... Ms. Bertha FELIX-MATA
37 Director of Financial Aid .... Ms. Mary MELLO
04 Administrative Asst to President .... Ms. Lorna DAVIS
08 Head Librarian .... Mr. Matthew MAGNUSON
18 Dir of Maintenance & Operations .... Mr. Shaun BAILEY
39 Director of Residential Living .... Mr. Alex VILLALOBOS

*West Hills College Lemoore (E)

555 College Avenue, Lemoore CA 93245-9248
County: Kings FICE Identification: 041113
Unit ID: 448594
Telephone: (559) 925-3000 Carnegie Class: Assoc/HT-High Trad
FAX Number: (559) 924-1243 Calendar System: Semester
URL: www.westhillscollege.com/lemoore
Established: 2002 Annual Undergrad Tuition & Fees (In-District): $1,380
Enrollment: 3,976 Coed
Affiliation or Control: State/Local IRS Status: 501(c)3
Highest Offering: Associate Degree
Accreditation: WJ

02 President .... Dr. Kristin CLARK
05 Vice President of Educational Svcs .... Mr. Dave BOLT
32 Vice President of Student Services .... Ms. Sylvia DORSEY-ROBINSON
20 Dean of Educational Svcs .... Mr. James PRESTON
35 Dean of Student Services .... Mr. Joel RUBLE
88 Director of Upward Bound .... Mr. Oscar VILLARREAL
37 Director of Financial Aid .... Ms. Deborah SORIA
88 Assoc Dean of Categorical Programs .... Ms. Lataria HALL
04 Administrative Asst to President .... Ms. Amber AVITIA
08 Head Librarian .... Mr. Ron OXFORD
18 Dir of Maintenance & Operations .... Vacant
41 Associate Dean of Athletics .... Vacant

---

*West Valley-Mission Community College District (F)

14000 Fruitvale Avenue, Saratoga CA 95070-5698
County: Santa Clara FICE Identification: 029139
Unit ID: 125222
Telephone: (408) 741-2011 Carnegie Class: N/A
FAX Number: (408) 867-8273
URL: www.wvm.edu

01 Chancellor .... Dr. Patrick SCHMITT
11 Vice Chancellor Admin Services .... Mr. Ed MADULI
15 Vice Chanc Human Resources .... Mr. Albert MOORE
30 Dean Advancement .... Ms. Cynthia SCHELCHER
13 Director Information Systems .... Mr. Ron SMITH
18 Director of Facilities .... Mr. Javier CASTRUITA
19 Chief of Police .... Mr. Kenneth TANAKA

*Mission College (G)

3000 Mission College Boulevard, Santa Clara CA 95054-1897
County: Santa Clara FICE Identification: 021191
Unit ID: 118930
Telephone: (408) 988-2200 Carnegie Class: Assoc/HT-High Non
FAX Number: (408) 496-0462 Calendar System: Semester
URL: www.missioncollege.org
Established: 1976 Annual Undergrad Tuition & Fees (In-District): $1,174
Enrollment: 8,435 Coed
Affiliation or Control: State/Local IRS Status: 501(c)3
Highest Offering: Associate Degree
Accreditation: WJ

02 President .... Mr. Daniel A. PECK
05 Vice Pres of Instruction .... Dr. Leandra MARTIN
32 Vice President Student Services .... Dr. John MOSBY
11 Vice Pres Administrative Services .... Mr. Rick BENNETT
35 Dean of Student Support Services .... Mr. Daniel SANIDAD
20 Dean of Instruction .... Mr. Danny NGUYEN
26 Dir of Public Info & Graphic Design .... Vacant
20 Director of Marketing .... Mr. Niall ADLER
81 Dean Applied Science .... Ms. Mina JAHAN
19 Chief of Police .... Lt. Kenneth TANAKA
18 Manager of Facilities .... Mr. Don HOUSTON
07 Director of Admissions .... Mr. Asmare TADESSE
09 Director of Institutional Research .... Ms. Inge BOND
37 Dir Student Enroll & Financial Aid .... Ms. Rita GROGAN
04 Exec Assistant to the President .... Ms. Milani ZEPEDA
88 Language Arts Division .... Ms. Kathy HENDERSON
60 Communications Dept .... Mr. Rob DEWIS
81 Mathematics and Science Division .... Mr. Rick HOBBS
83 Liberal Studies Division .... Mr. Keith JOHNSON
35 Student Services Division .... Ms. Thuy TRANG

*West Valley College (H)

14000 Fruitvale Avenue, Saratoga CA 95070-5698
County: Santa Clara FICE Identification: 001338
Unit ID: 125499
Telephone: (408) 867-2200 Carnegie Class: Assoc/HT-High Non
FAX Number: (408) 867-5033 Calendar System: Semester
URL: www.westvalley.edu
Established: 1963 Annual Undergrad Tuition & Fees (In-District): $1,186
Enrollment: 9,062 Coed
Affiliation or Control: State/Local IRS Status: 501(c)3
Highest Offering: Associate Degree
Accreditation: WJ

02 President .... Mr. Bradley DAVIS
05 VP Instruction .... Ms. Kuni HAY
32 VP Student Services .... Dr. Victoria HINDES
11 VP Administrative Services .... Mr. Patrick FENTON
20 Dean Instruction .... Ms. Stephanie KASHIMA
30 Dean Advancement .... Ms. Cindy SCHELCHER
36 Dean Career Pgm/Wrkforce Dev .... Mr. Bradley WEISBERG
26 Director Marketing/Communications .... Mr. Scott LUDWIG
35 Dean of Student Services .... Dr. Matais POUNCIL
100 Associate Vice Chancellor .... Mr. Albert MOORE
57 Dean School of Art & Design .... Mr. Andrew CHANDLER
88 Director Student Equity & Success .... Ms. Herlisa HAMP
18 Chief Facilities/Physical Plant .... Mr. Bill TAYLOR
37 Dir Student Financial Aid/Admiss .... Ms. Maritza CANTARERO
09 Research Analyst .... Mr. Miqueas DIAL
35 Director Student Development .... Dr. Sean PEPIN
29 Director Alumni Relations .... Ms. Cindy SCHELCHER
106 Coord Instruct Tech/Distance Lrng .... Ms. Lisa KAAZ
04 Sr Executive Assistant to the Presi .... Ms. Gloria GUTIERREZ
41 Athletic Director .... Mr. John VLAHOS

Westcliff University (I)

4199 Campus Drive #650, Irvine CA 92612
County: Orange Identification: 667203
Telephone: (888) 491-8686 Carnegie Class: Not Classified
FAX Number: (888) 409-7306 Calendar System: Trimester
URL: www.westcliff.edu
Established: 1993 Annual Undergrad Tuition & Fees: N/A
Enrollment: N/A Coed
Affiliation or Control: Proprietary IRS Status: Proprietary
Highest Offering: Master's
Accreditation: DEAC

01 CEO/President .... Dr. Anthony LEE
05 Provost/CAO .... Dr. David C. MCKINNEY
10 Chief Financial Officer .... Mr. Sean MURRAY

Western State University College of Law (J)

1 Banting, Irvine CA 92618-3601
Telephone: (714) 459-1101 FICE Identification: 010832
Accreditation: &WC, LAW

† Regional accreditation is carried under the parent institution, Argosy University in Orange, CA.

Western University of Health Sciences (K)

309 E 2nd Street, Pomona CA 91766-1854
County: Los Angeles FICE Identification: 024827
Unit ID: 112525
Telephone: (909) 623-6116 Carnegie Class: Spec-4-yr-Med
FAX Number: N/A Calendar System: Semester
URL: www.westernu.edu
Established: 1977 Annual Graduate Tuition & Fees: N/A
Enrollment: 3,842 Coed
Affiliation or Control: Independent Non-Profit IRS Status: 501(c)3
Highest Offering: Doctorate; No Undergraduates
Accreditation: WC, ARCPA, DENT, NURSE, OPT, OSTEO, PHAR, POD, PTA, VET

01 President .... Dr. Daniel R. WILSON
05 Provost/COO .... Dr. Gary GUGELCHUK
10 Treasurer/Chief Financial Officer .... Mr. Kevin SHAW
46 Exec Vice Provost for Academic Dev .... Dr. Elizabeth REGA
03 Senior Vice President .... Dr. Thomas FOX
20 Vice Provost .... Dr. Sheree ASTON
32 Vice Pres Student Affs/Enroll Mgt .... Dr. Beverly SANKS GUIDRY
25 Asst VP Spnsrd Pgms/Contract Mgt .... Mr. Matthew KATZ
84 Asst VP Enroll Mgmt/Registrar .... Ms. Kimberly DEKRUIF
15 Executive Director Human Resources .... Ms. Linda EMILIO
18 Exec Dir Facilities/Physical Plant .... Mr. Todd CLARK
07 Director Admiss COP/CGN .... Ms. Kathy FORD
07 Director Admissions COMP/MSHS .... Ms. Susan HANSON
07 Director Admissions CO/CPM/CDM .... Ms. Marie ANDERSON
07 Director Admissions CVM/PT/PA .... Ms. Karen HUTTON-LOPEZ
11 Chief Administrative Officer .... Mr. Steve JASPERSON
08 Director of University Library .... Ms. Patricia VADER
37 Director Financial Aid .... Mr. Otto REYER
88 Dir Ctr Disability Issues/Hlth Prof .... Ms. Brenda PREMO
13 Exec Director Information Tech .... Ms. Denise WILCOX
96 Director of Procurement Services .... Mr. Michael BUTLER
26 Exec Director of Public Affs/Mrktg .... Mr. Jeff KEATING
88 Dir Learning Enhancement/Acad Devel .... Ms. Dagmar COFER
09 Director of Institutional Research .... Dr. Juan RAMIREZ
40 Bookstore Director .... Ms. Elizabeth GUERRA
52 Dean College of Dental Medicine .. Dr. Steven W. FRIEDRICHSEN
67 Dean College of Pharmacy .... Dr. Daniel C. ROBINSON
88 Founding Dean College of Optometry .... Dr. Elizabeth HOPPE
88 Founding Dean College of Podiatry .... Dr. Lawrence HARKLESS
76 Dean College Allied Health Profess .... Dr. Stephanie BOWLIN
66 Int Dean Col of Graduate Nursing .... Dr. Mary LOPEZ
58 Dean Grad Col Biomedical Sciences .... Dr. Michel BAUDRY
74 Dean College of Veterinary Medicine .... Dr. Phil NELSON
63 Chr Dept Osteopath Manipulative Med .... Dr. Michael SEFFINGER
88 Chair Dept of Physical Therapy .... Dr. Denise SCHILLING
76 Chair Dept of Health Sciences .... Dr. Tina MEYER
88 Chair Physician Assistant Program .... Mr. Roy GUIZADO
63 Chair Department Family Medicine .... Dr. Alan CUNDARI
06 Registrar .... Ms. Kimberly DEKRUIF
19 Director Security/Safety .... Ms. Brett BOSTON
29 Director Alumni Relations .... Mr. Russel HESKIN

Westminster Theological Seminary in California (L)

1725 Bear Valley Parkway, Escondido CA 92027-4128
County: San Diego FICE Identification: 022768
Unit ID: 125718
Telephone: (760) 480-8474 Carnegie Class: Spec-4-yr-Faith
FAX Number: (760) 480-0252 Calendar System: Semester
URL: www.wscal.edu
Established: 1979 Annual Graduate Tuition & Fees: N/A
Enrollment: 149 Coed
Affiliation or Control: Independent Non-Profit IRS Status: 501(c)3

Highest Offering: Master's; No Undergraduates
Accreditation: WC, THEOL

01 President ... Dr. W. Robert GODFREY
11 Vice President for Administration ... Dr. Marcus MCARTHUR
05 Academic Dean ... Dr. John FESKO
30 Vice President for Advancement ... Ms. Dawn DOORN
84 VP for Enrollment Management ... Mr. Mark MACVEY
10 Chief Financial Officer ... Ms. Phyllis PIZZUTO
32 Dean of Students ... Dr. Julius KIM
08 Library Director ... Mr. James LUND
06 Registrar ... Mr. Danny MARRIOTT

Westmont College (A)

955 La Paz Road, Santa Barbara CA 93108-1089
County: Santa Barbara FICE Identification: 001341
Unit ID: 125727
Telephone: (805) 565-6000 Carnegie Class: Bac-A&S
FAX Number: (805) 565-7006 Calendar System: Semester
URL: www.westmont.edu
Established: 1937 Annual Undergrad Tuition & Fees: $41,360
Enrollment: 1,300 Coed
Affiliation or Control: Independent Non-Profit IRS Status: 501(c)3
Highest Offering: Baccalaureate
Accreditation: WC, MUS

01 President ... Dr. Gayle D. BEEBE
05 Provost/Dean of Faculty ... Dr. Mark L. SARGENT
10 Vice President Finance ... Mr. Douglas W. JONES
11 Vice President for Administration ... Mr. Christopher D. CALL
32 VP Student Life/Dean of Students ... Mrs. Edee SCHULZE
30 Vice President for Advancement ... Dr. Reed L. SHEARD
88 Vice President External Relations ... Mr. Cliff LUNDBERG
13 VP Information Technology & CIO ... Dr. Reed SHEARD
07 Dean of Admissions ... Mr. Silvio VAZQUEZ
35 Associate Dean of Students ... Mr. Timothy B. WILSON
88 Assoc Dean of Students for Res Life ... Mr. Stu CLEEK
06 Registrar ... Mrs. Michelle M. HARDLEY
08 Director Library/Information Svcs ... Mrs. Debra QUAST
09 Assoc Provost/Dir of Inst Research ... Dr. William A. WRIGHT
15 Director of Human Resources ... Ms. Beth CAUWELS
18 Director of Physical Plant ... Mr. Thomas BEVERIDGE
21 Controller ... Mr. Paul V. LARSON
23 Director of Student Health Services ... Dr. David HERNANDEZ
19 Public Safety Director ... Mr. Thomas G. BAUER
26 Director of Public Events ... Ms. Joan M. WIMBERLY
29 Exec Director Alumni & Parent Rels ... Mrs. Teri BRADFORD ROUSE
36 Director of Career/Development ... Mr. Paul BRADFORD
44 Senior Director of Gift Planning ... Mrs. Kati BUEHLER
88 Director of Campus Life ... Ms. Angela L. D'AMOUR
88 Director of Internships/Practica ... Mrs. Jennifer TAYLOR
37 Director of Financial Aid ... Mr. Sean SMITH
38 Director Counseling Services ... Mr. Eric NELSON
39 Director of Housing/Parking ... Mr. David W. KING
40 Asst Director Bookstore ... Mrs. Joanne GISH
41 Athletic Director ... Mr. David ODELL
42 Campus Pastor ... Rev. Ben PATTERSON
45 Director of Campus Planning ... Mr. Randy JONES
96 Assc Dir Procurement/Auxiliary Svcs ... Mr. Bill GROENEVELD
28 Director of Intercultural Programs ... Mr. Jason CHA
43 College Counsel ... Ms. Toya COOPER
20 Associate Academic Officer ... Dr. Tatiana NAZARENKO
24 Coord Media Services/Asst Librarian ... Ms. Mary LOGUE

Whittier College (B)

13406 E Philadelphia St, PO Box 634,
Whittier CA 90608-4413
County: Los Angeles FICE Identification: 001342
Unit ID: 125763
Telephone: (562) 907-4200 Carnegie Class: Bac-A&S
FAX Number: (562) 907-4242 Calendar System: 4/1/4
URL: www.whittier.edu
Established: 1887 Annual Undergrad Tuition & Fees: $43,280
Enrollment: 2,259 Coed
Affiliation or Control: Independent Non-Profit IRS Status: 501(c)3
Highest Offering: Doctorate
Accreditation: WC, LAW, SW

01 President ... Dr. Sharon D. HERZBERGER
10 Vice Pres Finance & Administration ... Mr. James DUNKELMAN
05 VP Academic Affs/Dean of Faculty ... Dr. Darrin GOOD
61 Dean of Whittier Law School ... Ms. Judith DAAR
30 VP for Advancement ... Mr. Steve DELGADO
84 Vice President Dean of Enrollment ... Mr. Kieron MILLER
32 Dean of Students ... Dr. Joel JOEL PEREZ
37 Director of Student Financial Aid ... Mr. David CARNEVALE
08 Library Director ... Mrs. Laurel CRUMP
20 Dir Whtr Scholar Pgm/Assc Acad Dean ... Ms. Doreen O'CONNOR-GOMEZ
26 Dir Public Relations/Communications ... Ms. Ana Lilia BARRAZA
13 Director of Computing Services ... Mr. Troy GREENUP
09 Dir of Institutional Research ... Mr. Gary WHISENAND
41 Director of Athletics ... Mr. Rob COLEMAN
53 Dir Lib Educ Pgm/Assoc Acad Dean ... Dr. Fritz SMITH
15 Director of Human Resources ... Ms. Cynthia JOSEPH
19 Director of Campus Safety ... Mr. Jose PADILLA

William Jessup University (C)

2121 University Avenue, Rocklin CA 95765-3707
County: Placer FICE Identification: 001281
Unit ID: 122728
Telephone: (916) 577-2200 Carnegie Class: Bac-Diverse
FAX Number: (916) 577-2203 Calendar System: Semester
URL: www.jessup.edu
Established: 1939 Annual Undergrad Tuition & Fees: $26,480
Enrollment: 1,212 Coed
Affiliation or Control: Independent Non-Profit IRS Status: 501(c)3
Highest Offering: Master's
Accreditation: WC, BI

01 President ... Dr. John JACKSON
05 Provost/Chief Academic Officer ... Dr. Dennis JAMESON
84 Vice Provost Enrollment Mgmt ... Dr. Todd ERICKSON
10 Chief Financial Officer ... Mr. David PUNT
30 Chief Development Officer ... Mr. Eric HOGUE
13 Chief Information Officer ... Mrs. Judy RENTZ
88 Accreditation Liaison Officer ... Dr. Kay LLOVIO
107 School of Professional Studies Dir ... Ms. Nancy THOMPSON
15 Director of Human Resources ... Vacant
21 Controller ... Ms. Diane KIM
08 University Librarian ... Mr. Kevin PISCHKE
88 Director of Church Relations ... Mr. Jim JESSUP
32 Dean of Students ... Mr. Jonathan SAMPSON
06 Registrar ... Mrs. Tina PETERSEN
07 Director of Admission ... Mr. Steve JIN
09 Institutional Research Director ... Mrs. Karen LAMBRECHTSEN
42 Campus Pastor ... Mr. Ryan HAYNES
41 Athletic Director ... Mr. Lance VON VOGT
18 Facilities Director ... Vacant
35 Chief Student Life Officer ... Dr. Kay LLOVIO
12 Academic Director Bay Area Center ... Dr. Daniel ALBRECHT
04 Executive Asst to President ... Ms. Janice NEWMAN
19 Director Security/Safety ... Mr. Dean CROSS
36 Director Student Placement ... Ms. Christy JEWELL
106 Dir Online Education/E-learning ... Ms. Sandra WOODSON
37 Director Student Financial Aid ... Mr. John SWAN

Woodbury University (D)

7500 North Glenoaks Boulevard, Burbank CA 91504-7520
County: Los Angeles FICE Identification: 001343
Unit ID: 125897
Telephone: (818) 767-0888 Carnegie Class: Masters/M
FAX Number: (818) 767-3470 Calendar System: Semester
URL: www.woodbury.edu
Established: 1884 Annual Undergrad Tuition & Fees: $36,408
Enrollment: 1,588 Coed
Affiliation or Control: Independent Non-Profit IRS Status: 501(c)3
Highest Offering: Master's
Accreditation: WC, ACBSP, ART, BUS, CIDA

01 President ... David M. STEELE-FIGUEREDO
101 Secretary of the Institution/Board ... Seta JAVOR
05 Interim Senior Vice President ... Randy STAUFFER
10 VP Administration & Human Resources ... Natalie AVALOS
84 VP Enrollment Management ... Michael TRUSCHKE
30 VP University Relations ... Vacant
13 VP Information Technology ... Eric WANG
32 Vice Pres Student Development ... Phyllis A. CREMER
35 Dean of Student Success ... Rebecca DEVEREAUX
50 Dean School of Business ... Vacant
48 Interim Dean School of Architecture ... Ingalill WAHLROOS-RITTER
06 Assistant Registrar ... Tamara L. BLOK
07 Director of Enrollment Services ... Celeastia WILLIAMS
20 Dean of Faculty ... Will MCCONNELL
88 Dean Institute of Transdisciplinary ... Douglas CREMER
09 Director of Institutional Research ... Christie RAINEY
29 Director of University Relations ... Michael SEYMOUR

World Mission University (E)

500 Shatto Place, Suite 600, Los Angeles CA 90020-1789
County: Los Angeles FICE Identification: 038683
Unit ID: 401223
Telephone: (213) 385-2322 Carnegie Class: Spec-4-yr-Faith
FAX Number: (213) 385-2332 Calendar System: Semester
URL: www.wmu.edu
Established: 1989 Annual Undergrad Tuition & Fees: $5,380
Enrollment: 282 Coed
Affiliation or Control: Independent Non-Profit IRS Status: 501(c)3
Highest Offering: First Professional Degree
Accreditation: BI, THEOL, TRACS

01 President ... Dr. John M. SONG
05 Exec Vice Pres/Chief Acad Officer ... Dr. Sung Jin LIM
32 Dean of Student Svcs/Financial Aid ... Mrs. Kristin KIM
30 Director of Development ... Ms. Keum Hee LEE
10 Director of Business ... Mr. Paul LIM
06 Registrar ... Mrs. Jin Joo NAM

The Wright Institute (F)

2728 Durant Avenue, Berkeley CA 94704-1796
County: Alameda FICE Identification: 008846
Unit ID: 126012
Telephone: (510) 841-9230 Carnegie Class: Spec-4-yr-Other Health
FAX Number: (510) 841-0167 Calendar System: Trimester
URL: www.wi.edu
Established: 1969 Annual Graduate Tuition & Fees: N/A
Enrollment: 445 Coed
Affiliation or Control: Independent Non-Profit IRS Status: 501(c)3
Highest Offering: Doctorate; No Undergraduates
Accreditation: WC, CLPSY

01 President ... Mr. Peter DYBWAD
05 Dean ... Dr. Gilbert NEWMAN
10 VP of Finance & Administrative Affs ... Ms. Tricia O'REILLY
32 Dean of Students/Registrar ... Ms. Ginny MORGAN
07 Dir of Admissions/Student Services ... Mr. John PITTS
08 Library Director ... Mr. Jason STRAUSS
37 Director of Financial Aid ... Ms. Julia KALYAYEVA

Yeshiva Ohr Elchonon Chabad/ West Coast Talmudical Seminary (G)

7215 Waring Avenue, Los Angeles CA 90046-7660
County: Los Angeles FICE Identification: 022624
Unit ID: 126076
Telephone: (323) 937-3763 Carnegie Class: Spec-4-yr-Faith
FAX Number: (323) 937-9456 Calendar System: Semester
URL: www.yoec.edu
Established: 1953 Annual Undergrad Tuition & Fees: $13,900
Enrollment: 163 Male
Affiliation or Control: Independent Non-Profit IRS Status: 501(c)3
Highest Offering: Baccalaureate
Accreditation: RABN

01 Chief Executive Officer ... Rabbi Ezra B. SCHOCHET
03 Executive Vice President ... Rabbi Mendel SPALTER
05 Curriculum Suprv/Education Counsel ... Rabbi Shimon RAICHIK
37 Director Student Financial Aid ... Mrs. Hendy TAUBER
06 Registrar ... Rabbi Chaim CITRON
38 Director Student Counseling ... Rabbi Mendel SCHAPIRO
08 Head Librarian ... Rabbi Ben Zion OSTER

Yo San University of Traditional Chinese Medicine (H)

13315 W Washington Boulevard, Los Angeles CA 90066
County: Los Angeles FICE Identification: 030982
Unit ID: 401250
Telephone: (310) 577-3000 Carnegie Class: Spec-4-yr-Other Health
FAX Number: (310) 577-3033 Calendar System: Trimester
URL: www.yosan.edu
Established: 1989 Annual Undergrad Tuition & Fees: N/A
Enrollment: 219 Coed
Affiliation or Control: Independent Non-Profit IRS Status: 501(c)3
Highest Offering: Doctorate; No Lower Division
Accreditation: ACUP

01 President/CEO ... Lois GREEN
05 Vice Pres Acad & Clinical Educ/CAO ... Lawrence LAU
06 Director Operations & Registrar ... Tora FLINT
10 Chief Finance Officer/VP Finance ... Tracy WANG
11 VP Advancement/Student Affs/COO ... Scott SIVLEY
63 Dean Clinical Education ... Brian LEE
84 Director of Enrollment Management ... Lisa GRIDLEY
37 Financial Aid ... Ed MERVINE
21 Controller/Bursar ... Mariani MAY
88 Interim Dean Doctoral Program ... Laraine CRAMPTON

*Yosemite Community College District (I)

PO Box 4065, Modesto CA 95352-4065
County: Stanislaus FICE Identification: 009146
Unit ID: 126100
Telephone: (209) 575-6509 Carnegie Class: N/A
FAX Number: (209) 575-6565
URL: www.yosemite.edu

01 Chancellor ... Dr. Joan E. SMITH
10 Exec Vice Chancellor Fiscal Service ... Ms. Teresa M. SCOTT
15 Vice Chancellor Human Resources ... Ms. Gina LEGURIA
13 Assistant Vice Chancellor Info Tech ... Mr. Martin (Marty) GANG

*Columbia College (J)

11600 Columbia College Drive, Sonora CA 95370-8580
County: Tuolumne FICE Identification: 007707
Unit ID: 112561
Telephone: (209) 588-5100 Carnegie Class: Assoc/MT-VT-Mix Trad/Non
FAX Number: (209) 588-5104 Calendar System: Semester
URL: www.gocolumbia.edu
Established: 1968 Annual Undergrad Tuition & Fees (In-District): $1,162
Enrollment: 2,397 Coed
Affiliation or Control: State/Local IRS Status: 501(c)3
Highest Offering: Associate Degree
Accreditation: WJ, ACFEI

02 President ... Dr. Angela FAIRCHILDS
05 Vice Pres Instruction ... Dr. Brian SANDERS
11 VP College & Administrative Svcs ... Vacant
20 Dean Instruct Svcs/Career Tech Edu ... Dr. Klaus TENBERGEN
49 Dean of Instruction/Arts & Sciences ... Dr. Joseph RYAN
24 Director of Info Tech & Media Svcs ... Mrs. Margo GUZMAN
41 Athletic Director ... Mr. Nate RIEN
37 Financial Aid Manager ... Ms. Marnie SHIVELY

26 Public Information Officer .... Vacant
31 Director Community Services .... Vacant
30 Director of Development .... Ms. Amy NILSON
09 Dir of Institutional Rsrch & Plng .... Ms. Diana SUNDAY
40 Bookstore Manager .... Mr. Jeff WHALEN
18 Manager Facilities/Operations .... Mr. Dave KEENER

*Modesto Junior College (A)

435 College Avenue, Modesto CA 95350-9977
County: Stanislaus FICE Identification: 001240
Unit ID: 118976
Telephone: (209) 575-6498 Carnegie Class: Assoc/MT-VT-High Trad
FAX Number: (209) 575-6630 Calendar System: Semester
URL: www.mjc.edu
Established: 1921 Annual Undergrad Tuition & Fees (In-District): $1,162
Enrollment: 17,578 Coed
Affiliation or Control: State/Local IRS Status: 501(c)3
Highest Offering: Baccalaureate
Accreditation: WJ, COARC, MAC

02 President .... Dr. Jill STEARNS
05 Vice President for Instruction .... Ms. Brenda THAMES
32 Vice Pres for Student Services .... Dr. James TODD
11 VP College & Administrative Svcs .... Dr. Albert ALT
57 Div Dean Arts/Humanites/Comm .... Mr. Mike SUNDQUIST
83 Div Dean Business/Behav/Social Sci .... Dr. Jennifer HAMILTON
76 Div Dean Inst/All Hlth/Fam/Con Sci .. Mr. Patrick BETTENCOURT
79 Div Dean Literature/Language Arts .... Ms. Jillian DALY
54 Div Dean Science/Math/Engineering .... Dr. Brian SANDERS
47 Dean Agri/Envir Science/Tech Ed .... Dr. Donald BORGES
88 Dean Public Safety/Tech Ed/Cmty Ed .... Mr. Pedro MENDEZ
25 Int Dir Planning/Grants Development .... Ms. Jenni ABBOTT
09 Director of Institutional Research .... Vacant
37 Director Student Financial Aid .... Ms. Peggy FIKSE
26 Marketing/Public Information Ofcr .... Ms. Linda HOILE

*Yuba Community College District (B)

2088 North Beale Road, Marysville CA 95901
County: Yuba Identification: 666478
Unit ID: 126119
Telephone: (530) 741-6700 Carnegie Class: N/A
FAX Number: (530) 634-7704
URL: www.yccd.edu

01 Chancellor .... Dr. Douglas B. HOUSTON
05 VC Educ Planning & Services .... Vacant
13 Chief Technology Officer .... Mr. Roger CLAGUE
102 Grants/Research/Development Officer .... Ms. Tonya MACK
15 Chief Human Resources Officer .... Mr. Jacques WHITFIELD
10 Chief Business Officer .... Mrs. Kuldeep KAUR

*Woodland Community College (C)

2300 East Gibson Road, Woodland CA 95776-5156
County: Yolo FICE Identification: 041438
Unit ID: 455512
Telephone: (530) 661-5700 Carnegie Class: Assoc/HT-High Trad
FAX Number: (530) 666-9028 Calendar System: Semester
URL: www.yccd.edu/woodland/
Established: 2008 Annual Undergrad Tuition & Fees (In-District): $1,144
Enrollment: 2,554 Coed
Affiliation or Control: State/Local IRS Status: 501(c)3
Highest Offering: Associate Degree
Accreditation: WJ

02 President .... Dr. Michael WHITE
05 Vice Pres Academic/Student Svcs .... Dr. Alfred B. KONUWA
04 Administrative Asst to President .... Ms. Ana L. VILLAGRANA

*Yuba College (D)

2088 N Beale Road, Marysville CA 95901-7699
County: Yuba FICE Identification: 001344
Unit ID: 126119
Telephone: (530) 741-6700 Carnegie Class: Not Classified
FAX Number: (530) 741-3541 Calendar System: Semester
URL: https://yc.yccd.edu/
Established: 1927 Annual Undergrad Tuition & Fees (In-District): N/A
Enrollment: N/A Coed
Affiliation or Control: State/Local IRS Status: 501(c)3
Highest Offering: Associate Degree
Accreditation: WJ, #RAD

02 President .... Dr. G. H JAVAHERIPOUR
10 Chief Business Officer .... Ms. Kuldeep KAUR
05 VP Academic/Student Services .... Dr. Sonja LOLLARD
06 Registrar .... Ms. Sonya HORN
32 Dean Student Services .... Dr. Delmy SPENCER
88 Interim Director TRIO Programs .... Mr. Julio DELGADO
50 Dean Applied Academics .... Dr. Daren OTTEN
88 Int Dir Child Dev Ctr/Foster Care .... Ms. Karen STANIS
66 Int Director Nursing/Allied Health .... Dr. Clark SMITH
18 Chief Facilities/Physical Plant .... Mr. David WILLIS
19 Director Public Safety .... Mr. Pete VILLARREAL
79 Dean of Humanities & Education .... Vacant
07 Dir Admissions/Records/Fin Aid .... Mr. Martin GUTIERREZ
15 Chief Human Resources Officer .... Dr. Jacques WHITFIELD
68 Director Athletics/Health/PE .... Mr. Erick BURNS
81 Dean STEM & Counseling Centers .... Dr. Karsten STEMMANN
88 Director Academic Excellence .... Ms. Kristina VANNUCCI

Zaytuna College (E)

2401 Le Conte Avenue, Berkeley CA 94709
County: Alameda Identification: 667230
Telephone: (510) 356-4760 Carnegie Class: Not Classified
FAX Number: (510) 327-2688 Calendar System: Semester
URL: www.zaytuna.edu
Established: 2009 Annual Undergrad Tuition & Fees: N/A
Enrollment: N/A Coed
Affiliation or Control: Independent Non-Profit IRS Status: 501(c)3
Highest Offering: Baccalaureate
Accreditation: WC

01 President .... Hamza YUSUF
05 Dean of Faculty .... Dr. Mark Damien DELP
10 Vice Pres Finance & Admin Services .... Waheed RASHEED
108 Dir of Assessment & Accreditation .... Sumaira AKHATAR

COLORADO

Academy of Natural Therapy (F)

625 8th Avenue, Greeley CO 80631
County: Weld FICE Identification: 040933
Unit ID: 449454
Telephone: (970) 352-1181 Carnegie Class: Spec 2-yr-Health
FAX Number: (970) 352-1906 Calendar System: Quarter
URL: www.natural-therapy.com
Established: 1989 Annual Undergrad Tuition & Fees: N/A
Enrollment: 54 Coed
Affiliation or Control: Proprietary IRS Status: Proprietary
Highest Offering: Associate Degree
Accreditation: COMTA

01 President .... Mr. Jeremiah James MONGAN

Adams State University (G)

208 Edgemont Boulevard, Alamosa CO 81101-2320
County: Alamosa FICE Identification: 001345
Unit ID: 126182
Telephone: (719) 587-7011 Carnegie Class: Masters/L
FAX Number: (719) 587-7522 Calendar System: Semester
URL: www.adams.edu
Established: 1921 Annual Undergrad Tuition & Fees (In-State): $8,574
Enrollment: 3,154 Coed
Affiliation or Control: State IRS Status: 501(c)3
Highest Offering: Doctorate
Accreditation: #NH, CACREP, MUS, NURSE

01 President .... Dr. Beverlee J. MCCLURE
05 Vice President for Academic Affairs .... Dr. Chris GILMER
10 VP for Administration and Finance .... Mr. Kurt CARY
84 Dir of Marketing & Enrollment Mgmt .... Ms. Karla HARDESTY
30 VP Institutional Advancement .... Vacant
18 Director of Facilities Services .... Mr. Scott TRAVIS
56 Asst VP Extended Campus - Academics .... Mr. Walter ROYBAL
21 Asst VP for Admin & Finance .... Ms. Heather HEERSINK
20 Asst VP for Academic Affairs .... Ms. Margaret DOELL
32 VP for Student Services .... Mr. Kenneth L. MARQUEZ
09 Senior Research Analyst .... Mr. Victor SOE
08 Director Library .... Ms. Carol SMITH
37 Director Student Financial Aid .... Mr. Philip SCHROEDER
35 Asst VP for Student Services .... Mr. Eric CARPIO
06 Registrar .... Ms. Belen MAESTAS
31 Exec Dir Community Partnerships .... Ms. Mary HOFFMAN
13 Chief Information Officer .... Mr. Kevin S. DANIEL
41 Athletic Director .... Mr. Larry MORTENSEN
26 Asst to President Communications .... Ms. Julie WAECHTER
109 Director of Auxiliary Services .... Mr. Bruce DEL TONDO
38 Director Counseling/Career Services .... Ms. Elisabeth TOMLIN
15 Director Human Resources .... Ms. Tracy ROGERS
102 Executive Director ASU Foundation .... Ms. Tammy L. LOPEZ
29 Director Alumni and Donor Relations .... Ms. Lori L. LASKE
96 Director of Purchasing .... Ms. Renee VIGIL
19 Dir Adams State Univ Police Dept .... Mr. Paul GROHOWSKI
40 Director Bookstore .... Mr. Darrell MEIS
27 Director of Creative Relations .... Mr. Mark SCHOENECKER
57 Chair English/Theatre/Communication .. Dr. David MACWILLIAMS
50 Chair Business & Economics .... Dr. Patrica ROBBINS
53 Chair Education .... Dr. Edward CROWTHER
77 Chair Chemistry/Computer Sci/Math .... Dr. Christina MILLER
81 Chair Biology/Earth Science .... Dr. Benita BRINK

Aims Community College (H)

Box 69, Greeley CO 80632-0069
County: Weld FICE Identification: 007582
Unit ID: 126207
Telephone: (970) 330-8008 Carnegie Class: Assoc/HVT-Mix Trad/Non
FAX Number: N/A Calendar System: Semester
URL: www.aims.edu
Established: 1967 Annual Undergrad Tuition & Fees (In-District): $1,835
Enrollment: 5,001 Coed
Affiliation or Control: Local IRS Status: 501(c)3
Highest Offering: Associate Degree
Accreditation: NH, ADNUR, EMT, IFSAC, SURGT

01 President .... Dr. Leah L. BORNSTEIN
10 Vie President Admin Services .... Mr. Bob COX
05 Vice President Academic Affairs .... Ms. Deborah KISH
20 Academic Dean .... Mr. Jeff SMITH
20 Academic Dean .... Mr. Robert ABERNATHY
32 Vice President Student Affairs .... Dr. Patricia MATIJEVIC
88 Vice President CCR .... Dr. Geri ANDERSON
35 Dean of Students .... Ms. Shannon MCCASLAND
30 Executive Director Foundation .... Ms. Julie BUDERUS
07 Exec Dir Admissions/Records .... Ms. Sarah ENER
15 Exec Director Human Resources .... Ms. Dee SHULTZ
09 Exec Dir Inst Research/Assessment .... Mr. William BROWN
21 Budget Director/Asst Controller .... Ms. Kailey BLOCK
18 Exec Director Facilities/Operations .... Mr. Michael MILLSAPPS
37 Executive Director Financial Aid .... Ms. Nancy GRAY
06 Registrar .... Mr. Stuart THOMAS
13 Exec Director IT Admin Services .... Ms. Andria ROGERS
21 Controller .... Ms. Kara ODELL
31 Exec Director Cmty & PIO .... Ms. Laura COALE
35 Exec Dir Student Leadership & Dev .... Dr. Ryan BARONE
12 Director Loveland Campus .... Ms. Heather LELCHOOK
88 Exec Campus Dir Transp/Public Svc .... Ms. Mary GABRIEL
12 Exec Campus Dir Fort Lupton .... Ms. Brenda RASK
103 Dean Workforce Dev/Cmty Prtnrshps .... Mr. Eli MERCER
89 Assoc Dean Early College .... Ms. Libby KLINGSMITH
49 Dean Arts & Sciences .... Dr. Richard HANKS

American Sentinel University (I)

2260 South Xanadu Way, Ste 310, Aurora CO 80014
County: Arapahoe FICE Identification: 041277
Unit ID: 460738
Telephone: (303) 991-1575 Carnegie Class: Not Classified
FAX Number: (303) 991-1577 Calendar System: Other
URL: www.americansentinel.edu
Established: 2000 Annual Undergrad Tuition & Fees: $9,315
Enrollment: 3,173 Coed
Affiliation or Control: Proprietary IRS Status: Proprietary
Highest Offering: Doctorate
Accreditation: @NH, DEAC, NUR, NURSE

01 President .... Ms. Mary A. ADAMS
84 Sr VP Enrollment Services .... Mr. Mark COBB
66 Dean of Nursing .... Dr. Judy BURCKHARDT
06 Registrar .... Ms. Sandie HUBBARD

Arapahoe Community College (J)

5900 S Santa Fe Drive, PO Box 9002,
Littleton CO 80160-9002
County: Arapahoe FICE Identification: 001346
Unit ID: 126289
Telephone: (303) 797-4222 Carnegie Class: Assoc/HVT-High Non
FAX Number: (303) 797-5935 Calendar System: Semester
URL: www.arapahoe.edu
Established: 1965 Annual Undergrad Tuition & Fees (In-State): $3,334
Enrollment: 10,401 Coed
Affiliation or Control: State IRS Status: 501(c)3
Highest Offering: Associate Degree
Accreditation: NH, ADNUR, CAHIIM, EMT, FUSER, MLTAD, PTAA

01 President .... Dr. Diana M. DOYLE
11 Vice President Admin Services .... Dr. Cindy SOMERS
05 Vice President Instruction .... Dr. Diane HEGEMAN
10 Chief Financial Officer .... Mr. Joseph LORENZO, JR.
103 Dean Community/Workforce Partnershp .... Mr. Matt MCKEEVER
32 Vice President of Student Services ... Dr. Lisa MATYE-EDWARDS
38 Director of Advising and Retention .... Mr. Michael MCMANUS
07 Director Admissions & Records .... Ms. Darcy BRIGGS
37 Dir of Student Financial Services .... Ms. Gail MCKINNEY
31 Exec Dir of Community/Workforce Pgm .... Ms. Kim LARSON-COONEY
83 Dean Legal/Comm/Soc & Behav Sci .... Dr. Vanessa ANDERSON
81 Dean Health/Math & Science .... Dr. Samuel DEVRIES
49 Dean Arts/Human/Business & Tech .... Ms. Rebecca WOULFE
102 Executive Director Foundation .... Ms. Courtney LOEHFELM
21 Controller .... Ms. Jill BECKER-LUTZ
19 Chief of Police .... Mr. Joseph MORRIS
09 Director Institutional Research .... Mr. Yared BELETE
08 Director Learning Resource Center .... Ms. Lisa GRABOWSKI
26 Dir of Marketing/Public Relations .... Ms. Tina GRIESHEIMER
35 Assoc Dean of Judicial Affairs .... Ms. Heather WILCOX
96 Purchasing Coordinator .... Mr. Daniel HOHN
18 Facilities Director .... Mr. David CRAWFORD
13 Chief Info Technology Officer (CIO) .... Mr. Joseph MCCORMICK
15 Director Personnel Services .... Ms. Angela WILLIAMS
04 Administrative Asst to President .... Ms. Carol PATTERSON

Argosy University, Denver (K)

7600 East Eastman Avenue, Denver CO 80231
Telephone: (303) 923-4110 Identification: 666654
Accreditation: &WC, ACBSP, CACREP, MFCD

† Regional accreditation is carried under the parent institution in Orange, CA.

The Art Institute of Colorado (L)

1200 Lincoln Street, Denver CO 80203-2172
County: Denver FICE Identification: 020789
Unit ID: 126702
Telephone: (303) 837-0825 Carnegie Class: Spec-4-yr-Arts
FAX Number: (303) 860-8520 Calendar System: Quarter
URL: www.artinstitutes.edu/denver
Established: 1952 Annual Undergrad Tuition & Fees: $17,628

Enrollment: 1,414 Coed
Affiliation or Control: Proprietary IRS Status: Proprietary
Highest Offering: Baccalaureate
Accreditation: NH, ACFEI, CIDA

01 President .... Mr. James O. CALDWELL
05 Vice President/Dean Academic Affs ....Dr. Benjamin A. VALDEZ
07 Senior Director of Admissions ....Ms. Judith JOCHEMS
32 Director of Student Services ....Mr. John RICHARDSON
10 Director Financial Services ....Ms. Tanya TAMIM
37 Director of Financial Aid ....Ms. Debra SARTAIN
06 Registrar ....Mr. David WESSLER
15 Human Resource Generalist ....Ms. Shandra ADAIR

Aspen University (A)

1660 S. Albion Street Suite 525, Denver CO 80222
County: Denver FICE Identification: 040803
Unit ID: 454829
Telephone: (303) 823-4025 Carnegie Class: DU-Mod
FAX Number: (303) 200-7428 Calendar System: Other
URL: www.aspen.edu
Established: 1987 Annual Undergrad Tuition & Fees: $3,750
Enrollment: 1,488 Coed
Affiliation or Control: Proprietary IRS Status: Proprietary
Highest Offering: Doctorate
Accreditation: DEAC, NURSE

01 Chairman & CEO ....Mr. Michael MATHEWS
05 Chief Academic Officer ....Dr. Cheri ST. ARNAULD
10 CFO ....Ms. Janet GILL
06 Registrar ....Ms. Ashley MOSS

Augustine Institute (B)

6160 S. Syracuse Way #310,
Greenwood Village CO 80111
County: Arapahoe Identification: 667219
Telephone: (303) 937-4420 Carnegie Class: Not Classified
FAX Number: (303) 468-2933 Calendar System: Semester
URL: augustineinstitute.org
Established: 2005 Annual Graduate Tuition & Fees: N/A
Enrollment: N/A Coed
Affiliation or Control: Roman Catholic IRS Status: 501(c)3
Highest Offering: Master's; No Undergraduates
Accreditation: THEOL

01 President ....Mr. Tim GRAY
05 Academic Dean ....Dr. Christopher BLUM

Bel-Rea Institute of Animal Technology (C)

1681 S Dayton Street, Denver CO 80247-3048
County: Arapahoe FICE Identification: 012670
Unit ID: 126359
Telephone: (800) 950-8001 Carnegie Class: Spec 2-yr-Health
FAX Number: (303) 751-9969 Calendar System: Quarter
URL: www.bel-rea.com
Established: 1971 Annual Undergrad Tuition & Fees: $11,588
Enrollment: 489 Coed
Affiliation or Control: Proprietary IRS Status: Proprietary
Highest Offering: Associate Degree
Accreditation: ACCSC

01 Director ....Paulette KAUFMAN
05 Dean of Education ....Nolan RUCKER
37 Director Student Financial Aid ....Stasi BONTINELLI
32 Director Student Services ....Cynthia MEDINA

College for Financial Planning (D)

9000 E. Nichols Avenue #200, Centennial CO 80112
County: Denver Identification: 666809
Unit ID: 126526
Telephone: (303) 220-1200 Carnegie Class: Not Classified
FAX Number: (303) 220-4940 Calendar System: Other
URL: www.cffp.edu
Established: 1972 Annual Graduate Tuition & Fees: N/A
Enrollment: N/A Coed
Affiliation or Control: Proprietary IRS Status: Proprietary
Highest Offering: Master's; No Undergraduates
Accreditation: NH

01 President ....Mr. John SEARS
05 Vice President Academic Affairs ....Mr. Jim PASZTOR
10 Vice President Business Development ....Mr. Dirk PANTONE
84 Director of Enrollment ....Ms. Alicia MEAD
06 Registrar ....Ms. Katie PEDERSON
38 Director Student Service Center ....Mr. Spencer CAMERON

CollegeAmerica Colorado Springs (E)

2020 N Academy Boulevard, Ste 100,
Colorado Springs CO 80909
Telephone: (719) 622-3600 Identification: 666293
Accreditation: ACCSC

† Branch campus of CollegeAmerica Denver, Denver, CO.

CollegeAmerica Denver (F)

1385 S Colorado Blvd. 5th Floor, Denver CO 80222
County: Denver FICE Identification: 025943
Unit ID: 126872
Telephone: (303) 300-8740 Carnegie Class: Spec-4-yr-Other Health
FAX Number: (303) 692-9156 Calendar System: Other
URL: www.collegeamerica.edu
Established: 1964 Annual Undergrad Tuition & Fees: $16,968
Enrollment: 407 Coed
Affiliation or Control: Independent Non-Profit IRS Status: 501(c)3
Highest Offering: Baccalaureate
Accreditation: ACCSC

01 Executive Director ....Ms. Suzanne SCALES
05 Academic Director ....Ms. Kacey JECHURA
37 Director of Financial Aid ....Ms. Sonia MARTINEZ
07 Director of Admissions ....Ms. Mary GORDY
06 Registrar ....Ms. Lauren ELI

CollegeAmerica Fort Collins (G)

4601 S Mason, Fort Collins CO 80525-3740
Telephone: (970) 225-4860 Identification: 666362
Accreditation: ACCSC

† Branch campus of CollegeAmerica Denver, Denver, CO.

Colorado Academy of Veterinary Technology (H)

2766 Janitell Road, Colorado Springs CO 80906
County: El Paso FICE Identification: 041850
Unit ID: 461953
Telephone: (719) 219-9636 Carnegie Class: Spec 2-yr-Health
FAX Number: (719) 302-5577 Calendar System: Quarter
URL: www.cavt.edu
Established: 2007 Annual Undergrad Tuition & Fees: $11,435
Enrollment: 75 Coed
Affiliation or Control: Proprietary IRS Status: Proprietary
Highest Offering: Associate Degree
Accreditation: COE

01 CEO/Admissions Officer/Registrar ....Dr. Steve RUBIN
05 Chief Academic Officer ....Vacant
38 Dir Student Counseling/Fin Aid ....Mrs. Traci THOMPSON

Colorado Christian University (I)

8787 W Alameda Avenue, Lakewood CO 80226-7499
County: Jefferson FICE Identification: 009401
Unit ID: 126669
Telephone: (303) 963-3000 Carnegie Class: Masters/M
FAX Number: (303) 963-3001 Calendar System: Semester
URL: www.ccu.edu
Established: 1914 Annual Undergrad Tuition & Fees: $27,986
Enrollment: 5,787 Coed
Affiliation or Control: Independent Non-Profit IRS Status: 501(c)3
Highest Offering: Master's
Accreditation: NH, CACREP, MUS, NURSE

01 President ....Mr. William L. ARMSTRONG
10 VP for Business Affairs & CFO ....Mr. Daniel L. COHRS
05 VP Acad Affairs College UG Studies ....Dr. Cherri S. PARKS
30 VP for Development ....Mr. Paul ELDRIDGE
32 VP for Student Development ....Mr. Jim S. MCCORMICK
20 VP of Acad Affairs/Dean CAGS ....Dr. Sarah SCHERLING
35 Asst VP Stdnt Pgm/Dean of Students ....Ms. Sharon M. FELKER
84 VP Enrollment for CAGS ....Ms. Allison SIEVERS
88 VP of Student Success ....Mr. Roger CHANDLER
50 Dean School of Business ....Dr. Gary EWEN
72 Dean of Business and Technology ....Dr. Melani J. DAY
53 Dean School of Education ....Dr. Debora SCHEFFEL
53 Dean of Ed/Curriculum & Instruction ....Dr. Wendy WENDOVER
79 Dean Sch Humanities & Sciences ....Dr. William R. SAXBY
64 Dean School of Music ....Mr. Steven T. TAYLOR
73 Dean School of Theology ....Dr. David KOTTER
66 Dean of Nursing & Sciences ....Dr. Barbara WHITE
73 Dean of Biblical Studies & Theology ....Dr. Earl WAGGONER
07 Director of Admissions ....Ms. Jo Leda MARTIN
43 University Counsel ....Mr. Steven MILLER
21 Controller ....Ms. Karen FARRAND
06 Registrar ....Ms. Linda K. PERCIANTE
41 Athletic Director ....Mr. Darren A. RICHIE
38 Director of Counseling Services ....Dr. Joannie L. DEBRITO
44 Director of Development ....Ms. Kathy PETTIT
18 Director of Facilities ....Mr. Mathew J. GOTHARD
37 Director of Financial Aid ....Mr. Steve M. WOODBURN
23 Director of Health Services ....Ms. Mandy WILLIAMS
15 Director of Human Resources ....Mr. Rick GARRIS
13 Dir of Information Systems/Tech ....Mr. Bryan SHOLTEN
08 Library Director ....Ms. Gayle C. GUNDERSON
36 Director of Life Directions Center ....Ms. Joy STRICKLAND
39 Director of Residence Life ....Mr. Joseph BROOKS
19 Director of Security ....Mr. Steven BELECKY
26 Dir of University Communications ....Ms. Lisa L. ZELLER
29 Director Alumni Relations ....Ms. Missy SMITH
105 Director of Web Development ....Mr. Chris FRANZ
04 Executive Assistant to President ....Ms. Kerry BLEIKAMP

Colorado College (J)

14 E Cache La Poudre St.,
Colorado Springs CO 80903-3294
County: El Paso FICE Identification: 001347
Unit ID: 126678
Telephone: (719) 389-6000 Carnegie Class: Bac-A&S
FAX Number: (719) 634-4180 Calendar System: Other
URL: www.coloradocollege.edu
Established: 1874 Annual Undergrad Tuition & Fees: $48,996
Enrollment: 2,067 Coed
Affiliation or Control: Independent Non-Profit IRS Status: 501(c)3
Highest Offering: Master's
Accreditation: NH

01 President ....Dr. Jill TIEFENTHALER
05 Dean of College & Faculty ....Dr. Sandra WONG
100 Chief of Staff ....Ms. Mary Frances KERR
10 Sr VP Business/Finance & Treas ....Mr. Robert G. MOORE
30 Vice Pres for Advancement ....Mr. Sean PIERI
84 Sr Vice Pres Enrollment Management ....Mr. Mark HATCH
32 VP Student Life/Dean of Students ....Mr. Mike EDMONDS
13 VP for Information Management/CTO ....Mr. Brian YOUNG
45 Asst VP for Institutional Planning ....Ms. Lyrae WILLIAMS
88 Assoc Dean of Academic Programs ....Dr. Emily CHAN
41 Asst VP Advancement Operations ....Ms. Molly BODNAR
39 Sr Assc Dn Stdnts/Dir Resident Life ....Mr. John LAUER
20 Associate Dean of the College ....Dr. Regula M. EVITT
20 Assoc Dean of the Faculty ....Dr. Mike SIDDOWAY
35 Associate Dean of Students ....Ms. Rochelle MASON
37 Director of Financial Aid ....Vacant
06 Registrar ....Mr. Phillip C. APODACA
26 Vice President for Communications ....Ms. Jane TURNIS
41 Director of Athletics ....Mr. Ken RALPH
104 Director International Programs ....Dr. Inger BULL
15 Director Human Resources ....Ms. Barbara WILSON
18 Director of Facilities ....Mr. Chris COULTER
19 Director Campus Safety ....Ms. Maggie SANTOS
08 Library Director ....Vacant
96 Director Administrative Svcs ....Mr. Don DAVIDSON
36 Director Career Center ....Ms. Megan NICKLAUS
28 Asst VP/Director of Butler Ctr ....Mr. Paul BUCKLEY
29 Director Alumni & Parent Relations ....Ms. Anita PARISEAU
91 Director Enterprise Info Svcs ....Mr. Vishvas PARADKAR
09 Dir Assessment/Program Review .....Ms. Amanda UDIS-KESSLER
21 Controller/Asst Treasurer ....Ms. Stacy LUTZ-DAVIDSON
24 Director of Enterprise Technology ....Mr. Vish PARADKAR
105 Director Web Communications ....Ms. Karen TO
21 Senior Budget Analyst ....Ms. Enid RUIZ-MATTEI
38 Counseling Sup/Clin Psychologist ....Mr. Bill DOVE
22 Director Disability Services ....Ms. Jan EDWARDS
27 College News Director ....Ms. Leslie WEDDELL
90 Director Educational Tech Svcs ....Mr. Chad SCHOENWILL
88 Director of Innovative Technology ....Mr. Matt GOTTFRIED
88 Dir Collab Cmty Engagement ....Mr. David HARKER
46 College Research Professor ....Dr. Kevin RASK
42 Chaplain ....Dr. Kate HOLBROOK
101 Special Assistant Board of Trustees ....Ms. Caitlin APIGIAN
04 Executive Asst to the President ....Ms. Lori HAMACHER

Colorado Heights University (K)

3001 S Federal Boulevard, Denver CO 80236-2711
County: Denver FICE Identification: 032893
Unit ID: 367839
Telephone: (303) 937-4225 Carnegie Class: Spec-4-yr-Bus
FAX Number: (303) 937-4224 Calendar System: Other
URL: www.chu.edu
Established: 1990 Annual Undergrad Tuition & Fees: $7,146
Enrollment: 154 Coed
Affiliation or Control: Independent Non-Profit IRS Status: 501(c)3
Highest Offering: Master's
Accreditation: ACICS

01 President ....Mr. Fred VAN LIEW
05 Dean of Academic Affairs ....Dr. Tracey TERNAM
10 VP of Finance & Administration ....Mr. Dave BOYLL
32 Dean of Student Affs/Enrollment Mgt ....Mr. Bryan CICERO
50 Dir of MBA and BA Intl Business ....Mr. Jon WILKERSON
06 Registrar ....Ms. Julie GORDON
15 Director of Human Resources ....Ms. Debra POWELL
37 Director of Financial Aid ....Ms. Beba PREDIC
39 Director of Public Safety ....Mr. Daniil YUSUFOV
13 Director Information Technology ....Mr. Mayer SALFITI
18 Director of Facilities ....Mr. Jose GALLEGOS

Colorado Mesa University (L)

1100 North Avenue, Grand Junction CO 81501-3122
County: Mesa FICE Identification: 001358
Unit ID: 127556
Telephone: (970) 248-1020 Carnegie Class: Bac-Diverse
FAX Number: (970) 248-1076 Calendar System: Semester
URL: www.coloradomesa.edu
Established: 1925 Annual Undergrad Tuition & Fees (In-State): $7,474
Enrollment: 9,116 Coed
Affiliation or Control: State IRS Status: 501(c)3
Highest Offering: Doctorate
Accreditation: NH, ADNUR, CAATE, MLTAD, MUS, NURSE, PNUR, RAD, @SW

01 President ....Mr. Tim FOSTER
05 Vice Pres Academic Affairs ....Dr. Cynthia PEMBERTON

10 Vice President Financial/Admin Svcs ... Ms. Laura GLATT
31 Vice Pres Community College Affairs ... Vacant
109 Asst Vice Pres Auxiliary Services ... Mr. Andy RODRIGUEZ
32 Vice Pres Student Services ... Mr. John MARSHALL
13 Exec Dir InformationTechnology/Comm ... Mr. Jeremy BROWN
20 Provost ... Dr. Carol FUTHEY
08 Library Director ... Ms. Sylvia RAEL
30 Director of Development ... Ms. Liz MEYER
37 Director Financial Aid ... Mr. Curt MARTIN
26 Director of Media Relations ... Ms. Dana NUNN
06 Registrar ... Ms. Holly TEAL
09 Dir of Inst Research/Assessment ... Ms. Sonia BRANDON
18 Chief Facilities/Physical Plant ... Mr. Kent MARSH
29 Director Alumni Relations ... Mr. Jared MEIER
84 Director Enrollment Management ... Mr. Michael POLL

Colorado Mesa University-Montrose Campus (A)

245 South Cascade Avenue, Montrose CO 81401
Telephone: (970) 249-7009 Identification: 770031
Accreditation: &NH

† Regional accreditation is carried under the parent institution in Grand Junction, CO

Colorado Mountain College (B)

802 Grand Avenue, Glenwood Springs CO 81602-3961
County: Garfield FICE Identification: 004506
Unit ID: 126711
Telephone: (970) 945-8691 Carnegie Class: Bac/Assoc-Mixed
FAX Number: (970) 947-8385 Calendar System: Semester
URL: www.coloradomtn.edu
Established: 1965 Annual Undergrad Tuition & Fees (In-District): $1,556
Enrollment: 5,705 Coed
Affiliation or Control: Local IRS Status: 501(c)3
Highest Offering: Baccalaureate
Accreditation: NH, ADNUR, EMT, NUR

01 President ... Dr. Carrie BESNETTE HAUSER
05 VP Academic Affairs ... Ms. Kathy KISER-MILLER
10 CFO ... Ms. Linda ENGLISH
09 VP Institutional Effectiveness ... Dr. Debra LOPER
32 VP Student Affairs ... Mr. Shane LARSON
15 Vice President of Human Resources ... Vacant
26 Public Relations Officer ... Ms. Debbie CRAWFORD
13 Chief Information Officer ... Vacant
07 Dir Pre-Enrollment Svcs/Registrar ... Mr. Shane LARSON
37 Director of Financial Aid ... Mr. Thomas VALLER
18 Director of College Facilities ... Mr. Peter WALLER
27 Director of Marketing/Publications ... Mr. Doug STEWART
96 Director of Purchasing ... Mr. Steve BOYD
20 Developmental Education Coordinator ... Ms. A. Yvette MYRICK
04 Administrative Asst to President ... Ms. Debbie NOVAK
100 Chief of Staff ... Mr. Matt GIANNESCHI
43 Dir Legal Services/General Counsel ... Mr. Richard GONZALES

Colorado Mountain College Alpine Campus (C)

1275 Crawford Avenue, Steamboat Springs CO 80487
Telephone: (970) 870-4444 Identification: 770038
Accreditation: &NH

† Regional accreditation is carried under the parent institution in Glenwood Springs, CO

Colorado Mountain College Aspen Campus (D)

0255 Sage Way, Aspen CO 81611
Telephone: (970) 925-7740 Identification: 770032
Accreditation: &NH

† Regional accreditation is carried under the parent institution in Glenwood Springs, CO

Colorado Mountain College Roaring Fork Campus-Spring Valley (E)

690 Colorado Avenue, Carbondale CO 81623
Telephone: (970) 963-2172 Identification: 770035
Accreditation: &NH

† Regional accreditation is carried under the parent institution in Glenwood Springs, CO

Colorado Mountain College Summit Campus-Breckinridge Campus (F)

PO Box 2208, Breckinridge CO 80424
Telephone: (970) 453-6757 Identification: 770033
Accreditation: &NH

† Regional accreditation is carried under the parent institution in Glenwood Springs, CO

Colorado Mountain College Timberline Campus (G)

27900 County Road 319, PO Box 897,
Buena Vista CO 81211
Telephone: (719) 395-8419 Identification: 770036
Accreditation: &NH

† Regional accreditation is carried under the parent institution in Glenwood Springs, CO

Colorado Mountain College Vail/Eagle Valley Campus (H)

150 Miller Ranch Road, Edwards CO 81632
Telephone: (970) 569-2900 Identification: 770034
Accreditation: &NH, MAC

† Regional accreditation is carried under the parent institution in Glenwood Springs, CO

Colorado Mountain College West Garfield Campus (I)

3695 Airport Road, Rifle CO 81650
Telephone: (970) 625-1871 Identification: 770037
Accreditation: &NH

† Regional accreditation is carried under the parent institution in Glenwood Springs, CO

Colorado Northwestern Community College (J)

500 Kennedy Drive, Rangely CO 81648-3598
County: Rio Blanco FICE Identification: 001359
Unit ID: 126748
Telephone: (970) 675-2261 Carnegie Class: Assoc/MT-VT-High Non
FAX Number: (970) 675-5046 Calendar System: Semester
URL: www.cncc.edu
Established: 1962 Annual Undergrad Tuition & Fees (In-District): $3,554
Enrollment: 1,145 Coed
Affiliation or Control: State/Local IRS Status: 170(c)1
Highest Offering: Associate Degree
Accreditation: NH, ADNUR, DH

01 President ... Mr. Russell GEORGE
12 Vice Pres Craig/Student Services ... Ms. Janell OBERLANDER
05 Vice Pres Instruction ... Dr. Holly BOOMER
10 Vice Pres Business/Administration ... Mr. Roger FICKEN
84 Director of Admissions/Registrar ... Ms. Kelly SCOTT
08 Library Director ... Ms. Leana COX
15 Human Resource Specialist ... Ms. Kim BENSE
26 Marketing Director ... Vacant
18 Facilities Director ... Mr. Roger FICKEN
09 Director of Institutional Research ... Ms. Susan BOLES
38 Director Student Counseling ... Ms. Caitlan MOORE
37 Financial Aid Technician ... Ms. Merrie BYERS
20 Dean of Instruction in Rangely ... Vacant
20 Dean of Instruction in Craig ... Ms. Donna THEIMER

Colorado Northwestern Community College Craig (K)

2801 W 9th Street, Craig CO 81625
Telephone: (970) 824-1101 Identification: 770039
Accreditation: &NH

† Regional accreditation is carried under the parent institution in Rangely, CO

Colorado School of Healing Arts (L)

7655 W Mississippi, Suite 100, Lakewood CO 80226-4332
County: Jefferson FICE Identification: 035844
Unit ID: 381732
Telephone: (303) 986-2320 Carnegie Class: Spec 2-yr-Health
FAX Number: (303) 980-6594 Calendar System: Quarter
URL: www.csha.net
Established: 1986 Annual Undergrad Tuition & Fees: $13,200
Enrollment: 176 Coed
Affiliation or Control: Proprietary IRS Status: Proprietary
Highest Offering: Associate Degree
Accreditation: ACCSC

01 Executive Director & Owner ... Mr. Dennis SIMPSON
03 Director ... Ms. Gina SIMPSON
13 Director IT Dept ... Mr. Dan GOLDEN
53 Director of Education Cert Pgm ... Ms. Chris SMITH
08 Head Librarian ... Ms. Kris WILL
11 Office Manager ... Mr. Chase MAURER
40 Bookstore Manager ... Mr. Greg SENICH
07 Admissions Representative ... Ms. Amy CHAVEZ

Colorado School of Mines (M)

1500 Illinois Street, Golden CO 80401-1843
County: Jefferson FICE Identification: 001348
Unit ID: 126775
Telephone: (303) 273-3000 Carnegie Class: DU-Higher
FAX Number: (303) 273-3278 Calendar System: Semester
URL: www.mines.edu
Established: 1874 Annual Undergrad Tuition & Fees (In-State): $17,353
Enrollment: 5,962 Coed
Affiliation or Control: State IRS Status: 501(c)3
Highest Offering: Doctorate
Accreditation: NH, ENG

01 President ... Dr. Paul C. JOHNSON
05 Provost ... Dr. Thomas BOYD
10 Executive Vice Pres Admin & Ops ... Ms. Kirsten VOLPI
88 Sr Vice Pres Strat Enterprises ... Dr. Nigel T. MIDDLETON
32 Vice Pres Student Life ... Dr. Dan FOX
30 Pres for Institutional Advancement ... Mr. Brian WINKELBAUER
84 AVP Enrollment Management ... Ms. Heather BOYD
100 Chief of Staff ... Mr. Peter HAN
06 Registrar ... Ms. Lara MEDLEY
07 Asst Director of Admissions ... Ms. Louisa DULEY
08 Interim Librarian ... Ms. Lisa DUNN
13 Chief Information Officer ... Mr. Michael ERICKSON
26 Exec Dir Integrated Marketing Comm ... Ms. Jake KUPIEC
37 Director of Financial Aid ... Ms. Jill ROBERTSON
51 Director of Special Programs ... Dr. Barry MARTIN
20 Associate Provost ... Dr. Thomas BOYD
18 Director of Plant Facilities ... Mr. Gary BOWERSOCK
22 Affirmative Action Officer ... Mr. Michael DOUGHERTY
35 AVP Student Svcs & Admin ... Ms. Rebecca FLINTOFT
38 Director Student Counseling ... Ms. Sandra SIMMS
41 Athletic Director ... Mr. David HANSBURG
04 Spec Assistant to the President ... Vacant
09 Director of Institutional Research ... Ms. Tricia DOUTHIT
15 Director Personnel Services ... Mr. Michael DOUGHERTY
35 Director Student Affairs ... Mr. Derek MORGAN
36 Director Student Placement ... Ms. Jean MANNING-CLARK
19 Director Public Safety ... Mr. Greg BOHLEN
94 Exec Dir Women in Sci Eng & Math ... Ms. Deb LASICH
92 Director Honors Program ... Dr. Ken OSGOOD
45 Dir Financial Planning & Budget ... Ms. Vicki NICHOL
93 Director Minority Engineering Pgm ... Ms. Andrea MORGAN
91 Director Enterprise Systems ... Mr. David LEE
29 Director Alumni Relations ... Vacant
104 Director of International Programs ... Ms. Kay GODEL-GENGENBACH
108 Director of Assessment ... Ms. Kay SCHNEIDER
43 Dir Legal Services/General Counsel ... Ms. Anne WALKER
88 Sr VP Research & Tech Transfer ... Dr. Tony DEAN
88 Dean Earth Resource Sci & Engr ... Dr. Romana GRAVES
54 Dean Engr & Computer Science ... Dr. Kevin MOORE
88 Dean Applied Sci & Engineering ... Dr. Michael KAUFMAN

Colorado School of Trades (N)

1575 Hoyt Street, Lakewood CO 80215-2996
County: Jefferson FICE Identification: 011572
Unit ID: 126784
Telephone: (800) 234-4594 Carnegie Class: Spec 2-yr-Tech
FAX Number: (303) 233-4723 Calendar System: Other
URL: www.schooloftrades.edu
Established: 1947 Annual Undergrad Tuition & Fees: N/A
Enrollment: 196 Coed
Affiliation or Control: Proprietary IRS Status: Proprietary
Highest Offering: Associate Degree
Accreditation: ACCSC

01 President ... Mr. Robert E. MARTIN

Colorado School of Traditional Chinese Medicine (O)

1441 York Street, Suite 202, Denver CO 80206-2127
County: Denver FICE Identification: 036863
Unit ID: 381352
Telephone: (303) 329-6355 Carnegie Class: Spec-4-yr-Other Health
FAX Number: (303) 388-8165 Calendar System: Trimester
URL: www.cstcm.edu
Established: 1989 Annual Undergrad Tuition & Fees: N/A
Enrollment: 130 Coed
Affiliation or Control: Proprietary IRS Status: Proprietary
Highest Offering: Master's
Accreditation: ACUP

01 Administrative Director ... Vladimir DIBRIGIDA
05 Academic Dean ... Camille RODRIQUEZ
20 Assistant Academic Dean ... Christopher SHIFLETT
20 Assistant Academic Dean ... Abigail MENSAH-BONSU
88 Clinic Director ... Parago JONES
37 Financial Aid Administrator ... Joel SPENCER
06 Registrar ... William WALLIN
07 Recruiting Director ... Chris DUXBURY-EDWARDS
88 Receptionist ... Kirsten WEEKS

*Colorado State University System Office (P)

475 17th Street, Suite 1550, Denver CO 80202
County: Denver FICE Identification: 033437
Telephone: (303) 534-6290 Carnegie Class: N/A
FAX Number: (303) 534-6298
URL: www.csusystem.edu

01 Chancellor ... Dr. Tony FRANK
05 Chief Academic Officer ... Dr. Rick MIRANDA
43 General Counsel ... Mr. Michael D. NOLSER
10 Chief Financial Officer ... Mr. Lynn JOHNSON
26 Director of Public Relations ... Mr. Kyle HENLEY
86 Government Relations Coordinator ... Mr. Rich SCHWEIGERT
04 Executive Asst to Chancellor ... Ms. Melanie GEARY

*Colorado State University (Q)

200 W. Lake Street, Fort Collins CO 80523-0015
County: Larimer FICE Identification: 001350
Unit ID: 126818
Telephone: (970) 491-1101 Carnegie Class: DU-Highest
FAX Number: (970) 491-0501 Calendar System: Semester

URL: www.colostate.edu
Established: 1870 Annual Undergrad Tuition & Fees (In-State): $10,558
Enrollment: 31,354 Coed
Affiliation or Control: State IRS Status: 501(c)3
Highest Offering: Doctorate
Accreditation: NH, BUS, CACREP, CEA, CIDA, CONST, COPSY, DIETC, DIETD, ENG, ENGR, IPSY, JOUR, LSAR, MFCD, MUS, OT, PH, SW, TEAC, VET

02 President .... Dr. Anthony A. FRANK
05 Senior Executive VP/Provost .... Dr. Rick MIRANDA
46 Vice President for Research .... Dr. Alan S. RUDOLPH
32 Vice Pres Student Affairs .... Ms. Blanche M. HUGHES
10 Assoc VP for Finance and Budgets .... Ms. Lynn JOHNSON
11 VP for University Operations .... Ms. Lynn JOHNSON
30 VP Advancement/Strategic Initiative .... Mr. Brett B. ANDERSON
84 Vice Pres for Enrollment/Access .... Dr. Robin C. BROWN
26 VP for External Relations .... Mr. Tom MILLIGAN
56 VP Engagement/Dir CO State Univ Ext .... Dr. Louis SWANSON
20 Vice Prov for Undergraduate Affairs .... Dr. Kelly LONG
58 Vice Provost Graduate Affairs .... Dr. Jodie R. HANZLIK
91 Director of Acad Comp/Network Svc .... Mr. Scott BAILY
15 Dir Human Resource Svcs .... Ms. Diana PRIETO
36 Director Career Services .... Mr. Jeremy PODANY
08 Exec Assoc Dean of Libraries .... Vacant
07 Assoc VP Enroll/VP for Diversity .... Ms. Mary R. ONTIVEROS
29 Exec Director Alumni Relations .... Ms. Kristi BOHLENDER
41 Athletic Director .... Mr. Joe PARKER
43 Deputy General Counsel .... Mr. Jason L. JOHNSON
47 Dean Agriculture Sciences .... Dr. Ajay MENON
88 Dean Applied Human Sciences .... Dr. Jeff MCCUBBIN
50 Dean of Business .... Dr. Beth WALKER
54 Dean of Engineering .... Dr. David MCLEAN
49 Dean of Liberal Arts .... Dr. Ann M. GILL
62 VP for IT/Dean of Libraries .... Dr. Patrick BURNS
65 Dean of Natural Resources .... Dr. John HAYES
81 Dean of Natural Sciences .... Dr. Janice L. NERGER
74 Dean of Veterinary Med & Biomed Sci .... Dr. Mark STETTER
06 Registrar .... Mr. Chris SENG
18 Chief Facilities/Physical Plant .... Mr. Steve R. HULTIN
22 Dir of Equal Opportunity .... Ms. Diana PRIETO
37 Director of Student Financial Aid .... Mr. Thomas BIEDSCHEID
39 Exec Dir Housing & Dining Services .... Dr. James DOLAK
40 Director of Bookstore .... Mr. John PARRY
96 Director of Purchasing .... Mr. Frank KRAPPES
92 Director University Honors Program .... Dr. Donald MYKLES
94 Dir Women & Gender Advocacy Center .... Ms. Kathy SISNEROS
09 Director of Institutional Research .... Dr. Laura JENSEN
100 Chief of Staff Office of the Pres .... Mr. Mark GILL

*Colorado State University-Global Campus (A)

7800 E Orchard Road, Suite 200, Greenwood Village CO 80111
County: Arapahoe FICE Identification: 042087
Unit ID: 476975
Telephone: (800) 462-7845 Carnegie Class: Masters/L
FAX Number: N/A Calendar System: Trimester
URL: https://csuglobal.edu
Established: 2008 Annual Undergrad Tuition & Fees (In-State): N/A
Enrollment: 9,259 Coed
Affiliation or Control: State IRS Status: 170(c)1
Highest Offering: Master's
Accreditation: NH, ACBSP

02 President & CEO .... Dr. Becky TAKEDA-TINKER

*Colorado State University-Pueblo (B)

2200 Bonforte Boulevard, Pueblo CO 81001-4901
County: Pueblo FICE Identification: 001365
Unit ID: 128106
Telephone: (719) 549-2100 Carnegie Class: Masters/M
FAX Number: (719) 549-2650 Calendar System: Semester
URL: www.csupueblo.edu
Established: 1933 Annual Undergrad Tuition & Fees (In-State): $8,282
Enrollment: 7,256 Coed
Affiliation or Control: State IRS Status: 501(c)3
Highest Offering: Master's
Accreditation: NH, BUS, CAATE, ENG, ENGT, MUS, NUR, SW, TEAC

02 President .... Dr. Lesley DI MARE
05 Provost/Exec VP for Academic Affs .... Dr. Rick KREMINSKI
10 VP Finance & Administration .... Mr. Karl SPIECKER
84 VP Enrollment Mgmt/Student Affairs .... Vacant
20 Asst Provost Assess/Student Lrng .... Dr. Helen CAPRIOGLIO
08 Dean Library .... Ms. Rhonda GONZALES
50 Dean Hasan School of Business .... Dr. Bruce RAYMOND
79 Dean Col of Humanities/Soc Sci .... Dr. William FOLKESTAD
54 Dean Engr/Educ/Profess Studies .... Dr. Sylvester KALEVELA
81 Dean Science/Math .... Dr. David LEHMPUHL
102 Executive Director Foundation .... Mr. Todd KELLY
26 Exec Director External Affairs .... Ms. Cora ZALETEL
09 Interim Dir Inst Research/Analysis .... Sixian YANG
21 Controller .... Mr. Robert GONZALES
37 Director Student Financial Services .... Vacant
06 Registrar .... Ms. Amy ROBERTSHAW
36 Director Career Center .... Mrs. Michelle B. GJERDE
13 Dir Info Tech Svcs/Chief Tech Ofcr .... Mr. Erich MATOLA
41 Director Athletics .... Mr. Joe FOLDA
18 Dir Facilities/Construction/Plng .... Mr. Craig CASON
15 Director Human Resources .... Mr. Ralph JACOBS

39 Dir Residence Life & Housing .... Ms. Jamie HINSHAW
109 Int Director Auxiliary Services .... Mr. Chris FENDRICH
23 Dir Student Health/Counseling .... Ms. Carolyn DAUGHERTY
29 Director Alumni Relations .... Ms. Tracy SAMORA
88 Director Center for Acad Enrichment .... Dr. Derek LOPEZ
22 Director Affirmative Action .... Vacant
85 Dir International Programs .... Ms. Annie WILLIAMS
04 Int Exec Asst to the President .... Ms. Niki WHITAKER
07 Director of Admissions .... Ms. Chrissy HOLLIDAY
28 Director of Diversity .... Ms. Jennifer DELUNA
32 Dean of Students & Residence Life .... Dr. Marie HUMPHREY

Colorado Technical University (C)

3151 South Vaughn Way, Suite 400, Aurora CO 80014
Telephone: (303) 632-2300 Identification: 666732
Accreditation: &NH, ACBSP

† Regional accreditation is carried under the parent institution in Colorado Springs, CO.

Colorado Technical University (D)

4435 N Chestnut Street, Colorado Springs CO 80907-3896
County: El Paso FICE Identification: 010148
Unit ID: 126827
Telephone: (719) 598-0200 Carnegie Class: Masters/L
FAX Number: (719) 598-3740 Calendar System: Quarter
URL: www.coloradotech.edu
Established: 1965 Annual Undergrad Tuition & Fees: $11,297
Enrollment: 1,566 Coed
Affiliation or Control: Proprietary IRS Status: Proprietary
Highest Offering: Doctorate
Accreditation: NH, ACBSP, ENG

00 Interim CEO .... Mr. Jack KOEHN
01 Campus President .... Mr. Andrew HURST
05 Chief Academic Officer/Provost .... Dr. Connie JOHNSON
07 Vice President of Admissions .... Mr. Keith ARMSTRONG
88 VP Univ Academic Services .... Mr. Brian DUFFY
20 Vice Provost .... Dr. Douglas STEIN
20 Vice Provost .... Dr. Emma ZONE
10 Dir Financial Planning/Analysis .... Ms. Erin KRAFT
36 Director of Career Services .... Ms. Belinda NICHOLS-ZONNO
08 Library Manager .... Ms. Nicole HULT
13 Manager of Information Systems .... Mr. Thomas LEIGH
53 Program Director General Education .... Dr. Tonya TROKA

Community College of Aurora (E)

16000 E Centre Tech Parkway, Aurora CO 80011-9036
County: Arapahoe FICE Identification: 022769
Unit ID: 126863
Telephone: (303) 360-4700 Carnegie Class: Assoc/MT-VT-High Non
FAX Number: (303) 360-4761 Calendar System: Semester
URL: www.ccaurora.edu
Established: 1983 Annual Undergrad Tuition & Fees (In-State): $3,538
Enrollment: 7,617 Coed
Affiliation or Control: State IRS Status: 501(c)3
Highest Offering: Associate Degree
Accreditation: NH, EMT

01 President .... Dr. Elizabeth OUDENHOVEN
05 Vice President of Academic Affairs .... Ms. Janel BRANDAU
10 VP of Administrative Services .... Mr. Duane RISSE
32 Vice President of Student Affairs .... Dr. Elena SANDOVAL-LUCERO
45 VP of Institutional Effectiveness .... Dr. Chris WARD
15 Director of Human Resources .... Ms. Cindy HESSE
21 Controller .... Ms. Lisa LEFEVRE
35 Dean of Students .... Ms. Tamara WHITE
20 Dean Academic Affairs .... Mr. Victor VIALPANDO
20 Dean Academic Affairs .... Dr. Ted SNOW
19 Director of Security .... Vacant
20 Dean Academic Affairs .... Vacant
36 Director of Career Services .... Ms. Barbara LINDSAY
13 Director Information Technology .... Mr. Sam THOMAS
18 Facilities Director .... Mr. Mike DAVIS
26 Director of Marketing .... Mr. Ethan RUZZANO
37 Director Financial Aid .... Mr. John YOUNG
06 Director Admissions & Registrar .... Ms. Kristen CUSACK
08 Director Library Services .... Vacant
09 Director of Institutional Research .... Ms. Catherine TROUTH
84 Dean of Retention & Student Success .... Dr. Derrick HAYNES
27 Director Public & Media Relations .... Vacant
102 Exec Dir CCA Foundation .... Mr. John WOLFKILL

Community College of Denver (F)

Campus Box 250, PO Box 173363, Denver CO 80217-3363
County: Denver FICE Identification: 009542
Unit ID: 126942
Telephone: (303) 556-2400 Carnegie Class: Assoc/MT-VT-Mix Trad/Non
FAX Number: (303) 556-8555 Calendar System: Semester
URL: www.ccd.edu
Established: 1967 Annual Undergrad Tuition & Fees (In-State): $3,509
Enrollment: 10,296 Coed
Affiliation or Control: State IRS Status: 501(c)3
Highest Offering: Associate Degree
Accreditation: NH, CSHSE, DH, RAD

01 President .... Dr. Everette FREEMAN

05 Provost/Chief Academic Officer .... Dr. Rhonda EPPER
10 Vice Pres Finance & Admin/CFO .... Mr. Robert BROWNING
32 Vice Pres Student Affairs .... Ms. Judi DIAZ BONACQUISTI
75 Dean Career/Technical Education .... Mr. James KYNOR
49 Dean Language/Arts/Behavioral Sci .... Ms. Ruthanne ORIHUELA
35 Dean Student Development/Retention .... Mrs. Tina GARCIA
84 Dean of Enrollment Services .... Dr. Tami SELBY
35 Dean of Student Life .... Ms. Meloni RUDOLPH
37 Director Financial Aid .... Vacant
07 Director Recruit/Student Outreach .... Mr. Nahum KISNER
15 Director Human Resources .... Ms. Patty DAVIES
13 Director IT Services .... Mr. Chris ARCARESE
09 Director Inst Research & Planning .... Mr. Ulises ARNOLD
04 Executive Asst to President .... Ms. Ladora SANDERS
06 Registrar .... Vacant
18 Chief Facilities/Physical Plant .... Mr. Kevin SEILER

Concorde Career College (G)

111 N Havana Street, Aurora CO 80010-4314
County: Arapahoe FICE Identification: 008871
Unit ID: 126687
Telephone: (303) 861-1151 Carnegie Class: Spec 2-yr-Health
FAX Number: (303) 839-5478 Calendar System: Other
URL: www.concorde.edu
Established: 1969 Annual Undergrad Tuition & Fees: N/A
Enrollment: 761 Coed
Affiliation or Control: Proprietary IRS Status: Proprietary
Highest Offering: Associate Degree
Accreditation: ACCSC, COARC, DH, PTAA, RAD, SURGT

07 Campus President .... Ms. Staci HEGERTY
05 Academic Dean .... Vacant
37 Director of Financial Aid .... Ms. Nancy DISATE
07 Director of Admissions .... Mr. Nick HRUBY

Denver School of Nursing (H)

1401 19th Street, Denver CO 80202
County: Denver FICE Identification: 041483
Unit ID: 454856
Telephone: (303) 292-0015 Carnegie Class: Spec-4-yr-Other Health
FAX Number: (720) 974-0290 Calendar System: Quarter
URL: www.denverschoolofnursing.edu
Established: 2003 Annual Undergrad Tuition & Fees: N/A
Enrollment: 790 Coed
Affiliation or Control: Proprietary IRS Status: Proprietary
Highest Offering: Master's
Accreditation: NH, ADNUR, NUR

01 President .... Dr. Cathy MAXWELL
10 Director of Business Operations .... Ms. Renee MCMILLIN
32 Director of Student Services .... Mr. Michael RUSCHIVAL
05 Dean/Dir of Nursing Education Pgms .... Dr. Z. JoAnna HILL

Denver Seminary (I)

6399 S Santa Fe Drive, Littleton CO 80120-2912
County: Arapahoe FICE Identification: 001352
Unit ID: 126979
Telephone: (303) 761-2482 Carnegie Class: Spec-4-yr-Faith
FAX Number: (303) 761-8060 Calendar System: Semester
URL: www.denverseminary.edu
Established: 1950 Annual Graduate Tuition & Fees: N/A
Enrollment: 944 Coed
Affiliation or Control: Interdenominational IRS Status: 501(c)3
Highest Offering: Doctorate; No Undergraduates
Accreditation: NH, CACREP, PAST, THEOL

01 President .... Dr. Mark S. YOUNG
00 Chancellor .... Dr. Gordon MACDONALD
05 Provost/Dean .... Dr. Randolph M. MACFARLAND
10 Vice President of Finance .... Ms. Deborah KELLAR
30 Vice President of Advancement .... Mr. Chris JOHNSON
32 VP Student Life/Enrollment Mgmt .... Mr. Robert JONES
20 Associate Academic Dean .... Dr. W. David BUSCHART
06 Registrar .... Mrs. Sara RIESE
35 Dean of Students .... Mr. Rob FOLEY
07 Director of Admissions .... Vacant
44 Director of Development .... Mrs. Jessica MILLS
109 Director of Auxiliary Services .... Mr. Kent B. QUACKENBUSH
13 Director of Information Systems .... Mr. Jason ADAMS
25 Director of Communications .... Mrs. Katie LARIC
88 Dir Educational Technology .... Mr. Aaron JOHNSON
13 Director of Facilities .... Mr. Rob BACHMAN
37 Director of Financial Aid .... Mr. Michael MURPHY
08 Director of Library .... Dr. Keith P. WELLS
73 Director of DMin Program .... Dr. Marshall SHELLEY
21 Controller/Dir Financial Services .... Ms. Diana SMITH
15 Director of Human Resources .... Ms. Zandy WENNERSTROM

DeVry University - Westminster Campus (J)

1870 W 122nd Avenue, Westminster CO 80234-2010
Telephone: (303) 280-7400 Identification: 666227
Accreditation: &NH, ENGT

† Regional accreditation is carried under the parent institution in Downers Grove, IL.

Ecotech Institute (A)

1400 South Abilene Street, Aurora CO 80012
Telephone: (303) 586-5290 Identification: 770840
Accreditation: ACICS

† Branch campus of Virginia College, Birmingham, AL

Everest College (B)

1815 Jet Wing Drive, Colorado Springs CO 80916
County: El Paso FICE Identification: 004503
Unit ID: 126401
Telephone: (719) 638-6580 Carnegie Class: Assoc/HVT-Mix Trad/Non
FAX Number: (719) 638-6818 Calendar System: Quarter
URL: www.everest.edu
Established: 1897 Annual Undergrad Tuition & Fees: $11,520
Enrollment: 330 Coed
Affiliation or Control: Proprietary IRS Status: Proprietary
Highest Offering: Associate Degree
Accreditation: ACICS, MAC

01 Campus Director .... Mr. Eric BEARD
05 Dean of Education .... Ms. Ronda EVANS
07 Director Admissions .... Mr. Dan NOEL
32 Director Student Success .... Mr. Dan MILNE

Everest College (C)

9065 Grant Street, Denver CO 80229-4339
County: Adams FICE Identification: 004507
Unit ID: 127787
Telephone: (303) 457-2757 Carnegie Class: Assoc/HVT-High Non
FAX Number: (303) 457-4030 Calendar System: Other
URL: www.everest.edu
Established: 1895 Annual Undergrad Tuition & Fees: $11,686
Enrollment: 342 Coed
Affiliation or Control: Independent Non-Profit IRS Status: 501(c)3
Highest Offering: Associate Degree
Accreditation: ACICS, MAC, SURGT

01 Executive Director .... Ms. Carissa SERGER
05 Academic Dean .... Mr. Ivan NIKOLAEFF
32 Director of Student Success .... Ms. Kim MARTINEZ
37 Director of Student Finance .... Ms. Kim MARTINEZ
36 Director of Career Services .... Ms. Diane BOOREN
06 Registrar .... Ms. Cindy STEERMAN

Fort Lewis College (D)

1000 Rim Drive, Durango CO 81301-3999
County: La Plata FICE Identification: 001353
Unit ID: 127185
Telephone: (970) 247-7010 Carnegie Class: Bac-A&S
FAX Number: (970) 247-7175 Calendar System: Semester
URL: www.fortlewis.edu
Established: 1911 Annual Undergrad Tuition & Fees (In-State): $7,600
Enrollment: 3,791 Coed
Affiliation or Control: State IRS Status: 170(c)1
Highest Offering: Master's
Accreditation: NH, BUS, CAATE, ENG, MUS, TEAC

53 Director of Teacher Education .... Dr. Richard FULTON
108 Dir Academic Effectiveness & Eval .... Dr. Lisa M. SNYDER
49 Assoc Dean Arts & Sciences .... Dr. Peter MCCORMICK
01 President .... Dr. Dene Kay THOMAS
05 Provost/Vice Pres Academic Affairs .... Dr. Barbara MORRIS
10 Vice Pres Finance & Administration .... Mr. Steven J. SCHWARTZ
30 Vice President for Advancement .... Mr. Mark A. JASTORFF
84 Assoc Vice Pres Enrollment Mgmt .... Dr. Carol SMITH
32 Vice President Student Affairs .... Dr. Glenna W. SEXTON
20 Assoc Vice Pres Academic Affairs .... Dr. Kenneth PEPION
21 Assoc Vics Pres Finance & Admin .... Ms. Michele PETERSON
06 Registrar .... Vacant
21 Controller .... Ms. Cheryl WIESCAMP
25 Director of Grants Management .... Ms. Angela ROCHAT
37 Director Financial Aid .... Ms. Tracey PICCOLI
07 Director of Admission .... Mr. Andrew BURNS
38 Dir Counseling Center .... Ms. Deb ALLEM
08 Director of the Library .... Ms. Martha A. TALMAN
18 Dir Physical Plant/College Engr .... Mr. Bob SMITH
15 Dir Human Resources/Equal Opptnty .... Mr. Darren MATHEWS
39 Dir Stdnt Housing/Conferences Svcs .... Ms. Julie N. LOVE
41 Athletic Director .... Mr. Gary HUNTER
13 Director Computing & Telecomm .... Mr. Matt MCGLAMERY
29 Director Alumni Engagement .... Mrs. Suzanne CONNORS
96 Director of Purchasing .... Mr. Wayne J. HERMES
26 Chief Public Relations Officer .... Mr. Mitch DAVIS
40 Bookstore Manager .... Ms. Brooke INGLE
28 Coord Equal Opport/Judicial Affs .... Dr. Haeryon KIM
83 Dean Sch Natural & Behavioral Sci .... Dr. Maureen BRANDON
50 Interim Dean Sch of Business Admin .... Dr. Paul MCGURR
49 Assoc Dean Arts & Sciences .... Ms. Anne E. MCCARTHY
106 Dir Digital Innovation & eLearning .... Ms. Kelly M. STANLEY
101 Secretary of the Institution/Board .... Ms. Peggy SHARP

Front Range Community College (E)

3645 W 112th Avenue, Westminster CO 80031-2105
County: Adams FICE Identification: 007933
Unit ID: 127200
Telephone: (303) 404-5000 Carnegie Class: Assoc/MT-VT-High Non
FAX Number: (303) 466-1623 Calendar System: Semester
URL: www.frontrange.edu
Established: 1968 Annual Undergrad Tuition & Fees (In-State): $3,527
Enrollment: 18,761 Coed
Affiliation or Control: State IRS Status: 501(c)3
Highest Offering: Associate Degree
Accreditation: NH, ADNUR, CAHIIM, DA, MAC

01 President .... Mr. Andrew R. DORSEY
04 Asst to the President .... Ms. Kimberly STEFANSKI
05 Vice Pres Academic/Student Affairs .... Dr. Gillian MCKNIGHT-TUTEIN
10 Vice Pres Finance & Administration .... Dr. Joseph HARBOUK
12 VP Westminster Campus/Brighton Ctr .... Ms. Therese BROWN
12 Vice Pres Larimer Campus .... Dr. Jean RUNYON
12 Vice Pres Boulder County Campus .... Dr. Linda CURRAN
84 Assoc VP Enroll Mgmt & Student Svcs .... Dr. Kris BINARD
18 Assoc VP Facilities Planning/Mgmt .... Mr. Derek BROWN
20 Dean of Instruction Larimer .... Dr. Shashi UNNITHAN
106 Dean of Online Learning .... Ms. Tammy VERCAUTEREN
20 Dean of Instruction Larimer .... Ms. Darcy LITZMAN
20 Dean of Instruction Boulder County .... Mr. Matt JAMISON
20 Dean of Instruction Westminster .... Ms. Catherine PELLISH
32 Dean of Student Svcs Boulder County .... Ms. Carla STEIN
32 Dean of Student Svcs Westminster .... Mr. Aaron PRESTWICH
15 Exec Director of Human Resources .... Mr. Paul MEESE
09 Director of Institutional Research .... Ms. Kim WALLACE
21 Director of Budget & Auxiliary Svcs .... Ms. Patti ARROYO
06 Registrar .... Ms. Sonia GONZALES
37 Dir of Financial Aid Larimer .... Ms. Carolee GOLDSMITH
08 Librarian .... Ms. Courtney BRUCH
18 Director of Facilities Westminster .... Mr. Patrick O'NEILL
18 Director of Facilities Larimer .... Mr. Dennis DEREMER
35 Director Student Life Westminster .... Ms. Amy ROSDIL
35 Director Student Life Larimer .... Ms. Mary BRANTON-HOUSLEY
35 Dir Student Life Boulder County .... Ms. Amanda CLANCY
102 Exec Director of Foundation .... Mr. Ryan MCCOY
26 Lead Dir Marketing/Communications .... Ms. Marian MAHARAS
27 Public Information Officer .... Mr. John FEELEY
13 Dir of Information Technology Svcs .... Ms. Jeannine MENEFEE
19 Dir Campus Security/Preparedness .... Mr. Gordon GOLDSMITH

Front Range Community College-Boulder County Campus (F)

2190 Miller Drive, Longmont CO 80501
Telephone: (303) 678-3722 Identification: 770041
Accreditation: &NH

† Regional accreditation is carried under the parent institution in Westminster, CO

Front Range Community College Larimer Campus (G)

4616 S Shields Street, Fort Collins CO 80526
Telephone: (970) 226-2500 Identification: 770040
Accreditation: &NH, ADNUR

† Regional accreditation is carried under the parent institution in Westminster, CO

Heritage College (H)

4704 Harlan Street, Suite 100, Denver CO 80212
County: Jefferson FICE Identification: 026110
Unit ID: 262509
Telephone: (303) 477-7240 Carnegie Class: Assoc/HVT-Mix Trad/Non
FAX Number: (303) 477-7276 Calendar System: Other
URL: www.heritage-education.com
Established: 1986 Annual Undergrad Tuition & Fees: N/A
Enrollment: 482 Coed
Affiliation or Control: Proprietary IRS Status: Proprietary
Highest Offering: Associate Degree
Accreditation: ABHES

01 College Director Denver .... Dan SNYDER
05 Director of Education .... Kai HILLBERRY
07 Director of Admissions .... Natalie ALAMAT
06 Registrar .... Adriana BUSTOS
36 Director of Career Services .... Michelle TYMOCZKO
37 Director of Financial Aid .... Vacant

Holmes Institute of Consciousness Studies (I)

573 Park Point Drive, Golden CO 80401
County: Jefferson Identification: 666255
Telephone: (720) 496-1370 Carnegie Class: Not Classified
FAX Number: (303) 526-0913 Calendar System: Quarter
URL: www.holmesinstitute.org
Established: 1972 Annual Graduate Tuition & Fees: N/A
Enrollment: N/A Coed
Affiliation or Control: Other IRS Status: 501(c)3
Highest Offering: Master's; No Undergraduates
Accreditation: DEAC

01 Dir of HICS/Dir of Education .... Rev Dr. Robert DEEN
06 Registrar .... Ms. Maureen THURSTON
05 Academic Dean .... Rev Dr. Kim KAISER
56 Dean of Distance Education .... Rev Dr. Christina TILLOTSON

IBMC College (J)

6805 Corporate Drive, Suite 100, Colorado Springs CO 80919
County: El Paso FICE Identification: 008635
Unit ID: 127839
Telephone: (719) 596-7400 Carnegie Class: Spec 2-yr-Health
FAX Number: (719) 596-2464 Calendar System: Other
URL: www.ibmc.edu
Established: 1966 Annual Undergrad Tuition & Fees: N/A
Enrollment: 357 Coed
Affiliation or Control: Proprietary IRS Status: Proprietary
Highest Offering: Associate Degree
Accreditation: ABHES

01 Campus President .... Mr. Mitch THOMPSON

IBMC College (K)

3842 South Mason Street, Fort Collins CO 80526
County: Larimer FICE Identification: 030063
Unit ID: 372329
Telephone: (970) 223-2669 Carnegie Class: Spec 2-yr-Health
FAX Number: (970) 223-2796 Calendar System: Quarter
URL: www.ibmc.edu
Established: 1987 Annual Undergrad Tuition & Fees: $12,240
Enrollment: 341 Coed
Affiliation or Control: Proprietary IRS Status: Proprietary
Highest Offering: Associate Degree
Accreditation: ACICS

00 CEO .... Mr. Steven STEELE
01 President .... Ms. Pat SCHLOTTER

IBMC College (L)

2863 35th Avenue, Greeley CO 80634-9421
Telephone: (970) 356-4733 Identification: 770631
Accreditation: ACICS

Iliff School of Theology (M)

2323 E. Iliff Ave, Denver CO 80210-4798
County: Denver FICE Identification: 001354
Unit ID: 127273
Telephone: (303) 744-1287 Carnegie Class: Spec-4-yr-Faith
FAX Number: (303) 777-3387 Calendar System: Quarter
URL: www.iliff.edu
Established: 1892 Annual Graduate Tuition & Fees: N/A
Enrollment: 333 Coed
Affiliation or Control: United Methodist IRS Status: 501(c)3
Highest Offering: Doctorate; No Undergraduates
Accreditation: NH, THEOL

01 President .... Dr. Thomas V. WOLFE
05 Vice Pres/Dean Academic Affairs .... Dr. Albert HERNANDEZ
10 Vice President for Business Affairs .... Ms. Kelly L. MCCORMICK
30 VP Inst Advancement/Enrollment .... Mr. David WORLEY
26 VP of Marketing Communications .... Ms. Greta GLOVEN
06 Registrar .... Ms. Carmen E. BACA-DOSTER
13 Dir of Academic and Info Technology .... Mr. Michael HEMENWAY
07 Director Admission/Financial Aid .... Ms. Peggy J. BLOCKER
28 Associate Dean of Diversities .... Dr. Edward ANTONIO
04 Executive Asst to President .... Mrs. Alisha ENO
18 Dir of Facilities Management .... Mr. Jerry ENO
29 Donor and Alumni Relations Director .... Ms. Caran WARE JOSEPH

Institute of Business and Medical Careers (N)

2315 North Main Street, Longmont CO 80501
Telephone: (303) 651-6819 Identification: 770630
Accreditation: ACICS

Institute of Taoist Education and Acupuncture (O)

317 West South Boulder Road, Ste 5, Louisville CO 80027
County: Boulder FICE Identification: 041212
Unit ID: 454838
Telephone: (720) 890-8922 Carnegie Class: Spec-4-yr-Other Health
FAX Number: (720) 890-7719 Calendar System: Other
URL: www.itea.edu
Established: 1996 Annual Graduate Tuition & Fees: N/A
Enrollment: 31 Coed
Affiliation or Control: Independent Non-Profit IRS Status: 501(c)3
Highest Offering: Master's; No Undergraduates
Accreditation: ACUP

01 President .... Sandra LILLIE
05 Director .... Hilary SKELLON
06 Registrar .... Claudia O'NIELL
10 Financial Administrator .... Angela SMITH

IntelliTec College (P)

2315 E Pikes Peak Avenue, Colorado Springs CO 80909-6096
County: El Paso FICE Identification: 022537
Unit ID: 128179
Telephone: (719) 632-7626 Carnegie Class: Assoc/HVT-High Trad
FAX Number: (719) 632-7451 Calendar System: Quarter

URL: www.intellitec.edu
Established: 1965 Annual Undergrad Tuition & Fees: N/A
Enrollment: 828 Coed
Affiliation or Control: Proprietary IRS Status: Proprietary
Highest Offering: Associate Degree
Accreditation: ACCSC

01 Campus Director .... Raymond ADA

IntelliTec College (A)

772 Horizon Drive, Grand Junction CO 81506-3994
County: Mesa FICE Identification: 030669
Unit ID: 128188
Telephone: (970) 245-8101 Carnegie Class: Assoc/HVT-High Non
FAX Number: (970) 243-8074 Calendar System: Quarter
URL: www.intelliteccollege.com
Established: 1984 Annual Undergrad Tuition & Fees: N/A
Enrollment: 617 Coed
Affiliation or Control: Proprietary IRS Status: Proprietary
Highest Offering: Associate Degree
Accreditation: ACCSC

01 President .... Mr. Wayne ZELLNER
05 Director .... Ms. Cheryl MORRIS

IntelliTec College (B)

3673 Parker Boulevard, Pueblo CO 81008-2211
Telephone: (719) 542-3181 Identification: 666366
Accreditation: ACCSC

Johnson & Wales University - Denver Campus (C)

7150 Montview Boulevard, Denver CO 80220-1866
Telephone: (303) 256-9300 Identification: 666411
Accreditation: &EH, DIETD

† Regional accreditation is carried under the parent institution in Providence, RI.

Lamar Community College (D)

2401 S Main, Lamar CO 81052-3999
County: Prowers FICE Identification: 001355
Unit ID: 127389
Telephone: (719) 336-2248 Carnegie Class: Assoc/MT-VT-High Non
FAX Number: (719) 336-2448 Calendar System: Semester
URL: www.lamarcc.edu
Established: 1937 Annual Undergrad Tuition & Fees (In-State): $3,546
Enrollment: 839 Coed
Affiliation or Control: State IRS Status: 501(c)3
Highest Offering: Associate Degree
Accreditation: NH, ADNUR

01 President .... Mr. John MARRIN
05 VP Academic Services/Student Svcs .... Ms. Cheryl SANCHEZ
11 VP Admin Svcs/Institutional Rsrch .... Mr. Chad DE BONO
20 Dean of Academic Services .... Dr. Annessa STAGNER
26 Director of Communication .... Ms. Anne-Marie CRAMPTON
06 Registrar .... Ms. Amber THOMPSON
08 Library Tech .... Ms. Ellen LOVELL
18 Director of Facilities .... Mr. Sean LIRLEY
15 Director Personnel Services .... Ms. Jennifer MORTIMEYER
39 Director Student Housing .... Mr. Michael CLARK
27 Director of Marketing .... Ms. Kristin LUBBERS
38 Director Student Counseling .... Ms. Deanna SIEMSEN
96 Director of Purchasing .... Ms. Ava BAIR
41 Athletic Director .... Mr. Scott CRAMPTON
37 Director Financial Aid .... Ms. Teale HEMPHILL
07 Director of Admissions .... Ms. Jenna DAVIS
09 Coordinator Institutional Research .... Ms. Kim WALLACE
84 Coord for Concurrent Enrollment .... Mr. Del CHASE

Lincoln College of Technology (E)

11194 East 45th Avenue, Denver CO 80239
County: Denver FICE Identification: 007547
Unit ID: 126951
Telephone: (303) 722-5724 Carnegie Class: Spec 2-yr-Tech
FAX Number: (303) 778-8264 Calendar System: Other
URL: www.lincolnedu.com
Established: 1963 Annual Undergrad Tuition & Fees: N/A
Enrollment: 1,263 Coed
Affiliation or Control: Proprietary IRS Status: Proprietary
Highest Offering: Associate Degree
Accreditation: ACCSC

01 Campus President .... Ms. Kelly THUMM-MOORE
07 Senior Director Admissions .... Ms. Jennifer HASH
05 Director of Education .... Mr. Ivan SMITH
04 Administrative Asst to President .... Ms. Melinda K. COWGER
06 Registrar .... Mr. Craig FITZPATRICK

McKinley College (F)

2001 Lowe Street, Fort Collins CO 80525-3474
County: Larimer Identification: 666237
Telephone: (970) 207-4550 Carnegie Class: Not Classified
FAX Number: (877) 599-5863 Calendar System: Other
URL: www.mckinleycollege.edu
Established: 2004 Annual Undergrad Tuition & Fees: N/A
Enrollment: N/A Coed
Affiliation or Control: Proprietary IRS Status: Proprietary
Highest Offering: Associate Degree
Accreditation: DEAC

01 President .... Ann ROHR
32 Vice President of Student Affairs .... Joyce LINDQUIST
05 Dean of Faculty .... Nancy HAMPSON
108 Director of Compliance & Accred .... Janet PERRY
106 Dir Online Education/E-learning .... Leslie BALLENTINE
88 Applications Development Director .... Scott LYNCH
15 Human Resources Manager .... Joy DAVIS
26 Marketing Director .... Holly COOK
36 Graduate Services Supervisor .... Karen THOMPSON
37 Financial Aid Supervisor .... Jennifer BRIGGLE
84 Admissions Manager .... Jennifer MANNS

Metropolitan State University of Denver (G)

PO Box 173362, Denver CO 80217-3362
County: Denver FICE Identification: 001360
Unit ID: 127565
Telephone: (303) 556-2400 Carnegie Class: Masters/M
FAX Number: (303) 556-3912 Calendar System: Semester
URL: www.msudenver.edu
Established: 1963 Annual Undergrad Tuition & Fees (In-State): $6,420
Enrollment: 21,674 Coed
Affiliation or Control: State IRS Status: 501(c)3
Highest Offering: Master's
Accreditation: NH, ART, BUS, CAATE, CS, CSHSE, DIETD, ENGT, EXSC, MT, MUS, NRPA, NUR, SW, THEA

01 President .... Dr. Stephen M. JORDAN
05 Vice President Academic Affairs .... Dr. Vicki GOLICH
10 Vice Pres Admin/Finance/Facilities .... Mr. Steve KREIDLER
30 VP Univ Advancement .... Mr. John EURTNESS
43 Gen Counsel/Sec to Board .... Ms. Loretta P. MARTINEZ
13 AVP Info Technology Services/CIO .... Dr. James LYALL
15 Director Human Resources .... Dr. Joshua MACKEY
84 Assoc VP Enrollment Services .... Ms. Lori KESTER
26 Chief of Staff/Marketing & Comm .... Ms. Catherine LUCAS
29 Dir of Alumni Relations/Giving .... Ms. Jamie HURST
50 Dean School Business .... Dr. Ann B. MURPHY
107 Dean School Professional Studies .... Dr. Sandra HAYNES
32 AVP Stdnt Engage & Well/Dean Stdnts .... Ms. Braelin PANTEL
06 Registrar .... Vacant
37 Director Financial Aid .... Ms. Cindy HEJL
41 Athletic Director .... Dr. G. Anthony GRANT
35 Director Student Activities .... Ms. Angela LEVALLEY
36 Director Career Services .... Ms. Bridgette COBLE
28 Assoc to Pres Inst Diversity .... Dr. Myron ANDERSON

Morgan Community College (H)

920 Barlow Road, Fort Morgan CO 80701-4399
County: Morgan FICE Identification: 009981
Unit ID: 127617
Telephone: (970) 542-3100 Carnegie Class: Assoc/HVT-High Non
FAX Number: (970) 542-3115 Calendar System: Semester
URL: www.morgancc.edu
Established: 1967 Annual Undergrad Tuition & Fees (In-State): $3,536
Enrollment: 1,837 Coed
Affiliation or Control: State IRS Status: Exempt
Highest Offering: Associate Degree
Accreditation: NH, ADNUR

01 President .... Dr. Kerry HART
10 Vice Pres Finance/Admin Services .... Ms. Susan CLOUGH
05 Vice President of Instruction .... Vacant
84 Vice President of Student Success .... Mr. Kent BAUER
04 Assistant to the President .... Ms. Jane FRIES
12 Center Director .... Ms. Mary ANDERSEN
12 Center Director .... Ms. Jessica FOURNIER
12 Center Director .... Ms. Kellie OVERTURF
12 Center Director .... Ms. Valerie RHOADES
09 Dir of Institutional Effectiveness .... Mr. Derek GRUBB
26 Dir of Communications & Marketing .... Ms. Katie BARRON
30 Dir Community Relations/Development .... Ms. Kari LINKER
37 Director of Financial Aid .... Ms. Sally SHAWCROFT
07 Director of Admissions .... Ms. Kim MAXWELL
15 Director of Human Resources .... Ms. Andria KOPPELS
08 Director of Learning Resources .... Ms. April AMACK
96 Director of Purchasing .... Ms. Trisha KEMBEL
40 Director of Bookstore .... Ms. Debbie CASTENEDA
18 Coordinator of M & O .... Mr. Seth NOBLE
36 Voc Guidance/Placement Counselor .... Mr. Dan MARLER
13 Director Information Technology .... Mr. Mark FRASCO
66 Assoc Dean Health Occupations .... Ms. Kathy FRISBIE
49 Assoc Dean Arts & Sciences .... Mr. Todd SCHNEIDER
50 Assoc Dean Business & Applied Tech .... Ms. Jaylene EVANS

Naropa University (I)

2130 Arapahoe Avenue, Boulder CO 80302-6697
County: Boulder FICE Identification: 021175
Unit ID: 127653
Telephone: (303) 444-0202 Carnegie Class: Masters/L
FAX Number: (303) 444-0410 Calendar System: Semester
URL: www.naropa.edu
Established: 1974 Annual Undergrad Tuition & Fees: $30,580
Enrollment: 996 Coed
Affiliation or Control: Independent Non-Profit IRS Status: 501(c)3
Highest Offering: Master's
Accreditation: NH

01 President .... Mr. Charles G. LIEF
04 Assistant to the President .... Ms. Rachel SOLUM
10 Vice President Business Affs/CFO .... Vacant
05 Provost/Vice Pres Academic Affs .... Dr. Janet CRAMER
26 Director of University Relations .... Mr. Bill RIGLER
30 Director of Development .... Ms. Angela MADURA
84 VP Student Affairs/Enrollment Mgmt .... Ms. Cheryl BARBOUR
13 Director of IT .... Mr. David EDMINSTER
07 Dean of Admissions .... Ms. Janet ERICKSON
97 Dean Naropa College .... Ms. Carole CLEMENTS
32 Dean of Students .... Mr. Learie NURSE
35 Director of Student Life .... Vacant
28 Dir of Diversity & Inclusion .... Ms. Regina SMITH
38 Director Counseling Center .... Ms. Anne COWARDIN
39 Resident Hall Manager .... Vacant
06 Registrar .... Ms. Keely PRESTON
08 Library Director .... Mr. Nicolas WEISS
18 Director of Safety/Facilities & Ops .... Mr. Aaron COOK
37 Dir Student Financial Services .... Ms. Nancy MORRELL
15 Director of Human Resources .... Mr. Randall ARNOLD
106 Director of Online Education .... Mr. Jirka HLADIS
29 Director of Alumni Relations .... Vacant
19 Asst Dir of Campus Security .... Ms. Karina SCOTT
36 Dir Career & Community Eng .... Ms. Sarah STEWARD

National American University-Centennial (J)

8242 S University Blvd, Suite 100, Centennial CO 80122
Telephone: (303) 542-7000 Identification: 770389
Accreditation: &NH, OTA

† Regional accreditation is carried under the parent institution in Rapid City, SD

National American University-Colorado Springs (K)

1915 Jamboree Drive, Suite 185,
Colorado Springs CO 80920
Telephone: (719) 590-8300 Identification: 770390
Accreditation: &NH, MAC

† Regional accreditation is carried under the parent institution in Rapid City, SD

National American University-Colorado Springs South (L)

1079 Space Center Drive, Unit 140,
Colorado Springs CO 80915
Telephone: (719) 208-3800 Identification: 770391
Accreditation: &NH

† Regional accreditation is carried under the parent institution in Rapid City, SD

National American University-Denver (M)

1325 South Colorado Blvd, Suite 100, Denver CO 80222
Telephone: (303) 876-7100 Identification: 770392
Accreditation: &NH, MAC

† Regional accreditation is carried under the parent institution in Rapid City, SD

Nazarene Bible College (N)

1111 Academy Park Loop,
Colorado Springs CO 80910-3704
County: El Paso FICE Identification: 013007
Unit ID: 127714
Telephone: (719) 884-5000 Carnegie Class: Spec-4-yr-Faith
FAX Number: (719) 884-5199 Calendar System: Trimester
URL: www.nbc.edu
Established: 1964 Annual Undergrad Tuition & Fees: $11,400
Enrollment: 762 Coed
Affiliation or Control: Church Of The Nazarene IRS Status: 501(c)3
Highest Offering: Baccalaureate
Accreditation: NH, BI

01 President .... Dr. Harold B. GRAVES
05 Vice President for Academic Affairs .... Dr. Alan D. LYKE
32 Dir Acad Advising/Student Success .... Mrs. Jan M. EDWARDS
10 Vice President for Finance .... Mrs. Shirley A. CADLE
84 VP for Enrollment Management .... Dr. David M. CHURCH
08 Library Director .... Prof. Ann M. ATTIG
37 Financial Aid Officer .... Ms. Jenny S. MADSEN
06 Registrar .... Mrs. Meg K. CURTIS
07 Director of Admissions .... Mr. Scott E. MCCONNAUGHEY
13 Chief Information Officer .... Mr. Fred R. PHILLIPS

Northeastern Junior College (O)

100 College Avenue, Sterling CO 80751-2399
County: Logan FICE Identification: 001361
Unit ID: 127732
Telephone: (970) 521-6600 Carnegie Class: Assoc/MT-VT-Mix Trad/Non
FAX Number: (970) 522-4945 Calendar System: Semester
URL: www.njc.edu
Established: 1941 Annual Undergrad Tuition & Fees (In-State): $3,708
Enrollment: 1,776 Coed

Affiliation or Control: State IRS Status: 501(c)3
Highest Offering: Associate Degree
Accreditation: NH, ADNUR

01 President ..... Mr. Jay LEE
05 Vice President Academic Services ..... Mr. Stanton GARTIN
10 Vice Pres Finance & Administration ..... Mr. Tyler KELSCH
32 Vice President Student Services ..... Mr. Steven SMITH
29 Alumni Director ..... Mr. Jack ANNAN
102 Executive Director NJC Foundation ..... Ms. Kathleen REINHARDT
06 Director Records/Admission Process ..... Ms. Lisa SCHAEFER
37 Director of Financial Aid ..... Ms. Alice WEINGARDT
35 Dir Resident Life & Student Activit ..... Vacant
18 Physical Plant Director ..... Mr. Tracey KNOX
15 Human Resources Director ..... Ms. Jeri ESTRADA
41 Athletic Director ..... Ms. Marci HENRY
96 Director of Purchasing ..... Ms. Erin WAITLEY
09 Dir of Inst Research/Plng/Devel ..... Ms. Leslie WEINSHEIM
26 Director of Marketing ..... Mr. Matt RUGGLES
21 Controller ..... Ms. Judy MCFADDEN
13 Director Information Technology ..... Ms. Cherie BRUNGARDT
40 Bookstore Director ..... Ms. Heather BRUNGARDT
04 Executive Asst to President ..... Ms. Shawn ROSE
07 Director of Admissions ..... Mr. Adam KUNKEL
106 Dir Online Education/E-learning ..... Ms. Cyndi VANDENBARK
108 Director Institutional Assessment ..... Ms. Misti PIERCE
25 Chief Contracts/Grants Admin ..... Ms. Rebecca ROMERO

Otero Junior College (A)

1802 Colorado Avenue, La Junta CO 81050-3346
County: Otero FICE Identification: 001362
Unit ID: 127778
Telephone: (719) 384-6831 Carnegie Class: Assoc/MT-VT-High Non
FAX Number: (719) 384-6933 Calendar System: Semester
URL: www.ojc.edu
Established: 1941 Annual Undergrad Tuition & Fees (In-State): $3,412
Enrollment: 1,434 Coed
Affiliation or Control: State IRS Status: 501(c)3
Highest Offering: Associate Degree
Accreditation: NH, ADNUR, PHLEB

01 President ..... Mr. James T. RIZZUTO
11 Vice Pres Administrative Services ..... Mr. Pat MALOTT
05 Vice Pres Instructional Services ..... Ms. Kim GRIMSLEY
32 Vice President Student Services ..... Mr. Jeff PAOLUCCI
20 Assoc VP Instructional Services ..... Mr. Ryan TROSPER
08 Director Learning Resources ..... Ms. Sue KEEFER
41 Athletic Director ..... Mr. Gary ADDINGTON
15 Director of Human Resources ..... Ms. Carol NOLL
18 Director of Physical Plant ..... Mr. John CANADAY, JR.
40 Bookstore Coordinator ..... Ms. Tiana EDDY
37 Director of Financial Aid ..... Ms. Angela BENFATTI
109 Director of Auxiliary Services ..... Ms. Genia SHORT
26 Dir of Communications/PR/Foundation ..... Mrs. Sue SAMANIEGO
13 Director of Computer Services ..... Mr. Mark ALLEN
09 Director of Institutional Research ..... Ms. Rebecca GRANTHAM
30 Dir Resource Development/Grants .. Ms. Audrey DEHDOUH-BERG
84 Assoc VP Enrollment Management ..... Mrs. Almabeth KAESS

Pikes Peak Community College (B)

5675 S Academy Boulevard,
Colorado Springs CO 80906-5498
County: El Paso FICE Identification: 008896
Unit ID: 127820
Telephone: (719) 502-2000 Carnegie Class: Assoc/MT-VT-Mix Trad/Non
FAX Number: (719) 502-2201 Calendar System: Semester
URL: www.ppcc.edu
Established: 1968 Annual Undergrad Tuition & Fees (In-State): $3,240
Enrollment: 13,947 Coed
Affiliation or Control: State IRS Status: 501(c)3
Highest Offering: Associate Degree
Accreditation: NH, ACFEI, ADNUR, DA, EMT

01 President ..... Dr. Lance BOLTON
04 Exec Assistant to the President ..... Ms. Kimberly BARNETT
05 Vice Pres Instructional Services ..... Dr. Josh BAKER
32 Vice President Student Services ..... Mr. Homer WESLEY
10 Vice Pres Administrative Services ..... Ms. Brenda LAUER
20 Director of Instructional Support ..... Ms. Julie HAZEL
84 Director Enrollment Services ..... Mr. Jeff HORNER
37 Director of Financial Aid ..... Mr. Ronald SWARTWOOD
08 Director of Libraries ..... Ms. Carole OLDS
15 Exec Dir of Human Resource Services ..... Mr. Carlton BROOKS
26 Exec Dir Marketing/Communications ..... Mr. Warren EPSTEIN
21 Director of Business Svcs ..... Ms. Eileen HOGUE
06 Registrar/Coordinator of Records ..... Ms. Twila HUMPHREY
102 Exec Dir Found/Res/Cmty Development ..... Ms. Lisa JAMES
18 Dir Facilities and Operations ..... Mr. Paul ROSS
13 Director of IT Support Services ..... Mr. Cyrille PARENT
19 Dir Public Safety/Emergency Mgmt ..... Mr. Jim BARRENTINE
88 Project Dir of Stdnt Spprt Svcs/Adj ..... Mr. Edmond QUESADA
88 Dir Military & Veteran Programs ..... Vacant
76 Dean Health and Science ..... Vacant
81 Dean Mathematics & English .. Ms. Jacquelyn GAITERS-JORDAN
50 Dean Business//Public Service/SS ..... Mr. Rob HUDSON
60 Dean Comm/Humanities/Tech Studies ..... Ms. Fran HETRICK
36 Dir of Career Planning & Advising ..... Mr. Lincoln WULF
32 Dean of Students ..... Ms. Jennifer SENGENBERGER
96 Director of Purchasing ..... Ms. Rockie HURRELL
38 Dir Stdnt Counseling/Resource Ctr ..... Ms. Yolanda HARRIS
88 Dean of High School Programs ..... Ms. Chelsy HARRIS
09 Exec Dir of Inst Effectiveness ..... Dr. Patrica DIWARA
103 Vice Pres of Workforce Development ..... Ms. Debbie SAGEN

Pima Medical Institute (C)

13750 E. Mississippi Avenue, Aurora CO 80012
County: Arapahoe FICE Identification: 041771
Unit ID: 461689
Telephone: (303) 368-7462 Carnegie Class: Spec 2-yr-Health
FAX Number: N/A Calendar System: Other
URL: pmi.edu
Established: 2012 Annual Undergrad Tuition & Fees: N/A
Enrollment: 315 Coed
Affiliation or Control: Proprietary IRS Status: Proprietary
Highest Offering: Associate Degree
Accreditation: ABHES

01 Campus Director ..... Mr. Michael BEATY

Pima Medical Institute-Colorado Springs (D)

3770 Citadel Drive North, Colorado Springs CO 80909
Telephone: (719) 482-7462 Identification: 770516
Accreditation: ABHES

† Branch campus of Pima Medical Institute-Tucson, Tucson, AZ

Pima Medical Institute-Denver (E)

7475 Dakin Street, Denver CO 80221
Telephone: (303) 426-1800 Identification: 666171
Accreditation: ABHES, COARC, OTA, PTAA, RAD

† Branch campus of Pima Medical Institute, Tucson, AZ.

Platt College (F)

3100 S Parker Road, Suite 200, Aurora CO 80014-3141
County: Arapahoe FICE Identification: 030149
Unit ID: 260813
Telephone: (303) 369-5151 Carnegie Class: Spec-4-yr-Other Health
FAX Number: (303) 745-1433 Calendar System: Quarter
URL: www.plattcolorado.edu
Established: 1986 Annual Undergrad Tuition & Fees: $19,286
Enrollment: 209 Coed
Affiliation or Control: Proprietary IRS Status: Proprietary
Highest Offering: Baccalaureate
Accreditation: ACCSC, NUR

01 President/CEO ..... Mr. Jerald B. SIRBU
05 Vice President of Academic Affairs ..... Dr. Julie BASLER
10 Director of Financial Services ..... Mr. Robert CRAVER
37 Director of Financial Aid/Registrar ..... Ms. Margie ROSE
08 Head Librarian ..... Ms. Laura CULLERTON
66 Dean College of Nursing ..... Ms. Hollie CALDWELL
06 Registrar ..... Ms. Katie DAHL
07 Admissions Representative ..... Ms. Rachael HORNBOSTEL

Pueblo Community College (G)

900 W Orman Avenue, Pueblo CO 81004-1499
County: Pueblo FICE Identification: 021163
Unit ID: 127884
Telephone: (719) 549-3200 Carnegie Class: Assoc/HVT-High Non
FAX Number: (719) 544-1179 Calendar System: Semester
URL: www.pueblocc.edu
Established: 1933 Annual Undergrad Tuition & Fees (In-State): $6,761
Enrollment: 6,203 Coed
Affiliation or Control: State IRS Status: 501(c)3
Highest Offering: Associate Degree
Accreditation: NH, ACFEI, ADNUR, COARC, DA, DH, EMT, OTA, PTAA, SURGT

01 President ..... Dr. Patricia ERJAVEC
10 Chief Business Officer ..... Mr. Jon BRUDE
05 Chief Academic Officer ..... Dr. Deborah SCHMITT
32 Dean of Student Success ..... Dr. Jose RIVERA
12 Exec Dean SWCCC Campus ..... Ms. Tonya NELSON
12 Dean Fremont Campus ..... Dr. Lana CARTER
76 Dean Health & Public Safety ..... Ms. Mary CHAVEZ
49 Dean of Arts & Science ..... Dr. Jeff ALEXANDER
50 Dean Business/Advance Technology ..... Dr. Jennifer SHERMAN
31 Exec Dir Pueblo Corporate College ..... Ms. Amanda CORUM
102 Director of PCC Foundation ..... Ms. Martha SIMMONS
07 Dir Admissions & Records/Registrar ..... Ms. Barbara BENEDICT
21 Controller ..... Ms. Emma ALCALA
37 Director Financial Aid ..... Ms. Monica HARDWICK
15 Director Human Resources ..... Mr. Ken NUFER
13 Director Information Technology ..... Mr. Bryan CRAWFORD
18 Director Facility Svcs/Capital Plng ..... Mr. Clifford KITCHEN
38 Director Learning Center ..... Mr. Ross BARNHART
08 Director Library Services ..... Ms. Chris MCGRATH
26 Director Marketing/Communications ..... Ms. Erin HERGERT
35 Dir Student & Judicial Affairs ..... Mr. Dennis JOHNSON
09 Dir Institutional Effectiveness ..... Mr. Corey SHILLING
96 Director of Purchasing ..... Mr. Edmond INIGUEZ
20 Director of Academic Advising ..... Mr. Gage MICHAEL
04 Administrative Asst to President ..... Ms. Julie JIMENEZ
106 Multimedia Tech Specialist ..... Mr. Robin LEACH

Pueblo Community College Fremont Campus (H)

51320 W Highway 50, Canon City CO 81212
Telephone: (719) 296-6100 Identification: 770042
Accreditation: &NH

† Regional accreditation is carried under the parent institution in Pueblo, CO

Red Rocks Community College (I)

13300 W Sixth Avenue, Lakewood CO 80228-1255
County: Jefferson FICE Identification: 009543
Unit ID: 127909
Telephone: (303) 914-6600 Carnegie Class: Assoc/HVT-High Non
FAX Number: (303) 914-6666 Calendar System: Semester
URL: www.rrcc.edu
Established: 1969 Annual Undergrad Tuition & Fees (In-State): $3,429
Enrollment: 8,112 Coed
Affiliation or Control: State IRS Status: 501(c)3
Highest Offering: Master's
Accreditation: NH, ARCPA, MAC, RAD

01 President ..... Dr. Michele HANEY
04 Exec Assistant to the President ..... Ms. Kathy SCHISSLER
10 Vice Pres Administrative Services ..... Ms. Peggy MORGAN
05 Vice President Instruction ..... Ms. Linda COMEAUX
32 Vice Pres Stdnt Svc/Enrollment Mgt ..... Vacant
35 Vice Pres Student Success ..... Dr. Lisa FOWLER
103 Vice Pres Workforce/Community Devel ..... Vacant
20 Dean Academic Services ..... Ms. Kelly CIRCLE
20 Dean Instructional Services ..... Ms. Nicole LACROIX
20 Dean Instructional Services ..... Mr. Mike COSTE
13 Dean Technology CTE ..... Mr. Bill MCGREEVY
88 Dean of Instruct/Exec Dir RMEC-OSHA ..... Ms. Joan SMITH
85 Director International Education ..... Ms. Linda YAZDANI
07 Dir Student Recruit/Advising/Admiss ..... Ms. Nancy CARLSON
21 Controller ..... Ms. Kathy KAOUDIS
37 Director Financial Aid ..... Ms. Linda CROOK
06 Registrar/Dir Enrollment Services ..... Dr. Dean RATHE
18 Director Facilities ..... Mr. Mark BANA
15 Interim Director Human Resources ..... Ms. Cynthia HIER
102 Assoc VP of Inst Advancement ..... Mr. Ron SLINGER
26 Director Marketing/Communications ..... Ms. Kim REIN
35 Director Student Activities ..... Ms. Carolyn MATTERN
88 Dir Childhood Ed & Support Svcs ..... Vacant
09 Director Institutional Research ..... Mr. Charles DUELL
28 Director of Diversity & Inclusion ..... Ms. Jennifer MACKEN
96 Coordinator Purchasing ..... Ms. Renee ARCHULETA
36 Director Student Outreach ..... Vacant
46 Exec Dir Planning/Rsrch/Inst Effect ..... Dr. Tim GRIFFIN

Red Rocks Community College Arvada Campus (J)

5420 Miller Street, Arvada CO 80002
Telephone: (303) 914-6010 Identification: 770045
Accreditation: &NH

† Regional accreditation is carried under the parent institution in Lakewood, CO

Redstone College (K)

10851 W 120th Avenue, Broomfield CO 80021-3401
County: Broomfield FICE Identification: 007297
Unit ID: 126605
Telephone: (303) 466-1714 Carnegie Class: Spec 2-yr-Tech
FAX Number: (303) 469-3797 Calendar System: Other
URL: www.redstone.edu
Established: 1965 Annual Undergrad Tuition & Fees: $15,743
Enrollment: 552 Coed
Affiliation or Control: Proprietary IRS Status: Proprietary
Highest Offering: Associate Degree
Accreditation: ACICS

01 Campus President ..... Mr. Glenn WILSON
05 Campus Academic Dean ..... Mr. Tim GUERRERO
07 Director of Admissions ..... Mr. Eric PACHECO
07 Director of Field Admissions ..... Ms. Kim VANDERWALL
11 Director of Campus Operations ..... Mr. Nicholas BROWN
06 Senior Registrar ..... Ms. Vicki MIDDEKER

Regis University (L)

3333 Regis Boulevard, Denver CO 80221-1099
County: Denver FICE Identification: 001363
Unit ID: 127918
Telephone: (303) 458-4100 Carnegie Class: Masters/L
FAX Number: (303) 964-5449 Calendar System: Semester
URL: www.regis.edu
Established: 1877 Annual Undergrad Tuition & Fees: $33,710
Enrollment: 9,208 Coed
Affiliation or Control: Roman Catholic IRS Status: 501(c)3
Highest Offering: Doctorate
Accreditation: NH, CACREP, CAHIIM, CS, MFCD, NURSE, PHAR, PTA

01 President ..... Rev. John P. FITZGIBBONS, SJ
43 Legal Counsel ..... Ms. Erika M. HOLLIS
05 Provost ..... Dr. Patricia A. LADEWIG
30 Vice President Advancement ..... Mr. Jason J. CANIGLIA

100 VP Mission/Chief of Staff .... Dr. Thomas E. REYNOLDS
10 Sr Vice President/CFO .... Dr. Salvador D. ACEVES
84 VP Enrollment Management .... Mr. Robert BLUST
84 Assoc VP Enrollment Services .... Mr. Bill HATHAWAY-CLARK
109 Assoc VP Auxiliary & Business Svcs .... Ms. Susan LAYTON
15 Assoc VP Human Resources .... Mr. Tony L. CROW
18 Assoc VP Physical Plant .... Mr. Michael J. REDMOND
20 Assistant Provost .... Mr. Steve JACOBS
29 Asst VP Alumn Engagement Pgms .... Ms. Sarah BEHUNEK
13 Chief Information Officer .... Mr. Jaganmohan GUDUR
107 Dean Professional Studies .... Dr. Elisa ROBYN
77 Dean Computer & Info Sciences .... Dr. Shari PLANTZ-MASTERS
76 Dean Health Professions .... Dr. Janet HOUSER
49 Dean of Regis College .... Dr. Thomas BOWIE
08 Dean of Libraries .... Dr. Janet LEE
32 Dean of Students .... Ms. Diane M. MCSHEEHY
07 Dean of Admissions .... Ms. Kim FRISCH
37 Director Financial Aid .... Ms. Elinor MILLER
06 Director Registration .... Ms. Cathy GORRELL
06 Director Academic Records .... Ms. Terry GAURMER
38 Director Counseling Personal Dev .... Dr. Chaney GIVENS
19 Director of Campus Safety .... Mr. Manuel AMADO
25 Director Academic Grants .... Mr. Donald BRIDGER
42 Director of University Ministry . Ms. Kristi GONSALVES-MCCABE
36 Director of Career Services .... Mr. Richard DELLIVENERI
41 Director Athletics .... Ms. Ann MARTIN
04 Administrative Asst to President .... Ms. Patti SCHOENINGER
09 Director of Institutional Research .... Ms. Cathy GORRELL
102 Dir Foundation/Corporate Relations .... Ms. Mary BROZOVICH
39 Director Student Housing .... Ms. Njal LUNDBERG
50 Dean of Business .... Dr. Timothy KEANE
90 Director Academic Computing .... Mr. Jeffrey GETCHELL
26 Chief Public Relations/Marketing .... Ms. Tara MOBERLY
44 Director Planned Giving .... Mr. Kurt BARTLEY

Rocky Mountain College of Art & Design (A)

1600 Pierce Street, Lakewood CO 80214-1433

County: Denver FICE Identification: 007649
Unit ID: 127945
Telephone: (303) 753-6046 Carnegie Class: Spec-4-yr-Arts
FAX Number: (303) 759-4970 Calendar System: Semester
URL: www.rmcad.edu
Established: 1963 Annual Undergrad Tuition & Fees: $16,370
Enrollment: 1,045 Coed
Affiliation or Control: Proprietary IRS Status: Proprietary
Highest Offering: Master's
Accreditation: NH, ART, CIDA

01 Chief Executive Officer .... Mr. Christopher MARCONI
11 Senior Vice President of Operations .... Mr. Chris MINCHEFF
05 Assistant Provost .... Ms. Neely PATTON
07 Vice President of Admissions .... Mr. Marc ABRAHAM
00 Chancellor .... Dr. Sage A. SCHEER
57 Dean .... Mr. Robert FLADRY
10 Senior Director of Finance .... Ms. Jane BAJAR
15 Director of Human Resources .... Ms. Carrie BRANCHEAU
06 Associate Registrar .... Mr. Jonathan EVES
32 Director of Student Affairs .... Mr. Yves NAVANT
08 Library Director .... Mr. Hugh THURLOW

Rocky Vista University (B)

8401 South Chambers Road, Parker CO 80134

County: Douglas Identification: 667002
Unit ID: 480790
Telephone: (303) 373-2008 Carnegie Class: Spec-4-yr-Med
FAX Number: N/A Calendar System: Other
URL: www.rvu.edu
Established: 2006 Annual Graduate Tuition & Fees: N/A
Enrollment: 623 Coed
Affiliation or Control: Proprietary IRS Status: Proprietary
Highest Offering: Doctorate; No Undergraduates
Accreditation: NH, OSTEO

01 President .... Dr. Clint ADAMS
04 Executive Administrative Assistant .... Ms. Linda TERPENNING
09 Exec Dir Inst Plng & Assessment .... Dr. Jennifer WILLIAMS
09 Asst Dir Compliance & Quality Assur .... Dr. Terence BRENNAN
05 Dean .... Dr. Thomas TOLD
10 Chief Operating Officer/CFO .... Mr. Peter FREYTAG
37 Dir Student Financial Svc .... Ms. Fran LATA
07 Exec Dir Admissions & Marketing .... Ms. Julie ROSENTHAL
32 Assoc Dean Student Affairs .... Ms. Amy SCHLUETER
06 Registrar .... Ms. Linda CAIRNS
08 Director of Library Services .... Mr. Brian SCHWARTZ
19 Director Security/Safety .... Mr. Dan HAVENS

St. John Vianney Theological Seminary (C)

1300 S Steele Street, Denver CO 80210-2526

County: Denver Identification: 666127
Telephone: (303) 282-3427 Carnegie Class: Not Classified
FAX Number: (303) 282-3453 Calendar System: Semester
URL: www.sjvdenver.edu
Established: 1999 Annual Graduate Tuition & Fees: N/A
Enrollment: N/A Male
Affiliation or Control: Roman Catholic IRS Status: 501(c)3
Highest Offering: Master's; No Undergraduates
Accreditation: THEOL

01 Rector .... V.Rev. Scott TRAYNOR
03 Vice Rector .... Rev. Jason WALLACE
05 Academic Dean .... Dr. Joel BARSTAD
10 Director of Finance .... Mr. Paul V LLAMARIA
08 Library Director .... Mr. Stephen SWEENEY
06 Registrar .... Ms. Denise SEERY

Southwest Acupuncture College (D)

6630 Gunpark Drive Suite 200, Boulder CO 80301-3339

Telephone: (303) 581-9955 Identification: 666618
Accreditation: ACUP

† Branch campus of Southwest Acupuncture College, Santa Fe, NM.

Southwest Colorado Community College-East (E)

701 Camino del Rio, Durango CO 81301

Telephone: (970) 247-2929 Identification: 770043
Accreditation: &NH

† Regional accreditation is carried under the parent institution in Pueblo, CO

Southwest Colorado Community College-West (F)

33057 Highway 160, Mancos CO 81328

Telephone: (970) 564-6200 Identification: 770044
Accreditation: &NH

† Regional accreditation is carried under the parent institution in Pueblo, CO

Trinidad State Junior College (G)

600 Prospect, Trinidad CO 81082-2396

County: Las Animas FICE Identification: 001368
Unit ID: 128258
Telephone: (719) 846-5011 Carnegie Class: Assoc/HVT-Mix Trad/Non
FAX Number: (719) 846-5667 Calendar System: Semester
URL: www.trinidadstate.edu
Established: 1925 Annual Undergrad Tuition & Fees (In-State): $4,530
Enrollment: 1,783 Coed
Affiliation or Control: State IRS Status: 501(c)3
Highest Offering: Associate Degree
Accreditation: NH, ADNUR, ENGR

01 President .... Dr. Carmen M. SIMONE
05 Vice President of Academic Affairs .... Ms. Lynette BATES
32 VP Stdnt Affairs & Sponsored Pgm .... Ms. Kerry GABRIELSON
10 Vice Pres of Business & Finance .... Mr. Bryan BRYANT
49 Dean Arts & Sciences .... Ms. Bonnie ORTEGA
35 Dean Student Services .... Mr. Robert MARTINEZ
15 Human Resources Director .... Ms. Lorrie VELASQUEZ
37 Director Financial Aid .... Ms. Wilma ATENCIO
06 Registrar/Institutional Research .... Ms. Annette LUJAN
18 Director Facilities/Physical Plant .... Mr. Louis MANTELLI
21 Controller .... Vacant
106 Distance Lrng/Audio Visual Coord .... Mr. Doug BAK
04 Administrative Asst to President .... Ms. Donna HADDOW
26 Director of Marketing .... Mr. Greg BOYCE
41 Athletic Director .... Mr. Mike SALBATO

Trinidad State Junior College San Luis Valley Campus (H)

1011 Main Street, Alamosa CO 81101

Telephone: (719) 589-7000 Identification: 770047
Accreditation: &NH

† Regional accreditation is carried under the parent institution in Trinidad, CO

UCH Memorial Hospital School Of Radiologic Technology (I)

1400 East Boulder Street, Colorado Springs CO 80909

County: El Paso Identification: 667097
Telephone: (719) 365-8291 Carnegie Class: Not Classified
FAX Number: N/A Calendar System: Semester
URL: www.uchealth.org
Established: 1969 Annual Undergrad Tuition & Fees: N/A
Enrollment: N/A Coed
Affiliation or Control: Independent Non-Profit IRS Status: 501(c)3
Highest Offering: Associate Degree
Accreditation: RAD

01 Director .... Elaine R. IVAN
05 Dean of Education .... Theresa TAYLOR
06 Registrar/Clinical Coordinator .... Karen GEORGE
07 Director of Admissions .... Elaine R. IVAN

*University of Colorado System Office (J)

1800 Grant Street, Suite 800, Denver CO 80203

County: Denver FICE Identification: 007996
Unit ID: 128300
Telephone: (303) 860-5600 Carnegie Class: N/A
FAX Number: (303) 860-5610
URL: www.cu.edu

01 President .... Mr. Bruce D. BENSON
05 Vice Pres Academic Affairs .... Dr. Michael LIGHTNER
100 Senior VP & Chief of Staff .... Mr. Leonard DINEGAR
10 VP & Chief Financial Officer .... Mr. Todd SALIMAN
43 VP University Counsel/Secy Board .... Mr. Pat O'ROURKE
15 Sr AVP/Chief Human Resource Ofcr .... Ms. Kathy NESBITT
86 VP Government Relations .... Ms. Tanya KELLY-BOWRY
26 Assoc VP University Relations .... Mr. Ken MCCONNELLOGUE
21 Asst VP & University Controller .... Mr. Robert KUEHLER
13 Asst VP & Chief Information Ofcr .... Mr. Scott MUNSON
31 Dir Business & Community Relations .... Ms. Elizabeth COLLINS
27 Assistant VP External Relations .... Ms. Michele MCKINNEY

*University of Colorado Boulder (K)

Boulder CO 80309-0001

County: Boulder FICE Identification: 001370
Unit ID: 126614
Telephone: (303) 492-1411 Carnegie Class: DU-Highest
FAX Number: N/A Calendar System: Semester
URL: www.colorado.edu
Established: 1876 Annual Undergrad Tuition & Fees (In-State): $11,091
Enrollment: 32,432 Coed
Affiliation or Control: State IRS Status: 501(c)3
Highest Offering: Doctorate
Accreditation: NH, AUD, BUS, CEA, CLPSY, CS, ENG, IPSY, JOUR, LAW, MUS, SP

02 Chancellor .... Dr. Phillip P. DISTEFANO
05 Provost & Exec VC for Acad Affairs .... Dr. Russell MOORE
10 Sr Vice Chanc/Chief Financial Ofcr .... Ms. Kelly L. FOX
46 Vice Chancellor for Research .... Dr. Terri FIEZ
11 Vice Chanc for Infrastruc/Safety .... Mr. David KANG
32 Vice Chanc for Student Affairs .... Ms. Christina GONZALES
28 Vice Chanc for Diversity/Equity .... Dr. Robert BOSWELL
26 Vice Chanc for Strategic Relations .... Ms. Frances DRAPER
21 Assoc VC for Budget & Planning .... Ms. Louise VALE
13 Assoc VC for IT/Chief Info Officer .... Dr. Lawrence M. LEVINE
04 Chief of Staff .... Ms. Catherine SHEA
30 Vice Chanc for Advancement .... Ms. Deb COFFIN
29 Asst Vice Chanc Alumni Relations .... Mr. Ryan CHREIST
58 Interim Dean of the Graduate School .... Dr. Ann SCHMIESING
61 Dean of Law .... Dr. James ANAYA
49 Dean of Arts & Sciences .... Dr. Steven R. LEIGH
54 Dean of Engineering .... Dr. Robert H. DAVIS
50 Dean of Business .... Dr. David L. IKENBERRY
53 Dean of Education .... Dr. Lorrie SHEPARD
64 Dean of Music .... Dr. Robert S. SHAY
60 Dean Media/Communications/Info .... Dr. Lori BERGEN
51 Dean of Division of Continuing Educ .... Dr. Sara THOMPSON
62 Dean of Libraries .... Mr. James F. WILLIAMS
35 Assoc VC/Dean of Students .... Ms. Akirah BRADLEY
37 Director of Financial Aid .... Ms. Gwen E. POMPER
07 Director of Admissions .... Mr. Kevin L. MACLENNAN
06 Registrar .... Dr. Kristi WOLD-MCCORMICK
22 Director Title IX Programs .... Ms. Valerie SIMONS
09 Dir of Institutional Research .... Mr. Robert STUBBS
25 Dir of Contracts and Grants .... Ms. Denitta D. WARD
15 Interim Chief Human Resources Ofcr .... Ms. Charlotte Katherine ERWIN
41 Athletic Director .... Mr. Rick GEORGE
19 Chief of Police .... Ms. Melissa A. ZAK
23 Interim Exec Dir Student Health Ctr .... Ms. Melissa LOWE
36 Director of Career Services .... Dr. Lisa SEVERY
39 Sr Asst VC/Exec Dir Housing Sevices .... Mr. Kambiz KHALILI
88 Director of Museum .... Dr. Patrick KOCIOLEK
104 Director Study Abroad .... Ms. Mary DANDO
43 Managing Sr Assoc Univ Counsel .... Ms. Elvira U. STREHLE-HENSON

*University of Colorado Colorado Springs (L)

1420 Austin Bluffs Parkway, Colorado Springs CO 80918

County: El Paso FICE Identification: 004509
Unit ID: 126580
Telephone: (719) 255-8227 Carnegie Class: Masters/L
FAX Number: (719) 255-3362 Calendar System: Semester
URL: www.uccs.edu
Established: 1965 Annual Undergrad Tuition & Fees (In-State): $7,692
Enrollment: 11,761 Coed
Affiliation or Control: State IRS Status: 501(c)3
Highest Offering: Doctorate
Accreditation: NH, BUS, CACREP, #CAEP, CLPSY, CS, DIETD, ENG, NURSE, SPAA

02 Chancellor .... Dr. Pam SHOCKLEY-ZALABAK
05 Interim Provost .... Dr. Terry SCHWARTZ
10 Vice Chanc Admin & Finance .... Susan SZPYRKA
32 Vice Chanc Student Success .... Vacant
30 Vice Chanc Univ Advancement .... Martin WOOD
20 Sr Vice Chanc Academic Affairs .... Dr. David MOON
106 Assoc Vice Chanc Online Education .... Venkateshwar REDDY
18 Chief Facilities/Physical Plant .... Gary REYNOLDS
21 Director Resource Management .... Gayanne SCOTT
43 Legal Counsel .... Jennifer GEORGE
13 Director of Information Technology .... Vacant
46 Assoc Vice Chanc Research .... Dr. Kelli KLEBE
28 Assoc Vice Chancellor Diversity .... Dr. Kee WARNER
25 Director of Sponsored Programs .... Gwen GENNARO
84 Director of Enrollment Mgmt .... Matthew COX
09 Director of Institutional Research .... Dr. Robyn MARSCHKE

15 Director of Human Resources ... Jeanne DURR
19 Director of Public Safety ... Brian MCPIKE
29 Director Alumni & Community Rels ... Jennifer HANE
37 Director Financial Aid ... Jevita ROGERS
26 Director Media Relations ... Tom HUTTON
38 Director Student Counseling ... Dr. Benek ALTAYLI
41 Director of Athletics ... Stephen KIRKHAM
35 Dean of Students ... Steve LINHART
49 Dean of Letters/Arts/Science ... Dr. Peter BRAZA
50 Dean of Business ... Dr. Venkateshwar REDDY
53 Dean of Education ... Dr. Valerie CONLEY
54 Dean of Engineering/Applied Science ... Dr. Ramaswami DANDAPANI
80 Dean of Public Affairs ... Dr. George REED
66 Dean Nursing/Health Sciences ... Dr. Nancy SMITH
58 Dean of Graduate School ... Dr. Kelli KLEBE
08 Dean of Library ... Dr. Martin GARNAR
39 Director Campus Housing ... Ralph GIESE
06 Registrar ... Tracy BARBER
04 Executive Asst to the Chancellor ... Brenda BONN
105 Director Web Services ... Craig DECKER
40 Director of Bookstore ... Paul DENISTON

*University of Colorado Denver|Anschutz Medical Campus (A)

1250 14th Street, Denver CO 80204
County: Denver FICE Identification: 004508
Unit ID: 126562
Telephone: (303) 556-2400 Carnegie Class: DU-Higher
FAX Number: N/A Calendar System: Semester
URL: www.ucdenver.edu
Established: 1912 Annual Undergrad Tuition & Fees (In-State): $8,692
Enrollment: 22,791 Coed
Affiliation or Control: State IRS Status: 501(c)3
Highest Offering: Doctorate
Accreditation: NH, AA, ARCPA, BUS, BUSA, CACREP, CLPSY, CS, DENT, DMS, ENG, HSA, IPSY, LSAR, MED, MIDWF, MUS, NURSE, PAST, PH, PHAR, PLNG, PTA, SPAA, TED

02 Chancellor ... Dr. Don ELLIMAN
03 VP Health Affairs/Exec VC AMC ... Ms. Lilly MARKS
46 Vice Chancellor for Research ... Dr. Richard TRAYSTMAN
10 Sr Vice Chanc Admin/Finance ... Ms. Terri C. CARROTHERS
17 VC Health Affairs/Dean of Medicine ... Dr. John REILLY
26 Vice Chanc of Univ Communications ... Ms. Leanna CLARK
05 Provost & VC Academic/Student Affs ... Dr. Roderick NAIRN
30 Vice Chanc of Development Anschutz ... Mr. Scott ARTHUR
30 Vice Chanc of Development Denver ... Mr. Matthew WASSERMAN
52 Dean School of Dental Medicine ... Dr. Denise KASSEBAUM
66 Dean College of Nursing ... Dr. Sarah THOMPSON
67 Dean School of Pharmacy ... Dr. Ralph ALTIERE
69 Dean CO School of Public Health ... Dr. David GOFF
58 Interim Dean Graduate School ... Dr. Terry POTTER
64 Dean College of Arts/Media ... Dr. Laurence KAPTAIN
80 Dean School of Public Affairs ... Dr. Paul TESKE
49 Dean College Liberal Arts & Sci ... Dr. Pamela JANSMA
48 Dean College of Arch/Planning ... Mr. Mark GELERNTER
50 Dean Business School ... Ms. Sueann AMBRON
53 Dean School of Education ... Dr. Rebecca KANTOR
54 Dean College of Engineering ... Dr. Marc INGBER
46 Assoc VC for Research ... Dr. Robert DAMRAUER
20 Assoc VC Academic Affairs ... Dr. Laura GOODWIN
32 Assoc VC Student Affairs ... Dr. Raul CARDENAS
28 Assoc VC Diversity/Inclusion ... Dr. Brenda ALLEN
21 Assoc VC Finance/Controller ... Ms. E. Kim HUBER
18 Assoc VC Facilities Management ... Mr. David C. TURNQUIST
88 Assoc VC of Academic Planning ... Dr. Terry POTTER
15 Asst VC Human Resources ... Mr. Kevin JACOBS
13 Asst VC Information Technology Svcs ... Mr. Russell POOLE
88 Asst VC Academic Tech/Extd Learning ... Mr. Robert TOLSMA
84 Asst VC UG Admissions/K-12 Outreach ... Mr. Chris DOWEN
09 Asst VC Institutional Research ... Dr. Christine STROUP-BENHAM
88 Asst VC Student Success ... Ms. Peggy LORE
88 Interim Asst VC University Life ... Mr. Sam KIM
06 Registrar ... Ms. Ingrid ESCHHOLZ
08 Director Auraria Library ... Dr. Mary SOMERVILLE
08 Interim Dir Health Sciences Library ... Ms. Melissa DESANTIS
27 Director PR/Media Relations ... Vacant
37 Interim Director Financial Aid Svcs ... Mr. Justin JARAMILLO
19 Chief of Police ... Mr. Doug ABRAHAM
29 Director Alumni Relations ... Ms. Joy FRENCH
43 Assistant University Counsel ... Mr. Christopher PUCKETT
35 Interim Dean of Students ... Dr. Kristin KUSHMIDER
104 Director International Education ... Mr. John SUNNYGARD
45 Chief Institutional Planning ... Mr. Michale DEL GIUDICE

University of Denver (B)

2199 S. University Blvd., Denver CO 80208-0001
County: Denver FICE Identification: 001371
Unit ID: 127060
Telephone: (303) 871-2000 Carnegie Class: DU-Higher
FAX Number: (303) 871-3301 Calendar System: Quarter
URL: www.du.edu
Established: 1864 Annual Undergrad Tuition & Fees: $44,178
Enrollment: 11,809 Coed
Affiliation or Control: Independent Non-Profit IRS Status: 501(c)3
Highest Offering: Doctorate
Accreditation: NH, ART, BUS, BUSA, CEA, CLPSY, COPSY, ENG, IPSY, LAW, LIB, MUS, SW

01 Chancellor ... Dr. Rebecca CHOPP
05 Provost ... Dr. Gregg O. KVISTAD
43 Vice Chanc Legal Affairs/Gen Couns ... Mr. Paul H. CHAN
32 Vice Chanc Campus Life/Inclus Excel ... Dr. Liliana RODRIGUEZ
10 Vice Chanc Business/Financial Affs ... Mr. Craig WOODY
41 Vice Chanc Athletics and Recreation ... Ms. Peg BRADLEY-DOPPES
30 Vice Chanc University Advancement ... Mr. Armin AFSAHI
26 Interim Vice Chanc Communications ... Ms. Barbara BROOKS
13 Assoc VC Tech/Chief Tech Officer ... Ms. Nancy ALLEN
84 Vice Chancellor for Enrollment ... Mr. Thomas WILLOUGHBY
37 Asst Vice Chanc Enroll/Dir Fin Aid ... Mr. John E. GUDVANGEN
04 Exec Assistant to the Chancellor ... Ms. Allison RIOLA
20 Associate Provost Academic Program ... Dr. Jennifer KARAS
07 Assoc Vice Chanc Enrollment ... Mr. Todd RINEHART
88 Assoc Vice Chanc IE/Exec Dir CME ... Ms. Johanna LEYBA
28 Sr Advisor to Chancellor/Provost ... Dr. Frank TUITT
58 Assoc Provost Graduate Studies ... Dr. Barbara WILCOTS
08 Interim Dean Libraries ... Mr. Michael LEVINE-CLARK
34 Interim Dean CO Women's College ... Dr. Linda OLSON
45 Interim Sr Assc Provost Plng/Budget ... Dr. Linda KOSTEN
102 Assc Vice Chanc Annual Giving/Found ... Vacant
44 Assoc Vice Chanc Major Gifts ... Mr. Mike MCCALL
06 Registrar ... Mr. Dennis M. BECKER
21 Controller/Assistant Treasurer ... Ms. Margaret HENRY
36 Exec Director Career Services ... Ms. Sue HINKIN
22 EO/ADA Compliance Director ... Ms. Jean MCALLISTER
18 Director Facilities Management ... Mr. Jeff BEMELEN
09 Interim Dir Institutional Research ... Mr. Mike FURNO
15 Vice Chancellor Human Resources ... Ms. Amy KING
19 Director Campus Safety ... Mr. Donald ENLOE
88 Dir Student Financial Services ... Ms. Janet BURKHARDT
88 Asst Vice Chanc Enterprise Services ... Ms. Susan LUTZ
23 Exec Dir of Univ Health Services ... Vacant
54 Dean Engr/Computer Science ... Mr. J.B HOLSTON
79 Dean Arts/Humanities/Social Science ... Dr. Daniel MCINTOSH
81 Dean Natural Science/Math ... Dr. Andrei KUTATELADZE
50 Dean College of Business ... Dr. Brent CHRITE
61 Dean College of Law ... Dr. Bruce SMITH
82 Dean Graduate Sch of Intl Studies ... Mr. Christopher R. HILL
70 Dean Graduate School of Social Work ... Vacant
55 Dean University College ... Mr. Michael MCGUIRE
53 Dean College of Education ... Dr. Karen RILEY
64 Director Lamont School of Music ... Ms. Nancy COCHRAN
31 Exec Dir Special Community Programs ... Dr. Cathy GRIEVE
57 Director School of Art/Art History ... Dr. Sarah GJERTSON
07 Director of Enrollment Services ... Ms. Anne GROSS
35 Exec Director of Campus Life ... Mr. Carl JOHNSON
101 Secretary of the Institution/Board ... Ms. Claire BROWNELL
104 Study Abroad Assistant Director ... Ms. Michelle REMBOLT
105 Senior Digital Design and Architect ... Mr. Matt ESCHENBAUM
106 Director of Web-based Learning ... Ms. Kathy KEAIRNS
108 Director of Assessment ... Vacant
39 Exec Dir Housing & Resident Educ ... Mr. Patrick CALL
96 Director of Business Services ... Mr. Bob MCVEIGH

University of Northern Colorado (C)

501 20th Street, Greeley CO 80639-6900
County: Weld FICE Identification: 001349
Unit ID: 127741
Telephone: (970) 351-1890 Carnegie Class: DU-Higher
FAX Number: (970) 351-1880 Calendar System: Semester
URL: www.unco.edu
Established: 1889 Annual Undergrad Tuition & Fees (In-State): $8,166
Enrollment: 12,050 Coed
Affiliation or Control: State IRS Status: 501(c)3
Highest Offering: Doctorate
Accreditation: NH, ART, AUD, BUS, BUSA, CAATE, CACREP, CEA, COPSY, CORE, DIETD, DIETI, IPSY, MUS, NURSE, PH, SCPSY, SP, TED, THEA

01 President ... Ms. Kay NORTON
05 Provost/Vice Pres Academic Affairs ... Ms. Robbyn WACKER
11 Vice President Administration ... Ms. Michelle QUINN
43 Vice President & University Counsel ... Mr. Dan SATRIANA
26 VP External & University Relations ... Mr. Dan WEAVER
30 Vice Pres Development/Alumni Rels ... Mr. Wayne WEBSTER
58 Dean Grad School ... Ms. Linda BLACK
20 Ast VP Undergrad Stds/Dean Univ Col ... Dr. Thomas SMITH
10 Asst Vice President Budgets/Analysi ... Ms. Susan SIMMERS
13 Asst Vice President Info Technology ... Mr. Bret NABER
84 Asst Vice Pres for Enrollment Mgmt ... Mr. Tobias GUZMAN
79 Dean Humanities/Social Sciences ... Dr. Laura CONNOLLY
50 Acting Dean Business ... Dr. Karen TURNER
53 Dean Education/Behavorial Sciences ... Dr. Eugene SHEEHAN
76 Dean Natural & Health Sciences ... Dr. Ellen GREGG
57 Dean Performing Visual Arts ... Dr. Leo WELCH
08 Dean University Libraries ... Ms. Helen REED
32 Dean of Students ... Dr. Katrina RODRIGUEZ
102 President University Foundation ... Mr. Rod ESCH
06 Registrar ... Mr. Charlie COUCH
07 Director of Admissions ... Dr. Sean M. BROGHAMMER
25 Actg AVP Sponsored Pgms/Research ... Dr. Robert HOUSER
37 Dir Student Financial Resources ... Mr. Marty SOMERO
36 Director of Career Services ... Ms. Renee WELCH
15 Director of Human Resources ... Mr. Marshall PARKS
29 Asst VP Alumni Relations ... Ms. Lyndsey CRUM
18 Director Facilities Management ... Mr. Kirk LEICHLITER
41 Director of NCAA Athletics ... Mr. Darren DUNN
39 Director of Residential Education ... Mr. Montez BUTTS
38 Director Student Counseling ... Ms. Kim WILCOX
19 Chief of University Police ... Mr. Dennis PUMPHREY
44 Director of Annual Giving ... Ms. Christina NICHOLS
27 Dir News & Public Relations ... Mr. Nate HAAS
96 Director of Purchasing ... Ms. Cristal SWAIN
104 Director Study Abroad ... Mr. Brent SPENCER
108 Director Institutional Assessment ... Ms. Kim BLACK
04 Administrative Asst to President ... Ms. Elaine QUAM
100 Chief of Staff ... Ms. Gloria REYNOLDS
101 Secretary of the Institution/Board ... Ms. Victoria NICCUM
105 Director Web Services ... Ms. Ronna JOHNSTON
106 Dir Online Education/E-learning ... Ms. Jeanie YORK

University of Phoenix Colorado Main Campus (D)

1000H Park Meadows Drive, Lone Tree CO 80124-5453
Telephone: (303) 755-9090 Identification: 770195
Accreditation: &NH, ACBSP

† Regional accreditation is carried under the parent institution in Tempe, AZ

University of the Rockies (E)

1201 16th Street, Suite 200, Denver CO 80202
County: Denver FICE Identification: 035453
Unit ID: 441308
Telephone: (866) 621-0124 Carnegie Class: Spec-4-yr-Other Health
FAX Number: (303) 446-5884 Calendar System: Other
URL: www.rockies.edu
Established: 1998 Annual Graduate Tuition & Fees: N/A
Enrollment: 1,639 Coed
Affiliation or Control: Proprietary IRS Status: Proprietary
Highest Offering: Doctorate; No Undergraduates
Accreditation: NH

01 President ... Dr. Dawn IWAMOTO
05 Provost ... Dr. Jeremy MORELAND
10 Vice Pres Finance & Operations ... Mr. Steve MANSDOERFER
21 Director of Financial Services ... Ms. Jamie ESQUIBEL
15 Director of Human Resources ... Ms. Barbara HENRY-QUINN
06 University Registrar ... Ms. Katina JORDAN
28 Director of Diversity ... Ms. Francesca GALARRAGA

U.S. Career Institute (F)

2001 Lowe Street, Fort Collins CO 80525
County: Larimer Identification: 666776
Telephone: (970) 207-4500 Carnegie Class: Not Classified
FAX Number: (970) 223-1678 Calendar System: Other
URL: www.uscareerinstitute.edu
Established: 1981 Annual Undergrad Tuition & Fees: N/A
Enrollment: N/A Coed
Affiliation or Control: Proprietary IRS Status: Proprietary
Highest Offering: Associate Degree
Accreditation: DEAC

01 President ... Ms. Ann ROHR
32 Vice President Student Affairs ... Ms. Joyce LINDQUIST
108 Director of Compliance & Retention ... Ms. Janet PERRY
106 Dean of Curriculum ... Ms. Leslie BALLENTINE
84 Admissions Manager ... Ms. Jennifer MANNS
15 Human Resources Manager ... Ms. Joy DAVIS
26 Director of Marketing ... Ms. Holly COOK

Western Colorado Community College-Tilman M. Bishop Campus (G)

2508 Blichmann Avenue, Grand Junction CO 81505
Telephone: (970) 255-2600 Identification: 770030
Accreditation: &NH

† Regional accreditation is carried under the parent institution in Grand Junction, CO

Western State Colorado University (H)

600 North Adams, Gunnison CO 81231-0001
County: Gunnison FICE Identification: 001372
Unit ID: 128391
Telephone: (970) 943-0120 Carnegie Class: Masters/S
FAX Number: (970) 943-7069 Calendar System: Semester
URL: www.western.edu
Established: 1901 Annual Undergrad Tuition & Fees (In-State): $8,451
Enrollment: 2,584 Coed
Affiliation or Control: State IRS Status: 501(c)3
Highest Offering: Master's
Accreditation: NH, MUS

01 President ... Dr. Greg SALSBURY
11 Exec Vice Pres and COO ... Mr. Brad BACA
05 Int Vice Pres for Academic Affairs ... Dr. Bill NIEMI
10 Chief Financial Officer ... Ms. Julie FEIER
32 Vice President for Student Affairs ... Mr. Gary PIERSON
26 Vice President Marketing/Enrollment ... Mr. John KAWAUCHI
20 Assoc Vice Pres Academic Affairs ... Dr. Kathleen KINKEMA
35 Assoc Vice Pres for Student Affairs ... Mr. Chris LUEKENGA
06 Registrar ... Ms. Ginny HAYES
37 Director of Financial Aid ... Ms. Carrie SHAW
104 Dir Intl Student Pgms/Study Abroad ... Ms. Katie WHEATON
41 Athletic Director ... Mr. Jason CARMICHAEL
15 Director of Human Resources ... Ms. Kim GAILEY
40 Director Retail Operations ... Ms. Teri HAUS
13 Chief Information Ofcr/IT Director ... Mr. Chad ROBINSON

08 Director Library Services ... Ms. Nancy GAUSS
51 Director Extended Studies ... Ms. Erica BOUCHER
39 Director of Residence Life ... Ms. Shelley JANSEN
36 Career Services Coordinator ... Ms. Mariah GREEN
26 Director of Public Relations ... Vacant
29 Director of Alumni Relations ... Ms. Tonya VANHEE
44 Director Annual & Special Gifts ... Vacant
09 Director Institutional Research ... Mr. Doug DRIVER
28 Director of Multicultural Center ... Ms. Sally ROMERO
96 Business Services Manager ... Ms. Sherry FORD

William Howard Taft University (A)

600 South Cherry Street, Office 525, Denver CO 80246
County: Denver FICE Identification: 041004
Unit ID: 454689
Telephone: (303) 867-1155 Carnegie Class: Spec-4-yr-Bus
FAX Number: (303) 867-1156 Calendar System: Other
URL: www.taft.edu
Established: 1976 Annual Undergrad Tuition & Fees: $4,170
Enrollment: 817 Coed
Affiliation or Control: Proprietary IRS Status: Proprietary
Highest Offering: Doctorate
Accreditation: DEAC

01 President ... Mr. Jerome ALLEY
03 Chief Operating Officer ... Mr. Robert K. STROUSE
11 Director of Administration ... Ms. Christine A. BALDWIN

† Tuition varies by degree program.

William Loveland College (B)

441 East 4th St., #101, Loveland CO 80537
County: Larimer Identification: 667234
Telephone: (970) 410-0456 Carnegie Class: Not Classified
FAX Number: (719) 452-3684 Calendar System: Semester
URL: wlcollege.ilm.edu
Established: 1973 Annual Graduate Tuition & Fees: N/A
Enrollment: N/A Coed
Affiliation or Control: Independent Non-Profit IRS Status: 501(c)3
Highest Offering: Master's; No Undergraduates
Accreditation: DEAC

01 Executive Director & Provost ... Mr. David E. LADY
05 Chief Academic Officer ... Dr. Randell ORNER
11 Vice Pres of Operations ... Mr. Jerry BOYLE
13 Chief Information Officer ... Mr. Mark RUPERT

CONNECTICUT

Albertus Magnus College (C)

700 Prospect Street, New Haven CT 06511-1189
County: New Haven FICE Identification: 001374
Unit ID: 128498
Telephone: (203) 773-8550 Carnegie Class: Masters/M
FAX Number: (203) 773-9539 Calendar System: Semester
URL: www.albertus.edu
Established: 1925 Annual Undergrad Tuition & Fees: $29,650
Enrollment: 1,550 Coed
Affiliation or Control: Independent Non-Profit IRS Status: 501(c)3
Highest Offering: Master's
Accreditation: EH, IACBE

01 Interim President ... Sr. Anne M. KILBRIDE, OP
05 Vice Pres Academic Affairs ... Dr. Sean O'CONNELL
10 Vice President Finance/Treasurer ... Mr. William C. GUERRERO
13 VP Information Technology Services ... Mr. Steven GSTALDER
29 VP Development/Alumni Relations ... Ms. Carolyn A. BEHAN KRAUS
32 Vice President for Student Services ... Mr. Andrew FOSTER
35 Asst Dean Campus Activities/Orien ... Ms. Erin MORRELL
06 Registrar ... Mrs. Melissa DELUCIA
08 Director Library/Information Svcs ... Ms. Anne LEENEY-PANAGROSSI
09 Inst Research & Assessment Analyst ... Ms. Viola SIMPSON
37 Director Financial Aid ... Mrs. Michelle COCHRAN
90 Director Academic Computing ... Vacant
41 Director of Athletics ... Mr. James ABROMAITIS
58 Director MALS Program ... Ms. Julia COASH
89 Director of Freshmen Advising ... Ms. Heather WOTTON
92 Director of Honors Program ... Dr. Christine ATKINS
96 Dir Purchas/Pub Sfty/Spec Projects ... Mr. James A. SCHAFRICK
15 Director Human Resources ... Ms. Renee SULLIVAN
26 Dir Communications/Community Rels ... Ms. Rosanne ZUDEKOFF
36 Director Career Services ... Mr. Patrick CLIFFORD
42 Coord of Dominican Ministries ... Mr. H. John HOFFMAN
18 Supervisor of Facilities Services ... Mr. Dan SECOR

Charter Oak State College (D)

55 Paul Manafort Drive, New Britain CT 06053-2142
County: Hartford FICE Identification: 029171
Unit ID: 128780
Telephone: (860) 515-3800 Carnegie Class: Bac-A&S
FAX Number: (860) 606-9615 Calendar System: Other
URL: www.charteroak.edu
Established: 1973 Annual Undergrad Tuition & Fees (In-State): N/A
Enrollment: 1,929 Coed
Affiliation or Control: State IRS Status: 501(c)3
Highest Offering: Master's
Accreditation: EH, CAHIIM

01 President ... Mr. Edward KLONOSKI
05 Provost ... Dr. Shirley M. ADAMS
20 Academic Dean Undergrad Programs ... Dr. Emily G. LEWIS
10 Chief Financial/Administrative Ofcr ... Mr. Clifford S. WILLIAMS
13 Chief Information Officer ... Mr. George F. CLAFFEY, JR.
09 Dir Institutional Effectiveness ... Mr. Michael BRODERICK
06 Registrar ... Ms. Jennifer WASHINGTON
37 Dir Financial Aid/Veterans Benefits ... Mr. Ralph BRASURE, III
20 Director Academic Services ... Ms. Linda LARKIN
07 Director Admissions ... Ms. Lori GAGNE PENDLETON
88 Coord Prior Learning Assessment Pgm ... Ms. Linda WILDER
26 Director Marketing/Public Relations ... Ms. Carolyn HEBERT
04 Administrative Asst to President ... Ms. Angela CHAPMAN
102 Dir Foundation/Corporate Relations ... Ms. Angela CHAPMAN
105 Director Web Services ... Mr. Daniel RUSSELL
15 Director Personnel Services ... Ms. Rowena MCGOLDRICK
29 Director Alumni Relations ... Ms. Angela CHAPMAN

*Connecticut Board of Regents for Higher Education (E)

39 Woodland Street, Hartford CT 06105-2337
County: Hartford Identification: 666656
Unit ID: 129011
Telephone: (860) 723-0000 Carnegie Class: N/A
FAX Number: (860) 723-0009
URL: www.ct.ed

01 President ... Mr. Mark E. OJAKIAN
05 Provost ... Dr. Jane McBride GATES
12 Vice President for CSU ... Dr. Elsa NUNEZ
12 Vice President for CCC ... Dr. David LEVINSON
15 VP for Human Resources ... Mr. Steve WEINBERGER
26 Director PR & Mktg ... Mr. Michael KOZLOWSKI
10 Chief Financial Officer ... Ms. Erika STEINER
13 Chief Information Officer ... Mr. Joseph TOLISANO
101 Assoc Board Affairs/Secy to BOT ... Ms. Erin FITZGERALD
04 Administrative Assistant ... Ms. Judith S. NOSAL
100 Chief of Staff ... Dr. Alice PRITCHARD
09 Director of Institutional Research ... Dr. William GAMMELL
18 Chief Facilities/Physical Plant ... Mr. Keith EPSTEIN
43 Dir Legal Services/General Counsel ... Ms. Ernestine WEAVER
27 Director of Communications ... Ms. Maribel LA LUZ

*Central Connecticut State University (F)

1615 Stanley Street, New Britain CT 06050-4010
County: Hartford FICE Identification: 001378
Unit ID: 128771
Telephone: (860) 832-3200 Carnegie Class: Masters/L
FAX Number: N/A Calendar System: Semester
URL: www.ccsu.edu
Established: 1849 Annual Undergrad Tuition & Fees (In-State): $9,300
Enrollment: 12,037 Coed
Affiliation or Control: State IRS Status: 501(c)3
Highest Offering: Doctorate
Accreditation: EH, BUS, CAATE, CACREP, CONST, COPE, CS, ENG, ENGT, EXSC, MFCD, MUS, NAIT, NURSE, SW, TED

02 Interim President ... Dr. Susan PEASE
04 Admin Assistant to the President ... Ms. Courtney MCDAVID
05 Provost/Vice Pres Academic Affs ... Dr. Carl R. LOVITT
30 Vice Pres Institutional Advancement ... Dr. Chris GALLIGAN
32 Vice President Student Affairs ... Dr. Laura TORDENTI
35 Associate Dean Student Affairs ... Mr. Ramon HERNANDEZ
20 Associate VP Academic Affairs ... Dr. Joseph P. PAIGE
58 Associate VP Graduate Studies ... Dr. Glynis A. FITZGERALD
26 Assoc VP Marketing/Communications ... Dr. Mark W. MCLAUGHLIN
43 University Counsel ... Ms. Carolyn MAGNAN
11 Chief Administrative Officer ... Dr. Richard R. BACHOO
10 Chief Financial Officer ... Mrs. Charlene CASAMENTO
15 Chief Human Resources Officer ... Mrs. Anna SUSKI-LENCZEWSKI
13 Chief Information Officer ... Ms. Jacquelynn BONESIO-PETERSON
28 Chief Diversity Officer ... Ms. Rosa RODRIGUEZ
49 Dean Liberal Arts Social Sciences ... Dr. Susan PEASE
50 Dean School of Business ... Dr. Ken COLWELL
53 Dean School Educ & Prof Studies ... Dr. Michael P. ALFANO
54 Dean School Engr/Science/Technology ... Dr. Faris MALHAS
82 Dir Center International Education ... Dr. Mamar NDIAYE
51 Dir Continuing Educ/Cmty Engagement ... Ms. Christa STERLING
07 Director Admissions & Recruitment ... Mr. Lawrence HALL
41 Director Athletics ... Mr. Paul SCHLICKMANN
39 Director Residence Life ... Ms. Jean ALICANDRO
19 Director Public Safety ... Mr. Gregory SNEED
37 Director Student Financial Aid ... Mr. Richard BISHOP
44 Director Institutional Advancement ... Ms. Cynthia B. CAYER
27 Media Relations Officer ... Ms. Janice PALMER
08 Director Library Services ... Mr. Carl ANTONUCCI
36 Int Dir Ctr Advisg/Career Exploratn ... Mr. Paul ROSSITTO
23 Dir Student Wellness Svcs ... Dr. Jacqueline HARRIS
06 Registrar ... Mr. Patrick TUCKER
38 Coordinator Office Wellness Educ ... Mr. Jonathan POHL
18 Asst Chief Admin Ofcr/Dir Facil Mgt ... Mr. Salvatore CINTORINO
21 University Controller ... Ms. Kimberly MARTOHUE
96 Purchasing Manager ... Mr. Thomas BRODEUR
09 Director of Institutional Research ... Ms. Yvonne KIRBY

*Eastern Connecticut State University (G)

83 Windham Street, Willimantic CT 06226-2295
County: Windham FICE Identification: 001425
Unit ID: 129215
Telephone: (860) 465-5000 Carnegie Class: Masters/S
FAX Number: (860) 465-4485 Calendar System: Semester
URL: www.easternct.edu
Established: 1889 Annual Undergrad Tuition & Fees (In-State): $10,016
Enrollment: 5,287 Coed
Affiliation or Control: State IRS Status: 501(c)3
Highest Offering: Master's
Accreditation: EH, SW, TED

02 President ... Dr. Elsa M. NUNEZ
05 Provost ... Dr. Dimitrios C. PACHIS
10 VP Finance/Administration ... Mr. James R. HOWARTH
32 Vice Pres Student Affairs ... Mr. Ken BEDINI
30 Vice Pres Institutional Advance ... Mr. Kenneth J. DELISA
28 Assoc VP Equity & Diversity ... Dr. Stacey CLOSE
35 Dean of Students ... Mr. Walter DIAZ
09 Asst Dir of Institutional Research ... Dr. Brian R. LASHLEY
41 Director of Athletics ... Ms. Lori RUNKSMEIER
08 Director of Library Services ... Ms. Patricia S. BANACH
84 Dir of Enrollment Mgmt/Fin Aid ... Dr. Jennifer HORNER
36 Director of Career Services ... Mr. Clifford MARRETT
29 Director of Alumni Affairs ... Mr. Michael STENKO
06 Registrar ... Ms. Jennifer HUOPPI
19 Director of Public Safety ... Mr. Jeffrey A. GAREWSKI
39 Director Housing/Residence Life ... Mr. Lamar COLEMAN
40 Director of Bookstore ... Ms. Allyson HALL
42 Director of Campus Ministry ... Rev. Laurence LAPOINTE
18 Dir of Facilities Mgmt/Planning ... Ms. Renee KEECH
26 Director University Relations ... Mr. Edward H. OSBORN
49 Dean of Arts & Sciences ... Dr. Carmen R. CID
51 Assoc Dean Continuing Education ... Dr. Indira PETOSKEY
58 Dean Educ/Prof Studies/Grad Pgm ... Dr. Jacob EASLEY
96 Assoc Dir Fiscal Affs/Acquisition ... Ms. Terry O'BRIEN
38 Director Counseling/Psych Svcs ... Vacant
15 Int Vice Pres for Human Resources ... Mr. Steven WEINBERGER
07 Director of Admissions ... Mr. Christopher DORSEY

*Southern Connecticut State University (H)

501 Crescent Street, New Haven CT 06515-0901
County: New Haven FICE Identification: 001406
Unit ID: 130493
Telephone: (203) 392-7278 Carnegie Class: Masters/L
FAX Number: N/A Calendar System: Semester
URL: www.southernct.edu
Established: 1893 Annual Undergrad Tuition & Fees (In-State): $9,600
Enrollment: 10,825 Coed
Affiliation or Control: State IRS Status: 501(c)3
Highest Offering: Doctorate
Accreditation: EH, CAATE, CACREP, CS, EXSC, MFCD, NURSE, PH, SP, SW, TED

53 Dean School Education ... Dr. Stephen HEGEDUS
02 President ... Dr. Mary A. PAPAZIAN
04 Admin Assistant to the President ... Ms. Charmaine R. LLOYD
100 Chief of Staff ... Ms. Jaye BAILEY
05 Provost/Vice Pres Acad Affairs ... Dr. Ellen DURNIN
10 EVP for Finance & Administration ... Mr. Mark ROZEWSKI
32 Vice Pres Student Affairs ... Dr. Tracy TYREE
30 Vice President Inst Advancement ... Mr. Robert L. STAMP
84 Assoc VP for Enrollment Management ... Dr. Terricita E. SASS
15 Chief Human Resources Officer ... Ms. Diane MAZZA
18 Assoc VP Capitol Budgeting/Fac Ops ... Mr. Robert G. SHEELEY
13 Chief Info Tech Officer ... Dr. Robert RENNIE
49 Dean School Arts & Sciences ... Mr. Steven BREESE
50 Dean School of Business ... Dr. Ellen DURNIN
58 Dean School Graduate Studies ... Dr. Gregory PAVEZA
70 Interim Dean School Health/Human Sv ... Dr. Sandra BULMER
41 Director of Athletics ... Mr. Jay MORAN
26 Director of Public Affairs ... Mr. Patrick DILGER
29 Director Alumni Affairs ... Ms. Michelle JOHNSTON
07 Director Admissions ... Ms. Alexis HAAKONSEN
06 Registrar ... Ms. Siham DOUGHMAN
08 Director of Library Services ... Dr. Christina BAUM
19 Director of Public Safety ... Mr. Joseph M. DOOLEY
25 Director of Sponsored Research ... Ms. Patricia M. ZIBLUK
37 Director of Financial Aid ... Ms. Gloria LEE
23 Director of Health Services ... Dr. Diane S. MORGENTHALER
35 Dean of Student Affairs ... Dr. Jules TETREAULT
46 AVP for Institutional Effectiveness ... Dr. Richard RICCARDI
38 Director of Counseling Services ... Dr. Jeffrey VANLONE
21 University Controller ... Ms. Lise M. BRULE
92 Director of Honors Program ... Dr. Terese GEMME
94 Director of Women's Studies ... Dr. Yi-Chun Tricia LIN
88 Dir of Academic & Career Advising ... Mr. Frank LADORE
39 Director of Residence Life ... Mr. Robert C. DEMEZZO

*Western Connecticut State University (I)

181 White Street, Danbury CT 06810-6885
County: Fairfield FICE Identification: 001380
Unit ID: 130776
Telephone: (203) 837-8200 Carnegie Class: Masters/M
FAX Number: (203) 837-8276 Calendar System: Semester
URL: www.wcsu.edu

Established: 1903 Annual Undergrad Tuition & Fees (In-State): $9,516
Enrollment: 5,952 Coed
Affiliation or Control: State IRS Status: 501(c)3
Highest Offering: Doctorate
Accreditation: EH, CACREP, MUS, NURSE, SW, TED

02 President ... Dr. John B. CLARK
05 Provost/Vice Pres Academic Affairs ... Dr. Jane MCBRIDE GATES
10 Assoc VP Finance & Administration ... Mr. Sean LOUGHRAN
30 Int VP Inst Advancement ... Dr. Keith BETTS
32 Vice Pres Student Affs ... Dr. Keith BETTS
88 Int Dean of Visual/Performing Arts ... Mr. Jamie BEGIAN
35 Dean of Student Affairs ... Dr. Walter CRAMER
49 Dean of Macricostas Arts & Sciences ... Dr. Mary STEWART ALEXANDER
50 Dean of Ancell Business ... Dr. David MARTIN
107 Dean of Professional Studies ... Dr. Jess HOUSE
15 Chief Human Resources Officer ... Mr. Frederic W. CRATTY
13 Int Chief Information Officer ... Mr. George CLAFFEY
21 Director Fiscal Affairs/Controller ... Mr. Peter ROSA
44 Director of Development ... Ms. Lynne LEBARRON
22 Chief Diversity Offficer ... Mr. Daryle DENNIS
06 Registrar ... Mr. Keith R. GAUVIN
08 Director of Library Services ... Ms. Veronica KENAUSIS
09 Director Inst Research/Assessment ... Dr. Jerry WILCOX
25 Director of Grant/Programs ... Ms. Gabrielle E. JAZWIECKI
38 Director of Counseling Svcs ... Dr. Rée GUNTER
37 Director of Financial Services ... Ms. Melissa STEPHENS
36 Director Career Development Center ... Ms. Kathleen LINDENMAYER
26 Director Univ & Cmty Relations ... Mr. Paul STEINMETZ
39 Director Housing & Residence Life ... Mr. Ron MASON
35 Director Student Life ... Dr. Paul M. SIMON
41 Int Director of Athletics ... Mr. Scott AMES
29 Int Director of Alumni Affairs ... Mr. Thomas CRUCITTI
07 Director of Admissions ... Vacant
45 Dir of Facilities Plng & Engr ... Mr. Peter VISENTIN
11 Director of Administrative Services ... Mr. Mark R. CASE
18 Assoc VP Facilities ... Mr. Luigi MARCONE
88 Dir Facil Utilization & Promotion ... Mr. John MURPHY
21 Director of Fin Planning & Budgets ... Ms. Mary Ann DEASE
27 Int Assoc Dir of Public Relations ... Ms. Sherri HILL
88 Chief of Police ... Mr. Roger CONNOR
04 Administrative Asst to President ... Ms. Janet MCKAY
84 Int Assoc VP Enrollment Services ... Mr. Jay MURRAY

*Asnuntuck Community College (A)

170 Elm Street, Enfield CT 06082-3800
County: Hartford FICE Identification: 011150
Unit ID: 128577
Telephone: (860) 253-3000 Carnegie Class: Assoc/HVT-Mix Trad/Non
FAX Number: (860) 253-3014 Calendar System: Semester
URL: www.asnuntuck.edu
Established: 1972 Annual Undergrad Tuition & Fees (In-State): $4,072
Enrollment: 1,603 Coed
Affiliation or Control: State IRS Status: 501(c)3
Highest Offering: Associate Degree
Accreditation: EH

02 President ... Mr. James P. LOMBELLA
05 Dean of Academic Affairs ... Mr. Michael STEFANOWICZ
10 Interim Dean of Administration ... Mr. Gennaro DEANGELIS
32 Interim Dean of Student Services ... Mr. Tim ST. JAMES
15 Interim Assoc Director of HR ... Ms. Cheryl A. CYR
84 Director of Enrollment Management ... Vacant
06 Registrar ... Ms. Diane CLOKEY
37 Interim Director of Financial Aid ... Ms. Beth-Anne EGAN
09 Director of Institutional Research ... Ms. Qing L. MACK
30 Director Institutional Advancement ... Mr. Keith MADORE
103 Dean Workforce Dev/Cont Educ ... Ms. Eileen PELTIER
18 Bldg Superintendent II/Phys Plant ... Mr. Joseph MULLER
26 Coord of Mktg/Business/Industry ... Mr. Gary CARRA
04 Executive Asst to President ... Ms. Margret G. VAN COTT
07 Interim Director of Admissions ... Ms. Jennifer ANILOWSKI
13 Director of Information Technology ... Ms. Lynn D. GREGOR
38 Dir Ctr for Advising/Stdnt Achieve ... Ms. Jill RUSHBROOK

*Capital Community College (B)

950 Main Street, Hartford CT 06103-1207
County: Hartford FICE Identification: 007635
Unit ID: 129367
Telephone: (860) 906-5000 Carnegie Class: Assoc/HT-Mix Trad/Non
FAX Number: (860) 520-7906 Calendar System: Semester
URL: www.ccc.commnet.edu
Established: 1967 Annual Undergrad Tuition & Fees (In-State): $4,102
Enrollment: 4,075 Coed
Affiliation or Control: State IRS Status: 501(c)3
Highest Offering: Associate Degree
Accreditation: EH, ADNUR, EMT, MAC, RAD

02 President ... Dr. Wilfredo NIEVES
05 Academic Dean ... Dr. Debbie THOMAS
32 Dean of Student Services ... Ms. Doris B. ARRINGTON
11 Dean of Administration ... Mr. Lester PRIMUS
51 Dean Continuing Educ/Community Svcs ... Ms. Linda GUZZO
09 Director of Institutional Research ... Ms. Jenny WANG
10 Director Finance/Administration ... Mr. Ted HALE
06 Registrar ... Mr. Argelio MARRERO
08 Director of Library Services ... Ms. Eileen RHODES
07 Director of Admissions ... Mr. Gregg GORNEAULT
37 Director of Financial Aid ... Ms. Margaret MALASPINA
13 Director of Computer Services ... Mr. Roger FERRARO
66 Dir Cont Educ Nurse/Allied Health ... Ms. Ruth KREMS
36 Dir of Career Planning/Development ... Ms. Linda DOMENITZ
26 Director of Information/Marketing ... Ms. Jane BRONFMAN
15 Director of Human Resources ... Ms. Josephine AGNELLO-VELEY
20 Associate Academic Officer ... Mr. C. Raymond HUGHES
30 Director Institutional Advancement ... Mr. John MCNAMARA

*Gateway Community College (C)

20 Church St., New Haven CT 06510-5970
County: New Haven FICE Identification: 008037
Unit ID: 130396
Telephone: (203) 285-2000 Carnegie Class: Assoc/HT-Mix Trad/Non
FAX Number: (203) 285-2018 Calendar System: Semester
URL: www.gwcc.commnet.edu
Established: 1968 Annual Undergrad Tuition & Fees (In-State): $4,032
Enrollment: 8,200 Coed
Affiliation or Control: State IRS Status: 501(c)3
Highest Offering: Associate Degree
Accreditation: EH, ADNUR, DIETT, NMT, RAD, RTT

02 President ... Dr. Dorsey L. KENDRICK
11 Dean of Administrative Services ... Mr. Louis S. D'ANTONIO
46 Dean of Devel/Community Partnership ... Ms. Mary Ellen CODY
05 Dean of Academics ... Dr. Mark KOSINSKI
51 Dean of Cont Educ/Workforce Develop ... Ms. Victoria BOZZUTO
15 Director Personnel/Contract Admin ... Ms. Lucille BROWN
04 Executive Assistant to President ... Vacant
09 Director Institutional Research ... Dr. Vincent P. TONG
26 Director Public Info & Marketing ... Ms. Evelyn GARD
10 Director Finance & Admin Svcs ... Ms. Jill MCDOWELL
30 Director Institutional Advancement ... Vacant
08 Director Library ... Ms. Clara OGBAA
84 Director of Enrollment Management ... Mr. Joseph CARBERRY
36 Director Career Development Center ... Ms. Kellie BYRD-DANSO
37 Director Financial Aid ... Mr. Raymond ZEEK
38 Director Student Counseling ... Mr. Michael BUCCILLI
32 Director of College Life ... Ms. Roberta PRIOR
24 Director Educational Technologies ... Ms. Wendy SAMBERG
25 Grants Facilitator ... Vacant
13 Director Computer Services ... Mr. Lawrence SALAY
24 Director Early Learning Center ... Ms. Sarah CHAMBERS
88 Coord Center for Education Svcs ... Ms. Clara MENA
50 Chair Business Department ... Mr. Richard REES
79 Chair Humanities Department ... Mr. Chester H. SCHNEPF
83 Chair Social Sciences Department ... Ms. Susan LONGSTON
88 Coord Early Childhood Education ... Ms. Carmelita E. VALENCIA-DAYE
88 Coord Drug/Alcohol Rehab Counseling ... Mr. Jonah COHEN
67 Coordinator Pharmacy Tech Program ... Ms. Louise A. PETROKA
81 Chair Math/Natural Sci Department ... Mr. Rocky TREMBLAY
50 Director Business & Industry Svcs ... Ms. Marilee BAKER-ROUSSAT
88 Director Dietetic Technician Pgm ... Ms. Marcia DORAN
76 Director Allied Health ... Ms. Sheila SOLERNOU
20 Associate Dean of Learning ... Vacant
54 Dir Engineering/Applied Technology ... Mr. Eric F. FLYNN
18 Chief Facilities/Physical Plant ... Mr. Lucian SIMONE
06 Registrar ... Ms. Maribel LOPEZ

*Housatonic Community College (D)

900 Lafayette Boulevard, Bridgeport CT 06604-4704
County: Fairfield FICE Identification: 004513
Unit ID: 129543
Telephone: (203) 332-5000 Carnegie Class: Assoc/HT-High Trad
FAX Number: (203) 332-5123 Calendar System: Semester
URL: www.housatonic.edu
Established: 1966 Annual Undergrad Tuition & Fees (In-State): $4,032
Enrollment: 5,286 Coed
Affiliation or Control: State IRS Status: 501(c)3
Highest Offering: Associate Degree
Accreditation: EH, OTA

02 President ... Dr. Paul BROADIE, II
05 Acting Academic Dean ... Dr. William Terry BROWN
11 Acting Dean of Administration ... Ms. Teresa ORAVETZ
32 Acting Dean of Students ... Mr. James D. CONNOLLY
20 Associate Dean Academics ... Vacant
06 Registrar ... Mr. James CONNOLLY
07 Director of Admissions ... Mr. Earl GRAHAM
08 Librarian ... Ms. Shelly STROHM
37 Director of Financial Aid ... Ms. Barbara SUROWIEC
26 Public Relations Associate ... Vacant
19 Director of Security ... Mr. Christopher GOUGH
09 Director Institutional Research ... Ms. Jan SCHAEFFLER
13 Director of Computer Services ... Mr. Anthony VITOLA
15 Director Personnel/Labor Relations ... Ms. Theresa EISENBACH
30 Exec Dir University Advancement ... Mr. Richard DUPONT
35 Director of Student Life ... Ms. Kelly HOPE
10 Director of Finance/Admin Svcs ... Ms. Teresa ORAVETZ
18 Coordinator of Facilities ... Mr. Richard HENNESSEY
04 Executive Asst to President ... Ms. Camilla COSTANTINI
38 Director Student Counseling ... Mr. Hernan YEPES

*Manchester Community College (E)

PO Box 1046, Great Path, Manchester CT 06045-1046
County: Hartford FICE Identification: 001392
Unit ID: 129695
Telephone: (860) 512-3000 Carnegie Class: Assoc/HT-High Trad
FAX Number: (860) 512-3631 Calendar System: Semester
URL: www.manchestercc.edu
Established: 1963 Annual Undergrad Tuition & Fees (In-State): $4,052
Enrollment: 7,300 Coed
Affiliation or Control: State IRS Status: 501(c)3
Highest Offering: Associate Degree
Accreditation: EH, ACFEI, COARC, DA, OTA, RAD, RTT, SURGT

02 President ... Dr. Gena GLICKMAN
05 Int Provost/Chief Academic Officer ... Ms. Marcia JEHNINGS
32 Dean of Student Affairs ... Dr. G. Duncan HARRIS
11 Dean of Administrative Affairs ... Mr. James MCDOWELL
30 Dean of Advancement ... Ms. Endia DECORDOVA
51 Dean of Continuing Education ... Ms. Melanie HABER
20 Associate Dean of Academic Affairs ... Dr. Pamela MITCHELL-CRUMP
10 Director Finance & Admin Services ... Ms. Regina FERRANTE
07 Assoc Director of Admissions ... Ms. Cynthia ZELDNER
06 Registrar ... Ms. Anita SPARROW
08 Dir Library Svcs/Educational Tech ... Ms. Deborah HERMAN
13 Director of Information Technology ... Mr. Barry GRANT
09 Director Plng/Research & Assessment ... Mr. David NIELSEN
15 Director of Human Resources ... Ms. Patricia LINDO
18 Dir Facilities Management/ Planning ... Ms. Darlene MANCINI-BROWN
26 Dir Marketing and Public Relations ... Ms. Charlene TAPPAN
37 Director of Financial Aid ... Ms. Ivette RIVERA-DREYER
72 Director Business/Engineering/Tech ... Vacant
83 Director Social Science/Hospitality ... Dr. Christopher PAULIN
81 Int Dir Math/Science/Health Careers ... Ms. Sharale GOLDING
79 Director of Liberal Arts ... Ms. Samantha GONZALEZ
35 Director of Student Life ... Mr. Trent J. BARBER
44 Development Associate ... Ms. Diana REID
38 Dir Counseling and Career Svcs ... Ms. Julia GREENE
84 Director of Enrollment Management ... Mr. Peter HARRIS
04 Executive Assistant to President ... Ms. Sara VINCENT
103 Int Director of Business & Industry ... Mr. Miguel PIGOTT
90 Director of Academic Support Ctr ... Mr. Brian CLEARY
85 Dir Multicultural/Intl Affairs ... Mr. Joseph MESQUITA
28 Director of Diversity ... Ms. Leah GLENDE
96 Assoc Director of Purchasing ... Mr. Paul MOUNDS

*Middlesex Community College (F)

100 Training Hill Road, Middletown CT 06457-4889
County: Middlesex FICE Identification: 008038
Unit ID: 129756
Telephone: (860) 343-5800 Carnegie Class: Assoc/HT-Mix Trad/Non
FAX Number: (860) 344-7488 Calendar System: Semester
URL: www.mxcc.commnet.edu
Established: 1966 Annual Undergrad Tuition & Fees (In-State): $4,032
Enrollment: 3,005 Coed
Affiliation or Control: State IRS Status: 501(c)3
Highest Offering: Associate Degree
Accreditation: EH, OPD, RAD

02 President ... Dr. Anna WASESCHA
05 Dean of Academics ... Dr. Steven MINKLER
11 Interim Dean of Administration ... Ms. Kimberly HOGAN
32 Dean of Students ... Dr. Adrienne MASLIN
51 Dean Continuing Education ... Vacant
06 Registrar ... Ms. Susan SALOWITZ
08 Director Library Services ... Ms. Lan LIU
37 Director Financial Aid ... Ms. Irene MARTIN
30 Associate Dean of Development ... Ms. Cheryl DUMONT-SMITH
07 Director of Admissions ... Ms. Gail BARRETT
09 Director of Institutional Research ... Dr. Paul CARMICHAEL
13 Director Information Technology ... Ms. Annie SCOTT
18 Chief Facilities/Physical Plant ... Mr. Steven CHESTER
15 Director Personnel Services ... Ms. Mary Lou PHILLIPS
88 Retention Specialist ... Ms. Judy MAZGULSKI
88 Disability Services Coordinator ... Ms. Hilary PHELPS
81 Division Director Math ... Vacant
79 Division Director Humanities ... Mr. Jaime FLORES

*Naugatuck Valley Community College (G)

750 Chase Parkway, Waterbury CT 06708-3089
County: New Haven FICE Identification: 006982
Unit ID: 129729
Telephone: (203) 575-8044 Carnegie Class: Assoc/MT-VT-High Trad
FAX Number: (203) 575-8096 Calendar System: Semester
URL: www.nv.edu
Established: 1964 Annual Undergrad Tuition & Fees (In-State): $4,072
Enrollment: 7,102 Coed
Affiliation or Control: State IRS Status: 501(c)3
Highest Offering: Associate Degree
Accreditation: EH, ADNUR, COARC, ENGT, PTAA, RAD

02 President ... Dr. Daisy Cocco DE FILIPPIS
05 Provost/Senior Dean Administration ... Mr. James TROUP
31 Director of Community Development ... Ms. Gina MARCANTONIO
32 Dean of Student Services ... Ms. Sarah GAGER
30 Dean of Community Engagement ... Mr. Waldemar KOSTRZEWA
13 Assoc Dean Information Technology ... Mr. Conal LARKIN
20 Dean of Academic Affairs ... Ms. Irene RIOS-KNAUF
06 Registrar ... Ms. Joan ARBUSTO
37 Director of Financial Aid ... Ms. Catherine HARDY
07 Director of Admissions ... Ms. Linda STANGO
22 Affirmative Action Officer ... Mr. Ron CLYMER
08 Director Learning Resource Ctr ... Ms. Jamie HAMMOND
10 Director of Finance/Admin Services ... Ms. Lisa PALEN
35 Director of Student Activities ... Ms. Karen BLAKE

18 Chief Facilities/Physical Plant .... Mr. Robert DIVJAK
09 Int Dir of Institutional Research .... Ms. Lisa RODRIGUES-DOOLABH
38 Actg Dir Student Development Svcs .... Ms. Bonnie GOULET
15 Director of Human Resources .... Ms. Kimberly CAROLINA
26 Director of Marketing .... Ms. Sydney VOGHEL-OCHS
27 Public Relations Associate .... Vacant

*Northwestern Connecticut Community-Technical College (A)

Park Place E, Winsted CT 06098-1798
County: Litchfield FICE Identification: 001398
Unit ID: 130040
Telephone: (860) 738-6300 Carnegie Class: Assoc/HT-Mix Trad/Non
FAX Number: (860) 738-6488 Calendar System: Semester
URL: www.nwcc.commnet.edu/
Established: 1965 Annual Undergrad Tuition & Fees (In-State): $4,047
Enrollment: 1,614 Coed
Affiliation or Control: State IRS Status: 501(c)3
Highest Offering: Associate Degree
Accreditation: EH, ADNUR, MAC

02 President .... Dr. Michael ROOKE
11 Dean of Administration .... Dr. Steven R. FRAZIER
05 Dean of Academic & Student Affairs .... Dr. Patricia A. BOUFFARD
07 Director of Admissions .... Ms. Joanne NARDI
08 Director of Library Services .... Mr. James PATTERSON
06 Registrar .... Ms. Debra ZAVATKAY
15 Director of Human Resources .... Ms. Wendy BOVIA
37 Financial Aid Officer .... Mr. Louis BRISTOL
13 Director of Computer Services .... Mr. Joseph DANAJOVITS
38 Dir of Student Development .... Ms. Ruth GONZALEZ
09 Director of Institutional Research .... Ms. Caitlin BOGER-HAWKINS
26 Director Marketing/Public Relations .... Mr. Grantley ADAMS
10 Director Financial/Admin Services .... Ms. Kimberly DRAGAN

*Norwalk Community College (B)

188 Richards Avenue, Norwalk CT 06854-1655
County: Fairfield FICE Identification: 001399
Unit ID: 130004
Telephone: (203) 857-7000 Carnegie Class: Assoc/HT-Mix Trad/Non
FAX Number: (203) 857-7287 Calendar System: Semester
URL: www.norwalk.edu
Established: 1961 Annual Undergrad Tuition & Fees (In-State): $4,052
Enrollment: 6,363 Coed
Affiliation or Control: State IRS Status: 501(c)3
Highest Offering: Associate Degree
Accreditation: EH, ADNUR, COARC, MAC, PTAA

02 President .... Dr. David L. LEVINSON
11 Dean of Administration .... Vacant
32 Dean of Students .... Dr. Calvin MCFADDEN
05 Dean of Academics .... Vacant
30 Executive Director of Development .... Ms. Ann ROGERS
103 Int Assoc Dn Ext Stds/Workforce Dev .... Dr. Kristina TESTA-BUZZEE
08 Director of Library Services .... Ms. Linda LERMAN
37 Director Financial Aid .... Mr. Luis GUAMAN
66 Int Director of Nursing Education .... Ms. Katherine FRIES
06 Registrar .... Ms. Danita BROWN
15 Director Human Resources .... Ms. Therese MARROCCO
26 Director of Public Relations .... Ms. Madeline K. BARILLO
38 Director Student Counseling .... Ms. Catherine MILLER
07 Acting Director of Admissions .... Mr. William CHAGNON
10 Director Finance/Administration .... Ms. Carrie MCGEE-YUROF
18 Chief Facilities/Physical Plant .... Mr. Craig CARLSON
28 Chief Diversity Officer .... Ms. Cheryl DEVONISH

*Quinebaug Valley Community College (C)

742 Upper Maple Street, Danielson CT 06239-1440
County: Windham FICE Identification: 010530
Unit ID: 130217
Telephone: (860) 932-4000 Carnegie Class: Assoc/MT-VT-High Trad
FAX Number: (860) 932-4306 Calendar System: Semester
URL: www.qvcc.edu
Established: 1971 Annual Undergrad Tuition & Fees (In-State): $4,062
Enrollment: 1,883 Coed
Affiliation or Control: State IRS Status: 501(c)3
Highest Offering: Associate Degree
Accreditation: EH, MAC

02 President .... Dr. Carlee DRUMMER
05 Dean Academic Affs & Student Svcs .... Mr. Alfred WILLIAMS
11 Dean of Administrative Services .... Mr. Paul MARTLAND
08 Director of Library Services .... Vacant
37 Director of Student Financial Aid .... Ms. Kim RICH
09 Director of Institutional Research .... Dr. Donna SOHAN
10 Dir Finance/Administrative Svcs .... Ms. Alessandra LUNDBERG
18 Chief Facilities/Physical Plant .... Mr. Martin CHARETTE
26 Chief Public Relations Officer .... Ms. Susan BREAULT
30 Dir of Institutional Advancement .... Ms. Monique WOLANIN
06 Registrar .... Ms. Amy KACERIK
27 Coordinator of Marketing .... Ms. Margie HUOPPI
07 Associate Director of Admissions .... Ms. Sarah HENDRICK
04 Administrative Asst to President .... Ms. Jennifer GREEN
103 Dir Workforce/Career Development .... Ms. Valerie NIGHTINGALE
13 Chief Info Technology Officer (CIO) .... Mr. Jarrod BOREK

*Three Rivers Community College (D)

574 New London Turnpike, Norwich CT 06360
County: New London FICE Identification: 009765
Unit ID: 129808
Telephone: (860) 215-9000 Carnegie Class: Assoc/HT-High Trad
FAX Number: (860) 215-9901 Calendar System: Semester
URL: www.trcc.commnet.edu
Established: 1963 Annual Undergrad Tuition & Fees (In-State): $4,072
Enrollment: 4,530 Coed
Affiliation or Control: State IRS Status: 501(c)3
Highest Offering: Associate Degree
Accreditation: EH, ACBSP, ADNUR

02 President .... Dr. Mary Ellen JUKOSKI
05 Academic Dean .... Dr. Jerry T. ICE
11 Dean of Administration and IT .... Mr. Stephen H. GOETCHIUS
84 Dn Student Svcs/Enrol Mgt/Wrkf Dev .... Mr. Stephen FINTON
13 Dir of Information Technology .... Mr. Larry DAVENPORT
30 Dir Institutional Advancement .... Ms. Betty BAILLARGEON
06 Interim Registrar .... Ms. Betty WILLIAMSON
10 Dir of Finance/Admin Svcs .... Ms. Gayle O'NEILL
38 Director of Student Development .... Dr. Jacqueline PHILLIPS
08 Director Library Services .... Ms. Mildred HODGE
15 Director Human Resources .... Ms. Louise C. SUMMA
37 Actg Dir Student Financial Aid .... Mr. Kenneth BRIGGS
18 Director of Facilities .... Mr. Arnie DE LA ROSSA
09 Office of Institutional Research .... Ms. Laura QIN
26 Dir of Marketing/Public Relations .... Ms. Kathryn GAFFNEY
14 Dir Information Tech Support .... Ms. Cathy DAVENPORT
14 Dir of Educational Technology .... Mr. Kem BARFIELD
35 Dir of Student Success .... Ms. Christine LANGUTH
04 Exec Assistant to President .... Ms. April HODSON
07 Director of Admissions .... Ms. Peg STROUP
32 Director of Student Programs .... Ms. Rhonda SPAZIANI
103 Assoc Dean Workforce Dev .... Ms. Marjorie VALENTIN

*Tunxis Community College (E)

271 Scott Swamp Road, Farmington CT 06032-3187
County: Hartford FICE Identification: 009764
Unit ID: 130606
Telephone: (860) 255-3500 Carnegie Class: Assoc/HT-Mix Trad/Non
FAX Number: N/A Calendar System: Semester
URL: www.tunxis.edu/
Established: 1969 Annual Undergrad Tuition & Fees (In-State): $3,866
Enrollment: 4,193 Coed
Affiliation or Control: State IRS Status: 501(c)3
Highest Offering: Associate Degree
Accreditation: EH, ACBSP, DA, DH

02 President .... Dr. Cathryn L. ADDY
05 Dean of Academic Affairs .... Dr. David ENGLAND
32 Dean of Student Affairs .... Dr. Kirk PETERS
11 Dean of Administration .... Mr. Charles CLEARY
10 Dir Finance/Administrative Services .... Ms. Nancy ESCHENBRENNER
30 Dir of Institutional Advancement .... Ms. Leigh E. KNOPF
15 Director Human Resources .... Vacant
08 Director Library Services .... Dr. Lisa LAVOIE
13 Director Information Technology .... Mr. Robert WAHL
07 Director of Admissions .... Ms. Tamika DAVIS
06 Registrar .... Ms. Susan WINN
35 Director Academic Support Center .... Ms. Kathleen SCHWAGER
09 Director of Institutional Research .... Vacant
37 Director Financial Aid Services .... Mr. David WELSH
18 Director of Facilities .... Mr. John LODOVICO
90 Coord Academic Info Technology .... Mr. Steven MEAD
91 Coord Admin Information Technology .... Mrs. Mary Ann DIORIO
26 Public Relations Associate .... Ms. Melissa LAMAR

Connecticut College (F)

270 Mohegan Avenue, New London CT 06320-4125
County: New London FICE Identification: 001379
Unit ID: 128902
Telephone: (860) 447-1911 Carnegie Class: Bac-A&S
FAX Number: (860) 439-2700 Calendar System: Semester
URL: www.conncoll.edu
Established: 1911 Annual Undergrad Tuition & Fees: $49,350
Enrollment: 1,900 Coed
Affiliation or Control: Independent Non-Profit IRS Status: 501(c)3
Highest Offering: Master's
Accreditation: EH

01 President .... Ms. Katherine BERGERON
05 Dean of the Faculty .... Ms. Abigail A. VANSLYCK
10 Vice Pres Finance and Admin .... Mr. Richard MADONNA
30 Vice President College Advancement .... Ms. Ann GOODWIN
08 Vice Pres of Info Svcs/Librarian .... Dr. W. Lee HISLE
26 Vice President Communications .... Ms. Pamela DUMAS SERFES
07 VP of Admission & Financial Aid .... Mr. Andrew STRICKLER
15 Asst VP HR/Professional Development .... Mrs. Cheryl L. MILLER
20 Dean of the College .... Jefferson SINGER
32 Dean of Student Life .... Dr. Victor J. ARCELUS
28 Dean of Institution Equity and Incl .... Mr. Jonathan MCNIGHT
20 Associate Dean of Faculty .... Prof. Jeffrey COLE
06 Registrar .... Ms. Elisabeth S. LABRIOLA
09 Director of Institutional Research .... Dr. John D. NUGENT
21 Controller .... Ms. Amanda B. MAYFIELD
37 Director of Financial Aid .... Mr. Sean MARTIN
41 Director of Athletics .... Mr. Francis SHIELDS

29 Director of Alumni Relations .... Ms. Bridget MCSHANE
38 Director Student Counseling .... Dr. Janet D. SPOLTORE
18 Chief Facilities/Physical Plant .... Mr. James NORTON
96 Director of Purchasing .... Vacant
88 Secretary of the College .... Ms. Bonnie WELLS

Fairfield University (G)

1073 N Benson Road, Fairfield CT 06824-5195
County: Fairfield FICE Identification: 001385
Unit ID: 129242
Telephone: (203) 254-4000 Carnegie Class: Masters/L
FAX Number: (203) 254-4101 Calendar System: Semester
URL: www.fairfield.edu
Established: 1942 Annual Undergrad Tuition & Fees: $44,875
Enrollment: 5,123 Coed
Affiliation or Control: Roman Catholic IRS Status: 501(c)3
Highest Offering: Doctorate
Accreditation: EH, ANEST, BUS, CACREP, ENG, MFCD, NURSE, TED

01 President .... Rev. Jeffrey P. VON ARX, SJ
42 Univ Chaplain/Special Asst to Pres .... Rev. Charles H. ALLEN, SJ
03 Exec VP & Chief Operating Officer .... Mr. Kevin P. LAWLOR
05 Provost/Sr Vice Pres Academic Affs .... Ms. Lynn BABINGTON
100 Exec Asst to Pres/Chief of Staff .... Mr. Michael TORTORA
10 Vice Pres Finance/Treasurer/CFO .... Mr. Michael TRAFECANTE
30 Vice Pres Univ Advancement .... Mr. Wally HALAS
15 Vice President of Human Resources .... Mr. Scott ESPOSITO
32 Sr Vice President Student Affairs .... Dr. Thomas C. PELLEGRINO
88 Vice Pres for Mission and Identity .... Dr. Nancy DALLAVALLE
26 VP Marketing and Communications .... Ms. Jennifer ANDERSON
20 Assoc Vice Pres Academic Affairs .... Dr. Mary Frances MALONE
20 Vice Provost/AVP Academic Affairs .... Dr. Christine SIEGEL
18 Assoc Vice Pres Facilities Mgmt .... Mr. David W. FRASSINELLI
38 Asst Vice Pres/Dir Counseling Svcs .... Dr. Susan N. BIRGE
21 Asst VP of Finance/Controller .... Mr. Kenneth FONTAINE
35 Asst Vice Pres Student Affairs .... Mr. James D. FITZPATRICK
09 Dir Institutional Research/Plng .... Ms. Amy BOCZER
84 Assoc Vice Pres/Dean of Enrollment .... Ms. Karen A. PELLEGRINO
07 Director of Graduate Admission .... Ms. Marianne L. GUMPPER
06 University Registrar .... Mr. Robert C. RUSSO
13 Chief Information Officer .... Vacant
37 Director of Financial Aid .... Ms. Diana M. DRAPER
36 Director of Career Planning Center .... Ms. Cathleen M. BORGMAN
29 Asst Vice Pres of Alumni Relations .... Ms. Janet A. CANEPA
42 Director of Campus Ministry .... Rev. Mark SCALESE
19 Director of Public Safety .... Mr. Todd A. PELAZZA
41 Director of Athletics .... Mr. Eugene P. DORIS
49 Dean College Arts & Science .... Dr. Yohuru WILLLIAMS
50 Dean Charles F Dolan Sch of Bus .... Dr. Donald E. GIBSON
54 Dean School of Engineering .... Dr. Bruce BERDANIER
66 Dean School of Nursing/Health Stds .... Dr. Meredith W. KAZER
53 Dean Grad Sch Educ/Allied Prof .... Dr. Robert HANNAFIN
35 AVP Student Affs/Dean of Students .... Ms. Karen A. DONOGHUE
88 Dir of Conference/Event Management .... Mr. Matthew A. DINNAN
35 Assoc Dean of Students .... Mr. William H. JOHNSON
28 Dir Student Diversity/Multicul Affs .... Ms. Chanel WARD
104 Director of Study Abroad .... Ms. Jennifer EWALD
92 Director of Honors Program .... Dr. John E. THIEL
08 Univ Librarian/Dir of Library Svcs .... Dr. Brent A. MAI
23 Director of Student Health Center .... Ms. Julia A. DUFFY
16 Director Human Resources .... Mr. Mark J. GUGLIELMONI
96 Purchasing Manager .... Mr. Peter PEREZ

Goodwin College (H)

One Riverside Drive, East Hartford CT 06118-2777
County: Hartford FICE Identification: 022449
Unit ID: 129154
Telephone: (860) 528-4111 Carnegie Class: Spec-4-yr-Other Health
FAX Number: (860) 291-9550 Calendar System: Semester
URL: www.goodwin.edu
Established: 1999 Annual Undergrad Tuition & Fees: $19,950
Enrollment: 3,440 Coed
Affiliation or Control: Independent Non-Profit IRS Status: 501(c)3
Highest Offering: Baccalaureate
Accreditation: EH, ADNUR, COARC, DH, EMT, HT, MAAB, MAC, #OTA

01 President .... Mr. Mark E. SCHEINBERG
03 Executive Vice President/Provost .... Ms. Ann B. CLARK
05 VP Academic Affs/Dean Faculty .... Ms. Danielle WILKEN
10 Vice President for Finance/CFO .... Mr. Eddie MEYER
45 Vice Pres for Inst Effectiveness .... Vacant
30 Vice Pres Economic/Strategic Dev .... Mr. Todd J. ANDREWS
18 Vice Pres Facilities/Technology .... Mr. Bryant L. HARRELL
84 Vice Pres Enrollment/Mrktg/Comm .... Mr. Daniel NOONAN
30 Vice President for Advancement .... Ms. Brooke PENDERS
20 Asst Vice Pres Academic Affairs .... Ms. Danielle S. WILKEN
13 Asst VP Information Technology .... Mr. Dan REGO
32 AVP Stdnt Affs/Dean of Students .... Dr. Sandy WIRTH
09 Asst VP Institutional Effectiveness .... Dr. Henriette M. PRANGER
88 Asst VP Strategy/Business Devel .... Dr. Clifford THERMER
84 Asst VP Enrollment Services .... Mr. Nicholas LENTINO
08 Director of Library Services .... Ms. Marilyn L. NOWLAN
56 Dean of Magnet Schools .... Mr. Alan KRAMER
36 Director of Career Services .... Mr. Lee HAMEROFF
26 Director of Communications .... Mr. Phil MOORE
44 Assoc Dir of Developmnt/Annual Fund .... Ms. Leia BELL
21 Director of Finance & Business Svcs .... Ms. Sharon N. DADDONA
37 Director of Financial Aid .... Ms. Bonnie SOLTZ-KNOWLTON
09 Dir Inst Research/Educ Assessment .... Dr. Alan J. STURTZ
106 Director of Online Learning .... Dr. Mark FAZIOLI
06 Registrar .... Ms. Allison MISKY

29 Alumni Relations Coordinator ... Ms. Vanessa PERGOLIZZI
04 Executive Assistant to President ... Ms. Ann ZAJCHOWSKI
66 Dept Chair/Director Nursing ... Ms. Janice COSTELLO

Hartford Seminary (A)

77 Sherman Street, Hartford CT 06105-2260
County: Hartford | FICE Identification: 001387
Unit ID: 129491
Telephone: (860) 509-9500 | Carnegie Class: Spec-4-yr-Faith
FAX Number: (860) 509-9509 | Calendar System: Semester
URL: www.hartsem.edu
Established: 1834 | Annual Graduate Tuition & Fees: N/A
Enrollment: 117 | Coed
Affiliation or Control: Independent Non-Profit | IRS Status: 501(c)3
Highest Offering: Doctorate; No Undergraduates
Accreditation: EH, THEOL

01 President ... Dr. Heidi HADSELL
05 Academic Dean ... Dr. Uriah KIM
11 Director of Admin and Facilities ... Ms. Roseann LEZAK JANOW
30 Chief Development Officer ... Mr. Samuel LOCKE
07 Director of Recruitment/Admissions ... Ms. Tina DEMO
88 Director Religion Research Inst ... Dr. Scott THUMMA
88 Director Doctor of Ministry Program ... Dr. Scott THUMMA
88 Director of Islamic Center ... Vacant
08 Library Director ... Dr. Steven BLACKBURN
44 Comm & Development Associate ... Mr. Patrick BYRNE
10 Chief Business Officer ... Mr. Michael SANDNER
06 Registrar ... Ms. Danielle LAVINE
04 Exec Assistant to the President ... Ms. Heather HOLDA
26 Director of Communications ... Ms. Susan SCHOENBERGER

Holy Apostles College and Seminary (B)

33 Prospect Hill Road, Cromwell CT 06416-2027
County: Middlesex | FICE Identification: 001389
Unit ID: 129534
Telephone: (860) 632-3010 | Carnegie Class: Spec-4-yr-Faith
FAX Number: (860) 632-3030 | Calendar System: Semester
URL: www.holyapostles.edu
Established: 1956 | Annual Undergrad Tuition & Fees: $7,750
Enrollment: 378 | Coed
Affiliation or Control: Roman Catholic | IRS Status: 501(c)3
Highest Offering: Beyond Master's But Less Than Doctorate
Accreditation: EH

01 President & Rector ... V.Rev. Douglas L. MOSEY
11 VP External Affs/Govt Compliance ... Dr. Sebastian MAHFOOD
05 Academic Dean/Chief Academic Ofcr ... Rev. Peter KUCER
32 Director of Student Services ... Mrs. Laura BROWN
10 Chief Financial Officer ... Mr. William RUSSELL
08 Director of Library Services ... Ms. Clare ADAMO
07 Director of Admissions ... Dr. Elizabeth REX

Lincoln College of New England (C)

2279 Mount Vernon Road, Southington CT 06489-1057
County: Hartford | FICE Identification: 009407
Unit ID: 128683
Telephone: (860) 628-4751 | Carnegie Class: Bac/Assoc-Assoc Dom
FAX Number: (860) 628-6444 | Calendar System: Semester
URL: www.lincolncollegene.edu
Established: 1966 | Annual Undergrad Tuition & Fees: $19,950
Enrollment: 715 | Coed
Affiliation or Control: Proprietary | IRS Status: Proprietary
Highest Offering: Baccalaureate
Accreditation: EH, CAHIIM, DA, DH, DIETT, FUSER, MAC, NURSE, OTA

01 President ... Ms. Denise LEWICKI
04 Executive Assistant to President ... Vacant
05 VP Academic Affairs ... Dr. Mark ANDERSON
11 VP Operations & Student Affairs ... Vacant
10 Dir Business Admin Services ... Mr. Stephen PERMAR
36 Director of Career Services ... Ms. Jenifer RAHUSEN
32 Assoc Dean of Student Services ... Mrs. Cynthia A. CLARK
20 Dean of Academic Affairs ... Mr. Chris DI STISO
06 Registrar ... Mr. Christopher DISTISO
07 Director of Admissions ... Ms. Edmund LIZOTTE
08 Director of Library Services ... Mr. Shawn FIELDS
37 Director of Financial Aid ... Mrs. Gina D. SWENTON
09 Director of Institutional Research ... Mr. Jon DALY
19 Director Campus Safety & Security ... Mr. David C. ALLING
13 IT Administrator-Southington ... Mr. Edward D. CONNELLY

Mitchell College (D)

437 Pequot Avenue, New London CT 06320-4498
County: New London | FICE Identification: 001393
Unit ID: 129774
Telephone: (860) 701-5000 | Carnegie Class: Bac-Diverse
FAX Number: (860) 701-5090 | Calendar System: Semester
URL: www.mitchell.edu
Established: 1938 | Annual Undergrad Tuition & Fees: $31,000
Enrollment: 778 | Coed
Affiliation or Control: Independent Non-Profit | IRS Status: 501(c)3
Highest Offering: Baccalaureate
Accreditation: EH

01 President ... Ms. Janet STEINMAYER
05 VP Acad Affs/Dean of the College ... Dr. Catherine WRIGHT
10 Vice Pres Administration & Finance ... Ms. Dyann J. BAKER
32 Vice Pres Student Affs/Dean Stdnts ... Ms. Sandra WIRTH
30 Vice Pres of Engagement ... Ms. Ruth SAUNDERS
15 Vice President for Human Resources ... Mr. Jonathan HOWELL
41 Director of Athletics ... Ms. Dana FULMER-GARFIELD
06 Registrar ... Ms. Amy VAN OOT
88 Director of Thames Academy ... Ms. Jacqueline JEWETT
08 Director of Library Services ... Vacant
13 Director of Academic Technologies ... Mr. Rich WALL
09 Dir Instl Research & Assessment ... Vacant
37 Director of Financial Aid ... Ms. Jacklyn C. STOLTZ
89 Assistant Dean 1st Year Experience ... Ms. Jennifer R. WELSH
27 Director of Communications ... Mrs. Colleen GRESH
36 Director of Integrative Learning ... Ms. Amanda LJUBICIC
39 Director of Residence Life ... Vacant
18 Director of Facilities ... Mr. Joseph PARDEE
88 Bursar ... Ms. Leah BRENNAN
07 Director of Admissions ... Mr. Bob MARTIN
04 Executive Assistant to President ... Ms. Karen BOURQUE
38 Director Health & Wellness ... Ms. Stacey TORPEY
19 Director Security/Safety ... Mr. George MARSHALL
26 Director of Marketing ... Ms. Lisa STINSON

Paier College of Art (E)

20 Gorham Avenue, Hamden CT 06514-3902
County: New Haven | FICE Identification: 007459
Unit ID: 130110
Telephone: (203) 287-3031 | Carnegie Class: Spec-4-yr-Arts
FAX Number: (203) 287-3021 | Calendar System: Semester
URL: www.paiercollegeofart.edu
Established: 1946 | Annual Undergrad Tuition & Fees: $15,450
Enrollment: 129 | Coed
Affiliation or Control: Proprietary | IRS Status: Proprietary
Highest Offering: Baccalaureate
Accreditation: ACCSC

01 President ... Mr. Jonathan E. PAIER
03 Vice President ... Mr. Daniel L. PAIER
05 Dean of the College ... Mr. Francis COOLEY
10 Director Finance ... Mrs. Maureen E. PAIER
57 Director Design/Graphics ... Mr. Peter MISERENDINO
102 Director Foundation/Arts ... Mr. Robert E. ZAPPALORTI
08 Librarian ... Ms. Beth HARRIS
37 Director Student Financial Aid ... Mr. John DE ROSE
32 Director of Student Services ... Mrs. Angela DEROSE
20 Assistant to the Dean ... Ms. Angela DEROSE
88 Director Interior Design ... Mr. Pierre STRAUCH
88 Director Photography ... Mr. Peter BENSON
07 Admissions Secretary ... Ms. Lynn PASCALE

Post University (F)

800 Country Club Road, Waterbury CT 06723-2540
County: New Haven | FICE Identification: 001401
Unit ID: 130183
Telephone: (203) 596-4500 | Carnegie Class: Masters/L
FAX Number: (203) 756-5810 | Calendar System: Semester
URL: www.post.edu
Established: 1890 | Annual Undergrad Tuition & Fees: $16,510
Enrollment: 8,366 | Coed
Affiliation or Control: Proprietary | IRS Status: Proprietary
Highest Offering: Master's
Accreditation: EH, ACBSP

00 Chief Executive Officer ... Mr. John L. HOPKINS
01 President ... Dr. Donald W. MROZ
11 Chief Operations Officer ... Mr. Bobby REESE
10 Chief Financial Officer ... Mr. Scott T. ALLEN
26 Chief Marketing Officer ... Mr. Richard SCHECHTER
13 Chief Information Officer ... Mr. Michael STATMORE
15 VP of Human Resources ... Mr. Donald KELLY
37 VP Student Finance ... Ms. Sharon SWEENEY
88 VP Operations Analysis ... Mr. Shane LIVELY
05 Provost ... Dr. Elizabeth JOHNSON
06 Registrar ... Ms. Mary Ann D'ENTREMONT
32 Dean of Students ... Ms. Erica PERYGA
88 Director of Acad Success & Ret ... Mr. Jeffrey OLSEN
07 Director Admissions Main Campus ... Ms. Kathryn REILLY
07 Director Admissions-ADP ... Ms. Jeanna SINN
07 Director Grad Admiss-ADP ... Ms. Gina TRICARICO
88 Dir of Military Field Enrollment ... Mr. Charles YOUNG
41 Director of Athletics ... Mr. Ronnie PALMER
49 Dean of School of Arts & Sciences ... Dr. Jeremi BAUER
50 Acting Dean of School of Business . Mr. Christopher SZPRYNGEL
80 Dean John P Burke Sch Pub Svcs & Ed ... Dr. Richard STROMPF
08 Library Director ... Ms. Tracy RALSTON
37 Director Financial Aid ... Mr. Robert ANDRUK
37 Director of Student Accounts ... Ms. Michelle ORBE
88 Director of Compliance ... Ms. Jillian DIAZ
37 Director of Student Fin Operations ... Ms. Michelle GAMBACINI
04 Executive Asst to the CEO ... Ms. Melissah KOCHERA
04 Executive Asst to the President ... Ms. Patricia JENNINGS
16 Human Resources Director ... Ms. Madelaine KELSEY
19 Director of Campus Safety ... Mr. Robert TANSLEY
38 Director Student Counseling ... Ms. Lisa ANTEL
36 Director Career Services ... Dr. Mary RIGALI
108 Director of Assessment ... Dr. Zvi GOLDMAN
18 Facilities Manager ... Mr. Bill DAVIS
46 Asst Provost Research/Innovation ... Vacant

Quinnipiac University (G)

275 Mount Carmel Avenue, Hamden CT 06518-1908
County: New Haven | FICE Identification: 001402
Unit ID: 130226
Telephone: (203) 582-8200 | Carnegie Class: Masters/L
FAX Number: (203) 582-4703 | Calendar System: Semester
URL: www.quinnipiac.edu
Established: 1929 | Annual Undergrad Tuition & Fees: $42,270
Enrollment: 9,035 | Coed
Affiliation or Control: Independent Non-Profit | IRS Status: 501(c)3
Highest Offering: First Professional Degree
Accreditation: EH, AA, ANEST, ARCPA, BUS, CAATE, CS, LAW, #MED, NURSE, OT, PA, PERF, PTA, RAD, SW, TED

01 President ... Dr. John L. LAHEY
04 Vice President/Exec Assoc to Pres ... Ms. Jean L. HUSTED
05 Executive Vice President/Provost ... Dr. Mark A. THOMPSON
10 VP Finance/Chief Financial Ofcr ... Mr. Mark VARHOLAK
26 Vice President for Public Affairs ... Ms. Lynn M. BUSHNELL
18 Vice Pres Facilities & Capital Plng ... Mr. Salvatore FILARDI
15 VP for Human Resources ... Ms. Jean L. HUSTED
07 Vice Pres for Admissions & Fin Aid ... Ms. Joan I. MOHR
84 Assoc VP for Admissions & Fin Aid ... Mr. Gregory E. EICHHORN
21 Assoc VP Budget & Fin Planning ... Mr. Sandip PATEL
30 Vice Pres Devel & Alumni Affairs ... Mr. Donald J. WEINBACH
32 Vice President & Dean of Students ... Dr. Monique DRUCKER
13 VP/Chief Info & Tech Officer ... Mr. Fred E. TARCA
20 Assoc VP Academic & Strategic Plng ... Dr. Annalisa ZINN
27 VP & Chief Digital Comm Officer ... Mr. Keith RHODES
27 Assoc VP for Public Relations ... Mr. John MORGAN
06 Registrar ... Mr. Joshua BERRY
106 VP & COO for QU Online ... Ms. Cynthia GALLATIN
28 AVP Acad Affs/Chief Diversity Ofcr ... Dr. Diane M. ARIZA
35 Assoc VP Student Affairs ... Ms. Cindy LONG PORTER
39 Director of Resident Life ... Vacant
35 Asst Dean & Director Student Center ... Mr. Daniel W. BROWN
23 Dir of Student Health Services ... Ms. Christy CHASE
38 Director of Health & Wellness ... Ms. Kerry PATTON
19 Chief of Public Safety ... Mr. Edgar RODRIGUEZ
08 Director of Arnold Bernhard Library ... Mr. Robert JOVEN
41 Director of Athletics & Recreation ... Mr. Greg AMODIO
40 Campus Store Manager ... Ms. Margaret SAMUL
104 Director for Global Education ... Ms. Andrea HOGAN
21 Assoc VP for Finance/Controller ... Mr. Daniel R. JOHNSON
96 Director of Shared Services ... Vacant
109 Assoc VP for Auxiliary Services ... Mr. John MERIANO
29 Sr Dir Parent/Family Development ... Ms. Melinda FORMICA
44 Sr Assoc VP Devel & Alumni Affairs ... Ms. Dianna PATEGAS
37 Assoc VP & Univ Director of Fin Aid ... Mr. Dominic YOIA
108 Assoc Dir Acad Assessment/Research ... Ms. Sungah KIM
90 Director of Academic Technology ... Ms. Lauren ERARDI
66 Dean School of Nursing ... Dr. Jean LANGE
50 Dean School of Business ... Dr. Matthew L. O'CONNOR
49 Dean College of Arts & Sciences ... Dr. Robert SMART
76 Dean School of Health Sciences ... Dr. William C. KOHLHEPP
61 Dean School of Law ... Ms. Jennifer BROWN
61 Associate Dean School of Law ... Mr. Neal R. FEIGENSON
60 Dean School of Communications ... Mr. Lee KAMLET
53 Dean School of Education ... Dr. Kevin BASMADJIAN
63 Dean School of Med & VP Health Affs ... Dr. Bruce KOEPPEN
54 Dean School of Engineering ... Dr. Justin KILE
94 Director of Women's Studies ... Dr. Jennifer SACCO

Rensselaer at Hartford (H)

275 Windsor Street, Hartford CT 06120-2991
Telephone: (860) 548-2400 | FICE Identification: 002804
Accreditation: &M

† Regional accreditation is carried under the parent institution, Rensselaer Polytechnic Institute, NY.

Sacred Heart University (I)

5151 Park Avenue, Fairfield CT 06825-1000
County: Fairfield | FICE Identification: 001403
Unit ID: 130253
Telephone: (203) 371-7999 | Carnegie Class: Masters/L
FAX Number: (203) 365-7652 | Calendar System: Semester
URL: www.sacredheart.edu
Established: 1963 | Annual Undergrad Tuition & Fees: $37,170
Enrollment: 7,781 | Coed
Affiliation or Control: Independent Non-Profit | IRS Status: 501(c)3
Highest Offering: Doctorate
Accreditation: EH, #ARCPA, BUS, CAATE, CEA, NURSE, OT, PTA, @SP, SW, TED

01 President ... Dr. John J. PETILLO
11 Sr VP Finance & Administration ... Mr. Michael J. KINNEY
05 Acting Provost/VP Academic Affairs ... Dr. Rupendra PALIWAL
32 Sr VP Student Affairs & Athletics ... Mr. James M. BARQUINERO
15 VP Human Resources ... Mr. Robert M. HARDY
26 VP Marketing & Communication ... Mr. Michael L. IANNAZZI
88 VP Mission & Catholic Identity ... Dr. Michael J. HIGGINS
10 VP Finance ... Mr. Philip J. MCCABE
13 VP Information Tech & Security ... Mr. Michael D. TRIMBLE
30 VP University Advancement ... Mr. William REIDY
20 Vice Provost Special Acad Programs ... Ms. Mary Lou DEROSA
43 University General Counsel ... Mr. Michael D. LAROBINA
49 Dean College of Arts & Sciences ... Mrs. Robin CAUTIN
50 Dean College of Business ... Dr. John CHALYKOFF

76 Dean College of Health Professions .... Dr. Patricia W. WALKER
53 Dean College of Education .... Dr. James C. CARL
66 Dean College of Nursing .... Ms. Mary Alice DONIUS
108 President University Acad Assembly .... Dr. Antoinette BRUCIATI

St. Vincent's College (A)

2800 Main Street, Bridgeport CT 06606-4292
County: Fairfield FICE Identification: 006191
Unit ID: 130448
Telephone: (203) 576-5235 Carnegie Class: Spec-4-yr-Other Health
FAX Number: (203) 576-5893 Calendar System: Semester
URL: www.stvincentscollege.edu
Established: 1991 Annual Undergrad Tuition & Fees: $14,630
Enrollment: 751 Coed
Affiliation or Control: Independent Non-Profit IRS Status: 501(c)3
Highest Offering: Baccalaureate
Accreditation: **EH**, ADNUR, MAC, NUR, RAD

01 President/CEO .... Dr. Michael GARGANO, JR.
10 Chief Financial Officer .... Mr. Christopher GIVEN
05 VP Academic Affairs/Dean of Faculty .... Dr. Susan CAPASSO
13 Director MIS/Student Affairs .... Mrs. Anet SURRRUSCO
09 Institutional Researcher .... Mrs. Sandra SHARP
11 Director of Administrative Services .... Vacant
29 Director Alumni Relations/Devel .... Mrs. Sharon BEASLEY
84 Director Enrollment Mgmt & Fin Svcs .... Mrs. Dorothy MARTIN-HATCHER
06 Registrar .... Mr. Vincent B. CATAUDELLA
51 Director of Continuing Education .... Ms. Tatiana RAMPINO
08 Librarian .... Ms. Vicky JACOBSON
66 Dean of Nursing .... Dr. Karen L. BARNETTT
88 Chair of Radiography .... Ms. Terry HINE
97 Chair of General Education .... Dr. Susan CAPASSO
88 Chair of Medical Assisting .... Ms. Holly MULRENAN
21 Director Student Accounts .... Vacant
88 Chair of Healthcare Administration .... Mr. William INGERSOLL

Trinity College (B)

300 Summit Street, Hartford CT 06106-3100
County: Hartford FICE Identification: 001414
Unit ID: 130590
Telephone: (860) 297-2000 Carnegie Class: Bac-A&S
FAX Number: (860) 297-5359 Calendar System: Semester
URL: www.trincoll.edu
Established: 1823 Annual Undergrad Tuition & Fees: $50,776
Enrollment: 2,408 Coed
Affiliation or Control: Independent Non-Profit IRS Status: 501(c)3
Highest Offering: Master's
Accreditation: **EH**, ENG

01 President .... Dr. Joanne BERGER-SWEENEY
05 Dean of the Faculty .... Dr. Timothy CRESSWELL
10 Vice Pres Finance & Ops/Treasurer .... Mr. Dan HITCHELL
13 Vice Pres Information Svcs/CIO .... Ms. Suzanne AEER
30 Vice Pres College Advancement .... Mr. Jack FRACASSO
32 Vice Pres Stdnt Affs/Dean Stdnts .... Mr. Joseph DICHRISTINA
84 Vice Pres Enrollment/Stdnt Success .... Dr. Angel B. PEREZ
101 Secretary of the College .... Mr. Dickens MATHIEU
07 Director of Admissions .... Mr. Anthony T. BERRY
20 Associate Academic Dean .... Dr. Sonia CARDENA
20 Associate Academic Dean .... Dr. Melanie STEIN
27 Director of Media Relations .... Vacant
31 Director of Community Relations .... Mr. Jason ROJAS
37 Director of Financial Aid .... Ms. Kelly O'BRIEN
06 Registrar .... Ms. Patricia MCGREGOR
18 Dir of Facilities Mgmt/Plng & Svcs .... Mr. Gary BRICHER
15 Director of Human Resources .... Ms. Beth IACAMPO
21 Director of Business Operations .... Mr. Michael ELLIOTT
21 Budget Director .... Ms. Marcia PHELAN JOHNSON
19 Director of Campus Safety .... Mr. Francisco ORTIZ
44 Director of Development .... Mr. Christopher FRENCH
44 Director of Annual Giving .... Mr. William KNAPP
36 Director of Career Development .... Ms. Violet GANNON
21 Comptroller .... Mr. Guy DRAPEAU
41 Director of Athletics .... Mr. Michael D. RENWICK
09 Director of Institutional Research .... Dr. James J. HUGHES
35 Director of Campus Life .... Ms. Amy DEBAUN
42 College Chaplain .... Rev. Allison READ
28 Dean Multicultural Affs/Sr Div Ofcr .... Ms. Karla SPURLOCK-EVANS
38 Director Student Counseling .... Dr. Randolph LEE
96 Director of Purchasing .... Mr. Michael S. ELLIOTT
88 Dean of Urban and Global Studies .... Dr. Xiangming CHEN
29 Acting Director of Alumni Relations .... Ms. Aliza FINN-WELCH
08 Head Librarian .... Dr. Richard S. ROSS
26 VP of Marketing/Communications .... Ms. Angela SCHAEFFER
04 Administrative Asst to President .... Ms. Patrice A. LEMOINE

University of Bridgeport (C)

126 Park Avenue, Bridgeport CT 06604-5620
County: Fairfield FICE Identification: 001416
Unit ID: 128744
Telephone: (203) 576-4000 Carnegie Class: Masters/L
FAX Number: (203) 576-4653 Calendar System: Semester
URL: www.bridgeport.edu
Established: 1927 Annual Undergrad Tuition & Fees: $30,850
Enrollment: 5,191 Coed
Affiliation or Control: Independent Non-Profit IRS Status: 501(c)3
Highest Offering: Doctorate
Accreditation: **EH**, ACBSP, ACUP, ARCPA, ART, CHIRO, DH, ENG, MT, NATUR

01 President .... Mr. Neil Albert SALONEN
04 Executive Assistant to President .... Ms. Joan E. FLORCZAK
05 Provost & VP for Academic Affairs .... Dr. Stephen E. HEALEY
10 VP Administration & Finance .... Dr. Susan D. WILLIAMS
88 Vice Pres International Programs .... Dr. Thomas J. WARD
30 Vice Pres for University Relations .... Vacant
18 VP of Facilities .... Mr. George ESTRADA
09 Exec Asst Pres Plng/Inst Research ... Ms. Barbara A. GABIANELLI
07 Associate VP for Enrollment .... Ms. Karissa L. PECKHAM
32 Dean of Students .... Ms. Edina R. OESTREICHER
08 University Librarian .... Ms. Deborah L. DULEPSKI
15 Dir Human Resources/Affirm Act Ofcr .. Dr. Melitha R. PRZYGODA
21 Controller .... Mr. Thomas A. DEBRIZZI, JR.
13 Systems Architect & CIO .... Mr. Matanya ELCHANANI
37 Director Student Financial Services . Ms. Christine E. FALZERANO
90 Director of Academic Computing . Mr. Abdelshakour A. ABUZNEID
19 Exec Director of Campus Security .... Ms. April J. VOURNELIS
38 Director of Counseling Services .... Ms. Amy L. SCEERY
06 University Registrar .... Mr. Christian HANSEN
85 Director of Intl Student Affairs .... Ms. Yumin WANG
39 Dir Housing/Res Life/Comm Standards .... Mr. Robert VASS
96 Director of Purchasing .... Ms. Jacqueline A. REEVES
35 Dir Campus Activity & Civic Engmt .... Ms. Kelli A. MEYER
12 Director of Waterbury Center .... Ms. Karen K. RINGWOOD
12 Director of Stamford Center .... Ms. Maureen L. MALONEY
29 Director Alumni Relations .... Vacant
26 Dir Public Info & Media Affairs .... Ms. Leslie H. GEARY
43 University Counsel .... Ms. Carolyn R. LINSEY
41 Athletic Director .... Mr. Anthony VITTI
51 Dean Continuing/Profess Studies .... Mr. Michael J. GIAMPAOLI
23 Director of Health Center .... Ms. Melissa H. LOPEZ
88 Director of Acupuncture Institute .... Dr. Jennifer BRETT
40 Manager of the Bookstore .... Ms. Jessica RALLIS
36 Director of Career Services .... Mr. Keith HASSELL
54 VP Grad Stds/Research & Dean Engr .... Dr. Tarek M. SOBH
49 Dean Arts & Sciences .... Dr. Manyul IM
53 Dean School of Education .... Dr. Allen P. COOK
88 Dean College of Chiropractic .... Dr. Michael A. CIOLFI
88 Dean College Naturopathic Medicine .. Dr. Marcia A. PRENGUBER
50 Dean School of Business .... Dr. Lloyd G. GIBSON
17 Vice Provost Div of Health Science .... Dr. David M. BRADY
97 Director Div of General Studies .... Dr. Edward V. GEIST
88 Director Academic Resource Center .... Ms. Roxie L. RAY
52 Dean Fones Sch of Dental Hygiene ..... Dr. Marcia H. LORENTZEN
56 Director for Distance Learning .... Mr. Kris BICKELL
24 Media Services Coordinator .... Ms. Lynn DORSEY
57 Dir Shintaro Akatsu Sch of Design .... Mr. Richard W. YELLE
88 Dir Physician Assistant Institute .... Dr. Monica LOCKWOOD
44 Director Annual Giving .... Vacant

University of Connecticut (D)

352 Mansfield Road, Storrs CT 06269
County: Tolland FICE Identification: 001417
Unit ID: 129020
Telephone: (860) 486-2000 Carnegie Class: DU-Highest
FAX Number: (860) 486-2627 Calendar System: Semester
URL: www.uconn.edu
Established: 1881 Annual Undergrad Tuition & Fees (In-State): $13,366
Enrollment: 26,541 Coed
Affiliation or Control: State IRS Status: 501(c)3
Highest Offering: Doctorate
Accreditation: **EH**, ART, AUD, BUS, BUSA, CAATE, CACREP, CEA, CGTECH, CLPSY, CS, DIETC, DIETD, DIETI, DMOLS, ENG, IPSY, JOUR, LAW, LSAR, MFCD, MT, MUS, NURSE, PHAR, PTA, SCPSY, SP, SPAA, SW, TED

01 President .... Susan HERBST
100 Chief of Staff .... Rachel RUBIN
05 Provost/Exec VP Academic Affairs .... Mun CHOI
17 Exec VP for Health Affairs .... Andrew AGWUNOBI
10 Exec VP for Admin and CFO .... Scott JORDAN
32 Vice President for Student Affairs .... Michael GILBERT
46 Vice President for Research .... Jeffrey SEEMANN
101 Executive Secretary to the Board .... Rachel RUBIN
26 Vice Pres for Communications .... P. Tysen KENDIG
41 Director of Athletics .... David BENEDICT
43 Asst Attorney General .... Holly BRAY
43 Vice President and General Counsel .... Richard ORR
13 Vice Provost & Chief Info Officer .... Michael MUNDRANE
45 Assoc VP for Budget & Planning .... Katrina SPENCER
19 Int Dir Pub Safety/Chief of Police .... Hans RHYNHART
28 Assoc VP & Chief Diversity Officer .... Joellle MURCHISON
88 Assoc VP for Institutional Equity .... Elizabeth CONKLIN
46 Int Asst VPrv for Inst Rsrch Effect .... Sally REIS
102 Pres Univ of Connecticut Foundation .... Joshua NEWTON
20 Vice Provost for Academic Affairs .... Sally REIS
20 Vice Provost fr Academic Operations .... Amy DONAHUE
84 VP Enrollment Planning & Mgmt .... Wayne LOCUST
08 Vice Prov for University Libraries .... Martha BEDARD
12 Director Stamford Campus .... Terrence CHENG
12 Director Avery Point Campus .... Joseph MADAUS
12 Director Waterbury Campus .... William J. PIZZUTO
12 Director Hartford Campus .... Michael MENARD
92 AVProv Enrich Pgms/Dir Honors Pgms .... Jennifer LEASE BUTTS
25 AVP Research/Sponsored Pgms Svcs .... Michael GLASGOW
20 Asst Vice Provost Acad Affairs .... Vacant
86 Sr Director Government Relations .... Joann LOMBARDO
86 Dir Govt Relations/Health Affairs .... Andrea KEILTY
06 Registrar .... Lauren DIGRAZIA
07 Director Undergrad Admissions .... Nathan FUERST
37 Director Student Financial Aid .... Mona LUCAS
29 Asst Vice Pres Alumni Relations .... Montique COTTON KELLY
23 Exec Director Student Health Svcs .... Suzanne ONORATO
15 Director of Human Resources .... Aliza WILDER
96 Dir Procurement/Logistical Svcs .... Matthew LARSON
47 Dean Col of Agric/Natural Resources .... Gregory WEIDEMANN
50 Dean School of Business .... John ELLIOTT
53 Dean Neag School of Education .... Richard SCHWAB
54 Dean of Engineering .... Kazem KAZEROUNIAN
88 Assoc Vice Prov Excell Teach/Lrng .... Peter DIPLOCK
57 Dean of Fine Arts .... Anne D'ALLEVA
58 Vice Prov Grad Ed/Dean Grad Sch .... Kent HOLSINGER
61 Dean School of Law .... Timothy FISHER
49 Dean College of Lib Arts/Sciences .... Jeremy TEITELBAUM
66 Dean School of Nursing .... Regina CUSSON
67 Dean School of Pharmacy .... James HALPERT
70 Interim Dean School of Social Work .... Nina ROVINELLI HELLER
52 Dean of Dental Medicine .... R. Lamont MACNEIL
63 Dean School of Medicine .... Bruce LIANG
38 Dir Student Counslg/Mental Hlth Svc .... Elizabeth CRACCO
39 Executive Director Residential Life .... Pamela SCHIPANI
88 Deputy Chief of Staff .... Michael KIRK
88 Master Planner/Chief Architect .... Laura CRUICKSHANK
88 Vice Provost for Global Affairs .... Daniel WEINER
36 Asst VProv/Exec Dir Career Services .... James R. LOWE
88 Asst VProvost for Student Success .... Maria D. MARTINEZ
88 Director Marketing Communications .... Patricia FAZIO
88 Ombuds .... James WOHL
88 Dir Institute for Materials Science .... Steven L. SUIB
04 Administrative Asst to President .... Debra MERRITT
104 Director Study Abroad .... Kevin BRENNAN
18 Assoc VP Facilities Ops & Bldg Svcs .... P. Michael JEDNAK
30 Vice President for Development .... Brian OTIS
44 Director of Planned Giving .... Gregory KNOTT
106 Dir Online Education/E-learning .... Peter DIPLOCK
88 Dir Vet Affs & Military Programs .... Alyssa KELLEHER

University of Connecticut Health Center (E)

263 Farmington Avenue, Farmington CT 06030-1827
Telephone: (860) 679-2000 FICE Identification: 009867
Accreditation: **&EH**, DENT, MED, PH

† Regional accreditation is carried under the parent institution in Storrs, CT.

University of Connecticut School of Law (F)

55 Elizabeth Street, Hartford CT 06105-2290
Telephone: (860) 570-5000 Identification: 770108
Accreditation: **&EH**, LAW

† Regional accreditation is carried under the parent institution in Storrs, CT

University of Hartford (G)

200 Bloomfield Avenue, West Hartford CT 06117-1599
County: Hartford FICE Identification: 001422
Unit ID: 129525
Telephone: (860) 768-4100 Carnegie Class: DU-Mod
FAX Number: (860) 768-4070 Calendar System: Semester
URL: www.hartford.edu
Established: 1877 Annual Undergrad Tuition & Fees: $36,460
Enrollment: 6,817 Coed
Affiliation or Control: Independent Non-Profit IRS Status: 501(c)3
Highest Offering: Doctorate
Accreditation: **EH**, ART, EUS, CLPSY, COARC, DANCE, ENG, ENGT, MUS, NURSE, OPE, PTA, RAD, TED, THEA

01 President .... Dr. Walter HARRISON
05 Interim Provost .... Dr. Frederick SWEITZER
10 Vice Pres Finance & Administration .... Mr. Arosha JAYAWICKREMA
30 Int Vice Pres Institutional Advance .... Ms. Kate PENDERGAST
32 Vice Pres Student Affs/Dean Stdnts .... Dr. J. Lee PETERS
26 Vice Pres of Univ Relations .... Mr. John J. CARSON
21 Asst Vice Pres Finance/Controller .... Ms. Laura WHITNEY
35 Asst Vice Pres Student Development .... Ms. DeLois LINDSEY
04 Senior Advisor to the President .... Ms. Susan FITZGERALD
35 Assoc Vice Pres for Student Life .... Mr. Irwin NUSSBAUM
21 Assoc Vice Pres/Treasurer .... Mr. Brett CARROLL
43 Vice Pres/Gen Counsel & Secretary .... Vacant
84 Sr Assoc Provost/Dean Enroll Mgmt .... Dr. Guy C. COLARULLI
58 Int Assoc Prov/Dean of Grad Studies .... Dr. Clark SAUNDERS
07 Dean of Admission .... Mr. Richard A. ZEISER
04 Exec Assistant to the President .... Ms. Ilena ROSENSTEIN
15 Exec Dir Human Resources & Devel .... Ms. Lisa BELANGER
08 Director University Libraries .... Ms. Randi L. ASHTON-PRITTING
37 Director Student Financial Aid .... Ms. Victoria HAMPTON
06 Registrar .... Ms. Natalie DURANT
38 Dir Counsel & Personal Development .... Mr. Nick PINKERTON
36 Director Career Center .... Mr. John KNIERING
13 Chief Information Officer .... Mr. Andrew HILLBERRY
19 Director Public Safety .... Mr. John SCHMALTZ
23 Director Health Services .... Ms. Mary NORRIS
24 Director User Services .... Mr. Sebastian SORRENTINO
25 Dir Inst Prtnrshp/Sponsored Rsrch .... Dr. Peter LISI
29 Director Alumni Relations .... Ms. Heather CORBETT
18 Assoc Vice Pres for Facilities/Mgmt .... Mr. Norman YOUNG
41 Director Athletics .... Mr. Anton GOFF
104 Director International Studies .... Ms. Sarah O'LEARY
09 Dir Institutional Effectiveness .... Ms. Nichole PETERSON
94 Director of Women's Center .... Ms. Kenna GRANT

88 Director of Judicial Process ... Ms. Kristy SEVERINO
96 Director of Purchasing ... Ms. Lisa CONDON
92 Director of University Honors ... Dr. Donald JONES
106 Asst Prov Online Lrng/Dean Univ Pgm ... Dr. R. J. MCGIVNEY
57 Dean Hartford Art School ... Dr. Nancy M. STUART
72 Dean College Engineer/Tech/Arch ... Dr. Louis MANZIONE
49 Dean College Arts & Science ... Dr. Katherine BLACK
50 Dean Barney School of Business ... Dr. Martin ROTH
12 Dean Hillyer Col/Int Dean Ungrd St .. Dr. David H. GOLDENBERG
53 Dean College of Education ... Vacant
88 Dean Hartt School ... Vacant
39 Asst Vice Pres for Residential Life ... Mr. Michael MALONE
27 Dir of Marketing/Communications .. Mr. Jonathan EASTERBROOK
101 Secretary of the Institution/Board ... Ms. Susan FITZGERALD
102 Dir Foundation/Corporate Relations ... Ms. Keeley PATRICK
103 Dir Workforce/Career Development ... Ms. Linda SCHULTZ
44 Director Annual or Planned Giving ... Ms. Jenn KEYO

University of New Haven (A)

300 Boston Post Road, West Haven CT 06516-1916
County: New Haven FICE Identification: 001397
Unit ID: 129941
Telephone: (203) 932-7000 Carnegie Class: Masters/L
FAX Number: (203) 931-6060 Calendar System: 4/1/4
URL: www.newhaven.edu
Established: 1920 Annual Undergrad Tuition & Fees: $35,650
Enrollment: 6,811 Coed
Affiliation or Control: Independent Non-Profit IRS Status: 501(c)3
Highest Offering: Doctorate
Accreditation: EH, ART, BUS, CS, DH, DIETD, @DIETI, ENG, FEPAC

01 President ... Dr. Steven H. KAPLAN
05 Provost/Vice Pres Academic Affs ... Dr. Daniel MAY
10 Vice Pres Finance/Treasurer of Univ ... Mr. George S. SYNODI
30 Vice President Univ Advancement ... Mr. Stephen J. MORIN
84 Vice Pres Enrollment Management ... Mr. Walter F. CAFFEY
15 Vice President Human Resources ... Ms. Caroline KOZIATEK
100 Chief of Staff & Univ Secretary ... Ms. Gayle S. TAGLIATELA
18 Assoc Vice President for Facilities ... Mr. Louis ANNINO
20 Assoc Provost Strategic Initiatives ... Dr. Stuart SIDLE
21 Assoc Vice Pres for Finance ... Mr. Patrick TORRE
13 Assoc VP Institutional Technology ... Mr. Vincent P. MANGIACAPRA
32 Assc VP Stdnt Affs/Dean of Students .. Ms. Rebecca D. JOHNSON
07 Assoc VP Enrollment Management ... Mr. Kevin J. PHILLIPS
41 Assoc Vice Pres Athletics/Recreation ... Ms. Deborah CHIN
37 Assoc Vice Pres Financial Aid ... Ms. Karen FLYNN
88 Asst Provost Undergrad Stds/Assess ... Dr. Gordon SIMERSON
08 University Librarian ... Ms. Hanko H. DOBI
44 Assoc VP for Development ... Ms. Roslyn REABACK
06 University Registrar ... Ms. Lynn KOHRN
30 Exec Dir of Advancement Operations ... Mr. Carl PITRUZZELLO
07 Associate VP of Graduate Enrollment .... Mr. Sean-Michael GREEN
85 Dir Intercult Rels/Intl Svcs Ofc ....Ms. Kathy KAUTZ DE ARANGO
29 Director of Alumni Events ... Ms. Jennifer PJATAK
38 Associate Director of Counseling ... Dr. Deborah EVERHART
09 Director Institutional Research ... Ms. Susan TURNER
19 Chief of University Police ... Chief Tracy MOONEY
85 Director of Intl Student Services ... Ms. Kathy KAUTZ
35 Director Student Activities ... Mr. Gregory OVEREND
96 Director of Procurement Services ... Mr. Robert STEVENS
85 Director International Admissions ... Mr. Joseph SPELLMAN
88 Dir Student Accounts/Risk Manager ... Mr. Marc MANIATIS
26 Assoc VP Communications/Pub Affairs ... Mr. Dean GOLEMBESKI
49 Dean College Arts & Sciences ... Dr. Lourdes ALVAREZ
50 Dean College Business ... Dr. Brian KENCH
54 Dean Tagliatela Col Engineering ... Dr. Ronald HARICHANDRAN
88 Dean Col Crim Justice/Forensic Sci ... Dr. Mario GABOURY
103 Exec Director of Career Development ... Mr. Matthew CAPORALE
104 Director International Study ... Ms. Jennie SHAMASNA
39 Associate Dean of Residential Life ... Ms. Nicole MCGRATH
108 Director of Academic Assessment ... Dr. Kristy HUNTLEY
04 President's Office Coordinator ... Ms. Jennifer FAZEKAS
91 Dir Enterprise Applications ... Mr. Todd MCINERNEY

University of Saint Joseph (B)

1678 Asylum Avenue, West Hartford CT 06117-2791
County: Hartford FICE Identification: 001409
Unit ID: 130314
Telephone: (860) 232-4571 Carnegie Class: Masters/L
FAX Number: (860) 232-6927 Calendar System: Semester
URL: www.usj.edu
Established: 1932 Annual Undergrad Tuition & Fees: $36,200
Enrollment: 2,565 Female
Affiliation or Control: Roman Catholic IRS Status: 501(c)3
Highest Offering: Doctorate
Accreditation: EH, CACREP, DIETD, DIETI, MFCD, NURSE, PHAR, SW, TED

01 President ... Dr. Rhona C. FREE
05 Provost ... Dr. Michelle KALIS
10 Sr VP Finance and Strategy ... Mr. Shawn M. HARRINGTON
30 VP Inst Advancement ... Ms. Marjorie PINNEY
84 VP Enrollment Management ... Ms. Kimberly CRONE
32 VP Student Affairs/Dean of Students ... Dr. Cheryl A. BARNARD
21 Assoc VP of Finance/Controller ... Mr. William HAWKINS
15 Director of Human Resources ... Ms. Deborah SPENCER
58 Dean Sch of Grad & Prof Studies ... Dr. Daniel NUSSBAUM
67 Dean School of Pharmacy ... Dr. Joseph OFOSU
53 Dean School of Education ... Dr. Ann MONROE-BAILLARGEON
76 Dean School of Health/Nat Sci ... Dr. Raouf BOULES
79 Dean School of Humanities/Soc Sci ... Dr. Wayne STEELY
08 Librarian ... Ms. Linda O. GEFFNER
06 Registrar ... Mr. Patrick MARTIN
41 Dir of Athletics/AVP Student Affair ... Mr. William CARDARELLI
26 Dir of Marketing & Communications ... Vacant
18 Director of Facilities ... Mr. Andrew LEVESQUE
29 Dir of Alumni Rels/Annual Giving ... Ms. Sarah BLANCHARD
37 Director of Financial Aid ... Ms. Ashley DUTTON
36 Director of Career Services ... Vacant
39 Director of Residential Life ... Mr. Frank KUSTER
35 Asst Dean Student Leadership ... Ms. Tracy LAKE
09 Director of Institutional Research ... Ms. Kathleen NEAL
13 Director of Info Tech (CIO) ... Mr. Joe GLEASON
19 Director of Public Safety ... Mr. Paul LOMBARDO
38 Director of Counseling & Wellness ... Dr. Meredith YUHAS
23 Director of Health Services ... Ms. Elizabeth COCOLA

Wesleyan University (C)

45 Wyllys Avenue, Middletown CT 06459
County: Middlesex FICE Identification: 001424
Unit ID: 130697
Telephone: (860) 685-2000 Carnegie Class: Bac-A&S
FAX Number: (860) 685-2001 Calendar System: Semester
URL: www.wesleyan.edu
Established: 1831 Annual Undergrad Tuition & Fees: $49,274
Enrollment: 3,224 Coed
Affiliation or Control: Independent Non-Profit IRS Status: 501(c)3
Highest Offering: Doctorate
Accreditation: EH

01 President ... Dr. Michael S. ROTH
05 Provost/Vice Pres Academic Affairs ... Dr. Joyce JACOBSEN
10 Vice Pres Finance/Administration ... Dr. Nathan D. PETERS
26 Vice President University Relations ... Ms. Barbara-Jan WILSON
28 Vice President for Equity and Incl ... Mr. Antonio FARIAS
32 Vice Pres of Student Affairs ... Mr. Michael J. WHALEY
13 VP Information Technology/CIO ... Dr. David BAIRD
29 Assoc VP External Relations ... Ms. Gemma F. EBSTEIN
30 Assoc Asst Vice Pres Development ... Vacant
20 Senior Associate Provost ... Dr. Mark HOVEY
18 Asst Vice President for Facilities ... Ms. Joyce TOPSHE
35 Asst Vice Pres/Dean of Students ... Mr. Richard CULLITON
07 Dean of Admissions & Financial Aid ... Ms. Nancy HARGRAVE MEISLAHN
58 Dir Cont Stds/Graduate Liberal Stds ... Ms. Jennifer CURRAN
06 Registrar ... Ms. Anna VAN DER BURG
08 University Librarian ... Mr. Dan CHERUBIN
09 Director of Institutional Research ... Mr. Michael E. WHITCOMB
37 Director Financial Aid ... Mr. John GUDVANGEN
36 Director Career Development ... Ms. Sharon CASTONGUAY
15 Director Human Resources ... Ms. Julia HICKS
19 Director Public Safety ... Mr. Scott ROHDE
31 Dir Community Svcs/Volunteerism ... Ms. Catherine CRIMMINS LECHOWICZ
41 Director of Athletics ... Mr. Michael WHALEN
45 Director of Strategic Initiatives ... Dr. Charles G. SALAS

Yale University (D)

New Haven CT 06520
County: New Haven FICE Identification: 001426
Unit ID: 130794
Telephone: (203) 432-4771 Carnegie Class: DU-Highest
FAX Number: N/A Calendar System: Semester
URL: www.yale.edu
Established: 1701 Annual Undergrad Tuition & Fees: $47,600
Enrollment: 12,336 Coed
Affiliation or Control: Independent Non-Profit IRS Status: 501(c)3
Highest Offering: Doctorate
Accreditation: EH, ARCPA, BUS, CLPSY, ENG, IPSY, LAW, MED, MIDWF, NURSE, PAST, PH, THEOL

01 President ... Peter SALOVEY
05 Provost ... Benjamin POLAK
86 Vice Pres & Dir New Haven/State Aff ... Bruce D. ALEXANDER
32 Secretary & VP Student Affairs ... Kimberly GOFF-CREWS
10 Vice Pres Finance & CFO ... Stephen MURPHY
30 Vice President Development ... Joan E. O'NEILL
43 Vice President & General Counsel ... Alexander DREIER
15 Vice Pres/Chief HR Officer ... Michael A. PEEL
20 Deputy Provost Science & Tech ... Steven M. GIRVIN
20 Deputy Provost Arts and Humanities ... Emily P. BAKEMEIER
20 Deputy Prov Health Affairs ... Stephanie SPANGLER
20 Deputy Provost Academic Resources ... J. Lloyd SUTTLE
11 Deputy VP of HR & Admin ... Janet E. LINDNER
18 Assoc VP Facilities ... John H. BOLLIER
26 Chief Comm Ofcr/Dir Ofc Public Affs ... Vacant
96 Assoc VP & Chief Procurement Ofcr ... John A. MAYES
102 Assoc VP/Dir Corp & Found Rels ... Patricia E. PEDERSEN
08 Univ Librarian & Deputy Provost ... Susan GIBBONS
09 Acting Dir Institutional Research ... Russell K. ADAIR
13 Chief Information Officer ... Leonard PETERS
19 Chief University Police ... Ronnell A. HIGGINS
06 University Registrar ... Gabriel G. OLSZEWSKI
07 Dean Undergraduate Admissions ... Jeremiah QUINLAN
35 Dean Student Affairs ... Vacant
29 Exec Director Assoc of Yale Alumni ... Vacant
37 Director University Financial Aid ... Caesar T. STORLAZZI
22 Dir Ofc Equal Opportunities ... Valarie J. STANLEY
23 Director University Health Services ... Dr. Paul GENECIN
90 Deputy CIO Academic IT ... Gary KIDNEY
25 Interim Dir Grants & Contract Admn .. Alice TANGREDI-HANNON
36 Director Career Services ... Jeanine DAMES
44 Univ Director Planned Giving ... Eileen B. DONAHUE
39 Dir Grad & Prof Student Housing ... George E. LONGYEAR, JR.
41 Director Athletics ... Thomas A. BECKETT
42 University Chaplain ... Sharon KUGLER
85 Director Intl Students & Scholars ... Ann KUHLMAN
84 Director of Enrollment Management ... Danielle CURTIS
48 Dean of the School of Architecture ... Robert A M. STERN
49 Dean of Yale College ... Jonathan HOLLOWAY
50 Dean School of Management ... Edward A. SNYDER
54 Dean School of Engineering ... Ms. T. Kyle VANDERLICK
57 Dean of the School of Art ... Robert STORR
58 Dean of Grad Sch Arts & Science ... Lynn COOLEY
57 Dean of the School of Drama ... James A. BUNDY
61 Dean of the Law School ... Robert C. POST
64 Dean of the School of Music ... Robert L. BLOCKER
65 Dean Sch of Forestry & Environ Stds ... Sir Peter CRANE
73 Dean of the Divinity School ... Gregory E. STERLING
88 Director Inst of Sacred Music ... Martin D. JEAN
63 Dean of School of Medicine ... Dr. Robert J. ALPERN
66 Dean of the School of Nursing ... Margaret GREY
69 Dean of Public Health ... Paul C. CLEARY
28 Chief Diversity Officer ... Deborah STANLEY-MCAULAY
104 Dean Intl & Professional Experience ... Jane EDWARDS

DELAWARE

Delaware College of Art and Design (E)

600 N Market Street, Wilmington DE 19801-3007
County: New Castle FICE Identification: 041398
Unit ID: 432524
Telephone: (302) 622-8000 Carnegie Class: Spec 2-yr-A&S
FAX Number: (302) 622-8870 Calendar System: Semester
URL: www.dcad.edu
Established: 1997 Annual Undergrad Tuition & Fees: $23,990
Enrollment: 185 Coed
Affiliation or Control: Independent Non-Profit IRS Status: 501(c)3
Highest Offering: Associate Degree
Accreditation: M, ART

01 President ... Mr. Stuart BARON
06 Registrar ... Ms. Krista ROTHWELL
08 Head Librarian ... Ms. Helena RICHARDSON
13 Information Technology Coordinator ... Mr. Bates CARTER
30 Director of Development ... Ms. Renee GARNICK
37 Director Student Financial Aid ... Ms. Nicole LITTLE
32 Director of Student Services ... Mr. Jason MOKAR
26 Director of Communications ... Ms. Amanda CURRY
11 Chief Administrative Officer ... Mr. Bill SCHOELL
07 Director of Admissions ... Vacant
108 Director Institutional Assessment ... Ms. Pamela MACPHERSON

Delaware State University (F)

1200 N DuPont Highway, Dover DE 19901-2275
County: Kent FICE Identification: 001428
Unit ID: 130934
Telephone: (302) 857-6001 Carnegie Class: Masters/M
FAX Number: (302) 857-6069 Calendar System: Semester
URL: www.desu.edu
Established: 1891 Annual Undergrad Tuition & Fees (In-State): $7,531
Enrollment: 4,397 Coed
Affiliation or Control: State IRS Status: 501(c)3
Highest Offering: Doctorate
Accreditation: M, BUS, @DIETC, DIETD, NUR, SW, TED

01 President ... Dr. Harry L. WILLIAMS
04 Executive Asst to the President ... Ms. Georgeann HAYWOOD
05 Int Vice Pres Div of Academic Affs ... Dr. Saundra DELAUDER
10 Sr VP & Chief Operating Officer ... Dr. Teresa HARDEE
30 VP Inst Advancement ... Dr. Vita C. PICKRUM
32 Vice Pres Student Affairs ... Dr. Stacy L. DOWNING
46 Vice President for Research ... Vacant
13 Assoc VP Information Technology ... Vacant
09 AVP Inst Research/Planning/Analysis ... Dr. Kimberly R. SUDLER
15 Vice Pres Human Resources ... Ms. Irene HAWKINS
43 General Counsel ... Mr. David SHEPPARD
18 Director of Facilities ... Mr. Randy JONES
06 Registrar ... Mr. Terrell HOLMES
07 Director of Admissions ... Vacant
62 Dean of Library Services ... Ms. Rebecca BATSON
37 Director of Financial Aid ... Vacant
29 Executive Director Alumni Relations ... Mrs. Trayce WILLIAMS
36 Director Career Services ... Vacant
19 Director of Public Safety ... Mr. Harry W. DOWNES
38 Director of Student Counseling ... Mr. Ralph ROBINSON
26 News Director ... Mr. Carlos HOLMES
41 Director of Athletics ... Mr. Louis PERKINS
44 Director Annual Giving ... Mrs. Charity SHOCKLEY
86 Director Government Relations ... Mr. Victor SANTOS

Delaware Technical Community College, George Campus (G)

300 N. Orange Street, Wilmington DE 19801
Telephone: (302) 571-5300 Identification: 770855
Accreditation: &M, ACBSP, CAHIIM, COARC, DMS, MAC, OTA, PTAA

† Regional accreditation is carried under the parent institution in Dover, DE

Delaware Technical Community College, Owens Campus (A)

21179 College Drive, Georgetown DE 19947-0610
Telephone: (302) 259-6000 FICE Identification: 007053
Accreditation: &M, ACBSP, ADNUR, COARC, CSHSE, DMS, ENGT, MLTAD, OTA, PNUR, PTAA, RAD

† Regional accreditation is carried under the parent institution in Dover, DE

Delaware Technical Community College, Stanton Campus (B)

400 Stanton-Christiana Road, Newark DE 19713-2197
Telephone: (302) 454-3900 FICE Identification: 021449
Accreditation: &M, ACFEI, ADNUR, CSHSE, ENGT, HT, NMT, RAD

† Regional accreditation is carried under the parent institution in Dover, DE

Delaware Technical Community College, Terry Campus (C)

100 Campus Drive, Dover DE 19904-1383
County: Kent FICE Identification: 011727
Unit ID: 130907
Telephone: (302) 857-1000 Carnegie Class: Assoc/HT-High Trad
FAX Number: (302) 857-1096 Calendar System: Semester
URL: www.dtcc.edu/terry
Established: 1972 Annual Undergrad Tuition & Fees (In-State): $3,632
Enrollment: 2,939 Coed
Affiliation or Control: State IRS Status: 501(c)3
Highest Offering: Baccalaureate
Accreditation: M, ACBSP, ACFEI, ADNUR, CSHSE, EMT, PNUR, SURGT

01 Vice President & Campus Director .... Dr. June S. TURANSKY
05 Dean Instruction .... Mr. John M. BUCKLEY
32 Dean Student Affairs .... Ms. Jennifer P. PIRES
04 Director Communication and Planning .... Ms. Dana L. SAWYER
103 Director Workforce Development .... Dr. Lisa S. STRUSOWSKI
15 Director of Human Resources .... Ms. Charlotte T. LISTER
11 Director of Administrative Services .... Mr. Ray PARSONS
37 Director Student Financial Aid .... Ms. Jennifer J. GRUNDEN
08 Head Librarian .... Dr. Margaret R. PROUSE
10 Director Business Services .... Ms. Noelle SUGALSKI
06 Registrar/Admissions Coordinator .... Ms. Nauleen A. PERRY
88 Asst Director of Admin Services .... Mr. Allan NELSON
20 Assistant Dean of Instruction .... Mr. Bill J. MORROW

Goldey-Beacom College (D)

4701 Limestone Road, Wilmington DE 19808-0551
County: New Castle FICE Identification: 001429
Unit ID: 130989
Telephone: (302) 998-8814 Carnegie Class: Spec-4-yr-Bus
FAX Number: (302) 998-8631 Calendar System: Semester
URL: www.gbc.edu
Established: 1886 Annual Undergrad Tuition & Fees: $22,950
Enrollment: 2,012 Coed
Affiliation or Control: Independent Non-Profit IRS Status: 501(c)3
Highest Offering: Master's
Accreditation: M, ACBSP, IACBE

01 President .... Dr. Gary L. WIRT
03 Executive Vice President .... Ms. Kristine M. SANTOMAURO
05 Vice President for Academic Affairs .... Ms. Alison Boord WHITE
10 Exec Dir of Finance/HR .... Ms. Susan M. MANNERING
32 Dean of Students .... Ms. Bernadette H. WIMBERLEY
84 Dean Enrollment Mgmt/Registrar .... Ms. Jane H. LYSLE
13 Dean of Information Technology/ACC .... Ms. Emily S. JACKSON
07 Director of Admissions .... Mr. Larry EBY
39 Director of Residence/Student Life .... Mr. Kevin MARTIN
41 Director of Athletics .... Mr. Charles A. HAMMOND
44 Director of External Affairs .... Ms. Janine SORBELLO
18 Director of Facilities/Operations .... Mr. Meezie FOSTER
08 Director of Library/Learning Center .... Mr. Russell MICHALAK
72 Director of Information Technology .... Mr. Peter RYSAVY
09 Dir Institutional Research/Training .... Dr. Monica RYSAVY
36 Career Service Coordinator .... Ms. Elizabeth KIRKER

Irish American University (E)

404 East Savannah Road, Lewes DE 19958
County: Sussex Identification: 667120
Telephone: (302) 793-1101 Carnegie Class: Not Classified
FAX Number: (808) 334-0443 Calendar System: Semester
URL: www.acd.ie
Established: 1993 Annual Undergrad Tuition & Fees: N/A
Enrollment: N/A Coed
Affiliation or Control: Independent Non-Profit IRS Status: 501(c)3
Highest Offering: Master's
Accreditation: M

01 President/CEO .... Dr. Donald E. ROSS
03 Executive Vice President .... Mr. Christopher SARAFIAN
05 Academic Dean .... Dr. Rory MCENTERGART
30 Provost Institutional Advancement .... Mr. Joseph A. ROONEY

University of Delaware (F)

104 Hullihen Hall, Newark DE 19716
County: New Castle FICE Identification: 001431
Unit ID: 130943
Telephone: (302) 831-2000 Carnegie Class: DU-Highest
FAX Number: (302) 831-8000 Calendar System: 4/1/4
URL: www.udel.edu
Established: 1743 Annual Undergrad Tuition & Fees (In-State): $12,520
Enrollment: 22,680 Coed
Affiliation or Control: State Related IRS Status: 501(c)3
Highest Offering: Doctorate
Accreditation: M, BUS, BUSA, CAATE, CEA, CLPSY, CSHSE, DIETD, DIETI, ENG, IPSY, MT, MUS, NURSE, PCSAS, PTA, @SP, SPAA, TED

01 President .... Dr. Dennis ASSANIS
05 Provost .... Dr. Domenico GRASSO
03 Interim EVP & Univ Treasurer .... Mr. Alan BRANGMAN
30 Vice Pres Development & Alum Rels .... Ms. Monica M. TAYLOR LOTTY
26 Interim VP Comm & Public Affairs .... Mr. John BRENNAN
13 Interim VP Information Technologies .... Mr. Jason CASH
43 Vice Pres and General Counsel .... Ms. Laure ERGIN
18 Interim VP Fac/Real Est/Aux Svcs .... Mr. Peter KRAWCHYK
46 Deputy Prov Research & Schlrship .... Dr. Charles RIORDAN
107 Senior Vice Prov Grad/Prof Educ .... Dr. Ann ARDIS
88 Vice Provost for Faculty Affairs .... Dr. Matt KINSERVIK
28 Vice Provost for Diversity .... Dr. Carol E. HENDERSON
20 Deputy Provost Academic Affairs .... Dr. Lynn OKAGAKI
101 Vice Pres & Univ Secretary .... Mr. Jeffrey W. GARLAND
08 Interim Vice Prov/Dir of Libraries .... Ms. Sandra MILLARD
32 Vice Pres for Student Life .... Ms. Dawn M. THOMPSON
84 Vice Pres Enrollment Management .... Mr. Christopher LUCIER
10 Vice Pres Finance/Dept Treasurer .... Mr. Gregory S. OLER
88 Assoc Provost & Chief of Staff .... Ms. Margaret B. BOTTORFF
51 Assoc Vice Prov Prof Cont Studies .... Dr. James K. BROOMALL
86 Director of Government Relations .... Mr. Derrick DEADWYLER, JR.
88 Assoc Provost Research & Effec .... Dr. John E. SAWYER
09 Director Institutional Research .... Dr. Heather A. KELLY
108 Int Director Ctr for Educ Effectiv .... Ms. Kathleen L. PUSECKER
29 AVP Alumni Engagement/Annual Giving .... Mr. Michael SCLAFANI
104 Int Assoc Dep Prov Intl Programs .... Mr. Ravi AMMIGAN
37 Director Student Financial Services .... Ms. Melissa STONE
36 Director Career Services .... Mr. Nathan ELTON
19 Exec Dir Campus & Public Safety .... Mr. Albert J. HOMIAK, JR.
47 Dean Agric & Natural Resources .... Dr. Mark RIEGER
49 Dean Arts & Sciences .... Dr. George H. WATSON
50 Dean Lerner Col Business & Econ .... Dr. Bruce W. WEBER
54 Dean Engineering .... Dr. Babatunde A. OGUNNAIKE
65 Interim Dean Earth Ocean & Environ .... Dr. Mohsen BADIEY
76 Dean Health Sciences .... Dr. Kathleen S. MATT
53 Interim Dean Educ & Human Develop .... Dr. Carol VUKELICH
92 Director University Honors Program .... Dr. Michael A. ARNOLD
07 Director Undergraduate Admissions .... Dr. William D. ZANDER
58 Director of Graduate Admissions .... Mr. Michael ALEXO
15 Chief Human Resources Officer .... Mr. Thomas LAPENTA
96 Director Procurement Services .... Vacant
06 University Registrar .... Mr. Jeff L. PALMER
21 Chief Budget Officer .... Ms. Kathy L. DETTLOFF
22 Dir Inst Diversity/Title IX Coord .... Dr. Susan L. GROFF
35 Dean of Students .... Dr. José-Luis RIERA
38 Director Ctr for Couns/Student Dev .... Dr. Charles L. BEALE
39 Exec Director Res Life & Housing .... Dr. Kathleen G. KERR
85 Director Intl Students & Scholars .... Mr. Ravi AMMIGAN
41 Dir Intercol Athletics & Rec Svcs .... Ms. Christine RAWAK
23 Director Student Health Services .... Dr. Timothy F. DOWLING
04 Assistant to the President .... Ms. Susan L. WILLIAMS

Wesley College (G)

120 N State Street, Dover DE 19901-3876
County: Kent FICE Identification: 001433
Unit ID: 131098
Telephone: (302) 736-2300 Carnegie Class: Bac-Diverse
FAX Number: (302) 736-2301 Calendar System: Semester
URL: www.wesley.edu
Established: 1873 Annual Undergrad Tuition & Fees: $25,020
Enrollment: 1,615 Coed
Affiliation or Control: United Methodist IRS Status: 501(c)3
Highest Offering: Master's
Accreditation: M, NUR, TED

01 President .... Mr. Robert E. CLARK, II
05 Provost & VP for Academic Affairs .... Dr. Jeffrey GIBSON
10 VP Finance/COO/CFO .... Dr. Christine GIBSON
30 Vice Pres Institutional Advancement .... Mr. Chris WOOD
84 VP of Enrollment Management .... Mr. Christopher DEARTH
32 Dean of Students .... Ms. Wanda ANDERSON
42 Dir Spiritual Life and Comm Involv .... Vacant
21 CPA/Controller .... Mr. James LEWIS
43 General Counsel .... Vacant
06 Registrar/Dir Student Acad Records .... Ms. Patricia SEUNARINE
12 Admin Coord DAFB .... Ms. Tracey LUNDBLAD
08 Director of Parker Library .... Ms. Jessica OLIN
07 Dir of Admissions Operations .... Ms. Sue HOUSER
07 Dir of Admissions Communication .... Ms. Cassandra HYNSON
35 Ex Dir Student Success/Retention .... Ms. Charlene STEPHENS
88 Dir Academic Support .... Ms. Christine MCDERMOTT
26 Dir Communications & Marketing .... Ms. Jessica COOK
09 Director of Institutional Research .... Ms. Jessica HANSEN
46 Data & Strat Res Specialist .... Mr. Abdul HAMEED
07 Assoc Director of Admissions .... Mr. Christopher JESTER
41 Exec Dir of Sports & Recreation .... Mr. Mike DRASS
18 Director of the Physical Plant .... Mr. Rick RICHARDSON
40 Director of the Bookstore .... Mr. Kris MCGLOTHIN
19 Director of Safety/Security .... Mr. Walter BEAUPRE
23 Director Student Health Services .... Dr. Jill MASER
44 Dir of Development .... Ms. Cathy NOSEL
44 Dir of Advancement Services .... Ms. Amanda DOWNES
39 Asst Dean of Students/Dir Res Life .... Ms. Melissa ELLIOTT
35 Director of Campus Life .... Ms. Carol KING
37 Dir of Student Financial Planning .... Mr. Michael HALL
38 Director of Counseling Service .... Ms. Ann ROGGE
85 Director of International Programs .... Ms. Rebecca MILLER
29 Director Alumni Affairs .... Ms. Laura MAYSE
41 Assoc Athletic Dir/Field Hockey .... Ms. Tracey SHORT
04 Assistant to the President .... Ms. Ellen COLEMAN
88 Supervisor Business Operations .... Ms. Adele FLAMM
103 Dir for Career Development .... Mr. Nicholas LANTZ
13 Chief Info Technology Officer (CIO) .... Mr. Paul COPELAND
15 Human Resources Director .... Ms. Heather SCHALK

Widener University Delaware Law School (H)

PO Box 7474, Wilmington DE 19803-0474
Telephone: (302) 477-2100 FICE Identification: 012962
Accreditation: &M, LAW

† Branch campus of Widener University in Pennsylvania. This listing reflects the administrators for the school of law for the Harrisburg (PA) and Delaware campuses.

Wilmington University (I)

320 N Dupont Highway, New Castle DE 19720-6491
County: New Castle FICE Identification: 007948
Unit ID: 131113
Telephone: (302) 356-4636 Carnegie Class: DU-Mod
FAX Number: (302) 328-5902 Calendar System: Trimester
URL: www.wilmu.edu
Established: 1967 Annual Undergrad Tuition & Fees: $10,430
Enrollment: 14,467 Coed
Affiliation or Control: Independent Non-Profit IRS Status: 501(c)3
Highest Offering: Doctorate
Accreditation: M, CACREP, IACBE, NURSE, TED

01 President .... Dr. Jack P. VARSALONA
04 Executive Asst to President .... Ms. Donna M. QUINN
101 Secretary of the Institution/Board .... Ms. Donna M. QUINN
03 Executive Vice President .... Dr. LaVerne T. HARMON
10 Senior VP/CFO Financial Affairs .... Ms. Heather A. O'CONNELL
88 Senior Vice President .... Dr. Erin DIMARCO
88 University Vice President .... Ms. Carole D. PITCHER
88 Vice President External Affairs .... Dr. Peter A. BAILEY
05 Vice President Academic Affairs .... Dr. James D. WILSON, JR.
11 Vice Pres Admin & Legal Affairs .... Dr. Christian A. TROWBRIDGE
84 Vice Pres Enrollment Management .... Dr. Eileen G. DONNELLY
88 Asst Vice Pres/Dean of Locations .... Dr. Bonnie L. KIRKPATRICK
21 Asst Vice President/Controller .... Mr. David R. LEWIS
43 Asst VP of Admin & Legal Affairs .... Mr. P. Donald HAGERMANN
26 Asst Vice Pres Public Relations .... Mr. Christopher G. PITCHER
108 Asst Vice President .... Dr. Angela C. SUCHANIC
106 Asst VP Admin Affs/Dean Online .... Dr. Sallie A. REISSMAN
32 Asst VP Student Affairs/Alumni Rel .... Dr. Tina M. BARKSDALE
20 Asst Vice Pres Academic Affairs .... Dr. Sheila M. SHARBAUGH
19 Asst VP/University Safety/Athletic .... Dr. Jack L. CUNNINGHAM
88 Asst VP Univ Relations/Admission .... Dr. Jacque R. VARSALONA
88 Asst VP Academic Support Services .... Ms. Peg P. MITCHELL
15 Chief Human Resources Officer .... Dr. Nicole ROMANO
18 Sr Director Buildings/Maintenance .... Mr. William P. QUINN
105 Sr Director of Web Communications .... Mr. Kevin G. BARRY
36 Sr Dir Career Svcs/Student Life .... Dr. Regina C. ALLEN-SHARPE
37 Sr Dir Student Financial Services .... Ms. Trudy E. HITE
88 Sr Dir University Partnership Ctr .... Dr. Stefanie A. WHITBY
44 Sr Director Annual Fund .... Ms. Gloria R. JOHNSON
06 Registrar .... Dr. Elizabeth P. JORDAN
08 Director Library .... Mr. James M. MCCLOSKEY
88 Dir Administrative Services .... Mr. Bryan E. STEINBERG
41 Director Athletics .... Ms. Linda M. ANDRZEJWSKI
07 Director of Admissions .... Ms. Laura M. MORRIS
78 Director Cooperative Learning .... Mr. David C. CAFFO
09 Director of Institutional Research .... Ms. Dana S. EGGLESTON
86 Director Government Relations .... Ms. Simone M. GEORGE
96 Purchasing Specialist .... Mr. Mark S. PARIS
50 Dean College of Business .... Dr. Robert W. RESCIGNO
53 Dean College of Education .... Dr. John C. GRAY
76 Dean College of Health Professions .... Ms. Denise Z. WESTBROOK
49 Dean College of Arts and Sciences .... Dr. Doreen B. TURNBO
83 Dean College of Soc & Beh .... Dr. Edward L. GUTHRIE
72 Dean College of Technology .... Dr. Mary Ann K. WESTERFIELD

DISTRICT OF COLUMBIA

American University (J)

4400 Massachusetts Avenue, NW, Washington DC 20016
FICE Identification: 001434
Unit ID: 131159
Telephone: (202) 885-1000 Carnegie Class: DU-Higher
FAX Number: N/A Calendar System: Semester
URL: www.american.edu
Established: 1893 Annual Undergrad Tuition & Fees: $43,103
Enrollment: 13,061 Coed
Affiliation or Control: United Methodist IRS Status: 501(c)3
Highest Offering: Doctorate

Accreditation: M, BUS, CLPSY, IPSY, JOUR, LAW, MUS, SPAA, TED

01 President ... Dr. Cornelius M. KERWIN
05 Provost ... Dr. Scott A. BASS
30 Vice President Development & Alumni ... Ms. Courtney SURLS
10 Vice President Finance & Treasurer ... Mr. Douglas KUDRAVETZ
32 Vice President Campus Life ... Dr. Gail S. HANSON
43 Vice President General Counsel ... Ms. Mary E. KENNARD
11 Vice Provost for Academic Admin ... Ms. Violeta ETTLE
18 Asst VP Facilities Management ... Mr. Vincent HARKINS
35 Asst Vice Pres and Dean of Students ... Dr. Robert HRADSKY
35 Asst Vice President Campus Life ... Dr. Fanta AW
108 Asst Provost Inst Research/ Assess ... Ms. Karen L. FROSLID JONES
29 Asst Vice Pres of Alumni Relations ... Ms. Raina LENNEY
21 Asst Vice President of Treasury ... Ms. Laura MCANDREW
84 Vice Provost Undergrad Enrollment ... Dr. Sharon ALSTON
13 Vice President and CIO ... Mr. David L. SWARTZ
100 Chief of Staff Office of President ... Mr. David E. TAYLOR
20 Dean Acad Affs/Sr Vice Provost ... Dr. Mary CLARK
58 Vice Provost Res/Dean Grad Studies ... Dr. Jonathan G. TUBMAN
20 Vice Provost Undergrad Studies ... Dr. Jessica WATERS
49 Dean College Arts & Sciences ... Dr. Peter STARR
60 Dean Sch of Communication ... Dr. Jeffrey RUTENBECK
50 Dean Kogod Sch of Business ... Dr. John T. DELANEY
61 Dean Washington College of Law ... Dr. Camille A. NELSON
82 Dean School of Intl Service ... Dr. James GOLDGEIER
107 Dean School of Prof & Extended Stds ... Dr. Carola WEIL
80 Dean School of Public Affairs ... Dr. Barbara ROMZEK
15 Asst VP of Human Resources ... Ms. Beth MUHA
36 Exec Director Career Center ... Mr. Gihan FERNANDO
88 Assoc Vice Provost/Acad Admin ... Ms. Prita PATEL
26 Vice President of Communication ... Dr. Teresa (Terry) FLANNERY
06 University Registrar ... Mr. Charles (Doug) MCKENNA
08 University Librarian ... Ms. Nancy DAVENPORT
21 Controller ... Ms. Nicole BRESNAHAN
88 Dir Student Account Operations ... Mr. Darrell COOK
21 Asst VP Budget & Finance Res Ctr ... Ms. Nana AN
42 Interim University Chaplain ... Rev. Mark SCHAEFER
19 Exec Dir Risk/Safety/Transportation ... Mr. Daniel NICHOLS
37 Asst Vice Provost Financial Aid ... Mr. Brian LEE SANG
38 Director of Counseling Center ... Dr. Traci CALLANDRILLO
25 Director of Procurement & Contracts ... Mr. Brian BLAIR
07 Asst Vice Provost UG Admissions ... Vacant
85 Director Intl Student/Scholar Svcs ... Ms. Senem BAKAR
92 Dir Univ Honors Program ... Dr. Christopher TUDGE
41 Director Athletics & Recreation ... Dr. William (Billy) WALKER
28 Sr Dir Ctr Diversity & Inclusion ... Ms. Tiffany SPEAKS
104 Director AU Abroad ... Ms. Sara E. DUMONT
45 Asst VP Planning/Project Mgmt ... Mr. David DOWER
88 Asst VP Univ Programs/Development ... Ms. Lee HOLSOPPLE
39 Asst VP Housing and Dining Programs ... Mr. Chris MOODY
07 Asst Vice Provost Ops/Enrollment ... Mr. Robert LINSON
04 Exec Assistant to the President ... Ms. Margaret CLEMMER
22 Sr Dir Employee Relations/Recruitr ... Ms. Deadre JOHNSON
90 Assoc Chief Information Officer ... Ms. Kamalika SANDELL
88 Dir Office of Sponsored Programs ... Mr. James CASEY
09 Asst Provost Inst Research/ Assess ... Ms. Karen L. FROSLID JONES
103 Dir Performance & Learning ... Ms. Sheila WAY
44 Exec Director Planned Giving ... Mr. Seth SPEYER
53 Dean School of Education ... Dr. Anastasia (Stacey) SNELLING
86 Asst VP External Rel/Auxillary Svcs ... Ms. Linda ARGO
91 Director Network Operations ... Mr. Hassan MARVI

The Catholic University of America (A)

620 Michigan Avenue, NE, Washington DC 20064-0002
FICE Identification: 001437
Unit ID: 131283
Telephone: (202) 319-5100 Carnegie Class: DU-Higher
FAX Number: (202) 319-4441 Calendar System: Semester
URL: www.cua.edu
Established: 1887 Annual Undergrad Tuition & Fees: $40,932
Enrollment: 6,699 Coed
Affiliation or Control: Roman Catholic IRS Status: 501(c)3
Highest Offering: Doctorate
Accreditation: M, CLPSY, CS, ENG, IPSY, LAW, LIB, MUS, NURSE, SW, TED, THEOL

01 President ... Mr. John H. GARVEY
100 VP University Rels/Chief of Staff ... Mr. Frank G. PERSICO
05 Provost ... Dr. Andrew V. ABELA
10 Vice Pres Finance & Treasurer ... Mr. Robert M. SPECTER
32 Vice President Student Affairs ... Dr. Michael S. ALLEN
84 Vice Pres Enroll Mgmt/Marketing ... Mr. Christopher P. LYDON
108 Vice Provost/Dean of Assessment ... Dr. Duilia DE MELLO
88 Vice Provost for Policy ... Ms. Lucia SILECCHIA
88 Vice Prov for Strategic Initiatives ... Dr. Binh TRAN
11 Vice Provost for Administration ... Mr. Victor NAKAS
35 Assoc VP Student Life/Dean Students ... Mr. Jonathan C. SAWYER
43 University Counsel ... Mr. Lawrence J. MORRIS
15 Assoc VP/Chief Human Resources ... Ms. Maureen BROOKBANK
18 Assoc VP Facilities Operations ... Ms. Margaret CARNEY
41 Assoc VP & Director Athletics ... Mr. Sean M. SULLIVAN
88 Executive Director for Housing ... Mr. Timothy CARNEY
30 Vice Pres for Univ Advancement ... Mr. Scott REMBOLD
44 Assoc VP Univ Advancement ... Ms. Nancy MURRAY
44 Assoc VP University Advancement ... Mr. William WARREN
25 Assoc Prov Sponsored Research ... Mr. Ralph ALBANO
26 Assoc VP Marketing/Communications ... Ms. Jacquelyn MALCOLM
106 Assoc Vice Prov Online Education ... Dr. James MONAGHAN
58 Dean Graduate Studies ... Dr. J. Steven BROWN
48 Dean of Architecture ... Mr. Randall OTT
49 Dean of Arts & Sciences ... Dr. Aaron DOMINGUEZ
50 Dean School of Business/Economics ... Mr. William BOWMAN
54 Dean of Engineering ... Dr. Charles C. NGUYEN
61 Dean of Law ... Mr. Daniel F. ATTRIDGE
64 Dean of Music ... Dr. Grayson WAGSTAFF
70 Dean Natl Catholic Sch Social Svcs ... Dr. William RAINFORD
66 Dean of Nursing ... Dr. Patricia MCMULLEN
73 Dean Theology/Religious Studies ... VRev. Mark MOROZOWICH
107 Dean Metro Sch Professional Studies ... Dr. Vincent KIERNAN
79 Dean of Philosophy ... Dr. John C. MCCARTHY
88 Dean of Canon Law ... Rev. Robert J. KASLYN, SJ
07 Dean of Undergrad Admissions ... Mr. James DEWEY-ROSENFELD
13 Chief Information Officer ... Mr. Matthew MCNALLY
27 Exec Director Univ Communications ... Ms. Elise ITALIANO
08 Director of Libraries ... Mr. Stephen CONNAGHAN
06 Registrar ... Ms. Julie ISHA
36 Director of Career Services ... Mr. Anthony CHIAPPETTA
29 Asst VP Alumni Relations & Univ Adv ... Ms. Kyra A. LYONS
19 Assoc VP Public Safety & Emergency ... Ms. Thomasine JOHNSON
38 Director of Counseling Center ... Dr. T. Monroe RAYBURN
23 Medical Director of Health Center ... Dr. Loretta STAUDT
37 Dir Student Financial Assistance ... Mr. Joe DOBROTA
39 Assoc Dean of Students ... Ms. Heidi E. ZEICH
44 Director of the CUA Fund ... Mr. Patrick DAVEY
42 Dir Univ Campus Ministry ... Rev. Jude DEANGELO, OFM CONV
09 Assoc VP Fin Plng/Inst Res/Assess ... Mr. Brian A. JOHNSTON
88 Vice Provost & Assoc Dean Undergrad ... Dr. Lynn MAYER
96 Assoc VP for Strategic Sourcing ... Ms. Debbie JACKSON
22 Dir of Employee Relations & EOO ... Ms. Lisa WOOD
88 Compliance and Ethics Officer ... Mr. Vincent A. LACOVARA
40 Manager Bookstore ... Mr. Jonathan HOWARD

Chicago School of Professional Psychology-Washington DC (B)

901 15th Street NW, Washington DC 20005
Telephone: (202) 706-5000 Identification: 770493
Accreditation: &WC, CLPSY

† Regional accreditation is carried under the parent institution in Los Angeles, CA

Gallaudet University (C)

800 Florida Avenue, NE, Washington DC 20002-3695
FICE Identification: 001443
Unit ID: 131450
Telephone: (202) 651-5000 Carnegie Class: Masters/M
FAX Number: (202) 651-5508 Calendar System: Semester
URL: www.gallaudet.edu
Established: 1864 Annual Undergrad Tuition & Fees: $15,604
Enrollment: 1,488 Coed
Affiliation or Control: Independent Non-Profit IRS Status: 501(c)3
Highest Offering: Doctorate
Accreditation: M, ACBSP, AUD, CACREP, CEA, CLPSY, SP, SW, TED

01 President ... Dr. Roberta (Bobbi) CORDANO
05 Provost ... Dr. Carol J. ERTING
10 Vice Pres Admin & Finance ... Mr. Paul KELLY
30 Vice Pres Dev & Alumni Relations ... Mr. Paul JULIN
20 VP Laurent Clerc Nat Deaf Ed Ctr ... Dr. Ronald STERN
101 Spec Asst to Pres/Board Liaison ... Ms. Rita JENOURE
84 Chief Enrollment Management Officer ... Vacant
28 Executive Director Diversity/Equity ... Mr. Edgar PALMER
53 Int Dean Sch Educ/Bus/Human Svcs ... Dr. Isaac AGBOOLA
58 Int Dean Graduate School ... Dr. Guarav MATHUR
32 Dean Student Affs/Academic Support ... Mr. Dwight BENEDICT
49 Dean College Arts & Sciences ... Dr. Genie GERTZ
88 Exec Director Academic Quality ... Dr. Patricia HULSEBOSCH
21 Executive Director Finance ... Ms. Jean CIBUZAR
45 Director University Budget ... Vacant
96 Exec Dir Business Support Services ... Mr. Gary ALLER
18 Director Facilities ... Mr. Amon BROWN
11 Asst Vice Pres Administration ... Mr. Fred WEINER
102 Dir Corporate/Foundations Relations ... Vacant
26 Exec Dir Community/Public Relations ... Ms. Catherine MURPHY
09 Director Institutional Research ... Ms. Lindsay BUCHKO
29 Director Alumni Relations ... Mr. Samuel SONNENSTRAHL
15 Director Human Resources Svcs ... Ms. Christina SHEN-AUSTIN
13 Exec Director Technology Services ... Mr. Earl PARKS
14 Dir Technology Services Enterprise ... Mr. Harvey GROSSINGER
08 Director Library Public Services ... Ms. Sarah HAMRICK
88 University Ombuds ... Ms. Elizabeth STONE
08 Dir Library Deaf Collection/Archive ... Mr. Michael OLSON
22 Director Equal Opportunity Programs ... Ms. Sharrell MCCASKILL
06 Registrar ... Ms. Elice PATTERSON
07 Director of Admissions ... Mr. Young Hae PARK

George Washington University (D)

2121 I Street, NW, Washington DC 20052-0002
FICE Identification: 001444
Unit ID: 131469
Telephone: (202) 994-1000 Carnegie Class: DU-Highest
FAX Number: (202) 994-0458 Calendar System: Semester
URL: www.gwu.edu
Established: 1821 Annual Undergrad Tuition & Fees: $50,435
Enrollment: 25,613 Coed
Affiliation or Control: Independent Non-Profit IRS Status: 501(c)3
Highest Offering: Doctorate
Accreditation: M, ARCPA, ART, BUS, BUSA, CACREP, CIDA, CLPSY, CORE, CS, ENG, FEPAC, HSA, IPSY, LAW, MED, MT, NURSE, PH, PTA, SP, SPAA, TED

01 President ... Dr. Steven KNAPP
100 Chief of Staff President's Office ... Ms. Barbara A. PORTER
05 Provost & Exec VP Academic Affairs ... Dr. Forrest MALTZMAN
30 Vice Pres for Dev/Alumni Relations ... Mr. Aristide J. COLLINS
10 Exec Vice President & Treasurer ... Mr. Louis H. KATZ
43 Senior Vice Pres & General Counsel ... Ms. Beth NOLAN
26 Vice President External Relations ... Ms. Lorraine A. VOLES
20 Deputy Provost Academic Affairs ... Dr. Teresa MURPHY
84 Vice Provost for Enrollment Mgmt ... Ms. Laurie KOEHLER
21 Vice Provost of Budget and Finance ... Ms. Rene S. O'NEAL
28 Vice Provost Diversity & Inclusion ... Ms. Caroline LAGUERRE-BROWN
88 Sen Assoc Prov for Intl Strategy ... Dr. Douglas B. SHAW
15 Int Chief Human Resources Officer ... Mr. Dale a. MCLEOD
13 Chief Information Officer ... Mr. David STEINOUR
20 Vice Provost Faculty Affairs ... Dr. Diane C. MARTIN
11 Senior Assoc VP of Operations ... Ms. Alicia M. O'NEIL KNIGHT
32 Senior Assoc VP & Dean of Students ... Dr. Peter A. KONWERSKI
89 Assoc VP & Dean of Freshmen ... Ms. Helen CANNADAY SAULNY
90 Assoc VP for Acad Technologies ... Ms. P. B. GARRETT
88 Assoc VP of Acad Plang & Assessment ... Dr. Cheryl BEIL
46 Vice President for Research ... Dr. Leo M. CHALUPA
21 AVP Budget & Financial Mgmt ... Ms. Stella G. APEKEY
21 University Comptroller ... Ms. Sharon HEINLE
09 Director Inst Research & Planning ... Mr. Joachim W. KNOP
86 Assistant Vice President DC Affairs ... Mr. Bernard DEMCZUK
87 Associate VP for International Pgms ... Dr. Donna SCARBORO
08 University Librarian ... Ms. Geneva HENRY
27 Asst VP for Communications ... Ms. Sarah GEGENHEIMER BALDASSARO
27 Exec Director of Media Relations ... Ms. Candace E. SMITH
29 Sr Associate VP Development ... Mr. David B. ANDERSON
06 Registrar ... Ms. Elizabeth A. AMUNDSON
07 Director of Undergrad Admissions ... Dr. Costas SOLOMOU
38 Director Counseling Center ... Vacant
37 Assoc VP & Director Financial Aid ... Mr. Daniel E. SMALL
36 Asst Provost Career Center ... Ms. Rachel A. BROWN
18 Exec Director Facilities ... Mr. James D. SCHROTE
85 Director International Services ... Ms. Jennifer H. DONAGHUE
19 Sr Assoc VP Safety & Security ... Mr. Darrell L. DARNELL
22 Dir EEO & Affirmative Action ... Ms. Vickie FAIR
23 Director Student Health Services ... Dr. Isabel GOLDENBERG
40 Director GW Bookstore ... Mr. Robert C. BLAKE
107 Dean Col of Professional Studies ... Dr. Ali ESKANDARIAN
49 Dean Columbian Col Arts/Sciences ... Dr. Ben VINSON
63 Dean Medicine & Health Sciences ... Dr. Jeffrey S. AKMAN
69 Dean School of Public Health ... Dr. Lynn R. GOLDMAN
61 Dean Law School ... Dr. Blake D. MORANT
54 Dean Engineer/Applied Science ... Dr. David DOLLING
53 Dean Education/Human Development ... Dr. Michael J. FEUER
50 Dean School of Business ... Dr. Linda A. LIVINGSTONE
82 Dean Elliott School Intl Affairs ... Dr. Reuben E. BRIGETY
66 Dean School of Nursing ... Dr. Pamela R. JEFFRIES
12 Dean GW Virginia Sci/Tech Campus ... Dr. Ali ESKANDARIAN
41 Director Athletics/Recreation ... Mr. Patrick NERO
84 Asst VP Grad Student Enroll Mgmt ... Dr. Kristin WILLIAMS
92 Director University Honors Program ... Dr. Maria H. FRAWLEY
93 Director Multicultural Student Svc ... Mr. Michael R. TAPSCOTT
104 Director Study Abroad ... Mr. Robert HALLWORTH
39 Director Student Housing ... Mr. Seth D. WEINSHEL

Georgetown University (E)

37th & O Streets, NW, Washington DC 20057-1947
FICE Identification: 001445
Unit ID: 131496
Telephone: (202) 687-0100 Carnegie Class: DU-Highest
FAX Number: N/A Calendar System: Semester
URL: www.georgetown.edu
Established: 1789 Annual Undergrad Tuition & Fees: $48,611
Enrollment: 17,858 Coed
Affiliation or Control: Roman Catholic IRS Status: 501(c)3
Highest Offering: Doctorate
Accreditation: M, ANEST, BUS, CEA, HSA, LAW, MED, MIDWF, NURSE, PAST

01 President ... Dr. John (Jack) J. DEGIOIA
46 Sr VP Research/Chief Technology Off ... Dr. Spiros DIMOLITSAS
101 Secretary of the University ... Mr. Edward M. QUINN
100 Chief of Staff ... Mr. Joseph FERRARA
05 Provost ... Dr. Robert M. GROVES
17 Exec Vice Pres Health Sciences ... Dr. Edward B. HEALTON
61 Exec Vice Pres/Dean of Law School ... Dr. William M. TREANOR
30 Vice Pres for Advancement ... Mr. R. Bartley MOORE
42 Vice Pres for Mission and Ministry ... Rev. Kevin O'BRIEN, SJ
11 Sr Vice Pres and COO ... Mr. Christopher L. AUGOSTINI
10 Vice Pres Finance & Univ Treasurer ... Mr. David RUBENSTEIN
13 Interim Vice Pres/CIO ... Mr. Judd NICHOLSON
15 VP Human Resources ... Ms. Brenda R. MALONE
26 VP Public Affairs & Strategic Dev ... Mr. Erik SMULSON
27 Assoc VP Communications ... Ms. Stacy KERR
18 VP Planning & Facilities Mgmt ... Mr. Robin MOREY
32 VP Student Affairs ... Dr. Todd OLSON
28 VP for Inst Diversity & Equity ... Ms. Rosemary KILKENNY
19 Chief of Police Dept Public Safety ... Mr. Jay GRUBER
43 VP & General Counsel ... Ms. Lisa M. BROWN
88 VP for Global Engagement ... Dr. Thomas BANCHOFF
29 Associate VP Alumni Relations ... Mr. William G. REYNOLDS
109 Assoc VP for Auxiliary Services ... Ms. Joelle D. WIESE
88 Assc VP Benefits/Chief Benefits Off ... Mr. Charles E. DESANTIS
14 Interim Deputy CIO ... Ms. Beth BERGSMARK
91 Assoc VP Enterprise Apps ... Vacant
20 Vice Provost Education ... Dr. Randall BASS
20 Vice Provost Research ... Dr. Janet MANN

20	Vice Provost Faculty	Dr. Adriana KUGLER
21	VP Finance Accounting & Systems	Ms. Pim THUKRAL
21	Assoc VP Financial Operations	Vacant
21	Asst VP Finance Planning & Budget	Mr. Matthew C. GREAVES
06	Assoc VP & University Registrar	Ms. Annamarie BIANCO
21	VP & COO Main Campus	Mr. Darryl E. CHRISTMON
07	Dean Undergraduate Admissions	Mr. Charles A. DEACON
90	AVP University Information Sys	Ms. Ardoth HASSLER
35	Assoc VP Student Affairs	Dr. Jeanne F. LORD
23	Asst VP for Student Health	Dr. Vince C. WINKLERPRINS
08	University Librarian	Ms. Artemis G. KIRK
88	Ex Dir Ctr New Designs Lrng/Schlrs	Dr. Edward J. MALONEY
37	Dean Student Financial Svcs	Ms. Patricia A. MCWADE
25	Director of Sponsored Programs	Ms. Mary E. SCHMIEDEL
49	Dean Georgetown College	Dr. Chester GILLIS
82	Dean School Foreign Service	Dr. Joel HELLMAN
50	Dean School of Business	Dr. David A. THOMAS
63	Dean Medical School	Dr. Stephen R. MITCHELL
66	Dean Sch of Nurs/Health Stds	Dr. Patricia CLOONAN
51	Dean Continuing Studies	Dr. Kelly OTTER
58	Dean of Grad School	Dr. Norberto M. GRZYWACZ
80	Dean McCourt School Public Policy	Dr. Edward B. MONTGOMERY
86	Asst to President Federal Relations	Mr. Scott S. FLEMING
31	Director Partnerships & Cmty Engage	Ms. Brenda ATKINSON-WILLOUGHBY
96	Asst VP Procurement	Mr. O.T WELLS
85	Director of Global Services	Ms. Vanessa MEYERS
104	Director of Global Education	Mr. Craig RINKER
36	Exec Director Career Center	Dr. Mike SCHAUB
22	Director Affirmative Action Pgm	Mr. Michael W. SMITH
24	Exec Dir Classroom Educ/Tech Svcs	Mr. Mark J. COHEN
38	Director Counseling Center	Dr. Philip W. MEILMAN
41	Director Athletics	Mr. Lee REED
39	Director of Residence Life	Ms. Stephanie J. LYNCH
108	Asst Dir CNDLS/Assessment	Ms. Mindy MCWILLIAMS
25	Dir Spons Projects Financial Ops	Vacant
102	Dir Found & Corp Relations	Ms. Carma FAUNTLEROY
44	Exec Director Gift Planning	Mr. Stephen LINK

Howard University (A)

2400 Sixth Street, NW, Washington DC 20059-0001

FICE Identification: 001448
Unit ID: 131520

Telephone: (202) 806-6100 | Carnegie Class: DU-Higher
FAX Number: (202) 806-5934 | Calendar System: Semester
URL: www.howard.edu
Established: 1867 | Annual Undergrad Tuition & Fees: $23,970
Enrollment: 10,265 | Coed
Affiliation or Control: Independent Non-Profit | IRS Status: 501(c)3
Highest Offering: Doctorate
Accreditation: M, ARCPA, ART, BUS, BUSA, CLPSY, COPSY, CS, DENT, DH DIETC, ENG, IPSY, JOUR, LAW, MED, MT, MUS, NURSE, OT, PHAR, #PTA, RTT, SP, SW, TED, THEA, THEOL

01	President	Dr. Wayne FREDERICK
05	Provost/Chief Academic Officer	Dr. Anthony K. WUTOH
101	Interim Secretary of University	Ms. Florence PRIOLEAU
43	General Counsel	Ms. Florence PRIOLEAU
10	Chief Financial Officer	Mr. Michael MASCH
26	Vice President for External Affairs	Ms. Gracia HILLMAN
15	VP for Human Resources	Ms. Carrolyn J. BOSTICK
30	Vice President Development	Ms. Laura JACK
17	CEO University Hospital	Mr. James EDWARDS
46	Assoc Provost Research & Graduates	Dr. Gary L. HARRIS
20	Assistant Provost	Dr. Mary HILL
20	Assoc Provost Undergraduate Studies	Dr. Melanie CARTER
32	Vice President Student Affairs	Mr. Kenneth M. HOLMES
88	AVP Regulatory/Research Compliance	Dr. Thomas O. OBISESAN
88	AVP for Research and Faculty	Dr. Kristy F. WOODS
13	Chief Information Officer	Mr. Carlos DE LA ROSA
100	Chief of Staff	Ms. LaRue BARKWELL
58	Dean Graduate School	Dr. Gary L. HARRIS
49	Dean College Arts/Sciences	Dr. Bernard A. MAIR
50	Dean School of Business	Dr. Barron H. HARVEY
61	Dean School of Law	Ms. Danielle R. HOLLEY-WALKER
63	Dean Medicine/VP Clinical Affairs	Dr. Hugh E. MIGHTY
52	Dean College of Dentistry	Dr. Dexter A. WOODS
54	Dean Col Engr/Arch/Comp Sc	Dr. Achille MESSAC
53	Interim Dean School of Education	Dr. Dawn WILLIAMS
60	Dean School Communications	Dr. Gracie LAWSON-BORDERS
88	Dean Nursing/Allied Hlth Sc	Dr. Gina S. BROWN
70	Dean School of Social Work	Dr. Sandra CREWE
73	Dean School of Divinity	Dr. Alton B. POLLARD, III
67	Interim Dean School of Pharmacy	Dr. Daphne BUCHANAN BERNARD
48	Director School of Architecture	Prof. Victor DZIDZIENYO
76	Assoc Dean/Div Allied Health Sci	Dr. Shirley J. JACKSON
66	Assoc Dean/Div of Nursing	Ms. Tammi L. DAMAS
57	Assoc Dean/Division of Fine Arts	Dr. Gwendolyn H. EVERETT
81	Assoc Dean/Div Natural Sciences	Dr. Robert CATCHINGS
83	Interim Assoc Dean/Social Sciences	Dr. Terri ADAMS
79	Associate Dean Humanities	Dr. James J. DAVIS
23	Associate VP for Clinical Affairs	Dr. Feseha WOLDU
06	Registrar	Ms. LaTrice BYAM
37	Interim Director Financial Aid	Ms. Dolapo OGUNMAKIN
07	Director of Admissions	Ms. Latrice BYAM
42	Dean Andrew Rankin Chapel	Dr. Bernard L. RICHARDSON
35	Dean Student Life & Activities	Ms. Tonya L. GUILLORY
39	Dean of Residence Life	Mr. Wilson T. BLAND
36	Director Career Services Office	Dr. Joan M. BROWNE
08	Interim Director Libraries	Ms. Carrie M. HACKNEY
88	Director Health Sciences Library	Ms. Fatima BARNES
88	Director Law Library	Ms. Rhea BALLARD-THROWER
24	Dir Teaching Learning & Assmnt Ctr	Dr. Helen BOND
16	Senior Director Human Resources	Mr. Michael MCFADDEN
22	Dir Equal Employment Opportunity	Mr. Antwan LOFTON
30	Director for Advancement Services	Mr. Jeremy C. RANDALL
29	Senior Director Alumni Relations	Mr. Charles GIBBS
44	Senior Director of Annual Giving	Mr. Keith D. MILES
27	AVP of External Affairs	Ms. Cynthia BROCK-SMITH
18	AVP Facilities	Mr. Eric COARD
88	Director Campus Planning	Mr. Derek NIEC-WILLIAMS
19	Chief of Campus Police	Mr. Brian K. JORDAN
31	Director HU Community Association	Ms. Maybelle T. BENNETT
109	Director Auxiliary Enterprises	Mr. Antwan L. CLINTON
92	Director of Honors Program	Dr. Daniel A. WILLIAMS, III
41	Athletics Director	Mr. Kery DAVIS
23	Director Student Health Center	Dr. David BOWMAN
40	Gen Manager Barnes & Noble at HU	Mr. Alex BAMFO
94	Director of Women's Studies	Vacant
18	Director Physical Facilities	Mr. Victor MCNAUGHTON
108	Director Institutional Assessment	Dr. Gerunda B. HUGHES
88	Director Events & Protocol	Mr. Andrew RIVERS

The Institute of World Politics (B)

1521 16th Street, NW, Washington DC 20036-1464

FICE Identification: 041144
Unit ID: 455804

Telephone: (202) 462-2101 | Carnegie Class: Spec-4-yr-Other
FAX Number: (202) 464-0335 | Calendar System: Semester
URL: www.iwp.edu
Established: 1990 | Annual Graduate Tuition & Fees: N/A
Enrollment: 136 | Coed
Affiliation or Control: Independent Non-Profit | IRS Status: 501(c)3
Highest Offering: Master's; No Undergraduates
Accreditation: M

01	President	Dr. John LENCZOWSKI
03	Executive Vice President	Lawrence COSGRIFF
05	Academic Dean	Dr. MacKubin OWENS
10	Chief Financial Officer	Elaine PINDER
30	VP Institutional Advancement	Tom ATWOOD
32	VP Student Affairs and Admissions	Jason JOHNSRUD
06	Registrar & Institutional Research	Hasanna BENSON-TYUS
88	Director Professional Affiliations	Dr. Tania MASTRAPA
84	Director Student Recruitment	Tim STEBBINS
29	Alumni/Communications Officer	Katie BRIDGES
36	Director Career Services	Derrick DORTCH
37	Director Financial Aid	Thelbert SNOWDEN
26	Director Marketing and Comm	MaryAnne GARNER
08	Library Manager	Dmitry KULIK
04	Asst to President/Development Ofcr	Kathy CARROLL

Inter-American Defense College (C)

210 B Street SW, Bldg 52, Ft McNair, Washington DC 20319

Identification: 667275

Telephone: (202) 646-1337 | Carnegie Class: Not Classified
FAX Number: N/A | Calendar System: Semester
URL: www.colegio-id.org
Established: 1962 | Annual Graduate Tuition & Fees: N/A
Enrollment: N/A | Coed
Affiliation or Control: Independent Non-Profit | IRS Status: 501(c)3
Highest Offering: Master's; No Undergraduates
Accreditation: ACICS

01	Director	RAdm. Martha HERB

Pontifical Faculty of the Immaculate Conception at the Dominican House of Studies (D)

487 Michigan Avenue, NE, Washington DC 20017-1585

FICE Identification: 012803
Unit ID: 131405

Telephone: (202) 495-3820 | Carnegie Class: Spec-4-yr-Faith
FAX Number: (202) 495-3873 | Calendar System: Semester
URL: www.dhs.edu
Established: 1902 | Annual Graduate Tuition & Fees: N/A
Enrollment: 95 | Coed
Affiliation or Control: Roman Catholic | IRS Status: 501(c)3
Highest Offering: Master's; No Undergraduates
Accreditation: M, THEOL

01	President	Fr. John LANGLOIS, OP
05	Vice President/Academic Dean	Fr. Thomas PETRI, OP
20	Secretary of Studies	Fr. Brian CHRZASTEK, OP
08	Librarian	Fr. John Martin RUIZ, OP
18	Director of Facilities	Ms. Shauna ROYE
42	Chaplain to Commuter Students	Fr. John Martin RUIZ, OP
06	Registrar	Fr. Albert TRUDEL, OP
10	Treasurer/Director of Financial Aid	Ms. Shauna ROYE
30	Assistant Director of Advancement	Mr. George CERVANTES
13	IT Director	Mr. Carlos MOLINA
36	Director of Career Placement	Dr. Jem SULLIVAN
04	Executive Assistant	Mrs. Patricia WORK
88	Administrative Secretary	Ms. Sharon SMITH

Pontifical John Paul II Institute for Studies on Marriage and Family (E)

620 Michigan Ave, NE, McGivney Hall, Washington DC 20064

FICE Identification: 041427
Unit ID: 455813

Telephone: (202) 526-3799 | Carnegie Class: Spec-4-yr-Faith
FAX Number: (202) 269-6090 | Calendar System: Other
URL: www.johnpaulii.edu
Established: 1988 | Annual Graduate Tuition & Fees: N/A
Enrollment: 64 | Coed
Affiliation or Control: Roman Catholic | IRS Status: 501(c)3
Highest Offering: Doctorate; No Undergraduates
Accreditation: M

01	President	RevMsg. Pierangelo SEQUERI
03	Vice President	Carl A. ANDERSON
05	Provost/Dean	Fr. Antonio LOPEZ
20	Associate Dean for Academic Affairs	David S. CRAWFORD
11	Assoc Dean Programs & Administration	Nick J. BAGILEO
07	Director of Admissions	Sara L. TRUDEAU

† Affiliated with The Catholic University of America, DC.

Strayer University (F)

1133 15th Street, NW, Washington DC 20005-2710

FICE Identification: 001459
Unit ID: 131803

Telephone: (202) 408-2400 | Carnegie Class: Masters/M
FAX Number: (202) 419-1423 | Calendar System: Quarter
URL: www.strayer.edu
Established: 1892 | Annual Undergrad Tuition & Fees: $12,975
Enrollment: 1,192 | Coed
Affiliation or Control: Proprietary | IRS Status: Proprietary
Highest Offering: Master's
Accreditation: M, ACBSP, TEAC

01	President	Mr. Brian W. JONES
05	Provost/Chief Academic Ofcr	Dr. Andrea BACKMAN
20	Vice Provost of Academic Admin	Ms. Lily GARCIA
32	Senior Vice Provost Student Affairs	Ms. Chandra QUAYE
08	University Librarian	Mr. David A. MOULTON
06	University Registrar	Ms. Laurie KOHSMANN
106	Global Online Campus Dean	Dr. Linda NOBIS
20	Chamblee Campus Dean	Ms. Jocelyn WILLIAMS
12	Chamblee Campus Director	Mr. Rick WYLIE
20	Chesterfield Campus Dean	Dr. Carol WILLIAMS
12	Chesterfield Campus Director	Ms. Amy BREEDEN
20	Christiana Campus Dean	Ms. Cornelia ZAVADSKY
12	Christiana Campus Director	Mr. Alex HARRIS
20	Charleston Campus Dean	Dr. Deborah HILL
12	Charleston Campus Director	Ms. Colette REID
20	Cobb County Campus Dean	Ms. Donna KILGORE LY
12	Cobb County Campus Director	Ms. Kedicia RITCHIE-MITCHELL
20	Columbia Campus Dean	Ms. Piper LORICK
12	Columbia Campus Director	Ms. Nedra BROWN
20	Delaware County Campus Dean	Ms. Cornelia ZAVADSKY
12	Delaware County Campus Director	Mr. Alex HARRIS
20	Fredericksburg Campus Dean	Dr. Peter DEDOMINICI
12	Fredericksburg Campus Director	Mr. Duan BUTLER
20	Greensboro Campus Dean	Dr. Joel GOLDSTEIN
12	Greensboro Campus Director	Ms. Dorenda CRAIGG
20	Henrico Campus Dean	Dr. Carol T. WILLIAMS
12	Henrico Campus Director	Ms. Amy BREEDEN
20	Lower Bucks Campus Dean	Dr. Byron WESS
12	Lower Bucks Campus Director	Ms. Lauren PLINER
20	Greenville Campus Dean	Dr. William DUERR
12	Greenville Campus Director	Ms. Ashley MILLS
20	Loudoun Campus Dean	Ms. Katie BRUNSWICK
12	Loudoun Campus Director	Ms. Shirin SAGHAFI
20	Manassas Campus Dean	Ms. Katie BRUNSWICK
12	Manassas Campus Director	Mr. Rizwan CHOUDHRY
20	North Raleigh Campus Dean	Dr. Pang-Jen CRAIG KUNG
12	North Raleigh Campus Director	Ms. Sharon POMEROY
20	Morrow Campus Dean	Dr. Angela WILLIAMS
12	Morrow Campus Director	Ms. Stephanie GOWER
20	Nashville Campus Dean	Dr. Aikyna FINCH
12	Nashville Campus Director	Ms. Marilyn MAYE
20	Newport News Campus Dean	Mr. Terrell MASON
12	Newport News Campus Director	Mr. Ryan ALLEN
20	North Charlotte Campus Dean	Dr. Jeffrey ROMANCZUK
12	North Charlotte Campus Director	Ms. Christine VITO
20	Owings Mills Campus Dean	Ms. Latoya HALE
12	Owings Mills Campus Director	Ms. Candy COLLINS
20	Roswell Campus Dean	Ms. Donna KILGORE LY
12	Roswell Campus Director	Ms. Kedicia RITCHIE-MITCHELL
20	Shelby Oaks Campus Dean	Dr. Clinton MILLER
12	Shelby Oaks Campus Director	Mr. Sam THOMAS
20	Prince Georges Campus Dean	Ms. Shanee MAJOR-KELLY
12	Prince Georges Campus Director	Ms. Candy COLLINS
20	Research Triangle Park Campus Dean	Dr. William DENNING
12	Research Triangle Park Campus Dir	Pashuan ARMOND
20	Rockville Campus Dean	Dr. Twila LINDSAY
12	Rockville Campus Director	Ms. Shirin SAGHAFI
20	South Charlotte Campus Dean	Dr. Miranda CARLTON-CAREW
12	South Charlotte Campus Director	Ms. Janet BEAMER
20	Virginia Beach Campus Dean	Ms. Ashley CASTLE
12	Virginia Beach Campus Director	Mr. Tom LOTITO
12	Takoma Park Campus Director	Ms. Carolene BLOOMFIELD
20	Takoma Park Campus Dean	Dr. Twila LINDSAY

20 Tampa East Campus Dean .... Ms. Nell MESHCHERYAKOV
12 Tampa East Campus Director ....Mr. Jeffrey KEITH
20 Tampa Westshore Campus Dean ..... Ms. Nell MESHCHERYAKOV
12 Tampa Westshore Campus Director ....Mr. Jeffrey KEITH
20 Woodbridge Campus Dean .... Dr. Ras ACOLASTE
12 Woodbridge Campus Director .... Mr. Haroon MOKEL
12 Thousand Oaks Campus Director ....Mr. Sam THOMAS
20 Thousand Oaks Campus Dean ....Dr. William CARMICHAEL
20 Washington Campus Dean .... Dr. Christy KARNES
12 Washington Campus Director ....Ms. Ashley COLLINS
20 White Marsh Campus Dean .... Ms. Tafadzwa NHIRA
12 White Marsh Campus Director ....Leator KNUCKLES
20 Arlington Campus Dean .... Dr. Christy KARNES
12 Arlington Campus Director ....Ms. Breanne WINTER
20 Alexandria Campus Dean ....Dr. Angela AGBOLI-ESEDEBE
12 Alexandria Campus Director .... Ms. Tamara DORSEY
20 Center City Campus Dean ....Ms. Saadia OULAMINE
12 Center City Campus Director ....Mr. Isaac WALTERS
20 Anne Arundel Campus Dean .... Ms. Aerin GILBERT
12 Anne Arundel Campus Director ....Ms. Cristen JONES
12 Birmingham Campus Director .... Ms. Kendra GOODE
20 Birmingham Campus Dean ....Mr. Keith JOHNSON
20 Chesapeake Campus Dean ....Ms. Ashley CASTLE
12 Chesapeake Campus Director .... Ms. Jeanne POINDEXTER
20 Assoc Huntsville Campus Dean ....Mr. Keith JOHNSON
12 Huntsville Campus Director ....Ms. Julie PRYOR
20 Little Rock Campus Dean ....Ms. Dana EVANS
12 Little Rock Campus Director ....Ms. Angela MILLER
20 Assoc Baymeadows Campus Dean .....Ms. Sunshine JINOGOZIAN
12 Baymeadows Campus Director ....Ms. Kristina HILLIARD
20 Assoc Brickell Campus Dean ....Mr. Nate SMITH
12 Brickell Campus Director ....Ms. Trish ADIA
20 Assoc Doral Campus Dean ....Mr. Nate SMITH
12 Doral Campus Director ....Ms. Trish ADIA
20 Assoc Ft. Lauderdale Campus Dean ....Mr. Nate SMITH
12 Ft. Lauderdale Campus Director .... Mr. Geoffrey RAMGOLAM
20 Assoc Maitland Campus Dean .... Ms. Sunshine JINGOZIAN
12 Maitland Campus Director .... Ms. Ann POHIRA VIETH
20 Miramar Campus Dean ....Dr. Joann RAPHAEL
12 Miramar Campus Director ....Ms. Trish ADIA
20 Assoc Orlando East Campus Dean .... Ms. Sunshine JINGOZIAN
12 Orlando East Campus Director .... Ms. Kristin HILLIARD
20 Palm Beach Gardens Campus Dean ....Dr. Joann RAPHAEL
12 Palm Beach Gardens Campus Director ....Ms. Trish ADIA
20 Assoc Sand Lake Campus Dean .... Ms. Sunshine JINGOZIAN
12 Sand Lake Campus Director .... Ms. Ann POHIRA VIETH
20 Augusta Campus Dean ....Dr. Amona WASHINGTON
12 Augusta Campus Director ....Mr. Steven HOGG
20 Columbus GA Campus Dean ....Dr. Robert E. CULVER
12 Columbus GA Campus Director ....Mr. Steven HOGG
20 Douglasville Campus Dean ....Dr. Timothy SHERMAN
12 Douglasville Campus Director .... Ms. Tracey MARTIN
20 Lithonia Campus Dean .... Dr. Tonya MOORE
12 Lithonia Campus Director ....Mr. Paul LAWSON
20 Savannah Campus Dean ....Dr. Denise OGDEN
12 Savannah Campus Director .... Ms. Lendozia EDWARDS
20 Jackson Campus Dean .... Dr. Dana EVANS
12 Jackson Campus Director ....Ms. Angela MILLER
20 Cherry Hill Campus Dean ....Dr. R. Renee THOMPSON
12 Cherry Hill Campus Director .... Ms. Mary Kate HODOWANEC
20 Lawrenceville Campus Dean .... Dr. Scott HOLTZCLAW
12 Lawrenceville Campus Director .... Ms. Amanda MALICZYSZYN
20 Piscataway Campus Dean .... Dr. Scott HOLTZCLAW
12 Piscataway Campus Director .... Ms. Amanda MALICZYSZYN
20 Willingboro Campus Dean ....Dr. R. Renee THOMPSON
12 Willingboro Campus Director .... Ms. Mary Kate HODOWANEC
20 Huntersville Campus Dean ....Dr. Jonita HENRY POWELL
12 Huntersville Campus Director ....Ms. Stephanie JOHNSON
20 Assoc South Raleigh Campus Dean .... Ms. Kimberly WILLIAMS
12 South Raleigh Campus Director .... Ms. Mara JEFFERSON
20 Assoc Allentown Campus Dean ....Ms. Holli QUINN
12 Allentown Campus Director .... Ms. Lauren PLINER
20 Knoxville Campus Dean ....Dr. Aikyna FINCH
12 Knoxville Campus Director ....Ms. Marilyn MAYE
20 Cedar Hill Campus Dean ....Dr. Marilyn CARROLL
12 Cedar Hill Campus Director .... Mr. Brian CHRISTIE
20 Irving Campus Dean ....Dr. Marilyn CARROLL
12 Irving Campus Director .... Mr. Brian CHRISTIE
20 Katy Campus Dean ....Ms. Charity LANIER
12 Katy Campus Director .... Mr. Brian CHRISTIE
20 North Austin Campus Dean .... Dr. Samuel GOODING
12 North Austin Campus Director ....Mr. Sean HOFER
20 North Dallas Campus Dean ....Dr. Marilyn CARROLL
12 North Dallas Campus Director .... Mr. Brian CHRISTIE
20 Northwest Houston Campus Dean .... Ms. Charity LANIER
12 Northwest Houston Campus Director .... Mr. Brian CHRISTIE
20 Plano Campus Dean ....Dr. Marilyn CARROLL
12 Plano Campus Director .... Mr. Brian CHRISTIE
20 San Antonio Campus Dean .... Dr. Samuel GOODING
12 San Antonio Campus Director ....Mr. Sean HOFER
20 Stafford Campus Dean ....Dr. Charity LANIER
12 Stafford Campus Director .... Mr. Brian CHRISTIE
20 Teays Valley Campus Dean ....Dr. Joel GOLDSTEIN
12 Teays Valley Campus Director .... Mr. David GORA

Trinity Washington University (A)

125 Michigan Avenue, NE, Washington DC 20017-1090

FICE Identification: 001460
Unit ID: 131876
Telephone: (202) 884-9000 Carnegie Class: Masters/L
FAX Number: (202) 884-9229 Calendar System: Semester
URL: www.trinitydc.edu
Established: 1897 Annual Undergrad Tuition & Fees: $22,780
Enrollment: 2,267 Female
Affiliation or Control: Roman Catholic IRS Status: 501(c)3
Highest Offering: Master's
Accreditation: M, NURSE, OTA, TED

01 President .... Ms. Patricia A. MCGUIRE
04 Special Assistant to the President .... Dr. Kim ELDRIDGE
05 Vice President Academic Affairs ....Dr. Carlota OCAMPO
84 Vice Pres Enrollment Development ....Dr. Stephanie L. KRUSEMARK
30 Vice Pres Institutional Advancement ....Ms. Ann PAULEY
11 Vice President Administration ....Mr. Michael MALEWICKI
32 Vice President for Student Affairs ....Dr. Karen GERLACH
44 Vice President of Development .... Ms. Kathleen ZEIFANG
15 Vice President for Human Resources ....Ms. Carole KING
49 Dean College of Arts & Science ....Dr. Pamela BARNETT
53 Dean School of Education ....Dr. Janet STOCKS
107 Dean School of Professional Studies ....Ms. Nevada WINROW
66 Dean Sch Nursing/Health Professions ....Dr. Mary ROMANELLO
35 Dean of Student Services ....Ms. Michelle BOWIE
41 Athletic Director ....Ms. Amy OLSON
42 Director of Campus Ministry ....Ms. Lynn MYRICK
18 Exec Director Facilities Services ....Mr. Tim KNIGHT
29 Director Alumnae Affairs ....Ms. Margy REAGAN
06 Registrar ....Ms. Susie POWERS
07 Director of Admissions .... Ms. Germel CLARKE
08 Head Librarian ....Ms. Trisha SMITH
10 Chief Business Officer ....Ms. Barbara LETTIERE
13 Chief Info Technology Officer (CIO) .... Mr. Michael BURBACK

University of the District of Columbia (B)

4200 Connecticut Avenue, NW,
Washington DC 20008-1174

FICE Identification: 001441
Unit ID: 131399
Telephone: (202) 274-5000 Carnegie Class: Masters/S
FAX Number: (202) 274-5304 Calendar System: Semester
URL: www.udc.edu
Established: 1976 Annual Undergrad Tuition & Fees (In-District): $5,251
Enrollment: 4,803 Coed
Affiliation or Control: Local IRS Status: 501(c)3
Highest Offering: Master's
Accreditation: M, ACBSP, CACREP, COARC, CS, DIETD, ENG, FUSER, LAW, NUR, SP, SW, TED

01 President ....Mr. Ronald MASON, JR.
05 Provost/Vice Pres Academic Affairs .... Dr. Rachel PETTY
32 Vice President for Student Affairs .... Dr. Valerie EPPS
15 Vice President Human Resources ....Ms. Myrtho BLANCHARD
18 Acting VP Facilities & Real Estate .... Mr. Erik THOMPSON
30 Vice Pres University Advancement ....Mr. Michael C. ROGERS
88 Executive Asst to the Provost .... Mr. Herman PRESCOTT
10 Chief Financial Officer .... Ms. Shaina COOPER
49 Dean Arts & Sciences .... Dr. April MASSEY
50 Dean Sch Business & Public Admin ....Dr. Sandra YATES
61 Dean School of Law ....Ms. Shelley BRODERICK
54 Dean Engineering/Applied Scis ....Dr. Devdas SHETTY
56 Dean Agric/Urban Sustainabilty ....Dr. Sabine O'HARA
06 University Registrar .... Ms. LaVerne M. HILL-FLANAGAN
37 Director Student Financial Aid ....Mr. James CONTRERAS
26 Dir Marketing & Communications ....Mr. Michael C. ROGERS
08 Interim Dean Learning Resources .... Ms. Melba BROOME
25 Director Grants Administration ....Ms. Cassandra PARKER
41 Athletic Director ....Ms. Patricia A. THOMAS
43 General Counsel ....Ms. Karen M. HARDWICK
88 General Manager UDC Cable TV ....Mr. Edward JONES, JR.
18 Dir of Operations and Maintenance ....Mr. Alvin VENSON
30 Exec Director of Development ....Ms. Felicia BRANT
09 Director of Institutional Research .... Mrs. Jackie XU
38 Director Student Counseling ....Dr. Sislena LEDBETTER
96 Director of Procurement .... Ms. Mary A. HARRIS
27 Director of Communications ....Mr. John GORDON
88 Dean Student Achievement .... Ms. Hermina P. PETERS
103 Dean Workforce Development .... Ms. Kim R. FORD
19 Dir Public Safety/Chief of Police ....Mr. Larry E. VOLTZ
36 Director Career Services .... Mr. Jared E. MOFFETT
86 Director State & Local Affairs ....Mr. Thomas E. REDMOND
21 Director Financial Operations .... Mr. David FRANKLIN
88 Director STEM .... Ms. Barbara J. HOLMES
29 Director Alumni Affairs .... Mr. Joseph LIBERTELLI
89 Director of Advising and Retention ....Ms. Kimberly CREWS
102 Director Sponsored Programs .... Ms. Jovita WELLS
13 Dir Information Technology ....Mr. Michael ROGERS
07 Director Admissions/TRIO Programs .... Ms. Saundra CARTER
101 Exec Secretary Office the Board ....Ms. Beverly FRANKLIN
28 Director of Labor & Employee Rels .... Ms. Jennifer MATTHEWS
84 Director Office of Retention .... Mr. Timothy L. HATCHETT

University of Phoenix Washington DC Campus (C)

25 Massachusetts Avenue, NW,
Washington DC 20001-1431
Telephone: (202) 423-2520 Identification: 770196
Accreditation: &NH, ACBSP

† Regional accreditation is carried under the parent institution in Tempe, AZ

University of the Potomac (D)

1401 H Street NW, Suite 100, Washington DC 20005

FICE Identification: 032183
Unit ID: 384412
Telephone: (202) 274-2303 Carnegie Class: Spec-4-yr-Bus
FAX Number: N/A Calendar System: Semester
URL: www.potomac.edu
Established: 1991 Annual Undergrad Tuition & Fees: $13,884
Enrollment: 264 Coed
Affiliation or Control: Proprietary IRS Status: Proprietary
Highest Offering: Master's
Accreditation: M

01 President/Chief Executive Officer ....Dr. Clinton GARDNER
108 VP Assessment/Inst Effectiveness .... Walter PERSON
08 Director of Learning Resource Ctr .... Edward ROBINSON
07 Director of Admissions .... Nerissa CONN-KULLING
26 Chief Marketing Officer ....Ron HENDRICKS

Wesley Theological Seminary (E)

4500 Massachusetts Avenue, NW,
Washington DC 20016-5690

FICE Identification: 001464
Unit ID: 131973
Telephone: (202) 885-8600 Carnegie Class: Spec-4-yr-Faith
FAX Number: (202) 885-8605 Calendar System: Semester
URL: www.wesleyseminary.edu
Established: 1882 Annual Graduate Tuition & Fees: N/A
Enrollment: 564 Coed
Affiliation or Control: United Methodist IRS Status: 501(c)3
Highest Offering: Doctorate; No Undergraduates
Accreditation: M, THEOL

01 President ....Dr. David MCALLISTER-WILSON
04 Exec Assistant to the President ....Dr. Josie HOOVER
10 Vice Pres Finance/CFO ....Mr. Jeffrey STRAITS
11 Vice President for Administration ....Rev. Terry BRADFIELD
24 Director of Educational Technology ....Ms. Berkeley COLLINS
30 Vice President for Development .... Rev. Laura NORVELL
05 Dean .... Dr. Robert MARTIN
32 Assoc Dean for Community Life .... Dr. Asa LEE
35 Director of Student Affairs ....Ms. Anne HOTTEL-COX
07 Associate Dean of Admissions ....Rev. William D. ALDRIDGE
88 Vice President of Int'l Relations .... Dr. Kyunglim SHIN LEE
88 Vice Pres of Strategic Initiatives ....Rev. Beth LUDLUM
06 Registrar ....Ms. Vanessa TERZAGHI
15 Director Human Resources ....Ms. Yasmin LEWIS-WHITE
18 Chief Facilities/Physical Plant .... Mr. Randall ADAMS
37 Director Student Financial Aid .... Ms. Mary VIBERT
08 Director of Library ....Rev. James ESTES
26 Director of Communications/Marketin .... Ms. Sheila GEORGE
44 Director of Annual Giving ....Ms. Kristin SCHOL
39 Director of Housing ....Ms. Monica PETTY

FLORIDA

Academy for Five Element Acupuncture (F)

305 SE Second Avenue, Gainesville FL 32601-6811
County: Alachua FICE Identification: 035243
Unit ID: 451079
Telephone: (352) 335-2332 Carnegie Class: Spec-4-yr-Other Health
FAX Number: (352) 337-2535 Calendar System: Trimester
URL: www.acupuncturist.edu
Established: 1998 Annual Graduate Tuition & Fees: N/A
Enrollment: 71 Coed
Affiliation or Control: Independent Non-Profit IRS Status: 501(c)3
Highest Offering: Master's; No Undergraduates
Accreditation: ACUP

01 President ....Ms. Misti OXFORD-PICKERAL
11 Vice President Administration .... Ms. Joanne EPSTEIN
05 Academic Dean .... Mr. Chuck GRAHAM
10 Finance Director .... Ms. Odalis CRUZ
37 Financial Aid Director .... Mr. Glenn MORRIS
06 Registrar ....Ms. Sarah THOMPSON
07 Admissions Counselor .... Mr. Jim BROOKS

Academy for Nursing and Health Occupations (G)

5154 Okeechobee Blvd #201, West Palm Beach FL 33417
County: Palm Beach FICE Identification: 033463
Unit ID: 412173
Telephone: (561) 683-1400 Carnegie Class: Spec 2-yr-Health
FAX Number: (561) 683-6773 Calendar System: Other
URL: www.anho.edu
Established: 1978 Annual Undergrad Tuition & Fees: N/A
Enrollment: 424 Coed
Affiliation or Control: Independent Non-Profit IRS Status: 501(c)3
Highest Offering: Associate Degree
Accreditation: COE

01 President ....Dr. Lois M. GACKENHEIMER
05 Assistant Director/Dean ....Renee WERNER
06 Registrar ....Elizabeth RODRIGUEZ
07 Admissions Specialist ....Angela STILES

Acupuncture & Massage College (A)

10506 N Kendall Drive, Miami FL 33176-1509
County: Miami-Dade　FICE Identification: 034145
Unit ID: 439969
Telephone: (305) 595-9500　Carnegie Class: Spec-4-yr-Other Health
FAX Number: (305) 595-2622　Calendar System: Semester
URL: www.amcollege.edu
Established: 1983　Annual Undergrad Tuition & Fees: $10,425
Enrollment: 158　Coed
Affiliation or Control: Proprietary　IRS Status: Proprietary
Highest Offering: Master's
Accreditation: ACCSC, ACUP

01 President ... Dr. Gabriel GLIKSBERG
05 Academic Dean ... Dr. Sylvia SANTANA
17 Clinic Director ... Dr. Hailan WU
37 Financial Aid Director ... Ms. Christy WOOD
07 Admissions Director ... Mr. Joe CALARESO
06 Registrar/Student Services ... Ms. Maria GARCIA

Advance Science Institute (B)

3750 West 12 Avenue, Hialeah FL 33012
County: Miami-Dade　FICE Identification: 037573
Unit ID: 444334
Telephone: (305) 827-5452　Carnegie Class: Not Classified
FAX Number: (305) 557-2268　Calendar System: Semester
URL: asimedschool.com
Established: 1998　Annual Undergrad Tuition & Fees: N/A
Enrollment: 34　Coed
Affiliation or Control: Proprietary　IRS Status: Proprietary
Highest Offering: Associate Degree
Accreditation: ACCSC

01 President ... Pablo PEREZ

Adventist University of Health Sciences (C)

671 Winyah Drive, Orlando FL 32803-1204
County: Orange　FICE Identification: 031155
Unit ID: 133872
Telephone: (407) 303-9798　Carnegie Class: Spec-4-yr-Other Health
FAX Number: (407) 303-5671　Calendar System: Trimester
URL: www.adu.edu
Established: 1992　Annual Undergrad Tuition & Fees: $13,030
Enrollment: 2,090　Coed
Affiliation or Control: Seventh-day Adventist　IRS Status: 501(c)3
Highest Offering: Doctorate
Accreditation: SC, ANEST, #ARCPA, DMS, NMT, NUR, OT, OTA, @PTA, RAD

01 President ... Dr. David E. GREENLAW
05 Provost ... Dr. Edwin HERNANDEZ
10 Sr VP for Finance/CFO ... Mr. Ruben O. MARTINEZ
32 VP for Student Services ... Mr. Stephen H. ROCHE
26 VP Marketing & Public Relations ... Mr. Lonnie MIXON
106 VP Educational Tech/Distance Educ ... Dr. Dan LIM
20 Associate VP for Academic Admin ... Dr. Len ARCHER
09 Dir of Institutional Effec & Accred ... Dr. Roy LUKMAN
37 Director of Financial Aid ... Ms. Rebecca VALENCIA
06 Registrar ... Dr. Janet CALDERON
88 Dir Ctr for Academic Achievement ... Dr. Ndala BOOKER
08 Library Director ... Ms. Deanna L. FLORES
88 Office of Mission ... Dr. Don WILLIAMS
07 Director of Enrollment Services ... Vacant
21 Chief Accountant ... Mr. Grayson GOODMAN
39 Director of Residence Hall ... Mr. David A. BRYANT
30 Director of Philanthrophy ... Dr. Carol BRADFIELD
15 Director of Human Resources ... Mr. Fred W. STEPHENS
13 Director of Information Technology ... Mr. Travis WOOLEY
04 Executive Asst to the President ... Mrs. Dawn H. CREFT
88 Chief Compliance Officer ... Ms. Starr S. BENDER

American College for Medical Careers (D)

5959 Lake Ellenor Drive, Orlando FL 32809
Telephone: (407) 738-4488　Identification: 770842
Accreditation: ACICS, #COARC, DMS

† Branch campus of Salter College, West Boylston, MA

American Medical Academy (E)

12215 SW 112th Street, Miami FL 33186
County: Miami-Dade　FICE Identification: 041921
Unit ID: 475714
Telephone: (305) 271-6555　Carnegie Class: Spec 2-yr-Health
FAX Number: (305) 271-6556　Calendar System: Semester
URL: www.ama.edu
Established: 2006　Annual Undergrad Tuition & Fees: N/A
Enrollment: 247　Coed
Affiliation or Control: Proprietary　IRS Status: Proprietary
Highest Offering: Associate Degree
Accreditation: ABHES

01 Chief Executive Officer ... Mr. Eduardo GUTIERREZ

Ana G. Mendez University System Metro Orlando Campus (F)

5601 S Semoran Boulevard, #55, Orlando FL 32822
Telephone: (407) 207-3363　Identification: 770921
Accreditation: &M

† Regional accreditation is carried under the parent institution in Rio Piedras, PR.

Ana G. Mendez University System South Florida Campus (G)

3520 Enterprise Way, Miramar FL 33025
Telephone: (954) 885-5595　Identification: 770922
Accreditation: &M

† Regional accreditation is carried under the parent institution in Rio Piedras, PR.

Ana G. Mendez University System Tampa Bay Campus (H)

3655 West Waters Avenue, Tampa FL 33614
Telephone: (813) 932-7500　Identification: 770923
Accreditation: &M

† Regional accreditation is carried under the parent institution in Rio Piedras, PR.

Argosy University, Sarasota (I)

5250 17th Street, Sarasota FL 34235-8246
Telephone: (941) 379-0404　FICE Identification: 025906
Accreditation: &WC, ACBSP, CACREP

† Regional accreditation is carried under the parent institution in Orange, CA.

Argosy University, Tampa (J)

1403 N. Howard Avenue, Tampa FL 33607
Telephone: (813) 393-5290　Identification: 666082
Accreditation: &WC, ACBSP, CLPSY

† Regional accreditation is carried under the parent institution in Orange, CA.

The Art Institute of Fort Lauderdale (K)

1799 SE 17th Street, Fort Lauderdale FL 33316-3000
County: Broward　FICE Identification: 010195
Unit ID: 132338
Telephone: (954) 463-3000　Carnegie Class: Spec-4-yr-Arts
FAX Number: (954) 523-7676　Calendar System: Quarter
URL: www.aifl.edu
Established: 1968　Annual Undergrad Tuition & Fees: $17,700
Enrollment: 1,514　Coed
Affiliation or Control: Proprietary　IRS Status: Proprietary
Highest Offering: Baccalaureate
Accreditation: #ACICS, ACFEI, CIDA

01 President ... Carolyn PIERCE
32 Dean of Student Affairs ... Yojana RODRIGUEZ-HUMBERT
05 Dean of Academic Affairs ... Eric WATSON
10 Director of Accounting ... Maria V. BARRON
06 Registrar ... Della PACK
07 Senior Director of Admissions ... Debra BARTKOWSKI
37 Director Student Financial Services ... Anita ROBERTS
36 Director of Career Services ... Wendy WAGNER-LIND
15 Human Resources Generalist ... Samantha GORDON

The Art Institute of Tampa (L)

4401 North Himes Avenue, Suite 150, Tampa FL 33614
Telephone: (813) 873-2112　Identification: 770935
Accreditation: &SC, ACFEI

† Branch campus of Miami International University of Art & Design, Miami, FL.

ATA Career Education-Spring Hill (M)

7351 Spring Hill Drive, Suite 11, Spring Hill FL 34606
Telephone: (352) 684-3007　Identification: 770521
Accreditation: ABHES

† Branch campus of ATA College, Louisville, KY

Atlantic Institute of Oriental Medicine (N)

100 E Broward Boulevard, Suite 100,
Fort Lauderdale FL 33301-3510
County: Broward　FICE Identification: 034296
Unit ID: 439446
Telephone: (954) 763-9840　Carnegie Class: Spec-4-yr-Other Health
FAX Number: (954) 763-9844　Calendar System: Trimester
URL: www.atom.edu
Established: 1994　Annual Graduate Tuition & Fees: N/A
Enrollment: 139　Coed
Affiliation or Control: Independent Non-Profit　IRS Status: 501(c)3
Highest Offering: Doctorate; No Undergraduates
Accreditation: ACUP

01 President ... Johanna C. YEN
11 Executive Director ... Dort BIGG
05 Academic Dean ... Yan CHENG
03 Executive Vice President ... Di FU
10 Financial Officer ... Celia MUNOZ
06 Registrar ... Milagros FERREIRA
08 Head Librarian ... Jeanne THOMAS

† Granted candidacy at the Doctorate level.

Atlantis University (O)

1442 Biscayne Boulevard, Miami FL 33132
County: Miami-Dade　FICE Identification: 042339
Telephone: (305) 377-8817　Carnegie Class: Not Classified
FAX Number: (305) 377-9557　Calendar System: Semester
URL: www.atlantisuniversity.edu
Established: 1975　Annual Undergrad Tuition & Fees: N/A
Enrollment: N/A　Coed
Affiliation or Control: Proprietary　IRS Status: Proprietary
Highest Offering: Master's
Accreditation: ACCSC

01 Executive Director ... Ms. Carol PALACIOS

Ave Maria School of Law (P)

1025 Commons Circle, Naples FL 34119
County: Collier　FICE Identification: 036914
Unit ID: 442295
Telephone: (239) 687-5300　Carnegie Class: Spec-4-yr-Law
FAX Number: (239) 353-3173　Calendar System: Semester
URL: www.avemarialaw.edu
Established: 2000　Annual Graduate Tuition & Fees: N/A
Enrollment: 269　Coed
Affiliation or Control: Roman Catholic　IRS Status: 501(c)3
Highest Offering: First Professional Degree; No Undergraduates
Accreditation: LAW

01 President and Dean ... Mr. Kevin CIEPLY
04 Executive Assistant to the Dean ... Ms. Pamela KRAMER
05 Assoc Dean Academic Affairs ... Mr. Timothy TRACEY
08 Director of the Law Library ... Mr. Ulysses JAEN
42 Chaplain ... Msgr. Frank MCGRATH
06 Registrar ... Ms. Dairys WHITE
37 Director of Financial Aid ... Mr. Kevin MCGOWAN
30 Chief Advancement/Comm Officer ... Ms. Donna HEISER
07 Director of Admissions ... Ms. Claire O'KEEFE
36 Director of Career Services ... Ms. Jennifer LUCAS-ROSS
10 Assoc Dean Student/Admin Affairs ... Ms. Kaye CASTRO
40 Bookstore Manager ... Ms. Kathryn LOVE

Ave Maria University (Q)

5050 Ave Maria Boulevard, Ave Maria FL 34142-9505
County: Collier　FICE Identification: 039413
Unit ID: 446048
Telephone: (239) 280-2500　Carnegie Class: Bac-A&S
FAX Number: (239) 352-2392　Calendar System: Semester
URL: www.avemaria.edu
Established: 2003　Annual Undergrad Tuition & Fees: $18,479
Enrollment: 1,081　Coed
Affiliation or Control: Independent Non-Profit　IRS Status: 501(c)3
Highest Offering: Doctorate
Accreditation: SC

00 Chancellor ... Mr. Thomas S. MONAGHAN
01 President/CEO ... Mr. James TOWEY
03 Executive Vice President ... Mr. Dennis GRACE
05 VP Academic Affairs ... Dr. Seana SUGRUE
13 Chief Information Officer ... Mr. Eddie DEJTHAI
30 VP Institutional Advancement ... Mr. Brian COUCH
32 VP Student Affairs ... Ms. Julie COSDEN
10 Chief Financial Officer ... Mr. Robert FARNHAM
07 Director of Admissions ... Ms. Karen FULL
06 Registrar ... Ms. Stephanie E. NEGIP
09 Coordinator Institutional Research ... Mrs. Helen N. ALTOMARI
37 Managing Financial Aid Director ... Mrs. Anne HART
41 Athletic Director ... Mrs. Kimberly KING
42 Director of Campus Ministry ... Fr. Robert GARRITY
44 Director Planned Giving ... Mr. Jeffrey MCMANUS
35 Director of Student Life ... Ms. Julie COSDEN
88 Director of Mission/Outreach ... Ms. Grace CHEFFERS
08 Director of Library Services ... Ms. Jennifer NODES
15 Human Resources & Privacy Ofcr ... Ms. Kathy PHELPS
18 Director Physical Plant & Security ... Mr. Jason SYLVESTER
38 Mental Health Counselor ... Ms. Sharon O'REILLY
39 Director Resident Life ... Mrs. Vivian CROCKETT
19 Director Security/Safety ... Mr. Peter VAN DE VOORDE
43 General Counsel ... Mr. William KIRK

Aviator College of Aeronautical Science & Technology (R)

3800 St. Lucie Boulevard, Fort Pierce FL 34946
County: Saint Lucie　FICE Identification: 039863
Unit ID: 447847
Telephone: (772) 466-4822　Carnegie Class: Spec 2-yr-Tech
FAX Number: (772) 462-4886　Calendar System: Semester
URL: www.aviator.edu

Established: 1984 Annual Undergrad Tuition & Fees: $73,132
Enrollment: 176 Coed
Affiliation or Control: Proprietary IRS Status: Proprietary
Highest Offering: Associate Degree
Accreditation: ACCSC, CEA

01 President ... Mr. Michael E. COHEN
10 Sr Vice Pres/Chief Financial Ofcr ... Ms. T.J METE
05 Director of Education ... Mr. Pierre LAVIAL
06 Registrar/Director Student Services ... Ms. Lisa KREAMER
37 Financial Aid Officer ... Ms. Amy ROTH

Azure College (A)

2900 North Military Trail #227, Boca Raton FL 33431
Telephone: (561) 401-0000 Identification: 770981
Accreditation: ABHES

Azure College (B)

2940 US 27 South, Sebring FL 33876
County: Highlands Identification: 667116
Unit ID: 483762
Telephone: (863) 774-3535 Carnegie Class: Not Classified
FAX Number: N/A Calendar System: Quarter
URL: www.azure.edu
Established: 2004 Annual Undergrad Tuition & Fees: $17,449
Enrollment: 397 Coed
Affiliation or Control: Proprietary IRS Status: Proprietary
Highest Offering: Baccalaureate
Accreditation: ABHES

11 Assoc VP of Regional Opers ... Ms. Shirley SAWYER

The Baptist College of Florida (C)

5400 College Drive, Graceville FL 32440-3306
County: Jackson FICE Identification: 021596
Unit ID: 132408
Telephone: (850) 263-3261 Carnegie Class: Spec-4-yr-Faith
FAX Number: (850) 263-9026 Calendar System: Semester
URL: www.baptistcollege.edu
Established: 1943 Annual Undergrad Tuition & Fees: $10,000
Enrollment: 486 Coed
Affiliation or Control: Southern Baptist IRS Status: 501(c)3
Highest Offering: Master's
Accreditation: SC, MUS

01 President ... Dr. Thomas A. KINCHEN
30 Vice President for Development ... Dr. Charles R. PARKER
05 Academic Dean ... Dr. G. Robin JUMPER
06 Registrar ... Ms. Stephanie W. ORR
26 Director of Marketing ... Mrs. Sandra K. RICHARDS
09 Director of Institutional Research ... Dr. Ed SCOTT
37 Director of Financial Aid & VA ... Mrs. Stephanie E. POWELL
32 Dean of Students ... Dr. Roger C. RICHARDS
07 Director of Admissions ... Mrs. Sandra K. RICHARDS
18 Maintenance Director ... Mr. Huie G. WILSON
10 Associate Business Officer ... Ms. Polly K. FLOYD
04 Administrative Asst to President ... Ms. Laura L. TICE
08 Head Librarian ... Mr. John E. SHAFFETT
84 Director Enrollment Management ... Ms. Sandra K. RICHARDS

Barry University (D)

11300 NE Second Avenue, Miami Shores FL 33161-6695
County: Dade FICE Identification: 001466
Unit ID: 132471
Telephone: (305) 899-3000 Carnegie Class: DU-Mod
FAX Number: (305) 899-3054 Calendar System: Semester
URL: www.barry.edu
Established: 1940 Annual Undergrad Tuition & Fees: $28,800
Enrollment: 8,518 Coed
Affiliation or Control: Roman Catholic IRS Status: 501(c)3
Highest Offering: Doctorate
Accreditation: SC, ANEST, ARCPA, BUS, CAATE, CACREP, HT, LAW, MACTE, MT, NURSE, OT, PERF, POD, SW, THEOL

01 President ... Sr. Linda BEVILACQUA
04 Executive Asst to the President ... Ms. Mary Ellen LETSCHE
00 President Emerita ... Sr. Jeanne O'LAUGHLIN
05 Provost ... Dr. John D. MURRAY
10 Vice Pres Business & Finance ... Mrs. Susan ROSENTHAL
15 Vice Pres Human Resources ... Mrs. Jennifer N. BOYD-PUGH
30 VP Inst Adv & External Affairs ... Mrs. Sara B. HERALD
88 VP Mission & Inst Effectiveness ... Dr. Christopher STARRATT
32 Vice President Student Affairs ... Dr. Scott F. SMITH
13 VP Technology/CIO ... Ms. Yvette BROWN
43 General Counsel ... Mr. David DUDGEON
49 Dean College of Arts/Sciences ... Dr. Karen A. CALLAGHAN
50 Dean School of Business ... Dr. Tomislav MANDAKOVIC
53 Dean School of Education ... Dr. Jill FARRELL
76 Dean College of Health Sciences ... Dr. John MCFADDEN
88 Dean Human Perf/Leisure Sci ... Dr. Darlene KLUKA
61 Dean School of Law ... Dr. Leticia M. DIAZ
63 Dean School of Pod Med ... Dr. Albert ARMSTRONG
51 Dean School of Prof & Career Educ ... Dr. Andrea KEENER
70 Dean School of Social Work ... Dr. Phyllis SCOTT
35 Assoc VP Student Affs/Dean Students ... Dr. Maria L. ALVAREZ
35 Assoc Vice Pres Student Affairs ... Dr. Eileen MCDONOUGH
18 Assoc Vice Pres Facilities Mgmt ... Mr. Julian ANGEL
29 Assoc VP Alum Rels & Annual Giving ... Mr. Matthew BLAIR
84 Assoc Vice Pres Enrollment Services ... Ms. Angela SCOTT
105 Assoc VP Enrollment Mkt Strategy ... Mr. Michel SILY
19 Director Public Safety & Emerg Mgt ... Mr. John BUHRMASTER
08 Interim Dir Library Svcs/Libr Dir ... Mr. Rodrigo CASTRO
42 Chaplain ... Fr. Cristobal TORRES
44 Assoc VP Major Gifts Develop ... Ms. Margaret HUBBARD
44 Director Annual Giving ... Mrs. Kristy HENRY
06 University Registrar ... Ms. Cynthia A. CHRUSZCZYK
39 Director Housing and Residence Life ... Mr. Matthew R. CAMERON
36 Director Career Services ... Mr. John MORIARTY
37 Director Financial Aid ... Mr. Howard D. HUMESTON
92 Director Honors Program ... Dr. Pawena SIRIMANGKALA
38 Director Student Counseling Center ... Dr. James SCOTT
26 Assoc VP Brand Mkt & Communications ... Ms. Kim COX
07 Director of Undergraduate Admission ... Ms. Sarah RILEY
09 Director Institutional Research ... Ms. Shaunette GRANT
14 Associate CIO ... Mr. Hernan LONDONO
41 Director of Athletics ... Mr. Michael COVONE
86 Dir External & Governmental Affairs ... Mrs. Elizabeth BESADE
102 Director Foundation Relations ... Ms. Shannon BROWN
105 Director Digital Media Strat & Dev ... Mr. Miguel RAMIREZ
109 Dir Student Union & Food Services ... Mr. Mickie VOUTSINAS
25 Director Grant & Sponsored Programs ... Mrs. Sandra L. MANCUSO
40 Manager Bookstore ... Ms. Claudia HADJEZ

Bay Medical Center (E)

615 N Bonita Avenue, Panama City FL 32401-3600
County: Bay FICE Identification: 011127
Unit ID: 439464
Telephone: (800) 422-2418 Carnegie Class: Not Classified
FAX Number: (850) 747-6115 Calendar System: Semester
URL: www.baymedical.org/Career-Center/
Established: 1969 Annual Graduate Tuition & Fees: N/A
Enrollment: N/A Coed
Affiliation or Control: Independent Non-Profit IRS Status: 501(c)3
Highest Offering: Master's; No Undergraduates
Accreditation: ANEST

01 Interim CEO ... Mr. Steve GRUBBS
10 Chief Financial Officer ... Mr. Ron PATRICK
05 Chief Nursing Officer ... Ms. Jeanne REEVES

Beacon College (F)

105 E Main Street, Leesburg FL 34748-5162
County: Lake FICE Identification: 033733
Unit ID: 384254
Telephone: (352) 787-7660 Carnegie Class: Bac-Diverse
FAX Number: (352) 787-0721 Calendar System: Semester
URL: www.beaconcollege.edu
Established: 1989 Annual Undergrad Tuition & Fees: $34,680
Enrollment: 223 Coed
Affiliation or Control: Independent Non-Profit IRS Status: 501(c)3
Highest Offering: Baccalaureate
Accreditation: SC

01 President ... Dr. George J. HAGERTY
05 Provost ... Dr. Shelly CHANDLER
32 Dean of Student Affairs ... Dr. Kerry GREENSTEIN
30 VP of Institutional Development ... Mr. Stephen MULLER
10 VP of Finance & Administration ... Mr. Otis VANCE
09 VP Institutional Effectiveness ... Dr. Shelly CHANDLER
06 Registrar ... Mr. David BROWN
18 Director of Facilities ... Vacant
37 Director of Financial Aid ... Ms. Shawna WELLS-BOOTH
08 Director of Library Resources ... Ms. Tiffany REITZ
13 Director of Information Technology ... Mr. Tim PAIGE
04 Exec Assistant to the President ... Ms. Tamara SYNDER
15 Director of Human Resources ... Mr. Tom BROWN
07 Dean of Admissions Enrollment Mgmt ... Ms. Dale HEROLD
101 Admin Asst to the Board ... Ms. Tamara SNYDER
103 Dir Workforce/Career Development ... Dr. Andrea BRODE
29 Director Alumni Relations ... Ms. Chelsea EUBANK
38 Director Student Counseling ... Mr. Josh GROVER
19 Chief of Campus Security ... Mr. Ryan NESBITT
39 Director Student Housing ... Ms. Carrie SANTAW

Bethesda College of Health Sciences (G)

3800 South Congress Ave Ste 9,
Boynton Beach FL 33426
County: Palm Beach Identification: 667258
Telephone: (561) 364-3064 Carnegie Class: Not Classified
FAX Number: (561) 364-3059 Calendar System: Semester
URL: www.BethesdaCollege.net
Established: 2011 Annual Undergrad Tuition & Fees: N/A
Enrollment: N/A Coed
Affiliation or Control: Independent Non-Profit IRS Status: 501(c)3
Highest Offering: Associate Degree
Accreditation: ACICS, RAD

01 Dean ... Jeanette KAMCIYAN

Bethune Cookman University (H)

640 Dr. Mary McLeod Bethune Blvd,
Daytona Beach FL 32114-3099
County: Volusia FICE Identification: 001467
Unit ID: 132602
Telephone: (386) 481-2000 Carnegie Class: Bac-A&S
FAX Number: (386) 481-2010 Calendar System: Semester
URL: www.cookman.edu
Established: 1904 Annual Undergrad Tuition & Fees: $14,410
Enrollment: 4,044 Coed
Affiliation or Control: United Methodist IRS Status: 501(c)3
Highest Offering: Master's
Accreditation: SC, ENG, MUS, NUR, TED

01 President ... Dr. Edison O. JACKSON
10 Vice President Fiscal Affairs ... Mr. George GALL
32 VP Student Affairs ... Mr. Jason E. GLENN
30 Vice Pres Institutional Advancement ... Dr. Hakim J. LUCAS
43 VP/General Counsel ... Mr. Hubert GRIMES
13 VP Info Tech/Chief Info Officer ... Mr. Franklin PATTERSON
05 Provost for Academic Affairs ... Dr. Helena WALROND
21 Assoc Vice Pres Finance/Budget ... Mr. Gabe CASSANOVA
84 Associate VP Enrollment Management ... Mr. Warren HEUSNER
100 Chief of Staff ... Mr. Fontaine DAVIS
39 Asst VP Resident Education and Comm ... Vacant
30 Director of Advancement ... Ms. Sophia HUGER
26 Director of Communications ... Mrs. Keisha BOYD
36 Dir Academic and Career Development ... Ms. Davita BONNER
08 Chief Librarian Dean of Library/ LRC ... Dr. Tasha LUCAS-YOUMANS
06 Registrar ... Ms. Patricia KRESL
07 Director Admissions ... Ms. Manicia FINCH
37 Director Financial Aid ... Ms. Salina HAMILTON
23 Director Health Services ... Vacant
41 Athletics Director ... Mr. Lynn THOMPSON
42 Chaplain/Dir of Religious Life ... Rev. John BALDWIN
19 Director of Security ... Chief Melvin WILLIAMS
18 VP Capital Assets and Planning ... Mr. Graham GILCHRIST
66 Dean School of Nursing ... Dr. Sandra TUCKER
50 Dean School of Business ... Dr. Ida WRIGHT
53 Dean School of Education ... Dr. Willis WALTER
49 Dean School of Liberal Arts ... Dr. Janice ALLEN-KELSEY
81 Dean Sch Science/Engineering/Math ... Dr. Herbert THOMPSON
107 Dean School of Professional Studies ... Dr. Arletha MCSWAIN
58 Dean of Graduate Studies ... Dr. Adrienne COOPER
97 Dean of Undergrad Studies ... Dr. Kimberly BURGESS
04 Executive Asst to President ... Mrs. Valerie WILT
90 Director Academic Computing ... Ms. Anna HEIN
76 Exec Dean/School of Health Sci ... Dr. Deanna WATHINGTON
88 Dean of Chapel ... Rev. David ALLEN, JR.
31 VP Business & Community Development ... Dr. Aubrey LONG
31 VP Community Affairs/K-16 Initiat ... Dr. Willis WALTER
15 Vice President Human Resources ... Dr. Nan FISHER-WILLIAMS
20 Associate Provost ... Dr. Adrienne COOPER
35 Asst Vice Pres for Student Life ... Dr. Clyde WILSON, JR.
38 Asst VP Counseling & Disability Svc ... Ms. Nadine HEUSNER
88 Director of Testing ... Mr. James LAI
108 Executive Director of Assessment ... Mr. Cory POTTER
29 Alumni Affairs Manager ... Ms. Marah BELTZ
44 Annual Giving Manager ... Ms. Ashley PORTERFIELD

Broward College (I)

111 E Las Olas Boulevard,
Fort Lauderdale FL 33301-2298
County: Broward FICE Identification: 001500
Unit ID: 132709
Telephone: (954) 201-7350 Carnegie Class: Bac/Assoc-Assoc Dom
FAX Number: (954) 201-7576 Calendar System: Trimester
URL: www.broward.edu
Established: 1959 Annual Undergrad Tuition & Fees (In-State): $2,753
Enrollment: 44,119 Coed
Affiliation or Control: State IRS Status: 501(c)3
Highest Offering: Baccalaureate
Accreditation: SC, ADNUR, CAHIIM, COARC, DA, DH, DMS, EMT, MAC, MUS, NMT, NUR, NURSE, OPD, PTAA

01 President ... Mr. J. David ARMSTRONG, JR.
05 Sr Vice Pres Acad Affairs/Provost ... Dr. Linda HOWDYSHELL
10 Sr Vice Pres Finance/Administration ... Mr. Thomas OLLIFF
84 Vice Pres Enrollment Mgmt ... Dr. Marielena DESANCTIS
26 VP Public Affairs and Marketing ... Mr. Don COOK
11 Vice President of Operations ... Mr. John DUNNUCK
102 VP Advanc/Exec Dir BC Foundation ... Ms. Nancy BOTERO
13 Vice President Info Technology ... Ms. Patti BARNEY
86 VP Govt Policy/Regulatory Affairs ... Mr. Gregory A. HAILE
103 Executive Director Workforce Educ ... Ms. Mildred COYNE
100 Chief of Staff ... Ms. Adriana FAZZANO FICANO
12 Campus President BC Online ... Dr. David SHULMAN
12 Campus President Central Campus ... Dr. Marielena DESANCTIS
12 Campus President North Campus ... Dr. Avis PROCTOR
12 Campus President South Campus ... Dr. Rolando GARCIA
21 Chief Financial Officer ... Mr. Jayson IROFF
18 Chief Facilities/Physical Plant ... Mr. Sean DEVANEY
09 Dean Institutional Research ... Ms. Pauline ANDERSON
45 Dean Inst Planning/Effectiveness ... Dr. Deborah POSNER
08 Dean of Libraries/Learning Res ... Ms. Sarah WIGGINS
37 Director of Student Financial Svcs ... Ms. Theresa COWAN
15 Exec Director Human Res & Equity ... Dr. Denese EDSALL
06 Registrar ... Ms. Rochelle MOORE
29 Director Alumni Relations ... Ms. Mary WORKMAN
04 Sr Exec Asst to the President ... Mrs. Avis M. MCCOY
19 Director Security/Safety ... Mr. Peter AGNESI
25 Int Chief Contracts/Grants Admin ... Ms. Kareen TORRES
96 Director of Purchasing ... Dr. Judy SCHMELZER

Brown Mackie College-Miami (J)

3700 Lakeside Drive, Miramar FL 33027
Telephone: (305) 341-6600 Identification: 666110

Accreditation: ACICS

† Branch campus of Brown Mackie College, Cincinnati, OH.

Cambridge College (A)

5150 Linton Boulevard, Suite 340, Delray Beach FL 33484
County: Palm Beach FICE Identification: 040834
Unit ID: 454865
Telephone: (561) 381-4990 Carnegie Class: Spec 2-yr-Health
FAX Number: (561) 381-4992 Calendar System: Other
URL: www.cambridgehealth.edu
Established: Annual Undergrad Tuition & Fees: N/A
Enrollment: 210 Coed
Affiliation or Control: Proprietary IRS Status: Proprietary
Highest Offering: Associate Degree
Accreditation: ABHES, DMS

01 President .... Mr. Terry LAPIER

Cambridge Institute of Allied Health & Technology-Altamonte Springs (B)

460 E. Altamonte Drive, Third Floor,
Altamonte Springs FL 32701
County: Seminole FICE Identification: 038425
Unit ID: 446109
Telephone: (407) 265-8383 Carnegie Class: Not Classified
FAX Number: (407) 265-8384 Calendar System: Other
URL: www.cambridgehealth.edu
Established: Annual Undergrad Tuition & Fees: N/A
Enrollment: 188 Coed
Affiliation or Control: Proprietary IRS Status: Proprietary
Highest Offering: Associate Degree
Accreditation: ABHES

01 President .... Dr. Terrance LAPIER
12 Campus Director .... Vicente QUINONES
07 Director of Admissions .... Gordon HUNT
06 Registrar .... Kristie MCCARTHY
37 Financial Aid Manager .... Silvana JUNIKE
36 Careers Services Director .... Theresa MANTOVANI

Carlos Albizu University Miami Campus (C)

2173 NW 99th Avenue, Miami FL 33172-2209
Telephone: (305) 593-1223 Identification: 666814
Accreditation: &M, CLPSY, SP

† Regional accreditation is carried under the parent institution in San Juan, PR.

Center of Cinematography, Art & Television (D)

1637 NW 27th Avenue, Miami FL 33125
Telephone: (305) 634-0550 Identification: 770562
Accreditation: ACCSC

† Branch campus of Colegio de Cinematografia, Artes y Television, Bayamon, PR

Chamberlain College of Nursing-Jacksonville Campus (E)

5200 Belfort Road, Suite 100, Jacksonville FL 32256
Telephone: (904) 251-8100 Identification: 770501
Accreditation: &NH, NURSE

† Regional accreditation is carried under the parent institution in Addison, IL

Chamberlain College of Nursing-Miramar (F)

2300 SW 145th Avenue, Miramar FL 33027
Telephone: (954) 885-3510 Identification: 770498
Accreditation: &NH, NURSE

† Regional accreditation is carried under the parent institution in Addison, IL

Chipola College (G)

3094 Indian Circle, Marianna FL 32446-3065
County: Jackson FICE Identification: 001472
Unit ID: 133021
Telephone: (850) 526-2761 Carnegie Class: Bac/Assoc-Mixed
FAX Number: (850) 718-2388 Calendar System: Semester
URL: www.chipola.edu
Established: 1947 Annual Undergrad Tuition & Fees (In-District): $3,120
Enrollment: 2,080 Coed
Affiliation or Control: State/Local IRS Status: 501(c)3
Highest Offering: Baccalaureate
Accreditation: SC, ADNUR, NUR

01 President .... Dr. Jason HURST
05 Sr VP Instructional/Student Svcs .... Dr. Sarah CLEMMONS
10 Vice Pres of Admin & Business Svcs .... Mr. Steve YOUNG
32 Vice Pres of Student Affairs .... Dr. Jayne ROBERTS
15 Assoc VP of HR & Equity .... Mrs. Karan P. DAVIS
13 Associate VP Information Systems .... Mr. Dennis F. EVERETT
108 Dean Assessment/Compliance & Grant .... Dr. Matthew HUGHES
18 Dir Facilities & Capital Projects .... Mr. Nolan BAKER
26 Director Public Relations .... Dr. Bryan C. CRAVEN
37 Director of Financial Aid .... Ms. Beverly HAMBRIGHT
41 Director of Athletics .... Mr. Jeffrey JOHNSON
06 Registrar .... Ms Kathy REHBERG
04 Administrative Asst to President .... Ms. Alice PENDERGRASS
103 Dir Workforce/Career Development .... Mr. Darwin GILMORE
106 Dir Online Education/E-learning .... Ms. Vikki MILTON

City College (H)

177 Montgomery Road, Altamonte Springs FL 32714
County Seminole FICE Identification: 030799
Unit ID: 417327
Telephone: (407) 831-9816 Carnegie Class: Assoc/HVT-Mix Trad/Non
FAX Number: (407) 831-1147 Calendar System: Quarter
URL: www.citycollegeorlando.edu
Established 1997 Annual Undergrad Tuition & Fees: $13,068
Enrollment: 410 Coed
Affiliation or Control: Independent Non-Profit IRS Status: 501(c)3
Highest Offering: Associate Degree
Accreditation: ACICS, EMT, SURTEC

01 President .... Mrs. Esther FIKE-CURRY
05 Executive Director .... Mr. Paul CASTELLANO
06 Registrar .... Ms. Jackie MORALES

City College (I)

2000 W Commercial Boulevard,
Fort Lauderdale FL 33309-1916
County Broward FICE Identification: 025154
Unit ID: 244233
Telephone: (954) 492-5353 Carnegie Class: Bac/Assoc-Mixed
FAX Number: (954) 491-1965 Calendar System: Quarter
URL: www.citycollege.edu
Established 1983 Annual Undergrad Tuition & Fees: $13,068
Enrollment: 575 Coed
Affiliation or Control: Independent Non-Profit IRS Status: 501(c)3
Highest Offering: Baccalaureate
Accreditation: ACICS, EMT, SURTEC

01 President .... Esther FIKE-CURRY
03 Executive Director .... Doug GOODWIN
36 Director of Career Development .... Vacant
05 Director of Education .... Anie BONILLA
07 Director of Admissions .... Patricia TATE
13 Director of Technologies .... Jeffrey CLAYTON
08 Director of Library .... Torri KELLOG
06 Registrar .... Sanchia WILLIAMS
15 Human Resources Generalist .... Petricia BURKHART
37 Director Student Financial Aid .... Patty PATTERSON

City College (J)

7001 NW Fourth Boulevard, Gainesville FL 32607
Telephone: (352) 335-4000 Identification: 666413
Accreditation: ACICS, EMT

† Branch campus of City College, Fort Lauderdale, FL.

City College (K)

6565 Taft Street, Hollywood FL 33024
Telephone: (954) 744-1777 Identification: 770674
Accreditation: ACICS

City College (L)

9300 S Dadeland Blvd, Suite 200, Miami FL 33156
Telephone: (305) 666-9242 Identification: 666414
Accreditation: ACICS, EMT, SURTEC

† Branch campus of City College, Fort Lauderdale, FL.

College of Business and Technology (M)

8700 W. Flagler Street, Miami FL 33174
County: Miami-Dade FICE Identification: 030716
Unit ID: 417318
Telephone: (305) 273-4499 Carnegie Class: Bac/Assoc-Mixed
FAX Number: (305) 270-0779 Calendar System: Semester
URL: www.cbt.edu
Established: 1988 Annual Undergrad Tuition & Fees: $17,870
Enrollment: 63 Coed
Affiliation or Control: Proprietary IRS Status: Proprietary
Highest Offering: Associate Degree
Accreditation: ACICS

00 CEO .... Mr. Fernando N. LLERENA
01 President .... Ms. Monica LLERENA
26 Director Marketing & Development .... Mr. Luis E. LLERENA
05 Regional Director of Education .... Mrs. Gladys P. LLERENA
10 Finance Director .... Ms. Maricel SPEZZACATENA
37 Financial Aid Director .... Mrs. Yazmin PALMA
36 Career Services Director .... Vacant
12 Acting Campus Director .... Mr. Hector DUENAS
84 Regional Director of Enrollment Op .... Mr. Hamlet ARIAS
20 Director of Academic Operations .... Mr. Hector DUENAS
20 Asst Director Academic Operations .... Ms. Carolyn SMITH
06 Registrar .... Vacant
08 Head Librarian .... Ms. Jennifer ROMA
15 HR Manager .... Ms. Alma TROCHE
13 IT Manager .... Mr. Julo GONZALEZ
88 Compliance Manager .... Mr. Ken KISTNER

College of Business and Technology - Cutler Bay (N)

19151 South Dixie Highway, Cutler Bay FL 33157
Telephone: (305) 273-4499 Identification: 770677
Accreditation: ACICS, CAHIIM

College of Business and Technology - Flagler (O)

8230 W Flagler Street, Miami FL 33144
Telephone: (305) 273-4499 Identification: 770676
Accreditation: ACICS

College of Business and Technology - Hialeah Campus (P)

935 West 49th Street, Hialeah FL 33012
Telephone: (305) 273-4499 Identification: 770675
Accreditation: ACICS

College of Business and Technology - Miami Gardens (Q)

5190 NW 167 Street, Suite 200, Miami Gardens FL 33014
Telephone: (786) 693-8801 Identification: 770612
Accreditation: ACICS

College of Central Florida (R)

3001 S.W. College Road, Ocala FL 34474
County: Marion FICE Identification: 001471
Unit ID: 132851
Telephone: (352) 237-2111 Carnegie Class: Bac/Assoc-Assoc Dom
FAX Number: (352) 291-4450 Calendar System: Semester
URL: www.cf.edu
Established: 1957 Annual Undergrad Tuition & Fees (In-District): $2,570
Enrollment: 7,931 Coed
Affiliation or Control: Local IRS Status: 501(c)3
Highest Offering: Baccalaureate
Accreditation: SC, ADNUR, CAHIIM, DA, EMT, NUR, PTAA, SURGT

01 President .... Dr. James D. HENNINGSEN
10 Vice Pres Administration & Finance .... Mr. Francis J. MAZUR, III
05 Vice President Academic Affairs .... Dr. Mark PAUGH
32 Vice President Student Affairs .... Dr. Saul REYES
12 Citrus Campus Vice President .... Dr. Vernon LAWTER, JR.
43 General Counsel & Dir Govt Rels .... Mr. Robert BATSEL
09 VP Inst Effectiveness/College Rels .... Dr. Jillian RAMSAMMY
26 Director Marketing/Public Relations .. Ms. Lois BRAUCKMULLER
102 Executive Director Foundation .... Mr. Christopher KNIFE
21 Assistant VP for Finance .... Mr. Steven ASH
12 Provost Levy Center .... Dr. Rayanne GIDDIS
88 Dean Public Service/Criminal Just .... Mr. Charles MCINTOSH
75 Dean Bus Tech Careers & Tech Educ .... Dr. Rob WOLF
35 Dean Student Services .... Dr. Henri BENLOLO
49 Dean Liberal Arts & Sciences .... Mr. Allan DANUFF
35 Dean Student Success .... Ms. Debbie BOWE
53 Dean Arts and Education .... Dr. Jennifer FRYNS
84 Dean Enrollment Management .... Ms. Lyn POWELL
76 Dean Health Sciences .... Dr. Gwen ALCORN
106 Dean E-learning & Learning Resource .... Dr. Tamara VIVIANO-BRODERICK
37 Director Financial Aid .... Ms. Maureen ANDERSON
09 Dir Institutional Effectiveness .... Dr. Lawrence J. KUSZYNSKI
07 Director Admissions/Records .... Mrs. Teri LITTLE-BERRY
18 Director Facilities .... Mr. Tommy MORELOCK
15 Director Human Resources .... Vacant
35 Director Student Life .... Ms. Marjorie MCGEE
88 Director Student Support Services .... Ms. Lisa SMITH
41 Director Athletics/Wellness .... Mr. Bob ZELINSKI
88 Director Access and Counsel Service .... Ms. Victoria COLLELI
88 Dir Stdnt Success & Educ Outreach .... Dr. Leonard EVERETT
88 Director Appleton Museum of Art .... Ms. Cindi MORRISON
25 Director Grants Funding .... Mr. Matt MATTHEWS
08 Library Director .... Ms. Teresa FAUST
19 Manager Public Safety .... Mr. Doug PREVATT
109 Manager Printing & Postal Service .... Mr. Andrew LOWERY
109 Manager Conference & Food Service .... Ms. Cheryl CROSBY
13 Associate VP Information Technology .... Mr. Hank GLASPIE
06 Registrar .... Ms. Devona SEWELL
30 Director of Development .... Ms. Traci MASON

Concorde Career Institute (S)

7259 Salisbury Road, Jacksonville FL 32256
County: Duval FICE Identification: 020896
Unit ID: 133845
Telephone: (904) 725-0525 Carnegie Class: Spec 2-yr-Health
FAX Number: (904) 721-9944 Calendar System: Semester
URL: www.concorde.edu
Established: 1988 Annual Undergrad Tuition & Fees: N/A
Enrollment: 552 Coed
Affiliation or Control: Proprietary IRS Status: Proprietary
Highest Offering: Associate Degree

Accreditation: ACCSC, COARC, PTAA, SURGT

01 Campus President .... Melissa RYAN

Concorde Career Institute (A)

10933 Marks Way, Miramar FL 33025
County: Broward FICE Identification: 022751
Unit ID: 133854
Telephone: (954) 731-8880 Carnegie Class: Spec 2-yr-Health
FAX Number: (954) 484-2961 Calendar System: Other
URL: www.concorde.edu
Established: 1989 Annual Undergrad Tuition & Fees: N/A
Enrollment: 640 Coed
Affiliation or Control: Proprietary IRS Status: Proprietary
Highest Offering: Associate Degree
Accreditation: ACCSC, COARC, OTA, PTAA, SURGT

01 Campus President .... Matthew DIACONT

Concorde Career Institute (B)

3444 McCrory Place, Orlando FL 32803
Telephone: (407) 812-3060 Identification: 770563
Accreditation: ACCSC, #COARC, SURGT

Concorde Career Institute (C)

4202 West Spruce Street, Tampa FL 33607-4127
County: Hillsborough FICE Identification: 021727
Unit ID: 133863
Telephone: (813) 874-0094 Carnegie Class: Spec 2-yr-Health
FAX Number: (813) 872-6884 Calendar System: Other
URL: www.concorde.edu
Established: 1978 Annual Undergrad Tuition & Fees: N/A
Enrollment: 411 Coed
Affiliation or Control: Proprietary IRS Status: Proprietary
Highest Offering: Associate Degree
Accreditation: ACCSC, COARC, SURGT

01 Campus President .... Mr. Rod KIRKWOOD

Daytona College (D)

425 South Nova Road, Ormond Beach FL 32174-8449
County: Volusia FICE Identification: 039396
Unit ID: 447014
Telephone: (386) 267-0565 Carnegie Class: Spec 2-yr-Health
FAX Number: (386) 267-0567 Calendar System: Semester
URL: www.daytonacollege.edu
Established: 1996 Annual Undergrad Tuition & Fees: N/A
Enrollment: 276 Coed
Affiliation or Control: Proprietary IRS Status: Proprietary
Highest Offering: Associate Degree
Accreditation: ACCSC

01 President .... Mr. Roger BRADLEY
05 Director .... Mr. Justin BERKOWITZ

Daytona State College (E)

PO Box 2811, Daytona Beach FL 32120-2811
County: Volusia FICE Identification: 001475
Unit ID: 133386
Telephone: (386) 506-3000 Carnegie Class: Bac/Assoc-Mixed
FAX Number: (386) 506-4440 Calendar System: Semester
URL: www.DaytonaState.edu
Established: 1958 Annual Undergrad Tuition & Fees (In-District): $3,282
Enrollment: 13,248 Coed
Affiliation or Control: State/Local IRS Status: 501(c)3
Highest Offering: Baccalaureate
Accreditation: SC, ADNUR, CAHIIM, COARC, DA, DH, EMT, ENGT, MAC, NUR, OTA, PTAA, SURGT

49 AVP Arts & Science .... Dr. Alycia EHLERT
53 AVP College of Education .... Dr. Alycia EHLERT
01 President .... Dr. Thomas LOBASSO
03 Executive Vice President .... Mr. Brian T. BABB
05 Provost .... Dr. Amy LOCKLEAR
10 Chief Business Officer .... Ms. Isalene MONTGOMERY
13 VP Information Technology .... Mr. Roberto LOMBARDO
15 AVP Human Resources .... Ms. Robin BARR
84 VP Enrollment Services .... Mr. Kenneth MATTHEWS
46 AVP Institutional Effectiveness .... Dr. Nancy MORGAN
08 Head Librarian .... Ms. Mercedes CLEMENT
69 Interim AVP College of Health .... Dr. Linda MILES
106 Exec Dir Instructional Resources .... Dr. Rob SAUM
32 VP Student Development .... Mr. Keith KENNEDY
18 Exec Director Facilities Planning .... Mr. Steven ECKMAN
09 Exec Dir Inst Research .... Mr. Robert WILKINSON
37 Dean Financial Aid .... Mr. Kevin MCCRARY
88 Dean School of Health & Wellness .... Mr. Will DUNNE
19 Director Campus Safety .... Mr. Bill TILLARD
12 Dean DeLand & Deltona Campuses .... Mr. Neil CLEMONS
12 Dean New Smryna Beach Campus .... Mr. Clarence MCCLOUD
43 College Counsel .... Mr. Brian BABB
51 Director Ctr for Business/Industry .... Mr. Frank MERCER
32 Asst Dean Student Activities .... Mr. Bruce COOK
38 Director Academic Advising .... Ms. LeeAnn DAVIS
07 Director Admissions/Recruitment .... Ms. Karen SANDERS
22 Director of Equity & Inclusion .... Mr. Lonnie THOMPSON
21 AVP Accounting .... Ms. Tina MYERS
06 Director Student Accounts .... Ms. Amy IVERSON
26 Director of Marketing .... Ms. Laurie WHITE
09 Dean Institutional Effectiveness .... Dr. Karla MOORE
102 Executive Director Foundation .... Ms. Kay BURNISTON
29 Director Alumni Relations .... Ms. Suzette CAMERON
96 Director of Purchasing .... Ms. Elaine ROSENGARTEN

DeVry University - Miramar Campus (F)

2300 SW 145th Avenue, Miramar FL 33027-4150
Telephone: (954) 499-9775 Identification: 666196
Accreditation: &NH, ENGT

† Regional accreditation is carried under the parent institution in Downers Grove, IL.

DeVry University - Orlando Campus (G)

7352 Greenbriar Pkwy, Orlando FL 32819-8934
Telephone: (407) 345-2800 Identification: 666112
Accreditation: &NH, ENGT

† Regional accreditation is carried under the parent institution in Downers Grove, IL.

Digital Media Arts College (H)

5400 Broken Sound Blvd, Suite 100,
Boca Raton FL 33487
County: Palm Beach FICE Identification: 041274
Unit ID: 451060
Telephone: (561) 391-1148 Carnegie Class: Bac-Diverse
FAX Number: (561) 998-3430 Calendar System: Semester
URL: www.dmac.edu
Established: 2002 Annual Undergrad Tuition & Fees: $13,968
Enrollment: 317 Coed
Affiliation or Control: Proprietary IRS Status: Proprietary
Highest Offering: Master's
Accreditation: ACICS

01 President .... Mr. Sunny SHARMA
10 Director Accounting & Finance .... Ms. Angela NOVATON

Dragon Rises College of Oriental Medicine (I)

1000 NE 16th Ave., Building F, Gainesville FL 32601-4557
County: Alachua FICE Identification: 038883
Unit ID: 449481
Telephone: (352) 371-2833 Carnegie Class: Not Classified
FAX Number: (352) 244-0003 Calendar System: Semester
URL: www.dragonrises.edu
Established: 2001 Annual Undergrad Tuition & Fees: N/A
Enrollment: N/A Coed
Affiliation or Control: Independent Non-Profit IRS Status: 501(c)3
Highest Offering: Master's
Accreditation: ACUP

01 Director/CEO .... Dr. George VALCOURT
05 Academic Dean .... Dr. George VALCOURT
23 Clinic Director .... Ms. Laisha CANNER-WARD
32 Director of Student Services .... Ms. Ruth HAYES-MORRISON
37 Financial Aid Administrator .... Ms. Karen MARTIN-BROWN

East West College of Natural Medicine (J)

3808 N Tamiami Trail, Sarasota FL 34234-5362
County: Sarasota FICE Identification: 034297
Unit ID: 439394
Telephone: (941) 355-9080 Carnegie Class: Spec-4-yr-Other Health
FAX Number: (941) 355-3243 Calendar System: Trimester
URL: www.ewcollege.edu
Established: 1994 Annual Undergrad Tuition & Fees: N/A
Enrollment: 128 Coed
Affiliation or Control: Proprietary IRS Status: Proprietary
Highest Offering: Master's
Accreditation: ACICS, ACUP

01 President/CEO .... Mr. Russell BATTIATA
05 Academic Dean .... Mr. Kevin PIERCE
07 Director of Admissions .... Mr. Russ BATTIATA

Eastern Florida State College (K)

3865 N. Wickham Road, Melbourne FL 32935
County: Brevard FICE Identification: 001470
Unit ID: 132693
Telephone: (321) 632-1111 Carnegie Class: Bac/Assoc-Assoc Dom
FAX Number: (321) 633-4565 Calendar System: Semester
URL: www.easternflorida.edu
Established: 1960 Annual Undergrad Tuition & Fees (In-District): $2,496
Enrollment: 15,931 Coed
Affiliation or Control: Local IRS Status: 501(c)3
Highest Offering: Baccalaureate
Accreditation: SC, COARC, DA, DH, EMT, MLTAD, @PTAA, RAD, SURGT

01 President .... Dr. James H. RICHEY
10 Chief Financial Officer .... Mr. Mark CHERRY
13 VP Financial & Technology Services .... Mr. Richard LAIRD
05 VP Academic Affairs/CLO .... Dr. Linda L. MIEDEMA
04 Exec Advisor to the President .... Dr. Joe L. SMITH
20 Assoc Vice Pres Academic Programs .... Dr. Kathy COBB
41 Assoc Vice Pres of Athletics .... Mr. Jeffrey CARR
18 Assoc Vice Pres Facilities .... Dr. Richard PARADISE
15 AVP/Exec Dir Human Resources .... Ms. Darla FERGUSON
19 AVP Public Safety Inst/Security .... Mr. Jack PARKER
31 AVP Communications .... Mr. John GLISCH
12 Provost Palm Bay Campus .... Dr. Wayne STEIN
12 Provost Melbourne Campus .... Ms. Sandy HANDFIELD
12 Provost Cocoa Campus .... Dr. Ethel NEWMAN
12 Provost Titusville Campus .... Dr. Philip SIMPSON
12 Provost eBrevard .... Dr. Kathy COBB
103 Dean/Workforce Trng & Devel .... Mr. Frank MARGIOTTA
37 Director Student Financial Aid .... Ms. Eileen BRZOZOWSKI
07 Dir Collegewide Admiss/Advsmnt/Test .... Ms. Michelle LOUFEK
04 Executive Asst to the President .... Ms. Gina CLINE
06 Registrar .... Ms. Stephanie BURNETTE
09 Director of Institutional Research .... Dr. Mark QUATHAMER
108 Director Institutional Assessment .... Dr. Jayne GORHAM
22 Dir Affirmative Action/EEO .... Ms. Darla FERGUSON
29 Director Alumni & Donor Relations .... Ms. Jennie KRIETE
36 Director Student Placement .... Dr. Cathy CADY

Eckerd College (L)

4200 54th Avenue S, Saint Petersburg FL 33711-4700
County: Pinellas FICE Identification: 001487
Unit ID: 133492
Telephone: (727) 867-1166 Carnegie Class: Bac-A&S
FAX Number: (727) 864-1877 Calendar System: 4/1/4
URL: www.eckerd.edu
Established: 1958 Annual Undergrad Tuition & Fees: $40,020
Enrollment: 2,083 Coed
Affiliation or Control: Presbyterian Church (U.S.A.) IRS Status: 501(c)3
Highest Offering: Baccalaureate
Accreditation: SC

01 President .... Dr. Donald R. EASTMAN, III
05 Exec Vice Pres/Provost/Dean Faculty .... Dr. Suzan HARRISON
10 VP Business and Finance .... Mr. Christopher P. BRENNAN
03 VP and Secretary of the College .... Dr. Lisa A. METS
30 Vice President Advancement .... Mr. Matthew S. BISSET
51 Vice Pres/Dean Executive Education .... Mr. Kelly KIRSCHNER
32 Vice Pres/Dean for Student Life .... Dr. James J. ANNARELLI
84 VP Enrollment Management .... Mr. John SULLIVAN
20 Assoc Dean Faculty Development .... Dr. Kathryn J. WATSON
26 VP Marketing and Communications .... Ms. Valerie GLIEM
21 Associate VP Business and Finance .... Ms. Luz ARCILA
30 Assoc VP Advancement .... Mr. Tom SCHNEIDER
88 Academic Director of PEL .... Dr. Margret SKAFTADOTTIR
105 Dir Web/Marketing/Communication .... Mr. Michel FOUGERES
88 Director of ASPEC .... Mr. Ken WOLFE
88 Director of CALA .... Dr. Norman SMITH
104 Director of International Education .... Ms. Diane L. FERRIS
85 Dir International Student Programs .... Mr. Olivier DEBURE
13 Director of Information Technology .... Dr. John A. DUFF
09 Exec Director Instl Effectiveness .... Ms. Jacqueline MACNEIL
06 Acting Registrar .... Ms. Amy APICERNO
08 Director of Library .... Ms. Lisa JOHNSTON
38 Director Counseling Services .... Dr. Scott C. STRADER
29 Director Alumni Relations .... Ms. Jessica FUGATE
19 Director Campus Safety .... Mr. Adam COLBY
36 Assoc Dean Career Planning .... Mr. Andrew BLACK
37 Director Financial Aid .... Dr. Pat E. WATKINS
41 Athletic Director .... Dr. Robert FORTOSIS
07 Director of Admission .... Mr. Jacob BROWNE
42 Chaplain .... Rev. Doug MCMAHON
46 Director of Sponsored Research .... Vacant
21 Controller .... Ms. Robin SMALLEY
88 Asst Dean Students for Campus Act .... Mr. Fred SABOTA
88 Assoc Dean Students Cmty Initiative .... Ms. Martie NEWBOLD
87 Dir Conferences and Summer School .... Ms. Cheryl GOLD
04 Administrative Asst to President .... Ms. JoAnn TOWNSEND

ECPI University College of Nursing (M)

660 Century Point, Lake Mary FL 32746
Telephone: (407) 562-9100 Identification: 770566
Accreditation: &SC, NURSE

† Regional accreditation is carried under the parent institution in Virginia Beach, VA

Edward Waters College (N)

1658 Kings Road, Jacksonville FL 32209-6199
County: Duval FICE Identification: 001478
Unit ID: 133526
Telephone: (904) 470-8000 Carnegie Class: Bac-Diverse
FAX Number: (904) 470-8039 Calendar System: Semester
URL: www.ewc.edu
Established: 1866 Annual Undergrad Tuition & Fees: $12,525
Enrollment: 929 Coed
Affiliation or Control: African Methodist Episcopal IRS Status: 501(c)3
Highest Offering: Baccalaureate
Accreditation: SC, IACBE

01 President .... Dr. Nathaniel GLOVER
03 Executive Vice President/COO .... Dr. Anna HAMMOND
88 Special Asistant to the President .... Mr. George DANDELAKE
05 VP Academic Affairs .... Dr. Marvin GRANT

10 VP Business & Finance .... Mr. Randolph MITCHELL
32 Int VP Student Affs/Enrollment Mgmt .... Dr. Eric JACKSON
30 VP Institutional Advancement .... Ms. Wanda WILLIS
21 Assoc VP/Business and Finance .... Ms. Jacqueline DOWDY
15 Director Human Resources .... Ms. Ernestine ROBINSON
88 Accreditation Coordinator .... Dr. Phyllis WALKER
25 Dir Title III & Sponsored Pgms .... Mrs. Lisa WILLIAMS
06 Registrar .... Ms. Maretta LATIMER
20 Asst VP Academic Affairs .... Dr. Stephanie CAMPBELL
37 Dir Financial Aid .... Ms. Janice NOWAK
09 Dir Inst Research & Assessment .... Ms. Bernice PARKER-BELL
88 Dir Upward Bound .... Dr. Delacy SANFORD
36 Career Services Director .... Mr. Antonio STARKE
44 Director of Development .... Ms. Anita WALTON
36 Dir Counseling Center .... Ms. Ragan SUMMERS
07 Dir of Admissions .... Mr. Joel WALKER
88 Dir of TRIO .... Mr. Selah BISHOP
31 Dir Community Resource Center .... Mrs. Marie HEATH
88 Dir of CTL .... Dr. Kenesha BRACELY
88 Dir of FAME .... Mrs. Gladys CLAY
41 Dir of Athletics .... Mr. Johnny REMBERT
13 Dir IT .... Mr. David SIMFUKWE
08 Library Director .... Ms. Carmella MARTIN
101 Secy of the College/Clerk of Board .... Mrs. Linda FOSTER
26 Coordinator of Public Relations .... Ms. Dee REGISTRE
29 Director of Alumni Affairs .... Ms. Anita WALTON
38 Director Counseling Cener .... Ms. Ragan SUMMERS
39 Dean of Students/Residence Life .... Dr. Karen BUCKMAN
96 Purchasing Clerk .... Ms. Susie MATTISON

Embry-Riddle Aeronautical University (A)

600 S Clyde Morris Boulevard,
Daytona Beach FL 32114-3900

County: Volusia FICE Identification: 001479
Unit ID: 133553
Telephone: (386) 226-6000 Carnegie Class: Masters/L
FAX Number: (386) 226-6459 Calendar System: Semester
URL: www.erau.edu
Established: 1926 Annual Undergrad Tuition & Fees: $33,218
Enrollment: 5,538 Coed
Affiliation or Control: Independent Non-Profit IRS Status: 501(c)3
Highest Offering: Doctorate
Accreditation: SC, AAB, ACBSP, CEA, CS, ENG, IFSAC

01 Interim President .... Dr. Karen A. HOLBROOK
05 SVP Academic Affairs & Research .... Dr. Richard HEIST
10 SVP for Finance and CFO .... Dr. Randy B. HOWARD
15 VP/Chief Human Resources Officer .... Brandon L. YOUNG
26 SVP External Relations .... William HAMPTON
13 Chief Information Officer .... Becky L. VASQUEZ
09 Director of Institutional Research .... Maria FRANCO
29 Exec Director of Alumni Relations .... William G. THOMPSON
39 Director of Housing .... Steven LOGAN
41 Director of Athletics .... John PHILLIPS
43 General Counsel .... Charlie W. SEVASTOS
84 Dean of Enrollment Management .... Robert J. ADAMS

Embry-Riddle Aeronautical University-Worldwide (B)

600 S Clyde Morris Boulevard,
Daytona Beach FL 32114-3900

Telephone: (800) 522-6787 Identification: 666089
Accreditation: &SC, AAB, ACBSP

† Regional accreditation is carried under the parent institution in Daytona Beach, FL.

Everest University-Brandon Campus (C)

3924 Coconut Palm Drive, Tampa FL 33619-1354

Telephone: (813) 621-0041 Identification: 666416
Accreditation: ACICS, ADNUR, SURTEC

† In teach-out mode; Branch campus of Everest University, Tampa, FL.

Everest University-Largo (D)

1199 East Bay Drive, Largo FL 33770-2556

Telephone: (727) 725-2688 FICE Identification: 025998
Accreditation: ACICS

† In teach-out mode. Branch campus of Everest University, Tampa, FL.

Everest University-Melbourne Campus (E)

2190 Sarno Road, Melbourne FL 32935

Telephone: (321) 253-2929 Identification: 666417
Accreditation: ACICS

† In teach-out mode. Branch campus of Everest University, Tampa, FL.

Everest University-Orange Park (F)

805 Wells Road, Orange Park FL 32073-2301

Telephone: (904) 264-9122 Identification: 666590
Accreditation: ACICS, MAAB

† Branch campus of Everest University, Tampa, FL.

Everest University-Pompano Beach Campus (G)

225 N Federal Highway, Pompano Beach FL 33062

Telephone: (954) 783-7339 FICE Identification: 008146
Accreditation: ACICS, MAAB

† In teach out mode. Branch campus of Everest University, Tampa, FL.

Everest University-South Orlando Campus (H)

9200 Southpark Center Loop, Orlando FL 32819-8606

Telephone: (407) 851-2525 Identification: 666418
Accreditation: ACICS

† In teach-out mode. Branch campus of Everest University, Tampa, FL.

Everest University-Tampa Campus (I)

3319 W Hillsborough Avenue, Tampa FL 33614-5801

Telephone: (813) 879-6000 FICE Identification: 007735
Accreditation: ACICS, MAC

† Branch campus of Everest University-North Orlando Campus, Orlando, FL.

Everglades University (J)

5002 T-Rex Avenue, Suite 100,
Boca Raton FL 33431-4493

County: Palm Beach FICE Identification: 031085
Unit ID: 385619
Telephone: (888) 772-6077 Carnegie Class: Bac-Diverse
FAX Number: (561) 912-1191 Calendar System: Semester
URL: www.evergladesuniversity.edu
Established: 1990 Annual Undergrad Tuition & Fees: $16,648
Enrollment: 1,451 Coed
Affiliation or Control: Independent Non-Profit IRS Status: 501(c)3
Highest Offering: Master's
Accreditation: SC

01 President/CEO .... Ms. Kristi L. MOLLIS
05 Vice President of Academic Affairs .... Dr. Jayne MOSCHELLA
37 Regional Director of Financial Aid .... Mrs. Seeta SINGH MOONILALL
26 Director of Marketing .... Mrs. Shay LAWRENCE
09 Director Inst Effectiveness .... Dr. Rachel ASKEW
08 Director of Library Services .... Ms. Anisa HITT
12 Vice President Boca Raton Campus .... Dr. Arlette PETERSSON
107 Vice President Online Division .... Mr. David SHELPMAN, JR.
12 Vice President Sarasota Campus .... Ms. Caroline KING
12 Vice President of Orlando Campus .... Mr. Paul HINKSMAN
20 Dean of Academics Online .... Dr. Maryruth HICKS
20 Dean of Academics Sarasota .... Dr. Melanie YERK
20 Dean of Academics Orlando .... Dr. Rosemarie BRANCIFORTE
20 Dean of Academics Boca Raton .... Dr. Lori KAUFMAN
07 Director of Admissions Boca .... Ms. Patricia RAMIREZ
07 Director of Admissions Online .... Mr. Scott BACKMAN
07 Director of Admissions Orlando .... Ms. Maria CONTREAS
07 Director of Admission Sarasota .... Ms. Barbara BEASLEY
04 Executive Asst to the President .... Mrs. Christina OAKLEY
37 Financial Aid Director Online .... Vacant
37 Financial Aid Director Sarasota .... Mrs. Courtney ROBERTSON
37 Financial Aid Director Orlando .... Mr. Anthony CHAMBERS
37 Asst Financial Aid Director Boca .... Ms. Anne RODNE
06 Head Registrar .... Mr. Adrian KACZOR
06 Registrar Online Division .... Ms. Dana NGUYEN
06 Registrar Boca .... Mrs. Pamela QUINTANA
06 Registrar Orlando .... Mrs. Jane STINIS
06 Registrar Sarasota .... Ms. Donna BARANOWSKI
20 Program Dir of Business .... Dr. Gerard JOHN WILLIAMS
88 Program Dir of Aviation .... Mr. Michael VAN DUSEN
76 Program Dir of Allied Health .... Dr. Christopher MENDEZ
76 Program Dir of Allied Health Online .... Dr. Michele VERMIGLIO
88 Librarian Boca Raton .... Ms. Victoria NIKOLOV
88 Librarian Sarasota .... Ms. Anisa HITT
88 Librarian Orlando .... Mr. Adam BRODY
32 Dir of Student Services Online .... Vacant
32 Dir of Student Services Boca Raton .. Ms. Jacqueline STODDART
32 Dir of Student Services Sarasota .... Ms. Melinda WALLER
32 Dir of Student Services Orlando .... Ms. Janie DICKEY
88 Bursar Online Division .... Ms. Latoya MYERS
88 Bursar Online Division .... Ms. Tangela ANDREWS
40 Bursar/Bookstore Manager Boca .... Ms. Kesha PAUL
40 Bookstore Manager Online Division .... Ms. Pamela PETERSON
40 Bursar/Bookstore Manager Sarasota .... Ms. Anita WENDZEL
40 Bursar/Bookstore Manager Orlando .... Ms. Camille BALABUER
88 Online Trainer .... Mr. Ronnie ABUKHALAF
88 Dir of Teaching & Learning .... Mr. Jared BEZET

Express Training Services (K)

3911 Newberry Rd Ste B, Gainesville FL 32607

County: Alachua Identification: 667276
Telephone: (352) 338-1193 Carnegie Class: Not Classified
FAX Number: (352) 240-1530 Calendar System: Other
URL: www.expresstrainingservices.com
Established: 2004 Annual Undergrad Tuition & Fees: N/A
Enrollment: N/A Coed
Affiliation or Control: Proprietary IRS Status: Proprietary
Highest Offering: Associate Degree
Accreditation: ACICS

07 Director of Admissions .... Tony KALISHMAN

FCC-Anthem College (L)

989 N Semoran Boulevard, Orlando FL 32807

Telephone (888) 852-7272 Identification: 770613
Accreditation: ACICS

Flagler College (M)

74 King Street, Saint Augustine FL 32084-4342

County: Saint Johns FICE Identification: 007893
Unit ID: 133711
Telephone (904) 829-6481 Carnegie Class: Bac-Diverse
FAX Number: (904) 824-6017 Calendar System: Semester
URL: www.flagler.edu
Established: 1968 Annual Undergrad Tuition & Fees: $16,830
Enrollment: 2,782 Coed
Affiliation or Control: Independent Non-Profit IRS Status: 501(c)3
Highest Offering: Master's
Accreditation: SC

01 President .... Dr. William T. ABARE, JR.
00 Chancellor .... Dr. William L. PROCTOR
10 Vice President Business Services .... Mr. David L. CARSON
30 Vice President Inst Advancement ..... Dr. Beverly C. CARMICHAEL
05 Vice President Academic Affairs .... Dr. Alan WOOLFOLK
26 Exec Director College Relations .... Ms. Donna DELORENZO
21 Executive Director of Finance .... Mr. Jeff KNIGHT
09 Director Analytics/Planning/Rsrch .... Dr. Will MILLER
27 Director of News and Information .... Mr. Brian L. THOMPSON
84 Vice Pres for Enrollment Mgmt .... Ms. Deborah L. THOMPSON
32 Vice President of Student Services .... Mr. Daniel P. STEWART
20 Assoc VP of Academic Affairs .... Mr. Yvan J. KELLY
35 Dean of Student Services .... Dr. Dirk HIBLER
38 Director of Counseling .... Dr. Amy FALVO
06 Registrar .... Mrs. Miriam C. ROBERSON
37 Director of Financial Aid .... Ms. Sheia I. PLEASANT-DOINE
36 Director of Career Services .... Ms. Tara STEVENSON
08 Director of Library Services .... Mr. Brian NESSELRODE
41 Director Intercollegiate Athletics .... Mr. Jud DAMON
19 Director of Safety & Security .... Mr. Kerry DAVIS
40 Bookstore Manager .... Mr. Bob SMITH
24 Director Educational Media Services .... Mr. Steven I. SKIPP
13 Director Technology Services .... Mr. Joseph S. PROVENZA
39 Director of Residence Life .... Ms. Michelle HOLLAND
35 Director of Student Activities .... Mr. Timothy MELLON
12 Dean Flagler College - Tallahassee .... Dr. Donald K. PARKS
22 Dir of Disability Services .... Ms. Eva Lynn FRANCISCO
18 Superintendent of Plant & Grounds .... Mr. Victor CHENEY
04 Exec Assistant to the President .... Ms. Mary Jane DILLON
21 Director of Business Services .... Mr. Larry D. WEEKS
29 Director Alumni Relations .... Ms. Margo BROWN
44 Director Annual Fund .... Mr. Jeffrey DAVITT
15 Director Human Resources .... Ms. Tricia KRISTOFF-RAMPATA
31 Director of College Relations ..... Ms. Laura STEVENSON-DUMAS
88 Senior Woman Admin Athletic Dept .... Ms. Karen HUDGINS
07 Director of Admissions .... Ms. Rachel U. BRANCH
101 Secretary of the Institution/Board .... Ms. Mary Jane DILLON
104 Director Study Abroad .... Ms. Barbara OTTAVIANI-JONES
105 Director Web Services .... Ms. Holly L. HILL

Florida Career College (N)

1743 N Congress Avenue, Boynton Beach FL 33426

Telephone: (561) 634-7400 Identification: 770678
Accreditation: ACICS

Florida Career College (O)

3750 West 18th Avenue, Hialeah FL 33012-7028

Telephone: (786) 534-0940 Identification: 666624
Accreditation: ACICS

Florida Career College (P)

6600 Youngerman Circle, Jacksonville FL 32244

Telephone: (904) 573-1900 Identification: 770679
Accreditation: ACICS

Florida Career College (Q)

3383 North State Road 7,
Lauderdale Lakes FL 33319-5617

Telephone: (954) 908-4700 Identification: 666622
Accreditation: ACICS

Florida Career College - Margate Campus (R)

3271 North State Road 7, Margate FL 33063

Telephone: (954) 935-7921 Identification: 770681
Accreditation: ACICS

Florida Career College (S)

1321 SW 107th Avenue, Suite 201B,
Miami FL 33174-2521

County: Miami-Dade FICE Identification: 023058
Unit ID: 133997
Telephone: (786) 534-0500 Carnegie Class: Bac/Assoc-Assoc Dom
FAX Number: N/A Calendar System: Quarter
URL: www.careercollege.edu
Established: 1982 Annual Undergrad Tuition & Fees: N/A
Enrollment: 6,227 Coed

Affiliation or Control: Proprietary IRS Status: Proprietary
Highest Offering: Associate Degree
Accreditation: ACICS

01 President/CEO .... Mr. David KNOBEL
03 Executive Director .... Mr. Dwayne ORE
06 Registrar .... Ms. Cheyla DAVILA

Florida Career College (A)
11731 Mills Drive, Bldg #2, Miami FL 33183
Telephone: (305) 384-7900 Identification: 770680
Accreditation: ACICS

Florida Career College (B)
7891 Pines Boulevard, Pembroke Pines FL 33024-6916
Telephone: (954) 399-4800 Identification: 666025
Accreditation: ACICS

Florida Career College (C)
9950 Princess Palm Ave, Suite 100, Tampa FL 33619
Telephone: (813) 621-5775 Identification: 770682
Accreditation: ACICS

Florida Career College (D)
6058 Okeechobee Boulevard, West Palm Beach FL 33417
Telephone: (561) 689-0550 Identification: 770683
Accreditation: ACICS

Florida Coastal School of Law (E)
8787 Baypine, Jacksonville FL 32256-8528
County: Duval FICE Identification: 033743
Unit ID: 434715
Telephone: (904) 680-7700 Carnegie Class: Spec-4-yr-Law
FAX Number: (904) 680-7777 Calendar System: Semester
URL: www.fcsl.edu
Established: 1995 Annual Graduate Tuition & Fees: N/A
Enrollment: 1,115 Coed
Affiliation or Control: Proprietary IRS Status: Proprietary
Highest Offering: First Professional Degree; No Undergraduates
Accreditation: LAW

01 President .... Mr. Dennis STONE
05 Dean .... Mr. Scott DEVITO
07 Associate Dean of Admissions .... Mr. Tony CARDENAS
30 Dir of Institutional Advancement .... Vacant
32 Assistant Dean of Student Affairs .... Mr. James ARTLEY
20 Associate Dean of Academic Affairs .... Ms. Jennifer REIBER
15 Sr Director of Human Resources .... Mrs. Susie PONTIFF STRINGER
62 Assoc Dean of Library & Technology .. Ms. Korin MUNSTERMAN
106 Assoc Dean of Strategy & Innovation .... Ms. Margaret IOANNIDES
28 Dir of Diversity/Equity/Inclusion .... Ms. Tammy HODO
88 Director of Experiential Learning .... Ms. Ericka CURRAN
09 Mgr of Institutional Effectiveness .... Ms. Karen EUBANKS
37 Asst Dir of Financial Aid .... Ms. Leslie TIGNOR
18 Dir of Security & Facilities .... Mr. Bill BREEN
88 Process Partner .... Ms. Lisa VERVYNCK
04 Exec Asst to the Dean & President .... Ms. Heather NUANES

Florida College (F)
119 N Glen Arven Avenue,
Temple Terrace FL 33617-5578
County: Hillsborough FICE Identification: 001482
Unit ID: 133809
Telephone: (813) 988-5131 Carnegie Class: Bac/Assoc-Mixed
FAX Number: (813) 899-6772 Calendar System: Semester
URL: www.floridacollege.edu
Established: 1944 Annual Undergrad Tuition & Fees: $16,074
Enrollment: 555 Coed
Affiliation or Control: Independent Non-Profit IRS Status: 501(c)3
Highest Offering: Baccalaureate
Accreditation: SC, MUS

01 President .... Dr. Harry E. PAYNE, JR.
05 Vice Pres of Acad & Student Affairs .... Dr. Daniel W. PETTY
20 Dean of Academics .... Dr. Brian L. CRISPELL
32 Dean of Student Services .... Dr. Jason S. LONGSTRETH
10 Chief Business Officer .... Mr. Ronnie STACKPOLE
37 Director Student Financial Aid .... Mr. Stephen BLAYLOCK
07 Dir of Admissions & Retention Svcs .... Mr. Paul CASEBOLT
09 Director of Institutional Research .... Dr. M. Thaxter DICKEY
88 Director of Advising .... Mrs. Shannon MCKINNEY
06 Registrar .... Mrs. Beth A. GRANT
08 Director of Library .... Mrs. Wanda DICKEY
90 Director of Academic Computing .... Mr. M. Ray HINDS
91 Director of Information Technology .... Mr. Jon RAE
30 Director of Development .... Mr. David L. CURRY
29 Director of Alumni Relations .... Mr. Adam J. OLSON
26 Director of Marketing/Info Officer .... Mr. Jared M. BARR
40 Manager of Bookstore .... Mrs. Amy CASEBOLT
88 Events Coordinator .... Mrs. Sharon L. CLARK

Florida College of Health Science (G)
6000 South Rio Grande Ave, Orlando FL 32809
County: Orange Identification: 667265
Telephone: (407) 601-0411 Carnegie Class: Not Classified
FAX Number: (407) 601-6983 Calendar System: Quarter
URL: www.floridacollegeofhealth.com
Established: Annual Undergrad Tuition & Fees: N/A
Enrollment: N/A Coed
Affiliation or Control: Proprietary IRS Status: Proprietary
Highest Offering: Associate Degree
Accreditation: ABHES

01 President .... Ms. Carole VALENTINE

Florida College of Integrative Medicine (H)
7100 Lake Ellenor Drive, Orlando FL 32809-5721
County: Orange FICE Identification: 032383
Unit ID: 434441
Telephone: (407) 888-8689 Carnegie Class: Spec-4-yr-Other Health
FAX Number: (407) 888-8211 Calendar System: Semester
URL: www.fcim.edu
Established: 1990 Annual Undergrad Tuition & Fees: N/A
Enrollment: 116 Coed
Affiliation or Control: Proprietary IRS Status: Proprietary
Highest Offering: Master's; No Lower Division
Accreditation: ACUP

01 President .... Mr. Larry L. HAN
03 Vice President .... Ms. Jenjen HAN
108 Chief Quality Officer .... Ms. Yuan-Yuan HAN
05 Dean of Academic Affairs .... Ms. Tara REED
11 Chief Administrative Officer .... Mr. Robert P. LYNCH
10 Director of Finance .... Ms. Susan HOEH
07 Admissions Advisor .... Ms. Michelle COLON
37 Director of Financial Aid .... Ms. Mary SIMMONS

Florida College of Natural Health (I)
2600 Lake Lucien Drive, Suite 140,
Maitland FL 32751-7253
Telephone: (407) 261-0319 Identification: 666513
Accreditation: ACCSC

† Branch campus of Florida College of Natural Health, Pompano Beach, FL.

Florida College of Natural Health (J)
7925 NW 12th Street, Suite 201, Miami FL 33126-1821
Telephone: (305) 597-9599 Identification: 666514
Accreditation: ACCSC

† Branch campus of Florida College of Natural Health, Pompano Beach, FL.

Florida College of Natural Health (K)
2001 W Sample Road, Suite 100,
Pompano Beach FL 33064-1342
County: Broward FICE Identification: 030086
Unit ID: 387925
Telephone: (954) 975-6400 Carnegie Class: Assoc/HVT-High Non
FAX Number: (954) 975-9633 Calendar System: Other
URL: www.fcnh.com
Established: 1986 Annual Undergrad Tuition & Fees: N/A
Enrollment: 203 Coed
Affiliation or Control: Proprietary IRS Status: Proprietary
Highest Offering: Associate Degree
Accreditation: ACCSC

01 President .... Mr. Stephen LAZARUS
05 Vice President of Education .... Ms. Dawnette CABALUNA
10 Controller .... Mr. Jeff ROSEN
22 Vice President of Compliance .... Ms. Melissa WADE

Florida Gateway College (L)
149 SE College Place, Lake City FL 32025-2007
County: Columbia FICE Identification: 001501
Unit ID: 135160
Telephone: (386) 752-1822 Carnegie Class: Bac/Assoc-Assoc Dom
FAX Number: (386) 755-1521 Calendar System: Semester
URL: www.fgc.edu
Established: 1947 Annual Undergrad Tuition & Fees (In-State): $3,100
Enrollment: 2,912 Coed
Affiliation or Control: State IRS Status: 501(c)3
Highest Offering: Baccalaureate
Accreditation: SC, ADNUR, EMT, NURSE, PTAA

01 President .... Dr. Lawrence BARRETT
10 Vice President Business Services .... Mr. Stephen BENSON
04 Assistant to the President .... Ms. Karyn CONGRESSI
05 Vice President for Academic Pgms .... Dr. Brian DOPSON
84 Vice President Enrollment Mgmt .... Ms. Jennifer PRICE
32 Vice President for Student Services .... Dr. Linda CROLEY
20 Dean of Academic Pgm & Bacc Liason .... Dr. Paula GAVIN
13 Exec Dir Info Technology/CIO .... Mr. Mike DAVIS
47 Exec Dir of Industrial & Agricult .... Mr. John PIERSOL
15 Executive Director Human Resources .... Ms. Sharon BEST
53 Exec Dir Ctr for Excell in Teaching .... Ms. Pamela CARSWELL
102 Executive Director Foundation .... Mr. Mike LEE
26 Exec Dir Media & Community Info .... Mr. Mike MCKEE
37 Director Financial Aid .... Mrs. Becky WESTBERRY
84 Director Enrollment Management .... Ms. Sandra JOHNSTON
06 Registrar .... Ms. Gayle HUNTER
21 Director Business Services .... Ms. Michelle HOLLOWAY
25 Director of Grants .... Mr. Daniel CRONRATH
09 Director of Research/Institutional .... Ms. Patty ANDERSON
66 Exec Director Nursing .... Ms. Melody CORSO
18 Director Facilities .... Mr. Ed D'AVI
96 Director of Purchasing .... Ms. Misty TAYLOR
36 Director Advising/Student Dev .... Dr. Margaret MCLAUGHLIN
88 Director for Water Resources .... Ms. Pam MURAWSKI
88 Director for Criminal Justice .... Mr. John JEWETT
62 Director Library Services .... Ms. Christine BOATRIGHT

Florida Institute of Technology (M)
150 W University Boulevard, Melbourne FL 32901-6975
County: Brevard FICE Identification: 001469
Unit ID: 133881
Telephone: (321) 674-8000 Carnegie Class: DU-Higher
FAX Number: (321) 984-8461 Calendar System: Semester
URL: www.fit.edu
Established: 1958 Annual Undergrad Tuition & Fees: $39,290
Enrollment: 6,393 Coed
Affiliation or Control: Independent Non-Profit IRS Status: 501(c)3
Highest Offering: Doctorate
Accreditation: SC, AAB, CLPSY, CS, ENG, IACBE

01 President .... Dr. T. Dwayne MCCAY
04 Exec Asst to Pres .... Ms. Rebecca CROOK
05 Sr VP Accred/Acad/Student Affs/CAO .... Dr. Monica BALOGA
11 Sr VP Operations/Global Initiatives .... Dr. Gaby HAWAT
10 Sr Vice Pres Financial Affairs/CFO .... Ms. Cathy WOOD
30 Sr Vice Pres/Chief Development Ofcr .... Dr. Susan ST. ONGE
86 Sr VP Ext Relations/Economic Dev .... Capt. Winston SCOTT
100 Chief of Staff/Govt Relations .... Mr. Frank KINNEY
88 Dean College of Aeronautics .... Dr. Korhan OYMAN
50 Dean College of Business .... Dr. Theodore RICHARDSON
54 Dean College of Engineering .... Dr. Martin GLICKSMAN
83 Dean Col of Psychology/Liberal Arts .... Dr. Mary Beth KENKEL
81 Dean College of Science .... Dr. Hamid RASSOUL
08 Dean of Libraries .... Dr. Sohair WASTAWY
29 VP Alum Rel/Exec Dir Alum Assn .... Mr. Albino P. CAMPANINI
30 Vice President Development .... Mr. Michael SEELEY
84 Vice Pres Enrollment Mgmt .... Mr. Gary HAMME
18 Vice Pres Facilities .... Vacant
13 Vice Pres IT/CIO .... Mr. Eric KLEDZIK
26 Vice Pres Marketing & Communication .. Mr. Wesley D. SUMNER
106 Vice Pres Online Learning .... Mr. Brian EHRLICH
88 Vice President Orlando Center .... Ms. Leslie HIELEMA
46 Vice President Research .... Dr. S. Ann BECKER
32 Vice President Student Affairs .... Dr. Randall L. ALFORD
102 Assoc VP Corp Sponsored Programs ... Ms. Gretchen SAUERMAN
21 Assoc Vice Pres Financial Services .... Ms. Brenda BROWN
35 Assoc VP Student Affs/Dean of Stdnt .... Mr. Rodney BOWERS
109 Asst VP Business & Ret Operation .... Mr. Greg GRAHAM
28 Chief Diversity Officer/Title IX .... Dr. Joni OGLESBY
06 Registrar .... Mr. David MICUS
88 Director Academic Support Services .... Mr. Rodd NEWCOMBE
41 Director Athletics .... Mr. William K. JURGENS
19 Director Campus Security .... Mr. Kevin GRAHAM
36 Director Career Services .... Ms. Dona E. GAYNOR
38 Dir Counseling/Psychological Svcs .... Dr. Robyn TAPLEY
88 Director Creative Services .... Ms. Judith E. TINTERA
88 Dir Environ & Regulatory Compliance .... Mr. Henry PEEBLES
18 Director Facilities Operations .... Mr. John M. MILBOURNE
37 Director Financial Aid .... Mr. Jay LALLY
07 Director Graduate Admissions .... Ms. Cheryl-Ann BROWN
07 Director Grad Adm Online/Off-Campus .. Ms. Carolyn P. FARRIOR
58 Director Graduate Programs .... Dr. Rosemary LAYNE
15 Director Human Resources .... Ms. Karen GATHERCOLE
09 Director Institutional Research .... Ms. Leslie L. SAVOIE
85 Director Intl Students/Scholar Svcs .... Ms. Judith BROOKE
104 Director Study Abroad .... Ms. Heather EMMERT
07 Director Undergraduate Admission .... Mr. Michael PERRY
88 Director University Museums .... Ms. Carla FUNK
90 Executive Director Ellucian .... Ms. Rebecca ARCHER

Florida Keys Community College (N)
5901 College Road, Key West FL 33040-4397
County: Monroe FICE Identification: 001485
Unit ID: 133960
Telephone: (305) 296-9081 Carnegie Class: Assoc/MT-VT-Mix Trad/Non
FAX Number: (305) 292-5155 Calendar System: Trimester
URL: www.fkcc.edu
Established: 1963 Annual Undergrad Tuition & Fees (In-District): $3,276
Enrollment: 1,033 Coed
Affiliation or Control: State/Local IRS Status: 501(c)3
Highest Offering: Associate Degree
Accreditation: SC

01 President .... Dr. Jonathan GUEUERRA
05 Vice President Academic Affairs .... Mrs. Brittany SYNDER
10 Vice Pres Business & Admin Svcs .... Ms. Jean MAUK
30 Vice President Advancement .... Dr. Frank WOOD
35 Dean Student Affairs .... Vacant
32 Manager Enrollment Management .... Mrs. Michelle CHERRY
51 Dir Cont Ed/Workforce/Testing .... Mrs. Cathy TORRES
04 Director President's Office .... Mrs. Debbie LEONARD
26 Dir College and Public Relations .. Mrs. Amber ERNST-LEONARD
06 Registrar .... Vacant
08 Director Learning Resources .... Ms. Lori KELLY
37 Director Financial Aid .... Ms. Beryl MORGAN

18 Dir Purchasing & Plant Operations ... Mr. Douglas PRYOR
13 Director of IT ... Mrs. Michelle ADAM
15 Director Human Resources ... Ms. Kathleen DANIEL
25 Director Sponsored Research ... Mr. Samuel PETERSON
21 Interim Controller ... Ms. Heather GARCIA
09 Director Institutional Research ... Ms. Linda MACMINN
30 Director Development/Alumni Rels ... Vacant
76 Dean of Science & Nursing ... Mr. Mark ROEY
103 Dean Business and Marine Tech ... Mr. Jack SUEBERT
49 Dean Arts & Sciences ... Mr. Michael MCPHERSON
39 Director of Campus Life ... Mr. Christopher DELISLE

Florida Memorial University (A)

15800 NW 42nd Avenue, Miami Gardens FL 33054-6199

County: Miami-Dade FICE Identification: 001486
Unit ID: 133979
Telephone: (305) 626-3600 Carnegie Class: Bac-Diverse
FAX Number: (305) 626-3769 Calendar System: Semester
URL: www.fmuniv.edu
Established: 1879 Annual Undergrad Tuition & Fees: $15,280
Enrollment: 1,528 Coed
Affiliation or Control: Independent Non-Profit IRS Status: 501(c)3
Highest Offering: Master's
Accreditation: SC, AAB, ACBSP, CS, MUS, SW

01 President ... Dr. Roslyn CLARK ARTIS
05 Executive VP and Provost ... Dr. Michelle HOWARD-VITAL
20 Associate Provost ... Dr. Denise CALLWOOD-BRATHWAITE
04 Assistant to President ... Ms. Rachel TURNER
49 Dean of Arts and Sciences ... Dr. Keshia N. ABRAHAM
10 Exec VP Finance/Administration ... Ms. Cynthia CURRY
84 Asst VP of Enrollment Mgmt ... Mr. Reynolda BROWN
30 Vice Pres University Advancement ... Mr. Marcus BURGESS
45 Assc VP Institutional Effectiveness ... Dr. William E. HOPPER
88 Chair Aviation and Safety ... Dr. Arnold J. TOLBERT
50 Dean School of Business ... Dr. Abbass ENTESSARI
53 Dean School of Education ... Dr. Idriss ABDOULAYE
81 Chair Health and Natural Sciences ... Dr. Rose Mary STIFFIN
83 Interim Chair Social Sciences ... Dr. Tameka HOBBS
64 Interim Chair Visual/Perf Arts ... Mr. Melvin WHITE
77 Chair Comp Science/Math & Tech ... Dr. Ben WONGSAROJ
79 Chair Humanities ... Dr. Keshia N. ABRAHAM
88 Dir Ctrs Acad Support & Reten ... Mr. Jae JACKSON
08 Director of Library Services ... Mr. Otis ALEXANDER
37 Acting Director Financial Aid ... Ms. Faye RODNEW
06 Registrar ... Mrs. Lelia EFFORD
09 Director of Institutional Research ... Dr. Carlos CANAS
15 Director Human Resources Management ... Ms. JaRenae WHITEHEAD
41 Director Intercollegiate Athletics ... Mr. Robert SMITH
36 Director Career Development ... Ms. Athena JACKSON
39 Director Residential Life ... Vacant
19 Chief of Campus Safety ... Chief Latrice ANDERSON
18 Dir Facility Mgmt/Plant Operations ... Mr. David JACCARINO
42 Dean of Campus Ministry ... Dr. Jeffrey D. SWAIN
29 Director Alumni Affairs ... Mrs. Sheila POWELL-COHEN
35 Director Student Activities ... Mr. C. Vernon MARTIN, JR.
85 International Student Advisor ... Mr. Trevor LEWIS
13 CIO ... Mr. Christopher BROMFIELD
32 Dean of Students ... Mrs. Valerie HALL
108 Director Institutional Assessment ... Dr. Richard YAKLICH

Florida National University Hialeah Campus (B)

4425 W. Jose Regueiro (20th) Ave,
Hialeah FL 33012-4108

County: Dade FICE Identification: 025476
Unit ID: 408844
Telephone: (305) 821-3333 Carnegie Class: Bac/Assoc-Mixed
FAX Number: (305) 362-0595 Calendar System: Semester
URL: www.fnu.edu
Established: 1982 Annual Undergrad Tuition & Fees: $13,250
Enrollment: 2,401 Coed
Affiliation or Control: Proprietary IRS Status: Proprietary
Highest Offering: Master's
Accreditation: SC, #COARC, NURSE, PTAA

01 President/CEO ... Dr. Maria C. REGUEIRO
09 VP of Assessment & Research/FA Dir ... Mr. Omar SANCHEZ
11 Vice President of Operations ... Mr. Frank ANDREU
05 Vice President of Academic Affairs ... Dr. Caridad HERNANDEZ
10 Controller ... Dr. Lourdes NIEVES
88 Accreditation Liaison ... Dr. Barbara J. RODRIGUEZ
07 Director of Admissions ... Mr. Robert LOPEZ
06 University Registrar ... Mr. Jose L. VALDES
32 Director of Student Services ... Mrs. Maria HOFFMAN
106 Director of Distance Learning ... Mrs. Sandra LOMENA
12 Campus Dean ... Dr. Jorge ALFONSO
50 Business & Economics Division Head ... Dr. James BULLEN
76 Allied Health Division Head ... Dr. Loreto ALMONTE
66 RN Program Nursing Division Dir ... Mrs. Maida BURGOS
79 Humanities and Fine Arts Division ... Dr. Barbara RODRIGUEZ
88 ESL Division Head ... Mr. Oscar PEREZ
66 MSN/BSN Program Director ... Mr. Ruben COLL
15 Human Resources Director ... Mr. Edward ZALDIVAR
41 Athletic Director ... Mr. Avery SWARN
88 Assistant Campus Dean ... Mrs. Olga RODRIGUEZ
88 Assistant Campus Dean ... Mrs. Yedi CEPERO
07 Admissions Supervisor Distance ... Mrs. Yolanda NAVARRO
07 Admissions Supervisor ... Mrs. Virginia RABELO

88 Academic Advisor ... Mrs. Carol ROMERO
88 Academic Advisor ... Mrs. Hazel RIVERA
31 Director Community Relations ... Mrs. Rachel TOURGEMAN
36 Job Placement Officer ... Mrs. Vanessa PEREZ
26 Social Media/Marketing Rep ... Mrs. Levanis DIAZ

Florida National University South Campus (C)

11865 SW 26th Street Unit H-3, Miami FL 33175

Telephone: (305) 226-9999 Identification: 666691
Accreditation: &SC

† Regional accreditation is carried under the parent institution Florida National College, Hialeah, FL.

Florida National University Training Center (D)

4206 West 12th Avenue, Hialeah FL 33012

Telephone: (305) 231-3326 Identification: 666690
Accreditation: &SC

† Regional accreditation is carried under the parent institution Florida National College, Hialeah, FL.

Florida Southern College (E)

111 Lake Hollingsworth Drive, Lakeland FL 33801-5698

County: Polk FICE Identification: 001488
Unit ID: 134079
Telephone: (863) 680-4111 Carnegie Class: Masters/S
FAX Number: (863) 680-4112 Calendar System: Semester
URL: www.flsouthern.edu
Established: 1883 Annual Undergrad Tuition & Fees: $31,460
Enrollment: 2,670 Coed
Affiliation or Control: United Methodist IRS Status: 501(c)3
Highest Offering: Doctorate
Accreditation: SC, EUS, #CAATE, MUS, NURSE

01 President ... Dr. Anne B. KERR
05 Provost ... Dr. Kyle FEDLER
07 Director of Admissions ... Ms. Arden MITCHELL
55 Director of Adult & Graduate Educ ... Ms. Kristen PLACEK
36 Director of Career Development ... Ms. Cara CIMA
39 Director of Community Living ... Mr. Marc A. TUSCHEN
23 Director of Health Services ... Ms. Jessica J. HODGSON
92 Director of Honors Program ... Dr. Gabriel J. LANGFORD
15 Director of Human Resources ... Ms. Katherine PAWLAK
09 Dir Inst Research/Effectiveness ... Dr. Kenneth M. REAVES
08 Director of the Library ... Mr. Randall M. MACDONALD
28 Director Life and Cultural Center ... Ms. Brenda LEWIS
26 Director of Marketing and Comm ... Ms. Katherine WHITAKER
18 Director of Operations ... Mr. Jon P. CAMP
06 Registrar ... Ms. Sally L. THISSEN
19 Director of Security/Safety ... Mr. William CAREW
38 Director of Student Counseling ... Dr. Carol BALLARD
37 Director of Student Financial Aid ... Mr. William L. HEALY
105 Director of Web Services ... Mr. James JARRETT
10 Vice President Finance & Admin ... Mr. Terry DENNIS
84 VP Enrollment Management ... Mr. John GRUNDIG
30 Vice President Advancement ... Dr. Robert H. TATE
41 Athletic Director ... Mr. Peter E. MEYER
42 Chaplain Director Campus Ministry ... Rev. Timothy S. WRIGHT
13 Chief Information Officer ... Mr. John L. THOMAS
104 Coordinator Student Travel ... Ms. Bridgette MCARTHUR
29 Coordinator of Alumni Services ... Vacant
20 Assoc Provost Experiential Educ ... Dr. Mary L. CROWE
44 Asst VP for Annual Giving ... Ms. Kathy ELLIS
102 Asst VP Advancement ... Ms. Heather PHARRIS
21 Controller ... Ms. Judy ROBINSON
49 Dean Art and Sciences ... Dr. Brad E. HOLLINGSHEAD
50 Dean Business and Free Enterprise ... Dr. William RHEY
40 Manager Bookstore ... Ms. Ashley LORD
53 Dean Education ... Dr. Tracey D. TEDDER
04 Executive Asst to President ... Ms. Lynn M. DENNIS
66 Dean Nursing and Health Science ... Dr. Linda S. COMER
71 Dean of Student Success ... Dr. Susan FREEMAN
32 Dean of Student Development ... Mr. Bill C. LANGSTON, II
35 Asst Dean of Student Development ... Mr. Mike CRAWFORD

Florida SouthWestern State College (F)

8099 College Parkway, SW, Fort Myers FL 33919-5566

County: Lee FICE Identification: 001477
Unit ID: 133508
Telephone: (239) 489-9300 Carnegie Class: Bac/Assoc-Mixed
FAX Number: (239) 489-9103 Calendar System: Semester
URL: www.fsw.edu
Established: 1961 Annual Undergrad Tuition & Fees (In-State): $3,401
Enrollment: 15,389 Coed
Affiliation or Control: State IRS Status: 501(c)3
Highest Offering: Baccalaureate
Accreditation: SC, ADNUR, CAHIIM, COARC, CVT, DH, EMT, NUR, RAD

01 President ... Dr. Jeffery ALLBRITTEN
100 Chief of Staff ... Dr. Henry PEEL
12 Regional VP/Pres Charlotte Campus ... Dr. Denis WRIGHT
12 Regional VP/Pres Collier Campus ... Dr. Robert JONES
05 Interim Provost & VP Acad Affairs ... Dr. Jeff STEWART
32 VP Student Affairs & Enroll Mgmt ... Dr. Christine DAVIS
10 VP Administrative Services ... Dr. Gina DOEBLE
30 VP Institutional Advancement ... Dr. Lou TRAINA

20 Associate VP Academic Affairs ... Dr. Eileen DELUCA
43 General Counsel ... Mr. Mark LUPE
50 Dean Business & Technology ... Dr. John MEYER
76 Dean Health Professions ... Dr. Marie COLLINS
53 Dean Education and Charter Schools ... Dr. Lawrence MILLER
49 Dean Arts/Humanities & Social Sci ... Dr. Emery ALFORD
49 Dean Pure & Applied Sciences ... Dr. Martin MCCLINTON
88 Exec Director International Ed ... Dr. Laura WEIR
86 Director Governmental Relations ... Mr. Matthew HOLLIDAY
41 Athletic Director ... Mr. Carl MCALOOSE
21 Asst VP Budget & Financial Svcs ... Mr. Tobias DISCENZA
84 Asst VP Enrollment/Student Success ... Dr. Laura ANTCZAK
88 Campus Dean Stdnt Affs & Acad Svcs ... Dr. Christy GILFERT
88 Campus Dean Stdnt Affs & Acad Svcs ... Ms. Gail MURPHY
35 Assoc Dean Student Life/Orientation ... Ms. Linda RICKMAN
88 Assoc Dean Bacc Pgm & Acad Svcs ... Ms. Michelle FANSLAU
35 Associate Dean of Students ... Mr. Mark BUKOWSKI
06 Registrar ... Mr. Garnett SALMON
13 Chief Information Officer ... Mr. Jason DUDLEY
08 Library Coordinator/Head Librarian ... Mr. William SHULUK
102 Sr Director Admin & Dev/Foundation ... Mr. Kevin MILLER
102 Senior Director Foundation Dev ... Ms. Susan ELLIS
26 Dir Comm & Public Info Officer ... Ms. Teresa MORGENSTERN
108 Dir Effectiveness & Accountability ... Dr. Susan HIBBARD
09 Director of Institutional Research ... Ms. Abby WILLCOX
12 Director Hendry/Glades Center ... Mr. Jeffery GIBBS
88 Bursar ... Mr. Dwain KEDDO
19 Director Public Safety ... Mr. Richard PARFITT
109 Director Auxiliary Services ... Ms. Judith PULTRO
37 Interim Director Financial Aid ... Mr. Al HERMSEN
15 Director Human Resources ... Ms. Susan BRONSTEIN
07 Director Admissions ... Ms. Amber MCCOWN
18 Interim Dir Facilities Plng & Dev ... Mr. Ron COPASS
88 Director Academic Support Programs ... Ms. Monica MOORE
39 Director Student Housing ... Mr. Justin LONG
88 Director Academic Assessment ... Dr. Joseph VAN GAALEN
88 Director Dual Enrollment ... Ms. Kristin CORKHILL
88 Director Adaptive Services ... Ms. Angela HARTSELL
88 Director Academic Advising ... Mr. Andrae JONES
96 Director of Procurement Services ... Ms. Lisa TUDOR
88 Director Testing Services ... Ms. Denise SWAFFORD
29 Coordinator Alumni Relations ... Mr. Joseph TURNER

Florida State College at Jacksonville (G)

501 W State Street, Jacksonville FL 32202-4097

County: Duval FICE Identification: 001484
Unit ID: 133702
Telephone: (904) 646-2300 Carnegie Class: Bac/Assoc-Mixed
FAX Number: N/A Calendar System: Semester
URL: www.fscj.edu
Established: 1965 Annual Undergrad Tuition & Fees (In-District): $2,830
Enrollment: 25,514 Coed
Affiliation or Control: Local IRS Status: Exempt
Highest Offering: Baccalaureate
Accreditation: SC, ACBSP, ACFEI, ADNUR, CAHIIM, COARC, CVT, DA, DH, EMT, FUSER, HT, MLTAD, NUR, OTA, PTAA, SURGT

01 College President ... Dr. Cynthia A. BIOTEAU
45 Acting VP for Inst Advancement ... Dr. Carrie HENDERSON
10 Vice Pres of Business Services ... Mr. Albert LITTLE
43 College General Counsel ... Dr. Colin C. MAILLOUX
05 Provost/Vice President of Academic ... Dr. John WALL
32 Vice President Student Services ... Dr. Christopher HOLLAND
12 Campus President North ... Dr. Sandy ROBINSON
12 Campus President Downtown ... Dr. Marie F. GNAGE
12 Campus President South ... Dr. Ian NEUHARD
12 Campus President Open/Deerwood ... Ms. Jana KOOI
12 Campus President Kent ... Dr. Cedrick GIBSON
84 AVP Enrollment Management ... Mr. Rich TURNER
49 AVP Arts & Sciences & Articulation ... Dr. Nancy K. WEBSTER
20 Executive Dean Academic Foundations ... Dr. Kathleen CIEZ-VOLZ
21 AVP Finance ... Ms. Anita KOVACS
35 AVP Student Success ... Ms. Melanie MILLER
103 AVP Workforce Educ/Econ Development ... Ms. Linda WOODARD
15 Chief Human Resources Officer ... Mr. Mark LACEY
21 Chief Business Affairs Officer ... Mr. Laurence I. SNELL
13 Chief Information Tech Officer ... Ms. Christy CAMPBELL
22 Ex Dir Employee Rel/Equity Officer ... Ms. Lisa J. MOORE
18 Exec Dir Facilities & Const Mgmt ... Mr. Charles M. STRATMANN
88 Exec Director Cultural Programs ... Dr. Milton A. RUSSOS
88 Executive Director College Data Rep ... Ms. Theresa LOTT
88 Executive Director Talent Acquis ... Ms. Barbara HUNTER
88 Executive Director Enterprise App ... Mr. Chris MARTIN
62 Executive Dean of Library Svcs ... Dr. Tom MESSNER
14 Deputy Chief Technology Officer ... Mr. Ron SMITH
19 Exec Dir Public Safety/Security ... Mr. James E. STEVENSON
92 Associate Provost ... Dr. Margo MARTIN
12 Executive Director of Nassau Center ... Ms. Donna MARTIN
102 Executive Director Foundation ... Mr. Cleve WARREN
12 Executive Director Cecil Center ... Mr. Paul MCNAMARA
96 Executive Director Purchasing ... Ms. Randi BROKVIST
86 Dir Government/Cmty Engagement ... Ms. Jennifer SILVA
88 Director of Student Onboarding ... Dr. Roland BULLARD
19 Director of Security ... Mr. Gordon BASS
37 Director Financial Aid ... Vacant
41 Director of Athletics ... Ms. Ginny ALEXANDER
25 Director of Resource Development ... Ms. Jennifer PETERSON
06 Registrar ... Vacant
09 Director Student Analytics/Research ... Mr. Greg MICHALSKI
26 Director Marketing/Communications ... Ms. Jill K. JOHNSON

Florida Technical College (A)
1199 S Woodland Boulevard, Deland FL 32720-7415
Telephone: (386) 734-3303 Identification: 666419
Accreditation: ACICS, MAAB

Florida Technical College (B)
3837 West Vine Street, Kissimmee FL 34741
Telephone: (407) 483-5700 Identification: 770684
Accreditation: ACICS, MAAB

Florida Technical College (C)
4715 South Florida Avenue, Suite 4,
Lakeland FL 33813-2101
Telephone: (866) 967-8822 FICE Identification: 025981
Accreditation: ACICS, MAAB

Florida Technical College (D)
12900 Challenger Parkway, Orlando FL 32826
County: Orange FICE Identification: 022187
Unit ID: 134112
Telephone: (407) 447-7300 Carnegie Class: Bac/Assoc-Assoc Dom
FAX Number: (407) 447-7301 Calendar System: Quarter
URL: www.ftccollege.edu
Established: 1982 Annual Undergrad Tuition & Fees: N/A
Enrollment: 2,977 Coed
Affiliation or Control: Proprietary IRS Status: Proprietary
Highest Offering: Baccalaureate
Accreditation: ACICS, MAAB

00 President/CEO .... Mr. David RUGGIERI
01 Executive Director .... Mr. John BUCK
11 Executive Administrator .... Ms. Helmi ACEVEDO
05 Director of Education .... Dr. David PENN
07 Director of Admissions .... Vacant
37 Director of Financial Aid .... Ms. Ivette LUGO

Florida Technical College (E)
12520 Pines Boulevard, Pembroke Pines FL 33027
Telephone: (954) 556-1900 Identification: 770685
Accreditation: ACICS, MAAB

Fortis College (F)
700 Blanding Boulevard, Suite 16, Orange Park FL 32065
County: Clay FICE Identification: 034343
Unit ID: 439792
Telephone: (904) 269-7086 Carnegie Class: Spec 2-yr-Health
FAX Number: (904) 269-6664 Calendar System: Semester
URL: www.fortis.edu
Established: 1985 Annual Undergrad Tuition & Fees: $14,322
Enrollment: 312 Coed
Affiliation or Control: Proprietary IRS Status: Proprietary
Highest Offering: Associate Degree
Accreditation: ACICS, SURGT

01 Campus President .... Mr. Wyman DICKEY

Fortis Institute-Pensacola (G)
4081 East Olive Road, Suite B, Pensacola FL 32514
Telephone: (850) 476-7607 Identification: 770513
Accreditation: ABHES

† Branch campus of Fortis College, Mobile, AL

Fortis Institute-Port St. Lucie (H)
9022 South Federal Highway/US-1,
Port St. Lucie FL 34952
Telephone: (772) 221-9799 Identification: 770527
Accreditation: ABHES

† Branch campus of Fortis Institute, Baton Rouge, LA.

Full Sail University (I)
3300 University Boulevard, Winter Park FL 32792
County: Orange FICE Identification: 023621
Unit ID: 134237
Telephone: (407) 679-0100 Carnegie Class: Masters/L
FAX Number: (407) 679-9685 Calendar System: Other
URL: www.fullsail.edu
Established: 1979 Annual Undergrad Tuition & Fees: $23,117
Enrollment: 19,285 Coed
Affiliation or Control: Proprietary IRS Status: Proprietary
Highest Offering: Master's
Accreditation: ACCSC

01 President .... Mr. Garry JONES
07 Vice President of Admissions .... Mr. Matt PENGRA

Galen College of Nursing (J)
11101 Roosevelt Blvd N, Suite 100,
St. Petersburg FL 33716
Telephone: (727) 577-1497 Identification: 770539
Accreditation: &SC, ADNUR

† Regional accreditation is carried under the parent institution in Louisville, KY

Golf Academy of America (K)
510 South Hunt Club Blvd., Apopka FL 32703
Telephone: (800) 342-7342 Identification: 666186
Accreditation: ACICS

† Branch campus of Virginia College, Birmingham, AL.

Gordon-Conwell Theological Seminary-Jacksonville (L)
118 East Monroe Street, Jacksonville FL 32202-3214
Telephone: (904) 354-4800 Identification: 770111
Accreditation: &EH, THEOL

† Regional accreditation is carried under the parent institution in South Hamilton, MA

Gulf Coast State College (M)
5230 W Highway 98, Panama City FL 32401-1058
County: Bay FICE Identification: 001490
Unit ID: 134343
Telephone: (850) 769-1551 Carnegie Class: Bac/Assoc-Assoc Dom
FAX Number: (850) 913-3319 Calendar System: Semester
URL: www.gulfcoast.edu
Established: 1957 Annual Undergrad Tuition & Fees (In-State): $2,765
Enrollment: 5,926 Coed
Affiliation or Control: State Related IRS Status: 501(c)3
Highest Offering: Baccalaureate
Accreditation: SC, ACFEI, ADNUR, COARC, DA, DH, EMT, NURSE, PTAA, RAD, SURGA, SURGT

01 President .... Dr. John R. HOLDNAK
10 Vice Pres Administration & Finance .... Mr. John D. MERCER
05 Acting VP Academic Affairs .... Dr. Holly KUEHNER
32 VP Student Affairs .... Dr. Melissa LAVENDER
45 VP Institutional Effect/Stratg Plng .... Dr. Cheryl L. FLAX-HYMAN
13 Chief Information Officer .... Ms. Rhonda BARKER
08 Director of Library .... Ms. Lori DRISCOLL
84 Director of Enrollment Services .... Ms. Sharon O. TODD
15 Exec Director of Human Resources .... Ms. Mary NICHOLSON
26 Exec Director Media & Community Rel .... Mr. Christopher P. THOMES
96 Coordinator of Purchasing .... Mr. Fred BROWN
37 Exec Director Student Financial Svc .... Mr. Christopher J. WESTLAKE
09 Institutional Research Analyst .... Ms. Amber COKER
04 Executive Asst to President .... Ms. Eileen WILKES

Health Career Institute (N)
1764 N. Congress Avenue, West Palm Beach FL 33409
County: Palm Beach Identification: 667104
Telephone: (561) 586-0121 Carnegie Class: Not Classified
FAX Number: (561) 471-4010 Calendar System: Semester
URL: www.hci.edu
Established: 1993 Annual Undergrad Tuition & Fees: N/A
Enrollment: N/A Coed
Affiliation or Control: Proprietary IRS Status: Proprietary
Highest Offering: Associate Degree
Accreditation: ACCSC

01 President .... Brenda GREEN
10 Business Manager .... Angela MOECKES

Heritage Institute-Fort Myers (O)
6630 Orion Drive, Suite 200, Fort Myers FL 33912-7130
County: Lee FICE Identification: 025971
Unit ID: 135124
Telephone: (239) 936-5822 Carnegie Class: Spec 2-yr-Health
FAX Number: (239) 225-9117 Calendar System: Other
URL: www.heritage-education.com
Established: 2001 Annual Undergrad Tuition & Fees: N/A
Enrollment: 738 Coed
Affiliation or Control: Proprietary IRS Status: Proprietary
Highest Offering: Associate Degree
Accreditation: ABHES

01 Director .... Mr. Mike SCHAFER

Heritage Institute-Jacksonville (P)
4130 Salisbury Road, Suite 1100, Jacksonville FL 32216
County: Duval FICE Identification: 030358
Unit ID: 372772
Telephone: (904) 332-0910 Carnegie Class: Spec 2-yr-Health
FAX Number: (904) 332-0920 Calendar System: Other
URL: www.heritage-education.com/campus_jacksonville.htm
Established: 2001 Annual Undergrad Tuition & Fees: N/A
Enrollment: 285 Coed
Affiliation or Control: Proprietary IRS Status: Proprietary
Highest Offering: Associate Degree
Accreditation: ABHES

01 Director .... Ms. Jennifer MULLINS

Herzing University (Q)
1865 SR 436, Winter Park FL 32792
Telephone: (407) 478-0500 Identification: 666422
Accreditation: &NH, ADNUR, NURSE, PTAA

† Regional accreditation is carried under the parent institution in Madison, WI.

Hillsborough Community College (R)
PO Box 31127, 39 Columbia Drive, Tampa FL 33631-3127
County: Hillsborough FICE Identification: 007870
Unit ID: 134495
Telephone: (813) 253-7000 Carnegie Class: Assoc/HT-High Trad
FAX Number: (813) 253-7183 Calendar System: Semester
URL: www.hccfl.edu
Established: 1968 Annual Undergrad Tuition & Fees (In-State): $2,506
Enrollment: 27,298 Coed
Affiliation or Control: State IRS Status: 501(c)3
Highest Offering: Associate Degree
Accreditation: SC, ACFEI, ADNUR, COARC, CSHSE, DA, DH, DIETT, DMS, EMT, MUS, NMT, OPD, RAD, RTT

01 President .... Dr. Ken ATWATER
10 VP Administration/CFO .... Mr. Al ERDMAN
05 VP for Academic Affairs .... Mr. Craig JOHNSON
13 VP Information Technology .... Mr. Daya PENDHARKAR
32 VP Student Services/Enrollment Mgt .... Dr. Ken RAY
12 Campus President Dale Mabry .... Dr. Robert CHUNN
12 Campus President Ybor City Campus .... Dr. Shawn ROBINSON
12 Campus President Plant City Campus .... Dr. Martyn CLAY
12 Campus President Brandon Campus .... Dr. Nancee SORENSON
12 Campus President South Shore Campus .... Dr. Allen WITT
22 Asst to Pres Equity/Special Pgms .... Dr. Joan HOLMES
26 Exec Dir Marketing/Public Relations .... Ms. Ashley CARL
09 Spc Asst to Pres Strat Plng & Analy .... Dr. Paul NAGY
102 Exec Director HCC Foundation .... Mr. Stephen SHEAR
43 College Attorney .... Ms. Martha Kaye KOEHLER
15 Exec Dir Human Resources .... Ms. Kristin SMUDER
21 Controller .... Ms. Kimberly MCMILLON
103 VP of Workforce Trainining .... Dr. Ginger CLARK
75 Director Technical Programs .... Dr. Brian MANN
88 Director Assoc in Arts Programs .... Dr. Karen GRIFFIN
90 Director of Academic Technology .... Mr. Mark LEWIS
20 Dean of Academic Affairs .... Dr. Keith BERRY
88 Dean of Acad Affairs - Plant City .... Dr. Anthony BORRELL
88 Dean of AS Programs - Brandon .... Dr. Alessandro ANZALONE
88 Dean of Arts & Sciences-Dale Mabry .... Dr. Mary BENDICKSON
88 Dean of AS Programs - Dale Mabry .... Dr. Elizabeth JOHNSON
81 Dean AA Math/Science - Dale Mabry .... Dr. James WYSONG
76 Dean Health/Wellness & Sports Tech .... Mr. Leif PENROSE
37 Financial Aid Director .... Ms. Tierra SMITH
06 Registrar .... Ms. Jennifer WILLIAMS
18 Director Facilities/Physical Plant .... Mr. Ben MARSHALL
96 Director of Purchasing .... Ms. Vonda MELCHIOR
31 Dir of Community & Govt Relations .... Mr. Eric JOHNSON
19 Director Security/Safety .... Mr. Jeff COPELAND

Hobe Sound Bible College (S)
PO Box 1065, Hobe Sound FL 33475-1065
County: Martin FICE Identification: 021889
Unit ID: 134510
Telephone: (772) 546-5534 Carnegie Class: Spec-4-yr-Faith
FAX Number: (772) 545-1422 Calendar System: Semester
URL: www.hsbc.edu
Established: 1960 Annual Undergrad Tuition & Fees: $6,320
Enrollment: 251 Coed
Affiliation or Control: Independent Non-Profit IRS Status: 501(c)3
Highest Offering: Baccalaureate
Accreditation: BI

01 President .... Dr. P. Daniel STETLER
05 Academic Dean .... Dr. Clifford W. CHURCHILL
10 Director of Finances .... Mr. Rick HUFF
11 Director of Administration .... Mr. Wesley HOLDEN
32 Dean of Students .... Mr. John S. JONES
33 Dean of Men .... Mr. Jonathan STRATTON
08 Librarian .... Mr. Phil JONES
26 Public Relations Director .... Mr. Paul STETLER
06 Registrar .... Mr. Lucas RYDER
07 Director of Admissions .... Ms. Pam DAVIS
51 Dean of External Studies .... Mr. Dalbert N. WALKER

Hodges University (T)
2655 Northbrooke Drive, Naples FL 34119-7932
County: Collier FICE Identification: 030375
Unit ID: 367884
Telephone: (239) 513-1122 Carnegie Class: Masters/S
FAX Number: (239) 598-6253 Calendar System: Trimester
URL: www.hodges.edu
Established: 1990 Annual Undergrad Tuition & Fees: $13,220
Enrollment: 1,892 Coed
Affiliation or Control: Independent Non-Profit IRS Status: 501(c)3
Highest Offering: Master's
Accreditation: SC, CACREP, CAHIIM, IACBE, MAC, PTAA

01 President .... Dr. Donald WORTHAM
32 Senior Vice Pres of Student Svcs .... Ms. Carol MORRISON
03 Exec Vice Pres of Operations .... Ms. Erica VOGT

07 Vice Pres of Enrollment Management .... Mr. Brent PASSEY
35 Dean of Students .... Dr. Marcia TURNER
30 Vice Pres of Relations/Stewardship .... Mr. Phil MEMOLI
26 Chief Marketing Officer .... Ms. Karen GREBING
09 Dir Institutional Effective/Rsrch .... Dr. Diane BALL
28 Chief Diversity Officer .... Ms. Gail WILLIAMS
29 Director of Alumni Affairs .... Mr. Brian HAWKINS
76 Dean School of Allied Health .... Dr. William GRIZ
72 Dean Fisher School of Technology .... Dr. Al BALL
50 Dean Johnson School of Business .... Dr. Aysegul TIMUR
107 Dean Nichols School of Prof Studies .... Dr. Mary NUOSCE
97 Dean School of Liberal Studies .... Dr. Elsa ROGERS

Hope College of Arts & Sciences (A)

1200 SW 3rd St, Pompano Beach FL 33317
County: Broward FICE Identification: 042517
Telephone: (954) 532-9614 Carnegie Class: Not Classified
FAX Number: N/A Calendar System: Other
URL: www.hcas.us
Established: 2011 Annual Undergrad Tuition & Fees: N/A
Enrollment: N/A Coed
Affiliation or Control: Proprietary IRS Status: Proprietary
Highest Offering: Associate Degree
Accreditation: **ACICS**

05 Dean of Academic Affairs .... Dr. Chantal DESIR

Indian River State College (B)

3209 Virginia Avenue, Fort Pierce FL 34981-5596
County: Saint Lucie FICE Identification: 001493
Unit ID: 134608
Telephone: (772) 462-4772 Carnegie Class: Bac/Assoc-Mixed
FAX Number: (772) 462-4796 Calendar System: Semester
URL: www.irsc.edu
Established: 1960 Annual Undergrad Tuition & Fees (In-District): $2,764
Enrollment: 17,665 Coed
Affiliation or Control: Local IRS Status: 501(c)3
Highest Offering: Baccalaureate
Accreditation: **SC**, ADNUR, CAHIIM, COARC, DA, DH, DT, EMT, MAC, MLTAD, NUR, PTAA, RAD, SURGT

01 President .... Dr. Edwin MASSEY
12 Vice President/Provost Fort Pierce .... Vacant
88 Vice President Science & Tech .... Mr. Jose FARINOS
45 Vice Pres Institutional Effectiv .... Dr. Christina HART
05 Vice President Academic Affairs .... Dr. Anthony IACONO
10 Vice President Financial Services .... Ms. Sheryl VITTITOE
32 Vice President Student Affairs .... Mr. Frank WATKINS
13 Vice President Institutional Tech .... Mr. Paul O'BRIEN
17 Dean Health Science .... Ms. Jane CEBELAK
12 Dean Northwest Center .... Mr. Andre HAWKINS
08 Dean Learning Resources .... Ms. Patricia PROFETA
75 Dean Industrial Education .... Ms. Donna RIVETT
12 Provost Pt St Lucie/St Lucie W .... Dr. Harvey ARNOLD
12 Provost Okeechobee County .... Mr. Russ BROWN
12 Provost Martin County .... Ms. Elizabeth GASKIN
12 Provost Indian River County .... Mr. Casey LUNCEFORD
102 Executive Director Foundation .... Ms. Ann DECKER
83 Dean Communication & Social Science .... Dr. Bruce FRASER
66 Dean Nursing .... Ms. Ann HUBBARD
11 Dean Administrative Services .... Ms. Jan PAGANO
80 Dean Public Service Education .... Mr. Evan BERRY
50 Dean Business Technology .... Mr. Ray CARPENTER
72 Dean Advanced Technology .... Mr. Kevin COOPER
53 Dean School of Education .... Dr. Marta CRONIN
15 Dean Human Resources .... Ms. Nancy CUNNINGHAM
18 Dean Facilities & Sustainability .... Mr. Sean DONAHUE
07 Dean Enrollment & Student Services .... Ms. Eileen STORCK
49 Dean Arts & Sciences .... Mr. Paul HORTON
21 Dean Finance .... Ms. Edith PACACHA
14 Dean Enterprise Systems .... Mr. Anthony VIA
41 Director Athletics .... Mr. Scott KIMMELMAN
88 Director Virtual Campus .... Ms. Kendall ST. HILAIRE
93 Director Minority Affairs .... Mr. Danny HOEY
26 Director Executive Communications ...... Mr. Andrew TREADWELL
30 Director Institutional Advancement .... Ms. Michelle ABALDO
84 Director Enrollment Management .... Mr. Douglas DORAN
88 Director Instructional Advising .... Ms. Dale HAYES
36 Director Student Success Services .... Ms. Flossie JACKSON
37 Director Financial Aid .... Ms. Mary LEWIS
35 Director Student Affairs .... Ms. Sharon LOWE
22 Equity Officer .... Ms. Adriene JEFFERSON
96 Purchasing Agent .... Mr. Don WINDHAM
19 Director Safety/Security .... Mr. Alan MONTGOMERY

International College of Health Sciences (C)

2300 S. Congress Avenue #105, Boynton Beach FL 33426
County: Palm Beach Identification: 667238
Telephone: (561) 202-6333 Carnegie Class: Not Classified
FAX Number: (561) 296-9647 Calendar System: Semester
URL: www.ihep.edu
Established: Annual Undergrad Tuition & Fees: N/A
Enrollment: N/A Coed
Affiliation or Control: Proprietary IRS Status: Proprietary
Highest Offering: Associate Degree
Accreditation: **ACICS**

01 Campus President .... Karyn VIDAL

Jacksonville University (D)

2800 University Boulevard N, Jacksonville FL 32211-3394
County: Duval FICE Identification: 001495
Unit ID: 134945
Telephone: (904) 256-8000 Carnegie Class: Masters/L
FAX Number: N/A Calendar System: Semester
URL: www.ju.edu
Established: 1934 Annual Undergrad Tuition & Fees: $32,620
Enrollment: 4,085 Coed
Affiliation or Control: Independent Non-Profit IRS Status: 501(c)3
Highest Offering: Doctorate
Accreditation: **SC**, AAB, BUS, DANCE, DENT, MUS, NURSE, @SP

01 President .... Mr. Timothy P. COST
05 Senior VP Univ & Academic Affairs .... Dr. Donnie HORNER
10 Senior VP Finance .... Mr. David HEALY
07 Chief Admissions Officer .... Mr. Tom TAGGART
32 Senior VP Student Affairs .... Dr. Kristie GOVER
30 Chief Advancement Officer .... Ms. Kimberly JONES
84 Sr VP Enroll Mgmt/Communications .... Ms. Margaret DEES
13 Chief Information Officer .... Mr. Tom HALL
04 Exec Assistant to the President .... Ms. Dolores STARR
06 Registrar .... Ms. Carolyn BARRETT
09 Director of Institutional Research .... Dr. Logan CROSS
08 Director of the Library .... Ms. Jessica COLLOGAN
35 Associate Dean of Students .... Mr. Luke MORRILL
36 Director of Career Development .... Ms. Toni HIGGS
37 Financial Aid Director .... Ms. Karen LAVERDIERE
21 Controller .... Ms. Liza MULLINS
11 Exec Dir Budgets/Business Opers .... Ms. Ellen M. PAIGE
96 Director of Purchasing .... Mr. Michael J. BOBBIN
40 Director of the Bookstore .... Mr. Patrick JONES
42 Campus Minister .... Mr. Lance BEAUCHAMP
15 Director of Human Resources .... Mr. James V. WILLIAMS
57 Dean of Col of Fine Arts .... Dr. Henry RINNE
49 Int Dean Col of Arts & Sciences .... Dr. Lee Ann CLEMENTS
50 Dean College of Business .... Dr. Don CAPENER
76 Brooks Col of HealthCare Sciences .... Dr. Christine SAPIENZA
64 Chairman Division of Music .... Dr. Tim SNYDER
79 Chair Div of Humanitites .... Dr. Scott KIMBROUGH
81 Chair Division of Science & Math .... Dr. Brian LANE
38 Director Student Counseling .... Ms. Kristin R. ALBERTS
83 Chair Division of Social Science .... Dr. Sherry JACKSON
88 Chair Division of Naval Science .... Capt. Neil KARNES
88 Chair Div of Theatre Arts & Dance .... Mr. Brian PALMER
57 Chair Division Art/Art History .... Mr. Eric KUNZENDORF
18 Chief Facilities/Physical Plant .... Ms. Teri SCHULTHEIS
19 Director Security/Safety .... Mr. Kevin BENNETT
102 Dir Foundation/Corporate Relations .... Ms. Michele QUERRY
29 Director Alumni Relations .... Ms. Kim GRANT
39 Director of Residential Life .... Mr. Lucas MULLIN
44 Director Annual or Planned Giving .... Ms. Maria YOKITIS
25 Dir Research & Sponsored Pgms .... Ms. Renee ROSSI

Johnson & Wales University (E)

1701 NE 127th Street, North Miami FL 33181-2518
Telephone: (305) 892-7000 Identification: 666423
Accreditation: **&EH**

† Regional accreditation is carried under the parent institution in Providence, RI.

Johnson University Florida (F)

1011 Bill Beck Boulevard, Kissimmee FL 34744-5301
Telephone: (407) 847-8966 FICE Identification: 021567
Accreditation: **&SC**, BI

† Regional accreditation is carried under the parent institution in Knoxville, TN

Jones College (G)

1195 Edgewood Ave., South, Jacksonville FL 32205
County: Duval FICE Identification: 001497
Unit ID: 135063
Telephone: (904) 743-1122 Carnegie Class: Bac/Assoc-Mixed
FAX Number: (904) 371-1127 Calendar System: Trimester
URL: www.jones.edu
Established: 1918 Annual Undergrad Tuition & Fees: $7,650
Enrollment: 495 Coed
Affiliation or Control: Independent Non-Profit IRS Status: 501(c)3
Highest Offering: Baccalaureate
Accreditation: **ACICS**

00 Corporate President & CEO .... Dorothy D. JONES
01 President of the College .... Dr. Mayra NUNEZ
38 Compliance Auditor .... Frank MCCAFFERTY
07 Director of Admissions .... Dalia KENNEDY
08 Librarian .... Marie LANIER
103 Dir Workforce/Career Development .... Allison ADAMS
104 Dir of Admin Support Intl Studies .... Mary BARBER
37 Director Student Financial Aid .... Becky DAVIS
43 Dir Legal Services/General Counsel .... Meredith BRASCA
53 Dean/Director Education .... Charles JONES
90 Director Academic Computing .... Kenneth JONES

Jose Maria Vargas University (H)

10131 Pines Boulevard, Pembroke Pines FL 33026
County: Broward FICE Identification: 041620
Unit ID: 461281
Telephone: (954) 322-4460 Carnegie Class: Spec-4-yr-Other
FAX Number: (954) 322-4131 Calendar System: Semester
URL: www.jmvu.edu
Established: 2003 Annual Undergrad Tuition & Fees: $10,480
Enrollment: 147 Coed
Affiliation or Control: Proprietary IRS Status: Proprietary
Highest Offering: Master's
Accreditation: **ACICS**

01 President .... Dr. Alicia F. PARRA
06 Registrar .... Ms. Lelis ORTIZ PARRA

Keiser University (I)

1800 Business Park Blvd, Daytona Beach FL 32114
Telephone: (386) 274-5060 Identification: 770900
Accreditation: **&SC**, ACBSP, DMS, MAC, OTA, RAD

† Regional accreditation is carried under the parent institution in Fort Lauderdale, FL

Keiser University (J)

1500 NW 49th Street, Fort Lauderdale FL 33309-3700
County: Broward FICE Identification: 021519
Unit ID: 135081
Telephone: (954) 776-4476 Carnegie Class: Bac/Assoc-Mixed
FAX Number: N/A Calendar System: Semester
URL: www.keiseruniversity.edu
Established: 1977 Annual Undergrad Tuition & Fees: $17,664
Enrollment: 19,110 Coed
Affiliation or Control: Independent Non-Profit IRS Status: 501(c)3
Highest Offering: Doctorate
Accreditation: **SC**, ACBSP, ADNUR, ARCPA, CAHIIM, COARC, @DIETI, DMS, MLTAD, NURSE, OTA, PTAA, RAD

01 Chancellor .... Dr. Arthur KEISER
03 Executive Vice Chancellor .... Mr. Peter CROCITTO
05 Vice Chancellor of Academic Affairs .... Dr. John SITES
31 Vice Chancellor of Community Rels .... Mrs. Belinda KEISER
84 Vice Chancellor of Enrollment Mgmt .... Mr. Brian WOODS
10 Sr Vice Chancellor of Finance .... Mr. Joseph BERARDINELLI
85 Vice Chancellor International Affs .... Mr. Zhanjun YANG
26 Reg Dir Media & Public Relations .... Ms. Kimberly DALE

Keiser University (K)

9100 Forum Corporate Pkwy, Fort Myers FL 33905
Telephone: (239) 277-1336 Identification: 770901
Accreditation: **&SC**, ACBSP, DMS, OTA

† Regional accreditation is carried under the parent institution in Fort Lauderdale, FL

Keiser University (L)

6430 Southpoint Pkwy, Jacksonville FL 33216
Telephone: (904) 296-3440 Identification: 770902
Accreditation: **&SC**, ACBSP, ADNUR, OTA, PTAA, RAD

† Regional accreditation is carried under the parent institution in Fort Lauderdale, FL

Keiser University (M)

2400 Interstate Drive, Lakeland FL 33805
Telephone: (863) 682-6020 Identification: 770903
Accreditation: **&SC**, ACBSP, ADNUR, DIETC, NMT, PTAA, RAD

† Regional accreditation is carried under the parent institution in Fort Lauderdale, FL

Keiser University (N)

900 South Babcock Street, Melbourne FL 32901
Telephone: (321) 409-4800 Identification: 770904
Accreditation: **&SC**, ACBSP, ACFEI, ADNUR, @DIETC, DMS, OTA, RAD

† Regional accreditation is carried under the parent institution in Fort Lauderdale, FL

Keiser University (O)

2101 NW 117th Avenue, Miami FL 33172
Telephone: (305) 596-2226 Identification: 770905
Accreditation: **&SC**, ACBSP, ADNUR, OTA, PTAA, RAD

† Regional accreditation is carried under the parent institution in Fort Lauderdale, FL

Keiser University (P)

6014 US Hwy 19 North, Ste 250,
New Port Richey FL 34652
Telephone: (727) 484-3110 Identification: 770854
Accreditation: **&SC**, DMS

† Regional accreditation is carried under the parent institution in Fort Lauderdale, FL

Keiser University (Q)

5600 Lake Underhill Road, Orlando FL 32807
Telephone: (407) 381-1233 Identification: 770906

Accreditation: &SC, ACBSP, ADNUR, HT, OTA

† Regional accreditation is carried under the parent institution in Fort Lauderdale, FL

Keiser University (A)
1640 SW 145th Avenue, Pembroke Pines FL 33027
Telephone: (954) 431-4300 Identification: 770907
Accreditation: &SC, ACBSP, DIETC, HT, OTA

† Regional accreditation is carried under the parent institution in Fort Lauderdale, FL

Keiser University (B)
6151 Lake Osprey Drive, Sarasota FL 34240
Telephone: (941) 907-3900 Identification: 770908
Accreditation: &SC, ACBSP, ACFEI, ADNUR, PTAA, RAD

† Regional accreditation is carried under the parent institution in Fort Lauderdale, FL

Keiser University (C)
1700 Halstead Blvd, Bldg 2, Tallahassee FL 32309
Telephone: (850) 906-9494 Identification: 770909
Accreditation: &SC, ACBSP, ACFEI, ADNUR, OTA

† Regional accreditation is carried under the parent institution in Fort Lauderdale, FL

Keiser University (D)
5002 West Waters Ave, Tampa FL 33634
Telephone: (813) 885-4900 Identification: 770910
Accreditation: &SC, ACBSP, ADNUR, OTA, SURGT

† Regional accreditation is carried under the parent institution in Fort Lauderdale, FL

Keiser University (E)
2085 Vista Parkway, West Palm Beach FL 33411-2719
Telephone: (561) 471-6000 Identification: 667032
Accreditation: &SC, ACBSP, ADNUR, OTA, PTAA

† Regional accreditation is carried under the parent institution Keiser University, Fort Lauderdale, FL.

Keiser University at Clearwater (F)
16120 US Hwy 19 N, Clearwater FL 33764
Telephone: (727) 576-6500 Identification: 666758
Accreditation: SC, SURGT

Key College (G)
225 E Dania Beach Blvd, Suite 130,
Dania Beach FL 33004-3042
County: Broward FICE Identification: 023251
Unit ID: 134422
Telephone: (954) 923-4440 Carnegie Class: Spec 2-yr-Other
FAX Number: (954) 923-9226 Calendar System: Quarter
URL: www.keycollege.edu
Established: 1982 Annual Undergrad Tuition & Fees: $11,085
Enrollment: 59 Coed
Affiliation or Control: Proprietary IRS Status: Proprietary
Highest Offering: Associate Degree
Accreditation: ACICS

01 President .... Mr. Ronald DOOLEY
05 Director of Academic Affairs .... Ms. Marella DOOLEY
07 Director of Admissions .... Mr. Ron DOOLEY
37 Director of Financial Aid .... Ms. Traci ANDREWS
06 Registrar .... Mr. Guy ETIENNE

Knox Theological Seminary (H)
5555 N Federal Highway, Fort Lauderdale FL 33308-3209
County: Broward FICE Identification: 039923
Unit ID: 484288
Telephone: (954) 771-0376 Carnegie Class: Not Classified
FAX Number: (954) 351-3343 Calendar System: Semester
URL: www.knoxseminary.edu
Established: 1989 Annual Undergrad Tuition & Fees: N/A
Enrollment: 287 Coed
Affiliation or Control: Independent Non-Profit IRS Status: 501(c)3
Highest Offering: Doctorate
Accreditation: THEOL

01 President & CEO .... Dr. Samuel LAMERSON
11 Vice President of Administration .... Dr. Timothy SANSBURY
05 Dean of Faculty/Dean of Students .... Dr. Scott MANOR
106 Dean of Distance Education .... Dr. John MARKLEY
26 Director of Communications .... Ms. Ivey Rose SMITH
30 Director of Development .... Mr. Charles BURGE
06 Registrar .... Ms. Lori GOTTSHALL
08 Head Librarian .... Mr. Alan WIBBELS
10 Director of Finance .... Mr. David LEGATE
04 Administrative Asst to President .... Ms. Laura KASTENSMIDT

Lake Erie College of Osteopathic Medicine Bradenton (I)
5000 Lakewood Rance Boulevard, Bradenton FL 34211
Telephone: (941) 756-0690 Identification: 770160
Accreditation: &M, DENT, OSTEO, PHAR

† Regional accreditation is carried under the parent institution in Erie, PA

Lake-Sumter State College (J)
9501 US Highway 441, Leesburg FL 34788-8751
County: Lake FICE Identification: 001502
Unit ID: 135188
Telephone: (352) 787-3747 Carnegie Class: Bac/Assoc-Assoc Dom
FAX Number: (352) 365-3548 Calendar System: Semester
URL: www.lssc.edu
Established: 1962 Annual Undergrad Tuition & Fees (In-District): $3,172
Enrollment: 4,470 Coed
Affiliation or Control: State/Local IRS Status: 501(c)3
Highest Offering: Baccalaureate
Accreditation: SC, ADNUR, CAHIIM

01 President .... Dr. Stanley SIDOR
10 Sr VP Business Affairs .... Mr. Richard M. SCOTT
05 VP Academic Affairs .... Dr. Douglas A. WYMER
84 VP Enrollment & Student Affairs .... Ms. Claire BRADY
21 Assoc VP for Business Affairs .... Ms. Vicki WARD
97 Assoc VP General Studies .... Mr. Thom KIEFT
15 Exec Director Human Resources .... Ms. Fran PISTILLI
13 Chief Information Officer .... Mr. Douglas GUILER
09 Exec Dir Planning & IE .... Mr. Dave WEBER
30 Exec Dir Inst Advance & Foundation .... Ms. Rosanne BRANDEBURG
18 Director College Facilities .... Mr. David MARTIN
08 Director Libraries .... Ms. Katie SACCO
32 Dean of Students .... Ms. Carolyn SCOTT
21 Director Accounting .... Ms. Diana BILLINGHAM
66 Interim Director Nursing .... Ms. Nicole TINNY
08 Interim Director Learning Center .... Ms. Wendy ERSKINE
26 Director College Relations .... Vacant
37 Director Financial Aid .... Ms. Audrey WILLIAMS
06 Registrar .... Ms. Alba RODRIGUEZ
41 Athletic Director .... Mr. Michael K. MATULIA
88 Int Dir Youth Outreach Programs .... Ms. Delrita MEISNER
106 Director Distance Learning .... Mr. Mike NATHANSON
07 Director Admissions .... Mr. Bryan ANDERSON
28 Equity Officer .... Vacant
96 Asst Director of Purchasing .... Mr. Bill PONKO
102 Coord Foundation/Alumni Scholarship .... Ms. Claudia MORRIS
103 Assoc Dean Workforce Programs .... Dr. Eugene JONES

Larkin Health Sciences Institute (K)
18301 North Miami Ave, Ste 1, Miami FL 33169
County: Miami-Dade Identification: 667288
Telephone: (305) 760-7500 Carnegie Class: Not Classified
FAX Number: N/A Calendar System: Semester
URL: ularkin.org
Established: Annual Graduate Tuition & Fees: N/A
Enrollment: N/A Coed
Affiliation or Control: Independent Non-Profit IRS Status: 501(c)3
Highest Offering: Doctorate; No Undergraduates
Accreditation: @PHAR

01 President .... Ms. Sandy SOSA-GUERRERO
03 Vice President .... Dr. Gary M. LEVIN
13 Director of Technology .... Dr. Jorge E. MACHADO

Le Cordon Bleu College of Culinary Arts in Miami (L)
3221 Enterprise Way, Miramar FL 33025-3929
Telephone: (954) 438-8882 Identification: 666369
Accreditation: ACCSC, ACICS, ACFEI

† In teach-out mode through September 2017. Branch campus of Le Cordon Bleu Institute of Culinary Arts, Pittsburgh, PA.

Le Cordon Bleu College of Culinary Arts in Orlando (M)
8511 Commodity Circle, Orlando FL 32819-9002
Telephone: (407) 888-4000 Identification: 666064
Accreditation: ACCSC, ACICS, ACFEI

† In teach-out mode through September 2017. Branch campus of International Academy of Design & Technology, Tampa, FL.

Lincoln College of Technology (N)
2410 Metrocentre Boulevard,
West Palm Beach FL 33407-3155
County: Palm Beach FICE Identification: 022808
Unit ID: 136066
Telephone: (561) 842-8324 Carnegie Class: Bac/Assoc-Mixed
FAX Number: (561) 842-9503 Calendar System: Other
URL: www.lincolncollegeoftechnology.com
Established: 1982 Annual Undergrad Tuition & Fees: $15,650
Enrollment: 713 Coed
Affiliation or Control: Proprietary IRS Status: Proprietary
Highest Offering: Baccalaureate
Accreditation: ACICS, ACFEI

01 President .... Mr. Mike CLULING

Lynn University (O)
3601 N Military Trail, Boca Raton FL 33431-5598
County: Palm Beach FICE Identification: 001505
Unit ID: 132657
Telephone: (561) 237-7000 Carnegie Class: Masters/L
FAX Number: (561) 237-7100 Calendar System: Semester
URL: www.lynn.edu
Established: 1962 Annual Undergrad Tuition & Fees: $35,200
Enrollment: 2,613 Coed
Affiliation or Control: Independent Non-Profit IRS Status: 501(c)3
Highest Offering: Doctorate
Accreditation: SC, IACBE, MUS

01 President .... Dr. Kevin M. ROSS
00 President Emeritus .... Dr. Donald E. ROSS
11 Sr Vice President Administration .... Mr. Gregory J. MALFITANO
05 Vice President Academic Affairs .... Dr. Gregg COX
84 Vice Pres Enrollment Management .... Dr. Gareth FOWLES
10 Vice President Business & Finance .... Ms. Laurie LEVINE
32 Vice President for Student Life .... Dr. Phil RIORDAN
30 Vice Pres Development/Alumni Affs .... Mr. Gregory J. MALFITANO
13 Chief Information Officer .... Mr. Chris G. BONIFORTI
26 Chief Marketing Officer .... Mrs. Sherrie WELDON
88 Dean of Administration .... Mr. Thomas J. HEFFERNAN
35 Dean of Students .... Mr. Gary MARTIN
43 General Counsel .... Mr. Michael ANTONELLO
88 Exec Dir Stdnt Administrative Svcs .... Ms. Evelyn C. NELSON
39 Director Housing & Residence Life .... Ms. Meagan ELSBERRY
36 Executive Director Career Develop .... Ms. Barbara CAMBIA
41 Director of Athletics .... Dr. Kristen L. MORAZ
109 Director Auxiliary Services .... Mr. Matthew P. CHALOUX
23 Director Health Center .... Ms. Rita ALBERT
27 Director of Marketing and Comm .... Ms. Stephanie BROWN
44 Director of Major Gifts .... Mr. Jay J. BRANDT
29 Director Alumni Affairs .... Mr. Matthew R. ROOS
42 Chaplain .... Fr. Martin C. DEVEREAUX
07 Dir Undergraduate Admissions .... Mr. Stefano PAPALEO
37 Dir Student Financial Assistance .... Mrs. Chan J. PARK
38 Director of the Counseling Center .... Ms. Nicole R. OVEDIA
96 Director of Purchasing .... Mr. Alfredo H. BONIFORTI
06 Registrar .... Ms. Jenifer MOSLEY
21 Director of Accounting .... Mr. Michael C. BOLDUC
07 Dir Graduate & UG Evening Admiss .... Mr. Steven PRUITT
09 Director of Institutional Research .... Mrs. Lara MARTIN
15 Director of Employee Services .... Mr. Aaron GREENBERG
40 Bookstore Manager .... Ms. Rita D. LOUREIRO
50 Dean College Business & Management .... Mr. RT GOOD
49 Dean College of Arts & Sciences .... Dr. Katrina CARTER-TELLISON
88 Dean School of Aeronautics .... Dr. Jeffrey C. JOHNSON
53 Dean Ross College of Education .... Dr. Kathleen WEIGEL
60 Dean College Intl Communications .... Dr. David L. JAFFE
64 Dean Conservatory of Music .... Dr. Jon H. ROBERTSON
88 Exe Dir Inst Achievement Learning .... Mr. Shaun EXSTEEN
08 Director of the Library .... Ms. Amy FILIATREAU
104 Director Center for Learning Abroad .... Mr. Brian PIRTTIMA
19 Chief .... Mr. Larry RICKARD

Med-Life Institute-Lauderdale Lakes (P)
4000 N. State Road 7, Suite 301,
Lauderdale Lakes FL 33319
County: Broward Identification: 667221
Telephone: (954) 943-8667 Carnegie Class: Not Classified
FAX Number: (954) 943-0984 Calendar System: Quarter
URL: www.medlifeinstitute.com
Established: 2003 Annual Undergrad Tuition & Fees: N/A
Enrollment: N/A Coed
Affiliation or Control: Proprietary IRS Status: Proprietary
Highest Offering: Associate Degree
Accreditation: ABHES

01 President/CEO .... Dr. Lemuel PIERRE

Med-Life Institute-Naples (Q)
4995 Tamiami Trail E, Naples FL 34113
County: Collier Identification: 667220
Telephone: (239) 732-1300 Carnegie Class: Not Classified
FAX Number: (239) 417-5110 Calendar System: Semester
URL: www.medlifeinstitute.com
Established: 2003 Annual Undergrad Tuition & Fees: N/A
Enrollment: N/A Coed
Affiliation or Control: Proprietary IRS Status: Proprietary
Highest Offering: Associate Degree
Accreditation: ABHES

01 President .... Mr. Cleophat TANIS

Medical Career Institute (R)
27975 Old 41 Road, Ste 201, Bonita Springs FL 34135
County: Lee Identification: 667266
Telephone: (239) 992-4624 Carnegie Class: Not Classified
FAX Number: (239) 405-8024 Calendar System: Semester
URL: www.medicalcareerinstitute.org
Established: 2008 Annual Undergrad Tuition & Fees: N/A

Enrollment: N/A Coed
Affiliation or Control: Proprietary IRS Status: Proprietary
Highest Offering: Associate Degree
Accreditation: ABHES

01 President/CEO .... Mr. Richard GONZALEZ

Medical Prep Institute (A)

2304 Busch Blvd, Tampa FL 33613
County: Hillsborough Identification: 667267
Telephone: (813) 932-1710 Carnegie Class: Not Classified
FAX Number: (813) 932-1721 Calendar System: Other
URL: www.medicalprepinstitute.org
Established: Annual Undergrad Tuition & Fees: N/A
Enrollment: N/A Coed
Affiliation or Control: Proprietary IRS Status: Proprietary
Highest Offering: Baccalaureate
Accreditation: ABHES

05 Dean of Academics .... Rochelle L. LEFLER

Mercy Hospital College of Nursing (B)

3663 South Miami Ave Ste 1500, Miami FL 33133
County: Miami-Dade Identification: 667222
Unit ID: 419217
Telephone: (305) 285-2777 Carnegie Class: Not Classified
FAX Number: (305) 285-2671 Calendar System: Semester
URL: www.mercymiami.com/professionals/college-of-nursing
Established: Annual Undergrad Tuition & Fees: N/A
Enrollment: 91 Coed
Affiliation or Control: Proprietary IRS Status: Proprietary
Highest Offering: Associate Degree
Accreditation: ABHES, ADNUR, PNUR

66 Dean .... Ms. Elizabeth HERNANDEZ

Meridian College (C)

7020 Professional Pkwy E, Sarasota FL 34240
County: Sarasota FICE Identification: 023268
Unit ID: 244279
Telephone: (941) 377-4880 Carnegie Class: Spec 2-yr-Health
FAX Number: (941) 378-2842 Calendar System: Other
URL: www.meridian.edu
Established: 1982 Annual Undergrad Tuition & Fees: N/A
Enrollment: 182 Coed
Affiliation or Control: Proprietary IRS Status: Proprietary
Highest Offering: Associate Degree
Accreditation: ACCSC

01 Campus Director .... Mr. Patrick MCDERMOTT
03 Executive Vice President .... Mr. Lenny DAVIS
05 Director of Education .... Mr. André DODSON
07 Director of Admissions .... Ms. Kim MILES
36 Director Student Placement .... Ms. Tracy FORDHAM

Miami Dade College (D)

300 NE Second Avenue, Miami FL 33132-2204
County: Miami-Dade County FICE Identification: 001506
Unit ID: 135717
Telephone: (305) 237-8888 Carnegie Class: Bac/Assoc-Assoc Dom
FAX Number: (305) 237-7913 Calendar System: Semester
URL: www.mdc.edu/main/
Established: 1960 Annual Undergrad Tuition & Fees (In-State): $2,834
Enrollment: 66,046 Coed
Affiliation or Control: State IRS Status: 501(c)3
Highest Offering: Baccalaureate
Accreditation: SC, ADNUR, ARCPA, ART, CAHIIM, COARC, DANCE, DH, DMS, EMT, FUSER, HT, MLTAD, MUS, NUR, OPD, PTAA, RAD, THEA

01 College President .... Dr. Eduardo J. PADRON
05 Provost Academic & Student Affairs .... Dr. Lenore RODICIO
11 Provost Operations .... Dr. Rolando MONTOYA
10 Sr Vice Provost Business Affairs .... Mr. E. H. LEVERING
13 Vice Provost Information Technology .... Dr. Wendy CHANG
18 Interim Vice Provost Facilities .... Ms. Neyda OTERO
15 Vice Provost Human Resources .... Ms. Iliana CASTILLO-FRICK
09 Vice Provost Inst Effectiveness .... Dr. Archieval CUBARRUBIA
12 Campus President Hialeah .... Vacant
12 Campus President Kendall .... Dr. Beverly MOORE-GARCIA
12 Campus President Medical .... Dr. Mark EVERETT
12 Campus President Wolfson .... Dr. Richard SOFIA
12 Campus President North .... Ms. Malou HARRISON
12 Campus President Homestead .... Dr. Jeanne JACOBS
12 Campus President InterAmerican .... Dr. Joanne BASHFORD
12 Campus President West .... Dr. Roger RAMSAMMY
21 Assoc Vice Prov Business Affs .... Ms. Delilah ALMEDA
35 Vice Provost Student Services .... Dr. Kathy MAALOUF
102 Executive Dir MDC Foundation .... Mr. Mark COLE
37 Assoc VP Student Financial Services .... Ms. Mercedes AMAYA
93 Director Employee Relations/EOP/ADA .... Dr. Joy C. RUFF
07 Interim Collegewide Dir Admissions .... Ms. Ferne CREARY
26 Chief Public Rels Officer/Dir Comm .... Mr. Juan MENDIETA
29 Director Annual Giving/Alumni Rels .... Ms. Nairobi ABRAMS
32 Director Student Life .... Ms. Nicole BRYANT
36 Dir Testing Admin/Pgm Evaluation .... Mr. Silvio RODRIGUEZ
28 Director of Diversity .... Dr. Joy C. RUFF
38 Director Student Advisement .... Mr. Jose RODRIGUEZ
84 Director Enrollment Management .... Vacant
96 Director of Purchasing .... Mr. Roman MARTINEZ
41 Director Athletics & Student Life .... Mr. Anthony FIORENZA
09 Director of Institutional Research .... Dr. Silvio RODRIGUEZ
43 Legal Counsel .... Ms. Carmen DOMINGUEZ
86 Director Governmental Affairs .... Ms. Victoria HERNANDEZ
100 Chief of Staff .... Mr. George ANDREWS
103 Exec Dir Workforce Educ & Partnrshp .... Ms. Cheryl BALDWIN
104 Director Study Abroad .... Ms. Carol REYES
105 College Webmaster .... Mr. Andrew SEAGA
08 Head Librarian/Dir Lrng Resources .... Mr. Erick DOMINICIS
85 Director Intl Student Services .... Ms. Anoush MCNAMEE
22 Dir Affirmative Action/EEO .... Dr. Joy C. RUFF

Miami International University of Art & Design (E)

1501 Biscayne Boulevard, Suite 100,
Miami FL 33132-1418
County: Miami-Dade FICE Identification: 008878
Unit ID: 134811
Telephone: (305) 428-5700 Carnegie Class: Spec-4-yr-Arts
FAX Number: (305) 374-7946 Calendar System: Quarter
URL: www.artinstitutes.edu/miami
Established: 1965 Annual Undergrad Tuition & Fees: $17,700
Enrollment: 2,846 Coed
Affiliation or Control: Proprietary IRS Status: Proprietary
Highest Offering: Master's
Accreditation: SC, CIDA

01 President .... Ms. Erika FLEMING
05 Dean of Academic Affairs .... Dr. Paul COX
10 Dir Admin & Financial Services .... Ms. Leslie THEROULDE
32 Dean of Student Affairs .... Mr. John OSBORNE
07 Senior Director of Admissions .... Mr. Kevin RYAN
08 Librarian .... Ms. Kiara NOLAN

Miami Regional University (F)

700 S. Royal Poinciana Blvd, Miami Springs FL 33166
County: Miami-Dade FICE Identification: 041284
Unit ID: 451103
Telephone: (305) 442-9223 Carnegie Class: Spec 2-yr-Health
FAX Number: (305) 442-8723 Calendar System: Other
URL: www.mru.edu
Established: 1996 Annual Undergrad Tuition & Fees: N/A
Enrollment: 708 Coed
Affiliation or Control: Proprietary IRS Status: Proprietary
Highest Offering: Master's
Accreditation: ACICS

01 President & CEO .... Ophelia SANCHEZ
03 Executive Vice President .... Ophelia VALLS
05 Chief Academic Officer .... Jay OBER
07 Director of Admissions .... Fernando MACHADO
08 Librarian .... Tammy OLIVERA
10 Chief Business Officer .... Henry BABANI
15 VP Employment Affairs .... Mitsy SOUSA
36 Director Student Placement .... Randy BREITER
37 Director Student Financial Aid .... Marcie SILVA

Millennia Atlantic University (G)

3801 NW 97th Avenue, Doral FL 33178
County: Miami-Dade FICE Identification: 041825
Unit ID: 461883
Telephone: (786) 331-1000 Carnegie Class: Spec-4-yr-Bus
FAX Number: (305) 503-9680 Calendar System: Semester
URL: www.maufl.edu
Established: Annual Undergrad Tuition & Fees: $9,332
Enrollment: 239 Coed
Affiliation or Control: Proprietary IRS Status: Proprietary
Highest Offering: Master's
Accreditation: ACICS

01 President .... Dr. Aristides MAZA-DUERTO
00 Chancellor .... Mr. Luis E. MARTINEZ
10 CFO .... Mrs. Orianna M. MOSS
05 Director of Academic Program .... Mrs. Teresa FITZGERALD
06 Registrar .... Ms. Natasha ALEONG
37 Financial Aid Manager .... Mrs. Karen TERRY
26 Coord of Marketing & Public Rels .... Vacant
36 Student Services and Placement Mgr .... Mrs. Kimberly SABOURIN
07 Director of Admissions .... Mrs. Anna HERNANDEZ
08 Librarian .... Mr. James SWANER
88 Bursar .... Mrs. Jenice MAZA

North Florida Community College (H)

325 NW Turner Davis Drive, Madison FL 32340-1610
County: Madison FICE Identification: 001508
Unit ID: 136145
Telephone: (850) 973-2288 Carnegie Class: Assoc/MT-VT-Mix Trad/Non
FAX Number: (850) 973-1696 Calendar System: Semester
URL: www.nfcc.edu
Established: 1958 Annual Undergrad Tuition & Fees (In-State): $3,054
Enrollment: 1,289 Coed
Affiliation or Control: State IRS Status: 501(c)3
Highest Offering: Associate Degree
Accreditation: SC

01 President .... Mr. John GROSSKOPF
05 Dean of Academic Affairs/CAO .... Ms. Frances ADLEBURG
10 Dean Administrative Svcs & CBO .... Mr. Andrew BARNES
07 Dean of Enrollment/Student Services .... Ms. Kay HOGAN
09 Manager of Networking Systems .... Mr. John SIRMON
15 Director of Personnel Services .... Mr. Bill HUNTER
08 Head Librarian .... Ms. Lynn WYCHE
88 SSS and Disability Coordinator .... Dr. Suzie CASHWELL
88 Director of Public Safety Academy .... Mr. Rick DAVIS
06 Registrar .... Ms. Lori PLEASANT
18 Chief Facilities/Physical Plant .... Mr. Dale HACKLE
26 Public Information Officer .... Ms. Kim SCARBORO
29 Dir Foundation Alumni Relations .... Dr. Cheryl JAMES
37 Director Student Financial Aid .... Ms. Amelia MULKEY
28 Director of Diversity .... Ms. Denise BELL
96 Director of Purchasing .... Ms. Sarah NEWSOME
04 Executive Asst to President .... Ms. Cindy M. GAYLARD
103 Dir Workforce/Career Development .... Mr. David DUNKLE
19 Director Security/Safety .... Mr. Skip JAMES

Northwest Florida State College (I)

100 College Boulevard, Niceville FL 32578-1295
County: Okaloosa FICE Identification: 001510
Unit ID: 136233
Telephone: (850) 678-5111 Carnegie Class: Bac/Assoc-Mixed
FAX Number: (850) 729-5215 Calendar System: Semester
URL: www.nwfsc.edu
Established: 1963 Annual Undergrad Tuition & Fees (In-State): $3,123
Enrollment: 6,295 Coed
Affiliation or Control: State IRS Status: 501(c)3
Highest Offering: Baccalaureate
Accreditation: SC, ADNUR, DA, EMT, NURSE

01 Interim President .... Dr. Sasha JARRELL
05 Acting VP for Academic Affairs .... Dr. Anne JARRELL
11 Vice Pres Administrative Services .... Mr. Randy WHITE
30 Vice Pres College Advancement .... Mrs. Cristie KEDROSKI
13 Chief Information Officer .... Mr. Greg ELLER
09 Director of Institutional Research .... Dr. Diane W. HODGINS
15 Director Human Resources/Diversity .... Ms. Nancy MURPHY
07 Director of Admissions .... Ms. Karyn COOPER
29 Assoc Director for Resource/Alumni .... Ms. Carla REINLIE
41 Athletic Director .... Mr. Ramsey ROSS
37 Director Financial Aid/Veteran Affs .... Ms. Patricia BENNETT
18 Facilities Director .... Mr. Sam JONES
88 Director Academic Advising .... Ms. Marlayna GOOSBY
08 Director Learning Resources Center .... Ms. Janice HENDERSON
26 Director Marketing/Public Relations .... Ms. Stephanie PETTIS
96 Coordinator of Purchasing .... Ms. Dedria LUNDERMAN
32 Dean of Students .... Dr. Aimee WATTS
04 Admin Assistant to President .... Ms. Carolyne LAUX
06 Registrar .... Ms. Bree DURHAM
106 Director of Online Education .... Mr. Syed HASNAIN
75 Dean of Career & Technical Educ .... Mr. Dennis SHERWOOD
97 Acting Dean of Education .... Dr. Deborah FONTAINE
35 Assoc Dean of Students .... Ms. Olivia MONET
19 Director Security/Safety .... Mr. William LOOPER
25 Grants Admin .... Dr. Anne SOUTHARD

Nova Southeastern University (J)

3301 College Avenue, Fort Lauderdale FL 33314-7796
County: Broward FICE Identification: 001509
Unit ID: 136215
Telephone: (954) 262-7300 Carnegie Class: DU-Higher
FAX Number: (954) 262-3800 Calendar System: Trimester
URL: www.nova.edu
Established: 1964 Annual Undergrad Tuition & Fees: $27,660
Enrollment: 24,148 Coed
Affiliation or Control: Independent Non-Profit IRS Status: 501(c)3
Highest Offering: Doctorate
Accreditation: SC, AA, ACAE, ARCPA, AUD, CAATE, CLPSY, #COARC, CVT, DENT, DMS, IACBE, IPSY, LAW, MFCD, NURSE, OPT, OPTR, OSTEO, OT, PH, PHAR, PTA, SCPSY, SP, SPAA, TED

01 President & CEO .... Dr. George L. HANBURY, II
05 Provost & Exec VP Academic Affairs .... Dr. Ralph V. ROGERS
11 Exec Vice President/COO .... Ms. Jacqueline A. TRAVISANO
10 VP Finance/CFO .... Ms. Alyson SILVA
00 Chancellor Nova Southeastern Univ .... Mr. Ray FERRERO, JR.
00 University President Emeritus .... Dr. Abraham FISCHLER
17 Chancellor Health Professions Div .... Dr. Fred LIPPMAN
20 Exec Dean for Administration .... Dr. Irving ROSENBAUM
88 SVP Transitional Rsrch & Econ Dev .... Dr. H. Thomas TEMPLE
08 VP Info Svcs/Univ Librarian .... Ms. Lydia M. ACOSTA
43 VP Legal Affairs .... Mr. Joel BERMAN
46 VP Research Tech Transfer .... Dr. Gary S. MARGULES
32 VP Student Affairs/Dean UG Studies .... Dr. Brad WILLIAMS
30 VP Inst Advancement .... Dr. Jennifer O'FLANNERY ANDERSON
13 VP Info Tech/Chief Info Ofcr .... Mr. Tom WEST
15 VP Human Resources .... Mr. Robert J. PIETRYKOWSKI
37 VP Enrollment and Stdnt Svcs .... Dr. Stephanie BROWN
21 VP Business Services .... Mr. Marc CROCQUET
106 VP Reg Campus & Online Educ .... Mr. Ricardo BELMAR
18 Interim VP Facilities Mgmt .... Mrs. Jessica BRUMLEY
26 Int Exec Director Univ Relations .... Mr. Brandon HENSLER
19 Director Public Safety .... Mr. James EWING
09 VP Institutional Effectiveness .... Dr. Donald J. RUDAWSKY
20 Associate Provost .... Dr. Ronald CHENAIL
88 Director Accreditation .... Ms. Jane DUNCAN
24 Exec Dir Ed Tech/Digital Media Prod .... Ms. Diane LIPPE

25 Director Sponsored Programs .... Ms. Cathy HARLAN
86 Exec Dir Licensure/State Relations .... Dr. Greg F. STIBER
12 Headmaster University School .... Mr. William KOPAS
27 Director University Publications .... Mr. Ron RYAN
27 Director Public Affairs .... Ms. Julie SPECHLER
36 Director of Career Development .... Ms. Shari SAPERSTEIN
29 Director of Alumni Relations .... Mr. R.J STAMPER
06 Dir University Registrar's Office .... Ms. G. Elaine N. POFF
41 Director Athletics .... Mr. Michael MOMINEY
88 Director Campus Recreation .... Mr. Tom VITUCCI
88 Executive Dir Internal Auditing .... Mr. Ron MIDEI
31 Exec Dir Inst & Comm Engagement ... Dr. Barbara PACKER-MUTI
88 VP Compliance/Chief Integrity Ofcr .... Ms. Robin SUPLER
88 Dir Museum of Art .... Ms. Bonnie CLEARWATER
63 Dean College Osteopathic Medicine .... Ms. Elaine WALLACE
67 Dean College Pharmacy .... Dr. Lisa DEZIEL
23 Vice Pres Clinical Operations .... Mr. Kelly GREGG
88 Dean College Optometry .... Dr. David LOSHIN
76 Dean College of Hlth Care Sciences .... Dr. Stanley WILSON
77 Dean Grad Sch Computer/Info Sci .... Dr. Amon SEAGULL
61 Dean Shepard Broad Law Center .... Mr. Jon GARON
65 Dean Oceanographic Center .... Dr. Richard DODGE
66 Dean College of Nursing .... Dr. Marcella M. RUTHERFORD
50 Dn W Huizenga Grad Sch Bus/Entr .... Dr. J. Preston JONES
92 Dean Farquhar Honors College .... Dr. Donald ROSENBLUM
88 Dean Center Psychological Stds .... Dr. Karen GROSBY
83 Dean Grad Sch Humanities/Social Sci .... Dr. Honggang YANG
88 Dean Mailman Ctr for Human Devel .... Dr. Roni LEIDERMAN
63 Dean College of Medical Sciences .... Dr. Harold LAUBAUCH
83 Dean Inst Study Hum Svcs/Hlth/Just .... Dr. Kimberly DURHAM
52 Dean of Dental Medicine .... Dr. Linda NIESSEN
53 Dean Fischler College of Educ .... Dr. Lynne SCHRUM
88 Dean College Allopathic Med .... Dr. Johannes VIEWEG

Orion College (A)

51 North State Road 7, Plantation FL 33317
County: Broward FICE Identification: 041359
Unit ID: 454883
Telephone: (866) 251-3244 Carnegie Class: Spec 2-yr-Health
FAX Number: (877) 493-7416 Calendar System: Other
URL: www.orioncollege.org
Established: 2004 Annual Undergrad Tuition & Fees: $12,304
Enrollment: 441 Coed
Affiliation or Control: Proprietary IRS Status: Proprietary
Highest Offering: Associate Degree
Accreditation: ABHES

01 President .... Jennifer ANGLIN
03 Vice President .... Sondra GERHOFF

Orlando Medical Institute (B)

6220 S. Orange Blossom Tr, Ste 410, Orlando FL 32809
County: Orange Identification: 667127
Telephone: (407) 251-0007 Carnegie Class: Not Classified
FAX Number: (407) 251-0352 Calendar System: Semester
URL: www.omi.edu
Established: 2004 Annual Undergrad Tuition & Fees: N/A
Enrollment: N/A Coed
Affiliation or Control: Proprietary IRS Status: Proprietary
Highest Offering: Associate Degree
Accreditation: ABHES

01 President .... Felix J. MARQUEZ, JR.
11 Vice Pres/Director Operations .... Abigail MARQUEZ

Palm Beach Atlantic University (C)

901 S. Flagler Drive, West Palm Beach FL 33401
County: Palm Beach FICE Identification: 008849
Unit ID: 136330
Telephone: (561) 803-2000 Carnegie Class: Masters/L
FAX Number: (561) 803-2186 Calendar System: Semester
URL: www.pba.edu
Established: 1968 Annual Undergrad Tuition & Fees: $27,150
Enrollment: 3,865 Coed
Affiliation or Control: Interdenominational IRS Status: 501(c)3
Highest Offering: Doctorate
Accreditation: SC, #CAATE, IACBE, MUS, NURSE, PHAR

01 President .... Mr. William M. FLEMING
05 Provost .... Dr. Gene FANT, JR.
10 Sr VP for Finance Admin & Plng .... Mr. John KAUTZ, III
30 Vice President Development .... Mrs. Vicki PUGH
07 Vice President for Admissions .... Mr. Tim WORLEY
04 Executive Asst to President .... Vacant
09 Asst Provost Rsrch/Effectiveness .... Mrs. Carolanne BROWN
13 Assoc VP Campus Information Svcs .... Mr. Phillip MAJOR
26 Assoc VP Univ Relations & Marketing .... Mrs. Rebecca PEELING
51 Dean MacArthur School of Leadership .... Dr. Craig DOMECK
49 Dean School of Arts & Sciences .... Dr. Robert LLOYD
50 Dean School of Business .... Dr. Leslie TURNER
53 Dean School of Education .... Dr. Gene SALE
57 Dean School of Music/Fine Arts .... Dr. Lloyd MIMS
66 Dean School of Nursing .... Dr. Joanne MASELLA
67 Dean Gregory School of Pharmacy .... Dr. Jeff LEWIS
60 Dean School Communication/Media .... Dr. J. Duane MEEKS
73 Dean School of Ministry .... Dr. Randy RICHARDS
06 Registrar .... Ms. Audrey SCHOFIELD
08 Dean of the Library .... Mr. Steven BAKER
20 Dean of Faculty .... Vacant
15 Assoc VP of Human Resources .... Ms. Mona L. HICKS
32 Dean of Students .... Mr. Kevin ABEL
18 Director of Physical Plant .... Mr. Matt STEVENS
21 Controller .... Mrs. Carla CROW
29 AVP Alumni Relations/Annual Fund .... Mrs. Delesa MORRIS
31 Dir of Campus and Community Events .... Mrs. Mary WARD
35 Assistant Dean of Students .... Mr. Bob LUTZ
37 Director of Financial Aid .... Mrs. Jen MCMAHON
40 Director of Campus Store .... Mrs. Abbie ROSEMEYER
41 Director of Athletics .... Mrs. Carolyn STONE
42 Director of Campus Ministries .... Mr. Mark KAPRIVE
92 Director of Supper Honors Program .... Dr. Tom ST. ANTOINE

Palm Beach State College (D)

4200 Congress Avenue, Lake Worth FL 33461-4796
County: Palm Beach FICE Identification: 001512
Unit ID: 136358
Telephone: (561) 967-7222 Carnegie Class: Bac/Assoc-Assoc Dom
FAX Number: (561) 868-3504 Calendar System: Semester
URL: www.palmbeachstate.edu
Established: 1933 Annual Undergrad Tuition & Fees (In-State): $2,444
Enrollment: 28,517 Coed
Affiliation or Control: State IRS Status: 501(c)3
Highest Offering: Baccalaureate
Accreditation: SC, ADNUR, CAHIIM, COARC, DA, DH, DMS, EMT, MAC, NUR, RAD, SURGT

01 President .... Ms. Ava L. PARKER
05 Vice President Academic Affairs .... Dr. Roger YOHE
10 Vice President Admin/Business Svcs .... Mr. Richard A. BECKER
32 Vice President Student Services .... Dr. Peter BARBATIS
13 Vice President Information Svcs .... Dr. Ginger L. PEDERSEN
31 Exec Director Community Engagement .... Ms. Rachael E. ONDRUS
43 General Counsel .... Mr. Kevin A. FERNANDER
30 Exec Director Foundation .... Ms. Suellen MANN
12 Provost Belle Glade .... Dr. Maria M. VALLEJO
12 Provost Boca Raton .... Dr. Bernadette MENDONEZ RUSSELL
12 Provost Palm Beach Gardens .... Dr. Holly L. BENNETT
12 Provost Lake Worth .... Dr. Jean WIHBEY
75 Dean Business/Trade & Industry .... Ms. Patricia V. RICHIE
76 Dean Health Science & Publ Safety .... Dr. Jacqueline ROGERS
97 Dean Academic Affairs Lake Worth .... Dr. Irving BERKOWITZ
97 Dean Academic Affairs PB Gardens .... Mr. Edward W. WILLEY
97 Dean Academic Affairs Belle Glade .... Dr. Roy M. VARGAS
97 Dean Academic Affairs Boca Raton .... Dr. Tunjarnika L. COLEMAN-FERRELL
88 Dean Bachelor Degree Programs .... Dr. Anita S. KAPLAN
20 Interim Dean Curriculum/Educ Tech .... Ms. Susan BIERSTER
35 Dean Student Services Lake Worth .... Ms. Penny J. MCISAAC
35 Dean Student Services Boca Raton .... Dr. Sheri E. GOLDSTEIN
35 Dean Student Services PB Gardens .... Mr. Scott MACLACHLAN
35 Asst Dean Student Svc Belle Glade .... Ms. Latanya L. MCNEAL
84 Dean Enrollment Management .... Mr. Chuck H. ZETTLER
37 Director Financial Aid .... Mr. Eddie VIERA
41 Athletics Director .... Dr. David HOLSTEIN
09 Exec Dir Inst Rsrch/Effectiveness .... Dr. Donald W. TAYLOR
18 Facilities Director .... Mr. John T. WASUKANIS
15 Exec Director Human Resources .... Ms. Barbara MATIAS
26 Dir College Relations & Marketing .... Dr. Grace H. TRUMAN
21 Controller .... Mr. James E. DUFFIE
06 College Registrar .... Ms. Amy L. MCDONALD
96 Procurement Director .... Mr. David CHOJNACKI
13 Chief Information Officer .... Vacant
25 Dir Resource & Grant Development .... Ms. Maureen CAPP
106 E-Learning Director .... Mr. Sidney BEITLER
108 Assessment Director .... Dr. Karen D. PAIN
19 Security & Risk Management Director .... Mr. John E. SMITH

Palmer College of Chiropractic, Port Orange Campus (E)

4777 City Center Parkway, Port Orange FL 32129-4153
Telephone: (386) 763-2709 Identification: 666330
Accreditation: &NH, &CHIRO

† Regional accreditation is carried under the parent institution in Davenport, IA.

Pasco-Hernando State College (F)

10230 Ridge Road, New Port Richey FL 34654-5199
County: Pasco FICE Identification: 010652
Unit ID: 136400
Telephone: (727) 847-2727 Carnegie Class: Bac/Assoc-Assoc Dom
FAX Number: (727) 816-1815 Calendar System: Semester
URL: www.phsc.edu
Established: 1972 Annual Undergrad Tuition & Fees (In-District): $3,155
Enrollment: 11,263 Coed
Affiliation or Control: State/Local IRS Status: 501(c)3
Highest Offering: Baccalaureate
Accreditation: SC, ADNUR, DH, EMT, NURSE

01 President .... Dr. Timothy L. BEARD
05 VP Acad Affs & Fac Dev/Col Provost .... Dr. Stanley M. GIANNET
32 VP Stdnt Affairs/Enrollment Mgmt .... Dr. Robert E. BADE
10 Vice Pres Administration & Finance .... Mr. Kenneth R. BURDZINSKI
12 Provost of the East Campus .... Dr. Lisa A. RICHARDSON
12 Provost North Campus .... Dr. Donna R. BURDZINSKI
12 Provost Spring Hill Campus .... Dr. Amy ANDERSON
12 Provost Porter Campus at Wiregrass .... Vacant
103 Dean of Workforce Development .... Mr. Edwin G. GOOLSBY
13 VP of Technology & Distance Educ .... Dr. Melissa L. HARTS
35 Dean Stdnt Dev & Enroll Mgmt .... Ms. Chiquita A. HENDERSON
20 Assoc Dean of Acad Aff & Inst Accr .... Dr. Kevin F. O'FARRELL
49 Dean Arts and Sciences .... Vacant
21 Asst VP Admin/Finance/Comptroller .... Mr. Brian S. HORN
09 Dean Institutional Effectiveness .... Dr. Gerardine K. COCHRAN
13 Exec Dir Management Info Svcs .... Ms. Janice L. SCOTT
30 Asst VP Inst Advance/Exec Dir Fnd .... Dr. William J. SHUSTOWSKI, JR.
66 Associate Dean of Nursing .. Dr. Barbara SOUTHWORTH-FISHER
07 Dir Admissions & Student Records .... Mr. Chris BIBBO
37 Dean Financial Aid .... Ms. Rebecca SHANAFELT
43 Asst VP of Policy/General Counsel . Mr. Stephen C. SCHROEDER
08 Director of Libraries .... Mr. Raymond J. CALVERT
41 Athletics Director/Instructor .... Mr. Stephen A. WINTERLING
26 Exec Dir Marketing/Public Relation .... Ms. Lucy T. MILLER
18 Director of Facilities .... Mr. Keith V. BRAUN
15 Exec Director of Human Resources .... Ms. Vivian M. FRIEND
109 Auxiliary Services Manager .... Mr. John D. COLLINS
35 Asst Dean Stdnt Aff/Engage/Spec Svc .... Dr. Katie M. BOWMAN
22 Dir of Global & Multi Aware & Spec .... Mr. Imani D. ASUKILE
96 Purchasing Agent .... Ms. Michelle L. SWINGLE
04 Executive Asst to President & DBOT .... Ms. Rhonda M. DODGE
29 Director Alumni & Donor Relations .... Ms. Michelle L. BULLWINKEL

Pensacola Christian College (G)

250 Brent Lane, Pensacola FL 32503
County: Escambia Identification: 667101
Telephone: (850) 478-8496 Carnegie Class: Not Classified
FAX Number: (850) 479-6577 Calendar System: Semester
URL: www.pcci.edu
Established: 1974 Annual Undergrad Tuition & Fees: N/A
Enrollment: N/A Coed
Affiliation or Control: Independent Non-Profit IRS Status: 501(c)3
Highest Offering: Doctorate
Accreditation: TRACS, ENG, NURSE

01 President .... Dr. Troy SHOEMAKER
03 Vice President/Exec Asst to Pres .... Dr. Joel MULLENIX
32 Vice Pres Student Life .... Dr. Paul OHMAN
10 Chief Financial Officer .... Mr. Gary EAST
06 Registrar .... Ms. Linda TROUTMAN

Pensacola State College (H)

1000 College Boulevard, Pensacola FL 32504-8998
County: Escambia FICE Identification: 001513
Unit ID: 136473
Telephone: (850) 484-1000 Carnegie Class: Bac/Assoc-Assoc Dom
FAX Number: (850) 484-1826 Calendar System: Semester
URL: www.pensacolastate.edu
Established: 1948 Annual Undergrad Tuition & Fees (In-District): $2,704
Enrollment: 10,317 Coed
Affiliation or Control: Local IRS Status: 501(c)3
Highest Offering: Baccalaureate
Accreditation: SC, ACFEI, ADNUR, CAHIIM, DH, EMT, MAC, NUR, NURSE, PNUR, PTAA, RAD, SURGT

01 President .... Dr. Ed MEADOWS
05 Vice Pres for Academic Affairs .... Dr. Erin SPICER
32 Vice President Student Affairs .... Mr. Tom GILLIAM
10 Vice President for Business .... Mrs. Gean Ann EMOND
103 Dean Workforce Educ/Vocational Supp .... Mr. Dan BUSSE
12 Dean Milton Campus .... Ms. Anthea AMOS
12 Dean Warrington Campus .... Ms. Frances DUNCAN
28 Assoc Vice Pres Inst Diversity .... Dr. Gael FRAZER
102 Exec Director College Foundation .... Mr. Aaron WEST
13 Executive Director ITS .... Mr. Bert MERRITT
86 Director of Govt Relations .... Ms. Sandy RAY
26 Director Marketing & College Info .... Ms. Sheila NICHOLS
06 Registrar .... Ms. Martha CAUGHEY
09 Dean Inst Research & Grants .... Dr. Debbie DOUMA
18 Director Physical Plant .... Mr. Walt WINTER
14 Director Technology Support .... Ms. Liz GOMEZ
15 Director Human Resources/EA/EO .... Ms. Tammy HENDERSON
37 Dir Fin Aid/Veteran Affairs/Scholar .... Ms. Karen KESSLER
36 Coordinator Student Job Services .... Ms. Sherry DUFFEY
19 Public Safety Director .... Mr. Hank SHIRAH
43 General Counsel .... Mr. Thomas J. GILLIAM
08 District Dept Head Libraries .... Ms. Lisa Marie BARTUSIK
96 Director of Purchasing .... Ms. Cassie BOATWRIGHT
21 Associate Business Officer .... Ms. Jackie PADILLA
29 Exec Director Alumni Affairs .... Ms. Patrice WHITTEN
07 Director of Admissions .... Ms. Martha CAUGHEY
38 Director Student Counseling .... Ms. Monique COLLINS
41 Director Athletics .... Mr. Bill HAMILTON
84 Dean Enrollment Services .... Ms. Kathy DUTREMBLE
12 Director South Santa Rosa Center .... Ms. Michele HORTON
12 Director Century Center .... Ms. Paula BYRD
31 Coordinator Community Education .... Ms. Frances YEO
04 Executive Asst to President .... Ms. Patricia S. CREWS
106 Dir Online Education/E-learning .... Dr. Bill WATERS
108 Director Institutional Research .... Mr. Michael JOHNSTON

Polk State College (I)

999 Avenue H, NE, Winter Haven FL 33881-4299
County: Polk FICE Identification: 001514
Unit ID: 136516
Telephone: (863) 297-1000 Carnegie Class: Bac/Assoc-Mixed
FAX Number: (863) 297-1065 Calendar System: Trimester

URL: www.polk.edu
Established: 1964 Annual Undergrad Tuition & Fees (In-District): $3,366
Enrollment: 11,060 Coed
Affiliation or Control: Local IRS Status: 501(c)3
Highest Offering: Baccalaureate
Accreditation: SC, ADNUR, COARC, CVT, DMS, EMT, NUR, OTA, PTAA, RAD

01 President Dr. Eileen HOLDEN
10 Vice Pres Administrative Svcs/CFO Mr. Peter ELLIOTT
05 Vice Pres Academic Affairs Dr. Ken ROSS
32 Vice Pres Student Services Mr. Reginal WEBB
30 Vice Pres Inst Advanc/Exec Dir PSCF Ms. Tracy PORTER
12 Campus Provost-LK Mr. Stephen HULL
12 Campus Provost-WH Dr. Martha SANTIAGO
88 AVP Strategic Initiatives Dr. Naomi BOYER
26 AVP Communications & Public Affs Ms. Tamara SAKAGAWA
20 District Dean Academic Affairs Dr. Orathai NORTHERN
15 Director Human Resources Ms. Jill HALL
35 Dean Student Services-WH Mr. Lawrence PAKOWSKI
35 Dean Student Services-LK Mr. Sylvester LITTLE
20 Dean Academic Affairs-WH Ms. April ROBINSON
20 Dean Academic Affairs-LK Mr. Donald PAINTER
21 Controller Ms. Teresa VOROUS
06 Director Stdnt Enrollment/Registrar Ms. Kathy BUCKLEW
37 Director Student Financial Svcs Ms. Marcia CONLIFFE
66 Director Nursing Dr. Annette HUTCHERSON
102 Director Financial Affs/PSC Found Mr. Lynn WILSON
18 Director Facilities Mr. George URBANO
22 Director Equity & Diversity Ms. Valparisa BAKER
103 Director Corporate College Mr. Robert CLANCEY
88 Principal Chain of Lakes CHS Ms. Bridget FETTER
88 Principal Lakeland Col HS Mr. Rick JEFFRIES
88 Center Director JDA Dr. Martha SANTIAGO
88 Associate Dean Student Svcs-LK Ms. Michelle SAMS
88 Associate Dean Student Svcs-WH Ms. Yulonda BELL
88 Associate Dean Academic Affs-LK Ms. Gerene THOMPSON
88 Associate Dean Academic Affs-WH Vacant
41 Athletic Director Mr. Bing TYUS
96 Director Purchasing Mr. Mark LILLQUIST
86 Director Government Relations Vacant

Polytechnic University of Puerto Rico (A)

8180 NW 36th Street, Suite 401, Miami FL 33166-6674
Telephone: (305) 418-8000 Identification: 666238
Accreditation: &M

† Regional accreditation is carried under the parent institution, Universidad Politecnica de Puerto Rico, San Juan, PR.

Polytechnic University of Puerto Rico-Orlando Campus (B)

550 N Econlockhatchee Trail, Orlando FL 32825
Telephone: (407) 677-7000 Identification: 770172
Accreditation: &M

† Regional accreditation is carried under the parent institution in San Juan, PR

The Praxis Institute (C)

1850 SW 8th Street, 4th Floor, Miami FL 33135
County: Miami-Dade FICE Identification: 031147
Unit ID: 430532
Telephone: (305) 642-4104 Carnegie Class: Not Classified
FAX Number: N/A Calendar System: Semester
URL: the-praxisinstitute.com
Established: 1988 Annual Undergrad Tuition & Fees: N/A
Enrollment: 365 Coed
Affiliation or Control: Proprietary IRS Status: Proprietary
Highest Offering: Associate Degree
Accreditation: COE, OTA, PTAA

01 Executive Director Rebeca ALFIE

Premiere International College (D)

2055 Central Avenue, Fort Myers FL 33901
County: Palm Beach Identification: 667295
Telephone: (239) 454-5000 Carnegie Class: Not Classified
FAX Number: (239) 454-0456 Calendar System: Quarter
URL: www.premierecollege.com
Established: 2009 Annual Undergrad Tuition & Fees: N/A
Enrollment: N/A Coed
Affiliation or Control: Proprietary IRS Status: Proprietary
Highest Offering: Associate Degree
Accreditation: ACICS

01 President Cynthia RUE

Professional Hands Institute (E)

3383 NW 7th Street, Suite 200, Miami FL 33125
County: Miami-Dade FICE Identification: 041431
Unit ID: 454908
Telephone: (305) 442-6011 Carnegie Class: Not Classified
FAX Number: (305) 442-6013 Calendar System: Semester
URL: www.prohands.edu
Established: 2004 Annual Undergrad Tuition & Fees: N/A
Enrollment: 37 Coed
Affiliation or Control: Proprietary IRS Status: Proprietary
Highest Offering: Associate Degree
Accreditation: COE

12 Campus Director Ms. Caridad TRIANA

Rasmussen College - Fort Myers (F)

9160 Forum Corporate Parkway, Fort Myers FL 33905
Telephone: (239) 477-2100 Identification: 667062
Accreditation: &NH, MAAB

† Regional accreditation is carried under the parent institution in Saint Cloud, MN. The tuition figure is an average, actual tuition may vary.

Rasmussen College - Land O'Lakes (G)

18600 Fernview Street, Land O'Lakes FL 34638
Telephone: (813) 435-3601 Identification: 770488
Accreditation: &NH, PNUR

† Regional accreditation carried under the parent institution in Saint Cloud, MN. The tuition figure is an average, actual tuition may vary.

Rasmussen College - New Port Richey (H)

8661 Citizens Drive, Suite 300, New Port Richey FL 34654
Telephone: (727) 942-0069 Identification: 666425
Accreditation: &NH, ADNUR, MAAB

† Regional accreditation is carried under parent institution in Saint Cloud, MN. The tuition figure is an average, actual tuition may vary.

Rasmussen College - Ocala (I)

4755 SW 46th Court, Ocala FL 34474
Telephone: (352) 629-1941 FICE Identification 008501
Accreditation: &NH, ADNUR, MAAB

† Regional accreditation carried under the parent institution in Saint Cloud, MN. The tuition figure is an average, actual tuition may vary.

Rasmussen College - Tampa/Brandon (J)

4042 Park Oaks Boulevard, Tampa FL 33610
Telephone: (813) 246-7600 Identification 667067
Accreditation: &NH, MAAB

† Regional accreditation is carried under the parent institution in Saint Cloud, MN. The tuition figure is an average, actual tuition may vary.

Reformed Theological Seminary (K)

1231 Reformation Drive, Oviedo FL 32765-7197
Telephone: (407) 366-9493 Identification 666628
Accreditation: &SC, THEOL

† Regional accreditation is carried under the parent institution in Jackson, MS.

Remington College Online (L)

500 International Pkwy, Suite 200, Heathrow FL 33612-5627
Telephone: (407) 562-5671 Identification 770567
Accreditation: ACCSC, OTA

† Branch campus of Remington College-Dallas Campus, Garland, TX

Ringling College of Art and Design (M)

2700 N Tamiami Trail, Sarasota FL 34234-5895
County Sarasota FICE Identification: 012574
Unit ID: 136774
Telephone: (941) 351-5100 Carnegie Class: Spec-4-yr-Arts
FAX Number: (941) 359-7517 Calendar System Semester
URL: www.ringling.edu
Established 1931 Annual Undergrad Tuition & Fees: $42,020
Enrollment: 1,219 Coed
Affiliation or Control: Independent Non-Profit IRS Status: 501(c)3
Highest Offering: Baccalaureate
Accreditation: SC, ART, CIDA

01 President Dr. Larry R. THOMPSON
04 Exec Assistant to President Ms. Cathy GAGLIARDI
05 Co-Int VP Academic Affairs/Dean Fac Mr. Jeff SCHWARTZ
05 Co-Int VP Academic Affairs/Dean Fac Mr. David H. JACKSON
30 Vice Pres Advancement Ms. Stacey CORLEY
10 Vice President for Finance & Admin Ms. Tracy A. WAGNER
15 VP Human/Organizational Development Ms. Christine C. DEGEORGE
32 Vice Pres Student Life/Dean Stdnts Dr. Tammy S. WALSH
20 Assoc VP Academics/Faculty Affairs Mr. David H. JACKSON
21 Asst VP for Fin & Admn/Controller Ms. Monica K. WAID
18 Asst VP/Dir Facilities Operations Mr. Jeffrey A. POLESHEK
07 Dean of Admissions Mr. James H. DEAN
51 Asst VP/Dir Continuing Stds/Sp Pgms Mr. Jerry BLADDICK
06 Registrar Mr. Justin SELPH
90 Director Institutional Technology Ms. Kris PEGAH
36 Director Career Services Mr. Charles KOVACS
19 Director of Public Safety Mr. Richard E. TUBBS

The Robert E. Webber Institute for Worship Studies (N)

4001 Hendricks Ave, Jacksonville FL 32207
County: Duval Identification: 666616
Telephone: (904) 264-2172 Carnegie Class: Not Classified
FAX Number: (904) 278-2878 Calendar System: Semester
URL: www.iws.edu
Established: 1998 Annual Graduate Tuition & Fees: N/A
Enrollment: N/A Coed
Affiliation or Control: Independent Non-Profit IRS Status: 501(c)3
Highest Offering: Doctorate; No Undergraduates
Accreditation: BI

01 Chief Executive Officer Dr. James R. HART
05 Chief Academic Officer Dr. Eric H. OHLMANN
10 Chief Financial Officer Ms. Christi G. MATTESON
06 Registrar Vacant
84 VP of Enrollment Management Mr. Mark J. MURRAY
08 Library Director Ms. Susan A. MASSEY
29 Director Alumni Relations Dr. Kent L. WALTERS
42 Dean of the Chapel Dr. Darrell A. HARRIS
88 Dir of Technical Services Mr. Samuel L. HOROWITZ
04 Asst to the President Vacant
32 Dir Student Services/Office Admin Ms. Sandy E. DINKINS
45 Dir Strategic Plng/Accreditation Dr. Steve E. HUNTLEY
13 Coordinator of Info Technology Dr. James Kenneth RUSHING
26 Dir of Missional Relations Dr. Frank FORTUNATO
30 Director of Advancement Vacant

Rollins College (O)

1000 Holt Avenue, Winter Park FL 32789-4499
County: Orange FICE Identification: 001515
Unit ID: 136950
Telephone: (407) 646-2000 Carnegie Class: Masters/L
FAX Number: (407) 646-2600 Calendar System: Semester
URL: www.rollins.edu
Established: 1885 Annual Undergrad Tuition & Fees: $44,760
Enrollment: 3,207 Coed
Affiliation or Control: Independent Non-Profit IRS Status: 501(c)3
Highest Offering Doctorate
Accreditation: SC, BUS, CACREP, MUS

01 President Dr. Grant H. CORNWELL
05 VP Acad Affairs/Provost Dr. Susan R. SINGER
32 Vice President Student Affairs Dr. Mamta M. ACCAPADI
10 Vice President Business/Finance Mr. Jeffrey EISENBARTH
30 Interim VP for Inst Advancement Ms. Amanda R. HOPKINS
13 Chief Information Officer Dr. Pat SCHOKNECHT
49 Interim Dean of Arts & Sciences Dr. Jennifer CAVENAUGH
107 Dean of Professional Studies Dr. Debra WELLMAN
51 Dean of Hamilton Holt School Dr. David C. RICHARD
35 Asst VP Stdnt Affs & Dean of Stdnts Dr. Meghan HARTE WEYANT
84 VP of Enrollment Mgmt and Marketing Dr. Faye F. TYDLASKA
50 Dean Crummer Grad Sch of Bus Dr. Deborah F. CROWN
42 Dean of Religious Life Rev. Katrina JENKINS
21 Assoc VP Finance/Asst Treasurer Mr. William SHORT
26 Assoc VP Marketing & Communications Mr. Douglas L. CLARK
15 Assoc VP Human Res/Risk Management Ms. Maria MARTINEZ
108 Asst Provost Inst Effectiveness Dr. Toni STROLLO HOLBROOK
08 Director of Olin Library Dr. Jonathan MILLER
41 Athletic Director Ms. Pennie PARKER
37 Director of Financial Aid Mr. Steve BOOKER
09 Director of Institutional Research Mr. Udeth LUGO
104 Director of International Programs Ms. Giselda BEAUDIN
07 Director of Admission Ms. Holly POHLIG
39 Sr Dir Res Life & Explorations Mr. Leon HAYNER
36 Asst VP of Career & Life Planning Ms. Lisa JOHNSON
18 Director of Facilities Management Mr. Scott BITIKOFER
96 Asst VP of Business Services Dr. Pat SCHOKNECHT
19 Assistant VP Public Safety Mr. Ken MILLER
29 Senior Director of Alumni Relations Ms. Caitlin HACKENBERG
44 Assistant VP of Development Ms. Amanda HOPKINS
102 Director of Foundation Relations Mr. Joseph MONTI
06 Registrar Ms. Robin MATEO
40 Manager of Bookstore Ms. Mary VITELLI
04 Exec Assistant to the President Dr. Lorrie KYLE
23 Director of Wellness Ms. Connie BRISCOE
25 Director Contracts/Grants Admin Ms. Devon MASSOT
35 Asst VP Student Affairs/Community Ms. Michele MEYER
16 Director of Human Resources Mr. Matt HAWKS

Saber College (P)

3990 West Flagler Street, Ste 103, Miami FL 33134
County: Miami-Dade FICE Identification: 036964
Unit ID: 449506
Telephone: (305) 443-9170 Carnegie Class: Spec 2-yr-Health
FAX Number: (305) 443-8441 Calendar System: Other
URL: www.sabercollege.com
Established: 1972 Annual Undergrad Tuition & Fees: N/A
Enrollment: 600 Coed
Affiliation or Control: Independent Non-Profit IRS Status: 501(c)3
Highest Offering: Associate Degree
Accreditation: COE, @PTAA

01 Director Ms. Angela GAUD

St. John Vianney College Seminary (A)

2900 SW 87th Avenue, Miami FL 33165-3244
County: Miami-Dade FICE Identification: 008075
Unit ID: 137272
Telephone: (305) 223-4561 Carnegie Class: Spec-4-yr-Faith
FAX Number: (305) 223-0650 Calendar System: Semester
URL: www.sjvcs.edu
Established: 1959 Annual Undergrad Tuition & Fees: $21,100
Enrollment: 108 Male
Affiliation or Control: Roman Catholic IRS Status: 501(c)3
Highest Offering: Baccalaureate
Accreditation: SC

01 Rector & President ....RevMsg. Roberto GARZA
32 Vice Rector/Dean of Students ....Rev. Scott CIRCE
05 Academic Dean ....Dr. Ramon SANTOS
06 Registrar/Office Manager ....Mrs. Bonnie DE ANGULO
10 Comptroller ....Mr. Carlos CALMET
08 Head Librarian ....Mrs. Maria RODRIGUEZ
38 Director of Counseling ....Vacant
42 Spiritual Director ....Rev. Joseph KOTTOYIL

St. Johns River State College (B)

5001 St. Johns Avenue, Palatka FL 32177-3897
County: Putnam FICE Identification: 001523
Unit ID: 137281
Telephone: (386) 312-4200 Carnegie Class: Bac/Assoc-Assoc Dom
FAX Number: (386) 312-4229 Calendar System: Semester
URL: www.sjrstate.edu
Established: 1958 Annual Undergrad Tuition & Fees (In-District): $2,830
Enrollment: 7,114 Coed
Affiliation or Control: State/Local IRS Status: 501(c)3
Highest Offering: Baccalaureate
Accreditation: SC, ADNUR, CAHIIM, COARC, NUR

01 President ....Mr. Joe PICKENS
43 Senior VP/General Counsel ....Dr. Melissa C. MILLER
32 Vice President Student Affairs ....Dr. Gilbert L. EVANS, JR.
05 VP & CAO/Exec Dir St Augustine ....Dr. Melanie A. BROWN
10 Vice President Finance & Admin/CFO ....Dr. Lynn POWERS
30 Vice Pres Develop/External Affairs ....Mrs. Caroline D. TINGLE
108 VP Assessment/Research & Tech ....Dr. Rosalind M. HUMERICK
103 VP Workforce/Exec Dir Orange Park ....Dr. Anna M. LEBESCH
20 Associate VP Academic Affairs ....Dr. Edward K. JORDAN
13 Chief Information Officer ....Mr. Paul M. HAWKINS
49 Dean of Arts & Sciences ....Dr. Laura L. BOILINI
19 Dean of Crim Justice/Public Safety ....Ms. Angela A. SOCKWELL
57 Dean of Florida School of the Arts ....Mr. Alain R. HENTSCHEL
08 Dean of Library Services ....Dr. Christina WILL
66 Dean Nursing ....Dr. Mary A. LANEY
55 Dean of Adult Education ....Dr. Melissa PERRY
53 Dean of Teacher Education ....Dr. Myrna L. ALLEN
84 Dean of Enrollment Management ....Mr. Daniel BARKOWITZ
76 Associate Dean of Allied Health ....Dr. Holly COULLIETTE
88 Exec Dir TH Center for the Arts ....Mr. Denton J. YOCKEY
50 Director of Business Education ....Mr. Joel C. ABO
103 Director of Workforce Services ....Mrs. Melissa E. O'CONNELL
51 Dir of Dual Enroll & College Access ....Mrs. Meghan DEPUTY
26 Director of Public Relations ....Mrs. Susan B. KESSLER
38 Dir Counseling/Acad Advising ....Ms. Karen THOMAS
88 Director of Testing & Stdnt Support ....Mr. Todd DIXON
06 Registrar ....Mrs. Susanne B. LINEBERGER
15 Dir of Benefits/Employee Relations ....Mrs. Ginger C. STOKES
21 Controller ....Mr. Randall PETERSON
106 Director of eLearning ....Mr. Jack C. HALL

Saint Leo University (C)

33701 State Road 52 W, Saint Leo FL 33574-6665
County: Pasco FICE Identification: 001526
Unit ID: 137032
Telephone: (352) 588-8200 Carnegie Class: Masters/L
FAX Number: (352) 588-8654 Calendar System: Semester
URL: www.saintleo.edu
Established: 1889 Annual Undergrad Tuition & Fees: $20,830
Enrollment: 16,349 Coed
Affiliation or Control: Roman Catholic IRS Status: 501(c)3
Highest Offering: Doctorate
Accreditation: SC, ACBSP, CEA, IACBE, SW

01 President ....Dr. William J. LENNOX, JR.
05 VP Academic Affairs ....Dr. Michael NASTANSKI
32 VP Student Affairs/Campus Operation ....Dr. Edward DADEZ
106 VP Enrollment & Online Services ....Ms. Kathryn MCFARLAND
10 VP Business Affairs ....Mr. Eric WEEKES
30 VP University Advancement ....Mr. Denny MOLLER
88 VP Business Development ....Mr. Robert QUINN
88 VP Saint Leo Univ Worldwide ....Ms. Melanie STORMS
04 Assistant to the President ....Ms. Molly-Dodd ADAMS
13 Assoc VP/Chief Information Officer ....Mr. Vijay SONTY
20 Associate VP Academic Affairs ....Dr. Jeffrey ANDERSON
20 Assoc VP Learning & Innovation ....Dr. Jeff BORDEN
88 Associate VP Regional Accreditation ....Dr. Patricia PARRISH
108 Director Academic Assessment ....Dr. Robert LUCIO
43 Associate VP/General Counsel ....Ms. Kelly HILL
84 Assistant Vice Pres Enrollment ....Mr. Reggie HILL
88 Asst VP Academic Worldwide Liaison ....Dr. Carol WALKER
42 Chaplain for University Ministries ....Fr. Kyle SMITH
35 Associate VP Student Affairs ....Mr. Kenneth POSNER
38 Director Counseling Services ....Mr. Lawson JOLLY
49 Dean School of Arts & Sciences ....Dr. Mary SPOTO
53 Dean School of Educ/Social Svcs ....Dr. Susan KINSELLA
50 Dean School of Business ....Dr. Balbir BAL
58 Dir Grad Studies Criminal Justice ....Dr. Robert DIEMER
58 Dir Grad Studies in Education ....Dr. Fern AEFSKY
58 Dir Grad Studies in Social Work ....Dr. Cindy LEE
58 Dir Graduate Studies in Theology ....Dr. Randall WOODARD
58 Director Graduate Creative Writing ....Dr. Steven KISTULENTZ
06 Registrar ....Mrs. Karen HATFIELD
08 Director Library Services ....Mr. Brent SHORT
07 Assoc VP of Enrollment/Support Svcs ....Mr. Jeffrey WALSH
88 Director Enrollment Info Systems ....Mr. Mark JONES
88 Asst VP of Learning Design ....Dr. Karen HAHN
88 Asst Director Disability Services ....Ms. Christine GEORGALLIS
39 Director of Residence Life ....Mr. Sean VAN GUILDER
11 Director Academic Administration ....Mr. Joseph TADEO
41 Director Intercollegiate Athletics ....Mr. Francis REIDY
26 Assoc VP Integrated Marketing ....Mr. Greg TEMNICK
88 Director Market Research ....Mr. William HAMILTON
18 Director Plant Operations ....Mr. Jose CABAN
19 Director Campus Security & Safety ....Mr. Vincent D'AMBROSIO
23 Director Health Services ....Ms. Teresa DADEZ
22 Asst Director Disability Services ....Ms. Christine GEORGALLIS
35 Assoc VP for Student Success ....Ms. Ana DI DONATO
29 Director Alumni Engagement ....Ms. Elizabeth BARR
44 Exec Director Development ....Ms. Dawn PARISI
88 Director Advancement Services ....Mr. Stephen KUBASEK
88 Grant & Scholarship Officer ....Ms. Victoria REECE
85 Director International Services ....Ms. Paige RAMSEY-HAMACHER
88 Director of Veteran Student Svcs ....Ms. Pamela MARTIS
15 Associate VP Human Resources ....Ms. Sheri NESHIEM
36 Director of Career Planning ....Mr. Robert LIDDELL
21 Assoc VP Finance ....Mr. James DETUCCIO
96 Mgr Accounts Payable/Procurement ....Ms. Laura SOLBERG
88 Director of Budgets ....Mr. Mark WILLIAMS
88 Director Internal Audit Services ....Ms. Monica MOYER
12 Asst VP Miltary Center Operations ....Mr. John CAIN
12 Asst VP Central Region ....Ms. Candis WHITFIELD
12 Asst VP Tampa Region ....Mr. Tyler UPSHAW
12 Asst VP Florida Region ....Ms. Katie DEGNER
103 Director Talent Development ....Mr. Joseph ARNER
109 Director Dining Services ....Mr. Rich VOGEL
88 Senior Executive Assistant ....Ms. Marcia MALIA
37 Associate VP of Financial Aid ....Ms. Melinda CLARK
27 Director University Communication ....Ms. Lucia RAATMA

St. Petersburg College (D)

PO Box 13489, Saint Petersburg FL 33733-3489
County: Pinellas FICE Identification: 001528
Unit ID: 137078
Telephone: (727) 341-4772 Carnegie Class: Bac/Assoc-Mixed
FAX Number: (727) 341-3318 Calendar System: Semester
URL: www.spcollege.edu
Established: 1927 Annual Undergrad Tuition & Fees (In-District): $3,352
Enrollment: 32,681 Coed
Affiliation or Control: Local IRS Status: 501(c)3
Highest Offering: Baccalaureate
Accreditation: SC, ADNUR, CAHIIM, CEA, COARC, DH, EMT, FUSER, NURSE, OPE, PTAA, RAD

01 President ....Dr. William D. LAW
05 Sr VP Instruction/Academic Pgm ....Dr. Anne M. COOPER
32 Sr Vice Pres Student Affairs ....Dr. Tonjua L. WILLIAMS
10 Sr VP Admin/Bus Svcs & Info Tech ....Vacant
18 Assoc VP Facilities Plng/Inst Svcs ....James WAECHTER
15 Human Resources/Dir of Operations ....Desiree WORONER
30 VP Inst Advance/Exec Dir Foundation ....Frances NEU
21 Acting Budget/Compliance Director ....Janette HUNT
84 Assoc VP Enrollment Services ....Dr. Pat RINARD
37 Assoc VP Financial Asst Svcs ....Michael J. BENNETT
20 Assoc VP Academic Affs/Partnership ....Catherine C. KENNEDY
20 Assoc Provost ....Heather DISLER
26 Exec Dir Marketing/Public Info ....Diana SABINO
103 Director Workforce Services ....Dr. Jason KRUPP
43 Acting General Counsel ....Suzanne GARDNER
12 Provost Allstate Center ....Dr. Scott FRONRATH
12 Provost Clearwater Campus ....Dr. Stanley VITTETOE
12 Provost/Health Education Center ....Dr. Eric CARVER
12 Provost St Petersburg Campus ....Jamelle CONNER
12 Provost Seminole Campus/eCampus ....Mark STRICKLAND
12 Provost Tarpon Springs Campus ....Dr. Marvin BRIGHT
12 Provost Downtown Center ....Dr. Kevin GORDON
22 Dir Equal Access/Equal Opp/Title IX ....Pam SMITH
96 Dir Procurement & Asset Mgmt ....Joe C. SMITH
38 Dir Student Success ....Joe DVORACSEK
88 Dean College of Public Safety Admin ....Dr. Brian FRANK
88 Dean Col of Policy Ethics/Leg Stds ....Dr. Susan S. DEMERS
83 Dean Social & Behavioral Sciences ....Dr. Joseph SMILEY
88 Principal St Pete Collegiate High ....Starla METZ
88 President Faculty Senate ....Dr. Richard MERCADANTE
50 Dean College of Business ....Dr. Greg NENSTIEL
81 Dean Mathematics ....Jimmy CHANG
65 Dean Natural Science ....Dr. John CHAPIN
79 Dean Humanities/Fine Arts ....Dr. Jonathan STEELE
53 Dean College of Education ....Dr. Kimberly HARTMAN
60 Dean Communications ....Joseph LEOPOLD
76 Dean College of Health Sciences ....Dr. Rebecca LUDWIG
74 Dean Sch of Veterinary Technology ....Dr. Richard FLORA
72 Dean College of Comp & Info Tech ....Dr. Sharon SETTERLIND
66 Dean College of Nursing ....Dr. Susan BAKER
08 Director Learning Resources ....Vacant
04 Executive Admin Svcs Specialist ....Rebecca TURNER
07 Director of Admissions and Records ....Eva CHRISTENSEN
09 Director of Institutional Research ....Dr. Edward SIEGEL
100 Chief of Staff ....Deborah BOYLE
104 Director International Programs ....Ramona KIRSCH
106 Associate VP Online Learning/Svcs ....Dr. Susan COLARIC
108 Director Assessment ....Magaly TYMMS
13 Senior Director Enterprise Systems ....Zoran STANISIC
19 Director College Security Services ....Daniel BARTO
25 Exec Dir of Grants Development ....Jackie SKRYD
86 Director Government Relations ....Edward W. WOODRUFF, JR.

St. Thomas University (E)

16401 NW 37th Avenue, Miami Gardens FL 33054-6498
County: Miami-Dade FICE Identification: 001468
Unit ID: 137476
Telephone: (305) 625-6000 Carnegie Class: Masters/L
FAX Number: (305) 628-6510 Calendar System: Semester
URL: www.stu.edu
Established: 1961 Annual Undergrad Tuition & Fees: $27,960
Enrollment: 2,217 Coed
Affiliation or Control: Roman Catholic IRS Status: 501(c)3
Highest Offering: Doctorate
Accreditation: SC, LAW

01 President ....Msgr. Franklyn M. CASALE
05 Provost & Chief Academic Officer ....Dr. Irma BECERRA
10 VP Administration/Chief Exec Ofcr ....Mr. Terrence L. O'CONNER
61 Dean of Law School ....Mr. Alfredo GARCIA
30 Vice Pres University Advancement ....Ms. Hilda FERNANDEZ
45 Vice Pres for Planning & Enrollment ....Vacant
20 Associate Provost ....Dr. Susan ANGULO
84 Dean Enrollment ....Mr. Celso ALVAREZ
26 Director University Marketing ....Burcu AYRIM
06 Executive Associate Registrar ....Mrs. Maria ABDEL
37 Assoc Director Financial Aid ....Ms. Yaidany RIVERO
08 University Librarian ....Mr. Lawrence TREADWELL, IV
21 Controller ....Mrs. Maribel SMITH
18 Director Facilities/Physical Plant ....Mr. Juan M. ZAMORA
09 Director Institutional Research ....Dr. Jerry WEINBERG
88 Assoc Dir Emergency/Risk Management ....Ms. Monique BRIJBASI
41 Athletic Director ....Mrs. Laura J. COURTLEY-TODD
07 Director of Admissions ....Mr. Celso J. ALVAREZ
32 Dean of Students ....Vacant
15 Assoc Director Human Resources ....Ms. Lenore M. PRADO
25 Director for Prospect Research ....Ms. Jacqueline HOUSE
38 Assoc Director Health & Wellness ....Vacant
73 Dean School of Theology ....RevMsg. Terrance E. HOGAN
12 Dean Biscayne College ....Vacant
13 Chief Information Officer ....Mr. Rudy IBARRA
29 Director Alumni Affairs ....Ms. Yisel CABRERA
44 Director Annual Giving ....Vacant
11 Director for Administration ....Mrs. Sylvia L. RODRIGUEZ

St. Vincent De Paul Regional Seminary (F)

10701 S Military Trail, Boynton Beach FL 33436-4899
County: Palm Beach FICE Identification: 008223
Unit ID: 136701
Telephone: (561) 732-4424 Carnegie Class: Spec-4-yr-Faith
FAX Number: (561) 737-2205 Calendar System: Semester
URL: www.svdp.edu
Established: 1963 Annual Graduate Tuition & Fees: N/A
Enrollment: 120 Coed
Affiliation or Control: Roman Catholic IRS Status: 501(c)3
Highest Offering: Master's; No Undergraduates
Accreditation: SC, THEOL

01 Rector/President ....Rev. David L. TOUPS
03 Vice Rector ....Rev. Remek BLASZKOWSKI
05 Academic Dean ....Rev. Alfredo HERNANDEZ
10 Treasurer ....Mr. Keith PARKER
08 Director of the Library ....Mr. Arthur QUINN
04 Administrative Asst to President ....Mrs. Herminia C. GARCIA
09 Dir Inst Research/Assessment ....Dr. Mary FROEHLE
30 Chief Development/Advancement ....Ms. Daniella COY
06 Registrar ....Mrs. Alicia RUEFF

San Ignacio University (G)

10395 NW 41st Street, Suite 125, Doral FL 33178
County: Miami-Dade Identification: 667130
Telephone: (305) 629-2929 Carnegie Class: Not Classified
FAX Number: (305) 629-2910 Calendar System: Semester
URL: www.sanignaciocollege.edu
Established: 2007 Annual Undergrad Tuition & Fees: N/A
Enrollment: N/A Coed
Affiliation or Control: Proprietary IRS Status: Proprietary
Highest Offering: Master's
Accreditation: ACICS

01 President ....Luciana DE LA FUENTE
03 Vice President ....Dr. Omar PAGAN
05 Chief Academic Officer ....Michael FLORES
06 Registrar ....Oscar CABRERA
08 Head Librarian ....Silvia LOPEZ
15 Human Resources Director ....Ligia BARROS
37 Financial Aid Director ....Elba CASTANOS
07 Admissions/Marketing Director ....Sergio CUBILLOS

Sanford-Brown College Tampa (A)

3725 West Grace Street, Tampa FL 33607

County: Hillsborough FICE Identification: 030314
Unit ID: 134680
Telephone: (813) 881-0007 Carnegie Class: Spec-4-yr-Arts
FAX Number: (813) 884-9327 Calendar System: Quarter
URL: www.sanfordbrown.edu/tampa
Established: 1984 Annual Undergrad Tuition & Fees: N/A
Enrollment: 426 Coed
Affiliation or Control: Proprietary IRS Status: Proprietary
Highest Offering: Baccalaureate
Accreditation: **ACICS**, CIDA, CVT

01 President .... Dr. Robert SWAIN
05 Dean .... Phil BULONE
36 Director of Career Services .... Matchez CHERSILS
08 Learning Resource Center Coord .... Vashba GREEN

† School is in teach-out plan through late 2016.

Sanford-Brown Institute (B)

10255 Fortune Parkway, Suite #501,
Jacksonville FL 32256-0757

County: Duval FICE Identification: 026164
Unit ID: 404505
Telephone: (904) 363-6221 Carnegie Class: Spec 2-yr-Health
FAX Number: (904) 363-6824 Calendar System: Other
URL: www.sanfordbrown.edu/Jacksonville
Established: 1977 Annual Undergrad Tuition & Fees: N/A
Enrollment: 340 Coed
Affiliation or Control: Proprietary IRS Status: Proprietary
Highest Offering: Associate Degree
Accreditation: **ACICS**, DH

01 President .... Mr. Ben SEDRINE
05 Director of Education .... Ms. Jennifer MULLINGS

† School is in teach-out plan.

Santa Fe College (C)

3000 NW 83rd Street, Gainesville FL 32606-6200

County: Alachua FICE Identification: 001519
Unit ID: 137096
Telephone: (352) 395-5000 Carnegie Class: Bac/Assoc-Assoc Dom
FAX Number: (352) 395-5581 Calendar System: Semester
URL: www.sfcollege.edu
Established: 1965 Annual Undergrad Tuition & Fees (In-District): $2,539
Enrollment: 15,055 Coed
Affiliation or Control: Local IRS Status: 501(c)3
Highest Offering: Baccalaureate
Accreditation: **SC**, ADNUR, CAHIIM, COARC, CONST, CVT, DA, DH, DMS, EMT, MT, NMT, NURSE, POLYT, RAD, SURGT

01 President .... Dr. Jackson N. SASSER
05 Provost/Vice Pres Academic Affairs .... Dr. Edward BONAHUE
10 Chief Financial Ofcr/VP Admin Affs .... Ms. Ginger GIBSON
32 Vice President Student Affairs .... Dr. Naima BROWN
30 Vice President Development .... Mr. Chuck CLEMONS
108 VP Assessment/Research/Technology .... Dr. Lisa ARMOUR
04 Assistant to the President .... Ms. Cathy KEEN
20 Associate VP Academic Affairs .... Dr. Jodi LONG
13 Assoc VP Information Tech Services .... Mr. Bill PENNEY
18 Assoc VP Facilities Services .... Vacant
35 Assoc VP Student Affs/Financial Aid .... Dr. Dan RODKIN
88 Assoc Vice Pres Educational Centers .... Dr. Cheryl CALHOUN
25 Asst VP/Development/Grants/Projects .... Vacant
20 Assoc Vice Pres Academic Affairs .... Dr. Stefanie WASCHULL
35 Asst Vice Pres Student Affairs .... Dr. Beatrice AWONIYI
43 Legal Counsel .... Ms. Patti P. LOCASCIO
06 College Registrar .... Mr. Mike HUTLEY
88 Dir High Sch Dual Enrollment Pgm .... Ms. Jennifer HOMARD
88 Director Advisement Center .... Ms. Kimberly FUGATE-ROBERTS
41 Athletic Director .... Mr. Jim KEITES
08 Director Library Service .... Ms. Myra STERRETT
19 Director Institute of Public Safety .... Mr. Tom ACKERMAN
35 Director of Student Life .... Dr. Tracey REEVES
96 Director of Purchasing .... Mr. David SHLAFER
28 Coordinator of Diversity .... Ms. Elizabeth O'REGGIO
37 Director Student Financial Aid .... Ms. Kamia MWANGO
15 Director Human Resources .... Ms. Lela FRYE
09 Director of Institutional Research .... Mr. Gary HARTGE
07 Coordinator for Admissions .... Ms. Gayle JONES
26 Chief Public Relations/Marketing .... Mr. John CARMEAN

Schiller International University (D)

8560 Ulmerton Road, Largo FL 33771

County: Pinellas FICE Identification: 023141
Unit ID: 404338
Telephone: (727) 736-5082 Carnegie Class: Spec-4-yr-Bus
FAX Number: (727) 734-0359 Calendar System: Semester
URL: www.schiller.edu
Established: 1964 Annual Undergrad Tuition & Fees: $21,540
Enrollment: 50 Coed
Affiliation or Control: Proprietary IRS Status: Proprietary
Highest Offering: Master's
Accreditation: **ACICS**

01 Campus Director .... Mr. Fabian FERNANDEZ
05 Provost .... Dr. Andrea BRZENIK
07 Director of Admissions .... Mr. Keith TOMLINSON

Seminole State College of Florida (E)

100 Weldon Boulevard, Sanford FL 32773-6199

County: Seminole FICE Identification: 001520
Unit ID: 137209
Telephone: (407) 708-4722 Carnegie Class: Bac/Assoc-Assoc Dom
FAX Number: (407) 708-2139 Calendar System: Semester
URL: www.seminolestate.edu
Established: 1965 Annual Undergrad Tuition & Fees (In-District): $3,131
Enrollment: 18,399 Coed
Affiliation or Control: Local IRS Status: 501(c)3
Highest Offering: Baccalaureate
Accreditation: **SC**, ADNUR, CAHIIM, COARC, EMT, PTAA

01 President .... Dr. E. Ann MCGEE
10 Executive VP/CFO .... Dr. Joseph SARNOVSKY
05 VP Academic Affairs/CAO .... Dr. Laura ROSS
32 VP Student Affairs/CSAO .... Vacant
13 VP Information Resources/CIO .... Dr. Dick T. HAMANN
102 Executive Director Foundation .... Dr. John GYLLIN
21 AVP Finance & Budget .... Ms. Judi COOPER
30 AVP Student Development .... Dr. Jan LLOYD
12 Dean of Students Altamonte Springs .... Ms. Lynn GARRETT
12 Dean of Students Oviedo Campus .... Mr. Randy PAWLOWSKI
08 Dean Learning Resources .... Ms. Barbara HILDEBRAND
36 AVP Career Programs .... Dr. Angela M. KERSENBROCK
54 Dean Engineering and Design .... Mr. Michael STALEY
51 Dean Academic Foundations .... Dr. Terri DANIELS
26 Dir College & Community Relations .... Ms. Deborah RICHARD
86 Director Government Relations .... Vacant
91 Director Networks .... Mr. Julio VALENTIN
38 Director Counseling and Advising .... Ms. Deborah LYNCH
20 Director Curriculum .... Ms. Carlene MCNEIL
15 AVP Human Resources .... Ms. Mae KLINE
07 Dir Enrollment Svcs/Registrar .... Ms. Kathy VOUDRY
37 Director Student Financial Aid .... Ms. Roseann AMATO
09 AVP Institutional Effectiveness .... Dr. Mark MORGAN
41 Director Intercollegiate Athletics .... Mr. John SCARPINO
84 AVP Student Recruitment .... Mrs. Pamela MENNECHEY
36 Director Career Development .... Ms. Heather ENGELKING
14 AVP Information Technology .... Ms. Pilar ACOSTA
106 Dir Online Education/E-learning .... Dr. Christine BROEKER
28 Director of Diversity .... Ms. Janet BALANOFF

South Florida Bible College (F)

1100 South Federal Highway, Deerfield Beach FL 33441

County: Broward FICE Identification: 032643
Unit ID: 366003
Telephone: (954) 545-4500 Carnegie Class: Spec-4-yr-Faith
FAX Number: (954) 719-3780 Calendar System: Semester
URL: www.sfbc.edu
Established: 1985 Annual Undergrad Tuition & Fees: $6,200
Enrollment: 116 Coed
Affiliation or Control: Interdenominational IRS Status: 501(c)3
Highest Offering: Master's
Accreditation: **BI**

01 President .... Dr. Mary A. DRABIK
03 Vice President .... Josiah STEPHAN
05 Chief Academic Officer .... Dr. John STEVENSON
10 Chief Financial Officer .... Zil WENCESLAU
06 Registrar .... Dr. Becky PRASAD
08 Librarian .... Paula STEVENSON
20 Dean of Faculty .... Dr. Esa AUTERO
32 Dean of Students .... Carol RICHARDSON
29 Director Alumni Relations .... George T. SHARP
84 Director Enrollment Management .... John MEZZACAPPA
13 Chief Info Technology Officer (CIO) .... Joshua DRABIK
30 Chief Development/Advancement .... Wayne RICHARDSON
04 Administrative Asst to President .... Deanna STEPHAN

South Florida State College (G)

600 W College Drive, Avon Park FL 33825-9399

County: Highlands FICE Identification: 001522
Unit ID: 137315
Telephone: (863) 453-6661 Carnegie Class: Bac/Assoc-Assoc Dom
FAX Number: (863) 453-0165 Calendar System: Trimester
URL: www.southflorida.edu
Established: 1965 Annual Undergrad Tuition & Fees (In-District): $3,165
Enrollment: 2,780 Coed
Affiliation or Control: Local IRS Status: 501(c)3
Highest Offering: Baccalaureate
Accreditation: **SC**, ADNUR, DA, DH, EMT, NUR, RAD

01 President .... Dr. Thomas C. LEITZEL
05 Vice Pres Educational/Stdnt Svcs .... Dr. Sidney VALENTINE
10 Controller .... Ms. Melissa LEE
11 Vice Pres Administrative Services .... Mr. Glenn W. LITTLE
75 Dean Applied Science & Tech .... Mr. Eric CHRISTENSEN
49 Int Dean Arts & Sciences .... Mr. Lynn MACNEILL
88 Director Cultural Programs .... Ms. Cynthia GARREN
45 Dean Resource Development .... Mrs. Jamie EATEMAN
32 Dean Student Services .... Dr. Timothy WISE
12 Director DeSoto Campus .... Mrs. Suzanne DEMERS
12 Director Hardee Campus .... Ms. Teresa CRAWFORD
12 Director Lake Placid Center .... Mr. Randall K. FAEPLOW
26 Director Community Relations .... Ms. Deborah LATTER
106 Director eLearning .... Mrs. Melanie M. JACKSON
15 Director Human Res/EA-EO & ADA Ofcr .... Mrs. Susie HALE
18 Dir Remodeling/Reno & Maint .... Mr. Robert E. FLORES
06 Registrar .... Dr. Deborah M. FUSCHETTI
41 Athletic Director .... Mr. Richard J. HITT
36 Director Career Development Center .... Mrs. Colleen RAFATTI
37 Director Financial Aid .... Mr. Jerry DONNA
13 Chief Information Officer .... Dr. Christopher VAN DER KAAY
38 Chair Counseling .... Mrs. Charla ELLERKER
08 Library Services .... Ms. Lena PHELPS
96 Coordinator Purchasing .... Mrs. Deborah OLSON
07 Director of Admissions .... Ms. Lynn HINTZ
76 Dean Division of Health Services .... Mrs. Rebecca SRODA

South University (H)

9801 Belevedere Road, Royal Palm Beach FL 33411

Telephone: (561) 273-6500 Identification: 666117
Accreditation: **&SC**, ACBSP, CACREP, NURSE, OTA, PTAA

† Regional accreditation is carried under the parent institution in Savannah, GA.

South University (I)

4401 North Himes Ave Ste 175, Tampa FL 33614-7095

Telephone: (813) 393-3800 Identification: 770913
Accreditation: **&SC**, ACBSP, ARCPA, NURSE, OTA, PTAA

† Regional accreditation is carried under the parent institution in Savannah, GA.

Southeastern College (J)

17395 NW 59th Avenue, Miami Lakes FL 33015-5111

Telephone: (305) 820-5003 Identification: 666290
Accreditation: **ACCSC**, MAAB, SURGT

† Branch campus of Southeastern College, West Palm Beach, FL.

Southeastern College (K)

2081 Vista Parkway, Suite 100B,
West Palm Beach FL 33411

County: Palm Beach FICE Identification: 031239
Unit ID: 428170
Telephone: (561) 433-2330 Carnegie Class: Spec 2-yr-Health
FAX Number: (561) 433-9025 Calendar System: Other
URL: www.sec.edu
Established: 1988 Annual Undergrad Tuition & Fees: $17,584
Enrollment: 1,013 Coed
Affiliation or Control: Proprietary IRS Status: Proprietary
Highest Offering: Associate Degree
Accreditation: **ACCSC**, MAAB, SURGT

01 Vice President .... Ms. Dana HUPPON

Southeastern University (L)

1000 Longfellow Boulevard, Lakeland FL 33801-6099

County: Polk FICE Identification: 001521
Unit ID: 137564
Telephone: (863) 667-5000 Carnegie Class: Masters/M
FAX Number: (863) 667-5200 Calendar System: Semester
URL: www.seu.edu
Established: 1935 Annual Undergrad Tuition & Fees: $22,840
Enrollment: 3,834 Coed
Affiliation or Control: Assemblies Of God Church IRS Status: 501(c)3
Highest Offering: Doctorate
Accreditation: **SC**, ACBSP, NURSE, SW

01 President .... Dr. Kent INGLE
03 Executive Vice President .... Dr. Brian CARROLL
05 Provost .... Dr. William C. HACKET, JR.
32 VP for Student Development .... Dr. James (Chris) OWEN
84 VP for Enrollment Management .... Mr. Roy ROWLAND, IV
09 VP for Institutional Research & EE .... Dr. Andrew H. PERMENTER
08 Dean of Library Services .... Mrs. Grace VEACH
06 Dir Student Records/Registrar .... Mrs. Linda M. KELSO
37 Exec Dir Student Financial Services .... Mr. Michael YOHE
88 Director of Hispanic Learning Ctr .... Ms. Betania TORRES
07 Director of Admissions .... Mrs. Sarah E. CLARK
15 Director Human Resources .... Ms. Betty KELLEY
26 Director External Relations .... Mr. Edward L. MANER
18 Exec Dir Facilities/Physical Plant .... Mr. Norman M. ALDERMAN
20 Director Academic Auxiliary Svcs .... Mrs. Ramona CARROLL
36 Sr Dir Center for Calling & Career .... Mrs. Pamela CROSBY
10 Exec Director of Finance .... Mr. Frederick S. GORE
84 Director Enrollment Marketing .... Mr. Brandt MERRITT
38 Dir Counseling/Health & Wellness .... Mrs. Paula WHITAKER
56 Exec Dir School of Extended Educ .... Mr. Andrew MILLER
13 Chief Info Technology Officer (CIO) .... Mr. Jerry RAINS
19 Director Security/Safety .... Mr. Richard DAVIS

Southern Technical College (M)

1685 Medical Lane, Fort Myers FL 33907-1158

County: Lee FICE Identification: 022788
Unit ID: 366553
Telephone: (239) 939-4766 Carnegie Class: Bac/Assoc-Mixed
FAX Number: (239) 790-2118 Calendar System: Quarter
URL: www.southerntech.edu
Established: 1974 Annual Undergrad Tuition & Fees: $14,400

Enrollment: 1,259 Coed
Affiliation or Control: Proprietary IRS Status: Proprietary
Highest Offering: Baccalaureate
Accreditation: ACICS, CAHIIM, SURTEC

01 President ... Mr. Pedro DEGUZMAN
05 VP of Academic Affairs ... Ms. Ilia MATOS

Southern Technical College (A)

2910 South Orlando Drive, Sanford FL 32773
County: Seminole FICE Identification: 039035
Unit ID: 446552
Telephone: (407) 323-4141 Carnegie Class: Not Classified
FAX Number: (407) 323-4221 Calendar System: Semester
URL: www.southerntech.edu
Established: 1956 Annual Undergrad Tuition & Fees: N/A
Enrollment: N/A Coed
Affiliation or Control: Proprietary IRS Status: Proprietary
Highest Offering: Associate Degree
Accreditation: ACICS

01 Dean ... Mr. David BRAME

Southern Technical College-Auburndale (B)

298 Havendale Boulevard, Auburndale FL 33823
Telephone: (407) 438-6000 Identification: 770705
Accreditation: ACICS

Southern Technical College-Brandon (C)

608 E Bloomingdale Avenue, Brandon FL 33511
Telephone: (813) 654-8800 Identification: 770707
Accreditation: ACICS

Southern Technical College-Mount Dora (D)

2799 W Old US Highway 441, Mount Dora FL 32757
Telephone: (352) 383-4242 Identification: 770706
Accreditation: ACICS

Southern Technical College-Orlando (E)

1485 Florida Mall Avenue, Orlando FL 32809
Telephone: (407) 438-6000 Identification: 770704
Accreditation: ACICS

Southern Technical College-Port Charlotte (F)

950 Tamiami Trail, Unit 109, Port Charlotte FL 33953
Telephone: (239) 274-5860 Identification: 770709
Accreditation: ACICS, SURTEC

Southern Technical College-Tampa (G)

3910 RIGA Boulevard, Tampa FL 33619-1269
Telephone: (813) 630-4401 Identification: 770708
Accreditation: ACICS, DMS, SURTEC

State College of Florida, Manatee-Sarasota (H)

PO Box 1849, Bradenton FL 34206-7046
County: Manatee FICE Identification: 001504
Unit ID: 135391
Telephone: (941) 752-5000 Carnegie Class: Bac/Assoc-Assoc Dom
FAX Number: (941) 727-6230 Calendar System: Semester
URL: www.scf.edu
Established: 1957 Annual Undergrad Tuition & Fees (In-District): $3,074
Enrollment: 10,314 Coed
Affiliation or Control: Local IRS Status: 501(c)3
Highest Offering: Baccalaureate
Accreditation: SC, ADNUR, DH, NUR, OTA, PTAA, RAD

01 President ... Dr. Carol F. PROBSTFELD
04 Exec Assistant to President ... Ms. Susan MARROCCO
10 VP Finance/Admin Services ... Ms. Julie JAKWAY
05 VP Academic Affairs ... Mr. Gary T. RUSSELL
84 VP Strategic Enrollment ... Dr. Richard BARNHOUSE
32 Dean Student Services ... Ms. Jaquelyn MCNEIL
12 Dean Venice ... Mr. Ryan HALE
35 Director Student Services ... Ms. MariLynn J. LEWY
12 Dean Bradenton ... Mr. Mike KIEFER
102 Executive Director SCF Foundation ... Ms. Cassandra HOLMES
38 Director Student Development ... Ms. Lynn DREES
12 Dean Lakewood Ranch ... Ms. Daisy VULOVICH
45 Director Planning & Inst Effect ... Mr. Bradley W. DAVIS
18 Director Facilities Manager ... Mr. Chris WELLMAN
103 Director Workforce Services ... Ms. Lee KOTWICKI
21 Director Business Services ... Mr. Josef RILL
22 Equity Officer ... Ms. Erika PERDUE
08 Director Library Services ... Ms. Margaret E. HAWKINS
09 Director Institutional Research ... Ms. Su-hua MEN
13 Director IT Operations ... Ms. Karla LAUER
37 Director Financial Aid ... Mr. Thomas VO
07 Director of Admissions ... Ms. Stacey SHARPLES
36 Director Career Resource Center ... Ms. Denise D. GATCH
41 Director Athletics ... Mr. Matt ENNIS
43 General Counsel ... Mr. Steve PROUTY
88 Head of SCF Collegiate School ... Ms. Kelly MONOD
106 Director Online Learning ... Mr. Gary BAKER
26 Director Communications & Marketing ... Ms. Jamie M. SMITH
19 Manager Public Safety ... Mr. Shawn PATTEN

*State University System of Florida, Board of Governors (I)

325 W Gaines Street, Suite 1614, Tallahassee FL 32399-0400
County: Leon FICE Identification: 008068
Unit ID: 137449
Telephone: (850) 245-0466 Carnegie Class: N/A
FAX Number: (850) 245-9685
URL: www.flbog.edu

01 Chancellor ... Mr. Marshall M. CRISER, III
05 Vice Chanc Academic/Student Affairs ... Dr. Jan IGNASH
10 Vice Chanc Budget & Finance ... Mr. Tim JONES
43 General Counsel ... Ms. Vikki SHIRLEY
22 Inspector General & Compliance ... Mr. Joseph MALESZEWSKI
101 Corporate Secretary ... Ms. Vikki SHIRLEY
86 Assoc Vice Chanc Govt Relations ... Vacant
04 Assistant to the Chancellor ... Ms. Shannon M. TRUE
26 Director of Communications ... Ms. Brittany DAVIS
13 Chief Info Technology Officer (CIO) ... Mr. Gene KOVACS
15 Director Personnel Services ... Ms. Abigail MARTIN
18 Chief Facilities/Physical Plant ... Mr. Chris KINSLEY

*Florida Agricultural and Mechanical University (J)

1601 S. Martin Luther King Jr. Blvd, Tallahassee FL 32307
County: Leon FICE Identification: 001480
Unit ID: 133650
Telephone: (850) 599-3000 Carnegie Class: DU-Higher
FAX Number: (850) 599-3952 Calendar System: Semester
URL: www.famu.edu
Established: 1887 Annual Undergrad Tuition & Fees (In-State): $5,785
Enrollment: 10,241 Coed
Affiliation or Control: State IRS Status: 501(c)3
Highest Offering: Doctorate
Accreditation: SC, ACBSP, CAHIIM, COARC, CS, ENG, ENGT, JOUR, LAW, NUR, OT, PH, PHAR, PTA, SW, TED

02 President (Chief Executive Officer) ... Dr. Elmira MANGUM
05 Provost/VP Academic Affairs ... Ms. Marcella DAVID
10 Actg VP Finance & Administration ... Ms. Angela POOLE
32 Vice President Student Affairs ... Dr. William HUDSON, JR.
25 VP Research & Govt Relations ... Dr. Timothy E. MOORE
30 VP University Advancement ... Mr. George COTTON
88 VP Audit and Compliance ... Mr. Richard GIVENS
43 VP Legal Affairs/General Counsel ... Ms. Shira THOMAS
20 Assoc Provost for Undergrad Educ ... Vacant
100 Chief of Staff ... Mr. Jimmy MILLER
35 Associate VP Student Affairs ... Dr. Angela COLEMAN
13 Associate VP/CIO Info Tech Svcs ... Mr. David CANTRELL
21 Associate VP/University Controller ... Ms. Tiffany HOLMES
35 Associate VP Student Life ... Mr. Thomas ALEXANDER
15 Associate VP Human Resources ... Ms. Joyce A. INGRAM
44 Actg Assoc VP Univ Development ... Ms. Juanita JOHNSON
102 Assoc VP University Advancement ... Ms. Mechelle ENGLISH
84 Assoc VP Enrollment Management ... Mr. Nigel EDWARDS
18 Assoc VP Facilities/Construction ... Mr. Sameer KAPILESHWARI
53 Dean Education ... Dr. Traki L. TAYLOR
47 Dean Agriculture & Food Sciences ... Dr. Robert TAYLOR
67 Dean Pharmacy & Pharm Sciences ... Dr. Michael THOMPSON
72 Dean Science & Technology ... Dr. Maurice EDINGTON
51 Director Continuing Education ... Ms. Phyllis WATSON
83 Dean Social Sci/Arts & Humanities ... Dr. Valencia E. MATTHEWS
50 Dean Business and Industry ... Dr. Shawnta FRIDAY-STROUD
54 Dean FAMU-FSU Engineering ... Dr. J. Murray GIBSON
61 Dean College of Law ... Ms. Angela F. EPPS
66 Dean Nursing ... Dr. Ruena NORMAN
76 Dean Allied Health Sciences ... Dr. Cynthia HUGHES HARRIS
48 Dean Architecture & Engr Technology ... Mr. Rodner WRIGHT
60 Dean Journalism & Graphic Comm ... Dr. Ann KIMBROUGH
65 Dean School of the Environment ... Dr. Victor IBEANUSI
58 Assoc Provost & Dean Grad Studies ... Dr. David JACKSON, JR.
08 Dean University Libraries ... Ms. Faye WATKINS
04 Assistant to the President ... Ms. Jacqueline HIGHTOWER
26 Assistant VP Communications ... Ms. Elise DURHAM
06 University Registrar ... Dr. Agatha ONWUNLI
07 Director Admissions & Enroll Mgmt ... Ms. Barbara COX
19 Chief of Police/Dir Public Safety ... Mr. Terence CALLOWAY
104 Asst VP International Ed & Dev ... Dr. William HYNDMAN, III
109 Asst VP Administrative Services ... Ms. Rebecca BROWN
09 Asst VP Institutional Research ... Dr. Kwadwo OWUSU-ADUEMIRI
88 Special Assistant to the President ... Mr. Dee GAMBLE
37 Director Financial Aid ... Ms. Lisa STEWART
88 Director Technology Transfer ... Mr. Reis ALSBERRY
88 Director Sponsored Programs ... Ms. Glory BROWN
88 Director Title III Programs ... Dr. Wanda FORD
88 Executive Dir Sustainability Inst ... Ms. Abena OJETAYO
88 Director Office of Animal Welfare ... Dr. Tanise JACKSON
36 Actg Director Career Center ... Ms. Kacey LOWE
88 University Ombudsman & Spec Asst VP ... Mr. Bryan F. SMITH
86 Director Governmental Relations ... Mr. Tola THOMPSON
25 Director Contracts & Grants ... Ms. Pamela BLOUNT
39 Director Student Housing ... Mr. Oscar CRUMITY
38 Int Director Counsel Services ... Ms. Quantina WASHINGTON
96 Director Purchasing ... Ms. Stephany FALL
23 Director Student Health Services ... Ms. Tanya TATUM
108 Actg Director Univ Assessment ... Dr. Franz RENEAU
29 Executive Director Alumni Affairs ... Ms. Carmen CUMMINGS
22 Director EEO ... Ms. Carrie GAVIN
41 Director Athletics ... Mr. Milton OVERTON
106 Director Instr Tech & Distance Ed ... Ms. Franzetta FITZ
109 Director Business & Auxiliary Svc ... Mr. Bryon WILLIAMS
105 Director ITS Services & Telecomm ... Mr. Ronald HENRY
101 Board of Trustees Liaison ... Ms. Linda BARGE-MILES
88 Director Veteran and Military Affs ... Mr. Raymond SPAULDING
88 Director Center for Disability ... Mr. Jovany FELIX

*Florida Atlantic University (K)

PO Box 3091, 777 Glades Road, Boca Raton FL 33431-0991
County: Palm Beach FICE Identification: 001481
Unit ID: 133669
Telephone: (561) 297-3000 Carnegie Class: DU-Higher
FAX Number: (561) 297-3942 Calendar System: Semester
URL: www.fau.edu
Established: 1961 Annual Undergrad Tuition & Fees (In-State): $4,831
Enrollment: 30,297 Coed
Affiliation or Control: State IRS Status: 501(c)3
Highest Offering: Doctorate
Accreditation: SC, BUS, CACREP, CAEP, CORE, CS, ENG, IPSY, MED, MUS, NURSE, PLNG, SP, SPAA, SW

02 President ... Dr. John KELLY
05 Provost/VP Academic Affairs ... Dr. Gary W. PERRY
10 VP Finance/Chief Fiscal Officer ... Ms. Dorothy RUSSELL
32 Vice Pres Student Affairs ... Dr. Corey KING
46 Vice President Research ... Dr. Daniel FLYNN
11 VP Admin Affairs ... Ms. Stacy VOLNICK
102 Int VP Cmty Engag/Exec Dir FAU Fdn ... Ms. Joanne DAVIS
13 Assoc Provost IT/CIO ... Mr. Jason BALL
29 Asst Vice Pres Alumni Relations ... Mr. Bradford W. CREWS
35 Assoc VP Student Affairs ... Ms. Claire E. GOOD
43 General Counsel ... Mr. David KIAN
22 Exec Dir Equity/Inclusion/Compl ... Mr. Ande DUROJAIYE
84 Asst Provost Enrollment Mgmt ... Ms. Tracy BOULUKOS
63 Dean C E Schmidt Col of Medicine ... Dr. David J. BJORKMAN
20 Vice Provost Academic Affairs ... Dr. Michele HAWKINS
80 Int Dean of Design/Social Inquiry ... Dr. Wesley E. HAWKINS
49 Dean of Arts & Letters ... Dr. Heather COLTMAN
50 Dean of Business ... Dr. Daniel GROPPER
53 Dean of Education ... Dr. Valerie BRISTOR
54 Dean of Engineering/Comp Sci ... Dr. Mohammad ILYAS
66 Dean of Nursing ... Dr. Marlaine SMITH
92 Dean of Honors College ... Dr. Jeff BULLER
20 Dean Undergraduate Studies ... Dr. Edward E. PRATT
81 Int Dean College of Science ... Dr. Janet BLANKS
58 Dean of Graduate Studies ... Dr. Deborah FLOYD
88 Asst Dean/PK-12 Sch/Educational Pgm ... Mr. Joel HERBST
90 Director Enterprise Computing Svcs . Mr. Mehran BASIRATMAND
91 Dir Univ Administrative Systems ... Ms. Kay RECKTENWALD
25 Int Dir Sponsored Programs ... Ms. Camille COLEY
09 Asst Prov Inst Effective/Analysis ... Mr. Jeffery HOYT
06 Registrar ... Mr. Brian HODGE
08 Dean University Libraries ... Ms. Carol HIXSON
15 Asst Vice Pres Human Resources ... Mr. David TOMANIO
41 Vice Pres for Athletics ... Mr. Patrick CHUN
39 Exec Director Student Housing ... Dr. Larry FAERMAN
36 Dir Career Devel Ctr/Student Place ... Ms. Sandra JAKUBOW
85 Director Intl Students/Scholar Svcs ... Dr. Mihaela METIANU
37 Director Student Financial Aid ... Ms. Tracy BOULUKOS

*Florida Gulf Coast University (L)

10501 FGCU Boulevard S, Fort Myers FL 33965-6565
County: Lee FICE Identification: 032553
Unit ID: 433660
Telephone: (239) 590-1000 Carnegie Class: Masters/L
FAX Number: (239) 590-1166 Calendar System: Semester
URL: www.fgcu.edu
Established: 1991 Annual Undergrad Tuition & Fees (In-State): $6,118
Enrollment: 14,473 Coed
Affiliation or Control: State IRS Status: 501(c)3
Highest Offering: Doctorate
Accreditation: SC, ANEST, BUS, CAATE, CACREP, ENG, MT, MUS, NURSE, OT, PTA, SPAA, SW, TED

02 President ... Dr. Wilson G. BRADSHAW
05 Provost & VP Academic Affairs ... Dr. Ronald B. TOLL
10 Vice Pres Admin Services/Finance ... Mr. Steve L. MAGIERA
30 VP Univ Advance/Exec Dir Foundation ... Mr. Christopher (Chris) J. SIMONEAU
32 Vice President Student Affairs ... Dr. J. Michael ROLLO
100 Vice President & Chief of Staff ... Ms. Susan EVANS
43 Vice President & General Counsel ... Ms. Vee LEONARD
20 Assoc VP Academic/Curriculum Sppt ... Dr. Cathy DUFF
45 Sr Asc Prov/Asc VP Plng & Inst Perf ... Dr. Paul SNYDER
58 Assoc VP Research/Dean Grad Studies ... Dr. T. C YIH
26 AVP Communications & Marketing ... Ms. Deborah WILTROUT
04 Asst to Pres/University Ombudsman ... Vacant
88 Asst Vice Pres Business Services ... Mr. Joseph MCDONALD
13 Asst VP Business Technology Svcs ... Ms. Mary BANKS
15 Asst Vice Pres Human Resources ... Ms. Christine LLOYD
21 Controller ... Ms. June GUTKNECHT
35 Dean Student Affairs ... Dr. Michele YOVANOVICH
49 Dean College Arts & Sciences ... Dr. Robert (Bob) GREGERSON
20 Dean of Undergraduate Studies ... Dr. Dawn LATTA KIRBY

50 Dean Lutgert College of Business .... Dr. Robert BEATTY
53 Dean College of Education .... Dr. Eunsook HYUN
76 Dean College Health Professions .... Dr. Mitchell CORDOVA
54 Dean U.A. Whitaker Col Engineering .... Dr. Richard A. BEHR
62 Dean Library Services .... Dr. Kathleen MILLER
45 Asst Dir Planning/Inst Performance .... Ms. Kristen VANSELOW
38 Dir Counseling/Student Health Svcs .... Dr. Jon L. BRUNNER
43 Asst Dean Judicial Affairs .... Mr. Chad TRISLER
07 Director of Admissions .... Mr. Marc LAVIOLETTE
96 Director of Procurement Services .... Ms. Maryan EGAN
19 Director Campus Police & Safety .... Chief Steven C. MOORE
18 Director Facilities Planning .... Mr. Tom MAYO
37 Director Student Financial Aid .... Mr. Jorge LOPEZ-ROSADO
06 University Registrar .... Ms. Susan BYARS
23 Dir Student Health Services/Med Dir .... Dr. Kevin COLLINS
41 Director Intercollegiate Athletics .... Mr. Kenneth KAVANAGH
28 Director Title IX Compliance .... Mr. Brandon WASHINGTON
85 Director International Services .... Dr. Elaine HOZDIK
106 Dir Web/E-learning/Publication Svcs .... Mr. David JAEGER
72 Director Academic & Event Tech ... Ms. Pat O'CONNOR-BENSON
36 Director Career Development Svcs .... Mr. Reid LENNERTZ
31 Dir Cmty Engagement/Svc Learning .... Ms. Jessica RHEA
29 Director Alumni Relations .... Ms. Kimberly WALLACE
92 Director Honors Program .... Dr. Clay MOTLEY
09 Director Inst Research/Analysis .... Dr. Robert VINES
21 Director University Budgets .... Mr. David VAZQUEZ
39 Director University Housing .... Dr. Brian FISHER
86 Director Government Relations .... Ms. Jennifer GOEN
88 Dir Environmental Health/Safety .... Ms. Rhonda HOLTZCLAW
51 Exec Dir Cont Educ/Off-Campus Pgms .... Dr. Paul THORNTON
88 General Manager/WGCU .... Mr. Rick JOHNSON
40 Manager The University Store .... Ms. Laura JENSEN
88 Dir Emergent Technologies Inst .... Dr. John WOOLSCHLAGER
88 Dir Ctr for Academic Achievement .... Dr. Lindsey SINGH
88 Dir Compliance/Risk Management .... Vacant

*Florida International University (A)

University Park, 11200 SW 8 Street, Miami FL 33199-0001

County: Miami-Dade FICE Identification: 009635
Unit ID: 133951
Telephone: (305) 348-2000 Carnegie Class: DU-Highest
FAX Number: N/A Calendar System: Semester
URL: www.fiu.edu
Established: 1965 Annual Undergrad Tuition & Fees (In-State): $6,556
Enrollment: 49,610 Coed
Affiliation or Control: State IRS Status: 501(c)3
Highest Offering: Doctorate
Accreditation: SC, ANEST, #ARCPA, ART, BUS, BUSA, CAATE, CACREP, CIDA, CLPSY, CONST, CS, DIETC, DIETD, ENG, FEPAC, HSA, IPSY, JOUR, LAW, LSAR, MED, MUS, NURSE, OT, PH, PTA, SP, SPAA, SW, TED, THEA

02 President .... Dr. Mark ROSENBERG
100 Chief of Staff .... Mr. Javier MARQUES
03 Executive VP & COO .... Dr. Kenneth FURTON
88 VP for Engagement .... Mr. Saif ISHOOF
05 Vice President Academic Affairs .... Dr. Elizabeth BEJAR
10 CFO & Sr VP for Administration .... Dr. Kenneth JESSELL
30 Vice President for Advancement .... Mr. Howard LIPMAN
32 VP Student Affairs .... Dr. Larry LUNSFORD
09 Interim VP Analysis/Info Mgmt .... Dr. Joyce ELAM
46 Vice President of Research .... Dr. Andres GIL
13 Vice President/CIO .... Mr. Robert GRILLO
12 Vice Prov Biscayne Bay Campus .... Mr. Stephen MOLL
84 VP Enrollment Management .... Dr. Luisa HAVENS
35 Assoc VP and Dean of Students .... Dr. Cathy AKENS
15 Vice President Human Resources .... Dr. Jaffus HARDRICK
18 Assoc VP Facilities Operations .... Mr. John CAL
07 Dir Undergraduate Admissions .... Ms. Jody GLASSMAN
49 Dean Col Arts/Sciences/Educ .... Dr. Michael HEITHAUS
50 Int Dean College Business Admin .... Dr. Jose ALDRICH
54 Dean Col Engineering/Computing .... Dr. Ranu JUNG
53 Director College of Education .... Dr. Laura DINEHART
88 Dean Sch Hospitality Management .... Dr. Mike HAMPTON
82 Dean School Intl/Pub Affairs .... Dr. John STACK
66 Dean Col Nursing/Health Science .... Dr. Ora STRICKLAND
69 Dean College of Public Health .... Dr. Tomas GUILARTE
61 Dean College of Law .... Dr. R. Alexander ACOSTA
63 Dean College of Medicine .... Dr. John ROCK
92 Dean Honors College .... Dr. Lesley NORTHUP
48 Dean Col Comm/Architecture/Arts .... Dr. Brian SCHRINER
77 Dir Sch Computing/Info Sciences .... Dr. Sundararaj IYENGAR
38 Asst VP Stdnt Hlth & Counseling .... Dr. Cheryl NOWELL
22 Director Equal Opportunity
Program .... Ms. Shirlyon J. MCWHORTER
88 Director School Accounting .... Dr. Ruth MCEWEN
88 Dir Multicultural Programs Admin .... Dr. Dorret SAWYERS
62 Dean of Libraries .... Dr. Anne PRESTAMO
41 Athletics Director .... Mr. Pete GARCIA
86 VP for Government Relations .... Ms. Michelle PALACIO
06 University Registrar .... Dr. Kevin COUGHLIN
31 AVP Community Rel/Special Events .... Ms. Dania ADAMS
37 Director Student Financial Aid .... Mr. Francisco VALINES
36 Director Career Services .... Dr. Fernando FIGUEREDO
23 Director Univ Health Services .... Dr. Oscar LOYNAZ
39 Dir of Housing/Residential Life .... Ms. Lynn HENDRICKS, JR.
22 Director Disability Student Svcs .... Ms. Amanda NIGUIDULA
88 Director Internal Audit .... Mr. Allen VANN
24 Dir University IT/Media Support .... Mr. Matthew HAGOOD
21 Associate VP and Univ Controller .... Ms. Cecilia HAMILTON
88 Dir Environmentl Health/Safety .... Ms. Yenny FARINAS
19 Chief of Police .... Chief Alexander CASAS
26 Director Media Relations .... Ms. Maydel SANTANA-BRAVO
43 General Counsel .... Ms. Kristina RAATTAMA
85 Interim Director Intl Student Svcs .... Ms. Nancy HERNANDEZ
25 Assistant VP for Research .... Mr. Roberto GUTIERREZ
04 Assistant Chief of Staff .... Ms. Claudia GONZALEZ
44 Exec Dir Dev Found Relations .... Ms. Nicole GLASGOW
102 Sr Dir Corporate/Found Relations .... Ms. Karla HERNANDEZ

*Florida Polytechnic University (B)

4700 Research Way, Lakeland FL 33805-8531

County: Polk Identification: 667279
Telephone: (863) 583-9050 Carnegie Class: Not Classified
FAX Number: N/A Calendar System: Semester
URL: www.floridapolytechnic.org
Established: 2012 Annual Undergrad Tuition & Fees (In-State): N/A
Enrollment: N/A Coed
Affiliation or Control: State IRS Status: 501(c)3
Highest Offering: Master's
Accreditation: @SC

02 President .... Dr. Randy K. AVENT

*Florida State University (C)

600 W. College Avenue, Tallahassee FL 32306

County: Leon FICE Identification: 001489
Unit ID: 134097
Telephone: (850) 644-2525 Carnegie Class: DU-Highest
FAX Number: (850) 644-9936 Calendar System: Semester
URL: www.fsu.edu
Established: 1851 Annual Undergrad Tuition & Fees (In-State): $6,507
Enrollment: 41,226 Coed
Affiliation or Control: State IRS Status: 501(c)3
Highest Offering: Doctorate
Accreditation: SC, AAFCS, ANEST, ART, BUS, BUSA, CAATE, CACREP, CIDA, CLPSY, CS, DANCE, DIETD, DIETI, ENG, IPSY, LAW, LIB, MED, MFCD, MUS, NURSE, PH, PLNG, PSPSY, SP, SPAA, SW, TED, THEA

02 President .... Mr. John E. THRASHER
05 Prov/Exec VP Academic Affairs .... Dr. Sally E. MCRORIE
10 Vice Pres Finance & Admin .... Mr. Kyle CLARK
32 Vice President Student Affairs .... Dr. Mary E. COBURN
46 Vice President Research .... Dr. Gary K. OSTRANDER
26 Vice Pres University Relations .... Ms. Kathleen DALY
45 VP Planning and Programs .... Vacant
30 VP University Advancement .... Mr. Thomas W. JENNINGS
102 Exec VP FSU Foundation .... Mr. Andy A. JHANJI
20 Vice Pres Faculty Development .... Dr. Janet KISTNER
100 Chief of Staff to President .... Mr. David COBURN
88 Assoc Vice President for Research .... Dr. Ross ELLINGTON
18 Associate VP for Facilities .... Mr. Dennis A. BAILEY
21 Assoc VP Budget/Planning/Fin Svcs .... Vacant
20 Asst VP for Academic Affairs .... Mr. Paul HARLACHER
15 Asst Vice Pres for Human Resources .... Ms. Renisha L. GIBBS
11 Asst VP for Administrative Services .... Dr. Perry CROWELL
84 Asst VP Enrollment Mgmt .... Mr. John EARNHILL
27 Asst VP of University Communication .... Ms Browning BROOKS
88 Dir Academic Pgm Professional Svcs .... Mr. Bill LINDNER
49 Dean Arts & Sciences .... Dr. Sam HUCKABA
50 Dean Business .... Dr. Michael HARTLINE
53 Dean Education .... Dr. Marcy P. DRISCOLL
59 Dean Human Sciences .... Dr. Michael DELP
88 Dean Communication & Information .... Dr. Larry DENNIS
66 Dean Nursing .... Dr. Judith MCFETRIDGE-DURDLE
88 Dean Criminology .... Dr. Thomas BLOMBERG
61 Dean Law .... Mr. Donald WEIDNER
83 Dean Social Sciences .... Dr. David W. RASMUSSEN
70 Dean Social Work .... Dr. Clark JAMES
88 Dean Motion Picture Arts .... Mr. Frank PATTERSON
64 Dean Music .... Dr. Patricia J. FLOWERS
57 Dean Fine Arts .... Mr. Peter WEISHAR
54 Int Dean Engineering .... Dr. Bruce LOCKE
63 Dean Medicine .... Dr. John FOGARTY
58 Dean Graduate Studies .... Dr. Nancy MARCUS
88 Dean Undergraduate Studies .... Dr. Karen L. LAUGHLIN
35 Dean of Students .... Dr. Jeanine WARD-ROOF
12 Dean Panama City Branch Campus .... Dr. Carol EDWARDS
06 University Registrar .... Dr. Kimberly BARBER
07 Director Admissions .... Ms. Hege FERGUSON
92 Int Dir University Honors Program .... Ms. Allen PEGGY
37 Director Student Financial Aid .... Mr. Darryl MARSHALL
08 Director Libraries .... Ms. Julia ZIMMERMAN
13 Chief Information Officer .... Mr. Michael BARRETT
90 Dir University Computing Services .... Mr. Byron MENCHION
43 General Counsel .... Ms. Carolyn EGAN
104 Director International Programs .... Dr. James E. PITTS
88 Chief Budget Officer .... Mr. Michael P. LAKE
09 Director Institutional Research .... Dr. Richard BURNETTE
86 Director Governmental Relations .... Ms. Kathleen M. DALY
41 Athletic Director .... Mr. Stan WILCOX
38 Director Student Counseling .... Dr. Carlos J. GOMEZ
19 Director Public Safety .... Mr. David L. PERRY
23 Director Student Health Services .... Dr. Lesley SACHER
36 Director Career Center .... Ms. Myrna HOOVER
29 President Alumni Association .... Mr. Scott ATWELL
88 Chief Audit Officer .... Mr. Sam MCCALL
28 Dir Diversity/Equal Opportunity .... Vacant
96 Director of Purchasing .... Mr. Ian ROBBINS
39 Director Student Housing .... Ms. Shannon STATEN
88 Director Business Services .... Mr. Harvey BUCHANAN
106 Director Distance Learning .... Dr Susann RUDASILL
25 Director Sponsored Research .... Ms. Pamela RAY
88 Director Information Technology .... Mr Kenneth JOHNSON

*New College of Florida (D)

5800 Bay Shore Road, Sarasota FL 34243-2109

County: Sarasota FICE Identification: 001507
Unit ID: 262129
Telephone: (941) 487-4100 Carnegie Class: Bac-A&S
FAX Number: (941) 487-4101 Calendar System: 4/1/4
URL: www.ncf.edu
Established: 1960 Annual Undergrad Tuition & Fees (In-State): $6,916
Enrollment: 834 Coed
Affiliation or Control: State IRS Status: 501(c)3
Highest Offering: Master's
Accreditation: SC

02 President .... Dr. Donal E. O'SHEA
05 Provost .... Dr. Stephen MILES
10 Vice Pres Finance & Administration .... Mr. John U. MARTIN
79 Chair of Humanities .... Dr. Miriam WALLACE
81 Chair of Natural Sciences .... Dr. Katherine WALSTROM
83 Chair of Social Sciences .... Dr. Richard COE
08 Dean Cook Library .... Dr. Brian DOHERTY
84 Dean of Enrollment & Info Tech .... Ms. Kathleen KILLION
32 Dean of Students .... Dr. Robin WILLIAMSON
07 Associate Dean of Admissions .... Ms. Sonia WU
20 Associate Academic Officer .... Dr. Robert ZAMSKY
21 Associate Business Officer .... Ms. Kimberly BENDICKSON
13 Chief Information Officer .... Mr. Ben FOSS
14 Director of Information Support .... Mr. Jeff SMITH
29 Director Alumnae/i Association .... Ms. Jessica ROGERS
06 Registrar .... Mr. Brian SCHOLTEN
26 Director Public Affairs .... Ms. Jessica ROOD
38 Director Counseling .... Dr. Anne E. FISHER
09 Director of Institutional Research .... Ms. Hui-Men WEN
108 Dir of Institutional Assessment .... Dr. Bradley THIESSEN
15 Director Personnel Services .... Mr. Daniel RICHARDSON
18 Chief Facilities/Physical Plant .... Mr. Alan BURR
28 Director of Diversity .... Vacant
96 Director of Purchasing .... Ms. Jean HARRIS
37 Director Student Financial Aid .... Ms. Tara KARAS
43 Director Legal Svcs/General Counsel .... Mr. Mike PIERCE
25 Contract Administrator .... Ms. Lee Ann RODRIGUEZ
72 Director of Technology Support .... Mr. Jeff SMITH
30 Chief Development .... Ms. MaryAnne YOUNG
19 Chief of Police .... Sgt. Michael KESSIE
39 Director Student Housing .... Dr. Mark STIER
41 Athletic Director .... Mr. Colin JORDAN
86 Director Government Relations .... Ms. Suzanne JANNEY
04 Administrative Asst to President .... Ms. Shelley WILBUR

*University of Central Florida (E)

PO Box 160000, Orlando FL 32816-0001

County: Orange FICE Identification: 003954
Unit ID: 132903
Telephone: (407) 823-2000 Carnegie Class: DU-Highest
FAX Number: N/A Calendar System: Semester
URL: www.ucf.edu
Established: 1963 Annual Undergrad Tuition & Fees (In-State): $6,368
Enrollment: 60,767 Coed
Affiliation or Control: State IRS Status: 501(c)3
Highest Offering: Doctorate
Accreditation: SC, BUS, BUSA, CAATE, CACREP, CAHIIM, CEA, CLPSY, CS, ENG, HSA, IPSY, MED, MT, MUS, NURSE, PTA, SP, SPAA, SW, TED, THEA

02 President .... Dr. John C. HITT
05 Provost/Executive Vice President .... Dr. A. Dale WHITTAKER
100 Vice President and Chief of Staff .... Dr. John SCHELL
10 Vice Pres Admin & Finance/CFO .... Mr. William F. MERCK, II
26 Vice President University Relations .... Dr. Daniel HOLSENBECK
43 Vice President/General Counsel .... Mr. W. Scott COLE
46 VP Research and Commercialization .... Dr. M. J. SOILEAU
32 VP Student Dev/Enrollment Svcs .... Dr. Maribeth EHASZ
30 VP Dev/Alum Rels/Foundation
CEO .... Mr. Michael J. MORSBERGER
31 Vice President Emerita Comm Rels .... Ms. Helen DONEGAN
63 VP Medical Affairs/Dean Med College .... Dr. Deborah GERMAN
41 Vice Pres & Dir of Athletics .... Mr. Danny WHITE
49 Dean College of Arts & Humanities .... Mr. Jeffrey MOORE
50 Dean College of Business Admin .... Dr. Paul JARLEY
53 Dean College of Education .... Dr. Pamela S. CARROLL
54 Dean College of Engr/Comp Sci .. Dr. Michael GEORGIOPOULOS
76 Dean College of Hlth/Pub Affs .... Dr. Michael FRUMKIN
88 Dean Rosen College Hospitality Mgt .... Dr. Abraham PIZAM
66 Dean College of Nursing .... Dr. Mary L. SOLE
88 Dean/Dir Col of Optics & Photonics .... Dr. Bahaa SALEH
81 Dean College of Sciences .... Dr. Michael D. JOHNSON
92 Dean Burnett Honors College .... Dr. Alvin WANG
13 Vice Provost & CIO Info Tech/Res .... Dr. Joel L. HARTMAN
12 Vice Provost Regional Campuses .... Dr. Jeff JONES
58 Int Vice Provost/Dean Grad Studies .... Dr. Mubarak SHAH
97 Vice Provost/Dean Undergrad Studies ..... Dr. Elizabeth A. DOOLEY
82 VPrv Fac Exc & Intl Affs/Glbl Strat .... Dr. Cynthia Y. YOUNG
88 Assoc Prov APQ and Assoc VP IKM .... Dr. M. Paige BORDEN
18 Assoc VP Facilities and Safety .... Ms. Lee KERNEK
29 Assoc Vice Pres Alumni Relations .... Ms. Julie C. STROH
86 Assoc VP for University Relations .... Mr. Fred KITTINGER
30 AVP of Col/Univ Advancement .... Mr. Jeff COATES
88 Assoc VP Rsrch & Commercialization .... Mr. Tom O'NEAL
07 Assoc VP Enrollment Services .... Dr. Gordon CHAVIS
27 VP Communications & Marketing .... Mr. Grant HESTON
37 Dir Student Financial Asst .... Ms. Alicia KEATON
06 University Registrar .... Mr. Brian BOYD
08 Director Libraries .... Mr. Barry BAKER

15 Int Assoc VP HR/Chief HR Officer ... Ms. Shelia DANIELS
19 Assoc VP Safety & Chief of Police ... Mr. Richard BEARY
93 Director Multicul Acad Suppt Svcs ... Mr. Wayne JACKSON
14 Chief Technology Officer ... Mr. Robert YANCKELLO
38 Director Counseling Center ... Dr. Karen HOFMANN
22 Director EEO Affirmative Action ... Ms. Maria BECKMAN
23 Director Health Services ... Dr. Michael G. DEICHEN
39 Exec Dir Housing and Residence Life ... Mrs. Christi HARTZLER
28 Chief Diversity Officer ... Ms. Karen MORRISON
96 Director of Purchasing ... Mr. Gregory ROBINSON
36 Exec Director Career Services ... Ms. Lynn HANSEN

*University of Florida (A)

235 Tigert Hall, Gainesville FL 32611-9500
County: Alachua FICE Identification: 001535
Unit ID: 134130
Telephone: (352) 392-3261 Carnegie Class: DU-Highest
FAX Number: (352) 392-8735 Calendar System: Semester
URL: www.ufl.edu
Established: 1853 Annual Undergrad Tuition & Fees (In-State): $6,381
Enrollment: 49,459 Coed
Affiliation or Control: State IRS Status: 501(c)3
Highest Offering: Doctorate
Accreditation: SC, ARCPA, ART, AUD, BUS, BUSA, CAATE, CACREP, CEA, CIDA, CLPSY, CONST, COPSY, DANCE, DENT, DIETD, DIETI, ENG, ENGR, HSA, IPSY, JOUR, LAW, LSAR, MED, MIDWF, MUS, NURSE, OT, PH, PHAR, PLNG, PTA, SCPSY, SP, TED, THEA, VET

02 President ... Dr. W. Kent FUCHS
05 Provost & Senior Vice President ... Dr. Joseph GLOVER
47 Sr Vice Pres Agric/Natural Res ... Dr. Jack M. PAYNE
17 Sr Vice Pres Health Affairs ... Dr. David S. GUZICK
10 VP/Chief Financial Ofcr ... Mr. Michael MCKEE
11 Sr Vice Pres/Chief Operating Ofcr ... Dr. Charles E. LANE
30 Vice President Advancement ... Mr. Thomas J. MITCHELL
21 Vice President Business Affairs ... Mr. Curtis REYNOLDS
32 Vice President Student Affairs ... Mr. David PARROTT
26 Vice President Univ Relations ... Ms. Jane A. ADAMS
15 Vice Pres Human Resources ... Ms. Jodi D. GENTRY
46 Vice President Research ... Dr. David P. NORTON
43 Vice President/General Counsel ... Ms. Jamie L. KEITH
13 Vice President & CIO ... Mr. Elias G. ELDAYRIE
84 Vice Pres Enroll Mgmt/Assoc Provost ... Dr. Zina EVANS
86 Assoc VP Government Relations ... Ms. Marion S. HOFFMAN
88 Associate Provost Teaching & Tech ... Dr. William A. MCCOLLOUGH
27 Asst Vice Pres Marketing ... Ms. Nicole YUCHT
27 Asst VP Media Rels/Public Affairs ... Ms. Janine SIKES
27 Senior Director Media Relations ... Mr. Stephen F. ORLANDO
16 Asst Vice Pres Human Resources ... Vacant
21 Business Affs/Finance/Admin AVP ... Mr. Craig R. HILL
18 Asst VP/Fac/Plng/Construction ... Mr. Carlos DOUGNAC
20 Associate Provost Academic Affairs ... Dr. Angel KWOLEK-FOLLAND
20 Assoc Provost Undergrad Affairs ... Dr. Angela LINDNER
09 Asst Provost/Dir Inst Research/Plng ... Dr. Marie ZEGLEN
35 Dean Students/Assoc VP Student Affs ... Dr. Jen D. SHAW
08 Dean University Libraries ... Ms. Judith RUSSELL
50 Dean of Business Administration ... Dr. John KRAFT
49 Dean of Liberal Arts & Science ... Mr. David E. RICHARDSON
68 Dean of Health/Human Performance ... Dr. Michael B. REID
61 Dean of Law ... Ms. Laura A. ROSENBURY
66 Dean of Nursing ... Dr. Anna M. MCDANIEL
67 Dean of Pharmacy ... Dr. Julie A. JOHNSON
54 Dean of Engineering ... Dr. Cammy ABERNATHY
47 Dean Agricultural/Life Sciences ... Dr. R. Elaine TURNER
60 Dean of Journalism/Communications ... Ms. Diane H. MCFARLIN
76 Dean Pub Health/Health Professions ... Dr. Michael PERRI
53 Dean of Education ... Dr. Glenn GOOD
47 Dean IFAS Extension ... Dr. Nick T. PLACE
74 Dean of Veterinary Medicine ... Dr. James W. LLOYD
57 Dean of Fine Arts ... Ms. Lucinda LAVELLI
48 Dean Design Construction Planning ... Dr. Chimay ANUMBA
63 Dean of Medicine ... Dr. Michael L. GOOD
46 Dean of IFAS Research ... Dr. Jacqueline BURNS
52 Dean of Dentistry ... Dr. Isabel GARCIA
58 Dean Graduate School ... Dr. Henry T. FRIERSON
65 Dir School Natural Res/Envir ... Dr. Thomas K. FRAZER
06 University Registrar ... Mr. Stephen J. PRITZ
23 Director of Student Health ... Dr. Guy NICOLETTE
38 Director of Counseling Center ... Dr. Sherry BENTON
37 Director Student Financial Aid ... Mr. Richard D. WILDER
36 Director of Career Resource Center ... Ms. Heather B. WHITE
14 Director of Computer Center ... Mr. Timothy J. FITZPATRICK
19 Director of University Police ... Ms. Linda J. STUMP
24 Director of Academic Technology ... Dr. Fedro S. ZAZUETA
65 Director of Forestry ... Dr. Timothy L. WHITE
39 Director of Housing ... Mr. Norbert W. DUNKEL
41 Athletic Director ... Mr. Jeremy N. FOLEY
29 Exec Director Alumni Affairs ... Ms. Danita NIAS
28 Director of Diversity ... Ms. Tamara COHEN
96 Director of Purchasing ... Ms. Lisa DEAL
07 Director of Admissions ... Mr. Patrick C. HERRING
04 Executive Asst to President ... Ms. Beth BOONE
106 Dir Online Education/E-learning ... Ms. Evangeline CUMMINGS
108 Director Institutional Assessment ... Dr. Timothy S. BROPHY

*University of North Florida (B)

1 UNF Drive, Jacksonville FL 32224-7699
County: Duval FICE Identification: 009841
Unit ID: 136172
Telephone: (904) 620-1000 Carnegie Class: Masters/L
FAX Number: (904) 620-2414 Calendar System: Semester
URL: www.unf.edu
Established: 1965 Annual Undergrad Tuition & Fees (In-State): $6,394
Enrollment: 15,984 Coed
Affiliation or Control: State IRS Status: 501(c)3
Highest Offering: Doctorate
Accreditation: SC, ANEST, BUS, BUSA, CAATE, CACREP, CONST, CS, DIETD, DIETI, ENG, ENGR, EXSC, HSA, MT, MUS, NURSE, PH, PTA, SPAA, SW, TED

02 President ... Mr. John A. DELANEY
05 Provost ... Dr. Earle C. TRAYNHAM
20 Associate Provost ... Dr. Bob J. COLEMAN
100 VP/Chief of Staff ... Dr. Thomas S. SERWATKA
86 VP Governmental Affairs ... Ms. Janet D. OWEN
43 VP/General Counsel ... Ms. Karen J. STONE
15 VP Human Resources ... Ms. Rachelle GOTTLIEB
10 VP Administration/Finance ... Ms. Shari A. SHUMAN
30 VP Development Alumni Aff ... Mr. Joshua D. MERCHANT
32 VP Student & International Affairs ... Dr. Mauricio GONZALEZ
84 Assoc VP Enrollment Svs ... Dr. Albert N. COLOM
07 Director of Admissions ... Ms. Karen LUCAS
88 Assoc VP/Compliance Officer ... Dr. Joann N. CAMPBELL
21 Assoc VP Admin & Finance ... Mr. Scott BENNETT
13 Assoc VP Chief Info Officer ... Mr. Reggie BRINSON
44 Dir for Major Gifts ... Ms. Christina LEVINE
35 Assoc VP Student Affairs ... Mr. Everett J. MALCOLM, III
45 Asst VP Research ... Dr. John KANTNER
88 Asst VP Development ... Ms. Ann S. MCCULLEN
26 VP Public Relations ... Ms. Sharon ASHTON
88 Asst VP Student Affairs ... Dr. Lucy S. CROFT
49 Int Dean College of Arts and Sci ... Dr. Daniel C. MOON
58 Dean of the Graduate School ... Dr. John KANTNER
08 Dean of the Library ... Dr. Elizabeth A. CURRY
88 Dean of Undergraduate Studies ... Dr. Karen B. PATTERSON
50 Dean Coggin College of Business ... Dr. Mark DAWKINS
53 Dean College of Education ... Dr. Diane YENDOL-HOPPEY
76 Dean Brooks College of Health ... Dr. Pam CHALLY
77 Dean Computing Engineering & Constr ... Dr. Mark A. TUMEO
51 Dean Continuing Education ... Mr. Robert WOOD
16 Dir Human Resources ... Mr. Greg CATRON
88 Internal Auditing ... Mr. Khareem D. GORDON
22 Dir Equal Opportunity Programs ... Ms. Cheryl N. GONZALEZ
88 Dir Professional Dev Training ... Ms. Kelly G. HARRISON
21 Chief Budget Officer ... Mr. Ricky B. ARJUNE
21 Controller ... Ms. Valerie O. STEVENSON
88 Dir of Compliance ... Ms. Donna R. KIRK
88 Dir Environment Health/Safety ... Mr. Daniel D. ENDICOTT
22 Dir ADA Compliance ... Ms. Rocelia T. GONZALEZ
14 Dir IT Networking ... Mr. Jeffrey A. DURFEE
21 Treasurer ... Mr. Michael S. NEGLIA
18 Dir Univ Facilities Planning ... Mr. Zak OVADIA
88 Dir University Center ... Mr. George ANDROUIN
29 Asst VP Alumni Engagement ... Mr. Christopher M. DECENT
19 Dir Safety Security ... Mr. Francis J. MACKESY
36 Dir Career Development Services ... Mr. Rick ROBERTS
85 Dir Intercultural Ctr for Peace ... Dr. Oupa SEANE
88 Dir Child Development Ctr ... Ms. Mahreen N. MIAN
23 Chief Medical Officer ... Dr. Lisa DYNAN-DOBBERTIEN
38 Dir Univ Counseling Center ... Dr. Andrew B. KING
34 Dir Women's Center ... Ms. Sheila D. SPIVEY
85 Dir The International Center ... Dr. Timothy ROBINSON
39 Dir Housing Residence Life ... Mr. Robert J. BOYLE
41 Athletic Director ... Mr. Lee L. MOON
88 Dir Faculty Enhancement ... Dr. Dan RICHARD
108 Director of Assessment ... Ms. Megan S. POSSINGER
92 Dir Honors Program ... Dr. Jeff MICHELMAN
37 Dir Student Financial Aid ... Mrs. Anissa AGNE
06 Registrar ... Mrs. Megan R. KUEHNER
09 Interim Dir Institutional Research ... Dr. Fen YU
88 Exec Dir FL Inst of Education ... Dr. Cheryl A. FOUNTAIN
88 Dir Small Business Dev Ctr ... Ms. Janice W. DONALDSON
88 Dir Disability Resource Center ... Dr. Russell G. DUBBERLY
96 Dir Purchasing ... Ms. Kathy RITTER
51 Dir Continuing Education ... Mr. John E. YANCEY
106 Dir Center for Instr & Res Tech ... Ms. Deb MILLER
90 Director Academic Technology ... Dr. Gordon F. RAKITA

*University of South Florida (C)

4202 E Fowler Avenue, Tampa FL 33620-6100
County: Hillsborough FICE Identification: 001537
Unit ID: 137351
Telephone: (813) 974-2011 Carnegie Class: DU-Highest
FAX Number: (813) 974-5530 Calendar System: Semester
URL: www.usf.edu
Established: 1956 Annual Undergrad Tuition & Fees (In-State): $6,410
Enrollment: 41,938 Coed
Affiliation or Control: State IRS Status: 501(c)3
Highest Offering: Doctorate
Accreditation: SC, ANEST, ART, AUD, BUS, BUSA, CAATE, CACREP, CEA, CLPSY, CORE, CS, DANCE, @DIETI, ENG, ENGR, HSA, IPSY, LIB, MED, MUS, NURSE, PCSAS, PH, PHAR, PTA, SCPSY, SP, SPAA, SW, TED, THEA

02 President ... Dr. Judy L. GENSHAFT
04 Special Assistant to the President ... Mr. John L. PRUGH, JR.
11 Chief Operating Officer & Sr VP ... Mr. John W. LONG
100 Chief of Staff/President's Office ... Dr. Cynthia S. VISOT
43 General Counsel ... Mr. Gerard SOLIS
05 Prov/Exec Vice Pres Academic Affs ... Dr. Ralph WILCOX
20 Vice Provost for HR and Space Plan ... Dr. Kofi GLOVER
20 Vice Provost for Plng/Perf & Acct ... Dr. Theresa H. CHISOLM
20 Vice Provost and AVP USF World ... Dr. Roger BRINDLEY
104 Director Education Abroad ... Dr. Amanda C. MAURER
46 Sr Vice Pres Research & Innovation ... Dr. Paul SANBERG
17 Sr Vice Pres USF Health ... Dr. Charles LOCKWOOD
23 VP & COO USF Health ... Dr. Edmund F. FUNAI
58 Sr Vice Provost/Dean Grad School ... Dr. Dwayne SMITH
10 Vice Pres Business & Finance ... Mr. Nick TRIVUNOVICH
88 Assistant Treasurer ... Ms. Dawn M. RODRIGUEZ
11 Vice Pres Administrative Services ... Mr. Calvin WILLIAMS
18 Asst VP Physical Plant ... Mr. Chris DUFFY
30 Sr Vice Pres University Advancement ... Mr. Joel MOMBERG
32 Vice President Student Affairs ... Dr. Thomas E. MILLER
13 Vice Pres Information Technology ... Mr. Sidney FERNANDES
14 AVP Information Technology ... Ms. Jenny PAULSEN
14 AVP Information Technology ... Swapna CHACKRAVARTHY
105 Director Web Services ... Mr. Christopher L. AKIN
29 Assoc Vice Pres Alumni Affairs ... Mr. Bill MCCAUSLAND
14 Assoc Vice Pres Info Technologies ... Mr. George W. ELLIS
22 Chief Diversity Officer ... Dr. Jose HERNANDEZ
20 Vice Provost for Student Success ... Dr. Paul J. DOSAL
15 Assoc Vice Pres Human Resources ... Ms. Donna KEENER
86 Asst Vice Pres Government Rels ... Mr. Mark WALSH
35 Asst Vice Pres/Dean of Students ... Dr. Danielle MCDONALD
35 Asst Vice Pres Student Affairs ... Mr. Guy CONWAY
88 University Ombuds ... Mr. Steven D. PREVAUX
39 Asst VP Housing/Residential Educ ... Ms. Ana HERNANDEZ
83 Dean Behavioral/Community Sci ... Dr. Julianne SEROVICH
50 Dean Business Administration ... Dr. Moez LIMAYEM
53 Int DeanCollege of Education ... Dr. Roger BRINDLEY
54 Dean Engineering ... Dr. Robert H. BISHOP
57 Dean College of the Arts ... Dr. James S. MOY
67 Dean College of Pharmacy ... Dr. Kevin B. SNEED
49 Dean Arts & Sciences ... Dr. Eric EISENBERG
92 Dean Honors College ... Dr. Charles H. ADAMS
66 Dean Nursing ... Dr. Dianne MORRISON-BEEDY
88 Dean Marine Science ... Dr. Jacqueline DIXON
69 Dean Public Health ... Dr. Donna PETERSEN
88 Int Dean Global Sustainability ... Dr. Richard BERMAN
89 Dean of Undergraduate Studies ... Dr. W. Robert SULLINS
106 Asst Vice Provost Innovative Educ ... Dr. Cynthia A. DELUCA
48 Dir Sch of Architecture/Cmty Design ... Mr. Robert MACLEOD
12 Regional Chanc Sarasota-Manatee ... Dr. Sandra STONE
12 Regional Chanc USF St Petersburg ... Dr. Sophia WISNIEWSKA
21 Controller ... Ms. Jennifer CONDON
26 Director of Media Relations ... Ms. Lara WADE
07 Director Admissions ... Mr. David HENRY
06 Registrar ... Ms. Lois PALMER
21 University Budget Officer ... Ms. Nell PETERSON
84 Assoc VP Enrollment Management ... Ms. Billie Jo HAMILTON
38 Director Counseling Center ... Dr. Ann JARONSKI
36 Asst Vice President Career Services ... Mr. Russ COUGHENAIR
19 Interim Chief University Police ... Mr. Chris DANEIL
08 USF Libraries Dean ... Dr. Todd CHAVEZ
41 Director of Athletics ... Mr. Mark HARLAN
28 Director of Diversity & Inclusion ... Ms. Patsy FELICIANO
96 Int Director Purchasing & Property ... Mr. George COTTER
09 Asst VP Office of Decision Support ... Dr. Valeria GARCIA

*University of South Florida St. Petersburg (D)

140 7th Avenue S, Saint Petersburg FL 33701-5016
County: Pinellas FICE Identification: 009016
Unit ID: 448840
Telephone: (727) 873-4873 Carnegie Class: Masters/M
FAX Number: (727) 873-4131 Calendar System: Semester
URL: www.usfsp.edu
Established: 1956 Annual Undergrad Tuition & Fees (In-District): $5,821
Enrollment: 4,491 Coed
Affiliation or Control: State/Local IRS Status: 501(c)3
Highest Offering: Master's
Accreditation: SC, BUS, BUSA, JOUR, TED

02 Regional Chancellor ... Dr. Sophia T. WISNIEWSKA
04 Special Asst to Regional Chancellor ... Dr. Vivian FUEYO
05 Reg Vice Chanc Academic Affairs ... Dr. Martin TADLOCK
10 Reg Vice Chanc Admin/Financial Svcs ... Dr. Joseph TRUBACZ
44 Reg Vice Chanc Univ Advancement ... Dr. Helen LEVINE
32 Reg Assoc Vice Chanc Student Affs ... Dr. Patricia HELTON
11 Reg Asst Vice Chanc Administration ... Dr. Chitra IYER
49 Dean College of Arts & Sciences ... Dr. Frank BIAFORA
50 Dean College of Business ... Dr. Sridhar SUNDARAM
53 Dean College of Education ... Dr. William HELLER
08 Dean of the Library ... Ms. Catherine CARDWELL
19 Chief of Police ... Dr. David HENDRY
13 Director of Campus Computing ... Mr. Jeff REISBERG
15 Assoc Director Human Resources ... Ms. Denelta ADDERLY-HENRY
37 Director of Financial Aid ... Ms. Erin DUNN
06 Director Records and Registration ... Ms. Linda CROSSMAN
07 Director Admissions & Marketing ... Ms. Holly KICKLITER
18 Dir Facil Plng/Construction Svcs ... Mr. John DICKSON
96 Purchasing Manager ... Mr. Bill BENJAMIN
21 Budget Director ... Mr. David EVERINGHAM
31 Communications Director ... Ms. Jessica BLAIS
30 Asst Director Development ... Ms. Alexis SEARFOSS
105 Director Web Services ... Mr. Edgardo DANGOND

*University of South Florida Sarasota-Manatee (E)

8350 Tamiami Trail, Sarasota FL 34243-2049
County: Manatee Identification: 667058
Unit ID: 451671
Telephone: (941) 359-4200 Carnegie Class: Masters/S
FAX Number: N/A Calendar System: Semester
URL: www.usfsm.edu

Established: 1956 Annual Undergrad Tuition & Fees (In-State): $5,587
Enrollment: 1,903 Coed
Affiliation or Control: State IRS Status: 501(c)3
Highest Offering: Master's; No Lower Division
Accreditation: SC, TED

02	Regional Chancellor	Dr. Sandra STONE
10	Vice Chancellor Business & Finance	Mr. Ben ELLINOR
05	Vice Chancellor Academic Affairs	Dr. Terry OSBORN
30	Vice Chancellor Advancement	Mr. Dennis L. STOVER
09	AVP Institutional Research	Dr. Bonnie J. JONES
49	Dean College of Arts & Sciences	Dr. Jane ROSE
50	Dean College of Business	Dr. James CURRAN
53	Director School of Education	Dr. Patricia HUNSADER
88	Dean Sch Hotel & Restaurant Mgt	Dr. Patrick MOREO
06	Registrar	Ms. Lynn LYNCH
09	Director of Institutional Research	Ms. Laura HOFFMAN
13	Chief Info Technology Officer (CIO)	Mr. Bryan MUDD
07	Director of Admissions	Mr. Andrew TELATOVICH
96	Director of Purchasing	Ms. Michelle KRUEGER
04	Administrative Asst to President	Ms. Tiffany JACKSON
08	Head Librarian	Ms. Diane FULKERSON

*University of West Florida (A)

11000 University Parkway, Pensacola FL 32514-5750
County: Escambia FICE Identification: 003955
Unit ID: 138354
Telephone: (850) 474-2000 Carnegie Class: DU-Mod
FAX Number: (850) 474-3131 Calendar System: Semester
URL: uwf.edu
Established: 1963 Annual Undergrad Tuition & Fees (In-State): $6,360
Enrollment: 12,602 Coed
Affiliation or Control: State IRS Status: 501(c)3
Highest Offering: Doctorate
Accreditation: SC, BUS, CAATE, ENG, MT, MUS, NURSE, PH, SW, TED

02	President	Dr. Judith A. BENSE
05	Provost & Executive VP	Dr. Martha D. SAUNDERS
32	Vice President Student Affairs	Dr. Kevin BAILEY
30	Vice Pres University Advancement	Dr. Brendan KELLY
20	Vice Provost	Dr. George B. ELLENBERG
35	Sr Assoc Vice Pres Student Affairs	Dr. James R. HURD
84	Assoc Vice Pres Enrollment Affairs	Dr. Joffery GAYMON
18	Assoc VP Facilities Dev/Operations	Dr. James R. BARNETT
21	Asc VP Internal Audit/Mgmt Consultg	Ms. J. Betsy BOWERS
15	Associate Director Human Resources	Mr. Jeff COMEAU
15	Assoc Director Human Resources	Ms. Jamie SPRAGUE
16	Asst Director HR	Ms. Christine DILLARD
96	Director Procurment & Contracts	Ms. Angela JONES
43	General Counsel	Ms. Patricia D. LOTT
35	Assistant VP/Dean of Students	Dr. Brandon FRYE
50	Dean of Business	Dr. Timothy O'KEEFE
49	Dean Arts/Social Sci/Humanities	Dr. Steven BROWN
107	Dean Education & Prof Studies	Dr. William CRAWLEY
08	Dean University Libraries	Mr. Robert DUGAN
35	Associate Dean of Students	Dr. LuSharon WILEY
10	Vice President and CFO	Dr. Steven CUNNINGHAM
21	Asst VP Financial Services	Ms. Colleen M. ASMUS
13	Executive Director & CTO ITS	Mrs. Melanie J. HAVEARD
26	Exec Dir University Communication	Ms. Megan GONZALEZ
07	Director of Admissions	Ms. Katherine CONDON
92	Director of Kugleman Honors Program	Dr. Greg LANIER
37	Director of Financial Aid	Ms. Shana GORE
19	Director of University Police	Mr. John S. WARREN
39	Director of Housing/Residence Life	Dr. Ruth L. DAVISON
38	Assistant VP Counseling Center	Dr. Rebecca E. KENNEDY
29	Director of Alumni Relations	Ms. Melissa H. GRACE
41	Athletic Director	Mr. David L. SCOTT
81	Dean Science/Engineering/Health	Dr. Michael HUGGINS
76	Dean College of Health	Dr. Ermalynn KIEHL
50	Dean University College	Dr. Kimberly LEDUFF
44	Assoc Vice Pres of Development	Vacant
109	Director Business/Auxiliary Svcs	Ms. Ellen P. TILL
06	Registrar	Ms. Kelly BRUNDAGE
86	Asst VP Govt & Community Relations	Ms. Janice GILLEY

Stetson University (B)

421 N Woodland Boulevard, DeLand FL 32723-0001
County: Volusia FICE Identification: 001531
Unit ID: 137546
Telephone: (386) 822-7000 Carnegie Class: Masters/M
FAX Number: (386) 822-8832 Calendar System: 4/1/4
URL: www.stetson.edu
Established: 1883 Annual Undergrad Tuition & Fees: $41,590
Enrollment: 4,137 Coed
Affiliation or Control: Independent Non-Profit IRS Status: 501(c)3
Highest Offering: Doctorate
Accreditation: SC, BUS, BUSA, CACREP, CAEP, LAW, MUS, TED

01	President	Dr. Wendy B. LIBBY
05	Interim Exec VP & Provost	Dr. Noel PAINTER
10	Exec Vice Pres & CFO	Mr. F. Robert HUTH
30	VP for Devel & Alumni Engagement	Mr. Jeffrey ULMER
84	VP Enrollment Management	Mr. Joel BAUMAN
26	VP for University Marketing	Mr. Bruce CHONG
32	Vice Pres for Student Affairs	Dr. Lua HANCOCK
61	Dean College of Law	Mr. Christopher PIETRUSZKIEWICZ
49	Dean of College of Arts & Sciences	Dr. Karen RYAN
50	Dean of School of Business Admin	Dr. Neal P. MERO
64	Dean of School of Music	Dr. Thomas G. MASSE
08	Dean of duPont-Ball Library	Ms. Susan RYAN
20	Assoc Provost for Faculty Devlpmnt	Dr. Rosalie RICHARDS
20	Assoc VP Academic Affairs	Vacant
06	Registrar	Mr. Robert BERWICK
41	Director of Athletics	Mr. Jeffrey F. ALTIER
13	Assoc VP & CIO	Dr. Jose BERNIER
15	Assoc VP for Human Resources	Ms. Drew MACAN
18	Assoc Vice Pres Facilities Mgmt	Mr. Al ALLEN
21	Assoc Vice Pres for Finance	Mr. Jeffrey MARGHEIM
21	Assoc VP Budget	Ms. Melissa PETERS
51	Assoc VP Boundless Learning	Dr. Joy MCGUIRL-HADLEY
88	Spec Advsr to Pres for Philanthropy	Ms. Linda P. DAVIS
35	Dean of Students	Ms. Lynn SCHOENBERG
36	Exec Dir Career Dev & Advising	Mr. Timothy STILES
42	University Chaplain	Rev. Michael R. FRONK
09	Dir Institutional Research	Dr. Resche HINES
104	Director of International Learning	Ms. Paula HENTZ
44	Assoc VP Development	Dr. Paul GLEASON
44	Asst VP Development	Ms. Katheryn P. PEARCE
44	Asst VP for Development	Ms. Rina TOVAR
44	Asst VP Dev & Communications	Ms. Amy GIPSON
29	Exec Dir Alumni Engagement	Mr. Woody O'CAIN
07	Exec Dir of Admissions	Ms. Alejandra SOSA PIERONI
37	Interim Dir Student Financial Aid	Ms. Alejandra SOSA PIERONI
39	Dir of Res Educ & Housing	Dr. Larry CORRELL-HUGHES
16	Director Human Resources	Ms. Betty WHITEMAN
96	Director of Purchasing	Ms. Valinda WIMER
19	Chief Pubic Safety	Mr. Robert MATUSICK
04	Executive Asst to President	Ms. Joan BEASLEY
102	Dir Ofc of Grants/Sponsored Rsrch	Ms. Carol BUCKELS
38	Director Counseling Ctr	Ms. Rachel BOLDMAN

Sullivan and Cogliano Training Centers (C)

4760 NW 167th Street, Miami FL 33014
County: Miami-Dade FICE Identification: 040393
Unit ID: 433466
Telephone: (305) 694-2401 Carnegie Class: Not Classified
FAX Number: (786) 871-7525 Calendar System: Other
URL: sctrain.edu
Established: 1997 Annual Undergrad Tuition & Fees: N/A
Enrollment: 627 Coed
Affiliation or Control: Proprietary IRS Status: Proprietary
Highest Offering: Associate Degree
Accreditation: COE

01	President & CEO	Herb COGLIANO

Suncoast College of Health (D)

6513 14th Street West #103, Bradenton FL 34207
County: Manatee Identification: 667296
Telephone: (941) 727-2273 Carnegie Class: Not Classified
FAX Number: N/A Calendar System: Quarter
URL: www.suncoastcollege.com
Established Annual Undergrad Tuition & Fees: N/A
Enrollment: N/A Coed
Affiliation or Control: Proprietary IRS Status: Proprietary
Highest Offering: Baccalaureate
Accreditation: ACICS

01	President	Lori BARNES

Tallahassee Community College (E)

444 Appleyard Drive, Tallahassee FL 32304-2895
County: Leon FICE Identification: 001533
Unit ID: 137759
Telephone: (850) 201-6200 Carnegie Class: Assoc/HT-High Trad
FAX Number: (850) 201-8682 Calendar System: Semester
URL: www.tcc.fl.edu
Established: 1966 Annual Undergrad Tuition & Fees (In-District): $2,026
Enrollment: 13,049 Coed
Affiliation or Control: Local IRS Status: 501(c)3
Highest Offering: Baccalaureate
Accreditation: SC, ADNUR, COARC, DA, DH, EMT, SURGT

01	President	Dr. Jim MURDAUGH
10	Vice Pres Administrative Svcs/CFO	Dr. Barbara WILLS
13	VP Information Technology	Mr. Bret INGERMAN
05	Provost and VP for Academic Affairs	Dr. Felecia MOORE-DAVIS
32	Vice President for Student Affs	Dr. Sheri ROWLAND
103	Vice Pres Workforce Development	Ms. Kimberly MOORE
26	VP Communications and Marketing	Mr. Al MORAN
88	Assoc VP Inst Effectiveness	Dr. Lei WANG
100	Chief of Staff	Mr. Scott BALOG
57	Dean Communications & Humanities	Dr. Tracy WOODARD-MEYERS
83	Dean Behavioral/Social Sciences	Dr. Monte FINKELSTEIN
72	Dean Business Industry & Technology	Vacant
88	Dean Transitional Studies	Ms. Sharisse TURNER
08	Director of Library Services	Ms. Deborah P. ROBINSON
76	Dean Health Care Professions	Vacant
37	Director of Financial Aid	Mr. William SPIERS
84	Dir of Student Success & Retention	Dr. Shanna AUTRY
15	Director of Human Resources	Ms. Audrey MATHEWS
102	Director of TCC Foundation	Ms. Heather MITCHELL
41	Director of Athletics	Mr. Rob CHANEY
35	Dir of Campus & Civic Engagement	Mr. Mike COLEMAN
88	Exec Dir Florida Public Safety Inst	Mr. E. E. EUNICE
18	Dir Facilities/Construction/Plng	Vacant
21	Controller	Ms. Patricia MANNING
45	Director of Educational Research	Dr. Barbara J. GILL
09	Director of Institutional Research	Ms. Margaret WINGATE
106	Dir Center for Distance Learning	Dr. Marilyn DICKEY
88	Dir Ctr for Teach/Learn/Ldrshp	Dr. Karinda BARRETT
18	Construction Coordinator	Mr. Bill HUNTER
85	International Students Coordinator	Ms. Betty JENSEN
14	Director of User Services	Mr. Chip SINGLETARY
14	Director of Enterprise Systems	Mr. Mike ROBECK
25	Contracts and Grants Manager	Ms. Vanessa WRIGHT
88	Director Grants & Special Projects	Mr. Steven SOLOMON
96	Purchasing Manager	Mr. Bobby HINSON
19	Chief of Police	Mr. Christopher SUMMERS
06	Registrar	Ms. Brenda KNIGHT
20	Dean of Curriculum and Instruction	Mrs. Calandra STRINGER
36	Director of Career Services	Ms. Catie GOODMAN
04	Administrative Asst to President	Ms. Lenda KLING
43	Dir Legal Services/General Counsel	Mr. Craig KNOX

Talmudic College of Florida (F)

4000 Alton Road, Miami Beach FL 33140
County: Dade FICE Identification: 025089
Unit ID: 137777
Telephone: (305) 534-7050 Carnegie Class: Spec-4-yr-Faith
FAX Number: (305) 534-8444 Calendar System: Semester
URL: www.talmudicu.edu
Established: 1974 Annual Undergrad Tuition & Fees: $13,250
Enrollment: 61 Male
Affiliation or Control: Independent Non-Profit IRS Status: 501(c)3
Highest Offering: Doctorate
Accreditation: RABN

01	President	Rabbi Yitzchak ZWEIG
05	Dean/Vice President	Rabbi Yochanan ZWEIG
06	Registrar	Rabbi Yitzchak WINKLER
37	Director Student Financial Aid	Ms. Sharon BRECHER
20	Director Educational Programs	Rabbi Yeshaya GREENBERG
07	Director of Admissions	Rabbi Yaakov BURSTYN

Taylor College (G)

5190 SE 125th Street, Belleview FL 34420
County: Marion FICE Identification: 041166
Unit ID: 449524
Telephone: (352) 245-4119 Carnegie Class: Spec 2-yr-Health
FAX Number: (352) 245-0276 Calendar System: Other
URL: taylorcollege.edu
Established: 1999 Annual Undergrad Tuition & Fees: $11,216
Enrollment: 150 Coed
Affiliation or Control: Proprietary IRS Status: Proprietary
Highest Offering: Associate Degree
Accreditation: COE, PTAA

01	President	Dianne HAMMOND

Thomas M. Cooley Law School Tampa Bay Campus (H)

9445 Camden Field Parkway, Riverview FL 33578
Telephone: (813) 419-5100 Identification: 770290
Accreditation: &NH

† Regional accreditation is carried under the parent institution in Lansing, MI

Touro College South (I)

1701 Washington Avenue, Miami Beach FL 33139
Telephone: (305) 535-1066 Identification: 770147
Accreditation: &M

† Regional accreditation is carried under the parent institution in New York, NY

Trinity Baptist College (J)

800 Hammond Boulevard, Jacksonville FL 32221-1398
County: Duval FICE Identification: 031019
Unit ID: 137953
Telephone: (904) 596-2400 Carnegie Class: Spec-4-yr-Faith
FAX Number: (904) 596-2532 Calendar System: Semester
URL: www.tbc.edu
Established: 1974 Annual Undergrad Tuition & Fees: $11,040
Enrollment: 389 Coed
Affiliation or Control: Baptist IRS Status: 501(c)3
Highest Offering: Master's
Accreditation: TRACS

00	Chancellor	Dr. Thomas C. MESSER
01	President/CEO	Mr. Mac HEAVENER
03	Senior Vice President	Dr. Matthew BEEMER
32	Dean of Students	Mr. Jeremiah STANLEY
84	Director of Enrollment Management	Mrs. Melissa GIBSON
37	Director of Financial Aid	Mr. Mark ELKINS
04	Administrative Asst to President	Mrs. Sherry LENTZ
06	Registrar	Dr. John CASH
08	Head Librarian	Dr. John LUCY
10	Chief Business Officer	Mr. Mike AKINS
41	Athletic Director	Mr. John JONES
18	Chief Facilities/Physical Plant	Mr. Roger CHASTAIN

19 Director Security/Safety ..... Mr. John CASH, JR.
29 Director Alumni Relations ..... Mrs. Jenny STANLEY
30 Chief Development/Advancement ..... Mr. Matthew HEAVENER

Trinity College of Florida (A)

2430 Welbilt Boulevard, Trinity FL 34655-4401
County: Pasco FICE Identification: 030282
Unit ID: 137962
Telephone: (727) 376-6911 Carnegie Class: Spec-4-yr-Faith
FAX Number: (727) 376-0781 Calendar System: Semester
URL: www.trinitycollege.edu
Established: 1932 Annual Undergrad Tuition & Fees: $15,690
Enrollment: 229 Coed
Affiliation or Control: Independent Non-Profit IRS Status: 501(c)3
Highest Offering: Baccalaureate
Accreditation: BI

01 President ..... Dr. Mark T. O'FARRELL
32 Vice President Student Affairs ..... Rev. Al DEPOUTOT
05 Vice President Academic Affairs ..... Dr. Dennis COX
30 Vice President for Advancement ..... Dr. Charlie MARTIN
10 Vice Pres for Business & Finance ..... Mr. Paul S. WILLARD
06 Registrar ..... Mrs. Shannon T. RANES
26 Asst VP Marketing/Communications ..... Vacant
07 Director of Admissions ..... Mrs. Rachel NOBLE
04 Administrative Asst to President ..... Mrs. Billie SKINNER
08 Head Librarian ..... Mrs. Cindy T. HYER

Trinity International University, Florida Regional Center (B)

8190 W State Road 84, Davie FL 33324-4611
Telephone: (954) 382-6400 FICE Identification: 012314
Accreditation: &NH

† Regional accreditation is carried under the parent institution in Deerfield, IL.

UAC School of Global Management (C)

7955 NW 12th St, Ste 119, Miami FL 33126
County: Miami-Dade Identification: 667277
Telephone: (305) 325-9090 Carnegie Class: Not Classified
FAX Number: (305) 507-4344 Calendar System: Other
URL: www.uac.edu
Established: Annual Undergrad Tuition & Fees: N/A
Enrollment: N/A Coed
Affiliation or Control: Proprietary IRS Status: Proprietary
Highest Offering: Master's
Accreditation: ACICS

01 President ..... Ramses VARGAS

Ultimate Medical Academy-Clearwater (D)

1255 Cleveland Street, Clearwater FL 33756
County: Pinellas FICE Identification: 035493
Unit ID: 441371
Telephone: (727) 298-8685 Carnegie Class: Spec 2-yr-Health
FAX Number: (727) 446-2489 Calendar System: Semester
URL: www.ultimatemedical.edu
Established: 1998 Annual Undergrad Tuition & Fees: N/A
Enrollment: 332 Coed
Affiliation or Control: Proprietary IRS Status: Proprietary
Highest Offering: Associate Degree
Accreditation: ABHES

01 Campus Director ..... Mr. Samuel HUTKIN

Ultimate Medical Academy Online-Tampa (E)

3101 W Martin Luther King Boulevard, Tampa FL 33607
Telephone: (813) 386-6350 Identification: 770528
Accreditation: ABHES, CAHIIM

Unilatina International College (F)

3130 Commerce Pkwy, Miramar FL 33025
County: Broward Identification: 667155
Telephone: (954) 607-4344 Carnegie Class: Not Classified
FAX Number: (954) 357-1766 Calendar System: Quarter
URL: www.unilatina.edu
Established: 2001 Annual Undergrad Tuition & Fees: N/A
Enrollment: N/A Coed
Affiliation or Control: Proprietary IRS Status: Proprietary
Highest Offering: Associate Degree
Accreditation: ACICS

01 President ..... Lydia B. BAUTISTA MOLLER
05 Academic Director ..... Angelica MOYANO

University of Fort Lauderdale (G)

4069 NW 16th Street, Lauderhill FL 33313-5809
County: Broward FICE Identification: 041563
Unit ID: 457402
Telephone: (954) 486-7728 Carnegie Class: Spec-4-yr-Faith
FAX Number: (954) 486-7667 Calendar System: Other
URL: www.uftl.edu
Established: Annual Undergrad Tuition & Fees: $7,410
Enrollment: 43 Coed
Affiliation or Control: Non-denominational IRS Status: 501(c)3
Highest Offering: Doctorate
Accreditation: TRACS

01 Chancellor and CEO ..... Dr. Henry B. FERNANDEZ
11 Chief Operating Officer ..... Mr. Maurice HERRING
10 Chief Financial Officer ..... Mr. Brian HANKERSON
05 Vice Pres for Academic Affairs ..... Dr. C. Racquel CAREW
09 VP Institutional Effect/Compliance ..... Ms. Chloris UNDERWOOD
06 Registrar ..... Ms. Lenice BARNETT
07 Director of Admissions ..... Vacant

University of Miami (H)

1252 Memorial Drive, Coral Gables FL 33124
County: Miami-Dade FICE Identification: 001536
Unit ID: 135726
Telephone: (305) 284-2211 Carnegie Class: DU-Highest
FAX Number: N/A Calendar System: Semester
URL: www.miami.edu
Established: 1925 Annual Undergrad Tuition & Fees: $45,724
Enrollment: 16,674 Coed
Affiliation or Control: Independent Non-Profit IRS Status: 501(c)3
Highest Offering: Doctorate
Accreditation: SC, ANEST, BUS, BUSA, CAATE, CEA, CLPSY, COPSY, DENT, ENG, HSA, IPSY, LAW, MED, MUS, NURSE, PH, PTA

01 President ..... Dr. Julio FRENK
05 Executive Vice President & Provost ..... Dr. Thomas J. LEBLANC
10 Sr VP Business & Finance and CFO ..... Mr. Joseph T. NATOLI
30 Sr VP Advancement/External Affairs ..... Mr. Sergio M. GONZALEZ
84 VP Enrollment Management ..... Mr. John G. HALLER
21 VP Finance & Treasurer ..... Mr. Geoffrey E. KIRLES
18 VP Real Estate & Facilities ..... Mr. Larry D. MARBERT
26 VP University Communications ..... Ms. Jacqueline R. MENENDEZ
15 VP Human Resources ..... Ms. Nerissa E. MORRIS
43 VP/General Counsel and Secretary ..... Ms. Aileen M. UGALDE
32 VP Student Affairs ..... Dr. Patricia A. WHITELY
00 Chairman Board of Trustees ..... Mr. Richard D. FAIN
100 President's Chief of Staff ..... Mr. Rodolfo J. FERNANDEZ
20 Sr Vice Provost/Dean Undergrad Educ ..... Dr. William S. GREEN
46 Vice Provost Research ..... Dr. John L. BIXBY
20 Vice Provost Faculty Affairs ..... Dr. David J. BIRNBACH
41 Director Athletics ..... Mr. Blake JAMES
29 Assoc VP Advancement & Alumni Rels ..... Ms. Donna A. ARBIDE
31 AVP Community Relations ..... Ms. Sarah N. ARTECONA
17 Sr VP Health Affairs/CEO Uhealth ..... Dr. Steve M. ALTSCHULER
105 AVP Communications and Marketing ..... Mr. Todd M. ELLENBERG
16 Associate Vice President/Med HR ..... Ms. Oona A. JORGENSEN
27 Executive Director Comm & PR ..... Mrs. Rosemary RAVINAL
19 Chief of Police ..... Major David A. RIVERO
63 Dean School of Medicine ..... Vacant
49 Dean College of Arts & Sciences ..... Dr. Leonidas G. BACHAS
48 Dean School of Architecture ..... Dr. Rodolphe EL-KHOURY
50 Dean Business Administration ..... Dr. Eugene ANDERSON
60 Dean School Communication ..... Dr. Gregory J. SHEPHERD
53 Dean Education/Human Development ..... Dr. Isaac PRILLELTENSKY
54 Dean College of Engineering ..... Dr. Jean Pierre BARDET
61 Dean School of Law ..... Ms. Patricia WHITE
64 Dean School of Music ..... Dr. Shelton G. BERG
65 Dean Marine & Atmospheric Science ..... Dr. Roni AVISSAR
66 Dean Nursing & Health Studies ..... Dr. Nilda P. PERAGALLO
58 Dean Graduate School ..... Dr. Guillermo PRADO
35 AVP Stdnt Affs & Dean of Students ..... Dr. Ricardo D. HALL
07 Associate Dean Enrollment ..... Mr. Mark REID
38 Director Student Counseling ..... Dr. Rene MONTEAGUDO
85 Director Intl Services ..... Ms. Teresa S. DE LA GUARDIA
39 Exec Director Student Housing ..... Mr. James G. SMART
96 Executive Director Purchasing ..... Ms. Susan R. MONTES
14 Associate VP Enterprise App ..... Mr. Jack J. GEORGE
14 Assoc VP and CISO ..... Mr. Timothy C. RAMSAY
90 Asst VP Chief Academic Tech Offic ..... Mr. Allan GYORKE
91 Assoc VP Information Technology ..... Mr. Brad ROHRER
109 Executive Director Auxiliary Svcs ..... Ms. Sandra REDWAY
51 Dean Continuing Education ..... Dr. Rebecca MACMILLAN FOX
40 Director Bookstore ..... Ms. Wendy SMITH
06 Registrar ..... Ms. Karen J. BECKETT
08 Dean Libraries ..... Dr. Charles ECKMAN
101 Assistant University Secretary ..... Ms. Leslie DELLINGER ACEITUNO
102 Exec Director Foundation Relations ..... Ms. Joanna DE VELASCO
36 Assoc Dean Career Services ..... Mr. Christian GARCIA
104 Director Study Abroad ..... Ms. Devika M. MILNER
22 AVP Workplace Equity ..... Ms. Beverly PRUITT
25 AVP Business Services ..... Mr. Humberto M. SPEZIANI
37 Assoc Dean Financial Aid ..... Mr. Raymond E. HIX
13 VP Information Technology & CIO ..... Mr. Steve CAWLEY
44 Executive Director Annual Giving ..... Mr. Troy ODOM
21 VP Budget & Planning ..... Mr. Mark DIAZ
04 Administrative Manager to President ..... Ms. Alicia BLATCHFORD
86 VP Government & Community Relations ..... Mr. Rodolfo J. FERNANDEZ
88 VP and Chief Compliance Officer ..... Mr. Rudolph H. GREEN

University of Phoenix Central Florida Main Campus (I)

8325 South Park Circle Ste 100, Orlando FL 32819
Telephone: (407) 345-8868 Identification: 770932
Accreditation: &NH, ACBSP

† Branch campus of University of Phoenix, Tempe, AZ.

University of Phoenix North Florida Campus (J)

4500 Salisbury Road, Jacksonville FL 32216-0959
Telephone: (904) 636-6645 Identification: 770197
Accreditation: &NH, ACBSP

† Regional accreditation is carried under the parent institution in Tempe, AZ

University of Phoenix South Florida Main Campus (K)

2400 SW 145th Avenue, Miramar FL 33207-4145
Telephone: (954) 382-5303 Identification: 770237
Accreditation: &NH, ACBSP

† Regional accreditation is carried under the parent institution in Tempe, AZ

University of St. Augustine for Health Sciences (L)

One University Boulevard, St. Augustine FL 32086
Telephone: (904) 826-0084 Identification: 770939
Accreditation: &WC, OT, PTA

† Branch campus of University of St. Augustine for Health Sciences, San Marcos, CA.

University of Tampa (M)

401 W Kennedy Boulevard, Tampa FL 33606-1490
County: Hillsborough FICE Identification: 001538
Unit ID: 137847
Telephone: (813) 253-3333 Carnegie Class: Masters/L
FAX Number: (813) 258-7207 Calendar System: Other
URL: www.ut.edu
Established: 1931 Annual Undergrad Tuition & Fees: $27,044
Enrollment: 7,683 Coed
Affiliation or Control: Independent Non-Profit IRS Status: 501(c)3
Highest Offering: Master's
Accreditation: SC, BUS, CAATE, CS, FEPAC, MUS, NUR

01 President ..... Dr. Ronald L. VAUGHN
05 Provost/Vice Pres Academic Affairs ..... Dr. David STERN
10 Vice Pres Administration/Finance ..... Mr. Richard W. OGOREK
84 Vice President Enrollment ..... Mr. Dennis L. NOSTRAND
30 Vice Pres Develop & Univ Relations ..... Mr. Gary B. GRANT
44 Vice Pres Capital Campaign ..... Mr. Daniel T. GURA
45 Vice Pres Operations & Planning ..... Dr. Linda W. DEVINE
88 Chief Information Security Officer ..... Ms. Tammy L. CLARK
21 Assistant Vice Pres Admin/Finance ..... Mr. T. Kevin LAFFERTY
32 Dean of Students ..... Ms. Stephanie R. KREBS
20 Assoc Provost & Dean of Acad Svcs ..... Dr. Katharine H. COLE
06 Registrar ..... Ms. Michelle PELAEZ
08 Director of the Library ..... Ms. Marlyn PETHE-COOK
29 Director of Alumni Relations ..... Mr. James HARDWICK
37 Director of Financial Aid ..... Ms. Jacqueline LATORELLA
26 Director of Public Information ..... Mr. Eric D. CARDENAS
18 Director of Facilities Management ..... Mr. David RAMSEY
15 Exec Director of Human Resources ..... Ms. Donna B. POPOVICH
07 Dir Enr Management/Admissions ..... Mr. Brent W. BENNER
41 Athletic Director ..... Mr. Larry J. MARFISE
40 Manager Campus Store ..... Ms. Angela M. O'CONNOR
39 Director of Residence Life ..... Vacant
22 Affirmative Action Officer ..... Ms. Donna B. POPOVICH
19 Director Safety & Security ..... Mr. Kevin A. HOWELL
23 Dir Health Center/Stdnt Counseling ..... Ms. Sharon P. SCHAEFER
38 Director Student Counseling ..... Ms. Sharon P. SCHAEFER
96 Director of Procurement ..... Ms. Cyn D. EZELL
09 Dir Institutional Effectiveness ..... Dr. Jeanne M. ROBERTS
92 Director of Honors Program ..... Dr. Gary S. LUTER
50 Dean College of Business ..... Dr. F. Frank GHANNADIAN
83 Dean Social Science/Math Education ..... Dr. Jack M. GELLER
81 Dean College Natural/Health Sci ..... Dr. James A. GORE
57 Dean College of Arts/Letters ..... Dr. Haig MARDIROSIAN
51 Assoc Dean Graduate/Continuing Stds ..... Dr. Donald D. MORRILL
89 Dir First Year/Baccalaureate Exp ..... Ms. Edesa SCARBOROUGH
36 Assoc Dean Career Dev & Engagement ..... Mr. Timothy HARDING
104 Assoc Dean International Programs ..... Dr. Marca BEAR
04 Executive Asst to President ..... Ms. Madelyn CASTRO

Valencia College (N)

PO Box 3028, Orlando FL 32802-3028
County: Orange FICE Identification: 006750
Unit ID: 138187
Telephone: (407) 299-5000 Carnegie Class: Bac/Assoc-Assoc Dom
FAX Number: (407) 426-8970 Calendar System: Semester
URL: www.valenciacollege.edu
Established: 1967 Annual Undergrad Tuition & Fees (In-State): $2,474
Enrollment: 43,217 Coed
Affiliation or Control: State IRS Status: 501(c)3
Highest Offering: Baccalaureate
Accreditation: SC, ADNUR, CEA, COARCP, CVT, DH, DMS, EMT, RAD

01 President ..... Dr. Sanford C. SHUGART
05 VP Academic Affairs & Planning ..... Dr. Susan E. LEDLOW
32 Vice President Student Affairs ..... Dr. Joyce C. ROMANO
10 Vice Pres Business Ops & Finance ..... Mr. Loren J. BENDER
30 Vice Pres Institutional Advancement ..... Vacant

43 Vice Pres Policy & General Counsel .... Dr. William J. MULLOWNEY
15 VP Org Dev & Human Resources .... Dr. Amy N. BOSLEY
26 VP Public Affairs & Marketing .... Mr. James R. GALBRAITH
12 Campus President East Campus .... Dr. Stacey R. JOHNSON
12 Campus President Osceola Campus .... Dr. Kathleen A. PLINSKE
12 Campus President West Campus .... Dr. Falecia D. WILLIAMS
13 VP Info Technology and CIO .... Mr. William J. SLOT
102 Foundation President and CEO . Ms. Geraldine M. P. GALLAGHER
16 Asst VP Human Resources .... Mr. Joe A. LIVINGSTON
18 Asst VP Fac Plng/Real Est Dev .... Mr. Eugene A. BOTTORFF
103 Asst VP Career & Workforce Educ .... Dr. Nasser HEDAYAT
21 Asst VP Financial Services .... Ms. Jacqueline D. LASCH
35 Asst VP Student Affairs .... Dr. Sonya F. JOSEPH
88 Asst VP College Transition .... Ms. Amy KLEEMAN
07 Asst VP Admissions & Records .... Ms. Linda K. HERLOCKER
28 Asst VP Diversity & Inclusion .... Vacant
19 Asst VP Operations .... Mr. Paul ROONEY
09 Asst VP IE & Planning .... Vacant
108 Asst VP Curriculum & Assessment .... Dr. Karen M. BORGLUM
88 Asst VP Budgets & Analysis .... Mr. Oscar J. CRISTANCHO MERCADO
102 Foundation VP & COO .... Ms. Michelle D. MATIS
25 Asst VP Resource Development .... Ms. Kristeen R. CHRISTIAN
88 Asst VP Teaching & Learning .... Ms. Wendi M. DEW
35 Dean of Students East .... Mr. Joseph M. SARRUBBO
35 Dean of Students West .... Dr. Benjamin C. LION
35 Dean of Students Osceola .... Ms. Jillian M. SZENTMIKLOSI
35 Dean of Students Winter Park .... Vacant
40 Director College Bookstore .... Mr. Todd A. HUNT
92 Director Honors Program .... Dr. Cheryl ROBINSON
105 Director Web and Portal Services .... Mr. James FLANAGAN
04 Senior Executive Assistant .... Ms. Barbara HALSTEAD
08 Campus Director Library W .... Ms. Ruth S. SMITH
88 Director Curriculum Initiatives .... Ms. Robyn BRIGHTON
37 Asst VP Financial Aid & Vet Affairs .... Mr. Christen L. CHRISTENSEN
84 Director Enrollment Services .... Ms. Jacquelyn F. THOMPSON
14 Assistant Chief Info Officer .... Ms. Patricia T. SMITH
27 Director Public Relations .... Ms. Carol E. TRAYNOR
96 Managing Director Procurement .... Ms. Rhonda S. ULMER
08 Campus Director Library E .... Vacant
08 Campus Director Library WP .... Ms. Katherine A. MILLER
106 Assoc Dir Online Teaching/Learning .... Ms. Page A. JERZAK
22 Dir Affirmative Action/EEO .... Mr. Ryan D. KANE

Virginia College (A)

5940 Beach Boulevard, Jacksonville FL 32207
Telephone: (904) 520-7400 Identification: 770839
Accreditation: ACICS, ACFEI, MAAB

† Branch campus of Virginia College, Birmingham, AL

Virginia College (B)

312 East Nine Mile Road, Suite 34, Pensacola FL 32514-1475
Telephone: (850) 436-8444 FICE Identification: 031005
Accreditation: ACICS, MAAB, SURGT

† Branch campus of Virginia College, Birmingham, AL.

Warner University (C)

13895 Highway 27, Lake Wales FL 33859-2549
County: Polk FICE Identification: 008848
Unit ID: 138275
Telephone: (863) 638-1426 Carnegie Class: Bac-Diverse
FAX Number: (863) 638-1472 Calendar System: Semester
URL: www.warner.edu
Established: 1968 Annual Undergrad Tuition & Fees: $19,754
Enrollment: 1,161 Coed
Affiliation or Control: Church Of God IRS Status: 501(c)3
Highest Offering: Master's
Accreditation: SC, SW

01 President .... Dr. David A. HOAG
88 Asst to the President/SACS Liaison .... Dr. James G. MOYER
05 VP and Chief Academic Officer .... Dr. Steven DARR
10 Vice Pres for Finance & Business .... Mr. Greg A. RODDEN
30 Vice President for Advancement .... Mrs. Doris B. GUKICH
84 VP for Enrollment Mgmt & Marketing .... Mrs. Dawn M. RAFOOL
32 Dean of Students .... Rev. Dawn MEADOWS
43 General Counsel .... Dr. Norman WHITE
06 Registrar .... Mrs. Sara F. KANE
07 Dean of Admissions .... Mr. Bob MOBLEY
37 Director Student Financial Aid .... Mrs. Lorrie STEEDLEY
21 Controller .... Mr. Dean MEADOWS
08 Librarian .... Mrs. Sherill HARRIGER
29 Director Alumni Relations .... Miss Kareen PICKETT
09 Director of Institutional Research .... Mrs. Lisa B. MURPHY
18 Chief Facilities/Physical Plant .... Mr. Bill BROWN
97 Director of General Studies .... Mrs. Kelly MILLS
88 Chair Ministry .... Dr. Michael SANDERS
40 Director Bookstore .... Ms. Monica HAMILTON
13 Director of Institutional Tech .... Mr. Mark THOMAS
19 Director Campus Security .... Mr. Brian ROWLES
36 Director Career Counseling .... Mrs. Dawn MEADOWS
88 Director Academic Skills Ctr .... Mrs. Kelly MORGAN
106 Director Online Services .... Mr. Shawn TAYLOR
107 Dean Adult Prof Division .... Mr. Thomas MALCOLM
88 Dean Adult Ministry Division .... Mr. Thomas MALCOLM
04 Administrative Asst to President .... Mrs. Alane RICHARDVILLE
41 Athletic Director .... Mr. Kevin JONES

Webber International University (D)

1201 Scenic Highway N/P.O. Box 96, Babson Park FL 33827-0096
County: Polk FICE Identification: 001540
Unit ID: 138293
Telephone: (863) 638-1431 Carnegie Class: Bac-Diverse
FAX Number: (863) 638-2823 Calendar System: Semester
URL: www.webber.edu
Established: 1927 Annual Undergrad Tuition & Fees: $24,792
Enrollment: 732 Coed
Affiliation or Control: Independent Non-Profit IRS Status: 501(c)3
Highest Offering: Master's
Accreditation: SC, IACBE

01 President .... Dr. H. Keith WADE
05 Academic Dean .... Dr. Charles SHIEH
10 Vice President Finance .... Ms. Christina JORDON
32 Dean of Student Life .... Mr. Jay CULVER
06 Registrar/Dir of Financial Aid .... Mrs. Kathy A. WILSON
31 Director Cmty Rels & Marketing .... Mrs. Devyn MONTALVO
08 Head Librarian .... Ms. Sue DUNNING
26 Dir Public Relations/Athletic Dir .... Mr. Bill HEATH
13 Director Information Technology .... Mr. Bob M. WEIS
18 Director of Campus Svcs/Maintenance .... Mr. Matt YENTES
40 Director of Bookstore .... Ms. Ruby FERNANDEZ
07 Director of Admissions .... Mr. Ryan PICARD
09 Director of Institutional Effectiv .... Dr. Nelson MARQUEZ
50 Chair of Business Education .... Dr. Jeanette EBERLE
53 Chair of General Education Division .... Dr. Charles WUNKER
04 Executive Asst to President .... Ms. Gerlinde DANCY
19 Director Security/Safety .... Mr. Michael RITTER
29 Dir Annual Fund/Alumni Relations .... Ms. Jennifer MUELLER

West Coast University - Miami (E)

9250 NW 36th Street, Doral FL 33178
Telephone: (786) 501-7070 Identification: 770936
Accreditation: &WC

† Branch campus of West Coast University, North Hollywood, CA.

Wolford College (F)

1336 Creekside Boulevard, Suite 2, Naples FL 34108-1931
County: Collier FICE Identification: 039393
Unit ID: 451130
Telephone: (239) 513-1135 Carnegie Class: Spec-4-yr-Other Health
FAX Number: (239) 513-1368 Calendar System: Semester
URL: www.wolford.edu
Established: 2004 Annual Graduate Tuition & Fees: N/A
Enrollment: 208 Coed
Affiliation or Control: Independent Non-Profit IRS Status: 501(c)3
Highest Offering: Master's; No Undergraduates
Accreditation: ANEST

01 President/CEO .... Ms. Lynda WATERHOUSE
00 Chancellor .... Dr. Thomas COOK
37 Director of Financial Aid Services .... Mr. Gilbert CHANG
84 Dir Enrollment & Student Services .... Ms. Lori ELLISON
04 Administrative Asst/Accred Coord .... Ms. Jessica GARCIA

WyoTech (G)

470 Destination Daytona Lane, Ormond Beach FL 32174
County: Volusia FICE Identification: 023462
Unit ID: 132268
Telephone: (386) 255-0295 Carnegie Class: Spec 2-yr-Tech
FAX Number: (386) 252-3523 Calendar System: Quarter
URL: www.wyotech.edu
Established: Annual Undergrad Tuition & Fees: N/A
Enrollment: 400 Coed
Affiliation or Control: Proprietary IRS Status: Proprietary
Highest Offering: Associate Degree
Accreditation: ACCSC

01 Campus Director/Academic Dean .... Mr. Chris BARTON

Yeshiva Gedolah Rabbinical College (H)

1140 Alton Road, Miami Beach FL 33139-4708
County: Dade FICE Identification: 032563
Unit ID: 363712
Telephone: (305) 653-8770 Carnegie Class: Not Classified
FAX Number: (305) 653-6790 Calendar System: Semester
URL: www.lecfl.com
Established: 1973 Annual Undergrad Tuition & Fees: $8,400
Enrollment: 52 Male
Affiliation or Control: Independent Non-Profit IRS Status: 501(c)3
Highest Offering: Master's
Accreditation: @RABN

01 Executive Vice President .... Rabbi Benzion KORF
05 Dean .... Rabbi Abraham KORF
06 Registrar .... Ayelet BORTUNK
07 Director of Admissions .... Rabbi Bentche KORF

GEORGIA

Abraham Baldwin Agricultural College (I)

ABAC 1 - 2802 Moore Highway, Tifton GA 31793-2601
County: Tift FICE Identification: 001541
Unit ID: 138558
Telephone: (229) 391-5050 Carnegie Class: Bac/Assoc-Mixed
FAX Number: (229) 391-5051 Calendar System: Semester
URL: www.abac.edu
Established: 1908 Annual Undergrad Tuition & Fees (In-State): $3,453
Enrollment: 3,458 Coed
Affiliation or Control: State IRS Status: 501(c)3
Highest Offering: Baccalaureate
Accreditation: SC, ADNUR

01 President .... Dr. David BRIDGES
05 Interim VP for Academic Affairs .... Dr. Gail DILLARD
10 VP for Fiscal Affairs & Opers .... Mr. Paul WILLIS
30 Interim VP Ext Affairs/Advancement .... Mr. Paul WILLIAMS
08 Director of Library Services .... Vacant
32 Dean of Students .... Ms. Bernice HUGHES
41 Athletic Director .... Mr. Alan KRAMER
06 Registrar .... Dr. Amy WILLIS
38 Director of Student Development .... Dr. Maggie MARTIN
37 Director of Student Financial Svcs .... Mr. Michael WRIGHT
15 Director of Human Resources .... Mr. Richard SPANCAKE
26 Director of Public Relations .... Ms. Lindsey ROBERTS
108 Director of Assessment .... Vacant
84 Director Enrollment Management .... Ms. Donna WEBB
96 Director of Procurement .... Ms. Teri MATHIS
19 Chief of Police .... Mr. Frank STRICKLAND
04 Administrative Asst to President .... Ms. Pam LEONARD
39 Director of Student Housing .... Dr. Chris S. KINSEY
13 Chief Info Technology Officer .... Mr. Robert GERHART

† Part of the University System of Georgia.

Agnes Scott College (J)

141 E. College Avenue, Decatur GA 30030-3770
County: DeKalb FICE Identification: 001542
Unit ID: 138600
Telephone: (404) 471-6000 Carnegie Class: Bac-A&S
FAX Number: (404) 471-6067 Calendar System: Semester
URL: www.agnesscott.edu
Established: 1889 Annual Undergrad Tuition & Fees: $37,236
Enrollment: 873 Female
Affiliation or Control: Presbyterian Church (U.S.A.) IRS Status: 501(c)3
Highest Offering: Baccalaureate
Accreditation: SC

01 President .... Dr. Elizabeth KISS
05 VP for Academic Affairs .... Dr. Kerry E. PANNELL
32 Interim VP for Student Life .... Dr. Kijua SANDERS-MCMURTRY
10 VP Business & Finance .... Mr. John P. HEGMAN
30 VP for College Advancement .... Dr. Robiaun R. CHARLES
84 VP Enrollment & Dean of Admission .... Ms. Laura MARTIN-FEDICH
26 Associate VP Marketing & PR .... Vacant
101 Associate VP & Board Secretary .... Ms. Lea Ann HUDSON
13 Assoc VP Technology .... Ms. LaNeta COUNTS
20 Assoc Dean of the College .... Dr. Lilia HARVEY
56 Associate VP Extended Programs .... Dr. Patricia SZYMURSKI
06 Registrar .... Ms. Gail N. MEIS
08 Director of Library Services .... Ms. Elizabeth BAGLEY
29 Senior Director Alumnae Relations .... Ms. Kimberly VICKERS
18 Director of Facilities .... Mr. Tim BLANKENSHIP
15 Associate VP for Human Resources .... Ms. Karen GILBERT
41 Associate Dean for Athletics & SA .... Ms. Joeleen AKIN
42 Chaplain .... Rev. Kate COLUSSY-ESTES
37 Director of Financial Aid .... Mr. Patrick BONONES
09 Director of Institutional Research .... Dr. Corey DUNN
07 Director of Admissions .... Ms. Alexa GAETA
23 Executive Director Wellness Center .... Ms. Juanita G. MOTTLEY
19 Director of Public Safety .... Mr. Henry HOPE
36 Director Student Placement .... Ms. Dawn KILLENBERG

Albany State University (K)

504 College Drive, Albany GA 31705-2796
County: Dougherty FICE Identification: 001544
Unit ID: 138716
Telephone: (229) 430-4600 Carnegie Class: Masters/M
FAX Number: (229) 430-4830 Calendar System: Semester
URL: www.asurams.edu
Established: 1903 Annual Undergrad Tuition & Fees (In-State): $5,490
Enrollment: 3,910 Coed
Affiliation or Control: State IRS Status: 501(c)3
Highest Offering: Beyond Master's But Less Than Doctorate
Accreditation: SC, ACBSP, CACREP, FEPAC, NUR, SPAA, SW, TED

01 President .... Dr. Arthur N. DUNNING
100 Senior Advisor/Spec Asst to Pres .... Ms. Cynthia HOKE
26 Spec Asst to Pres .... Mrs. Wendy WILSON
43 Legal Counsel/Title IX Coord .... Ms. Rowena DANIELS
05 Provost/VP Academic Affairs .... Dr. Olufunke FONTENOT
10 Vice President Fiscal Affairs .... Mr. Shawn MCGEE
13 VP Information Technology .... Mr. Del KIMBROUGH
30 VP Institutional Advancement .... Dr. Cynthia GEORGE

32 VP Student Affairs & Success .... Dr. Danette SAYLOR
46 Assoc Prov Sponsored Pgms .... Dr. Louise WRENSFORD
88 Graduate School Dean .... Dr. Louise WRENSFORD
84 Assoc VP Enrollment Management .... Vacant
45 Asst VP Inst Effect/Research & Plng .... Dr. Kellei SAMUELS
06 Registrar .... Ms. Victoria EILAND
19 Chief of Police .... Mr. John FIELDS
21 Controller .... Ms. Dorothy MARTIN
83 Dean Arts & Humanities .... Dr. Marilyn SPEARMAN
50 Dean College of Business .... Dr. Alicia JACKSON
53 Interim Dean College of Education .... Dr. Thomas THOMPSON
88 Dean Sciences & Health Professions .... Dr. Joyce JOHNSON
41 Director of Athletics .... Dr. Richard WILLIAMS
88 Director Internal Audits .... Ms. Katherine LASTER
88 Director Title III .... Ms. Saundrette MOODY
88 Director Budgets and Contracts .... Mrs. Marion RYANT
109 Director Business Services .... Ms. Lori W. BURNETT
18 Interim Dir Facilities Management .... Mr. Robert LAWSON
15 Interim Dir Human Resources Mgmt .... Ms. Kimberly CARTER
16 Asst Director Human Resources Mgmt .... Ms. Cassandra ALEXANDER
88 Director Infrastructure Services .... Mr. Lonnie WORMLEY
91 Director Application Services .... Mr. Amitabh SINGH
88 Dir Academic On-Line Instruction .... Ms. LaQuata SUMTER
92 Director Honors Program .... Dr. Melvin SHELTON
104 Director Global Programs .... Dr. Nneka-Nora OSAKWE
26 Director University Communications .... Ms. Landera CARROLL
29 Director Alumni Affairs .... Ms. Sue POLITE-SOLOMON
36 Director Career Services .... Ms. Tracy S. WILLIAMS
88 Director Sports Information .... Mr. Stanley MCCORMICK
35 Interim Dir Student Life .... Ms. Charity STARR
88 Director Judicial Affairs .... Ms. Angelnique JORDAN
38 Director Counseling/Disability Svcs .... Dr. Stephanie HARRIS-JOLLY
23 Director Student Health Services .... Dr. Vicki PHILLIPS
88 Exec Asst Ctr African American Male .... Mr. Antonio LEROY
07 Interim Director of Admissions .... Mr. Allan CASE
37 Director Financial Aid .... Mrs. Stephanie LAWRENCE
88 Dir of Academic Advising/Retention .... Dr. Ouida MCAFEE
25 Director Sponsored Programs .... Mrs. Melissa WIDNER
88 Director Undergrad Research Ctr .... Dr. Zephyrinus OKONKWO
08 Director Library Services .... Dr. LaVerne MCLAUGHLIN
88 Director Academic Success Unit .... Mrs. Flo HILL
88 Director Quality Enhancement Plan .... Dr. Clancy THOMAS
88 Director Water Policy Center .... Dr. Mark MASTERS
09 Director Institutional Research .... Dr. Frank ARCHER, III
44 Director of Development .... Mr. Andrew FLOYD
40 Director Bookstore .... Ms. Tara JOHNSON
88 Food Service Director .... Mr. Henry WARD

† Part of the University System of Georgia.

Albany Technical College (A)

1704 S Slappey Boulevard, Albany GA 31701-3587
County: Dougherty FICE Identification: 005601
Unit ID: 138682
Telephone: (229) 430-3500 Carnegie Class: Assoc/HVT-Mix Trad/Non
FAX Number: (229) 430-3594 Calendar System: Semester
URL: www.albanytech.edu
Established: 1961 Annual Undergrad Tuition & Fees (In-State): $2,652
Enrollment: 3,640 Coed
Affiliation or Control: State IRS Status: 501(c)3
Highest Offering: Associate Degree
Accreditation: SC, DA, EMT, MAC, RAD, SURGT

01 President .... Dr. Anthony O. PARKER
05 Exec Vice Pres Academic Affairs .... Dr. Tanjula PETTY
32 VP Student Affairs/Enrollment Mgmt .... Dr. Sherry AAKER
46 Vice President Economic Development .... Mr. Matt TRICE
10 Vice Pres Administrative Services .... Mrs. Kathy SKATES
45 Vice Pres of Inst Effectiveness .... Dr. Kimberly LEE
55 Vice Pres of Adult Education .... Mrs. Linda COSTON
04 Special Assistant to the President .... Mr. Joe NAJJAR
06 Registrar .... Ms. Suzann CULPEPPER
37 Director of Financial Aid .... Ms. Helen CATT
36 Dir of Job Placement/Career Svcs .... Ms. Judy JIMMERSON
21 Director of Accounting Services .... Ms. Janet HAYES
20 Dean of Academic Affairs .... Dr. Debra JONES
20 Dean of Academic Affairs .... Ms. Joy KNIGHTON
20 Dean of Academic Affairs .... Dr. Emmett GRISWOLD
55 Dean of Evening Administration .... Dr. Ed COOPER
88 Director of Business & Industry Svc .... Vacant
51 Director of Continuing Education .... Ms. Valerie WILLIAMS
09 Director of Institutional Research .... Mr. Joe NAJJAR
26 Exec Dir Public Relations/Marketing .... Ms. Wendy HOWELL
13 Director of Computer/Info Systems .... Mr. Bruce HOPKINS
88 Director of Special Programs .... Vacant
18 Director of Facilities .... Mr. Lavon ACKLEY
56 Dir Spec Proj/Tech in Curriculum .... Ms. Troycia WEBB
35 Director Student Activities .... Dr. Mary RICHARDSON
07 Director of Admissions .... Dr. Alexander EDWARD

American InterContinental University (B)

6600 Pchtree-Dunwdy Rd, 500 Embassy,
Atlanta GA 30328
Telephone: (404) 965-6500 Identification: 666723
Accreditation: &NH, ACBSP, CIDA

† Regional accreditation is carried under the parent institution in Hoffman Estates, IL.

Andrew College (C)

501 College Street, Cuthbert GA 39840-5550
County: Randolph FICE Identification: 001545
Unit ID: 138761
Telephone: (229) 732-2171 Carnegie Class: Assoc/HT-High Trad
FAX Number: (229) 732-2176 Calendar System: Semester
URL: www.andrewcollege.edu
Established: 1854 Annual Undergrad Tuition & Fees: $14,924
Enrollment: 303 Coed
Affiliation or Control: United Methodist IRS Status: 501(c)3
Highest Offering: Associate Degree
Accreditation: SC

01 President .... Dr. Linda R. BUCHANAN
05 Int Dean of Academic Affairs .... Dr. Richard MCCALLUM
10 Vice President for Finance .... Mr. Bobby MOYE
30 Vice President for Advancement .... Mr. Andy BRUBAKER
84 Vice President for Enrollment .... Mr. Andy GEETER
21 Controller .... Mrs. Julie CADLE
32 Dean of Student Affairs .... Ms. Whitney MOSLEY
41 Athletic Director .... Mr. Blake WILLIAMS
42 Chaplain .... Rev. Peter VERMEULEN
08 Director of Library Services .... Mrs. Karan PITTMAN
40 Director of Bookstore .... Ms. McKenzie RAGAN
26 Dir of Communications & Marketing .... Ms. Sheri MICHAELS
06 Registrar .... Ms. Tekesha JACKSON
18 Director of Maintenance .... Mr. Andrew LOWERY
19 Chief of Police .... Mr. Freddie JENKINS
39 Director of Residence Life .... Ms. Shaqualyn DAVIS
105 Web Services .... Mr. Brice HERRIN
88 FOCUS Director .... Mrs. Bennie MATTOX
09 Director of Student Success Ctr/IR .... Ms. Terri CRAFT
37 Director of Financial Aid .... Mrs. Daquiri TYSON
15 Director of Human Resources .... Mrs. Lola MOSES

Argosy University, Atlanta (D)

980 Hammond Drive, Suite 100, Atlanta GA 30328-6162
Telephone: (770) 671-1200 Identification: 666735
Accreditation: &WC, ACBSP, CACREP, CLPSY

† Regional accreditation is carried under the parent institution in Orange, CA.

Armstrong State University (E)

11935 Abercorn Street, Savannah GA 31419-1997
County: Chatham FICE Identification: 001546
Unit ID: 138789
Telephone: (912) 344-2576 Carnegie Class: Masters/L
FAX Number: N/A Calendar System: Semester
URL: www.armstrong.edu
Established: 1935 Annual Undergrad Tuition & Fees (In-State): $5,360
Enrollment: 7,094 Coed
Affiliation or Control: State IRS Status: 501(c)3
Highest Offering: Doctorate
Accreditation: SC, COARC, CS, DMS, HSA, MT, MUS, NMT, NURSE, PH, PTA, RAD, RTT, SP, TED

01 President .... Dr. Linda M. BLEICKEN
05 Provost & VP Academic Affairs .... Dr. Robert SMITH
10 Vice President Business & Finance ... Mr. Christopher CORRIGAN
32 Vice President Student Affairs .... Dr. Georj LEWIS
30 Vice President for Advancement .... Mr. William KELSO
100 Chief of Staff .... Dr. Amy HEASTON
43 University Counsel .... Mr. Lee DAVIS
13 CIO .... Mr. Timothy MOODY
14 Associate CIO .... Ms. Pamela CULBERSON
21 Associate VP Business & Finance .... Mr. Cam REAGIN
84 Associate VP Enrollment Services .... Dr. Joy HAMM
20 Dean College of Health Professions .... Dr. David WARD
53 Dean College of Education .... Dr. Janet BUCKENMEYER
49 Dean College of Liberal Arts .... Dr. Chris CURTIS
72 Interim Dean Science and Technology .... Dr. Delana NIVENS
08 University Librarian .... Mr. Doug FRAZIER
06 Interim Registrar .... Ms. Kathleen PLATT
19 Chief Campus Police .... Mr. Wayne WILLCOX
41 Athletic Director .... Ms. Lisa SWEANY
07 Director of Admissions .... Ms. Tobe FRIERSON
88 Director Faculty Development .... Dr. Nancy REMLER
37 Director Financial Aid .... Ms. Kaye O'NEAL
89 Director First Year Experience .... Mr. Gregory ANDERSON
92 Director Honors Program .... Dr. Jonathan ROBERTS
36 Interim Director of Career Services .... Mr. Glenn GIBNEY
09 Director Institutional Research .... Ms. Laura J. MILLS
85 Director of Intl Education .... Dr. Dorothee MERTZ-WEIGEL
104 Asst Director International Educ .... Dr. Kristin KASTING
35 Interim Dean of Students .... Mr. Andrew DIES
12 Interim Director Liberty Center .... Ms. Dorothy KEMPSON
106 Int Dir Online & Blended Learning .... Dr. Nancy REMLER
15 Director of Human Resources .... Mr. John BROOKS
18 Director Facility Services .... Ms. Katie TWINING
38 Director Counseling Services .... Ms. Jeanne MCGOWAN
39 Director Housing & Residence Life .... Mr. Nick SHRADER
28 Director Multicultural Affairs .... Ms. Nashia WHITTENBURG
35 Assistant Dean of Students .... Ms. Kate STEINER
29 Director Alumni Development .... Ms. Cheryl ANDERSON
44 Assistant Vice President of Develop .... Ms. Julie GERBSCH
26 Director Marketing & Communications .... Dr. Allison HERSH
105 Manager of Web Communications .... Ms. Janice STANFORD
04 Executive Asst to President .... Ms. Trina SMITH
108 Director Assessment .... Ms. Angeles EAMES
22 Dir Affirmative Action/EEO .... Ms. Deidra DENNIE
25 Dir Grants & Sponsored Research .... Ms. Susan ARSHACK
86 Director Government Relations .... Col. Peter HOFFMAN

† Part of the University System of Georgia.

The Art Institute of Atlanta (F)

6600 Peachtree Dunwoody Road, Atlanta GA 30328-1635
County: Fulton FICE Identification: 009270
Unit ID: 138813
Telephone: (770) 394-8300 Carnegie Class: Spec-4-yr-Arts
FAX Number: (770) 394-0008 Calendar System: Quarter
URL: www.artinstitutes.edu/atlanta/
Established: 1949 Annual Undergrad Tuition & Fees: $17,592
Enrollment: 2,623 Coed
Affiliation or Control: Proprietary IRS Status: Proprietary
Highest Offering: Baccalaureate
Accreditation: SC, ACFEI, CIDA

01 President .... Mr. Newton MYVETT
10 Director of Accounting .... Mr. Shane PATILLA
15 Director of Human Resources .... Ms. Michele DAVIS
07 Senior Director of Admissions .... Mr. Doug LOCHBAUM
05 Dean of Academic Affairs .... Dr. Ameeta JADAV
32 Dean of Student Affairs .... Mr. Michael DIXON
37 Director of Student Financial Svcs .... Ms. Kimberly PANCHANA
09 Dir of Inst Effectiveness/Research .... Vacant
08 Librarian .... Ms. Clara WILLIAMS
13 Director of Technology .... Mr. Patrick SLUDER
06 Registrar .... Ms. Diana HILL
36 Director of Career Services .... Ms. Sharon CLAY
26 Director of Communications .... Ms. Devra PRANSKY
18 Director of Facilities .... Ms. Stacey CARMICHAEL
39 Director of Residence Life/Housing .... Ms. Dominique CONTEH
04 Exec Assistant to the President .... Ms. Precious PRENDERGAST

Ashworth College (G)

6625 The Corners Parkway, Suite 500,
Norcross GA 30092-3406
County: Gwinnett Identification: 666106
Telephone: (770) 729-8400 Carnegie Class: Not Classified
FAX Number: (770) 729-9296 Calendar System: Semester
URL: www.ashworthcollege.edu
Established: 2000 Annual Undergrad Tuition & Fees: N/A
Enrollment: N/A Coed
Affiliation or Control: Proprietary IRS Status: Proprietary
Highest Offering: Master's
Accreditation: DEAC

01 President .... Mr. Robert KLAPPER
05 Chief Academic Officer .... Mr. William KAKISH

Athens Technical College (H)

800 US Highway 29 N, Athens GA 30601-1500
County: Clarke FICE Identification: 005600
Unit ID: 246813
Telephone: (706) 355-5000 Carnegie Class: Assoc/HVT-Mix Trad/Non
FAX Number: (706) 369-5753 Calendar System: Semester
URL: www.athenstech.edu
Established: 1958 Annual Undergrad Tuition & Fees (In-State): $2,684
Enrollment: 4,336 Coed
Affiliation or Control: State IRS Status: 501(c)3
Highest Offering: Associate Degree
Accreditation: SC, ACBSP, ADNUR, CAHIIM, DA, DH, EMT, PTAA, RAD, SURGT

01 President .... Dr. Andrea D. DANIEL
05 Vice President for Academic Affairs .... Ms. Caroline ANGELO
32 Vice President for Student Affairs .... Ms. Jennifer BENSON
10 Vice Pres Administrative Services .... Ms. Kathryn S. THOMAS
45 Vice Pres Economic Development .... Dr. Ilka MCCONNELL
12 Vice President of Off Campus Sites .... Vacant
13 Vice Pres Information Technology .... Mr. Dennis ASHWORTH
09 Vice President Adult Education .... Ms. Stephanie G. BENSON
72 Dean Technology/Engineering/Math .... Dr. Margaret MORGAN
76 Dean Life Sciences/Public Safety .... Mr. Glenn HENRY
50 Dean Business/Educ/Humanities .... Vacant
06 Director Registration & Records .... Ms. Kala MCNAIR
07 Director Admissions .... Ms. Justin MCCALLA
08 Director Library Services .... Ms. Carol STANLEY
08 Distance Educ & Outreach Librarian .... Ms. Beth THORNTON
36 Director Student Support/Career Dev .... Ms. Keli FEWOX
37 Director Financial Aid .... Ms. Wanda HICKS
12 Exec Dir Walton County Campus .... Mr. Lenzy REID, III
12 Director Greene County Campus .... Mr. Sibley BRYAN
35 Student Activities Director .... Mr. Alvie COES
15 Director Human Resources .... Ms. Becky BURTON
18 Facilities Director .... Mr. Jim WALTER
30 Director Institutional Advancement .... Vacant
21 Director of Accounting .... Mr. Ryan STANLEY
106 Dean General Ed and Online Learning .... Dr. Mary Clare DIGIACOMO
19 Director Security/Safety .... Mr. Jeff STRICKLAND
26 Director Public Relations .... Mr. Antoine BOYNTON

Atlanta Metropolitan State College (I)

1630 Metropolitan Parkway, SW, Atlanta GA 30310-4498
County: Fulton FICE Identification: 012165
Unit ID: 138901
Telephone: (404) 756-4000 Carnegie Class: Bac/Assoc-Assoc Dom
FAX Number: (404) 756-4460 Calendar System: Semester

URL: www.atlm.edu
Established: 1974 Annual Undergrad Tuition & Fees (In-State): $3,250
Enrollment: 2,977 Coed
Affiliation or Control: State IRS Status: 501(c)3
Highest Offering: Baccalaureate
Accreditation: SC, ACBSP

01 President Dr. Gary A. MCGAHA, SR.
05 Vice Pres Academic Affairs Dr. Michael HEARD
10 Vice President Fiscal Affairs Mr. Freddie JOHNSON
32 Vice President Student Affairs Vacant
30 Vice Pres Institutional Advancement Vacant
21 Assoc VP Fiscal Affairs Mrs. Michelle ALSTON-BROWN
50 Dean Div Business/Computer Sci Vacant
79 Dean Div Humanities/Fine Arts Dr. Frank JOHNSON
81 Dean Div of Sci/Math/Health Profess Dr. Bryan MITCHELL
83 Dean Div of Social Sciences Dr. Vance GRAY
06 Dir Enrollment Services/Registrar Mrs. Candace PERRY
15 Director of Human Resources Ms. Regina Ray SIMMONS
08 Director of the Library Mr. Robert QUARLES
35 Director of Student Activities Ms. Iris SHANKLIN
37 Director of Financial Aid Dr. Michelle CHAPMAN
38 Director Counseling/Disability Svcs Ms. Dorothy WILLIAMS
13 Chief Information Officer Mr. Antonio TRAVIS
09 Director Inst Effectiveness Dr. Mark CUNNINGHAM
19 Director of Campus Safety Mr. Antonio LONG
35 Dir of Student Outreach & Access Mr. Stephen WOODALL
18 Dir Plant Operations/Facilities Mr. E. Keith WILLIAMS
40 Bookstore Manager Ms. Gloria MCCLAIN
26 Media Relations Director/Marketing Ms. Sheila TENNEY
41 Athletic Director Mr. Robert PRICHETT

† Part of the University System of Georgia.

Atlanta Technical College (A)

1560 Metropolitan Parkway, SW, Atlanta GA 30310-4446
County: Fulton FICE Identification: 008543
Unit ID: 138840
Telephone: (404) 225-4400 Carnegie Class: Assoc/HVT-Mix Trad/Non
FAX Number: (404) 225-4445 Calendar System: Semester
URL: www.atlantatech.edu
Established: 1967 Annual Undergrad Tuition & Fees (In-State): $2,746
Enrollment: 4,282 Coed
Affiliation or Control: State IRS Status: 501(c)3
Highest Offering: Associate Degree
Accreditation: SC, ACFEI, CAHIIM, DA, DH, DT, EMT, MAC, #PTAA, RAD, SURGT

01 President Dr. Alvetta P. THOMAS
05 Vice President Academic Affairs Dr. Murray WILLIAMS
11 Vice Pres Administrative Services Ms. Teresa BROWN
32 Vice President Student Affairs Dr. Rushton JOHNSON
30 Vice President Economic Development Ms. Yulonda BEAUFORD
04 Assistant to the President Dr. Joni WILLIAMS
26 Director Communications & Marketing Ms. Lauretta ADAMS
37 Director of Financial Aid Mr. Lamario PRIMAS
84 Director of Enrollment Management Mr. Vory BILLUPS
20 Assoc VP IE/Academic Affairs Dr. Kimberly FRAZIER
88 Dean Industrial and Transportation Vacant
51 Director of Continuing Education Vacant
36 Director Career Placement Mr. Michael BURNSIDE
50 Dean Business and Public Services Ms. Phoebe COQUEREL
88 Dean Health and Public Safety Dr. Queenston THORPE
06 Registrar Ms. Niya EADY
15 Director Human Resources Ms. Marilyn SMITH-ROBINSON
18 Director of Facilities Vacant
09 Director of Institutional Research Vacant
49 Interim Dean Arts and Sciences Ms. Sonya MCCOY-WILSON
08 Director of Library Services Ms. Tosha BUSSEY
106 AVP of Evening/Weekend/Online Mr. Shawn ADAMS
13 Director of Information Technology Dr. Shannon THOMAS
19 AVP of Operations Mr. Fred HAMMETT
25 Director of Sponsored Programs Ms. Faye EVANS
96 Procurement Officer Ms. Ella SIZEMORE

Atlanta's John Marshall Law School (B)

1422 West Peachtree Street NW, Atlanta GA 30309
County: Fulton FICE Identification: 031733
Unit ID: 138929
Telephone: (404) 872-3593 Carnegie Class: Spec-4-yr-Law
FAX Number: (404) 873-3802 Calendar System: Semester
URL: www.johnmarshall.edu
Established: 1933 Annual Graduate Tuition & Fees: N/A
Enrollment: 505 Coed
Affiliation or Control: Proprietary IRS Status: Proprietary
Highest Offering: First Professional Degree; No Undergraduates
Accreditation: LAW

01 Dean/CEO Mr. Malcolm L. MORRIS
32 Assoc Dean of Students Ms. Sheryl E. HARRISON-MERCER
10 Assoc Dean of Finance Mr. Allan BREZEL
06 Registrar Ms. Cheryl FEREBEE
26 Asst Dir Marketing & Communications Ms. Hilary WALDO
07 Director of Admissions Mrs. Rebecca MILTER
37 Director of Financial Aid Mr. Montre EVERETT
29 Alumni Director Mrs. Virginia ARNOLD
36 Asst Dean of Career Development Mrs. Ivonne BETANCOURT
05 Assoc Dean for Academic Program Mr. M. Scott BOONE
20 Assoc Dean of Academic Admin Ms. Browning JEFFRIES
08 Director of Law Library Mr. Michael LYNCH

Augusta Technical College (C)

3200 Augusta Tech Drive, Augusta GA 30906-3399
County: Richmond FICE Identification: 005599
Unit ID: 138956
Telephone: (706) 771-4000 Carnegie Class: Assoc/HVT-High Trad
FAX Number: (706) 771-4016 Calendar System: Semester
URL: www.augustatech.edu
Established: 1961 Annual Undergrad Tuition & Fees (In-District): $2,644
Enrollment: 4,269 Coed
Affiliation or Control: State/Local IRS Status: 501(c)3
Highest Offering: Associate Degree
Accreditation: SC, COARC, CVT, DA, ENGT, MAC, OTA, PNUR, RAD, SURGT

01 President Mr. Terry D. ELAM
05 Sr Vice President Academic Affairs Dr. C. Rick HALL
10 Vice Pres Administrative Services Ms. Sheila M. HILL
32 Vice Pres Student Affairs Dr. Nicole KENNEDY
88 Vice President Economic Development Dr. Lisa PALMER
12 Dean/Director Waynesboro Campus Mr. Greg COURSEY
37 Director Financial Aid Ms. Beverly SMYRE HINES
07 Director Admissions Ms. Christine BALL
30 Director Institutional Advancement Ms Beverly PELTIER
06 Registrar Mr. Mike VIOLETTE
45 Sr Vice Pres Inst Effectiveness Dr. Melissa F. ALSTON
21 Director Accounting Ms. Sherrick L. JOHNSON
26 Director Marketing/Public Relations Ms. Kimberly HOLDEN
15 Director Human Resources Ms. Shannon PATTERSON
12 Dean Director Thomson Campus Ms. Julie LANGHAM
84 Enrollment Manager Ms. Jeanette LOWE
36 Director Career Services Ms. Donna WENDT
88 High School Coordinator Mrs. Evett DAVIS
76 Dean Allied Health Science Dr. Gwen TAYLOR
50 Dean Business/Public Safety Ms. Elizabeth A. JULIAN
97 Dean Gen Educ & Learning Support Mr. John RICHARDSON
54 Dean Industrial & Engineering Tech Mr. James PRICE
08 Head Librarian Mrs. Bonnie OWEN
106 Dir Online Education/E-learning Mrs. Tammy O'BRIEN
18 Chief Facilities/Physical Plant Mr. Garry STEPHENS
19 Director Security/Safety Mr. Mike ANCHOR

Augusta University (D)

1120 Fifteenth Street, Augusta GA 30912-0004
County: Richmond FICE Identification: 001579
Unit ID: 482149
Telephone: (706) 721-0211 Carnegie Class: Not Classified
FAX Number: N/A Calendar System: Semester
URL: www.augusta.edu
Established: 1828 Annual Undergrad Tuition & Fees (In-State): $8,282
Enrollment: 7,988 Coed
Affiliation or Control: State IRS Status: 501(c)3
Highest Offering: Doctorate
Accreditation: SC, ANEST, ARCPA, ART, BUS, CACREP, CAHIIM, COARC, DENT, DH, IPSY, MED, MIL, MT, MUS, NMT, NURSE, OT, PH, PTA, FTT, SPAA, SW, TED

01 President Dr. Brooks A. KEEL
05 Exec VP for Acad Affairs/Provost Dr. Gretchen CAUGHMAN
10 Chief Business Ofcr/EVP Admin & Fin Mr. Anthony E. WAGNER
26 EVP Strategic Comm/Chf Mrktng Ofcr Ms. Karla LEEPER
31 Exec VP External Rel/Chief of Staff Mr. Russell KEEN
43 EVP Legal Affairs/General Counsel Mr. Chris MELCHER
17 VP Clinical Affs/Dean Medicine Dr. Peter F. BUCKLEY
86 VP Govt Rels/Chief Advocacy Officer Mr. W. Michael SHAFFER
46 Senior Vice President for Research Dr. Michael DIAMOND
30 Sr VP Advance/Cmty Relations/CDO Vacant
15 Enterprise VP Human Resources Ms. Susan A. NORTON
20 VP Academic & Faculty Affairs Dr. Carol RYCHLY
28 VP Acad Plng/Strategic Initiative Dr. Quincy BYRDSONG
32 VP for Student Affairs/Enrollment Dr. Mark Allen POISEL
09 VP Institutional Effectiveness Mrs. Beth P. BRIGDON
18 VP Facilities Service Mr. Philip HOWARD
27 VP Communications & Marketing Mr. Jack EVANS
21 Vice Pres Finance Mr. Lee FRUITTICHER
58 Dean The Graduate School Dr. Mitchell WATSKY
76 Dean College of Allied Health Dr. E. Andrew BALAS
52 Dean College of Dental Med Dr. Carol LEFEBVRE
66 Dean College of Nursing Dr. Lucy N. MARION
50 Int Dean Hull College of Business Dr. Mark THOMPSON
49 Dean College of Arts/Hum/Soc Sci Dr. Charles CLARK
53 Dean College of Education Dr. Zach KELEHEAR
81 Dean College of Science & Math Dr. Rickey P. HICKS
88 Chief Audit Officer Mr. Clay SPROUSE
88 Chief Integrity Officer Mr. James RUSH, JR.
13 VP Information Technology/CIO Mr. Charles ENICKS
88 Director Cancer Center Dr. Samir KHLEIF
06 Registrar Vacant
88 Bursar Ms. Beth WELSH
41 Director of Athletics Mr. Clint BRYANT
19 Int Director of Public Safety Maj. Eugene MAXWELL
08 Director of Libraries Dr. Brenda SEAGO
88 Director of Supply Chain Mgmt Mr. Clay TROVER
109 Director of Auxiliary Services Mr. Karl MUNSCHY
37 Director of Financial Aid Ms. Cynthia PARKS
07 Interim Director of Admissions Mr. Scott ARGO

† Part of the University System of Georgia.

Bainbridge State College (E)

2500 E Shotwell Street, PO Box 990, Bainbridge GA 39818-0990
County: Decatur FICE Identification: 011074
Unit ID: 139010
Telephone: (229) 243-6000 Carnegie Class: Assoc/HVT-High Trad
FAX Number: (229) 248-2623 Calendar System: Semester
URL: www.bainbridge.edu
Established: 1970 Annual Undergrad Tuition & Fees (In-State): $3,227
Enrollment: 2,470 Coed
Affiliation or Control: State IRS Status: 501(c)3
Highest Offering: Baccalaureate
Accreditation: SC, ADNUR

01 Interim President Dr. Stuart RAYFIELD
05 Vice Pres Academic & Student Affs Dr. Rodney CARR
10 Interim VP of Business & Operations Mr. Gordon PRETTELT
49 Dean School of Arts & Sciences Ms. Joann SIMPSON
107 Int Dean Sch Hlth Sci/Profess Stds Mr. Jason RUBENBAUER
32 Associate Dean of Student Affairs Mr. Spencer STEWART
08 Director Library Ms. Michelle BARSOM
26 Chief Public Relations Officer Vacant
37 Interim Director of Financial Aid Ms. Haley HOOKS
21 Interim Comptroller Ms. Leslie JUDKINS
18 Director of Plant Operations Mr. Wayne QUINN
91 Director of Technology Services Mr. Scott DUNN
35 Assistant Dean of Student Affairs Mr. Sam MAYHEW
30 Exec Director of Inst Advancement Ms. Lauren HARRELL
07 Director of Admissions Ms. Melanie CLEVELAND
19 Director of Public Safety Mr. James SPOONER
06 Assistant Registrar Mr. Robert THOMPSON

† Part of the University System of Georgia.

Berry College (F)

2277 Martha Berry Highway, NW, Mount Berry GA 30149-0001
County: Floyd FICE Identification: 001554
Unit ID: 139144
Telephone: (706) 232-5374 Carnegie Class: Masters/S
FAX Number: (706) 236-2238 Calendar System: Semester
URL: www.berry.edu
Established: 1902 Annual Undergrad Tuition & Fees: $31,996
Enrollment: 2,177 Coed
Affiliation or Control: Independent Non-Profit IRS Status: 501(c)3
Highest Offering: Beyond Master's But Less Than Doctorate
Accreditation: SC, BUS, MUS, NURSE

01 President Dr. Stephen R. BRIGGS
05 Vice President & Provost Dr. Andrew BRESSETTE
10 Vice President Finance Mr. Brian I. ERB
32 VP Student Affairs and Enrollment Ms. Debbie HEIDA
30 Vice Pres Institutional Advancement Ms. Bettyann O'NEILL
84 VP of Enrollment Management Dr. Gary WATERS
100 Chief of Staff Vacant
42 Chaplain Rev. Jonathan HUGGINS
35 Assoc Vice Pres Student Affairs Ms. Lindsey TAYLOR
20 Assistant Provost Dr. Thomas D. KENNEDY
50 Dean Campbell School of Business Dr. Joyce HEAMES
53 Dean Charter School of Education Dr. Jackie MCDOWELL
79 Dean School Humanities/Arts/Soc Sci Dr. Thomas D. KENNEDY
66 Dean of Nursing Dr. Vanice ROBERTS
81 Dean School of Math/Nat Sci Dr. Gary BRETON
78 Dean Stdnt Work/Experiential Lrng Mr. Rufus MASSEY
88 Dean Academic Services Dr. David SLADE
07 Asst Vice Pres Admissions Mr. Brett E. KENNEDY
26 Dir Marketing & Communications Mr. Cameron JORDAN
08 Director of the Library Ms. Sherre Lee HARRINGTON
29 Director of Alumni Affairs Ms. Jennifer SCHAKNOWSKI
13 Chief Information Officer Ms. Penny EVANS-PLANTS
38 Director of Counseling Center Dr. J. Marshall JENKINS
37 Director of Financial Aid Ms. Donna CHILDRES
36 Director of Career Center Mrs. Sue TARPLEY
09 Dir Institutional Research Dr. Bryce DURBIN
46 Dir Research & Sponsored Programs Mrs. Donna DAVIN
18 Director Physical Plant Mr. Mark HOPKINS
89 Director First Year Experience Mrs. Katherine POWELL
92 Director Honors Program Dr. Lara WHELAN
94 Director Women's Studies Dr. Susan CONRADSEN
96 Director Purchasing Mr. Brad BARRIS
85 Director International Programs Ms. Sarah EGERER
15 Director Human Resources Mr. Wayne PHIPPS
43 Director of Legal Services Mr. Danny PRICE
28 Director of Multicultural Affairs Dr. Tasha TOY
78 Dir Stdnt Work/Experiential Lrng Mr. Michael BURNES
88 Director of Employee Development Mr. Mark KOZERA
06 Registrar Dr. Bryce DURBIN
41 Director of Athletics Mr. Todd BROOKS

Beulah Heights University (G)

892 Berne Street, SE, PO Box 18145, Atlanta GA 30316-1873
County: Fulton FICE Identification: 030763
Unit ID: 139153
Telephone: (404) 627-2681 Carnegie Class: Spec-4-yr-Faith
FAX Number: (404) 627-0702 Calendar System: Semester
URL: www.beulah.org
Established: 1918 Annual Undergrad Tuition & Fees: $9,390
Enrollment: 673 Coed
Affiliation or Control: Other Protestant IRS Status: 501(c)3

Highest Offering: Doctorate
Accreditation: BI, TRACS

01 President .... Dr. Benson M. KARANJA
04 Administrative Asst to President .... Ms. Kimberly WIGLEY
11 Vice Pres Operations .... Mr. Peter KARANJA
05 Vice Pres/Dean Academic Affairs .... Dr. Wes WILSON
32 Sr Dir Student Life/Enrollment Mgmt .... Dr. Iria ABRAM
106 Dean of Distance Learning .... Dr. Mark HARDGROVE
108 Director of Assessment .... Mr. Dennis C. MALONE
06 University Registrar .... Ms. NaTanya F. DOWELL
10 Director of Finance/Comptroller .... Ms. Bernadette ASHER
37 Director of Financial Aid .... Ms. Alyssa TAKATORI
07 Director of Admissions .... Mr. Arthur BRELAND
88 Vice Pres Asian Affairs .... Dr. John KIM
73 Asst Chair Religious Studies .... Mr. Walter TURNER
50 Chair Business/Leadership Studies .... Dr. Kenneth MILLER
26 Director of Marketing .... Ms. Alison KIM
08 Director of Library Services .... Mr. Pradeep K. DAS
15 Director Personnel Services (HR) .... Ms. Trish STATON
42 Dean of Chapel .... Rev. Billy JOHNSON

Brenau University (A)

500 Washington Street, SE, Gainesville GA 30501-3668
County: Hall FICE Identification: 001556
Unit ID: 139199
Telephone: (770) 534-6299 Carnegie Class: Masters/L
FAX Number: (770) 534-6114 Calendar System: Semester
URL: www.brenau.edu
Established: 1878 Annual Undergrad Tuition & Fees: $25,878
Enrollment: 2,789 Coed
Affiliation or Control: Independent Non-Profit IRS Status: 501(c)3
Highest Offering: Doctorate
Accreditation: SC, ACBSP, CIDA, NURSE, OT, @PTA, TED

01 President .... Dr. Ed L. SCHRADER
03 Sr VP/Chief Financial Ofcr .... Dr. David L. BARNETT
05 Provost & VP For Academic Affairs .... Dr. Nancy F. KRIPPEL
100 Chief of Staff .... Ms. Jody Y. WALL
10 Vice President Financial Services .... Mr. Toby R. HINTON
84 Vice Pres Enrollment Management .... Mr. Ray TATUM
30 Vice Pres External Relations .... Mr. J. Matthew THOMAS
13 Vice Pres Information Technology .... Mr. Chip L. ANDREWS
09 Director of Research & Planning .... Dr. Robert E. CUTTINO
37 Assoc VP & Dir Financial Aid .... Ms. Pam J. BARRETT
21 Asst VP Financial Svcs/Controller .... Ms. Holly REYNOLDS
15 Director of Human Resources .... Ms. Kelley L. MADDOX
18 Director Facilities & Logistics .... Mr. Mike HOLLIMON
26 VP Communications/Publications .... Mr. David MORRISON
32 Dean of Student Success & Retention .... Ms. Valerie SIMMONS-WALSTON
36 Director of Career Services .... Mr. George BAGEL
24 Director of Learning Center .... Dr. Vince J. YAMILKOSKI
41 Athletic Director .... Mr. Mike LOCHSTAMPFOR
23 Chaplain .... Dr. Don HARRISON
53 Dean College of Education .... Dr. Eugene WILLIAMS
76 Dean College of Health Sciences .... Dr. Gale H. STARICH
50 Dean College Business/Mass Comm .... Dr. Suzanne ERICKSON
79 Dean College of Fine Arts & Human .... Dr. Andrea C. BIRCH
08 Dean of Library Svcs & SACS Liaison .... Ms. Marlene GIGUERE
88 Executive Director for Admissions .... Mr. Nathan R. GOSS
06 Registrar & Dir of Student Records .... Ms. Barbara WILSON
29 Exec Director Alumni .... Ms. Ashley CARTER
19 Director Campus Safety & Security .... Ms. Paula DAMPIER

Brewton-Parker College (B)

201 David-Eliza Fountain Circle,
Mount Vernon GA 30445-0197
County: Montgomery FICE Identification: 001557
Unit ID: 139205
Telephone: (912) 583-2241 Carnegie Class: Bac-Diverse
FAX Number: (912) 583-4498 Calendar System: Semester
URL: www.bpc.edu
Established: 1904 Annual Undergrad Tuition & Fees: $16,180
Enrollment: 638 Coed
Affiliation or Control: Baptist IRS Status: 501(c)3
Highest Offering: Baccalaureate
Accreditation: SC, @TRACS

01 President .... Dr. Steven F. ECHOLS
04 Administrative Asst to President .... Mrs. Jennifer J. BLAYLOCK
43 General Counsel .... Mr. Thomas EVERETT
10 Chief Financial Officer .... Dr. Nicole SHEPARD
05 Provost .... Dr. Robert M. BRIAN
30 VP College Advancement .... Vacant
32 VP of Student Services and Athletic .... Mr. Daniel PREVETT
07 VP of Enrollment Services .... Mr. Chris DOOLEY
11 Director of Operations .... Mr. Jim WAMPLER
15 Director Human Resources .... Ms. Nikki BELL
37 Director of Financial Aid .... Ms. Loretta WATSON
07 Director of Admissions .... Mrs. Kim BELL
38 Dir Counseling Services .... Mr. Thadeus HOLLOWAY
08 Librarian .... Mr. Daryl FLETCHER
06 Registrar .... Mrs. Elizabeth ADAMS
09 Dir of IER .... Dr. Patti WILLIAMS
26 Dir Public Relations and Marketing .... Ms. Amanda CORBIN
88 Textbook Coordinator .... Mrs. Lynn ADDISON
29 Director Alumni Relations .... Ms. Kim LAJINESS
22 Dir Affirmative Action/EEO .... Mr. Forrest RICH
50 Chair Business and Communication .... Dr. James WEST
53 Chair Education and Behav Sci .... Mrs. Sky JOYCE
79 Chair Christian Studies Humanities .... Dr. Grant LILFORD
81 Chair Math and Natural Sci .... Dr. Helene PETERS
42 Campus Pastor .... Mr. Steve EDWARDS
88 Director of Baptist Col Ministry .... Ms. Lauren PARNELL

Brown College of Court Reporting (C)

1100 Spring Street NW, Suite 101, Atlanta GA 30309
County: Fulton FICE Identification: 020609
Unit ID: 139214
Telephone: (404) 876-1227 Carnegie Class: Not Classified
FAX Number: (404) 876-4415 Calendar System: Quarter
URL: www.bccr.edu
Established: 1972 Annual Undergrad Tuition & Fees: $12,900
Enrollment: 208 Coed
Affiliation or Control: Proprietary IRS Status: Proprietary
Highest Offering: Associate Degree
Accreditation: COE

01 President .... Russell FREEMAN
03 Director .... Marita CAREY
07 Director of Admissions .... Carlette JENNINGS
05 Director of Education .... Julie MORRIS
06 Registrar .... Lisa LOWE

Brown Mackie College-Atlanta (D)

4370 Peachtree Road NE, Atlanta GA 30319
Telephone: (404) 799-4500 FICE Identification: 026214
Accreditation: ACICS, OTA

† Branch campus of The Art Institute of Phoenix, Phoenix, AZ

Cambridge Institute of Allied Health & Technology (E)

5673 Peachtree Dunwoody Rd, Ste 450, Atlanta GA 30342
Telephone: (404) 255-4500 Identification: 770938
Accreditation: ABHES

† Branch campus of Cambridge Institute of Allied Health and Technology, Delray Beach, FL.

Carver College (F)

3870 Cascade Road SW, Atlanta GA 30331-2184
County: Fulton FICE Identification: 036353
Unit ID: 139287
Telephone: (404) 527-4520 Carnegie Class: Spec-4-yr-Faith
FAX Number: (404) 527-4524 Calendar System: Semester
URL: www.carver.edu
Established: 1943 Annual Undergrad Tuition & Fees: $9,860
Enrollment: 88 Coed
Affiliation or Control: Independent Non-Profit IRS Status: 501(c)3
Highest Offering: Baccalaureate
Accreditation: #BI

01 President and CEO .... Mr. Robert W. CRUMMIE
05 Academic Dean .... Mr. Joseph MILLER
30 Director of Advancement .... Mrs. Carla M. CRUMMIE
32 Dean of Students .... Mr. Thomas B. CAIN
84 Dir Enrollment Management .... Ms. Tonya CANNON
06 Registrar .... Mrs. Olive JACKS
09 Dir Institutional Effectiveness .... Mrs. Marriane GREENFIELD
29 Director Alumni Affairs .... Ms. Cathy REYNOLDS
42 Director of Chapel Services .... Mr. Teddy WRIGHT
73 Director of Bible/Theology Studies .... Dr. Benjamin JACKS
97 Director of General Studies .... Mrs. Amber BOGLIN
107 Director of Professional Studies .... Dr. John A. JENKINS
08 Director of Library Services .... Ms. Debra A. MILLIGAN
83 Director of Psychology Studies .... Ms. Patricia WESLEY
50 Director of Business Division .... Dr. Wynton HEYLIGER
18 Director of Physical Plant .... Mr. Herman PATE
41 Athletic Director .... Mr. Martin CARTER
40 Director of Bookstore .... Mr. Willie KITCHENS
04 Assistant to the President .... Ms. Iverna SHELTON
19 Chief of Police .... Capt. Ray COLLINS
26 Public Relations/Sports Information .... Mr. Augustus HOWARD

Central Georgia Technical College (G)

3300 Macon Tech Drive, Macon GA 31206
County: Bibb FICE Identification: 005763
Unit ID: 140304
Telephone: (478) 757-3400 Carnegie Class: Not Classified
FAX Number: (478) 757-3454 Calendar System: Quarter
URL: www.centralgatech.edu
Established: 1966 Annual Undergrad Tuition & Fees (In-State): N/A
Enrollment: N/A Coed
Affiliation or Control: State IRS Status: 501(c)3
Highest Offering: Associate Degree
Accreditation: SC, CVT, DH, EMT, MLTAD, POLYT, RAD, SURGT

01 President .... Dr. Ivan ALLEN
05 Vice President Academic Affairs .... Dr. Amy HOLLOWAY
10 Vice President Admin/Fin Svcs .... Ms. Michelle SINIARD
32 Vice President Student Affairs .... Mr. Craig JACKSON
31 Vice President Economic Development .... Ms. Andrea GRINER
11 AVP Facilities/Ancillary Svcs .... Mr. Jimmy FAIRCLOTH
13 Chief Information Officer .... Mr. Brian SNELGROVE
12 VP for Satellite Operations South .... Dr. Joan THOMPSON
35 Dean of Student Affairs .... Vacant
06 Registrar .... Ms. Sonja JENKINS
30 Asst VP for Advancement .... Ms. Tonya MCCLURE
08 Director Library & Media Services .... Mr. Neil MCARTHUR
37 Director of Financial Aid .... Ms. Jackie WHITE
15 Executive Director Human Resources .... Ms. Carol JONES
18 Facilities Director .... Mr. Robert DOMINY
51 Director of Continuing Education .... Mr. Clay TEAGUE

Central Georgia Technical College (H)

80 Cohen Walker Drive, Warner Robins GA 31088-2729
County: Houston FICE Identification: 025086
Unit ID: 483045
Telephone: (478) 988-6800 Carnegie Class: Not Classified
FAX Number: (478) 988-6813 Calendar System: Quarter
URL: www.centralgatech.edu
Established: 1973 Annual Undergrad Tuition & Fees (In-State): $2,674
Enrollment: 7,625 Coed
Affiliation or Control: State IRS Status: 501(c)3
Highest Offering: Associate Degree
Accreditation: SC, DH, RAD, SURGT

01 President .... Dr. Ivan H. ALLEN
03 Executive Vice President .... Mr. Jeffrey SCRUGGS
05 Vice President for Academic Affairs .... Dr. Amy L. HOLLOWAY
32 Vice President for Student Affairs .... Mr. Craig JACKSON
09 VP Economic Development .... Ms. Andrea GRINER
11 VP Administrative Financial Svcs .... Mrs. Michelle SINIARD
88 Vice President for Adult Education .... Ms. Brenda L. BROWN
26 Asst VP Enrol Svcs/Marketing/PR .... Mrs. Janet H. KELLY
07 Director of Admissions .... Mr. Dann WEBB
37 Director of Financial Aid .... Ms. Shirley GLOVER
06 Registrar .... Ms. Sonja JENKINS
08 Director of Library Services .... Dr. Dumont C. BUNN
15 Exec Director of Human Resources .... Ms. Carol F. JONES
30 Asst VP of Advancement .... Ms. Tonya L. MCCLURE
18 Asst VP Facilities/Ancillary Svcs .... Mr. Jimmy FAIRCLOTH

Chamberlain College of Nursing-Atlanta (I)

5775 Peachtree-Dunwoody Rd NE,A100,
Atlanta GA 30342
Telephone: (404) 250-8500 Identification: 770504
Accreditation: &NH, NURSE

† Regional accreditation is carried under the parent institution in Addison, IL

Chattahoochee Technical College (J)

980 South Cobb Drive, Marietta GA 30060
County: Cobb FICE Identification: 030290
Unit ID: 140331
Telephone: (770) 528-4545 Carnegie Class: Assoc/HVT-Mix Trad/Non
FAX Number: (770) 975-4126 Calendar System: Quarter
URL: www.chattahoocheetech.edu
Established: 1981 Annual Undergrad Tuition & Fees (In-State): $2,682
Enrollment: 9,942 Coed
Affiliation or Control: State IRS Status: 501(c)3
Highest Offering: Associate Degree
Accreditation: SC, ACFEI, ADNUR, EMT, MAC, MLTAD, OTA, PTAA, RAD, SURGT

01 President .... Dr. Ron NEWCOMB
04 Administrative Asst to President .... Ms. Tammy COLLUM
05 Vice President for Academics .... Dr. Jason TANNER
11 Vice Pres for Administrative Svcs .... Ms. Catrice HUFSTETLER
32 VP Student Affairs/Technology .... Dr. Trina BOTELER
31 Vice Pres External Affairs .... Ms. Jennifer NELSON
18 Vice President for Facilities .... Mr. David SIMMONS
15 Vice President Human Resources .... Mr. Ron PRICE
30 Vice Pres Economic Development .... Mr. Rex BISHOP
26 Exec Dir External Affs/Brd Liaison .... Ms. Jennifer NELSON
27 Specialist for Public Relations .... Ms. Rebecca LONG

Clark Atlanta University (K)

223 James P. Brawley Drive, SW, Atlanta GA 30314-4391
County: Fulton FICE Identification: 001559
Unit ID: 138947
Telephone: (404) 880-8000 Carnegie Class: DU-Higher
FAX Number: N/A Calendar System: Semester
URL: www.cau.edu
Established: 1988 Annual Undergrad Tuition & Fees: $21,945
Enrollment: 3,485 Coed
Affiliation or Control: United Methodist IRS Status: 501(c)3
Highest Offering: Doctorate
Accreditation: SC, BUS, CACREP, SPAA, SW, TED

01 President .... Dr. Ronald A. JOHNSON
05 Provost/VP for Acad Affairs .... Dr. Peter O. NWOSU
30 Int VP for Inst Advance/Univ Rels .... Ms. Marilynn A. DAVIS
10 Exec VP and CFO .... Ms. Lucille MAUGE
32 Int Asst VP of Student Affairs .... Dr. Cynthia CLEM
46 Assoc VP Research/Sponsored Pgms .... Dr. Olugbemiga O. OLATIDOYE
20 Assoc VP for Academic Affairs .... Dr. LeVon E. WILSON
13 Assoc VP/Chief Info Ofcr .... Vacant
21 Interim Assoc VP/Controller .... Mr. Leighton O'SULLIVAN
35 Dean of Students .... Ms. Ernita HEMMITT
09 Asst VP Planning Assess/Inst Rsrch .... Dr. Narendra H. PATEL
43 General Counsel .... Mr. Lance DUNNINGS

06 University Registrar .... Ms. Susan GIBSON
26 Assoc VP Strategic Communications .... Ms. Donna BROCK
29 Director Alumni Relations .... Ms. Gay-linn JASHO
15 EVP Human Resources .... Ms. Debra HOYT
07 Dir Recruitment & Admissions .... Ms. Lori RICE-SADDLER
38 Director University Counseling Ctr .... Dr. Joy BRADFORD
36 Career Planning/Placement .... Mr. Andre MCKINNEY
37 Director Student Financial Aid .... Mr. James STOTTS
96 Director of Purchasing .... Ms. Donna BYRD
41 Director of Athletics .... Mr. J. Lin DAWSON
49 Dean Arts & Sciences .... Dr. Danille K. TAYLOR
50 Interim Dean School of Business .... Dr. Ed L. DAVIS
53 Dean School of Education .... Dr. Moses NORMAN
70 Dean School of Social Work .... Dr. Jenny L. JONES
58 Dean Graduate Studies .... Vacant
19 Chief of Public Safety .... Chief Thomas TRAWICK
23 Director Health Services .... Ms. Janet SINGLETON
25 Dir Accts Payable Grants/Contracts .... Ms. Rotesha HARRIS
39 Interim Director of Residence Life .... Ms. Joy OSORIO
88 Director Instructional Media .... Mr. Frank EDWARDS
101 Coordinator for Board Relations .... Ms. Natalie BAKER
104 Coordinator Multicultural Affairs .... Ms. Gwen WADE
22 University Compliance Officer .... Mr. Robert CLARK
18 Asst Director of Facilities .... Mr. Steve LESTER
108 Exec Dir Institutional Assessment .... Dr. Tia MINNIS
04 Executive Asst to President .... Ms. Rita HARDY
100 Chief of Staff .... Ms. Marilyn DAVIS

Clayton State University (A)

2000 Clayton State Boulevard, Morrow GA 30260-0285
County: Clayton FICE Identification: 008976
Unit ID: 139311
Telephone: (678) 466-4000 Carnegie Class: Masters/M
FAX Number: (770) 961-3700 Calendar System: Semester
URL: www.clayton.edu
Established: 1969 Annual Undergrad Tuition & Fees (In-State): $5,340
Enrollment: 7,022 Coed
Affiliation or Control: State IRS Status: 501(c)3
Highest Offering: Master's
Accreditation: SC, BUS, DH, MUS, NURSE, TED

01 President .... Dr. Thomas HYNES
05 Provost/Vice Pres Academic Affairs .... Dr. Kevin DEMMITT
10 VP for Operations/Planning/Budget .... Ms. Corlis CUMMINGS
32 Vice President for Student Affairs .... Dr. Elaine MANGLITZ
26 Vice President External Affairs .... Ms. Kate TROELSTRA
13 Vice Pres Information Tech & Svcs .... Mr. Bill GRUSZKA
20 AVP Academic Planning/Assessment .... Dr. Jill L. LANE
35 Assistant Vice Pres Student Affairs .... Dr. Allen WARD
84 Asst VP Enroll Mgmt/Acad Success .... Dr. Stephen SCHULTHEIS
41 Executive Director of Athletics .... Mr. Tim DUNCAN
88 Executive Director of Spivey Hall .... Mr. Samuel DIXON
15 Exec Dir Human Resources & Services .... Mr. Tom GAUSVIK
49 Dean of Arts & Sciences .... Dr. Nasser MOMAYEZI
36 Director Retention& Stdnt Placement .... Mr. Eric TACK
50 Dean of Business .... Dr. Avinandan MUKHERJEE
76 Dean of Health Sciences .... Dr. Lisa EICHELBERGER
81 Dean Information/Mathematical Sci .... Dr. Lila ROBERTS
08 Dean of Library Services .... Dr. Gordon BAKER
88 Dir Center for Instructional Dev .... Mr. Justin MAYS
51 Director of Continuing Education .... Ms. Karen LAMARSH
06 University Registrar .... Ms. Rebecca GMEINER
07 Director of Admissions .... Mr. Stephen JENKINS
109 Director of Auxiliary Services .... Ms. Carolina AMERO
27 Asst VP Marketing/Communications .... Ms. Maritza FERREIRA
18 Director of Plant Operations .... Mr. Harun BISWAS
19 Director of Public Safety .... Mr. Bobby HAMIL
30 Director of Development .... Mr. Thomas GIFFIN
09 Director of Institutional Research .... Dr. Narem REDDY
24 Director Media Services .... Mr. Paul BAILEY
38 Director of Counseling Services .... Dr. Christine SMITH
37 Director Student Financial Aid .... Ms. Pat BARTON
96 Director of Purchasing .... Ms. Marcia JONES
29 Director Alumni Relations .... Ms. Leila TATUM
21 Comptroller .... Mr. Donal CHRISTIAN

† Part of the University System of Georgia.

Coastal Pines Technical College (B)

1701 Carswell Avenue, Waycross GA 31503-4016
County: Ware FICE Identification: 005511
Unit ID: 485458
Telephone: (912) 287-6584 Carnegie Class: Not Classified
FAX Number: (912) 287-4865 Calendar System: Semester
URL: www.coastalpines.edu
Established: 1965 Annual Undergrad Tuition & Fees (In-State): $4,770
Enrollment: 2,431 Coed
Affiliation or Control: State IRS Status: 501(c)3
Highest Offering: Associate Degree
Accreditation: SC, COARC, EMT, MAC, MLTAD, RAD, SURGT

01 President .... Dr. Glenn DEIBERT
05 Vice Pres for Academic Affairs .... Vacant
11 VP of Administrative Services .... Ms. Monica O'QUINN
46 Vice Pres for Economic Development .... Dr. Pete SNELL
32 Vice President for Student Affairs .... Ms. Karla EUBANKS
06 Registrar .... Ms. Tara EICHFIELD
30 Vice President for Advancement .... Ms. Cindy TANNER
18 Facilities Director .... Mr. Chad BOYETT
36 Career Placement & Develop Coord .... Mr. Buck THIGPEN
37 Director Student Financial Aid .... Ms. Tina MANNING
09 VP for Institutional Effectiveness .... Dr. Teresa ALLEN
07 Director of Admissions .... Mr. Chris JEANCAKE
15 Human Resources Coordinator .... Ms. Cynthia LINDER
04 Administrative Asst to President .... Ms. Natasha KING
08 Director of Library Services .... Ms. Cassie CLEMONS
13 Chief Info Technology Officer (CIO) .... Mr. Derrell HARRIS
38 Director Student Counseling .... Ms. Cathy MONTGOMERY

College of Coastal Georgia (C)

One College Drive, Brunswick GA 31520-3632
County: Glynn FICE Identification: 001558
Unit ID: 139250
Telephone: (912) 279-5700 Carnegie Class: Bac/Assoc-Mixed
FAX Number: (912) 262-3072 Calendar System: Semester
URL: www.ccga.edu
Established: 1961 Annual Undergrad Tuition & Fees (In-State): $3,971
Enrollment: 3,008 Coed
Affiliation or Control: State IRS Status: 501(c)3
Highest Offering: Baccalaureate
Accreditation: SC, ACFEI, ADNUR, MLTAD, NUR, RAD, TED

01 President .... Dr. Gregory F. ALOIA
05 Vice President Academic Affairs .... Dr. Tracy PELLETT
30 Vice President Advancement .... Vacant
10 Vice President Business Affairs .... Mr. Jeffrey H. PRESTON
32 Vice President Student Affairs .... Dr. Jason W. UMFRESS
20 Asst VP Academic Affairs .... Dr. German VARGAS
20 Asst VP Academic Affairs .... Dr. Andrea WALLACE
21 Asst VP Business Affairs .... Mr. C. Tom SAUNDERS
84 Asst VP Enrollment Management .... Mr. Clayton DANIELS
13 Chief Information Officer .... Mr. Alan OURS
19 Chief of Police .... Mr. Bryan SIPE
08 Dean of Library Services .... Ms. Debra HOLMES
35 Dean of Students .... Dr. Michael BUTCHER
49 Dean School of Arts and Sciences .... Dr. Keith E. BELCHER
50 Dean Sch of Business & Public Affs .... Dr. William MOUNTS
53 Dean School of Education & Teacher .... Dr. Michael HAZELKORN
66 Dean School of Nursing & Health Sci .... Vacant
41 Director of Athletics .... Dr. William CARLTON
12 Director Camden Center .... Vacant
106 Director of E-Learning .... Dr. Lisa MCNEAL
09 Director Institutional Effectivenes .... Dr. James LYNCH
104 Dir of International Initiatives .... Vacant
15 Director of Human Resources .... Ms. Phyllis BROADWELL
18 Director of Facilities and Plant Op .... Mr. Gary STRICKLAND
26 Director of Marketing & Public Rels .... Mr. John CORNELL
37 Director Student Financial Aid .... Ms. Terral HARRIS
06 Registrar .... Ms. Lisa LESSEIG
07 Associate Director of Admissions .... Ms. Aerial DICKERSON
04 Executive Assistant President's Off .... Ms. Judy JOHNSTON
88 Coordinator Faculty & Admin Svcs .... Ms. Connie HIOTT
96 Purchasing Officer .... Ms. Karen C. MARTIN

† Part of the University System of Georgia.

Columbia Theological Seminary (D)

P.O. Box 520, 701 S Columbia Drive,
Decatur GA 30031-0520
County: DeKalb FICE Identification: 001560
Unit ID: 139348
Telephone: (404) 378-8821 Carnegie Class: Spec-4-yr-Faith
FAX Number: (404) 377-9696 Calendar System: 4/1/4
URL: www.ctsnet.edu
Established: 1828 Annual Graduate Tuition & Fees: N/A
Enrollment: 213 Coed
Affiliation or Control: Presbyterian Church (U.S.A.) IRS Status: 501(c)3
Highest Offering: Doctorate; No Undergraduates
Accreditation: SC, THEOL

01 President .... Dr. Leanne VAN DYK
05 Interim VP Academic Affairs .... Dr. Christine R. YODER
28 VP Equity/Diversity & Inclusion .... Dr. Deborah F. MULLEN
10 VP Business and Finance .... Mr. Martin SADLER
32 Dean of Students .... Vacant
30 VP Institutional Advancement .... Mr. Steven P. MILLER
20 Assoc Dean Academic Administration .... Dr. Ann Clay ADAMS
08 Director of Library .... Dr. Kelly D. CAMPBELL
107 Assoc Dean Advanced Prof Studies .... Dr. Kevin PARK
06 Registrar .... Mr. Mike MEDFORD
07 Director Recruitment and Admission .... Ms. Betsy LYLES
26 Director of Communications .... Mr. Michael THOMPSON

Columbus State University (E)

4225 University Avenue, Columbus GA 31907-5645
County: Muscogee FICE Identification: 001561
Unit ID: 139366
Telephone: (706) 507-8800 Carnegie Class: Masters/L
FAX Number: (706) 568-2123 Calendar System: Semester
URL: www.columbusstate.edu
Established: 1958 Annual Undergrad Tuition & Fees (In-State): $6,011
Enrollment: 8,192 Coed
Affiliation or Control: State IRS Status: 501(c)3
Highest Offering: Doctorate
Accreditation: SC, ART, BUS, CACREP, MUS, NURSE, TED, THEA

01 President .... Dr. Chris MARKWOOD
05 Interim Provost/VP Academic Affairs .... Dr. Tina BUTCHER
10 Vice President Business & Finance .... Mr. Tom HELTON
32 VP Student Affairs & Enrollment Mgt .... Dr. Gina SHEEKS
30 VP University Advancement .... Dr. Rocky KETTERING
13 Chief Information Officer .... Mr. Abraham GEORGE
84 Asst VP for Enrollment Mgmt .... Mr. John MCELVEEN
26 Assoc VP for University Relations .... Mr. John LESTER
50 Dean College of Business & Comp Sci .... Dr. Linda HADLEY
08 Dean of Libraries .... Mr. Mark FLYNN
35 AVP Student Affs/Dean of Students .... Mr. Aaron J. REESE
15 Human Resources Director .... Ms. Laurie S. JONES
09 Director Institutional Research .... Dr. Sri SITHARAMAN
41 Athletic Director .... Mr. Todd REESER
37 Director Financial Aid .... Mr. Russ ROMANDINI
07 Director of Admissions .... Ms. Viola ALEXANDER

† Part of the University System of Georgia.

Columbus Technical College (F)

928 Manchester Expressway, Columbus GA 31904-6572
County: Muscogee FICE Identification: 005624
Unit ID: 139357
Telephone: (706) 649-1800 Carnegie Class: Assoc/HVT-Mix Trad/Non
FAX Number: (706) 649-1885 Calendar System: Semester
URL: www.columbustech.edu
Established: 1961 Annual Undergrad Tuition & Fees (In-State): $2,694
Enrollment: 3,594 Coed
Affiliation or Control: State IRS Status: 501(c)3
Highest Offering: Associate Degree
Accreditation: SC, ADNUR, COARC, DA, DH, DMS, MAC, RAD, SURGT

01 President .... Ms. Lorette M. HOOVER
10 VP Admin/Chief Financial Svcs .... Ms. Karen THOMAS
05 Vice President Academic Affairs .... Dr. Melanie THORNTON
32 Vice President Student Affairs .... Ms. Tara ASKEW
18 Vice President Operations .... Mr. Tommy WILSON
46 VP Institutional Effectiveness .... Ms. Monique BAUCHAM
88 Vice President Economic Development .... Mr. James LOYD
51 Assoc VP of Adult Education .... Ms. April HOPSON
15 Director of Human Resources .... Ms. Patricia HOOD
26 Director of Communications .... Ms. Cheryl MYERS
37 Associate VP of Financial Aid .... Ms. Debbie HENSHAW
38 Director Student Counseling .... Ms. Olive VIDAL-KENDALL
30 Director Institutional Advancement .... Mr. David FLETCHER

Covenant College (G)

14049 Scenic Highway, Lookout Mountain TN 30750-4164
County: Dade FICE Identification: 003484
Unit ID: 139393
Telephone: (706) 820-1560 Carnegie Class: Bac-A&S
FAX Number: (706) 820-2165 Calendar System: Semester
URL: www.covenant.edu
Established: 1955 Annual Undergrad Tuition & Fees: $31,320
Enrollment: 1,173 Coed
Affiliation or Control: Presbyterian Church In America IRS Status: 501(c)3
Highest Offering: Master's
Accreditation: SC

01 President .... Dr. J. Derek HALVORSON
05 Vice Pres of Academic Affairs .... Dr. Jeffrey B. HALL
30 Vice President of Development .... Mr. Jeff SANDHOFF
32 Vice Pres of Student Development .... Mr. Brad VOYLES
10 Vice Pres of Finance & Operations .... Mr. Dan WYKOFF
08 Director of Library Services .... Mr. John HOLBERG
06 Dean of Records and Registrar .... Mr. Rodney E. MILLER
42 Chaplain .... Mr. Grant LOWE
58 Dean of Master of Education Pgm .... Dr. Jim DREXLER
21 Controller .... Mr. Robert E. HARBERT
88 Campus Architect .... Mr. David NORTHCUTT
37 Director of Financial Aid .... Mrs. Beth BAILEY
15 Senior HR Partner .... Ms. Judy PENNYMAN
41 Director of Athletics .... Mr. Kyle TAYLOR
13 Director of Technology Services .... Ms. Marjorie CROCKER
29 Director of Alumni Relations .... Ms. Kim COLLINS
23 Director of Health Services .... Ms. Tina HOLT
07 Director of Admissions .... Mr. Scott SCHINDLER
09 Director of Institutional Research .... Dr. Karen NELSON
26 Dir of Marketing & Communications .... Mr. David PETERSON
20 Director of Academic Support .... Mrs. Janet HULSEY
36 Dir of Center for Calling & Career .... Mr. John PLATING
04 Admin Asst to Office of President .... Mrs. Cassandra JONES
19 Director of Safety & Security .... Mr. Kevin PATTY
109 Director of Business Operations .... Mr. Tom SCHREINER
100 Dir of Admin Office of President .... Ms. Jen ALLEN
104 Director of Global Education .... Ms. Christiana FITZPATRICK

Dalton State College (H)

650 College Drive, Dalton GA 30720-3797
County: Whitfield FICE Identification: 003956
Unit ID: 139463
Telephone: (706) 272-4436 Carnegie Class: Bac/Assoc-Mixed
FAX Number: (706) 272-4588 Calendar System: Semester
URL: www.daltonstate.edu
Established: 1963 Annual Undergrad Tuition & Fees (In-State): $4,052
Enrollment: 4,854 Coed
Affiliation or Control: State IRS Status: 501(c)3
Highest Offering: Baccalaureate
Accreditation: SC, ADNUR, BUS, COARC, MAC, MLTAD, NUR, PHLEB, RAD, SW, TED

01 President .... Dr. Margaret VENABLE
05 VP for Academic Affairs .... Dr. Pat CHUTE

10 Vice President Fiscal Affairs ... Mr. Nick HENRY
84 Vice Pres Enrollment & Student Svcs ... Dr. Jodi S. JOHNSON
20 Assoc VP Academic Affairs ... Dr. Andy MEYER
37 Director of Financial Aid/Vet Svcs ... Ms. Carol JONES
08 Interim Librarian ... Ms. Melissa WHITESELL
09 Director Inst Research & Planning ... Dr. Henry M. CODJOE
18 Interim Director Plant Opers ... Mr. George BREWER
26 Director Marketing & Communication ... Ms. Pam PARTAIN
102 Director Foundation ... Mr. David ELROD
32 Dean of Students ... Ms. Jami HALL
15 Director Human Resources ... Ms. Lori MCCARTY
96 Purchasing Coordinator ... Ms. Penny CORDELL
13 Director Computing & Info Services ... Mr. Terry BAILEY
19 Director Public Safety ... Mr. Michael MASTERS
29 Director Alumni Relations ... Mr. Josh WILSON
39 Director Student Housing ... Mrs. Natalie BATES
50 Dean School of Business ... Dr. Larry JOHNSON
53 Dean School of Education ... Dr. Sharon HIXON
49 Dean School of Liberal Arts ... Ms. Mary NIELSEN
81 Dean School of Science/Tech/Math ... Mr. Randall GRIFFUS
76 Dean Health Professions ... Dr. Gina KERTULIS-TARTAR
06 Registrar ... Mr. Rob WINGFIELD
04 Administrative Asst to President ... Mrs. Elizabeth CHADWICK
07 Director of Admissions ... Mrs. Katherine LOGAN

† Part of the University System of Georgia.

Darton State College (A)

2400 Gillionville Road, Albany GA 31707-3098
County: Dougherty FICE Identification: 001543
Unit ID: 138691
Telephone: (229) 317-6000 Carnegie Class: Bac/Assoc-Assoc Dom
FAX Number: (229) 317-6604 Calendar System: Semester
URL: www.darton.edu
Established: 1963 Annual Undergrad Tuition & Fees (In-State): $3,395
Enrollment: 5,623 Coed
Affiliation or Control: State IRS Status: 501(c)3
Highest Offering: Baccalaureate
Accreditation: **SC**, ADNUR, CAHIIM, COARC, DH, EMT, HT, MLTAD, NUR, OTA, PTAA, RAD

01 Interim President ... Dr. Richard CARVAJAL
10 Interim Assoc VP for Fiscal Affairs ... Mr. John CLEMENS
05 Interim VP Academic Affairs ... Dr. Elizabeth PERKINS
32 Interim Vice Pres Student Affairs ... Dr. Danette SAYLOR
21 Asst VP Business/Financial Svcs ... Mr. Stan BROWN
08 Director Learning Resources Ctr ... Mrs. Mary WASHINGTON
07 Director Admissions ... Mr. Allan CASE
13 Dir Office of Info Tech/CIO ... Mr. Del KIMBROUGH
18 Director Physical Plant ... Mr. Lee HOWELL
26 Interim Director College Relations ... Ms. Cynthia GEORGE
41 Interim Athletic Director ... Ms. Lea HENRY
06 Registrar ... Mrs. Frances CARR
37 Asst Director Financial Aid ... Ms. Haley HOOKS
15 Interim Dir Human Resources Officer ... Ms. Kimberly CARTER
85 International Coordinator ... Ms. Sue Ann BALCH
29 Director Alumni Relations ... Vacant
36 Director Student Placement ... Ms. Gloria RIDGEWAY
96 Director of Purchasing ... Mrs. Joy CAUSEY
89 Director Freshmen Studies ... Ms. Gloria RIDGEWAY
92 Coordinator Honors Program ... Ms. Shani CLARK
93 Director Minority Students ... Mr. Rocco CAPPELLO
09 Director of Institutional Research ... Dr. Shavecca SNEAD
106 Dir Online Education/E-learning ... Ms. Renita LUCK
19 Major of Police/Public Safety ... Mr. James BRACKIN
22 Dir Affirmative Action/EEO ... Ms. Kimberly CARTER
25 Interim Director of Grants ... Ms. Shalonda HEARD
28 Director of Diversity ... Vacant
30 Interim Chief Advancement Officer ... Ms. Cynthia GEORGE
39 Director Residence Life ... Mr. Rocco CAPPELLO
84 Interim Asst VP Enrollment Mgmt ... Mr. Frank MALINOWSKI
43 Legal Affairs Officer ... Ms. Claudia LYERLY

† Part of the University System of Georgia.

DeVry University - Decatur Campus (B)

One West Court Square, Ste. 100,
Decatur GA 30030-2556
Telephone: (404) 270-2700 FICE Identification: 009224
Accreditation: **&NH**, CAHIIM, ENGT

† Regional accreditation is carried under the parent institution in Downers Grove, IL.

East Georgia State College (C)

131 College Circle, Swainsboro GA 30401-3643
County: Emanuel FICE Identification: 010997
Unit ID: 139621
Telephone: (478) 289-2000 Carnegie Class: Bac/Assoc-Assoc Dom
FAX Number: (478) 289-2038 Calendar System: Semester
URL: www.ega.edu
Established: 1973 Annual Undergrad Tuition & Fees (In-State): $3,067
Enrollment: 2,910 Coed
Affiliation or Control: State IRS Status: 501(c)3
Highest Offering: Baccalaureate
Accreditation: **SC**

01 President ... Dr. Robert G. BOEHMER
05 Vice President for Academic Affairs ... Dr. Timothy D. GOODMAN
10 Vice President for Business Affairs ... Mr. Cliff GAY
32 Vice Pres for Student Affairs ... Dr. Donald AVERY
13 Vice Pres Information Technology ... Mr. Mike ROUNTREE
100 Chief of Staff/Legal Counsel ... Mrs. Mary C. SMITH
04 Executive Assistant to President ... Mrs. Susan GRAY
08 Librarian ... Mrs. Amanda MCKENZIE
06 Registrar ... Ms. Tabithia ROSS
12 Director of EGSC -Augusta ... Ms. Jordyn NAIL
09 Director of Institutional Research ... Mr. David GRIBBIN
84 Assoc Vice Pres Enrollment Mgmt ... Mrs. Karen S. JONES
15 Director of Human Resources ... Mrs. Tracy WOODS
30 Vice Pres Institutional Advancement ... Ms. Elizabeth GILMER
11 Director of Business Operations ... Mrs. Michelle GOFF
44 Assoc VP Institutional Advancement ... Ms. Norma KENNEDY
12 Director of EGSC-Statesboro ... Ms. Caroline JOYNER
19 Dir Public Safety/Chief of Police ... Mr. Wiley GAMMON
35 Director of Student Life ... Ms. Vicki SHERROD
07 Director of Admissions ... Ms. Georgia EDMOND
38 Dir Counseling/Disability Services ... Dr. Odey P. EGBE
39 Director of Housing ... Ms. Missie CRAWFORD
41 Director of Athletics ... Mr. Chuck WIMBERLY
88 Dir Sudie A Fulford Cmty Lrng Ctr ... Mrs. Jean D. SCHWABE
18 Director of Plant Operations ... Mr. David STEPTOE
21 Director of Accounting Services ... Ms. Becky FOSKEY
106 Director of Distance Education ... Dr. Dee MCKINNEY
88 Director of Academic Advisement ... Ms. Deborah KITTRELL-MIKELL
88 Director Learning Support ... Ms. Jill KIRKLAND
109 Director of Auxiliary Services ... Ms. Ruth UNDERWOOD
88 Director of Student Conduct ... Ms. Sherrie HELMS
81 Dean of Mathematics & Sciences ... Dr. Jim WEDINCAMP
79 Dean of Humanities ... Dr. Carmine PALUMBO
83 Dean of Social Sciences ... Dr. Lee CHEEK
81 Chair of Biology Department ... Dr. David CHEVALIER
88 Dir of Ctr for Teaching & Learning ... Vacant
88 Dir of Military Resource Center ... Ms. Stacey KING

† Part of the University System of Georgia.

Emmanuel College (D)

181 Springs Street, Franklin Springs GA 30639
County: Franklin FICE Identification: 001563
Unit ID: 139630
Telephone: (706) 245-7226 Carnegie Class: Bac-Diverse
FAX Number: (706) 245-4424 Calendar System: Semester
URL: www.ec.edu
Established: 1919 Annual Undergrad Tuition & Fees: $18,870
Enrollment: 816 Coed
Affiliation or Control: Pentecostal Holiness Church IRS Status: 501(c)3
Highest Offering: Baccalaureate
Accreditation: **SC**

01 President ... Dr. Ronald WHITE
32 Vice President for Student Life ... Dr. Tracy REYNOLDS
05 Vice President for Academic Affairs ... Dr. John R. HENZEL, JR.
10 Vice President for Finance ... Mr. Greg K. HEARN
30 Vice President for Development ... Mr. W. Brian JAMES
84 Vice Pres Enrollment Mgmt/Marketing ... Ms. Wendy VINSON
08 Director of Library Services ... Ms. Austina JORDAN
06 Registrar ... Mrs. Debra F. GRIZZLE
37 Director of Financial Aid ... Mrs. Niki STINSON
13 Director of Information Technology ... Mr. Glenn TONEY
11 Assoc VP of Campus Operations ... Mr. Matt MCREE
41 Athletics Director ... Mr. Nate MOORMAN
42 Dir Spiritual Life/Campus Pastor ... Mr. Chris MAXWELL
15 Director of Human Resources ... Mrs. Joann HARPER
26 Chief Public Relations Officer ... Mrs. Ashley WESTBROOK
96 Director of Accounting Services ... Mrs. Anita RAY
18 Physical Plant Director ... Mr. Wayne CRIDER
09 Director of Institutional Research ... Dr. Brian PEEK
29 Director Alumni Relations ... Mr. Harrell W. QUEEN
36 Dir Career Svcs/Student Counseling ... Mr. Jason CROY
04 Administrative Asst to President ... Mrs. Mary BEADLES
19 Director Security/Safety ... Mr. Joel SWAILS
39 Director Student Housing ... Mrs. Ginni MAXWELL

Emory University (E)

201 Dowman Drive, Atlanta GA 30322-0001
County: DeKalb FICE Identification: 001564
Unit ID: 139658
Telephone: (404) 727-6123 Carnegie Class: DU-Highest
FAX Number: (404) 727-5997 Calendar System: Semester
URL: www.emory.edu
Established: 1836 Annual Undergrad Tuition & Fees: $46,314
Enrollment: 14,769 Coed
Affiliation or Control: United Methodist IRS Status: 501(c)3
Highest Offering: Doctorate
Accreditation: **SC**, AA, ARCPA, BUS, CLPSY, DENT, IPSY, LAW, MED, MIDWF, NURSE, PAST, PCSAS, PH, PTA, RAD, THEOL

01 President ... Dr. Claire E. STERK
05 Interim Provost/Exec VP Acad Affs ... Dr. Stuart M. ZOLA
11 Interim Exec VP for Business/Admin ... Mr. Peter BARNES
17 Exec Vice Pres Health Affairs ... Dr. Jonathan S. LEWIN
101 VP/Secretary of the University ... Ms. Alllison K. DYKES
04 VP/Deputy to the President ... Dr. Gary S. HAUK
43 Sr Vice Pres & General Counsel ... Mr. Stephen D. SENCER
30 Sr Vice Pres Devel/Alumni Rels ... Ms. Susan CRUSE
32 Sr Vice President/Dean Campus Life ... Dr. Ajay NAIR
88 Vice Provost International Affairs ... Dr. Philip WAINWRIGHT
46 Vice President for Research Admin ... Dr. David L. WYNES
10 Vice President for Finance/CFO ... Ms. Carol KISSAL
58 Vice Provost/Dean Graduate Sch ... Dr. Lisa A. TEDESCO
15 Co Vice President Human Resources ... Ms. Theresa MILAZZO
15 Co Vice President Human Resources ... Ms. Del KING
26 Senior VP Comm/Public Affairs ... Mr. Jerry LEWIS
88 VP Strategic Research Initiatives ... Dr. Lanny S. LIEBESKIND
86 Vice Pres Govt and Cmty Affairs ... Ms. Cameron TAYLOR
18 Vice President Campus Services ... Mr. Matthew EARLY
29 Sr Assoc Vice Pres Alumni Affairs ... Ms. Sarah COOK
25 Assoc Vice Pres for Research Admin ... Ms. Kathleen BIENKOWSKI
21 Assoc VP Finance & Controller ... Ms. Allison S. BERG
28 Assoc Vice Provost Equity/Inclusion ... Ms. Lynell CADRAY
20 Sr Vice Prov Academic Affairs ... Dr. Lynn ZIMMERMAN
84 Assoc Vice Prov Enrollment Svcs ... Ms. Heather MUGG
08 Enterprise CIO/Sr VP Lib Svcs ... Mr. Richard A. MENDOLA
07 AVP Undergrad Enroll/Dean of Admiss ... Dr. John LATTING
21 Chief Univ Budget Officer ... Mr. Michael ANDRECHAK
49 Interim Dean of Emory College ... Dr. Michael A. ELLIOTT
12 Dean & CEO Oxford College ... Dr. Douglas A. HICKS
63 Dean of Medicine ... Dr. Christian P. LARSEN
66 Dean of Nursing ... Dr. Linda MCCAULEY
73 Dean of Theology ... Dr. Jan LOVE
61 Dean of Law ... Mr. Robert SCHAPIRO
50 Dean of Business School ... Ms. Erika JAMES
69 Dean of Public Health ... Dr. James W. CURRAN
85 Dir Intl Student Scholar Program ... Ms. Shinsaeng KO
80 Pres & CEO of the Carter Center ... Ms. Mary Ann PETERS
42 Dean of the Chapel & Spiritual Life ... Rev. Bridgette YOUNG ROSS
06 University Registrar ... Ms. JoAnn MCKENZIE
27 AVP Communications & Marketing ... Mr. David JOHNSON
36 Exec Director Career Service ... Mr. Paul FOWLER
19 Assistant VP Public Safety ... Mr. Craig T. WATSON
41 Director Athletics/Recreation ... Dr. Michael VIENNA
12 Director Yerkes Research Ctrs ... Dr. Paul JOHNSON
49 Director Institute Liberal Arts ... Dr. Kevin CORRIGAN
88 Director M C Carlos Museum ... Ms. Bonnie SPEED
40 Director Bookstore ... Mr. Bruce COVEY
39 Service Supervisor Housing ... Mr. Kenneth JONES, JR.
38 Assistant VP Counseling/Psych Svcs ... Dr. Wanda COLLINS
09 Director Institutional Research ... Dr. Melissa BOLYARD
96 Director Contract Admin/Compliance ... Mr. Rex HARDAWAY
44 Executive Director of Annual Giving ... Ms. Kimberly JULIAN BOWDEN
45 Vice Provost University Strategies ... Mr. Michael SACKS
88 Director Operations ... Ms. Carol A. FLOWERS
37 Director Student Financial Aid ... Mr. John LEACH

Fort Valley State University (F)

1005 State University Drive, Fort Valley GA 31030-4313
County: Peach FICE Identification: 001566
Unit ID: 139719
Telephone: (478) 825-6211 Carnegie Class: Masters/S
FAX Number: (478) 825-6394 Calendar System: Semester
URL: www.fvsu.edu
Established: 1895 Annual Undergrad Tuition & Fees (In-State): $5,594
Enrollment: 2,594 Coed
Affiliation or Control: State IRS Status: 501(c)3
Highest Offering: Beyond Master's But Less Than Doctorate
Accreditation: **SC**, AAFCS, CACREP, CORE, ENGT, TED

01 President ... Dr. Paul JONES
05 Provost/VP for Academic Affairs ... Dr. Ramon STUART
10 VP Business & Finance ... Ms. Mary LOOMIS
31 Interim VP External Affairs ... Dr. Chanta HAYWOOD
84 Vice Pres Enroll Mgmt/Stdnt Success ... Dr. B. Donta TRUSS
09 VP Inst Research/Plng & Effec ... Dr. B. Donta TRUSS
88 Assoc VP for Land Grant Affair ... Dr. Mark LATTIMORE
49 Dean Arts & Sciences ... Dr. Uppinder MEHAN
21 Interim Comptroller ... Ms. Akwai AGOONS
06 Registrar ... Mrs. Sharee LAWRENCE
43 Chief Legal Officer/Dir Govt Rels ... Mr. Charles JONES
13 Director for Information Technology ... Mr. Gary MILLER
08 Director Hunt Memorial Library ... Mr. Frank MAHITAB
07 Director Admissions ... Ms. Calandra WRIGHT
37 Director Financial Aid ... Ms. Cynthia PARKS
29 Director Alumni Affairs ... Mr. Ed BOSTON
15 Director of Human Resources ... Ms. Tricia ADDISON
19 Director Campus Safety ... Mr. Ken MORGAN
47 Dean Agriculture ... Dr. Gavindarajan KANNAN
23 Dir Student Health & Behav Coun ... Mrs. Jacqueline CASKEY-JAMES
18 Director Plant & Maintenance ... Dr. Dwayne CREW
36 Director Counsel/Career Development ... Ms. Simmons ROMELDA
26 Director Marketing/Communications ... Mrs. Pamela BERRY-JOHNSON
41 Director of Athletics ... Dr. Darryl POPE
88 Exec Dir Retention Services ... Dr. Stevie LAWRENCE
53 Int Dean College of Education ... Dr. Rebecca MCMULLEN
22 Dir Affirmative Act/EEO/Diversity ... Mrs. Denise W. EADY
25 Director of Sponsored Programs ... Mrs. Lisa WILSON
30 Development Director ... Mr. Robert STEPHENS
39 Director Student Housing ... Mr. Shawn MODENA
102 Director Foundation ... Mrs. Kristie KENNEY
50 Director Business ... Dr. Samuel GYAPONG
54 Director Engineering ... Mr. Archie WILLIAMS
96 Director of Purchasing ... Ms. Becky HORTON

† Part of the University System of Georgia.

Georgia Christian University (G)

6789 Peachtree Industrial Boulevard, Atlanta GA 30360
County: DeKalb FICE Identification: 041565
Unit ID: 461236

Telephone: (770) 279-0507 Carnegie Class: Bac-Diverse
FAX Number: (770) 279-0308 Calendar System: Semester
URL: www.gcuniv.edu
Established: 1993 Annual Undergrad Tuition & Fees: $5,125
Enrollment: 265 Coed
Affiliation or Control: Independent Non-Profit IRS Status: 501(c)3
Highest Offering: Doctorate
Accreditation: @THEOL, TRACS

00 Chancellor ... Dr. Paul C. KIM
01 President ... Dr. Paul KIM
07 Director of Admissions ... Ms. Mi Hee LEE
05 Vice President for Academic Affairs ... Dr. Howoo LEE
88 Assistant of Academic Affairs ... Dr. Mia KANG
10 Vice President for Business Affairs ... Dr. Hee Sook SONG
20 Dean Academic Affairs ... Dr. Eun Moo LEE
45 Director Of Planning ... Mr. Matthew LEWIS
21 Chief Financial Officer ... Ms. Eunice KIM
12 Director of New Jersey TS Campus ... Ms. Sun Hee CHOI
12 Director of Virginia TS Campus ... Dr. Nam Hong CHO
12 Director of California TS Campus ... Dr. Haejinn HAHN
13 Senior Director of IT ... Mr. Deok Joo MOO
14 Assistant of IT ... Mr. William QUEIROZ
24 Director of Literature & Infomation ... Dr. Young Hwan KIM
18 Chief Facilities/Physical Plant ... Rev. Min Soo KIM
19 Director Security/Safety ... Mr. Samuel KIM
21 Director of Business Affairs ... Mr. Daniel KIM
88 Assistant of Business Affairs ... Mr. Hyun Seok JO
88 Director of ESOL ... Mr. Alain GALLIE
29 Director Alumni Relations ... Dr. Chang Sun PYO
26 Chief Public Relations Officer ... Dr. Sam Young KIM
06 Registrar ... Ms. Sara KIM
37 Director Student Financial Aid ... Ms. Ji Hyun KIM
25 Director of IPEDS ... Dr. Mija WOO
50 Dean School of Business ... Dr. Kyung-il GHYMN
73 Dean School of Christianity ... Dr. Young Jun KIM
73 Dean School of Divinity ... Dr. Ho Woo LEE
64 Dean School of Music ... Dr. Joo Won JUN
88 Dean Mission/World Christianity ... Dr. Eun Moo LEE
63 Dean School of Oriental Medicine ... Dr. Byeong HYUN
88 International Student Advisor ... Ms. Jy Hyun KIM
09 Dir of Institutional Effectiveness ... Dr. Heung Sung NOH
42 Chaplain ... Dr. Hyun Sung CHO
08 Director of the Library ... Ms. Hyongsig SONG
04 Administrative Asst to President ... Ms. Chawook BAE
32 Director of Student Affairs ... Dr. Hyun Sung CHO

Georgia College & State University (A)

231 West Hancock Street, Milledgeville GA 31061-0490
County: Baldwin FICE Identification: 001602
Unit ID: 139861
Telephone: (478) 445-5004 Carnegie Class: Masters/L
FAX Number: (478) 445-1191 Calendar System: Semester
URL: www.gcsu.edu
Established: 1889 Annual Undergrad Tuition & Fees (In-State): $9,170
Enrollment: 6,772 Coed
Affiliation or Control: State IRS Status: 501(c)3
Highest Offering: Doctorate
Accreditation: SC, BUS, CAATE, CS, MUS, NUR, NURSE, SPAA, TED

01 President ... Dr. Steve M. DORMAN
04 Special Assistant to the President ... Ms. Monica STARLEY
05 Interim Provost/VP for Acad Affairs ... Dr. Costas SPIROU
10 VP Finance/Administration ... Ms. Susan ALLEN
32 Vice President for Student Affairs ... Dr. Bruce HARSHBARGER
30 VP for University Advancement ... Ms. Monica DELISA
88 Dir of Econ Dev/External Relations ... Mr. Johnny GRANT
20 Interim Associate Provost ... Dr. Dale YOUNG
88 Assoc Provost for Student Success ... Dr. Carolyn DENARD
45 Assoc VP for Strategic Initiatives ... Dr. Mark PELTON
35 Dean of Students ... Dr. Andy LEWTER
26 Assoc VP Strategic Communications ... Mr. Omar ODEH
84 Assoc VP for Enrollment Management ... Ms. Suzanne PITTMAN
109 Asst VP for Auxiliary Services ... Mr. Kyle CULLARS
21 Sr Dir for Budget Planning & Admin ... Mr. Russ WILLIAMS
49 Dean College of Arts & Sciences ... Mr. Ken PROCTER
50 Dean College of Business ... Dr. Jim PAYNE
53 Dean College of Education ... Dr. Joseph PETERS
76 Dean College of Health Sciences ... Dr. Sandra GANGSTEAD
39 Exec Director of University Housing ... Mr. Larry CHRISTENSON
88 Univ Architect/Dir Facilities Plng ... Mr. Michael RICKENBAKER
18 Director of Facilities Operations ... Mr. Mark DUCLOS
19 Interim Chief of Police ... Mr. Mitchell JONES
09 Asst VP of Institutional Research ... Dr. Chris FERLAND
12 Director Macon Graduate Center ... Vacant
13 Chief Information Officer ... Mr. Robert ORR
08 Director of Libraries ... Dr. Joe MOCNIK
36 Director Career Center ... Ms. Mary ROBERTS
40 Bookstore Manager ... Ms. Barresa ADAMS
15 Chief Human Resources Officer ... Ms. Leslie PIERCE
28 Chief Diversity Officer ... Dr. Veronica WOMACK
07 Director of Admissions ... Mr. Ramon BLAKLEY
06 Registrar ... Ms. Kay ANDERSON
41 Director of Athetics ... Mr. Wendell STATON
29 Dir Alumni Relations/Annual Giving ... Mrs. Mindy MILLER
43 Director of Legal Affairs ... Ms. Qiana WILSON
38 Director of Counseling Services ... Dr. Stephen WILSON
37 Director of Financial Aid ... Ms. Cathy CRAWLEY
88 Sr Dir Materials Mgmt/Central Svcs ... Mr. Mark MEEKS
88 Dir for Internal Audit/Advisory Ser ... Vacant
35 Director of Campus Life ... Mr. Tom MILES
104 Asst VP for International Educ ... Dr. Eric SPEARS

Georgia Gwinnett College (B)

1000 University Center Lane, Lawrenceville GA 30043
County: Gwinnett FICE Identification: 041429
Unit ID: 447689
Telephone: (678) 407-5000 Carnegie Class: Bac-Diverse
FAX Number: N/A Calendar System: Semester
URL: www.ggc.edu
Established: 2005 Annual Undergrad Tuition & Fees (In-District): $5,648
Enrollment: 10,828 Coed
Affiliation or Control: State/Local IRS Status: 501(c)3
Highest Offering: Baccalaureate
Accreditation: SC, TED

01 President ... Dr. Stanley PRECZEWSKI
05 SVP for Academic Affairs/Provost ... Dr. TJ ARANT
11 Vice Pres Operations ... Mr. Eddie BEAUCHAMP
13 Vice Pres Educational Technology ... Dr. Mark IKEN
10 VP of Business & Finance/CFO ... Ms. Laura MAXWELL
30 Vice Pres Strategic Communications ... Ms. Renee BYRD-LEWIS
100 Chief of Staff ... Mr. Dan NOLAN
32 Sr Assoc Provost Student Affairs ... Dr. Jim B. FATZINGER
15 Assoc VP Human Resources ... Mrs. Katherine KYLE
19 AVP of Public Safety/Police Chief ... Mr. Terrance SCHNEIDER
41 Athletic Director ... Dr. Darin WILSON
07 Associate Director Admissions ... Mrs. Kristi L. MCBRIDE
04 Administrative Asst to President ... Mrs. Luann CAUSLAND
06 Registrar ... Ms Nancy GRATTAN
08 Dean of Library Services ... Mr. Gene RUFFIN
09 Director of Institutional Research ... Dr. Lily HWANG
108 Exec Director Instl Effectiveness ... Dr. Juliana LANCASTER
46 Dir Research & Sponsored Programs ... Dr. Cathy HAKES
26 Director for Public Relations ... Vacant
28 Exec Dir Legal/Diversity Affairs ... Mr Marc CARDINALLI
29 Director Alumni Relations ... Mr. Andrew SCHMIDT
37 Director Student Financial Aid ... Ms. Kimberly JORDAN
38 Director Student Counseling ... Dr. Tamara D'ANJOU TURNER
50 Dean School of Business ... Vacant
53 Dean School of Education ... Dr. Cathy E. MOORE

Georgia Highlands College (C)

3175 Cedartown Highway SE, Rome GA 30161-3897
County: Floyd FICE Identification: 009507
Unit ID: 139700
Telephone: (706) 802-5000 Carnegie Class: Bac/Assoc-Assoc Dom
FAX Number: (706) 295-6341 Calendar System: Semester
URL: www.highlands.edu
Established: 1970 Annual Undergrad Tuition & Fees (In-State): $3,115
Enrollment: 5,365 Coed
Affiliation or Control: State IRS Status: 501(c)3
Highest Offering: Baccalaureate
Accreditation: SC, ADNUR, DH, NUR

01 President ... Dr. Donald J. GREEN
05 Vice President Academic Affairs ... Dr. Renva WATTERSON
10 Vice Pres Finance/Administration ... Mr. Jeff DAVIS
32 Vice President Student Affairs ... Dr. Todd JONES
15 Vice President Human Resources ... Ms. Ginni SILER
30 VP/Advanc/Exec Dir GHS Foundation ... Ms. Mary TRANSUE
13 VP/Information Technology/CIO ... Mr. Jeff PATTY
37 Director Financial Aid ... Ms. Megan SIMPSON
07 Director of Admissions & Registrar ... Ms. Sandie DAVIS
08 Dean Libraries/College Testing ... Mr. Elijah SCOTT
12 Dean Marietta ... Mr. Ken REAVES
12 Dean Paulding/Douglasville ... Ms. Connie WATJEN
12 Dean Floyd ... Dr. Todd JONES
12 Dean Cartersville ... Ms Leslie JOHNSON
04 Executive Asst to the President ... Ms. Tammy NICHOLSON
41 Director of Athletics ... Mr. Phillip GAFFNEY
18 Director Plant Operations ... Mr. Phillip KIMSEY

† Part of the University System of Georgia.

Georgia Institute of Technology (D)

225 North Avenue, NW, Atlanta GA 30332-0002
County: Fulton FICE Identification: 001569
Unit ID: 139755
Telephone: (404) 894-2000 Carnegie Class: DU-Highest
FAX Number: (404) 894-1277 Calendar System: Semester
URL: www.gatech.edu
Established: 1885 Annual Undergrad Tuition & Fees (In-State): $12,204
Enrollment: 23,109 Coed
Affiliation or Control: State IRS Status: 501(c)3
Highest Offering: Doctorate
Accreditation: SC, ART, BUS, CEA, CONST, CS, ENG, IPSY, OPE, PLNG

01 President ... Dr. G. P. (Bud) PETERSON
05 Provost/Exec VP Academic Affairs ... Dr. Rafael BRAS
10 Exec VP Administration/Finance ... Mr. Steven SWANT
46 Executive Vice President Research ... Dr. Stephen CROSS
100 Assistant Vice Pres/Chief of Staff ... Ms. Lynn DURHAM
30 Vice President Development ... Mr Barrett H. CARSON
26 Vice Pres Communications/Marketing ... Mr. Michael L. WARDEN
32 VP Student Life & Dean of Students ... Mr. John STEIN
88 VP/Director GA Tech Res Inst ... Dr. Andrew GERBER
46 Vice President Research ... Ms. Jilda GARTON
86 Vice Pres Government/Cmty Relations ... Mr. Dene SHEHEANE
88 VP Enterprise Innovation Inst ... Mr. Chris DOWNING
29 President Georgia Tech Alumni Assoc ... Mr. Joseph IRWIN
58 Vice Prov Grad Educ/Faculty Affairs ... Dr. Susan COZZENS
84 Vice Prov Enrollment Services ... Dr. Paul KOHN
20 Vice Prov Undergraduate Education ... Dr. Colin POTTS
43 Vice Pres Legal Affairs/Risk Mgmt ... Mr. Patrick MCKENNA
28 Vice President Institute Diversity ... Dr. Archie ERVIN
15 Assoc VP Human Resources ... Dr. Kim HARRINGTON
18 Vice President Facilities ... Mr. Charles G. RHODE
11 Senior Vice Pres Admin/Finance ... Dr. Jeffrey SCOTT
31 Vice President Campus Services ... Mr. Paul STROUTS
13 Vice President Information Tech/CIO ... Mr. James O'CONNOR
41 Director of Athletics ... Mr. Michael BOBINSKI
22 Sr Director Diversity Management ... Ms. Pearl ALEXANDER
12 Dean Ivan Allen Col Liberal Arts ... Dr. Jacqueline J. ROYSTER
48 Dean College of Design ... Dr. Steve FRENCH
77 Dean College of Computing ... Dr. Zvi GALIL
54 Dean College of Engineering ... Dr. Gary S. MAY
08 Dean Libraries/Vice Prov Acad Eff ... Ms. Catherine MURRAY-RUST
82 Dean Scheller College of Business ... Dr. Maryam ALAVI
81 Dean College of Sciences ... Dr. Paul GOLDBART
06 Registrar ... Ms. Reta PIKOWSKY
40 Director Bookstore ... Mr. Gerald J. MALONEY
19 Director of Security & Police ... Mr. Robert CONNOLLY
107 Dean Professional Education ... Dr. Nelson BAKER
36 Executive Director Career Develop ... Dr. Michelle TULLIER
37 Director Student Financial Aid ... Ms. Marie MONS
23 Sr Director Student Health Svcs ... Dr. Gregory MOORE
39 Executive Director Housing ... Mr. Michael BLACK
09 Exec Dir Inst Research/Decision Spt ... Ms. Sandra J. BRAMBLETT
85 Vice Prov International Initiatives ... Dr. Yves BERTHELOT
104 Exec Dir International Education ... Ms. Amy HENRY
38 Director Counseling Center ... Dr. Ruperto PEREZ
109 Senior Director Auxiliary Services ... Mr. Richard STEELE
07 Director Undergraduate Admission ... Mr. Richard CLARK
96 Director of Procurement Services ... Mr. Frans BARENDS
88 Exec Dir Inst Budget Plng & Admin ... Mr. James KIRK
88 Dir Capital Planning/Space Mgmt ... Mr. Howard WERTHEIMER
88 Exec Director Strategic Consulting ... Dr. Sonia ALVAREZ-ROBINSON
88 Bursar ... Mr. Terry FAIR
21 Assoc Vice Pres Financial Services ... Mr. James FORTNER

† Part of the University System of Georgia.

Georgia Military College (E)

201 E Greene Street, Milledgeville GA 31061-3398
County: Baldwin FICE Identification: 001571
Unit ID: 485111
Telephone: (478) 387-4900 Carnegie Class: Not Classified
FAX Number: N/A Calendar System: Quarter
URL: www.gmc.edu
Established: 1879 Annual Undergrad Tuition & Fees: $5,940
Enrollment: 7,262 Coed
Affiliation or Control: Independent Non-Profit IRS Status: 501(c)3
Highest Offering: Baccalaureate
Accreditation: SC

01 President ... LtGen. William B. CALDWELL, IV
03 Executive Vice President/COO ... BGEN. Curt RAUHUT
05 Chief Academic Ofcr/Dn of Faculty ... Dr. Phillip M. HOLMES
10 Chief Financial Officer ... COL. James WATKINS
32 Commandant/Dean of Students ... COL. Patrick BEER
30 Chief College Relations Officer ... Mr. Mark STROM
13 VP Info Technology/Online Campus ... Mr. Jody YEARWOOD
15 VP Human Resources ... Ms. Jill ROBBINS
21 Assoc Vice Pres Resource Management ... Ms. Susan MEEKS
09 Director Institutional Research ... Dr. Susan ISAAC
41 Athletic Director ... Mr. Bert WILLIAMS
18 Director Facilities/Engineer ... Mr. Jeff GRAY
06 Associate VP Academic Records ... Mrs. Robin KNIGHT
08 Director of Library Services ... Ms. Erin NEWTON
19 Chief of Security/Safety ... Mr. James HODNETT
20 Associate Academic Officer ... Mr. Derek STONE
84 Director of Enrollment Management ... Mr. Jody YEARWOOD
04 Administrative Asst to President ... Ms. Joelle TRUMBO
100 Chief of Staff ... Dr. Jeannie ZIPPERER
26 Chief Public Relations/Marketing ... Mr. Jay BENTLEY
37 Director Student Financial Aid ... Ms. Alisa STEPHENS

Georgia Northwestern Technical College (F)

One Maurice Culberson Drive, Rome GA 30161
County: Floyd FICE Identification: 005257
Unit ID: 139384
Telephone: (706) 295-6963 Carnegie Class: Assoc/HVT-Mix Trad/Non
FAX Number: (706) 295-6944 Calendar System: Semester
URL: www.gntc.edu
Established: 1956 Annual Undergrad Tuition & Fees (In-State): $2,684
Enrollment: 5,816 Coed
Affiliation or Control: State IRS Status: 501(c)3
Highest Offering: Associate Degree
Accreditation: SC, ADNUR, CAHIIM, COARC, DA, DMS, EMT, MAC, OTA, RAD, SURGT

01 President ... Dr. Pete MCDONALD
05 Provost ... Vacant
11 Vice Pres Administrative Services ... Ms. Kelly BARNES
30 Vice Pres Econ Development ... Dr. Pete MCDONALD
20 Vice President Academic Affairs ... Dr. Mindy MCCANNON
09 Vice Pres Inst Effectiveness ... Ms. Heidi POPHAM
51 Actg Vice President Adult Education ... Ms. Kerri HOSMER

32	Vice Pres Student Affairs	Mr. Stuart PHILLIPS
06	Registrar	Ms. Selena MAGNUSSON
08	Director of Library Services	Mr. John LASSITER
19	Director Safety & Security	Mr. Bill BYARS
37	Exec Director of Financial Aid	Mr. Stephen ANDERSEN
18	Director Facilities Management	Mr. Jeffrey AGAN
26	Dir Marketing/Public Relations	Ms. Amber JORDAN
15	Director of Human Resources	Ms. Peggy CORDELL

Georgia Piedmont Technical College (A)

495 N Indian Creek Drive, Clarkston GA 30021-2397

County: DeKalb FICE Identification: 005622
Unit ID: 244446
Telephone: (404) 297-9522 Carnegie Class: Assoc/HVT-Mix Trad/Non
FAX Number: (404) 297-4234 Calendar System: Semester
URL: www.gptc.edu
Established: 1961 Annual Undergrad Tuition & Fees (In-State): $2,840
Enrollment: 4,050 Coed
Affiliation or Control: State IRS Status: 501(c)3
Highest Offering: Associate Degree
Accreditation: SC, EMT, ENGT, MAC, MLTAD

01	President	Dr. Jabari SIMAMA
04	Exec Dir & Spec Asst to President	Mr. Keith SAGERS
05	Exec Vice Pres Academic/Stdnt Affs	Dr. Ivan HARRELL
10	Vice Pres Business/Financial Svcs	Mr. Mark KOMDAT
46	Vice Pres of Economic Development	Dr. Jeff STEVENSON
31	VP Econonic Devel/Cmty Engagement	Ms. Cynthia EDWARDS
30	VP Institutional Advancement	Mr. Anthony NEAL
32	Int Vice President Student Affairs	Dr. Candice JONES
20	Assoc Vice Pres Academic Affairs	Dr. Debra GORDON
37	Assistant VP of Financial Aid	Ms. Lakisha SANDERS
20	Dean of Academic Programs	Mr. Marcus HICKS
88	Dean of Adult Literacy	Dr. Jacqueline ECHOLS
35	Dean of Student Affairs	Ms. Candice JONES
108	Dean of Quality Initiatives	Dr. Catrenia MCLENDON
15	Director of Human Resources	Ms. Lolita MORRISON
26	Dir Marketing/Public Relations	Ms. Martha PACINI
06	Registrar	Ms. Joana BLANKSON
07	Director of Admissions/Records	Mr. Corey PARKER
51	Director Continuing Education	Ms. Loretta HICKS
18	Int Dir Facilities/Auxiliary Svcs	Mr. Raymond CLUNIE
36	Dir Adv/Career & Retention Svcs	Ms. Angela CUMMINGS
13	Director of Information Technology	Mr. Keith PERRY

Georgia Southern University (B)

PO Box 8033, Statesboro GA 30460-8033

County: Bulloch FICE Identification: 001572
Unit ID: 139931
Telephone: (912) 478-4636 Carnegie Class: DU-Mod
FAX Number: N/A Calendar System: Semester
URL: www.georgiasouthern.edu
Established: 1906 Annual Undergrad Tuition & Fees (In-State): $6,273
Enrollment: 20,517 Coed
Affiliation or Control: State IRS Status: 501(c)3
Highest Offering: Doctorate
Accreditation: SC, ART, BUS, BUSA, CAATE, CACREP, CIDA, CLPSY, CONST, CS, DIETD, @DIETI, ENG, ENGT, MUS, NRPA, NURSE, PH, TED, THEA

01	President	Dr. Jaimie HEBERT
05	Provost	Dr. Jean E. BARTELS
10	Vice Pres Business & Finance	Mr. Rob WHITAKER
32	VP Student Affairs & Enroll Mgmt	Dr. Teresa THOMPSON
30	VP Univ Advance/GSU Foundation Pres	Ms. Salinda ARTHUR
13	Interim Chief Technology Officer	Mr. Ron STALNAKER
86	VP for External Affairs	Mr. Trip ADDISON
46	Interim Vice Pres for Research	Dr. Don MCLEMORE
09	Assoc VP Strategic Rsrch & Analysis	Dr. Jayne PERKINS BROWN
20	Associate Provost	Dr. Diana CONE
35	Dean of Students	Ms. Patrice BUCKNER JACKSON
43	Assoc Vice Pres for Legal Affairs	Ms. Maura COPELAND
44	Assoc VP University Advancement	Mr. Michael SHIPPAM
04	Exec Associate to the President	Ms. Leigh PRICE
07	Director of Admissions	Ms. Amy SMITH
58	Dean College of Graduate Studies	Vacant
50	Dean College Business Admin	Dr. Allen AMASON
53	Dean College Education	Dr. Thomas KOBALLA
76	Dean College Health/Human Sci	Dr. Barry JOYNER
49	Dean Col Liberal Arts/Social Sci	Dr. Curtis RICKER
81	Dean College Science & Mathematics	Dr. Martha ABELL
54	Dean AEP Col Engr/Info Tech	Dr. Mohammad DAVOUD
51	Exec Director Continuing Educ	Dr. Belkis CAPELES
69	Dean College of Public Health	Dr. R. Gregory EVANS
62	Dean University Library	Dr. Bede MITCHELL
88	Dir NCAA Compliance	Mr. Keith ROUGHTON
88	Chief Audit & Advisory Services	Ms. Jana BRILEY
43	Associate University Attorney	Mr. Geoffrey CARSON
26	Assoc VP Mktg & Comm	Ms. Jan BOND
88	Director Academic Success Center	Vacant
37	Director Financial Aid	Ms. Tracey MINGO
06	Registrar	Dr. Velma BURDEN
109	Assoc VP Auxiliary Services	Mr. Edward D. MILLS
21	Senior Assoc VP/Controller	Ms. Kim THOMPSON BROWN
15	Assoc VP Human Resources	Ms. Rebecca CARROLL
41	Athletic Director	Mr. Tom KLEINLEIN
18	Assoc VP Facilities	Mr. Marvin MILLS
19	Director Public Safety	Ms. Laura MCCULLOUGH
36	Director Career Services	Mr. Philip BRUCE
38	Director Counseling Services	Dr. Jodi K. CALDWELL
88	Director Educ Opportunity Programs	Dr. Joyya SMITH
23	Director Health Services	Ms. Elissa NORRIS
39	Director University Housing	Mr. Peter BLUTREICH
28	Dir Multicultural Student Center	Ms. Dorsey BALDWIN
88	Director Leadership/Outreach Pgms	Dr. Todd DEAL
88	Director Advancement IT	Ms. Jill GERIG
29	Sr Director Alumni Relations	Mr. Wendell TOMPKINS, JR.
88	Director Botanic Garden	Ms. Carolyn ALTMAN
14	Director Technical Services	Mr. Joey REEVES
90	Director Info Tech for Acad Affairs	Ms. Pamela DEAL
88	Director Museum	Dr. Brent THARP
88	Director Wildlife Educ/Raptor Ctr	Mr. Steven M. HEIN
96	Director of Procurement & Contract	Mr. John OGLESBY
28	Dir Equal Opp/Title IX	Mr. Joel WRIGHT
89	Director First-Year Experience	Dr. Chris CAPLINGER
92	Director Univ Honors Program	Dr. Steven ENGEL
13	Chief Information Tech Security Ofc	Mr. Michael FOX
88	Director Centers for Teaching & Tec	Dr. Rachel SCHWARTZ
22	Dir Stdnt Affs/Disability Res Ctr	Mrs. Deborah J. PEREZ-LOPEZ
102	Director Foundation Acct	Ms. Jodi COLLINS

† Part of the University System of Georgia.

Georgia Southwestern State University (C)

800 GA Southwestern State Univ Dr,
Americus GA 31709-4693

County: Sumter FICE Identification: 001573
Unit ID: 139764
Telephone: (877) 871-4594 Carnegie Class: Masters/M
FAX Number: N/A Calendar System: Semester
URL: www.gsw.edu
Established: 1906 Annual Undergrad Tuition & Fees (In-State): $5,262
Enrollment: 2,666 Coed
Affiliation or Control: State IRS Status: 501(c)3
Highest Offering: Beyond Master's But Less Than Doctorate
Accreditation: SC, BUS, NUR, NURSE, TED

01	Interim President	Dr. Charles E. PATTERSON
05	Vice President Academic Affairs	Dr. Brian U. ADLER
10	Vice Pres Business & Finance	Mr. W. Cody KING
32	Vice President for Student Affairs	Dr. Samuel T. MILLER
84	Vice Pres Enroll Mgmt/Dir Admiss	Dr. Gaye HAYES
09	Director Institutional Research	Dr. Lisa A. COOPER
08	Dean Library Services	Ms. Ru STORY-HUFFMAN
13	Dir Information Technology/CIO	Mr. Royce HACKETT
102	GSW Foundation Executive Director	Ms. Reda K. ROWELL
06	Registrar	Ms. Krista SMITH
36	Director Career Services Center	Ms. Sandra FOWLER
37	Director Student Financial Aid	Ms. Angela V. BRYANT
26	Director University Relations	Mr. Stephen E. SNYDER
35	Assistant Dean of Students	Dr. Darcy BRAGG
41	Athletic Director	Mr. Mike LEEDER
29	Coord Alumni Relations/Annual Fund	Ms. Kimberly COMER
15	Director of Human Resources	Ms. Gena WILSON
19	Director of Public Safety	Mr. Michael TRACY

† Part of the University System of Georgia.

Georgia State University (D)

PO Box 3999, Atlanta GA 30302-3999

County: Fulton FICE Identification: 001574
Unit ID: 139940
Telephone: (404) 413-2000 Carnegie Class: DU-Highest
FAX Number: (404) 413-1380 Calendar System: Semester
URL: www.gsu.edu
Established: 1913 Annual Undergrad Tuition & Fees (In-State): $8,974
Enrollment: 32,556 Coed
Affiliation or Control: State IRS Status: 501(c)3
Highest Offering: Doctorate
Accreditation: SC, ART, BUS, BUSA, CACREP, CEA, CLPSY, COARC, COPSY, CORE, DIETC, DIETD, EXSC, HSA, IPSY, LAW, MUS, NURSE, PH, PTA, SCPSY, SP, SPAA, SW, TED

01	President	Dr. Mark P. BECKER
05	Sr VP Academic Affairs & Provost	Dr. Risa I. PALM
10	Sr VP Finance & Administration	Dr. Jerry J. RACKLIFFE
84	Vice Provost & VP Enroll Mgt	Dr. Timothy M. RENICK
12	Vice Provost/Dean Perimeter College	Dr. Peter LYONS
46	Vice President Research & Econ Dev	Dr. James A. WEYHENMEYER
32	Vice President Student Affairs	Dr. Douglass F. COVEY
30	Vice President Development	Mr. Walter T. MASSEY
26	VP PR & Mktg Communications	Mr. Don HALE
43	University Attorney	Dr. Kerry L. HEYWARD
49	Dean Arts & Sciences	Vacant
50	Dean Business	Dr. Richard D. PHILLIPS
53	Dean Education	Dr. Paul A. ALBERTO
66	Dean Nursing/Health Professions	Dr. Nancy P. KROPF
69	Dean Public Health	Dr. Michael P. ERIKSEN
61	Dean Law	Dr. Steven J. KAMINSHINE
80	Dean Policy Studies	Dr. Mary Beth WALKER
92	Dean Honors College	Dr. Larry S. BERMAN
08	Dean Libraries	Mr. Jeff STEELY
88	Assoc Provost Strategic Initiatives	Dr. Robert D. MORRIS
58	Interim Assoc Provost Grad Programs	Dr. Lisa P. ARMISTEAD
09	Assoc Provost Inst Effectiveness	Dr. Jonathan GAYLES
82	Assc Prov International Initiatives	Vacant
20	Assoc Provost Faculty Affairs	Dr. Kavita PANDIT
88	Assistant Provost Admin Operations	Mr. Christopher D. HILL
45	Assoc VP Research Integrity	Dr. Brenda J. CHAPMAN
88	Assoc VP Tech Lic/Commercial	Dr. Chester A. BISBEE
88	Chief Innovation Officer for IT	Mr. Phil VENTIMIGLIA
13	Assoc VP IS&T/Chief Technology Ofc	Mr. Dennis ROSE
18	Assoc VP Facilities	Mr. Ramesh VAKAMUDI
21	Assoc Vice President Finance	Ms. Elizabeth R. JONES
21	Assoc VP Finance & Comptroller	Mr. Bruce R. SPRATT
30	Assoc VP Central Development	Vacant
30	Assoc VP Constituent Programs Dev	Mr. Michael J. WORLEY
88	Asst VP Campaign Strategy	Ms. Susan BOYETTE
102	Assoc VP GSU Foundation	Mr. Dale J. PALMER
35	Assoc VP Stdnt Affs/Dean Students	Dr. Darryl B. HOLLOMAN
27	Assoc VP Public Relations	Ms. Andrea JONES
07	Asst VP Undergraduate Admissions	Mr. Scott M. BURKE
84	Asst VP Student Retention	Dr. Allison CALHOUN-BROWN
29	Asst VP Alumni Relations	Ms. Christina C. MILLION
15	Asst VP Human Resources	Ms. Linda J. NELSON
22	Asst VP Opp Dev/Diversity Educ	Ms. Linda J. NELSON
19	Asst VP/Chief University Police	Vacant
06	Registrar	Ms. Shari P. SCHWARTZ
85	Dir Intl Students/Scholars Svcs	Ms. Heather L. HOUSLEY
39	Director University Housing	Mr. Randy D. BROWN, JR.
38	Director Psychological & Health Svc	Dr. Jill LEE-BARBER
28	Director Diversity Programs	Mr. John R. DAY
54	Director Application Engineering	Mr. John M. BANDY, JR.
14	Director Technology Engineering	Mr. Keith E. CAMPBELL
77	Interim Dir Research Computing	Mr. Davide GAETANO
36	Director University Career Svcs	Vacant
37	Director Financial Aid	Mr. Louis B. SCOTT
96	Director of Business Services	Mr. Michael E. DAVIDSON
88	Dir Univ Auditing & Advisory Svcs	Mr. Sterling ROTH
88	Director Design/Construction Svcs	Ms. Kimberly P. BAUER
88	Director Emergency Management	Mr. Keith P. SUMAS
31	Director Govt & Community Affairs	Ms. Julia M. KERLIN
41	Athletic Director	Mr. Charles G. COBB
88	Special Advisor to President	Mr. Thomas C. LEWIS
04	Assistant to the President	Ms. Ethel M. BROWN

† Part of the University System of Georgia.

Gordon State College (E)

419 College Dr., Barnesville GA 30204-1746

County: Lamar FICE Identification: 001575
Unit ID: 139968
Telephone: (678) 359-5555 Carnegie Class: Bac/Assoc-Mixed
FAX Number: (678) 359-5080 Calendar System: Semester
URL: www.gordonstate.edu
Established: 1852 Annual Undergrad Tuition & Fees (In-State): $3,551
Enrollment: 4,047 Coed
Affiliation or Control: State IRS Status: 501(c)3
Highest Offering: Baccalaureate
Accreditation: SC, ADNUR, NUR, TED

01	President	Dr. Max BURNS
05	Provost & VP Academic Affairs	Dr. Jeffery KNIGHTON
10	VP Finance and Administration	Mrs. Kristen ALBRITTON
32	VP Student Affairs	Dr. Dennis R. CHAMBERLAIN
30	VP Institutional Advancement	Mrs. Rhonda TOON
04	Administrative Asst to President	Mrs. Dolores BELL
20	Associate VP Academic Affairs	Dr. Richard BASKIN
88	Asst VP Institutional Effectiveness	Mrs. Teresa BETKOWSKI
08	Library Director	Dr. Sonya GAITHER
09	Director of Institutional Research	Mr. Britt LIFSEY
49	Int Dean School of Arts & Sciences	Dr. Susan FINAZZO
53	Dean School of Education	Dr. Michael MAHAN
66	Dean School of Nursing	Dr. Anne PURVIS
20	Director of Student Success Center	Mr. Peter J. HIGGINS
21	Assistant VP/Controller	Mr. Walter GREEN
15	Asst VP Human Resources	Ms. Laura BOWEN
21	Bursar	Mr. Kenneth HUTTO
21	Dir of Budgets & Aux Operations	Mr. Justin WHITE
18	Director of Facilities	Mr. Richard VEREEN
37	Director of Financial Aid	Mrs. Jody DEFORE
13	Director of Information Technology	Mr. Jeff HAYES
19	Director of Public Safety	Chief Jeff MASON
07	Int Director of Admissions	Mr. Nathan BELL
41	Interim Athletic Director	Mr. Gary SHARPE
38	Director of Counseling Services	Ms. Alicia DORTON
39	Director of Residence Life	Ms. Tonya R. COLEMAN
35	Director of Student Activities	Ms. Sharon LLOYD
06	Registrar	Mrs. Janet BARRAS
30	Development Officer	Mr. Skipper BURNS
29	Director of Alumni Relations	Vacant
26	Chief Public Information Officer	Mrs. Tamara BOATWRIGHT
40	Bookstore Manager	Mrs. Connie H. WADE

† Part of the University System of Georgia.

Gupton Jones College of Funeral Service (F)

5141 Snapfinger Woods Drive, Decatur GA 30035-4022

County: DeKalb FICE Identification: 010771
Unit ID: 139995
Telephone: (770) 593-2257 Carnegie Class: Spec 2-yr-A&S
FAX Number: (770) 593-1891 Calendar System: Quarter
URL: www.gupton-jones.edu
Established: 1920 Annual Undergrad Tuition & Fees: $11,100
Enrollment: 162 Coed
Affiliation or Control: Independent Non-Profit IRS Status: 501(c)3
Highest Offering: Associate Degree

Accreditation: **FUSER**

01 President ... Mr. Antonio WALLACE
05 Dean ... Mr. Duane PIEL
06 Registrar ... Ms. Felicia SMITH

Gwinnett College (A)

4230 Highway 29, Suite 11, Lilburn GA 30047-3447
County: Gwinnett FICE Identification: 025830
Unit ID: 140003
Telephone: (770) 381-7200 Carnegie Class: Assoc/HVT-High Non
FAX Number: (770) 381-0454 Calendar System: Other
URL: www.gwinnettcollege.com
Established: 1976 Annual Undergrad Tuition & Fees: $9,925
Enrollment: 325 Coed
Affiliation or Control: Proprietary IRS Status: Proprietary
Highest Offering: Associate Degree
Accreditation: **ACICS**

01 President ... Mr. Michael DAVIS

Gwinnett College-Marietta (B)

1130 North Chase Parkway, Suite 100, Marietta GA 30067
County: Cobb FICE Identification: 038044
Unit ID: 444714
Telephone: (770) 859-9779 Carnegie Class: Spec 2-yr-Health
FAX Number: (770) 859-9778 Calendar System: Quarter
URL: www.medtech.edu
Established: Annual Undergrad Tuition & Fees: N/A
Enrollment: 320 Coed
Affiliation or Control: Proprietary IRS Status: Proprietary
Highest Offering: Associate Degree
Accreditation: **COE**

01 Campus President ... Mr. Michael DAVIS

Gwinnett College-Sandy Springs (C)

6690 Roswell Rd, NE, Ste 2200, Sandy Springs GA 30328
FICE Identification: 034183
Unit ID: 425250
Telephone: (770) 457-2021 Carnegie Class: Not Classified
FAX Number: (404) 574-2234 Calendar System: Other
URL: www.risingspirit.edu
Established: 1994 Annual Undergrad Tuition & Fees: N/A
Enrollment: 84 Coed
Affiliation or Control: Proprietary IRS Status: Proprietary
Highest Offering: Associate Degree
Accreditation: **ACCSC**

Gwinnett Technical College (D)

5150 Sugarloaf Parkway, Lawrenceville GA 30043-5702
County: Gwinnett FICE Identification: 022884
Unit ID: 140012
Telephone: (770) 962-7580 Carnegie Class: Assoc/HVT-High Trad
FAX Number: (770) 962-7985 Calendar System: Semester
URL: www.gwinnetttech.edu
Established: 1984 Annual Undergrad Tuition & Fees (In-State): $2,796
Enrollment: 7,234 Coed
Affiliation or Control: State IRS Status: 501(c)3
Highest Offering: Associate Degree
Accreditation: **SC**, ACFEI, ADNUR, CAHIIM, COARC, CVT, DA, DMS, EMT, MAC, RAD, SURGT

01 President ... Dr. Glen D. CANNON
10 Executive VP Finance/Administration ... Mr. David WELDEN
05 VP of Academic Affairs ... Dr. Victoria SEALS
26 VP of Economic Development ... Mr. Dave MCCULLOCH
32 VP of Student Affairs ... Dr. Julie POST
30 VP of Institutional Advancement ... Ms. Mary Beth BYERLY
103 Director State Workforce Programs ... Ms. Ann SECHRIST
15 Director of Human Resources ... Ms. Debbie GERARDO
06 Dir of Admissions & Registrar ... Dr. Jymmyca WYATT
36 Director of Career Services ... Ms. Ave MILLER
37 Director of Financial Aid ... Ms. Lisa MARTIN
53 Dean of Adult Education ... Ms. Stephanie ROOKS
07 Exec Dir Enrollment Processing ... Ms. Brenda PYLE
18 Supervisor of Facilities Operation ... Ms. Janice BOLTON
19 Chief of Campus Police & Security ... Mr. Mike BLOUIN
08 Manager of Library Services ... Ms. Elissa CHECOV
09 Dir Inst Research & Effectiveness ... Dr. Carla MORELON
04 Exec Assistant to the President ... Ms. Melissa FLANAGAN

Herzing University (E)

3393 Peachtree Road NE, Suite 1003,
Atlanta GA 30326-1332
Telephone: (404) 816-4533 FICE Identification: 020897
Accreditation: **&NH**, NURSE

† Regional accreditation is carried under the parent institution in Madison, WI.

Interactive College of Technology (F)

5303 New Peachtree Road, Chamblee GA 30341-2818
County: DeKalb FICE Identification: 022843
Unit ID: 138655
Telephone: (770) 216-2960 Carnegie Class: Assoc/HVT-High Trad
FAX Number: (770) 216-2988 Calendar System: Semester
URL: www.ict.edu
Established: 1986 Annual Undergrad Tuition & Fees: $9,113
Enrollment: 346 Coed
Affiliation or Control: Proprietary IRS Status: Proprietary
Highest Offering: Associate Degree
Accreditation: **#COE**

01 President ... Mr. Elmer R. SMITH
03 Executive Vice President ... Mr. Michael E. POWER
05 Dean of the College ... Mr. Thomas A. BLAIR
12 Campus Director Pasadena Texas ... Mr. Michael SAN FILIPO
12 Campus Dir SW Houston Texas ... Ms. Cynthia BRYSON
12 Campus Dir North Houston Texas ... Mr. Harry MAUZ
12 Campus Director - Newport KY ... Mr. Rich ELLISON
12 Campus Director - Morrow GA ... Mr. Greg KOCH
12 Campus Director - Gainesville GA ... Ms. Sofia LUKAS
04 Administrative Asst to President ... Ms. Karen A. MILLER
06 Registrar ... Ms. Rosalind HOLT
26 Chief Public Relations/Marketing ... Mr. Jim C. HARRIS
36 Director Student Placement ... Mr. Andre GIPSON

Interactive College of Technology (G)

2323-C Browns Bridge Road, Gainesville GA 30504
Telephone: (678) 456-0550 Identification: 770533
Accreditation: **COE**

Interactive College of Technology (H)

1580 Southdale Parkway, Suite C, Morrow GA 30260
Telephone: (770) 960-1298 Identification: 770534
Accreditation: **COE**

Interdenominational Theological Center (I)

700 Martin L. King, Jr. Drive, SW, Atlanta GA 30314-4143
County: Fulton FICE Identification: 001568
Unit ID: 140146
Telephone: (404) 527-7700 Carnegie Class: Spec-4-yr-Faith
FAX Number: (404) 527-0901 Calendar System: Semester
URL: www.itc.edu
Established: 1958 Annual Graduate Tuition & Fees: N/A
Enrollment: 306 Coed
Affiliation or Control: Interdenominational IRS Status: 501(c)3
Highest Offering: Doctorate; No Undergraduates
Accreditation: **SC**, THEOL

01 President ... Dr. Edward LORENZA WHEELER
05 Provost/VP for Academic Services ... Dr. Maisha HANDY
11 Vice Pres of Admin Services ... Dr. Charles E. THOMAS, JR.
10 Vice Pres Financial Services ... Mr. Alfred NORRIS
30 VP for Institutional Advancement ... Mr. Charles WARD
84 AVP Enrollment Management/Registrar ... Ms. Bobbie HALL
37 Financial Aid Director ... Mr. Johnny NIMES
15 Director Human Resource ... Ms. Idell HENDERSON
29 Director Alumni Relations ... Ms. Timi C. SIMPSON
07 Director of Admissions/Recruitment ... Ms. Michelle DAVIS
42 Chaplain ... Dr. Keith SLAUGHTER

Kennesaw State University (J)

585 Cobb Avenue NW, MD #0101,
Kennesaw GA 30144-5563
County: Cobb FICE Identification: 001577
Unit ID: 140164
Telephone: (470) 578-6033 Carnegie Class: DU-Mod
FAX Number: N/A Calendar System: Semester
URL: www.kennesaw.edu
Established: 1963 Annual Undergrad Tuition & Fees (In-State): N/A
Enrollment: 25,714 Coed
Affiliation or Control: State IRS Status: 501(c)3
Highest Offering: Doctorate
Accreditation: **SC**, ART, BUS, BUSA, CGTECH, CONST, CS, ENG, ENGR, ENGT, MACTE, MUS, NURSE, SPAA, SW, TED, THEA

01 President ... Mr. Sam OLENS
10 Interim Chief Financial Officer ... Ms. Julie PETERSON
05 Provost/Vice Pres Academic Affs ... Dr. W. Ken HARMON
30 VP University Advancement & Devel ... Mr. Michael HARDERS
32 Vice Pres Student Affairs ... Dr. Kathleen WHITE
11 Vice President for Operations ... Vacant
58 VP Research/Dean Graduate College ... Dr. Charles J. AMLANER
26 VP Strategic Comm & Marketing ... Ms. Arlethia PERRY-JOHNSON
31 VP Economic Dev/Community Engage ... Mr. Charles ROSS
20 Senior Vice Provost Academic Affs ... Dr. John OMACHONU
43 Interim General Counsel ... Mr. Andrew NEWTON
04 Faculty Exec Assistant to President ... Dr. Jon PRESTON
20 Assoc Vice Pres for Curriculum ... Dr. Valerie D. WHITTLESEY
21 Assoc Vice Pres for Operations ... Vacant
20 Interim Dean University College ... Dr. Lynn STALLINGS
15 Int Chief Human Resources Officer ... Ms. Alicia STIGNANI
13 Interim Chief Information Officer ... Ms. Lectra LAWHORNE
84 Assoc Vice Pres Enrollment Services ... Mr. Kim WEST
106 AVP Technology Enhanced Learning ... Dr. Elke LEEDS
08 Asst Vice Pres for Library Services ... Dr. J. David EVANS
18 Asst Vice Pres Facilities Services ... Mr. John A. ANDERSON
27 Asst VP Strategic Comm//Marketing ... Mr. Ronald RAMOS
46 Asst VP Enterprise Info Mgmt ... Dr. Robert SMITH
35 Asst VP Student Life Operations ... Ms. Katherine E. ALDAY
79 Dean Humanities/Social Science ... Dr. Robert DORFF
81 Dean Science & Mathematics ... Dr. Mark R. ANDERSON
53 Dean Bagwell College of Education ... Dr. Arlinda EATON
50 Dean Coles College of Business ... Dr. Kathy S. SCHWAIG
76 Dean WellStar Col Health/Human Svcs ... Dr. Mark TILLMAN
49 Dean College of the Arts ... Dr. Patricia S. POULTER
48 Dean Architecture/Construction Mgmt ... Dr. Richard COLE
77 Dean Computing/Software Engineering ... Dr. Eun K. PARK
58 Interim Dean Graduate College ... Dr. Mike DISHMAN
92 Dean Honors College ... Dr. Rita BAILEY
51 Dean Continuing/Professional Educ ... Ms. Barbara S. CALHOUN
35 Assoc VP Student Affairs ... Dr. Michael L. SANSEVIRO
07 Sr Exec Director Enrollment Svcs ... Ms. Susan N. BLAKE
38 Assoc VP/Dir Student Success Svcs ... Dr. Robert J. MATTOX
28 Chief Diversity Officer ... Dr. Erik MALEWSKI
06 Registrar ... Mr. Kim WEST
14 Assoc CIO/CTO ... Dr. John L. ISENHOUR
91 Exec Dir Enterprise Systems & Svcs ... Ms. Rifka MAYANI
37 Director Student Financial Aid ... Mr. Rondall H. DAY
07 Dir Student Recruitment/Admissions ... Dr. Angela J. EVANS
25 Director Procurement & Contracting ... Ms. Laura MCMILLAN
36 Int Dir of Career Services Center ... Ms. Ana BAIDA
41 Athletics Director ... Mr. Vaughn A. WILLIAMS
29 Director Alumni Affairs ... Ms. Pierrette MAILLET
44 Director Annual Giving ... Dr. Joan DUNCAN
19 AVP Public Safety/Chief of Police ... Mr. Roger STEARNS
88 Dir Enterprise Academic Reporting ... Ms. Donna R. HUTCHESON
96 Director Procurement & Contracting ... Ms. Laura MCMILLAN
100 Exec Admin to Pres/Chf of Protocol ... Ms. Lynda K. JOHNSON
103 Dir Workforce/Career Development ... Vacant
104 Education Abroad Progam Coordinator ... Ms. Nicole MEANOR
105 Dir Web Services/Mobile Development ... Mr. Chris WARD
108 Vice Provost Inst Effectiveness ... Dr. Jorge PÉREZ
39 Director University Housing ... Mr. Christopher BRUNO
54 Dean of Engineering/Eng Technology ... Dr. Thomas CURRIN
86 Director Government Relations ... Ms. Amanda SEALS

† Part of the University System of Georgia.

LaGrange College (K)

601 Broad Street, La Grange GA 30240-2999
County: Troup FICE Identification: 001578
Unit ID: 140234
Telephone: (706) 880-8000 Carnegie Class: Bac-A&S
FAX Number: (706) 880-8358 Calendar System: 4/1/4
URL: www.lagrange.edu
Established: 1831 Annual Undergrad Tuition & Fees: $27,540
Enrollment: 964 Coed
Affiliation or Control: United Methodist IRS Status: 501(c)3
Highest Offering: Master's
Accreditation: **SC**, ACBSP, NUR

01 President ... Dr. Dan MCALEXANDER
04 Executive Assistant to President ... Mrs. Carla RHODES
31 Events Coordinator ... Ms. Tammy ROGERS
41 VP of Athletics ... Mrs. Jennifer D. CLAYBROOK
05 Provost ... Dr. David GARRISON
32 VP of Student Engagement ... Dr. Mark SHOOK
06 Registrar ... Ms. Cindy SAINES
08 Co-Director Library ... Mr. Joseph MARCINIAK
08 Co-Director Library ... Ms. Charlene BAXTER
55 Dir Graduate/Degree Completion ... Mr. Jeff LUKKEN
09 Director Inst Effectiveness ... Dr. Carol YIN
36 Director Career Development Center ... Dr. Karen PRUETT
38 Director Counseling Center ... Mrs. Pamela TREMBLAY
20 Associate Provost ... Dr. Maranah SAUTER
104 Associate Provost and Professor ... Mrs. Sarah Beth MALLORY
39 Director Res Educ & Housing ... Mr. Vernon JAMES
30 VP of External Relations ... Mrs. Rebecca ROTH
26 Sr Director Communications/Mktg ... Mr. Dean A. HARTMAN
37 Director Student Financial Aid ... Mrs. Michelle REEVES
44 Senior Director Development ... Vacant
29 Director Alumni & Cmty Relations ... Mrs. Martha PIRKLE
84 VP of Enrollment ... Mr. Joseph C. MILLER
44 Major Gift Officer ... Mr. Mark DAVIS
07 Director of Admission ... Mr. David MCGREAL
105 Asst Director Communications & Mktg ... Mr. David BEARD
10 VP of Finance & Operations ... Mr. Martin E. PIRRMAN
21 Director of Finance ... Mrs. Patti D. HOXSIE
15 VP of Human Resources ... Mrs. Dawn COKER
13 Chief Information Officer ... Vacant
18 Manager Facilities/Physical Plant ... Mr. Michael CONIGLIO
19 Director of Security ... Mr. Michael A. THOMAS
14 Director Information Technology ... Mr. James BLACKWOOD
42 Director Spiritual Life & Chaplain ... Mr. Adam ROBERTS
106 Director Online Instruction ... Dr. Jon ERNSTBERGER
91 Database Administrator ... Mr. Brandon MOBLEY

Lanier Technical College (L)

2990 Landrum Education Drive, Oakwood GA 30566-3405
County: Hall FICE Identification: 005254
Unit ID: 140243
Telephone: (770) 533-7000 Carnegie Class: Assoc/HVT-High Trad
FAX Number: (678) 989-3107 Calendar System: Semester
URL: www.laniertech.edu
Established: 1964 Annual Undergrad Tuition & Fees (In-State): $3,164
Enrollment: 3,695 Coed
Affiliation or Control: State IRS Status: 501(c)3
Highest Offering: Associate Degree
Accreditation: **SC**, DA, DH, EMT, MAC, PTAA, RAD, SURGT

01 President ....Dr. Ray PERREN
03 Executive Vice President ....Mr. Tim MCDONALD
103 Vice President Economic Development ....Mr. Carl ROGERS
05 Vice President Academic Affairs ....Dr. Tavarez HOLSTON
45 Vice President IE & Operations ....Dr. Joanne P. TOLLESON
32 Vice President Student Affairs ....Ms. Nancy BEAVER
10 Vice Pres Administrative Services ....Mr. Les SALTER
13 Vice Pres Information Technology ....Mr. Robbie VICKERS
04 Executive Assistant to President ....Ms. Karen MINOR
75 Dean of Professional Programs ....Ms. Donna BRINSON
76 Dean of Allied Health ....Dr. Deanne COLLINS
50 Dean of Business & Computer Science ....Ms. Lisa MALOOF
72 Dean of Technical & Industrial Pgm ....Mr. Troy LINSEY
97 Dean of General Education ....Dr. Howard LEDFORD
09 Dir of Institutional Effectiveness ....Mr. Brad GADBERRY
30 Exec Dir Institutional Advancement ....Mr. Dennis STOCKTON
26 Director of Marketing ....Mr. Dave PARRISH
07 Director of Admissions ....Ms. Sue CRONIC
06 Registrar ....Ms. Caroline FRICK
37 Director Student Financial Aid ....Ms. Kimberly KELLEY
21 Director Administrative Services ....Ms. Mary FOWLER
15 Director of Human Resources ....Ms. Jill CANTRELL
18 Director of Facilities ....Mr. Guy ABBS
36 Career Services Specialist ....Ms. Melissa LAWRENCE
28 Disability Services Coordinatore ....Ms. Mallory SAFLEY
08 Library Services Director ....Ms. Kathryn S. THOMPSON
19 College Police Chief ....Mr. Jeff STRICKLAND
96 Purchasing Agent ....Ms. Kathy PHAGAN

Le Cordon Bleu College of Culinary Arts in Atlanta (A)

1927 Lakeside Parkway, Tucker GA 30084-5865
Telephone: (770) 938-4711 Identification: 666298
Accreditation: ACICS, ACFEI

† In teach-out mode through September 2017. Branch campus of Le Cordon Bleu College of Culinary Arts, Portland, OR.

Life University (B)

1269 Barclay Circle, Marietta GA 30060-2996
County: Cobb FICE Identification: 020748
Unit ID: 140252
Telephone: (770) 426-2600 Carnegie Class: Spec-4-yr-Other Health
FAX Number: (770) 429-4819 Calendar System: Quarter
URL: www.life.edu
Established: 1974 Annual Undergrad Tuition & Fees: $10,860
Enrollment: 2,754 Coed
Affiliation or Control: Independent Non-Profit IRS Status: 501(c)3
Highest Offering: Doctorate
Accreditation: SC, CAATE, CHIRO, DIETD, DIETI

01 President ....Dr. Guy F. RIEKEMAN
10 Exec VP for Finance ....Mr. William JARR
05 Provost and VP of Academic Affairs ....Dr. Rob SCOTT
20 Vice Provost/Interim VPAA ....Dr. Tim GROSS
44 VP of University Advancement ....Mr. Greg HARRIS
32 VP for Student Services ....Dr. Marc SCHNEIDER
11 VP of Operations ....Mr. John MCGEE
84 VP of Enrollment & Mktg ....Dr. Cynthia BOYD
88 VP of Professional Relations ....Dr. Gilles LAMARCHE
41 Director of Athletics ....Mr. Dan PAYNE
15 Director of Human Resources ....Ms. Stella PETERSON
13 Chief Information Officer ....Mr. John ALTIKULAC
14 Director Information Technology ....Mr. Thorton MUIR
104 Director of Global Initiatives ....Dr. John DOWNES
76 Dean College of Chiropractic ....Dr. Leslie KING
88 Dean College of Grad and Undergrad ....Dr. Jana W. HOLWICK
88 Assoc Dean Grad & Undergrad Studies ....Dr. Michael D. SMITH
23 Assistant Dean for Clinics ....Dr. Bernadette LAVENDER
88 Assoc Dean College of Chiropractic ....Dr. Michael CLUSSERATH
06 Registrar ....Ms. Heather HOFFMAN
07 Director of Admissions Operations ....Ms. Stephanie BUCHANAN
106 Assoc Dean Online Education ....Ms. Camille KARLSON
08 Director of Learning Resources ....Ms. Karen PRESTON
46 Director of Research ....Dr. Stephanie SULLIVAN
29 Alumni Relations Manager ....Ms. Mary Ellen LEFFARD
108 Director of Inst Effectiveness ....Dr. Vince ERARIO
09 Director of Institutional Research ....Dr. Howard WRIGHT
18 Director Facilities/Physical Plant ....Mr. Larry RIDDLE
38 Director Student Success ....Dr. Lisa RUBIN
37 Director Student Financial Aid ....Ms. Melissa WATERS
35 Exec Dir of Student Services ....Ms. Jennifer VALTOS
36 Director of Career Planning ....Ms. Susan DUDT
88 Dir of Student Administrative Svcs ....Ms. Kay FREELAND
26 Director of Communications ....Mr. Will BROOKS
21 Budget Director ....Ms. Amy MCILVANE
30 Director of Development ....Ms. Erin DANCER
27 Director of Marketing ....Ms. Shelly BATCHER
44 Director of Advancement Services ....Ms. Lauren NELSON
88 Director of Life Force ....Dr. Cierra HOFFMAN
101 Board Secretary ....Ms. Nita LOONEY
96 Director of Purchasing ....Mr. Mel BURTON

Luther Rice College and Seminary (C)

3038 Evans Mill Road, Lithonia GA 30038-2454
County: DeKalb FICE Identification: 031009
Unit ID: 135364
Telephone: (770) 484-1204 Carnegie Class: Spec-4-yr-Faith
FAX Number: (770) 484-1155 Calendar System: Semester
URL: www.lutherrice.edu
Established: 1962 Annual Undergrad Tuition & Fees: $6,336
Enrollment: 1,218 Coed
Affiliation or Control: Independent Non-Profit IRS Status: 501(c)3
Highest Offering: Doctorate
Accreditation: BI, TRACS

01 President ....Dr. James L. FLANAGAN
10 Vice President Financial Affairs ....Mr. Louis B. HARDCASTLE
32 Director for Student Development ....Mr. Steve PRAY
05 Vice President for Academic Affairs ....Dr. Ralph J. MCCANN
26 Director of Marketing ....Mr. Russell L. SORROW
09 VP for Institutional Effectiveness ....Dr. Ralph J. MCCANN
08 Director of Library Services ....Mr. Prasada SAJJA
37 Director Student Financial Aid ....Mr. Casey W. KUFFREY
85 Asst to the Pres Global Strategy ....Dr. Ronald B. LONG
58 Director Doctor of Ministry Program ....Dr. Ron K. COBB
20 Acting Assoc VP Academic Affairs ....Mr. Evan POSEY
11 VP for Administration ....Mr. Steven STEINHILBER
07 Director of Admissions ....Mr. Gary COOK
13 Chief Info Technology Officer (CIO) ....Mr. Ken STOKES

Mercer University (D)

1501 Mercer University Drive, Macon GA 31207-0003
County: Bibb FICE Identification: 001580
Unit ID: 140447
Telephone: (478) 301-2700 Carnegie Class: DU-Mod
FAX Number: (478) 301-2108 Calendar System: Semester
URL: www.mercer.edu
Established: 1833 Annual Undergrad Tuition & Fees: $34,450
Enrollment: 8,552 Coed
Affiliation or Control: Independent Non-Profit IRS Status: 501(c)3
Highest Offering: Doctorate
Accreditation: SC, ARCPA, BUS, CACREP, CS, ENG, LAW, MED, MFCD, MUS, NURSE, PH, PHAR, PTA, THEOL

01 President and CEO ....Mr. William D. UNDERWOOD
00 Chancellor ....Dr. R. Kirby GODSEY
100 Senior VP and Chief of Staff ....Mr. Larry D. BRUMLEY
05 Provost ....Dr. D. Scott DAVIS
10 Executive VP for Admin & Finance ....Dr. James S. NETHERTON
30 Sr VP for University Advancement ....Mr. John A. PATTERSON
84 Sr Vice Pres Enrollment Management ....Dr. Penny L. ELKINS
43 Vice President and General Counsel ....Mr. William G. SOLOMON
13 Chief Technology Officer ....Mr. Michael R. BELOTE
17 Sr VP Health Sciences/Dean Phar/HS ....Dr. Hewitt MATTHEWS
32 Vice President & Dean of Students ....Dr. Doug R. PEARSON
46 Sr V Prov Research/Dean Grad Stds ....Dr. Wayne C. GLASGOW
09 Vice Provost for Inst Effectiveness ....Dr. Susan C. MALONE
21 Treasurer & Assoc VP Finance ....Ms. Julia T. DAVIS
18 Assoc Vice President for Facilities ....Mr. Russell VULLO
15 Associate Vice Pres Personnel Admin ....Ms. Rhonda W. LIDSTONE
26 Sr Asst VP Marketing Communications ....Mr. Richard L. CAMERON
37 Assoc VP Student Financial Planning ....Ms. Maria A. HAMMETT
49 Dean College of Liberal Arts ....Dr. Anita O. GUSTAFSON
61 Dean School of Law ....Ms. Daisy H. FLOYD
63 Dean School of Medicine ....Dr. Jean R. SUMNER
54 Dean School of Engineering ....Dr. Wade H. SHAW
50 Dean Sch Business/Econ ....Dr. Susan P. GILBERT
73 Dean School of Theology ....Dr. Jeffrey G. WILLETTS
53 Dean College of Education ....Dr. James J. BARTA
66 Dean College of Nursing ....Dr. Linda A. STREIT
51 Dean College Cont/Prof Studies ....Dr. Priscilla R. DANHEISER
64 Dean School of Music ....Dr. C. David KEITH
76 Dean Col of Health Professions ....Dr. Lisa M. LUNDQUIST
08 Dean of University Libraries ....Ms. Elizabeth D. HAMMOND
06 Registrar ....Ms. Lucy P. WILSON
41 Athletic Director ....Mr. Jim COLE
19 Chief Police Department ....Mr. Gary COLLINS
09 Director of Institutional Research ....Ms. Sarah E. MAY
96 Director of Purchasing ....Mr. Charles MIZE
04 Administrative Asst to President ....Ms. Vonne SHEFFIELD
29 Director Alumni Relations ....Ms. Jill H. KINSELLA
86 Director Government Relations ....Mr. Hugh D. SOSEBEE, JR.

Middle Georgia State University (E)

100 University Parkway, Macon GA 31206-5145
County: Bibb FICE Identification: 007728
Unit ID: 482158
Telephone: (478) 471-2700 Carnegie Class: Bac-Diverse
FAX Number: (478) 471-2846 Calendar System: Semester
URL: www.mga.edu
Established: 1884 Annual Undergrad Tuition & Fees (In-State): $3,890
Enrollment: 7,927 Coed
Affiliation or Control: State IRS Status: 501(c)3
Highest Offering: Master's
Accreditation: SC, ADNUR, COARC, CS, NUR, OTA, TED

01 President ....Dr. Christopher BLAKE
05 Provost ....Dr. Melanie HATCH
10 Exec VP Finance & Operations ....Ms. Nancy STROUD
32 VP Student Affairs ....Ms. Jennifer BRANNON
30 VP Univ Advancement/Exec Dir Fdn ....Mr. Raymond CARNLEY
20 Vice Provost Academic Initiatives ....Dr. Pamela BEDWELL
20 Vice Provost for Acad Integrity ....Mr. Andy CLARK
88 Assoc Provost Regional Campus Coord ....Dr. Deepa ARORA
108 Asst Provost Acad Planning/Policy ....Dr. Mary WEARN
20 Asst Provost for Student Success ....Dr. Sheri ROWLAND
31 Asst Provost Innovative Outreach ....Dr. Art RECESSO
100 Chief of Staff ....Mr. Albert J. ABRAMS
13 Chief Information Officer ....Mr. Roger DIXON
43 Dir Legal Services/General Counsel ....Ms. Frances DAVIS
26 VP Recruit/Mktg-Chief Mktg Officer ....Ms. Cheryl CARTY
15 Interim Exec Dir Human Resources ....Ms. Vicky SMITH
44 Exec Dir Major and Planning Giving ....Ms. Julie DAVIS
35 Asst VP Student Affairs ....Mr. Michael STEWART
18 Asst VP Facilities ....Mr. David SIMS
19 Asst VP Risk Mgmt and Police Svcs ....Mr. Shawn DOUGLAS
21 Controller ....Mr. Brian STANLEY
06 Registrar ....Ms. Brenda HOGAN
07 Director of Admissions ....Ms. Margo WOODHAM
29 Director Alumni Relations ....Ms. Natalie RISCHBIETER
41 Director Athletics/Rec/Wellness ....Mr. Charles MULLIS
109 Director Auxiliary Services ....Mr. Kevin REID
40 Director Campus Stores ....Ms. Ashley EVANS
38 Director Counseling ....Ms. Predita HOWARD
37 Director Financial Aid ....Ms. LeeAnn KIRKLAND
25 Director Grants and Contracts ....Ms. Barbara RATZLAFF
09 Interim Dir Institutional Research ....Dr. Michael GIBBONS
104 Interim Director International Educ ....Dr. Laura THOMASON
08 Director Library Services ....Ms. Pat BORCK
96 Director Purchasing ....Ms. Barbara BURNS
39 Director of Residence Life ....Mr. Brian HARRELL
12 Director Cochran/Eastman Campuses ....Mr. Henry WHITFIELD
12 Director Warner Robins Campus ....Ms. Pella MURPHY
58 Interim Dean Graduate Studies ....Dr. Loretta CLAYTON
49 Dean Arts & Sciences ....Dr. Ron WILLIAMS
88 Interim Dean Aviation ....Mr. Adon CLARK
50 Dean of Business ....Dr. Varkey K. TITUS
53 Dean of Education ....Dr. David FULLER
76 Dean Health Sciences ....Dr. Rebecca J. CORVEY
72 Dean Information Technology ....Dr. Alex KOOHANG
04 Administrative Asst to President ....Ms. Carrie WIMBERLEY

† Part of the University System of Georgia.

Miller-Motte Technical College (F)

621 NW Frontage Road, Augusta GA 30907
Telephone: (706) 396-8000 Identification: 770710
Accreditation: ACICS

† Branch campus of Miller-Motte Technical College, Clarksville, TN

Miller-Motte Technical College (G)

1800 Box Road, Columbus GA 31907
Telephone: (706) 225-5000 Identification: 770711
Accreditation: ACICS

† Branch campus of Miller-Motte Technical College, Clarksville, TN

Miller-Motte Technical College (H)

175 Tom Hill Sr Boulevard, Macon GA 31210
Telephone: (478) 803-4800 Identification: 770844
Accreditation: ACICS

† Branch campus of McCann School of Business & Technology, Pottsville, PA

Morehouse College (I)

830 Westview Drive SW, Atlanta GA 30314-3773
County: Fulton FICE Identification: 001582
Unit ID: 140553
Telephone: (404) 681-2800 Carnegie Class: Bac-A&S
FAX Number: (404) 681-2650 Calendar System: Semester
URL: www.morehouse.edu
Established: 1867 Annual Undergrad Tuition & Fees: $26,742
Enrollment: 2,109 Male
Affiliation or Control: Independent Non-Profit IRS Status: 501(c)3
Highest Offering: Baccalaureate
Accreditation: SC, BUS, MUS

01 President ....Dr. John S. WILSON, JR.
05 Provost/SVP Academic Affairs ....Dr. Garikai CAMPBELL
18 Assoc Vice Pres Campus Operations ....Mr. Andre E. BERTRAND
30 Int VP Institutional Advancement ....Dr. John P. BROWN
11 Chief Operating Officer ....Mr. William TAGGART
32 Vice Pres Student Development ....Dr. Timothy SAMS
10 Vice Pres Business Affairs/CFO ....Dr. Alan D. ROBERTSON, SR.
15 AVP Human Resource ....Mrs. Amanda BAILEY
44 Special Asst Pres-Capital Campaign ....Ms. Kathleen L. JOHNSON
42 Dean Martin Luther King Jr Chapel ....Dr. Lawrence E. CARTER
06 Interim Dean/Registrar ....Ms. Kasi ROBINSON
07 Director Admissions & Recruitment ....Mr. Darryl ISOM
37 Director of Financial Aid ....Ms. Sheryl SPIVEY
29 Dir Alumni Rels/Annual Giving Pgm ....Mr. Henry GOODGAME
26 Interim Director of Communications ....Ms. Elise DURHAM
36 Director of Placement ....Mr. Doug COOPER
41 Athletic Director ....Mr. Andre PATTILLO
39 Director Student Housing ....Mr. Maurice WASHINGTON
19 Chief of Campus Police ....Chief Valerie DALTON
85 Interim Dir Andrew Young Ctr ....Mr. Julius COLES
20 Special Assistant to Provost ....Dr. Tafaya RANSOM
35 Director Student Services ....Mr. Kevin BOOKER
38 Director of Student Counseling ....Dr. Gary WRIGHT
96 Assoc VP/Chief Procurement Mgr ....Mr. Ralph JOHNSON
27 Publications Manager ....Ms. Vickie HAMPTON
84 Assoc VP of Enrollment Management ....Mr. Terrance DIXON
21 Director of Budgets ....Mr. David LERCH
21 Controller ....Ms. Robbie BISHOP-MONROE
13 Chief Information Officer ....Mr. Clifford RUSSELL
43 General Counsel & Chief of Staff ....Ms. Lacrecia CADE
88 Chief Internal Auditor ....Ms. Undria STALLINGS

Morehouse School of Medicine (A)

720 Westview Drive, SW, Atlanta GA 30310-1495

County: Fulton FICE Identification: 024821
Unit ID: 140562
Telephone: (404) 752-1500 Carnegie Class: Spec-4-yr-Med
FAX Number: (404) 752-1027 Calendar System: Semester
URL: www.msm.edu
Established: 1975 Annual Graduate Tuition & Fees: N/A
Enrollment: 398 Coed
Affiliation or Control: Independent Non-Profit IRS Status: 501(c)3
Highest Offering: Doctorate; No Undergraduates
Accreditation: SC, MED, PH

01 President .... Dr. Valerie MONTGOMERY RICE
05 Dean .... Dr. Valerie MONTGOMERY RICE
86 Exec Director of Government Affairs .... Mr. Daniel DAWES
43 General Counsel .... Ms. Almeta COOPER
30 Sr Vice President of Institutional .... Dr. Bennie L. HARRIS
46 VP/Exec Vice Dean Rsrch/Acad Admin .... Dr. Sandra HARRIS-HOOKER
26 VP of Marketing & Communications .... Ms. Pamela SIMMONS
15 Associate VP of Human Resources .... Ms. Denise BRITT
102 Assoc VP Development/Advance .... Dr. Ernie HUGHES
20 Sr Assoc Dean Educational Affairs .... Dr. Martha ELKS
88 Sr Assoc Dean for Clinical Affairs .... Dr. Derrick BEECH, JR.
20 Assoc Dean Faculty Affairs .... Dr. Erika BROWN
37 Director Student Fiscal Affairs .... Ms. Cynthia H. HANDY
08 Library Manager .... Mr. Joe SWANSON, JR.
09 Director II Planning & IR/Title 3 .... Vacant
25 Exec Director of Grants & Contracts .... Ms. Sandi PHILLIPS
29 Director Alumni Affairs .... Ms. Samra COOTE
07 Director Admissions .... Vacant
96 Director Purchasing .... Mr. Philmon THOMAS
44 Major Gifts Officer .... Vacant
22 Chief Compliance Officer .... Ms. Desiree RAMIREZ
06 Registrar .... Ms. Angela FREEMAN
13 Chief Information Officer .... Vacant
19 Chief of Police .... Mr. Joseph CHEVALIER, JR.

North Georgia Technical College (B)

PO Box 65, Clarkesville GA 30523-0065

County: Habersham FICE Identification: 005619
Unit ID: 140678
Telephone: (706) 754-7700 Carnegie Class: Assoc/HVT-High Trad
FAX Number: (706) 754-7777 Calendar System: Semester
URL: www.northgatech.edu
Established: 1943 Annual Undergrad Tuition & Fees (In-State): $2,724
Enrollment: 2,663 Coed
Affiliation or Control: State IRS Status: 501(c)3
Highest Offering: Associate Degree
Accreditation: SC, ACFEI, MAC, MLTAD

01 President .... Dr. Mark IVESTER
05 Vice President for Academic Affairs .... Kathie IVESTER
32 Vice President for Student Affairs .... Dr. Michael KING
11 Vice President for Administration .... Carol CARSON
30 Vice Pres of Economic Development .... Rick STORY
06 Registrar .... Michele SHIRLEY
07 Director of Admissions .... Michele SHIRLEY
15 Human Resources Coordinator .... Lorna CHAPMAN
18 Chief Facilities/Physical Plant .... Michael BOYD
26 Chief Public Relations Officer .... Amy HULSEY
29 Director Alumni Relations .... Cynthia BROWN
35 Campus Life Director .... Sherry SEAL
36 Director for Job Placement .... Patrick LEDFORD
37 Financial Aid Director .... Audra JIMENEZ
96 Procurement Officer .... Jeannie BARRETT
09 Institutional Research Analyst .... Hamilton SCOTT
46 Institutional Effectiveness Dir .... Janet HENDERSON
20 Dean for Academic Affairs .... Dan PRESSLEY
20 Dean for Academic Affairs .... Leslie MCFARLIN
20 Dean for Academic Affairs .... Mindy GLANDER
106 Distance Education Specialist .... Dr. Renee DEIBERT
13 Information Technology Director .... Savonda TURNER
19 Chief of Police .... Stan LOVEL

Oconee Fall Line Technical College-North Campus (C)

1189 Deepstep Road, Sandersville GA 31082-9337

County: Washington FICE Identification: 031555
Unit ID: 420431
Telephone: (478) 553-2050 Carnegie Class: Assoc/HVT-High Non
FAX Number: (478) 553-2118 Calendar System: Semester
URL: www.oftc.edu
Established: 1996 Annual Undergrad Tuition & Fees (In-State): $2,614
Enrollment: 1,659 Coed
Affiliation or Control: State IRS Status: 501(c)3
Highest Offering: Associate Degree
Accreditation: SC, COE

01 President .... Dr. Lloyd HORADAN
05 Vice Pres Academic/Student Affs .... Ms. Erica HARDEN
10 Vice Pres Administrative Services .... Ms. Rosemary SELBY
30 Vice Pres Economic Development .... Ms. Kim DAVID
49 Dean Arts & Sciences/Business Svcs .. Ms. Michele STRICKLAND
32 Dean Student Affairs .... Ms. Johnnie EDGE
06 Registrar .... Ms. Geri CLEMENTS
07 Director of Admissions .... Ms. Raydor CONEWAY
15 Director Human Resources .... Ms. Sharon O'NEAL
21 Director of Administrative Services .... Ms. Penny KITCHENS
18 Director Facilities/Physical Plant .... Mr. Jim HARRISON
26 Exec Director Marketing .... Ms. Lakeshia POOLE
37 Financial Aid Director .... Ms. Betty YOUNG
28 Dir of Spec Populations/Stdnt Life .... Ms. Susan HAMMOCK

Oconee Fall Line Technical College-South Campus (D)

560 Pinehill Road, Dublin GA 31021-1599

County: Laurens FICE Identification: 022795
Unit ID: 140076
Telephone: (478) 275-6589 Carnegie Class: Not Classified
FAX Number: (478) 275-6642 Calendar System: Semester
URL: www.oftc.edu
Established: 1984 Annual Undergrad Tuition & Fees (In-State): N/A
Enrollment: N/A Coed
Affiliation or Control: State IRS Status: 501(c)3
Highest Offering: Associate Degree
Accreditation: SC, COE, COARC, MAC, RAD

01 President .... Dr. Lloyd HORADAN
09 Vice Pres Inst Effectiveness .... Dr. Katie DAVIS
32 Dean Student Affairs .... Mr. Jay MULLIS
06 Assistant Registrar .... Ms. Kimberly NOLES
18 Director Facilities .... Mr. Ragan GREEN
30 Exec Dir Institutional Advancement .... Mrs. Jenny SHUMAN
19 Chief Security & Facilities .... Mr. Mark ROGERS
36 Director of Career Development .... Vacant
76 Dean Allied Health/Prof Svcs .... Ms. Tammy BAYTO
37 Asst Director Financial Aid .... Ms. Teresa CRAFTON
08 Director Library Services .... Ms. Wendi MORRIS
07 Director of Admissions .... Mr. Raydor CONEWAY

Ogeechee Technical College (E)

One Joseph E. Kennedy Boulevard,
Statesboro GA 30458-8049

County: Bulloch FICE Identification: 030300
Unit ID: 366465
Telephone: (912) 681-5500 Carnegie Class Assoc/HVT-High Trad
FAX Number: (912) 486-7704 Calendar System: Semester
URL: www.ogeecheetech.edu
Established: 1986 Annual Undergrad Tuition & Fees (In-State): $2,862
Enrollment: 2,340 Coordinate
Affiliation or Control: State IRS Status: 170(c)1
Highest Offering: Associate Degree
Accreditation: SC, CAHIIM, DA, DMS, FUSER, MAC, OPD, RAD, SURGT

01 President .... Ms. Lori S. DURDEN
04 Exec Assistant to the President .... Ms. Karen MOBLEY
05 Exec Vice Pres for Academic Affairs .... Dr. Charlene LAMAR
06 Vice President Economic Development .... Ms. Jan MOORE
108 VP Institutional Effectiveness .... Ms. Brandy TAYLOR
32 Vice President Student Affairs .... Dr. Ryan FOLEY
10 Vice President for Administration .... Ms. Eyvonne HART
13 VP Technology & Institutional Supp .... Mr. Jeff DAVIS
30 VP for College Advancement .... Mr. Barry TURNER
09 Director Inst Research & Planning .... Ms. YLonne HODGES
08 Director for Library Services .... Ms. Lisa LANIER
51 Dir Continuing Educ & Ind Training ...... Ms. Kathleen KOSMOSKI
07 Director for Admissions .... Ms. Molly BICKERTON
06 Registrar .... Ms. Michelle STUBBS
37 Director for Financial Aid .... Ms. Letrel THOMAS
15 Director for Human Resources .... Mr. Steve MILLER
109 Exec Director to Auxiliary Services .... Mr. J.J ALTMAN
18 Director for Plant Operations .... Mr. Buddy SAPP
19 Director Campus Safety & Security .... Mr. Stan YORK
20 Dean for Academic Affairs .... Dr. Paul MIZELL
97 Dean Distance & General Education .... Ms. Jennifer WITHERINGTON
20 Dean for Academic Affairs .... Ms. Kelly KINGRY
21 Asst VP for Administration .... Ms. Tonya VICKERS

Oglethorpe University (F)

4484 Peachtree Road, NE, Atlanta GA 30319-2797

County: DeKalb FICE Identification: 001586
Unit ID: 140696
Telephone: (404) 261-1441 Carnegie Class: Bac-A&S
FAX Number: (404) 364-8500 Calendar System: Semester
URL: www.oglethorpe.edu
Established: 1835 Annual Undergrad Tuition & Fees: $33,800
Enrollment: 1,094 Coed
Affiliation or Control: Independent Non-Profit IRS Status: 501(c)3
Highest Offering: Master's
Accreditation: SC

01 President .... Dr. Lawrence M. SCHALL
05 Provost/VP Academic Affairs .... Dr. Glenn SHARFMAN
10 Vice Pres for Business & Finance .... Mr. Norman MCKAY
30 Vice Pres Devel & Alumni Relations .... Ms. Robyn FURNESS-FALLIN
84 VP Enrollment/FinancialAid .... Ms. Lucy LEUSCH
32 Dean of Students .... Ms. Michelle HALL
20 Assoc Provost .... Dr. Keith AUFDERHEIDE
04 Exec Assistant to the President .... Ms. Colleen D'ALESSANDRO
08 Univ Librarian/Library Director .... Ms. Anne SALTER
06 Registrar .... Mr. Brian COLDREN
09 Director of Institutional Research .... Mr. Todd CRAIG
26 Exec Dir University Communications .... Mr. Todd BENNETT
41 Athletic Director .... Ms. Becky HALL
37 Director of Financial Aid .... Mr. Chris SUMMERS
39 Director of Residence Life .... Dr. Amy PALDER
21 Director of Finance/Controller .... Vacant
13 Chief Information Officer .... Mr. Michael GONSALVES
27 Dir University Communications .... Ms. Renee VARY KEELE
29 Director of Alumni/Donor Relations ...... Ms. Mary RINALDI WINN
36 Director of Career Development .... Ms. Amy CLEMENTE
44 Director of Major Gifts .... Mr. John CARR
15 Director Human Resources .... Ms. Sandy BUTLER
31 Dir Center for Civic Engagement .... Vacant
18 Director Facilities/Physical Plant .... Mr. Lance KNIGHT
07 Associate Director of Admissions .... Ms. Whitney LEWIS
40 Bookstore Manager .... Vacant

Pacific Institute of Technology (G)

1388 Southlake Plaza Drive, Morrow GA 30260

County: Clayton Identification: 667239
Telephone: (678) 610-5900 Carnegie Class: Not Classified
FAX Number: (678) 610-5008 Calendar System: Quarter
URL: www.pacifictech.edu
Established: 1999 Annual Undergrad Tuition & Fees: N/A
Enrollment: N/A Coed
Affiliation or Control: Proprietary IRS Status: Proprietary
Highest Offering: Associate Degree
Accreditation: ACICS

01 President .... Mr. Frank WEBSTER

Paine College (H)

1235 Fifteenth Street, Augusta GA 30901-3182

County: Richmond FICE Identification: 001587
Unit ID: 140720
Telephone: (706) 821-8200 Carnegie Class: Bac-A&S
FAX Number: (706) 821-8373 Calendar System: Semester
URL: www.paine.edu
Established: 1882 Annual Undergrad Tuition & Fees: $14,224
Enrollment: 848 Coed
Affiliation or Control: Multiple Protestant Denominations
IRS Status: 501(c)3
Highest Offering: Baccalaureate
Accreditation: #SC, ACBSP, TED

01 President .... Dr. Samuel SULLIVAN
04 Office Manager/President's Office .... Mrs. Juanita HARPS
05 Provost/VP Academic Affairs .... Dr. Cheryl EVANS JONES
32 VP Student Affairs .... Dr. Elias ETINGE
10 VP Administrative & Fiscal Affairs .... Ms. Mary MORALE
30 VP of Institutional Advancement .... Ms. Sunya YOUNG
42 Campus Pastor .... Dr. Luther FELDER
41 Director of Athletics .... Mrs. Selina KOHN
20 Exec Asst Provost/VP Acad Affairs .... Ms. Frances WIMBERLY
50 Chair Business Dept .... Dr. Okoroafor NZEH
53 Chair Education Dept .... Dr. LaShawnda LINDSAY-DENNIS
79 Chair Humanities Dept .... Dr. Catherine ADAMS
81 Chair Math Sci Tech Dept .... Dr. Raul PETERS
60 Chair Media Studies Dept .... Ms. Teri BURNETTE
83 Chair Social Sciences Dept .... Dr. Lawanda CUMMINGS
55 Pgm Coord Ctr for Adv Prof Studies .... Mrs. Symphoni WIGGINS
09 Dir Inst Research/Qual Enhance Plng ..... Mrs. Alice M. SIMPKINS
08 Director Library/LRC .... Mrs. Alana LEWIS
06 Registrar .... Mrs. Tanika BEARD
36 Director Career Services .... Mrs. April EWING
38 Director Counseling & Wellness Ctr ..... Ms. Brooke ROBERTSON
39 Dir Residence Life/Stdnt Activities .... Ms. Lauren DEVILLE
19 Chief of Police .... Chief Leroy MORGAN, JR.
21 Controller .... Ms. Veronica STREETMAN
18 Dir Facilities Mgmt/Environ Svcs .... Mr. Clarence CANADA
37 Interim Director Financial Aid .... Ms. Consuelo QUINN
15 Director Human Resources .... Vacant
13 Chief Information Officer .... Mr. Michael HICKS
88 Manager The Lion's Internet Cafe .... Mr. C. Keith BROWN
44 Asst VP of Inst Advancement .... Ms. Helene CARTER
44 Director Institutional Development .... Mr. Darnell HOLSTON
29 Director Alumni Relations .... Mrs. Mildred KENDRICK
26 Dir Communications & Marketing .... Ms. Tonya WILLIAMS
25 Director Sponsored Progms/Title III .... Vacant
88 Director of Tutorial Services .... Dr. Sezilee REID
108 Director of Assessment & Eval .... Ms. Amanda GUSTAFSON
24 LRC Manager .... Mrs. Rosa L. MARTIN
07 Asst Dir Admissions/Recruit Coord .... Mr. Charles SINGLEY, III
88 Sr Women's Athletics Administrator .... Ms. Kisha LUCETTE
88 Asst Ath Dir Compliance/Stdnt Svcs .... Mr. Nathan COCHRAN
88 Asst Ath Dir External Relations .... Mr. Jonavon STEPHENS

Philadelphia College of Osteopathic Medicine Georgia Campus (I)

625 Old Peachtree Road NW, Suwanee GA 30024

Telephone: (678) 225-7500 Identification: 770165
Accreditation: &M, CSTEO, PHAR

† Regional accreditation is carried under the parent institution in Philadelphia, PA

Piedmont College (J)

PO Box 10, Demorest GA 30535-0010

County: Habersham FICE Identification: 001588
Unit ID: 140818
Telephone: (706) 778-3000 Carnegie Class: Masters/L

FAX Number: (706) 776-0701 Calendar System: Semester
URL: www.piedmont.edu
Established: 1897 Annual Undergrad Tuition & Fees: $21,990
Enrollment: 2,120 Coed
Affiliation or Control: United Church Of Christ IRS Status: 501(c)3
Highest Offering: Doctorate
Accreditation: SC, ACBSP, NUR

01 President Dr. James F. MELLICHAMP
05 Vice Pres Academic Affairs Dr. Perry RETTIG
10 Vice Pres Administration & Finance Mr. Kenneth JONES
30 Vice President for Advancement Ms. Amy AMASON
21 Asst VP Finance/Human Resources Ms. Margie MEANS
13 AVP of Information Technology Dr. Shahryar HEYDARI
88 Special Assistant to the President Ms. Jane KIDD
04 Assistant to the President Ms. Kristen GRAY
32 Dean of Student Engagement Ms. Emily PETTIT
07 Dean of Admiss/Undergrad Enrol Mgmt Ms. Cynthia L. PETERSON
08 Dean of Libraries/College Librarian Mr. Robert GLASS, JR.
06 Registrar Mr. Anthony COX
09 Director of Institutional Research Ms. Kim LOVELL
84 Director Graduate Enrollment Mgmt Ms. Kathleen CARTER
07 Director Undergraduate Admissions Ms. Brenda BOONSTRA
37 Director of Financial Aid Mr. David MCMILLION
42 Campus Minister Rev. Timothy GARVIN-LEIGHTON
15 Human Resources Manager Ms. Elaina COCHRAN
26 Director of Public Relations Mr. David E. PRICE
41 Dir of Intercollegiate Athletics Mr. Jim PEEPLES
21 Compliance & Treasury Officer Ms. Leesa P. ANDERSON
19 Director Security/Campus Police Ms. Chanon PRITCHARD
66 Dean School of Nursing/Health Sci Dr. Julie BEHR
50 Dean School of Business Admin Dr. Edward TAYLOR
49 Dean School of Arts & Sciences Dr. Steven NIMMO
53 Dean School of Education Dr. Donald GNECCO

Point University (A)

507 West 10th St, West Point GA 31833
County: Troup FICE Identification: 001547
Unit ID: 138868
Telephone: (706) 385-1000 Carnegie Class: Bac-Diverse
FAX Number: (706) 645-9473 Calendar System: Semester
URL: www.point.edu
Established: 1937 Annual Undergrad Tuition & Fees: $18,500
Enrollment: 1,522 Coed
Affiliation or Control: Christian Churches And Churches of Christ
IRS Status: 501(c)3
Highest Offering: Master's
Accreditation: SC, TED

01 President Mr. Dean C. COLLINS
05 Chief Academic Officer Dr. W. Darryl HARRISON
108 Vice Pres for Inst Effectiveness Dr. Dennis E. GLENN
10 Vice Pres of Finance Mr. Dan FRAZIER
08 Library Director Mr. Michael L. BAIN
84 Vice Pres for Enrollment Management Dr. Stacy BARTLETT
07 Asst Vice President of Enrollment Mrs. Tiffany WOOD
06 Registrar Ms. Caley MOTES
07 Executive Director of Enrollment Mr. Rusty HASSELL
37 Director of Financial Aid Ms. Janifer MORGAN
88 Director of Student Accounts Ms. Yolanda STEELE
32 Dean of Students Ms. Laura SCHAAF
11 Chief Operations Officer Mr. Lance FRANCIS
15 Director of Human Resources Ms. Margaret HODGE
42 Vice Pres for Spiritual Formation Mr. Wye HUXFORD
30 Vice President of Advancement Mr. Joshua HARRELSON
44 Director of Development Mr. Richard BUMPERS
29 Director of Alumni Relations Ms. Pam ROSS
26 Communications Manager Mrs. Katherine HAMILTON
13 Vice Pres for Info Technology Mr. Bill DORMINY
41 Athletic Director Mr. Alan WILSON
18 Dir of Facilities and Maintenance Mr. Jim ALDRIDGE
19 Director of Security Mr. Fred BERKELEY
88 Director of Student Finance Mr. John LANIER
106 Vice Pres Graduate & Prof Studies Mr. Chris DAVIS
39 Residence Life Manager Ms. Kasey BODINE

† Formerly Atlanta Christian College

Reformed University (B)

1700 North Brown Road, Suite 104,
Lawrenceville GA 30043
County: Gwinnett Identification: 667247
Telephone: (770) 232-2717 Carnegie Class: Not Classified
FAX Number: N/A Calendar System: Semester
URL: www.trsusa.org
Established: 1992 Annual Undergrad Tuition & Fees: N/A
Enrollment: N/A Coed
Affiliation or Control: Presbyterian Church In America IRS Status: Exempt
Highest Offering: Master's
Accreditation: @TRACS

01 President Dr. Joshua PARK

Reinhardt University (C)

7300 Reinhardt Circle, Waleska GA 30183-2981
County: Cherokee FICE Identification: 001589
Unit ID: 140872
Telephone: (770) 720-5600 Carnegie Class: Bac-Diverse
FAX Number: (770) 720-5602 Calendar System: Semester
URL: www.reinhardt.edu
Established: 1883 Annual Undergrad Tuition & Fees: $20,266
Enrollment: 1,422 Coed
Affiliation or Control: United Methodist IRS Status: 501(c)3
Highest Offering: Master's
Accreditation: SC, MUS

01 President Dr. Kina S. MALLARD
04 Executive Assistant to President Mrs. Bonnie H. DEBORD
05 VP & Dean for Academic Affairs Dr. Mark A. ROBERTS
10 Vice Pres Finance & Administration Mr. David R. LEOPARD
30 VP for Advancement & Marketing Mr. Timothy A. NORTON
32 VP Student Affairs/Dean of Students Dr. Roger R. LEE
84 VP for Enrollment Mgmt Mrs. Julie C. FLEMING
41 Director of Athletics Mr. William C. POPP
58 Assoc VP Acad Svcs/Grad Studies Dr. Margaret M. MORLIER
101 Asst Secretary Board of Trustees Mrs. Bonnie H. DEBORD
18 Director of Physical Plant Mrs. Missy H. DAYOUB
26 Director of Marketing Mr. W. Huitt RABEL
13 Dir of Info Tech/Chief Tech Officer Mr. David G. DOSTER
88 Exec Director of Funk Heritage Ctr Dr. Joseph H. KITCHENS
07 Director of Admissions Ms. Lacey L. SATTERFIELD
06 Registrar Ms. Janet M. RODNING
09 Dir Inst Research/Effectiveness Mr. Daniel TEODORESCU
08 Director of Library Services Mr. Joel C. LANGFORD
19 Interim Director of Public Safety Ms. Susan A. MILLER
29 Dir Alumni Rel & Alumni Giving Vacant
42 Minister to Students Rev. Ted GOSHORN
21 Controller Vacant
37 Director Student Financial Aid Mrs. Angie D. HARLOW
15 Director Human Resources Mrs. Kelly M. MORRIS
39 Director Residence Life Mr. Eric W. BOOTH
23 University Nurse Mrs. Alicia C. MILES
35 Asst Dean of Students/Dir Stdnt Act Dr. Walter P. MAY
38 Director of Counseling Svcs Mr. Derek L. STRUCHTEMEYER
88 Dir Center for Student Success Dr. Catherine B. EMANUEL
36 Dir Career & Professional Dev Svcs Mrs. Peggy C. FEEHERY
40 Bookstore Manager Mrs. Janet SWEENEY
106 Coordinator Online Education Dr. Katherine E. HYATT
49 Dean School of Arts & Humanities Dr. Arthur W. GLOWKA
81 Dean School of Maths & Sciences Dr. Jake P. HARNEY
50 Dean McCamish School Business Dr. Katherine E. HYATT
53 Dean Price School of Education Dr. Cindy M. KIERNAN
64 Dean School of Performing Arts Dr. Fredrick A. TARRANT
107 Int Dean Sch Professional Studies Mr. Lester W. DRAWDY
66 Dean School of Nursing/Health Svcs Dr. Glynis D. BLACKARD

SAE Institute Atlanta (D)

215 Peachtree Street NE, Suite 300,
Atlanta GA 30303-1739
County: Fulton FICE Identification: 042066
Unit ID: 476948
Telephone: (404) 526-9366 Carnegie Class: Spec 2-yr-Tech
FAX Number: (404) 526-9367 Calendar System: Semester
URL: atlanta.sae.edu
Established: 1976 Annual Undergrad Tuition & Fees: N/A
Enrollment: 374 Coed
Affiliation or Control: Proprietary IRS Status: Proprietary
Highest Offering: Associate Degree
Accreditation: ACICS

01 Campus Director Mr. Ken WADE
05 Director of Education Dr. Sheila WILLIAMS

Savannah College of Art and Design (E)

342 Bull Street, PO Box 3146, Savannah GA 31402-6263
County: Chatham FICE Identification: 021415
Unit ID: 140951
Telephone: (912) 525-5000 Carnegie Class: Spec-4-yr-Arts
FAX Number: (912) 525-6263 Calendar System: Quarter
URL: www.scad.edu
Established: 1978 Annual Undergrad Tuition & Fees: $34,970
Enrollment: 11,347 Coed
Affiliation or Control: Independent Non-Profit IRS Status: 501(c)3
Highest Offering: Master's
Accreditation: SC, CIDA

01 President Mrs. Paula WALLACE
03 COO Vacant
10 Senior VP for Finance Mr. J.J WALLER
88 VP for Student Financial Services Mr. Scott LINZEY
21 VP for Business Operations Mr. Steve MINEO
46 Sr Vice Pres University Resources Mr. Glenn E. WALLACE, JR.
05 Chief Academic Officer Dr. Gokhan OZAYSIN
20 AVP for Acad Support/Legal Affairs Ms. Hannah FLOWER
12 Vice President for SCAD Atlanta Dr. Teresa GRIFFIS
12 Vice President for SCAD Hong Kong Mr. David PUGH
88 Dir of Strategic Content Ms. Cassandra HANDLEY
32 Vice President for Student Success Dr. Philip ALLETTO
13 VP for Information Technology Mr. Brad GRANT
106 VP for Strategy & Innovation Mr. John Paul ROWAN
07 Associate Vice President Admission Ms. Laura KENNEDY
15 VP for HR and Auxiliary Operations Mr. Jeff HARRIS
09 VP Special Projects and IE Ms. Erin O'LEARY
20 Dean of Academic Svcs Atlanta Mr. Dale CLIFFORD
26 Director of Univ Communications Ms. Ally HUGHES
18 Exec Dir of Physical Resources Ms. Helen MORGAN
08 Senior Director of Library Services Mr. Darrell NAYLOR-JOHNSON
37 Director of Financial Aid Ms. Kim BEVERIDGE
07 Exec Dir Adm Recruitment Ms. Jenny JAQUILLARD
19 Exec Director of Security Mr. John BUCKOVICH
41 Athletics Director Mr. Doug WOLLENBURG
38 Dir Counseling/Student Support Svc Mr. Christopher CORBETT
58 Sr Dir of Grad Studies & Registrar Ms. Sarah MCCARN
88 Dean of School of Building Arts Mr. Christian SOTTILE
88 Dean of School Communication Arts Mr. Anthony FISHER
88 Dean of School of Design Mr. Victor ERMOLI
88 Dean of School of Digital Media Ms. Tina O'HAILEY
57 Dean of School of Fine Arts Mr. Steve BLISS
49 Dean of School of Liberal Arts Dr. Beth CONCEPCION
88 Dean School of Fashion Mr. Michael FINK
88 Dean School of Foundation Studies Ms. Maureen GARVIN
88 Dean of Entertainment Arts Mr. Gregory BECK
36 Exec Dir of Career & Alumni Success Ms. Kimberly LOPEZ
44 Exec Director of Giving Ms. Tish CAMPBELL
20 Exec Dean of Academic Services Mr. Jesus ROJAS
108 AVP Inst Effectiv & Assessment Dr. Tara OVIEDO
35 Dean of Students Atlanta Mr. Art MALLOY

Savannah State University (F)

3219 College Street, Savannah GA 31404-5308
County: Chatham FICE Identification: 001590
Unit ID: 140960
Telephone: (912) 358-3004 Carnegie Class: Masters/S
FAX Number: N/A Calendar System: Semester
URL: www.savannahstate.edu
Established: 1890 Annual Undergrad Tuition & Fees (In-State): $5,644
Enrollment: 4,915 Coed
Affiliation or Control: State IRS Status: 501(c)3
Highest Offering: Master's
Accreditation: SC, BUS, ENGT, JOUR, SPAA, SW

01 University President Dr. Cheryl DOZIER
05 Interim Provost/VP Academic Affairs Dr. Kimberly HOLMES
10 Vice Pres Business & Finance Mr. Edward B. JOLLEY, JR.
32 Vice President Student Affairs Dr. Carl WALTON
30 VP Advancement/Exec Dir SSU Found Mr. Phillip D. ADAMS
13 Chief Information Officer Dr. Mable MOORE
50 Dean College Business Admin Dr. Mostafa SARHAN
81 Dean Col Science & Technology Dr. Jonathan LAMBRIGHT
49 Int Dean Col Liberal Arts/Soc Sci Dr. Julius SCIPIO
53 Dean School of Teacher Education Vacant
84 Assistant VP for Enrollment Mr. Descatur POTIER
26 Director Marketing/Communications Ms. Loretta HEYWARD
15 Assistant VP Human Resources Dr. Sandra M. BEST
08 Librarian Mrs. MaryJo FAYOYIN
19 Chief of Police Mr. James BARNWELL
18 Director Facilities/Physical Plant Mr. Ervin OGDEN
43 Dir Legal Services/General Counsel Mr. Joseph STEFFEN
09 Dir Inst Research/Plng/Assessment Dr. Michael G. CROW
29 Director Alumni Relations Ms. Barbara S. MYERS
37 Director Financial Aid Mr. Kenneth WILSON
41 Director Athletics Mr. Sterling STEWARD, JR.
35 Director of Student Development Ms. Jacqueline AWE
06 Registrar Ms. Wendy MERKOUSKO
04 Exec Asst to President Ms. Lisa SCIPIO
39 Director Student Housing Dr. Priscilla WILLIAMS

† Part of the University System of Georgia.

Savannah Technical College (G)

5717 White Bluff Road, Savannah GA 31405-5521
County: Chatham FICE Identification: 005618
Unit ID: 140942
Telephone: (912) 443-5700 Carnegie Class: Assoc/HVT-Mix Trad/Non
FAX Number: (912) 443-5705 Calendar System: Semester
URL: www.savannahtech.edu
Established: 1967 Annual Undergrad Tuition & Fees (In-State): $2,654
Enrollment: 4,644 Coed
Affiliation or Control: State IRS Status: 501(c)3
Highest Offering: Associate Degree
Accreditation: SC, ACFEI, DA, DH, ENGT, MAC, SURGT

01 President Dr. Kathy S. LOVE
05 Vice Pres Academic Affairs Dr. Ken BOYD
11 Vice Pres Administrative Services Ms. Sue Z. TURNER
32 Vice President Student Affairs Ms. Terrie O. SELLERS
45 Vice Pres Economic Development Mr. Kevin WERNTZ
84 Exec Director Enroll Mgmt/Marketing Ms. Gail EUBANKS
13 Exec Director Information Tech Mr. Jamie DAVIS
07 Director Admissions Ms. Gwendolyn MOORE
37 Director Financial Aid Ms. Faith ANDERSON
06 Registrar Ms. Regina THOMAS-WILLIAMS
18 Director Facilities/Operations Dr. Vic BURKE
37 Exec Dir Student Financial Services Ms. Teresa POTTS
15 Director Human Resources Ms. Melissa BANKS
88 Director Learning Enrichment Center Dr. Ethel BERKSTEINER
08 Library Services Director Mr. Jim BURCH
26 Director of Communications Ms. Amy SHAFFER
12 Campus Dean Liberty Campus Mr. Lonnie GRIFFIN
12 Campus Dean Effingham Campus Mr. Robert SOLOMON
96 Purchasing Manager Mr. Kevin CHIEVES
88 Dean Public Services Mr. Anthony FAUST
76 Dean Health Science Vacant
50 Dean Business and Technology Mr. Brendan FERRARA
97 Dean General Studies Mr. Brent STUBBS
88 Dean Industrial Technology Mr. Joseph POWELL
20 Dean Curriculum/Special Projects Dr. Kathleen MERRIGAN
88 Dean Aviation Mr. Tal LOOS
56 Adult Education Coordinator Dr. Charlene FORD

88 Military Outreach Coordinator .... Mr. Jeff ASHMEN
88 Student Navigator .... Mr. Mark STUMP

Shorter University (A)

315 Shorter Avenue, Rome GA 30165-4298
County: Floyd FICE Identification: 001591
Unit ID: 140988
Telephone: (706) 291-2121 Carnegie Class: Bac-Diverse
FAX Number: (706) 236-1515 Calendar System: Semester
URL: www.shorter.edu
Established: 1873 Annual Undergrad Tuition & Fees: $20,846
Enrollment: 1,566 Coed
Affiliation or Control: Baptist IRS Status: 501(c)3
Highest Offering: Master's
Accreditation: SC, MUS, NURSE

01 President .... Dr. Donald V. DOWLESS
05 Executive Vice President & Provost .... Dr. Donald L. MARTIN
11 VP for Administrative Affairs .... Vacant
10 VP for Finance & CFO .... Ms. Susan ZEIRD
84 Vice Pres Enrollment Management .... Dr. Emily MESSER
30 Vice President for Advancement .... Vacant
32 VP Student Affairs/Dean of Students .... Mr. Corey HUMPHRIES
26 Assoc VP University Communications .... Dr. Dawn C. TOLBERT
104 Asst Vice Pres International Pgms .... Mrs. Linda PALUMBO-OLSZANSKI
06 Registrar .... Mr. Justin MITCHELL
29 Director of Alumni Relations .... Mrs. Melissa WILLIAMS
35 Director of Student Life & Conduct .... Mr. Anthony CHATMAN
08 Director of Libraries .... Ms. Linda FLOYD
09 Director of Inst Planning/Research .... Mr. Matthew LE HEW
37 Director of Financial Aid .... Ms. Colleen LASSITER
15 Director Human Resources .... Mr. Tommy CURTIS
90 Director of Academic Computing .... Mr. Anthony J. NICHOLS
56 Director Special Programs .... Vacant
13 Director of Information Technology .... Mr. Jeff BRAMLETTE
18 Director of Facilities Management .... Mr. Bob BAGLEY
38 Director of Student Support Svcs .... Ms. Sara COLLIER
23 Director of Health Services .... Mrs. Mary SHOTWELL SMITH
41 Athletic Director .... Mr. Donald Kim GRAHAM
44 Director of Annual Giving .... Vacant
07 Director of Admissions .... Mr. Patrick MCELHANEY
39 Director Residence Life .... Mr. Anthony CHATMON
40 Bookstore Manager .... Ms. Cassie POTTS
57 Dean School of the Arts .... Dr. John REAMS
50 Interim Dean College of Business .... Mr. Heath HOOPER
49 Dean College of Arts & Sciences .... Dr. Kathi VOSEVICH
53 Dean School of Education .... Dr. Norma HARPER
56 Dean Coll Adult/Professional Pgms .... Dr. Amy AUSTIN
66 Dean School of Nursing .... Dr. Roxanne JOHNSTON
106 Director of Online Programs .... Vacant
81 Chair of Natural Sciences .... Mr. Clint HELMS
73 Chair Dept of Christian Studies .... Dr. Earle KELLETT
77 Chair Dept of Mathematics .... Dr. Diana SWANAGAN
60 Chair Dept of Communication Arts .... Dr. Cassandra JOHNSON
83 Chair Dept of Social Sciences .... Dr. Barsha PICKELL
42 Campus Minister .... Rev. David E. ROLAND

South Georgia State College (B)

100 W College Park Drive, Douglas GA 31533-5098
County: Coffee FICE Identification: 001592
Unit ID: 482699
Telephone: (912) 260-4394 Carnegie Class: Bac/Assoc-Assoc Dom
FAX Number: (912) 260-4454 Calendar System: Semester
URL: www.sgsc.edu
Established: 1906 Annual Undergrad Tuition & Fees (In-State): $3,211
Enrollment: 2,611 Coed
Affiliation or Control: State IRS Status: 501(c)3
Highest Offering: Baccalaureate
Accreditation: SC, ADNUR, NUR

01 Interim President .... Dr. Ingrid THOMPSON-SELLERS
05 Vice Pres Academic Affairs .... Dr. Robert PAGE
32 Vice President for Student Success .... Ms. Lynn MCCRANEY
10 Vice President for Fiscal Affairs .... Mr. Mark LATHAM
30 Vice President for External Affairs .... Ms. Walda KIGHT
18 Vice President for Operations .... Mr. Keith NEWELL
20 Asst Vice Pres for Academic Affairs .... Dr. Rick REIMAN
13 Chief Info Technology Officer .... Mr. Jimmy HARPER
08 Director of Libraries .... Ms. Jacqueline VICKERS
06 Registrar .... Ms. Ame WILKERSON
37 Director of Financial Aid .... Vacant
15 Director of Human Resources .... Mr. Ryan SCONYERS
07 Director of Admissions .... Ms. Angela WASDIN
12 Dir of Entry Programs and Planning .... Ms. Valerie WEBSTER
40 Bookstore Manager .... Ms. Daphne FRENCH
35 Dean of Students .... Dr. Greg TANNER
09 Dir of Institutional Effectiveness .... Ms. Danielle SUTLIFF
19 Campus Poilice Chief .... Ms. Sonja MCCULLOCH
26 Marketing Coordinator .... Ms. Courtney SEARS

† Part of the University System of Georgia.

South Georgia Technical College (C)

900 South Georgia Tech Parkway,
Americus GA 31709-8167
County: Sumter FICE Identification: 005617
Unit ID: 141006
Telephone: (229) 931-2394 Carnegie Class: Assoc/HVT-Mix Trad/Non
FAX Number: (229) 931-2924 Calendar System: Semester
URL: www.southgatech.edu
Established: 1948 Annual Undergrad Tuition & Fees (In-State): $2,724
Enrollment: 1,658 Coed
Affiliation or Control: State IRS Status: 501(c)3
Highest Offering: Associate Degree
Accreditation: SC

01 President .... Dr. John WATFORD
11 Vice Pres Administrative Services .... Lea COE
10 Vice Pres Business & Industry Svcs .... Wally SUMMERS
05 Vice President for Academic Affairs .... David KUIPERS
09 Vice Pres of Institutional Support .... Karen J. WERLING
04 Special Assistant to the President .... Don SMITH
20 Dean of Academic Affairs .... Raymond HOLT
20 Dean of Academic Affairs .... Vanessa WALL
20 Dean of Academic Affairs .... Dr. Andrea OATES
20 Dean of Academic Affairs .... Dr. David FINLEY
26 Vice Pres Institutional Advancement .... Su Ann BIRD
13 Technology Director .... Wray SKIPPER
37 Director of Financial Aid .... Carrie WILDER
15 Director Personnel Services .... Sancy LARSON
32 Director of Campus Life .... Cynthia CARTER
21 Director of Accounting .... Robin BELL
88 Director of Administrative Services .... Mark BROOKS
06 Registrar .... Julie PARTAIN
08 Librarian .... Jerry STOVALL
07 Director of Admissions .... Whitney CRISP
41 Athletic Director .... James FREY
29 Director Alumni Relations .... SuAnn BIRD
38 Director Student Counseling .... LaKenya JOHNSON
84 Director Enrollment Management .... Whitney CRISP
18 Chief Facilities/Physical Plant .... Don SMITH
96 Purchasing Agent .... Gail CLARY
19 Director Security/Safety .... Sammy STONE

South University (D)

709 Mall Boulevard, Savannah GA 31406-4881
County: Chatham FICE Identification: 013039
Unit ID: 139579
Telephone: (912) 201-8000 Carnegie Class: Masters/M
FAX Number: (912) 201-8070 Calendar System: Quarter
URL: www.southuniversity.edu
Established: 1899 Annual Undergrad Tuition & Fees: $16,761
Enrollment: 1,490 Coed
Affiliation or Control: Proprietary IRS Status: Proprietary
Highest Offering: Doctorate
Accreditation: SC, AA, ACBSP, ARCPA, CACREP, MAC, NURSE, PHAR, PTAA

01 Chancellor .... Mr. John T. SOUTH, III
12 President At Charlotte Campus .... Mr. Mark MARTIN
12 President At Raleigh-Durham Campus .... Mr. Christopher MESECAR
12 President At Dallas Campus .... Ms. Barbara JANOWSKI
12 President At Fort Worth Campus .... Vacant
12 President Montgomery Campus .... Mr. Victor K. BIEBIGHAUSER
12 President West Palm Beach Campus .... Mr. Thomas CREOLA
12 President Columbia Campus .... Dr. David SHOOP
12 President Novi Campus .... Ms. Sheila MALEWSKA
12 President Richmond Campus .... Mr. Troy RALSTON
12 President Tampa Campus .... Dr. Bob BOHMAN
12 President Virginia Beach Campus .... Vacant
12 President Austin Campus .... Ms. Shelby FRUTCHEY
12 President Cleveland Campus .... Mr. Scott BEHMER
12 President High Point Campus .... Mr. Michael TREMBLEY
12 President Savannah Campus .... Dr. Todd CELLINI
13 Assoc Chanc Information Technology .... Mr. James FREYBURGER
14 Regional Campus Technology Manager .... Mr. Dustin BARRETT
11 Vice Chanc South Campuses .... Mr. David MCGURE
106 Vice Chanc Online & Strat Operation .... Mr. Steven READ
05 Vice Chancellor Academic Affairs .... Dr. Jay STUBBLEFIELD
20 Assoc Vice Chanc Academic Affairs .... Dr. Destini COPP
20 Assoc Vice Chan Academic Affairs .... Vacant
20 Assoc Vice Chan Academic Affairs .... Dr. Devin BYRD
08 Interim Asst Vice Chanc Univ Libr .... Ms. Nancy SPEISSER
06 University Registrar .... Ms. Anita MACIAS
20 Asst Vice Chanc Academic Services .... Dr. Tamara AVANT
09 Sr Director Inst Effectiveness .... Dr. Frances W. OBLANDER
108 Director for Academic Assessment .... Ms. Elizabeth DEVITA
20 Dir QEP & Academic Project Manager .... Dr. Reinhold GERBSCH
49 Dean College of Arts and Sciences .... Vacant
50 Dean College of Business .... Dr. Cheryl NOLL
107 Dean College of Health Professions .... Dr. Scott MCPHEE
66 Dean College of Nursing .... Dr. Mable H. SMITH
67 Dean School of Pharmacy .... Dr. Curtis JONES
57 Dean College Creative Art & Design .... Dr. Leslie BAUGHMAN
73 Dean College of Theology .... Dr. Robert R. REDMAN, JR.
07 Vice Chancellor for Admissions .... Mr. Matthew MILLS
84 Regional Director of Admissions .... Mr. Matt SWANSON
84 Regional Director of Admissions .... Ms. Ashley WEEKS
28 ADA Training Manager .... Ms. Ashley JOHNSON
15 Assoc Chancellor of Human Resources .... Ms. Lynne HAINES
16 Senior Human Resources Generalist .... Ms. Christy SHAPARD
88 Human Resources Generalist .... Ms. Jamie FRAZIER-HELD
32 Asst Chancellor for Student Affairs .... Ms. Alisa KROUSE
36 University Director Career Services .... Ms. Paula REISING
10 Vice Chancellor for Finance .... Mr. John PAPP
37 Asst Chanc Student Financial Svcs .... Ms. Kacey ATKINSON
26 Associate Chancellor for Marketing .... Mr. Jeff BEAMON
27 Digital Marketing Director .... Ms. Kalani ROBINSON
27 Marketing Director SU Online .... Mr. John MAASS

Southeastern Technical College (E)

3001 E First Street, Vidalia GA 30474-8817
County: Toombs FICE Identification: 030665
Unit ID: 368911
Telephone: (912) 538-3100 Carnegie Class: Assoc/HVT-Mix Trad/Non
FAX Number: (912) 538-3156 Calendar System: Semester
URL: www.southeasterntech.edu
Established: 1989 Annual Undergrad Tuition & Fees (In-State): $2,774
Enrollment: 1,623 Coed
Affiliation or Control: State IRS Status: 501(c)3
Highest Offering: Associate Degree
Accreditation: SC, DH, EMT, MAC, MLTAD, RAD

01 President .... Mr. Larry CALHOUN
05 Vice Pres Academic Affairs .... Ms. Teresa COLEMAN
11 Vice Pres Administrative Services .... Ms. Denise POWELL
10 Vice President Fiscal Affairs .... Vacant
32 Vice President Student Affairs .... Dr. Barry DOTSON
84 Director Enrollment Services .... Mr. Brad HART
06 Registrar .... Ms. Karen VEREEN
37 Director Financial Aid .... Mr. Mitchell FAGLER
36 Director Job Placement .... Mr. Lance HELMS
103 Special Populations Coordinator .... Ms. Helen THOMAS
40 Bookstore Manager .... Ms. Stacy FREEMAN
26 Dir Marketing & Public Relations .... Ms. Krysta RUSHING
08 Head Librarian .... Mrs. Leah DASHER
19 Director Security/Safety .... Mr. Travis AKRIDGE

Southern Crescent Technical College (F)

501 Varsity Road, Griffin GA 30223-2042
County: Spalding FICE Identification: 005621
Unit ID: 139986
Telephone: (770) 228-7348 Carnegie Class: Assoc/HVT-Mix Trad/Non
FAX Number: (770) 229-3227 Calendar System: Semester
URL: www.sctech.edu
Established: 1963 Annual Undergrad Tuition & Fees (In-State): $4,122
Enrollment: 4,898 Coed
Affiliation or Control: State IRS Status: 501(c)3
Highest Offering: Associate Degree
Accreditation: SC, CAHIIM, COARC, COARCP, DA, EMT, MAC, SURGT

01 President .... Dr. Randall PETERS
03 Executive Vice President .... Mr. Mark ANDREWS
05 Vice Pres for Academic Affairs .... Dr. Dawn HODGES
32 Vice Pres for Student Affairs .... Dr. Xenia JOHNS
10 Vice Pres Administrative Services .... Ms. Miriam CASLIN
18 Vice Pres Facilities/Operations .... Mr. Jim BROWN
30 Vice President Advancement .... Ms. Barbara Jo COOK
46 Vice Pres Inst Effectiveness .... Ms. Melissa GORDON
06 Registrar .... Ms. Kathlyn BURDEN
26 Dir Marketing & Public Relations .... Ms. Anna TAYLOR
37 Director of Financial Aid .... Ms. Kimberly MORRIS
49 Dean Business Tech Arts & Sciences/ .... Ms. Rebecca JOHNSON
76 Dean Allied Health .... Mr. Michael MELVIN
75 Dean Personal Svcs/Public Safety .... Mr. Lemuel MERCADO
75 Dean Industrial Technical Studies .... Mr. Alan STANFIELD
106 Dean Computer Info Services .... Ms. Tempie KITCHENS
84 Director of Enrollment Management .... Dr. Jasper FOUST
15 Director of Human Resources .... Ms. Sharon IRBY
35 Director of Student Affairs .... Ms. Cherryl GILBERT
21 Director of Administrative Services .... Ms. Gina BYRD
36 Director of Career Services .... Ms. Susan MURRAY
19 Campus Police Chief .... Mr. Kenneth TROISI
13 Chief Information Officer .... Mr. Michael SHIVER
75 Dean Adult Education .... Ms. Sharon CLOUD
88 Dean Film Technology .... Mr. Douglas BRUCE

Southern Regional Technical College (G)

15689 US Highway 19 N, Thomasville GA 31792-2622
County: Thomas FICE Identification: 005615
Unit ID: 141158
Telephone: (229) 225-4096 Carnegie Class: Assoc/HVT-Mix Trad/Non
FAX Number: (229) 225-4330 Calendar System: Semester
URL: www.southernregional.edu
Established: 2015 Annual Undergrad Tuition & Fees (In-State): N/A
Enrollment: 1,541 Coed
Affiliation or Control: State IRS Status: 501(c)3
Highest Offering: Associate Degree
Accreditation: SC, ADNUR, EMT, MAC, MLTAD, SURGT

01 President .... Dr. Craig R. WENTWORTH
11 Vice Pres Administrative Services .... Mr. Ross COX
05 Vice Pres Academic Affairs .... Dr. Annie L. MCELROY
32 Vice President Student Affairs .... Ms. Leigh WALLACE
30 Vice President Economic Development .... Mr. Dennis LEE
09 VP Institutional Effectiveness .... Dr. Debbie GOODMAN
76 Dean School of Health Sciences .... Ms. Carla BARROW
50 Dean School of Bus/Industrial Tech .... Ms. Abby CARTER
107 Dean School of Professional Svcs .... Ms. Tina STRICKLAND
49 Dean School of Art and Sciences .... Ms. Kathryn KENT
37 Executive Director Financial Aid .... Ms. Judi LOVVORN
26 VP Marketing/Inst Devel/Pub Rels .... Ms. Amy MAISON
88 Director Adult Education .... Ms. Melissa BURTLE
07 Director of Admissions .... Ms. Wanda HANCOCK
35 Director Student Affairs .... Ms. Lisa GRIFFIN
06 Registrar .... Ms. Wendi TOSTENSON

08 Executive Director Library Services ... Ms. Udella SPICER
36 Dir Career Services & Counseling ... Dr. Jeanine LONG
15 Director Human Resources ... Mr. Michael HEARD
18 VP Operations ... Mr. David EVANS

Spelman College (A)

350 Spelman Lane, SW, Atlanta GA 30314-4399
County: Fulton FICE Identification: 001594
Unit ID: 141060
Telephone: (404) 681-3643 Carnegie Class: Bac-A&S
FAX Number: N/A Calendar System: Semester
URL: www.spelman.edu
Established: 1881 Annual Undergrad Tuition & Fees: $26,388
Enrollment: 2,135 Female
Affiliation or Control: Independent Non-Profit IRS Status: 501(c)3
Highest Offering: Baccalaureate
Accreditation: SC, MUS, TED

01 President ... Dr. Mary SCHMIDT CAMPBELL
05 Int Provost & VP Academic Affairs ... Dr. Myra BURNETT
88 Special Assistant to the Provost ... Dr. Dolores BRADLEY BRENNAN
10 VP Business/Financial Affairs/ Treas ... Mr. Robert D. FLANIGAN, JR.
32 Vice President for Student Affairs ... Dr. Darnita KILLIAN
26 Vice President College Relations ... Ms. Jane SMITH
84 Vice Pres Enrollment Management ... Ms. Ingrid HAYES
30 Associate VP for Development ... Ms. Reshunda MAHONE
88 Director of Budgets & Contracts ... Ms. Rhonda HONEGAN
21 Controller ... Ms. April AUSTIN
101 Secretary of College ... Dr. Terri REED
27 Director Marketing & Communications ... Ms. Joyce E. DAVIS
04 Executive Assistant ... Ms. Jarvis RIDGES
13 VP of MIT & Chief Info Officer ... Ms. Delores BARTON
105 Dir Bonner Comm Svcs/Student Dev ... Ms. Jilo TISDALE
20 Dean of Undergraduate Studies ... Dr. Desiree PEDESCLEAUX
42 Director Sisters Center for WISDOM ... Rev. Lisa D. RHODES
06 Registrar ... Mr. John BROWN
07 Director of Admissions ... Ms. Tiffany NELSON
27 Director Publications ... Ms. Jo Moore STEWART
29 Director of Alumnae Affairs ... Ms. Sharon OWENS
37 Assoc Dir of Financial Aid ... Ms. Thresa GAY
36 Director Career Planning/Devel ... Mr. Harold BELL
78 Director of Cooperative Education ... Mr. Keith WEBB
15 Director Human Resources ... Ms. Bernadette COHEN
38 Director Counseling Services ... Dr. Ave MARSHALL
09 Dir Inst Rsrch/Assessment/Planning ... Ms. Jill TRIPLETT
88 Director Women's Resource Center ... Dr. Beverly GUY-SHEFTALL
18 Director Facilities/Mgmt & Svcs ... Mr. Arthur E. FRAZIER, III
19 Director of Public Safety ... Mr. Steve BOWSER
24 Educational Technology Coordinator ... Ms. Natasha BROWN
46 Associate Provost of Research ... Vacant
102 Dir of Corp & Foundation Relations ... Ms. Shelese LANE
88 Director of Special Events ... Ms. Heather HAWES
39 Director Housing & Residential Life ... Ms. Alison CUMMINGS
86 Director Title III/Government Rels ... Ms. Helga GREENFIELD
88 Coordinator of Inclusion Division ... Ms. Letitia J. DENARD
85 Council on Intl Educ Exchange ... Ms. Theresa METZGER
08 Library Director/CEO ... Ms. Loretta PARHAM
23 Director Health Services ... Ms. Brenda DALTON
25 Director Sponsored Programs ... Dr. Claudia SCHOLZ
35 Dean of Students ... Ms. Fran'Cee BROWN MCCLURE
40 Bookstore Manager ... Ms. Tiffani HODGE
41 Int Dir Physical Educ & Athletics ... Ms. Joyce TERRELL
96 Dir Administrative Support Svcs ... Ms. Jacqueline JAMES
44 Director of Donor Relations ... Ms. Stacy LYONS
88 Director of Budgets & Contracts ... Ms. Dawn ALSTON

Thomas University (B)

1501 Millpond Road, Thomasville GA 31792-7499
County: Thomas FICE Identification: 001555
Unit ID: 141167
Telephone: (229) 226-1621 Carnegie Class: Masters/S
FAX Number: (229) 226-1653 Calendar System: Semester
URL: www.thomasu.edu
Established: 1950 Annual Undergrad Tuition & Fees: $16,400
Enrollment: 1,138 Coed
Affiliation or Control: Independent Non-Profit IRS Status: 501(c)3
Highest Offering: Master's
Accreditation: SC, #CORE, IACBE, MT, NUR, SW

01 President ... Dr. Andy SHEPPARD
05 Provost & Exec Vice President ... Dr. Ann LANDIS
30 Vice Pres Institutional Advancement ... Dr. Grady ENLOW
08 Univ Librarian/Dir Info Services ... Ms. Lynn KELLY
06 Registrar ... Mr. Richard VAUPEL
09 Director of Institutional Research ... Danae JOHNSON
84 Assoc VP Enrollment Management ... Dr. Jill DENNIS
37 Director of Financial Aid ... Ms. Chrissy GAINOUS
41 Director of Athletics ... Mr. Michael D. LEE
10 Controller ... Ms. Sue STONE
32 Student Life/Athletics Coordinator ... Vacant
44 Director of Annual Fund ... Ms. Heather CAIRNS
26 Director of Communications ... Mrs. Cindy MONTGOMERY
04 Assistant to the President ... Mrs. Linda M. HERNDON

Toccoa Falls College (C)

107 Kincaid Drive, Toccoa Falls GA 30598-0068
County: Stephens FICE Identification: 001596
Unit ID: 141185
Telephone: (706) 886-6831 Carnegie Class: Bac-Diverse
FAX Number: (706) 282-6005 Calendar System: Semester
URL: www.tfc.edu
Established: 1907 Annual Undergrad Tuition & Fees: $20,710
Enrollment: 920 Coed
Affiliation or Control: The Christian And Missionary Alliance
IRS Status: 501(c)3
Highest Offering: Baccalaureate
Accreditation: SC, MUS

01 President ... Dr. Robert M. MYERS
04 Sr Exec Administrative Assistant ... Mrs. Paula S. ELKINS
32 VP Student Affairs ... Dr. Ken W. GASSIOT
30 VP for Advancement ... Mr. Lee P. YOWELL
10 Vice President for Finance ... Mr. R. Gregg SCHULTE
05 Provost/VP for Academic Affairs ... Dr. W. Brian SHELTON
84 VP for Enrollment Services ... Mr. James ZUGELDER
42 Director Spiritual Formation ... Mr. Chris STRATTON
09 Director Institutional Research ... Dr. Kieran CLEMENTS
106 Director of Distance Education ... Ms. Anna MCCLATCHY
39 Director Residence/Community Life ... Mrs. Emily SPROWLS
29 Director Alumni Assoc/Col Relations ... Mrs. Deborah WILKES
38 Dir Stdnt Health/Career Servs ... Mr. Johnathan C. KERR
37 Director Student Financial Aid ... Mr. Stuart SPIRES
07 Director of Admissions ... Mr. Zack WHITT
06 Registrar ... Mr. Kelly G. VICKERS
41 Athletic Director ... Mr. Mac INGMIRE
18 Chief Facilities/Physical Plant ... Mr. Merlin SCHENCK
19 Director of Security/Safety ... Mr. Stephen JOHANNES
15 Director Human Resources ... Ms. Mary Kaye RITCHEY
40 Director of Business Services ... Mrs. Helen GENTRY

Truett McConnell College (D)

100 Alumni Drive, Cleveland GA 30528-1264
County: White FICE Identification: 001597
Unit ID: 141237
Telephone: (706) 865-2134 Carnegie Class: Bac-Diverse
FAX Number: (706) 243-4968 Calendar System: Semester
URL: www.truett.edu
Established: 1946 Annual Undergrad Tuition & Fees: $18,000
Enrollment: 1,681 Coed
Affiliation or Control: Baptist IRS Status: 501(c)3
Highest Offering: Master's
Accreditation: SC, MUS, NURSE

01 President ... Dr. Emir CANER
05 Vice Pres Academic Services ... Dr. Brad REYNOLDS
11 Vice Pres Administrative Svcs ... Dr. David ARMSTRONG
32 Vice President of Student Services ... Mr. Chris EPPLING
10 VP Finance/Operations/Gen Counsel ... Dr. Joe WIEGAND
04 Executive Assistant to President ... Ms. Cindy ERBELE
41 Athletic Director ... Dr. Stacy HALL
06 Registrar/Dir Inst Research ... Mrs. Melissa FORTNER
37 Director of Financial Aid ... Mr. Truitt FRANKLIN
08 Director of Library Resources ... Mrs. Teresa HAYMORE
29 Director of Alumni Relations ... Dr. John YARBROUGH
07 Admissions Diector ... Mr. Andrew GAILEY
42 Director of Church Relations ... Dr. David DRAKE
40 Campus Store Director ... Mr. Eddie O'BRIEN

University of Georgia (E)

Athens GA 30602-0001
County: Clarke FICE Identification: 001598
Unit ID: 139959
Telephone: (706) 542-3000 Carnegie Class: DU-Highest
FAX Number: N/A Calendar System: Semester
URL: www.uga.edu
Established: 1785 Annual Undergrad Tuition & Fees (In-State): $11,622
Enrollment: 35,197 Coed
Affiliation or Control: State IRS Status: 501(c)3
Highest Offering: Doctorate
Accreditation: SC, AAFCS, ART, BUS, BUSA, CAATE, CACREP, CIDA, CLPSY, COPSY, CS, DANCE, DIETD, DIETI, ENG, JOUR, LAW, LSAR, MFCD, MUS, PCSAS, PH, PHAR, SCPSY, SP, SPAA, SW, TED, THEA, VET

01 President ... Dr. Jere W. MOREHEAD
100 Chief of Staff ... Dr. Kathy R. PHARR
04 Assistant to the President ... Dr. Kyle TSCHEPIKOW
04 Assistant to the President ... Mr. Arthur TRIPP, JR.
05 Sr VP Academic Affs/Provost ... Dr. Pamela WHITTEN
10 Sr Assoc VP Finance & Admin ... Mr. James SHORE
20 Vice Provost Academic Affairs ... Dr. Russ MUMPER
11 Vice Pres for Finance & Admin ... Mr. Ryan A. NESBIT
26 Vice Pres for Develop & Alumni Rel ... Mr. Kelly K. KERNER
20 Vice President for Instruction ... Dr. Rahul SHRIVASTAV
46 Vice President for Research ... Dr. David C. LEE
88 Vice Pres Public Svc/Outreach ... Dr. Jennifer L. FRUM
32 Vice President Student Affairs ... Dr. Victor K. WILSON
86 Vice President for Govt Relations ... Mr. J. Griffin DOYLE
27 Vice President for Marketing & Comm ... Ms. Karri HOBSON-PAPE
92 Assoc Prov/Dir of Honors Program ... Dr. David S. WILLIAMS
104 Int Assoc Prov International Educ ... Dr. Noel FALLOWS
28 Assoc Prov/Chief Diversity Officer ... Dr. Michelle G. COOK
20 Assoc Provost Academic Programs ... Dr. Margaret AMSTUTZ
13 VP for Information Technology ... Dr. Timothy M. CHESTER
08 Assoc Provost/University Librarian ... Dr. Toby GRAHAM
88 Assoc Provost Faculty Affairs ... Ms. Sarah COVERT
07 Assoc VP Admissions/Enroll Mgmt ... Mr. Patrick WINTER
21 Assoc VP & Controller ... Ms. Holley W. SCHRAMSKI
18 Assoc VP Facilities Management ... Mr. Ralph F. JOHNSON
15 Associate VP Human Resources ... Mr. Juan JARRETT
43 Executive Director Legal Affairs ... Mr. Michael RAEBER
49 Dean of Arts & Sciences ... Dr. Alan T. DORSEY
47 Dean of Agricultural & Environ Sci ... Dr. Samuel PARDUE
61 Dean of Law ... Mr. Peter RUTLEDGE
67 Dean of Pharmacy ... Dr. Svein OIE
65 Dean Forestry & Natural Resources ... Dr. Dale GREENE
53 Dean of Education ... Dr. Craig H. KENNEDY
58 Dean of the Graduate School ... Dr. Suzanne BARBOUR
50 Dean of Business ... Dr. Benjamin C. AYERS
60 Dean Journalism & Mass Comm ... Dr. Charles N. DAVIS
59 Dean of Family & Consumer Sci ... Dr. Linda K. FOX
74 Dean of Veterinary Medicine ... Dr. Sheila W. ALLEN
70 Dean of Social Work ... Dr. Maurice C. DANIELS
48 Dean of Environment & Design ... Mr. Daniel J. NADENICEK
80 Dean of Public/International Affs ... Dr. Stefanie A. LINDQUIST
69 Dean of Public Health ... Dr. Phillip L. WILLIAMS
88 Dean School of Ecology ... Dr. John L. GITTLEMAN
88 Dean GHSU/UGA Medical ... Dr. Shelley NUSS
54 Dean of Engineering ... Dr. Donald LEO
41 Athletic Director ... Mr. William G. MCGARITY
22 Director of Equal Opportunity ... Ms. E. Janyce DAWKINS
06 Registrar ... Dr. Jan M. HATHCOTE
19 Chief of Police ... Chief James E. WILLIAMSON
37 Director of Student Financial Aid ... Ms. Bonnie C. JOERSCHKE
36 Director of Career Services Center ... Mr. Scott T. WILLIAMS
39 Executive Director of Housing ... Dr. Gerard J. KOWALSKI
23 Exec Director of Health Services ... Dr. Jean E. CHIN
35 Dean of Students ... Dr. William M. MCDONALD
38 Dir Counseling/Psychological Svcs ... Dr. Gayle M. ROBBINS
88 Interim Director Georgia Center ... Dr. Lawrence S. DEMPSEY
29 Exec Dir of Alumni Relations ... Ms. Meredith G. JOHNSON
30 Sr Assoc VP for Dev & Alumni Rel ... Mr. Jay STROMAN
09 Director of Institutional Research ... Mr. Paul KLUTE
88 Interim Dir of Academic Enhancement ... Dr. Naomi NORMAN
94 Director Inst of Women's Studies ... Dr. Juanita JOHNSON-BAILEY
96 Director of Purchasing ... Ms. Annette EVANS
106 Dir Online Education/E-learning ... Dr. Keith BAILEY
108 Sr Director for Accreditation ... Mr. Allan AYCOCK
44 Exec Dir Annual or Planned Giving ... Mr. David JONES
88 Director Office of Economic Dev ... Mr. Sean MCMILLAN

† Part of the University System of Georgia.

University of North Georgia (F)

82 College Circle, Dahlonega GA 30597-1001
County: Lumpkin FICE Identification: 001585
Unit ID: 482680
Telephone: (706) 864-1400 Carnegie Class: Masters/M
FAX Number: (706) 864-1478 Calendar System: Semester
URL: ung.edu
Established: 1873 Annual Undergrad Tuition & Fees (In-State): $4,403
Enrollment: 16,064 Coed
Affiliation or Control: State IRS Status: 501(c)3
Highest Offering: Doctorate
Accreditation: SC, ART, BUS, CAATE, CACREP, CSHSE, NUR, PTA, TED

01 President ... Dr. Bonita JACOBS
05 Provost & Sr VP Academic Affairs ... Dr. Tom ORMOND
10 Sr VP Business & Finance ... Mr. Frank J. MCCONNELL
11 Sr VP Leadership & Global Engage ... Dr. Billy WELLS
32 VP Student Affairs ... Dr. Janet MARLING
12 VP of Gainesville Campus ... Dr. Richard OATES
30 VP of University Advancement ... Mr. Jeff TARNOWSKI
20 Int Assoc Provost Academic Affairs ... Dr. Chaudron GILLE
108 Assoc Provost Inst Effectiveness ... Dr. Denise YOUNG
46 Assoc Prov & Chief Research Officer ... Dr. Andy NOVOBILSKI
88 Assoc VP & Dean Univ College ... Dr. Carol ADAMS
58 Assoc VP Graduate Studies ... Dr. Bill GASH
21 Assoc VP Finan Srvcs & Comptroller ... Ms. Donna CALDWELL
109 Assoc VP Aux Services & Real Estate ... Mr. Gerald SULLIVAN
13 Chief Information Officer ... Mr. Brandon HAAG
84 Assoc VP Enrollment Management ... Ms. Sallie MCMULLIN
35 Assoc VP Stdnt Aff & Dean of Stdnts ... Dr. Cara RAY
35 Asst VP Stdnt Affs & Dean of Stdnts ... Dr. Michelle BROWN
35 Asst VP Stdnt Affs & Dean of Stdnts ... Ms. Alyson PAUL
29 Director Alumni Relations & Annual ... Ms. Wendy HUGULEY
106 Dir Distance Educ/Tech Integration ... Dr. Irene KOKKALA
07 Int Exec Director UG Admissions ... Ms. Molly POTTS
07 Director of Cadet Admissions ... Mr. Tony MOSS
92 Dean of Honors Program ... Dr. Tanya BENNETT
41 Director of Athletics ... Ms. Lindsay REEVES
88 Director of Internal Audit ... Ms. Jill HOLMAN
06 University Registrar ... Mr. Steve STUBBS
25 Director of Grants & Contracts ... Ms. Kelley ROBERTS
37 Director of Financial Aid ... Ms. Jill RAYNER
09 Director Institutional Research ... Ms. Linda ROWLAND
08 Dean of Libraries ... Dr. Deborah PROSSER
49 Dean College of Arts & Letters ... Dr. Christopher JESPERSEN
50 Dean M C College of Business ... Dr. Donna MAYO
53 Dean of College of Education ... Dr. Susan AYRES
81 Dean College of Sci & Mathematics ... Dr. Michael BODRI
76 Dean College of Health Sciences ... Dr. Teresa CONNER-KERR
104 Assoc VP International Programs ... Dr. John WILSON
15 Assoc VP Human Resources ... Ms. Beth ARBUTHNOT
18 Asst VP of Facilities ... Mr. Todd BERMANN
19 Director of Public Safety ... Mr. Justin GAINES
14 Deputy CIO ... Mr. Steve MCLEOD
26 Assoc VP of University Relations ... Ms. Kate MAINE
20 Commandant Corp of Cadets ... Col. James PALMER
36 Director of Career Services ... Vacant
38 Director Counseling Services ... Dr. Simon CORDERY
39 Director of Residence Life ... Ms. Treva SMITH
23 Director of Student Health Services ... Ms. Karen TOMLINSON

12 Exec Dir Cumming Campus .... Mr. Jason PRUITT
12 CEO Oconee Campus .... Vacant
108 Dir Accreditation & Assessment .... Ms. Betsy CANTRELL
88 Director of Estate & Gift Planning .... Mr. Jeff BOGGAN
51 Director Continuing Education .... Dr. Wendy ESTES
86 Assoc VP Econ Dev & Cmty Engagement .... Dr. Edward MIENIE
43 General Counsel & Dir Gov Relations .... Ms. Jenna COLVIN
96 Director Purchasing .... Ms. Beverly LONG
22 Dir Student Disability Services .... Mr. Thomas MCCOY
85 Dir Multicultural Student Affairs .... Mr. Robert ROBINSON
04 Admin Asst to the President .... Ms. Linda SMITH
28 Diversity Advisor to President .... Ms. Sheila CALDWELL
105 Director Web Services .... Ms. Joanie CHEMBARS
91 Director Administrative Computing .... Mr. Rick CRAIN

† Part of the University System of Georgia.

University of Phoenix Atlanta Campus (A)

8200 Roberts Drive, Sandy Springs GA 30350-4147
Telephone: (678) 731-0555 Identification: 770200
Accreditation: &NH, ACBSP

† Regional accreditation is carried under the parent institution in Tempe, AZ

University of Phoenix Augusta Campus (B)

3150 Perimeter Parkway, Augusta GA 30909-4583
Telephone: (706) 868-2000 Identification: 770198
Accreditation: &NH, ACBSP

† Regional accreditation is carried under the parent institution in Tempe, AZ

University of Phoenix Columbus GA Campus (C)

7200 North Lake Drive, Columbus GA 31909
Telephone: (706) 320-1266 Identification: 770199
Accreditation: &NH, ACBSP

† Regional accreditation is carried under the parent institution in Tempe, AZ

University of Phoenix Savannah Campus (D)

8001 Chatham Center Drive, Savannah GA 31405-7400
Telephone: (912) 232-0531 Identification: 770201
Accreditation: &NH, ACBSP

† No longer accepting campus-based students.

University of West Georgia (E)

1601 Maple Street, Carrollton GA 30118-0001
County: Carroll FICE Identification: 001601
Unit ID: 141334
Telephone: (678) 839-5000 Carnegie Class: DU-Mod
FAX Number: N/A Calendar System: Semester
URL: www.westga.edu
Established: 1906 Annual Undergrad Tuition & Fees (In-State): $6,143
Enrollment: 12,206 Coed
Affiliation or Control: State IRS Status: 501(c)3
Highest Offering: Doctorate
Accreditation: SC, ART, BUS, BUSA, CACREP, CS, MUS, NURSE, SP, SPAA, TED, THEA

01 President .... Dr. Kyle MARRERO
05 Provost & VP for Academic Affairs .... Dr. Michael CRAFTON
10 Exec VP for Business & Finance .... Mr. Jim SUTHERLAND
32 VP for Student Affairs & Enroll Mgt .... Dr. Scott LINGRELL
26 VP for University Advancement .... Mr. Dave FRABONI
30 Director of Development .... Ms. Diane HOMESLEY
84 AVP for Enrollment Management .... Dr. John HEAD
20 Associate VP for Academic Affairs .... Dr. Myrna GANTNER
21 University Controller .... Mr. Richard SEARS
83 Dean Social Sciences .... Dr. N. Jane MCCANDLESS
50 Dean Richards College of Business .... Dr. Faye S. MCINTYRE
53 Dean Education .... Dr. Dianne HOFF
79 Interim Dean Arts & Humanities .... Dr. Pauline GAGNON
81 Interim Dean Science & Mathematics .... Dr. Scott GORDON
92 Dean Honors College .... Dr. Janet DONOHOE
06 Registrar .... Ms. Donna HALEY
07 Director Admissions .... Mr. Justin BARLOW
08 Dean of Libraries .... Ms. Lorene FLANDERS
37 Director Financial Aid .... Dr. Philip HAWKINS
36 Director Career Services .... Ms. Keri BURNS
13 Chief Information Officer .... Mrs. Kathy KRAL
51 Director Continuing Education .... Mr. Marty DAVIS
15 Dir of Human Resources .... Ms. Juanita HICKS
18 Asst VP Campus Planning/Facilities .... Mr. Brendan BOWEN
19 Chief of University Police .... Mr. Thomas J. MACKEL
23 Director Health Services .... Dr. Leslie COTTRELL
39 Director Housing & Residence Life .... Mr. Stephen WHITLOCK
41 Director of Athletics .... Mr. Daryl DICKEY
07 Director Counseling Center .... Dr. Lisa ADAMS SOMERLOT
109 Asst VP Auxiliary Services .... Mr. Mark REEVES
108 AVP Inst Effectiveness & Assessment .... Dr. Catherine JENKS
29 Director of Alumni Relations .... Mr. H. Franklin PRITCHETT
27 Asst Vice President of UA .... Ms. Jami BOWER
25 Int AVP Research & Sponsored Proj .... Dr. Denise OVERFIELD
106 Dean USG eCore .... Dr. Melanie N. CLAY
44 Assoc Director of Legacy Giving .... Mr. Baylor BASSETT
24 Asst Director for Classroom Support .... Mr. Brian MCCRARY
43 University General Counsel .... Ms. Jane SIMPSON
102 Assoc Exec Dir of WG Foundation .... Mr. Bart GILLESPIE
66 Dean Tanner School of Nursing .... Dr. Jennifer SCHUESSLER
14 Director of User Services .... Mr. Blake ADAMS
16 Asst Director of Human Resources .... Mr. Rodney BYRD
96 Director of Purchasing .... Ms. Shelly PARKER
22 Social Equity Officer .... Mr. Willie BLACK
86 Govt & External Relations Spec .... Mr. Russell CRUTCHFIELD
12 Chief Admin Officer Off Campus Pgm .... Dr. Robert HEABERLIN
105 Manager Web Innovations .... Mr. Denny CHASTEEN
16 Asst Director of Human Resources .... Ms. Laquana MARRABLE
40 Bookstore Manager .... Ms. Bettina A. ROBINSON
85 Dir International Services & Pgms .... Dr. Maria DOYLE

† Part of the University System of Georgia.

*University System of Georgia Office (F)

270 Washington Street, SW, Atlanta GA 30334-9007
County: Fulton FICE Identification: 008290
Telephone: (404) 962-3049 Carnegie Class: N/A
FAX Number: (404) 962-3013
URL: www.usg.edu

01 Chancellor .... Mr. Henry M. HUCKABY
04 Executive Assistant to Chancellor .... Ms. Bertha L. HARRIS
11 Exec Vice Chanc Administration .... Mr. Steve WRIGLEY
05 Exec Vice Chanc/Chief Academic Ofcr .... Dr. Houston DAVIS
45 Assoc VC Planning & Implementation .... Ms. Shelley C. NICKEL
10 Vice Chancellor Fiscal Affairs .... Ms. Shelley C. NICKEL
21 Chief Audit Officer .... Mr. John M. FUCHKO, III
18 Vice Chancellor Facilities .... Mr. Jim JAMES
43 Vice Chancellor Legal Affairs .... Mr. Sam BURCH
26 Vice Chanc Comm & Govt Relations .... Mr. Charles SUTLIVE
13 Vice Chanc/Chief Information Ofcr .... Dr. Robert LAURINE

Valdosta State University (G)

1500 N Patterson Street, Valdosta GA 31698-0010
County: Lowndes FICE Identification: 001599
Unit ID: 141264
Telephone: (229) 333-5800 Carnegie Class: DU-Mod
FAX Number: (229) 333-7400 Calendar System: Semester
URL: www.valdosta.edu
Established: 1906 Annual Undergrad Tuition & Fees (In-State): $6,297
Enrollment: 11,563 Coed
Affiliation or Control: State IRS Status: 501(c)3
Highest Offering: Doctorate
Accreditation: SC, ART, BUS, CAATE, CACREP, CAEP, CS, EXSC, LIB, MFCD, MUS, NURSE, SP, SPAA, SW, THEA

01 Interim President .... Dr. Kelli BROWN
05 Interim Provost & VPAA .... Dr. Brian L. GERBER
10 Vice President for Finance & Admin .... Ms. Traycee F. MARTIN
30 Vice President for Advancement .... Mr. John D. CRAWFORD
32 VP for Student Affairs .... Dr. Vince MILLER
58 Asst VP Rsrch & Grad Dean .... Dr. James T. LAPLANT
20 Assoc Provost Academic Affairs .... Dr. Sharon L. GRAVETT
20 Dean Undergrad Studies AA .... Dr. Lai K. ORENDUFF
88 Asst VP for Development .... Ms. Hilary H. GIBBS
86 Exec Asst to Pres & VP Ext Affairs .... Mr. Philip D. ALLEN
49 Dean College of Arts & Sciences .... Dr. Connie L. RICHARDS
50 Dean College of Business Admin .... Dr. Wayne L. PLUMLY
57 Dean College of the Arts .... Mr. Arthur E. PEARCE
53 Int Dean College of Educ & Hum Svc .... Dr. Lynn C. MINOR
66 Dean College of Nursing .... Dr. Sheri R. NOVIELLO
92 Dean of Honors College .... Dr. Michael P. SAVOIE
08 University Librarian .... Dr. Alan BERNSTEIN
06 Registrar .... Mr. Stanley JONES
106 Dir of Office of Extended Learning .... Ms. Meg H. GIDDINGS
27 Chief Information Officer .... Mr. Brian A. HAUGABROOK
13 Chief Technology Officer .... Mr. Joseph A. NEWTON
07 Exec Dir of Enrollment Services .... Mr. Tee MITCHELL
39 Int Dir Housing & Residence Life .... Ms. Niki W. TURLEY
88 Director of Off-Campus Learning .... Dr. Joseph WEAVER
41 Director of Athletics .... Mr. Herb REINHARD
37 Director of Financial Aid .... Mr. Douglas R. TANNER
88 Dir of Creative Design Services .... Mr. Jeff GRANT
36 Director of Career Opportunities .... Dr. Gerald WILLIAMS
29 Director Alumni Relations .... Ms. Melinda F. FUDGE
15 Director of Human Resources .... Dr. Denise BOGART
88 Director Division Aerospace Studies .... LtCol. Melvin GREEN, III
22 Director of Social Equity .... Dr. Maggie J. VIVERETTE
43 University Attorney .... Mr. Tony G. THOMAS
18 Dir Phys Plant & Facilities Plng .... Mr. Ray SABLE
26 Dir Univ Marketing & Cmty Relations .... Vacant
38 Director of Counseling Center .... Dr. Tricia A. HALE
88 Director of Centralized Advising .... Ms. Alicia ROBERSON
40 Manager of Bookstore .... Ms. Lee Ann JOHNSON
23 Director of Student Health Services .... Dr. Edwin L. HIATT
19 Int Dir Public Safety/Police Chief .... Mr. Alan ROWE
108 Director of Inst Effectiveness .... Dr. Michael M. BLACK
44 Director Info Technology Svcs .... Ms. Amelia REAMS
04 Exec Admin Asst to President .... Ms. Melinda CUTCHENS
96 Int Asst Director of Procurement .... Mr. Matthew R. WALL
09 Director Inst Research .... Mr. Barrie D. FITZGERALD

† Part of the University System of Georgia.

Virginia College (H)

2807 Wylds Road Extension, Suite B, Augusta GA 30909
Telephone: (706) 288-2500 Identification: 770833
Accreditation: ACICS, MAAB, SURGT

† Branch campus of Virginia College, Birmingham, AL

Virginia College (I)

5601 Veterans Parkway, Columbus GA 31904
Telephone: (762) 207-1600 Identification: 770835
Accreditation: ACICS, MAAB, SURGT

† Branch campus of Virginia College, Birmingham, AL

Virginia College (J)

1901 Paul Walsh Drive, Macon GA 31206
Telephone: (478) 803-4600 Identification: 770834
Accreditation: ACICS, MAAB

† Branch campus of Virginia College, Birmingham, AL

Virginia College (K)

14045 Abercorn Street, Suite 1503, Savannah GA 31419
Telephone: (912) 721-5600 Identification: 770836
Accreditation: ACICS, ACFEI, MAAB, SURGT

† Branch campus of Virginia College, Birmingham, AL

Wesleyan College (L)

4760 Forsyth Road, Macon GA 31210-4462
County: Bibb FICE Identification: 001600
Unit ID: 141325
Telephone: (478) 477-1110 Carnegie Class: Bac-A&S
FAX Number: (478) 757-4030 Calendar System: Semester
URL: www.wesleyancollege.edu
Established: 1836 Annual Undergrad Tuition & Fees: $20,290
Enrollment: 711 Female
Affiliation or Control: United Methodist IRS Status: 501(c)3
Highest Offering: Master's
Accreditation: SC, MUS, NURSE

01 President .... Ms. Ruth A. KNOX
05 Provost/VP for Academic Affairs .... Dr. Vivia L. FOWLER
30 VP Institutional Advancement .... Ms. Andrea G. WILLIFORD
10 Vice Pres Finance/Treasurer .... Mr. Richard P. MAIER
32 Vice Pres for Student Affairs .... Ms. Patricia M. GIBBS
84 Vice Pres for Enrollment Services .... Ms. Danielle LODGE
06 Assistant Dean/Registrar .... Ms. Angie WRIGHT
04 Assistant to the President .... Mrs. Denise W. HOLLOWAY
04 Assistant to the President .... Mrs. Carol A. PAYTON
08 Library Director .... Ms. Kristi PEAVY
13 Director of Information Services .... Mr. Kevin L. ULSHAFER
29 Director of Alumnae Affairs .... Ms. Cathy C. SNOW
26 Director of Communications .... Ms. Mary Ann HOWARD
44 Director of Annual Fund .... Ms. Whitney DAVIS
37 Director of Financial Aid .... Mr. Stephen PURVIS
39 Director of Residence Life .... Ms. Stefanie SWANGER
18 Director of Physical Plant .... Ms. Kelly BLEDSOE
41 Athletic Director .... Ms. Patty GIBBS
42 Director of Campus Ministry .... Rev. Debra C. WILLIAMS
19 Director Security/Safety .... Mr. Lionel DOSS
15 Director Human Resources .... Ms. Meagon DAVIS
07 Director of Admissions .... Ms. Lisa SLOBEN
09 Director of Institutional Research .... Ms. Thelma SEXTON
35 Chief Student Life Officer .... Ms. Stefanie SWANGER
36 Director Career Development .... Ms. Kathleen CROWNOVER
38 Director Student Counseling .... Ms. Jamie THAMES
96 Director of Purchasing .... Mr. Brandon GOULD
20 Associate Academic Officer .... Dr. Matthew R. MARTIN
21 Associate Business Officer .... Ms. Dawn P. NASH
40 Bookstore Manager .... Mr. Brandon GOULD

West Georgia Technical College (M)

176 Murphy Campus Boulevard, Waco GA 30182-2407
County: Haralson FICE Identification: 010487
Unit ID: 139278
Telephone: (770) 537-6000 Carnegie Class: Assoc/HVT-Mix Trad/Non
FAX Number: (770) 537-7976 Calendar System: Semester
URL: www.westgatech.edu
Established: 1968 Annual Undergrad Tuition & Fees (In-State): $2,724
Enrollment: 6,536 Coed
Affiliation or Control: State IRS Status: 501(c)3
Highest Offering: Associate Degree
Accreditation: SC, ACBSP, ADNUR, CAHIIM, DH, MAC, MLTAD, RAD, SURGT

01 President .... Mr. Steve G. DANIEL
05 Provost/COO .... Dr. Perrin ALFORD
11 Vice President Administrative Svcs .... Mr. Rick LEVEILLE
20 Vice President Academic Affairs .... Dr. Kristen DOUGLAS
32 Vice President Student Affairs .... Dr. Tonya F. WHITLOCK
30 Exec Dir Institutional Advancement .... Ms. Kim LEARNARD
09 VP Institutional Effectiveness .... Vacant
20 Asst Vice Pres For Curriculum .... Dr. Sindi MCGOWAN
08 Exec Director Library Services .... Mr. Emanuel MITCHELL
06 Registrar .... Mrs. Laura THORNTON
13 Exec Dir Information Technology .... Mr. Sam JENKINS
07 Director of Admissions .... Mrs. Mary ADERHOLD

18 Director Facilities .... Mr. Michael JILES
04 Administrative Asst to President .... Mrs. Julia WATSON
36 Manager Career Services .... Ms. Dawne WHITE
37 Director Student Financial Aid .... Mrs. Anna ENGLISH
41 Interim Athletic Director .... Mr. Todd PRATT
10 Chief Business Officer .... Ms. Carol REID
103 Dir Workforce/Career Development .... Ms. Laura B. GAMMAGE
15 Director Personnel Services .... Ms. Susan DANHAUSER
19 Chief of Police .... Mr. James PERRY
50 Dean Sch of Business & Public Svcs .... Ms. Babs RUSSELL
53 Dean Sch of Arts & Sciences .... Mr. Brian BARKLEY
54 Dean Sch of Trade & Technology .... Ms. Linda SULLIVAN

Wiregrass Georgia Technical College (A)

4089 Val Tech Road, Valdosta GA 31602

County: Lowndes FICE Identification: 005256
Unit ID: 141255
Telephone: (229) 333-2100 Carnegie Class: Assoc/HVT-High Non
FAX Number: (229) 333-2129 Calendar System: Semester
URL: www.wiregrass.edu
Established: 1963 Annual Undergrad Tuition & Fees (In-State): $2,734
Enrollment: 3,629 Coed
Affiliation or Control: State IRS Status: 501(c)3
Highest Offering: Associate Degree
Accreditation: **SC**, CAHIIM, DA, DH, EMT, MAC, RAD, SURGT

01 President .... Dr. Tina K. ANDERSON
05 Exec Vice Pres Academic Affairs .... Dr. Shawn UTLEY
10 Vice President Operations .... Ms. Lisa TOMBERLIN
46 VP Research/Strategic Initiatives .... Dr. Ron O'MEARA
11 VP for Administrative Services .... Ms. Keren WYNN
84 VP for Enrollment Management .... Ms. Angela HOBBY
09 Exec Dir for Inst Effectiveness .... Dr. Bonnie KELLY
31 VP for Community Affairs .... Mr. Alvin PAYTON
46 VP for Economic Development .... Ms. Lidell GREENWAY
13 Chief Info Technology Officer (CIO) .... Mr. Jarrod BROGDON
18 Chief of Facilities .... Mr. Michael FLETCHER
30 Exec Dir Advancement/Res Devel .... Dr. Penelope SCHMIDT
32 Dean of Student Affairs .... Ms. Shannon POLLOCK
26 Dir for Cmty/College Relations .... Ms. Lydia HUBERT
07 Director Recruitment .... Ms. Brooke JARAMILLO
04 Administrative Asst to President .... Ms. Cheryl ACREE
06 Assistant Registrar .... Ms. Julie SCOTT
08 Head Librarian .... Vacant
105 Director Web Services .... Vacant
106 Exec Director Online Education .... Ms. Sally DORMINY
15 Exec Dir of Human Resources .... Ms. Shalonda SANDERS
19 Chief of Police .... Mr. Mike KELLY
36 Director Student Placement .... Ms. Kay MORRIS
37 Financial Aid Coordinator .... Ms. Paula HERRING
96 Director of Purchasing .... Mr. Jim RAGO
50 Dean of Business/Education .... Ms. Lynn BOWEN
49 Dean of Arts and Science .... Ms. Lynn BOWEN

Young Harris College (B)

1 College Street, Young Harris GA 30582-0098

County: Towns FICE Identification: 001604
Unit ID: 141361
Telephone: (706) 379-3111 Carnegie Class: Bac-A&S
FAX Number: (706) 379-4319 Calendar System: Semester
URL: www.yhc.edu
Established: 1886 Annual Undergrad Tuition & Fees: $28,012
Enrollment: 1,218 Coed
Affiliation or Control: United Methodist IRS Status: 501(c)3
Highest Offering: Baccalaureate
Accreditation: **SC**, MUS

01 President .... Ms. Cathy COX
05 Vice Pres for Academic Affairs .... Dr. Gary MYERS
11 Senior VP for Finance & Admin .... Dr. Brooks SEAY
10 Controller .... Mr. Wade M. BENSON
32 Vice President for Student Affairs .... Ms. Angi SMITH
84 Vice Pres for Enrollment Management .... Mr. Clinton G. HOBBS
30 Vice President of Advancement .... Mr. Jimmy OWEN
45 VP for Planning and Assessment .... Ms. Rosemary R. ROYSTON
13 Vice President of Campus Technology .... Mr. Ken FANEUFF
29 Director of Alumni Relations .... Ms. Dana ENSLEY
20 Assoc VP for Academic Services .... Dr. Keith DEFOOR
08 Dean of Library Services .... Ms. Debra MARCH
38 Dir of Counseling & Psycholigical .... Ms. Lynne GRADY
06 Registrar .... Ms. Tammy GIBSON
37 Director of Financial Aid .... Ms. Linda ADAMS
15 Human Resources Director .... Mr. Vince ROBELOTTO
26 Dir of Communication & Marketing .... Ms. LeAnn WALDROUP
18 Facilities General Manager .... Mr. Jim RAWSKI
19 Director of Safety & Compliance .... Vacant
41 Director of Athletics .... Mr. Randy DUNN
42 Chaplain & Dean of the Chapel .... Rev. Blair TOLBERT
04 Administrative Asst to President .... Ms. Teresa KELLEY
39 Asst Dean of Students .... Mr. Stuart MILLER

HAWAII

Argosy University, Hawaii (C)

400 ABS Tower, 1001 Bishop Street, Honolulu HI 96813

Telephone: (808) 536-5555 Identification: 666787
Accreditation: &WC, ACBSP, CLPSY

† Regional accreditation is carried under the parent institution in Orange, CA.

Babel University Professional School of Translation (D)

1833 Kalakaua Avenue, #208, Honolulu HI 96815

County: Honolulu Identification: 666350
Telephone: (808) 946-3773 Carnegie Class: Not Classified
FAX Number: (808) 946-3993 Calendar System: Other
URL: www.babel.edu
Established: 2000 Annual Graduate Tuition & Fees: N/A
Enrollment: N/A Coed
Affiliation or Control: Proprietary IRS Status: Proprietary
Highest Offering: Master's; No Undergraduates
Accreditation: **DEAC**

01 Chancellor .... Dr. Miyoko YUASA
03 Vice Chancellor/Educational Dir .... Mr. Tomoki HOTTA
05 Head of Deans .... Mr. Yoshiharu ISHIDA

Brigham Young University Hawaii (E)

55-220 Kulanui Street, Laie Oahu HI 96762-1294

County: Honolulu FICE Identification: 001606
Unit ID: 230047
Telephone: (808) 675-3211 Carnegie Class: Bac-Diverse
FAX Number: (808) 675-3329 Calendar System: Semester
URL: www.byuh.edu
Established: 1955 Annual Undergrad Tuition & Fees: $5,100
Enrollment: 2,787 Coed
Affiliation or Control: Latter-day Saints IRS Status: 501(c)3
Highest Offering: Baccalaureate
Accreditation: **WC**, SW, TEAC

01 President .... Dr. John S. TANNER
05 Vice President for Academics .... Dr. John D. BELL
11 VP Administrative Services .... Mr. Norman S. BLACK
32 VP for Student Development & Svcs .... Dr. Debbie HIPPOLITE WRIGHT
04 Admin Assistant to the President .... Mrs. Lisa FAONELUA
108 Assoc Academic VP for Assessment .... Dr. Rosalind RAM
20 Assoc Academic VP for Instruction .... Dr. David BYBEE
20 Assoc Academic VP for Curriculum .... Dr. Jennifer LANE
81 Dean College of Math and Sciences .... Dr. Mark B. CANNON
50 Dean College of Bus/Computing/Govt .... Dr. James D. LEE
88 Dean College of Human Development .... Dr. Mark WOLFERSBERGER
88 Dean College of Lang/Culture & Arts .... Dr. Phillip MCARTHUR
13 University Technology Officer .... Mr. Kevin SCHLAG
07 Director Enrollment Services .... Mr. Arapata MEHA
41 Director of Athletics .... Mr. Ken WAGNER
08 University Librarian .... Mr. Michael ALDRICH
21 Director Budget Services .... Mr. Steven TUELLER
96 Director of Purchasing & Travel .... Mr. Robert OWAN
19 Director Safety/Security & Risk Mgt .... Mr. Earl MORRIS
15 Director of Human Resources .... Mrs. Tessie FAUSTINO
18 Director Facilities Management .... Mr. Randy SHARP
10 Director Financial Services .... Mr. Eric MARLER
23 Director Health Center .... Dr. P. Douglas NIELSON
88 Dir Compliance & Internal Audit .... Mr. Christopher BEARD
36 Director Career Services .... Mr. Mark MACDONALD
38 Director of Counseling Services .... Mrs. Leilani AUNA
35 Director Student Leadership & Honor .... Ms. Alison WHITING
109 Director Food Services .... Mr. David KEALA
26 Director Communications .... Mr. Michael JOHANSON
88 Director Testing and Assessment .... Mr. Christopher WRIGHT
06 Registrar .... Mr. Daryl WHITFORD
39 Director Housing & Residential Life .... Mr. Edwin ROGERS
51 Manager of Educational Outreach .... Mrs. Edna OWAN
40 Manager Bookstore .... Mr. David FONOIMOANA

† Affiliated with Brigham Young University, Provo, UT.

Chaminade University of Honolulu (F)

3140 Waialae Avenue, Honolulu HI 96816-1578

County: Honolulu FICE Identification: 001605
Unit ID: 141486
Telephone: (808) 735-4711 Carnegie Class: Masters/L
FAX Number: (808) 735-4870 Calendar System: Semester
URL: www.chaminade.edu
Established: 1955 Annual Undergrad Tuition & Fees: $21,780
Enrollment: 2,756 Coed
Affiliation or Control: Independent Non-Profit IRS Status: 501(c)3
Highest Offering: Master's
Accreditation: **WC**, CIDA, IACBE, MACTE, NURSE, TEAC

01 President .... Bro. Bernard PLOEGER, SM
88 Exec Director of Compliance & Pers .... Ms. Christine DENTON
05 Provost .... Dr. Helen WHIPPY
30 VP for Institutional Advancement .... Ms. Diane PETERS-NGUYEN
10 Vice President Finance/Facilities .... Ms. Aulani KAANOI
13 Dean of Info Technologies & Support .... Mr. Kyle JOHNSON
84 Dean of Enrollment Management .... Ms. Joy BOUEY
32 Dean of Students .... Ms. Allison JEROME
90 Director Network/Desktop Services .... Mr. Eddie PANG
51 Dir Professional & Continuing Educ .... Ms. Cindy JANUS
29 Director of Alumni Relations .... Ms. Be-Jay KODAMA
41 Director of Athletics .... Mr. William VILLA
42 Director of Campus Ministry .... Mr. Danny O'REGAN
36 Dir Career Develop/Job Placement .... Ms. Angela COLORETTI
18 Director of Facilities Operations .... Mr. Michael HAISEN
11 Director of Administrative Services .... Ms. Elaine OISHI
21 Director of Finance .... Mr. Choong LIM
08 Director of Library .... Ms. Sharon LEPAGE
19 Director of Security .... Mr. Robert WONG
38 Director of Student Counseling .... Dr. June YASUHARA
06 Registrar .... Mr. John MORRIS
37 Director of Financial Aid .... Ms. Amy TAKIGUCHI
09 Dir of Institutional Research .... Mr. Hieu NGUYEN
26 Senior Dir of Univ Communications .... Ms. Lisa FURUTA

Hawaii Medical College (G)

1221 Kapiolani Blvd PH 35, Honolulu HI 96814

County: Honolulu FICE Identification: 041822
Unit ID: 460756
Telephone: (808) 237-5140 Carnegie Class: Not Classified
FAX Number: N/A Calendar System: Other
URL: www.hmi.edu
Established: 2007 Annual Undergrad Tuition & Fees: $16,508
Enrollment: 503 Coed
Affiliation or Control: Proprietary IRS Status: Proprietary
Highest Offering: Associate Degree
Accreditation: **CNCE**

01 Executive Director .... Guy BENJAMIN
05 Director of Education .... Anita GRAHAM-ROY

Hawaii Pacific University (H)

1164 Bishop Street, Suite 800, Honolulu HI 96813-2882

County: Honolulu FICE Identification: 007279
Unit ID: 141644
Telephone: (808) 544-0200 Carnegie Class: Masters/L
FAX Number: (808) 544-1136 Calendar System: Semester
URL: www.hpu.edu
Established: 1965 Annual Undergrad Tuition & Fees: $22,440
Enrollment: 5,827 Coed
Affiliation or Control: Independent Non-Profit IRS Status: 501(c)3
Highest Offering: Master's
Accreditation: **WC**, NURSE, SW, TEAC

01 President .... Mr. John GOTANDA
00 President Emeritus .... Mr. Chatt G. WRIGHT
11 Exece Vice Pres Admin/Gen Counsel .... Ms. Janet S. KLOENHAMER
05 Provost & VP Academic Affairs .... Mr. Matthew LIAO-TROTH
10 VP/Chief Financial Officer .... Mr. Bruce EDWARDS
84 Vice Pres Enrollment Management .... Mr. Greg GRAUMAN
30 Vice Pres University Relations .... Mr. Samuel MOKU
20 Assoc VP Academic Affairs .... Mr. Joe SCHMIEDL
15 Int AVP of Human Resources .... Ms. Diana NILES-HANSEN
21 Associate VP/Controller .... Mr. James BRESE
50 Int Dean Business Administration .... Dr. Warren WEE
76 Dean College of Health/Sciences .... Dr. Lynette LANDRY
81 Dean Natural/Computational Sciences .... Dr. Brenda JENSEN
49 Int Dean College of Liberal Arts .... Dr. J. William POTTER, JR.
89 Dean of Students .... Ms. Marites MCKEE
106 Asst Dean Distance Education Policy .... Dr. Asoke DATTA
07 Assoc Dir International Admissions .... Mr. Jimmi HEMMENBACH
97 Assistant Dean General Education .... Dr. Valentina ABORDONADO
07 Director of Admissions .... Ms. Marissa BRATTON
104 Director Intl Exchange/Study Abroad .... Ms. Melissa MATSUBARA
36 Director Career Svcs Ctr/Co-op Educ .... Mr. Michael VAN LEAR
06 University Registrar .... Ms. Jean LANG
37 Assoc Director Financial Aid .... Ms. Alyson MACHADO
41 Executive Athletic Director .... Mr. Vince BALDEMOR
51 Assoc Dir Adult Learning Program .... Ms. Jill MERL
105 Director Web Services .... Vacant
08 Director of Libraries .... Ms. Nori LEONG
42 University Chaplain .... Rev. Dale BURKE
13 Director Computing Services .... Ms. Lisa CARPENTER
19 Assoc Director Security and Safety .... Mr. Wayne FERNANDEZ
18 Director Facilities Management .... Mr. John RUSSELL
29 Alumni/Parent Relations Coordinator .... Vacant
38 Dir Counseling/Behavioral Health .... Dr. Kevin BOWMAN
96 Procurement Director .... Mr. Kevin WETTER
26 Chief Information Ofcr/Vice Pres .... Dr. Sharon BLANTON
100 Chief of Staff .... Mr. Mark E. DELOS REYES DAVIS

Hawaii Tokai International College (I)

91-971 Farrington Hwy, Kapolei HI 96707

County: Honolulu FICE Identification: 037603
Telephone: (808) 983-4000 Carnegie Class: Not Classified
FAX Number: (808) 983-4107 Calendar System: Quarter
URL: www.hawaiitokai.edu
Established: 1992 Annual Undergrad Tuition & Fees: N/A
Enrollment: N/A Coed
Affiliation or Control: Independent Non-Profit IRS Status: 501(c)3
Highest Offering: Associate Degree
Accreditation: **WJ**

01 Chancellor .... Mr. Takuya YOSHIMURA
03 Vice Chancellor .... Mr. Mark HAMILTON
10 Exec Director of Administration .... Mr. Tsuyoshi TSURUMI
05 Dean of Instruction .... Mr. Mark ANTHONY
08 Librarian .... Ms. Sharrese CASTILLO
32 Director of Student Services .... Dr. Yukari KUNISUE
15 Human Resources Specialist .... Ms. Jeremy BURCH
21 Finance Department .... Ms. Miho BRADLEY
88 Academic Liaison Officer .... Ms. Erin FUKUMOTO

Institute of Clinical Acupuncture and Oriental Medicine (A)

100 N Beretania Street, Suite 203 B,
Honolulu HI 96817-4709
County: Honolulu FICE Identification: 037353
Unit ID: 444899
Telephone: (808) 521-2288 Carnegie Class: Spec-4-yr-Other Health
FAX Number: (808) 521-2271 Calendar System: Semester
URL: www.orientalmedicine.edu
Established: 1996 Annual Graduate Tuition & Fees: N/A
Enrollment: 54 Coed
Affiliation or Control: Proprietary IRS Status: Proprietary
Highest Offering: Master's; No Undergraduates
Accreditation: **ACUP**

01 President .... Dr. Wai Hoa LOW
05 Chancellor Academic Affairs .... Dr. Edmund BERNAUER
32 Director of Student Affairs .... Dr. Craig TWENTYMAN
63 Clinic Director .... Dr. Catherine Yu-Ling LOW

Pacific Rim Christian University (B)

290 Sand Island Access Road, Honolulu HI 96819
County: Honolulu Identification: 667010
Unit ID: 457484
Telephone: (808) 853-1040 Carnegie Class: Bac-Diverse
FAX Number: (808) 853-1042 Calendar System: Semester
URL: hawaii.newhope.edu/
Established: 1998 Annual Undergrad Tuition & Fees: $10,080
Enrollment: 108 Coed
Affiliation or Control: Independent Non-Profit IRS Status: 501(c)3
Highest Offering: Master's
Accreditation: **BI**

00 Founder .... Dr. Wayne CORDEIRO
01 President .... Dr. Kent KEITH
58 Dean Grad Sch/Pres Emeritus .... Dr. Randall FURUSHIMA
05 Vice Pres Academic Affairs .... Martha STINTON
32 Vice Pres Student Services .... Craig PANKOW
07 Director of Admissions .... Jade RANESES
08 Library Director .... Cari RYAN
37 Director of Financial Aid .... Michael THOMPSON

Remington College-Honolulu Campus (C)

1111 Bishop Street, Suite 400, Honolulu HI 96813-2811
Telephone: (808) 942-1000 Identification: 666028
Accreditation: **ACCSC**

† Branch campus of Remington College, Mobile, AL.

*University of Hawaii System (D)

2444 Dole Street, Honolulu HI 96822
County: Honolulu FICE Identification: 007885
Unit ID: 141963
Telephone: (808) 956-8207 Carnegie Class: N/A
FAX Number: (808) 956-5286
URL: www.hawaii.edu

01 President .... Dr. David K. LASSNER
05 VP for Academic Planning & Policy .... Dr. Risa E. DICKSON
46 VP for Research and Innovation .... Dr. Vassilis L. SYRMOS
43 VP for Legal Affs/Univ Gen Counsel .... Ms. Carrie K. OKINAGA
10 VP for Budget and Finance/CFO .... Mr. Kalbert K. YOUNG
88 VP for Community Colleges .... Dr. John F. MORTON
11 VP for Administration .... Ms. Jan N. GOUVEIA
13 VP for Information Tech/CIO .... Mr. Garret T. YOSHIMI
32 Interim Assoc VP Student Affairs .... Dr. Farrah-Marie GOMES
102 President & CEO UH Foundation .... Ms. Donna VUCHINICH
21 Director of Budget .... Mr. Michael M. NG
15 System Director Human Resources .... Ms. Debra A. ISHII
14 Director Management Info Systems .... Ms. Susan K. INOUYE
45 Director Ofc of Research Services .... Ms. Yaa-Yin FONG
21 Dir Fin Mgmt & Controller .... Ms. Susan X. LIN
09 Director Data Govt & Operations .... Ms. Sandra K. FURUTO
22 Director EEO/AA .... Ms. Mie WATANABE
88 Director Media Production .... Mr. Dan T. MEISENZAHL
26 Director of Communications .... Ms. Diane E. CHANG
100 Executive Asst to President .... Mr. David W. LONBORG
101 Exec Administrator/Sec to the BOR .... Ms. Cynthia D. QUINN
86 Director Government Relations .... Ms. Stephanie C. KIM
100 Executive Asst to President .... Ms. Lynne K. MONACO
04 Administrative Asst to President .... Ms. Janelle L. MURAKAWA

*University of Hawaii at Hilo (E)

200 W Kawili Street, Hilo HI 96720-4091
County: Hawaii FICE Identification: 001611
Unit ID: 141565
Telephone: (808) 932-7348 Carnegie Class: Masters/S
FAX Number: (808) 932-7338 Calendar System: Semester
URL: www.hilo.hawaii.edu
Established: 1947 Annual Undergrad Tuition & Fees (In-State): $7,332
Enrollment: 3,924 Coed
Affiliation or Control: State IRS Status: 501(c)3
Highest Offering: Doctorate
Accreditation: **WC, BUS, CEA, NUR, NURSE, PHAR**

02 Chancellor .... Dr. Donald O. STRANEY
05 Vice Chancellor Academic Affairs .... Dr. Matthew PLATZ
10 Vice Chanc Administrative Affs .... Dr. Marcia SAKAI
46 Vice Chancellor for Research .... Vacant
32 Interim VC Student Affairs .... Ms. Gail MAKUAKANE-LUNDIN
20 Asst VC for Academic Affairs .... Vacant
21 Budget Director .... Ms. Lois M. FUJIYOSHI
88 Director University Disability Svcs .... Ms. Susan SHIRACHI
15 Director Human Resources .... Mr. Keleihi'ikapo i RAPOZA
18 Director Facilities Planning .... Mr. Lo-Li CHIH
26 Director University Relations .... Mr. Jerry CHANG
08 Interim University Librarian .... Ms. Helen ROGERS
24 Director Media Relations .... Ms. Alyson Y. KAKUGAWA-LEONG
07 Interim Director Admissions .... Mr. Zach STREET
38 Int Asst Director Counseling .... Mr. Andrew POLLOI
39 Exec Director Housing & Dining Svs .... Mr. Miles H. NAGATA
35 Director Campus Center .... Ms. Ellen L KUSANO
37 Director Financial Aid .... Ms. Sherrie PADILLA
06 Interim University Registrar .... Ms. Chelsea KAY-WONG
49 Dean College of Arts & Sciences .... Dr. Susan BROWN
50 Dean College of Business/Economics .... Dr. Krishna DHIR
67 Interim Dean College of Pharmacy .... Dr. Carolyn MA
47 Int Dean Col Agri/For/Nat Res Mgmt .... Dr. Bruce MATHEWS
51 Int Dean Cont Educ/Community Svcs .... Dr. Farrahmarie GOMES
41 Director of Athletics .... Mr. Patrick J GUILLEN
40 Bookstore Manager .... Mr. Jason K. TANAKA
85 Exex Dir Internatl Student Services .... Mr. James P. MELLON
36 Exec Director Career Services .... Ms. Kainoa ARIOLA-SUKISAKI
22 Director EEO/AA .... Dr. Jennifer STOTTER
09 Institutional Research Analyst .... Ms. Kelli OKUMURA
29 Director Marketing & Alumni .... Ms. Yu Yok PEARRING
30 Exec Director of Development .... Ms. Mariko MIHO
94 Coordinator Women's Center .... Ms. Leslie MCCLUNG
23 Asst Director Medical Services .... Ms. Heather HIRATA
88 Dir College of Hawaiian Language .... Ms. Keiki KAWAI'AE'A
19 Director Security/Safety .... Mr. Darrell MAYFIELD

*University of Hawaii at Manoa (F)

2500 Campus Road, Honolulu HI 96822-2217
County: Honolulu FICE Identification: 001610
Unit ID: 141574
Telephone: (808) 956-8111 Carnegie Class: DU-Highest
FAX Number: N/A Calendar System: Semester
URL: www.manoa.hawaii.edu
Established: 1907 Annual Undergrad Tuition & Fees (In-State): $11,164
Enrollment: 19,507 Coed
Affiliation or Control: State IRS Status: 501(c)3
Highest Offering: Doctorate
Accreditation: **WC, BUS, CAATE, CEA, CLPSY, CORE, DH, DIETD, ENG, IPSY, LAW, LIB, MED, MT, MUS, NURSE, PH, PLNG, SP, SW, TED**

02 Chancellor .... Dr. Robert BLEY-VROMAN
10 Vice Chanc Admin/Finance/ Operations .... Ms. Kathleen D. CUTSHAW
05 Vice Chanc Academic Affairs .... Dr. Reed W. DASENBROCK
32 Int Vice Chancellor for Students .... Ms. Lori IDETA
06 University Registrar .... Mr. Stuart LAU
08 University Librarian .... Dr. Irene HEROLD
37 Director Financial Aid Services .... Ms. Jodie M. KUBA
38 Director Counsel/Student Devel Ctr .... Dr. Allyson M. TANOUYE
23 Director University Health Center .... Dr. Andrew W. NICHOLS
39 Director Student Housing .... Mr. Michael W. KAPTIK
40 Director Campus Svcs (Bookstore) .... Ms. Deborah T. HEUBLER
41 Athletic Director .... Mr. David MATLIN
86 Director of Cmty/Govt Affairs .... Mr. Elmer KAAI
28 Dir Stdnt Equity/Exclnce/Diversity .... Dr. Amefil AGBAYANI
36 Interim Dir Manoa Career Center .... Ms. Wendy SORA
15 Director Human Resources .... Ms. Tammy KUNIYOSHI
88 Director Cancer Center .... Dr. Michele CARBONE
88 Director Institute for Astronomy .... Dr. Guenther HASINGER
88 Director Waikiki Aquarium .... Dr. Andrew ROSSITER
88 Int Assc Dr Pac Biosci Research Ctr .... Dr. Marilyn DUNLAP
56 Int Dean Outreach College .... Dr. William G. CHISMAR
50 Dean Shidler College of Business .... Dr. V. Vance ROLEY
58 Dean Graduate Education .... Dr. Krystyna AUNE
88 Int Dean Sch of Travel Industry Mgt .... Dr. Tom BINGHAM
53 Dean College of Education .... Dr. Donald B. YOUNG
54 Dean College of Engineering .... Dr. Peter E. CROUCH
47 Dean Col Trop Agric & Human Res .... Dr. Maria GALLO
63 Dean John A Burns Sch of Med .... Dr. Jerris R. HEDGES
66 Dean Sch Nursing & Dental Hygiene .... Dr. Mary G. BOLAND
70 Dean M P Thompson Sch of Soc Work .... Dr. Noreen K MOKUAU
61 Dean Wm S Richardson Sch of Law .... Mr. Aviam SOIFER
48 Dean School of Architecture .... Mr. Daniel S. FRIEDMAN
49 Dean College Arts & Humanities .... Mr. Peter ARNADE
65 Int Dean College Natural Sciences .... Dr. Kristin KUMASHIRO
83 Dean College Social Sciences .... Dr. Denise E. KONAN
79 Int Dean College Lang Ling & Lit .... Dr. Jeffrey G. CARROLL
88 Dean Sch Ocean & Earth Sci & Tech .... Dr. Brian TAYLOR
88 Dean Pacific and Asian Studies .... Dr. R. Anderson SUTTON
88 Dn Hawaiinuiakea Sch Hawn Knowledge .... Dr. Maenette BENHAM
09 Director of Institutional Research .... Dr. Yang ZHANG

*University of Hawaii - West Oahu (G)

91-1001 Farrington Highway, Kapolei HI 96707
County: Honolulu FICE Identification: 021078
Unit ID: 141981
Telephone: (808) 689-2770 Carnegie Class: Bac-Diverse
FAX Number: (808) 689-2771 Calendar System: Semester
URL: www.uhwo.hawaii.edu
Established: 1976 Annual Undergrad Tuition & Fees (In-State): $7,152
Enrollment: 2,661 Coed
Affiliation or Control: State IRS Status: 501(c)3
Highest Offering: Baccalaureate
Accreditation: **WC, TED**

02 Interim Chancellor .... Dr. Doris CHING
05 Vice Chanc Academic Affairs .... Dr. Jeffrey MONIZ
32 Vice Chanc for Student Affairs .... Dr. Judy OLIVEIRA
11 Vice Chanc for Administration .... Mr. Kevin ISHIDA
20 Director Strategic Initiatives .... Ms. Sherry PROPER
84 Director for Enrollment Management .... Mr. Joseph MAREKO
09 Assoc Dir of Institutional Research .... Mr. John STANLEY
26 Director of Communications .... Ms. Leila SHIMOKAWA
08 Librarian .... Ms. Sara AIELLO
06 Registrar .... Ms. Robyn OSHIRO
37 Financial Aid Officer .... Mr. Lester ISHIMOTO
15 Director of Human Resources .... Ms. Nancy K. NAKASONE
18 Facilities/Mgmt/Operation Mgr .... Mr. Dan FURUYA
10 Director of Business Affairs .... Ms. Linda SAIKI

*University of Hawaii Community Colleges (H)

2444 Dole Street, Honolulu HI 96822-2411
County: Honolulu FICE Identification: 006751
Unit ID: 420592
Telephone: (808) 956-7038 Carnegie Class: N/A
FAX Number: (808) 956-9219
URL: www.hawaii.edu

01 Vice Pres for Community Colleges .... Dr. John F. MORTON
05 Assoc Vice Pres Academic Affairs .... Dr. Peter QUIGLEY
11 Assoc Vice Pres Admin/Cmty Col Oper .... Mr. Michael T. UNEBASAMI
04 Executive Assistant to the VP & Dir .... Ms. Deborah NAKAGAWA
10 Director Budget & Planning .... Mr. Lance YAMAMOTO
108 Director Academic Plng Assessment .... Ms. Cheryl CHAPPELL-LONG
15 Director Personnel Services .... Ms. Sandra UYENO
18 Director Facilities/Physical Plant .... Ms. Denise YOSHIMORI-YAMAMOTO
22 Dir Affirmative Action/EEO .... Ms. Mary PERREIRA
26 Public Relations/Marketing .... Ms. Susan LEE

*Kapiolani Community College (I)

4303 Diamond Head Road, Honolulu HI 96816-4496
County: Honolulu FICE Identification: 001613
Unit ID: 141796
Telephone: (808) 734-9000 Carnegie Class: Assoc/HT-Mix Trad/Non
FAX Number: (808) 734-9162 Calendar System: Semester
URL: www.kcc.hawaii.edu
Established: 1957 Annual Undergrad Tuition & Fees (In-State): $2,940
Enrollment: 7,994 Coed
Affiliation or Control: State IRS Status: 501(c)3
Highest Offering: Associate Degree
Accreditation: **WJ, ACBSP, ACFEI, ADNUR, COARC, DA, EMT, MAC, MLTAD, OTA, PHLEB, FTAA, RAD, SURGT**

02 Interim Chancellor .... Dr. Louise PAGOTTO
05 Interim VC Academic Affairs .... Ms. Susan KAZAMA
10 Vice Chancellor for Admin Services .... Mr. Brian FURUTO
32 Vice Chanellor for Student Affairs .... Dr. Brenda IVELISSE
49 Dean Arts and Sciences .... Mr. Nawa?a NAPOLEON
50 Dean Hospitality/Business/Legal .... Mr. John RICHARDS
66 Dean Health Programs .... Dr. Patricia O'HAGAN
51 Dir Continuing Educ & Training .... Ms. Ann ISHIDA-HO
04 Special Asst to the Chancellor .... Ms. Joanne WHITAKER
88 Dir Culinary Inst of the Pacific .... Mr. Conrad NONAKA
09 Dir Institutional Effectiveness .... Dr. Robert FRANCO
08 Librarian .... Vacant
06 Registrar .... Ms. Jerilyn ENOKAWA
37 Financial Aid Officer .... Ms. Jennifer BRADLEY
109 Auxiliary Services Officer .... Mr. Gordon MAN
26 Dean College & Community Relations .... Dr. Carol HOSHIKO
30 Development Officer .... Ms. Linh HOANG POE
15 Director Personnel Office .... Ms. Kelli BRANDVOLD
21 Fiscal Officer .... Mr. Justin KASHIWAEDA

*University of Hawaii Hawaii Community College (J)

1175 Manono Street, Hilo HI 96720-4091
County: Hawaii FICE Identification: 005258
Unit ID: 383190
Telephone: (808) 934-2500 Carnegie Class: Assoc/MT-VT-High Trad
FAX Number: (808) 934-2501 Calendar System: Semester
URL: www.hawaii.hawaii.edu
Established: 1941 Annual Undergrad Tuition & Fees (In-State): $2,940
Enrollment: 3,186 Coed
Affiliation or Control: State IRS Status: 501(c)3
Highest Offering: Associate Degree
Accreditation: **WJ, ACFEI, ADNUR**

02 Chancellor .... Dr. Rachel H. SOLEMSAAS
05 Vice Chanc Academic Affairs .... Ms. Joni Y. ONISHI
10 Vice Chanc Administrative Affairs .... Mr. James M. YOSHIDA
32 Vice Chanc Student Affairs .... Mr. Jason S. CIFRA
51 Int Dir Continuing Educ/Training .... Ms. Deborah S. SHIGEHARA
37 Student Financial Aid Officer .... Ms. Vivian LAMOTHE
12 Director UH Center at West Hawaii .... Dr. Kenneth Marty FLETCHER
15 Human Resource Manager .... Ms. Mari CHANG

07 Registrar/Admissions/Records Mgr Ms. Dorinna MANUEL-CORTEZ
21 Budget Analyst Ms. Jodi MINE

*University of Hawaii Honolulu Community College (A)

874 Dillingham Boulevard, Honolulu HI 96817-4598
County: Honolulu FICE Identification: 001612
Unit ID: 141680
Telephone: (808) 845-9211 Carnegie Class: Assoc/HVT-Mix Trad/Non
FAX Number: (808) 845-9173 Calendar System: Semester
URL: www.honolulu.hawaii.edu
Established: 1920 Annual Undergrad Tuition & Fees (In-State): $2,910
Enrollment: 4,144 Coed
Affiliation or Control: State IRS Status: 501(c)3
Highest Offering: Associate Degree
Accreditation: **WJ**

02 Chancellor Ms. Erika LACRO
11 Vice Chancellor of Admin Svcs Mr. Derek INAFUKU
05 Vice Chancellor of Academic Affairs Ms. Katy HO
88 Director PCATT Mr. Steven AUERBACH
88 Dean Transport & Trades Mr. Keala CHOCK
08 Librarian in Charge Ms. Irene MESINA
37 Financial Aid Officer Ms. Jannine OYAMA
15 Human Resources Mgr/EEO/AA Coord Ms. Monique TINGKANG
32 Director Student Affairs Ms. Emily Ann KUKULIES
06 Registrar Ms. Josephine STENBERG
09 Director Management Info & Research Mr. Steven SHIGEMOTO
36 Dir Student Placement/Counselor Ms. Silvan CHUNG
20 Dean University College Ms. Marcia ROBERTS-DEUTSCH
07 Director of Admissions Ms. Josephine STENBERG
10 Acting Chief Business Officer Ms. Myrna PATTERSON
26 Chief Public Relations Officer Ms. Billie LUEDER
38 Director Student Counseling Ms. Lara SUGIMOTO
88 Dean of Academic Support Mr. Wayne SUNAHARA
96 Acting Director of Purchasing Ms. Myrna PATTERSON
88 Director Secondary Education Pgms Ms. Lara SUGIMOTO
13 Chief Info Technology Officer (CIO) Mr. Michael MEYER
35 Dean of Student Services Ms. Lara SUGIMOTO

*University of Hawaii Kauai Community College (B)

3-1901 Kaumualii Highway, Lihue HI 96766-9500
County: Kauai FICE Identification: 001614
Unit ID: 141802
Telephone: (808) 245-8311 Carnegie Class: Assoc/MT-VT-High Trad
FAX Number: (808) 245-8220 Calendar System: Semester
URL: kauai.hawaii.edu/
Established: 1964 Annual Undergrad Tuition & Fees (In-State): $2,988
Enrollment: 1,424 Coed
Affiliation or Control: State IRS Status: 501(c)3
Highest Offering: Associate Degree
Accreditation: **WJ**, ACFEI, ADNUR

02 Chancellor Dr. Helen COX
05 Vice Chanc Academic Affairs Dr. James DIRE
32 Int Vice Chanc Student Affairs Mr. Isaiah KAAUWAI
11 Vice Chanc Administrative Services Mr. Brandon SHIMOKAWA
20 Int Dir Acad Support/Univ Ctr Dir Ms. Colleen KAIMINAAUAO
51 Director Continuing Educ/Training Mr. Calvin SHIRAI
08 Librarian Mr. Robert KAJIWARA
10 Chief Financial Officer Mr. Leighton ORIDE
37 Financial Aid Officer Mr. Jeff ANDERSON
15 Human Resource Specialist Ms. JoRae BAPTISTE
35 Counselor Mr. John CONSTANTINO
09 Institutional Researcher Mr. Jonathan KALK

*University of Hawaii - Leeward Community College (C)

96-045 Ala Ike, Pearl City HI 96782-3393
County: Honolulu FICE Identification: 004549
Unit ID: 141811
Telephone: (808) 455-0011 Carnegie Class: Assoc/HT-Mix Trad/Non
FAX Number: (808) 455-0471 Calendar System: Semester
URL: www.leeward.hawaii.edu
Established: 1968 Annual Undergrad Tuition & Fees (In-State): $2,935
Enrollment: 7,742 Coed
Affiliation or Control: State IRS Status: 501(c)3
Highest Offering: Associate Degree
Accreditation: **WJ**, ACFEI, TEAC

02 Chancellor Mr. Manuel J. CABRAL
05 Int Vice Chancellor Academic Affs Ms. Della TERAOKA
11 Vice Chancellor Admin Services Mr. Mark LANE
10 Fiscal Manager Ms. Cecilia LUCAS
49 Dean Arts & Sciences Mr. James GOODMAN
72 Dean Career & Tech Education Mr. Ron UMEHIRA
32 Dean Student Services Dr. Curtis WASHBURN
20 Dean of Academic Services Mr. Paul KUEHN
08 Librarian Mr. Wayde OSHIRO
06 Registrar Mr. Grant HELGESON
37 Financial Aid Officer Mr. Gregg YOSHIMURA
18 Aux & Facilities Services Mgr Ms. Sandy MAEDA
09 Dir Policy/Planning/Assessment Vacant
26 Marketing Director Ms. Kathleen CABRAL
15 Human Resources/EEO/AA Officer Mr. Michael WONG

13 Information Technology Coord Ms. Jennifer DEGIACINTO
12 Int Coord Waianae Education Center Mr. Danny WYATT
24 Media Coordinator Ms. Leanne CHUN
35 Student Activities Coordinator Ms. Lexer CHOU
36 Placement Officer Vacant

*University of Hawaii Maui College (D)

310 Kaahumanu Avenue, Kahului HI 96732-1644
County: Maui FICE Identification: 001615
Unit ID: 141839
Telephone: (808) 984-3500 Carnegie Class: Bac/Assoc-Assoc Dom
FAX Number: (808) 984-3546 Calendar System: Semester
URL: maui.hawaii.edu
Established: 1931 Annual Undergrad Tuition & Fees (In-State): $3,006
Enrollment: 3,809 Coed
Affiliation or Control: State IRS Status: 501(c)3
Highest Offering: Baccalaureate
Accreditation: **WC**, ACFEI, ADNUR, DH

02 Chancellor Dr. Lui HOKOANA
05 Vice Chanc Academic Affairs Dr. Jonathon MCKEE
32 Vice Chancellor of Student Affs Ms. Debra NAKAMA
10 Vice Chanc of Administrative Affs Mr. David TAMANAHA
20 Int Assistant Dean of Instruction Mr. David GROOMS
51 Director Continuing Educ/Training Ms. Karen HANADA
08 Librarian Ms. Ellen PETERSON
12 Director University Center Maui Ms. Tamone Karen HANADA
07 Director of Admissions/Registrar Ms. Flora MORA
09 Director of Institutional Research Dr. Jeannie PEZZOLI
15 Director Personnel Services Ms. Susan TOKUNAGA
18 Chief Facilities/Physical Plant Mr. Robert BURTON
21 Associate Fiscal Officer Ms. Cindy YAMAMOTO
30 Chief Development Ms. Cordy MACLAUGHLIN
36 Director Student Placement Ms. Debra NAKAMA
37 Interim Financial Aid Officer Mr. Kilohana MILLER
38 Director Student Counseling Mr. Shane PAYBA

*University of Hawaii Windward Community College (E)

45-720 Keaahala Road, Kaneohe HI 96744-3598
County: Honolulu FICE Identification: 011220
Unit ID: 141990
Telephone: (808) 235-7400 Carnegie Class: Assoc/HT-High Non
FAX Number: (808) 247-5362 Calendar System: Semester
URL: www.wcc.hawaii.edu
Established: 1972 Annual Undergrad Tuition & Fees (In-State): $2,920
Enrollment: 2,661 Coed
Affiliation or Control: State IRS Status: 501(c)3
Highest Offering: Associate Degree
Accreditation: **WJ**

02 Chancellor Mr. Doug DYKSTRA
05 Vice Chancellor Academic Affs Dr. Ardis ESHENBERG
32 Vice Chancellor Student Affairs Ms. Amy ROZEK
11 Vice Chanc Administrative Services Mr. Brian PACTOL
20 Int Dean of Academic Affairs Div I Ms. Linka MULLIKIN
20 Dean of Academic Affairs Div II Mr. Charles SASAKI
75 Dir Vocational/Cmty Education Mr. Mike MOSER
08 Head Librarian Ms. Sarah Gilman SUR
06 Registrar Ms. Geri IMAI
09 Director of Institutional Research Mr. Jeffrey HUNT
37 Director Student Financial Aid Mr. Steven CHIGAWA
15 Personnel Officer Ms. Karen CHO
26 Marketing/Public Relations Dir Ms. Bonnie BEATSON

University of Phoenix Hawaii Campus (F)

745 Fort Street, Suite 2000, Honolulu HI 96813-3800
Telephone: (808) 536-2686 Identification: 770202
Accreditation: **&NH**, ACBSP, TED

† Regional accreditation is carried under the parent institution in Tempe, AZ

World Medicine Institute (G)

1073 Hind Iuka Drive, Honolulu HI 96821
County: Honolulu FICE Identification: 030725
Unit ID: 141936
Telephone: (808) 373-2849 Carnegie Class: Spec-4-yr-Other Health
FAX Number: (808) 373-4341 Calendar System: Semester
URL: www.wmi.edu
Established: 1970 Annual Graduate Tuition & Fees: N/A
Enrollment: 49 Coed
Affiliation or Control: Independent Non-Profit IRS Status: 501(c)3
Highest Offering: Master's; No Undergraduates
Accreditation: **ACUP**

01 President Dr. Lillian CHANG
05 Academic Dean Dr. Wasim SIDDIQUI
10 Chief Operating Officer Dr. Eric ONO
09 Director of Institutional Research Dr. Catharina ANG
37 Director Student Financial Aid Mr. Hansford CHOCK
07 Dir Admissions/Registrar/Enr Mgmt Dr. Gayle TODOKI
15 Chief Human Resources Officer Dr. Patricia BRADY
18 Chief Facilities/Physical Plant Mr. Conrad LOMMEN
20 Associate Academic Officer Dr. Ellen CACHOLA
29 Director of Alumni Affairs Ms. Tia KLUG-WESSERL
32 Chief Student Affairs Officer Mr. Frank GONZALES
38 Director of Student Counseling Dr. Eric ONO

IDAHO

Boise Bible College (H)

8695 W Marigold Street, Boise ID 83714-1220
County: Ada FICE Identification: 022345
Unit ID: 142090
Telephone: (208) 376-7731 Carnegie Class: Spec-4-yr-Faith
FAX Number: (208) 376-7743 Calendar System: Semester
URL: www.boisebible.edu
Established: 1945 Annual Undergrad Tuition & Fees: $11,665
Enrollment: 175 Coed
Affiliation or Control: Christian Churches And Churches of Christ
IRS Status: 501(c)3
Highest Offering: Baccalaureate
Accreditation: **BI**

01 President Mr. Terry E. STINE
05 Academic Dean Mr. Charles FABER
32 Dean of Students Mr. Cody CHRISTENSEN
10 Business Officer Mr. Mark STEVENS
30 Director of Development Mr. David DAVOLT
06 Registrar Mr. Ross KNUDSEN
07 Director of Admissions Mr. Mike MAGLISH
08 Librarian Ms. Amber GROVE
37 Financial Aid Director Mrs. Joyce ANDERSON
18 Supt of Building & Grounds Mr. Jon SHINGLER
04 Executive Assistant Mrs. Mary REICH

Boise State University (I)

1910 University Drive, Boise ID 83725-1000
County: Ada FICE Identification: 001616
Unit ID: 142115
Telephone: (208) 426-1000 Carnegie Class: DU-Mod
FAX Number: (208) 426-3765 Calendar System: Semester
URL: www.boisestate.edu
Established: 1932 Annual Undergrad Tuition & Fees (In-State): $6,876
Enrollment: 22,227 Coed
Affiliation or Control: State IRS Status: 501(c)3
Highest Offering: Doctorate
Accreditation: **NW**, ART, BUS, BUSA, CAATE, CACREP, COARC, CONST, CS, DMS, ENG, MUS, RAD, SPAA, SW, TED, THEA

01 President Dr. Robert W. KUSTRA
05 Provost/Vice Pres Academic Affairs Dr. Martin E. SCHIMPF
10 Vice Pres Finan/Administration Ms. Stacy PEARSON
32 Interim Vice Pres Student Affairs Dr. Leslie DURHAM
30 Vice Pres University Advancement Ms. Laura SIMIC
43 Vice Pres Gen Counsel & Campus Op Mr. Kevin SATTERLEE
20 Vice Provost for Acad Planning Dr. James MUNGER
20 Vice Provost for Undergrad Studies Dr. Sharon PATERSON
21 Associate Vice Pres for Finance Ms. Jo Ellen DI NUCCI
35 Assoc Vice Pres Student Life Dr. Leslie WEBB
18 Acting Assoc VP Campus Plng/Facil Michael SUMPTER
46 Vice Pres for Research & Econ Devel Dr. Mark RUDIN
13 Assoc Vice Pres of IT Mr. Max DAVIS-JOHNSON
08 Dean of University Library Ms. Tracy BICKNELL-HOLMES
35 Dean of Students Dr. Chris WUTHRICH
84 Assoc Vice Pres Enrollment Services Mr. James ANDERSON
15 Asst VP Human Resources Mr. Jay STEPHENS
29 Executive Director Alumni Affairs Ms. Lisa GARDNER
17 Medical Services Director Dr. Vincent SERIO
06 Registrar Ms. Kristine COLLINS
18 Exec Director Campus Security Mr. John KAPLAN
40 Interim Director Bookstore Ms. Nicole R. GOUVEA
09 Director Institutional Research Dr. Shari ELLERTSON
07 Director of Admissions Dr. Kelly TALBERT
26 Assoc Vice Pres Comm & Market Mr. Greg HAHN
41 Exec Director Athletics Mr. Curt APSEY
22 Affirmative Action/EEO Ms. Jean SOLECKI
38 Director Counseling Services Dr. Karla WEST
37 Dir Financial Aid & Scholarships Ms. Diana FAIRCHILD
96 Director of Purchasing Ms. Terri SPINAZZA
51 Dean Extended Studies Mr. Mark WHEELER
49 Dean of Arts & Sciences Dr. Tony ROARK
50 Dean of Business & Economics Dr. Kenneth J. PETERSEN
53 Dean of Education Dr. Richard OSGUTHORPE
58 Dean of the Graduate College Dr. Jack PELTON
76 Dean of Health Sciences Dr. Tim DUNNAGAN
54 Dean of College of Engineering Dr. Amy MOLL
88 Dean Col of Innovation & Design Mr. Gordon JONES
92 Dean Honors College Dr. Andrew FINSTUEN
88 Dean School of Public Service Dr. Corey COOK
04 Exec Asst to President Ms. Melissa JENSEN
100 Chief of Staff Ms. Randi MCDERMOTT
104 Director Intl Learn Opps Ms. Corrine HENKE
39 Director Housing and Res Life Dr. Dean KENNEDY
86 Director Government Relations Mr. Bruce C. NEWCOMB
88 Director of IDEA Dr. Leslie MADSEN-BROOKS
103 Dir Workforce/Career Development Ms. Debbie KAYLOR
106 Dir Online Education/E-learning Ms. Janet ATKINSON
28 Director of Student Diversity Mr. Francisco SALINAS
102 Dir of Corporate & Foundation Rels Ms. Virginia PELLEGRINI
44 Sr Director Annual Giving Ms. Gertrude L. ARNOLD

Brigham Young University-Idaho (J)

525 South Center Street, Rexburg ID 83460
County: Madison FICE Identification: 001625
Unit ID: 142522
Telephone: (208) 496-1411 Carnegie Class: Bac-Diverse
FAX Number: (208) 496-1103 Calendar System: Semester

URL: www.byui.edu
Established: 1888 Annual Undergrad Tuition & Fees: $3,830
Enrollment: 36,624 Coed
Affiliation or Control: Latter-day Saints IRS Status: 501(c)3
Highest Offering: Baccalaureate
Accreditation: NW, EMT, ENG, MAC, MUS, NUR, PTAA, SW

01 President Dr. Clark G. GILBERT
05 Academic Vice President Dr. Henry J. EYRING
46 University Resources Vice President Mr. Jeffrey R. MORRIN
32 Student Svcs & Activities Vice Pres Mr. Kevin T. MIYASAKI
20 Assoc Academic VP Instruction Mr. Kelly T. BURGENER
106 Assoc Acad VP Curriculum & Online Dr. Van D. CHRISTMAN
20 Assoc Acad VP Support Services Dr. Richard K. PAGE
20 Assoc Acad VP Student Connections Dr. Ralph M. KERN
35 Dean of Students Mr. Kip B. HARRIS
88 Student Well Being Mng Director Mr. Wynn N. HILL
13 Chief Information Officer Mr. Joe TAYLOR
09 Inst Research & Assessment Director Dr. Scott J. BERGSTROM
06 Student Records & Registration Mr. Kyle R. MARTIN
37 Student Fin Aid/Scholarship Dir Mr. Aaron D. SANNS
08 University Librarian Mrs. Laurie S. FRANCIS
10 Univ Operations Managing Director Mr. Wayne N. CLARK
15 Human Resources Director Mr. Kevin L. PRICE
23 Student Health Services Director Mr. Shaun ORR
38 Student Counseling Center Director Mr. Reed J. STODDARD
19 University Security & Safety Dir Mr. Garth M. GUNDERSON
07 Admissions Director Mr. Tyler R. WILLIAMS
29 Alumni Director Mr. Steven J. DAVIS
35 Student Activities Mng Director Mr. Derek R. FAY
26 University Relations Mng Director Mr. Merv R. BROWN
30 Philanthropies Director Mr. Christopher W. MOORE
39 Housing & Student Living Director Dr. Troy J. DOUGHERTY
43 Legal Counsel Mr. Stephen CRAIG
21 Financial Services Mng Director Mr. Shane WEBSTER
88 Academic Discovery Center Director Mrs. Jill EVANS
96 Purchasing & Travel Director Mr. Mike B. THUESON
88 Student Svcs Managing Director Mr. Ben PACKER
88 University Store Manager Mr. Brett COOK
104 International Services Manager Mr. Mike R. OSWALD
04 Asst to Pres Strategy & Planning Mrs. Betty A. OLDHAM

Broadview University (A)

2750 East Gala Court, Meridian ID 83642
Telephone: (208) 577-2900 Identification: 770712
Accreditation: ACICS, MAAB

† Branch campus of Broadview University, West Jordan, UT

Brown Mackie College-Boise (B)

9050 West Overland Road, Ste. 101, Boise ID 83709
Telephone: (208) 321-8800 Identification: 666780
Accreditation: ACICS, OTA

† Branch campus of Brown Mackie College, South Bend, IN.

Carrington College - Boise (C)

1122 N Liberty Street, Boise ID 83704-8741
Telephone: (208) 377-8080 FICE Identification: 022180
Accreditation: &WJ, DA, DH, MAAB, PNUR, PTAA

† Regional accreditation is carried under the parent institution in Sacramento, CA.

The College of Idaho (D)

2112 Cleveland Boulevard, Caldwell ID 83605-9990
County: Canyon FICE Identification: 001617
Unit ID: 142294
Telephone: (208) 459-5011 Carnegie Class: Bac-A&S
FAX Number: (208) 454-2077 Calendar System: Other
URL: www.collegeofidaho.edu
Established: 1891 Annual Undergrad Tuition & Fees: $26,155
Enrollment: 1,144 Coed
Affiliation or Control: Independent Non-Profit IRS Status: 501(c)3
Highest Offering: Master's
Accreditation: NW

01 President Dr. Charlotte G. BORST
05 Vice President Academic Affairs Dr. John OTTENHOFF
10 Vice Pres Finance/Administration Mr. Richard ERNE
32 Vice President Student Affairs Dr. Paul BENNION
30 Vice President for Advancement Mr. Michael VANDERVELDEN
84 Vice President for Enrollment Dr. Lorna HUNTER
20 Associate Dean of Faculty Dr. Paul MOULTON
06 Registrar Ms. Susan HINES
41 Director of Athletics Mr. Marty HOLLY
26 Dir of Marketing & Communications Mr. Jordan RODRIGUEZ
29 Director of Alumni Ms. Sally SKINNER
44 Director of Boone Fund Ms. Kylie REAGAN
08 Director of Library Ms. Christine SCHUTZ
18 Director of Facilities Mr. Kyle ABRAHAMSON
21 Controller Mr. Jesse HARRIS
37 Director of Financial Services Ms. Jennifer WORDEN
15 Human Resources Director Ms. Nancy JOHNSON-CASSULO
36 Director Student Placement Ms. Jennifer RIDDLE
92 Director of Honors Program Dr. Sue SCHAPER
39 Director of Residential Life Ms. Jen NELSON
93 Director of Multicultural Affairs Mr. Arnold HERNANDEZ
42 Campus Minister/Asc Dean Students Dr. Phil ROGERS
19 Director of Campus Safety Mr. Allan LAIRD
13 Director of Information Technology Mr. Fred WARR
09 Director Institutional Research Mr. Mark HEIDRICH
30 Director Development Mr. Jack CAFFERTY
07 Associate Director of Admissions Mr. Mike BURDINE
40 Bookstore Manager Ms. Susan HUNSPERGER
38 Counselor Ms. Cynthia MAUZERALL
04 Executive Asst to President Ms. Anitra L. TOWNSEND

College of Southern Idaho (E)

PO Box 1238, 315 Falls Avenue,
Twin Falls ID 83303-1238
County: Twin Falls FICE Identification: 001619
Unit ID: 142559
Telephone: (208) 733-9554 Carnegie Class: Assoc/MT-VT-High Non
FAX Number: (208) 736-3015 Calendar System: Semester
URL: www.csi.edu
Established: 1965 Annual Undergrad Tuition & Fees (In-District): $2,880
Enrollment: 8,473 Coed
Affiliation or Control: Local IRS Status: 501(c)3
Highest Offering: Associate Degree
Accreditation: NW, ADNUR, DH, EMT, MAC, PTAA, RAD, SURGA, SURGT

01 President Dr. D. Jeff FOX
00 Chairman of the Board Mr. Karl KLEINKOPF
05 Exec VP/Chief Academic Officer Dr. Todd SCHWARZ
10 Vice President of Administration Mr. Jeff HARMON
13 Chief Technology Officer Mr. Kevin MARK
32 Assoc VP Student Services Dr. Michelle SCHUTT
09 Assoc Dean of IE/ALO Mr. Chris BRAGG
88 Assoc Dean of Student Success Mr. John HUGHES
04 Exec Admin Asst to President Ms. Kathy S. DEAHL
21 Chief Financial Officer Ms. Kristy CARPENTER
20 Instructional Dean Dr. Cindy R. BOND
20 Instructional Dean Mr. Terry L. PATTERSON
20 Instructional Dean HSHS Mr. Jayson LLOYD
35 Dean of Students Vacant
56 Assoc Dean of Extended Studies Mr. Cesar PEREZ
15 Director Human Resources Mr. Eric NIELSON
06 Registrar Dr. Michele MCFARLANE
07 Director of Admissions Ms. Gail SCHULL
37 Director of Student Financial Aid Ms. Jennifer J. ZIMMERS
08 Director Library Ms. Teri L. FATTIG
102 Executive Director Foundation Ms. Debra J. WILSON
103 Director Workforce Development Ms. Brandi TURNIPSEED
14 Dir Application/Data Architecture Mr. Ed DITLEFSEN
14 Dir Systems/Network Architecture Mr. Bruce NUKAYA
41 Athletic Director Mr. Joel C. BATE
18 Director Physical Plant Mr. Allen SCHERBINSKE
19 Director Security & Safety Mr. James MUNN
26 Public Information Director Mr. Doug L. MAUGHAN
27 Public Information Specialist Ms. Kim LAPRAY
40 Bookstore Manager Ms. Jayme KETTERLING
92 Coordinator Honors Program Mr. Brian DOBBS
39 Director Student Housing Ms. Angela URSENBACH

College of Western Idaho (F)

6056 Birch Lane, Nampa ID 83687
County: Canyon FICE Identification 042118
Unit ID: 455114
Telephone: (208) 562-3000 Carnegie Class: Assoc/MT-VT-Mix Trad/Non
FAX Number: (888) 562-3216 Calendar System: Semester
URL: cwidaho.cc
Established: 2007 Annual Undergrad Tuition & Fees (In-District): $3,264
Enrollment: 10,217 Coed
Affiliation or Control: Local IRS Status: 501(c)3
Highest Offering: Associate Degree
Accreditation: @NW, ACFEI, ADNUR, DA, EMT, #PTAA, SURGT

01 President Dr. Bert GLANDON
05 Exec VP Instruction/Student Svcs Mr. David SHELLBERG
10 VP Finance & Administration Ms. Cheryl WRIGHT
45 VP Resource Development Mr. Craig BROWN
20 Asst VP Academic Affairs Ms. Brenda PETTINGER
32 Int Dean Stdnt Affairs/Enroll Svcs Mr. Eric STUDEBAKER
75 Dean Career & Technical Education Mr. Will FANNING
13 Chief Information Officer Dr. David HUNTER
21 Comptroller Mr. Tony MEATTE
106 Dean Intructional Support Mr. James JANSEN
57 Dean Languages & Arts Ms. Laura STAVOE
81 Dean STEM Ms. Kae JENSEN
83 Dean Social Sciences & Public Aff Ms. Courtney SANTILLAN
50 Asst Dean Business/Info Tech Ms. Kelly STEELY
76 Asst Dean Health Professions Ms. Cathleen CURRIE
72 Asst Dean Trades & Technology Mr. Pat NEAL
88 Asst Dean Transportation Mr. Jeff SCHROEDER
21 Associate Controller Ms. Mary Jo HAYES
102 Executive Director CWI Foundation Mr. Mitch MINNETTE
18 Executive Director Facilities Mgmt Mr. Jeff FLYNN
15 Executive Director Human Resources Ms. Lillian TALLEY
26 Exec Dir Marketing/Advancement Ms. Jennifer COUCH
103 Executive Director Workforce Devel Ms. Christi ROOD
07 Director of Admissions & One Stop Mr. Luis CALOCA
88 Director Adult Basic Education Mr. Jac WEBB
88 Director Advising & New Students Ms. Autumn BRACKLEY
88 Director Center for Teach/Learn Ms. Courtney COLBY-BOND
88 Director Dual Cr/College Readiness Mr. Stephen CRUMRINE
37 Director Financial Aid Ms. Nicole MCMILLIN
09 Director Inst Effectiveness Mr. Doug DEPRIEST
08 Director Library Services Ms. Kim REED
88 Director Math Solutions Center Ms. Susan KNIGHTS
35 Director Student Affairs & Programs Mr. Shane OSTERMEIER
88 Director WD Business & Manufact Mr. Marc SWINNEY
06 Registrar Ms. Connie BLACK

Eastern Idaho Technical College (G)

1600 S 25th E, Idaho Falls ID 83404-5788
County: Bonneville FICE Identification: 011133
Unit ID: 142179
Telephone: (208) 524-3000 Carnegie Class: Assoc/HVT-High Non
FAX Number: (208) 524-3007 Calendar System: Semester
URL: www.eitc.edu
Established: 1969 Annual Undergrad Tuition & Fees (In-State): $2,780
Enrollment: 686 Coed
Affiliation or Control: State IRS Status: 501(c)3
Highest Offering: Associate Degree
Accreditation: NW, MAC, SURGT

01 President Dr. Rick K. AMAN
10 Vice President of Finance and Admin Dr. Christian GODFREY
05 VP of Instruction & Student Affairs Dr. Sharee ANDERSON
06 Registrar Mrs. Rae Lynn PATTERSON
21 Controller Mr. Don E. BOURNE
103 Mgr Workforce Trng/Cmty Education Mr. Kenneth W. ERICKSON
37 Financial Aid Director Mrs. Shayna SHARP
04 President Administrative Assistant Mrs. Kristina BUCHAN
26 Director of College Relations Mr. Todd WIGHTMAN
102 Foundation Director Mrs. Natalie J. HEBARD
07 Director of Admissions/Placement Mrs. Hailey MACK
50 Business/Office/Technology Div Mgr Mr. Leslie JERNBERG
97 General Education Division Manager Mrs. Peggy L. NELSON
76 Health Care Technology Div Manager Mr. Jared L. GARDNER
88 Trades/Industry Division Manager Mr. Kent E. BERGGREN
88 Adult Basic Education Div Manager Mrs. Theresa GROENEWOLD
09 Director of Institutional Research Mr. Lee STIMPSON
13 Chief Info Technology Officer (CIO) Mrs. Karen FOSTER

Idaho State University (H)

921 S 8th, Pocatello ID 83209-0009
County: Bannock FICE Identification: 001620
Unit ID: 142276
Telephone: (208) 282-0211 Carnegie Class: DU-Mod
FAX Number: (208) 282-4000 Calendar System: Semester
URL: www.isu.edu
Established: 1901 Annual Undergrad Tuition & Fees (In-State): $6,784
Enrollment: 13,429 Coed
Affiliation or Control: State IRS Status: 501(c)3
Highest Offering: Doctorate
Accreditation: NW, ADNUR, ARCPA, AUD, BUS, BUSA, CAATE, CACREP, CAHIIM, CLPSY, COARC, COMTA, DENT, DH, DIETD, DIETI, EMT, ENG, ENGR, ENGT, MAC, MT, MUS, NAIT, NURSE, OT, PH, PHAR, PTA, PTAA, RAD, SP, SW, TED, THEA

01 President Dr. Arthur C. VAILAS
05 Provost/VP for Acad Affairs Dr. Laura WOODWORTH-NEY
10 Vice President for Finance & Admin Mr. James A. FLETCHER
30 Vice Pres University Advancement Dr. Kent M. TINGEY
32 Vice Pres of Student Affairs Dr. Patricia TERRELL
46 Vice President for Research Dr. Cornelis VAN DER SCHYF
43 University Legal Counsel Ms. Joanne HIRASE-STACEY
41 Athletic Director Mr. Jeff TINGEY
20 Vice Provost Dr. Lyle CASTLE
20 AVP/Exec Dean Div Health Sciences Dr. Linda HATZENBUEHLER
20 AVP for Academic Affairs Dr. Margaret JOHNSON
20 AVP for Academic Affairs Ms. Selena GRACE
30 AVP for Development Ms. Pauline THIROS
18 AVP for Facilities Services Mr. Phillip MOESSNER
58 Dean of Graduate School Dr. Cornelis VAN DER SCHYF
54 Interim Dean College Science & Eng Dr. Richard BREY
67 Dean College of Pharmacy Dr. Paul S. CADY
50 Dean College of Business Dr. Thomas OTTAWAY
49 Dean College of Arts & Letters Dr. Kandi TURLEY-AMES
53 Interim Dean College of Education Dr. Karen APPLEBY
75 Dean College of Technology Dr. Scott RASMUSSEN
12 Dean of Academic Pgm ISU-Meridian Dr. Bessie KATSILOMETES
12 Dean of Academic Pgm ISU-Id Falls Dr. Lyle W. CASTLE
08 Dean & University Librarian Mr. Karl BRIDGES
06 Registrar & Dir of Undergrad Admiss Ms. Laura MCKENZIE
13 Chief Information Officer Mr. Randy GAINES
29 Director Alumni Relations Ms. K.C FELT
09 Director Institutional Research Mr. Vince MILLER
37 Director Student Financial Aid Mr. James MARTIN
15 Director Human Resources Mr. Brian SAGENDORF
23 Director Student Health Center Dr. Ronald SOLBRIG
22 Dir EEO/Affirm Action & Diversity Ms. Stacey GIBSON
19 Director Public Safety Mr. Lewis EAKINS
26 Director Marketing & Communication Mr. Stuart SUMMERS
86 Director Government Relations Mr. Kent KUNZ
88 Director Events Management Mr. George CASPER
35 Director of Student Life Dr. Jane COE-SMITH
38 Director of Counseling & Testing Dr. Don PAULSON
85 Interim Asst Dir of Intl Programs Mr. Shawn BASCOM
84 Director of Enrollment Services/IF Ms. Ann HOWELL
07 Interim Director of Admissions Ms. Nicole ROSEBERG
39 Director University Housing Mr. Craig THOMPSON
96 Director of Purchasing Services Mr. David BUCK

Lewis-Clark State College (A)

500 8th Avenue, Lewiston ID 83501-2698
County: Nez Perce FICE Identification: 001621
Unit ID: 142328
Telephone: (208) 792-5272 Carnegie Class: Bac-Diverse
FAX Number: (208) 792-2831 Calendar System: Semester
URL: www.lcsc.edu
Established: 1893 Annual Undergrad Tuition & Fees (In-State): $7,224
Enrollment: 4,304 Coed
Affiliation or Control: State IRS Status: 501(c)3
Highest Offering: Baccalaureate
Accreditation: NW, EMT, IACBE, MAC, NURSE, #PTAA, RAD, SW, TED

01 President .... Dr. J. Anthony FERNANDEZ
05 Provost/VP Academic Affairs .... Dr. Lori STINSON
10 VP Finance and Administration .... Mr. Todd KILBURN
75 Dean Professional/Technical Pgms .... Dr. Robert LOHRMEYER
51 Dean Community Programs .... Ms. Kathy MARTIN
20 Dean Academic Programs .... Ms. Mary FLORES
32 Vice President Student Affairs .... Dr. Andrew HANSON
08 Director of Library Services .... Ms. Susan NIEWENHOUS
103 Director of Workforce Training .... Dr. Linda STRICKLIN
07 Director of Admissions/Registrar .... Ms. Nikol ROUBIDOUX
09 Dir Planning/Research/Assessment .... Mr. Sean GEHRKE
13 Chief Technology Officer .... Mr. Allen SCHMOOCK
41 Athletic Director .... Mr. Gary PICONE
15 Director of Human Resources .... Ms. Vikki SWIFT
26 Director of College Communications .... Mr. Logan FOWLER
29 Director of Alumni Relations .... Ms. Renee OLSEN
37 Director of Student Financial Aid .... Ms. Laura HUGHES
30 Director of College Advancement .... Ms. Erika ALLEN
18 Director of Physical Plant .... Mr. Matt GRAVES
36 Director Career & Advising Services .... Ms. Debra LYBYER
96 Director of Purchasing .... Ms. Sheila KOM

New Saint Andrews College (B)

PO Box 9025, Moscow ID 83843-1525
County: Latah Identification: 666166
Unit ID: 440396
Telephone: (208) 882-1566 Carnegie Class: Not Classified
FAX Number: (208) 882-4293 Calendar System: Other
URL: www.nsa.edu
Established: 1994 Annual Undergrad Tuition & Fees: $11,800
Enrollment: N/A Coed
Affiliation or Control: Independent Non-Profit IRS Status: 501(c)3
Highest Offering: Master's
Accreditation: TRACS

01 President .... Dr. Ben MERKLE
05 Academic Dean .... Dr. Timothy EDWARDS
73 Director MA Program .... Mr. Douglas WILSON
53 Dir Classical Christian Studies Pgm .... Mr. Christopher SCHLECT
10 Chief Financial Officer .... Mr. Thomas BRAINERD
08 Head Librarian .... Mrs. Helen HOWELL
06 Registrar .... Mr. Jacob MOYA
07 Director of Recruitment .... Mrs. Brenda SCHLECT
30 Director Development .... Mr. Nicholas ROZIER
32 Manager New Student Services .... Mr. John SAWYER

North Idaho College (C)

1000 W Garden Avenue, Coeur d'Alene ID 83814-2199
County: Kootenai FICE Identification: 001623
Unit ID: 142443
Telephone: (208) 769-3300 Carnegie Class: Assoc/MT-VT-High Trad
FAX Number: (208) 765-2761 Calendar System: Semester
URL: www.nic.edu
Established: 1933 Annual Undergrad Tuition & Fees (In-District): $3,214
Enrollment: 5,768 Coed
Affiliation or Control: Local IRS Status: 501(c)3
Highest Offering: Associate Degree
Accreditation: NW, ADNUR, MAC, #PTAA, RAD

01 President .... Dr. Richard L. MACLENNAN
05 Vice President for Instruction .... Dr. Lita BURNS
10 VP for Finance & Business Affairs .... Mr. Christopher MARTIN
32 Vice President for Student Services .... Mr. Graydon STANLEY
31 VP Cmty & Governmental Relations .... Mr. Mark BROWNING
103 Dean of Career Tech/Workforce Educ .... Ms. Kassie SILVAS
97 Dean of General Studies .... Dr. Larry BRIGGS
66 Dean of Nursing & Health Prof .... Ms. Christy DOYLE
06 Director of Admissions/Registrar .... Ms. Tami HAFT
09 Director of Inst Effectiveness .... Ms. Ann LEWIS
08 Library Director .... Mr. George MCALISTER
13 Chief Information Officer .... Mr. Ken WARDINSKY
37 Director of Financial Aid .... Ms. Stephanie HOUSE
18 Asst Director of Facilities .... Mr. Garry STARK
26 Director of Comm & Marketing .... Ms. Stacy HUDSON
30 Development Director .... Ms. Rayelle ANDERSON
35 Director Student Development .... Mr. Alex HARRIS
21 Controller .... Ms. Sarah GARCIA
72 Technology Coordinator .... Mr. Andy FINNEY
29 Alumni Relations Coordinator .... Mr. Taylor FORE
04 Sr Executive Assistant .... Ms. Shannon GOODRICH
106 Director of E-learning .... Mr. Thomas SCOTT
25 Grants Development Manager .... Ms. Sara FLADELAND
41 Athletic Director .... Mr. Alvin WILLIAMS
19 Supervisor Security .... Mr. Patrick MURRAY

Northwest Nazarene University (D)

623 S. University Boulevard, Nampa ID 83686-5897
County: Canyon FICE Identification: 001624
Unit ID: 142461
Telephone: (208) 467-8011 Carnegie Class: Masters/L
FAX Number: (208) 467-8099 Calendar System: Semester
URL: www.nnu.edu
Established: 1913 Annual Undergrad Tuition & Fees: $28,150
Enrollment: 2,249 Coed
Affiliation or Control: Church Of The Nazarene IRS Status: 501(c)3
Highest Offering: Doctorate
Accreditation: NW, ACBSP, CACREP, ENG, MUS, NURSE, SW, TED

01 President .... Mr. Joel K. PEARSALL
05 Vice Pres Academic Affairs/Dean .... Dr. Ed ROBINSON
10 Vice Pres Financial Affairs .... Mr. David S. TARRANT
84 Vice Pres Enrollment & Marketing .... Vacant
32 Vice President Student Development .... Dr. Carey W. COOK
88 Vice Pres Spiritual & Ldrshp Dev .... Dr. Fred C. FULLERTON
30 AVP of Development .... Mr. Mark WHEELER
06 Registrar .... Mrs. Nancy A. AYERS
08 Director of the Library .... Dr. Sharon I. BULL
29 Director of Alumni Relations .... Mr. Darl L. BRUNER
51 Dir Center for Professional Devel .... Mr. Dave R. COVINGTON
42 Dean of the Chapel .... Rev. Dustin METCALF
42 Director of Campus Ministry .... Ms. Julene M. TEGERSTRAND
40 Bookstore Manager .... Ms. Gail D. WALKER
39 Director of Residential Life .... Mrs. Karen L. PEARSON
38 Director of Wellness Center .... Mrs. Terri BLACKBURN
07 Director of Admissions .... Mr. Shawn A. BLENKER
21 Controller .... Mrs. Macey CROW
26 Director of Marketing & Media .... Vacant
35 Director of Community Life .... Mr. Grant T. MILLER
36 Director of Career Center .... Ms. Amanda F. MARBLE
13 Exec Director of Info Technology .... Mr. Sal SIMILI
24 Director of Tech & Media Resources .... Vacant
37 Director of Financial Aid .... Mrs. Ann CRABB
15 Director of Human Resources .... Ms. Sherry L. HARTMAN
41 Athletic Director .... Ms. Kelli LINDLEY
91 Dir of Administrative Computing .... Mr. Brian C. STILLMAN
18 Chief Facilities/Physical Plant .... Mr. Jade ANDERSON
04 Administrative Asst to President .... Ms. Jill D. JONES

Stevens-Henager College (E)

901 Pier View Drive, Suite 105, Idaho Falls ID 83404
Telephone: (205) 522-0887 Identification: 770573
Accreditation: ACCSC

† Branch campus of Stevens-Henager College, Ogden, UT

Stevens-Henager College-Boise (F)

1444 S. Entertainment Avenue, Boise ID 83709
Telephone: (208) 383-4540 Identification: 666329
Accreditation: ACCSC, COARC

† Branch campus of Stevens-Henager College, Ogden, UT

University of Idaho (G)

875 Perimeter Drive MS 3151, Moscow ID 83844-3151
County: Latah FICE Identification: 001626
Unit ID: 142285
Telephone: (208) 885-6111 Carnegie Class: DU-Higher
FAX Number: N/A Calendar System: Semester
URL: www.uidaho.edu
Established: 1889 Annual Undergrad Tuition & Fees (In-State): $7,020
Enrollment: 11,702 Coed
Affiliation or Control: State IRS Status: 501(c)3
Highest Offering: Doctorate
Accreditation: NW, ART, BUS, BUSA, CAATE, CEA, CIDA, CORE, CS, DIETC, ENG, IPSY, JOUR, LAW, LSAR, MUS, NAIT, NRPA, TED

01 President .... Dr. Chuck A. STABEN
05 Provost & Executive VP .... Dr. John M. WIENCEK
10 VP Finance .... Mr. Brian R. FOISY
30 VP University Advancement .... Ms. Mary Kay MCFADDEN
03 VP Infrastructure .... Mr. Dan EWART
46 VP Research & Econ Dev .... Dr. John MCIVER
84 Asst Vice Pres Enrollmnt Managemnt .... Vacant
88 Special Assistant/Prnc Gft Officer .... Mr. Michael C. PERRY
88 Special Asst/Agriculture Initiative .... Dr. John FOLTZ
26 Executive Dir of Mktg & Comm .... Ms. Stefany BALES
41 Athletic Director .... Dr. Robert SPEAR
43 General Counsel .... Mr. Kent E. NELSON
86 Special Asst State Govt Relations .... Mr. Joe STEGNER
28 Chief Diversity Officer .... Dr. Yolanda BISBEE
08 Dean Library Services .... Ms. Lynn N. BAIRD
49 Dean Col of Letters/Arts Soc Sci .... Dr. Andrew KERSTEN
47 Dean College of Agric/Life Sci .... Dr. Michael PARRELLA
50 Dean College of Business & Econ .... Dr. Marc CHOPIN
53 Dean College of Education .... Dr. Alison CARR-CHELLMAN
54 Dean College of Engineering .... Dr. Larry STAUFFER
58 Dean Graduate Studies .... Dr. Jerry MCMURTY
65 Dean College of Natural Resources .... Dr. Kurt PREGITZER
61 Dean College of Law .... Mr. Mark ADAMS
48 Dean College of Art & Architecture .... Vacant
81 Assoc Dean College of Science .... Dr. Mark NIELSEN
20 Vice Provost Academic Affairs .... Dr. Jeanne M. STEVENSON
32 Vice Provost of Student Affairs .... Vacant
109 Asst VP Auxiliary Services .... Mr. Alan COKER
15 Executive Director Human Resources .... Mr. Wesley MATTHEWS
45 Budget Director .... Ms. Trina MAHONEY
12 Executive Officer Couer d'Alene .... Dr. Charles BUCK
12 Executive Officer Boise Center .... Mr. Michael SATZ
12 Exectuive Office Idaho Falls Center .... Dr. Marc SKINNER
18 Assistant Vice President Facilities .... Mr. Brian D. JOHNSON
13 AVP ITS/CIO .... Mr. Daniel EWART
19 Director Public Security/Safety .... Mr. Matt DORSCHEL
108 Director Inst Research & Assessment .... Dr. Dale PIETRZAK
37 Director Student Financial Aid .... Dr. Daniel D. DAVENPORT
07 Director of Admissions .... Mr. Cezar MESQUITA
38 Director Counseling & Testing Ctr .... Dr. Joan PULAKOS
42 Director Campus Christian Center .... Ms. Sharon A. KEHOE
39 Director University Residences .... Ms. Dee Dee KANIKKEBERG
44 Director Annual Giving .... Mr. James BROWNSON
92 Director Honors Program .... Dr. Alton CAMPBELL
93 Dir Multicultural Affairs .... Mr. Jesse MARTINEZ
94 Director Women's Center .... Ms. Lysa SALSBURY
40 Director Bookstore .... Mr. John BALES
96 Director Purchasing Services .... Ms. Julia MCILROY
36 Director Career Services .... Mr. Eric ANDERSON
25 Director Research Admin .... Ms. Deborah SHAVER
35 Dean of Students .... Dr. Blaine ECKLES
103 Dir Academic Support and Access Pgm .... Ms. Cynthia CASTRO
06 Registrar .... Ms. Heather A. CHERMAK
29 Executive Dir Alumni Relations .... Ms. Kathy BARNARD
102 Dir Foundation/Corporate Relations .... Ms. Bobbi HUGHES
106 Dir Distance & Extended Educ .... Mr. Terry RATCLIFF
87 Coord Summer & Dual Credit Pgm .... Ms. Linda GOLLBERG
22 Assc Dir Human Rights/Access/Inclus .... Ms. Erin AGIDIUS
105 Director Enterprise Applications .... Mr. Brian BORCHERS
104 Exec Dir International Programs .... Ms. Susan BENDER
100 Chief of Staff President's Office .... Ms. Brenda HELBLING

University of Phoenix Idaho Campus (H)

1420 South Tech Lane, Meridian ID 83642-5114
Telephone: (208) 898-2000 Identification: 770204
Accreditation: &NH, ACBSP

† No longer accepting campus-based students.

ILLINOIS

Adler University (I)

17 North Dearborn Street, Chicago IL 60602
County: Cook FICE Identification: 020681
Unit ID: 142832
Telephone: (312) 662-4000 Carnegie Class: Spec-4-yr-Other Health
FAX Number: (312) 662-4099 Calendar System: Semester
URL: www.adler.edu
Established: 1952 Annual Graduate Tuition & Fees: N/A
Enrollment: 1,004 Coed
Affiliation or Control: Independent Non-Profit IRS Status: 501(c)3
Highest Offering: Doctorate; No Undergraduates
Accreditation: NH, CACREP, CLPSY, CORE, IPSY

01 President .... Dr. Raymond E. CROSSMAN
101 Board Secy/Dir Ofc of the Pres .... Ms. Mitzi NORTON
11 Vice President Administration .... Ms. Jo Beth CUP
05 Vice President Academic Affairs .... Dr. Wendy PASZKIEWICZ
10 Vice President Finance & IT .... Mr. Jeffrey GREEN
30 VP for Institutional Advancement .... Ms. Mary Jo LAMPARSKI
07 Vice President Admissions .... Mr. Craig HINES
26 Assoc Vice President Marketing .... Mr. Mark BRANSON
06 Registrar .... Ms. Sheba JONES
32 Assoc Vice President Student Affair .... Mr. Greg MACVARISH
88 Ex Dir Inst Pub Safety/Soc Justice .... Dr. Elena QUINTARA
35 Asst Director Student Affairs .... Ms. Jennifer POPE
37 Director Student Financial Aid .... Mr. David NELSON
13 Associate VP Technology .... Mr. Paul COLLINS
08 Director Library .... Ms. Kerry COCHRANE
09 Director of Institutional Research .... Mr. Don HUFFMAN
12 Dean Vancouver Campus .... Mr. Bradley O'HARA
106 Executive Dean Online Campus .... Ms. Greta FERKEL
15 AVP Human Resources .... Ms. Susan YASECKO
29 Director Alumni Relations .... Mr. Michael ZAROBE
44 Director Annual Giving .... Ms. Anna KULSETH

Ambria College of Nursing (J)

5210 Trillium Boulevard, Hoffman Estates IL 60192
County: Cook FICE Identification: 041247
Unit ID: 457527
Telephone: (847) 397-0300 Carnegie Class: Spec 2-yr-Health
FAX Number: (847) 397-0313 Calendar System: Other
URL: www.ambria.edu
Established: 2006 Annual Undergrad Tuition & Fees: N/A
Enrollment: 432 Coed
Affiliation or Control: Proprietary IRS Status: Proprietary
Highest Offering: Baccalaureate
Accreditation: ACICS

01 President .... Jon OLIVEROS

American Academy of Art (K)

332 S Michigan Avenue, Chicago IL 60604-4302
County: Cook FICE Identification: 001628
Unit ID: 142887
Telephone: (312) 461-0600 Carnegie Class: Spec-4-yr-Arts
FAX Number: (312) 294-9570 Calendar System: Semester

URL: www.aaart.edu
Established: 1923　Annual Undergrad Tuition & Fees: $31,220
Enrollment: 365　Coed
Affiliation or Control: Independent Non-Profit　IRS Status: 501(c)3
Highest Offering: Baccalaureate
Accreditation: **NH**, ACCSC

01 Director ... Mr. Richard H. OTTO
05 Academic Dean ... Mr. Duncan WEBB
06 Registrar ... Ms. Marcia R. THOMAS
36 Career Services Coordinator ... Ms. Lindsay SANDBOTHE
37 Financial Aid Director ... Ms. Ione FITZGERALD
88 Cultural Coordinator ... Ms. Lou Ann BURKHARDT
07 Director of Admissions ... Mr. Stuart ROSENBLOOM

American InterContinental University (A)

231 North Martingale Rd, 6th Floor, Schaumburg IL 60173
County: Cook　FICE Identification: 021136
Unit ID: 445027
Telephone: (877) 701-3800　Carnegie Class: Masters/L
FAX Number: N/A　Calendar System: Quarter
URL: www.aiuonline.edu
Established: 1970　Annual Undergrad Tuition & Fees: $11,004
Enrollment: 11,900　Coed
Affiliation or Control: Proprietary　IRS Status: Proprietary
Highest Offering: Master's
Accreditation: **NH**, ACBSP, TEAC

00 Chancellor ... Dr. George P. MILLER
01 President ... Mr. John KLINE
05 Provost/Chief Academic Officer ... Dr. Ruki JAYARAMAN
32 Vice President Student Affairs ... Ms. Betsy BALACHANDRAN
10 VP Finance/Strategy/Univ Operations ... Mr. John SPRINGER
07 Vice President Admissions ... Ms. Trisha GANGER
09 Dir of Institutional Effectiveness ... Mr. Chris PERRY

Argosy University, Chicago (B)

225 North Michigan Ave., Suite 1300, Chicago IL 60601
Telephone: (312) 777-7600　Identification: 666736
Accreditation: **&WC**, ACBSP, CACREP, CLPSY

† Regional accreditation is carried under the parent institution in Orange, CA.

Argosy University, Schaumburg (C)

999 N. Plaza Drive, Suite 111, Schaumburg IL 60173-5403
Telephone: (847) 969-4900　Identification: 666789
Accreditation: **&WC**, ACBSP, CACREP, CLPSY

† Regional accreditation is carried under the parent institution in Orange, CA.

Augustana College (D)

639 38th Street, Rock Island IL 61201-2296
County: Rock Island　FICE Identification: 001633
Unit ID: 143084
Telephone: (309) 794-7000　Carnegie Class: Bac-A&S
FAX Number: (309) 794-7422　Calendar System: Trimester
URL: www.augustana.edu
Established: 1860　Annual Undergrad Tuition & Fees: $38,466
Enrollment: 2,497　Coed
Affiliation or Control: Evangelical Lutheran Church In America
IRS Status: 501(c)3
Highest Offering: Baccalaureate
Accreditation: **NH**, MUS, TED

01 President ... Mr. Steven C. BAHLS
05 Dean of College ... Dr. Pareena G. LAWRENCE
10 Vice Pres Business & Finance ... Mr. Kirk D. ANDERSON
30 Vice President Advancement ... Ms. Julie E. CROCKETT
32 Vice Pres/Dean of Student Services ... Dr. Evelyn S. CAMPBELL
84 VP Enrollment/Communication/Plng ... Mr. W. Kent BARNDS
20 Associate Dean of the College . Dr. Wendy S. HILTON-MORROW
20 Associate Dean of the College ... Dr. Kristin DOUGLAS
20 Associate Dean of the College ... Dr. Jeffrey RATLIFF-CRAIN
42 Chaplain ... Rev. Richard W. PRIGGIE
06 College Registrar ... Ms. Liesl A. FOWLER
09 Asst Dean/Director Inst Research ... Mr. Mark SALISBURY
08 Director of the Library ... Ms. Carla B. TRACY
36 Associate VP Careers & Prof Devel ... Vacant
13 Director of ITS ... Mr. Chris VAUGHAN
37 Director of Student Financial Aid ... Ms. Susan STANDLEY
96 Director of Purchasing ... Vacant
19 Chief of Public Safety ... Mr. Thomas M. PHILLIS
41 Director of Athletics ... Mr. Mike ZAPOLSKI
15 Director Human Resources ... Mrs. Laura C. FORD
18 Director Facilities Services ... Mr. Joe SCIFO
38 Director Student Counseling ... Mr. Michael W. TENDALL
35 Assistant Dean of Student Life ... Ms. Laura L. SCHNACK
26 Assistant VP for Comm & Marketing ... Ms. Keri RURSCH
28 Director of Multicultural & Intl ... Mr. Samuel PAYAN
29 Director Alumni/Parent Relations ... Ms. Kelly NOACK
07 Director of Admissions/Recruitment ... Ms. Meghan M. COOLEY
04 Administrative Asst to President ... Ms. Jennifer MOON
104 Director Study Abroad ... Dr. Allen P. BERTSCHE
43 Dir Legal Services/General Counsel ... Ms. Sheri L. CURRAN
100 Chief of Staff ... Mr. Kai SWANSON
102 Dir Foundation/Corporate Relations ... Ms. Lori FODERICK
44 Associate VP of Development ... Ms. Nancy A. JOHNSON
39 Director of Residential Life ... Mr. Christopher BEYER

Aurora University (E)

347 S Gladstone Avenue, Aurora IL 60506-4892
County: Kane　FICE Identification: 001634
Unit ID: 143118
Telephone: (630) 892-6431　Carnegie Class: Masters/L
FAX Number: (630) 844-5463　Calendar System: Semester
URL: www.aurora.edu
Established: 1893　Annual Undergrad Tuition & Fees: $22,080
Enrollment: 5,084　Coed
Affiliation or Control: Independent Non-Profit　IRS Status: 501(c)3
Highest Offering: Doctorate
Accreditation: **NH**, CAATE, NURSE, SW, TED

01 President ... Dr. Rebecca L. SHERRICK
30 Executive Vice President ... Mr. Theodore C. PARGE
05 Vice President for Academic Affairs ... Dr. Frank M. BUSCHER
10 Vice President for Finance ... Ms. Sharon MAXWELL
84 Sr Vice President for Enrollment ... Dr. Donna DE SPAIN
32 Sr Vice President for Student Life ... Dr. Lora DE LACEY
26 VP Univ Communications/Admin ... Mr. Steven MCFARLAND
31 Vice President Community Relations ... Ms. Sarah R. RUSSE
30 VP for Development/Alumni Relations ... Ms. Teri TOMASZKIEWICZ
15 Vice President of Human Resources ... Ms. Mary WEIS
35 Asst Vice Pres for Student Life ... Dr. Amy GRAY
37 Dean of Student Financial Services ... Ms. Heather L. GRANART
13 Vice President for Technology ... Mr. David W. DIEHL
06 Registrar ... Ms. Lisa WISNIOWICZ
08 Director University Library ... Ms. Kathy CLARK
19 Director of Campus Safety ... Mr. Gary BOLT
44 Director Special Gifts ... Mr. Roger K. PAROLINI
41 Athletic Director ... Mr. James HAMAD
38 Director of Counseling Center ... Dr. Marcie WISEMAN
66 Exec Dir Sch of Nursing/Allied Hlth ... Dr. Brenda SHOSTROM
70 Exec Dir of School of Social Work ... Dr. Fred R. MCKENZIE
88 Dean of Faculty Development ... Dr. Alicia C. COSKY
49 Dean College of Art and Sciences ... Dr. Carmella MORAN
53 Exec Director School of Education ... Dr. Jocelyn BOOTH
68 Exec Dir Sch Human Perf/Recreation ... Dr. Jennifer BUCKLEY
50 Exec Dir Dunham Sch Bus/Public Pol ... Dr. Toby ARQUETTE
51 Dean of Online Enroll/Cont Educ ... Dr. Donna LILJEGREN
106 Academic Dean of Online Programs ... Dr. Portia RANSOM
20 Dean Academic Administration ... Dr. Mary TARLING

Benedictine University (F)

5700 College Road, Lisle IL 60532-0900
County: DuPage　FICE Identification: 001767
Unit ID: 145619
Telephone: (630) 829-6000　Carnegie Class: DU-Mod
FAX Number: (630) 960-1126　Calendar System: Semester
URL: www.ben.edu
Established: 1887　Annual Undergrad Tuition & Fees: $27,465
Enrollment: 6,307　Coed
Affiliation or Control: Roman Catholic　IRS Status: 501(c)3
Highest Offering: Doctorate
Accreditation: **NH**, DIETD, DIETI, NURSE, PH

01 President ... Dr. Michael S. BROPHY
03 Campus Executive Officer ... Mr. Charles GREGORY
05 Provost/Vice Pres Academic Affs ... Dr. Maria DE LA CAMARA
10 VP Business & Finance ... Ms. Miroslava MEJIA KRUG
30 Vice President of Development ... Mr. Leonard A. BERTOLINI
32 Vice Pres Student Life ... Mr. Marco MASINI
09 Assoc Provost ... Dr. David SONNENBERGER
42 Director University Ministry ... Ms. Carrie ROBERTS
84 VP for Enrollment Services ... Ms. Kari GIBBONS
06 Registrar ... Ms. Janet HULSEY
08 Director Library Services ... Mr. Jack FRITTS
37 Sr Associate Dean Financial Aid ... Ms. Diane BATTISTELLA
09 Vice Pres of Institutional Research ... Dr. Robert STANLEY
36 Director Career Development ... Ms. Julie COSIMO
23 Director Health Services ... Ms. Janet DEELY
26 Exec Dir Marketing/Communications ... Ms. Mercy ROBB
50 Dean College of Business ... Dr. Sandra GILL
81 Dean College of Science ... Dr. Bart NG
49 Dean College of Liberal Arts ... Dr. Susan MIKULA
51 National Moser Center Adult Lrng ... Ms. Michele KOPPITZ
53 Dean Col Education/Health Services ... Dr. Ethel RAGLAND
19 Chief of Police ... Mr. Michael SALATINO
18 Director Campus Services ... Mr. Chet ILDEFONSO
31 Director Community Development ... Ms. Denise WEST
15 Director of Personnel Resources ... Ms. Betsy RH NESMITH
35 Student Activ & Commuter Svcs Coord ... Ms. Katie BUELL
13 Chief Information Officer ... Mr. Rodney FOWLKES
07 Director of Admissions ... Mr. Anthony SCOLA
04 Administrative Asst to President ... Ms. Elizabeth HILL
102 Dir Foundation/Corporate Relations ... Ms. Anna HANSON
104 Director Study Abroad ... Ms. Jennifer ERICKSON
105 Director Web Services ... Mr. Kevin SHERMAN
108 Director Institutional Assessment ... Mr. Thomas WANGLER
29 Director Alumni Relations ... Ms. Trente ARENS
38 Director Student Counseling ... Ms. Karen CAMPANA
39 Director Student Housing ... Mr. Jon MILLER
41 Athletic Director ... Mr. Mark MCHORNEY
43 Dir Legal Services/General Counsel ... Ms. Nancy STOECKER
44 Director Annual or Planned Giving ... Ms. Jill POSKIN
45 Chief Institutional Planning ... Mr. Chad TREISCH
86 Director Government Relations ... Mr. Kevin RAPPEL

Benedictine University at Springfield (G)

1500 N 5th Street, Springfield IL 62702
Telephone: (217) 525-1420　Identification: 770067
Accreditation: **&NH**

† Regional accreditation is carried under the parent institution in Lisle, IL

Bexley Seabury (H)

1407 E 60th St, Chicago IL 60637
County: Cook　FICE Identification: 001754
Unit ID: 148724
Telephone: (773) 380-6780　Carnegie Class: Spec-4-yr-Faith
FAX Number: (773) 380-6788　Calendar System: Semester
URL: www.bexleyseabury.edu
Established: 1858　Annual Graduate Tuition & Fees: N/A
Enrollment: 45　Coed
Affiliation or Control: Protestant Episcopal　IRS Status: 501(c)3
Highest Offering: Doctorate; No Undergraduates
Accreditation: **THEOL**

01 President ... Rev. Roger A. FERLO
05 Academic Dean ... Dr. Therese DELISIO
30 Vice Pres Advancement/Church Rels ... Mr. Conrad SELNICK
10 Director of Finance ... Mr. Robert DOAK
04 Exec Assistant to the President ... Br. Ronald A. FOX, BSG
08 Director United Library ... Ms. Lucy CHUNG
06 Recruiter/Digital Missioner ... Mr. Jaime BRICENO
42 Dir of Congregational Development ... Rev. Suzann HOLDING
15 Mgr Acct/Human Resource/Spec Events ... Ms. Lynn BOWERS
44 Annual Campaign Coordinator ... Ms. Susan QUIGLEY

Black Hawk College (I)

6600 34th Avenue, Moline IL 61265-5899
County: Rock Island　FICE Identification: 001638
Unit ID: 143279
Telephone: (309) 796-5000　Carnegie Class: Assoc/MT-VT-High Non
FAX Number: (309) 792-5976　Calendar System: Semester
URL: www.bhc.edu
Established: 1946　Annual Undergrad Tuition & Fees (In-District): $4,050
Enrollment: 6,307　Coed
Affiliation or Control: Local　IRS Status: 501(c)3
Highest Offering: Associate Degree
Accreditation: **NH**, ADNUR, EMT, PTAA

01 President ... Dr. Bettie TRUITT
05 VP of Instruction/Student Svcs ... Dr. Amy MAXEINER
10 VP Finance/Admin & Board Treasurer ... Mr. Steve FROMMELT
50 Executive Dean ... Dr. Betsey MORTHLAND
15 Director of Human Resources ... Ms. Stacey CARY
19 Chief of Police ... Mr. Shawn CISNA
09 Director Plng & Inst Effectiveness ... Ms. Kathy MALCOLM
26 Director Marketing/Public Relations ... Mr. John MEINEKE
13 Co-CIO/IT Systems Manager ... Mr. Ryan WHITE
13 Co-CIO/Manager of Admin Systems ... Ms. Sandy COX
102 Exec Dir BHC Foundation EC Campus ... Ms. Liz BREEDLOVE
102 Exec Dir BHC Foundation QC Campus ... Ms. Jessica MALCHEFF
49 Academic Dean ... Dr. Lee WEIMER
51 Dean Adult/Continuing Educ ... Ms. Glenda NICKE
32 Dean of Student Services ... Mr. Luis MORENO
81 Academic Dean ... Mr. Ken NICKELS
66 Assistant Academic Dean ... Ms. Karen BABER
04 Executive Asst to the President ... Ms. Heather BENNETT
36 Director Career Services Center ... Dr. Bruce STOREY
37 Director of Financial Aid ... Ms. Joanna DYE
41 Division Director Athletics/Coach ... Mr. Gary HUBER
08 Librarian ... Ms. Ashtin TRIMBLE
51 Director Adult Education ... Ms. Bianca PERKINS
06 Registrar ... Ms. Heather BJORGAN
40 Bookstore Manager Quad Cities ... Ms. Aimee MUHLEMAN
96 Purchasing Manager ... Mr. Mike MELEG
50 Dept Chair Business & Technology ... Ms. Carrie DELCOURT
57 Dept Chair Comm & Fine Arts .. Ms. Melissa HEBERT-JOHNSON
79 Dept Chair Human/Languages/Journal ... Mr. Bill DESMOND
81 Dept Chair Mathematics ... Ms. Connie MCLEAN
54 Dept Chair Natural Science/Engrng ... Mr. Brian GLASER
83 Dept Chair Social Sciences ... Mr. Mark ESPOSITO
47 Department Chair Agriculture ... Dr. Jeffrey HAWES
66 Dept Chair Nursing ... Ms. Trudy STARR
76 Dept Chair Allied Health/HPE ... Ms. Diane ABELS
88 Dept Chair Counseling ... Ms. Wendy BOCK
62 Dept Chair Lrg Resource Center ... Vacant
53 Dept Chair Psych/Sociology/Educ ... Dr. Traci DAVIS
72 Dept Chair Career Technologies ... Ms. Jamie HILL
18 Chief Facilities/Physical Plant ... Mr. Bob MCCHURCH

Black Hawk College East Campus (J)

26230 Black Hawk Road, Galva IL 61434
Telephone: (309) 854-1700　Identification: 770069
Accreditation: **&NH**

† Regional accreditation is carried under the parent institution in Moline, IL

Blackburn College (K)

700 College Avenue, Carlinville IL 62626-1498
County: Macoupin　FICE Identification: 001639
Unit ID: 143288
Telephone: (217) 854-3231　Carnegie Class: Bac-Diverse
FAX Number: (217) 854-5700　Calendar System: Semester

URL: www.blackburn.edu
Established: 1837 Annual Undergrad Tuition & Fees: $20,364
Enrollment: 585 Coed
Affiliation or Control: Presbyterian Church (U.S.A.) IRS Status: 501(c)3
Highest Offering: Baccalaureate
Accreditation: NH

01 President .... Dr. John COMERFORD
05 Provost .... Dr. John MCCLUSKY
10 Vice Pres Administration & Finance .... Mr. Steve MORRIS
30 VP for Institutional Advancement .... Ms. Sheryl RAY
32 Vice Pres of Student Affairs .... Ms. Heidi HEINZ
101 Exec Asst to Pres/Sec Bd Trustees .... Ms. Shawna POE
07 Director of Admissions .... Ms. Alisha KAPP
88 Director of Transfer Admissions .... Mr. Brian HERRMANN
29 Sr Develop Ofcr/Alumni/Staff Rels .... Mr. Nate RUSH
37 Director of Financial Aid .... Ms. Jane KELSEY
08 Head Librarian .... Mr. Spencer BRAYTON
38 College Counselor .... Mr. Tim MORENZ
06 College Registrar .... Ms. Dianna RUYLE
15 Director Personnel Services .... Ms. Melissa JONES
36 Director Student Placement .... Ms. Suzanne KRUPICA
18 Director Physical Plant .... Vacant
41 Dir of Athletics/Recreational Pgms .... Mr. John MALIN
42 Chaplain .... Vacant
26 Director of Public Relations .... Mr. Peter OSWALD
09 Director of Institutional Research .... Dr. Kristi NELMS
21 Controller .... Ms. Dawn SHRYOCK
44 Director of Annual Giving .... Dr. Mark ZOBEL
84 Enrollment Services Administrator .... Ms. Kathy RUITER
19 Director Security/Safety .... Mr. Morrison FRASER
28 Director of Diversity .... Mr. Jarrod GRAY
13 Chief Info Technology Officer (CIO) .... Mr. Jason CLONINGER

Blessing-Rieman College of Nursing (A)

11th & Oak, PO Box 7005, Quincy IL 62305-7005
County: Adams FICE Identification: 006214
Unit ID: 143297
Telephone: (217) 228-5520 Carnegie Class: Spec-4-yr-Other Health
FAX Number: (217) 223-4661 Calendar System: Semester
URL: www.brcn.edu
Established: 1891 Annual Undergrad Tuition & Fees: N/A
Enrollment: 253 Coed
Affiliation or Control: Independent Non-Profit IRS Status: 501(c)3
Highest Offering: Master's
Accreditation: NH, #COARC, NURSE

01 President/CEO .... Dr. Brenda BESHEARS
05 Academic Dean .... Dr. Jan AKRIGHT
06 Registrar .... Ms. Rachel CRAMSEY

Bradley University (B)

1501 W Bradley Avenue, Peoria IL 61625-0001
County: Peoria FICE Identification: 001641
Unit ID: 143358
Telephone: (309) 676-7611 Carnegie Class: Masters/M
FAX Number: N/A Calendar System: Semester
URL: www.bradley.edu
Established: 1897 Annual Undergrad Tuition & Fees: $31,480
Enrollment: 5,300 Coed
Affiliation or Control: Independent Non-Profit IRS Status: 501(c)3
Highest Offering: Doctorate
Accreditation: NH, ART, BUS, BUSA, CACREP, CONST, DIETD, DIETI, ENG, ENGT, MUS, NUR, PTA, SW, TED, THEA

01 President .... Dr. Gary R. ROBERTS
05 Provost/Vice Pres Academic Affs .... Dr. Walter R. ZAKAHI
20 Assistant Provost Academic Affairs .... Mrs. Linda J. PIZZUTI
10 Vice President Business Affairs .... Mr. Gary M. ANNA
30 Vice President Advancement .... Mr. Jacob HEUSER
32 Vice President Student Affairs .... Mr. Nathan THOMAS
84 VP Enrollment Management .... Vacant
26 Exec Dir Public Relations .... Ms. Renee CHARLES
88 Assoc VP Enrollment Management .... Mr. Justin BALL
58 Assoc Provost/Dean Res/Grad School .... Dr. Jeffrey BAKKEN
21 Assoc Business Officer/Controller .... Mrs. Pratima N. GANDHI
50 Dean Foster Col Business .... Dr. Darrell J. RADSON
57 Dean Slane Col Commun/Fine Arts .... Dr. Jeffrey H. HUBERMAN
53 Dean Educ & Health Sciences .... Dr. Joan SATTLER
54 Dean Engineering & Technology .... Dr. Lex A. AKERS
49 Dean Liberal Arts & Sciences .... Dr. Christopher JONES
13 Int Assoc Provost Info Res & Tech .... Mrs. Sandra BURY
08 Exec Director of the Library .... Ms. Barbara GALIK
39 Dir Ctr Residential Lvng/Ldrshp .... Mr. Ryan BAIR
88 Exec Dir Student Involvement .... Mr. Mike KEUP
36 Exec Dir Smith Career Center .... Mr. Jon NEIDY
14 Exec Dir Computing Services .... Ms. Sandra BURY
24 Ex Dir Instruct Tech/Media Svcs .... Mr. Nial L. JOHNSON
29 Director of Alumni Relations .... Ms. Tory JENNETTEN
51 Executive Director Continuing Educ .... Ms. Janet LANGE
06 Registrar .... Mr. Andreas KINDLER
37 Director Financial Aid .... Ms. Debra JACKSON
19 Chief of Campus Police .... Mr. Brian JOSCHKO
15 Director of Human Resources .... Ms. Nena PEPLOW
18 Director Facilities Management .... Vacant
23 Medical Director Health Services .... Dr. Jessica HIGGS
27 Senior Director Public Relations .... Ms. Kathleen CONVER
41 Director Athletics .... Dr. Chris REYNOLDS
78 Director Springer Center .... Mrs. Dawn KOELTZOW
87 Dir Summer/Interim Sessions .... Ms. Janet LANGE
25 Exec Dir Sponsored Programs .... Ms. Sandra SHUMAKER
22 Director Affirmative Action/EEO .... Ms. Nena PEPLOW
28 Exec Dir Diversity/Inclusion .... Mr. Norris CHASE
92 Director of Honors Program .... Dr. Kyle DZAPO
94 Dir of Women's Studies & Gender .... Dr. Amy SCOTT
09 Dir of Institutional Improvement .... Ms. Jennifer G. BURGE
40 Manager Bookstore .... Mr. Paul KROENKE
88 Dir of PreProfessional Health Adv .... Dr. Valerie BENNETT
88 Dir Pre-Law Center .... Ms. Jerelyn MAHER
07 Asst Dir Admissions .... Mr. Joshua JONES
104 Director Study Abroad .... Dr. Christine BLOUCH
38 Dir of Health Services .... Ms. Jessica HIGGS

Carl Sandburg College (C)

2400 Tom L. Wilson Boulevard, Galesburg IL 61401-9576
County: Knox FICE Identification: 007265
Unit ID: 143613
Telephone: (309) 344-2518 Carnegie Class: Assoc/MT-VT-High Non
FAX Number: (309) 344-1395 Calendar System: Semester
URL: www.sandburg.edu
Established: 1966 Annual Undergrad Tuition & Fees: $4,250
Enrollment: 2,200 Coed
Affiliation or Control: Independent Non-Profit IRS Status: 501(c)3
Highest Offering: Associate Degree
Accreditation: NH, ADNUR, DH, FUSER, PNUR

01 President .... Dr. Lori L. SUNDBERG
05 VP of Academic Services .... Ms. Julie GIBB
32 VP of Student Services .... Mr. Steve NORTON
04 Sr Exec Assistant to President .... Ms. Lisa ZUCCO
45 Dean HR/Institutional Effectiveness .... Dr. Constance THURMAN
10 Chief Financial Officer/Treasurer .... Ms. Lisa BLAKE
26 Director Marketing/Public Relations .... Ms. Robin DEMOTT
35 Dean of Student Success .... Ms. Misty LYON
19 Director of Public Safety .... Mr. Kipton CANFIELD
15 Director of Human Resources .... Ms. Gina KRUPPS
08 Coordinator of Library Services .... Ms. Amy CAULKINS
27 Public Relations Specialist .... Mr. Aaron FREY
20 Dean of Career & Corporate Dev .... Dr. Kyle CECIL
12 Dean of Extension Services .... Ms. Debra MILLER
109 Director of Business Services .... Ms. Lisa BLAKE
37 Director Financial Aid .... Ms. Lisa HANSON
30 Exec Director of Advancement .... Ms. Stephanie ACKERMANN
88 Director TRIO Upward Bound .... Mr. Tony BENTLEY
07 Director of Recruitment .... Ms. Antoinette MURPHY
66 Associate Dean of Nursing .... Ms. Mischelle MONAGLE
07 Director of Admissions & Records .... Mr. Rick EDDY
41 Athletic Director .... Mr. Mike BAILEY
79 Assoc Dean Humanities/Fine Arts .... Ms. Carol PETERSEN
81 Assoc Dean Math/Natural Sciences .... Mr. Dave BURNS
83 Assoc Dean Social & Behavioral Sci .... Ms. Jill JOHNSON
75 Interim Assoc Dean CTHE .... Ms. Diana HIGGINS
09 Coordinator of Institutional Rsrch .... Ms. Sara CREE

Carl Sandburg College The Branch Campus (D)

305 Sandburg Drive, Carthage IL 62321
Telephone: (217) 357-3129 Identification: 770071
Accreditation: &NH

† Regional accreditation is carried under the parent institution in Galesburg, IL

Carl Sandburg College The Extension Center (E)

380 E Main Street, Bushnell IL 61422
Telephone: (309) 772-2177 Identification: 770070
Accreditation: &NH

† Regional accreditation is carried under the parent institution in Galesburg, IL

Catholic Theological Union (F)

5401 S Cornell Avenue, Chicago IL 60615-5698
County: Cook FICE Identification: 009232
Unit ID: 143659
Telephone: (773) 371-5400 Carnegie Class: Spec-4-yr-Faith
FAX Number: (773) 324-8490 Calendar System: Semester
URL: www.ctu.edu
Established: 1968 Annual Graduate Tuition & Fees: N/A
Enrollment: 410 Coed
Affiliation or Control: Roman Catholic IRS Status: 501(c)3
Highest Offering: Doctorate; No Undergraduates
Accreditation: THEOL

01 President .... Rev. Mark R. FRANCIS, CSV
05 Vice President/Academic Dean .... Sr. Barbara E. REID, OP
10 Vice Pres Administration & Finance .... Mr. Michael W. CONNORS
30 Director of Development .... Ms. Colleen KENNEDY
26 Dir of Marketing & Communications .... Mr. Jeff KRAFT
08 Director of the Library .... Ms. Melody L. MCMAHON
06 Registrar .... Mrs. Maria De Jesus LEMUS
07 Asst Director Admissions/Retention .... Mr. Patrick MCGOWAN
13 Director of Information Technology .... Mr. Darnell PAYNE
04 Assistant to the President .... Sr. Pam PAULOSKI, SP
84 Director Enrollment Management .... Ms. Christine HENDERSON

*Chamberlain College of Nursing-Administrative Office (G)

3005 Highland Parkway, Downers Grove IL 60515
County: DuPage Identification: 667149
Telephone: (888) 556-8226 Carnegie Class: N/A
FAX Number: (630) 512-8888
URL: www.chamberlain.edu

01 President .... Dr. Susan GROENWALD
11 Sr Dir Campus Operations .... Elizabeth DUNLEVY
11 Sr Dir Campus Operations .... Kimberly LAMAR
11 Sr Dir Campus Operations .... Patrick ROMBALSKI
05 VP Academic Affairs .... Dr. Richard COWLING
10 VP Finance .... Sonya EVANOSKY
26 VP Marketing .... Thomas WILLIAMS
07 VP Enrollment Management .... Larry VENSEY
32 VP Student Services .... June MARLOWE

† Part of DeVry University, IL.

*Chamberlain College of Nursing-Addison (H)

1221 N. Swift Road, Addison IL 60101
County: DuPage FICE Identification: 006385
Unit ID: 454227
Telephone: (630) 953-3660 Carnegie Class: Not Classified
FAX Number: (630) 628-1154 Calendar System: Semester
URL: www.chamberlain.edu
Established: 1889 Annual Undergrad Tuition & Fees: $18,000
Enrollment: 18,665 Coed
Affiliation or Control: Proprietary IRS Status: Proprietary
Highest Offering: Doctorate
Accreditation: NH, NURSE

02 Campus President .... Dr. Jan SNOW
05 Dean Academic Affairs .... Terry BRENNAN
32 Manager Student Services .... Lisa PETSCHENKO
07 Director Admissions .... Roz CASTRO

† Master's and Doctorate programs are only offered online.

**Chamberlain College of Nursing-Chicago* (I)

3300 North Campbell Avenue, Chicago IL 60618
Telephone: (773) 961-3000 Identification: 770495
Accreditation: &NH, NURSE

† Regional accreditation is carried under the parent institution in Addison, IL

**Chamberlain College of Nursing-Tinley Park* (J)

18624 West Creek Drive, Tinley Park IL 60477
Telephone: (708) 560-2000 Identification: 770496
Accreditation: &NH, NURSE

† Regional accreditation is carried under the parent institution in Addison, IL

Chicago ORT Technical Institute (K)

5440 W. Fargo Avenue, Skokie IL 60077
County: Cook FICE Identification: 041184
Unit ID: 393180
Telephone: (847) 324-5588 Carnegie Class: Spec 2-yr-Other
FAX Number: (847) 324-5580 Calendar System: Other
URL: www.ortchicagotech.edu
Established: 1991 Annual Undergrad Tuition & Fees: N/A
Enrollment: 433 Coed
Affiliation or Control: Independent Non-Profit IRS Status: 501(c)3
Highest Offering: Associate Degree
Accreditation: CNCE

01 Executive Director .... Michelle MOVITZ
07 Director of Admissions .... Michael THORNBER

Chicago School of Professional Psychology-Chicago (L)

325 N Wells Street, Chicago IL 60654-8158
Telephone: (312) 329-6600 Identification: 770349
Accreditation: &WC, CLPSY

† Regional accreditation is carried under the parent institution in Los Angeles, CA

Chicago State University (M)

9501 S King Drive, Chicago IL 60628-1598
County: Cook FICE Identification: 001694
Unit ID: 144005
Telephone: (773) 995-2000 Carnegie Class: Masters/M
FAX Number: (773) 995-2563 Calendar System: Semester
URL: www.csu.edu
Established: 1867 Annual Undergrad Tuition & Fees (In-State): $9,994
Enrollment: 5,211 Coed
Affiliation or Control: State IRS Status: 501(c)3
Highest Offering: Doctorate
Accreditation: NH, ACBSP, ART, CACREP, CAHIIM, MUS, NRPA, NUR, OT, PHAR, SW, TED

01 President .... Dr. Thomas J. CALHOUN, JR.
05 Provost/Sr VP for Academic Affairs .... Dr. Angela HENDERSON
43 VP Gen Counsel for Labor/Legal Affs .... Mr. Patrick CAGE
10 Int VP of Administration & Finance .... Mr. Cecil LUCY
21 Executive Director Budget/Resource ... Mrs. Arrileen PATAWARAN
13 Chief Information Officer .... Mr. Prashant SHINDE
84 Vice Pres of Enrollment Management .... Dr. Carol CORTILET-ALBRECHT
09 Dir Inst Effectiveness & Research .... Dr. Latrice E. EGGLESTON WILLIAMS
32 Dean of Student Affairs & FYE .... Ms. Sheila COLLINS
49 Dean Arts & Sciences .... Dr. Leroy JONES, II
53 Dean Education .... Dr. Satasha GREEN
67 Int Dean College of Pharmacy .... Dr. Carmita COLEMAN
76 Dean College of Health Sciences .... Dr. Leslie A. ROUNDTREE
50 Dean College of Business .... Mr. Derrick K. COLLINS
08 Dean of Library/Instruct Services .... Dr. Richard DARGA
51 Dean Cont Educ Nontrad Pgms .... Ms. Nelly MAYNARD
06 Registrar .... Mrs. Shawnice AVILEZ
21 Bursar .... Vacant
37 Int Director of Financial Aid .... Mr. James LUCKE
07 Director of Admissions and Outreach .... Mrs. Nancy BHATIA
29 Exec Director Alumni Affairs .... Mr. Louis WRIGHT
26 Dir of Marketing & Communications .... Mrs. Sabrina LAND
15 Assoc VP Director Human Resources .... Dr. Renee D. MITCHELL
36 Director of Career Development .... Dr. Renee D. MITCHELL
96 Director of Purchasing .... Vacant
18 Int Dir Facilities/Physical Plant .... Mrs. Monique HORTON
20 Interim Assoc VP Academic Affairs .... Dr. Bernard ROWAN
35 Dir of Student Act & Leadership Dev .... Ms. MaToya MARSH
38 Director Counseling Center .... Dr. Yvonne PATTERSON
27 Dir Public Relations/Communications .... Vacant
108 Asst Provos Curriculum & Assessment .... Vacant
25 Int Assoc VP of Sponsored Programs .... Dr. David KANIS
88 Assoc VP Gen Counsel/Ethics Officer .... Ms. Robin HAWKINS
86 Director Intergovernmental Affs .... Vacant
19 Chief of Police .... Ms. Patricia WALSH
39 Director Student Housing .... Mr. Timothy LEE
41 Assoc VP/Athletic Director .... Dr. Denisha HENDRICKS

Chicago Theological Seminary (A)

1407 East 60th Street, Chicago IL 60637-1284

County: Cook | FICE Identification: 001661 | Unit ID: 144014
Telephone: (773) 896-2400 | Carnegie Class: Spec-4-yr-Faith
FAX Number: (773) 643-1284 | Calendar System: Semester
URL: www.ctschicago.edu
Established: 1855 | Annual Graduate Tuition & Fees: N/A
Enrollment: 249 | Coed
Affiliation or Control: United Church Of Christ | IRS Status: 501(c)3
Highest Offering: Doctorate; No Undergraduates
Accreditation: NH, THEOL

01 President .... Dr. Alice HUNT
05 Academic Dean .... Dr. Ken STONE
10 Vice President for Finance & Admin .... Ms. Julie FISHER
30 Vice President for Advancement .... Ms. Rhonda BROWN
06 Registrar .... Ms. Elena JIMENEZ
08 Head Librarian .... Vacant
07 Director Recruitment/Admission .... Rev. Lisa SEIWERT
04 Assistant to the President .... Ms. Kim M. JOHNSON
26 Director of Marketing .... Ms. Susan CUSICK
18 Facilities Coordinator .... Ms. Shauna WARREN

Christian Life College (B)

400 E Gregory Street, Mount Prospect IL 60056-2522

County: Cook | FICE Identification: 031993 | Unit ID: 260947
Telephone: (847) 259-1840 | Carnegie Class: Spec-4-yr-Faith
FAX Number: (847) 259-3888 | Calendar System: Semester
URL: www.christianlifecollege.edu
Established: 1950 | Annual Undergrad Tuition & Fees: $11,000
Enrollment: 38 | Coed
Affiliation or Control: Pentecostal/Charismatic Non-Denominational | IRS Status: 501(c)3
Highest Offering: Baccalaureate
Accreditation: TRACS

01 President .... Mr. Harry R. SCHMIDT
05 Academic Dean .... Mr. Wayne R. WACHSMUTH
08 Director of Library Services .... Vacant
10 Director of Finance .... Mr. Roger K. STEVENS
32 Dean of Students .... Vacant
06 Registrar .... Miss Haley BENSON

*City Colleges of Chicago (C)

226 W Jackson Boulevard, Chicago IL 60606-6998

County: Cook | FICE Identification: 001647 | Unit ID: 144500
Telephone: (312) 553-2500 | Carnegie Class: N/A
FAX Number: (312) 553-2699
URL: www.ccc.edu

01 Chancellor .... Ms. Cheryl L. HYMAN
10 Vice Chanc Finance/Business/CFO .... Ms. Joyce CARSON
13 Vice Chanc/Chief Information Ofcr .... Mr. Jerrold MARTIN
09 Exec Vice Chanc/Chief Strategy Ofcr .... Mr. Rasmus LYNNERUP
11 Vice Chanc Administrative Services .... Ms. Diane MINOR
43 General Counsel .... Mr. Eugene MUNIN
30 Exec Vice Chancellor/Sr Advisor .... Mr. Laurent PERNOT

*City Colleges of Chicago Harold Washington College (D)

30 E Lake Street, Chicago IL 60601-2449

County: Cook | FICE Identification: 001652 | Unit ID: 144209
Telephone: (312) 553-5600 | Carnegie Class: Assoc/HT-Mix Trad/Non
FAX Number: (312) 553-5964 | Calendar System: Semester
URL: www.ccc.edu
Established: 1962 | Annual Undergrad Tuition & Fees (In-District): $3,506
Enrollment: 9,392 | Coed
Affiliation or Control: State/Local | IRS Status: 501(c)3
Highest Offering: Associate Degree
Accreditation: NH, ACBSP

02 President .... Dr. Margaret J. MARTYN
05 Interim Vice Pres Academic Affairs .... Mr. Armen SARRAFIAN
10 Exec Dir of Business/Operations .... Mr. Kent LUSK
37 Director of Financial Aid .... Mr. Norberto VALENTIN
18 Chief Facilities/Physical Plant .... Mr. Richard WREN
88 Dean of College to Careers .... Mr. Paul THOMPSON, III
08 Librarian .... Mr. John KIERALDO
15 Human Resources Admin .... Ms. Valerie GOODE
20 Dean of Instruction .... Vacant
32 Dean of Student Services .... Mr. Wendell BLAIR
20 Associate Dean of Instruction .... Dr. Cynthia CERRENTANO
13 Director Information Technology .... Ms. Ewa BEJNAROWICZ
35 Assoc Dean of Student Services .... Ms. Patricia CUEVAS
46 Asst Director Research/Planning .... Dr. George W. CALISTO
06 Registrar .... Ms. Courtney O'BRIEN
19 Director of Security .... Mr. Milton OWENS
09 Director Strategy/Initiatives .... Vacant

*City Colleges of Chicago Harry S Truman College (E)

1145 W Wilson Avenue, Chicago IL 60640-5691

County: Cook | FICE Identification: 001648 | Unit ID: 144184
Telephone: (773) 907-4700 | Carnegie Class: Assoc/MT-VT-High Non
FAX Number: (773) 907-4464 | Calendar System: Semester
URL: www.trumancollege.edu
Established: 1956 | Annual Undergrad Tuition & Fees (In-District): $3,506
Enrollment: 10,601 | Coed
Affiliation or Control: State/Local | IRS Status: 501(c)3
Highest Offering: Associate Degree
Accreditation: NH, ADNUR

02 President .... Dr. Reagan F. ROMALI
03 Vice President .... Dr. Pervez RAHMAN
05 Dean of Instruction .... Ms. Susan MARCUS
06 Registrar .... Ms. My Linh TRAN
32 Dean of Student Services .... Ms. Maryann SOLEY
35 Associate Dean of Student Services .... Mr. Quincy PADEN
56 Dean of Adult Education .... Mr. Armanda MATA
51 Director of Continuing Education .... Ms. Kyla WILSON
20 Associate Dean of Instruction .... Ms. DeShaunta STEWART
20 Associate Dean of Instruction .... Ms. Maggie RICE AYALA
10 Exec Director Business Services .... Mr. Thomas DUNHAM
19 Director of Security .... Mr. Andres DURBAK
37 Director of Financial Aid .... Mr. Robert EVANS
15 Director Human Resource .... Mr. Michael ROBERTS
26 Director Public Relations/Marketing .... Mr. R. Scott BRIGHAM
109 Director Auxiliary Services .... Ms. Penelope VARNAVA
72 Director Information Technology .... Mr. Anthony GAMBOA
24 Director Lakeview Learning Center .... Vacant
09 Asst Dir of Research & Planning .... Ms. Maureen PYLMAN
21 Business Manager .... Ms. Nina CAO
20 Director of Developmental Education .... Ms. Elizabeth ROSENTHAL

*City Colleges of Chicago Kennedy-King College (F)

6301 South Halsted Street, Chicago IL 60621-3798

County: Cook | FICE Identification: 001654 | Unit ID: 144157
Telephone: (773) 602-5000 | Carnegie Class: Assoc/HVT-High Non
FAX Number: N/A | Calendar System: Semester
URL: www.ccc.edu/colleges/kennedy
Established: 1934 | Annual Undergrad Tuition & Fees (In-District): $3,506
Enrollment: 5,313 | Coed
Affiliation or Control: State/Local | IRS Status: 501(c)3
Highest Offering: Associate Degree
Accreditation: NH, DH

02 President .... Ms. Arshele STEVENS
05 Vice President for Academic Affairs .... Dr. Kristy LISLE
32 Dean Student Services .... Dr. Johnny CRAIG
12 Dean-Dawson Tech Institute .... Mr. Robert BARNETT
36 Dean College to Careers .... Mr. Marshall SHAFKOWITZ
51 Dean Adult/Continuing Education .... Ms. Chadra LANG
20 Dean of Instruction .... Mr. Eddie PHILLIPS
35 Assoc Dean Student Services .... Ms. Zalika LANDRUM
35 Assoc Dean Student Services .... Mr. Isaac ZUNIGA
88 Dean Washburne Culinary Institute .... Ms. Jori ORSINI
37 Director Financial Aid .... Ms. Tabitha O'NEIL
20 Director Academic Support Services .... Ms. Shandria HOLMES
10 Exec Dir Business/Operations .... Mr. Baha AWADALLAH
06 Registrar .... Mr. Eric HAYES
09 Director of Institutional Research .... Vacant

18 Chief Facilities/Physical Plant .... Mr. Jerome DABNEY
26 Marketing Director .... Vacant
15 Director Human Resources .... Mrs. Araceli CABRALES-MEDINA
27 Senior Director of Communications .... Ms. Katheryn HAYES
04 Assistant to the President .... Mrs. Roxanne BROWN
109 Director of Auxiliary Services .... Mr. Robert GRAHAM
45 Director Strategic Initiatives .... Mr. Patrick GIPSON

*City Colleges of Chicago Olive-Harvey College (G)

10001 S Woodlawn Avenue, Chicago IL 60628-1645

County: Cook | FICE Identification: 009767 | Unit ID: 144175
Telephone: (773) 291-6100 | Carnegie Class: Assoc/HVT-High Non
FAX Number: (773) 291-6304 | Calendar System: Semester
URL: www.ccc.edu/colleges/olive-harvey/pages/default.aspx
Established: 1970 | Annual Undergrad Tuition & Fees (In-District): $3,506
Enrollment: 4,572 | Coed
Affiliation or Control: State/Local | IRS Status: 501(c)3
Highest Offering: Associate Degree
Accreditation: NH

02 President .... Ms. Angelia N. MILLENDER
04 Executive Office Manager .... Ms. Lexie TRIPP
05 VP Academic Affairs .... Dr. Susan MALEKPOUR
88 Dean STEM/Ctr Teaching & Lrng .... Dr. Vera AVERYHART-FULLARD
32 Dean Student Services .... Ms. Michelle ADAMS
51 Dean Adult & Continuing Education .... Mr. Robert REIMER
36 Dean of College to Career .... Mr. Martin KAPLAN
35 Interim Dean of Student Services .... Ms. Tania WITTGENFELD
20 Dean of Instruction .... Dr. Stephanie DECICCO
35 Assoc Dean of Student Services .... Dr. Ria PINKSTON-MCKEE
36 Assoc Dean of College to Career .... Ms. Joanne IVORY
10 Exec Dir Bus/Admin/Auxiliary Svcs .... Ms. Angela ARRINGTON-JONES
09 Director of Strategic Initiative .... Ms. Nicole HOBBS
13 Director Information Technology .... Mr. Savio PINTO
36 Dir Career Planning/ Placement .... Ms. Kassandra MCGHEE JOHNSON
12 Director of South Chicago Lrng Ctr .... Mr. John ROSALES
37 Director Financial Aid .... Ms. Jolander JEFFRIES
06 Registrar .... Ms. Dorian THOMAS
19 Director Security .... Mr. Louis TORRES
88 Director Child Development Center .... Ms. Tiffany CARTER
41 Director of Athletics .... Mr. James COOPER
15 Director Human Resources .... Ms. Latasha LARRY
26 Director Public Relations .... Vacant
38 Manager Wellness Center .... Ms. TeraKesha HAMMOND
18 Chief Engineer .... Mr. Tom SIEFERT

*City Colleges of Chicago Richard J. Daley College (H)

7500 S Pulaski Road, Chicago IL 60652-1299

County: Cook | FICE Identification: 001649 | Unit ID: 144193
Telephone: (773) 838-7500 | Carnegie Class: Assoc/HVT-High Non
FAX Number: (773) 838-7524 | Calendar System: Semester
URL: daley.ccc.edu
Established: 1960 | Annual Undergrad Tuition & Fees (In-District): $3,506
Enrollment: 8,914 | Coed
Affiliation or Control: State/Local | IRS Status: 501(c)3
Highest Offering: Associate Degree
Accreditation: NH

02 President .... Dr. Jose M. AYBAR
05 Vice Pres Academic/Student Affs .... Dr. Keith MCCOY
20 Dean of Instruction .... Mr. Michael CRAWFORD
36 Dean of College to Careers .... Vacant
55 Dean Adult Education .... Mr. Victor CASTILLO
32 Dean of Student Services .... Dr. Edwardo GARZA
51 Dean Continuing Education .... Mrs. Jean JOHNSON
10 Exec Director Business Operations .... Ms. Crystal WASHINGTON
18 Chief Engineer/Physical Plant .... Mr. Tim SMITH
19 Director Security .... Mr. Ronald MARTIN
35 Assoc Dean Student Services .... Ms. Maria ACOSTA
35 Assoc Dean Student Services .... Ms. Eileen LYNCH
06 Assistant Registrar .... Mr. Victor SANCHEZ
15 Director Human Resources .... Ms. Elinore MOORE
13 Director of Information Technology .... Mr. Ronald VERSETTO
26 Senior Director of Marketing .... Vacant
37 Director Student Financial Aid .... Dr. Loucynda WHITE

*City Colleges of Chicago Wilbur Wright College (I)

4300 N Narragansett Avenue, Chicago IL 60634-1591

County: Cook | FICE Identification: 001655 | Unit ID: 144218
Telephone: (773) 777-7900 | Carnegie Class: Assoc/MT-VT-High Non
FAX Number: (773) 481-8185 | Calendar System: Semester
URL: www.ccc.edu/wright
Established: 1934 | Annual Undergrad Tuition & Fees (In-District): $3,506
Enrollment: 12,146 | Coed
Affiliation or Control: State/Local | IRS Status: 501(c)3
Highest Offering: Associate Degree
Accreditation: NH, ACBSP, OTA, RAD

02 President Dr. David POTASH
05 VP of Academic & Student Affairs Ms. Nicole REAVES
32 Dean of Student Services Ms. Romell MURDEN-WOLDU
20 Dean of Instruction Mr. James HOWLEY
35 Assoc Dean Student Svcs Ms. Maria LLOPIZ
35 Assoc Dean Student Svcs Ms. Linda HUERTAS
20 Associate Dean of Instruction Ms. Nancy KOLL
88 Director Developmental Education Ms. Sara SCHUPACK
10 Executive Business Director Ms. Phoebe WOOD
37 Director of Financial Aid Ms. Inesha KELLY
09 Dir Institutional Research/Plng Mr. Brian TRZEBIATOWSKI
13 Director Information Technology Mr. Anthony GAMBOA
18 Director of Facilities Ms. Dina LEILER
26 Director of Public Relations Mr. Stefan MAISNIER
15 Human Resources Manager Ms. Griselda SILVA
38 Director of Wellness Center Ms. Anne WYSOGLAD
19 Director of Security Mr. Jack MURPHY
06 Registrar Ms. Mai ALY
41 Athletic Director Mr. John MCDONNELL
88 Interim Dean of Adult Education Ms. Jeffrey TINLEY
51 Dean Professional & Personal Dev Ms. Alba PEZZAROSSI
12 Dean of Humboldt Park Center Mr. Kenneth SANTIAGO
31 Community Affairs Liaison Ms. Iris MILLAN
04 Administrative Asst to President Ms. Margaret KLUZA

*Malcolm X College, One of the City Colleges of Chicago (A)

1900 W. Jackson Boulevard, Chicago IL 60612-3197

County: Cook FICE Identification: 001650
Unit ID: 144166
Telephone: (312) 850-7000 Carnegie Class: Assoc/HVT-High Non
FAX Number: (312) 850-7039 Calendar System: Semester
URL: www.ccc.edu/malcolmx
Established: 1911 Annual Undergrad Tuition & Fees (In-District): $3,506
Enrollment: 6,245 Coed
Affiliation or Control: State/Local IRS Status: 501(c)3
Highest Offering: Associate Degree
Accreditation: NH, ADNUR, COARC, EMT, FUSER, RAD, SURGT

02 Interim President Mr. David A. SANDERS
05 Int Vice Pres Acad/Student Affairs Dr. Kimberly HOLLINGSWORTH
32 Dean Student Services Dr. Tasha WILLIAMS
10 Exec Director Business Operations Ms. Tiffany DIXON
04 Executive Office Manager Mrs. Alanna S. WITHERSPOON
15 Director of Human Resources Mr. Stanley BEAMON
20 Interim Dean Instruction Mr. William O'DONNELL
20 Assoc Dean Instruction Mr. Byron A. JAVIER
13 Director Information Technology Mr. Lonnie WASHINGTON
06 Registrar Mr. Jeffery WONDERS
35 Assoc Dean Student Services Mr. Mario DIAZ
37 Director Financial Aid Ms. Tamika CARSON
88 Director Child Care Center Ms. Aisha RUTHER
19 Director Security/Public Safety Mrs. Angela HEARTS-GLASS
18 Chief Facilites/Physical Plant Mr. John MORLEY
08 Librarian Vacant
21 Business Manager Mr. Richard SLATER
76 Int Dean Health Sciences Programs Mr. Roy WALKER
20 Assoc Dean Instruction Ms. Yoriel MARCANO
56 Dean Adult Education Programs Ms. Pamela LYNCH
51 Dean Continuing Education Vacant
66 Dean City Col Chicago/Nursing Pgm Dr. Marsha ATKINS
88 Assoc Dean Student Development Ms. Lisa WILLIS
76 Assoc Dean Health Careers Vacant
36 Dir Career Planning/Placement Ms. Toya JOHNSON
103 Director Workforce Partnerships Ms. Rhonda HARDEMON
26 Director of Public Relations Vacant
46 Director of Strategic Initiatives Ms. Dhyia THOMPSON
109 Director of Auxiliary Services Mrs. Jessica HOLLOWAY

College of DuPage (B)

425 Fawell Boulevard, Glen Ellyn IL 60137-6599

County: DuPage FICE Identification: 006656
Unit ID: 144865
Telephone: (630) 942-2800 Carnegie Class: Assoc/MT-VT-High Non
FAX Number: (630) 858-9399 Calendar System: Semester
URL: www.cod.edu
Established: 1965 Annual Undergrad Tuition & Fees (In-District): $5,275
Enrollment: 29,476 Coed
Affiliation or Control: State/Local IRS Status: 501(c)3
Highest Offering: Associate Degree
Accreditation: #NH, ACFEI, ADNUR, ART, CAHIIM, COARC, CONST, CSHSE, DH, DMS, MAC, NMT, POLYT, #PTAA, RAD, SURGT

01 President Dr. Ann RONDEAU
03 Executive Vice President Dr. Joseph COLLINS
05 Vice President Academic Affairs Dr. Jean V. KARTJE
10 Interim VP Administration Ms. Kim MICHAEL-LEE
13 Vice Pres Information Technology Mr. Chuck CURRIER
45 VP Planning & Inst Effectiveness Mr. James BENTE
15 Vice President Human Resources Ms. Linda SANDS-VANKERK
30 Interim Exec Dir COD Foundation Ms. Karen KUHN
24 Asst VP Info Sys/Multimedia Svcs Ms. Donna BERLINER
20 Assoc VP Academic Affairs Mr. Emmanuel AWUAH
26 Vice Pres Marketing & Communication Mr. Joseph MOORE
32 Vice President Student Affairs Mr. Earl DOWLING
49 Dean Liberal Arts Dr. Daniel LLOYD
75 Dean Health & Sciences Mr. Thomas CAMERON
51 Dean Cont Ed/Extended Learning Dr. Joseph CASSIDY
08 Dean Learning Resources Ms. Ellen SUTTON
35 Dean Student Affairs Ms. Susan M. MARTIN
21 Interim Controller Mr. Scott BRADY
18 Dir Facilities Planning and Dev Mr. Bruce SCHMIEDL
06 Dean Admiss/Registration/Records Ms. Jane L. SMITH
09 Director Research & Analytics Mr. Eugene YE
88 Internal Auditor Mr. James E. MARTNER
57 Director Performing Arts Mrs. Diana MARTINEZ
41 Director Athletics Mr. Paul ZAKOWSKI
25 Director of Grants Ms. Barbara ABROMITIS
86 Director Legislative Relations Ms. Mary Ann MILLUSH
19 Director & Chief COD Police Dept Mr. Joseph MULLIN
18 Director Facilities Operations Mr. Jim MA
79 Associate Dean Humanities Dr. Sandra MARTINS
60 Associate Dean English & Acad ESL Mr. Sheldon WALCHER
27 Dir Marketing & Creative Svcs Ms. Laurie JORGENSEN
16 Director Labor & Emp Relations Ms. Mia IGYARTO
72 Assoc Dean Technology Mr. John KRONENBURGER
83 Assoc Dean Social & Behav Sciences Ms. Marianne HUNNICUTT
81 Assoc Dean Math & Physical Sciences Mr. Thomas SCHRADER
88 Assoc Dean Health & Bio Sciences Ms. Karen SOLT
88 Assoc Dean Learn Resource Mr. Blakely WALTER
07 Manager Admissions & Outreach Ms. Tamara MCCLAIN

College of Lake County (C)

19351 W Washington Street, Grayslake IL 60030-1198

County: Lake FICE Identification: 007694
Unit ID: 146472
Telephone: (847) 543-2000 Carnegie Class: Assoc/HVT-High Non
FAX Number: (847) 223-1017 Calendar System: Semester
URL: www.clcillinois.edu
Established: 1967 Annual Undergrad Tuition & Fees (In-District): $3,612
Enrollment: 15,410 Coed
Affiliation or Control: Local IRS Status: 501(c)3
Highest Offering: Associate Degree
Accreditation: NH, ADNUR, CAHIIM, DH, MAC, PHLEB, RAD, SURGT

01 President Dr. Jerry W. WEBER
05 Vice President Educ Affairs Dr. Richard J. HANEY
11 Vice Pres Administrative Affs Mr. Kenneth GOTSCH
32 Assoc Vice Pres of Student Devel Ms. Karen HLAVIN
20 Asst Vice Pres Educational Affairs Ms. Alyssa O'BRIEN
88 Asst Dir Student Develop Operation Ms. Jennifer MALLER
12 Dean Southlake Campus Ms. Vicky CVITKOVIC
12 Dean Lakeshore Campus Dr. Alphonso BALDWIN
08 Dean Libraries/Instruction Svcs Mr. Brian BEECHER
21 Controller Mr. Andy WILLIAMS
50 Dean of Business/Social Science Div Dr. Jeffrey STOMPER
76 Dean Biological/Health Sciences Mr. Steven HOLMAN
79 Dean Comm Arts/Humanities/Fine Arts Mr. Roland G. MILLER
54 Int Dean Engr/Math/Physical Science Mr. Rob TWARDOCK
51 Dean Adult Basic Education/GED/ESL Dr. Arlene SANTOS-GEORGE
38 Dean Counsel/Advising/Transfer Ctr Ms. Christina CARPENTER
31 Assoc Dean Community Education Vacant
103 Exec Dir Workforce/Prof Dev Inst Ms. Roneida MARTIN
26 Exec Dir Public Relations & Mktg Ms. Evelyn R. SCHIELE
35 Int Executive Director Student Life Ms. Teresa AGUINALDO
102 Executive Director CLC Foundation Ms. Karen SCHMIDT
15 Exec Director Human Resources Ms. Julia GUINEY
88 Exec Dir James Lumber Ctr Perf Arts Ms. Gwethalyn BRONNER
09 Exec Dir/Inst Effect/Plan/Research Dr. Sean HOGAN
41 Director of Athletics/Title IX Mr. Nic SCANDRETT
86 Dir Resource Dev/Legislative Affrs Mr. Nick C. KALLIERIS
13 Chief Info Ofcr/Info Tech Svcs Ms. Lynn BUTLER
14 Director User Services/User Spport Mr. David AYKROID
10 Dir Business & Auxiliary Services Ms. Michele REYNOLDS
88 Dir Application Svcs/Applic Develop Mr. Jay MEYER
88 Director Student Services Lakeshore Mr. David WEATHERSPOON
18 Director Facilities Administration Mr. Mike WELCH
88 Dir Children's Learning Center Ms. Sandra GROENINGER
22 Dir Ofc Students with Disabilities Mr. Thomas CROWE
19 Chief of Police/CLC Police Dept Mr. Thomas GUENTHER
36 Exec Dir Career/Placement Services Ms. Sylvia M. JOHNSON JONES
88 Asst Dir Educational Affairs Ops Ms. Arlene SANTOS-GEORGE
66 Director Nursing Education Dr. Deborah JEZUIT
88 Director Judicial Services Ms. Margaret C. MILLER
23 Director Health Services Ms. Michelle M. GRACE
37 Director Financial Aid Ms. Erin FOWLES
88 Dir Active Learning Technologies Mr. Scott RIAL
88 Dir Continuing Professional Devel Ms. Carol EWING
88 Asst Director of Business Services Vacant
84 Asst Director Enrollment Services Ms. Debra MICHELINI
88 Director Green Jobs Initiative Mr. Stephen BELL
88 Director Student Support Services Ms. Zandra GENOUS
88 Director Technical Services Mr. James SENFT
38 Dir of Advising/New Student Pgms Ms. Christine LEWIS
88 Project Dir IGEN Career Pathways Dr. Theresa BERRYMAN
100 Chief of Staff Mr. Derrick HARDEN
07 Director Admissions/Recruitment Mr. Jason SARNA

College of Lake County Lakeshore Campus (D)

33 North Genesee Street, Waukegan IL 60085

Telephone: (847) 543-2191 Identification: 770073
Accreditation: &NH

† Regional accreditation is carried under the parent institution in Grayslake, IL

College of Lake County Southlake Campus (E)

1120 South Milwaukee Avenue, Vernon Hills IL 60061

Telephone: (847) 543-6501 Identification: 770072
Accreditation: &NH

† Regional accreditation is carried under the parent institution in Grayslake, IL

Columbia College Chicago (F)

600 S Michigan Avenue, Chicago IL 60605-1996

County: Cook FICE Identification: 001665
Unit ID: 144281
Telephone: (312) 369-1000 Carnegie Class: Masters/M
FAX Number: (312) 369-8069 Calendar System: Semester
URL: www.colum.edu
Established: 1890 Annual Undergrad Tuition & Fees: $24,344
Enrollment: 9,440 Coed
Affiliation or Control: Independent Non-Profit IRS Status: 501(c)3
Highest Offering: Master's
Accreditation: NH, CIDA

01 President Dr. Kwang-Wu KIM
05 Sr VP Academic Affairs/Provost Dr. Stanley WEARDEN
10 Interim VP Business Affairs/CFO Mr. Richard DOWSEK
43 Senior Counsel Ms. Patricia BERGESON
30 Vice Pres Development Vacant
88 Vice President Campus Environment Ms. Alicia M. BERG
32 Vice President Student Affairs Mr. Mark KELLY
49 Int Dean Sch Liberal Arts/Sciences Dr. Steven COREY
57 Dean School of Fine/Performing Arts Mr. John GREEN
45 Assoc VP/Planning and Compliance Ms. Anne FOLEY
18 Assoc VP Facilities/Operations Mr. John KAVOURIS
35 Assoc Vice Pres/Dean of Students Ms. Sharon WILSON-TAYLOR
19 Assoc Vice Pres Safety & Security Mr. Robert KOVERMAN
15 Assoc Vice Pres of Human Res Ms. Patricia RIOS
09 AVP Institutional Effectiveness Mr. Royal DAWSON
84 AVP Enrollment Management Mr. Jeffrey MEECE
37 AVP Student Financial Svcs Ms. Jennifer WATERS
35 Asst Dean of Student Development Mr. William FRIEDMAN
26 Senior Director of Public Relations Mr. Steve KAUFFMAN
96 Director of Purchasing Mr. Thomas RUSSELL
28 Exec Director Multicultural Affs Ms. Sheila CARTER
85 Dir International Student Affairs Ms. Gigi POSEJPAL
06 Director of Records/Registrar Mr. Marvin COHEN
39 Director of Residence Life Ms. Mary OAKES

Concordia University Chicago (G)

7400 Augusta Street, River Forest IL 60305-1499

County: Cook FICE Identification: 001666
Unit ID: 144351
Telephone: (708) 771-8300 Carnegie Class: Spec-4-yr-Other
FAX Number: (708) 209-3176 Calendar System: Semester
URL: www.cuchicago.edu
Established: 1864 Annual Undergrad Tuition & Fees: $29,520
Enrollment: 5,038 Coed
Affiliation or Control: Lutheran Church - Missouri Synod
IRS Status: 501(c)3
Highest Offering: Doctorate
Accreditation: NH, CACREP, MUS, TED

01 President Dr. Daniel GARD
05 Sr Vice President for Academics Dr. John ZILLMAN
102 President for Foundation Mr. James M. MILLER
45 Sr VP for Planning & Research Dr. Alan E. MEYER
10 Vice President for Finance Mr. Tom HALLETT
11 Vice President for Administration Dr. Dennis E. WITTE
84 Sr VP Enrollment/Student Svcs Ms. Evelyn P. BURDICK
32 Vice President Student Services Mr. Jeff HYNES
84 Asst Vice President for Enrollment Ms. Gwen E. KANELOS
26 Asst Vice Pres Marketing Mr. Eric MATANYI
49 Dean College Arts & Sciences Dr. Rachel EELLS
53 Dean College Education Dr. Kevin BRANDON
50 Dean College of Business Dr. Claudia SANTIN
107 Dean Col of Innovation & Prof Pgms Dr. Thomas JANDRIS
09 Director Institutional Research Ms. Elizabeth OWOLABI
37 Director Student Financial Planning Ms. Aida ASENCIO-PINTO
06 Registrar Ms. Connie PETTINGER
08 Director of Library Services Ms. Yana V. SERDYUK
88 Director of Degree Completion Dr. Carol J. REISECK
36 Director Career Services Mr. Gerald PINOTTI
15 Director of Human Resources Ms. Peg O'BRIEN
18 Director of Physical Plant Ms. Linda HOLOWICKI
11 Assistant VP of Administration Mr. Glen D. STEINER
29 Director of Alumni Relations Ms. Paige CRAIG
38 Director Schmieding Counseling Ctr Dr. Carol A. JABS
109 Director of Auxiliary Services Mr. Pete D. BECKER
41 Director of Athletics Mr. Peter D. GNAN
21 Director of Business Services Ms. Aileen POL
88 Director of Budget Services Ms. Tina NEPOMUCENO
39 Director University Housing Ms. Jessica KLINGBERG
42 University Pastor Rev. Jeffrey LEININGER
24 Dir of Media Production Services Mr. James A. KOSINSKY
19 Director of Public Safety Mr. David WITKEN
88 Director of Academic Advising Ms. Rosemarie GARCIA-HILLS
96 Director of Purchasing Ms. Denise JAMES
91 Manager of Admin Information System Ms. Linda C. BERRY
85 International Student Coordinator Ms. Chyvonne GIBSON
07 Exec Director Graduate Admissison Ms. Deborah NESS

Coyne College (A)

330 North Green Street, Chicago IL 60607-1300
County: Cook FICE Identification: 007549
Unit ID: 144485
Telephone: (773) 577-8100 Carnegie Class: Assoc/HVT-High Non
FAX Number: (312) 226-3818 Calendar System: Other
URL: www.coynecollege.edu
Established: 1899 Annual Undergrad Tuition & Fees: N/A
Enrollment: 611 Coed
Affiliation or Control: Proprietary IRS Status: Proprietary
Highest Offering: Associate Degree
Accreditation: ACCSC, MAAB

01 President ... Mr. Russell T. FREEMAN
05 Director of Education ... Virginia HANSON
07 Director of Admissions ... Claudia MACIAS-SILVERMAN
06 Registrar ... Tina FANUCCHI
08 Librarian ... Diana BARTHELEMY
36 Director of Career Services ... Jenny GONZALEZ
37 Director of Financial Aid ... Ashley TUCHTEN

Danville Area Community College (B)

2000 E Main Street, Danville IL 61832-5199
County: Vermilion FICE Identification: 001669
Unit ID: 144564
Telephone: (217) 443-3222 Carnegie Class: Assoc/HVT-High Non
FAX Number: (217) 443-8560 Calendar System: Semester
URL: www.dacc.edu
Established: 1949 Annual Undergrad Tuition & Fees (In-District): $4,125
Enrollment: 3,207 Coed
Affiliation or Control: State/Local IRS Status: 501(c)3
Highest Offering: Associate Degree
Accreditation: NH, ADNUR, CAHIIM, RAD

01 President ... Dr. Alice M. JACOBS
04 Admin Asst to the Pres/Board Sec ... Ms. Kerri L. THURMAN
05 VP Instruction & Student Svcs ... Mr. David L. KIETZMANN
15 Director Human Resources/AA Ofcr ... Ms. Jill A. CRANMORE
10 Chief Financial Officer ... Ms. Tammy L. CLARK-BETANCOURT
11 Director Administrative Services ... Mr. R. Michael CUNNINGHAM
84 Dean Student Services ... Ms. Stacy L. EHMEN
102 Foundation Executive Director ... Ms. Tracy D. WAHLFELDT
26 Director Marketing/Col Relations ... Ms. Lara L. CONKLIN
09 Dir Institutional Effectiveness ... Mr. Bob MATTSON
103 Executive Director of JTP ... Mr. Brian C. HENSGEN
21 Controller ... Ms. Debra L. KNIGHT
37 Director of Financial Aid ... Ms. Janet M. INGARGIOLA
91 Director of Admin Data Systems ... Mr. Kim H. COLWELL
90 Director Computer & Network Svcs ... Mr. Mark BARNES
88 Director of Adult Education ... Ms. Laura M. WILLIAMS
50 Dean Business & Technology ... Mr. Bruce M. RAPE
49 Dean Liberal Arts and Library Servi ... Dr. Penny J. MCCONNELL
81 Dean Math & Sciences ... Ms. Kathy R. STURGEON
41 Athletic Director ... Mr. Tim M. BUNTON
88 Director Small Business Development ... Ms. Carol NICHOLS
07 Director Admissions & Registrar ... Ms. Cindy J. PECK
38 Director Student Support Services ... Ms. Shanay M. WRIGHT
36 Coordinator Career Services ... Ms. Carla M. BOYD
88 Coordinator Recruitment ... Ms. Dawn S. NASSER
19 Director Security/Safety ... Mr. Greg FEGETT

DePaul University (C)

1 E Jackson Boulevard, Chicago IL 60604-2287
County: Cook FICE Identification: 001671
Unit ID: 144740
Telephone: (312) 362-8610 Carnegie Class: DU-Mod
FAX Number: (312) 362-5322 Calendar System: Quarter
URL: www.depaul.edu
Established: 1898 Annual Undergrad Tuition & Fees: $36,361
Enrollment: 23,799 Coed
Affiliation or Control: Roman Catholic IRS Status: 501(c)3
Highest Offering: Doctorate
Accreditation: NH, ANEST, BUS, BUSA, CEA, CLPSY, LAW, MUS, NURSE, PH, SPAA, SW

01 President ... Rev. Dennis H. HOLTSCHNEIDER
00 Chancellor ... Rev. John T. RICHARDSON, CM
05 Provost ... Dr. Marten L. DEN BOER
10 Executive Vice President ... Mr. Jeffrey BETHKE
101 Sec of Univ/VP Teaching & Learning ... Rev. Edward R. UDOVIC
32 VP Student Affairs ... Dr. Gene ZDZIARSKI
84 Sr Vice Pres Enroll Mgmt/Marketing ... Dr. David H. KALSBEEK
30 Sr Vice Pres for Advancement ... Ms. Erin MINNE
15 Vice President Human Resources ... Ms. Stephanie SMITH
18 Vice President Facilities Operation ... Mr. Robert J. JANIS
43 Vice President & General Counsel ... Dr. Jose D. PADILLA
29 Asst VP Alumni Engagement/Outreac ... Ms. Tracy KRAHL
28 VP Inst Diversity & Equity ... Dr. Elizabeth F. ORTIZ
26 VP Public Relations & Communication ... Ms. Linda BLAKLEY
20 Assoc Provost Academic Affairs ... Dr. Caryn CHADEN
106 Assoc VP Academic Affairs Online ... Dr. GianMario BESANA
45 VP Planning & Presidential Admin ... Dr. Jay BRAATZ
13 VP Information Services ... Mr. Robert MCCORMICK
35 Assoc Vice Pres Student Development ... Dr. Peggy BURKE
22 Assoc VP Diversity ... Mr. Rico TYLER
09 AVP Inst Research/Market Analytics ... Dr. Liz SANDERS
84 AVP Enrollment Management/ Marketing ... Mr. Jon BOECKENSTEDT
36 AVP Div Planning & Mgmt/Career Ctr ... Ms. Jane MCGRATH
42 Assoc VP University Ministry ... Mr. Mark LABOE
108 AVP Planning/Opers & Assess ... Dr. Ellen MEENTS-DECAIGNY
27 Assoc VP Univ Marketing Comm ... Ms. Gwyn FRIEND
27 AVP Strategic Marketing & Branding ... Ms. Verna DONOVAN
27 Exec Dir News & Integrated Content ... Ms. Caro HUGHES
88 Senior Executive University Mission ... Rev. Edward R. UDOVIC, CM
88 Treasurer ... Mr. Santino CARINGELLA
21 Controller ... Ms. Sherri SIDLER
90 Dir Faculty Instructional Tech Svcs ... Dr. Sharon GUAN
37 Assoc Vice Pres Financial Aid ... Ms. Paula LUFF
25 VP for Research Services ... Dr. Lawrence HAMER
07 Associate Director of Admission ... Ms. Cass JOHNSON
19 Director Public Safety ... Mr. Robert WACHOWSKI
38 Director Student Counseling ... Dr. Jeffery LANFEAR
39 Director of Housing Operations ... Mr. Rick MORECI
41 Athletics Director ... Ms. Jean PONSETTO
06 Director of Registration/Records ... Ms. Patricia HUERTA
104 Director Study Abroad ... Ms. Nobi HAYASHI
88 Asst VP Grad & Adult Recruit & Adm ... Ms. Suzanne DEPEDER
07 Dean of Undergraduate Admission ... Ms. Carlene KLAAS
77 Dean Computing & Digital Media ... Dr. David MILLER
49 Dean Liberal Arts & Social Sciences ... Dr. Guillermo VASQUEZ DE VELASCO
50 Dean Driehaus Business College ... Dr. Ray WHITTINGTON
60 Dean Col of Communication ... Dr. Salma GHANEM
64 Dean School of Music ... Dr. Ronald CALTABIANO
61 Dean College of Law ... Ms. Jennifer R. PEREA
57 Dean Theatre School ... Mr. John CULBERT
53 Dean School of Education ... Dr. Paul ZIONTS
51 Dean School for New Learning ... Dr. Marisa ALICEA
76 Dean Col of Science & Health ... Dr. Gerald P. KOOCHER
08 Head Librarian ... Dr. Scott WALTER
04 Administrative Asst to President ... Ms. Phyllis GREGG
100 Deputy Chief of Staff ... Ms. Annette WILSON
86 Assoc VP Community & Govt Relations ... Mr. Peter COFFEY

*DeVry University - Home Office (D)

3005 Highland Parkway, Downers Grove IL 60515-5799
County: DuPage FICE Identification: 001672
Unit ID: 144777
Telephone: (800) 733-3879 Carnegie Class: N/A
FAX Number: (630) 571-0317
URL: www.devry.edu

00 President & Chief Executive Officer ... Ms. Lisa WARDELL
01 President of DeVry University ... Mr. Robert PAUL
86 SVP External Relations ... Ms. Lisa SODEIKA
26 Chief Marketing Officer ... Ms. Melissa ESBENSHADE
32 VP of Student & Career Services ... Ms. Madeleine SLUTSKY
10 SVP/CFO/Treasurer ... Mr. Patrick UNZICKER
106 President DeVry Online Services ... Mr. Eric DIRST
43 SVP/General Counsel/Corp Secretary ... Mr. Gregory DAVIS
84 VP Enrollment Management ... Ms. Elise AWWAD
88 VP Enrollment Management - Online ... Mr. Mark BUCK
05 Associate Provost ... Ms. Donna REKAU
15 SVP Human Resources ... Ms. Donna JENNINGS
88 VP Regulatory Compliance Officer ... Mr. Thomas BABEL
88 President Prof & Intl Education ... Mr. Steven RIEHS
07 Vice President Admissions ... Mr. Russell GILL
07 Group Director Admissions ... Mr. Matt DEARSMAN
07 Group Director Admissions ... Mr. David WOOD

*DeVry University - Chicago Campus (E)

3300 N Campbell Avenue, Chicago IL 60618-5916
County: Cook FICE Identification: 010727
Unit ID: 482477
Telephone: (773) 929-8500 Carnegie Class: Not Classified
FAX Number: (773) 348-1780 Calendar System: Semester
URL: www.devry.edu
Established: 1931 Annual Undergrad Tuition & Fees: $19,568
Enrollment: 24,220 Coed
Affiliation or Control: Proprietary IRS Status: Proprietary
Highest Offering: Master's
Accreditation: NH, CAHIIM, ENGT

02 Campus Dean ... Mr. Piotr LECHOWSKI
05 Group Dean Acad Excellence ... Mr. Timothy ZOREK
07 Group Director Admissions ... Ms. Tanya DI IULIO
32 Manager Student Services ... Ms. Cilvia OSBORNE
08 Regional Librarian ... Mr. Jason ROSSI

† Regional accreditation is carried under the parent institution in Downers Grove, IL.

Dominican University (F)

7900 W Division Street, River Forest IL 60305-1099
County: Cook FICE Identification: 001750
Unit ID: 148496
Telephone: (708) 366-2490 Carnegie Class: Masters/L
FAX Number: (708) 524-5990 Calendar System: Semester
URL: www.dom.edu
Established: 1901 Annual Undergrad Tuition & Fees: $30,670
Enrollment: 3,498 Coed
Affiliation or Control: Roman Catholic IRS Status: 501(c)3
Highest Offering: Doctorate
Accreditation: NH, BUS, DIETC, DIETD, LIB, SW, TED

01 President ... Dr. Donna M. CARROLL
05 Provost ... Dr. Jeffrey BREESE
20 Associate Provost ... Dr. David H. KRAUSE
10 Sr VP for Finance & Administration ... Dr. Amy MCCORMACK
42 Vice Pres for Mission & Ministry ... Dr. Claire NOONAN
30 Vice Pres University Advancement ... Ms. Grace J. CICHOMSKA
84 Interim VP Enrollment Management ... Ms. Pam JOHNSON
13 VP Info Tech/Chief Information Ofcr ... Ms. Jill ALBIN-HILL
07 AVP Enroll Mgt/Dir Undergrad Admiss ... Mr. Glenn HAMILTON
26 Dir Media & Markeing ... Ms. Christina HAMILTON
32 Dean of Students ... Ms. Trudi GOGGIN
50 Dean Brennan School of Business ... Dr. Roberto CURCI
62 Dean Grad School Library Science ... Ms. Kate MAREK
53 Dean School of Education ... Dr. Victoria CHOU
70 Dean Graduate School Social Work ... Dr. Charles STOOPS
49 Dean College of Arts & Science ... Dr. Jeffrey CARLSON
88 Assistant Provost ... Mr. Matthew J. HLINAK
08 University Librarian ... Ms. Felice E. MACIEJEWSKI
06 Registrar ... Mr. Michael Patrick MILLER
36 Director Career Development ... Ms. Keli WOJCIECHOWSKI
29 Dir Alumnae/i Relations ... Ms. Alysha COMSTOCK
88 Promoter of Mission Integration ... Sr. Mary Ann MEUNINGHOFF, OP
09 Dir Institutional Rsch & Assessment ... Ms. Elizabeth SILK
15 Director Human Resources ... Ms. Roberta MCMAHON
18 Director/Physical Plant ... Mr. Daniel BULOW
07 Director Transfer/Adult Admission ... Mr. Michael MORSOVILLO
37 Director Financial Aid ... Ms. Victoria SPIVAK
23 Director Wellness Center ... Ms. Elizabeth RITZMAN
41 Director Athletics ... Mr. Erick BAUMANN
104 Director International Studies ... Dr. Sue PONREMY

East-West University (G)

816 S Michigan Avenue, Chicago IL 60605-2185
County: Cook FICE Identification: 021686
Unit ID: 144883
Telephone: (312) 939-0111 Carnegie Class: Bac-A&S
FAX Number: (312) 939-0083 Calendar System: Quarter
URL: www.eastwest.edu
Established: 1980 Annual Undergrad Tuition & Fees: $20,145
Enrollment: 555 Coed
Affiliation or Control: Independent Non-Profit IRS Status: 501(c)3
Highest Offering: Baccalaureate
Accreditation: #NH

01 Chancellor ... Dr. M. Wasiullah KHAN
05 Provost ... Dr. Madhu JAIN
20 Associate Provost ... Dr. Ekkehard T. WILKE
88 Assistant Provost for Acad Quality ... Dr. Lawrence J. GORMAN
30 Dean Development/Univ Relations ... Mr. Zafar A. MALIK
32 Director Counseling/Student Affairs ... Ms. Sonja M. SIMS
07 Director of Admissions ... Mr. Raul ANDRADE
37 Director of Financial Aid ... Mr. Cesar CAMPOS
06 Registrar ... Ms. Denise MORALES
04 Assistant to the Chancellor ... Dr. Karen HUNT-AHMED
19 Director of Security ... Mr. Tasleem RAJA
10 Director of Business ... Dr. Madhu JAIN
44 Dir Devel/Univ Rels/Publications ... Ms. Barbara ABRAJANO
26 Manager Public Relations ... Vacant
18 Facilities Manager ... Mr. Tasleem RAJA
38 Academic Counselor ... Ms. Nancy HALL
85 International Student Advisor ... Mr. Rashed JAHANGIR

Eastern Illinois University (H)

600 Lincoln Avenue, Charleston IL 61920-3099
County: Coles FICE Identification: 001674
Unit ID: 144892
Telephone: (217) 581-5000 Carnegie Class: Masters/L
FAX Number: (217) 581-2722 Calendar System: Semester
URL: www.eiu.edu
Established: 1895 Annual Undergrad Tuition & Fees (In-State): $11,312
Enrollment: 8,913 Coed
Affiliation or Control: State IRS Status: 501(c)3
Highest Offering: Beyond Master's But Less Than Doctorate
Accreditation: NH, AAFCS, ART, BUS, BUSA, #CAATE, CACREP, DIETD, DIETI, JOUR, MUS, NAIT, NRPA, NURSE, SP, TED, THEA

01 President ... Dr. David M. GLASSMAN
05 Provost/Vice Pres Academic Affairs ... Dr. Blair M. LORD
10 Int Vice Pres Bus Affairs/Treasurer ... Mr. Paul A. MCCANN
32 Int Associate VP Student Affairs ... Ms. Lynette DRAKE
30 Vice Pres University Advancement ... Vacant
20 Associate VP Academic Affairs ... Mr. Jeffrey F. CROSS
35 Special Asst to VP Student Affairs ... Ms. Jennifer L. SIPES
13 Int Asst VP for InfoTech Svcs ... Mr. Brian MURPHY
26 Asst VP Integ Marketing/Communic ... Vacant
08 Dean of Library Services ... Dr. Allen K. LANHAM
92 Dean Honors College ... Dr. Richard ENGLAND
15 Director Human Resources ... Vacant
43 General Counsel ... Mr. Robert L. MILLER
22 Int Director Civil Rights ... Dr. Shawn PEOPLES
45 Dir Planning/Budgeting/Research ... Mr. Michael S. MAURER
07 Assoc Director of Admissions ... Ms. Kara HADLEY-SHAKYA
37 Int Sr Assoc Dir of Financial Aid ... Ms. Amanda STARWALT
06 Registrar ... Ms. Amy J. LYNCH
29 Director Alumni Svc/Community Rels ... Mr. Steven W. RICH
18 Dir Facilities/Planning Mgmt ... Mr. Timothy P. ZIMMER
96 Dir Procur/Disburs/Contract Svc ... Ms. Kay E. MCELWEE
38 Director of Counseling Center ... Vacant
25 Director of Research & Grants ... Dr. Robert W. CHESNUT

41 Director of Athletics ... Mr. Thomas R. MICHAEL
93 Director of Minority Affairs ... Ms. Mona DAVENPORT
39 Director of Housing/Dining Service ... Mr. Mark A. HUDSON
21 Interim Director Business Services ... Ms. Linda C. HOLLOWAY
36 Asst Dir of Career Services ... Ms. Allison L. FREES-WILLIAMS
51 Dean Continuing Education ... Dr. Regis M. GILMAN
58 Int Dean Graduate School ... Dr. Ryan C. HENDRICKSON
81 Int Dean College Sciences ... Dr. Doug KLARUP
50 Dean Lumpkin Col Bus/Appl Sci ... Dr. Mahyar IZADI
79 Int Dean College Arts/Humanities ... Dr. Anita SHELTON
53 Dean College Education ... Dr. Diane H. JACKMAN

Elgin Community College (A)

1700 Spartan Drive, Elgin IL 60123-7193
County: Kane FICE Identification: 001675
Unit ID: 144944
Telephone: (847) 697-1000 Carnegie Class: Assoc/HVT-High Non
FAX Number: (847) 214-7995 Calendar System: Semester
URL: www.elgin.edu
Established: 1949 Annual Undergrad Tuition & Fees (In-District): $2,868
Enrollment: 10,929 Coed
Affiliation or Control: Local IRS Status: 501(c)3
Highest Offering: Associate Degree
Accreditation: NH, ADNUR, COMTA, CSHSE, DA, HT, MLTAD, PTAA, RAD, RADMAG, SURGT

01 President ... Dr. David SAM
10 Vice Pres Business/Finance ... Ms. Sharon KONNY
05 VP Teaching/Learning/Student Dev ... Ms. Rose DIGERLANDO
20 Asst VP Teach/Lrng/Stdnt Dev ... Ms. Marcy THOMPSON
20 Dean Academic Dev/Learning Resource ... Dr. Mi HU
88 Dean Sustain/Safety & Career Tech ... Dr. Ileo LOTT
83 Dean Comm/Behavioral Sciences ... Dr. Ruixuan MAO
57 Dean Liberal/Visual/Performing Arts ... Ms. Mary HATCH
32 Dean of Student Services ... Dr. Gregory ROBINSON
88 Dean Adult Basic Education ... Ms. Peggy HEINRICH
76 Dean Hlth Prof/Int Dn Math/Sci/Eng ... Ms. Wendy MILLER
84 Assoc Dean Enrollment Management ... Dr. Mary PERKINS
106 Assoc Dean Inst Improve/Dist Lrng ... Mr. Timothy MOORE
88 Asc Dean TRIO/Reten/Stdnt Outreach ... Dr. L. Bruce AUSTIN
18 Managing Director Facilities ... Mr. Cal BYRD
15 Chief Human Resources Officer ... Dr. Richard ENYARD
13 Chief Information Officer ... Mr. Ned COONEN
26 Exec Director Communications ... Ms. Toya WEBB
30 Exec Dir Inst Advance/ECC Found ... Ms. Katherine SAWYER
88 Managing Dir Inst Comp/Curr ... Ms. Annamarie SCHOPEN
45 Sr Exec Dir Planning/Inst Effect ... Dr. Philip GARBER
09 Managing Dir Institutional Research ... Mr. David RUDDEN
37 Director Financial Aid/Scholarships ... Ms. Amy PERRIN
19 Chief of Police ... Mr. Emad EASSA
21 Controller ... Ms. Heather SCHOLL
84 Managing Director Enrollment Svcs ... Dr. Jennifer MCCLURE
90 Director Academic Computing ... Ms. Karin STACY
22 Paralegal/EEO/AA Title IX/FOIA Ofcr ... Ms. Marilyn PRENTICE
41 Director Athletics & Wellness ... Mr. Kent PAYNE
96 Director Business Services ... Ms. Melissa TAIT
36 Acad Advising/Transfer/Career Svcs ... Ms. Peggy GUNDRUM
27 Director of Marketing ... Ms. Heidi HEALY
35 Director Orientation/Student Life ... Ms. Amybeth MAURER
88 Dir Small Business Devel Center ... Ms. Sybil EGE
14 Sr Director Technology Services ... Mr. Phil HOWARD
86 Dir Cmty Engagemnt/Legislative Affs ... Ms. Paula AMENTA
04 Sr Exec Asst to Pres/Board Recorder ... Ms. Diane KERRUISH

Ellis University (B)

2 Mid America Plaza, Suite 824AB,
Oakbrook Terrace IL 60181
County: DuPage FICE Identification: 041433
Unit ID: 452133
Telephone: (877) 366-0321 Carnegie Class: Not Classified
FAX Number: (630) 873-3487 Calendar System: Semester
URL: www.ellis.edu
Established: 2008 Annual Undergrad Tuition & Fees: N/A
Enrollment: N/A Coed
Affiliation or Control: Proprietary IRS Status: Proprietary
Highest Offering: Master's
Accreditation: DEAC

01 President ... Dr. Virginia A. CARLIN
10 Chief Financial Officer ... Randy WILLY
05 Chair of Academic Programs ... Dr. Russell RADFORD
06 Director of Registrar Functions ... Yahana TEGEGNE

Elmhurst College (C)

190 Prospect, Elmhurst IL 60126-3296
County: DuPage FICE Identification: 001676
Unit ID: 144962
Telephone: (630) 279-4100 Carnegie Class: Masters/M
FAX Number: (630) 617-3282 Calendar System: 4/1/4
URL: www.elmhurst.edu
Established: 1871 Annual Undergrad Tuition & Fees: $34,450
Enrollment: 3,257 Coed
Affiliation or Control: United Church Of Christ IRS Status: 501(c)3
Highest Offering: Master's
Accreditation: NH, NURSE, @SP

01 President ... Dr. Troy VANAKEN
10 VP of Finance & Administration&CFO ... Ms. Karen KISSEL
05 Int VP Acad Affs/Dean of Faculty ... Dr. Heather HALL
13 VP and Chief Information Officer ... Mr. Kurt ASHLEY
29 VP for Development/Alumni Relations ... Mr. Joseph R. EMMICK
32 Interim Dean of Students ... Ms. Christine SMITH
107 Dean School for Professional Stds ... Dr. Timothy RICORDATI
20 Associate Dean of Faculty ... Dr. Theodore LERUD
88 Exec Dir Center for Pro Excellence ... Dr. Lawrence B. CARROLL
18 Exec Director Facilities Management ... Mr. Bruce J. MATHER
42 Chaplain ... Rev. H. Scott MATHENEY
06 Registrar ... Mr. S. Dean ELLENS
26 Int Dir Communications/Public Affs ... Ms. Desiree CHEN-MENICHINI
08 Director of the Library ... Ms. Susan S. STEFFEN
36 Director of Career Education ... Ms. Peggy KILLIAN
21 Controller ... Mr. James STUART
38 Director of Counseling Services ... Dr. Amy SWARR
28 Director of Intercultural Education ... Vacant
88 Director Development Services ... Ms. Emily TELFORD
29 Director of Alumni Engagement ... Ms. Samantha KILEY
15 Director of Human Resources ... Ms. Lynita GEBHARDT
19 Exec Director of Campus Security ... Mr. Jeff KEDROWSKI
37 Director of Financial Aid ... Ms. Ruth PUSICH
07 Executive Director of Admissions ... Ms. Stephanie LEVENSON
07 Managing Dir Adult/Grad Admission ... Mr. Tim PANFIL
39 Director of Residence Life ... Ms. Christine J. SMITH
41 Director Intercollegiate Athletics ... Mr. Paul KROHN
04 Administrative Asst to President ... Ms. Donna STALKER
101 Assistant to the Board of Trustees ... Ms. Armaline MIRRETTI
104 Director Study Abroad ... Ms. Alice NIZIOLEK
25 Chief Contracts/Grants Admin ... Ms. Jill MCWILLIAMS
30 Chief Development/Advancement ... Ms. Meg HOWES
44 Director of Annual Giving ... Ms. Lori STEINER
50 Dir Ctr for Business & Economics ... Dr. Gary WILSON
53 Dept Chair Education ... Dr. Jeanne WHITE
96 Director of Purchasing ... Ms. Donna MALANCA

Erikson Institute (D)

451 N. Lasalle Street, Chicago IL 60654
County: Cook FICE Identification: 035103
Unit ID: 409254
Telephone: (312) 755-2250 Carnegie Class: Spec-4-yr-Other
FAX Number: (312) 755-0928 Calendar System: Semester
URL: www.erikson.edu
Established: 1966 Annual Graduate Tuition & Fees: N/A
Enrollment: 256 Coed
Affiliation or Control: Independent Non-Profit IRS Status: 501(c)3
Highest Offering: Master's; No Undergraduates
Accreditation: NH, SW

01 President/CEO ... Geoffrey A. NAGLE
05 Sr VP Academic Affs/Dean of Faculty ... Jie-Qi CHEN
10 Vice President Finance/Admin/CFO ... Patricia LAWSON
30 Vice Pres Institutional Advancement ... Randy L. HOLGATE
84 Dean of Enrollment Management ... Michel FRENDIAN
32 Dean of Students ... Colette DAVISON
13 Chief Information Officer ... Jonathan FRANK
26 Chief Communications Officer ... Bonita BRODT
44 Asst Dir Data Systems/Donor Svcs ... Madeleine HOLDSWORTH
29 Dir Development/Alumni Relations ... Joan CLAFFEY

Eureka College (E)

300 E College Avenue, Eureka IL 61530-1500
County: Woodford FICE Identification: 001678
Unit ID: 144971
Telephone: (309) 467-3721 Carnegie Class: Bac-Diverse
FAX Number: (309) 467-6386 Calendar System: Semester
URL: www.eureka.edu
Established: 1855 Annual Undergrad Tuition & Fees: $20,510
Enrollment: 664 Coed
Affiliation or Control: Christian Church (Disciples Of Christ)
IRS Status: 501(c)3
Highest Offering: Baccalaureate
Accreditation: NH

01 President ... Dr. Jamel WRIGHT
04 Administrative Asst to President ... Ms. Jyl ZUBIATE
05 Provost & Dean of the College ... Dr. Daniel BLANKENSHIP
10 VP Fin/Fac/Chief Financial Officer ... Mr. Marc PASTERIS
32 Dean of Students ... Dr. Jeffrey COATS
30 Vice Pres of Institutional Advance ... Mr. Michael MURTAGH
06 Registrar ... Ms. Kendi ONNEN
08 Library Director ... Mr. Tony GLASS
18 Director of Physical Plant ... Mr. Daryle EGE
42 Chaplain ... Rev. Bruce M. FOWLKES
36 Director of Career Services ... Mrs. Kelly HARRIS
13 Director of Computer Services ... Dr. Kanaka VIJITHA-KUMARA
37 Director of Financial Aid ... Mrs. Erin BLINE
41 Athletic Director ... Mr. Steve THOMPSON
29 Director Alumni Relations ... Mrs. Shellie SCHWANKE
15 Director Personnel Services ... Mrs. Lori GUTH
39 Director Student Housing ... Ms. Lisa FISCHER
28 Chief Diversity Officer ... Ms. Jess BROWN
26 Director of Communications ... Ms. Katherine TELLEZ
07 Dean of Admissions/Fin Aid ... Mrs. Anne LEANOS

Fox College (F)

6640 South Cicero Avenue, Bedford Park IL 60638
County: Cook FICE Identification: 025228
Unit ID: 145239
Telephone: (708) 444-4500 Carnegie Class: Spec 2-yr-Health
FAX Number: (708) 802-6585 Calendar System: Semester
URL: www.foxcollege.edu
Established: 1932 Annual Undergrad Tuition & Fees: $15,080
Enrollment: 360 Coed
Affiliation or Control: Proprietary IRS Status: Proprietary
Highest Offering: Associate Degree
Accreditation: NH, MAAB, PTAA

01 President ... Mr. Carey CRANSTON
11 Operations Administrator ... Ms. Nicole BROWN
05 Chief Academic Officer ... Mr. Jeff MARCUM
08 Head Librarian ... Ms. Sierra CAMPBELL
36 Director Student Placement ... Ms. Lisa FENTON
37 Director Student Financial Aid ... Ms. Kerry DEMARS

Garrett-Evangelical Theological Seminary (G)

2121 Sheridan Road, Evanston IL 60201-3298
County: Cook FICE Identification: 001682
Unit ID: 145275
Telephone: (847) 866-3900 Carnegie Class: Spec-4-yr-Faith
FAX Number: (847) 866-3884 Calendar System: Semester
URL: www.garrett.edu
Established: 1853 Annual Graduate Tuition & Fees: N/A
Enrollment: 365 Coed
Affiliation or Control: United Methodist IRS Status: 501(c)3
Highest Offering: Doctorate; No Undergraduates
Accreditation: NH, THEOL

01 President ... Dr. Lallene J. RECTOR
11 VP for Administration ... Dr. James A. NOSEWORTHY
05 Vice Pres Academic Affairs/Dean ... Dr. Luis J. RIVERA
30 Vice President for Development ... Dr. David L. HEETLAND
84 Vice Pres for Enrollment Management ... Rev. Becky J. EBERHART
10 Vice President Business Affairs/CFO ... Mr. Dale MCCLAIN
32 Asst VP Student Life/Dean Students ... Rev. Cynthia A. WILSON
42 Dean of the Chapel ... Rev. Tercio JUNKER
04 Dir of the President's Office ... Ms. Erin B. MOORE
21 Controller ... Mr. Bob SUTTON
06 Registrar/Dir of Academic Studies ... Rev. Vince MCGLOTHIN-ELLER
08 Director of United Library ... Dr. Lucy CHUNG
18 Director of Buildings & Grounds ... Ms. Cheryl LARSEN
39 Director of Housing & Food Service ... Ms. Barbara B. ADAMS
29 Dir Annual Gvg/Alum Rel/ Hospitality ... Mrs. April MCGLOTHIN-ELLER
88 Director of Stewardship ... Ms. Ceciley AKINS
37 Director of Financial Aid ... Mr. Jason GILL
26 Director of Communications ... Mr. Shane NICHOLS

Governors State University (H)

1 University Parkway, University Park IL 60484-0975
County: Will FICE Identification: 009145
Unit ID: 145336
Telephone: (708) 534-5000 Carnegie Class: Masters/L
FAX Number: (708) 534-4107 Calendar System: Semester
URL: www.govst.edu
Established: 1969 Annual Undergrad Tuition & Fees (In-State): $10,246
Enrollment: 5,776 Coed
Affiliation or Control: State IRS Status: 501(c)3
Highest Offering: Doctorate
Accreditation: NH, ACBSP, CACREP, HSA, NUR, OT, PTA, SP, SPAA, SW, TED

53 Dean College Education ... Dr. Andrea EVANS
38 Dir Student Devel/Counseling Center ... Ms. Kelly MCCARTHY
01 President ... Dr. Elaine P. MAIMON
05 Provost/VP Academic Affairs ... Dr. Deborah BORDELON
30 VP Advancement/CEO Foundation ... Mr. William DAVIS
84 VP Enrollment Mgmt & Marketing ... Mr. Charles NOLLEY
13 Assoc VP/CIO Information Tech Svcs ... Mr. John BUENGER
43 Legal Counsel ... Ms. Alexis KENNEDY
22 Affirmative Action/EO ... Ms. Alexis KENNEDY
45 Director Budget Planning/Inst Rsrch ... Dr. Jeffrey SLOVAK
09 Assoc Dir of Institutional Research ... Mr. Marco KRCATOVICH, II
10 Director Budget & Financial Plng ... Ms. Kim LAMBERT-THOMAS
29 Director of Alumni Assoc ... Ms. Cheri GAREY
26 Asst VP of Marketing/Communication ... Ms. Keisha DYSON
50 Dean Col Business/Public Admin ... Dr. Ellen FOSTER CURTIS
49 Dean College Arts Sciences ... Dr. Reinhold HILL
76 Dean Col Health Professions ... Dr. Elizabeth CADA
32 Dean Student Affairs & Services ... Dr. Aurelio VALENTE
08 Dean University Library ... Lydia MORROW RUETTEN
06 Registrar ... Mr. Christopher HUANG
37 Director Financial Aid ... Mr. John PERRY
20 Associate Provost/AVP Academic Affs ... Dr. Colleen SEXTON
15 Director Human Resources ... Ms. Joyce COLEMAN
18 Director Physical Plant ... Mr. Sajid MAIN
19 Int Director Dept Public Safety ... Mr. James MCGEE
36 Director of Career Services ... Ms. Darcie R. CAMPOS
96 Dir of Procurement/Auxiliary Svcs ... Ms. Tracy SULLIVAN
04 Executive Asst to President ... Ms. Penny PERDUE
39 Director Student Housing ... Dr. Elizabeth JOSEPH
41 Athletic Director ... Mr. Anthony BATES
86 Director Government Relations ... Ms. Maureen KELLY

Greenville College (I)

315 E College, Greenville IL 62246
County: Bond FICE Identification: 001684
Unit ID: 145372
Telephone: (618) 664-2800 Carnegie Class: Masters/S
FAX Number: (618) 664-6841 Calendar System: 4/1/4
URL: www.greenville.edu

Established: 1892 Annual Undergrad Tuition & Fees: $25,088
Enrollment: 1,307 Coed
Affiliation or Control: Free Methodist IRS Status: 501(c)3
Highest Offering: Master's
Accreditation: NH, @SW, TEAC

01	President	Dr. Ivan FILBY
101	Executive Assistant to the Board	Mrs. Kim FITCH
05	Provost & Chief Operating Officer	Dr. Edwin ESTEVEZ
30	Vice Pres for Development	Mrs. Linda MYETTE
10	Vice President for Finance	Mr. Tim DIETZ
29	Sr Advis to Pres for Alumni Rels	Dr Norman D. HALL
07	Dean of Undergraduate Admissions	Mr. Karl HATTON
88	Dean of Adult Studies	Dr. Dave HOLDEN
08	Interim Director of Library	Mrs. Georgann KURTZ-SHAW
06	Registrar	Mrs. Michelle SUSSENBACH
37	Director of Financial Aid	Mrs. Marilae LATHAM
44	Director of Major & Planned Gifts	Mr. Kent KROBER
42	Dean Chapel & Dir Spiritual Form	Mrs. Lori GAFFNER
18	Director of Facilities	Mr. Mark OWENS
26	Director of Marketing	Vacant
49	Dean School Arts & Sciences	Dr. Teresa HOLDEN
53	Dean School of Education	Dr. Mark LAMB
41	Dean of Athletics	Dr. Doug FAULKNER
28	Dean of Diversity	Dr. Eugene DUNKLEY
50	Dean of School of Business	Dr. Suzanne DAVIS

Harper College (A)

1200 W Algonquin Road, Palatine IL 60067-7398
County: Cook FICE Identification: 003961
Unit ID: 149842
Telephone: (847) 925-6000 Carnegie Class: Assoc/MT-VT-High Non
FAX Number: (847) 925-6034 Calendar System: Semester
URL: www.harpercollege.edu
Established: 1965 Annual Undergrad Tuition & Fees (In-District): $3,228
Enrollment: 14,957 Coed
Affiliation or Control: State/Local IRS Status: 501(c)3
Highest Offering: Associate Degree
Accreditation: NH, ACBSP, ADNUR, CAHIIM, DH, DIETT, DMS, MAC, MUS, RAD

01	President	Dr. Kenneth L. ENDER
100	Chief of Staff/VP Wkfc Plng/Inst	Dr. Maria COONS
05	Provost	Dr. Judith MARWICK
10	Exec VP Finance & Admin Services	Dr. Ron ALLY
30	VP and Chief Advancement Officer	Ms. Laura BROWN
28	Assoc Provost/Spc Asst/Div & Inclus	Ms. Michele SMITH
26	Chief Media/Community Rel Officer	Mr. Phil BURDICK
20	Assoc Provost/Interdis Student Succ	Mr. Brian KNETL
15	Chief Human Resources Officer	Mr. Roger SPAYER
13	Chief Information Officer	Mr. Patrick BAUER
21	Controller	Mr. Bret BONNSTETTER
18	Exec Dir of Facilities Management	Vacant
84	Asst Provost/Dean Enrollment Svcs	Ms. Maria MOTEN
32	Asst Provost/Dean Student Dev	Ms. Sheryl OTTO
103	Exec Dean/Asst VP Workfrc/Strat All	Dr. Mark MROZINSKI
45	Exec Dir Plng/Research/Inst Eff	Ms. Darlene SCHLENBECKER
75	Dean Career & Technical Programs	Dr. Mary Beth OTTINGER
76	Dean Health Careers	Ms. Kimberly CHAVIS
08	Dean Resources for Learning	Ms. Njambi KAMOCHE
35	Dean Student Affairs	Dr Travaris HARRIS
50	Dean Business & Social Science	Ms. Kathryn ROGALSKI
81	Dean Mathematics & Sciences	Ms. Kathy BRUCE
88	Assoc Dean Academy of Teaching Exce	Dr. Michael BATES
103	Dean Workforce & Economic Devel	Dr. Rebecca LAKE
49	Dean Liberal Arts/Interim Dean AEE	Dr. Jennifer BERNE
102	Asc Exec Dir Found/Dir Major Gifts	Ms Heather ZOLDAK
88	Assoc Dean Interdisc Stdnt Success	Ms. Darice TROUT
88	Int Asst Dean Acad Enrich/Engage	Ms. Marjorie ALLEN
35	Assoc Dean Student Affairs	Dr. Keith O'NEILL
23	Director Health Services	Dr. Bridget CAHILL
88	Dir New Student Programs/Retention	Ms Vicki ATKINSON
14	Director IT Enterprise Systems	Dr. Mike BABB
27	Director Marketing Services	Mr. Mike BARZACCHINI
36	Director Job Placement Resource Ctr	Ms. Kathleen CANFIELD
91	Director IT Client Services	Ms. Sue CONTARINO
09	Director Institutional Research	Dr. Katherine COY
88	Director Adult Educational Dev	Ms. Andrea FIEBIG
88	Dir One Million Degrees Pgm	Ms. Kristin HOFFHINES
88	Dir One Stop Center/Student Svcs	Ms. Paula HANLEY
88	Dir Phys Plant/Int Exec Dir Facil	Mr. Darryl KNIGHT
37	Dir Student Financial Assistance	Ms. Laura MCGEE
66	Director Nursing	Ms. Julie D'AGOSTINO
07	Dir Student Recruitment & Outreach	Mr. Robert PARZY
38	Dir Academic Advising & Counseling	Dr. Eric ROSENTHAL
41	Director of Athletics & Fitness	Mr. Doug SPIWAK
19	Chief of Police	Mr. Paul LEBRECK
88	Campus Architect	Mr. Steve PETERSEN

Harrington College of Design (B)

200 W Madison, 2nd Floor, Chicago IL 60606-3433
County: Cook FICE Identification: 020552
Unit ID: 145460
Telephone: (312) 939-4975 Carnegie Class: Spec-4-yr-Arts
FAX Number: (312) 939-8005 Calendar System: Semester
URL: www.harrington.edu
Established: 1931 Annual Undergrad Tuition & Fees: N/A
Enrollment: 516 Coed
Affiliation or Control: Proprietary IRS Status: Proprietary
Highest Offering: Master's
Accreditation: NH

01	President	Mr. Max S. SHANGLE
05	Director of Academic Affairs	Ms. Gretchen FRICKX
07	Director of Admissions	Ms. Jessie MCEWEN
10	Regional Controller	Ms. Gladys CHINCHILLA
13	Manager of IT & Facilities	Mr. Hector DORINO
36	Director Career Services	Ms. Camille HARRIS
08	Head Librarian	Ms. Leigh GATES
21	Campus Business Operations Manager	Mr. Ryan FROEHLE
06	Registrar	Mr. Sam DELAROSA
32	Director Student Services	Mr. Sam DELAROSA

† School is in teach-out plan and plans to close in May, 2018. All of Harrington's classes have been transferred to Columbia College Chicago.

Heartland Community College (C)

1500 W Raab Road, Normal IL 61761-9446
County: McLean FICE Identification: 030838
Unit ID: 384342
Telephone: (309) 268-8000 Carnegie Class: Assoc/HT-High Non
FAX Number: (309) 268-7999 Calendar System: Semester
URL: www.heartland.edu
Established: 1990 Annual Undergrad Tuition & Fees (In-District): $4,260
Enrollment: 5,286 Coed
Affiliation or Control: State/Local IRS Status: 501(c)3
Highest Offering: Associate Degree
Accreditation: NH, ADNUR, @PTAA, RAD

01	President	Mr. Robert E. WIDMER
05	Vice Pres Learning/Student Success	Dr. Rick PEARCE
10	Vice President Business Services	Mr. Douglas MINTER
30	Vice Pres Cont Educ/Advancement	Ms. Kelli HILL
20	Assoc VP for Academic Affairs	Dr. Sarah DIEL-HUNT
88	Dean Student Success	Ms. Anita MOORE
84	Dean Enrollment Services	Mr. Fadriac SHINVILLE
18	Executive Director of Facilities	Mr. James HUBBARD
11	Director of Administrative Services	Ms. Valerie CRAWFORD
13	Chief Information Officer	Mr. Scott BROSS
21	Controller	Ms. Sharon MCDONALD
37	Director of Financial Aid	Mr. Todd BURNS
15	Exec Director Human Resources	Mrs. Barb LEATHERS
09	Exec Director Inst Effectiveness	Vacant
41	Director of Athletics	Mr. Ryan KNOX
29	Director College Engagement	Ms. Colleen REYNOLDS
36	Director Student Success	Ms. Kimberly KELLEY
06	Director of Records	Ms. Cindy ALFANO
26	Director of Marketing	Ms. Amy HUMPHREYS
32	Director of Student Engagement	Mr. Marvin RASCH
38	Dir Advisement/Career Services	Ms. Lindsay EICKHORST
07	Director of Admissions	Ms. Candace BROWNLEE

Hebrew Theological College (D)

7135 N Carpenter Road, Skokie IL 60077-3263
County: Cook FICE Identification: 001685
Unit ID: 145497
Telephone: (847) 982-2500 Carnegie Class: Spec-4-yr-Faith
FAX Number: (847) 674-6381 Calendar System: Semester
URL: www.htc.edu
Established: 1922 Annual Undergrad Tuition & Fees: $19,900
Enrollment: 468 Coordinate
Affiliation or Control: Independent Non-Profit IRS Status: 501(c)3
Highest Offering: Master's
Accreditation: NH

01	Interim Chancellor	Rabbi Shmuel SCHUMAN
05	Chief Academic Officer	Dr. Zev ELEFF
100	Chief of Staff	Ms. Cheryl KARP
20	Rosh Hayeshiva	Rabbi Avraham FRIEDMAN
11	Vice President for Administration	Rabbi Sender KUTNER
33	Mashgiach Ruchani-Dean	Rabbi Zvi ZIMMERMAN
34	Menahel Ruchani-Dean	Rabbi Binyamin OLSTEIN
34	Assistant Dean Blitstein Institute	Ms. Rita LIPSHITZ
06	Registrar	Rabbi Gavriel BACHRACH
07	Director of Admissions	Rabbi Joshua ZISOOK
30	Director of Development	Rabbi Gershon SEIF
44	Development Coordinator	Rabbi Yaakov FRIEDMAN
08	Librarian	Ms. Eti BERLAND

† Separate campuses for male and female students. Part of the Touro College and University System.

Highland Community College (E)

2998 W Pearl City Road, Freeport IL 61032-9341
County: Stephenson FICE Identification: 001681
Unit ID: 145521
Telephone: (815) 235-6121 Carnegie Class: Assoc/MT-VT-High Non
FAX Number: (815) 235-6130 Calendar System: Semester
URL: www.highland.edu
Established: 1962 Annual Undergrad Tuition & Fees (In-District): $3,423
Enrollment: 1,730 Coed
Affiliation or Control: State/Local IRS Status: 501(c)3
Highest Offering: Associate Degree
Accreditation: NH, MAC

01	President	Mr. Tim HOOD
03	Executive Vice President	Ms. Chris KUBERSKI
10	Vice Pres Administrative Services	Ms. Jill M. JANSSEN
32	Vice Pres Student Dev & Support Svc	Ms. Elizabeth L. GERBER
15	Associate VP Human Resources	Ms. Rose A. FERGUSON
50	Dean Business & Technology	Mr. Scott R. ANDERSON
79	Int Dean Humanities/Social Sci	Mr. Jim PHILLIPS
81	Int Dean Natural Science & Math	Dr. Brendan C. DUTMER
66	Int Dean Nursing & Allied Health	Ms. Jennifer GROBE
51	Director Adult Education	Mr. Mark JANSEN
41	Director Athletics	Mr. Peter E. NORMAN
07	Director of Enrollment & Records	Mr. Jeremy BRADT
18	Director Facilities & Safety	Mr. Kurt SIMPSON
37	Director Financial Aid	Ms. Kathy BANGASSER
13	Director ITS	Mr. Nathan HENSAL
09	Director Institutional Research	Dr. Michelle THRUMAN
88	Dir Learning & Transitional Educ	Ms. Carolyn PETSCHE
31	Director Marketing & Cmty Relations	Mr. Pete WILLGING
88	Director Retired & Senior Vol Pgm	Ms. Cindi MIELKE
88	Director Title IV Student Support	Mr. Anthony SAGO
21	Manager Accounting	Ms. Mary J. LLOYD
40	Manager Bookstore	Ms. Madonna KEENEY
101	Exec Asst to President/Board Sec	Ms. Terri A. GRIMES
102	Executive Director Foundation	Mr. James M. BERBERET

Illinois Central College (F)

1 College Drive, East Peoria IL 61635-0001
County: Tazewell FICE Identification: 006753
Unit ID: 145682
Telephone: (309) 694-5422 Carnegie Class: Assoc/MT-VT-Mix Trad/Non
FAX Number: (309) 694-5450 Calendar System: Semester
URL: www.icc.edu
Established: 1966 Annual Undergrad Tuition & Fees (In-District): $4,050
Enrollment: 10,296 Coed
Affiliation or Control: State/Local IRS Status: 501(c)3
Highest Offering: Associate Degree
Accreditation: NH, ADNUF, COARC, DH, EMT, MAC, MLTAD, MUS, OTA, PTAA, RAD, SURGT

01	President	Dr. Sheila QUIRK-BAILEY
10	Exec VP Administration/Finance	Mr. Bruce BUDDE
26	Vice President of Marketing & Comm	Dr. Cheryl FLIEGE
05	Interim Provost	Dr. Margaret A. SWANSON
102	Int Exec Dir Education Foundation	Ms. Stephanie HOLMES
15	Vice President of Human Resources	Ms. Marti BLOODSAW
28	VP of Diversity/Intl & Adult Educ	Dr. Rita ALI
32	Vice President Student Services	Dr. Tracy MORRIS
09	Exec Dir Inst Research & Planning	Mr. David COOK
35	Dean of Students	Ms. Emily POINTS
37	Dean of Enrollment Management	Ms. Beth MCCLAIN
35	Dean of Student Services	Ms. Angela DREESSEN
51	Dean Corporate/Community Education	Ms. Ellen GEORGE
88	Assoc Dean Organizational Learning	Ms. Janice KINSINGER
83	Dean of Social Sciences	Dr. Marwin SPILLER
79	Dean Eng/Humanities/Lang	Ms. Jennifer SWARTOUT
81	Dean Math/Science/Engineering	Mr. Joe BERGMAN
50	Dean Business/Hospitality/Info Sys	Ms. Julie HOWAR
57	Dean Arts & Communications	Ms. Kari SCHIMMEL
47	Dean Agriculture/Industrial Tech	Ms. Stacy GEHRIG
31	Dean Comm Outreach/Career Readiness	Ms. Kay SUTTON
76	Dean Health Careers	Ms. Wendee GUTH
106	Associate Dean Online Learning	Dr. Patrice HESS
21	Director Business Services	Ms. Kim MALCOLM
06	Registrar	Ms. Nikisha WRIGHTANDERSON
29	Coordinator Alumni Relations	Vacant
04	Administrative Asst to President	Ms. Paula FRALEY
08	Director Library Services	Ms. Cathryne KAUFMAN
19	Campus Police Chief	Mr. Thomas LARSON
22	Dir Affirmative Action/EEO	Dr. Rita ALI
25	Grants Development Officer	Dr. Herbert DACOSTA
41	Athletic Director	Ms. Sue SINCLAIR
104	Dir International Educ Program	Dr. Barbara BURTON
88	Controller	Mr. Ed BABCOCK
101	Secretary of the Institution/Board	Ms. Paula FRALEY
86	Legislative Liaison	Ms. Valerie WELSH

Illinois College (G)

1101 W College Avenue, Jacksonville IL 62650-2299
County: Morgan FICE Identification: 001688
Unit ID: 145691
Telephone: (217) 245-3000 Carnegie Class: Bac-A&S
FAX Number: (217) 245-3034 Calendar System: Semester
URL: www.ic.edu
Established: 1829 Annual Undergrad Tuition & Fees: $31,660
Enrollment: 965 Coed
Affiliation or Control: Independent Non-Profit IRS Status: 501(c)3
Highest Offering: Master's
Accreditation: NH

01	President	Dr. Barbara A. FARLEY
05	Provost and Dean of the College	Dr. Catharine E. O'CONNELL
10	Vice President of Business Affairs	Vacant
30	Vice President Development & Alumni	Mr. William JOHNSON
84	Vice President of Enrollment	Ms. Stephanie CHIPMAN
32	Dean of Students	Dr. Malinda L. CARLSON
20	Dean of the Faculty	Dr. Adam PORTER
20	Dean of Student Success	Dr. Andrew JONES
09	Exec Dir for Inst Research	Dr. Robert A. SWEATMAN
06	Registrar	Ms. Helen KUHN
13	Chief Info Technology Officer (CIO)	Mr. Patrick BROWN
07	Senior Assoc Director Admissions	Mr. Richard L. BYSTRY
37	Director of Financial Aid	Ms. Katherine A. TAYLOR
88	Associate Director of Admissions	Ms. Kristen REED
29	Dir Annual Giving/Alumni Relations	Ms. Kristin E. JAMISON
26	Director Marketing/Communications	Mr. Bryan LEONARD
08	Library Director	Mr. Luke BEATTY
18	Director of Campus Facilities	Mr. Al DILLOW

36 Director of Career Services ..... Ms. Susan K. DRAKE
21 Controller ..... Ms. Melissa J. DYSON
35 Dir Center for Student Involvement ..... Ms. Karen K. HOMOLKA
42 Chaplain ..... Rev. Katrina E. JENKINS
15 Director of Human Resources ..... Ms. Angela VALUCK
38 Dir Templeton Counseling Center ..... Mr. William TENNILL
28 Director of Diversity ..... Vacant
41 Athletic Director ..... Mr. Mike SNYDER

Illinois College of Optometry (A)

3241 S Michigan Avenue, Chicago IL 60616-3878
County: Cook FICE Identification: 001689
Unit ID: 145628
Telephone: (312) 225-1700 Carnegie Class: Spec-4-yr-Other Health
FAX Number: (312) 225-1724 Calendar System: Quarter
URL: www.ico.edu
Established: 1872 Annual Graduate Tuition & Fees: N/A
Enrollment: 638 Coed
Affiliation or Control: Independent Non-Profit IRS Status: 501(c)3
Highest Offering: First Professional Degree; No Undergraduates
Accreditation: NH, OPT, OPTR

01 President ..... Dr. Arol R. AUGSBURGER
05 Vice Pres for Academic Affairs/Dean ..... Dr. Stephanie MESSNER
10 VP for Finance & Business/CFO ..... Mr. John BUDZYNSKI
11 Vice President Administration ..... Mrs. Laura L. ROUNCE
17 Vice Pres for Patient Care Services ..... Dr. Leonard V. MESSNER
30 VP Student/Alumni/College Devel ..... Dr. Mark COLIP
22 VP Compliance/Cmty Based Services ..... Dr. Valarie CONRAD
06 Asst Dean Academic Admin/Registrar ..... Mrs. Lavern YOUNG
07 Director of Admissions ..... Ms. Teisha JOHNSON
32 Sr Director Student Development ..... Ms. Beth KARMIS
37 Director Student Financial Aid ..... Ms. Melissa BARTOLD
29 Director Alumni Relations ..... Ms. Connie M. SCAVUZZO
18 Chief Facilities/Physical Plant ..... Mr. Opie NIMON
26 Director of Communications ..... Ms. Jennifer SOPKO

*Illinois Eastern Community Colleges System Office (B)

233 E Chestnut Street, Olney IL 62450-2298
County: Richland FICE Identification: 009135
Unit ID: 443368
Telephone: (618) 393-2982 Carnegie Class: N/A
FAX Number: (618) 392-4816
URL: www.iecc.edu

01 Chief Executive Officer ..... Mr. Terry BRUCE
05 Chief Academic Officer ..... Mrs. Chris CANTWELL
10 Chief Finance Officer/Treasurer ..... Mr. Roger BROWNING
103 Dean Workforce Education ..... Mr. Michael THOMAS
30 Assoc Dean Grants/Inst Development ..... Vacant
20 Pgm Director College Support Svcs ..... Ms. Rita S. ADAMS
85 Pgm Dir Intl Std/Dir Dist Std Rctmt ..... Ms. Pamela SWANSON-MADDEN
15 Director of Human Resources ..... Mrs. Tara BUERSTER
88 Director TRIO Upward Bound ..... Ms. Samantha WEIDNER
88 Pgm Dir Student Learning Assessment ..... Mr. Brandon WEGER
88 Director TRIO Student Support Svcs ..... Mr. Wain DAVIS
88 Director TRIO Talent Search ..... Ms. Elizabeth OLIVER

*Illinois Eastern Community Colleges Frontier Community College (C)

Frontier Drive, Fairfield IL 62837-9801
County: Wayne FICE Identification: 020744
Unit ID: 403469
Telephone: (618) 842-3711 Carnegie Class: Assoc/HVT-High Non
FAX Number: (618) 842-4425 Calendar System: Semester
URL: www.iecc.edu/fcc
Established: 1976 Annual Undergrad Tuition & Fees (In-District): $3,146
Enrollment: 2,218 Coed
Affiliation or Control: State/Local IRS Status: 501(c)3
Highest Offering: Associate Degree
Accreditation: &NH, ADNUR

02 President ..... Dr. Gerald EDGREN, JR.
05 Dean of Instruction ..... Mr. Paul BRUINSMA
32 Asst Dean of Student Services ..... Mrs. Jan WILES
51 Director of Adult Education ..... Ms. Cheryl HOLDER
10 Director of Business ..... Mrs. Mary JOHNSTON
08 Director of Learning Resource Ctr ..... Ms. Merna YOUNGBLOOD
41 Athletic Director ..... Mr. Thomas KENT
88 Pgm Dir Emergency Preparedness Mgmt ..... Mr. Scott MESEROLE
18 Supervisor of Building & Grounds ..... Mr. Galen DUNN
37 Coordinator of Financial Aid ..... Ms. Lori NOE
88 Coord Literary Development Program ..... Vacant
06 Coordinator of Registration/Records ..... Ms. Amy LOSS

† Regional accreditation is carried under the parent institution Illinois Eastern Community Colleges System Office in Olney, IL.

*Illinois Eastern Community Colleges Lincoln Trail College (D)

11220 State Highway 1, Robinson IL 62454-5707
County: Crawford FICE Identification: 009786
Unit ID: 403478
Telephone: (618) 544-8657 Carnegie Class: Assoc/MT-VT-High Non
FAX Number: (618) 544-7423 Calendar System: Semester
URL: www.iecc.edu/ltc
Established: 1969 Annual Undergrad Tuition & Fees (In-District): $3,146
Enrollment: 1,031 Coed
Affiliation or Control: State/Local IRS Status: 501(c)3
Highest Offering: Associate Degree
Accreditation: &NH, ADNUR

02 President ..... Dr. Ryan GOWER
05 Dean of the College ..... Mr. David CARPENTER
37 Director of Financial Aid ..... Mr. Aaron WHITE
32 Asst Dean of Student Services ..... Ms. Megan SCOTT
08 Director of Learning Resource Ctr ..... Ms. Vicky BONELLI
10 Director of Business ..... Ms. Jamie HENRY
41 Athletic Director ..... Mr. Kevin BOWERS
18 Groundskeeper ..... Mr. Dan LEGGITT
26 Coord Public Information/Marketing ..... Mr. Christopher FORDE

† Regional accreditation is carried under the parent institution Illinois Eastern Community Colleges System Office in Olney, IL.

*Illinois Eastern Community Colleges Olney Central College (E)

305 North West Street, Olney IL 62450-1099
County: Richland FICE Identification: 001742
Unit ID: 145707
Telephone: (618) 395-7777 Carnegie Class: Assoc/MT-VT-High Non
FAX Number: (618) 392-3293 Calendar System: Semester
URL: www.iecc.edu/occ
Established: 1962 Annual Undergrad Tuition & Fees (In-District): $3,146
Enrollment: 1,398 Coed
Affiliation or Control: State/Local IRS Status: 501(c)3
Highest Offering: Associate Degree
Accreditation: &NH, ADNUR, RAD

02 President ..... Mr. Rodney RANES
05 Dean of Instruction ..... Mr. Jeff CUTCHIN
32 Assistant Dean Student Services ..... Vacant
76 Assoc Dean Nursing Allied Health ..... Ms. Theresa MARCOTTE
08 Director Learning Skills Center/LRC ..... Ms. Linda SHIDLER
88 Director Cosmetology ..... Ms. Linda MILLER
10 Director Business ..... Mr. Doug SHIPMAN
41 Athletic Director/Coach ..... Mr. Dennis CONLEY
37 Financial Aid Coordinator ..... Ms. Andie PAMPE

† Regional accreditation is carried under the parent institution Illinois Eastern Community Colleges System Office in Olney, IL.

*Illinois Eastern Community Colleges Wabash Valley College (F)

2200 College Drive, Mount Carmel IL 62863-2657
County: Wabash FICE Identification: 001779
Unit ID: 403487
Telephone: (618) 262-8641 Carnegie Class: Assoc/MT-VT-High Non
FAX Number: (618) 262-5347 Calendar System: Semester
URL: www.iecc.edu/wvc
Established: 1960 Annual Undergrad Tuition & Fees (In-District): $3,146
Enrollment: 4,240 Coed
Affiliation or Control: State/Local IRS Status: 501(c)3
Highest Offering: Associate Degree
Accreditation: &NH, ADNUR

02 President ..... Mr. Matt FOWLER
05 Dean of Instruction ..... Mr. Robert CONN
32 Assistant Dean Student Services ..... Mrs. Tiffany COWGER
20 Director of Academic Advising ..... Mr. Tim ZIMMER
08 Director of LRC ..... Ms. Sandy CRAIG
60 Director of Broadcasting ..... Mr. Kyle PEACH
41 Athletic Director ..... Mr. Mike CARPENTER
10 Director of Business ..... Mrs. Reilly BAUMGART
37 Financial Aid Coordinator ..... Ms. Mary JOHNSON
18 Groundskeeper ..... Mr. Adam ROESCH

† Regional accreditation is carried under the parent institution Illinois Eastern Community Colleges System Office in Olney, IL.

The Illinois Institute of Art (G)

350 N Orleans, Suite 136, Chicago IL 60654-1514
County: Cook FICE Identification: 012584
Unit ID: 148177
Telephone: (312) 280-3500 Carnegie Class: Spec-4-yr-Arts
FAX Number: (312) 777-8780 Calendar System: Quarter
URL: www.artinstitutes.edu/chicago
Established: 1916 Annual Undergrad Tuition & Fees: $17,592
Enrollment: 1,807 Coed
Affiliation or Control: Proprietary IRS Status: Proprietary
Highest Offering: Baccalaureate
Accreditation: NH, ACFEI, CIDA

01 President/Chicago ..... David W. RAY
05 Vice President Academic Affairs ..... Dr. Donna L. GRAY
20 Associate Dean of Academic Affairs ..... Karen JANKO
07 Senior Director of Admissions ..... Summer TOOMEY
06 Registrar ..... Michael DONOHUE
08 Librarian ..... Sean MCCARTHY
79 Program Coordinator Humanities ..... Karine BRAVAIS-SLYMAN
81 Program Coordinator Math/Science ..... Deann GROSSI
10 Regional Director of Finance ..... Daniel LEAVITT
37 Director Student Financial Aid ..... Terry LEPPELLERE
32 Dean of Student Affairs ..... Catherine BROKENSHIRE
35 Asst Dean Student Affs/Dir Housing ..... Valarie RAND
38 Student Support Coordinator ..... Sara SPIEGEL
40 Supply Store Manager ..... Ricardo OLAVE
36 Director of Career Services ..... Vanessa JACKSON
15 Human Resources Generalist ..... Rae DEROSE
13 Director of Technology ..... Terence HAHN
29 Director Alumni Relations ..... Anne CAMPION

The Illinois Institute of Art-Schaumburg (H)

1000 Plaza Drive, Suite 100, Schaumburg IL 60173-4913
Telephone: (847) 619-3450 Identification: 770074
Accreditation: &NH, CIDA

† Regional accreditation is carried under the parent institution in Chicago, IL

Illinois Institute of Technology (I)

10 West 35th Street, Chicago IL 60616-3793
County: Cook FICE Identification: 001691
Unit ID: 145725
Telephone: (312) 567-3000 Carnegie Class: DU-Higher
FAX Number: (312) 567-3004 Calendar System: Semester
URL: www.iit.edu
Established: 1890 Annual Undergrad Tuition & Fees: $43,680
Enrollment: 7,898 Coed
Affiliation or Control: Independent Non-Profit IRS Status: 501(c)3
Highest Offering: Doctorate
Accreditation: NH, BUS, CACREP, CLPSY, CORE, CS, ENG, LSAR

01 President ..... Dr. Alan CRAMB
05 Provost ..... Ms. Frances BRONET
10 VP Finance & Administration ..... Dr. Pat LAUGHLIN
21 Deputy Controller ..... Mr. Ken JOHNSTON
18 VP Facilities & Public Safety ..... Mr. Bruce WATTS
30 Vice Pres Institutional Advancement ..... Ms. Betsy HUGHES
88 Vice Pres International Affairs ..... Dr. Darsh T. WASAN
86 Vice President External Affairs ..... Mr. David E. BAKER
43 Vice President General Counsel ..... Mr. Anthony D'AMATO
31 VP Community Affairs & Outreach ..... Mr. Leroy E. KENNEDY
88 Sr VP & Dir IIT Research Inst ..... Dr. David MCCORMICK
88 VP & Dir Inst Food Safety & Health ..... Dr. Robert BRACKETT
13 Chief Information Officer ..... Mr. Ophir TRIGALO
04 Director President's Office ..... Ms. Sandra LAPORTE
28 Vice Provost Student Diversity ..... Mr. Gerald DOYLE
15 Associate VP Human Resources ..... Ms. Antoinette MURRIL
07 Vice Pres Admissions/Financial Aid ..... Dr. Mike GOSZ
20 Vice Provost Academic Affairs ..... Dr. Chris WHITE
88 Vice Provost for Research ..... Dr. Chris WHITE
32 Vice Provost Student Affairs ..... Ms. Katherine MURPHY-STETZ
61 Dean Chicago-Kent College of Law ..... Mr. Hal J. KRENT
49 Dean College of Science & Letters ..... Dr. Russell BETTS
54 Dean Armour Col of Engineering ..... Dr. Natacha DEPAOLA
50 Dean Stuart School of Business ..... Dr. Harvey KAHALAS
48 Dean College of Architecture ..... Mr. Wiel ARETS
83 Dean Lewis Col of Human Sciences ..... Dr. Christine HIMES
12 Dean Institute of Design ..... Mr. Patrick F. WHITNEY
58 Dean Graduate Col & VP Research ..... Dr. Ali CINAR
72 Dean School of Applied Technology ..... Dr. Bob CARLSON
08 Dean of Libraries ..... Ms. Sharon BOSTICK
88 Assoc Vice Provost UG Acad Affairs ..... Ms. Carole ORZE
88 Assoc Vice Provost Grad Acad Affs ..... Ms. Holli PRYOR-HARRIS
37 Assoc Vice President Enrollment Svc ..... Ms. Abby MCGRATH
84 Assoc Vice President Enrollment ..... Ms. Caryn SCHNIERLE
06 Interim Registrar ..... Ms. Carole ORZE
45 AVP Strategic Initiatives ..... Ms. April WELCH
25 Director Sponsored Research ..... Ms. Domenica G. PAPPAS
14 Director Enterprise Systems ..... Mr. Vince BATTISTA
07 Director UG Admissions ..... Ms. Toni RILEY
07 Director Graduate Admissions ..... Mr. Rishab MALHOTRA
108 Director of Assessment ..... Dr. Carol-Ann EMMONS
29 Sr Director Alumni & Donor Rels ..... Mr. James ACTON
41 AVP Director of Athletics ..... Mr. Joseph HAKES
19 Director Public Safety ..... Mr. Carl DOBRICH
22 Associate General Counsel ..... Ms. Candida MIRANDA
96 Director of Purchasing ..... Mr. Frank FIORITO
28 Director Student Ctr for Diversity ..... Ms. Lisa MONTGOMERY
39 AVP Residence & Greek Life ..... Ms. Slandie DIEUJUSTE
88 Dir Environmental Health & Safety ..... Ms. Cynthia CHAFFEE
38 Director Student Health & Wellness ..... Ms. Anita OPDYCKE
105 Director Web Development/Services ..... Mr. Brian BAILEY
106 Dir IIT Online Tech Svcs ..... Ms. Lauren WOODS
90 Manager Academic Computing ..... Mr. Bill ORNT

Illinois Institute of Technology Chicago-Kent College of Law (J)

565 W Adams Street, Chicago IL 60661
Telephone: (312) 906-5000 Identification: 770075
Accreditation: &NH, LAW

† Regional accreditation is carried under the parent institution in Chicago, IL

Illinois Institute of Technology Institute of Design (K)

350 N LaSalle Street, Chicago IL 60610
Telephone: (312) 595-4900 Identification: 770076
Accreditation: &NH

† Regional accreditation is carried under the parent institution in Chicago, IL

Illinois Institute of Technology Rice Campus (A)

201 East Loop Road, Wheaton IL 60189
Telephone: (630) 682-6000　Identification: 770077
Accreditation: &NH

† Regional accreditation is carried under the parent institution in Chicago, IL

Illinois State University (B)

School and North Streets, Normal IL 61790-0001
County: McLean　FICE Identification: 001692
Unit ID: 145813
Telephone: (309) 438-2111　Carnegie Class: DU-Higher
FAX Number: (309) 438-2768　Calendar System: Semester
URL: www.ilstu.edu
Established: 1857　Annual Undergrad Tuition & Fees (In-State): $13,666
Enrollment: 20,615　Coed
Affiliation or Control: State　IRS Status: 501(c)3
Highest Offering: Doctorate
Accreditation: NH, AAFCS, ART, AUD, BUS, BUSA, CAATE, CAHIIM, CIDA, CONST, CS, DIETD, DIETI, ENGR, IPSY, MT, MUS, NAIT, NRPA, NURSE, SCPSY, SP, SW, TED, THEA

01 President .... Dr. Larry DIETZ
05 VP Academic Affairs & Provost .... Dr. Janet KREJCI
10 VP Finance & Planning .... Mr. Greg ALT
32 VP Student Affairs .... Dr. Levester JOHNSON
26 VP University Advancement .... Mr. Pat VICKERMAN
20 Associate Provost .... Dr. Jim JAWAHAR
35 Interim Asst VP Student Affairs .... Dr. Danielle MILLER-SCHUSTER
21 Sr Assoc VP Finance & Planning .... Ms. Debra K. SMITLEY
91 Chief Academic Technology Officer .... Dr. Mark WALBERT
58 Int Asc VP Grad Std/Rsrch/Intl Educ .... Dr. John BAUR
84 Assoc VP Enrollment Management .... Dr. Troy JOHNSON
15 Asst VP Human Resources .... Ms. Tammy CARLSON
08 Dean University Libraries .... Dr. Dane WARD
06 University Registrar .... Mr. Jess D. RAY
07 Director Admissions .... Mr. Jeff MAVROS
20 Director University College .... Ms. Amelia NOEL-ELKINS
30 Exec Director of Development .... Ms. Joy D. HUTCHCRAFT
21 Senior Associate Comptroller .... Ms. JoEllen BAHNSEN
37 Director Financial Aid .... Ms. Jana ALBRECHT
29 Exec Director Alumni Engagement .... Ms. Doris GROVES
18 Exec Director Facilities Management .... Mr. Charles SCOTT
19 Chief University Police .... Mr. Aaron WOODRUFF
28 Dir Ofc of Eq Opportunity & Access .... Mr. Shane MCCREERY
23 Director Student Health Services .... Ms. Laura KNOBLAUCH
39 Director University Housing .... Ms. Stacey MWILAMBWE
41 Director Intercollegiate Athletics .... Mr. Larry LYONS
85 Director International Studies .... Dr. Luis CANALES
92 Interim Director Honors Program .... Dr. Rocio RIVADENEYRA
94 Director Women's Studies .... Dr. Alison BAILEY
96 Director of Purchasing .... Ms. Judy JOHNSON
49 Dean College Arts & Sciences .... Dr. Gregory B. SIMPSON
50 Dean College Business .... Mr. Ajay SAMANT
53 Acting Dean College Education .... Mr. Albert AZINGER
72 Int Dean College Applied Sci/Tech .... Dr. Jan MURPHY
57 Dean College Fine Arts .... Ms. Jean M K. MILLER
66 Dean Mennonite College .... Dr. Judy NEUBRANDER
100 Chief of Staff .... Mr. Jay GROVES
35 Acting Dean of Students .... Dr. John DAVENPORT
88 Asst VP Acad Admin .... Dr. Sam CATANZARO
88 Interim Assoc VP Acad Fiscal Mgmt .... Dr. Alan LACY
88 Asst VP Administrative Technologies .... Mr. Charles EDAMALA
21 Dir of Budget Planning/Operations .... Ms. Sandra CAVI
44 Exec Dir Annual Giving .... Ms. Lora WEY
88 Chief Operations Ofcr Advancement .... Ms. Jill JONES
27 Exec Dir University Marketing/Comm .... Mr. Brian BEAM
45 Dir Planning/Rsch/Policy Analysis .... Ms. Angela ENGEL
108 Director University Assessment .... Dr. Ryan SMITH
38 Director Student Counseling .... Dr. Sandy COLBS
43 General Counsel .... Ms. Lisa HUSON
105 Director Web & Interactive Comm .... Mr. Arturo RAMIREZ
86 Director State Government Relations .... Dr. Jonathan LACKLAND
90 AVP Academic Technologies .... Dr. Mark WALBERT

Illinois Valley Community College (C)

815 N Orlando Smith Road, Oglesby IL 61348-9692
County: La Salle　FICE Identification: 001705
Unit ID: 145831
Telephone: (815) 224-2720　Carnegie Class: Assoc/HVT-High Non
FAX Number: (815) 224-3033　Calendar System: Semester
URL: www.ivcc.edu
Established: 1966　Annual Undergrad Tuition & Fees (In-District): $3,818
Enrollment: 3,525　Coed
Affiliation or Control: Local　IRS Status: 501(c)3
Highest Offering: Associate Degree
Accreditation: NH, ADNUR, DA

01 President .... Dr. Jerry M. CORCORAN
05 Vice Pres for Academic Affairs .... Dr. Deborah L. ANDERSON
10 Vice Pres Business Svcs/Finance .... Ms. Cheryl E. ROELFSEMA
20 AVP Academic Affs/Dean Wrkfce Devel .... Ms. Sue L. ISERMANN
32 Assoc Vice Pres Student Svcs .... Mr. Mark J. GRZYBOWSKI
24 Director of Learning Technologies .... Ms. Emily B. VESCOGNI
31 Director Cmty Relations & Marketing .... Mr. Francis R. BROLLEY
13 Dir of Information Technology Svcs .... Mr. Harold B. BARNES
51 Interim Dir Cont Educ/Business Svcs .... Ms. Jennifer C. SCHERI
15 Director Human Resources .... Ms. Glenna S. JONES
37 Director of Financial Aid .... Ms. Patricia A. WILLIAMSON
07 Director of Admissions/Records .... Mr. Quintin M. OVEROCKER
08 Head Librarian .... Ms. Frances A. WHALEY
30 Director of Development .... Mr. Francis R. BROLLEY
96 Director of Purchasing .... Ms. Michelle L. CARBONI
18 Director of Facilities .... Mr. Scott CURLEY
09 Director of Institutional Research .... Mr. Matthew P. SUERTH
81 Dean Natural Science/Business .... Mr. Ron W. GROLEAU
66 Dean Health Professions/ Nursing .... Ms. Bonnie L. BENNETT-CAMPBELL
79 Dn Humanities/Fine Arts/Soc Sci .... Mr. Brian R. HOLLOWAY
53 Dean English/Mathematics/Educ .... Dr. Robyn L. SCHIFFMAN

Illinois Wesleyan University (D)

PO Box 2900, 1312 Park Street, Bloomington IL 61702-2900
County: McLean　FICE Identification: 001696
Unit ID: 145646
Telephone: (309) 556-1000　Carnegie Class: Bac-A&S
FAX Number: (309) 556-3411　Calendar System: Other
URL: www.iwu.edu
Established: 1850　Annual Undergrad Tuition & Fees: $42,490
Enrollment: 1,893　Coed
Affiliation or Control: Independent Non-Profit　IRS Status: 501(c)3
Highest Offering: Baccalaureate
Accreditation: NH, MUS, NURSE

01 President .... Dr. Eric R. JENSEN
05 Provost & Dean of Faculty .... Dr. Jonathan D. GREEN
10 Vice President Business & Finance .... Mr. Daniel P. KLOTZBACH
30 Int Vice President for Advancement .... Mr. Steve SEIBRING
26 Int Vice Pres for Communications .... Ms. Ann AUBRY
32 VP Student Affairs/Dean Students .... Dr. Karla CARNEY-HALL
07 Dean of Admissions .... Mr. Robert MURRAY
09 AVP Instl Research/Plng/Evaluation .... Dr. Michael THOMPSON
86 Dir Government/Community Relations .... Mr. Carl F. TEICHMAN
04 Exec Assistant to the President .... Dr. Molly MUNSON-DRYER
20 Assoc Provost Acad Plng/Standards .... Dr. Frank A. BOYD
20 Assoc Dean Curricular/Faculty Devel .... Prof. Lynda DUKE
15 Assoc VP for Human Resources .... Ms. Catherine SPITZ
13 Asst Provost/Chief Technology Ofcr .... Mr. Trey SHORT
44 Associate Vice Pres Gift Planning .... Mr. Steve D. SEIBRING
35 Assoc Dean of Students .... Ms. Darcy L. GREDER
38 Asst Dean/Dir Student Counseling .... Dr. Annorrah MOORMAN
35 Asst Dean Students/Dir Campus Life .... Dr. Brandon COMMON
08 University Librarian .... Dr. Karen SCHMIDT
06 Registrar .... Dr. Leslie BETZ
42 University Chaplain .... Rev. Elyse NELSON WINGER
21 Controller .... Mr. John BRYANT
37 Director of Financial Aid .... Mr. Scott SEIBRING
64 Director of School of Music .... Dr. Mario J. PELUSI
57 Director of School of Art .... Prof. Julie JOHNSON
57 Director of School of Theatre Arts .... Dr. Thomas QUINN
66 Director of School of Nursing .... Dr. Victoria FOLSE
41 Director of Athletics .... Prof. Mike WAGNER
29 Director of Alumni Relations .... Ms. Adriane POWELL
102 Dir Grants/Foundation Relations .... Mr. Dick FOLSE
44 Dir of Wesleyan Annual Fund .... Mr. Van MILLER
36 Director of Career Center .... Mr. Warren KISTNER
18 Director of Physical Plant .... Mr. James J. BLUMBERG
88 Director of Sports Information .... Mr. Stewart I. SALOWITZ
93 Director of Diversity & Inclusion .... Vacant
35 Int Dir of Student Act/Leadership Pgms .... Ms. Liz HINDERKS
94 Dir of Women's & Gender Studies .... Dr. Carole MYSCOFSKI
104 Director of International Office .... Ms. Stacey SHIMIZU
40 Bookstore Manager .... Mr. Thaddeus SUTTER

Institute for Clinical Social Work (E)

401 South State Street, Suite 822, Chicago IL 60605
County: Cook　FICE Identification: 025737
Unit ID: 145886
Telephone: (312) 935-4232　Carnegie Class: Spec-4-yr-Other Health
FAX Number: (312) 935-4255　Calendar System: Semester
URL: www.icsw.edu
Established: 1981　Annual Graduate Tuition & Fees: N/A
Enrollment: 124　Coed
Affiliation or Control: Independent Non-Profit　IRS Status: 501(c)3
Highest Offering: Doctorate; No Undergraduates
Accreditation: NH

01 Dean/President .... Dr. Scott H. ROSE
05 Associate Dean .... Dr. Jennifer TOLLESON
11 Vice President of Operations .... Lynne GORDON
20 Director of Academic Administration .... Elizabeth OLLER
37 Director of Student Financial Svcs .... Sebastien BEAUDET
08 Librarian .... Vacant
07 Director of Admissions .... Jennifer TOLLESON

John A. Logan College (F)

700 Logan College Road, Carterville IL 62918-2500
County: Williamson　FICE Identification: 008076
Unit ID: 146205
Telephone: (618) 985-3741　Carnegie Class: Assoc/HVT-High Non
FAX Number: (618) 985-2248　Calendar System: Semester
URL: www.jalc.edu
Established: 1967　Annual Undergrad Tuition & Fees (In-District): $3,270
Enrollment: 6,718　Coed
Affiliation or Control: State/Local　IRS Status: 501(c)3
Highest Offering: Associate Degree
Accreditation: NH, CAHIIM, CONST, DA, DH, DMS, MLTAD, OTA, SURGT

01 President .... Dr. Ron HOUSE
05 Vice President Instruction Services .... Vacant
10 VP Business Svcs/College Facilities .... Mr. Brad MCCORMICK
11 VP Administration .... Dr. Larry PETERSON
32 Dean Student Services .... Mr. Tim WILLIAMS
21 Dean Financial Operations .... Ms. Stacy BUCKINGHAM
20 Dean Academic Affairs .... Ms. Melanie PECORD
103 Dean Workforce Dev/Adult Education .... Ms. Kay FLLEMING
88 Dir for Term Faculty Instruction .... Ms. April STANLY
72 Dean for Career and Technical Educ .... Vacant
51 Dean for Continuing Education .... Dr. Barry HANCOCK
88 Assoc Dr Adult Basic/Secondary Educ .... Vacant
13 Assoc Dean Information Technology .... Vacant
07 Assoc Director of Admissions .... Ms. Christy STEWART
37 Director of Student Financial Asst .... Ms. Sherry SUMMARY
08 Assoc Dean for Library Services .... Vacant
30 Dean for Institutional Effectivenes .... Dr. Valerie BARKO
84 Dir Recruit/Retention/Acad Advisor .... Dr. Steve O'KEEFE
35 Director of Student Activities .... Ms. Adrienne BARKLEY-GIFFIN
36 Director of Career Services .... Ms. Lisa HUDGENS
102 Executive Director of Foundation .... Ms. Staci SHAFER
66 Director of Nursing .... Ms. Marilyn FALASTER
36 Director of Testing Services .... Ms. Christy MCBRIDE
15 Exec Dir of Human Resources/AAO .... Dr. Clay BREWER
18 Dir Buildings and Grounds .... Mr. Tim GIBSON
09 Director Institutional Research .... Mr. Eric PULLEY
04 Administrative Asst to President .... Ms. Sondra WALKER
101 Admin Asst Pres/Board of Trustees .... Ms. Susan MAY
28 Director of Diversity & Inclusion .... Ms. Toyin FOX
41 Athletic Director .... Vacant
88 Dir of Emergency Plng & Risk Mgmt .... Mr. Don PRIDDY
88 Bus Function Analyst in Stdnt Svcs .... Mr. Terry CRAIN
38 Director of Student Success .... Ms. Carolyn GALLEGLY
88 Director Academic Advisement .... Ms. Stacy HOLLOWAY
96 Dir of Purchasing/Auxilary Svcs .... Ms. Sue ZAMORA
88 CCR & R Director .... Ms. Lori LONGUEVILLE
88 Director of ASE .... Ms. Crystal HOSSELTON
56 Director of Adult Education .... Ms. Karla TABING
50 Director of Business & Industry .... Mr. Dennis WHITE
88 Director of Corporate Education .... Ms. Michelle HAMILTON
88 Exec Dir of Integrated Technology .... Mr. Scott ELLIOTT
88 Director of CHEC .... Mr. Bradley GRIFFITH
51 Director of Continuing Education .... Mr. Greg STETTLER
18 Director of Facility Services .... Mr. Chris NAEGELE

John Marshall Law School (G)

315 S Plymouth Court, Chicago IL 60604-3968
County: Cook　FICE Identification: 001698
Unit ID: 146241
Telephone: (312) 427-2737　Carnegie Class: Spec-4-yr-Law
FAX Number: (312) 427-8307　Calendar System: Semester
URL: www.jmls.edu
Established: 1899　Annual Graduate Tuition & Fees: N/A
Enrollment: 1,307　Coed
Affiliation or Control: Independent Non-Profit　IRS Status: 501(c)3
Highest Offering: First Professional Degree; No Undergraduates
Accreditation: NH, LAW

01 Dean .... Mr. John E. CORKERY
05 Assoc Dean Academic Affairs .... Mr. Anthony NIEDWIECKI
07 Assoc Dean Admissions/Student Affs .... Mr. William B. POWERS
10 Chief Financial Officer .... Ms. Cynthia SAH
30 Exec Dir Development/Alum Rels .... Mr. John D. BERGHOLZ
13 Dir Library & IT Operations .... Mr. Ramsey DONNELL
20 Asst Dean for Academic Services .... Ms. Jodie NEEDHAM
15 Asst Dean Human Resources .... Mr. Martin D'AMBROSE
36 Asst Dean Career Services .... Ms. Chante SPANN
06 Registrar .... Ms. Jodie NEEDHAM
26 Dir Marketing/Communications .... Mr. Michael HUGGINS
37 Director Student Financial Aid .... Ms. Yara SANTANA
09 Exec Dir of Institutional Affairs .... Ms. Anna KRUG
88 Assoc Dean for Advanced Studies .... Ms. Kathryn KENNEDY
88 Assoc Dn Professional/Career Strat .... Hon. Margaret O'Mara FROSSARD, RET.
28 Chief Diversity/Inclusion Officer .... Mr. Troy RIDDLE
19 Director Security/Safety .... Mr. Ali HALEEM
88 Assoc Dean Faculty Affairs .... Ms. Julie SPANBAUER
11 Asst Dean for Administration .... Ms. Teresa DO

John Wood Community College (H)

1301 S 48th Street, Quincy IL 62305-8736
County: Adams　FICE Identification: 012813
Unit ID: 146278
Telephone: (217) 224-6500　Carnegie Class: Assoc/MT-VT-High Non
FAX Number: (217) 224-4208　Calendar System: Semester
URL: www.jwcc.edu
Established: 1974　Annual Undergrad Tuition & Fees (In-District): $4,410
Enrollment: 1,900　Coed
Affiliation or Control: State/Local　IRS Status: 501(c)3
Highest Offering: Associate Degree
Accreditation: NH, SURGT

01 President .... Mr. Michael ELBE
05 Vice President for Instruction .... Dr. Laurel KLINKENBERG
10 Dean Business Svcs/Inst Effective .... Mr. Josh WELKER
32 Dean Student Services .... Vacant
49 Dean Arts and Sciences .... Mr. Mike TERRY
75 Dean Careers/Tech/Health Education .... Mr. William STUFFLICK

84 Dean Enrollment Svcs/Dir Finan Aid ... Ms. Melanie LECHTENBERG
07 Director Admissions ... Mr. William SCHAFFER
06 Registrar/Dean of Students ... Mr. Cody BAGGETT
21 Director Fiscal Services ... Ms. Susan FIFER
35 Director Support Services ... Mr. Robert HODGSON
13 Director Information Technology ... Mr. Joshua BRUECK
08 Director Learning Resource Center ... Ms. Barbara LIEBER
26 Director Public Relations/Marketing ... Ms. Tracy ORNE
30 Director Advancement ... Ms. Barbara HOLTHAUS
15 Director Human Resources ... Ms. Dana KEPPNER
18 Director Physical Plant ... Mr. Lou BARTA
37 Director Financial Aid ... Ms. Melanie LECHTENBERG
19 Dean of Ops/Chief of Campus Police ... Mr. Bill LATOUR
41 Manager Athletics & Intramurals ... Mr. Brad HOYT
40 Manager Campus Services ... Ms. Lynn BLICKHAN
96 Purchasing Coordinator ... Ms. Darla SNYDER
47 Dept Chair Ag Sciences ... Mr. Gary SHUPE
77 Dept Chair Ofc Technology/Comp Sci ... Mr. Nick KRIZMANIC
50 Dept Chair Business ... Ms. Cathy STEPHENS
81 Department Chair Mathematics ... Ms. Shari HARRIS
65 Dept Chair Natural Sciences ... Dr. Ivan PAUL
79 Dept Chair Lang/Lit/Hum/Fine Arts ... Ms. Christine WIEWEL
88 Dept Chair Developmental Education ... Ms. Elizabeth ONIK
83 Dept Chair Social/Behavior Science ... Dr. Randall EGDORF
04 Administrative Asst to President ... Ms. Leah BENZ
102 Dir Foundation/Corporate Relations ... Ms. Barbara HOLTHAUS

Joliet Junior College (A)

1215 Houbolt Road, Joliet IL 60431-8938
County: Will FICE Identification: 001699
Unit ID: 146296
Telephone: (815) 729-9020 Carnegie Class: Assoc/MT-VT-High Non
FAX Number: N/A Calendar System: Semester
URL: www.jjc.edu
Established: 1901 Annual Undergrad Tuition & Fees (In-District): $3,450
Enrollment: 15,776 Coed
Affiliation or Control: State/Local IRS Status: 501(c)3
Highest Offering: Associate Degree
Accreditation: NH, ACBSP, ACFEI, ADNUR, CAHIIM, MUS

01 Interim President ... Dr. Judy MITCHELL
10 Interim VP Administrative Services ... Mr. Jeff HEAP
13 Exec Dir Information Technology ... Mr. Jim SERR
32 VP Student Development ... Dr. Yolanda ISAACS
31 Dean Community/Economic Development ... Vacant
07 Director Admissions & Recruitment ... Ms. Jennifer KLOBERDANZ
88 Dir Adult & Family Services ... Ms. Emilie MCCALLISTER
37 Director Financial Aid ... Vacant
15 Int Exec Director Human Resources ... Ms. Judy CONNELLY
06 Registrar ... Mr. Keith TILLMAN
18 Director Facility Services ... Mr. Patrick VAN DUYNE
21 Director Business/Auxiliary Svcs ... Ms. Janice REEDUS
26 Dir Communications/External Rels ... Ms. Kelly ROHDER
36 Director Career Services ... Ms. Bridgett LARKIN-BEENE
41 Director Athletics ... Mr. Wayne KING
21 Director Financial Svcs/Controller ... Mr. Jeffrey HEAP
19 Dir Campus Safety & Police Chief ... Mr. Peter COMANDA
30 Ex Dir Inst Adv Exec Dir JJC Found ... Ms. Kristin MULVEY
08 Director Library ... Vacant
09 Director of Institutional Research ... Mr. Joseph OFFERMANN
29 Director Alumni Relations ... Ms. Kelly LARSON
40 Manager Bookstore ... Vacant
88 Coord GSD ... Dr. Angie KAYSEN-LUZBETAK
74 Dept Chair Veterinary Medicine Tech ... Dr. Scott KELLER
38 Counselor/Dept Chair ... Ms. Jennifer KIMBAROVSKY
04 Senior Admin Asst to President ... Ms. Jennifer TENN
100 Chief of Staff ... Ms. Linda SMITH
101 Secretary of the Institution/Board ... Ms. Joan TIERNEY
103 Dir Workforce Development ... Ms. Caroline PORTLOCK
104 Coordinator Study Abroad ... Ms. Tamara BRATTOLI
106 Dir Online Education/E-learning ... Mr. Chris OSTWINKLE
84 Dean of Enrollment Management ... Mr. Trevell EDDINS

Judson University (B)

1151 N State Street, Elgin IL 60123-1498
County: Kane FICE Identification: 001700
Unit ID: 146339
Telephone: (847) 628-2500 Carnegie Class: Masters/S
FAX Number: (847) 628-1027 Calendar System: Semester
URL: www.judsonu.edu
Established: 1913 Annual Undergrad Tuition & Fees: $28,170
Enrollment: 1,288 Coed
Affiliation or Control: American Baptist IRS Status: 501(c)3
Highest Offering: Doctorate
Accreditation: NH

01 President ... Dr. Gene CRUME
04 Exec Assistant to the President ... Mrs. Tena ROBOTHAM
05 Provost/Chief Academic Officer ... Dr. Wilbert FRIESEN
10 CFO & VP for Business Affairs ... Mr. Jeff EDER
06 Assoc VP and Univ Registrar ... Ms. Virginia GUTH
84 VP for Enrollment & Strategic Plan ... Ms. Nancy BINGER
91 VP for University Technology ... Mrs. Hasi SMITH
49 Dean Liberal Arts/Sciences & Educ ... Dr. Lanette POTEETE-YOUNG
48 Interim Dean Art/Design & Arch ... Dr. Jhennifer AMUNDSON
50 Dean Business & Professional Stds ... Dr. David COOK
32 VP for Student Life ... Mrs. Lisa JAROT
08 Library Director ... Mr. Larry WILD
13 Exec Dir for Information Technology ... Mr. Brent RICHARDSON
44 Senior VP for External Relations ... Mr. Devlin DONALDSON
88 Director of Advancement ... Mr. Dan DICK
29 Director of Alumni Relations ... Mrs. Bonnie BIENERT
37 Director of Financial Aid ... Ms. Diana WINTON
07 Director of Admissions ... Mr. Nate MCNEELY
26 Director of Comm & Marketing ... Ms. Mary DULABAUM
36 Director of Career Development ... Mrs. Doris HAUGEN
38 Dir of Student Health & Wellness ... Mr. Elliott ANDERSON
19 Director of Campus Safety ... Mr. Nick SALZMANN
41 Athletic Director ... Mr. Chad GASSMAN
88 Director of Retention/Student Advoc ... Miss Jaimee BARTHA
85 International Advisor ... Mr. Rafael HECK
35 Associate Dean of Students ... Ms. Casey SUNDSTEDT
23 Director of Health Center ... Ms. Susan WEBER
88 Tutor/ADA Compliance Coordinator ... Ms. Gineen VARGAS
92 Honors Director ... Dr. Craig KAPLOWITZ
15 Director of Human Resources ... Mr. Jeremiah THOMPSON
101 Asst Sec to Board of Trustees ... Mrs. Tena ROBOTHAM
105 Webmaster ... Mr. Eric SECKER
28 Asst for Diversity/Spiritual Dev ... Dr. Curtis SARTOR
09 Director of Institutional Research ... Mr. Chad BRIGGS

Kankakee Community College (C)

100 College Drive, Kankakee IL 60901-6505
County: Kankakee FICE Identification: 007690
Unit ID: 146348
Telephone: (815) 802-8100 Carnegie Class: Assoc/HVT-High Non
FAX Number: (815) 802-8101 Calendar System: Semester
URL: www.kcc.edu
Established: 1966 Annual Undergrad Tuition & Fees (In-District): $4,050
Enrollment: 3,378 Coed
Affiliation or Control: State/Local IRS Status: 501(c)3
Highest Offering: Associate Degree
Accreditation: NH, ADNUR, COARC, MLTAD, PHLEB, PTAA

01 President ... Dr. John AVENDANO
04 Executive Secretary to President ... Ms. Karen SLAGER
05 VP of Instructional & Stdnt Success ... Dr. Michael BOYD
10 VP for Finance & Administration ... Ms. Vicki GARDNER
06 Registrar ... Mr. David HERMANN
32 Dean of Student Development ... Ms. Julia WASKOSKY
09 Director Institutional Research ... Dr. Purva DEVOL
31 Director Adult & Community Educ ... Ms. Margaret WOLF
103 Director of Workforce Development ... Ms. Dana WASHINGTON
37 Director Financial Aid ... Ms. Deanna THOMPSON
35 Coordinator Student Life ... Ms. Linh WILLIAMS
88 Director Fitness Center ... Mr. Dennis CLARK
41 Director Athletics ... Mr. Todd POST
15 Director Human Resources ... Mr. David CAGLE
10 Director Financial Affairs ... Ms. Beth NUNLEY
50 Assoc Dean Business & Technology ... Mr. Paul CARLSON
51 Asst Dean Cont Educ & Career Svcs ... Ms. Mary POSING
18 Dir Campus Facilities & Security ... Mr. Rich SODERQUIST
88 Coordinator Small Business Devel ... Mr. Ken CRITE
81 Assoc Dean Math/Science Division ... Vacant
76 Assoc Dean Health Careers Div ... Ms. Sheri CAGLE
88 Director Student Advisement ... Ms. Meredith PURCELL
76 Director Respiratory Therapist Pgm ... Ms. Nancy OZEE
76 Director Medical Lab Technology ... Ms. Glenda FORNERIS
83 Assoc Dean Humanities/Social Sci ... Vacant
76 Director Radiology Technology Pgm ... Ms. Darla JEPSON
13 Director Information Tech Svcs ... Mr. Michael O'CONNOR
102 Exec Director of KCC Foundation ... Ms. Kelly MYERS
07 Coord Admissions & Recruitment ... Ms. Laura GARDNER
88 Director Institutional Tech/Fac Dev ... Mr. Craig KEIGHER
62 Director Learning Resource Center ... Ms. Karen BECKER
26 Director Marketing ... Ms. Kari NUGENT
101 Board Recording Secretary ... Ms. Karen SLAGER

Kaskaskia College (D)

27210 College Road, Centralia IL 62801-7878
County: Clinton FICE Identification: 001701
Unit ID: 146366
Telephone: (618) 545-3000 Carnegie Class: Assoc/HVT-High Non
FAX Number: (618) 532-1990 Calendar System: Semester
URL: www.kaskaskia.edu
Established: 1940 Annual Undergrad Tuition & Fees (In-District): $4,192
Enrollment: 4,906 Coed
Affiliation or Control: State/Local IRS Status: 501(c)3
Highest Offering: Associate Degree
Accreditation: NH, ADNUR, COARC, DA, MLTAD, OTA, PTAA, RAD, SURGT

01 President ... Dr. Penny QUINN
11 Vice Pres Administrative Services ... Mrs. Nancy KINSEY
05 Vice Pres Instructional Services ... Dr. Gregory LABYAK
32 Vice President of Student Services ... Mrs. Susan BATCHELOR
75 Dean Career & Technical Education ... Mr. George EVANS
49 Dean of Arts & Sciences ... Ms. Kellie HENEGAR
66 Dean of Nursing ... Mrs. Janet GARRETSON
09 Dean Institutional Effectiveness ... Mr. Jeffrey EBEL
43 Dir Legal CounselRisk Mgt/Plan Giv ... Ms. Rhonda BOEHNE
15 Director of Human Resources ... Ms. Anna MOYER
18 Director Facilities/Physical Plant ... Mr. Jennings CARTER
96 Director Purchasing/Auxiliary Svcs ... Mr. Craig ROPER
37 Director of Financial Aid ... Ms. Jill KLOSTERMANN
76 Director of Radiologic Technology ... Mrs. Mimi POLCZYNSKI
76 Dir Physical Therapist Asst Pgm ... Ms. Jane HERRMANN
13 Dean of Information Technology ... Ms. Gina SCHUETZ
27 Director of Public Information ... Ms. Cathy KARRICK
26 Director of Marketing ... Mr. Travis HENSON
40 Bookstore Manager ... Ms. Cheryl JOHNSON
51 Dean of Adult Education ... Vacant
41 Athletic Director ... Mr. Adam ESSES
10 Controller ... Ms. Judy HEMKER
88 Director of Student Recruitment ... Ms. Amy TROUTT
07 Dir Admissions/Records & Dual Cred ... Mrs. Cheryl BOEHNE
30 Dir Inst Advancement Programs ... Mrs. Suzanne CHRIST

Kendall College (E)

900 N North Branch Street, Chicago IL 60642
County: Cook FICE Identification: 001703
Unit ID: 146393
Telephone: (312) 752-2000 Carnegie Class: Bac-Diverse
FAX Number: (312) 752-2021 Calendar System: Quarter
URL: www.kendall.edu
Established: 1934 Annual Undergrad Tuition & Fees: $19,459
Enrollment: 1,516 Coed
Affiliation or Control: Proprietary IRS Status: Proprietary
Highest Offering: Baccalaureate
Accreditation: NH, ACFEI

01 President ... Ms. Kimberly SHAMBROOK
05 Provost ... Dr. Agueda BENITO
84 Director of Domestic Enrollment ... Ms. Genevieve BURKE
04 Executive Assistant to President ... Mr. Scott BRANDEL
10 Senior Finance Manager ... Mr. Kene CHIDUME
06 Registrar ... Ms. Amanda MOLLER
15 Manager of Human Resources ... Ms. Crystal KAMINSKI
29 Alumni Affairs ... Vacant
32 Director of Student Operations ... Mr. Frank ARCE
08 Library Technician ... Ms. Alexis CARSCADDEN
88 Director of Intl Enrollment ... Mr. Ken KASEE
37 Director of Financial Aid ... Mr. Lauren WALKER
39 Director of Housing ... Vacant
97 Director of General Education ... Mr. Ryan BARTELMAY
19 Director Campus Safety ... Ms. Jeanette KONIECZKA
09 Manager of Institutional Research ... Mr. Todd BOTTOM
96 Senior Procurement Manager ... Ms. Lara ENGERT
07 Director of Admissions & Records ... Ms. Daniela LEOPALDI

Kishwaukee College (F)

21193 Malta Road, Malta IL 60150-9600
County: De Kalb FICE Identification: 007684
Unit ID: 146418
Telephone: (815) 825-2086 Carnegie Class: Assoc/MT-VT-High Non
FAX Number: (815) 825-2072 Calendar System: Semester
URL: www.kishwaukeecollege.edu
Established: 1968 Annual Undergrad Tuition & Fees (In-District): $3,990
Enrollment: 4,475 Coed
Affiliation or Control: State/Local IRS Status: 501(c)3
Highest Offering: Associate Degree
Accreditation: NH, RAD

01 President ... Dr. Laurie BOROWICZ
05 Vice President Instruction ... Mr. Mark LANTING
10 Chief Financial Officer ... Ms. Beth YOUNG
32 Vice President Student Services ... Mr. Sedgwick HARRIS
09 VP Institutional Effectiveness ... Mr. Kevin J. FUSS
83 Dean Arts/Communic/Social Science ... Ms. Jaime LONG
72 Dean Career Technologies ... Mr. Matt FEUERBORN
76 Dean Health & Education ... Ms. Bette CHILTON
35 Dean of Student Services ... Ms. Nancy PARTCH
81 Dean Math/Science/Business ... Ms. Sara POHL
51 Dean Adult Educ/Transition Pgms ... Ms. Joanne KANTNER
103 Strategic Partnerships ... Mr. Bill NICKLAS
102 Exec Dir Kish Col Foundation Devel ... Mr. Marshall HAYES
07 Dir Admissions/Registration/Records .. Ms. Michelle ROTHMEYER
26 Dir of Marketing & Public Relations ... Ms. Kayte HAMEL
37 Director Student Financial Aid ... Ms. Cynthia STONESIFER
13 Director Information Technology ... Mr. Robert MCGARRY
40 Bookstore Manager ... Ms. Jessica ANDERSON
08 Director Library Services ... Ms. Anne-Marie GREEN
15 Director Human Resources ... Mr. Eric HERMONSON
41 Athletic Director ... Mr. Craig JACKSON
18 Chief Facilities/Physical Plant ... Mr. Michael KUROPAS
04 Executive Assistant to President ... Ms. Cindy MCCLUSKEY
108 Director Institutional Assessment ... Mr. Matthew CRULL
28 Coord Access/Equity and Diversity ... Vacant
96 Purchasing Coordinator ... Ms. Kathleen JONES

Knowledge Systems Institute (G)

3420 Main Street, Skokie IL 60076-2453
County: Cook FICE Identification: 026227
Unit ID: 260956
Telephone: (847) 679-3135 Carnegie Class: Spec-4-yr-Other Tech
FAX Number: (847) 679-3166 Calendar System: Semester
URL: www.ksi.edu
Established: 1978 Annual Graduate Tuition & Fees: N/A
Enrollment: 193 Coed
Affiliation or Control: Independent Non-Profit IRS Status: 501(c)3
Highest Offering: Master's; No Undergraduates
Accreditation: NH

01 President ... Dr. Daniel GRAUPE
10 Vice Pres Operations ... Ms. Judy CHANG
05 Dean of Academic Affairs ... Dr. Hector HERNANDEZ
88 Department Chair ... Dr. Cheng-Yuan HSIEH
11 Administrative Manager ... Ms. Noorjhan ALI

Knox College (A)

2 E South Street, Galesburg IL 61401-4999
County: Knox FICE Identification: 001704
Unit ID: 146427
Telephone: (309) 341-7000 Carnegie Class: Bac-A&S
FAX Number: (309) 341-7090 Calendar System: Trimester
URL: www.knox.edu
Established: 1837 Annual Undergrad Tuition & Fees: $41,847
Enrollment: 1,399 Coed
Affiliation or Control: Independent Non-Profit IRS Status: 501(c)3
Highest Offering: Baccalaureate
Accreditation: NH

01 President .... Dr. Teresa L. AMOTT
101 Secretary of the College .... Ms. Peggy J. WARE
05 VP Acad Affairs/Dean of College .... Dr. Laura L. BEHLING
10 Vice Pres for Finance & Admin Svcs .... Mr. Keith A. ARCHER
30 Vice President for Advancement .... Ms. Beverly HOLMES
07 Vice Pres Enrollment/Dean of Admiss .... Mr. Paul R. STEENIS
32 VP for Student Development .... Dr. Anne R. EHRLICH
26 VP Communications .... Ms. Megan SCOTT
06 Registrar .... Dr. Chuck SCHULZ
32 Dean of Students .... Ms. Debbie SOUTHERN
20 Associate Dean of College .... Dr. Lori SCHROEDER
37 Director Financial Aid .... Ms. Ann BRILL
08 Librarian .... Mr. Jeffrey A. DOUGLAS
36 Director Ctr Career Pre-Prof Dev .... Ms. Terrie SALINE
13 VP/CIO Information Technology Svcs .... Mr. Steven HALL
15 AVP Director Human Resources .... Ms. Crystal D. BOHN
18 Director Facilities Services .... Mr. Scott MAUST
21 Controller .... Ms. Bobby Jo MAURER
86 Dir Government & Community Relation .... Ms. Karrie HEARTLEIN
29 Dir Alumni & Constituent Programs .... Ms. Carol J. BROWN
38 Director of Counseling Services .... Vacant
41 Director of Athletics .... Mr. Chad EISELE
19 Director Campus Safety .... Mr. Mark A. WELKER
09 Dir Institutional Research/Assess .... Mr. Charles L. CLARK
102 Dir Corporate/Foundation Relations .... Ms. Anne-Marie BERK
43 Dir Legal Services/General Counsel .... Vacant
44 Director Annual or Planned Giving .... Mr. Scott PARK

Lake Forest College (B)

555 N Sheridan Road, Lake Forest IL 60045-2338
County: Lake FICE Identification: 001706
Unit ID: 146481
Telephone: (847) 234-3100 Carnegie Class: Bac-A&S
FAX Number: (847) 735-6291 Calendar System: Semester
URL: www.lakeforest.edu
Established: 1857 Annual Undergrad Tuition & Fees: $42,644
Enrollment: 1,626 Coed
Affiliation or Control: Independent Non-Profit IRS Status: 501(c)3
Highest Offering: Master's
Accreditation: NH

01 President .... Mr. Stephen D. SCHUTT
05 Provost/Dean of Faculty .... Dr. Michael ORR
10 VP for Finance/Planning & Treasurer .... Ms. Lori SUNDBERG
30 VP of Development & Alumni Pgms .... Mr. Philip HOOD
07 VP of Enrollment .... Mr. Chris ELLERTSON
32 Vice President for Student Affairs .... Mr. Rob FLOT
21 Controller and Payroll .... Ms. Doris DUMAS
04 Executive Assistant to President .... Ms. Elizabeth A. PALM
35 Assoc Dean Dir of Residence Life .... Mr. Andrew POLLOM
28 Director Intercult Relelations .... Ms. Erin HOFFMAN
20 Asc Dean Facul/Dir Ctr Chicago Pgms .... Dr. Davis SCHNEIDERMAN
20 Assoc Dean Facul/Dir Lrng/Tchng Ctr .... Dr. Ann ROBERTS
31 Director of Community Education .... Mr. Dan LEMAHIEU
37 Associate VP of Financial Aid .... Mr. Gerard J. CEBRZYNSKI
41 Athletic Director .... Ms. Jacqueline SLAATS
08 Librarian & Director Info Svcs/Tech .... Mr. James R. CUBIT
06 Registrar .... Ms. Ruthane I. BOPP
38 Director of Counseling Services .... Dr. Jennifer JEZIORSKI
29 Assoc Vice Pres for Alumni Relation .... Ms. Kim FEIGH
09 Director of Institutional Research .... Ms. Lori H. SUNDBERG
15 Director of Human Resources .... Ms. Agnes STEPEK
36 Director of Career Services .... Ms. Lisa HINKLEY
18 Director of Facilities Management .... Mr. David J. SIEBERT
26 Assoc VP for Comm//Mktg .... Ms. Elizabeth LIBBY
19 Director of Public Safety .... Mr. Richard L. COHEN
101 Secretary of the Institution/Board .... Ms. Carol LUEDERS
104 Director Study Abroad .... Ms. Ashley SINCLAIR
44 Director Annual Giving .... Ms. Katie ROTH

Lake Forest Graduate School of Management (C)

1905 W Field Court, Lake Forest IL 60045-4824
County: Lake FICE Identification: 023192
Unit ID: 146490
Telephone: (847) 234-5005 Carnegie Class: Spec-4-yr-Bus
FAX Number: (847) 295-3656 Calendar System: Semester
URL: www.lakeforestmba.edu
Established: 1946 Annual Graduate Tuition & Fees: N/A
Enrollment: 470 Coed
Affiliation or Control: Independent Non-Profit IRS Status: 501(c)3
Highest Offering: Master's; No Undergraduates
Accreditation: NH

01 President .... Mr. Jeffrey J. ANDERSON
05 VP and Chief Academic Officer .... Dr. Bryan J. WATKINS
10 VP Finance & CFO .... Mr. Thomas PEROZZI
26 Senior Director of Marketing .... Ms. Barb SIEGEL
20 VP Corporate Learning Solutions .... Ms. Carrie BUCHWALD
15 VP External Relations & HR .... Ms. Stasia ZWISLER
13 VP IT & CIO .... Mr. Gregory KOZAK
20 Dean Faculty & Degree Programs .... Dr. Cheryl BONCUORE
20 Dean Corporate Learning Solutions .... Dr. Neil HOLMAN
09 Mgr Institutional Research .... Ms. Jeanne KUETER
06 Registrar .... Ms. Christine L. PERLSTROM
37 Associate Director of Financial Aid .... Ms. Rebecca KIM
07 Senior Director of Admissions .... Ms. Carolyn BRUNE
32 Director of Student Services .... Ms. Currie GASCHE
04 Administrative Asst to President .... Ms. Dana KAECHELE

Lake Land College (D)

5001 Lake Land Boulevard, Mattoon IL 61938-9366
County: Coles FICE Identification: 007644
Unit ID: 146506
Telephone: (217) 234-5253 Carnegie Class: Assoc/HVT-High Non
FAX Number: (217) 234-5400 Calendar System: Semester
URL: www.lakeland.cc.il.us
Established: 1966 Annual Undergrad Tuition & Fees (In-District): $3,459
Enrollment: 5,593 Coed
Affiliation or Control: State/Local IRS Status: 501(c)3
Highest Offering: Associate Degree
Accreditation: NH, ADNUR, DH, PNUR, PTAA

01 President .... Dr. Josh BULLOCK
100 Senior Executive to the President .... Ms. Jean Anne GRUNLOH
04 Admin Asst to the President's Ofc .... Ms. Seirra LAUGHHUNN
10 VP for Business Services .... Mr. Bryan GLECKLER
05 VP for Academic Services .... Dr. Jim HULL
32 Vice President for Student Services .... Dr. Tina STOVALL
20 Assoc Vice Pres of Instruction .... Ms. Leslie DEVORE
88 Dean of Correctional Pgms-South .... Mr. Brandon YOUNG
20 Assoc Vice Pres Educational Svcs .... Dr. Deb HUTTI
07 Dean of Admissions Services .... Mr. Jon VAN DYKE
88 Assoc Dean Corrections-Taylorville .... Mr. Robert EIFERT
88 Assoc Dean Corrections-Graham .... Vacant
88 Assoc Dean Corrections-Western .... Ms. Malea HARNEY
88 Assoc Dean Correction-IL River .... Mr. Michael CHASE
88 Assoc Dean Corrections-Southwestern .... Mr. Harvey GROENNERT
88 Assoc Dean Corrections-Jacksonville .... Mr. Steve BAHNEY
88 Assoc Dean Corrections-Lawrence .... Ms. Valerie PRATSCHER
88 Assoc Dean Corrections-Robinson .... Vacant
88 Assc Dean Corrections-Vandalia .... Mr. Steve DRAKE
44 Exec Dir College Advance/Foundation .... Ms. Jacqueline JOINES
88 Site Director Corrections-Hill .... Vacant
88 Site Director Corr-Vienna & Shawnee .... Mr. Blake MCCONNELL
21 Comptroller .... Ms. Madge SHOOT
50 Dir Center for Business & Industry .... Ms. Bonnie MOORE
08 Director of Library Services .... Mr. Scott DRONE-SILVERS
26 Dir of Marketing/Public Relations .... Mrs. Kelly ALLEE
13 Dir of Information Systems/Services .... Mr. Lee SPANIOL
37 Dir of Financial Aid/Veteran Svcs .... Ms. Paula CARPENTER
18 Director of Facilities Planning .... Mr. Michael KASDORF
15 Director of Human Resources .... Ms. Dawn SCHLECHTE
88 Director of Learning Technologies .... Mr. Steve GARREN
25 Director of Grants Development .... Ms. Emily RAMAGE
35 Director Student Life .... Ms. Valerie LYNCH
109 Director of Auxiliary Services .... Ms. Christina KRAMER
29 Dir of Alumni Rels/Annual Giving .... Mr. Dave COX
36 Director of Career Services .... Ms. Tina MOORE
38 Chair of Counseling/Judicial Affs .... Ms. Emily HARTKE
18 Dir of Physical Plant Operations .... Mr. Scott RAWLINGS
41 Director of Athletics .... Mr. William JACKSON
09 Director of Institutional Research .... Dr. Mary BREER
84 Coordinator of Enrollment Services .... Ms. Paula SMITH

Lakeview College of Nursing (E)

903 N Logan Avenue, Danville IL 61832-3788
County: Vermilion FICE Identification: 010501
Unit ID: 146533
Telephone: (217) 709-0920 Carnegie Class: Spec-4-yr-Other Health
FAX Number: (217) 709-0954 Calendar System: Semester
URL: www.lakeviewcol.edu
Established: 1987 Annual Undergrad Tuition & Fees: N/A
Enrollment: 317 Coed
Affiliation or Control: Independent Non-Profit IRS Status: 501(c)3
Highest Offering: Baccalaureate
Accreditation: NH, NURSE

01 President .... Ms. Sheila MINGEE
05 Interim Dean of Nursing .... Ms. Jessica SOTIRIOU
06 Registrar/Director of Enrollment .... Ms. Connie YOUNG
08 Library Director/IT Coordinator .... Ms. Miranda SHAKE

Le Cordon Bleu College of Culinary Arts in Chicago (F)

361 W Chestnut Street, Chicago IL 60610
County: Cook FICE Identification: 023522
Unit ID: 144467
Telephone: (312) 944-0882 Carnegie Class: Spec 2-yr-A&S
FAX Number: (312) 944-8557 Calendar System: Quarter
URL: www.chefs.edu/chicago
Established: 1983 Annual Undergrad Tuition & Fees: $13,796
Enrollment: 1,086 Coed
Affiliation or Control: Proprietary IRS Status: Proprietary
Highest Offering: Associate Degree
Accreditation: NH, ACFEI

01 Campus President .... Mrs. Maegan K. MURPHY
07 Director of Admissions .... Mr. Kevin FERGUSON
08 Regional Librarian .... Ms. Laura RICE
108 Director Institutional Effectivenes .... Ms. Julianna DHANIE
36 Director of Career Services .... Ms. Mona YAEAGER
37 Business Operations Manager .... Ms. Christina NELSON
53 Director of Education .... Mr. Michael RILEY

† In teach-out mode through December 2017.

Lewis and Clark Community College (G)

5800 Godfrey Road, Godfrey IL 62035-2466
County: Madison FICE Identification: 010020
Unit ID: 146603
Telephone: (618) 468-7000 Carnegie Class: Assoc/MT-VT-High Non
FAX Number: (618) 466-2798 Calendar System: Semester
URL: www.lc.edu
Established: 1970 Annual Undergrad Tuition & Fees (In-District): $3,072
Enrollment: 7,903 Coed
Affiliation or Control: State/Local IRS Status: 501(c)3
Highest Offering: Associate Degree
Accreditation: NH, ADNUR, DA, DH, OTA

01 President .... Dr. Dale T. CHAPMAN
05 Vice President Academic Affairs .... Dr. Linda CHAPMAN
84 Vice President Enrollment Services .... Mr. Kent SCHEFFEL
32 Vice Pres Student Engagement .... Dr. Sean HILL
11 Vice President Administration .... Ms. Lori ARTIS
10 Vice President Finance .... Mrs. Mary SCHULTE
21 Chief Budget Officer .... Mrs. Nancy KAISER
88 Director Corp & Comm Learning .... Mrs. Kathy WILLIS
13 Chief Information Officer .... Vacant
09 Dir Institutional Res/Library Svcs .... Mr. Dennis KRIEB
06 Registrar .... Ms. Heidi SCOTT
41 Director Athletics .... Mr. Doug STOTLER
07 Director of Enrollment Center .... Ms. Delfina DORNES
15 Director Human Resources .... Mr. Gabe SPRINGER
18 Facilities Manager .... Mr. Mike RANDALL
19 Director Security .... Mr. Brad RAISH
26 Manager Media Services .... Ms. Laura INLOW
28 Coordinator Diversity & Inclusion .... Ms. Adrienne REED
30 Director of Development .... Ms. Debbie EDELMAN
37 Director Financial Aid .... Ms. Angela WEAVER

Lewis University (H)

One University Parkway, Romeoville IL 60446-2200
County: Will FICE Identification: 001707
Unit ID: 146612
Telephone: (815) 838-0500 Carnegie Class: Masters/L
FAX Number: (815) 838-9456 Calendar System: Semester
URL: www.lewisu.edu
Established: 1932 Annual Undergrad Tuition & Fees: $29,040
Enrollment: 6,689 Coed
Affiliation or Control: Roman Catholic IRS Status: 501(c)3
Highest Offering: Doctorate
Accreditation: NH, ACBSP, #CAATE, NURSE, SW, TED

01 President .... Dr. David J. LIVINGSTON
05 Provost .... Dr. Stephany SCHLACHTER
32 Sr Vice President Student Services .... Mr. Joseph FALESE
10 Senior Vice Pres/CFO .... Mr. Robert DEROSE
84 Sr VP Enrollment Mgmt/Marketing .... Mr. Raymond KENNELLY
30 Interim VP University Advancement .... Mr. Luigi AMENDOLA
07 Director of Admission .... Mr. Ryan COCKERILL
35 Dean of Student Services .... Ms. Katheryn SLATTERY
28 VP Mission & Academic Services .... Dr. Kurt SCHACKMUTH
49 Dean College Arts & Sciences .... Dr. Bonnie BONDAVALLI
50 Dean College Business .... Dr. Rami KHASAWNEH
66 Dean Col Nursing/Health Professions .... Dr. Peggy RICE
53 Dean College of Education .... Dr. Pamela JESSEE
15 Assoc Vice Pres Human Resources .... Ms. Graciela DUFOUR
09 Assoc VP Inst Research/Planning .... Dr. Kang BAI
08 Director of Library .... Mr. Thomas URBANSKI
06 Registrar .... Ms. Jacqueline SCHMIDT
37 Director of Financial Aid .... Ms. Janeen DECHARINTE
26 Director Marketing/Communications .... Dr. Ramona LAMONTAGNE
41 Director of Athletics .... Dr. John PLANEK
38 Director of Counseling Services .... Ms. Michele MANASSAH
19 Chief of Police .... Mr. James MONTANARI
42 Director of University Ministry .... Mr. Steve ZLATIC
31 Dir of Meetings/Events/Conferences .... Ms. Julie PENNER
85 Director International Student Svcs .... Mr. Michael FEKETE
11 Director of Administrative Systems .... Mr. Charles PUSTZ
13 Associate Vice Pres/Technology .... Dr. LeRoy BUTLER
29 Dir Alumni Relations/Advancement .... Mr. Bustinza REYNALDO
96 Director of Opers and Purchasing .... Ms. Jennifer SKVARLA
36 Exec Director of Career Services .... Ms. Mary MYERS
04 Administrative Asst to President .... Ms. Margaret KIENTOP
102 Dir Foundation & Corp Relations .... Ms. Jennifer DOHERTY
104 Director Study Abroad .... Mr. Christopher SWANSON
105 Director Web Services .... Mr. Sylvain GOYETTE
18 Assoc VP Facilities/Physical Plant .... Mr. Donald CASTELLO
25 Director of Sponsored Programs .... Mr. Jeffrey RITCHIE
23 Director Health Services .... Ms. Michele RONCHETTI
39 Director of Residence Life .... Mr. Fredrick GANDY

Lincoln Christian University (A)

100 Campus View Drive, Lincoln IL 62656-2167
County: Logan FICE Identification: 001708
Unit ID: 146667
Telephone: (217) 732-3168 Carnegie Class: Spec-4-yr-Faith
FAX Number: (217) 732-5914 Calendar System: Semester
URL: www.lincolnchristian.edu
Established: 1944 Annual Undergrad Tuition & Fees: $12,900
Enrollment: 940 Coed
Affiliation or Control: Christian Churches And Churches of Christ
IRS Status: 501(c)3
Highest Offering: Doctorate
Accreditation: NH, BI, CACREP, THEOL

01 President ... Dr. Donald GREEN
10 Vice President of Finance ... Mr. G. Steve POPENFOOSE
84 Vice Pres of Enrollment Services ... Dr. Silas MCCORMICK
32 VP of Student Services ... Mr. Randall INGMIRE
05 Interim Vice President of Academics ... Dr. Rochelle SCHEUERMANN
30 VP of University Advancement ... Vacant
29 VP of Alumni Services ... Mr. Lynn LAUGHLIN
35 Dean of Students ... Mr. Steve COLLINS
06 Registrar ... Mr. Shawn SMITH
08 Director of Library Services ... Ms. Nancy OLSON
37 Director of Financial Aid ... Ms. Nancy SIDDENS
101 Admin Asst to Pres/Secy Bd of Gov ... Mrs. Linda SEGGELKE
13 Director of Campus Technology ... Mr. Larry WOOLARD
15 Director of Human Resources ... Mrs. Marla BENNETT
41 Athletic Director ... Vacant
18 Chief Facilities/Physical Plant ... Mr. Freddie TEDRICK
26 Chief Public Relations/Marketing ... Ms. Christine THOMAS

Lincoln College (B)

300 Keokuk Street, Lincoln IL 62656-1699
County: Logan FICE Identification: 001709
Unit ID: 146676
Telephone: (217) 732-3155 Carnegie Class: Bac/Assoc-Mixed
FAX Number: (217) 732-8859 Calendar System: Semester
URL: www.lincolncollege.edu
Established: 1865 Annual Undergrad Tuition & Fees: $17,700
Enrollment: 1,264 Coed
Affiliation or Control: Independent Non-Profit IRS Status: 501(c)3
Highest Offering: Baccalaureate
Accreditation: NH, IACBE

01 President ... Dr. David M. GERLACH
05 Vice President for Academic Affairs ... Dr. A. Gigi FANSLER
30 Vice President for Advancement ... Ms. Debbie ACKERMAN
84 VP for Enroll Mgmt & Student Svcs ... Ms. Susan BOEHLER
10 Vice Pres Finance & Administration ... Mr. Greg A. EIMER
07 Dean of Enrollment Management ... Mr. Joe HENDRIX
32 Dean of Students ... Mrs. Bridgett THOMAS
107 Exec Dir Center for Adult Learning ... Mr. Vance LAINE
88 Director of Academic Advising ... Mr. Todd LAFRENZ
06 Registrar ... Mrs. Debra J. HARMON
08 Head Librarian ... Ms. Dorothy RYAN
13 Director of Information Technology ... Mr. David LOLLING
21 Controller ... Mrs. Katherine PAPESCH
15 Director of Human Resources ... Ms. Sara SCHWANTZ
18 Director of Building & Grounds ... Ms. Ronda PIATT
37 Director of Financial Aid ... Mr. Chris STECKMANN
41 Athletic Director ... Mr. Dave KLEMM
40 Bookstore Manager ... Mrs. Donna HUTCHISON

Lincoln College - Normal (C)

715 W Raab Road, Normal IL 61761
Telephone: (309) 452-0500 Identification: 770078
Accreditation: &NH

† Regional accreditation is carried under the parent institution in Lincoln, IL

Lincoln College of Technology (D)

8317 West North Avenue, Melrose Park IL 60160-1605
County: Cook FICE Identification: 010316
Unit ID: 146700
Telephone: (708) 344-4700 Carnegie Class: Spec 2-yr-Tech
FAX Number: (708) 345-4065 Calendar System: Semester
URL: www.lincolntech.edu
Established: 1950 Annual Undergrad Tuition & Fees: N/A
Enrollment: 717 Coed
Affiliation or Control: Proprietary IRS Status: Proprietary
Highest Offering: Associate Degree
Accreditation: ACCSC

01 Campus President ... Karen M. CLARK
05 Campus VP of Education ... Larry KESHNER
11 Director Administrative Services ... Karen STEPINA
36 Director of Career Services ... Latasha ROBY
37 Director of Financial Aid ... Cliff DAVIS
04 Administrative Asst to President ... Mindy GUARINO
07 Director of Admissions ... Kevin FERGUSON
08 Head Librarian ... Karen MCELWAIN

Lincoln Land Community College (E)

5250 Shepherd Road, PO Box 19256,
Springfield IL 62794-9256
County: Sangamon FICE Identification: 007170
Unit ID: 146685
Telephone: (217) 786-2200 Carnegie Class: Assoc/HVT-High Non
FAX Number: (217) 786-2468 Calendar System: Semester
URL: www.llcc.edu
Established: 1967 Annual Undergrad Tuition & Fees (In-District): $2,904
Enrollment: 7,006 Coed
Affiliation or Control: Local IRS Status: 501(c)3
Highest Offering: Associate Degree
Accreditation: NH, ADNUR, COARC, NDT, OTA, PNUR, RAD, SURGT

01 President ... Dr. Charlotte J. WARREN
11 Vice President Administrative Svcs ... Mr. Todd MCDONALD
05 Vice President Academic Services ... Dr. Eileen G. TEPATTI
32 Vice President Student Services ... Ms. Lesley J. FREDERICK
103 VP Workforce Dev/Cmty Educ ... Dr. Judy JOZAITIS
13 Chief Information Officer ... Mr. Esteban CRUZ
15 AVP Human Resources ... Ms. Junell A. RANSDELL
84 AVP Enrollment Services ... Ms. Lisa COLLIER
10 AVP Finance ... Ms. Karie L. LONGHTA
86 Asst VP Corp/Govt Trng & Econ Devel ... Ms. Paula J. LUEBBERT
18 Assistant VP Construction ... Mr. Hugh GARVEY
12 AVP LLCC Outreach ... Mr. Scott R. STALLMAN
102 Exec Director LLCC Foundation ... Ms. Karen A. SANDERS
26 Exec Dir Public Relations/Marketing ... Ms. Lynn WHALEN
88 Exec Director Academic Success ... Mrs. Julie CLEVENGER
88 Director Small Business Devel Ctr ... Mr. Kevin LUST
07 Director Admissions/Records ... Mrs. Shanda R. BYER
22 Dir Employ Bnft Svc/Eq Opty Cmpl Of ... Ms. Nicole M. RALPH
09 Director Institutional Research ... Ms. Susan SIMPSON
45 Dir Institutional Effectiveness ... Ms. Tricia A. KUJAWA
19 Police Chief ... Mr. Bradley D. GENTRY
50 Dean Business & Technologies ... Mr. David A. GREEN
83 Dean Social Sciences ... Dr. Victor K. BRODERICK
20 AVP Academic Services ... Ms. Wendy L. HOWERTER
57 Dean Arts & Humanities ... Mr. J. Timothy HUMPHREY
81 Dean Mathematics and Sciences ... Mr. William D. BADE
76 Dean Health Professions ... Dr. Cynthia L. MASKEY
08 Assoc Dean Library ... Mrs. Tamara KUHN-SCHNELL
106 Dean ITDE ... Mrs. Becky PARTON
14 Director IT and Infrastructure ... Mr. Ben ROTH
14 Director IT Service and Support ... Mrs. Joni BERNAHL
41 Director Athletics ... Mr. Ron RIGGLE
109 Director Campus Services ... Mr. Andrew BLAYLOCK
35 Assistant VP Student Success ... Ms. Leslie R. JOHNSON
38 Dir Advising/Counseling/Career Svcs ... Ms. Mary Beth RAY
18 Director Facilities ... Mr. David BRETSCHER

Lindenwood University Belleville Campus (F)

2600 West Main Street, Belleville IL 62226
Telephone: (618) 239-6000 Identification: 770322
Accreditation: &NH, ACBSP

† Regional accreditation is carried under the parent institution in Saint Charles, MO

Loyola University Chicago (G)

1032 W. Sheridan Road, Chicago IL 60660
County: Cook FICE Identification: 001710
Unit ID: 146719
Telephone: (773) 274-3000 Carnegie Class: DU-Higher
FAX Number: (312) 915-7003 Calendar System: Semester
URL: www.luc.edu
Established: 1870 Annual Undergrad Tuition & Fees: $40,426
Enrollment: 15,902 Coed
Affiliation or Control: Roman Catholic IRS Status: 501(c)3
Highest Offering: Doctorate
Accreditation: NH, BUS, BUSA, CLPSY, COPSY, DENT, DIETI, EMT, #FEPAC, LAW, MED, NURSE, PH, SCPSY, SW, TED, THEA

00 Chancellor ... Rev. Michael J. GARANZINI, SJ
01 President ... Dr. Jo Ann ROONEY
17 Provost Health Sciences ... Dr. Margaret F. CALLAHAN
05 Provost ... Dr. John P. PELISSERO
10 Sr Vice President Finance & CFO ... Mr. Robert A. MUNSON
85 Vice Provost Acad Ctrs/Global Inits ... Dr. Patrick M. BOYLE
20 Vice Provost Academic & Faculty Res ... Dr. David P. PRASSE
30 Interim VP Advancement ... Ms. Jamie ORSINI
45 Sr VP Cap Planning & Campus Mgmt ... Mr. Wayne MAGDZIARZ
11 Sr VP Admin Svcs ... Mr. Thomas M. KELLY
96 Manager of Purchasing ... Mr. Sam J. PERRY
90 Director Academic Tech Services ... Mr. Bruce A. MONTES
88 Asst Prov Dir Academic Business Ops ... Ms. Joanna PAPPAS
88 Dir Enrollment Systems & Analysis ... Mr. Timothy HEUER
28 Dir Student Diversity & Multicultur ... Mr. Joseph SAUCEDO
29 Director Alumni Relations HSD ... Ms. Krista GIUFFI
37 Interim Director of Financial Aid ... Mr. Tobyn L. FRIAR
15 Director of Human Resources ... Ms. Joan C. STASIAK
90 Dir of System Implementation & Cons ... Mr. Kevin J. SMITH
102 Dir of Corporate & Foundation Rels ... Ms. Angela LIEGEL
06 Director of Registration & Records ... Ms. Clare M. KORINEK
88 Dir Advancement Info Services ... Vacant
21 Treasurer & Chief Inv Officer ... Mr. Eric JONES
09 Director Institutional Research ... Dr. Richard S. HURST
07 Director Undergraduate Admissions ... Ms. Erin T. MORIATY
39 Director Residence Life ... Ms. Debrah SCHMIDT-ROGERS
101 Asst VP/Asst to Pres/Chairman ... Dr. Donna B. CURIN
104 Executive Director Intl Programs ... Dr. Jennifer ENGEL
106 Director Online Learning ... Ms. Sarah DYSART
18 Director Infrastructure Services ... Mr. Dan VONDER HEIDE
25 Assoc VP Finance Sponsored Pgm Acc ... Ms. Donna QUIRK
88 Dir Enterprise Architecture & Promo ... Mr. Jim SIBENALLER
36 Director Career Development Center ... Ms. Kathryn JACKSON
43 Vice President & General Counsel ... Ms. Pam COSTAS
38 Director Wellness Center ... Ms. Diane C. ASARO
28 Dir Cultural Affairs & LUMA ... Ms. Pam AMBROSE
88 Dir Facilities WTC ... Mr. Mark FEIEREISEL
32 Vice President Student Development ... Ms. Jane NEUFELD
42 Director Campus Ministry ... Dr. Lisa REITER
54 Director Engineering Sciiences ... Dr. Gail BAURA
41 Athletic Director ... Mr. Steve WATSON
85 Director Chicago Center ... Mr. Jason OBIN
88 Director Compensation & Benefits ... Ms. Debra MEISTER
21 Dir General Accounting ... Ms. Maria ARAQUE
88 Director Faculty Admin-HSD ... Ms. Martha KING
88 Exec Dir Research Admin & Dev HSD ... Ms. Kelly FEEHAN
88 Research Services Director ... Dr. William SELLERS
102 Executive Director Corp Engagement ... Dr. Janet DEATHERIDGE
88 Dir Inst Environmental Sustain ... Dr. Nancy TUCHMAN
15 Vice President HR & CDO ... Dr. Winifred WILLIAMS
88 Director Strategic Financing/Risk ... Ms. Susan BODIN
24 Dir Communication & Media ... Mr. Steve CHRISTENSON
65 Director Environmental Services ... Mr. William CURTIN
88 Dir of Capital Business Operations ... Mr. David BEALL
88 Dir Institute Pastoral Studies ... Dr. Brian SCHMISEK
84 Dir Graduate/Professional Admiss ... Vacant
51 Director Adult & Transfer Center ... Ms. Jill SCHUR
88 Director Enrollment Marketing ... Ms. Heather TAYLOR
19 Director Campus Safety ... Mr. Thomas MURRAY
29 Director Alumni Relations ... Ms. Leticia NIETO
88 Dir of Advancement Communication ... Mr. Brendan KEATING
105 Director of Web Communication ... Mr. John DREVS
88 Director of Student Complex ... Ms. Dawn M. COLLINS
21 Director Financial Svcs & Payroll ... Ms. Rebecca GOMEZ
96 Director of Cash Management ... Mr. Corey O'BRIEN
18 Director of Facilities-HSD ... Mr. Tom EARLY
12 Interim VP & Director Rome Ctr ... Rev. Michael J. GARANZINI
12 General Manager LUREC & Cuneo ... Mr. Kevin GINTY
86 Vice President Government Affairs ... Mr. Philip P. HALE
13 Vice President Information Services ... Ms. Susan M. MALISCH
03 Vice Chancellor ... Rev. John COSTELLO, SJ
26 VP Marketing & Communications ... Ms. Kelly SHANNON
88 Sr VP for Health Sciences ... Mr. Steve BERGFELD
88 Assoc VP Finance - HSD ... Ms. Lauren HAGAN
44 Assoc VP Advancement ... Vacant
88 Assoc VP Informatics/System Devel ... Mr. Ronald N. PRICE
21 Assoc VP Finance & Controller ... Ms. Andrea SABITSANA
109 Associate VP Campus Services ... Vacant
31 Assoc VP Campus/Community Planning ... Ms. Jennifer R. CLARK
21 Assoc VP for Budget & Finance ... Mr. Ben SMIGIELSKI
18 Associate VP of Capital Projects ... Ms. Kana WIBBENMEYER
88 Dir Retail/Residential Property Ast ... Mr. Brian T. O'LEARY
35 Asst VP & Dean of Students ... Mr. Kenechukwu MMEJE
35 Assistant VP Student Development ... Dr. Jack MCLEAN
27 Asst VP Brand Marketing ... Ms. Katie HESSION
84 Assoc Provost Enrollment Management ... Mr. Paul G. ROBERTS
46 Dean Graduate School & Research ... Dr. Patricia MOONEY-MELVIN
88 Assoc Provost Academic Admin ... Dr. Marian A. CLAFFEY
88 Assoc Provost for Mission & Identit ... Dr. John HARDT
62 Assoc Provost & Dir HSD Library ... Ms. Gail HENDLER
88 Assoc Provost Curriculum Dev ... Dr. Jo Beth D'AGOSTINO
96 Dir Special Projects ... Mr. Brian R. SLAVINKAS
88 Asst Provost & Dir Faculty Admin ... Ms. Anne C. REULAND
88 Asst Prov Educ Resources HSD ... Rev. Keith MUCCINO, SJ
88 Assistant Provost Academic Advising ... Dr. Dale TAMPKE
100 Special Assistant to the President ... Ms. Lorraine G. FITZGERALD
08 Interim Dean University Libraries ... Mr. Frederick D. BARNHART
50 Dean School of Business Admin ... Dr. Kevin STEVENS
49 Dean Arts & Sciences ... Mr. Thomas J. REGAN
62 Dean Libraries ... Mr. Robert A. SEAL
51 Dean Continuing & Professional Educ ... Dr. Walter PEARSON
60 Dean School of Communication ... Dr. Donald B. HEIDER
61 Dean School of Law ... Mr. Michael J. KAUFMAN
63 Dean School of Medicine ... Dr. Linda BRUBAKER
66 Dean School of Nursing ... Dr. Vicki A. KEOUGH
70 Interim Dean School of Social Work ... Dr. Susan GROSSMAN
72 Dir Procedure Improvement & Tech Ad ... Ms. Danielle HANSON
16 Dean Faculty Rome Center ... Dr. Alexander EVERS
53 Dean School of Education ... Dr. Teri PIGOTT
88 Dean & Exec Dir Arrupe College ... Rev. Stephen N. KATSOUROS, SJ
18 Superintendent Lakeside Facilities ... Mr. William SHERRY
88 Exec Director Conference Services ... Mr. Dana ADAMS

Loyola University Health Sciences Campus (H)

2160 S First Avenue, Maywood IL 60153
Telephone: (708) 216-9000 Identification: 770080
Accreditation: &NH, PAST

† Regional accreditation is carried under the parent institution in Chicago, IL

Loyola University Water Town Campus (I)

820 N Michigan Avenue, Chicago IL 60611
Telephone: (312) 915-6000 Identification: 770079
Accreditation: &NH

† Regional accreditation is carried under the parent institution in Chicago, IL

Lutheran School of Theology at Chicago (A)

1100 E 55th Street, Chicago IL 60615-5199

County: Cook | FICE Identification: 001712 | Unit ID: 146728
Telephone: (773) 256-0700 | Carnegie Class: Spec-4-yr-Faith
FAX Number: (773) 256-0782 | Calendar System: Semester
URL: www.lstc.edu
Established: 1860 | Annual Graduate Tuition & Fees: N/A
Enrollment: 228 | Coed
Affiliation or Control: Evangelical Lutheran Church In America | IRS Status: 501(c)3
Highest Offering: Doctorate; No Undergraduates
Accreditation: NH, THEOL

Code	Title	Name
01	President	Dr. James NIEMAN
04	Assistant to the President	Ms. Patti DEBIAS
108	Exec for Administration/Assess/Plng	Ms. Laura WILHELM
05	Dean/Vice Pres for Academic Affairs	Dr. Esther MENN
88	Director of the MDiv Programs	Dr. Kathleen BILLMAN
88	Director of the MA Programs	Rev. Jan RIPPENTROP
58	Director of Advanced Studies	Dr. Ben STEWART
42	Pastor to the Community	Dr. Harvard STEPHENS, JR.
11	Vice President for Operations	Mr. Bob BERRIDGE
30	Vice President for Advancement	Mr. Mark H. VAN SCHARREL
10	Vice President for Finance	Mr. Robert EDER
32	Dean of Student Services	Dr. Scott CHALMERS
06	Registrar	Ms. Patricia A. BARTLEY
26	Director of Communications/Mktg	Ms. Janet BODEN
08	Director of Library	Dr. Christine WENDEROTH
13	Dir of Information Technology Svcs	Mr. Kenesa DEBELA

MacCormac College (B)

29 E Madison Street 2nd Floor, Chicago IL 60602-4405

County: Cook | FICE Identification: 001716 | Unit ID: 146816
Telephone: (312) 922-1884 | Carnegie Class: Assoc/HVT-High Trad
FAX Number: (312) 922-4286 | Calendar System: Semester
URL: www.maccormac.edu
Established: 1904 | Annual Undergrad Tuition & Fees: $12,660
Enrollment: 216 | Coed
Affiliation or Control: Independent Non-Profit | IRS Status: 501(c)3
Highest Offering: Associate Degree
Accreditation: NH

Code	Title	Name
00	Chancellor	Dr. Marnelle ALEXIS
01	Interim President	Mr. Matt GAWENDA
05	Dean of Academic & Student Affairs	Mr. Roberto D. TORRES
06	Registrar	Ms. Mariza SILVA
37	Director of Financial Aid	Ms. Alexandra GRANT
07	Assoc Dir Admission	Mr. Marcus TROUTMAN
26	Dir Communications/Public Relations	Ms. Natasha MEEAJANE

MacMurray College (C)

447 E College Avenue, Jacksonville IL 62650-2590

County: Morgan | FICE Identification: 001717 | Unit ID: 146825
Telephone: (217) 479-7000 | Carnegie Class: Bac-Diverse
FAX Number: (217) 245-0405 | Calendar System: 4/1/4
URL: www.mac.edu
Established: 1846 | Annual Undergrad Tuition & Fees: $24,172
Enrollment: 554 | Coed
Affiliation or Control: United Methodist | IRS Status: 501(c)3
Highest Offering: Baccalaureate
Accreditation: #NH, NURSE, SW

Code	Title	Name
01	President	Dr. Mark J. TIERNO
10	CFO	Ms. Kimberly STREIB
05	Interim Provost	Dr. John COX
32	Dean of Student Life	Ms. Beth OBERG
30	Exec Dir Institutional Advancement	Vacant
07	Enrollment Manager	Mr. Tressman GOODE
21	Controller	Mr. Andrew SIDOCK
13	Director of IT/System Administrator	Ms. Nancy SULLIVAN
06	Registrar	Vacant
08	Librarian	Ms. Susan EILERING
37	Director of One-Stop Student Svcs	Ms. Laci ENGELBRECHT
36	Director of Career Services	Ms. Anne GODMAN
29	Director Alumni Relations	Ms. Rikki LANGAN
09	Director of Institutional Research	Vacant
18	Director of Facilities	Mr. Jonathan JUMPER
26	Director of Public Relations	Mr. Ted ROTH
04	Executive Asst to President	Ms. Sharon SEYMOUR
41	Athletic Director	Mr. Justin FUHLER

McCormick Theological Seminary (D)

5460 S University Avenue, Chicago IL 60615-5108

County: Cook | FICE Identification: 001721 | Unit ID: 146977
Telephone: (773) 947-6300 | Carnegie Class: Spec-4-yr-Faith
FAX Number: (773) 288-2612 | Calendar System: 4/1/4
URL: www.mccormick.edu
Established: 1829 | Annual Graduate Tuition & Fees: N/A
Enrollment: 181 | Coed
Affiliation or Control: Presbyterian Church (U.S.A.) | IRS Status: 501(c)3
Highest Offering: Doctorate; No Undergraduates
Accreditation: NH, THEOL

Code	Title	Name
01	President	Rev. Frank M. YAMADA
10	Exec Vice Pres/Chief Business Ofcr	Mr. David CRAWFORD
05	Vice Pres Acad Affs/Dean Faculty	Dr. Theodore HIEBERT
32	Vice President for Student Affairs	Vacant
30	Vice Pres Seminary Rels/Development	Ms. Lisa M. DAGHER
06	Registrar	Ms. Chandra WADE
29	Dir of Alumni/ae & Church Rels	Rev. Nannette BANKS
08	Director of JKM Library	Dr. Christine WENDEROTH
15	Director Human Resources	Ms. Ashley WOODFAULK
37	Dir Student Financial Aid/Planning	Ms. Tabitha HIGHTOWER
07	Sr Director Admissions/Enrollment	Ms. Veronica JOHNSON

McHenry County College (E)

8900 US Highway 14, Crystal Lake IL 60012-2796

County: McHenry | FICE Identification: 007691 | Unit ID: 147004
Telephone: (815) 455-3700 | Carnegie Class: Assoc/MT-VT-High Non
FAX Number: (815) 455-3999 | Calendar System: Semester
URL: www.mchenry.edu
Established: 1967 | Annual Undergrad Tuition & Fees (In-District): $3,314
Enrollment: 6,567 | Coed
Affiliation or Control: State/Local | IRS Status: 501(c)3
Highest Offering: Associate Degree
Accreditation: NH, OTA

Code	Title	Name
01	President	Dr. Clinton E. GABBARD
30	InterimVP Institutional Advancement	Ms. Christina HAGGERTY
10	CFO/Treasurer	Mr. Bob TENUTA
05	VP Academic & Student Affairs	Vacant
20	Interim AVP for Arts and Science	Dr. Brock FISHER
20	Interim AVP Career Technical Ed	Dr. Terri BERRYMAN
13	Chief Information Officer	Dr. Allen P. BUTLER
04	Asst to the President/Board Liaison	Mrs. Pat KRIEGERMEIER
19	Exec Dir Public Safety/Facilities	Mr. Michael CLESCERI
26	Chief Communications Officer	Mrs. Christina HAGGERTY
32	AVP Academic & Student Affairs	Ms. Julietta PATRICK
21	AVP of Finance	Ms. Lynn COWLIN
15	AVP of Human Resources	Ms. Angelina CASTILLO
79	Exec Dean Humanities & Soc Sciences	Mr. Brock FISCHER
81	Exec Dean Math/Sciences Health Pgm	Vacant
103	Exec Dean Workforce Comm	Ms. Terri BERRMAN
75	Exec Dean Educ/Career/Technical Ed	Vacant
102	Int Exec Director MCC Foundation	Ms. Brenda STIFF
103	Exec Dir Workforce Community Pgm	Mr. David MATTS
88	Exec Director of Adult Education	Mr. Julio CAPELES-DELGADO
20	Dean of Academic Development	Ms. Adriane HUTCHINSON
84	Dean Enrollment Services	Ms. Marianne DEVENNY
08	Dean of Library	Ms. Kate HARGER
88	Dean of Student Development	Dr. Flecia THOMAS
66	Director Nursing	Ms. Betsy SCHNOWSKE
88	Director Recruitment & Staffing	Ms. Sandra HESS MOLL
88	Director Institutional Effectivenes	Ms. Patricia STEJSKAL
14	Director Software Solutions	Mr. Todd SMITH
14	Director Technology Support Service	Mr. Geary SMITH
40	Director Bookstore	Ms. Karen SMITH
41	Director Athletics-Intramural & Rec	Ms. Karen WILEY
51	Dir of Continuing Education	Ms. Dori SULLINS
25	Director of Resource Development	Mr. Mark DOUGHER
23	Director of Health and Wellness	Ms. Lena KALEMBA
88	Director of Sustainability	Ms. Kim HANKINS
88	Director of Learning Support	Ms. Emma HENDRIETH
109	Director Food Services	Ms. Sandra JOHNSTON
96	Director of Business Services	Ms. Jennifer JONES
37	Director of Financial Aid	Ms. Leana DAVIS
06	Director of Registration & Records	Ms. Amy HALLER
14	Director Infrastructure Operations	Mr. Rob RASMUSSEN
106	Director of Online Learning	Dr. Raymond LAWSON
09	Director of Institutional Research	Dr. Amy HUMKE
18	Director Facilities	Mr. Todd WHEELAND
88	Dir Fieldwork Occ Therapy Asst Pgm	Ms. Marlene VOGT
88	Dir Health Info Technology Programs	Ms. Chris COCLANIS-LODING
88	Dir Physcial Therapy Asst Program	Mr. Donald SCHMIDT
72	Assoc Dean Educ Career/Tech Educ	Ms. Diana SHARP
79	Assoc Dean Humanities/Social Sci	Dr. Loreen KELLER
81	Assoc Dean Math/Science/Health	Vacant
88	Assoc Dean College/Career Readiness	Mr. Tony CAPALBO
88	Mgr IL Small Business Development	Ms. Kristi PATTERSON
88	Manager of Customer Service	Mr. Frank GELASI
88	Manager of Nursing Laboratory	Ms. Ann STAUCHE
07	Manager New Student Transitions	Ms. Kellie CARPER
35	Mgr of Student Conduct/Campus Life	Ms. Talia KORONKIEWICZ
16	Director of Human Resources	Ms. Anita ROEWER
88	Manager Accounts & Production	Mr. Ryan KLOS
22	Manager Access & Disability Service	Ms. Lil O'CONNELL

McKendree University (F)

701 College Road, Lebanon IL 62254-9990

County: Saint Clair | FICE Identification: 001722 | Unit ID: 147013
Telephone: (618) 537-4481 | Carnegie Class: Masters/L
FAX Number: (618) 537-6259 | Calendar System: Semester
URL: www.mckendree.edu
Established: 1828 | Annual Undergrad Tuition & Fees: $27,930
Enrollment: 3,131 | Coed
Affiliation or Control: United Methodist | IRS Status: 501(c)3
Highest Offering: Doctorate
Accreditation: NH, #CAATE, IACBE, NURSE

Code	Title	Name
01	President	Dr. James M. DENNIS
03	Senior Vice President	Ms. Victoria A. DOWLING
04	Assistant to the President	Ms. Patti J. DANIELS
05	Provost/Dean of the University	Dr. Christine M. BAHR
10	Vice Pres Finance/Administration	Mrs. Sally A. MAYHEW
07	Vice Pres Admission & Financial Aid	Mr. Chris HALL
32	Vice President Student Affairs	Dr. Joni BASTIAN
09	Vice Pres Research Plng & Tech	Vacant
20	Associate Dean of the University	Dr. Tami EGGLESTON
12	Assoc Dean McKendree-at-Scott	Mrs. Tia CROWDER
56	External Programs	Dr. Joseph J. CIPFL
13	Director Technology Information	Mr. George KRISS
06	Registrar/Asst Dean	Ms. Debra LARSON
08	Librarian	Vacant
21	Accounting Manager	Mrs. Shari B. KEFFER
26	Exec Dir Marketing/Communications	Mrs. Krysti H. CONNELLY
29	Director Alumni Relations	Mr. PJ THOMPSON
44	Director of Annual Giving	Mr. Vincent PIAZZA
37	Director Financial Aid	Mrs. Elizabeth JUEHNE
36	Director Career Services	Ms. Jennifer K. PICKERELL
18	Director of Operations	Mr. Tom P. JENSEN
15	Director Human Resources	Ms. Shirley A. BAUGH
27	Director Media Relations	Ms. Lisa K. BRANDON
39	Director of Residence Life	Vacant
35	Director of Campus Activities	Mr. Craig L. ROBERTSON
41	Athletic Director	Mr. Chuck BRUEGGEMANN
42	Chaplain/Director Church Relations	Rev Dr. B. Timothy HARRISON
40	Bookstore Director	Vacant
30	Director of Advancement Services	Mr. Scott L. BILLHARTZ
19	Director Safety & Security	Mr. Ranodore M. FOGGS
44	Director of Major Gifts	Ms. Heidi BAGWELL
88	Director of Student Accounts	Mrs. Marsha GILES
28	Director of Diversity	Mr. Brent W. REEVES

Meadville Lombard Theological School (G)

610 South Michigan Avenue, Chicago IL 60605

County: Cook | FICE Identification: 001723 | Unit ID: 147031
Telephone: (773) 256-3000 | Carnegie Class: Spec-4-yr-Faith
FAX Number: (312) 327-7002 | Calendar System: Semester
URL: www.meadville.edu
Established: 1844 | Annual Graduate Tuition & Fees: N/A
Enrollment: 85 | Coed
Affiliation or Control: Unitarian Universalist | IRS Status: 501(c)3
Highest Offering: Doctorate; No Undergraduates
Accreditation: THEOL

Code	Title	Name
01	President	Dr. Lee BARKER
05	Provost	Dr. Sharon WELCH
10	Vice Pres Finance & Administration	Ms. Deborah BIEBER
06	Registrar	Ms. Valencia PENN-HARGROVE

Methodist College (H)

7600 N. Academic Dr, Peoria IL 61615

County: Peoria | FICE Identification: 006228 | Unit ID: 147129
Telephone: (309) 672-5513 | Carnegie Class: Spec-4-yr-Other Health
FAX Number: (309) 671-8303 | Calendar System: Semester
URL: www.methodistcol.edu
Established: 2000 | Annual Undergrad Tuition & Fees: $20,140
Enrollment: 595 | Coed
Affiliation or Control: Independent Non-Profit | IRS Status: 501(c)3
Highest Offering: Baccalaureate
Accreditation: NH, NURSE

Code	Title	Name
01	President	Dr. Kimberly JOHNSTON
05	Vice Pres Academic Affairs	Dr. Deborah GARRISON
84	Dean Enrollment Management	Dr. Keith BRANHAM
10	Director of Finance	Mr. Tim DIETZ
20	Director of Educational Tech	Mr. Matthew HERTZOG
15	Director Human Resources	Ms. Linda MOORE
13	Dir Information/Instruct Technology	Dr. Matthew HERTZOG
06	Registrar	Ms. Melissa EARNEST
07	Director Admissions & Advisement	Ms. Alissa SELBURG
37	Director Financial Aid	Ms. Angela ROBINSON
09	Institutional Research Coordinator	Ms. Kristin WOIWODE

Midstate College (I)

411 W Northmoor Road, Peoria IL 61614-3558

County: Peoria | FICE Identification: 004568 | Unit ID: 147165
Telephone: (309) 692-4092 | Carnegie Class: Bac/Assoc-Mixed
FAX Number: (309) 692-3893 | Calendar System: Quarter
URL: www.midstate.edu
Established: 1888 | Annual Undergrad Tuition & Fees: $16,230
Enrollment: 521 | Coed
Affiliation or Control: Proprietary | IRS Status: Proprietary
Highest Offering: Baccalaureate
Accreditation: NH, CAHIIM, MAC

Code	Title	Name
01	President and CEO	Meredith N. BUNCH
05	Dean of Academics	Ruth E. SHAFFER
32	Dean of Students	Vicki DRAKSLER
10	Controller	Angie HATTEN
06	Registrar	Angela K. KEPLER
37	Director of Financial Assistance	Linda SCOTT
26	Exec Dir of Marketing/Enrollment	Ashley SPAIN
35	Director of Student Affairs	Rhonda P. URBAN

36 Director of Career Services ... Jennie GREENAN
08 Director of Library Services ... Jane BRADBURY

Midwest College of Oriental Medicine (A)

1601 Sherman Avenue, Suite 300, Evanston IL 60202
Telephone: (773) 975-1295 Identification: 666090
Accreditation: ACUP

† Branch campus of Midwest College of Oriental Medicine, Racine, WI

Midwestern Career College (B)

20 N. Wacker Dr, Ste 3800, Chicago IL 60606
County: Cook FICE Identification: 041390
Unit ID: 457536
Telephone: (312) 236-9000 Carnegie Class: Not Classified
FAX Number: (312) 277-1007 Calendar System: Other
URL: mccollege.edu
Established: 2004 Annual Undergrad Tuition & Fees: N/A
Enrollment: 85 Coed
Affiliation or Control: Proprietary IRS Status: Proprietary
Highest Offering: Associate Degree
Accreditation: COE

Midwestern University (C)

555 31st Street, Downers Grove IL 60515-1200
County: DuPage FICE Identification: 001657
Unit ID: 143853
Telephone: (630) 969-4400 Carnegie Class: Spec-4-yr-Med
FAX Number: N/A Calendar System: Quarter
URL: www.midwestern.edu
Established: 1900 Annual Undergrad Tuition & Fees: N/A
Enrollment: 2,917 Coed
Affiliation or Control: Independent Non-Profit IRS Status: 501(c)3
Highest Offering: Doctorate
Accreditation: NH, ARCPA, CLPSY, DENT, @OPT, OSTEO, OT, PHAR, PTA, @SP

01 President/CEO ... Dr. Kathleen H. GOEPPINGER
03 Exec VP/Chief Operating Officer ... Dr. Arthur G. DOBBELAERE
10 Sr VP/Chief Financial Officer ... Mr. Gregory J. GAUS
21 Vice President Finance ... Mr. Dean P. MALONE
46 VP Research & Strategic Initiatives ... Dr. Theresa W. FOSSUM
26 Vice President University Relations ... Dr. Karen D. JOHNSON
05 VP/CAO Dental/Med/Veterinary Educ ... Dr. Dennis J. PAULSON
05 VP/CAO Pharmacy & Optometry ... Dr. Mary W L. LEE
05 VP/CAO Health Sci Ed & VP Clinic Op ... Dr. Kathleen N. PLAYER
11 VP Human Resources & Administration ... Ms. Angela L. MARTY
43 VP & General Counsel ... Ms. Barbara L. MCCLOUD
63 Dean Chicago Col of Osteo Medicine ... Dr. Karen J. NICHOLS
67 Dean Chicago College of Pharmacy ... Dr. Nancy F. FJORTOFT
76 Dean Col Health Sci Dowers Grove ... Dr. Fred D. ROMANO
88 Dean Optometry ... Dr. Sunny M. SANDERS
52 Dean College of Dental Medicine IL ... Dr. M. A. J. Lex MACNEIL
88 Dean Basic Sciences ... Dr. Kyle H. RAMSEY
58 Dean Postdoctoral Education ... Dr. Thomas A. BOYLE
32 Dean Student Services ... Dr. Teresa A. DOMBROWSKI
07 Director of Admissions ... Mr. Michael J. LAKEN
18 Director Campus Facilities ... Mr. Kevin M. MCCORMICK
30 Director Development/Alumni ... Ms. Barbara WYSOCKI
15 Director Human Resources ... Ms. Amy B. GIBSON
13 Director Information Technology Svc ... Mr. Erik P. CARROLL
09 Director of Institutional Research ... Dr. Kevin P. HYNES
62 Director Library ... Ms. Rebecca A. CATON
24 Director Media Resources ... Ms. Kathleen A M. DOOLEY
06 Registrar ... Ms. Betty N. MORRISON
46 Director Research & Sponsored Pgms ... Dr. James M. WOODS
19 Director Security/Safety ... Mr. Paul R. CREEKMORE
37 Director Student Financial Services ... Mr. Nathan ERNST
27 Director of Communications ... Ms. Dana FAY

† Tuition varies by degree program.

Millikin University (D)

1184 W Main Street, Decatur IL 62522-2084
County: Macon FICE Identification: 001724
Unit ID: 147244
Telephone: (217) 424-6211 Carnegie Class: Bac-Diverse
FAX Number: (217) 424-3993 Calendar System: Semester
URL: www.millikin.edu
Established: 1901 Annual Undergrad Tuition & Fees: $30,630
Enrollment: 2,190 Coed
Affiliation or Control: Presbyterian Church (U.S.A.) IRS Status: 501(c)3
Highest Offering: Doctorate
Accreditation: NH, ACBSP, ANEST, #CAATE, MUS, NURSE

01 President ... Dr. Patrick E. WHITE
05 Provost ... Dr. Jeffery P. APER
10 Vice Pres Finance/Business Affs ... Mrs. Ruby F. JAMES
30 Vice Pres University Development ... Mr. Dave E. BRANDON
84 Vice President Enrollment/Marketing ... Ms. Sarah SHUPENUS
32 Dean of Student Development ... Mrs. Raphaella PRANGE
100 Chief of Staff/Board Secretary ... Ms. Marilyn S. DAVIS
49 Dean of Arts & Sciences ... Dr. Randy M. BROOKS
57 Dean of Fine Arts ... Ms. Laura LEDFORD
107 Dean Col of Professional Studies ... Dr. Deborah L. SLAYTON
50 Dean Tabor School Business ... Dr. Najiba BENABESS
06 Registrar ... Mr. Jason WICKLINE
29 Sr Director Alumni/Donor Engagement ... Vacant
44 Director of Major Gifts/Grant Devel ... Ms. Dawn SANDONE
36 Director of Career Center ... Ms. Pamela M. FOLGER
13 Director of Technology ... Mrs. Amy BRILLEY
08 Director of the Library ... Ms. Cindy FULLER
44 Sr Director of Development ... Mrs. Amanda PODESCHI
41 Director of Athletics ... Dr. Craig WHITE
53 Director of School of Education ... Dr. Christina MAGOULIAS
88 Director Kirkland Fine Arts Center ... Mrs. Janiece L. SADDORIS-TRAUGHBER
28 Dir Inclusion/Student Engagement ... Mrs. Molly BERRY
104 Director Center for Intl Education ... Ms. Carrie TRIMBLE
15 Director Human Resources ... Ms. Diane L. LANE
21 Controller ... Mrs. Vicki A. WRIGLEY
38 Director of Counseling Services ... Mr. Kevin C. GRAHAM
92 Director of Honors Program ... Dr. Michael HARTSOCK
35 Director Student Development ... Mr. Z. Paul REYNOLDS
37 Director of Financial Aid ... Ms. Cheryl L. HOWERTON
58 Director of MBA Program ... Dr. Anthony F. LIBERATORE
64 Director School of Music ... Dr. Stephen B. WIDENHOFER
87 Director of Summer School ... Dr. Randy M. BROOKS
19 Dir Dept Public Safety/Chief Police ... Mr. Chris BALLARD
66 Director School of Nursing ... Dr. Pamela L. LINDSEY
07 Dean of Admission ... Mr. Kevin MCINTYRE
39 Director of Residence Life ... Mr. Paul LIDY
18 Director of Facilities Services ... Mr. Michael KUROPAS
26 Director of Marketing ... Vacant
09 Coord of Institutional Research ... Mrs. Laura A. BIRCH
105 Web Developer ... Ms. Jessica LANDGREBE

Monmouth College (E)

700 E Broadway, Monmouth IL 61462-1963
County: Warren FICE Identification: 001725
Unit ID: 147341
Telephone: (800) 747-2687 Carnegie Class: Bac-A&S
FAX Number: (309) 457-2141 Calendar System: Semester
URL: www.monmouthcollege.edu
Established: 1853 Annual Undergrad Tuition & Fees: $34,200
Enrollment: 1,300 Coed
Affiliation or Control: Presbyterian Church (U.S.A.) IRS Status: 501(c)3
Highest Offering: Baccalaureate
Accreditation: NH

01 President ... Dr. Clarence R. WYATT
05 Dean of Faculty ... Dr. David M. TIMMERMAN
10 Vice President Finance & Business ... Mr. Richard A. MARSHALL
30 Vice Pres Devel/College Relations ... Col. Stephen M. BLOOMER
32 Vice Pres Student Life/Dn Students ... Ms. Jacquelyn S. CONDON
84 Vice President for Enrollment Mgmt ... Mr. Trent GILBERT
06 Registrar ... Ms. Kristi HIPPEN
08 Director Hewes Library ... Mr. Richard SAYRE
37 Director of Financial Aid ... Ms. Jayne A. SCHRECK
29 Director of Alumni Engagement ... Ms. Hannah MAHER
26 Director College Communications ... Mr. Duane BONIFER
07 Director of Admissions ... Mr. Nick SPAETH
44 Asst Director of Annual Giving ... Ms. Jennifer SANBERG
15 Director of Personnel Services ... Mr. Mike MCNALL
18 Director Facilities Management ... Ms. Sarah YOUNG
20 Associate Dean of the Faculty ... Dr. Frank GERSICH
21 Controller ... Ms. Debbie CLARK

Moody Bible Institute (F)

820 N LaSalle Boulevard, Chicago IL 60610-3263
County: Cook FICE Identification: 001727
Unit ID: 147369
Telephone: (312) 329-4000 Carnegie Class: Spec-4-yr-Faith
FAX Number: (312) 329-4109 Calendar System: Semester
URL: www.moody.edu
Established: 1886 Annual Undergrad Tuition & Fees: $12,284
Enrollment: 3,967 Coed
Affiliation or Control: Independent Non-Profit IRS Status: 501(c)3
Highest Offering: First Professional Degree
Accreditation: NH, BI, MUS, THEOL

01 President ... Dr. J. Paul NYQUIST
05 Provost & Dean of Education ... Dr. Junias V. VENUGOPAL
11 Exec VP & Chief Operating Officer ... Mr. Steven A. MOGCK
10 Chief Financial Officer ... Mr. Ken HEULITT
43 VP & General Counsel ... Mrs. Janet A. STIVEN
20 VP & Associate Provost of Faculty ... Dr. Larry J. DAVIDHIZAR
13 VP of Information Systems ... Mr. Frank W. LEBER
15 VP of Human Resources ... Ms. Debbie ZELINSKI
26 VP of Corporate Communications ... Mrs. Christine GORZ
20 VP & Dean of Undergraduate School ... Dr. James G. SPENCER
58 VP/Dean of Theol Sem & Grad School ... Dr. John A. JELINEK
106 VP & Dean of Dist Learning School ... Vacant
32 VP & Dean of Student Life ... Dr. Timothy E. ARENS
84 VP/Dean of Student/Enrollment Svcs ... Mr. Anthony TURNER
08 Department Manager Library ... Mr. James PRESTON
09 Director of Change Management ... Mr. Daniel M. HASSLER
108 Dir of Accreditation & Assessment ... Ms. Camille WARD
06 Registrar/Director of Acad Records ... Mr. George MOSHER
29 Exec Director Alumni Association ... Mrs. Nancy HASTINGS
39 Associate Dean Residence Life ... Mr. Bruce R. NORQUIST
88 Associate Dean of Students ... Ms. Rachel MONFETTE
36 Assoc Dean of Career Development ... Mr. Patrick FRIEDLINE
38 Associate Dean Counseling Services ... Mr. Steve BRASEL
35 Associate Dean for Student Programs ... Mr. Joseph M. GONZALES, JR.
104 Dean of International Study Program ... Dr. Gregg QUIGGLE
12 Campus Dean MBI Spokane WA ... Dr. Jack LEWIS
88 Dean of Student Srvcs Spokane WA ... Mr. Daniel R. WARD
88 Pgm Mgr of Missionary Aviation Tech ... Mr. James A. CONRAD
88 Dir of Programs and Instruction MDL ... Mrs. Janet RANDERSON
88 Dir of Instructional Design MDL ... Mr. Kevin MAHAFFY
88 Director of Student Experience MDL ... Mr. John ENGELKEMIER
12 Campus Dean MTS Plymouth MI ... Mr. Christopher BROOKS
44 VP of Donor Dev & Channel Strategy ... Mr. Bruce EVERHART
30 VP of Stewardship ... Mr. James ELLIOTT
96 Manager of Procurement Services ... Mr. Paul BRACKLEY
102 Dir Foundation/Corporate Relations ... Ms. Mollie BOND
21 Controller ... Ms. Linda WAHR
37 Director of Financial Aid ... Mrs. Heather SHALLEY
14 Technology Services Director ... Mr. Michael JANCHENKO
18 Division Manager of Facilities ... Mr. Bill BIELAWSKI
19 Deputy Chief of Public Safety ... Mr. Brian M. STOFFER
41 Athletic Director ... Mr. Daniel DUNN
23 Admin of Health Service ... Ms. Ann MEYER
04 Executive Assistant to President ... Ms. Mary OLIVA

† Tuition is paid through donor contributions. Fees are $1,950.00 per year.

Moraine Valley Community College (G)

9000 W College Parkway, Palos Hills IL 60465-0937
County: Cook FICE Identification: 007692
Unit ID: 147378
Telephone: (708) 974-4300 Carnegie Class: Assoc/MT-VT-High Non
FAX Number: (708) 974-1184 Calendar System: Semester
URL: www.morainevalley.edu
Established: 1967 Annual Undergrad Tuition & Fees (In-District): $3,996
Enrollment: 15,286 Coed
Affiliation or Control: State/Local IRS Status: 501(c)3
Highest Offering: Associate Degree
Accreditation: NH, ACFEI, ADNUR, CAHIIM, COARC, COMTA, MAC, PHLEB, POLYT, RAD

01 President ... Dr. Sylvia JENKINS
05 Vice President Academic Affairs ... Dr. Pamela HANEY
32 Vice President Student Devel ... Dr. Normah SALLEH-BARONE
11 Vice Pres Administrative Services ... Vacant
10 Vice Pres Financial & Business Svcs ... Mr. Robert STERKOWITZ
13 Chief Information Officer ... Mr. Kamlesh SANGHVI
50 Dean Science/Business/Comp Tech ... Dr. Ryen NAGLE
49 Dean Liberal Arts ... Dr. Walter FRONCZEK
38 Dean Student Engagement ... Dr. Scott FRIEDMAN
84 Dean Enrollment Services ... Mr. Severo BALASON
51 Dean Corporate/Cmty & Cont Educ ... Vacant
36 Dean Career Programs ... Ms. Kiana BATTTLE
35 Dean Student Services ... Mr. Chester SHAW
88 Dean Learn Enrich & Col Readiness ... Mr. Michael MORSCHES
35 Dean of Students/Compliance Officer ... Mr. Kent MARSHALL
37 Director Financial Aid ... Ms. Carissa DAVIS
09 Dir Institutional Research/Planning ... Dr. Sadya KHAN
19 Chief of Police ... Mr. Patrick O'CONNOR
15 Director Human Resources ... Ms. Lynn HARRINGTON
07 Director of Admissions/Recruitment ... Mr. Andrew SARATA
18 Director Campus Operations ... Mr. Rick BRENNAN
109 Director Auxiliary Services ... Mr. Kashif SHAH
88 Director Health Education Well Ctr ... Mr. William FINN
85 Asst Dean Intl Student Admissions ... Ms. Diane VIVERITO
26 Director Marketing & Communications ... Ms. Clare BRINER
44 Dir Res Devel/Extended Programs ... Dr. Sharon KATTERMAN
21 Controller ... Ms. Theresa O'CARROLL
22 Director Center Disability Services ... Ms. Debbie SIEVERS
96 Director of Purchasing ... Ms. Jane BENTLEY
102 Executive Director Foundation ... Ms. Kristy MCGREAL
20 Dean Academic Development/Outreach ... Dr. Cynthia ANDERSON
20 Dean Academic Services ... Ms. Jennifer DAVIDSON
88 Dean Learning Resource Center ... Ms. Terra JACOBSON
88 Dean Student Success ... Dr. Jo Ann JENKINS

Morrison Institute of Technology (H)

701 Portland Avenue, Morrison IL 61270-2959
County: Whiteside FICE Identification: 008880
Unit ID: 147396
Telephone: (815) 772-7218 Carnegie Class: Spec 2-yr-Tech
FAX Number: (815) 772-7584 Calendar System: Semester
URL: www.morrisontech.edu
Established: 1973 Annual Undergrad Tuition & Fees: $15,600
Enrollment: 86 Coed
Affiliation or Control: Independent Non-Profit IRS Status: 501(c)3
Highest Offering: Associate Degree
Accreditation: COE, ENGT

01 Chief Executive Officer ... Mr. Christopher D. SCOTT
05 Vice President of Academic Affairs ... Mr. Greg J. TULLY
10 Vice President for Finance ... Mr. Richard PARKINSON
06 Registrar ... Ms. Dana VERDICK
07 Director of Admissions ... Mr. Larry LIBBERTON

Morthland College (I)

202 East Oak St, PO Box 429, West Frankfort IL 62896
County: Franklin FICE Identification: 042279
Telephone: (618) 937-2127 Carnegie Class: Not Classified
FAX Number: (618) 937-2137 Calendar System: Semester
URL: www.morthland.edu
Established: 2009 Annual Undergrad Tuition & Fees: N/A
Enrollment: N/A Coed
Affiliation or Control: Independent Non-Profit IRS Status: 501(c)3
Highest Offering: Baccalaureate

Accreditation: TRACS

01 President .... Dr. Tim MORTHLAND
03 Executive Vice President .... Ms. Emily HAYES
05 Provost .... Dr. Randy CARNEY
30 VP Campus Development .... Ms. Stephanie PARTON
32 Dean of Student Affairs .... Ms. Cathie MIELDEZIS
41 Athletic Director .... Mr. Reid CURE

Morton College (A)

3801 S Central Avenue, Cicero IL 60804-4398
County: Cook FICE Identification: 001728
Unit ID: 147411
Telephone: (708) 656-8000 Carnegie Class: Assoc/MT-VT-High Non
FAX Number: (708) 656-3297 Calendar System: Semester
URL: www.morton.edu
Established: 1924 Annual Undergrad Tuition & Fees (In-District): $3,668
Enrollment: 4,653 Coed
Affiliation or Control: State/Local IRS Status: 501(c)3
Highest Offering: Associate Degree
Accreditation: NH, ADNUR, PTAA

01 President .... Dr. Stanley FIELDS
05 Provost .... Dr. Muddassir SIDDIQI
45 VP of Inst Plng & Effectiveness .... Dr. Keith MCLAUGHLIN
51 Dean Adult & Continuing Education .... Dr. Tom PIERCE
32 Director Student Activities .... Ms. Marisol VELASQUEZ
08 Director of Library .... Ms. Jennifer BUTLER
15 Exec Director of Human Resources .... Mr. Anthony RAY
31 Director of Continuing Education .... Ms. Susan FELICE
09 Director Institutional Research .... Ms. Magda BANDA
18 Director of Facilities & Operations .... Mr. John POTEMPA
37 Director of Financial Aid .... Ms. Yolanda FREEMON
06 Registrar .... Ms. Marlena AVALOS-THOMPSON
10 Director of Business Services .... Ms. Mireya PEREZ
11 Exec Director of Operations .... Mr. Frank MARZULLO

National-Louis University (B)

122 S Michigan Avenue, Chicago IL 60603
County: Cook FICE Identification: 001733
Unit ID: 147536
Telephone: (888) 658-8632 Carnegie Class: DU-Mod
FAX Number: N/A Calendar System: Quarter
URL: www.nl.edu
Established: 1886 Annual Undergrad Tuition & Fees: $10,617
Enrollment: 4,582 Coed
Affiliation or Control: Independent Non-Profit IRS Status: 501(c)3
Highest Offering: Doctorate
Accreditation: NH, CACREP, IACBE, TED

01 President .... Dr. Nivine MEGAHED
05 Provost .... Dr. Alison HILSABECK
30 Vice Pres Institutional Advancement .... Ms. Carole WOOD
15 Vice President Human Resources .... Mr. Tom BERGMANN
10 Vice Pres Finance & Administration .... Mr. Marty MICKEY
84 Vice Pres Enrollment Mgmt .... Ms. Bobbi BIRINGER
26 Vice Pres Marketing/Communications .... Mr. Tom EHRHARDT
09 Vice Provost Institutional Effect .... Dr. Marsha WATSON
20 Vice Prov Acad Pgm & Fac Dev .... Dr. Ignacio LOPEZ
88 Exec Dir of Advising/Retention .... Mr. Stephen NEER
50 Dean CPSA .... Dr. Judah VIOLA
53 Dean NCE .... Dr. Robert MULLER
08 Dean University Library .... Dr. Robert MORRISON
32 VP Student Services .... Mr. Steve DIBENEDETTO
12 Exec Director Florida Regional .... Dr. Karen O'DONNELL
28 Director of Employment/Diversity .... Ms. Erin HAULOTTE
37 Director of Student Finance .... Ms. Rathenia HUNTER
07 Director of Admissions .... Mr. Ken KASPRZAK
51 Director Outreach Academic Pgm .... Ms. Karen HAWORTH
35 Director of Student Experience .... Ms. Danielle LABAN
04 Administrative Asst to President .... Ms. Diane M. TRAUSCH
06 Registrar .... Ms. Shannon MEGGERT
108 Director Institutional Assessment .... Vacant
13 Chief Info Technology Officer (CIO) .... Mr. Michael GRAHAM
18 Chief Facilities/Physical Plant .... Mr. Richard SORENSON
25 Assoc Dir of Grant Operations .... Ms. Lucille MORGAN
29 Director Alumni & Outreach Programs .... Vacant
90 Director Academic Computing .... Vacant
91 Technical Director .... Mr. John MAZARIEGOS
96 Purchasing Coordinator .... Ms. Caryn SMITH
102 Dir Foundation/Corporate Relations .... Mr. Brian RUSSELL

National-Louis University Elgin Campus (C)

620 Tollgate Road, Elgin IL 60123
Telephone: (800) 443-5522 Identification: 770083
Accreditation: &NH

† Regional accreditation is carried under the parent institution in Chicago, IL

National-Louis University Lisle Campus (D)

850 Warrenville Road, Lisle IL 60532
Telephone: (800) 443-5522 Identification: 770084
Accreditation: &NH

† Regional accreditation is carried under the parent institution in Chicago, IL

National-Louis University North Shore Campus (E)

5202 Old Orchard Road, Skokie IL 60077
Telephone: (800) 443-5522 Identification: 770085
Accreditation: &NH

† Regional accreditation is carried under the parent institution in Chicago, IL

National-Louis University Wheeling Campus (F)

1000 Capitol Drive, Wheeling IL 60090
Telephone: (800) 443-5522 Identification: 770086
Accreditation: &NH

† Regional accreditation is carried under the parent institution in Chicago, IL

National University of Health Sciences (G)

200 E Roosevelt Road, Lombard IL 60148-4583
County: DuPage FICE Identification: 001732
Unit ID: 147590
Telephone: (630) 629-2000 Carnegie Class: Spec-4-yr-Other Health
FAX Number: (630) 889-6600 Calendar System: Trimester
URL: www.nuhs.edu
Established: 1906 Annual Undergrad Tuition & Fees: N/A
Enrollment: 705 Coed
Affiliation or Control: Independent Non-Profit IRS Status: 501(c)3
Highest Offering: First Professional Degree
Accreditation: NH, ACUP, CHIRO, COMTA, NATUR

01 President .... Dr. Joseph P D. STIEFEL
05 Vice President Academic Services .... Dr. Randy L. SWENSON
10 Vice President Business Services .... Mr. Ron MENSCHING
11 Vice Pres Administrative Services .... Ms. Tracy MCHUGH
76 Dean College Allied Health Sciences .... Dr. Randy L. SWENSON
51 Dean Col Postprofessional Educ .... Dr. Jenna GLENN
23 Dean of Clinics .... Dr. Theodore JOHNSON
107 Dean Col Professional Studies FL .... Dr. Daniel STRAUSS
107 Dean Col Professional Studies IL .... Dr. Robert SHIEL
46 Dean of Research .... Dr. Gregory D. CRAMER
32 Dean of Students .... Dr. Daniel R. DRISCOLL
108 Dean Academic Assessment .... Vacant
88 Dean Accreditation .... Vacant
08 Director Learning Resource Center .... Ms. Patricia GENARDO
06 University Registrar .... Ms. Izabela DUBAK
07 Dir Communication/Enrollment Svcs .... Ms. Victoria SWEENEY
21 Director of Financial Services .... Ms. Sue UNGER
37 Director of Financial Aid .... Mr. Marc YAMBO
18 Director Maintenance & Facilities .... Mr. Mark GALVANONI
15 Director of Human Resources .... Mr. Andrew WOZNIAK
26 Chief Public Relations Officer .... Ms. Marie OLBRYSH
30 Dir Alumni Rels & Development .... Mrs. Lynn NELSON
13 Dir Management Information Services .... Mr. Ron MENSCHING
40 Bookstore Manager .... Ms. Sue ROBERTSON
39 Coordinator of Housing .... Ms. Marilyn FREAD

North Central College (H)

30 N Brainard Street, Naperville IL 60540-4607
County: DuPage FICE Identification: 001734
Unit ID: 147660
Telephone: (630) 637-5100 Carnegie Class: Masters/M
FAX Number: (630) 637-5121 Calendar System: Trimester
URL: www.northcentralcollege.edu
Established: 1861 Annual Undergrad Tuition & Fees: $35,421
Enrollment: 3,043 Coed
Affiliation or Control: United Methodist IRS Status: 501(c)3
Highest Offering: Master's
Accreditation: NH, CAATE

01 President .... Dr. Troy D. HAMMOND
04 Exec Secy/Assistant to President .... Ms. Kimberly SALZBRUNN
05 Provost/VP Academic Affairs .... Dr. Abiodun GOKE-PARIOLA
10 Vice President of Finance/CFO .... Ms. Maryellen SKERIK
30 Vice Pres Institutional Advancement .... Mr. Rick E. SPENCER
84 VP Enrollment Management/Athletics .... Mr. Marty R. SAUER
32 VP Student Affairs/Dean of Students .... Ms. Kimberly SLUIS
11 Vice President for Operations .... Mr. Michael J. HUDSON
13 VP/Chief Information Officer .... Mr. Matthew BURDEN
15 Asst Vice Pres Human Resources .... Mr. John ACARDO
26 Asst Vice Pres Mktg/Communications .... Mr. James GODO
20 Associate Academic Dean .... Dr. Marti S. BOGART
07 Dean of Admissions .... Ms. Martha A. STOLZE
58 Dean Graduate Pgms/Continuing Educ .... Dr. Pamela MONACO
06 Registrar .... Mr. Joel WELLS
08 Director of the Library .... Mr. John J. SMALL
36 Director of Career Development .... Mr. Jeffrey D. DENARD
37 Director of Financial Aid .... Vacant
23 Director of the Wellness Center .... Ms. Tatiana SIFRI
31 Director of Cmty Educ/Conf/Camps .... Mr. Troy BRISTOW
41 Athletic Director .... Mr. James MILLER
21 AVP Finance/Controller .... Mr. David S. MISSURELLI
39 Director of Residence Life .... Ms. Sarah E. AVERY
42 Campus Chaplain .... Rev. Eric DOOLITTLE
44 Director of Planned Giving .... Mr. Bruce NORTELL
09 Director of Institutional Research .... Mr. Peter S. BARGER
29 Director Alumni/Dev Relations .... Mr. Adrian M. ALDRICH
28 Director of Multicultural Affairs .... Ms. Dorothy J. PLEAS

North Park University (I)

3225 W Foster Avenue, Chicago IL 60625-4895
County: Cook FICE Identification: 001735
Unit ID: 147679
Telephone: (773) 244-6200 Carnegie Class: Masters/L
FAX Number: N/A Calendar System: Semester
URL: www.northpark.edu
Established: 1891 Annual Undergrad Tuition & Fees: $25,860
Enrollment: 3,185 Coed
Affiliation or Control: Evangelical Covenant Church Of America
IRS Status: 501(c)3
Highest Offering: Doctorate
Accreditation: NH, #CAATE, IACBE, MUS, NURSE, THEOL

01 President .... Dr. David L. PARKYN
10 Executive Vice President/CFO .... Mr. Carl E. BALSAM
05 Provost .... Dr. Michael O. EMERSON
84 Vice Pres for Enrollment/Marketing .... Mr. Genaro BALCAZAR
30 Vice President for Development .... Ms. Mary K. SURRIDGE
73 Seminary Dean .... Dr. David W. KERSTEN
49 Dean of College of Arts & Sciences .... Dr. Gregor THUSWALDNER
51 Dean School of Adult Learning .... Dr. Lori SCREMENTI
50 Dean School of Business & NFP Mgmt .... Dr. Wesley LINDAHL
53 Dean School of Education .... Dr. Rebecca NELSON
64 Dean School of Music .... Dr. Craig JOHNSON
66 Dean School of Nursing .... Dr. Linda DUNCAN
28 Dean of Diversity & Intercult Pgm .... Vacant
32 VP for Student Engagement .... Dr. Jodi KOSLOW MARTIN
08 Dean Library & Academic Technology .... Ms. Kathryn MAIER-O'SHEA
07 Director Undergraduate Enrollment .... Ms. Amanda NOASCONO
23 Director Health Services .... Ms. Hannah AZEVEDO
37 Director Financial Aid Services .... Ms. Carolyn LACH
13 Director of Information Technology .... Mr. Jeffrey K. LUNDBLAD
15 Director of Human Resources .... Ms. Ingrid K. TENGLIN
18 Director of Physical Plant .... Mr. Carl H. WISTROM
19 Director of Security .... Mr. Daniel GOORIS
21 Director of Finance .... Mr. Lester H. CARLSTROM
26 Dir Univ Marketing & Communications .... Mr. Christopher CHILDERS
41 Athletic Director .... Mr. Jack F. SURRIDGE
42 Director University Ministries .... Mr. Anthony ZAMBLE
36 Senior Director of Career Planning .... Ms. Pamela BOZEMAN-EVANS
06 Registrar .... Mr. Aaron D. SCHOOF
29 Alumni Relations Director .... Ms. Melissa VELEZ LUCE
04 Assistant to the President .... Mrs. Karen P. MEARS
104 Director of International Office .... Dr. Sumie SONG
39 Director Student Housing .... Mr. Aidan HOWORTH
44 Annual Fund Manager .... Mr. Justin PREVOST-SCHULTZ
108 Director Institutional Assessment .... Ms. Hannah ANTHONY

Northeastern Illinois University (J)

5500 N Saint Louis Avenue, Chicago IL 60625-4699
County: Cook FICE Identification: 001693
Unit ID: 147776
Telephone: (773) 583-4050 Carnegie Class: Masters/L
FAX Number: (773) 442-4900 Calendar System: Semester
URL: www.neiu.edu
Established: 1867 Annual Undergrad Tuition & Fees (In-State): $9,351
Enrollment: 10,275 Coed
Affiliation or Control: State IRS Status: 501(c)3
Highest Offering: Master's
Accreditation: NH, ART, BUS, CACREP, CORE, MUS, SW, TED

01 President .... Dr. Sharon K. HAHS
05 Provost & VP Academic Affairs .... Dr. Richard J. HELLDOBLER
10 Vice Pres Finance & Administration .... Mr. Michael J. PIERICK
32 Vice President for Student Affairs .... Dr. Daniel LOPEZ, JR.
30 Vice President Inst Advancement .... Ms. Liesl V. DOWNEY
35 Dean of Students .... Mr. Matthew F. SPECHT
07 Associate VP Enrollment Services .... Dr. Janice M. HARRING-HENDON
21 Director of Univ Budgets .... Ms. Ann M. MCNABB
08 Dean Libraries & Learning Res .... Mr. Carlos MELIAN
09 Exec Dir Inst Rsrch & Assessment .... Mr. Blase E. MASINI
15 Dir of HR Empl & Labor Relations .... Ms. Marta E. MASO
25 Director Sponsored Programs .... Ms. Sharon K. TODD
26 Chief Communication Officer/Dir .... Mr. Michael M. DIZON
37 Director Financial Aid .... Ms. Maureen T. AMOS
50 Dean College Bus/Management .... Dr. Michael D. BEDELL
58 Dean College Graduate Studies & Res .... Dr. Michael J. STERN
53 Dean College of Education .... Vacant
49 Dean College of Arts & Sciences .... Vacant
18 Asst Vice Pres Facilities Mgmt .... Ms. Nancy MEDINA
19 Director University Police Dept .... Vacant
21 Director Controller's Office .... Ms. Fe L. LENON
22 Dir Equal Opportunity/AA & Ethics .... Ms. Leah HEINECKE-KRUMHUS
86 Executive Dir Government Relations .... Dr. Suleyma PEREZ
06 University Registrar .... Mr. Daniel R. WEBER
29 Director of Alumni Relations .... Ms. Damaris TAPIA
38 Dir Student Health & Counseling .... Dr. Susan R. STOCK
96 Asst VP Procurement & Support Svcs .... Mr. Robert B. FILIPP
44 Director Institutional Advancement .... Mr. John L. BUTLER-LUDWIG
96 Director Purchasing .... Ms. Rosalinda CASTILLO

Northern Illinois University (A)

1425 W. Lincoln Way, De Kalb IL 60115-2828
County: De Kalb FICE Identification: 001737
Unit ID: 147703
Telephone: (815) 753-1000 Carnegie Class: DU-Higher
FAX Number: (815) 753-0198 Calendar System: Semester
URL: www.niu.edu
Established: 1895 Annual Undergrad Tuition & Fees (In-State): $14,295
Enrollment: 20,611 Coed
Affiliation or Control: State IRS Status: 501(c)3
Highest Offering: Doctorate
Accreditation: NH, ART, AUD, BUS, BUSA, CAATE, CACREP, CLPSY, CORE, DIETD, DIETI, ENG, ENGT, IPSY, LAW, MFCD, MT, MUS, NAIT, NURSE, PH, PTA, SCPSY, SP, SPAA, TED, THEA

01 President .... Douglas D. BAKER
05 Executive Vice Pres & Provost .... Lisa FREEMAN
20 Vice Provost Academic Planning/Dev .... Carolinda DOUGLASS
10 VP Administration & Finance .... Alan PHILLIPS
45 Vice Prov Resource Planning .... Susan MINI
51 VP University Outreach .... Anne C. KAPLAN
32 Vice Pres Student Affs/Enroll Mgmt .... Eric WELDY
46 VP Research/Innovative Partnership .... Jerry BLAZEY
26 Int VP Marketing & Communications .... Harlan TELLER
43 VP/General Counsel/Legal Svcs .... Jerry D. BLAKEMORE
102 Vice Pres University Advancement .... Catherine SQUIRES
13 VP Chief Information Officer .... Brett CORYELL
18 VP Facilities Planning & Opers .... Alan PHILLIPS
84 VP Enrollment Mgmt & Dir of Admin .... Dani ROLLINS
15 AVP Administration/HR .... Celeste LATHAM
35 Assoc VP Stdnt Affs & Dean of Stdnt .... Kelley WESENER-MICHAEL
23 Director Health Services .... Andrew DIGATE
28 Asst Vice Pres Diversity/Equity .... Katrina CALDWELL
20 Vice Provost .... Anne BIRBERICK
50 Dean of Business .... Balaji RAJAGOPALAN
53 Dean of Education .... Laurie ELISH-PIPER
54 Dean of Engineering/Engr Tech .... Promod VOHRA
61 Dean of Law .... Mark CORDES
49 Dean Liberal Arts & Sciences .... Christopher MCCORD
76 Dean Health & Human Sciences .... Derryl BLOCK
57 Dean Visual & Performing Arts .... Paul BAUER
58 Dean Grad Sch/AVP Grad Studies .... Bradley BOND
85 Interim Sr International Affairs .... Bradley BOND
88 Asst VP Outreach Rockford .... Rena COTSONES
12 Director Lorado Taft Field Campus .... Diana DENNIS
12 Director NIU Naperville .... Gina KENYON
06 Director Registration & Records .... Jerry MONTAG
09 Director of Institutional Research .... J. Daniel HOUSE
25 Director of Sponsored Projects .... David STONE
36 Acting Exec Dir of Career Services .... Brandon T. LAGANA
37 Director of Student Financial Aid .... Rebecca BABEL
38 Exec Dir Counseling/Consultation .... Brooke RUXTON
40 University Bookstore Manager .... Don TURK
19 Police Chief/Public Safety .... Thomas R. PHILLIPS, SR.
41 Athletic Director .... Sean FRAZIER
91 Director Enterprise Info Systems .... Vacant
39 Acting Exec Dir Housing & Dining .... Patricia MARTINEZ
22 Dir Disability Resources Center .... Debra MILLER
29 Director Alumni Relations .... Joseph MATTY
96 Director of Purchasing .... Vacant

Northern Seminary (B)

660 E Butterfield Road, Lombard IL 60148-5698
County: DuPage FICE Identification: 001736
Unit ID: 147697
Telephone: (630) 620-2180 Carnegie Class: Spec-4-yr-Faith
FAX Number: (630) 620-2190 Calendar System: Quarter
URL: www.seminary.edu
Established: 1913 Annual Graduate Tuition & Fees: N/A
Enrollment: 205 Coed
Affiliation or Control: American Baptist IRS Status: 501(c)3
Highest Offering: Doctorate; No Undergraduates
Accreditation: THEOL

01 President .... Dr. William SHIELL
04 Executive Assistant to President .... Vacant
05 Vice President of Academic Affairs .... Dr. Karen WALKER FREEBURG
20 Associate Dean .... Dr. Jason GILE
30 Vice President of Advancement .... Mr. David KRAUSE
10 Exec Dir of Finance & Operations .... Mr. Joshua CARNEY
07 Executive Director of Enrollment .... Mr. Joshua MOORE
06 Registrar .... Ms. Marilyn R. MAST HEWITT
88 Director Doctoral Studies .... Dr. Karen WALKER-FREEBURG
32 Dean of Students .... Mr. Josiah BLACK
08 Director of Brimson Grow Library .... Mr. Scott ERDENGERG

Northwest Suburban College (C)

5999 S. New Wilke Road, Rolling Meadows IL 60008
County: Cook Identification: 667240
Telephone: (847) 290-6425 Carnegie Class: Not Classified
FAX Number: (847) 290-1441 Calendar System: Semester
URL: www.nwsc.edu
Established: 2008 Annual Undergrad Tuition & Fees: N/A
Enrollment: N/A Coed
Affiliation or Control: Independent Non-Profit IRS Status: 501(c)3
Highest Offering: Associate Degree
Accreditation: ACICS

01 President .... Dr. M. T. ALINIAZEE
05 Provost/Dean of Acad & Student Affs .... Dr. Maksood AKBAR
20 Associate Dean .... Dr. Shazia ILYAS
07 Admissions Representative .... Mr. Luke MANGOGNIA

Northwestern College (D)

9501 Technology Blvd; Suite 425, Rosemont IL 60018
County: Cook FICE Identification: 012362
Unit ID: 147749
Telephone: (847) 233-7700 Carnegie Class: Assoc/HVT-Mix Trad/Non
FAX Number: (847) 233-7705 Calendar System: Quarter
URL: www.nc.edu
Established: 1902 Annual Undergrad Tuition & Fees: $17,860
Enrollment: 338 Coed
Affiliation or Control: Proprietary IRS Status: Proprietary
Highest Offering: Associate Degree
Accreditation: NH, ACBSP, CAHIIM, MAC, RAD

01 President .... Mr. Lawrence SCHUMACHER
03 Executive VP of Operations .... Mrs. Gail SCHUMACHER
11 Chief Operations Officer .... Mr. Dimitrios KRIARAS
10 Chief Financial Officer .... Mr. Daniel AMBROSE
10 Controller .... Ms. Leslie RODRIGUEZ
108 VP of Accreditation and Compliance .... Mrs. Diane MAREK
05 VP of Academic Success .... Mr. William BELL
09 Dean of Institutional Research .... Mr. John N. MOYE
13 Chief Information & Digital Officer .... Mr. David HOMAN
32 VP of Student Affairs .... Mrs. Barbara ANDERSON-SAPATA
86 Government and Public Relations Dir .... Ms. Laura POLLASTRINI
08 Director of Library Services .... Ms. Sarah DULAY
12 Director of Bridgeview Campus .... Mrs. Mary REYNOLDS
12 Director of Chicago Campus .... Mrs. Jill MAKSYMEC
15 Director of Human Resources .... Mrs. Margie BENNECKE
37 Director of Financial Assistance .... Ms. Patricia KILIAN
105 Institutional Initiatives Director .... Ms. Lauren SCHUMACHER
38 Director of Counseling .... Vacant
106 Dean of Academic Operations .... Ms. Rakisha SLOANE
07 Enrollment Services Manager .... Ms. Theresa VALDES
66 Dean of Nursing .... Vacant
06 Registrar .... Ms. Tina MARFOE
36 Career Development Coordinator .... Ms. Amy BUOSCIO
36 Career Development Coordinator .... Mr. Greg NORTON
97 Program Director - GE .... Mr. David COOPER
61 Program Director - LS .... Vacant
50 Program Director - SC&T .... Ms. Sheila ROE-BOSTON
76 Program Director - SHS .... Ms. Chandra HURT
04 Executive Asst to President .... Ms. Vilma FRANCO

Northwestern College-SW Campus (E)

7725 S Harlem Avenue, Bridgeview IL 60455
Telephone: (888) 205-2283 Identification: 770089
Accreditation: &NH

† Regional accreditation is carried under the parent institution in Rosemont, IL

Northwestern University (F)

633 Clark Street, Evanston IL 60208-3854
County: Cook FICE Identification: 001739
Unit ID: 147767
Telephone: (847) 491-8400 Carnegie Class: DU-Highest
FAX Number: (847) 491-7364 Calendar System: Quarter
URL: www.northwestern.edu
Established: 1851 Annual Undergrad Tuition & Fees: $49,047
Enrollment: 21,554 Coed
Affiliation or Control: Independent Non-Profit IRS Status: 501(c)3
Highest Offering: Doctorate
Accreditation: NH, ARCPA, AUD, BUS, CACREP, CLPSY, ENG, IPSY, JOUR, LAW, MED, MFCD, MUS, OPE, PCSAS, PH, PTA, SP

01 President .... Dr. Morton O. SCHAPIRO
05 Provost .... Dr. Daniel I. LINZER
10 Executive Vice President .... Mr. Nim S. CHINNIAH
32 Vice President Student Affairs .... Dr. Patricia TELLES-IRVIN
26 Vice President University Relations .... Mr. Alan K. CUBBAGE
45 Vice Pres Administration & Planning .... Ms. Marilyn MCCOY
13 Vice Pres Information Technology .... Mr. Sean B. REYNOLDS
30 Vice Pres for Alumni Rel & Devel .... Mr. Robert MCQUINN
46 Vice President Research .... Mr. Joseph T. WALSH
88 Vice Pres/Chief Investment Officer .... Mr. William H. MCLEAN
43 Vice President/General Counsel .... Mr. Philip L. HARRIS
18 VP for Facilities .... Mr. John DÖANGELO
84 Associate Provost Univ Enrollment .... Mr. Michael E. MILLS
53 Associate Provost Undergrad Educ .... Dr. Ronald R. BRAEUTIGAM
20 Associate Provost Faculty Affairs .... Vacant
20 Assoc VP & Assoc Provost Academic .... Mr. Jake JULIA
21 Assoc Prov Budget/Facil/Analysis .... Ms. Jean E. SHEDD
86 Spec Asst to Pres for Govt Rels .... Mr. Bruce LAYTON
04 Assistant to the President .... Mr. Eugene Y. LOWE, JR.
100 Director Office of the President .... Ms. Judith V. REMINGTON
41 Vice Pres Athletics and Recreation .... Mr. James J. PHILLIPS
72 Dean Sch Engr/Applied Science .... Dr. Julio M. OTTINO
50 Dean Graduate School of Management .... Dr. Sally E. BLOUNT
60 Dean School of Journalism .... Dr. Bradley J. HAMM
64 Dean School of Music .... Dr. Toni-Marie MONTGOMERY
63 Lewis Landsberg Deanship/Deans Ofc .... Dr. Eric G. NEILSON
51 Dean/Assoc Prov SPS .... Dr. Thomas F. GIBBONS
58 Dean Graduate School .... Mr. Dwight A. MCBRIDE
60 Dean School of Communication .... Dr. Barbara J. O'KEEFE
53 Dean School of Educ & Social Policy .... Dr. Penelope L. PETERSON
49 Dean College Arts & Science .... Mr. Adrian RANDOLPH
61 Dean School of Law .... Dr. Daniel B. RODRIGUEZ
08 University Librarian .... Ms. Sarah M. PRITCHARD
36 Exec Dir of Univ Career Svcs .... Mr. Mark PRESNELL
35 Assistant VP of Student Engagement .... Ms. Kelly SCHAEFER
29 Assoc VP Alumni Relations & Develop .... Mr. David LIVELY
88 Assoc Vice President for Research .... Mr. Lewis SMITH
88 Assoc Vice President for Research .... Mr. Jian CAO
88 Assoc VP for Rsrch Innov & New Vent .... Ms. Alicia LOFFLER
88 Assoc Vice President for Research .... Ms. Ann ADAMS
88 Dean for Research .... Mr. Rex CHISHOLM
21 Assoc Vice Pres Budget Planning .... Mr. James M. HURLEY
18 Assoc Vice Pres Facilities Mgmt .... Mr. Ronald NAYLER
15 Assoc Vice Pres for Human Resources .... Ms. Pamela BEEMER
21 Assoc Vice Pres Finance/Controller .... Ms. Ingrid S. STAFFORD
07 Dean of Undergraduate Admissions .... Mr. Christopher WATSON
88 Exec Dir Intl Research Partnerships .... Ms. Indrani MUKHARJI
23 Exec Director Health Services .... Dr. John ALEXANDER
39 Asst Dean of Students .... Ms. Mary GOLDENBERG
38 Director of Counseling/Psych Svcs .... Dr. John H. DUNKLE
42 University Chaplain .... Dr. Timothy S. STEVENS
88 Asst VP for Information .... Mr. Amit PRACHAND
88 Dir Program Review/Spec Project .... Mr. Jeremy HUNSUCKER
88 Asst VP for Planning .... Ms. Eileen MCCARTHY
06 University Registrar .... Ms. Jacqualyn CASAZZA
37 Director Financial Aid .... Ms. Carolyn V. LINDLEY
16 Dir HR Consulting Svcs/Staffing .... Vacant
19 Chief of University Police .... Mr. Bruce LEWIS
21 Assoc VP of Audit & Advisory Svcs .... Ms. Betty L. MCPHILIMY
22 Dir Equal Emply Opprty/Affirm Act .... Ms. Tasha SHELTON
96 Director University Svcs Purchasing .... Mr. Jim KONRAD
28 Asst Provost Diversity & Inclusion .... Ms. Dona CORDERO

Oakton Community College (G)

1600 E Golf Road, Des Plaines IL 60016-1256
County: Cook FICE Identification: 009896
Unit ID: 147800
Telephone: (847) 635-1600 Carnegie Class: Assoc/MT-VT-High Non
FAX Number: (847) 635-1992 Calendar System: Semester
URL: www.oakton.edu
Established: 1969 Annual Undergrad Tuition & Fees (In-District): $3,285
Enrollment: 10,589 Coed
Affiliation or Control: Local IRS Status: 501(c)3
Highest Offering: Associate Degree
Accreditation: NH, ADNUR, CAHIIM, MLTAD, PTAA

01 President .... Dr. Joianne L. SMITH
05 Vice President Academic Affairs .... Dr. Thomas HAMEL
20 Assistant VP Academic Affairs .... Dr. Nancy PRENDERGAST
20 Assistant VP Academic Affairs .... Dr. Michael CARR
32 Vice President Student Affairs .... Dr. Karl BROOKS
28 AVP for Access/Equity & Diversity .... Vacant
10 Vice President Business & Finance .... Vacant
51 AVP Cont Ed/Trng/Wrkfrc Dev .... Dr. Colette HANDS
13 Vice Pres Information Technology .... Ms. Bonnie LUCAS
76 Dean Science & Health Careers .... Ms. Ruth WILLIAMS
81 Dean Math & Technology .... Dr. Robert SOMPOLSKI
60 Dean Language/Humanities & the Arts .... Ms. Linda KORBEL
83 Dean Social Science/Business .... Mr. Bradley WOOTEN
26 Director of College Relations .... Mr. Paul PALIAN
09 Executive Director Research .... Dr. Maya EVANS
08 Dean Library & On-line Learning .... Vacant
84 Dir of Student Recruitment/Outreach .... Ms. Michele BROWN
06 Director of Registrar Services .... Mr. Bruce OATES
35 Director of Student Life .... Ms. Ann Marie BARRY
88 Dean of Student Success .... Mr. Sebastian CONTRERAS, JR.
88 Dir of Student Learning/Engagement .... Ms. Leana CUELLAR
41 Director of Athletics .... Mr. Bruce OATES
103 Dir Workforce Dev & Corp Training .... Dr. Colette HANDS
21 Controller .... Mr. Andy WILLIAMS
21 Director of Business Services .... Ms. Doreen SCHWARTZ
15 Chief Human Resources Officer .... Ms. Mums MARTENS
18 Director of Facilities .... Ms. Leah SWANQUIST
14 Director Systems & Network Svcs .... Mr. John WADE
14 Dir of Educ Computing/End User Svcs .... Ms. Renee KOZIMOR
07 Director of Enrollment Services .... Ms. Cheryl WARMANN
25 Dir of Grants & Alternative Funding .... Ms. Roxann MARSHBURN
51 Dir of Operations and Admin .... Ms. Robyn BAILEY
28 Ethics Officer .... Ms. Mum MARTENS
38 Director of Counseling .... Dr. Mark KIEL
19 Chief of Police .... Mr. Dale GUSTAFSON
30 Executive Director of Development .... Dr. Mary KNIGHT

Oakton Community College Ray Hartstein Campus (H)

7701 N Lincoln Avenue, Skokie IL 60077
Telephone: (847) 635-1600 Identification: 770091
Accreditation: &NH

† Regional accreditation is carried under the parent institution in Des Plaines, IL

Olivet Nazarene University (I)

One University Avenue, Bourbonnais IL 60914-2345
County: Kankakee FICE Identification: 001741
Unit ID: 147828
Telephone: (815) 939-5011 Carnegie Class: Masters/L
FAX Number: (815) 935-4998 Calendar System: Semester
URL: www.olivet.edu
Established: 1907 Annual Undergrad Tuition & Fees: $32,790

Enrollment: 4,861 Coed
Affiliation or Control: Church Of The Nazarene IRS Status: 501(c)3
Highest Offering: Doctorate
Accreditation: NH, #CAATE, DIETD, ENG, MUS, NURSE, SW, TED

01 President .... Dr. John C. BOWLING
05 Vice President Academic Affairs .... Dr. Carol MAXSON
10 Vice President for Finance .... Dr. Douglas E. PERRY
32 Vice President Student Development .... Dr. Walter W. WEBB
26 Vice Pres Institutional Advancement .... Dr. Brian ALLEN
88 Vice Pres of Strategic Expansion .... Mr. Ryan SPITTAL
49 Dean College of Arts & Sciences .... Dr. Stephen LOWE
73 Dn Sch Theology/Christian Ministry .... Dr. Mark QUANSTROM
53 Dean School of Education .... Dr. Robert HULL
20 Assoc VP for Academic Affairs .... Dr. Houston THOMPSON
29 Acting Dir Alumni & University Rels .... Mr. Erinn PROEHL
07 Director of Admissions .... Mrs. Susan WOLFF
06 Dean of Inst Effect & Registrar .... Mr. Jonathan PICKERING
08 Interim Dean of Library Services .... Mrs. Pam GREENLEE
37 Director of Financial Aid .... Mr. Greg BRUNER
13 Chief Information Officer .... Mr. Dennis SEYMOUR
41 Athletic Director .... Mr. Gary NEWSOME
42 Chaplain .... Rev. Mark HOLCOMB
30 Director of Development .... Mr. John MONGERSON
35 Director Student Activities .... Mrs. Kathy STEINACKER
38 Director Student Counseling .... Mrs. Lisa VANDER VEER
15 Director of Human Resources .... Mr. David PICKERING
18 Chief Facilities/Physical Plant .... Mr. Matt WHITIS
40 Bookstore Manager .... Mrs. Rachel PIAZZA
36 Assoc Director of Career Services .... Miss Poppy MILLER
85 International Student Advisor .... Dr. Mark MOUNTAIN
27 Director of Marketing .... Mr. Remington ANKSORUS
19 Director Security/Safety .... Mr. Dale NEWSOME
76 Dean School of Life/Health Sciences .... Mrs. Amber RESIDORI
64 Dean School of Music .... Dr. Don REDDICK
50 Dean School of Business .... Dr. Glen REWERTS
54 Dean School of Engineering .... Dr. Shane RITTER
58 Dean School Grad/Continuing Studies .... Dr. Jonathan BARTLING

Pacific College of Oriental Medicine (A)

65 East Wacker Place 21st Floor, Chicago IL 60601
Telephone: (888) 729-4811 Identification: 666615
Accreditation: &WC, ACUP

† Branch campus of Pacific College of Oriental Medicine, San Diego CA.

Parkland College (B)

2400 W Bradley Avenue, Champaign IL 61821-1899
County: Champaign FICE Identification: 007118
Unit ID: 147916
Telephone: (217) 351-2200 Carnegie Class: Assoc/HVT-High Non
FAX Number: (217) 351-2581 Calendar System: Semester
URL: www.parkland.edu
Established: 1966 Annual Undergrad Tuition & Fees (In-District): $3,945
Enrollment: 8,443 Coed
Affiliation or Control: State/Local IRS Status: 501(c)3
Highest Offering: Associate Degree
Accreditation: NH, ADNUR, COARC, DH, EMT, OTA, RAD, SURGT

01 President .... Dr. Thomas R. RAMAGE
04 Asst to President/Board of Trustees .... Ms. Nancy R. WILLAMON
05 Vice President Academic Svcs .... Dr. Pam LAU
32 Vice President Student Services .... Dr. Mike TRAME
10 Vice Pres Administrative Svcs/ CFO .... Mr. Christopher M. RANDLES
30 Vice Pres Institutional Advancement .... Dr. Seamus REILLY
35 Dean of Students .... Ms. Marietta TURNER
09 Dean Institutional Effectiveness .... Mr. Kevin KNOTT
106 Dean Adult Basic Educ/Workforce Dev .... Ms. Tawanna NICKENS
75 Dean of Career & Transfer Prgms .... Mr. Randy FLETCHER
50 Dept Chair Bus & Agri Industries .... Mr. Bruce HENRIKSON
77 Department Chair Comp Science & IT .... Ms. Maria MOBASSERI
54 Dept Chair Engineering Science/Tech .... Ms. Catherine STALTER
79 Dept Chair Humanities .... Mr. Tom BARNARD
57 Dept Chair Fine & Applied Arts .... Ms. Nancy SUTTON
76 Dept Chair Health Professions .... Ms. Roberta SCHOLZE
81 Department Chair Mathematics .... Mr. Geoffrey GRIFFITHS
65 Dept Chair Natural Sciences .... Ms. Sheryl DRAKE
83 Dept Chair Social Sci & Human Svcs .... Mr. Paul SARANTAKOS
88 Dir Center for Academic Success .... Vacant
26 Dir Marketing & Public Relations .... Vacant
103 Exec Director Workforce Development .... Mr. Tawanna NICKENS
102 Exec Dir Foundation/Alumni Affairs .... Ms. Ellen SCHMIDT
08 Director Library .... Ms. Anna Maria S. WATKIN
31 Director Community Education .... Ms. Amy FLESHNER
25 Director Grants and Contracts .... Mr. Joshua BIRKY
07 Director Admissions/Enrollment Mgmt .... Mr. Reo WILHOUR
35 Director Student Life .... Dr. Thomas M. CAULFIELD
41 Director Athletics .... Mr. Rod M. LOVETT
36 Director Career Center .... Ms. Sandra L. SPENCER
38 Dir Counseling & Advising Center .... Mr. John SHEAHAN
37 Director Financial Aid .... Mr. Tim WENDT
19 Director Public Safety .... Mr. William COLBROOK
18 Director Physical Plant .... Mr. James BUSTARD
15 Director Human Resources .... Ms. Kathleen MCANDREW
21 Controller .... Mr. Dave DONSBACH
40 Manager of Bookstore .... Ms. Diane M. KIEST
88 Director Assessment Center .... Dr. Michael TRAME

Prairie State College (C)

202 S Halsted Street, Chicago Heights IL 60411-8226
County: Cook FICE Identification: 001640
Unit ID: 148007
Telephone: (708) 709-3500 Carnegie Class: Assoc/HVT-High Non
FAX Number: (708) 755-2587 Calendar System: Semester
URL: www.prairiestate.edu
Established: 1957 Annual Undergrad Tuition & Fees (In-District): $3,432
Enrollment: 4,574 Coed
Affiliation or Control: State/Local IRS Status: 501(c)3
Highest Offering: Associate Degree
Accreditation: NH, ADNUR, DH, SURGT

01 President .... Dr. Terri L. WINFREE
10 Vice Pres Finance & Administration .... Dr. Thomas SABAN
05 Vice Pres Acad Affs/Dean Faculty .... Dr. Marie C. HANSEL
31 Vice Pres Community/Economic Devel .... Mr. Craig D. SCHMIDT
32 VP Student Affairs/Dean of Students .... Dr. Gregory A. THOMAS
49 Dean Liberal Arts .... Mr. Elighie WILSON
50 Dean Business/Mathematics & Science .... Dr. Debra L. PRENDERGAST
72 Dean Health/Industrial Tech .... Ms. Patty ZUCCARELLO
15 Exec Dir Human Resources .... Mr. David CRONAN
16 Asst Dir of Human Resources .... Mr. Leo ALEXANDER
13 Exec Dir Info Technology Resources .... Mr. Gregory KAIN
56 Dean Adult Education .... Ms. Kim M. KUNCE
21 Controller/Dir of Business Svcs .... Ms. Marina KIBARDINA
08 Assoc Dean/Library .... Ms. Kristina HOWARD
51 Dean Corporate/Continuing Education .... Ms. Kelly LAPETINO
35 Dean Student Dev/Campus Life .... Mr. Felix SIMPKINS
18 Exec Dir Facilities and Operations .... Mr. Timothy L. KOSIEK
26 Exec Dir Public Relations/Marketing .... Vacant
102 Executive Director Foundation .... Ms. Deborah S. HAVIGHORST
07 Exec Dir Enrollment/Fin Aid Svcs .... Ms. Jaime M. MILLER
19 Dir Police/Campus Safe/Chief Police .... Mr. George PFOTENHAUER
37 Director Financial Aid .... Ms. Grace MCGINNIS
09 Director Inst Research/Planning .... Dr. Adane G. KASSA
88 Director Institutional Support Svcs .... Ms. Paulette A. MAURER
41 Director of Athletics .... Mr. Christopher ZORICH
04 Admin Dir Pres Office/Board .... Ms. Patricia G. TROST
89 Director First Year Experience .... Dr. Stephanie COLEMAN
20 Associate Dean Academic Affairs .... Vacant

Prince Institute - Southeast (D)

1300 East Woodfield Road, Suite 110, Schaumburg IL 60173
FICE Identification: 022960
Unit ID: 101958
Telephone: (847) 592-6600 Carnegie Class: Not Classified
FAX Number: N/A Calendar System: Quarter
URL: www.princeinstitute.edu
Established: 1976 Annual Undergrad Tuition & Fees: $10,485
Enrollment: 84 Coed
Affiliation or Control: Proprietary IRS Status: Proprietary
Highest Offering: Associate Degree
Accreditation: ACICS

01 Campus Director .... Mr. Gerald C. ACEVEDO
05 Dean of Academic Affairs .... Ms. Candace H. SHEPARD
10 Director Campus Operations .... Mr. Keith WEROSH
07 Admissions Representative .... Ms. Sherry HILL

Principia College (E)

1 Maybeck Place, Elsah IL 62028-9799
County: Jersey FICE Identification: 001744
Unit ID: 148016
Telephone: (618) 374-2131 Carnegie Class: Bac-A&S
FAX Number: (618) 374-5500 Calendar System: Semester
URL: www.principiacollege.edu
Established: 1898 Annual Undergrad Tuition & Fees: $27,440
Enrollment: 493 Coed
Affiliation or Control: Independent Non-Profit IRS Status: 501(c)3
Highest Offering: Baccalaureate
Accreditation: NH

01 President .... Dr. Jonathan PALMER
05 Provost .... Dr. Joseph RITTER
88 Chief Investment Officer .... Mr. Howard E. BERNER, JR.
10 Vice President Finance & Operations .... Mr. Doug GIBBS
11 Vice President Administration .... Mrs. Karen D. GRIMMER
30 Vice President External Relations .... Mr. Peter STEVENS
20 Associate Dean of Academics .... Dr. Libby SCHEIERN
71 Dir Acad Special Programs .... Mr. James HEGARTY
06 Registrar .... Ms. Alice DERVIN
32 Dean of Students .... Ms. Debra JONES
08 Director of Libraries .... Mrs. Lisa ROBERTS
13 Director Information Technology .... Mr. Chris HUFFORD
104 Director of Principia Abroad .... Dr. Gregory W. SANDFORD
41 Director of Athletics .... Mr. Lee ELLIS
15 Human Resources Director .... Ms. SharonAnn SMITH
18 Director of Facilities .... Mr. Ed GOEWERT
21 Controller .... Mr. Don MILLER
29 Dir Alumni/Field Rels/Ann Giving .... Mrs. Donna GIBBS
07 Dir Admissions/Col Financial Aid .... Mrs. Tami GAVALETZ
96 Purchasing Agent .... Mrs. Susan CURRY
38 Director Academic Career Advising .... Mrs. Midge BROWNING
09 Institutional Research Officer .... Ms. Roz HIBBS
26 Dir Marketing & Communications .... Ms. Laurel WALTERS

Quincy University (F)

1800 College Avenue, Quincy IL 62301-2699
County: Adams FICE Identification: 001745
Unit ID: 148131
Telephone: (217) 222-8020 Carnegie Class: Masters/M
FAX Number: (217) 228-5257 Calendar System: Semester
URL: www.quincy.edu
Established: 1860 Annual Undergrad Tuition & Fees: $26,998
Enrollment: 1,279 Coed
Affiliation or Control: Roman Catholic IRS Status: 501(c)3
Highest Offering: Master's
Accreditation: NH

01 President .... Dr. Robert GERVASI
05 VP for Academic Affairs .... Dr. Ann BEHRENS
42 VP for Mission & Ministry .... Fr. John DOCTOR, OFM
10 VP for Business/Finance .... Mr. Tim WEIS
84 VP Student Enrollment & Engagement .... Dr. Soumitra GHOSH
41 VP for Athletics/Athletic Dir .... Mr. Marty BELL
30 VP for Univ Advancement .... Mrs. Julie BELL
13 Chief Information Officer .... Mr. Tony HAYES
04 Exec Assistant to the President .... Mrs. Julie BUDINE
101 Corporate Secretary .... Fr. John DOCTOR, OFM
21 Assoc VP for Finance/Controller .... Mrs. Jean GREEN
06 Registrar .... Ms. Barbara WELLMAN
50 Dean School of Business .... Dr. Cynthia HALIEMUN
53 Dean School of Education .... Dr. Bruce SPITZER
08 Dean Library/Info Resources .... Ms. Patricia TOMCZAK
79 Chair Division of Humanities .... Dr. Daniel STRUDWICK
81 Chair Division Science & Technology .... Dr. Lee ENGER
83 Chair Div Behavioral/Social Sci .... Dr. Wendy BELLER
57 Chair Div Communication/Fine Arts .... Mr. Karl WARMA
32 Acting Dean of Students .... Mrs. Crystal SUTTER
108 Director of Assessment .... Dr. David SHINN
92 Director Honors Program .... Dr. Daniel STRUDWICK
42 Director Campus Ministry .... Mr. Ray HEILMANN
29 Dir Development/Alumni/Cmty Service .... Mr. Matthew BERGMAN
37 Director Financial Aid .... Ms. Lisa FLACK
18 Director Facilities Management .... Mr. Kevin BUSSEY
39 Director Residence Life/Community .... Mr. Jason AMEZCUA
19 Director Safety & Security .... Mr. Sam LATHROP
15 Director Human Resources .... Mrs. Tanya MOORE
38 Director Counseling Center .... Mrs. Molly DUNN-STEINKE
07 Director of Admissions .... Mrs. Abby WAYMAN
88 Director Student Success Center .... Mrs. Christine TRACY
36 Director Career Services .... Mrs. Kristen LIESEN
96 Purchasing .... Ms. Jennifer TRUITT
25 Grant Writer .... Mrs. Julie BOLL
40 Manager Bookstore .... Mr. Ben MEANS

Rasmussen College - Aurora (G)

2363 Sequoia Drive, Suite 131, Aurora IL 60506
Telephone: (630) 888-3500 Identification: 667060
Accreditation: &NH, CAHIIM, MAAB

† Regional accreditation is carried under the parent institution in Saint Cloud, MN. The tuition figure is an average, actual tuition may vary.

Rasmussen College - Mokena/Tinley Park (H)

8650 W. Spring Lake Drive, Mokena IL 60448
Telephone: (815) 534-3300 Identification: 667064
Accreditation: &NH, MAAB

† Regional accreditation carried under the parent institution in Saint Cloud, MN. The tuition figure is an average, actual tuition may vary.

Rasmussen College - Rockford (I)

6000 E. State Street, 4th Floor, Rockford IL 61108
Telephone: (815) 316-4800 Identification: 667065
Accreditation: &NH, CAHIIM, MAAB

† Regional accreditation carried under the parent institution in Saint Cloud, MN. The tuition figure is an average, actual tuition may vary.

Rasmussen College - Romeoville/Joliet (J)

1400 West Normantown Road, Romeoville IL 60446
Telephone: (815) 306-2600 Identification: 667066
Accreditation: &NH, MAAB

† Regional accreditation carried under the parent institution in Saint Cloud, MN. The tuition figure is an average, actual tuition may vary.

Realtor University (K)

430 North Michigan Ave, Chicago IL 60611
County: Cook Identification: 667270
Telephone: (855) 786-6546 Carnegie Class: Not Classified
FAX Number: N/A Calendar System: Semester
URL: www.realtors.edu
Established: 2003 Annual Graduate Tuition & Fees: N/A
Enrollment: N/A Coed
Affiliation or Control: Proprietary IRS Status: Proprietary
Highest Offering: Master's; No Undergraduates
Accreditation: DEAC

01 President .... Dale A. STINTON

Rend Lake College (A)

468 N Ken Gray Parkway, Ina IL 62846-9801
County: Jefferson FICE Identification: 007119
Unit ID: 148256
Telephone: (618) 437-5321 Carnegie Class: Assoc/HVT-High Non
FAX Number: (618) 437-5677 Calendar System: Semester
URL: www.rlc.edu
Established: 1967 Annual Undergrad Tuition & Fees (In-District): $3,000
Enrollment: 2,970 Coed
Affiliation or Control: State/Local IRS Status: 501(c)3
Highest Offering: Associate Degree
Accreditation: NH, CAHIIM, EMT, MLTAD, OTA, RAD, SURGT

01 President .... Mr. Terry WILKERSON
05 VP Career Technical Education .... Mrs. Lori RAGLAND
10 VP of Finance & Administration .... Mrs. Angie KISTNER
09 VP of Institutional Effectiveness .... Mrs. Andrea WITTHOFT
32 VP of Student Services .... Mrs. Lisa PRICE
26 Director Marketing & Information .... Mr. Chad COPPLE
37 Director Student Financial Aid .... Ms. Cheri RUSHING
41 Athletic Director .... Mr. Tim WILLS
18 Director Physical Plant .... Mr. Donnie MILLENBINE
102 CEO of RLC Foundation .... Mrs. Kathleen ZIBBY-DAMRON
06 Director of Student Records .... Mrs. Kelly DOWNES
09 Director of Institutional Research .... Mrs. Vickie SCHULTE

Resurrection University (B)

1431 N. Claremont Street, 6th Floor, Chicago IL 60622
County: Cook FICE Identification: 006250
Unit ID: 149763
Telephone: (773) 252-6464 Carnegie Class: Spec-4-yr-Other Health
FAX Number: (773) 227-5134 Calendar System: Semester
URL: www.resu.edu
Established: 1982 Annual Undergrad Tuition & Fees: N/A
Enrollment: 508 Coed
Affiliation or Control: Independent Non-Profit IRS Status: 501(c)3
Highest Offering: Master's
Accreditation: NH, CAHIIM, NURSE, RAD

01 President .... Dr. Therese A. SCANLAN
05 Chief Academic Officer .... Vacant
26 VP Marketing & Enrollment Mgmt .... Ms. Jeri BINGHAM
10 Chief Operating Officer .... Vacant
32 Director of Student Development .... Ms. Esther WALLEN
90 Network Support Analyst .... Mr. Zbigniew KUSNIERZ
37 Student Financial Aid .... Ms. Shirley HOWELL
06 Registrar .... Mr. Michael SHERMAN
84 Director of Enrollment Mgmt .... Mr. Ron DE LOS SANTOS
08 Manager of Library Services .... Ms. Liesl COTTRELL
15 VP Student & Employee Affairs .... Mr. Brian BOLLENBACHER
66 Interim Dean of Nursing .... Dr. Kathleen MUGLIA

Richland Community College (C)

One College Park, Decatur IL 62521-8513
County: Macon FICE Identification: 010879
Unit ID: 148292
Telephone: (217) 875-7200 Carnegie Class: Assoc/MT-VT-High Non
FAX Number: (217) 875-6961 Calendar System: Semester
URL: www.richland.edu
Established: 1971 Annual Undergrad Tuition & Fees (In-District): $3,744
Enrollment: 3,369 Coed
Affiliation or Control: State/Local IRS Status: 501(c)3
Highest Offering: Associate Degree
Accreditation: NH, ACFEI, ADNUR, CAHIIM, RAD, SURGT

01 President .... Dr. Cristobal (Cris) VALDEZ
10 Vice President of Finance & Admin .... Mr. Greg E. FLORIAN
05 Vice Pres Academic Services .... Dr. Denise CREWS
32 Vice Pres of Student Success .... Mr. Marcus BROWN
103 VP Econ Dev/Innov Wkfce Solutions .... Dr. Douglas BRAUER
106 Director Online Learning .... Mrs. Kona JONES
30 Exec Director Foundation & Devel .... Vacant
29 Dir Scholarships/Alumni Development .... Mrs. Tricia CORDULACK
26 Exec Dir Public Info/Chief of Staff .... Ms. Lisa GREGORY
07 Dean Enrollment Services .... Mr. Marcus BROWN
06 Director Advising & Registrar .... Mr. Richard KERR
35 Director Student Success .... Ms. Kathryn MAST
38 Director Student Development .... Mrs. Deborah MCGEE
36 Director Career Services .... Mr. Michael DIGGS
15 Director Human Resources .... Mr. Richard GSCHWEND
37 Asst Dir Financial Aid/Veteran Affs .... Ms. Jody BURTNETT
81 Dean of Math & Sciences .... Dr. Andy HYNDS
72 Dean of Business & Technology .... Dr. Jack ADWELL
51 Dean Continuing & Prof Educ Div .... Mrs. Darbe BRINKOETTER
57 Int Dean Comm/Fine Arts/Educ/Hum .... Dr. John CORDULACK
76 Dean of Health Professions .... Ms. Ellen COLBECK

Robert Morris University - Illinois (D)

401 South State Street, Chicago IL 60605-1225
County: Cook FICE Identification: 001746
Unit ID: 148335
Telephone: (312) 935-6800 Carnegie Class: Masters/L
FAX Number: (312) 935-6660 Calendar System: Other
URL: www.robertmorris.edu
Established: 1913 Annual Undergrad Tuition & Fees: $25,200
Enrollment: 3,205 Coed
Affiliation or Control: Independent Non-Profit IRS Status: 501(c)3
Highest Offering: Master's
Accreditation: NH, IACBE, MAC, SURGT

00 Chancellor .... Michael P. VIOLLT
01 President .... Mablene KRUEGER
03 Executive Vice President .... Nicole CAFILLIO
10 Sr VP/Chief Financial Officer .... Arlene REGNERUS
13 VP of Information Systems .... Lisa CONTRERAS
32 VP of Student Affairs .... Angela JORDAN
37 VP of Financial Services .... Leigh BRINSON
41 VP of Extracurricular Activities .... Megan SMITH-EGGERT
15 VP of Human Resources .... Ann BRESINGHAM
21 Controller .... Melanie CARLIN
05 VP of Academic Administration .... Kathleen SUHAJDA
88 VP of Brand and Image/Advancement .... Christine FISHER
26 VP of Marketing & Recruitment .... Danielle NAFFZIGER
109 VP of Auxiliary Operations .... Nick JARMUZ
66 Dean College of Nurs & Health Stds .... Lora TIMMONS
106 Dean of Experiential Technology .... Deanna HO
97 Dean of College of Liberal Arts .... Jill MCCINTY
72 Dean of Inst of Technology & Media .... Basim KHARTABIL
06 Dean of Student Information .... Stella MACH
49 Dean of Professional Arts .... Shelley LAMANTIA-WRIGHT
50 Dean of Business Administration .... Larry NIEMAN
58 Dean of Morris Grad School of Mgmt .... Kayed AKKAWI
88 Dean of Academics MGSM .... Diane ALLEN
07 Dean of Admissions .... Betsy VANHOFF
88 Dean of FP & Scholarship Int .... Caitlin LEEDS
107 Dean for Academic Initiatives .... Paula DIAZ
19 Director Security/Safety .... Paul HUERTA
11 Director of Administration .... Michelle HAYES
40 Director of Bookstore Operations .... Julie MELLER
88 Dir of Graduate Relations .... Anastasios GOULOS
102 Dir of Corporate Advancement .... Michelle CASINI
102 Dir of Corporate Relations .... Elizabeth O'LEARY
53 Director of Education .... Kimberly WARFORD
53 Director of Education .... Jane WENDORFF-CRAPS
39 Dir of Student Life and Housing .... Janely RIVERA
08 Institutional Library Director .... Sue DUTLER
18 Institutional Operations Director .... Nino RANDAZZO
14 Director of Networking Services .... Adrian CEPEDA
27 Director of Public Relations .... Nancy DONOHOE
88 Dir of Admissions Info Systems .... Damaris RIVERA
91 Director of Data Administration .... Deana MUNOZ
88 Sr Dir of Academic Administration .... Kathleen VIOLLT
35 Dir of Student Support Services .... Angelica CASTANDEA
88 Director of Grant Advancement .... Lauren MILLER
88 Dir of Upward Bound and ETS .... Carolyn BASLEY
90 Director of Academic Programming .... Carmen CUEVAS

Rock Valley College (E)

3301 N Mulford Road, Rockford IL 61114-5699
County: Winnebago FICE Identification: 001747
Unit ID: 148380
Telephone: (815) 921-7821 Carnegie Class: Assoc/MT-VT-High Non
FAX Number: N/A Calendar System: Semester
URL: www.rockvalleycollege.edu
Established: 1964 Annual Undergrad Tuition & Fees (In-District): $3,044
Enrollment: 7,737 Coed
Affiliation or Control: Local IRS Status: 501(c)3
Highest Offering: Associate Degree
Accreditation: NH, COARC, DH, SURGT

01 President .... Mr. Michael MASTROIANNI
05 Provost/Chief Academic Officer .... Vacant
11 Vice Pres Administrative Services .... Mr. Christopher BLACK, JR.
32 Interim Dean of Students .... Mr. Rick DANIELS
51 VP Career & Technical Education .... Mr. Ronald GEARY
15 Vice President of Human Resources .... Ms. Jessica JONES
09 VP Institutional Effectiveness .... Dr. Lisa MEHLIG
30 VP/Chief Development Officer .... Ms. Susan GLENN
84 AVP Enrollment Management/Retention .... Mr. Howard SPEARMAN
13 Chief Information Officer .... Ms. Diann JABUSCH
18 Director Facilities Planning & POM .... Vacant
26 Exec Dir Col Comm/Marketing .... Vacant
88 Director Theatre & Arts Park .... Mr. Michael WEBB
19 Director Public Safety .... Mr. Joe DROUGHT
06 Registrar/Director Records/Rgstn .... Mr. Brooke JOHNSON
36 Manager Career Svcs/Placement .... Ms. Kelly COOPER
04 Assistant to the President .... Ms. Ann KERWITZ
41 Athletic Director .... Ms. Misty OPAT

Rockford Career College (F)

1130 S. Alpine Road, Suite 100, Rockford IL 61108
County: Winnebago FICE Identification: 008545
Unit ID: 148399
Telephone: (815) 965-8616 Carnegie Class: Assoc/HVT-High Non
FAX Number: (815) 965-0360 Calendar System: Quarter
URL: www.rockfordcareercollege.edu
Established: 1862 Annual Undergrad Tuition & Fees: $11,684
Enrollment: 434 Coed
Affiliation or Control: Proprietary IRS Status: Proprietary
Highest Offering: Associate Degree
Accreditation: ACICS, MAC

01 President/CEO .... Mr. Stephen TAVE
10 Vice President/Dir of Finance .... Mr. Guary BERNADELLE
05 Academic Dean .... Mr. Tom LEU
12 Campus President .... Mr. Mick O'HERRON
32 Student Services Director .... Ms. Danielle HARRIOTT
06 Registrar/Director of Compliance .... Ms. Christine LOTT
07 Director of Admissions .... Mr. Kevin PARTELOW
15 Director of Human Resources .... Mr. Kent SHEPLER
36 Director Career Services .... Ms. Ann STITES
37 Director of Financial Aid .... Mr. La'Zarvius FERGUSON
26 Director of College Relations .... Mr. Jeff SWANBERG
27 Marketing Coordinator .... Mr. Dusten CARLSON

Rockford University (G)

5050 E State Street, Rockford IL 61108-2393
County: Winnebago FICE Identification: 001748
Unit ID: 148405
Telephone: (815) 226-4000 Carnegie Class: Masters/S
FAX Number: (815) 226-4119 Calendar System: Semester
URL: www.rockford.edu
Established: 1847 Annual Undergrad Tuition & Fees: $28,330
Enrollment: 1,277 Coed
Affiliation or Control: Independent Non-Profit IRS Status: 501(c)3
Highest Offering: Master's
Accreditation: NH, IACBE, NUR

01 President .... Dr. Eric W. FULCOMER
05 VP of Academic Affairs/Provost .... Dr. Belinda WHOLEBEN
30 VP for Institutional Advancement .... Mr. Bernard SUNDSTEDT
88 Senior Development Officer .... Mr. John MCNAMARA
10 Sr VP for Business/Operations/CFO .... Ms. Christina ANDERSON
21 Business Office Accounting Manager .... Mr. Justin KRUEGER
84 Int VP Enrollment Management .... Mr. Matthew PHILLIPS
07 Assoc VP Undergraduate Admission .. Ms. Jennifer NORDSTROM
37 Assistant VP for SAS .... Mr. Todd FISCHER-FREE
11 Associate Vice President Operations .... Vacant
13 Director of Information Technology .... Mr. Ryan CUSHING
32 Dean of Students .... Ms. Lisa HETZEL
58 Director of MBA .... Mr. Jeffrey FAHRENWALD
58 Director of MAT .... Vacant
06 Registrar .... Ms. Anna J. JATTKOWSKI-HUDSON
04 Exec Assistant to the President .... Ms. Brenda PERRONE
04 Special Assistant to the President .... Ms. Teddy PHILLIPS
41 Athletic Director .... Mrs. Kristyn KING
15 Director of Human Resources .... Ms. Monique LINDSTEDT
36 Director Career Services .... Mr. Maurice WEST, II
26 Director of Communications .... Ms. Rita ELLIOTT
09 Coordinator of IR .... Mr. Todd FISCHER-FREE
88 Director of Global Affairs .... Mr. Sam BANDY
38 Director Counseling .... Mrs. Sallyann ROBERTS
23 Director Health Services .... Mrs. Cecelia M. BRISTOL
18 Director Facilities/Custodial Svcs .... Mr. Matthew MCGAUGHEY
19 Director Campus Safety & Security .... Mr. Jeffrey SCHELLING
08 Head Librarian .... Ms. Kelly JAMES

Roosevelt University (H)

430 S Michigan Avenue, Chicago IL 60605-1394
County: Cook FICE Identification: 001749
Unit ID: 148487
Telephone: (312) 341-3500 Carnegie Class: Masters/L
FAX Number: (312) 341-3655 Calendar System: Semester
URL: www.roosevelt.edu
Established: 1945 Annual Undergrad Tuition & Fees: $27,300
Enrollment: 6,069 Coed
Affiliation or Control: Independent Non-Profit IRS Status: 501(c)3
Highest Offering: Doctorate
Accreditation: NH, ACBSP, CACREP, CLPSY, MUS, PHAR, TED

01 President .... Dr. Ali MALEKZADEH
05 Exec Vice President/Univ Provost .... Dr. Lois BECKER
20 Vice Provost Academic Affairs .... Dr. Samuel ROSENBERG
10 Interim Sr VP of Fin/Admin and CFO .... Ms. Tangella MADDOX
84 VP Enrollment Mgmt .... Mr. Paul MCGUINNESS
100 Chief of Staff & Asst Secy to BOT .... Mr. Michael FORD
30 VP Inst Advancement .... Mr. Don JONES
29 Asst VP Alumni Relations/Campaigns .... Ms. Janice PARKIN
26 Asst VP Public Relations .... Mr. Thomas R. KAROW
32 Int AVP Stdnt Affairs/Dean Students .... Ms. Sharron EVANS
09 Assoc Provost Inst Research .... Mr. Joseph P. REGAN
21 Associate VP Finance .... Vacant
18 Assoc VP Campus Planning & Op .... Mr. Steven A. HOSELTON
88 Asst Provost Adult & Exp Learning .... Ms. Laurie CASHMAN
85 Asst Dir of International Programs .... Ms. Dawn HOUGLAND
13 Chief Information Officer .... Mr. Neeraj KUMAR
58 Assoc Provost Research & Grad Stds .... Dr. Kimberly N. RUFFIN
49 Dean College Arts & Sciences .... Dr. Bonnie GUNZENHAUSER
50 Dean College Business Admin .... Dr. Joe CHAN
64 Dean College of Performing Arts .... Mr. Henry FOGEL
107 Dean College of Professional Stds .... Dr. Deb ORR
53 Dean College of Education .... Dr. Thomas PHILION
67 Interim Dean College of Pharmacy .... Dr. Melissa HOGAN
88 Exec Dir of Auditorium Theatre/ CEO .... Ms. Tania CASTROVERDE MOSKOLENKO
08 Head Pub Svcs/Dir Rob Lib .... Ms. Linda WILKINSON
06 University Registrar .... Ms. Lakisha YOUNG
38 Director Counseling Center .... Dr. Mary GRIGAR
36 Director Career & Prof Development .... Ms. Jennifer WONDERLY
04 Senior Exec Asst to President .... Ms. Christine SPENCER
19 Director Security/Safety .... Ms. Maureen FRONCEK
41 Assoc VP Enroll Mgmt .... Mr. Michael CASSIDY
07 Director of Admissions .... Mr. Al NUNEZ
105 Senior Web Developer .... Ms. Vickie BERTINI
96 Director of Purchasing .... Mr. Calvin LYONS

Roosevelt University Albert A. Robin Campus (I)

1400 N Roosevelt Boulevard, Schaumburg IL 60173
Telephone: (847) 619-7300 Identification: 770092

Accreditation: &NH

† Regional accreditation is carried under the parent institution in Chicago, IL

Rosalind Franklin University of Medicine & Science (A)

3333 Green Bay Road, North Chicago IL 60064-3095
County: Lake FICE Identification: 001659
Unit ID: 145558
Telephone: (847) 578-3000 Carnegie Class: Spec-4-yr-Med
FAX Number: (847) 578-3401 Calendar System: Quarter
URL: www.rosalindfranklin.edu
Established: 1912 Annual Undergrad Tuition & Fees: N/A
Enrollment: 2,191 Coed
Affiliation or Control: Independent Non-Profit IRS Status: 501(c)3
Highest Offering: Doctorate; No Lower Division
Accreditation: NH, ANEST, ARCPA, CLPSY, MED, PA, PHAR, POD, PTA

01 President/CEO ... Dr. Michael WELCH
05 Provost ... Dr. Wendy RHEAULT
10 VP Finance & Admin ... John NYLEN
67 Dean Col of Pharmacy ... Dr. Marc ABEL
107 Dean College Health Professions ... Dr. James CARLSON
58 Dean Sch Grad PostDoc Stds ... Dr. Joseph X. DIMARIO
63 Dean Medical School ... Dr. James RECORD
63 Dean Scholl Col Podiatric Med ... Dr. Nancy L. PARSLEY
46 Exec VP Research ... Dr. Ronald S. KAPLAN
26 VP Marketing/Brand Management ... Ms. Lee CONCHA
32 VP Student Affairs & Inclusion ... Ms. Rebecca DURKIN
17 Assoc Prov/Clinical Partnerships ... Dr. Sandra LARSON
13 Chief Information Officer ... Mr. Richard LOESCH
43 Chief Compliance Officer ... Mr. Bret MOBERG
84 VP Strategic Enrollment Management ... Dr. Bruce C. NEIMEYER
30 VP Institutional Advancement ... Mr. Chad RUBACK
20 VP Academic/Faculty Affairs ... Dr. Judith STOECKER
37 AVP Student Financial Services ... Ms. Maryann DECAIRE
106 AVP Online Learning/Instruct Design ... Ms. Marilyn HANSON
108 AVP Accreditation/Assessment ... Dr. Glenda GALLISATH
88 AVP Faculty Development ... Dr. Rea KATZ
29 Exec Dir Alumni Relations ... Ms. Martha KELLY BATES
35 Exec Dir Campus Life ... Ms. Shelly BRZYCKI
21 Controller ... Mr. Thomas J. BUNS
100 Dir Office of the President ... Ms. Donna AGNEW
19 Dir Campus Security ... Mr. Gordon BLANCHARD
96 Dir Materials Management ... Mr. Vince BUTERA
06 Registrar ... Mr. Timothy CARROLL
28 Dir Training/Educational Programs ... Dr. Monica CUMMINGS
25 Dir Sponsored Research ... Ms. Dora ESPINOZA
09 Dir Institutional Research ... Ms. Renee FRANCISCO
88 Dir Academic Support ... Ms. Elizabeth FRIEDMAN
18 Dir Facilities Management ... Mr. Robert D. JACKSON
15 Dir of Human Resources ... Ms. Sally J. MADDEN
44 Dir Annual Giving ... Mr. Mark RUSSELL
102 Dir Foundation & Grant Relations ... Ms. Shella BLUE
07 Dir Admissions/Enrollment ... Ms. Tonishea TERRY-JACKSON
39 Coordinator for Residence Life ... Ms. Amber WOYAK
04 Executive Administrative Assistant ... Ms. Jean MINA

Rush University (B)

600 S Paulina, Chicago IL 60612-3832
County: Cook FICE Identification: 009800
Unit ID: 148511
Telephone: (312) 942-7100 Carnegie Class: Spec-4-yr-Med
FAX Number: (312) 942-2219 Calendar System: Quarter
URL: www.rushu.rush.edu
Established: 1971 Annual Undergrad Tuition & Fees: N/A
Enrollment: 2,457 Coed
Affiliation or Control: Independent Non-Profit IRS Status: 501(c)3
Highest Offering: Doctorate
Accreditation: NH, ANEST, ARCPA, AUD, BBT, COARC, DIETI, DMS, HSA, IPSY, MED, MT, NURSE, OT, PAST, PERF, SP

01 CEO RUMC & Pres Rush University ... Dr. Larry J. GOODMAN
17 President & COO RUMC ... Mr. Michael DANDORPH
05 Provost ... Dr. Thomas A. DEUTSCH
26 Vice Pres Corp/External Affairs ... Mr. Terry PETERSON
10 Senior Vice President Finance ... Mr. John MORDACH
30 Senior Vice President Philanthropy ... Ms. Diane M. MCKEEVER
13 Sr Vice Pres/Chief Information Ofcr ... Vacant
43 Vice President Legal Affairs ... Mr. Carl BERGETZ
15 Sr Vice President Human Resource ... Ms. Mary E. SCHOPP
25 Vice Pres Chief Compliance Office ... Dr. Cynthia E. BOYD
22 Dir Student Diversity & Multicultu ... Dr. LeManuel BITSOI
32 Assoc Provost Student Affairs ... Dr. Gayle WARD
108 Assoc Prov Inst Res/Assess/Accred ... Dr. Rosemarie SUHAYDA
76 Dean Col of Health Sciences ... Dr. Charlotte ROYEEN
58 Acting Dean Graduate College ... Dr. James L. MULSHINE
66 Dean College of Nursing ... Dr. Marquis D. FOREMAN
63 Dean Rush Medical College ... Dr. Ranga KRISHNAN
20 Sr Assoc Dean Med/Student Pgm ... Dr. Keith BOYD
27 Assoc VP Marketing & Comm ... Mr. Ryan NAGDEMAN
08 Interim Director Library ... Ms. Sandra WENNER
35 Director Student Life & Engagement ... Ms. Angela BRANSON
37 Asst Dir Student Financial Aid ... Mr. Michael BIEL
09 Director of Institutional Research ... Dr. Joshua JACOBS
38 Director Student Counsel Center ... Dr. Hilarie TEREBESSY
29 Director Alumni Relations ... Mr. Roscoe CRAMPTON
85 International Student Coordinator ... Mr. Melvin HARRIS
96 Director of Purchasing ... Mr. Michael MULROE
106 Director METC ... Mr. Frank TOMSIC
21 Manager of Financial Affairs ... Mr. Patrick MCNULTY
06 Registrar ... Ms. Brenda WEDDINGTON
102 Dir Foundation/Corporate Relations ... Ms. Sophia WOROBEC
105 Assoc VP IS Clinical Systems ... Mr. Steven P. WIGHTKIN
19 Director Security Services ... Mr. Laurs FREIDENFELDS
50 Director Business ... Mr. Richard K. DAVIS
54 Director Med Ctr Engineering ... Mr. Mike WISNIEWSKI
101 Secretary of the Institution/Board ... Ms. Diane M. MCKEEVER

SAE Institute Chicago (C)

820 N. Orleans St., Ste 125, Chicago IL 60610
Telephone: (312) 300-5685 Identification: 770970
Accreditation: ACCSC, ACICS

† Branch campus of SAE Institute Nashville, Nashville, TN

Saint Anthony College of Nursing (D)

5658 E State Street, Rockford IL 61108-2425
County: Winnebago FICE Identification: 009987
Unit ID: 149028
Telephone: (815) 395-5091 Carnegie Class: Spec-4-yr-Other Health
FAX Number: (815) 395-2275 Calendar System: Semester
URL: www.sacn.edu
Established: 1915 Annual Undergrad Tuition & Fees: N/A
Enrollment: 309 Coed
Affiliation or Control: Roman Catholic IRS Status: 501(c)3
Highest Offering: Doctorate
Accreditation: NH, NURSE

01 President ... Dr. Sandie S. SOLDWISCH
66 Dean Undergraduate Affairs ... Dr. Elizabeth M. CARSON
58 Dean Graduate Affairs & Research ... Dr. Shannon K. LIZER
32 Associate Dean Support Services ... Ms. Nancy A. SANDERS
08 Library Supervisor ... Ms. Heather A. KLEPITSCH
37 Financial Aid Officer ... Ms. Serrita WOODS

St. Augustine College (E)

1333-45 W Argyle Street, Chicago IL 60640-3501
County: Cook FICE Identification: 021854
Unit ID: 148876
Telephone: (773) 878-8756 Carnegie Class: Bac/Assoc-Mixed
FAX Number: (773) 878-0937 Calendar System: Semester
URL: www.staugustine.edu
Established: 1980 Annual Undergrad Tuition & Fees: $9,840
Enrollment: 1,529 Coed
Affiliation or Control: Independent Non-Profit IRS Status: 501(c)3
Highest Offering: Baccalaureate
Accreditation: NH, COARC, SW

01 President ... Dr. Andrew C. SUND
05 Dean of Academic & Student Affairs ... Dr. Bruno BONDAVALLI
20 Dean of Instruction ... Ms. Madeline ROMAN-VARGAS
10 VP for Finance ... Ms. Saundra K. FLEMING
30 VP for Marketing/Advancement ... Mr. David CORDOVA
103 VP Institute Workforce Development ... Mr. Norman RUANO
09 VP Technology/Research & Systems ... Mr. Paul HECK
37 Director of Financial Aid ... Ms. Maria ZAMBONINO
15 Director Human Resources ... Mr. Teofilo CALERO
18 Director of Physical Facilities ... Mr. Francisco MICHEL
07 Director of Admission ... Ms. Gloria QUIROZ
12 Director West Satellite ... Ms. Carmen RIVERA
12 Director South Satellite ... Ms. Gloria QUIROZ
12 Director of Southeast Satellite ... Ms. Patricia VEGA
12 Director of Aurora Satallite ... Ms. Elizabeth CARDENAS
24 Dir of Learning Resources Center ... Ms. Elizabeth GRUBY

Saint Francis Medical Center College of Nursing (F)

511 NE Greenleaf Street, Peoria IL 61603-3783
County: Peoria FICE Identification: 006240
Unit ID: 148575
Telephone: (309) 655-2201 Carnegie Class: Spec-4-yr-Other Health
FAX Number: (309) 624-8973 Calendar System: Semester
URL: www.sfmccon.edu
Established: 1985 Annual Undergrad Tuition & Fees: N/A
Enrollment: 682 Coed
Affiliation or Control: Roman Catholic IRS Status: 501(c)3
Highest Offering: Doctorate
Accreditation: NH, NUR

01 President of the College ... Dr. Patricia A. STOCKERT
05 Dean Undergraduate Program ... Dr. Sue C. BROWN
58 Dean Graduate Program ... Dr. Kimberly A. MITCHELL
32 Asst Dean of Support Services ... Mr. Kevin N. STEPHENS
07 Director of Admissions/Registrar ... Ms. Janice E. FARQUHARSON
08 Librarian ... Mr. William KOMANECKI
38 College Counselor ... Mrs. Jennifer CARLOCK
37 Coord Student Fin/Financial Assist ... Mrs. Nancy S. PERRYMAN
10 Coord Student Finance/Accts Rec ... Ms Laura L. SIMMONS
04 Administrative Assistant ... Ms. Luann MORELOCK
108 Inst Effectiveness/Assess Specialst ... Mr Ryan A. WILLIAMS

St. John's College (G)

729 E. Carpenter Street, Springfield IL 62702-5317
County: Sangamon FICE Identification: 030980
Unit ID: 148593
Telephone: (217) 525-5628 Carnegie Class: Spec-4-yr-Other Health
FAX Number: (217) 757-6870 Calendar System: Semester
URL: www.stjohnscollegespringfield.edu
Established: 1991 Annual Undergrad Tuition & Fees: N/A
Enrollment: 119 Coed
Affiliation or Control: Independent Non-Profit IRS Status: 501(c)3
Highest Offering: Baccalaureate
Accreditation: NH, NUR

01 Chancellor ... Dr. Charlene S. AARON
05 Dean of Academic Affairs ... Dr. Jane DIERS
07 Admissions Officer/Registrar ... Ms. Britni CARUSO
30 Student Development Officer ... Ms. Holly R. BLANDFORD
51 Director of Continuing Education ... Dr. Mary Jo BROWN
37 Financial Aid Officer ... Mr. Timothy MARTEN

Saint Xavier University (H)

3700 W 103rd Street, Chicago IL 60655-3105
County: Cook FICE Identification: 001768
Unit ID: 148627
Telephone: (773) 298-3000 Carnegie Class: Masters/L
FAX Number: (773) 779-9061 Calendar System: Semester
URL: www.sxu.edu
Established: 1846 Annual Undergrad Tuition & Fees: $30,920
Enrollment: 4,073 Coed
Affiliation or Control: Roman Catholic IRS Status: 501(c)3
Highest Offering: Master's
Accreditation: NH, BUS, MUS, NURSE, SP, TED

01 President ... Ms. Christine M. WISEMAN
05 Interim Provost ... Dr. Kathleen ALAIMO
10 Vice President Business & Finance ... Mr. Robert H. FISHER
32 Vice President Student Affairs ... Mr. John P. PELRINE, JR.
09 Exec Dir Institutional Research ... Dr. Kathleen CARLSON
35 Asst Vice Pres Student Affairs ... Ms. Carrie SCHADE
18 Director of Facilities Management ... Mr. Peter SKACH
20 Associate Provost ... Dr. Richard VENNERI
20 Asst Provost/Director Retention ... Ms. Maureen WOGAN
35 Dean of Students ... Dr. Eileen DOHERTY
109 Director Auxiliary Services ... Ms. Linda MORENO
37 Director Financial Aid ... Ms. Susan SWISHER
21 Controller ... Ms. Diane STALLMANN
43 General Counsel ... Ms. Kathleen A. RINEHART
07 Director of Admission ... Mr. Brian HOTZFIELD
26 Executive Director Media Relation ... Ms. Karla THOMAS
24 Director CIDAT ... Mr. Christopher ZAKREWSKI
08 Director Library ... Mr. David STERN
06 Director Records/Registration Svcs ... Ms. Barbara SUTTON
19 Dir Public Safety/Chief of Police ... Mr. Jack TOUHY
41 Director Athletics ... Mr. Robert HALLBERG
42 VP University Mission & Ministry ... Mr. Graziano MARCHESCHI
85 Dir Center International Education ... Ms. Kelly REIDY-FOX
36 Director of Career Services ... Ms. Jean RIORDAN
49 Dean College Arts/Sciences ... Dr. Kathleen ALAIMO
53 Dean School of Education ... Dr. Suzanne LEE
50 Dean Graham School of Management ... Dr. Asghar SABBAGHI
66 Dean School of Nursing ... Dr. Gloria JACOBSON
04 Executive Assistant to President ... Ms. Gail B. YOUNG

Saint Xavier University Orland Park Campus (I)

18230 Orland Parkway, Orland Park IL 60467
Telephone: (708) 802-6200 Identification: 770093
Accreditation: &NH

† Regional accreditation is carried under the parent institution in Chicago, IL

Sanford-Brown College (J)

1 N State Street, Suite 500, Chicago IL 60602-9736
County: Cook FICE Identification: 021603
Unit ID: 146010
Telephone: (312) 980-9200 Carnegie Class: Spec-4-yr-Arts
FAX Number: (312) 541-3929 Calendar System: Quarter
URL: www.sanfordbrown.edu
Established: 1977 Annual Undergrad Tuition & Fees: N/A
Enrollment: 229 Coed
Affiliation or Control: Proprietary IRS Status: Proprietary
Highest Offering: Baccalaureate
Accreditation: ACICS

01 President ... Mr. Anthony WILLIAMS
05 Campus Director of Education ... Mr. Michael GORMAN
08 Regional Director Library Services ... Ms. Amanda HENDERSON
36 Director of Career Services ... Mr. Elliott REASONER
10 Business Operations Manager ... Mr. Willis JORDAN

† School is in teach-out plan through November 2017.

Sauk Valley Community College (K)

173 Illinois Route 2, Dixon IL 61021-9188
County: Lee FICE Identification: 001752
Unit ID: 148672
Telephone: (815) 288-5511 Carnegie Class: Assoc/HVT-High Non
FAX Number: (815) 288-1880 Calendar System: Semester
URL: www.svcc.edu
Established: 1965 Annual Undergrad Tuition & Fees (In-District): $3,258
Enrollment: 2,211 Coed
Affiliation or Control: State/Local IRS Status: 501(c)3
Highest Offering: Associate Degree
Accreditation: NH, RAD

01 President ....Dr. David M. HELLMICH
05 Vice Pres Academics/Student Svcs ....Mr. Jon D. MANDRELL
09 Vice Pres Research Plng/Info Affs ....Mr. Steve C. NUNEZ
76 Dean Health Professions ....Ms. Janet L. LYNCH
10 Dean of Business Services ....Ms. Melissa DYE
18 Director Facilities ....Mr. Frank J. MURPHY
15 Director of Human Resources ....Ms. Kathryn C. SNOW
84 Director Enrollment Mgmt/Registrar ....Ms. Pamela S. MEDEMA
102 Foundation Manager ....Ms. Sharri K. MILLER
13 Dean of Information Services ....Ms. Chris A. SHELLEY
41 Director of Athletics ....Mr. Russ K. DAMHOFF
37 Director of Financial Assistance ....Ms. Jennifer A. SCHULTZ
91 Instructional Technology Sppt Spec ....Ms. Kathleen M. DIRKS

School of the Art Institute of Chicago (A)

37 S Wabash, Chicago IL 60603-3103
County: Cook FICE Identification: 001753
Unit ID: 143048
Telephone: (312) 899-5100 Carnegie Class: Spec-4-yr-Arts
FAX Number: (312) 263-0141 Calendar System: Semester
URL: www.saic.edu
Established: 1866 Annual Undergrad Tuition & Fees: $43,960
Enrollment: 3,599 Coed
Affiliation or Control: Independent Non-Profit IRS Status: 501(c)3
Highest Offering: Master's
Accreditation: NH, ART

01 President ....Dr. Elissa TENNY
05 Provost ....Mr. Craig BARTON
84 Vice Pres Enrollment Management ....Ms. Rose MILKOWSKI
30 VP for Institutional Advancement ....Ms. Cheryl JESSOGNE
10 Vice Pres Finance & Administration ....Mr. Brian ESKER
15 Vice President for Human Resources ....Mr. Michael NICOLAI
32 Vice Pres/Dean of Student Affairs ....Dr. Felice DUBLON
20 Vice Provost ....Mr. Paul COFFEY
18 Vice Pres Campus Operations ....Mr. Thomas BUECHELE
20 Dean of Faculty/VP Acad Affs ....Ms. Lisa WAINWRIGHT
35 Dean of Student Life ....Ms. Deborah MARTIN
21 Exec Dir Academic Accounting ....Ms. Sherry MISGEN
26 Exec Dir Enroll Mktg & Operations ....Ms. Maryann SCHAEFER
29 Assoc Director Alumni Relations ....Vacant
38 Exec Director Wellness Center ....Dr. Joseph BEHEN
84 Exec Director Enrollment Services ....Ms. Jane BRUMITT
06 Director Registration & Records ....Mr. Brad ERZ
08 Exec Director of School Library ....Ms. Claire EIKE
36 Dean Career & Prof Experience ....Dr. Terri LONIER
07 Director of Undergrad Admissions ....Ms. Asia MITCHELL
07 Director of Graduate Admissions ....Ms. Nicole HALL
37 Director of Student Financial Svcs ....Mr. Patrick JAMES
28 Director of Multicultural Affairs ....Ms. Rashayla BROWN
88 Director of Learning Center ....Ms. Valerie ST. GERMAIN
49 Dean of Undergraduate Studies ....Ms. Tiffany HOLMES
58 Dean of Graduate Studies ....Mr. Arnold KEMP
28 Dir of Acad Affairs/Diversity/Incl ....Dr. Christina GOMEZ

Shawnee Community College (B)

8364 Shawnee College Road, Ullin IL 62992-2206
County: Pulaski FICE Identification: 007693
Unit ID: 148821
Telephone: (618) 634-3200 Carnegie Class: Assoc/MT-VT-High Non
FAX Number: (618) 634-3300 Calendar System: Semester
URL: www.shawneecc.edu
Established: 1967 Annual Undergrad Tuition & Fees (In-District): $3,264
Enrollment: 1,799 Coed
Affiliation or Control: Local IRS Status: 501(c)3
Highest Offering: Associate Degree
Accreditation: NH, CAHIIM, MLTAD, OTA, SURGT

01 President ....Dr. Tim BELLAMEY
05 Vice Pres Instructional Services ....Dr. Vickie ARTMAN
32 Vice President Student Svcs ....Ms. Jipaum ASKEW-ROBINSON
04 Asst to President ....Ms. Becky CASPER LYNN
20 Dean Instructional Services ....Ms. Gabriele FARNER
51 Dean Adult Educ/Alternative Instruc ....Vacant
10 Chief Financial Officer ....Ms. Tiffiney RYAN
38 Student Support Services Director ....Ms. Amber SUGGS
35 Dean of Student Services ....Ms. Dee BLAKELY
37 Dir Fin Aid/Coord Vet & Mil Personl ....Dr. Tammy CAPPS
41 Athletic Director ....Mr. John SPARKS
13 Director MIS ....Mr. Chris CLARK
12 Director Metro Center ....Ms. Faye JOYNER-KEENE
66 Director of Nursing ....Ms. Denise GRIFFITH
08 Head Librarian ....Ms. Tracey JOHNSON
06 Registrar ....Ms. Danielle BOYD
102 Dir Resource Development/Foundation ....Vacant
21 Director of Business Services ....Ms. Brandy WOODS
18 Facilities Director ....Mr. Don KOCH
09 Director of Institutional Research ....Mr. Chris BARR
40 Bookstore Manager ....Ms. Erica POAT
88 Special Needs Counselor ....Ms. Lee Ann GEORGE
88 Coord Ctr for Cmty/Economic Devel ....Ms. Candy EASTWOOD
26 Public Relations Coordinator ....Ms. Katelynn ARMSTRONG
36 Career Services Coordinator ....Ms. Leslie WELDON
50 Div Chair Business/Occup/Tech Dp ....Ms. Ruth SMITH
81 Division Chair Math/Science ....Ms. Rhonda DILLOW
79 Div Chr Social Stds/Humanities/Comm ....Ms. Sharon WALKER
76 Div Chair Allied Health ....Ms. Tracy LOHSTROH
15 Human Resources Director ....Ms. Emily FORTHMAN

Shimer College (C)

3424 S State Street, Second Floor,
Chicago IL 60616-3893
County: Cook FICE Identification: 001756
Unit ID: 148849
Telephone: (312) 235-3500 Carnegie Class: Bac-A&S
FAX Number: (312) 235-3502 Calendar System: Semester
URL: www.shimer.edu
Established: 1853 Annual Undergrad Tuition & Fees: $34,004
Enrollment: 74 Coed
Affiliation or Control: Independent Non-Profit IRS Status: 501(c)3
Highest Offering: Baccalaureate
Accreditation: NH

01 President ....Dr. Susan HENKING
11 Chief Operating Officer ....Mr. James ULRICH
05 Dean of the College ....Dr. Harold STONE
32 Director of Student Life ....Ms. Samantha BENNETT
30 Director of Development ....Vacant
37 Director of Financial Aid ....Ms. Janet HENTHORN
84 Dean of Enrollment Management ....Mr. Adam ASHER
10 Chief Financial Officer ....Ms. Phyllis DOBBS
06 Registrar ....Mr. James ULRICH
26 Director of Communications ....Ms. Alex ROSENBERG

SOLEX College (D)

350 East Dundee Road, Wheeling IL 60090
County: Cook FICE Identification: 045816
Unit ID: 459356
Telephone: (847) 229-9595 Carnegie Class: Spec 2-yr-Other
FAX Number: (847) 229-1919 Calendar System: Other
URL: www.solex.edu
Established: 1995 Annual Undergrad Tuition & Fees: N/A
Enrollment: 91 Coed
Affiliation or Control: Proprietary IRS Status: Proprietary
Highest Offering: Associate Degree
Accreditation: ACICS, COMTA, PTAA

01 Executive Director ....Mr. Leon E. LINTON

South Suburban College of Cook County (E)

15800 S State Street, South Holland IL 60473-1270
County: Cook FICE Identification: 001769
Unit ID: 149365
Telephone: (708) 596-2000 Carnegie Class: Assoc/MT-VT-High Non
FAX Number: (708) 210-5710 Calendar System: Semester
URL: www.ssc.edu
Established: 1927 Annual Undergrad Tuition & Fees (In-District): $4,583
Enrollment: 4,329 Coed
Affiliation or Control: State/Local IRS Status: 501(c)3
Highest Offering: Associate Degree
Accreditation: NH, OTA, PHLEB

01 College President ....Mr. Don MANNING
05 Vice President Academic Services ....Dr. Linda STOKES-WILSON
11 Vice Pres Administration ....Mr. Martin LAREAU
32 Vice President Student Development ....Ms. Songie ADEBIYI
84 VP Enrollment/Community Education ....Mrs. Jane Ellen STOCKER
35 Dean Student Services ....Ms. Patrice BURTON
20 AVP Academic Svcs/Instl Effect ....Mr. Ronald KAWANNA, JR.
50 Dean Business & Technology ....Mr. James COATES
76 Dean Allied Health/Career Programs ....Mr. Jeff WADDY
57 Dean Fine Arts/Soc & Behav Sci/Bus ....Mr. Tom GOVAN, JR.
66 Dean Nursing/Fine Arts/English/Hum ....Ms. Miriam ANTHONY
51 Director Continuing Education ....Ms. Shirley DREWENSKI
10 Treasurer/Controller ....Mr. Tim POLLERT
26 Director Public Rels/Pub & Found ....Mr. Patrick RUSH
13 Director Information Technology ....Mr. John SPEHAR
88 Dir New Student Ctr & Retenion Svcs ....Mrs. Jazaer FARRAR
84 Director Enrollment Services ....Mrs. Robin RIHACEK
37 Director of Financial Aid ....Mr. John SEMPLE
18 Director Physical Plant Services ....Mr. Justin PAPP
24 Dir Communication Svcs/Media Design ....Mrs. Lisa MILLER
41 Athletic Director ....Mr. Steve RUZICH
09 Director of Institutional Research ....Mr. Kevin RIORDAN
15 Director Human Resources ....Ms. Kimberly PIGATTI
06 Manager for Registration/Records ....Ms. Tenial WHITTED
07 Mgr of Admissions/Recruitment ....Ms. Tiffane JONES

South Suburban College of Cook County University and College Center (F)

16333 Kilbourne Avenue, Oak Forest IL 60452
Telephone: (708) 225-6029 Identification: 770094
Accreditation: &NH

† Regional accreditation is carried under the parent institution in South Holland, IL

Southeastern Illinois College (G)

3575 College Road, Harrisburg IL 62946-4925
County: Saline FICE Identification: 001757
Unit ID: 148937
Telephone: (618) 252-5400 Carnegie Class: Assoc/MT-VT-High Non
FAX Number: (618) 252-3156 Calendar System: Semester
URL: www.sic.edu
Established: 1960 Annual Undergrad Tuition & Fees (In-District): $3,120
Enrollment: 1,834 Coed
Affiliation or Control: State/Local IRS Status: 501(c)3
Highest Offering: Associate Degree
Accreditation: NH, MLTAD, OTA, SURGT

01 President ....Dr. Jonah RICE
05 Vice President Instruction ....Dr. Karen WEISS
10 Dean Administration/Business Affs ....Mr. David WRIGHT
32 Dean Student Servicess/Enrollment ....Mr. Chad FLANNERY
103 Assoc Dean Workforce & Cmty Educ ....Mrs. Lori COX
08 Librarian/LRC Director ....Mr. Gary JONES
84 Director Enrollment Services ....Ms. Kyla BURFORD
26 Marketing Coordinator ....Ms. Angela WILSON
37 Financial Aid Director ....Ms. Emily HENSON
13 Chief Information Officer ....Mr. Greg MCCULLOCH
76 Director Allied Health & Nursing ....Ms. Amy MURPHY
15 Exec Asst to Pres/Human Res Mgr ....Mrs. Barbara POTTER
06 Registrar ....Ms. Kyla BURFORD
18 Director of Environmental Services ....Mr. Ed FITZGERALD

*Southern Illinois University System (H)

Stone Center - 1400 Douglas Drive, Carbondale IL 62901
County: Jackson FICE Identification: 008237
Unit ID: 149240
Telephone: (618) 536-3331 Carnegie Class: N/A
FAX Number: (618) 536-3404
URL: www.siusystem.edu

01 President ....Dr. Randy J. DUNN
05 Interim VP Academic Affairs ....Dr. James ALLEN
10 Sr VP Financial/Admin Affs/Bd Treas ....Dr. Duane STUCKY
88 Director Risk Management ....Ms. Chris GLIDEWELL
86 Exec Dir Governmental/Public Affs ....Mr. John CHARLES
21 Exec Dir of Internal Audits ....Ms. Kim LABONTE
43 General Counsel ....Mr. Lucas CRATER
04 Assistant to the President ....Ms. Paula S. KEITH

*Southern Illinois University Carbondale (I)

1265 Lincoln Drive, Carbondale IL 62901-6899
County: Jackson FICE Identification: 001758
Unit ID: 149222
Telephone: (618) 453-2121 Carnegie Class: DU-Higher
FAX Number: (618) 453-3250 Calendar System: Semester
URL: siu.edu
Established: 1869 Annual Undergrad Tuition & Fees (In-State): $13,137
Enrollment: 17,989 Coed
Affiliation or Control: State IRS Status: 501(c)3
Highest Offering: Doctorate
Accreditation: NH, AAB, ARCPA, ART, BUS, BUSA, CACREP, CEA, CIDA, CLPSY, COPSY, CORE, CS, DH, DIETD, DIETI, DMS, ENG, ENGT, FUSER, IFSAC, IPSY, JOUR, LAW, MED, MUS, NAIT, PH, PTAA, RAD, RADDOS, RADMAG, RTT, SP, SPAA, SW, TED, THEA

02 Interim Chancellor ....Dr. William B. COLWELL
05 Interim Provost & Vice Chancellor ....Dr. Susan FORD
32 Dean of Students ....Vacant
30 VC for Development & Alumni Rels ....Mr. Jim SALMO
10 VC for Administration and Finance ....Mr. Kevin BAME
46 Interim VC for Research ....Dr. James GARVEY
28 Associate Chancellor for Diversity ....Vacant
102 CFO SIU Foundation ....Mr. Stephen NAGLE
13 Interim Chief Info Officer ....Mr. Scott D. BRIDGES
84 Asst Provost Enrollment Mgmt ....Vacant
20 Assoc Provost for Academic Admin ....Dr. David DILALLA
20 Assoc Provost for Academic Programs ....Dr. James S. ALLEN
04 Assistant to the Chancellor ....Mr. Matthew BAUGHMAN
49 Dean Liberal Arts ....Dr. Meera KOMARRAJU
50 Dean College of Business ....Dr. Terry CLARK
53 Dean Educ & Human Services ....Dr. Matthew W. KEEFER
54 Dean Engineering ....Dr. John J. WARWICK
58 Dean Graduate School ....Dr. Yueh-Ting LEE
61 Dean School of Law ....Dr. Cynthia FOUNTAINE
81 Dean College of Science ....Dr. Laurie ACHENBACH
63 Dean School of Medicine ....Dr. Jerry E. KRUSE
47 Dean Agricultural Sciences ....Dr. Mickey A. LATOUR
72 Dean Col Applied Sciences & Arts ....Dr. JuAn WANG
57 Dean Mass Comm/Media Arts ....Dr. Dafna P. LEMISH
08 Dean Library Affairs ....Vacant
07 Director Undergrad Admissions ....Vacant
37 Director Student Financial Aid ....Ms. Terry HARFST
29 Associate VC Alumni Services ....Ms. Michelle SUAREZ
88 Interim Budget Director ....Ms. Judith MARSHALL
09 Dir Institutional Research ....Vacant
21 Executive Director for Finance ....Ms. Judith MARSHALL
26 Chief Marketing & Comm Officer ....Ms. Rae GOLDSMITH
15 Director Human Resources ....Ms. Jennifer WATSON
39 Interim Director University Housing ....Mr. Jon L. SHAFFER
36 Director Univ Career Services ....Mr. Douglas C. REICHENBERGER
85 Int Director International Educ ....Mr. Andrew CARVER
18 Director Plant/Service Operations ....Vacant
19 Director of Public Safety ....Mr. Benjamin NEWMAN
23 Director Student Health Services ....Dr. Ted W. GRACE
41 Dir Intercollegiate Athl ....Mr. Tommy BELL
106 Director Distance Education ....Dr. Mandara SAVAGE
06 Director Registrar's Office ....Ms. Tamara WORKMAN
38 Asst Dir Student Counseling Cntr ....Dr. Frank KOSMICKI
96 Int Director Procurement Services ....Ms. Debbie ABELL
35 Assoc Dean of Students ....Vacant
25 Dir Office of Sponsored Projects ....Mr. Wayne GLASS

*Southern Illinois University Edwardsville (A)

Edwardsville IL 62026
County: Madison FICE Identification: 001759
Unit ID: 149231
Telephone: (618) 650-2000 Carnegie Class: Masters/L
FAX Number: (618) 650-2270 Calendar System: Semester
URL: www.siue.edu
Established: 1957 Annual Undergrad Tuition & Fees (In-State): $10,247
Enrollment: 13,972 Coed
Affiliation or Control: State IRS Status: 501(c)3
Highest Offering: Doctorate
Accreditation: NH, ANEST, ART, BUS, BUSA, CONST, CS, DENT, ENG, EXSC, JOUR, MUS, NURSE, PHAR, SP, SPAA, SW, TED, THEA

02 Chancellor .... Dr. Randall G. PEMBROOK
05 Interim Provost & VC for Acad Affs .... Dr. P. Denise COBB
10 Interim Vice Chancellor for Admin .... Mr. Richard WALKER
30 VC Univ Adv & CEO SIUE Foundation .... Ms. Rachel C. STACK
32 Vice Chanc for Student Affairs .... Dr. Jeffrey N. WAPLE
100 Chief of Staff .... Ms. Kimberly H. DURR
22 Dir Equal Opp/Access & Title IX .... Mr. Chad MARTINEZ
20 Assoc Prov for Acad Plng & Pgm Dev .... Vacant
20 Assoc Prov Rsch/Dean Grad Sch .... Dr. Jerry B. WEINBERG
35 Assoc VC Stdnt Affs/Dean of Stdnts .... Dr. James W. KLENKE
35 Assoc VC for Student Affairs .... Ms. Lora MILES
13 Interim Assoc VC for IT & CIO .... Mr. Steven HUFFSTUTLER
28 Asc Chanc Inst Diversity/Inclusion .... Dr. Venessa BROWN
88 Asst Prov for Acad Innov & Eff .... Dr. Erin BEHNEN
41 Asst VC Athletic Dev/Dir Athletics .... Dr. Bradley L. HEWITT
84 Assoc VC for Enrollment Mgmt .... Mr. Scott BELOBRAJDIC
45 Asst VC for Planning & Budgeting .... Vacant
49 Dean College of Arts & Sciences .... Dr. Gregory BUDZBAN
50 Interim Dean School of Business .... Dr. Timothy SCHOENECKER
52 Dean Sch of Dental Medicine .... Dr. Bruce E. ROTTER
53 Dean Sch of Educ/Hlth & Human Behav .... Dr. Curt LOX
54 Dean School of Engineering .... Dr. Cem KARACAL
66 Dean School of Nursing .... Dr. Laura BERNAIX
67 Dean School of Pharmacy .... Dr. Gireesh V. GUPCHUP
62 Dean Library & Information Services .... Dr. Regina MCBRIDE
21 Budget Director .... Mr. William F. WINTER, JR.
26 Exec Dir Univ Mktg & Comm .... Mr. Doug MCILHAGGA
88 Dir Grant Funded Pgm East StL Ctr .... Mr. Jesse DIXON
88 Director Academic Advising .... Vacant
07 Director Admissions .... Mr. Todd C. BURRELL
29 Dir Constituent Rel & Special Proj .... Ms. Cathy TAYLOR
36 Director Career Dev Center .... Ms. Susan SEIBERT
38 Director Counseling Services .... Dr. James LINSIN
18 Director Facilities Management .... Mr. Paul FULIGNI
23 Director Health Service .... Ms. Riane B. GREENWALT
15 Director Human Resources .... Ms. Sherrie SENKFOR
09 Dir Institutional Rsrch & Studies .... Mr. Phillip M. BROWN
85 Exec Dir International Affairs .... Dr. Mary WEISHAAR
96 Director of Purchasing .... Ms. Nancy J. UFERT FAIRLESS
37 Dir Student Financial Aid .... Ms. Sally MULLEN
102 Dir Univ Advancement/Foundation Ops .... Mr. Kevin MARTIN
39 Director University Housing .... Mr. Michael J. SCHULTZ
19 Director University Police .... Mr. Kevin SCHMOLL
06 Registrar .... Ms. Laura A. STROM

*Southern Illinois University Carbondale School of Medicine (B)

PO Box 19620, Springfield IL 62794-9620
Telephone: (217) 545-8000 Identification: 770181
Accreditation: &NH

† Regional accreditation is carried under the parent institution in Carbondale, IL

Southwestern Illinois College (C)

2500 Carlyle Avenue, Belleville IL 62221-5899
County: Saint Clair FICE Identification: 001636
Unit ID: 143215
Telephone: (618) 235-2700 Carnegie Class: Assoc/HVT-High Non
FAX Number: (618) 277-0631 Calendar System: Semester
URL: www.swic.edu
Established: 1946 Annual Undergrad Tuition & Fees (In-District): $3,420
Enrollment: 10,545 Coed
Affiliation or Control: State/Local IRS Status: 501(c)3
Highest Offering: Associate Degree
Accreditation: NH, ACFEI, ADNUR, CAHIIM, COARC, EMT, MAC, MLTAD, PTAA, RAD

01 President - District .... Dr. Georgia COSTELLO
10 VP Administrative Svcs/Treasurer .... Mr. Bernie J. YSURSA, JR.
05 Vice Pres Instruction .... Mr. Clay L. BAITMAN
31 Vice Pres Community Svcs .... Dr. Mark P. EICHENLAUB
26 Vice Pres Mktg/Institutional Adv .... Mr. Mike R. FLEMING
15 Director Human Resources .... Ms. Sherry FAVRE
21 Controller .... Ms. Missy ROCHE
32 Vice Pres Student Development .... Ms. Staci G. CLAYBORNE
20 Assoc Dean Instructional Services .... Ms. Patricia POU
12 Executive Director SWGCC .... Ms. Nancy LEVAULT
12 Executive Director Red Bud Campus .... Mr. Mike REED
08 Dean Learning Resources .... Mrs. Laurie A. BINGEL
37 Director of Financial Aid/Placement .... Mr. Robert TEBBE
13 Chief Information Officer .... Dr. James RIHA
18 Director of Physical Plant .... Mr. Ron R. HENDERSON
19 Director of Public Safety .... Mr. Mark A. GREEN
96 Director of Purchasing .... Mr. Mike R. THOMAS
76 Dean Hlth Sci and Homeland Security .... Ms. Julie A. MUERTZ
50 Dean of Business Division .... Dr. Janet S. FONTENOT
72 Dean of Technical Education .... Mr. Brad SPARKS
81 Dean of Math & Science .... Mr. Steve L. HOLMAN
49 Dean of Liberal Arts .... Mr. Richard SPENCER
51 Director Adult Education/Cont Educ .... Dr. Lea MAUE
84 Dean of Enrollment Services .... Ms. Michelle L. BIRK
88 Dean of Success Programs .... Ms. Deborah ALFORD
88 Treasurer IL Green Economy Network .... Mr. Robert J. HILGENBRINK
06 Specialist for Registration/Records .... Ms. Debra RAHN

Southwestern Illinois College Red Bud Campus (D)

500 W South 4th Street, Red Bud IL 62278
Telephone: (618) 282-6682 Identification: 770096
Accreditation: &NH

† Regional accreditation is carried under the parent institution in Belleville, IL

Southwestern Illinois College Sam Wolf Granite City Campus (E)

4950 Maryville Road, Granite City IL 62040
Telephone: (618) 931-0600 Identification: 770095
Accreditation: &NH

† Regional accreditation is carried under the parent institution in Belleville, IL

Spertus Institute for Jewish Learning and Leadership (F)

610 S Michigan Avenue, Chicago IL 60605-1994
County: Cook FICE Identification: 001663
Unit ID: 148982
Telephone: (312) 322-1700 Carnegie Class: Spec-4-yr-Other
FAX Number: (312) 922-6406 Calendar System: Quarter
URL: www.spertus.edu
Established: 1924 Annual Graduate Tuition & Fees: N/A
Enrollment: 185 Coed
Affiliation or Control: Independent Non-Profit IRS Status: 501(c)3
Highest Offering: Doctorate; No Undergraduates
Accreditation: NH

01 President .... Dr. Hal M. LEWIS
05 Provost/Vice President .... Dr. Dean BELL
20 Assistant Dean .... Ms. Beth SCHENKER
10 Controller .... Mr. Doug PETERSON
88 Director Nonprofit Admin Program .... Dr. Karen BAIRD
37 Financial Aid Mgr .... Ms. Pamela FELTON
88 Dir Center for Jewish Leadership .... Mr. Tal ROSEN

Spoon River College (G)

23235 N County Road 22, Canton IL 61520-9801
County: Fulton FICE Identification: 001643
Unit ID: 148991
Telephone: (309) 647-4645 Carnegie Class: Assoc/MT-VT-High Non
FAX Number: (309) 649-6235 Calendar System: Semester
URL: www.src.edu
Established: 1959 Annual Undergrad Tuition & Fees (In-District): $4,200
Enrollment: 1,667 Coed
Affiliation or Control: Local IRS Status: 501(c)3
Highest Offering: Associate Degree
Accreditation: NH

01 President .... Mr. Curt OLDFIELD
05 Vice Pres Inst/Student Services .... Vacant
10 Vice Pres Administrative Services .... Mr. Brett STOLLER
04 Executive Asst to the President .... Ms. Julie HAMPTON
36 Dean Career & Technical Education .... Mr. Brad O'BRIEN
32 Dean Student Services .... Ms. Missy WILKINSON
66 Director Nursing .... Ms. Tamatha SCHLEICH
88 Dean Transfer Education .... Ms. Holly NORTON
06 Dir of Records & Admissions .... Ms. Melissa WILKINSON
18 Director Facilities .... Mr. Bob A. HAILE
55 Dir Adult and Outreach Education .... Mr. Chad MURPHY
08 Librarian .... Ms. Marla TURGEON
13 Chief Information Officer .... Mr. Raj SIDDARAJU
41 Director Athletics/Student Life .... Mr. John BASSETT
109 Director Business & Auxil Services .... Ms. Sarah GRAY
37 Director Financial Aid .... Ms. Salinda Jo BRANSON
15 Director Human Resources .... Ms. Michelle L. BUGOS
14 Director Technology Services .... Mr. Dean CLARY
84 Director Enrollment Services .... Ms. Janet MUNSON
09 Coord Institutional Reporting .... Mr. Aaron ROE
26 Director Marketing .... Ms. Sherri RADER
27 Coordinator Public Information .... Ms. Sally SHIELDS
102 Director Foundation .... Mr. Colin DAVIS
30 Director Institutional Advancement .... Vacant

Spoon River College-Macomb Campus (H)

208 S Johnston Street, Macomb IL 61455
Telephone: (309) 837-5727 Identification: 770097
Accreditation: &NH

† Regional accreditation is carried under the parent institution in Canton, IL

Taylor Business Institute (I)

318 W Adams Street, Suite 500, Chicago IL 60606
County: Cook FICE Identification: 011810
Unit ID: 149310
Telephone: (312) 658-5100 Carnegie Class: Assoc/MT-VT-High Non
FAX Number: (312) 658-0867 Calendar System: Quarter
URL: www.tbiil.edu
Established: 1962 Annual Undergrad Tuition & Fees: $14,175
Enrollment: 280 Coed
Affiliation or Control: Proprietary IRS Status: Proprietary
Highest Offering: Associate Degree
Accreditation: @NH, ACICS

01 President .... Mrs. Janice C. PARKER

Telshe Yeshiva-Chicago (J)

3535 W Foster Avenue, Chicago IL 60625-5598
County: Cook FICE Identification: 020732
Unit ID: 149329
Telephone: (773) 463-7738 Carnegie Class: Spec-4-yr-Faith
FAX Number: (773) 463-2849 Calendar System: Semester
Established: 1960 Annual Undergrad Tuition & Fees: $12,000
Enrollment: 79 Male
Affiliation or Control: Independent Non-Profit IRS Status: 501(c)3
Highest Offering: Second Talmudic Degree
Accreditation: RABN

01 President .... Rabbi Avrohom C. LEVIN
03 Executive Vice President .... Rabbi Yitzchok LEVIN
05 Vice President .... Rabbi Chaim D. KELLER
05 Vice President .... Rabbi Moshe SCHMELCZER
11 Administrative Director/Secretary .... Rabbi Shmuel ADLER

Toyota Technological Institute at Chicago (K)

6045 South Kenwood Avenue, Chicago IL 60637
County: Cook Identification: 666367
Unit ID: 445054
Telephone: (773) 834-2500 Carnegie Class: Not Classified
FAX Number: (773) 834-9881 Calendar System: Quarter
URL: www.ttic.edu
Established: 2003 Annual Graduate Tuition & Fees: N/A
Enrollment: N/A Coed
Affiliation or Control: Independent Non-Profit IRS Status: 501(c)3
Highest Offering: Doctorate; No Undergraduates
Accreditation: NH

01 President .... Dr. Sadaoki FURUI
05 Chief Academic Officer .... Dr. David MCALLESTER
10 Chief Financial Officer .... Ms. Jessica JOHNSTON
58 Admin Director of Graduate Studies .... Ms. Christina NOVAK

Tribeca Flashpoint Media Arts Academy (L)

28 North Clark Street, Suite 500, Chicago IL 60602
County: Cook Identification: 667083
Unit ID: 460747
Telephone: (312) 487-4743 Carnegie Class: Bac/Assoc-Assoc Dom
FAX Number: (312) 506-0708 Calendar System: Semester
URL: www.tribecaflashpoint.edu
Established: 2007 Annual Undergrad Tuition & Fees: $25,665
Enrollment: 353 Coed
Affiliation or Control: Proprietary IRS Status: Proprietary
Highest Offering: Baccalaureate
Accreditation: ACICS

01 President .... Bill VAN HUIS
05 Exec VP/Dean Academic Affairs .... Peter HAWLEY
10 Exec VP/Chief Financial Officer .... Erik PARKS
32 Vice President Student Affairs .... Kelly PARKER
30 VP Strategy/Development .... Kyle O'MEARA
26 Chief Marketing Officer .... Cheni VEGA
106 Director Online Education .... David DUNWORTH

Trinity Christian College (M)

6601 W College Drive, Palos Heights IL 60463-0929
County: Cook FICE Identification: 001771
Unit ID: 149505
Telephone: (708) 597-3000 Carnegie Class: Bac-Diverse
FAX Number: (708) 385-5665 Calendar System: 4/1/4
URL: www.trnty.edu
Established: 1959 Annual Undergrad Tuition & Fees: $26,665
Enrollment: 1,406 Coed
Affiliation or Control: Independent Non-Profit IRS Status: 501(c)3
Highest Offering: Master's
Accreditation: NH, ACBSP, NURSE, SW

01 President .... Mr. Kurt D. DYKSTRA
05 Provost .... Dr. Aaron KUECKER
10 Vice Pres for Finance & Admin .... Mr. James E. BELSTRA
32 Vice Pres for Student Life .... Mrs. Rebekah L. STARKENBURG
30 Vice Pres for Advancement .... Vacant
08 Director of Library Services .... Mrs. Cathy MAYER
06 Registrar .... Ms. Jaynn TOBIAS-JOHNSON

07 Vice Pres for Enrollment .... Mr. Rick RIDDERING
36 Director of Vocation and Career Dev .... Mr. Jeff TIMMER
55 Dean Adult Studies & Grad Programs .... Dr. Rhoda MATTSON
29 Director of Alumni Relations .... Mr. Bill DERUITER
26 Dir of Marketing and Communications .... Vacant
88 Senior Graphic Designer .... Mr. Pete VEGA
13 Director of Computer Services .... Mr. Joe VELDERMAN
41 Director of Athletics .... Mr. Bill SCHEPEL
31 Dir of Cmty Engage & Diversity Pgm .... Vacant
42 Chaplain .... Dr. Willis VAN GRONINGEN
85 Director of Off-Campus Programs .... Dr. Burton J. ROZEMA
37 Director Financial Aid .... Mr. Ryan ZANTINGH
18 Director of Building/Grounds .... Mr. Tim TIMMONS
44 Director of Planned Giving .... Mr. Ken BOSS
21 Controller .... Mr. Mike TROCHUCK
28 Dir of Diversity/Dir AS Psychology .... Dr. Tiffany KING
92 Director of Honors Program .... Dr. Craig MATTSON
38 Director Cooper Ctr Counseling .... Dr. Dan SARTOR
84 Exec Director of College Enrollment .... Vacant
09 Asst Registar for Inst Research .... Ms. Kimberly WILLIAMS
15 Human Resources Manager .... Ms. Julia FOUST
20 Assoc Dean Academics .... Dr. John FRY
04 Executive Assistant to President .... Ms. Deborah S. VINCENT
19 Director Security/Safety .... Mr. Tom KAZEN
102 Dir Foundation/Corporate Relations .... Mr. Dennis HARMS

Trinity College of Nursing & Health Sciences (A)

2122 25th Avenue, Rock Island IL 61201-5317
County: Rock Island FICE Identification: 006225
Unit ID: 146755
Telephone: (309) 779-7700 Carnegie Class: Spec-4-yr-Other Health
FAX Number: (309) 779-7748 Calendar System: Semester
URL: www.trinitycollegeqc.edu
Established: 1994 Annual Undergrad Tuition & Fees: $27,067
Enrollment: 246 Coed
Affiliation or Control: Independent Non-Profit IRS Status: 501(c)3
Highest Offering: Master's
Accreditation: NH, ADNUR, COARC, NURSE, RAD

01 Chancellor .... Dr. Tracy L. POELVOORDE
05 Int Dean of Nursing & Health Sci .... Dr. Christine KESSEL
06 Registrar .... Ms. Cara BANKS

Trinity International University (B)

2065 Half Day Road, Deerfield IL 60015-1284
County: Lake FICE Identification: 001772
Unit ID: 149514
Telephone: (847) 945-8800 Carnegie Class: DU-Mod
FAX Number: (847) 317-8090 Calendar System: Semester
URL: www.tiu.edu
Established: 1897 Annual Undergrad Tuition & Fees: $28,700
Enrollment: 2,202 Coed
Affiliation or Control: Evangelical Free Church Of America
IRS Status: 501(c)3
Highest Offering: Doctorate
Accreditation: NH, CAATE, THEOL

01 President .... Dr. David S. DOCKERY
03 Exec Vice President & Provost .... Vacant
05 VP Education/Dean TEDS .... Dr. Graham COLE
05 VP Academic Admin/Dean TC & TGS .... Dr. Thomas CORNMAN
84 Sr VP Univ Svcs/Strat Initiatives .... Mr. Rich GRIMM
32 VP Student Life/Dean of Students .... Mr. Feliy THEONUGRAHA
13 Sr VP Information Technology/Plng .... Mr. Steven GEGGIE
30 Sr Vice Pres University Advancement .... Dr. David HOAG
10 Sr VP of Business & Finance/CFO .... Mr. Mike PICHA
20 Spec Asst to Pres Academic Admin .... Ms. Jeanette HSIEH
26 VP for University Communication .... Mr. Mark KAHLER
21 VP for Fin/Inst Research/Controller .... Mr. Paul EISENMENGER
42 Vice Pres University Ministries .... Mr. Felix THEONUGRAHA
27 Asst VP University Communication .... Mr. Chris DONOTO
73 Assoc Academic Dean Divinity School .... Dr. H. Wayne JOHNSON
51 Director Adult Academic Programs .... Mr. Jay SIMALA
35 Assoc Dean of Undergraduate Stdnts .... Ms. Karen WROBBEL
90 Director of Acad/Desktop Computing .... Mr. Chris MILLER
91 Director Administrative Computing .... Ms. Katie KEMP
58 Assoc Dean of Graduate School .... Dr. Don HEDGES
61 Dean of Law School .... Mr. Myron R. STEEVES
07 Director Undergraduate Admissions .... Mr. Jordan BRYANT
19 Director of Security Services .... Mr. Bob TOPOREK
96 Director of Facilities .... Ms. Julie WONG
15 Interim Director of Human Resources .... Mrs. Linda BRUNDIDGE
06 University Registrar .... Ms. Tiffany SELL
37 Executive Director Student Services .... Ms. Rachel RUSSIAKY
36 Director of Career Services .... Ms. Jan VICTOR
36 Director of Placement .... Dr. Phil SELL
08 University Librarian .... Dr. Robert H. KRAPOHL
29 Director of Alumni Relations .... Mr. Michael GORSLINE
92 Director of Honors Program .... Dr. Matt HELLER
35 Director of Student Activities .... Ms. Heather CORDERO

Triton College (C)

2000 Fifth Avenue, River Grove IL 60171-1995
County: Cook FICE Identification: 001773
Unit ID: 149532
Telephone: (708) 456-0300 Carnegie Class: Assoc/MT-VT-High Non
FAX Number: (708) 583-3112 Calendar System: Semester
URL: www.triton.edu
Established: 1964 Annual Undergrad Tuition & Fees (In-District): $3,870
Enrollment: 11,577 Coed
Affiliation or Control: Local IRS Status: 501(c)3
Highest Offering: Associate Degree
Accreditation: NH, ADNUR, DMS, NMT, RAD, SURGT

01 President .... Ms. Mary-Rita MOORE
05 VP Academic and Student Affairs .... Dr. Douglas OLSON
10 Vice President Business Services .... Mr. Sean SULLIVAN
26 Senior Executive of Public Affairs .... Mr. Randy BARNETTE
101 Secretary for Brd of Trustees .... Ms. Susan PAGE
13 Assoc VP Information Systems .... Mr. Michael GARRITY
21 Assoc VP Finance & Business .... Mr. Garrick ABEZETIAN
21 Assoc VP Business Operations .... Mr. Kevin KENNEDY
18 Assoc VP of Facilities .... Mr. John LAMBRECHT
15 Assoc VP Human Resources .... Mr. Joe KLINGER
32 Assoc VP of Student Affairs .... Dr. Quincy MARTIN, III
20 Assoc VP Academic Affairs .... Ms. Cheryl ANTONICH
35 Dean of Student Services .... Mr. Corey WILLIAMS
84 Dean of Enrollment Services .... Dr. Amanda TURNER
49 Dean of Arts & Sciences .... Mr. Kevin LI
72 Dean of Business & Technology .... Dr. Henry "Chuck" BOHLEKE
51 Dean of Continuing Education .... Mr. Paul JENSEN
09 Dean of Academic Success .... Dr. Deborah BANESS KING
55 Dean of Adult Education .... Dr. Virginia CABASA-HESS
49 Assoc Dean of Arts & Sciences .... Mr. Evan BROWN
37 Assoc Dean of Financial Aid .... Ms. Patricia ZINGA
21 Executive Director of Finance .... Mr. James REYNOLDS
27 Executive Director of Marketing .... Mr. Sam TOLIA
09 Executive Director of Research .... Dr. Kurian THARAKUNNEL
25 Exec Dir Grants Development .... Ms. Sacella SMITH
51 Asst Dean Continuing Education .... Ms. Colleen ROCKAFELLOW
14 Sr Data and System Admin .... Ms. Elise RAPALA
86 Director Public Affairs .... Ms. Audrey JONAS
88 Public Relations Associate .... Ms. Brenda JONES WATKINS
72 Instructional Technologist .... Ms. Marie-Ange ZICHER

University of Chicago (D)

5801 S Ellis Avenue, Chicago IL 60637-1496
County: Cook FICE Identification: 001774
Unit ID: 144050
Telephone: (773) 702-1234 Carnegie Class: DU-Highest
FAX Number: N/A Calendar System: Quarter
URL: www.uchicago.edu
Established: 1890 Annual Undergrad Tuition & Fees: $51,351
Enrollment: 15,097 Coed
Affiliation or Control: Independent Non-Profit IRS Status: 501(c)3
Highest Offering: Doctorate
Accreditation: NH, BUS, IPSY, LAW, MED, SW, THEOL

01 President .... Mr. Robert J. ZIMMER
05 Provost .... Mr. Daniel D. DIERMEIER
03 Executive Vice Provost .... Ms. Sian BEILOCK
03 Executive Vice President .... Mr. David B. FITHIAN
17 EVP for Medical Affairs/Dean of BSD .... Dr. Kenneth POLONSKY
100 VP and Chief of Staff .... Ms. Katie CALLOW-WRIGHT
101 VP/Sec of the University .... Mr. Darren REISBERG
46 EVP for Research/Natl Lab .... Mr. Eric D. ISAACS
10 VP of Operations/CFO .... Mr. Rowan MIRANDA
30 VP for Alumni Rels & Development .... Mr. Ken MANOTTI
43 Vice President & General Counsel .... Ms. Kim TAYLOR
88 Vice Pres/Chief Investment Officer .... Mr. Mark A. SCHMID
88 Assoc VP for Global Initiatives .... Mr. Michael KULMA
07 VP for Enroll/Admissions/Aid .... Mr. James NONDORF
32 VP/Campus Life Student Services .... Ms. Michele RASMUSSEN
31 Vice President for Civic Engagement .... Mr. Derek DOUGLAS
26 Vice Pres for Communications .... Mr. John LONGBRAKE
49 Dean of the College .... Mr. John W. BOYER
81 Dean Physical Sciences Division .... Mr. Edward W. KOLB
83 Dean of Social Sciences Division .... Mr. David NIRENBERG
42 Dean Rockefeller Memorial Chapel .... Ms. Elizabeth DAVENPORT
79 Dean of Humanities Division .... Vacant
54 Dean of Molecular Engineering .... Mr. Matthew TIRRELL
50 Dean of Booth School of Business .... Mr. Sunil KUMAR
61 Dean of the Law School .... Mr. Thomas MILES
73 Interim Dean of the Divinity School .... Mr. Richard A. ROSENGARTEN
51 Dean of Graham School .... Mr. Mark R. NEMEC
63 Dean Medicine .... Mr. Kenneth POLONSKY
80 Dean Harris Sch of Public Policy .... Vacant
70 Dean Social Svcs Admin .... Mr. Neil GUTERMAN
21 Senior Advisor for Finance & Admin .... Mr. John R. KROLL
20 Assoc Provost and Budget Director .... Mr. David L. MURPHY
13 VP and CIO .... Mr. Cole W. CAMPLESE
15 Interim Associate VP HR .... Mr. Mike KNITTER
20 Senior Associate Provost .... Mr. Larry HILL
28 Vice Provost for Diversity .... Dr. Melissa GILLIAM
88 Vice Provost for Acad Initiatives .... Ms. Melina HALE
06 Registrar .... Mr. Scott CAMPBELL
37 Executive Director University Aid .... Ms. Amanda FIJAL
57 Deputy Provost for the Arts .... Mr. Lawrence ZBIKOWSKI
22 Asst Provost/Affirm Action Ofcr .... Ms. Sarah WAKE
09 Dir Institutional Research .... Mr. William GREENLAND
29 Senior AVP Alumni Rels & Develop .... Mr. Damon CATES
36 Exec Dir Career Advancement .... Ms. Meredith DAW
41 Athletic Director .... Ms. Erin MCDERMOTT
08 Director University Library .... Ms. Brenda JOHNSON
38 Dir Student Counseling Services .... Mr. David ALBERT
96 Exec Dir Payroll/Procurement .... Mr. Mark FEHLBERG
39 Exec Director Student Housing .... Ms. Jennifer LUTTIG-KOMROSKY

*University of Illinois System (E)

506 S Wright Street, Urbana IL 61801-3689
County: Champaign FICE Identification: 008001
Unit ID: 149587
Telephone: (217) 333-6400 Carnegie Class: N/A
FAX Number: (217) 333-5733
URL: www.uillinois.edu

01 President .... Dr. Timothy L. KILLEEN
12 Chancellor/Vice President (Chicago) .... Dr. Michael AMIRIDIS
12 Chancellor/Vice President (Sprfld) .... Dr. Susan KOCH
12 Chancellor/Vice President (Urbana) .... Dr. Robert J. JONES
10 VP & Chief Financial Officer .... Mr. Walter KNORR
05 Vice Pres for Academic Affairs .... Vacant
09 Vice Pres for Research .... Vacant
43 University Counsel .... Mr. Thomas R. BEARROWS
26 Exec Dir for University Relations .... Mr. Thomas P. HARDY
13 CIO & Sr Assoc VP .... Dr. Michael HITES
15 Interim Assoc VP Human Resources .... Ms. Jami PAINTER
101 Secretary Board of Trustees/Univ .... Ms. Dedra M. WILLIAMS
102 President/CEO Univ Foundation .... Mr. James H. MOORE, JR.
29 Pres/CEO Univ Alumni Association .... Mr. Loren R. TAYLOR

*University of Illinois at Chicago (F)

601 S Morgan, M/C 102, Chicago IL 60607-7128
County: Cook FICE Identification: 001776
Unit ID: 145600
Telephone: (312) 996-7000 Carnegie Class: DU-Highest
FAX Number: (312) 413-3393 Calendar System: Semester
URL: www.uic.edu
Established: 1896 Annual Undergrad Tuition & Fees (In-State): $13,664
Enrollment: 27,969 Coed
Affiliation or Control: State IRS Status: 501(c)3
Highest Offering: Doctorate
Accreditation: NH, BUS, BUSA, CAHIIM, CEA, CLPSY, CS, DENT, DIETC, DIETD, ENG, ENGR, FEPAC, HSA, IPSY, MED, MIDWF, MIL, NURSE, OT, PAST, PH, PHAR, PLNG, PTA, SPAA, SW

02 Chancellor .... Dr. Michael AMIRIDIS
05 Provost and Vice Chanc Acad Affs .... Dr. Susan POSER
32 Vice Chancellor Student Affairs .... Dr. Barbara HENLEY
11 Vice Chanc for Administrative Svcs .... Mr. Mark DONOVAN
46 Vice Chancellor for Research .... Dr. Mitra DUTTA
26 Exec Assoc Chanc External Affairs .... Mr. Michael REDDING
17 CEO Hospital Administration .... Dr. Avijit GHOSH
29 Vice President Alumni Relations .... Ms. Arlene NORSYM
30 Vice Chancellor Development .... Mr. Jeff NEARHOOF
84 Vice Prov Acad/Enrollment Svcs .... Mr. Kevin BROWNE
15 Vice Provost for Faculty Affairs .... Dr. Renee TAYLOR
20 Int Vice Prov Undergrad Affairs .... Dr. Emanuel POLLACK
45 Vice Provost Planning & Programs .... Dr. Saul WEINER
21 Vice Provost Resource Plng/Mgmt .... Ms. Janet PARKER
35 Assoc Vice Chanc/Dean Student Affs .... Dr. Linda DEANNA
27 Senior Exec Director Public Affairs .... Ms. Sherri MCGINNIS GONZALEZ
23 Vice Chancellor Health Affairs .... Dr. Robert BARISH
10 Interim Asst VP Business/Finance .... Ms. Vanessa PEOPLES
48 Dean Col of Architect/Design/Arts .... Dr. Steve EVERETT
50 Dean College of Business Admin .... Dr. Michael B. MIKHAIL
52 Dean College of Dentistry .... Dr. Clark STANFORD
53 Dean College of Education .... Dr. Alfred TATUM
54 Dean College of Engineering .... Dr. Peter C. NELSON
76 Dean Col Applied Health Sciences .... Dr. Bo FERNHALL
58 Dean Graduate College .... Dr. Karen COLLEY
92 Dean Honors College .... Dr. Ralph KEEN
49 Dean College Liberal Arts/Sciences .... Dr. Astrida O. TANTILLO
63 Dean College of Medicine .... Dr. Dimitri AZAR
66 Dean College of Nursing .... Dr. Terri E. WEAVER
67 Dean College of Pharmacy .... Dr. Jerry BAUMAN
70 Dean College of Social Work .... Dr. Creasie HAIRSTON
69 Dean School of Public Health .... Dr. Paul BRANDT-RAUF
27 Dean Urban Planning/Public Affairs .... Dr. Michael A. PAGANO
43 University Counsel .... Mr. Thomas R. BEARROWS
08 University Librarian .... Ms. Mary CASE
88 Asst Univ Librarian Health Sciences .... Ms. Kathryn H. CARPENTER
07 Managing Director Admissions .... Ms. Malinda LORKOVICH
41 Director Athletics .... Mr. James W. SCHMIDT
38 Director Counseling Services .... Dr. Joseph HERMES
37 Interim Director Financial Aid .... Ms. Shirley RODRIGUEZ-VEGA
09 Director of Institutional Research .... Mr. William C. HAYWARD
16 Assoc Vice Provost Faculty Affairs .... Ms. Angela L. YUDT
22 Director Access/Equity .... Ms. Caryn A. BILLS-WINDT
36 Director Career Services .... Mr. Thy NGUYEN
13 CIO/Exec Dir Acad Computing .... Ms. Cynthia E. HERRERA LINDSTROM
56 Exec Dir Extended Campus .... Ms. Gayla M. STONER
06 Registrar .... Mr. Robert DIXON
96 Director of Purchasing .... Ms. Debra MATLOCK
18 Exec Dir Operations/Maintenance .... Mr. Clarence F. BRIDGES
28 Vice Provost for Diversity .... Dr. Tyrone A. FORMAN

*University of Illinois at Springfield (G)

One University Plaza, Springfield IL 62703-5407
County: Sangamon FICE Identification: 009333
Unit ID: 148654
Telephone: (217) 206-6600 Carnegie Class: Masters/L
FAX Number: (217) 206-6511 Calendar System: Semester
URL: www.uis.edu
Established: 1969 Annual Undergrad Tuition & Fees (In-State): $11,413
Enrollment: 5,431 Coed
Affiliation or Control: State IRS Status: 501(c)3

Highest Offering: Doctorate
Accreditation: NH, BUS, CACREP, MT, SPAA, SW

02 Chancellor .... Dr. Susan KOCH
05 Interim Vice Chancellor Acad Affs .... Dr. James ERMATINGER
32 Interim Vice Chanc Student Affairs .... Dr. Clarice FORD
20 Assc Vice Chanc Undergrad Education .... Ms. Karen MORANSKI
29 Assoc Vice Chanc for Alumni Rels .... Mr. Charles SCHRAGE
30 Vice Chanc Dev/Sr VP UL Found .... Dr. Jeffrey D. LORBER
35 Asst Vice Chanc for Student Service .... Dr. Van VIEREGGE
18 Exec Dir Facility Services .... Mr. David BARROWS
22 Asc Chanc Access/Equal Opportunity .... Ms. Deanie BROWN
27 Assoc Chancellor for Public Affairs .... Mr. Ryan CROKE
49 Actg Dean Col Liberal Arts/Science .... Dr. Lucia VAZQUEZ
50 Dean College Business/Management .... Dr. Ronald D. MCNEIL
80 Acting Dean Col Public Affs/Admin .... Dr. James ERMATINGER
53 Dean College Educ/Human Svcs .... Dr. Hanfu MI
15 Interim Sr Dir HR .... Mr. Ryan CROKE
84 Director of Enrollment Management .... Vacant
43 Legal Counsel .... Ms. Rhonda PERRY
08 Interim Dean of Libray .... Dr. Hanfu MI
26 Director Public Information .... Mr. Derek SCHNAPP
10 Assc Provost Budget and Admin Plng .... Dr. Jerry JOSEPH
19 Chief Campus Police Department .... Mr. Donald MITCHELL
06 Registrar .... Mr. Brian CLEVENGER
35 Director of Student Life .... Ms. Cynthia THOMPSON
41 Interim Director of Athletics .... Ms. Hayley TREADWAY
90 Director Campus Technology Service .... Vacant
09 Director Institutional Research .... Ms. Laura DORMAN
96 Director of Purchasing .... Mr. Michael BLOECHLE
37 Acting Dir Financial Assistance .... Ms. Carolyn SCHLOEMANN
38 Exec Director Counseling Center .... Dr. Judith SHIPP
85 Director International Programs .. Dr. Jonathan GOLDBERGBELLE
13 Assoc Prov Information Technology .... Mr. Farokh ESLAHI
39 Director Campus Housing .... Mr. John RINGLE
07 Director of Admissions .... Mr. Fernando PLANAS
21 Sr Business/Financial Coordinator .... Mr. Jason BANE

*University of Illinois at Urbana-Champaign (A)

601 E John Street, Champaign IL 61820-5711
County: Champaign — FICE Identification: 001775
Unit ID: 145637
Telephone: (217) 333-6677 — Carnegie Class: DU-Highest
FAX Number: (217) 244-5639 — Calendar System: Semester
URL: www.illinois.edu
Established: 1867 — Annual Undergrad Tuition & Fees (In-State): $15,054
Enrollment: 45,140 — Coed
Affiliation or Control: State — IRS Status: 501(c)3
Highest Offering: Doctorate
Accreditation: NH, ART, AUD, BUS, BUSA, CEA, CLPSY, COPSY, CS, DANCE, DIETD, DIETI, ENG, IPSY, JOUR, LAW, LIB, LSAR, MUS, NRPA, PCSAS, PH, PLNG, SP, SW, THEA, VET

00 Chief Executive Officer (President) .... Dr. Timothy L. KILLEEN
02 Chancellor .... Dr. Robert J. JONES
05 Int Prov/Vice Chanc Academic Affs .... Dr. Edward FESER
46 Vice Chancellor Research .... Dr. Peter E. SCHIFFER
32 Vice Chancellor Student Affairs .... Dr. C. Renee ROMANO
30 Int VC Inst Advancement/Fndn Admin .... Mr. Edward EWALD
31 Associate Chanc Corp Intl Relations .... Dr. Pradeep KHANNA
20 Vice Provost Academic Affairs .... Dr. Elabbas BENMAMOUN
88 Associate Chancellor .... Mr. Michael DELORENZO
28 Associate Chancellor for Diversity .... Dr. Assata ZERAI
26 Associate Chanc Public Affairs .... Ms. Robin KALER
03 Associate Chancellor .... Ms. Katherine GALVIN
15 Associate Provost Human Resources .... Ms. Elyne COLE
84 Assoc Prov Enrollment Mgmt .... Mr. Keith MARSHALL
104 Vice Provost Intl Pgms/Studies .... Ms. Reitumetse MABOKELA
20 Vice Provost for Undergrad Educ .... Dr. Charles L. TUCKER
21 Exec Assoc Provost Budget Planning .... Ms. Vicky GRESS
09 Asst Provost Management Info .... Dr. Amy EDWARDS
49 Dean Liberal Arts & Sciences .... Dr. Barbara WILSON
61 Dean Law .... Dr. Vikram AMAR
74 Dean Veterinary Medicine .... Dr. Peter CONSTABLE
54 Dean Engineering .... Dr. Andreas C. CANGELLARIS
47 Dean Agric/Consumer/Environ Sci .... Dr. Robert HAUSER
50 Dean Business .... Dr. Jeffrey BROWN
57 Acting Dean Fine & Applied Arts .... Ms. Kathleen HARLEMAN
70 Dean School of Social Work .... Dr. Wynne S. KORR
68 Dean Col Applied Health Sciences .... Dr. Tanya M. GALLAGHER
60 Int Dean College of Media .... Dr. Wojciech CHODZKO-ZAJKO
58 Dean Graduate College .... Dr. Wojciech CHODZKO-ZAJKO
62 Dean School of Info Sciences .... Dr. Allen H. RENEAR
53 Dean Education .... Dr. Mary KALANTZIS
63 Reg Dean Col Med/Urbana-Champ .... Dr. Michele MARISCALCO
16 Dean Labor & Employment Rels .... Dr. Fritz DRASGOW
08 University Librarian & Dean .... Mr. John P. WILKIN
13 Chief Information Officer .... Mr. Mark HENDERSON
35 Dean of Students .... Dr. Kenneth BALLOM
56 Assoc Dean Extension & Outreach .... Dr. George CZAPAR
41 Director Athletics .... Mr. Josh WHITMAN
10 Asst Vice Pres Bus/Fin Affairs .... Ms. Ginger VELAZQUEZ
43 Campus Legal Counsel .... Mr. Scott RICE
88 Deputy CIO Information Technology .... Mr. John M. ROSSI
22 Dir Equal Opportunity & Access .... Ms. Heidi JOHNSON
19 Director Public Safety .... Mr. Jeffrey T. CHRISTENSEN
18 Int Exec Director Facilities .... Ms. Helen COLEMAN
23 Director McKinley Health Center .... Dr. Robert D. PALINKAS
36 Director Career Services Center .... Dr. Gail ROONEY
37 Director Student Financial Aid .... Mr. Daniel R. MANN
38 Director Counseling Center .... Dr. Carla MCCOWAN

39 Director Housing Division .... Ms. Alma SEALINE
88 Dir Ctr Innovative Teaching/Lrng .... Dr. Michel BELLINI
06 Registrar .... Ms. Meghan HAZEN
07 Director of Admissions .... Ms. Nancy WALSH
101 Secretary of the Institution/Board .... Ms. Dedra WILLIAMS
108 Assistant Provost for Assessment .... Dr. Staci J. PROVEZIS

*University of Illinois at Chicago College of Medicine at Peoria (B)

Box 1649, Peoria IL 61656-1649
Telephone: (309) 671-3000 — Identification: 770182
Accreditation: &NH

† Regional accreditation is carried under the parent institution in Chicago, IL

*University of Illinois College of Medicine at Rockford (C)

1601 Parkview Avenue, Rockford IL 61107
Telephone: (815) 395-0600 — Identification: 770183
Accreditation: &NH, PHAR

† Regional accreditation is carried under the parent institution in Chicago, IL

*University of Illinois at Chicago College of Medicine at Urbana (D)

506 South Matthews Avenue, Urbana IL 61801
Telephone: (217) 333-5465 — Identification: 770184
Accreditation: &NH

† Regional accreditation is carried under the parent institution in Chicago, IL

University of Phoenix Chicago Campus (E)

1500 McConnor Parkway, Suite 700, Schaumburg IL 60173-4395
Telephone: (847) 413-1922 — Identification: 770205
Accreditation: &NH, ACBSP

† No longer accepting campus-based students.

University of St. Francis (F)

500 N Wilcox Street, Joliet IL 60435-6188
County: Will — FICE Identification: 001664
Unit ID: 148584
Telephone: (815) 740-3400 — Carnegie Class: Masters/L
FAX Number: (815) 740-4285 — Calendar System: Semester
URL: www.stfrancis.edu
Established: 1920 — Annual Undergrad Tuition & Fees: $29,950
Enrollment: 3,762 — Coed
Affiliation or Control: Roman Catholic — IRS Status: 501(c)3
Highest Offering: Doctorate
Accreditation: NH, ACBSP, NRPA, NURSE, RTT, SW, TED

01 President .... Dr. Arvid C. JOHNSON
05 Provost/VP Academic Affairs .... Dr. Frank H. PASCOE
10 VP Administration & Finance .... Ms. Julee A. GARD
84 VP Admissions/Mktg/Enrollment Svcs .... Mr. Charles W. BEUTEL
88 VP Mission Int & Univ Ministry .... Sr. Mary Elizabeth IMLER
32 VP Student & Alumni Affairs .... Mr. Damon N. SLOAN
13 VP Operations & IT .... Mr. Terrance L. COTTRELL
31 Exec Dir Mktg & Communications .Ms. Mary Lin L. MISCOLINO
30 Chief Development Officer .... Ms. Regina M. BLOCK
49 Dean Col Arts & Sciences .... Dr. Robert KASE
50 Dean Col Business/Health .... Dr. Orlando GRIEGO
53 Dean Col Education .... Dr. John S. GAMBRO
66 Dean Leach Col Nursing .... Dr. Carol J. WILSON
20 Dean Teaching & Learning Outcomes .... Dr. Pamela K. STEINKE
37 Exec Dir Financial Aid .... Mr. Bruce FOOTE
29 Dir Alumni Relations .... Ms. Aubrey L. KNIGHT
41 Dir Athletics .... Mr. Dave LAKETA
36 Dir Career Success Center .... Ms. Maribeth HEARN
38 Dir Counseling & Wellness .... Mr. Carlos AQUINO
15 Dir Human Resources .... Ms. Mary L. SPREITZER
28 Dir Institutional Diversity .... Vacant
07 Dir Undergrad Admissions .... Ms. Cynthia A. LAMBERT
07 Dir Grad/Degree Completion Admiss .... Ms. Sandra L. SLOKA
104 Dir Intl Programs Office .... Ms. Angie MAFFEO
26 Dir Marketing Services .... Ms. Julie FUTTERER
14 Dir Network Support Services .... Mr. Mark T. SNODGRASS
18 Dir Operations & Facilities .... Mr. Mike DECMAN
39 Dir Residence Education .... Ms. Mollie ROCKAFELLOW
19 Dir Safety/Security & Transport .... Mr. Joseph W. KRIPP
42 Dir University Ministry .... Mr. Joseph T. WYSOCKI
06 Registrar .... Ms. Laura A. KOGA
08 Head Librarian .... Ms. Shannon WENZEL
23 Coordinator of Health Services .... Ms. Phyllis M. PETERSON
09 Asst Dir Institutional Research .... Ms. Rebecca R. GARLAND

University of Saint Mary of the Lake-Mundelein Seminary (G)

1000 E Maple Avenue, Mundelein IL 60060-1174
County: Lake — FICE Identification: 001765
Unit ID: 148885
Telephone: (847) 566-6401 — Carnegie Class: Spec-4-yr-Faith
FAX Number: (847) 566-7330 — Calendar System: Semester
URL: www.usml.edu
Established: 1844 — Annual Graduate Tuition & Fees: N/A
Enrollment: 284 — Male
Affiliation or Control: Roman Catholic — IRS Status: 501(c)3
Highest Offering: Doctorate; No Undergraduates
Accreditation: THEOL

00 Chancellor .... ArBish. Blase CUPICH
01 Rector/President .... Rev. John KARTJE
03 Vice Rector for Formation .... Rev. Brian WELTER
05 Vice Rector for Academic Affairs .... Rev. Thomas A. BAIMA
73 Pres/Pontifical Faculty of Theology .... Rev. Brendan LUPTON
10 Vice President for Finance .... Mr. John F. LEHOCKY
30 Vice President Inst Advancement .... Mr. Ryan BUTTS
20 Assoc Acad Dean Sem/Grad Sch .... Dr. Christopher MCATEE
73 Director Pre-Theology Program .... Rev. Dennis SPIES
08 Library Director .... Mrs. Lorraine OLLEY EUSTICE
06 Registrar .... Mrs. Mary Ann ULZ
88 Director of Pastoral Internships .... Rev. Martin BARNUM
88 Director of Liturgy .... Rev. Bradley ZAMORA
88 Director of Spiritual Life .... Rev. Carlos RODRIGUEZ
85 Director of International Students .... Rev. Martin BARNUM
18 Chief Facilities/Physical Plant .... Mr. Clayton KALWEIT
07 Director of Admissions .... Rev. Edward PELRINE

VanderCook College of Music (H)

3140 S Federal Street, Chicago IL 60616-3731
County: Cook — FICE Identification: 001778
Unit ID: 149639
Telephone: (312) 225-6288 — Carnegie Class: Spec-4-yr-Arts
FAX Number: (312) 225-5211 — Calendar System: Semester
URL: www.vandercook.edu
Established: 1909 — Annual Undergrad Tuition & Fees: $26,300
Enrollment: 176 — Coed
Affiliation or Control: Independent Non-Profit — IRS Status: 501(c)3
Highest Offering: Master's
Accreditation: NH, MUS

01 President .... Dr. Charles T. MENGHINI
08 Head Librarian .... Mr. Robert DELAND
05 Dean of Undergraduate Studies .... Ms. Stacey L. DOLAN
58 Dean of Graduate Studies .... Mr. Robert L. SINCLAIR
07 Director of Admissions & Retention .... Ms. LeeAnn MEYER
10 Chief Financial Officer .... Ms. Michelle ANDERSON
37 Director of Financial Aid .... Ms. Sirena COVINGTON
13 Director Information Technologies .... Mr. Rick MALIK
04 President's Assistant .... Ms. Cindy TOVAR
51 Director of Continuing Education .... Mr. Patrick BENSON
09 Director of Institutional Reports .... Mr. Gregor MEYER
06 Registrar/EPO Director .... Mrs. Carolyn BERGHOFF
29 Director Alumni Relations .... Ms. Cindy TOVAR

Vatterott College-Fairview Heights (I)

110 Commerce Lane, Fairview Heights IL 62208
Telephone: (618) 489-2400 — Identification: 770943
Accreditation: ACCSC

† Branch campus of Vatterott College-NorthPark, Berkeley, MO

Vatterott College-Quincy (J)

3609 North Marx Drive, Quincy IL 62305
County: Adams — FICE Identification: 020693
Unit ID: 148140
Telephone: (217) 224-0600 — Carnegie Class: Assoc/HVT-High Non
FAX Number: (217) 223-6771 — Calendar System: Other
URL: www.vatterott-college.edu
Established: 1995 — Annual Undergrad Tuition & Fees: $12,534
Enrollment: 140 — Coed
Affiliation or Control: Proprietary — IRS Status: Proprietary
Highest Offering: Associate Degree
Accreditation: ACCSC

01 Campus Director .... Mr. Tom LOCKETT
05 Director of Education .... Vacant
30 VP Regulatory Affs/Strategic Devel .... Mr. Aaron LACEY
43 General Counsel/Chief Administrator .... Mr. Scott CASANOVER

Waubonsee Community College (K)

Route 47 at Waubonsee Drive, Sugar Grove IL 60554-9799
County: Kane — FICE Identification: 006931
Unit ID: 149727
Telephone: (630) 466-7900 — Carnegie Class: Assoc/MT-VT-High Non
FAX Number: (630) 466-7550 — Calendar System: Semester
URL: www.waubonsee.edu
Established: 1966 — Annual Undergrad Tuition & Fees (In-District): $2,832
Enrollment: 10,904 — Coed
Affiliation or Control: Local — IRS Status: 501(c)3
Highest Offering: Associate Degree
Accreditation: NH, ADNUR, ART, CAHIIM, EMT, MAC, SURGT

01 President .... Dr. Christine J. SOBEK
05 Exec VP Educ Affs/Chief Lrng Ofcr .... Vacant
10 Exec VP Finance & Operations .... Mr. David QUILLEN
45 VP Strategic Development .... Dr. Jamal SCOTT
32 Vice Pres of Student Development .... Dr. Melinda L. TEJADA
21 Asst Vice President of Finance .... Ms. Darla S. CARDINE
106 Asst VP Online Lrng/Instruction Sup .... Dr. Renee TONIONI
36 Asst VP Workforce Sol/Comm Learning .... Mr. Gary KECSKÉS

75 Asst VP Career/Technical Education ... Ms. Suzette MURRAY
88 Asst VP Transfer/Development Educ ... Dr. Jonathan PAVER
13 Chief Information Officer ... Mr. Terence FELTON
35 Dean for Students ... Dr. Scott PESKA
15 Exec Director Human Resources ... Ms. Michele NEEDHAM
26 Exec Dir Marketing/Communications ... Ms. Amanda GEIST
76 Dean Health Professions/Public Svc ... Dr. Jess TOUSSAINT
83 Dean Social Sciences/Edu/World Lang ... Dr. Laura ORTIZ
79 Dean Communic/Humanities/Fine Arts ... Ms. Cynthia SPARR
88 Dean Development Ed/Coll Read ... Dr. Medea RAMBISH
81 Dean Mathematics/Sciences ... Ms. Mary Edith BUTLER
38 Dean Counseling/Careers/Student Sup ... Ms. Kelli SINCLAIR
56 Dean Adult Education ... Ms. Jeri L. DIXON
30 Chief Advancement Officer ... Mr. Robert BARTO
50 Dean Business/Career Technologies ... Ms. Ne'Keisha STEPNEY
103 Dean Workforce Development ... Ms. Lesa NORRIS
84 Dean Enrollment Management ... Ms. Faith LASHURE
31 Dean Community Education ... Mr. Douglas L. GRIER
04 Dir Pres Communications/Operations ... Ms. Kimberly CAPONI
37 Dir Student Financial Aid Services ... Dr. Charles BOUDREAU
09 Dir Inst Effective/Title V Proj Dir ... Dr. Stacey RANDALL
28 Dir Governmental/Cmty Engagement ... Dr. Lourdes BLACKSMITH
19 Dir Emergency Management/Safety ... Mr. John WU
88 Dir Accounting/Business Services ... Mr. Bruce HARTMANN
18 Director Campus Operations ... Mr. Daniel LARSEN
06 Dir Registration/Records/Registrar ... Mr. Marc DALE
07 Admissions Manager ... Ms. Joy SANDERS

Western Illinois University (A)

1 University Circle, Macomb IL 61455-1390
County: McDonough FICE Identification: 001780
Unit ID: 149772
Telephone: (309) 298-1414 Carnegie Class: Masters/L
FAX Number: (309) 298-2400 Calendar System: Semester
URL: www.wiu.edu
Established: 1899 Annual Undergrad Tuition & Fees (In-State): $12,889
Enrollment: 11,458 Coed
Affiliation or Control: State IRS Status: 501(c)3
Highest Offering: Doctorate
Accreditation: NH, ART, BUS, BUSA, CAATE, CACREP, CEA, DIETD, ENG, MUS, NAIT, NRPA, NURSE, SP, SW, TED, THEA

01 President ... Dr. Jack THOMAS
05 Interim Provost/Academic VP ... Dr. Kathleen NEUMANN
20 Assoc Prov/Assoc VP Acad Affs ... Dr. Russell MORGAN
20 Asst VP for Academic Affairs ... Dr. Ronald WILLIAMS
20 Assoc Provost/Undergrad & Grad ... Dr. Nancy P. PARSONS
10 VP Administrative Services ... Mr. Matthew J. BIERMAN
32 Vice President Student Services ... Dr. Ronald C. WILLIAMS
30 Vice Pres Advancement/Public Svcs ... Mr. Bradley BAINTER
29 Director Alumni Programs ... Ms. Amy SPELMAN
23 General Counsel Attorney ... Ms. Rica CALHOUN
39 Assoc Vice Pres Student Services ... Mr. John BIERNBAUM
45 VP for QC & Planning ... Dr. Joseph RIVES
86 Asst to Pres Government Relations ... Ms. Jeanette MALAFA
49 Dean College Arts/Sciences ... Dr. Susan MARTINELLI-FERNANDEZ
50 Interim Dean College Business/Tech ... Dr. William C. BAILEY
53 Dean Col Educ & Human Svcs ... Dr. Erskine SMITH
57 Dean Fine Arts & Comm ... Mr. William T. CLOW
08 Dean University Libraries ... Dr. Michael LORENZEN
92 Dir Illinois Centennial Honors Col ... Dr. Richard J. HARDY
64 Director School of Music ... Dr. Tami WALKER
06 Registrar ... Dr. Angela LYNN
21 Interim Director Business Services ... Mr. Matthew J. BIERMAN
13 Exec Dir University Technology/CIO ... Mr. Stephen L. FRAZIER
26 Director University Relations ... Ms. Darcie R. SHINBERGER
09 Director Inst Research & Planning ... Ms. Angela BONIFAS
22 Director Equal Opportunity & Access ... Ms. Andrea HENDERSON
37 Director Financial Aid ... Ms. Terri HARE
36 Director Placement ... Mr. Martin J. KRAL
15 Director Human Resources ... Ms. Pamela L. BOWMAN
18 Director Physical Plant ... Mr. Scott A. COKER
19 Director Public Safety ... Mr. Scott HARRIS
23 Director Health Center ... Ms. John W. SMITH
31 Dir Distance Learning and Outreach ... Dr. Richard CARTER
40 Interim Dir University Bookstore ... Ms. Ann COMERFORD
41 Interim Director Athletics ... Mr. Matt TANNEY
102 Director WIU Foundation ... Mr. Bradley BAINTER
07 Interim Director Admissions ... Ms. Sara LYTLE
38 Director Student Counseling ... Mr. James E. DITULIO
85 Dir Center International Studies ... Dr. Richard CARTER
88 Director Budget ... Mr. Matthew J. BIERMAN

Western Illinois University Quad Cities (B)

3300 River Drive, Moline IL 61265
Telephone: (309) 762-9481 Identification: 770100
Accreditation: &NH

† Regional accreditation is carried under the parent institution in Macomb, IL

Wheaton College (C)

501 College Avenue, Wheaton IL 60187-5593
County: DuPage FICE Identification: 001781
Unit ID: 149781
Telephone: (630) 752-5000 Carnegie Class: Bac-A&S
FAX Number: (630) 752-5555 Calendar System: Semester
URL: www.wheaton.edu
Established: 1860 Annual Undergrad Tuition & Fees: $32,950
Enrollment: 2,914 Coed
Affiliation or Control: Independent Non-Profit IRS Status: 501(c)3
Highest Offering: Doctorate
Accreditation: NH, CACREP, CLPSY, MFCD, MUS, TED

01 President ... Dr. Philip G. RYKEN
05 Provost ... Dr. Margaret DIDDAMS
10 Vice President for Finance ... Mr. Dale A. KEMP
32 Vice President Student Development ... Mr. Paul O. CHELSEN
30 VP Advancement/Alumni Rels ... Mr. Kirk FARNEY
13 Chief Information Officer ... Ms. Wendy WOODWARD
29 Sr Dir Vocation & Alum Engagement ... Ms. Cindra STACKHOUSE TAETZSCH
04 Exec Asst to the President ... Miss Marilee A. MELVIN
58 Dean of the Graduate School ... Dr. Nicholas PERRIN
79 Dean Humanities/Theol Studies ... Dr. Jill P. BAUMGAERTNER
49 Dean Conservatory/Arts & Comm ... Dr. Michael WILDER
83 Dean Natural & Social Sciences ... Dr. Dorothy F. CHAPPELL
104 Dean Global & Exper Learning ... Dr. Laura M. MONTGOMERY
35 Dean of Student Engagement ... Dr. Steve IVESTER
08 College Librarian ... Mrs. Lisa T. RICHMOND
21 Controller ... Mr. Craig SQUIRE
20 Executive Dir Billy Graham Center ... Dr. Ed STETZER
09 Dir Inst Research & Acad Support ... Dr. Gary N. LARSON
06 Registrar ... Mrs. Peggy KING
109 Dir of Planning and Budget ... Mr. Scott OKESSON
24 Dir Academic and Media Tech ... Mr. J. R. SMITH
36 Interim Dir Ctr Vocation & Career ... Ms. Dee PIERCE
15 Director of Human Resources ... Mrs. Karen TUCKER
07 Director Undergraduate Admissions ... Ms. Shawn B. LEFTWICH
07 Director Graduate Admissions ... Mr. Dusty DI SANTO
37 Director of Student Financial Aid ... Ms. Karen BELLING
41 Director of Athletics ... Ms. Julie DAVIS
39 Associate Dean of Residence Life ... Mr. Justin HETH
38 Director of Counseling ... Dr. Toussaint WHETSTONE
42 Chaplain ... Rev. Timothy BLACKMON
23 Director of Student Health Services ... Ms. Britt BLACK
26 Director Marketing Communications ... Ms. Kimberly MEDAGLIA
27 Director of Media Relations ... Ms. LaTonya TAYLOR
40 Manager of Bookstore ... Ms. Jennifer HAMPTON
18 Director of Facilities Management ... Mr. James M. JOHNSON
19 Chief of Public Safety ... Mr. Robert F. NORRIS
93 Director Multicultural Development ... Mr. Rodney K. SISCO
96 Director of Purchasing ... Mr. John GLASS
88 Director Risk Management ... Mr. Daniel CLARK
105 Director Web Communications ... Mrs. Rebecca LARSON
25 Academic Grants Officer ... Mrs. Virginia SHAFFER

Worsham College of Mortuary Science (D)

495 Northgate Parkway, Wheeling IL 60090-2646
County: Cook FICE Identification: 001783
Unit ID: 369455
Telephone: (847) 808-8444 Carnegie Class: Spec 2-yr-A&S
FAX Number: (847) 808-8493 Calendar System: Quarter
URL: www.worshamcollege.com
Established: 1911 Annual Undergrad Tuition & Fees: N/A
Enrollment: 108 Coed
Affiliation or Control: Proprietary IRS Status: Proprietary
Highest Offering: Associate Degree
Accreditation: FUSER

01 Director ... Ms. Stephanie J. KANN

INDIANA

American College of Education (E)

101 West Ohio Street, Suite 1200, Indianapolis IN 46204
County: Marion Identification: 666242
Unit ID: 449889
Telephone: (800) 280-0307 Carnegie Class: Spec-4-yr-Other
FAX Number: (877) 470-5896 Calendar System: Semester
URL: www.ace.edu
Established: 2005 Annual Undergrad Tuition & Fees: N/A
Enrollment: 2,589 Coed
Affiliation or Control: Proprietary IRS Status: Proprietary
Highest Offering: Doctorate
Accreditation: NH, TEAC

01 Interim President ... Dr. Shawntel D. LANDRY
05 Provost ... Dr. Shawntel D. LANDRY
26 Chief Operating Officer ... Mr. Dan HOLESTINE
84 VP Enrollment Operations ... Ms. Monica CARSON
88 VP Regulatory Affairs & Compliance ... Ms. Karen SWENSON
07 Director of Admissions ... Ms. Courtney SHELTON
06 Registrar ... Ms. Stephanie HINSHAW
09 Dir Inst Research/Effectiveness ... Dr. Kathryn TALLEY
04 Administrative Asst to President ... Ms. Jill ALGATE
08 Librarian ... Dr. Sandra QUIATKOWSKI
10 Chief Financial Officer ... Ms. Tiffany NEVILLE
13 Information Technology ... Mr. James ALDRIDGE
15 Director Human Resources ... Ms. KK BYLAND
53 Acad Dean & Dir Grad Programs ... Dr. Lee TINCHER
108 Director Assessment & Accreditation ... Ms. Alison GILLINGS

American National University (F)

6060 Castleway West Drive, Indianapolis IN 46250
County: Marion FICE Identification: 010489
Telephone: (317) 578-7353 Carnegie Class: Not Classified
FAX Number: (317) 578-7721 Calendar System: Quarter
URL: www.an.edu
Established: 1886 Annual Undergrad Tuition & Fees: N/A
Enrollment: N/A Coed
Affiliation or Control: Proprietary IRS Status: Proprietary
Highest Offering: Master's
Accreditation: ACICS, CAHIIM, MAC, SURGT

01 Campus Director ... Vacant
03 Regional Vice Pres of Operations ... Mr. Paul WOEF
04 Admin Asst to Campus Director ... Ms. Paula PYNM

American National University (G)

1030 E Jefferson Boulevard, South Bend IN 46617
Telephone: (574) 307-7100 Identification: 770695
Accreditation: ACICS, MAC

Anabaptist Mennonite Biblical Seminary (H)

3003 Benham Avenue, Elkhart IN 46517-1999
County: Elkhart FICE Identification: 001823
Unit ID: 151865
Telephone: (574) 295-3726 Carnegie Class: Spec-4-yr-Faith
FAX Number: (574) 295-0092 Calendar System: 4/1/4
URL: www.ambs.edu
Established: 1946 Annual Graduate Tuition & Fees: N/A
Enrollment: 106 Coed
Affiliation or Control: Mennonite Church IRS Status: 501(c)3
Highest Offering: Master's; No Undergraduates
Accreditation: NH, THEOL

01 President ... Dr. Sara W. SHENK
05 Academic Dean ... Dr. Rebecca SLOUGH
10 Vice President and CFO ... Mr. Ron RINGENBERG
30 Director of Development ... Ms. Missy K. SCHROCK
06 Registrar ... Mr. Scott JANZEN
08 Director of Library Services ... Mr. Karl STUTZMAN
84 Dir Enrollment Mgmt/Financial Aid ... Mr. Daniel GRIMES
73 Director of Inst Mennonite Studies ... Dr. Mary H. SCHERTZ

Ancilla College (I)

PO Box 1, Donaldson IN 46513-0001
County: Marshall FICE Identification: 001784
Unit ID: 150048
Telephone: (574) 936-8898 Carnegie Class: Assoc/HT-High Trad
FAX Number: (574) 935-1773 Calendar System: Semester
URL: www.ancilla.edu
Established: 1937 Annual Undergrad Tuition & Fees: $14,330
Enrollment: 400 Coed
Affiliation or Control: Roman Catholic IRS Status: 501(c)3
Highest Offering: Associate Degree
Accreditation: NH

01 President ... Dr. Ken ZIRKLE
04 Assistant to the President ... Ms. Diana CALDWELL
05 VP of Academic Affairs ... Dr. Joanna BLOUNT
10 VP of Finance & Admin ... Mr. Mike BROWN
30 Vice President of Development ... Mr. Todd ZELTWANGER
84 Vice President of Enrollment Mgmt ... Mr. Eric WIGNALL
42 Vice President Mission Integration ... Sr. Jolise MAY, PHJC
21 Director of Business Affairs ... Ms. Marcella HOPPLE
37 Director of Financial Aid ... Vacant
41 Athletic Director ... Mr. Robert REESE
30 Development & Alumni Relations Mgr ... Ms. Emily HUTSELL
13 Director of Information Technology ... Mr. John LINBACK
18 Chief Facilities/Physical Plant ... Mr. Tom NOWAK
06 Registrar/Institutiional Research ... Ms. Tiffany FISHER
40 Bookstore Manager ... Ms. Kim WEHR
08 Librarian ... Ms. Cassaundra BASH
17 Director Nursing & Health Science ... Ms. Ann FITZGERALD
26 Dir of Marketing & Social Media ... Ms. Amanda PETRUCELLI
39 Director Student Services ... Mr. Scott HORCH

Anderson University (J)

1100 E Fifth Street, Anderson IN 46012-3495
County: Madison FICE Identification: 001785
Unit ID: 150066
Telephone: (765) 649-9071 Carnegie Class: Masters/M
FAX Number: (765) 641-3851 Calendar System: Semester
URL: www.anderson.edu
Established: 1917 Annual Undergrad Tuition & Fees: $27,680
Enrollment: 2,399 Coed
Affiliation or Control: Church Of God IRS Status: 501(c)3
Highest Offering: Doctorate
Accreditation: NH, ACBSP, CAATE, MUS, NURSE, SW, THEOL

01 President ... Mr. John PISTOLE
05 Provost ... Dr. Marie MORRIS
10 Vice President Finance/Treasurer ... Mrs. Dana STUART
30 Vice President for Advancement ... Mr. Hudson AKIN
84 VP Enrollment & Marketing ... Ms. Rebecca FULLER BEELER
73 Dean Sch of Theology/Christian Min ... Dr. MaryAnn HAWKINS
50 Dean Falls School of Business ... Dr. Terry TRUITT
53 Dean School of Education ... Dr. Merribeth BRUNING
81 Dean Sch Humanities/Behavioral Sci ... Dr. Joel SHROCK
64 Dean School Music/Theatre & Dance ... Dr. Jeffrey WRIGHT
66 Dean Sch Nursing & Kinesiology ... Dr. Lynn SCHMIDT
54 School of Science & Engineering ... Dr. Chad WALLACE
42 Campus Pastor ... Rev. Tamara SHELTON

33 Dean of Students .... Dr. Christopher CONFER
06 University Registrar .... Mr. Arthur LEAK
08 Director of Libraries .... Dr. Janet BREWER
07 Director of Admissions .... Ms. Kynan SIMISON
21 Assistant Treasurer/Controller .... Mrs. Vanessa TIJERINA
36 Director of Career Development .... Vacant
13 Director of Info Technology Svcs .... Mr. Michael TUCKER
37 Student Financial Services .... Mrs. Gayla ROBERTS
18 Exec Dir Facilities & Property Mgmt .... Mr. Joseph ROYER
15 Director of Human Resources .... Ms. Shanna MCCLURE
19 Director Police & Security Services .... Mr. Rick GARRETT
40 Bookstore Manager .... Mr. Dustin MARTIN
41 Athletic Director .... Ms. Marcie TAYLOR
38 Director Counseling Services .... Ms. Christal HELVERING
29 Director of Alumni Engagement .... Vacant
109 Manager Business & Auxiliary Svcs .... Mrs. Suahil HOUSHOLDER
04 Administrative Asst to President .... Mrs. Ronda REEMER
104 Director Study Abroad .... Mrs. Aurora DOSTER
108 Director Institutional Assessment .... Dr. Jaye ROGERS
39 Student Housing Coordinator .... Mrs. Alex JONES

The Art Institute of Indianapolis (A)

3500 Depauw Boulevard Suite 1010,
Indianapolis IN 46268
Telephone: (317) 613-4800 Identification: 666247
Accreditation: #ACICS

† Branch campus of The Art Institute of Phoenix, AZ.

Ball State University (B)

2000 W. University Avenue, Muncie IN 47306-1099
County: Delaware FICE Identification: 001786
Unit ID: 150136
Telephone: (765) 289-1241 Carnegie Class: DU-Higher
FAX Number: (765) 285-1461 Calendar System: Semester
URL: www.bsu.edu
Established: 1918 Annual Undergrad Tuition & Fees (In-State): $9,498
Enrollment: 20,655 Coed
Affiliation or Control: State IRS Status: 501(c)3
Highest Offering: Doctorate
Accreditation: NH, AAFCS, ART, AUD, BUS, BUSA, CAATE, CACREP, CEA, CIDA, COARC, CONST, COPSY, CORE, DANCE, DIETD, DIETI, IPSY, JOUR, LSAR, MUS, NURSE, PLNG, RAD, SCPSY, SP, SW, TED, THEA

01 Interim President .... Dr. Terry S. KING
05 Acting Provost/EVP Academic Affairs .... Dr. Robert MORRIS
10 VP Business Affairs & Treasurer .... Mr. Bernard M. HANNON
32 VP Stdnt Aff/Enr Mgt/Dean of Stdnts .... Dr. Kay BALES
43 VP & General Counsel .... Ms. Sali K. FALLING
13 Interim VP for IT .... Mr. Loren MALM
86 VP Govt Relations Cmty Engagement .... Ms. Julie HALBIG
102 President and CEO BSU Foundation .... Ms. Cheri E. O'NEILL
41 Dir Intercollegiate Athletics .... Mr. Mark SANDY
20 Assoc Provost/Dean Univ College .... Dr. Marilyn M. BUCK
28 Associate Provost Diversity .... Dr. Charlene ALEXANDER
88 Int Assoc Prov Learning Initiatives .... Dr. Marilyn BUCK
50 Assoc Prov Entrepreneurial Learning .... Ms. Jennifer BLACKMER
108 Asst Provost Inst Effectiveness .... Dr. William KNIGHT
39 AVP Student Affairs/Dir of Housing .... Dr. Alan HARGRAVE
103 Assoc VP Econ Dev/Community Engage . Dr. John A. FALLON, III
26 Assoc VP Strategic Communications .... Ms. Joan TODD
18 Assoc VP Facilities Planning/Mgmt .... Mr. James LOWE
21 Assoc VP Finance/Asst Treasurer .... Vacant
109 Assoc VP Business/Auxiliary Svcs .... Ms. Julie HOPWOOD
14 Asst VP IT for Strategic/Fiscal Mgt .... Mr. Donald KING, JR.
07 AVP of Enrollment/Ex Dir of Admiss .... Mr. Christopher T. MUNCHEL
08 Dean University Libraries .... Mr. Matthew SHAW
48 Interim Dean Architecture/Planning .... Mr. Phillip REPP
49 Int Dean Col of Science/Humanities .... Dr. Jeffry GRIGSBY
50 Dean Miller College of Business .... Dr. Jennifer P. BOTT
53 Dean of Teachers College .... Dr. John E. JACOBSON
57 Dean College of Fine Arts .... Dr. Robert A. KVAM
58 Acting Dean of Graduate School .... Dr. Carolyn KAPINUS
60 Dean Col of Comm/Info/Media .... Mr. Roger LAVERY
72 Int Dean Col Applied Science/Tech .... Dr. Marilyn BUCK
90 Founding Dean College of Health .... Dr. Mitchell WHALEY
92 Dean of Honors College .... Dr. James S. RUEBEL
50 Chief Entrepreneurship Officer .... Dr. Michael GOLDSBY
06 Reg/Dir Registration/Acad Pgms .... Mrs. Nancy L. CRONK
37 Director Scholarships/Financial Aid .... Dr. John MCPHERSON
15 Director of Human Resources Svcs .... Ms. Kate STOSS
19 Director Public Safety .... Mr. James DUCKHAM
25 Director Contracts & Grants .... Ms. Kathy A. LUCAS
100 President's Chief of Staff .... Vacant
44 Director Annual or Planned Giving .... Mr. Phillip PURCELL
30 Senior VP for Development .... Mr. Mark HELMUS
88 VP of Strategic Engagement and Com .... Ms. Jean CROSBY
22 Assoc Dean of Students/Title IX .... Ms. Katie SLABAUGH
106 Dir Online Education/E-learning .... Ms. Staci DAVIS
38 Director Counseling/Health Services .... Dr. Tim HESS
88 Dir Unified Techonology Support .... Mr. Dan LUTZ
36 Director Career Center .... Mr. Jim MCATEE
96 Director of Purchasing Services .... Mr. Roger HASSENZAHL
24 Dir of University Media Services .... Mr. Allen GORDON
88 Dir of Economic Development Policy .... Mr. David R. TERRELL
88 Dir Econ and Community Development .... Mr. Dick HEUPEL
104 Exec Dir International Programs .... Mr. Imara DAWSON
04 Exec Dir of Presidential Operations .... Ms. Stephanie K. ARRINGTON
101 Secretary to the Board of Trustees .... Ms. Anita KELSEY
105 Interim Chief Creative Officer .... Ms. Mary BARR

Bethany Theological Seminary (C)

615 National Road W, Richmond IN 47374-4019
County: Wayne FICE Identification: 001637
Unit ID: 143233
Telephone: (800) 287-8822 Carnegie Class: Spec-4-yr-Faith
FAX Number: (765) 983-1840 Calendar System: Semester
URL: www.bethanyseminary.edu
Established: 1905 Annual Graduate Tuition & Fees: N/A
Enrollment: 67 Coed
Affiliation or Control: Church Of The Brethren IRS Status: 501(c)3
Highest Offering: Master's; No Undergraduates
Accreditation: NH, THEOL

01 President .... RevDr. Jeffrey W. CARTER
05 Academic Dean .... Dr. Steven J. SCHWEITZER
10 Exec Director of Business Services .... Ms. Brenda J. REISH
30 Exec Dir Institutional Advancement .... Mr. Mark A. LANCASTER
20 Director of Academic Services .... Ms. April VANLONDEN
26 Director of Communications .... Ms. Jennifer L. WILLIAMS
32 Int Exec Dir Admiss/Dir Student Dev . Ms. Amy S. GALL RITCHIE
12 Exec Director Brethren Academy .... Ms. Julie M. HOSTETTER
88 Director Inst Ministry with Youth .... Mr. Russell HAITCH
88 Dir Peace/Cross Cultural Studies .... Mr. Scott HOLLAND
88 Director of the MA Program .... Ms. Denise KETTERING-LANE
88 Dir of Educational Technology .... Mr. Dan POOLE

Bethel College (D)

1001 Bethel Circle, Mishawaka IN 46545-5509
County: Saint Joseph FICE Identification: 001787
Unit ID: 150145
Telephone: (574) 807-7000 Carnegie Class: Masters/S
FAX Number: (574) 807-7957 Calendar System: Semester
URL: www.bethelcollege.edu
Established: 1947 Annual Undergrad Tuition & Fees: $26,590
Enrollment: 1,792 Coed
Affiliation or Control: Missionary Church IRS Status: 501(c)3
Highest Offering: Master's
Accreditation: NH, ADNUR, MUS, NUR, TED

01 President .... Dr. Gregg A. CHENOWETH
05 VP for Academic Services .... Dr. Barbara H. BELLEFEUILLLE
30 VP for Institutional Advancement .... Mr. Richard A. MUNROE
10 Interim VP for Business Affairs .... Dr. Raymond E. WHITEMAN
32 VP for Student Development .... Dr. Shawn M. HOLTGREN
36 Director of Student Success .... Vacant
84 Asst VP for Enrollment/Marketng .... Vacant
13 Senior Director of IT .... Ms. Patti J. FISHER
66 Dean of Nursing .... Dr. Deborah GILLUM
49 Dean of Arts & Sciences .... Dr. Janna MCLEAN
53 Dean of Education .... Vacant
83 Dean of Humanities/Social Sciences .... Dr. Bradley D. SMITH
35 Director of Student Life .... Mrs. Julie BEAM
06 Registrar .... Mrs. Jeanne E. FOX
36 Director Student Enrichment .... Vacant
37 Director Financial Aid .... Mrs. Jody P. WALKER
26 Director Public Relations .... Mrs. Erin C. KINZEL
41 Director Athletics .... Dr. Thomas VISKER
08 Director Library Services .... Mr. Mark J. ROOT
88 Director Teacher Certification .... Mrs. Kimberly J. MEYER
109 Sr Dir Auxiliary Svcs/Phys Plant .... Mr. Edward E. BERNHARD
09 Director Institutional Research .... Dr. Raymond E. WHITEMAN
19 Director Campus Safety .... Mr. Paul E. NEEL
85 Director International Students .... Mrs. Susan A. MATTESON
91 Director Administrative Computing .... Mr. Harold E. RODGERS
29 Director Alumni Services .... Mrs. Emily S. SHERWOOD
84 AVP of Traditional Enroll/Fin Aid .... Ms. Andrea M. HELMUTH
15 Director Human Resources .... Mr. Mike L. NICHOLAS
04 Administrative Asst to President .... Mrs. Barbara J. RODGERS
104 Director Study Abroad .... Vacant
44 Director Annual or Planned Giving .... Ms. Stephen J. MATTESON

Brightwood College (E)

7833 Indianapolis Boulevard, Hammond IN 46324-3347
County: Lake FICE Identification: 022018
Unit ID: 152415
Telephone: (219) 844-0100 Carnegie Class: Not Classified
FAX Number: (219) 844-0105 Calendar System: Quarter
URL: www.brightwood.edu
Established: 1969 Annual Undergrad Tuition & Fees: N/A
Enrollment: 299 Coed
Affiliation or Control: Proprietary IRS Status: Proprietary
Highest Offering: Associate Degree
Accreditation: ACICS

01 Campus President .... Chris ARTIM
07 Director of Admissions .... Wayne HAMPTON
36 Director Student Placement .... Jennifer ROSS-ANDERSON
37 Director Student Financial Aid .... MelodyAnn CLARK
05 Academic Dean .... Andrea MONTELLA

Brightwood College (F)

4200 South East Street, Indianapolis IN 46227
Telephone: (317) 782-0315 Identification: 770575
Accreditation: ACICS, MAAB

Brown Mackie College-Fort Wayne (G)

3000 E Coliseum Boulevard, Ste 100,
Fort Wayne IN 46805-1565
Telephone: (260) 484-4400 Identification: 666435
Accreditation: ACICS, OTA, #PTAA

† Branch campus of Brown Mackie-South Bend, South Bend, IN.

Brown Mackie College-Indianapolis (H)

1200 N. Meridian Street, Suite 100, Indianapolis IN 46204
Telephone: (317) 554-8300 Identification: 666394
Accreditation: ACICS, OTA

† Branch campus of Brown Mackie College-Findlay, Findlay, OH.

Brown Mackie College-Merrillville (I)

1000 E 80th Place, Suite 205M, Merrillville IN 46410-5602
Telephone: (219) 769-3321 FICE Identification: 021032
Accreditation: ACICS, OTA

† Branch campus of Brown Mackie College-Cincinnati, Cincinnati, OH.

Brown Mackie College-South Bend (J)

3454 Douglas Road, South Bend IN 46635
Telephone: (574) 237-0774 FICE Identification: 004583
Accreditation: ACICS, OTA, PTAA

† Branch campus of The Art Institute of Phoenix, Phoenix, AZ

Butler University (K)

4600 Sunset Avenue, Indianapolis IN 46208-3443
County: Marion FICE Identification: 001788
Unit ID: 150163
Telephone: (317) 940-8000 Carnegie Class: Masters/L
FAX Number: (317) 940-9930 Calendar System: Semester
URL: www.butler.edu
Established: 1855 Annual Undergrad Tuition & Fees: $37,010
Enrollment: 4,848 Coed
Affiliation or Control: Independent Non-Profit IRS Status: 501(c)3
Highest Offering: Doctorate
Accreditation: NH, ARCPA, BUS, CACREP, DANCE, IPSY, MUS, PHAR, TED, THEA

01 President .... Mr. James M. DANKO
05 Provost/VP Academic Affairs .... Dr. Kathryn MORRIS
10 Vice President for Finance .... Mr. Bruce E. ARICK
30 VP University Advancement .... Ms. Jaci THIEDE
26 VP Marketing & Communication .... Mr. Matthew S. MINDRUM
32 Vice President of Student Affairs .... Dr. Anne FLAHERTY
41 VP & Director of Athletics .... Mr. Barry S. COLLIER
84 VP of Enrollment Management .... Ms. Lori GREENE
100 Chief of Staff/Exec Dir Pub Safety .... Mr. Ben D. HUNTER
43 General Counsel .... Ms. Claire KONOPA AIGOTTI
20 Assoc Provost .... Mr. Thomas PARADIS
57 Dean Jordan College Fine Arts .... Dr. Ronald CALTABIANO
50 Dean College of Business .... Dr. Stephen STANDIFIRD
49 Dean Liberal Arts & Science .... Dr. Jay R. HOWARD
53 Dean Education .... Dr. Ena M. SHELLEY
67 Dean Pharmacy & Health Sciences .... Dr. Mary H. GRAHAM
60 Dean College of Communication .... Dr. Gary EDGERTON
08 Dean of Libraries .... Dr. Julie L. MILLER
35 Dean Student Services .... Dr. Sally E. CLICK
35 Dean Student Life .... Dr. Anne G. FLAHERTY
38 Asst Dean & Director Counseling Ctr .... Dr. Keith B. MAGNUS
18 Executive Director of Facilities .... Mr. Richard MICHAL
44 Exec Dir Major Gifts .... Mr. Sean DUNLAVY
15 VP of Human Resources .... Mr. James GALLAHER
88 Exec Director Clowes Memorial Hall .... Mr. Ty SUTTON
21 Executive Budget Director .... Mr. Robert J. MARCUS
37 Director Financial Aid .... Ms. Melissa J. SMURDON
88 Dir Confs & Events .... Ms. Beth A. ALEXANDER
39 Director Residence Life .... Ms. Karla K. CUNNINGHAM
09 Director Institutional Research .... Dr. Nandini RAMASWAMY
85 Director Global Education .... Ms. Jill MCKINNEY
36 Director Career Services .... Mr. Gary R. BEAULIEU
27 Director of Creative Services .... Ms. Nancy LYZUN
28 Director of Diversity Programs .... Ms. Valerie J. DAVIDSON
31 Director of Exernal Relations .... Mr. Michael KALTENMARK
07 Director of Admission .... Ms. Aimee SCHEUERMANN
06 Registrar .... Ms. Michele NEARY
13 Chief Information Officer .... Mr. Peter WILLIAMS
21 Controller .... Ms. Susan M. WESTERMEYER
40 Manager Bookstore .... Ms. Janine L. FRAINIER
96 Manager of Purchasing .... Ms. Shelly S. RABIDEAU
04 Exec Assistant to the President .... Ms. Emily KENNEY

Calumet College of Saint Joseph (L)

2400 New York Avenue, Whiting IN 46394-2195
County: Lake FICE Identification: 001834
Unit ID: 150172
Telephone: (219) 473-7770 Carnegie Class: Masters/S
FAX Number: (219) 473-4259 Calendar System: Semester
URL: www.ccsj.edu
Established: 1951 Annual Undergrad Tuition & Fees: $17,000
Enrollment: 1,072 Coed
Affiliation or Control: Roman Catholic IRS Status: 501(c)3
Highest Offering: Master's

Accreditation: NH, TED

01 President .... Dr. Daniel LOWERY
05 Vice President Academic Affairs .... Dr. Ginger RODRIGUEZ
30 Dir of Institutional Advancement .... Ms. Ester DIAZ
10 VP Business & Finance .... Ms. Lynn MISKUS
32 VP of Student Affairs & Retention .. Ms. Dionne JONES-MALONE
06 Registrar .... Ms. Diana FRANCIS
08 Director of Library Services .... Ms. Qi CHIN
09 Institutional Researcher .... Mr. Darren HENDERSON
26 Dir of Marketing & Public Relations .... Ms. Linda GAJEWSKI
41 Athletic Director .... Mr. Enrique TORRES
42 Director of Campus Ministry .... Br. Jerry SCHWIETERMAN
18 VP of Facilities & Technology .... Mr. Gene KESSLER
84 Director of Enrollment Management .... Mr. Carl CUTTONE
37 Dir Financial Aid/Business Ofc Ops .... Ms. Gina PIRTLE
13 Director of Computer Services .... Mr. Kevin KRIEPS
29 Alumni Relations .... Ms. Angela HUGHES
38 Director of Academic Advising .... Ms. Sally LOBO-TORRES
105 Director Web Services .... Mr. Jesus AVALOS

Chamberlain College of Nursing-Indianapolis Campus (A)

9100 Keystone Crossing, Suite 600, Indianapolis IN 46240
Telephone: (317) 816-7335 Identification: 770503
Accreditation: &NH, NURSE

† Regional accreditation is carried under the parent institution in Addison, IL

Christian Theological Seminary (B)

1000 W. 42nd Street, Indianapolis IN 46208-3301
County: Marion FICE Identification: 001789
Unit ID: 150215
Telephone: (317) 924-1331 Carnegie Class: Spec-4-yr-Faith
FAX Number: (317) 923-1961 Calendar System: Semester
URL: www.cts.edu
Established: 1925 Annual Graduate Tuition & Fees: N/A
Enrollment: 172 Coed
Affiliation or Control: Christian Church (Disciples Of Christ)
IRS Status: 501(c)3
Highest Offering: Doctorate; No Undergraduates
Accreditation: NH, MFCD, THEOL

01 President .... Dr. Matthew M. BOULTON
03 Executive Vice President .... Rev. Verity JONES
05 Vice Pres of Academics .... Dr. Leah GUNNING-FRANCIS
30 Vice President Development .... Rev. Sarah LUND
32 Dean of Students .... Rev. Mary HARRIS
10 Vice President Finance and Business .... Mr. Curtis SHORT
11 Director Finance & Administration .... Mr. Patrick ZULKOWSKI
04 Executive Administrator .... Ms. Sarah EVANS
07 Director of Admissions .... Rev. Brenda FREIJE
44 Director Annual Fund .... Ms. Aimee LARAMORE
21 Director of Business Affairs .... Mr. Chuck CORBIN
08 Director of Library .... Mr. Anthony ELIA
06 Registrar .... Mr. Matt SCHLIMGEN
75 Director of Field Education .... Dr. William KINCAID
18 Director of Facilities .... Mr. Richard DAVIS
37 Int Dir of Student Financial Aid .... Mr. Rodney DUNN
26 Director of Communications .... Ms. Liz JOSS
40 Bookstore Manager .... Mr. Nick BUCK

College of Court Reporting, Inc. (C)

111 W 10th, Suite 111, Hobart IN 46342-5969
County: Lake FICE Identification: 026158
Unit ID: 150251
Telephone: (866) 294-3974 Carnegie Class: Spec 2-yr-Other
FAX Number: (219) 942-1631 Calendar System: Semester
URL: www.ccr.edu
Established: 1984 Annual Undergrad Tuition & Fees: $7,250
Enrollment: 218 Coed
Affiliation or Control: Proprietary IRS Status: Proprietary
Highest Offering: Associate Degree
Accreditation: ACICS

01 President .... Mr. Jeff T. MOODY
03 Executive Director .... Mr. Jay VETTICKAL
05 Director of Education .... Ms. Kay MOODY
07 Director of Admissions .... Ms. Nicky M. RODRIQUEZ
37 Director of Financial Aid .... Ms. Lisa MORTON
32 Director of Student Services .... Ms. Kathleen LAZART

Concordia Theological Seminary (D)

6600 N Clinton Street, Fort Wayne IN 46825-4996
County: Allen FICE Identification: 020876
Unit ID: 150288
Telephone: (260) 452-2100 Carnegie Class: Spec-4-yr-Faith
FAX Number: (260) 452-2121 Calendar System: Quarter
URL: www.ctsfw.edu
Established: 1846 Annual Graduate Tuition & Fees: N/A
Enrollment: 322 Male
Affiliation or Control: Lutheran Church - Missouri Synod
IRS Status: 501(c)3
Highest Offering: Doctorate; No Undergraduates
Accreditation: NH, THEOL

01 President .... Dr. Lawrence R. RAST
05 Academic Dean .... Dr. Charles A. GIESCHEN
36 Dean Pastoral Education/Placement .... Dr. Carl C. FICKENSCHER, II
32 Dean of Students .... Rev. Thomas P. ZIMMERMAN
10 Vice President of Operations .... Rev. Jon SCICLUNA
06 Registrar .... Mrs. Barbara A. WEGMAN
07 Director of Admissions .... Rev. John M. DREYER
08 Head Librarian .... Prof. Robert V. ROETHEMEYER

Crossroads Bible College (E)

601 N Shortridge Road, Indianapolis IN 46219-4912
County: Marion FICE Identification: 034567
Unit ID: 439613
Telephone: (317) 789-8255 Carnegie Class: Spec-4-yr-Faith
FAX Number: (317) 789-8253 Calendar System: Semester
URL: www.crossroads.edu
Established: 1980 Annual Undergrad Tuition & Fees: $12,400
Enrollment: 241 Coed
Affiliation or Control: Independent Non-Profit IRS Status: 501(c)3
Highest Offering: Baccalaureate
Accreditation: BI

01 President .... Dr. A. Charles WARE
03 Executive Vice President .... Dr. John A. CRABTREE, JR.
05 Dean of Educational Svcs .... Dr. Joel BADAL
11 Dean of Administration .... Mr. Marcus SCHRADER
84 Dean of Enrollment Management .... Mr. Richard GREEN
07 Director of Admission/Retention .... Ms. Annetta COLEMAN
18 Facilities Director .... Mr. Nelson POYNTER

DePauw University (F)

313 S Locust Street, Greencastle IN 46135-1772
County: Putnam FICE Identification: 001792
Unit ID: 150400
Telephone: (765) 658-4800 Carnegie Class: Bac-A&S
FAX Number: (765) 658-4177 Calendar System: 4/1/4
URL: www.depauw.edu
Established: 1837 Annual Undergrad Tuition & Fees: $44,678
Enrollment: 2,215 Coed
Affiliation or Control: United Methodist IRS Status: 501(c)3
Highest Offering: Baccalaureate
Accreditation: NH, MUS

01 President .... Dr. Mark MCCOY
04 Executive Assistant to President .... Ms. Elizabeth DEMMINGS
100 Chief of Staff/Assoc VP for Comm .... Dr. Cindy BABINGTON
05 VP for Academic Affairs .... Dr. Anne HARRIS
32 VP Student Academic Life .... Mr. Alan P. HILL
10 VP for Finance/Administration .... Mr. Bradley A. KELSHEIMER
84 VP for Enrollment Management .... Mr. Anthony JONES
30 VP for Development .... Ms. Melanie NORTON
20 Dean of the Faculty .... Dr. Carrie F. KLAUS
88 Dean of Experiential Learning .... Mr. Alan HILL
64 Dean of the School of Music .... Dr. Ayden ADLER
13 Chief Information Officer .... Ms. Carol L. SMITH
35 Dean of Campus Life .... Mr. Dorian SHAGER
06 Registrar .... Dr. Kenneth J. KIRKPATRICK
89 Director of First Year Programs .... Ms. Cara SETCHELL
20 Dean of Academic Life .... Dr. David A. BERQUE
15 Director of Human Resources .... Ms. Amy HAUG
37 Director of Financial Aid .... Mr. Craig A. SLAUGHTER
41 Director of Athletics .... Ms. Stevie BAKER-WATSON
29 Associate VP for Alumni Engagement .... Mr. Steven J. SETCHELL
21 Assoc VP for Finance .... Mr. Travis W. LINNEWEBER
08 Director of Libraries .... Mr. Rick E. PROVINE
44 Director of Annual Giving .... Ms. Kristin CHAMPA
19 Director of Public Safety .... Ms. Angela D. NALLY
07 Director of Admission .... Vacant
96 Director of Purchasing .... Mr. Richard SHUCK
18 Assoc VP for Facilities .... Mr. Richard N. VANCE
26 Exec Director of Media Relations .... Mr. Ken OWEN
09 Director of Institutional Research .... Dr. William M. TOBIN
38 Director of Student Counseling .... Dr. Julie D'ARGENT
39 Director of Housing .... Ms. Myrna HERNANDEZ
28 Director of Diversity .... Ms. Renee MADISON
36 Director Student Placement .... Vacant

Earlham College and Earlham School of Religion (G)

801 National Road W, Richmond IN 47374-4095
County: Wayne FICE Identification: 001793
Unit ID: 150455
Telephone: (765) 983-1200 Carnegie Class: Bac-A&S
FAX Number: (765) 983-1304 Calendar System: Semester
URL: www.earlham.edu
Established: 1847 Annual Undergrad Tuition & Fees: $44,390
Enrollment: 1,076 Coed
Affiliation or Control: Friends IRS Status: 501(c)3
Highest Offering: Master's
Accreditation: NH, THEOL

01 President .... John David DAWSON
05 Vice President Academic Affairs .... Greg MAHLER
10 Vice President Business Affairs .... Sena LANDEY
30 Vice President Advancement .... Avis STEWART
88 Vice President School of Religion .... Jay MARSHALL
07 VP of Enrollment & Communications .... Jonathan STROUD
32 VP/Dean of Student Life .... Laura HUTCHINSON
20 Associate Academic Dean .... Lori WATSON
44 Assoc VP for Institutional Advance .... Kim TANNER
29 Director of Alumni Relations .... Gail CLARK
21 Controller .... Cathy HABSCHMIDT
06 Registrar .... Stanley HILL
88 Director Academic Support Services .... Donna KEESLING
84 Director of Admissions .... Vacant
73 Admissions School of Religion .... Matt HISRICH
41 Athletic Director .... Mike BERGUM
13 Director of Computing Services .... Thomas STEFFES
37 Director of Financial Aid .... Katherine GOTTSCHALK
23 Director of Health Services .... Mary Ann STIENBARGER
15 Director of Human Resources/Ops .... Dana NORTH
85 Director of International Programs .... Patty O'MALEY-LAMSON
18 Director of Physical Plant .... Ian SMITH
26 AVP for Marketing & Communications .... Susanna TANNER
27 Director of Media Relations .... Brian ZIMMERMAN
19 Director of Public Safety .... Tom KEARNS
08 Director of Library .... Neal BAKER
35 Director Student Leadership .... Tracy DUBS
28 Director of Diversity & Inclusion .... Susan LEE
36 Director Center Integrated Learning .... Jay ROBERTS
04 Administrative Asst to President .... Lyn THOMAS
25 Chief Contracts/Grants Admin .... Vacant
39 Director Residence Life .... Shane PETERS
09 Director of Institutional Research .... Polly ALBRIGHT
38 Director Student Counseling .... Jessica SANFORD
102 Dir Foundation/Corporate Relations .... Sara PAULE
104 Director Study Abroad .... Patty LAMSON

Faith Bible Seminary (H)

5526 State Road 26 East, Lafayette IN 47905
County: Tippecanoe Identification: 667250
Telephone: (765) 448-1986 Carnegie Class: Not Classified
FAX Number: N/A Calendar System: Other
URL: www.faithlafayette.org/seminary
Established: 2005 Annual Graduate Tuition & Fees: N/A
Enrollment: N/A Coed
Affiliation or Control: Independent Non-Profit IRS Status: 501(c)3
Highest Offering: Master's; No Undergraduates
Accreditation: @BI

01 President .... Dr. Brent AUCOIN
06 Registrar .... Mr. Kirk FATOOL

Fortis College (I)

9001 N Wesleyan Road, Indianapolis IN 46268
Telephone: (317) 808-4800 Identification: 770574
Accreditation: ACCSC, ADNUR, MAAB

† Branch campus of Fortis Colleg, Winter Park, FL.

Franklin College of Indiana (J)

101 Branigin Boulevard, Franklin IN 46131-2623
County: Johnson FICE Identification: 001798
Unit ID: 150604
Telephone: (317) 738-8000 Carnegie Class: Bac-A&S
FAX Number: (317) 736-6030 Calendar System: 4/1/4
URL: www.franklincollege.edu
Established: 1834 Annual Undergrad Tuition & Fees: $29,025
Enrollment: 1,075 Coed
Affiliation or Control: American Baptist IRS Status: 501(c)3
Highest Offering: Master's
Accreditation: NH, CAATE, TED

01 President .... Dr. Thomas J. MINAR
04 Assistant to the President .... Ms. Janet D. SCHANTZ
10 Vice President Business/Finance .... Mr. Daniel SCHLUGE
05 Interim Provost & Dean of College .... Dr. Timothy L. GARNER
07 Interim Dean of Admission & Fin Aid . Mrs. Kathryn D. COFFMAN
30 VP of Development/Alumni Engagement .... Mrs. Gail LOWRY
20 Acting Associate Dean .... Dr. Denise BAIRD
32 VP Stdnt Affs/Dean of Students .... Mr. Ellis F. HALL
29 Dean Alumni/Student Engagement .... Mrs. Brooke A. WORLAND
06 Registrar .... Ms. Lisa MAHAN
18 Dir Facilities/Energy Management .... Mr. Thomas PATZ
39 Director of Residence Life .... Mr. Jacob E. KNIGHT
38 Director of Counseling Center .... Dr. John R. SHAFER
35 Asst Dean Student Involvement .... Ms. Keri ELLINGTON
46 Dir of Development Research .... Ms. Betsy SCHMIDT
44 Sr Dir Development/Planned Giving .... Mr. Thomas W. ARMOR
37 Director of Financial Aid .... Mrs. Elizabeth SAPPENFIELD
42 Campus Minister .... Rev. Leah PARSELL RUMSEY
41 Athletic Director .... Mr. Kerry N. PRATHER
13 Dir of Information Tech Services .... Mr. Larry J. STOFFEL
36 Dir Career Svcs/Asst Dean Students .... Mr. Kirk J. BIXLER
88 Director of Leadership Development .... Mr. Dale REBHORN
104 Dir Intercultural/Off-Campus Stds .... Ms. Jennifer CATALDI
109 Director of Dining Services-Sodexo .... Mr. Les PETROFF
44 Annual Fund Director .... Mrs. Jane HOWARD
07 Director of Admissions .... Ms. Jennifer BOSTROM
27 Director of Communications .... Ms. Deidra BAUMGARDNER
26 Director of Marketing .... Ms. Theresa LEHMAN
08 Director of Library Services .... Ms. Denise SHOREY
19 Director of Campus Security .... Mr. Steve LEONARD
105 Website Administrator .... Ms. Ann KISH
15 Manager of Employee Resources .... Mrs. Maureen PINNICK
22 Director Physical Facilities .... Mr. Thomas PATZ
40 Asst Bookstore Manager .... Mrs. Janet DOWTY
21 Business Office Manager .... Mr. Bradley JONES

23 Coordinator Student Health Center .... Ms. Catherine DECLEENE
28 Coord Multicultural/Diversity Svcs .... Ms. Terri L. ROBERTS-LEONARD
50 Head Business/Computing/Math Div .... Mr Kerry D. SMITH
53 Head Education Division .... Dr. Linda AIREY
79 Head Humanities Division .... Dr. Susan CRISAFULLI
60 Head Journalism Division .... Mr. Joel CRAMER
65 Head Natural Sciences Division .... Dr. Steven K. BROWDER
83 Head Social Sciences Division .... Dr. Denise M. BAIRD
57 Head Fine Arts Division .... Mr. Robin ROBERTS

Goshen College (A)

1700 S Main Street, Goshen IN 46526-4794
County: Elkhart — FICE Identification: 001799
Unit ID: 150668
Telephone: (574) 535-7000 — Carnegie Class: Bac-Diverse
FAX Number: (574) 535-7060 — Calendar System: Semester
URL: www.goshen.edu
Established: 1894 — Annual Undergrad Tuition & Fees: $30,900
Enrollment: 843 — Coed
Affiliation or Control: Mennonite Church — IRS Status: 501(c)3
Highest Offering: Master's
Accreditation: NH, NURSE, SW, TED

01 President .... Dr. James E. BRENNEMAN
03 Executive Vice President .... Dr. Ken F. NEWBOLD
05 VP Academic Affairs/Academic Dean .... Dr. Ross PETERSON-VEATCH
10 Vice President for Finance .... Vacant
30 Vice Pres Institutional Advancement .... Mr. James K. CASKEY
84 VP for Enroll Management/Marketing .... Vacant
28 Director of Intercultural Dev .... Mr. Gilberto PEREZ, JR.
66 Director of Undergraduate Nursing .... Ms. Brenda SROF
58 Director of Graduate Nursing .... Dr. Ruth STOLTZFUS
70 Director of Social Work .... Dr. Jeanne M. LIECHTY
53 Director of Elementary Teacher Educ .... Dr. Kathryn MEYER REIMER
08 Librarian .... Vacant
82 Director of International Education .... Dr. Tom J. MEYERS
88 Director of Secondary Education .... Ms. Suzanne EHST
13 Director of Information Tech Svcs .... Mr. Michael SHERER
09 Director of Institutional Research .... Mr. Justin HEINZEKEHR
06 Registrar .... Ms. Jan KAUFFMAN
37 Director Student Financial Aid .... Mr. Joel D. SHORT
26 Director of Communications .... Ms. Jodi BEYELER
29 Director of Alumni/Parent Relations .... Mr. Dan LIECHTY
42 Campus Minister .... Mr. Robert E. YODER
36 Director of Career Services .... Ms. Melissa KINSEY
18 Director of Facilities .... Mr. Clay E. SHETLER
15 Director of Human Resources .... Mr. Norm BAKHIT
106 Director of Adult/Online Pgms .... Mr. Phil MASON
39 Director of Residence Life .... Mr. Chad COLEMAN
04 Exec Assistant to the President .... Ms Kathleen YODER
108 Director Institutional Assessment .... Mr. Justin HEINZEKEHR
41 Athletic Director .... Mr. Josh GLEASON
38 Director Student Counseling .... Ms. Launa ROHR
07 Dean of Admissions .... Ms Adela HUFFORD

Grace College and Seminary (B)

200 Seminary Drive, Winona Lake IN 46590-1294
County: Kosciusko — FICE Identification: 001800
Unit ID: 150677
Telephone: (574) 372-5100 — Carnegie Class: Masters/S
FAX Number: (574) 372-5139 — Calendar System: Semester
URL: www.grace.edu
Established: 1937 — Annual Undergrad Tuition & Fees: $22,450
Enrollment: 2,185 — Coed
Affiliation or Control: Fellowship Of Grace Brethren Churches — IRS Status: 501(c)3
Highest Offering: Doctorate
Accreditation: NH, CACREP, TED, THEOL

01 President .... Dr. William J. KATIP
04 Exec Assistant to the President .... Mrs. Rhonda K. RABER
05 Exec VP Academic Affairs .... Dr. John R. LILLIS
83 Exec Assistant Academic Affairs .... Mrs. Elma C. SHERMAN
20 Exec Officer Academic Affairs .... Vacant
73 VP & Dean Seminary & School of Min .... Dr. Jeffery A. GILL
30 VP Advancement .... Mr. Andrew R. FLAMM
11 VP Administration & Compliance .... Dr. Carrie A. YOCUM
84 VP Enrollment Management/Marketing .... Mrs. Cindy N. SISSON
10 VP Financial Affairs/CFO .... Mr. Paul G. BLAIR
45 VP Strategic Initiatives & Planning .... Vacant
32 VP Student Affairs .... Dr. James E. SWANSON
51 Dean of Community Education .... Dr. Stephen A. GRILL
49 Dean of School of Arts & Sciences .... Dr. Mark M. NORRIS
83 Dean of Sch of Behavioral Science .... Dr. Thomas J. EDGINGTON
50 Dean of School of Business .... Dr. Jeffrey K. FAWCETT
53 Dean of School of Education .... Dr. Laurinda A. OWEN
106 Exec Dean School of Prof/Online Ed .... Mr. Timothy J. ZIEBARTH
42 Dean of Chapel .... Mr. Brent MENCARELLI
06 Registrar .... Mr. Steven T. CARLSON
08 Dir Library Services .... Mrs. Tonya L. FAWCETT
13 Dir Information Technology .... Mr. Donald W. FLUKE
23 Dir Student Health & Counseling .... Dr. Debra S. MUSSER
37 Dir Student Financial Aid .... Mrs. Charlette R. SAUDERS
15 Dir of Human Resource .... Mrs. Lisa F. HARMAN
26 Dir of Marketing .... Mr. Steven BREEDEN
18 Director Physical Plant .... Mr. Randy KLEINHANS
29 Director Alumni Engagement .... Mr. Dennis L. DUNCAN
41 Director of Athletics .... Mr. Chad BRISCOE
36 Director Career Connections .... Ms. Denise TERRY
09 Dir Institutional Effectiveness .... Dr Mark H RAIKES
100 Chief of Staff .... Dr. Carrie A YOCUM

Hanover College (C)

PO Box 108, Hanover IN 47243-0108
County: Jefferson — FICE Identification: 001801
Unit ID: 150756
Telephone: (812) 866-7000 — Carnegie Class: Bac-A&S
FAX Number: (812) 866-2164 — Calendar System: Other
URL: www.hanover.edu
Established: 1827 — Annual Undergrad Tuition & Fees: $34,514
Enrollment: 1,145 — Coed
Affiliation or Control: Presbyterian Church (U.S.A.) — IRS Status: 501(c)3
Highest Offering: Baccalaureate
Accreditation: NH, TED

01 President .... Dr. Lake LAMBERT, III
04 Executive Asst to the President .... Treva SHELTON
10 Vice President Business Affairs .... Michael BRUCE
41 Director of Athletics .... Lynn HALL
30 Vice President College Advancement .... Velba RODRIGUEZ
05 Vice President Academic Affairs .... Dr. Steve JOBE
84 Vice Pres Enrollment Management .... Jon RIESTER
32 Vice President Student Life .... Dr. Dewain LEE
88 Exec Dir Business Scholars Program .... Jerry JOHNSON
88 Special Asst to the President .... Chris GAGE
06 Registrar .... Dr. Ken PRINCE
13 Chief Technology Officer .... John COLLINS
35 Associate Dean of Students .... Katy LOWE-SCHNEIDER
42 Chaplain .... Catherine KNOTT
29 Interim Dir of Alumni Engagement .... Christy HUGHES
19 Director of Campus Safety .... Jim HICKERSON
36 Director of Career Center .... Margaret KRANTZ
26 Dir of Communications & Marketing .... Rhonda BURCH
08 Director of Duggan Library .... Kelly JOYCE
37 Director of Financial Aid .... Richard NASH
23 Director of Health Services .... Sandi ALEXANDER-LEWIS
15 Director of Human Resources .... Shelley PREOCANIN
18 Director of Physical Plant .... Scott KLEIN
104 Director of Study Abroad .... Usch APPELT
38 Director of Student Counseling .... Catherine LE SAUX
39 Director of Student Housing .... Lindsay FAULSTICK
96 Director of Purchasing .... Kevin BROWN

Harrison College - Anderson Campus (D)

140 E 53rd Street, Anderson IN 46013-17[illegible]
Telephone: (765) 644-7514 — Identification: 666030
Accreditation: ACICS, MAC

† Regional accreditation is carried under the parent institution in Indianapolis (Downtown Campus), IN.

Harrison College - Columbus Indiana Campus (E)

2222 Poshard Drive, Columbus IN 47203-1[illegible]43
Telephone: (812) 379-9000 — Identification: 666428
Accreditation: ACICS, MAC

† Regional accreditation is carried under the parent institution in Indianapolis (Downtown Campus), IN.

Harrison College - Elkhart Campus (F)

56075 Parkway Avenue, Elkhart IN 46516-9325
Telephone: (574) 522-0397 — Identification: 666143
Accreditation: ACICS, MAC

† Regional accreditation is carried under the parent institution in Indianapolis (Downtown Campus), IN.

Harrison College - Evansville Campus (G)

4601 Theater Drive, Evansville IN 47715-3901
Telephone: (812) 476-6000 — Identification: 666429
Accreditation: ACICS, MAC

† Regional accreditation is carried under the parent institution in Indianapolis (Downtown Campus), IN.

Harrison College - Fort Wayne Campus (H)

6413 N Clinton Street, Fort Wayne IN 46825-4911
Telephone: (260) 471-7667 — Identification: 666029
Accreditation: ACICS, MAC, SURGT

† Regional accreditation is carried under the parent institution in Indianapolis (Downtown Campus), IN.

Harrison College - Indianapolis Downtown Campus (I)

550 E Washington Street, Indianapolis IN 46204-2611
County: Marion — FICE Identification: 021584
Unit ID: 151166
Telephone: (317) 447-6200 — Carnegie Class: Bac/Assoc-Mixed
FAX Number: (317) 686-9190 — Calendar System: Quarter
URL: www.harrison.edu
Established: 1902 — Annual Undergrad Tuition & Fees: $17,100
Enrollment: 3,498 — Coed
Affiliation or Control: Proprietary — IRS Status: Proprietary
Highest Offering: Baccalaureate
Accreditation: ACICS, ACFEI, MAC, NURSE

01 President .... Dr. James D. HUTTON
12 Campus President .... Mr. Ryon KAOPUIKI

† Includes online and The Chef's Academy.

Harrison College - Indianapolis East Campus (J)

8150 Brookville Road, Indianapolis IN 46239-8903
Telephone: (317) 375-8000 — Identification: 666430
Accreditation: ACICS, ADNUR, MAC, MLTAD, SURGT

† Regional accreditation is carried under the parent institution in Indianapolis (Downtown Campus), IN.

Harrison College - Indianapolis Northwest Campus (K)

6300 Technology Center Drive, Indianapolis IN 46278-6022
Telephone: (317) 873-6500 — Identification: 666388
Accreditation: ACICS

† Regional accreditation is carried under the parent institution in Indianapolis (Downtown Campus), IN.

Harrison College - Lafayette Campus (L)

4705 Meijer Court, Lafayette IN 47905-4859
Telephone: (765) 447-9550 — Identification: 666431
Accreditation: ACICS, MAC

† Regional accreditation is carried under the parent institution in Indianapolis (Downtown Campus), IN.

Harrison College - Terre Haute Campus (M)

1378 S State Road 46, Terre Haute IN 47803-9787
Telephone: (812) 877-2100 — Identification: 666433
Accreditation: ACICS, MAC

† Regional accreditation is carried under the parent institution in Indianapolis (Downtown Campus), IN.

Holy Cross College (N)

PO Box 308, Notre Dame IN 46556-0308
County: Saint Joseph — FICE Identification: 007263
Unit ID: 150774
Telephone: (574) 239-8400 — Carnegie Class: Bac-A&S
FAX Number: (574) 239-8323 — Calendar System: Semester
URL: www.hcc-nd.edu
Established: 1966 — Annual Undergrad Tuition & Fees: $27,950
Enrollment: 520 — Coed
Affiliation or Control: Roman Catholic — IRS Status: 501(c)3
Highest Offering: Baccalaureate
Accreditation: NH

01 President .... Bro. John R. PAIGE, CSC
11 VP for Administration .... Vacant
30 VP for Advancement .... Mr. Michael BRACH
04 Executive Assistant .... Ms. Jodie L. SWEET
05 VP for Academic Affairs .... Dr. Justin WATSON
32 VP for Student Affairs .... Dr. Kelly JORDAN
26 Director of Communications .... Ms. Kristina BARROSO-BURRELL
45 VP for Strategic Initiatives .... Bro. Jesus ALONSO, CSC
06 Registrar .... Mrs. Hiroko TEZUKA
84 Director of Enrollment Management .... Bro. Jesus ALONSO, CSC
37 Director of Financial Aid .... Mr. Michael SCHMALTZ
38 Director of Student Counseling Svcs .... Mr. Thomas DEHORN
13 Director of Campus Technology .... Mr. Doug BLAIR
39 Director of Residence Life .... Mr. William MCKENNEY
08 Director of Library Services .... Mrs. Mary Ellen HEGEDUS
36 Director of Career Development .... Mr. Alan JONES
42 Director of Campus Ministry .... Mr. Andrew POLANIECKI
41 Athletic Director .... Ms. Aimee NIESPODZIANY
09 Director of Institutional Research .... Bro. Charles DREVON
10 Chief Financial/Business Officer .... Mrs. Deanna COLEMAN
15 Chief Human Resources Officer .... Mrs. Gwen DEMAEGD
18 Chief Facilities/Physical Plant .... Mr. Mark HILL
21 Associate Business Officer .... Ms. Cathy OSOWSKI
29 Director of Alumni Affairs .... Ms. Judeann HASTINGS
44 Director of Annual Giving .... Ms. Elizabeth FULNECKY
19 Chief Security Officer .... Mr. Greg RUNNELS

Huntington University (O)

2303 College Avenue, Huntington IN 46750-9986
County: Huntington — FICE Identification: 001803
Unit ID: 150941
Telephone: (260) 356-6000 — Carnegie Class: Bac-Diverse
FAX Number: (260) 359-4086 — Calendar System: 4/1/4
URL: www.huntington.edu
Established: 1897 — Annual Undergrad Tuition & Fees: $24,822
Enrollment: 1,209 — Coed
Affiliation or Control: United Brethren Church — IRS Status: 501(c)3
Highest Offering: Doctorate
Accreditation: NH, NURSE, OT, SW, TED

01 President .... Dr. Sherilyn R. EMBERTON

05 Vice President Academic Affairs ....Dr. Michael K. WANOUS
10 VP for Business/Finance/Treasurer ....Mr. Gregory A. SMITLEY
84 VP Enrollment Mgmt & Marketing ....Mr. Daniel SOLMS
45 VP Strategy & Grad/Professionl Pgms ...Dr. Ann C. MCPHERREN
30 Vice President for Advancement ....Mr. Vincent D. HAUPERT
32 Vice President for Student Life ....Dr. Ron L. COFFEY
04 Administrative Secy to President ....Mrs. Cindy H. GEDERS
42 Campus Pastor ....Rev. Arthur L. WILSON
58 Dir of Grad & Professional Programs ....Mrs. Julie K. GOETZ
36 Assoc Dean Student Life/Career Dev ....Ms. Martha J. SMITH
35 Assoc Dean of Student Development ....Mr. Jesse M. BROWN
21 Controller/Dir of Fin Services ....Mrs. Connie C. BONNER
37 Director of Financial Aid ....Mr. Jerry W. DAVIS
06 Registrar ....Mrs. Sarah J. HARVEY
08 Director of Library Services ....Ms. Anita GRAY
13 Dir Information/Technology Services ....Mr. Adam L. SKILES
38 Director of Learning Assistance ....Mrs. Kris L. CHAFIN
41 Athletic Director ....Ms. Lori L. CULLER
18 Director of Physical Plant ....Mr. Jerry A. GRESSLEY
29 Director of Alumni Relations ....Mrs. Marcy T. HAWKINS
19 Director of Campus Police ....Mr. Barry A. COCHRAN
88 Dir of Horizon Leadership Program ....Mr. Jesse M. BROWN

Indiana State University (A)

200 N 7th Street, Terre Haute IN 47809-1902
County: Vigo FICE Identification: 001807
Unit ID: 151324
Telephone: (812) 237-6311 Carnegie Class: DU-Mod
FAX Number: (812) 237-2291 Calendar System: Semester
URL: web.indstate.edu
Established: 1865 Annual Undergrad Tuition & Fees (In-State): $8,580
Enrollment: 13,183 Coed
Affiliation or Control: State IRS Status: 501(c)3
Highest Offering: Doctorate
Accreditation: NH, AAFCS, #ARCPA, ART, BUS, CAATE, CACREP, CIDA, CLPSY, CONST, COPSY, DIETC, ENGR, ENGT, MUS, NAIT, NUR, OT, @PTA, SCPSY, SP, SW, TED

01 President ....Dr. Daniel J. BRADLEY
100 Chief of Staff ....Ms. Teresa D. EXLINE
86 Exec Dir of Government Relations ....Mr. Greg J. GOODE
88 Exec Dir Strat Initiat/Dir Ent Svc ....Dr. Monica LOVE
05 Provost/Vice Pres Academic Affs ....Dr. Michael J. LICARI
10 Sr VP Finance & Admin/Univ Treas ....Ms. Diann E. MCKEE
84 Sr VP Enrollment Mgmt/Mktg/Comm ....Mr. John BEACON
32 VP Student Affairs ....Dr. Willie BANKS
88 Vice Pres Univ Engagement ....Dr. Nancy B. ROGERS
43 General Counsel Legal Affairs ....Ms. Bridget K. BUTWIN
20 Assoc VP Academic Affairs ....Dr. Joshua POWERS
13 Assoc VP Chief Info Officer ....Dr. Lisa SPENCE
18 Assoc VP Univ Facilities Management ....Mr. Kevin L. RUNION
26 Asst VP Comm/Marketing ....Mr. Santhana NAIDU
07 Assoc VP Enroll/Mgmt/Adm/HS Rel ....Mr. Richard J. TOOMEY
29 Director of Alumni Affairs ....Mr. Rex KENDALL
15 Assoc VP Human Resources ....Mr. Wil DOWNS
14 Exec Dir Information Technology ....Mr. Yancy PHILLIPS
21 Business Officer ....Ms. Diann E. MCKEE
06 Registrar ....Ms. April HAY
22 Assoc VP Equal Opp &Title IX Dir ....Dr. Leah REYNOLDS
22 Spec Asst to Prov Inclusive Exc ....Vacant
28 Exec Dir Multicultural Svcs & Pgms ....Ms. Elonda ERVIN
41 Director of Athletics ....Mr. Sherard CLINKSCALES
36 Executive Dir Career Svcs ....Dr. Darby C. SCISM
25 Director Sponsored Programs ....Ms. Dawn UNDERWOOD
09 Director of Institutional Research ....Ms. Patty MCCLINTOCK
19 Director of Public Safety ....Mr. Joseph M. NEWPORT
96 Dir Purchasing/Central Receiving ....Mr. Kevin BARR
39 Executive Dir of Residential Life ....Ms. Amanda KNERR
38 Director of Student Counseling ....Dr. Kenneth CHEW
37 Director Student Financial Aid ....Ms. Crystal BAKER
49 Interim Dean of Arts & Sciences ....Dr. Christopher OLSEN
50 Dean of Business ....Dr. Brien N. SMITH
53 Dean of Education ....Dr. Kandi HILL-CLARKE
68 Interim Dean Health & Human Svcs ....Dr. Eliezer BERMUDEZ
72 Dean of Technology ....Dr. Robert ENGLISH
58 Dean of Grad/Professional Studies ....Dr. Lynn MAURER
08 Dean of Library Services ....Dr. Robin CRUMRIN
56 Dean of Extended Learning ....Dr. Ken BRAUCHLE

Indiana Tech (B)

1600 E Washington Boulevard, Fort Wayne IN 46803-1297
County: Allen FICE Identification: 001805
Unit ID: 151290
Telephone: (260) 422-5561 Carnegie Class: Spec-4-yr-Bus
FAX Number: (260) 420-1453 Calendar System: Semester
URL: www.IndianaTech.edu
Established: 1930 Annual Undergrad Tuition & Fees: $25,600
Enrollment: 7,192 Coed
Affiliation or Control: Independent Non-Profit IRS Status: 501(c)3
Highest Offering: Doctorate
Accreditation: NH, CAHIIM, ENG, #LAW

01 President ....Dr. Arthur E. SNYDER
15 Human Resources Director ....Mr. Christopher B. BLACK
100 Executive Operations Director ....Ms. Jennifer A. ROSS
04 Executive Operations Coordinator ....Ms. Penny J. EGLY
10 Exec VP Finance & Administration ....Ms. Judy K. ROY
21 Controller ....Ms. Shelly R. MUSOLF
13 Director of Information Technology ....Mr. Jeff S. LEICHTY
18 Dir Security & Facilities Mgmt ....Mr. R. Michael TOWNSLEY
37 Financial Aid Director ....Mr. Scott W. THUM
05 Vice President for Academic Affairs ....Dr. John F. SHANNON
54 Dean of Engineering/Computer Sci ....Mr. David A. ASCHLIMAN
50 Dean of Business ....Vacant
97 Dean of General Studies ....Dr. Joshua C. FRANCIS
58 Director Global Leadership Program ....Dr. Kenneth E. RAUCH
09 Director of Academic Research ....Mr. Christopher D. DOUSE
08 Director McMillen Library ....Ms. Constance E. SCOTT
06 Registrar ....Mr. Esaeas J. RODRIGUEZ
108 Director of Institutional Planning ....Mr. Henry D. KING
77 Assoc Dean of Computer Sciences ....Mr. Gary A. MESSICK
61 Dean Law School ....Mr. Charles P. CERCONE
08 Associate Dean for Library Affairs ....Ms. Phebe E. POYDRAS
84 VP for Enrollment Management ....Mr. Steve A. HERENDEEN
84 Enrollment Manager-Fort Wayne ....Mr. Yiani DEMITSAS
106 Director of Online Learning ....Dr. Y. Ben LEE
11 Associate VP for Operations ....Ms. Sharon LOKUTA
07 CPS Director of Admissions .... Mr. Duncan L. MCCORQUODALE
32 VP for Student Affairs ....Dr. Daniel J. STOKER
41 Athletic Director ....Ms. Debra P. WARREN
39 Assoc VP Student Services ....Mr. Chris M. DICKSON
35 Director Student Life ....Ms. Andrea G. CHECK
36 Director Career Center ....Ms. Cynthia P. VERDUCE
42 Faith Services Coordinator ....Mr. Gregory P. BYMAN
26 VP University Relations ....Mr. Brian W. ENGELHART
30 Associate VP Advancement ....Ms. Mary V. SLAFKOSKY
29 Dir Annual Fund & Alumni Relations ......Ms. Arienne B. JULIANO
88 Exec Dir C3 ....Ms. Crystal E. VANN WALLSTROM
102 Dir Foundation/Corporate Relations ....Ms. Tracina A. SMITH
44 Director Annual or Planned Giving ....Ms. Lisa M. BIERS

Indiana Tech-Elkhart (C)

3333 Middleburg Street, Elkhart IN 46516
Telephone: (574) 296-7075 Identification: 770102
Accreditation: &NH

† Regional accreditation is carried under the parent institution in Fort Wayne, IN

Indiana Tech-Indianapolis (D)

3500 DePaul W Boulevard, Indianapolis IN 46268
Telephone: (317) 466-2121 Identification: 770103
Accreditation: &NH

† Regional accreditation is carried under the parent institution in Fort Wayne, IN

*Indiana University (E)

107 S. Indiana Ave., Bryan Hall 200,
Bloomington IN 47405-7000
County: Monroe FICE Identification: 008002
Unit ID: 151351
Telephone: (812) 855-4613 Carnegie Class: N/A
FAX Number: (812) 855-9586
URL: www.indiana.edu

01 President ....Dr. Michael A. MCROBBIE
05 Exec Vice President/Provost IUB ....Ms. Lauren ROBEL
03 Exec Vice President IU ....Dr. Nasser PAYDAR
21 Exec VP Univ Academic Affairs ....Mr. John APPLEGATE
46 Vice Pres for Research ....Dr. Fred CATE
28 VP Diversity/Equity/Multicultural ....Dr. James WIMBUSH
18 Vice Pres Capital Planning & Facil ....Dr. Thomas MORRISON
10 Interim Vice President/CFO ....Ms. Joan HAGEN
86 Vice Pres Government Relations ....Mr. Michael SAMPLE
100 Chief of Staff ....Dr. Karen H. ADAMS
13 Vice President Info Tech/CIO ....Dr. Brad C. WHEELER
43 Vice Pres and University Counsel ... Ms. Jacqueline A. SIMMONS
104 Vice Pres for International Affairs ....Dr. David ZARET
88 Vice President for Engagement ....Mr. William B. STEPHAN
41 VP & Dir of Intercoll Athletics ....Mr. Fred GLASS
63 VP Univ Clinical Affs/Dean Sch Med ....Dr. Jay HESS
21 University Treasurer ....Mr. Don LUKES
22 Director of Affirmative Action ....Ms. Julie KNOST
29 Exec Dir IU Alumni Association ....Mr. J. Thomas FORBES
102 President IU Foundation ....Dr. Dan SMITH
04 Administrative Asst to President ....Ms. Nicole TODD
19 AVP Public Safety & Inst Assurance ....Mr. Mark S. BRUHN
25 Exec Dir Grant & Contract Services ....Mr. James BECKER
32 Dean of Students ....Dr. Lori RIESER
37 Dir of Ops Student Financial Aid ....Ms. Jenny STEPHENS

*Indiana University Bloomington (F)

107 S. Indiana Avenue, Bloomington IN 47405-7000
County: Monroe FICE Identification: 001809
Unit ID: 151351
Telephone: (812) 855-4848 Carnegie Class: Not Classified
FAX Number: (812) 855-5678 Calendar System: Semester
URL: www.iub.edu
Established: 1820 Annual Undergrad Tuition & Fees (In-State): N/A
Enrollment: N/A Coed
Affiliation or Control: State IRS Status: 501(c)3
Highest Offering: Doctorate
Accreditation: NH, ART, AUD, BUS, BUSA, CAATE, CACREP, CEA, CIDA, CLPSY, COPSY, DIETD, IPSY, JOUR, LAW, LIB, MUS, NRPA, OPT, OPTR, OPTT, PCSAS, PH, SCPSY, SP, SPAA, TED, THEA

02 President ....Dr. Michael MCROBBIE
05 Exec VP & Provost ....Ms. Lauren ROBEL
03 Exec VP & Chanc IUPUI ....Mr. Nasser PAYDAR
05 Exec VP Univ Academic Affairs ....Mr. John S. APPLEGATE
10 Acting VP & CFO ....Ms. Joan HAGEN
63 VP University Clinical Affairs ....Dr. Jay HESS
18 VP Capital Planning & Facilities ....Mr. Tom MORRISON
28 VP Diversity/Equity & Multicul Affs ....Mr. James WIMBUSH
46 VP for Research ....Mr. Fred H. CATE
26 VP for Public Affs & Govt Relations ....Mr. Mike SAMPLE
88 VP for Engagement ....Mr. William B. STEPHAN
88 VP Development IU Foundation ....Mr. Jonathan D. PURVIS
20 Vice Prov for Undergraduate Educ ....Mr. Dennis GROTH
20 Vice Prov Faculty & Academic Affs ....Ms. Eliza PAVALKO
09 Exec Dir of Institutional Research ....Mr. Todd SCHMITZ
84 Vice Prov Enrollment Mgmt ....Mr. David JOHNSON
88 Vice Prov Grad Educ & Health Sci ....Mr. David DALEKE
88 Vice Prov Strategic Initiatives ....Dr. Munirpallam VENKATARAMANAN
30 Exec Vice Pres Development/IU Fdn ....Mr. Richard K. DUPREE
28 Vice Prov Educ Inclusion/Diversity ....Mr. Martin MCCRORY
21 Assoc VP & Univ Controller ....Ms. Joan HAGEN
15 Assoc VP Univ Human Resources ....Mr. John WHELAN
13 VP Info Technology & CIO ....Mr. Brad WHEELER
58 Dean University Graduate School ....Mr. James WIMBUSH
102 Pres & CEO IU Foundation ....Mr. Daniel C. SMITH
85 Assoc VP for International Svcs ....Mr. Christopher VIERS
27 Assoc VP and Deputy CIO ....Ms. Laurie G. ANTOLOVIC
88 Assoc VP & Chief Audit Officer ....Mr. Stewart COBINE
49 Dean College Arts & Sciences ....Mr. Larry SINGELL
08 Ruth Lilly Dean Univ Libraries ....Ms. Carolyn WALTERS
32 Dean of Students ....Mr. Pete GOLDSMITH
63 Dean of Medical Sciences ....Dr. John B. WATKINS
50 Dean Kelley School of Business ....Ms. Idalene KESNER
53 Interim Dean School of Education ....Mr. Terrence C. MASON
68 Dean School of Public Health ....Dr. Mohammed TORABI
88 Dean School of Optometry ....Dr. Joseph BONANNO
61 Dean School of Law ....Mr. Austen L. PARRISH
64 Dean Jacobs School of Music ....Mr. Gwyn RICHARDS
60 Dean Media School ....Mr. James SHANAHAN
88 Int Dean Sch Informatics and Comp ....Mr. Brad WHEELER
88 Dean School of Global and Intl Stds ....Mr. Lee FEINSTEIN
80 Dean SPEA ....Dr. John D. GRAHAM
66 Int Dean School of Nursing ....Ms. Desiree HENSEL
82 VP International Affairs ....Mr. David ZARET
92 Dean Hutton Honors College ....Ms. Andrea CICCARELLI
70 Director School of Social Work ....Ms. Karen ALLEN
29 Exec Dir IU Alumni Association ....Mr. J.T FORBES
39 Exec Dir Residential Pgm & Svcs ....Mr. Pat CONNOR
16 Bloomington Dir Employee Rels Svcs ....Ms. Suzanne RYAN
06 Assoc Vice Provost/Registrar ....Mr. Mark MCCONAHAY
23 Exec Dir IU Health Center ....Dr. Pete GROGG
43 VP & General Counsel ....Ms. Jacqueline SIMMONS
22 Director Affirmative Action ....Ms. Julie KNOST
19 Chief of Police ....Ms. Laury FLINT
88 Exec Dir Indiana Memorial Union ....Mr. Hank WALTER
88 Exec Dir Radio/TV Services ....Mr. Perry METZ
88 Director IU Auditorium ....Mr. Doug BOOHER
38 Director Counseling & Psych Svs ....Dr. Nancy STOCKTON
41 VP & Dir Intercollegiate Athletics ....Mr. Fred GLASS
96 Asst VP Procurement Services ....Ms. Jill SCHUNK
88 Director IU Art Museum ....Mr. David BRENNEMAN
07 Director of Admissions ....Ms. Sacha THIEME
100 Chief of Staff ....Ms. Karen ADAMS
101 Secretary of the Institution/Board ....Ms. Deborah A. LEMON
104 Assoc VP Overseas Study ....Ms. Kathleen SIDELI
106 Asst VP & Dir Online Education ....Mr. Chris FOLEY
88 Director of Healthy IU ....Ms. Patricia HOLLINGSWORTH
88 University Treasurer ....Mr. Don LUKES
88 Dir Office of Sustainability ....Mr. William BROWN
103 Dir Workforce/Career Development ....Mr. Patrick DONAHUE
37 Director Student Financial Aid . Ms. Jackie KENNEDY-FLETCHER
86 Director Government Relations ....Ms. Becca POLCZ
44 Assoc VP Gift Planning Svcs ....Mr. Brian D. YELEY

*Indiana University East (G)

2325 Chester Boulevard, Richmond IN 47374-1289
County: Wayne FICE Identification: 001811
Unit ID: 151388
Telephone: (765) 973-8200 Carnegie Class: Masters/S
FAX Number: N/A Calendar System: Semester
URL: www.iue.edu
Established: 1946 Annual Undergrad Tuition & Fees (In-State): $6,930
Enrollment: 4,573 Coed
Affiliation or Control: State IRS Status: 501(c)3
Highest Offering: Master's
Accreditation: NH, ACBSP, NUR, TED

02 Chancellor ....Dr. Kathyrn CRUZ-URIBE
05 Vice Chanc Academic Affairs ....Dr. Michelle MALOTT
26 Vice Chanc External Affs/Marketing ....Mr. Jason TROUTWINE
10 Vice Chancellor Admin & Finance ....Mr. Dan DOOLEY
32 Dean Students/Academic Affairs ....Dr. Mary BLAKEFIELD
13 Director Information Technology ....Mr. Todd DUKE
30 Director of Gift Development ....Ms. Paula Kay KING
06 Registrar ....Mr. Dennis HICKS
08 Director Library/Media Services ....Dr. Frances YATES
15 Interim Director Human Resources ....Mr. James SUMMERS
36 Career and Internship Coordinator ....Ms. Sally SAYDSHOEV
07 Director of Admissions ....Ms. Molly VANDERPOOL
37 Dir Fin Aid & Scholarships ....Ms. Sarah SOPER
20 Director University College ....Ms. Carrie REISNER
40 Manager of Barnes & Noble Bookstore ....Ms. Kristy FRASHER
35 Director of Campus Life ....Ms. Rebeckah HESTER

21 Interim Bursar ... Ms. Shelley DODSON
70 Director Social Work/Human Services ... Mr. Ed FITZGERALD
27 Director Communications & Marketing ... Mr. John DALTON
29 Director Alumni Relations ... Ms. Terry WIESEHAN
50 Dean Business/Technology ... Dr. Bob MULLIGAN
79 Dean Humanities & Social Sciences ... Dr. Ross ALEXANDER
81 Dean Natural Science & Math ... Dr. Neil SABINE
66 Dean of Nursing ... Ms. Karen CLARK
53 Dean of Education ... Dr. Jerry WILDE

*Indiana University Kokomo (A)

2300 S Washington, Box 9003, Kokomo IN 46904-9003
County: Howard FICE Identification: 001814
Unit ID: 151333
Telephone: (765) 453-2000 Carnegie Class: Bac-Diverse
FAX Number: (765) 455-9444 Calendar System: Semester
URL: www.iuk.edu
Established: 1945 Annual Undergrad Tuition & Fees (In-State): $6,941
Enrollment: 4,180 Coed
Affiliation or Control: State IRS Status: 501(c)3
Highest Offering: Master's
Accreditation: NH, BUS, NUR, NURSE, RAD, TED

53 Int Dean School of Education ... Dr. Shirley AAMIDOR
02 Chancellor ... Dr. Susan SCIAME-GIESECKE
05 Vice Chanc Academic Affairs ... Dr. Mark CANADA
20 Assoc VC for Acad Aff/Stdnt Success ... Dr. Christina DOWNEY
20 Asst VC for Acad Affs/Fac Dev ... Dr. Julie SAAM
20 Asst Vice Chanc Academic Affairs ... Dr. Scott JONES
32 Vice Chanc Student Affs/Enroll Mgmt ... Dr. Todd GAMBILL
30 Vice Chancellor for Advancement ... Ms. Jan HALPERIN
72 Director Purdue Polytechnic Inst ... Mr. Jeff GRIFFIN
08 Dean of the Library ... Ms. Polly BORUFF-JONES
37 Director Financial Aid ... Ms. Karen SHAW
10 Director of Budget Administration ... Dr. Philemon YEBEI
31 Dir External Rels/Public Affairs ... Ms. Catherine VALCKE
06 Registrar ... Ms. Stacey THOMAS
100 Chief of Staff ... Ms. Gerry G. STROMAN
36 Manager Career/Accessibility Center ... Ms. Tracy SPRINGER
26 Director Media & Marketing ... Ms. Marie RADEL
07 Director of Admissions ... Ms. Angie SIDERS
23 Coord Stdnt Life & Campus Diversity ... Ms. Maria AHMAD
35 Dean of Students ... Ms. Sarah SARBER
18 Director Facilities/Physical Plant ... Mr. John SARBER
50 Dean School of Business ... Dr. Alan KRABBENHOFT
49 Dean Sch Humanities/Social Sciences ... Vacant
66 Dean School of Nursing ... Dr. Linda WALLACE
81 Dean School of Sciences ... Dr. Christian CHAURET
09 Director of Institutional Research ... Ms. Angela SMITH
13 Chief Info Technology Officer (CIO) ... Ms. Beth VANGORDON
15 Director Personnel Services ... Ms. Gabby VANALSTINE
41 Athletic Director ... Mr. Greg COOPER

*Indiana University Northwest (B)

3400 Broadway, Gary IN 46408-1197
County: Lake FICE Identification: 001815
Unit ID: 151360
Telephone: (219) 980-6500 Carnegie Class: Masters/M
FAX Number: (219) 980-6670 Calendar System: Semester
URL: www.iun.edu
Established: 1921 Annual Undergrad Tuition & Fees (In-State): $6,963
Enrollment: 6,052 Coed
Affiliation or Control: State IRS Status: 501(c)3
Highest Offering: Master's
Accreditation: NH, BUS, CAHIIM, DA, DH, NUR, RAD, RTT, SPAA, TED

02 Chancellor ... Dr. William J. LOWE
04 Exec Asst to the Chancellor ... Mrs. Kathy MALONE
05 Exec Vice Chanc Academic Affairs ... Dr. Mark MCPHAIL
11 Exec Dir of Facilities/Operations ... Mr. Andrew KAPOCIUS
32 Vice Chanc Student Svcs/Enroll Mgmt ... Dr. Alexis S. MONTEVIRGEN
10 Campus Chief Financial Officer ... Mrs. Marianne MILICH
26 Vice Chanc Advancement & Ext Affs ... Ms. Jeri Pat GABBERT
13 Chief Information Officer ... Ms. Beth VAN GORDON
20 Assoc Vice Chanc Academic Affs ... Dr. Cynthia O'DELL
09 Asst VC Inst Effectiveness & Rsrch ... Mr. John NOVAK
49 Dean College of Arts & Sciences ... Dr. Mark HOYERT
88 Dean Col of Health & Human Svcs ... Dr. Patrick BANKSTON
50 Dean School of Business & Economics ... Dr. Anna ROMINGER
53 Interim Dean School of Education ... Dr. Charles HOBSON
80 Dir Public & Environ Affs ... Dr. Karl BESEL
70 Director Social Work ... Dr. Darlene LYNCH
06 Registrar ... Mr. Craig DEMYER
88 Director Pre-Professional Pgm ... Dr. Michael LAPOINTE
07 Director of Admissions ... Ms. Dorothy FRINK
37 Director Financial Aid ... Mr. Harold BURTLEY
36 Director Career & Placement ... Ms. Sharese DUDLEY
35 Director Student Activities ... Mr. Scott FULK
19 Director Security ... Mr. Wayne JAMES
29 Director Alumni Relations ... Ms. Paulette LAFATA-JOHNSON
66 Director Division of Nursing ... Dr. Linda DELUNAS
24 Director Instr Media ... Mr. Aaron PIGORS
08 Director Library ... Mr. Timothy SUTHERLAND
18 Director Physical Plant ... Mr. Otto JEFIMENKO
21 Manager Student Accounts ... Ms. Sandra MENDOZA
25 Director Research/Sponsored Pgms ... Ms. T.J STOOPS
15 Interim Director Human Resources ... Ms. Mianta' DIMING
28 Director Diversity Programming ... Mr. James WALLACE, JR.
38 Director of Counseling Services ... Ms. Barbara A. DAHL
22 Director Affirmative Action ... Ms. Ida GILLIS

38 Dir Schlrshp in Teaching & Learning ... Dr. Christopher YOUNG
88 Dir Urban & Regional Excellence ... Dr. Ellen SZARLETA
105 Director Web Services ... Ms. Myriam YOUNG
106 Dir Online Education/E-learning ... Mr. Christopher YOUNG
41 Athletic Director ... Mr. Kristofer SCHNATZ

*Indiana University-Purdue University Fort Wayne (C)

2101 E Coliseum Boulevard, Fort Wayne IN 46805-1499
County: Allen FICE Identification: 001828
Unit ID: 151102
Telephone: (260) 481-6100 Carnegie Class: Masters/L
FAX Number: (260) 481-6880 Calendar System: Semester
URL: www.ipfw.edu
Established: 1964 Annual Undergrad Tuition & Fees (In-State): $8,080
Enrollment: 13,214 Coed
Affiliation or Control: State IRS Status: 501(c)3
Highest Offering: Doctorate
Accreditation: NH, ART, BUS, CS, DA, DH, DT, ENG, ENGT, MUS, NAD, TED, THEA

02 Chancellor ... Dr. Vicky L. CARWEIN
05 Vice Chanc Academic Affairs ... Dr. Carl DRUMMOND
10 Vice Chanc Financial/Admin Affairs ... Dr. David WESSE
32 Vice Chancellor Student Affairs ... Dr. George S. MCCLELLAN
30 Vice Chancellor for Advancement ... Vacant
13 Chief Information Officer ... Mr. Mitch DAVIDSON
18 Director Physical Plant ... Mr. Jay H. HARRIS
29 Interim Director Alumni Relations ... Ms. Melissa EASTMAN
08 Library Dean ... Ms. Cheryl B. TRUESDELL
15 Director Human Resources ... Ms. Tamarah D. BROWNLEE
41 Director of Athletics ... Ms. Kelley HARTLEY
06 Registrar ... Mr. Patrick A. MCLAUGHLIN
96 Director Purchasing ... Ms. Cynthia M. ELICK
19 Chief University Police ... Ms. Julie YUNKER
22 Director Institutional Equity ... Ms. Christine M. MARCUCCILLI
85 Director International Program ... Mr. Brian MYLREA
37 Director Financial Aid ... Mr. David PETERSON
07 Director of Admissions ... Ms. Tonishea JACKSON
49 Dean Arts & Sciences ... Dr. Eric C. LINK
76 Dean Health Sciences ... Dr. Ann OBERGFELL
51 Exec Director Continuing Stds ... Ms. Karen VANGORDER
26 Director of Marketing ... Mr. Jack PATTON
72 Interim Dean Engr Tech/Computer Sc ... Dr. Carlos POMALAZA-RAEZ
53 Dean Educ & Public Policy ... Dr. James BURG
50 Interim Dean Business ... Dr. Joseph KHAMALAH
57 Dean Visual/Performing Arts ... Dr. John O'CONNELL
46 Assoc Vice Chanc Rsrch Ext Support ... Vacant
35 Dean of Students ... Dr. Eric M. NORMAN
28 Assoc Vice Chancellor Diversity ... Mr. Kenneth C. CHRISTMON
100 Chief of Staff ... Ms. Kimberly WAGNER
09 Director of Institutional Research ... Vacant

*Indiana University-Purdue University Indianapolis (D)

301 University Blvd., Suite 5010, Indianapolis IN 46202-5146
County: Marion FICE Identification: 001813
Unit ID: 151111
Telephone: (317) 274-5555 Carnegie Class: DU-Higher
FAX Number: N/A Calendar System: Semester
URL: www.iupui.edu
Established: 1969 Annual Undergrad Tuition & Fees (In-State): $9,056
Enrollment: 30,690 Coed
Affiliation or Control: State IRS Status: 501(c)3
Highest Offering: Doctorate
Accreditation: NH, #ARCPA, ART, CACREP, CAHIIM, CIDA, CLPSY, COARC, CS, CYTO, DA, DENT, DH, DIETI, EMT, ENG, ENGT, FEPAC, HSA, HT, IPSY, LAW, MED, MT, MUS, NMT, NURSE, OT, PA, PAST, PH, PTA, RAD, RADDOS, RTT, SPAA, SW

02 Chancellor ... Dr. Nassar H. PAYDAR
100 Chief of Staff ... Ms. Christine FITZPATRICK
28 Vice Chanc Diversity/Equity/Incl ... Dr. Karen L. DACE
04 Assistant to Chancellor for Comm ... Dr. Becky WOOD
05 Int Exec Vice Chanc/Chief Acad Ofcr ... Dr. Kathy E. JOHNSON
10 Int Vice Chanc Admin & Finance ... Ms. Camy BROEKER
26 Vice Chancellor External Affairs ... Ms. Amy C. WARNER
32 Int Vice Chancellor Student Affairs ... Dr. Tralicia POWELL LEWIS
46 Interim Vice Chancellor Research ... Dr. Simon ATKINSON
13 Dean Information Technologies ... Dr. Anastasia MORRONE
08 Dean University Library ... Mr. David W. LEWIS
84 Int Director Enrollment Services ... Ms. Mary Beth MYERS
06 Registrar ... Ms. Mary Beth MYERS
21 Bursar ... Mr. Dan YOUNGBLOOD
22 Director Equal Opportunity ... Ms. Kim D. KIRKLAND
38 Director Student Counseling ... Dr. Julie LASH
39 Director Campus Housing ... Mr. Aaron HART
40 Bookstore Manager ... Mr. Neil SCARBOROUGH
36 Career Services Council ... Mr. Joshua D. KILLEY
41 Athletic Director ... Dr. Roderick PERRY
29 Director Alumni Relations ... Mr. Stefan S. DAVIS
27 Director News & Media ... Ms. Margie SMITH-SIMMONS
09 Director Institutional Research ... Dr. Gary PIKE
07 Dir of Undergraduate Admissions ... Ms. Yohlunda MOSLEY
37 Director Student Financial Aid ... Mr. Marvin L. SMITH
15 Asst Vice Chanc Human Resources ... Ms. Carlene M. THOMPSON

23 Medical Director Student Health Svc ... Dr. Stephen F. WINTERMEYER
18 Director Campus Facility Services ... Ms. Emily C. WREN
19 Chief Campus Police ... Mr. Robert L. TRUE
92 Dean Honors College ... Dr. E. Jane LUZAR
96 Director Purchasing ... Mr. Robert HALTER
45 Senior Advisor/Academic Planning ... Dr. Trudy W. BANTA
12 Dean Columbus Campus ... Dr. Reinhold R. HILL
76 Int Dean School Health/Rehab Sci ... Dr. Becky PORTER
57 Dean Herron School of Art ... Ms. Valerie EICKMEIER
52 Dean School of Dentistry ... Dr. John N. WILLIAMS
54 Dean School of Engr/Technology ... Dr. David J. RUSSOMANNO
88 Exec Assoc Dean of Informatics ... Dr. Mathew J. PALAKAL
61 Dean McKinney Sch of Law ... Mr. Andrew R. KLEIN
49 Dean School of Liberal Arts ... Dr. Thomas J. DAVIS
63 Dean School of Medicine ... Dr. Jay L. HESS
66 Dean School of Nursing ... Dr. Robin P. NEWHOUSE
68 Dean School of Physical Education ... Dr. James M. GLADDEN
81 Dean School of Science ... Dr. Simon RHODES
70 Dean School of Social Work ... Dr. Michael PATCHNER
69 Dean Fairbanks Sch of Public Health ... Dr. Paul K. HALVERSON
88 Dean Lilly Fam Sch of Philanthropy ... Dr. Amir PASIC
53 Exec Assoc Dean School of Education ... Dr. Robin L. HUGHES
80 Exec Assoc Dean Public/Environ Affs ... Dr. Lilliard RICHARDSON
85 Assoc Vice Chanc International Affs ... Dr. Gil LATZ
50 Assoc Dean School of Business ... Dr. Philip L. COCHRAN
58 Associate Dean Graduate School ... Dr. Janice S. BLUM
89 Interim Dean University College ... Dr. Stephen HUNDLEY
43 Dir Legal Services/General Counsel ... Mr. Joseph M. SCODRO

*Indiana University South Bend (E)

1700 Mishawaka Avenue, South Bend IN 46634-7111
County: Saint Joseph FICE Identification: 001816
Unit ID: 151342
Telephone: (574) 520-4872 Carnegie Class: Masters/M
FAX Number: (574) 520-4334 Calendar System: Semester
URL: www.iusb.edu
Established: 1940 Annual Undergrad Tuition & Fees (In-State): $6,986
Enrollment: 7,859 Coed
Affiliation or Control: State IRS Status: 501(c)3
Highest Offering: Master's
Accreditation: NH, BUS, CACREP, DH, MUS, NURSE, RAD, SPAA, TED

02 Chancellor ... Dr. Terry L. ALLISON
05 Exec Vice Chanc Acad Affairs ... Dr. Jann JOSEPH
10 Vice Chancellor Finance & Admin ... Mr. Philip IAPALUCCI
26 Vice Chanc Public Affs/Univ Advance ... Dr. Ilene SHEFFER
13 Regional Chief Information Officer ... Ms. Elizabeth VAN GORDON
20 Int Assoc Vice Chanc Academic Affs ... Dr. Linda CHEN
32 Assoc Vice Chanc Student Services ... Ms. Karen L. WHITE
84 Assoc Vice Chanc Enrollment Svcs ... Ms. Cathy M. BUCKMAN
06 Registrar ... Mr. Keith DAWSON
35 Dir Student Activit Ctr/Athletics ... Mr. Steve BRUCE
18 Director Facilities Management ... Mr. Michael PRATER
19 Director of Safety & Security ... Mr. Martin L. GERSEY
15 Dir of Human Resources/Career Svcs ... Ms. Deb SCHMITT
24 Dir of Instructional Media Svcs ... Mr. Jim YOCOM
29 Dir Alumni Affs/Campus Ceremonies ... Vacant
27 Director Communications/Marketing ... Mr. Kenneth W. BAIERL
52 Director of Dental Auxiliary Educ ... Ms. Kristyn QUIMBY
51 Director of Extended Learning ... Mr. Mike MANCINI
97 Director of General Studies ... Dr. David A. VOLLRATH
85 Director of International Programs ... Dr. Scott SERNAU
38 Director Student Counseling Ctr ... Mr. Kevin GRIFFITH
07 Director of Admissions ... Ms. Connie PETERSON-MILLER
09 Director of Institutional Research ... Mr. Biniam TESFAMARIAM
28 Director of Diversity ... Ms. Martha (Marty) MCCAMPBELL
30 Director of Development ... Ms. Dina HARRIS
39 Director of Student Housing ... Vacant
21 Director of Accounting ... Ms. Kathleen PIZANA
37 Associate Director of Financial Aid ... Ms. Cyndi LANG
49 Dean of Liberal Arts & Science ... Dr. Elizabeth E. DUNN
50 Dean of Business & Economics ... Vacant
53 Dean of Education ... Dr. Marvin LYNN
57 Dean of the Arts ... Dr. Marvin CURTIS
66 Dean of Nursing/Health Profess ... Vacant
08 Dean of Library Services ... Ms. Vicki BLOOM

*Indiana University Southeast (F)

4201 Grant Line Road, New Albany IN 47150-2158
County: Floyd FICE Identification: 001817
Unit ID: 151379
Telephone: (812) 941-2333 Carnegie Class: Masters/L
FAX Number: (812) 941-2475 Calendar System: Semester
URL: www.ius.edu
Established: 1941 Annual Undergrad Tuition & Fees (In-State): $6,949
Enrollment: 6,442 Coed
Affiliation or Control: State IRS Status: 501(c)3
Highest Offering: Master's
Accreditation: NH, BUS, NURSE, TED

02 Chancellor ... Dr. Ray WALLACE
05 Executive VC Academic Affairs ... Dr. Uric DUFRENE
10 VC Administration/Finance ... Mr. Dana C. WAVLE
84 VC Enrollment Mgmt/Student Affairs ... Dr. Jason L. MERIWETHER
30 VC Advancement ... Ms. Betty S. RUSSO
20 Int Assoc VC Academic Affairs ... Dr. Angela M. SALAS
20 Asst VC Academic Affairs ... Dr. Annette M. WYANDOTTE
32 Asst VC Retention/Student Services ... Ms. Amanda G. STONECIPHER
13 Chief Information Officer ... Ms. Elizabeth VAN GORDON

07 Director Admissions ... Mr. Chris CREWS
04 Exec Secretary to the Chancellor ... Ms. Sarah R. JAMES
35 Dean for Student Life ... Dr. Seuth CHALEUNPHONH
06 Registrar ... Mr. James (Jay) MCTYIER
37 Director Student Financial Aid ... Ms. Traci ARMES
08 Director Library Services ... Mr. C. Martin ROSEN
36 Director Career Development ... Ms. Danielle LEFFLER
18 Exec Dir of Facility Operations ... Mr. Robert C. POFF
14 Dir IT Communications & Support ... Mr. Nicholas T. RAY
41 Director Athletics ... Mr. Joseph M. GLOVER
72 Dir Purdue College of Technology ... Andrew B. TAKAMI
15 Director Human Resources ... Mr. Ray KLEIN
09 Dir Institutional Effectiveness ... Mr. Ronald E. SEVERTIS, JR.
19 Chief Safety & Security ... Mr. Charles EDELEN
38 Dir Personal Counseling ... Dr. Michael DAY
26 Int Dir Mktg & Communications ... Mr. Joseph M. GLOVER
97 Manager General Studies ... Ms. Saundra E. GORDON
79 Dean School Arts & Letters ... Mr. James HESSELMAN
81 Dean School Natural Sciences ... Dr. Elaine HAUB
83 Dean School Social Sciences ... Dr. Kelly A. RYAN
50 Dean School Business ... Dr. David EPLION
53 Dean School Education ... Dr. Doyin COKER-KOLO
66 Interim Dean School Nursing ... Dr. Donna J. BOWLES
46 Dean for Research ... Dr. Diane E. WILLE
28 Director Staff Equity & Diversity ... Ms. Darlene P. YOUNG
29 Dir Alumni and Community Relations ... Mr. J. T. DOUGLAS
88 Dir Advising Ctr Explrtry Students ... Ms. Rebecca TURNER
88 Director Academic Accting Services ... Ms. Melissa D. HILL
88 Director Student Accting Services ... Ms. Ashley M. MCKAY
88 Interim Acad Information Officer ... Mr. Steven KROLAK

*Indiana University-Purdue University Columbus (A)

4601 Central Avenue, Columbus IN 47203
Telephone: (812) 348-7271 Identification: 770185
Accreditation: &NH, NURSE

† Regional accreditation is carried under the parent institution in Indianapolis, IN

Indiana Wesleyan University (B)

4201 S Washington Street, Marion IN 46953-4999
County: Grant FICE Identification: 001822
Unit ID: 151801
Telephone: (765) 674-6901 Carnegie Class: Masters/L
FAX Number: (765) 677-2499 Calendar System: 4/1/4
URL: www.indwes.edu
Established: 1920 Annual Undergrad Tuition & Fees: $24,728
Enrollment: 14,943 Coed
Affiliation or Control: Wesleyan Church IRS Status: 501(c)3
Highest Offering: Doctorate
Accreditation: NH, #CAATE, CACREP, EXSC, MFCD, MUS, NURSE, SW, TED, THEOL

01 President ... Dr. David WRIGHT
05 Chief Academic Officer/Provost ... Dr. Stacy HAMMONS
88 CEO for Residential Education ... Dr. Keith NEWMAN
88 CEO for Non-Residential Education ... Mrs. Audrey HAHN
28 VP for Multicultural Enrichment ... Mrs. Diane MCDANIEL
10 Vice President Business Affs/CFO ... Mrs. Nancy SCHOONMAKER
88 VP Wesley Seminary ... Vacant
20 VP for Academic Affairs/CAPS ... Dr. Brock REIMAN
20 VP for Academic Affairs/SON ... Dr. Barbara IHRKE
30 VP for Advancement ... Dr. Brian GARDNER
20 Associate Provost ... Dr. Don SPROWL
26 VP Enroll Mgmt & Mktg/Residential ... Vacant
84 VP Enroll Mgmt & Mktg/Non-Resident ... Mr. David ROSE
88 VP Life Calling & Integrative Lrng ... Dr. Brandon HILL
11 VP of Operations/Residential Campus ... Mr. John JONES
04 Sr Counsel to the President/Ombudsm ... Mrs. Karen ROORBACH
58 Dean Graduate School ... Dr. Joanne BARNES
88 Dean of the Seminary ... Dr. David SMITH
76 Dean School of Health Sciences ... Dr. Martin RICE
88 Dean of Developmental Learning ... Mr. Andrew PARKER
37 Associate VP Financial Aid ... Mr. Thomas RATLIFF
08 Director Library Resources ... Mrs. Shelia CARLBLOM
08 Director Off-campus Library Svcs ... Mrs. Jule KIND
29 Director of Alumni ... Mr. Rick CARDER
07 Dir Admissions/Residential Educ ... Mr. Adam FARMER
36 Exec Dir Ctr for Student Success ... Mr. Nathan HERRING
15 Exec Director Human Resources ... Mr. Mark PEDERSON
06 University Registrar ... Mrs. Kim NICHOLSON
43 University Counsel ... Mr. Shawn MATTER
21 Controller ... Mrs. Tiffany LEWIS
41 Athletic Director ... Mr. Mark DEMICHAEL
42 Dean of the Chapel ... Dr. John BRAY
92 Exec Director of Honors College ... Mr. David RIGGS
09 Director Institutional Research ... Mr. Tony PARANDI
18 AVP Facilities Services ... Mr. Don ROWLEY
19 Director Campus Police ... Mr. Mario RANGEL
25 Director of Research Support ... Dr. Ken BIELEN

International Business College (C)

5699 Coventry Lane, Fort Wayne IN 46804-9990
County: Allen FICE Identification: 004579
Unit ID: 151458
Telephone: (260) 459-4500 Carnegie Class: Bac/Assoc-Mixed
FAX Number: (260) 436-1896 Calendar System: Semester
URL: www.ibcfortwayne.edu
Established: 1889 Annual Undergrad Tuition & Fees: $13,920
Enrollment: 372 Coed
Affiliation or Control: Proprietary IRS Status: Proprietary
Highest Offering: Baccalaureate
Accreditation: ACICS, MAC

01 President ... Vacant
05 Director of Education ... Ms. Amee AUGENSTEIN
07 Director of Admissions ... Ms. Gena HOPKINS
32 Student Services Director ... Ms. Roxanna SHULL
36 Director of Placement ... Vacant
06 Registrar ... Ms. Christine ELLIS

International Business College (D)

7205 Shadeland Station, Indianapolis IN 46256-3997
Telephone: (317) 813-2300 Identification: 666929
Accreditation: ACICS, DA, MAC

*Ivy Tech Community College of Indiana-Central Office (E)

50 W Fall Creek Parkway N Drive, Indianapolis IN 46208-5752
County: Marion FICE Identification: 008546
Unit ID: 363563
Telephone: (317) 921-4882 Carnegie Class: N/A
FAX Number: (317) 921-4753
URL: www.ivytech.edu

01 President ... Dr. Sue J. ELLSPERMANN
05 Provost/Sr Vice President ... Dr. Steven TINCHER
102 Sr Vice Pres Ivy Tech Foundation ... Mr. John MURPHY
10 Sr Vice President/CFO ... Mr. Chris RUHL
26 Sr Vice Pres Mktg/Comm/Stdnt Exp ... Mr. Jeff FANTER
20 Vice Pres Academic Affairs ... Dr. Russell D. BAKER
18 Vice President Facilities Planning ... Ms. Amanda WILSON
84 VP for Student Experience/Cust Svc ... Ms. Anne P. VALENTINE
06 Asst VP Student Records ... Mrs. Ann YATER
37 Chief Fin Student Resources Ofcr ... Mr. Ben BURTON
15 Executive Director Human Resources ... Mrs. Julie LORTON-ROWLAND
45 Assoc VP Planning/Research ... Mrs. Jill KRAMER
21 Assistant Treasurer ... Mr. Mark A. HUSK
13 Chief Technology Officer ... Mrs. Anne BRINSON
07 Asst VP Admissions/Enrollment ... Ms. Seana MURPHY

*Ivy Tech Community College of Indiana-Central Indiana (F)

50 W Fall Creek Parkway North Drive, Indianapolis IN 46208-5752
County: Marion FICE Identification: 009917
Unit ID: 150987
Telephone: (317) 921-4882 Carnegie Class: Assoc/MT-VT-High Non
FAX Number: (317) 921-4753 Calendar System: Semester
URL: www.ivytech.edu/indianapolis/
Established: 1966 Annual Undergrad Tuition & Fees (In-State): $4,115
Enrollment: 91,179 Coed
Affiliation or Control: State IRS Status: 501(c)3
Highest Offering: Associate Degree
Accreditation: NH, ACBSP, ACFEI, ADNUR, ART, CAHIIM, COARC, CSHSE, ENGT, FUSER, MAC, NAIT, PNUR, RAD, SURGT

02 Chancellor ... Dr. Kathleen F. LEE
05 VC of Academic Affairs ... Dr. Frank MOMAN
32 Vice Chancellor of Student Affairs ... Dr. Darrell CAIN
10 Executive Director of Finance ... Mr. Corey BACK
15 Exec Director of Human Resources ... Ms. Sara MCKEE
11 Exec Dir of Administrative Services ... Mr. James N. BARNEY
103 Exec Dir Workforce & Economic Devel ... Vacant
30 Exec Dir Institutional Advancement ... Mr. Thomas KILIAN
35 Asst Vice Chanc Student Affairs ... Mr. Jerry H. HARRELL
35 Asst Vice Chanc Student Affairs ... Dr. Tracy FUNK
84 Assoc Vice Pres Enrollment ... Ms. Anne P. VALENTINE
37 Director of Financial Aid ... Ms. Chaunta REDFIELD
06 Interim Registrar ... Ms. Katrina OWENS
09 Director of Institutional Research ... Dr. Jeff CORNETT
36 Director of Career Services ... Ms. Rebecca PATTEN-LEMONS
96 Director of Purchasing ... Mr. Jerry L. KOENIG
20 Asst Vice Chanc Academic Affairs ... Mr. Gary PELLICO
26 Director Marketing/Communications ... Ms. Kelli FORD
46 Director of Resource Development ... Ms. Sherry MCGOWAN

*Ivy Tech Community College of Indiana-Anderson (G)

104 West 53rd Street, Anderson IN 46013-1502
Telephone: (800) 644-4882 Identification: 770239
Accreditation: &NH

† Regional accreditation is carried under the parent institution in Indianapolis, IN

*Ivy Tech Community College of Indiana-Bloomington (H)

200 N Daniels Way, Bloomington IN 47404-9772
Telephone: (812) 332-1559 FICE Identification: 035213
Accreditation: &NH, ACBSP, ACFEI, ADNUR, COARC, CSHSE, EMT, NAIT, PNUR, RTT

† Regional accreditation is carried under the parent institution in Indianapolis, IN

*Ivy Tech Community College of Indiana-Columbus (I)

4475 Central Avenue, Columbus IN 47203-1868
Telephone: (812) 372-9925 FICE Identification: 010038
Accreditation: &NH, ART, ACBSP, ADNUR, CSHSE, DA, EMT, MAC, NAIT, PNUR, SURGT

† Regional accreditation is carried under the parent institution in Indianapolis, IN

*Ivy Tech Community College of Indiana-East Central (J)

4301 Cowan Road, Muncie IN 47302-9448
Telephone: (765) 289-2291 FICE Identification: 009924
Accreditation: &NH, ACBSP, ACFEI, ADNUR, CSHSE, DA, DH, MAC, NAIT, PNUR, PTAA, RAD, SURGT

† Regional accreditation is carried under the parent institution in Indianapolis, IN

*Ivy Tech Community College of Indiana-East Chicago (K)

410 East Columbus Drive, East Chicago IN 46312
Telephone: (219) 392-3600 Identification: 770240
Accreditation: &NH

† Regional accreditation is carried under the parent institution in Indianapolis, IN

*Ivy Tech Community College of Indiana-Elkhart (L)

22531 County Road 18, Goshen IN 46528
Telephone: (574) 830-0375 Identification: 770241
Accreditation: &NH

† Regional accreditation is carried under the parent institution in Indianapolis, IN

*Ivy Tech Community College of Indiana-Kokomo (M)

1815 E Morgan Street, Box 1373, Kokomo IN 46903-1373
Telephone: (765) 459-0561 FICE Identification: 010041
Accreditation: &NH, ACBSP, ADNUR, CSHSE, DA, EMT, MAC, NAIT, PNUR, SURGT

† Regional accreditation is carried under the parent institution in Indianapolis, IN

*Ivy Tech Community College of Indiana-Lafayette (N)

3101 S Creasy Lane, Box 6299, Lafayette IN 47903-6299
Telephone: (765) 269-5000 FICE Identification: 010039
Accreditation: &NH, ACBSP, ADNUR, COARC, CSHSE, DA, MAC, NAIT, PNUR, SURGT

† Regional accreditation is carried under the parent institution in Indianapolis, IN

*Ivy Tech Community College of Indiana-Lawrenceburg-Riverfront (O)

50 Walnut Street, Lawrenceburg IN 47025
Telephone: (812) 537-4010 Identification: 770242
Accreditation: &NH, MAC

† Regional accreditation is carried under the parent institution in Indianapolis, IN

*Ivy Tech Community College of Indiana-Logansport (P)

1 Ivy Tech Way, Logansport IN 46947
Telephone: (866) 753-5102 Identification: 770243
Accreditation: &NH

† Regional accreditation is carried under the parent institution in Indianapolis, IN

*Ivy Tech Community College of Indiana-Marion (Q)

261 S Commerce Drive, Marion IN 46953
Telephone: (800) 554-1159 Identification: 770244
Accreditation: &NH, MAC

† Regional accreditation is carried under the parent institution in Indianapolis, IN

*Ivy Tech Community College of Indiana-Michigan City (R)

3714 Franklin Drive, Michigan City IN 46360
Telephone: (219) 879-9137 Identification: 770245
Accreditation: &NH, ACFEI, MAC

† Regional accreditation is carried under the parent institution in Indianapolis, IN

* Ivy Tech Community College of Indiana-North Central (A)

220 Dean Johnson Boulevard, South Bend IN 46601-3415
Telephone: (574) 289-7001 FICE Identification: 008423
Accreditation: &NH, ART, ACBSP, ACFEI, ADNUR, COARC, CSHSE, DA, DH, EMT, MAC, MLTAD, NAIT, PNUR

† Regional accreditation is carried under the parent institution in Indianapolis, IN

* Ivy Tech Community College of Indiana-Northeast (B)

3800 N Anthony Boulevard, Fort Wayne IN 46805-1489
Telephone: (260) 482-9171 FICE Identification: 009926
Accreditation: &NH, ACBSP, ACFEI, ADNUR, CAHIIM, COARC, CSHSE, EMT, MAC, NAIT, PNUR

† Regional accreditation is carried under the parent institution in Indianapolis, IN

* Ivy Tech Community College of Indiana-Northwest (C)

1440 E 35th Avenue, Gary IN 46409-1499
Telephone: (219) 981-1111 FICE Identification: 010040
Accreditation: &NH, ACBSP, ADNUR, COARC, CSHSE, FUSER, MAC, NAIT, PNUR, PTAA, SURGT

† Regional accreditation is carried under the parent institution in Indianapolis, IN

* Ivy Tech Community College of Indiana-Richmond (D)

2357 Chester Boulevard, Richmond IN 47374-1298
Telephone: (765) 966-2656 FICE Identification: 010037
Accreditation: &NH, ACBSP, ADNUR, COARC, CSHSE, MAC, NAIT, PNUR

† Regional accreditation is carried under the parent institution in Indianapolis, IN

* Ivy Tech Community College of Indiana-Southeast (E)

590 Ivy Tech Drive, Madison IN 47250-1883
Telephone: (812) 265-2580 FICE Identification: 009923
Accreditation: &NH, ACBSP, ADNUR, CSHSE, EMT, MAC, PNUR

† Regional accreditation is carried under the parent institution in Indianapolis, IN

* Ivy Tech Community College of Indiana-Southern Indiana (F)

8204 Highway 311, Sellersburg IN 47172-1897
Telephone: (812) 246-3301 FICE Identification: 010109
Accreditation: &NH, ACBSP, ADNUR, ART, COARC, CSHSE, MAC, MLTAD, NAIT, PNUR, PTAA

† Regional accreditation is carried under the parent institution in Indianapolis, IN

* Ivy Tech Community College of Indiana-Southwest (G)

3501 First Avenue, Evansville IN 47710-1881
Telephone: (812) 426-2865 FICE Identification: 009925
Accreditation: &NH, ACBSP, ADNUR, CSHSE, EMT, MAC, NAIT, PNUR, SURGT

† Regional accreditation is carried under the parent institution in Indianapolis, IN

* Ivy Tech Community College of Indiana-Valparaiso (H)

3100 Ivy Tech Drive, Valparaiso IN 46383
Telephone: (219) 464-8514 Identification: 770246
Accreditation: &NH

† Regional accreditation is carried under the parent institution in Indianapolis, IN

* Ivy Tech Community College of Indiana-Wabash (I)

277 N Thorne Street, Wabash IN 46992
Telephone: (260) 563-8828 Identification: 770247
Accreditation: &NH

† Regional accreditation is carried under the parent institution in Indianapolis, IN

* Ivy Tech Community College of Indiana-Wabash Valley (J)

8000 S. Education Drive, Terre Haute IN 47802-4833
Telephone: (812) 299-1121 FICE Identification: 008547
Accreditation: &NH, ACBSP, ADNUR, ART, COARC, CSHSE, DMS, EMT, MAC, MLTAD, NAIT, PNUR, RAD, SURGT

† Regional accreditation is carried under the parent institution in Indianapolis, IN

* Ivy Tech Community College of Indiana-Warsaw (K)

2545 Silreus Crossing, Warsaw IN 46582
Telephone: (574) 267-5428 Identification: 770248
Accreditation: &NH

† Regional accreditation is carried under the parent institution in Indianapolis, IN

Lincoln College of Technology (L)

7225 Winton Drive, Building 128,
Indianapolis IN 46268-4198
County: Marion FICE Identification: 007938
Unit ID: 151661
Telephone: (317) 632-5553 Carnegie Class: Spec 2-yr-Tech
FAX Number: (317) 851-3273 Calendar System: Semester
URL: www.lincolntech.edu
Established: 1962 Annual Undergrad Tuition & Fees: N/A
Enrollment: 1,199 Coed
Affiliation or Control: Proprietary IRS Status: Proprietary
Highest Offering: Associate Degree
Accreditation: ACCSC

01 Campus President .... Stephanie MILLER
05 Academic Dean .... Bill THOMPSON
11 Director Administrative Services .... Linda WILKINS
37 Director Student Financial Aid .... Sheila ANDREWS
07 Director of Adult Admissions .... Vacant
07 Director of High School Admissions .... John MARTIN
36 Director of Career Services .... Bryan FEILEN
13 IT Administrator .... Blake BROOKS
18 Facilities Manager .... Roger PARK
21 Business Office Coordinator .... Dawn KEMP

Manchester University (M)

604 E College Avenue, North Manchester IN 46962-1225
County: Wabash FICE Identification: 001820
Unit ID: 151777
Telephone: (260) 982-5000 Carnegie Class: Bac-Diverse
FAX Number: (260) 982-5043 Calendar System: 4/1/4
URL: www.manchester.edu
Established: 1889 Annual Undergrad Tuition & Fees: $29,910
Enrollment: 1,488 Coed
Affiliation or Control: Church Of The Brethren IRS Status: 501(c)3
Highest Offering: Doctorate
Accreditation: NH, CAATE, PHAR, SW, TED

01 President .... Dr. David F. MCFADDEN
05 Vice President Academic Affairs .... Dr. Tim MCELWEE
10 Vice Pres Financial Affairs/Treas .... Mr. Jack A. GOCHENAUR
30 Vice President College Advancement .... Mrs. Melanie HARMON
84 VP Enrollment & Marketing .... Ms. Whitney CAUDILL
84 Asst VP for Enrollment/Marketing .... Mr. Adam HOHMAN
20 Associate Academic Dean .... Vacant
29 Director of Alumni Relations .... Ms. Jennifer SHEPHERD
08 Director of the Library .... Ms. Jill LICHTSINN
06 Registrar .... Ms. Lila D. HAMMER
24 Director of Audio-Visual Services .... Mr. Stanley G. PITTMAN
38 Director of Counseling .... Ms. Danette NORMAN TILL
36 Director of Career Services .... Vacant
39 Director of Residence Life .... Mr. Allen J. MACHIELSON
42 Campus Pastor .... Mr. Walt WILTSCHEK
41 Director of Athletics .... Mr. Rick ESPESET
13 Director of Mgmt Info Services .... Mr. Michael CASE
19 Director of Security .... Mr. Harold NAPIER
44 Director of the Manchester Fund .... Ms. Janeen W. KOOI
37 Director of Student Financial Aid .... Ms. Sherri L. SHOCKEY
85 Director of Multicultural Affairs .... Mr. Michael G. DIXON
26 Director of Public Relations .... Ms. Anne GREGORY
18 Director of Physical Plant .... Vacant
23 Director of Health Services .... Ms. Anna C. RICHISON
21 Senior Accountant .... Mr. Michael J. LECKRONE
32 Director Student Affairs .... Ms. Shanon L. FAWBUSH
96 Director of Purchasing .... Mr. Quentin J. MOUDY
40 Bookstore Manager .... Ms. Heather K. GOCHENAUR
04 Administrative Asst to President .... Mrs. Karen K. BRACE

Marian University (N)

3200 Cold Spring Road, Indianapolis IN 46222-1997
County: Marion FICE Identification: 001821
Unit ID: 151786
Telephone: (317) 955-6000 Carnegie Class: Masters/M
FAX Number: (317) 955-6448 Calendar System: Semester
URL: www.marian.edu
Established: 1851 Annual Undergrad Tuition & Fees: $30,500
Enrollment: 2,771 Coed
Affiliation or Control: Roman Catholic IRS Status: 501(c)3
Highest Offering: Doctorate
Accreditation: NH, IACBE, NURSE, @OSTEO, TED

01 President .... Mr. Daniel J. ELSENER
05 Executive VP and Provost .... Dr. Thomas ENNEKING
45 Interim VP Mission & Identity .... Mr. Adam SETMEYER
10 SVP for Personnel/Fin/Facil/Tech .... Mr. Greg GINDER
26 VP for Marketing Communications .... Mr. Mark APPLE
30 SVP Tchr Lrng Excel/Dn The Educ Col .... Dr. Kenith BRITT
32 VP Student Life and Success .... Ms. Ruth RODGERS
63 VP and Dean College of Osteopathic .... Dr. Don SEFCIK
84 VP Enrollment Management .... Dr. Paul (PJ) WOOLSTON
37 Dean Financial Aid/Enroll Mgmt .... Mr. Chad BIR
20 Dean for Academic Affairs .... Mr. William HARTING
18 Exec Dir Facilities/Procurement .... Mr. Evan HAWKINS
41 Director of Athletics .... Mr. Steve DOWNING
29 Dir Alumni/Parent Engagement .... Ms. Cathy SILER
06 Registrar .... Ms. Jennifer SCHWARTZ
08 Library Director .... Ms. Rhonda HUISMAN
35 Director of Student Act/Orientation .... Mr. Ben BRAKSICK
19 Director of Safety & Police Svcs .... Mr. Scott RALPH
13 AVP & Chief Information Officer .... Mr. Ray STANLEY
27 Manager of Event Marketing and Spon .... Ms. Maggie KUCIK
36 Executive Director The Exchange .... Ms. Ellen WHITT
38 Director Academic Support Services .... Mrs. Marjorie BATIC
07 AVP for Enrollment Management .... Vacant
55 Exec Director Adult Programs .... Ms. Amy BENNETT
38 Director of Counseling Services .... Dr. Marla SMITH
88 Director of Advancement Information .... Vacant
23 Director of Health & Wellness Svcs .... Ms. Jan CARNAGHI
09 Director of Institutional Research .... Mr. William HARTING
15 Director of Human Resources .... Vacant
21 Director of Business Services .... Ms. Alice SHELTON
40 Bookstore Manager .... Ms. Allison BONEZ
04 Executive Asst to President .... Ms. Cyndi KAMP
11 VP of Administration/General Counse .... Ms. Deborah LAWRENCE

Martin University (O)

2186 North Sherman Drive, Indianapolis IN 46218
County: Marion FICE Identification: 021408
Unit ID: 151810
Telephone: (317) 543-3235 Carnegie Class: Bac-A&S
FAX Number: (317) 543-3257 Calendar System: Semester
URL: www.martin.edu
Established: 1977 Annual Undergrad Tuition & Fees: $12,536
Enrollment: 402 Coed
Affiliation or Control: Independent Non-Profit IRS Status: 501(c)3
Highest Offering: Master's
Accreditation: #NH

01 President .... Dr. Eugene WHITE
05 VP Academic Affs/Student Svc .... Dr. Charlesetta SMITH STALEY
09 VP of Institutional Effectiveness .... Dr. Brian STEUERWALD
10 VP Fiscal Affairs .... Mr. Michael MOOS
37 Director Financial Aid .... Ms. Virginia GOODWIN
32 Director Student Services .... Ms. Dana L. MUDROW
26 Dir of Univ Res/Communications .... Ms. Jennifer MCCLOUD
21 Bursar .... Ms. Angela HARRINGTON-MARTIN
06 Registrar .... Ms. Dana DODSON

Mid-America College of Funeral Service (P)

3111 Hamburg Pike, Jeffersonville IN 47130-9630
County: Clark FICE Identification: 010618
Unit ID: 151962
Telephone: (812) 288-8878 Carnegie Class: Spec-4-yr-Other
FAX Number: (812) 288-5942 Calendar System: Quarter
URL: www.mid-america.edu
Established: 1980 Annual Undergrad Tuition & Fees: $11,150
Enrollment: 58 Coed
Affiliation or Control: Independent Non-Profit IRS Status: 501(c)3
Highest Offering: Baccalaureate
Accreditation: FUSER

01 President .... Ms. Lauren M. BUDROW
32 Dean of Students/Financial Aid .... Ms. Alisa PERKINS
06 Registrar .... Ms. Angela PERSINGER
29 Director Alumni Relations .... Vacant
07 Director of Admissions .... Mr. Michael MOELLER

Mid-America Reformed Seminary (Q)

229 Seminary Drive, Dyer IN 46311-1069
County: Lake FICE Identification: 039893
Unit ID: 373030
Telephone: (219) 864-2400 Carnegie Class: Not Classified
FAX Number: (219) 864-2410 Calendar System: Semester
URL: www.midamerica.edu
Established: 1981 Annual Graduate Tuition & Fees: N/A
Enrollment: N/A Coed
Affiliation or Control: Independent Non-Profit IRS Status: 501(c)3
Highest Offering: Master's; No Undergraduates
Accreditation: THEOL, TRACS

01 President .... Dr. Cornelius VENEMA
32 Dean of Students .... Rev. Alan STRANGE
30 Vice President of Advancement .... Mr. Mike DECKINGA
11 Vice President of Operations .... Mr. Keith LEMAHIEU
36 Director of Apprenticeship Program .... Rev. Mark VANDERHART
07 Director of Admissions .... Rev. Jeffrey DEBOER
09 Director Institutional Assessment .... Rev. Marcus MININGER

MJS College School of Nursing (R)

8401 Ohio Street, Merrillville IN 46410
County: Lake Identification: 667272
Telephone: (219) 769-2047 Carnegie Class: Not Classified
FAX Number: (888) 522-9313 Calendar System: Semester
URL: www.mjscollege.net
Established: Annual Undergrad Tuition & Fees: N/A
Enrollment: N/A Coed
Affiliation or Control: Proprietary IRS Status: Proprietary

Highest Offering: Associate Degree
Accreditation: ACICS

01	President	Oranu IBEKIE
05	Dean of Academics	Annette MURRAY

National American University-Indianapolis (A)

3600 Woodview Terrace, Suite 200, Indianapolis IN 46268
Telephone: (800) 609-1430 Identification: 770393
Accreditation: &NH

† Regional accreditation is carried under the parent institution in Rapid City, SD

Oakland City University (B)

138 N Lucretia Street, Oakland City IN 47660-1099
County: Gibson FICE Identification: 001824
Unit ID: 152099
Telephone: (812) 749-4781 Carnegie Class: Bac-Diverse
FAX Number: (812) 749-1233 Calendar System: Semester
URL: www.oak.edu
Established: 1885 Annual Undergrad Tuition & Fees: $22,800
Enrollment: 2,086 Coed
Affiliation or Control: Baptist IRS Status: 501(c)3
Highest Offering: Doctorate
Accreditation: NH, IACBE, TED, THEOL

01	President	Dr. Ray G. BARBER
11	Vice Pres Administration & Finance	Dr. Robert E. YEAGER
05	Provost	Dr. Daniel DUNIVAN
10	Chief Financial Officer	Mrs. Elizabeth BARBER
30	Director of Advancement	Mr. Brian BAKER
73	Dean Religious Studies	Dr. Daniel DUNIVAN
50	Dean School of Business	Dr. Cathy ROBB
53	Dean School of Education	Dr. Steven DEGEORGE
49	Dean School of Arts & Sciences	Dr. Claudine CUTCHIN
108	Director of Assessment	Mrs. Katheryn WEBB
32	Director of Campus Life	Mr. Brad KNOTTS
106	Coordinator of Online Learning	Dr. Mark SIMPSON
37	Director of Financial Aid	Mrs. Nicole SHARP
56	Coordinator Adult Extend Learning	Dr. Cathy ROBB
22	Compliance Officer	Ms. Patricia ENDICOTT
88	Director of Correctional Education	Mr. Theodore PEARSON
06	Registrar	Mrs. Linda TIPTON
08	Director of Library	Mrs. Denise PINNICK
26	Director of Mktg/Athletic Director	Dr. Mike SANDIFAR
42	Campus Minister	Rev. Marc GRIMES
18	Director of Maintenance	Mr. Greg BURKE
88	Payroll Coordinator	Mrs. Cheryl YATES
15	Human Resources Coordinator	Mrs. Cheryl YATES
13	Director of Information Technology	Mr. Clint WOOLSEY
19	Chief of Security	Mr. Alec HENSLEY
29	Director of Alumni Affairs	Ms. Susan SULLIVAN
36	Director of Directions Program	Mrs. Charity JULIAN
35	Director Student Support Services	Mrs. Tamara MILEY
21	Assistant Chief Financial Officer	Mrs. Elizabeth CARLISLE
88	Supervisor of Collections	Mrs. Anita MISKELL
88	Director of Housekeeping	Mrs. Dorothy GRAPER

Ottawa University Jeffersonville (C)

287 Quarter Master Court, Jeffersonville IN 47130-3669
Telephone: (785) 242-5200 Identification: 666088
Accreditation: &NH

† Regional accreditation is carried under the parent institution in Ottawa, KS.

Purdue University Main Campus (D)

610 Purdue Mall, West Lafayette IN 47907-2040
County: Tippecanoe FICE Identification: 001825
Unit ID: 243780
Telephone: (765) 494-4600 Carnegie Class: DU-Highest
FAX Number: N/A Calendar System: Semester
URL: www.purdue.edu
Established: 1869 Annual Undergrad Tuition & Fees (In-State): $10,002
Enrollment: 39,752 Coed
Affiliation or Control: State IRS Status: 501(c)3
Highest Offering: Doctorate
Accreditation: NH, AAB, ART, AUD, BUS, CAATE, CACREP, CIDA, CLPSY, CONST, COPSY, CS, DIETC, DIETD, ENG, ENGR, ENGT, IPSY, LSAR, NAIT, NURSE, PHAR, SP, TED, THEA, VET

01	President	Mr. Mitchell E. DANIELS, JR.
10	Exec Vice President & Treasurer	Mr. William E. SULLIVAN
05	Provost/Exec VP for Acad Affairs	Dr. Debasish DUTTA
21	Sr VP Business Svcs/Asst Treas	Mr. James S. ALMOND
13	Vice Pres Information Technology	Dr. William G. MCCARTNEY
15	Vice President Human Resources	Mr. Trent KLINGERMAN
26	Vice President for Public Affairs	Ms. Julie K. GRIFFITH
20	Int Vice Prov Student Acad Affairs	Dr. Frank J. DOOLEY
20	Vice Pres Faculty Affairs	Dr. Peter HOLLENBECK
08	Dean of Libraries	Dr. James L. MULLINS
29	President & CEO Alumni Association	Mr. Ralph AMOS
07	Dean Admiss/VP Enroll Mgmt	Dr. Pamela T. HORNE
37	Director Financial Aid	Mr. Ted E. MALONE

Purdue University North Central Campus (E)

1401 S US 421, Westville IN 46391-9542
Telephone: (219) 785-5200 FICE Identification: 001826
Accreditation: &NH, ACBSP, ENG, ENGR, ENGT, NUR, TED

† Branch campus of Purdue University Northwest, Hammond, IN

Purdue University Northwest (F)

2200 169th Street, Hammond IN 46323-2094
County: Lake FICE Identification: 001827
Unit ID: 152248
Telephone: (219) 989-2204 Carnegie Class: Masters/L
FAX Number: (219) 989-2581 Calendar System: Semester
URL: www.pnw.edu
Established: 1946 Annual Undergrad Tuition & Fees (In-State): $6,868
Enrollment: 9,501 Coed
Affiliation or Control: State IRS Status: 501(c)3
Highest Offering: Doctorate
Accreditation: NH, BUS, CACREP, CEA, CS, ENG, ENGR, ENGT, MFCD, NAIT, NUR, TED

01	Chancellor	Dr. Thomas L. KEON
05	Vice Chanc Acad Affs & Provost	Dr. Ralph O. MUELLER
10	Vice Chanc Finance & Admin	Mr. Steve TURNER
30	Vice Chanc for Inst Advancement	Dr. Regina D. BIDDINGS-MURO
13	Vice Chanc Info Services	Mr. Tim WINDERS
32	Vice Chanc Enroll Mgmt & Stdnt Affs	Dr. Carmen PANLILIO
46	Director of Reserch & Grad Stds	Dr. Joy COLWELL
26	Assoc Vice Chanc Marketing	Ms. Kris FALZONE
09	Int AVC Accreditation & Assessment	Dr. Becky STANKOWSKI
11	Asst Vice Chancellor for Admin Svcs	Mr. Michael KULL
27	Asst Vice Chanc Advance/Univ Rels	Mr. Wes K. LUKOSHUS
35	Assoc Vice Chanc Stdnt Affs/EOP	Mr. Roy HAMILTON
21	Asst VC Business Svcs/Comptroller	Mr. Phillip JANKOWSKI
15	Asst Vice Chanc Human Resources	Ms. Susan MILLLER
49	Int Dean Col Human/Educ/Soc Sci	Dr. Ronald CORTHELL
54	Int Dean Col of Engr & Science	Dr. Chris HOLFORD
72	Dean College of Technology	Dr. Niaz LATIF
50	Dean College of Business	Dr. Jane MUTCHLER
66	Dean College of Nursing	Dr. Lisa HOPP
53	Interim Dir School of Education	Dr. Rex MORROW
06	Registrar	Ms. Cheryl ARROYO
21	Assc Comptroller Accnt/Budget Svcs	Ms. Donna ADELSPERGER
37	Int Exec Dir Fin Student Svcs	Ms. Freda WHISENTON-COMER
41	Director of Athletics	Mr. Richard J. COSTELLO
38	Director Counseling Center	Dr. Kenneth JACKSON
08	Dir Research/Learning & Res Svcs	Ms. Tammy GUERRERO
29	Dir Alumni Affairs & Advancement	Ms. Megan DAVIS-OCHI
19	University Police	Chief Patricia NOWAK
85	Asst Vice International Affairs	Dr. Dallas KENNY
96	Dir of Procurement/General Services	Mr. Philip BROWN
39	Director of Housing Residental Educ	Ms. Scott IVERSON
92	Dean Honors Program	Dr. Rowan JOHN
84	Assoc Dean Enroll Mgmt & Grad Pgms	Dr. Lori FELDMAN
04	Sr Exec Asst Strategic Initiatives	Ms. Daphne D. ROBINSON
102	Dir Advance Resource/Donor Steward	Ms. Mary Jane DOPP
104	Education Abroad Coordinator	Ms. Judy MOORE
105	Int Dir Tech Infrastruc Services	Ms. Heather ZAMOJSKI
25	Exec Director CVIS	Dr. Chenn ZHOU
28	Director Ofc Equity & Diversity	Ms. Linda B. KNOX
36	Director Career Dev & Services	Ms. Natalie CONNORS
90	Asst Vice Chanc Lrng Tech	Ms. Heather ZAMOJSKI
07	Asst Vice Chan Enrollmnt Mgmt	Vacant
88	Dir of Procurement/General Services	Ms. Elizabeth DEPEW
88	Director of Public Safety	Mr. Brian MILLER
88	Sr Direct Space Mgmt	Ms. Michelle GRANT
88	Manager Strategic Events	Ms. Ashley GERODIMOS
88	Lead Security Analyst	Ms. Katie GUTIERREZ
88	Exec Dir Enterprise App Svcs	Mr. Paul JOHANSEN
18	Chief Facilities/Physical Plant	Mr. Steve TURNER
22	Dir Affirmative Action/EEO	Ms. Linda B. KNOX

Radiological Technologies University-VT (G)

100 E. Wayne St., Ste 140, South Bend IN 46601
County: St. Joseph Identification: 667156
Telephone: (574) 232-2408 Carnegie Class: Not Classified
FAX Number: (574) 232-2200 Calendar System: Semester
URL: www.rtuvt.com
Established: 2009 Annual Undergrad Tuition & Fees: N/A
Enrollment: N/A Coed
Affiliation or Control: Proprietary IRS Status: Proprietary
Highest Offering: Master's
Accreditation: ACICS, RADDOS

01	President	Brent D. MURPHY
11	Dir of Administrative Services	Betsy DATEMA

Rose-Hulman Institute of Technology (H)

5500 Wabash Avenue, Terre Haute IN 47803-3920
County: Vigo FICE Identification: 001830
Unit ID: 152318
Telephone: (812) 877-1511 Carnegie Class: Spec-4-yr-Eng
FAX Number: (812) 877-9925 Calendar System: Quarter
URL: www.rose-hulman.edu
Established: 1874 Annual Undergrad Tuition & Fees: $45,141
Enrollment: 2,388 Coed
Affiliation or Control: Independent Non-Profit IRS Status: 501(c)3
Highest Offering: Master's
Accreditation: NH, CS, ENG

01	President	Dr. James C. CONWELL
10	Senior VP/Chief Admin Officer	Mr. Robert A. COONS
05	Vice Pres Academic Affairs	Dr. Anne HOUTMAN
30	VP Inst Advancement	Mr. Steven BRADY
32	Vice President Student Affairs	Mr. Erik Z. HAYES
26	VP Communications/Marketing	Mr. James A. GOECKER
21	Assoc VP for Finance/Controller	Mr. Matthew D. DAVIS
84	Vice President Enrollment Mgmt	Mr. James A. GOECKER
88	Vice Pres of Corp Eng/Ventures	Dr. Elizabeth M. HAGERMAN
88	Dean of Innovation/Engagement	Dr. William KLINE
20	Interim Dean of Faculty	Dr. Jameel AHMED
20	Associate Dean of Faculty	Dr. Azad SIAHMAKOUN
88	Int Dept Head of BBE	Dr. Kay C. DEE
104	Dir of Study Abroad/Intl Exchanges	Mr. Christopher DIXON
13	Vice Pres Info Tech and CIO	Dr. Wayne DENNISON
18	Sr Director Facilities Operations	Mr. Michael A. TAYLOR
36	Dir Career Services/Employer Rels	Mr. Kevin L. HEWERDINE
07	Dean of Admissions	Ms. Lisa M. NORTON
29	Executive Director Alumni Affairs	Vacant
45	Exec Dir Inst Rsrch/Plng/Assessment	Dr. Julia M. WILLIAMS
15	Director of Human Resources	Ms. Kimberly D. MILLER
37	Director of Financial Aid	Ms. Melinda L. MIDDLETON
41	Director of Athletics	Mr. Jeffrey L. JENKINS
28	Director Center for Diversity	Ms. Janice FENN
44	Sr Director of Planned Giving	Mr. Chris AIMONE
44	Annual Fund Coordinator	Ms. Jennifer KENZOR
06	Registrar	Ms. Jan LIND
08	Library Director	Ms. Bernadette EWEN
19	Director of Public Safety	Mr. John S. WOLFE
40	Bookstore Manager	Ms. Sheryl E. FULK
85	Dir Intl Stdnt Svcs/Disability Svcs	Ms. Karen A. DEGRANGE
04	Exec Assistant to the President	Ms. Kerry SCHAFFER
25	Dir Fin Svcs/Sponsored Programs	Ms. Linda L. PRICE
109	Director Administrative Services	Mr. Bryan T. BROMSTRUP
09	Director of Institutional Research	Dr. Timothy CHOW
102	Director of Corporate Relations	Mr. Brandon M. ZOLLNER
35	Assoc VP & Dean of Student Affairs	Mr. Thomas D. MILLER
35	Dean of Student Services	Ms. Kristen J. LOYD
101	Dir Donor Relations/Exec Asst Board	Ms. Tammy SHAFFER
24	Instructional Technology Manager	Ms. Cheryl CLAPP
24	Emerging Digital Technologies Mgr	Mr. Alan WARD
38	Director of Counseling Services	Dr. Michael LATTA

St. Anthony School of Echocardiography (I)

1201 S. Main Street, Crown Point IN 46307
County: Lake Identification: 667119
Telephone: (219) 757-6132 Carnegie Class: Not Classified
FAX Number: (219) 681-6725 Calendar System: Semester
URL: www.franciscanalliance.org/hospitals/crownpoint
Established: 2004 Annual Undergrad Tuition & Fees: N/A
Enrollment: N/A Coed
Affiliation or Control: Independent Non-Profit IRS Status: 501(c)3
Highest Offering: Associate Degree
Accreditation: DMS

01	Co-Program Director	Lori HULT
01	Co-Program Director	Karin KOLISZ

Saint Joseph's College (J)

PO Box 870, US Highway 231, Rensselaer IN 47978-0870
County: Jasper FICE Identification: 001833
Unit ID: 152363
Telephone: (219) 866-6000 Carnegie Class: Bac-Diverse
FAX Number: (219) 866-6100 Calendar System: Semester
URL: www.saintjoe.edu
Established: 1889 Annual Undergrad Tuition & Fees: $28,690
Enrollment: 1,166 Coed
Affiliation or Control: Roman Catholic IRS Status: 501(c)3
Highest Offering: Master's
Accreditation: NH, IACBE, NURSE, TED

01	President	Dr. Robert A. PASTOOR
04	Admin Asst to the President	Mrs. Sheila K. HANEWICH
05	Vice Pres for Academic Affairs	Dr. Chad A. PULVER
10	Vice President Business Affairs	Mr. Spencer CONROY
30	Vice Pres Inst Advancement/Mrktng	Mr. Gregory ROBERTS
44	Asst VP Institutional Advancement	Mrs. Elizabeth GRAF
32	VP Student Development	Vacant
06	Registrar	Mrs. Maureen HEALEY
84	Vice Pres Enrollment Management	Mrs. Beth TERRELL
08	Librarian	Mr. Timothy SALM
13	VP Information Technology/CIO	Mr. G. Scott GILREATH
38	Director of Counseling Services	Ms. Laura WAGNER
18	Chief Facilities/Physical Plant	Mr. Randal FLINN
15	Director Human Resources	Ms. Nancy STUDER
26	Director of Integrated Marketing	Mr. Gregory GILL
29	Director Alumni Relations	Mrs. Kendra ILLINGWORTH
37	Director Student Financial Services	Mrs. Becky SHIDE
28	Director of Diversity	Mr. Ernest WATSON
36	Director Career Development	Vacant
41	Athletic Director	Mr. William MASSOELS
40	Director Bookstore	Mrs. Rhonda ELIJAH
42	Chaplain/Director Campus Ministry	Vacant

Saint Mary-of-the-Woods College (K)

1 St Mary of Woods College,
St Mary of the Woods IN 47876-1099
County: Vigo FICE Identification: 001835
Unit ID: 152381
Telephone: (812) 535-5151 Carnegie Class: Bac-Diverse

FAX Number: (812) 535-5231 Calendar System: Semester
URL: www.smwc.edu
Established: 1840 Annual Undergrad Tuition & Fees: $28,932
Enrollment: 931 Coed
Affiliation or Control: Roman Catholic IRS Status: 501(c)3
Highest Offering: Master's
Accreditation: NH, MUS, TED

01 President .... Dr. Dottie KING
30 VP for Advancement .... Ms. Karen DYER
10 Controller .... Ms. Jaclyn WALTER
05 Vice President for Academic Affairs .... Dr. Janet CLARK
11 Vice President for Operations .... Ms. Vicki KOSOWSKY
84 Vice Pres for Enrollment Management ... Mr. Brennan RANDOLPH
06 Registrar .... Ms. Deanna BABCOCK
08 Director of the Library .... Ms. Judy TRIBBLE
29 Senior Dir Advancement/Alumni Rels .... Ms. Susan TURNER
26 Executive Dir of College Relations .... Ms. Dee REED
07 Exec Director of Campus Admissions .... Mr. Ryan MCDONALD
106 Director Woods Online Program .... Ms. Gwen HAGEMEYER
13 Sr Dir Information & Academic Svcs .... Ms. Mary SAMM
36 Director of Career Development .... Ms. Susan GRESHAM
15 Director Human Resources .... Ms. Diana WARREN
32 Director Campus Life .... Mr. Jeffrey MALLOY
37 Director Financial Aid .... Ms. Darla HOPPER
44 Dir Major and Planned Gifts .... Vacant
64 Dir Grad Pgm Music Therapy .... Ms. Tracy RICHARDSON
88 Dir Grad Pgm Art Therapy .... Ms. Kathy GOTSHALL
88 Dir Grad Pgm Leadership Development .... Ms. Susan DECKER
09 Director of Institutional Research .... Mr. Mike KING

Saint Mary's College (A)

Notre Dame IN 46556
County: Saint Joseph FICE Identification: 001836
Unit ID: 152390
Telephone: (574) 284-4000 Carnegie Class: Bac-A&S
FAX Number: (574) 284-4716 Calendar System: Semester
URL: www.saintmarys.edu
Established: 1844 Annual Undergrad Tuition & Fees: $37,400
Enrollment: 1,519 Female
Affiliation or Control: Roman Catholic IRS Status: 501(c)3
Highest Offering: Doctorate
Accreditation: NH, ART, MUS, NURSE, @SP, SW, TED

01 President .... Ms. Janice A. CERVELLI
04 Special Asst to the President .... Vacant
05 Provost/Sr VP Academic Affairs .... Dr. Patricia A. FLEMING
26 Vice President College Relations .... Ms. Shari M. RODRIGUEZ
32 Vice President for Student Affairs .... Ms. Karen A. JOHNSON
10 Vice Pres Finance & Administration .... Ms. Susan BOLT
84 Vice Pres for Enrollment Management .... Ms. Mona BOWE
83 Vice President for Mission .... Ms. Judith FEAN
83 Associate Dean for Advising .... Ms. Susan VANEK
06 Registrar .... Mr. Todd NORRIS
07 Director of Admission .... Ms. Sarah DVORAK
08 Director of Library .... Ms. Janet S. FORE
09 Director of Institutional Research .... Mr. Daniel FLOWERS
29 Director of Alumnae Relations .... Ms. Kara O'LEARY
37 Director of Financial Aid .... Ms. Kathleen M. BROWN
27 Director of Media Relations .... Ms. Gwen O'BRIEN
38 Director of Women's Health .... Ms. Elizabeth FOURMAN
13 Chief Information Officer .... Mr. Michael BOEHM
15 Director of Human Resources .... Ms. Kris URSCHEL
19 Director of Safety & Security .... Mr. David GARIEPY
40 Manager Bookstore .... Vacant
41 Director of Athletics .... Ms. Julie SCHROEDER-BIEK
42 Director of Campus Ministry .... Ms. Regina WILSON
18 Director of Facilities .... Mr. Benjamin BOWMAN
96 Director of Purchasing .... Ms. Kathleen CARLSON
88 Director of Student Involvement .... Ms. Brittany HOUSE
85 Director of Multicultural Program .... Ms. Gloria JENKINS
43 College Counsel .... Mr. Richard NUGENT

Saint Meinrad School of Theology (B)

200 Hill Drive, St. Meinrad IN 47577-1030
County: Spencer FICE Identification: 007276
Unit ID: 152451
Telephone: (812) 357-6611 Carnegie Class: Spec-4-yr-Faith
FAX Number: (812) 357-6964 Calendar System: Semester
URL: www.saintmeinrad.edu
Established: 1861 Annual Graduate Tuition & Fees: N/A
Enrollment: 217 Coed
Affiliation or Control: Roman Catholic IRS Status: 501(c)3
Highest Offering: Master's; No Undergraduates
Accreditation: NH, THEOL

01 President & Rector .... Rev. Denis ROBINSON, OSB
03 Vice Rector .... Rev. Tobias COLGAN, OSB
05 Academic Dean .... Dr. Robert ALVIS
84 Director of Enrollment .... Rev. Luke WAUGH, OSB
42 Director of Spiritual Formation .... Rev. Peter MARSHALL
20 Director of Lay Degree Programs .... Sr. Jeana VISEL, OSB
30 Vice President of Development .... Mr. Michael ZIEMIANSKI
10 Business Manager & Treasurer .... Mrs. Lisa CASTLEBURY
08 Library Director .... Dr. Daniel KOLB
06 Registrar .... Mrs. Donna BALBACH
88 Dir of Clergy Formation Pgm .... Dr. Patrick COOPER
21 Director of Budget .... Mrs. Pam DOWLAND
37 Director of Student Financial Aid .... Mrs. Ruth KRESS
26 Director of Communications .... Mrs. Mary Jeanne SCHUMACHER
29 Director of Alumni Relations .... Mr. Christian MOCEK
38 Director of Student Counseling Ctr .... Sr. Diane PHARO, SCN
09 Director of Institutional Research .... Mr. John SCHLACHTER
23 Director of Health Services .... Ms. Ann ROHLEDER
04 Executive Secretary .... Mrs. Karen SCHERZER
13 Chief Info Technology Officer
(CIO) .... Mr. Dave GRAMELSPACHER
18 Chief Facilities/Physical Plant .... Mr. Andy HAGEDORN
44 Director Annual or Planned Giving .... Mr. Darren SROUFE
105 Director Web Services .... Mrs. Mary Jeanne SCHUMACHER
106 Dir Online Education/E-learning .... Sr. Jeana VISEL, OSB
15 Director Human Resources .... Mr. Mike GRAMELSPACHER
19 Director Security/Safety .... Mr. Gary GUY

Taylor University (C)

West 236 Reade Avenue, Upland IN 46989-1001
County: Grant FICE Identification: 001838
Unit ID: 152530
Telephone: (765) 998-2751 Carnegie Class: Bac-Diverse
FAX Number: (765) 998-4910 Calendar System: 4/1/4
URL: www.taylor.edu
Established: 1846 Annual Undergrad Tuition & Fees: $30,270
Enrollment: 2,146 Coed
Affiliation or Control: Independent Non-Profit IRS Status: 501(c)3
Highest Offering: Master's
Accreditation: NH, CEA, ENG, MUS, SW, TED

01 President .... Mr. Lowell HAINES
05 Provost .... Dr. Jeffrey MOSHIER
11 VP Business Administration .... Mr. Ronald SUTHERLAND
30 Interim VP Univ Advancement .... Ms. Sherri HARTER
32 VP Student Development .... Dr. Skip TRUDEAU
84 VP Enroll Mgmt & Marketing .... Mr. Stephen MORTLAND
10 VP Finance & CFO .... Mr. Stephen OLSON
20 Vice Provost .... Dr. Jeff GROELING
49 Dean Sch Hum/Arts & Biblical Stds .... Dr. Michael HAMMOND
83 Dean Sch of Soc Sci/Educ & Bus .... Dr. Rhoda SOMMERS
81 Dean Sch Natural & Applied Sciences .... Dr. William TOLL
104 Dean International Programs .... Dr. Charles BRAINER
13 Chief Information Officer .... Mr. Rob LINEHAN
41 Interim Director of Athletics .... Ms. Amy STUCKY
20 Dean Faculty Development/Dir BCTLE .... Dr. Faye CHECHOWICH
88 Senior Director for Campaigns .... Mr. David RITCHIE
44 Exec Director of Development .... Mr. Mike FALDER
29 Exec Dir for Alumni Relations .... Ms. Dara BERKHALTER
37 Assoc Dean Enroll Mgmt/Dir Fin Aid .... Mr. Timothy NACE
08 University Librarian .... Mr. Daniel BOWELL
35 Dean of Students .... Mr. Steve MORLEY
44 Director Taylor Scholarship Fund .... Mr. Andre PAYNE
39 Dir Residence Life .... Mr. Scott BARRETT
06 Registrar .... Ms. Janet ROGERS
106 Director of Online Learning .... Ms. Carrie MEYER
42 Campus Pastor .... Mr. Jon CAVANAGH
15 Asst Director of Human Resources .... Ms. April EVANS
07 Exec Director Admissions .... Ms. Amy BARNETT
18 Director of Physical Plant .... Mr. Greg ELEY
38 Interim Dir of Counseling Ctr .... Ms. Caroline POLAND
19 Chief of Police/Taylor Police .... Mr. Jeff WALLACE
09 Director IR/Assoc Registrar .... Dr. Edwin WELCH
21 Controller .... Mr. David LLOYD
108 Director Assessment/Quality Improv .... Dr. Kim CASE
88 Payroll Manager .... Ms. Toni NEWLIN
88 University Bursar .... Ms. Cathy MOORMAN
24 Director of Tech & Learning Ctr .... Dr. Ken BOYD
103 Dn Exper Lrng/Dir Calling/Career .... Dr. Drew MOSER
105 Assoc Dir of Enterprise Systems .... Mr. Corey COOPER

TCM International Institute (D)

6337 Hollister Drive, Indianapolis IN 46224
County: Marion Identification: 666333
Telephone: (317) 299-0333 Carnegie Class: Not Classified
FAX Number: (317) 290-8607 Calendar System: Semester
URL: www.tcmi.org
Established: 1991 Annual Graduate Tuition & Fees: N/A
Enrollment: N/A Coed
Affiliation or Control: Independent Non-Profit IRS Status: 501(c)3
Highest Offering: Master's; No Undergraduates
Accreditation: NH

01 President .... Dr. Tony TWIST
05 Academic Affairs Manager .... Ms. Victoria BOJONCA
06 Registrar .... Ms. Victoria BOJONCA
10 Director of Finance .... Ms. Julie RICE

Trine University (E)

1 University Avenue, Angola IN 46703-1764
County: Steuben FICE Identification: 001839
Unit ID: 152567
Telephone: (260) 665-4100 Carnegie Class: Bac-Diverse
FAX Number: (260) 665-4292 Calendar System: Semester
URL: www.trine.edu
Established: 1884 Annual Undergrad Tuition & Fees: $30,350
Enrollment: 2,831 Coed
Affiliation or Control: Independent Non-Profit IRS Status: 501(c)3
Highest Offering: Doctorate
Accreditation: NH, ACBSP, ENG, @PTA, TED

01 President .... Dr. Earl D. BROOKS, II
03 Senior Vice President .... Mr. Mike BOCK
05 Vice President for Academic Affairs .... Dr. Allen HERSEL
10 Vice President Finance .... Ms. Jody GREER
30 Vice Pres for Alumni & Development .... Mr. Kent D. STUCKY
84 Vice Pres Enrollment Management .... Mr. Scott GOPLIN
32 Vice President for Student Services .... Mr. Randy WHITE
51 Asst Vice Pres for Adult Learning .... Dr. Jean DELLER
49 Dean Jannen School of Arts & Sci .... Mr. Craig LAKER
107 Dean of Professional Studies .... Ms. Mersiha ALIC
15 Human Resources .... Ms. Jamie NORTON
41 Athletic Director .... Mr. Matt LAND
06 Registrar .... Ms. Debra F. HELMSING
26 Dir Integrated & Brand Marketing .... Mr. Dave JARZYNA
04 Assistant to the President .... Ms. Gretchen MILLER
37 Director Student Financial Planning .... Ms. Kim BENNETT
08 Director of the Library .... Ms. Kristina BREWER
36 Int Director of Placement/Coop Educ .... Ms. Linda COOPER
09 Director Inst Planning/Analysis .... Ms. Christina ZUMBRUN

Trine University-Fort Wayne Regional Campus (F)

9910 Dupont Circle Dr East, Ste 130,
Fort Wayne IN 46825
Telephone: (260) 483-4949 Identification: 770105
Accreditation: &NH

† Regional accreditation is carried under the parent institution in Angola, IN

Trine University-South Bend Regional Campus (G)

4101 Edison Lakes Parkway, Ste 250,
Mishawaka IN 46545
Telephone: (574) 243-0500 Identification: 770106
Accreditation: &NH

† Regional accreditation is carried under the parent institution in Angola, IN

Union Bible College (H)

PO Box 900, Westfield IN 46074
County: Hamilton Identification: 667253
Telephone: (317) 896-9324 Carnegie Class: Not Classified
FAX Number: (317) 867-0784 Calendar System: Semester
URL: www.ubca.org
Established: 1911 Annual Undergrad Tuition & Fees: N/A
Enrollment: N/A Coed
Affiliation or Control: Interdenominational IRS Status: 501(c)3
Highest Offering: Baccalaureate
Accreditation: @BI

01 President .... C. Adam BUCKLER
05 Academic Dean .... John WHITAKER
10 Finance Director .... Lanae WHITAKER
11 Director of Operations .... Greg HOBELMAN
32 Dean of Student Affairs .... Joe CAREY
09 Director of Institutional Research .... Isabel RUNDELL
06 Registrar .... Lisa BURKET

University of Evansville (I)

1800 Lincoln Avenue, Evansville IN 47722-1586
County: Vanderburgh FICE Identification: 001795
Unit ID: 150534
Telephone: (812) 488-2000 Carnegie Class: Masters/S
FAX Number: (812) 488-2320 Calendar System: Semester
URL: www.evansville.edu
Established: 1854 Annual Undergrad Tuition & Fees: $32,946
Enrollment: 2,567 Coed
Affiliation or Control: United Methodist IRS Status: 501(c)3
Highest Offering: Doctorate
Accreditation: NH, BUS, CAATE, CS, ENG, MUS, NUR, PTA, PTAA

01 President .... Dr. Thomas A. KAZEE
05 Exec VP Academic Affairs .... Dr. Michael AUSTIN
30 VP Development .... Ms. Abigail WERLING
10 Vice President Fiscal Affairs/Admin .... Mr. Jeffery M. WOLF
32 VP Student Affairs/Dean of Students .... Dr. Dana CLAYTON
84 Vice President Enrollment Services .... Dr. Shane DAVIDSON
26 VP Marketing and Communication .... Mr. Donald JONES
25 Assoc VP Academic Affs .... Vacant
35 Asst VP Student Affs/Dir Res Life .... Mr. Michael A. TESSIER
21 Asst VP for Fiscal Affairs .... Ms. Donna O. TEAGUE
13 Dir of Technology Services .... Mr. Michael SMITH
49 Dean of Arts & Sciences .... Dr. Ray LUTGRING
50 Dean of Business Administration .... Dr. Greg RAWSKI
53 Dean of Educ/Health Science .... Ms. Mary KESSLER
54 Dean Engineering/Computer Science .... Dr. Phillip M. GERHART
51 Director of Adult Education .... Ms. Kristie BYRNS
85 Exec Dir International Programs .... Dr. Wesley MILNER
41 Director of Athletics .... Mr. Mark SPENCER
88 Dir of Content Development .... Ms. Amanda CAMPBELL
09 Dir Institutional Effectiveness .... Mr. Chul LEE
06 University Registrar .... Ms. Jennifer BRIGGS
08 University Librarian .... Mr. Robb WALTNER
42 University Chaplain .... Rev. Tammy GIESELMAN
11 Director of Administrative Services .... Mr. Mark J. LOGEL
29 Director of Alumni/Parent Relations .... Ms. Sylvia Y. DEVAULT
36 Director of Career Svcs/Placement .... Mr. C. Gene WELLS
38 Director of Counseling/Health Educ .... Ms. Sylvia T. BUCK

37 Director of Financial Aid .... Ms. Cathleen WRIGHT
15 Director of Human Resources .... Mr. Keith GEHLHAUSEN
18 Dir of Facilities Mgmt & Planning .... Mr. Chad MILLER
19 Director of Safety & Security .... Mr. Harold P. MATTHEWS
104 Director of Harlaxton Programs .... Ms. Holly CARTER
40 Director of Bookstore .... Mr. Douglas GUSTWILLER
28 Director of Diversity .... Ms. LaNeeca WILLIAMS
44 Director of Development .... Mr. Scott A. GILREATH
88 Director of Academic Advising ... Ms. Deborah A. KASSENBROCK
37 Director of Student Engagement .... Mr. Geoffrey M. EDWARDS
07 Dean of Admissions .... Mr. Scott HENNE
04 Assistant to the President .... Ms. Patricia A. LIPPERT
101 Assistant Secretary of the Board .... Ms. Rebecca SIMPSON

University of Indianapolis (A)

1400 E Hanna Avenue, Indianapolis IN 46227-3697
County: Marion FICE Identification: 001804
Unit ID: 151263
Telephone: (317) 788-3368 Carnegie Class: Masters/L
FAX Number: (317) 788-3300 Calendar System: Semester
URL: www.uindy.edu
Established: 1902 Annual Undergrad Tuition & Fees: $26,290
Enrollment: 5,442 Coed
Affiliation or Control: United Methodist IRS Status: 501(c)3
Highest Offering: Doctorate
Accreditation: NH, ACBSP, ART, CAATE, CLPSY, COARC, EXSC, MIDWF, MUS, NURSE, OT, PTA, PTAA, SW, TED

01 President .... Dr. Robert L. MANUEL
05 Exec VP Academic Affairs/Provost .... Dr. Deborah Ware BALOGH
84 Exec VP for Campus Affs/Enroll Svcs .... Mr. Mark T. WEIGAND
10 VP of Business & Finance/Treasurer .... Mr. Michael L. HOLSTEIN
26 VP Communications & Marketing .... Dr. Jeanette DEDIEMAR
30 Vice President for Univ Advancement .... Mr. Christopher H. MOLLOY
31 Assoc VP of Community Relations .... Dr. David W. WANTZ
41 VP for Intercollegiate Athletics .... Dr. Sue C. WILLEY
42 Dean Ecumenical and Interfaith Pgm .... Dr. Michael G. CARTWRIGHT
43 Vice President & General Counsel .... Ms. Samantha KARN
32 VP for Stdnt/Campus Affs/Dn of Std .... Ms. Kory M. VITANGELI
100 Special Asst to the President .... Ms. Lara G. MANN
04 Executive Administrative Asst .... Ms. Angela PRESNELL
36 Assoc VP of Professional Edge .... Mr. Corey L. WILSON
09 Asst VP of Inst Planning & Rsrch .... Dr. Patrick ALLES
35 Assistant Dean of Students .... Mr. Joseph THOMAS
06 Registrar .... Ms. Kristine L. DOZIER
13 Associate VP Information Systems .... Mr. Steven R. HERRIFORD
49 Dean of College of Arts & Sciences .... Dr. Jennifer A. DRAKE
50 Dean School of Business .... Dr. Lawrence BELCHER
53 Dean School of Education .... Dr. Kathryn A. MORAN
66 Dean School of Nursing .... Dr. Anne C. THOMAS
76 Dean College of Health Sciences .... Dr. Stephanie KELLY
51 Dean School of Adult Learning ..... Dr. Judy APPLE VANALSTINE
55 Dean Psychological Sciences .... Dr. Anita J. THOMAS
20 Assoc Provost for Academic Systems .... Dr. Mary Beth BAGG
20 Int Assoc Prov Rsrch/Grad/Acad Ptnr .... Ms. Ellen MILLER
108 Assoc VP for Accreditation .... Dr. Mary C. MOORE
07 Associate VP for Admissions .... Mr. Ronald W. WILKS
08 Library Director .... Vacant
15 Director Human Resources .... Mrs. Erin P. FARRELL
37 Assoc VP or Financial Aid .... Mrs. Linda B. HANDY
58 Director Graduate Business Pgms .... Mr. Stephen A. TOKAR
18 Executive Director Physical Plant .... Mrs. Pamela L. FOX
19 Director Safety & Police Services .... Mr. David K. SELBY
31 Director of Service Learning .... Dr. Marianna K. FOULKROD
42 Chaplain/Dir Lantz Center .... Rev. Jeremiah GIBBS
29 Assoc VP Alumni Engagement .... Mr. Andy M. KOCHER
85 Director International Division .... Ms. Marilyn O. CHASE
24 Asst VP of Information Systems .... Mr. Robert A. JONES
38 Director Counseling Center .... Dr. Kelly M. MILLER
40 Bookstore Manager .... Vacant
45 Director of Facilities & Planning .... Ms. Andrea NEWSOM

University of Notre Dame (B)

400 Main Building, Notre Dame IN 46556
County: Saint Joseph FICE Identification: 001840
Unit ID: 152080
Telephone: (574) 631-5000 Carnegie Class: DU-Highest
FAX Number: (574) 631-6700 Calendar System: Semester
URL: www.nd.edu
Established: 1842 Annual Undergrad Tuition & Fees: $47,929
Enrollment: 12,179 Coed
Affiliation or Control: Roman Catholic IRS Status: 501(c)3
Highest Offering: Doctorate
Accreditation: NH, ART, BUS, BUSA, CS, ENG, IPSY, LAW, THEOL

01 President .... Rev. John I. JENKINS, CSC
05 Provost .... Dr. Thomas G. BURISH
03 Executive Vice President .... Dr. John F. AFFLECK-GRAVES
20 Vice Pres/Sr Associate Provost .... Dr. Christine M. MAZIAR
20 Vice Pres/Associate Provost .... Dr. Maura A. RYAN
89 VP/Assoc Prov/Dean First Year Stdts .... Dr. Hugh R. PAGE, JR.
82 VP/Provost Internationalization .... Dr. Nicholas ENTRIKIN
32 Vice President for Student Affairs .... Ms. Erin HOFFMANN HARDING
10 Vice President for Finance .... Mr. John A. SEJDINAJ
46 Vice President for Research .... Dr. Robert J. BERNHARD
43 Vice President & General Counsel .... Ms. Marianne CORR
88 Vice Pres/Chief Investment Ofcr .... Mr. Scott C. MALPASS
41 Vice Pres & Director of Athletics .... Mr. John 'Jack' B. SWARBRICK, JR.
15 Vice Pres Human Resources .... Mr. Robert K. MCQUADE
26 Vice President University Relations .... Mr. Louis M. NANNI
13 VP & Chief Information Officer .... Mr. Ronald D. KRAEMER
88 VP Mission Engagmnt/Church Affairs .Rev. William M. LIES, CSC
58 VP/Assoc Prov/Dean Graduate Sch .... Dr. Laura CARLSON
100 Chief of Staff .... Ms. Ann M. FIRTH
28 Chief Diversity Officer .... Mr. Eric LOVE
84 Assoc VP Undergraduate Enrollment .... Mr. Donald C. BISHOP
18 Assoc VP Facilities & Design .... Mr. Douglas K. MARSH
06 Registrar .... Mr. Charles T. HURLEY
96 Director Procurement .... Mr. Vaibhav AGARWAL
50 Dean of College of Business .... Dr. Roger D. HUANG
61 Dean of Law School .... Prof. Nell J. NEWTON
54 Dean College of Engineering .... Dr. Peter K. KILPATRICK
49 Dean of Arts & Letters .... Dr. John T. MCGREEVY
81 Dean of Science .... Dr. Mary E. GALVIN
48 Dean of Architecture .... Dr. Michael N. LYKOUDIS
88 Dean First Year of Studies .... Dr. Hugh R. PAGE
29 Exec Director Alumni Assoc .... Ms. Dolly DUFFY
08 Dir of University Libraries .... Ms. Diane PARR WALKER
27 Chief Communications Executive .... Mr. Paul BROWNE
42 Director of Campus Ministry .... Rev. Peter M. MCCORMICK, CSC
37 Dir of Student Financial Aid .... Ms. Mary B. NUCCIARONE
36 Director of Career Center .... Mr. Lee J. SVETE
38 Director of Counseling Center ...Dr. Susan C. STEIBE-PASALICH
45 Assoc VP Strategic Planning .... Mr. David C. BAILEY
19 Director of Security/Police .... Mr. Phillip A. JOHNSON
07 Director of Admissions .... Mr. Robert MUNDY
101 Secretary of the Institution/Board .... Ms. Beth SWIFT
09 Director of Institutional Research .... Ms. Eva NANCE
102 Dir Foundation/Corporate Relations .... Mr. Rudy REYES
104 Director Study Abroad .... Ms. Kathleen OPEL
39 Director Student Housing .... Ms. Karen M. KENNEDY
04 Administrative Asst to President .... Ms. Sarah A. GOTSCH
86 Director Government Relations .... Mr. Timothy D. SEXTON

University of Phoenix Indianapolis Campus (C)

7999 Knue Road, Indianapolis IN 46250-1932
Telephone: (317) 585-8610 Identification: 770206
Accreditation: &NH, ACBSP

† No longer accepting campus-based students.

University of Saint Francis (D)

2701 Spring Street, Fort Wayne IN 46808-3994
County: Allen FICE Identification: 001832
Unit ID: 152336
Telephone: (260) 399-7700 Carnegie Class: Masters/M
FAX Number: N/A Calendar System: Semester
URL: www.sf.edu
Established: 1890 Annual Undergrad Tuition & Fees: $27,220
Enrollment: 2,308 Coed
Affiliation or Control: Roman Catholic IRS Status: 501(c)3
Highest Offering: Master's
Accreditation: NH, ACBSP, ADNUR, ARCPA, ART, @DIETC, MLTAD, NURSE, PTAA, RAD, SURGT, SW, TED

01 President .... Sr. M. Elise KRISS, OSF
05 Vice President Academic Affairs .... Dr. J. Andrew PRALL
11 Vice President Administration .... Mrs. Teresa A. SORDELET
30 Vice Pres Institutional Advancement .... Dr. Matthew J. SMITH
10 Vice President Finance & Operations .... Mr. Richard A. BIENZ
20 Assoc VP Academic Affairs .... Dr. Joseph M. FRIONA
84 Assoc VP Enrollment Management .... Mr. Jean Paul SPAGNOLO
45 Assoc VP Inst Research/Planning .... Dr. Stephanie J. OETTING
26 Assoc Vice President Marketing .... Mrs. Trois K. HART
88 Assistant VP Mission Integration ..... Sr. M. Anita HOLZMER, OSF
50 Dean Keith Busse School of Business .... Dr. Robert W. LEE
57 Dean School of Creative Arts .... Mr. Rick E. CARTWRIGHT
17 Dean School of Health Sciences .... Dr. Mindy J. YODER
49 Dean School Liberal Arts & Sciences .... Dr. Lance D. RICHEY
12 Dean Crown Point Site .... Dr. Marsha M. KING
32 Dean of Students .... Mr. Donald B. APPIARIUS
35 Associate Dean Campus Life .... Mrs. Elizabeth A. GROMAN
21 Controller .... Mr. Craig M. TEETSEL
06 Registrar .... Mr. Francis P. CONNOR
29 Dir Alumni Relations .... Ms. Melissa S. EASTMAN
15 Dir Human Resources & Org Devel .... Ms. Jennifer M. FAWBUSH
07 Executive Dir Enrollment Services .... Ms. Jamie M. MCGRATH
08 Assoc Dir Information/Instruc Svcs ..Mrs. Maureen E. MCMAHAN
53 Chair Department of Education .... Dr. Daniel J. TORLONE
106 Dir Adult/Online Enrollment Svcs ..Mrs. Michelle L. KUHLHORST
44 Director Annual Fund .... Mrs. Alexandra ELLIS KREAGER
41 Director Athletics .... Mr. Michael H. MCCAFFREY
42 Director Campus Ministry .... Mr. Scott R. OPPERMAN
42 Chaplain .... Fr. David L. MEINZEN
102 Dir Corp/Found Relations and Grants .... Mrs. Lynnette M. MCKENNA FRAZIER
44 Director Development .... Mr. Matthew C. ROWAN
88 Director Employer Relations .... Mrs. Natalie M. WAGONER
88 Dir Environ Health/Safety/Risk Mgt .... Mr. Randy D. TROY
37 Director Financial Aid .... Mrs. Michelle L. NISUN
88 Dir Hlth Sci Strategic Initiatives .... Dr. Lorene R. ARNOLD
92 Director Honors Program .... Dr. Kenneth A. BUGAJSKI
16 Assistant Director Human Resources .... Mr. Andy MCKEE
105 Dir Marketing & Creative Services .... Mrs. Carla S. PYLE
28 Dir Retention/Diversity Programming .... Mr. Garien L. HUDSON
88 Director Service & Social Action .... Mrs. Katrina P. BOEDEKER
88 Director Sports Information .... Mr. William J. SCOTT
88 Assistant Dean Student Success .... Mrs. Tricia J. VANDERLEE BUGAJSKI
91 Interim Exec Dir Univ Technology .... Mr. Mark ROBBINS
13 Dir Enterprise Applications .... Mr. A. Drew REPP
19 Supervisor Campus Safety/Security ..... Mr. Edward A. LAROCQUE
18 Supervisor Maintenance/Grounds .... Mr. Rex A. BERCOT
09 Research/Assessment Analyst .... Mrs. Kim E. DIETRICH
04 Admin Liaison Office of Pres .... Miss Vicki L. JACOBS, OFS
109 Mgr & Exec Chef AVI Food Service .... Mr. Brian D. SMITH
40 Mgr Barnes & Noble Campus Shoppe .... Mrs. Robin HUFFMAN

University of Southern Indiana (E)

8600 University Boulevard, Evansville IN 47712-3596
County: Vanderburgh FICE Identification: 001808
Unit ID: 151306
Telephone: (812) 464-8600 Carnegie Class: Masters/L
FAX Number: (812) 464-1960 Calendar System: Semester
URL: www.usi.edu
Established: 1965 Annual Undergrad Tuition & Fees (In-State): $7,178
Enrollment: 9,364 Coed
Affiliation or Control: State IRS Status: 501(c)3
Highest Offering: Doctorate
Accreditation: NH, ART, BUS, BUSA, COARC, DA, DH, DIETD, DMS, ENG, NURSE, OT, OTA, RAD, SW

01 President .... Dr. Linda L M. BENNETT
100 Exec Assistant to the President .... Ms. Miekka M. COX
05 Provost .... Dr. Ronald S. ROCHON
10 Vice President for Finance & Admin .... Mr. Steven J. BRIDGES
86 Vice Pres Govt and Univ Relations .... Ms. Cynthia S. BRINKER
84 VP for Enrollment Management .... Mr. Andrew W. WRIGHT
26 Assoc VP Marketing/Communications .... Ms. Kindra STRUPP
56 Assoc Provost Outreach Engagement .... Dr. Mark C. BERNHARD
20 Asst Provost for Academic Affairs .... Dr. Shelly B. BLUNT
32 Assoc Provost for Student Affairs .... Dr. Marcia K. KIESSLING
21 Assoc Vice Pres Budget and Planning .... Ms. Mary A. HUPFER
09 Exec Director Plng/Research/Assess .Dr. Katherine A. DRAUGHON
58 Director of Graduate Studies .... Dr. Mayola ROWSER
06 Registrar .... Ms. Sandy K. FRANK
07 Director of Undergrad Admission .... Mr. Rashad E. SMITH
08 Director of Library Svcs .... Ms. Marna M. HOSTETLER
30 Director of Development/USI Fndtn .... Mr. David A. BOWER
92 Director Honors Program .... Dr. Antonia D. BAMBINA
38 Director of Counseling .... Dr. B. Thomas LONGWELL
29 Director of Alumni $ Volunteer Svcs .... Mrs. Janet L. JOHNSON
37 Director of Student Financial Asst .... Ms. Mary J. HARPER
15 Exec Director of Human Resources ..... Mr. Andrew R. LENHARDT
36 Director Career Svcs & Internships .... Mr. Philip L. PARKER
35 Dean of Students .... Dr. Bryan RUSH
85 Asst Provost Intl Programs & Svcs .... Mrs. Heidi GREGORI-GAHAN
28 Director Multicultural Center .... Ms. Pamela F. HOPSON
13 Exec Dir of Information Technology .... Mr. Richard TOENISKOETTER
90 Academic Services Coordinator .... Mr. Juzar AHMED
18 Dir of Facility Operations & Plng .... Mr. James E. WOLFE
96 Director Procurement Services .... Mr. Daniel R. MARTENS
27 Director of Univ Communication .... Mr. John A. FARLESS
19 Director of Public Safety .... Mr. Stephen WOODALL
39 Director of Residence Life .... Ms. Amy S. PRICE
40 Campus Store Manager .... Mr. Michael J. GOELZHAUSER
41 Athletic Director .... Mr. Jon Mark HALL
50 Dean Romain College of Business .... Dr. Mohammed KHAYUM
49 Dean College of Liberal Arts .... Dr. James M. BEEBY
66 Dean College Nursing/Health Profess .... Dr. Ann H. WHITE
81 Int Dean College of Sci/Engr/Educ .... Dr. Zane W. MITCHELL
51 Exec Dir Continuing Education .... Ms. Dawn M. STONEKING
106 Asst Provost for Distance Learning .... Ms. Megan W. LINOS

Valparaiso University (F)

1700 Chapel Drive, Valparaiso IN 46383-9978
County: Porter FICE Identification: 001842
Unit ID: 152600
Telephone: (219) 464-5000 Carnegie Class: Masters/L
FAX Number: (219) 464-5381 Calendar System: Semester
URL: valpo.edu
Established: 1859 Annual Undergrad Tuition & Fees: $36,160
Enrollment: 4,507 Coed
Affiliation or Control: Lutheran IRS Status: 501(c)3
Highest Offering: Doctorate
Accreditation: NH, BUS, CACREP, ENG, LAW, MUS, NURSE, SW, TED

01 President .... Dr. Mark A. HECKLER
05 Provost/Exec VP for Acad Affs .... Dr. Mark BIERMANN
20 Assoc Prov International Affairs .... Dr. Jaishankar RAMAN
32 VP for Student Affairs .... Dr. Bonnie L. HUNTER
84 VP for Enrollment Mgt & Mktg .... Mr. Michael JOSEPH
58 Dean Grad School/Cont Educ .... Dr. Jennifer ZIEGLER
30 VP for Advancement .... Ms. Lisa HOLLANDER
43 VP University Counsel .... Mr. Darron C. FARHA
10 VP for Finance & Administration .... Ms. Susan SCROGGINS
92 Dean of Christ College .... Dr. Peter KANELOS
49 Dean College Arts & Sciences .... Dr. Jon T. KILPINEN
61 Dean School of Law .... Dr. Andrea LYON
54 Dean College of Engineering .... Dr. Eric JOHNSON
50 Dean College of Business Admin .... Dr. James BRODZINSKI
66 Dean College of Nursing .... Dr. Janet M. BROWN
08 Dean Library Services .... Dr. Bradford L. EDEN
35 Dean of Students .... Dr. Timothy S. JENKINS
84 AVP Enrollment Management .... Mr. David FEVIG

42 AVP for Mission & Ministry .... Rev. Brian T. JOHNSON
06 Registrar .... Ms. Stephanie MARTIN
19 Chief University Police .... Ms. Rebecca A. WALKOWIAK
39 Asst Dean Students/Residential Life .... Mr. Ryan BLEVINS
104 Assoc Dir of Study Abroad .... Ms. Erin KUNERT
85 Assoc Dir of International Program .... Ms. Janice LIN
29 Director Alumni Relations .... Ms. Linda ROETTGER
15 Dir Human Resource Services .... Mr. Scott HARRISON
18 Exec Dir of Facilities .... Mr. Jon VARNELL
36 Director Career Center .... Mr. Tom CATH
38 Director of Counseling Services .... Dr. Stewart E. COOPER
41 Director Athletics .... Mr. Mark LABARBERA
20 Asst Provost for Faculty Affairs .... Dr. Rick GILLMAN
21 Controller .... Ms. Diana BLANEY
28 Director of Multicultural Programs .... Mr. Byron MARTIN
96 Director of Procurement .... Ms. Nancy K. MURRAY
09 Exec Dir Instl Effectiveness .... Mr. Greg STINSON
42 University Pastor .... Rev. Charlene COX
42 University Pastor .... Rev. James WETZSTEIN
37 Director of Financial Aid .... Ms. Karen KLIMCZYK
100 Chief of Staff .... Mr. Rick AMRHEIN
04 Administrative Asst to President .... Ms. Gwen GRAHAM
07 Director of Admissions .... Ms. Barb LIESKE
101 Secretary of the Institution/Board .... Mr. Darron FARHA
102 Dir Foundation/Corporate Relations .... Ms. Kathy GROTH
13 Chief Info Technology Officer (CIO) .... Mr. Rick AMRHEIN
44 Director Annual or Planned Giving .... Mr. David NOVAK
88 Director of Operations .... Ms. Diane NOE

Vincennes University (A)

1002 N First Street, Vincennes IN 47591-1504
County: Knox FICE Identification: 001843
Unit ID: 152637
Telephone: (812) 888-8888 Carnegie Class: Bac/Assoc-Assoc Dom
FAX Number: (812) 888-5868 Calendar System: Semester
URL: www.vinu.edu
Established: 1801 Annual Undergrad Tuition & Fees (In-State): $5,375
Enrollment: 19,205 Coed
Affiliation or Control: State IRS Status: 501(c)3
Highest Offering: Baccalaureate
Accreditation: NH, ACBSP, ADNUR, ART, CAHIIM, EMT, FUSER, NUR, PNUR, PTAA, SURGT, TED, THEA

01 President .... Dr. Charles R. JOHNSON
05 Provost/Vice Pres Institutional Svc .... Dr. Laurel A. SMITH
10 Vice Pres Financial Svcs/Govt Rels .... Mr. Phillip S. RATH
103 VP Workforce Dev/Comm Services .... Mr. David A. TUCKER
12 Assistant VP/Dean Jasper Campus .... Dr. Chris GRAY
21 Associate Vice President/Controller .... Ms. Linda L. WALDROUP
32 Asst Provost Student Affairs .... Vacant
20 Asst Provost Curriculum & Inst .... Mr. Michael GRESS
35 Interim Dean of Students .... Ms. Taja DAVIDSON
26 Sr Director External Relations .... Ms. Kristi R. DEETZ
07 Director of Admissions .... Ms. Heidi M. WHITEHEAD
08 Director of Learning Resources/Tech .... Mr. David M. PETER
09 Director of Institutional Research .... Ms. Kimela A. MEEKS
13 Director of Mgmt Information Center .... Mr. Carmin A. SCHNARR
27 Director Public Information .... Mr. Duane H. CHATTIN
88 Director of University Events .... Ms. Cynthia A. BEAMAN
36 Dir Ctr for Career & Empl Relations .... Mr. Richard A. COLEMAN
37 Director of Student Financial Aid .... Mr. Stanley J. WERNE
22 Director Disability Services .... Ms. Leslie M. SMITH
38 Director of Student Counseling .... Dr. Lisa J. BISHOP
40 Manager of Bookstore .... Mr. Alan RAGGO
102 President of VU Foundation .... Mr. Bumper R. HOSTETLER
41 Athletic Director .... Mr. Harry L. MEEKS
88 Sr Dir Dual Credit Partnerships .... Ms. Heather MOFFAT
29 Director of Alumni Programs .... Ms. Jennifer D. GILMORE
85 Director Multicultural Affairs .... Vacant
18 Director of Physical Plant .... Mr. Andrew YOUNG
19 Director of Campus Police .... Mr. James M. JONES
88 Bursar .... Ms. Lori J. HOSTETLER
24 Director of Media Services .... Mr. Jay D. WOLF
06 Registrar .... Ms. Rebecca K. LITTLE
39 Director Residential Life .... Ms. Dawn M. BREWER
88 Director Marketing Services .... Ms. Andrea G. TSCHERTER
96 Director of Procurement .... Mr. Michael L. MORRISON
38 Director Student Success Ctr .... Ms. Michelle CUMMINS
88 Director Architectural Services .... Mr. Andrew YOUNG
15 Director Human Resources/ AAO .... Ms. Regina L. MCCORD-FITHIAN
76 Dean College Health Sci/Human Perf .... Dr. Jana L. VIECK
50 Dean College of Business/Public Svc .... Ms. Anna MILLER
72 Int Dean College of Technology .... Mr. Dean ACKERMAN
81 Dean College of Science/Engr/Math .... Dr. Paul J. WILDER
83 Dean Soc Sci/Perf Arts/Comm .... Vacant
88 Budget Director .... Mr. Tim EATON
79 Dean College of Humanities .... Ms. Joan PUCKETT
88 Dir Avia Tech Ctr Indianapolis .... Mr. Michael D. GEHRICH
88 Director Marketing Communications .... Ms. Krystal F. SPENCER
88 Dir Institutional Effectiveness .... Vacant
20 Director Early College .... Ms. Nicole SHANKLE
88 Asst VP Outreach & Engagement .... Mr. Matthew J. SCHWARTZ
88 Director Veterans Affairs .... Ms. Kristen PHILLIPS
88 Dir Gibson Ctr Adv Mfg/Logistics .... Vacant
88 Dir Plainfield Logistics Center .... Mr. James E. DOLAN
04 Administrative Asst to President .... Ms. Patricia A. KONKLE
88 Director International Recruitment .... Ms. Valerie M. ALLEN
23 Dir Univ Primary Care Clinic .... Ms. Denah PERRY

Vincennes University-Jasper Center (B)

850 College Avenue, Jasper IN 47546
Telephone: (812) 482-3030 Identification: 770107
Accreditation: &NH

† Regional accreditation is carried under the parent institution in Vincennes, IN

Wabash College (C)

301 W Wabash, PO Box 352, Crawfordsville IN 47933-0352
County: Montgomery FICE Identification: 001844
Unit ID: 152673
Telephone: (765) 361-6100 Carnegie Class: Bac-A&S
FAX Number: (765) 361-6461 Calendar System: Semester
URL: www.wabash.edu
Established: 1832 Annual Undergrad Tuition & Fees: $39,980
Enrollment: 926 Male
Affiliation or Control: Independent Non-Profit IRS Status: 501(c)3
Highest Offering: Baccalaureate
Accreditation: NH

01 President .... Dr. Gregory D. HESS
05 Dean of the College .... Dr. Scott FELLER
10 Chief Financial Officer & Treasurer .... Mr. Larry GRIFFITH
32 Dean of Students .... Mr. Michael E. RATERS
30 Dean for Advancement .... Ms. Michelle L. JANSSEN
84 Dean for Enrollment Management .... Dr. Michael F. THORP
36 Dean for Professional Development .... Mr. Alan P. HILL
100 Chief of Staff .... Mr. James L. AMIDON
20 Sr Associate Dean of the College .... Dr. Todd F. MCDORMAN
08 Head Librarian & Dir Lilly Library .... Mr. John E. LAMBORN
06 Registrar and Assoc Dean .... Dr. Jonathan D. JUMP
13 Director of IT Services .... Mr. Bradley K. WEAVER
37 Director of Financial Aid .... Ms. Heidi A. CARL
35 Associate Dean of Students .... Mr. Marc WELCH
36 Director of Career Development .... Mr. R. Scott CRAWFORD
29 Dir of Alumni & Parent Relations .... Mr. Steve HOFFMAN
109 Director of Business Auxiliaries .... Mr. Thomas E. KEEDY
41 Dir of Athletics & Campus Wellness .... Mr. Joseph R. HAKLIN
44 Associate Dean for Advancement .... Mr. Joseph R. KLEN
15 Director of Human Resources .... Ms. Catherine A. METZ
18 Director of Campus Services .... Mr. David MORGAN
21 Controller .... Ms. Cathy VANARSDALL
38 Director of Counseling Services .... Mr. Kevin C. SWAIM
28 Int Director of Malcolm X Institute .... Mr. Alan HILL
88 Director of Inquiries CILA .... Dr. Charles F. BLAICH
88 Dir Wabash Ctr Teaching/Learning .... Dr. Nadine S. PENCE
19 Director of Safety and Security .... Mr. Richard G. WOODS
09 Director of Institutional Research .... Dr. Preston R. BOST
101 Secretary of the Institution/Board .... Mr. James L. AMIDON, JR.
102 Dir Foundation/Corporate Relations .... Ms. Deborah WOODS
104 Director International Programs .... Ms. Amy WEIR
26 Chief Public Relations/Marketing .... Ms. Kimberly JOHNSON
96 Director of Purchasing .... Mr. Thomas E. KEEDY

IOWA

Allen College (D)

1825 Logan Avenue, Waterloo IA 50703-1999
County: Black Hawk FICE Identification: 030691
Unit ID: 152798
Telephone: (319) 226-2000 Carnegie Class: Spec-4-yr-Other Health
FAX Number: (319) 226-2010 Calendar System: Semester
URL: www.allencollege.edu
Established: 1989 Annual Undergrad Tuition & Fees: $17,373
Enrollment: 575 Coed
Affiliation or Control: Independent Non-Profit IRS Status: 501(c)3
Highest Offering: Doctorate
Accreditation: NH, DMS, MT, NMT, NURSE, RAD

01 Chancellor .... Dr. Jerry DURHAM
05 Vice Chancellor of Academic Affairs .... Dr. Nancy KRAMER
10 Dir Business/Administrative Svcs .... Ms. Denise HANSON
66 Dean School of Nursing .... Dr. Kendra WILLIAMS-PEREZ
76 Dean School of Health Sciences .... Dr. Peggy FORTSCH
32 Dean of Student Services .... Dr. Joanna RAMSDEN-MEIER
37 Director of Financial Aid .... Ms. Jobyna JOHNSTON
37 Financial Aid Coordinator .... Ms. Molly CORDES
24 Media Specialist .... Ms. Robin NICHOLSON
06 Registrar .... Ms. Michelle KOEHN
08 Director of Library Services .... Dr. Ruth YAN
07 Director of Admissions .... Ms. Molly QUINN
09 Coord Inst Research/Effectiveness .... Vacant

Antioch School of Church Planting and Leadership Development (E)

2400 Oakwood Road, Ames IA 50014
County: Story Identification: 667026
Telephone: (515) 292-9694 Carnegie Class: Not Classified
FAX Number: (515) 292-1933 Calendar System: Other
URL: www.antiochschool.edu
Established: 2006 Annual Undergrad Tuition & Fees: N/A
Enrollment: N/A Coed
Affiliation or Control: Independent Non-Profit IRS Status: 501(c)3
Highest Offering: Doctorate
Accreditation: DEAC

01 President .... Jeff REED
05 Academic Dean .... Stephen KEMP

*Board of Regents, State of Iowa (F)

11260 Aurora Avenue, Urbandale IA 50322-7905
County: Polk FICE Identification: 033443
Telephone: (515) 281-3934 Carnegie Class: N/A
FAX Number: (515) 281-6420
URL: www.regents.iowa.gov

01 Executive Director & CEO .... Dr. Bob DONLEY
05 Chief Academic Officer .... Dr. Diana GONZALEZ
10 Chief Operating Officer .... Mr. Mark BRAUN
43 Board Counsel .... Mrs. Aimee K. CLAEYS
04 Administrative Asst to President .... Mrs. Laura M. DICKSON

*Iowa State University (G)

Ames IA 50011-0002
County: Story FICE Identification: 001869
Unit ID: 153603
Telephone: (515) 294-4111 Carnegie Class: DU-Highest
FAX Number: (515) 294-2592 Calendar System: Semester
URL: www.iastate.edu
Established: 1858 Annual Undergrad Tuition & Fees (In-State): $7,736
Enrollment: 34,435 Coed
Affiliation or Control: State IRS Status: 501(c)3
Highest Offering: Doctorate
Accreditation: NH, ART, BUS, BUSA, CAATE, CIDA, COPSY, CS, DIETD, DIETI, ENG, IPSY, JOUR, LSAR, MUS, NAIT, PLNG, VET

02 President .... Dr. Steven LEATH
100 Chief Financial Off/Chief of Staff .... Mr. Miles LACKEY
04 Assistant to the President .... Ms. Shirley J. KNIPFEL
43 University Counsel .... Mr. Michael E. NORTON
05 Sr Vice President and Provost .... Dr. Jonathan A. WICKERT
10 Sr Vice Pres for University Svcs .... Ms. Katherine GREGORY
32 Sr Vice Pres for Student Affairs .... Dr. Martino HARMON
88 Vice Pres for Ec Dev/Bus Engagement .... Dr. Michael R. CRUM
46 Vice Pres Research .... Dr. Sarah M. NUSSER
56 Vice Pres Extension/Outreach .... Dr. Cathann A. KRESS
13 Vice President Info Tech Svcs .... Dr. Jim KURTENBACH
28 Vice Pres for Diversity & Inclusion .... Dr. Reginald C. STEWART
20 Associate Provost Academic Programs .... Dr. David K. HOLGER
20 Assoc Prov Faculty .... Dr. Dawn BRATSCH-PRINCE
21 Associate Vice President/Univ Sec .... Ms. Pam ELLIOTT CAIN
18 Assoc Vice Pres Facilities .... Mr. David J. MILLER
15 Int Vice President Human Resources .... Ms. Kristi DARR
84 Assoc Vice Pres Student Affairs .... Dr. Martino HARMON
38 Int Dir for Student Counseling Svcs .... Dr. Joyce DAVIDSON
30 President of ISU Foundation .... Ms. Larissa HOLTMYER-JONES
29 President of Alumni Association .... Dr. Jeffrey W. JOHNSON
41 Director of Athletics .... Mr. Jamie B. POLLARD
26 Exec Director of University Rels .... Mr. John F. MCCARROLL
06 Registrar .... Ms. Laura J. DOERING
37 Director of Financial Aid .... Ms. Roberta L. JOHNSON
07 Director of Admissions .... Ms. Katharine JOHNSON SUSKI
22 Director of Equal Opportunity .... Ms. Margo FOREMAN
09 Int Director of Inst Research .... Sandra W. GAHN
19 Int Director of Public Safety .... Mr. Aaron V. DELASHMUTT
35 Int Dean of Students .... Dr. Keith E. ROBINDER
23 Director of Student Health .... Ms. Erin BALDWIN
104 Director Study Abroad .... Dr. Trevor NELSON
39 Director of Residence .... Dr. Peter D. ENGLIN
91 Associate CIO .... Mr. David M. POPELKA
25 Assoc Director/Sponsored Pgm Admin .... Ms. Tamara R. POLASKI
88 Director Ames Laboratory .... Dr. Adam SCHWARTZ
96 Director of Purchasing .... Ms. Nancy S. BROOKS
40 Director University Bookstore .... Ms. Rita M. PHILLIPS
58 Dean Graduate College .... Dr. David K. HOLGER
08 Dean of Library Services .... Ms. Mary E. MCNEIL
47 Dean College of Agriculture .... Dr. Wendy WINTERSTEEN
50 Dean College of Business .... Mr. David P. SPALDING
48 Dean College of Design .... Mr. Luis C. RICO-GUTIERREZ
53 Dean College of Human Sciences .... Dr. Laura JOLLY
54 Dean College of Engineering .... Dr. Sarah RAJALA
49 Dean Col of Lib Arts & Sciences .... Dr. Beate SCHMITTMANN
74 Dean College of Veterinary Medicine .... Dr. Lisa K. NOLAN
106 Assoc Director for Online Education .... Dr. Ralph E. NAPOLITANO
102 Sr Dir Dev/Corporate Relations .... Mr. Mark BOECK
102 Sr Dir Dev/Foundation Relations .... Ms. Donna VAN PELT
44 Exec Dir of Annual & Special Giving .... Ms. Melissa ROWAN
27 Director of University Marketing .... Ms. Carole A. CUSTER

*University of Iowa (H)

Iowa City IA 52242-0001
County: Johnson FICE Identification: 001892
Unit ID: 153658
Telephone: (319) 335-3500 Carnegie Class: DU-Highest
FAX Number: (319) 335-0807 Calendar System: Semester
URL: www.uiowa.edu
Established: 1847 Annual Undergrad Tuition & Fees (In-State): $8,104
Enrollment: 29,970 Coed
Affiliation or Control: State IRS Status: 501(c)3
Highest Offering: Doctorate
Accreditation: NH, ANEST, ARCPA, AUD, BUS, BUSA, CAATE, CACREP, CEA, CLPSY, COPSY, CORE, DANCE, DENT, DIETI, DMS, EMT, ENG, ENGR, HSA, IPSY, JOUR, LAW, LIB, MED, MUS, NMT, NURSE, PAST, PCSAS, PERF, PH, PHAR, PLNG, PTA, RAD, RTT, SCPSY, SP, SW, THEA

02 President ... Mr. Bruce HARRELD
05 Exec Vice President & Provost ... Dr. Patrick B. BUTLER
46 VP Research & Economic Development ... Dr. Daniel REED
10 SVP Fin & Ops/Chief Financial Ofcr ... Mr. Rod LEHNERTZ
32 VP Student Life ... Dr. Thomas R. ROCKLIN
17 VP Med Affairs/Dean College of Med ... Dr. Jean E. ROBILLARD
30 Vice Pres & Development Officer ... Mr. David R. DIERKS
26 Asst VP External Affairs ... Ms. Jeneane BECK
26 Interim Sr Director Marketing Comm ... Mr. Ben HILL
20 Associate Provost Faculty ... Dr. Kevin KREGEL
28 Chief Diversity Officer/AP ... Dr. Georgina DODGE
88 Assoc Provost/Dean Univ College ... Mr. Lon MOELLER
45 Assoc Vice President Research ... Dr. Richard D. HICHWA
11 Assoc VP/Dir of Admin and Planning .. Mr. Donald J. SZESZYCKI
15 Int Assoc VP Finance/Dir HR ... Mr. Kevin WARD
18 Assoc VP/Dir Facilities Management ... Mr. Donald J. GUCKERT
13 Assoc Vice President & CIO ... Mr. Steven R. FLEAGLE
23 Assoc VP/CEO Univ Hosp & Clinics ... Mr. Kenneth KATES
25 Exec Director Sponsored Programs ... Ms. Jennifer LASSNER
19 Interim Director Public Safety ... Mr. David VISIN
85 Dean International Programs ... Dr. Downing THOMAS
43 VP Legal Affairs & General Counsel ... Ms. Carroll REASONER
08 University Librarian ... Mr. John P. CULSHAW
29 Exec Director Alumni Association ... Mr. Jeffrey D. KUETER
102 President University Foundation ... Ms. Lynette L. MARSHALL
07 Director Admissions/Enrollment ... Mr. Kirk R. KLUVER
37 Director Student Financial Aid ... Mr. Mark S. WARNER
06 Registrar ... Mr. Lawrence J. LOCKWOOD
36 Director Career Center ... Mr. David A. BAUMGARTNER
38 Director Univ Counseling Services ... Dr. Sam V. COCHRAN, III
39 Director Residence Services ... Mr. Von STANGE
41 Director Athletics Administration ... Mr. Gary BARTA
49 Dean Col of Liberal Arts & Sciences ... Dr. Chaden DJALALI
50 Dean College of Business Admin ... Dr. Sarah GARDIAL
52 Dean College of Dentistry ... Dr. David C. JOHNSEN
53 Dean College of Education ... Dr. Daniel CLAY
54 Dean College of Engineering ... Dr. Alec SCRANTON
58 Dean Graduate College ... Dr. John C. KELLER
61 Dean College of Law ... Dr. Gail B. AGRAWAL
66 Dean College of Nursing ... Dr. Rita A. FRANTZ
67 Dean College of Pharmacy ... Dr. Donald E. LETENDRE
69 Dean College of Public Health ... Dr. Susan CURRY
04 Special Assistant to President ... Dr. Thomas K. DEAN
22 Dir Equal Opportunity/Diversity ... Ms. Jennifer A. MODESTOU
86 Director State Relations ... Mr. Keith SAUNDERS
40 Director University Bookstore ... Mr. George E. HERBERT
96 Director Purchasing ... Ms. Deborah J. ZUMBACH
92 Director Honors Program ... Dr. Art L. SPISAK
87 Director Summer Session ... Dr. Marlys BOOTE
35 Dean of Students ... Dr. Lyn REDINGTON
84 Assoc VP/Enrollment Management ... Dr. Brent GAGE
100 Chief of Staff ... Mr. Peter MATTHES
104 Director Study Abroad ... Mr. Douglas LEE
09 Director of Institutional Research ... Mr. Daniel REED
44 Director Annual or Planned Giving ... Ms. Erin ALLEN

*University of Northern Iowa (A)

1227 W 27th Street, Cedar Falls IA 50614-0001

County: Black Hawk — FICE Identification: 001890
Unit ID: 154095
Telephone: (319) 273-2311 — Carnegie Class: Masters/L
FAX Number: (319) 273-2885 — Calendar System: Semester
URL: www.uni.edu
Established: 1876 — Annual Undergrad Tuition & Fees (In-State): $7,817
Enrollment: 11,928 — Coed
Affiliation or Control: State — IRS Status: 501(c)3
Highest Offering: Doctorate
Accreditation: NH, BUS, CAATE, CACREP, CEA, CIDA, ENGT, MUS, NAIT, NRPA, SP, SW, THEA

02 Interim President ... Dr. A. James WOHLPART
05 Interim Exec VP & Provost ... Dr. Brenda L. BASS
10 Sr VP Admin/Financial Svcs ... Dr. Michael A. HAGER
32 Interim VP for Student Affairs ... Dr. Jan M. HANISH
30 Vice President for Univ Advancement ... Ms. Lisa B. BARONIO
84 Assoc VP for Enrollment Management . Mr. Matthew D. KROEGER
18 Director Physical Plant Admin ... Mr. Michael W. ZWANZIGER
26 Director Univ Relations ... Mr. Scott A. KETELSEN
39 Asst VP & Exec Dir of Residence ... Mr. Glenn P. GRAY
20 Assoc Provost for Acad Affairs ... Dr. Kavita R. DHANWADA
20 Assoc Provost for Faculty ... Dr. Nancy H. COBB
13 Chief Information Officer ... Ms. Marty L. MARK
09 Dir Inst Research & Effectiveness ... Dr. Kristin M. MOSER
62 Dean of Library Services ... Mr. Christopher N. COX
06 University Registrar ... Mr. Philip L. PATTON
29 Director Alumni Relations ... Ms. Leslie J. PRIDEAUX
37 Director of Financial Aid ... Ms. Joyce MORROW
15 Dir Human Resource Services ... Ms. Michelle C. BYERS
36 Exec Dir Stdnt Engagement/Outrch ... Mr. Robert J. FREDERICK
83 Interim Dean Col Soc/Behav Sciences ... Dr. Patrick P. PEASE
53 Dean Col Education ... Dr. Gaëtane JEAN-MARIE
49 Dean Col Hum/Arts & Science ... Dr. John E. FRITCH
51 Dean Cont Educ/Special Programs ... Dr. Kent M. JOHNSON
58 Dean Graduate College ... Dr. Kavita R. DHANWADA
50 Dean Col Business Admin ... Dr. Leslie K. WILSON
35 Dean of Students ... Dr. Leslie K. WILLIAMS
38 Counseling Center Director ... Dr. David C. TOWLE
22 Asst to Pres Compliance/Equity Mgmt .. Ms. Leah K. GUTKNECHT
41 Athletic Director ... Mr. David W. HARRIS
21 Treas/Asst VP Finance & Operations ... Ms. Kelly A. FLEGE
86 State Relations Officer ... Ms. Mary C. BRAUN
104 Exec Director Intl Programs ... Mr. Philip D. PLOURDE
88 Director Undergraduate Studies ... Dr. Deirdre A. HEISTAD
19 Chief of Police/Dir Public Safety ... Ms. Helen M. HAIRE
25 Grants and Contracts Administrator ... Mr. Tolif R. HUNT
43 University Counsel ... Mr. Timothy J. MCKENNA
88 Controller/Secretary/Director ... Ms. Tonya L. GERBACHT
07 Director of Admissions ... Ms. Kara M. HADLEY-SHAKYA
28 Asst to Pres/Chief Div Officer ... Ms. Gwennette C. BERRY
106 Dir Student Success and Retention ... Dr. Kristin L. WOODS
44 VP for Principal Gifts ... Ms. Noreen M. HERMANSEN

Briar Cliff University (B)

3303 Rebecca Street, Sioux City IA 51104-2324

County: Woodbury — FICE Identification: 001846
Unit ID: 152992
Telephone: (712) 279-5321 — Carnegie Class: Bac-Diverse
FAX Number: (712) 279-5410 — Calendar System: 4/1/4
URL: www.briarcliff.edu
Established: 1929 — Annual Undergrad Tuition & Fees: $28,090
Enrollment: 1,135 — Coed
Affiliation or Control: Roman Catholic — IRS Status: 501(c)3
Highest Offering: Doctorate
Accreditation: NH, NURSE, @PTA, SW

01 President ... Dr. Hamid A. SHIRVANI
05 Interim VP Academic Affairs ... Dr. Todd KNEALING
10 Vice President Finance & Treasurer ... Mrs. Beth GRIGSBY
30 Vice Pres University Relations ... Mrs. Tina STROUD
84 Vice Pres Enrollment Management ... Mr. Brian EBEN
32 Vice President Student Development ... Mrs. Louise PASKEY
06 Registrar ... Mrs. Deidre ENGEL
08 Librarian/Dir Information Services ... Mr. Julius FLESCHNER
13 Director Computer Center ... Ms. Leah WARD
29 Activities/Events & E-Coordinator ... Ms. Lorna KOHN
36 Director Career Development ... Mr. Joshua COBBS
37 Director Financial Aid ... Mrs. Shelby REED
40 Director Bookstore ... Ms. Nancy WATSON
41 Athletic Director ... Mr. Steve GAST
42 Director Campus Ministry ... Sr. Janet MAY
18 Director Physical Plant ... Mr. Eric HOLMQUIST
26 Director Marketing & Communications ... Mrs. Amanda MAYO
07 Director of Admissions ... Vacant
15 Director Human Resources ... Mr. Beau SUDTELGTE
39 Director Residence Life ... Mr. Dave ARENS
38 Director Student Counseling ... Mrs. Jeanette TOBIN
09 Director of Institutional Research ... Ms. Deidre ENGEL
44 Director of Philanthropy ... Mrs. Carolyn ELLWANGER
19 Director Security/Safety ... Mr. Marty POTTEBAUM

Brown Mackie College-Quad Cities (C)

2119 East Kimberly Road, Bettendorf IA 52722

Telephone: (563) 344-1500 — Identification: 666792
Accreditation: ACICS, OTA

† Branch campus of The Art Institute of Phoenix, Phoenix, AZ

Buena Vista University (D)

610 W Fourth Street, Storm Lake IA 50588-1798

County: Buena Vista — FICE Identification: 001847
Unit ID: 153001
Telephone: (712) 749-2351 — Carnegie Class: Bac-Diverse
FAX Number: (712) 749-2037 — Calendar System: 4/1/4
URL: www.bvu.edu
Established: 1891 — Annual Undergrad Tuition & Fees: $31,318
Enrollment: 2,295 — Coed
Affiliation or Control: Presbyterian Church (U.S.A.) — IRS Status: 501(c)3
Highest Offering: Master's
Accreditation: NH, #CAATE, SW

01 President ... Mr. Frederick V. MOORE
04 Assistant to the President ... Ms. Emily A. WILLIAMS
05 VP Academic Affairs/Dean of Faculty ... Dr. James SALVUCCI
10 Vice President Business Services ... Ms. Suzette RADKE
84 Vice Pres for Enrollment Management ... Mr. Michael FRANTZ
32 VP Student Affairs/DOS ... Mr. Dale SCULLY
30 Vice Pres for Inst Advancement ... Mr. Kenneth L. CONVERSE
81 Dean School of Science ... Mr. Ben DONATH
50 Dean HWS School of Business ... Vacant
53 Dean School of Education ... Dr. Julie FINNERN
60 Dean School Communication & Arts ... Dr. Anna ELSDEN
83 Dean School Social Sci/Phil/Relig ... Dr. Dixee BARTHOLOMEW-FEIS
20 Associate Dean of Faculty ... Dr. Peter K. STEINFELD
20 AVP Acad Affs/Dn Graduate/Prof Stds ... Dr. Jill RHEA
06 Registrar ... Ms. Nila HOUSKA
07 Director of Admissions ... Mr. Mike FOX
15 Human Resources Manager ... Ms. Meghann HENRICH
08 Actg Dir of Library/Ref Librarian ... Ms. Jodie MORIN
26 Dir University Marketing & Comm ... Ms. Jennifer FELTON
29 Director of Alumni Rels/Annual Fund ... Ms. Amy J. JONES
13 Managing Director Univ Info Svcs ... Mr. Bob WALKER
18 Director of Physical Plant ... Mr. Keith E. SCHMIDT
36 Director of Career Services ... Mr. Jeff STOCCO
37 Director of Financial Assistance ... Ms. Leanne VALENTINE
28 Dir of Multicultural Engagement ... Ms. Ebony KING
41 Athletic Director ... Ms. Jack DENHOLM
42 Chaplain ... Rev. Ken MEISSNER
19 Director of Campus Security ... Mr. Mark KIRKHOLM
38 Director of Counseling Services ... Vacant
09 Institutional Researcher ... Mr. James E. HEWETT
96 Purchasing Administrator ... Ms. Tanya LANDGRAF

Central College (E)

812 University, Pella IA 50219-1999

County: Marion — FICE Identification: 001850
Unit ID: 153108
Telephone: (641) 628-9000 — Carnegie Class: Bac-A&S
FAX Number: (641) 628-5316 — Calendar System: Semester
URL: www.central.edu
Established: 1853 — Annual Undergrad Tuition & Fees: $33,345
Enrollment: 1,411 — Coed
Affiliation or Control: Reformed Church In America — IRS Status: 501(c)3
Highest Offering: Baccalaureate
Accreditation: NH, CAATE, MUS

01 President ... Dr. Mark L. PUTNAM
05 VP Academic Affairs/Dean of Faculty ... Dr. Mary M. STREY
30 Vice President Advancement ... Mr. Bill NORTHUP
84 Vice Pres Enrollment Management ... Mrs. Carol WILLIAMSON
32 Vice Pres Student Development ... Dr. Peggy FITCH
10 Vice Pres for Finance & Admin ... Mr. Thomas JOHNSON
20 Director of Academic Resources ... Mr. Eric JONES
35 Dean of Students ... Mr. Charles STREY
07 Director of Admission ... Mr. Chevy FREIBURGER
38 Director of Counseling ... Ms. Michelle KELLAR
39 Assistant Dean of Students ... Ms. Melissa SHARKEY
08 Director of Geisler Library ... Ms. Beth MCMAHON
88 Associate Dean for Global Education ... Ms. Lyn R. ISAACSON
36 Director of Career Center ... Mrs. Patricia JOACHIM KITZMAN
29 Director of Alumni Relations ... Ms. Kathy THOMPSON
37 Director Financial Aid ... Mr. Wayne DILLE
104 Director of Study Abroad ... Mr. Blaire MODIC
13 Chief Information Officer ... Ms. Debra BRUXVOORT
42 Chaplain ... Rev. Joe BRUMMEL
44 Dir Development/Planned Giving ... Mr. Don MORRISON
15 Director of Human Resources ... Ms. Paula RYAN
41 Athletics Director ... Mr. Eric VAN KLEY
18 Dir Facilities Planning/Management ... Mr. Mike LUBBERDEN
06 Registrar ... Ms. Stephanie HENNING
04 Administrative Asst to President ... Ms. Carma STURTZ
09 Institutional Research Director ... Mr. Thomas WALKER

Clarke University (F)

1550 Clarke Drive, Dubuque IA 52001-3198

County: Dubuque — FICE Identification: 001852
Unit ID: 153126
Telephone: (563) 588-6300 — Carnegie Class: Bac-Diverse
FAX Number: (563) 588-6789 — Calendar System: Semester
URL: www.clarke.edu
Established: 1843 — Annual Undergrad Tuition & Fees: $29,940
Enrollment: 1,200 — Coed
Affiliation or Control: Roman Catholic — IRS Status: 501(c)3
Highest Offering: Doctorate
Accreditation: NH, CAATE, MUS, NURSE, PTA, SW

01 President ... Dr. Joanne M. BURROWS, SC
04 Exec Admin Assistant to President ... Ms. Kathy TEIG
05 Vice Pres Academic Affs ... Dr. Susan R. BURNS
30 Vice Pres Institutional Advancement ... Mr. Bill BIEBUYCK
32 Vice President Student Life ... Ms. Kate ZANGER
10 Vice President Business & Finance ... Ms. Daisy HALVORSON
84 Vice President Enrollment Mgmt ... Mr. Jay FEDJE
88 Assistant to the President ... Ms. Megan STULL
06 Registrar ... Ms. Kristi BAGSTAD
08 Director of Library ... Ms. Susanne LEIBOLD
20 Dean of Undergraduate Studies ... Dr. Graciela CANEIRO-LIVINGSTON
58 Acad Dean of Adult & Grad Studies ... Dr. Jo LOBERTINI
37 Director of Financial Aid ... Ms. Amy NORTON
26 Exec Director of Marketing & Comm ... Mr. Ken BROWN
13 Chief Technology Officer ... Mr. Andy BELLINGS
18 Exec Dir of Facilities Management ... Mr. Chris DRESSLER
38 Asst Dir of Counseling/Career Svcs ... Ms. Becky HERRIG
15 Director of Human Resources ... Ms. Megan LUCAS
41 Director of Athletics ... Mr. Curt LONG
42 Director of Campus Ministry ... Vacant
40 Director of the Bookstore ... Ms. Sarah MERZ
23 Director of Health Services ... Ms. Julie BURGMEIER
90 Asst Dean Acad Affairs/Inst Supp ... Mr. Pat MADDUX
07 Asst Director of Admissions ... Vacant
44 Director of Development ... Ms. Kari NICKOL
29 Assoc Dir of Alumni Relations ... Ms. Alissa RIEGLER
85 International Students Advisor ... Ms. Evelyn NADEAU
39 Dean of Students ... Mr. Kevin UTT

Coe College (G)

1220 1st Avenue, NE, Cedar Rapids IA 52402-5092

County: Linn — FICE Identification: 001854
Unit ID: 153144
Telephone: (319) 399-8000 — Carnegie Class: Bac-A&S
FAX Number: (319) 399-8830 — Calendar System: Semester
URL: www.coe.edu
Established: 1851 — Annual Undergrad Tuition & Fees: $39,080
Enrollment: 1,436 — Coed
Affiliation or Control: Independent Non-Profit — IRS Status: 501(c)3
Highest Offering: Master's
Accreditation: NH, CAATE, MUS, NURSE

01 President ... Dr. David W. MCINALLY
03 Executive Vice President ... Mr. Michael L. WHITE
05 Provost/Dean of Faculty ... Dr. Paula O'LOUGHLIN

32 Vice President for Student Affairs .... Mr. Erik ALBINSON
30 Vice President for Advancement .... Mr. David HAYES
07 Associate VP/Dean of Admission .... Ms. Julie STAKER
06 Registrar .... Mr. Jason CLAPP
08 Director Library Services .... Ms. Jill JACK
29 Director Alumni Programs .... Ms. Jean A. JOHNSON
09 Director of Institutional Research .... Dr. Wendy L. DUNN
26 Dir of Marketing/Public Relations .... Mr. Rod PRITCHARD
37 Director of Financial Aid .... Ms. Barbara HOFFMAN
20 Associate Dean .... Dr. Dan LEHN
35 Dean of Students .... Mr. Tom HICKS
85 International Student Advisor .... Mr. Peter GERLACH
42 Chaplain .... Rev. Kristin E. HUTSON
23 Director of Health Services .... Ms. Lindsay SHEDEK
41 Director of Athletics .... Mr. John M. CHANDLER
18 Director of Physical Plant .... Ms. Lisa CIHA
36 Career Services Coordinator .... Ms. Michelle MCILLECE
36 Dir of Internships/Career Services .... Vacant
15 Director of Human Resources .... Ms. Kristina BRIDGES
04 Administrative Asst to President .... Ms. Kim PRIBYL
13 Chief Info Technology Officer .... Mr. Anthony BATA
19 Director Security/Safety .... Mr. Carlos VELEZ
44 Director Annual/Planned Giving .... Ms. Barb TUPPER

Cornell College (A)

600 First Street SW, Mount Vernon IA 52314-1098
County: Linn FICE Identification: 001856
Unit ID: 153162
Telephone: (319) 895-4000 Carnegie Class: Bac-A&S
FAX Number: (319) 895-4492 Calendar System: Other
URL: www.cornellcollege.edu
Established: 1853 Annual Undergrad Tuition & Fees: $38,700
Enrollment: 1,086 Coed
Affiliation or Control: United Methodist IRS Status: 501(c)3
Highest Offering: Baccalaureate
Accreditation: NH

01 President .... Mr. Jonathan BRAND
05 VP Acad Affairs/Dean of College .... Dr. R. Joseph DIEKER
10 Vice President Business Affairs .... Ms. Kay LANGSETH
84 Vice President for Enrollment .... Ms. Colleen MURPHY
32 Vice President Student Affairs .... Mr. John W. HARP
44 VP for Alumni & College Advancement .... Ms. Pam GERARD
35 Dean of Students .... Dr. Gwendolyn SCHIMEK
20 Associate Dean of the College .... Dr. Benjamin GREENSTEIN
09 Director of Institutional Research .... Dr. Becki S. ELKINS
37 Director of Student Financial Asst .... Ms. Shannon AMUNDSON
06 Registrar .... Dr. Becki ELKINS
08 College Librarian .... Mr. Paul WAELCHLI
29 Director of Alumni & Annual Giving .... Mr. RJ HOLMES-LEOPOLD
30 Senior Director of Development .... Ms. Kristi COLUMBUS
26 Senior Dir Marketing/Communications .... Ms. Jen VISSER
42 Chaplain .... Ms. Catherine M. QUEHL-ENGEL
22 Affirmative Action Officer .... Ms. Lindsey HOTZ
41 Athletics Director .... Mr. John T. COCHRANE
18 Director of Facilities .... Mr. Joel C. MILLER
36 Director Career Engagement Center .... Mr. Jason NAPOLI
38 Director Student Counseling .... Dr. Brenda C. LOVSTUEN
15 Human Resource Coordinator .... Ms. Lindsey HOTZ
07 Director of Admission .... Ms. Marie SCHOFER
13 Director of Information Technology .... Mr. Jeff GIBSON
40 Manager Bookstore .... Ms. Lee Ann GRIMLEY
04 Administrative Asst to President .... Ms. RuthAnn SCHEER
101 Secretary to the Board of Trustees .... Ms. RuthAnn SCHEER
19 Campus Safety Director .... Mr. Mark WINDER

Des Moines Area Community College (B)

2006 S Ankeny Boulevard, Ankeny IA 50023-3993
County: Polk FICE Identification: 007120
Unit ID: 153214
Telephone: (515) 964-6200 Carnegie Class: Assoc/MT-VT-High Non
FAX Number: N/A Calendar System: Semester
URL: www.dmacc.edu
Established: 1966 Annual Undergrad Tuition & Fees (In-District): $3,913
Enrollment: 23,526 Coed
Affiliation or Control: State/Local IRS Status: 501(c)3
Highest Offering: Associate Degree
Accreditation: NH, ACBSP, ACFEI, ADNUR, COARC, DA, DH, FUSER, MAC, MLTAD, SURGT

01 President/CEO .... Dr. Rob DENSON
05 Exec Vice Pres Academic Affairs .... Dr. Kim LINDUSKA
10 Vice President Business Svcs .... Mr. Greg MARTIN
13 Exec Dir Information Solutions .... Mr. Mark CLARK
12 Provost Urban Campus .... Dr. Laura DOUGLAS
12 Provost Boone Campus .... Mr. Tom LEE
12 Provost Carroll Campus .... Mr. Joel LUNDSTROM
12 Provost Newton Campus .... Ms. Mary ENTZ
12 Provost West Campus .... Dr. Tony PAUSTIAN
32 Exec Dean Student Services .... Dr. Laurie WOLF
15 Executive Director Human Resources .... Dr. Sandy TRYON
102 Executive Director Foundation .... Ms. Tara CONNOLLY
09 Exec Director Inst Effectiveness .... Dr. Joe DEHART
51 Exec Dir Continuing Education .... Mr. Michael HOFFMAN
50 Exec Dir Business Resources .... Ms. Kim DIDIER
37 Director Financial Aid .... Mr. Ean FREELS
26 Director of Marketing .... Mr. Todd JONES
25 Director Grants/Contracts .... Ms. Deb KCUA
06 Registrar .... Ms. Rachel ERKKILA
18 Chief Facilities/Physical Plant .... Mr. Ned MILLER
38 Director of Student Development .... Vacant
96 Director of Purchasing .... Mr. Tim HAGER
27 Media Liaison .... Mr. Dan IVIS
70 Dean Sciences & Humanities .... Mr. Jim STICK
72 Dean Industrial & Technology .... Mr. Scott OCKEN
76 Dean Health Service & Science .... Mr. Art BROWN
50 Dean Business/Mgmt/Information Tech .... Mr. MD ISLEY
55 Dean Evening & Weekend College .... Ms. Andrea ISEMINGER
08 Head Librarian .... Ms. Rebecca FUNKE
41 Athletic Director .... Mr. Orv SALMON
101 Secretary of the Institution/Board .... Ms. Carolyn FARLOW

Des Moines Area Community College Boone Campus (C)

1125 Hancock Drive, Boone IA 50036
Telephone: (515) 432-7203 Identification: 770048
Accreditation: &NH

† Regional accreditation is carried under the parent institution in Ankeny, IA

Des Moines Area Community College Carroll Campus (D)

906 North Grant Road, Carroll IA 51401-2525
Telephone: (712) 792-1755 Identification: 770049
Accreditation: &NH

† Regional accreditation is carried under the parent institution in Ankeny, IA

Des Moines Area Community College Newton Campus (E)

600 N 2nd Avenue West, Newton IA 50208
Telephone: (641) 791-3622 Identification: 770051
Accreditation: &NH

† Regional accreditation is carried under the parent institution in Ankeny, IA

Des Moines Area Community College Urban Campus (F)

1100 7th Street, Des Moines IA 50314
Telephone: (515) 244-4226 Identification: 770050
Accreditation: &NH

† Regional accreditation is carried under the parent institution in Ankeny, IA

Des Moines Area Community College West Des Moines Campus (G)

5959 West Grand Avenue, West Des Moines IA 50266
Telephone: (515) 633-2407 Identification: 770052
Accreditation: &NH

† Regional accreditation is carried under the parent institution in Ankeny, IA

Des Moines University (H)

3200 Grand Avenue, Des Moines IA 50312-4198
County: Polk FICE Identification: 001855
Unit ID: 154156
Telephone: (515) 271-1400 Carnegie Class: Spec-4-yr-Med
FAX Number: (515) 271-1532 Calendar System: Other
URL: www.dmu.edu
Established: 1898 Annual Graduate Tuition & Fees: N/A
Enrollment: 1,662 Coed
Affiliation or Control: Independent Non-Profit IRS Status: 501(c)3
Highest Offering: First Professional Degree; No Undergraduates
Accreditation: NH, #ARCPA, HSA, OSTEO, PH, POD, PTA

01 President/CEO .... Dr. Angela L. WALKER FRANKLIN
05 Provost .... Dr. Karen P. MCLEAN
32 VP Enrollment Mgmt/Student Svcs .... Ms. Kimberly BROWN
86 Chief External & Govt Affs Officer .... Ms. Susan HUPPERT
46 Vice President for Research .... Dr. Jeffrey GRAY
06 Registrar .... Ms. Kathy L. SCAGLIONE
08 Director of Library .... Ms. Natalie HUTCHINSON
15 Chief Human Resources Officer .... Ms. Becky LADE
13 Chief Information Officer .... Ms. Carolyn WEAVER
37 Director of Financial Aid .... Ms. Mary PAYNE
18 Director of Facilities Management .... Mr. David MCNERNEY
19 Director University Services .... Mr. John BRUECKEN
88 Chief Compliance Officer .... Ms. Erika LINDEN
10 Chief Financial Officer .... Mr. Mark J. PEIFFER
69 Director Public Health Program .... Dr. Rachel REIMER
76 Director Healthcare Administration .... Dr. Carla STEBBINS
26 Int Dir Marketing & Communication .... Ms. Barbara BOOSE
38 Dir Center for Teaching & Learning .... Dr. Kerry GREGORYK
76 Dean College Health Sciences .... Dr. Jodi CAHALAN
63 Dean Col Podiatric Medicine/Surg .... Dr. Robert YOHO
63 Interim Dean COM .... Dr. Bret RIPLEY
04 Executive Asst to President .... Ms. Christina HENDERSON
07 Director of Admissions/Recruitment .... Ms. Molly MOELLER
28 Director of Multicultural Affairs .... Dr. Richard SALAS
29 Director Alumni Relations .... Ms. Bonnette VONDRAK
30 Chief Development Officer .... Ms. Stephanie GREINER
101 Secretary of the Institution/Board .... Ms. Linda KADING
09 Institutional Research Manager .... Mr. Josh KVINLAUG

† Tuition varies by degree program.

Divine Word College (I)

102 Jacoby Drive, SW, PO Box 380,
Epworth IA 52045-0380
County: Dubuque FICE Identification: 001858
Unit ID: 153241
Telephone: (563) 876-3353 Carnegie Class: Spec-4-yr-Faith
FAX Number: (563) 876-3407 Calendar System: Semester
URL: www.dwci.edu
Established: 1918 Annual Undergrad Tuition & Fees: $12,600
Enrollment: 96 Male
Affiliation or Control: Roman Catholic IRS Status: 501(c)3
Highest Offering: Baccalaureate
Accreditation: NH

01 President .... Fr. Timothy A. LENCHAK
05 Academic Dean/Vice President .... Dr. Mathew KANJIRATHINKAL
10 Vice Pres for Finances/Fin Aid Dir .... Mr. Mark PASKER
32 Dean of Students .... Rev. Bang TRAN
07 Director Admissions/VP Recruitment .... Mr. Len UHAL
30 Development Director .... Mr. Terrance SYKORA
26 Public Relations Director .... Ms. Sandy WILGENBUSCH
08 Librarian .... Vacant
06 Registrar .... Mr. Paul STAMM
38 Counselor .... Mrs. Nan PECK
104 Director Study Abroad .... Rev. Kenneth ANICH
13 Chief Info Technology Officer (CIO) .... Mr. Brad FLORENCE
45 Chief Institutional Planning .... Rev. John SZUKALSKI, SVD

Dordt College (J)

498 4th Avenue, NE, Sioux Center IA 51250-1697
County: Sioux FICE Identification: 001859
Unit ID: 153250
Telephone: (712) 722-6000 Carnegie Class: Bac-Diverse
FAX Number: (712) 722-6035 Calendar System: Semester
URL: www.dordt.edu
Established: 1955 Annual Undergrad Tuition & Fees: $28,280
Enrollment: 1,459 Coed
Affiliation or Control: Christian Reformed Church IRS Status: 501(c)3
Highest Offering: Master's
Accreditation: NH, ENG, NURSE, SW

01 President .... Dr. Erik HOEKSTRA
05 Provost .... Dr. Eric A. FORSETH
30 Vice President College Advancement .... Mr. John BAAS
10 Exec Dir of Finance & Facilities .... Mr. Arlan NEDERHOFF
11 Vice President for Administration .... Mr. Howard WILSON
88 Director of Global Education .... Mr. Adam ADAMS
37 Director Financial Aid .... Mr. Harlan HARMELINK
06 Registrar .... Mr. James BOS
88 Director for Research & Scholarship .... Dr. Nathan TINTLE
20 Dean for Curriculum & Instruction .... Dr. Leah ZUIDEMA
58 Director Graduate Education .... Dr. Timothy VAN SOELEN
36 Career Services Coordinator .... Mrs. Sarah MOSS
26 Marketing and Public Relations .... Ms. Sonya JONGSMA KNAUSS
18 Director Physical Plant .... Mr. Stan OORDT
32 Dean of Campus Life .... Mr. Robert TAYLOR
42 Dean of Chapel .... Rev. Aaron BAART
41 Director of Athletics .... Mr. Glenn BOUMA
40 Director Bookstore/Purchasing .... Ms. Lora DEVRIES
44 Director of Planned Giving .... Mr. Dave VANDER WERF
29 Director Alumni/External Relations .... Mr. Brandon HUISMAN
15 Director Human Resources .... Mrs. Sue DROOG
96 Director of Purchasing .... Mr. Fred HAAN
91 Director of Computer Services .... Mr. Brian VAN DONSELAAR
08 Director of Library Services .... Ms. Jennifer BREEMS
23 Director of Health Sciences .... Ms. Deb BOMGAARS
88 Director Academic Skills Center .... Ms. Sharon ROSENBOOM
04 Administrative Asst to President .... Mrs. LeeAnn MOERMAN
07 Director of Admissions .... Mr. Greg VAN DYKE

Drake University (K)

2507 University Avenue, Des Moines IA 50311-4505
County: Polk FICE Identification: 001860
Unit ID: 153269
Telephone: (515) 271-2011 Carnegie Class: Masters/L
FAX Number: (515) 271-3016 Calendar System: Semester
URL: www.drake.edu
Established: 1881 Annual Undergrad Tuition & Fees: $33,696
Enrollment: 5,062 Coed
Affiliation or Control: Independent Non-Profit IRS Status: 501(c)3
Highest Offering: Doctorate
Accreditation: NH, ART, CACREP, CORE, JOUR, LAW, MUS, PHAR

01 President .... Mr. Earl F. MARTIN
05 Provost .... Dr. Sue MATTISON
10 Chief Financial Officer .... Ms. Teresa KREJCI
11 Chief Administrative Officer .... Ms. Venessa MACRO
30 Vice Pres Alumni and Development .... Mr. John SMITH
07 Dean of Admission .... Vacant
20 Associate Provost of Curriculum .... Mr. Art SANDERS
32 Associate Prov Student Affairs .... Ms. Melissa STURM-SMITH
35 Dean of Students .... Dr. Sentwali BAKARI
15 Human Resources Director .... Mr. Gary JOHNSON
13 Chief Tech Information Officer .... Mr. Chris GILL

18 Director Facility Services ... Ms. Jolene SCHMIDT
09 Dir of Inst Research & Assessment ... Mr. Kevin SAUNDERS
06 Director of Student Records ... Mr. Kevin P. MOENKHAUS
08 Dean Cowles Library ... Mr. Rodney N. HENSHAW
85 Int Assoc Provost of Intl Programs ... Dr. Annique KIEL
91 Director Campus Information Svcs ... Vacant
19 Chief Campus Security Services ... Mr. Scott LAW
26 VP University Communications ... Ms. Debra LUKEHART
29 Alumni/Parent Programs ... Vacant
49 Dean Arts & Sciences ... Dr. Joseph LENZ
53 Dean School Education ... Dr. Janet M. MCMAHILL
61 Dean Law School ... Mr. Jerry ANDERSON
50 Dean Business/Public Administration ... Ms. Terri VAUGHAN
67 Dean Pharmacy/Health Science ... Dr. Renae CHESNUT
60 Dean Journ/Mass Communications ... Ms. Kathleen RICHARDSON
41 Director Intercollegiate Athletics ... Ms. Sandy Hatfield CLUBB
37 Director Financial Aid ... Ms. Susan K. LADD
38 Director University Counseling Ctr ... Dr. Mark KLOBERDANZ
92 Assistant Director Honors Program ... Ms. Charlene SKIDMORE
94 Director Women's Studies ... Dr. Nancy REINCKE
31 Neighborhood & Comm Rel Mgr ... Mr. Nick VALDEZ
39 Director Office of Residence Life ... Ms. Lorissa LIEURANCE
04 Asst to President ... Ms. Cheryle ANANIA
100 Chief of Staff ... Ms. Shannon COFIELD
44 Director of Development ... Mr. John AMATO
96 Director of Purchasing ... Ms. Caron FINDLEY

*Eastern Iowa Community College District (A)

306 W River Drive, Davenport IA 52801-1221
County: Scott FICE Identification: 004075
Unit ID: 153311
Telephone: (563) 336-3300 Carnegie Class: N/A
FAX Number: (563) 336-3350
URL: www.eicc.edu

01 Chancellor ... Dr. Donald S. DOUCETTE
30 Exec Dir Resource Development ... Dr. Ellen KABAT LENSCH
05 Vice Chanc for Education & Training ... Dr. Joan KINDLE
26 Associate Director for Marketing ... Ms. Karen FARLEY
09 Dir Institutional Effectiveness ... Ms. Laurie ADOLPH
27 Associate Director Communications ... Mr. Alan CAMPBELL
10 Chief Business Officer ... Mr. Suteesh TANDON
101 Secretary of the Institution/Board ... Ms. Honey BEDELL
15 Director Personnel Services ... Ms. Deb SULLIVAN
18 Chief Facilities/Physical Plant ... Mr. Matt SCHMIT
84 Director Enrollment Management ... Ms. Erin SNYDER

*Clinton Community College (B)

1000 Lincoln Boulevard, Clinton IA 52732-6299
County: Clinton FICE Identification: 001853
Unit ID: 153135
Telephone: (563) 244-7001 Carnegie Class: Not Classified
FAX Number: (563) 244-7107 Calendar System: Semester
URL: www.eicc.edu
Established: 1966 Annual Undergrad Tuition & Fees (In-District): N/A
Enrollment: N/A Coed
Affiliation or Control: State/Local IRS Status: 501(c)3
Highest Offering: Associate Degree
Accreditation: &NH, EMT

02 President ... Dr. Karen VICKERS
05 Dean of the College ... Mr. Ron SERPLISS
32 Dean of Student Development ... Ms. Lisa MILLER
102 Asst to Pres/Exec Dir Sharar Found ... Ms. Ann EISENMAN
04 Assistant to President/Admin ... Ms. Deborah RICHTER

† Regional accreditation is carried under the parent institution Eastern Iowa Community College District in Davenport, IA.

*Muscatine Community College (C)

152 Colorado Street, Muscatine IA 52761-5396
County: Muscatine FICE Identification: 001882
Unit ID: 154040
Telephone: (563) 288-6001 Carnegie Class: Not Classified
FAX Number: (563) 288-6074 Calendar System: Semester
URL: www.eicc.edu
Established: 1929 Annual Undergrad Tuition & Fees (In-District): N/A
Enrollment: N/A Coed
Affiliation or Control: State/Local IRS Status: 501(c)3
Highest Offering: Associate Degree
Accreditation: &NH, EMT

02 President ... Dr. Naomi DEWINTER
04 Assistant to the President ... Ms. Lisa WIEGEL
05 Dean of the College ... Dr. Jeremy PICKARD
32 Dean of Student Development ... Ms. Shelly CRAM-RAHLF
31 Director Business/Industry Center ... Mr. Marvin SMITH
06 Registrar ... Ms. Robin MITCHELL
08 Library Specialist ... Ms. Nancy LUIKART

† Regional accreditation is carried under the parent institution Eastern Iowa Community College District in Davenport, IA.

*Scott Community College (D)

500 Belmont Road, Bettendorf IA 52722-6804
County: Scott FICE Identification: 001885
Unit ID: 154314
Telephone: (563) 441-4001 Carnegie Class: Not Classified
FAX Number: (563) 441-4154 Calendar System: Semester
URL: www.eicc.edu
Established: 1966 Annual Undergrad Tuition & Fees (In-District): N/A
Enrollment: N/A Coed
Affiliation or Control: State/Local IRS Status: 501(c)3
Highest Offering: Associate Degree
Accreditation: &NH, CAHIIM, DA, EMT, NDT, RAD, SURGT

02 President ... Dr. Teresa A. PAPER
32 Dean of Student Development/Affs ... Ms. LaDrina WILSON
103 Dean Career Assistance Center ... Mr. Scott SCHNEIDER
05 Dean of the College ... Dr. Gerald WICKHAM
08 Librarian ... Ms. Michelle BAILEY
11 Asst to President Administration ... Mr. Matt SCHMIT
06 Registrar ... Mr. Arnold THODE
37 Director Student Financial Aid ... Ms. Jeannine INGELSON
36 Job Placement Specialist ... Mr. Wayne COLE

† Regional accreditation is carried under the parent institution Eastern Iowa Community College District in Davenport, IA.

Emmaus Bible College (E)

2570 Asbury Road, Dubuque IA 52001-3096
County: Dubuque FICE Identification: 023289
Unit ID: 153302
Telephone: (563) 588-8000 Carnegie Class: Spec-4-yr-Faith
FAX Number: (563) 588-1216 Calendar System: Semester
URL: www.emmaus.edu
Established: 1941 Annual Undergrad Tuition & Fees: $15,920
Enrollment: 216 Coed
Affiliation or Control: Independent Non-Profit IRS Status: 501(c)3
Highest Offering: Baccalaureate
Accreditation: NH, BI

01 President ... Mr. Philip BOOM
10 VP for Administration and Finance ... Mr. Mark A. PRESSON
05 Vice President for Academic Affairs ... Mrs. Lisa L. BEATTY
30 Vice President for Advancement ... Mr. Jon W. GLOCK
32 Dean for Student Development ... Mr. Israel CHAVEZ
88 Dean for Biblical Studies ... Dr. David J. MACLEOD
08 Librarian ... Mr. John H. RUSH
37 Financial Aid Officer ... Mr. Steve C. SEEMAN
21 Controller ... Mr. Steve M. JENSEN
06 Registrar ... Mrs. Janice G. BENNETT
106 Dir Online Education/E-learning ... Mr. Tom KOOK
108 Director Institutional Assessment ... Ms. Sherri L. POLL
29 Director Alumni Relations ... Mr. Jonathan J. ROUTLEY
41 Athletic Director ... Vacant
84 Director Enrollment Management ... Ms. Laurel R. RASMUSSEN

Faith Baptist Bible College and Seminary (F)

1900 NW 4th Street, Ankeny IA 50023-2152
County: Polk FICE Identification: 007121
Unit ID: 153320
Telephone: (515) 964-0601 Carnegie Class: Spec-4-yr-Faith
FAX Number: (515) 964-1638 Calendar System: Semester
URL: www.faith.edu
Established: 1921 Annual Undergrad Tuition & Fees: $16,600
Enrollment: 292 Coed
Affiliation or Control: Independent Non-Profit IRS Status: 501(c)3
Highest Offering: First Professional Degree
Accreditation: NH, BI

01 President ... Dr. James R. TILLOTSON
05 VP for Academic Services ... Dr. Kenneth D. RATHBUN
73 Dean of Seminary ... Dr. Douglas E. BROWN
10 VP for Business/CFO ... Mr. Daniel H. BJOKNE
30 VP for Advancement/Church Rels ... Vacant
34 Dean of Women ... Mrs. Carrie A. AUGSBURGER
32 Dean of Students ... Mr. Lance A. AUGSBURGER
26 Director of Communications ... Mr. Don K. ANDERSON
06 Registrar ... Dr. Christopher E. ELLIS
37 Director Student Financial Aid ... Mr. Breck H. APPELL
08 Head Librarian ... Dr. Paul A. HARTOG
04 Administrative Asst to President ... Miss Briana K. HARRIER
07 VP for Enrollment and Student Life ... Mr. Mark L. DAVIS
106 Dir Online Education/E-learning ... Dr. Christopher E. ELLIS
41 Athletic Director ... Mr. Brian S. FINCHAM
108 Director Institutional Assessment ... Dr. Donald LONG

Graceland University (G)

1 University Place, Lamoni IA 50140-1699
County: Decatur FICE Identification: 001866
Unit ID: 153366
Telephone: (641) 784-5000 Carnegie Class: Masters/M
FAX Number: (641) 784-5480 Calendar System: Trimester
URL: www.graceland.edu
Established: 1895 Annual Undergrad Tuition & Fees: $25,890
Enrollment: 2,406 Coed
Affiliation or Control: Other IRS Status: 501(c)3
Highest Offering: Doctorate
Accreditation: NH, #CAATE, NURSE, TED

01 President ... Dr. John SELLARS
05 Vice Pres Acad Affs/Dean of Faculty ... Dr. Tammy EVERETT
09 VP Institutional Effectiveness ... Dr. Kathleen M. CLAUSON BASH
10 CIO/Vice Pres Business & Admin Svc ... Mr. Paul DAVIS
32 VP Student Life/Dean of Students ... Mr. Dave SCHAAL
84 Vice Pres Enrollment ... Mr. Scott BRIELL
30 Vice Pres Institutional Advancement ... Mr. Kelly EVERETT
51 Director Graduate/Continuing Educ ... Mr. Paul BINNICKER
39 Director of Residence Life ... Ms. Deb SKINNER
06 Registrar ... Mrs. M. Joyce LIGHTHILL
29 Director of Alumni Relations ... Mr. Paul DAVIS
36 Director Career/Acad/CAP Couns Ctr ... Ms. Catharine CRAIG
15 Director Human Resources ... Mrs. Ondrea DORY
04 Executive Asst to President ... Mrs. Jodi L. SEYMOUR
44 Director of Annual Fund/Stewardship ... Mrs. Peggy STURDEVANT
85 Director International Programs ... Ms. Diana JONES
50 Dean School of Business ... Dr. Robert POULTON
53 Acting Dean School of Education ... Dr. Lee BASH
66 Dean School of Nursing ... Dr. Claudia HORTON
07 Director of Admissions ... Mr. Kevin BROWN
09 Director of Institutional Research ... Mr. James UHLENKAMP

Grand View University (H)

1200 Grandview Avenue, Des Moines IA 50316-1599
County: Polk FICE Identification: 001867
Unit ID: 153375
Telephone: (515) 263-2800 Carnegie Class: Bac-Diverse
FAX Number: (515) 263-6095 Calendar System: Semester
URL: www.grandview.edu
Established: 1896 Annual Undergrad Tuition & Fees: $24,614
Enrollment: 2,064 Coed
Affiliation or Control: Evangelical Lutheran Church In America
IRS Status: 501(c)3
Highest Offering: Master's
Accreditation: NH, NURSE, @SW

01 President ... Mr. Kent L. HENNING
04 Exec Admin Asst to the President ... Ms. Corinna KING
05 Provost/Vice Pres Academic Affairs ... Dr. Carl MOSES
79 Dean College of Humanities & Educ ... Dr. Ross WASTVEDT
83 Dean College of Social/Nat Science ... Dr. Paul RIDER
10 Vice Pres Administration & Finance ... Mr. Adam J. VOIGTS
30 Vice President Advancement ... Mr. William H. BURMA
84 Vice Pres Enrollment Management ... Ms. Debbie M. BARGER
26 Vice Pres Marketing/Communications ... Ms. Kendall DILLON
32 Vice President Student Affairs ... Dr. Jay B. PRESCOTT
37 Director Financial Aid ... Ms. Michele A. DUNNE
20 Special Assistant to the Provost . Ms. Pamela M. CHRISTOFFERS
51 Dean Graduate/Adult Programs ... Dr. Patricia A. WILLIAMS
35 Associate VP for Student Affairs ... Mr. Jason K. BAUER
06 Registrar ... Ms. Debbie K. GANNON
42 Senior Campus Pastor ... Rev. Russell L. LACKEY
09 Director Inst Planning/Research ... Ms. Debbie M. BARGER
36 Director Career Center ... Ms. Susan M. STEARNS
91 Vice President Information Svcs/CIO ... Mr. Tim T. WHEELDON
08 Director of the Library ... Ms. Pamela D. REES
40 Director Bookstore & Campus Svcs ... Mr. Michael D. SHUPP
07 Director of Admissions ... Mr. Ryan THOMPSON
18 Director Buildings & Grounds ... Ms. Kim I. BUTLER
38 Director Leadership & Counseling ... Mr. Kent A. SCHORNACK
28 Dir Multicultural & Cmty Outreach ... Mr. Alex H. PIEDRAS
41 Athletic Director ... Mr. Troy A. PLUMMER
15 Human Resources Manager ... Ms. Erica L. KLUVER
88 Special Assistant to the President ... Mr. Robert BARRON

Grinnell College (I)

1121 Park Street, Grinnell IA 50112-1690
County: Poweshiek FICE Identification: 001868
Unit ID: 153384
Telephone: (641) 269-4000 Carnegie Class: Bac-A&S
FAX Number: (641) 269-3408 Calendar System: Semester
URL: www.grinnell.edu
Established: 1846 Annual Undergrad Tuition & Fees: $46,990
Enrollment: 1,734 Coed
Affiliation or Control: Independent Non-Profit IRS Status: 501(c)3
Highest Offering: Baccalaureate
Accreditation: NH

01 President ... Raynard S. KINGTON
100 Chief of Staff/VP Planning ... Angela VOOS
05 Vice Pres Acad Affs/Dean Col ... Michael LATHAM
30 Vice President Dev/Alumni Rel ... Shane JACOBSON
88 Chief Investment Officer ... Scott L. WILSON
10 Vice President for Finance/Treas ... Kate E. WALKER
20 Associate Dean of College ... Maria TAPIAS
20 Associate Dean of College ... Karla ERICKSON
07 VP Enroll/Dean Adm & Fin Aid ... Joseph P. BAGNOLI
30 Director of Development Operations ... Adam LAUG
37 Director of Student Financial Aid ... Brad LINDBERG
15 Assistant VP of Human Resources ... Mary GREINER
26 Director of Communication ... Vacant
06 Registrar ... Jason MAHER
08 Librarian ... Vacant
29 Director of Alumni Relations ... Jayn CHANEY
13 Chief Information Tech Officer ... Dave ROBINSON
09 Assoc VP Analytics/Inst Rsch ... Randall STILES
85 Director Intl Student Services ... Karen K. EDWARDS
40 Manager/Bookstore ... Cassandra J. WHERRY
41 Athletic Director ... Andrew HAMILTON
23 Dir Stdnt Health & Counsel Service ... Deb SHILL
38 Dean Student Success/Acad Advising ... Joyce STERN
18 Director Facilities Mgmt ... Richard WHITNEY
19 Interim Dir of Safety & Security ... Scott KINNIE
42 Chaplain/Dean of Rel Life ... Deanna SHORB
102 Director Corp/Found/Govt Rels ... Susan FERRARI

32 Assoc VP Student Affairs .... Andrea CONNER
35 Dean of Students .... Sarah MOSCHENROSS
31 Dir Community Enhancement/Engagemnt . Monica CHAVEZ-SILVA
36 Dean & Director/Career Life & Svcs .... Mark PELTZ
04 Executive Asst to President .... Tammy PRUSHA
101 Secretary of the College .... Susan SCHOEN
104 Director Study Abroad .... Richard BRIGHT
28 Director of Diversity .... Lakeshia JOHNSON
39 Director Residence Life .... John ROLON
44 Director Annual Giving .... Mae PARKER
22 Chief Diversity Officer .... Lakesia JOHNSON
96 Procurement Manager .... Amanda JONES

Hamilton Technical College (A)

1011 E 53rd Street, Davenport IA 52807-2616

County: Scott FICE Identification: 012064
Unit ID: 153427
Telephone: (563) 386-3570 Carnegie Class: Spec-4-yr-Other Tech
FAX Number: (563) 386-6756 Calendar System: Semester
URL: www.hamiltontechcollege.com
Established: 1969 Annual Undergrad Tuition & Fees: $12,165
Enrollment: 153 Coed
Affiliation or Control: Proprietary IRS Status: Proprietary
Highest Offering: Baccalaureate
Accreditation: ACCSC

01 President .... Mrs. Maryanne HAMILTON
32 Dean of Students .... Mr. Brian BEERT

Hawkeye Community College (B)

Box 8015, Waterloo IA 50704-8015

County: Black Hawk FICE Identification: 004595
Unit ID: 153445
Telephone: (319) 296-2320 Carnegie Class: Assoc/MT-VT-High Non
FAX Number: (319) 296-2874 Calendar System: Semester
URL: www.hawkeyecollege.edu
Established: 1966 Annual Undergrad Tuition & Fees (In-District): $4,466
Enrollment: 5,291 Coed
Affiliation or Control: State/Local IRS Status: 501(c)3
Highest Offering: Associate Degree
Accreditation: NH, COARC, DA, DH, MLTAD, OTA, PTAA

01 President .... Dr. Linda A. ALLEN
05 Vice Pres Academic Affairs .... Dr. Jane BRADLEY
10 Vice Pres Administration & Finance .... Mr. Dan GILLEN
30 Vice Pres Institutional Advancement .... Ms. Kathy A. FLYNN
102 Executive Director Foundation .... Ms. Holly JOHNSON
15 Exec Dir Human Resource Services .... Mr. John D. CLOPTON
81 Dean Math/Natural & Social Sciences .... Dr. Cynthia BOTTRELL
79 Dean Comm/Humanities/Educ/Fine Arts . Ms. Catharine FREEMAN
75 Dean Applied Science/Eng Technology .... Mr. David GRUNKLEE
76 Dean Health Sciences .... Mr. Eugene LEUTZINGER
50 Dean Business & Public Services .... Mr. Bryan RENFRO
32 Dean of Students .... Ms. Nancy HENDERSON
07 Director Admissions & Recruitment .... Mr. Dave BALL
21 Director Business Services .... Ms. Julie THOMAS
13 Director Communication/Info Systems .... Mr. Brian MCCORMICK
62 Director Library Services .... Ms. Candace HAVELY
51 Exec Director Busines & Cmty Educ .... Mr. Aaron SAUERBREI
18 Director Plant & Facilities .... Ms. Lindsey NISSEN
06 Dir Student Records & Registration .... Ms. Patricia A. EAST
24 Director Teaching/Learning Services .... Mr. Robin GALLOWAY
09 Director Institutional Research .... Ms. Connie BUHR
26 Director Public Relations/Marketing .... Ms. Mary Pat MOORE
28 Director of Inclusion & Diversity .... Ms. Rhonda MCRINA
35 Assoc Director of Student Life .... Ms. Stephanie CHERRY
44 Development Officer .... Ms. Karen GEBEL
101 Board Secretary .... Ms. Denise A. DUNN
19 Dir Public Safety/Emergency Mgr .... Mr. John BECKMAN
88 Director Urban Ctrs/Adult Literacy .... Ms. Sandra JENSEN
88 Dean of Transitional Programs .... Mr. Tom MUELLER
103 Dir Workforce/Career Development .... Ms. Christina MASON
37 Director Student Financial Aid .... Ms. Gisella BAKER
04 Assistant to President .... Ms. Donna S. MCNULTY

Indian Hills Community College (C)

525 Grandview Avenue, Ottumwa IA 52501-1398

County: Wapello FICE Identification: 008403
Unit ID: 153472
Telephone: (641) 683-5111 Carnegie Class: Assoc/MT-VT-High Non
FAX Number: (641) 683-5184 Calendar System: Quarter
URL: www.indianhills.edu
Established: 1966 Annual Undergrad Tuition & Fees (In-District): $3,840
Enrollment: 4,412 Coed
Affiliation or Control: State/Local IRS Status: 501(c)3
Highest Offering: Associate Degree
Accreditation: NH, ACFEI, CA, CAHIIM, DA, DH, EMT, MLTAD, OTA, PTAA, RAD

01 President .... Dr. Marlene SPROUSE
10 Chief Financial Officer .... Mr. Bill MECK
05 Vice Pres Acad Affs/Instl Effect .... Dr. Matt THOMPSON
49 Executive Dean Arts & Sciences .... Ms. Darlas SHOCKLEY
103 Exec Dean Reg Economic Advancement .... Mr. Tom RUBEL
32 Exec Dean Student Services .... Mr. Chris BOWSER
76 Exec Dean Health Sciences .... Dr. Jill BUDDE
12 Dean Centerville Campus .... Mr. Joe STARCEVICH
86 Assoc Dean Govt Affs/Information .... Ms. Martha WICK
102 Exec Dir Foundation/Cmty Rels .... Ms. Rachelle KARSTENS
15 Director Human Resources .... Ms. Bonnie CAMPBELL
18 Director Maintenance .... Mr. Rick FOSDYCK
06 Registrar .... Ms. Jon KELLEY
41 Athletic Director .... Mr. Mike HAGEN
26 Director for Media/Public Rels .... Mr. Kevin PINK
88 Chair Aviation Programs .... Mr. Darren GRAHAM
07 Director of Admissions .... Mr. Mark THOMPSON
09 Director of Institutional Research .... Dr. Stephanie HOLLIMAN
29 Director of Alumni Relations .... Dr. Bianca MYERS
35 Chief Development .... Ms. Rhonda CONRAD

Indian Hills Community College Centerville (D)

721 N First Street, Centerville IA 52544

Telephone: (641) 856-2143 Identification: 770054
Accreditation: &NH

† Regional accreditation is carried under the parent institution in Ottumwa, IA

Inste Bible College (E)

2302 SW 3rd Street, Ankeny IA 50023-2453

County: Polk Identification: 666461
Telephone: (515) 289-9200 Carnegie Class: Not Classified
FAX Number: (515) 289-9201 Calendar System: Semester
URL: www.inste.edu
Established: 1982 Annual Undergrad Tuition & Fees: N/A
Enrollment: N/A Coed
Affiliation or Control: Interdenominational IRS Status: 501(c)3
Highest Offering: Baccalaureate
Accreditation: DEAC

01 President .... Dr. Nicholas VENDITTI
05 Vice President .... Dr. Leona VENDITTI
20 Assistant Dean .... Rev. Victor COLÓN

Iowa Central Community College (F)

One Triton Circle, Fort Dodge IA 50501

County: Webster FICE Identification: 001865
Unit ID: 153524
Telephone: (515) 576-7201 Carnegie Class: Assoc/MT-VT-Mix Trad/Non
FAX Number: (515) 576-7207 Calendar System: Semester
URL: www.iowacentral.edu
Established: 1966 Annual Undergrad Tuition & Fees (In-District): $4,890
Enrollment: 5,686 Coed
Affiliation or Control: Local IRS Status: 501(c)3
Highest Offering: Associate Degree
Accreditation: NH, DH, EMT, MAC, MLTAD, RAD

01 President .... Dr. Daniel P. KINNEY
04 Assistant to the President .... Mrs. Karen L. LOMBARD
05 Vice President of Instruction .... Dr. Dreand R. JOHNSON
32 Vice Pres Enroll Mgmt/Student Devel .... Mr. Thomas J. BENEKE
10 Vice President of Business Affairs .... Mrs. Angela A. MARTIN
86 VP External Affairs/Govt Rels .... Mr. James B. KERSTEN
30 VP Development/Alumni Rels .... Mrs. Laurie M. HENDRICKS
72 Business & Ind Technology Dean .... Mr. Neale J. ADAMS
66 Health Sciences Dean .... Mrs. Trina J. STATON
49 Liberal Arts & Sciences Dean .... Mrs. Jennifer M. CONDON
106 Distance Learning Dean .... Mr. Timothy J. MARTIN
09 Institutional Effective Exec Dir .... Dr. Stacy L. MENTZER
103 Econ Workforce Dev & Cont Educ .... Mrs. Shelly R. BLUNK
06 Registrar .... Ms. Courtney A. KOPP
07 Enrollment Management Director .... Mrs. Sara A. SCHARF
88 Retention Center Director .... Mrs. Tracy L. CRIPPEN-HAAKE
37 Financial Aid Director .... Mrs. Lindsey M. CHRISTIE
21 Business Office Director .... Mr. Luke J. GROVE
15 Human Resources Director .... Mrs. Kimberly N. WHITMORE
16 Human Resources Coordinator .... Ms. Sandi J. PIEPER
41 Intercollegiate Athletics Director .... Mr. Rick A. SANDQUIST
39 Housing Director .... Mr. Jeremy C. CONLEY
38 Mental Health Counselor .... Mrs. Kelli A. REUTER
35 Student Life & Activities Director .... Mr. David L. PEARSON
88 Academic Resource Services Director .... Ms. Lori L. WALTON
18 Physical Facilities Director .... Mr. Shan L. BEECHER
12 Storm Lake Center Director .... Mr. Dan J. ANDERSON
12 Webster City Center Director .... Mrs. Kelly J. WIRTZ
26 Public Information Director .... Mr. Paul A. DECOURSEY
13 Institutional Technology Director .... Mr. Jeff A. NELSEN
13 Institutional Technology Director .... Mr. Troy D. CRAMPTON
14 Computer System Analyst .... Mr. Warren K. BAUER
40 Bookstore Manager .... Mrs. Samantha E. MCCLAIN

Iowa Lakes Community College (G)

19 S Seventh Street, Estherville IA 51334-2234

County: Emmet FICE Identification: 001864
Unit ID: 153533
Telephone: (712) 362-2604 Carnegie Class: Assoc/MT-VT-High Non
FAX Number: (712) 362-8363 Calendar System: Semester
URL: www.iowalakes.edu
Established: 1967 Annual Undergrad Tuition & Fees (In-District): $5,676
Enrollment: 2,340 Coed
Affiliation or Control: State/Local IRS Status: 501(c)3
Highest Offering: Associate Degree
Accreditation: NH, MAC, SURGT

01 President .... Ms. Valerie K. NEWHOUSE
03 Vice President of Administration .... Mr. Scott M. STOKES
12 Exec Dean Emmetsburg Campus .... Mr. Thomas S. BROTHERTON
26 Exec Director of Marketing .... Ms. Jane S. CAMPBELL
18 Exec Dir of Facilities Management .... Ms. Delaine S. HINEY
12 Exec Dean Estherville Campus .... Mr. Robert A. LEIFELD
15 Exec Director Human Resources .... Ms. Kathy A. MULLER
31 Exec Dir Cmty & Business Relations .... Ms. Jolene R. ROGERS
10 Chief Financial Officer .... Mr. Jeff D. SOPER
32 Executive Dean of Students .... Ms. Julie R. WILLIAMS

Iowa Lakes Community College Emmetsburg Campus (H)

3200 College Drive, Emmetsburg IA 50536

Telephone: (712) 852-3554 Identification: 770055
Accreditation: &NH

† Regional accreditation is carried under the parent institution in Estherville, IA

Iowa Lakes Community College Spencer Campus (I)

Gateway N 1900 Grand Ave, Ste B-1, Spencer IA 51301

Telephone: (712) 262-7141 Identification: 770056
Accreditation: &NH

† Regional accreditation is carried under the parent institution in Estherville, IA

*Iowa Valley Community College District (J)

3702 S Center Street, Marshalltown IA 50158-4760

County: Marshall FICE Identification: 033436
Telephone: (641) 752-4643 Carnegie Class: N/A
FAX Number: (641) 754-1336
URL: www.iavalley.edu

01 Chancellor .... Mr. Christopher DUREE
11 Vice Chanc Administrative Services .... Ms. Colleen SPRINGER
51 Vice Chanc Continuing Educ/Training .... Ms. Jacque GOODMAN
10 Chief Financial Officer .... Ms. Kathleen PINK
13 Chief Information Officer .... Mr. Jim WILSON
12 Provost of ECC .... Dr. Martin REIMER
12 Provost of MCC .... Dr. Robin SHAFFER LILIENTHAL
12 Dean of Iowa Valley Grinnell .... Ms. Mary Anne NICKLE
26 Director of Marketing .... Ms. Robin ANCTIL
09 Institutional Researcher .... Dr. Lisa BREJA
04 Admin Assistant to the Chancellor .... Ms. Barbara JENNINGS
86 Director Government Relations .... Ms. Cynthia SCHULTE

*Ellsworth Community College (K)

1100 College Avenue, Iowa Falls IA 50126-1199

County: Hardin FICE Identification: 001862
Unit ID: 153296
Telephone: (641) 648-4611 Carnegie Class: Assoc/HT-High Trad
FAX Number: (641) 648-3128 Calendar System: Semester
URL: https://www.iavalley.edu/
Established: 1890 Annual Undergrad Tuition & Fees (In-District): $4,416
Enrollment: 949 Coed
Affiliation or Control: State/Local IRS Status: 501(c)3
Highest Offering: Associate Degree
Accreditation: &NH, MAC

02 Provost .... Dr. Nancy MUECKE
05 Dean of Students & Academic Affairs .... Dr. Lisa STOCK
08 Director of Libraries .... Ms. Sandra GREUFE
32 Director of Athletics/Student Life .... Mr. Nate FORSYTH
37 Director Financial Aid .... Ms. Tara MILLER
44 Dir Annual Plan Giving/Dir Alum Rel .... Ms. Kaitlyn BARTLING
07 Director of Admissions .... Ms. Adriane SIETSEMA
84 Dean Enrollment Mgmt/Registrar .... Dr. Barb KLEIN

† Regional accreditation is carried under the parent institution Iowa Valley Community College District in Marshalltown, IA.

*Marshalltown Community College (L)

3700 S Center Street, Marshalltown IA 50158-4760

County: Marshall FICE Identification: 001875
Unit ID: 153922
Telephone: (641) 752-7106 Carnegie Class: Assoc/MT-VT-High Non
FAX Number: (641) 752-8149 Calendar System: Semester
URL: www.mcc.iavalley.edu
Established: 1927 Annual Undergrad Tuition & Fees (In-District): $4,416
Enrollment: 2,041 Coed
Affiliation or Control: State/Local IRS Status: 501(c)3
Highest Offering: Associate Degree
Accreditation: &NH, DA

02 Chancellor .... Dr. Christopher A. DUREE
05 Provost .... Dr. Robin SHAFFER LILIENTHAL
11 Vice Chanc Administrative Services .... Ms. Colleen SPRINGER
10 Chief Financial Officer .... Ms. Kathy PINK
51 Vice Chancellor of Cont Educ/Trng .... Jacque GOODMAN
20 Dean of Academic Affairs .... Mr. Patrick KENNEDY
32 Dean of Student Affairs .... Dr. Chris A. RUSSELL
20 Dir of Retention/Learning Svcs/TRIO .... Mr. Nate CHUA
06 Registrar/Dir of Operations .... Ms. Mandy BROWN
76 Assoc Dean of Health Occupations .... Ms. Linda HANSON
102 Executive Director MCC Foundation .... Ms. Carol GEIL
84 Dean Enrollment/Student Life .... Ms. Angie REDMOND
37 Director Student Financial Aid .... Mr. Matt DANIELS

26 Director of Marketing ... Vacant
09 Dir of Institutional Research ... Vacant
41 Athletic Director ... Ms. Kathleen BROWN
35 Dir Student Engagement/Res Life ... Mr. Chris BREES
38 Senior Student Success Specialist ... Mr. Dan KEY
08 Library Services Manager ... Ms. Joanna PRIMUS
40 MCC Bookstore Associate ... Mr. Aaron DEBOER

† Regional accreditation is carried under the parent institution Iowa Valley Community College District in Marshalltown, IA.

Iowa Wesleyan University (A)

601 N Main, Mount Pleasant IA 52641-1398
County: Henry FICE Identification: 001871
Unit ID: 153621
Telephone: (319) 385-8021 Carnegie Class: Bac-Diverse
FAX Number: (319) 385-6296 Calendar System: Semester
URL: www.iw.edu
Established: 1842 Annual Undergrad Tuition & Fees: $27,286
Enrollment: 473 Coed
Affiliation or Control: United Methodist IRS Status: 501(c)3
Highest Offering: Baccalaureate
Accreditation: NH, NUR

01 President ... Dr. Steven E. TITUS
10 VP for Finance and Treasurer ... Ms. Chris PLUNKETT
84 VP for Enrollment Management ... Vacant
05 VP Academic Affairs ... Dr. DeWayne FRAZIER
30 VP for Strategic Initiatives ... Ms. Meg RICHTMAN
32 VP for Student Development ... Dr. Wes BROOKS
13 Assoc VP/Chief Information Officer ... Dr. Kit NIP
06 Registrar ... Ms. Catherine ASHTON
37 Director of Financial Aid ... Ms. Julie DUPLESSIS
07 Director of Admissions ... Vacant
21 Controller ... Ms. Deb LILLIE
20 Asst VP for Academic Affairs ... Ms. Paula KINNEY
15 Director of Human Resources ... Ms. Kathy MOOTHART
44 Director of Wesleyan Fund ... Vacant
26 Director of Marketing/Communication ... Ms. Ashlee WHIPPLE
27 Publications Manager ... Vacant
29 Director of Alumni/Parent Relations ... Ms. Holly JONES
41 Athletic Director ... Mr. Steve WILLIAMSON
18 Director of Physical Plant ... Mr. Bob VITALE
35 Director of Student Activities ... Ms. Kat NIEMANN
36 Director of Career Development ... Mr. Jack BRUNS
40 Bookstore Director ... Ms. Amy MABEUS
04 Asst to the President ... Ms. Mary NOTESTEIN
105 Webmaster ... Ms. Cindee VANDIJK
09 Director of Institutional Research ... Vacant
102 Dir Corporate/Foundation Relations ... Mr. Jim PEDRICK

Iowa Western Community College (B)

2700 College Road, Council Bluffs IA 51503-0567
County: Pottawattamie FICE Identification: 004598
Unit ID: 153630
Telephone: (712) 325-3200 Carnegie Class: Assoc/MT-VT-Mix Trad/Non
FAX Number: (712) 325-3424 Calendar System: Semester
URL: www.iwcc.edu
Established: 1966 Annual Undergrad Tuition & Fees (In-District): $5,216
Enrollment: 6,547 Coed
Affiliation or Control: State/Local IRS Status: 501(c)3
Highest Offering: Associate Degree
Accreditation: NH, ACFEI, DA, DH, EMT, #MAC, PTAA, SURGT

01 President ... Dr. Dan KINNEY
04 Assistant to the President ... Ms. Erin STOPAK
05 Vice President for Academic Affairs ... Dr. Marjorie WELCH
10 Vice President of Finance ... Mr. Edwin HOLTZ
32 Vice President for Student Services ... Mrs. Tori CHRISTIE
26 Vice Pres of Marketing/Public Rels ... Mr. Donald KOHLER
30 Vice Pres Institutional Advancement ... Mrs. Molly NOON
103 VP Economic/Workforce Devel ... Mr. Mark STANLEY
09 Dean Institutional Research/Accred ... Mrs. Barb GODDEN
07 Dean Admissions & Records ... Mr. Chris LAFERLA
84 Dean of Advising/Academic Support ... Mrs. Keri ZIMMER
35 Dean Student Life/Student Success ... Ms. Kimberly HENRY
106 Dean Distance Educ/Pathway Dev ... Mr. Matthew MANCUSO
81 Dean Science/Tech/Engineering/Math ... Mrs. Kim CARTER
79 Dean of Comm/Education/Fine Arts ... Mrs. Jenny KRUGER
76 Dean of Health & Sports Sciences ... Dr. Gina SCHOCHENMAIER
51 Dean of Continuing Education ... Mrs. Pam SOUTHWORTH
50 Dean Ag/Bus/Computer Info/Soc Sci ... Mr. Rick MCFAYDEN
06 Registrar ... Mrs. Jill CLARK
15 Director of Human Resources ... Mrs. Kelly FISCHER
29 Director of Alumni Relations ... Mrs. Stacy SHOCKEY
37 Director of Student Financial Aid ... Ms. Laura THAYER-MENCKE
21 Director Accounting ... Ms. Randi PAPE
13 Dir Information Technology ... Mr. James A. MAHLBERG
41 Athletic Director ... Mr. Jeremy CAPO
39 Director of Residence Life ... Mrs. Elizabeth LUIKEN
18 Director Physical Plant ... Mr. Brian SUTTER
96 Director of Purchasing ... Mrs. Diane OSBAHR
40 College Store Manager ... Mrs. Maggie SOBCZYK-BARRON
88 Food Service Manager ... Mr. Bradley GROESSER

Iowa Western Community College Clarinda Center (C)

923 East Washington Street, Clarinda IA 51632
Telephone: (712) 542-5117 Identification: 770057
Accreditation: &NH

† Regional accreditation is carried under the parent institution in Council Bluffs, IA

Kaplan University (D)

3165 Edgewood Parkway SW,
Cedar Rapids IA 52404-2998
Telephone: (319) 363-0481 FICE Identification: 004220
Accreditation: &NH, ACBSP, MAC

† Regional accreditation is carried under the parent institution in Davenport, IA.

Kaplan University (E)

1801 East Kimberly Road, Suite 1,
Davenport IA 52807-2095
County: Scott FICE Identification: 004586
Unit ID: 260901
Telephone: (563) 355-3500 Carnegie Class: Masters/L
FAX Number: (563) 355-1320 Calendar System: Quarter
URL: www.kaplanuniversity.edu/davenport-iowa.aspx
Established: 1937 Annual Undergrad Tuition & Fees: $14,241
Enrollment: 52,018 Coed
Affiliation or Control: Proprietary IRS Status: Proprietary
Highest Offering: Doctorate
Accreditation: NH, ACBSP, MAC, NURSE

01 Campus President ... Ms. Liza ZERBONIA
31 Campus Relations Manager ... Ms. Angela BOWERS
32 Director of Student Services ... Vacant
37 Director of Financial Aid ... Ms. Sharon BARBER
07 Director of Admissions ... Mr. Jason WILEBSKI
36 Employment Search Coordinator ... Ms. Sandra WAKEFIELD
08 Librarian ... Ms. Marlene METZGAR
06 Registrar ... Ms. Janet GEHRLS

Kaplan University (F)

Plaza West 2570 4th Street, SW,
Mason City IA 50401-3102
Telephone: (641) 423-2530 Identification: 666438
Accreditation: &NH, ACBSP

† Regional accreditation is carried under the parent institution in Davenport, IA.

Kaplan University (G)

4655 121st Street, Urbandale IA 50323-2311
Telephone: (515) 727-2100 Identification: 666437
Accreditation: &NH, ACBSP, MAC

† Regional accreditation is carried under the parent institution in Davenport, IA.

Kaplan University-Cedar Falls (H)

7009 Nordic Drive, Cedar Falls IA 50613
Telephone: (319) 277-0220 Identification: 770058
Accreditation: &NH, ACBSP, MAC

† Regional accreditation is carried under the parent institution in Davenport, IA

Kirkwood Community College (I)

6301 Kirkwood Blvd. SW, Cedar Rapids IA 52406
County: Linn FICE Identification: 004076
Unit ID: 153737
Telephone: (319) 398-5411 Carnegie Class: Assoc/MT-VT-High Non
FAX Number: (319) 398-1037 Calendar System: Semester
URL: www.kirkwood.edu
Established: 1966 Annual Undergrad Tuition & Fees (In-District): $4,194
Enrollment: 14,190 Coed
Affiliation or Control: Local IRS Status: 501(c)3
Highest Offering: Associate Degree
Accreditation: NH, ACFEI, CAHIIM, COARC, DA, DH, DT, EMT, MAC, NDT, OTA, PTAA, SURGT

01 President ... Dr. Mick STARCEVICH
51 VP Cont Education/Training Svcs ... Dr. Kim BECICKA
10 Vice President/Chief Fin/Oper Ofcr ... Mr. Jim CHOATE
30 Vice President Development ... Ms. Kathy HALL
05 Vice President Academic Affairs ... Dr. Bill LAMB
32 Vice President Student Services ... Mr. Jon BUSE
20 Assoc Vice President Acad Affairs ... Mr. John HENIK
12 Dean Iowa City Campus ... Dr. Ann VALENTINE
35 Dean of Students ... Ms. Melissa PAYNE
15 Director Human Resources ... Mr. Mike ROBERTS
13 Associate VP IT ... Mr. Jon NEFF
09 Associate VP Institutional Research ... Mr. Al ROWE
106 Dean Distance Lrng & Secondary Pgm ... Mr. Todd PRUSHA
84 Director Enrollment Management ... Mr. Patrick CLEMENCE
08 Director Library ... Mr. Arron WINGS
07 Director Admissions ... Mr. Douglas F. BANNON
18 Associate VP Facilities & Security ... Mr. Troy MCQUILLEN
25 Director Grants & Fed Programs ... Ms. Heather CONLEY
41 Athletic Director ... Mr. Doug WAGEMESTER
06 Registrar ... Ms. Dena RAUCH
29 Scholarship & Alumni Director ... Ms. Jody DONALDSON
37 Director Student Financial Aid ... Mr. Patrick CLEMENCE
47 Dean Agriculture ... Mr. Scott ERMER
72 Dean Industrial Technology ... Mr. Dan MARTIN
79 Dean Humanities & English ... Ms. Jennifer BRADLEY
76 Dean Allied Health ... Ms. Nicky CLINE
83 Dean Social Sciences/Career Option ... Dr. Brooke STRAHN-KOLLER
81 Dean Math/Science ... Mr. Marvin BAUSMAN
66 Dean Nursing ... Dr. Kathryn DOLTER
76 Dean Health Occupations ... Dr. Mike MCLAUGHLIN
50 Dean Business & Information Tech ... Ms. Colette ATKINS
88 Dean Learning Services ... Mr. Arron WINGS
04 Administrative Asst to President ... Ms. Carrie ANDERSON
104 Director Study Abroad ... Ms. Dawn WOOD
19 Director Security/Safety ... Ms. Melissa JENSEN
26 Chief Public Relations/Marketing ... Mr. Kevin HANSEN
44 Director Annual or Planned Giving ... Ms. Susan OVEL

Kirkwood Community College Iowa City (J)

1816 Lower Muscatine Road, Iowa City IA 52240
Telephone: (819) 887-3658 Identification: 770062
Accreditation: &NH

† Regional accreditation is carried under the parent institution in Cedar Rapids, IA

Loras College (K)

1450 Alta Vista, Dubuque IA 52004-0178
County: Dubuque FICE Identification: 001873
Unit ID: 153825
Telephone: (563) 588-7100 Carnegie Class: Bac-Diverse
FAX Number: (563) 588-7964 Calendar System: Semester
URL: www.loras.edu
Established: 1839 Annual Undergrad Tuition & Fees: $30,628
Enrollment: 1,569 Coed
Affiliation or Control: Roman Catholic IRS Status: 501(c)3
Highest Offering: Master's
Accreditation: NH, #CAATE, ENG, SW

01 President ... Mr. James E. COLLINS
05 Interim Academic Dean ... Rev. Douglas O. WATHIER
10 Interim VP Finance/Admin Svcs ... Mr. Michael H. DOYLE
03 Senior Vice President ... Dr. Mary Ellen CARROLL
30 VP Institutional Advancement ... Mr. Michael H. DOYLE
32 VP Student Development ... Dr. Arthur W. SUNLEAF
04 Executive Assistant to President ... Ms. Heather L. JUNGBLUT
42 Dean of Campus Spiritual Life ... Rev. William M. JOENSEN
91 Sr Dir Technology Services ... Mr. Thomas D. KRUSE
29 Exec Dir Alumni/Communications ... Ms. Bobbi L. EARLES
15 Dir Human Resources ... Mr. Troy M. WRIGHT
09 Director of Institutional Research ... Mr. Scott J. BAUMLER
38 Director Center for Counseling ... Ms. Tricia S. BORELLI
07 Admiss Dir of Recruit & Retention .. Mr. Kyle J. KLAPATAUSKAS
88 Dir of Academic Resource Ctr ... Ms. Joyce A. MELDREM
35 Assistant Dean of Students ... Ms. Molly A. BURROWS-SCHUMACHER
30 Assoc VP Institutional Advance ... Mr. Joshua D. BOOTS
41 Dir Intercollegiate Athletics ... Ms. Denise A. UDELHOFEN
18 Asst VP Physical Resources ... Mr. John R. MCDERMOTT
40 Director of Bookstore ... Ms. Renee A. MENNE
23 Director of Health Center ... Ms. Tammy S. MARTI
42 Campus Ministry/P&J Coordinator ... Ms. Anastacia M. MCDERMOTT
06 Interim Registrar ... Ms. Jane A. MOURING
19 Dir Res Life & Campus Safety ... Ms. Molly A. BURROWS-SCHUMACHER
35 Assoc Dean of Students ... Ms. Kimberly A. WALSH
37 Director of Financial Planning ... Ms. Julie A. DUNN
102 Dir Foundation/Gov Support ... Ms. Valorie A. WOERDEHOFF
26 Dir Communications/Marketing ... Ms. Susan P. HAFKEMEYER
96 Controller for Business Office ... Ms. Rennie A. ROOT
36 Academic Internship Coordinator ... Ms. Jennifer WEBER

Luther College (L)

700 College Drive, Decorah IA 52101-1045
County: Winneshiek FICE Identification: 001874
Unit ID: 153834
Telephone: (563) 387-2000 Carnegie Class: Bac-A&S
FAX Number: (563) 387-2158 Calendar System: 4/1/4
URL: www.luther.edu
Established: 1861 Annual Undergrad Tuition & Fees: $39,190
Enrollment: 2,385 Coed
Affiliation or Control: Evangelical Lutheran Church In America
IRS Status: 501(c)3
Highest Offering: Baccalaureate
Accreditation: NH, CAATE, MUS, NURSE, SW, TED

01 President ... Dr. Paula J. CARLSON
05 Vice Pres Acad Affs/Dean of College ... Dr. Kevin KRAUS
20 Assistant Dean ... Ms. Arleen ORVIS
30 Vice President for Development ... Vacant
10 Vice President for Finance & Admin ... Mr. Eric RUNESTAD
32 Vice Pres/Dean for Student Life ... Mr. Corey LANDSTROM
84 Vice Pres Enrollment Management ... Mr. Scot SCHAEFFER
26 Vice Pres Communications/Marketing ... Dr. Rob K. LARSON
13 Exec Dir Library & Information Svcs ... Mr. Paul R. MATTSON
21 Controller ... Ms. Peggy LENSING
18 Director of Facilities Services ... Mr. Jay L. UTHOFF
91 Director Information Systems ... Ms. Marcia A. GULLICKSON
44 Senior Development Officer ... Mr. Doug NELSON
06 Registrar ... Dr. Kristin SWANSON
20 Associate Dean/Dir Faculty Devel ... Dr. Jeffrey WILKERSON
15 Director Human Resources ... Ms. Marsha WENTHOLD
41 Director Intercollegiate Athletics ... Ms. Renae HARTL

29 Exec Director of Alumni Relations ....Ms. Sherry B. ALCOCK
27 Director of Publications ....Mr. Michael BARTELS
27 Director of Media Relations ....Ms. Julie TRYTTEN
04 Assistant to the President ....Ms. Susan LYNDON
35 Assistant Dean Student Life ....Ms. Kelsey BOYCE
36 Director Career Center ....Ms. Brenda RANUM
38 Director Counseling Service ....Ms. Meg HAMMES
37 Director Student Financial Planning ....Ms. Janice K. CORDELL
42 Dir Campus Ministry & Cong Rels ....Rev. Michael R. BLAIR
40 Director Book Shop/Union Services ......Ms. Deanna CASTERTON
39 Assistant Dean & Dir Res Life ....Ms. Kristine FRANZEN
85 Exec Dir Ctr Global Learn & Int Adm ....Mr. Jon LUND
23 Director Health Services ....Ms. Diane TAPPE
19 Director Security/Safety ....Mr. Robert HARRI
88 Director Campus Programing ....Ms. Tanya M. GERTZ
28 Interim Dir of Diversity Ctr ....Ms. Wintlett TAYLOR-BROWNE
09 Director Assessment/Inst Research ....Dr. Jon A. CHRISTY
07 Senior Assoc Director of Admissions ....Mr. Kirk NEUBAUER
35 Coordinator Student Activities ....Ms. Trish NEUBAUER
88 Asst Dean & Health Res Adv ....Ms. Janet HUNTER

Maharishi University of Management (A)

1000 N 4th Street, Fairfield IA 52557-0001
County: Jefferson FICE Identification: 011113
Unit ID: 153861
Telephone: (641) 472-7000 Carnegie Class: Masters/L
FAX Number: (641) 472-1179 Calendar System: Semester
URL: www.mum.edu
Established: 1971 Annual Undergrad Tuition & Fees: $26,530
Enrollment: 1,454 Coed
Affiliation or Control: Independent Non-Profit IRS Status: 501(c)3
Highest Offering: Doctorate
Accreditation: NH, IACBE

01 President ....Dr. Bevan H. MORRIS
03 Executive Vice President ....Dr. Craig PEARSON
45 Vice President of Expansion ....Mr. Thomas BROOKS
05 Dean of Faculty ....Dr. Cathy GORINI
10 Treasurer ....Mr. Michael SPIVAK
88 International Vice President ....Dr. Michael DILLBECK
88 International Vice President ....Dr. Susan DILLBECK
11 Chief Administrative Officer ....Mr. David TODT
43 Legal Counsel/Dean Global Develop ....Mr. Bill GOLDSTEIN
07 Fellow-Dean of Admissions ....Ms. Gwendolyn STOWE
07 Fellow-Dean of Admissions ....Ms. Aster HESSE
32 Dean of Students ....Mr. Rod EASON
33 Associate Dean of Men ....Vacant
34 Associate Dean of Women ....Ms. Amellia HESSE
06 Registrar ....Ms. Mary KING
26 Media Relations ....Mr. Norman ZIEROLD
51 Dir Distance Educ/Intl Programs ....Mr. Dennis HEATON
27 Director of Press ....Mr. Harry BRIGHT
39 Director of Housing ....Mr. Mahmood ALI
37 Director of Student Financial Aid ....Mr. Dan WASIELEWSKI
13 Director of Information Services ....Mr. Simon RODRIGUEZ
09 Director Evaluation ....Dr. Chris JONES
15 Director/Human Resources ....Mr. Stan LAMOTHE
29 Director Alumni ....Mr. Joshua WILSON
30 Co-Exec Director Inst Advancement ....Mr. Nick ROSANIA
30 Co-Exec Director Inst Advancement ....Ms. Sandra ROSANIA
36 Director Career Services ....Dr. Steve LANGERUD
18 Chief Facilities/Physical Plant ....Mr. Craig WAGNER
49 Dean College of Arts & Sciences ....Dr. Chris JONES
77 Dean College of Computer Sci & Math ......Mr. Gregory GUTHRIE
58 Dean of Graduate School ....Dr. Frederick TRAVIS
04 Administrative Asst to President ....Ms. Jane AIKENS
08 Head Librarian ....Ms. Rouzanna VARDANYAN
41 Athletic Director ....Mr. Ken DALEY
44 Director of Major Gifts ....Mr. Brad MYLETT
101 Secretary of the Board of Trustees ....Ms. Susan TRACY
19 Director of Security and Safety ....Ms. Beata NACSA
106 Dir Online Education/E-learning ....Ms. Cheryl MICHIE
38 Director Student Support Services ....Mr. Jonathan SHAPIRO

Mercy College of Health Sciences (B)

928 Sixth Avenue, Des Moines IA 50309-1239
County: Polk FICE Identification: 006273
Unit ID: 153977
Telephone: (515) 643-3180 Carnegie Class: Spec-4-yr-Other Health
FAX Number: (515) 643-6698 Calendar System: Semester
URL: www.mchs.edu
Established: 1995 Annual Undergrad Tuition & Fees: $16,268
Enrollment: 774 Coed
Affiliation or Control: Roman Catholic IRS Status: 501(c)3
Highest Offering: Baccalaureate
Accreditation: NH, ADNUR, DMS, EMT, MAC, MT, NURSE, PTAA, RAD, SURGT

01 President ....Dr. Barbara Q. DECKER
05 VP of Academic Affairs and Provost ....Dr. Steven D. LANGDON
26 VP of External Affairs ....Mr. Brian P. TINGLEFF
10 VP of Business & Regulatory Affairs ....Dr. Thomas LEAHY
84 VP Enroll Mgmt & Student Affairs ....Dr. Karen ANDERSON
66 Dean of Nursing ....Dr. Nancy KERTZ
49 Dean of Liberal Arts & Sciences ....Dr. Jeannine MATZ
76 Dean of Allied Health ....Dr. Robert LOCH
09 Dean Inst Rsrch & Effectiveness ....Dr. Jeanette MCGREEVY
08 Dir of Library and Media Services ....Mr. Roy MEADOR
06 Registrar ....Ms. Carolyn BUCKLIN
15 Human Resources Business Partner ....Ms. Anne DENNIS

37 Director of Financial Aid ....Mr. Joe BROOKOVER
38 Director of Student Success ....Dr. Kristine OWENS
13 Director of Information Technology ....Mr. David VON ARB
18 Facilities Manager ....Mr. David STEENHOEK
07 Director of Admissions ....Ms. Heather GAUMER
27 Marketing Coordinator ....Mr. Jim TAGYE
04 Administrative Asst to President ....Ms. Carole ADAMS

Morningside College (C)

1501 Morningside Avenue, Sioux City IA 51106-1751
County: Woodbury FICE Identification: 001879
Unit ID: 154004
Telephone: (712) 274-5000 Carnegie Class: Masters/M
FAX Number: (712) 274-5101 Calendar System: Semester
URL: www.morningside.edu
Established: 1894 Annual Undergrad Tuition & Fees: $28,155
Enrollment: 2,823 Coed
Affiliation or Control: United Methodist IRS Status: 501(c)3
Highest Offering: Master's
Accreditation: NH, MUS, NURSE

01 President ....Mr. John C. REYNDERS
05 Provost ....Dr. William C. DEEDS
10 Vice President Business & Finance ....Mr. Ronald A. JORGENSEN
32 Vice Pres Student Life & Enrollment ....Mrs. Terri A. CURRY
30 Vice Pres Institutional Advancement ..Mrs. Kari L. WINKLEPLECK
35 Dean of Students ....Ms. Karmen TEN NAPEL
20 Associate Dean for Acad Affairs ....Dr. Bethany HINGA
09 Assoc VP Grad Pgm & Inst Assessment ....Dr. John PINTO
88 Vice President Advising ....Dr. Lillian LOPEZ
06 Registrar ....Mrs. Jen DOLPHIN
37 Director Student Financial Planning ....Ms. Karen GAGNON
13 Exec Dir of Information Services ....Mr. Mike HUSMANN
26 Vice Pres Communications & Mktg ....Mr. Rick G. WOLLMAN
29 Director of Alumni Relations ....Mr. Shiran NATHANIEL
07 Director of Admissions ....Ms. Steph PETERS
18 Director of Physical Plant ....Mr. Kirk JOHNSON
19 Director of Security ....Mr. Brett LYON
23 Director of Student Health ....Ms. Carol GARVEY
36 Director of Career Services ....Ms. Stacie HAYS
40 Director of Bookstore ....Mr. Duane BENSON
41 Athletic Director ....Mr. Tim JAGER
42 Campus Ministry ....Mr. Ryan M. RUSSELL
44 Director of Gift Planning ....Mr. Jonathan BLUM
15 Director Human Resources ....Ms. Cindy WELP
21 Controller ....Mr. Paul TREFT
04 Administrative Asst to President ....Mrs. Lisa KROHN
102 Senior Writer & Foundation Mgr ....Ms. Laura L. FLORIO
105 Digital Communications Mgr ....Mr. Kevin PETTEBAUM
39 Asst Director Residence Life ....Ms. Sheri HINEMAN
08 Library Director ....Mr. Adam FULLERTON
38 Personal Counselor ....Ms. Bobbi MEISTER
101 Secretary of the Institution/Board ....Mrs. Lisa KROHN
104 Director Study Abroad ....Dr. Bethany HINGA
108 Director Institutional Assessment ....Dr. John PINTO
91 Director Administrative Computing ....Ms. Carla GREGG
106 Dir Online Education/E-learning ....Ms. Michelle E. LAUGHLIN

Mount Mercy University (D)

1330 Elmhurst Drive NE, Cedar Rapids IA 52402-4797
County: Linn FICE Identification: 001880
Unit ID: 154013
Telephone: (319) 363-8213 Carnegie Class: Masters/M
FAX Number: (319) 363-5270 Calendar System: 4/1/4
URL: www.mtmercy.edu
Established: 1928 Annual Undergrad Tuition & Fees: $28,226
Enrollment: 1,762 Coed
Affiliation or Control: Roman Catholic IRS Status: 501(c)3
Highest Offering: Master's
Accreditation: NH, MFCD, NURSE, SW

01 President ....Ms. Laurie HAMEN
05 Provost ....Dr. Janet HANDLER
10 VP of Finance ....Mr. Doug BROCK
84 VP Admin/Enrollment/Student Svcs ....Dr. Robert CALLAHAN
30 VP of Development/Alumni Relations ....Ms. Brenda DUELLO
42 VP of Mission and Ministry ....Sr. Shari SUTHERLAND
20 Assoc Prov/Exec Dir Acad Innovation ....Dr. Tom CASTLE
07 Dean of Admissions ....Ms. Terri CRUMLEY
06 Registrar ....Mr. Chance MCWORTHY
08 Director of Library Services ....Ms. Marilyn MURPHY
36 Director of Career Services ....Ms. Cheryl TABARELLA-REED
44 Assistant VP for Alumni Development ......Ms. Donna DREWELOW
37 Director of Financial Aid ....Ms. Bethany RINDERKNECHT
26 Asst VP Communications/Marketing ....Vacant
41 Director of Athletics ....Mr. Paul GAVIN
32 Dean of Students ....Ms. Malinda JENSEN
88 Director of Faculty Development ....Dr. Edy PARSONS
38 Director of Counseling ....Ms. Karol WHITE
13 Exec Dir of Technology Operations ....Ms. Connie SNITKER
19 Director of Public Safety ....Mr. Nicholas HEINTZ
24 Academic Technology Librarian ....Ms. Nadia GILLITZER
15 Director of Human Resources ....Mr. Thomas DOERMANN
18 Director of Facilities ....Mr. Dave DENNIS
92 Director of Honors Program ....Dr. Joy OCHS
40 Bookstore Manager ....Ms. Janie MILLS
04 Assistant to the President ....Ms. Kim BLANKENHEIM
09 Exec Dir of Institutional Research ....Ms. Lori HEYING

North Iowa Area Community College (E)

500 College Drive, Mason City IA 50401-7299
County: Cerro Gordo FICE Identification: 001877
Unit ID: 154059
Telephone: (641) 423-1264 Carnegie Class: Assoc/HVT-Mix Trad/Non
FAX Number: (641) 423-1711 Calendar System: Semester
URL: www.niacc.edu
Established: 1917 Annual Undergrad Tuition & Fees (In-District): $4,793
Enrollment: 2,950 Coed
Affiliation or Control: State/Local IRS Status: 501(c)3
Highest Offering: Associate Degree
Accreditation: NH, ADNUF, MAC, PTAA

01 President ....Dr. Steven D. SCHULZ
05 Vice President Academic Affairs ....Mr. David J. MASSEY
10 Vice Pres Administrative Services ....Mrs. Kathy M. GROVE
32 Vice President of Student Services ....Dr. Terri L. EWERS
30 Director of Inst Advancement ....Mrs. Molly H. KNOLL
88 Director of JPEC ....Mr. Timothy J. PUTNAM
15 VP Organiz Develop & Human Resource ....Dr. Shelly M. SCHMIT
06 Registrar ....Mrs. Michelle L. PETZNICK
83 Chair Humanities & Social Science ....Mr. Joe D. DAVIS
81 Chair Math & Wellness ....Dr. Kathy M. ROGOTZKE
76 Chair Health and Natural Science ....Vacant
72 Interim Chair Industrial Division ....Ms. Laura L. WOOD
50 Chair Business/Ag Division ....Ms. Laura L. WOOD
51 Dean of Continuing Education ....Mr. Terry W. SCHUMAKER
37 Director of Financial Aid ....Mrs. Mary E. BLOOMINGDALE
20 Director Learning Services ....Ms. Dalila A. SAJADIAN
13 Chief Information Officer ....Mr. Josh C. MACK
103 Regional WIA Director ....Mr. Christopher M. HANNAN
38 Dir Student Develop/Counselor ....Ms. Trudy G. LABARR
40 Bookstore Manager ....Mrs. Rhonda K. NESHEIM-KAUFFMAN
41 Director of Athletics ....Mr. Dan J. MASON
18 Director of Facilities Management ....Mr. Tony A. PAPPAS
21 Director Business Services ....Ms. Mindy R. EASTMAN
39 Director Student Housing ....Mr. Travis J. HERGERT
08 Librarian ....Ms. Jennie VER STEEG
26 Dir Marketing/Public Rel/Govt Affs ....Mrs. Valerie F. ZAHORSKI-SCHMIDT
88 Director Accelerator/Incubator ....Mr. Daniel J. WINEGARDEN
88 Director SBDC ....Mr. Brook S. BOEHMLER
88 Director of School Partnerships ....Mr. Brian M. WOGEN
88 Dir of Operations/Continuing Educ ..Mrs. Constance J. GLANDON
88 Director of Sales & Programming ....Mrs. Jody L. EAST
09 Director of Institutional Research ....Dr. Shelly M. SCHMIT
102 Grant Writer/Inst Fund Develop Spec ......Ms. Jana T. BARRACKS
106 Instructional Tech Coordinator ....Mr. Bruce G. MCKEE
29 Director Alumni Relations ....Mrs. Molly H. KNOLL
07 Director of Admissions ....Mrs. Rachel L. MCGUIRE
28 Director of Diversity ....Dr. Shelly M. SCHMIT
04 Administrative Asst to President ....Ms. Ronda L. SMITH
101 Secretary of the Institution/Board ....Mrs. Kathy M. GROVE
22 Dir Affirmative Action/EEO ....Dr. Shelly M. SCHMIT

Northeast Iowa Community College (F)

Box 400, Calmar IA 52132-0400
County: Winneshiek FICE Identification: 004587
Unit ID: 154110
Telephone: (563) 562-3263 Carnegie Class: Assoc/HVT-High Non
FAX Number: (563) 562-3719 Calendar System: Semester
URL: www.nicc.edu
Established: 1966 Annual Undergrad Tuition & Fees (In-District): $4,676
Enrollment: 4,934 Coed
Affiliation or Control: Local IRS Status: 501(c)3
Highest Offering: Associate Degree
Accreditation: NH, CAHIIM, COARC, DA

01 President ....Dr. Liang C. WEE
10 Vice Pres Finance & Administration ....Mr. David W. DAHMS
05 Chief Acad Ofcr/VP Academic Affairs ....Dr. Kathy J. NACOS-BURDS
46 Vice Pres Bus & Community Solutions ....Dr. Wendy A. MIHM-HEROLD
12 Assoc Vice President for Operations ....Ms. Rhonda K. SEIBERT
51 Exec Dir of Inst Effectiveness ....Ms. Wendy S. KNIGHT
102 Exec Director of NICC Foundation ....Ms. Julie A. WURTZEL
21 Executive Director of Finance ....Mr. Thomas M. RIDOUT
15 Exec Director of Human Resources ....Ms. Connie KUENNEN
106 Director Distance Learning ....Mr. Kyle T. COLLINS
13 Director Computer Information Sys ....Mr. Craig R. MEIRICK
09 Director of Institutional Research ....Ms. Dolores M. MILLER
88 Director Economic Devel/Peosta ....Mr. Gregory A. WILLGING
37 Director of Financial Aid ....Mr. Randy D. MASHEK
06 District Registrar ....Ms. Karla R. WINTER
06 Dir of Advising/Registr/Persistence ....Ms. Sheila R. BECKER
36 Career Services Manager ....Mr. Chris E. ENTRINGER
07 Director of Admissions ....Ms. Kristi L. STRIEF
26 Dir Marketing/News/Publications ....Ms. Shea A. HERBST

Northwest Iowa Community College (G)

603 W Park Street, Sheldon IA 51201-1046
County: Sioux FICE Identification: 004600
Unit ID: 154129
Telephone: (712) 324-5061 Carnegie Class: Assoc/HVT-High Non
FAX Number: (712) 324-4136 Calendar System: Semester
URL: www.nwicc.edu

Established: 1966 Annual Undergrad Tuition & Fees (In-District): $5,550
Enrollment: 1,568 Coed
Affiliation or Control: State/Local IRS Status: 501(c)3
Highest Offering: Associate Degree
Accreditation: NH, CAHIIM

01 President .... Dr. Alethea F. STUBBE
05 VP Student & Academic Services .... Dr. John HARTOG
30 VP Inst Adv & External Affairs .... Dr. Jan E. SNYDER
10 VP Operations & Finance .... Mr. Mark BROWN
49 Dean Arts & Sci/Business/Health .... Dr. Rhonda R. PENNINGS
72 Dean Applied Technology .... Mr. Steve WALDSTEIN
53 Dean Center for Teaching & Learning .... Ms. Gretchen G. BARTELSON
21 Director of Business Services .... Ms. Jessica WILLIAMS
37 Director Financial Aid .... Ms. Karna HOFMEYER
84 Director Enrollment Management .... Ms. Lisa L. STORY
08 Director of Library Services .... Ms. Molly D. GALM
13 Director of Technology & Info Svcs .... Mr. Mike OLDENKAMP
88 Director of TRIO .... Ms. Laurie L. EDWARDS
06 Registrar/Assoc Dean of Students .... Ms. Beth SIBENALLER-WOODALL
15 Director of Human Resources .... Ms. Sandy BRUNS
88 Director of Alt HS/Learning Center .... Ms. Susan SCHMIDT
26 Director Community Relations .... Ms. Kristin E. KOLLBAUM
18 Director Physical Facilities .... Mr. Doug RODGER

Northeast Iowa Community College Peosta Campus (A)

8342 NICC Drive, Peosta IA 52068
Telephone: (800) 728-7367 Identification: 770063
Accreditation: &NH, EMT, MAC, RAD

† Regional accreditation is carried under the parent institution in Calmar, IA

Northwestern College (B)

101 Seventh Street, SW, Orange City IA 51041-1996
County: Sioux FICE Identification: 001883
Unit ID: 154101
Telephone: (712) 707-7000 Carnegie Class: Bac-Diverse
FAX Number: (712) 707-7247 Calendar System: Semester
URL: www.nwciowa.edu
Established: 1882 Annual Undergrad Tuition & Fees: $28,950
Enrollment: 1,205 Coed
Affiliation or Control: Reformed Church In America IRS Status: 501(c)3
Highest Offering: Master's
Accreditation: NH, CAATE, IACBE, NURSE, SW

01 President .... Mr. Gregory E. CHRISTY
32 Dean of Student Life .... Dr. Julie VERMEER ELLIOTT
10 Vice President Financial Affairs .... Mr. Doug D. BEUKELMAN
30 Vice President Advancement .... Mr. Jay WIELENGA
84 Dean of Enrollment Management .... Mr. Mark BLOEMENDAAL
42 Assoc Dean of Spiritual Formation .... Ms. Barb DEWALD
41 Director of Athletics .... Mr. Earl WOUDSTRA
08 Director of the Library .... Ms. Greta GROND
06 Registrar .... Ms. Sandy VAN KLEY
37 Director of Financial Aid .... Mr. Eric ANDERSON
13 Director of Computing Services .... Mr. Harlan R. JORGENSEN
26 Director of Public Relations .... Mr. Duane L. BEESON
36 Director of Career Development .... Mr. William C. MINNICK
38 Dir Student Counseling Services .... Dr. Sally EDMAN
18 Director of Maintenance/Operations .... Mr. Scott K. SIMMELINK
29 Director Alumni Relations .... Mr. Corky KOERSELMAN
15 Director of Human Resources .... Mrs. Deb SANDBULTE
09 Director of Institutional Research .... Mr. Michael WALLINGA
04 Administrative Asst to President .... Ms. Jill HAARSMA
19 Director Security/Safety .... Mr. Andrew VAN OMMEREN
07 Director of Admissions .... Ms. Jackie DAVIS

Palmer College of Chiropractic (C)

1000 Brady Street, Davenport IA 52803-5287
County: Scott FICE Identification: 012300
Unit ID: 154174
Telephone: (563) 884-5000 Carnegie Class: Spec-4-yr-Other Health
FAX Number: (563) 884-5409 Calendar System: Trimester
URL: www.palmer.edu
Established: 1897 Annual Undergrad Tuition & Fees: $8,748
Enrollment: 2,181 Coed
Affiliation or Control: Independent Non-Profit IRS Status: 501(c)3
Highest Offering: First Professional Degree
Accreditation: NH, CHIRO

01 Chancellor .... Dr. Dennis M. MARCHIORI
05 College Provost .... Dr. Daniel J. WEINERT
108 Vice Chancellor for Inst Effect .... Dr. Robert E. PERCUOCO
32 Vice Chancellor Student Success .... Dr. Kevin A. CUNNINGHAM
84 Vice Chancellor for Enrollment .... Mr. Thomas STEMPEK
10 Vice Chancellor for Administration .. Dr. James A. CHRISTOPHER
46 Vice Chancellor for Research .... Dr. Christine GOERTZ
26 Vice Chancellor for Mktg & Comm .... Mr. James O'CONNOR
29 Exec Director Alumni & Development .... Dr. Mickey G. BURT
20 Dean of Academic Affairs .... Dr. Kevin PAUSTIAN
88 Assoc Dean of Academic Affairs .... Dr. Michelle BARBER
88 Assoc Dean of Academic Affairs .... Dr. Michael TUNNING
23 Dean of Clinics .... Dr. Ron BOESCH
88 Director of Undergrad Studies .... Ms. Cathy EBERHART
06 Senior Director/Registrar .... Ms. Mindy S. LEAHY
09 Sr Dir Institutional Research & Eff .... Dr. Dustin C. DERBY
21 Senior Dir for Financial Affairs .... Ms. Alexis A. VANDER HORN
13 Senior Dir Information Services .... Mr. Mark WISELEY
15 Senior Director of Human Resources .... Ms. Michelle K. WALKER
18 Senior Director of Facilities .... Mr. Earl WILFONG
07 Sr Dir of Admissions & Recruitment .... Ms. Julie BEHN
37 Senior Dir of Financial Planning .... Ms. Abbey NAGLE-KUCH
108 Senior Director for Assessment .... Dr. Andrea HAAN
24 Sr Dir/Center for Teaching/Lrng .... Dr. Dana J. LAWRENCE
38 Sr Dir of Academic Support Services .... Dr. Ann MARGRAVE
08 Senior Director of Library .... Ms. Chabha HOCINE
88 Sr Dir Quality Assurance/Sys Organ .... Ms. Earlye A. JULIEN
101 Exec Director Board Affairs .... Ms. Lynne LINDSTROM
104 Sr Director Clinic Administration .... Dr. Julie SCHRAD
19 Sr Dir Campus Safety and Security .... Mr. Brian SHARKEY

St. Ambrose University (D)

518 W Locust Street, Davenport IA 52803-2898
County: Scott FICE Identification: 001889
Unit ID: 154235
Telephone: (563) 333-6000 Carnegie Class: Masters/L
FAX Number: (563) 333-6243 Calendar System: Semester
URL: www.sau.edu
Established: 1882 Annual Undergrad Tuition & Fees: $28,380
Enrollment: 3,508 Coed
Affiliation or Control: Roman Catholic IRS Status: 501(c)3
Highest Offering: Doctorate
Accreditation: NH, ACBSP, #ARCPA, ENG, NURSE, OT, PTA, SP, SW, TEAC

01 President .... Sr. Joan LESCINSKI, CSJ
05 Provost & VP for ASA .... Dr. Paul KOCH
10 Vice President Finance .... Mr. Michael C. POSTER
42 Chaplain .... Rev. Charles A. ADAM
30 Vice President Advancement .... Mr. James R. STANGLE
84 Vice Pres Enrollment Management .... Mr. John D. COOPER
46 Assoc Vice Pres Assess/Research .... Dr. Tracy SCHUSTER-MATLOCK
11 Director Administrative Services .... Ms. Carol A. GLINES
26 Asst Vice Pres Communications/Mktg .... Ms. Linda R. HIRSCH
32 Assoc VP Student Svs/Dean of Stdnts .... Mr. Timothy PHILLIPS
15 Director Human Resources .... Ms. Audrey D. BLAIR
13 Exec Dir of Information Resources .... Ms. Mary B. HEINZMAN
29 Director Alumni Rels & Spec Project .... Ms. Anne A. GANNAWAY
37 Director Financial Aid .... Ms. Julie A. HAACK
38 Director Counseling .... Ms. Amy M. SCOTT
18 Director Physical Plant .... Mr. Jim M. HANNON
06 Registrar .... Mr. Dan L. ZEIMET
23 Director of Health Services .... Ms. Nancy A. HINES
19 Director of Security .... Mr. Robert CHRISTOPHER
39 Director of Resident Life .... Mr. Matt B. HANSEN
08 Director Library .... Ms. Mary B. HEINZMAN
36 Director Career Development .... Ms. Angela P. ELLIOTT
41 Athletic Director .... Mr. Raymond J. SHOVLAIN
94 Director of Women's Studies .... Ms. Katy A. STRZEPEK
40 Manager of Bookstore .... Mr. Cory W. SAMBDMAN
85 Asst VP International Education .... Dr. Ryan D. DYE
88 Chair Masters Pastoral Studies .... Dr. Micah KIEL
88 Chair Masters Criminal Justice .... Dr. Patrick C. ARCHER
49 Dean College Arts & Sciences .... Dr. Paula M. MCNUTT
50 Dean College Business .... Dr. William J. LESCH
71 Dean Health & Human Services .... Dr. Sandra L. CASSADY
88 Dean Academic Adult & Graduate Pgm .... Dr. Regina M. MATHESON
54 Dir Industrial & Mechinical Engr .... Dr. Jodi E. PROSISE
57 Director Fine Arts .... Mr. Lance A. SADLEK
88 Director Occupational Therapy .... Dr. Lynn J. KILBURG
88 Director Masters of Accounting .... Dr. Rebekah A. HEATH
58 Director MBA Pgm .... Dr. David J. O'CONNELL
58 Director Graduate Student Recruit .... Ms. Michelle L. KRONFELD
28 Director of Diversity .... Mr. Ryan C. SADDLER
04 Senior Asst to President .... Ms. Kathleen M. ANDERSON
09 Director Institutional Research .... Ms. Clare M. HOLLADAY
44 Assoc VP Legacy Giving/Campaign Dir .... Ms. Sally E. CRINO
53 Director Education .... Dr. Thomas CARPENTER
86 Director Government Relations .... Mr. Paul J. FOLEY
101 Secretary of the Institution/Board .... Sr. Joan LESCINSKI, CSJ
102 Dir Foundation/Corporate Relations .... Ms. Nikki J. DEFAUW
104 Director Study Abroad .... Dr. Ryan D. DYE
106 Dir Online Education/E-learning .... Dr. Regina M. MATHESON
108 Director Institutional Assessment .... Dr. Tracy SCHUSTER-MATLOCK
96 Director of Purchasing .... Ms. Carol A. GLINES
43 Dir Compliance & Title IX Coord .... Ms. Megan LEVETZOW

St. Luke's College (E)

2720 Stone Park Boulevard, Sioux City IA 51104-0010
County: Woodbury FICE Identification: 007291
Unit ID: 154262
Telephone: (712) 279-3149 Carnegie Class: Spec-4-yr-Other Health
FAX Number: (712) 233-8017 Calendar System: Semester
URL: www.stlukescollege.edu
Established: 1995 Annual Undergrad Tuition & Fees: $19,360
Enrollment: 254 Coed
Affiliation or Control: Independent Non-Profit IRS Status: 501(c)3
Highest Offering: Baccalaureate
Accreditation: NH, ADNUR, COARC, MT, RAD

01 Chancellor .... Mr. Michael D. STILES
05 Chief Academic Officer .... Dr. Susan BOWERS
32 Dean Student Services .... Ms. Danelle D. JOHANNSEN
66 Dean Nursing Education .... Dr. Susan BOWERS
76 Dean Health Sciences .... Dr. Dan JENSEN
06 Registrar .... Ms. Michelle FITCH
10 Bursar .... Ms. Lori MEIER
26 Director of Communications .... Vacant
07 Enrollment Mgmt/Marketing Coord .... Ms. Sherry MCCARTHY
08 Dept Chair/Library .... Ms. Nancy ZUBROD
29 Alumni/Events Coordinator .... Ms. Monica HARVEY
37 Director Student Financial Aid .... Ms. Danelle JOHANNSEN

Shiloh University (F)

100 Shiloh Drive, Kalona IA 52247
County: Washington Identification: 667095
Unit ID: 480499
Telephone: (319) 656-2447 Carnegie Class: Spec-4-yr-Faith
FAX Number: (319) 656-2448 Calendar System: Trimester
URL: www.shilohuniversity.edu
Established: 2006 Annual Undergrad Tuition & Fees: $4,510
Enrollment: 46 Coed
Affiliation or Control: Independent Non-Profit IRS Status: 501(c)3
Highest Offering: Doctorate
Accreditation: DEAC

00 Chancellor .... Mr. Gary HARGRAVE
01 President .... Mr. Christopher REEVES
05 Vice President of Academics .... Dr. Wesley PINKHAM
24 Vice President of Instructional Svc .... Dr. Daniel SALVADOR
13 Vice President of Technology .... Mr. James WIRTHLIN
58 Dean .... Dr. John BUCKINGHAM
06 Registrar .... Mrs. Judy BREWER
07 Admissions Coordinator .... Mr. Andy THOMPSON
08 Library Director .... Ms. Julie MCPHAIL

Simpson College (G)

1450 SW Vintage Pkwy, Ankeny IA 50023
Telephone: (515) 965-9355 Identification: 770849
Accreditation: &NH

† Regional accreditation is carried under the parent institution in Indianola, IA

Simpson College (H)

701 North C Street, Indianola IA 50125-1297
County: Warren FICE Identification: 001887
Unit ID: 154350
Telephone: (515) 961-6251 Carnegie Class: Bac-A&S
FAX Number: (515) 961-1498 Calendar System: Other
URL: www.simpson.edu
Established: 1860 Annual Undergrad Tuition & Fees: $34,175
Enrollment: 1,725 Coed
Affiliation or Control: United Methodist IRS Status: 501(c)3
Highest Offering: Master's
Accreditation: NH, CAATE, MUS

01 President .... Dr. Jay K. SIMMONS
05 Vice Pres/Dean Academic Affairs .... Dr. Kent EATON
10 Vice President Business/Finance .... Mr. Kenneth I. BIRKENHOLTZ
30 Vice President College Advancement .... Mr. Robert J. LANE
32 Vice President Student Development .... Dr. Heidi LEVINE
84 Vice President Enrollment .... Ms. Deborah J. TIERNEY
13 VP Info Svcs/Chief Info Officer .... Ms. Kelley L. BRADDER
37 Asst VP Enrollment/Financial Aid .... Ms. Tracie PAVON
06 Registrar & Associate Dean .... Ms. Jody RAGAN
35 Dean of Students .... Mr. Luke BEHAUNEK
26 Vice President Marketing and PR .... Ms. Jill JOHNSON
08 Director of Library .... Ms. Cynthia M. DYER
44 Director of Annual Giving .... Ms. Brenna STOFFA
15 Director of Human Resources .... Ms. Mary E. BARTLEY
36 Director of Career Services .... Vacant
07 Director of Admissions .... Ms. Alison SWANSON
41 Athletic Director .... Mr. Brian NIEMUTH
96 Director of Procurement .... Ms. Marilyn J. LEEK
35 Assistant Dean of Students .... Mr. Richard O. RAMOS
42 Chaplain .... Rev. Mara BAILEY
18 Director Campus Services .... Mr. John HARRIS
21 Controller .... Mr. Logan EDEL
19 Coordinator of Campus Security .... Mr. Chris FRERICHS
51 Associate Dean Adult Learning .... Dr. Rosemary J. LINK
28 International Educ Coordinator .... Mr. Jay WILKINSON
04 Administrative Asst to President .... Ms. Brenda K. WICKETT
29 Director Alumni Relations .... Mr. Andy ENGLISH

Simpson College West Des Moines (I)

1415 28th Street, #250, West Des Moines IA 50266
Telephone: (515) 309-3099 Identification: 770064
Accreditation: &NH

† Regional accreditation is carried under the parent institution in Indianola, IA

Southeastern Community College (J)

1500 W Agency Road, PO Box 180,
West Burlington IA 52655-0180
County: Des Moines FICE Identification: 001848
Unit ID: 154378
Telephone: (319) 752-2731 Carnegie Class: Assoc/MT-VT-Mix Trad/Non
FAX Number: (319) 752-4957 Calendar System: Semester
URL: www.scciowa.edu
Established: 1966 Annual Undergrad Tuition & Fees (In-District): $4,950
Enrollment: 2,987 Coed

Affiliation or Control: State/Local IRS Status: 501(c)3
Highest Offering: Associate Degree
Accreditation: NH, COARC, EMT, MAC

01 President ... Dr. Michael ASH
05 Vice Pres of Academic Affairs ... Dr. Carole RICHARDSON
32 Vice President of Student Services ... Ms. Joan WILLIAMS
11 Vice Pres Administrative Services ... Mr. Kevin CARR
30 Exec Director for Inst Advancement ... Ms. Rebecca RUMP
37 Financial Aid Officer ... Ms. Renae ARMENTROUT
84 Enrollment Coordinator ... Ms. Dana CHRISMAN
06 Registrar ... Mr. Tim GRAY
15 Director Human Resources ... Ms. Michelle FOSTER
49 Dean Arts and Sciences ... Vacant
12 Executive Dean of Keokuk Campus ... Dr. Teresa GARCIA
75 Dean Career/Tech/Health Educ ... Vacant
26 Dir Marketing/Communications ... Mr. Jeff EBBING

Southeastern Community College Keokuk Campus (A)

335 Messenger Road, PO Box 6007, Keokuk IA 52632
Telephone: (319) 524-3221 Identification: 770065
Accreditation: &NH

† Regional accreditation is carried under the parent institution in West Burlington, IA

Southwestern Community College (B)

1501 W Townline Street, Creston IA 50801-1098
County: Union FICE Identification: 001857
Unit ID: 154396
Telephone: (641) 782-7081 Carnegie Class: Assoc/MT-VT-High Non
FAX Number: (641) 782-3312 Calendar System: Semester
URL: www.swcciowa.edu
Established: 1966 Annual Undergrad Tuition & Fees (In-State): $5,360
Enrollment: 1,600 Coed
Affiliation or Control: State IRS Status: 501(c)3
Highest Offering: Associate Degree
Accreditation: NH

01 President/CEO ... Dr. Barbara J. CRITTENDEN
03 Vice President Economic Development ... Mr. Thomas L. LESAN
10 Chief Financial Officer ... Mrs. Tia SAMO
05 Vice President Instruction ... Mr. Bill TAYLOR
32 Dean Stdnt Svcs/Dir Inst Advance ... Ms. Beth KULOW
20 Asst Vice Pres of Instruction ... Mrs. Lindsay STOAKS
106 Director of Distance Education ... Mr. Doug GREENE
15 Director of Human Resources ... Mrs. Jolene GRIFFITH
26 Director of Marketing ... Mrs. Terri HIGGINS
08 Head Librarian ... Mrs. Ann COULTER
13 Director of Information Technology ... Mr. Scott HELM
37 Director of Financial Aid ... Mrs. Sarah FREESTONE
06 Registrar ... Ms. Sandy WEBB
04 Administrative Asst to President ... Mrs. Mary Jo SKARDA
07 Director of Admissions ... Ms. Caitlyn LESAN

University of Dubuque (C)

2000 University Avenue, Dubuque IA 52001-5099
County: Dubuque FICE Identification: 001891
Unit ID: 153278
Telephone: (563) 589-3000 Carnegie Class: Masters/S
FAX Number: (563) 589-3682 Calendar System: 4/1/4
URL: www.dbq.edu
Established: 1852 Annual Undergrad Tuition & Fees: $27,895
Enrollment: 2,121 Coed
Affiliation or Control: Presbyterian Church (U.S.A.) IRS Status: 501(c)3
Highest Offering: Doctorate
Accreditation: NH, AAB, #ARCPA, NURSE, THEOL

01 President ... Dr. Jeffrey F. BULLOCK
04 Exec Assistant to the President ... Mrs. Deborah L. BUOL
05 Vice President/Dean of the College ... Dr. Mark WARD
10 Vice Pres Finance/Auxiliary Servs ... Mr. James D. STEINER
84 Vice Pres Enrollment/Univ Rels ... Mr. Peter L. SMITH
20 Vice Pres/Dean of Seminary ... Dr. Bradley J. LONGFIELD
32 Vice President/Dean of Student Life ... Dr. Michael H. MIYAMOTO
13 Director of Technology ... Ms. Sherry CUSICK
30 Sr AVP Enroll Mgmt/Univ Relations ... Mr. Jesse L. JAMES
06 Registrar ... Ms. Kim BAUMLER
08 Director of Libraries ... Ms. Mary Anne KNEFEL
15 Director of Human Resources ... Ms. Julie MACTAGGART
37 Dean of Student Financial Planning ... Mr. Timothy KREMER
09 Dir Institutional Research ... Ms. Keri SAMSON
36 Director of Career Services ... Dr. Amy BAUS
29 Director for Alumni Engagement ... Ms. Katie KRAUS
40 Director Bookstore ... Ms. Margo KETELS
41 Athletic Director ... Mr. Dan RUNKLE
18 Director of Facilities ... Mr. Craig KLOFT
04 Special Assistant to the President ... Dr. John R. STEWART
88 Exec Dir Heritage Center ... Mr. Thomas J. ROBBINS
07 Director of First-year Admissions ... Mr. Robert D. BROSHOUS

Upper Iowa University (D)

605 Washington, Box 1857, Fayette IA 52142-1857
County: Fayette FICE Identification: 001893
Unit ID: 154493
Telephone: (563) 425-5200 Carnegie Class: Masters/M
FAX Number: (563) 425-5271 Calendar System: Semester
URL: www.uiu.edu
Established: 1857 Annual Undergrad Tuition & Fees: $28,073
Enrollment: 5,162 Coed
Affiliation or Control: Independent Non-Profit IRS Status: 501(c)3
Highest Offering: Master's
Accreditation: NH, CAATE, NURSE

01 President ... Dr. William R. DUFFY, II
05 Provost/Executive Vice Presidenet ... Dr. Kurt WOOD
10 CFO ... Vacant
82 VP Student Life/International Pgms ... Mr. Ismael J. BETANCOURT VELEZ
84 VP Enrollment Management ... Ms. Kathy FRANKEN
30 VP of External Affairs ... Mr. Andrew WENTHE
09 Assoc Provost ... Ms. Janet SHEPHERD
88 AVP for Military Affs/Business Dev ... Mr. Wayne CONVERSE
56 Asst VP Center for Distance Educ ... Ms. Barb SCHULTZ
32 Int Dean of Student Development ... Dr. Nadia KOROBOVA
36 Assoc Dean Stdnts/Dir Res Life ... Ms. Jean MERKLE
12 Dir Mid-West/South Central Region ... Mr. Walter BEMBRY
12 Dir North Central/Mid-Central Reg ... Ms. Jen WEBB
07 Exec Director of Admissions ... Mr. Anthony DIJOHN
06 Registrar ... Mrs. Holly STREETER
08 Director Library Services ... Mrs. Becky WADIAN
41 Director Athletics ... Mr. David MILLER
04 Exec Assistant to the President ... Ms. Holly D. WOLFF
105 Director Internet Development ... Mr. Joel KUNZE
21 Associate Business Ofcr/Controller ... Ms. Kathy FRANKEN
36 Director of Career Development ... Ms. Hope TRAINOR
35 Director Student Activities ... Mr. Darryl GROVE
26 Exec Dir for Comm and Marketing ... Mr. Karl EASTTORP
86 Director External Affairs ... Mr. Andrew WENTHE
29 Director of Alumni Relations ... Mr. Jasem DIAZ
13 Director Information Technology ... Mr. Terry SMID
15 Director Human Resources ... Ms. Tiffany ADAMS
88 Director Sports Info Services ... Mr. Howard THOMPSON
18 Exec Director of Facilities ... Mr. Scott JUSTASON
40 Bookstore Manager ... Ms. Becky WISSMILLER

Vatterott College-Des Moines (E)

7000 Fleur Drive, Des Moines IA 50321-2414
County: Polk FICE Identification: 026092
Unit ID: 373058
Telephone: (515) 309-9000 Carnegie Class: Assoc/HVT-High Non
FAX Number: (515) 309-0366 Calendar System: Other
URL: www.vatterott-college.edu
Established: 1997 Annual Undergrad Tuition & Fees: $12,920
Enrollment: 194 Coed
Affiliation or Control: Proprietary IRS Status: Proprietary
Highest Offering: Associate Degree
Accreditation: ACCSC, DA, MAAB

01 Interim Campus Director ... Ms. Debra LENIHAN

Waldorf College (F)

106 S 6th Street, Forest City IA 50436-1713
County: Winnebago FICE Identification: 001895
Unit ID: 154518
Telephone: (641) 585-2450 Carnegie Class: Bac-Diverse
FAX Number: (641) 585-8194 Calendar System: Semester
URL: www.waldorf.edu
Established: 1903 Annual Undergrad Tuition & Fees: $20,884
Enrollment: 1,426 Coed
Affiliation or Control: Proprietary IRS Status: Proprietary
Highest Offering: Master's
Accreditation: NH

01 President ... Dr. Robert ALSOP
05 Dean of Col/Vice Pres Acad Affs ... Dr. Vince BEACH
10 Vice President Business Affairs ... Mr. Mason HARMS
04 Assistant to the President ... Ms. Cindy CARTER
32 Dean of Students ... Mr. Jason RAMAKER
92 Dean of Honors Program ... Dr. Suzanne FALCK-YI
07 Director Admissions ... Mr. Scott PITCHER
08 Library Director ... Mr. Derrick BURTON
29 Director of Alumni Affairs ... Ms. Amy THORSON
06 Registrar ... Mr. Darrell BARBOUR
37 Director of Financial Aid ... Mr. Duane POLSDOFER
18 Director of Facilities Services ... Vacant
26 Marketing Director ... Ms. Nanci ELDER
44 Director of Annual Fund ... Ms. Nancy OLSON
38 Counselor ... Mr. James AMELSBERG
41 Athletic Director ... Mr. Bart GRAY
36 Director Student Placement ... Ms. Mary REISETTER
40 Bookstore Manager ... Ms. Karla SCHAEFER
15 Director Human Resources ... Ms. Dawn RAMAKER

Wartburg College (G)

PO Box 1003, 100 Wartburg Boulevard, Waverly IA 50677-0903
County: Bremer FICE Identification: 001896
Unit ID: 154527
Telephone: (319) 352-8200 Carnegie Class: Bac-A&S
FAX Number: (319) 352-8514 Calendar System: Other
URL: www.wartburg.edu
Established: 1852 Annual Undergrad Tuition & Fees: $37,190
Enrollment: 1,661 Coed
Affiliation or Control: Evangelical Lutheran Church In America
IRS Status: 501(c)3
Highest Offering: Baccalaureate
Accreditation: NH, MUS, SW, TED

01 President ... Dr. Darrel D. COLSON
05 VP Acad Affairs/Dean Faculty ... Dr. Brian ERNSTING
32 VP Student Life/Dean Students ... Dr. Daniel KITTLE
10 VP for Finance and Administration ... Mr. Richard SEGGERMAN
30 Vice Pres Institutional Advancement ... Mr. Scott C. LEISINGER
84 Vice Pres Enrollment Management ... Dr. Edith J. WALDSTEIN
07 Asst VP Admiss/Alumni/Parent Pgms ... Mr. Jay T. COLEMAN
06 Registrar ... Ms. Sheree S. COVERT
26 VP for Marketing & Communications ... Vacant
91 Dir of Info Technology Svcs/CIO ... Mr. Gary L. WIPPERMAN
08 College Librarian ... Mr. Curtis BRUNDY
29 Dir Alumni/Parent Rel/Annual Giving ... Ms. Renee VOVES
37 Director of Financial Aid ... Ms. Jen L. SASSMAN
41 Exec Dir of Athletics and Wellness ... Mr. Eric R. WILLIS
42 Dean of the Chapel ... Rev. Ramona S. BOUZARD
18 Director of Physical Plant ... Mr. Scott SHARAR
39 Dir Res Life/Chief Student Conduct ... Ms. Cassie HALES
36 Dir of Pathways/Career Svcs ... Mr. Derek N. SOLHEIM
38 Director of Counseling Svcs ... Mrs. Stephanie R. NEWSOM
40 Bookstore Manager ... Ms. Janet HUEBNER
85 Director of International Programs ... Ms. Helen LEONG
35 Director of Campus Programming ... Ms. Ashley LANG
88 Campus Pastor ... Rev. Brian A. BECKSTROM
21 Chief Business Officer & Treasurer ... Mr. Richard W. SEGGERMAN
15 Director of Human Resources ... Ms. Jamie HOLLAWAY
30 Director of Development ... Mr. Donald J. MEYER
09 Dir of Inst Research/Prof of Psych ... Vacant
92 Director Honors Program ... Dr. Leilani ZART
04 Assistant to the President ... Ms. Janeen K. STEWART
20 Asst Dean for Academic Affairs ... Mr. Douglas D. KOSCHMEDER
28 Dir Student Diversity Programs ... Ms. Krystal MADLOCK

Wartburg Theological Seminary (H)

333 Wartburg Place, Dubuque IA 52003
County: Dubuque FICE Identification: 001897
Unit ID: 154536
Telephone: (563) 589-0200 Carnegie Class: Spec-4-yr-Faith
FAX Number: (563) 589-0333 Calendar System: 4/1/4
URL: www.wartburgseminary.edu
Established: 1854 Annual Graduate Tuition & Fees: N/A
Enrollment: 123 Coed
Affiliation or Control: Evangelical Lutheran Church In America
IRS Status: 501(c)3
Highest Offering: Master's; No Undergraduates
Accreditation: NH, THEOL

01 President ... Rev. Louise N. JOHNSON
05 Academic Dean of the Seminary ... Dr. Craig L. NESSAN
10 Vice Pres for Finance & Operations ... Mr. Andy B. WILLENBORG
30 Vice President for Mission Support ... Ms. Janelle KOEPKE
88 Dean for Vocation ... Rev. Amy L. CURRENT
08 Library Director ... Ms. Susan J S. EBERTZ
06 Registrar/Admin Assistant to Dean ... Dr. Kevin L. ANDERSON
13 Director of Information Technology ... Mr. Richard ROBLEDO
04 Asst to President ... Ms. Lynne BAUMHOVER

Western Iowa Tech Community College (I)

PO Box 5199, 4647 Stone Avenue, Sioux City IA 51102-5199
County: Woodbury FICE Identification: 007316
Unit ID: 154572
Telephone: (712) 274-6400 Carnegie Class: Assoc/HVT-High Non
FAX Number: (712) 274-6412 Calendar System: Semester
URL: www.witcc.edu
Established: 1966 Annual Undergrad Tuition & Fees (In-District): $4,104
Enrollment: 6,399 Coed
Affiliation or Control: State/Local IRS Status: 501(c)3
Highest Offering: Associate Degree
Accreditation: NH, DA, EMT, MAC, PNUR, PTAA, SURGT

01 President ... Dr. Terry MURRELL
05 VP Learning ... Ms. Juline ALBERT
10 VP Finance/Administrative Svcs ... Mr. Troy JASMAN
15 Exec Director Human Resources ... Ms. Brenda BRADLEY
13 Dean of Information Technologies ... Mr. Mike LOGAN
84 Dean of Completion/Students ... Dr. Tricia SUTHERLAND
88 Dean of Outreach ... Ms. Janet GILL
20 Executive Dean of Instruction ... Mr. Darin MOELLER
32 Director of Student Support ... Ms. Sara KLATT
30 Exec Director College Development ... Mr. Jim BRAUNSCHWEIG
08 Library Manager ... Ms. Sharon DYKSHOORN
88 KWIT/KOJI-FM General Manager ... Ms. Gretchen GONDEK
88 Director Small Business Devel Ctr ... Mr. Todd RAUSCH
18 Director Physical Plant ... Mr. Kyle HUESER
06 Registrar ... Ms. Lora VANDER ZWAAG
26 Director Marketing/Publications ... Ms. Emma HEWITT
37 Director of Financial Aid ... Ms. LeAnn HOFFMAN

William Penn University (J)

201 Trueblood Avenue, Oskaloosa IA 52577-1799
County: Mahaska FICE Identification: 001900
Unit ID: 154590
Telephone: (641) 673-1001 Carnegie Class: Masters/S
FAX Number: (641) 673-1396 Calendar System: Semester
URL: www.wmpenn.edu
Established: 1873 Annual Undergrad Tuition & Fees: $23,930
Enrollment: 1,791 Coed
Affiliation or Control: Friends IRS Status: 501(c)3

Highest Offering: Master's
Accreditation: NH, NURSE

01 President .... Mr. John OTTOSSON
05 Vice Pres for Academic Affairs .... Dr. Noel STAHLE
30 Vice Pres for Advancement .... Ms. Marsha RIORDAN
10 VP Financial Operations .... Ms. Bonnie JOHNSON
11 VP of Operations .... Mr. Greg HAFNER
84 VP for Enrollment Management .... Ms. Kerra STRONG
56 Vice Pres of Col of Working Adults .... Ms. Linda PARKER
29 Assoc Vice Pres Alumni Relations .... Vacant
108 Director of Assessment .... Dr. Jared PEARCE
06 Registrar .... Ms. DeAnne DOLL
37 Director of Financial Aid .... Ms. Cyndi PEIFFER
36 Career Services Coordinator .... Ms. Debbie STEVENS
08 Head Librarian .... Ms. Julie HANSEN
15 Human Resource Director .... Vacant
32 Director of Student Activities .... Mr. Levi TARBELL
09 Director of Institutional Research .... Mr. Michael EDWARDS
42 Campus Minister .... Vacant
40 Bookstore Manager .... Ms. Heidi PARKER
18 Director of Buildings & Grounds .... Mr. Milt CAMPBELL
83 Chair Div of Social/Behavioral Sci .... Dr. Michael COLLINS
72 Co-Chair Div of Applied Technology .... Dr. Jim DROST
72 Co-Chair Div of Applied Technology .... Mr. Jim HOEKSEMA
53 Co-Chair Division of Education .... Ms. Susan BOXLER
53 Co-Chair Division of Education .... Ms. Cathy WILLIAMSON
50 Chair Div of Business Admin .... Dr. Lance EDWARDS
79 Chair Division of Humanities .... Dr. Anita MEINERT
76 Chair Div of Health & Life Sciences .... Dr. Gary CHRISTOPHER
66 Chair Div of Nursing .... Dr. Brenda KROGH-DUREE
04 Executive Asst to President .... Ms. Angella DURIAN-GAMBELL
13 Director of Information Services .... Mr. Mike FOSTER
19 Director of Security .... Mr. Tim REYNOLDS
38 Campus Counselor .... Ms. Tyne SMITH
39 Co-Director of Residence Life .... Ms. Dianne BURNS
39 Co-Director of Residence Life .... Mr. Matt CROONQUIST
41 Athletic Director .... Mr. Greg HAFNER

KANSAS

Allen County Community College (A)

1801 N Cottonwood, Iola KS 66749-1698
County: Allen FICE Identification: 001901
Unit ID: 154642
Telephone: (620) 365-5116 Carnegie Class: Assoc/HVT-Mix Trad/Non
FAX Number: (620) 365-7406 Calendar System: Semester
URL: www.allencc.edu
Established: 1923 Annual Undergrad Tuition & Fees (In-District): $2,910
Enrollment: 2,628 Coed
Affiliation or Control: State/Local IRS Status: 501(c)3
Highest Offering: Associate Degree
Accreditation: NH

01 President .... Mr. John A. MASTERSON
05 Vice Pres for Academic Affairs .... Mr. Jon MARSHALL
10 Vice Pres for Finance & Operations .... Mr. Brian COUNSIL
32 Vice Pres Student Affairs .... Ms. Cynthia JACOBSON
12 Dean for the Iola Campus .... Mrs. Tosca HARRIS
12 Dean for the Burlingame Campus .... Mr. Bob REAVIS
106 Dean for Online Learning .... Mrs. Regena BAILEY-AYE
08 Director of Library .... Mrs. Sandy MOORE
13 Director of MIS .... Mr. Doug DUNLAP
37 Director of Financial Aid .... Mrs. Kim MURRY
18 Director of Physical Plant Opers .... Mr. Kent TOMSON
07 Director of Admissions .... Ms. Rebecca BILDERBACK
41 Director of Athletics .... Dr. Doug DESMARTEAU
40 Director of Bookstore .... Mrs. Donna CASON
76 Allied Health Director .... Ms. Kattia ANDREWS
85 Foreign Student Advisor .... Mrs. Nichole PETERS
90 Director Academic Computing .... Mrs. Christy CUTSHAW
09 Director Inst Research/Assessment .... Vacant
35 Director Student Life .... Mr. Ryan BILDERBACK
06 Registrar .... Mrs. Bobbie HAVILAND
26 Public Relations Coordinator .... Mrs. Nancy FORD

Allen County Community College Burlingame Campus (B)

100 Bloomquist, Burlingame KS 66413
Telephone: (785) 654-2416 Identification: 770249
Accreditation: &NH

† Regional accreditation is carried under the parent institution in Iola, KS

The Art Institutes International - Kansas City (C)

8208 Melrose Drive, Lenexa KS 66214
Telephone: (913) 217-4600 Identification: 666765
Accreditation: #ACICS

† Branch campus of The Art Institute of Phoenix, AZ. School is in teach-out plan.

Baker University (D)

618 Eighth Street, Baldwin City KS 66006-0065
County: Douglas FICE Identification: 001903
Unit ID: 154688
Telephone: (785) 594-6451 Carnegie Class: Masters/L
FAX Number: (785) 594-2522 Calendar System: 4/1/4
URL: www.bakeru.edu
Established: 1858 Annual Undergrad Tuition & Fees: $27,160
Enrollment: 2,957 Coed
Affiliation or Control: United Methodist IRS Status: 501(c)3
Highest Offering: Doctorate
Accreditation: NH, ACBSP, MUS, NURSE, TED

01 President .... Dr. Lynne MURRAY
05 Interim Provost .... Dr. Tes MEHRING
84 VP of Enrollment/Marketing .... Ms. Danielle YEAROUT
13 CIO/VP Strateg Plng & Academic Res .... Mr. Andy JETT
10 VP of Finance .... Mr. David HOUCHEN
53 Dean School of Education .... Dr. Marc CHILDRESS
66 Dean of School of Nursing .... Dr. Bernadette M. FETTEROLF
49 Dean of CAS .... Ms. Martha HARRIS
107 Dean SPGS .... Dr. Jake BUCHER
41 Director Of Athletics .... Ms. Theresa YETMAR
84 Director of Admissions .... Ms. Cheryl MCCRARY
26 Director of Marketing & Comm .... Mr. Chris SMITH
31 Director of Corporate Relations .... Mr. Ivan HUNTOON
06 University Registrar .... Ms. Ruth MILLER
21 Chief Accounting Officer/Controller .... Ms. Melissa VAN LEIDEN
18 Dir of Physical Plant & Facility Op .... Mr. Jeremy PORTLOCK
42 Minister to the University .... Rev. Kevin HOPKINS
37 Senior Director of Financial Aid .... Ms. Jeanne MOTT
15 Chief Human Resources Officer .... Ms. Connie DEEL
32 Dean of Students .... Dr. Cassy BAILEY
30 Senior Dir of Development .... Ms. Amy PIERSOL
09 Dir of Institutional Research .... Mr. Eric HAYS
35 Assoc Dean Students & Dir Diversity .... Dr. Teresa CLOUNCH
29 Dir of Alumni Relations .... Mr. Doug BARTH
36 Director of Career Services .... Ms. Susan WADE
38 Dir of Health & Counseling Center .... Dr. Tim HODGES
08 Director of Library Services .... Mr. Ray WALLING

Baker University School of Professional and Graduate Studies (E)

7301 College Boulevard, Suite 120,
Overland Park KS 66210-1856
Telephone: (913) 491-4432 Identification: 770250
Accreditation: &NH

† Regional accreditation is carried under the parent institution in Baldwin City, KS

Barclay College (F)

607 N Kingman, Haviland KS 67059-0288
County: Kiowa FICE Identification: 001917
Unit ID: 155070
Telephone: (620) 862-5252 Carnegie Class: Spec-4-yr-Faith
FAX Number: (620) 862-5242 Calendar System: Semester
URL: www.barclaycollege.edu
Established: 1917 Annual Undergrad Tuition & Fees: $14,390
Enrollment: 251 Coed
Affiliation or Control: Independent Non-Profit IRS Status: 501(c)3
Highest Offering: Master's
Accreditation: @NH, BI

01 President .... Dr. Royce FRAZIER
00 Chancellor .... Dr. Adrian HALVERSTADT
05 VP Academics .... Dr. Jim LE SHANA
10 VP Business Services .... Mr. Lee ANDERS
32 VP Student Services .... Ms. Tiffany VAN DAME
30 VP Institutional Advancement .... Mr. Larry LEWIS
06 VP Registration and Records .... Dr. Glenn W. LEPPERT
37 Director Student Financial Aid .... Mr. Ryan HAASE
07 Admissions Counselor .... Mr. Justin KENDALL
08 Librarian .... Mr. Pat HALL
29 Alumni Relations .... Dr. Herb FRAZIER
106 Dir Online Education/E-learning .... Mr. Aaron STOKES
13 Chief Info Technology Officer (CIO) .... Mr. Trent MAGGARD
15 Director Personnel Services .... Mrs. Gayle MORTIMER
18 Chief Facilities/Physical Plant .... Mr. CD FITCH
19 Director Security/Safety .... Ms. Tiffany VAN DAME
41 Athletic Director .... Mr. Royce BRYAN
09 Director of Institutional Research .... Dr. Keith WHITE
25 Chief Contracts/Grants Admin .... Mr. Larry LEWIS

Barton County Community College (G)

245 NE 30th Road, Great Bend KS 67530-9107
County: Barton FICE Identification: 004608
Unit ID: 154697
Telephone: (620) 792-2701 Carnegie Class: Assoc/MT-VT-High Non
FAX Number: (620) 792-5624 Calendar System: Semester
URL: www.bartonccc.edu
Established: 1965 Annual Undergrad Tuition & Fees (In-District): $3,200
Enrollment: 5,292 Coed
Affiliation or Control: State/Local IRS Status: 501(c)3
Highest Offering: Associate Degree
Accreditation: NH, ADNUR, EMT, MLTAD

01 President .... Dr. Carl R. HEILMAN
05 VP of Instruction & Student Svcs .... Dr. Robin GARRETT
11 Dean of Administration .... Mr. Mark E. DEAN
13 Dean of Information Services .... Mr. Charles PERKINS
32 Dean of Student Services .... Mrs. Angela M. MADDY
20 Dean of Academics .... Mr. Brian HOWE
88 Dean Ft Riley Lrng Svcs/Mil Ops .... Ms. Ashley ANDERSON
103 Dean Workforce Training & Cmty Educ .... Mrs. Elaine R. SIMMONS
37 Asst Dean Stndt Svcs/Dir Fin Aid .... Mrs. Myrna L. PERKINS
30 Exec Dir Institutional Advancement .... Ms. Coleen CAPE
66 Exec Dir Nursing & Healthcare Educ .... Dr. Kathy KOTTAS
50 Exec Dir of Business/Tech/Cmty Educ .... Ms. Jane HOWARD
103 Exec Dir Workforce Trng & Cmty Educ .... Ms. Mary FOLEY
26 Dir of Public Relations & Marketing .... Mr. Brandon STEINERT
04 Assistant to President .... Mrs. Amye SCHNEIDER
41 Director of Athletics .... Mr. Trevor ROLFS
08 Director of Learning Resources .... Mrs. ReGina REYNOLDS-CASPER
15 Director of Human Resources .... Mrs. Julie A. KNOBLICH
07 Director of Admissions .... Ms. Tana COOPER
19 Coordinator of Facility Management .... Mr. Jim D. IRELAND
25 Director of Grants .... Ms. Cathie R. OSHIRO
06 Registrar .... Mrs. Lori D. CROWTHER
40 Bookstore Manager .... Mrs. Connie M. KERNS
09 Coord of Instruct & Instnl Research .... Mrs. Caicey L. CRUTCHER
39 Coordinator of Student Housing .... Mr. Jonathan DIETZ

Barton County Community College Fort Riley Campus (H)

PO Box 2463, Bldg 211, Room 211, Fort Riley KS 66442
Telephone: (877) 620-6606 Identification: 770251
Accreditation: &NH

† Regional accreditation is carried under the parent institution in Great Bend, KS

Benedictine College (I)

1020 N 2nd Street, Atchison KS 66002-1499
County: Atchison FICE Identification: 010256
Unit ID: 154712
Telephone: (913) 367-5340 Carnegie Class: Bac-Diverse
FAX Number: (913) 367-6566 Calendar System: Semester
URL: www.benedictine.edu
Established: 1858 Annual Undergrad Tuition & Fees: $26,200
Enrollment: 2,138 Coed
Affiliation or Control: Roman Catholic IRS Status: 501(c)3
Highest Offering: Master's
Accreditation: NH, #CAATE, ENG, MUS, NURSE, TED

01 President .... Mr. Stephen D. MINNIS
05 Dean of the College .... Dr. Kimberly C. SHANKMAN
10 Chief Financial Officer .... Mr. Ronald J. OLINGER
30 Vice President Advancement .... Ms. Kelly J. VOWELS
84 Dean of Enrollment Management .... Mr. Pete HELGESEN
32 Vice President of Student Life .... Dr. Linda HENRY
35 Dean of Students .... Dr. Joseph WURTZ
42 Director for Mission and Ministry .... Mr. David TROTTER
41 Athletic Director .... Mr. Charles GARTENMAYER
26 Vice President for College Rels .... Mr. Tom HOOPES
20 Assoc Dean & Registrar .... Sr. Linda HERNDON, OSB
09 Director of Institutional Research .... Ms. Mary T. HYNEK
58 Exec Dir of Grad Business Programs .... Mr. Dave GEENENS
58 Director of MASL/Asst Prof Educ .... Dr. Cheryl REDING
37 Director of Student Financial Aid .... Mr. Tony TANKING
27 Dir of Marketing & Communications .... Mr. Steve JOHNSON
38 Director of Counseling Center .... Mr. Kerry A. MARVIN
23 Director of Student Health Services .... Ms. Janet ADRIAN
18 Director of Operations .... Mr. Matt FASSERO
13 Dir of Tech & Information Sys .... Mr. Randy ROWLAND
88 Director of International Program .... Mr. Daniele MUSSO
08 Librarian .... Mr. Steven GROMATZKY
39 Director of Residence Life .... Mr. Sean MULCAHY
21 Bursar .... Ms. Becky MILLER
36 Director of Career Development .... Ms. Katie MCDOWELL
29 Director of Planned Giving & Alumni .... Mr. Tim ANDREWS
04 Executive Asst to President .... Ms. Brianna SLUDER
15 Int Director of Human Resources .... Ms. Carolyn SANDERS
19 Security Account Manager .... Mr. Danny FAIRLEY
53 Chair Education Department .... Dr. Matthew RAMSEY
54 Chair Engineering Department .... Dr. Darrin MUGGLI

Bethany College (J)

335 E Swensson Street, Lindsborg KS 67456-1895
County: McPherson FICE Identification: 001904
Unit ID: 154721
Telephone: (785) 227-3311 Carnegie Class: Bac-Diverse
FAX Number: (785) 227-2004 Calendar System: 4/1/4
URL: www.bethanylb.edu
Established: 1881 Annual Undergrad Tuition & Fees: $25,900
Enrollment: 717 Coed
Affiliation or Control: Evangelical Lutheran Church In America
IRS Status: 501(c)3
Highest Offering: Baccalaureate
Accreditation: #NH, CAATE, MUS, TED

01 President .... Mr. William JONES
05 Provost & Dean of the College .... Mr. Robert CARLSON
30 VP for Advancement .... Vacant
44 Assoc Vice Pres for Development .... Mr. Warren OLSON
10 VP for Finance and Operations .... Ms. Jean HALL
21 Controller .... Ms. Angela MARTIN
32 Dean of Athletics/Student Develop .... Mr. Dane PAVLOVICH
35 Assoc Dean for Student Development .... Mr. Matthew RIORDAN
84 Dean of Admissions/Financial Aid .... Mr. Matt PHANNENSTIEL
37 Director of Financial Aid .... Ms. Amy HOSS
06 Registrar .... Ms. Cathy BRITTON
08 Dir of Wallerstedt Learning Center .... Ms. Denise K. CARSON

41 Dean of Athletics .... Mr. Dane PAVLOVICH
18 Director of Campus Facilities .... Mr. Randy JIRAK
13 Director of Technology Services .... Mr. Matthew CARVER
88 Director of Information Services .... Ms. Christi PAULSEN
26 Director of Communications & Mktg .... Ms. Tina M. GOODWIN
29 Director Alumni Relations .... Ms. Molly B. JOHNSON
36 Director Career Services .... Vacant
39 Residential Education Director .... Mr. Matt RIORDAN
42 Campus Pastor .... Mr. Tyler ATKINSON
35 Director Campus Activities .... Ms. Roxie L. SJOGREN
88 Program Dir Athletic Training .... Mr. David SLACK
53 Program Director Teacher Education .... Prof. Gail KONZEM
64 Music Department Co-Chair .... Dr. Dan MASTERSON
65 Music Department Co-Chair .... Dr. Mark LUCAS
15 Director of Human Resources .... Ms. Lisa EASTER
09 Institutional Research Analyst .... Ms. Sarah B. ZEHNDER
40 Bookstore Manager .... Ms. Brenda C. SMITH
92 Honors Program Coordinator .... Dr. Kristin VAN TASSEL
38 Student Counselor .... Mr. David OLSEN
85 Coord Student Dev & Intl Program .... Ms. Charlotte ANDERSON
04 Admin Assistant to President .... Ms. Linda BALL
108 Institutional Assessment .... Dr. Duke ROGERS
07 Asst Dir of Admissions/Operations .... Ms. Vicki CORNETT

Bethel College (A)

300 E 27th Street, North Newton KS 67117-0531

County: Harvey FICE Identification: 001905
Unit ID: 154749
Telephone: (316) 283-2500 Carnegie Class: Bac-A&S
FAX Number: (316) 284-5286 Calendar System: 4/1/4
URL: www.bethelks.edu
Established: 1887 Annual Undergrad Tuition & Fees: $25,400
Enrollment: 483 Coed
Affiliation or Control: Mennonite Church IRS Status: 501(c)3
Highest Offering: Baccalaureate
Accreditation: NH, CAATE, NURSE, SW, TED

01 President .... Dr. Perry D. WHITE
04 Assistant to the President .... Ms. Rosa M. BARRERA
05 Vice President Academic Affairs .... Dr. Robert W. MILLIMAN
32 Vice President Student Life .... Mr. Aaron L. AUSTIN
41 Athletic Director .... Mr. Kent ALLSHOUSE
30 Vice President Advancement .... Ms. Pamela TIESZEN
10 Vice President for Business Affairs .... Mr. Allen WEDEL
26 VP for Marketing and Communications .... Ms. Lori LIVENGOOD
06 Registrar .... Ms. Marcia K. MILLER
44 Director of Development .... Mr. Matt HEIN
07 Vice President for Admissions .... Mr. Andrew W. JOHNSON
37 Director of Financial Aid .... Mr. Clark OSWALD
29 Director of Alumni Relations .... Mr. Bradley KOHLMAN
08 Head Librarian .... Ms. Gail STUCKY
42 Director of Church Relations .... Mr. Peter GOERZEN
18 Chief Facilities/Physical Plant .... Mr. Les GOERZEN
13 Chief Info Technology Officer (CIO) .... Mr. Rus ROGERS
36 Dir Student Placement/Counseling .... Ms. Joanna BJERUM
84 Enrollment Activities Coordinator .... Ms. Jane SCHMIDT

Brown Mackie College-Kansas City (B)

9705 Lenexa Drive, Lenexa KS 66215-1345

Telephone: (913) 768-1900 Identification: 666091
Accreditation: &NH, OTA, SURTEC

† Regional accreditation is carried under the parent institution in Salina, KS.

Brown Mackie College-Salina (C)

2106 S 9th Street, Salina KS 67401-7307

County: Saline FICE Identification: 006755
Unit ID: 154776
Telephone: (785) 825-5422 Carnegie Class: Spec-4-yr-Other Health
FAX Number: (785) 827-7623 Calendar System: Other
URL: www.brownmackie.edu
Established: 1892 Annual Undergrad Tuition & Fees: $12,672
Enrollment: 452 Coed
Affiliation or Control: Proprietary IRS Status: Proprietary
Highest Offering: Baccalaureate
Accreditation: NH, OTA

01 President .... Ms. Judy HOLMES
05 Dean of Academic Affairs .... Ms. Ralynn ERNEST
06 Registrar .... Ms. Kristi HAYS
36 Director of Career Services .... Ms. Robin NASH

Bryan University (D)

1527 SW Fairlawn Road, Topeka KS 66604

County: Shawnee FICE Identification: 030662
Unit ID: 154794
Telephone: (785) 272-0889 Carnegie Class: Assoc/MT-VT-High Non
FAX Number: (785) 272-4538 Calendar System: Other
URL: www.bryanu.edu
Established: 1982 Annual Undergrad Tuition & Fees: $15,448
Enrollment: 63 Coed
Affiliation or Control: Proprietary IRS Status: Proprietary
Highest Offering: Associate Degree
Accreditation: ACICS

01 Executive Director .... Mr. Wayne MAJOR

Butler Community College (E)

901 S. Haverhill Road, El Dorado KS 67042-3225

County: Butler FICE Identification: 001906
Unit ID: 154800
Telephone: (316) 321-2222 Carnegie Class: Assoc/HT-Mix Trad/Non
FAX Number: (316) 322-3109 Calendar System: Semester
URL: www.butlercc.edu
Established: 1927 Annual Undergrad Tuition & Fees (In-District): $3,235
Enrollment: 9,003 Coed
Affiliation or Control: Local IRS Status: 501(c)3
Highest Offering: Associate Degree
Accreditation: NH, ACBSP, ADNUR, ENGT

01 President .... Dr. Kimberly KRULL
05 Vice President of Academics .... Ms. Lori WINNINGHAM
10 Vice President of Finance .... Mr. Kent WILLIAMS
32 Vice President of Student Services .... Mr. Bill RINKENBAUGH
30 Vice President for Inst Advancement .... Ms. Stacy COFER
08 Reference Librarian .... Ms. Judy BASTIN
06 Registrar .... Ms. Willow DEAN
09 Director of Institutional Research .... Dr. Gene GEORGE
15 Director Personnel Services .... Ms. Vicki LONG
21 Associate Business Officer .... Ms. Edith WAUGH
29 Director Alumni Relations .... Vacant
36 Director Student Placement .... Vacant
37 Director Student Financial Aid .... Ms. Heather WARD
35 Associate VP of Student Services .... Ms. Jessica OHMAN
26 Director of Institutional Marketing .... Ms. Kelly SNEDDEN
18 Director Facilities .... Mr. Lynn UMHOLTZ
96 Director of Purchasing .... Ms. Yolanda HACKLER
07 Director of Admissions .... Ms. Kirsten ALLEN
38 Director Student Counseling .... Ms. Jessica OHMAN
13 Chief Info Technology Officer (CIO) .... Mr. Tom ERWIN
19 Director Security/Safety .... Mr. James BRYAN
39 Director Residence Life .... Ms. Cary BROCK
41 Athletic Director .... Mr. Todd CARTER

Butler of Andover (F)

1810 N Andover Road, Andover KS 67002

Telephone: (316) 733-0071 Identification: 770253
Accreditation: &NH

† Regional accreditation is carried under the parent institution in El Dorado, KS

Butler of Council Grove (G)

131 West Main, Council Grove KS 66846

Telephone: (620) 767-5158 Identification: 770254
Accreditation: &NH

† Regional accreditation is carried under the parent institution in El Dorado, KS

Butler of Marion (H)

412 N Second Street, Marion KS 66861

Telephone: (620) 382-2183 Identification: 770255
Accreditation: &NH

† Regional accreditation is carried under the parent institution in El Dorado, KS

Butler of McConnell (I)

Ed Ctr, Bldg 412, 53474 Lawrence Ct,
McConnell AFB KS 67221

Telephone: (316) 681-3522 Identification: 770257
Accreditation: &NH

† Regional accreditation is carried under the parent institution in El Dorado, KS

Butler of Rose Hill (J)

712 Rose Hill Road, Rose Hill KS 67133

Telephone: (316) 776-9429 Identification: 770256
Accreditation: &NH

† Regional accreditation is carried under the parent institution in El Dorado, KS

Central Baptist Theological Seminary (K)

6601 Monticello Road, Shawnee KS 66226-3513

County: Johnson FICE Identification: 001907
Unit ID: 154837
Telephone: (913) 667-5700 Carnegie Class: Spec-4-yr-Faith
FAX Number: (913) 371-8110 Calendar System: Semester
URL: cbts.edu
Established: 1901 Annual Graduate Tuition & Fees: $9,140
Enrollment: 391 Coed
Affiliation or Control: Baptist IRS Status: 501(c)3
Highest Offering: Doctorate; No Undergraduates
Accreditation: NH, THEOL

01 President .... Dr. Molly T. MARSHALL
05 Dean of the Seminary .... Dr. Robert E. JOHNSON
03 Executive Vice President .... Mr. George TOWNSEND
30 VP for Institutional Advancement .... Dr. John W. GRAVLEY
06 Associate Dean/Registrar .... Mr. Stephen GUINN
26 Director of Seminary Relations .... Ms. Robin SANDBOTHE
07 Director of Recruitment .... Rev. Debra SERMONS

Central Christian College of Kansas (L)

1200 S Main, PO Box 1403, McPherson KS 67460

County: McPherson FICE Identification: 001908
Unit ID: 154855
Telephone: (620) 241-0723 Carnegie Class: Bac-Diverse
FAX Number: (620) 241-6032 Calendar System: 4/1/4
URL: www.centralchristian.edu
Established: 1884 Annual Undergrad Tuition & Fees: $14,501
Enrollment: 1,165 Coed
Affiliation or Control: Free Methodist IRS Status: 501(c)3
Highest Offering: Baccalaureate
Accreditation: NH

01 President .... Col. Hal HOXIE
05 Provost .... Dr. Leonard FAVARA, JR.
30 Director of Advancement .... Mrs. Michelle BARREIRO
32 Chief Student Affairs Officer .... Rev. Chris SMITH
10 Chief Financial Officer .... Mr. Chris STOCKLIN
11 Chief Operations Officer .... Mr. Tom GRECO
41 Athletic Director .... Mr. Steve REED
06 Registrar .... Mrs. Michele AUGUST
26 Marketing Director .... Mr. Tracy CASS
21 Business Office Manager .... Mr. Phil NELSON
37 Int Director of Financial Aid .... Mrs. Nicole CARVER
08 Head Librarian .... Ms. Bev KELLEY
20 Associate Academic Officer .... Mr. Cheyenne KROEKER
18 Chief Facilities/Physical Plant .... Mr. Bob BAILEY
42 Dir of Spiritual Formation .... Mr. Justin MOURN
04 Administrative Asst to President .... Mrs. Amanda ANDERSON
07 Deputy Director of Admissions .... Mrs. Tina GOLDEN
13 Chief Info Technology Officer (CIO) .... Mr. Doug VANDERHOOF
104 Dir International Student Progams .... Ms. Hatsue AIZAWA

Cleveland University - Kansas City (M)

10850 Lowell Avenue, Overland Park KS 66210

County: Johnson FICE Identification: 020907
Unit ID: 177038
Telephone: (913) 234-0600 Carnegie Class: Spec-4-yr-Other Health
FAX Number: (913) 234-0904 Calendar System: Trimester
URL: www.cleveland.edu
Established: 1922 Annual Undergrad Tuition & Fees: $9,120
Enrollment: 483 Coed
Affiliation or Control: Independent Non-Profit IRS Status: 501(c)3
Highest Offering: First Professional Degree
Accreditation: NH, CHIRO

01 President .... Dr. Carl S. CLEVELAND, III
10 Chief Operating Officer .... Mr. Jeff KARP
05 Int Provost/DeanClinical Education .... Dr. Julia BARTLETT
84 VP Enrollment Management .... Mr. Alex BACH
26 VP of Campus and Alumni Relations .... Dr. Clark BECKLEY
15 Vice Pres HR/Organizational Devel .... Mr. Dale MARRANT
20 Dean of Pre-Clinical Education .... Dr. Paul BARLETT
20 Dean of Chiropractic Education .... Dr. Julia BARTLETT
21 Controller .... Ms. Marla COPE
06 Director of Academic Records .... Mr. David FOOSE
37 Director of Financial Aid .... Ms. Caprice CALAMAIO
09 Dir Inst Reporting/Corporate Rels .... Dr. Christena NICHOLSON
09 Director of Research .... Dr. Mark T. PFEFER
32 Director of Student Services .... Ms. Jalonna BOWIE
07 Director of Admissions .... Ms. Melissa DENTON
08 Library Director .... Ms. Simone BRIAND
13 Systems Administrator .... Mr. Calvin DANIELS
04 Assistant to the President .... Ms. Marjorie BRADSHAW
18 Director of Facilities Mgmt .... Mr. Frank HANEY

Cloud County Community College (N)

2221 Campus Drive, Concordia KS 66901-1002

County: Cloud FICE Identification: 001909
Unit ID: 154907
Telephone: (785) 243-1435 Carnegie Class: Assoc/HVT-High Non
FAX Number: (785) 243-1459 Calendar System: Semester
URL: www.cloud.edu
Established: 1965 Annual Undergrad Tuition & Fees (In-District): $2,820
Enrollment: 2,439 Coed
Affiliation or Control: State/Local IRS Status: 501(c)3
Highest Offering: Associate Degree
Accreditation: NH, ADNUR

01 President .... Dr. Danette TOONE
05 Vice President for Academic Affairs .... Dr. Brenda EDLESTON
32 Vice Pres Student Services .... Ms. Kimberly REYNOLDS
11 Vice Pres for Administrative Svcs .... Ms. Amy LANGE
13 Vice Pres Information Technology .... Mr. Shawn WALDEN
30 Director Institutional Advancement .... Vacant
07 Director of Admissions .... Mr. Shane OLSON
08 Director of Library Services .... Ms. Jennifer SCHROEDER
41 Athletic Director .... Mr. Matthew BECHARD
06 Registrar .... Mrs. Linda PETERSEN
18 Chief Facilities/Physical Plant .... Mr. Rex E. SICARD
26 Chief Public Relations Officer .... Ms. Jenny ACREE
102 Ex Dir Cloud County Cmty Col Found .... Ms. Kimberly REYNOLDS

37 Director Student Financial Aid .... Ms. Suzi KNOETTGEN
38 Director Advising & Retention .... Ms. Amber KNOETTGEN
15 Director of Human Resources .... Ms. Christine WILSON
09 Director Institutional Research .... Dr. Mitch STIMERS

Cloud County Community College Geary County Campus (A)

631 Caroline Avenue, Junction City KS 66441
Telephone: (785) 238-8010 Identification: 770258
Accreditation: &NH

† Regional accreditation is carried under the parent institution in Concordia, KS

Coffeyville Community College (B)

400 W 11th Street, Coffeyville KS 67337-5064
County: Montgomery FICE Identification: 001910
Unit ID: 154925
Telephone: (620) 251-7700 Carnegie Class: Assoc/HVT-High Non
FAX Number: (620) 252-7098 Calendar System: Semester
URL: www.coffeyville.edu
Established: 1923 Annual Undergrad Tuition & Fees (In-District): $2,304
Enrollment: 1,508 Coed
Affiliation or Control: State/Local IRS Status: 501(c)3
Highest Offering: Associate Degree
Accreditation: NH, EMT, MAC

01 President .... Ms. Linda MOLEY
05 Vice President for Academic Service .... Ms. Aron POTTER
10 Vice Pres for Operations & Finance .... Mr. Jeff MORRIS
88 VP for Innovation/Bus Initiatives .... Mr. Marlon THORNBURG
12 Director Columbus Technical Campus .... Mrs. Cindy HARROLD
102 Exec Director-CCC Foundation .... Mr. Dickie ROLLS
32 Dean of Student Life .... Mr. Ryan MCCUNE
09 Dean Institutional Research/Records ..... Mrs. Deborah OESTMANN
26 Director of Marketing .... Ms. Kris ADAMS
20 Director Academic Advising/SSC .... Mrs. Kim LAY
45 Director Institutional Effectivenes .... Mr. Marty EVENSVOLD
37 Director of Financial Aid .... Mrs. Pam FEERER
15 Director of Human Resources .... Mrs. Kelli BAUER
41 Athletics Director .... Mr. Jeff LEIKER
18 Director of Maintenance .... Ms. Vivian FROST
106 Director of Distance Learning .... Mr. Brad WEBER
40 Bookstore Manager .... Mrs. Karen STRIMPLE
07 Admissions Representative .... Ms. Kristin HORNER

Colby Community College (C)

1255 S Range, Colby KS 67701-4099
County: Thomas FICE Identification: 001911
Unit ID: 154934
Telephone: (785) 462-3984 Carnegie Class: Assoc/MT-VT-Mix Trad/Non
FAX Number: (785) 460-4699 Calendar System: Semester
URL: www.colbycc.edu
Established: 1964 Annual Undergrad Tuition & Fees (In-District): $3,150
Enrollment: 1,508 Coed
Affiliation or Control: State/Local IRS Status: 501(c)3
Highest Offering: Associate Degree
Accreditation: #NH, ADNUR, PTAA

01 President .... Mr. Seth M. CARTER
05 Vice President of Academic Affairs .... Mr. Bradley BENNETT
32 Vice President of Student Affairs .... Dr. George MCNULTY
10 Vice President of Business Affairs .... Ms. Carolyn KASDORF
06 Registrar .... Mr. Christopher LEE
08 Librarian .... Mrs. Tara SCHROER
26 Director of Public Information .... Mr. Doug JOHNSON
09 Director of Data Management .... Mrs. Angel MORRISON
07 Director of Admissions .... Mrs. Amy MELIKOVA
37 Director of Financial Aid .... Mrs. Cindi KRISS
29 Director Alumni Relations .... Ms. Jennifer SCHOENFELD
41 Athletic Director .... Mr. Ryan STURDY
13 Director of IT .... Mr. Douglass MCDOWALL
04 Administrative Asst to President .... Ms. Penny CLINE

Cowley County Community College (D)

125 S Second, PO Box 1147,
Arkansas City KS 67005-1147
County: Cowley FICE Identification: 001902
Unit ID: 154952
Telephone: (620) 442-0430 Carnegie Class: Assoc/HT-Mix Trad/Non
FAX Number: (620) 441-5350 Calendar System: Semester
URL: www.cowley.edu
Established: 1922 Annual Undergrad Tuition & Fees (In-District): $2,604
Enrollment: 3,376 Coed
Affiliation or Control: Local IRS Status: 501(c)3
Highest Offering: Associate Degree
Accreditation: NH, EMT

01 President .... Dr. Dennis C. RITTLE
20 AVP Secondary Partnerships/Acad .... Ms. Janice STOVER
05 Vice President of Academic Affairs .... Dr. Harold ARNETT
10 Vice Pres of Finance/Administration .... Dr. Gloria WALKER
13 Vice Pres Information Technology .... Mr. Paul ERDMANN
30 Vice Pres Institutional Development .... Vacant
84 Exec Director Enrollment Management .... Mr. Josh COBBLE
32 Executive Director of Student Life .... Mr. Jason O'TOOLE
41 Athletic Director .... Mr. Shane LARSON
35 Director of Student Affairs .... Ms. Kristi SHAW
103 AVP Business/Industry Advancement .... Ms. Stephanie JOHNS-HINES
106 AVP Distance Learning & Site Mgmt .... Mr. Eddie ANDREO
26 Dir Inst Comm/Public Relations .... Mr. Rama PEROO
06 Registrar .... Mr. Devin GRAVES
15 Director of Human Resources .... Ms. Linda KREUTZER

Dodge City Community College (E)

2501 N 14th Avenue, Dodge City KS 67801-2399
County: Ford FICE Identification: 001913
Unit ID: 154998
Telephone: (620) 225-1321 Carnegie Class: Assoc/MT-VT-High Non
FAX Number: (620) 227-9366 Calendar System: Semester
URL: www.dc3.edu
Established: 1935 Annual Undergrad Tuition & Fees (In-District): $2,100
Enrollment: 1,768 Coed
Affiliation or Control: State/Local IRS Status: 501(c)3
Highest Offering: Associate Degree
Accreditation: NH, ADNUR

01 President .... Dr. Harold E. NOLTE, JR.
05 Exec VP Academic Affairs .... Mr. Danny GILLUM
10 Vice Pres of Operations & Finance .... Ms. Vada HERMON
31 VP Community & Industry Relations .... Mr. Anthony LYONS
32 Dean of Students .... Ms. Stephanie LANNING
102 Exec Director of DCCC Foundation .... Vacant
51 Dir Bus/Technology/Continuing Educ .... Vacant
24 Director Adult Learning Center .... Mrs. Brandi FERGUSON
15 Director or Human Resources .... Mr. David WETMORE
07 Director of Admissions .... Mr. James KUMM
08 Director Learning Resource Center .... Mrs. Shelly HUELSMAN
66 Director Nursing Allied Health .... Ms. Carolyn WRIGHT
41 Athletic Director .... Mr. Casey MALEK
37 Director of Financial Aid .... Mr. Russ MCBEE
21 Director of Business Services .... Ms. Debbie BISCH
40 Director Bookstore .... Mrs. Debby MALEK
13 Director Information Technology .... Mrs. Judith MAXFIELD
39 Director of Residence Life .... Mrs. Carol KUMM
18 Director of Facilities & Operations .... Mr. Tim RIEKENBERG
16 Asst Director of Human Resources .... Ms. Sheila BERGKAMP
04 Exec Assistant to the President .... Mrs. Carla PATEE
20 Dean of Instruction & Outreach .... Mr. Ryan AUSMUS
106 VP of Online & Outreach Learning .... Dr. Adam JOHN
103 Dean of Innovation/Workforce Dev .... Vacant
09 Dir of Inst Research/Accreditation .... Ms. Deanna MANN
21 Comptroller .... Ms. Sandy MOORE
19 Director Security/Safety .... Vacant

Donnelly College (F)

608 N 18th Street, Kansas City KS 66102-4298
County: Wyandotte FICE Identification: 001914
Unit ID: 155007
Telephone: (913) 621-8700 Carnegie Class: Bac/Assoc-Mixed
FAX Number: (913) 621-8719 Calendar System: Semester
URL: www.donnelly.edu
Established: 1949 Annual Undergrad Tuition & Fees: $6,822
Enrollment: 463 Coed
Affiliation or Control: Roman Catholic IRS Status: 501(c)3
Highest Offering: Baccalaureate
Accreditation: NH

01 President .... Msgr. Stuart SWETLAND
05 Vice President of Academics/Stdnts .... Mr. Pedro LEITE
30 Vice President of Advancement .... Mrs. Emily BUCKLEY
10 Vice President of Business Affairs .... Ms. Laurie LOETHEN
32 Director Student Success .... Dr. Mary PFLANZ
06 Registrar .... Ms. Jennifer BALES
36 Career Center Coord/Library Dir .... Mrs. Jane BALLAGH DE TOVAR
37 Director of Financial Aid .... Mr. Michael PEPPLE
09 Dir Institutional Rsrch/Plng/Assess .... Mrs. Frances SANDERS
13 Director of Computer Services .... Mr. Jaime FUENTES
29 Alumni Relations .... Mr. Roger BERG

Emporia State University (G)

1 Kellogg Circle, Emporia KS 66801-5415
County: Lyon FICE Identification: 001927
Unit ID: 155025
Telephone: (620) 341-1200 Carnegie Class: Masters/L
FAX Number: (620) 341-5553 Calendar System: Semester
URL: www.emporia.edu
Established: 1863 Annual Undergrad Tuition & Fees (In-State): $5,936
Enrollment: 6,114 Coed
Affiliation or Control: State IRS Status: 501(c)3
Highest Offering: Doctorate
Accreditation: NH, ART, BUS, CAATE, CACREP, CEA, CORE, LIB, MUS, NUR, TED

01 President .... Dr. Allison GARRETT
05 Provost/VP for Academic Affairs .... Dr. David CORDLE
11 Vice President Admin & Fiscal Affs .... Mr. Werner GOLLING
32 Vice President Student Affairs .... Dr. James E. WILLIAMS
13 Assoc Vice Pres Info Technology .... Mr. Cory FALLDINE
09 Asst Provost Inst Research/Assess .... Dr. JoLanna KORD
85 Dean of International Education .... Mr. Gonzalo BRUCE
35 Dean of Students .... Ms. Lynn M. HOBSON
10 Assoc Vice Pres Fiscal Affairs .... Ms. Diana E. KUHLMANN
102 President ESU Foundation .... Mr. Shane SHIVLEY
29 Director of Alumni/Govt Rels .... Mr. K. Tyler CURTIS
88 Director Natl Teachers Hall of Fame .... Ms. Carol STRICKLAND
22 Affirmative Action Officer .... Ms. Judy ANDERSON
53 Dean/The Teachers College .... Dr. Kenneth WEAVER
49 Dean College of Liberal Arts/Sci .... Dr. R. Brent THOMAS
50 Dean School of Business .... Dr. Ed BASHAW
62 Dean School of Library/Info Mgmt .... Dr. Wooseob JEONG
58 Dean Graduate Studies .... Dr. James SPOTSWOOD
88 Exec Dir Jones Inst Educ Excel .... Dr. Roger CASWELL
06 Registrar .... Ms. M. Elaine HENRIE
08 Dean University Libraries/Archives .... Dr. Michelle HAMMOND
106 Director Distance Education .... Dr. James SPOTSWOOD
37 Director Student Financial Aid .... Ms. M. Elaine HENRIE
07 Director Admissions .... Ms. Laura M. EDDY
36 Director Career Services .... Ms. June COLEMAN
38 Director Stdnt Wellness/ Counseling .... Ms. Sally CRAWFORD-FOWLER
26 Exec Dir Marketing & Media Relation .... Mr. Umair ABBASI
41 Director Athletics .... Mr. Kent L. WEISER
18 Director Facilities/Physical Plant .... Mr. Mark S. RUNGE
15 Director Human Resources .... Ms. Judy ANDERSON
23 Director Health Services .... Ms. Mary MCDANIEL
39 Dir Residential Life/Orientation .... Ms. Cass COUGHLIN
40 Manager Bookstore .... Mr. Michael MCRELL
19 Director Police & Safety .... Capt. Chris HOOVER
43 General Counsel .... Mr. Kevin JOHNSON
21 Controller .... Ms. Mary MINGENBACK
92 Associate Provost Honors College .... Dr. Gary WYATT
28 Director Diversity & Inclusion .... Mr. Jason BROOKS
04 Administrative Asst to President .... Ms. Sarah MCKERNAN
86 Director Government Relations .... Mr. Brian DENTON
91 Assoc CIO Academic & User Support .... Dr. Rob GIBSON

Flint Hills Technical College (H)

3301 W 18th Avenue, Emporia KS 66801-5957
County: Lyon FICE Identification: 005264
Unit ID: 155052
Telephone: (620) 343-4600 Carnegie Class: Assoc/HVT-Mix Trad/Non
FAX Number: (620) 343-4610 Calendar System: Semester
URL: www.fhtc.edu
Established: 1965 Annual Undergrad Tuition & Fees (In-District): $5,720
Enrollment: 836 Coed
Affiliation or Control: State/Local IRS Status: 501(c)3
Highest Offering: Associate Degree
Accreditation: NH, DA, DH

01 President .... Dr. Dean HOLLENBECK
05 Vice Pres Instructional Services .... Mr. Steve LOEWEN
32 Vice Pres Student Services .... Ms. Lisa KIRMER
10 Vice Pres Business Services .... Mrs. Nancy THOMPSON
15 Director Personnel Services .... Mrs. Jacinda KAHLE
37 Director Student Financial Aid .... Ms. Sandra SCHROEDER
84 Director Enrollment Management .... Mrs. Brenda CARMICHAEL
04 Administrative Asst to President .... Ms. Jacqui ANDERSON
30 Chief Development/Advancement .... Mr. Mike CROUCH

Fort Hays State University (I)

600 Park Street, Hays KS 67601-4099
County: Ellis FICE Identification: 001915
Unit ID: 155061
Telephone: (785) 628-4000 Carnegie Class: Masters/L
FAX Number: (785) 628-4096 Calendar System: Semester
URL: www.fhsu.edu
Established: 1902 Annual Undergrad Tuition & Fees (In-State): $4,654
Enrollment: 13,825 Coed
Affiliation or Control: State IRS Status: 501(c)3
Highest Offering: Doctorate
Accreditation: NH, CAATE, MUS, NURSE, RAD, SP, SW, TED

01 President .... Dr. Mirta M. MARTIN
05 Provost .... Dr. Graham GLYNN
10 Vice Pres Administration & Finance .... Mr. Mike BARNETT
32 Vice Pres Student Affairs .... Dr. Joseph G. LINN
13 Vice President for Technology .... Dr. Joy HATCH
35 Assoc Vice Pres Student Affairs .... Ms. Keegan NICHOLS
88 Assoc Vice Pres Innovation/LrngTech .... Dr. Andrew FELDSTEIN
104 Int Assoc VicePres Intl Programs .... Dr. Yaprak DALAT-WARD
09 Asst Provost Quality Improvement .... Vacant
58 Dean Graduate Studies and Research ... Dr. Chapman RACKAWAY
04 Assistant to the President .... Ms. Lisa M. KARLIN
35 Asst Vice Pres Student Affairs .... Dr. Kenton OLLIFF
06 Registrar .... Mr. Craig KARLIN
07 Admissions Director .... Ms. Tricia CLINE
29 Exec Director Alumni & Govt Rels .... Ms. Debra K. PRIDEAUX
45 Director Budget & Planning .... Mr. Larry R. GETTY
36 Director Career Services .... Mr. Daniel B. RICE
37 Dir Student Financial Aid .... Ms. Wendy ROHLEDER-SOOK
26 Director University Relations .... Mr. Lisa L. KARLIN
08 Director Library .... Ms. Deborah LUDWIG
15 Director Personnel Services .... Ms. Shannon LINDSEY
51 Dean Virtual College .... Mr. Dennis KING
53 Dean College Education .... Dr. Paul ADAMS
49 Dean Col Arts/Humanities/Soc Sci .... Dr. Paul W. FABER
50 Dean Col Business/Entrepreneurship .... Dr. Mark BANNISTER
76 Dean Col Health/Behavioral Science .... Dr. Jeff BRIGGS
18 Co-Dir Chief Facil/Physical Plant .... Mr. Jim SCHREIBER
18 Co-Dir Chief Facil/Physical Plant .... Mr. Ken JACOBS
38 Dir Acad Advis/Career Exploration .... Dr. Patricia L. GRIFFIN
28 Diversity Coordinator .... Vacant
19 Director Security/Safety .... Mr. Ed HOWELL

22 Dir Affirmative Action/EEO .... Ms. Carrie LANE
102 President Foundation .... Mr. Jason WILLIBY
25 Chief Contracts/Grants Admin .... Ms. Leslie PAIGE
41 Athletic Director .... Mr. Curtis HAMMEKE
104 Director Study Abroad .... Ms. Andree BRISSON-FARLEY
43 General Counsel .... Ms. Kerry WASINGER
54 Dean College of Science/Tech/Math .... Dr. Greg FARLEY
84 Asst Vice Pres Enrollment Mgmt .... Mr. Dennis KING
91 Manager New Dev Technologies .... Ms. Jackie RUDER
96 Director of Purchasing .... Ms. Kathy HERRMAN

Fort Scott Community College (A)

2108 S Horton, Fort Scott KS 66701-3140
County: Bourbon FICE Identification: 001916
Unit ID: 155098
Telephone: (620) 223-2700 Carnegie Class: Assoc/HVT-High Non
FAX Number: (620) 223-4927 Calendar System: Semester
URL: www.fortscott.edu
Established: 1919 Annual Undergrad Tuition & Fees (In-District): $2,820
Enrollment: 1,816 Coed
Affiliation or Control: State/Local IRS Status: 501(c)3
Highest Offering: Associate Degree
Accreditation: NH, ADNUR

01 President .... Alysia JOHNSTON
05 Vice President of Academic Affairs .... Regena LANCE
32 Vice President of Students .... Robert GOLTRA
10 Vice Pres of Finance and Operations .... Julie EICHENBERGER
13 Director of Research & Technology .... Jacob REICHARD
07 Director Admissions .... Matt GLADES
08 Director of Library .... Susie ARVIDSON
06 Registrar .... Courtney METCALF
26 Director Public Relations .... Heather CUTSHALL
66 Director Nursing .... Bill RHOADS
41 Athletic Director .... Tom HAVRON
14 Information Technology Director .... Jason SIMON
12 Dean Crawford County .... Santos MANRIQUE
12 Dean of Miami County Campus .... Buddy Jo TANCK
38 Director of Advising .... Janet FANCHER
15 Human Resource Director .... Juley MCDANIEL
30 Director of Development/Alumni .... Bailey LYONS
37 Director Student Financial Aid .... Lillie GRUBB
88 Director of Gordon Parks Museum .... Jill WARFORD
35 Director of Student Life .... Marci MYERS
21 Director Business Operations .... Mindy RUSSELL
04 Administrative Asst to President .... Darlene WOOD
101 Secretary of the Institution/Board .... Juley MCDANIEL
22 Dir Affirmative Action/EEO .... Juley MCDANIEL
39 Director Student Housing .... Marci MYERS
88 Program Industry Coordinator .... Nacoma OEHME
25 Director Grants & Special Projects .... Ralph BEACHAM

Friends University (B)

2100 W University Avenue, Wichita KS 67213-3397
County: Sedgwick FICE Identification: 001918
Unit ID: 155089
Telephone: (316) 295-5000 Carnegie Class: Masters/L
FAX Number: (316) 295-5060 Calendar System: Semester
URL: www.friends.edu
Established: 1898 Annual Undergrad Tuition & Fees: $25,965
Enrollment: 1,882 Coed
Affiliation or Control: Independent Non-Profit IRS Status: 501(c)3
Highest Offering: Master's
Accreditation: NH, MFCD, MUS, TED

01 President .... Dr. Amy CAREY
04 Executive Asst to the President .... Ms. Natasha PEREZ
05 VP of Academic Affairs .... Dr. Jasper LESAGE
10 VP of Finance .... Ms. Marsha BEWERSDORF
32 VP of Student Affairs .... Dr. Carole OBERMEYER
30 VP of University Advancement .... Vacant
26 Assoc VP Marketing & Communications .... Ms. Deb STOCKMAN
11 VP of Administration .... Ms. Kelley WILLIAMS
84 VP of Enrollment Management .... Mr. Ken FAFFLER
06 University Registrar .... Mr. Mark BRITTON
49 Dean Col of Bus/Art/Sci & Educ .... Dr. Bill ALLAN
107 Dean Col of Adult and Prof Studies .... Dr. David HOFMEISTER
58 Dean Graduate School .... Dr. David HOFMEISTER
50 Chair Business & IT .... Dr. Arlen HONTS
57 Chair Fine Arts .... Vacant
81 Chair Natural Science/Math .... Dr. Nora STRASSER
73 Chair Religion/Humanities .... Dr. Jeremy GALLEGOS
53 Chair Teacher Education .... Dr. Jan WILSON
83 Chair Social/Behavioral Science .... Dr. Tor WYNN
08 Director Library .... Ms. Anne CRANE
18 Chief Facilities/Physical Plant .... Mr. Paul WINCHESTER
96 Director of Business Operations .... Mr. Ryan ARCHER
07 Sr Dir Admissions & Fin Aid .... Mr. Brandon PIERCE
41 Director Athletics .... Dr. Carole OBERMEYER
37 Director Financial Aid .... Mr. Tony LUBBERS
42 Pastor & Dean Campus Ministries .... Dr. Guy CHMIELESKI
39 Dir Community & Res Development .... Ms. Kelley MARTIN
26 Director of Marketing .... Ms. Gisele MCMINIMY
29 Director of Alumni Relations .... Ms. Brie BOULANGER
12 Site Director - Topeka .... Vacant
12 Site Manager - Kansas City .... Ms. Monica HASHEMI-BOZARTH
44 Director of Planned Giving .... Mr. Eric LITWILLER
09 Director of Institutional Research .... Mr. Aidan DUNLEAVY
19 Director Security/Safety .... Mr. Richard VINROE

Garden City Community College (C)

801 Campus Drive, Garden City KS 67846-6398
County: Finney FICE Identification: 001919
Unit ID: 155104
Telephone: (620) 276-7611 Carnegie Class: Assoc/MT-VT-Mix Trad/Non
FAX Number: (620) 276-9573 Calendar System: Semester
URL: www.gcccks.edu
Established: 1919 Annual Undergrad Tuition & Fees (In-District): $2,816
Enrollment: 2,072 Coed
Affiliation or Control: Local IRS Status: 501(c)3
Highest Offering: Associate Degree
Accreditation: NH, ADNUR, EMT

01 President .... Dr. Herbert SWENDER
11 Exec Vice Pres Admin Svcs .... Ms. Dee WIGNER
05 VP Instruction & Student Svcs/CAO .... Mr. Ryan RUDA
07 Director of Admissions .... Vacant
84 Director of Enrollment Management .... Ms. Tammy TABOR
06 Registrar .... Ms. Nancy UNRUH
13 Director of Information Technology .... Mr. Jeff SOUTHERN
15 Director of Human Resources .... Ms. Sara KOEHN
18 Director of Facilities .... Mr. Derek RAMOS
26 Director Marketing & PR .... Ms. Kristi TEMPEL
37 Director Student Financial Aid .... Ms. Melinda HARRINGTON
39 Director Residential Life .... Ms. Christine DILLINGHAM
32 Dean of Student Services/Asst AD .... Mr. Colin LAMB
103 Director of Workforce Development .... Mr. Jerrad WEBB
04 Executive Assistant to President .... Ms. Debra ATKINSON
09 Director of Institutional Research .... Vacant
10 Comptroller .... Ms. Debra NICHOLSON
19 Campus Police Chief .... Mr. Rodney DOZIER
08 Director Library Services .... Mr. Trent SMITH
41 Athletic Director .... Mr. John GREEN
44 Executive Director Endowment .... Mr. Jeremy GIGOT

Grantham University (D)

16025 W 113th Street, Lenexa KS 66219
County: Johnson FICE Identification: 004283
Unit ID: 442569
Telephone: (888) 947-2684 Carnegie Class: Masters/L
FAX Number: (913) 309-4949 Calendar System: Other
URL: www.grantham.edu
Established: 1951 Annual Undergrad Tuition & Fees: $6,500
Enrollment: 12,577 Coed
Affiliation or Control: Proprietary IRS Status: Proprietary
Highest Offering: Master's
Accreditation: DEAC, ENGT, IACBE

01 Campus President/COO .... Steve WALDRON
30 Chief Development Officer .... Brad GIBBS
10 Chief Financial Officer .... Lily CARPIO
05 Chief Academic Officer/Provost .... Dr. Cheryl HAYEK
45 Vice Pres of Strategic Initiatives .... Dr. Jeffrey CROPSEY
22 Vice President of Compliance .... Harry DOTSON
84 Vice Pres Student Enrollment .... Jared PARLETTE
15 Vice President of Human Resources .... Kip ESRY
13 Chief Information Officer .... Anthony SCHLINSOG
06 Associate Registrar .... Joshua CARCOPA
103 Director University Outreach .... Tabitha DAVIS

Haskell Indian Nations University (E)

155 Indian Avenue, #5030, Lawrence KS 66046-4800
County: Douglas FICE Identification: 010438
Unit ID: 155140
Telephone: (785) 749-8404 Carnegie Class: Tribal
FAX Number: (785) 749-8406 Calendar System: Semester
URL: www.haskell.edu
Established: 1884 Annual Undergrad Tuition & Fees: $580
Enrollment: 808 Coed
Affiliation or Control: Federal IRS Status: Exempt
Highest Offering: Baccalaureate
Accreditation: NH, TED

01 President .... Dr. Venida CHENAULT
05 Acting Vice Pres Academic Affairs .... Ms. Julia GOOD FOX
11 Vice President University Services .... Ms. Tonia SALVINI
10 Chief Finance Officer .... Ms. Brenda FACEHORSE
13 Chief Information Officer .... Mr. Joshua ARCE
08 Acting Dir Academic Support Ctr .... Ms. Beverly FORTNER
39 Dir Resident Housing/Mgr Stdnt Life .... Mr. Jim TUCKER
37 Financial Aid Officer .... Ms. Carlene MORRIS
06 Registrar .... Ms. Lou HARA
07 Director of Admissions .... Ms. Dorothy D. STITES
09 Dir Instl Research/Sponsored Pgms .... Ms. Cynthia GROUNDS
36 Career Development Specialist .... Vacant
38 Director Student Counseling .... Vacant
15 Human Resources Liaison .... Ms. Mona FRANKLIN
96 Acquisitions .... Ms. Janice BEGAY
26 Executive Asst/Public Relations .... Mr. Stephen PRUE
18 Director Facilities Management .... Mr. Lee PAHCODDY, JR.

Heritage College-Wichita (F)

2800 South Rock Road, Wichita KS 67210
Telephone: (316) 681-1615 Identification: 770529
Accreditation: ABHES

† Branch campus of Heritage College, Denver, CO

Hesston College (G)

Box 3000, Hesston KS 67062-2093
County: Harvey FICE Identification: 001920
Unit ID: 155177
Telephone: (620) 327-4221 Carnegie Class: Assoc/HT-High Trad
FAX Number: (620) 327-8300 Calendar System: Semester
URL: www.hesston.edu
Established: 1909 Annual Undergrad Tuition & Fees: $25,234
Enrollment: 428 Coed
Affiliation or Control: Mennonite Church IRS Status: 501(c)3
Highest Offering: Baccalaureate
Accreditation: NH, ADNUR

01 Interim President .... Mr. Ben SPRUNGER
05 Vice Pres of Academics .... Mr. Brent YODER
07 Vice President of Admissions .... Mrs. Rachel S. MILLER
10 Vice Pres Finance & Auxiliary Svcs .... Mr. Mark LANDES
32 Vice Pres of Student Development .... Mr. Rob RAMSEYER
29 Director of Alumni & Church Rels .... Mr. Dallas STUTZMAN
06 Registrar .... Mrs. Angie BROCKMUELLER
21 Business Manager .... Mr. Karl BRUBAKER

Highland Community College (H)

606 W Main, Highland KS 66035-0068
County: Doniphan FICE Identification: 001921
Unit ID: 155186
Telephone: (785) 442-6000 Carnegie Class: Assoc/HVT-High Non
FAX Number: (785) 442-6100 Calendar System: Semester
URL: www.highlandcc.edu
Established: 1858 Annual Undergrad Tuition & Fees (In-District): $3,134
Enrollment: 3,217 Coed
Affiliation or Control: Local IRS Status: 501(c)3
Highest Offering: Associate Degree
Accreditation: NH

01 President .... Mr. David REIST
05 Vice President for Academic Affairs .... Ms. Peggy FORSBERG
32 Vice President for Student Services .... Dr. Cheryl RASMUSSEN
10 Vice Pres for Finance/Operations .... Mr. Daniel ERBERT
88 Director of Technical Education .... Mr. Lucas HUNZIGER
30 Vice Pres Institutional Advancement .... Dr. Craig E. MOSHER
06 Registrar .... Ms. Alice HAMILTON
37 Financial Aid Director .... Mr. Joshua NORTH
13 Director of Information Systems .... Mr. Josh BERRY
09 Director of Institutional Research .... Mr. Jeffrey HURN
38 Director Student Counseling .... Ms. Kristin WOODRUFF
41 Athletic Director .... Mr. Tyler NORDMAN
08 Library Director .... Ms. Penny DONALDSON
18 Supervisor of Buildings & Grounds .... Mr. Rick BLEVINS
26 Chief Public Relations Officer .... Dr. Craig MOSHER
29 Director Alumni Relations .... Dr. Craig MOSHER
35 Director of Student Life .... Vacant
15 Human Resource Manager .... Ms. Eileen C. GRONNIGER
40 Bookstore Coordinator .... Ms. Stephanie HARSHBERGER
07 Director of Admissions .... Ms. Stephanie PETERSON
106 Dir Online Education/E-learning .... Ms. Denise PETERS

Hutchinson Community College (I)

1300 N Plum Street, Hutchinson KS 67501-5894
County: Reno FICE Identification: 001923
Unit ID: 155195
Telephone: (620) 665-3500 Carnegie Class: Assoc/MT-VT-High Non
FAX Number: (620) 665-3310 Calendar System: Semester
URL: www.hutchcc.edu
Established: 1928 Annual Undergrad Tuition & Fees (In-District): $2,848
Enrollment: 5,718 Coed
Affiliation or Control: State/Local IRS Status: 501(c)3
Highest Offering: Associate Degree
Accreditation: NH, ACBSP, ADNUR, CAHIIM, #COARC, EMT, PNUR, PTAA, RAD, SURGT

01 President .... Dr. Carter FILE
05 Vice President of Academic Affairs .... Dr. Cindy HOSS
10 Vice President Finance/Operations .... Ms. Julie BLANTON
103 VP Workforce Development/Outreach .... Mr. Steve PORTER
32 Vice President of Students .... Mr. Brett BRIGHT
26 Director of Marketing & Info .... Mr. Denny STOECKLEIN
13 Director of Data Processing .... Mr. Loren L. MORRIS
06 Registrar .... Mrs. Christina LONG
41 Athletic Director .... Mr. Josh GOOCH
15 Director of Personnel .... Mr. Brooks E. MANTOOTH
37 Financial Aid Officer .... Mr. Nathan BUCHE
07 Director of Admissions .... Mr. Corbin STROBEL
18 Director of Plant Facilities .... Mr. Don ROSE
39 Director of Residence Life .... Ms. Dana HINSHAW
29 Director Alumni Relations .... Mrs. Cindy KEAST
08 Coordinator of Library Services .... Mr. Robert KELLY
09 Coord of Institutional Research .... Mr. Rex CHEEVER

Independence Community College (J)

1057 West College Avenue,
Independence KS 67301-0708
County: Montgomery FICE Identification: 001924
Unit ID: 155201
Telephone: (620) 331-4100 Carnegie Class: Assoc/HVT-High Non
FAX Number: (620) 331-5344 Calendar System: Semester
URL: www.indycc.edu
Established: 1925 Annual Undergrad Tuition & Fees (In-District): $3,376
Enrollment: 945 Coed

Affiliation or Control: State/Local IRS Status: 501(c)3
Highest Offering: Associate Degree
Accreditation: NH

01 President .... Dr. Daniel W. BARWICK
10 Contoller .... Ms. Wendy ISLE
05 VP Academic Affairs .... Vacant
32 VP Student Affairs/Athletics .... Ms. Tammie GELDENHUYS
13 IT Director .... Mr. Eric MONTGOMERY
26 Marketing Director/Instructor .... Mr. Brad HENDERSON
102 Foundation Director .... Ms. Lori SHAW
20 Dean of Instruction .... Mr. David SMITH
06 Registrar .... Ms. Sonja CONLEY
08 Director Library/Lrng Resource Ctr .... Mr. Drew BEISSWENGER
18 Maintenance/Custodial Supervisor .... Ms. Chris MCDIARMID
07 Director of Admissions .... Ms. Brittany THORNTON
37 Financial Aid Director .... Ms. Laura ALLISON
09 Dir of Institutional Research .... Ms. Debbie PHELPS
04 Executive Asst to President .... Ms. Beverly HARRIS
40 Bookstore Manager .... Ms. Teresa VESTAL
88 Upward Bound Program Director .... Ms. Stacia KAYLOR
15 Human Resources Coordinator .... Ms. Keli TUSCHMAN
51 Associate Dean On-line/Cont Educ .... Ms. Kara WHEELER
88 Associate Dean Acad Support Svcs .... Ms. Taylor CRAWSHAW

Johnson County Community College (A)

12345 College Boulevard, Overland Park KS 66210-1299
County: Johnson FICE Identification: 008244
Unit ID: 155210
Telephone: (913) 469-8500 Carnegie Class: Assoc/MT-VT-High Non
FAX Number: (913) 469-2559 Calendar System: Semester
URL: www.jccc.edu
Established: 1969 Annual Undergrad Tuition & Fees (In-District): $2,730
Enrollment: 19,429 Coed
Affiliation or Control: State/Local IRS Status: 501(c)3
Highest Offering: Associate Degree
Accreditation: NH, ACBSP, ACFEI, ADNUR, COARC, DH, EMT, IFSAC

01 President .... Dr. Joe SOPCICH
10 Exec Vice Pres Finance & Admin Svcs .... Dr. Barbara LARSON
05 Exec VP Instruction/Operations .... Dr. Judy KORB
11 Exec VP Administrative Services .... Ms. Barbara LARSON
32 Vice Pres Student Success/Engagemnt .... Dr. Randy WEBER
13 Vice President Information Services .... Mr. Tom PAGANO
20 Vice Pres Instruction/CAO .... Dr. Mickey MCCLOUD
04 Exec Asst to the President & Board .... Ms. Terri SCHLICHT
21 AVP Financial Services .... Ms. Rachel LIERZ
18 AVP Campus Services .... Mr. Rex HAYS
96 AVP Business Services .... Mr. Mitch BORCHERS
31 AVP College & Community Relations .... Vacant
50 Dean Business & Technology .... Mr. Mike WEST
14 Director Admin Computing Services .... Ms. Sandra WARNER
26 Exec Dir Mktg/Communications .... Mr. Chris GRAY
35 Dean Student Success .... Mr. Paul KYLE
41 Asst Dean Athletics .... Mr. Carl HEINRICH
84 Asst Dean Enrollment Management .... Ms. MargE SHELLEY
35 Asst Dean Student Life/Ldrshp Dev .... Ms. Pam VASSAR
37 Director Student Financial Aid .... Ms. Christal WILLIAMS
36 Director Testing and Assessment .... Ms. Mary Ann DICKERSON
06 Registrar .... Ms. Leslie QUINN
08 Director Library Services .... Mr. Mark DAGANAAR
07 Director of Admissions .... Mr. Peter BELK
92 Program Facilitator Honors .... Ms. Anna PAGE
09 Director of Institutional Research .... Ms. Natalie ALLEMAN-BEYERS
38 Dean Learner Engagement & Success .... Mr. Richard MOEHRING

Kansas Christian College (B)

7401 Metcalf, Overland Park KS 66204-1995
County: Johnson Identification: 667134
Telephone: (913) 722-0272 Carnegie Class: Not Classified
FAX Number: (913) 403-0595 Calendar System: Semester
URL: www.kansaschristian.edu
Established: 1938 Annual Undergrad Tuition & Fees: N/A
Enrollment: N/A Coed
Affiliation or Control: Independent Non-Profit IRS Status: 501(c)3
Highest Offering: Baccalaureate
Accreditation: @BI

01 President .... Mr. Delbert L. SCOTT
05 VP Academic Affairs/CAO .... Ms. Dorothy PURTLE
10 Chief Business Officer .... Mr. Bill LEE
06 Registrar .... Mr. Christopher SUMPTER
08 Head Librarian .... Ms. Dorie SCOFIELD

Kansas City Kansas Community College (C)

7250 State Avenue, Kansas City KS 66112-3003
County: Wyandotte FICE Identification: 001925
Unit ID: 155292
Telephone: (913) 334-1100 Carnegie Class: Assoc/HVT-Mix Trad/Non
FAX Number: (913) 288-7609 Calendar System: Semester
URL: www.kckcc.edu
Established: 1923 Annual Undergrad Tuition & Fees (In-District): $3,240
Enrollment: 6,198 Coed
Affiliation or Control: State/Local IRS Status: 501(c)3
Highest Offering: Associate Degree
Accreditation: NH, ACBSP, ADNUR, COARC, EMT, FUSER, MAC, PTAA

01 President .... Dr. Doris F. GIVENS
10 Chief Financial Ofc/Chief Oper Ofc .... Dr. Susan LINDAHL
05 VP Academic Affairs & Student Svcs .... Dr. Michael VITALE
81 Dean Math/Sci/CompTech/Bus/CEB .... Dr. Edward KREMER
84 Interim Dean Enrollment Management .... Dr. Michael BURNS
36 Dean Academic Workforce Programs .... Ms. Leota MARKS
103 Director of Workforce Development .... Ms. Marisa GRAY
88 Director of Entrepreneurship .... Ms. Alicia HOOKS
79 Dean Arts/Humanities/Social Science .... Dr. Cherilee WALKER
13 VP Information Services .... Mr. Baz ABOUELENEIN
09 Dean Institutional Services .... Dr. Sangki MIN
66 Dean Nursing/Allied Health .... Dr. Tiffany BOHM
32 Dean of Student Services .... Dr. Jonathan LONG
75 Dean Technical Operations .... Mr. Cliff SMITH
88 Exec Director Leavenworth Center .... Vacant
88 Director of Academic Resource Ctr .... Dr. Michael BURNS
41 Director of Athletics .... Mr. Anthony (Tony) TOMPKINS
40 Director of Bookstore Operations .... Vacant
18 Director of Buildings/Grounds .... Mr. Jeff SIXTA
19 Director of Campus Police .... Mr. Greg SCHNEIDER
14 Director of Computing .... Mr. James BENNETT
51 Director of Cont Educ & Cmty Svcs .... Ms. Rosemary L. LISCHKA
38 Director of Student Advising .... Mr. Shawn DERRITT
88 Director Counseling-Advocacy Ctr .... Ms. Linda WARNER
37 Director of Financial Aid .... Ms. Mary I. DORR
21 Director of Financial Records .... Ms. Marie BRANSTETTER
92 Director of Honors/Phi Theta Kappa .... Dr. Stacy TUCKER
28 Director of Intercultural Center .... Ms. Barbara CLARK-EVANS
08 Director of Library .... Vacant
24 Director Media Services Technology .... Mr. Randy ROYER
106 Director of Online Services .... Ms. Susan STUART
35 Director of Student Activities .... Ms. Andrica WILCOXEN
07 Director of Admissions .... Ms. Tami A. BARTUNEK
06 Registrar .... Ms. Theresa HOLLIDAY
15 Director Human Resources .... Mr. Alfonso ZARATE
88 Director Forensic Laboratory .... Ms. D.C BROIL
88 Director Wellness Center .... Mr. Rob M. CRANE
103 Director of Cultural Outreach .... Mr. Brian PATRICK
66 Director Nursing .... Dr. Tiffany BOHM
66 Director Practical Nursing .... Ms. Susan K. WHITE
88 Assistant Director Student Develop .... Ms. Tamara D. MILLER
88 Director Technical Programs .... Mr. Richard PIPER
88 Director Technical Programs Perkins .... Ms. Donna S. SHAWN
88 Asst Director Academic Resources .... Ms. Amanda WILLIAMS
88 Director Performing Arts Center .... Dr. Cherilee WALKER
04 Administrative Asst to President .... Ms. Peggy L. FRIEDMANN
105 Director Web Services .... Mr. Matthew FOWLER
22 Dir Affirmative Action/EEO .... Ms. Leota MARKS
39 Director Student Housing .... Dr. Jonathan LONG
43 Dir Legal Services/General Counsel .... Vacant
102 Dir Foundation/Corporate Relations .... Mr. Lacy WARD

Kansas State University (D)

919 Mid-Campus Drive North, Manhattan KS 66506
County: Riley FICE Identification: 001928
Unit ID: 155399
Telephone: (785) 532-6250 Carnegie Class: DU-Highest
FAX Number: (785) 532-2120 Calendar System: Semester
URL: www.k-state.edu
Established: 1863 Annual Undergrad Tuition & Fees (In-State): $9,350
Enrollment: 24,766 Coed
Affiliation or Control: State IRS Status: 501(c)3
Highest Offering: Doctorate
Accreditation: NH, ART, BUS, BUSA, CAATE, CACREP, CEA, CIDA, CONST, CS, DIETC, DIETD, ENG, IPSY, JOUR, LSAR, MFCD, MUS, NRPA, PH, PLNG, SP, SPAA, SW, TED, THEA, VET

01 Interim President .... Mr. Richard B. MYERS
04 Exec Asst to the President .... Ms. Dana M. HASTINGS
05 Provost and Senior Vice President .... Dr. April C. MASON
10 VP Admin & Finance .... Ms. Cindy A. BONTRAGER
46 VP for Research .... Dr. Peter K. DORHOUT
32 VP Student Life/Dean of Students .... Dr. Pat J. BOSCO
26 VP for Communications & Marketing .... Mr. Jeffery B. MORRIS
15 VP Human Capital .... Ms. Cheryl L. JOHNSON
102 President/CEO of Foundation .... Mr. Greg WILLEMS
29 Alumni Association President .... Ms. Amy Button RENZ
41 Athletic Director .... Mr. John CURRIE
31 Chief of Staff/Dir Community Rels .... Dr. Jackie L. HARTMAN
86 Dir for Governmental Relations .... Dr. Susan K. PETERSON
88 Exec Dir Military/Veterans Affairs .... Mr. Arthur S. DE GROAT
43 General Counsel .... Ms. Cheryl G. STRECKER
20 Senior Vice Provost .... Dr. Ruth DYER
13 Interim Vice Provost Info Tech Svcs .... Mr. Rob CAFFEY
108 Assoc Prov Institutional Effectiv .... Dr. Brian A. NIEHOFF
28 Interim Assoc Prov for Diversity .... Dr. Zelia Z. WILEY
09 Director Planning & Analysis .... Ms. Kelli S. COX
08 Dean of Libraries .... Dr. Lori A. GOETSCH
47 Dean of Agriculture .... Dr. John FLOROS
48 Dean Architecture/Planning/Design .... Mr. Timothy DE NOBLE
49 Interim Dean of Arts & Sciences .... Dr. Amitabha CHAKRABARTI
50 Dean of Business Admin .... Dr. Kevin P. GWINNER
51 Dean of Continuing Education .... Dr. Sue C. MAES
53 Dean of Education .... Dr. Debbie K. MERCER
54 Dean of Engineering .... Dr. Darren M. DAWSON
58 Dean of Graduate School .... Dr. Carol SHANKLIN
59 Dean of Human Ecology .... Dr. John B. BUCKWALTER
72 CEO/Dean of Technology & Aviation .... Dr. Verna M. FITZSIMMONS
74 Dean of Veterinary Medicine .... Dr. Tammy R. BECKHAM
12 Interim CEO K-State Olathe .... Dr. Ralph C. RICHARDSON
56 Dir Research and Extension .... Dr. John FLOROS
18 Assoc VP Facilities Planning/Mgmt .... Mr. Ryan F. SWANSON
21 Asst VP for Budget Planning .... Mr. Ethan E. ERICKSON
19 Asst VP Univ Police & Public Safety .... Mr. Ronnie D. GRICE
96 Director of Purchasing .... Ms. Carla BISHOP
07 Assoc VP/Director of Admissions .... Mr. Lawrence E. MOEDER
06 Registrar .... Dr. Monty E. NIELSEN
37 Assoc VP/Dir Student Fin Assist .... Mr. Lawrence E. MOEDER
39 Asst VP/Dir Housing & Dining Svcs .... Mr. Derek A. JACKSON
36 Exec Dir Career & Employment Svcs .... Ms. Kerri D. KELLER

Kansas State University Polytechnic, College of Technology and Aviation (E)

2310 Centennial Road, Salina KS 67401-8196
Telephone: (785) 826-2601 FICE Identification: 004611
Accreditation: &NH, AAB, ENGT

† Regional accreditation is carried under the parent institution in Manhattan, KS.

Kansas Wesleyan University (F)

100 E Claflin Avenue, Salina KS 67401-6196
County: Saline FICE Identification: 001929
Unit ID: 155414
Telephone: (785) 827-5541 Carnegie Class: Bac-Diverse
FAX Number: (785) 827-0927 Calendar System: Semester
URL: www.kwu.edu
Established: 1886 Annual Undergrad Tuition & Fees: $26,600
Enrollment: 710 Coed
Affiliation or Control: United Methodist IRS Status: 501(c)3
Highest Offering: Master's
Accreditation: NH

01 President and CEO .... Dr. Matthew R. THOMPSON
04 Executive Assistant to President .... Ms. Jan M. SHIRK
03 Executive Vice President .... Vacant
10 Vice Pres Finance/Administration .... Mr. Wayne R. SCHNEIDER
21 Controller/Business Officer .... Mr. John W. COYKENDALL
84 Vice Pres Enrollment Management .... Dr. Mark A. BANDRE
37 Director Student Financial Planning .... Mrs. Lois MADSEN
06 Interim Registrar .... Mrs. Karissa L. SWENSON
07 Director of Admissions .... Mr. Esteban PAREDES
05 Interim Provost .... Dr. Bill BACKLIN
20 Interim Assistant Provost .... Dr. Damon KRAFT
88 Admin Assistant to EVP/Provost .... Ms. Kristan HERNANDEZ
30 Vice Pres Institutional Advancement .... Mrs. Melanie B. OVERTON
29 Director of Alumni Relations .... Mr. Bryan L. MCCULLAR
26 Sr Dir Advancement & Communications .... Mrs. Paula HERMANN
27 Dir of Marketing & Communications .... Mr. John ELMORE
32 Exec Director Student Development .... Ms. Bridget R. WEISER
36 Career Planning & Exper Educ Spec .... Vacant
39 Director of Residence Life .... Mr. Nate THIES
38 Dir Student Success/Testing Center .... Mrs. Jennifer BARRETT
88 Dir of Spiritual Development .... Vacant
08 Director of Library Svcs .... Ms. Ruth MIRTZ
24 Production Manager .... Mr. Paul GREEN
13 Director of Information Systems .... Mr. Jay C. KROB
19 Director of Emergency Management .... Dr. Lonnie BOOKER
18 Director of Plant Operations .... Mr. Darrell D. VICTORY
40 Manager Yotee's Bookstore .... Mr. Steve G. CARRIER
42 Chaplain Univ United Meth Church .... Vacant
41 Athletic Director .... Mr. Michael HERMANN
58 Director of MBA Program .... Dr. Damon KRAFT
66 Division Nursing Education Chair .... Dr. Debra LOGAN
53 Director of Teacher Education .... Dr. Kristine RODRIGUEZ
79 Division Chair Humanities .... Dr. Michael RUSSELL
49 Div Chair Applied Art & Sciences .... Prof. Bryan K. MINNICH
83 Division Chair Social Sciences .... Dr. Paul HEDLUND
57 Division Chair Fine Arts .... Prof. Barbara J. NICKELL
81 Division of Natural Sciences Chair .... Dr. Stephanie WELTER
15 Human Resources Director .... Mr. Frank ROTH

Labette Community College (G)

200 S 14th, Parsons KS 67357-4299
County: Labette FICE Identification: 001930
Unit ID: 155450
Telephone: (620) 421-6700 Carnegie Class: Assoc/MT-VT-High Non
FAX Number: (620) 421-0921 Calendar System: Semester
URL: www.labette.edu
Established: 1923 Annual Undergrad Tuition & Fees (In-District): $2,670
Enrollment: 1,891 Coed
Affiliation or Control: Local IRS Status: 501(c)3
Highest Offering: Associate Degree
Accreditation: NH, ADNUR, COARC, DA, DMS, PTAA, RAD

01 President .... Dr. George C. KNOX
04 Executive Assistant to President .... Ms. Megan A. FUGATE
05 Vice President Academic Affairs .... Mr. Joe BURKE
10 Vice President Finance & Operations .... Ms. Leanna J. DOHERTY
32 Vice President Student Affairs .... Ms. Tammy FUENTEZ
84 Assoc Dean Enrollment Mgmt .... Ms. Kathy JOHNSTON
20 Dean of Instruction .... Mr. Mark WATKINS
13 Director of Information Technology .... Mrs. Jody BURZINSKI
30 Dir Resource Devel/Alumni Rels .... Mrs. Lindi D. FORBES
08 Director of Library Services .... Mr. Scott M. ZOLLARS
18 Director of Physical Plant .... Mr. Kevin DOHERTY
66 Director of Nursing .... Mrs. Delyna BOHNENBLUST
41 Athletic Director .... Mr. Aaron J. KEAL
26 Director of Public Relations .... Mrs. Bethany KENDRICK
06 Registrar/Dir Student Financial Aid .... Ms. Kathy JOHNSTON

15 Director of Human Relations .... Ms. Janice S. GEORGE
37 Director Student Financial Aid .... Ms. Kathy JOHNSTON
35 Student Life Coordinator .... Mrs. Melissa NANCE
40 Bookstore Specialist .... Mrs. Lois D. HEMBREE

Manhattan Area Technical College (A)

3136 Dickens Avenue, Manhattan KS 66503-2499
County: Riley　FICE Identification: 005500
Unit ID: 155487
Telephone: (785) 587-2800　Carnegie Class: Assoc/HVT-High Non
FAX Number: (785) 587-2804　Calendar System: Semester
URL: www.manhattantech.edu
Established: 1965　Annual Undergrad Tuition & Fees (In-District): $4,900
Enrollment: 766　Coed
Affiliation or Control: State/Local　IRS Status: 501(c)3
Highest Offering: Associate Degree
Accreditation: NH, ADNUR, DH, MLTAD

01 President/CEO ....Dr. Jim J. GENANDT
05 Vice Pres of Instructional Affairs .... Ms. Marilyn MAHAN
10 Vice President of Business Services ...... Mr. Keith ZACHARIASEN
32 Vice President of Student Services .... Ms. Sarah PHILLIPS
30 Assoc VP Institutional Advancement ....Dr. Richard FOGG
21 Chief Financial Officer ....Ms. Carmela JACOBS
13 Chief Information Officer ....Mr. Josh GFELLER
06 Registrar ....Ms. Rachel SHERLEY
15 Director Human Resources ....Ms. Trysta WILLIAMS
07 Director of Admissions ....Mr. Neil ROSS
37 Director Financial Aid .... Ms. Laura WEISS-COOK

Manhattan Christian College (B)

1415 Anderson, Manhattan KS 66502-4081
County: Riley　FICE Identification: 001931
Unit ID: 155496
Telephone: (785) 539-3571　Carnegie Class: Spec-4-yr-Faith
FAX Number: (785) 539-0832　Calendar System: Semester
URL: www.mccks.edu
Established: 1927　Annual Undergrad Tuition & Fees: $14,290
Enrollment: 311　Coed
Affiliation or Control: Christian Churches And Churches of Christ
IRS Status: 501(c)3
Highest Offering: Baccalaureate
Accreditation: NH, BI

01 President ....Mr. J. Kevin INGRAM
05 Int Vice President Academic Affairs .... Dr. Greg DELORT
10 Vice President Business Affairs ....Ms. Lori J. STANFIELD
32 Vice President Student Life ....Dr. Rick L. WRIGHT
06 Registrar ....Mr. Jeff DAVIS
30 Director Institutional Advancement ....Mrs. Jolene K. RUPE
08 Director of Library Services ....Mrs. Mary Ann BUHLER
41 Athletic Director ....Mr. Shawn M. CONDRA
29 Alumni Relations Director .... Mrs. Genae DENVER
04 Admin Asst to President ....Ms. Shalin KLEIN
07 Director of Admissions ....Mr. Nick BROWN
37 Financial Aid Counselor ....Ms. Jenna KECK

McPherson College (C)

1600 E Euclid, PO Box 1402, McPherson KS 67460-1402
County: McPherson　FICE Identification: 001933
Unit ID: 155511
Telephone: (620) 242-0400　Carnegie Class: Bac-Diverse
FAX Number: (620) 241-8443　Calendar System: 4/1/4
URL: www.mcpherson.edu
Established: 1887　Annual Undergrad Tuition & Fees: $25,236
Enrollment: 659　Coed
Affiliation or Control: Church Of The Brethren　IRS Status: 501(c)3
Highest Offering: Master's
Accreditation: NH, TED

01 President ....Mr. Michael P. SCHNEIDER
05 Provost/VP Academic Affairs .... Dr. Bruce CLARY
30 Vice President for Advancement ....Mr. Steve GUSTAFSON
10 Vice President for Finance ....Mr. Rick TUXHORN
84 Vice Pres Enrollment Management ....Ms. Christi HOPKINS
100 Chief of Staff ....Ms. Abby ARCHER-RIERSON
32 Assoc Dean of Students/Student Life ....Mr. Ben COFFEY
41 Athletic Director ....Mr. Doug QUINT
06 Registrar ....Ms. Tricia HARTSHORN
37 Director Financial Aid/Admissions ....Ms. Sara BRUBAKER
08 Director of Library Services ....Ms. Mary HESTER
29 Director Alumni Relations ....Mrs. Karlene TYLER

MidAmerica Nazarene University (D)

2030 E College Way, Olathe KS 66062-1899
County: Johnson　FICE Identification: 007032
Unit ID: 155520
Telephone: (913) 782-3750　Carnegie Class: Masters/M
FAX Number: (913) 971-3290　Calendar System: Semester
URL: www.mnu.edu
Established: 1966　Annual Undergrad Tuition & Fees: $26,150
Enrollment: 1,870　Coed
Affiliation or Control: Church Of The Nazarene　IRS Status: 501(c)3
Highest Offering: Master's
Accreditation: NH, ACBSP, #CAATE, CACREP, MUS, NURSE, TED

01 President ....Dr. David J. SPITTAL
05 Provost and Chief Academic Officer ....Dr. Mary JONES
10 Interim Vice President Finance ....Mr. Michael B. STOWELL
30 Vice Pres University Advancement ....Mr. Jon D. NORTH
32 VP Student Development ....Mrs. Kristi KEETON
42 University Chaplain ....Mr. Brady J. BRAATZ
58 Vice Provost/Dean SPGS ....Dr. Mark C. FORD
13 Associate VP for Instructional Tech .... Dr. Martin CROSSLAND
84 Assoc VP Enrollment Management ....Mr. Darcy EBERT
09 Dir Institutional Effectiveness ....Mrs. Patricia J. WALSH
66 Dean Sch Nursing/Health Sci ....Dr. Karen D. WIEGMAN
50 Dean School of Business ....Mrs. Jamie MYRTLE
83 Dean Sch Behav Sci/Counseling ....Dr. Todd FRYE
49 Dean College of Arts & Sciences ....Dr. Nancy DAMRON
06 Registrar ....Mr. James R. GARRISON
08 Director Library ....Mr. Bruce FLANDERS
30 Assoc VP University Advancement ....Mr. Tim KEETON
29 Director of Alumni Relations ....Mr. Kevin S. GARBER
37 Director of Student Financial Svcs ......Mr. Cathy L. COLAPIETRO
41 Athletic Director ....Mr. Kevin L. STEELE
15 Director of Human Resources ....Mrs. Nancy S. MERIMEE
26 Director of Marketing ....Mrs. Kimberly CAMPBELL
18 Director of Facility Services ....Mr. Jon N. SPENCE
40 Director MERC/Postmaster ....Mr. Nikos KELLEPOURIS
19 Director of Campus Safety ....Mr. Richard M. PACHECO
90 Associate VP Academic/Prof Success ....Dr. Richard HANSEN

National American University-Overland Park (E)

10310 Mastin Street, Overland Park KS 66212
Telephone: (913) 981-8700　Identification: 770394
Accreditation: &NH, MAC

† Regional accreditation is carried under the parent institution in Rapid City, SD

National American University-Wichita (F)

7309 E 21st Street, Suite G40, Wichita KS 67206
Telephone: (316) 448-5400　Identification: 770395
Accreditation: &NH, MAC

† Regional accreditation is carried under the parent institution in Rapid City, SD

National American University-Wichita West (G)

8428 W 13th Street N, Suite 120, Wichita KS 67212
Telephone: (316) 448-3150　Identification: 770396
Accreditation: &NH

† Regional accreditation is carried under the parent institution in Rapid City, SD

Neosho County Community College (H)

800 W 14th Street, Chanute KS 66720-2699
County: Neosho　FICE Identification: 001936
Unit ID: 155566
Telephone: (620) 431-2820　Carnegie Class: Assoc/HVT-High Non
FAX Number: (620) 431-0082　Calendar System: Semester
URL: www.neosho.edu
Established: 1935　Annual Undergrad Tuition & Fees (In-District): $4,352
Enrollment: 2,212　Coed
Affiliation or Control: Local　IRS Status: 501(c)3
Highest Offering: Associate Degree
Accreditation: NH, ACBSP, ADNUR, CAHIIM, OTA, SURGT

01 President ....Dr. Brian L. INBODY
05 Vice President Student Learning ....Ms. Sarah ROBB
11 Vice President for Operations ....Mr. Benjamin J. SMITH
10 Chief Financial Officer ....Ms. Sondra K. SOLANDER
103 Dean Outreach/Workforce Development ..... Ms. Brenda L. KRUMM
12 Dean Ottawa Campus ....Vacant
32 Dean of Student Services ....Ms. Kerrie COOMES
15 Director of Human Resources ....Ms. Karin JACOBSON
106 Dean for Ottawa & Online Campuses ....Ms. Marie GARDNER
13 Dean for Operations/CIO ....Mr. Kerry D. RAMABARGAR
30 Director of Development/Alumni
Rels ....Ms. Claudia CHRISTIANSEN
08 Coordinator of Library Services ....Mr. Todd KNISPEL
37 Director Student Financial Aid ....Ms. Jennifer DAISY
66 Director of Nursing ....Ms. Pamela COVAULT
105 Dir of Tech Services/Webmaster ....Mr. Jon SEIBERT
46 Director of Assessment/Research ....Mr. Ethan SMILIE
41 Athletic Director ....Mr. Mike SADDLER
85 Dir International Student Services ....Ms. Sarah CADWALLADER
06 Registrar ....Ms. Amy MORRIS
09 Coordinator/Institutional Research ....Ms. LuAnn HAUSER
40 Chanute Bookstore Coordinator ....Ms. Kara HALE
40 Ottawa Bookstore Coordinator ....Ms. Julie VINEYARD
26 Advertising/Media Coordinator ....Ms. Nancy ISAAC
39 Director of Residence/Student Life .... Ms. Allison OUELLETTE
04 AA to the President/Board Clerk ....Ms. Denise GILMORE
18 Director of Facilities ....Mr. Kyle SEUFERT
07 Director of Admissions ....Ms. Tristan JONES

Newman University (I)

3100 McCormick, Wichita KS 67213-2097
County: Sedgwick　FICE Identification: 001939
Unit ID: 155335
Telephone: (316) 942-4291　Carnegie Class: Masters/M
FAX Number: (316) 942-4483　Calendar System: Semester
URL: www.newmanu.edu
Established: 1933　Annual Undergrad Tuition & Fees: $26,030
Enrollment: 3,687　Coed
Affiliation or Control: Roman Catholic　IRS Status: 501(c)3
Highest Offering: Master's
Accreditation: NH, ANEST, COARC, NURSE, OTA, RAD, SW, TED

01 President ....Dr. Noreen CARROCCI
04 Exec Assistant to the President ....Ms. Tracy MCGAREY
05 Provost & Vice Pres Acad
Affairs ....Dr. Kimberly MCDOWALL LONG
30 Vice Pres University Advancement ....Mr. J.V JOHNSTON
10 Vice Pres Finance/Administration ....Ms. Jennifer GANTZ
32 VP Student Affairs/Dir Athletics ....Mr. Victor TRILLI
84 Vice Pres Enrollment Management ....Mr. Norm JONES
20 Assoc VP Acad Svcs/Student Dev .... Ms. Rosemary NIEDENS
42 Director of Campus Ministry ....Fr. John FOGLIASSO
29 Director of Alumni Relations ....Vacant
09 Director of Institutional Research ....Dr. Lori STEINER
08 Library Director ....Mr. Steve HAMERSKY
06 Registrar ....Ms. Shirley RUEB
37 Director of Financial Aid .... Ms. Myra PFANNENSTIEL
40 Director of Bookstore ....Mr. Larry WILLIAMS
13 Chief Information Officer ....Mr. Icer VAUGHAN
19 Director of Security ....Mr. Morris FLOYD
21 Controller ....Ms. Diana GRIBLIN
35 Dean of Students ....Mr. Levi ESSES
58 Dean College of Grad/Cont Studies ....Fr. Joseph GILE
49 Dean College of Undergrad Studies ....Dr. David SHUBERT
50 Dean School of Business ....Dr. Brett ANDREWS
104 Director Study Abroad ....Dr. Cheryl GOLDEN
18 Chief Facilities/Physical Plant .... Mr. Bruce SANDERSON
26 Chief Public Relations/Marketing .... Mr. Clark SCHAFER

North Central Kansas Technical College (J)

PO Box 507, Beloit KS 67420-0507
County: Mitchell　FICE Identification: 005265
Unit ID: 155593
Telephone: (785) 738-2276　Carnegie Class: Assoc/HVT-High Non
FAX Number: (785) 738-2903　Calendar System: Semester
URL: www.ncktc.edu
Established: 1964　Annual Undergrad Tuition & Fees (In-District): $5,180
Enrollment: 819　Coed
Affiliation or Control: State/Local　IRS Status: 501(c)3
Highest Offering: Associate Degree
Accreditation: NH, ADNUR

01 President ....Mr. Eric BURKS
05 Dean of Instruction ....Mr. Corey ISBELL
11 Dean of Administrative Services .... Mrs. Brandi ZIMMER
12 Dean of Hays Campus .... Mrs. Sandy GOTTSCHALK
06 Registrar ....Mrs. Judy HEIDRICK
09 Coordinator Institutional Research ....Mrs. Jennifer BROWN
32 Dean of Student Services ....Ms. Angel PRESCOTT
37 Director Student Financial Aid ....Mr. Gary ODLE
04 Administrative Asst to President ....Ms. Bobette ROESTI
102 Dir Foundation/Marketing ....Ms. Nicole RAINEY
101 Secretary of the Institution/Board ....Ms. Bobette ROESTI
13 Chief Info Technology Officer (CIO) ....Mr. Ian DRAEMEL

North Central Kansas Technical College (K)

2205 Wheatland Avenue, Hays KS 67601
Telephone: (785) 625-2437　Identification: 770259
Accreditation: &NH

† Regional accreditation is carried under the parent institution in Beloit, KS

Northwest Kansas Technical College (L)

1209 Harrison Street, PO Box 668,
Goodland KS 67735-3441
County: Sherman　FICE Identification: 005267
Unit ID: 155618
Telephone: (785) 890-3641　Carnegie Class: Assoc/HVT-Mix Trad/Non
FAX Number: (785) 899-5711　Calendar System: Semester
URL: www.nwktc.edu
Established: 1964　Annual Undergrad Tuition & Fees (In-District): N/A
Enrollment: 647　Coed
Affiliation or Control: State/Local　IRS Status: 501(c)3
Highest Offering: Associate Degree
Accreditation: NH, COARC, MAC

01 President ....Dr. Ben SCHEARS
05 Vice Pres Academic/Student Affairs ......Ms. Brenda L. CHATFIELD
20 Asst Vice Pres Academic Affairs ....Mr. Scott SEARCY
10 Chief Financial Officer ....Ms. Sherri KNITIG
13 Chief Information Officer ....Mr. Brad BERGSMA
06 Registrar ....Ms. Sylvia SHORES

Ottawa University (M)

1001 S Cedar Street, Ottawa KS 66067-3399
County: Franklin　FICE Identification: 001937
Unit ID: 155627
Telephone: (785) 242-5200　Carnegie Class: Bac-Diverse
FAX Number: (785) 229-1020　Calendar System: Semester
URL: www.ottawa.edu
Established: 1865　Annual Undergrad Tuition & Fees: $26,204
Enrollment: 618　Coed

Affiliation or Control: American Baptist IRS Status: 501(c)3
Highest Offering: Master's
Accreditation: NH, ACBSP, NURSE, TED

01 President ... Mr. Kevin EICHNER
05 Exec VP & University Provost ... Dr. Terry HAINES
76 Dean of Health Sciences ... Dr. Dennis TYNER
10 Exec VP & Chief Financial Officer ... Mr. J. Clark RIBORDY
26 VP & Chief Marketing Officer ... Ms. Nancy WINGER
30 Vice Pres University Advancement ... Mr. Paul BEAN
32 Dean Student Affairs ... Mr. Tom TALDO
07 Director of Admissions ... Mr. Andy STILES
06 University Registrar ... Ms. Karen ADAMS
21 Director Finance/Controller ... Ms. Noelle TESTA
21 Director Business Operations ... Mr. Thomas CORLEY
15 Director Human Resources ... Ms. Joanna WALTERS
37 Director Financial Aid ... Mr. Howard FISCHER
29 Director Alumni Programs ... Ms. Janice TRIGG
08 Director Library Services ... Ms. Gloria CREED-DIKEOGU
41 Director Athletics ... Ms. Arabie CONNER
18 Chief Facilities/Physical Plant ... Mr. Herb ORR
04 Executive Assistant to President ... Ms. Gaynia MENNINGER
11 Chief Operations Officer ... Mr. Keith JOHNSON
20 Dean of Instruction ... Dr. Teresa KELLEY
53 Dean School of Education ... Dr. Amy HOGAN
84 Director of Enrollment Management ... Ms. Lydia MATLOCK
50 Dean Angell Snyder Sch of Business ... Dr. Orville BLACKMAN
49 Dean School of Arts & Sciences ... Dr. Beverly RODGERS
86 Director Govt/Reg & Legal Affairs ... Ms. Carrie STEVENS

† The Online division is included in the institution's enrollment count.

Ottawa University Kansas City (A)

4370 W. 109th Street, Suite 200,
Overland Park KS 66211-1302
Telephone: (913) 266-8600 Identification: 666083
Accreditation: &NH

† Regional accreditation is carried under the parent institution in Ottawa, KS.

Pinnacle Career Institute (B)

1601 W. 23rd Street, Ste 200, Lawrence KS 66046
County: Douglas FICE Identification: 026130
Unit ID: 367097
Telephone: (785) 841-9640 Carnegie Class: Spec 2-yr-Health
FAX Number: (785) 841-4854 Calendar System: Quarter
URL: www.pcitraining.edu
Established: 1953 Annual Undergrad Tuition & Fees: N/A
Enrollment: 113 Coed
Affiliation or Control: Proprietary IRS Status: Proprietary
Highest Offering: Associate Degree
Accreditation: ACICS

01 Executive Director ... Ms. Colleen SCHNEIDER

Pittsburg State University (C)

1701 S Broadway, Pittsburg KS 66762-7500
County: Crawford FICE Identification: 001926
Unit ID: 155681
Telephone: (620) 231-7000 Carnegie Class: Masters/L
FAX Number: (620) 235-4080 Calendar System: Semester
URL: www.pittstate.edu
Established: 1903 Annual Undergrad Tuition & Fees (In-State): $6,508
Enrollment: 7,479 Coed
Affiliation or Control: State IRS Status: 501(c)3
Highest Offering: Doctorate
Accreditation: NH, BUS, CACREP, CEA, ENGR, ENGT, MUS, NRPA, NURSE, SW, TED

01 President ... Dr. Steven A. SCOTT
05 Provost & VP for Academic Affairs ... Dr. Lynette OLSON
11 VP Administration & Finance ... Mr. John D. PATTERSON
30 VP University Advancement ... Ms. Kathleen FLANNERY
06 Registrar ... Ms. Debbie GREVE
32 VP Student Life ... Dr. Steve ERWIN
88 Assoc VP for Communication & Mktg ... Mr. Chris KELLY
84 Assoc VP Enroll Mgmt/Stdnt Success ... Mr. Lee YOUNG
51 Dean Graduate & Continuing Studies ... Dr. Pawan KAHOL
49 Interim Dean of Arts & Sciences ... Dr. Mary Carol POMATTO
50 Dean of Business ... Dr. Paul GRIMES
53 Dean of Education ... Dr. Howard W. SMITH
72 Dean of Technology ... Dr. Tim DAWSEY
08 Dean of Library Services ... Mr. Randy ROBERTS
108 Director of Assessment ... Ms. Nora HATTON
26 Director of Media Relations ... Mr. Ron WOMBLE
29 Dir Alumni Rels/Constituent Svcs ... Mr. Jon A. BARTLOW
13 Chief Information Officer ... Ms. Angela NERIA
15 Director Human Resource Svcs/Budget ... Dr. Michele D. SEXTON
85 Director of International Affairs ... Dr. Cathy L. ARCUINO
04 Dir of Community & Govt Relations ... Dr. Shawn NACCARATO
18 Director of Trades & Landscape Svcs ... Mr. Tom AMERSHEK
18 Director Gen & Custodial Services ... Mr. Tim SENECAUT
19 Director of University Police ... Mr. Mike MCCRACKEN
22 Director of Institutional Equity ... Ms. Cindy JOHNSON
37 Director of Financial Aid ... Ms. Tammy HIGGINS
41 Direct of Intercollegiate Athletics ... Mr. Jim JOHNSON
07 Director of Admissions ... Ms. Melinda A. ROELFS
36 Director Career Services ... Ms. Mindy E. CLONINGER
09 Director of Institutional Research ... Dr. Dai LI
38 Dir University Counseling Services ... Dr. Steven MAYHEW
96 Director of Purchasing ... Mr. Jim HUGHES
28 Director of Diversity ... Ms. Deatrea ROSE
10 Controller ... Ms. Barbara J. WINTER
39 Director of University Housing ... Ms. Connie D. MALLE
88 Exec Dir Innovation & Bus Dev ... Dr. Shawn NACCARATO

Pratt Community College (D)

348 NE SR 61, Pratt KS 67124-8432
County: Pratt FICE Identification: 001938
Unit ID: 155715
Telephone: (620) 672-5641 Carnegie Class: Assoc/HVT-High Non
FAX Number: (620) 672-5288 Calendar System: Semester
URL: www.prattcc.edu
Established: 1938 Annual Undergrad Tuition & Fees (In-District): $3,168
Enrollment: 1,383 Coed
Affiliation or Control: State/Local IRS Status: 501(c)3
Highest Offering: Associate Degree
Accreditation: NH, ACBSP

01 President ... Dr. Mike CALVERT
05 Vice President Instruction ... Dr. Michael FITZPATRICK
10 Vice President Finance/Operations ... Mr. Kent ADAMS
84 Vice Pres Student Enroll Management ... Ms. Lisa MILLER
30 Vice Pres of Inst Advancement ... Mr. Kurt MCAFEE
41 Director of Athletics ... Mr. Bill WILSON
07 Director of Admissions ... Ms. Jackie MUNDT
06 Registrar ... Ms. Erin LACIO
13 Director of Information Technology ... Mr. Jerry SANKO
37 Director of Financial Aid ... Ms. Alicia NOVOTNY
08 Dir Linda Hunt Memorial Library ... Ms. Sandra WAGNER
15 Director of Personnel ... Ms. Rita PINKALL
38 Director Student Success Center ... Ms. Amy JACKSON
21 Controller ... Ms. Christy WRIGHT
18 Director of Buildings & Grounds ... Mr. Dan PETZ
39 Director of Residence Life ... Mr. Scott GOODHEART
04 Administrative Asst to President ... Ms. Donna MEIER PFEIFER
29 Director Alumni Relations ... Mr. Kurt MCAFEE
108 Director of Planning & Assessment ... Mr. David SCHMIDT

Rasmussen College-Kansas City/Overland Park (E)

11600 College Boulevard, Overland Park KS 66210
Telephone: (913) 491-7870 Identification: 770489
Accreditation: &NH, MAAB

† Regional accreditation carried under the parent institution in Saint Cloud, MN. The tuition figure is an average, actual tuition may vary.

Rasmussen College Topeka (F)

620 SW Governor View, Topeka KS 66606
Telephone: (785) 228-7320 Identification: 770490
Accreditation: &NH, MAAB

† Regional accreditation carried under the parent institution in Saint Cloud, MN. The tuition figure is an average, actual tuition may vary.

Saint Paul School of Theology (G)

4370 West 109th Street, Suite 300,
Overland Park KS 66211
County: Johnson FICE Identification: 002509
Unit ID: 179317
Telephone: (913) 253-5000 Carnegie Class: Spec-4-yr-Faith
FAX Number: (913) 253-5075 Calendar System: Semester
URL: www.spst.edu
Established: 1958 Annual Graduate Tuition & Fees: N/A
Enrollment: 153 Coed
Affiliation or Control: United Methodist IRS Status: 501(c)3
Highest Offering: Doctorate; No Undergraduates
Accreditation: NH, THEOL

01 President ... Rev. Neil B. BLAIR
05 Interim VP Academic Affairs/Dean ... Dr. Elaine A. ROBINSON
30 Vice President for Advancement ... Vacant
12 Academic Dean for OCU Site ... Dr. Elaine A. ROBINSON
32 Associate Dean of Students ... Rev. Margaretta S. NARCISSE
15 Director of Human Resources ... Mr. Barney BARRY
06 Registrar ... Ms. Tahmeka THOMPSON
37 Dir of Student Financial Services ... Ms. Kim WARREN
07 Dir of Student Recruitment Services ... Mr. Brian GREEN-YOUNG
26 Director of Communications ... Ms. Heather SNODGRASS
108 Assessment & Compliance Coordinator ... Ms. Jayme LAWLOR
08 Librarian ... Ms. Maggie MUELLER
04 Executive Assistant to President ... Ms. Melissa WHALEN
10 CFO ... Mr. Barney BARRY
101 Secretary of the Institution/Board ... Ms. Julie ROBINSON
36 Director Student Recruitment Svcs ... Mr. Brian GREEN-YOUNG

Salina Area Technical College (H)

2562 Centennial Road, Salina KS 67401
County: Saline FICE Identification: 005499
Unit ID: 155830
Telephone: (785) 309-3100 Carnegie Class: Assoc/HVT-High Non
FAX Number: (785) 309-3101 Calendar System: Semester
URL: www.salinatech.edu
Established: 1965 Annual Undergrad Tuition & Fees (In-District): $5,518
Enrollment: 537 Coed
Affiliation or Control: State/Local IRS Status: 501(c)3
Highest Offering: Associate Degree
Accreditation: @NH, DA

01 President ... Mr. Gregory A. NICHOLS
05 Vice Pres of Instruction ... Ms. Stephani JOHNS-HINES
11 Vice Pres of Administrative Svcs ... Mr. Andrew MANLEY
32 Vice Pres of Student Services ... Mrs. Susan EBERWEIN
09 Director of Inst Research/Registrar ... Mrs. Denise R. HOEFFNER
15 Director Human Resources ... Mrs. Tamera WILCOX
18 Director of Facilities ... Vacant
25 Director of Grants and Planning ... Vacant
102 Exec Dir of SATC Foundation ... Ms. Morgan POWELL
37 Director Student Financial Aid ... Mrs. Susan EBERWEIN
07 Recruiting Coordinator ... Mr. Patrick HILL

Seward County Community College (I)

1801 N Kansas Avenue, Liberal KS 67901-2054
County: Seward FICE Identification: 008228
Unit ID: 155858
Telephone: (620) 624-1951 Carnegie Class: Assoc/MT-VT-High Trad
FAX Number: (620) 417-1169 Calendar System: Semester
URL: www.sccc.edu
Established: 1967 Annual Undergrad Tuition & Fees (In-District): $2,688
Enrollment: 1,852 Coed
Affiliation or Control: State/Local IRS Status: 501(c)3
Highest Offering: Associate Degree
Accreditation: NH, ACBSP, ADNUR, COARC, MLTAD, SURGT

01 President ... Dr. Ken J. TRZASKA
05 Vice President of Academic Affairs ... Dr. Todd CARTER
10 VP of Finance & Operations ... Mr. Dennis M. SANDER
32 Vice President of Student Services ... Ms. Celeste DONOVAN
88 Dean of Career & Technical Educ ... Vacant
06 Registrar ... Ms. Alaina M. RICE
13 Director of Information Technology ... Mr. J. J. WIDENER
37 Director of Financial Aid ... Mrs. Donna M. FISHER
26 Exec Dir of Marketing & PR ... Ms. Rachel C. COLEMAN
50 Director of Business & Industry ... Mrs. Norma Jean DODGE
24 Director of Multi-media Technology ... Mr. Doug BROWNE
08 Director of Library ... Mr. Matthew PANNKUK
41 Director of Athletics ... Mr. Galen W. MCSPADDEN
18 Director of Facilities ... Mr. Roger SCHEIB
40 Director of Bookstore ... Ms. Jerri L. LYDDON
30 Executive Dir of Development ... Ms. Tammy DOLL
39 Director of Student Living Center ... Ms. Kate A. MULLIGAN
09 Institutional Research/Data Analyst ... Ms. Teresa WEHMEIER
19 Dir of Safety and Security ... Mr. Dennis K. MULANAX
15 Director of Human Resources ... Ms. Tanya DOWELL
07 Admissions Coordinator/Recruiting ... Ms. Alyson CALL
07 Coordinator of Admissions/Marketing ... Mr. Chandler KIRKHART
38 Dir Counseling/Advising/Career Svcs ... Ms. Mariah CLINE
35 Dir of Student Life & Leadership ... Mr. Wade LYON
04 Executive Assistant ... Mrs. Lois B. MAGNER
66 Director of Nursing ... Ms. Susan INGLAND
75 Dean of Industrial Technology ... Mr. Larry A. MCLEMORE
105 Website and Portal Manager ... Mr. Craig DUSEK
108 Director of Research and Assessment ... Vacant
84 Director of Admissions ... Mr. Bert LUALLEN
29 Exec Dir Alum Engagement/Grant Dev ... Ms. Charity HORINEK

Southwestern College (J)

100 College Street, Winfield KS 67156-2499
County: Cowley FICE Identification: 001940
Unit ID: 155900
Telephone: (620) 229-6000 Carnegie Class: Masters/M
FAX Number: (620) 229-6224 Calendar System: Semester
URL: www.sckans.edu
Established: 1885 Annual Undergrad Tuition & Fees: $25,946
Enrollment: 1,627 Coed
Affiliation or Control: United Methodist IRS Status: 501(c)3
Highest Offering: Doctorate
Accreditation: NH, CAATE, #CAEP, MUS, NURSE

01 President ... Dr. Bradley J. ANDREWS
05 Interim Provost ... Dr. Tracy H. FREDERICK
10 Vice President Finance ... Ms. Sheila R. KRUG
88 VP Student Retention & Success ... Dr. Dawn E. PLEAS-BAILEY
88 VP Enroll Mgmt for Prof Studies ... Ms. Susan BACKOFEN
45 VP Planning/New Programs ... Dr. Stephen K. WILKE
30 Vice Pres Institutional Advancement ... Ms. DeAnn DOCKERY
26 Vice President Communications ... Ms. Sara S. WEINERT
13 Vice Pres Information Technology ... Mr. Ben LIM
32 Assoc VP Student Life/Dean Students ... Mr. Dan FALK
29 Director Alumni Programs ... Ms. Susan G. LOWE
08 Library Director ... Ms. Dalene MCDONALD
84 VP Enroll Mgmt Main Campus ... Mr. Dean T. CLARK
37 Director Financial Aid ... Ms. Brenda D. HICKS
06 Registrar ... Ms. Linda WEIPPERT
09 Director of Institutional Research ... Ms. Joni RANKIN
41 Director Athletics ... Mr. Matthew A. SHELTON
15 Director Human Resources ... Ms. Lonnie BOYD
96 Director of Purchasing ... Mr. David H. DOLSEN
04 Exec Asst to President & Provost ... Ms. Becky S. MANGUS
107 Acad Dean Prof Studies ... Dr. Amy M. LASH ESAU
53 Acad Dean Education ... Dr. Cameron B. CARLSON
20 Acad Dean Main Campus ... Dr. Peter G. HECKMAN
42 Campus Minister ... Rev. Benjamin C. HANNE

Southwestern College Wichita East (K)

2040 S Rock Road, Wichita KS 67207
Telephone: (316) 684-5335 Identification: 770260

Accreditation: &NH

† Regional accreditation is carried under the parent institution in Winfield, KS

Sterling College (A)

125 W Cooper Street, Sterling KS 67579-1533
County: Rice FICE Identification: 001945
Unit ID: 155937
Telephone: (620) 278-2173 Carnegie Class: Bac-Diverse
FAX Number: (620) 278-4411 Calendar System: 4/1/4
URL: www.sterling.edu
Established: 1887 Annual Undergrad Tuition & Fees: $22,950
Enrollment: 720 Coed
Affiliation or Control: Presbyterian IRS Status: 501(c)3
Highest Offering: Baccalaureate
Accreditation: NH, CAATE, TED

01 President .... Mr. Scott RICH
05 Vice President Academic Affairs .... Dr. Ken BROWN
30 Vice President for Inst Advancement .... Mr. Scott CARTER
32 Vice President Student Life .... Ms. Kimberly CHRISTIAN
11 Vice Pres Admin/Inst Initiatives .... Mr. David LANDIS
41 Athletic Director .... Mr. Gary KEMPF
26 Dir Marketing/Pres Communications .... Mr. Brad EVENSON
10 Director of Finance & Admin .... Ms. Rita OWNBEY
37 Director of Financial Aid .... Ms. Mitzi SUHLER
06 Registrar .... Ms. Janet CAYWOOD
44 Director of Planned Giving .... Ms. Sheila BIRD
29 Alumni & Marketing Manager .... Ms. Teryn IRVIN
18 Chief Facilities/Physical Plant .... Mr. Steven CAYWOOD
38 Director Student Counseling .... Ms. Loida LEONE
08 Library Director .... Vacant
36 Director of Career Services .... Mr. Terry EHRESMAN
07 Vice President Enrollment .... Mr. Dennis DUTTON
04 Administrative Asst to President .... Ms. Erica FOSS
42 Chaplain .... Mr. Christian DASHIELL
108 Director Institutional Assessment .... Dr. Spencer WAGLEY
13 Chief Info Technology Officer (CIO) .... Mr. Mykeal PITTS
15 Director Personnel Services .... Ms. Terri RIDGE

Tabor College (B)

400 S Jefferson Street, Hillsboro KS 67063-1753
County: Marion FICE Identification: 001946
Unit ID: 155973
Telephone: (620) 947-3121 Carnegie Class: Bac-Diverse
FAX Number: (620) 947-2607 Calendar System: 4/1/4
URL: www.tabor.edu
Established: 1908 Annual Undergrad Tuition & Fees: $25,320
Enrollment: 766 Coed
Affiliation or Control: Mennonite Brethren Church IRS Status: 501(c)3
Highest Offering: Master's
Accreditation: NH, #CAATE, MUS, NURSE, @SW, TED

01 President .... Dr. Jules GLANZER
05 Vice President Academic Affairs .... Dr. Frank JOHNSON
10 Sr Vice President Business/Finance .... Mr. Kirby FADENRECHT
30 Vice President Advancement .... Mr. Ronald BRAUN
41 Vice President of Athletics .... Mr. Rusty ALLEN
32 Vice President of Student Life .... Dr. Jim PAULUS
06 Registrar .... Mr. Scott FRANZ
08 Director of Library Services .... Ms. Janet WILLIAMS
84 Director Enrollment Management .... Mr. Rusty ALLEN
37 Dir of Student Financial Services .... Ms. Sommer SMITH
29 Director Alumni Relations .... Mr. Rod HAMM
26 Director of Communications .... Ms. Katrina HANCOCK
18 Director Facilities/Physical Plant .... Mr. Doug GRABER
35 Director Student Success .... Vacant
09 Institutional Research .... Mrs. Deborah PENN
13 Director of Information Technology .... Mr. Chris GLANZER
14 Chief Information Officer .... Mrs. Joy MARK
15 Human Resources Coordinator .... Mrs. Ruth FUNK

University of Kansas Edwards Campus (C)

12600 Quivira Road, Overland Park KS 66213
Telephone: (913) 897-8400 Identification: 770261
Accreditation: &NH

† Regional accreditation is carried under the parent institution in Lawrence, KS

University of Kansas Main Campus (D)

1450 Jayhawk Boulevard, Room 230,
Lawrence KS 66045-7518
County: Douglas FICE Identification: 001948
Unit ID: 155317
Telephone: (785) 864-3131 Carnegie Class: DU-Highest
FAX Number: (785) 864-4120 Calendar System: Semester
URL: www.ku.edu
Established: 1866 Annual Undergrad Tuition & Fees (In-State): $10,825
Enrollment: 27,180 Coed
Affiliation or Control: State IRS Status: 501(c)3
Highest Offering: Doctorate
Accreditation: NH, ART, BUS, BUSA, CAATE, CEA, CLPSY, COPSY, CS, ENG, HSA, IPSY, JOUR, LAW, MUS, PH, PHAR, PLNG, SCPSY, SF, SPAA, SW, TED

01 Chancellor .... Dr. Bernadette GRAY-LITTLE
05 Exec Vice Chancellor/Provost .... Dr. Neeli BENDAPUDI
12 Vice Chancellor/Dean Edwards Campus .... Dr. David COOK
26 Vice Chancellor for Public Affairs .... Dr. Timothy CABONI
04 Executive Assistant to Chancellor .... Ms. Mary G. BURG
43 General Counsel .... Mr. James P. POTTORFF, JR.
20 Sr Vice Provost Academic Affairs .... Dr. Sara ROSEN
20 Vice Provost .... Dr. Mary Lee HUMMERT
20 Vice Provost .... Ms. Diane H. GODDARD
32 Vice Provost for Student Affairs .... Dr. Tammara DURHAM
46 Vice Prov Research/Grad Studies .... Dr. James W. TRACY
28 Vice Provost Diversity & Equity .... Dr. E. Nathan THOMAS, III
84 VP Enrollment Management .... Dr. Matt MELVIN
13 Chief Information Officer .... Mr. Bob LIM
45 Asst Vice Provost Research .... Ms. Kristi M. BILLINGER
58 Assoc VP/Dean Research & Grad Stds .... Dr. Michael C. ROBERTS
104 Assoc VP International Programs .... Ms. Susan GRONBECK-TEDESCO
11 Assoc Vice Provost of Operations .... Mr. Barry K. SWANSON
30 President Endowment Association .... Mr. Dale SEUFERLING
29 President Alumni Association .... Mr. Heath J. PETERSON
07 Director Admissions .... Ms. Lisa P. KRESS
10 Chief Business/Financial Plng Ofcr .... Ms. Leisa JULIAN
21 Comptroller .... Ms. Karina M. YOAKUM
21 Director Budget Office .... Mr. Richard L. MCKINNEY
06 University Registrar .... Ms. Cindy SANDERS
09 Univ Director Inst Research Plng .... Ms. Deborah J. TEETER
15 AVP for Human Resource Management .... Mr. Michael ROUNDS
85 Director International Student Svcs .... Dr. Chuck OLCESE
38 Director Counseling/Psych Services .... Dr. Michael LYNCH MAESTAS
18 Director Design & Construction Mgmt .... Mr. James E. MODIG
37 Director Student Financial Aid .... Ms. Brenda MAIGAARD
36 Director Career/Employment Svcs .... Mr. David GASTON
41 Director Intercollegiate Athletics .... Dr. Sheahon ZENGER
18 Interim Director Facilities Service .... Mr. Vince AVILA
22 Director Inst Oppty & Access .... Mr. Joshua JONES
28 Director Multicultural Affairs .... Ms. Precious PORRAS
23 Director Student Health Services .... Dr. Douglas C. DECHARIO
14 Asst Director Information Tech .... Ms. Anne MADDEN JOHNSON
39 Director Housing .... Dr. Diana ROBERTSON
86 Director State Relations .... Ms. Kelly M. REYNOLDS
92 Director Honors Program .... Dr. C. Bryan YOUNG
86 Director Federal Relations .... Mr. Jack CLINE
40 Director Bookstores .... Ms. Jen O'CONNOR
51 Exec Dir Continuing Education .... Ms. Sharon D. GRAHAM
25 Manager Contract Negotiations .... Ms. Lucille MARINO
91 Project Coord Information Systems .... Mr. David M. GARDNER
49 Dean Liberal Arts/Science .... Dr. Carl W. LEJUEZ
61 Dean of Law .... Mr. Stephen W. MAZZA
54 Dean of Engineering .... Dr. Michael BRANICKY
48 Dean Architecture/Design/Planning .... Dr. Mahesh DAAS
50 Dean of Business .... Dr. James GUTHRIE
67 Dean of Pharmacy .... Dr. Kenneth L. AUDUS
60 Dean of Journalism .... Dr. Ann M. BRILL
53 Dean of Education .... Dr. Rick GINSBERG
64 Dean of Music .... Dr. Robert L. WALZEL, JR.
70 Acting Dean of Social Welfare .... Dr. Stephen KAPP
08 Dean Libraries .... Mr. Kevin L. SMITH
57 Assoc Dean School of the Arts .... Dr. Henry BIAL
19 Director Security/Safety .... Mr. Chris KEARY

† Medical Center and Main campus enrollments should be combined for the total institution enrollment.

University of Kansas Medical Center (E)

3901 Rainbow Boulevard, Kansas City KS 66160-0001
Telephone: (913) 588-5000 FICE Identification: 024579
Accreditation: &NH, ANEST, AUD, CAHIIM, COARC, DIETI, DMOLS, DMS, MED, MIDWF, MT, NMT, NURSE, OT, PTA

† Enrollment at the Medical Center is included within the published enrollment for the University of Kansas Main Campus. Regional accreditation is carried under the parent institution in Lawrence, KS.

University of Saint Mary (F)

4100 S 4th Street Trafficway, Leavenworth KS 66048-5082
County: Leavenworth FICE Identification: 001943
Unit ID: 155812
Telephone: (913) 682-5151 Carnegie Class: Masters/M
FAX Number: (913) 758-6140 Calendar System: Semester
URL: www.stmary.edu
Established: 1923 Annual Undergrad Tuition & Fees: $25,620
Enrollment: 1,436 Coed
Affiliation or Control: Roman Catholic IRS Status: 501(c)3
Highest Offering: Doctorate
Accreditation: NH, CAHIIM, IACBE, NURSE, PTA, TED

01 President .... Sr. Diane STEELE
05 Academic Vice President .... Dr. Bryan LEBEAU
10 Vice President for Finance .... Ms. Nancy BRAMLETT
30 Vice President of Development .... Ms. Karolyn DREILING
07 VP Admissions & Marketing .... Mr. John SHULTZ
32 Vice President for Student Life .... Mr. Daniel DENTINO
88 Director Operations of Enrollment .... Mrs. Kitti O'DONNELL
06 Registrar .... Mr. Russell PERKINS
08 Director of the Library .... Ms. Danielle DION
09 Data Analyst .... Ms. Veronica DONOVAN
29 Alumni and Events Coordinator .... Ms. Sharon CLAY
37 Director of Financial Aid .... Ms. Annissa EPPERSON
42 Director of Campus Ministry .... Mr. Robert KILLION
44 Development Officer Planned Giving .... Ms. Jane LIEBERT

41 Athletic Director .... Mr. Rob MILLER
15 Director Human Resources .... Ms. Kelly GRISNIK
39 Director of Residence Life .... Mr. Tyler GADWOOD
21 Controller .... Ms. Sherry WELLS
38 Counselor .... Ms. Deborah SHADDY
18 Plant Manager .... Mr. Mark GIESEMAN
40 Bookstore Manager .... Ms. Cynthia FORRESTER
12 Site Coordinator Johnson County .... Ms. Patricia HOWARD
13 Coordinator of Computer Operations .... Mr. Kevin GANTT
04 Executive Administrative Assistant .... Ms. Kathy TATOM
35 Director of Student Activities .... Ms. Lisa POTOKA
19 Director of Campus Security .... Mr. Donald STUBBINGS

Vatterott College - Wichita (G)

8853 East 37th Street North, Wichita KS 67226-2018
Telephone: (316) 634-0066 Identification: 666583
Accreditation: ACCSC

† Branch campus of Vatterott College-North Park, Berkeley, MO.

Washburn University (H)

1700 SW College Avenue, Topeka KS 66621-0001
County: Shawnee FICE Identification: 001949
Unit ID: 156082
Telephone: (785) 670-1010 Carnegie Class: Masters/M
FAX Number: (785) 670-1089 Calendar System: Semester
URL: www.washburn.edu
Established: 1865 Annual Undergrad Tuition & Fees (In-District): $6,350
Enrollment: 6,722 Coed
Affiliation or Control: Local IRS Status: 501(c)3
Highest Offering: Doctorate
Accreditation: NH, ART, BUS, CAATE, CAHIIM, CEA, COARC, DMS, LAW, MUS, NURSE, OTA, PTAA, RAD, SW, TED

01 President .... Dr. Jerry B. FARLEY
05 Interim Vice Pres Academic Affairs .... Dr. JuliAnn MAZACHEK
10 Vice Pres Admin & Treasurer .... Mr. Rick L. ANDERSON
32 Vice President for Student Life .... Dr. Eric GROSPITCH
04 Special Assistant to the President .... Vacant
84 Director Enrollment Management .... Dr. Richard W. LIEDTKE
43 University Legal Counsel .... Mr. Marc FRIED
35 Assoc Vice Pres of Student Life .... Mr. Joel BLUML
20 Assoc Vice Pres Acad Affairs .... Dr. Nancy A. TATE
21 Assoc Vice Pres & Dir of Finance .... Mr. Chris LEACH
102 President WU Foundation .... Dr. Julliann MAZACHEK
06 Registrar .... Ms. Kelly RUSSELL
08 Dean of Libraries .... Dr. Alan BEARMAN
37 Director Student Financial Aid .... Ms. Kandace MARS
07 Director of Admissions .... Ms. Kris KLIMA
15 Director of Human Resources .... Ms. Teresa LEE
90 Director Info Systems & Services .... Vacant
09 Director Strategic Analysis & Rep .... Dr. Robert L. HANDLEY
49 Dean College Arts/Sciences .... Dr. Laura STEPHENSON
88 Dean School Applied Studies .... Dr. Pat MUNZER
61 Dean School of Law .... Mr. Thomas J. ROMIG
50 Dean School of Business .... Dr. David SOLLARS
66 Dean School of Nursing .... Dr. Monica S. SCHEIBMEIR
41 Director of Athletics .... Mr. Loren FERRE
35 Director Student Services .... Vacant
22 Director Equal Opportunity .... Dr. Pam FOSTER
18 Director Facilities Services .... Mr. Rich CONNELL
23 Director Health Services .... Dr. Shirley DINKEL
29 Alumni Association Director .... Ms. Susie HOFFMANN
92 Dean Honors Program .... Dr. Michael J. MCGUIRE
39 Director Student Housing .... Ms. Mindy P. RENDON
40 Director Bookstore .... Vacant
35 Director Student Activities .... Ms. Jessica BARRACLOUGH
38 Director Student Counseling .... Ms. Jamie OLSEN
26 Director of University Relations .... Mr. Patrick EARLY
36 Director Student Placement .... Mr. Kent MCANALLY
19 Interim Director of Police .... Mr. Chris ENOS

Wichita Area Technical College (I)

4004 N Webb Road, Wichita KS 67226-8101
County: Sedgwick FICE Identification: 005498
Unit ID: 156107
Telephone: (316) 677-9400 Carnegie Class: Assoc/HVT-High Non
FAX Number: (316) 677-9510 Calendar System: Semester
URL: www.watc.edu
Established: 1965 Annual Undergrad Tuition & Fees (In-District): $7,317
Enrollment: 3,373 Coed
Affiliation or Control: State/Local IRS Status: 501(c)3
Highest Offering: Associate Degree
Accreditation: NH, DA, MAC, SURGT

01 President .... Ms. Sheree UTASH
05 Chief of Academic Affairs .... Mr. Scott LUCAS
10 Vice Pres Finance/Administration .... Mr. Greg UNRUH
32 Vice President Student Services .... Mr. Justin PFEIFER
26 Dir Marketing/Community Outreach .... Mr. Andy MCFAYDEN
13 Exec Dir Tech/Inst Effectiveness .... Mr. Randy ROEBUCK
15 Exec Director Human Resources .... Ms. Judy MOUNT
30 Director Advancement .... Ms. Danielle SCHWEIGER

Wichita State University (J)

1845 N Fairmount, Wichita KS 67260-0001
County: Sedgwick FICE Identification: 001950
Unit ID: 156125
Telephone: (316) 978-3456 Carnegie Class: DU-Higher
FAX Number: (316) 978-3770 Calendar System: Semester

URL: www.wichita.edu
Established: 1895 Annual Undergrad Tuition & Fees (In-State): $7,528
Enrollment: 14,995 Coed
Affiliation or Control: State IRS Status: 501(c)3
Highest Offering: Doctorate
Accreditation: NH, ARCPA, ART, AUD, BUS, BUSA, CAATE, CLPSY, CS, DANCE, DENT, DH, ENG, ENGT, IPSY, MT, MUS, NURSE, PTA, SP, SPAA, SW, TED

01 President ... Dr. John W. BARDO
05 Provost/Senior VP Academic Affairs ... Dr. Anthony VIZZINI
10 VP Administration & Finance ... Ms. Mary L. HERRIN
32 VP Student Affairs ... Dr. Eric L. SEXTON
43 General Counsel ... Mr. David MOSES
26 VP Strategic Communications ... Mr. Lou HELDMAN
20 Assoc VP Academic Affairs ... Dr. David WRIGHT
20 Assoc VP Academic Affairs ... Dr. Richard D. MUMA
13 Chief Information Officer ... Mr. Toney FLACK
20 Assoc VP Academic Affairs ... Dr. Linnea GLENMAYE
46 VP Research & Technology Transfer ... Dr. John S. TOMBLIN
49 Dean Liberal Arts & Sciences ... Dr. Ronald R. MATSON
50 Dean Barton School of Business ... Dr. Anand DESAI
53 Dean Education ... Dr. Shirley LEFEVER-DAVIS
54 Dean Engineering ... Dr. Royce BOWDEN
57 Dean Fine Arts ... Dr. Rodney E. MILLER
76 Dean Health Professions ... Dr. Sandra BIBB
58 Dean Graduate School ... Dr. Dennis LIVESAY
08 Interim Dean Libraries ... Ms. Kathy DOWNES
35 Dean of Students ... Ms. Christine SCHNEIKART-LUEBBE
86 Exec Director Government Relations ... Mr. Andrew SCHLAPP
24 Dir Media Resources Center ... Mr. John JONES
102 CEO & President WSU Foundation ... Ms. Elizabeth H. KING
41 Interim Athletic Director ... Mr. Darron BOATRIGHT
88 Director Creative Services ... Mr. Craig LINDEMAN
15 Director Human Resources ... Mrs. Frankie M. KIRKENDOLL
21 Director Budgets ... Mr. David MILLER
06 Registrar ... Ms. Gina D. CRABTREE
07 Director Admissions ... Mr. Bobby GANDU
37 Director Financial Aid ... Ms. Sheelu M. SURENDER
36 Director Placement/Career Services ... Ms. Jill M. PLETCHER
38 Director Counseling & Testing ... Dr. Maureen DASEY-MORALES
18 Director Physical Plant ... Mr. Woodrow DEPONTIER
45 Director of Facilities Planning ... Mr. Eric KING
19 Campus Police Chief ... Ms. Sara B. MORRIS
23 Director Student Health Services ... Ms. Camille CHILDERS
39 Director Stdnt Housing & Resid Life ... Mr. Scott JENSEN
28 Director Diversity & Inclusion ... Ms. Alicia SANCHEZ
40 Manager Bookstore ... Mr. Kevin J. KONDA
21 Assoc VP Financial Operations ... Ms. Lois TATRO
42 Campus Minister ... Rev. Christopher ESHELMAN
96 Director of Purchasing ... Mr. Steven WHITE
29 Executive Director Alumni Assoc ... Ms. Courtney MARSHALL
22 Director of EEO ... Ms. Jane J. LINK
04 Assistant to President ... Ms. Anna LANIER WEYERS
106 Dir Online Education/E-learning ... Mr. Mark D. PORCARO

Wichita Technical Institute (A)

2051 South Meridian Avenue, Wichita KS 67213-1927
County: Sedgwick FICE Identification: 010503
Unit ID: 156134
Telephone: (316) 943-2241 Carnegie Class: Spec 2-yr-Tech
FAX Number: (316) 943-5438 Calendar System: Quarter
URL: www.wti.edu
Established: Annual Undergrad Tuition & Fees: N/A
Enrollment: 1,000 Coed
Affiliation or Control: Proprietary IRS Status: Proprietary
Highest Offering: Associate Degree
Accreditation: ACCSC

01 Director ... Mr. Rod MOORE

KENTUCKY

Alice Lloyd College (B)

Purpose Road, Pippa Passes KY 41844-9703
County: Knott FICE Identification: 001951
Unit ID: 156189
Telephone: (606) 368-2101 Carnegie Class: Bac-A&S
FAX Number: (606) 368-6212 Calendar System: Semester
URL: www.alc.edu
Established: 1923 Annual Undergrad Tuition & Fees: $11,460
Enrollment: 657 Coed
Affiliation or Control: Independent Non-Profit IRS Status: 501(c)3
Highest Offering: Baccalaureate
Accreditation: SC

01 President ... Dr. Joe A. STEPP
03 Executive Vice President ... Dr. Jim STEPP
05 Vice President Academic Affairs ... Dr. Claude CRUM
10 Vice President of Business Affairs ... Mr. David JOHNSON
32 Dean of Students & Community Life ... Mr. Scott CORNETT
07 Director of Admissions ... Ms. Angela PHIPPS
06 Registrar ... Ms. Dana DOTSON
08 Director of Library ... Mr. Andrew BUSROE
37 Director of Financial Aid ... Mrs. Jacqueline STEWART
88 Director of Student Work Program ... Mr. Kerry RATLIFF
53 Director of Teacher Education ... Mr. Norman BISHOP
18 Director of Physical Plant ... Mr. Ryan GIBSON
39 Director of Student Housing ... Mr. John MILLS
29 Director of Alumni Relations ... Mrs. Teresa GRENDER
35 Director of Student Activities ... Ms. Christine STUMBO
26 Dir of Marketing & Communications ... Ms. Katelin HYLTON
09 Director of Institutional Research ... Mr. Norman BISHOP
30 Director of Development ... Mrs. Margo SPARKMAN
102 Dir Foundation/Corporate Relations ... Ms. Priscilla FRALEY
41 Athletic Director ... Mr. Gary STEPP

† Cost of tuition is guaranteed for students from 108 county territories.

American National University (C)

115 E Lexington Avenue, Danville KY 40422-1517
Telephone: (859) 236-6991 Identification: 666441
Accreditation: ACICS, MAC

† Branch campus of American National University, Indianapolis, IN

American National University (D)

8095 Connector Drive, Florence KY 41042-1466
Telephone: (859) 525-6510 Identification: 666442
Accreditation: ACICS, MAC, SURGT

† Branch campus of American National University, Indianapolis, IN

American National University (E)

2376 Sir Barton Way, Lexington KY 40509-2256
Telephone: (859) 253-0621 Identification: 667202
Accreditation: ACICS, MAC, SURGT

† Branch campus of American National University, Indianapolis, IN

American National University (F)

4205 Dixie Highway, Louisville KY 40216-4147
Telephone: (502) 447-7634 Identification: 666443
Accreditation: ACICS, CAHIIM, MAC, SURGT

† Branch campus of American National University, Indianapolis, IN

American National University (G)

50 National College Boulevard, Pikeville KY 41501-3176
Telephone: (606) 478-7200 Identification: 666444
Accreditation: ACICS, MAC

† Branch campus of American National University, Indianapolis, IN

American National University (H)

125 S Killarney Lane, Richmond KY 40475-2309
Telephone: (859) 623-8956 Identification: 666445
Accreditation: ACICS, MAC

† Branch campus of American National University, Indianapolis, IN

Asbury Theological Seminary (I)

204 N Lexington Avenue, Wilmore KY 40390-1199
County: Jessamine FICE Identification: 001953
Unit ID: 156222
Telephone: (859) 858-3581 Carnegie Class: Spec-4-yr-Faith
FAX Number: N/A Calendar System: 4/1/4
URL: www.asburyseminary.edu
Established: 1923 Annual Graduate Tuition & Fees: N/A
Enrollment: 1,470 Coed
Affiliation or Control: Independent Non-Profit IRS Status: 501(c)3
Highest Offering: Doctorate; No Undergraduates
Accreditation: SC, CACREP, THEOL

01 President ... Dr. Timothy C. TENNENT
11 Vice President/COO ... Mr. Robert S. LANDREBE
05 Provost/VP Academic for Affairs ... Dr. Douglas K. MATTHEWS
10 Vice Pres Finance/Admin/CFO ... Mr. Bryan P. BLANKENSHIP
30 Vice President for Advancement ... Mr. Jay MANSUR
31 Vice President Community Formation ... Dr. Marilyn ELLIOTT
84 Vice Pres Enrollment Management ... Mr. Kevin BISH
13 Chief Technology Officer ... Mr. Patrick GARDELLA
06 Registrar ... Dr. Christine L. JOHNSON
07 Director of Admissions ... Mr. Randy OZAN
37 Director of Student Financial Aid ... Mrs. Jenny BURKHART
18 Director of Physical Plant ... Mr. Lanny SPEARS
09 Dir Inst Effectiveness/Assessment ... Dr. Alexandra HENCHY
15 Director of Human Resources ... Mrs. Barbara ANTROBUS
29 Director Alumni/Church Relations ... Ms. Tammy CESSNA
73 Dean School of Theology & Formation ... Dr. James THOBABEN
88 Dean Beeson Center ... Dr. David GYERTSON
88 Dean ESJ School World of Missions ... Dr. Gregg OKESSON
88 Dean School Biblical Interpretation ... Dr. David BAUER
73 Actg Dean School Practical Theology ... Dr. Chris KIESLING
88 Dean Advanced Research Programs ... Dr. Lalsangkima PACHUAU
04 Executive Asst to President ... Ms. Angela CLOYD

Asbury University (J)

1 Macklem Drive, Wilmore KY 40390-1198
County: Jessamine FICE Identification: 001952
Unit ID: 156213
Telephone: (859) 858-3511 Carnegie Class: Masters/S
FAX Number: (859) 858-3921 Calendar System: Semester
URL: www.asbury.edu
Established: 1890 Annual Undergrad Tuition & Fees: $27,934
Enrollment: 1,879 Coed
Affiliation or Control: Independent Non-Profit IRS Status: 501(c)3
Highest Offering: Beyond Master's But Less Than Doctorate
Accreditation: SC, MUS, SW, TED

01 President ... Dr. Sandra C. GRAY
05 Provost ... Dr. Jon S. KULAGA
10 Vice Pres Business Affs & Treasurer ... Mr. Glenn R. HAMILTON
84 Vice Pres of Enrollment Management ... Dr. Mark J. TROYER
32 Vice Pres Student Dev/Dean Students ... Dr. Sarah T. BALDWIN
30 Vice Pres Institutional Advancement ... Mr. Charles SHEPARD
20 Academic Dean ... Dr. Timothy G. CAMPBELL
49 Dir of College of Arts & Sciences ... Dr. Stephen K. CLEMENTS
53 Dean of School of Education ... Dr. Sherry W. POWERS
60 Dean of School of Comm Arts ... Dr. James R. OWENS
58 Dean School of Grad & Prof Studies ... Dr. William HALL, JR.
51 Dir of Adult Professional Studies ... Mr. T. Joshua FEE
106 Director of Online Education ... Dr. William HALL, JR.
44 Senior Advancement Director ... Rev. Stuart A. SMITH
37 Director of Financial Aid ... Mr. Ronald M. ANDERSON
42 Assoc Dean for Campus Ministries ... Rev. Gregory K. HASELOFF
39 Assoc Dean for Residence Life ... Mr. Joe W. BRUNER
06 Registrar ... Mrs. Sheryl VOIGTS
29 Dir of Alumni Relations/Parents Pgm ... Mrs. Lisa D. HARPER
08 Director of Library Services ... Mr. Morgan A. TRACY
13 Director of Information Services ... Mr. Paul J. DUPREE
07 Director of Admissions ... Mr. Brandon COMBS
26 Dir of Marketing & Communications ... Mr. Brad JOHNSON
18 Director of Physical Plant ... Mr. Eric C. MCMILLION
23 Supervisor of Clinic ... Miss Carol J. AMEY
36 Dir Center for Career & Calling ... Ms. Michelle KRATZER
38 Assoc Dean of Wholeness & Wellness ... Mr. Kevin BELLEW
19 Dir of Security & Environ Safety ... Mr. David HAY
40 Manager of Bookstore ... Mr. C. David TRAMMELL
21 Associate Business Officer ... Mr. Gary E. HOWARD
04 Exec Assistant to the President ... Ms. Michelle CLARK
85 Coordinator of Intercultural Pgms ... Rev. Esther JADHAV
41 Athletics Director ... Mr. Mark PERDUE
09 Director of Institutional Research ... Dr. Gay HOLCOMB
104 Coordinator Global Engagement Ofc ... Mrs. Tina WEI SMITH
15 Dir of Human Resources/Risk Mgt ... Mrs. Jan CRAIGMILES
45 Director Institutional Planning ... Mr. Paul STEPHENS
50 Dean Howard Dayton Sch Business ... Dr. Michael KANE

ATA College (K)

10180 Linn Station Road, Ste A-200, Louisville KY 40223
County: Jefferson FICE Identification: 040383
Unit ID: 447935
Telephone: (502) 371-8330 Carnegie Class: Spec 2-yr-Health
FAX Number: (502) 371-8598 Calendar System: Quarter
URL: www.ata.edu
Established: 1994 Annual Undergrad Tuition & Fees: $11,545
Enrollment: 439 Coed
Affiliation or Control: Proprietary IRS Status: Proprietary
Highest Offering: Associate Degree
Accreditation: ABHES

01 President ... Mr. Donald A. JONES

Baptist Seminary of Kentucky (L)

400 E. College St, Box 358, Georgetown KY 40324
County: Scott Identification: 667211
Telephone: (502) 863-8300 Carnegie Class: Not Classified
FAX Number: (502) 863-8300 Calendar System: Semester
URL: www.bsky.org
Established: 2002 Annual Graduate Tuition & Fees: N/A
Enrollment: N/A Coed
Affiliation or Control: Independent Non-Profit IRS Status: 501(c)3
Highest Offering: Master's; No Undergraduates
Accreditation: THEOL

01 President ... Dr. Greg C. EARWOOD
05 Academic Dean ... Dr. Dalen C. JACKSON
07 Director of Admissions ... Mr. Jarrod LOPEZ

Beckfield College (M)

16 Spiral Drive, Florence KY 41042-4866
County: Boone FICE Identification: 024911
Unit ID: 247065
Telephone: (859) 371-9393 Carnegie Class: Bac/Assoc-Assoc Dom
FAX Number: (859) 371-5096 Calendar System: Quarter
URL: www.beckfield.edu
Established: 1984 Annual Undergrad Tuition & Fees: $13,281
Enrollment: 712 Coed
Affiliation or Control: Proprietary IRS Status: Proprietary
Highest Offering: Baccalaureate
Accreditation: ACICS

00 Corporate College President/CFO ... Ms. Diane G. WOLFER
01 President Florence Campus ... Ms. Mia GRANACHER
05 Dean of Academic Affairs ... Dr. Rachel A. MCARTHUR
12 Campus Director of Florence ... Mr. Keith GRANT
32 Director of Student Services ... Ms. Katina SCHLIMM
37 Director of Financial Aid ... Ms. Patricia A. NETTLETON
13 Director of Information Technology ... Mr. James BRUN
07 Director Admissions ... Mr. Jeff BAKER
36 Director Career Services ... Ms. Karen SHELDON
22 Director of Compliance ... Mr. Peter NETTLETON
06 Registrar ... Vacant
08 Librarian ... Ms. Gayle ECABERT

50 Dean of Business/Technology ... Dr. Erica OKERE
66 Dean of Nursing ... Dr. Deborah SMITH
76 Dean of Allied Health ... Ms. Dolores DOMINGUEZ
97 Dean of General Education ... Ms. Mindy HODGES
88 Dean of Criminal Justice ... Ms. Brandy EXELER
04 Assistant to the President ... Ms. Cheryl A. KUNKEL

Bellarmine University (A)

2001 Newburg Road, Louisville KY 40205-0671
County: Jefferson FICE Identification: 001954
Unit ID: 156286
Telephone: (502) 272-8000 Carnegie Class: Masters/L
FAX Number: (502) 272-8033 Calendar System: Semester
URL: www.bellarmine.edu
Established: 1950 Annual Undergrad Tuition & Fees: $37,650
Enrollment: 3,609 Coed
Affiliation or Control: Independent Non-Profit IRS Status: 501(c)3
Highest Offering: Doctorate
Accreditation: SC, BUS, COARC, MT, NURSE, PTA, TED

01 Interim President ... Dr. Doris A. TEGART
05 Provost ... Dr. Carole PFEFFER
20 Vice Provost ... Dr. Graham ELLIS
20 Vice Provost ... Dr. Jay D. GATRELL
20 Vice Provost ... Dr. Anne BUCALOS
10 Vice President for Admin & Finance ... Mr. Robert L. ZIMLICH
32 Vice President for Student Affairs ... Dr. Helen G. RYAN
30 VP for Dev & Alumni Relations ... Mr. Glenn F. KOSSE
26 VP for Comm & Public Affairs ... Mr. Hunt C. HELM
84 Vice President for Enrollment Mgmt ... Dr. Sean J. RYAN
100 Exec Assistant to the President ... Ms. Marisa ZOELLER
04 Administrative Asst to President ... Ms. Lucy BURNS
66 Dn Lansing Sch of Nursing/Hlth Sci ... Dr. Mark WIEGAND
50 Dean Rubel School of Business ... Dr. Robert BROWN
107 Dean of Continuing and Prof Studies ... Dr. Sean J. RYAN
53 Dean Annsley Frazier Thornton Educ ... Dr. Robert B. COOTER
65 Dean Sch of Environmental Studies ... Dr. Robert KINGSOLVER
49 Dean Bellarmine College ... Dr. William E. FENTON
15 Chief Human Resources Officer ... Ms. Lynn M. BYNUM
21 Asst VP Business Affairs ... Ms. Denise BROWN-CORNELIUS
44 Associate VP Development ... Ms. Tina KAUFFMAN
28 Asst VP Stdnt & Multicultural Affs ... Mr. Patrick ENGLERT
85 Chief International Officer ... Ms. Gabriele BOSLEY
35 Dean of Students ... Dr. Sean MCGREEVEY
92 Director Honors Program ... Dr. Jonathan W. BLANDFORD
41 Athletic Director ... Mr. Scott P. WIEGANDT
18 Asst VP Facilities Management ... Mr. Jeffrey DEAN
07 Dean of Admission ... Mr. Timothy A. STURGEON
08 Director of the Library ... Mr. John K. STEMMER
19 Director of Safety & Security ... Mr. Joseph FRYE
07 Dean of Graduate Admission ... Dr. Sara Y. PETTINGILL
06 Registrar ... Ms. Ann E. OLSEN
96 Purchasing Manager ... Mr. Patrick COONS
42 Director Campus Ministry ... Dr. Melanie P. SULLIVAN
39 Associate Dean Residence Life ... Ms. Leslie M. MAXIE-ASHFORD
13 Vice Provost Information Technology ... Mr. Eric SATTERLY
37 Director Student Financial Aid ... Ms. Heather BOUTELL
36 Director of Career Services ... Dr. Lilly MASSA-MCKINLEY
29 Executive Director Alumni Relations ... Mr. Peter W. KREMER
27 Director of News/Media/Social Netwk ... Mr. Jason A. CISSELL
38 Director of Counseling Center ... Dr. Gary PETIPRIN
104 Study Abroad Advisor ... Ms. Bridget KLEIN
92 Director of Brown Scholars Program ... Dr. Conor A. PICKEN

Berea College (B)

101 Chestnut Street, Berea KY 40404-0003
County: Madison FICE Identification: 001955
Unit ID: 156295
Telephone: (859) 985-3000 Carnegie Class: Bac-A&S
FAX Number: (859) 985-3917 Calendar System: Semester
URL: www.berea.edu
Established: 1855 Annual Undergrad Tuition & Fees: $24,370
Enrollment: 1,621 Coed
Affiliation or Control: Independent Non-Profit IRS Status: 501(c)3
Highest Offering: Baccalaureate
Accreditation: SC, NURSE, TED

01 President ... Dr. Lyle D. ROELOFS
10 Vice President Finance ... Mr. Jeff S. AMBURGEY
29 VP Alumni & College Relations ... Ms. Bernadine DOUGLAS
32 VP Labor and Student Life ... Mr. Virgil BURNSIDE
11 VP Operations and Sustainability ... Mr. Derrick SINGLETON
30 Associate VP for Development ... Ms. Joanne SINGH
04 Assistant to President ... Ms. Rebecca PARRISH
35 Asst Vice Pres for Student Life ... Mr. Gus GERASSIMIDES
05 Academic VP/Dean of the Faculty ... Dr. Chad BERRY
37 Dir of Student Financial Aid Svcs ... Ms. Theresa LOWDER
38 Dir Counseling/Psychological Svcs ... Ms. Sue REIMONDO
44 Director of Gift Planning ... Ms. Amy SHEHEE
108 Director of Academic Assessment ... Dr. Robert SMITH
20 Dean of Curriculum/Student Learning ... Dr. Scott STEELE
13 Chief Information Officer ... Ms. Huapei CHEN
07 Director of Admissions Operations ... Mr. Luke HODSON
88 Associate VP of Alumni Relations ... Ms. Jackie COLLIER
15 Director of Human Resources ... Mr. Steve LAWSON
18 Director of Facilities Management ... Mr. Wayne ORR
88 Director of Appalachian Center ... Mr. Chris GREEN
09 Director of Inst Rsrch/Assessment ... Ms. Judith WECKMAN
26 Publications and Project Manager ... Mr. J. MORGAN
08 Director of Library Services ... Ms. Anne CHASE
41 Dir Athletics/Seabury Ctr Complex ... Mr. Mark CARTMILL
42 Director Campus Christian Center ... Rev. Gail BOWMAN
43 General Counsel ... Mr. Judge WILSON
19 Director of Public Safety ... Mr. V Lavoyed HUDGINS
28 Director Black Cultural Center ... Ms. Monica JONES
88 Dean of Labor ... Mr. David E. TIPTON
85 Director International Center ... Dr. Richard CAHILL
40 Retail Manager College Store ... Ms. Susan BUCKMASTER
96 Purchasing Manager ... Ms. Aurelia BRANDENBURG
24 Media Services Coordinator ... Mr. Rob LEWIS
06 Director of Academic Services ... Mr. Curtis SANDBERG
88 Center for Transformative Learning ... Ms. Leslie OFTQUIST-AHRENS
88 Woodson Center for Interracial Educ ... Dr. Alicestyne TURLEY
88 Director of CELTS ... Ms. Ashley COCHRANE
23 Director of Health and Wellness ... Ms. Jill GURTATOWSKI
88 Director of Internships ... Ms. Esther LIVINGSTON
103 Director of Career Development ... Ms. Amarica TUDOR
104 Education Abroad Adviser ... Ms. Ann BUTWELL
22 VP for Diversity and Inclusion ... Dr. Linda LEEK

Brescia University (C)

717 Frederica Street, Owensboro KY 42301-3023
County: Daviess FICE Identification: 001958
Unit ID: 156356
Telephone: (270) 685-3131 Carnegie Class: Bac-Diverse
FAX Number: (270) 686-6422 Calendar System: Semester
URL: www.brescia.edu
Established: 1950 Annual Undergrad Tuition & Fees: $20,440
Enrollment: 1,056 Coed
Affiliation or Control: Roman Catholic IRS Status: 501(c)3
Highest Offering: Master's
Accreditation: SC, SW

01 President ... Rev. Larry HOSTETTER
05 Vice President & Academic Dean ... Dr. Cheryl CLEMONS
10 Vice President Business & Finance ... Mr. Dale CECIL
84 Vice President of Enrollment ... Mr. Christopher HOUK
30 Vice Pres Institutional Advancement ... Ms. Tracy NAYLOR
32 Vice Pres/Dean Student Development ... Mr. Joshua R. CLARY
39 Director Residence Life ... Mr. Issac DUNCAN
35 Director Stdnts Act/Leadership Dev ... Ms. Patricia LOVETT
06 Registrar ... Sr. Helena FISCHER, OSU
106 Director of BU Online ... Ms. Shanda LARUE
38 Director of Counseling Center ... Ms. Eva G. ATKINSON
08 Director of Library Services ... Sr. Judith N. RINEY, OSU
88 Director of UCTL ... Dr. Anna KUTHY
15 Director of Human Resources ... Ms. Tammy S. KELLER
13 Director of Information Technology ... Mr. Chris FORD
18 Director of Physical Plant ... Mr. Mike WARD
37 Director of Financial Aid ... Ms. Kristi EIDSON
41 Director of Athletics ... Mr. Brian SKORTZ
26 Director of Public Relations ... Ms. Kayla CRUSE
29 Sr Director of Alumni & Donor Rels ... Mr. Mike GOETZ
44 Director of Annual Giving ... Ms. Sydney WARREN
09 Director of Institutional Research ... Ms. Stephanie CLARY
58 Director of Graduate Program-MBA ... Dr. Sandra O. OBILADE
58 Director of Graduate Program-MSCI ... Dr. Patricia A. AKOJIE
42 Director of Campus Ministry ... Sr. Pam MUELLER, OSU
07 Director of Admissions ... Ms. Christy ROHNER
21 Asst Director Business & Finance ... Ms. Nancy W. REYNOLDS
36 Coordinator of Career Services ... Ms. Sarah JACKSON
20 Associate Academic Dean for Online ... Mr. Jeffrey BARNETTE
40 Bookstore Manager ... Ms. Beverly MCCANDLESS
25 Grants Writer/Special Asst to Pres ... Vacant

Brown Mackie College-Hopkinsville (D)

4001 Fort Campbell Boulevard,
Hopkinsville KY 42240-4948
Telephone: (270) 886-1302 Identification: 666516
Accreditation: ACICS, OTA

† Branch campus of Brown Mackie College-Findlay, Findlay, OH.

Brown Mackie College-Louisville (E)

3605 Fern Valley Road, Louisville KY 40219-1916
Telephone: (502) 810-6000 FICE Identification: 021082
Accreditation: ACICS, OTA

† Branch campus of Brown Mackie College-Findlay, Findlay, OH.

Brown Mackie College-Northern Kentucky (F)

309 Buttermilk Pike, Fort Mitchell KY 41017-2191
Telephone: (859) 341-5627 Identification: 666446
Accreditation: ACICS, OTA

† School is in teach-out plan. Branch campus of Brown Mackie College, Cincinnati, OH.

Campbellsville University (G)

1 University Drive, Campbellsville KY 42718-2799
County: Taylor FICE Identification: 001959
Unit ID: 156365
Telephone: (270) 789-5000 Carnegie Class: Masters/L
FAX Number: (270) 789-5050 Calendar System: Semester
URL: www.campbellsville.edu
Established: 1906 Annual Undergrad Tuition & Fees: $23,828
Enrollment: 3,427 Coed
Affiliation or Control: Baptist IRS Status: 501(c)3
Highest Offering: Master's
Accreditation: SC, IACBE, MUS, NUR, SW, TED

01 President ... Dr. Michael CARTER
10 Vice Pres Finance & Administration ... Mr. Otto TENNANT
05 Vice President Academic Affairs ... Dr. Donna HEDGEPATH
30 Vice President for Development ... Mr. Benji KELLY
07 VP Admiss/Stdnt Svcs & Dean Stdnts ... Mr. Dave WALTERS
20 Associate Academic Officer ... Dr. Jeanette PARKER
21 Controller ... Mr. Tim JUDD
09 Director of Institutional Research ... Mrs. Anna PAVY
38 Director of Student Counseling ... Vacant
92 Director of Honors Program ... Dr. Craig L. ROGERS
41 Director of Athletics ... Mr. Rusty HOLLINGSWORTH
40 Director of Bookstore ... Mrs. Donna WRIGHT
42 Director of Campus Ministries ... Mr. Edwin C. PAVY
13 Director of Computing/Communication ... Mr. Eric SMITH
37 Director of Financial Aid ... Mrs. Chris MAPES
29 Director of Alumni Relations ... Vacant
08 Director of Library Services ... Mr. John BURCH
15 Director of Personnel Services ... Mr. Terry VANMETER
18 Director of Maintenance ... Mr. Steve MORRIS
26 Director of News Information ... Mrs. Joan C. MCKINNEY
06 Director of Student Records ... Mrs. Rita A. CREASON
04 Secretary to the President ... Mrs. Kellie VAUGHN
96 Director of Purchasing ... Mrs. Lisa FERGUSON
88 Director of Custodial Services ... Mr. Bob STOTTS

Centre College (H)

600 W Walnut Street, Danville KY 40422-1394
County: Boyle FICE Identification: 001961
Unit ID: 156408
Telephone: (859) 238-5200 Carnegie Class: Bac-A&S
FAX Number: (859) 238-6977 Calendar System: Other
URL: www.centre.edu
Established: 1819 Annual Undergrad Tuition & Fees: $38,200
Enrollment: 1,387 Coed
Affiliation or Control: Independent Non-Profit IRS Status: 501(c)3
Highest Offering: Baccalaureate
Accreditation: SC

01 President ... Dr. John A. ROUSH
05 Vice President & Dean of College ... Dr. Stephanie L. FABRITIUS
10 Int Vice Pres Finance & Treasurer ... Mr. John R. FARRIS
26 Vice President College Relations ... Dr. Richard W. TROLLINGER
32 Vice Pres/Dean of Student Life ... Mr. Wm. Randy HAYS
30 Assoc VP Development/Alumni Affairs ... Mr. Shawn LYONS
43 Assoc VP for Legal Affs/Gift Plng ... Mr. James P. LEAHEY
53 Professor of Education ... Dr. Donna M. PLUMMER
28 Assoc Vice Pres Diversity/Acad Affs ... Dr. Rodmon KING
07 Dean of Admissions & Financial Aid ... Mr. Robert M. NESMITH
20 Associate Dean of the College ... Dr. Brian CUSATO
38 Director of Counseling Services ... Ms. Ann E. GOODWIN
45 Asst to the President for Planning ... Dr. J. Patrick NOLTEMEYER
104 Director of International Programs ... Dr. Milton M. REIGELMAN
08 Director of Library Services ... Mr. Stanley R. CAMPBELL
04 Exec Assistant to the President ... Ms. Yvonne Y. MORLEY
37 Director of Financial Aid ... Mr. Kevin D. LAMB
06 Registrar ... Mr. Timothy P. CULHAN
15 Director Human Resources/Admin Svcs ... Mrs. Kay L. DRAKE
27 Director of Communications ... Dr. Michael P. STRYSICK
36 Director of Career Services ... Ms. Joy ASHER
39 Director Student Life & Housing ... Ms. Ann S. YOUNG
41 Director of Athletics & Recreation ... Mr. W. Bradley FIELDS
19 Co-Director of Public Safety ... Mr. Kevin S. MILBY
19 Co-Director of Public Safety ... Mr. Gary D. BUGG
09 Director of Institutional Research ... Mr. J. Patrick NOLTEMEYER
13 Director of Info Technology Service ... Mr. J. Keith FOWLKES
24 Director Ctr for Teaching/Learning ... Dr. Sarah E. LASHLEY
18 Director of Facilities Management ... Mr. D. Wayne KING
21 Controller ... Mr. R. Scott OWENS
42 College Chaplain ... Dr. Richard D. AXTELL
96 Dir Purchasing/Campus Interiors ... Ms. Ann T. SMITH
29 Director of Alumni Affairs ... Ms. Megan H. MILBY
57 Director Norton Center for Arts ... Mr. Steven A. HOFFMAN

Clear Creek Baptist Bible College (I)

300 Clear Creek Road, Pineville KY 40977-9754
County: Bell FICE Identification: 025356
Unit ID: 156417
Telephone: (606) 337-3196 Carnegie Class: Spec-4-yr-Faith
FAX Number: (606) 337-2372 Calendar System: Semester
URL: www.ccbbc.edu
Established: 1926 Annual Undergrad Tuition & Fees: $6,792
Enrollment: 156 Coed
Affiliation or Control: Southern Baptist IRS Status: 501(c)3
Highest Offering: Baccalaureate
Accreditation: SC, BI

01 President ... Dr. Donnie S. FOX
05 Academic Dean ... Dr. Jay SULFRIDGE
32 Dean of Student Affairs ... Rev. Charlie GOODMAN
11 Administrative Dean ... Mr. Jeremy ANDERSON
30 Dean of Institutional Advancement ... Mr. Shannon BENEFIEL
08 Director of Library ... Mrs. Marge CUMMINGS
42 Christian Service Director ... Rev. Richard BARTELS
18 Director of Physical Plant ... Mr. Ronnie WASHAM
37 Director Financial Aid ... Mr. Sam RISNER
06 Registrar ... Mr. Jacob YATES
07 Director of Admissions ... Mr. Greg YOUNG
26 Director of College Relations ... Rev. Richard L. WITHERITE
13 Dir of Information Technologies ... Mr. Shane KAKHOLA
56 Director of Distance Education ... Dr. Jay BARNETT

Daymar College Online (A)

4112 Fern Valley Road, Louisville KY 40219
Telephone: (502) 495-1040 Identification: 770615
Accreditation: ACICS

Daymar College-Bellevue (B)

119 Fairfield Avenue, Bellevue KY 41073
Telephone: (859) 291-0800 Identification: 666390
Accreditation: ACICS

† Branch campus of Daymar College, Owensboro, KY.

Daymar College-Bowling Green (C)

2421 Fitzgerald Industrial Drive,
Bowling Green KY 42101-4071
Telephone: (270) 843-6750 Identification: 666439
Accreditation: ACICS

† Branch campus of Daymar College, Nashville, TN.

Daymar College-Madisonville (D)

1105 National Mine Drive, Madisonville KY 42431
Telephone: (270) 643-0312 Identification: 667079
Accreditation: ACICS

† In teach-out mode. Branch campus of Daymar College, Owensboro, KY.

Daymar College-Owensboro (E)

3361 Buckland Square, Owensboro KY 42301
County: Daviess FICE Identification: 009313
Unit ID: 157465
Telephone: (270) 926-4040 Carnegie Class: Spec-4-yr-Other Health
FAX Number: (270) 685-4090 Calendar System: Quarter
URL: www.daymarcollege.edu
Established: 1963 Annual Undergrad Tuition & Fees: $17,000
Enrollment: 94 Coed
Affiliation or Control: Proprietary IRS Status: Proprietary
Highest Offering: Baccalaureate
Accreditation: ACICS

01 Area President .... Tina LYNCH
66 Director of Nursing .... Dr. Michael RAGER

† In teach-out mode.

Eastern Kentucky University (F)

521 Lancaster Avenue, Richmond KY 40475-3102
County: Madison FICE Identification: 001963
Unit ID: 156620
Telephone: (859) 622-1000 Carnegie Class: Masters/L
FAX Number: (859) 622-1020 Calendar System: Semester
URL: www.eku.edu
Established: 1906 Annual Undergrad Tuition & Fees (In-State): $8,150
Enrollment: 16,305 Coed
Affiliation or Control: State IRS Status: 501(c)3
Highest Offering: Doctorate
Accreditation: SC, AAFCS, ADNUR, BUS, CAATE, CACREP, CAHIIM, CONST, CS, DIETD, DIETI, EMT, ENGT, FEPAC, IFSAC, MT, MUS, NAIT, NRPA, NURSE, OT, PH, SP, SPAA, SW, TED

01 President .... Dr. Michael BENSON
05 Provost/Vice Pres Academic Affairs .... Dr. Janna VICE
32 Dean of Students .... Ms. Kenna MIDDLETON
10 VP of Finance & Administration .... Mr. Barry POYNTER
30 Vice Pres University Advancement .... Mr. Nick PERLICK
84 Act VP Enrol Mgt/Mrktng/Univ Rels .... Mr. Brett MORRIS
45 Assoc VP University Programs .... Dr. Sara ZEIGLER
26 Asst VP Branding & Marketing .... Mr. Doug CORNETT
35 Exec Director Student Affairs .... Dr. Salome NNOROMELE
76 Dean Health Sciences .... Dr. Deborah WHITEHOUSE
49 Dean Arts & Sciences .... Dr. John WADE
50 Dean Business & Technology .... Dr. Thomas EREKSON
53 Dean Education .... Vacant
88 Dean Justice & Safety .... Dr. Victor KAPPELER
86 Exec Dir Government Relations .... Mr. David MCFADDIN
43 University Counsel .... Dr. Laurie CARTER
19 Chief of Police .... Mr. Brian MULLINS
08 Director Libraries .... Ms. Betina GARDNER
06 Registrar .... Ms. Tina DAVIS
27 Director Advising .... Mr. Benton SHIREY
07 Director Admissions .... Mr. Brett MORRIS
36 Director Career Services .... Mrs. Gladys MILLER
25 Director Sponsored Programs .... Mr. Gus BENSON
92 Director Honors Program .... Dr. David COLEMAN
09 Asst VP Inst Research/Effectiveness .... Ms. Tanlee WESSON
85 Director International Education .... Vacant
38 Director Counseling Center .... Dr. Jen C. WALKER
39 Exec Director Housing .... Mr. Billy MARTIN
88 Director Judicial Affairs/Disabled .... Mrs. Betsy BOHANNON
37 Dir Student Financial Assistance .... Mr. Bryan ERSLAN
23 Director Student Health Services .... Dr. Pradeep BOSE
40 Director Bookstore .... Mr. Timothy GOGNAT
15 Interim Director Equity/Inclusion .... Mr. Brandon WILLIAMS
90 Director Info Tech/Delivery Svcs .... Ms. Jean MARLOW
29 Asst VP Alumni/Donor Engagement .... Mrs. Kari MARTIN
109 Exec Dir Stdnt Life/Auxiliary Svcs .... Mr. Billy MARTIN
18 Director Facilities Services .... Mr. David WILLIAMS
28 Interim Chief Diversity Officer .... Mr. Sherwood THOMPSON
41 Athletic Director .... Mr. Stephen LOCHMUELLER
96 Director of Purchasing .... Ms. Lora SNIDER
42 Chaplain .... Dr. Patrick C. NNOROMELE
04 Admin Asst to the President .... Ms. Lisa KELLEY
04 Exec Asst to the President & BOR .... Mr. Jeremy RAINES

Frontier Nursing University (G)

195 School Street, Hyden KY 41749
County: Leslie FICE Identification: 030070
Unit ID: 156727
Telephone: (606) 672-2312 Carnegie Class: Spec-4-yr-Other Health
FAX Number: (606) 672-3776 Calendar System: Quarter
URL: www.frontier.edu
Established: 1939 Annual Graduate Tuition & Fees: N/A
Enrollment: 1,478 Coed
Affiliation or Control: Independent Non-Profit IRS Status: 501(c)3
Highest Offering: Doctorate; No Undergraduates
Accreditation: SC, MIDWF, NUR

01 President & Dean .... Dr. Susan STONE
05 Associate Dean of Academic Affairs .... Dr. Anne COCKERHAM
66 Dean of Nursing .... Dr. Julie MARFELL
46 Associate Dean of Research .... Vacant
88 PM-DNP Program Director .... Dr. Susan YOUNT
88 Bridge Option Director .... Dr. Trish VOSS
37 Director of Financial Aid .... Ms. Rainie BOGGS

Galen College of Nursing (H)

1031 Zorn Avenue, Louisville KY 40207-1064
County: Jefferson FICE Identification: 030837
Unit ID: 156471
Telephone: (502) 410-6200 Carnegie Class: Spec 2-yr-Health
FAX Number: (502) 568-1271 Calendar System: Quarter
URL: www.galencollege.edu
Established: 1989 Annual Undergrad Tuition & Fees: N/A
Enrollment: 879 Coed
Affiliation or Control: Proprietary IRS Status: Proprietary
Highest Offering: Baccalaureate
Accreditation: SC, ADNUR, NURSE

01 Chief Executive Officer .... Mr. Mark A. VOGT
05 Interim Academic President .... Dr. Joan L. FREY
06 Director of Academic Records .... Ms. Jonda BRINNER
106 Dean of Online Programs .... Dr. Kathy BURLINGAME
66 ADN Program Director of Main Campus .... Dr. Constance COOPER
88 Executive VP of Prelicensure Nurs .... Dr. Audria DENKER
11 VP of Operations and Reg Affairs .... Ms. Kathleen DWYER
84 VP of Enrollment Management .... Mr. Carter SMITH
66 Dean of Main Campus .... Dr. Joan L. FREY
10 VP of Finance .... Mr. Thomas DWYER
14 Director of Information Technology .... Mr. Duane HELLUMS
20 Executive VP and Provost .... Dr. Steve HYNDMAN
26 Director of Marketing .... Ms. Anna KITSON
15 Director of Human Resources .... Vacant
88 Executive VP of Post-licensure Nsg .... Dr. Tracy ORTELLI
66 PN Program Director of Main Campus .... Ms. Lisa PEAK
37 Director of Financial Aid .... Ms. Joni M. PENLAND
03 Executive VP and CAO .... Mr. Joseph R. PETERS
13 VP of Technology and Planning .... Mr. David RAY
108 Director of Inst Effectiveness .... Dr. Carissa SHAFTO
07 Director of Admissions .... Ms. Terri THOMAS

Georgetown College (I)

400 E College Street, Georgetown KY 40324-1696
County: Scott FICE Identification: 001964
Unit ID: 156745
Telephone: (502) 863-8000 Carnegie Class: Bac-A&S
FAX Number: (502) 868-8891 Calendar System: Semester
URL: www.georgetowncollege.edu
Established: 1829 Annual Undergrad Tuition & Fees: $34,280
Enrollment: 1,262 Coed
Affiliation or Control: Baptist IRS Status: 501(c)3
Highest Offering: Master's
Accreditation: #SC, CAATE, TED

01 President .... Dr. Dwaine GREENE
05 Provost/Dean of the College .... Dr. Rosemary ALLEN
10 Vice President/CFO/Treasurer .... Mr. David WILHITE
101 Asst to President/Board Secretary .... Mr. Robin OLDHAM
30 VP Institutional Advancement .... Dr. Todd RASBERRY
32 Dean of Students/Title IX Coord .... Ms. Laura JOHNSON
84 Vice President for Enrollment .... Dr. Jonathan SANDS WISE
13 Assoc VP for Info Tech Services .... Mr. Donald L. BLAKEMAN
26 Assoc VP for Comm & Marketing .... Mr. Jim ALLISON
21 Controller .... Vacant
88 Bursar .... Vacant
06 Registrar .... Mr. Jason SNIDER
88 Dir Ctr for Culturally Rel Pedagogy .... Dr. Rebecca POWELL
15 Director of Human Resources .... Ms. Tracie SHAPIRO
53 Dean of Education .... Dr. Joy BOWERS-CAMPBELL
07 Director of Admissions .... Mr. Jeremiah TUDOR
37 Dir of Student Financial Planning .... Mr. Bob FULTZ
30 Director of Development .... Vacant
09 Director of Institutional Research .... Dr. Jessica HEARN
08 Director of Library Services .... Mr. Benjamin RAWLINS
29 Director of Alumni Relations .... Ms. Laura OWSLEY
41 Director of Athletics .... Mr. Brian EVANS
88 Dir Comm/Mktg & Church Relations .... Mr. H.K KINGKADE
36 Dir Graves Ctr for Calling & Career .... Ms. Holly JAMES
19 Director Campus Safety .... Mr. Dan BROWN
38 Director of Counseling/Health Svcs .... Ms. Megan REDDITT
18 Dir Facilities and Grounds .... Mr. Bart HORNE
28 Director of Diversity Initiatives .... Ms. Beth ORTEGON

Indiana Tech-Louisville (J)

11855 Commonwealth Drive, Louisville KY 40299
Telephone: (502) 708-2363 Identification: 770104
Accreditation: &NH

† Regional accreditation is carried under the parent institution in Fort Wayne, IN

Interactive College of Technology (K)

76 Caruthers Road, Newport KY 41071
Telephone: (859) 282-8989 Identification: 770535
Accreditation: COE

† Branch campus of Interactive College of Technology, Chamblee, GA

Kentucky Christian University (L)

100 Academic Parkway, Grayson KY 41143-2205
County: Carter FICE Identification: 001965
Unit ID: 157100
Telephone: (606) 474-3000 Carnegie Class: Bac-Diverse
FAX Number: (606) 474-3189 Calendar System: Semester
URL: www.kcu.edu
Established: 1919 Annual Undergrad Tuition & Fees: $17,810
Enrollment: 658 Coed
Affiliation or Control: Christian Churches And Churches of Christ
IRS Status: 501(c)3
Highest Offering: Master's
Accreditation: SC, NURSE, SW

01 President/CEO .... Dr. Jeff K. METCALF
05 Executive Vice President .... Dr. Marvin L. ELLIOTT
30 Director of Development .... Mr. Monty COOPER
88 Director of Church Relations .... Mr. Jeff W. GREENE
06 Registrar .... Mrs. Andrea L. STAMPER
13 Director of Campus Technology .... Mr. Greg C. RICHARDSON
08 Library Director .... Mrs. Naulayne R. ENDERS
108 Director Institutional Assessment .... Vacant
32 Director of Student Services .... Mr. William B. BAUMGARDNER
42 Campus Minister .... Mr. Larry W. MARSHALL
37 Director Financial Aid .... Mrs. Jennie M. BENDER
15 Human Resource Officer .... Mr. Terry L. YANKEY
38 Student Counseling Coordinator .... Mrs. Lori A. SMITH-WARD
41 Athletic Director .... Mr. Bruce W. DIXON
39 Director of Residence Services .... Vacant
18 Director of Facilities .... Mr. John R. SEAGRAVES
29 Alumni Relations Officer .... Mr. Jeff W. GREENE
58 Dean of the Graduate School .... Dr. David A. FIENSY
07 Director of Enrollment Services .... Mrs. Sheree GREER
40 Manager of Retail Operations .... Mrs. Patty J. SERHAL
105 Website Manager .... Mr. David A. BENNETT
10 Director of Business .... Mr. Daniel R. WHITE

*Kentucky Community and Technical College System (M)

300 N Main Street, Versailles KY 40383-1245
County: Woodford FICE Identification: 006724
Unit ID: 157854
Telephone: (859) 256-3100 Carnegie Class: N/A
FAX Number: (859) 256-3119
URL: www.kctcs.edu

01 President .... Dr. Jay BOX
00 Chancellor .... Dr. Rhonda TRACY
05 VC Academic Affairs .... Dr. Paul BLANKENSHIP
10 Vice President .... Mr. Wendell FOLLOWELL
13 Vice President .... Dr. Paul CZARAPATA
30 Vice President .... Mr. Timothy R. BURCHAM, CFRE
32 Vice President .... Dr. Gloria MCCALL
103 VC Econ Dev/Workforce Solutions .... Dr. Paul SCHREFFLER
09 VC Research and Analysis .... Dr. Alicia CROUCH
04 Sr Exec Assistant to the President .... Ms. Beth HILLIARD

*Ashland Community and Technical College (N)

1400 College Drive, Ashland KY 41101-3617
County: Boyd FICE Identification: 001990
Unit ID: 156231
Telephone: (606) 326-2000 Carnegie Class: Assoc/HVT-Mix Trad/Non
FAX Number: (606) 326-2187 Calendar System: Semester
URL: www.ashland.kctcs.edu
Established: 1938 Annual Undergrad Tuition & Fees (In-State): $3,624
Enrollment: 3,345 Coed
Affiliation or Control: State IRS Status: 501(c)3
Highest Offering: Associate Degree
Accreditation: SC, ADNUR, COARC, EMT, IFSAC, SURGT

02 President & CEO .... Dr. Kay ADKINS
05 Dean of Academic Affairs .... Dr. Janie KITCHEN
32 Dean Student Success/Enroll Svcs .... Mr. Steven WOODBURN

10 Dean of Business Affairs .... Ms. Karen BLEVINS
30 Dean Resource Dev/External Affairs ...... Ms. Willie MCCULLOUGH
09 Dean Inst Plng/Research/Effective .... Mr. Steve FLOUHOUSE
86 Dean of Public Service .... Mr. John MCGLONE
26 Director of Marketing .... Ms. Allison GOBLE
08 Director of Library Services .... Ms. Pamela KLINEPETER
07 Director of Admissions/Registrar .... Ms. Robin LEWIS
13 Assoc Dean Information Technology .... Mr. Farnoosh RAFIEE
28 Director of Cultural Diversity .... Mr. Alvin BAKER
15 Director of Human Resources .... Ms. Kellie ALLEN
25 Director of Grants & Contracts .... Ms. Sarah DIAMOND BURROWAY
37 Director of Financial Aid .... Mr. Adam ABSHIRE
76 Division Chair Health Sciences .... Ms. Elizabeth MCGINNIS
49 Division Chair Arts & Sciences ...... Ms. Nicole GRIFFITH-GREEN
50 Div Chair Bus/Prof Svcs/Technology .... Ms. Molly WEBB
88 Div Chair Manuf/Transp/Ind Tech .... Dr. Keith BRAMMELL
103 Director of Workforce Solutions .... Dr. Karen COBURN
88 Director of Student Support Svcs .... Ms. Megan HORNE
51 Director of Adult Education .... Ms. Penny QUALLS

*Big Sandy Community and Technical College (A)

1 Bert T. Combs Drive, Prestonburg KY 41653-9502
County: Floyd FICE Identification: 001996
Unit ID: 157553
Telephone: (606) 886-3863 Carnegie Class: Assoc/HVT-High Non
FAX Number: (606) 886-2677 Calendar System: Semester
URL: www.bigsandy.kctcs.edu
Established: 1964 Annual Undergrad Tuition & Fees (In-State): $3,624
Enrollment: 4,638 Coed
Affiliation or Control: State IRS Status: 501(c)3
Highest Offering: Associate Degree
Accreditation: SC, COARC, DH

02 President/CEO .... Dr. Devin STEPHENSON
03 Chief Institutional Officer .... Mr. Bobby MCCOOL
05 Provost .... Vacant
32 Dean of Student Affairs .... Mr. Jimmy WRIGHT
10 Chief Business Affairs Officer .... Ms. Michelle MEEK
08 Director of Library Services .... Ms. Kathy LOWE
15 Director of Human Resources .... Ms. Bryen GOBLE
06 Registrar .... Mr. Jeffrey T. HOCKS
37 Director of Financial Aid .... Ms. Cathy HURD-CRANK
09 Dean of Institutional Effectiveness .... Dr. Chris DANIEL
13 Dean of Information Technology .... Vacant
18 Dir Facil/Safety/Auxiliary Svcs .... Mr. John HERALD
40 Bookstore Manager .... Ms. Stephanie WEST
26 Public Relations .... Mr. Joshua BALL
30 Director of Advancement .... Vacant
20 Dean of Academic Affairs .... Ms. Myra ELLIOTT
28 Director of Cultural Diversity .... Ms. Tina TERRY
103 Director Workforce Solutions .... Ms. Kelli HALL

*Bluegrass Community and Technical College (B)

470 Cooper Drive, Lexington KY 40506-0001
County: Fayette FICE Identification: 009707
Unit ID: 156392
Telephone: (859) 246-6200 Carnegie Class: Assoc/HVT-High Trad
FAX Number: (859) 246-4664 Calendar System: Semester
URL: www.bluegrass.kctcs.edu
Established: 1965 Annual Undergrad Tuition & Fees (In-State): $3,704
Enrollment: 10,952 Coed
Affiliation or Control: State IRS Status: 501(c)3
Highest Offering: Associate Degree
Accreditation: SC, ADNUR, COARC, DH, IFSAC, MAC, NMT, RAD, SURGT

02 President & CEO .... Dr. Augusta A. JULIAN
13 VP of Information Technology .... Mr. Ren BATES
05 VP of Academics/WFS .... Dr. Gregory FEENEY
32 VP Student Dev/Enrollment Svcs .. Dr. Palisa WILLIAMS RUSHIN
10 VP Finance & Administration .... Ms. Lisa G. BELL
28 VP Multiculturalism & Inclusion .... Ms. Charlene WALKER
30 VP Advancement & Org Development .... Mr. Mark MANUEL
20 Dean Academics .... Dr. Karen MAYO
20 Dean Academics .... Ms. Tammy LILES
103 Dean of Academics/Workforce Devel .... Ms. Pam HATCHER
20 Dean of Academic Support .... Ms. Rebecca SIMMS
06 Registrar .... Ms. Becky HARP-STEPHENS
37 Financial Aid Director .... Ms. Runan PENDERGRAST
07 Admissions Director .... Ms. Shelbie HUGLE
15 Associate VP Institutional Develop .... Ms. Deborrah L. CATLETT
26 PR and Marketing Coordinator .... Ms. Jennifer TYSON
38 Director of Advising & Assessment .... Ms. Pamela BATES
88 Associate Vice President for Advanc .... Ms. Laurel MARTIN
79 Assistant Dean Humanities .... Ms. Angella KING
76 Asst Dean Allied Health/Nat Science .... Dr. Yasemin CONGLETON
66 Assistant Dean Nursing .... Ms. Susan HAYES
81 Asst Dean Mathematics/Statistics .... Ms. Jackie WISEMAN
77 Asst Dean Business/CIS .... Ms. Melanie WILLIAMSON
72 Asst Dean Advanced Mfg and Trade .... Mr. Ralph POTTER
83 Asst Dean Comm/Hist/Lang/Social Sci .... Dr. Steven WHITE
08 Director Learning Resources Center .... Mr. Steve STONE
51 Director Adult Education .... Mr. David STURGILL
106 Assistant Dean Distance Learning .... Vacant
18 Director of Maintenance/Operations .... Mr. Michael BALL

*Elizabethtown Community and Technical College (C)

600 College Street Road, Elizabethtown KY 42701
County: Hardin FICE Identification: 001991
Unit ID: 156648
Telephone: (270) 769-2371 Carnegie Class: Assoc/HVT-Mix Trad/Non
FAX Number: (270) 769-0736 Calendar System: Semester
URL: www.elizabethtown.kctcs.edu
Established: 1963 Annual Undergrad Tuition & Fees (In-State): $3,624
Enrollment: 7,314 Coed
Affiliation or Control: State IRS Status: 501(c)3
Highest Offering: Associate Degree
Accreditation: SC, ADNUR, CCARC, IFSAC, RAD

02 President .... Dr. Thelma WHITE
05 Provost/CAO .... Dr. Tiffany EVANS
32 Chief Student Affairs Officer .... Dr. Dale BUCKLES
11 Chief Operations .... Mr. Keith JOHNSON
12 Campus Education Center Director .... Mr. Darrin POWELL
103 Dean of Workforce Development .... Dr. Thomas DAVENPORT
10 Dean of Business Affairs .... Mr. John WHITE
20 Dean of Instruction/Prof Develop .... Ms. Sue FRENCH
08 Library Director .... Ms. Ann THOMPSON
15 Director of Human Resources .... Ms. Kris WOOD
06 Registrar .... Mr. Bryan SMITH
13 Director of Information Technology .... Mr. Chris LEE
37 Director of Financial Aid .... Mr. Michael BARLOW
30 Chief Development .... Mr. Ronald HARRELL
26 Director of Public Relations .... Ms. Mary Jo KING
24 Learning Center Coordinator .... Ms. Pam HARPER
36 Counselor .... Ms. Sharon SPRATT
38 Counselor .... Ms. Suzanne DARLAND
40 Bookstore Manager .... Mr. Michael GESSNER
46 Director Inst Effectiveness .... Ms. Sarah EDWARDS
18 Maintenance/Operations Supervisor .... Mr. Charles COBB
57 Chair Div of Arts/Humanities .... Ms. Jacqueline HAWKINS
81 Chair Div of Biological Science ...... Ms. Tiffany MCFALLS-SMITH
81 Chair Div of Physical Science .... Mr. Paul STURGEON
75 Chair Div Occupational Technology .... Mr. Mike HAZZARD
83 Chair Div Social & Behavioral Sci .... Ms. Ramona BARROW
28 Director of Diversity .... Ms. Felicia TOLIVER
109 Campus Administrative Coordinator .... Dr. David DONATHAN

*Gateway Community and Technical College (D)

500 Technology Way, Florence KY 41042
County: Boone FICE Identification: 005273
Unit ID: 157438
Telephone: (859) 441-4500 Carnegie Class: Assoc/HVT-Mix Trad/Non
FAX Number: (859) 341-6859 Calendar System: Semester
URL: www.gateway.kctcs.edu
Established: 1961 Annual Undergrad Tuition & Fees (In-State): $3,704
Enrollment: 4,594 Coed
Affiliation or Control: State IRS Status: 501(c)3
Highest Offering: Associate Degree
Accreditation: SC, CAHIIM, IFSAC

02 Interim President/CEO .... Dr. Vic ADAMS
04 Executive Assistant to President .... Ms. Sharon POORE
03 Executive Vice President .... Dr. Patricia GOODMAN
09 Associate VP for Knowledge Mgt .... Mr. Jeremy BERBERICH
05 VP Academic Affairs .... Dr. Teri VONHANDORF
49 Dean of Arts and Sciences .... Dr. Susan SANTOS
50 Dean of Business/IT/Prof Services .... Dr. Amy CARRINO
76 Dean of Health Professions .... Ms. Amber CARTER
72 Dean of Manufacturing & Technology .... Mr. Dee WRIGHT
75 Dean of Transportation Technologies .... Mr. Sam COLLIER
30 VP Devel & Strategic Partnerships .... Dr. Amber DECKER
32 VP Student Development .... Ms. Ingrid WASHINGTON
35 Associate VP for Student Dev .... Ms. Mallis GRAVES
20 Associate VP Academic Services .... Mr. Doug PENIX
38 Director of Counseling .... Ms. Tiffany MINARD
10 VP Admin & Business Affairs .... Mr. James YOUNGER
103 VP Corporate College .... Ms. Carissa SCHUTZMAN
84 Dean of Enrollment Services .... Mr. Andre WASHINGTON
06 Registrar .... Vacant
15 Director of Human Resources .... Ms. Phyllis YEAGER
18 Director Maintenance & Operations .... Mr. George HALL
19 Director Security/Safety .... Mr. Tim CHESSER
26 Director of Communications .... Ms. Michelle SJOGREN
37 Director of Financial Aid .... Ms. Zana SMITH
13 Director of Information Services .... Ms. Melissa SEARS
66 Director of Nursing .... Ms. Melani STALLKAMP
89 Director Early College Initiatives .... Ms. Shelby KRENTZ
08 Director Library/Information Svcs .... Ms. Denise FRITSCH
25 Director of Grants/Special Projects .... Ms. Sandy ORTMAN-TOMLIN
27 Creative Strategies Coordinator .... Mr. Patrick LAMPING
105 Web Services Manager .... Vacant

*Hazard Community and Technical College (E)

One Community College Drive, Hazard KY 41701-2402
County: Perry FICE Identification: 006962
Unit ID: 156790
Telephone: (606) 436-5721 Carnegie Class: Assoc/HVT-High Trad
FAX Number: (606) 439-2988 Calendar System: Semester
URL: www.hazard.kctcs.edu
Established: 1968 Annual Undergrad Tuition & Fees (In-State): $3,624
Enrollment: 3,462 Coed
Affiliation or Control: State IRS Status: 501(c)3
Highest Offering: Associate Degree
Accreditation: SC, CAHIIM, DMS, IFSAC, PTAA, RAD, SURGT

02 President/CEO .... Dr. Jennifer LINDON
05 Int Provost/Vice Pres of Acad Svcs .... Ms. Germaine SHAFFER
32 Vice President of Student Affairs .... Ms. Germaine SHAFFER
10 Chief Financial Officer .... Ms. Connie WATTS
04 Asst to President Special Projects .... Ms. Delcie COMBS
13 Chief Information Officer .... Ms. Donna ROARK
15 Senior Director of Human Resources .... Ms. Vickie COMBS
21 Dean of Business Services .... Ms. Jackie HALL
08 Director Library Services .... Mrs. Cathy BRANSON
97 Dean General Education .... Ms. Leila SMITH
103 Dean Occup Tech & Workforce Sol .... Ms. Jennifer LINDON
76 Dean Allied Health Science Tech .... Ms. Anna NAPIER
56 Dean Distance Learning .... Ms. Ella STRONG
26 Director of Public Relations .... Mrs. Evelyn WOOD
37 Director of Financial Aid .... Mr. Charles ANDERSON, JR.
06 Registrar .... Ms. Libby PETERS
07 Director of Admissions .... Mr. Scott GROSS
108 Dir of Effect/Planning & Research .... Ms. Alexis MALEPEAI
18 Dir of Maintenance and Operations .... Mr. Stu FUGATE

*Henderson Community College (F)

2660 S Green Street, Henderson KY 42420-4699
County: Henderson FICE Identification: 001993
Unit ID: 156851
Telephone: (270) 827-1867 Carnegie Class: Assoc/MT-VT-High Non
FAX Number: (270) 831-9600 Calendar System: Semester
URL: www.henderson.kctcs.edu
Established: 1960 Annual Undergrad Tuition & Fees (In-State): $3,624
Enrollment: 2,000 Coed
Affiliation or Control: State IRS Status: 501(c)3
Highest Offering: Associate Degree
Accreditation: SC, ADNUR, DH, MAC, MLTAD

02 President .... Dr. Kris WILLIAMS
05 Interim Chief Academic Officer .... Mr. Paul KASENOW
32 Chief Student Officer .... Mr. Keith SAYLES
10 Chief Business Affairs Officer .... Mr. Jerry H. GENTRY
08 Library Director .... Mr. Mike W. KNECHT
13 Chief Information Technology Ofcr .... Ms. Kimberley S. CONLEY
15 Director of Human Resources .... Ms. Doris J. LAKE
57 Director of Fine Arts Center .... Ms. Rachael BAAR
06 Registrar .... Mr. Chad PHILLIPS
66 Interim Director of Nursing .... Ms. Debbie WHITAKER
88 Dean Success Grants .... Ms. Pamala P. WILSON
28 Director of Cultural Diversity .... Mr. William DIXON
30 Chief Advancement Officer .... Ms. Jennifer PRESTON
09 Dir Institutional Research & Effect .... Mr. Brian MCMURTRAY
18 Maintenance/Oper Supervisor .... Mr. Lance CONYERS
35 Student Activities Coordinator .... Mr. Larry TUTT
36 Career Services Coordinator .... Ms. Angela WATSON
37 Director Financial Aid .... Mr. Andrew ZELLERS
84 Assoc Dean for Enrollment Mgmt .... Mr. Cary CONLEY
88 Professional Development Coord .... Ms. Katie GRIFFIS
49 Div Chair Liberal Arts/Prof Studies .... Ms. Sharon BURTON
76 Div Chair Allied Health .... Ms. Kim DEAN
81 Div Chair STEM .... Mr. Eugene PATSALIDES
04 Administrative Asst to President .... Ms. Malinda S. HUDSON
103 Dir Community/Workforce/Econ Dev .... Vacant

*Hopkinsville Community College (G)

720 North Drive, PO Box 2100,
Hopkinsville KY 42241-2100
County: Christian FICE Identification: 001994
Unit ID: 156860
Telephone: (270) 707-3700 Carnegie Class: Assoc/MT-VT-High Trad
FAX Number: (270) 886-0237 Calendar System: Semester
URL: www.hopkinsville.kctcs.edu
Established: 1965 Annual Undergrad Tuition & Fees (In-State): $3,624
Enrollment: 3,566 Coed
Affiliation or Control: State IRS Status: 501(c)3
Highest Offering: Associate Degree
Accreditation: SC, ADNUR

02 President .... Dr. Jay S. ALLEN
04 Exec Admin Asst to President .... Ms. Janice JONES
05 Chief Academic Affairs Officer .... Dr. Alissa YOUNG
06 Registrar .... Ms. Melissa STEVENSON
08 Library Services Director .... Ms. Ann NICHOLS
09 Dir Institutional Effectiveness .... Vacant
10 Chief Business Affairs Officer .... Mr. Jeff HORTON
12 Campus/Educ Center Director FTC .... Ms. Allisha LEE
13 Information Technology Director .... Mr. Tony NELSON
15 Human Resources Director .... Ms. Yvonne GLASMAN
18 Maintenance/Operations Director .... Mr. Dan HAMBY
19 Safety and Security Director .... Mr. Bill BESSETTE
21 Business Affairs Associate Dean .... Ms. Ann T. HOLLAND
26 Marketing & Communication Director .... Ms. Rena YOUNG
28 Cultural Diversity Director .... Ms. Tracey Y. FOLDEN
30 Chief Institutional Advancement Ofc .... Ms. Yvette EASTHAM
32 Chief Student Affairs Officer .... Dr. Jason D. WARREN
36 Career & Transfer Director .... Ms. Kanya ALLEN
37 Financial Aid Director .... Ms. Janet GUNTHER
38 Advising Center Director .... Ms. Deloria SCOTT
40 Bookstore Director .... Ms. Diane CUNNINGHAM
57 Arts and Sciences Division Chair .... Dr. Ken CASEY

72 Professional & Technical Studies .... Mr. Gregory BRIDGEMAN
76 Allied Health Div Chair ....Ms. Peggy I. BOZARTH
81 Mathmatics & Sciences Div Chair ....Mr. Ted H. WILSON
103 Chief CWED Officer ....Ms. Carol KIRVES

*Jefferson Community and Technical College (A)

109 E Broadway, Louisville KY 40202-2000
County: Jefferson FICE Identification: 006961
Unit ID: 156921
Telephone: (502) 213-5333 Carnegie Class: Assoc/HVT-High Trad
FAX Number: (502) 213-2115 Calendar System: Semester
URL: www.jefferson.kctcs.edu
Established: 1967 Annual Undergrad Tuition & Fees (In-State): $3,704
Enrollment: 13,550 Coed
Affiliation or Control: State IRS Status: 501(c)3
Highest Offering: Associate Degree
Accreditation: SC, ACFEI, ADNUR, CAHIIM, COARC, IFSAC, MAC, MLTAD, OTA, PTAA, RAD, SURGT

02 President ....Dr. Ty J. HANDY
05 VP of Academic & Student Affairs .Dr. Diane CALHOUN-FRENCH
10 Controller ....Ms. Norma NORTHERN
20 Int Dean Academic Affs Tech Pgms .... Dr. Telly SELLARS
20 Dean of General Education/Transfer .... Dr. Randy DAVIS
12 Dean of Bullitt and Shelby Campuses .... Dr. Denise GRAY
32 Dean Student Affairs Downtown ....Dr. Laura SMITH
08 Library Services Director .... Ms. Sheree WILLIAMS
13 Chief Information Technology Office ....Mr. Thomas ROGERS
09 Institutional Effectiveness ....Dr. Jo ZAUSCH
06 Registrar ....Ms. Amanda TINDALL
26 Chief of Staff/PR Marketing .... Ms. Lisa BROSKY
15 Director of Human Resources .... Ms. Toni WHALEN
18 Facilities Director .... Mr. Craig TURPIN
37 Director of Financial Aid ....Ms. Angela JOHNSON
30 Inst Advance/Development Coord ....Ms. Karla HALL
103 VP Workforce Sol CE/CS/Bus/ Industry ....Ms. Mary Ann HYLAND-MURR
38 Student Counseling ....Ms. Rhonda GUMMER
96 Director of Purchasing .... Ms. Pamela DUMM
12 Director of Carrollton Campus .... Ms. Susan CARLISLE
12 Dean of Extended Campuses/Academic .... Ms. Donna MILLER
24 Learning Center Coord Downtown ....Ms. Reneau WAGGONER
04 Administrative Asst to President ....Ms. Teresa B. HARPER
106 Dir Online Education/E-learning .... Mr. Adam ELIAS
25 Chief Contracts/Grants Admin ....Ms. Joanna LYNCH

*Madisonville Community College (B)

2000 College Drive, Madisonville KY 42431-9199
County: Hopkins FICE Identification: 009010
Unit ID: 157304
Telephone: (270) 824-8562 Carnegie Class: Assoc/HVT-High Non
FAX Number: (270) 824-1866 Calendar System: Semester
URL: www.madisonville.kctcs.edu
Established: 1968 Annual Undergrad Tuition & Fees (In-State): $3,624
Enrollment: 4,433 Coed
Affiliation or Control: State IRS Status: 501(c)3
Highest Offering: Associate Degree
Accreditation: SC, ADNUR, COARC, IFSAC, MLTAD, OTA, PTAA, RAD, SURGA, SURGT

02 President .... Dr. Cynthia S. KELLEY
05 Chief Academic Officer ....Dr. Deborah M. COX
10 Chief Business Affairs Officer ....Mr. Ray GILLASPIE
32 Chief Student Affairs Officer ....Dr. Jay V. PARRENT
72 Division Chair Applied Technology .... Mr. Matt LUCKETT
66 Div Chr Nursing/Related Tech ....Ms. Shannon ALLEN
79 Div Chr Humanities/Related Tech ....Dr. Mary B. WERNER
83 Div Chr Social Science/Related Tech ....Ms. Natalie F. COOPER
81 Div Chr Mathematics and Sciences ....Dr. John D. LOWBRIDGE
76 Div Chr Allied Health/Related Tech ...... Ms. Stephanie A. TAYLOR
08 Director of Library Services ....Ms. Cherry L. BERGES
06 Registrar ....Ms. Tiffanie WITT
15 Director of Human Resources ....Ms. May F. WRIGHT
36 Director of Counseling Services .... Ms. Cathy A. VAUGHAN
30 Director of Advancement .... Mr. Chris WOODALL
37 Director of Financial Aid ....Ms. Martha PHELPS
26 Public Relations Director ....Ms. Joyce RIGGS
56 Extended Campus Director ....Ms. Betsy ALLEN
25 Dir Grants/Planning & Effectiveness ... Mr. David A. SCHUERMER
28 Director of Cultural Diversity ....Mr. James H. BOWLES
103 Director Workforce Solutions ....Mr. Mike DAVENPORT
20 Dean of Academic Affairs .... Ms. Lisa A. HOWERTON
21 Dean of Business Affairs ....Mr. Michael L. JOHNSON
40 Bookstore Manager ....Ms. Sonya L. PARKER
84 Director of Enrollment Management ....Ms. Aimee J. WILKERSON

*Maysville Community and Technical College (C)

1755 US Highway 68, Maysville KY 41056-8910
County: Mason FICE Identification: 006960
Unit ID: 157331
Telephone: (606) 759-7141 Carnegie Class: Assoc/HVT-High Non
FAX Number: (606) 759-7176 Calendar System: Semester
URL: www.maysville.kctcs.edu
Established: 1966 Annual Undergrad Tuition & Fees (In-State): $3,624
Enrollment: 3,478 Coed
Affiliation or Control: State IRS Status: 501(c)3
Highest Offering: Associate Degree
Accreditation: SC, COARC, IFSAC, MAC

02 President ....Dr. Steve VACIK
05 Provost ....Dr. Juston PATE
10 Chief Finance & Facilities Officer ....Mr. George A. JONES
84 Chief Ofcr Enrollment/Student Svc ....Ms. Jessica KERN
20 Assoc Dean Academic Support Svc .... Dr. Dana CALLAND
09 Assoc Dean Institutional Rsch/Plng ....Ms. Pam STAFFORD
08 Director Library Services ....Ms. Sonja EADS
13 Director Information Technology .... Mr. Henry JEFFERSON
30 Dir Resource Development/Foundation .... Ms. Cara CLARKE
103 Chief Officer Workforce Solutions .... Ms. Barbara CAMPBELL
37 Director Student Financial Aid ....Ms. Sandy POWER
06 Registrar ....Ms. Lori GAUNCE
26 Dir Marketing & Public Relations ....Ms. Jessica KERN
28 Director of Diversity .... Ms. Millicent HARDING
15 Director of Human Resources .... Ms. Sandi L. ESTILL
25 Director Grants & Contracts .... Ms. Andrea CALLAND
106 Coordinator Distance Learning ....Ms. Kim SPARKS
20 Coordinator of Academic Programs .... Mr. Stanley CLICK
50 Div Chr Business/Info Technologies ....Ms. Tara THORNBERRY
49 Div Chair Liberal Arts/Education ....Ms. Kathleen MELLENKAMP
81 Div Chair Math/Science/Agriculture ....Dr. Angela FULTZ
66 Division Chair of Health Sciences ....Ms. Deborah NOLDER
72 Division Chair Industrial Tech .... Mr. Tony WALLACE

*Owensboro Community and Technical College (D)

4800 New Hartford Road, Owensboro KY 42303-1899
County: Daviess FICE Identification: 030345
Unit ID: 247940
Telephone: (270) 686-4400 Carnegie Class: Assoc/HVT-Mix Trad/Non
FAX Number: (270) 686-4496 Calendar System: Semester
URL: www.octc.kctcs.edu
Established: 1986 Annual Undergrad Tuition & Fees (In-State): $3,624
Enrollment: 4,156 Coed
Affiliation or Control: State IRS Status: 501(c)3
Highest Offering: Associate Degree
Accreditation: SC, ACBSP, EMT, IFSAC, RAD, SURGT

02 President .... Dr. Scott WILLIAMS
04 Assistant to the President .... Ms. Kittridge MIDKIFF
05 Interim VP of Academic Affairs ....Mr. Mike RODGERS
32 VP of Student Affairs .... Mr. Kevin BEARDMORE
30 VP Institutional Advancement ....Vacant
10 VP of Business Affairs .... Ms. Sarah PRICE
13 VP Information Technology .... Mr. James HARTZ
103 VP Workforce Solutions .... Ms. Cynthia FIORELLA
35 Assoc Dean of Student Affairs .... Ms. Sandy CARDEN
08 Library Services Director ....Ms. Donna ABELL
06 Registrar .... Ms. Sandy CARDEN
15 Director of Human Resources .... Ms. Victoria HOHIEMER
09 Director of Institutional Research .... Mr. Kevin BEARDMORE
29 Dir Advancement/Alumni Relations ....Vacant
37 Financial Aid Director ....Ms. Bernice AYER
26 Director of Public Relations ....Ms. Bernadette TOYE-HALE
28 Director of Diversity .... Mr. Lewatis MCNEAL
38 Director Student Counseling .... Ms. Barbara TIPMORE
84 Director Enrollment Management .... Mr. Kevin BEARDMORE
96 Director of Purchasing .... Ms. Sarah PRICE
24 Dir of Teaching & Learning Center ....Vacant
40 Bookstore Manager ....Ms. Sonya SOUTHARD
88 TV Production Manager ....Mr. John BRYENTON
07 Senior Admissions Advisor ....Ms. Linda CALHOUN
36 Career Resource/Placemnt Ctr Coord .... Ms. Katie BALLARD
79 Associate Dean Humanities ....Dr. Julia LEDFORD
83 Assoc Dean Soc Sci/Bus/Public Svc .... Dr. Marc MALTBY
81 Assoc Dean Math/Sci/Allied Health .... Dr. Veena SALLAN
75 Assoc Dean Advanced Technologies .... Mr. Dean AUTRY
66 Associate Dean Nursing .... Ms. Terri LANHAM
88 Assc Dean Personal Svc/Skill Trades ....Mr. Mike RODGERS
20 Assoc Dean Academic Affairs ....Dr. Stacy EDDS-ELLIS
09 Coord Institutional Effectiveness .... Ms. Joy BOWLDS
19 Director Security/Safety .... Mr. Jeff WILLIAMS

*Somerset Community College (E)

808 Monticello Street, Somerset KY 42501-2973
County: Pulaski FICE Identification: 001997
Unit ID: 157711
Telephone: (877) 629-9722 Carnegie Class: Assoc/HVT-High Trad
FAX Number: N/A Calendar System: Semester
URL: somerset.kctcs.edu
Established: 1965 Annual Undergrad Tuition & Fees (In-State): $3,624
Enrollment: 6,995 Coed
Affiliation or Control: State IRS Status: 501(c)3
Highest Offering: Associate Degree
Accreditation: SC, ADNUR, COARC, IFSAC, MLTAD, PTAA, RAD, SURGT

02 President/CEO ....Dr. Jo MARSHALL
05 Provost ....Dr. Tony L. HONEYCUTT
10 Chief Business Affairs Officer ....Dr. Timothy ZIMMERMAN
11 Chief Operations Officer .... Mr. Larry ABBOTT
49 Dean of Arts and Sciences ....Vacant
76 Dean for Health Sciences ....Ms. Nancy L. POWELL
88 Dean of Applied Technology .... Mr. Roger L. ANGEVINE
09 Dir of Institutional Effectiveness ....Dr. Clint HAYES
32 Dean of Student Affairs .... Ms. Tracy L. CASADA
106 Assoc Dean for Distance Education .... Ms. Linda D. BOURNE
103 Chief Cmty Wkfc & Economic Dev Ofc ....Ms. Alesa JOHNSON
79 Assoc Dean Humanities/Fine Arts/SS .... Mr. Jon BURLEW
83 Assoc Dean Math/Natural Science ....Dr. Clint R. HAYES
88 Assoc Dean Const/Manuf/Trans ....Mr. Daniel C. BURNETT
50 Assoc Dean Bus/IT/Crim Just/Ed/ Cons ....Ms. Lois A. MCWHORTER
88 Dean Academic Support Services .... Mr. Bruce GOVER
30 Chief Inst Advancement Officer .... Ms. Cindy D. CLOUSE
20 Assoc Dean for Learning ....Vacant
37 Int Director of Financial Aid ....Mr. Patrick MAYER
06 Registrar ....Ms. Paula J. LATHAM
15 Director of Human Resources ....Ms. Jill N. MEECE
26 Director of Public Relations .... Ms. Cindy D. CLOUSE
28 Director of Cultural Diversity ....Ms. Elaine WILSON
12 Director of McCreary Center .... Mr. Steve HAMMONS
12 Director of Clinton Center ....Ms. Judy TALLENT
12 Director of Casey Center ....Ms. Judy SAPP
12 Director of Russell Center .... Ms. Winfrey BATES

*Southcentral Kentucky Community and Technical College (F)

1845 Loop Drive, Bowling Green KY 42101-9202
County: Warren FICE Identification: 005271
Unit ID: 156338
Telephone: (270) 901-1000 Carnegie Class: Assoc/HVT-Mix Trad/Non
FAX Number: (270) 901-1145 Calendar System: Semester
URL: www.bowlinggreen.kctcs.edu
Established: 1939 Annual Undergrad Tuition & Fees (In-State): $3,624
Enrollment: 4,014 Coed
Affiliation or Control: State IRS Status: 501(c)3
Highest Offering: Associate Degree
Accreditation: SC, ACFEI, COARC, DMS, IFSAC, RAD, SURGT

02 President & CEO ....Dr. Phillip W. NEAL
05 Provost ....Dr. Maggie SHELTON
32 Int VP Student/Organization Success ....Ms. Brooke JUSTICE
10 Vice President Finance/Admin .... Mr. Chris CUMENS
31 Int Vice Pres Outreach/Cmty Dev .... Dr. James B. MCCASLIN
06 Interim Registrar .... Ms. Amy CANNON
15 Director of Human Resources ....Ms. Sherri L. FORESTER
26 Director of Public Relations .... Mr. Mark D. BROOKS
30 Director of Inst Advancement ....Ms. Heather ROGERS
37 Director of Financial Aid ....Ms. Jennifer WELLS
09 Director Institution Effectiveness .... Mr. Mark GARRETT

*Southeast Kentucky Community and Technical College (G)

700 College Road, Cumberland KY 40823-1099
County: Harlan FICE Identification: 001998
Unit ID: 157739
Telephone: (606) 589-2145 Carnegie Class: Assoc/HVT-High Non
FAX Number: (606) 589-3175 Calendar System: Semester
URL: www.southeast.kctcs.edu
Established: 1960 Annual Undergrad Tuition & Fees (In-State): $3,624
Enrollment: 3,660 Coed
Affiliation or Control: State IRS Status: 501(c)3
Highest Offering: Associate Degree
Accreditation: SC, ADNUR, COARC, FUSER, MLTAD, PTAA, RAD, SURGT

02 President ....Dr. Lynn MOORE
05 Chief Academic Officer ....Dr. Elijah BUELL
30 VP Advancement ....Mr. Scott SHERMAN
10 Chief Business Affairs Officer ....Ms. Angela SIMPSON
15 Director Human Resources ....Ms. Billie FRANKS
08 Head Librarian ....Mr. Warren GRAY
13 Director of Information Technology .... Mr. Merrill GALLOWAY
28 Director of Diversity ....Ms. Carolyn SUNDY
32 Chief Student Affairs Officer ....Dr. Rebecca PARROTT
07 Director of Admissions ....Ms. Veria BALDWIN
37 Coordinator Financial Aid ....Ms. Charlotte LOCKABY

*West Kentucky Community and Technical College (H)

4810 Alben Barkley Drive, Paducah KY 42002-7380
County: McCracken FICE Identification: 001979
Unit ID: 157483
Telephone: (270) 554-9200 Carnegie Class: Assoc/HVT-Mix Trad/Non
FAX Number: (270) 554-6217 Calendar System: Semester
URL: www.westkentucky.kctcs.edu
Established: 1909 Annual Undergrad Tuition & Fees (In-State): $3,624
Enrollment: 6,402 Coed
Affiliation or Control: State IRS Status: 501(c)3
Highest Offering: Associate Degree
Accreditation: SC, ACBSP, ACFEI, ADNUR, DA, DMS, IFSAC, MLTAD, PNUR, PTAA, RAD, SURGT

02 President .... Dr. Barbara VEAZEY
103 VP of Workforce Solutions ....Mr. Jim PAPE
05 VP of Academic Affairs ....Dr. Tena PAYNE
32 VP of Student Development ....Dr. Belinda DALTON-RUSSELL
11 VP of Administrative Services .... Mr. John CARRICO
10 VP Business Affairs .... Ms. Susan GRAVES
30 VP Institutional Advancement ....Ms. Ashley WRIGHT
84 VP of Enrollment ....Mr. Nate SLATON
08 Interim Library Services Director ....Ms. Amy SULLIVAN
37 Financial Aid Director .... Ms. Angel RHODES
26 Public Relations Director ....Ms. Janett BLYTHE
13 Director Information Technology ....Ms. Ruby RODGERS
15 Director Human Resources .... Ms. Bridget CANTER

40 Bookstore Manager .... Mr. Todd MITCHELL
06 Registrar/Dir of Admissions .... Ms. Jess PUFFENBARGER
35 Student Activities Coordinator .... Ms. Amy ELMORE
79 Dean Humanities/Fine Arts/Soc Sci .... Mr. Britton SHURLEY
66 Dean Nursing Division .... Ms. Shari GHOLSON
50 Dean Business/Comp Related Tech Div .... Ms. Tammy POTTER
76 Dean Allied Health Division .... Ms. Peggy BLOCK
75 Dean Applied Tech Division .... Ms. Stephanie MILLIKEN
81 Dean Science & Math Division .... Dr. Karen HLINKA
97 Dean Transition Education Div .... Ms. Sanci TEAGUE
09 Associate VP of IE .... Dr. Renea AKIN
04 Administrative Asst to President .... Ms. Barbara MAXEY
19 Director Security/Safety .... Mr. David WALLACE

Kentucky Mountain Bible College (A)

855 Highway 541, Jackson KY 41339
County: Breathitt FICE Identification: 030021
Unit ID: 157030
Telephone: (606) 693-5000 Carnegie Class: Spec-4-yr-Faith
FAX Number: (606) 693-4884 Calendar System: Semester
URL: www.kmbc.edu
Established: 1931 Annual Undergrad Tuition & Fees: $7,440
Enrollment: 84 Coed
Affiliation or Control: Independent Non-Profit IRS Status: 501(c)3
Highest Offering: Baccalaureate
Accreditation: BI

01 President .... Dr. Philip E. SPEAS
05 Academic Dean/Exec Vice Pres .... Rev. Thomas H. LORIMER
10 Chief Business Manager/Director IT .... Mr. Steve A. LORIMER
32 Dean of Student Affairs .... Mr. Jim NELSON
08 Head Librarian .... Ms. Patricia A. BOWEN
06 Registrar .... Dr. Richard E. ENGLEHARDT
07 Chief Admissions Counselor .... Mr. David W. LORIMER
37 Director Student Financial Aid .... Ms. Rosita MARSHALL
26 Dir PR/Foreign Stdnts/Dean of Men .... Mr. James H. NELSON
34 Dean of Women .... Vacant
18 Chief Facilities/Physical Plant .... Mr. Jonathan MATHES
20 Associate Academic Officer .... Mrs. Sara BAGBY
29 Director of Alumni Relations .... Ms. Donna WOODRING
106 Dir Online Education/E-learning .... Mr. Jason GOBEN
88 Title 9 Coordinator .... Mr. Robert ENGLAND
108 Director Institutional Assessment .... Mr. Zane DARLAND
96 Director of Purchasing .... Mr. David BOLERATZ

Kentucky State University (B)

400 E Main Street, Frankfort KY 40601-2355
County: Franklin FICE Identification: 001968
Unit ID: 157058
Telephone: (502) 597-6000 Carnegie Class: Bac-Diverse
FAX Number: (502) 597-6490 Calendar System: Semester
URL: www.kysu.edu
Established: 1886 Annual Undergrad Tuition & Fees (In-State): $7,754
Enrollment: 1,895 Coed
Affiliation or Control: State IRS Status: 501(c)3
Highest Offering: Doctorate
Accreditation: SC, ACBSP, ADNUR, MUS, NUR, SPAA, SW, TED

01 President .... Dr. Raymond M. BURSE
05 Acting VP Academic Affairs .... Dr. Candice JACKSON
10 VP for Business Affairs .... Mr. Curtis E. CREAGH
32 VP Student Affairs .... Dr. Vernell A. BENNETT
30 Interim VP External Relations & Dev .... Mr. Max A. MAXWELL
43 General Counsel .... Ms. Lori A. DAVIS
13 Interim Chief Information Officer .... Ms. Wendy D. DIXIE
45 Special Asst to Pres Strategic Plng .... Ms. Melinda A. IMPELLIZZERI
20 Dean of the University .... Dr. Lorna L. SHAW
19 Asst to Pres for Risk and Police .... Mr. George R. BAKER
06 Interim Registrar .... Ms. Yolanda C. BENSON
07 Director of Admissions .... Vacant
25 Associate VP Grants Sponsored Pgm .... Dr. Mary W. SPOR
21 Assistant VP Business Affairs .... Mr. Paul S. EDWARDS
47 Assoc VP Land Grant & Dean CAFSS .... Dr. Teferi D. TSEGAYE
26 Assistant to the VP Public Relation .... Ms. Felicia Y. LEWIS
18 Acting Facilities Director .... Mr. Russell L. SMITH
15 Director Human Resource Services .... Ms. Rayla SMOOT
37 Director Student Financial Aid .... Ms. Victoria G. OWENS
41 Interim Director Athletics .... Mr. Harry O. STINSON, III
08 Director Library .... Ms. Sheila A. STUCKEY
96 Purchasing Manager .... Ms. Tonya Y. MONTGOMERY
58 Graduate Studies Director .... Dr. James B. OBIELODAN
39 Director Residence Life .... Vacant
23 Director Health Services .... Ms. Floarine A. WILSON
36 Director Counsel & Placement .... Mr. Ronald BANKS
29 Director Alumni Affairs .... Mr. Wendell C. THOMAS
56 Associate Extension Admin .... Dr. Javiette V. SAMUEL
09 Int Dir Institutional Research Eff .... Ms. Yuliana SUSANTO
46 Associate Director Research .... Dr. Kirk W. POMPER
109 Int Director Auxiliary Enterprise .... Ms. Kathy O. PEALE
106 Academic Technology Trainer .... Ms. Jennifer P. MILES
16 Asst Director HR/Disability Svcs .... Dr. Lloyd CLARK
50 Chair Business .... Dr. Abdul M. TURAY
53 Chair Education .... Dr. Sylvia A. MASON
57 Interim Chair Fine Arts .... Dr. Roosevelt O. SHELTON
66 Chair Nursing .... Dr. Indira D. TYLER
77 Chair Computer Sciences .... Dr. Chi SHEN
80 Interim Chair Public Administration .... Dr. Stephen GRAHAM-HILL
81 Chair Mathematics .... Dr. Fariba BIGDELI-JAHED
83 Acting Chair Social Sciences .... Dr. Tierra M. FREEMAN
92 Chair Whitney Young Honors .... Dr. Thomas J. MCPARTLAND

Kentucky Wesleyan College (C)

3000 Frederica Street, Owensboro KY 42301
County: Daviess FICE Identification: 001969
Unit ID: 157076
Telephone: (270) 926-3111 Carnegie Class: Bac-Diverse
FAX Number: (270) 926-3112 Calendar System: Semester
URL: www.kwc.edu
Established: 1858 Annual Undergrad Tuition & Fees: $23,120
Enrollment: 709 Coed
Affiliation or Control: United Methodist IRS Status: 501(c)3
Highest Offering: Baccalaureate
Accreditation: #SC, IACBE

01 President .... Dr. Bart DARRELL
05 VP Acad Affairs/Dean of the College .... Dr. Paula DEHN
10 Vice President of Finance .... Ms. Cindra K. STIFF
32 VP of Exec Initiatives & Retention .... Mr. Scott E. KRAMER
35 Assoc Dean of Student Services .... Ms. Rebecca MCQUEEN
13 Dir Information Tech Services .... Mr. Kevin PAYNE
30 Vice President for Advancement .... Mr. Thomas W. KEITH
07 Director of Admissions .... Vacant
06 Registrar .... Ms. Lou Ann BOWERSOX
09 Dir of Institutional Effective/Rsch .... Vacant
15 Director of Human Resources .... Mrs. Linda E. KELLER
37 Director of Financial Aid .... Ms. Samantha HAYS
89 Director of the PLUS Center .... Vacant
08 Director of Library Learning Center .... Mrs. Patricia G. MCFARLING
41 Director of Athletics .... Mr. Rob MALLORY
21 Controller .... Ms. Stephanie SNYDER
26 Director of Public Relations .... Ms. Kathy RUTHERMAN
42 KWC Chaplain/Dir Church Relations .... Vacant
30 Dir Development/Donor Rels .... Mr. M. Blake HARRISON
04 Assistant to President .... Ms. Chanda F. PRATER
106 Assoc Dean/Dir Online Education .... Mrs. Rebecca FRANCIS
35 Assistant Dean of Student Services .... Ms. Louise CLAUSEN
36 Dir of Career Dev & Service Learn .... Ms. Margaret CAMBRON

Lexington Theological Seminary (D)

230 Lexington Green Circle, Ste 300, Lexington KY 40503
County: Fayette FICE Identification: 001971
Unit ID: 157207
Telephone: (859) 252-0361 Carnegie Class: Spec-4-yr-Faith
FAX Number: (859) 281-6042 Calendar System: Semester
URL: www.lextheo.edu
Established: 1865 Annual Graduate Tuition & Fees: N/A
Enrollment: 87 Coed
Affiliation or Control: Christian Church (Disciples Of Christ)
IRS Status: 501(c)3
Highest Offering: Doctorate; No Undergraduates
Accreditation: THEOL

01 President .... Dr. Charisse L. GILLETT
05 VP Academic Affairs/Dean .... Dr. Richard WEIS
30 Vice President for Advancement .... Mr. Mark V. BLANKENSHIP
10 Chief Financial Officer .... Mrs. Karen C. WAGERS
06 Registrar .... Ms. Windy KIDD
08 Librarian .... Ms. Dolores YILIBUW
13 Director Information Services .... Mr. Ben WYATT
07 Director Admission .... Rev. Erin CASH
15 Director Personnel Services .... Ms. Karen C. WAGERS
18 Chief Facilities/Physical Plant .... Ms. Karen C. WAGERS
29 Director Alumni Relations .... Mr. Mark V. BLANKENSHIP
37 Director Student Financial Aid .... Ms. Windy KIDD
96 Director of Purchasing .... Ms. Robin VARNER

Lindsey Wilson College (E)

210 Lindsey Wilson Street, Columbia KY 42728-1298
County: Adair FICE Identification: 001972
Unit ID: 157216
Telephone: (270) 384-2126 Carnegie Class: Masters/L
FAX Number: (270) 384-8200 Calendar System: Semester
URL: www.lindsey.edu
Established: 1903 Annual Undergrad Tuition & Fees: $23,162
Enrollment: 2,641 Coed
Affiliation or Control: United Methodist IRS Status: 501(c)3
Highest Offering: Doctorate
Accreditation: SC, CACREP, IACBE, NURSE, TED

01 President .... Dr. William T. LUCKEY, JR.
00 Chancellor .... Dr. John B. BEGLEY
05 Vice President Academic Affairs .... Dr. Bettie C. STARR
10 Vice President Administration .... Mr. Mark COLEMAN
30 Vice President Advancement .... Mr. Kevin A. THOMPSON
04 Executive Assistant .... Mrs. Nancy SINCLAIR
32 Vice Pres Student Svcs/Enroll Mgmt .... Dr. Dean ADAMS
37 VP Educ Outreach/Stdnt Finan Svcs .... Mrs. Denise G. FUDGE
35 Dean of Students .... Mr. Christopher SCHMIDT
20 Associate Academic Dean .... Vacant
88 Dean of Chapel .... Dr. Terry W. SWAN
07 Dean of Admissions .... Mrs. Traci M. POOLER
07 Director of Admissions .... Mrs. Charity F. FERGUSON
55 Director of Evening College .... Ms. Regina HAUGEN
41 Athletic Director .... Mr. Willis POOLER, III
06 Registrar .... Mrs. Sue B. COOMER
15 Director of Human Resources .... Mrs. Karen F. WRIGHT
31 Dir of Civic Engagement & Std Ldrsp .... Mrs. Amy C. THOMPSON-WELLS
36 Director Career Services .... Mrs. Ashley MILLER
08 Librarian .... Mr. C. Phil HANNA

18 Director of Physical Plant .... Mr. Michael L. NEWTON
109 Director of Auxiliary Services .... Mr. Jeff WILLIS
40 Bookstore Manager .... Mrs. Amy M. COOPER
35 Director of Student Activities .... Ms. Lafawn NETTLES
85 Dir International Student Programs .... Ms. Sabine EASTHAM
14 Director Information Services .... Mrs. Harriet B. GOLD
13 Director of Information Systems .... Mr. Anthony MOORE
26 Public Relations Officer .... Mrs. Venus POPPLEWELL
29 Assistant to Pres Alumni Affairs .... Mr. Randy BURNS
19 Director Safety/Security .... Mr. Michael STATEN
42 Chaplain .... Rev. Troy A. ELMORE
37 Director Student Financial Services .... Ms. Marilyn RADFORD
38 Director Student Counseling .... Dr. Jeff CRANE
66 Director of Nursing .... Mrs. Marian SMITH

Louisville Presbyterian Theological Seminary (F)

1044 Alta Vista Road, Louisville KY 40205-1798
County: Jefferson FICE Identification: 001974
Unit ID: 157298
Telephone: (502) 895-3411 Carnegie Class: Spec-4-yr-Faith
FAX Number: (502) 895-1096 Calendar System: 4/1/4
URL: www.lpts.edu
Established: 1853 Annual Graduate Tuition & Fees: N/A
Enrollment: 169 Coed
Affiliation or Control: Presbyterian Church (U.S.A.) IRS Status: 501(c)3
Highest Offering: Doctorate; No Undergraduates
Accreditation: SC, MFCD, THEOL

01 President .... Dr. Michael JINKINS
30 Int Vice Pres Inst Advancement .... Ms. Sally PENDLETON
10 Vice President & CFO .... Mr. Patrick A. CECIL
05 Dean of the Seminary .... Dr. Susan R. GARRETT
32 Dean of Students .... Rev. Kilen GRAY
06 Registrar/OIRE .... Dr. Steve COOK
29 Director of Church Relations .... Ms. Sandra MOON
44 Director of Seminary Fund .... Ms. Erin HAMILTON
14 Director of Data Management .... Ms. Heather GRIFFIN
26 Director of Communications .... Mr. Chris WOOTON
08 Director of Library Services .... Dr. Matthew COLLINS
21 Controller .... Ms. Angela TRAYLOR
51 Director of DMin & Continuing Ed .... Vacant
07 Director of Recruitment & Admiss .... Ms. Emily MILLER
13 Director of IT Services .... Mr. Jack SHARER
18 Director of Facilities .... Mr. Tim WILLIAMS
04 Administrative Asst to President .... Ms. Susan A. DILUCA

Midway University (G)

512 E Stephens Street, Midway KY 40347-1120
County: Woodford FICE Identification: 001975
Unit ID: 157377
Telephone: (859) 846-4421 Carnegie Class: Masters/S
FAX Number: (859) 846-5349 Calendar System: Semester
URL: www.midway.edu
Established: 1847 Annual Undergrad Tuition & Fees: $22,250
Enrollment: 1,140 Coed
Affiliation or Control: Christian Church (Disciples Of Christ)
IRS Status: 501(c)3
Highest Offering: Master's
Accreditation: SC, ADNUR, MAAB, NUR

01 President .... Dr. John P. MARSDEN
05 VP of Academic Affairs .... Dr. Mary E. STIVERS
04 Exec Assistant to the President .... Ms. Sheila K. HOLSCLAW
10 Vice Pres of Finance and Admin .... Mrs. Heather BIGARD
30 Vice President of Advancement .... Mr. Scott B. FITZPATRICK
84 VP of Enrollment Management .... Ms. Kelly S. GOSNELL
26 Vice Pres of Marketing & Comm .... Mrs. Ellen D. GREGORY
20 Associate VP Academic Affairs .... Dr. William (Bill) BROWN
32 Asst VP of Student Affairs .... Ms. Sarah G. MUDD
07 Dir of Data and Reporting/Admiss .... Mrs. Jessica NEALEY
58 Int Dir of Adult Undergr & Grad Adm .... Mrs. Rebeccca MATTINGLY
13 Chief Information Officer .... Dr. Salah SHAKIR
06 Registrar .... Mrs. Linda P. ELDRIDGE
08 Director of Library Services .... Ms. Catherine L. REILENDER
41 Athletic Director .... Mr. William "Rusty" KENNEDY, II
14 Technical Support Specialist .... Mr. Eric ASHCRAFT
15 Director of Human Resources .... Ms. Trish JONES
29 Development Officer .... Ms. Mary Jean THOMAS
37 Director Student Financial Planning .... Mrs. Kate WARE
18 Director of Facilities .... Mr. Sherman ADAMS
09 Director Compliance & Research .... Dr. Johnie DEAN
28 Dir Ofc of Multicultural & Int Affs .... Ms. Emily EVANS
50 Dean Business/Equine/Sport Stds .... Vacant
49 Dean School of Arts & Sciences .... Dr. Charles H. ROBERTS
76 Dean School of Health Sciences .... Dr. Barbara KITCHEN

Morehead State University (H)

150 University Boulevard, Morehead KY 40351-1689
County: Rowan FICE Identification: 001976
Unit ID: 157386
Telephone: (800) 585-6781 Carnegie Class: Masters/L
FAX Number: N/A Calendar System: Semester
URL: www.moreheadstate.edu
Established: 1887 Annual Undergrad Tuition & Fees (In-State): $8,098
Enrollment: 11,052 Coed
Affiliation or Control: State IRS Status: 501(c)3
Highest Offering: Doctorate

Accreditation: SC, ADNUR, ART, BUS, COARC, DMS, MUS, NAIT, NURSE, RAD, RADMAG, SPAA, SW, TED, THEA

01 President ....Dr. Wayne D. ANDREWS
05 Provost & VP Academic Affairs ....Dr. Steven M. RALSTON
10 Chief Financial Officer/VP AFS ....Ms. Beth G. PATRICK
32 Vice President Student Life ....Ms. Madonna B. WEATHERS
30 Vice Pres for Univ Advancement ....Mr. James A. SHAW
45 Executive Assistant to President ....Dr. John P. ERNST
20 Assoc VP Academic Affairs/Programs ..Dr. Clarenda M. PHILLIPS
04 Assistant to the President ....Ms. Sharon S. REYNOLDS
06 Interim Registrar ....Ms. Deborah ROSS
58 AVP & Dean of Graduate School ....Dr. Michael C. HENSON
51 Asst VP Adult Educ & College Access ....Dr. Dan J. CONNELL
84 Asst Vice Pres Enrollment Services ....Mr. Jeffrey R. LILES
20 Asst VP Academic Affs/Inst Effectiv ....Ms. Jill C. RATLIFF
26 Asst VP Communication & Marketing ....Ms. Jami M. HORNBUCKLE
18 Asst VP Facilities Management ....Mr. Rick T. LINIO
109 Asst Vice Pres Auxiliary Services ....Mr. William REDWINE
29 Asst VP Alumni Relations & Develop ....Ms. Melinda C. HIGHLEY
13 Asst VP Technology ....Mr. Steve RICHMOND
35 AVP Student Life/Dean of Students ....Vacant
08 Dean of Library Services ....Dr. David L. GREGORY
07 Dir of Undergraduate Admissions ....Ms. Holly L. POLLOCK
09 Dir Inst Research & Analysis ....Dr. Jennifer S. TISON
15 Director of Human Resources ....Mr. Harold D. NALLY
19 Chief of Police ....Mr. Merrell J. HARRISON
21 Director Accounting/Financial Svcs ....Mrs. Kelli D. OWEN
21 Exec Dir Budgets & Financial Plng ....Ms. Teresa C. LINDGREN
88 Dir Stdnt Act Inclusion/Ldrshp Dev ....Mr. Ricardo NAZARIO-COLON
37 Director Financial Aid ....Ms. Denise M. TRUSTY
36 Director Career Services ....Ms. Julia L. HAWKINS
39 Director of Housing/Residence Educ ....Dr. Christopher A. SUMMERLIN
41 Director of Athletics ....Mr. Brian A. HUTCHINSON
43 General Counsel ....Dr. Jane FITZPATRICK
27 Media Relations Director ....Mr. Jason BLANTON
79 Director of DIIS ....Dr. Philip KRUMMRICH
96 Director Procurement Services ....Ms. Ladonna M. PURCELL
38 Director of Counseling & Health Svc ....Dr. Shannon L. SMITH-STEPHENS
50 Dean Col of Business & Technology ....Dr. Robert ALBERT
53 Int Dean College of Education ....Dr. Chris MILLER
81 Dean College of Science ....Dr. Wayne C. MILLER
79 Dean Col of Arts/Human/Soc Studies ....Dr. Scott MCBRIDE
105 Web Marketing Director ....Ms. April H. NUTTER
106 Director Distance Education & Instr ....Ms. Misty HANKS

Murray State University (A)

218 Wells Hall, Murray KY 42071-3318
County: Calloway FICE Identification: 001977
Unit ID: 157401
Telephone: (270) 809-3011 Carnegie Class: Masters/L
FAX Number: (270) 809-3413 Calendar System: Semester
URL: www.murraystate.edu
Established: 1922 Annual Undergrad Tuition & Fees (In-State): $7,608
Enrollment: 11,207 Coed
Affiliation or Control: State IRS Status: 501(c)3
Highest Offering: Doctorate
Accreditation: SC, ANEST, ART, BUS, #CAATE, CACREP, DIETD, DIETI, ENG, ENGR, ENGT, EXSC, JOUR, MUS, NURSE, SP, SW, THEA

01 President ....Dr. Robert O. DAVIES
101 Sr Exec Coord for Pres/Coord Bd Rel ....Ms. Jill HUNT
05 Acting Provost/VP Academic Affairs ....Dr. Renae DUNCAN
10 VP Finance & Admin Svcs ....Ms. Jacklyn K. DUDLEY
32 VP Student Affairs ....Dr. Don E. ROBERTSON
30 VP Marketing & Outreach ....Dr. Adrienne KING
20 Assoc Provost Grad Educ & Research ....Dr. Robert PERVINE
20 Assoc Provost Undergrad Education ....Dr. Renae D. DUNCAN
35 Interim Assoc VP Student Affairs ....Mr. Michael E. YOUNG
26 Communications Director ....Mr. Shawn TOUNEY
43 General Counsel ....Mr. John P. RALL
50 Dean College of Business ....Dr. Timothey TODD
53 Dean Col of Education & Human Svcs ....Dr. David WHALEY
79 Interim Dean Col Humanities & Arts ....Dr. Staci STONE
81 Dean Col Science/Engineering & Tech ....Dr. Stephen H. COBB
47 Dean Hutson School of Agriculture ....Dr. Tony L. BRANNON
66 Dean School Nursing & Health Profes ....Dr. Marcia B. HOBBS
08 Dean University Libraries ....Ms. Asheley IRELAND
51 Dean Regional Academic Outreach ....Dr. Brian W. VAN HORN
106 Asst Dean RAO/Dir Dist Learning ....Mr. Daniel A. LAVIT
97 Coordinator University Studies ....Dr. Peter F. MURPHY
92 Director Honors College ....Dr. Warren EDMINSTER
85 Exec Dir Institute for Intl Studies ....Dr. Guangming ZOU
104 Assoc Director Education Abroad ....Ms. Melanie C. MCCALLON
84 Assoc VP Enrollment Mgmt ....Mr. Fred K. DIETZ
07 Dir Undgrad Admissions Svcs ....Ms. Lesa C. HARRIS
06 Registrar ....Ms. Tracy ROBERTS
37 Dir Student Financial Aid ....Ms. Janet BALOK
39 Director Housing ....Dr. J. David WILSON
38 Dir University Counseling Services ....Dr. Angie TRZEPACZ
28 Dir Multicultural Affairs ....Mr. Sidney G. CARTHELL
36 Director Career Services ....Dr. Ross B. MELOAN
23 Director Health Services ....Ms. Kimberly S. PASCHALL
21 Dir Fiscal Plng/Analysis/Budget ....Vacant
96 Director Procurement Services ....Ms. Jan R. FUQUA
22 Ex Dir Inst Diversity/Equity/Access ....Ms. Cami DUFFY
13 Chief Information Officer ....Mr. Keith WEBER
91 Dir Enterprise Application Services ....Mr. Brantly D. TRAVIS
90 Dir Ctr Teaching/Learning/Tech ....Mr. Howard T. RICE
09 Dir Institutional Effectiveness ....Dr. Kelley C. WEZNER
41 Athletic Director ....Mr. C. Allen WARD
18 Interim Chief Facilities Officer ....Mr. David BURDETTE
19 Dir Public Safety/Emergency Mgmt ....Mr. Jamie HERRING
40 Director University Store ....Ms. R. Karol HARDISON
25 Director Sponsored Programs ....Mr. John A. ROARK
29 Assoc Director Alumni Affairs ....Ms. Katie W. PAYNE
105 Manager Web Services ....Ms. Charley B. ALLEN
100 Pres Advisor Strategic Initiative ....Dr. K. Renee FISTER
102 President MSU Foundation ....Dr. Robert JACKSON
86 Director Government Relations ....Mr. Jordan SMITH
15 Director Human Resources ....Ms. Joyce GORDON

Northern Kentucky University (B)

Nunn Drive, Highland Heights KY 41099-0000
County: Campbell FICE Identification: 009275
Unit ID: 157447
Telephone: (859) 572-5100 Carnegie Class: Masters/L
FAX Number: (859) 572-5566 Calendar System: Semester
URL: www.nku.edu
Established: 1968 Annual Undergrad Tuition & Fees (In-State): $9,120
Enrollment: 15,090 Coed
Affiliation or Control: State IRS Status: 501(c)3
Highest Offering: Doctorate
Accreditation: SC, BUS, CAATE, CACREP, COARC, CONST, ENGT, LAW, MUS, NUR, NURSE, RAD, SPAA, SW, TED

01 President ....Mr. Geoffrey S. MEARNS
04 Exec Asst to President ....Dr. Kathryn J. HERSCHEDE
05 Provost/Exec VP Academic Affairs ....Ms. Sue OTT ROWLANDS
10 Sr Vice Pres Admin & Finance ....Dr. Sue HODGES MOORE
32 Vice Pres Student Affairs ....Dr. Daniel NADLER
30 Vice Pres University Advancement ....Mr. Eric C. GENTRY
43 VP Legal Affairs & General Counsel ....Ms. Joan GATES
20 Vice Prov Undergrad Academic Affs ....Dr. Idna CORBETT
84 VP Enrollment/Degree Management ....Ms. Kimberly SCRANAGE
58 Vice Prov Grad Educ/Rsrch/ Outreach ....Ms. Samantha LANGLEY-TURNBAUGH
20 Assoc Provost Academic Affs/Admin ....Ms. Beth SWEENEY
13 Chief Information Officer ....Mr. Timothy FERGUSON
08 Assoc Provost Library Services ....Mr. Arne J. ALMQUIST
35 AVP Student Engage/Dean of Students ....Vacant
29 AVP Development & Alumni Relations ....Ms. Julie DIALS
49 Dean College of Arts & Sciences ....Vacant
50 Dean College of Business ....Dr. Rebecca PORTERFIELD
88 Dean College of Informatics ....Dr. Kevin KIRBY
53 Dean College of Ed/Human Svcs ....Dr. Cynthia REED
61 Dean Chase College of Law ....Mr. Jeffrey STANDEN
66 Dean College of Health Professions ....Dr. Dale SCALISE-SMITH
11 Director of Administration ....Ms. Karen SULLIVAN
18 Asst VP Facilities Management ....Mr. Syed ZAIDI
18 Director Operations & Maintenance ....Mr. Ray MIRIZZI
26 Asst VP Marketing & Communications ....Ms. Kelly MARTIN
21 Dir Fin & Operational Auditing ....Mr. Larry MEYER
109 Dir BusinessOps/Auxiliary Services ....Mr. Andy MEEKS
88 Dir Univ Architect/Design/Const Mgt ....Mr. Steve NIENABER
88 Director Campus Space and Planning ....Ms. Mary Paula SCHUH
15 Senior Director Human Resources ....Ms. Lori SOUTHWOOD
21 Comptroller ....Mr. Russell A. KERDOLFF
19 Director University Police ....Mr. Leslie KACHUREK
96 Director Procurement Services ....Mr. Jeffrey STRUNK
92 Interim Director Honors Program ....Ms. Belle ZEMBRODT
07 Director Undergraduate Admissions ....Ms. Melissa GORBANDT
104 Exec Dir Intl Education Center ....Dr. Francois LEROY
06 Registrar ....Mr. W. Allen COLE, III
37 AVP Enrollment & Financial Aid ....Ms. Leah STEWART
78 Exec Dir Ctr for Civic Engagement ....Mr. Mark NEIKIRK
51 Director Community Connections ....Ms. Melinda SPONG
25 Director Research/Grants/Contracts ....Ms. Mary UCCI
89 Director First Year Programs ....Ms. Jeanne PETTIT
21 Chief Financial Officer ....Mr. Mike HALES
09 AVP Planning/Institutional Research ....Ms. Vickie NATALE
88 Assoc Dir Institutional Research ....Mr. Shawn RAINEY
88 Director Campus Recreation ....Mr. Matthew HACKETT
38 Assoc Dir Health/Counseling/Prev ....Ms. Lisa BARRESI
35 Director of Student Engagement ....Ms. Tiffany MAYSE
22 Dir Hlth/Counseling/Stdnt Wellness ....Mr. Ben ANDERSON
39 AVP Student Engagement/Business Ops ....Mr. Arnie SLAUGHTER
36 Director Career Services ....Mr. Bill FROUDE
41 Dir of Intercollegiate Athletics ....Mr. Ken BOTHOF
22 Sr Advisor to Pres Inclusive Excell ....Dr. Kathleen ROBERTS

Simmons College of Kentucky (C)

1018 South 7th Street, Louisville KY 40203-3322
County: Jefferson FICE Identification: 041780
Unit ID: 461759
Telephone: (502) 776-1443 Carnegie Class: Spec-4-yr-Faith
FAX Number: (502) 776-2227 Calendar System: Semester
URL: www.simmonscollegeky.edu
Established: 1879 Annual Undergrad Tuition & Fees: $5,330
Enrollment: 261 Coed
Affiliation or Control: Baptist IRS Status: 501(c)3
Highest Offering: Baccalaureate
Accreditation: BI

01 President ....Dr. Kevin W. COSBY
03 Executive Vice President ....Dr. Frank M. SMITH, JR.
03 Executive Vice President ....Dr. Ken B. JOBST
05 Vice Pres Academic Affairs ....Dr. Brian J. WELLS
32 Vice Pres Student Affs/Dir Admiss ....Dr. Christine COSBY-GAITHER
06 Registrar ....Ms. Deborah THOMAS

The Southern Baptist Theological Seminary (D)

2825 Lexington Road, Louisville KY 40280-2899
County: Jefferson FICE Identification: 001982
Unit ID: 157748
Telephone: (502) 897-4011 Carnegie Class: Spec-4-yr-Faith
FAX Number: (502) 899-1770 Calendar System: Other
URL: www.sbts.edu
Established: 1859 Annual Undergrad Tuition & Fees: $17,080
Enrollment: 3,416 Coed
Affiliation or Control: Southern Baptist IRS Status: 501(c)3
Highest Offering: Doctorate
Accreditation: SC, MUS, THEOL

01 President ....Dr. R. Albert MOHLER, JR.
100 Chief of Staff to the President ....Dr. Thomas HELLAMS
04 Sr Admin Asst Office of President ....Mrs. Celeste EAGLE
05 Sr VP Academic Administration ....Dr. Randy STINSON
11 Sr VP Institutional Administration ....Mr. Dan DUMAS
10 Vice Pres of Business & Strategy ....Mr. Geoff DENNIS
11 Vice President of Operations ....Mr. Andrew VINCENT
26 Vice President Communications ....Mr. Steve WATTERS
13 VP CampusTechnology ....Mr. Jason HEATH
30 VP Institutional Advancement ....Mr. Craig PARKER
20 Vice President Academic Services ....Dr. Adam GREENWAY
106 Assoc VP Online Education ....Dr. Timothy Paul JONES
108 Assoc VP Institutional Assessment ....Dr. Joseph C. HARROD
84 Assoc VP Enrollment Management ....Mr. Matt MINIER
15 Director Human Resources ....Mr. Richard MCRAE
18 Chief Facilities/Physical Plant ....Mr. Ken RICHARDSON
41 Director of Health & Recreation ....Mr. Blake ROGERS
07 Director of Admissions ....Mr. Kody GIBSON
08 Librarian ....Dr. Berry DRIVER
37 Manager of Financial Aid ....Mrs. Erin JOINER
73 Dean of School of Theology ....Dr. Greg WILLS
88 Dean Missions Evang Ch Growth ....Mr. Adam GREENWAY
12 Dean Boyce College ....Dr. Matthew HALL
06 Registrar ....Mr. Norm CHUNG
39 Director Student Housing ....Mrs. Kari PAYTON

Spalding University (E)

845 S Third Street, Louisville KY 40203-2213
County: Jefferson FICE Identification: 001960
Unit ID: 157757
Telephone: (502) 585-9911 Carnegie Class: DU-Mod
FAX Number: (502) 585-7158 Calendar System: Other
URL: www.spalding.edu
Established: 1814 Annual Undergrad Tuition & Fees: $24,000
Enrollment: 2,311 Coed
Affiliation or Control: Independent Non-Profit IRS Status: 501(c)3
Highest Offering: Doctorate
Accreditation: SC, CLPSY, IACBE, NURSE, OT, SW, TED

01 President ....Ms. Tori MURDEN MCCLURE
05 Provost ....Dr. Randy STRICKLAND
30 Chief Advancement Officer ....Mr. Bert GRIFFIN
32 Dean of Students ....Dr. Richard HUDSON
10 Chief Financial Officer ....Mr. Rush SHERMAN
43 General Counsel ....Ms. Emily NORRIS
84 Dean of Enrollment Management ....Mr. Chris HART
53 Dean of College of Education ....Dr. Beverly C. KEEPERS
83 Assoc Dean College Social Sci/Hum ....Dr. Melissa CHASTAIN
88 Director Adult Accelerated Program ....Ms. Katherine WALKER-PAYNE
76 Dean Kosair Col Health & Nat Sci ....Dr. Joanne BERRYMAN
26 Chief Marketing Officer ....Mr. Rick BARNEY
88 Director Academic Resource Center ....Mr. Sam MEYER
88 Director Academic Advising Center ....Ms. Katherine WALKER-PAYNE
06 Registrar ....Ms. Jennifer GOHMANN
13 Chief Information Officer ....Mr. Ezra KRUMHANSL
08 Director Library ....Mr. Tony HOPKINS
37 Director Financial Aid ....Ms. Michelle STANDRIDGE
15 Human Resources Manager ....Ms. Jennifer BROCKHOFF
09 Dir of Institutional Effectiveness ....Ms. Kay VETTER
27 Director of Executive Communication ....Ms. Beth NEWBERRY
41 Director of Athletics ....Mr. Roger BURKMAN
88 Admin Dir/Mstr Fine Arts in Writing ....Ms. Karen MANN
21 Controller ....Ms. Anne-Marie HOGAN
18 JLL Facilities Manager ....Mr. Kevin WEBER
40 Bookstore Manager ....Vacant
50 Dir Masters Business Communications ....Dr. Robin HINKLE
07 Director of Admissions ....Mr. Matthew ELDER

Spencerian College (F)

2355 Harrodsburg Rd, Lexington KY 40504
Telephone: (859) 223-9608 Identification: 666448
Accreditation: ACICS, MAC, MLTAB, RAD

† Branch campus of Spencerian College, Louisville, KY.

Spencerian College (G)

4627 Dixie Highway, Louisville KY 40216-2605
County: Jefferson FICE Identification: 004618
Unit ID: 157766
Telephone: (502) 447-1000 Carnegie Class: Spec-4-yr-Other Health

FAX Number: (502) 447-4574 Calendar System: Quarter
URL: www.spencerian.edu
Established: 1892 Annual Undergrad Tuition & Fees: $18,540
Enrollment: 500 Coed
Affiliation or Control: Proprietary IRS Status: Proprietary
Highest Offering: Baccalaureate
Accreditation: **ACICS**, COARC, COMTA, CVT, MAC, MLTAB RAD, SURGT

01 Executive Director .... Ms. Jan M. GORDON
05 Academic Dean .... Ms. Linda BLAIR
06 Registrar .... Mr. Rob SUKALA
37 Director of Financial Planning .... Ms. Jill SCHULER
07 Director of Admissions .... Ms. Charmaine POWELL
36 Director of Career Services .... Ms. Annette CALHOUN
32 Director of Student Services .... Ms. Amanda HICKERSON

Sullivan College of Technology and Design (A)

3901 Atkinson Square Drive, Louisville KY 40218-4549
County: Jefferson FICE Identification: 012088
Unit ID: 157270
Telephone: (502) 456-6509 Carnegie Class: Spec-4-yr-Arts
FAX Number: (502) 456-2341 Calendar System: Quarter
URL: www.sctd.edu
Established: 1961 Annual Undergrad Tuition & Fees: $20,680
Enrollment: 365 Coed
Affiliation or Control: Proprietary IRS Status: Proprietary
Highest Offering: Baccalaureate
Accreditation: **ACICS**, CIDA

00 Chancellor .... Dr. A. R. SULLIVAN
01 President .... Mr. Glenn D. SULLIVAN
11 Chief Operations Officer .... Mr. Thomas F. DAVISSON
05 Dean of Academic Affairs .... Mr. Robert MITCHELL
10 Vice President Finance .... Mr. Shelton BRIDGES
84 Vice Pres Enrollment Management .... Mr. James CRICK
12 Executive Director .... Mr. Chris ERNST
13 Chief Technology Officer .... Ms. Jody GILLENWATER
55 Evening Division Dean .... Ms. Brittany LEACH
06 Registrar .... Mr. Ryan SEARS
07 Director of Admissions .... Ms. Ashley AUSTIN
37 Dir of Student Financial Planning .... Ms. Michelle SMITH
08 Head Librarian .... Ms. Jill SHERMAN
36 Director Career Services .... Ms. Donna REED
21 Business Officer .... Mr. Frank SALVAGNE
29 Director Alumni Relations .... Ms. Hazel MATTHEWS

Sullivan University (B)

3101 Bardstown Road, Louisville KY 40205-3000
County: Jefferson FICE Identification: 004619
Unit ID: 157793
Telephone: (502) 456-6504 Carnegie Class: Masters/L
FAX Number: (502) 456-0040 Calendar System: Quarter
URL: www.sullivan.edu
Established: 1962 Annual Undergrad Tuition & Fees: $19,740
Enrollment: 4,394 Coed
Affiliation or Control: Proprietary IRS Status: Proprietary
Highest Offering: Doctorate
Accreditation: **SC**, ACFEI, #ARCPA, MAC, NURSE, PHAR

00 Chancellor .... Dr. A. R. SULLIVAN
01 President .... Mr. Glenn D. SULLIVAN
03 Chief Executive Officer .... Dr. Jay MARR
05 Provost .... Dr. Ken MILLER
88 Senior Vice President .... Mr. Thomas F. DAVISSON
10 Vice President Finance .... Mr. Shelton BRIDGES
84 Vice Pres Enrollment Management .... Mr. James CRICK
07 Vice President of Admissions .... Ms. Nina MARTINEZ
58 Assoc Provost/Dean Graduate School .... Dr. Tim SWENSON
32 Dean of Students .... Mr. Gabe GHAMMACHI
88 Dir Natl Ctr Hospitality Studies .... Mr. David DODD
06 Registrar .... Ms. Kim MITCHELL
08 Librarian .... Mr. Charles BROWN
13 Chief Technology Officer .... Mr. Mike GROSSE
36 Director of Career Services .... Mr. Sam MANNINO
37 Director Student Financial Planning .... Ms. Amanda MCANINCH
55 Director Evening Division .... Mr. James TAYLOR
40 Bookstore Manager .... Mr. Bryan NEEDY
12 Director Lexington Branch .... Mr. David KEENE
96 Director of Purchasing .... Ms. Ann VEST
56 Director of Extension Campus .... Ms. Barbara DEAN
88 University Ombudsman .... Mr. Jim KLEIN
29 Director Alumni Relations .... Ms. Hazel MATTHEWS
09 Director Institutional Research .... Dr. Mark WILJANEN
18 Manager Campus Facilities .... Mr. Mike FOWLER
35 Student Life Coordinator .... Ms. Kim ATWOOD
67 Dean College of Pharmacy .... Dr. Cindy STOWE
50 Dean College of Business Admin .... Dr. Ken MORAN
72 Dean Col Information/Computer Tech .... Dr. Emmanuel UDOH

Thomas More College (C)

333 Thomas More Parkway,
Crestview Hills KY 41017-3495
County: Kenton FICE Identification: 002001
Unit ID: 157809
Telephone: (859) 341-5800 Carnegie Class: Masters/S
FAX Number: (859) 344-3345 Calendar System: Semester
URL: www.thomasmore.edu
Established: 1921 Annual Undergrad Tuition & Fees: $29,153
Enrollment: 1,655 Coed
Affiliation or Control: Roman Catholic IRS Status: 501(c)3
Highest Offering: Master's
Accreditation: **SC**, ACBSP, NUR, TED

01 President .... Mr. David A. ARMSTRONG
04 Assistant to the President .... Ms. Charlene BARLOW
10 CFO .... Mr. Jeff BRIGGS
05 Vice President for Academic Affairs .... Dr. Kathleen JAGGER
30 Vice Pres for Inst Advancement .... Vacant
11 Vice Pres of Operations/Cmty Affs .... Vacant
32 Dean of Students .... Ms. Amy WYLIE
09 Dir of Inst Planning/Effectiveness .... Ms. Kelly FRENCH
06 Registrar .... Ms. Michelle VEZINA
08 Director of Library .... Ms. Leoma DUNN
37 Director of Financial Aid .... Ms. Dyane FOLTZ
13 Director of IT .... Mr. Sean KAPSAL
26 Dir Communications/Media Relations .... Ms. Marita SALKOWSKI
38 Director of Counseling .... Ms. Veronica A. LUBBE
42 Chaplain .... Rev. Gerald E. TWADDELL
84 AVP of Enrollment Management .... Dr. Christopher POWERS
41 Athletic Director .... Mr. Terry E. CONNOR
19 Director of Campus Safety .... Mr. William WILSON
15 Director of Human Resources .... Ms. Laura CUSTER
18 Director of Facilities .... Mr. Eric WILKYMACKY
29 Director of Alumni .... Ms. Monica GINNEY
36 Dir of Career Planning/Coop Educ .... Ms. Julie MUELLER
73 Director of Campus Ministry .... Mr. Andrew COLE
21 Controller .... Ms. Beth MALEY
51 Director of Lifelong Learning .... Mr. Nathan HARTMAN
92 Director of Honors Program .... Dr. Catherine SHERRON
44 Dir Annual Giving/Special Events .... Vacant
07 Associate Director of Admissions .... Mr. Justin VOGEL
35 Director of Student Engagement .... Mr. Kevin REYNOLDS
39 Coordinator of Residence Life .... Vacant

Transylvania University (D)

300 N Broadway, Lexington KY 40508-1797
County: Fayette FICE Identification: 001987
Unit ID: 157818
Telephone: (859) 233-8300 Carnegie Class: Bac-A&S
FAX Number: (859) 233-8797 Calendar System: Other
URL: www.transy.edu
Established: 1780 Annual Undergrad Tuition & Fees: $34,370
Enrollment: 1,014 Coed
Affiliation or Control: Christian Church (Disciples Of Christ)
IRS Status: 501(c)3
Highest Offering: Baccalaureate
Accreditation: **SC**, TED

01 President .... Dr. Seamus CAREY
05 Vice Pres & Dean of the University .... Dr. Laura BRYAN
10 Vice President Finance & Business .... Mr. Marc MATHEWS
07 VP for Enrollment & Student Affairs .... Dr. Holly SHEILLEY
30 VP for Advancement .... Mr. Martin SMITH
13 VP for Information Technology .... Mr. Jason WHITAKER
26 Vice President for Marketing & Comm .... Ms. Michele SPARKS
28 Dir Diversity/Incl & Intl Students .... Ms. Serenity WRIGHT
04 Executive Asst to President .... Ms. Rachel MILLARD
06 Registrar .... Ms. Michelle RAWLINGS
08 Librarian .... Ms. Susan M. BROWN
09 Director of Institutional Research .... Mr. Ryan M. CONYERS
104 Director of Study Abroad .... Ms. Kathryn C. SIMON
36 Director of Career Development .... Ms. Susan S. RAYER
15 Assoc VP & Director Human Resources .... Mr. Jeff MUDRAK
18 Chief Facilities/Physical Plant .... Mr. Charlie L. REDMON
19 Director Security/Safety .... Mr. Gregg MLRAVCHICK
96 Director of Purchasing .... Ms. Shawn T. SINGLETON
39 Director Student Housing .... Mr. Bob BROWN
37 Director of Financial Aid .... Mr. David J. CECIL
29 Director Alumni Relations .... Ms. Natasa PAJIC

Union College (E)

310 College Street, Barbourville KY 40906-1499
County: Knox FICE Identification: 001988
Unit ID: 157863
Telephone: (606) 546-4151 Carnegie Class: Masters/M
FAX Number: (606) 546-1217 Calendar System: Other
URL: www.unionky.edu
Established: 1879 Annual Undergrad Tuition & Fees: $24,000
Enrollment: 1,139 Coed
Affiliation or Control: United Methodist IRS Status: 501(c)3
Highest Offering: Master's
Accreditation: **SC**, #CAATE, NURSE, TED

01 President .... Dr. Marcia HAWKINS
05 VP for Academic Affairs .... Dr. David JOHNS
30 Vice President of Advancement .... Mr. Michael R. MCPHERSON
84 Director Undergraduate Enrollment .... Mr. Craig GROOMS
32 Dean of Students .... Mr. Justin KITTS
53 Head of Educational Studies Dept .... Dr. Jason REEVES
35 Associate Dean Student Life .... Vacant
10 Chief Business Officer .... Mr. Steve HOSKINS
21 Controller .... Ms. Elisabeth RICHARDSON
06 Registrar .... Ms. Kathy INKSTER
18 Director of Physical Plant (NMRC) .... Mr. James JAMERSON
41 Athletic Director .... Mr. Tim CURRY
29 Director of Alumni Relations .... Mr. Brian STRUNK
09 Director of Institutional Research .... Ms. Anisa JAMES
26 Director of Public Relations .... Mr. Jay STANCIL
88 Director of Sports Information .... Mr. John GATTO
88 Associate Dean for Student Success .... Ms. Stephanie SMITH
08 Head Librarian .... Ms. Tara L. COOPER
42 College Minister .... Rev. David MILLER
31 Director of Center for Civic Engage .... Vacant
37 Director of Financial Aid .... Ms. Andra BUTLER
15 Benefits Coordinator .... Ms. Lynn SMITH
19 Safety Team Leader .... Mr. Jurgin MCRIGHT
50 Chair Department of Business .... Dr. Carolyn PAYNE
88 Chair Dept Wellness/Human Perf/Rec .... Dr. Larry INKSTER
79 Chair Dept Engr/Comm/Language .... Dr. Jimmy D. SMITH
57 Chr Dpt Hist/Relig Std/Fn/Perf Arts .... Dr. Russell SISSON
81 Chair Dept of Natural Sciences .... Dr. Dan COVINGTON
83 Chair Dept Social/Behav Science .... Dr. Robert ARMOUR
04 Assistant to the President .... Ms. Sherry PARTIN
88 Events Coordinator .... Ms. Bobbie DOOLIN
102 Dir Foundation/Corporate Relations .... Ms. Monica CLOUSE
105 Director Web Services .... Mr. Kevin SIMPSON
108 Director Institutional Effectivenes .... Dr. Barry PELPHREY

University of the Cumberlands (F)

6191 College Station Drive, Williamsburg KY 40769-1372
County: Whitley FICE Identification: 001962
Unit ID: 156541
Telephone: (606) 549-2200 Carnegie Class: DU-Mod
FAX Number: (606) 539-4280 Calendar System: Semester
URL: www.ucumberlands.edu
Established: 1888 Annual Undergrad Tuition & Fees: $21,000
Enrollment: 5,736 Coed
Affiliation or Control: Baptist IRS Status: 501(c)3
Highest Offering: Doctorate
Accreditation: **SC**, #ARCPA, CACREP, NURSE, TED

01 President .... Dr. Larry L. COCKRUM
30 Vice Pres Institutional Advancement .... Ms. Jamirae HAMMONS
05 Vice President Academic Affairs .... Dr. Barbara KENNEDY
32 Vice President Student Services .... Dr. Emily COLEMAN
23 Vice President Medical Services .... Dr. Eddie PERKINS
10 Chief Financial Officer .... Mr. Chris ROLPH
11 Director .... Mr. Travis WILSON
37 Vice Pres Student Financial Plng .... Mr. Steve ALLEN
41 Vice Pres Athletics/Athletic Dir .... Mr. Chris KRAFTICK
13 VP for Information Technology .... Dr. Donnie GRIMES
84 VP for Enrollment & Communication .... Dr. Jerry JACKSON
06 Registrar .... Mr. Charles DUPIER
20 Associate Dean .... Dr. Thomas E. FISH
26 Director of Communications .... Mrs. Leslie RYSER
35 Dean Student Life .... Ms. Linda CARTER
15 Director of Human Resources .... Ms. Pearl BAKER
42 Dir International Pgm/Church Rels .... Dr. Rick FLEENOR
36 Director of Career Services .... Ms. Debbie HARP
08 Director of Library .... Ms. Jan WREN
58 Director of Graduate Advising .... Mrs. Shonda POWERS
29 Director Alumni Relations .... Mr. Paul STEPP
18 Director of Physical Plant .... Mr. David ROOT
21 Bursar .... Ms. Jo DUPIER

University of Kentucky (G)

101 Main Building, Lexington KY 40506-0003
County: Fayette FICE Identification: 001989
Unit ID: 157085
Telephone: (859) 257-9000 Carnegie Class: DU-Highest
FAX Number: (859) 257-4000 Calendar System: Semester
URL: www.uky.edu
Established: 1865 Annual Undergrad Tuition & Fees (In-State): $10,936
Enrollment: 29,203 Coed
Affiliation or Control: State IRS Status: 501(c)3
Highest Offering: Doctorate
Accreditation: **SC**, AAFCS, ARCPA, ART, BUS, BUSA, CAATE, CIDA, CLPSY, COPSY, CORE, CS, DENT, DIETC, DIETD, DIETI, ENG, HSA, IPSY, JOUR, LAW, LIB, LSAR, MED, MFCD, MT, MUS, NURSE, PAST, PCSAS, PH, PHAR, PTA, SCPSY, SP, SPAA, SW, TED, THEA

01 President .... Dr. Eli I. CAPILOUTO
46 Vice President Research .... Dr. Lisa A. CASSIS
05 Provost .... Dr. Tim S. TRACY
100 Chief of Staff .... Dr. Bill K. SWINFORD
11 Exec VP Finance/Administration .... Mr. Eric N. MONDAY
17 Executive VP for Health Affairs .... Dr. Michael KARPF
13 Interim Chief Information Officer .... Ms. Karen WILLMOTT
32 Int VP Stdnt Affs/Dean of Students .... Dr. Victor A. HAZARD
28 Interim VP Institutional Diversity .... Mr. Terry D. ALLEN
30 Vice President for Development .... Dr. D. Michael RICHEY
10 VP Health Affs/Chief Financial Ofcr .... Mr. Murray B. CLARK
45 VP Financial Planning & CBO .... Ms. Angela S. MARTIN
18 VP Facilities Mgmt & Chief Facil .... Ms. Mary S. VOSEVICH
22 Assoc VP Institutional Equity .... Mr. Terry D. ALLEN
26 VP University Relations .... Mr. Thomas W. HARRIS
15 VP Human Resources Admin & CHRO .... Ms. Kimberly P. WILSON
88 Asst Vice Pres Public Safety .... Mr. Anthony BEATTY
109 Interim Assoc VP Auxiliary Services .... Ms. Sarah F. NIKIRK
25 Assoc VP Res Admin & Fiscal Affs .... Mr. Jack SUPPLEE, JR.
25 Exec Director Sponsored Projects .... Ms. Kim C. CARTER
88 Assoc VP Clinical Network Devel .... Mr. Joe CLAYPOOL
58 Dean of Graduate School .... Vacant
20 Assoc Provost Undergrad Education .... Vacant
20 Assoc Provost Faculty Advancement .... Dr. Gene T. LINEBERRY
84 Assoc Provost Enroll Mgmt/Registrar .... Mr. Don E. WITT
08 Dean of Libraries .... Dr. Terry L. BIRDWHISTELL
27 Exec Director Public Relations .... Mr. Jay D. BLANTON
27 Director University Press .... Dr. Stephen M. WRINN
43 General Counsel .... Mr. William E. THRO

41 Director Athletics .... Mr. Mitch S. BARNHART
37 Director Student Financial Aid .... Dr. Nimmi K. WIGGINS
09 Director of Institutional Research .... Dr. Roger P. SUGARMAN
36 Asst Dean for Career & Academic Exp .... Mr. Ray R. CLERE
38 Director Counseling & Testing .... Dr. Mary C. BOLIN
29 Director Alumni Affairs .... Mr. Stan R. KEY
21 Controller .... Ms. Ronda S. BECK
47 Dean of Agriculture/Food & Envir .... Dr. Nancy M. COX
19 Chief of Police .... Mr. Joseph W. MONROE
88 Dean of Design .... Ms. Mitzi VERNON
88 Exec Director Student Center .... Mr. John H. HERBST
49 Dean of Arts & Sciences .... Dr. Mark L. KORNBLUH
50 Dean of Business & Economics .... Dr. David W. BLACKWELL
53 Dean of Education .... Dr. Mary John O'HAIR
54 Dean of Engineering .... Dr. John Y. WALZ
57 Dean of Fine Arts .... Dr. Michael TICK
60 Dean of Communication/Information .... Dr. H. Dan O'HAIR
61 Dean of Law .... Dr. David A. BRENNEN
70 Interim Dean of Social Work .... Dr. Ann VAIL
76 Dean of Health Sciences .... Dr. Scott M. LEPHART
52 Dean of Dentistry .... Dr. Stephanos KYRKANIDES
63 Dean of Medicine/VP Clinical Affs .... Dr. Robert DIPAOLA
66 Dean of Nursing .... Dr. Janie H. HEATH
67 Interim Dean of Pharmacy .... Dr. Kelly M. SMITH
69 Dean Public Health .... Dr. Donna ARNETT
96 Exec Director Purchasing & CPO .... Mr. William L. HARRIS
108 Director of Assessment .... Ms. Tara A. ROSE
44 Director Annual Giving .... Ms. Anne V. LICHTENBERG

University of Louisville (A)

2301 S Third Street, Louisville KY 40292-0001
County: Jefferson FICE Identification: 001999
Unit ID: 157289
Telephone: (502) 852-5555 Carnegie Class: DU-Highest
FAX Number: (502) 852-7013 Calendar System: Semester
URL: www.louisville.edu
Established: 1798 Annual Undergrad Tuition & Fees (In-State): $10,744
Enrollment: 21,561 Coed
Affiliation or Control: State IRS Status: 501(c)3
Highest Offering: Doctorate
Accreditation: SC, #AUD, BUS, BUSA, CACREP, #CIDA, CLPSY, COPSY, CS, DENT, DH, ENG, EXSC, IPSY, LAW, MED, MFCD, MUS, NURSE, PAST, PH, PLNG, SP, SPAA, SW, THEA

01 President .... Dr. James R. RAMSEY
05 Int Exec Vice Pres/University Prov .... Dr. Neville G. PINTO
17 Exec Vice Pres for Health Affairs .... Vacant
46 Executive VP for Research .... Dr. Bill PIERCE
10 Sr VP Finance & Admin & COO .... Mr. Harlan SANDS
32 Acting VP Student Affairs .... Dr. Michael MARDIS, JR.
30 Vice Pres Univ Advancement .... Mr. Keith INMAN
13 Vice Pres Information Tech .... Vacant
86 VP for Community Engagement .... Mr. Daniel HALL
15 Vice Pres Human Resources .... Vacant
41 Vice President for Athletics .... Mr. Tom JURICH
44 Sr Assoc VP Advancement .... Ms. Rebecca SIMPSON
18 Assoc VP Facilities/Physical Plant .... Mr. Larry DETHERAGE
29 Assoc VP for Alumni Relations .... Ms. Deborah DIETZLER
100 Chief of Staff for the President .... Ms. Kathleen M. SMITH
43 Interim University Counsel .... Ms. Dana B. MAYTON
20 Vice Prov Undergraduate Affairs .... Dr. Dale B. BILLINGSLEY
58 Dean Graduate School .... Dr. Beth A. BOEHM
28 Vice Prov for Diversity/Intl Affs ... Dr. Mordean TAYLOR-ARCHER
09 Vice Provost IR Effect & Analytics .... Mr. Robert S. GOLDSTEIN
106 Assoc Univ Provost Distance Ed/Delp .... Dr. Gale RHODES
88 Asst Prov for Accreditation .... Ms. Connie C. SHUMAKE
21 Controller .... Mr. Larry W. ZINK
07 Executive Director Admissions .... Ms. Jenny L. SAWYER
06 University Registrar .... Mr. Scott A. BURKS
37 Director Financial Aid .... Ms. Sandra NEEL
26 Director of Comm/Marketing .... Ms. Cindy HESS
25 Director Contract Admin/Risk Mgmt .... Mr. David MARTIN
16 Dir of Staff Dev/Employee Rel .... Ms. Mary E. MILES
19 Director Public Safety .... Mr. Wayne HALL
09 Exec Director Inst Res & Plng .... Ms. Becky PATTERSON
45 Exec Director Inst Effectiveness .... Dr. Cheryl B. GILCHRIST
39 Director Student Housing .... Ms. Shannon D. STATEN
105 Director of Digital Media .... Mr. Jeffery A. RUSHTON
27 Director Media Relations .... Mr. Mark HEBERT
88 Assoc Vice Pres for Audit Services .... Mr. David F. BARKER
14 Exec Dir IT Infrastructure .... Ms. Brenda B. GOMBOSKY
92 Exec Director of Honors Program .... Dr. Joy HART
96 Director Purchasing .... Mr. David MARTIN
88 Dir Planning/Design & Construction .... Mr. Kenneth DIETZ
36 Director Career Development .... Mr. Trey LEWIS
38 Director Counseling Center .... Ms. Aesha TYLER
08 Dean of University Libraries .... Mr. Robert FOX
49 Dean College Arts & Sciences .... Dr. Kimberly KEMPF-LEONARD
50 Int Dean College of Business ..... Dr. Rohan M. CHRISTIE-DAVID
52 Dean School of Dentistry .... Dr. John J. SAUK
53 Dean Col of Educ/Human Develop .... Dr. Ann LARSON
70 Dean Kent School Social Work .... Dr. Terry L. SINGER
64 Dean School of Music .... Dr. Christopher DOANE
61 Dean Brandeis School of Law .... Ms. Susan DUNCAN
66 Dean School of Nursing .... Dr. Marcia J. HERN
54 Dean Speed School of Engineering .... Dr. Neville PINTO
63 Dean School of Medicine .... Dr. Toni GANZEL
69 Dean Public Health/Information Sci .... Dr. Craig H. BLAKELY
35 Dean of Students/Assoc VP Stdnt Aff .... Dr. Michael MARDIS
04 Assistant to the President .... Ms. Debra K. DOUGHERTY

University of Phoenix Louisville Campus (B)

10400 Linn Station Road, Louisville KY 40223-3839
Telephone: (502) 423-0149 Identification: 770207
Accreditation: &NH, ACBSP

† No longer accepting campus-based students.

University of Pikeville (C)

147 Sycamore Street, Pikeville KY 41501-1194
County: Pike FICE Identification: 001980
Unit ID: 157535
Telephone: (606) 218-5250 Carnegie Class: Bac-A&S
FAX Number: (606) 218-5269 Calendar System: Semester
URL: www.upike.edu
Established: 1889 Annual Undergrad Tuition & Fees: $18,840
Enrollment: 2,458 Coed
Affiliation or Control: Presbyterian Church (U.S.A.) IRS Status: 501(c)3
Highest Offering: Doctorate
Accreditation: SC, NUR, @OPT, OSTEO, SW

00 Chancellor .... Mr. Paul E. PATTON
01 President .... Dr. Burton J. WEBB
05 Provost .... Dr. Lori WERTH
49 Dean College Arts/Sciences .... Dr. Thomas R. HESS
88 Dean College of Optometry .... Dr. Andrew BUZZELLI
50 Dean College of Business .... Dr. Howard V. ROBERTS
10 Vice Pres Finance/Business Affairs .... Mr. Barry BENTLEY
30 Vice President for Advancement .... Mr. David HUTCHENS
26 Asst Vice President Public Affairs .... Mrs. Lucy HOLMAN
63 VP Health Affairs/Dean KYCOM .... Dr. Boyd R. BUSER
32 Dean of Students .... Vacant
84 Dean of Enrollment Management .... Mrs. Teresa LOCKHART
07 Director Admissions .... Mrs. Teresa LOCKHART
08 Director of Library Services .... Ms. Karen S. CHAFIN-EVANS
06 Asst VP Academic Affairs/Registrar .... Mrs. Gia POTTER
09 Director of Institutional Research .... Dr. Meg SIDLE
13 Senior Info Services Administrator .... Mr. Randy SCARBERRY
18 Asst VP for Facilities .... Mr. John HOLMAN
37 Director of Student Financial Svcs .... Vacant
15 Director of Human Resources .... Mr. Michael PACHECO
04 Executive Asst to President .... Mrs. Sherrie MARRS
19 Director Security/Safety .... Mr. Allen ABSHIRE
41 Athletic Director .... Mr. Robert STAGGS
105 Director of New Media .... Dr. Bruce PARSONS
105 Coordinator of New Media .... Mr. Jacob STRATTON
25 Chief Contracts/Grants Admin .... Mrs. Tiffany THACKER
29 Director Alumni Relations .... Ms. Lisa BLACKBURN
38 Director Student Success .... Ms. Ambria RAY
39 Housing Operations Supervisor .... Mr. Chris ROBINSON
44 Director Annual or Planned Giving .... Mr. Ronald DAMRON
53 Dean College of Education .... Dr. David BARNETT
90 Director Academic Computing .... Mrs. Corrine BOLT

Western Kentucky University (D)

1906 College Heights Blvd, Bowling Green KY 42101-3576
County: Warren FICE Identification: 002002
Unit ID: 157951
Telephone: (270) 745-0111 Carnegie Class: Masters/L
FAX Number: (270) 745-5387 Calendar System: Semester
URL: www.wku.edu
Established: 1906 Annual Undergrad Tuition & Fees (In-State): $9,482
Enrollment: 20,171 Coed
Affiliation or Control: State IRS Status: 501(c)3
Highest Offering: Doctorate
Accreditation: SC, ADNUR, ART, BUS, BUSA, CACREP, CAHIIM, CONST, DANCE, DH, DIETD, @DIETI, ENG, JOUR, MUS, NAIT, NRPA, NURSE, PH, PTA, SP, SPAA, SW, TED, THEA

01 President .... Dr. Gary A. RANSDELL
05 Provost/VP Academic Affairs .... Dr. David LEE
46 Int Assoc Provost for Research .... Dr. Cheryl DAVIS
26 VP for Public Affairs .... Ms. Robbin M. TAYLOR
30 VP Development & Alumni Rels .... Mr. Marc ARCHAMBAULT
32 Vice President Student Affairs .... Mr. Brian KUSTER
10 Vice President Finance & Admin .... Ms. K. Ann MEAD
100 Chief of Staff/General Counsel .... Ms. Deborah T. WILKINS
20 Vice Provost Academic Affairs .... Dr. Richard C. MILLER
84 Chief Enrollment/Grad Officer .... Dr. Brian MEREDITH
106 Assoc VP Ext Learning & Outreach .... Dr. Beth LAVES
79 Dean Arts & Letters .... Dr. Larry SNYDER, JR.
50 Dean Business .... Dr. Jeffrey KATZ
53 Dean Education/Behavioral Sci .... Dr. Sam EVANS
76 Dean Health & Human Services .... Dr. Neale R. CHUMBLER
81 Dean Science/Engineering .... Dr. Cheryl L. STEVENS
58 Interim Dean Grad Studies .... Dr. Eric REED
97 Assc Provost Regional Hgh Ed/Dean .... Dr. Dennis K. GEORGE
62 Dean Libraries .... Ms. Connie FOSTER
88 Assoc VP Enrichment & Effectiveness .... Dr. Doug MCELROY
88 Assoc VP Planning & Program Develop .... Dr. Sylvia GAIKO
21 Chief Financial Officer .... Mr. Jim CUMMINGS
21 Budget Director .... Ms. Kimberly REED
07 Director Recruitment & Admissions .... Dr. Jace T. LUX
88 Assoc VP Academic Budgets & Admin .... Mrs. Ladonna L. HUNTON
06 University Registrar .... Ms. Tiffany ROBINSON
13 Chief Information Tech Officer .... Mr. Gordon L. JOHNSON
15 Director Human Resources .... Mr. Tony L. GLISSON
18 Director Facilities Management .... Mr. Trent BLAIR
12 Regional Chancellor .... Dr. Sally RAY
12 Regional Chancellor .... Dr. Gene E. TICE
90 Director Academic Technology .... Mr. John BOWERS
88 Assoc Dir Advising & Retention Ctr .... Mr. Christopher JENSEN
28 Director Diversity & Inclusion .... Ms. Andrea GARR-BARNES
39 Director Housing & Residence Life .... Ms. Kit TOLBERT
19 Chief of Police .... Mr. Robert DEANE
102 President College Heights Found .... Mr. Donald SMITH
44 Associate VP Major Gifts .... Mr. John P. BLAIR
36 Director Ctr for Career & Prof Dev .... Mr. Robert UNSELD, JR.
37 Dir Student Financial Assistance .... Ms. Cindy BURNETTE
88 Director Student Support Svcs .... Mr. Chris GEORGE
40 Director WKU Store .... Ms. Ann FLORESCA
09 Director Institutional Research .... Dr. Tuesdi HELBIG
22 Equal Oppty/ADA/Compliance Director .... Mr. Joshua HAYES
24 Director Public Radio Services .... Mr. David BRINKLEY
41 Dir Intercollegiate Athletics .... Mr. Todd M. STEWART
85 Dir Intl Enrollment Mgmt .... Ms. Stephanie SIEGGREEN
92 Executive Director Honors College .... Dr. Craig COBANE
96 Director Purchasing/Accts Payable .... Mr. Ken BAUSHKE
101 Assistant to the President .... Ms. Julia J. MCDONALD
101 Executive Administrative Assistant .... Ms. Torie COCKRIEL
104 Dir Study Abroad/Global Learning .... Ms. Laura M. MONARCH
27 Director of Media Relations .... Mr. Bob SKIPPER
86 VP/Dir Govt & Community Relations .... Ms. Jennifer B. SMITH
04 Executive Administrative Assistant .... Ms. Shelia E. HOUCHINS

LOUISIANA

Baton Rouge School of Computers (E)

9352 Interline Avenue, Baton Rouge LA 70809-1909
County: East Baton Rouge FICE Identification: 021975
Unit ID: 158343
Telephone: (225) 923-2524 Carnegie Class: Spec 2-yr-Tech
FAX Number: (225) 923-2979 Calendar System: Other
URL: www.brsc.edu
Established: 1979 Annual Undergrad Tuition & Fees: N/A
Enrollment: 78 Coed
Affiliation or Control: Proprietary IRS Status: Proprietary
Highest Offering: Associate Degree
Accreditation: ACCSC

01 President/Director .... Mrs. Betty D. TRUXILLO
05 Chief Academic Officer .... Ms. Pauline ROBERTS
06 Registrar .... Ms. Diane MCNABB

Blue Cliff College (F)

3200 Cleary Avenue, Metairie LA 70002-5714
County: Jefferson FICE Identification: 032943
Unit ID: 434821
Telephone: (504) 456-3141 Carnegie Class: Not Classified
FAX Number: (504) 456-7849 Calendar System: Quarter
URL: www.bluecliffcollege.edu
Established: 1987 Annual Undergrad Tuition & Fees: N/A
Enrollment: 892 Coed
Affiliation or Control: Proprietary IRS Status: Proprietary
Highest Offering: Associate Degree
Accreditation: ACCSC

01 President/CEO .... Mr. Reggie MOORE
05 Campus Director .... Mr. Doug ROBERTSON

Cameron College (G)

2740 Canal Street, New Orleans LA 70119-5500
County: Orleans FICE Identification: 022340
Unit ID: 158440
Telephone: (504) 821-5881 Carnegie Class: Spec 2-yr-Health
FAX Number: (504) 822-3467 Calendar System: Other
URL: www.cameroncollege.com
Established: 1981 Annual Undergrad Tuition & Fees: N/A
Enrollment: 20 Coed
Affiliation or Control: Proprietary IRS Status: Proprietary
Highest Offering: Associate Degree
Accreditation: COE

01 Director .... Ms. Heather GUIDRY

Career Technical College (H)

1227 Shreveport-Barksdale Highway, Shreveport LA 71105
Telephone: (318) 629-2889 Identification: 770723
Accreditation: ACICS, MAC, SURGT

Centenary College of Louisiana (I)

PO Box 41188, Shreveport LA 71134-1188
County: Caddo FICE Identification: 002003
Unit ID: 158477
Telephone: (318) 869-5011 Carnegie Class: Bac-A&S
FAX Number: (318) 869-5010 Calendar System: Semester
URL: www.centenary.edu
Established: 1825 Annual Undergrad Tuition & Fees: $33,900
Enrollment: 619 Coed
Affiliation or Control: United Methodist IRS Status: 501(c)3
Highest Offering: Master's
Accreditation: #SC, MUS, TEAC, TED

01 President .... Dr. Christopher HOLOMAN
04 Exec Assistant to the President .... Mrs. Connie WHITTINGTON
05 Provost & Dean of the College .... Dr. Jenifer WARD
10 Vice President for Finance/Admin .... Mr. Bob BLUE
50 Dean of the School of Business .... Vacant
64 Dean of the School of Music .... Dr. Gale ODOM
30 Vice Pres for Development .... Mr. Fred LANDRY
84 Vice President for Enrollment .... Mr. Calhoun ALLEN
20 Vice Provost for Academic Affairs .... Dr. Karen SOUL
13 Director of Information Technology .... Mr. Scott MERRITT
21 Business Manager .... Mrs. Monica POWELL
41 Director of Athletics & Wellness .... Mr. Robert BUNNELL
32 Dean of Students .... Mr. Mark MILLER
38 Director of Counseling .... Ms. Tina FELDT
37 Director of Financial Aid .... Mrs. Lynette VISKOZKI
06 Director of Re-Enrollment .... Ms. Nicole SHELBY
08 Librarian .... Ms. Christy WRENN
26 Dir of Strategic Communications .... Mrs. Kate PEDROTTY
29 Director Alumni/Family Relations .... Ms. Saige SOLOMON
38 Director of Professional Success .... Mrs. Rachael PETERS
18 Director of Facilities .... Mr. Chris SAMPITE
46 Director Sponsored Research .... Ms. Patty J. ROBERTS
44 Sr Director of Philanthropy .... Vacant
07 Assoc Dir Admissions/Recruitment .... Ms. Lauren CARLETON
15 Human Resources Director .... Ms. Edie CUMMINGS
19 Director of Public Safety .... Mr. Eddie WALKER

Delta School of Business & Technology, DBA Delta Tech (A)

517 Broad Street, Lake Charles LA 70601-4334
County: Calcasieu　　FICE Identification: 020555
Unit ID: 158723
Telephone: (337) 439-5765　　Carnegie Class: Assoc/HVT-Mix Trad/Non
FAX Number: (337) 436-5151　　Calendar System: Quarter
URL: www.deltatech.edu
Established: 1970　　Annual Undergrad Tuition & Fees: $9,685
Enrollment: 208　　Coed
Affiliation or Control: Proprietary　　IRS Status: Proprietary
Highest Offering: Associate Degree
Accreditation: **ACICS**

01 Chief Executive Officer .... Mr. Jeff EDWARDS
10 Chief Fiscal Officer/Corp Secretary .... Mrs. Nina LEBLANC
05 Dean of Academics .... Ms. Michelle EDWARDS
11 Director of Operations .... Mr. Allen MCLAUGHLIN

Dillard University (B)

2601 Gentilly Boulevard, New Orleans LA 70122-3097
County: Orleans　　FICE Identification: 002004
Unit ID: 158802
Telephone: (504) 283-8822　　Carnegie Class: Bac-A&S
FAX Number: N/A　　Calendar System: Semester
URL: www.dillard.edu
Established: 1869　　Annual Undergrad Tuition & Fees: $16,252
Enrollment: 1,200　　Coed
Affiliation or Control: United Methodist　　IRS Status: 501(c)3
Highest Offering: Baccalaureate
Accreditation: **SC**, NUR

01 President .... Dr. Walter M. KIMBROUGH
03 Executive Vice President .... Mr. Marc BARNES
05 Provost/Sr VP for Academic Affairs .... Dr. Yolanda PAGE
32 Vice President for Student Success .... Vacant
43 VP for Legal Affairs .... Dr. Denise WALLACE
10 VP for Business & Finance .... Mrs. Janel GREEN
20 Associate Provost .... Dr. Christopher JEFFRIES
07 Asst VP of Admissions & Programming .... Ms. Monica WHITE
18 Assoc Vice Pres Facilities Mgmt .... Mr. Adonis WOODS
36 Director of Career/Prof Services .... Ms. Caretta COOKE
06 Dir of Records & Registration .... Mr. Robert MITCHELL, JR.
37 Int Dir Financial Aid/Scholarships .... Ms. Shannon NEAL
102 Assoc VP Research & Spons Programs .... Mr. Theodore CALLIER
30 Director of Development .... Mr. El Cabrel LEE
04 ExecutiveAssistant to the President .... Ms. Kathy TAYLOR
09 Director of Institutional Research .... Dr. Willie KIRKLAND
31 Director Community Development .... Mr. Nick L. HARRIS
19 Chief of Police .... Mr. Julian COAXUM
15 Director of Human Resources .... Mrs. Brittany RICHARDSON
26 Dir of Marketing Communications .... Mr. David GRUBB
97 Dean of College of General Studies .... Vacant
08 Interim Dean of Library/Learning .... Ms. Cynthia CHARLES
49 Dean of College of Arts & Sciences .... Dr. John WILSON
96 Purchasing Officer .... Ms. Anlatear KIRKLIN
103 Dir Workforce/Career Development .... Ms. Caretta COOKE
105 Director Web Services .... Mr. Norward SEARS
13 Chief Info Technology Officer (CIO) .... Mr. Cederic KONYAOLE
22 Dir Affirmative Action/EEO .... Ms. Denise WALLACE
25 Chief Contracts/Grants Admin .... Mr. Theodore CALLIER
39 Director Student Housing .... Dr. Demetrius JOHNSON
41 Athletic Director .... Dr. Kiki BAKER-BARNES
50 Dean of Business .... Dr. Richard IGWIKI
29 Director Alumni Relations .... Mrs. Adrian GUY-ANDERSON
44 Director Annual or Planned Giving .... Mr. Christian PRYOR
84 Director Enrollment Management .... Mr. David PAGE

Fortis College (C)

9255 Interline Avenue, Baton Rouge LA 70809
County: East Baton Rouge　　FICE Identification: 034803
Unit ID: 439738
Telephone: (225) 248-1015　　Carnegie Class: Spec 2-yr-Health
FAX Number: (225) 248-9517　　Calendar System: Other
URL: www.fortis.edu
Established: 1991　　Annual Undergrad Tuition & Fees: $14,226
Enrollment: 382　　Coed
Affiliation or Control: Proprietary　　IRS Status: Proprietary
Highest Offering: Associate Degree
Accreditation: **ABHES**, MLTAD, RAD, SURGT, SURTEC

01 Campus Director .... Vacant
11 Office Manager .... Ms. Mary RICAUD

Herzing University (D)

2500 Williams Boulevard, Kenner LA 70062
Telephone: (504) 733-0074　　Identification: 666450
Accreditation: **&NH**, MAAB, SURTEC

† Regional accreditation is carried under the parent institution in Madison, WI.

ITI Technical College (E)

13944 Airline Highway, Baton Rouge LA 70817-5998
County: East Baton Rouge　　FICE Identification: 021662
Unit ID: 159197
Telephone: (225) 752-4230　　Carnegie Class: Spec 2-yr-Tech
FAX Number: (225) 756-0903　　Calendar System: Quarter
URL: www.iticollege.edu
Established: 1973　　Annual Undergrad Tuition & Fees: $10,575
Enrollment: 691　　Coed
Affiliation or Control: Proprietary　　IRS Status: Proprietary
Highest Offering: Associate Degree
Accreditation: **ACCSC**

01 President .... Mr. Earl Joe MARTIN, III
03 Vice President .... Mr. Mark WORTHY
05 Dean of Education .... Ms. Lisa LAUNEY
88 Director of Compliance .... Mr. Michael CHAMPAGNE
06 Registrar .... Ms. Teresa MAYEUX
07 Director of Admissions .... Mr. Shawn NORRIS
37 Director Student Financial Aid .... Ms. Connie ROUBIQUE

Louisiana College (F)

1140 College Drive, Pineville LA 71359-0001
County: Rapides　　FICE Identification: 002007
Unit ID: 159568
Telephone: (318) 487-7000　　Carnegie Class: Masters/M
FAX Number: (318) 487-7191　　Calendar System: Semester
URL: www.lacollege.edu
Established: 1906　　Annual Undergrad Tuition & Fees: $15,070
Enrollment: 1,256　　Coed
Affiliation or Control: Southern Baptist　　IRS Status: 501(c)3
Highest Offering: Master's
Accreditation: **SC**, ACBSP, #CAATE, MUS, NURSE, PTAA, SW, TEAC

01 President .... Dr. Rick BREWER
03 VP Integration Faith/Learning .... Dr. Philip CAPLES
05 Interim Vice Pres Academic Affairs .... Dr. Cheryl CLARK
10 Vice President for Business Affairs .... Mr. Randall HARGIS
30 VP Inst Advancement/New Projects .... Mr. Byron MCGEE
32 Dean of Students .... Vacant
06 Registrar .... Ms. Eileen DEBOER
84 VP Enrollment Mgmt/Admissions .... Dr. Brandon BANNN
37 Director of Financial Aid .... Mr. David BARNARD
08 Director of the Library .... Mr. Terry MARTIN
26 Exec Asst to Pres Comm/Marketing .... Mr. Norm MILLER
13 Director Computer Services .... Mr. Shane DAVIS
18 Director of Physical Plant .... Mr. Randall HARGIS
21 Director of Business Office .... Ms. Beverly INGRAM
39 Director of Housing .... Mr. Dayne REEVES
41 Athletic Director .... Mr. Dennis DUNN
42 Baptist Student Union Director .... Mr. Thomas WORSHAM
44 Director Constituent Relations .... Vacant
35 Director Student Activities .... Ms. K. B THOMAS
36 Director Career Development .... Mrs. Lenei MERCER
09 Coor of Institutional Research .... Mr. Jeremy TREME
38 Director Student Counseling .... Ms. Lenei MERCER
07 Asst Director of Admissions .... Ms. Renee MELDER
15 Director Personnel Services .... Ms. Shannon TASSIN
40 Bookstore Manager .... Ms. Linda BILLINGSLEY
29 Director of Alumni Relations .... Ms. Kathy OVERTURF
19 Coordinator of Safety & Security .... Mr. Charles ROBERTSON
23 Coordinator of Health Services .... Ms. Janel SANDERS
04 Executive Asst to the President .... Ms. Karen WATKINS

*Louisiana Community & Technical College System (G)

265 S Foster Drive, Baton Rouge LA 70806-4104
County: East Baton Rouge　　Identification: 666188
Telephone: (225) 922-2800　　Carnegie Class: N/A
FAX Number: (225) 922-2392
URL: www.lctcs.edu

01 President .... Dr. Monty SULLIVAN
10 Chief Operations Officer .... Mr. Joseph F. MARIN
05 Chief Content Officer .... Dr. Paul CARLSEN
30 Chief External Affairs Officer .... Mr. David HELVESTON
26 Exec Director Media Relations .... Mr. Quintin TAYLOR

*Baton Rouge Community College (H)

201 Community College Drive,
Baton Rouge LA 70806-4156
County: East Baton Rouge　　FICE Identification: 037303
Unit ID: 437103
Telephone: (225) 216-8000　　Carnegie Class: Assoc/HT-Mix Trad/Non
FAX Number: (225) 216-8100　　Calendar System: Semester
URL: www.mybrcc.edu
Established: 1998　　Annual Undergrad Tuition & Fees (In-District): $3,872
Enrollment: 7,740　　Coed
Affiliation or Control: State/Local　　IRS Status: 501(c)3
Highest Offering: Associate Degree
Accreditation: **SC**, ACBSP, ACFEI, ADNUR, DMS, NAIT, SURGT

02 Interim Chancellor .... Dr. Dennis F. MICHAELIS
04 Asst to the Chancellor .... Ms. Tuesday A. GRAY
26 Exec Dir of PR & Marketing .... Ms. Kizzy PAYTON
84 Interim VC for Student Affairs .... Mr. Brad BANKHEAD
103 Vice Chanc for Workforce Developmen . Mr. Charles FREEBURGH
30 Vice Chanc for Inst Adv/Foundation .... Mr. Philip L. SMITH, JR.
09 Interim Dir of Inst Research .... Ms. Rebecca LOVELL
46 Dir of Business Process Improv .... Ms. Dionne ANDRUS
05 Interim Vice Chanc Acad Affairs .... Dr. Joann LINVILLE
10 Vice Chanc for Finance & Admin .... Ms. Helen HARRIS
21 Director of Acct & Finance .... Mr. Corlin LEBLANC
23 Director of Budgets .... Ms. Quintesah SYAS
13 Chief Information Officer .... Mr. Ronald SOLOMON
15 Director of HR/Payroll .... Ms. Gail PERRY
19 Chief of Police .... Ms. Genoria TILLEY
25 Dir Grants Resource Center .... Ms. Ann ZANDERS
18 Exec Dir of Facilities/Env Safety .... Mr. Bill SMITH
29 Alumni Relations Manager .... Ms. Georgia SCOBEE
32 Exec Dir of Student Services .... Dr. Teresa A. JONES
88 Assoc Dir of Student Engagement .... Ms. Stacia HARDY
36 Director of Career Services .... Ms. Lisa HIBNER
37 Interim Director of Financial Aid .... Ms. Kimberly ZANDERS
41 Athletic Director .... Mr. Neil HAYHURST
38 Director of Student Success .... Ms. Wendy DEVALL
88 Dir of Academic Learning Center .... Ms. Jeanne STACY
88 Upward Bound Program Director .... Ms. Darica SIMON
88 Director of Student Services .... Mr. Johnny MANELA
96 Director of Purchasing .... Mr. Michael CONSTANTIN
06 Dir of Enrollment Svcs/Registrar .... Ms. Erin BLAKE

*Bossier Parish Community College (I)

6220 E Texas Street, Bossier City LA 71111-6922
County: Bossier　　FICE Identification: 020554
Unit ID: 158431
Telephone: (318) 678-6000　　Carnegie Class: Assoc/HT-Mix Trad/Non
FAX Number: (318) 678-6389　　Calendar System: Semester
URL: www.bpcc.edu
Established: 1966　　Annual Undergrad Tuition & Fees (In-District): $4,070
Enrollment: 8,693　　Coed
Affiliation or Control: State/Local　　IRS Status: 501(c)3
Highest Offering: Associate Degree
Accreditation: **SC**, ACFEI, ADNUR, COARC, EMT, MAC, NAIT, OTA, PHLEB, PTAA, SURGT

02 Chancellor .... Dr. Douglas R. BATEMAN
05 VC for Academic Affairs .... Ms. Lesa TAYLOR DUPREE
11 Exec VC Business Affs .... Mr. Tom WILLIAMS
32 VC of Student Services .... Ms. Karen RECCHIA
103 VC of Econ & Workforce Devl .... Ms. Gayle FLOWERS
10 Assoc VC Finance .... Mr. Raymond ABRAHAM
45 Assoc VC Inst Planning & Assessment .. Dr. Holly FRENCH-HART
51 Dean of Workforce Develop/Cont Educ .... Ms. Lisa WARGO
08 Dean of Learning Resources .... Ms. Brenda BRANTLEY
88 Assoc VC for Innov Learning .... Ms. Donna WOMACK
21 Comptroller .... Ms. Carol BATES
37 Director Student Financial Aid .... Ms. Vicki TEMPLE
06 Registrar .... Mr. Richard COCKERHAM
26 Director of Public Relations .... Ms. Tracy MCGILL
15 Director of Human Resources .... Ms. Teri BASHARA
35 Director of Student Life .... Ms. Marjoree HARPER
13 Chief Information Officer .... Mr. Gary HOLLATZ
22 Diversity/Multicultural Affairs .... Ms. Cindy DARBY
72 Director of Educational Technology .... Mr. Charley CAMERON
18 Dir Physical Plant & Maintenance .... Mr. Joe ST. ANDRE
30 Director Institutional Advancement .... Ms. Stephanie ROGERS
25 Director of Grants .... Ms. Jennifer LAWRENCE
96 Director of Purchasing .... Ms. Gayle DOUCET
04 Exec Assistant to Chancellor .... Ms. Christy MOORE
07 Dean of Enrollment Management .... Ms. Kathy VERCHER
108 Dir Institutional Effectiveness .... Ms. Allison MARTIN
19 Director Security/Safety .... Mr. Mike MAY
60 Dean of Comm & Performing Arts .... Dr. Ray Scott CRAWFORD
50 Dean of Business .... Ms. Peggy FULLER
54 Dean of TEM .... Ms. Sandra PARTAIN
66 Dean of Sci/Nursing/Allied Health .... Ms. Carolyn BURROUGHS
49 Dean of Liberal Arts .... Ms. Vicki DENNIS
83 Dean of Behavioral Social Sciences .... Vacant
88 Dean of Acad Advising .... Ms. Peggy FULLER
09 Int Dir of Inst Research/Assesment .... Ms. Staci PHILLIPS
41 Athletic Director .... Mr. John RENNIE

*Central Louisiana Technical College Avoyelles Campus (J)

508 Choupique Street, Cottonport LA 71327-3743
County: Avoyelles　　FICE Identification: 008317
Unit ID: 158237
Telephone: (318) 876-2401　　Carnegie Class: Not Classified

FAX Number: (318) 876-2634 Calendar System: Semester
URL: www.cltcc.edu
Established: 1938 Annual Undergrad Tuition & Fees (In-District): N/A
Enrollment: N/A Coed
Affiliation or Control: State/Local IRS Status: 501(c)3
Highest Offering: Associate Degree
Accreditation: COE

02 Campus Dean .... Ms. Jacqueline AUSBON

*Central Louisiana Technical College Oakdale Campus (A)

117 Highway 1152, Oakdale LA 71463-3536
County: Allen FICE Identification: 030026
Unit ID: 160047
Telephone: (318) 335-3944 Carnegie Class: Not Classified
FAX Number: (318) 335-3347 Calendar System: Quarter
URL: www.cltcc.edu
Established: 1999 Annual Undergrad Tuition & Fees (In-District): N/A
Enrollment: N/A Coed
Affiliation or Control: State/Local IRS Status: 501(c)3
Highest Offering: Associate Degree
Accreditation: COE

02 Campus Dean .... Ms. Kim ANDREWS

*Central Louisiana Technical Community College (B)

4311 S. Macarthur Drive, Alexandria LA 71301
County: Rapides FICE Identification: 005489
Unit ID: 158088
Telephone: (318) 487-5443 Carnegie Class: Assoc/HVT-High Non
FAX Number: (318) 487-5970 Calendar System: Trimester
URL: www.cltcc.edu
Established: 1965 Annual Undergrad Tuition & Fees (In-State): $3,921
Enrollment: 2,049 Coed
Affiliation or Control: State IRS Status: 501(c)3
Highest Offering: Associate Degree
Accreditation: COE

02 Chancellor .... Dr. James (Jimmy) R. SAWTELLE, III
05 Int Vice Chanc Academic Affairs .... Mr. William TULAK
10 Vice Chanc of Finance/Admin .... Ms. Lee MOORE
32 Vice Chanc Student Affs/Enrol Mgmt .... Ms. Heather POOLE

*Central Louisiana Technical & Community College-Huey P. Long Campus (C)

5960 Highway 167 N, Winnfield LA 71483-5075
County: Winn FICE Identification: 005480
Unit ID: 159090
Telephone: (318) 628-4342 Carnegie Class: Not Classified
FAX Number: (318) 628-7768 Calendar System: Semester
URL: www.cltcc.edu
Established: 1938 Annual Undergrad Tuition & Fees (In-District): N/A
Enrollment: N/A Coed
Affiliation or Control: State/Local IRS Status: 501(c)3
Highest Offering: Associate Degree
Accreditation: COE

02 Campus Dean .... Mr. Jeff JOHNSON

*Delgado Community College (D)

615 City Park Avenue, New Orleans LA 70119-4399
County: Orleans FICE Identification: 004625
Unit ID: 158662
Telephone: (504) 671-5000 Carnegie Class: Assoc/MT-VT-High Trad
FAX Number: (504) 361-6699 Calendar System: Semester
URL: www.dcc.edu
Established: 1921 Annual Undergrad Tuition & Fees (In-District): $3,911
Enrollment: 17,152 Coed
Affiliation or Control: State/Local IRS Status: 501(c)3
Highest Offering: Associate Degree
Accreditation: SC, ACBSP, ACFEI, ADNUR, CAHIIM, COARC, DIETT, DMS, EMT, ENGT, FUSER, MLTAD, NAIT, NMT, OTA, PHLEB, POLYT, PTAA, RAD, RTT, SURGT

02 Chancellor .... Ms. Joan Y. DAVIS
10 Int VC Business/Admin Affairs .... Mr. Steven H. CAZAUBON
05 Vice Chanc Acad Affs/Col Provost .... Dr. Kathleen CURPHY
103 Vice Chanc Workforce Dev/Tech Educ .... Dr. Larissa LITTLETON-STEIB
30 VC Inst Advancement/Public Rels .... Dr. Stanton F. MCNEELY, III
66 Exec Dean Charity School/Nursing .... Dr. Cheryl MYERS
76 Dean Allied Health .... Mr. Harold GASPARD
50 Dean Business & Technology .... Mr. Warren PUNEKY
60 Dean Communication Division .... Dr. Lester ADELSBERG
81 Dean Science & Math .... Mr. Thomas GRUBER
79 Dean Arts and Humanities .... Ms. Patrice MOORE
106 Dean Dist Lrng and Instr Tech .... Ms. Jeanne SAMUEL
12 Exec Dean Northshore .... Ms. Ashley CHITWOOD
12 Exec Dean West Bank Campus .... Dr. Peter CHO
32 Exec Dean City Park/VC Stdnt Affs .... Dr. Arnel COSEY
15 Asst Vice Chanc for Human Resources .... Ms. Carla MAJOR
13 Exec Dean S Collier/AVC Info Tech .... Mr. Thomas LOVINCE
21 Asst VC Financial Services .... Mr. Ronald RUSSO
18 Asst VC Facilities & Planning .... Mr. James ROYER
21 Interim Asst VC/Controller .... Ms. Garnette LISTI
04 Executive Asst to the Chancellor .... Ms. Traci SMOTHERS
72 Int Asst Dean Business & Technology .... Ms. Karen MUHSIN
09 Int Exec Dir Planning & Research .... Ms. Juan REN
88 Exec Dir Curriculum & Pgm Devel .... Mr. Timothy STAMM
08 Dean Library .... Mr. Timothy STAMM
37 Director Financial Aid .... Ms. Rhonda KING
41 Athletic Director .... Mr. Joe SCHEUERMANN
06 College Registrar .... Ms. Maria CISNEROS
07 Director Admissions/Enrollment Svcs .... Ms. Gwen BOUTTE
44 Director Restricted Funds .... Vacant
35 Director Student Life .... Mrs. Michelle GRECO
88 Director Advising & Testing .... Ms. Tania CARRADINE
96 Director Purchasing .... Ms. Susan VARBLE
19 Director Campus Police .... Ms. Julie LEA

*L.E. Fletcher Technical Community College (E)

1407 Highway 311, Schriever LA 70395
County: Terrebonne FICE Identification: 005761
Unit ID: 160481
Telephone: (985) 448-7900 Carnegie Class: Assoc/HVT-High Non
FAX Number: (985) 446-3308 Calendar System: Semester
URL: www.fletcher.edu
Established: 1948 Annual Undergrad Tuition & Fees (In-State): $3,951
Enrollment: 1,777 Coed
Affiliation or Control: State IRS Status: Exempt
Highest Offering: Associate Degree
Accreditation: SC, ADNUR, COARC, NAIT, PHLEB, PNUR

02 Chancellor .... Dr. Kristine STRICKLAND
03 Executive Vice Chancellor .... Dr. Derrick MANNS
10 Vice Chancellor of Finance .... Vacant
103 Vice Chancellor of Workforce .... Ms. Cindy POSKEY
05 Vice Chancellor of Academic Affairs .... Dr. Derrick MANNS
06 Registrar .... Ms. Lisa HIDALGO
09 Director of Inst Research & Effect .... Ms. Carrie CORTEZ
21 Director of Accounting .... Mr. Andrew BOYNE
32 Associate VC Student Services .... Dr. Becky MCBRIDE
75 Director of Business and Drafting .... Ms. Fathia WILLIAMS
66 Dean of Nursing and Allied Health .... Ms. Sonia CLARKE
07 Director of Admissions .... Ms. Ana NANNEY
15 HR Manager .... Ms. Gina MARCEL
37 Director of Financial Aid .... Mr. Derrick PROCELL
04 Assistant to the Chancellor .... Ms. Brenda FAUCHEUX
08 Head Librarian .... Mrs. Jasmine RICHARD
30 Exec Dir of Inst Advancement .... Vacant
49 Dean Art and Sciences .... Ms. Donna ESTRADA
88 Director of Workforce Education .... Mrs. Catherine BARBER
88 Director of Technical Education .... Mr. Breck CHAISSON
75 Dean of LAMPI .... Mr. Carl MOORE
96 Director of Purchasing .... Ms. Nancy CLEMENT

*Louisiana Delta Community College (F)

7500 Millhaven Road, Monroe LA 71203
County: Ouachita Parish FICE Identification: 041301
Unit ID: 483212
Telephone: (318) 345-9000 Carnegie Class: Assoc/HVT-High Trad
FAX Number: N/A Calendar System: Semester
URL: www.ladelta.edu
Established: 2001 Annual Undergrad Tuition & Fees (In-District): $4,767
Enrollment: 3,081 Coed
Affiliation or Control: State/Local IRS Status: 501(c)3
Highest Offering: Associate Degree
Accreditation: SC, ADNUR, NAIT

02 Chancellor .... Vacant
05 Vice Chanc of Academic Affairs .... Vacant
10 VC of Finance & Administration .... Mr. Troy CASERTA
84 Dir of Enrollment Mgmt/Registrar .... Mr. Adam ABERCROMBIE
32 Vice Chanc of Student Affairs .... Mr. John TURNER
30 Exec Dir of Dev/Alumni Relations .... Mr. James JOPLING
13 Chief Information Officer .... Mr. Bradley MASTERS

*Northshore Technical Community College (G)

1710 Sullivan Drive, Bogalusa LA 70427-5866
County: Washington FICE Identification: 006756
Unit ID: 160667
Telephone: (985) 732-6640 Carnegie Class: Assoc/HVT-High Non
FAX Number: (985) 732-6603 Calendar System: Semester
URL: www.northshorecollege.edu
Established: 1930 Annual Undergrad Tuition & Fees (In-District): $3,935
Enrollment: 3,752 Coed
Affiliation or Control: State/Local IRS Status: 501(c)3
Highest Offering: Associate Degree
Accreditation: COE

02 Chancellor .... Dr. William S. WAINWRIGHT
10 Vice Chancellor Finance & Admin .... Mr. Marc CHAUVIN
32 Vice Provost of Student Affairs .... Ms. Christy MONTGOMERY
108 VProv Assess & Plng/Dn Campus Admin .... Ms. Shelia SINGLETARY
08 Director of Library Services .... Ms. Margaret KELLER
72 Dean of Technical Studies .... Mr. Dewayne LAMBERT
76 Dean of Health Sciences & Nursing .... Ms. Katherine M. LYONS
81 Dean of Academic and STEM Programs .... Dr. Tina TINNEY
12 Interim Dean of Campus Admin .... Ms. Kim FINCH
12 Dean of Campus Administration .... Ms. Bridget LABORDE
103 Executive Director of Workforce Dev .... Mr. David LLOYD
15 Human Resources Director .... Ms. Joanna DILLMAN
06 Registrar .... Ms. Kim FINCH
18 Chief Facilities/Physical Plant .... Mr. Gerald BLAPPERT
96 Director of Purchasing .... Mr. Danny STEWART
37 Financial Aid Director .... Nichole LABAT

*Northwest Louisiana Technical College Northwest Campus (H)

9500 Industrial Drive, Minden LA 71055
County: Webster FICE Identification: 009975
Unit ID: 160010
Telephone: (318) 371-3035 Carnegie Class: Assoc/HVT-High Non
FAX Number: (318) 371-3026 Calendar System: Trimester
URL: www.nwltc.edu
Established: 1952 Annual Undergrad Tuition & Fees (In-District): $2,817
Enrollment: 3,283 Coed
Affiliation or Control: State/Local IRS Status: 501(c)3
Highest Offering: Associate Degree
Accreditation: COE

02 Interim Director .... Ms. Dianne CLARK
03 Dean Main Campus/Facilities .... Mr. Charles SCOTT PRICE
15 Chief Human Resources Officer .... Ms. Amber SAUNDERS
10 Chief Financial Officer .... Ms. Jennifer PYE
37 Director of Financial Aid .... Ms. Annette CHANLER
32 Director of Student Services .... Ms. Cindy MAGGIO
09 Director of Institutional Research .... Ms. Haley HOLDER
103 Director of Workforce Development .... Mr. Curtis STORMS
05 Chief Academic Officer .... Ms. Laurie MORROW
12 Dean Shreveport Campus .... Mr. David RHODES

*Nunez Community College (I)

3710 Paris Road, Chalmette LA 70043-1297
County: Saint Bernard FICE Identification: 021661
Unit ID: 158884
Telephone: (504) 278-6200 Carnegie Class: Assoc/HVT-High Non
FAX Number: (504) 278-6480 Calendar System: Semester
URL: www.nunez.edu
Established: 1992 Annual Undergrad Tuition & Fees (In-District): $3,945
Enrollment: 2,617 Coed
Affiliation or Control: State/Local IRS Status: 501(c)3
Highest Offering: Associate Degree
Accreditation: SC, NAIT

02 Chancellor .... Dr. Thomas R. WARNER
05 Vice Chanc Academic & Student Affs .... Vacant
30 VC for Institutional Advancement .... Ms. Teresa L. SMITH
10 Chief Financial Officer .... Mr. Louis LEHR
15 Dir Human Res/Exec Asst to Chanc .... Mr. Richard GREENE
20 Dean of Academic Affairs .... Ms. Tonia LORIA
32 Dean for Student Affairs .... Ms. Becky MAILLET
45 Dean Planning/Inst Effectiveness .... Mr. Leonard UNBEHAGEN
103 Director Workforce Development .... Mr. Ernest T. FRAZIER, JR.
06 Registrar .... Ms. Meg GREENFIELD
07 Director of Admissions .... Mrs. Brittney BARRAS
37 Director Financial Aid .... Mr. John WHISNANT
26 Public Information Officer .... Ms. Lindsay JAKIEL DIULUS
18 Coordinator of Facilities .... Ms. Dawn HART-THORE
25 Director of Sponsored Programs .... Ms. Kimberly RUTHERFORD
13 IT Manager .... Mr. Jason HOSCH

*River Parishes Community College (J)

PO Box 2367, Gonzales LA 70707
County: Ascension FICE Identification: 037894
Unit ID: 436304
Telephone: (225) 743-8500 Carnegie Class: Assoc/MT-VT-High Non
FAX Number: (225) 644-8210 Calendar System: Semester
URL: www.rpcc.edu
Established: 1999 Annual Undergrad Tuition & Fees (In-District): $3,911
Enrollment: 1,981 Coed
Affiliation or Control: State/Local IRS Status: 501(c)3
Highest Offering: Associate Degree
Accreditation: SC, NAIT

02 Chancellor .... Dr. Dale DOTY
10 VC Business/Finance/Administration .... Khalli HAGAN
05 VC of Academic Studies .... Dr. Crystal LEE
103 VC Workforce Development .... Dr. Bruce WAGUESPACK
21 Director of Accounting & Payroll .... Lisa JACKSON
30 Director Institutional Advancement .... Glen DUCAN
37 Director Financial Aid .... Terry MARTIN
38 Director Student Counseling .... Jennifer KLEINPETER
08 Director of Library Services .... Wendy JOHNSON
15 Human Resource Manager .... Donna WHITTINGTON
09 Director of Institutional Research .... Melba KENNEDY

*South Central Louisiana Technical College Young Memorial Campus (K)

900 Youngs Road, Morgan City LA 70380-2931
County: Saint Mary FICE Identification: 005526
Unit ID: 160913
Telephone: (985) 380-2957 Carnegie Class: Spec 2-yr-Tech

FAX Number: (985) 380-2440 Calendar System: Semester
URL: www.scl.edu
Established: 1965 Annual Undergrad Tuition & Fees (In-District): $2,526
Enrollment: 2,039 Coed
Affiliation or Control: State/Local IRS Status: 501(c)3
Highest Offering: Associate Degree
Accreditation: COE

02 College Director .... Mr. Earl W. MEADOR
05 Chief Academic Officer .... Ms. Melanie HENRY
07 Dir of Admissions/Student Affairs .... Ms. Tammie L. MOORE
09 Director of Institutional Research .... Ms. Katherine FALGOUT
15 Director Human Resources .... Ms. Pam MILLER
103 Chief Workforce Development Ofcr .... Mr. Anthony L. BAHAM

*South Louisiana Community College (A)

1101 Bertrand Drive, Lafayette LA 70506-4124
County: Lafayette FICE Identification: 039563
Unit ID: 434061
Telephone: (337) 521-9000 Carnegie Class: Assoc/HVT-High Non
FAX Number: (337) 521-9061 Calendar System: Semester
URL: www.solacc.edu
Established: 1998 Annual Undergrad Tuition & Fees (In-District): $3,974
Enrollment: 6,332 Coed
Affiliation or Control: State/Local IRS Status: 501(c)3
Highest Offering: Associate Degree
Accreditation: SC, ACFEI, EMT, MLTAD, NAIT, SURGT

02 Chancellor .... Dr. Natalie HARDER
04 Sr Exec Assistant to the Chancellor .... Ms. Allison DUFFY
09 Vice Chanc Strategic Initiatives .... Dr. Micheal GLISSON
10 Vice Chanc Finance & Administration .... Mr. Bryan GLATTER
103 Vice Chanc Economic & Workforce Dev .... Dr. Willie SMITH
32 Vice Chanc for Student Services .... Dr. Vincent JUNE
07 Int Director of Admissions .... Ms. Lisa KIRK
37 Asst Director of Financial Aid .... Ms. Janelle MANUEL
08 Director of Library Services .... Ms. Katherine ROLFES
21 Business Manager .... Ms. Janet LAGRANGE
96 Director of Accounting .... Ms. Carla ORTEGO
18 Director of Facilities .... Mr. Edwin LOPEZ
15 Dir Administration/Human Resources .... Ms. Alicia HULIN

*Sowela Technical Community College (B)

PO Box 16950, Lake Charles LA 70616-6950
County: Calcasieu FICE Identification: 005467
Unit ID: 160579
Telephone: (337) 421-6565 Carnegie Class: Assoc/HVT-High Trad
FAX Number: (337) 491-2135 Calendar System: Semester
URL: www.sowela.edu
Established: 1938 Annual Undergrad Tuition & Fees (In-District): $4,077
Enrollment: 3,411 Coed
Affiliation or Control: State/Local IRS Status: 501(c)3
Highest Offering: Associate Degree
Accreditation: SC, ACFEI, COE, NAIT

02 Chancellor .... Dr. Neil ASPINWALL
04 Assistant to the Chancellor .... Ms. Mary REEDER
05 Vice Chancellor Academic Affairs .... Ms. Paula HELLUMS
10 Vice Chancellor Finance .... Ms. Jeanine NEWMAN
46 Vice Chancellor Workforce Solutions .... Vacant
13 Int Chief Info Res & Tech Officer .... Dr. Martha J. SCHEXNEIDER
84 Int Exec Dir Enroll Mgmt/Stdnt Affs .... Ms. Anna DAIGLE
21 Controller .... Mr. Francis PORCHE, JR.
37 Director of Financial Aid .... Ms. Anna DAIGLE
08 Director of Library Services .... Ms. Mary Frances SHERWOOD
15 Director of Human Resources .... Dr. FitzPatrick ANYANWU
103 Director of Workforce Development .... Mr. William E. MAYO
32 Director of Student Support Svcs .... Ms. Christine COLLINS
18 Director Facilities Planning & Mgmt .... Mr. Davidson DARBONE
09 Exec Director Planning & Analysis .... Dr. Fitzpatrick U. ANYANWU
30 Exec Dir Institutional Advancement .... Ms. Marianne WHITE

*Northwest Louisiana Technical College Natchitoches Campus (C)

6587 Highway 1 Bypass, Natchitoches LA 71458-0657
Telephone: (318) 357-3162 FICE Identification: 021602
Accreditation: COE

† Branch campus of Northwest Louisiana Technical College Northwest Campus, Minden, LA.

*Northwest Louisiana Technical College Shreveport Campus (D)

Box 78527, 2010 N Market Street,
Shreveport LA 71137-8527
Telephone: (318) 676-7811 FICE Identification: 005469
Accreditation: COE

† Branch campus of Northwest Louisiana Technical College Northwest Campus, Minden, LA.

*South Central Louisiana Technical College Lafourche Campus (E)

1425 Tiger Drive, Thibodaux LA 70301-4336
Telephone: (985) 447-0924 FICE Identification: 030091
Accreditation: COE, SURGT

† Branch campus of South Central Louisiana Technical College Young Memorial Campus.

*South Central Louisiana Technical College Reserve Campus (F)

PO Drawer AQ, 181 Regala Park Road,
Reserve LA 70084-0542
Telephone: (985) 536-4418 FICE Identification: 023334
Accreditation: COE, NAIT

† Branch campus of South Central Louisiana Technical College Young Memorial Campus.

Louisiana Culinary Institute (G)

10550 Airline Highway, Baton Rouge LA 70816-4109
County: East Baton Rouge FICE Identification: 041123
Unit ID: 449612
Telephone: (225) 769-8820 Carnegie Class: Spec 2-yr-A&S
FAX Number: (225) 769-8792 Calendar System: Semester
URL: www.lci.edu
Established: 2002 Annual Undergrad Tuition & Fees: $14,575
Enrollment: 208 Coed
Affiliation or Control: Proprietary IRS Status: Proprietary
Highest Offering: Associate Degree
Accreditation: ACICS, COE, ACFEI

01 Chief Executive Officer .... Keith RUSH

*Louisiana State University Administration (H)

3810 W Lakeshore Drive, Baton Rouge LA 70808-4600
County: East Baton Rouge FICE Identification: 002009
Unit ID: 159638
Telephone: (225) 578-2111 Carnegie Class: N/A
FAX Number: (225) 578-5524
URL: www.lsu.edu

01 President .... Dr. F. King ALEXANDER
05 VP Academic Affairs/Tech Trans .... Dr. Carolyn H. HARGRAVE
17 Exec VP HC/Med Educ Redesign .... Dr. Frank OPELKA
88 Asst Vice Pres for System Relations .... Dr. Robert H. RASMUSSEN
10 Assoc Vice Pres Finance/Admin .... Mrs. Wendy S MONEAUX
18 System Director Facility Planning .... Mr. Danny MAHAFFEY
43 LSU Lead Counsel .... Mr. W. Shelby MCKENZIE
15 System Dir Human Resource/Risk Mgt .... Ms. Sharyon LIPSCOMB
21 System Director Internal Audit .... Mr. Chad BRACKIN

*Louisiana State University and Agricultural and Mechanical College (I)

Baton Rouge LA 70803-0100
County: East Baton Rouge FICE Identification: 002010
Unit ID: 159391
Telephone: (225) 578-3202 Carnegie Class: DU-Highest
FAX Number: (225) 578-6400 Calendar System: Semester
URL: www.lsu.edu
Established: 1860 Annual Undergrad Tuition & Fees (In-State): $9,714
Enrollment: 31,044 Coed
Affiliation or Control: State IRS Status: 501(c)3
Highest Offering: Doctorate
Accreditation: SC, ART, BUS, CAATE, CACREP, CIDA, #CLPSY, CONST, CS, DIETD, ENG, IPSY, JOUR, LAW, LIB, LSAR, MUS, SCPSY, SP, SPAA, SW, TED, THEA, VET

02 President .... Dr. King ALEXANDER
05 Exec Vice Pres/Provost .... Dr. Richard KOUBEK
43 General Counsel .... Mr. Thomas SKINNER
26 Int VP Strategic Communication .... Mr. Jason DRODDY
10 Vice Pres Finance & Admin .... Mr. Daniel LAYZELL
46 Vice Pres Research & Econ Dev .... Dr. Kalliat T. VALSARAJ
45 Vice Pres Strategic Initiatives .... Dr. Isiah M. WARNER
32 Vice Pres Student Life & Acad Svcs .... Dr. Kurt J. KEPPLER
102 President/CEO LSU Foundation .... Mr. Stephen MORET
28 Vice Prov Office of Diversity .... Mr. Dereck ROVARIS
20 Sr Vice Prov Academic Affairs .... Dr. Jane CASSIDY
20 Assoc Vice Pres Academic Planning .... Dr. Gilmore REEVE
15 Assoc VP Human Resources Mgmt .... Mr. A.G. MONACO
84 Assoc VP Enrollment Management .... Ms. Charlotte TULLOS
30 Exec Director Inst Advancement .... Ms. Bunnie CANNON
86 Exec Dir Pub Policy & Ext Affairs .... Dr. Jason DRODDY
85 Assoc VP International Programs .... Dr. Hector ZAPATA
37 Assoc Dir Student Aid/Scholarships .... Ms. Amy MARIX
08 Dean LSU Libraries .... Mr. Stanley WILDER
79 Dean College of Hum & Soc Sciences .... Dr. Stacia HAYNIE
58 Dean of Graduate School .... Dr. Michelle MASSE
54 Int Dean College of Engineering .... Dr. Judy WORNAT
47 Dean College of Agriculture .... Dr. William RICHARDSON
50 Dean Ourso College of Business .... Dr. Richard D. WHITE
64 Dean College Music & Dramatic Arts .... Mr. Todd QUEEN
81 Dean College of Science .... Dr. Cynthia PETERSON
62 Dean Sch of Library & Info Science .... Dr. Carol BARRY
53 Dean College of Human Sci & Educ .... Dr. Damon P. ANDREW
57 Dean College of Art & Design .... Mr. Alkis TSOLAKIS
74 Dean Veterinary Medicine .... Dr. Joel D. BAINES
60 Dean Manship Sch of Mass Comm .... Dr. Jerry CEPPOS
92 Dean Honors College .... Dr. Jonathan H. EARLE
65 Dean Sch of Coast & Environ .... Dr. Christopher D'ELIA
88 Exec Director University College .... Mr. Paul IVEY
35 Assc Dean of Student/Dir Greek Life .... Ms. Angela GUILLORY
88 Sr Ex Dir SN Ctr Security Rsch Trng .... Mr. Jim FERNANDEZ
88 Exec Director Center Energy Stds .... Mr. David DISMUKES
51 Exec Director Continuing Education .... Mr. Douglas P. WEIMER
29 President LSU Alumni Association .... Mr. Cliff VANNOY
59 Director School Human Ecology .... Dr. Roy J. MARTIN
88 Exec Director LSU Museum of Art .... Dr. Daniel STETSON
18 Exec Director Facility Services .... Mr. Tony LOMBARDO
13 Assoc VP Admin & Info Tech Services .... Mr. Brian NICHOLS
75 Int Dir Sch Human Res Ed & Wk Dev .... Dr. Reid BATES
80 Director Public Admin Institute .... Dr. James A. RICHARDSON
88 Director LSU Press .... Ms. MaryKatherine CALLAWAY
41 Vice President/Athletic Director .... Mr. Joe ALLEVA
06 Assoc Vice Provost & Univ Registrar .... Mr. Robert K. DOOLOS
36 Director Olinde Career Center .... Mr. Jesse G. DOWNS
09 Director of Institutional Research .... Mr. Bernie BRAUN
93 Director Multicultural Affairs .... Vacant
94 Director Women's Center .... Ms. Summer STEIB
65 Director Museum of Natural Science .... Mr. Robb T. BRUMFIELD
88 Director Rural Life Museum .... Mr. David FLOYD
96 Exec Director Purchasing & Property .... Ms. Sally MCKECHNIE
07 Assoc Director of Admissions .... Ms. Lupe LAMADRID
19 Chief of LSU Police .... Mr. Lawrence RABALAIS
39 Exec Director Residential Life .... Mr. Steve WALLER

*Louisiana State University at Alexandria (J)

8100 Highway 71 S, Alexandria LA 71302-9121
County: Rapides FICE Identification: 002011
Unit ID: 159382
Telephone: (318) 445-3672 Carnegie Class: Bac-A&S
FAX Number: (318) 473-6418 Calendar System: Semester
URL: www.lsua.edu
Established: 1959 Annual Undergrad Tuition & Fees (In-State): $6,158
Enrollment: 2,702 Coed
Affiliation or Control: State IRS Status: 501(c)3
Highest Offering: Baccalaureate
Accreditation: SC, ADNUR, MLTAD, NUR, RAD, TED

02 Chancellor .... Dr. Daniel HOWARD
05 Vice Chanc Academic & Student Affs .... Dr. Barbara S. HATFIELD
10 Int Vice Chanc Finance/Admin Svcs .... Mr. Deron THAXTON
30 Director Institutional Advancement .... Ms. Melinda F. ANDERSON
20 Asst VC Academic/Student Affairs .... Dr. Eamon HALPIN
21 Asst VC Finance/Admin Services .... Vacant
50 Int Dept Chair Business Admin .... Dr. Haywood JOINER
49 Dept Chair Arts/English/Humanities .... Dr. Holly WILSON
83 Dept Chair Behavioral & Social Sci .... Dr. Jerry SANSON
81 Dept Chair Math & Physical Sciences .... Dr. Nathan PONDER
53 Department Chair Education .... Dr. Patsy JENKINS
76 Department Chair Allied Health .... Dr. Haywood JOINER
66 Department Chair Nursing .... Dr. Cathy CORMIER
49 Dept Chair Biological Sciences .... Dr. Carol CORBAT
18 Exec Director of Facility Services .... Vacant
08 Director Library Services .... Dr. Bonnie HINES
37 Director of Financial Aid .... Vacant
13 Exec Dir Info Educational Tech Svcs .... Mr. Deron THAXTON
15 Director Human Resource Management .... Ms. Lynette BURLEW
51 Director Continuing Education .... Vacant
88 Director of Advising .... Dr. Eamon HALPIN
09 Dir Inst Research/Effectiveness .... Vacant
96 Dir Procurement Svcs/Property Mgmt .... Vacant
41 Director Athletics .... Vacant
07 Director of Admissions & Recruiting .... Ms. Shelly KIEFFER
06 Registrar .... Ms. Stephanie CAGE
19 Dir Public Safety/Chief of Police .... Mr. Dwayne ROGERS

*Louisiana State University at Eunice (K)

2048 Johnson Highway, Eunice LA 70535-6726
County: Acadia FICE Identification: 002012
Unit ID: 159407
Telephone: (337) 457-7311 Carnegie Class: Assoc/HT-High Trad
FAX Number: (337) 546-6620 Calendar System: Semester
URL: www.lsue.edu
Established: 1964 Annual Undergrad Tuition & Fees (In-State): $3,828
Enrollment: 2,738 Coed
Affiliation or Control: State IRS Status: 501(c)3
Highest Offering: Associate Degree
Accreditation: SC, ADNUR, #COARC, DMS, RAD

02 Chancellor .... Dr. Kimberly A. RUSSELL
05 Vice Chancellor Academic Affairs .... Dr. Renee ROBICHAUX
84 Vice Chancellor Enrollment Mgmt .... Mr. Jerrett D. PHILLIPS
10 Vice Chancellor Business Affairs .... Ms. Arlene C. TUCKER
26 Director of Public Relations .... Mr. Van REED
08 Director of the Library .... Mr. Gerald PATOUT
06 Registrar/Dir of Admissions .... Dr. Kenneth ELLIOTT
37 Director of Financial Aid .... Ms. Jacqueline LA CHAPELLE
30 Dir Foundation & Institutional Dev .... Vacant
09 Dir Inst Effect/Devel Educ .... Dr. Paul FOWLER

51 Int Director Continuing Education ....Mr. Launey P. GRIFFITH
18 Director Physical Plant ....Mr. Michael BROUSSARD
25 Director Grants ....Vacant
15 Director Personnel Services ....Ms. Angel MCGEE
81 Head Division of Sciences ....Dr. John HAMLIN
50 Head Div Bus/Nursing/Allied Health ....Ms. Dotty MCDONALD
49 Head Division of Liberal Arts ....Vacant
13 Chief Info Technology Officer (CIO) ....Vacant
41 Athletic Director ....Mr. Jeff WILLIS

*Louisiana State University Health Sciences Center-New Orleans (A)

433 Bolivar Street, New Orleans LA 70112-2223
County: Orleans FICE Identification: 002014
Unit ID: 159373
Telephone: (504) 568-4808 Carnegie Class: Spec-4-yr-Med
FAX Number: N/A Calendar System: Semester
URL: www.lsuhsc.edu
Established: 1931 Annual Undergrad Tuition & Fees (In-State): N/A
Enrollment: 2,828 Coed
Affiliation or Control: State IRS Status: 501(c)3
Highest Offering: Doctorate
Accreditation: SC, ANEST, #ARCPA, AUD, CACREP, COARC, CORE, CVT, DENT, DH, DT, IPSY, MED, MT, NURSE, OT, PH, PTA, SP

02 Chancellor ....Dr. Larry H. HOLLIER
05 Vice Chanc Acad Aff/Dean Grad Stds ....Dr. Joseph M. MOERSCHBAECHER
10 Vice Chancellor Finance/Admin ....Ms. Wendy SIMONEAUX
31 Vice Chanc Cmty/Minority Affairs ....Mr. Edwin MURRAY
17 Vice Chanc Clinic Affairs ....Dr. J. Chris WINTERS
43 General Counsel ....Ms. Katherine MUSLOW
63 Dean Medicine NO ....Dr. Steve NELSON
52 Dean School of Dentistry ....Dr. Henry GREMILLION
66 Dean of Nursing ....Dr. Demetrius PORCHE
69 Dean of Public Health ....Dr. Dean SMITH
76 Dean Allied Health Professions ....Dr. Jim R. CAIRO
04 Assistant to the Chancellor ....Mrs. Christine MANALLA
86 Director of International Services ....Ms. Remy E. ALLEN
14 Director Computer Services ....Ms. Bettina OWENS
13 Director Information Services ....Ms. Leslie L. CAPO
08 Director Library Administration ....Ms. Debra H. SIBLEY
15 Director Human Resource Mgmt ....Mr. Danielle LOMBARD-SIMS
06 Registrar ....Mr. William Bryant FAUST
37 Assoc Dir Student Financial Aid ....Ms. Kimberly BRUNO
09 Director of Institutional Research ....Dr. Ken KRATZ
18 Chief Facilities/Physical Plant ....Mr. John BALL
96 Exec Director of Purchasing ....Mr. Brent HEROLD
26 Director of External Relations ....Mr. Christopher VIDRINE

*Louisiana State University Health Sciences Center at Shreveport (B)

1501 Kings Highway, Shreveport LA 71103
County: Caddo FICE Identification: 008067
Unit ID: 435000
Telephone: (318) 675-5241 Carnegie Class: Spec-4-yr-Med
FAX Number: (318) 675-5244 Calendar System: Semester
URL: www.lsuhscshreveport.edu
Established: 1969 Annual Undergrad Tuition & Fees: N/A
Enrollment: 870 Coed
Affiliation or Control: Other IRS Status: Exempt
Highest Offering: Doctorate
Accreditation: SC, ARCPA, COARC, DENT, MED, MT, OT, PH, PTA, SP

02 Interim Chancellor & Dean SOM ....Dr. Ghali E. GHALI
11 Vice Chancellor Administration ....Mr. Victor YICK
46 Vice Chancellor Research Affairs ....Dr. Daniel N. GRANGER
05 Vice Chancellor Academic Affairs ....Dr. Jane EGGERSTEDT
10 Chief Financial Officer ....Ms. Sheila FAOUR
43 Senior Legal Counsel ....Ms. Susan ARMSTRONG
76 Dean Sch Allied Health Professions ....Dr. Joseph MCCULLOCH
58 Dean School of Graduate Studies ....Dr. Sandra C. ROERIG
88 Exec Director of Campus Operations ....Mr. Joseph MICIOTTO
86 Exec Dir Government Affairs ....Ms. Mimi HEDGCOCK
26 Exec Dir Comm/Public Relations ....Ms. Sally CROOM
13 Chief Info Technology Officer (CIO) ....Dr. Timothy MAGNER
07 Asst Dean for Admissions SOM ....Dr. Frank S. KENNEDY
32 Asst Dean for Student Affairs SOM ....Dr. Mark PLATT
15 Exec Director of Human Resources ....Ms. Lisa EBARB
88 Executive Director-Medical Services ....Ms. Leisa OGLESBY
18 Chief Facilities/Physical Plant ....Mr. Marc GIBSON
19 Director Security/Safety ....Mr. Willie BUFFINGTON
09 Director of Institutional Planning ....Mr. Jeffrey D. HOWELLS
25 Director of Sponsored Programs ....Ms. Annella NELSON
06 Registrar ....Ms. Kim CARMEN
08 Head Librarian ....Ms. Dixie JONES
37 Director Student Financial Aid ....Ms. Sherry GLADNEY
28 Director of Diversity ....Mr. Roosevelt SEABERRY
29 Director Alumni Relations ....Ms. Marianne COMEGYS
16 Asst Director of Human Resources ....Mr. Michael DONLEY

† Tuition varies by degree program.

*Louisiana State University in Shreveport (C)

One University Place, Shreveport LA 71115-2399
County: Caddo FICE Identification: 002013
Unit ID: 159416
Telephone: (318) 797-5000 Carnegie Class: Masters/M
FAX Number: (318) 797-5180 Calendar System: Semester
URL: www.lsus.edu
Established: 1967 Annual Undergrad Tuition & Fees (In-State): $6,903
Enrollment: 4,186 Coed
Affiliation or Control: State IRS Status: 501(c)3
Highest Offering: Doctorate
Accreditation: SC, BUS, CS, PH, TED

02 Chancellor ....Mr. Lawrence S. CLARK
05 Provost/VC Academic Affairs ....Dr. John S. VASSAR
10 Vice Chancellor Business Affairs ....Mr. Michael T. FERRELL
32 Assoc VC Student Affairs ....Mrs. Paula B. ATKINS
102 Executive Director LSUS Foundation ....Ms. Laura PERDUE
29 Director Alumni Affairs ....Ms. Dianne B. HOWELL
09 Director Planning/Inst Research ....Vacant
06 Registrar ....Ms. Darlenna M. ATKINS
15 Director of Human Resource Mgmt ....Mr. Bill WOLFE
08 Interim Dean Noel Memorial Library ....Mr. Brian SHERMAN
37 Director of Student Financial Aid ....Ms. Chelsea CHANCE
07 Director of Admissions ....Mr. David D. STANFORD
36 Dir Student Devel & Counseling ....Vacant
13 Assoc VC & CIO/IT ....Mr. Shelby C. KEITH
18 Interim Dir of Facility Services ....Mr. Harry HARPER, JR.
40 Director of Bookstore ....Ms. Brenda P. BARTLEBAUGH
96 Director of Purchasing ....Mr. Bill WOLFE
26 Director of Media/Public Relations ....Mrs. Brooke H. RINAUDO
04 Assistant to the Chancellor ....Vacant
19 Dir of University Police ....Mr. Donald W. WRAY
41 Athletic Director ....Mr. Lucas MORGAN
49 Dean of Arts and Sciences ....Dr. Larry ANDERSON
58 Dean of Graduate Studies ....Dr. Sanjay T. MENON
51 Exec Dir Continuing Education ....Mr. Brent WALLACE
53 Dean Business/Ed/Human Dev ....Dr. Nancy MILLER

*University of New Orleans (D)

2000 Lakeshore Drive, New Orleans LA 70148-2000
County: Orleans FICE Identification: 002015
Unit ID: 159939
Telephone: (504) 280-6000 Carnegie Class: DU-Higher
FAX Number: (504) 280-5522 Calendar System: Semester
URL: www.uno.edu
Established: 1958 Annual Undergrad Tuition & Fees (In-State): $8,004
Enrollment: 9,234 Coed
Affiliation or Control: State IRS Status: 501(c)3
Highest Offering: Doctorate
Accreditation: SC, ART, BUS, BUSA, CACREP, CS, ENG, MUS, PLNG, SPAA, TED, THEA

02 President ....Dr. John W. NICKLOW
05 Interim Provost/VP Academic Affairs ....Dr. Norm WHITLEY
10 VP Business Affairs ....Dr. Gregg LASSEN
32 Dean of Students ....Dr. Brett KEMKER
13 Chief Information Officer ....Mr. David DUPREE
85 Asst VP/Director International Educ ....Ms. Alea COT
19 Asst Vice Chanc for Public Safety ......Mr. Thomas HARRINGTON
50 Dean of Business Administration ....Dr. John A. WILLIAMS
54 Dean of Engineering ....Dr. Emir MACARI
49 Int Dean Liberal Arts & Education ....Dr. Kevin GRAVES
08 Interim Dean of Library ....Dr. Lora AMSBERRYAUGIER
81 Dean of Sciences ....Dr. Steve JOHNSON
06 University Registrar ....Mr. Matt MOORE
29 Director Alumni Affairs ....Ms. Pamela MEYER
26 Chief Communications Officer ....Mr. Adam NORRIS
96 Associate Director of Purchasing ....Ms. Heather CASSELL
41 Director Athletics ....Mr. Derek MOREL
39 Director Student Housing ....Mr. Mike BRAUNINGER

Loyola University New Orleans (E)

6363 Saint Charles Avenue, New Orleans LA 70118-6195
County: Orleans FICE Identification: 002016
Unit ID: 159656
Telephone: (504) 865-2011 Carnegie Class: Masters/L
FAX Number: (504) 865-3851 Calendar System: Semester
URL: www.loyno.edu
Established: 1912 Annual Undergrad Tuition & Fees: $37,830
Enrollment: 4,330 Coed
Affiliation or Control: Roman Catholic IRS Status: 501(c)3
Highest Offering: Doctorate
Accreditation: SC, BUS, CACREP, JOUR, LAW, MUS, NURSE

01 President ....Rev. Kevin W. WILDES, SJ
101 Exec Asst to Pres for Board Rels ....Ms. Kristine D. LELONG
04 Executive Assistant to President ....Ms. Gail HOWARD
05 Provost/Vice Pres Academic Affs ....Dr. Marc MANGANARO
10 Vice Pres Finance/Administration ....Mr. John J. CALAMIA
30 Vice Pres Institutional Advance ....Mr. William BISHOP
32 VP Student Affairs/Assoc Provost ....Dr. Marcia L. PETTY
88 Vice Pres for Mission & Ministry ....Dr. John SEBASTIAN
84 Vice Pres for Enrollment Management ....Ms. Roberta KASKEL
13 Vice Prov Information Tech/CIO ....Mr. Bret JACOBS
21 Assoc Vice Pres Financial Affairs ....Mr. Leon MATHES
44 Assoc Vice Pres Development ....Mr. Chris WISEMAN
26 VP Marketing/Communications ....Ms. Laura KURZU
11 Asst Vice Pres Administration ....Mr. Paul C. FLEMING
35 Asst Vice Pres of Student Affairs ....Mr. Robert A. REED
09 Sr Dir Inst Rsrch/Student Success ....Dr. Brad PETITFILS
42 Director of University Ministry ....Mr. Kurt BINDEWALD
108 Coord Internal Reporting/Assessment ......Ms. Donna BOURGEOIS
27 Assoc Dir Public Affs/External Rels ....Ms. Patricia MURRET
43 General Counsel ....Vacant
29 Director Alumni Engagement ....Ms. Laurie LEIVA
06 Dir Stdnt Records/Registration Svcs ....Ms. Kathy R. GROS
15 Director of Human Resources ....Mr. Ross D. MATTHEWS
40 Bookstore Manager ....Ms. Maleta WILSON
41 Director Athletics & Wellness ....Mr. Brett SIMPSON
36 Director Career Development Center ....Ms. Tamara BAKER
23 Director of Student Health Services ....Dr. Alicia BOURQUE
19 Director University Police ....Mr. Patrick X. BAILEY
37 Director Scholarships/Financial Aid ....Ms. Carrie GLASS
08 Director of the Law Library ....Mr. P. Michael WHIPPLE
104 Dir Center for International Educ ....Ms. Debra DANNA
86 Dir Govt Relations & Legal Affairs ....Mr. Tommy SCREEN
38 Director Student Counseling ....Dr. Alicia BOURQUE
96 Director of Purchasing ....Mr. Robert NELSON
06 Dir Admin Services-Student Records ....Mr. Michael RACHAL
39 Director of Residential Life ....Ms. Amy BOYLE
08 Dean of Libraries ....Ms. Deborah POOLE
79 Dean Humanities/Natural Science ....Dr. Maria CALZADA
61 Interim Dean of Law ....Rev. Lawrence MOORE, SJ
64 Dean of Music and Fine Arts ....Mr. Anthony DECUIR
50 Dean of Business ....Dr. William LOCANDER
83 Dean of Social Sciences ....Dr. Roger WHITE
88 Int Director of Service Learning ....Ms. Jennifer N. JEANFREAU
88 Director of Women's Resource Ctr ....Ms. Patricia BOYETT
92 Dir of University Honors Program ....Ms. Naomi YAVNEH
88 Dir of Common Curriculum ....Dr. Lydia VOIGT
35 Director of Student Services ....Ms. Maria MCBRIDE
109 Director of Campus Dining ....Ms. Heather BACQUE
07 Director of Admissions ....Ms. Susan OAKES
18 Chief Facilities/Physical Plant ....Mr. Thomas J. RAYMOND
25 Chief Contracts/Grants Admin ....Dr. Heidi L. DAVIS
28 Interim Chief Diversity Officer ....Dr. Liv KNEWMAN

McCann School of Business and Technology (F)

2319 Louisville Avenue, Monroe LA 71201-6126
County: Ouachita FICE Identification: 026068
Unit ID: 367112
Telephone: (318) 323-2889 Carnegie Class: Assoc/HVT-High Non
FAX Number: (318) 324-9883 Calendar System: Quarter
URL: www.careertc.edu
Established: 1988 Annual Undergrad Tuition & Fees: $9,858
Enrollment: 623 Coed
Affiliation or Control: Proprietary IRS Status: Proprietary
Highest Offering: Associate Degree
Accreditation: ACICS, MAC, SURGT

01 Campus Director ....Ms. Cheryl P. LOKEY

NationsUniversity (G)

650 Poydras St., Ste 1400, PMB 133,
New Orleans LA 70130
County: Orleans Identification: 667257
Telephone: (866) 617-6446 Carnegie Class: Not Classified
FAX Number: N/A Calendar System: Other
URL: www.nationsu.edu
Established: 1996 Annual Undergrad Tuition & Fees: N/A
Enrollment: N/A Coed
Affiliation or Control: Independent Non-Profit IRS Status: 501(c)3
Highest Offering: Master's
Accreditation: DEAC

01 President/CEO ....Dr. Mac LYNN

New Orleans Baptist Theological Seminary (H)

3939 Gentilly Boulevard, New Orleans LA 70126
County: Orleans FICE Identification: 002019
Unit ID: 159948
Telephone: (504) 282-4455 Carnegie Class: Spec-4-yr-Faith
FAX Number: (504) 283-3631 Calendar System: Semester
URL: www.nobts.edu
Established: 1917 Annual Undergrad Tuition & Fees: $6,900
Enrollment: 2,806 Coed
Affiliation or Control: Southern Baptist IRS Status: 501(c)3
Highest Offering: Doctorate
Accreditation: SC, MUS, THEOL

01 President ....Dr. Charles S. KELLEY, JR.
05 Provost ....Dr. Steve W. LEMKE
09 Dir Institutional Effectiveness ....Dr. Jimmy DUKES
10 Vice President for Business Affairs ....Mr. Clay L. CORVIN
30 Vice President for Development ....Mr. Randy DRIGGERS
58 Dean Graduate Studies ....Dr. Mike EDENS
12 Dean Leavell College ....Dr. L. Thomas STRONG, III
32 Dean of Students ....Dr. J. Craig GARRETT
07 Dean of Admissions & Registrar ....Dr. Paul E. GREGOIRE, JR.
08 Dean of Libraries ....Dr. Jeff D. GRIFFIN
18 Associate VP of Facilities ....Dr. Jim O. PARKER
13 Assoc VP Information Technology ....Dr. Laurie S. WATTS
73 Assoc Dean Prof Doctoral Pgms ....Dr. Reggie R. OGEA
106 Associate Dean of Online Learning ....Dr. W. Craig PRICE
58 Assoc Dean Research Doctoral Pgms ....Dr. Charles A. RAY, JR.
35 Assoc Dean of Students ....Dr. Judi JACKSON
15 Director of Human Resources ....Ms. Pattie SHOENER
26 Chief Public Relations Officer ....Mr. Gary D. MYERS
29 Director of Alumni Relations ....Dr. Dennis L. PHELPS
36 Director of Student Enlistment ....Dr. Jonathan C. KEY
37 Director of Student Financial Aid ....Mr. Michael WANG

38 Director of Testing & Counseling ....Dr. Jeffery W. NAVE
88 Director of Innovative Learning ....Dr. Donna B. PEAVEY
39 Director Student Housing ....Mrs. Julie BARENTINE
41 Athletic Director ....Mr. Brad WINTER

Notre Dame Seminary, Graduate School of Theology (A)

2901 S Carrollton Avenue, New Orleans LA 70118-4391
County: Orleans FICE Identification: 002022
Unit ID: 160029
Telephone: (504) 866-7426 Carnegie Class: Spec-4-yr-Faith
FAX Number: (504) 866-3119 Calendar System: Semester
URL: www.nds.edu
Established: 1923 Annual Undergrad Tuition & Fees: N/A
Enrollment: 189 Coed
Affiliation or Control: Roman Catholic IRS Status: 501(c)3
Highest Offering: Master's
Accreditation: SC, THEOL

01 President - Rector ....V.Rev. James A. WEHNER, STD
05 Academic Dean ....Dr. Thomas J. NEAL
08 Director of Library ....Mr. Thomas B. BENDER, IV
09 Director IE/Planning/Faculty Devel ....Dr. Rebecca S. MALONEY
10 Business Manager ....Ms. Michelle W. KLEIN

Our Lady of the Lake College (B)

5414 Brittany Drive, Baton Rouge LA 70808
County: East Baton Rouge FICE Identification: 031062
Unit ID: 160074
Telephone: (225) 768-1700 Carnegie Class: Spec-4-yr-Other Health
FAX Number: (225) 768-0811 Calendar System: Semester
URL: www.ololcollege.edu
Established: 1923 Annual Undergrad Tuition & Fees: $11,444
Enrollment: 1,722 Coed
Affiliation or Control: Roman Catholic IRS Status: 501(c)3
Highest Offering: Master's
Accreditation: SC, ANEST, ARCPA, COARC, MT, NUR, PTAA, RAD

01 President ....Dr. Tina HOLLAND
05 Vice Pres for Academic Affairs ....Dr. Edward VIOLETT
30 VP for Institutional Advancement ....Ms. Judith ROBERSON
10 Vice Pres Operations & Finance ....Ms. Beverly SONNIER-PLAISANCE
84 VP Stdnt Affairs/Enrollment Mgmt ....Ms. Rebecca CANNON
88 VP for Mission Identity ....Sr. Martha Ann ABSHIRE
66 Dean School of Nursing ....Dr. Phyllis PEDERSEN
76 Dean School of Health Professions ....Dr. Katherine KRIEG
32 Dean of Students ....Dr. Alison WELLS
49 Dean of School of Arts & Sciences ....Dr. Brian RASH
37 Director Financial Aid ....Ms. Barrye BAILEY
06 Registrar ....Ms. Kimberly JONES-JAMES
88 Interim Dir Physician Asst Studies ....Ms. Lena OSBORNE
88 Director Nurse Anesthesia Program ....Dr. Aimee BADEAUX
76 Director Radiologic Technology ....Mr. Mark MARTONE
76 Director Clinical Lab Sciences ....Dr. Debbie FOX
76 Director Physical Therapist Asst ....Ms. Leah GEHEBER
88 Dir Health Service Administration ....Dr. Riaz FERDAUS
76 Director Respiratory Therapy ....Ms. Sue DAVIS
88 Director Writing Center ....Mr. Angus WOODWARD
13 Director of Information Systems ....Mr. Edward LEWIS
07 Director of Admissions ....Ms. Kimberly DUDLEY
09 Dir Institutional Effectiveness ....Ms. Candi MCELHENY
91 Manager Student Info System ....Mr. Janssen BURRIS
04 Executive Asst to President ....Ms. Kimberly MELANCON

Remington College-Baton Rouge Campus (C)

4520 S Sherwood Forrest Blvd #001,
Baton Rouge LA 70816
Telephone: (225) 236-3200 Identification: 666449
Accreditation: ACCSC

† Branch campus of Remington College, Cleveland, OH.

Remington College-Lafayette Campus (D)

303 Rue Louis XIV, Lafayette LA 70508-5700
Telephone: (337) 981-4010 FICE Identification: 005203
Accreditation: ACCSC

† Branch campus of Remington College, Cleveland, OH.

Remington College-Shreveport (E)

2106 Bert Kouns Industrial Loop, Shreveport LA 71118
Telephone: (318) 239-4309 Identification: 666302
Accreditation: ACCSC

† Branch campus of Remington College, Cleveland, OH.

Saint Joseph Seminary College (F)

75376 River Road, Saint Benedict LA 70457-9999
County: Saint Tammany FICE Identification: 002027
Unit ID: 160409
Telephone: (985) 867-2232 Carnegie Class: Spec-4-yr-Faith
FAX Number: (985) 867-2270 Calendar System: Semester
URL: www.sjasc.edu
Established: 1891 Annual Undergrad Tuition & Fees: $16,913
Enrollment: 135 Male
Affiliation or Control: Roman Catholic IRS Status: 501(c)3
Highest Offering: Baccalaureate
Accreditation: SC

01 President - Rector ....V.Rev. Gregory M. BOQUET, OSB
05 Academic Dean ....Dr. Daniel P. BURNS
03 Vice-Rector ....Rev. Matthew CLARK, OSB
08 Librarian ....Ms. Bonnie WOOD
10 Business Officer ....Mrs. Jennifer WHITEHOUSE
37 Director Financial Aid ....Ms. Caroline BIZOT
29 Director of Alumni Affairs ....Rev. Matthew CLARK, OSB
30 Director of Development ....Mrs. Leslie TATE
26 Director of Communications ....Vacant
32 Dean of Students ....Rev. Jonathan WALLIS, OSB
06 Registrar ....Mr. Casey EDLER
108 Director Institutional Assessment ....Dr. Dianna LAURENT
13 Chief Info Technology Officer (CIO) ....Mr. Todd RUSSELL
18 Chief Facilities/Physical Plant ....Mr. Jim ROBEAUU

*Southern University and Agricultural & Mechanical College System Office (G)

JS Clark Admin Building, 4th Floor,
Baton Rouge LA 70813-0001
County: East Baton Rouge Parish FICE Identification: 009637
Unit ID: 160533
Telephone: (225) 771-4680 Carnegie Class: N/A
FAX Number: (225) 771-5522
URL: www.sus.edu

01 President/Chancellor ....Dr. Ray L. BELTON
10 System VP/Finance/Business Affairs ....Mr. Flandus MCCLINTON
13 Assoc VP/Information Technology ....Dr. Gabriel FAGBEYIRO
15 System VP/Human Resources ....Mr. Lester A. FOURCIAU
84 System Dir Enroll/Online Processes ....Ms. Michelle HILL
30 System Dir Dev/Exec Dir Foundation ....Mr. Alfred E. HARRELL, III
43 General Counsel to the System/Board ....Ms. Tracie L. WOODS
04 Exec Assoc to President/Chancellor ....Ms. Robyn M. MERRICK
26 System Director of Communications ....Mr. Henry J. TILLMAN
18 System Dir of Facilities Planning ....Mr. Eli GUILLORY
21 System Director of Internal Audit ....Ms. Linda H. CATALON
09 System Dir/Institutional Research ....Vacant

*Southern University and A&M College (H)

Harding Boulevard, Baton Rouge LA 70813-0001
County: East Baton Rouge FICE Identification: 002025
Unit ID: 160621
Telephone: (225) 771-4500 Carnegie Class: Masters/L
FAX Number: (225) 771-2018 Calendar System: Semester
URL: www.subr.edu
Established: 1880 Annual Undergrad Tuition & Fees (In-State): $7,346
Enrollment: 6,330 Coed
Affiliation or Control: State IRS Status: 501(c)3
Highest Offering: Doctorate
Accreditation: SC, AAFCS, BUS, CORE, CS, #DIETD, DIETI, ENG, ENGT, JOUR, MUS, NURSE, SP, SPAA, SW, TED

02 President/Chancellor ....Dr. Ray BELTON
05 EVP for Academic Affairs & Provost ....Dr. M. Christopher BROWN
32 Vice Chanc Stdnt Affs/Enroll Mgmt ....Dr. Brandon DUMAS
10 Vice Chanc of Finance & Admin ....Mr. Benjamin PUGH
46 VC Research & Strategic Initiative ....Dr. Michael A. STUBBLEFIELD
20 Assoc Vice Chanc/Dn Honors College ....Vacant
21 AVP Finance/Admin/Controller ....Vacant
26 Director of Communications ....Mr. Henry TILLMAN
45 Dir Planning Assess/Inst Research ....Dr. Christopher GUILLORY
29 Dir Alumni Aff/Exec Dir SU Alum Fed ....Vacant
15 Director Human Resources ....Mr. Lester FOURCIAU
06 Registrar ....Mrs. Carolnda BEAN
07 Exec Dir Admissions/Recruitment ....Mr. Anthony JACKSON
35 Dean of Students ....Mr. Marcus A. COLEMAN
39 Director Residential Housing ....Ms. Tracie A. ABRAHAM
37 Director of Financial Aid ....Ms. Ursula SHORTY
13 AVP for IT/Chief Information Ofcr ....Dr. Gabriel FAGBEYIRO
51 Dir Intl Educ/Dir Svc Learning/CE ....Dr. Barbara CARPENTER
41 Athletic Director ....Mr. Roman BANKS
18 Dir Facilities Svcs/Physical Plant ....Mr. Eli G. GUILLORY, III
88 Director School of Accountancy ....Ms. Mary A. DARBY
96 Director of Purchasing ....Mrs. Linda B. ANTOINE
38 Director Student Counseling ....Dr. VaraRay IRVIN
62 Dean of Libraries ....Mrs. Emma BRADFORD-PERRY
88 Dean University College ....Dr. Dana CARPENTER
92 Dean of Honors College ....Dr. Diola BAGAYOKO
58 Dean of the Graduate School ....Dr. Damien D. EJIGIRI
54 Dean College of Engineering ....Dr. Habib P. MOHAMADIAN
50 Dean College of Business ....Dr. Donald R. ANDREWS
53 Dean College of Education ....Dr. Verjanis PEOPLES
59 Chair Dept Family/Consumer Sciences ....Dr. Kasundra CYRUS
83 Int Dean Col Social/Behavioral Sci ....Dr. Albert SAMUELS
48 Coordinator School of Architecture ....Mr. Lonnie WILKINSON
66 Dean College of Nursing/Allied Hlth ....Dr. Janet RAMI
47 Int Dn Col of Sciences/Agriculture ....Dr. Robert H. MILLER

*Southern University at New Orleans (I)

6400 Press Drive, New Orleans LA 70126-1009
County: Orleans FICE Identification: 002026
Unit ID: 160630
Telephone: (504) 286-5000 Carnegie Class: Masters/M
FAX Number: (504) 286-5131 Calendar System: Semester
URL: www.suno.edu
Established: 1956 Annual Undergrad Tuition & Fees (In-State): $5,827
Enrollment: 2,103 Coed
Affiliation or Control: State IRS Status: 501(c)3
Highest Offering: Master's
Accreditation: SC, AAFCS, BUS, CAHIIM, SW, TED

02 Interim Chancellor ....Dr. Lisa MIMS-DEVEZIN
04 Int Exec Assoc to the Chancellor ....Dr. Harry DOUGHTY
05 VC for Academic Affairs & SACS ....Dr. David S. ADEGBOYE
10 VC for Admin & Finance ....Mr. Jullin RENTHROPE
09 Dir IR/IE & Strategic Planning ....Vacant
09 Director Quality Enhancement Plan ....Mr. Ashu BENJAMIN
108 Learning Outcomes/Assessment Coord ....Ms. Mallory MARTIN
84 VC Student Affs & Enroll Services ....Dr. Donna GRANT
29 Vice Chan Cmty Outreach/Univ Advanc ....Mrs. Gloria B. MOULTRIE
21 Director of Facilities Management ....Mr. Shaun M. LEWIS
25 Dir Grants & Sponsored Programs ....Dr. William R. BELISLE
06 Registrar ....Ms. Gilda DAVIS
21 Comptroller ....Ms. Shawn M. CHARLES
08 Director of Library ....Mrs. Shatiqua A. MOSBY-WILSON
36 Dir Career Counseling & Vet Liaison ....Mr. Joseph MARION
13 Director of Information Technology ....Mr. Edmond M. CUMMINGS
15 Director of Human Resources ....Ms. Evelyn MASTERS-DUBUCLET
19 Police Captain Campus Police ....Mr. Bruce ADAMS
20 Assoc VC Academic Affairs Faculty ....Mr. Wesley T. BISHOP
41 Interim Director of Athletics ....Mr. Yhann PLUMMER
07 Asst VC for Enrollment Management ....Ms. Leatrice D. LATIMORE
26 Director of Public Relations ....Ms. Tammy BARNEY
96 Director of Purchasing ....Ms. Marilyn G. MANUEL
106 Director of E-Learning ....Ms. Shelia WOOD
70 Dean School of Social Work ....Dr. Ronald MANCOSKE
50 Dean College of Business/Pub Admin ....Dr. Igwe E. UDEH
88 Director of Museum Studies ....Mr. Haithum EID
58 Dean of Graduate Studies ....Vacant
49 Int Dean College of Arts & Sciences ....Dr. Evelyn HARRELL
53 Int Dean College Educ & Human Dev ....Dr. Willie JONES
22 Dir Services for Students w/Disab ....Ms. Yolanda L. MIMS
32 Dir of Student Activities/Orgs ....Vacant
38 Dir of Student Development Center ....Mrs. Josephine OKORONKWO
88 Director of Title III Programs ....Dr. Brenda W. JACKSON
88 Dir Student Support Services Pgm ....Ms. Linda D. FREDERICK
88 Dir Ctr for African & American Stds ....Ms. Linda HILL

*Southern University at Shreveport-Louisiana (J)

3050 Martin Luther King Drive, Shreveport LA 71107-4795
County: Caddo FICE Identification: 007686
Unit ID: 160649
Telephone: (318) 670-6000 Carnegie Class: Assoc/MT-VT-High Trad
FAX Number: (318) 670-6374 Calendar System: Semester
URL: www.susla.edu
Established: 1964 Annual Undergrad Tuition & Fees (In-State): $3,987
Enrollment: 2,952 Coed
Affiliation or Control: State IRS Status: 501(c)3
Highest Offering: Associate Degree
Accreditation: SC, ADNUF, CAHIIM, COARC, DH, MLTAD, PHLEB, RAD, SURGT

02 Chancellor ....Dr. Rodney ELLIS
26 Spec Asst to Chanc IR/Div Univ Rels ....Theron JACKSON
04 Exec Associate to the Chancellor ....Ms. Melva WILLIAMS
05 Vice Chanc Academic/Student Affs ....Dr. Rosetta JONES
10 Int Vice Chanc Finance/Admi ....Ms. Brandy JACOBSEN
103 VC Cmty Outreach/Workforce Develop ....Mrs. Janice B. SNEED
32 Asst Vice Chanc Student Affairs ....Dr. Fatina ELLIOTT
84 Asst Vice Chanc Enrollment Mgmt ....Mr. Terence VINSON
20 Asst Vice Chanc for Academic Affs ....Dr. Regina ROBINSON
21 Comptroller ....Mrs. Brandy JACOBSEN
21 Bursar ....Ms. Tomeka K. BROWN
06 Registrar ....Dr. Lalita ROGERS
08 Library Director ....Mrs. Jane O'RILEY
35 Director of Student Activities ....Mrs. Rebecca GILLIAM
51 Director of Continuing Education ....Mrs. Beverly J. PARKER
07 Director of Admission & Recruitment ....Ms. Annie MOSS
37 Director of Financial Aid ....Ms. Katraya WILLIAMS
27 Dir Office of University Relations ....Ms. Krystle GRINDLEY
19 Chief University Police ....Mr. Marshall NELSON
13 Dir Information Technology Center ....Dr. Gabriel FAGBEYIRO
88 Director Student Support Services ....Ms. Karen COCO
75 Director Aerospace Technology ....Mr. David FOGLEMAN
38 University Counselor ....Ms. Kaye L. WASHINGTON
15 Director Human Resources ....Mr. Wayne H. BRYANT
96 Director of Purchasing ....Ms. Sophia JACKSON-LEE
18 Dir Physical Plant Facilities ....Mr. Joseph LACOUR
21 University Budget Officer ....Ms. Regina WINN
72 Director Radiologic Technology ....Ms. Sheila SWIFT
88 Exec Dir TRIO Community Outreach ....Ms. Betty C. FAGBEYIRO
88 Director Dental Hygiene ....Mrs. Kheysia H. WASHINGTON
88 Director Biomedical Research Devel ....Dr. Joseph ORBAN
09 Director Inst Plng/Assessment/Rsrch ....Mr. Martin FORTNER
66 Director of Nursing ....Dr. Tiffany VARNER
50 Division Chair Business Studies ....Vacant
79 Division Chair for Humanities ....Ms. Wanda M. WALLER
72 Div Chair Science & Technology ....Dr. Barry C. HESTER
76 Div Chair Allied Health Sci ....Mrs. JoAnn BROWN
83 Div Ch Behav Sci/Educ/Bus Standards ....Dr. Rosalyn J. HOLT

*Southern University Law Center (A)

PO Box 9294, Baton Rouge LA 70813

County: East Baton Rouge Identification: 667233
Unit ID: 440916
Telephone: (225) 771-2552 Carnegie Class: Spec-4-yr-Law
FAX Number: N/A Calendar System: Semester
URL: www.sulc.edu
Established: 1947 Annual Graduate Tuition & Fees: N/A
Enrollment: 644 Coed
Affiliation or Control: State IRS Status: 501(c)3
Highest Offering: First Professional Degree; No Undergraduates
Accreditation: SC, LAW

02 Chancellor .... Mr. John K. PIERRE
05 Chief Academic Officer .... Mr. Roederick C. WHITE
06 Registrar .... Mrs. D'Andrea J. LEE
07 Director of Admissions .... Ms. Andrea LOVE
09 VC Inst Accountability/Assessment .... Ms. Alfreda DIAMOND
10 Assoc Vice Chanc for Financial Affs .... Mr. Terry HALL
18 Chief Facilities/Physical Plant .... Ms. Angela GAINES
26 Chief Public Relations Officer .... Ms. Rachel EMANUEL
29 Director of Alumni Affairs .... Ms. Cynthia REED
30 Chief Development Officer .... Ms. Tonya FREEMAN
32 Chief Student Affairs Officer .... Mr. Roederick WHITE
36 Director of Student Placement .... Mr. Tavares WALKER
37 Director of Student Financial Aid .... Ms. Calaundra CLARKE
84 Director Enrollment Management .... Ms. D'Andrea J. LEE

Southwest University (B)

2200 Veterans Memorial Boulevard,
Kenner LA 70062-4005

County: Jefferson Identification: 666310
Telephone: (504) 468-2900 Carnegie Class: Not Classified
FAX Number: (504) 468-3213 Calendar System: Semester
URL: www.southwest.edu
Established: 1982 Annual Undergrad Tuition & Fees: N/A
Enrollment: N/A Coed
Affiliation or Control: Proprietary IRS Status: Proprietary
Highest Offering: Master's
Accreditation: DEAC

01 President .... Dr. Grayce LEE
11 Chief Administrative Officer .... Mr. Neil FESER
07 Admissions .... Mrs. Lydia OCMAND

Tulane University (C)

6823 St. Charles Avenue, New Orleans LA 70118-5698

County: Orleans FICE Identification: 002029
Unit ID: 160755
Telephone: (504) 865-5000 Carnegie Class: DU-Highest
FAX Number: (504) 865-5202 Calendar System: Semester
URL: www.tulane.edu
Established: 1834 Annual Undergrad Tuition & Fees: $49,638
Enrollment: 12,603 Coed
Affiliation or Control: Independent Non-Profit IRS Status: 501(c)3
Highest Offering: Doctorate
Accreditation: SC, BUS, DIETI, ENG, ENGR, HSA, IPSY, LAW, MED, PH, SCPSY, SW, TEAC

01 President .... Mr. Michael A. FITTS
05 Sr Vice Pres Acad Affairs/Provost .... Prof. Robin FORMAN
30 Sr Vice Pres for Advancement .... Vacant
108 Sr VP Strategic Init/Inst Effectiv .... Mr. Richard MATASAR
11 Chief Operating Officer .... Mr. Patrick NORTON
63 Sr Vice Pres/Dn School of Medicine .... Dr. L. L. HAMM
43 General Counsel .... Ms. Victoria D. JOHNSON
13 VP Information Technology/CTO .... Mr. Charles P. MCMAHON
10 Chief Investment Officer .... Mr. Jeremy T. CRIGLER
20 Senior Associate Provost .... Dr. Ana LOPEZ
32 VP Student Affairs .... Dr. J. Davidson PORTER
20 Assoc Provost Health Sciences .... Dr. M. A. 'Tonette' KROUSEL-WOOD
58 Assoc Prov Graduate Studies .... Dr. Michael CUNNINGHAM
100 Chief of Staff & Vice President .... Ms. Tania TETLOW
22 VP Inst Equity/Asst to Pres Dvrsity .... Ms. Deborah E. LOVE
84 Vice Pres Enrollment Mgmt .... Mr. Satya DATTAGUPTA
18 VP Facilities Management .... Mr. Randolph PHILIPSON
26 Vice Pres University Communications .... Ms. Deborah L. GRANT
46 Vice President for Research .... Dr. Laura LEVY
30 Vice Pres Constituency Programs .... Ms. Luann D. DOZIER
86 Assoc VP Government Relations .... Ms. Sharon P. COURTNEY
109 Assoc VP Auxiliary Svcs/Student Ctr .... Mr. Robert C. HAILEY
18 Assoc Vice President Facilities .... Mr. Sylvester C. JOHNSON
37 Assoc Vice President Financial Aid .... Mr. Michael GOODMAN
21 Director Budget .... Mr. Gene MEYERS
29 VP for Alumni Affairs .... Mr. James STOFAN
21 Controller .... Mr. Frank (Doug) HARRELL
19 Director of Public Safety .... Mr. Jon BARNWELL
08 Dean Library & Academic Information .... Mr. David BANUSH
38 Exec Dir Educ Resources/Couns .... Dr. Donna BENDER
36 Exec Director Career Svcs Ctr .... Dr. Amjad AYOUBI
12 Dir Tulane Natl Primate Res Ctr .... Dr. Andrew LACKNER
24 Executive Director Publications .... Ms. Carol J. SCHLUETER
39 Assoc VP Housing Services/Residence .... Dr. Brian JOHNSON
96 Director Central Procurement Svcs .... Mr. William VAN CLEAVE
91 Asst VP Academic & Admin Computing .... Ms. Mary T. WALSH
41 Director Athletics .... Mr. Troy DANNEN
51 Dean Sch Cont Stds/Summer Sch .... Dr. Suri DUITCH
49 Dean School of Liberal Arts .... Dr. Carole HABER
49 Dean Newcomb-Tulane College .... Dr. James MACLAREN
61 Dean School of Law .... Mr. David D. MEYER
69 Dean Sch Public Health/Trop Med .... Dr. Pierre BUEKENS
54 Dean School Science & Engineering .... Dr. Nicholas J. ALTIERO
48 Dean School of Architecture .... Mr. Kenneth SCHWARTZ
50 Dean AB Freeman School of Business .... Dr. Ira SOLOMON
70 Dean School of Social Work .... Dr. Patrick BORDNICK
09 Director of Institutional Research .... Mr. Shawn POTTER
88 Exec Dir of CELT .... Dr. Susann LUSNIA
85 Assoc Dean Ctr for Global Education .... Dr. Scott PENTZER
35 Assoc VP Student Affairs .... Dr. John NONNAMAKER
20 Assoc Provost International Affairs .... Vacant
88 CPS Executive Director .... Dr. Agnieszka NANCE
04 Administrative Asst to President .... Ms. Jennifer JUMONVILLE
07 Director of Admissions .... Mr. Jeffrey SCHIFFMAN

University of Holy Cross (D)

4123 Woodland Drive, New Orleans LA 70131-7399

County: Orleans FICE Identification: 002023
Unit ID: 160065
Telephone: (504) 394-7744 Carnegie Class: Bac-Diverse
FAX Number: (504) 391-2421 Calendar System: Semester
URL: www.olhcc.edu
Established: 1916 Annual Undergrad Tuition & Fees: $11,510
Enrollment: 1,095 Coed
Affiliation or Control: Roman Catholic IRS Status: 501(c)3
Highest Offering: Doctorate
Accreditation: SC, CACREP, IACBE, NUR, RAD, TED

01 President .... Dr. David M. LANDRY
05 Provost/VP Academic Affairs .... Dr. Victoria DAHMES
10 Vice Pres for Finance & Operations .... Mrs. Arlean WEHLE
30 Vice Pres for Philanthropy/Planning .... Mr. David CATHERMAN
84 VP for Enrollment Management .... Ms. Meredith REED
88 VP for Mission Integration .... Sr. Rochelle PERRIER
08 Director of Library Services .... Ms. Diana SCHAUBHUT
83 Dean Couns/Educ/Business .... Dr. Carolyn WHITE
66 Dean Nursing/Allied Health .... Dr. Patricia PRECHTER
49 Dean Liberal Arts and Science .... Dr. Michael LABRANCHE
32 Chief Student Affairs/Student Life .... Mr. Andre CARPENTER
06 Registrar .... Ms. Traci REES
09 Director Inst Research & Planning .... Dr. Jacques DETIEGE
42 Director of Campus Ministry .... Vacant
15 Human Resources Manager .... Ms. Cathy WAGUESPACK
44 Director of Annual Fund .... Mr. David CATHERMAN
13 Director of Technology Services .... Ms. Rosalind CHESTER
37 Director of Financial Aid .... Mr. Hayden WAGAR
04 Administrative Asst to President .... Ms. Peggy BOURGEOIS
07 Director of Admissions .... Ms. Megan WAITE
19 Director Security/Safety .... Mr. Bernard NELSON
26 Chief Public Relations/Marketing .... Ms. Erin SULLIVAN
29 Director Alumni Relations .... Mr. Steve MORGAN
106 Online Education Coordinator .... Dr. Tess O'NEILL

*University of Louisiana System Office (E)

1201 N Third Street, Suite 7-300,
Baton Rouge LA 70802-5243

County: East Baton Rouge FICE Identification: 033444
Unit ID: 247083
Telephone: (225) 342-6950 Carnegie Class: N/A
FAX Number: (225) 342-6473
URL: www.ulsystem.net

01 Interim President .... Dr. Daniel D. RENEAU
05 VP or Academic Affairs .... Dr. Jeannine KAHN
10 VP for Business and Finance .... Dr. Edwin LITOLFF
26 VP of External Affairs .... Ms. Rachel KINCAID

*Grambling State University (F)

403 Main Street, Grambling LA 71245

County: Lincoln FICE Identification: 002006
Unit ID: 159009
Telephone: (318) 247-3811 Carnegie Class: Masters/L
FAX Number: (318) 274-6172 Calendar System: Semester
URL: www.gram.edu
Established: 1901 Annual Undergrad Tuition & Fees (In-State): $7,063
Enrollment: 4,504 Coed
Affiliation or Control: State IRS Status: 501(c)3
Highest Offering: Doctorate
Accreditation: SC, BUS, CS, ENGT, JOUR, MUS, NRPA, NUR, SPAA, SW, TED, THEA

02 Acting President .... Dr. Leon SANDERS
05 Int Provost/VP Academic Affairs .... Dr. Janet GUYDEN
10 Vice President for Finance and Admn .... Mr. Leon SANDERS
84 VP Inst Effect & Dir Enroll Mgmt .... Dr. Damon R. WADE
32 Assoc Vice Pres Student Affairs .... Dr. David C. PONTON, JR.
30 Int VP Research Advanc/Econ Dev .... Mr. Otto MEYERS, III
18 Director of Facilties Management .... Mr. Kevin TALLAKSEN
13 Interim Assoc VP of Info Technology .... Ms. Peggy HANLEY
09 Director of Institutional Research .... Ms. Ulrica S. EDWARDS
19 University Police Chief .... Mr. Howard CAVINESS
15 AVP of Human Resources .... Mrs. Monica BRADLEY
53 Dean Col of Educ/Prof & Grad Stds .... Dr. Larnell FLANNAGAN
50 Interim Dean College of Business .... Dr. Erick VALENTINE
58 Dean Division Grad Studies/Research .... Dr. Larnell FLANNAGAN
49 Interim Dean College of Arts & Sci .... Dr. King D. GODWIN
92 Assistant Dean Honors College .... Dr. Ellen SMILEY
41 Interim Director of Athletics .... Dr. Obadiah SIMMONS
22 EEO Officer & Wage & Salary Officer .... Mrs. Monica BRADLEY
07 Director of Admissions .... Mr. Latari FLEMING
06 University Registrar .... Mrs. Patricia J. HUTCHERSON
37 Dir Student Financial Aid .... Mr. Gavin HAMM
91 Dir of Administrative Computing .... Vacant
04 Executive Asst to the President .... Dr. Adriel HILTON
29 Exec Director of Alumni Affairs .... Ms. Carolyn COLLIER
23 Director of Health Services .... Mrs. Patrice OUTLEY
38 Director Counseling Center .... Dr. Coleen SPEED
39 Interim Dir of Residential Life .... Ms. Dana K. HOWARD
42 Director of Campus Ministry .... Vacant
96 Director of Purchasing .... Mr. Alvin BRADLEY
40 Manager University Bookstore .... Mr. Elliot JONES
106 Director of Distance Learning .... Mr. Eldrie HAMILTON
88 Special Assistant to Provost and VP .... Mrs. Catina CROWE
36 Director of Career Services .... Dr. Shelia FOBBS

*Louisiana Tech University (G)

PO Box 3168, Ruston LA 71272-0001

County: Lincoln FICE Identification: 002008
Unit ID: 159647
Telephone: (318) 257-0211 Carnegie Class: DU-Mod
FAX Number: (318) 257-2928 Calendar System: Quarter
URL: www.latech.edu
Established: 1894 Annual Undergrad Tuition & Fees (In-State): $8,854
Enrollment: 11,225 Coed
Affiliation or Control: State IRS Status: 501(c)3
Highest Offering: Doctorate
Accreditation: SC, AAB, AAFCS, ADNUR, ART, AUD, BUS, BUSA, CACREP, CAHIIM, CIDA, COPSY, CS, DIETD, DIETI, ENG, ENGT, MUS, SP, TED

02 President .... Dr. Leslie K. GUICE
05 Vice Pres Academic Affairs .... Dr. Terry M. MCCONATHY
32 Vice Pres for Student Advancement .... Dr. Jim M. KING
11 AVP of Administration & Facilities .... Mr. Sam G. WALLACE
30 Vice President for Univ Advancement .... Vacant
10 AVP of Finance & Comptroller .... Mrs. Lisa L. COLE
50 Dean of Business .... Dr. Chris MARTIN
49 Dean of Liberal Arts .... Dr. Don KACZVINSKY
53 Dean of Education .... Dr. Don N. SCHILLINGER
54 Dean of Engineering & Science .... Dr. Hisham HEGAB
65 Dean of Applied & Natural Sciences .... Dr. Gary A. KENNEDY
84 Dean of Enrollment Management .... Mrs. Pamela R. FORD
26 Exec Dir University Communications .... Dr. David GUERIN
07 Interim Director of Admissions .... Mrs. Joan B. EDINGER
13 Director of Computer Center .... Mr. Roy S. WATERS
37 Director Student Financial Aid .... Ms. Aimee F. BAXTER
09 Director Institutional Research .... Mrs. Lori C. THEIS
06 Registrar .... Mr. Robert D. VENTO
08 Interim Director of Libraries .... Ms. Rita FRANKS
15 Director of Human Resources .... Mrs. Sheila TRAMMEL
29 Director of Alumni Relations .... Mr. Wesley CAVIN
36 Dir Career Ctr/Student Counseling .... Mr. Ron CATHEY
89 Director of Freshmen Studies .... Vacant
92 Director of Honors Program .... Dr. Rick SIMMONS
93 Director of Multicultural Affairs .... Vacant
96 Director of Purchasing .... Ms. Melissa HUGHES
18 Chief Facilities/Physical Plant .... Vacant
41 Athletics Director .... Mr. Thomas H. MCCLELLAND, II

*McNeese State University (H)

4205 Ryan Street, Lake Charles LA 70609-4510

County: Calcasieu FICE Identification: 002017
Unit ID: 159717
Telephone: (337) 475-5000 Carnegie Class: Masters/L
FAX Number: (337) 475-5012 Calendar System: Semester
URL: www.mcneese.edu
Established: 1939 Annual Undergrad Tuition & Fees (In-State): $7,290
Enrollment: 8,237 Coed
Affiliation or Control: State IRS Status: 501(c)3
Highest Offering: Beyond Master's But Less Than Doctorate
Accreditation: SC, ADNUR, ART, BUS, #CAATE, CACREP, CS, DIETD, DIETI, ENG, MT, MUS, NURSE, RAD, TED

02 President .... Dr. Philip C. WILLIAMS
05 Provost/VP Academic & Student Affs .... Dr. Jeanne M. DABOVAL
10 VP Business Affairs/University Svcs .... Mr. Eddie P. MECHE
30 Vice Pres University Advancement .... Mr. Richard H. REID
84 Assoc VP Enrollment Management .... Ms. Stephanie B. TARVER
32 AVP University Services .... Dr. Christopher THOMAS
81 Dean College of Science .... Dr. George F. MEAD, JR.
50 Dean College Business .... Dr. Musa M. ESSAYYAD
53 Dean of College of Education .... Dr. Wayne R. FETTER
49 Dean College Liberal Arts .... Dr. Ray MILES
54 Dean Col of Engr & Engr Technology .... Dr. Nikos KIRITSIS
66 Dean of College of Nursing .... Dr. Peggy L. WOLFE
18 Director Facilities & Plant Opers .... Mr. Richard R. RHODEN
13 Chief Information Technology .... Mr. Chad THIBODEAUX
31 Dir Community Service and Outreach .... Mrs. Betty H. ANDERSON
15 Dir Human Res/Student Employment .... Ms. Charlene R. ABBOTT
09 Director Institutional Research .... Vacant
37 Director Student Financial Aid .... Ms. Taina J. SAVOIT
08 Director of Library .... Ms. Debbie L. JOHNSON-HOUSTON
19 University Police Chief .... Mr. Robert SPINKS
29 Director Alumni Affairs .... Ms. Joyce D. PATTERSON
88 Director of Scholarships .... Ms. Ralynn F. CASTETE
07 Dir of Admissions and Recruiting .... Ms. Kourtney ISTRE
41 Athletic Director .... Mr. F. Bruce HEMPHILL
45 Dir Inst Research and Effectiveness .... Ms. Jessica HUTCHINGS

96 Director Purchasing/Property Cntrl .... Ms. Roxane FONTENOT
92 Director of Honors College .... Dr. Scott E. GOINS
14 Director of Univ Computing Services .... Mr. Stanley HIPPLER
46 Dir Ofc of Research/Sponsored Pgm .... Vacant
85 Internat Stdnt Advisor/Dir Int Pgm .... Ms. Preble GIRARD
26 Director Public Relations .... Ms. Candace V. TOWNSEND
23 RN Supervisor-Student Health .... Vacant
40 Bookstore Manager .... Ms. Donna LUNDQUIST
106 Director of Electronic Learning .... Ms. Helen B. WARE
28 Chief Diversity Officer .... Dr. Michael T. SNOWDEN
04 Administrative Asst to President .... Ms. Lisa SULLIVAN
06 Registrar .... Ms. Catrina BOENIG
38 Director Student Counseling/Health .... Ms. Ramie THIBODEAUX

*Nicholls State University (A)

University Station, Thibodaux LA 70310-0001
County: Lafourche FICE Identification: 002005
Unit ID: 159966
Telephone: (985) 446-8111 Carnegie Class: Masters/M
FAX Number: (985) 448-4920 Calendar System: Semester
URL: www.nicholls.edu
Established: 1948 Annual Undergrad Tuition & Fees (In-State): $7,348
Enrollment: 6,292 Coed
Affiliation or Control: State IRS Status: 501(c)3
Highest Offering: Beyond Master's But Less Than Doctorate
Accreditation: SC, AAFCS, ART, BUS, BUSA, CAATE, CACREP, DIETD, ENGR, JOUR, MUS, NAIT, NURSE, TED

02 President .... Dr. Bruce T. MURPHY
05 Provost/VP for Academic Affairs .... Dr. Lynn GILLETTE
32 Vice Pres Student Affairs .... Dr. Eugene A. DIAL
30 VP for University Advancement .... Dr. Neal WEAVER
18 Superint Facility/Proj Manager .... Mr. Stan SILVERII
10 Assoc Vice Pres for Finance/CFO .... Vacant
45 Exec Dir of Planning/Effectiveness .... Mrs. Renee G. HICKS
49 Dean of Arts & Sciences .... Dr. John DOUCET
66 Dean of Nursing and Allied Health .... Dr. Velma S. WESTBROOK
50 Int Dean Business Administration .... Dr. Marilyn MACIK-FREY
53 Dean of Education .... Dr. Leslie JONES
20 Director of Academic Services .... Mr. David ZERANGUE
09 Dir Assess/Institutional Research .... Mrs. Leslie B. DISHMAN
08 Co-Director of Library .... Dr. Van VIATOR
08 Co-Director of Library .... Ms. Anke TONN
08 Co-Director of Library .... Mr. Clifton THERIOT
19 Director of University Police .... Mr. Craig M. JACCUZZO
36 Director of Career Services .... Ms. Kristie R. TAUZIN
37 Director of Student Financial Aid .... Ms. Casie TRICHE
13 Director of Computing Center .... Mr. Charles R. ORDOYNE
15 Director of Human Resources .... Ms. Annette ARBONEAUX
26 Director of University Relations .... Ms. Stephanie VERDIN
51 Dir of Continuing Education .... Mr. Jason EIERMANN
41 Athletic Director .... Mr. Robert BERNARDI
29 Exec Dir Alumni & External Affairs .... Miss Monique CROCHET
06 Director Records & Registration .... Mr. Kelly J. RODRIGUE
07 Director of Admissions .... Mrs. Becky L. DUROCHER
23 Director University Health Services .... Vacant
35 Dean of Student Services .... Dr. Michele E. CARUSO
39 Director Residence Life .... Vacant
84 Director of Enrollment Services .... Mrs. Courtney CASSARD
96 Director of Purchasing .... Mr. Terry G. DUPRE
46 Director Research & Sponsored Pgms .... Mrs. Debra BENOIT
58 Director of Graduate Programs .... Mrs. DesLey PLAISANCE
88 Director of Printing & Design .... Mr. Bruno RUGGIERO
109 Director of Auxiliary Services .... Mrs. Brenda HASKINS
88 Coordinator of Veterans Services .... Mr. Gilberto BURBANTE
106 Dir Online Education/E-learning .... Dr. Andrew SIMONCELLI
100 Chief of Staff .... Mr. Alex ARCENEAUX

*Northwestern State University (B)

310 Sam Sibley Drive, Suite 223,
Natchitoches LA 71497-0002
County: Natchitoches FICE Identification: 002021
Unit ID: 160038
Telephone: (318) 357-6011 Carnegie Class: Masters/L
FAX Number: (318) 357-4223 Calendar System: Semester
URL: www.nsula.edu
Established: 1884 Annual Undergrad Tuition & Fees (In-State): $7,006
Enrollment: 9,002 Coed
Affiliation or Control: State IRS Status: 501(c)3
Highest Offering: Doctorate
Accreditation: SC, AAFCS, ADNUR, ART, BUS, CACREP, ENGT, MUS, NURSE, RAD, SW, TED, THEA

02 President .... Dr. James B. HENDERSON
05 Chief Academic Officer .... Dr. Vickie GENTRY
11 Vice Pres for University Affairs .... Dr. Marcus JONES
30 Vice President for External Affairs .... Mr. Jerry D. PIERCE
46 VP for Tech/Innovation/Eco Dev .... Dr. Darlene WILLIAMS
10 Vice President Business Affairs .... Mr. Carl JONES
32 Interim VP for Student Experience .... Dr. Chirs MAGGIO
35 Dean of Students .... Mrs. Frances CONINE
53 Dean Col of Education/Human Dev .... Dr. Vickie GENTRY
49 Interim Dean Col of Arts & Sciences .... Dr. Greg HANDEL
66 Dean Col of Nursing & Allied Health .... Dr. Dana CLAWSON
50 Interim Dean Col of Business & Tech .... Dr. Margaret KILCOYNE
88 Director Scholars' College .... Dr. Kirsten BARTELS
12 Director CENLA Campus .... Mr. Jason PARKS
09 Director Institutional Research .... Vacant
06 Registrar .... Mrs. Lillie F. BELL
08 Director of Libraries .... Ms. Abbie LANDRY

29 Asst VP External Affs/Univ Advance .... Mr. Drake OWENS
37 Director Student Financial Aid .... Ms. Lauren JACKSON
88 Dir Creative & Performing Arts .... Dr. Greg HANDEL
26 Director NSU Press .... Mrs. Leah JACKSON
36 Director Counseling & Career Svcs .... Mrs. Rebecca BOONE
41 Athletic Director .... Mr. Greg BURKE
23 Director of Health Services .... Mrs. Stephanie CAMPBELL
07 Director of University Recruiting .... Mrs. Jana LUCKY
15 Director Human Resources .... Mr. Cecil KNOTTS
18 Physical Plant Director .... Mr. Dale WOHLETZ
96 Director of Purchasing .... Mr. Dale MARTIN
21 Associate Business Officer .... Ms. Rita GRAVES

*Southeastern Louisiana University (C)

548 Ned McGehee Drive, Hammond LA 70402-0001
County: Tangipahoa FICE Identification: 002024
Unit ID: 160612
Telephone: (985) 549-2000 Carnegie Class: Masters/L
FAX Number: (985) 549-2061 Calendar System: Semester
URL: www.southeastern.edu/
Established: 1925 Annual Undergrad Tuition & Fees (In-State): $7,280
Enrollment: 14,487 Coed
Affiliation or Control: State IRS Status: 501(c)3
Highest Offering: Doctorate
Accreditation: SC, AAFCS, ART, BUS, BUSA, #CAATE, CACREP, CS, ENGR, ENGT, MUS, NAIT, NURSE, SP, SW, TED

02 President .... Dr. John L. CRAIN
05 Interim Provost/VP Academic Affairs .... Dr. Tena GOLDING
10 VP Administration/Finance .... Mr. Sam DOMIANO
30 Vice Pres University Advancement .... Ms. Wendy LAUDERDALE
32 Vice President Student Affairs .... Dr. Marvin L. YATES
20 Asst VP Academic Affairs .... Dr. Debora JOHNSON
13 Chief Information Officer .... Dr. Mike M. ASOODEH
86 Exec Asst Public & Govt Affairs .... Ms. Erin K. COWSER
21 Controller .... Ms. Nettie L. BURCHFIELD
06 Director Records & Registration .... Ms. Paulette M. POCHE
08 Director of Library .... Mr. Eric W. JOHNSON
36 Director Career Development Svcs .... Mr. Ken W. RIDGEDELL
109 Interim Director Auxiliary Services .... Ms. Connie DAVIS
29 Interim Director of Alumni Services .... Ms. Julie PERISE
39 Dir Student Housing & Resident Svcs .... Dr. Kay MAURIN
15 Director Human Resources .... Ms. Tara DUPRE
19 Director University Police .... Mr. Harold TODD
46 Dir Sponsored Research/Programs .... Ms. Cheryl HALL
41 Athletic Director .... Mr. Jay ARTIGUES
18 Director Facility Planning .... Mr. Ken D. HOWE
92 Director Honors Program .... Dr. Kent NEUERBURG
23 Director Health Services .... Ms. Michelle REED
38 Director Counseling Center .... Vacant
07 Director Admissions .... Vacant
37 Director Financial Aid .... Mr. Charles CAMBRE
09 Director Inst Research/Assessment .... Dr. Michelle HALL
26 Director Public Information .... Mr. Rene G. ABADIE
96 Dir Purchasing/Property Control .... Mr. Richard HIMBER
85 Dir Multicultural/Intl Stdnt Affs .... Mr. Eric J. SUMMERS
22 Coordinator EEO/ADA .... Mr. Gene E. PREGEANT
49 Int Dn Col Arts/Human/Soc Sciences .... Dr. Karen FONTENOT
50 Int Dean of College of Business .... Dr. Antoinette PHILLIPS
53 Interim Dean College Education .... Dr. Shirley JACOB
66 Dean Col of Nursing & Health Sci .... Dr. Ann CARRUTH
72 Dean Col of Science & Technology .... Dr. Daniel MCCARTHY

*University of Louisiana at Lafayette (D)

104 University Circle, Lafayette LA 70503-0001
County: Lafayette FICE Identification: 002031
Unit ID: 160658
Telephone: (337) 482-1000 Carnegie Class: DU-Higher
FAX Number: (337) 482-6195 Calendar System: Semester
URL: www.louisiana.edu
Established: 1898 Annual Undergrad Tuition & Fees (In-State): $8,256
Enrollment: 17,195 Coed
Affiliation or Control: State IRS Status: 501(c)3
Highest Offering: Doctorate
Accreditation: SC, ART, BUS, BUSA, #CAATE, CACREP, CAHIIM, CIDA, CS, DIETD, DIETI, ENG, JOUR, MUS, NAIT, NURSE, SP, TED

02 President .... Dr. E. Joseph SAVOIE
05 Provost/VP for Academic Affairs .... Dr. David DANAHAR
10 VP Administration & Finance .... Mr. Jerry L. LEBLANC
32 VP for Student Affairs .... Ms. Patricia COTTONHAM
30 VP University Advancement .... Mr. John BLOHM
46 Vice Pres for Research .... Dr. Ramesh KOLLURU
84 VP for Enrollment Mgmt .... Dr. DeWayne BOWIE
13 Chief Information Officer .... Mr. Gene FIELDS
11 Director of Administrative Services .... Ms. Lisa C. LANDRY
21 Asst Vice Pres Financial Services .... Ms. Debra CALAIS
21 Comptroller .... Vacant
108 Asst VP Institutional Plng & Effect .... Vacant
20 Asst VP Academic Affairs .... Ms. Ellen D. COOK
35 Dean of Students .... Ms. Margarita PEREZ
35 Assoc Dean Students/Dir Stdnt Life .... Ms. Heidie LINDSEY
25 Assoc Dir Research/Sponsored Pgms .... Ms. Abby GUILLORY
91 Director of Information Systems .... Mr. Sam F. BULLARD
14 Director Computing Support Services .... Mr. Patrick LANDRY
08 Dean of University Libraries .... Dr. Charles W. TRICHE, III
07 Dir of UN Admissions & Recruitment .... Mr. Andy BENOIT
88 Director Information Networks .... Mr. Stephen J. MAHLER
09 Director of Institutional Research .... Ms. Lisa LORD

55 Director University Connection .... Ms. Amanda DOYLE
37 Director of Financial Aid .... Ms. Cindy SHOWS-PEREZ
96 Director Purchasing .... Ms. Marie FRANK
27 Assoc Director Publications .... Ms. Kathleen A. THAMES
36 Director Career Services .... Ms. Kim A. BILLEAUDEAU
19 Chief of Police .... Chief Joey STURM
23 Director Student Health Svcs .... Ms. Madeline HUSBAND-ARDOIN
49 Dean Liberal Arts .... Dr. Jordan KELLMAN
54 Dean of Engineering .... Dr. Mark E. ZAPPI
53 Dean of Education .... Dr. Gerald P. CARLSON
66 Dean of Nursing .... Dr. Gail P. POIRRIER
58 Dean of Graduate School .... Dr. Mary FARMER-KAISER
50 Dean of Business Administration .... Ms. Gwen FONTENOT
81 Dean of Sciences .... Dr. Azmy ACKLEH
97 Dean of University College .... Dr. Bobbie DECUIR
57 Dean College of the Arts .... Mr. H. Gordon BROOKS, II
77 Director Ctr Adv Computer Studies .... Dr. Magdy A. BAYOUMI
18 Director Physical Plant .... Mr. William J. CRIST
22 Director Operational Review/EEO Off .... Ms. Christine BRASHER
39 Director Housing .... Mr. Jules BREAUX
40 Manager Bookstore .... Mr. Robert RICHARD
24 Director Univ Media/Printing Svcs .... Mr. Steve MAHLER
41 Athletic Director .... Mr. Scott FARMER
85 Director Office of Intl Affairs .... Dr. Rose HONEGGER
51 Director of Continuing Education .... Ms. Dawn PROVOST
31 Dean of Community Service .... Mr. David YARBROUGH
86 Coordinator Governmental Relations .... Vacant
26 Dir of Communication and Marketing .... Mr. Aaron MARTIN
29 Director Alumni Affairs .... Ms. Jennifer LEMEUNIER
44 Planned Giving Officer .... Mr. David P. COMEAUX
38 Director Counseling and Testing .... Mr. Brian FREDERICK
15 Director of Human Resources .... Mr. Paul THOMAS
06 Registrar .... Mr. Mickey DIEZ
106 Director of Distance Learning .... Dr. Luke DOWDEN
92 Director of Honors Program .... Dr. Julia FREDERICK
89 Director of First-Year Experience .... Dr. Jennifer FAUST
28 Director of Diversity .... Ms. Taniecea MALLERY
108 Director Institutional Assessment .... Ms. Alise HAGAN

*University of Louisiana at Monroe (E)

700 University Avenue, Monroe LA 71209-0001
County: Ouachita FICE Identification: 002020
Unit ID: 159993
Telephone: (318) 342-1000 Carnegie Class: DU-Mod
FAX Number: (318) 342-5161 Calendar System: Semester
URL: www.ulm.edu
Established: 1931 Annual Undergrad Tuition & Fees (In-State): $7,658
Enrollment: 8,517 Coed
Affiliation or Control: State IRS Status: 501(c)3
Highest Offering: Doctorate
Accreditation: SC, BUS, BUSA, CACREP, CONST, CS, DH, EXSC, MFCD, MT, MUS, NURSE, OT, OTA, PHAR, RAD, SP, SW, TED

02 President .... Dr. Nick J. BRUNO
03 Executive VP .... Dr. Stephen P. RICHTERS
10 Chief Business Officer .... Mr. William T. GRAVES
32 Vice President for Student Affairs .... Mr. Camile CURRIER
05 Vice President for Academic Affairs .... Dr. Eric A. PANI
84 Asst VP for Mktg/Recruit/Cmty Engag .... Mrs. Lisa R. MILLER
07 Director Enrollment & Scholarship .... Ms. Mary SCHMEER
41 Director of Athletics .... Mr. Brian WICKSTROM
26 Director Marketing/Communications .... Dr. Julia LETLOW
88 Director Internal Audit .... Mr. Kirby D. CAMPBELL
49 Dean Arts/Education & Sciences .... Dr. Sandra M. LEMOINE
50 Dean Business and Social Sciences .... Dr. Ronald BERRY
67 Dean Health and Pharmaceutical Sci .... Dr. Benny BLAYLOCK
58 Director Graduate School .... Dr. Leonard CLARK
108 Director Assessment and Evaluation .... Mrs. Allison L. THOMPSON
09 Exec Dir Univ Planning/Analysis .... Mr. Jeffrey HENDRIX
08 Interim Dean of the Library .... Mrs. Cynthia ROBERTSON
51 Director eULM .... Ms. Paula THORNHILL
06 Registrar .... Mr. Anthony MALTA
37 Director Financial Aid Services .... Mrs. Frankie EVERETT
85 Dir Intl Student Program and Svcs .... Mrs. Sami OWENS
88 Director of University Retention .... Mrs. Barbara MICHAELIDES
102 Executive Director Foundation .... Mrs. Susan CHAPPELL
39 Director Residential Life .... Ms. Tresea L. BUCKHAULTS
45 Budget Officer .... Mrs. Gail C. PARKER
21 Controller .... Ms. Sarah WALKER
15 Director Human Resources .... Ms. Melissa DUCOTE
13 Director Computer Center .... Mr. Chance W. EPPINETTE
109 Exec Dir Auxiliary Enterprises .... Mr. Tommy WALPOLE
40 Manager University Bookstore .... Ms. Heather DAMRON
18 Director Physical Plant Admin .... Mr. Robert KARAM
18 Facilities Planning Officer .... Mr. Michael DAVIS
35 Spec Projects Ofcr/Title IX Coord .... Ms. Treina LANDRUM
38 Director Counseling Center .... Ms. Karen FOSTER
19 Director of University Police .... Mr. Tom TORREGROSSA
36 Director Career Connections .... Ms. Roslynn POGUE
88 Dir Recreational Svcs/Facilities .... Mr. Brandon BRUSCATO
88 Technology and Comm Liaison .... Mr. Lindsey S. WILKERSON
29 Director of Alumni Affairs .... Ms. Robin S. UNDERWOOD
30 Senior Development Officer .... Mrs. Anne LOCKHART

University of Phoenix Baton Rouge Campus (F)

2431 S Acadian Thruway, Baton Rouge LA 70808-2300
Telephone: (225) 927-4443 Identification: 770208
Accreditation: &NH, ACBSP

† No longer accepting campus-based students.

Virginia College (A)

9501 Cortana Place, Baton Rouge LA 70815-8604
Telephone: (225) 236-3900 Identification: 770826
Accreditation: ACICS, ACFEI, MAAB, SURGT

† Tuition varies by degree program.

Virginia College (B)

2950 East Texas Street, Suite C, Bossier City LA 71111
Telephone: (888) 342-0014 Identification: 770827
Accreditation: ACICS, MAAB

† Branch campus of Virginia College, Birmingham, AL

Xavier University of Louisiana (C)

One Drexel Drive, New Orleans LA 70125-1098
County: Orleans FICE Identification: 002032
Unit ID: 160904
Telephone: (504) 486-7411 Carnegie Class: Masters/S
FAX Number: (504) 520-7904 Calendar System: Semester
URL: www.xula.edu
Established: 1925 Annual Undergrad Tuition & Fees: $22,349
Enrollment: 2,976 Coed
Affiliation or Control: Roman Catholic IRS Status: 501(c)3
Highest Offering: Doctorate
Accreditation: SC, ACBSP, CACREP, MUS, PHAR, TED

01 President Dr. C. Reynold VERRET
11 Sr Vice Pres for Administration Mr. Ralph JOHNSON
05 Provost and Sr VP Academic Affairs Dr. Ann MCCALL
46 Assoc VP Research/Sponsored Pgms Dr. Deborah MARSHALL
32 Vice President for Student Services Mr. Joseph K. BYRD
30 Vice President for Inst Advancement Mrs. Gia SOUBLET
10 Vice President for Finance Mr. Edward PHILLIPS
13 VP for Office of Technology Mr. Tony MOORE
45 VP Planning Inst Res & Assessment Dr. Ronald R. DURNFORD
18 Vice President Facilities Planning Mr. Marion BRACY
20 Assoc VP for Academic Affairs Dr. Marguerite GIGUETTE
109 Assoc Vice Pres Auxiliary Services Mr. William JEFFRION
07 Dean of Admissions Mr. Winston D. BROWN
06 Registrar Ms. Avis STUARD
42 University Chaplain Fr. Etido S. JEROME
21 Director of Accounting Ms. Joyce SANDIFER
21 Director of Operations Ms. Lori GIE
21 Dir Fin Reporting & External Audit Mrs. Ingenue S. SCHEXNIDER-FIELDS
15 Director of Human Resources Mr. Larry CALVIN
49 Dean of Arts & Sciences Dr. Anil KUKREJA
67 Dean of College of Pharmacy Dr. Kathleen KENNEDY
89 Director of Freshmen Studies Dr. Wendy GAUDIN
108 Dir of Inst Effectiv & Assessment Dr. Danielle DUFFOURC
09 Director for Institutional Research Dr. Clair WILKINS GREEN
88 Dir Inst Compliance & Plng Init Dr. Treva A. LEE
08 Director of the Library Dr. Lynette RALPH
36 Director of Career Services Mrs. Carolyn D. THOMAS
37 Director of Financial Aid Ms. Emily LONDON-JONES
19 Director of Campus Police Mr. Duane CARKUM
23 Med Dir Student Health Services Dr. Robert MERCADEL
38 Director of Counseling Services Dr. Brian TURNER
29 Director of Alumni Relations Ms. Kimberly REESE
40 Manager Bookstore Ms. Rose NAQUIN
41 Athletic Director Mr. Jason HORN
04 Administrative Asst to President Mrs. Amelia JENKINS
101 Secretary of the Institution/Board Mrs. Isabella THOMPSON
104 Director Study Abroad Mr. Torian LEE
106 Dir Online Education/E-learning Dr. Karen NICHOLS
39 Director Student Housing Mrs. Judy BRACY
44 Director Annual or Planned Giving Ms. Lacrecia JAMES
105 Director Web Services Mr. Brian BOWERS
26 Chief Public Relations/Marketing Mr. Richard TUCKER

MAINE

Bates College (D)

2 Andrews Road, Lewiston ME 04240-6047
County: Androscoggin FICE Identification: 002036
Unit ID: 160977
Telephone: (207) 786-6255 Carnegie Class: Bac-A&S
FAX Number: (207) 786-6123 Calendar System: Other
URL: www.bates.edu
Established: 1855 Annual Undergrad Tuition & Fees: $48,435
Enrollment: 1,773 Coed
Affiliation or Control: Independent Non-Profit IRS Status: 501(c)3
Highest Offering: Baccalaureate
Accreditation: EH

01 President Dr. A. Clayton SPENCER
05 VP Academic Affairs/Dean of Faculty Dr. Matthew R. AUER
10 VP Finance & Admin/Treasurer Mr. Geoffrey SWIFT
08 VP Info & Libr Services/Librarian Ms. Katie VALE
30 VP Advancement Ms. Sarah R. PEARSON
32 Dean of Students Mr. Joshua MCINTOSH
21 Asst Vice Pres Financial Planning Mr. Douglas W. GINEVAN
20 Associate Dean of Faculty Dr. Kathryn G. LOW
20 Assoc Dean of Faculty Dr. Margaret A. IMBER
31 Director of Community Partnerships Ms. Darby K. RAY
06 Registrar Ms. Mary MESERVE
09 Dir Inst Rsch/Analysis and Planning Ms. Anne Marie T. RUSSELL
15 Asst VP Human Resources Vacant
18 Dir of Facilities Svcs Operations Mr. Jay PHILLIPS
88 Dir Capital Planning/Construction Ms. Pamela J. WICHROSKI
07 Dean of Admissions & Financial Aid Ms. Leigh WEISENBURGER
19 Dir Security & Campus Safety Mr. Thomas P. CAREY
23 Dir Health Services Vacant
26 Asst VP Communications/Media Rels Mr. Sean T. FINDLEN
37 Dir Student Financial Services Ms. Wendy G. GLASS
40 Dir Bookstore/Contract Officer Ms. Gail S. ST. PIERRE
36 Dir of Career Services Mr. David MCDONOUGH
91 Dir Sys Development & Integration Ms. Eileen P. ZIMMERMAN
24 Dir of Academic Technology Services Mr. Andrew W. WHITE
41 Athletic Director Mr. Kevin MCHUGH
42 College Chaplain Ms. Brittany LONGSDORF
39 Asst Dean of Students/Housing Ms. Erin FOSTER ZSIGA
102 Dir of the Office for External Grnt Ms. Rachel WRAY
104 Assoc Dean of Students/Study Abroad Vacant
100 Chief of Staff Mr. Michael HUSSEY
28 AVP and Chief Diversity Officer Ms. Crystal WILLIAMS
84 Asst Dean of Admis/Intl Enrollment Ms. Misha GARG
04 Exec Assistant to the President Ms. Claire B. SCHMOLL
101 Secretary of the Institution/Board Mr. Michael HUSSEY

† Tuition figure is a comprehensive fees figure.

Beal College (E)

99 Farm Road, Bangor ME 04401-6831
County: Penobscot FICE Identification: 005204
Unit ID: 160995
Telephone: (207) 947-4591 Carnegie Class: Assoc/HVT-High Non
FAX Number: (207) 947-0208 Calendar System: Other
URL: www.bealcollege.edu
Established: 1891 Annual Undergrad Tuition & Fees: N/A
Enrollment: 429 Coed
Affiliation or Control: Proprietary IRS Status: Proprietary
Highest Offering: Associate Degree
Accreditation: ACICS, CAHIIM, MAC

01 President Ms. Sheryl L. DEWALT
11 Director of Operations Mr. Corey LEIGHTON
10 Director of Finance Ms. Renee DUNTON
05 Director of Education Ms. Deborah CROCKETT
07 Director of Admissions Ms. Sue BORDEN
37 Director Student Financial Aid Ms. Maggie MAGEE
32 Director of Student Affairs Ms. Stephanie MISHOU
08 Chief Librarian Ms. Tegan C. MILLS
18 Superintendent Physical Plant Mr. Kevin HARDY
88 Dir Early Child Ed/Hospitality Svcs Ms. Susan XIRINACHS
76 Director Allied Health Ms. Barbara MARCHELLETTA
40 Director Bookstore Ms. Wandamae CLEAVES
36 Director Student Placement Ms. Donna GILLETTE
06 Registrar Ms. Ellen EDWARDS
50 Director Business Studies Ms. Katrin TEEL
83 Director Social & Human Svcs Asst Ms. Susan POLYOT
75 Director Welding Technology Mr. Jesse CROSBY
03 Chief Operations Officer Mr. Stephen H. VILLETT

Bowdoin College (F)

3500 College Station, Brunswick ME 04011-8448
County: Cumberland FICE Identification: 002038
Unit ID: 161004
Telephone: (207) 725-3000 Carnegie Class: Bac-A&S
FAX Number: (207) 725-3123 Calendar System: Semester
URL: www.bowdoin.edu
Established: 1794 Annual Undergrad Tuition & Fees: $48,212
Enrollment: 1,805 Coed
Affiliation or Control: Independent Non-Profit IRS Status: 501(c)3
Highest Offering: Master's
Accreditation: EH

01 President Dr. Clayton ROSE
11 Int Sr VP Finance/Admin/Treasurer Mr. Matthew ORLANDO
46 Sr VP Devel & Alumni Relations Mr. Rick GANONG
26 Sr VP Communications/Public Affairs Mr. Scott W. HOOD
13 SVP/Chief Information Officer Mr. Mitchel W. DAVIS
10 Vice Pres Finance/Administration Mr. Matthew ORLANDO
15 Vice President of Human Resources Ms. Tamara D. SPOERRI
32 Dean of Student Affairs Mr. Timothy W. FOSTER
05 Dean for Academic Affairs Dr. Jennifer SCANLON
07 Dean of Admissions/Financial Aid Ms. E.Whitney SOULE
09 VP Inst Rsrch/Analytics Consulting Dr. Christina M. FINNERAN
29 Director Alumni Relations Ms. Rodie F. LLOYD
08 College Librarian Ms. Marjorie HASSEN
37 Director of Student Aid Mr. Michael D. BARTINI
06 Registrar Ms. Martina DUNCAN
19 Director of Security Mr. Randall NICHOLS
36 Director of Career Planning Mr. Timothy DIEHL
38 Director of Counseling Service Dr. Bernie HERSHBERGER
41 Director of Athletics Mr. Timothy M. RYAN
23 Director of Health Services Dr. Birgit POLS
18 Director Facilities Ops/Maintenance Mr. Theodore R. STAM
24 Instructional Media Librarian Ms. Carmen M. GREENLEE
21 Director of Finance & Campus Svcs Mr. Delwin C. WILSON
39 Director of Residential Life Ms. Meadow DAVIS
109 Dir Dining & Bookstore Services Ms. Mary M. KENNEDY
35 Director of Student Activities Dr. Allen W. DELONG
35 Sr Associate Dean Student Affairs Ms. Kimberly A. PACELLI
88 Co-Dir of the Museum of Art Ms. Anne GOODYEAR
88 Co-Dir of the Musuem of Art Mr. Frank GOODYEAR
18 Director of Capital Projects Mr. Donald V. BORKOWSKI
20 Assoc Dean for Academic Affairs Dr. Barry LOGAN

Colby College (G)

4000 Mayflower Hill, Waterville ME 04901-8840
County: Kennebec FICE Identification: 002039
Unit ID: 161086
Telephone: (207) 859-4000 Carnegie Class: Bac-A&S
FAX Number: (207) 859-4603 Calendar System: 4/1/4
URL: www.colby.edu
Established: 1813 Annual Undergrad Tuition & Fees: $49,120
Enrollment: 1,847 Coed
Affiliation or Control: Independent Non-Profit IRS Status: 501(c)3
Highest Offering: Baccalaureate
Accreditation: EH

01 President Dr. David A. GREENE
05 Provost and Dean of Faculty Dr. Lori G. KLETZER
10 Vice President Admin & CFO Mr. Douglas C. TERP
30 VP College & Student Advancement Dr. Daniel LUGO
32 Dean of the College Dr. Karlene A. BURRELL-MCRAE
26 Vice President for Communications Ms. Ruth JACKSON
07 Vice Pres/Dean Admiss & Fin Aid Dr. Matthew PROTO
20 Assoc Provost & Dean of Faculty Dr. Margaret T. MCFADDEN
32 Asst Vice Pres/Sr Associate Dean Ms. Barbara E. MOORE
35 Sr Assoc/DOS/Dir Campus Life Vacant
06 Registrar Ms. Elizabeth N. SCHILLER
08 Director of Libraries Mr. Clement P. GUTHRO
36 Director of Career Center Ms. Alisa M. JOHNSON
88 Director of Special Programs Mr. Jacques MOORE
37 Director of Financial Aid Mr. Elreo CAMPBELL
29 Director of Alumni Relations Vacant
15 Director Human Resources Mr. Mark CROSBY
19 Director of Security Mr. Peter S. CHENEVERT
13 Chief Information Officer Ms. Cindy J. MITCHELL
18 Asst VP Facilities and Campus Plng Ms. Minakshi M. AMUNDSEN
23 Medical Director Dr. Paul D. BERKNER
38 Director of Counseling Services Mr. Eric S. JOHNSON
41 Director of Athletics Mr. Timothy W. WHEATON
09 Dir Inst Research & Assessment Ms. Rebecca H. BRODIGAN
21 Controller Mr. Ruben L. RIVERA
40 Director of the Bookstore Ms. Barbara C. SHUTT
104 Director of Off-Campus Study Dr. Nancy DOWNEY
102 Director of Grants Mr. William C. LAYTON, III
04 Asst to the Pres/Dir of Planning Mr. Brian J. CLARK
100 VP and Secretary of the College Dr. C. Andrew MCGADNEY

College of the Atlantic (H)

105 Eden Street, Bar Harbor ME 04609-1198
County: Hancock FICE Identification: 011385
Unit ID: 160959
Telephone: (207) 288-5015 Carnegie Class: Bac-A&S
FAX Number: (207) 288-3780 Calendar System: Trimester
URL: www.coa.edu
Established: 1969 Annual Undergrad Tuition & Fees: $42,084
Enrollment: 386 Coed
Affiliation or Control: Independent Non-Profit IRS Status: 501(c)3
Highest Offering: Master's
Accreditation: EH

01 President Dr. Darron COLLINS
05 Academic Dean Dr. Ken HILL
10 Administrative Dean Mr. Andy GRIFFITHS
32 Dean for Student Life Ms. Sarah LUKE
30 Dean Institutional Advancement Ms. Lynn BOULGER
07 Dean of Admission Ms. Heather ALBERT-KNOPP
06 Registrar Ms. Judy ALLEN
08 Director of Thorndike Library Ms. Jane HULTBERG
21 Comptroller Mrs. Melissa COOK
37 Director of Financial Aid Mr. Bruce HAZAM
36 Director of Internship/Career Svcs Ms. Jill BARLOW-KELLEY
26 Public Relations Manager Mr. Rob LEVIN

Husson University (I)

1 College Circle, Bangor ME 04401-2929
County: Penobscot FICE Identification: 002043
Unit ID: 161165
Telephone: (207) 941-7000 Carnegie Class: Masters/M
FAX Number: (207) 941-7139 Calendar System: Semester
URL: www.husson.edu
Established: 1898 Annual Undergrad Tuition & Fees: N/A
Enrollment: 3,415 Coed
Affiliation or Control: Independent Non-Profit IRS Status: 501(c)3
Highest Offering: Doctorate
Accreditation: EH, CACREP, IACBE, NURSE, OT, PHAR, PTA

01 President Dr. Robert A. CLARK
05 VP for Academic Affairs/Provost Dr. Lynne COY-OGAN
10 VP Finance & Admin/Treasurer Craig HADLEY
30 Vice President for Advancement Sara C. ROBINSON
84 VP Enrollment Management Jonathan HENRY
50 Dean College of Business Dr. Marie HANSEN
67 Dean School of Pharmacy Dr. Rodney LARSON
53 Dean College of Health & Education Dr. Rhonda WASKIEWICZ
49 Dean Science/Humanities Dr. Patricia BIXEL
26 Exec Dir of Marketing and Comm Eric GORDON
32 Dean of Student Life Carl STILES

53 Director School of Education ... Barbara MOODY
07 Director of Admissions ... John CHAMPOLI
37 Director of Financial Aid ... Anne TABOR
13 Exec Dir of Information Resources ... Garth CORMIER
06 Registrar ... Nancy FENDERS
09 Director of Institutional Research ... Dr. Gail TUDOR
108 Director Institutional Assessment ... Travis E. ALLEN
106 Dir Online and Extended Learning ... Vacant
36 Director Career Services ... James WESTHOFF
41 Director of Athletics ... Francis PERGOLIZZI
27 Dir of Comm and Student Engagement ... Julia GREEN
15 Human Resources Director ... Janet KELLE
29 Director of Alumni Relations ... Amanda CUMMINGS
18 Director of Maintenance ... Gary GEROW
08 Librarian ... Susanna PATHAK
31 Dir of Special Programs ... Mike FOSTER
44 Director of Advancement Services ... Lynda ROHMAN
04 Administrative Asst to President ... Kandi HALE
100 Chief of Staff ... Mary Ann HAAS
19 Director Safety and Security ... Ray BESSETTE
38 Director of Counseling Services ... Colleen OWENS
105 Website Manager & Social Media Dir .Matthew GREEN-HAMANN
109 Assoc Vice President for Auxil ... Thomas WARREN

Institute for Doctoral Studies in the Visual Arts (A)

130 Neal Street, Portland ME 04102
County: Cumberland FICE Identification: 041888
Unit ID: 462044
Telephone: (207) 879-8757 Carnegie Class: Bac-A&S
FAX Number: N/A Calendar System: Semester
URL: www.idsva.org
Established: 2007 Annual Graduate Tuition & Fees: N/A
Enrollment: 52 Coed
Affiliation or Control: Independent Non-Profit IRS Status: 501(c)3
Highest Offering: Doctorate; No Undergraduates
Accreditation: EH

01 President ... George SMITH
03 Executive Vice President ... Amy CURTIS

Kaplan University-Augusta (B)

14 Marketplace Drive, Augusta ME 04330
Telephone: (207) 213-2500 Identification: 770060
Accreditation: &NH, MAC

† Regional accreditation is carried under the parent institution in Davenport, IA

Kaplan University-Lewiston (C)

475 Lisbon Street, Lewiston ME 04240
Telephone: (207) 333-3300 Identification: 770061
Accreditation: &NH, MAC

† Regional accreditation is carried under the parent institution in Davenport, IA

Kaplan University-Maine (D)

265 Western Avenue, South Portland ME 04106
Telephone: (207) 774-6126 FICE Identification: 009292
Accreditation: &NH, ACBSP, MAC

† Regional accreditation is carried under the parent institution in Davenport, IA.

The Landing School (E)

286 River Road, Arundel ME 04046
County: York FICE Identification: 023613
Unit ID: 161208
Telephone: (207) 985-7976 Carnegie Class: Spec 2-yr-Tech
FAX Number: (207) 985-7942 Calendar System: Semester
URL: www.landingschool.edu
Established: 1978 Annual Undergrad Tuition & Fees: $21,694
Enrollment: 78 Coed
Affiliation or Control: Independent Non-Profit IRS Status: 501(c)3
Highest Offering: Associate Degree
Accreditation: ACCSC

01 President ... Dr. Richard J. SCHUHMANN
05 Director of Education ... Mr. Richard WOODMAN
10 Dir of Administration & Finance ... Ms. Kristy LANK
07 Director of Admissions ... Mr. Matthew BARRY
37 Director Student Financial Aid ... Ms. Jennifer BECHARD

Maine College of Art (F)

522 Congress St, Portland ME 04101
County: Cumberland FICE Identification: 011673
Unit ID: 161509
Telephone: (207) 699-5521 Carnegie Class: Spec-4-yr-Arts
FAX Number: (207) 775-5087 Calendar System: Semester
URL: www.meca.edu
Established: 1882 Annual Undergrad Tuition & Fees: $32,290
Enrollment: 459 Coed
Affiliation or Control: Independent Non-Profit IRS Status: 501(c)3
Highest Offering: Master's
Accreditation: EH, ART

01 President ... Mr. Donald TUSKI
03 Executive Vice President ... Ms. Beth ELICKER
05 Dean/Vice Pres Academic Affairs ... Mr. Ian ANDERSON
30 VP for Institutional Advancement ... Ms. Rebecca CONRAD
06 Registrar ... Ms. Anne DENNISON
32 Director of Student Life ... Ms. Adrea JAEHNIG
07 Director of Admissions ... Ms. Megan LLOYD
13 Director Technology ... Mr. Seth CLAYTER
26 Dir of Marketing & Communications ... Mr. Rafi DER SIMONIAN
10 Director of Business Services ... Mr. Phil STEVENS
37 Director of Financial Aid ... Ms. Carri FRECHETTE
51 Director Continuing Studies ... Ms. Courtney COOK
18 Chief Facilities/Physical Plant ... Mr. Douglas DOERING
08 Library Director ... Ms. Moira STEVENS
04 Executive Assistant ... Ms. Melissa SULLIVAN
29 Director Alumni Relations ... Ms. Jill DALTON
36 Director of Artists at Work ... Ms. Jessica TOMLINSON

Maine College of Health Professions (G)

70 Middle Street, Lewiston ME 04240-7027
County: Androscoggin FICE Identification: 006305
Unit ID: 161022
Telephone: (207) 795-2840 Carnegie Class: Spec 2-yr-Health
FAX Number: (207) 795-2849 Calendar System: Semester
URL: www.mchp.edu
Established: 1891 Annual Undergrad Tuition & Fees: $11,400
Enrollment: 210 Coed
Affiliation or Control: Independent Non-Profit IRS Status: 501(c)3
Highest Offering: Associate Degree
Accreditation: EH, ADNUR, NMT, RAD

01 President ... Dr. Monika BISSELL
10 Director of Financial Affairs ... Ms. Lesa ROSE
05 Director of General Education ... Mrs. Judith RIPLEY
07 Director of Admissions ... Ms. Erica WATSON
06 Registrar ... Mrs. Kathleen C. JACQUES
37 Student Financial Aid Specialist ... Mrs. Nicole DEBLOIS
66 Interim Director of Nursing ... Ms. Heather FRASER

*Maine Community College System (H)

323 State Street, Augusta ME 04330-7131
County: Kennebec Identification: 666092
Unit ID: 409713
Telephone: (207) 629-4000 Carnegie Class: N/A
FAX Number: (207) 629-4048
URL: www.mccs.me.edu/

01 President ... Mr. Derek LANGHAUSER
05 Chief Academic Officer ... Ms. Janet SORTOR
10 Chief Financial Officer ... Mr. David DAIGLER

*Central Maine Community College (I)

1250 Turner Street, Auburn ME 04210-6498
County: Androscoggin FICE Identification: 005276
Unit ID: 161077
Telephone: (207) 755-5100 Carnegie Class: Assoc/MT-VT-High Trad
FAX Number: (207) 755-5491 Calendar System: Semester
URL: www.cmcc.edu
Established: 1964 Annual Undergrad Tuition & Fees (In-State): $3,750
Enrollment: 3,162 Coed
Affiliation or Control: State IRS Status: 501(c)3
Highest Offering: Associate Degree
Accreditation: EH, ADNUR

02 President ... Dr. Scott E. KNAPP
05 Dean Academic Affairs ... Ms. Betsy LIBBY
06 Registrar ... Ms. Sonya SAMPSON
10 Dean of Finance and General Service ... Ms. Pamela FEMIERES-MORIN
37 Director of Financial Aid ... Mr. John BOWIE
31 Dean Corporate/Community Services ... Ms. Diane DOSTIE
32 Dean of Student Services ... Mr. Nicholas HAWEL
26 Dean of Planning & Public Affairs ... Mr. Roger PHILIPPON
07 Director of Admissions ... Mr. Andrew MORONG
08 Head Librarian ... Ms. Judith FROST
18 Chief Physical Plant ... Mr. Raymond MASSE
22 Affirmative Action Officer ... Ms. Barbara OWEN
39 Director of Housing/Athletic Dir ... Mr. David GONYEA
40 Director of Bookstore ... Ms. Christine MORIN
15 Dean of Human Resources ... Ms. Barbara OWEN
27 Director of Communications ... Ms. Heather B. SEYMOUR

*Eastern Maine Community College (J)

354 Hogan Road, Bangor ME 04401-4280
County: Penobscot FICE Identification: 005277
Unit ID: 161138
Telephone: (207) 974-4600 Carnegie Class: Assoc/HVT-High Non
FAX Number: (207) 974-4608 Calendar System: Semester
URL: www.emcc.edu
Established: 1966 Annual Undergrad Tuition & Fees (In-State): $3,810
Enrollment: 2,613 Coed
Affiliation or Control: State IRS Status: 501(c)3
Highest Offering: Associate Degree
Accreditation: EH, ADNUR, EMT, MAC, RAD, SURGT

02 President ... Dr. Lisa LARSON
05 Academic Dean ... Ms. Elizabeth RUSSELL
10 Dir Finance & Auxiliary Services ... Mr. Jerry HAYMAN
09 Dean Inst Research/Enrollment Mgmt ... Mr. Daniel CROCKER
88 Professional Services Coordinator ... Mr. Matt MCLAUGHLIN
07 Director of Admissions ... Ms. Stacy GREEN
15 Director of Human Resources ... Ms. Jody VAIL
08 Librarian ... Ms. Janet ELVIDGE
37 Director of Financial Aid ... Ms. Candace WARD
13 Dean of Communication/Info Tech ... Mr. Timothy CONROY
18 Dir Facilities Mgmt/Student Life ... Vacant
20 Assistant Academic Dean ... Vacant
30 Dir of Institutional Advancement ... Ms. Jenn KHAVARI

*Kennebec Valley Community College (K)

92 Western Avenue, Fairfield ME 04937-1367
County: Somerset FICE Identification: 009826
Unit ID: 161192
Telephone: (207) 453-5000 Carnegie Class: Assoc/MT-VT-High Non
FAX Number: (207) 453-5010 Calendar System: Semester
URL: www.kvcc.me.edu
Established: 1970 Annual Undergrad Tuition & Fees (In-State): $3,385
Enrollment: 2,401 Coed
Affiliation or Control: State IRS Status: 501(c)3
Highest Offering: Associate Degree
Accreditation: EH, ACBSP, ADNUR, CAHIIM, COARC, EMT, MAC, OTA, PTAA, RAD

02 President ... Dr. Richard HOPPER
05 Academic Dean ... Ms. Erica MAZZEO
13 Dean of Tech/Chief Security Officer ... Mr. Kevin CASEY
32 VP of Student Affairs/Public Rels ... Ms. Karen NORMANDIN
10 Dean of Finance & Administration ... Ms. Monett WILSON
84 Asst Dean of Enrollment Management ... Mr. Crichton MCKENNA
06 Registrar ... Mrs. Lisa YORK-LEMELIN
30 Director of Development ... Ms. Michelle WEBB
37 Director of Financial Aid ... Ms. Anne CONNORS
09 Director of Institutional Research ... Ms. Karen GLEW

*Northern Maine Community College (L)

33 Edgemont Drive, Presque Isle ME 04769-2099
County: Aroostook FICE Identification: 005760
Unit ID: 161484
Telephone: (207) 768-2700 Carnegie Class: Assoc/HVT-Mix Trad/Non
FAX Number: (207) 768-2831 Calendar System: Semester
URL: www.nmcc.edu
Established: 1961 Annual Undergrad Tuition & Fees (In-State): $3,376
Enrollment: 1,079 Coed
Affiliation or Control: State IRS Status: 501(c)3
Highest Offering: Associate Degree
Accreditation: EH, ACBSP, ADNUR, EMT, MAC

02 President ... Mr. Timothy D. CROWLEY
05 Academic Dean ... Dr. Dorothy MARTIN
32 Dean of Students ... Dr. William G. EGELER
10 Dean of Finance ... Mr. Michael WILLIAMS
51 Asst Dean Continuing Education ... Ms. Leah BUCK
30 Dean of Development/Public Affairs ... Ms. Sue BERNARD
07 Director of Admissions ... Mr. Eugene MCCLUSKEY
06 Registrar ... Ms. Betsy A. HARRIS
37 Director for Financial Aid ... Ms. Norma M. SMITH
39 Director of Housing & Resident Life ... Mr. Jon A. BLANCHARD
38 Director of Counseling ... Ms. Tammy NELSON
18 Dean of Tech and Facilities ... Mr. Barry INGRAHAM
21 Business Manager ... Mr. Philip R. BROWN
40 College Store Manager ... Ms. Rebecca A. MAYNARD
08 Head Librarian ... Ms. Gail ROY
19 College Safety/Security Officer ... Mr. Glenn TAGGETT
15 Human Resource Coordinator ... Ms. Beth HUMMEL

*Southern Maine Community College (M)

2 Fort Road, South Portland ME 04106-1698
County: Cumberland FICE Identification: 005525
Unit ID: 161545
Telephone: (207) 741-5500 Carnegie Class: Assoc/MT-VT-High Trad
FAX Number: (207) 741-5751 Calendar System: Semester
URL: www.smccme.edu
Established: 1946 Annual Undergrad Tuition & Fees (In-State): $3,694
Enrollment: 6,734 Coed
Affiliation or Control: State IRS Status: 501(c)3
Highest Offering: Associate Degree
Accreditation: EH, ACFEI, ADNUR, COARC, DIETT, EMT, RAD

02 President/CEO ... Ronald G. CANTOR
05 Interim Dean of Academics ... Charles J. GREGORY
32 Dean of Student Life/Affirm Action ... Tiffanie L. BENTLEY
26 Dean of Effectiveness & Engagement ... Kaylene MITCHELL
04 Asst to the Pres/Strategic Initiat ... Darla JEWETT
04 Exec Assistant to the President ... Lori HALL
12 Dean of the Midcoast Campus ... James WHITTEN
10 Dean of Finance ... Robert COOMBS
13 Dean of Information Technology/CIO ... Timothy DUNNE
88 Int Dean Bus & Cmty Partnerships ... Julie CHASE
20 Associate Dean of Academic Affairs ... Paul CHARPENTIER
06 Asst Dean of Records/Retention ... Jeremy DILL

21 Director of Budget & Financial Rpt ... Shaun GRAY
37 Director of Financial Aid Systems ... Michel LUSSIER
07 Director of Admissions ... Amy LEE
88 Assistant Dean of Student Success ... Kathleen DOAN
39 Dir of Residence Life & Stdnt Dev ... Shane LONG
19 Director Campus Security ... Joseph MANHARDT
41 Director of Athletics ... Matthew RICHARDS
18 Plant Maintenance Engineer III ... James RENY
40 Manager Campus Store ... Cherie BRYANT
21 Business Mgr Student Billing/Bursar ... Leslie GUERRETTE
15 HR & Benefits Manager ... Denise RENY
38 Dir Counseling & Disability Svcs ... Sandra LYNHAM
27 Director of Communications ... Clarke CANFIELD
102 Dir Foundation Corporate Relations ... Joan COHEN
105 Director Web Services ... Ken POOLEY
103 Dir Workforce/Career Development ... Brenda DOWNEY
106 Dir Online Education/E-learning ... Michael HART

*Washington County Community College (A)

One College Drive, Calais ME 04619-9704
County: Washington FICE Identification: 009231
Unit ID: 161581
Telephone: (207) 454-1000 Carnegie Class: Assoc/HVT-Mix Trad/Non
FAX Number: (207) 454-1092 Calendar System: Semester
URL: www.wccc.me.edu
Established: 1969 Annual Undergrad Tuition & Fees (In-State): $3,630
Enrollment: 491 Coed
Affiliation or Control: State IRS Status: 501(c)3
Highest Offering: Associate Degree
Accreditation: EH, MAC

02 President ... Mr. Joseph CASSIDY
05 Dean of Academic Affairs ... Mr. Alexander CLIFFORD
10 Dean of Finance ... Ms. Desiree THOMPSON
15 Dir of HR/Devel/Communications ... Mrs. Tina ERSKINE
84 Dean Enrollment Mgmt/Student Svcs ... Mrs. Susan MINGO
37 Financial Aid Director ... Ms. Linda WINCHESTER
07 Director of Admissions ... Mrs. Susan MINGO
39 Director Student Housing ... Ms. Karen GOOKIN

*York County Community College (B)

112 College Drive, Wells ME 04090-0529
County: York FICE Identification: 031229
Unit ID: 420440
Telephone: (207) 646-9282 Carnegie Class: Assoc/HT-Mix Trad/Non
FAX Number: (207) 646-9675 Calendar System: Semester
URL: www.yccc.edu
Established: 1994 Annual Undergrad Tuition & Fees (In-State): $3,480
Enrollment: 1,699 Coed
Affiliation or Control: State IRS Status: 501(c)3
Highest Offering: Associate Degree
Accreditation: EH

02 President ... Dr. Barbara FINKELSTEIN
05 Vice President/Academic Dean ... Ms. Paula GAGNON
32 Dean of Students ... Mr. Jason AREY
10 Dean of Finance & Administration ... Mr. Samuel ELLIS
26 Dir of Marketing/Communications ... Ms. Stacy CHILICKI
31 Dir of Business/Community Programs ... Ms. Paulette MILLETTE
04 Exec Assistant to the President ... Ms. Erin HAYE
20 Associate Academic Dean ... Ms. Doreen ROGAN
08 Director Library/Learning Resources ... Ms. Amber TATNALL
88 Faculty Development Coordinator ... Ms. Stefanie FORSTER
07 Director of Admissions ... Mr. Fred QUISTGARD
84 Director of Enrollment Services ... Ms. Jessica MASI
37 Director Financial Aid ... Mr. David DAIGLE
13 Director of Technology ... Mr. Eric BOURQUE
21 Business Manager ... Vacant
15 Human Resources & Benefits Manager ... Ms. Ellen HARFORD
18 Manager of Facilities ... Mr. Dana PETERSEN
09 Assoc Dean of Inst Research ... Mr. Nicholas GILL

Maine Maritime Academy (C)

Pleasant Street, Castine ME 04420-0001
County: Hancock FICE Identification: 002044
Unit ID: 161299
Telephone: (207) 326-4311 Carnegie Class: Bac-Diverse
FAX Number: (207) 326-2218 Calendar System: Semester
URL: www.mma.edu
Established: 1941 Annual Undergrad Tuition & Fees (In-State): $12,788
Enrollment: 1,060 Coed
Affiliation or Control: State IRS Status: 501(c)3
Highest Offering: Master's
Accreditation: EH, ENG, ENGT

01 President ... Dr. William J. BRENNAN
05 Provost ... Dr. David GARDNER
11 VP Financial & Institutional Svcs ... Ms. Petra CARVER
84 VP Stdnt Svcs/Enrollment Mgmt ... Dr. Elizabeth TRUE
30 Vice President for Advancement ... Mr. Christopher HALEY
15 Human Resource Officer ... Mrs. Carrie MARGRAVE
32 Chief Student Life Officer ... Ms. Amanda NGUYEN
35 Dean of Student Services ... Ms. Deidra DAVIS
36 Placement Director ... Mr. Timothy LEACH
07 Director of Admissions ... Vacant
06 Registrar ... Ms. Christina STEPHENS
29 Director Alumni Relations ... Mr. Jeff WRIGHT
37 Director Student Financial Aid ... Ms. Kathy HEATH
38 Director Student Counseling ... Mr. Paul FERREIRA
08 Head Librarian ... Ms. Wendy GIRVEN
10 Chief Business Officer ... Ms. Diana SNAPP
18 Chief Facilities/Physical Plant ... Mr. Adam POTTER
20 Associate Academic Dean ... Dr. Susan LOOMIS
26 Chief Public Relations Officer ... Mrs. Jennifer DEJOY
09 Director of Institutional Research ... Mr. Ryan KING
96 Director of Purchasing ... Mrs. Alice HERRICK
28 Dir Policy/Institutional Equity ... Vacant
04 Executive Asst to President ... Ms. Rhonda VARNEY
13 Chief Info Technology Officer (CIO) ... Mrs. Lisa ROY
19 Director Security/Safety ... Mr. Ryan KUHL
41 Athletic Director ... Mr. Stephen PEED

Saint Joseph's College of Maine (D)

278 Whites Bridge Road, Standish ME 04084-5236
County: Cumberland FICE Identification: 002051
Unit ID: 161518
Telephone: (207) 892-6766 Carnegie Class: Masters/L
FAX Number: (207) 893-7861 Calendar System: Semester
URL: www.sjcme.edu
Established: 1912 Annual Undergrad Tuition & Fees: $32,620
Enrollment: 2,933 Coed
Affiliation or Control: Roman Catholic IRS Status: 501(c)3
Highest Offering: Master's
Accreditation: EH, NURSE

01 President ... Dr. James S. DLUGOS
05 VP & Chief Officer of Learning ... Dr. Michael PARDALES
30 VP & Chief Advancement Officer ... Ms. Joanne BEAN
84 VP Enrollment ... Ms. Lynne ROBINSON
88 VP for Sponsorship & Mission ... Vacant
10 VP & Chief Financial Officer ... Mr. Stuart KOOP
13 AVP Chief Information Officer ... Mr. Chip STILES
32 Asst Director Student Activities ... Mr. Matthew GAWEL
06 Director Academic Records/Registrar ... Mr. Kevin PAQUETTE
08 Director Library ... Ms. Shelly DAVIS
23 Director of Student Health Center ... Ms. Sheri PIERS
15 AVP/Chief Human Resources Officer ... Ms. Kristine AVERY

Thomas College (E)

180 W River Road, Waterville ME 04901-5097
County: Kennebec FICE Identification: 002052
Unit ID: 161563
Telephone: (207) 859-1111 Carnegie Class: Masters/S
FAX Number: (207) 859-1114 Calendar System: Semester
URL: www.thomas.edu
Established: 1894 Annual Undergrad Tuition & Fees: $24,300
Enrollment: 1,404 Coed
Affiliation or Control: Independent Non-Profit IRS Status: 501(c)3
Highest Offering: Master's
Accreditation: EH

01 President ... Ms. Laurie G. LACHANCE
03 Executive Vice President ... Mr. Bernie OUELLETTE
05 Provost ... Dr. Thomas EDWARDS
10 Senior Vice President/CFO/Treasurer ... Ms. Beth B. GIBBS
30 Vice Pres Advancement ... Mr. Robert M. MOORE
32 Vice President Student Affairs ... Ms. Lisa DESAUTELS-POLIQUIN
13 Vice Pres Information Services/CIO ... Mr. Christopher RHODA
84 Vice Pres Enrollment Management ... Mr. Jonathan KENT
44 Assistant Vice Pres Advancement ... Ms. Erin BALTES
35 Dean of Students ... Ms. Hannah GLADSTONE
20 Assistant Academic Dean ... Ms. Merlene SANBORN
15 Chief Human Resources Officer ... Ms. Michelle JOLER-LABBE
08 Director Library Services ... Ms. Lisa AURIEMMA
37 Director Student Financial Services ... Ms. Jeannine BOSSE
29 Director Alumni/Career Services ... Mr. Corey PELLETIER
18 Director Physical Plant ... Mr. James PARSONS
06 Registrar ... Ms. Lindsey NELSON
45 Director of Stategic Initiatives ... Ms. Mikaela ZIOBRO
04 Executive Asst to President ... Ms. Leta BILODEAU
41 Director of Athletics ... Mr. David ROUSSEL
26 Director of Publications ... Ms. Jennifer BUKER

Unity College (F)

90 Quaker Hill Road, Unity ME 04988-9502
County: Waldo FICE Identification: 006858
Unit ID: 161572
Telephone: (207) 509-7100 Carnegie Class: Bac-Diverse
FAX Number: (207) 512-1192 Calendar System: Semester
URL: www.unity.edu
Established: 1965 Annual Undergrad Tuition & Fees: $26,800
Enrollment: 601 Coed
Affiliation or Control: Independent Non-Profit IRS Status: 501(c)3
Highest Offering: Master's
Accreditation: EH

01 President ... Dr. Melik Peter KHOURY
100 Chief of Staff ... Dr. John ZAVODNY
05 Int Chief Academic Officer ... Dr. Rob SCOTT
10 Chief Business Officer ... Mr. Brent E. WEST
30 Chief Fundraising Ofcr/Development ... Mrs. Erica HUTCHINSON
13 Chief Information Officer ... Mr. Bert AUDETTE
26 Chief Marketing Officer (CMO) ... Ms. Diane RAY
106 Chief Distance Education Officer ... Dr. Michelle CAMINOS
88 Chief Sustainability Officer ... Ms. Jennifer DEHART
101 Secretary to Board ... Ms. Chris MELANSON
04 Executive Assistant ... Ms. Kimberly SHEFF
06 Registrar ... Ms. Heather A. MCANIRLIN
32 Dean of Student Affairs ... Mr. Gary ZANE
07 Director of Admissions ... Mr. Joseph SALTALAMACHIA
09 Director of Institutional Research ... Ms. Holly HEIN
41 Director of Athletics ... Mr. Chris KEIN
109 Director Dining Services ... Ms. Lorey DUPREY
36 Director Career Services ... Ms. Nicole COLLINS
18 Director Facilities & Public Safety ... Mr. Daniel LAFORGE
37 Director Financial Aid ... Mr. Rand E. NEWELL
23 Director Health & Wellness Center ... Ms. Anna MCGALLIARD
15 Director Human Resources ... Ms. Bethany DRIGGS
24 Director Learning Resource Center ... Dr. James HECK
08 Director Quimby Library ... Ms. Sandra ABBOTT-STOUT
88 Director Outdoor Adventure Center ... Ms. Jessica STEELE
39 Director Residence Life ... Mr. Stephen S. NASON
35 Director Student Accounts ... Ms. Jeri ROBERTS
88 Director Writing Center ... Ms. Judy WILLIAMS
53 Director of Teacher Education ... Dr. Jennifer CARTIER
27 Assoc Dir College Communications ... Mr. Bob MENTZINGER
19 Chief Public Safety Officer ... Mr. Dean BESSEY
88 Community-Based/Internship Coord ... Ms. Reeta BENEDICT
40 Manager Bookstore ... Ms. Leigh JUSKEVICE

*University of Maine System Office (G)

16 Central Street, Bangor ME 04401-5106
County: Penobscot FICE Identification: 008012
Unit ID: 161280
Telephone: (207) 973-3200 Carnegie Class: N/A
FAX Number: (207) 973-3296
URL: www.maine.edu

01 Chancellor ... Dr. James H. PAGE
10 CFO & Treasurer ... Mr. Ryan LOW
43 University Counsel ... Mr. James B. THELEN
86 Asst Dir of Comm/Governmental Rels ... Ms. Alison P. SUCY
101 Clerk of the Board ... Ms. Tracy BIGNEY
32 Chief Student Affairs Officer ... Ms. Rosa REDONNETT
13 Chief Information Officer ... Mr. Dick THOMPSON
18 Chief General Services Officer ... Mr. M. F. Chip GAVIN
15 Chief Human Resources Officer ... Ms. Lynda DEC
26 Exec Director of Public Affairs ... Mr. Daniel DEMERITT

*University of Maine (H)

Orono ME 04469-0001
County: Penobscot FICE Identification: 002053
Unit ID: 161253
Telephone: (207) 581-1110 Carnegie Class: DU-Higher
FAX Number: (207) 581-1604 Calendar System: Semester
URL: www.umaine.edu
Established: 1865 Annual Undergrad Tuition & Fees (In-State): $10,610
Enrollment: 11,286 Coed
Affiliation or Control: State IRS Status: 501(c)3
Highest Offering: Doctorate
Accreditation: EH, ART, BUS, CAATE, CEA, CLPSY, CS, DIETD, DIETI, ENG, ENGT, IPSY, MUS, NURSE, SP, SW, TED

02 President ... Dr. Susan J. HUNTER
05 Exec VP Academic Affairs/Provost ... Dr. Jeffrey E. HECKER
10 Assoc VC & Chief Financial Officer ... Mr. Ryan LOW
102 Pres Univ of Maine Foundation ... Dr. Jeffery N. MILLS
32 VP Student Affs/Dean of Students ... Dr. Robert Q. DANA
46 Vice President for Research ... Dr. Carol H. KIM
84 Int VP Enrollment Management ... Mr. Joel WINCOWSKI
88 VP Innovation/Economic Development ... Mr. James WARD, IV
15 Interim Director of Human Resources ... Mr. Larry LEWELLEN
21 Chief Business Officer ... Mrs. Claire I. STRICKLAND
20 Sr Assoc Prov/Dean Undergrad Educ ... Dr. Jeffrey E. ST. JOHN
100 Chief of Staff ... CAPT. Jim D. SETTELE
08 Dean of Libraries ... Ms. Joyce V. RUMERY
13 Assoc Chief Information Officer ... Ms. Cindy MITCHELL
18 Exec Dir Facilities/Capital Mgt Svc ... Mr. Stewart A. HARVEY
26 Sr Dir Univ Relations/Operations ... Ms. Margaret A. NAGLE
109 Exec Director of Auxiliary Services ... Mr. Daniel H. STURRUP
25 Dir Research & Sponsored Programs ... Mr. Michael M. HASTINGS
06 Registrar ... Ms. Kimberly D. PAGE
07 Asst Dir Graduate Enrollment Svcs ... Ms. Sharon M. OLIVER
37 Director of Financial Aid ... Ms. Sarah DOHENY
36 Director of Career Center ... Ms. Crisanne BLACKIE
09 Director Institutional Studies ... Mr. Ted T. COLADARCI
85 Int Director International Programs ... Ms. Sarah JOUGHIN
41 Athletic Director ... Mr. Karlton W. CREECH
28 Director Equal Employment Diversity ... Ms. Jacqueline D. HYMES
19 Chief Police Dept ... Chief Roland J. LACROIX
29 President/Exec Dir Alumni Assn ... Mr. John N. DIAMOND
40 Interim Director of Bookstore ... Mr. Richard YOUNG
96 Director of Procurement Services ... Mr. Kevin CARR
38 Director Student Counseling ... Mr. Douglas P. JOHNSON
27 Director Strategic Communications ... Ms. Jen O'LEARY
49 Dean Liberal Arts & Sciences ... Dr. Emily A. HADDAD
50 Dean Maine Business School ... Dr. Ivan M. MANEV
53 Dean Educ/Human Development ... Dr. Timothy G. REAGAN
54 Dean Engineering ... Dr. Dana N. HUMPHREY
65 Dean Natural Science/Forestry/Agric ... Dr. Edward N. ASHWORTH
51 Dean Lifelong Learning ... Dr. Monique M. LAROCQUE
58 Dean Graduate School ... Dr. Carol KIM

*University of Maine at Augusta (I)

46 University Drive, Augusta ME 04330-9410
County: Kennebec FICE Identification: 006760
Unit ID: 161217
Telephone: (207) 621-3000 Carnegie Class: Bac-Diverse

FAX Number: (207) 621-3116 Calendar System: Semester
URL: www.uma.edu
Established: 1965 Annual Undergrad Tuition & Fees (In-State): $7,448
Enrollment: 4,664 Coed
Affiliation or Control: State IRS Status: 501(c)3
Highest Offering: Baccalaureate
Accreditation: EH, ADNUR, DA, DH, MLTAD, NUR

02 President ... Dr. James CONNEELY
05 Vice President/Provost ... Dr. Joe S. SZAKAS
10 Chief Business Officer ... Mr. Tim BROKAW
11 Exec Director of Admin Services ... Ms. Sheri R. STEVENS
30 VP for Univ Advance/Chief of Staff ... Ms. Joyce BLANCHARD
84 VP Stdnt Engagement/Enroll Mgt ... Dr. Claire GOOD
08 Int Director of UMA Library Svcs ... Mr. Ben TREAT
32 Dean of Students ... Ms. Sheri FRASER
107 Dean College of Prof Studies ... Ms. Brenda MCALEER
37 Director of Financial Aid ... Ms. Sherry MCCOLLETT
06 Registrar ... Ms. Ann CORBETT
15 Director of Human Resources ... Mr. David LANE
18 Chief Facilities/Physical Plant ... Mr. Peter ST. MICHEL
38 Director of Counseling ... Ms. Jennifer MASCARO
07 Dir of Enrollment Svcs & Advising ... Ms. Tricia DYER
40 Director Bookstore ... Mr. Jerry GARTHOFF
26 Exec Dir of Marketing & Pub Rel ... Mr. Mark TARDIF
09 Senior Strategy Advisor for Org Eff ... Mr. Gregory LAPOINTE
49 Dean College of Arts & Sciences ... Mr. Greg FAHY

*University of Maine at Farmington (A)

224 Main Street, Farmington ME 04938-1911
County: Franklin FICE Identification: 002040
Unit ID: 161226
Telephone: (207) 778-7000 Carnegie Class: Bac-Diverse
FAX Number: (207) 778-7247 Calendar System: Semester
URL: www.umf.maine.edu
Established: 1864 Annual Undergrad Tuition & Fees (In-State): $9,217
Enrollment: 1,960 Coed
Affiliation or Control: State IRS Status: 501(c)3
Highest Offering: Master's
Accreditation: EH, TED

02 President ... Dr. Kathryn A. FOSTER
05 Vice Pres Academic Affairs/Provost ... Dr. Joseph P. MCGINN
10 Exec Dir Finance & Administration ... Ms. Laurie A. GARDNER
32 Vice Pres Student & Community Svcs ... Ms. Celeste BRANHAM
84 Vice Pres for Enrollment ... Mr. Jared CASH
88 Sustainability Coordinator ... Dr. Lucas C. KELLETT
53 Assoc Provost & Dean of Education ... Dr. Katherine W. YARDLEY
20 Assoc Provost ... Dr. Jonathan COHEN
92 Director of Honors Program ... Dr. Eric BROWN
88 Dir of Learning Assistance Center ... Ms. Jessica BERRY
37 Financial Aid Director ... Mr. Ronald P. MILLIKEN
21 Director of Finance ... Ms. Kathleen P. FALCO
88 Dir Center for Student Development ... Mr. Robert A. PEDERSON
26 Assoc Director of Media Relations ... Ms. April C. MULHERIN
13 IT Operations Manager ... Ms. Nicole HAGGAN
41 Dir Athletics/Fitness & Recreation ... Ms. Julie A. DAVIS
88 Dir Fitness & Recreation Center ... Mr. James D. TONER
35 Director Student Life ... Mr. Brian K. UFFORD
23 Director Student Health Center ... Dr. Susan E. COCHRAN
18 Director of Facilities Management ... Mr. Jeffrey MCKAY
19 Director of Public Safety ... Mr. Brock E. CATON
27 Dir of Marketing and Communications ... Ms. Jennifer A. ERIKSEN

*University of Maine at Fort Kent (B)

23 University Drive, Fort Kent ME 04743-1292
County: Aroostook FICE Identification: 002041
Unit ID: 161235
Telephone: (207) 834-7500 Carnegie Class: Bac-Diverse
FAX Number: (207) 834-7503 Calendar System: Semester
URL: www.umfk.maine.edu
Established: 1878 Annual Undergrad Tuition & Fees (In-State): $7,575
Enrollment: 1,327 Coed
Affiliation or Control: State IRS Status: 501(c)3
Highest Offering: Baccalaureate
Accreditation: EH, IACBE, NURSE

02 Interim President ... Dr. John N. SHORT
05 Vice President Academic Affairs ... Dr. Steven GAMMON
10 Vice President for Administration ... Mr. John D. MURPHY
31 Dean of Community Education ... Mr. Scott A. VOISINE
84 Dean Enrollment Svcs/Student Life ... Ms. Ellia SABLAN-ZEBEDY
36 Assistant Dean of Student Success ... Ms. Christine NUNEMAKER
06 Registrar ... Mr. Mark SCHENK
15 Senior HR Business Partner ... Mr. Douglas HISE
66 Nursing Division Director ... Ms. Erin SOUCY
08 Dir of Information Svcs/Library ... Ms. Leslie E. KELLY
07 Director of Admissions ... Ms. Jill CAIRNS
37 Director of Financial Aid ... Ms. Lisa M. LIPE
18 Director of Facilities Management ... Mr. Andrew C. JACOBS
22 Director of Administrative Services ... Ms. Pamela ASHBY
29 Director Alumni Relations ... Vacant
32 Assoc Dean Student Life/Development ... Mr. Raymond R. PHINNEY
09 Assoc Dir of Institutional Research ... Mr. Joseph R. BJERKLIE
30 Development Officer ... Ms. Linda DEPREY

*University of Maine at Machias (C)

116 O'Brien Avenue, Machias ME 04654-1397
County: Washington FICE Identification: 002055
Unit ID: 161244
Telephone: (207) 255-1200 Carnegie Class: Bac-A&S
FAX Number: (207) 255-4864 Calendar System: Semester
URL: www.umm.maine.edu
Established: 1909 Annual Undergrad Tuition & Fees (In-State): $7,480
Enrollment: 810 Coed
Affiliation or Control: State IRS Status: 501(c)3
Highest Offering: Baccalaureate
Accreditation: EH, NRPA

02 Interim President ... Dr. Sue HUSEMAN
05 Vice Pres Academic Affairs/Provost ... Dr. Stuart G. SWAIN
10 Chief Financial Officer ... Mr. Mark HATT
32 Dean of Students and Admissions ... Dr. Melvin ADAMS
06 Registrar ... Ms. Mary STOVER
08 Director Library ... Ms. Marianne THIBODEAU
15 Director Human Resources ... Ms. Kim PAGE
37 Director Student Financial Aid ... Mrs. Katie KURZ
18 Director Physical Facilities ... Mr. Robert FARRIS
26 Director Public Relations ... Ms. Sharon K. MACK
41 Director Athletics ... Ms. Betsy HAYDEN
13 IT Operations Manager ... Mr. Alan KRYSZAK

*University of Maine at Presque Isle (D)

181 Main Street, Presque Isle ME 04769-2888
County: Aroostook FICE Identification: 002033
Unit ID: 161341
Telephone: (207) 768-9400 Carnegie Class: Bac-Diverse
FAX Number: (207) 768-9608 Calendar System: Semester
URL: www.umpi.edu
Established: 1903 Annual Undergrad Tuition & Fees (In-State): $7,300
Enrollment: 1,138 Coed
Affiliation or Control: State IRS Status: 501(c)3
Highest Offering: Baccalaureate
Accreditation: EH, #CAATE, MLTAD, PTAA, SW

02 Interim President ... Dr. Raymond J. RICE
05 Vice President Academic Affairs ... Dr. Raymond J. RICE
10 Campus Business Officer ... Mr. Benjamin SHAW
37 Dir Financial Services/Operations ... Mr. Christopher BELL
32 Dean of Students ... Mr. James D. STEPP
07 Director of Admissions ... Ms. Erin V. BENSON
06 Registrar ... Ms. Kathy K. DAVIS
15 HR Senior Business Partner/AA/EEO ... Mr. Douglas HISE
08 Director of Library Services ... Mr. Roger GETZ
36 Director of Career Preparation ... Ms. Nicole FOURNIER
39 Interim Director Residence Life ... Mr. James D. STEPP
41 Director of Athletics ... Mr. Michael S. HOLMES
26 Director of Media Relations ... Ms. Rachel RICE
30 Exec Dir of University Advancement ... Ms. Debbie ROARK
40 Bookstore Manager ... Mr. Greg DOAK
18 Director of Facilities Management ... Mr. Gregg BOUCHARD
19 Director Security/Safety ... Mr. Frederick A. THOMAS
88 Director of Student Success ... Ms. Vanessa PEARSON

*University of Southern Maine (E)

96 Falmouth Street, PO Box 9300,
Portland ME 04101-9300
County: Cumberland FICE Identification: 002054
Unit ID: 161554
Telephone: (207) 780-4141 Carnegie Class: Masters/L
FAX Number: (207) 780-4933 Calendar System: Semester
URL: www.usm.maine.edu
Established: 1878 Annual Undergrad Tuition & Fees (In-State): $7,796
Enrollment: 8,428 Coed
Affiliation or Control: State IRS Status: 501(c)3
Highest Offering: Doctorate
Accreditation: EH, ART, BUS, CAATE, CACREP, CORE, CS, ENG, EXSC, HSA, LAW, MUS, NAIT, NURSE, OT, SW, TEAC

02 President ... Dr. Glenn T. CUMMINGS
05 Provost/VPAA ... Dr. Jeannine UZZI
10 Chief Financial Officer/VP Admin ... Mr. Buster NEEL
84 VP Enrollment Management ... Ms. Nancy E. GRIFFIN
30 Vice President for Advancement ... Mr. George CAMPBELL
09 Assoc Dir Institutional Research ... Ms. Patricia DAVIS
18 Exec Director Facilities Management ... Mr. Adam THIBODEAU
96 Director of Purchasing and Payables ... Vacant
08 University Librarian ... Mr. David NUTTY
108 Director Academic Assessment Ctr ... Ms. Susan L. KING
38 Director of Health & Counseling ... Dr. Kristine BERTINI
15 Chief Human Resources Office ... Ms. Natalie JONES
26 Executive Director Public Affairs ... Mr. Bob STEIN
37 Director of Financial Aid ... Mr. Keith DUBOIS
32 Executive Director Student Success ... Ms. Elizabeth HIGGINS
07 Director Admissions ... Mr. Andrew KING
06 Registrar ... Ms. Karin PIRES
22 Director of Equal Opportunity ... Vacant
72 Director CTEL ... Mr. Paul COCHRANE
31 Director of Community Standards ... Ms. Joy PUFHAL
41 Director of Athletics & Rec Sports ... Mr. Al BEAN
39 Director of Residential Life ... Mr. Jason SAUCIER
40 Director of USM Bookstore ... Vacant
61 Dean School of Law ... Ms. Danielle CONWAY
50 Int Dean College of Mgmt/Human Svcs ... Dr. Joanne WILLIAMS
72 Dean College of Sci/Tech & Health ... Dr. James GRAVES
49 Int Dean Arts/Humanities/Soc Sci ... Dr. Adam TUCHINSKY
12 Dean Lewiston-Auburn College ... Dr. Joyce GIBSON
88 Director of Community-Based Lrng ... Dr. Susan MCWILLIAMS
24 Manager Audiovisual/Media Services ... Ms. Angela COOK
94 Director of Women's Studies ... Dr. Lisa WALKER
85 Coordinator Multicultural Affairs ... Mr. Reza JALALI
29 Director of Alumni Relations ... Ms. Betsy UHUAD
27 Director of Marketing ... Ms. Traci ST. PIERRE
102 President & CEO USM Foundation ... Mr. George CAMPBELL
46 Director of Research ... Ms. Kris SAHONCHIK

University of New England (F)

11 Hills Beach Road, Biddeford ME 04005-9988
County: York FICE Identification: 002050
Unit ID: 161457
Telephone: (207) 283-0171 Carnegie Class: Masters/L
FAX Number: (207) 282-6379 Calendar System: Semester
URL: www.une.edu
Established: 1831 Annual Undergrad Tuition & Fees: $34,760
Enrollment: 6,429 Coed
Affiliation or Control: Independent Non-Profit IRS Status: 501(c)3
Highest Offering: Doctorate
Accreditation: EH, ACBSP, ANEST, ARCPA, CAATE, DENT, DH, NUR, OSTEO, OT, PH, PHAR, PTA, SW

01 President ... Dr. Danielle RIPICH
04 Executive Asst to the President ... Ms. Holly HAMMOND NASS
05 Provost & Senior Vice President ... Dr. James KOELBL
06 Registrar ... Vacant
07 Dean of University Admissions ... Mr. Scott STEINBERG
23 Sr Vice Pres for Health Affairs ... Dr. Douglas WOOD
58 VP Strategic Initiatives ... Dr. Ellen BEAULIEU
18 Vice Pres of Operations ... Mr. William BOLA
88 Vice President Clinical Affairs ... Dr. Dora MILLS
10 Vice Pres Finance and Admin ... Ms. Nicole TRUFANT
30 Vice Pres Institutional Advancement ... Mr. Bill CHANCE
32 Vice Pres Student Affairs ... Vacant
15 Exec Dir Human Resources ... Ms. Sharen BEAULIEU
82 VP Global Affairs & Communications ... Dr. Anouar MAJID
46 VP for Research & Scholarship ... Dr. Edward BILSKY
106 Dean College of Grad/Prof Studies ... Dr. Martha WILSON
49 Dean College Arts & Sciences ... Dr. Jeanne HEY
17 Dean College Health Professions ... Dr. Elizabeth FRANCIS-CONNOLLY
63 Dean College Osteopathic Medicine ... Dr. Douglas WOOD
67 Dean College of Pharmacy ... Dr. Gayle BRAZEAU
52 Dean of College Dental Medicine ... Dr. Jon RYDER
62 Dean Library Services ... Mr. Andrew GOLUB
35 Dean of Students ... Vacant
88 Asst Dean Student Support Svcs ... Dr. John LANGEVIN
17 Assoc Dean College Health Prof ... Dr. Karen PARDUE
49 Assoc Dean College Arts & Sciences ... Dr. Susan GRAY
29 Director Alumni Relations ... Ms. Amy HAIL
39 Asst Dean of Students Res Life ... Ms. Jennifer DEBURRO
41 Assoc VP & Director of Athletics ... Mr. Jack MCDONALD
09 Director for Institutional Research ... Ms. Margaret MOREMEN
88 Director Campus Planning ... Mr. Alan THIBEAULT
19 Director Campus Safety & Security ... Mr. Donald CLARK
96 Director Purch/Risk Mgmt/Contract ... Mr. William BOLA
62 Director Reference Services ... Ms. Barbara SWARTZLANDER
28 Assoc Dir Multi-Cult Affs/Diversity ... Mr. Richard ANDERSON MARTINEZ
25 Director Sponsored Programs ... Mr. Nicholas GERE
38 Director Student Counseling ... Dr. John LANGEVIN
57 Exec Director Student Fiscal Svcs ... Mr. Paul HENDERSON
100 Senior Advisor to the President and ... Mr. John TUMIEL
104 Director Study Abroad/Global Educa ... Ms. Emily DRAGON
108 Director Institutional Assessment ... Ms. Margy MOREMEN
13 Chief Info Technology Officer (CIO) ... Mr. Craig LOFTUS
36 Director Career Services ... Dr. Mary JONES

MARYLAND

Allegany College of Maryland (G)

12401 Willowbrook Road, SE,
Cumberland MD 21502-2596
County: Allegany FICE Identification: 002057
Unit ID: 161688
Telephone: (301) 784-5000 Carnegie Class: Assoc/MT-VT-High Trad
FAX Number: (301) 784-5050 Calendar System: Semester
URL: www.allegany.edu
Established: 1961 Annual Undergrad Tuition & Fees (In-District): $3,660
Enrollment: 3,227 Coed
Affiliation or Control: Local IRS Status: 501(c)3
Highest Offering: Associate Degree
Accreditation: M, ADNUR, COARC, COMTA, CSHSE, DH, MAC, MLTAD, OTA, PTAA, RAD

01 President ... Dr. Cynthia S. BAMBARA
05 Vice Pres Instructional Affairs ... Dr. David HINDS
10 Vice President Finance ... Mr. David DEWITT
30 VP Col Advancement/Enroll Mgmt ... Mrs. Linda A. PRICE
11 VP Administrative Services ... Dr. Mona CLITES
32 VP Student Services ... Dr. B. Renee CONNER
51 VP of Continuing Education ... Mr. Jeff KIRK
13 Assoc Dean Computer Services ... Vacant
09 Assoc Dean Institutional Research ... Mr. Scott HARRAH
30 Vice Pres of Grants & Development ... Mr. David R. JONES
37 Director Student Financial Aid ... Mrs. Vicki SMITH
07 Director Admissions/Registration ... Ms. Carol KAUFFMAN
18 Director of Physical Plant ... Mr. Adam PHIPPS
08 Director Learning Resources ... Mr. Matthew HAY
26 Dir Public Relations/Recruitment ... Ms. Shauna N. MCQUADE
41 Athletic Director ... Mr. Steve BAZARNIC
51 Director Professional Cont Educ ... Mrs. Becky L. RUPPERT

69 Director Health Prof Cont Education .... Ms. Linda ATKINSON
38 Director Student Counseling ....Vacant
15 Director Human Resources ....Mr. Chris EVERETT

Ana G. Mendez University System Capital Area Campus (A)

11006 Veirs Mill Road, Wheaton MD 20902
Telephone: (301) 949-2224 Identification: 770924
Accreditation: &M

† Regional accreditation is carried under the parent institution in Rio Piedras, PR

Anne Arundel Community College (B)

101 College Parkway, Arnold MD 21012-1895
County: Anne Arundel FICE Identification: 002058
Unit ID: 161767
Telephone: (410) 777-2222 Carnegie Class: Assoc/HT-Mix Trad/Non
FAX Number: (410) 777-2489 Calendar System: Semester
URL: www.aacc.edu
Established: 1961 Annual Undergrad Tuition & Fees (In-District): $4,464
Enrollment: 15,274 Coed
Affiliation or Control: State/Local IRS Status: 501(c)3
Highest Offering: Associate Degree
Accreditation: M, ACFEI, ADNUR, ARCPA, CAHIIM, CSHSE, EMT, MAC, MLTAD, PTAA, RAD, SURGT

01 President ....Dr. Dawn S. LINDSAY
05 VP for Learning ....Dr. Michael H. GAVIN
10 VP Learning Resources Management .... Ms. Melissa A. BEARDMORE
03 VP for Learner Support Services .... Ms. Felicia L. PATTERSON
106 Dean of Virtual Campus ....Ms. Frances TURCOTT
20 Associate VP for Learning ....Dr. Claire L. SMITH
30 Director of Development ....Mr. Vollie D. MELSON
32 Dean of Student Services ....Dr. Jacqueline S. JACKSON
76 Dean School Health/Wellness/Phys Ed ....Dr. Elizabeth H. APPEL
66 Director of Nursing ....Ms. Beth Anne BATTURS
49 Dean School of Liberal Arts .... Dr. Alicia MORSE
50 Dean School of Business & Law ....Ms. Karen COOK
81 Dean School of Science & Technology ..... Dr. Bruce A. BOWMAN
51 Dean Sch Cont Educ & Workforce Dev ....Dr. Faith A. HARLAND-WHITE
22 Controller ....Ms. Martha D. ROTHSCHILD
21 Executive Director of Finance ....Mr. Andrew P. LITTLE
13 Chief Technology Officer/Info Svcs ....Ms. Shirin M. GOODARZI
08 Director of Library ....Ms. Cynthia K. STEINHOFF
06 Registrar ....Ms. Nancy A. BEIER
09 Dean Plng/Rsrch/Inst Assess ....Dr. Ricka K. FINE
15 Exec Director of Human Resources ....Ms. Suzanne L. BOYER
26 Exec Director PR & Marketing ....Mr. Daniel B. BAUM
37 Director of Financial Aid ....Mr. Richard C. HEATH
07 Dir Admissions/Enroll Development ... Mr. Thomas J. MCGINN, III
11 Exec Dir of Administrative Services ...Mr. Maury L. CHAPUT, JR.
35 Asst Dean Student Devel & Success ....Vacant
84 Dean Enrollment Services ....Dr. John F. GRABOWSKI
36 Dir Counseling/Advising/Reten Svcs ....Ms. Bonnie J. GARRETT
35 Director of Student Life ....Ms. Christine M. STORCK
22 Federal Compliance Officer ....Ms. Suzanne L. BOYER
40 College Bookstore Manager ....Mr. Steven M. PEGG
19 Director Public Safety ....Mr. J. Gary LYLE
96 Director Purchasing/Contracting ....Ms. Melanie L. SCHERER
29 Manager Major Giving .... Ms. Jenny CRAWFORD
23 Coordinator Health Services ....Ms. Beth A. MAYS
41 Athletic Director ....Mr. Duane HERR
28 Coordinator of Minority Recruitment ....Mr. James T. JACKSON, JR.
94 Coordinator of Women's Studies ....Dr. Suzanne J. SPOOR
88 Director of Environmental Center ....Dr. M. Stephen AILSTOCK
88 Director Center Study Local Issues ....Dr. Daniel D. NATAF
88 Dir Homeland Sec/Crim Justice Inst ....Dr. Tyrone POWERS
53 Director TEACH Institute ....Ms. Colleen K. EISENBEISER
88 Director Hosp/Cul Arts/Tourism Inst .... Ms. Mary Ellen MASON
38 Coordinator Inst for the Future ....Mr. Steven T. HENICK
88 Dir Sarbanes Center/Pub & Cmty Svc ..... Ms. Cathleen H. DOYLE
28 Chief Diversity Officer ....Mr. James A. FELTON, III
04 Administrative Asst to President ....Ms. Judy HEATH
18 Dir Facilities Planning & Construc ....Mr. James TAYLOR
25 Director Sponsored Programs ....Ms. Deborah A. MERCADO

Bais HaMedrash & Mesivta of Baltimore (C)

6823 Old Pimlico Road, Baltimore MD 21209
County: Baltimore FICE Identification: 041884
Unit ID: 476601
Telephone: (410) 486-0006 Carnegie Class: Spec-4-yr-Faith
FAX Number: (410) 602-9738 Calendar System: Semester
Established: 1997 Annual Undergrad Tuition & Fees: $12,450
Enrollment: 59 Male
Affiliation or Control: Independent Non-Profit IRS Status: 501(c)3
Highest Offering: First Talmudic Degree
Accreditation: RABN

01 Rosh Yeshiva .... Rabbi Zvi Dov SLANGER

Baltimore City Community College (D)

2901 Liberty Heights Avenue, Baltimore MD 21215-7893
County: Baltimore City FICE Identification: 002061
Unit ID: 161864
Telephone: (410) 462-8300 Carnegie Class: Assoc/HT-Mix Trad/Non
FAX Number: (410) 462-7795 Calendar System: Semester
URL: www.bccc.edu
Established: 1947 Annual Undergrad Tuition & Fees (In-State): $2,578
Enrollment: 5,024 Coed
Affiliation or Control: State IRS Status: 501(c)3
Highest Offering: Associate Degree
Accreditation: M, ACBSP, ADNUR, COARC, DH, PTAA, SURGT

01 President and CEO ....Dr. Gordon F. MAY
10 VP Business & Finance ....Mr. Calvin HARRIS, JR.
32 Interim VP for Student Affairs ....Dr. Tonja RINGGOLD
05 VP Academic Affairs ....Dr. Tonja RINGGOLD
51 Vice Pres Business & Cont Educ .... Mr. Gregory MASON
84 Dean of Enrollment Management ....Vacant
30 InteVP of Institutional Advancement .... Dr. Nassim EBRAHIMI
18 Dir Facilities/Plng/Operations ....Vacant
21 Controller/Chief of Accounting ....Ms. Sabina SILKWORTH
37 Director Student Financial Aid ....Ms. Vera BROOKS
13 Int Chief Information Tech Officer ....Dr. Tom WAMALWA
08 Director Library/Media Services ....Vacant
06 Exec Director Records/Registrar .... Ms. Sylvia ROCHESTER
15 Executive Director of HR ....Vacant
09 Director of Institutional Research ....Ms. Eileen HAWKINS
96 Chief Procurement Officer ....Mr. Daniel COLEMAN
04 Executive Asst to the President .... Ms. Valerie MCQUEEN-BEY
07 Director of Admissions ....Ms. Deneen DANGERFIELD
101 Asst to President Board Relations ..... Ms. Valerie MCQUEEN-BEY
106 Director of E-Learning ....Dr. Diana ZILBERMAN
19 Director of Public Safety ....Vacant
36 Coordinator Job Placement ....Mr. Vincent WHITMORE
41 Director Intercollegiate Athletics ....Ms. Tara OWENS
86 Director Government Relations .... Ms. Shanetta PASKEL
100 Chief of Staff ....Mr. Bryan PERRY

Brightwood College (E)

1520 S Caton Avenue, Baltimore MD 21227-1063
County: Baltimore City FICE Identification: 007491
Unit ID: 163736
Telephone: (410) 644-6400 Carnegie Class: Spec 2-yr-Tech
FAX Number: (410) 644-6481 Calendar System: Quarter
URL: www.brightwood.edu
Established: 1956 Annual Undergrad Tuition & Fees: N/A
Enrollment: 582 Coed
Affiliation or Control: Proprietary IRS Status: Proprietary
Highest Offering: Associate Degree
Accreditation: ACICS

01 Campus President .... Mr. Kevin BEAVER
05 Director of Education .... Ms. Greta BONAPARTE

Brightwood College (F)

4600 Powder Mill Road, Suite 500, Beltsville MD 20705-2649
County: Prince Georges FICE Identification: 020836
Unit ID: 164058
Telephone: (301) 937-8448 Carnegie Class: Assoc/HVT-Mix Trad/Non
FAX Number: (301) 937-5327 Calendar System: Quarter
URL: www.brightwood.edu
Established: 1956 Annual Undergrad Tuition & Fees: N/A
Enrollment: 388 Coed
Affiliation or Control: Proprietary IRS Status: Proprietary
Highest Offering: Associate Degree
Accreditation: ACICS

01 Campus President ....Mr. Karl E. JEFFERSON

Brightwood College (G)

803 Glen Eagles Court, Towson MD 21286-2201
County: Baltimore FICE Identification: 010410
Unit ID: 161776
Telephone: (410) 828-2600 Carnegie Class: Assoc/HVT-Mix Trad/Non
FAX Number: (410) 296-5356 Calendar System: Quarter
URL: www.brightwood.edu
Established: 1956 Annual Undergrad Tuition & Fees: N/A
Enrollment: 318 Coed
Affiliation or Control: Proprietary IRS Status: Proprietary
Highest Offering: Associate Degree
Accreditation: ACICS

01 President ....Mr. Jeremiah STAROPOLI
07 Director of Admissions .... Mr. Dru YOKUM

Capitol Technology University (H)

11301 Springfield Road, Laurel MD 20708-9759
County: Prince Georges FICE Identification: 001436
Unit ID: 162061
Telephone: (301) 369-2800 Carnegie Class: Spec-4-yr-Eng
FAX Number: (301) 953-1442 Calendar System: Semester
URL: www.captechu.edu
Established: 1927 Annual Undergrad Tuition & Fees: $23,508
Enrollment: 793 Coed
Affiliation or Control: Independent Non-Profit IRS Status: 501(c)3
Highest Offering: Doctorate
Accreditation: M, ENG, ENGT, IACBE

01 President ....Dr. Michael T. WOOD
05 Vice President for Academic Affairs ....Dr. W. Vic MACONACHY
10 Vice Pres Finance/Administration ....Jeffrey L. WILLIAMS
84 Vice Pres for Enrollment & Student ....Dianne M. O'NEILL
30 Vice President Advancement ....Dr. Donna THOMAS
20 Dean of Academics ....Dr. Helen G. BARKER
32 Dean Student Life & Retention ...... Melinda A. BUNNELL-RHYNE
54 Dean Engineering/Computer Sci/Tech ....Vacant
06 Director of Registration & Records ....Greg HUGHES
08 Dir Library/Information Literacy ....Vacant
11 Dir Administration/Human Resources ....Tammy VOLBERDING
07 Senior Director Admissions ....George H. WALLS
26 Director Communications ....Robert HERSCHBACH
29 Assistant Dir Development ....Vacant
07 Dir Admissions Operations ....Meghan YOUNG
37 Director of Financial Aid ....Kim WITTLER
21 Director of Finance ....Kathleen WERNER
51 Director of Continuing Education ....Vacant
90 Director Academic Computing ....Allen EXNER
18 Director of Maintenance ....Bruce RIBB
04 Administrative Asst to President ....Aletha R. WADE

Carroll Community College (I)

1601 Washington Road, Westminster MD 21157-6913
County: Carroll FICE Identification: 031007
Unit ID: 405872
Telephone: (410) 386-8000 Carnegie Class: Assoc/HT-High Trad
FAX Number: (410) 386-8181 Calendar System: Semester
URL: www.carrollcc.edu
Established: 1993 Annual Undergrad Tuition & Fees (In-District): $3,619
Enrollment: 3,645 Coed
Affiliation or Control: Local IRS Status: 501(c)3
Highest Offering: Associate Degree
Accreditation: M, PTAA

01 President ....Dr. James D. BALL
10 Exec Vice Pres Administration ....Mr. Alan M. SCHUMAN
05 VP of Academic & Student Affairs ....Dr. Jan OHLEMACHER
45 VP Planning Marketing & Assessment ....Dr. Craig A. CLAGETT
51 VP Continuing Education/Training ....Ms. Karen L. MERKLE
30 Exec Dir Inst Devel/College Found ....Mr. Steven WANTZ
88 Integrity & Judicial Affairs Advoc ....Mr. Joel M. HOSKOWITZ
26 Dir of Communication & Media Rels ....Ms. Sylvia BLAIR
50 Div Chair Business & Technology ....Mr. Robert BROWN
60 Div Chair English & Modern Language ......Ms. Siobhan WRIGHT
76 Div Chair Allied Health ....Dr. Nancy PERRY
83 Div Chair Social Sciences ....Dr. Michael STOVALL
54 Div Chair Mathematics/Engineer ....Ms. Maria BURNESS
81 Div Chair Sciences ....Dr. Raza KHAN
53 Div Chair Educ & Trans Studies ....Ms. Susan SIES
97 Div Chair Humanities & Perf Arts ....Dr. Robert YOUNG
57 Div Chair Fine Arts ....Mr. Scott GORE
88 Sr Dir Student Engagement/Compl ....Dr. Kristie CRUMLEY
06 Registrar ....Ms. Elizabeth WINGERT
38 Dir Advise/Transfer/Stdnt Placement ..... Ms. Janenne CORCORAN
88 Director Transfer ....Mr. Paul HUNTER
07 Sr Director Enrollment Development ....Ms. Candace EDWARDS
37 Director of Financial Aid ....Mr. John GAY
08 Sr Dir Library/Media/Dist Learning ....Mr. Alan BOGAGE
106 Director Distance Learning Programs ....Vacant
27 Director Publications/Comm Design .... Dr. Maya DEMISHKEVICH
09 Director Institutional Research ....Ms. Janet NICKELS
103 Sr Dir CET/Wkforce Trng & Bus Svcs ....Ms. Libby TROSTLE
31 Sr Dir Lifelong Lrng/Pgm Supp Sys ....Ms. Jean MARRIOTT
105 Director of Network & Tech Services ....Ms. Patti DAVIS
21 Director Fiscal Affairs ....Mr. Timothy LEAGUE
15 Director Human Resources ....Ms. Donna MARRIOTT
18 Director Facilities Management ....Ms. Terry BOWEN
19 Chief of Public Safety & Security ....Mr. Wayne LIVESAY
22 Director Disability Support Svcs ....Mr. Joseph TATELA
86 Chief Compliance & Integrity Ofcr ....Dr. Michael KIPHART

Cecil College (J)

One Seahawk Drive, North East MD 21901-1999
County: Cecil FICE Identification: 008308
Unit ID: 162104
Telephone: (410) 287-6060 Carnegie Class: Assoc/HT-High Trad
FAX Number: (410) 287-1026 Calendar System: Semester
URL: www.cecil.edu
Established: 1968 Annual Undergrad Tuition & Fees (In-District): $3,660
Enrollment: 2,551 Coed
Affiliation or Control: State/Local IRS Status: 501(c)3
Highest Offering: Associate Degree
Accreditation: M, ADNUR, EMT, MAC, PTAA

01 President ....Dr. Mary WAY BOLT
05 Vice President Academic Programs ....Dr. Kimberly BATTY-HERBERT
10 Vice President Finance ....Mr. Daniel THOMPSON
32 VP Students/Inst Effectiveness ....Dr. Diane C. LANE
13 Interim CIO ....Mr. Peter LUNDBERG
30 Vice Pres Institutional Advancement ....Ms. Chris Ann SZEP
15 Executive Director Human Resources .... Ms. Colleen CASHILL
20 Dean of Academic Programs .... Dr. Dave ORE
31 Dean of Career/Community Education ....Mr. Miles DEAN
66 Dean Nursing Ed/Alld Hlth/Hlth Sci ....Dr. Christy DRYER
18 Director of Facilities ....Ms. Jaclyn CANCELLIERE
37 Director of Financial Aid Services ....Ms. Amanda SOLECKI
26 Director of Marketing ....Ms. Charlene CONOLLY
84 Director of Enrollment Management .... Ms. Cindy MISHOE
93 Director Minority Student Services ....Ms. Laney HOXTER
09 Director of Institutional Research ....Mr. Dan STOICESCU
06 Director of Records & Registration ....Ms. S. Tomeka SWAN

08 Director of Library Services .... Ms. Lorraine MARTORANA
41 Director Athletics .... Mr. Ed DURHAM
29 Coordinator Alumni Relations .... Ms. Mary MOORE
04 Exec Assistant to the President .... Ms. Sherry PISTOR
21 Controller .... Mr. Craig WHITEFORD
19 Director Security/Safety .... Mr. John CAPOZZOLI

Chesapeake College (A)

PO Box 8, 1000 College Circle, Wye Mills MD 21679-0008
County: Queen Annes FICE Identification: 004650
Unit ID: 162168
Telephone: (410) 822-5400 Carnegie Class: Assoc/HT-High Trad
FAX Number: (410) 827-5875 Calendar System: Semester
URL: www.chesapeake.edu
Established: 1965 Annual Undergrad Tuition & Fees (In-District): $3,676
Enrollment: 2,426 Coed
Affiliation or Control: State/Local IRS Status: 501(c)3
Highest Offering: Associate Degree
Accreditation: M, ADNUR, EMT, PTAA, RAD, SURGT

01 President .... Dr. Barbara A. VINIAR
05 Vice President for Academic Affairs .... Dr. Clay RAILEY
11 VP for Administrative Services .... Mr. Tim JONES
32 Vice President for Student Success .... Dr. Richard D. MIDCAP
72 VP Technology & Academic Support .... Mr. Douglass P. GRAY
30 VP of Institutional Advancement .... Ms. Lucie HUGHES
18 Director of Facilities .... Mr. Paul RENSHAW
49 Dean for Liberal Arts & Sciences .... Dr. Eleanor WELSH
107 Dean for Career & Professional Stds .... Vacant
08 Dean of Learning Resources .... Ms. Chandra M. GIGLIOTTI
15 Director of Human Resources .... Ms. Susan A. CIANCHETTA
37 Director of Financial Aid .... Ms. Mindy M. SCHAFFER
51 Dean of Continuing Education .... Vacant
09 Dir Inst Planning/Research & Assmnt .... Mr. Vincent MARUGGI
07 Dean for Admissions/
Recruitment .... Ms. Kathleen J. PETRICHENKO
26 Director of Public Information .... Ms. Marcie A. MOLLOY
06 Registrar .... Mr. James A. DAVIDSON
35 Dean for Student Development .... Ms. Joan M. SEITZER
04 Exec Assoc to President/Board .... Mrs. Jane THOMAS

College of Southern Maryland (B)

PO Box 910, La Plata MD 20646-0910
County: Charles FICE Identification: 002064
Unit ID: 162122
Telephone: (301) 934-2251 Carnegie Class: Assoc/HT-High Trad
FAX Number: (301) 934-7698 Calendar System: Semester
URL: www.csmd.edu
Established: 1958 Annual Undergrad Tuition & Fees (In-District): $3,542
Enrollment: 8,411 Coed
Affiliation or Control: Local IRS Status: 501(c)3
Highest Offering: Associate Degree
Accreditation: M, ACBSP, ADNUR, EMT, MLTAD, PNUR, PTAA

01 President .... Dr. Bradley GOTTFRIED
05 Vice Pres Academic Affairs .... Dr. Eileen ABEL
12 Vice President Leonardtown Campus .... Dr. Tracy HARRIS
12 VP Prince Frederick Campus .... Dr. Richard FLEMING
103 VP Cmty Educ & Workforce Dev .... Dr. Daniel MOSSER
10 VP Financial & Admin Services .... Mr. Tony JERNIGAN
32 VP Student/Instruc Support Svcs .... Dr. William COMEY
30 Vice President for Advancement .... Ms. Michelle GOODWIN
43 Vice President/General Counsel .... Mr. Craig PATENAUDE
20 Assoc VP Academic Affairs .... Mr. Rob FARINELLI
09 Assoc VP Plng/Inst Effective/Rsrch .... Dr. Kelly MCMURRAY
84 Assoc VP Enrollment Mgmt Team .... Vacant
13 Assoc VP Info Management .... Mr. James FINGER
18 Director of Facilities .... Mr. Ron TOWARD
15 Assoc VP of Human Resources .... Dr. Mychal COLEMAN
26 Asst Vice Pres Community Relations ..... Ms. Karen SMITH-HUPP
37 Director Financial Assistance .... Mr. Christian ZIMMERMANN
06 Registrar .... Ms. Carol HARRISON
08 Director of Library .... Mr. Thomas REPENNING
66 Chair Nursing Dept .... Dr. Laura POLK
35 Director of Athletics/Student Life .... Ms. Michelle RUBLE
40 General Mgr College Store .... Ms. Marcy GANNON
07 Director Admissions Department .... Mr. Brian HAMMOND
38 Director Advisement/Career Services .... Ms. Helene CAMERON
96 Director of Procurement .... Mr. Joe PICCOLO
28 Assoc VP Diversity/Equal Oppty .... Ms. Danelle MCCLANAHAN
04 Exec Asst to President & Board .... Ms. Kim YELLMAN
19 Exec Director Security/Safety .... Mr. Don FRICK
25 Grants Coordinator .... Ms. Becky COCKERHAM
44 Director Development .... Ms. Chelsea BROWN
27 Marketing Director .... Ms. Theresa JOHNSON

The Community College of Baltimore County (C)

7201 Rossville Blvd., Baltimore MD 21237-3899
County: Baltimore FICE Identification: 002063
Unit ID: 434672
Telephone: (443) 840-2222 Carnegie Class: Assoc/HT-High Trad
FAX Number: (443) 840-1100 Calendar System: Semester
URL: www.ccbcmd.edu
Established: 1957 Annual Undergrad Tuition & Fees (In-District): $3,712
Enrollment: 22,887 Coed
Affiliation or Control: Local IRS Status: 501(c)3
Highest Offering: Associate Degree
Accreditation: M, ACBSP, ADNUR, ART, CAHIIM, COARC, COMTA, CSHSE, DH, EMT, FUSER, MAC, MLTAD, MUS, OTA, POLYT, RAD, RTT, SURGT, THEA

01 President .... Dr. Sandra L. KURTINITIS
30 Vice Pres Institutional Advancement .... Mr. Kenneth WESTARY
10 Vice Pres Finance/Administration .... Ms. Melissa HOPP
05 Vice Pres Instruction .... Dr. Mark MCCOLLOCH
84 VP Enrollment & Student Services .... Dr. Richard LILLEY
26 Sr Director for Public Relations .... Ms. Mary DELUCA
15 Senior Director Human Resources .... Ms. Penny MILSOM

Faith Theological Seminary (D)

529 Walker Avenue, Baltimore MD 21212
County: Baltimore City Identification: 667016
Unit ID: 212452
Telephone: (410) 323-6211 Carnegie Class: Spec-4-yr-Faith
FAX Number: (410) 323-6331 Calendar System: Semester
URL: www.faiththeological.org
Established: 1937 Annual Undergrad Tuition & Fees: $5,870
Enrollment: 142 Coed
Affiliation or Control: Non-denominational IRS Status: 501(c)3
Highest Offering: Doctorate; No Lower Division
Accreditation: #TRACS

01 President .... Rev.Dr. Norman J. MANOHAR
05 Academic Dean .... Dr. Stephen T. HAGUE
06 Registrar .... Mrs. Aruna S. MANOHAR
07 Dir Admissions/Distance Education .... Dr. Michael DEWALT
08 Head Librarian .... Mrs. Anita TAYLOR
108 Director Institutional Assessment .... Mrs. Margaret P. PROCH
10 Business Manager/DSO .... Mrs. Susan J. WOOD
13 IT Manager/Financial Aid Advisor .... Mr. John MANOHAR

Fortis College (E)

4351 Garden City Drive, Landover MD 20785
Telephone: (301) 459-3650 Identification: 770731
Accreditation: ACICS, DH, MLTAD

† Branch campus of Fortis Institute, Erie, PA

Frederick Community College (F)

7932 Opossumtown Pike, Frederick MD 21702-2097
County: Frederick FICE Identification: 002071
Unit ID: 162557
Telephone: (301) 846-2400 Carnegie Class: Assoc/HT-High Trad
FAX Number: (301) 846-2498 Calendar System: Semester
URL: www.frederick.edu
Established: 1957 Annual Undergrad Tuition & Fees (In-District): $3,364
Enrollment: 6,031 Coed
Affiliation or Control: State/Local IRS Status: 501(c)3
Highest Offering: Associate Degree
Accreditation: M, ADNUR, COARC, NMT, SURGT

01 President .... Ms. Elizabeth BURMASTER
11 Chief of Operations .... Mr. John WICHSER
05 Provost/VP for Academic Affairs .... Dr. Tony HAWKINS
51 VP for CE/Workforce Development .... Mr. David CROGHAN
10 VP for Finance & Human Resources .... Ms. Dana MCDONALD
32 VP for Learning Support .... Dr. Wayne BARBOUR
30 Exec Dir Institutional Advancement .... Ms. Deborah POWELL
13 Chief Technology Officer .... Mr. Wayne KELLER
28 Director Diversity/Equity & Incl .... Ms. Shezwae FLEMING
20 AVP of Academic Affairs .... Dr. Alanka BROWN
84 AVP for Enrollment Management .... Ms. Laura MEARS
15 AVP for Human Resources .... Ms. Maryrose WILSON
21 Assistant Director Fiscal Services .... Ms. Angela LUDEMAN
21 AVP for Fiscal Services .... Mr. Bill GRUTZKUHN
06 Exec Dir of Welcome Center/Registar . Ms. Deidre WEILMINSTER
49 AVP/Dean of Arts & Science .... Dr. Brian STIPELMEAN
20 AVP Teaching/Learning .... Dr. Kelly TRIGGER
35 AVP/Dean of Students .... Mr. Jerry HAYNES
35 Dir Center for Student Engagement . Ms. Jeanni WINSTON-MUIR
38 Spec Asst to President Inst Effect .... Mr. Gerald L. BOYD
18 Exec Dir Facilities Planning .... Mr. John ANZINGER
08 Exec Director Library .... Vacant
09 Exec Dir Assessment and Research .... Dr. Gohar FARAHANI
26 Director of Marketing .... Mr. Michael BAISEY
38 Director of Special Projects .... Mr. Michael PRITCHARD
37 Exec Dir Financial Aid .... Ms. Brenda DAYHOFF
04 Exec Assoc to the President & BOT .... Ms. Kari MELVIN
36 Exec Director Workforce Training .... Ms. Patricia MEYER
38 Exec Director Emergency Management .... Ms. Kathy FRANCIS
14 Exec Dir of Enterprise Application .... Mr. Adam RENO
41 Director of Athletics .... Mr. Rodney BENNETT
38 Director Children's Center .... Ms. Teri BICKEL
106 Exec Director Distributed Learning .... Mr. Jurgen HILKE
38 Exec Dir Counseling & Advising .... Dr. Chad ADERO
38 Director Office of Adult Services .... Ms. Janice BROWN
22 Director Students w/Disabilities .. Ms. Kate KRAMER-JEFFERSON
07 Director of Admissions .... Ms. Lisa FREEL
14 Exec Dir Network Services .... Mr. Joe MARSHALL
105 Director Web Services .... Ms. Cindy OSBON
38 Coordinator Veterans Services .... Ms. Rachel NACHLAS
109 Exec Director Auxiliary Services .... Mr. Frederick HOCKENBERRY
38 Director Administrative Projects .... Ms. Linda SEEK
102 Asst Dir Scholarships & Grants ...... Ms. Michelle NUSUM-SMITH
109 Director Dining Services .... Ms. Donna S. SOWERS
29 Asst Dir of Alumni Relations .... Ms. Christina PETERMAN

Garrett College (G)

687 Mosser Road, McHenry MD 21541-1265
County: Garrett FICE Identification: 010014
Unit ID: 162609
Telephone: (301) 387-3000 Carnegie Class: Assoc/HT-High Trad
FAX Number: (301) 387-3038 Calendar System: Semester
URL: www.garrettcollege.edu
Established: 1966 Annual Undergrad Tuition & Fees (In-District): $3,584
Enrollment: 713 Coed
Affiliation or Control: State/Local IRS Status: 501(c)3
Highest Offering: Associate Degree
Accreditation: M, EMT

01 President .... Dr. Richard MACLENNAN
04 Executive Assistant to President .... Ms. Marcia KNEPP
10 VP of Administration & Finance .... Ms. Josephine GILMAN
05 VP of Academic & Student Affairs .... Dr. Sarah GARRETT
20 AVP of Instruction & Student Svcs .... Mr. Alexander TUEL
51 Dean of Cont Educ/Workforce Devel .... Ms. Julie YODER
13 Director of IT .... Ms. Jami REYNOLDS
30 Dir Develop/Exec Dir Foundation .... Ms. Cherie KRUG
06 Director of Records & Registration .... Ms. Kim DEGIOVANNI
37 Director of Financial Aid .... Ms. Cissy VANSICKLE
08 Interim Library Director .... Ms. Ellen SHEAFFER
21 Director of Business Office .... Ms. Katherine BROWNING
18 Plant Manager .... Mr. Hugh SCHRIER
15 Director of Human Resources .... Ms. Linda K. FIKE
32 Director of Student Life .... Ms. Tracie ELLIS
65 Dir of Natural Res/Wildlife Tech .... Mr. Kevin DODGE
41 Director of Athletics .... Mr. Dennis GIBSON
50 Director of Business/Info Tech .... Dr. Qing YUAN
36 Coordinator of Academic Support .... Ms. Rhonda SCHWINABART
96 Purchasing/Accounts Payable .... Ms. Bonnie BROADWATER
09 Coord of Institutional Research .... Ms. Kelli SISLER
40 Interim Bookstore Manager .... Ms. Lois ANDERSON
84 Director of Enrollment Management .... Ms. Rachelle DAVIS
45 Dean of Inst Effectiveness .... Mr. James ALLEN, JR.
105 Webmaster .... Vacant
88 Director of Adventure Sports .... Mr. Michael LOGSDON
106 Coordinator of Distance Learning .... Ms. Denise FRIEND
19 Coordinator of Security/Safety .... Ms. Shelley MENEAR
26 Coordinator of Marketing and PR .... Ms. Stacy HOLLER

Goucher College (H)

1021 Dulaney Valley Road, Towson MD 21204-2780
County: Baltimore FICE Identification: 002073
Unit ID: 162654
Telephone: (410) 337-6000 Carnegie Class: Bac-A&S
FAX Number: (410) 337-6123 Calendar System: Semester
URL: www.goucher.edu
Established: 1885 Annual Undergrad Tuition & Fees: $42,180
Enrollment: 2,120 Coed
Affiliation or Control: Independent Non-Profit IRS Status: 501(c)3
Highest Offering: Master's
Accreditation: M

01 President .... Dr. Jose A. BOWEN
05 Provost & Chief Academic Officer .... Dr. Leslie W. LEWIS
45 Sr VP for Strategic Initiatives .... Mr. Marty SWEIDEL
32 Vice Pres/Dean of Students .... Dr. Bryan F. COKER
30 Vice Pres Advancement .... Ms. Trishana E. BOWDEN
10 VP for Finance & Administration .... Ms. Lynne LOCHTE
26 Exec Dir Marketing & Communications . Ms. Stephanie COLDREN
13 VP for Technology and Planning .... Mr. Bill LEIMBACH
43 General Counsel .... Ms. Barbara STOB
20 Associate Provost for UG Affairs .... Ms. La Jerne CORNISH
82 Assoc Dean International Studies .... Mr. Eric SINGER
35 Asst VP for Student Affairs .... Ms. Emily PERL
15 Vice President for Human Resources .... Ms. Deborah LUPTON
21 Controller .... Mr. Alex ANTKOWIAK
07 Director of Admissions .... Mr. Carlton E. SURBECK, III
08 Librarian .... Ms. Nancy MAGNUSON
29 Exec Dir for Alumnae/i
Engagement .... Ms. Jennifer PAWLO - JOHNSTONE
36 Director of Career Development .... Ms. Traci MARTIN
58 Director Grad Program in Education .... Ms. Phyllis SUNSHINE
06 Registrar .... Mr. Andrew WESTFALL
09 Dir for Institutional Effectiveness .... Ms. Shuang LIU
10 Dir Business/Auxiliary Services .... Mr. Calvin GLADDEN
18 Dir Facilities Management Services ..... Mr. Terence MCCANN, JR.
37 Director Financial Aid .... Ms. Stephanie BENDER
105 Webmaster .... Mr. John PERRELLI
106 Dir Online Education/E-learning .... Ms. Linda BRUCE
28 Asst Dean Stdnts Intercultural Affs .... Ms. Luz BURGOS-LOPEZ
39 Director Student Housing .... Mr. Pavan PURSWANI
41 Athletic Director .... Mr. Geoff MILLER

Hagerstown Community College (I)

11400 Robinwood Drive, Hagerstown MD 21742-6590
County: Washington FICE Identification: 002074
Unit ID: 162690
Telephone: (240) 500-2000 Carnegie Class: Assoc/MT-VT-Mix Trad/Non
FAX Number: (301) 393-3682 Calendar System: Semester
URL: www.hagerstowncc.edu
Established: 1946 Annual Undergrad Tuition & Fees (In-District): $3,564
Enrollment: 4,615 Coed
Affiliation or Control: State/Local IRS Status: 501(c)3
Highest Offering: Associate Degree
Accreditation: M, ADNUR, DA, DH, EMT, PNUR, RAD

01 President ... Dr. Guy ALTIERI
05 VP of Academic Affs & Student Svcs ... Dr. David WARNER
10 Vice Pres Administration/Finance ... Ms. Christina S. KILDUFF
32 Dean of Students ... Vacant
09 Dean of Plng/Inst Effectiveness ... Ms. Barbara E. MACHT
51 Dean Continuing Educ/Bus Svcs ... Ms. Theresa M. SHANK
18 Dir Facilities Management & Plng ... Mr. Jonathan G. METCALF
07 Dir of Admissions & Enrollment Mgmt ... Mr. Kevin CRAWFORD
30 Exec Director College Advancement ... Ms. Stacey L. LOWMAN
26 Director Marketing/Public Info ... Ms. Elizabeth L. KIRKPATRICK
37 Director of Financial Aid & Records ... Ms. Carolyn S. COX
106 Dean Academic Services/Online Educ ... Dr. Julian K. HORTON
21 Director of Finance ... Mr. David C. BITTORF
21 Director of Business Services ... Ms. Lita J. ORNER
66 Director of Nursing ... Ms. Karen S. HAMMOND
15 Director of Human Resources ... Ms. Jennifer A. KNIGHT
41 Dir Athletics/Phys Ed/Leisure Stds ... Vacant
13 Director of Information Technology ... Mr. Craig M. FENTRESS

Harford Community College (A)

401 Thomas Run Road, Bel Air MD 21015-1698
County: Harford FICE Identification: 002075
Unit ID: 162706
Telephone: (443) 412-2000 Carnegie Class: Assoc/HT-High Trad
FAX Number: (443) 412-2120 Calendar System: Semester
URL: www.harford.edu
Established: 1957 Annual Undergrad Tuition & Fees (In-District): $3,341
Enrollment: 6,714 Coed
Affiliation or Control: Local IRS Status: 501(c)3
Highest Offering: Associate Degree
Accreditation: M, ADNUR, HT, MAC

01 President ... Dr. Dianna G. PHILLIPS
05 Int Vice President Academic Affairs ... Mr. Avery W. WARD
10 Vice President Finance & Operations ... Mr. Fredrick P. JOHNSON
32 VP Student Affairs/Inst Effective ... Dr. Deborah J. CRUISE
31 VP External Relations and HR ... Ms. Brenda M. MORRISON
13 Chief Information Officer ... Dr. Thomas FRANZA
96 Asst Vice Pres Procurement ... Vacant
84 Assoc VP Enrollment Services ... Dr. Alexandra ADAMS
35 Assoc VP Student Development ... Dr. Diane L. RESIDES
21 Assoc VP Finance & Budget ... Mr. Stephen S. PHILLIPS
51 Assoc VP Continuing Educ & Training ... Dr. Zoann J. PARKER
18 Assoc VP Campus Operations ... Mr. Stephen P. GAREY
37 Director Financial Aid ... Ms. Amy R. SPINNATO
06 Assistant Registrar ... Vacant
26 Dir Marketing & Public Relations ... Ms. Nancy J. DYSARD
15 Dir Human Resources/Employee Dev ... Ms. Kathleen M. CALLAN
29 Director College/Alumni Development ... Ms. Denise M. DREGIER
08 Director Library & Info Resources ... Ms. Carol M. ALLEN
106 Dir eLearning & Instr Resources ... Dr. Karen M. REGE
09 Dir Inst Research/Plng/Effective ... Ms. Valerie T. SWAIN
38 Dir Advising/Career/Transfer Svcs ... Ms. J. Bonnie SULZBACH
40 Coordinator College Store ... Ms. Linda L. FIFE
07 Dir for Admissions and Registrar ... Ms. Megan CORNETT
29 Alumni Coordinator ... Ms. JeanMarie KRYGOWSKI
81 Dean Science/Tech/Engr/Math ... Ms. Deborah R. WROBEL
83 Dean Behavioral & Social Sciences ... Mr. Avery W. WARD
79 Dean Humanities ... Dr. Leroy HAMILTON
57 Dean Visual/Performing/Applied Arts ... Mr. Paul E. LABE
50 Dean Bus/Ed/Computing/Applied Tech ... Mr. John F. MAYHORNE
66 Dean Nursing & Allied Health Profs ... Ms. Laura C. PRESTON

Hood College (B)

401 Rosemont Avenue, Frederick MD 21701-8575
County: Frederick FICE Identification: 002076
Unit ID: 162760
Telephone: (301) 663-3131 Carnegie Class: Masters/L
FAX Number: (301) 694-7653 Calendar System: Semester
URL: www.hood.edu
Established: 1893 Annual Undergrad Tuition & Fees: $35,150
Enrollment: 2,365 Coed
Affiliation or Control: Independent Non-Profit IRS Status: 501(c)3
Highest Offering: Doctorate
Accreditation: M, ACBSP, CS, NURSE, SW, TED

01 President ... Dr. Andrea E. CHAPDELAINE
05 Provost/VP Academic Affairs ... Dr. Deborah RICKER
10 Vice Pres Finance ... Mr. Charles G. MANN
30 VP for Institutional Advancement ... Ms. Nancy E. GILLECE
32 VP Student Life/Dean of Students ... Dr. Olivia G. WHITE
84 VP Undergrad/Grad Enrollment ... Mr. William BROWN
07 Director of Admissions ... Ms. Jennifer DECKER
58 Interim Dean of Graduate School ... Dr. April BOULTON
20 Director CAAR ... Mr. Matthew HOLSAPPLE
26 Exec Dir Marketing/Communications ... Mr. Dave DIEHL
29 Sr Director of Alumnae/i Programs ... Ms. Linda ROTH
06 Registrar ... Mrs. Nanette MARKEY
08 Interim Director of Library Service ... Mr. Toby PETERSON
37 Director of Financial Aid ... Ms. Brenda DISORBO
15 Director of Human Resources ... Ms. Carol M. WUENSCHEL
18 Director of Facilities ... Mr. James THOMAS
13 Chief Technology Officer ... Vacant
09 Director of Institutional Research ... Ms. Cynthia EMORY
04 Executive Asst to President ... Ms. Diane K. WISE
104 Director Study Abroad ... Vacant
19 Director Security/Safety ... Mr. Thurmond MAYNARD
38 Director Student Counseling ... Ms. Delores GRIGSBY
39 Director Student Housing ... Mr. Matthew TROUTMAN
41 Athletic Director ... Mr. Tom DICKMAN

Howard Community College (C)

10901 Little Patuxent Parkway, Columbia MD 21044-3197
County: Howard FICE Identification: 008175
Unit ID: 162779
Telephone: (443) 518-1000 Carnegie Class: Assoc/HT-High Trad
FAX Number: N/A Calendar System: Semester
URL: www.howardcc.edu
Established: 1966 Annual Undergrad Tuition & Fees (In-District): $3,698
Enrollment: 9,920 Coed
Affiliation or Control: State/Local IRS Status: 501(c)3
Highest Offering: Associate Degree
Accreditation: M, ACFEI, ADNUR, CVT, DH, DMS, EMT, MLTAD, MUS, PNUR, PTAA, RAD

01 President ... Dr. Kathleen B. HETHERINGTON
32 Vice President of Student Services ... Dr. Cynthia J. PETERKA
05 Interim VP of Academic Affairs ... Dr. Jean M. SVACINA
10 Vice Pres of Administration/Finance ... Ms. Lynn C. COLEMAN
13 Vice Pres Information Technology ... Mr. Thomas J. GLASER
51 AVP Cont Education/Workforce Dev ... Mr. Edgar SWAIN
84 Assoc Vice Pres Enrollment Services ... Ms. Alison BUCKLEY
35 Assoc Vice Pres for Student Devel ... Ms. Janice L. MARKS
15 Associate Vice Pres Human Resources ... Mr. Dave JORDAN
21 Associate Vice Pres of Finance ... Ms. Janet L. CULLISON
09 Exec Dir Plng/Research & Org Dev ... Ms. Zoe A. IRVIN
18 Exec Dir Capital Proj/Facilities ... Mr. Charles NIGHTINGALE
101 Executive Associate to President ... Ms. Linda EMMERICH
26 Exec Dir Public Relations/Mktg ... Ms. Elizabeth HOMAN
88 Director of Finance ... Ms. Amanda HUFFMAN
30 Director of Development ... Ms. Melissa MATTEY
109 Director Auxiliary Services ... Mr. Kevin COLLINS
19 Director of Public Safety ... Mr. Ken MCGLYNN
35 Interim Director Student Life ... Ms. Schnell R. GARRETT
04 Exec Assistant to the President ... Ms. Farida P. GUZDAR
96 Director of Purchasing ... Ms. Elizabeth H. MOSS
06 Registrar ... Ms. Catherine MUND
07 Director of Admissions & Advising ... Ms. Dorothy B. PLANTZ
104 Director of International Education ... Ms. Christele N. CAIN
105 Web Enterprise Services Manager ... Mr. Roger F. STOTT
37 Director of Financial Aid Services ... Ms. Dawn LOWE
41 Athletics Director ... Ms. Diane E. SCHUMACHER

Johns Hopkins University (D)

3400 N. Charles Street, Baltimore MD 21218-2680
County: Independent City FICE Identification: 002077
Unit ID: 162928
Telephone: (410) 516-8000 Carnegie Class: DU-Highest
FAX Number: N/A Calendar System: Semester
URL: www.jhu.edu
Established: 1876 Annual Undergrad Tuition & Fees: $48,710
Enrollment: 21,372 Coed
Affiliation or Control: Independent Non-Profit IRS Status: 501(c)3
Highest Offering: Doctorate
Accreditation: M, BBT, CACREP, CS, DIETC, DMS, ENG, ENGR, HSA, IPSY, MED, MIL, NMT, NURSE, PDPSY, PH, TED

01 President ... Mr. Ronald J. DANIELS
100 Sr Vice President/Chief of Staff ... Ms. Kerry A. ATES
05 Provost & Sr VP Acad Affs ... Dr. Sunil KUMAR
17 CEO Johns Hopkins Medicine ... Dr. Paul D. ROTHMAN
10 Sr VP Finance & Administration ... Mr. Daniel G. ENNIS
29 VP for Development & Alum Relations ... Mr. Fritz SCHROEDER
45 Vice Pres Strategic Initiatives ... Mr. Phillip SPECTOR
26 Vice Pres Comm/Public Affairs ... Mr. Glenn M. BIELER
43 Vice Pres/General Counsel ... Mr. Mark B. ROTENBERG
43 Deputy General Counsel ... Mr. Frederick SAVAGE
86 Vice Pres Govt/Community Affairs ... Mr. Thomas LEWIS
18 Vice Pres Real Estate/Campus Svcs ... Mr. Alan FISH
15 Vice Pres Human Resources ... Ms. Charlene M. HAYES
21 Vice Pres Finance & CFO ... Ms. Helene GRADY
21 Vice Pres Chief Investment Officer ... Dr. Kathryn J. CRECELIUS
21 Chief Risk Officer ... Dr. Jonathan LINKS
32 Vice Provost for Student Affairs ... Dr. Kevin SHOLLENBERGER
20 Vice Provost Faculty Affairs ... Dr. Cheryl HOLCOMB-MCCOY
20 Vice Provost Academic Services ... Mr. Philip TANG
07 Vice Provost for Admiss & Fin Aid ... Mr. David PHILLIPS
88 Vice Provost Education ... Dr. Kelly GEBO
13 Vice Provost Info Technology/CIO ... Ms. Stephanie REEL
22 Vice Provost Institutional Equity ... Ms. Caroline LAGUERRE-BROWN
46 Vice Provost Research ... Dr. Denis WIRTZ
09 Asst Provost Institutional Research ... Dr. Cathy J. LEBO
88 Asst Prov International Services ... Mr. James BRAILER
88 Vice Provost for Digital Initiative ... Vacant
06 Registrar ... Ms. Mary Ellen FLAHERTY
82 Dean Nitze School Adv Intl Studies ... Dr. Vali NASR
49 Dean Krieger School Arts & Sciences ... Dr. Beverly WENDLAND
50 Dean Carey Business School ... Dr. Bernard FERRARI
53 Dean School of Education ... Dr. David W. ANDREWS
54 Dean Whiting Sch Engineering ... Dr. Ed SCHLESINGER
63 Dean School of Medicine ... Dr. Paul ROTHMAN
66 Dean School of Nursing ... Dr. Patricia DAVIDSON
69 Dean Bloomberg School Public Health ... Dr. Michael J. KLAG
08 Dean Sheridan Libraries and Museums ... Mr. Winston G. TABB
64 Director Peabody Institute ... Mr. Fred BRONSTEIN
81 Director Applied Physics Lab ... Mr. Ralph SEMMEL
96 Director Purchasing ... Mr. Paul N. BEYER
21 Controller ... Mr. Scott JONES
19 Exec Director Safety & Security ... Mr. Leroy "Lee" JONES
21 Exec Director Internal Audits ... Mr. James JARRELL
27 Exec Director Comm & Public Affairs ... Mr. Dennis O'SHEA
88 Exec Director JH Real Estate ... Mr. Brian B. DEMBECK
04 Administrative Asst to President ... Ms. Gillian RATHBONE-WEBBER
104 Director Study Abroad ... Dr. Lori A. CITTI
28 Chair Diversity Leadership Council ... Mr. Ashley J. LLORENS
36 Executive Director Career Center ... Ms. Trudy VAN ZEE
41 Athletic Director ... Mr. Tom CALDER

Kaplan University (E)

18618 Crestwood Drive, Hagerstown MD 21742-2797
Telephone: (301) 766-3600 FICE Identification: 007946
Accreditation: &NH, ACBSP, MAC, PHLEB

† Regional accreditation is carried under the parent institution in Davenport, IA.

Lincoln College of Technology (F)

9325 Snowden River Parkway, Columbia MD 21046
County: Howard FICE Identification: 007936
Unit ID: 163028
Telephone: (410) 290-7100 Carnegie Class: Assoc/HVT-Mix Trad/Non
FAX Number: (410) 290-7880 Calendar System: Quarter
URL: www.lincolntech.com
Established: 1978 Annual Undergrad Tuition & Fees: N/A
Enrollment: 647 Coed
Affiliation or Control: Proprietary IRS Status: Proprietary
Highest Offering: Associate Degree
Accreditation: ACCSC

01 Campus President ... Mr. Glen JOHANNESEN

Loyola University Maryland (G)

4501 N Charles Street, Baltimore MD 21210-2694
County: Independent City FICE Identification: 002078
Unit ID: 163046
Telephone: (410) 617-2000 Carnegie Class: Masters/L
FAX Number: (410) 322-2768 Calendar System: Semester
URL: www.loyola.edu
Established: 1852 Annual Undergrad Tuition & Fees: $45,200
Enrollment: 5,967 Coed
Affiliation or Control: Roman Catholic IRS Status: 501(c)3
Highest Offering: Doctorate
Accreditation: M, BUS, BUSA, CACREP, CLPSY, CS, ENG, SP, TED

01 President ... Rev. Brian F. LINNANE, SJ
03 Executive Vice President ... Dr. Susan DONOVAN
04 Executive Asst to the President ... Mr. Darryl COWARD
05 Vice President for Academic Affairs ... Dr. Amy WOLFSON
10 Vice Pres for Finance & Treasurer ... Mr. Randall GENTZLER
30 Vice President Advancement ... Dr. Terrence SAWYER
32 VP Student Devel/Dean of Students ... Dr. Sheilah SHAW HORTON
84 Vice Pres Enrollment Management ... Mr. Marc CAMILLE
20 Assoc Vice Pres Academic Affairs ... Ms. Jenny LOWRY
28 Asst VP Academic Affrs/Diversity ... Dr. Martha L. WHARTON
37 Asst Vice Pres of Financial Aid ... Mr. Mark L. LINDENMEYER
09 Asst VP of Institutional Research ... Ms. Terra SCHEHR
18 Assoc VP Facilities/Campus Services ... Ms. Helen SCHNEIDER
13 Asst VP of Technology Services/CIO ... Ms. Louise FINN
26 Dir Marketing and Communications ... Ms. Rita BUETTNER
15 Asst Vice Pres for Human Resources ... Ms. Kathleen PARNELL
21 Asst Vice Pres for Administration ... Mr. Joan FLYNN
27 Asst VP Marketing/Communications ... Ms. Sharon HIGGINS
41 Asst VP/Director of Athletics ... Mr. James PAQUETTE
38 Assoc VP Student Development ... Dr. Donelda COOK
102 Dir Corporation & Foundation Rels ... Mr. Thomas BRUSH
07 Director Undergraduate Admissions ... Vacant
07 Director of Graduate Admissions ... Ms. Maureen FAUX
06 Director of Records ... Ms. Rita L. STEINER
85 Dean of International Programs ... Dr. Andre COLOMBAT
08 Director of Library ... Ms. Barbara PREECE
42 Director of Campus Ministry ... Mr. Sean BRAY
88 Dir Ctr Comm Svc/Justice & YRI ... Ms. Erin O'KEEFE
36 Director of the Career Center ... Ms. Jennifer KACZKOWSKI
88 Sexual Violence Prev & Educ Coord ... Ms. Melissa LEES
88 Director Recreational Sports ... Mr. Bryan HAUNERT
35 Director Student Activities ... Mr. Mark C. BRODERICK
88 Director ALANA Services ... Mr. Rodney PARKER
21 Asst VP Controller ... Vacant
45 Director Budget & Planning ... Mr. Sean FRANCIS
109 Director Event Svcs/Auxiliary Mgmt ... Mr. Joseph BRADLEY
88 Director of Project Management ... Mr. Laszlo PELY
88 Director Environment Health/Safety ... Mr. Thomas HETTLEMAN
19 Dir of Public Safety/Campus Police ... Mr. Timothy FOX
29 Director Alumni Relations ... Mr. Thomas BRUSH
30 Asst VP Advancement ... Ms. Jo Ann DOLAN
88 Director of Creative Services ... Mr. Brian HATCHER
88 Director Advancement Services ... Mr. Ian WEBSTER
49 Dean College of Arts & Sciences ... Dr. Amanda THOMAS
50 Dean Sellinger Sch Business & Mgmt ... Dr. Kathleen GETZ
49 Assoc Dean Social Sciences/Graduate ... Dr. Jeffrey BARNETT
50 Asst Dean for Business Programs ... Ms. Susan HASLER
88 Associate Dean of Students ... Ms. Michelle CHEATEM
18 Dir Facilities Management ... Ms. Kiki WILLIAMS
44 Director of Annual Giving ... Ms. Dianne THOMPSON
88 Director Budget & Data Management ... Ms. Lorie HOLTGRAVE
88 Director of Bangkok Programs ... Vacant
105 Dir Web Communications ... Ms. Amy FILARDO

Maple Springs Baptist Bible College & Seminary (A)

4130 Belt Road, Capitol Heights MD 20743-5712
County: Prince Georges FICE Identification: 038224
Unit ID: 446394
Telephone: (301) 736-3631 Carnegie Class: Spec-4-yr-Faith
FAX Number: (301) 735-6507 Calendar System: Semester
URL: www.msbbcs.edu
Established: 1986 Annual Undergrad Tuition & Fees: $4,590
Enrollment: 99 Coed
Affiliation or Control: Baptist IRS Status: 501(c)3
Highest Offering: Doctorate
Accreditation: TRACS

01 President Dr. Larry W. JORDAN
05 Vice President Academic Affairs Dr. Vivian BESS
11 Vice Pres Administration & Finance Vacant
73 Academic Dean College Division Dr. Carl KEELS
06 Director Records and Admissions Dr. Esther BIRCH
09 Dir Institutional Plng/Assessment Dr. David CLARK
10 Director Business Affairs Mrs. Fannie G. THOMPSON
32 Director Student Affairs Dr. Jerrye FELICIANA
08 Dir Library/Instrnl Resource Center Mr. Darren JONES
37 Financial Aid Coordinator Mrs. Patricia JONES

Maryland Institute College of Art (B)

1300 W. Mount Royal Avenue, Baltimore MD 21217-4191
County: Independent City FICE Identification: 002080
Unit ID: 163295
Telephone: (410) 669-9200 Carnegie Class: Spec-4-yr-Arts
FAX Number: (410) 669-9206 Calendar System: Semester
URL: www.mica.edu
Established: 1826 Annual Undergrad Tuition & Fees: $43,370
Enrollment: 2,262 Coed
Affiliation or Control: Independent Non-Profit IRS Status: 501(c)3
Highest Offering: Master's
Accreditation: M, ART

01 President Mr. Samuel HOI
05 Vice Pres Academic Affairs/Provost Dr. David BOGEN
10 Vice Pres Operations/Finance/COO Mr. Douglas MANN
30 Vice Pres Advancement Ms. Rita WALTERS
32 Vice Pres Student Affairs Mr. Michael PATTERSON
07 VP Admissions/Financial Aid Ms. Theresa BEDOYA
13 Vice Pres Technology Systems & Svcs Mr. Tom HYATT
11 Vice Pres Strategic Iniatives Mr. Mike MOLLA
97 Vice Provost Open Studies Mr. David GRACYALNY
46 Vice Provost Research/Grad Studies Ms. Gwynne KEATHLEY
04 Executive Assistant to President Ms. Lisa SHEPPLEY
37 Assoc VP Financial Aid Ms. Diane PRENGAMAN
44 Assoc VP Dev/Constituent Rels Ms. Lillian BURKE
14 Assoc VP Tech/Systems/Services Ms. Susan MILTENBERGER
18 Assoc VP Facilities Management Mr. Timothy MILLNER
15 Human Resources Director Ms. Laura ROSSI
20 Dean Academic Services Ms. Cynthia BARTH
53 Dean Art Education Ms. Karen CARROLL
35 Assoc Dean Stdnt Life/Judicial Affs Ms. Kelly HOOVER
88 Assoc Dean Student Health Wellness Vacant
07 Assoc Dean Undergraduate Admissions Vacant
07 Director of Graduate Admissions Mr. Christopher HARRING
51 Assoc Dn Cont Studies/Open Studies Mr. Peter DUBEAU
06 Assoc Dean Enrollment Svs/Registrar Ms. Christine PETERSON
28 Asst Dean Diversity Intercultur Dev Mr. Clyde JOHNSON, JR.
21 Director Accounting Ms. Jessica RURKA
88 Director Budget Ms. Brigitte SULLIVAN
26 VP for Strategic Communications Ms. Debra RUBINO
39 Director Residence Life Mr. Scott STONE
36 Director Career Development Ms. Megan MILLER
31 Director Community Engagement Ms. Karen STULTS
38 Director Counseling Center Ms. Patricia FARRELL
35 Director Student Activities Ms. Karol MARTINEZ-DOANE
88 Director Admissions Operations Ms. Cheryl ISSOD
08 Director & Head Librarian Vacant
88 Director Annual Fund Vacant
88 Director Advancement Services Ms. Dana COSTELLO
88 Research & Stewardship Manager Ms. Nayeli MOWBRAY
88 Director Exhibitions Mr. Gerald ROSS
85 Director International Affairs Ms. Mary ALLEN
88 Director Writing St/Learn Res Ctr Mr. Daniel GUTSTEIN
88 Dir Data Mgmt/Registration Cont Std Ms. Sarah MARAVETZ
84 Dir Enroll Svcs/Stdnt Records/Rsrch Mr. Hadley GARBART
19 Director of Campus Safety Mr. Marlon BYRD
88 Director Events Mr. Jon LIPITZ
88 Director Operation Services Mr. Chris BOHASKA
29 Director Alumni & Parent Relations Ms. Lindsay DORRANCE
102 Director Corp/Found/Govt Relations Ms. Sara WARREN
105 Director of Web Communications Mr. Justin CODD
24 Director Technical Support Services Mr. John RHODES
91 Director Administrative Systems Vacant
105 Director Network Services Mr. David APAW
90 Dir Instructional Advance & Tech Ms. Pamela STEFANUCA
40 Manager College Store Ms. Kerri LITZ

Maryland University of Integrative Health (C)

7750 Montpelier Road, Laurel MD 20723-6010
County: Howard FICE Identification: 025784
Unit ID: 164085
Telephone: (410) 888-9048 Carnegie Class: Spec-4-yr-Other Health
FAX Number: (410) 888-9004 Calendar System: Trimester
URL: www.muih.edu
Established: 1981 Annual Graduate Tuition & Fees: N/A
Enrollment: 780 Coed
Affiliation or Control: Independent Non-Profit IRS Status: 501(c)3
Highest Offering: Doctorate; No Undergraduates
Accreditation: M, ACUP

01 President & CEO Mr. Frank VITALE
05 Provost/VP Academic Affairs Dr. Christina SAX
11 VP Administration Ms. Louise GUSSIN
30 VP Inst Adv & Chief Values Officer Ms. Cheryl WALKER SHAPERO
32 VP University/Student Affairs Ms. Gail DOERR
10 VP/CFO & Treasurer Mr. Marc LEVIN
106 Assoc Provost Digital Learning Ms. Mary Ellen HRUTKA
108 Asst Provost Acad Assessment & Accr Ms. Deneb FALABELLA
09 Asst Provost Research Mr. James SNOW
84 Assoc VP Enrollment Management Mr. Chad EGRESI
76 Acad Dir Acupuncture/Oriental Med Mr. Jeffrey MILLISON
76 Academic Director Herbal Programs Dr. Michael TIMS
76 Academic Director Nutrition Dr. Kathleen WARNER
37 Director Student Financial Aid Ms. Kristina DEAN
08 Director of Library Services Ms. Jennifer KIRIN
29 Director Alumni Affairs Ms. Patricia DELORENZO
06 Assoc Registrar Ms. Ashley ANDERSON
04 Administrative Asst to President Ms. Olga MADIOU-BEALE
43 General Counsel Ms. Louise GUSSIN
07 Assoc Director of Admissions Mr. Nicholas HOWLEY
26 Director Marketing Ms. Beth HANDY
13 Director IT Mr. Lesly ELVARD
19 Manager Security/Safety Ms. Jennifer YOCUM
35 Director Student Affairs Mr. Jan SHERRILL

McDaniel College (D)

2 College Hill, Westminster MD 21157-4390
County: Carroll FICE Identification: 002109
Unit ID: 164270
Telephone: (410) 848-7000 Carnegie Class: Bac-A&S
FAX Number: (410) 857-2279 Calendar System: Semester
URL: www.mcdaniel.edu
Established: 1867 Annual Undergrad Tuition & Fees: $39,500
Enrollment: 3,206 Coed
Affiliation or Control: Independent Non-Profit IRS Status: 501(c)3
Highest Offering: Master's
Accreditation: M, SW, TED

01 President Dr. Roger N. CASEY
100 Chief of Staff Mr. Geoff PEARSON
05 Provost/Dean of Faculty Dr. Julia JASKEN
10 Vice Pres Administration & Finance Mr. Thomas PHIZACKLEA
30 Interim Vice President Advancement Ms. Vicky SHAFFER
32 Vice Pres/Dean of Student Affairs Ms. Beth R. GERL
84 VP Enroll Mgt/Dean of Admissions Ms. Florence W. HINES
13 Chief Information Officer Dr. Greg DUMONT
26 Assoc Vice Pres Comm/Marketing Ms. Gina PELLUSCH
58 Dean Graduate/Professional Stds Dr. Michael TYLER
20 Assoc Dean/International Programs Dr. Amy MCNICHOLS
88 Assoc Dean/Student Academic Life Ms. Lisa BRESLIN
89 Assoc Dean/First Year Program Ms. Karen VIOLANTI
35 Assoc Dean/Student Affairs Ms. Elizabeth TOWLE
44 Executive Director of Major/Planned Mr. Robert CONRAD
29 Executive Director of Alumni Relati Ms. Heather WILENSKY
102 Dir Corp & Foundation Relations Ms. Bonnie CATON
08 Director of Library Ms. Jessame E. FERGUSON
37 Director Financial Aid Ms. Zhanna GOLTSER
06 Registrar Ms. Sandra CLARK
41 Director Athletics Mr. Paul MOYER
36 Director Center for Exper and Opp Ms. Constance SGARLATA
38 Director Counseling Vacant
35 Director Student Engagement Ms. Christine WORKMAN
39 Director of Residence Life Mr. Michael ROBBINS
21 Director Financial Services/Treas Mr. Arthur S. WISNER
15 Director Human Resources Ms. Jennifer GLENNON
45 Dir Facility Plng/Capital Projects Mr. Edgar S. SELL, JR.
18 Director Physical Plant Mr. Stafford TORGESEN
19 Director of Campus Safety Mr. James HAMRICK
40 Manager Bookstore Mr. Kyle MELOCHE
109 Dir Conferences/Auxiliary Services Ms. Mary J. COLBERT
28 Director of Diversity and Inclusion Vacant
92 Director of Honors Program Dr. Bryn UPTON
96 Director of Purchasing/Receiving Ms. Ellen RUGEMER
88 Coord of Deaf Education Program Dr. Mark M. RUST
09 Director Institutional Research Vacant
86 Director of Government Relations Dr. Herbert C. SMITH
07 Director of Admissions Ms. Heidi REIGEL
104 Director of International Programs Ms. Elizabeth DAVIS
105 Director Digital Comm/Social Media Mr. Vince BUSCEMI
25 Director Academic/Government Grants Ms. Robin DEWEY

Montgomery College (E)

900 Hungerford Drive, Rockville MD 20850-1733
County: Montgomery FICE Identification: 006911
Unit ID: 163426
Telephone: (240) 567-5000 Carnegie Class: Assoc/HT-Mix Trad/Non
FAX Number: (240) 567-6397 Calendar System: Semester
URL: www.montgomerycollege.edu
Established: 1946 Annual Undergrad Tuition & Fees (In-District): $4,728
Enrollment: 25,517 Coed
Affiliation or Control: Local IRS Status: 501(c)3
Highest Offering: Associate Degree
Accreditation: M, ADNUR, CAHIIM, DMS, MUS, POLYT, PTAA, RAD, SURGT

01 President Dr. DeRionne P. POLLARD
05 Sr VP for Academic Affairs Dr. Sanjay RAI
32 Sr VP for Student Affairs Dr. Monica R. BROWN
11 Sr VP for Admin & Fiscal Svcs Dr. Janet WORMACK
30 Sr VP for Advance & Comm Engagement Mr. David SEARS
100 Chief of Staff/Chief Strategy Ofcr Dr. Stephen D. CAIN
88 Deputy Chief of Staff and Strategy Dr. Michelle T. SCOTT
35 Assoc SVP for Student Affairs Dr. Melissa GREGORY
88 Assoc SVP for Admin & Fiscal Svcs Ms. Donna SCHENA
20 Assoc SVP for Academic Affairs Ms. Carolyn TERRY
86 Chief Government Relations Officer Ms. Susan MADDEN
43 Acting General Counsel Mr. Timothy D. DIETZ
04 Assistant to the President Ms. Ida BRITTON
101 Board Relations Coordinator Ms. Arlean GRAHAM
101 Board Relations Coordinator Ms. Lily LEE
12 VP/Prov Rockville Campus Dr. Kimberly KELLEY
12 VP/Prov Germantown Campus Ms. Margaret LATIMER
12 VP/Prov Takoma Park Campus Dr. Brad J. STEWART
103 VP/Prov Workforce Dev & Cont Educ Mr. George M. PAYNE
45 VP of Planning & Inst Effectiveness Ms. Kathleen WESSMAN
13 VP of Instructional & IT/CIO Mr. Carl E. WHITMAN
15 VP of Human Res/Dev & Engagement Ms. Nadine PORTER
18 Interim VP of Facilities & Security Mr. John MCLEAN
26 VP of Communications Mr. Ray GILMER
10 VP of Finance/CFO Ms. Ruby SHERMAN
88 VP of Audit & Business Process Mgmt Mr. Robert PRESTON
106 VP E-Learning/Innov/Teaching Exc Dr. Michael MILLES
50 Instructional Dean of Business Ms. Katherine MICHAELIAN
54 Collegewide Dean Science/Engr/Tech Dr. Muhammad KEHNEMOUYI
53 Instructional Dean Education Ms. Debra POESE
41 Athletic Director Mr. Derek A. CARTER
102 Dir of MC Foundation/Dir of Dev Ms. Carol ROGNRUD
44 Major and Planned Gifts Director Ms. Francene WALKER
102 Exec Dir Hercules Pinkney Life SP Ms. Martha SCHOONMAKER
09 Dir Institutional Rsrch & Analysis Dr. Robert LYNCH
96 Dir of Procurement Mr. Patrick JOHNSON
37 Collegewide Dir of Financial Aid Ms. Judith M. TAYLOR
06 Dir Enroll Svcs & College Registrar Mr. Ernest CARTLEDGE
19 Dir Public Safety/Emergency Mgmt Ms. Shawn HARRISON
108 Dir of Assessment Dr. Cassandra JONES
25 Dir Corporate/Foundation Relations Ms. Rose GARVIN AQUILINO
29 Alumni Coordinator Mr. John LIBBY
08 Dir College Libraries & Info Svcs Mr. Tanner WRAY
104 Coord of Travel & Study Abroad Dr. Gregory MALVEAUX

Morgan State University (F)

1700 East Cold Spring Lane, Baltimore MD 21251-0001
County: Independent City FICE Identification: 002083
Unit ID: 163453
Telephone: (443) 885-3333 Carnegie Class: DU-Mod
FAX Number: (443) 885-3698 Calendar System: Semester
URL: www.morgan.edu
Established: 1867 Annual Undergrad Tuition & Fees (In-State): $7,508
Enrollment: 7,698 Coed
Affiliation or Control: State IRS Status: 501(c)3
Highest Offering: Doctorate
Accreditation: M, BUS, BUSA, DIETD, ENG, ENGR, LSAR, MT, MUS, NURSE, PH, PLNG, SW, TED

53 Dean School of Education Dr. Patricia WELCH
01 President Dr. David WILSON
05 Provost/Vice Pres Academic Affs Dr. Gloria GIBSON
88 VP Academic Outreach and Engagement Dr. Maurice TAYLOR
10 Vice Pres Finance & Management Mr. Sidney EVANS
13 Chief Information Officer Dr. Adebisi OLADIPUPO
32 Vice Pres Student Affairs Dr. Kevin BANKS
30 Vice Pres Institutional Advancement Ms. Cheryl Y. HITCHCOCK
20 Assoc VP for Academic Affairs Dr. Kara TURNER
21 Asst Vice President for Finance Mr. Bickram JANAK
35 Associate VP Student Affairs Ms. Tanya RUSH
100 Chief of Staff Dr. Don-Terry VEAL
49 Acting Dean College of Liberal Arts Dr. Pamela SCOTT-JOHNSON
50 Dean School Business & Management Dr. Fikru BOGHOSSIAN
54 Dean School of Engineering Dr. Eugene DELOATCH
58 Dean of the Graduate School Dr. Mark GARRISON
48 Dean School of Architecture Dr. Mary Anne AKERS
70 Dean School of Social Work Dr. Anna MCPHATTER
69 Dean School of Community Health Dr. Kim SYDNOR
37 Director of Financial Aid Ms. Tanya WILKERSON
38 Director of Counseling Services Ms. Nina DOBSON-HOPKINS
08 Director of Library Dr. Richard BRADBERRY
06 Director of Records/Registration Mr. Hans COOPER
07 Director of Admissions Ms. Shonda GRAY
36 Director of Placement Ms. Seana COULTER
15 Director Human Resources Ms. Armada GRANT
29 Director Alumni Association Mrs. Joyce BROWN
14 Director Computer Center Mr. Gilbert MORGAN
86 Director State Relations Mr. Claude E. HITCHCOCK
09 Director of Institutional Research Ms. Cheryl ROLLINS
18 Acting Director Physical Plant Mr. Premdat KOKILEPERSAUD
26 Director Public Relations Mr. Clinton R. COLEMAN
84 Director Enrollment Management Vacant
96 Interim Director of Purchasing Ms. Lois WHITAKER
28 Director of Diversity Ms. Tanyka BARBER

Mount St. Mary's University (G)

16300 Old Emmitsburg Road,
Emmitsburg MD 21727-7799
County: Frederick FICE Identification: 002086
Unit ID: 163462

Telephone: (301) 447-6122 Carnegie Class: Masters/M
FAX Number: (301) 447-5634 Calendar System: Semester
URL: www.msmary.edu
Established: 1808 Annual Undergrad Tuition & Fees: $37,500
Enrollment: 2,305 Coed
Affiliation or Control: Roman Catholic IRS Status: 501(c)3
Highest Offering: Master's
Accreditation: M, IACBE, TED, THEOL

01 Interim President ... Dr. Timothy W. TRAINOR
03 Vice President/Rector ... Msgr. Andrew R. BAKER
84 VP Enrollment Mgmt/Stdnt Affairs ... Mr. Michael POST
88 Vice President University Affairs ... Ms. Pauline ENGLESTATTER
05 Interim Provost ... Dr. Jenny HUNTER-CEVERA
10 Vice Pres for Business & Finance ... Mr. William E. DAVIES
30 Vice President for Advancement ... Mr. Robert J. BRENNAN
20 Assoc Provost ... Dr. David MCCARTHY
50 Dean Richard J Bolte Sr Sch of Bus ... Dr. Karl W. EINOLF
53 Dean Sch Education & Human Services ... Dr. Barbara MARTIN PALMER
81 Dean School Natural Science & Math ... Dr. Jeffrey SIMMONS
49 Dean College of Liberal Arts ... Dr. Peter DORSEY
41 Director of Athletics ... Ms. Lynne P. ROBINSON
42 Chaplain ... Fr. Brian NOLAN
32 Interim Dean of Students ... Mr. Kenneth MCVEARRY
12 Dean Frederick Campus ... Mr. Joe LEBHERZ
08 Dean of the Library ... Mr. Charles KUHN
09 Director Institutional Research ... Ms. Linda K. SITES
06 Registrar ... Mr. Chris WEBER
50 Asst Director Grad/Adult Business ... Ms. Carol RINKOFF
88 Manager Conferences/Special Pgms ... Ms. Danielle GRACE
23 Director of Health Services ... Dr. Bonnie PORTIER
24 Director of Media Systems ... Mr. John B. BREWER, JR.
37 Director of Financial Aid ... Mr. David C. REEDER
36 Director Career Center ... Ms. Claire TAURIELLO
88 Chief Transformation Officer ... Mr. Simon BLACKWELL
26 Director of University Marketing ... Ms. Hilary DOUWES
44 Director of Annual Giving ... Ms. Emily MYERS
15 Director of Human Resources ... Vacant
19 Director of Public Safety ... Mr. Rodney GRAYS
29 Director of Alumni Relations ... Ms. Maureen C. PLANT
18 Director of Physical Plant ... Ms. Kimberly KLABE
88 Director Office of Social Justice ... Mr. Ian VANANDEN
28 Director Ctr for Student Diversity ... Ms. Chianti BLACKMON
35 Dir Campus Activ/Student Ldrshp ... Mr. Joe ENSTE
92 Director of the Honors Program ... Dr. Jennifer STAIGER
40 Manager of College Store ... Ms. Amanda CASALE
96 Purchasing Agent ... Ms. Maria L. TOPPER

Ner Israel Rabbinical College (A)

400 Mount Wilson Lane, Baltimore MD 21208-1198
County: Baltimore FICE Identification: 002087
Unit ID: 163532
Telephone: (410) 484-7200 Carnegie Class: Spec-4-yr-Faith
FAX Number: (410) 484-3060 Calendar System: Semester
Established: 1933 Annual Undergrad Tuition & Fees: $10,900
Enrollment: 512 Male
Affiliation or Control: Independent Non-Profit IRS Status: 501(c)3
Highest Offering: Doctorate
Accreditation: RABN

01 President ... Rabbi Sheftel M. NEUBERGER
05 Chief Academic Officer ... Rabbi Aharon FELDMAN
03 Executive Director ... Mr. Jerome H. KADDEN
04 Assistant to the President ... Rabbi Boruch NEUBERGER
07 Director of Admissions ... Rabbi Beryl WEISBORD
13 Director of Administrative Services ... Mr. Larry RIBAKOW
06 Registrar ... Rabbi Chaim D. LAPIDUS
37 Director Student Financial Aid ... Rabbi Shmuel SCHACHTER
85 Foreign Student Advisor ... Rabbi Eliyahu HAKKAKIAN
30 Director of Development ... Rabbi Louis HOFFMAN
45 Director of Planning ... Rabbi Leonard OBERSTEIN
26 Director Community Relations ... Rabbi Jonathan SEIDEMANN
18 Chief Physical Plant ... Mr. David FRIEDMAN
08 Head Librarian ... Rabbi Avrohom SHNIDMAN
39 Director of Student Housing ... Rabbi Emanuel GOLDFEIZ
29 Associate Director Alumni Relations ... Rabbi Eli GREENGART

Notre Dame of Maryland University (B)

4701 N Charles Street, Baltimore MD 21210-2404
County: Independent City FICE Identification: 002065
Unit ID: 163578
Telephone: (410) 435-0100 Carnegie Class: Masters/L
FAX Number: (410) 532-5791 Calendar System: Semester
URL: www.ndm.edu
Established: 1873 Annual Undergrad Tuition & Fees: $33,670
Enrollment: 2,764 Female
Affiliation or Control: Roman Catholic IRS Status: 501(c)3
Highest Offering: Doctorate
Accreditation: M, NUR, PHAR, TED

01 President ... Dr. Marylou YAM
05 Int Vice President Academic Affairs ... Dr. Clarenda PHILLIPS
32 Vice President Student Life ... Dr. Rebecca SAWYER
30 Vice Pres Institutional Advancement ... Dr. Tanya EASTON
84 Vice Pres Enrollment Management ... Mr. Terry WHITTUM
10 Vice Pres for Finance & Admin ... Mr. Herbert HANSEN
20 Associate VP Academic Affairs ... Dr. Kathryn DOHERTY
88 Assoc VP Enrollment Mgmt ... Ms. Sharon BOGDAN
100 Chief of Staff ... Mr. Gregory FITZGERALD
06 Registrar ... Ms. Irma WILLIAMS
37 Director of Financial Aid ... Ms. Audrey BROOKS
36 Director Career Center ... Mr. Ammad SHEIKH
13 Director Information Technology ... Mr. Warren SZELISTOWSKI
29 Director of Alumnae Relations ... Ms. Emilia POITER
08 Librarian ... Ms. Barbara PREECE
85 Director International Program ... Mr. Eleftherios MICHAEL
07 Director of Admissions ... Ms. Angela BAUMLER
09 Dir Inst Research/Effectiveness ... Ms. Luz CACEDA
15 Director of Human Resources ... Ms. Theresa ARNOVE
18 Director of Facility Management ... Mr. Martin KAJIC
21 Controller ... Ms. Barbara MORRIS
38 Director Counseling Center ... Ms. Amy PROVAN
19 Director of Public Safety ... Mr. Jeff MUNCHEL
40 Bookstore Manager ... Ms. Emily WARNER
41 Athletic Director ... Ms. Erin FOLEY
42 Director Campus Ministry ... Vacant
67 Dean School of Pharmacy ... Dr. Anne LIN
07 Director Pharmacy Admissions ... Mr. Larry SHATTUCK
25 Chief Contracts/Grants Admin ... Mr. Carroll GALVIN
26 Chief Public Relations/Marketing ... Mr. Christian KENDZIERSKI

Prince George's Community College (C)

301 Largo Road, Largo MD 20774-2199
County: Prince Georges FICE Identification: 002089
Unit ID: 163657
Telephone: (301) 546-7422 Carnegie Class: Assoc/HT-High Trad
FAX Number: N/A Calendar System: Semester
URL: www.pgcc.edu
Established: 1958 Annual Undergrad Tuition & Fees (In-District): $3,650
Enrollment: 13,678 Coed
Affiliation or Control: Local IRS Status: 501(c)3
Highest Offering: Associate Degree
Accreditation: M, ADNUR, CAHIIM, COARC, EMT, NMT, RAD

01 President ... Dr. Charlene M. DUKES
05 Vice Pres Academic Affairs ... Dr. Sandra F. DUNNINGTON
32 Vice Pres Student Services ... Dr. Tyjaun A. LEE
10 Vice Pres Administrative Services ... Mr. Thomas E. KNAPP
103 Int VP Workforce Devel/Cont Educ ... Mr. Joseph L. MARTINELLI
72 Vice Pres Technology Services ... Dr. Joseph G. ROSSMEIER
20 Sr Acad Admin to VP for Acad Affs ... Ms. Catherine LAPALOMBARA
38 Dean Student Development Svcs ... Dr. Scheherazade W. FORMAN
84 Dean of Enrollment Services ... Ms. Cindy D. CHILDS
09 Int Dean Planning/Instl Research ... Mr. William RICHMAN
51 Dean Wrkfrce Dev/Cont Educ Pgms ... Mr. Joseph I. MARTINELLI
15 Dean Human Resources ... Ms. Lark T. DOBSON
88 Dean of Learning Foundations ... Dr. Beverly S. REED
21 Dean Financial Affairs ... Ms. Sabrina WELLS
100 Chief of Staff ... Ms. Alonia C. SHARPS
08 Dir Library/Learning Resources ... Ms. Priscilla C. THOMPSON
06 Registrar ... Ms. Nilaya BACCUS-HAIRSTON
07 Director Recruitment ... Vacant
18 Dean Facilities Management ... Dr. David C. MOSBY
88 Director Physical Facilities ... Mr. John DETISTH
86 Dir Community & Government Affairs ... Vacant
30 Exec Dir Institutional Advancement ... Ms. Brenda S. MITCHELL
26 Director Marketing & Creative Svcs ... Ms. Joyce X. BENTZMAN
13 Chief Technology Officer ... Mr. William L. ANDERSON
96 Interim Director of Procurement ... Mrs. LaTonya HOLLAND
37 Director Financial Aid ... Vacant
36 Manager Career & Job Services ... Ms. Stephanie S. PAIR-CUNNINGHAM
79 Dean of Liberal Arts ... Dr. Carolyn F. HOFFMAN
35 Dean College Life Services ... Mr. Malverse A. NICHOLSON, JR.
76 Dean of Health Science ... Ms. Angela D. ANDERSON
81 Dean Science/Tech/Engr/Math ... Dr. Christine E. BARROW
83 Int Dean Soc Sci/Bus Studies Div ... Dr. Lorraine P. BASSETTE

St. John's College (D)

60 College Avenue, Annapolis MD 21401
County: Anne Arundel FICE Identification: 002092
Unit ID: 163976
Telephone: (410) 263-2371 Carnegie Class: Bac-A&S
FAX Number: (410) 626-2886 Calendar System: Semester
URL: www.sjc.edu
Established: 1784 Annual Undergrad Tuition & Fees: $49,119
Enrollment: 472 Coed
Affiliation or Control: Independent Non-Profit IRS Status: 501(c)3
Highest Offering: Master's
Accreditation: M

01 President ... Mr. Christopher B. NELSON
30 Vice Pres Advancement Annapolis ... Ms. Barbara GOYETTE
05 Dean of College ... Dr. Joseph MACFARLAND
10 Treasurer/Financial Officer ... Mr. Joseph SMOLSKIS
06 Registrar ... Ms. Melissa STEINER
07 Director of Admissions ... Mr. Benjamin BAUM
102 Director Corporate/Foundation Rels ... Ms. Susan BORDEN
37 Director of Financial Aid ... Ms. Dana KENNEDY
08 Library Director ... Ms. Catherine DIXON
15 Director of Human Resources ... Ms. Deborah ANAWALT
18 Supt of Buildings & Grounds ... Mr. Sid PHIPPS
19 Chief of Security ... Mr. Timon LINN
23 Director of Student Health ... Ms. Nancy CALABRESE
26 Director of Communications ... Ms. Patricia DEMPSEY
32 Director of Student Services ... Ms. Taylor WATERS
20 Assistant Dean ... Ms. Heather LATHAM
36 Director of Career Services ... Ms. Jaime DUNN
40 Bookstore Manager ... Mr. Robin DUNN
41 Director of Athletics ... Mr. Michael MCQUARRIE
58 Director of Graduate Institute ... Mr. Jeff BLACK
21 Controller ... Ms. Diane SAWYER
29 Director of Alumni Relations ... Mr. Leo PICKENS
04 Executive Asst to President ... Ms. Ashleigh CADMUS

† See Affiliate: St. John's College at Santa Fe, NM.

St. Mary's College of Maryland (E)

47645 College Drive, Saint Mary's City MD 20686-3001
County: Saint Mary's FICE Identification: 002095
Unit ID: 163912
Telephone: (240) 895-2000 Carnegie Class: Bac-A&S
FAX Number: (240) 895-4462 Calendar System: Semester
URL: www.smcm.edu
Established: 1840 Annual Undergrad Tuition & Fees (In-State): $13,895
Enrollment: 1,721 Coed
Affiliation or Control: State IRS Status: 501(c)3
Highest Offering: Master's
Accreditation: M

01 President ... Dr. Tuajuanda C. JORDAN
05 Provost/Dean of Faculty ... Dr. Michael R. WICK
10 VP Business & Finance ... Mr. Charles C. JACKSON
30 VP for Institutional Advancement ... Ms. Carolyn S. CURRY
84 Vice Pres Enrollment Management ... Mr. Gary L. SHERMAN
21 Asst Vice President for Finance ... Mr. Christopher J. TRUE
11 Asst VP for Campus Operations ... Mr. Derek K. THORNTON
101 Exec Assoc to President ... Ms. Cynthia A. GROSS
26 Asst VP of Marketing/Communication ... Mr. Michael L. BRUCKLER
29 Director Alumni Relations ... Mr. David M. SUSHINSKY
09 Assoc Dir Institutional Research ... Mr. Ross P. CONOVER
06 Registrar ... Mr. Nickolas B. TULLEY
20 Interim Assoc Dean of Faculty ... Dr. Katherine L. GANTZ
37 Director of Financial Aid ... Ms. Nadine L. HUTTON
07 Director of Admissions ... Vacant
32 VP for Student Affairs ... Mr. Leonard E. BROWN, JR.
38 Exec Dir of the Wellness Center ... Dr. Kyle K. BISHOP
41 Director of Athletics/Recreation ... Mr. Scott W. DEVINE
20 Int Assoc Dean of Curriculum ... Dr. Christine A. WOOLEY
20 Assoc Dean of Academic Services ... Dr. Donald R. STABILE
18 Assoc VP Planning & Facilities ... Vacant
19 Director of Public Safety ... Ms. Tressa A. SETLAK
40 Director of the Campus Store ... Mr. Richard T. WAGNER
15 Director of Human Resources ... Ms. Shannon K. JARBOE
23 Director of Health Services ... Ms. Linda L. SKUTKA
35 Assoc Dean Retention/Stdnt Success ... Ms. Joanne A. GOLDWATER
13 Asst VP of Information Technology ... Mr. Christopher L. BURCH
44 Sr Devel Ofcr Annual Giving ... Mr. Richard J. EDGAR
08 Director of the Library/Media Svcs ... Ms. Katherine E. PITCHER
102 Director of Corporate and Found ... Ms. Lauren K. SAMPSON
21 Comptroller/Director of Accounting ... Mr. Gabriel A. MBOMEH
43 Assistant Attorney General ... Ms. Allison J. BOYLE
22 Affirm Act/Equal Opportunity Office ... Mr. Melvin A. MCCLINTOCK
25 Director of Sponsored Research ... Dr. Sabine DILLINGHAM
96 Procurement Ofcr/Dir of Auxiliary ... Mr. Patrick G. HUNT
71 Director DeSousa Brent Scholars Pgm ... Dr. Frederico J. TALLEY
88 Director Events and Conferences ... Ms. Linda T. JONES
44 Sr Devel Ofcr Major Gifts ... Ms. Karen C. RALEY
104 Director of International Education ... Vacant
36 Interim Dir of Career Development ... Ms. Kate A. SHIREY
04 Administrative Asst to President ... Ms. Vivian R. JORDAN
90 Senior Learning Technologist ... Mr. Benjamin P. CASTO
91 Director Administrative Computing ... Ms. Emily J. CARTER
39 Director of Residence Life ... Mr. Derek M. YOUNG
88 Dir of Title IX Compliance ... Mr. Michael K. DUNN

Saint Mary's Seminary and University (F)

5400 Roland Avenue, Baltimore MD 21210-1994
County: Independent City FICE Identification: 002096
Unit ID: 163842
Telephone: (410) 864-4000 Carnegie Class: Not Classified
FAX Number: (410) 864-4278 Calendar System: Semester
URL: www.stmarys.edu
Established: 1791 Annual Undergrad Tuition & Fees: N/A
Enrollment: N/A Coed
Affiliation or Control: Roman Catholic IRS Status: 501(c)3
Highest Offering: First Professional Degree
Accreditation: M, THEOL

01 President/Rector ... Rev. Phillip J. BROWN
10 Vice President for Finance ... Mr. Richard G. CHILDS
30 Vice Pres Advancement/Human Res ... Mrs. Elizabeth L. VISCONAGE
05 Dean School Theology ... Rev. Thomas BURKE
73 Dean Ecumenical Institute Theology ... Dr. D. Brent LAYTHAM
73 Dean Ecclesiastical Faculty ... Rev. Thomas BURKE
06 University Registrar ... Ms. Paula M. THIGPEN
37 Director Financial Aid ... Ms. Victoria F. GAUNT
08 Director of Knott Library ... Mr. Thomas RASZEWSKI
13 Director Information Services ... Mr. Arryn MILNE

The SANS Technology Institute (G)

8120 Woodmont Avenue, Suite 310, Bethesda MD 20814
County: Montgomery Identification: 667006
Telephone: (301) 654-7267 Carnegie Class: Not Classified

FAX Number: (301) 951-0140 Calendar System: Other
URL: www.sans.edu
Established: 2006 Annual Graduate Tuition & Fees: N/A
Enrollment: N/A Coed
Affiliation or Control: Proprietary IRS Status: Proprietary
Highest Offering: Master's; No Undergraduates
Accreditation: M

01 President ....Mr. Alan PALLER
03 Executive Director ....Mr. Bill LOCKHART
05 Provost ....Dr. Toby GOUKER

Stevenson University (A)

1525 Greenspring Valley Road,
Stevenson MD 21153-0641
County: Baltimore FICE Identification: 002107
Unit ID: 164173
Telephone: (410) 486-7000 Carnegie Class: Masters/M
FAX Number: (410) 486-3552 Calendar System: Semester
URL: www.stevenson.edu
Established: 1947 Annual Undergrad Tuition & Fees: $30,998
Enrollment: 4,322 Coed
Affiliation or Control: Independent Non-Profit IRS Status: 501(c)3
Highest Offering: Master's
Accreditation: M, CSHSE, MT, NURSE, TED

01 President ....Dr. Kevin J. MANNING
04 Assistant to President ....Ms. Ruth HUBBARD
05 Executive VP for Academic Affairs ....Dr. Paul D. LACK
10 Exec Vice Pres/Chief Financial Ofcr ..Mr. Timothy M. CAMPBELL
30 Vice Pres University Advancement ....Mr. Steve CLOSE
84 Vice Pres Enrollment Management ....Mr. Mark J. HERGAN
32 Vice President Student Affairs ....Ms. Claire E. MOORE
26 Int VP Marketing & Digital Comm ....Mr. John BUETTNER
15 Vice Pres for Human Resources ....Ms. Pamela BARKETT
100 Vice President & Chief of Staff ....Ms. Sue KENNEY
20 Associate VP for Academic Affairs ....Dr. Jo-Ellen ASBURY
36 VP for Career Services ....Ms. Anne SCHOLL-FIEDLER
58 Dean Graduate/Professional Studies ....Ms. Joyce K. BECKER
50 Interim Dean School of Business ....Mr. Aris MELISSARATOS
81 Dean School of Science ....Dr. Meredith DURMOWICZ
83 Dean Sch of Humanities/Social Sci ....Vacant
88 Dean School of Design ....Ms. Amanda HOSTALKA
53 Dean School of Education ....Dr. Deborah KRAFT
18 Asst VP Fac & Campus Svcs ....Mr. Leland BEITEL
21 Asst VP Finan Affs/Controller ....Ms. Melanie M. EDMONDSON
37 Director of Financial Aid ....Ms. Barbara MILLER
35 Assoc VP/Dean of Students ....Dr. Jeffrey M. KELLY
13 Chief Information Officer/Asst VP ....Mr. Tom ALLEN
09 Director Institutional Research ....Dr. Bonnie THOMAS
108 Director for Assessment ....Dr. Natasha MILLER
23 Assoc Dean/Dir of Wellness Center ....Ms. Linda REYMANN
66 Associate Dean GPS Nursing ....Dr. Judith FEUSTLE
66 Dept Chair Nursing Education ....Ms. Ellen CLAYTON
106 Associate Dean Distance Education ....Dr. Barbara ZIRKIN
08 Director of Library Services ....Ms. Susan BONSTEEL
06 Registrar ....Ms. Tracy L. BOLT
19 Director of Safety & Security ....Mr. Timothy OSTENDARP
41 Athletic Director ....Mr. Brett C. ADAMS
109 Director Auxiliary Services ....Mr. Robert REED
28 Director of Multicultural Affairs ....Vacant
29 Director Alumni Relations ....Mr. James MYERS
88 Dir of Disability Services ....Ms. Abigail S. HURSON

Stratford University Baltimore Campus (B)

219 S. Central Avenue, Baltimore MD 21202
Telephone: (410) 752-4710 Identification: 770616
Accreditation: ACICS, ACFEI

† Branch campus of Stratford University, Falls Church, VA

University of Phoenix Maryland Campus (C)

8830 Stanford Boulevard, Suite 100,
Columbia MD 21045-5423
Telephone: (410) 872-9001 Identification: 770210
Accreditation: &NH, ACBSP

† No longer accepting campus-based students.

*The University System of Maryland Office (D)

3300 Metzerott Road, Adelphi MD 20783
County: Prince George's FICE Identification: 007959
Unit ID: 164146
Telephone: (301) 445-2740 Carnegie Class: N/A
FAX Number: N/A
URL: www.usmd.edu

01 Chancellor ....Dr. Robert L. CARET
05 Sr VC Academic Affairs ....Dr. Joann BOUGHMAN
10 COO/Vice Chanc Admin & Finance ....Mr. Joseph F. VIVONA
30 VC Advancement & CEO USM Foundation ....Mr. Leonard R. RALEY
86 VC Governmental Relations ....Mr. Patrick N. HOGAN
26 VC for Communications ....Ms. Anne MOULTRIE
100 USM Chief of Staff ....Ms. Janice B. DOYLE
20 Assoc Vice Chanc Academic Affairs ....Ms. Teri HOLLANDER
13 Assoc VC & CIO ....Mr. Donald Z. SPICER
21 Director Internal Audit ....Mr. David MOSCA
21 Director Budget Analysis ....Ms. Monica WEST

*University of Maryland College Park (E)

1101 Main Administration Building,
College Park MD 20742
County: Prince Georges FICE Identification: 002103
Unit ID: 163286
Telephone: (301) 405-1000 Carnegie Class: DU-Highest
FAX Number: (301) 314-9560 Calendar System: Semester
URL: www.umd.edu
Established: 1856 Annual Undergrad Tuition & Fees (In-State): $9,996
Enrollment: 37,610 Coed
Affiliation or Control: State IRS Status: 501(c)3
Highest Offering: Doctorate
Accreditation: M, AUD, BUS, CEA, CLPSY, COPSY, DIETD, DIETI, ENG, IACEE, IPSY, JOUR, LIB, LSAR, MFCD, MUS, PH, PLNG, SCPSY, SP, SPAA, TED

02 President ....Dr. Wallace D. LOH
100 Asst Pres & Chief of Staff ....Ms. Michele A. EASTMAN
05 Sr Vice President & Provost ....Dr. Mary Ann RANKIN
10 Vice President Admin & Finance ....Mr. Carlo COLELLA
43 Vice President and General Counsel ...Mr. Michael R. FOTERALA
30 Vice President University Relations ....Mr. Peter E. WEILER
32 Vice President Student Affairs ....Dr. Linda M. CLEMENT
13 Vice Pres Info Tech & CIO ....Dr. Eric DENNA
46 Vice President Research ....Dr. Patrick G. O'SHEA
47 Dean Col Agric/Natural Resources ....Dr. Craig BEYROUTY
48 Dean Sch Architecture/Plng/Preserv ....Mr. David CRONRATH
79 Dean College Arts & Humanities ....Dr. Bonnie T. DILL
83 Dean Col Behavioral/Social Sciences ....Dr. Gregory F. BALL
50 Dean Smith School of Business ....Dr. Alexander J. TRIANTIS
81 Dean Computer/Math/Natural Science ....Dr. Jayanth R. BANAVAR
53 Dean of College of Education ....Dr. Donna L. WISEMAN
54 Dean Clark School of Engineering ....Dr. Darryl J. PINES
69 Dean School of Public Health ....Dr. Jane E. CLARK
60 Dean Merrill College of Journalism ....Ms. Lucy A. DALGLISH
62 Dean College Info Studies ....Dr. Keith MARZULLO
80 Dean School Public Policy ....Dr. Robert C. ORR
20 Dean Undergraduate Studies ....Dr. William A. COHEN
58 Dean Graduate School ....Vacant
08 Interim Dean of Libraries ....Dr. Babak HAMIDZADEH
104 Assoc VP International Affairs ....Dr. Ross D. LEWIN
09 Asst VP/Inst Research & Planning ....Ms. Sharon A. LA VOY
18 Assoc VP & Chief Facilities Officer ....Mr. Charles R. REUNING
28 Assoc VP & Chief Diversity Officer ....Dr. Kumea SHORTER-GOODEN
39 Director Resident Life ....Dr. Deborah F. GRANDNER
88 Assoc Vice Pres for Research ....Ms. Denise CLARK
35 Asst Vice Pres Student Affairs ....Dr. John ZACKER
84 Assoc VP Enrollment Mgmt ....Ms. Barbara A. GILL
07 Director of Undergrad Admissions ....Ms. Shannon GUNDY
37 Director Student Financial Aid ....Ms. Monique BOYD
56 Assoc VP Extended Studies ....Mr. Chuck A. WILSON
06 University Registrar ....Dr. Adrian R. CORNELIUS
21 Assoc Vice Pres & CFO ....Mr. Paul S. DWORKIS
26 Asst VP Marketing & Communications ....Mr. Brian ULLMANN
20 Professor/Assoc Prov Faculty Affs ....Dr. John BERTOT
29 Exec Director Alumni Association ....Ms. Amy EICHHORST
36 Director University Career Center ....Mr. Kelley BISHOP
64 Director School of Music ....Dr. Robert L. GIBSON
85 Dir Intl Student & Scholar Services ....Ms. Susan-Ellis DOUGHERTY
41 Director Athletics ....Mr. Kevin ANDERSON
109 Director Stamp Student Union ....Dr. Marsha A. GUENZLER-STEVENS
23 Director University Health Center ....Dr. David MCBRIDE
38 Director Counseling Center ...Dr. Sharon E. KIRKLAND-GORDON
19 Dir Pub Safety/Chief Campus Police ....Mr. David B. MITCHELL
15 Asst VP University Human Resources ...Ms. Jewel WASHINGTON
92 Director University Honors Program ....Dr. Susan J. DWYER
31 Asst Director Community Service ....Dr. Craig SLACK
86 Exec Director Government Relations ....Mr. Ross STERN
96 Asst VP Procurement Str Sourcing ....Mr. James P. HALEY, SR.
106 Assoc Provost Learning Initiatives ....Dr. Ben BEDERSON
108 Assoc Provost Acad Planning & Pgms ....Dr. Elizabeth J. BEISE

*University of Maryland Baltimore (F)

620 W. Lexington Street, Baltimore MD 21201-1508
County: Independent City FICE Identification: 002104
Unit ID: 163259
Telephone: (410) 706-7004 Carnegie Class: Spec-4-yr-Med
FAX Number: (410) 706-0500 Calendar System: Semester
URL: www.umaryland.edu
Established: 1807 Annual Undergrad Tuition & Fees (In-State): N/A
Enrollment: 6,276 Coed
Affiliation or Control: State IRS Status: 501(c)3
Highest Offering: Doctorate
Accreditation: M, ANEST, DENT, DH, DIETI, IPSY, LAW, MED, MT, NURSE, PA, PH, PHAR, PTA, RADDOS, SW

02 President ....Dr. Jay A. PERMAN
05 Sr VP/Chief Acad & Research Officer ....Dr. Bruce E. JARRELL
11 VP Operations & Planning/Vice Dean ....Dr. Roger J. WARD
17 Vice President Medical Affairs/Dean ....Dr. E. Albert REECE
10 Chief Admin & Finance Officer/VP ....Ms. Dawn M. RHODES
25 VP/Chf Enterprise & Econ Dev Ofc ....Mr. James L. HUGHES
13 VP/Chief Information Officer ....Dr. Peter J. MURRAY
46 Sr VP/Chief Acad & Research Officer ....Dr. Bruce E. JARRELL
26 Chief Communications Officer/VP ....Ms. Jennifer B. LITCHMAN
30 Chief Development Officer/VP ....Mr. Michael B. DOWDY
86 Chief Govt Affairs Officer/AVP ....Mr. Kevin P. KELLY
43 Chief University Counsel ....Ms. Susan GILLETTE
19 Chief of Police/AVP Public Safety ....Mr. Antonio WILLIAMS
88 Chief Accountability Officer ....Dr. Roger J. WARD
32 Sr Assoc Dean/AVP Acad & Stdnt Affs ....Mr. Flavius R. LILLY
18 Assoc VP Facilities & Operations ....Mr. Robert M. ROWAN
15 Assoc VP Human Resources ....Mr. Matthew LASECKI
37 Assoc VP Student Financial Asst ....Ms. Patricia A. SCOTT
44 Assoc VP Development ....Mr. Thomas HOFSTETTER
21 Assoc VP Budget & Finance ....Mr. Scott BITNER
88 Deputy Chief Accountability Ofc AVP ....Ms. Susan BUSKIRK
14 Asst VP Information Technology ....Mr. Christopher G. PHILLIPS
09 Asst VP Institutional Research ....Mr. Gregory C. SPENGLER
108 Asst VP Inst Res & Accountability ....Mr. Gregory C. SPENGLER
27 Asst VP Communications & Public Aff ....Ms. Laura A. KOZAK
88 AVP Sponsored Projects Accounting ....Ms. Lynn M. MCGINLEY
88 AVP ORD Marketing & Operations ....Ms. Linda CASSARD
88 AVP ORD Sponsored Programs Admin ....Mr. Dennis PAFFRATH
88 AVP ORD Technology Transfer ....Mr. Philip ROBILOTTO
88 AVP ORD Center for Clinical Trials ....Mr. Michael ROLLOR
88 AVP ORD Economic Development ....Ms. Jane SHAAB
102 Treasurer & Dir of Operations UMBF ....Ms. Pamela HECKLER
08 Exec Dir Health Sci/Human Svc Libr ....Ms. Mary J. TOOEY
90 Exec Dir Enterprise Applications ....Mr. Michael SMITH
31 Exec Dir Cmty Initiatives/Engage ....Ms. Ashley R. VALIS
06 Director Records & Registration ....Mr. Ryan HOLTZ
88 Director Benefits & Compensation ....Ms. Patricia HOFFMAN
22 Director EEO/Affirmative Action ....Ms. Sheila GREENWOOD-BLACKSHEAR
28 Dir Diversity & Inclusion Init ....Ms. Rahel DENBOBA
85 Director International Services ....Ms. Amy RAMIREZ
38 Director Counseling ....Ms. Emilia K. PETRILLO
41 Director Univ Recreation & Fitness ....Mr. William P. CROCKETT
23 Director Student Health Center ....Dr. James BARONAS
35 Director Student Services ....Ms. Cynthia E. RICE
39 Director of UM Housing ....Ms. Margaret SCHOTTO
88 Director of Financial Services ....Ms. Susan E. MCKECHNIE
96 Director of Procurement Services ....Mr. Joseph EVANS
45 Dir of Capital Budget and Planning ....Ms. Angela FOWLER-YOUNG
105 Dir Web Dev Interactive Media ....Mr. Amir CHAMSAZ
52 Dean School of Dentistry ....Dr. Mark A. REYNOLDS
58 Dean Graduate School ....Dr. Bruce E. JARRELL
61 Dean School of Law ....Mr. Donald TOBIN
63 Dean School of Medicine ....Dr. E. Albert REECE
66 Dean School of Nursing ....Dr. Jane M. KIRSCHLING
67 Dean School of Pharmacy ....Dr. Natalie D. EDDINGTON
70 Dean School of Social Work ....Dr. Richard P. BARTH

*University of Maryland Baltimore County (G)

1000 Hilltop Circle, Baltimore MD 21250-0001
County: Baltimore FICE Identification: 002105
Unit ID: 163268
Telephone: (410) 455-1000 Carnegie Class: DU-Higher
FAX Number: (410) 455-1210 Calendar System: 4/1/4
URL: www.umbc.edu
Established: 1966 Annual Undergrad Tuition & Fees (In-State): $11,006
Enrollment: 13,979 Coed
Affiliation or Control: State IRS Status: 501(c)3
Highest Offering: Doctorate
Accreditation: M, CLPSY, CS, DANCE, DMS, EMT, ENG, IPSY, MUS, SW, TED

02 President ....Dr. Freeman A. HRABOWSKI
05 Provost/Sr Vice Pres Acad Affs ....Dr. Philip ROUS
10 Vice Pres Finance/Administration ....Ms. Lynne SCHAEFER
32 Vice President Student Affairs ....Dr. Nancy YOUNG
30 Vice Pres Institutional Advancement ....Mr. Gregory SIMMONS
13 Vice Pres Information Technology ....Mr. Jack J. SUESS
46 Vice President of Research ....Dr. Karl V. STEINER
49 Dean Col of Arts/Humanities/Soc Sci ....Dr. Scott CASPER
81 Dean Col Natural/Math Sciences ....Dr. William LACOURSE
54 Dean College of Engr/Info Tech ....Dr. Julia ROSS
84 Asst Dean Graduate Enrollment Mgmt ....Ms. K. Jill BARR
20 Vice Provost/Dean Undergrad Educ ....Dr. Diane M. LEE
107 Int Vice Provost for Prof Studies ....Dr. Christopher STEELE
20 Vice Provost Academic Affairs ....Dr. Antonio R. MOREIRA
58 Dean/Vice Provost for Graduate Educ ....Dr. Janet RUTLEDGE
15 Vice Provost Faculty Affairs ....Dr. Patrice MCDERMOTT
84 Vice Provost Enrollment Mgmt ....Dr. Yvette MOZIE-ROSS
21 Assoc VP Financial Services ....Mr. Benjamin LOWENTHAL
26 Assistant to Pres/Assoc VP Mktg/PR ....Ms. Lisa G. AKCHIN
11 Assoc VP Administrative Services ....Ms. Terry COOK
16 Associate VP for Human Resources ....Ms. Valerie A. THOMAS
29 Director Alumni Relations ....Ms. Stanyell BRUCE
88 Asst VP New Media/Instruction Tech ....Mr. John FRITZ
18 Asst VP Facilities Management ....Mr. Rusty POSTLEWATE
04 Senior Advisor to the President ....Dr. Peter HENDERSON
96 Director of Procurement ....Ms. Sharon QUINN
92 Director Honors College ....Dr. Simon STACEY
41 Director Physical Educ & Recreation ....Dr. Tim HALL
19 Director University Police ....Mr. Mark SPARKS
36 Asst VP Career & Corp Partnership ....Ms. Caroline BAKER
23 Int Director Health Services ....Dr. Bruce HERMAN
37 Director Financial Aid ....Ms. Jane HICKEY
25 Asst Director Sponsored Programs ....Mr. Stanley JACKSON
40 Director of UMBC Bookstore ....Mr. Robert J. SOMERS
85 Director International Educ Svcs ....Dr. Arlene WERGIN ODENWALD
08 Director Library ....Mr. Patrick DAWSON

06 Registrar .... Ms. Pamela HAWLEY
35 Int Director Student Life .... Ms. Jennifer DRESS
43 General Counsel .... Mr. David GLEASON
07 Assistant Vice Provost .... Mr. Dale BITTINGER
39 Director Residential Life .... Mr. John FOX
09 Director of Institutional Research .... Dr. Connie PIERSON
38 Director Student Counseling .... Dr. Bruce HERMAN
100 Chief of Staff President's Office .... Ms. Elyse ASHBURN

*University of Maryland Center for Environmental Science (A)

PO Box 775, Cambridge MD 21613

County: Dorchester Identification: 667159
Telephone: (410) 228-9250 Carnegie Class: Not Classified
FAX Number: (410) 228-3843 Calendar System: Semester
URL: www.umces.edu
Established: 1925 Annual Graduate Tuition & Fees: N/A
Enrollment: N/A Coed
Affiliation or Control: State IRS Status: 501(c)3
Highest Offering: Doctorate; No Undergraduates
Accreditation: M

02 President .... Dr. Donald BOESCH
05 Vice Pres for Education .... Dr. Larry SANFORD

*University of Maryland Eastern Shore (B)

11868 Academic Oval, Princess Anne MD 21853-1299

County: Somerset FICE Identification: 002106
Unit ID: 163338
Telephone: (410) 651-2200 Carnegie Class: DU-Mod
FAX Number: (410) 651-6105 Calendar System: Semester
URL: www.umes.edu
Established: 1886 Annual Undergrad Tuition & Fees (In-State): $7,625
Enrollment: 4,279 Coed
Affiliation or Control: State IRS Status: 501(c)3
Highest Offering: Doctorate
Accreditation: M, BUS, CONST, CORE, DIETD, DIETI, ENG, PHAR, PTA, TED

02 President .... Dr. Juliette B. BELL
03 Executive Vice President .... Ms. Kimberly C. DUMPSON
05 Int Provost/VP Academic Affairs .... Dr. Alton THOMPSON
10 Vice Pres Administrative Affs/CFO .... Mr. Kevin APPLETON
30 Vice President Inst Advancement .... Mr. Stephen L. MCDANIEL
32 Vice President Student Affairs .... Vacant
88 VP Research/Economic Development .... Vacant
13 Chief Information Officer .... Vacant
20 Vice Provost Acad Affairs .... Dr. Kimberly D. WHITEHEAD
88 Asst to VP Administrative Affairs .... Dr. Maurice C. NGWABA
21 Asst VP Admin Affs/Budget Director .... Vacant
15 Asst VP Human Resources .... Ms. Marie H. BILLIE
35 Assoc VP Student Affairs .... Dr. James M. WHITE
91 Director Administrative Computing .... Mr. Kenneth GASTON
56 Int Assoc Extension Administrator .... Dr. Enrique N. ESCOBAR
29 Director Alumni Affairs .... Mr. James G. LUNNERMON, II
08 Dean Library Services .... Ms. Adrienne WEBBER
37 Director Financial Aid .... Mr. James W. KELLAM
23 Director Student Health Services .... Ms. Sharone V. GRANT
96 Director Procurement .... Ms. Jacqueline M. COLLINS
07 Actg Dir Admiss & Recruitment .... Ms. Jinawa A. MCNEIL
06 Registrar .... Ms. Cheryl HOLDEN-DUFFY
12 Gen Mgr Richard A Henson Center .... Ms. Kimberly A. MILLS
36 Director Career Services .... Dr. Theresa QUEENAN
09 Director Inst Research/Plng/Assess .... Dr. Stanley M. NYIRENDA
19 Director Public Safety .... Mr. Ernest LEATHERBURY, JR.
18 Director Physical Plant .... Mr. Kenny B. BELTON
39 Director Residence Life .... Mr. Marvin L. JONES
41 Athletic Director .... Mr. Keith S. DAVIDSON
21 Comptroller .... Ms. Bonita E. BYRD
46 Director Sponsored Research .... Ms. Catherine BOLEK
88 Director Student Retention & Svcs .... Dr. Angela L. WILLIAMS
88 Director Upward Bound .... Dr. Nicole L. GALE
35 Director Student Activities .... Ms. Qiana J. DRUMMOND
88 Director Title III Program .... Dr. Frances H. MCKINNEY
26 Director Public Relations .... Mr. William ROBINSON
44 Director Development .... Dr. Veronique L. DIRIKER
88 Director Advancement Services .... Ms. Chenita R. REDDICK
51 Coordinator Continuing Education .... Ms. Gretchen M. BOGGS
38 Coordinator Counseling Services .... Dr. Patricia E. TILGHMAN
58 Dean Graduate Studies .... Dr. Jennifer M. KEANE-DAWES
47 Dean School Agric/Natural Sciences .... Dr. Moses T. KAIRO
49 Dean School of Arts & Professions .... Dr. Ray J. DAVIS
50 Dean School Business & Technology .... Dr. Ayodele J. ALADE
67 Int Dean Sch Pharmacy/Health Prof .... Dr. Rondall E. ALLEN

*University of Maryland University College (C)

3501 University Boulevard East, Adelphi MD 20783-7998

County: Prince Georges FICE Identification: 011644
Unit ID: 163204
Telephone: (301) 985-7000 Carnegie Class: Masters/L
FAX Number: (301) 985-7678 Calendar System: Semester
URL: www.umuc.edu
Established: 1947 Annual Undergrad Tuition & Fees (In-State): $7,056
Enrollment: 47,906 Coed
Affiliation or Control: State IRS Status: 501(c)3
Highest Offering: Doctorate
Accreditation: M, CAHIIM, NURSE, TED

02 President .... Mr. Javier MIYARES
11 SVP/Chief Operating Officer .... Mr. George SHOENBERGER
10 Vice Pres Chief Financial Officer .... Mr. Eugene D. LOCKETT, JR.
05 Provost/Sr Vice Pres Academic Affs .... Dr. Marie CINI
26 Sr Vice President Communications .... Mr. Michael FREEDMAN
45 Sr VP Institutional Effectiveness .... Vacant
88 Sr VP Military & Veteran Operations .... Mr. Lloyd MILES
13 Sr Vice Pres Analytics/Plng/Tech .... Mr. Peter C. YOUNG
43 Vice President & General Counsel .... Ms. Maureen DAVID
15 VP/Chief Human Resources Officer .... Mr. John PETROV
86 Vice Pres Federal Govt Relations .... Ms. Sarah DUFENDACH
30 Vice Pres Inst Advancement .... Ms. Cathy SWEET
28 Ombudsman/VP Diversity Programs .... Dr. Blair HAYES
18 Associate Vice President Facilities .... Mr. George TRUJILLO
88 Director of State Govt Relations .... Vacant
37 AVP Student Financial Aid .... Ms. Cheryl STORIE
58 Vice Prov/Dean The Graduate School .... Mr. Aric KRAUSE
08 Assoc Provost of Library Services .... Mr. Stephen MILLER
06 Assoc Vice Provost/Registrar .... Ms. Joellen SHENDY
49 Dean The Undergrad School .... Dr. Matthew PRINEAS
09 Sr Director Institutional Research .... Wei ZHOU
07 Director of Admissions .... Vacant
84 Sr VP Strategic Enrollment Mgmt .... Ms. Erika ORRIS

*Bowie State University (D)

14000 Jericho Park Road, Bowie MD 20715-3318

County: Prince Georges FICE Identification: 002062
Unit ID: 162007
Telephone: (301) 860-4000 Carnegie Class: Masters/L
FAX Number: (301) 860-3510 Calendar System: Semester
URL: www.bowiestate.edu
Established: 1865 Annual Undergrad Tuition & Fees (In-State): $7,660
Enrollment: 5,695 Coed
Affiliation or Control: State IRS Status: 501(c)3
Highest Offering: Doctorate
Accreditation: M, ACBSP, CS, NUR, SPAA, SW, TED

02 President .... Dr. Mickey L. BURNIM
05 Provost/Vice Pres Academic Affs .... Dr. Weldon JACKSON
10 Vice Pres Finance & Administration .... Dr. Karl B. BROCKENBROUGH
30 Vice Pres Institutional Advancement .... Dr. Richard LUCAS, JR.
32 VP Student Affairs/Campus Life .... Dr. Artie L. TRAVIS
43 Vice Pres & General Counsel .... Ms. Karen JOHNSON SHAHEED
35 Student Code of Conduct .... Mrs. Thomaice BOARDLEY
13 VP Office of Information Technology .... Mr. E. Wayne ROSE
84 Asst VP Enrollment Management .... Mr. Troy MILLER
88 Asst to Prov Institutional Effec .... Ms. Gayle M. FINK
06 University Registrar .... Ms. Patricia MITCHELL
08 Assoc Library Dir/Interim Dean .... Ms. Marian RUCKER-SHAMU
36 Director Career Services .... Ms. April JOHNOSON
15 Sr Director of Human Resources .... Ms. Sheila HOBSON
19 Chief of Campus Police .... Mr. Ernest WAITERS
58 Int Dean Sch of Grad Stds/Research .... Dr. Cosmos NWOKEAFOR
49 Dean College of Arts & Sciences .... Dr. George ACQUAAH
50 Dean College of Business .... Dr. Anthony NELSON
53 Interim Dean College of Education .... Dr. Rhonda JETER-TWILLEY
107 Dean College of Professional Stds .... Dr. Jerome H. SCHIELE
92 Director UCE Honors Program .... Dr. Monika GROSS
23 Director University Wellness Center .... Dr. Rita WUTOH
41 Director Athletics .... Mr. Clyde DOUGHTY, JR.
26 Dir University Relations/ Marketing .... Ms. Cassandra M. ROBINSON
88 Director University Wiseman Centre .... Mr. Frank WALLER
37 Director Financial Aid .... Ms. Angela ISAAC
18 Director Facilities .... Mr. Darryl WILLIFORD
07 Director Undergraduate Admissions .... Mr. Derrick DAVIS
29 Director of Alumni Relations .... Ms. Anette WEDDERBURN
96 Director of Purchasing .... Mr. Steve A. JOST
09 Director of Institutional Research .... Ms. Shama AKHTAR
100 Chief of Staff .... Ms. Tammi L. THOMAS
04 Administrative Asst to President .... Ms. Denise WARD
108 Director Institutional Assessment .... Dr. Becky VERZINSKI
38 Director Student Counseling .... Dr. Tonya SWANSON
39 Director Student Housing .... Ms. Gladys WATSON

*Coppin State University (E)

2500 W North Avenue, Baltimore MD 21216-3698

County: Baltimore City FICE Identification: 002068
Unit ID: 162283
Telephone: (410) 951-3000 Carnegie Class: Masters/S
FAX Number: (410) 333-5369 Calendar System: Semester
URL: www.coppin.edu
Established: 1900 Annual Undergrad Tuition & Fees (In-State): $7,346
Enrollment: 3,133 Coed
Affiliation or Control: State IRS Status: 501(c)3
Highest Offering: Doctorate
Accreditation: M, ACBSP, CAHIIM, CORE, NURSE, SW, TED

02 President .... Dr. Maria THOMPSON
05 Int Provost/VP Academic Affairs .... Dr. Beverly DOWNING
30 VP Institutional Advancement .... Mr. Douglas DALZELL
10 VP Administration & Finance .... Mr. Steve DANIK
32 Vice Pres Student Affairs .... Dr. Michael FREEMAN
13 VP Information Systems/CIO .... Dr. Ahmed EL-HAGGAN
84 Assoc VP Enrollment Management .... Mr. Troy MILLER
45 Assoc VP Planning/Assessment .... Vacant
20 Actg Assoc Vice Pres Academic Affs .... Dr. Habtu BRAHA
21 Assoc Vice Pres Admin/Finance .... Vacant
18 Assoc VP Capital Plng/Constr & Cont .... Mr. Maqbool PATEL
86 Assoc VP of Pub Policy & Govt Rel .... Dr. Monica E. RANDALL
15 Assoc VP of Human Resorces .... Mrs. Lisa EARLY
07 Director of Admissions .... Ms. Michelle R. GROSS
06 Interim Registrar .... Ms. Karen BARLAND
21 Controller .... Mrs. Crystal MOSLEY
08 Director of the Library .... Dr. Mary WANZA
37 Director of Financial Aid .... Ms. Thelma ROSS
36 Director of Career Services Center .... Mrs. Linda BOWIE
19 Chief of Public Safety .... Chief Leonard HAMM
39 Director of Housing/Residence Life .... Mrs. Vallyn MERRICK
41 Int Director of Athletics .... Mrs. Alecia SHIELDS-GADSON
35 Director Student Support Services .... Ms. Leila WASHINGTON
44 Director Major Gifts/Planned Giving .... Ms. Tara TURNER
96 Director of Purchasing .... Mr. Thomas E. DAWSON, JR.
26 Director of University Relations .... Vacant
88 Director Client Computing Services .... Mr. Emmanuel OWUSU-SEKYERE
88 Director Coppin Academy .... Vacant
35 Director of Student Activities .... Mrs. Jocelyn BRYANT
14 Director Telecommunications .... Mr. Claude K. RADER
105 Director Web & Multimedia .... Mr. Andrew C. BAIN
31 Exec Dir of Community Partnerships .... Vacant
92 Dean Honors College & McNair Pgms .... Mr. Ronnie L. COLLINS, SR.
58 Dean Graduate School .... Dr. Mary E. OWENS-SOUTHHALL
66 Dean of Nursing .... Dr. Tracey L. MURRAY
04 Executive Assistant to President .... Mrs. Sherie JOHNSON
88 Chair Interdisciplinary Studies .... Ms. Tondelaya BLACKSTONE
97 Chair General & Adult Education .... Dr. Jacqueline H. WILLIAMS
88 Int Chr Applied Psych/Rehab Counsel .... Mr. James STEWART
61 Chair Crim Justice/Law Enforcement .... Dr. Dilip DAS
53 Chair Curriculum & Instruction .... Dr. Glynis BARBER
57 Chair Fine Arts .... Dr. Garey HYATT
82 Chair History Geography/Global Stds .... Dr. Katherine BANKOLE-MEDINA
79 Interim Chair Humanities .... Dr. Seth FORREST
50 Chr Mgmt Sci & Economics (Business) .... Dr. Habtu BRAHA
77 Int Chair Math & Computer Science .... Dr. Sean BROOKS
65 Chair Natural Sciences .... Dr. Gilbert OGONJI
83 Chair Social Sciences .... Dr. John L. HUDGINS
70 Chair Social Work .... Dr. Errol BOLDEN
68 Chair Health/Physical Education .... Vacant
88 Chair Special Education .... Dr. Daniel P. JOSEPH

*Frostburg State University (F)

101 Braddock Road, Frostburg MD 21532-2303

County: Allegany FICE Identification: 002072
Unit ID: 162584
Telephone: (301) 687-4000 Carnegie Class: Masters/L
FAX Number: (301) 687-4737 Calendar System: Semester
URL: www.frostburg.edu
Established: 1898 Annual Undergrad Tuition & Fees (In-State): $8,488
Enrollment: 5,645 Coed
Affiliation or Control: State IRS Status: 501(c)3
Highest Offering: Doctorate
Accreditation: M, BUS, CAATE, ENG, NRPA, NURSE, SW, TED

02 President .... Dr. Ronald NOWACZYK
05 Int Provost & VP Academic Affairs .... Dr. Ahmad TOOTOONCHI
32 VP Student/Education Svcs .... Dr. Thomas BOWLING
10 Vice President for Admin & Finance .... Mr. David C. ROSE
30 Vice Pres Univ Advancement .... Mr. John SHORT
84 Assoc VP for Enrollment Management .... Mr. Wray BLAIR
100 Int VP for Intl & Govt Affairs .... Dr. John BOWMAN
15 Vice President Human Resources .... Ms. Katherine SNYDER
43 University Counsel .... Ms. Karen A. TREBER
20 Associate Provost .... Vacant
20 Interim Asst Provost .... Dr. Doris SANTAMARIA-MAKANG
21 Assoc VP Finance & Controller .... Mr. Richard A. REPAC
35 Asst VP Student Svcs/Dean of Stdnts .... Vacant
88 Associate VP Univ Advancement .... Ms. Colleen STUMP
45 Assoc Director Budget & Planning .... Ms. Denise MURPHY
49 Dean Col Liberal Arts & Science .... Dr. Joseph M. HOFFMAN
50 Int Dean College of Business .... Dr. Sudhir SINGH
53 Dean College of Education .... Dr. Clarence GOLDEN
08 Director of the Library .... Ms. Lea MESSMAN-MANDICOTT
37 Director of Financial Aid .... Mrs. Angela L. HOVATTER
108 Director of PAIR .... Ms. SaraBeth BITTINGER
25 Dir of Research/Sponsored Programs .... Mr. Aaron HOEL
58 Director of Graduate Services .... Ms. Vickie MAZER
18 Director Facilities/Physical Plant .... Mr. Robert BOYCE
26 Director News & Media Services .... Ms. Elizabeth MEDCALF
36 Director Career Services .... Dr. Robbie L. CORDLE
38 Assoc Dir Counseling & Psyc Svcs .... Dr. Shawn F. GOLDEN-LLEWELLYN
40 Asst Mgr Bookstore & ID Services .... Mr. Kenneth EMERICK
41 Athletic Director .... Mr. Troy DELL
19 Chief University Police .... Col. Cynthia SMITH
13 Chief Information Officer .... Mr. Troy DONOWAY
91 Director of Technology Services .... Ms. Beth KENNEY
29 Director of Alumni .... Ms. Shannon L. GRIBBLE
22 Director of AA/EEO .... Mrs. Beth HOFFMAN
07 Director of Admissions .... Ms. Trisha GREGORY
28 Director of Diversity .... Ms. Robin WYNDER
44 Major Gifts Officer .... Mr. Jason ANDRICK
14 Dir Networking/Telecommunications .... Mr. Brian JENKINS
96 Coord Procurement/Material Handling .... Mr. Alan R. SNYDER
23 Director Health Services .... Ms. Darlene SMITH
39 Director Residence Life .... Mr. Dana A. SEVERANCE
06 Registrar .... Dr. Jay HEGEMAN

*Salisbury University (A)

1101 Camden Avenue, Salisbury MD 21801-6860
County: Wicomico — FICE Identification: 002091
Unit ID: 163851
Telephone: (410) 543-6000 — Carnegie Class: Masters/L
FAX Number: (410) 548-2587 — Calendar System: Semester
URL: www.salisbury.edu
Established: 1925 — Annual Undergrad Tuition & Fees (In-State): $9,086
Enrollment: 8,770 — Coed
Affiliation or Control: State — IRS Status: 501(c)3
Highest Offering: Doctorate
Accreditation: M, BUS, BUSA, CAATE, COARC, EXSC, MT, MUS, NURSE, SW, TED

02 President .... Dr. Janet E. DUDLEY-ESHBACH
05 Provost & Sr VP of Acad Affairs .... Dr. Diane D. ALLEN
100 Chief of Staff .... Ms. Amy S. HASSON
10 Interim VP Admin and Finance .... Mr. Marvin PYLES
32 Vice Pres of Student Affairs .... Dr. Dane R. FOUST
30 Vice Pres Advancement/External Affs .... Mr. T. Greg PRINCE
84 Asst VP of Enrollment Management .... Mr. Aaron M. BASKO
28 Chief Diversity Officer .... Mr. Humberto X. ARISTIZABAL
35 Associate VP of Student Affairs .... Ms. Mentha A. HYNES-WILSON
20 Interim Associate Provost .... Dr. Jason MCCARTNEY
20 Assoc Vice Pres Academic Affairs .... Ms. Melissa M. BOOG
18 Assoc VP Facilities & Cap Mgmt .... Mr. Eric J. BERKHEIMER
35 Asst VP Student Affs/Dean Students .... Ms. Valerie J. RANDALL-LEE
13 Chief Information Officer .... Mr. Ken KUNDELL
26 Director of Public Relations .... Mr. Richard W. CULVER
41 Interim Director of Athletics .... Dr. Gerard DIBARTOLO
92 Director Honors Program .... Dr. James J. BUSS
06 Registrar .... Ms. Jacqueline M. MAISEL
07 Director of Admissions .... Ms. Elizabeth A. SKOGLUND
09 Special Asst to Pres/UARA .... Dr. Kara O. SIEGERT
08 Dean of Libraries & Instr Resources .... Dr. Beatriz B. HARDY
38 Director of Counseling Center .... Dr. Kathleen J. SCOTT
36 Director of Career Services .... Dr. Kevin FALLON
37 Director of Financial Aid .... Ms. Barri ZIMMERMAN
15 Assoc VP for HR .... Vacant
29 Dir Alumni Relations & Gift Develop .... Mr. Jayme E. BLOCK
23 Director of Student Health Services .... Ms. Victoria A. LENTZ
35 Director of Student Activities .... Ms. Tricia G. SMITH
86 Dir of Govt & Community Relations .... Mr. Robert J. SHEEHAN
43 General Counsel .... Ms. Susan A. GRIISSER
39 Director Housing/Residence Life .... Mr. David P. GUTOSKEY
19 Director of Public Safety .... Mr. Edwin L. LASHLEY
40 Director of Bookstore .... Ms. Lisa G. GRAY
18 Director of Physical Plant .... Mr. Kevin J. MANN
96 Director of Purchasing .... Vacant
75 Dean Henson Sch Science/Tech .... Dr. Karen L. OLMSTEAD
50 Dean Perdue School of Business .... Dr. Christy H. WEER
49 Dean Fulton School of Liberal Arts .... Dr. Maarten L. PEREBOOM
53 Int Dean Seidel Sch Ed/Prof Studies .... Dr. Kelly FIALA
58 Dean Graduate Studies/Research .... Dr. Clifton P. GRIFFIN
88 Dir Ctr for Student Achievement .... Dr. Heather W. HOLMES
19 Asst VP Public Sfty/Chief of Police .... Chief Bernard GERST
53 Dean College of Education .... Dr. Laurie MULLEN
50 Dean College of Business/Economics .... Dr. Shohreh A. KAYNAMA
49 Dean College of Liberal Arts .... Dr. Terry COONEY
81 Dean J&M Fisher Col of Science/Math .... Dr. David VANKO
57 Dean Col Fine Arts/Communications .... Ms. Susan PICINICH
76 Dean College of Health Professions .... Dr. Lisa PLOWFIELD
92 Interim Dean Honors College .... Dr. Terry COONEY
43 University Counsel .... Ms. Traevena BYRD
08 Dean of University Libraries .... Ms. Deborah NOLAN
104 Director Study Abroad .... Ms. Liz SHEARER
94 Chair Women's & Gender Studies .... Dr. Cindy H. GISSENDANNER
09 Director Institutional Research .... Mr. Tim BIBO, JR.
27 Dir Communications/Media Relations .... Mr. Raymond C. FELDMANN
41 Director of Athletics .... Mr. Timothy LEONARD
23 Director of Health Services .... Dr. Matthias GOLDSTEIN
40 Director of University Store .... Ms. Stacey ELOFIR
96 Director of Procurement .... Ms. Lucy SLAICH
38 Director Counseling Center .... Dr. Gregory REISING
36 Director of Career Center .... Ms. Lorie LOGAN-BENNETT
06 Assoc Director Records/Registration .... Ms. Susan HYMAN

*Towson University (B)

8000 York Road, Baltimore MD 21252-0001
County: Baltimore — FICE Identification: 002099
Unit ID: 164076
Telephone: (410) 704-2000 — Carnegie Class: Masters/L
FAX Number: N/A — Calendar System: 4/1/4
URL: www.towson.edu
Established: 1866 — Annual Undergrad Tuition & Fees (In-State): $9,182
Enrollment: 22,285 — Coed
Affiliation or Control: State — IRS Status: 501(c)3
Highest Offering: Doctorate
Accreditation: M, ARCPA, AUD, BUS, BUSA, CAATE, CS, DANCE, FEPAC, IPSY, MUS, NURSE, OT, SP, TED, THEA

02 President .... Dr. Kim SCHATZEL
05 Provost/Vice Pres Acad Affairs .... Dr. Timothy CHANDLER
10 Vice Pres Admin & Finance .... Mr. Joseph J. OSTER
30 Vice Pres University Advancement .... Dr. Gary N. RUBIN
32 Vice President Student Affairs .... Dr. Deb MORIARTY
46 Interim VP Innovation/Applied Rsrch .... Ms. Daraius IRANI
100 Chief of Staff .... Ms. Jennifer GAJEWSKI
88 Deputy Chief of Staff .... Ms. Marina COOPER
22 VP of Equity and Inclusion .... Vacant
20 Vice Provost .... Dr. S. Maggie REITZ
84 Assoc VP Enrollment Mgmt/Registrar .... Mr. Robert GIORDANI
44 Assoc Vice President Development .... Mr. Michael CATHER
26 VP Univ Marketing/Communications .... Ms. Josianne E. PENNINGTON
29 Assoc Vice Pres Alumni Relations .... Ms. Lori B. ARMSTRONG
13 Assoc Vice President OTS/CIO .... Mr. Jeffrey SCHMIDT
109 Assoc Vice Pres Auxiliary Svcs .... Mr. Daniel SLATTERY
18 Assoc VP Facilities Management .... Mr. Kevin PETERSEN
21 Assoc VP Fiscal Planning & Svcs .... Mr. Robert CAMPBELL
15 Assoc Vice Pres Human Resources .... Mr. Phillip ROSS, III
35 Assoc Vice Pres Student Affairs .... Dr. Jana VARWIG
45 Assoc Prov Academic Res & Plng .... Dr. Gary LEVY
88 Assoc Vice President Campus Life .... Dr. Teresa HALL
28 Asst VP Student Affairs/Diversity .... Mr. L. Victor COLLINS
39 Asst VP Housing & Residence Life .... Ms. Antoinette CANDIA-BAILEY
37 Director for Financial Aid .... Mr. David HORNE
25 Asst VP Sponsored Programs/Research .... Ms. Amy L. TAYLOR
07 Director of Admissions .... Mr. David FEDORCHAK

*University of Baltimore (C)

1420 N Charles Street, Baltimore MD 21201-5779
County: Independent City — FICE Identification: 002102
Unit ID: 161873
Telephone: (410) 837-4200 — Carnegie Class: Masters/L
FAX Number: N/A — Calendar System: Semester
URL: www.ubalt.edu
Established: 1925 — Annual Undergrad Tuition & Fees (In-State): $8,326
Enrollment: 6,422 — Coed
Affiliation or Control: State — IRS Status: 501(c)3
Highest Offering: Doctorate
Accreditation: M, BUS, LAW, SPAA

02 President .... Mr. Kurt L. SCHMOKE
05 Executive Vice President & Provost .... Ms. Darlene B. SMITH
10 Sr VP Admin & Finance .... Mr. Harry SCHUCKEL
32 Vice Pres Student Affairs .... Ms. Shelia BURKHALTER
84 Chief Enrollment Manager .... Vacant
30 Vice Pres Institutional Advancement .... Ms. Theresa SILANSKIS
27 Vice Pres University Advance/Comm .... Vacant
86 VP Government & Community Relations .... Ms. Anita HAREWOOD
18 VP Facil Mgmt/Capital Planning .... Mr. Neb SERTSU
13 Vice Pres Technology/CIO .... Mr. David BOBART
15 Asst Vice Pres Human Resources .... Ms. Mary MAHER
07 AVP Admissions .... Vacant
20 Vice Provost .... Ms. Catherine ANDERSEN
09 Asst Provost Institutional Research .... Mr. Paul MONIODIS
35 Dean of Students .... Ms. Kathleen ANDERSON
28 Dir Diversity and Culture Center .... Ms. Karla M. SHEPHERD
07 Actg Executive Director Admissions .... Ms. Janet WHELAN
08 Dean of Llibrary .... Ms. Lucy HOLMAN
19 Chief of Police .... Mr. Samuel D. TRESS
84 AVP Enrollment Services .... Mr. Mark JACQUE
96 Director of Procurement & Supply .... Mr. Blair BLANKINSHIP
44 Dir Annual Giving/Alumni Relations .... Ms. Kate CRIMMINS
38 Director Counseling Services .... Dr. Myra WATERS
36 Director Career & Professional Dev .... Ms. Lakeisha MATHEWS
06 Assistant Registrar .... Mr. Ramal JENKINS
09 Director Institutional Research .... Vacant
26 Manager Public Information .... Mr. Chris HART
80 Dean College of Public Affairs .... Dr. Roger HARTLEY
49 Interim Dean College of Arts & Sci .... Dr. Christine SPENCER
61 Dean of the School of Law .... Dr. Ronald WEICH
50 Dean School of Business .... Mr. Murray DALZIEL
88 Dir Center for Education Access .... Ms. Karyn SCHULZ
21 AVP Admin & University Budget Dir .... Ms. Barbara AUGHENBAUGH
29 Director Alumni Relations .... Ms. Al HEDDEN
37 Director Student Financial Aid .... Mr. Joe BLEVINS

Washington Adventist University (D)

7600 Flower Avenue, Takoma Park MD 20912-7794
County: Montgomery — FICE Identification: 002067
Unit ID: 162210
Telephone: (301) 891-4000 — Carnegie Class: Masters/M
FAX Number: (301) 270-1618 — Calendar System: Semester
URL: www.wau.edu
Established: 1904 — Annual Undergrad Tuition & Fees: $22,790
Enrollment: 1,057 — Coed
Affiliation or Control: Seventh-day Adventist — IRS Status: 501(c)3
Highest Offering: Master's
Accreditation: M, MUS, RAD

01 President .... Dr. Weymouth SPENCE
05 Provost .... Dr. Cheryl HARRIS KISUNZU
10 Exec Vice Pres Finance .... Mr. Patrick FARLEY
11 Chief of Operations & Compliance .... Ms. Janette NEUFVILLE
32 Vice Pres Student Life .... Mr. Bruce PEIFER
84 VP Marketing & Enrollment .... Mr. William JACKSON
42 Vice President Ministry .... Dr. Baraka MUGANDA
13 VP Information Technology .... Vacant
15 Assoc VP of Human Resources .... Ms. Ryhee JONES
58 Dean Sch Grad/Professional Studies .... Ms. Nicole CURRIER
88 Dean of Student Success .... Dr. Ralph JOHNSON
06 Registrar .... Ms. Juanita WOMACK
33 Dean of Men .... Mr. Tim NELSON
34 Dean of Women .... Ms. Sabrina ETIENNE
08 Library Director .... Mr. Don ESSEX
30 Director of Development .... Vacant
19 Director Safety & Security .... Mr. Edwin MONGE
41 Athletic Director .... Mr. Patrick CRAREY, II
07 Director of Admissions & Recruitmen .... Ms. Wanda COLON-CANALES
29 Director of Alumni .... Ms. Ellie BARKER
26 Director Corporate Communications .... Ms. Angie CREWS
78 Dir Coop Educ/Acad Support & Test .... Mr. Fitzroy THOMAS
18 Chief Facilities/Physical Plant .... Mr. Steve LAPHAM
37 Director Student Financial Aid .... Ms. Sharon CONWAY
38 Campus Counseling .... Dr. Grethel BRADFORD
40 Manager the College Bookstore .... Mr. Lloyd YUTUC
85 Director of International Students .... Dr. Beulah MANUEL
66 Director of Nursing .... Dr. Nancie CRESPIE
04 Administrative Asst to President .... Ms. Lydée BATTLE
09 Director of Institutional Research .... Mr. Jonathan PETER

Washington College (E)

300 Washington Avenue, Chestertown MD 21620-1197
County: Kent — FICE Identification: 002108
Unit ID: 164216
Telephone: (410) 778-2800 — Carnegie Class: Bac-A&S
FAX Number: (410) 778-7850 — Calendar System: Semester
URL: www.washcoll.edu
Established: 1782 — Annual Undergrad Tuition & Fees: $43,850
Enrollment: 1,485 — Coed
Affiliation or Control: Independent Non-Profit — IRS Status: 501(c)3
Highest Offering: Master's
Accreditation: M

01 President .... Ms. Sheila C. BAIR
05 Provost/Dean of College .... Dr. Emily CHAMLEE-WRIGHT
100 Chief of Staff .... Mr. Joseph L. HOLT
10 Vice Pres Finance/Administration .... Dr. Mark C. HAMPTON
30 Vice Pres College Advancement .... Vacant
44 Sr AVP College Advancement .... Mrs. Barbara H. HECK
84 Vice Pres Enrollment Mgmt .... Mr. Satyajit DATTAGUPTA
26 AVP Col Rels/Marketing/Media Rels .... Mr. Michael O'CONNOR
32 Vice President & Dean of Students .... Dr. Xavier A. COLE
35 Assoc Vice Pres Student Affairs .... Dr. Sarah R. FEYERHERM
29 Dir Alumni Rels/Ldrship Annual Gvng .... Ms. Rebekah L. HARDY
09 Asst Provost Inst Research & Assmt .... Mr. Victor SENSENIG
20 Asst Dean Academic Initiatives .... Dr. Andrea G. LANGE
31 Director of Campus Special Events .... Mrs. Laura J. WILSON
41 Director of Athletics .... Dr. Bryan L. MATTHEWS
06 Registrar .... Ms. Ashley TURLINGTON
08 Director of Miller Library .... Dr. Ruth C. SHOGE
27 Chief Information Officer .... Mr. Scott COWDREY
91 Director of Admin Computing .... Mr. Kenneth W. SUTTON
58 Director of Graduate Program .... Dr. Andrea G. LANGE
21 Controller .... Ms. Penelope L. FARLEY
18 Director of Physical Plant .... Mr. Reid C. RAUDENBUSH
15 Director of Human Resources .... Vacant
19 Director of Public Safety .... Mr. Gerald K. RODERICK
07 Director of Admissions .... Mr. Bradly BOOKE
37 Director of Financial Aid .... Ms. Jeani M. NARCUM
39 Dir Resid Life/Assoc Dean of Stdnts .... Mr. Carl CROWE
85 Director International Programs .... Vacant
23 Clinical Director Health Services .... Mrs. Lisa M. MARX
38 Director of Counseling Center .... Ms. Miranda ALTMAN
36 Director of Career Development .... Mr. James M. ALLISON, JR.
28 Asst Dean for Multi-Cultural Affs .... Vacant
40 Bookstore Manager .... Ms. Shannon WYBLE

Women's Institute of Torah Seminary (F)

6602 Park Heights Ave, Baltimore MD 21215
County: Baltimore — Identification: 667271
Telephone: (410) 358-3144 — Carnegie Class: Not Classified
FAX Number: (866) 990-1983 — Calendar System: Semester
URL: www.maalotbaltimore.org
Established: 1998 — Annual Undergrad Tuition & Fees: N/A
Enrollment: N/A — Female
Affiliation or Control: Jewish — IRS Status: 501(c)3
Highest Offering: Baccalaureate
Accreditation: AIJS

Wor-Wic Community College (G)

32000 Campus Drive, Salisbury MD 21804-1486
County: Wicomico — FICE Identification: 020739
Unit ID: 164313
Telephone: (410) 334-2800 — Carnegie Class: Assoc/HT-High Trad
FAX Number: (410) 334-2951 — Calendar System: Semester
URL: www.worwic.edu
Established: 1975 — Annual Undergrad Tuition & Fees (In-District): $2,880
Enrollment: 3,104 — Coed
Affiliation or Control: Local — IRS Status: 501(c)3
Highest Offering: Associate Degree
Accreditation: M, ACFEI, EMT, OTA, @PTAA, RAD

01 President .... Dr. Murray K. HOY
05 Sr Vice Pres Academic Affairs .... Dr. Stephen L. CAPELLI
84 Vice Pres Enroll Mgmt & Student Aff .... Mr. Bryan NEWTON
10 Vice Pres Administrative Services .... Ms. Jennifer A. SANDT
26 Vice Pres Institutional Affairs .... Dr. Reenie MCCORMICK
51 Dean Continuing Education .... Mrs. Ruth E. BAKER
97 Dean General Education .... Dr. Colleen C. DALLAM
75 Dean Occupational Education .... Dr. Trevor H. JONES

07 Director Admissions ....Mr. Richard C. WEBSTER
13 Director Information Technology ....Ms. Ruth GILL
36 Director Career Services ....Ms. Lori SMOOT
37 Director Financial Aid ....Ms. Deborah D. JENKINS
21 Director Accounting ....Mr. Thomas N. TYSON
15 Director Human Resources ....Ms. Karen BERKHEIMER
38 Director Counseling ....Ms. Annette BROWN
27 Director Marketing ....Ms. Janet S. KENNINGTON
09 Director Institutional Research ....Ms. Carol A. MENZEL
30 Director Development ....Ms. Janice MURPHY
06 Registrar ....Ms. Kelly HEWETT
32 Sr Director of Student Development ....Ms. Deirdra G. JOHNSON
35 Director Student Engagement ....Ms. Nicole BUCCALO
08 Director of Library Services ....Ms. Cheryl MICHAEL
18 Director Facilities Management ....Mr. Angelo FONTANAZZA
96 Director Purchasing & Auxiliary Svc ....Ms. Allison M. CANADA
105 Webmaster ....Mr. Joshua W. TOWNSEND
19 Director Public Safety ....Mr. Linnie VANN

Yeshiva College of the Nation's Capital (A)

1216 Arcola Avenue, Silver Spring MD 20902-3408

County: Montgomery FICE Identification: 039373
Unit ID: 434937
Telephone: (301) 649-7077 Carnegie Class: Spec-4-yr-Faith
FAX Number: (301) 649-7053 Calendar System: Semester
Established: 1995 Annual Undergrad Tuition & Fees: $9,700
Enrollment: 35 Male
Affiliation or Control: Independent Non-Profit IRS Status: 501(c)3
Highest Offering: Second Talmudic Degree
Accreditation: RABN

01 President ....Rabbi Yitzchok MERKIN
05 Rosh Yeshiva ....Rabbi Aaron LOPIANSKY
37 Financial Aid Director ....Ms. Maryanna WALLS
11 Administrator ....Rabbi Yitzy LABELL

MASSACHUSETTS

American International College (B)

1000 State Street, Springfield MA 01109-3155

County: Hampden FICE Identification: 002114
Unit ID: 164447
Telephone: (413) 737-7000 Carnegie Class: DU-Mod
FAX Number: (413) 205-3084 Calendar System: Semester
URL: www.aic.edu
Established: 1885 Annual Undergrad Tuition & Fees: $31,870
Enrollment: 3,629 Coed
Affiliation or Control: Independent Non-Profit IRS Status: 501(c)3
Highest Offering: Doctorate
Accreditation: EH, IACBE, NURSE, OT, PTA

01 President ....Dr. Vincent M. MANIACI
05 Exec Vice Pres of Academic Affairs ....Dr. Raj PARIKH
11 Exec VP Administration ....Mr. Mark R. BERMAN
13 Chief Information Officer ....Ms. Mimi ROYSTON
15 Vice President for Human Resources ....Ms. Nicolle M. CESTERO
09 VP for Institutional Effectiveness ....Dr. Gregory T. SCHMUTTE
10 Vice President for Finance ....Mr. Thomas DYBICK
30 VP for Institutional Advancement ....Vacant
18 VP for Facilities ....Vacant
07 Dean of UG Admissions ....Ms. Kerry BARNES
07 Dean of Graduate Admissions ....Mr. Jonathan SCULLY
41 Athletic Director ....Mr. Matthew JOHNSON
76 Dean Health Sciences ....Dr. Cesarina THOMPSON
49 Dean Business/Arts/Sciences ....Dr. Susanne SWANKER
53 Dean of Education ....Dr. Sylvia MASON
32 Dean of Students ....Mr. Brian J. O'SHAUGHNESSY
06 Registrar ....Mr. Paul KLESCHICK
08 Director of Library ....Ms. Estelle H. SPENCER
26 Dir for Marketing & Communications ....Mr. Robert COLE
38 Director Counseling Center ....Dr. Rose L. ANDREJCZYK
36 Dir of Career Services ....Mr. J. A. MARSHALL
76 Director Physical Therapy Program ....Dr. Cindy BUCHANAN
66 Director of Division of Nursing ....Dr. Karen S. ROUSSEAU
50 Director of Business ....Dr. Rob POOLE
37 Director for Financial Aid ....Ms. Sage CRARY-STACHOWIAK
21 Comptroller ....Mr. Christopher GARRITY
04 Admin Asst to President ....Ms. Lani KRETSCHMAR
19 Director Security/Safety ....Mr. David KUZMESKI
91 Director Academic Computing ....Vacant
29 Director Alumni Relations ....Ms. Heather CAHILL
39 Director Student Housing ....Mr. Matthew SCOTT

Amherst College (C)

PO Box 5000, Amherst MA 01002-5000

County: Hampshire FICE Identification: 002115
Unit ID: 164465
Telephone: (413) 542-2000 Carnegie Class: Bac-A&S
FAX Number: (413) 542-2621 Calendar System: Semester
URL: www.amherst.edu
Established: 1821 Annual Undergrad Tuition & Fees: $50,562
Enrollment: 1,792 Coed
Affiliation or Control: Independent Non-Profit IRS Status: 501(c)3
Highest Offering: Baccalaureate
Accreditation: EH

01 President ....Dr. Carolyn (Biddy) A. MARTIN
100 Chief of Staff/Sec of the Board ....Ms. Susan PIKOR
05 Dean of the Faculty ....Dr. Catherine A. EPSTEIN
32 Chief Student Affairs Officer ....Dr. Suzanne R. COFFEY
07 Dean Admission/Financial Aid ....Ms. Katharine L. FRETWELL
37 Dean of Financial Aid ....Ms. Gail W. HOLT
20 Associate Dean of the Faculty ....Dr. John CHENEY
20 Associate Dean of the Faculty ....Dr. Austin D. SARAT
10 Chief Financial Officer ....Mr. Kevin C. WEINMAN
30 Chief Advancement Officer ....Ms. Megan MOREY
43 Chief Policy Ofcr/General Counsel ....Ms. Lisa H. RUTHERFORD
29 Exec Dir Alumni Pgms/Annual Giving ....Ms. Elizabeth A. ANEMA
06 Registrar ....Ms. Kathleen KILVENTON
15 Director of Human Resources ....Ms. Maria-Judith RODRIGUEZ
21 Controller ....Mr. Stephen M. NIGRO
09 Director of Institutional Research ....Mr. Jesse D. BARBA
26 Chief Communications Officer ....Dr. Peter F. MACKEY
08 College Librarian ....Mr. Bryn GEFFERT
13 Chief Information Officer ....Mr. David L. HAMILTON
23 Director of Student Health Services ....Dr. Warren H. MORGAN
38 Director of Counseling Center ....Dr. Jacqueline ALVAREZ
36 Director of the Career Center ....Vacant
41 Director of Athletics ....Mr. Donald R. FAULSTICK
18 Chief of Campus Operations ....Mr. James D. BRASSORD
19 Chief of Campus Police ....Mr. John B. CARTER
109 Director of Dining Services ....Mr. Charles G. THOMPSON

Andover Newton Theological School (D)

210 Herrick Road, Newton Centre MA 02459-2243

County: Middlesex FICE Identification: 002116
Unit ID: 164474
Telephone: (617) 964-1100 Carnegie Class: Spec-4-yr-Faith
FAX Number: (617) 965-9756 Calendar System: Semester
URL: www.ants.edu
Established: 1807 Annual Graduate Tuition & Fees: N/A
Enrollment: 260 Coed
Affiliation or Control: Independent Non-Profit IRS Status: 501(c)3
Highest Offering: Doctorate; No Undergraduates
Accreditation: EH, THEOL

01 President ....Rev. Martin COPENHAVER
05 Dean of the Faculty ....Dr. Sarah B. DRUMMOND
10 Vice President for Finance ....Mr. Brian BOYCE
30 Interim Vice Pres Inst Advance ....Ms. Davida Foy CRABTREE
06 Registrar ....Ms. Nayda G. AGUILA
08 Co-Director of the Library ....Rev. Nancy LOIS
32 Dean of Students ....Dr. Nancy E. NIENHUIS
04 Assistant to the President ....Mr. David AMES
18 Director Physical Plant ....Mr. Frank CAVACO
13 Chief Information Officer ....Mr. Mugur ROZ
37 Coordinator Financial Aid ....Ms. Rosemary TURANO
39 Director Housing & Events Planning ....Mr. Frank NOVO

Anna Maria College (E)

50 Sunset Lane, Paxton MA 01612-1198

County: Worcester FICE Identification: 002117
Unit ID: 164492
Telephone: (508) 849-3300 Carnegie Class: Masters/M
FAX Number: (508) 849-3334 Calendar System: 4/1/4
URL: www.annamaria.edu
Established: 1946 Annual Undergrad Tuition & Fees: $35,074
Enrollment: 1,430 Coed
Affiliation or Control: Roman Catholic IRS Status: 501(c)3
Highest Offering: Beyond Master's But Less Than Doctorate
Accreditation: EH, MUS, NUR, SW

01 President ....Ms. Mary Louise RETELLE
03 Executive Vice President ....Vacant
10 Vice President/Chief Financial Ofcr ....Mr. David M. ROSATI
11 Vice Pres/Chief Operations Officer ....Mr. David K. BREEN
05 VP for Academic Affairs ....Dr. Christine L. HOLMES
32 VP for Student Affairs ....Mr. Andrew O. KLEIN
30 VP for Institutional Advancement ....Ms. Sharon M. DAVENPORT
26 Director of College Relations ....Vacant
09 Director of Institutional Research ....Ms. Irene IRUDAYAM
06 Registrar ....Ms. Barbara ZAWALICH
88 Director of the Learning Center ....Mr. Dennis VANASSE
23 Director of Health Services ....Ms. Linda ARONSON
08 Director of Library ....Ms. Janice WILBUR
29 Director Alumni Relations ....Mr. Wesley DUNHAM
36 Director Career Counsel/Placement ....Vacant
37 Director Financial Aid ....Ms. Sandra PEREIRA
13 Chief Information Officer ....Mr. Michael MIERS
04 Executive Asst to the President ....Ms. Kay FLICK
18 Director Physical Plant ....Mr. Matthew SIMPSON
41 Athletic Director ....Ms. Laura HABACKER
42 Director Campus Ministry ....Fr. Manuel CLAVIJO
15 Director of Human Resources ....Vacant
88 Dean of Mission Effectiveness ....Sr. Rollande QUINTAL
07 Dean of Admission & Financial Aid ....Mr. Peter J. MILLER
35 Dean of Student Life ....Ms. Lisa SAVERESE
28 Director of Multicultural Affairs ....Mr. Joshua DODDS
51 Director Grad/Continuing Educ ....Mr. William PURNELL
19 Director Security/Safety ....Lt. Mark SAVASTA

Assumption College (F)

500 Salisbury Street, Worcester MA 01609-1296

County: Worcester FICE Identification: 002118
Unit ID: 164562
Telephone: (508) 767-7000 Carnegie Class: Bac-A&S
FAX Number: (508) 767-7169 Calendar System: Semester
URL: www.assumption.edu
Established: 1904 Annual Undergrad Tuition & Fees: $36,160
Enrollment: 2,719 Coed
Affiliation or Control: Roman Catholic IRS Status: 501(c)3
Highest Offering: Beyond Master's But Less Than Doctorate
Accreditation: EH, CORE

01 President ....Dr. Francesco C. CESAREO
10 VP for Finance and Administration ....Mr. Peter D. WELLS
05 Provost/Academic Vice Pres ....Dr. Louise Carroll KEELEY
32 Vice President for Student Affairs ....Dr. Catherine M. WOODBROOKS
30 Vice Pres Institutional Advancement ....Mr. Timothy R. STANTON
42 Vice President Mission ....Rev. Dennis M. GALLAGHER, AA
84 Vice Pres for Enrollment Management ....Mr. Evan E. LIPP
43 General Counsel ....Dr. Michael H. RUBINO
20 Associate Provost ....Dr. Kimberly A. SCHANDEL
51 Dir of Career & Continuing Educ ....Mr. Dennis BRAUN
07 Dean of Admissions ....Ms. Kathleen M. MURPHY
20 Dean of Undergraduate Studies ....Dr. Eloise KNOWLTON
58 Assistant Provost/Dean of Grad Stds ....Mr. Joseph B. MORRISON
89 Assistant Dean for the First Year ....Dr. Jennifer K. MORRISON
42 Director of Campus Ministry ....Mr. Paul F. COVINO
35 Dean of Student Development ....Dr. Khym Isaac DE BARROS
08 Director of Library Services ....Ms. Doris Ann SWEET
10 Director of Finance ....Ms. Cathleen R. CULLEN
09 Director Inst Research and Ac Asst ....Mr. Stuart J. MUNRO
107 Director Opers Grad & Prof Studies ....Vacant
06 Registrar ....Mr. David W. AALTO
13 Exec Dir Info Tech & Media Svcs ....Dr. Dawn M. THISTLE
15 Director of Human Resources/AAO ....Ms. Grace BLUNT
26 Executive Director of Communication ....Mr. Michael K. GUILFOYLE
29 Director of Alumni Relations ....Ms. Diane LASKA-NIXON
44 Director of Assumption Fund ....Mr. Timothy R. MARTIN
88 Director of Academic Support Center ....Dr. Allen A. BRUEHL
35 Dean of Campus Life ....Mr. Conway CAMPBELL
39 Assoc Dean Campus Life/Dir Res Life ....Mr. Joseph ZITO
41 Director of Athletics ....Mr. Nichloas A. SMITH
19 Director of Public Safety ....Mr. Steven B. CARL
23 Director of Health Services ....Ms. Elizabeth DREXLER-HINES
24 Director of Media Services ....Mr. Ted HALEY
37 Director of Financial Aid ....Mr. William C. SMITH
21 Director of Business Services ....Mr. Todd DERDERIAN
25 Director of Grant Development ....Dr. Landy C. JOHNSON
35 Dean of Students ....Mr. Robert G. RAVENELLE
28 Director Cross Cultural Center ....Ms. Beatriz PATINO
96 Director of Purchasing ....Ms. Gail M. RACINE
86 Exec Asst for Govt/Cmty Relations ....Mr. Daniel F. DITULLIO
36 Director of Career Services ....Ms. Nicole DIORIO
04 Exec Admin Asst to President ....Ms. Sharon A. MAHONEY

Babson College (G)

231 Forest Street, Babson Park MA 02457-0310

County: Norfolk FICE Identification: 002121
Unit ID: 164580
Telephone: (781) 235-1200 Carnegie Class: Spec-4-yr-Bus
FAX Number: (781) 239-5231 Calendar System: Semester
URL: www.babson.edu
Established: 1919 Annual Undergrad Tuition & Fees: $46,784
Enrollment: 3,049 Coed
Affiliation or Control: Independent Non-Profit IRS Status: 501(c)3
Highest Offering: Master's
Accreditation: EH, BUS

01 President ....Dr. Kerry MURPHY HEALEY
12 CEO Babson Global ....Dr. Shahid ANSARI
05 Acting Provost ....Dr. Gordon PRICHETT
10 Chief Administrative Officer ....Ms. Katherine CRAVEN
45 Chf of Stf/VP Strategic Initiatives ....Mr. Steve MOORE
18 AVP Facilities Mgmt & Contruction ....Ms. Janet FISHSTEIN
101 VP for Governance ....Ms. Jane EDMONDS
44 Senior VP for Advancement ....Mr. Edward CHIU
30 Vice President of Development ....Ms. Diana P. ZAIS
29 VP Alumni and Friends Network ....Ms. Carol J. HACKER
15 Vice Pres Human Resources ....Ms. Donna BONAPARTE
43 VP and General Counsel ....Mr. Jonathan MOLL
36 Dir Graduate Center for Career Dev ....Ms. Cheri PAULSON
06 Registrar ....Ms. Linda KEAN
36 Dir Ungrad Center for Career Dev ....Ms. Donna SOSHOWSKI
27 Director of Public Relations ....Mr. Michael CHMURA
13 Chief Information Officer ....Mr. Phillip KNUTEL
26 VP/Chief Marketing Officer ....Ms. Sarah SYKORA
32 VP/Dean of Students ....Dr. Lawrence P. WARD
20 Dean of Faculty ....Ms. Carolyn HOTCHKISS
07 Dean Undergraduate Admissions ....Ms. Courtney MINDEN
97 Interim Dean Undergraduate School ....Dr. Henry DENEAULT
107 Dean of Babson Exec Education ....Ms. Elaine EISENMAN
37 Assoc Dean UG Sch/Dir Std Fin Svcs ....Ms. Melissa J. SHAAK
94 Exec Dir Ctr for Wms Entrep Lshp ....Dr. Susan DUFFY
07 Director Graduate Admissions ....Ms. Petia WHITMORE
09 Director of Institutional Research ....Ms. Anne Marie DELANEY
96 Director of Business Services ....Ms. Teresa PITARO
28 Chief Diversity & Inclusion Officer ....Dr. Sadie BURTON-GOSS
58 Dean Graduate School ....Dr. Will LAMB
19 Director Public Safety ....Mr. James POLLARD
41 Director of Athletics ....Mr. Josh MACARTHUR

Bard College at Simon's Rock (H)

84 Alford Road, Great Barrington MA 01230-9702

County: Berkshire FICE Identification: 009645
Unit ID: 167792
Telephone: (413) 644-4400 Carnegie Class: Bac-A&S

FAX Number: (413) 528-7365 Calendar System: Semester
URL: www.simons-rock.edu
Established: 1964 Annual Undergrad Tuition & Fees: $50,209
Enrollment: 329 Coed
Affiliation or Control: Independent Non-Profit IRS Status: 501(c)3
Highest Offering: Baccalaureate
Accreditation: EH

01 President .... Dr. Leon BOTSTEIN
03 Executive Vice President .... Mr. Dimitri PAPADIMITRIOU
05 Vice President/Provost .... Dr. Ian BICKFORD
04 Asst to Vice President & Provost .... Ms. Lisa CLAYTON
32 Dean of the College .... Ms. Leslie DAVIDSON
20 Dean of Academic Affairs .... Dr. Patricia SHARPE
35 Dean of Campus Life .... Mr. Robert GRAVES
10 Director of Finance/Admin/HR .... Mr. Bryant MORGAN
20 Dean of Academic Engagement .... Dr. Sue LYON
26 Director of Communications .... Ms. Kimberly ROCK
30 Chief Development/Advancement .... Vacant
07 Director of Admissions .... Ms. Chandra JOOS DEKOVEN
06 Registrar .... Ms. Heidi ROTHBERG
08 Library Director .... Mr. Brian MIKESELL
37 Director of Financial Aid .... Ms. Ellen MAMMEN
18 Director Physical Plant .... Mr. Gerard NESEL
38 Director Campus Wellness Ctr .... Ms. Sharon HARTUNIAN
13 Director of Information Technology .... Ms. Janice GILDAWIE
19 Director of Security .... Mr. Kenneth GEREMIA
39 Director of Residence Life .... Mr. Ali GONZALEZ TORRES
44 Director of Annual Fund/Alumni .... Mr. Richard MONTONE
41 Athletic Center Manager .... Mr. David COLLOPY
57 Division Head Arts .... Mr. Ben KRUPKA
81 Division Head Science/Math/Computer .... Dr. David MYERS
83 Division Head Social Studies .... Dr. Brian CONOLLY
79 Division Head Language/Literature .... Dr. Brendan MATHEWS
103 Dir of Academic Trans & Career Dev .... Ms. Manat WOOTEN
28 Dir of Equity & Inclusion .. Ms. Gwendolyn HAMPTON VANSANT

Bay Path University (A)

588 Longmeadow Street, Longmeadow MA 01106-2292
County: Hampden FICE Identification: 002122
Unit ID: 164632
Telephone: (413) 565-1000 Carnegie Class: Masters/L
FAX Number: (413) 565-1105 Calendar System: Semester
URL: www.baypath.edu
Established: 1897 Annual Undergrad Tuition & Fees: $31,785
Enrollment: 2,587 Female
Affiliation or Control: Independent Non-Profit IRS Status: 501(c)3
Highest Offering: Master's
Accreditation: EH, ARCPA, OT

01 President .... Dr. Carol A. LEARY
05 Vice Pres Academic Affairs/ Provost .... Dr. Melissa MORRISS-OLSON
10 VP Finance/Administrative Services .... Mr. Michael GIAMPIETRO
30 VP for Institutional Advancement .... Ms. Kathleen BOURQUE
45 Chief Strategy Officer Springfield .... Ms. Caron T. HOBIN
04 Assistant to the President .... Ms. Barbara KOCHON
21 Associate Vice President Finance .... Ms. Donna GUERTIN
46 Founding Dean of Research .... Ms. Ann DOBMEYER
12 Director of the Burlington Campus .... Ms. Amy CARMACK
12 Director of CMC Campus .... Ms. Laura HUNTER
26 Director of Communications .... Ms. Kathleen WROBLEWSKI
37 Director of Student Financial Svcs .... Ms. Stephanie KING
36 Exec Dir Career & Life Planning .... Ms. Laureen CIRILLO
08 Director of the Library .... Mr. Michael MORAN
06 Registrar .... Ms. Stephanie SANCHEZ
29 Dir of Alumni Relations .... Ms. Amanda SBRISCIA
23 Director of Health Services .... Vacant
19 Captain Campus Public Safety .... Mr. Danilo FELICIANO
15 Asst VP & Dir of Human Resources .... Ms. Kathleen HALPIN-ROBBINS
18 Director Facilities/Campus Svcs .... Mr. Paul E. STANTON
13 Exec Director Info Technology .... Mr. Brian BASGEN
14 Mgr of Info Systems and Telecommun .... Mrs. Linda A. SIMONDS
41 Director of Athletics .... Mr. Steven J. SMITH
77 Dir Masters of Sci Commun/Info Mgmt .... Mr. Richard BRIOTTA
32 Director of Student Life .... Ms. Natalie STOTHART
88 Sr Dir Bus Pgm Online/Ongrnd Spfld .... Vacant
88 Dir MBA Entrepr Thnkg/Innov Practic .... Mr. Mo SATTAR
88 Dir Grad Pgms Nonprofit Mgmt/Philan .... Mr. Jeffrey GREIM
20 Assistant Provost .... Ms. Kathleen MARTIN
76 Director of Health & Wellness .... Ms. Katie JONES
88 Dir Center for Teaching & Learning .... Dr. Charlotte BRIGGS
17 Director of Clinical Education .... Vacant
96 Exec Dir of Purchasing/Office Svcs .... Mr. Ted LETH-STEENSEN
102 Dir Foundation/Corporate Relations .... Ms. Janine MCVAY
53 Assoc Prov Sch Educ/Human/Hlth Sci .... Dr. Elizabeth FLEMING
49 Dean School Art/Science/Mgmt .... Dr. Thomas LOPER
107 Chief Learning Officer Springfield .... Dr. Vana NESPOR
35 Dean of Planning & Student Develop .... Mr. Dave YELLE
83 Found Dean Sch Health Sci/Hum Behav .... Vacant
88 Dir Occupational Therapy Program .... Dr. Lori VAUGHN
07 Dean Graduate Admissions .... Ms. Diane RANALDI
108 Exec Dir Academic Ops/Assessment .... Vacant
88 Deputy Chief Operational Effect .... Ms. Amanda GOULD
57 Director MFA Program .... Ms. Leanna JAMES BLACKWELL
53 Director ABA Program .... Dr. Susan AINSLEIGH
88 Director PA Program .... Ms. Theresa RIETHLE
44 Dir of Annual Giving & Alumni Rel .... Ms. Amanda SBRISCIA
88 Director of Cybersecurity Program .... Mr. Lawrence SNYDER

Bay State College (B)

122 Commonwealth Avenue, Boston MA 02116-2975
County: Suffolk FICE Identification: 003965
Unit ID: 164641
Telephone: (617) 217-9000 Carnegie Class: Bac/Assoc-Mixed
FAX Number: (617) 249-0400 Calendar System: Semester
URL: www.baystate.edu
Established: 1946 Annual Undergrad Tuition & Fees: $21,524
Enrollment: 1,108 Coed
Affiliation or Control: Proprietary IRS Status: Proprietary
Highest Offering: Baccalaureate
Accreditation: EH, ADNUR, MAAB, PTAA

01 President .... Dr. Stacy L. SWEENEY
05 Vice President of Academic Affairs .... Dr. William CARROLL
10 Vice Pres Administration & Finance .... Meg TRANT
32 Vice Pres Student Affs/Dean Stdnts .... Kate O'HARA
84 Vice Pres Enrollment Management .... Sentil KUMAR
26 VP of Marketing/Communications .... Chip BERGSTROM
37 Director Student Financial Services .... Jeanne DEVANI
06 Registrar .... Sarah WOOD
08 Librarian .... Jessica NEAVE
07 Director of Admissions .... Clancy KRUEGER
21 Student Account Administrator .... Melissa PEDERSEN
36 Director Career Services .... Diann LLOYD-DENNIS
38 Director Student Counseling .... Cheryl RAICHE
15 Director Human Resources .... Donna GAFFEY
35 Asst Dir Student Activities .... Kristin STAINE
18 Facilities Manager .... Vacant

Bay State College (C)

101 Industrial Park Road, Taunton MA 02780
Telephone: (617) 217-9829 Identification: 770927
Accreditation: &EH, MAAB

† Main campus is Bay State College in Boston, MA

Becker College (D)

61 Sever Street, Worcester MA 01609-2165
County: Worcester FICE Identification: 002123
Unit ID: 164720
Telephone: (508) 791-9241 Carnegie Class: Bac-Diverse
FAX Number: (508) 796-2693 Calendar System: Semester
URL: www.becker.edu
Established: 1784 Annual Undergrad Tuition & Fees: $34,080
Enrollment: 2,021 Coed
Affiliation or Control: Independent Non-Profit IRS Status: 501(c)3
Highest Offering: Master's
Accreditation: EH, ADNUR, NUR

01 President .... Dr. Robert E. JOHNSON
10 Executive Vice President & CFO .... Dr. David A. ELLIS
05 Sr VP/Chief Acad & Stdnt Affs Ofcr .... Dr. Nancy P. CRIMMIN
30 Vice President Inst Advancement .... Dr. Colleen L. BIELITZ
84 Vice President Enrollment Mgmt .... Mr. Greg W. POTTS
26 Chief Marketing Officer .... Ms. Janet DAVENPORT
13 Chief Information Officer .... Ms. Patricia L. PATRIA
19 Campus Police Chief .... Mr. David J. BOUSQUET
100 Chief of Staff/Spec Asst to Pres .... Ms. Anne A. SROKA
15 Associate VP Human Resources .... Ms. Kathleen M. GARVEY
20 Asst VP for Curriculum & Instruct .... Dr. Amber L. VAILL
41 Asst VP & Athletic Director .... Mr. Francis E. MILLERICK
11 Assistant VP for Administration .... Mr. Kenneth CAMERON
07 Dean of Admissions .... Mr. Michael PERRON
57 Dean School of Design & Technology .... Mr. Alan RITACCO
66 Dean Sch of Nursing & Beh Sciences .... Dr. Judith PARE
74 Dean School of Animal Studies .... Dr. Julie A. BAILEY
32 Assistant Dean of Student Affairs .... Dr. Tracey A. PAKSTIS
88 Executive Director MassDIGI .... Mr. Timothy LOEW
55 Exec Dir Accelerated/Prof Studies .... Mr. Robert OUTERBRIDGE, JR.
88 Exec Director of Global Initiatives .... Dr. Debra PALLATTO-FONTAINE
36 Exec Dir Career Eucd & Advising .... Mr. Richard DAVINO
38 Director of Counseling Services .... Dr. Chantelle PSEEKOS
96 Dir Budget & Business Services .... Mr. Michael MONGEON
08 Director of the Libraries .... Ms. Donna M. SIBLEY
27 Communications Director .... Ms. Sandy LASHIN-CUREWITZ
29 Dir Alumni Relations & Annual Fund .... Ms. Elizabeth FLEMING
53 Director of Education Programs .... Ms. Nina MAZLOFF
88 Director of Equestrian Center .... Ms. Nicole EASTMAN
09 Dir Inst Research & Assessment .... Ms. Vera MAUK
39 Dir Resid Life & Student Conduct .... Mr. Joseph A. LOMASTRO
37 Director Financial Aid .... Ms. Heather E. RULAND
18 Director of Facilities .... Mr. Richard ROODBEEN
109 Director of Dining Services .... Mr. Robert WILDER
88 Director Yunis Social Bus Centre .... Mr. David A. JORDAN
88 Dir Col Learning Ctr/ADA/Disability .... Ms. Mary-Lou ROBERTS
50 Director of Business Programs .... Dr. Vaughn A. CALHOUN
85 Dir Intl Students & Title IX .... Ms. Michelle FATCHERIC
88 Director of Student Accounts/Bursar .... Mr. Alexander M. HARTMAN
23 Director of Health Services .... Ms. Catherine MELOCHE
16 Associate Director Human Resources .... Mr. Steven J. BOURGAULT
88 Manager Creative Services .... Ms. Judith TONELLI-BROWN
40 General Manager Bookstore .... Ms. Randie FARMELANT
90 Helpdesk Manager .... Mr. Steven J. BIGDA
88 Mgr Auxiliary & Safety Services .... Ms. Diana JOHNSON
104 Coordinator of Study Abroad .... Mr. Daniel W. CHAPMAN
06 Registrar .... Ms. Nikki ANDREWS
21 Controller .... Mr. Richard N. NAYLOR
04 Exec Asst to Pres/Liason to Board .... Ms. Patricia KALINOWSKI

Benjamin Franklin Institute of Technology (E)

41 Berkeley Street, Boston MA 02116-6296
County: Suffolk FICE Identification: 002151
Unit ID: 165884
Telephone: (617) 588-1368 Carnegie Class: Spec-4-yr-Other Tech
FAX Number: (617) 482-3706 Calendar System: Semester
URL: www.bfit.edu
Established: 1908 Annual Undergrad Tuition & Fees: $16,950
Enrollment: 507 Coed
Affiliation or Control: Independent Non-Profit IRS Status: 501(c)3
Highest Offering: Baccalaureate
Accreditation: EH, OPD

01 President .... Anthony BENOIT
05 Dean of Academic Affairs .... Brian BICKNELL
32 Dean of Student Services .... Mike BOSCO
10 Chief Financial & Admin Officer .... Maureen JOYCE
06 Registrar .... James KLASEN
08 Librarian .... Sharon B. BONK
07 Associate Dean of Admissions .... Marvin LOISEAU
30 Chief Development Officer .... Kimberly FREEDMAN
20 Director of Student Success .... Ashley MANSFIELD
09 Director of Institutional Research .... James KLASEN
15 Director Human Resources .... Shelley DROPKIN
19 Director of Facilities .... Myftar MYRTAJ
36 Director of Career Services .... Emily LEOPOLD
37 Director Student Financial Services .... Jamie SANTIAGO
04 Administrative Asst to President .... Carole ANDREOTTI

Bentley University (F)

175 Forest Street, Waltham MA 02452-4705
County: Middlesex FICE Identification: 002124
Unit ID: 164739
Telephone: (781) 891-2000 Carnegie Class: Masters/L
FAX Number: (781) 891-2569 Calendar System: Semester
URL: www.bentley.edu
Established: 1917 Annual Undergrad Tuition & Fees: $44,085
Enrollment: 5,565 Coed
Affiliation or Control: Independent Non-Profit IRS Status: 501(c)3
Highest Offering: Doctorate
Accreditation: EH, BUS, BUSA

01 President .... Ms. Gloria C. LARSON
43 General Counsel/Secretary to Corp .... Ms. Judith MALONE
05 Acting Co-Provost .... Dr. Daniel EVERETT
05 Acting Co-Provost .... Dr. Roy WIGGINS
102 Dir Corp Foundation Relations .... Mr. Paul CARBERRY
10 VP Admin/Finance/Treas .... Mr. Kenneth CODY
30 VP University Advancement .... Mr. William TORREY
32 VP Student Affairs .... Dr. J. Andrew SHEPARDSON
13 Chief Information Officer .... Mr. Bob WITTSTEIN
37 Int VP Enrollment Management .... Ms. Donna KENDALL
49 Dean of Arts and Sciences .... Dr. Daniel EVERETT
50 Dean of Business/Grad Sch .... Dr. Roy WIGGINS
20 Associate Provost .... Dr. Vicki LAFARGE
88 Assoc Dean Academic Services .... Ms. Catherina CARLSON
58 Asst Dean/Director GSAS .... Vacant
29 Exec Director of Adv Relations .... Ms. Leigh GASPAR
26 Chief Marketing Officer .... Ms. Val FOX
15 Assoc VP of Human Resources .... Ms. Ann DEXTER
11 Assoc Dean of Business Programs .... Dr. Dorothy FELDMANN
21 Assoc VP Finance .... Ms. Nancy ANTUNES
06 Registrar .... Ms. Patricia ROGERS
22 Spec Advisor to the Pres/Ombudsman .... Dr. Earl AVERY
38 Director of Counseling Center .... Dr. Peter FORKNER
41 Director of Athletics .... Mr. Robert DEFELICE
09 Director of Institutional Research .... Ms. Kelly GIARDULLO
39 Assoc Dean Student Affairs/Res Cent .... Mr. John PIGA
90 Dir Academic Tech/Library/Rsch Svcs .... Ms. Laurie SUTCH
31 Director Service-Learning Center .... Dr. Jonathon WHITE
19 Executive Director of Public Safety .... Mr. Ernest LEFFLER
27 Dir News/Communications Relations .... Ms. Michele WALSH
36 Assoc VP Univ Career Services .... Ms. Susan BRENNAN
23 Asst Dean/Dir Health & Wellness .... Ms. Geraldine TAYLOR
25 Director of Sponsored Programs .... Ms. Susan RICHMAN
07 Exec Director Undergrad Admission .... Ms. Suzanne CUCCURULLO
07 Asst Dean/Dir of Grad Admission .... Ms. Sharon HILL
88 Director of MBA Programs .... Dr. David SCHWARZKOPF
18 Exec Director Facilities Management .... Mr. Thomas KANE
96 Exec Dir Purchasing/Adm & Camp Svcs .... Ms. Julianne BRITT
44 Sr Assoc Dir Annual Giving .... Mr. Brian READ
35 Dir of Student Prog & Engagement .... Ms. Nicole CHABOT-WIEFERICH
04 Administrative Asst to President .... Ms. Sharon M. WILLIAMS-DYER
104 Director of International Education .... Ms. Natalie SCHLEGEL

Berklee College of Music (G)

1140 Boylston Street, Boston MA 02215-3693
County: Suffolk FICE Identification: 002126
Unit ID: 164748
Telephone: (617) 266-1400 Carnegie Class: Spec-4-yr-Arts
FAX Number: (617) 247-6878 Calendar System: Semester
URL: www.berklee.edu
Established: 1945 Annual Undergrad Tuition & Fees: $40,082
Enrollment: 4,908 Coed
Affiliation or Control: Independent Non-Profit IRS Status: 501(c)3
Highest Offering: Master's

Accreditation: EH

01 President ... Roger H. BROWN
100 Chief of Staff ... Melissa HOWE
12 Pres Boston Conservatory Berklee ... Richard ORTNER
05 Sr Vice Pres Academic Affs/Provost ... Lawrence J. SIMPSON
84 Sr VP Student Enrollment/Engagement ... Betsy NEWMAN
102 Sr VP Institutional Advancement ... Cindy ALBERT LINK
10 Chief Financial Officer ... Richard M. HISEY
13 Sr VP Innovation/Strategy/Tech ... David MASH
14 Assoc VP Information Technology ... Scott V. STREET
15 Vice Pres Human Resources ... Eileen ALVITI
88 VP Educ Outreach/Social Entrepren ... Lee WHITMORE
88 Assoc Vice Pres Global Initiatives ... Matthew NICHOLL
20 VP Academic Affs/Vice Provost ... S. Jay KENNEDY
26 Asst VP for External Affairs ... Rob HAYES
88 Dean of Profes Performance Division ... Matt MARVUGLIO
88 Dean Prof Writing Div/Music Tech ... Kari JUUSELA
53 Dean of Prof Education Division ... Darla S. HANLEY
06 Registrar ... Michael HAGERTY
39 Director of Housing ... Marguerite SHARKEY
37 Asst VP Student Financial Services ... Tod OLIVIERE
38 Director of Counseling ... Toni BLACKWELL
07 Dean of Admissions ... Damien S. BRACKEN
36 Director Career Development Center ... Peter SPELLMAN
18 Senior Director of Physical Plant ... Kevin ANDERSON

Boston Architectural College (A)

320 Newbury Street, Boston MA 02115-2795
County: Suffolk FICE Identification: 003966
Unit ID: 164872
Telephone: (617) 262-5000 Carnegie Class: Spec-4-yr-Arts
FAX Number: (617) 585-0111 Calendar System: Semester
URL: www.the-bac.edu
Established: 1889 Annual Undergrad Tuition & Fees: $20,666
Enrollment: 876 Coed
Affiliation or Control: Independent Non-Profit IRS Status: 501(c)3
Highest Offering: Master's
Accreditation: EH, CIDA, LSAR

01 President ... Mr. Glen S. LEROY
05 Interim Provost ... Ms. Diana RAMIREZ-JASSO
10 Vice President for Finance/Admin ... Ms. Kathleen C. ROOD
30 VP Institutional Advancement ... Mr. Evan GALLIVAN
84 VP of Enrollment Management ... Mr. James RYAN
18 Associate VP of Facilities ... Mr. Arthur BYERS
32 Assoc Vice Pres/Dean of Students ... Mr. Richard M. GRISWOLD
88 Dean of School of Interior Design ... Mr. Crandon GUSTAFSON
88 Dean School of Landscape Architect ... Ms. Maria BELLALTA
88 Dean School of Design Studies ... Mr. Donald HUNSICKER
48 Dean School of Architecture ... Ms. Karen L. NELSON
88 Dean & Faculty of Practice ... Mr. Len CHARNEY
13 Chief Information Officer ... Mr. Timothy OGAWA
88 Dir of Master's Thesis Arch ... Mr. Ian TABERNER
88 Director of Design Media ... Mr. Aidan ACKERMAN
88 Director of Foundation Instruction ... Ms. Beth GARVER
88 Director of Media Arts ... Mr. Luis MONTALVO
30 Director of Development ... Ms. Lindsey CIMOCHOWSKI
08 Library Director ... Ms. Susan A. LEWIS
07 Director of Admissions ... Ms. Meredith SPINNATO
37 Director of Financial Aid ... Mr. Janice WILKOS-GREENBERG
06 Assoc Registrar ... Mr. Joseph DIDONATO
11 Dir of Administrative Operations ... Ms. Patti VAUGHN
88 Dean of Advising Services ... Ms. Rebecca CHABOT-WIEFERICH
88 Director of Foundation Studies ... Mr. Lee PETERS
35 Dean of Student Svcs & Registrar ... Mrs. Bethany FANTASIA
88 Exec Asst Governance & Development ... Mr. Johnny REDMOND
15 Director of Human Resources ... Ms. Jondelle DEVEAUX
29 Alumni & Development Officer ... Ms. Catalina IANETTA
21 Controller ... Ms. Patricia FARINO
88 Director Foundation Student Support ... Mr. Michael DANIELS
88 Director of Liberal Studies ... Ms. Victoria HALLINAN

Boston Baptist College (B)

950 Metropolitan Avenue, Boston MA 02136-4000
County: Suffolk FICE Identification: 032483
Unit ID: 164614
Telephone: (617) 364-3510 Carnegie Class: Spec-4-yr-Faith
FAX Number: (775) 245-1498 Calendar System: Semester
URL: www.boston.edu
Established: 1976 Annual Undergrad Tuition & Fees: $12,600
Enrollment: 94 Coed
Affiliation or Control: Baptist IRS Status: 501(c)3
Highest Offering: Baccalaureate
Accreditation: TRACS

01 President ... Rev. David V. MELTON
32 Vice President for Student Services ... Rev. Kenneth D. GILLMING
11 Vice President for Operations ... Mr. Randall WARD
84 Director of Enrollment Services ... Mr. Scott MAIDEN
07 Director of Admissions ... Mr. Scott MAIDEN
08 Head Librarian ... Mr. Fred TATRO

Boston College (C)

140 Commonwealth Avenue, Chestnut Hill MA 02467-3934
County: Middlesex FICE Identification: 002128
Unit ID: 164924
Telephone: (617) 552-8000 Carnegie Class: DU-Highest
FAX Number: (617) 552-8828 Calendar System: Semester
URL: www.bc.edu
Established: 1863 Annual Undergrad Tuition & Fees: $49,324
Enrollment: 14,317 Coed
Affiliation or Control: Roman Catholic IRS Status: 501(c)3
Highest Offering: Doctorate
Accreditation: EH, ANEST, BUS, COPSY, LAW, NURSE, SW, TEAC, THEOL

01 President ... Rev. William P. LEAHY, S.J.
00 Chancellor ... Rev. J. Donald MONAN, S.J.
05 Provost & Dean of Faculties ... Dr. David QUIGLEY
03 Executive Vice President ... Mr. Michael J. LOCHHEAD
30 Senior VP University Advancement ... Mr. James J. HUSSON
04 Executive Assistant to President ... Mr. Kevin J. SHEA
10 Financial Vice President/Treasurer ... Mr. John D. BURKE
101 Vice President/University Secretary ... Rev. Terrence P. DEVINO, S.J.
32 Vice Pres Student Affairs ... Dr. Barbara JONES
15 Vice President for Human Resources ... Mr. David P. TRAINOR
13 Vice Pres Information Technology ... Mr. Michael J. BOURQUE
88 Vice Pres Univ Mission & Ministry ... Rev. John T. BUTLER, S.J.
86 Vice Pres Govt/Community Affairs ... Mr. Thomas J. KEADY
18 Vice Pres Facilities Management ... Mr. Daniel F. BOURQUE
45 Vice Pres Planning & Assessment ... Dr. Kelli J. ARMSTRONG
20 Vice Provost for Undergrad Affairs ... Dr. Akua SARR
46 Vice Provost for Research ... Dr. Thomas CHILES
84 Vice Prov for Enrollment Management ... Ms. Nanci TESSIER
20 Vice Provost for Faculties ... Dr. Billy SOO
44 Vice President for Development ... Ms. Beth MCDERMOTT
20 Assoc Vice Provost Undergrad Acad ... Dr. J. Joseph BURNS
18 Assoc VP Capital Projects ... Ms. Mary S. NARDONE
29 Associate VP Alumni Relations ... Ms. Joy MOORE
16 Assoc VP Human Resources ... Mr. William MURPHY
109 Assoc VP Auxiliary Services ... Ms. Patricia A. BANDO
49 Dean College Arts & Sciences ... Rev. Gregory KALSCHEUR, S.J.
87 Dean Col Adv Stds/Summer Session ... Rev. James R. BURNS
53 Dean School of Education ... Dr. Stanton WORTHAM
61 Dean Law School ... Mr. Vincent D. ROUGEAU
50 Dean School of Management ... Dr. Andrew C. BOYNTON
66 Dean of School of Nursing ... Dr. Susan GENNARO
70 Dean Grad School of Social Work ... Dr. Gautam N. YADAMA
73 Dean School of Theology & Ministry ... Vacant
84 Dean of Enrollment Management ... Mr. Robert S. LAY
35 Assoc VP Student Affairs Engagement ... Dr. Katherine G. O'DAIR
08 University Librarian ... Dr. Thomas WALL
28 Exec Dir Institutional Diversity ... Mr. Richard P. JEFFERSON
06 Exec Director Student Services ... Dr. Louise M. LONABOCKER
07 Director of Admission ... Mr. John L. MAHONEY, JR.
26 Exec Dir/Special Asst to Pres/Mktg ... Mr. Ben BIRNBAUM
27 Dir Office of News & Public Affairs ... Mr. John B. DUNN
102 Exec Director School Development ... Mrs. Ginger K. SAARIAHO
41 Director Athletic Department ... Dr. Brad BATES
36 Assoc VP Career Center ... Mr. Joseph DUPONT
42 Director Campus Ministry ... Rev. Anthony PENNA
31 Director of Community Affairs ... Mr. William R. MILLS
38 Assoc VP Univ Counseling Svcs ... Dr. Thomas P. MCGUINNESS
37 Director Financial Aid ... Ms. Mary S. MCGRANAHAN
23 Director Health Services ... Dr. Thomas I. NARY
39 Assoc VP Residential Life ... Mr. George A. AREY
25 Dir Pre-Award Admin Sponsored Pgms ... Mrs. Sharon COMVALIUS-GODDARD
19 Dir Public Safety/Chief of Police ... Mr. John M. KING
40 Director Bookstore ... Mr. Robert STEWART
43 General Counsel ... Mr. Joseph M. HERLIHY
24 Director Media Technology Services ... Mr. David CORKUM
85 Director International Programs ... Dr. Nick GOZIK
88 Director Presidential Scholars Pgms ... Rev. James F. KEENAN, SJ
93 Director AHANA Student Programs ... Dr. Ines MATURANA SENDOYA
86 Director Governmental Relations ... Ms. Jeanne LEVESQUE
96 Director Procurement Services ... Mr. Paul MCGOWAN
09 Director Inst Research & Assessment ... Dr. Jessica A. GREENE

Boston Graduate School of Psychoanalysis (D)

1581 Beacon Street, Brookline MA 02446-4602
County: Norfolk FICE Identification: 031943
Unit ID: 164915
Telephone: (617) 277-3915 Carnegie Class: Spec-4-yr-Other Health
FAX Number: (617) 277-0312 Calendar System: Semester
URL: www.bgsp.edu
Established: 1973 Annual Graduate Tuition & Fees: N/A
Enrollment: 136 Coed
Affiliation or Control: Independent Non-Profit IRS Status: 501(c)3
Highest Offering: Doctorate; No Undergraduates
Accreditation: EH

01 President ... Dr. Jane SYNDER
10 Vice President Finance ... Dr. Carol PANETTA
58 Dean of Graduate Studies ... Dr. Lynn PERLMAN
07 Director of Admissions ... Dr. Paula BERMAN
06 Registrar ... Ms. Allison WILLIAMS
37 Director of Financial Aid ... Ms. Stephanie WOOLBERT
21 Controller ... Ms. Gayle DOLAN
08 Head Librarian ... Ms. Amy COHEN-ROSE
09 Director of the Center for Research ... Dr. Stephen SOLDZ

Boston University (E)

One Silber Way, Boston MA 02215-1700
County: Suffolk FICE Identification: 002130
Unit ID: 164988
Telephone: (617) 353-2000 Carnegie Class: DU-Highest
FAX Number: (617) 353-2053 Calendar System: Semester
URL: www.bu.edu
Established: 1839 Annual Undergrad Tuition & Fees: $48,436
Enrollment: 32,112 Coed
Affiliation or Control: Independent Non-Profit IRS Status: 501(c)3
Highest Offering: Doctorate
Accreditation: EH, #ARCPA, ART, BUS, CAATE, CACREP, CEA, CLPSY, DENT, DIETD, DIETI, ENG, FEPAC, HSA, IPSY, LAW, MED, MUS, OT, PH, PTA, SP, SW, THEOL

01 President ... Robert A. BROWN
05 University Provost ... Jean MORRISON
17 Provost Med Campus/Dean Sch of Med ... Karen H. ANTMAN
100 VP & Chief of Staff to President ... Douglas SEARS
49 Dean Col/Grad Sch Arts & Sciences ... Ann CUDD
60 Dean College of Communication ... Thomas FIEDLER
53 Dean School of Education ... Hardin L. COLEMAN
54 Dean College of Engineering ... Kenneth R. LUTCHEN
57 Interim Dean College of Fine Arts ... Lynne ALLEN
97 Dean College General Studies ... Natalie MCKNIGHT
88 Dean School of Hospitality Admin ... Arun UPNEJA
61 Dean of School of Law ... Maureen A. O'ROURKE
50 Dean Questrom School of Business ... Kenneth W. FREEMAN
42 Dean of Marsh Chapel ... Robert A. HILL
51 Dean Metropolitan College/Ext Ed ... Tanya ZLATEVA
76 Dean SAR Health & Rehab Science ... Christopher A. MOORE
70 Dean School of Social Work ... Gail STEKETEE
73 Dean School of Theology ... Mary Elizabeth MOORE
52 Dean School of Dental Medicine ... Jeffery W. HUTTER
69 Dean School of Public Health ... Sandro GALEA
32 Associate Provost/Dean of Students ... Kenneth ELMORE
88 VP/Assoc Provost Global Programs ... Willis G. WANG
84 VP Enrollment & Student Affairs ... Laurie POHL
46 VP & Assoc Provost Research ... Gloria WATERS
20 Assoc Provost Graduate Affairs ... Timothy BARBARI
20 Assoc Provost Budget & Planning ... Patricia O'BRIEN
20 Assoc Provost Strategic Initiatives ... Nicole HAWKES
20 Assoc Provost Undergraduate Affairs ... Elizabeth LOIZEAUX
20 Assoc Provost for Faculty Affairs ... Julie SANDELL
18 Senior Vice President Operations ... Gary W. NICKSA
10 Senior Vice Pres/CFO & Treasurer ... Martin J. HOWARD
26 Senior VP External Affairs ... Stephen P. BURGAY
101 Sr VP/Sr Counsel & Board Secy ... Todd L C. KLIPP
43 VP & General Counsel ... Erika GEETTER
30 Senior VP Devel/Alumni Relations ... Scott G. NICHOLS
13 VP Information Services & Tech ... Tracy SCHROEDER
88 Chief Investment Officer ... Lila HUNNEWELL
88 Dean Pardee School of Global Pgms ... Adil NAJAM
45 Vice President Budget and Planning ... Derek HOWE
109 Vice President Auxiliary Services ... Peter SMOKOWSKI
18 VP for Real Estate & Facility Serv ... Michael DONOVAN
86 VP Government & Community Rel ... Robert DONAHUE
86 Vice President Federal Relations ... Jennifer GRODSKY
27 VP For Marketing And Creative Svcs ... Amy HOOK
11 Vice Pres Administrative Services ... Peter FIEDLER
29 VP Alumni Relations ... Steven A. HALL
88 Vice President Development ... Karen ENGELBOURG
88 Assoc VP Budget & Planning ... Ines GARRANT
07 Assoc VP/Exec Dir Undergraduate Adm ... Kelly WALTER
25 Assoc VP Sponsored Programs ... Diane BALDWIN
35 Assoc VP Enroll & Student Affairs ... Denise MOONEY
37 Assoc VP/Exec Dir Financial Assist ... Christine MCGUIRE
44 Assoc VP Sch-based Dev & Alum Rels ... Adam K. WISE
09 Asst VP Institutional Research ... Melanie MADAIO-O'BRIEN
44 Asst VP Annual Giving ... Daniel ALLENBY
41 Asst VP & Director of Athletics ... Drew MARROCHELLO
09 Director Institutional Research ... Linette DECARIE
23 Director Student Health Services ... Judy PLATT
28 Director Howard Thurman Center ... Katherine KENNEDY
103 Director Career Planning Services ... Vacant
85 Director Intl Student/Scholars Ofc ... Jeanne KELLEY
35 Asst Dean/Exec Dir Student Affairs ... John BATTAGLINO
96 Exec Director Sourcing/Procurement ... Walter WICKERSHAM
39 Exec Director of Housing/Dining ... Marc ROBILLARD
68 Exec Director Physical Education ... Timothy MOORE
104 Exec Director Study Abroad ... Gareth MCFEELY
06 University Registrar ... Christine PAAL
08 University Librarian ... Robert HUDSON
15 Chief Human Resource Officer ... Diane P. TUCKER
19 Chief of Police ... Thomas G. ROBBINS
87 Assistant Dean Summer Term ... Donna SHEA
35 Assoc Director Student Activities ... Raul FERNANDEZ
46 VP Research Finance & Operations ... Vacant
88 General Manager Agganis Arena ... Kristoffer W. BRASSIL

Brandeis University (F)

415 South Street, Waltham MA 02453
County: Middlesex FICE Identification: 002133
Unit ID: 165015
Telephone: (781) 736-2000 Carnegie Class: DU-Highest
FAX Number: (781) 736-8699 Calendar System: Semester
URL: www.brandeis.edu
Established: 1948 Annual Undergrad Tuition & Fees: $49,598
Enrollment: 5,945 Coed
Affiliation or Control: Independent Non-Profit IRS Status: 501(c)3
Highest Offering: Doctorate
Accreditation: EH, BUS

01 President ... Dr. Ronald D. LIEBOWITZ
05 Interim Provost ... Dr. Irving R. EPSTEIN
11 Senior Vice President and COO ... Mr. Steve MANOS
101 Sr Advisor to Pres/Asst Sec BOT ... Dr. Peter GIUMETTE
30 Sr Vice Pres Inst Advancement ... Ms. Nancy K. WINSHIP
84 Sr Vice Pres for Students/Enroll ... Mr. Andrew FLAGEL
43 Sr VP and General Counsel ... Mr. Steven S. LOCKE

88 Chief Legal Officer .... Mr. David A. BUNIS
10 Exec VP for Finance/Administration .... Mr. Stewart URETSKY
13 CIO/Vice Provost Univ Librarian .... Mr. John UNSWORTH
18 Vice Pres for Operations .... Mr. James GRAY
15 Vice Pres Human Resources .... Ms. Robin NELSON-BAILEY
45 VP Planning/Institutional Research .... Mr. Dan FELDMAN
49 Dean of Arts & Sciences .... Dr. Susan J. BIRREN
70 Int Dn Heller Sch Social Pol & Mgt .... Dr. Marty KRAUSS
50 Int Dean International Business Sch .... Dr. Matthew SHEEHY
06 University Registrar .... Dr. Mark S. HEWITT

Cambridge College (A)

1000 Massachusetts Avenue, Cambridge MA 02138-5304
County: Middlesex FICE Identification: 021829
Unit ID: 165167
Telephone: (800) 877-4723 Carnegie Class: Masters/L
FAX Number: (617) 349-3545 Calendar System: Trimester
URL: www.cambridgecollege.edu
Established: 1971 Annual Undergrad Tuition & Fees: $14,004
Enrollment: 2,841 Coed
Affiliation or Control: Independent Non-Profit IRS Status: 501(c)3
Highest Offering: Doctorate
Accreditation: EH, TEAC

01 President .... Deborah C. JACKSON
05 Provost/Vice Pres Academic Affairs .... Dr. Catherine KOVEROLA
10 CFO/Vice President of Finance .... John SPINARD
43 Acting General Counsel .... Judith SIZER
30 Vice Pres Institutional Advancement .... Carson BERGLUND
26 VP Marketing/Communications and PR .... Jacqueline CONRAD
45 VP of Innovation/Strat Initiatives .... Mark ROTONDO
86 Vice President of Strategic Partner .... Phillip PAGE
15 Director of Human Resources .... Lauretta SIGGERS
37 Director of Financial Aid .... Frank LAUDER
21 Controller .... Lynn WOOD
06 Registrar .... Amy CAVALIER
20 Associate Provost .... Dr. Gilda GELY
88 Dir of Student Financial Services .... Sabrina HARLAN
90 Director of Information Technology .... Achal KHATRI
18 Director of Business Operations .... Vacant
12 Asst Director of Lawrence MA .... Melissa Sue FRASCA
12 Director Springfield MA .... Teresa (Terrie) FORTE
12 Director of Southern California .... Rita CLEMONS
12 Director of Puerto Rico .... Dr. Santiago MENDEZ-HERNANDEZ
04 Administrative Asst to President .... Robyn CARROLL
07 Director of Admissions .... Carol LOMBARDI
102 Dir Foundation/Corporate Relations .... Sonnya ESPINAL
29 Dir Alumni Relations/Annual Fund .... Kevin DRISCOLL
32 Dean Student Affairs/Student Life .... Regina ROBINSON
50 Dean School of Management .... Mary Ann JOSEPH
53 Dean School of Education .... Dr. Sheila WRIGHT
20 Dean Undergraduate Studies .... James LEE
54 Dean School of Psychology .... Dr. Niti SETH

Clark University (B)

950 Main Street, Worcester MA 01610-1477
County: Worcester FICE Identification: 002139
Unit ID: 165334
Telephone: (508) 793-7711 Carnegie Class: DU-Mod
FAX Number: (508) 793-7780 Calendar System: Semester
URL: www.clarku.edu
Established: 1887 Annual Undergrad Tuition & Fees: $41,940
Enrollment: 3,423 Coed
Affiliation or Control: Independent Non-Profit IRS Status: 501(c)3
Highest Offering: Doctorate
Accreditation: EH, BUS, CLPSY

01 President .... Dr. David P. ANGEL
03 Executive Vice President .... Ms. Julie L. DOLAN
10 Chief Investment Officer .... Mr. James E. COLLINS
05 Provost & Vice Pres Academic Affs .... Dr. Davis BAIRD
30 Vice Pres University Advancement .... Mr. Jeffrey GILLOOLY
26 Vice Pres Marketing & Communication .... Ms. Paula DAVID
13 Vice Pres for Information Tech/CIO .... Ms. Pennie TURGEON
86 VP Government/Cmty Affs/Campus Svcs .... Mr. John FOLEY
32 Dean of Students .... Dr. Frances MAGEE
46 Assoc Provost/Dean of Research .... Dr. Nancy BUDWIG
58 Assoc Provost/Dean Graduate Studies .... Dr. William FISHER
49 Assoc Provost/Dean of College .... Dr. Matthew MALSKY
20 Sr Assc Dean of Col & Dir Acad Ad .... Dr. Kevin MCKENNA
50 Dean Graduate School Mgmt .... Dr. Catherine USOFF
07 Dean of Admissions & Financial Aid .... Mr. Donald HONEMAN
37 Director of Financial Aid .... Ms. Mary Ellen SEVERANCE
08 University Librarian .... Dr. Gwendolynne ARTHUR
21 Controller .... Ms. Katherine CANNON
36 Director Career Services .... Ms. Victoria COX-LANYON
06 Registrar .... Ms. Rebecca HUNTER
15 Interim Dir of HR/Affirm Act .... Mr. David EVERITT
18 Director of Physical Plant .... Mr. Daniel RODERICK
41 Director of Athletics .... Ms. Trish CRONIN
19 Chief of Campus Police .... Mr. Stephen P. GOULET
23 Director of Health Services .... Ms. Robin MCNALLY
28 Chief Officer Diversity/Inclusion .... Ms. Sheree MARLOWE
04 Assistant to the President .... Ms. Joanne MILLER
21 Business Manager .... Mr. Paul WYKES
09 Manager of Institutional Research .... Mr. Jeffrey HIMMELBERGER
104 Director Study Abroad .... Ms. Adriane VAN GILS-PIERCE
39 Director Student Housing .... Mr. Adam KEYES
44 Director Annual or Planned Giving .... Ms. Lindsay ALLEN

College of the Holy Cross (C)

1 College Street, Worcester MA 01610-2322
County: Worcester FICE Identification: 002141
Unit ID: 166124
Telephone: (508) 793-2011 Carnegie Class: Bac-A&S
FAX Number: (508) 793-3030 Calendar System: Semester
URL: www.holycross.edu
Established: 1843 Annual Undergrad Tuition & Fees: $47,176
Enrollment: 2,787 Coed
Affiliation or Control: Roman Catholic IRS Status: 501(c)3
Highest Offering: Baccalaureate
Accreditation: EH, THEA

01 President .... Rev. Philip L. BOROUGHS, SJ
04 Special Assistant to the President .... Ms. Jane CORR
03 Senior Vice President .... Dr. Frank VELLACCIO
05 VP Academic Affairs/Dean of Col .... Dr. Margaret FREIJE
10 VP Admin & Finance/Treasurer .... Ms. Dottie HAUVER
88 Chief Investment Officer .... Mr. Timothy JARRY
32 VP Student Affairs/Dean of Students .... Ms. Jacqueline D. PETERSON
30 VP for Development/Alumni Relations .... Ms. Tracy BARLOK
42 Vice President for Mission .... Rev. William R. CAMPBELL, SJ
20 Associate Dean of the College .... Mr. Ronald JARRET
21 Director of Finance/Asst Treasurer .... Ms. Elizabeth DIONNE
06 Registrar .... Ms. Patricia RING
07 Director of Admissions .... Ms. Ann B. MCDERMOTT
08 Interim Dir of Library Services .... Ms. Karen REILLY
37 Director of Financial Aid .... Ms. Lynne M. MYERS
25 Director of Sponsored Research .... Ms. Stacy RISEMAN
42 Director Ofc of College Chaplains .... Ms. Marybeth KEARNS-BARRETT
71 Director Ctr Interdisc/Spec Studies .... Dr. Richard E. MATLAK
36 Director of Career Planning .... Ms. Amy MURPHY
13 Director Information Tech Services .... Dr. Ellen J. KEOHANE
26 Chief Marketing & Comm Officer .... Ms. Ellen RYDER
29 Director of Alumni Relations .... Ms. Kristyn M. DYER
19 Director of Public Safety .... Mr. Robert HART
35 Director of Campus Center .... Mr. Jeremiah O'CONNOR
18 Director of Physical Plant .... Mr. Scott M. MERRILL
41 Director of Athletics .... Mr. Nathan PINE
21 Controller .... Mr. Charles F. ESTAPHAN
45 Director of Planning .... Ms. Judy A. HANNUM
38 Director Counseling Center .... Dr. Paul GALVINHILL
23 Director Student Health Services .... Ms. Martha SULLIVAN
15 Director Human Resources .... Mr. David ACHENBACH
96 Manager of Purchasing .... Ms. Joan E. ANDERSON
09 Ofc of Assessment/Research .... Dr. Denise BELL
86 Dir of Govt/Cmty Relations .... Mr. Jamie D. HOAG
43 General Counsel .... Ms. Elizabeth SMALL
28 Chief Diversity Officer .... Mr. Amit TANEJA
88 Director of Title IX Initiatives .... Ms. Elizabeth CANNING

College of Our Lady of the Elms (D)

291 Springfield Street, Chicopee MA 01013-2839
County: Hampden FICE Identification: 002140
Unit ID: 167394
Telephone: (413) 594-2761 Carnegie Class: Masters/S
FAX Number: (413) 592-4871 Calendar System: Semester
URL: www.elms.edu
Established: 1928 Annual Undergrad Tuition & Fees: $32,280
Enrollment: 1,717 Coed
Affiliation or Control: Roman Catholic IRS Status: 501(c)3
Highest Offering: Doctorate
Accreditation: EH, IACBE, NURSE, SW

01 President .... Dr. Mary REAP
05 Vice President of Academic Affairs .... Dr. Walter C. BREAU
10 Vice Pres Finance/Administration .... Brian E. DOHERTY
32 Dean of Students .... Teresa WINTERS
30 Vice Pres of Instl Advancement .... Dr. Carla OLESKA
07 Director of Admissions .... Joseph WAGNER
28 Dir of Diversity & Inclusion .... Javier VENTURA
20 Dean of Stdnt Success & Strat Init .... Dr. Joyce HAMPTON
06 Registrar .... Frances BLISS
08 Director of Library .... Anthony FONSECA
26 Director of Institutional Marketing .... Nancy FARRELL
37 Director of Financial Aid .... Kristin HMIELESKI
13 Director Information Technology .... Mary KASELOUSKAS
15 Director Human Resources/Personnel .... Marie PHILLIPS
36 Dir of Career Development .... Phyllis WILLIAMS-THOMPSON
04 Administrative Asst to President .... Sandra C. TALBOT
09 Dir of Institutional Research .... Karalee YVON
101 Secretary of the Institution/Board .... Sandra TALBOT
108 Dir of Institutional Assessment .... Karalee YVON
102 Dir Foundation/Corporate Relations .... Vacant
44 Dir of Annual Giving .... Nicole SANTOS
18 Chief Facilities & Physical Plant .... Michael SULLIVAN
39 Dir of Student Housing .... Dominick LIGUCCIONI
19 Director Security & Safety .... Thomas FOLEY
29 Dir of Alumni Relations .... Jessica COLSON
36 Director Student Placement .... Vacant
41 Athletic Director .... Ellen MCEWEN
44 Dir of Dev & Legacy Giving .... Bernadette NOWAKOWSKI
66 Dean School of Nursing .... Dr. Kathleen SCOBLE
58 Dean Grad & Prof Studies .... Dr. Elizabeth HUKOWICZ

Conway School of Landscape Design (E)

332 S Deerfield Road, PO Box 179,
Conway MA 01341-0179
County: Franklin FICE Identification: 022743
Unit ID: 165495
Telephone: (413) 369-4044 Carnegie Class: Spec-4-yr-Arts
FAX Number: (413) 369-4032 Calendar System: Trimester
URL: www.csld.edu
Established: 1972 Annual Graduate Tuition & Fees: N/A
Enrollment: 17 Coed
Affiliation or Control: Independent Non-Profit IRS Status: 501(c)3
Highest Offering: Master's; No Undergraduates
Accreditation: EH

01 President/Director .... Mr. Paul C. HELLMUND
11 Int Administrative Director .... Mr. John BALDWIN
10 Director of Finance .... Mr. John BALDWIN
30 Director of Advancement .... Ms. Nina ANTONETTI

Curry College (F)

1071 Blue Hill Avenue, Milton MA 02186-2395
County: Norfolk FICE Identification: 002143
Unit ID: 165529
Telephone: (617) 333-0500 Carnegie Class: Masters/M
FAX Number: (617) 979-3540 Calendar System: Semester
URL: www.curry.edu
Established: 1879 Annual Undergrad Tuition & Fees: $36,765
Enrollment: 3,141 Coed
Affiliation or Control: Independent Non-Profit IRS Status: 501(c)3
Highest Offering: Master's
Accreditation: EH, NURSE

01 President .... Mr. Kenneth K. QUIGLEY, JR.
05 Vice President Academic Affairs .... Dr. David SZCZERBACKI
30 Vice Pres Institutional Advancement .... Mr. Christopher LAWSON
10 Chief Financial Officer .... Mr. Eric NORMAN
07 Dean of Admission .... Ms. Jane P. FIDLER
32 Dean of Student Affairs .... Ms. Maryellen M. KILEY
45 Dean for Institutional Planning .... Dr. Susan W. PENNINI
04 Assistant to the President .... Ms. Amy M. BIANCHI
08 Director Library .... Mr. Garrett EASTMAN
13 Interim Chief Information Officer .... Mr. Joseph M. BRUNO
35 VP of Human Resources .... Mirlen MAL
06 Registrar .... Ms. June KOUKOL
18 Chief Facilities/Physical Plant .... Mr. Robert G. O'CONNELL
26 Chief Public Relations Officer .... Ms. Frances L. JACKSON
36 Director of Student Placement .... Ms. Kerrie ABORN
37 Dir of Student Financial Services .... Ms. Stephanny J. ELIAS
38 Director of Student Counseling .... Dr. Alison W. MARKSON
09 Director of Institutional Research .... Ms. Jennifer DUNNE
105 Director Web Services .... Mr. John EAGAN
41 Athletic Director .... Mr. Vincent ERUZIONE
39 Director Student Housing .... Ms. Jennifer MAITINO

Dean College (G)

99 Main Street, Franklin MA 02038-1994
County: Norfolk FICE Identification: 002144
Unit ID: 165574
Telephone: (508) 541-1508 Carnegie Class: Bac/Assoc-Mixed
FAX Number: (508) 541-8726 Calendar System: Semester
URL: www.dean.edu
Established: 1865 Annual Undergrad Tuition & Fees: $35,420
Enrollment: 1,325 Coed
Affiliation or Control: Independent Non-Profit IRS Status: 501(c)3
Highest Offering: Baccalaureate
Accreditation: EH

01 President .... Dr. Paula M. ROONEY
04 Exec Assistant to President .... Ms. Sandra CAIN
05 VP Academic Affairs .... Dr. Michael FISHBEIN
10 Vice Pres Financial Svcs/Treasurer .... Mr. Dan MODELANE
84 VP Enrollment & Retention .... Ms. Cindy T. KOZIL
30 Vice Pres Institutional Advancement .... Ms. Coleen RESNICK
13 VP/Chief Information Officer .... Mr. Darrell KULESZA
15 VP/Chief Human Resources Officer .... Dr. Gary CONVERTINO
44 Assoc Vice Pres Leadership Gifts .... Mr. Ryan MCDONALD
21 Assoc VP/Controller/Asst Treasurer .... Ms. Kathleen MCGUIRE
07 Assoc VP Enrollment/Dean Admission .... Ms. Iris GODES
88 Assc VP Student Success/Career Plng .... Ms. Wendy ADLER
20 Asst VP Academic Affairs .... Ms. Melissa READ
18 Asst VP Capital Planning/Facilities .... Mr. Brian KELLY
26 VP Marketing & Business Development .... Mr. Gregg CHALK
32 Dean of Students .... Mr. David DRUCKER
51 Dean School of Continuing Studies .... Ms. Diletta MASIELLO
50 Dean School of Business .... Dr. Robert CUOMO
49 Dean Sch of Liberal Arts/Sciences .... Dr. Dawn POIRIER
57 Dean School of Dance .... Mr. Marc ARTENTSEN
57 Dean School of the Arts .... Dr. David KRASNER
06 Registrar .... Mr. Daniel O'DRISCOLL
19 Dir Law Enforcement Services .... Mr. Ken CORKRAN
08 Director of the Library .... Mr. Ted BURKE
41 Athletic Director .... Mr. Todd A. VASEY
39 Director of Residence Life .... Ms. Shannon VALVERDE
35 Dir Student Activities/Orientation .... Ms. Jennifer BOTHWELL
40 Director of Bookstore .... Ms. Jackie CALDERONE
37 Dean Student & Financial Plng/Svcs .... Mr. Frank MULLEN
88 Director Enrollment Operations .... Ms. Kathleen RYAN

36 Dir Career Planning/Internships ....Ms. Thea CERIO
38 Director of Counseling Services ....Ms. Mary Ann SILVESTRI
29 Director Alumni Relations ....Ms. Jodi BRIGGS

Eastern Nazarene College (A)

23 E Elm Avenue, Quincy MA 02170-2999
County: Norfolk FICE Identification: 002145
Unit ID: 165644
Telephone: (617) 745-3000 Carnegie Class: Masters/S
FAX Number: (617) 745-3907 Calendar System: 4/1/4
URL: www.enc.edu
Established: 1918 Annual Undergrad Tuition & Fees: $29,880
Enrollment: 1,211 Coed
Affiliation or Control: Church Of The Nazarene IRS Status: 501(c)3
Highest Offering: Master's
Accreditation: EH, SW

01 President ....Dr. Corlis A. MCGEE
05 Provost & Dean of the College ....Dr. Timothy T. WOOSTER
10 Vice President for Finance ....Mr. Jan G. WEISEN
32 Vice Pres Student Development ....Mr. Jeff KIRKSEY
84 Director of Enrollment ....Mr. Brian PARKER
30 Vice President Inst Advancement ....Dr. Larry BOLLINGER
39 Assoc Dean Students/Residence Life ....Mr. Marion MASON
06 Registrar ....Mrs. Margaret BALLARD
37 Director Financial Aid ....Ms. Delinda HALL
08 Director of Library Services ....Ms. Amy HWANG
19 Director Safety/Security/Risk Mgmt ....Mr. John GELORMINI
38 Dir Counseling & Career Services ....Mr. Bradford E. THORNE
58 Dean of Div of Graduate/Prof Stds ....Vacant
41 Athletic Director ....Mr. Bradford ZARGES
18 Maintenance Manager ....Mr. Mike JOHNSTON
45 Supervisor Instructional Resources ....Ms. Patricia VASQUEZ
21 Controller ....Mrs. Myrna GIBERTSON
42 Director Church Relations ....Mr. Stephen DILLMAN
22 Director Human Resources ....Ms. Lauren BOWEN
40 Director Bookstore ....Ms. Keri LEWIS
13 Chief Information Officer ....Mr. Charles BURT
04 Admin Assistant to the President ....Mrs. Sheryl WEISEN
39 Dir Resident Life/Multicultural Aff ....Mr. Robert BENJAMIN
09 Director of Institutional Research ....Mr. Kevin WELLS
29 Director Alumni Relations ....Ms. Rebecca SHAW
36 Director Student Placement ....Ms. Krista BOGERTMAN

Emerson College (B)

120 Boylston Street, Boston MA 02116-4624
County: Suffolk FICE Identification: 002146
Unit ID: 165662
Telephone: (617) 824-8500 Carnegie Class: Masters/L
FAX Number: (617) 824-8511 Calendar System: Semester
URL: www.emerson.edu
Established: 1880 Annual Undergrad Tuition & Fees: $41,052
Enrollment: 4,545 Coed
Affiliation or Control: Independent Non-Profit IRS Status: 501(c)3
Highest Offering: Doctorate
Accreditation: EH, SP

01 President ....Mr. M. Lee PELTON
43 Vice President & General Counsel ....Ms. Christine HUGHES
10 Vice President for Admin & Finance ....Ms. Maureen MURPHY
05 Vice President for Academic Affairs ....Ms. Michaele WHELAN
13 VP for Information Technology ....Dr. William GILLIGAN
26 Vice Pres Communications/Marketing ....Mr. Andrew TIEDEMANN
28 VP Diversity & Inclusion ....Ms. Sylvia SPEARS
84 Vice Pres Enrollment Management ....Ms. Ruthanne MADSEN
21 Assoc Vice Pres for Finance ....Mr. Marc MILLER
15 Assoc Vice Pres for Human Resources ....Ms. Alexa JACKSON
29 AVP Inst Advance/Dir Alumni Affrs ....Ms. Barbara RUTBERG
86 Assoc Vice Pres Govt/Community Rels ....Ms. Margaret Ann INGS
58 Dean Grad Studies/AVP Acad Affairs ....Ms. Carol PARKER
32 Vice Pres/Dean of Students ....Mr. James HOPPE
107 Exec Director Professional Studies ....Ms. Lesley NICHOLS
08 Exec Director of Library Services ....Mr. Robert FLEMING
07 Director of Graduate Admission ....Ms. Leanda FERLAND
36 Director of Career Services ....Ms. Carol SPECTOR
38 Director Counseling Center ....Dr. Elise HARRISON
41 Director Athletics ....Ms. Patricia NICOL
85 Director International Student Affs ....Ms. Virga MOHSINI
96 Director Purchasing/Risk Management ....Ms. Margaret ROGAN
39 Assoc Dean Housing/Residence Life ....Mr. David W. HADEN
21 Controller ....Mr. Jonathan PEARSALL
06 Registrar ....Mr. William DEWOLF
42 Chair Center for Spiritual Life ....Vacant
101 Exec Asst to the Board of Trustees ....Ms. Anne SHAUGHNESSY
18 Int Assoc Director of Facilities ....Mr. Joseph KNOLL
37 Director Financial Aid ....Ms. Angela GRANT
07 Dean of Admissions ....Mr. Eric SYKES
09 Director of Institutional Research ....Mr. Michael DUGGAR

Emmanuel College (C)

400 The Fenway, Boston MA 02115-5798
County: Suffolk FICE Identification: 002147
Unit ID: 165671
Telephone: (617) 277-9340 Carnegie Class: Bac-A&S
FAX Number: (617) 735-9877 Calendar System: Semester
URL: www.emmanuel.edu
Established: 1919 Annual Undergrad Tuition & Fees: $36,504
Enrollment: 2,311 Coed
Affiliation or Control: Roman Catholic IRS Status: 501(c)3
Highest Offering: Master's
Accreditation: EH, NURSE

01 President ....Sr. Janet EISNER, SND
03 Exec Asst to the President ....Ms. Michelle ERICKSON
04 Senior Assistant to the President ....Ms. Lori SIMMONS
10 VP of Finance/Treasurer (CFO) ....Sr. Anne DONOVAN, SND
05 VP Academic Affairs & Dean ....Dr. William LEONARD
32 VP of Student Affairs ....Dr. Patricia RISSMEYER
86 VP for Government & Cmty Relations ....Vacant
30 VP of Development & Alumni Rels ....Vacant
37 Assoc VP for Student Financial Svcs ....Ms. Jennifer PORTER
42 VP of Mission & Ministry ....Fr. John SPENCER, SJ
26 VP of Marketing & Communication ....Mr. Robert MCDONALD
07 Dean of Enrollment ....Ms. Sandra ROBBINS
35 Dean of Students ....Dr. Joseph ONOFRIETTI
06 Assoc VP for Inst Rsrch/Registrar ....Ms. Elizabeth ROSS
20 Assoc Dean Academic Administration ....Ms. Cindy O'CALLAGHAN
88 Asst Dean Cmty Stdrds & Family Pgms ....Ms. Mary Beth THOMAS
88 Assoc Dean of Academic Advising ....Sr. Susan THORNELL, SND
79 Assoc Dean Humanities/Soc Science ....Ms. Lisa STEPANSKI
66 Assoc Dean Nursing ....Ms. Diane SHEA
81 Assoc Dean Natural Sciences ....Dr. Josef KURTZ
08 Director of Library Services ....Vacant
15 Director of Human Resources ....Ms. Erin FARMER NOONAN
41 Director of Athletics & Recreation ....Ms. Alexis MASTRONARDI
38 Director of Counseling ....Dr. Brenda HAWKS
90 Director of Academic Resource Ctr ....Ms. Wendy LABRON
09 Director of Institutional Research ....Ms. Alison VALLEREUX
13 Chief Info Technology Officer (CIO) ....Mr. Sean PHILPOTT
19 Director Security/Safety ....Mr. John KELLY
29 Director Alumni Relations ....Ms. Molly M. ZUCCARINI

Endicott College (D)

376 Hale Street, Beverly MA 01915-2098
County: Essex FICE Identification: 002148
Unit ID: 165699
Telephone: (978) 927-0585 Carnegie Class: Masters/L
FAX Number: (978) 927-0084 Calendar System: 4/1/4
URL: www.endicott.edu
Established: 1939 Annual Undergrad Tuition & Fees: $30,492
Enrollment: 4,429 Coed
Affiliation or Control: Independent Non-Profit IRS Status: 501(c)3
Highest Offering: Doctorate
Accreditation: EH, ART, CAATE, CIDA, NUR

01 President ....Dr. Richard E. WYLIE
03 Executive Vice President ....Ms. Lynne O'TOOLE
05 Vice President & Academic Dean ....Dr. Laura ROSSI-LE
10 Vice President Finance ....Mr. Tony FERULLO
84 Vice Pres Admissions/Financial Aid ....Mr. Thomas J. REDMAN
58 VP/Dean Graduate & Prof Stds ....Dr. Mary HUEGEL
30 Vice Pres Institutional Advancement ....Mr. David VIGNERON
20 VP/Dean of Academic Resources ....Dr. Kathleen BARNES
26 Assistant Vice President PR ....Ms. Joanne L. WALDNER
90 Assoc Dean of Academic Technology ....Mr. Kent BARCLAY
07 Associate Dean of Admission ....Mr. George M. SHERMAN
45 Executive Director of Research ....Mr. Peter L. HART
15 Director Human Resources ....Ms. Sally ARNOLD
21 Controller ....Mr. Andy VIDAL
06 Registrar ....Ms. Rosa CADENA
08 Library Director ....Mr. Brian COURTEMANCHE
37 Dean of Financial Aid ....Ms. Marcia D. TOOMEY
41 Director of Athletics ....Dr. Brian WYLIE
91 Chief Information Systems Officer ....Mr. Gary F. KELLEY
38 Director Counseling Center ....Ms. Karen TOMPKINS
18 Director of Physical Plant ....Mr. Dennis MONACO
27 Director Communications ....Ms. Carol RAICHE
36 Director of Career Services ....Ms. Dale MCLENNAN
36 Dean of Internship & Career Center ....Mr. Eric HALL
09 Director of Institutional Research ....Mr. Donny FEMINO
96 Director of Purchasing ....Ms. Susan AYERS
85 Director of International Education ....Dr. Warren JAFERIAN
49 Dean of Arts & Sciences ....Dr. Gene WONG
53 Dean of Education ....Dr. Sara QUAY
57 Dean of Visual & Performing Arts ....Mr. Mark TOWNER
59 Dean of Hospitality Management ....Dr. William H. SAMENFINK
68 Dean of Sports Science/Fitness Stds ....Dr. Deborah SWANTON
66 Dean of Nursing ....Dr. Kelly FISHER
50 Dean of Business ....Dr. Michael PAIGE
60 Dean of Communication ....Dr. Laurel HELLERSTEIN
88 Director Internship ....Ms. Cindy RICHARD
101 Executive Administrative Assistant ....Ms. Amy ASTOLFI
105 Director Web Development ....Ms. Jeanne COMMETTE
19 Director of Public Safety/Chief ....Mr. Charles FEMINO
43 General Counsel ....Ms. Karen ABBOTT
104 Director Study Abroad ....Ms. Alicia VINAL
29 Director of Alumni Relations ....Ms. Jessica JACOBS
32 Dean of Students ....Ms. Brandi JOHNSON
44 Director of Annual Giving ....Ms. Sarah EARNEST

Episcopal Divinity School (E)

99 Brattle Street, Cambridge MA 02138-3494
County: Middlesex FICE Identification: 002149
Unit ID: 165705
Telephone: (617) 868-3450 Carnegie Class: Spec-4-yr-Faith
FAX Number: (617) 864-5385 Calendar System: Semester
URL: www.eds.edu
Established: 1857 Annual Graduate Tuition & Fees: N/A
Enrollment: 62 Coed
Affiliation or Control: Protestant Episcopal IRS Status: 501(c)3
Highest Offering: Doctorate; No Undergraduates
Accreditation: THEOL

01 Interim President ....Rev.Dr. William NELSEN
05 VP for Academic Affairs & Dean ....Dr. Angela BAUER-LEVESQUE
32 Dean of Student & Comm Life ....Rev. Thomas EOYANG
30 VP Institutional Advancement ....Ms. Janine DAILEY
08 Director of the Library ....Vacant
26 Dir of Communications & Marketing ....Mr. Justin AIER
10 Chief Financial and Planning Office ....Mr. William JUDGE
21 Comptroller ....Ms. Joanne MANNING
07 Mgr of Admissions & Recruitment ....Ms. Hillary KODY
06 Manager of Student Records/Registr ....Ms. Cecelia CULL
88 Director of Contextual Education ....Rev. Amy MCCREATH
18 Buildings & Grounds ....Ms. Denise MARDER
04 Exec Assistant to President & Dean ....Ms. Jane WAGNER
37 Director Student Financial Aid ....Ms. Valerie PATERSON
15 Director of Human Resources ....Ms. Samaria STALLINGS

FINE Mortuary College (F)

150 Kerry Place, Norwood MA 02062
County: Norfolk FICE Identification: 033164
Unit ID: 436599
Telephone: (781) 762-1211 Carnegie Class: Spec 2-yr-A&S
FAX Number: (781) 762-7177 Calendar System: Quarter
URL: www.fmc.edu
Established: 1996 Annual Undergrad Tuition & Fees: $19,575
Enrollment: 95 Coed
Affiliation or Control: Proprietary IRS Status: Proprietary
Highest Offering: Associate Degree
Accreditation: FUSER

01 President ....Mrs. Sherry JONES
03 Executive Vice President ....Mr. Kevin KOCH
05 Program Director ....Mr. Peter MASUZZO
11 Campus Manager ....Mr. Jason KELLER

Fisher College (G)

118 Beacon Street, Boston MA 02116-1500
County: Suffolk FICE Identification: 002150
Unit ID: 165802
Telephone: (617) 236-8800 Carnegie Class: Bac/Assoc-Mixed
FAX Number: (617) 236-8858 Calendar System: Semester
URL: www.fisher.edu
Established: 1903 Annual Undergrad Tuition & Fees: $28,942
Enrollment: 1,875 Coed
Affiliation or Control: Independent Non-Profit IRS Status: 501(c)3
Highest Offering: Master's
Accreditation: EH, CAHIIM, NURSE

01 President ....Dr. Thomas MCGOVERN
05 Vice President Academic Affairs ....Dr. Janet KUSER
10 VP for Finance ....Mr. Steven RICH
84 VP of Enrollment Management ....Mr. Robert MELARAGNI
11 General Counsel/VP Operations ....Ms. Carolina AVELLANEDA
32 Dean of Students ....Ms. Shiela LALLY
88 Dean Intl Acad Oper/Curriculum Dev ....Ms. Nancy PITHIS
49 Asst Dean School of Liberal Arts ....Dr. Dean WALTON
06 College Registrar ....Ms. Alissa BERTRAM
41 Director of Athletics ....Dr. Leonard NARDONE
21 Director of Accounting ....Mr. Jeffrey CONRAD
13 Director of Information Services ....Mr. Jonathan BARTSCH
18 Director of Facilities ....Mr. Paul MCBRINE
37 Director of Financial Aid ....Ms. Laura BIECHLER
45 VP of Strategy and Planning ....Dr. Melinda COOK
20 Assistant Dean for Academic Affairs ....Mr. Carla DELUCIA
35 Director Student Involvement ....Ms. Lisa JACKSON
19 Chief Dept of Public Safety ....Ms. Deborah CRAFTS
36 Director of Career Services ....Ms. Barbara ZERILLO
88 Director of Accessibility Service ....Dr. Wanda CAMACHO-MARON
21 College Bursar ....Ms. Kristen MARTINEZ
08 College Librarian ....Mr. Joshua MCKAIN
30 Assoc Dir Advancement & Alumni Rels ....Ms. Amanda MATARESE
09 Director of Institutional Research ....Mr. Alex WAGNER
58 Dean Grad Studies ....Dr. Neil TROTTA
39 Director Student Housing ....Mr. Kyle GRENIER
04 Manager Office of President/HR Mgr ....Ms. Ellen LYONS
26 Communications Manager ....Ms. Christina MARTIN

Franklin W. Olin College of Engineering (H)

Olin Way, Needham MA 02492-1200
County: Norfolk FICE Identification: 039463
Unit ID: 441982
Telephone: (781) 292-2300 Carnegie Class: Spec-4-yr-Eng
FAX Number: (781) 292-2210 Calendar System: Semester
URL: www.olin.edu
Established: 2002 Annual Undergrad Tuition & Fees: $48,181
Enrollment: 350 Coed
Affiliation or Control: Independent Non-Profit IRS Status: 501(c)3
Highest Offering: Baccalaureate
Accreditation: EH, ENG

01 President ....Dr. Richard K. MILLER
04 Asst to President ....Ms. Nancy SULLIVAN
05 Provost/Dean of Faculty ....Dr. Vincent P. MANNO
32 Dean of Student Affairs ....Ms. Rae-Anne BUTERA
06 Assoc Dean Student Life & Registrar ....Ms. Linda T. CANAVAN
07 Dean of Admission and Financial Aid ....Ms. Emily ROPER-DOTEN
37 Director of Financial Aid ....Ms. Jean RICKER

08 Library Director .... Mr. Jeff GOLDENSON
03 Executive Vice President .... Mr. Stephen P. HANNABURY
10 VP for Financial Affairs .... Ms. Patricia GALLAGHER
13 VP Operations/Chief Info Officer .... Ms. Joanne KOSSUTH
26 Chief Marketing Officer .... Ms. Michelle DAVIS
09 Asst Provost for Inst Research .... Mr. Jeremy GOODMAN
30 VP Development/Family & Alumni Rel .... Ms. Catherine DIDION
29 Director Family & Alumni Relations .... Ms. Kristina RAPOSA

† All admitted students who enroll at Olin College receive an Olin Scholarship covering half tuition during the eight semesters of the baccalaureate program.

Gordon College (A)

255 Grapevine Road, Wenham MA 01984-1899
County: Essex FICE Identification: 002153
Unit ID: 165936
Telephone: (978) 927-2300 Carnegie Class: Bac-A&S
FAX Number: (978) 867-4659 Calendar System: Semester
URL: www.gordon.edu
Established: 1889 Annual Undergrad Tuition & Fees: $35,386
Enrollment: 2,105 Coed
Affiliation or Control: Independent Non-Profit IRS Status: 501(c)3
Highest Offering: Master's
Accreditation: EH, MUS, SW

01 President .... Dr. D. Michael LINDSAY
03 Exec VP and Chief of Staff .... Mr. Daniel TYMANN
05 Provost .... Dr. Janel CURRY
10 VP for Finance and Administration .... Mr. Michael J. AHEARN
07 AVP Enrollment .... Ms. June BODONI
32 Vice President for Student Life .... Mrs. Jennifer JUKANOVICH
26 VP of Marketing and Communications .... Mr. Rick SWEENEY
08 Director of Library Services .... Mr. Myron SCHIRER-SUTER
06 Registrar .... Mrs. Alice A. FALCONE
13 AVP of Techonology & Operations .... Mr. Christopher JONES
37 Sr Dir of Student Financial Svcs .... Mr. Daniel O'CONNELL
15 Director of Human Resources .... Ms. Nancy ANDERSON
18 Dir of Plant Operations and Sustain .... Mr. Paul HELGESEN
21 Controller .... Ms. Kim MATHER
29 AVP College Relations & Annual Fund .... Mrs. Britt CARLSON
36 Director of Career Services .... Ms. Pam LAZARAKIS
96 Dir of Purchasing and Distribution .... Mr. Michael NAWOICHIK
09 Exec Dir Institutional Research .... Mr. Robert VAN CLEEF
19 Director Security/Safety .... Mr. Glenn DECKERT
30 Dir of Development Information Tech .... Mr. Rick HOUSTON
41 Director of Athletics .... Mr. Jon TYMANN
44 Chief Development Officer .... Mr. Paul EDWARD
105 Director of Web .... Mr. Stephen DAGLEY
28 Dr of Multicultural Initiatives .... Ms. Paulea MOONEY-MCCOY
39 Director of Residence Life .... Mr. Michael CURTIS

Gordon-Conwell Theological Seminary (B)

130 Essex Street, South Hamilton MA 01982-2317
County: Essex FICE Identification: 009747
Unit ID: 165945
Telephone: (978) 468-7111 Carnegie Class: Spec-4-yr-Faith
FAX Number: (978) 468-6691 Calendar System: Semester
URL: www.gordonconwell.edu
Established: 1884 Annual Graduate Tuition & Fees: N/A
Enrollment: 2,067 Coed
Affiliation or Control: Independent Non-Profit IRS Status: 501(c)3
Highest Offering: Doctorate; No Undergraduates
Accreditation: EH, THEOL

01 President .... Dr. Dennis HOLLINGER
10 Vice Pres Finance/Operations .... Mr. Jay S. TREWERN
05 Vice Pres for Academic Affairs .... Dr. Richard LINTS
30 Vice President of Advancement .... Mr. Kurt W. DRESCHER
12 Dean of Boston Campus .... Dr. Mark HARDEN
12 Academic Dean - Charlotte .... Dr. Timothy S. LANIAK
32 Dean of Students .... Ms. Michelle D. WILLIAMS
15 Exec Dir of Human Resources .... Ms. Robin HIGLE
13 Chief Information Officer .... Mrs. Amy E. DONOVAN
84 Dean Enrollment Mgmt/Registrar .... Mr. Scott B. POBLENZ
18 Director of Physical Plant .... Mr. Timothy INGRAHAM
08 Director of Goddard Library .... Mr. Meredith KLINE
42 Dir Doctor of Ministry Programs .... Mr. Dave CURRIE
88 Director of the Ockenga Institute .... Dr. David G. HORN
37 Director of Financial Aid .... Mr. Stacey T. GLIDDEN
40 Director of Support Services .... Mr. David SHOREY
19 Director of Campus Safety .... Mr. Cabot W. DODGE
26 Dir of Communications & Marketing .... Mr. Michael L. COLARERI
07 Asst Director of Admissions .... Ms. Jill M. BENSON
21 Controller & Dir Financial Svcs .... Mr. Gregg HANSEN
30 Chief Advancement Ofcr Charlotte .... Dr. Neely GASTON

Hampshire College (C)

893 West Street, Amherst MA 01002-3372
County: Hampshire FICE Identification: 004661
Unit ID: 166018
Telephone: (413) 549-4600 Carnegie Class: Bac-A&S
FAX Number: (413) 559-5584 Calendar System: 4/1/4
URL: www.hampshire.edu
Established: 1965 Annual Undergrad Tuition & Fees: $49,048
Enrollment: 1,376 Coed
Affiliation or Control: Independent Non-Profit IRS Status: 501(c)3
Highest Offering: Baccalaureate
Accreditation: EH

01 President .... Dr. Jonathan LASH
101 Secretary of the College .... Ms. Beth I. WARD
05 Vice President & Dean of Faculty .... Dr. Eva RUESCHMANN
32 VP Student Affairs/Dean of Students .... Mr. Byron MCCRAE
10 Vice Pres for Finance & Admin .... Mr. Mary MCENEANY
15 Assoc Vice Pres Human Resources .... Ms. Ann Michele RUOCCO
30 Chief Advancement Officer .... Mr. Clay BALLANTINE
84 Dean of Enrollment/Retention .... Ms. Meredith TWOMBLY
08 Director of Library/Info Services .... Ms. Jennifer KING
06 Director of Central Records .... Ms. Roberta P. STUART
37 Director of Financial Aid .... Ms. Jennifer G. LAWTON
09 Director of Institutional Research .... Ms. Meredith TWOMBLY
18 Director of Facilities and Grounds .... Mr. Larry ARCHEY
20 AVP of Academic Affairs .... Ms. Yaniris FERNANDEZ
26 Chief Creative Officer .... Mr. David GIBSON
29 Director Alumni & Family Relations .... Ms. Melissa MILLS-DICK
36 Director Student Placement .... Ms. Carin RANK
38 Director Student Counseling .... Dr. Eliza MCARDLE
100 Chief of Staff .... Ms. Joanna OLIN
28 Chief Diversity Officer .... Ms. Diana FERNANDEZ

Harvard University (D)

1350 Massachusetts Ave, Cambridge MA 02138-3800
County: Middlesex FICE Identification: 002155
Unit ID: 166027
Telephone: (617) 495-1000 Carnegie Class: DU-Highest
FAX Number: (617) 495-0500 Calendar System: Semester
URL: www.harvard.edu
Established: 1636 Annual Undergrad Tuition & Fees: $45,278
Enrollment: 28,791 Coed
Affiliation or Control: Independent Non-Profit IRS Status: 501(c)3
Highest Offering: Doctorate
Accreditation: EH, BUS, CLPSY, DENT, ENG, IPSY, LAW, LSAR, MED, PCSAS, PH, PLNG, THEOL

01 President .... Drew GILPIN FAUST
05 Provost .... Alan GARBER
49 Dean Arts and Sciences .... Michael D. SMITH
58 Dean Graduate School of A&S .... Xiao-Li MENG
50 Dean Harvard Business School .... Nitin NOHRIA
49 Dean Harvard College .... Rakesh KHURANA
56 Dean Continuing Educ and Extension .... Huntington D. LAMBERT
52 Dean School of Dental Medicine .... R. Bruce DONOFF
48 Dean Graduate School of Design .... Mohsen MOSTAFAVI
73 Dean Harvard Divinity School .... David N. HEMPTON
53 Dean Graduate School of Education .... James E. RYAN
54 Dean Engineering/Applied Sciences .... Francis J. DOYLE
80 Dean Kennedy School of Government .... Douglas ELMENDORF
61 Dean Harvard Law School .... Martha MINOW
63 Dean Harvard Medical School .... Vacant
69 Dean School of Public Health .... Vacant
88 Dean Inst for Advanced Studies .... Lizabeth COHEN
88 Treasurer .... Paul J. FINNEGAN
03 Executive Vice President .... Katherine N. LAPP
29 VP Alumni Affairs/Development .... Tamara ROGERS
10 VP for Finance and CFO .... Thomas HOLLISTER
101 VP and Secretary of the University .... Marc GOODHEART
88 VP for Strategy and Programs .... Leah ROSOVSKY
43 VP and General Counsel .... Robert IULIANO
26 VP Public Affairs and Communication .... Paul ANDREW
15 VP for Human Resources .... Marilyn HAUSAMMANN
45 VP Planning and Project Management .... Vacant
08 VP for the Harvard Library .... Sarah E. THOMAS
13 VP and CIO .... Anne MARGULIES
18 VP for Campus Services .... Meredith WEENICK

Hebrew College (E)

160 Herrick Road, Newton Centre MA 02459-2237
County: Middlesex FICE Identification: 002157
Unit ID: 166045
Telephone: (617) 559-8600 Carnegie Class: Spec-4-yr-Faith
FAX Number: (617) 559-8601 Calendar System: Semester
URL: www.hebrewcollege.edu
Established: 1921 Annual Undergrad Tuition & Fees: N/A
Enrollment: 146 Coed
Affiliation or Control: Independent Non-Profit IRS Status: 501(c)3
Highest Offering: Beyond Master's But Less Than Doctorate
Accreditation: EH

01 President .... Rabbi Daniel LEHMANN
10 Vice Pres Finance & Administration .... Mr. Keith DROPKIN
05 Provost .... Vacant
84 Director of Enrollment Management .... Mr. Bob GIELOW
06 Registrar/Dir Student Financial Aid .... Ms. Marilyn JAYE
15 Director Personnel Services .... Ms. Steffi BOBBIN
04 Assistant to the President .... Ms. Jessica EISENBERG

Hellenic College-Holy Cross Greek Orthodox School of Theology (F)

50 Goddard Avenue, Brookline MA 02445-7496
County: Norfolk FICE Identification: 002154
Unit ID: 166054
Telephone: (617) 731-3500 Carnegie Class: Spec-4-yr-Faith
FAX Number: (617) 850-1460 Calendar System: Semester
URL: www.hchc.edu
Established: 1937 Annual Undergrad Tuition & Fees: $22,490
Enrollment: 183 Coed
Affiliation or Control: Greek Orthodox IRS Status: 501(c)3
Highest Offering: Master's
Accreditation: EH, THEOL

01 President .... RevDr. Christopher T. METROPULOS
73 Dean School of Theology .... Dr. James SKEDROS
05 Dean Hellenic College .... Dr. Demetrios KATOS
32 Dean of Students .... Fr. Nicholas BELCHER
10 Chief Financial Officer .... Mr. Kevin DERRIVAN
07 Director of Admissions & Records .... Mr. Gregory FLOOR
08 Director Library .... Rev. Joachim COTSONIS
37 Financial Aid Director .... Mr. Michael KIRCHMAIER
06 Registrar .... Mr. Jay OSTROSKY
13 Director Computing/Information Mgmt .... Mr. Mugur ROZ
42 Chaplain .... Vacant
38 Director Student Counseling .... Vacant
30 Director Institutional Advancement .... Mr. Kosta ALEXIS
29 Director of Alumni Office .... Vacant
21 Controller .... Mr. Paul HUBBARD
40 Bookstore Manager .... Mr. Eric ROBERSON
39 Director of Housing/Security .... Vacant
15 Director of Human Resources .... Mr. David VOLZ
44 Director Annual or Planned Giving .... Ms. Frances LEVAS

Hult International Business School (G)

One Education Street, Cambridge MA 02141-1805
County: Middlesex FICE Identification: 041432
Unit ID: 164368
Telephone: (617) 746-1990 Carnegie Class: Spec-4-yr-Bus
FAX Number: (617) 746-1991 Calendar System: Other
URL: www.hult.edu
Established: 1964 Annual Undergrad Tuition & Fees: N/A
Enrollment: 814 Coed
Affiliation or Control: Proprietary IRS Status: Proprietary
Highest Offering: Master's
Accreditation: EH

01 President .... Dr. Stephen J. HODGES
05 Chief Academic Officer .... Prof. Johan ROOS
10 Chief Financial Officer .... Mr. Anders LJUNGDAHL
11 Chief Operations Officer .... Mr. Chris HOLMES
20 Dean of Faculty .... Mr. Nick AMDUR
12 Dean Boston Campus .... Dr. Emmett TRACY
12 Dean San Francisco Campus .... Mr. Larry LOUIE
84 Regional Director Enrollment .... Mr. Steve WYNN
36 Dir of Career Services Boston .... Ms. Joanne MARKOW
32 Dir Student Services Boston .... Ms. Emily BURKE
06 Senior Registrar Boston Campus .... Mr. Richard LESTAGE
06 Registrar San Francisco Campus .... Ms. Caroline CONNOR
37 Director Student Financial Aid .... Ms. Karen VAN DYNE

Laboure College (H)

303 Adams Street, Milton MA 02186-4253
County: Suffolk FICE Identification: 006324
Unit ID: 165264
Telephone: (617) 322-3500 Carnegie Class: Spec-4-yr-Other Health
FAX Number: (617) 296-7947 Calendar System: Semester
URL: www.laboure.edu
Established: 1892 Annual Undergrad Tuition & Fees: $34,410
Enrollment: 757 Coed
Affiliation or Control: Roman Catholic IRS Status: 501(c)3
Highest Offering: Baccalaureate
Accreditation: EH, ADNUF, CAHIIM, DIETT, NDT, NURSE, RTT

01 President .... Maureen A. SMITH
05 Vice President of Academic Affairs .... Albert DECICCIO
30 Vice Pres Institutional Advancement .... Catherine PHILBIN
84 Vice Pres Enrollment Management .... Nora SHERIDAN
04 Administrative Asst to President .... Megan D. COX
06 Registrar .... John SACCO
07 Director of Admissions .... Erin HANLON
08 Director of Library .... Andrew CALO
10 Chief Financial Officer .... Mark VIRELLO
13 Chief Info Technology Officer (CIO) .... Eric ELLIS
15 Chief Human Resource Officer .... Martha DOVE
19 Director Security/Safety .... Yvonne HALL
26 Chief Marketing Officer .... Katelyn DWYER
29 Director Alumni Relations .... Tramaine WEEKES
37 Director Student Financial Aid .... Erin HANLON

Lasell College (I)

1844 Commonwealth Avenue, Newton MA 02466-2716
County: Middlesex FICE Identification: 002158
Unit ID: 166391
Telephone: (617) 243-2000 Carnegie Class: Masters/M
FAX Number: (617) 243-2389 Calendar System: Semester
URL: www.lasell.edu
Established: 1851 Annual Undergrad Tuition & Fees: $32,000
Enrollment: 2,070 Coed
Affiliation or Control: Independent Non-Profit IRS Status: 501(c)3
Highest Offering: Master's
Accreditation: EH, ACBSF, CAATE, EXSC

01 President .... Michael B. ALEXANDER
04 Exec Assistant to the President .... Pamela FARIA
05 VP Academic Affairs .... James OSTROW
10 VP Admin & Finance/CFO .... Michael HOYLE
84 VP Enrollment Management .... Kathleen O'CONNOR
88 VP Lasell Village .... Anne DOYLE

32 VP Student Affairs ... Diane AUSTIN
26 VP Comm/Community & Govt Rels ... Vacant
30 VP Development & Alumni Relations ... Dean HICKEY
21 Assistant Vice President Finance ... Diane PARKER
20 Assoc VP/Dean Undergraduate Educ ... Steven BLOOM
07 Dean Undergraduate Admission ... James TWEED
58 Dean Grad & Prof Studies ... Joan DOLAMORE
89 Dean Advis & First Year Programs ... Helena SANTOS
35 Dean Student Affairs ... David HENNESSEY
37 Dir Student Financial Planning ... Michele KOSBOTH
09 Dir Institutional Research ... Eric LANTHIER
06 Registrar ... Dianne POLIZZI
18 Director Plant Operations ... Wayne LAMOUREUX
27 Dir Communications ... Michelle GASSEAU
30 Dir Development ... Mark LAFRANCE
29 Dir Alumni Relations/Annual Giving ... Lauren MCCAUSLIN
35 Dir Student Act & Orientation ... Jennifer GRANGER
23 Dir Health Center ... Lisa PEARLMAN
08 Dir Library ... Delritta HORNBUCKLE
41 Dir Athletics ... Kristy WALTER
15 Dir Human Resources ... Donna DANIELS
38 Dir Counseling Center ... Janice FLETCHER
07 Dir Graduate Admission ... Adrienne FRANCIOSI
42 Dir Center for Spirtual Life ... Thomas SULLIVAN
13 Chief Information Officer ... Deborah GELCH
44 Annual Giving Officer ... Rebecca BRENNER
39 Dir Residential Life ... Vacant

Le Cordon Bleu College of Culinary Arts in Cambridge (A)

215 First Street, Cambridge MA 02142
Telephone: (617) 218-8000 Identification: 770576
Accreditation: ACCSC, ACICS

† In teach-out mode through September 2017.

Lesley University (B)

29 Everett Street, Cambridge MA 02138-2790
County: Middlesex FICE Identification: 002160
Unit ID: 166452
Telephone: (617) 868-9600 Carnegie Class: DU-Mod
FAX Number: (617) 349-8717 Calendar System: Semester
URL: www.lesley.edu
Established: 1909 Annual Undergrad Tuition & Fees: $25,095
Enrollment: 4,859 Coed
Affiliation or Control: Independent Non-Profit IRS Status: 501(c)3
Highest Offering: Doctorate
Accreditation: EH, ART, TEAC

01 President ... Mr. Jeff A. WEISS
05 Provost ... Dr. Selase W. WILLIAMS
11 Vice President for Administration ... Ms. Marylou BATT
10 Vice President/CFO ... Ms. Bernice BRADIN
30 Vice President of Advancement ... Ms. Janis MARTINSON
84 VP of Enrollment Management ... Mr. Timothy ROBISON
21 VP for Budgeting & Fin Planning ... Ms. M. L. DYMSKI
43 General Counsel ... Ms. Shirin PHILIPP
100 Chief of Staff ... Dr. MaryPat LOHSE
20 Associate Provost ... Dr. Lisa IJIRI
58 Dean Grad Sch Arts & Social Sci ... Dr. David KATZ
53 Dean School of Education ... Dr. Jack GILLETTE
32 Dean of Student Life & Academic Dev ... Dr. Nathaniel MAYS
49 Dean College of Liberal Arts & Sci ... Dr. Steven SHAPIRO
57 Dean of College of Art and Design ... Dr. Richard ZAUFT
07 Director of Graduate Admissions ... Ms. Barbara SELMO
15 Director of Human Resources ... Ms. Jane JOYCE
37 Director of Financial Aid ... Mr. Scott JEWELL
21 Controller ... Mr. Stephen MICARELLI
08 Dean of Libraries ... Mr. Hedi BENAICHA
07 Dir Undergrad Admissions ... Ms. Deb KOCAR
09 Dir of Assessment/Inst Research ... Dr. Linda PURSLEY
04 Assistant to the President ... Ms. Kathleen SAMMARTINO
06 Registrar ... Ms. Adrianne ZONDERMAN
28 Dir Equal Opportunity & Inclusion ... Dr. Barbara ADDISON REID

Longy School of Music of Bard College (C)

27 Garden Street, Cambridge MA 02138
Telephone: (617) 876-0956 Identification: 770137
Accreditation: &M

† Regional accreditation is carried under the parent institution in Annandale-On-Hudson, NY

*Massachusetts Board of Higher Education (D)

One Ashburton Place, Room 1401,
Boston MA 02108-1696
County: Suffolk FICE Identification: 029283
Unit ID: 166531
Telephone: (617) 994-6950 Carnegie Class: N/A
FAX Number: (617) 727-6397
URL: www.mass.edu

01 Commissioner ... Dr. Carlos SANTIAGO
103 Assoc Comm of Workforce Development . Mr. David C. CEDRONE
05 Assoc Comm Academic Affs/Stdnt Succ ... Dr. Winifred M. HAGAN
09 Sr Comm Research/Planning ... Dr. Jonathan KELLER
43 General Counsel ... Ms. Constantia PAPANIKOLAOU
10 Dep Comm Administration and Finance ... Mr. Sean NELSON
37 Sr Dep Comm Student Financial Aid ... Dr. Clantha MCCURDY

*University of Massachusetts System Office (E)

One Beacon Street, 31st Floor, Boston MA 02108
County: Suffolk FICE Identification: 008017
Unit ID: 166665
Telephone: (617) 287-7050 Carnegie Class: N/A
FAX Number: (617) 287-7167
URL: www.umassp.edu

01 President ... Mr. Martin T. MEEHAN
03 Exec VP/Chief Operating Officer ... Mr. James JULIAN
05 Sr VP Acad Affs/Stdnt & Intl Affs ... Dr. Marcellette WILLIAMS
10 Sr VP Administration and Finance ... Ms. Christine WILDA
30 Vice President for Advancement ... Mr. Charles PAGNAM
26 VP Strategic Comm/Univ Spokesperson ... Mr. Robert CONNOLLY
104 Deputy Chief Operating Officer ... Ms. Susan KELLY
86 Special Asst to Pres Govt Relation ... Mr. David MCDERMOTT
43 General Counsel ... Ms. Deirdre HEATWOLE
13 Assoc VP and Chief Info Officer ... Mr. Robert SOLIS
101 Secretary to Board of Trustees ... Ms. Zunilka BARRETT
21 Director for University Auditing ... Mr. Kyle DAVID
15 Human Resources Officer ... Mr. Andrew RUSSELL
106 Interim CEO UMass Online ... Dr. John CUNNINGHAM

*University of Massachusetts (F)

Amherst MA 01003-0001
County: Hampshire FICE Identification: 002221
Unit ID: 166629
Telephone: (413) 545-0111 Carnegie Class: DU-Highest
FAX Number: N/A Calendar System: Semester
URL: www.umass.edu
Established: 1863 Annual Undergrad Tuition & Fees (In-State): $14,171
Enrollment: 28,635 Coed
Affiliation or Control: State IRS Status: 501(c)3
Highest Offering: Doctorate
Accreditation: EH, ART, AUD, BUS, BUSA, CLPSY, DIETD, DIETI, ENG, IPSY, LSAR, MUS, NURSE, PH, PLNG, SCPSY, SP, TED

02 Chancellor ... Dr. Kumble R. SUBBASWAMY
03 Deputy Chancellor ... Dr. Robert S. FELDMAN
05 Sr VC/Provost Academic Affairs ... Dr. Katherine S. NEWMAN
10 Vice Chancellor Admin/Finance ... Mr. Andrew MANGELS
30 VC Development & Alumni Relations ... Mr. Michael A. LETO
46 Vice Chancellor Research ... Dr. Michael F. MALONE
32 VC Student Affairs & Campus Life ... Ms. Enku GELAYE
26 Vice Chanc University Relations ... Mr. John KENNEDY
41 Director of Athletics ... Mr. Ryan BAMFORD
43 Senior Counsel ... Mr. Brian W. BURKE
13 VC Information Services & CIO ... Ms. Julie L. BUEHLER
22 Exec Dir EO&D/Chief Diversity Ofcr ... Ms. Debora D. FERREIRA
28 Faculty Adv Diversity & Excellence ... Dr. Anna BRANCH
100 Chief of Staff ... Ms. Natalie BLAIS
20 Vice Provost for Academic Affairs ... Dr. Elizabeth R. DUMONT
20 Vice Provost Undegrad & Cont Educ ... Dr. Carol A. BARR
58 Vice Provost/Dean of Grad School ... Dr. John J. MCCARTHY
88 Assoc Provost Academic Personnel ... Mr. John BRYAN
85 Assoc Prov International Programs ... Dr. Jack AHERN
84 Assoc Provost Enrollment Management ... Dr. James ROCHE
45 Assoc Chancellor/Chf Planning Ofcr ... Dr. Bryan C. HARVEY
20 Asst Provost Advising/Acad
Advising ... Dr. Pamela R. MARSH-WILLIAMS
09 Asst Chanc Institutional Research ... Dr. Marilyn H. BLAUSTEIN
108 Asst Provost Assessment/Educ Effect ... Dr. Martha L. STASSEN
51 Exec Director Continuing Education ... Mr. William S. MCCLURE
07 Director Undergraduate Admissions ... Vacant
37 Director Financial Aid Services ... Ms. Suzanne PETERS
06 University Registrar ... Mr. John LENZI
92 Dean Commonwealth Honors College ... Dr. Gretchen GERZINA
79 Dean Col Humanities & Fine Arts ... Dr. Julie C. HAYES
81 Dean Col Natural Science ... Dr. Steve GOODWIN
53 Dean School of Education ... Dr. Christine B. MCCORMICK
54 Dean College of Engineering ... Dr. Timothy J. ANDERSON
50 Dean School of Management ... Dr. Mark A. FULLER
66 Dean School of Nursing ... Dr. Stephen CAVANAGH
69 Dean Sch Public Health/Health Sci ... Dr. C. Marjorie AELION
08 Director of Libraries ... Dr. Simon NEAME
56 Director of Extension ... Ms. Nancy GARRABRANTS
47 Dir Stockbridge School Agriculture ... Dr. Wesley AUTIO
88 Director Fine Arts Center ... Dr. Willie L. HILL, JR.
15 Asst Vice Chanc Human Resources ... Ms. Marie H. BOWEN
21 Assoc VC Finance & Budget Director ... Mr. Andrew P. MANGELS
18 Assoc VC Facilities & Campus Svcs ... Ms. Juanita M. HOLLER
19 Director Public Safety/Chief Police ... Mr. Patrick T. ARCHBALD
96 Director Procurement & Campus Svcs ... Mr. John O. MARTIN
40 Manager Univ Store/Retail Services ... Mr. Ken KAHLER
35 VC Student Affairs/Campus Life ... Ms. Enku GELAYE
39 Exec Director Residential Life ... Mr. Edward C. HULL
23 Director University Health Services ... Dr. George A. COREY
38 Director Mental Health/Health
Svcs ... Dr. Harry S. ROCKLAND-MILLER
36 Interim Director Career Services ... Ms. Candice J. SERAFINO
29 Exec Director Alumni Relations ... Dr. JC SCHNABL
86 Exec Dir Public/Constituent Rels ... Mr. Christopher DUNN
31 Assoc VC for University Relations ... Dr. Nancy BUFFONE
25 Acting Dir Grant & Contract Admin ... Ms. Carol SPRAGUE
91 Deputy CIO/Dir Admin Applics ... Ms. Heidi DOLLARD
90 Assoc Dir OIT Academic Computing ... Mr. Fred ZINN
24 Director Educational Media ... Mr. Stephen PIELOCK
105 Web Manager ... Ms. Nina SOSSEN

*University of Massachusetts Boston (G)

100 Morrissey Boulevard, Boston MA 02125-3393
County: Suffolk FICE Identification: 002222
Unit ID: 166638
Telephone: (617) 287-5000 Carnegie Class: DU-Higher
FAX Number: (617) 265-7173 Calendar System: Semester
URL: www.umb.edu
Established: 1964 Annual Undergrad Tuition & Fees (In-State): $12,682
Enrollment: 16,756 Coed
Affiliation or Control: State IRS Status: 501(c)3
Highest Offering: Doctorate
Accreditation: EH, BUS, CACREP, CLPSY, COPSY, CORE, CS, MFCD, NURSE, SCPSY, TEAC

02 Chancellor ... Dr. J. Keith MOTLEY
88 Assistant Chancellor ... Dr. Theresa MORTIMER
100 Chief of Staff ... Mr. Christopher HOGAN
05 Provost ... Dr. Winston LANGLEY
10 Vice Chanc for Admin & Finance ... Ms. Ellen O'CONNOR
30 VC for University Advancement ... Vacant
84 Vice Chanc Enrollment Mgmt ... Ms. Lisa JOHNSON
32 Int Vice Chancellor for Student Aff ... Ms. Lisa BUENAVENTURA
32 Int Vice Chancellor for Student Aff ... Mr. James OVERTON
41 VC for Athletics & Special Projects ... Mr. Charlie TITUS
86 VC for Govt Rel/Public Aff ... Mr. Edward LAMBERT
13 Vice Provost Info Tech/CIO ... Mr. Robert WEIR
15 Asst Vice Chanc for Human Resources ... Ms. Becky HSU
29 Assoc VC Alumni
Relations ... Ms. Elizabeth FREEDMAN DOHERTY
31 Int Director Community Relations ... Mr. Philip J. CARVER
23 Exec Dir Univ Health Services ... Mr. Robert POMALES
20 Associate Provost ... Ms. Kristine ALSTER
20 Assoc Provost Assess and Planning ... Dr. Peter LANGER
84 Asst VC for Enrollment Mgmt ... Mr. John DREW
53 Dean Col of Educ & Human Dev ... Mr. Michael MIDDLETON
51 Dean of University College ... Dr. Philip DISALVIO
81 Dean of Math & Science ... Dr. Andrew GROSOVSKY
79 Dean of Liberal Arts ... Dr. David TERKLA
50 Dean College of Management ... Dr. Jorge HADDOCK
66 Int Dean College of Nursing ... Dr. Marion WINFREY
80 Int Dean of CPCS ... Dr. Anna MADISON
35 Dean of Students ... Vacant
43 Interim General Counsel ... Ms. Deirdre HEATWOLE
26 Director of Communications ... Mr. DeWayne LEHMAN
38 Director Univ Advising Center ... Ms. Gail STUBBS
09 Assoc Prov Institutional Research ... Mr. James J. HUGHES
06 Director of Registration & Records ... Mr. David R. CESARIO
37 Director Financial Aid Services ... Ms. Judy KEYES
08 Dean of University Libraries ... Dr. Daniel ORTIZ
22 Int Chief Diversity Officer-ODI ... Ms. Georgianna MELENDEZ
18 Director of Facilities Devel & Mgmt ... Ms. Dorothy RENAGHAN
19 Int Director of Public Safety ... Mr. Donald BAYNARD
40 Director of Campus Services ... Ms. Diane D'ARRIGO
41 Senior Assoc Director of Athletics ... Ms. Terry CONDON
36 Director of Career Services ... Mr. Mark KENYON
96 Director of Procurement ... Mr. Darryl MAYERS
92 Dean of Honors College ... Ms. Rajini SRIKANTH
20 Asst Vice Provost Undergrad Studies ... Ms. Maura MAST

*University of Massachusetts Dartmouth (H)

285 Old Westport Road, North Dartmouth MA 02747-2300
County: Bristol FICE Identification: 002210
Unit ID: 167987
Telephone: (508) 999-8000 Carnegie Class: DU-Higher
FAX Number: (508) 999-8901 Calendar System: Semester
URL: www.umassd.edu
Established: 1895 Annual Undergrad Tuition & Fees (In-State): $12,588
Enrollment: 9,111 Coed
Affiliation or Control: State IRS Status: 501(c)3
Highest Offering: Doctorate
Accreditation: EH, ART, BUS, CS, ENG, #LAW, MT, NURSE

02 Interim Chancellor ... Dr. Peyton HELM
05 Provost/VC Acad & Student Affairs ... Dr. Mohammad KARIM
10 VC Admin & Finance/CFO ... Mr. James SHEEHAN
30 Interim VC Advancement ... Mr. Joseph MEDINA
04 Executive Office Director ... Ms. Lori NICKERSON
51 Interim Exec Dir Univ Extension ... Mr. David PEDRO
20 Vice Provost for Academic Affairs ... Dr. Magali CARRERA
58 Assoc Provost Grad Studies ... Dr. Tesfay MERESSI
84 Assc VC Enrollment Management ... Mr. Ian DAY
21 Assoc Vice Chancellor Finance ... Ms. Mary Louise NUNES
18 Associate VC Facilities Management ... Mr. Peter DUFFY
58 Dir Graduate Studies/Admissions ... Mr. Scott WEBSTER
22 Assoc VC Diversity/Equity/Inc ... Ms. Deborah MAJEWSKI
88 Assistant VC Student Success ... Ms. Carol SPENCER
32 Assoc Vice Chanc Student Affairs ... Dr. David M. MILSTONE
13 Interim Assoc VC IT/CIO ... Mr. Holger DIPPEL
91 Asst VC IT System & Planning ... Vacant
88 Asst VC for Pgm Planning/Fiscal
Mgt ... Ms. Joanne ZANELLA-LITKE
49 Dean College Arts & Science ... Dr. Jeannette RILEY
50 Dean Charlton Col of Business ... Dr. Angappa GUNASEKARAN
54 Dean College of Engineering ... Dr. Robert PECK
66 Dean College of Nursing ... Dr. Kimberly CHRISTOPHER
57 Dean College Visual Perform Arts ... Mr. David KLAMEN
88 Dean School Marine Science/Tech ... Dr. Steven LOHRENZ
61 Dean School of Law ... Ms. Mary Lu BILEK

96 Asst VC for Administrative Services .... Mr. Michael LAGRASSA
21 Asst Financial Controller .... Ms. Suzanne AUDET
92 Director Honors Program .... Dr. Catherine GARDNER
94 Dir Center Women/Gender/Sexuality .... Dr. Juli PARKER
88 Dir Academic Advising Center .... Ms. Suzanne MELLONI
06 University Registrar .... Ms. Audra CALLAHAN
07 Director of Admissions .... Ms. Hanan KHAMIS
09 Director of Institutional Research .... Ms. Tammy A. SILVA
08 Dean Library Services .... Mr. Terrance BURTON
19 Dir Public Safety/Chief of Police .... Col. Emil FIORAVANTI
36 Director Career Development Center .... Ms. Linda KENT DAVIS
37 Director Financial Aid .... Vacant
38 Dir Counseling/Stdnt Develop Ctr .... Dr. Christine FRIZZELL
90 Exec Dir IT Quality Assurance .... Ms. Margaret S. DIAS
29 Asst VC Alumni Relations .... Vacant
29 Director of Alumni Relations .... Ms. Nancy VANASSE
15 Asst VC Human Resources .... Ms. Carol SANTOS
18 Director Facilities/Physical Plant .... Mr. Jeffrey LOURO
41 Director of Athletics .... Ms. Amanda VAN VOORHIS
23 Director of Health Services .... Ms. Sheila DORGAN
39 Director of Housing/Residence Life .... Ms. Lucinda POUDRIER-AARONSON
44 Director Annual Funds .... Ms. Leanne BARKLEY
26 Vice Chancellor for Univ Marketing .... Ms. Renee BUISSON
88 Bursar .... Ms. Kathleen L. EUBANKS
35 Asst VC Student Affairs .... Ms. Cynthia CUMMINGS
35 Associate Dean of Students .... Ms. Shelly METIVIER SCOTT
104 Dir International Programs Office .... Vacant
85 Dir International Student Center .... Ms. Christina M. BRUEN
93 Director Fred Douglas Unity House .... Ms. Nicole WILLIAMS
88 Director Academic Resource Center .... Mr. Sokratis KOUMAS
105 Webmaster .... Mr. Donald KING
108 Dir of Learning Assessment .... Vacant
100 Assistant Chancellor .... Mr. John HOEY
101 Senior VC Strategic Management .... Mr. Gerard KAVANAUGH
102 Public Affairs Specialist .... Mr. Joseph SULLIVAN
103 Dir Experiential Learning & Intern .... Ms. Amelia SCOTT
106 Dir Center for Access & Success .... Ms. Wendi CHAKA
25 Dir Sponsored Projects Admin .... Ms. Elena GLATMAN
28 Equal Opportunity Spec/Investigator .... Mr. David GOMES
45 Asst VC Campus Master Planning/Cap .... Mr. Michael HAYES

*University of Massachusetts Lowell (A)

1 University Avenue, Lowell MA 01854-2881

County: Middlesex | FICE Identification: 002161 | Unit ID: 166513
Telephone: (978) 934-4000 | Carnegie Class: DU-Higher
FAX Number: (978) 934-3000 | Calendar System: Semester
URL: www.uml.edu
Established: 1894 | Annual Undergrad Tuition & Fees (In-State): $13,427
Enrollment: 17,179 | Coed
Affiliation or Control: State | IRS Status: 501(c)3
Highest Offering: Doctorate
Accreditation: EH, ART, BUS, @DIETC, ENG, ENGR, ENGT, MT, MUS, NURSE, PTA, TED

02 Chancellor .... Dr. Jacqueline F. MOLONEY
05 Provost .... Dr. Michael E. VAYDA
10 Vice Chancellor Finance & Operation ... Ms. Joanne YESTRAMSKI
26 VC University Relations .... Ms. Patricia MCCAFFERTY
30 Vice Chancellor for Advancement .... Mr. John FEUDO
84 Dean Enrollment & Student Success .... Mr. Thomas TAYLOR
41 Director of Athletics .... Mr. Dana SKINNER
46 VC of Research & Administration .... Dr. Julie CHEN
15 Assoc VC Human Resources and EOO .... Ms. Lauren TURNER
106 Exec Dir Acad Svcs Online/Cont Ed .... Ms. Pauline CARROLL
21 Assoc Vice Chancellor for Finance .... Mr. Steven O'RIORDAN
106 Sr Exec Dir Online/Cont Educ .... Ms. Catherine KENDRICK
88 Vice Provost for Enrollment .... Dr. John TING
58 Vice Provost Grad & Internal Affs .... Dr. Kathryn CARTER
88 Special Assistant to Chancellor .... Dr. Donald PIERSON
18 Assoc VC Facilities Managment .... Mr. Thomas DREYER
88 Assoc VC Entrepreneurship Econ Dev .... Mr. Steven TELLO
49 Dean Col Fine Arts/Hum/Soc Sci .... Dr. Luis FALCON
81 Dean College of Sciences .... Dr. Mark HINES
53 Dean of Education .... Dr. Anita GREENWOOD
54 Dean College of Engineering .... Dr. Joseph HARTMAN
76 Dean College of Health Sciences .... Dr. Shortie MCKINNEY
50 Dean Manning School of Business .. Dr. Sandra RICHTERMEYER
09 Director of Institutional Research .... Dr. Julie ALIG
08 Director of Libraries .... Mr. George HART
06 Registrar .... Ms. Kerry DONOHOE
37 Assoc Dean Enrollment/Dir Fin Aid .... Ms. Joyce MCLAUGHLIN
32 Assoc VC Student Affs/Univ Events .... Mr. Larry SIEGEL
38 Director of Counseling Svcs .... Dr. John PAKSTIS
29 Dir of Alumni Relations .... Ms. Heather MAKREZ
19 Chief Univ Police Dir Public Safety .... Mr. Randolph BRASHEARS
88 Dir Graduate Admissions .... Ms. Linda SOUTHWORTH
96 Chief Procurement Officer .... Mr. Thomas HOOLE
88 Dir Outreach & Recruitment .... Mr. Michael BELCHER
07 Assoc Dean Enroll & Dir UG Admiss .... Ms. Kerri JOHNSTON
88 Assoc Director UCAPS .... Mr. Jon VICTORINE
28 Dir Equal Opportunity & Outreach .... Ms. Clara ORLANDO
36 Asst Dean Student Affs/Career Dev .... Mr. Gregory DENON
22 Dir Student Disability Services .... Ms. Jody GOLDSTEIN
35 Dean Student Affairs & Enrichment .... Mr. James KOHL
23 Assoc Dir Student Health Svcs .... Ms. Diana WALKER MOYER
108 Director of Assessment .... Ms. Paula HAINES
35 Dean Student Affairs & Event Svcs .... Ms. Brenda EVANS
13 Chief Information Officer .... Mr. Michael CIPRIANO
85 Exec Dir Intl Administration .... Ms. Maria CONLEY
104 Director Intl Exper/Study Abroad .... Ms. Fern MACKINNON

*University of Massachusetts Medical School (B)

55 Lake Avenue N, Worcester MA 01655-0001

County: Worcester | FICE Identification: 009756 | Unit ID: 166708
Telephone: (508) 856-8989 | Carnegie Class: Spec-4-yr-Med
FAX Number: (508) 856-8181 | Calendar System: Semester
URL: www.umassmed.edu
Established: 1962 | Annual Graduate Tuition & Fees: N/A
Enrollment: 1,103 | Coed
Affiliation or Control: State | IRS Status: 501(c)3
Highest Offering: Doctorate; No Undergraduates
Accreditation: EH, IPSY, MED, NURSE

02 Chancellor & SVP Health Sciences .... Dr. Michael F. COLLINS
05 Dean Provost & Exec Dep Chancellor .... Dr. Terence R. FLOTTE
10 Exec VC Administration & Finance .... Mr. Robert E. JENAL
88 Exec VC Innovation and Business Dev .... Dr. Brendan O'LEARY
30 VC for Advancement .... Mr. John J. HAYES
88 Exec Vice Chancellor MassBiologics .... Dr. Mark D. KLEMPNER
11 Exec VC Commonwealth Medicine .... Ms. Joyce A. MURPHY
15 VC Diversity & Inclusion .... Dr. Deborah L. PLUMMER
86 VC Government/Community Relations .... Mr. James LEARY
26 Vice Chancellor of Communications .... Ms. Jennifer BERRYMAN
88 Vice Provost Faculty Affairs .... Dr. Luanne THORNDYKE
88 Vice Provost School Services .... Dr. Deborah Harmon HINES
53 Sr Assoc Dean Educational Affairs .... Dr. Michele P. PUGNAIRE
63 Sr Assc Dean Clin Aff/Assc Dean GME .... Dr. Deborah DEMARCO
66 Dean Graduate School of Nursing .... Dr. Joan VITELLO
32 Assoc Dean Student Affairs .... Dr. Sonia CHIMIENTI
58 Dean Grad School Biomedical Science .... Dr. Anthony CARRUTHERS
06 Registrar .... Mr. Michael F. BAKER
13 Chief Information Officer .... Mr. Greg WOLF
07 Assoc Dean for Admissions .... Dr. Mariann M. MANNO
37 Director Financial Aid .... Mr. Shawn MORRISSEY
08 Director of Library .... Ms. Elaine R. MARTIN
100 Chancellor's Chief of Staff .... Mr. Brendan H. CHISHOLM
04 Spec Assistant to the Chancellor .... Mr. Ryan GLINES
88 Vice Provost for Clin/Trans Science .... Dr. Katherine LUZURIAGA
100 Chief of Staff .... Ms. Kristen MAKI
20 Exec Asst Dean Provost & Exec Dep .... Ms. Kimberly LAPERLE
88 Assc Provost Basic Sci Research .... Dr. Jean KING

*Bridgewater State University (C)

131 Summer Street, Bridgewater MA 02325-0001

County: Plymouth | FICE Identification: 002183 | Unit ID: 165024
Telephone: (508) 531-1000 | Carnegie Class: Masters/L
FAX Number: N/A | Calendar System: Semester
URL: www.bridgew.edu
Established: 1840 | Annual Undergrad Tuition & Fees (In-State): $8,903
Enrollment: 11,187 | Coed
Affiliation or Control: State | IRS Status: 501(c)3
Highest Offering: Master's
Accreditation: EH, AAB, ART, #CAATE, CACREP, CS, MUS, @SP, SPAA, SW, TED

02 President .... Mr. Frederick CLARK
05 Provost & VP Academic Affairs .... Dr. Barbara FELDMAN
88 Special Advisor to the President .... Dr. Karim ISMAILI
11 Sr Vice Pres Administration/Finance .... Mr. Miguel GOMES, JR.
32 Interim VP Student Affairs .... Dr. Margaret JABLONSKI
30 VP University Advancement .... Dr. Brenda MOLIFE
15 VP Human Resources & Talent Mgmt .... Ms. Keri POWERS
26 VP Marketing & Communication .... Mr. Paul JEAN
28 VP of Student Success & Diversity .... Dr. Sabrina GENTLEWARRIOR
10 Chief of Staff .... Dr. Deniz ZEYNEP LEUENBERGER
10 Assoc Vice President Finance .... Mr. Douglas SHROPSHIRE
22 Director Title IX Coordinator .... Ms. Erin DEBOBES
15 Director HR & Talent Management .... Mr. Brian SALVAGGIO
35 Assoc Vice Pres Student Affairs .... Ms. Derrine ROCCO
84 Assoc Vice Pres for Enrollment Svcs .... Dr. Heather C. SMITH
20 Assoc Provost Faculty Affs .... Dr. Pamela M. WITCHER
45 Assoc Provost Academic Plng/Admin .... Dr. Michael YOUNG
79 Dean Col of Humanities/Social Sci .... Dr. Paula M. KREBS
53 Dean Col Education/Allied Stds .... Dr. Lisa BATTAGLINO
51 Dean Col of Continuing Studies .... Dr. David CRANE
50 Dean Ricciardi College of Business .... Dr. Elmore ALEXANDER
100 Chief of Staff .... Dr. Deniz LEUENBERGER
07 Dean of University Admissions .... Mr. Gregg A. MEYER
13 VP & Chief Information Officer .... Mr. Raymond LEFEBVRE
06 Registrar .... Mr. Joseph WOLK
88 Director Academic Achievement Ctr .... Ms. Alicia D'OYLEY
29 Director Alumni Relations .... Ms. Shana MURRELL
30 Assistant VP for Development .... Mr. Todd AUDYATIS
41 Director Athletics/Recreation .... Dr. Marybeth LAMB
21 Director University Services .... Ms. Margarida VIEIRA
19 Chief of Police .... Mr. David TILLINGHAST
36 Director Career Services .... Mr. John PAGANELLI
88 Director Children's Center .... Vacant
37 Director of Financial Aid .... Ms. Janet GUMBRIS
23 Senior Director Wellness Center .... Dr. Mary Lou FRIAS
08 Director Library Administration .... Mr. Michael SOMERS
51 Direc Continuing/Distance Education .... Vacant
22 Director Multicultural Affairs .... Ms. Sydne M. MARROW
27 Director of Publications .... Ms. Marie MURPHY
25 Director Grants/Sponsored Projects .... Ms. Mia ZOINO
96 Director of Procurement Services .... Dr. Jennifer PACHECO

28 Director of Institutional Diversity .... Vacant
18 Assoc VP Facilities Management/Plng .... Ms. Karen JASON
81 Dean Bartlett Col Science & Math ..... Dr. Kristen PORTER-UTLEY
58 Int Dean College of Graduate Stds .... Dr. Wendy HAYNES
09 Director of Institutional Research .... Dr. Kate MCLAREN
88 Director Teaching and Learning .... Dr. Roben TOROSYAN
46 Director Undergraduate Research .... Dr. Jenny SHANAHAN
85 Dir International Students/Scholar .... Dr. Roopa RAWJEE
88 Dir Regional Partnerships .... Dr. Diana E. JENNINGS
104 Director Study Abroad .... Mr. Michael SANDY
88 Asst VP Applications & Development .... Vacant
91 Dir Administrative Systems .... Ms. Kelley BARAN
88 Asst VP Infrastructure Netwk Sy .... Mr. Steven ZUROMSKI
105 Director of Web Development .... Ms. Eileen O'SULLIVAN
26 Dir Integrated Marketing and Comm .... Ms. Eva GAFFNEY
27 Director of University News .... Mr. John WINTERS
38 Asst Clinical Dir Counseling Center .... Mr. Philip ROBERTS
39 Dir Residence Life and Housing .... Ms. Beth MORIARTY
88 Deputy Chief of Staff .... Ms. Mary DELGADO
108 Director of Assessment .... Dr. Ruth SLOTNICK
04 Staff Associate to the President .... Ms. Kelly HESS SALISBURY
43 General Counsel .... Vacant

*Fitchburg State University (D)

160 Pearl Street, Fitchburg MA 01420-2697

County: Worcester | FICE Identification: 002184 | Unit ID: 165820
Telephone: (978) 345-2151 | Carnegie Class: Masters/L
FAX Number: (978) 665-3693 | Calendar System: Semester
URL: www.fitchburgstate.edu
Established: 1894 | Annual Undergrad Tuition & Fees (In-State): $9,935
Enrollment: 6,810 | Coed
Affiliation or Control: State | IRS Status: 501(c)3
Highest Offering: Master's
Accreditation: EH, CS, CSHSE, IACBE, NURSE, TED

02 President .... Dr. Richard S. LAPIDUS
05 Provost/VP Academic Affairs .... Dr. Alberto CARDELLE
10 Vice Pres Finance & Administration .... Mr. Jay BRY
20 Associate VP Academic Affairs .... Dr. Catherine CANNEY
26 Exec Asst to Pres for External Affs .... Mr. Michael V. SHANLEY
32 Dean of Student & Academic Life .... Dr. Stanley BUCHOLC
53 Dean of Education .... Dr. Bruno HICKS
30 Vice President of Inst Advancement .... Mr. Christopher HENDRY
35 Assistant Dean for Student Devel ... Dr. Henry C. PARKINSON, III
06 Registrar .... Ms. Linda DUPELL
09 Director of Institutional Research .... Mr. Anthony WILCOX
08 Interim Director Library .... Dr. Sean GOODLETT
41 Director Athletics .... Ms. Sue M. LAUDER
07 Director of Admissions .... Mr. Sean GANAS
36 Director of Career Services .... Ms. Erin C. KELLEHER
38 Director Counseling .... Dr. Robert HYNES
23 Director Student Health Services .... Ms. Martha FAVRE
29 Asst Director of Alumni Relations .... Ms. Emily AUSTIN-BRUNS
19 Interim Director of Campus Police .... Chief Michael CLOUTIER
44 Director of Annual Giving .... Ms. Tanya CROWLEY
15 Asst VP of Human Resources/Payroll .... Ms. Jessica MURDOCH
18 Dir of Operations & Maint .... Mr. Richard MCCLUSKEY
18 Dir Capital Planning & Construction .... Mr. Doug THOMAS
25 Director Grants & Sponsored Pgm .... Ms. Karen FRANK MAYS
37 Director Financial Aid .... Ms. Denise BRINDLE
106 Dir Online Education/E-learning .... Dr. Michael B. LEAMY
108 Director Institutional Assessment .... Dr. Christopher CRATSLEY
13 Chief Info Technology Officer (CIO) .... Mr. Stephen E. SWARTZ
39 Director Student Housing .... Ms. Kristin MURPHY
04 Special Asst to President .... Ms. Gail M. DOIRON

*Framingham State University (E)

100 State Street, PO Box 9101, Framingham MA 01701-9101

County: Middlesex | FICE Identification: 002185 | Unit ID: 165866
Telephone: (508) 620-1220 | Carnegie Class: Masters/L
FAX Number: (508) 626-4592 | Calendar System: Semester
URL: www.framingham.edu
Established: 1839 | Annual Undergrad Tuition & Fees (In-State): $8,700
Enrollment: 6,499 | Coed
Affiliation or Control: State | IRS Status: 501(c)3
Highest Offering: Master's
Accreditation: EH, ART, DIETC, DIETD, NURSE, TED

02 President .... Dr. F. Javier CEVALLOS
03 Executive Vice President .... Dr. Dale M. HAMEL
05 Vice President Academic Affairs .... Dr. Linda VADEN-GOAD
88 Vice President Enrollment & Student .... Dr. Lorretta HOLLOWAY
43 Vice President/General Counsel .... Ms. Rita COLUCCI
20 Associate Vice President .... Dr. Scott B. GREENBERG
13 Associate Vice President .... Mr. Patrick LAUGHRAN
18 Assistant Vice President .... Mr. Warren FAIRBANKS
84 Dean of Enrollment Management .... Mr. Jeremy SPENCER
32 Dean of Student Affairs .... Dr. Melinda K. STOOPS
39 Associate Dean Student Affairs .... Mr. Glenn COCHRAN
07 Associate Dean Undergrad Admissions .... Ms. Shayna EDDY
35 Assistant Dean Student Affairs .... Mr. David N. BALDWIN
88 Assistant Dean Student Affairs .... Dr. Christopher GREGORY
06 Executive Director/Registrar .... Mr. Mark R. POWERS
15 Director Human Resources .... Ms. Erin NECHIPURENKO
19 Chief Public Safety .... Mr. Brad MEDEIROS
88 Director Academic Support .... Ms. LaDonna BRIDGES
108 Director Assessment .... Dr. Mark NICHOLAS

41 Director Athletics ... Mr. Thomas KELLEY
36 Director Career Services ... Mrs. Dawn ROSS
37 Director Financial Aid ... Ms. Deborah ALTSHER
10 Director Financial Services ... Ms. Rachel TRANT
89 Director First Year Programs ... Mr. Benjamin J. TRAPANICK
23 Director Health Services ... Ms. Ilene HOFRENNING
104 Director International Education ... Ms. Jane DECATUR
08 Director Library Services ... Mrs. Bonnie MITCHELL
38 Director Counseling Center ... Dr. Paul WELCH
35 Director Student Involvement ... Ms. Rachel LUCKING
88 Director Student Accounts ... Mr. Gregory JACKSON
30 Director Development ... Mr. Eric GUSTAFSON
25 Director Grants Sponsored Programs ... Mr. Jonathan LEE
09 Director Institutional Research ... Ms. Ann CASO
04 Administrative Assistant ... Ms. Katie RESTUCCIA
22 Director of Equal Opportunity ... Ms. Kimberly DEXTER
58 Dean of Graduate Studies ... Dr. Yasar NAJJAR
26 Chief Public Relations Officer ... Mr. Daniel MAGAZU
28 Chief Diversity & Inclusion Officer ... Mr. Sean HUDDLESTON
29 Director of Alumni Relations ... Mr. Steve WHITTEMORE

*Massachusetts College of Art and Design (A)

621 Huntington Avenue, Boston MA 02115-5882
County: Suffolk FICE Identification: 002180
Unit ID: 166674
Telephone: (617) 879-7000 Carnegie Class: Spec-4-yr-Arts
FAX Number: (617) 566-4034 Calendar System: Semester
URL: www.massart.edu
Established: 1873 Annual Undergrad Tuition & Fees (In-State): $11,725
Enrollment: 2,095 Coed
Affiliation or Control: State IRS Status: 501(c)3
Highest Offering: Master's
Accreditation: EH, ART

02 President ... Dr. David NELSON
10 Executive VP of Admin & Finance ... Mr. Kurt STEINBERG
03 Associate VP of Administration ... Mr. Robert PERRY
05 Provost/Vice Pres Academic Affairs ... Mr. Ken STRICKLAND
32 Vice President Student Development ... Dr. Maureen KEEFE
30 Vice Pres Institutional Advancement ... Ms. Marjorie O'MALLEY
09 Assoc VP for Planning/Research ... Ms. Kathleen KEENAN
21 Asst Vice Pres of Fiscal Affairs ... Mr. Donald ARPINO
100 Chief of Staff President's Office ... Ms. Susana SEGAT
07 Dean of Admissions/Enrollment ... Mr. Christopher WRIGHT
88 Assoc VP/Dean Multi-Cultural Affs ... Dr. Jamie COSTELLO
06 Registrar ... Mr. Jonathan RAND
37 Director of Financial Aid ... Mr. Aurelio RAMIREZ
88 Dir Curatorial Pgms/Prof Galleries ... Ms. Lisa TUNG
08 Director Library ... Ms. Rachel RESNICK
15 Director Human Resources ... Ms. Velda MCRAE-YATES
22 Dir Civil Rights Compliance/Dvrsty ... Ms. Mercedes EVANS
18 Exec Dir Facilities/Physical Plant ... Mr. Howie LAROSEE
11 Director of Administrative Services ... Mr. James MCDAID
26 Exec Dir Marketing/Communications ... Ms. Ellen CARR
13 Chief Info Technology Officer ... Mr. Patrick O'CONNOR
19 Director Security/Safety ... Mr. Dwayne FARLEY
104 Director Study Abroad ... Ms. Erica PUCCIO O'BRIEN
38 Director Student Counseling ... Dr. Betsy SMITH

*Massachusetts College of Liberal Arts (B)

375 Church Street, North Adams MA 01247-4100
County: Berkshire FICE Identification: 002187
Unit ID: 167288
Telephone: (413) 662-5000 Carnegie Class: Bac-A&S
FAX Number: (413) 662-5010 Calendar System: Semester
URL: www.mcla.edu
Established: 1894 Annual Undergrad Tuition & Fees (In-State): $9,475
Enrollment: 1,765 Coed
Affiliation or Control: State IRS Status: 501(c)3
Highest Offering: Master's
Accreditation: EH, #CAATE

02 President ... Dr. James F. BIRGE
03 Executive Vice President ... Ms. Denise RICHARDELLO
05 VP Academic Affairs ... Dr. Cynthia F. BROWN
10 VP Administration & Finance ... Mr. Lawrence M. BEHAN
32 VP Student Affairs ... Dr. Catherine B. HOLBROOK
30 VP Institutional Advancement ... Vacant
20 Dean Academic Affairs ... Dr. Monica JOSLIN
13 Chief Information Officer ... Mr. Curt KING
58 Dean Gradaute & Continuing Educ ... Dr. Howard EBERWEIN
35 Associate Dean Student Affairs ... Ms. Theresa M. O'BRYANT
08 Associate Dean Library Services ... Ms. Maureen HORAK
88 Associate Dean CSSE ... Vacant
20 Associate Dean Academic Affairs ... Dr. Adrienne WOOTTERS
04 Assistant to President ... Ms. Ginger MENARD
06 Assistant Dean Registrar ... Mr. Steven KING
07 Director Admissions ... Ms. Gina PUC
09 Institutional Research Analyst ... Mr. Jason G. CANALES
14 Director Information Technology ... Mr. Ian BERGERON
15 Director Human Resources ... Ms. Barbara CHAPUT
18 Director Facilities Management ... Mr. Charles L. KIMBERLING
19 Director Public Safety ... Mr. Daniel J. COLONNO
21 Director Fiscal Affairs ... Ms. Laura BROWN
21 Director Student Accounts/Bursar ... Ms. Bonnie J. HOWLAND
23 Director Health Services ... Ms. Jacki KRZANIK
26 Director Marketing & Communications ... Ms. Bernadette LUPO
29 Dir Alumni Relations & Development ... Ms. Christine NAUGHTON
37 Director Financial Aid ... Ms. Elizabeth PETRI
38 Director Counseling Services ... Ms. Heidi A. RIELLO
39 Director Residential Programs ... Ms. Dianne M. MANNING
41 Director Athletics ... Ms. Laura MOONEY
44 Annual Giving Program Manager ... Ms. Nikki LOTHER
105 Web and Applications Manager ... Mr. Steven J. PESOLA
108 Director Assessment ... Ms. Erin M. MILNE

*Massachusetts Maritime Academy (C)

101 Academy Drive, Buzzards Bay MA 02532-3400
County: Barnstable FICE Identification: 002181
Unit ID: 166692
Telephone: (508) 830-5000 Carnegie Class: Masters/S
FAX Number: (508) 830-5004 Calendar System: Semester
URL: www.maritime.edu
Established: 1891 Annual Undergrad Tuition & Fees (In-State): $7,630
Enrollment: 1,497 Coed
Affiliation or Control: State IRS Status: 501(c)3
Highest Offering: Master's
Accreditation: EH, IACBE

02 President ... RADM. Francis X. MCDONALD
05 Vice President/Dean ... CAPT. Brad LIMA
10 Vice Pres Finance ... Ms. Rose CASS
30 Vice Pres Advancement ... Ms. Holly KNIGHT
27 Vice President/CIO ... Ms. Anne Marie FALLON
32 Vice Pres Student Services ... CAPT. Edward ROZAK
36 Assoc Dir Career/Professional Svcs ... CDR. Maryanne RICHARDS
84 Vice Pres Enrollment Management ... CAPT. Elizabeth STEVENSON
06 Director Student Records/Registrar ... Mr. Michael CUFF
08 Director Library ... Ms. Susan BERTEAUX
108 Dir of Institutional Effectiveness ... Dr. Marlene CLAPP
15 Dean Human Resources ... Mrs. Elizabeth BENWAY
18 Vice President Operations ... Mr. Paul O'KEEFE
26 Chief Public Relations Officer ... Mr. Christopher RYAN
29 Director Alumni Relations ... Mr. Ian MACLEOD
37 Director Student Financial Aid ... Mrs. Cathy KEDSKI
96 Director of Purchasing ... Mr. Paul AIROZO
11 VP/Marine Operations ... CAPT. Thomas BUSHY
41 Athletic Director ... Mr. Garin VERIS

*Salem State University (D)

352 Lafayette Street, Salem MA 01970-5353
County: Essex FICE Identification: 002188
Unit ID: 167729
Telephone: (978) 542-6000 Carnegie Class: Masters/L
FAX Number: (978) 542-6970 Calendar System: Semester
URL: www.salemstate.edu
Established: 1854 Annual Undergrad Tuition & Fees (In-State): $9,246
Enrollment: 9,267 Coed
Affiliation or Control: State IRS Status: 501(c)3
Highest Offering: Master's
Accreditation: EH, ART, CAATE, CS, MUS, NMT, NURSE, OT, SW, TED, THEA

02 President ... Dr. Patricia M. MESERVEY
05 Provost & Academic VP ... Dr. David J. SILVA
84 VP Enrollment Mgmt & Student Life ... Dr. Scott JAMES
30 VP Institutional Advancement ... Ms. Cynthia MCGURREN
100 Chief of Staff ... Ms. Beth A. BOWER
26 Asst VP Marketing/Creative Svcs ... Mr. Corey CRONIN
13 CIO-CISO ... Ms. Patricia AINSWORTH
10 Assoc VP Financial Svcs ... Mr. Joseph DONOVAN
15 Assistant VP for HR & EEO ... Mr. Mark R. QUIGLEY
20 Assoc Provost and Dean Human Svcs ... Dr. Neal DECHILLO
20 Asst Provost ... Vacant
86 Director of External Affairs ... Ms. Adria LEACH
08 Interim Librarian & Lrng Support ... Mr. Zachary NEWELL
50 Interim Dean School of Business ... Dr. Linda NOWAK
53 Dean of Education ... Dr. Joseph CAMBONE
51 Dean Sch Cont & Prof Studies ... Dr. Mary CHURCHILL
49 Dean School of Arts & Sciences ... Dr. Gail GASPARICH
32 Dean of Student Life ... Dr. Carla THARP
44 Asst VP Institutional Advancement ... Ms. Eileen M. O'BRIEN
101 Sr Asst to Pres/Asst Secy to BOT ... Ms. Katrina SADOWSKI
19 Director Public Safety ... Mr. Gene R. LABONTE
41 Director Athletics ... Ms. Peggy CARL
06 Registrar ... Ms. Megan M. MILLER
84 Assistant VP for Enroll Mgmt ... Ms. Bonnie GALINSKI
18 Director of Facilities ... Mr. Gualter ALMEIDA
28 Dir Diversity & Multicult Affairs ... Ms. Rebecca COMAGE
29 Director Alumni Affairs ... Ms. Mandy RAY
37 Director of Financial Aid ... Ms. Judy CRAMER
38 Dir Counseling and Health Service ... Ms. Elisa CASTILLO
96 Director Purchasing & Vendor Rel ... Ms. Evelyn WILSON
25 Dir Sponsored Programs & Res Adm ... Ms. Mary MADER
07 Director of Admissions ... Ms. Mary DUNN
102 Dir Foundation/Corporate Relations ... Ms. Lisa MCFADDEN
39 Director Student Housing ... Mr. Neil ANDRITO
43 Dir Legal Services/General Counsel ... Mr. John KEENAN

*Westfield State University (E)

577 Western Avenue, Westfield MA 01086-1630
County: Hampden FICE Identification: 002189
Unit ID: 168263
Telephone: (413) 572-5300 Carnegie Class: Masters/M
FAX Number: (413) 572-8147 Calendar System: Semester
URL: www.westfield.ma.edu
Established: 1838 Annual Undergrad Tuition & Fees (In-State): $8,815
Enrollment: 6,321 Coed
Affiliation or Control: State IRS Status: 501(c)3
Highest Offering: Beyond Master's But Less Than Doctorate
Accreditation: EH, #CAATE, CS, EXSC, MUS, NURSE, SW, TED

02 President ... Dr. Ramon S. TORRECILHA
05 Interim Vice Pres Academic Affairs ... Dr. Marsha MAROTTA
32 Vice Pres Student Affairs ... Dr. Carlton PICKRON
84 VP Enrollment Management ... Vacant
10 VP Administration & Finance ... Mr. Stephen TAKSAR
30 VP Institutional Advancement ... Dr. Erica BROMAN
21 Assoc VP Administration/Finance ... Ms. Lisa FREEMAN
11 Assoc VP Facilities & Operations ... Dr. Curt ROBIE
15 Interim Asst VP Human Resources ... Ms. Evie SOUCIE
20 Dean of Faculty ... Dr. Stephen ADAMS
49 Interim Dean of Undergrad Studies ... Dr. Christina SWAIDAN
51 Interim Dean Graduate/Cont Educ ... Dr. Shelley TINKHAM
53 Dean of Education ... Dr. Cheryl STANLEY
35 Dean of Students ... Ms. Susan LAMONTAGNE
06 Registrar ... Mr. John OHOTNICKY
09 Assoc Dean Inst Research/Assess ... Dr. Lisa PLANTEFABER
88 Assoc Dean Academic Achievement ... Ms. Maureen MCCARTNEY
08 Dean Acad Info Svcs/Dir Library . Mr. Thomas RAFFENSPERGER
39 Exec Director Residential Life ... Dr. Jon CONLOGUE
19 Director Public Safety ... Mr. Tony CASCIANO
36 Director Career Services ... Mr. Junior DELGADO
90 Exec Director Acad Tech Services ... Mr. Christopher HIRTLE
72 Director Information Technology ... Mr. Alan BLAIR
91 Director Admin Systems ... Mr. Rudolph HEBERT
18 Director Facilities/Operations ... Mr. Terry FENSTAD
41 Director Athletics ... Mr. Richard LENFEST
38 Director Counseling Center ... Ms. Tammy BRINGAZE
23 Director Health Services ... Ms. Patricia BERUBE
37 Director of Financial Aid ... Ms. Catherine RYAN
07 Director of Admissions ... Dr. Kelly HART
96 Director of Purchasing ... Mr. Chris RAYMOND
25 Director Grants Sponsored Programs ... Ms. Louann D'ANGELO
102 Director of WSU Foundation ... Mr. Michael KNAPIK
04 Executive Assistant to President ... Ms. Dominique CHAPMAN
101 Admin Asst to Board of Trustees ... Ms. Michelle LOUBERT
104 Director of International Program ... Ms. Cynthia SIEGLER
28 Director of Diversity & Inclusion ... Ms. Lizette RIVERA
88 Veteran & Military Svcs Coord ... Ms. Lisa DUCHARME
100 Chief of Staff ... Dr. Diane PRUSANK
106 Dir Center for Instructional Tech ... Ms. Lynn ZAYAC
22 Dir Non-Discrimination Compliance ... Mr. Lawrence P. JOHNSON
26 Director of Campus Communications ... Ms. Tricia OLIVER

*Worcester State University (F)

486 Chandler Street, Worcester MA 01602-2597
County: Worcester FICE Identification: 002190
Unit ID: 168430
Telephone: (508) 929-8000 Carnegie Class: Masters/L
FAX Number: (508) 929-8191 Calendar System: Semester
URL: www.worcester.edu
Established: 1874 Annual Undergrad Tuition & Fees (In-State): $8,857
Enrollment: 6,350 Coed
Affiliation or Control: State IRS Status: 501(c)3
Highest Offering: Master's
Accreditation: EH, NMT, NURSE, OT, SP, TEAC

02 President ... Mr. Barry M. MALONEY
05 Provost/VP of Academic Affairs ... Dr. Lois A. WIMS
10 Vice Pres Administration & Finance ... Ms. Kathleen EICHELROTH
32 Dean of Student Affairs ... Ms. Julie KAZARIAN
30 Vice Pres University Advancement ... Mr. Thomas MCNAMARA
84 Vice Pres for Enrollment Management ... Dr. Ryan FORSYTHE
20 Assoc VP for Academic Affairs ... Vacant
21 Assoc VP Administration & Finance ... Ms. Robin QUILL
13 Assoc VP/CIO Univ Technology Svcs ... Dr. Anthony ADADE
58 Assoc VP CE & Dean Grad Stds ... Dr. Roberta KYLE
108 Asst VP for Assessment & Planning ... Vacant
22 Dir Diversity/Inclusion & Eq Op ... Mr. Isaac TESFAY
53 Dean Sch of Educ/Health/Nat Sci ... Dr. Linda LARRIVEE
79 Dean Sch of Human & Social Sciences ... Vacant
88 Assoc Dean Sch Educ/Heath/Nat Sci ... Dr. Raynold LEWIS
66 Associate Dean of Nursing ... Dr. Stephanie CHALUPKA
51 Assoc Dean of Grad/Cont Educ ... Ms. Sara GRADY
35 Assoc Dean & Dir Stdnt Ctr/Activ ... Mr. Timothy J. SULLIVAN
93 Asst Dean/Dir Multicultural Affairs ... Ms. Marcela URIBE-JENNINGS
19 Chief of Campus Police ... Mr. Michael NOCKUNAS
86 Asst to Pres for Intl/Cmty & Govt ... Mr. Carl HERRIN
26 Asst to Pres for Camp Communication ... Ms. Renae LIAS CLAFFEY
08 Executive Director of the Library ... Mr. Matthew BEJUNE
29 Exec Dir Univ Advancement & Alumni ... Ms. Karen SHARPE
15 Asst VP of HR/Payroll/Aff Act/Eq ... Ms. Stacey DEBOISE LUSTER
18 Director of Facilities ... Ms. Sandra OLSON
37 Director of Financial Aid ... Ms. Jayne MCGINN
07 Director of Admissions ... Mr. Joseph DICARLO
06 Registrar ... Ms. Julie CHAFEE
39 Director Residence Life & Housing ... Mr. Adrian GAGE
88 Manager of Student Accounts ... Ms. Julie CARMEL
96 Dir Procurement/Business Manager ... Ms. Brenda BUSSEY
09 Director of Institutional Research ... Mr. Kenneth SMITH
38 Director Student Counseling ... Ms. Laura MURPHY
85 Director of International Students ... Ms. Katey PALUMBO
36 Director of Career Services ... Ms. Jillian ANDERSON
41 Director of Athletics ... Mr. Michael A. MUDD
24 Director of Media Services ... Mr. Thomas R. WHITE
109 Director of Admin Support Services ... Ms. Nancy M. RAMSDELL

*Berkshire Community College (G)

1350 West Street, Pittsfield MA 01201-5786
County: Berkshire FICE Identification: 002167
Unit ID: 164775

Telephone: (413) 499-4660 Carnegie Class: Assoc/HT-High Trad
FAX Number: (413) 447-7840 Calendar System: Semester
URL: www.berkshirecc.edu
Established: 1960 Annual Undergrad Tuition & Fees (In-State): $4,866
Enrollment: 2,230 Coed
Affiliation or Control: State IRS Status: 501(c)3
Highest Offering: Associate Degree
Accreditation: EH, ADNUR, COARC, PTAA

02 President Dr. Ellen KENNEDY
05 Int Vice Pres for Academic Affairs Dr. Maura DELANEY
10 Vice Pres Admin/Finance/CFO Mr. John LAW
32 Vice Pres Student Affs/Enroll Svcs Mr. Michael BULLOCK
30 Vice Pres Institutional Advancement Mr. Craig SMITH
103 VP Community Educ/Workforce Devel Mr. William MULHOLLAND
15 VP Human Res/Affirm Action Officer Ms. Deborah COTE
66 Int Dean Nursing/Allied Health Dr. Chris AYLESWORTH
06 Registrar Mr. Adam EMERSON
102 Exec Dir BCC Foundation Mr. Craig SMITH
13 Director Information Technology Mr. Richard WIXSOM
07 Dir of Marketing/Stdnt Recruitment Ms. Christina BARRETT
37 Director Student Financial Aid Ms. Anne MOORE
38 Senior Academic Counselor Ms. Lisa MATTILA
04 Assistant to the President Ms. Kim BROOKMAN

*Bristol Community College (A)

777 Elsbree Street, Fall River MA 02720-7395
County: Bristol FICE Identification: 002176
Unit ID: 165033
Telephone: (508) 678-2811 Carnegie Class: Assoc/HT-High Trad
FAX Number: (508) 730-3270 Calendar System: Semester
URL: www.bristolcc.edu
Established: 1965 Annual Undergrad Tuition & Fees (In-State): $4,296
Enrollment: 9,189 Coed
Affiliation or Control: State IRS Status: 501(c)3
Highest Offering: Associate Degree
Accreditation: EH, ADNUR, CAHIIM, COMTA, DH, MAC, MLTAD, OTA

02 President Dr. John J. SBREGA
03 Executive Vice President Mr. David F. FEENEY
05 Vice President of Academic Affairs Mr. Greg SETHARES
50 Dean of Business & Info Tech Mr. William BERARDI
79 Dean of Humanities & Education Dr. Ulli RYDER
83 Dean of Behavioral & Soc Sciences Dr. Kathleen PEARLE
76 Dean of Health Sciences Ms. Patricia DENT
81 Dean of Math/Science & Engineering Dr. Sarmad SAMAN
10 VP of Administration & Finance Mr. Steven KENYON
30 VP of Resource Development Ms. Elizabeth K. MCCARTHY
84 VP of Students and Enrollment Mgt Mr. Steve OZUG
91 VP of Information Technology Ms. Jo-Ann M. PELLETIER
103 Acting VP of Workforce Development Mr. Paul VIGEANT
32 Director Student Engagement Ms. Kathleen BURNS
07 Dean of Admissions Vacant
12 Dean of New Bedford Campus Mr. Jim DANIELS
12 Dean of Attleboro Center Mr. Rodney CLARK
06 Registrar Mr. Benjamin BAUMANN
08 Associate Dean Library Sciences Mr. Robert REZENDES
25 Dean of Grant Development Ms. Jennifer MENARD
37 Dean of Financial Aid & Technology Mr. David ALLEN
38 Director Counseling Services Mr. Michael BENSINK
15 VP of Human Resources/Affirm Action Mr. Tafa AWOLAJU
18 Director of Facilities Management Mr. Leo RACINE
19 Director of Public Safety Mr. Wayne WOOD
21 Comptroller Mr. Keith TONI
11 Associate VP of Administration Ms. Linda DANZELL
20 Assoc VP of Academic Affairs Mr. Anthony UCCI
20 Assoc VP of Academic Affairs Dr. Ana GAILLAT
84 Acting VP Enrollment Services Ms. Kathleen TORPEY GARGANTA
26 VP College Communications Ms. Joyce BRENNAN
29 Assoc VP Development Alumni Affairs Ms. Katherine BREZINA
44 Assoc VP Major Gifts Annual Fund Ms. Jennifer RAXTER
22 Dean Disability Svcs & Student Engm Ms. Susan BOISSONEAULT
78 Director Coop Education Ms. Nicole HEANEY
31 Dean Ctr Workforce/Community Educ Ms. Carmen AGUILAR
23 Health Services Coordinator Ms. Carol CONSTANTINE
56 Asst Dean Instructional Lrng Tech Ms. April BELLAFIORE
09 VP Inst Research/Plng & Assessment Ms. Rhonda GABOVITCH
92 Director Honors Program Ms. Susan MCCOURT
96 Director of Purchasing Ms. Philicia PACHECO
36 Coord Career Planning Placement Ms. Patricia CONDON
41 Athletic Director Mr. Derek VIVEIROS
04 Executive Assistant to President Ms. Kathleen A. WORDELL
88 Dean Access and Transition Ms. Sarah MORRELL

*Bunker Hill Community College (B)

250 New Rutherford Avenue, Boston MA 02129-2925
County: Suffolk FICE Identification: 011210
Unit ID: 165112
Telephone: (617) 228-2000 Carnegie Class: Assoc/HT-Mix Trad/Non
FAX Number: (617) 228-2082 Calendar System: Semester
URL: www.bhcc.mass.edu
Established: 1973 Annual Undergrad Tuition & Fees (In-State): $3,576
Enrollment: 14,253 Coed
Affiliation or Control: State IRS Status: 501(c)3
Highest Offering: Associate Degree
Accreditation: EH, ADNUR, #COARC, DMS, MLTAD, RAD, SURGT

02 President Dr. Pam Y. EDDINGER
10 VP of Administration and Finance Mr. John PITCHER
05 VP Academic Affairs/Student Service Dr. James F. CANNIFF
28 Director Diversity & Inclusion Mr. Thomas L. SALTONSTALL
09 Exec Dean Inst Effectiveness Vacant
20 Associate Dean Academic Affairs Ms. Liya ESCALERA-KELLEY
32 Dean of Students Ms. Julie B. ELKINS
26 Exec Director of Communications Ms. Karen NORTON
18 Director Facilities Management Mr. Gary BIGELOW
81 Int Dean Mathematics/Behav Sciences Dr. Maria K. PUENTE
79 Dean of Humanities Ms. Lori A. CATALLOZZI
54 Dean Science/Engineering Dr. Laurie K. MCCORRY
107 Int Dean of Professional Studies Dr. Laurie K. MCCORRY
66 Dean Nurse Education Dr. Judith MANN
12 Associate Provost Chelsea Campus Dr. Alice MURILLO
21 Comptroller Mr. Weusi A. TAFAWA
25 Director of Grants Development Mr. Steven A. ROLLER
84 Director Enrollment Systems Ms. Debra A. BOYER
06 Interim Registrar Ms. Kim BUCKWALTER
08 Director Library/Info Center Dr. Vivica D. PIERRE
13 Chief Information Officer Ms. Laura GRANDGENETT
15 Dir Human Resources/Labor Relations Ms. Molly B. AMBROSE
27 Executive Director of Marketing Ms. Karen M. NORTON
19 Director of Public Safety Mr. Robert BARROWS
37 Director of Financial Aid Ms. Melissa HOLSTER
96 Manager Purchasing Mr. Mukti RAUT
07 Assoc Dean Enrollment Ms. Anne BROWN
30 Executive Director of Development Ms. Marilyn KUHAR
100 Exec Asst to the President Mr. George HALLSMITH
108 Exec Dir Institutional Research Mr. David LEAVITT

*Cape Cod Community College (C)

2240 Iyannough Road, West Barnstable MA 02668-1599
County: Barnstable FICE Identification: 002168
Unit ID: 165194
Telephone: (508) 362-2131 Carnegie Class: Assoc/HT-Mix Trad/Non
FAX Number: (508) 362-3988 Calendar System: Semester
URL: www.capecod.edu
Established: 1960 Annual Undergrad Tuition & Fees (In-State): $4,212
Enrollment: 3,818 Coed
Affiliation or Control: State IRS Status: 501(c)3
Highest Offering: Associate Degree
Accreditation: EH, ADNUR, DH, MAC

02 President Dr. John L. COX
05 Vice Pres Academic/Student Affairs Dr. Susan MILLER
10 Vice President Finance & Operations Mr. Walter T. BROOKS
21 Asst VP Administration & Finance Vacant
18 Director Facilities Mr. Jeffrey MARCOTTE
13 Asst VP Information Technology Vacant
49 Dean Arts & Humanities Dr. Lore DEBOWER
81 Dean Science/Tech/Math/Business Dr. Robert CODY
08 Dean Learning Res & Student Success Mr. David ZIEMBA
84 Dean Enroll Mgmt/Advising Services Ms. Christine MCCAREY
83 Dean Health/Social Sci/Human Svcs Ms. Susan MADDIGAN
15 Asst VP Human Resources Mr. Victor SANTOS
08 Assoc Dean Library Ms. Jeanmarie FRASER
07 Director Admissions Mr. Matthew CORMIER
37 Director of Financial Aid Ms. Sherry ANDERSEN
26 Director College Communications Mr. Michael GROSS
06 Registrar Ms. Lucina HOLMES
19 Chief Public Safety Ms. Karen AHERN
04 Exec Assistant to President Ms. Mia HAZLETT
36 Coord Career Plng & Placement Ms. Kristina IERARDI
09 Dir Institutional Research & Effec Ms. Maureen O'SHEA
41 Athletic Director Vacant

*Greenfield Community College (D)

1 College Drive, Greenfield MA 01301-9739
County: Franklin FICE Identification: 002169
Unit ID: 165981
Telephone: (413) 775-1000 Carnegie Class: Assoc/HT-High Trad
FAX Number: (413) 774-4676 Calendar System: Semester
URL: www.gcc.mass.edu
Established: 1962 Annual Undergrad Tuition & Fees (In-State): $5,210
Enrollment: 2,127 Coed
Affiliation or Control: State IRS Status: 501(c)3
Highest Offering: Associate Degree
Accreditation: EH, ADNUR, MAC

02 President Dr. Robert L. PURA
05 Chief Academic/Student Affairs Ofcr Dr. Catherine SEAVER
10 Chief Financial Officer Mr. Barry BRAIM
103 Dean of Workforce & Cmty Educ Ms. Alyce STILES
84 Dean of Enrollment Services Ms. Elaine LAPOMARDO
79 Dean Humanities Mr. Leo HWANG
81 Dean Engr/Math/Nurs & Sciences Ms. Mary Ellen FYDENKEVEZ
50 Dean Bus/IT/Soc Sci/Prof Stds Ms. Kathleen VRANOS
15 Exec Dir of Human Resources Mr. Peter SENNETT
30 Exec Director Resource Development Ms. Regina CURTIS
13 Chief Information Officer Mr. Michael ASSAF
28 Chief Diversity Officer Mr. Peter SENNETT
18 Director Physical Plant Mr. Jeffrey MARQUES
07 Admissions Director Mr. Mark HUDGIK
37 Director Financial Aid Ms. Linda DESJARDINS
19 Director Public Safety Mr. Louis SANTAMARIA
96 Director of Purchasing Mr. Ryan AIKEN
08 Director Library Ms. Deborah CHOWN
21 Comptroller Ms. Karen PHILLIPS
06 Registrar Ms. Holly FITZPATRICK
38 Co-Coord Learning Asst Programs Ms. Cynthia SNOW
38 Co-Coord Learning Asst Programs Mr. Norman BEEBE
36 Coordinator of Student Assessment Ms. Catherine DEVLIN
32 Coordinator of Student Activities Ms. Mary MCENTEE
04 Staff Assistant to President Ms. Shannon LARANGE
31 Interim Dir Cmty & Workforce Educ Mr. Jermiah RIORDON
108 Director Institutional Assessment Ms. Marie BREHENY
26 Marketing Coordinator Ms. Liz CARROLL

*Holyoke Community College (E)

303 Homestead Avenue, Holyoke MA 01040-1099
County: Hampden FICE Identification: 002170
Unit ID: 166133
Telephone: (413) 538-7000 Carnegie Class: Assoc/HT-High Trad
FAX Number: (413) 552-2045 Calendar System: Semester
URL: www.hcc.edu
Established: 1946 Annual Undergrad Tuition & Fees (In-State): $4,166
Enrollment: 6,604 Coed
Affiliation or Control: State IRS Status: 501(c)3
Highest Offering: Associate Degree
Accreditation: EH, ACFEI, ADNUR, MUS, RAD

02 President Dr. William F. MESSNER
11 Vice Pres Administration & Finance Mr. William FOGARTY
05 Vice President Academic Affairs Ms. Monica PEREZ
32 Vice President Student Affairs Ms. Yanina VARGAS
30 Vice Pres Institutional Development Ms. Erica BROMAN
28 Assistant Vice Pres of Diversity Ms. Idelia SMITH
08 Dean Library Ms. Mary DIXEY
84 Dean of Enrollment Management Ms. Renee TASTAD
15 Dean Human Resources Ms. Clara ELLIOTT
36 Dean Coop Education & Career Svcs Vacant
06 Registrar Ms. Christine HOLBROOK
37 Director of Financial Aid Ms. Karen DEROUIN
91 Director Administrative Computing Vacant
18 Dir Facilities & Engineering Svcs Mr. Dan CAMPBELL
10 Comptroller Ms. Marcia MITCHELL
13 Chief Information Officer Ms. Linda SZALANKIEWICZ
21 Dir Business Services/Purchasing Ms. Karen DESJEANS
09 Director Institutional Research Ms. Veena DHANKHER
26 Dir of Marketing/Public Relations Ms. JoAnne ROME
29 Dir Alumni Relations/Special Events Ms. Bonnie ZIMA DOWD
35 Dean of Student Services Mr. Tony SBALBI
20 Director of Academic Administration Ms. Idelia SMITH

*Massachusetts Bay Community College (F)

50 Oakland Street, Wellesley Hills MA 02481-5357
County: Norfolk FICE Identification: 002171
Unit ID: 166647
Telephone: (781) 239-3000 Carnegie Class: Assoc/MT-VT-Mix Trad/Non
FAX Number: (781) 237-1061 Calendar System: Semester
URL: www.massbay.edu
Established: 1961 Annual Undergrad Tuition & Fees (In-State): $4,496
Enrollment: 5,369 Coed
Affiliation or Control: State IRS Status: 501(c)3
Highest Offering: Associate Degree
Accreditation: EH, ADNUR, RAD, SURGT

02 President Dr. David PODELL
04 Assistant to the President Ms. Karen BRITTON
05 VP Academic Affairs/CAO Dr. Lynn HUNTER
10 VP Finance & Administrative Svcs Ms. Kathleen KIRLEIS
15 Int VP HR/Labor Rels/Compliance/AA Ms. Lisa BACON
30 VP of Inst Advance & Alumni Rels Ms. Mary SHIA
84 Asst VP Enrollment Management Ms. Lisa SLAVIN
32 Dean of Students Dr. Elizabeth BLUMBERG
45 Chief Strat Planning/Inst Effective Dr. Courtney JACKSON
13 Chief Information Officer Mr. Michael LYONS
50 Dean Business & Prof Studies Dr. Susan MAGGIONI
51 Dean Ctr Corp Training/Comm Educ Ms. Carol STAFFIER
76 Dean Health Sciences Division Dr. Lynne DAVIS
79 Dean Humanities & Social Sciences Dr. Christopher LA BARBERA
81 Dean STEM Division Dr. Chitra JAVDEKAR
06 Registrar Mr. Ali GUVENDIREN
21 Controller Ms. Eileen GERENZ
96 Budget Analyst Mr. Kevin FLYNN
88 Dir Academic Achievement Center Ms. Jennifer JEFFERSON
20 Director of Academic Advising Ms. Sarah READING
91 Director Administrative Computing Mr. Terry KRAMER
07 Director of Admissions Ms. Donna RAPOSA
41 Dir Ath/Rec/Wellness/Com Outreach Mr. Bill RAYNOR
36 Director of Career Services Ms. Julie FURBISH
38 Director of Counseling Mr. Jon EDWARDS
88 Director CTLTI Dr. Linda GRISHAM
37 Director of Financial Aid Ms. Roxanne DUMAS
18 Director of Facilities Ms. Lauren CURLEY
08 Director of Learning Services Mr. Timothy RIVARD
25 Director of Grants Development Ms. Laura BROWN
26 Dir Marketing & Inst Communications Mr. Lee KOH
19 Director of Public Safety Mr. Charles (Chuck) FURGAL
87 Director of Retention Mr. Richard WILLIAMS
35 Coordinator of Student Activities Ms. Julie SCHLEICHER

*Massasoit Community College (G)

1 Massasoit Boulevard, Brockton MA 02302-3996
County: Plymouth FICE Identification: 002177
Unit ID: 166823
Telephone: (508) 588-9100 Carnegie Class: Assoc/HT-Mix Trad/Non
FAX Number: (508) 427-1202 Calendar System: Semester
URL: www.massasoit.mass.edu

Established: 1966 Annual Undergrad Tuition & Fees (In-State): $4,488
Enrollment: 7,905 Coed
Affiliation or Control: State IRS Status: 501(c)3
Highest Offering: Associate Degree
Accreditation: EH, ADNUR, COARC, DA, MAC, RAD

02 President Dr. Charles WALL
05 VP Faculty & Instruction Dr. Barbara MCCARTHY
10 Chief Financial Officer Mr. William MITCHELL
32 Vice Pres Student Svcs/Enroll Mgmt Mr. David TRACY
12 Vice Pres/Dean of Canton Campus Mr. Nicholas PALANTZAS
15 Director of Human Resources Ms. Margaret GAZZARA HESS
09 Assoc Dean Institutional Research Ms. Mary GOODHUE LYNCH
25 Associate Dean of Grants Ms. Hollyce STATES
04 Exec Dir Extrnl Affs/Asst to Pres Mr. Phillip SHEPPARD
26 Public Relations Director Ms. Laurie MAKER
84 Dean of Enrollment Management Vacant
35 Dean Student Affairs Vacant
07 Director of Admissions Ms. Michelle HUGHES
37 Director Student Financial Aid Mr. Todd HUGHES
06 Registrar Ms. Jannie GILSON
38 Director Student Counseling Ms. Christine DYMENT
28 Director of Diversity Ms. Yolanda DENNIS
13 CIO Vacant
21 Comptroller Ms. Patricia MARCELLA
36 Director of Career Placement Ms. Kathyrn PRYLES
18 Director Facilities/Physical Plant Mr. Richard HADLEY
96 Director of Purchasing Vacant
41 Director of Athletics Ms. Julie MULVEY
29 Director Alumni Relations Mr. Steve MURPHY
50 Acting Dean Business & Technology Ms. Lynda THOMPSON
79 Dean Humanities/Social Science Ms. Deanna YAMEEN
76 Dean Allied Health Dr. Anne SCALZO-MCNEIL
83 Dean Public Svc/Social Science Ms. Karyn BOUTIN
81 Dean Science & Math Mr. Douglas BROWN
72 Dean of Emergent Technologies Ms. Carine SAUVIGNON
88 Dean of Academic Advising Mr. Peter JOHNSTON

*Middlesex Community College (A)

591 Springs Road, Bedford MA 01730-1197
County: Middlesex FICE Identification: 009936
Unit ID: 166887
Telephone: (781) 280-3200 Carnegie Class: Assoc/HT-High Trad
FAX Number: (781) 275-0741 Calendar System: Semester
URL: www.middlesex.mass.edu
Established: 1969 Annual Undergrad Tuition & Fees (In-State): $4,514
Enrollment: 9,205 Coed
Affiliation or Control: State IRS Status: 501(c)3
Highest Offering: Associate Degree
Accreditation: EH, ADNUR, DA, DH, DMS, DT, MAC, RAD

02 President Dr. James L. MABRY
05 Provost/VP of Academic Affairs Mr. Philip J. SISSON
03 Executive Vice President Vacant
84 VP Enrollment Svcs/Rsrch & Plng Vacant
10 Int VP Administration & Finance Ms. Gina SPAZIANI
04 Assistant to the President Ms. Lura SMITH
20 Associate Provost Vacant
32 Dean of Students Ms. Pamela B. FLAHERTY
79 Dean Humanities and Social Sciences Mr. Matthew OLSON
72 Dean of Business/Education & Publi Ms. Judith HOGAN
17 Dean of Health and STEM Ms. Kathleen J. SWEENEY
88 Dean Professional/Instructional Dev Ms. Susan ANDERSON
22 Asst Dir HR/Affirm Action Officer Ms. Darcy ORELLANA
12 Dean of Lowell Campus Ms. Colleen COX
12 Dir Fac Mgmt/Bedford Campus Mgr Mr. John LYONS
84 Dean of Enrollment Services Ms. Audrey NAHABEDIAN
26 Dean External Affs/Col Advancement Mr. Dennis MALVERS
07 Dean of Admissions Ms. Marilynn GALLAGAN
35 Associate Dean of Students Ms. Susan WOODS
09 Assoc Dean Institutional Planning Vacant
27 Exec Director Public Affairs Mr. Patrick COOK
27 Director Marketing Communication Ms. Jennifer M. ARADHYA
15 Interim Director Human Resources Ms. Mary CHATIGNY
37 Director of Financial Aid Mr. Robert BAUMAL
21 Comptroller Ms. Kathy RICH
21 Bursar Mr. Christopher FIORI
08 Director Library Services Ms. Maryann NILES
23 Director of Health Services Vacant
06 Registrar Mr. Daniel MOYNIHAN
96 Coordinator of Purchasing Ms. Maureen HUDSON

*Mount Wachusett Community College (B)

444 Green Street, Gardner MA 01440-1000
County: Worcester FICE Identification: 002172
Unit ID: 166957
Telephone: (978) 632-6600 Carnegie Class: Assoc/MT-VT-High Trad
FAX Number: (978) 632-6155 Calendar System: Semester
URL: www.mwcc.edu
Established: 1963 Annual Undergrad Tuition & Fees (In-State): $5,188
Enrollment: 4,336 Coed
Affiliation or Control: State IRS Status: 501(c)3
Highest Offering: Associate Degree
Accreditation: EH, ADNUR, DA, DH, MAC, MLTAD, PNUR, PTAA

02 President Dr. Daniel M. ASQUINO
84 Exec VP & VP of Enrollment Services Ms. Ann M. MCDONALD
05 Vice Pres of Academic Affairs Dr. Melissa FAMA
51 VP Lifelong Learning/Workforce Dev Ms. Jacqueline BELROSE
10 VP Finance & Administration Mr. Robert LABONTE
15 VP HR/Affirmative Action Officer Ms. Diane RUKSNAITIS
26 Vice Pres Marketing/Communications Vacant
30 Assoc VP Institutional Advancement Mr. Joseph STISO
12 Dean Leominster Campus Mr. John WALSH
72 Dean Academic & Inst Technology Mr. Vincent IALENTI
76 Dean School of Health Sciences Ms. Eileen COSTELLO
08 Dean Library and Academic Support Vacant
09 Asst Dean of Records/Instl Research Ms. Rebecca FOREST
36 Dir North Central Career Services Ms. Cynthia KRUSEN
18 Director Maintenance/Mechanical Sys Mr. William SWIFT
68 Director Fitness & Wellness Center Mr. Stephen WASHKEVICH
19 Chief Public Safety & Security Ms. Karen KOLIMAGA
32 Assistant Dean of Student Services Mr. Gregory CLEMENT
38 Director of Counseling Vacant
29 Dir Alumni Affairs/Annual Giving Ms. Carol JACOBSON
06 Registrar Ms. Rebecca FOREST

*North Shore Community College (C)

1 Ferncroft Road, PO Box 3340, Danvers MA 01923-0840
County: Essex FICE Identification: 002173
Unit ID: 167312
Telephone: (978) 762-4000 Carnegie Class: Assoc/MT-VT-High Trad
FAX Number: (978) 762-4020 Calendar System: Semester
URL: www.northshore.edu
Established: 1965 Annual Undergrad Tuition & Fees (In-State): $4,536
Enrollment: 7,412 Coed
Affiliation or Control: State IRS Status: 501(c)3
Highest Offering: Associate Degree
Accreditation: EH, ADNUR, COARC, MAC, OTA, PNUR, PTAA, RAD, SURGT

02 President Dr. Patricia A. GENTILE
05 Vice Pres Academic Affairs Dr. Karen HYNICK
10 Vice Pres Administration/Finance Ms. Janice M. FORSSTROM
32 Vice Pres Student Affairs Mr. Jermaine WILLIAMS
30 Vice Pres Institutional Advancement Mr. Mark REIMER
45 Asst Vice Pres Budget/Planning Ms. Mariflor UVA
15 Vice President Human Res/Affirm Act Ms. Madeline WALLIS
103 Dean Workforce Dev/Corp Educ Ms. Dianne PALTER-GILL
90 Dean Academic Technology Mr. Michael BADOLATO
07 Dean of Enrollment Services Mr. John DUFF
37 Asst VP Student Financial Svcs/Comp Mr. Stephen CREAMER
20 Assistant Dean Academic Affairs Vacant
08 Director Library/Tutoring Mr. Rex KRAJEWSKI
13 Dir of Networking/Info Services Mr. Gary HAM
37 Director of Financial Aid Ms. Susan SULLIVAN
09 Asst Vice Pres Planning & Research Ms. Laurie LACHAPELLE
18 Asst Vice Pres Facilities Mgmt Mr. Richard RENEY
19 Campus Police Chief Mr. Douglas P. PUSKA
21 Comptroller Ms. Patricia CALLAHAN
26 Director Public Relations/New Media Ms. Linda BRANTLEY
29 Director Alumni Relations Ms. Sandra ROCHON
35 Chief Student Life Officer Ms. Lisa MILSO
36 Director Student Placement Ms. Lynn MARCUS
07 Director of Recruitment Vacant
38 Director Student Support & Advising Mr. Daniel O'NEILL
27 Director Marketing Communications Ms. Samantha MCGILLOWAY
40 Bookstore Manager Mr. Shawn CRONIN
06 Registrar Ms. Mel POTOCZAK

*Northern Essex Community College (D)

100 Elliott Street, Haverhill MA 01830-2399
County: Essex FICE Identification: 002174
Unit ID: 167376
Telephone: (978) 556-3000 Carnegie Class: Assoc/HT-High Trad
FAX Number: (978) 556-3723 Calendar System: Semester
URL: www.necc.mass.edu
Established: 1960 Annual Undergrad Tuition & Fees (In-State): $4,560
Enrollment: 6,963 Coed
Affiliation or Control: State IRS Status: 501(c)3
Highest Offering: Associate Degree
Accreditation: EH, ADNUR, COARC, CSHSE, DA, MAC, MLTAD, PNUR, POLYT, RAD

02 President Dr. Lane A. GLENN
05 Vice President of Academic Affairs Dr. William HEINEMAN
30 Vice Pres Institutional Advancement Ms. Jean C. POTH
10 Vice Pres Finance & Administration Mr. Michael MCCARTHY
15 Vice President of Human Resources Mr. Stephen W. FABBRUCCI
07 Dean of Enroll Services Ms. Tina FAVARA
12 Exec Dir of Lawrence Campus Dr. Noemi CUSTODIA-LORA
09 Dean of Institutional Research Ms. Kelly SARETSKY
44 Dean of Development Ms. Wendy SHAFFER
88 Dean of Acad Support/Transfer Ms. Grace YOUNG
103 Exec Dir Workforce Devel/Cont Educ Mr. George MORIARTY
13 Chief Information Officer Mr. Jeffrey BICKFORD
06 Registrar Ms. Sue SHAIN
37 Director of Financial Aid Ms. Alexis FISHBONE
26 Director of Public Relations Ms. Ernestine GREENSLADE
29 Director Alumni Relations Ms. Lindsey GRAHAM
32 Chief Student Life Officer Ms. Nita LAMBORGHINI
35 Director Student Affairs Ms. Dina BROWN
18 Chief Facilities/Physical Plant Vacant
96 Director of Purchasing Vacant
04 Sr Exec Asst to President Ms. Cheryl GOODWIN

*Quinsigamond Community College (E)

670 W Boylston Street, Worcester MA 01606-2092
County: Worcester FICE Identification: 002175
Unit ID: 167534
Telephone: (508) 853-2300 Carnegie Class: Assoc/HT-High Trad
FAX Number: (508) 852-6943 Calendar System: Semester
URL: www.qcc.edu
Established: 1963 Annual Undergrad Tuition & Fees (In-State): $5,302
Enrollment: 8,452 Coed
Affiliation or Control: State IRS Status: 501(c)3
Highest Offering: Associate Degree
Accreditation: EH, ADNUR, COARC, CSHSE, DA, DH, MAC, OTA, PNUR, RAD, SURGT

02 President Dr. Gail E. CARBERRY
05 VP of Academic Affairs Ms. Patricia A. TONEY
10 VP of Administration Mr. Stephen T. MARINI
84 VP of Student Enrollment/Develop Dr. Lillian M. ORTIZ
15 VP of Human Resources Mr. William DARING
20 Assistant VP Academic Affairs Dr. Nancy SCHOENFELD
20 Assistant VP Academic Affairs Ms. Jane SHEA
04 Executive Assistant to President Ms. Selina M. BORIA
21 Asst VP for Finance/Comptroller Ms. Debra A. LAFLASH
79 Dean Humanities & Education Dr. Clarence ATES
76 Dean Health Care Dr. Jane JUNE
50 Dean Business/Engineer/Technology Ms. Kathleen RENTSCH
81 Dean Science & Mathematics Dr. Leslie HORTON
06 Assoc Dean Enrollment/Registrar Ms. Tara F. JENKINS
62 Dean of Library Services Ms. Andrea MACRITCHIE
09 Dean of Inst Research/Planning Dr. Ingrid SKADBERG
84 Dean of Enrollment Management Ms. Michelle TUFAU-AFRIYIE
13 Chief Technology Officer Mr. Ken DWYER
56 Asst VP Ext Campus Operations Mr. Victor SOMMA
32 Director Student Life Vacant
18 Director of Facilities Mr. Don HALL
37 Director Student Financial Aid Ms. Karen GRANT
96 Purchasing Manager Ms. Stacey TATA
19 Chief of Campus Police Mr. Kevin RITACCO
26 Dir Institutional Communications Mr. Joshua MARTIN
22 Dean for Employment & Equity Ms. Anita BOWDEN
38 Coordinator of Counseling Services Vacant
28 Director Disability Services Ms. Kristen PROCTOR
35 Dean of Students Ms. Elizabeth WOODS
07 Director of Admissions Ms. Mishawn DAVIS-EYENE

*Roxbury Community College (F)

1234 Columbus Avenue,
Roxbury Crossing MA 02120-3423
County: Suffolk FICE Identification: 011930
Unit ID: 167631
Telephone: (617) 427-0060 Carnegie Class: Assoc/HT-High Trad
FAX Number: (617) 541-5351 Calendar System: Semester
URL: rcc.mass.edu
Established: 1973 Annual Undergrad Tuition & Fees (In-State): $3,984
Enrollment: 2,393 Coed
Affiliation or Control: State IRS Status: 501(c)3
Highest Offering: Associate Degree
Accreditation: EH, ADNUR, RAD

02 President Dr. Valerie R. ROBERSON
04 Executive Asst to the President Ms. Martha LAMBERT
05 VP Academic And Student Affairs Ms. Cecile REGNER
30 VP Advancement/Cmty Engagement Ms. Lorita WILLIAMS
10 Vice President of Admin & Finance Mr. Kevin HEPNER
13 Chief Information Tech Officer Mr. Patrick JEAN-LOUIS
15 Chief Human Res/Affirm Action Ofcr Ms. Patricia WEST
41 Director of RLTAC Mr. A. Keith MCDERMOTT
08 Director of Library Mr. William HOAG
23 Director of Health Services Ms. Ruth HINES
30 Dir Development/Alumni/Foundation Mr. Richard M. IACOBUCCI
06 Registrar Ms. Cheryl MARTIN
32 Director of Student Life Ms. Elizabeth CLARK
26 Director Marketing/Communications Mr. Jordan SMOCK
57 Dir of Visual/Performing/Media Arts Mr. Marshall HUGHES
88 Director of the Writing Center Lab Ms. Judith KAHALAS
37 Assoc Director Financial Aid Mr. Alex JEAN-JACQUES
25 Grants Research Specialist Ms. Yvonne E. ANTHONY

*Springfield Technical Community College (G)

Armory Square, Springfield MA 01105-1296
County: Hampden FICE Identification: 008078
Unit ID: 167905
Telephone: (413) 781-7822 Carnegie Class: Assoc/HT-High Trad
FAX Number: (413) 755-6309 Calendar System: Semester
URL: www.stcc.edu
Established: 1967 Annual Undergrad Tuition & Fees (In-State): $5,436
Enrollment: 6,622 Coed
Affiliation or Control: State IRS Status: 501(c)3
Highest Offering: Associate Degree
Accreditation: EH, ADNUR, COARC, DA, DH, DMS, ENGT, MAC, MLTAD, OTA, PTAA, RAD, SURGT

02 President Dr. John B. COOK
05 VP of Academic Affairs Dr. Arlene RODRIGUEZ
10 VP of Administration/CFO Mr. Joseph DASILVA
20 Dean of Enrollment Management Mr. Matthew GRAVEL
32 Int VP Student/Multicultural Affs Mr. Kamari COLLINS

04 Assistant to the President ... Mr. Michael J. SUZOR
50 Dean Business/Info Tech ... Dr. Leona R. ITTLEMAN
66 Director of Nursing ... Ms. Lisa FUGIEL
72 Dean EngineeringTech/Mathematics ... Ms. Adrienne SMITH
76 Dean Health and Patient Simulation ... Mr. Michael C. FOSS
79 Interim Dean Arts/Hum/SocialSci ... Dr. Anne BONEMERY
81 Dean Sciences/Engineering Transfer ... Dr. Robert DICKERMAN
51 Dean of Business Services ... Dr. Debbie BELLUCCI
35 Dean of Students ... Ms. LaRue A. PIERCE
07 Dean of Admissions ... Ms. Louisa M. DAVIS FREEMAN
108 Dean of Institutional Effectiveness ... Dr. Barb CHALFONTE
06 Registrar ... Mrs. Theresa REMILLARD
41 Director of Athletics ... Mr. J. Vincent GRASSETTI
102 VP Foundation/Workforce Options ... Mr. Bob LEPAGE
19 Chief of Police/Dir Public Safety ... Ms. E. Shawn DEJONG
18 Sr Director of Facilities ... Mrs. Maureen SOCHA
20 Dean Acad Advising/Student Success ... Mr. Kamari COLLINS
23 Coordinator of Health Services ... Mr. Jonathan L. MILLER
26 Director of Marketing ... Ms. Joan THOMAS
36 Director of Coop/Career Placement ... Ms. Pamela WHITE
15 Senior Director of Human Resources ... Ms. Joan D. NADEAU
16 Director of Human Resources ... Ms. Cheryl ROGERS
37 Director Student Financial Aid ... Mr. Jeremy GREENHOUSE
88 Fiscal/Financial Project Manager ... Mr. Jason COHEN
35 Coord Student Activities/Devel ... Ms. Andrea TARPEY
27 Coordinator of Media Relations ... Ms. Carla POTTS
88 Senior Director Finance/Budgets ... Mrs. Cathy OLSON
14 Sr Director of IT Applications ... Mr. Clifton PORTER
13 Sr Director of IT Infrastructure ... Mr. Robert TRUSCH
62 Dean Library Services ... Ms. Barbara WURTZEL
88 Controller ... Mr. Jonathan TUDRYN
09 Director of Institutional Research ... Ms. Suzanne SMITH
108 Director of Assessment ... Dr. Tracey TROTTIER
88 Director of Grants ... Vacant
96 Director of Purchasing ... Mr. Roger BESSETTE
88 Director of Access/Student Success ... Mr. Roosevelt CHARLES
88 Director of Gateway to College ... Ms. Jennifer SANCHEZ
44 Dir Alumni Relations/Annual Giving ... Ms. Christina TUOHEY
76 Assistant Dean Health ... Mr. Christopher SCOTT
102 Director of Foundation ... Ms. Jessica PROKOP
88 Director of Great Ideas ... Ms. Kerri KANE
37 Director of Student Accounts ... Ms. Dorothy UNGERER

Massachusetts Institute of Technology (A)

77 Massachusetts Avenue, Cambridge MA 02139-4307
County: Middlesex — FICE Identification: 002178
Unit ID: 166683
Telephone: (617) 253-1000 — Carnegie Class: DU-Highest
FAX Number: N/A — Calendar System: 4/1/4
URL: web.mit.edu
Established: 1861 — Annual Undergrad Tuition & Fees: $46,704
Enrollment: 11,319 — Coed
Affiliation or Control: Independent Non-Profit — IRS Status: 501(c)3
Highest Offering: Doctorate
Accreditation: EH, BUS, CS, ENG, PLNG

01 President ... Dr. L. Rafael REIF
88 Chairman of the Corporation ... Mr. Robert B. MILLARD
05 Provost ... Prof. Martin SCHMIDT
00 Chancellor ... Prof. Cynthia BARNHART
03 Exec Vice President & Treasurer ... Mr. Israel RUIZ
46 Vice President for Research ... Prof. Maria T. ZUBER
43 Vice President & General Counsel ... Mr. Mark DIVINCENZO
20 Chancellor for Academic Advancement ... Mr. W. Eric L. GRIMSON
101 Vice President ... Dr. Kirk D. KOLENBRANDER
26 VP for Communications ... Mr. Nate NICKERSON
30 VP for Resource Development ... Ms. Julie LUCAS
88 Senior VP & Secretary of the Corp ... Mr. R. Gregory MORGAN
88 Deputy Executive Vice President ... Mr. Anthony P. SHARON
15 VP for Human Resources ... Ms. Lorraine GOFFE-RUSH
13 Vice President IS&T ... Mr. John CHARLES
10 Vice President for Finance ... Mr. Glen SHOR
29 Exec VP & CEO Alumni Association ... Ms. Judith M. COLE
88 President MIT Investment Mgmt Co ... Mr. Seth ALEXANDER
48 Dean Sch of Architecture & Planning ... Prof. Hashim SARKIS
54 Dean School of Engineering ... Prof. Ian A. WAITZ
79 Dean Sch Hum/Arts/Soc Sciences ... Prof. Melissa NOBLES
81 Dean School of Science ... Prof. Michael SIPSER
50 Dean Sloan School of Management ... Prof. David C. SCHMITTLEIN
20 Associate Provost ... Dr. Karen GLEASON
20 Associate Provost ... Prof. Philip S. KHOURY
20 Associate Provost ... Prof. Richard K. LESTER
08 Director of Libraries ... Mr. Chris BOURG
28 Institute Community & Equity Ofcr ... Prof. Edmund BERTSCHINGER
58 Interim Dean Graduate for Education ... Ms. Blanche E. STATON
88 Dean for Undergraduate Education ... Prof. Dennis FREEMAN
32 Vice President for Student Life ... Dr. Suzy NELSON
106 Vice President for Open Learning ... Prof. Sanjay SARMA
88 Director Lincoln Laboratory ... Dr. Eric D. EVANS
86 Director MIT Washington Office ... Mr. William B. BONVILLIAN
07 Dean of Admissions/Student Fin Svcs ... Mr. Stuart SCHMILL
23 Medical Dir & Head MIT Medical ... Dr. Cecilia Warpinski STUOPIS
18 Director Campus Services and Chief ... Chief John DI FAVA
45 Director of Campus Planning ... Mr. Dennis SWINFORD
102 Exec Dir Foundation Relations ... Ms. Lindley HUEY
25 Dir Office of Sponsored Programs ... Ms. Michelle D. CHRISTY
96 Asst Dir of Strategic Sourcing ... Ms. Sara MALCONIAN
41 Director of Athletics ... Ms. Julie SORIERO
09 Director of Institutional Research ... Mrs. Lydia S. SNOVER
85 Dir International Students Office ... Mr. David ELWELL
36 Exec Dir Global Educ/Career Dev Ctr ... Ms. Melanie L. PARKER
93 Associate Dean and Director OME ... Ms. DiOnetta CRAYTON
06 Registrar ... Ms. Mary CALLAHAN
40 Director MIT Press ... Ms. Amy BRAND
39 Director of Housing Operations ... Vacant
42 Chaplain to the Institute ... Dr. Robert M. RANDOLPH
38 Assoc Dean Student Support Services ... Mr. David RANDALL
94 Women's and Gender Studies Director ... Prof. Helen Elaine LEE
104 Associate Dean Global Education ... Ms. Malgorzata HEDDERICK
24 Manager Audio Visual ... Mr. Louis W. GRAHAM, JR.
90 Dir Platform & Systems Integration ... Mr. Garry P. ZACHEISS
04 Exec Assistant to the President ... Ms. Karla CASEY

Massachusetts School of Law at Andover (B)

500 Federal Street, Andover MA 01810-1094
County: Essex — FICE Identification: 032353
Unit ID: 369002
Telephone: (978) 681-0800 — Carnegie Class: Spec-4-yr-Law
FAX Number: (978) 681-6330 — Calendar System: Semester
URL: www.mslaw.edu
Established: 1988 — Annual Graduate Tuition & Fees: N/A
Enrollment: 408 — Coed
Affiliation or Control: Independent Non-Profit — IRS Status: 501(c)3
Highest Offering: Doctorate; No Undergraduates
Accreditation: EH

00 Dean Emeritus ... Mr. Lawrence R. VELVEL
01 Dean ... Prof. Michael COYNE
10 Chief Business Officer ... Prof. Paula KALDIS
37 Director Student Financial Aid ... Ms. Lynn BOWAB
06 Registrar ... Ms. Louise ROSE
07 Director of Admissions ... Ms. Paula COLBY CLEMENTS
26 Director of Media ... Ms. Kathryn VILLARE
36 Director of Career Services ... Ms. Ursula FURI-PERRY
29 Director of Alumni Relations ... Ms. Ursula FURI-PERRY

MCPHS University (C)

179 Longwood Avenue, Boston MA 02115-5896
County: Suffolk — FICE Identification: 002165
Unit ID: 166656
Telephone: (617) 732-2800 — Carnegie Class: Spec-4-yr-Other Health
FAX Number: (617) 732-2801 — Calendar System: Semester
URL: www.mcphs.edu
Established: 1823 — Annual Undergrad Tuition & Fees: $30,530
Enrollment: 6,935 — Coed
Affiliation or Control: Independent Non-Profit — IRS Status: 501(c)3
Highest Offering: Doctorate
Accreditation: EH, ARCPA, DH, NMT, NURSE, OPT, PHAR, PTA, RAD, RTT

01 President ... Mr. Charles F. MONAHAN, JR.
05 Interim VP Academic Affairs/Provost ... Dr. George HUMPHREY
10 Exec Vice President/COO & CFO ... Mr. Richard J. LESSARD
30 VP for Development & Chief of Staff ... Ms. Marguerite JOHNSON
20 Assoc VP Academic Affs/Assoc Prov ... Dr. Michael MONTAGNE
20 Assoc Prov Acad & Intl Affairs ... Dr. Caroline ZEIND
106 Assoc Provost Online Education/CEO ... Dr. Barbara MACAULAY
43 VP/General Counsel & CCO ... Ms. Deborah A. O'MALLEY
32 Dean of Students ... Dr. Craig MACK
67 Dean of Pharmacy Boston ... Dr. Paul DIFRANCESCO
67 Interim Dean of Pharmacy Wor/Man ... Dr. Anna MORIN
08 Dean Library & Learning Resources ... Mr. Richard KAPLAN
49 Dean School of Arts and Sciences ... Dr. Julia C. ANDERSON
66 Dean School of Nursing Graduate ... Dr. Carol ELIADI
66 Dean School of Nursing Undergrad ... Dr. Paula JAMES
52 Dean Forsyth Sch of Dental Hygiene ... Dr. Linda D. BOYD
88 Interim Director Physicial Therapy ... Dr. Janna KUCHARSKI HOWARD
88 Dean School of Rehabilitation Sci ... Vacant
88 Director of PA Studies Boston ... Mr. Christopher COOPER
88 Interim Dir of PA Studies Wor/Man ... Ms. Kristy ALTONEY-MAGEE
88 Chair Med Imaging & Therapeutics ... Dr. Lisa FANNING
88 Interim Dean of Optometry ... Dr. Lesley WALLS
88 Dean of Acupuncture & Oriental Med ... Ms. Meredith ST JOHN
88 Director of Occupational Therapy ... Dr. Douglas SIMMONS
15 Chief Human Resources Officer ... Ms. Mary LILLY
11 Admin Dean/Chief Retention Officer ... Ms. Stacey TAYLOR
06 Registrar ... Ms. Aen MEYERS
13 Director of Information Services ... Mr. Tom SCANLON
21 Chief Business Officer ... Mr. Keith BELLUCCI
12 Exec Director Wor/Manch Campuses ... Dr. Seth P. WALL
29 Exec Director Alumni Relations ... Ms. Dawn BALLOU
07 Chief Enrollment Officer ... Ms. Kathleen RYAN
96 Director of Purchasing ... Ms. Margaret EATON-CRAWFORD
38 Director Counseling Services ... Ms. Molly PAYNE
26 Director of Communications ... Mr. Michael RATTY
39 Asst Dean Residential Living ... Mr. Joshua CHENEY
35 Asst Dean Campus Life & Leadership ... Ms. Jennifer MICHAEL
18 Director of Facilities ... Mr. Jeff WARD
19 Chief of Public Safety ... Mr. Jack KELLY
105 Manager of Web Services ... Ms. Charlene ROBERTSON
09 Dir Inst Research & Assessment ... Mr. Rajiv MALHOTRA
04 Administrative Asst to President ... Ms. Sheryl CHEAL

MCPHS-Worcester Campus (D)

19 Foster Street, Worcester MA 01608-1715
Telephone: (508) 890-8855 — Identification: 770112
Accreditation: &EH

† Regional accreditation is carried under the parent institution in Boston, MA

Merrimack College (E)

315 Turnpike Street, North Andover MA 01845-5800
County: Essex — FICE Identification: 002120
Unit ID: 166850
Telephone: (978) 837-5000 — Carnegie Class: Masters/M
FAX Number: (978) 837-5222 — Calendar System: Semester
URL: www.merrimack.edu
Established: 1947 — Annual Undergrad Tuition & Fees: $37,670
Enrollment: 3,337 — Coed
Affiliation or Control: Roman Catholic — IRS Status: 501(c)3
Highest Offering: Master's
Accreditation: EH, CAATE, ENG

01 President ... Dr. Christopher E. HOPEY
100 Chief of Staff/Exec Vice President ... Mr. Jeffrey DOGGETT
04 Director Office of the President ... Ms. Lisa JEBALI
05 Provost & Sr VP Academic Affairs ... Dr. Carol GLOD
10 Vice Pres Finance & Budget/CFO ... Mr. William KLINE
04 Special Assistant to the President ... Dr. Russell MAYER
11 VP of Administration & Campus Svcs ... Mr. Mark COLLINS
84 VP for Enrollment & Retention ... Mr. David HAUTANEN
32 Vice Pres Mission/Student Affairs ... Rev. Raymond DLUGOS, OSA
30 VP Development and Alumni Affairs ... Ms. Sara BRAZDA
45 VP Planning/Research & Registrar ... Dr. Nancy LUDWIG
88 Assoc VP/Chief of Staff to Provost ... Mr. Mark GOULD
26 Assoc VP Communications ... Mr. James CHIAVELLI
86 AVP for External Affairs ... Mr. Felipe SCHWARZ
20 Senior Vice Provost ... Dr. Cynthia MCGOWAN
43 Internal General Counsel ... Mr. Nicholas MCDONALD
27 Asst VP for Marketing ... Ms. Zoe COHEN
21 Asst VP & Controller Fiscal Affair ... Ms. Paula CONNOLLY
29 Assoc VP Develop & Alumni Relations ... Ms. Joanne MERMELSTEIN
35 AVP Stdnt Engage/Dean 1st Yr Stdnts ... Ms. Allison GILL
104 AVP Intl/Grad/Multicul Students ... Ms. Lauren BENT
36 Assoc VP Corporate & Career Engage ... Dr. Heather MAIETTA
50 Dean Girard School of Business ... Dr. Mark CORDANO
54 Dean Science & Engineering ... Dr. Alan WEATHERWAX
49 Dean of Liberal Arts ... Dr. Kathleen TIEMANN
53 Dean School of Education ... Dr. Dan BUTIN
88 AVP for Wellness/Dean of Students ... Ms. Stephanie KENDALL
37 Director of Student Financial Aid ... Ms. Adrienne MONTGOMERY
13 Chief Information Officer ... Mr. Chip STILES
07 Director of Undergraduate Admission ... Mr. Darren CONINE
41 Director of Athletics ... Mr. Jeremy GIBSON
09 Dir Institutional Research & Plng ... Ms. Kristen SULLIVAN
15 Director Human Resources ... Ms. Denice BAKER
08 Director of the Library ... Ms. Kathryn GEOFFRION-SCANNELL
42 Director of Campus Ministry ... Rev. Keith HOLLIS
23 Director Counseling & Health Svcs ... Vacant
39 Director of Residence Life ... Mr. Cameron SMITH
19 Director of Police Services ... Mr. Michael DELGRECO
31 Dir of Stevens Service Learning Ctr ... Ms. Mary MCHUGH
24 Dir of Media Instructional Services ... Mr. Kevin SALEMME
96 Director of Purchasing ... Mr. Michael MAGNER
105 Director of Web Services ... Ms. Stacie BOWMAN
28 Director Diversity Education ... Mr. J. Scott GAGE
88 Special Asst Acad Affairs/Provost ... Mr. Michael ACCARDI

MGH Institute of Health Professions (F)

36 1st Avenue, Boston MA 02129-4557
County: Suffolk — FICE Identification: 022316
Unit ID: 166869
Telephone: (617) 726-2947 — Carnegie Class: Spec-4-yr-Other Health
FAX Number: (617) 726-3716 — Calendar System: Semester
URL: www.mghihp.edu
Established: 1977 — Annual Undergrad Tuition & Fees: N/A
Enrollment: 1,166 — Coed
Affiliation or Control: Independent Non-Profit — IRS Status: 501(c)3
Highest Offering: Doctorate
Accreditation: EH, #ARCPA, NURSE, PTA, SP

† Tuition varies by degree program.

Montserrat College of Art (G)

23 Essex Street, Beverly MA 01915-4508
County: Essex — FICE Identification: 020630
Unit ID: 166911
Telephone: (978) 921-4242 — Carnegie Class: Spec-4-yr-Arts
FAX Number: (978) 922-4268 — Calendar System: Semester
URL: www.montserrat.edu
Established: 1970 — Annual Undergrad Tuition & Fees: $29,550
Enrollment: 402 — Coed
Affiliation or Control: Independent Non-Profit — IRS Status: 501(c)3
Highest Offering: Baccalaureate
Accreditation: EH, ART

01 President ... Dr. Stephen D. IMMERMAN
05 Dean Faculty/Academic Affairs ... Ms. Laura TONELLI
32 Dean of Students ... Ms. Maureen WARK
30 Dean of Development ... Mr. Howard AMIDON
26 Dean College Rels/Spec Asst to Pres ... Ms. Jo BRODERICK
10 Chief Financial Officer ... Ms. Cara CALLANAN

13 Director of Information Technology .... Mr. Jake SYNDER
08 Librarian .... Ms. Cheri COE
06 Registrar .... Mrs. Theresa SKELLY
37 Director of Financial Aid .... Ms. Emma PUGLISI
15 Human Resources Generalist .... Ms. Christin BOURANIS
07 Director of Admissions .... Mr. Jeffrey NEWELL
04 Executive Asst to the President .... Ms. Margaret WAUGH

Mount Holyoke College (A)

50 College Street, South Hadley MA 01075-1424
County: Hampshire FICE Identification: 002192
Unit ID: 166939
Telephone: (413) 538-2000 Carnegie Class: Bac-A&S
FAX Number: (413) 538-2391 Calendar System: Semester
URL: www.mtholyoke.edu
Established: 1837 Annual Undergrad Tuition & Fees: $43,886
Enrollment: 2,255 Female
Affiliation or Control: Independent Non-Profit IRS Status: 501(c)3
Highest Offering: Master's
Accreditation: EH

01 President .... Sonya STEPHENS
05 Dean of Faculty/VP for Acad Affairs .... Jon WESTERN
10 VP for Finance and Administration .... Shannon GUREK
84 VP for Enrollment .... Gail BERSON
30 VP for Advancement .... Kassandra JOLLEY
32 Dean of the College/VP Student Affs .... Vacant
26 VP for Communications and Marketing .... Christine HUTCHINS
101 Sr Advisor/Secretary of the Board .... Lenore REILLY
06 Registrar .... Elizabeth PYLE
13 Chief Info Technology Officer (CIO) .... Alex WIRTH-CAUCHON

Mount Ida College (B)

777 Dedham Street, Newton MA 02459
County: Middlesex FICE Identification: 002193
Unit ID: 166948
Telephone: (617) 928-4500 Carnegie Class: Bac-Diverse
FAX Number: (617) 928-4746 Calendar System: Semester
URL: www.mountida.edu
Established: 1899 Annual Undergrad Tuition & Fees: $32,300
Enrollment: 1,320 Coed
Affiliation or Control: Independent Non-Profit IRS Status: 501(c)3
Highest Offering: Master's
Accreditation: EH, ART, CIDA, DH, FUSER

01 President .... Mr. Barry BROWN
05 Provost and Chief Academic Officer .... Mr. Ronald E. AKIE
30 Vice President for Advancement .... Ms. Jill WIERBICKI ABRAHAMS
10 Vice Pres & Chief Financial Officer .... Mr. Jason POTTS
32 Vice President of Student Affairs .... Ms. Laura DEVEAU
21 Interim Controller .... Ms. Diane WOLFF
88 Asst Dean Student Engage/ Leadership .... Mr. Patrick ROMERAO-ALDAZ
06 Registrar .... Ms. Kathy POSEY
22 Director of Disability Services .... Mr. Nick FARANDA
29 Dir Alumni Relations/Annual Giving .... Ms. Jeannette BUNTIN
37 Director Financial Aid .... Ms. Dyan TEEHAN
36 Director of Career Services .... Mr. Robert BROOKS
15 Interim Director of Human Resources .... Ms. Donna EHRLICH
26 Assoc VP Marketing & Communication .... Ms. Fran BERGER
85 Dir Ctr Gbl Connections/Cont Educ .... Ms. Robin MELAVALIN
41 Athletic Director .... Mr. Matthew BURKE
19 Acting Director of Public Safety .... Mr. John KENNEDY
18 Director of Facilities .... Mr. Andrew PAIGE
09 Director of Institutional Research .... Mr. Jerome DEAN
35 Dean of Student Services .... Ms. Mary Anne MILLER
24 Director of Educational Media .... Mr. Manouche MADANIPOUR
96 Director of Business Services .... Ms. Leah WEBBER
07 Dean of Admissions .... Mr. Jeff CUTTING
28 Asst Director Diversity & Inclusion .... Mr. James DULIN
42 College Chaplain .... Vacant
13 Director Network Services .... Mr. David VALENTINE
23 Director Student Health Services .... Ms. Beth GRAMPETRO
58 Assistant Dean Graduate Studies .... Mr. Scott BURKE
04 Administrative Asst to President .... Ms. Grace J. BELTRAME
43 Dir Legal Services/General Counsel .... Ms. Suzanne GALLAGHER

The National Graduate School of Quality Management (C)

186 Jones Road, Falmouth MA 02540-2908
County: Barnstable FICE Identification: 035043
Unit ID: 441478
Telephone: (800) 838-2580 Carnegie Class: Spec-4-yr-Bus
FAX Number: (508) 457-5347 Calendar System: Other
URL: www.ngs.edu
Established: 1993 Annual Undergrad Tuition & Fees: N/A
Enrollment: 239 Coed
Affiliation or Control: Independent Non-Profit IRS Status: 501(c)3
Highest Offering: Doctorate
Accreditation: EH

01 Interim President .... Dr. Robert V. ANTONUCCI
05 Dean of Academic Affairs .... Dr. Eileen SULLIVAN
10 Chief Financial Officer .... Mr. Charles RITCH
84 Dean Enrollment Management .... Mr. John ALONSO
19 Campus Security .... Mr. Jay BEIRNE
30 Director of Development .... Mr. Allan WILSON

New England College of Business and Finance (D)

10 High Street, Suite 204, Boston MA 02110
County: Suffolk FICE Identification: 039653
Unit ID: 164438
Telephone: (617) 603-6900 Carnegie Class: Spec-4-yr-Bus
FAX Number: (877) 469-6961 Calendar System: Other
URL: www.necb.edu
Established: 1909 Annual Undergrad Tuition & Fees: $10,525
Enrollment: 841 Coed
Affiliation or Control: Proprietary IRS Status: Proprietary
Highest Offering: Master's
Accreditation: EH

01 President .... Mr. Howard E. HORTON
05 Provost .... Ms. Debra LEAHY
10 Sr VP Operations/Finance .... Mr. Dennis J. MADIGAN
32 Sr Vice Pres of Student Services .... Ms. Paula BRAMANTE
21 Controller .... Ms. Cassie LAMPSHIRE
20 Asst Provost/Dean of UG Studies .... Mr. Roger PAO
88 Program Chair MBE .... Ms. Deborah SEMENTA
88 Program Chair MBA .... Dr. Carla PATALANO
04 Asst to the President/Office Mgr .... Ms. Kathy CANTALUPA
06 Registrar .... Mr. Robert WAGSTAFF
88 Dean of Students .... Ms. Caitrin BRISSON
84 Director of Enrollment .... Ms. Kirsten THOMPSON
37 Student Finance Supervisor .... Ms. Renee JORDON

New England College of Optometry (E)

424 Beacon Street, Boston MA 02115-1129
County: Suffolk FICE Identification: 002164
Unit ID: 167093
Telephone: (617) 266-2030 Carnegie Class: Spec-4-yr-Other Health
FAX Number: (617) 424-9202 Calendar System: Semester
URL: www.neco.edu
Established: 1894 Annual Undergrad Tuition & Fees: N/A
Enrollment: 519 Coed
Affiliation or Control: Independent Non-Profit IRS Status: 501(c)3
Highest Offering: Doctorate
Accreditation: EH, OPT, OPTR

01 President .... Dr. Clifford SCOTT
05 VP & Dean of Academic Affairs .... Dr. Robert DIMARTINO
10 Sr VP Finance/Admin/CFO .... Ms. Traci LOGAN
17 Chief Practice Management & Clinic .... Dr. David MILLS
30 VP of Institutional Advancement .... Ms. Nancy BROUDE
32 Assoc Dean Students/Dir Stdnt Svcs .... Ms. Barbara MCGINLEY
07 Director of Admissions .... Ms. Kristen TOBIN
37 Director Student Financial Aid .... Ms. Carol RUBEL
15 Director of Human Resources .... Ms. Patricia DAHILL
06 Registrar .... Ms. Glenda UNDERWOOD
08 Director of Library Services .... Ms. Kristin MOTTE
04 Executive Asst to the President .... Ms. Marie HILL

New England Conservatory of Music (F)

290 Huntington Avenue, Boston MA 02115-5018
County: Suffolk FICE Identification: 002194
Unit ID: 167057
Telephone: (617) 585-1100 Carnegie Class: Spec-4-yr-Arts
FAX Number: (617) 262-0500 Calendar System: Semester
URL: www.necmusic.edu
Established: 1867 Annual Undergrad Tuition & Fees: $43,055
Enrollment: 782 Coed
Affiliation or Control: Independent Non-Profit IRS Status: 501(c)3
Highest Offering: Doctorate
Accreditation: EH

01 Interim President .... Mr. Thomas NOVAK
05 Provost/Dean of the College .... Mr. Thomas NOVAK
10 Sr Vice Pres Finance/Operations .... Mr. Edward R. LESSER
30 Exec Vice Pres Institutional Advanc .... Mr. Don JONES
26 Vice Pres Marketing/Communications .... Ms. Carol PHELAN
100 Chief of Staff .... Ms. Kairyn RAINER
56 Dean/Exec Dir Sch Continuing Educ .... Ms. Leslie Wu FOLEY
32 Dean of Students .... Ms. Suzanne HEGLAND
07 Asst Dean for Admissions .... Mr. Alex POWELL
21 Controller .... Ms. Amanda GATES
18 Exec Dir Facilities/Engrng/Constr .... Mr. Michael RYAN
06 Registrar .... Mr. Robert WINKLEY
08 Director of Libraries .... Mr. Alan KARASS
37 Director Financial Aid .... Ms. Lauren URBANEK
35 Director Residence Life .... Ms. Allesandra C. PALMER
29 Senior Director of Alumni Relations ...... Ms. Katrina DEBONVILLE
15 Director of Human Resources .... Vacant
13 Director ITS .... Mr. Charles MEMBRINO
09 Director of Institutional Research .... Ms. Sarah DOW
20 Asst Dean of Stdnts/Dir Intl Stdnts .... Ms. Rebecca TEETERS
38 Director Student Counseling .... Ms. Jan LERBINGER
88 Dir of Entrepreneurial Musicianship .... Ms. Rachel ROBERTS

The New England Institute of Art (G)

10 Brookline Place West, Brookline MA 02445-7295
County: Norfolk FICE Identification: 007486
Unit ID: 167321
Telephone: (617) 739-1700 Carnegie Class: Spec-4-yr-Arts
FAX Number: (617) 582-4500 Calendar System: Semester
URL: www.artinstitutes.edu/boston
Established: 1952 Annual Undergrad Tuition & Fees: $18,636
Enrollment: 555 Coed
Affiliation or Control: Proprietary IRS Status: Proprietary
Highest Offering: Baccalaureate
Accreditation: EH

01 President .... Dr. John LAY
05 Dean of Academic Affairs .... Mr. Chris PREVITA
32 Dean of Student Affairs .... Ms. Michele TRACIA
06 Registrar .... Ms. Maria SARDINAS
13 Campus Technology Manager .... Mr. Sayed KHODIER
15 Human Resources Generalist .... Ms. Camile BATEMAN
36 Director of Career Services .... Mr. John LAY

† In teach-out mode.

New England Law | Boston (H)

154 Stuart Street, Boston MA 02116-5687
County: Suffolk FICE Identification: 008916
Unit ID: 167215
Telephone: (617) 451-0010 Carnegie Class: Spec-4-yr-Law
FAX Number: (617) 422-7333 Calendar System: Semester
URL: www.nesl.edu
Established: 1908 Annual Undergrad Tuition & Fees: N/A
Enrollment: 871 Coed
Affiliation or Control: Independent Non-Profit IRS Status: 501(c)3
Highest Offering: First Professional Degree
Accreditation: LAW

01 Dean .... Mr. John F. O'BRIEN
05 Associate Dean .... Mr. Victor M. HANSEN
11 Associate Dean of Administration .... Ms. Susan S. CALAMARE
20 Assistant Dean .... Ms. Sandra GOLDSMITH
07 Director of Admission .... Ms. Michelle L'ETOILE
10 Chief Financial Officer .... Mr. David M. ROSATI
08 Director of the Law Library .... Ms. Anne ACTON
30 Dir Career Svcs/Dev/Alumni Rels .... Ms. Mandie A. LEBEAU
37 Director of Financial Aid .... Mr. Eric A. KRUPSKI
06 Registrar .... Mr. David M. BERTI
18 Director of Facilities/Security .... Mr. Miguel ALVARADO
32 Director of Student Services .... Ms. Jacqueline PILGRIM

New England School of Acupuncture (I)

150 California Street, Newton MA 02458-1005
County: Middlesex FICE Identification: 025798
Unit ID: 167181
Telephone: (617) 558-1788 Carnegie Class: Spec-4-yr-Other Health
FAX Number: (617) 558-1789 Calendar System: Trimester
URL: www.nesa.edu
Established: 1975 Annual Undergrad Tuition & Fees: N/A
Enrollment: 160 Coed
Affiliation or Control: Independent Non-Profit IRS Status: 501(c)3
Highest Offering: Master's; No Lower Division
Accreditation: ACUP

01 Executive Director .... Susan L. GORMAN
05 Academic Dean .... Meredith ST. JOHN
10 Controller .... Katherine DECELLES
07 Asst Director of Recruitment .... Patrick CAMERON
06 Registrar .... Vacant

Newbury College (J)

129 Fisher Avenue, Brookline MA 02445-5796
County: Norfolk FICE Identification: 007484
Unit ID: 167251
Telephone: (617) 730-7000 Carnegie Class: Bac-Diverse
FAX Number: (617) 731-9618 Calendar System: Semester
URL: www.newbury.edu
Established: 1962 Annual Undergrad Tuition & Fees: $31,408
Enrollment: 874 Coed
Affiliation or Control: Independent Non-Profit IRS Status: 501(c)3
Highest Offering: Baccalaureate
Accreditation: EH

01 President .... Dr. Joseph L. CHILLO
05 Vice President Academic Affairs .... Dr. Frank SARGENT
10 Vice President Finance/CFO .... Ms. Joyce HANLON
100 Chief of Staff .... Mr. Paul MARTIN
30 Vice President for Advancement .... Ms. Clare MCCULLY
84 Vice Pres Enrollment Management .... Mr. Salvadore LIBERTO
88 Dean of Student Success .... Ms. Anne-Marie KENNEY
20 Assoc Dean for Academic Services .... Ms. Sara D'ANJOU
08 Director of Library Services .... Mr. Anthony VIOLA
37 Director of Student Financial Aid .... Ms. Jenny AGUIAR
06 Registrar .... Mr. Jesse AVALOS
15 Director Human Resources .... Ms. Amy DOWNING
36 Director of Career Services .... Ms. Sara SHECKELLS
38 Director Counseling/Health Educ .... Ms. Susan CHAMANDY
18 Director of Facilities .... Mr. Ron MINERVINI
41 Director of Athletics .... Mr. Jonathan HARPER
07 Associate Director of Admissions .... Ms. Shannon MCCARTHY
32 Interim Dean of Student Affairs .... Ms. Jennifer FORRY
04 Executive Asst to President .... Ms. Kori LANTAS
19 Director Campus Safety .... Mr. Daniel AMORIM

Nichols College (A)

Center Road, PO Box 5000, Dudley MA 01571-5000
County: Worcester — FICE Identification: 002197
Unit ID: 167260
Telephone: (508) 213-1560 — Carnegie Class: Spec-4-yr-Bus
FAX Number: N/A — Calendar System: Semester
URL: www.nichols.edu
Established: 1815 — Annual Undergrad Tuition & Fees: $33,300
Enrollment: 1,495 — Coed
Affiliation or Control: Independent Non-Profit — IRS Status: 501(c)3
Highest Offering: Master's
Accreditation: EH, IACBE

01 President ....Susan WEST ENGELKEMEYER
05 Provost and Senior Vice President ....Alan J. REINHARDT
10 Vice President Administration ....Michael J. STANTON
30 Vice President for Advancement ....William C. PIECZYNSKI
84 Vice President for Enrollment ....William BOFFI
32 Dean of Students ....Pamela J. BOGGIO
26 Assoc VP Marketing/Communications ....Cynthia G. BROWN
13 Chief Information Officer ....Kevin F. BRASSARD
58 Exec Dir Graduate & Prof Studies ....Kerry CALNAN
04 Assistant to the President ....Lynn S. LOOBY
06 Assoc Dean Academic Admin/Records ....Peter M. ENGH
41 Director of Athletics ....Christopher COLVIN
07 Asst Dean for Enrollment ....Paul O. BROWER
06 Registrar ....Betin ROBICHAUD
08 Director of Library ....Jim DOUGLAS
15 Asst Director of Human Resources ....Katie CUSHING
29 Director of Alumni Relations ....Molly THIENEL
21 Controller ....Jamie SKOWYRA
35 Dir Student Activities/Orientation ....Brian QUINLAN
36 Director of Career Services ....Elizabeth HORGAN
37 Director of Financial Aid ....Jennifer BIANCO
38 Director Mental Health Services . Monica GOODRICH PELLETIER
27 Director of Public Relations ....Lorraine MARTINELLE
18 Assoc VP for Facilities Management ....Robert W. LAVIGNE
07 Associate Director of Admissions ....Emily REARDON
96 Director Procurement & Contract Svc ....Kay F. YOUNG
19 Director Public Safety ....Jack CAULFIELD
23 Director Health Services ....Katherine NICOLETTI
39 Director Residence Life ....Marney BUSS
104 Director Study Abroad ....Susan WAYMAN
105 Director Web & Social Media ....Claudia SNELL

Northeastern University (B)

360 Huntington Avenue, Boston MA 02115-0195
County: Suffolk — FICE Identification: 002199
Unit ID: 167358
Telephone: (617) 373-2000 — Carnegie Class: DU-Highest
FAX Number: N/A — Calendar System: Semester
URL: www.northeastern.edu
Established: 1898 — Annual Undergrad Tuition & Fees: $45,530
Enrollment: 19,798 — Coed
Affiliation or Control: Independent Non-Profit — IRS Status: 501(c)3
Highest Offering: Doctorate
Accreditation: EH, ANEST, ARCPA, AUD, BUS, ENG, ENGT, LAW, NURSE, PH, PHAR, PSPSY, PTA, SCPSY, SP, SPAA

01 President ....Dr. Joseph E. AOUN
04 Executive Asst to the President ....Ms. Susie C. GUSZCZA
05 Sr VP Academic Affairs and Provost ....Dr. James C. BEAN
100 Chief of Staff ....Mr. James HACKNEY
88 Sr VP Enroll Mgmt & CEO NUGN ..Dr. Philomena V. MANTELLA
30 Sr VP University Advancement ......Ms. Diane N. MACGILLIVRAY
43 Sr VP and General Counsel ....Mr. Ralph C. MARTIN, II
26 Sr VP External Affairs ....Mr. Michael A. ARMINI
11 Sr VP & Chief Operating Officer ....Vacant
12 Seattle Campus Dean & CEO ....Mr. Scott MCKINLEY
12 Charlotte Campus Dean & CEO ....Dr. Cheryl RICHARDS
08 Dean University Libraries ....Mr. William M. WAKELING
46 Sr Vice Provost Research/Grad Educ ....Dr. Art KRAMER
88 Sr Vice Prov UG Ed & Exp Learning ....Dr. Susan AMBROSE
32 Chief Integrated Stdnt Engmt Ofcr ....Dr. Laura A. WANKEL
88 VP & Senior Counsel ....Mr. Vincent J. LEMBO
13 VP & CIO ....Mr. Rehan KHAN
84 VP Enrollment Management .... Mr. Sundar KUMARASAMY
35 VP Student Affs & Dean of Students ....Ms. Madeleine A. ESTABROOK
88 VP Development ....Ms. Luanne KIRWIN
15 VP Human Resources Management .... Ms. Katherine N. PENDERGAST
18 VP Facilities ....Ms. Nancy S. MAY
86 VP Government Relations ....Mr. Tim E. LESHAN
88 VP Public Affairs ....Vacant
88 VP Business Affs Graduate Campuses .Mr. M. Seamus HARREYS
88 VP Advancement & Campaign Director ....Mr. Joseph DONNELLY, JR.
31 VP City & Community Affairs ....Mr. John M. TOBIN
88 VP Enterprise Risk Management .... Ms. Sonya GRANAHAN
88 VP & Chief Campus Planning and Dev . Ms. Kathy SPIEGELMAN
20 Vice Provost Academic Affairs ....Vacant
20 Vice Provost Budget/Planning/Admin ....Dr. Anthony RINI
28 Vice Prov Inst Diversity & Inclsn ....Dr. John ARMENDARIZ
76 Interim Dean Health Sciences ....Mr. Jack REYNOLDS
37 Dean Student Financial Services ....Mr. Tony ERWIN
36 Assoc VP Career Services/Co-Op Educ ....Ms. Maria K. STEIN
88 Assoc VP & Deputy General Counsel ....Ms. Lisa SINCLAIR
58 AVP Graduate Affairs ....Dr. Phil HE
21 Assoc VP of Finance ....Mr. Greg CONDELL
88 AVP Research Administration ....Ms. Dana CARROLL
09 AVP Inst Rsrch & Data Admin ....Ms. Rana GLASGAL
06 Asst VP & University Registrar ....Ms. Linda D. ALLEN
27 Asst VP Communications ....Ms. Renata NYUL
88 AVP Interdisc Initiatives/Spec Proj ....Mr. Robert DIETRICH
44 Asst VP of Treasury Mgmt ....Ms. Alysa GERLACH
92 Director University Honors Program ....Ms. Laurie KRAMER
42 Exec Dir Spirituality & Dialogue ....Mr. Alexander KERN
19 Director of Public Safety ....Mr. Michael DAVIS
41 Director of Athletics ....Mr. Peter P. ROBY
10 Sr VP Finance & Treasurer ....Mr. Thomas NEDELL
88 Sr Advisor to the President ....Mr. Jack H. MCCARTHY
77 Dean Col Computer & Info Science ....Dr. Carla E. BRODLEY
54 Dean College of Engineering ....Dr. Nadine AUBRY
81 Dean College of Science ....Dr. Kenneth HENDERSON
50 Dean D'Amore-McKim School of Bus ....Dr. Hugh COURTNEY
57 Dean College of Arts/Media/Design ....Dr. Elizabeth HUDSON
61 Dean School of Law ....Dr. Jeremy PAUL
83 Dean Col of Soc Sci & Humanities ....Dr. Uta POIGER
107 Int Dean Col Prof Studies ....Dr. Mary LOEFFELHOLZ
12 Dean Toronto Campus ....Dr. John LABRIE
106 Dir Online Education/E-learning ....Mr. Chris MALLETT
29 Director Alumni Relations ....Mr. Rick DAVIS
39 Director Student Housing ....Mr. Robert JOSE

Northpoint Bible College (C)

320 South Main Street, Haverhill MA 01835
County: Essex — FICE Identification: 035705
Unit ID: 217606
Telephone: (978) 478-3400 — Carnegie Class: Spec-4-yr-Faith
FAX Number: (978) 478-3406 — Calendar System: Semester
URL: www.northpoint.edu
Established: 1924 — Annual Undergrad Tuition & Fees: $11,150
Enrollment: 312 — Coed
Affiliation or Control: Assemblies Of God Church — IRS Status: 501(c)3
Highest Offering: Master's
Accreditation: BI

01 President ....Rev Dr David J. ARNETT
05 Academic Dean ....Rev Dr. Daniel HOWELL
32 Dean of Student Affairs ....Rev. David HANSHUMAKER
10 Director of Finance ....Mrs. Jaime RAGSDALE
07 Director of Enrollment ....Rev. Jonathan RAGSDALE
08 Head Librarian ....Miss Ginger MCDONALD
37 Director of Financial Aid ....Miss Patricia STAUFFER
04 Administrative Asst to President ....Ms. Tanya BURKE
06 Registrar ....Mrs Amy MARANVILLE
13 Chief Info Technology Officer (CIO) ....Mr. Steve SIMMONS

Pine Manor College (D)

400 Heath Street, Chestnut Hill MA 02467-2332
County: Norfolk — FICE Identification 002201
Unit ID: 167455
Telephone: (617) 731-7000 — Carnegie Class: Bac-A&S
FAX Number: (617) 731-7199 — Calendar System: Semester
URL: www.pmc.edu
Established: 1911 — Annual Undergrad Tuition & Fees: $27,050
Enrollment 442 — Coed
Affiliation or Control: Independent Non-Profit — IRS Status: 501(c)3
Highest Offering: Master's
Accreditation: #EH

01 President ....Mr. Thomas O'REILLY
05 Dean of College ....Dr. Diane MELLO-GOLDNER
10 Exec VP/Dir Finance & Admin ....Mr. Richard M. REGAN
15 VP/Chief Human Resources Officer ....Mr. William OPAVA
30 Chief Development Officer ....Ms. Susan FUGLIESE
32 Dean of Student Affairs ....Ms. Staci WEBER
84 Vice President for Enrollment ....Vacant
06 Registrar/Dir Inst Research ....Mr. Jeffrey MEI
26 Dir Publications/Media Relations ....Ms. Efrat ZINNAR-SHAVIT
08 Library Director ....Ms. Sarah WOOLF

Pope St. John XXIII National Seminary (E)

558 South Avenue, Weston MA 02493-2699
County: Middlesex — FICE Identification: 002202
Unit ID: 167464
Telephone: (781) 899-5500 — Carnegie Class: Spec-4-yr-Faith
FAX Number: (781) 899-9057 — Calendar System: Semester
URL: www.psjs.edu
Established: 1964 — Annual Graduate Tuition & Fees: N/A
Enrollment: 65 — Male
Affiliation or Control: Roman Catholic — IRS Status: 501(c)3
Highest Offering: Master's; No Undergraduates
Accreditation: THEOL

01 Rector and President ....Rev. William B. PALARDY
05 Academic Dean ....Dr. Anthony KEATY
08 Librarian ....Sr. Jacqueline MILLER
10 Business Manager ....Mrs. Kyle RYAN
06 Registrar ....Dr. Anthony KEATY
30 Chief Development Officer ....Mr. Richard MURPHY
32 Chief Student Life Officer ....Rev. Paul MICELI

Quincy College (F)

1250 Hancock Street, Quincy MA 02169-4324
County: Norfolk — FICE Identification: 002205
Unit ID: 167525
Telephone: (617) 984-1700 — Carnegie Class: Assoc/HT-Mix Trad/Non
FAX Number: (617) 984-1779 — Calendar System: Semester
URL: www.quincycollege.edu
Established: 1958 — Annual Undergrad Tuition & Fees (In-District): $5,524
Enrollment: 4,705 — Coed
Affiliation or Control: Local — IRS Status: 501(c)3
Highest Offering: Associate Degree
Accreditation: EH, ADNUR, MLTAD, PNUR, @PTAA, SURGT

01 President ....Dr. Peter H. TSAFFARAS
05 SVP Academic Affairs ....Ms. Aundrea E. KELLEY
10 SVP Administration/Finance ....Mr. Joseph MERCURIO
100 Assistant to the President ....Mr. Stephen KEARNEY
04 Admin Asst to President ....Ms. Donna M. BRUGMAN
06 Dir of Student Records & Registrar ....Ms. Catherine MALONEY
66 Dean of Nursing ....Ms. Linda PENDERGAST
49 Dean of Liberal Arts ....Dr. Robert BAKER
50 Dean of Professional Programs ....Mr. William BRENNAN
81 Dean of Natural & Health Sciences .....Capt. Vincent VANJOOLEN
21 Director of Finance ....Mr. Martin AHERN
13 VP Technology & Mission Support ....Mr. Tom C. PHAM
20 VP Acad & Admin Affairs & Dean/PLY ....Ms. Mary BURKE
37 Assoc VP for Financial Aid ....Ms. Rose M. DEVITO
18 Dir of Admin Services & Facilities ....Mr. William C. HALL
32 Assoc VP for Student Development ....Ms. Susan G. BOSSA
15 Vice Pres for Human Resources ....Ms. Mary SCOTT
26 Assoc VP of Comm & Marketing ....Mr. Taggart BOYLE
07 Director of Admissions ....Mr. Eric CLARK
88 Director of Academic Advising ....Mr. David CICHOCKI
85 Director of Int'l Student Services ....Ms. Lisa STACK
30 Director Institutional Advancement ....Ms. Tina CAHILL
09 Assoc VP for Inst Research & Assess ....Dr. Kimberly PUHALA
35 Director of Student Development ....Ms. Amanda DECK
08 Director of Library Services ....Ms. Susan WHITEHEAD
106 Dean Online Programs & Inst Affairs ...Mr. Michael MARRAPODI
103 Dir Workforce Dev & Comm Engagement ....Ms. Kate LOPCI

Regis College (G)

235 Wellesley Street, Weston MA 02493-1571
County: Middlesex — FICE Identification: 002206
Unit ID: 167598
Telephone: (781) 768-7000 — Carnegie Class: Spec-4-yr-Other Health
FAX Number: (781) 768-8339 — Calendar System: Semester
URL: www.regiscollege.edu
Established: 1927 — Annual Undergrad Tuition & Fees: $37,540
Enrollment: 1,912 — Coed
Affiliation or Control: Independent Non-Profit — IRS Status: 501(c)3
Highest Offering: Doctorate
Accreditation: EH, ADNUR, NMT, NUR, RAD, SW

01 President ....Dr. Antoinette M. HAYS
10 Vice President Finance/Business ....Mr. Thomas G. PISTORINO
05 Vice President Academic Affairs ....Dr. Malcolm O. ASADOORIAN, III
07 Director of Admission ....Vacant
37 Director of Financial Aid ....Ms. Bonnie QUINN
06 Registrar ....Ms. Esther A. GHAZARIAN
09 Dean of Institutional Research ....Vacant
15 Director of Human Resources ....Ms. Joan D. SULLIVAN
18 Director of Physical Plant ....Mr. Joseph SHAUGHNESSY
21 Director Finance & Business ....Ms. Nancy PLASKER
29 Director of Alumni Relations ....Mrs. Christina DUGGAN
32 VP Student Affairs & UG Enrollment ....Dr. Kara KOLOMITZ
23 Director of Health Services ....Ms. Dianna JONES
04 Special Assistant to President ....Vacant
08 Director of Library ....Ms. Jane PECK
13 Chief Information Officer ....Ms. Kate KORZENDORFER
41 Director Athletics & Physical Educ ....Mr. Robert RILEY
42 Director Campus Ministry ....Mr. Daniel LEAHY
96 Director of Purchasing ....Ms. Diep SHEEHAN
31 Director of Community Living ....Ms. Kelly TRESELER
35 Director of Student Programs ....Mr. Paul MURPHY
30 Chief Development Officer ....Ms. Miriam FINN-SHERMAN

Saint John's Seminary (H)

127 Lake Street, Brighton MA 02135-3898
County: Suffolk — FICE Identification: 002214
Unit ID: 167677
Telephone: (617) 254-2610 — Carnegie Class: Spec-4-yr-Faith
FAX Number: (617) 787-2336 — Calendar System: Semester
URL: www.sjs.edu
Established: 1884 — Annual Undergrad Tuition & Fees: $22,650
Enrollment: 190 — Coed
Affiliation or Control: Roman Catholic — IRS Status: 501(c)3
Highest Offering: Master's
Accreditation: EH, THEOL

01 Rector ....Msgr. James MORONEY
03 Vice Rector ....Rev. Christopher K. O'CONNOR
05 Dean of Faculty ....Prof. Paul METILLY
32 Dean of Students ....Rev. Edward RILEY
07 Director of Admissions & Records ...Mrs. Maureen DEBERNARDI
08 Librarian ....Rev. Raymond VAN DE MOORTELL
10 Director Finance and Operations ....Mr. Richard A. FLAHERTY
73 Director Pre-Theology Program ....Rev. David PIGNATO
21 Asst Finance Director ....Mr. Armand DILANDO
108 Executive Institutional Assessment ....Mr. Kieran KELLY
44 Director Annual or Planned Giving ....Ms. Sandra BARRY

Salter College (A)

645 Shawinigan Drive, Chicopee MA 01020-3744
Telephone: (508) 853-1074 Identification: 770724
Accreditation: ACICS

Salter College (B)

184 West Boylston Street, West Boylston MA 01583
County: Worcester FICE Identification: 004666
Unit ID: 167738
Telephone: (508) 853-1074 Carnegie Class: Assoc/HVT-Mix Trad/Non
FAX Number: (508) 853-1674 Calendar System: Semester
URL: www.saltercollege-us.com
Established: 1937 Annual Undergrad Tuition & Fees: N/A
Enrollment: 555 Coed
Affiliation or Control: Proprietary IRS Status: Proprietary
Highest Offering: Associate Degree
Accreditation: ACICS, ACFEI, MAC

01 Campus Director ... Ms. Erin MCGRATH

Simmons College (C)

300 The Fenway, Boston MA 02115-5898
County: Suffolk FICE Identification: 002208
Unit ID: 167783
Telephone: (617) 521-2000 Carnegie Class: Masters/L
FAX Number: (617) 521-3065 Calendar System: Semester
URL: www.simmons.edu
Established: 1899 Annual Undergrad Tuition & Fees: $37,380
Enrollment: 4,802 Coordinate
Affiliation or Control: Independent Non-Profit IRS Status: 501(c)3
Highest Offering: Doctorate
Accreditation: EH, BUS, DIETD, DIETI, HSA, LIB, NURSE, PTA, SW

01 President ... Helen G. DRINAN
04 Assistant to the President ... Marianne FIGUEIREDO
05 Provost ... Sheila (Katie) CONBOY
10 Sr VP Finance/Administration ... Donna NG
26 VP Comm/Diversity & Inclusion ... Cheryl HOWARD
30 VP Advancement ... Marianne E. LORD
32 VP Student Affairs/Dean of Students ... Sarah NEILL
84 VP Enrollment Mgmt ... John F. DOLAN
20 Deputy Provost ... Stefan KRUG
62 Dean Grad Sch Library/Info Science ... Eileen G. ABELS
76 Dean Sch Nursing & Health Sciences ... Judy BEAL
50 Dean School of Management ... Cathy MINEHAN
49 Dean College of Arts & Sciences ... Renee WHITE
104 Director of Study Abroad ... Joseph STANLEY
06 Asst VP Acad Operations & Registrar ... Donna M. DOLAN
08 Director Library ... Daphne HARRINGTON
25 Director Sponsored Programs ... Jon KIMBALL
09 Director Institutional Research ... Lan GAO
36 Director Career Education Center ... Andrea WOLF
13 Executive Director Technology CIO ... Debra ORR
14 Sr Dir Enterprise Applications & Sv ... Michael PENNACHIO
19 Director Public Safety ... Sean COLLINS
96 Director Purchasing & Procurement ... Kathy PERONI-CALLAHAN
07 Director of Undergraduate Admission ... Ellen JOHNSON
07 Assistant VP Graduate Admissions ... Kristen HAACK
27 Sr Director Marketing ... Allyson IRISH
30 Assoc VP Advancement ... Laura BRINK
88 Event Strategist ... Janice TAYLOR
42 Spiritual Life Program Manager ... Bonnie-Jeanne CASEY
38 Clinical Director Counseling Svcs ... Sherri ETTINGER
39 Director Residence Life ... Jessica FAULK
41 Director Athletics ... Ali KANTOR
35 Assoc Dean Office for Student Life ... Vacant
43 VP & General Counsel ... Kathleen R. ROGERS
15 VP Talent & Human Capital Strategy ... Regina SHERWOOD
100 Chief of Staff ... Lynda CONNOLLY
28 Assistant Provost for Diversity ... Lisa SMITH-MCQUEENIE

Smith College (D)

Northampton MA 01063-0001
County: Hampshire FICE Identification: 002209
Unit ID: 167835
Telephone: (413) 584-2700 Carnegie Class: Bac-A&S
FAX Number: (413) 585-2123 Calendar System: Semester
URL: www.smith.edu
Established: 1871 Annual Undergrad Tuition & Fees: $46,288
Enrollment: 2,989 Female
Affiliation or Control: Independent Non-Profit IRS Status: 501(c)3
Highest Offering: Doctorate
Accreditation: EH, ENG, SW

01 President ... Kathleen MCCARTNEY
04 Secretary to the President ... Beth BERG
10 Vice Pres Finance & Administration ... Michael W. HOWARD
05 Provost & Dean of the Faculty ... Katherine ROWE
84 VP for Enrollment ... Audrey Y. SMITH
20 Dean for Academic Development ... Bill PETERSON
32 VP Campus Life/Dean of the College ... Donna LISKER
35 Dean of Students ... Julianne OHOTNICKY
70 Dean School for Social Work ... Marianne YOSHIOKA
39 Director of Residence Life ... Becky SHAW
85 Assoc Dean International Students ... Caitlin B. SZYMKOWICZ
30 VP for Development ... Beth BALMUTH RAFFELD
38 Assoc Dir Health Svcs/Stdnt Counsel ... Pamela MCCARTHY
26 VP for Public Affairs ... Laurie FENLASON
29 VP Alum Rels/Exec Dir Alumnae Assn ... Jennifer S. CHRISLER
13 VP Information Technology ... Samantha EARP
09 Exec Dir Inst Research ... Cate ROWEN
08 Director of Libraries ... Christopher LORING
15 Assoc VP for Human Resources ... Lawrence HUNT
07 Dean of Admission ... Debra D. SHAVER
37 Dir Student Financial Services ... David J. BELANGER
06 Registrar ... Gretchen B. HERRINGER
36 Director Career Development Office ... Stacie HAGENBAUGH
28 VP for Incl/Diversity and Equity ... Dwight K. HAMILTON
58 Dir Grad Pgms/Assoc Dean of Faculty ... Danielle D. RAMDATH
18 Assoc VP for Facilities Management ... Roger MOSIER
23 Director of Health Services ... Leslie R. JAFFE
41 Director of Athletics ... Krisin HUGHES
42 Dean of Religious Life ... Jennifer L. WALTERS
96 Procurement Director ... Linda HIESIGER
104 Dean for International Study ... Rebecca HOVEY
108 Assoc Director of Assessment ... Minh LY

Springfield College (E)

263 Alden Street, Springfield MA 01109-3797
County: Hampden FICE Identification: 002211
Unit ID: 167899
Telephone: (413) 748-3000 Carnegie Class: Masters/L
FAX Number: N/A Calendar System: Semester
URL: www.springfieldcollege.edu
Established: 1885 Annual Undergrad Tuition & Fees: $34,455
Enrollment: 3,178 Coed
Affiliation or Control: Independent Non-Profit IRS Status: 501(c)3
Highest Offering: Doctorate
Accreditation: EH, ARCPA, CAATE, COPSY, CORE, EMT, EXSC, IACBE, NRPA, OT, PTA, SW

01 President ... Dr. Mary-Beth A. COOPER
05 Provost & VP Academic Affairs ... Dr. Martha POTVIN
29 Vice President Devel & Alumni Rels ... Mr. John A. WHITE
10 Sr VP for Finance & Admin ... Mr. John MAILHOT
32 VP for Student Affairs ... Dr. Shannon FINNING
43 VP & General Counsel ... Mr. Christopher NERONHA
88 VP for Inclusion & Com Engagement ... Dr. Calvin R. HILL
20 Assoc VP Academic Affairs ... Dr. Mary Ann COUGHLIN
21 Director of Human Resources ... Ms. Miriam SIEGEL
30 Associate VP Development ... Vacant
84 VP of Enrollment Management ... Mr. Stuart JONES
06 Registrar ... Mr. Keith INGALLS
08 Director of Library ... Ms. Andrea S. TAUPIER
29 Director of Alumni Relations ... Ms. Tamie KIDESS LUCEY
37 Director of Financial Aid ... Mr. Edward CIOSEK
36 Director of Career Center ... Ms. Jeanette M. DOYLE
13 Chief Information Officer ... Mr. Danny DAVIS
90 Sr Dir Networking/AC & Clnt Comp ... Mr. Thomas F. LARKIN
26 Exec Dir Office of Communications ... Mr. Stephen ROULIER
38 Director of Counseling Center ... Mr. Brian KRYLOWICZ
19 Exec Dir Public Safety/Chief ... Ms. Karen LEARY
85 Director of International Center ... Dr. Deborah ALM
42 Director Campus Ministry ... Mr. David MCMAHON
18 Director of Facilities & Campus Svc ... Mr. Gregory WALTERS
41 Director of Athletics ... Dr. Craig POISSON
96 Director of Purchasing ... Ms. Lita ADAMS

Stonehill College (F)

320 Washington Street, Easton MA 02357-6110
County: Bristol FICE Identification: 002217
Unit ID: 167996
Telephone: (508) 565-1000 Carnegie Class: Bac-A&S
FAX Number: (508) 565-1500 Calendar System: Semester
URL: www.stonehill.edu
Established: 1948 Annual Undergrad Tuition & Fees: $38,550
Enrollment: 2,284 Coed
Affiliation or Control: Roman Catholic IRS Status: 501(c)3
Highest Offering: Baccalaureate
Accreditation: EH, BUS

01 President ... Rev. John F. DENNING, CSC
100 Chief of Staff ... Mrs. Heather L. HEERMAN
05 Provost/VP for Acad Affairs ... Dr. Joseph FAVAZZA
10 Vice Pres for Finance & Treasurer ... Ms. Jeanne FINLAYSON
30 Vice President for Advancement ... Mr. Francis X. DILLON
32 Vice President of Student Affairs ... Ms. Pauline DOBROWSKI
88 Vice President for Mission ... Rev. James LIES, CSC
84 VP for Enrollment Mgmt & Marketing ... Mrs. Catherine CAPOLUPO
21 AVP for Finance & Operations ... Mr. Craig BINNEY
35 Assoc VP for Students Affairs ... Mr. Kevin PISKADLO
37 Asst VP/Dir of Student Aid/Finance ... Mrs. Eileen K. O'LEARY
04 Sr Executive Asst to the President ... Mrs. Jessica L. GRACIA
20 Dean of the Faculty ... Dr. Maria CURTIN
43 General Counsel ... Mr. Thomas V. FLYNN
21 Controller ... Ms. Jennifer MATHEWS
07 Dean of Admissions ... Mr. Joe DACEY
06 Registrar ... Mr. John PESTANA
09 Dir of Inst Research/Assessment ... Mr. Brian M. OLES
08 Director of College Library ... Ms. Cheryl MCGRATH
26 Dir of Media Rels & Communications ... Mr. Martin P. MCGOVERN
29 Director of Alumni Affairs ... Ms. Anne M. SANT
15 Director of Human Resources ... Ms. Maryann B. BIEDAK
38 Dir of Counseling & Testing Center ... Ms. Maria A. KAVANAUGH
13 Chief Information Officer ... Ms. Tamara ANDERSON
19 Chief of Police ... Mr. Peter CARNES
42 Director Campus Ministry ... Rev. Anthony SZAKALY, CSC
90 Manager of Instructional Technology ... Ms. Janice HARRISON
45 Director of Academic Development ... Ms. Bonnie L. TROUPE
88 Dir of Enterprise Infrastructure ... Mr. Thomas MCGRATH
23 Director of Health Services ... Ms. Maria SULLIVAN
36 Director of Career Services ... Mrs. Christina M. BURNEY
41 Dir of Intercollegiate Athletics ... Mr. Dean R. O'KEEFE
92 Interim Director of Honors Program ... Prof. Allyson SHECKLER
44 Director of Development ... Mr. Douglas J. SMITH
20 Dir of Academic Svcs & Advising ... Ms. Eileen H. BELLEMORE
96 Director of Purchasing ... Mr. Gregory WOLFE
45 Asst VP for Planning & Budgeting ... Mr. Stephen BEAUREGARD
39 Director of Residence Life ... Ms. Kristen PIERCE
24 Dir of Media/Videography Services ... Mr. Michael PIETROWSKI
40 Manager of College Bookstore ... Mrs. Mary DUNCKLEE
88 Dean of Academic Achievement ... Dr. Craig ALMEIDA
97 Asst Dean Gen Educ & Acad Achievmnt ... Dr. Todd S. GERNES
18 Dir of Facilities Management ... Mr. Bruce BOYER
104 Director International Programs ... Vacant
31 Campus Minister Svc Immersion Pgm ... Ms. Mary Anne CAPPELLERI
28 Director of Intercultural Affairs ... Ms. Constanza CABELLO

Suffolk University (G)

8 Ashburton Place, Boston MA 02108-2770
County: Suffolk FICE Identification: 002218
Unit ID: 168005
Telephone: (617) 573-8000 Carnegie Class: DU-Mod
FAX Number: (617) 573-8353 Calendar System: Semester
URL: www.suffolk.edu
Established: 1906 Annual Undergrad Tuition & Fees: $33,934
Enrollment: 8,215 Coed
Affiliation or Control: Independent Non-Profit IRS Status: 501(c)3
Highest Offering: Doctorate
Accreditation: EH, ART, BUS, BUSA, CIDA, CLPSY, ENG, IPSY, LAW, RADDOS, RTT, SPAA

01 Acting President ... Dr. Marisa KELLY
05 Acting Provost ... Mr. Sebastian ROYO
10 Sr VP Finance/Admin/Treasurer ... Ms. Laura SANDER
30 Sr Vice Pres for Advancement ... Mr. Colm RENEHAN
84 Sr Vice Pres for Enrollment ... Mr. Michael CROWLEY
26 VP Marketing/Communications ... Mr. Greg GATLIN
86 Sr VP Government/Community Affairs ... Mr. John A. NUCCI
20 Vice Prov Faculty Devel/Curriculum ... Mr. Jeffrey POKORAK
37 AVP/Dir of Financial Aid ... Ms. Christine M. PERRY
100 Chief of Staff ... Dr. Carol S. STREIT
32 AVP/Dean of Students ... Dr. Ann C. COYNE
50 Dean Sawyer Business School ... Mr. William J. O'NEILL, JR.
61 Dean of the Law School ... Mr. Andrew PERLMAN
49 Dean College Arts & Science ... Dr. Maria TOYADA
22 Chief Diversity/Inclusion Officer ... Ms. Nicole G. PRICE
07 Director Undergraduate Admission ... Vacant
07 Director Graduate Admission ... Mr. Cory J. MEYERS
08 Director of Sawyer Library ... Ms. Sharon BRITTON
06 University Registrar ... Ms. Mary LALLY
36 Director Career Development Center ... Ms. Teresa DIMAGNO
15 Chief Human ResourcesOfficer ... Ms. Katherine WHIDDEN
29 Director of Alumni Affairs/Law Sch ... Ms. Kate GOGGINS
13 Chief Information Officer ... Mr. Thomas LYNCH, III
19 Cheif University Police ... Mr. Gerard COLETTA
35 Director of Student Activities ... Mr. John SILVERIA
41 Int Director of Athletics ... Mr. Cary MCCONNELL
18 Sr Dir Facilites Plng & Mgmt ... Mr. Gordon B. KING
88 Asst Dean for Acad Svcs Law School ... Ms. Lorraine D. COVE
08 Law Librarian ... Ms. Elizabeth MCKENZIE
09 Assoc Provost/Inst Research ... Ms. Melanie JENKINS

Tufts University (H)

Medford MA 02155-5555
County: Middlesex FICE Identification: 002219
Unit ID: 168148
Telephone: (617) 628-5000 Carnegie Class: DU-Highest
FAX Number: N/A Calendar System: Semester
URL: www.tufts.edu
Established: 1852 Annual Undergrad Tuition & Fees: $50,604
Enrollment: 10,907 Coed
Affiliation or Control: Independent Non-Profit IRS Status: 501(c)3
Highest Offering: Doctorate
Accreditation: EH, ARCPA, ART, CS, DENT, DIETI, ENG, IPSY, MED, OT, PH, PLNG, VET

01 President ... Dr. Anthony P. MONACO
100 Chief of Staff ... Mr. Michael BAENEN
03 Executive Vice President ... Ms. Patricia CAMPBELL
05 Provost & Senior Vice President ... Mr. David R. HARRIS
43 SVP Univ Relations & Gen Counsel ... Ms. Mary R. JEKA
30 SVP University Advancement ... Mr. Eric C. JOHNSON
11 Vice President for Operations ... Ms. Linda SNYDER
10 Vice President Finance/Treasurer ... Mr. Thomas S. MCGURTY
15 VP for Human Resources ... Mr. Julien C. CARTER
13 VP & Chief Information Officer ... Mr. David J. KAHLE
26 Vice Pres Communications/Marketing ... Ms. Christine SANNI
20 Vice Provost ... Mr. Kevin DUNN
46 Vice Provost for Research ... Vacant
09 Assoc Provost Inst Res & Eval ... Dr. Dawn G. TERKLA
21 Assistant Provost for Admin/Finance ... Ms. Celia K. CAMPBELL
29 Interim Exec Dir Alumni Relations ... Ms. Margot BIGGIN
22 Assoc Prov/Chief Diversity Officer ... Dr. Mark BRIMHALL-VARGAS
23 Sr Director Health/Wellness Svcs ... Ms. Michelle D. BOWDLER

37 Director of Financial Aid ... Ms. Patricia REILLY
27 Director Public Relations ... Ms. Kimberly M. THURLER
36 Executive Director Career Center ... Mr. Gregory J. VICTORY
08 Director Tisch Library ... Ms. Laura WOOD
18 Senior Facilities Director ... Mr. Stephen NASSON
28 Director Equal Opportunity ... Ms. Jill A. ZELLMER
38 Director Mental Health Services ... Dr. Julie S. ROSS
19 Director Public & Env Safety ... Mr. Kevin C. MAGUIRE
49 Dean Arts & Sciences ... Mr. James GLASER
54 Dean of Engineering ... Dr. Jianmin QU
60 Dean SMFA ... Ms. Nancy BAUER
58 Dean Grad School of A&S ... Mr. Robert G. COOK
82 Dean Fletcher Sch Law & Diplomacy ... Adm. James STAVRIDIS
52 Dean of Dental Medicine ... Dr. Huw F. THOMAS
74 Dean Cummings Sch of Veterinary Med . Dr. Deborah KOCHEVAR
63 Dean Medical School ... Dr. Harris BERMAN
88 Dean Sackler School ... Dr. Naomi ROSENBERG
88 Dean Friedman School ... Dr. Dariush MOZAFFARIAN
88 Dean Tisch College ... Mr. Alan SOLOMONT
53 Dean Undergrad & Grad Educ ... Mr. John BARKER
88 Dean Academic Adv & Undergrad Study ... Dr. Carmen LOWE
32 Dean of Student Affairs ... Ms. Mary Pat MCMAHON
35 Dean of Student Services/Art & Sci ... Mr. Paul STANTON
07 Dean Undergrad Admiss/Enroll Mgt .. Ms. Karen L. RICHARDSON
96 Purchasing Director ... Mr. John HOMICH
41 Director Athletics ... Mr. John MORRIS
42 University Chaplain ... Rev. Gregory MCGONIGLE
102 Sr Dir Corp & Foundation Relations ... Ms. Ippolita A. CANTUTI-CASTELVETRI
104 Associate Dean Programs Abroad ... Ms. Sheila BAYNE
39 Director Residential Life ... Ms. Yolanda M. KING
44 Senior Director Gift Planning ... Ms. Brooke ANDERSON
31 Director Community Relations ... Ms. Barbara G. RUBEL

University of Phoenix Boston Campus (A)

2 Adams Place, Suite 300, Quincy MA 02169
Telephone: (866) 867-3678 Identification: 770209
Accreditation: &NH, ACBSP

† No longer accepting campus-based students.

Urban College of Boston (B)

178 Tremont Street, Boston MA 02111-1006
County: Suffolk FICE Identification: 031305
Unit ID: 429128
Telephone: (617) 449-7070 Carnegie Class: Spec 2-yr-Other
FAX Number: (617) 423-4758 Calendar System: Semester
URL: www.urbancollege.edu
Established: 1993 Annual Undergrad Tuition & Fees: $7,124
Enrollment: 810 Coed
Affiliation or Control: Independent Non-Profit IRS Status: 501(c)3
Highest Offering: Associate Degree
Accreditation: EH

01 President ... Mr. Michael TAYLOR
05 Vice President Academic Affairs ... Ms. Nancy C. DANIEL
10 Dean of Administration/Finance ... Mr. Stephen LOZEN
84 Dean Enrollment Svcs & Registrar ... Mr. Avanti SEYMOUR
32 Dean of Students/Dir Student Affs ... Ms. Carmen PINEDA
37 Director of Financial Aid ... Ms. Mia TAYLOR
20 Instructional Coordinator ... Mr. Phoenix FENG
10 Business Manager ... Ms. Kathleen BARDELL

Wellesley College (C)

106 Central Street, Wellesley MA 02481-8203
County: Norfolk FICE Identification: 002224
Unit ID: 168218
Telephone: (781) 283-1000 Carnegie Class: Bac-A&S
FAX Number: (781) 283-3639 Calendar System: Semester
URL: www.wellesley.edu
Established: 1875 Annual Undergrad Tuition & Fees: $46,836
Enrollment: 2,323 Female
Affiliation or Control: Independent Non-Profit IRS Status: 501(c)3
Highest Offering: Baccalaureate
Accreditation: EH

01 President ... Paula A. JOHNSON
05 Provost & Dean of the College ... Andrew SHENNAN
30 VP for Resources & Public Affairs ... Cameran MASON
10 VP Finance Administration/Treasurer ... Ben HAMMOND
18 Asst VP Facilities Management/Plng ... David CHAKRABORTY
15 Asst VP/Director Human Resources/EO ... Carolyn SLABODEN
13 Chief Information Officer ... Ganesan RAVISHANKER
07 Dean of Admission/Financial Aid ... Joy ST. JOHN
32 Interim Dean of Students ... Carol BATE
42 Dean Religious/Spiritual Life ... Tiffany L. STEINWERT
20 Dean of Academic Affairs ... Ann VELENCHIK
20 Dean of Faculty Affairs ... Kathryn LYNCH
09 Assc Provost Institutional Planning ... Pamela L. TAYLOR
28 Assc Prov/Acad Dir Dvrsty/Inclusion ... Robbin CHAPMAN
06 Registrar ... Carol SHANMUGARATNAM
29 Executive Director Alumnae Assn ... Missy SHEA
37 Director of Student Financial Svcs ... Scott JUEDES
36 Assoc Prov/Dir Exec Ctr Work/Svc ... Christine CRUZVERGARA
26 Chief Public Relations Officer ... Elizabeth T. GILDERSLEEVE
35 Assoc Director Student Involvement ... Megan K. JORDAN
38 Administrative Counseling Svcs ... Robin COOK-NOBLES
101 Clerk Board of Trustees ... Marianne B. COOLEY
96 Purchasing Manager ... Tina M. DOLAN

Wentworth Institute of Technology (D)

550 Huntington Avenue, Boston MA 02115-5998
County: Suffolk FICE Identification: 002225
Unit ID: 168227
Telephone: (617) 989-4590 Carnegie Class: Masters/M
FAX Number: (617) 989-4591 Calendar System: Semester
URL: www.wit.edu
Established: 1904 Annual Undergrad Tuition & Fees: $32,500
Enrollment: 4,558 Coed
Affiliation or Control: Independent Non-Profit IRS Status: 501(c)3
Highest Offering: Master's
Accreditation: EH, ART, CIDA, CONST, CS, ENG, ENGT, IACBE

01 President ... Dr. Zorica PANTIC
100 Chief of Staff ... Ms. Amy INTILLE
05 Provost ... Dr. Richard HANSEN
10 Vice Pres Finance ... Mr. Robert TOTINO
21 Vice President Business ... Mr. David A. WAHLSTROM
30 Vice Pres Institutional Advancement ... Ms. Paula SAKEY
84 VP Enrollment Management ... Ms. Keiko BROOMHEAD
15 Vice Pres Human Resources ... Ms. Anne M. GILL
13 VP of Information Technology ... Mr. Mark STAPLES
88 Exec Asst to the Chief of Staff ... Ms. Rebecca COAKLEY
20 Assoc Provost ... Vacant
32 VP Student Affairs/Dean of Stdnts ... Ms. Annamarie WENNER
21 Assoc Vice President Finance ... Mr. David GILMORE
84 Assoc VP of Enrollment Management ... Ms. Dianne PLUMMER
31 Assoc VP Community Affairs ... Ms. Sandra E. PASCAL
14 Assoc VP Information Technology ... Mr. Leslie VAUGHAN
88 AVP Innovation & Entrepreneurship ... Ms. Monique FUCHS
20 Director Acad Operations ... Ms. Kelly PARRISH
51 Dean of College of Prof & Cont Educ ... Ms. Deborah WRIGHT
07 Executive Director of Admissions ... Ms. Maureen DISCHINO
06 Registrar ... Ms. Joan MONAHAN
08 Director of Library ... Mr. Kevin KIDD
35 Dir Student Financial Services ... Ms. Patricia OSGOOD
18 Associate VP Physical Facilities ... Mr. Michael PANKIEVICH
26 Director of Publications ... Mr. Caleb COCHRAN
35 Associate Dean of Students ... Mr. Peter FOWLER
102 Dir Corp Foundation/Govt Rels ... Ms. Lori FRIEDMAN
37 Director Financial Aid ... Ms. Anne-Marie CARUSO
38 Director of Counseling ... Ms. Maura MULLIGAN
19 Director of Public Safety ... Mr. William POWERS
41 Associate Athletic Director ... Mr. William P. GORMAN
36 Dir Of Cooperative Educ/Career Svcs ... Ms. Robbin BEAUCHAMP
39 Director Housing & Residential Life ... Mr. Philip BERNARD
41 Director of Athletics ... Ms. Cheryl AARON
96 Director of Purchasing ... Mr. Gerald INMAN
09 Institutional Researcher ... Mr. Alan T. WHITEMORE
49 Dean for Arts & Sciences ... Dr. Patrick HAFFORD
48 Dean for Arch/Design & Const Mgmt ... Dr. Charles HOTCHKISS
54 Dean for Engineering & Technology ... Mr. Frederick DRISCOLL
18 Director of Physical Plant ... Mr. Robert FERRO
88 Director Office of Campus Life ... Ms. Carissa DURFEE
108 Director of Accreditation ... Ms. Cidhinnia TORRES CAMPOS

Western New England University (E)

1215 Wilbraham Road, Springfield MA 01119-2684
County: Hampden FICE Identification: 002226
Unit ID: 168254
Telephone: (413) 782-3111 Carnegie Class: Masters/M
FAX Number: (413) 782-1746 Calendar System: Semester
URL: www.wne.edu
Established: 1919 Annual Undergrad Tuition & Fees: $34,030
Enrollment: 3,922 Coed
Affiliation or Control: Independent Non-Profit IRS Status: 501(c)3
Highest Offering: Doctorate
Accreditation: EH, BUS, ENG, LAW, PHAR, SW

01 President ... Dr. Anthony S. CAPRIO
04 Administrative Asst to President ... Ms. Marie IRZYK
05 Provost/Vice Pres Academic Affairs ... Dr. Linda E. JONES
26 Vice Pres Marketing & External Affs ... Mrs. Barbara A. MOFFAT
10 Vice Pres Finance & Administration ... Mr. William J. KELLEHER
84 Vice President for Enrollment Mgmt ... Mr. Bryan J. GROSS
32 VP Student Affairs/Dean of Students ... Dr. Jeanne S. HART-STEFFES
30 Vice President Advancement ... Ms. Beverly J. DWIGHT
88 Vice Pres for Strategic Initiatives ... Dr. Richard S. KEATING
13 Asst Vice Pres Information Tech ... Mr. Scott J. COOPEE
15 Asst VP & Dir of Human Resources ... Ms. Joanne OLLSON
61 Dean of the School of Law ... Prof. Eric J. GOUVIN
67 Dean of the College of Pharmacy ... Dr. Evan ROBINSON
49 Dean of the College of Arts & Sci ... Dr. Saeed GHAHRAMANI
50 Dean of the College of Business ... Dr. Julie SICILIANO
54 Dean of the College of Engineering ... Dr. S. Hossein CHERAGHI
89 Dean First Year/Transfer Students ... Ms. Kerri P. JARZABSKI
08 Assoc Dean Law Library/Info Res ... Ms. Patricia NEWCOMBE
39 Asst Dean of Students and Res Life ... Mr. Jerry ROEDER
28 Asst Dean of Diversity Programs ... Mrs. Yvonne BOGLE
06 Registrar ... Ms. Terese CHENIER
37 Director of Financial Aid ... Ms. Kathleen CHAMBERS
41 Director of Athletics ... Dr. Michael THEULEN
36 Director Career Development Center ... Ms. Andrea ST. JAMES
38 Director of Counseling Services ... Dr. Wayne D. CARPENTER
08 Director of D'Amour Library ... Mrs. Priscilla L. PERKINS
23 Director of Health Services ... Ms. Kathleen A. REID
18 Director of Facilities Management ... Mr. C. Michael DUNCAN
90 Dir Educational Technology Center ... Mr. Steven NARMONTAS
91 Dir of Administrative Info Systems ... Mr. Anthony MUTTI
29 Director of Alumni Relations ... Ms. Katherine PAPPAS

102 Dir of Foundation Relations ... Mr. Matthew VANHEYNIGEN
42 Spiritual Life Coordinator ... Ms. Sheila HANIFIN
19 Director of Public Safety ... Mr. Adam WOODROW
11 Director Administrative Services ... Ms. Arlene M. ROCK
07 Dir of Undergraduate Admissions ... Mr. Christopher WYSTEPEK
20 Academic Scheduling Controller ... Dr. Linda M. CHOJNICKI
09 Director Inst Research & Planning ... Dr. Richard A. WAGNER
43 General Counsel ... Mrs. Cheryl SMITH

Wheaton College (F)

26 E Main Street, Norton MA 02766-2322
County: Bristol FICE Identification: 002227
Unit ID: 168281
Telephone: (508) 286-8200 Carnegie Class: Bac-A&S
FAX Number: (508) 286-8270 Calendar System: Semester
URL: www.wheatoncollege.edu
Established: 1834 Annual Undergrad Tuition & Fees: $47,700
Enrollment: 1,587 Coed
Affiliation or Control: Independent Non-Profit IRS Status: 501(c)3
Highest Offering: Baccalaureate
Accreditation: EH

01 President ... Dr. Dennis HANNO
05 Provost ... Dr. Renée T. WHITE
10 VP Finance/Administration ... Mr. Brian DOUGLAS
30 Vice President College Advancement ... Ms. Merritt CROWLEY
84 Vice President Enrollment ... Mr. Grant GOSSELIN
32 VP Student Affairs/Dean of Students ... Ms. Kate E. KENNY
26 VP Marketing and Communications ... Mr. Gene P. BEGIN
37 Asst VP Enroll/Stdnt Finan Svcs ... Ms. Robin RANDALL
26 Assistant VP for Communications ... Mr. Michael GRACA
06 Registrar/Dean Academic Systems ... Vacant
29 Dir Alumni Rels/Annual Giving ... Ms. Courtney SHURTLEFF
15 Asst VP/Director Human Resources ... Ms. Barbara LEMA
38 Assoc Dean/Director Counseling Ctr ... Mr. Jeffrey KLUG
07 Director of Admission ... Ms. Judy PURDY
18 Asst VP Business Svcs/Phys Plant ... Mr. John M. SULLIVAN
09 Director of Institutional Research ... Dr. Polly PREWITT-FREILINO
39 Director Stdnt Life/Housing ... Mr. Edward T. BURNETT
19 Director Public Safety ... Chief Christopher SANTIAGO
101 Asst to President/Sec Brd Trustees ... Ms. Kristen TURCOTTE
41 Athletic Director ... Mr. John SUTYAK
104 Director Study Abroad ... Ms. Gretchen YOUNG
13 Chief Info Technology Officer (CIO) ... Ms. Susan V. WAWRZASZEK
91 Director Administrative Computing ... Ms. Susan A. MORGADO
36 Director of Career Services ... Ms. Lisa GAVIGAN

Wheelock College (G)

200 The Riverway, Boston MA 02215-4176
County: Suffolk FICE Identification: 002228
Unit ID: 168290
Telephone: (617) 879-2000 Carnegie Class: Masters/M
FAX Number: (617) 566-7369 Calendar System: Semester
URL: www.wheelock.edu
Established: 1888 Annual Undergrad Tuition & Fees: $33,835
Enrollment: 1,331 Coed
Affiliation or Control: Independent Non-Profit IRS Status: 501(c)3
Highest Offering: Beyond Master's But Less Than Doctorate
Accreditation: EH, SW, TED

01 President ... Dr. David CHARD
04 Sr Exec Asst to Pres/Corp Secretary ... Ms. Valerie THORNHILL-HUDSON
11 VP Admin/Inst Effect/Innovation ... Vacant
05 VP for Academic Affairs ... Vacant
30 VP for Development/Alumni Affairs ... Ms. Jennifer RICE
10 VP/Chief Financial Officer ... Ms. Anne Marie MARTORANA
84 VP Student Success and Engagement ... Dr. Adrian K. HAUGABROOK
07 AVP Undergrad Admissions ... Mr. Cory MEYERS
86 Dir of Government and Ext Affairs ... Ms. Marta ROSA
32 Dean of Students ... Ms. Barbara MORGAN
49 Interim Dean of Arts & Sciences ... Dr. Detris Honora ADELABU
104 Dean International Pgms/Prtnrshp ... Dr. Linda DAVIS
53 Assoc Dean of Education ... Dr. Donna MCKIBBENS
70 Assoc Dean of Social Work ... Dr. Hope HASLAM STRAUGHAN
07 Director of Graduate Admissions ... Mr. Brian MINCHELLO
06 Registrar ... Ms. Michelle ORMEROD
08 Interim Director of Library ... Ms. Ann GLANNON
15 Director of Human Resources ... Ms. Michele CREWS
13 Director of Information Technology ... Mr. Jonathan LAPIERRE
36 Dir Center for Career Development ... Vacant
18 Chief Facilities/Physical Plant ... Mr. Ed JACQUES
38 Director Counseling Center ... Ms. Eileen THOMPSON
29 Dir of Development/Alumni Relations ... Ms. Lauren MARQUIS
09 Institutional Research Analyst ... Mr. Lance ANGELL
26 Marketing Manager ... Mr. Stephen DILL
41 Athletic Director ... Mr. Dwight DATCHER
42 Spiritual Life Coordinator ... Dr. Adrienne KISNER
39 Director of Residence Life ... Ms. Darcy DUBOIS
27 Communications Manager ... Ms. Beth KAPLAN
107 Interim Dean of Grad/Prof Programs . Dr. Linda BANKS-SANTILLI

William James College (H)

1 Wells Avenue, Newton MA 02459-3211
County: Norfolk FICE Identification: 021636
Unit ID: 166717
Telephone: (617) 327-6777 Carnegie Class: Spec-4-yr-Other Health
FAX Number: (617) 327-4447 Calendar System: Semester
URL: www.williamjames.edu

Established: 1974 Annual Graduate Tuition & Fees: N/A
Enrollment: 700 Coed
Affiliation or Control: Independent Non-Profit IRS Status: 501(c)3
Highest Offering: Doctorate; No Undergraduates
Accreditation: EH, CLPSY, IPSY, SCPSY

01 President .... Dr. Nicholas COVINO
04 Executive Asst to the President .... Ms. Lilly MANOLIS
10 VP Finance & Operations .... Mr. Daniel BRENT
05 Vice Pres Academic Affairs .... Dr. Stanley BERMAN
46 Assoc VP for Research .... Dr. Edward DEVOS
37 Director Financial Aid .... Mrs. Elaine TOOMEY
06 Registrar .... Ms. Sonji PAIGE
32 Dean of Students .... Mr. Josh COOPER
88 Director of Multicultural Affairs .... Dr. Mari Carmen BENNASAR
07 Director of Admissions .... Mr. Mario MURGA
51 Director Continuing Prof Education .... Mr. Dean ABBY
27 Director of Marketing .... Mrs. Katie O'HARE
13 Dir Information Technology .... Mr. Jeff CHOO
08 Head Librarian .... Mr. Matt KRAMER
15 Human Resource Director .... Mrs. Ellen COLLINS
18 Facilities Manager .... Mr. Kevin COSTELLO
26 Chief Public Relations Officer .... Ms. Patti JACOBS
96 Director of Purchasing .... Ms. Marice NICHOLS
29 Director Alumni Relations .... Dr. Alan BECK
09 Director of Institutional Research .... Dr. Ed DEVOS
28 Director of Diversity .... Dr. Elana WOLCOFF
30 Director of Development .... Ms. Ann DOLYE

† Formerly Massachusetts School of Professional Psychology

Williams College (A)

880 Main Street, Williamstown MA 01267
County: Berkshire FICE Identification: 002229
Unit ID: 168342
Telephone: (413) 597-3131 Carnegie Class: Bac-A&S
FAX Number: N/A Calendar System: 4/1/4
URL: www.williams.edu
Established: 1793 Annual Undergrad Tuition & Fees: $50,070
Enrollment: 2,126 Coed
Affiliation or Control: Independent Non-Profit IRS Status: 501(c)3
Highest Offering: Master's
Accreditation: EH

01 President .... Adam F. FALK
05 Dean of Faculty .... Denise K. BUELL
45 Provost .... William C. DUDLEY
10 VP for Fin & Admin and Treasurer .... Frederick W. PUDDESTER
32 Vice President for Campus Life .... Stephen P. KLASS
28 VP for Inst Diversity & Equity .... Leticia HAYNES
26 Chief Communications Officer .... Angela P. SCHAEFFER
04 Asst to Pres/Secretary of the Col .... Keli A. GAIL
20 Dean of the College .... Marlene J. SANDSTROM
18 Exec Director Facilities Management .... Robert F. WRIGHT
06 Registrar .... Barbara A. CASEY
07 Director of Admission .... Richard L. NESBITT
37 Director of Financial Aid .... Paul J. BOYER
08 Librarian .... David M. PILACHOWSKI
21 Controller .... Susan S. HOGAN
29 Director Alumni Relations .... Brooks L. FOEHL
15 Director of Human Resources .... Martha R. TETRAULT
36 Director of Career Center .... Donald J. KJELLEREN
109 Director of Dining Services .... Robert P. VOLPI
13 Chief Technology Officer .... Barron KORALESKY
09 Director of Institutional Research .... Courtney WADE
23 Director of Health Admin Services .... Angie MARANO
35 Director Office of Student Life .... Douglas J. SCHIAZZA
41 Director of Athletics/PE .... Lisa M. MELENDY
42 Chaplain .... Richard E. SPALDING

Woods Hole Oceanographic Institution (B)

266 Woods Hole Road, Woods Hole MA 02543-1535
County: Barnstable FICE Identification: 002230
Unit ID: 166610
Telephone: (508) 289-2252 Carnegie Class: Not Classified
FAX Number: N/A Calendar System: 4/1/4
URL: www.whci.edu
Established: 1930 Annual Graduate Tuition & Fees: N/A
Enrollment: N/A Coed
Affiliation or Control: Independent Non-Profit IRS Status: 501(c)3
Highest Offering: Doctorate; No Undergraduates
Accreditation: EH

01 President and Director .... Dr. Mark R. ABBOTT
09 Exec Vice Pres/Director of Research .... Dr. Laurence P. MADIN
05 VP of Academic Programs and Dean .... Dr. James A. YODER
10 Vice Pres of Operations/CFO .... Mr. Jeffrey FERNANDEZ
18 VP Marine Facilities/Operations .... Mr. Robert MUNIER
43 VP Legal Affairs/General Counsel .... Mr. Christopher LAND
30 Chief Development Officer .... Mr. Charles GAUVIN
20 Associate Dean .... Dr. Margaret K. TIVEY
06 Registrar .... Ms. Julia WESTWATER
08 Research Librarian .... Ms. Holly N. MILLER

Worcester Polytechnic Institute (C)

100 Institute Road, Worcester MA 01609-2280
County: Worcester FICE Identification: 002233
Unit ID: 168421
Telephone: (508) 831-5000 Carnegie Class: DU-Higher
FAX Number: (508) 831-5753 Calendar System: Semester
URL: www.wpi.edu
Established: 1865 Annual Undergrad Tuition & Fees: $45,590
Enrollment: 6,381 Coed
Affiliation or Control: Independent Non-Profit IRS Status: 501(c)3
Highest Offering: Doctorate
Accreditation: EH, BUS, ENG

01 President .... Dr. Laurie LESHIN
05 Sr Vice President and Provost .... Dr. Bruce BURSTEN
10 Executive Vice President & CFO .... Mr. Jeffrey S. SOLOMON
30 VP for University Advancement .... Mr. William J. MCAVOY
26 Chief Marketing Officer .... Ms. Amy M. MORTON
13 Chief Information Officer (CIO) .... Ms. Deborah C. SCOTT
03 Senior Vice President .... Ms. Kristin R. TICHENOR
18 Asst Vice President for Facilities .... Mr. Alfred DIMAURO, JR.
15 VP Talent Development/CDO .... Ms. Michelle JONES-JOHNSON
20 VP Academic & Corporate Devel .... Mr. Stephen P. FLAVIN
32 Vice President of Student Affairs .... Mr. Philip N. CLAY
22 AVP/Chief Compliance Officer .... Mr. Jon C. BARTELSON
36 Exec Director Career Devel Center .... Mr. Stefan KOPPI
100 Asst VP/Chief of Staff .... Ms. Stephanie PASHA
07 Director of Admissions .... Ms. Jennifer A. CLUETT
06 University Registrar .... Ms. Sarah L. MILES
27 Director of Research Communications .... Mr. Michael W. DORSEY
96 Director of Procurement Services .... Ms. Laurie COLELLA
21 University Controller .... Ms. Charlene M. BELLOWS
09 Assistant VP of Budget Planning .... Ms. Judith L. TRAINOR
38 Asst Dean of Stdnt Dev/Dir SDCC .... Mr. Charles C. MORSE
88 Associate Director LSBC .... Mr. Andrew BUTLER
37 Executive Director Student Aid .... Ms. Monica M. BLONDIN
19 Dir Environmental Health & Safety .... Mr. Daniel T. SARACHICK
28 Director of Multicultural Affair .... Ms. Bonnie J. WALKER
29 Exec Director Lifetime Engagement .... Mr. Peter A. THOMAS

MICHIGAN

Adrian College (D)

110 S Madison Street, Adrian MI 49221-2575
County: Lenawee FICE Identification: 002234
Unit ID: 168528
Telephone: (517) 265-5161 Carnegie Class: Bac-Diverse
FAX Number: (517) 264-3331 Calendar System: Semester
URL: www.adrian.edu
Established: 1859 Annual Undergrad Tuition & Fees: $33,610
Enrollment: 1,641 Coed
Affiliation or Control: United Methodist IRS Status: 501(c)3
Highest Offering: Master's
Accreditation: NH, CAATE, SW, TEAC

01 President .... Dr. Jeffrey R. DOCKING
05 Vice Pres/Dean for Academic Affairs .... Dr. Agnes CALDWELL
30 Vice Pres Institutional Advancement .... Mr. James MAHONY
84 Vice President of Enrollment .... Mr. Frank J. HRIBAR
10 Vice Pres Business Affairs/CFO .... Mr. Jerry WRIGHT
32 Dean of Student Affairs .... Mr. Troy SCHMIDLI
20 Asst Dean of Academic Affairs .... Ms. Bridgette WINSLOW
21 Asst Vice Pres of Business Affairs .... Mr. David DREWS
44 Asst Vice President for Development .... Mr. Ryan EFF
07 Associate Director of Admissions .... Ms. Erin DESMET
42 Chaplain/Director Church Relations .. Dr. Christopher P. MOMANY
26 Director of Public Relations .... Vacant
06 Registrar .... Ms. Kristen MILLER
35 Associate Dean for Student Life . Ms. Megan VANDERKERKHOVE
21 Controller .... Ms. Nicole MEGALE
86 Dir of Govt & Foundation Relations .... Ms. Amy CAMPBELL
15 Director of Human Resources .... Mrs. Renee BURCK
40 Bookstore Manager .... Ms. Rachelle M. DUFFY
93 Dir Multicultural Cultural Programs .... Ms. Idali FELICIANO
29 Director Alumni Relations .... Mrs. Marsha FIELDER
41 Director of Athletics .... Mr. Michael DUFFY
19 Director of Campus Safety .... Mr. Wade BIETELCHIES
36 Director of Career Planning .... Mrs. Janna D'AMICO
88 Director of Conferences .... Ms. Denise HEIN
38 Director of Counseling .... Ms. Monique J. SAVAGE
08 Head Librarian .... Mr. David CRUSE
23 Director of Health Center .... Ms. Dawn MARSH
96 Director of Purchasing .... Ms. Donna WARD
37 Director of Financial Aid .... Mr. Matt RHEINECKER
18 Director of Facilities .... Mr. Chris STIVER
09 Director of Institutional Research .... Ms. Beth L. HEISS
88 Director of Academic Services .... Ms. Linda JACOBS
88 Asst Director of Academic Services .... Ms. Danielle WARD
13 Asst Dir of Information Services .... Vacant
04 Administrative Asst to President .... Mrs. Andrea BURT

Albion College (E)

611 E Porter Street, Albion MI 49224-1831
County: Calhoun FICE Identification: 002235
Unit ID: 168546
Telephone: (517) 629-1000 Carnegie Class: Bac-A&S
FAX Number: (517) 629-0509 Calendar System: Semester
URL: www.albion.edu
Established: 1835 Annual Undergrad Tuition & Fees: $39,313
Enrollment: 1,268 Coed
Affiliation or Control: United Methodist IRS Status: 501(c)3
Highest Offering: Baccalaureate
Accreditation: NH, CAATE, MUS, TEAC

01 President .... Dr. Mauri A. DITZLER
10 Vice Pres Business & Finance .... Mr. Jerry WHITE
05 Provost .... Dr. Marc ROY
30 Vice Pres Institutional Advancement .... Mr. Robert ANDERSON
84 Vice Pres Enrollment Management .... Mr. Steven KLEIN
32 Vice Pres & Dean Student Affairs .... Dr. Sally J. WALKER
13 Assoc Vice Pres Info Svcs/CIO .... Mr. Michael DEVER
07 Director of Admissions .... Ms. Mandy DUBIEL
39 Director Residential Life .... Ms. Julie MCMAHON
08 Director of Libraries .... Dr. Michael VAN HOUTEN
26 Director of Communications .... Mr. John THOMPSON
29 Director of Alumni Engagement .... Ms. Elinor MARSH
38 Director of Counseling .... Dr. Frank KELEMEN
37 Director of Financial Aid .... Ms. Ann WHITMER
06 Registrar .... Dr. Andrew M. DUNHAM
109 Director Dining & Hospitality Svcs .... Mrs. Pat MILLER
18 Director of Facilities Operations .... Mr. Donald MASTERNAK
19 Director of Campus Safety .... Mr. Kenneth SNYDER
41 Athletic Director .... Mr. Matthew AREND
42 College Chaplain .... Rev. Daniel MCQUOWN
15 Director of Human Resources .... Mrs. Lisa LOCKE
09 Director of Institutional Research .... Dr. Andrew DUNHAM
96 Director of Purchasing .... Mrs. Susan CLARK
20 Associate Academic Officer .... Dr. John WOELL
28 Assoc Director Multicultural Affs .... Ms. Keena WILLIAMS
40 Manager of Bookstore .... Vacant

Alma College (F)

614 W Superior, Alma MI 48801-1599
County: Gratiot FICE Identification: 002236
Unit ID: 168591
Telephone: (989) 463-7111 Carnegie Class: Bac-A&S
FAX Number: (989) 463-7277 Calendar System: Other
URL: www.alma.edu
Established: 1886 Annual Undergrad Tuition & Fees: $35,428
Enrollment: 1,396 Coed
Affiliation or Control: Independent Non-Profit IRS Status: 501(c)3
Highest Offering: Baccalaureate
Accreditation: NH, CAATE, MUS, TEAC

01 President .... Dr. Jeff ABERNATHY
05 Provost & Vice Pres for Acad Affs .... Dr. Michael L. SELMON
10 VP for Finance & Administration .... Mr. Todd FRIESNER
30 Vice President for Advancement .... Mr. Matt VANDENBERG
84 Vice President for Enrollment .... Mr. Bob GARCIA
32 Vice President for Student Life .... Dr. Nicholas A. PICCOLO
26 Vice Pres Communication/Marketing .... Ms. Ann HALL
04 Executive Asst to the President .... Ms. Sandee A. GADDE
06 Associate Provost & Registrar .... Ms. Julie WILLIAMS
20 Assistant Provost .... Ms. Susan M. DEEL
42 Chaplain .... Rev. Noel SNYDER
37 Dir Stdnt Financial Assistance .... Ms. Michelle MCNIER
08 Director of Library .... Ms. Carol ZEILE
27 Director of College Communications .... Mr. Mike SILVERTHORN
13 Chief Technology Officer .... Dr. Keith R. NELSON
18 Director Facilities & Service Mgmt .... Mr. Douglas DICE
15 Director Human Resources .... Mr. Kenneth L. BORGMAN
21 Controller .... Mr. Dan HENRIS
29 Director Alumni Relations .... Ms. Amanda SLENSKI
35 Director Campus Life .... Mr. David K. BLANDFORD
38 Director Counseling & Wellness .... Ms. Anne K. LAMBRECHT
07 Director Admissions .... Vacant
09 Research Analyst .... Mr. John MACARTHUR

Alpena Community College (G)

665 Johnson Street, Alpena MI 49707-1495
County: Alpena FICE Identification: 002237
Unit ID: 168607
Telephone: (989) 356-9021 Carnegie Class: Assoc/MT-VT-High Trad
FAX Number: (989) 358-7553 Calendar System: Semester
URL: www.alpenacc.edu
Established: 1952 Annual Undergrad Tuition & Fees (In-District): $4,140
Enrollment: 1,636 Coed
Affiliation or Control: Local IRS Status: 501(c)3
Highest Offering: Baccalaureate
Accreditation: NH, MAC

01 President .... Dr. Donald MACMASTER
05 Vice Pres of Instruction .... Ms. Kathleen MARSH
10 Vice President Admin & Finance .... Mr. Richard SUTHERLAND
32 Dean of Students .... Ms. Nancy SEGUIN
21 Controller .... Ms. Lyn KOWALEWSKY
20 Dean Learning Resource Center .... Ms. Wendy BROOKS
25 Director of TAACCT Grants .... Ms. Dawn STONE
13 Co-Director Mgmt Info Systems .... Ms. Vicky KROPP
13 Co-Director Mgmt Info Systems .... Mr. Mark GRUNDER
26 Dir Public Information/Marketing .... Mr. Jay WALTERREIT
40 Director of ACC Bookstore .... Mr. William MATZKE
102 Dir Dev/Exec Dir ACC Foundation .... Ms. Penny BOLDREY
18 Director of Facilities Management .... Mr. Nicholas BREGE
88 Volunteer Center Director .... Ms. Kathleen BRUSKI
06 Registrar .... Ms. Lori DZIESINSKI
15 Director Human Resources .... Ms. Carolyn DAOUST
07 Director of Admissions .... Mr. Mike KOLLIEN
37 Director Student Financial Aid .... Mr. Robert ROOSE

Andrews University (H)

8975 U.S. 31, Berrien Springs MI 49104-0001
County: Berrien FICE Identification: 002238
Unit ID: 168740
Telephone: (269) 471-7771 Carnegie Class: DU-Mod
FAX Number: (269) 471-6900 Calendar System: Semester

URL: www.andrews.edu
Established: 1874 Annual Undergrad Tuition & Fees: $27,000
Enrollment: 3,418 Coed
Affiliation or Control: Seventh-day Adventist IRS Status: 501(c)3
Highest Offering: Doctorate
Accreditation: NH, CACREP, CS, DIETD, DIETI, ENG, IACBE, MT, MUS, NUR, PTA, @SP, SW, TED, THEOL

01 President .... Dr. Andrea T. LUXTON
05 Provost .... Dr. Christon ARTHUR
20 Assistant Provost Inst Assessment .... Dr. Lynn MERKLIN
10 Vice President for Financial Admin .... Mr. Lawrence E. SCHALK
32 Vice President for Student Life .... Dr. Frances M. FAEHNER
26 Vice Pres Marketing & Communication .... Mr. Stephen D. PAYNE
84 Vice Pres for Enrollment Management .... Mr. Randy K. GRAVES
30 Vice President for Advancement .... Dr. David A. FAEHNER
43 General Counsel .... Ms. Gwendolyn POWELL BRASWELL
06 Registrar .... Ms. Aimee VITANGCOL REGOSO
49 Dean College Arts & Sciences .... Dr. Keith E. MATTINGLY
76 Dean School of Health Professions .... Dr. Emmanuel RUDATSIKIRA
50 Dean School of Business Admin .... Dr. Allen F. STEMBRIDGE
53 Dean School of Education .... Dr. Robson MARINHO
48 Dean Sch Architect & Interior Des .... Mr. Carey CARSCALLEN
73 Dean of Theological Seminary .... Dr. Jiri MOSKALA
58 Interim Dean Sch of Grad Studies .... Dr. Wagner KUHN
106 Dean Sch of Dist Educ/Intl Partners .... Dr. Alayne THORPE
08 Dean of Libraries .... Mr. Lawrence W. ONSAGER
21 Associate Business Officer .... Mr. Glenn A. MEEKMA
39 Dir of University Apartment Life .... Mr. Alfredo RUIZ
34 Dir of the Women's Residence Halls .... Ms. Jennifer R. BURRILL
33 Dir of the Men's Residence Halls .... Mr. Spencer D. CARTER
85 Dir of International Student Svcs .... Mr. Robert BENJAMIN
92 Director of Honors Program .... Dr. L. Monique PITTMAN
15 Director of Human Resources .... Mr. Daniel E. AGNETTA
37 Director Student Financial Aid .... Ms. Elynda A. BEDNEY
07 Director of Undergrad Admissions .... Ms. Shanna LEAK
07 Director of Graduate Admissions .... Ms. Monica WRINGER
88 Media Relations Specialist .... Ms. Becky ST. CLAIR
29 Director of Alumni Services .... Mr. Andriy KHARKOVYY
38 Dir of Counseling/Testing Center .... Dr. Judith FISHER
40 Manager of Bookstore .... Ms. Cynthia SWANSON
19 Director of Campus Safety .... Mr. Benjamin PANIGOT
23 Director of Medical Services .... Vacant
42 University Chaplain .... Ms. June M. PRICE
09 Director Institutional Research .... Mr. James R. MASSENA
18 Director of Facilities Management .... Mr. Paul ELDER
04 Executive Asst to President .... Ms. Dalry B. PAYNE
41 Athletic Director .... Mr. David JARDINE
44 Director of Planned Giving .... Ms. Tari POPP
104 Director Study Abroad .... Dr. Pedro NAVIA
105 Director Web Services .... Mr. Robert FUSTE
13 Chief Information Officer .... Ms. Lorena L. BIDWELL
28 Director of Diversity .... Vacant

Aquinas College (A)

1607 Robinson Road, SE, Grand Rapids MI 49506-1799
County: Kent FICE Identification: 002239
Unit ID: 168786
Telephone: (616) 632-8900 Carnegie Class: Masters/S
FAX Number: (616) 732-4469 Calendar System: Semester
URL: www.aquinas.edu
Established: 1886 Annual Undergrad Tuition & Fees: $28,320
Enrollment: 1,933 Coed
Affiliation or Control: Roman Catholic IRS Status: 501(c)3
Highest Offering: Master's
Accreditation: NH, CAATE, TEAC

01 President .... Dr. Juan OLIVAREZ
05 Provost/Dean of Faculty .... Dr. Stephen BARROWS
30 Vice Pres Institutional Advancement .... Ms. Patricia CASTIGLIONE
10 Vice President Finance .... Dr. Leonard KOGUT
84 Vice Pres Enrollment Management .... Ms. Paula T. MEEHAN
04 Assistant to President .... Ms. Monica EDISON
26 Assoc VP Marketing & Communication .... Mr. Carl APPLE
07 Assoc VP for Admissions .... Mr. Thomas MIKOWSKI
32 Assoc VP for Student Services .... Mr. Brian MATZKE
21 Controller .... Ms. Cathy LUCK
09 Dean of Institutional Effectiveness .... Dr. Susan ENGLISH
53 Dean of School of Education .... Vacant
06 Registrar .... Mrs. Cecelia MESLER
38 Director of Counseling Services .... Ms. Sharon E. SMITH
51 Director of Continuing Education .... Dr. Deborah WICKERING
104 Dir International Education Pgms .... Vacant
94 Director of Women's Studies .... Ms. Amy DUNHAM STRAND
92 Director of Honors Program .... Dr. Michelle DEROSE
58 Director of Graduate Management .... Mr. Brian DIVITA
08 Co-Director Woodhouse Library .... Ms. Shellie JEFFRIES
08 Co-Director Woodhouse Library .... Ms. Francine PAOLINI
18 Director of Maintenance .... Mr. Dale HAISMA
39 Director Residence Life .... Ms. Julie BLASZAK
07 Director of Admissions .... Ms. Angela SCHLOSSER-BACON
37 Director of Financial Aid .... Ms. Darcy KAMPFSCHULTE
41 Director Athletics .... Mr. Terry M. BOCIAN
42 Director Campus Ministry .... Vacant
13 Dir Information Technology & Svcs .... Vacant
29 Director of Alumni Relations .... Ms. Brigid AVERY
35 Director of Campus Life .... Ms. Heather HALL
44 Director of Major Gifts .... Ms. Cecelia CUNNINGHAM
44 Director of Corporate Giving .... Dr. Ali ERHAN
20 Director of Academic Advising .... Ms. Cecelia MESLER
28 Director of Diversity & Inclusion .... Ms. Latoya BOOKER

40 Director Bookstore .... Ms. Marian TODISH
24 Media Coordinator .... Ms. Francine PAOLINI
42 Campus Chaplain .... Rev. Stanley DRONGOWSKI, OP

The Art Institute of Michigan (B)

28175 Cabot Drive, Novi MI 48377
Telephone: (248) 675-3800 Identification: 666692
Accreditation: &NH, ACFEI

† Regional accreditation is carried under the parent institution The Illinois Institute of Art, Chicago, IL.

*Baker College System (C)

1050 W Bristol Road, Flint MI 48507-5508
County: Genesee Identification: 666923
Unit ID: 419572
Telephone: (810) 766-4280 Carnegie Class: N/A
FAX Number: (810) 766-4279
URL: www.baker.edu

00 Chairman of the Board .... Mr. Jim CUMMINS
01 CEO/President of System .... Dr. Bart DAIG
05 Vice President for Academics .... Dr. Denise A. BANNAN
13 Vice Pres Information Technology .... Ms. Jacqueline SPICER
15 Vice President of Human Resources .... Ms. Dana CLARK
26 Vice Pres Marketing/Admissions/PR .... Mr. Bruce LUNDEEN
10 Corporate Controller .... Mr. Michael MOORE
32 Vice President of Student Affairs .... Mr. Gerald MCCARTY
20 Assoc Provost of Academic Affairs .... Dr. Lesa LOUCH
36 Director of Career Services .... Mrs. Laura ZUCK
14 Director of IT Operations .... Mrs. Sheryl L. DEAN
08 Director of Library Services .... Mrs. Lynn STACEY
58 President Graduate Studies .... Dr. Jill LANGEN

*Baker College of Flint (D)

1050 W Bristol Road, Flint MI 48507-5508
County: Genesee FICE Identification: 004673
Unit ID: 168847
Telephone: (810) 766-4000 Carnegie Class: Bac/Assoc-Mixed
FAX Number: (810) 766-4293 Calendar System: Quarter
URL: www.baker.edu
Established: 1911 Annual Undergrad Tuition & Fees: $8,640
Enrollment: 3,726 Coed
Affiliation or Control: Independent Non-Profit IRS Status: 501(c)3
Highest Offering: Doctorate
Accreditation: NH, CAHIIM, CSHSE, ENG, IACBE, MAC, NURSE, OT, POLYT, PTAA, SURGT, TEAC

02 President .... Mrs. Wen HELMINGWAY
05 Director of Academic Affairs .... Dr. Jason YOUNG
07 Vice President of Admissions .... Mr. Kevin PNACEK
15 Vice President of Human Resources .... Ms. Dana CLARK
32 Vice President of Student Services .... Mr. Gerald MCCARTY, II
50 Dir Business Admin/Early Child Educ .... Dr. John C. COTE
76 Dean of Health/Human Services .... Vacant
08 Director of Library Services .... Vacant
06 Co-Registrar .... Ms. Judi LANGOLF
06 Co-Registrar .... Ms. Jill PRICE
13 Director of Computer Operations .... Mr. Michael MYERS
18 Director of Facilities .... Mr. Kim STODDARD
38 Director of Counseling/Assessment .... Mr. Paul ZANG
19 Director of Safety/Security .... Mr. John JOSEPH
40 Director of Bookstore .... Mr. Nick ANGLE
54 Dir Engineering/Computer Science .... Mrs. Anca SALA
26 Director Community Relations .... Vacant
10 Business Officer .... Mrs. Rebecca AYRE-BOGGS
36 Director of Career Services .... Ms. Janie STEWART
37 Director Student Financial Aid .... Ms. Veta NORRIS
31 Director Corporate/Community Svcs .... Mr. Jeff MALLETS
23 Director of Health and Fitness .... Mrs. Maureen MILLER
39 Housing Coordinator .... Ms. Lauren PHILLIPS

*Baker College of Allen Park (E)

4500 Enterprise Drive, Allen Park MI 48101-3033
Telephone: (313) 425-3700 Identification: 666996
Accreditation: &NH, CAHIIM, COMTA, CSHSE, IACBE, MAC, MLTAD, OPD, OTA, PTAA, SURGT

† Regional accreditation is carried under the parent institution in Flint, MI

*Baker College of Auburn Hills (F)

1500 University Drive, Auburn Hills MI 48326-2642
Telephone: (248) 340-0600 Identification: 666940
Accreditation: &NH, COARC, CSHSE, DA, DMS, IACBE, MAC, PHLEB, PTAA

† Regional accreditation is carried under the parent institution in Flint, MI

*Baker College of Cadillac (G)

9600 E 13th Street, Cadillac MI 49601-9600
Telephone: (231) 876-3100 Identification: 666941
Accreditation: &NH, COMTA, CSHSE, EMT, IACBE, MAC, SURGT

† Regional accreditation is carried under the parent institution in Flint, MI

*Baker College of Clinton Township (H)

34950 Little Mack Avenue,
Clinton Township MI 48035-4701
Telephone: (586) 791-6610 Identification: 666942
Accreditation: &NH, CAHIIM, COMTA, CSHSE, EMT, IACBE, MAC, RAD, SURGT

† Regional accreditation is carried under the parent institution in Flint, MI

*Baker College of Jackson (I)

2800 Springport Road, Jackson MI 49202-1290
Telephone: (517) 788-7800 FICE Identification: 004680
Accreditation: &NH, CAHIIM, COMTA, CSHSE, IACBE, MAC, RTT, SURGT

† Regional accreditation is carried under the parent institution in Flint, MI

*Baker College of Muskegon (J)

1903 Marquette Avenue, Muskegon MI 49442-1490
Telephone: (231) 777-5200 FICE Identification: 002296
Accreditation: &NH, ACFEI, ADNUR, COMTA, CSHSE, IACBE, MAC, OTA, PTAA, RAD, SURGT

† Regional accreditation is carried under the parent institution in Flint, MI

*Baker College of Owosso (K)

1020 S Washington Street, Owosso MI 48867-4400
Telephone: (989) 729-3370 Identification: 666937
Accreditation: &NH, CSHSE, DMS, IACBE, MAC, MLTAD, OTA, RAD

† Regional accreditation is carried under the parent institution in Flint, MI

*Baker College of Port Huron (L)

3403 Lapeer Road, Port Huron MI 48060-2597
Telephone: (810) 985-7000 Identification: 666943
Accreditation: &NH, CSHSE, DH, IACBE, MAC

† Regional accreditation is carried under the parent institution in Flint, MI

Bay College West Campus (M)

PO Box 130, Iron Mountain MI 49801
Telephone: (906) 774-8547 Identification: 770262
Accreditation: &NH

† Regional accreditation is carried under the parent institution in Escanaba, MI

Bay Mills Community College (N)

12214 W Lakeshore Drive, Brimley MI 49715-9750
County: Chippewa FICE Identification: 030666
Unit ID: 380359
Telephone: (906) 248-3354 Carnegie Class: Tribal
FAX Number: (906) 248-3351 Calendar System: Semester
URL: www.bmcc.edu
Established: 1984 Annual Undergrad Tuition & Fees: $3,040
Enrollment: 555 Coed
Affiliation or Control: Tribal Control IRS Status: 501(c)3
Highest Offering: Associate Degree
Accreditation: NH

01 President .... Michael C. PARISH
05 Vice President of Academic Affairs .... Samantha CAMERON
10 Vice Pres Business & Finance .... Laura POSTMA
32 Dean of Student Services .... Debra J. WILSON
13 Director Technology .... Chet KASPER
06 Registrar/Inst Info Systems Mgr .... Sherri SCHOFIELD
37 Director Student Financial Aid .... Tina MILLER
07 Director of Admissions .... Elaine LEHRE
88 Land Grant Director .... Stephen YANNI
30 Director of Development .... Kathy ADAIR
08 Library Director .... Megan CLARKE

Bay de Noc Community College (O)

2001 N Lincoln Road, Escanaba MI 49829-2510
County: Delta FICE Identification: 002240
Unit ID: 168883
Telephone: (906) 786-5802 Carnegie Class: Assoc/MT-VT-High Trad
FAX Number: (906) 789-6952 Calendar System: Semester
URL: www.baycollege.edu
Established: 1962 Annual Undergrad Tuition & Fees (In-District): $4,460
Enrollment: 2,024 Coed
Affiliation or Control: Local IRS Status: 501(c)3
Highest Offering: Associate Degree
Accreditation: NH, ADNUR

01 President .... Dr. Laura COLEMAN
11 VP of Operations .... Ms. Christine WILLIAMS
12 VP of Finance & West Campus .... Mr. Kevin CARLSON
49 Exec Dean of Arts/Sciences & AS .... Dr. Matthew BARRON
50 Exec Dean of Business/Tech/WD .... Mr. Mark KINNEY
30 VP of College Advancement .... Ms. Kim CARNE
37 Director of Financial Aid .... Ms. Laurie SPANGENBERG
07 Dean Admission Services .... Vacant
15 Director of Human Resources .... Mrs. Bridget DEGROOT
18 Director of Buildings & Grounds .... Mr. Ralph CURRY
76 Dean of Allied Health .... Ms. Jeanette STEBELTON
32 Director of Student Life .... Mr. Dave LAUR

103 Exec Dir Professional Workforce Dev .... Mr. Robert PONTIUS
08 Head Librarian .... Mr. Oscar DELONG
04 Exec Admin Asst to President .... Mrs. Laura JOHNSON
06 Registrar .... Vacant
106 Director of Online Learning .... Mr. Joseph MOLD
84 Executive Dean of Student Services .... Mr. Travis BLUME

Calvin College (A)

3201 Burton Street, SE, Grand Rapids MI 49546-4388
County: Kent FICE Identification: 002241
Unit ID: 169080
Telephone: (616) 526-6000 Carnegie Class: Bac-Diverse
FAX Number: (616) 526-8551 Calendar System: 4/1/4
URL: www.calvin.edu
Established: 1876 Annual Undergrad Tuition & Fees: $30,660
Enrollment: 3,993 Coed
Affiliation or Control: Christian Reformed Church IRS Status: 501(c)3
Highest Offering: Master's
Accreditation: NH, CS, ENG, MUS, NURSE, SP, SW, TEAC

01 President .... Dr. Michael K. LE ROY
05 Provost .... Dr. Cheryl BRANDSEN
10 Vice Pres Admin/Finance .... Ms. Sally VANDER PLOEG
30 Vice President for Advancement .... Mr. Kenneth ERFFMEYER
84 Vice Pres Enrollment Management .... Mr. Russell J. BLOEM
32 Vice President Student Life .... Dr. Sarah VISSER
15 Vice President People/Strategy & IT .... Mr. Todd K. HUBERS
13 Assoc Vice President for IT .... Mr. Brian PAIGE
28 Exec Assoc for Diversity/Inclusion .... Dr. Michelle LOYD-PAIGE
42 College Chaplain .... Dr. Mary HULST
21 Director of Finance .... Ms. Barbara BOERS
08 Dean of the Library .... Mr. David MALONE
29 Director Alumni/Parent Relations ..... Mr. Michael J. VAN DENEND
06 Director Academic Svcs/Registrar .... Mr. Thomas L. STEENWYK
39 Dean of Residence Life .... Mr. John WITTE
35 Dean of Student Development .... Mr. C. Robert CROW
88 Dean of Students for Judicial Affs ...... Ms. Jane E. HENDRIKSMA
46 Dean of Research & Scholarship .... Dr. Matthew WALHOUT
108 Dean Institutional Effectiveness .... Dr. Michael STOB
83 Acad Dean Lang/Soc Sci/Context Disc .. Dr. Elizabeth VANDERLEI
81 Acad Dean Educ/Kinesio/Nat Sci/Math .... Dr. Stanley L. HAAN
04 Senior Executive Associate .... Mr. Robert A. BERKHOF
36 Director of Career Development .... Ms. TaRita JOHNSON
09 Dir Institutional/Enroll Research .... Mr. Thomas A. VAN ECK
26 Dir Communications & Brand Strategy ..... Mr. Timothy L. ELLENS
27 Director of Marketing .... Ms. Jeanne NIENHUIS
88 Director Social Research Center .... Dr. Neil CARLSON
19 Director of Campus Safety .... Mr. William T. CORNER
18 Director Physical Plant .... Mr. Philip D. BEEZHOLD
24 Director Instruc Resources Center .... Mr. Randal G. NIEUWSMA
38 Director Broene Counseling Center .... Vacant
23 Director Health Services .... Dr. Laura CHAMPION
92 Director Honors Program .... Dr. Bruce BERGLUND
41 Athletic Director Men .... Dr. James TIMMER, JR.
41 Athletic Director Women .... Dr. Nancy L. MEYER
102 Dir Foundation/Corporate Relations .... Ms. Jodi OVERMAN
104 Director Study Abroad .... Dr. Donald DEGRAAF
105 Director Web Services .... Mr. Luke ROBINSON
37 Director Student Financial Aid .... Mr. Paul R. WITTE, III
44 Director Annual Giving & Engagement .... Mr. Rick TREUR
53 Dean of Education .... Dr. James ROOKS
07 Director of Admissions/Counseling .... Mr. Ben ARENDT

Calvin Theological Seminary (B)

3233 Burton Street, SE, Grand Rapids MI 49546-4387
County: Kent FICE Identification: 002242
Unit ID: 169099
Telephone: (616) 957-6036 Carnegie Class: Spec-4-yr-Faith
FAX Number: (616) 957-8621 Calendar System: Semester
URL: www.calvinseminary.edu
Established: 1876 Annual Graduate Tuition & Fees: N/A
Enrollment: 291 Coed
Affiliation or Control: Christian Reformed Church IRS Status: 501(c)3
Highest Offering: Doctorate; No Undergraduates
Accreditation: THEOL

01 President .... Rev. Julius T. MEDENBLIK
05 Dean of Academic Programs .... Dr. Ronald J. FEENSTRA
20 Assoc Academic Dean .... Ms. Mary L. VANDENBERG
06 Registrar .... Ms. Joan BEELEN
32 Dean of Students .... Rev. Jeff SAJDAK
08 Theological Librarian .... Rev. Lugene L. SCHEMPER
10 Chief Financial & Operations Ofcr .... Ms. Jinny DE JONG
30 Director of Development .... Mr. Robert KNOOR
36 Director of Mentored Ministries .... Rev. Alvern GELDER
07 Dir of Admissions/Enrollment Mgmt .... Mr. Aaron EINFELD
37 Director of Financial Aid .... Mrs. Jennifer SETTERGREN

Career Quest Learning Center (C)

3215 S. Pennsylvania Avenue, Lansing MI 48910
County: Ingham FICE Identification: 039153
Unit ID: 446136
Telephone: (517) 318-3330 Carnegie Class: Assoc/HVT-High Non
FAX Number: (517) 318-3331 Calendar System: Other
URL: www.careerquest.edu
Established: 1995 Annual Undergrad Tuition & Fees: N/A
Enrollment: 408 Coed
Affiliation or Control: Proprietary IRS Status: Proprietary
Highest Offering: Associate Degree
Accreditation: COE

01 President & CEO .... Robert MCCART

Central Michigan University (D)

1200 S. Franklin Street, Mount Pleasant MI 48859
County: Isabella FICE Identification: 002243
Unit ID: 169248
Telephone: (989) 774-4000 Carnegie Class: DU-Higher
FAX Number: (989) 774-3537 Calendar System: Semester
URL: www.cmich.edu
Established: 1892 Annual Undergrad Tuition & Fees (In-State): $11,850
Enrollment: 26,879 Coed
Affiliation or Control: State IRS Status: 501(c)3
Highest Offering: Doctorate
Accreditation: NH, ART, ARCPA, AUD, BUS, BUSA, CAATE, CIDA, CLPSY, DIETD, DIETI, ENG, JOUR, #MED, MUS, NAIT, NRPA, PTA, SCPSY, SP, SPAA, SW, TEAC

01 President .... Dr. George E. ROSS
05 Executive VP/Provost .... Dr. Michael A. GEALT
10 Vice Pres Finance/Admin Svcs .... Mr. Barrie J. WILKES
86 Vice Pres Govt & Ext Relations .... Ms. Kathleen M. WILBUR
84 Vice Pres Enrollment & Student Svcs ..... Mr. Steven L. JOHNSON
30 Vice Pres Advancement .... Mr. Robert K. MARTIN
88 Vice Provost Academic Development .... Mr. Peter G. ROSS
13 Vice President Info Technology/CIO .... Dr. Roger E. REHM
21 AVP Fin Svcs & Reporting/Controller .... Ms. Mary M. HILL
26 AVP University Communications .... Ms. Sherry S. KNIGHT
18 Assoc Vice Pres Facilities Mgmt .... Mr. Stephen P. LAWRENCE
109 Interim Exec Dir Auxiliary Services .... Mr. Calvin H. SEELYE
39 Director Residence Life .... Ms. Kathleen GARDNER
28 Assoc Vice Pres Diversity .... Ms. Carolyn M. DUNN
15 Assoc VP Human Resources .... Ms. Lori L. HELLA
20 Vice Provost Academic Effectiveness ... Dr. Claudia B. DOUGLASS
108 Director Curriculum & Assessment .... Mr. Michael A. CARSON
88 Sr Vice Provost Academic Admin .... Dr. Ray L. CHRISTIE
46 Interim VP Rsrch & Dean Grad Stds .... Dr. David E. ASH
44 Assoc Vice President Advancement .... Mr. Edward A. TOLCHER
08 Interim Dean of Libraries .... Ms. Kathy M. IRWIN
32 Assoc VP Student Affairs .... Mr. Anthony A. VOISIN
35 Executive Director Student Affairs .... Mr. Shaun HOLTGRIEVE
88 Exec Dir Acad Advis/Assistance .... Ms. Michelle L. HOWARD
29 Exec Dir of Alumni Relations .... Ms. Marcie M. OTTEMAN
09 Exec Dir Institutional Research .... Dr. Robert M. ROE
22 Exec Dir Civil Rights/Inst Equity .... Ms. Katherine M. LASHER
07 Director Undergraduate Admissions .. Mr. Thomas W. SPEAKMAN
43 Vice President & General Counsel .... Dr. Manuel R. RUPE
06 Registrar .... Mr. Keith J. MALKOWSKI
37 Director Scholarships/Financial Aid .... Mr. Kirk M. YATS
36 Director Career Services .... Ms. Julia B. SHERLOCK
41 Assoc VP/Director of Athletics .... Mr. David W. HEEKE, JR.
38 Director Counseling Center .... Mr. Ross J. RAPAPORT
25 Director Financial Plan & Budgets .... Mr. Joseph L. GARRISON
27 Sr Assoc Director Public Relations .... Ms. Heather L. SMITH
19 Chief of Police .... Mr. William YEAGLEY, JR.
40 Director CMU Bookstore .... Mr. Barry D. WATERS
81 Dean College of Sci & Engineering .... Dr. Ian R. DAVISON
76 Dean College of Health Professions .... Dr. Tom J. MASTERSON
63 Dean College of Medicine .... Dr. George E. KIKANO
83 Dean Col Hum/Soc/Behav Sci .... Dr. Pamela S. GATES
57 Dean College Comm/Fine Arts .... Dr. Janet HETHORN
50 Dean College of Business Admin .... Dr. Charles T. CRESPY
53 Dean College Education/Human Svcs .... Dr. Dale-Elizabeth PEHRSSON
04 Executive Assistant to President .... Ms. Mary Jane FLANAGAN
85 Exec Dir International Affairs .... Mr. William A. HOLMES
96 Dir Contract & Purchasing Svcs .... Mr. Thomas P. TRIONFI
92 Director Honors Program .... Dr. Phame M. CAMARENA
93 Exec Dir Ctr Inclusion & Diversity .... Dr. Traci L. GUINN
102 Dir Corp & Foundation Relations .... Ms. Kimberly R. HOUSTON-PHILPOT
104 Director Study Abroad .... Ms. Dianne S. DESALVO

Chamberlain College of Nursing-Troy (E)

200 Kirts Blvd, Ste C, Troy MI 48084
Telephone: (248) 817-4140 Identification: 770851
Accreditation: &NH, NURSE

† Regional accreditation is carried under the parent institution in Addison, IL

Cleary University (F)

3750 Cleary Drive, Howell MI 48843
County: Livingston FICE Identification: 002246
Unit ID: 169327
Telephone: (800) 686-1883 Carnegie Class: Spec-4-yr-Bus
FAX Number: N/A Calendar System: Semester
URL: www.cleary.edu
Established: 1883 Annual Undergrad Tuition & Fees: $20,000
Enrollment: 537 Coed
Affiliation or Control: Independent Non-Profit IRS Status: 501(c)3
Highest Offering: Master's
Accreditation: NH

01 President & CEO .... Mr. Jayson BOYERS
05 VP Academic Affairs & Provost .... Dr. Lance LEWIS
10 VP Finance & Administration .... Ms. Judy WALKER
26 VP Communications & Enrollment Mgmt .... Dr. Matt BENNETT
06 Asst VP Academic Svcs/Registrar .... Ms. Dawn M. FISER
04 Exec Asst to Pres/Board of Trustees .... Ms. Linda T. RENTZ
20 Dean College Undergrad Studies .... Ms. Dawn MARKELL
85 Dean International Students .... Ms. Sadhana ALANGAR
13 Exec Director/Chief Info Officer .... Mr. David G. BOWERS
09 Dir Institutional Research/Analysis .... Mr. Tim VEENSTRA
109 Chief Auxiliary Services Officer .... Mr. Gary BACHMAN
30 Exec Dir Development/Alumni Rel .... Ms. Janet FILIP
37 Director Financial Aid .... Ms. Vesta SMITH-CAMPBELL
36 Dir Career Services & Placement .... Ms. Peggy SIMPSON
40 Director Bookstore Services .... Ms. Sheila THOMPSON
07 Director of Admissions .... Ms. Carrie BONOFIGLIO
15 Chief Human Resource Officer .... Ms. Julie SVERID
41 Athletic Director .... Mr. Ward MULLENS
44 Director Annual or Planned Giving .... Ms. Josephine JABARA

College for Creative Studies (G)

201 E Kirby, Detroit MI 48202-4034
County: Wayne FICE Identification: 006771
Unit ID: 169442
Telephone: (313) 664-7400 Carnegie Class: Spec-4-yr-Arts
FAX Number: (313) 872-8377 Calendar System: Semester
URL: www.collegeforcreativestudies.edu
Established: 1906 Annual Undergrad Tuition & Fees: $38,950
Enrollment: 1,459 Coed
Affiliation or Control: Independent Non-Profit IRS Status: 501(c)3
Highest Offering: Master's
Accreditation: NH, ART, CIDA

01 President .... Mr. Richard L. ROGERS
100 Exec Asst to Pres & Sec to Board .... Ms. Sandra WILSON
04 Admin Assistant to the President .... Ms. Brigette NEAL
05 Provost & VP for Academic Affairs .... Mr. Sooshin CHOI
10 Vice Pres Administration & Finance .... Ms. Anne D. BECK
84 Vice Pres Enrollmnt & Student Svcs .... Ms. Julie HINGELBERG
30 Vice Pres Institutional Advancement .... Ms. Nina HOLDEN
20 Assoc Provost Faculty Affairs .... Ms. Sharon PROCTER
58 Dean Graduate Studies .... Ms. Joanne HEALY
57 Dean Undergraduate Studies .... Mr. Vince CARDUCCI
32 Dean of Students .... Mr. Daniel LONG
06 Registrar & Acad Advising Director .... Ms. Nadine ASHTON
07 Director of Admissions .... Ms. Carla GONZALEZ
37 Director Financial Aid .... Ms. Kristin MOSKOVITZ
35 Director Student Life .... Mr. Michael COLEMAN
85 Director Intl Student Services .... Mr. Francisco LOPEZ
28 Director of Multicultural Affairs .... Mr. Cliff HARRIS
51 Dir Continuing & Precollege Studies .... Ms. Jane STEWART
31 Dir of Community Arts Partnerships .... Mr. Mikel BRESEE
08 Director Library .... Ms. Beth WALKER
19 Director of Safety & Security .... Vacant
18 Director Facilities & Admin Svcs .... Vacant
13 Director Information Technology .... Mr. Greg FRASER
90 Director of Academic Technologies .... Ms. Laurie EVANS
21 Director Business Services .... Ms. Kerri MCKAY
15 Director Human Resources .... Ms. Gina FINNEY
26 Director Marketing & Communications ..... Mr. Marcus POPIOLEK
44 Dir Annual Giving/Donor Services .... Ms. Elizabeth KLOS
36 Director Career Services .... Ms. Terese NEHRA
29 Asst Dir Annual Giv/Alumni Rels .... Mr. Anthony SPANGLER
38 Personal Counselor .... Ms. Valerie WEISS
40 Manager Bookstore .... Ms. Glen MORREN
39 Director of Residence Life .... Mr. Ryan HARRISON
102 Dir Foundation/Corporate Relations .... Ms. Shannon MCPARTLON
108 Assoc Provost for Curriculum .... Ms. Donna LANTZ

Compass College of Cinematic Arts (H)

41 Sheldon Boulevard, SE, Grand Rapids MI 49503
County: Kent FICE Identification: 041633
Unit ID: 459417
Telephone: (616) 988-1000 Carnegie Class: Spec-4-yr-Arts
FAX Number: (616) 458-4676 Calendar System: Other
URL: www.compass.edu
Established: 2003 Annual Undergrad Tuition & Fees: $14,175
Enrollment: 96 Coed
Affiliation or Control: Independent Non-Profit IRS Status: 501(c)3
Highest Offering: Baccalaureate
Accreditation: ACCSC

01 President .... Keri LOWE
03 VP of Institutional Affairs .... Austin MORSE
05 Director of Education .... Dr. Mark VANDERMEER
10 Finance Manager .... Laura COULIER
26 Director Marketing & Recruiting .... Tom LOWE
07 Admissions Manager .... Amy HILLS

Concordia University Ann Arbor (I)

4090 Geddes Road, Ann Arbor MI 48105-2797
County: Washtenaw FICE Identification: 002247
Unit ID: 169363
Telephone: (734) 995-7300 Carnegie Class: Bac-Diverse
FAX Number: (734) 995-4610 Calendar System: Semester
URL: www.cuaa.edu
Established: 1962 Annual Undergrad Tuition & Fees: $26,910
Enrollment: 829 Coed
Affiliation or Control: Lutheran Church - Missouri Synod
IRS Status: 501(c)3
Highest Offering: Master's
Accreditation: NH, TED

01 President ....Rev. Patrick FERRY
03 Executive VP & Chief Oper Ofcr ....Mr. Allen PROCHNOW
11 VP of Admin/Campus Chief Exec ....Mr. Curt GIELOW
05 Sr VP Academic Affairs ....Dr. William CARIO
10 Vice Pres Finance/CFO ....Ms. Joan SCHOLZ
07 Director of Enrollment Services ....Mr. Jonathon BAHR
32 Executive Director Student Life ....Rev. John RATHJE
38 Director Student Counseling ....Mrs. Gina VERSEMAN
39 Director Residence Life ....Mr. Dauthan KEENER
41 Director of Athletics ....Mr. Lonnie PRIES
42 Director of Spiritual Life ....Mr. Robert MCKINNEY
18 Director Buildings & Grounds ....Mr. Jerry NOVAK
19 Director Security/Safety ....Mr. James STEPHENSON
13 Director IT Services ....Mr. Christopher RAASCH
30 Director of Development ....Mr. Martin MORO
09 Director of Institutional Research ....Dr. Mae KELLER
08 Coordinator of Library Services ....Mr. Michael O'LEARY
15 Human Resources Generalist ....Mrs. Barb WALTHER
53 Campus Dean School of Education ....Dr. Harvey SCHMIT
50 Campus Dean School of Business ....Dr. Suzanne SIEGLE
66 Campus Dean School of Nursing ....Dr. Cynthia FENSKE
49 Campus Dean School Arts & Sciences ...Dr. Robert MCCORMICK
09 Campus Coord of Acad Operations ....Dr. Kelsi ANDERSON

Cornerstone University (A)

1001 E Beltline Avenue, NE, Grand Rapids MI 49525-5897
County: Kent FICE Identification: 002266
Unit ID: 170037
Telephone: (616) 949-5300 Carnegie Class: Masters/L
FAX Number: (616) 222-1540 Calendar System: Semester
URL: www.cornerstone.edu
Established: 1941 Annual Undergrad Tuition & Fees: $26,100
Enrollment: 2,770 Coed
Affiliation or Control: Independent Non-Profit IRS Status: 501(c)3
Highest Offering: Doctorate
Accreditation: NH, MUS, SW, TEAC, THEOL

01 President ....Dr. Joseph M. STOWELL
03 Executive Vice President ....Mr. Marc FOWLER
05 Chief Academic Officer ....Dr. John VERBERKMOES
10 Chief Financial Officer ....Mrs. Dee MOONEY
88 Vice President of Broadcasting ....Mr. Chris LEMKE
32 Vice Pres Student Development ....Mr. Gerald LONGJOHN
30 VP of Advancement ....Mr. Bob SACK
20 Dean of Curriculum & Accreditation ....Dr. Pete MUIR
73 Dean Grand Rpds Theol Seminary ....Mr. John VER BERKMOES
108 Assoc Dean Assessment/Stdnt Success ....Mrs. Emily GRATSON
35 Director of Student Services ....Mr. Keith DEBOER
08 Director of Miller Library ....Mr. Fred SWEET
37 Director Financial Services ....Mrs. Carol CARPENTER
21 Controller ....Mr. Scott STEWART
88 Director of Retention ....Mrs. Kay LANDRUM
41 Athletic Director ....Mr. Chip HUBER
15 Director of Human Resources ....Mrs. Emilie AZKOUL
18 Director of Campus Services ....Mr. Bob PRIOLO
19 Director of Campus Safety ....Mr. Brandan BISHOP
29 Director of Alumni ....Mrs. Amanda LAWRENCE
06 Registrar ....Mrs. Gail DUHON
24 Director of Technical Support ....Mr. Dan MILLS
38 Director of the Counseling Center ....Mr. Scott COUREY
92 Director of Honors Program ....Mr. Michael STEVENS
07 Director of Admissions ....Mr. Dave EMERSON
04 Administrative Asst to President ....Mrs. Beth LONGJOHN

Cranbrook Academy of Art (B)

39221 Woodward Avenue, PO Box 801,
Bloomfield Hills MI 48303-0801
County: Oakland FICE Identification: 002248
Unit ID: 169424
Telephone: (248) 645-3300 Carnegie Class: Spec-4-yr-Arts
FAX Number: (248) 645-3591 Calendar System: Semester
URL: www.cranbrook.edu
Established: 1932 Annual Graduate Tuition & Fees: N/A
Enrollment: 156 Coed
Affiliation or Control: Independent Non-Profit IRS Status: 501(c)3
Highest Offering: Master's; No Undergraduates
Accreditation: NH, ART

01 Director ....Mr. Christopher SCOATES
06 Registrar/Fin Aid & Admiss Mgr ....Ms. Leslie TOBAKOS

Davenport University (C)

6191 Kraft Avenue, S.E., Grand Rapids MI 49512
County: Kent FICE Identification: 002249
Unit ID: 169479
Telephone: (616) 698-7111 Carnegie Class: Masters/L
FAX Number: N/A Calendar System: Semester
URL: www.davenport.edu
Established: 1866 Annual Undergrad Tuition & Fees: $15,952
Enrollment: 8,715 Coed
Affiliation or Control: Independent Non-Profit IRS Status: 501(c)3
Highest Offering: Master's
Accreditation: NH, CAHIIM, IACBE, MAC, NUR, NURSE, OT, PNUR

01 President ....Dr. Richard J. PAPPAS
30 Exec VP Advancement ....Ms. Peg LUY
46 Exec VP of Quality & Effectiveness ....Dr. Scott EPSTEIN
15 Exec VP Human/Organizational Devel ....Mr. Dave VENEKLASE
07 Exec VP Admission & Student Svcs ....Mr. Walter O'NEILL
10 Exec Vice President for Finance/CFO ....Mr. Michael S. VOLK
05 Exec VP Academics/Provost ....Dr. Linda RINKER
13 Vice Pres Information Technology ....Mr. Brian MILLER
09 VP for Institutional Research ....Dr. Kathy ABOUFADEL
50 Dean College of Business & Tech ....Dr. Pamela IMPERATO
76 Dean College of Health Professions ....Dr. Karen DALEY
49 Dean College of Arts and Sciences ....Vacant
106 Dean Online ....Mr. Brian MILLER
107 Dean College of Urban Education ....Ms. Susan GUNN
37 Exec Director Financial Aid ....Mr. David DE BOER
26 Executive Dir of Communications ....Mr. Robyn LUYMES
29 Director of Alumni Relations ....Mr. Jason MADDON
21 Controller ....Mr. Michael SLEVA
06 University Registrar ....Ms. Donna MILHAM
41 Director of Athletics ....Mr. Paul LOWDEN
04 Administrative Asst to President ....Ms. Rose KARSTEN
28 Director of Diversity ....Dr. RhaeArn BOOKER
19 Director Security/Safety ....Mr. Matt MILLER

Davenport University Holland (D)

643 S Waverly Road, Holland MI 49423
Telephone: (616) 395-4600 Identification: 770266
Accreditation: &NH

† Regional accreditation is carried under the parent institution in Grand Rapids, MI

Davenport University Lansing (E)

220 E Kalamazoo, Lansing MI 48933
Telephone: (517) 484-2600 Identification: 770268
Accreditation: &NH MAC

† Regional accreditation is carried under the parent institution in Grand Rapids, MI

Davenport University Livonia (F)

19499 Victor Parkway, Livonia MI 48152
Telephone: (734) 943-2800 Identification: 770269
Accreditation: &NH

† Regional accreditation is carried under the parent institution in Grand Rapids, MI

Davenport University Midland (G)

3555 E Patrick Road, Midland MI 48642
Telephone: (989) 835-5588 Identification: 770270
Accreditation: &NH

† Regional accreditation is carried under the parent institution in Grand Rapids, MI

Davenport University Warren (H)

27650 Dequindre Road, Warren MI 48092
Telephone: (586) 558-8700 Identification: 770272
Accreditation: &NH

† Regional accreditation is carried under the parent institution in Grand Rapids, MI

Delta College (I)

1961 Delta Rd., University Center MI 48710-0001
County: Bay FICE Identification: 002251
Unit ID: 169521
Telephone: (989) 686-9000 Carnegie Class: Assoc/MT-VT-Mix Trad/Non
FAX Number: (989) 667-0620 Calendar System: Semester
URL: www.delta.edu
Established: 1961 Annual Undergrad Tuition & Fees (In-District): $3,395
Enrollment: 9,842 Coed
Affiliation or Control: Local IRS Status: 501(c)3
Highest Offering: Associate Degree
Accreditation: NH, ADNUR, COARC, DA, DH, DMS, PTAA, RAD, SURGT

01 President ....Dr. Jean GOODNOW
10 Vice President Finance/Treasurer ....Ms. Debra K. LUTZ
32 Vice President Student & Educ Svcs ...Ms. Margarita MOSQUEDA
05 VP Instruction/Learning Svcs ....Dr. Reva CURRY
30 Ex Dir Delta Col Found/Inst Advance ....Ms. Pam CLARK
20 Dean of Teaching & Learning ....Mr. David PERUSKI
35 Dean of Students ....Mr. Jonathan MILLER
36 Dean Career Educ/Learning Part ....Ms. Ginny PRZYGOCKI
84 Dean of Enrollment Management ....Dr. Russell CURLEY
26 Marketing & Public Info Director ....Ms. Leanne GOVITZ
11 Dir Institutional Effectiveness ....Ms. Andrea L. URSUY
101 Assistant to Pres/Board Secretary ....Ms. Andrea URSUY
25 Director of Corporate Services ....Ms. Jennifer CARROLL
37 Director of Student Financial Aid ....Ms. Lisa MARTENS
15 Director of Human Resources ....Mr. Scott LEWLESS
18 Director of Facilities Management ....Mr. Larry E. RAMSEYER
07 Dir of Admissions & Recruitment ....Mr. Zachary WARD
19 Director of Public Safety ....Mr. Robert BATTINKOFF
88 Director of Learning Centers ....Ms. Kristy NELSON
38 Dir Counseling Advising/Career Svcs ....Ms. Diana GUTIERREZ
21 Business Services Director ....Ms. Barbara WEBB
09 Director of Institutional Research ....Mr. Wm. Michael WOOD
06 Registrar ....Ms. Terri GOULD
13 Chief Information Officer ....Mr. Jason STAHL
40 Bookstore Manager ....Ms. Barbara POWERS
08 Mgr of Library Programs & Services ....Ms. Michele PRATT

Eastern Michigan University (J)

Ypsilanti MI 48197-2207
County: Washtenaw FICE Identification: 002259
Unit ID: 169798
Telephone: (734) 487-1849 Carnegie Class: DU-Mod
FAX Number: (734) 481-1095 Calendar System: Semester
URL: www.emich.edu
Established: 1849 Annual Undergrad Tuition & Fees (In-State): $10,417
Enrollment: 22,401 Coed
Affiliation or Control: State IRS Status: 501(c)3
Highest Offering: Doctorate
Accreditation: NH, #ARCPA, BUS, #CAATE, CACREP, CEA, CIDA, CLPSY, CONST, DIETC, ENGT, MT, MUS, NURSE, OPE, OT, PLNG, SP, SPAA, SW, TED

01 President ....Dr. James M. SMITH
05 Interim Provost ....Dr. Rhonda LONGWORTH
10 Chief Financial Officer ....Mr. Michael VALDES
26 Vice President Communications ....Mr. Walter KRAFT
30 Interim VP Advancement ....Ms. Jill HUNSBERGER
101 VP & Sec to the Board of Regents ....Ms. Vicki REAUME
41 VP/Dir Intercollegiate Athletics ....Ms. Heather LYKE
32 Assoc Vice Pres Student Affairs ....Mr. Calvin PHILLIPS
20 Assoc Prov/Assoc VP Acad Pgm Svcs ....Dr. Rhonda KINNEY LONGWORTH
20 Assoc Prov/Assoc VP Admin ....Dr. James J. CARROLL, III
84 Assoc Vice Pres Enrollment Mgmt ....Mr. Kevin KUCERA
86 Int Exec Dir Govt/Cmty Relations ....Dr. Russ OLWELL
18 VP for Operations and Facilities ....Mr. John P. DONEGAN
15 VP for University Human Resources ....Mr. David TURNER
43 General Counsel/University Attorney ....Ms. Gloria HAGE
13 Asst VP/CIO Information Technolog ....Dr. Carl POWELL
19 Exec Dir Public Safety ....Mr. Robert HEIGHES
88 Advisor to the President ....Mr. Leigh GREDEN
88 Dir Univ House & Special Events ....Ms. Kelly BRENNAN
69 Dean Col Health & Human Svcs ....Dr. Murali NAIR
49 Dean Col of Art & Sciences ....Dr. Thomas VENNER
50 Dean Col of Business ....Dr. Michael TIDWELL
53 Dean Col of Education ....Dr. Michael SAYLER
72 Dean Col of Technology ....Dr. Mohamad QATU
58 Int Assc Prov/AVP Grad Studies/Rsrc ....Dr. Wade TORNQUIST
27 Assoc VP Marketing & Communication ....Mr. Theodore G. COUTILISH
27 Executive Director Media Relations ....Mr. Geoffrey LARCOM
23 Asst VP of Student Well-Being ....Ms. Ellen GOLD
09 Asst VP & Exec Dir Inst Rsrch/Info ....Dr. Bin NING
20 Asst VP for Academic Affairs ....Dr. David WOIKE
21 Asst VP Bus Oper/Student Svcs ....Mr. Brian KULPA
102 Exec Dir Foundation Operations/CFO ....Ms. Laura WILBANKS
88 Ombuds ....Dr. Chiara HENSLEY
29 Exec Dir Alumni Relations ....Ms. Ann THOMPSON
08 Interim University Librarian ....Dr. Susann DEVRIES
88 Dir Charter Schools Program ....Dr. Malverne WINBORNE
92 Director Honors College ....Dr. Rebecca SIPE
39 Dir Housing & Residence Life ....Ms. Jeanette ZALBA
21 Exec Dir Financial Plng & Budget ....Mr. Todd OHMER
88 Dir University Convocation Center ....Mr. Mark MONAHAN
44 Sr Development Officer/Central Svcs ....Ms. Susan RINK
88 Chief Development Officer ....Ms. Jill HUNSBERGER
88 Exec Dir Integrated Content ....Ms. Darcy GIFFORD
88 Gen Mgr WEMU-FM Public Rad ....Ms. Mary MOTHERWELL
06 Registrar ....Ms. Christina SHELL
37 Director Financial Aid ....Ms. Donna HOLUBIK
38 Dir Diversity & Affirmative Action ....Ms. Sharon ABRAHAM
96 Director Purchasing ....Mr. Dean BACKOS
88 Title IX Coordinator ....Dr. Melody A. WERNER
88 Senior Assoc to CFO ....Mr. Daniel KELLY
88 Controller ....Ms. Doris M. CELIAN
88 Director Business Services ....Mr. Bryan HOWARD
88 Dir Business Systems Support ....Mr. Kenneth R. ADKINS

Ecumenical Theological Seminary (K)

2930 Woodward Avenue, Detroit MI 48201-3035
County: Wayne FICE Identification: 040024
Unit ID: 247162
Telephone: (313) 831-5200 Carnegie Class: Spec-4-yr-Faith
FAX Number: (313) 831-1353 Calendar System: Quarter
URL: www.etseminary.edu
Established: 1980 Annual Undergrad Tuition & Fees: N/A
Enrollment: 103 Coed
Affiliation or Control: Independent Non-Profit IRS Status: 501(c)3
Highest Offering: Doctorate
Accreditation: THEOL

01 President ....Dr. Stephen B. MURRAY
05 Vice Pres Academic Affs/Acad Dean ....Dr. Kenneth E. HARRIS
10 Vice Pres Finance/Administration ....Mr. Andrew I. MELTON
30 Dir Inst Advancement/Marketing ....Mr. John CUNNINGHAM
06 Registrar/Coord Acad Initiatives ....Ms. Barbara PYE
08 Library Director ....Mr. Joshua PIKKA
07 Director of Admissions/Recruitment ....Dr. Patricia CHUNN
21 Finance Officer ....Ms. Porsha MALLETT

Ferris State University (L)

1201 S. State Street, Big Rapids MI 49307-2295
County: Mecosta FICE Identification: 002260
Unit ID: 169910
Telephone: (231) 591-2000 Carnegie Class: Masters/M
FAX Number: (231) 591-3592 Calendar System: Semester
URL: www.ferris.edu
Established: 1884 Annual Undergrad Tuition & Fees (In-State): $10,970
Enrollment: 14,600 Coed

Affiliation or Control: State IRS Status: 501(c)3
Highest Offering: First Professional Degree
Accreditation: NH, ACBSP, ART, CAHIIM, CIDA, COARC, CONST, DH, DMS, ENG, ENGT, MLTAD, MT, NMT, NUR, OPT, OPTR, PHAR, RAD, SW, TEAC

01 President ... Dr. David L. EISLER
05 Provost & VPAA ... Dr. Paul A. BLAKE
43 Vice President & General Counsel ... Mr. Miles J. POSTEMA
10 VP of Administration & Finance ... Mr. Jerry L. SCOBY
30 VP of Advancement & Mktg ... Ms. Shelly PEARCY
32 Vice President Student Affairs ... Dr. Jeanine WARD-ROOF
12 President of KCAD & VP of Ferris ... Dr. Leslie BELLAVANCE
12 Interim Dean Extended and Intl ... Ms. Cheryl CLUCHEY
28 VP for Diversity and Inclusion ... Dr. David PILGRIM
88 Assoc Provost of Accreditation ... Dr. Roberta TEAHEN
20 Assoc Provost Retention ... Dr. William POTTER
21 Assistant VP of Finance ... Mr. Mike GRANDY
30 Assoc Vice Pres Advancement ... Mr. David LEPPER
15 Assoc Vice Pres Human Resources ... Ms. Jan BLAIR
30 Assoc Vice Pres for Advancement ... Ms. Carla MILLER
18 Assoc Vice Pres Plant Management ... Mr. Mike HUGHES
84 Associate Dean Enrollment Services ... Ms. Kathy LAKE
07 Dean of Enrollment Services ... Dr. Kristen SALOMONSON
45 Director Budget Planning/Analysis ... Ms. Sally DEPEW
13 Chief Technology Officer ... Vacant
19 Director of Public Safety ... Mr. Bruce BORKOVICH
88 Mgr Stdnt Empl & Financial Aid Adv ... Mr. John RANDLE
88 Director of University Center ... Mr. Mark SCHUELKE
38 Director Counseling & Health Center . Ms. Renee VANDER MYDE
35 Interim Dean of Student Life ... Mr. Nick CAMPAU
88 Dir Multicultural Student Svcs ... Dr. Matthew CHANEY
88 Dir for CLACS ... Ms. Angela ROMAN
88 Director University Recreation ... Ms. Cindy HORN
29 Assoc VP for External Affairs ... Mr. Jeremy MISHLER
09 Dir of Inst Research & Testing ... Ms. Mitzi DAY
39 Director Residential Life ... Mr. Brian MARQUARDT
40 Director Bookstore ... Ms. Karen BOHREN
41 Director of Athletics ... Mr. Perk WEISENBURGER
44 Dir Annual Giving & Advance Svcs ... Ms. Jennifer YONTZ
96 Director Purchasing ... Mr. Michael PETHICK
49 Dean of Arts & Sciences ... Dr. Kristi HAIK
50 Dean of Business ... Dr. David NICOL
53 Dean Educ & Human Svcs ... Mr. Arrick JACKSON
67 Dean of Pharmacy ... Dr. Steve DURST
76 Dean of Health Professions ... Dr. Matthew ADEYANJU
63 Dean Michigan College Optometry ... Dr. David DAMARI
72 Dean of Engineering Technology ... Mr. Larry SCHULT
08 Dean of FLITE ... Dr. Scott GARRISON
04 Executive Asst to the President ... Ms. Elaine KAMPTNER
101 Secretary to the Board ... Ms. Karen HUISMAN
37 Director Financial Aid ... Ms. Sara DEW

Finlandia University (A)

601 Quincy Street, Hancock MI 49930-1882
County: Houghton FICE Identification: 002322
Unit ID: 172440
Telephone: (906) 482-5300 Carnegie Class: Bac-Diverse
FAX Number: (906) 487-7366 Calendar System: Semester
URL: www.finlandia.edu
Established: 1896 Annual Undergrad Tuition & Fees: $22,110
Enrollment: 493 Coed
Affiliation or Control: Evangelical Lutheran Church In America
IRS Status: 501(c)3
Highest Offering: Baccalaureate
Accreditation: NH, MAC, NURSE, PTAA

01 President ... Dr. Philip JOHNSON
10 Chief Financial Officer ... Ms. Angela PRICE
05 Vice Pres Academic & Student Affs ... Dr. Fredi DE YAMPERT
26 VP University Relations ... Ms. Karin VAN DYKE
30 Vice Pres Advancement & Enrollment ... Vacant
04 Executive Administrative Assistant ... Ms. Doreen KORPELA
27 Director Marketing/Communications ... Mr. Michael BABCOCK
102 Dir Grants and Foundation Affairs ... Ms. Terri MARTIN
08 Librarian ... Ms. Rebecca DALY
32 Dir Academic Success & Student Life ... Ms. Erin BARNETT
42 Campus Pastor ... Mr. Soren SCHMIDT
06 Registrar ... Mr. Jason SULLIVAN
13 Director Information Technology ... Mr. Scott BLAKE
41 Athletic Director ... Ms. Kristan SCHUSTER
18 Director of Plant and Facilities ... Mr. Curt HAHKA
21 Controller ... Ms. Lori BAAKKO
37 Director Student Financial Aid ... Ms. Sandra TURNQUIST
36 Career Services Manager ... Mr. Mark CAVIS
09 Institutional Research Analyst ... Mr. Hannu LEPPANEN
40 Bookstore Manager ... Ms. Alana NOLAN
96 Purchaser ... Ms. Janine NOTTKE
15 Human Resources Specialist ... Ms. Liz WILLIAMS
07 Director of Admissions ... Mr. Travis HANSON
19 Director of Campus Safety/Security ... Mr. Jim HARDEN
28 Director of Diversity ... Dr. Shana PORTEEN
39 Coordinator Residence Life ... Ms. Leann FOGLE
49 Dean College of Arts & Sciences ... Dr. Christine O'NEIL
57 Dean Intl School of Art & Design ... Ms. Denise VANDEVILLE
76 Dean College of Health Science ... Vacant
104 Dean Intl School of Business ... Mr. Kevin MANNINEN

Glen Oaks Community College (B)

62249 Shimmel Road, Centreville MI 49032-9719
County: Saint Joseph FICE Identification: 002263
Unit ID: 169974
Telephone: (269) 467-9945 Carnegie Class: Assoc/MT-VT-Mix Trad/Non
FAX Number: (269) 467-4114 Calendar System: Semester
URL: www.glenoaks.edu
Established: 1965 Annual Undergrad Tuition & Fees (In-District): $3,168
Enrollment: 1,104 Coed
Affiliation or Control: Local IRS Status: 501(c)3
Highest Offering: Associate Degree
Accreditation: NH, MAC

01 President ... Dr. David DEVIER
05 Dean of Academics/Extended Learning ... Dr. Patricia MORGENSTERN
10 Dean of Finance/Administrative Svcs ... Mr. Bruce ZAKRZEWSKI
32 Assistant Dean of Student Services ... Ms. Tonya HOWDEN
66 Dean of Nursing ... Mr. Bill LEDERMAN
84 Asst Dean Enrollment Svcs/Registrar ... Ms. Beverly ANDREWS
08 Director Learning Resources Center ... Ms. Betsy S. MORGAN
21 Accountant ... Ms. Jennifer DODSON
18 Director of Buildings/Grounds ... Mr. Jay PARKER
07 Director of Admissions ... Ms. Adrienne SKINNER
37 Dir of Financial Aid/Scholarships ... Ms. Jean ZIMMERMAN
41 Director of Athletics ... Ms. Courtney IVAN
09 Institutional Effect/Rsrch Analyst ... Ms. Tammy RUSSELL
15 Personnel Coordinator ... Ms. Candy BOHACZ
26 Public Relations/Marketing ... Ms. Valorie JUERGENS

Gogebic Community College (C)

E4946 Jackson Road, Ironwood MI 49938-1366
County: Gogebic FICE Identification: 002264
Unit ID: 169992
Telephone: (906) 932-4231 Carnegie Class: Assoc/MT-VT-High Trad
FAX Number: (906) 932-5541 Calendar System: Semester
URL: www.gogebic.edu
Established: 1931 Annual Undergrad Tuition & Fees (In-District): $4,344
Enrollment: 1,119 Coed
Affiliation or Control: Local IRS Status: 501(c)3
Highest Offering: Associate Degree
Accreditation: NH, MAC

01 President ... Mr. James A. LORENSON
05 Dean of Instruction/Dir Exten Pgm ... Vacant
10 Dean of Business Services ... Mr. Erik M. GUENARD
32 Dean of Student Services ... Ms. Jeanne GRAHAM
37 Dir Financial Aid/Veterans Svcs ... Ms. Suzetta R. FORBES
76 Director of Allied Health Program ... Ms. Nicole ROWE
88 Director of Ski Area Management ... Mr. James VANDERSPOEL
08 Dir Learning Resource/Instruct Tech .. Ms. Kathryn MACIEJEWSKI
13 Director of Computer Services ... Ms. Kathie A. MUNN
07 Dir of Admission/Public Information ... Ms. Kim ZECKOVICH
30 Dir of Institutional Development ... Ms. Kelly MARZCAK
15 Director of Human Resources ... Ms. Ashley PAQUETTE
88 Transfer Coordinator ... Ms. Jennifer FORSHEY
06 Asst Registrar/Institutional Rschr ... Ms. Miranda LAWVER
04 Administrative Asst to President ... Ms. Linda M. GUSTAFSON

Grace Bible College (D)

1011 Aldon Street, SW, Grand Rapids MI 49509-1998
County: Kent FICE Identification: 002265
Unit ID: 170000
Telephone: (616) 538-2330 Carnegie Class: Bac/Assoc-Mixed
FAX Number: (616) 538-0599 Calendar System: Semester
URL: www.gbcol.edu
Established: 1939 Annual Undergrad Tuition & Fees: $12,268
Enrollment: 700 Coed
Affiliation or Control: Independent Non-Profit IRS Status: 501(c)3
Highest Offering: Master's
Accreditation: NH, BI

01 President ... Dr. Kenneth B. KEMPER
05 Provost ... Mrs. Kim PILIECI
10 Vice Pres Finance/Bus Operations ... Mr. Douglas VRIESMAN
11 Exec Vice President Operations ... Mr. Brian P. SHERSTAD
32 Assoc Vice Pres Community Life ... Mr. Kyle BOHL
04 Executive Assistant to President ... Mrs. Joyce A. STORMS
06 Registrar ... Ms. Linda K. SILER
44 Fund Development Director ... Mr. Steve HILBRANDS
08 Director Library Services ... Mr. Jeff BRODRICK
37 Director of Financial Aid ... Mr. Kurt POSTMA
84 Assoc Vice Pres for Enrollment ... Mr. Kevin E. GILLIAM
13 Director of Information Technology ... Mr. Mark LOVE
18 Director of Maintenance ... Mr. Nathan JOHNSON
41 Athletic Director ... Mr. Gary BAILEY
42 Campus Ministry Coordinator ... Mr. Jim GAMBLE
26 Assoc Vice President of Marketing ... Mr. Zak SORENSEN
108 Director Institutional Assessment ... Mr. Timothy RUMLEY
15 Assoc Vice Pres of Human Resources ... Mrs. Sherea LACY
29 Alumni Services Coordinator ... Ms. Julianne POORT

Grand Rapids Community College (E)

143 Bostwick Avenue, NE, Grand Rapids MI 49503-3295
County: Kent FICE Identification: 002267
Unit ID: 170055
Telephone: (616) 234-4000 Carnegie Class: Assoc/HT-Mix Trad/Non
FAX Number: (616) 234-4005 Calendar System: Semester
URL: www.grcc.edu
Established: 1914 Annual Undergrad Tuition & Fees (In-District): $3,051
Enrollment: 15,668 Coed
Affiliation or Control: Local IRS Status: 501(c)3
Highest Offering: Associate Degree
Accreditation: NH, ACFEI, ADNUR, ART, DA, DH, MAC, MUS, OTA, PNUR, RAD

01 President ... Dr. Steven C. ENDER
05 Prov/Exec VP Academic Affairs ... Dr. Laurie CHESLEY
10 Exec VP Business/Financial Services ... Ms. Lisa FREIBURGER
13 VP & CIO Lrng Res/Tech Solutions ... Mr. David ANDERSON
30 Assoc VP Advancement/Exec Dir Found ... Dr. Kathryn MULLINS
88 Dean of Adult & Developmental Educ ... Mr. John COWLES
103 Director of Workforce Training ... Ms. Julie PARKS
32 Dean Student Affairs ... Ms. Tina OEN-HOXIE
09 Dean Inst Research & Planning ... Ms. Donna KRAGT
49 Dean School of Arts & Sciences ... Dr. Michael VARGO
72 Dean Instruct Design/Info Tech ... Ms. Patti TREPKOWSKI
07 Assoc Dean Admiss/Enrollment Mgmt ... Ms. Diane D. PATRICK
26 Director of Communications ... Ms. Leah NIXON
37 Director of Financial Aid ... Ms. Ann ISACKSON
15 Executive Director Human Resources ... Ms. Cathy WILSON
06 Registrar ... Ms. Diane PATRICK
35 Director Student Activities ... Mr. Eric MULLEN
36 Assoc Director Student Employment ... Ms. Luann WEDGE
08 Director of Library Services ... Ms. Pat INGERSOLL
18 Executive Director of Facilities ... Mr. Thomas J. SMITH
19 Chief of Campus Police ... Ms. Rebecca R. WHITMAN
43 General Counsel ... Ms. Kathy KEATING
96 Director Purchasing ... Mr. Mansfield MATTHEWSON
12 Dean of Lakeshore Campus & Outreach ... Mr. Daniel CLARK
22 Exec Dir Equity/Community/Legis ... Mr. Eric WILLIAMS
28 Dir Diversity Learning Center ... Ms. Christina ARNOLD

Grand Valley State University (F)

1 Campus Drive, Allendale MI 49401-9403
County: Ottawa FICE Identification: 002268
Unit ID: 170082
Telephone: (616) 331-5000 Carnegie Class: Masters/L
FAX Number: (616) 331-3503 Calendar System: Semester
URL: www.gvsu.edu
Established: 1960 Annual Undergrad Tuition & Fees (In-State): $11,363
Enrollment: 25,094 Coed
Affiliation or Control: State IRS Status: 501(c)3
Highest Offering: Doctorate
Accreditation: NH, ARCPA, ART, BUS, BUSA, CAATE, CS, CVT, @DIETC, DMS, ENG, IPSY, MT, MUS, NURSE, OT, PTA, RADDOS, RTT, @SP, SPAA, SW, TED

01 President ... Dr. Thomas J. HAAS
05 Provost/Exec VP Acad & Student Affs ... Dr. Gayle R. DAVIS
10 Interim VP for Finance/Admin ... Mr. D. Scott RICHARDSON
26 Vice President University Relations ... Mr. Matthew E. MCLOGAN
84 Vice President Enrollment Develop ... Ms. Lynn M. BLUE
30 Vice President for Development ... Ms. Karen M. LOTH
28 Vice President Inclusion and Equity ... Dr. Jesse M. BERNAL
43 Vice President and General Counsel ... Mr. Thomas A. BUTCHER
100 Exec Assoc to the President ... Ms. Teri L. LOSEY
32 V Prov/Dean Student Services ... Dr. Eileen SULLIVAN
88 V Prov for Research Admin ... Dr. Robert SMART
20 V Prov Instruct Develop & Innov ... Dr. Christine RENER
23 V Prov for Health ... Dr. Jean NAGELKERK
20 Assoc VP Academic Affairs ... Dr. Maria CIMITILE
20 Asst VP Academic Affairs ... Dr. Edward ABOUFADEL
20 Asst VP for Academic Affairs ... Dr. Suzeanne BENET
20 Asst VP Academic Affairs ... Dr. Chris PLOUFF
20 Asst VP Academic Affairs ... Ms. Kathleen GULEMBO
21 Assoc VP Business/Finance ... Mr. Brian COPELAND
21 Asst VP for University Budgets ... Mr. Jeff MUSSER
15 Assoc VP Human Resources ... Mr. D. Scott RICHARDSON
88 Assoc VP Institutional Marketing ... Ms. Rhonda LUBBERTS
27 Assoc VP for Univ Communications ... Ms. Mary Eilleen LYON
88 Assoc VP for Strategic Initiatives ... Mr. James BACHMEIER
18 Assoc VP Facilities Services ... Mr. Timothy THIMMESCH
88 Assoc VP for Facilities Planning ... Mr. James MOYER
12 Asst VP for Pew Campus Operations ... Ms. Lisa HAYNES
88 Asst VP for Inclusion & Equity ... Ms. Kathleen VANDERVEEN
35 Assoc VP Student Affs & Inclusion ... Dr. Marlene KOWALSKI-BRAUN
88 Assoc VP for Charter SChools ... Mr. Tim WOOD
49 Dean Col of Liberal Arts & Sciences ... Dr. Frederick ANTCZAK
50 Dean Seidman Col of Business ... Dr. Diana LAWSON
70 Dean College of Cmty/Public Service ... Dr. George GRANT
53 Dean College of Education ... Dr. Barry KANPOL
54 Dean Padnos Col Engr & Computing ... Dr. Paul PLOTKOWSKI
76 Dean College of Health Professions ... Dr. Roy OLSSON
88 Dean College Interdisciplin Studies ... Dr. Anne HISKES
66 Dean Kirkhof College of Nursing ... Dr. Cynthia MCCURREN
58 Dean of The Graduate School ... Dr. Jeffrey POTTEIGER
08 Dean University Libraries ... Dr. Lee VAN ORSDEL
07 Director of Admissions ... Ms. Jodi CHYCINSKI
29 Director of Alumni Relations ... Mr. Chris BARBEE
36 Director of Career Center ... Mr. Troy FARLEY
37 Director of Financial Aid ... Ms. Michelle RHODES
88 Director of Hauenstein Center ... Mr. Gleaves WHITNEY
39 Director of Housing & Res Life ... Dr. Andrew BEACHNAU
13 Director of Information Technology ... Ms. Sue KORZINEK
09 Director of Institutional Analysis ... Dr. Philip BATTY
28 Director of AA/EEO Equity Officer ... Mr. Gary GAWEL
96 Director of Procurement Services ... Mr. Kim PATRICK
19 Director Public Safety/Police Chief ... Ms. Renee FREEMAN
38 Director Univ Counseling Center ... Dr. Amber ROBERTS
41 Athletic Director ... Ms. Keri BECKER
40 Bookstore Manager ... Mr. Jerrod NICKELS
85 Chief International Officer ... Dr. Mark SCHAUB
88 Controller ... Ms. Pam BRENZING
88 General Manager WGVU ... Mr. Michael WALENTA
06 Registrar ... Dr. Sherril SOMAN
22 Title IX Coordinator ... Ms. Theresa ROWLAND

Grand Valley State University Meijer Campus (A)

515 South Waverly Road, Holland MI 49423
Telephone: (616) 331-3910 Identification: 770275
Accreditation: &NH

† Regional accreditation is carried under the parent institution in Allendale, MI

Grand Valley State University Pew Campus (B)

401 Fulton St W, Grand Rapids MI 49504
Telephone: (616) 331-5000 Identification: 770274
Accreditation: &NH

† Regional accreditation is carried under the parent institution in Allendale, MI

Great Lakes Christian College (C)

6211 Willow Highway, Lansing MI 48917-1299
County: Eaton FICE Identification: 002269
Unit ID: 170091
Telephone: (517) 321-0242 Carnegie Class: Spec-4-yr-Faith
FAX Number: (517) 321-5902 Calendar System: Semester
URL: www.glcc.edu
Established: 1949 Annual Undergrad Tuition & Fees: $14,540
Enrollment: 160 Coed
Affiliation or Control: Christian Churches And Churches of Christ
IRS Status: 501(c)3
Highest Offering: Baccalaureate
Accreditation: NH

01 President .... Mr. Lawrence L. CARTER
10 Vice President Finance/Operations .... Mr. James A. LOCKWOOD
05 Vice President of Academic Affairs .... Mr. David J. RICHARDS
30 Vice Pres Institutional Advancement .... Mr. Philip E. BEAVERS
84 Vice Pres of Enrollment Management .... Mr. Lloyd S. SCHARER
06 Registrar .... Mr. James ORME
08 Director of Library Services .... Mr. James ORME
37 Financial Aid Director .... Prof. Ryan APPLE
32 Dean of Students/Dir Student Life .... Mr. Ryan BUSHNELL
41 Athletic Director .... Ms. Sasha LOCKWOOD
88 Director of Outreach Ministries .... Mrs. Judy BEAVERS
18 Maintenance Supervisor .... Mr. Chris ADLEMAN

Henry Ford College (D)

5101 Evergreen Road, Dearborn MI 48128-1495
County: Wayne FICE Identification: 002270
Unit ID: 170240
Telephone: (313) 845-9615 Carnegie Class: Assoc/HT-Mix Trad/Non
FAX Number: (313) 845-9658 Calendar System: Semester
URL: www.hfcc.edu
Established: 1938 Annual Undergrad Tuition & Fees (In-District): $2,798
Enrollment: 13,790 Coed
Affiliation or Control: Local IRS Status: 501(c)3
Highest Offering: Baccalaureate
Accreditation: NH, ACFEI, ADNUR, COARC, MAC, PTAA, RAD, SURGT

01 President .... Dr. Stanley C. JENSEN
10 Vice President Financial Services .... Dr. John SATKOWSKI
32 Vice President Student Services .... Dr. Lisa COPPRUE
05 Vice Pres Academic/Career Education .... Vacant
30 Vice President of Development .... Mr. A. Reginald BEST, JR.
11 VP Admin Services/Chief of Staff .... Dr. Cynthia GLASS
26 Vice President Strategy and Info .... Ms. Becky J. CHADWICK
06 Exec Director Registration/Record .... Ms. Holly DIAMOND
38 Assoc Dean Counseling .... Mr. Imad NOURI
103 Director of Workforce Development .... Ms. Patricia CHATMAN
66 Assoc Dean of Nursing .... Ms. Susan SHUNKWILER
08 Director Library .... Mr. Terrence POTVIN
13 Exec Dir Information Technology .... Mr. Sandro SILVESTRI
27 Exec Dir Marketing/Communications .... Mr. Gary ERWIN
37 Exec Director Student Financial Aid .... Mr. Kevin J. CULLER
92 Director Honors Program .... Dr. Michael DAHER
96 Director Purchasing .... Mr. Fred STEINER
40 Manager of College Store .... Ms. Pamela HALL
04 Administrative Asst to President .... Ms. Kathy DIMITRIOU
09 Director of Institutional Research .... Mr. Chris BUCZYNSKI
15 Director Personnel Services .... Mr. William LODGE
19 Director Security/Safety .... Ms. Karen SCHOEN
41 Athletic Director .... Ms. Rochelle TAYLOR
43 Dir Legal Services/General Counsel .... Ms. Eileen HUSBAND

Hillsdale College (E)

33 East College Street, Hillsdale MI 49242-1298
County: Hillsdale FICE Identification: 002272
Unit ID: 170286
Telephone: (517) 437-7341 Carnegie Class: Bac-A&S
FAX Number: (517) 437-3923 Calendar System: Semester
URL: www.hillsdale.edu
Established: 1844 Annual Undergrad Tuition & Fees: $24,592
Enrollment: N/A Coed
Affiliation or Control: Independent Non-Profit IRS Status: 501(c)3
Highest Offering: Doctorate
Accreditation: NH

01 President .... Dr. Larry ARNN
05 Provost .... Dr. David WHALEN
11 VP & Chief Administrative Officer .... Mr. Rich PEWE
43 VP & General Counsel .... Mr. Robert NORTON
07 VP Admissions/Business Improvement .... Mr. Doug BANBURY
26 VP External Affairs .... Mr. Douglas JEFFREY
10 VP Finance .... Mr. Patrick FLANNERY
30 VP Institutional Advancement .... Mr. John CERVINI
88 VP Marketing .... Mr. Matt SCHLIENTZ
32 VP Student Affairs/Dean of Women .... Ms. Diane PHILIPP
27 Associate VP External Affairs .... Mr. Timothy CASPAR
100 Chief Staff Officer .... Mr. Mike HARNER
36 Executive Director Career Services .... Mr. Ken KOOPMANS
15 Executive Director HR .... Ms. Janet MARSH
90 Executive Director ITS .... Mr. Jason SHERRILL
29 Director Alumni Affairs .... Mr. Grigor HASTED
41 Director Athletics .... Mr. Don BRUBACHER
19 Director Campus Security .... Mr. William WHORLEY
40 Director College Bookstore .... Ms. Cindy WILLING
105 Director Digital and Social Media .... Mr. Brad LOWREY
37 Director Financial Aid .... Mr. Rich MOEGGENBERG
23 Director Health Services .... Mr. Brock LUTZ
08 Director Library .... Mr. Dan KNOCH
09 Director Institutional Research .... Mr. George ALLEN
27 Director Marketing .... Mr. Bill GRAY
18 Director Physical Plant .... Mr. Todd CLOW
35 Director Student Activities .... Mr. Anthony MANNO
42 Chaplain .... RtRev. Peter BECKWITH
21 Controller .... Ms. LeAnn CREGER
33 Dean of Men .... Mr. Aaron PETERSEN
06 Registrar .... Mr. Douglas MCARTHUR
04 Admin Assistant to the President .... Ms. Victoria BERGEN
20 Assistant to the Provost .... Mr. Mark MAIER

Hope College (F)

141 E 12th Street, Holland MI 49423-3607
County: Ottawa FICE Identification: 002273
Unit ID: 170301
Telephone: (616) 395-7000 Carnegie Class: Bac-A&S
FAX Number: (616) 395-7922 Calendar System: Semester
URL: www.hope.edu
Established: 1866 Annual Undergrad Tuition & Fees: $30,550
Enrollment: 3,455 Coed
Affiliation or Control: Reformed Church In America IRS Status: 501(c)3
Highest Offering: Baccalaureate
Accreditation: NH, ART, CAATE, DANCE, ENG, MUS, NURSE, SW, TEAC, THEA

01 President .... Dr. John C. KNAPP
05 Interim Provost .... Dr. Karen NORDELL-PEARSON
10 Vice Pres and Chief Fiscal Officer .... Mr. Thomas W. BYLSMA
07 Vice President for Admissions .... Mr. William VANDERBILT
30 VP for Develop & Alumni Engagement .... Mr. Jeffrey PUCKETT
32 VP Student Devel/Dean of Students .... Dr. Richard A. FROST
26 VP Public Affairs & Marketing .... Mrs. Jennifer FELLINGER
08 Librarian .... Ms. Kelly G. JACOBSMA
39 Dir of Residential Life & Housing .... Dr. John E. JOBSON
22 Director of Multicultural Life .... Ms. Vanessa GREENE
94 Director of Women's Studies .... Ms. Priscilla D. ATKINS
81 Dean for Natural Sciences .... Dr. David G. VANWYLEN
79 Interim Dean for Arts & Humanities .... Dr. Marc BAER
83 Dean for Social Sciences .... Dr. Scott D. VANDER STOEP
88 Dean of the Chapel .... Rev. Trygve D. JOHNSON
06 Registrar .... Ms. Carol DEJONG
37 Director of Financial Aid .... Ms. Jill NUTT
36 Director Career Services .... Mr. Dale F. AUSTIN
21 Director of Finance & Business Svcs .... Mr. Douglas VAN DYKEN
13 Director of Operations & Technology .... Mr. Greg MAYBURY
14 Director of Computing & Info Tech .... Mr. Carl E. HEIDEMAN
15 Director Human Resources .... Mrs. Lori MULDER
18 Director Physical Plant .... Mr. Greg MAYBURY
40 Manager of Bookstore .... Mr. Craig THELEN
29 Dir of Parent & Alumni Relations .... Mr. Scott TRAVIS
41 Co-Director of Athletics .... Mr. Tim SCHOONVELD
41 Co-Director of Athletics .... Ms. Melinda LARSON
42 Senior Chaplain .... Rev. Paul H. BOERSMA
38 Asst Dean/Director Counseling Ctr .... Dr. Kristen GRAY
04 Administrative Asst to President .... Mrs. Jan SOMMERVILLE
19 Director Security/Safety .... Mr. Jeffrey HERTEL
25 Chief Contracts/Grants Admin .... Ms. Tracey NALLY

Jackson College (G)

2111 Emmons Road, Jackson MI 49201-3399
County: Jackson FICE Identification: 002274
Unit ID: 170444
Telephone: (517) 787-0800 Carnegie Class: Bac/Assoc-Assoc Dom
FAX Number: (517) 796-8630 Calendar System: Semester
URL: www.jccmi.edu
Established: 1928 Annual Undergrad Tuition & Fees (In-District): $3,912
Enrollment: 5,487 Coed
Affiliation or Control: Local IRS Status: 501(c)3
Highest Offering: Baccalaureate
Accreditation: NH, ACBSP, COARC, DMS, MAC, RAD

01 President/CEO .... Dr. Daniel J. PHELAN
10 Vice President of Finance/CFO .... Mr. Darrell NORRIS
32 Executive Dean of Students .... Mrs. Kristi HOTTENSTEIN
05 Provost .... Dr. Rebekah WOODS
11 Vice Pres of Administration .... Ms. Cindy ALLEN
102 President of JCC Foundation .... Mr. Jason VALENTE
04 Administrative Asst to President .... Vacant
06 Registrar .... Mr. Zakary MCNITT
07 Director of Admissions .... Ms. Karen CUZYDLO
08 Head Librarian .... Ms. Stephanie DAVIS
09 Exec Director of Inst Effectivness .... Mr. Rob STIRTON
100 Chief of Staff .... Ms. Sara JOHNSON
103 Dir Workforce/Career Development .... Ms. Tina MATZ
18 Chief Facilities/Physical Plant .... Mr. Jim JONES
19 Director Security/Safety .... Mr. Jeffrey WHIPPLE
28 Director of Diversity .... Mr. Lee HAMPTON
29 Director Alumni Relations .... Ms. Brigette ROBINSON
37 Director Student Financial Aid .... Ms. Andrew SPOHN
39 Director Student Housing .... Ms. Tasha WARFIELD
41 Athletic Director .... Ms. Heather BATEMAN

Kalamazoo College (H)

1200 Academy Street, Kalamazoo MI 49006-3295
County: Kalamazoo FICE Identification: 002275
Unit ID: 170532
Telephone: (269) 337-7000 Carnegie Class: Bac-A&S
FAX Number: (269) 337-7251 Calendar System: Quarter
URL: www.kzoo.edu
Established: 1833 Annual Undergrad Tuition & Fees: $42,946
Enrollment: 1,461 Coed
Affiliation or Control: Independent Non-Profit IRS Status: 501(c)3
Highest Offering: Baccalaureate
Accreditation: NH

01 President .... Dr. Jorge G. GONZALEZ
05 Provost .... Dr. Michael A. MCDONALD
10 Vice President Business & Finance .... Mr. James E. PRINCE
30 Vice President College Advancement .... Mr. Albert J. DESIMONE
32 VP Student Devel & Dean of Students .... Dr. Sarah B. WESTFALL
85 Associate Provost for Intl Pgms .... Dr. Margaret WIEDENHOEFT
13 Associate Provost for Info Services .... Mr. Gregory S. DIMENT
09 Asst Provost Inst Support/Research .... Ms. Anne T. DUEWEKE
35 Assoc Dean of Stdnts/1st Yr Exper .... Ms. Dana JANSMA
06 Registrar .... Ms. Nicole KRAGT
15 Human Resources Manager .... Ms. Renee E. BOELCKE
07 Dean of Admission and Financial Aid .... Mr. Eric P. STAAB
37 Director of Financial Aid .... Ms. Marian STOWERS
26 Director of College Communication .... Mr. James A. VANSWEDEN
18 Director of Facilities Management .... Mr. Paul W. MANSTROM
40 Director Bookstore .... Ms. Deborah L. THOMPSON
29 Director of Alumni Relations .... Ms. Kimberly J. ALDRICH
38 Director of Student Counseling .... Dr. Kenlanna FERGUSON
88 Director of Advising .... Ms. Lesley J. CLINARD
36 Dir Ctr Career/Professional Devel .... Ms. Joan C. HAWXHURST
20 Associate Provost .... Dr. Laura L. FURGE
04 Administrative Asst to President .... Ms. Melanie K. WILLIAMS
08 Head Librarian .... Dr. Stacy A. NOWICKI
102 Dir Foundation/Corporate Relations .... Ms. Ann M. JENKS
19 Director Security/Safety .... Vacant
41 Athletic Director .... Ms. Kristen J. SMITH
84 Enrollment Data Specialist .... Ms. Linda WIRGAU
101 Secretary of the Institution/Board .... Ms. Melanie K. WILLIAMS

Kalamazoo Valley Community College (I)

6767 West O Avenue, PO Box 4070,
Kalamazoo MI 49003-4070
County: Kalamazoo FICE Identification: 006949
Unit ID: 170541
Telephone: (269) 488-4400 Carnegie Class: Assoc/MT-VT-Mix Trad/Non
FAX Number: (269) 488-4220 Calendar System: Semester
URL: www.kvcc.edu
Established: 1966 Annual Undergrad Tuition & Fees (In-District): $3,060
Enrollment: 9,489 Coed
Affiliation or Control: Local IRS Status: 501(c)3
Highest Offering: Associate Degree
Accreditation: NH, COARC, DH, EMT, MAC

01 President .... Dr. Marilyn J. SCHLACK
05 EVP Instruct/Student Success Svcs .... Dr. Dennis BERTCH
10 Vice President Finance & Business .... Ms. Louise ANDERSON
32 EVP Enrollment/Campus Operations .... Mr. Michael COLLINS
15 Vice President for Human Resources .... Ms. Sandra BOHNET
13 Vice Pres for Admin Svc/Info Tech .... Mr. Terrel F. HUTCHINS
45 VP for Strategic Business/Cmty Dev .... Mr. Craig JBARA
35 Assoc VP for Student Success .... Ms. Laura COSBY
86 Exec Dir Analytics/Special Projects .... Ms. Kathy JOHNSON
19 Director of Public Safety .... Mr. Richard IVES
08 Director of Libraries .... Vacant
07 Dir Admissions/Registration/Records .... Ms. Sarah HUBBELL
09 Dir Planning/Research/Assessment .... Mr. Stephen CANNELL
30 Director Development .... Mr. Steve DOHERTY
37 Director Financial Aid .... Mr. Roger MILLER
18 Dir Facilities/Construction Mgmt .... Mr. Daniel MALEY
96 Director of Purchasing .... Mr. Paul O'CONNELL
21 Business Manager .... Ms. Muriel HICE
66 Director of Nursing .... Vacant

Kalamazoo Valley Community College Arcadia Commons Campus (J)

202 North Rose St Kalamazoo MI 49007
Telephone: (269) 373-7800 Identification: 770276
Accreditation: &NH

† Regional accreditation is carried under the parent institution in Kalamazoo, MI

Kellogg Community College (A)

450 North Avenue, Battle Creek MI 49017-3397
County: Calhoun FICE Identification: 002276
Unit ID: 170550
Telephone: (269) 965-3931 Carnegie Class: Assoc/MT-VT-High Trad
FAX Number: (269) 962-4290 Calendar System: Semester
URL: www.kellogg.edu
Established: 1956 Annual Undergrad Tuition & Fees (In-District): $3,488
Enrollment: 5,929 Coed
Affiliation or Control: Local IRS Status: 501(c)3
Highest Offering: Associate Degree
Accreditation: NH, DH, EMT, PTAA, RAD

01 President Mr. Mark P. O'CONNELL
05 Vice President Instruction Mr. Kevin RABINEAU
11 Vice Pres Administration/Finance Vacant
32 Vice Pres Student & Community Svcs Dr. Kay KECK
10 Chief Financial Officer Mr. Richard SCOTT
13 Chief of Administrative Services Mr. Bob REYNOLDS
57 Chair Arts & Communication Dept Ms. Barbara SUDEIKIS
81 Chair Math & Science Dept Ms. Carole DAVIS
49 Dean Arts/Sciences/Regional Educ Vacant
102 Executive Director KCC Foundation Ms. Teresa DURHAM
96 Director Purchasing Ms. Angela CLEVELAND
06 Registrar Ms. Colleen WRIGHT
08 Director Library Services Ms. Martha STILWELL
41 Director Athletics & PE Mr. Tom SHAW
12 Director of Grahl Center Ms. Roberta GAGNON
12 Director of Fehsenfeld Center Mr. Colin MCCALEB
15 Director Human Resources Ms. Ali ROBERTSON
18 Dir Inst Facilities/Public Safety Mr. John DI PIERRO
51 Director Lifelong Learning Ms. Mary GREEN
09 Director Inst Compliance Reporting Ms. Naomi LIVENGOOD
21 Director of Finance Ms. Tracy BEATTY
12 Director Regional Mfg Tech Center Mr. Tom LONGMAN
35 Dean Student & Community Services Ms. Terah ZAREMBA
26 Dir Public Information & Marketing Mr. Eric GREENE
07 Director of Admissions Ms. Meredith STRAVERS
40 Bookstore Manager Ms. Catherine JAMES
28 Director of Diversity Dr. Jorge ZEBALLOS
04 Executive Asst to President Ms. Rebecca GALLIMORE
103 Dean Workforce Development Dr. Jan KARAZIM
36 Director Career & Emp Services Mr. Patrick CASEY
37 Director Financial Aid Ms. Nikki JEWELL
38 Manager Academic Advising Ms. Donna MALASKI

Kendall College of Art & Design of Ferris State University (B)

17 Fountain Street, NW, Grand Rapids MI 49503
Telephone: (800) 676-2787 Identification: 770273
Accreditation: &NH

† Regional accreditation is carried under the parent institution in Big Rapids, MI

Kettering University (C)

1700 University Avenue, Flint MI 48504-6214
County: Genesee FICE Identification: 002262
Unit ID: 169983
Telephone: (810) 762-9500 Carnegie Class: Masters/M
FAX Number: (810) 762-9837 Calendar System: Semester
URL: www.kettering.edu
Established: 1919 Annual Undergrad Tuition & Fees: $38,430
Enrollment: 2,079 Coed
Affiliation or Control: Independent Non-Profit IRS Status: 501(c)3
Highest Offering: Master's
Accreditation: NH, ACBSP, CS, ENG, ENGR

01 President Dr. Robert K. MCMAHAN
04 Executive Assistant to President Ms. Evelyn YAEGER
04 Assistant to President Ms. Megan HANSON
05 Provost & VP Academic Affairs Dr. James ZHANG
10 VP Administration & Finance Mr. Tom AYERS
84 VP Enrollment Services Mr. Kip DARCY
32 VP Student Life & Dean of Students Ms. Betsy E. HOMSHER
30 VP Univ Advancement/Ext Relations Ms. Susan DAVIES
13 VP Instruct/Admin & Info Technology Ms. Viola SPRAGUE
106 VP Kettering Global Ms. Christine WALLACE
20 Assoc VP Acad Services Vacant
15 Director Human Resources Ms. Beth EWALD
102 Dir of Philanthropy Corp/Found Mr. Thomas SOMMER
29 Dir of Alumni Engagement Mr. Steven BANDURSKI
88 Dir of Philanthropy Indiv Giving Ms. Caroline ETHINGTON
19 Director of Campus Safety Mr. Paul CRANE
37 Director Student Financial Aid Ms. Diane K. KIMES
21 Controller Ms. Beth A. COVERS
09 Director Institution Effectiveness Dr. Edwin IMASUEN
58 Director Graduate Programs Mr. Tom CREECH
18 Director Physical Plant Mr. Joseph ASPERGER
08 Director Library Services Dr. Charles D. HANSON
07 Director Intl & Undergrad Admiss Ms. Tracie JONES
41 Director Athletics/Rec Service Mr. Michael L. SCHAAL
93 Director Minority Student Affairs Mr. L.B MCCUNE
104 Director International Office Dr. Basem ALZAHABI
109 Director Auxiliary Services Ms. Nadine L. THOR
26 Director of Marketing Ms. Julie A. ULSETH
06 Registrar Mr. Michael MOSHER
23 Director Wellness Center Ms. Cristina REED
39 Director Residence Life Ms. Katherine BOSIO
78 Director Coop Educ & Career Svcs Ms. Venetia PETTEWAY
88 MI SBTDC Regional Director Ms. Marsha J. LYTTLE
96 Purchasing Manager Ms. Kathleen A. REMENDER
14 Director of IT Operations Mr. Daniel GARCIA
25 Contract/Grant Specialist Ms. Jodi L. DORR
105 Webmaster Ms. Donna WICKS
88 Dir Center Excellence Teach & Learn Dr. Terri LYNCH-CARIS
88 Dir Enrollment Events/Visitor Rels Ms. Sheila ADAMS COWES
88 Director Special Events Ms. Diane ALDERSON
88 Director Academic Service Center Dr. Natalie CANDELA

Keweenaw Bay Ojibwa Community College (D)

111 Beartown Rd, PO Box 519, Baraga MI 49908
County: Baraga FICE Identification: 041647
Unit ID: 461315
Telephone: (906) 353-4640 Carnegie Class: Tribal
FAX Number: (906) 353-8107 Calendar System: Semester
URL: www.kbocc.edu
Established: 1975 Annual Undergrad Tuition & Fees (In-District): $2,900
Enrollment: 89 Coed
Affiliation or Control: Local IRS Status: 501(c)3
Highest Offering: Associate Degree
Accreditation: NH

01 President Ms. Debra J. PARRISH
05 Dean of Instruction Dr. Lynn AHO
07 Admissions Officer Mr. Patrick RACETTE
10 Business Officer Ms. Megan SHANAHAN
32 Dean of Student Services Ms. Isabelle WELSH
37 Director Financial Aid Ms. Liz JULIO
88 Cultural Advisor Mr. Donald DOWD

Kirtland Community College (E)

10775 N Saint Helen Road, Roscommon MI 48653-9721
County: Roscommon FICE Identification: 007171
Unit ID: 170587
Telephone: (989) 275-5000 Carnegie Class: Assoc/MT-VT-High Trad
FAX Number: (989) 275-6706 Calendar System: Semester
URL: www.kirtland.edu
Established: 1966 Annual Undergrad Tuition & Fees (In-District): $3,725
Enrollment: 1,773 Coed
Affiliation or Control: Local IRS Status: 501(c)3
Highest Offering: Associate Degree
Accreditation: NH, CVT

01 President Dr. Thomas QUINN
05 Vice Pres of Instructional Services Dr. Julie LAVENDER
32 Vice Pres of Student Svcs/Registrar Ms. Michelle VYSKOCIL
10 Vice Pres of Business Services Mr. Jason BROGE
13 Chief Info Ofcr/Title III Proj Dir Mr. Tim SCHERER
97 Dean of General Education/Transfer Mr. Jason TETZLOFF
75 Dean of Occupational Programs Ms. Laura PERCIVAL
08 Director of Library & Tutoring Svcs Ms. Deb SHUMAKER
37 Director of Financial Aid Ms. Christin BATES
18 Director of Facilities Ms. Evelyn SCHENK
15 Dir of Human Resources/Talent Dev Mr. Dale SHANTZ
09 Director of Institutional Research Mr. Nick BAKER
102 Foundation Director Ms. Lynne RUDEN
26 Director of Public Information Ms. Sarah HOLECHECK
07 Admissions Coordinator Ms. Michelle DEVINE

Kuyper College (F)

3333 East Beltline Avenue, NE,
Grand Rapids MI 49525-9749
County: Kent FICE Identification: 002311
Unit ID: 171881
Telephone: (616) 222-3000 Carnegie Class: Bac-Diverse
FAX Number: (616) 988-3608 Calendar System: Semester
URL: www.kuyper.edu
Established: 1939 Annual Undergrad Tuition & Fees: $19,544
Enrollment: 270 Coed
Affiliation or Control: Independent Non-Profit IRS Status: 501(c)3
Highest Offering: Baccalaureate
Accreditation: NH, BI, SW

01 President Dr. Nicholas V. KROEZE
05 Provost Dr. Patricia R. HARRIS
06 Registrar Mr. Kyle WIGBOLDY
10 Vice Pres Business Administration Mr. Duane BRAS
30 Vice Pres College Advancement Mr. Ken CAPISCIOLTO
07 Assistant Director of Admissions Ms. Kirsten HERICH
37 Financial Aid Director Ms. Agnes M. RUSSELL
44 Director Annual/Planned Giving Ms. Teresa JANZEN
04 Assistant to the President Ms. Dawn A. LYNEMA
08 Librarian Ms. Dianne V. ZANDBERGEN
32 Director of Student Life Mr. Curt ESSENBURG
18 Director of Physical Plant Mr. Tim CHUPP
29 Director of Alumni/Public Relations Ms. Hannah SCHIERBEEK
15 Director Personnel Services Ms. Mary CARLSON
13 Director Computing/Info Management Mr. Keith TORNO
49 Arts and Sciences Ms. Teresa RENKEMA
64 Music Dr. Carol HOCHHALTER
70 Social Work Mr. Greg SCOTT
73 Theology Dr. Branson PARLER
85 International Student Services Mr. Josh RUMBARGER
50 Director of Business Leadership Mr. Marc ANDREAS
19 Director Security/Safety Mr. Randy WILLIAMSON

Lake Michigan College (G)

2755 E Napier, Benton Harbor MI 49022-1899
County: Berrien FICE Identification: 002277
Unit ID: 170620
Telephone: (269) 927-1000 Carnegie Class: Bac/Assoc-Assoc Dom
FAX Number: N/A Calendar System: Semester
URL: www.lakemichigancollege.edu
Established: 1946 Annual Undergrad Tuition & Fees (In-District): $4,140
Enrollment: 4,219 Coed
Affiliation or Control: Local IRS Status: 501(c)3
Highest Offering: Baccalaureate
Accreditation: NH, ADNUR, DA, DMS, RAD

01 President Dr. Robert P. HARRISON
11 VP Administrative Services Ms. Anne C. ERDMAN
30 VP Institutional Advance/Planning Vacant
10 Vice President Finance Ms. Kelli HAHN
04 Exec Assistant to the President Ms. Rebecca STEFFEN
05 VP Academics Dr. Leslie KELLOGG
103 Dean Career Education Workforce Dr. Ken FLOWERS
49 Dean Arts & Sciences Dr. Gary ROBERTS
76 Dean Health Sciences Ms. Marla CLARK
32 VP Student Services Mr. Doug SCHAFFER
31 VP Community Engagement Ms. Barbara CRAIG
88 Manager Mainstage Services Mr. Mike NADOLSKI
18 Director Facilities Management Mr. Lee H. VAN GINHOVEN
13 Exec Dir Informational Technology Mr. Randall MELTON
26 Director Marketing & Communications Ms. Candice ELDERS
06 Registrar Ms. Helen HAYS-THOMAS
44 Director Major Gifts/Estate Plng Vacant
102 President College Foundation Mr. Mike WELCH
96 Purchasing Manager Mr. Nathan MAIN
91 Network Administrator Vacant
90 Director Teaching/Learning Center Mr. Mark KELLY
84 Director Enrollment Mgmt Vacant
08 Head Librarian Ms. Diane BAKER
09 Director of Institutional Research Mr. John HULSEBUS
19 Director Security/Safety Mr. Steve SILCOX
39 Director Student Housing Mr. Matt KREVDA
41 Athletic Director Mr. Jason COOPER

Lake Michigan College Bertrand Crossing (H)

1905 Foundation Drive, Niles MI 49120
Telephone: (269) 695-1391 Identification: 770277
Accreditation: &NH

† Regional accreditation is carried under the parent institution in Benton Harbor, MI

Lake Michigan College South Haven (I)

125 Veterans Boulevard, South Haven MI 49090
Telephone: (269) 639-8442 Identification: 770278
Accreditation: &NH

† Regional accreditation is carried under the parent institution in Benton Harbor, MI

Lake Superior State University (J)

650 W Easterday Avenue,
Sault Sainte Marie MI 49783-1699
County: Chippewa FICE Identification: 002293
Unit ID: 170639
Telephone: (906) 632-6841 Carnegie Class: Bac-Diverse
FAX Number: (906) 635-2111 Calendar System: Semester
URL: www.lssu.edu
Established: 1946 Annual Undergrad Tuition & Fees (In-State): $10,580
Enrollment: 2,407 Coed
Affiliation or Control: State IRS Status: 501(c)3
Highest Offering: Master's
Accreditation: NH, ACBSP, CAATE, ENG, ENGT, IFSAC, NURSE, TEAC

01 President Dr. Thomas C. PLEGER
05 Int Provost/VP Academic Affairs Dr. David FINLEY
32 Vice Pres Stdnt Affs/Enroll Svcs Mr. Matt JURVELIN
10 Int Vice President Finance Mr. Morrie WALWORTH
108 Assoc Provost Assess/Grad/Educ Dr. David MYTON
49 Dean ALSS & Emerg Svcs Dr. Paige GORDIER
81 Dean Natural & Math Sciences Dr. Barbara KELLER
66 Interim Dean Nursing Mr. Ronald HUTCHINS
50 Dean Business & Engineering Dr. David FINLEY
53 Asst Dean Education Dr. Donna FIEBELKORN
13 Director IT/Network Admin Mr. Scott OLSON
18 Director Physical Plant Mr. Steve GREGORY
06 Registrar Ms. Nancy NEVE
07 Director of Admissions Mr. Allan CASE
15 Associate VP for Human Resources Mr. Philip ESPINOSA
36 Director of Career Services Ms. Theresa WEAVER
37 Director of Financial Aid Ms. Deborah FAUST
38 Director of Counseling Ms. Kristin LARSON
39 Director Housing/Residential Life Mr. Scott M. KORB
26 Director of Public Affairs Mr. Thomas A. PINK
29 Director Alumni Relations Ms. Susan FITZPATRICK
102 Director of Foundation Mr. Tom COATES
96 Director of Purchasing Ms. Colleen RYE
23 Director Health Services Ms. Karen STOREY
28 Dir Native American Ctr/Diversity Ms. Stephanie SABATINE
41 Athletic Director Ms. Kristin DUNBAR
35 Director Student Life Mr. Scott KORB
40 Bookstore Manager Ms. Amber MCLEAN
09 Institutional Research Analyst Vacant

Lansing Community College (A)

610 N Capitol Avenue, Lansing MI 48933

County: Ingham FICE Identification: 002278

Unit ID: 170657

Telephone: (517) 483-1200 Carnegie Class: Assoc/MT-VT-Mix Trad/Non

FAX Number: (517) 483-1845 Calendar System: Semester

URL: www.lcc.edu

Established: 1957 Annual Undergrad Tuition & Fees (In-District): $3,020

Enrollment: 16,031 Coed

Affiliation or Control: Local IRS Status: 501(c)3

Highest Offering: Associate Degree

Accreditation: NH, ADNUR, COMTA, DH, DMS, EMT, IFSAC, RAD, SURGT

01 President ... Dr. Brent KNIGHT
05 Provost ... Dr. Richard PRYSTOWSKY
10 Sr VP Finance/Admin & Advancement ... Dr. Lisa WEBB SHARPE
21 Chief Financial Officer ... Mr. Don WILSKE
13 Chief Information Officer ... Mr. Kevin BUBB
11 Exec Dir Administrative Svcs ... Ms. Patricia ENGLE
20 Associate VP Academic Affairs ... Dr. Vicki DEKETELAERE
30 Assoc VP External Affs/Development ... Ms. Elva REVILLA
88 Dean Health & Human Services ... Ms. Margie CLARK
103 Dean Community Educ/Workforce Dev ... Mr. Bo GARCIA
49 Dean Arts & Sciences ... Ms. Elaine POGONCHEFF
32 Dean Student Affairs ... Dr. Tanya MCFADDEN
72 Dean Technical Careers ... Mr. Mark COSGROVE
15 Exec Director Human Resources ... Ms. Ann KRONEMAN
28 Chief Diversity Officer ... Dr. Paul HERNANDEZ
26 Director Public Affairs ... Ms. Devon BRADLEY
77 Director Center for Data Science ... Mr. Matt FALL

Lawrence Technological University (B)

21000 W Ten Mile Road, Southfield MI 48075-1058

County: Oakland FICE Identification: 002279

Unit ID: 170675

Telephone: (248) 204-4000 Carnegie Class: Masters/L

FAX Number: (248) 204-3727 Calendar System: Semester

URL: www.ltu.edu

Established: 1932 Annual Undergrad Tuition & Fees: $30,300

Enrollment: 4,015 Coed

Affiliation or Control: Independent Non-Profit IRS Status: 501(c)3

Highest Offering: Doctorate

Accreditation: NH, ACBSP, ART, CIDA, ENG, IACBE

01 President ... Dr. Virinder K. MOUDGIL
04 Exec Assistant to the President ... Ms. Karen MCARDLE
05 Provost ... Dr. Maria J. VAZ
88 Exec Dir Marburger STEM Center ... Ms. Sibrina Nichelle COLLINS
10 Vice Pres Finance/Admin ... Ms. Linda L. HEIGHT
30 Vice Pres of University Advancement ... Ms. Kristen R. DEVRIES
88 Assoc VP Advance/Chief Dev Officer ... Mr. Dennis J. HOWIE
20 Assistant Provost ... Mr. Jim JOLLY
84 Asst Provost Enrollment Management ... Ms. Lisa R. KUJAWA
48 Dean of Architecture & Design ... Mr. Karl DAUBMANN
49 Dean of Arts & Sciences ... Dr. Hsiao-Ping H. MOORE
54 Dean of Engineering ... Dr. Nabil F. GRACE
50 Dean of Management ... Dr. Bahman MIRSHAB
32 Dean of Students ... Mr. Kevin FINN
26 Assoc Vice Pres Mktg & Public Affs ... Mr. Bruce J. ANNETT, JR.
13 Chief Information Officer IT Svcs ... Mr. Tim CHAVIS
07 Director Admissions ... Ms. Jane T. ROHRBACK
06 University Registrar ... Ms. Noreen FERGUSON
08 Director Library ... Mr. Gary R. COCOZZOLI
18 Director Campus Facilities ... Mr. Carey G. VALENTINE
14 Director Help Desk/Services ... Ms. Charlene RAMOS
37 Director of Financial Aid ... Ms. Susie POLI-SMITH
41 Athletic Director ... Mr. Scott TRUDEAU
36 Director of Career Services ... Ms. Peg PIERCE
35 Assistant Dean of Students ... Ms. Cyndi SPOTTS
24 Director Audio Visual Media Svcs ... Mr. Walter G. BIZON
39 Director Residence Life ... Ms. Kimberly OSANTOWSKI
86 Exec Dir Corp & Comm Partnerships ... Mr. Mark J. BRUCKI
102 Dir of Corp & Foundation Relations ... Mr. Howard DAVIS
44 Philanthropy Director ... Ms. Julie VULAJ
44 Philanthropy Director ... Vacant
28 Director of Diversity ... Mr. Kevin FINN
15 Exec Director of Human Resources ... Ms. Deshawn JOHNSON
40 Manager Campus Bookstore ... Ms. Adria RAHN
109 Manager Dining Services ... Ms. Nancy THOMAS
27 Dir Univ Comm & Academic Editor ... Ms. Anne M G. ADAMUS
27 Managing Editor News Bureau ... Mr. Matt ROUSH
19 Director of Campus Safety ... Mr. Steven J. BOGDALEK
29 Manager Alumni Rels/Alumni Giving ... Ms. Lauren N. MORRIS
31 Dir of University Special Events ... Ms. Robin LECLERC
44 Coordinator of Advancement Services ... Ms. Brande' OLIVER
88 University Architect ... Mr. Joseph C. VERYSER
88 Student Engagement Coordinator ... Mr. Phil LUCAS
88 Dir of Academic Achievement Center ... Dr. Gladys M. AVILES
09 Dir of Inst Research/Academic Plng ... Ms. Noreen FERGUSON
96 Purchasing Agent ... Ms. Michelle BUTKOVICH
105 Manager of Web Services ... Mr. Christian FORREST
106 Interim Dir Online Educ/E-learning ... Ms. Lynn MILLER-WIETECHA

Macomb Community College (C)

14500 Twelve Mile Road, Warren MI 48088-9838

County: Macomb FICE Identification: 008906

Unit ID: 170790

Telephone: (586) 445-7241 Carnegie Class: Assoc/MT-VT-High Non

FAX Number: (586) 445-7886 Calendar System: Semester

URL: www.macomb.edu

Established: 1954 Annual Undergrad Tuition & Fees (In-District): $3,169

Enrollment: 22,914 Coed

Affiliation or Control: Local IRS Status: 501(c)3

Highest Offering: Associate Degree

Accreditation: NH, ACFEI, ADNUR, CAHIIM, COARC, EMT, IFSAC, MAC, OTA, PTAA, SURGT

01 President ... Dr. James JACOBS
05 Senior VP/Provost Learning Unit ... Dr. James SAWYER
10 Vice President for Business ... Ms. Elizabeth ARGIRI
15 Vice President for Human Resources ... Ms. Denise WILLIAMS
30 VP College Adv/Community Relations ... Dr Casandra ULBRICH
88 Dean University Relations ... Ms. Donna PETRAS
32 Vice President for Student Services ... Ms. Jill M THOMAS-LITTLE
49 Dean Arts & Sciences ... Dr. Marie PRITCHETT
76 Dean Health/Public Services ... Ms. Charlene MCPEAK
54 Dean Engineering & Adv Tech ... Mr Joseph PETROSKY
50 Dean Business & Info Technology ... Mr. David CORBA
35 Dean of Student Success ... Dr. Susan BOYD
31 Dean Student & Community Services ... Mr. Geary MAIURI
45 Exec Director Planning & Research ... Ms. Cerri Lynn PAVONE
21 Director Finance & Investments ... Ms. Roberta REMIAS
19 Captain College Police ... Mr. Thomas WILK
88 Director Public Service Institute ... Mr. John CALABRESE
26 Director Marketing & Recruitment ... Ms. Audrey TAKACS
09 Director Institutional Research ... Ms. Deirdre SYMS
88 Director Special Research Projects ... Mr. Randal HICKMAN
06 Registrar/Dir Enrollment Services ... Ms. Carrie JEFFERS
102 Director Macomb College Foundation ... Ms. Dawn MAGRETTA
38 Dir Counseling & Academic Advising ... Ms. Michelle KOSS
96 Purchasing Administrator ... Mr. Dennis COSTELLO
41 Manager Athletics/Sports Clubs ... Mr. Randall NELSON
18 Director Facilities Management ... Mr. Stevan ALTON
37 Director of Financial Aid ... Mr. Douglas LEVY
36 Director Career Employment Services ... Mr. Robert PENKALA
51 Dir Workforce Continuing Education ... Ms. Elise JOHNSON
13 CIO/Exec Dir Communications & IT ... Mr. Michael ZIMMERMAN
08 Dean Libraries/Learning Resources ... Mr. Michael BALSAMO
43 General Counsel/Exec Dir Col Police ... Mr. Hunter WENDT

Madonna University (D)

36600 Schoolcraft Road, Livonia MI 48150-1176

County: Wayne FICE Identification: 002282

Unit ID: 170806

Telephone: (734) 432-5300 Carnegie Class: Masters/L

FAX Number: (734) 432-5333 Calendar System: Semester

URL: www.madonna.edu

Established: 1947 Annual Undergrad Tuition & Fees: $18,740

Enrollment: 3,947 Coed

Affiliation or Control: Roman Catholic IRS Status: 501(c)3

Highest Offering: Doctorate

Accreditation: NH, DIETD, DMS, FEPAC, NURSE, SW, TED

01 President ... Dr. Michael GRANDILLO
30 Vice Pres for Advancement ... Vacant
05 Provost and VP for Academic Admin ... Dr. Lewis WALKER
10 Vice Pres for Finance/Operations ... Mr. David BOYD
32 Vice President for Student Affairs ... Dr. Connie TINGSON-GATUZ
84 VP Enrollmnt Mgt & Univ Advancement ... Dr. Cameron CRUICKSHANK
42 Director of Campus Ministry ... Mr. Patrick WATERS
06 Registrar ... Ms. Dina DUBUIS
07 Director of Admissions ... Mr Mark SCHROEDER
28 Director of BLG Program ... Mr. Brett JORDAN
08 Director of Library Services ... Ms Joanne LUMETTA
37 Director of Financial Aid ... Mr. Chris ZIEGLER
13 Director Information Systems ... Vacant
15 Director of Human Resources ... Ms. Tracey DURDEN
36 Director of Career Services ... Ms. Christine BRANT
88 Director of Special Events ... Ms. Katie ALEXANDER
19 Director Public Safety ... Mr. David HAMMERSCHMIDT
41 Director Athletics ... Mr. Bryan RIZZO
40 Bookstore Manager ... Ms. Debbie MITCHELL
39 Director Residence Hall ... Ms. Tanisha MCINTOSH
24 Director Media Services ... Vacant
23 Director Instruction Center ... Ms. Susan GREEN
09 Director of Institutional Research ... Dr. Phillip OLLA
18 Chief Facilities/Physical Plant ... Vacant
29 Director Alumni Relations ... Ms. Carole BOOMS
26 Director of Marketing ... Ms. Karen SANBORN
79 Dean Arts & Humanities ... Dr. Kathleen EDELMAYER
50 Interim Dean Business ... Dr. Deborah DUNN
58 Dean Graduate Studies ... Dr. Deborah DUNN
66 Dean Nursing & Health ... Dr. Deborah VARGO
83 Dean Social Sciences ... Dr. Karen ROSS
53 Dean Education ... Dr. Karen OBSNIUK
101 Secretary of the Institution/Board ... Sr. Margaret KIJEK
102 Dir Foundation/Corporate Relations ... Vacant
104 Director Study Abroad ... Mr. John MAGEE
105 Director Web Services ... Ms. Sheryl HERRON
106 Dir Online Education/E-learning ... Vacant
91 Chief Info Technology Officer ... Ms. Carol HALL
04 Executive Asst to President ... Ms. Cheryll A. JOHNSON
100 Chief of Staff ... Mr. Neil NEIDHARDT

Marygrove College (E)

8425 W McNichols Road, Detroit MI 48221-2599

County: Wayne FICE Identification: 002284

Unit ID: 170842

Telephone: (313) 927-1200 Carnegie Class: Masters/L

FAX Number: (313) 927-1345 Calendar System: Semester

URL: www.marygrove.edu

Established: 1905 Annual Undergrad Tuition & Fees: $20,930

Enrollment: 1,774 Coed

Affiliation or Control: Roman Catholic IRS Status: 501(c)3

Highest Offering: Master's

Accreditation: NH, SW, TEAC

01 President ... Dr. Elizabeth A. BURNS
30 Int VP Institutional Advancement ... Dr. Gregory CASCIONE
04 Exec Assistant to the President ... Ms. Maryann S. KUMMER
05 Interim Provost ... Dr. Sally WELCH
84 Vice President for Enrollment Mgmt ... Dr. Denise MALLETT
10 Interim VP Finance/Admin & CFO ... Mr. James L. MURDOCK
06 Registrar ... Ms. Gladys SMITH
07 Director of Admissions ... Ms. Sharon M. TOLES
08 Interim Director of the Library ... Dr. Laura MANLEY
09 Director of Institutional Research ... Mr. John SENKO
11 Director of Administrative Services ... Mr. Horace DANDRIDGE
15 Director of Human Resources ... Ms. Tamiko OGBURN
20 Dean of Academic Programs ... Vacant
19 Lieutenant Campus Safety ... Mr. Roosevelt LAWRENCE, JR.
20 Dean of the Faculty ... Dr. Frank D. RASHID
21 Controller ... Mr. David OTIS
29 Dir of Alumni Relations/Annual Giv ... Ms. Janice M. MACHUSAK
32 Director Student Success Center ... Dr. Carolyn ROBERTS
36 Director of Career Services ... Vacant
37 Director Scholarships & Fin Aid ... Ms. Kimberly L. GOODEN
38 Assistant Dean for Student Devel ... Dr. Carolyn ROBERTS
41 Athletic Director ... Mr. Stephen BLOOMFIELD
42 Director of Mission Integration ... Mr. Jesse COX
51 Continuing Education Coordinator ... Ms. Theresa JORDAN
26 Mgr of Marketing and Communications ... Ms. Renee AHEE
106 Director Online Education ... Dr. Mitali CHAUDHERY

MIAT College of Technology (F)

2955 South Haggerty Road, Canton MI 48188

County: Wayne FICE Identification: 020603

Unit ID: 169655

Telephone: (734) 423-2139 Carnegie Class: Spec 2-yr-Tech

FAX Number: (734) 858-5000 Calendar System: Other

URL: www.miat.edu

Established: Annual Undergrad Tuition & Fees: $14,743

Enrollment: 382 Coed

Affiliation or Control: Proprietary IRS Status: Proprietary

Highest Offering: Associate Degree

Accreditation: ACCSC

01 Campus President ... Mr. Kevin BURCHETT

MIAT College of Technology (G)

533 Northpark Central Dr, Houston MI 77073

Telephone: (713) 401-3399 Identification: 770972

Accreditation: ACCSC

Michigan School of Professional Psychology (H)

26811 Orchard Lake Road, Farmington Hills MI 48334-4512

County: Oakland FICE Identification: 021989

Unit ID: 169220

Telephone: (248) 476-1122 Carnegie Class: Spec-4-yr-Other Health

FAX Number: (248) 476-1125 Calendar System: Semester

URL: www.mispp.edu

Established: 1981 Annual Graduate Tuition & Fees: N/A

Enrollment: 150 Coed

Affiliation or Control: Independent Non-Profit IRS Status: 501(c)3

Highest Offering: Doctorate; No Undergraduates

Accreditation: NH, CLPSY

01 President/Chief Executive Officer ... Dr. Diane BLAU
03 Vice President/Chief Operating Ofcr ... Ms. Diane ZALAPI
05 Program Director/Chief Academic Ofc ... Dr. Fran BROWN
13 Director of Info Tech & Bldg Svcs ... Mr. Jeffrey CROSS
08 Head Academic Librarian ... Ms. Michelle WHEELER
06 Registrar ... Ms. Amanda MING
07 Admissions/Recruitment Coordinator ... Ms. Tori HOLMES
11 Dir of Administrative Operations ... Ms. Laura LANE
88 Interim Dir of Clinical Training ... Dr. Jill CASTRO

Michigan State University (I)

426 Auditorium Road, East Lansing MI 48824-1046

County: Ingham FICE Identification: 002290

Unit ID: 171100

Telephone: (517) 355-1855 Carnegie Class: DU-Highest

FAX Number: N/A Calendar System: Semester

URL: www.msu.edu

Established: 1855 Annual Undergrad Tuition & Fees (In-State): $13,560

Enrollment: 50,081 Coed

Affiliation or Control: State IRS Status: 501(c)3

Highest Offering: Doctorate

Accreditation: NH, ANEST, BUS, BUSA, CAATE, CEA, CIDA, CLPSY, CONST, CORE, CS, DIETD, DIETI, ENG, FEPAC, IPSY, JOUR, LAW, LSAR, MED, MFCD, MT, MUS, NURSE, OSTEO, PLNG, SCPSY, SP, SW, TEAC, VET

01 President ... Dr. Lou Anna K. SIMON
05 Provost/Exec VP Academic Affairs ... Dr. June P. YOUATT
11 Exec Vice Pres for Admin Services ... Dr. Satish S. UDPA
101 Vice President/Secretary to Board ... Mr. William R. BEEKMAN

46 Vice President Research & Grad Stds ... Dr. Stephen HSU
32 VP Student Affairs & Svcs ... Dr. Denise B. MAYBANK
86 Vice President Governmental Affairs ... Mr. Mark A. BURNHAM
10 Vice Pres Finance Opers/Treasurer ... Mr. Mark HAAS
30 Vice Pres Univ Advancement ... Mr. Robert GROVES
43 VP Legal Affairs & General Counsel ... Mr. Robert A. NOTO
18 VP Infrastructure Planning & Facil ... Mr. Dan BOLLMAN
109 Vice President Auxiliary Services ... Mr. Vennie GORE
26 VP Communication & Brand Strategy ... Ms. Heather C. SWAIN
22 Dir Incl/Intrcult Init/Sr Adv P Dvr ... Ms. Paulette GRANBERRY-RUSSELL
88 Assoc VP Research/Graduate Studies ... Dr. Paul M. HUNT
58 Int Assoc Prov and Dean Grad School ... Dr. Judith STODDART
20 Assoc Prov & Dean Ungrad Educ ... Dr. Douglas ESTRY
88 Assoc Prov Univ Outreach/ Engagement ... Dr. Hiram E. FITZGERALD
88 Assoc Provost Academic Svcs ... Dr. John D. GABOURY
16 Assoc Prov/VP Academic Human Res ... Mr. Theodore H. CURRY, II
45 Asst VP & Director of Plng/Budgets ... Mr. David S. BYELICH
15 Asst Vice Pres for Human Resources ... Ms. Sharon BUTLER
13 CIO & VP of Information and Tech ... Ms. Joanna YOUNG
88 Asst VP Ofc of Sponsored Programs ... Dr. Twila REIGHLEY
21 Controller ... Mr. Greg DEPPONG
07 Director of Admissions ... Mr. James W. COTTER
29 Assoc VP for Alumni Relations ... Mr. W. Scott WESTERMAN, III
25 Director Contract & Grant Admin ... Mr. Daniel T. EVON
36 Assoc Dir Career Services/Placement ... Dr. Linda GROSS
38 Director Counseling Center ... Dr. Scott BECKER
88 Dir MI AgBioResearch ... Dr. Doug BUHLER
56 Assoc Dir MSU Extension ... Dr. Jeff DWYER
37 Director of Financial Aid ... Mr. Richard SHIPMAN
06 Registrar ... Dr. Nicole ROVIG
85 Director Intl Students/Scholars ... Mr. Peter F. BRIGGS
23 Director MSU Student Health Ctr ... Dr. Glynda M. MOORER
92 Dean Honors College ... Dr. Cynthia JACKSON-ELMOORE
41 Director Intercollegiate Athletics ... Mr. Mark J. HOLLIS
08 Director of Libraries ... Mr. Clifford H. HAKA
88 Dir Natl Supercond Cyclotron Lab ... Dr. Brad SHERRILL
19 Police Chf/Dir Police & Pub Safety ... Mr. James H. DUNLAP
88 Director Undergraduate Univ Div ... Dr. Bonita P. CURRY
47 Interim Dean Col Ag & Nat Resources ... Dr. Doug BUHLER
79 Dean College Arts & Letters ... Dr. Christopher P. LONG
79 Dean Res Col Arts/Humanities ... Dr. Stephen L. ESQUITH
50 Dean Eli Broad Col of Business ... Dr. Sanjay GUPTA
60 Dean Col Comm/Arts & Sci ... Dr. Prabu DAVID
53 Dean College of Education ... Dr. Robert FLODEN
54 Dean College of Engineering ... Dr. Leo KEMPEL
63 Interim Dean College Human Medicine ... Dr. Aron SOUSA
82 Dean James Madison College ... Dr. Sherman W. GARNETT
61 Dean College of Law ... Ms. Joan W. HOWARTH
81 Dean Lyman Briggs College ... Dr. Elizabeth H. SIMMONS
64 Dean College of Music ... Mr. James FORGER
81 Dean College Natural Science ... Dr. R. James KIRKPATRICK
66 Dean College of Nursing ... Dr. Randolph RASCH
63 Dean College Osteopathic Medicine ... Dr. William D. STRAMPEL
83 Interim Dean College of Social Sci ... Dr. Neal SCHMITT
74 Dean College Veterinary Medicine ... Dr. John C. BAKER
82 Dean Intl Studies & Programs ... Dr. Steven D. HANSON

Michigan Technological University (A)

1400 Townsend Drive, Houghton MI 49931-1295
County: Houghton FICE Identification: 002292
Unit ID: 171128
Telephone: (906) 487-1885 Carnegie Class: DU-Higher
FAX Number: (906) 487-2935 Calendar System: Semester
URL: www.mtu.edu
Established: 1885 Annual Undergrad Tuition & Fees (In-State): $14,286
Enrollment: 7,099 Coed
Affiliation or Control: State IRS Status: 501(c)3
Highest Offering: Doctorate
Accreditation: NH, BUS, CEA, CONST, CS, ENG, ENGT, TEAC

01 President ... Dr. Glenn D. MROZ
05 Provost/Vice Pres Academic Affairs ... Dr. Jacqueline E. HUNTOON
86 Vice Pres Governmental Relations ... Vacant
11 Vice President for Administration ... Ms. Ellen S. HORSCH
46 Vice President for Research ... Dr. David D. REED
32 VP for Student Affairs/Advancement ... Dr. Les P. COOK
84 Assc VP Enrollment & Univ Relations ... Dr. John B. LEHMAN
35 Dean of Students ... Dr. Bonnie B. GORMAN
10 Treasurer ... Ms. Julie SEPPALA
26 Director Marketing/Communications ... Mr. Ian REPP
08 Director of the Library ... Ms. Ellen MARKS
09 Institutional Analysis ... Mr. Richard ELENICH
29 Exec Director Alumni Relations ... Ms. Brenda RUDIGER
06 Registrar ... Ms. Theresa K. JACQUES
07 Director Undergraduate Recruitment ... Ms. Allison A. CARTER
15 Director Human Resources ... Ms. Renee HILLER
37 Director of Financial Aid ... Mr. Joe J. COOPER
36 Director University Career Center ... Mr. Steve PATCHIN
18 Dir Facilities/Physical Plant ... Ms. Kerri SLEEMAN
21 Director Planning & Budgeting ... Ms. Deborah L. SHELDEN
38 Director Counseling Services ... Mr. Donald S. WILLIAMS
19 Director Public Safety ... Mr. Brian J. CADWELL
22 Director Affirmative Programs ... Dr. Jill HODGES
96 Director of Purchasing ... Mr. Raymond E. LASANEN
58 Dean Graduate School ... Dr. Pushpalatha MURTHY
50 Interim Dean Business & Economics ... Dr. Dean L. JOHNSON
54 Dean of Engineering ... Dr. Wayne PENNINGTON
65 Dean of Forestry ... Dr. Terry SHARIK
49 Dean Sciences/Arts ... Dr. Bruce E. SEELY
72 Dean of Technology ... Dr. James FRENDEWEY, JR.
100 Chief of Staff ... Ms. Roberta M. DESSELLIER
13 Chief Info Technology Officer (CIO) ... Mr. Joshua OLSON
41 Athletic Director ... Ms. Suzanne SANREGRET
25 Chief Contracts/Grants Admin ... Ms. Julie SEPPALA
30 Chief Development/Advancement ... Dr. Les P. COOK
39 Director Student Housing ... Mr. Travis L. PIERCE

Mid Michigan Community College (B)

1375 S Clare Avenue, Harrison MI 48625-9447
County: Clare FICE Identification: 006768
Unit ID: 171155
Telephone: (989) 386-6622 Carnegie Class: Assoc/HT-Mix Trad/Non
FAX Number: (989) 386-2411 Calendar System: Semester
URL: www.midmich.edu
Established: 1965 Annual Undergrad Tuition & Fees (In-District): $3,609
Enrollment: 4,422 Coed
Affiliation or Control: State/Local IRS Status: 501(c)3
Highest Offering: Associate Degree
Accreditation: NH, MAC, PHLEB, PTAA, RAD

01 President ... Dr. Christine M. HAMMOND
05 Vice President of Academic Services . Dr. Michael W. JANKOVIAK
32 VP Community/Student Relations ... Dr. Matt MILLER
10 Vice President for Admin & Finance ... Ms. Lillian K. FRICK
04 Executive Assistant to President ... Ms. Tonya M. CLAYTON
15 Exec Director of Personnel Services ... Ms. Lori FASSETT
26 College Info/Org Dev Officer ... Mr. Anthony FREDS
35 Exec Dean of Student Services ... Ms. Kimberly BARNES
103 Exec Dir Econ/Workforce Dev ... Mr. Scott GOVITZ
81 Dean of Math & Science ... Mr. Peter VELGUTH
69 Dean of Health Sciences ... Dr. Maggie MAGOON
49 Dean Liberal Arts ... Dr. Scott MERTES
75 Dean of Occupational Studies ... Mr. Shawn TROY
06 Registrar ... Mr. Charles "Hank" BRYAN
21 Director of Accounting ... Ms. Susan CALL
88 SBDC Director ... Mr. Anthony FOX
07 Director of Marketing & Admissions ... Ms. Jessica GORDON
08 Dir Library/Learning Services ... Mr. Corey GOETHE
37 Director of Financial Aid ... Mr. Gale M. CRANDELL
109 Director Auxiliary Services ... Ms. Kelly KOCH
18 Director of Facilities ... Mr. William D. WHITMAN
14 IT Systems Manager ... Mr. Chris KLIEWONEIT
13 Director IT ... Mr. Kirk A. LEHR
76 Director Radiology ... Ms. LouAnn GOODWIN
88 Dir Grants Mgmt & Resource Dev ... Ms. Carol DARLINGTON
88 Dir Of Educational Talent Search ... Ms. Marilee KUJAT
09 Director of Institutional Research ... Mr. Kim OREN
35 Student Advancement Coordinator ... Ms. Tammy ALVARO

Monroe County Community College (C)

1555 S Raisinville Road, Monroe MI 48161-9746
County: Monroe FICE Identification: 002294
Unit ID: 171225
Telephone: (734) 242-7300 Carnegie Class: Assoc/HT-High Non
FAX Number: (734) 242-9711 Calendar System: Semester
URL: www.monroeccc.edu
Established: 1964 Annual Undergrad Tuition & Fees (In-District): $3,730
Enrollment: 3,482 Coed
Affiliation or Control: Local IRS Status: 170(c)1
Highest Offering: Associate Degree
Accreditation: NH, ADNUR, COARC

01 President ... Dr. Kojo QUARTEY
05 Vice President of Instruction ... Dr. Grace B. YACKEE
10 Vice Pres of Admin ... Ms. Suzanne M. WETZEL
32 Vice Pres Student & Information Svc ... Mr. Randell W. DANIELS
50 Dean of Business ... Mr. Paul L. KNOLLMAN
76 Dean of Health Sciences ... Ms. Kimberly LINDQUIST
79 Dean of Humanities/Social Science ... Dr. Paul HEDEEN
72 Dean of Applied Sci & Eng Tech ... Mr. Parmeshwar COOMAR
06 Registrar ... Ms. Tracy VOGT
07 Director of Admissions/Guidance ... Mr. Mark HALL
88 Director of Upward Bound ... Mr. Anthony QUINN
88 Director of Respiratory Therapy ... Mr. Nicholas PRUSH
21 Director of Financial Services ... Mr. Andrew FISCHER
18 Director Physical Plant ... Mr. Jack BURNS
96 Dir Auxiliary Services/Purchasing ... Ms. Jean FORD
14 Director Data Processing Services ... Mr. James A. ROSS
37 Director of Financial Aid ... Ms. Valerie CULLER
36 Dir Business Devel/Employment Svcs ... Mr. Barry C. KINSEY
88 Director of Lifelong Learning ... Ms. Tina PILLARELLI
13 Manager Information Services ... Mr. Brian K. LAY
26 Director of Marketing/Communication ... Mr. Joseph VERKENNES
15 Director of Human Resources ... Ms. Molly M. MCCUTCHAN
04 Executive Asst to President ... Ms. Penny R. DORCEY
09 Coord Inst Research/Eval & Assess ... Miss Jamie DELEEUW
102 Exec Director Foundation ... Mr. Joshua MYERS

Montcalm Community College (D)

2800 College Drive, Sidney MI 48885-9723
County: Montcalm FICE Identification: 002295
Unit ID: 171234
Telephone: (989) 328-2111 Carnegie Class: Assoc/HVT-High Trad
FAX Number: (989) 328-2950 Calendar System: Semester
URL: www.montcalm.edu
Established: 1965 Annual Undergrad Tuition & Fees (In-District): $3,540
Enrollment: 1,832 Coed
Affiliation or Control: Local IRS Status: 501(c)3
Highest Offering: Associate Degree
Accreditation: NH, MAC

01 President ... Mr. Robert C. FERRENTINO
05 Vice Pres for Student/Acad Affairs ... Mr. Robert SPOHR
10 VP Administrative Services ... Ms. Connie STEWART
102 Executive Director of Foundation ... Ms. Therese A. SMITH
32 Dean Student & Enrollment Svcs ... Ms. Debra ALEXANDER
37 Director of Financial Aid ... Ms. Traci NICHOLS
13 Director Information Tech Svcs ... Mr. Rodney C. MIDDLETON
09 Director Institutional Effectivenes ... Ms. Lisa LUND
26 Communications Director ... Ms. Shelly STRAUTZ-SPRINGBORN
15 Director of Human Resources ... Vacant
21 Director of Accounting ... Ms. Kire WIERDA
18 Director of Facilities ... Mr. George GERMAIN
76 Dean of Health Occupations ... Ms. Amy EADY
07 Director of Recruitment/Enrollment ... Mr. Ryan WILSON
103 Dean Workforce Education ... Ms. Susan HATTO
29 Director Alumni Relations ... Ms. Melissa CHRISTENSEN

Moody Theological Seminary-Michigan (E)

41550 E Ann Arbor Trail, Plymouth MI 48170-4308
Telephone: (734) 207-9581 FICE Identification: 031353
Accreditation: &NH, THEOL

† Regional accreditation is carried under the parent institution Moody Bible Institute, Chicago, IL.

Mott Community College (F)

1401 E Court Street, Flint MI 48503-2089
County: Genesee FICE Identification: 002261
Unit ID: 169275
Telephone: (810) 762-0200 Carnegie Class: Assoc/HT-Mix Trad/Non
FAX Number: (810) 762-0257 Calendar System: Semester
URL: www.mcc.edu
Established: 1923 Annual Undergrad Tuition & Fees (In-District): $3,668
Enrollment: 8,937 Coed
Affiliation or Control: Local IRS Status: 501(c)3
Highest Offering: Associate Degree
Accreditation: NH, ACBSP, ADNUR, COARC, DA, DH, OTA, PTAA

01 President ... Dr. Beverly WALKER-GRIFFEA
30 Assoc VP Institutional Advancement ... Mr. Dale WEIGHILL
05 Vice Pres Academic Affairs ... Dr. Amy FUGATE
32 VP Student Success ... Vacant
10 Chief Financial Officer ... Mr. Larry GAWTHROP
15 Associate Vice President of HR ... Mrs. Mary GMEINER
88 Exec Dean Regional Tech Ctr Project ... Mr. Tom CRAMPTON
51 Exec Dir Corporate Svcs & Cont Educ ... Vacant
35 Interim Exec Dean Student Services ... Mr. Troy BOQUETTE
37 Exec Dir Student Fin Svcs ... Ms. Jennifer DOW-MCDONALD
81 Dean of Math & Science ... Dr. Todd TROUTMAN
76 Dean of Health Sciences ... Dr. Rebecca MYSZENSKI
83 Dean Social Sciences & Fine Arts ... Ms. Mary CUSACK
50 Dean of Business ... Mr. Stephen SHUBERT
72 Dean of Technology ... Mr. Clark HARRIS
26 Exec Director Marketing & PR ... Vacant
13 Chief Technology Officer ... Ms. Cheryl BASSETT
06 Registrar ... Mr. Chris ENGLE
36 Exec Dir Career Ctr/Job Placement ... Vacant
62 Executive Director Library ... Ms. Jill SODT
18 Exec Dir Physical Plant/Architect ... Mr. Larry KOEHLER
41 Director Athletics/Campus Rec ... Mr. Tom HEALEY
09 Exec Dir Institutional Research ... Mrs. Lori HANCOCK
35 Director Student Life ... Ms. Dawn VANNIMAN
96 Director of Purchasing ... Ms. Jody MICHAEL
04 Administrative Asst to President ... Ms. Lisa M. POMA
101 Board Relations Coordinator ... Mr. Michael SIMON
103 Assoc VP Workforce & Economic Dev ... Mr. Robert MATTHEWS

Muskegon Community College (G)

221 S Quarterline Road, Muskegon MI 49442-1493
County: Muskegon FICE Identification: 002297
Unit ID: 171304
Telephone: (231) 773-9131 Carnegie Class: Assoc/HT-Mix Trad/Non
FAX Number: (231) 777-0440 Calendar System: Semester
URL: www.muskegoncc.edu
Established: 1926 Annual Undergrad Tuition & Fees (In-District): $5,030
Enrollment: 4,640 Coed
Affiliation or Control: Local IRS Status: Exempt
Highest Offering: Associate Degree
Accreditation: NH, ADNUR, COARC

01 President ... Dr. Dale K. NESBARY
05 VP of Academic Affairs and Finance ... Ms. Teresa STURRUS
32 VP Student Svcs and Administration ... Dr. John SELMON
06 Dean of Academic Svcs/Registrar ... Ms. Jean ROBERTS
20 Dean of Instruction & Assessment ... Dr. Edward BREITENBACH
31 Dean of Community Outreach ... Ms. Trynette Lottie HARPS
84 Dean of Enrollment Services ... Ms. Cindy REUSS
10 Director of Finance ... Mr. Kenneth LONG
13 Chief Information Officer ... Mr. Mike ALSTROM
37 Director Financial Aid ... Mr. Bruce WIERDA
09 Dir Institutional Research & Grants ... Mr. Eduardo BEDOYA
45 Director of Strategic Initiatives ... Ms. Tina DEE
15 Adm Dir of Human Resources ... Ms. Kristine ANDERSON
41 Athletic Director ... Mr. Marty MCDERMOTT
18 Physical Plant Director ... Mr. Gerald NYLAND
29 Alumni Relations Manager ... Ms. Julie WELLER
04 Executive Assistant to President ... Ms. Cindy S. DEBOEF

North Central Michigan College (A)

1515 Howard Street, Petoskey MI 49770-8717
County: Emmet FICE Identification: 002299
Unit ID: 171395
Telephone: (231) 348-6600 Carnegie Class: Assoc/HT-High Trad
FAX Number: (231) 348-6628 Calendar System: Semester
URL: www.ncmich.edu
Established: 1958 Annual Undergrad Tuition & Fees (In-District): $3,571
Enrollment: 2,581 Coed
Affiliation or Control: Local IRS Status: 501(c)3
Highest Offering: Associate Degree
Accreditation: NH

01 President .... Dr. Cameron BRUNET-KOCH
05 VP Academic Affairs/Student Success .... Dr. Peter OLSON
10 VP of Finance & Facilities .... David HARTNETT
32 VP of Student Services .... Renee DEYOUNG
102 Executive Director Foundation .... Dr. Lisa WATSON
08 Librarian .... Leland PARSONS
37 Director of Financial Aid .... Virginia PANOFF
18 Director of Physical Plant .... Vacant
84 Dir Enrollment Services/Registrar .... Joseph BALINSKI
21 Controller .... Troy SLATER
39 Dir Student Activities/Camp Housing .... Vacant
15 Human Resources .... Diana SOUZA
40 Bookstore Manager .... Julie WEAVER
09 Assoc Dean Research & Assessment .... Dr. Robert MARSH
49 Assoc Dean Liberal Arts .... Dr. Sara GLASGOW
66 Assoc Dean Nurs/Allied Hlth/Sci .... Rene BIEGANOWSKI
50 Assoc Dean Business/Manuf/Tech .... Vacant
26 Director of College Communications .... Carol LAENEN
07 Director of Student Outreach .... Wendy FOUGHT
13 Director of Information Services .... David BORING
88 Director of Resource Center .... Dallas CULVAHOUSE
04 Administrative Asst to President .... Megan VAN HORN

Northern Michigan University (B)

1401 Presque Isle Avenue, Marquette MI 49855-5301
County: Marquette FICE Identification: 002301
Unit ID: 171456
Telephone: (906) 227-1000 Carnegie Class: Masters/M
FAX Number: (906) 227-2204 Calendar System: Semester
URL: www.nmu.edu
Established: 1899 Annual Undergrad Tuition & Fees (In-State): $9,620
Enrollment: 8,781 Coed
Affiliation or Control: State IRS Status: 501(c)3
Highest Offering: Doctorate
Accreditation: NH, BUS, CA, CAATE, CGTECH, DMOLS, ENGT, MLTAD, MT, MUS, NURSE, RAD, SURGT, SW, TEAC

01 President .... Dr. Fritz J. ERICKSON
05 Provost/VP Academic Affairs .... Dr. Kerri SCHUILING
10 VP for Finance & Administration .... Mr. R. Gavin LEACH
30 Vice Pres Advancement .... Ms. Martha B. HAYNES
84 Vice Pres Enroll Mgmt/Student Svcs .... Dr. Steven NEIHEISEL
09 Assoc VP for Inst Research .... Dr. Linda WANG
31 VP Extended Lrng/Cmty Engagement .. Dr. Steve VANDENAVOND
20 Asc Provost Acad Affs/Undergrad Pgm .... Dr. Dale P. KAPLA
58 Asst Provost Graduate Educ/Research .... Dr. Brian CHERRY
90 Dean Academic Information Services .... Ms. Leslie A. WARREN
32 Assistant VP/Dean of Students .... Dr. Christine G. GREER
49 Dean of Arts & Sciences .... Dr. Michael J. BROADWAY
50 Dean Walker L Cisler Col Bus .... Dr. David RAYOME
107 Interim Dean College Prof Studies .... Dr. Charles MESLOH
06 Registrar .... Ms. Kim M. ROTUNDO
44 Director Major/Planned Giving .... Ms. Amy M. HUBINGER
45 Asst to Pres Strategic Initiatives .... Ms. Cindy L. PAAVOLA
36 Dir of Acad & Career Advisement .... Mr. James G. GADZINSKI
37 Director of Financial Aid .... Mr. Michael R. ROTUNDO
38 Acting Director Counseling Center .... Ms. Marie AHO
88 Director Glenn T Seaborg Center .... Ms. Chris STANDERFORD
41 Athletic Director .... Mr. Forrest KARR
19 Dir Public Safety/Police Services .... Mr. Michael J. BATH
39 Director Housing/Residence Life .... Mr. Gary BICE
07 Director of Admissions .... Ms. Gerri L. DANIELS
23 Chief of Staff/Physician .... Dr. David M. LUOMA
15 Director of Human Resources .... Ms. Rhea DEVER
26 Asst VP Marketing & Communications .... Mr. Derek HALL
28 Dir Multicult Educ/Resource Center .... Ms. Shirley A. BROZZO
85 Director International Programs .... Mr. Kevin J. TIMLIN
92 Director of Honors Program .... Dr. David H. WOOD
88 Director of Support/Consulting Svcs .... Ms. Felecia J. FLACK
24 Director Broadcast & AV Services .... Mr. Eric L. SMITH
29 Exec Dir Alumni Ops/Annual Giving .... Ms. Robyn L. STILLE
40 Bookstore Manager .... Mr. Michael J. KUZAK
18 Associate VP Eng & Plan/Facilities .... Ms. Kathy A. RICHARDS
13 Chief Technology Officer .... Mr. David W. MAKI
96 Manager of Purchasing .... Mr. Steven D. BROWN
86 Director of Government Relations .... Ms. Deanna HEMMILA
04 Executive Assistant to President .... Ms. Laura GLOVER
101 Secretary Board of Trustees .... Ms. Cathy NIEMI

Northwestern Michigan College (C)

1701 E Front Street, Traverse City MI 49686-3061
County: Grand Traverse FICE Identification: 002302
Unit ID: 171483
Telephone: (231) 995-1000 Carnegie Class: Bac/Assoc-Assoc Dom
FAX Number: (231) 995-1339 Calendar System: Semester
URL: www.nmc.edu
Established: 1951 Annual Undergrad Tuition & Fees (In-District): $3,330
Enrollment: 4,502 Coed
Affiliation or Control: Local IRS Status: 501(c)3
Highest Offering: Baccalaureate
Accreditation: NH, ACFEI, ADNUR, DA, PNUR

01 President .... Mr. Timothy J. NELSON
05 VP for Educational Services .... Dr. Stephen N. SICILIANO
107 VP Lifelong/Professional Learning .... Ms. Marguerite C. COTTO
10 VP of Finance & Administration .... Ms. Vicki COOK
37 Director Student Financial Services .... Ms. Linda BERLIN
13 VP for Student Svcs & Technology .... Mr. Todd NEIBAUER
84 Associate Dean Enrollment Services .... Ms. Pam PALERMO
32 Dean of Students .... Ms. Lisa THOMAS
04 Exec Assistant to President & Board .... Ms. Holly J. GORTON
15 Director of Human Resources .... Mr. Mark LIEBLING
88 Exec Dir of Dennos Museum Center ... Mr. Eugene A. JENNEMAN
24 Director Educational Media Tech .... Ms. Terri GUSTAFSON
12 Supt Great Lakes Maritime Academy .... RAdm. Gerard ACHENBACH, USMS
20 Dir Academic Affairs/Business Div .... Dr. Susan DECAMILLIS
56 Director Extended Educ Services .... Mr. Don CUNNINGHAM
06 Registrar .... Ms. Sheila RUPP
23 Director of Health Services .... Ms. Renee R. JACOBSON
09 Dir Research Planning Effectiveness .... Ms. Joy EVANS
18 Director of Campus Services .... Mr. Paul PERRY
26 Exec Dir of PR/Marketing/Communic .... Ms. Diana FAIRBANKS LAWSON
102 Exec Dir of Resource Dev & Found .... Ms. Rebecca M. TEAHEN
29 Director Alumni Relations .... Ms. Betsy COFFIA
62 Director of Library Services .... Ms. Tina J. ULRICH
88 Director Great Lakes Culinary Inst .... Mr. Frederick L. LAUGHLIN
88 Director Training & Research .... Mr. Richard R. WOLIN
21 Controller .... Ms. Cheryl SULLIVAN
96 Purchasing Manager .... Mr. Donald LOEFFLER
19 Asst Dir Campus Safety & Security .... Mr. Jim WHITE
07 Director of Admissions .... Ms. Cathryn CLAERHOUT
36 Director of Learning Services .... Ms. Kari L. KAHLER
68 Coordinator Physical Education .... Mr. Peter W. LACOURSE
75 Director of Technical Division .... Mr. Ed BAILEY
88 Director of Aviation .... Mr. Alex BLOYE

Northwood University (D)

4000 Whiting Drive, Midland MI 48640-2398
County: Midland FICE Identification: 004072
Unit ID: 171492
Telephone: (989) 837-4200 Carnegie Class: Spec-4-yr-Bus
FAX Number: (989) 837-4111 Calendar System: Semester
URL: www.northwood.edu
Established: 1959 Annual Undergrad Tuition & Fees: $24,170
Enrollment: 3,131 Coed
Affiliation or Control: Independent Non-Profit IRS Status: 501(c)3
Highest Offering: Master's
Accreditation: NH, ACBSP

01 President & Chief Executive Officer .... Dr. Keith A. PRETTY
05 EVP/CAO/COO .... Dr. Kristin STEHOUWER
10 Vice President Finance & Treasurer .... Mr. W. Karl STEPHAN
88 SVP Strategic/Corporate Alliances .... Dr. Timothy G. NASH
84 VP Enrollment Management .... Dr. Brian SANDUSKY
30 VP University Advancement & Alumni . Mr. Justin W. MARSHALL
12 President Northwood Texas .... Dr. Kevin G. FEGAN
26 VP Marketing/Communications/PR .... Ms. Rachel VALDISERRI
51 Associate Dean Adult Degree Program .... Ms. Rhonda C. ANDERSON
36 Director of Career Services .... Mr. Gregory S. STIFFLER
32 Dean of Students .... Mr. Stephen A. CRIPE
85 Dean International Programs .... Ms. Mamillo REEVES
96 Director of Asset Management .... Mr. David L. BENDER
06 Registrar .... Dr. Marisa L. TOSCHKOFF
37 System Financial Aid Director .... Mr. Mark A. MARTIN
15 Director of Human Resources .... Ms. Pamela L. CHRISTIE
21 Business Office Mgr/System Director .... Ms. Susan M. RIDGWAY
29 Executive Director Alumni Relations .... Ms. Julie L. FELSKE
04 Administrative Asst to President .... Ms. Sue A. NOWICKI
41 Athletic Director .... Mr. David F. MARSH
19 Director Security/Safety .... Mr. Jason VONRE CHBAUER

Oakland Community College (E)

2480 Opdyke Road, Bloomfield Hills MI 48304-2236
County: Oakland FICE Identification: 002303
Unit ID: 171535
Telephone: (248) 341-2000 Carnegie Class: Assoc/HT-High Non
FAX Number: (248) 341-2099 Calendar System: Semester
URL: www.oaklandcc.edu
Established: 1964 Annual Undergrad Tuition & Fees (In-District): $2,745
Enrollment: 24,031 Coed
Affiliation or Control: State/Local IRS Status: 501(c)3
Highest Offering: Associate Degree
Accreditation: NH, ACFEI, ADNUR, COARC, DH, DMS, MAC, RAD, SURGT

01 Chancellor .... Dr. Timothy R. MEYER
05 Vice Chanc Academic & Student Affs .... Dr. Mary C. MAZE
10 Int Vice Chanc of Business/Finance .... Mr. Charles THOMAS
11 Vice Chanc Administrative Svcs .... Mr. Peter PROVENZANO
26 Interim Vice Chanc External Affairs .... Ms. Janet ROBERTS
15 Vice Chancellor Human Resources .... Mr. William J. MACQUEEN
32 Assoc Vice Chanc Acad/Student Affs .... Dr. Timothy SHERWOOD
04 Exec Assistant to Chancellor .... Ms. Cherie A. FOSTER
12 President Highland Lakes Campus .... Dr. Cynthia ROMAN
12 President Royal Oak/Southfield Camp .... Dr. Steven J. REIF
12 President Auburn Hills Campus .... Dr. Timothy L. TAYLOR
12 Interim Pres Orchard Ridge Campus .... Dr. Steven J. REIF
09 Exec Dir Inst Research/Quality/Plng .... Ms. Nancy C. SHOWERS
88 Exec Dir Curriculum & Student Lrng .... Mr. Martin A. ORLOWSKI
13 Vice Chanc Info Technologies/CIO .... Mr. Robert MONTGOMERY
84 Exec Director Enrollment Mgmt .... Mrs. Carla R. SIMS
66 Acad Dean Nursing/Health Profession .... Ms. Rosalind WOODSON
27 Exec Dir Marketing/Communications .... Ms. Janet E. ROBERTS
72 Exec Dir Information Technologies .... Mr. Chuck S. FLAGG
06 Registrar .... Mr. Stephen M. LINDEN
18 Director Physical Facilities .... Mr. Daniel P. CHEREWICK
19 Director Public Safety .... Mr. Terry L. MCCAULEY
21 Director Financial Services .... Ms. Sharon K. CONVERSE
21 Director Budget & Financial Plng .... Mrs. Renee OSZUST
22 Director Employee Relations .... Mr. Gary S. CASEY
102 Interim Director OCC Foundation .... Ms. Candy GEETER
36 Director Placement/Coop Education .... Mr. Willie L. LLOYD
41 Interim Athletic Director .... Ms. Jamie CORONA
96 Int Director Purch/Auxiliary Svcs .... Ms. Sarah L. ROWLEY
37 Director Financial Res/Scholarships .... Ms. Wilma B. PORTER
16 Director Personnel Services .... Mrs. Margaret R. CARROLL
29 Director Alumni & Annual Giving .... Vacant
81 Academic Dean Math/Nat Life Sci .... Mr. Michael M. GOLDIN
54 Int Academic Dean Eng/Mfg/Ind Tech .... Ms. Deborah A. BAYER
80 Academic Dean Public Services/CREST .... Ms. Deborah A. BAYER
62 Academic Dean Learning Resources .... Ms. Mary Ann SHEBLE
83 Int Academic Dean Social Sciences .... Ms. Mary Ann SHEBLE
79 Acad Dean Humanities/Art & Design .... Mr. Henry Y. TANAKA
88 Academic Dean College Readiness .... Ms. Beverly J. STANBROUGH
60 Int Acad Dean English/Lit/Commun .... Ms. Beverly J. STANBROUGH
50 Acad Dean Bus & Info Technologies .... Mr. Tom M. HENDRICKS

Oakland Community College Auburn Hills (F)

2900Featherstone Road, Auburn Hills MI 48326-2845
Telephone: (248) 232-4100 Identification: 770281
Accreditation: &NH

† Regional accreditation is carried under the parent institution in Bloomfield Hills, MI

Oakland Community College Highland Lakes (G)

7350 Cooley Lake Road, Waterford MI 48327-4187
Telephone: (248) 942-3100 Identification: 770285
Accreditation: &NH

† Regional accreditation is carried under the parent institution in Bloomfield Hills, MI

Oakland Community College Orchard Ridge (H)

27055 Orchard Lake Road,
Farmington Hills MI 48334-4579
Telephone: (248) 522-3400 Identification: 770282
Accreditation: &NH

† Regional accreditation is carried under the parent institution in Bloomfield Hills, MI

Oakland Community College Royal Oak (I)

739 South Washington, Royal Oak MI 48067-3898
Telephone: (248) 246-2400 Identification: 770283
Accreditation: &NH

† Regional accreditation is carried under the parent institution in Bloomfield Hills, MI

Oakland Community College Southfield (J)

22322 Rutland Drive, Southfield MI 48075-4793
Telephone: (248) 233-2700 Identification: 770284
Accreditation: &NH

† Regional accreditation is carried under the parent institution in Bloomfield Hills, MI

Oakland University (K)

2200 N. Squirrel Road, Rochester MI 48309-4401
County: Oakland FICE Identification: 002307
Unit ID: 171571
Telephone: (248) 370-2100 Carnegie Class: DU-Mod
FAX Number: N/A Calendar System: Semester
URL: www.oakland.edu
Established: 1957 Annual Undergrad Tuition & Fees (In-State): $11,344
Enrollment: 20,519 Coed
Affiliation or Control: State IRS Status: 501(c)3
Highest Offering: Doctorate
Accreditation: NH, ANEST, BUS, BUSA, CACREP, CS, DANCE, ENG, ENGR, MED, MUS, NURSE, PTA, SPAA, SW, TEAC, THEA

01 President .... Dr. George W. HYND
05 Sr VP Academic Affairs/Provost .... Dr. James P. LENITNI
32 VP Student Affairs .... Mr. Glenn MCINTOSH
11 Chief Operating Officer .... Mr. Scott G. KUNSELMAN
30 VP Dev/Alumni Relations .... Ms. Angie SCHMUCKER
10 VP Finance & Administration .... Mr. John W. BEAGHAN
86 VP Government & Comm Relations .... Ms. Rochelle A. BLACK
12 Exec Dir OU Macomb .... Ms. Julie TRUBE
66 Interim Dean of Nursing .... Dr. Gary MOORE

54 Dean Engineering & Computer Science .... Dr. Louay M. CHAMRA
76 Interim Dean School Health Sciences .... Dr. Richard J. ROZEK
53 Dean Educ & Human Services .... Dr. Jon MARGERUM-LEYS
49 Dean College Arts & Sciences .... Dr. Kevin J. CORCORAN
50 Dean School of Business Admin .... Dr. Michael A. MAZZEO
63 Dean School of Medicine .... Dr. Robert FOLBERG
08 Dean University Library .... Mr. Stephen P. WEITER
20 Senior Associate Provost .... Dr. Susan M. AWBREY
46 Interim Vice Provost Research .... Dr. Arik DVIR
24 Asst VP Classrm Spprt/Instruct Tech .... Mr. George T. PREISINGER
20 Asst VP Academic Affairs .... Ms. Peggy S. COOKE
88 Dir Ctr Excellence Tchg Lrng .... Dr. Judith ABLESER
88 Dir Eye Research Institute .... Dr. Frank GIBLIN
88 Director FAJRI .... Dr. Sayed NASSAR
21 Asst VP Finance & Administration .... Mr. Thomas P. LEMARBE
18 Assoc VP Facilities Management .... Mr. Terry STOLLSTEIMER
15 Asst VP University Human Resources ...... Mr. Ronald P. WATSON
102 Interim Campaign Director .... Ms. Alison K. GAUDREAU
35 Asst VP SA/Dean Students .... Ms. Nancy A. SCHMITZ
19 Chief of Police .... Mr. Mark B. GORDON
06 Registrar .... Mr. Steven J. SHABLIN
44 Dir Annual Giving Program .... Ms. Kelly N. BRAULT
37 Director of Financial Aid .... Ms. Cindy L. HERMSEN
29 Sr Dir of Engagement/Alumni .... Ms. Sue HELDEROP
26 VP Univ Communications & Marketing .... Mr. John O. YOUNG
41 Director of Athletics .... Mr. Jeffrey F. KONYA
28 Dir Inclus Intercu Initiatives/Atty .... Ms. Joi M. CUNNINGHAM
39 Director of University Housing .... Mr. James R. ZENTMEYER
36 Director Career Services .... Mr. Wayne J. THIBODEAU
38 Director Counseling Center .... Dr. David J. SCHWARTZ
85 Director International Students .... Mr. David J. ARCHBOLD
22 Director Disability Support Svcs .... Ms. Linda G. SISSON
96 Director of Purchasing .... Ms. Paula S. REYES
28 Sr Adv to Pres/Div Equity Incl .... Dr. Patricia A. DOLLY
106 Int Dir E-Learning/Instr Support .... Mr. John COUGHLIN
108 Dir Inst Research & Assessment .... Ms. Laura A. SCHARTMAN
101 VP Legal Affairs & General Counsel ...... Mr. Victor A. ZAMBARDI
13 Chief Information Officer .... Ms. Theresa M. ROWE
07 Director of Admissions .... Ms. Dawn M. AUBRY
58 Dean Graduate Education .... Dr. Claudia A. PETRESCU

Olivet College (A)

320 S Main Street, Olivet MI 49076-9406
County: Eaton FICE Identification: 002308
Unit ID: 171599
Telephone: (269) 749-7000 Carnegie Class: Bac-Diverse
FAX Number: (269) 749-7600 Calendar System: Semester
URL: www.olivetcollege.edu
Established: 1844 Annual Undergrad Tuition & Fees: $24,816
Enrollment: 1,058 Coed
Affiliation or Control: Independent Non-Profit IRS Status: 501(c)3
Highest Offering: Master's
Accreditation: NH, TEAC

01 President .... Dr. Steven M. COREY
05 Provost and Dean of the College .... Dr. Maria DAVIS
10 Vice Pres Finance/Administration .... Ms. Jackie LOOSER
07 Vice Pres Admissions & Mktg .... Mr. Tim JOHNSTON
32 Vice President/Dean Student Life .... Dr. Linda LOGAN
30 Vice Pres Advancement .... Mr. William HULL
13 Asst Vice President Technology .... Mr. Suresh ACHARYA
06 Registrar .... Ms. Leslie SULLIVAN
41 Athletic Director .... Mr. Ryan SHOCKEY
42 Director of Campus Ministries .... Mr. Michael F. FALES
36 Dir Career Services Network .... Ms. Diane KIRKHAM
37 Director of Student Financial Aid .... Ms. Libby JEAN
18 Director of Facilities .... Mr. Frank SCHUMACHER
94 Director of Women's Resource Center .... Ms. Cynthia NOYES
39 Student Housing .... Ms. Shawn HOLT
15 Director of Human Resources .... Mrs. Terri GLASGOW
29 Director of Alumni Engagement .. Ms. Martha MASON JENNINGS
04 Executive Asst to President .... Ms. Barbara SPENCER

Puritan Reformed Theological Seminary (B)

2965 Leonard St NE, Grand Rapids MI 49525
County: Kent Identification: 667099
Telephone: (616) 977-0599 Carnegie Class: Not Classified
FAX Number: (616) 285-3246 Calendar System: Semester
URL: www.prts.edu
Established: 1995 Annual Graduate Tuition & Fees: N/A
Enrollment: N/A Coed
Affiliation or Control: Independent Non-Profit IRS Status: 501(c)3
Highest Offering: Master's; No Undergraduates
Accreditation: THEOL

01 President .... Dr. Joel R. BEEKE
05 Academic Dean/VP Academic Affairs .... Dr. Michael BARRETT
06 Registrar .... Mr. Jonathon BEEKE
10 Vice President for Operations .... Mr. Henk KLEYN
38 Dean of Students/Spiritual Form .... Rev. Mark KELDERMAN
04 Administrative Asst to President .... Ms. Ann C. DYKEMA
26 Chief Public Relations/Marketing .... Mr. Chris HANNA
07 Director of Admissions .... Mr. Jonathon D. BEEKE
08 Head Librarian .... Mrs. Laura LADWIG
106 Dir Online Education/E-learning .... Mr. Chris ENGELSMA

Rochester College (C)

800 W Avon Road, Rochester Hills MI 48307-2764
County: Oakland FICE Identification: 002288
Unit ID: 170967
Telephone: (248) 218-2000 Carnegie Class: Bac-Diverse
FAX Number: (248) 218-2025 Calendar System: Semester
URL: www.rc.edu
Established: 1959 Annual Undergrad Tuition & Fees: $21,028
Enrollment: 1,113 Coed
Affiliation or Control: Independent Non-Profit IRS Status: 501(c)3
Highest Offering: Master's
Accreditation: NH, NURSE

01 President .... Dr. John N. TYSON
05 Provost .... Dr. Brian STOGNER
07 Vice Pres Admissions/Athletic Dir .... Mr. Klint PLEASANT
30 Vice President Development .... Mr. Tom RELLINGER
10 Chief Financial Officer .... Mr. Tom RELLINGER
07 Dean of Enrollment .... Ms. Mackenzie RELLINGER
21 Controller .... Ms. Susan IDE
18 Director Operational Support .... Mr. Mark JOHNSON
50 Dir School of Bus/Prof Studies .... Mr. Danny CAGNET
79 Dean School of Humanities .... Dr. Catherine PARKER
15 Director of Human Resources .... Mrs. Ginny MAY
26 Dir of Communication Services .... Mr. Elliot JONES
32 Dean of Students .... Ms. Candace CAIN
37 Director of Student Financial Svcs .... Ms. Jessica BRISTOW
08 Director of Library Services .... Mrs. Allison JIMENEZ
06 Registrar .... Ms. Rebekah PINCHBACK
108 Director of Assessment .... Mr. J. Mark MANRY
29 Director of Alumni .... Mr. Larry STEWART
35 Student Life Specialist .... Mrs. Teri BUTCHER
41 Director of Athletics .... Mr. Klint PLEASANT
42 Campus Minister .... Mr. Chris SHIELDS
19 Director of Safety & Security .... Mr. Shawn WESTAWAY
04 Assistant to the President .... Ms. Karen HART

Sacred Heart Major Seminary (D)

2701 Chicago Boulevard, Detroit MI 48206-1799
County: Wayne FICE Identification: 002313
Unit ID: 172033
Telephone: (313) 883-8500 Carnegie Class: Spec-4-yr-Faith
FAX Number: (313) 868-6440 Calendar System: Semester
URL: www.shms.edu
Established: 1919 Annual Undergrad Tuition & Fees: $18,029
Enrollment: 424 Coed
Affiliation or Control: Roman Catholic IRS Status: 501(c)3
Highest Offering: Master's
Accreditation: NH, THEOL

01 Rector & President .... Msgr. Todd LAJINESS
32 Vice Rector/Dean of Seminarians .... Rev. Gerard BATTERSBY
05 Dean of Studies .... Rev. Timothy LABOE
73 Dean of the Institute for Ministry .... Vacant
10 Director Finance/Treasurer .... Ms. Ann Marie CONNOLLY
06 Registrar .... Mr. David TWELLMAN
35 Director Undergraduate Seminarians .... Rev. Stephen BURR
38 Graduate Spiritual Director .... Rev. Daniel TRAPP
08 Library Director .... Mr. Christopher SPILKER
38 Undergraduate Spiritual Director .... Rev. Robert SPEZIA
58 Dir Graduate Pastoral Formation .... Rev. John VANDENAKKER
13 Dir of Educational Technology .... Vacant
30 Dir Development/Stewardship .... Mr. David KELLEY
18 Facilities Director .... Mr. John DUNCAN
07 Director of Admissions .... Mr. Ryan CAHILL

Saginaw Chippewa Tribal College (E)

2274 Enterprise Drive, Mount Pleasant MI 48858-2335
County: Isabella FICE Identification: 037723
Unit ID: 441070
Telephone: (989) 775-4123 Carnegie Class: Tribal
FAX Number: (989) 775-4528 Calendar System: Semester
URL: www.sagchip.edu
Established: 1998 Annual Undergrad Tuition & Fees: $2,040
Enrollment: 141 Coed
Affiliation or Control: Tribal Control IRS Status: 501(c)3
Highest Offering: Associate Degree
Accreditation: NH

01 President .... Ms. Carla SINEWAY
05 Dean of Instruction .... Ms. Cheryl SWARTHOUT
32 Dean of Student Services .... Mr. Nathaniel LAMBERTSON
07 Admissions Officer/Registrar .... Ms. Amanda FLAUGHER
37 Financial Aid Officer .... Ms. Patricia ALONZO
09 Dean of Research .... Ms. Tracy REED
25 Grants and Special Projects Coord .... Ms. Gena QUALLS

Saginaw Valley State University (F)

7400 Bay Road, University Center MI 48710-0001
County: Saginaw FICE Identification: 002314
Unit ID: 172051
Telephone: (989) 964-4000 Carnegie Class: Masters/L
FAX Number: (989) 964-0180 Calendar System: Semester
URL: www.svsu.edu
Established: 1963 Annual Undergrad Tuition & Fees (In-State): $8,968
Enrollment: 9,829 Coed
Affiliation or Control: State IRS Status: 501(c)3
Highest Offering: Doctorate
Accreditation: NH, BUS, CAATE, CEA, ENG, MT, MUS, NURSE, OT, SW, TED

01 President .... Dr. Donald J. BACHAND
05 Provost/VP Academic Affairs .... Dr. Deborah R. HUNTLEY
10 Exec VP Admin & Business Affairs ..... Mr. James G. MULADORE
29 Executive Director Alumni Relations .... Mr. James P. DWYER
32 Assoc Prov Student Affs/Dn Students .... Mr. Sidney R. CHILDS
86 Director of External Affairs .... Dr. Eugene J. HAMILTON
28 Spec Asst to Pres/Diversity Pgms .... Dr. Mamie T. THORNS
83 Assoc Dean Arts/Behavioral Sciences .... Dr. Carlos RAMET
45 Assoc Provost Intl/Advanced Studies .... Dr. Marc H. PERETZ
21 Assoc VP Admin & Business Affairs .... Mr. Ronald E. PORTWINE
18 AVP Campus Facilities Plng/Const ..... Mr. Stephen L. HOCQUARD
21 Business & Financial Analyst .... Ms. Susan L. CRANE
13 Exec Dir Information Tech Svcs .... Mr. Larry K. EMMONS
07 Director of Admissions .... Ms. Jennifer K. PAHL
06 Registrar .... Dr. Clifford DORNE
36 Director Career Services .... Mr. Michael W. MAJOR
21 Director Business Services .... Ms. Connie J. SCHWEITZER
88 University Ombudsman .... Mr. Richard P. THOMPSON
29 Director of Alumni Relations .... Mr. Kevin J. SCHULTZ
14 Dir Enterprise Applications & Devel .... Mr. Patrick C. SAMOLEWSKI
31 Dir Media & Community Relations .... Mr. J. J BOEHM
08 Int Dir of Melvin J Zahnow Library .... Ms. Anita DEY
25 Dir Sponsored Pgms/IRB Rsrch Compl ..... Ms. Janet D. RENTSCH
15 Director of Human Resources .... Dr. Jack VANHOORELBEKE
19 Chief of University Police .... Mr. Ronald E. TREPKOWSKI
37 Director Scholarships/Financial Aid .... Mr. Robert L. LEMUEL
22 Director of Disability Services .... Ms. Monica B. REYES
38 Dir Student Counseling Center .... Mr. Eddie V. JONES
41 Athletic Director .... Mr. Michael E. WATSON
44 Director of Annual Giving .... Mr. Joseph A. VOGL
53 Dean College of Education .... Mr. Craig DOUGLAS
88 Dir Enviornmental Health & Safety .... Mr. Robert J. TUTSOCK
88 Exec Dir Ctr for Business/Econ Dev .... Mr. Harold L. LEAVER
93 Director Multicultural Services .... Mr. Shawn WILSON
20 Associate Provost .... Dr. David M. CALLEJO PEREZ
102 Executive Director SVSU Foundation .... Mr. Andrew J. BETHUNE
40 Bookstore Manager .... Mr. Chris J. PAWLOSKI
96 Purchasing Manager .... Mr. Joshua M. WEBB
35 Asst Dean Stdnt Life/Leadership Pgm .... Mr. Bryan E. CRAINER
88 Exec Asst to Dean Arts/Behav Sci .... Dr. Joni M. BOYE-BEAMAN
50 Dean Business & Management .... Dr. Rama YELKUR
76 Dean of Health & Human Services .... Dr. Judith P. RULAND
54 Assoc Dean College of Sci/Engr/Tech .... Dr. Andrew M. CHUBB

St. Clair County Community College (G)

323 Erie Street, PO Box 5015, Port Huron MI 48061-5015
County: St. Clair FICE Identification: 002310
Unit ID: 172291
Telephone: (810) 984-3881 Carnegie Class: Assoc/HT-High Trad
FAX Number: (810) 984-4730 Calendar System: Semester
URL: www.sc4.edu
Established: 1923 Annual Undergrad Tuition & Fees (In-District): $3,715
Enrollment: 4,127 Coed
Affiliation or Control: Local IRS Status: 501(c)3
Highest Offering: Associate Degree
Accreditation: NH, ADNUR, CAHIIM, RAD

01 President .... Dr. Deborah SNYDER
05 Chief Academic Officer .... Mr. James NEESE
10 Chief Operating Officer .... Mr. Kirk A. KRAMER
32 Vice President Student Services .... Mr. Pete LACEY
09 VP Institutional Effectiveness .... Ms. Linda DAVIS
66 Dean of Nursing/Health/Human Svcs .... Ms. Cindy NICHOLSON
37 Dir of Financial Assistance/Svcs .... Ms. Josephine R. CASSAR
06 Registrar .... Ms. Carrie BEARSS
21 Controller .... Ms. Mary K. BRUNNER
41 Dir Campus Activities/Athletics .... Mr. Dale R. VOS
08 Director of Library Services .... Mr. Christopher RENNIE

Schoolcraft College (H)

18600 Haggerty Road, Livonia MI 48152-2696
County: Wayne FICE Identification: 002315
Unit ID: 172200
Telephone: (734) 462-4400 Carnegie Class: Assoc/MT-VT-High Non
FAX Number: (734) 462-4507 Calendar System: Semester
URL: www.schoolcraft.edu
Established: 1961 Annual Undergrad Tuition & Fees (In-District): $3,564
Enrollment: 11,542 Coed
Affiliation or Control: Local IRS Status: 501(c)3
Highest Offering: Baccalaureate
Accreditation: NH, ACFEI, ADNUR, CAHIIM, MAC, PNUR

01 President .... Dr. Conway A. JEFFRESS
10 Vice Pres/Chief Financial Officer .... Dr. Glenn CERNY
05 Vice Pres/CAO .... Mr. Richard WEINKAUF
32 Vice Pres/Chief Student Affs Ofcr .... Ms. Cheryl M. HAGEN
26 VP & Chief Information Officer .... Mr. Patrick TURNER
49 Dean Liberal Arts & Sciences .... Dr. Cheryl HAWKINS
75 Dean Occupational Prog/Econ Dev .... Dr. Robert LEADLEY
20 Dean of Educ & Lrng Support .... Dr. Deborah DAIEK
88 Assoc Dean College Centers .... Dr. Bonnie HECKARD-FARMER
51 Assoc Dean Cont Educ/Prof Develop .... Dr. Leslie PETTY
38 Assoc Dean Counseling/Student Sppt .... Dr. Michael OLIVER
11 Assoc Dean Opers/Curriculum/Assess .... Ms. Cindy CICCHELLI
84 Assoc Dean Enroll Mgmt/Student Rels .... Mr. Martin HEATOR
53 Assoc Dean Education Programs .... Dr. Dennis GENIG

81 Assoc Dean Sciences .... Mr. Charles HAYES
88 Assoc Dean Public Safety Programs ...... Mr. Gerald CHAMPAGNE
88 Assoc Dean Advising & Partnerships .... Ms. Laurie KATTUAH-SNYDER
72 Asst Dean Occupational Programs .... Ms. Amy JONES
15 Exec Director of Human Resources .... Ms. Laura SENSING
06 Registrar .... Ms. Nicole WILSON-FENNELL
37 Exec Dir Student Financial Services .... Ms. Regina MOSLEY
19 Campus Police Authority Chief .... Mr. Steven KAUFMAN
96 Dir of Purchasing/Business Ops .... Mr. Matthew WILSON
21 Controller/Director of Finance .... Mr. Jon LAMB
13 Exec Dir of Information Technology .... Mr. Christopher DENNY
07 Assoc Dean Admissions/Stdnt Engage .... Ms. Stacey STOVER
88 Exec Dir Info Security & Networking .... Mr. Jeffrey BORTON
88 Exec Dir of Enterprise Applications .... Ms. Laura CULLEN
04 Executive Asst to President .... Ms. Karla W. FRENTZOS
18 Exec Dir/Facilities Operations .... Mr. John WRIGHT
27 Exec Dir Marketing & Advancement .... Mr. Frank RUGGIRELLO
41 Director of Athletics .... Mr. Sidney FOX
44 Director of Development .... Ms. Elizabeth KOHLER
91 Director Administrative Systems .... Mr. Scott HEUSNER

Siena Heights University (A)

1247 Siena Heights Drive, Adrian MI 49221-1796

County: Lenawee FICE Identification: 002316
Unit ID: 172264
Telephone: (517) 263-0731 Carnegie Class: Masters/M
FAX Number: (517) 264-7704 Calendar System: Semester
URL: www.sienaheights.edu
Established: 1919 Annual Undergrad Tuition & Fees: $23,750
Enrollment: 2,642 Coed
Affiliation or Control: Roman Catholic IRS Status: 501(c)3
Highest Offering: Beyond Master's But Less Than Doctorate
Accreditation: NH, ART, NURSE, SW, TEAC

01 President .... Dr. Peg ALBERT, OP
10 Sr Vice Pres for Business/Finance .... Dr. J. Lee JOHNSON
30 Vice President for Advancement .... Mr. Mitchell P. BLONDE
05 Vice President for Academic Affairs ..... Dr. Sharon R. WEBER, OP
84 Vice Pres of Enrollment Mgmt Svcs .... Mr. George WOLF
28 Director of Alumni Office .... Mrs. Jenny ENGLE
107 Dean of Professional Studies/Grad .... Dr. Cheri BETZ
49 Dean College of Arts and Science .... Dr. Matthew DRAUD
32 Dean for Students .... Mr. Michael ORLANDO
06 Registrar .... Ms. Joy GARROW
07 Director of Admissions .... Ms. Trudy MOHRE
08 Director of Library .... Ms. Jennifer DEAN
13 Chief Information Officer .... Mr. Robert C. METZ
41 Director of Athletics .... Mr. Frederick M. SMITH
15 Human Resource Director .... Mr. Michael L. KARABETSOS
42 Director of Campus Ministry .... Fr. John GRACE
38 Director of Counseling Services .... Mrs. Sandy MORLEY
20 Director of Academic Advising .... Ms. Wiona PORATH
18 Supt of Buildings & Grounds .... Mr. Brian BERTRAM
09 Director of Institutional Research .... Mr. Jason HARTZ
39 Director of Residence Life .... Ms. Rachel RICKINGER
19 Director of Campus Security .... Mrs. Cindy A. BIRDWELL
23 Director of Health Services .... Sr. Sharon SPANBAUER
29 Director of Alumni Relations .... Mrs. Jenny ENGLE
36 Director of Career Services .... Ms. Sarah A. CHRENKO
44 Director of Donor Relations .... Mrs. Jenn BROOKET
28 Director of Immersion & Diversity .... Mrs. Sharese MATHIS
88 Dir of Integrated Univ Marketing .... Mr. Doug GOODNOUGH
37 Director Student Financial Aid .... Mrs. Lori KOSARUE
21 Controller .... Ms. Mary KRUSE
44 Coordinator of Annual Fund .... Mrs. Sheri HARDCASTLE
04 Executive Assistant to President .... Ms. Deborah KELLER

South University (B)

41555 Twelve Mile Road, Novi MI 48377

Telephone: (248) 675-0200 Identification: 770914
Accreditation: &SC, ACBSP, NURSE, PTAA

† Regional accreditation is carried under the parent institution in Savannah, GA

Southwestern Michigan College (C)

58900 Cherry Grove Road, Dowagiac MI 49047-9793

County: Cass FICE Identification: 002317
Unit ID: 172307
Telephone: (269) 782-1000 Carnegie Class: Assoc/HT-High Trad
FAX Number: (269) 782-8414 Calendar System: Semester
URL: www.swmich.edu
Established: 1964 Annual Undergrad Tuition & Fees (In-District): $4,921
Enrollment: 2,567 Coed
Affiliation or Control: State/Local IRS Status: 501(c)3
Highest Offering: Associate Degree
Accreditation: NH, CAHIIM

01 President .... Dr. David MATHEWS
100 Chief of Staff .... Mr. Thomas ATKINSON
10 Vice President/Chief Business Ofcr .... Ms. Susan COULSTON
05 Vice President of Instruction .... Dr. David FLEMING
32 Vice President of Student Services .... Ms. Eileen CROUSE
13 Executive Dir Computing Services .... Ms. Jeanne LUTHJOHAN
35 Executive Dir Student Services .... Ms. Angela PALSAK
49 Dean of Arts and Sciences .... Dr. Scott TOPPING
50 Dean NAC/School of Business .... Dr. Stacy HORNER
66 Dean School Nursing/Human Services ..... Ms. Rebecca JELLISON
18 Director of Buildings & Grounds .... Mr. John EBERHART
44 Director of Development .... Ms. Eileen TONEY
88 Dir of Educational Talent Srch Pgm .... Ms. Amy ANDERSON
07 Director of Admissions .... Mr. Jason SMITH
35 Director of EXCEL .... Ms. Laura SKILLINGS
37 Director of Financial Aid .... Ms. Christine PASSER
15 Director of Human Resources .... Ms. Kate DORNER
09 Director of Institutional Research .... Dr. Angela EVANS
08 Director of Library Services .... Ms. Colleen WELSCH
12 Director of Niles Campus .... Mr. Brent BREWER
06 Director of Records/Registrar .... Ms. M'Isha STARKS
88 Dir of Student and Testing Services ...... Ms. Charlotte MCGOWAN
39 Director of Student Housing .... Mr. Jason WILT
88 Manager of Accounting .... Ms. Christy MANGUS
21 Controller .... Ms. Michelle KITE
26 Manager of Marketing .... Ms. Michelle BOGUE
88 Manager of Student Activity Center .... Ms. Bethany BALLARD

Southwestern Michigan College Niles Area Campus (D)

33890 U.S. Highway 12, Niles MI 49120

Telephone: (800) 456-8675 Identification: 770286
Accreditation: &NH

† Regional accreditation is carried under the parent institution in Dowagiac, MI

Spring Arbor University (E)

106 E Main Street, Spring Arbor MI 49283-9799

County: Jackson FICE Identification: 002318
Unit ID: 172334
Telephone: (517) 750-1200 Carnegie Class: Masters/L
FAX Number: (517) 750-6620 Calendar System: 4/1/4
URL: www.arbor.edu
Established: 1873 Annual Undergrad Tuition & Fees: $25,510
Enrollment: 3,733 Coed
Affiliation or Control: Free Methodist IRS Status: 501(c)3
Highest Offering: Master's
Accreditation: NH, CACREP, MUS, NURSE, SW, TEAC

01 University President .... Dr. Brent ELLIS
05 Provost/Chief Academic Officer .... Dr. Kimberly RUPERT
03 Executive Vice President .... Dr. Douglas A. WILCOXSON
10 Vice Pres Finance & Administration .... Mr. Kevin W. ROSE
32 VP Student Success & Calling .... Dr. Kimberly K. HAYWORTH
100 Chief of Staff .... Mr. Damon M. SEACOTT
07 VP Enroll & Marketing .... Mr. Malachi D. CRANE
12 Assistant Provost SAU Global .... Dr. Linda G. SHERRILL
15 Director of Human Resources .... Mrs. Melissa MONTGOMERY
91 Chief Technology Officer .... Vacant
20 Associate Provost .... Mr. Rod S. STEWART
30 Assistant VP Advancement Operations . Mrs. Rhonda R. SAURBEK
49 Dean School Arts & Sciences .... Vacant
50 Dean Gainey School of Business .... Dr. Caleb K. CHAN
53 Dean School of Education .... Dr. Linda G. SHERRILL
88 Dean School of Human Services .... Mrs. Tamara L. DINDOFFER
35 Asst VP Student Development .... Mr. Dan VANDERHILL
06 Registrar .... Vacant
84 Director of Enrollment Operations .... Mr. Kevin BROWN
21 Assistant VP Financial Services .... Mrs. Dawn I. SCHNITKEY
44 Executive Director of Development .... Mrs. Linda SCHAUB
41 Athletic Director .... Mr. Ryan T. COTTINGHAM
42 Chaplain .... Mr. Ronald L. KOPICKO
37 Director of Financial Aid .... Mr. Herbert K. ROTICH
09 Director Institutional Research .... Mr. Thomas P. KORMAN
108 Director of Assessment .... Vacant
08 Director Library .... Mr. Robert D. BOLTON
18 Director of Physical Plant .... Mr. Larry OUSLEY
89 Director Retention & Fresh Programs .... Vacant
104 Director Cross Cultural Studies .... Mrs. Diane L. KURTZ
23 Exec Dir Student Health/Wellness .... Mrs. Mary BRODA
39 Asst Dean Students/Dir of Housing .... Mr. Robert C. PRATT
36 Director Career Svcs/Acad Advising .... Vacant
19 Director Campus Safety .... Mr. Scott L. KREBILL
106 Assoc Dean External/SAUonline .... Mr. Gary R. TUCKER
28 Director Intercultural Relations .... Mr. Eric A. BEDA
29 Director Alumni Relations .... Mrs. Irene L. PRICE
105 Web Architect .... Mr. Peter J. SHACKELFORD
04 Dir Operations Pres/Provost Office .... Mrs. Sarah R. CRANE

SS. Cyril and Methodius Seminary (F)

3535 Indian Trail, Orchard Lake MI 48324-1623

County: Oakland FICE Identification: 037384
Unit ID: 260211
Telephone: (248) 683-0310 Carnegie Class: Not Classified
FAX Number: (248) 738-6735 Calendar System: Semester
URL: www.sscms.edu
Established: 1885 Annual Graduate Tuition & Fees: N/A
Enrollment: N/A Coed
Affiliation or Control: Roman Catholic IRS Status: 501(c)3
Highest Offering: Master's; No Undergraduates
Accreditation: THEOL

01 Rector/President .... RevMsg. Thomas MACHALSKI
05 Interim Academic Dean .... Rev. Leonard OBLOY
06 Registrar .... Ms. Joanna OLEJNICZAK-CAUSHAJ

University of Detroit Mercy (G)

4001 W McNichols Road, Detroit MI 48221-3038

County: Wayne FICE Identification: 002323
Unit ID: 169716
Telephone: (313) 993-1000 Carnegie Class: Masters/L
FAX Number: (313) 993-1229 Calendar System: Semester
URL: www.udmercy.edu
Established: 1877 Annual Undergrad Tuition & Fees: $38,626
Enrollment: 4,945 Coed
Affiliation or Control: Roman Catholic IRS Status: 501(c)3
Highest Offering: Doctorate
Accreditation: NH, ANEST, ARCPA, BUS, CACREP, CLPSY, DENT, DH, ENG, NURSE, SW, TEAC

01 President .... Dr. Antoine M. GARIBALDI
05 Provost and VP for Academic Affairs .... Ms. Pamela ZARKOWSKI
10 VP for Business & Finance and CFO . Mr. Vincent ABATEMARCO
30 VP for University Advancement .... Mr. Arnold D'AMBROSIO
84 VP Enrollment & Student Affairs .... Ms. Deborah STIEFFEL
101 University Secretary & Senior Atty .... Ms. Monica BARBOUR
18 Assoc Vice Pres Facil Management ...... Ms. Tamara BATCHELLER
15 Associate Vice Pres Human Resources ...... Mr. Steven J. NELSON
26 Assoc VP Marketing & Public Affairs .... Ms. Liz PATTERSON
13 Associate Vice President ITS .... Mr. Edward TRACY, II
06 Associate VP/Registrar .... Ms. Diane M. PRAET
44 Exec Director of Annual Giving .... Ms. Ann FISHER
88 Exec Director of Major Gifts .... Ms. Nikki BORGES
32 Dean of Students .... Ms. Monica WILLIAMS
08 Dean of Libraries .... Ms. Jennifer DEAN
09 Director of Institutional Research .... Ms. Shelley WAGNON
37 Director Scholarships & Aid .... Ms. Jenny MCALONAN
35 Associate Director of Student Life .... Ms. Dorothy STEWART
41 Director of Athletics .... Mr. Robert VOWELS
49 Dean College of Liberal Arts/Ed .... Dr. Mark DENHAM
61 Dean School of Law .... Ms. Phyllis CROCKER
54 Dean College Engineering & Science .... Dr. Gary KULECK
48 Dean School of Architecture .... Mr. William WITTIG
50 Dean Col Business Admin .... Dr. Joseph EISENHAUER
52 Dean School of Dentistry .... Dr. Mert AKSU
76 Dean CHP/Nursing .... Dr. Christine PACINI
88 Dean Coop Education/Career Ctr .... Ms. Sheryl JOHNSON-ROULHAC
39 Director Residence Life .... Ms. Lanae GILL
04 Exec Asst to the President .... Ms. Lisa MACDONNELL
85 Dir of International Services .... Ms. Weihong SUN
38 Director of Wellness Center .... Ms. Annamaria SILVERI
92 Director of Honors Program .... Mr. J. Todd HIBBARD
96 Director of Procurement Services .... Ms. Tina A. MAITLAND
88 Coordinator of Advancement Systems .... Ms. Stephanie JONES
07 Executive Director of Admissions .... Ms. Tyra ROUNDS
108 Director Institutional Assessment .... Dr. Elizabeth ROBERTS-KIRCHOFF
19 Director Public Safety .... Ms. Letitia WILLIAMS
25 Dir of Sponsored Research .... Ms. Catherine CALDWELL
53 Chair Education Department .... Dr. Lorri MACDONALD
106 Dir Online Education/E-learning .... Ms. Jennifer DEAN
102 Dir Foundation/Corporate Relations .... Ms. Yvonne LINDSTROM
22 Title IX & Equity/Compliance Coord .... Ms. Marjorie LANG
29 Director Alumni Relations .... Ms. Margaret PATTISON

University of Detroit Mercy Corktown Campus (H)

2700 Martin Luther King Jr. Blvd, Detroit MI 48208-2576

Telephone: (313) 494-6700 Identification: 770291
Accreditation: &NH

† Regional accreditation is carried under the parent institution in Detroit, MI

University of Detroit Mercy School of Law (I)

651 E Jefferson Avenue, Detroit MI 48226-4349

Telephone: (313) 596-0200 Identification: 770292
Accreditation: &NH, LAW

† Regional accreditation is carried under the parent institution in Detroit, MI

University of Michigan-Ann Arbor (J)

500 S. State Street, Ann Arbor MI 48109

County: Washtenaw FICE Identification: 002325
Unit ID: 170976
Telephone: (734) 764-1817 Carnegie Class: DU-Highest
FAX Number: N/A Calendar System: Trimester
URL: umich.edu
Established: 1817 Annual Undergrad Tuition & Fees (In-State): $13,856
Enrollment: 43,625 Coed
Affiliation or Control: State IRS Status: 501(c)3
Highest Offering: Doctorate
Accreditation: NH, ART, BUS, CAATE, CLPSY, CS, DANCE, DENT, DH, DIETD, DIETI, ENG, ENGR, HSA, IPSY, LAW, LIB, LSAR, MED, MIDWF, MUS, NURSE, PDPSY, PH, PHAR, PLNG, SW, TEAC

01 President .... Dr. Mark S. SCHLISSEL
05 Provost/Exec VP Academic Affs .... Dr. Martha E. POLLACK
10 Exec VP/CFO .... Mr. Kevin P. HEGARTY
17 Exec VP for Medical Affairs .... Dr. Marschall S. RUNGE
30 Vice President Development .... Mr. Jerry A. MAY
32 Vice President Student Life .... Dr. E. Royster HARPER
46 Vice President for Research .... Dr. S. Jack HU
86 Vice Pres Governmental Relations ...... Ms. Cynthia H. WILBANKS
26 Vice Pres Global Communications .... Ms. Lisa M. RUDGERS
43 Vice Pres/General Counsel .... Mr. Timothy G. LYNCH
101 Vice Pres/Sec of the University .... Ms. Sally J. CHURCHILL
04 Exec Asst to the President .... Ms. Erika J. HRABEC

100 Special Counsel to the Provost .... Ms. Kelly L. CUNNINGHAM
20 Vice Provost Acad/Budget Affairs .... Dr. Alfred FRANZBLAU
20 Vice Provost Acad & Faculty Affairs .... Dr. Lori J. PIERCE
20 Vice Provost Acad & Faculty Affairs .... Dr. Sara B. BLAIR
58 Vice Provost Acad Affs Grad Stds .... Dr. Janet A. WEISS
104 Vice Provost Global & Engaged Educ .. Dr. James P. HOLLOWAY
20 Vice Prov Equity/Inclus & Acad Affs .... Dr. Robert M. SELLERS
20 Vice Prov Dig Educ & Univ Librarian .... Dr. James L. HILTON
09 Assoc Vice Provost & Exec Dir OBP .... Ms. Tammy C. BIMER
07 Director Undergrad Admissions .... Ms. Erica L. SANDERS
15 Assoc Vice Provost & Sr Dr Acad HR .... Mr. Jeffery R. FRUMKIN
22 Assoc Vice Prov/Sr Dir Inst Equity .... Mr. Anthony J. WALESBY
18 Assoc VP Facilities/Operations .... Mr. Henry D. BAIER
21 Interim Assoc VP Finance .... Ms. Nancy A. HOBBS
88 Chief Investment Officer .... Mr. Erik LUNDBERG
30 Assoc VP for Development .... Mr. Dondi L. CUPP
17 Assoc VP for Medical Affairs .... Dr. John E. BILLI
46 Assoc VP for Research .... Dr. Volker SICK
46 Assoc VP for Research .... Dr. J. Brian FOWLKES
46 Assoc VP for Research .... Dr. Toni C. ANTONUCCI
46 Assoc VP for Research .... Mr. Daryl C. WEINERT
46 Assoc VP for Research .... Dr. Eric MICHIELSSEN
46 Assoc VP Research .... Mr. Kenneth J. NISBET
46 Assoc VP Research .... Dr. James A. ASHTON-MILLER
35 Assoc VP Student Life/Dean Stdnts .... Ms. Laura B. JONES
35 Assoc VP Student Life .... Ms. Anjali N. ANTURKAR
35 Assoc VP Student Life .... Dr. Simone HIMBEAULT-TAYLOR
35 Assoc VP Student Life .... Mr. Loren J. RULLMAN
16 Assoc VP for Human Resources .... Ms. Laurita E. THOMAS
13 Assoc VP Info Tech/Chief Info Ofcr .... Ms. Laura M. PATTERSON
06 University Registrar .... Mr. Paul A. ROBINSON
96 Interim Dir Procurement Services .... Mr. Colin T. ANDERSON
38 Director Counseling & Psych Service .... Dr. Todd D. SEVIG
39 Director University Housing .... Ms. Linda L. NEWMAN
23 Director University Health Service .... Dr. Robert A. WINFIELD
19 Exec Dir Pub Safety/Security .... Mr. Eddie L. WASHINGTON
37 Exec Director Financial Aid .... Ms. Pamela W. FOWLER
18 Executive Director Plant Operations .... Mr. Richard W. ROBBEN
41 Director of Athletics .... Mr. Warde MANUEL
48 Int Dn Col Architecture/Urban Plng .... Mr. Robert FISHMAN
49 Dean Col Literature/Science/Arts .... Dr. Andrew D. MARTIN
54 Dean College of Engineering .... Dr. David C. MUNSON
61 Dean Law School .... Mr. Mark D. WEST
63 Dean Medical School .... Dr. James O. WOOLLISCROFT
67 Dean College of Pharmacy .... Dr. James T. DALTON
65 Dean Sch Natural Resrc/Environ .... Dr. Marie L. MIRANDA
64 Dean School Music Theatre & Dance .... Mr. Aaron P. DWORKIN
57 Dean School of Art & Design .... Dr. Gunalan L. NADARAJAN
50 Dean School of Business .... Dr. Alison DAVIS-BLAKE
52 Dean School of Dentistry .... Dr. Laurie K. MCCAULEY
53 Dean School of Education .... Dr. Deborah L. BALL
62 Dean School of Information .... Dr. Jeffrey K. MACKIE-MASON
68 Dean School of Kinesiology .... Dr. Ronald F. ZERNICKE
66 Dean School of Nursing .... Dr. Kathleen M. POTEMPA
80 Dean School of Public Policy .... Dr. Susan M. COLLINS
70 Dean School of Social Work .... Dr. Laura LEIN
69 Dean School of Public Health .... Dr. Martin A. PHILBERT
29 President Alumni Association .... Mr. Steve C. GRAFTON

University of Michigan-Dearborn (A)

4901 Evergreen Road, Dearborn MI 48128-1491
County: Wayne FICE Identification: 002326
Unit ID: 171137
Telephone: (313) 593-5000 Carnegie Class: Masters/L
FAX Number: (313) 593-5452 Calendar System: Trimester
URL: www.umd.umich.edu
Established: 1959 Annual Undergrad Tuition & Fees (In-State): $11,304
Enrollment: 8,923 Coed
Affiliation or Control: State IRS Status: 501(c)3
Highest Offering: Doctorate
Accreditation: NH, BUS, CEA, CS, ENG, TEAC

01 Chancellor .... Dr. Daniel LITTLE
05 Prov/Vice Chanc Academic Affs .... Dr. Catherine A. DAVY
10 Vice Chancellor Business Affairs .... Mr. Jeffrey L. EVANS
84 Vice Chanc Enroll Mgmt .... Mr. Ray E. METZ
30 Vice Chanc Inst Advancement .... Ms. Mallory M. SIMPSON
31 Vice Chanc for External Relations .... Mr. Kenneth KETTENBEIL
21 Director of Financial Services .... Mr. Noel HORNBACHER
06 Registrar .... Ms. Janice LEWIS-BOYD
100 Chief of Staff .... Vacant
26 Director Communications/Marketing .... Ms. Beth MARMARELLI
86 Government Relations Manager .... Mr. Mike LATVIS
15 Director of Human Resources .... Ms. Keisha BLEVINS
29 Alumni Engagement .... Vacant
20 Associate Provost Undergraduate .... Dr. Mitchel SOLLENBERGER
20 Associate Provost Graduate .... Dr. Ilir MITEZA
13 Director IT Strategy/Operations .... Mr. Robert GOFFENEY
08 Director of Library .... Ms. Elaine LOGAN
09 Int Dir of Institutional Research .... Dr. Mitchel SOLLENBERGER
84 Asst VC for Enrollment Management .... Dr. Monica PORTER
07 Director of Admissions .... Ms. Deb PEFFER
37 Director of Financial Aid .... Ms. Katherine ALLEN
38 Director of Counseling .... Dr. Debra HUTTON
36 Director of Career Services .... Ms. Regina M. STORRS
85 Director of International Affairs .... Dr. Monica PORTER
32 Director of Student Engagement ... Ms. Reetha PERANANAMGAM
18 Exec Dir of Facilities Operations .... Ms. Carol GLICK
19 Chief of Police .... Mr. Kevin WILLIAMS
22 Institutional Equity Officer .... Ms. Anita GREEN
28 Sp Counsel to Chanc for Inclusion .... Dr. Ann LAMPKIN-WILLIAMS

49 Dean Col Arts/Science/Letters .... Dr. Martin HERSHOCK
54 Dean Col of Engr/Comp Sci .... Dr. A. W. ENGLAND
50 Dean College of Business .... Dr. Raju BALAKRISHNAN
53 Dean College of Ed/Health/HS .... Dr. Janine JANOSKY
88 Director of Enrollment Research .... Mr. Dan MERIAN
41 Athletic Director .... Mr. Matt BEAUDRY

University of Michigan-Flint (B)

303 E Kearsley Street, Flint MI 48502-1950
County: Genesee FICE Identification: 002327
Unit ID: 171146
Telephone: (810) 762-3000 Carnegie Class: Masters/L
FAX Number: (810) 762-5725 Calendar System: Semester
URL: www.umflint.edu
Established: 1956 Annual Undergrad Tuition & Fees (In-State): $9,936
Enrollment: 8,574 Coed
Affiliation or Control: State IRS Status: 501(c)3
Highest Offering: Doctorate
Accreditation: NH, ANEST, BUS, CEA, ENG, MUS, NURSE, PTA, RTT, SW, TED

01 Chancellor .... Dr. Susan E. BORREGO
05 Provost/VC Academic Affairs .... Dr. Douglas KNERR
32 VC Campus Inclusion & Student Life .... Dr. Barbara J. AVERY
10 Interim VC Business and Finance .... Mr. Michael J. HAGUE
21 Asst Vice Chanc Business & Finance .... Vacant
35 Assoc VC & Dean of Students .... Dr. Julie SNYDER
88 Asst VC for Student Success .... Dr. Jonathan GRADY
58 Sr Vice Provost/Dean Grad Pgms .... Dr. Vahid LOTFI
20 Asst Prov/Dean Undergrad Studies .... Vacant
26 Interim Exec Dir Univ Relations .... Ms. Marjory RAYMER
86 Director Government Relations .... Mr. David E. LOSSING
28 Exec Director Educational Oppty .... Vacant
08 Director of Library .... Mr. Robert L. HOUBECK, JR.
06 Registrar .... Ms. Karen A. ARNOULD
07 Admissions Director .... Mr. Jon DAVIDSON
37 Director Financial Aid .... Ms. Lori VEDDER
15 Director Human Res/Affirm Action .... Ms. Beth MANNING
49 Dean College Arts & Sciences .... Dr. Susan GANO-PHILLIPS
50 Dean School of Management .... Dr. Scott JOHNSON
66 Director Nursing Program .... Dr. Margaret ANDREWS
76 Dean Sch Health Prof & Studies .... Dr. Donna FRY
53 Dean Sch Education & Human Svcs .... Dr. Robert BARNETT
51 Director of Extended Learning .... Ms. Deborah WHITE
19 Director of Public Safety .... Mr. Raymond D. HALL
18 Dir Facilities Mgmt/Auxiliary Svcs .... Mr. George HAKIM
13 Director Info Technology Services .... Mr. Scott ARNST
36 Director Student Success Center .... Ms. Aimi MOSS
46 Director of Research .... Dr. Kenneth SYLVESTER
21 Director of Financial Svcs & Budget .... Mr. Gerald GLASCO
88 Interim Dir University Outreach .... Ms. Paula NAS
30 VC University Advancement .... Ms. Kristin LINDSEY
96 Procurement Agent Senior .... Ms. Brenda ROTH
09 Director of Institutional Analysis .... Ms. Fawn SKARSTEN
38 Director CAPS .... Ms. Tamara MCKAY
39 Director Student Housing .... Mr. William WASHINGTON
100 Chief of Staff .... Dr. Tess BARKER
04 Executive Asst to the Chancellor .... Ms. Dru A. DORAN
29 Director Alumni Relations .... Dr. Mary Jo SEKELSKY
44 Director of Development .... Mr. Jay NUSSEL
92 Director Honors Program .... Dr. Maureen THUM
88 Sr Dir of Student Involv & Ldrship .... Dr. Michelle ROSYNSKY
88 Dir of Adm Info Mgmt Services .... Ms. Jay GANDHI
88 Dir Women's Educational Center .... Dr. Rushika PATEL
88 Dir Thompson Center for T&L .... Dr. Tracy WACKER

University of Phoenix Detroit Main Campus (C)

26261 Evergreen Road, Southfield MI 48076-4400
Telephone: (248) 675-3700 Identification: 770211
Accreditation: &NH

† Regional accreditation is carried under the parent institution in Tempe, AZ

Van Andel Institute Graduate School (D)

333 Bostwick Avenue NE, Grand Rapids MI 49503
County: Kent Identification: 667085
Telephone: (616) 234-5708 Carnegie Class: Not Classified
FAX Number: (616) 234-5709 Calendar System: Semester
URL: vaei.vai.org/grad-school/
Established: 1996 Annual Graduate Tuition & Fees: N/A
Enrollment: N/A Coed
Affiliation or Control: Independent Non-Profit IRS Status: 501(c)3
Highest Offering: Doctorate; No Undergraduates
Accreditation: NH

01 President/Dean of the Graduate Sch . Dr. Steven J. TRIEZENBERG
05 Associate Dean of Graduate School .... Dr. Julie D. TURNER
06 Enrollment and Records Admin .... Ms. Carol RAPPLEY
04 Administrative Asst to President .... Ms. Kristie VANDERHOOF

Walsh College Novi Campus (E)

41500 Gardenbrook Road, Novi MI 48375-1313
Telephone: (248) 349-5454 Identification: 770293
Accreditation: &NH

† Regional accreditation is carried under the parent institution in Troy, MI

Walsh College of Accountancy and Business Administration (F)

3838 Livernois Road, Box 7006, Troy MI 48007-7006
County: Oakland FICE Identification: 004071
Unit ID: 172608
Telephone: (248) 689-8282 Carnegie Class: Spec-4-yr-Bus
FAX Number: (248) 689-9066 Calendar System: Semester
URL: www.walshcollege.edu
Established: 1922 Annual Undergrad Tuition & Fees: N/A
Enrollment: 2,753 Coed
Affiliation or Control: Independent Non-Profit IRS Status: 501(c)3
Highest Offering: Doctorate
Accreditation: NH, ACBSP

01 President & CEO .... Ms. Stephanie W. BERGERON
05 Interim Exec VP/Chief Academic Ofc .... Dr. Michael A. RINKUS
10 Vice President/CFO/Treasurer . Ms. Helen C. KIEBA-TOLKSDORF
26 Asst VP/Director of Marketing .... Ms. Brenda MELLER
15 VP/Chief Human Resources/Admin Ofcr .... Ms. Elizabeth A. BARNES
30 Vice President/Chief Devel Officer .... Ms. Audrey OLMSTEAD
04 Exec Assistant to the President .... Ms. Judie DZIERBICKI
32 Asst VP Student Services/Marketing .... Ms. Victoria R. SCAVONE
106 Director Office of Online Learning .... Mr. Thomas PETZ
20 Director Academic Administration .... Ms. Monique CARDENAS
37 Director Financial Aid .... Ms. Catherine BERRAHOU
18 Director Facilities/Auxiliary Svcs .... Ms. Chris STOUT
21 Controller .... Mr. Ryan KUNZELMAN
07 Director Admissions/Acad Advising .... Ms. Heather RIGBY
06 Director of Records/Registrar .... Ms. Stacy JOHNSON
13 Exec Dir Ofc of Info Technology .... Mr. Jacob KLEIN
12 Director Novi Campus .... Mr. Jason SWEET
36 Director Career Services .... Ms. Brenda PAINE
88 Chair Management .... Dr. Sheila R. RONIS
88 Chair Business Comm .... Dr. Linda HAGAN
88 Chair Marketing .... Dr. Michael LEVENS
88 Director Launchpad .... Ms. Carol GLYNN
29 Manager of Alumni Relations .... Ms. MiVida BURRUS
88 Chair Accounting/Taxation .... Mr. John BLACK
88 Chair Finance & Economics .... Mr. Greg TODD
72 Chair Decision Sciences .... Dr. Barbara CIARAMITARO

Washtenaw Community College (G)

4800 E Huron River Dr, Ann Arbor MI 48105-4800
County: Washtenaw FICE Identification: 002328
Unit ID: 172617
Telephone: (734) 973-3300 Carnegie Class: Assoc/MT-VT-High Non
FAX Number: (734) 677-5413 Calendar System: Semester
URL: www.wccnet.edu
Established: 1965 Annual Undergrad Tuition & Fees (In-District): $2,424
Enrollment: 12,295 Coed
Affiliation or Control: Local IRS Status: 501(c)3
Highest Offering: Associate Degree
Accreditation: NH, ACFEI, ADNUR, DA, PTAA, RAD, SURGT

01 President .... Dr. Rose BELLANCA
10 VP & Chief Financial Officer .... Mr. William JOHNSON
05 VP for Instruction .... Dr. Michael NEALON
15 VP Human Resources Mgmt .... Mr. Douglas KRUZEL
32 VP Student & Academic Services .... Ms. Linda BLAKEY
18 VP Facilities & Campus Safety .... Mr. Damon FLOWERS
30 Vice Pres of College Advancement .... Vacant
31 VP Economic/Community & College Dev .... Ms. Michelle MUELLER
07 AVP Recruitment & Enrollment .... Dr. Evan MONTAGUE
45 Exec Dir Inst Effect Plng & Accred .... Ms. Julie MORRISON
20 Dean Supp Svcs & Student Advocacy .... Dr. Elizabeth ORBITS
62 Dean Learning Resources .... Mr. Victor LIU
50 Dean Business & Computer Tech .... Dr. Kimberly HURNS
81 Dean Math & Natural Science .... Ms. Kristin GOOD
36 Dean Career Svc/UA Programs .... Ms. Marilyn DONHAM
28 Dean Diversity & Inclusion .... Mr. Arnett CHISHOLM
88 Dean Adv Tech/Public Service .... Mr. Brandon TUCKER
10 Controller .... Ms. Lynn MARTIN
96 Dir Budget Purchasing Auxiliary Svc .... Ms. Barbara FILLINGER
16 Director Human Resource Svcs .... Ms. Christine MIHALY
37 Director Financial Aid .... Ms. Lori TRAPP
09 Director Institutional Research .... Dr. Roger MOURAD
19 Director Safety & Security .... Mr. Jacques DESROSIERS
35 Dir Student Development/Activities .... Mr. Peter LESHKEVICH
84 Dean of Enrollment Management .... Mr. Larry AEILTS
86 Dir of Government Relations .... Vacant
43 General Counsel .... Mr. Larry BARKOFF
88 Exec Administrator to President/BOT .... Ms. Vanessa BROOKS
04 Executive Admin Asst to President .... Ms. Karen PERKETT
100 Chief of Staff .... Ms. Monique JAMES

Wayne County Community College District (H)

801 W Fort Street, Detroit MI 48226-3010
County: Wayne FICE Identification: 009230
Unit ID: 172635
Telephone: (313) 496-2600 Carnegie Class: Assoc/MT-VT-Mix Trad/Non
FAX Number: (313) 961-9439 Calendar System: Semester
URL: www.wcccd.edu
Established: 1967 Annual Undergrad Tuition & Fees (In-District): $2,813
Enrollment: 16,310 Coed
Affiliation or Control: State/Local IRS Status: 501(c)3
Highest Offering: Associate Degree

Accreditation: NH, DA, DH, EMT, SURGA, SURGT

01 Chancellor .... Dr. Curtis L. IVERY
05 Interim Dist VC Educ Affairs/DL .... Dr. George W. SWAN, III
32 Dist VC Student Svcs/Dual Enrollmnt .... Mr. Brian SINGLETON
51 Dist VC Sch Cont Ed/Wrkforce Dev .... Ms. Shawna FORBES
10 Dist VC Finance & Admin .... Ms. Kim DICARO
15 Dist VC HR/Accountability .... Mr. Mirza F. AHMED
09 Dist VC IE & Info Mgmt .... Ms. Johnesa HODGE
12 Campus President/CAO Downriver .... Mr. Anthony ARMINIAK
12 Campus President/CAO Downtown .... Ms. Denise SHANNON
12 Campus President/CAO Western .... Mr. Michael P. DOTSON
12 Campus President Northwest .... Dr. Letitia UDUMA
12 Campus President/CAO Eastern .... Ms. Mawine DIGGS
88 Dist Asst to Chanc Instr/Stdnt Succ .... Dr. Patrick J. MCNALLY
12 Provost University Center .... Dr. Sandra T. ROBINSON
72 Provost of Learning Technology .... Ms. Kiran SEKHRI
30 Dist VC Institutional Advancement .... Ms. Muna KHOURY

Wayne County Community College District Downriver Campus (A)

21000 Northline Road, Taylor MI 48180
Telephone: (734) 946-3500 Identification: 770297
Accreditation: &NH

† Regional accreditation is carried under the parent institution in Detroit, MI

Wayne County Community College District Downtown Campus (B)

1001 West Fort Street, Detroit MI 48226
Telephone: (313) 496-2758 Identification: 770926
Accreditation: &NH

Wayne County Community College District Eastern Campus (C)

5901 Conner, Detroit MI 48213
Telephone: (313) 922-3311 Identification: 770295
Accreditation: &NH

† Regional accreditation is carried under the parent institution in Detroit, MI

Wayne County Community College District Northwest Campus (D)

8200 West Outer Drive, Detroit MI 48219
Telephone: (313) 943-4000 Identification: 770296
Accreditation: &NH

† Regional accreditation is carried under the parent institution in Detroit, MI

Wayne County Community College District Western Campus (E)

9555 Haggerty Road, Belleville MI 48111
Telephone: (734) 699-7008 Identification: 770294
Accreditation: &NH

† Regional accreditation is carried under the parent institution in Detroit, MI

Wayne State University (F)

656 W. Kirby Street, Room # 4070, Detroit MI 48202-4095
County: Wayne FICE Identification: 002329
Unit ID: 172644
Telephone: (313) 577-2424 Carnegie Class: DU-Highest
FAX Number: (313) 577-8154 Calendar System: Semester
URL: www.wayne.edu
Established: 1868 Annual Undergrad Tuition & Fees (In-State): $11,314
Enrollment: 27,578 Coed
Affiliation or Control: State IRS Status: 501(c)3
Highest Offering: Doctorate
Accreditation: NH, ANEST, ARCPA, AUD, BUS, CACREP, CLPSY, CORE, DANCE, DIETC, ENG, ENGT, FUSER, LAW, LIB, MED, MIDWF, MT, MUS, NURSE, OT, PA, PH, PHAR, PLNG, PTA, RAD, RTT, SP, SPAA, SW, TEAC, THEA

01 President .... Dr. M. Roy WILSON
100 Chief of Staff/VP Marketing & Comm .... Mr. Michael G. WRIGHT
05 Provost .... Dr. Keith WHITFIELD
10 VP Finance & Business/Treasurer/CFO .... Mr. William DECATUR
43 Vice President and General Counsel .... Mr. Louis A. LESSEM
46 Vice President for Research .... Dr. Stephen M. LANIER
30 VP Development and Alumni Affairs .... Ms. Susan E. BURNS
86 VP Government and Community Affairs .... Mr. Patrick O. LINDSEY
20 Asscociate VP Undergraduate Affairs .... Mr. R. Darin ELLIS
88 VP for Economic Development .... Mr. Ned STAEBLER
84 Int Assoc VP for Enrollment Mgmt .... Mr. Ahmad EZZEDDINE
101 Secretary to the BOG .... Ms. Julie H. MILLER
04 Assistant to the President .... Ms. Allison GUILLIOM
29 Exec Dir Alumni Relations .... Mr. Peter CABORN
15 Associate VP of Human Resources .... Ms. Alicia PENDELTON
18 Assoc VP Facilities/Planning/Mgmt .... Mr. Mark ALLEN
21 Assoc VP Budget/Planning/Analysis .... Mr. Robert KOHRMAN
44 Associate VP of Individual Giving .... Ms. Tracy UTECH
32 Dean of Students .... Dr. David J. STRAUSS
07 Director Undergraduate Admissions .... Ms. Ericka JACKSON
26 Director of Communications .... Mr. Mathew T. LOCKWOOD
25 Asst VP Sponsored Program Admin .... Ms. Gail L. RYAN
37 Int Director Student Financial Aid .... Ms. Gayle REYNOLDS
62 Dean University Library System .... Dr. Sandra G. YEE
06 University Registrar .... Ms. Linda K. FALKIEWICZ
88 Asscciate VP for Research .... Dr. Gloria HEPPNER
49 Dean College of Liberal Arts/Sci .... Dr. Wayne RASKIND
61 Dean Law School .... Ms. Jocelyn BENSON
63 Dean School of Medicine .... Dr. Jack SOBEL
66 Dean College of Nursing .... Dr. Laurie LAUZON CLABO
54 Dean College of Engineering .... Dr. Farshad FOTOUHI
50 Dean Ilitch School of Business .... Dr. Robert E. FORSYTHE
70 Dean School of Social Work .... Dr. Cheryl E. WAITES
67 Dean College of Pharmacy & Health .... Dr. Semme S. LAU
53 Dean College of Education .... Dr. R. Douglas WHITMAN
57 Dean College Fine/Perf & Comm Arts .... Dr. Matthew SEEGER
92 Dean Honors College .... Dr. Jerry HERRON
58 Dean Graduate School .... Dr. Ambika MATHUR
96 Assistant VP of Procurement .... Mr. Kenneth DOHERTY
104 Asscciate VP Outreach & Intl Pgms .... Dr. Ahmad EZZEDDINE
21 Assoc VP Business & Auxiliary Ops .... Mr. Timothy MICHAEL
88 Assoc VP Tech Commercialization .... Dr. Joan DUNBAR
13 Asscciate VP CIO .... Mr. Daren HUBBARD
41 Director of Athletics .... Mr. Robert FOURNIER
105 Director of Web Communications .... Mr. Nick DENARDIS
19 Chief of Police .... Mr. Anthony HOLT
22 Interim Director Equal Opportunity .... Ms. Nikki WRIGHT
28 Assoc Provost Diversity & Inclusion .... Ms. Marquita CHAMBLEE
36 Director of Career Services .... Mr. Ronald KENT
39 Director Housing & Residential Life .... Ms. Jeanine BESSETTE
108 Director Institutional Assessment .... Dr. Catherine BARRETTE
38 Director Student Counseling .... Dr. Jeffrey KUENTZEL
09 Director Institutional Research .... Mr. Song YAN
102 Assoc VP Principal Gifts .... Mr. Jefferson PORTER

West Shore Community College (G)

3000 N. Stiles Road, Scottville MI 49454-0277
County: Mason FICE Identification: 007950
Unit ID: 172671
Telephone: (231) 845-6211 Carnegie Class: Assoc/MT-VT-Mix Trad/Non
FAX Number: (231) 843-5803 Calendar System: Semester
URL: www.westshore.edu
Established: 1967 Annual Undergrad Tuition & Fees (In-District): $2,478
Enrollment: 1,330 Coed
Affiliation or Control: Local IRS Status: 501(c)3
Highest Offering: Associate Degree
Accreditation: NH

01 President .... Dr. Kenneth URBAN
26 Exec Director of Communications .... Mr. Thomas A. HAWLEY
11 VP of Administrative Services .... Mr. Scott WARD
49 Dean of Arts and Sciences .... Dr. Brooke FORTMANN
75 Dean of Occupational Programs .... Ms. Christy CHRISTMAS
32 Dean of Student Services .... Mr. Chad E. INABINET
06 Registrar .... Ms. Jill SWEET
09 Director of Institutional Research .... Mr. Steve SPARLING
40 Director of Bookstore & Food Svcs .... Ms. Cheryl HOGAN
04 Exec Assistant to the President .... Ms. Lisa STANKOWSKI
37 Director Financial Aid .... Ms. Rebekah SCHAUB
91 Manager of Adm Computing Systems .... Ms. Bonnie CHALTRON
88 Director of Criminal Justice .... Mr. Dan DELLAR
88 Director of Recreational Services .... Mr. Michael A. MOORE
15 Director of Human Resources .... Ms. Debra CAMPBELL
88 Director Student Resources .... Ms. Carla E. SHAY
08 Director of Library Services .... Ms. Renee SNODGRASS
23 Director of Wellness Center .... Ms. Julie PAGE-SMITH
10 Director of Accounting .... Ms. Kristen BIGGS

Western Michigan University (H)

1903 W Michigan Avenue, Kalamazoo MI 49008-5202
County: Kalamazoo FICE Identification: 002330
Unit ID: 172699
Telephone: (269) 387-1000 Carnegie Class: DU-Higher
FAX Number: (269) 387-0958 Calendar System: Semester
URL: wmich.edu
Established: 1903 Annual Undergrad Tuition & Fees (In-State): $11,029
Enrollment: 23,914 Coed
Affiliation or Control: State IRS Status: 501(c)3
Highest Offering: Doctorate
Accreditation: NH, AAB, ARCPA, ART, AUD, BUS, BUSA, #CAATE, CACREP, CEA, CIDA, CLPSY, COPSY, CORE, CS, DANCE, DIETD, DIETI, ENG, ENGT, IPSY, MUS, NURSE, OT, SP, SPAA, SW, TED, THEA

01 President .... Dr. John M. DUNN
05 Provost/Vice Pres Academic Affairs .... Dr. Timothy J. GREENE
10 Vice Pres Business & Finance/CFO .... Ms. Jan VAN DER KLEY
32 VP Student Affairs/Dean of Students .... Dr. Diane K. ANDERSON
46 Vice President for Research .... Dr. Daniel M. LITYNSKI
30 VP Development & Alumni Relations .... Mr. James THOMAS
43 VP Legal Affairs & General Counsel .... Dr. Carol L. J. HUSTOLES
86 VP Govt Affairs & Univ Relations .... Mr. Gregory J. ROSINE
28 VP for Diversity and Inclusion .... Dr. Martha B. WARFIELD
27 Vice Prov Budget & Personnel/CIO .... Dr. James A. GILCHRIST
84 Assoc Prov for Enrollment Mgmt .... Vacant
09 Assoc Provost Inst Effectiveness .... Dr. Jody BRYLINSKY
108 Assoc Prov Assessmt/UG Studies .... Dr. David S. REINHOLD
21 Assoc Vice Pres for Bus & Finance .... Ms. Patti VANWALBECK
15 Assoc Vice Pres Human Resources .... Dr. Warren L. HILLS
18 Assoc Vice Pres Facilities Mgmt .... Mr. Peter J. STRAZDAS
35 Assoc VP for Student Affairs .... Dr. Suzie NAGEL
35 Assoc VP for Student Affairs .... Mr. Vernon PAYNE
45 Exec Dir University Budgets .... Ms. Colleen SCARFF
31 Assoc VP for Community Outreach .... Mr. Robert MILLER
101 Secretary Board of Trustees .... Mr. Kahler B. SCHUEMANN
58 Dean Graduate College .... Dr. Susan R. STAPLETON
49 Dean of Arts & Sciences .... Dr. Carla M. KORETSKY
88 Dean of Aviation .... Capt. David M. POWELL
50 Interim Dean of Business .... Dr. Satish DESHPANDE
53 Dean of Education & Human Dev .... Dr. Ming LI
54 Dean of Engineer & Applied Sciences .... Dr. Houssam TOUTANJI
57 Dean of Fine Arts .... Mr. Daniel GUYETTE
76 Dean Health & Human Services .... Dr. Earlie WASHINGTON
92 Interim Dean of Lee Honors College .... Ms. Jane BAAS
08 Dean of Libraries .... Ms. Julie A. GARRISON
26 Exec Dir of University Relations .... Ms. Cheryl ROLAND
36 Exec Dir Professional & Career Dev .... Ms. Lynn C. KELLY-ALBERTSON
06 Registrar .... Ms. Carrie CUMMING
07 Director Admissions/Orientation .... Ms. Dachea HILL
37 Int Dir Student Financial Aid .... Dr. Terrell L. HODGE
38 Dir Counseling Services .... Dr. Geniene M. GERSH
41 Dir Athletics .... Ms. Kathy B. BEAUREGARD
88 Assoc Prov for Global Education .... Dr. Wolfgang SCHLOER
85 Dir Intl Admissions & Services .... Mr. Juan TAVARES
106 Assoc Prov Extended Univ Programs .... Dr. Dawn M. GAYMER
13 Chief Technology Officer .... Mr. Thomas WOLF, JR.
22 Exec Dir Institutional Equity .... Dr. Evelyn B. WINFIELD-THOMAS

Western Michigan University Cooley Law School (I)

300 S Capitol Avenue, Lansing MI 48933
County: Ingham FICE Identification: 012627
Unit ID: 172477
Telephone: (517) 371-5140 Carnegie Class: Spec-4-yr-Law
FAX Number: (517) 334-5718 Calendar System: Semester
URL: www.cooley.edu
Established: 1972 Annual Graduate Tuition & Fees: N/A
Enrollment: 1,880 Coed
Affiliation or Control: Independent Non-Profit IRS Status: 501(c)3
Highest Offering: First Professional Degree; No Undergraduates
Accreditation: NH, LAW

01 President .... Don LEDUC
04 Executive Asst to the President .... Cherie BECK
05 Dean .... Don LEDUC
10 Chief Financial Officer/COO .... Kathleen CONKLIN
07 Associate Director of Admissions .... Julia DUHAN
08 Associate Dean Library/Info Svcs .... Duane STROJNY
20 Associate Dean Lansing Campus .... Christine CHURCH
108 Assoc Dean Planning/Accreditation .... Laura LEDUC
36 Assoc Dean Career Prof Development .... Charles TOY
32 Assoc Dean Students/Professionalism .... Amy TIMMER
43 Assoc Dean External Aff/Gen Counsel .... James ROBB
13 Assoc Dean for Information Tech/CIO .... Charles MICKENS
84 Assoc Dean for Enrollment Services .... Paul ZELENSKI
12 Associate Dean Grand Rapids .... Nelson MILLER
12 Associate Dean Tampa Bay .... Jeffrey MARTLEW
12 Associate Dean Auburn Hills Campus .... Joan VESTRAND
88 Assistant Dean Auburn Hills Campus .... Lisa HALUSHKA
88 Assistant Dean Lansing Campus .... Kathy SWEDLOW
88 Assistant Dean Grand Rapids Campus .... Tracey BRAME
88 Assistant Dean Tampa Bay Campus .... Ronald SUTTON
06 Registrar/Dir of Student Records .... Mohammad SOHAIL
37 Director Financial Aid .... Richard BORUSZEWSKI
40 Bookstore Manager .... Joelle TOPP
21 Controller .... Ronda BECK
29 Director Alumni Donor Relations .... Pamela HEOS
26 Director Communications .... Terry CARELLA
35 Director Student Services .... Christopher LEWIS

Western Michigan University Cooley Law School Auburn Hills Campus (J)

2630 Featherstone, Auburn Hills MI 48326
Telephone: (248) 751-7800 Identification: 770288
Accreditation: &NH

† Regional accreditation is carried under the parent institution in Lansing, MI

Western Michigan University Cooley Law School Grand Rapids Campus (K)

111 Commerce Avenue, SW, Grand Rapids MI 49503
Telephone: (606) 301-6800 Identification: 770289
Accreditation: &NH

† Regional accreditation is carried under the parent institution in Lansing, MI

Western Michigan University Homer Stryker MD School of Medicine (L)

1000 Oakland Dr, Kalamazoo MI 49008-8010
County: Kalamazoo Identification: 667287
Telephone: (269) 337-4400 Carnegie Class: Not Classified
FAX Number: N/A Calendar System: Semester
URL: med.wmich.edu
Established: 2012 Annual Graduate Tuition & Fees: N/A
Enrollment: N/A Coed
Affiliation or Control: Independent Non-Profit IRS Status: 501(c)3

Highest Offering: Doctorate; No Undergraduates
Accreditation: @NH, #MED

01 Founding Dean .... Dr. Hal B. JENSON

Western Theological Seminary (A)

101 E 13th Street, Holland MI 49423-3622
County: Ottawa FICE Identification: 002331
Unit ID: 172705
Telephone: (616) 392-8555 Carnegie Class: Spec-4-yr-Faith
FAX Number: (616) 392-7717 Calendar System: Semester
URL: www.westernsem.edu
Established: 1866 Annual Graduate Tuition & Fees: N/A
Enrollment: 272 Coed
Affiliation or Control: Reformed Church In America IRS Status: 501(c)3
Highest Offering: Doctorate; No Undergraduates
Accreditation: THEOL

01 President .... Dr. Timothy BROWN
05 Academic Dean/VP Academic Affairs .... Dr. Alvin PADILLA
30 Vice Pres of Operations/Advancement .... Rev. Jeffrey MUNROE
10 Vice President of Finance .... Mr. Norman DONKERSLOOT
08 Interim Director of the Library .... Mrs. Ann E. NIEUWKOOP
06 Registrar .... Mrs. Pat DYKHUIS
07 Director of Admissions .... Dr. Mark POPPEN

Yeshiva Beth Yehuda - Yeshiva Gedolah of Greater Detroit (B)

24600 Greenfield, Oak Park MI 48237-1544
County: Oakland FICE Identification: 023638
Unit ID: 247773
Telephone: (248) 968-3360 Carnegie Class: Spec-4-yr-Faith
FAX Number: (248) 968-8613 Calendar System: Semester
Established: 1985 Annual Undergrad Tuition & Fees: $6,200
Enrollment: 70 Male
Affiliation or Control: Independent Non-Profit IRS Status: 501(c)3
Highest Offering: Doctorate
Accreditation: RABN

01 Dean .... Rabbi Y. BAKST
05 Assistant Dean .... Rabbi M. S. BAKST
11 Executive Administrator .... Rabbi P. RUSHNAWITZ
37 Director of Financial Aid .... Rabbi Y. BLITZ

MINNESOTA

Academy College (C)

1600 W. 82nd Street, Suite 100, Bloomington MN 55431
County: Hennepin FICE Identification: 020503
Unit ID: 172866
Telephone: (952) 851-0066 Carnegie Class: Bac/Assoc-Mixed
FAX Number: (952) 851-0094 Calendar System: Quarter
URL: www.academycollege.edu
Established: 1936 Annual Undergrad Tuition & Fees: $17,450
Enrollment: 127 Coed
Affiliation or Control: Proprietary IRS Status: Proprietary
Highest Offering: Baccalaureate
Accreditation: ACICS, MAC

07 President .... Nancy GRAZZINI-OLSON
37 Director of Financial Aid .... Kellye MACLEOD

Adler Graduate School (D)

1550 E 78th Street, Richfield MN 55423
County: Hennepin FICE Identification: 030519
Unit ID: 374024
Telephone: (612) 861-7554 Carnegie Class: Spec-4-yr-Other Health
FAX Number: (612) 861-7559 Calendar System: Semester
URL: www.alfredadler.edu
Established: 1969 Annual Graduate Tuition & Fees: N/A
Enrollment: 368 Coed
Affiliation or Control: Independent Non-Profit IRS Status: 501(c)3
Highest Offering: Master's; No Undergraduates
Accreditation: NH

01 President .... Dr. Daniel HAUGEN
05 Academic Vice President .... Mr. Chris HELGESTAD
10 Director of Business .... Ms. Kathy BENGTSON
07 Director of Admissions .... Ms. Evelyn HAAS
37 Director of Student Financial Aid .... Ms. Jeanette MAYNARD NELSON
06 Registrar .... Ms. Debbie VELASCO
08 Head Librarian .... Ms. Nicole MARCHAND

American Academy of Acupuncture and Oriental Medicine (E)

1925 W County Road B2, Roseville MN 55113-2703
County: Ramsey FICE Identification: 038333
Unit ID: 446002
Telephone: (651) 631-0204 Carnegie Class: Spec-4-yr-Other Health
FAX Number: (651) 631-0361 Calendar System: Trimester
URL: www.aaaom.edu
Established: 1997 Annual Graduate Tuition & Fees: N/A
Enrollment: 57 Coed
Affiliation or Control: Proprietary IRS Status: Proprietary
Highest Offering: Master's; No Undergraduates
Accreditation: ACUP

01 President .... Dr. Changzhen GONG
11 Administrative Director .... Leila NIELSEN
37 Financial Aid Officer .... Cate LARSON

Argosy University, Twin Cities (F)

1515 Central Parkway, Eagan MN 55121-1756
Telephone: (888) 844-2004 FICE Identification: 007619
Accreditation: &WC, ACBSP, CLPSY, DH, DMS, HT, MAC, MFCD, MLTAD, MT, RTT

† Regional accreditation is carried under the parent institution in Orange, CA.

The Art Institutes International Minnesota (G)

15 S 9th Street, Minneapolis MN 55402-2808
County: Hennepin FICE Identification: 010248
Unit ID: 173887
Telephone: (612) 332-3361 Carnegie Class: Spec-4-yr-Arts
FAX Number: (612) 332-3934 Calendar System: Quarter
URL: www.artinstitutes.edu/minneapolis
Established: 1964 Annual Undergrad Tuition & Fees: $17,414
Enrollment: 932 Coed
Affiliation or Control: Proprietary IRS Status: Proprietary
Highest Offering: Baccalaureate
Accreditation: #ACICS, ACFEI

† School is in teach-out plan through 2019.

Association Free Lutheran Bible School and Seminary (H)

3134 East Medicine Lake Blvd, Plymouth MN 55441
County: Hennepin Identification: 667235
Telephone: (763) 544-9501 Carnegie Class: Not Classified
FAX Number: (763) 412-2047 Calendar System: Semester
URL: www.aflbs.org
Established: 1964 Annual Graduate Tuition & Fees: N/A
Enrollment: N/A Coed
Affiliation or Control: Independent Non-Profit IRS Status: 501(c)3
Highest Offering: Master's; No Undergraduates
Accreditation: @TRACS

01 President .... Wade MOBLEY
03 Vice President .... Joel ROLF
05 Vice President Academic Affairs .... Mark OLSON
11 Vice President of Operations .... Larry MYHRER

Augsburg College (I)

2211 Riverside Avenue, Minneapolis MN 55454-1398
County: Hennepin FICE Identification: 002334
Unit ID: 173045
Telephone: (612) 330-1000 Carnegie Class: Masters/L
FAX Number: (612) 330-1649 Calendar System: Semester
URL: www.augsburg.edu
Established: 1869 Annual Undergrad Tuition & Fees: $35,465
Enrollment: 3,548 Coed
Affiliation or Control: Evangelical Lutheran Church In America
IRS Status: 501(c)3
Highest Offering: Doctorate
Accreditation: NH, ARCPA, MUS, NURSE, SW, TED

01 President .... Dr. Paul C. PRIBBENOW
05 Provost and Chief Academic Officer .... Dr. Karen KAIVOLA
10 CFO/VP Finance & Admin .... Dr. Beth REISSENWEBER
30 VP Institutional Advancement .... Ms. Heather RIDDLE
84 VP Enrollment Management .... Dr. William MULLEN
32 VP Student Affairs .... Ms. Ann L. GARVEY
26 VP Marketing/Communication .... Ms. Rebecca JOHN
13 VP & Chief Information Officer .... Mr. Leif B. ANDERSON
29 AVP Institutional Advancement .... Ms. Kim STONE
88 AVP Major Gifts .... Mr. Keith STOUT
58 AVP/Dean Grad & Prof Studies .... Vacant
49 AVP/Dean of Arts & Sciences .... Dr. Amy GORT
88 Dean of Global Education .... Mr. Eric CANNY
35 Dean of Students .... Dr. Sarah GRIESSE
12 Director Rochester Program .... Vacant
41 Athletic Director .... Mr. Jeffrey F. SWENSON
42 Campus Pastor .... Rev. Sonja HAGANDER
28 Chief Diversity Officer/Dir CAO .... Ms. Joanne REECK
37 Interim Director of Financial Aid .... Ms. Amanda BURGESS
06 Registrar .... Ms. Crystal COMER
07 Director Undergraduate Admissions .... Mr. Rick ELLIS
07 Director Graduate Admissions .... Mr. Nathan GORR
18 Director of Facilities .... Mr. Dennis STUCKEY
14 Director of Information Technology .... Mr. Scott KRAJEWSKI
38 Director Ctr Wellness & Counseling . Ms. Nancy G. GUILBEAULT
15 Director & Chief HR Officer .... Ms. Lisa STOCK
08 Director Library Services .... Ms. Mary HOLLERICH
19 Director Public Safety & Risk Mgmt .... Mr. Scott BROWNELL
31 Director Community Relations .... Mr. Steve PEACOCK
88 Director Parent/Family Relations ..... Ms. Sally DANIELS HERRON
88 Director StepUp Program .... Ms. Patrice SALMERI
88 Director Advancement Services .... Vacant
44 Director of Leadership Gifts .... Ms. Amy ALKIRE
85 Director International Student Svc .... Mr. James TRELSTAD-PORTER
21 Controller .... Mr. Matthew KSEPKA
21 Director of Budget .... Mr. Tom CARROLL
88 Director Event & Conf Planning .... Ms. Jodi COLLEN
20 Director of Academic Administration .... Dr. Nathan HALLANGER
27 Director News and Media Services .... Ms. Stephanie WEISS
27 Director Marketing Communication .... Mr. Stephen JENDRASZAK
36 Director Strommen Career Center .... Mr. Keith MUNSON
39 Director Residence Life .... Ms. Amanda ERDMAN
104 Director Global Initiatives .... Ms. Leah SPINOSA DE VEGA
25 Director Sponsored Programs .... Ms. Erica SWIFT
102 Asst Dir Foundation/Corporate Rels .... Ms. Amanda SCHERER
04 Special Assistant to President .... Ms. Beth HELGEN
88 Operations Manager Admissions .... Ms. Keri VANOVERSCHELDE
40 Bookstore Manager .... Mr. Dustin ENOCKSON

Bethany Global University (J)

6820 Auto Club Road, Suite C, Bloomington MN 55438
County: Hennepin Identification: 667136
Telephone: (952) 944-2121 Carnegie Class: Not Classified
FAX Number: (952) 829-2753 Calendar System: Semester
URL: www.bcom.org
Established: 1948 Annual Undergrad Tuition & Fees: N/A
Enrollment: N/A Coed
Affiliation or Control: Interdenominational IRS Status: 501(c)3
Highest Offering: Master's
Accreditation: BI

01 President .... Dan BROKKE
03 Executive Vice President .... Tim FREEMAN
04 Administrative Asst to President .... Deb CHENEY
05 Chief Academic Officer .... Paul HARTFORD
06 Registrar .... Jason HACHE
07 Director of Admissions .... Lori BEYER
08 Head Librarian .... Roger VANOOSTEN
101 Secretary of the Institution/Board .... Theresa HARTFORD
106 Dir Online Education/E-learning .... Jim RAYMO
13 Chief Info Technology Officer (CIO) .... Chris ERICKSON
15 Director Personnel Services .... Chelsey HOFFMEISTER
18 Chief Facilities/Physical Plant .... Mike MORCOMB
19 Director Security/Safety .... Matt ADAIR
26 Chief Public Relations/Marketing .... Dan SANCHEZ
29 Director Alumni Relations .... Marnie FUJII
30 Chief Development/Advancement .... Randy DIRKS
32 Chief Student Affairs/Student Life .... Derek BROKKE
37 Director Student Financial Aid .... Aaron HARRIS
84 Director Enrollment Management .... Dave HASZ

Bethany Lutheran College (K)

700 Luther Drive, Mankato MN 56001-6163
County: Blue Earth FICE Identification: 002337
Unit ID: 173142
Telephone: (507) 344-7000 Carnegie Class: Bac-A&S
FAX Number: (507) 344-7376 Calendar System: Semester
URL: www.blc.edu
Established: 1911 Annual Undergrad Tuition & Fees: $25,170
Enrollment: 531 Coed
Affiliation or Control: Evangelical Lutheran Synod IRS Status: 501(c)3
Highest Offering: Baccalaureate
Accreditation: NH

01 President .... Dr. Gene R. PFEIFER
42 Dir Campus Spiritual Life/Chaplain .... Rev. Donald L. MOLDSTAD
05 Vice President of Academic Affairs .... Dr. Eric K. WOLLER
32 Vice President of Student Affairs .... Dr. Theodore E. MANTHE
10 VP of Finance & Administration .... Mr. Daniel L. MUNDAHL
30 Vice President of Advancement .... Mr. Arthur P. WESTPHAL
37 Director of Financial Aid .... Mr. Jeffrey W. YOUNGE
06 Registrar .... Ms. Mary Jo H. STARKSON
07 Vice President of Enrollment .... Mr. Daniel P. TOMHAVE
15 Manager of Human Resources ..... Ms. Paulette L. TONN BOOKER
08 Interim Dir of Library Services .... Ms. Alyssa K. INNIGER
13 Director of Information Technology .... Mr. John M. SEHLOFF
26 Dir of Institutional Communication .... Mr. Lance W. SCHWARTZ
41 Director of Athletics .... Mr. Donald M. WESTPHAL
29 Manager of Alumni Relations .... Mr. Jacob C. KRIER
09 Mgr Acad & Institutional Research .... Ms. Lisa A. SHUBERT
40 Bookstore Manager .... Mr. Paul G. WOLD
21 Controller .... Mr. Gregory W. COSTELLO
28 Coord Ctr for Intercultural Develop .... Vacant
38 Coord of Student Counseling .... Vacant
18 Director of Facilities .... Mr. Juel O. MERSETH
108 Director of Assessment .... Dr. Theodore E. MANTHE
04 Administrative Asst to President .... Ms. Lynette Y. MERSETH

Bethel University (L)

3900 Bethel Drive, Saint Paul MN 55112-6999
County: Ramsey FICE Identification: 009058
Unit ID: 173160
Telephone: (651) 638-6400 Carnegie Class: Masters/L
FAX Number: (651) 638-6001 Calendar System: Semester
URL: www.bethel.edu
Established: 1871 Annual Undergrad Tuition & Fees: $34,140
Enrollment: 3,979 Coed
Affiliation or Control: Baptist IRS Status: 501(c)3
Highest Offering: Doctorate

Accreditation: NH, ACBSP, #ARCPA, CAATE, MFCD, @MIDWF, NURSE, SW, TEAC, THEOL

01 President ... Dr. James H. BARNES, III
100 Executive Assistant to President ... Dr. Randy BERGEN
05 Executive Vice Pres and Provost ... Dr. Debra HARLESS
10 Chief Financial Officer ... Mr. Patrick BROOKE
46 Sr VP Strategic Plng & Opers Effect ... Mr. Joseph LALUZERNE
26 Chief Marketing Officer ... Ms. Carmen SHIELDS
30 Sr VP University Relations ... Mr. Mark MILES
46 Chief Inst Data/Research Officer ... Mr. Daniel NELSON
90 VP for Facilities & Technology ... Mr. Mark POSNER
29 Exec Minister for Church Relations ... Mr. Ralph GUSTAFSON
32 Vice President Student Life ... Dr. William WASHINGTON
49 Vice President & Dean of CAS ... Dr. Deborah SULLIVAN-TRAINOR
58 Vice Pres Dean Cont Stds/Grad Pgm ... Mr. Richard CROMBIE
73 VP and Dean BSSP ... Dr. David CLARK
84 VP for Enrollment Management ... Mr. Timothy EATON
79 Dean Arts & Humanities ... Dr. Barrett FISHER
108 Assoc Dean Inst Assess/Accred ... Dr. Joel FREDERICKSON
81 Dean Natural/Behavioral Sci ... Dr. Carole YOUNG
107 Dean Faculty Dev/Professional Pgms ... Dr. Pamela ERWIN
104 Assoc Dean Off-Campus Programs ... Mr. Vincent PETERS
12 Actg Dn/Exec Ofcr BU Sem San Diego ... Dr. Arnell MOTZ
35 Dean of Students ... Dr. Marie WISNER
08 Director of Libraries ... Mr. David R. STEWART
15 Director of Human Resources ... Ms. Cara WALD
41 Athletic Director ... Mr. Robert B. BJORKLUND
37 Financial Aid Officer ... Mr. Jeffery D. OLSON
42 Dean Campus Ministrs/Campus Pastor ... Ms. Laurel BUNKER
07 Director of CAS Admissions ... Mr. Bret HYDER
07 Dir Seminary Admissions ... Ms. Jennifer NISKA
07 Director of CAPS/GS Admissions ... Vacant
06 University Registrar ... Ms. Katrina CHAPMAN
36 Director Career Counsel/Placement ... Mr. Dave BROZA
19 Chief of Security and Safety ... Mr. Andrew LUCHSINGER
40 Director Campus Stores ... Ms. Jill SONSTEBY
23 Director of Health Services ... Mrs. Elizabeth K. MILLER
96 Director of Purchasing ... Vacant
38 Director Student Counseling ... Dr. Miriam HILL
18 Director of Facilities Admin Ops ... Ms. Molly HOLMES
18 Director Facilities Tech Ops ... Mr. Glenn HOFER
28 Chief Diversity Officer ... Dr. Ruben RIVERA
29 Director Alum & Family Relations ... Mr. Jim BENDER

† The marriage and family therapy master's program at Bethel Seminary San Diego is accredited by the Commission on Accreditation for Marriage and Family Therapy Education (COAMFTE) of the American Association for Marriage and Family Therapy (AAMFT)

Bethlehem College & Seminary (A)

720 13th Avenue South, Minneapolis MN 55415

County: Hennepin — Identification: 667249
Telephone: (612) 455-3420 — Carnegie Class: Not Classified
FAX Number: N/A — Calendar System: Semester
URL: bcsmn.edu
Established: 2009 — Annual Undergrad Tuition & Fees: N/A
Enrollment: N/A — Coed
Affiliation or Control: Independent Non-Profit — IRS Status: 501(c)3
Highest Offering: Master's
Accreditation: BI

01 President ... Dr. Timothy TOMLINSON
05 Academic Dean ... Dr. Brian TABB
11 VP of Administration ... Jason ABELL
30 VP of Advancement ... Rick SEGAL
07 Director of Admissions ... Daniel KLEVEN

Capella University (B)

225 S 6th Street, 9th Floor, Minneapolis MN 55402-4319

County: Hennepin — FICE Identification: 032673
Unit ID: 413413
Telephone: (888) 227-3552 — Carnegie Class: DU-Mod
FAX Number: (612) 977-5066 — Calendar System: Other
URL: www.capella.edu
Established: 1993 — Annual Undergrad Tuition & Fees: $13,176
Enrollment: 35,061 — Coed
Affiliation or Control: Proprietary — IRS Status: Proprietary
Highest Offering: Doctorate
Accreditation: NH, ACBSP, CACREP, CS, MFCD, NURSE, @SW, TED

01 Interim President ... Dr. Richard SENESE
05 VP Academic Affairs/CAO ... Dr. Richard SENESE
03 VP of Colleges & Univ Ops/COO ... Mr. Andrew WATT

Carleton College (C)

1 N College Street, Northfield MN 55057-4001

County: Rice — FICE Identification: 002340
Unit ID: 173258
Telephone: (507) 222-4000 — Carnegie Class: Bac-A&S
FAX Number: (507) 222-4204 — Calendar System: Trimester
URL: www.carleton.edu
Established: 1866 — Annual Undergrad Tuition & Fees: $49,263
Enrollment: 2,057 — Coed
Affiliation or Control: Independent Non-Profit — IRS Status: 501(c)3
Highest Offering: Baccalaureate
Accreditation: NH

01 President ... Mr. Steven G. POSKANZER, JR.
05 Dean of the College ... Ms. Beverly NAGEL
10 VP Business & Finance/Treasurer ... Mr. Fred A. ROGERS
30 Vice President External Relations ... Mr. Tommy BONNER
32 VP for Student Dev/Dean of Students ... Ms. Carolyn LIVINGSTON
07 VP and Dean of Admissions/Fin Aid ... Mr. Paul THIBOUTOT
100 Assoc Vice President/Chief of Staff ... Ms. Elise ESLINGER
26 Assoc VP External Relations ... Ms. Gayle MCJUNKIN
26 Assoc VP Ext Relations/Dir Col Comm ... Mr. Joe HARGIS
20 Associate Dean of the College ... Ms. Gretchen HOFMEISTER
20 Associate Dean of the College ... Mr. George SHUFFELTON
88 Director of Student Fellowships ... Ms. Marynel RYAN VAN ZEE
35 Associate Dean of Students ... Ms. Julie THORNTON
35 Associate Dean of Students ... Mr. Joseph BAGGOT
35 Associate Dean of Students ... Ms. Cathy CARLSON
37 Assoc Dean Admiss/Dir Stdnt Fin Svc ... Mr. Rod M. OTO
42 Chaplain ... Rev. Carolyn FURE-SLOCUM
06 Registrar ... Ms. Emy FARLEY
08 College Librarian ... Mr. Bradley SCHAFFNER
09 Dir of Inst Research and Assessment ... Mr. James FERGERSON
44 Asst VP Alum/Par Rel/Annual Giving ... Ms. Becky ZRIMSEK
29 Director of Alumni Relations ... Ms. Sarah FORSTER
44 Director of Alumni Annual Fund ... Ms. Maggie PATRICK
88 Director of Development ... Mr. Dan RUSTAD
44 Director of Gift Planning ... Ms. Lynne WILMOT
13 Chief Technology Officer ... Ms. Janet SCANNELL
105 Dir Marketing Comm/Content Dvlpmt ... Ms. Jaye LAWRENCE
27 Director of Media/Public Relations ... Mr. Eric SIEGER
15 Director of Human Resources ... Ms. Kerstin CARDENAS
39 Director of Residential Life ... Ms. Andrea ROBINSON
88 Dir Intercult/International Life ... Ms. Joy KLUTTZ
104 Director of Off-Campus Studies ... Ms. Helena KAUFMAN
36 Director of the Career Center ... Ms. Kimberly BETZ
23 Dir Student Health and Counseling ... Ms. Marit LYSNE
18 Dir of Facilities/Capital Planning ... Mr. Steven SPEHN
21 Comptroller ... Ms. Linda THORNTON
102 Dir Corporate/Foundation Relations ... Mr. Mark GLEASON
88 Dir of Educational Research ... Ms. Andrea NIXON
88 Dir Center for Learning/Teaching ... Ms. Melissa EBLEN-ZAYAS
109 Director of Auxiliary Services ... Mr. Daniel BERGESON
41 Athletic Director ... Mr. Gerald YOUNG
19 Director of Security Services ... Mr. Wayne E SENHUTH
105 Director of Web Services ... Ms. Julie ANDERSON
88 Dir of Enterprise Information Svcs ... Ms. Julie CREAMER
88 Director of Technology Support ... Mr. Austin ROBINSON-COOLIDGE

Central Baptist Theological Seminary of Minneapolis (D)

900 Forestview Lane N, Plymouth MN 55441-5934

County: Hennepin — Identification: 666050
Telephone: (763) 417-8250 — Carnegie Class: Not Classified
FAX Number: (763) 417-8258 — Calendar System: Semester
URL: www.centralseminary.edu
Established: 1956 — Annual Undergrad Tuition & Fees: N/A
Enrollment: N/A — Coed
Affiliation or Control: Baptist — IRS Status: 501(c)3
Highest Offering: Doctorate
Accreditation: TRACS

01 President ... Dr. Matthew D. MORRELL
03 Provost ... Dr. Brett WILLIAMS
05 VP of Academic Affairs ... Dr. Jonathan R. PRATT
06 Registrar ... Mr. Jeff F. STRAUB

*College of Medicine, Mayo Clinic (E)

200 First Street, Rochester MN 55905-3712

County: Olmsted — Identification: 666719
Telephone: (507) 284-2511 — Carnegie Class: N/A
FAX Number: (507) 284-0999
URL: www.mayo.edu

01 Chief Executive Officer ... Dr. John H. NOSEWORTHY
05 Exec Dean for Education Mayo Clinic ... Dr. Frederick B. MEYER
46 Exec Dean for Research Mayo Clinic ... Dr. Greg GORES
15 Chair of Human Resources ... Mr. Kenneth J. SCHNEIDER
26 Chief Marketing Officer ... Mr. John H. WESTON
30 Exec Dean of Development ... Dr. Michael CAMILLERI
86 Chair Government Relations ... Dr. Kathleen HARRINGTON
37 Financial Aid Officer ... Mr. David L. DAHLEN
08 Director of Libraries ... Ms. Anna Beth MORGAN
29 Director Mayo Clinic Alumni Center ... Ms. Judith ANDERSON

*Mayo Medical School (F)

200 1st Street SW, Rochester MN 55905-0001

County: Olmsted — FICE Identification: 011732
Unit ID: 173957
Telephone: (507) 538-4897 — Carnegie Class: Spec-4-yr-Med
FAX Number: (507) 284-2634 — Calendar System: Other
URL: www.mayo.edu/mms
Established: 1971 — Annual Undergrad Tuition & Fees: N/A
Enrollment: 228 — Coed
Affiliation or Control: Independent Non-Profit — IRS Status: 501(c)3
Highest Offering: First Professional Degree
Accreditation: NH, MED

02 Dean ... Dr. Fredric B. MEYER
05 Assoc Dean Academic Affairs ... Dr. Darcy A. REED
32 Assoc Dean Student Affairs ... Dr. Alexandra P. WOLANSKYJ
20 Assoc Dean Faculty Affairs ... Dr. Geoffrey B. THOMPSON
11 Administrator for Mayo Med School ... Ms. Marcia ANDRESEN REID
22 Chief Human Resources ... Ms. Cathryn FRASER
26 Chief Mktg Ofcr/Chair Public Affs ... Mr. Chris W. GADE
88 Internatl Personnel Practice Group ... Ms. Ann H. LANCE
37 Financial Aid Officer ... Mr. David L. DAHLEN
08 Head Librarian ... Ms. Anna Beth MORGAN

*Mayo Clinic College of Medicine-Mayo Graduate School (G)

200 First Street SW, Rochester MN 55905-0001

Telephone: (507) 538-1160 — FICE Identification: 011516
Accreditation: &NH, DENT, PDPSY

† Regional accreditation is carried under College of Medicine, Mayo Clinic.

*Mayo School of Health Sciences (H)

200 First St. SW, Siebens Bldg 3, Rochester MN 55905-0001

Telephone: (507) 284-3293 — FICE Identification: 008182
Accreditation: &NH, ANEST, COARC, CVT, CYTO, DIETI, DMS, HT, MT, NDT, NMT, PAST, PHLEB, PTA, RAD, RTT, SURGA

† Regional accreditation is carried under College of Medicine, Mayo Clinic.

College of Saint Benedict (I)

37 S College Avenue, Saint Joseph MN 56374-2099

County: Stearns — FICE Identification: 002341
Unit ID: 174747
Telephone: (320) 363-5011 — Carnegie Class: Bac-A&S
FAX Number: (320) 363-6099 — Calendar System: Semester
URL: www.csbsju.edu
Established: 1913 — Annual Undergrad Tuition & Fees: $40,846
Enrollment: 2,020 — Coordinate
Affiliation or Control: Roman Catholic — IRS Status: 501(c)3
Highest Offering: Baccalaureate
Accreditation: NH, DIETD, MUS, NURSE, TED

01 President ... Dr. Mary HINTON
05 Provost Academic Affairs ... Dr. Richard ICE
32 Vice President Student Development ... Ms. Mary A. GELLER
30 VP Institutional Advancement ... Ms. Kathy HANSEN
84 VP Planning and Public Affairs ... Mr. Jon D. MCGEE
10 Vice Pres Finance/Administration ... Ms. Susan M. PALMER
07 VP Admission & Financial Aid ... Dr. Calvin MOSLEY
18 Exec Director Facilities ... Mr. Brad SINN
20 Academic Dean ... Dr. Karen ERICKSON
26 Chief Mktg & Comm Officer ... Ms. Tammy MOORE
34 Dean of Students ... Ms. Jody L. TERHAAR
06 Registrar ... Ms. Julie E. GRUSKA
08 Director Library ... Ms. Kathy PARKER
37 Exec Director Financial Aid ... Mr. Stuart PERRY
15 Director Human Resources ... Ms. Carol ABELL
38 Director of Counseling ... Dr. Mike J. EWING
42 Director of Campus Ministry ... Sr. Sharon NOHNER, OSB
41 Athletic Director ... Ms. Glennis WERNER
13 Director of Info Technology Svc ... Ms. Casey GORDON
19 Director of Security ... Mr. Darren SWANSON
21 Controller ... Ms. Anne OBERMAN
36 Director of Career Services ... Dr. Heidi HARLANDER
09 Assoc Dir of Institutional Research ... Ms. Karen KNUTSON
40 Director of Bookstores ... Ms. Tina STREIT
100 Chief of Staff/Lead Title IX Coord ... Dr. Kathryn ENKE
88 Director/Student Human Rights ... Mr. Brandyn WOODARD
29 Asst Director Alumnae Relations ... Ms. Kristin LYMAN
44 Assoc VP Institutional Advancement ... Ms. Heather PIEPER-OLSON
27 Exec Director of Public Relations ... Mr. Michael HEMMESCH

The College of Saint Scholastica (J)

1200 Kenwood Avenue, Duluth MN 55811-4199

County: Saint Louis — FICE Identification: 002343
Unit ID: 174899
Telephone: (218) 723-6000 — Carnegie Class: Masters/L
FAX Number: (218) 723-6290 — Calendar System: Semester
URL: www.css.edu
Established: 1912 — Annual Undergrad Tuition & Fees: $33,994
Enrollment: 4,204 — Coed
Affiliation or Control: Roman Catholic — IRS Status: 501(c)3
Highest Offering: Doctorate
Accreditation: NH, CAATE, CAEP, CAHIIM, NURSE, OT, PTA, SW, TEAC

01 President ... Dr. Colette GEARY
10 Vice President Finance ... Ms. Susan KERRY
05 Vice Pres Academic Affairs ... Dr. Elizabeth DOMHOLDT
30 Vice Pres College Advancement ... Mr. John LABOSKY
32 Vice President for Student Affairs ... Mr. Steve LYONS
84 Vice Pres for Enrollment Management ... Mr. Eric BERG
15 VP for HR & Chief Diversity Officer ... Ms. Patricia PRATT-COOK
88 Assoc Vice Pres College Advancement ... Ms. Janet S. ROSEN
06 Registrar ... Mr. George A. BEATTIE
26 Exec Dir Public & Media Relations ... Mr. Robert J. ASHENMACHER
13 Chief Information Officer ... Mr. Xavier KNIGHT
08 Director of Library ... Mr. Kevin MCGREW

09 Director of Institutional Research Dr. Iwalani ELSE
18 Director of Facilities Services Mr. Tom BREKKE
88 Director OneStop Student Service Ms. Linda ROGENTINE
29 Director Alumni Relations Ms. Lisa ROSETH
07 Dir of Undergraduate Admissions Mr. Bryan KARL
07 Assoc Dir of Transfer Admissions Ms. Brenda PANGER
41 Athletic Director Mr. Don OLSON
42 Director of Campus Ministry Mr. Nathan LANGER
37 Director Student Financial Aid Mr. Jon ERICKSON
38 Dir Stdnt Ctr Health/Well-Being Mr. Tad SEARS
96 Purchasing Manager Ms. Lisa ANDERSON
79 Dean School of Arts & Letters Dr. Tammy OSTRANDER
50 Dean Sch of Buiness & Tech Dr. Lynne HAMRE
53 Dean School of Education Dr. Jo OLSEN
76 Dean School of Health Sciences Dr. Bruce LOPPNOW
66 Dean School of Nursing Dr. Julie ANDERSON
81 Dean School of Sciences Dr. Aileen BEARD
85 International Student Advisor Ms. Alison CHAMPEAUX
45 Vice Pres for Strategic Initiatives Vacant
04 Exec Admin Asst to President Ms. Joan HOLTER
19 Safety and Security Manager Mr. Michael TURNER
39 Director of Residential Life Mr. Elliott JOHNSTON
92 Director Honors Program Dr. Debra SCHROEDER
44 Exec Dir of Planned Giving Ms. Karen FINSETH
40 Bookstore Manager Ms. Ksenia OLSON
97 Director of General Education Dr. Bret AMUNDSON
88 Assoc VP of Mission Integration Sr. Kathleen DEL MONTE
88 Virtual Campus Director Mr. Craig BRIDGES
35 Dean of Students Ms. Megan PERRY-SPEARS
88 Asst Dean Advising & Retention Mr. David BAUMAN
28 Director of Institutional Diversity Vacant
101 Secretary of the Institution/Board Ms. Joan HOLTER
105 Director Web Services Ms. Chris JUGASEK
106 Dir Academic Tech & Online Learning Mr. Peter PRUEFER
36 Director Career Services Ms. Mary ANDERSON
102 Assoc Vice Pres College Advancement Ms. Janet ROSEN

Concordia College (A)

901 8th Street S, Moorhead MN 56562-0001
County: Clay FICE Identification: 002346
Unit ID: 173300
Telephone: (218) 299-4000 Carnegie Class: Bac-A&S
FAX Number: (218) 299-3947 Calendar System: Semester
URL: www.cord.edu
Established: 1891 Annual Undergrad Tuition & Fees: $35,464
Enrollment: 2,398 Coed
Affiliation or Control: Evangelical Lutheran Church In America
IRS Status: 501(c)3
Highest Offering: Master's
Accreditation: NH, #CAEP, DIETD, DIETI, MUS, NURSE, SW

01 President Dr. William J. CRAFT
05 Dean of College/VP Academic Affairs Dr. Eric J. ELIASON
10 Vice Pres Finance/Treasurer Ms. Linda J. BROWN
84 Vice Pres Enrollment and Marketing Mr. Karl A. STUMO
30 Vice Pres Advancement Ms. Teresa L. HARLAND
32 VP Student Affairs/Dean of Students Dr. J. Sue OATEY
04 Senior Associate to the President Ms. Tracey A. MOORHEAD
13 Chief Info Ofcr/Assoc Vice Pres Mr. Bruce W. VIEWEG
07 Exec Dir of Admission & Scholarship Ms. Carola THORSON
06 Registrar Ms. Ericka K. PETERSON
37 Assoc VP Enrollment & Financial Aid Mr. Eric J. ADDINGTON
08 Librarian Mrs. Laura K. PROBST
36 Assoc Dn of Col/Int Dir Career Ctr Dr. Lisa SETHRE-HOFSTAD
15 Director Human Resources Ms. Peggy L. TORRANCE
29 Director Alumni Relations Mr. Eric P. JOHNSON
26 Assoc VP Commun & Chf Mktg Officer Mr. Josh D. LYSNE
09 Dir of Institutional Effectiveness Ms. Jasi O'CONNOR
18 Director of Facilities Management Mr. Wayne R. FLACK
38 Director of Student Counseling Vacant
41 Interim Athletic Director Ms. Rachel D. BERGESON
42 Campus Pastor Rev. Elizabeth C. MCHAN
85 Director Intercultural Affairs Dr. Per ANDERSON
19 Director of Public Safety Mr. William MACDONALD

Concordia University, St. Paul (B)

1282 Concordia Ave, Saint Paul MN 55104-5494
County: Ramsey FICE Identification: 002347
Unit ID: 173328
Telephone: (651) 641-8278 Carnegie Class: Masters/L
FAX Number: (651) 659-0207 Calendar System: Semester
URL: www.csp.edu
Established: 1893 Annual Undergrad Tuition & Fees: $20,750
Enrollment: 4,081 Coed
Affiliation or Control: Lutheran Church - Missouri Synod
IRS Status: 501(c)3
Highest Offering: Doctorate
Accreditation: NH, ACBSP, OPE, @PTA

01 President Rev.Dr. Thomas Karl RIES
03 Executive Vice President Dr. Cheryl T. CHATMAN
05 Vice President Academic Affairs Dr. Marilyn REINECK
10 Vice President for Finance Rev.Dr. Michael H. DORNER
30 Vice President for Advancement Mr. Mark HILL
11 Sr Vice Pres for Administration Dr. Eric E. LAMOTT
84 Assoc VP Cohort Enrollment Mgmt Ms. Kim CRAIG
07 Assc VP Traditional Enrollment Mgmt Mrs. Kristin M. VOGEL
32 Assoc VP Sudent Life Mr. Jason M. RAHN
108 Assoc VP for Assessment/Accred Dr. Miriam LUEBKE
53 Dean College of Education & Science Mr. Lonn MALY
49 Dean College of Arts & Letters Dr. Paul HILLMER
58 Dean of Graduate School Dr. Michael WALCHESKI
50 Dean College of Business Dr. Kevin HALL
28 Dean of Diversity Dr. Cheryl T. CHATMAN
39 Associate Dean of Residence Life Ms. Sharon R. SCHEWE
06 Registrar Mrs. Toni SQUIRES
08 Director of Library Services Dr. Charlotte M. KNOCHE
26 Dir Univ Communications/Mrktng Mr. Jason DEBOER-MORAN
15 Director of Human Resources Mrs. Mary M. ARNOLD
37 Director of Financial Aid Ms. Jeanie PECK
04 Executive Assistant to President Ms. Jill K. SIMON
42 University Pastor Rev. Thomas GUNDERMANN
88 Director of Traditional Advising Ms. Gretchen WALTHER
09 Director of Institutional Research Ms. Beth C. PETER
29 Director of Alumni Relations Mrs. Rhonda K. PALMERSHEIM
41 Director of Athletics Mr. Mark MCKENZIE
18 Director of Operations Mr. James P. ORCHARD
36 Director of Placement/Prof Ms. Jacquelyn MAGNUSON
40 Bookstore Manager Mr. Chad L. MASTEL
90 Director of Computer Services Mr. Jonathan S. BREITBARTH
91 Director Administrative Computing Ms. Beth C. PETER
19 Risk Manager Mrs. Sara K. MULSO
24 Help Desk Coordinator Ms. Brianna TRAQUAIR

Crossroads College (C)

920 Mayowood Road, SW, Rochester MN 55902-2382
County: Olmsted FICE Identification: 002366
Unit ID: 174206
Telephone: (507) 288-4563 Carnegie Class: Spec-4-yr-Faith
FAX Number: (507) 288-9046 Calendar System: Semester
URL: www.crossroadscollege.edu
Established: 1913 Annual Undergrad Tuition & Fees: $16,040
Enrollment: 109 Coed
Affiliation or Control: Christian Churches And Churches of Christ
IRS Status: 501(c)3
Highest Offering: Baccalaureate
Accreditation: @TRACS

01 President Michael KILGALLIN
05 Vice President of Academics Mark KRAUSE
10 Vice Pres Administration & Finance Roger LANGSETH
32 VP of Student Development Brian DUNBAR
06 Registrar Sarah JORDE
08 Director of the Library Vacant
07 Director of Admissions Todd LOONEY
37 Director of Financial Aid Jason VAGT
21 Business Manager Roger W. LANGSETH

Crown College (D)

8700 College View Drive, Saint Bonifacius MN 55375-9001
County: Carver FICE Identification: 002383
Unit ID: 174862
Telephone: (952) 446-4100 Carnegie Class: Bac-Diverse
FAX Number: (952) 446-4149 Calendar System: Semester
URL: www.crown.edu
Established: 1916 Annual Undergrad Tuition & Fees: $23,740
Enrollment: 1,278 Coed
Affiliation or Control: The Christian And Missionary Alliance
IRS Status: 501(c)3
Highest Offering: Master's
Accreditation: NH, NURSE

01 President Dr. David J. WIGGINS
04 Exec Assistant to the President Mrs. Shirley M. GRANLUND
10 Acting VP Finance Dr. Scott MOATS
05 VP Academic Affairs/Provost Dr. Scott MOATS
32 VP Student Development Dr. Paul BLEZIEN
84 Int VP Enrollment & Marketing Svcs Dr. Paul BLEZIEN
30 Director of External Relations Ms. Jill OSBORN
20 Dean for Undergraduate Pgms Dr. Scott MOATS
66 Director of Nursing Mrs. Teresa NEWBY
21 Controller Mr. Ronald STRAKA
41 Interim Athletic Director Mr. Jamison ROSS
08 Director of Media Services Dr. Dennis INGOLFSLAND
06 Registrar Mrs. Cheryl FISK
37 Interim Director of Financial Aid Mrs. Judy BEDFORD
35 Dir Leadership Dev/Stdnt Activity Ms. Kate JONES
07 Director of Graduate Admissions Ms. Maggie UNGER
18 Director of Facilities Services Mr. Rick LARSON
40 Director of Campus Store Mrs. Alyssa GRIFFITH
58 Dean Sch Online Studies/Grad School Dr. Fawn MCCRACKEN
42 Chaplain Mr. Bill KUHN
07 Dean of SAS Enrollment Ms. Korey COMPAAN
15 Director of Human Resources Mrs. Amy LUESSE
36 Dir Career Services Mr. Darren NOBLE
13 Director of Technology Services Mr. Paul FLAGSTAD
26 Marketing/Communications Manager Ms. Jessica ARTIBEE
29 Alumni Relations Coordinator Mr. Adam JESKA

Duluth Business University, Inc. (E)

4724 Mike Colalillo Drive, Duluth MN 55807-2723
County: Saint Louis FICE Identification: 009892
Unit ID: 173489
Telephone: (218) 722-4000 Carnegie Class: Bac/Assoc-Assoc Dom
FAX Number: (218) 628-2127 Calendar System: Quarter
URL: www.dbumn.edu
Established: 1891 Annual Undergrad Tuition & Fees: $17,810
Enrollment: 182 Coed
Affiliation or Control: Proprietary IRS Status: Proprietary
Highest Offering: Baccalaureate
Accreditation: ACICS, MAC

01 President Mr. James R. GESSNER
12 Campus Director Mrs. Bonnie L. KUPCZYNSKI
05 Associate Director Mr. David LUTZKA
08 Librarian Ms. Joyce C. PETERSON
36 Career Services Manager Mr. David E. COOK
37 Financial Aid Advisor Mrs. Gloria G. COOLE

Dunwoody College of Technology (F)

818 Dunwoody Boulevard, Minneapolis MN 55403-1192
County: Hennepin FICE Identification: 004641
Unit ID: 175227
Telephone: (612) 374-5800 Carnegie Class: Bac/Assoc-Mixed
FAX Number: (612) 381-9620 Calendar System: Semester
URL: www.dunwoody.edu
Established: 1914 Annual Undergrad Tuition & Fees: $20,194
Enrollment: 1,070 Coed
Affiliation or Control: Independent Non-Profit IRS Status: 501(c)3
Highest Offering: Baccalaureate
Accreditation: NH, CIDA, ENGT, RAD

01 President Mr. Rich WAGNER
05 Provost Mr. Jeff YLINEN
20 Associate Provost Ms. Ann IVERSON
10 Chief Financial Officer Mr. James MCDONALD
84 Vice President Enrollment Mgmt Ms. Cynthia OLSON
30 VP of Institutional Advancement Mr. Stuart LANG
15 Vice President of Human Resources Ms. Patricia EDMAN

Globe University (G)

2777 34th Street South, Moorhead MN 56560
Telephone: (218) 422-1000 Identification: 770717
Accreditation: ACICS

Globe University (H)

80 South Eighth Street, Suite 51, Minneapolis MN 55402
Telephone: (651) 332-8042 Identification: 770734
Accreditation: ACICS

Globe University (I)

8089 Globe Drive, Woodbury MN 55125-3388
County: Washington FICE Identification: 004642
Unit ID: 173629
Telephone: (651) 730-5100 Carnegie Class: Bac-Diverse
FAX Number: (651) 730-5151 Calendar System: Quarter
URL: www.globeuniversity.edu
Established: 1885 Annual Undergrad Tuition & Fees: $14,040
Enrollment: 776 Coed
Affiliation or Control: Proprietary IRS Status: Proprietary
Highest Offering: Master's
Accreditation: ACICS, MAAB

01 Campus Director Ms. Lisa PALERMO
05 Dean of Education Ms. Kelley ALIFFI
37 Financial Aid Manager Ms. Holly WEBERG
07 Director of Admissions Ms. Jennifer PULLIN

Gustavus Adolphus College (J)

800 W College Avenue, Saint Peter MN 56082-1498
County: Nicollet FICE Identification: 002353
Unit ID: 173647
Telephone: (507) 933-8000 Carnegie Class: Bac-A&S
FAX Number: (507) 933-7041 Calendar System: Semester
URL: www.gustavus.edu
Established: 1862 Annual Undergrad Tuition & Fees: $41,620
Enrollment: 2,457 Coed
Affiliation or Control: Evangelical Lutheran Church In America
IRS Status: 501(c)3
Highest Offering: Baccalaureate
Accreditation: NH, CAATE, NURSE

01 President Ms. Rebecca M. BERGMAN
05 Interim Dean of the Faculty Dr. Brenda S. KELLY
10 VP for Finance and Treasurer Mr. Thomas J. ROONEY
07 AVP and Dean of Admission Mr. Richard S. AUNE
30 VP for Institutional Advancement Mr. Thomas W. YOUNG
32 VP for Student Life Dr. JoNes R. VANHECKE
26 VP Marketing & Communication Mr. Timothy R. KENNEDY
28 Director Diversity Center Ms. Jaime L. HOLLIS
09 Director Institutional Research Mr. David A. MENK
08 Head Librarian Mr. Daniel J. MOLLNER
88 Director Church Relations Rev. Grady I. ST. DENNIS
29 Dir Alumni and Parent Engagement Mr. Glen D. LLOYD
36 Director Career Development Ms. Cynthia L. FAVRE
06 Registrar Ms. Kristianne R. WESTPHAL
13 Dir Gustavus Technology Services Mr. Bruce N. AARSVOLD
18 Director Physical Plant Mr. Fath-Allah OUDGHIRI
37 AVP and Dean of Financial Aid Mr. Doug O. MINTER
39 Director Residential Life Mr. Lawrence C. POTTS
42 Chaplain Rev. Siri C. ERICKSON
42 Chaplain Rev. Brian E. KONKOL
35 Associate Dean of Students Dr. Stephen R. BENNETT
41 Athletics Director Mr. Thomas W. BROWN
15 Director Human Resources Ms. Julie KLINE
19 Director Campus Security Ms. Carol A. BREWER

40 Manager Book Mark .... Ms. Molly L. YONKERS
27 Dir Media Relations/Internal Comm .... Mr. JJ AKIN
04 Asst to the Pres & Sec of the Board .... Ms. Jolene D. CHRISTENSEN

Hamline University (A)

1536 Hewitt Avenue, Saint Paul MN 55104-1284
County: Ramsey | FICE Identification: 002354
Unit ID: 173665
Telephone: (651) 523-2800 | Carnegie Class: Masters/L
FAX Number: (651) 523-2899 | Calendar System: 4/1/4
URL: www.hamline.edu
Established: 1854 | Annual Undergrad Tuition & Fees: $37,886
Enrollment: 4,469 | Coed
Affiliation or Control: United Methodist | IRS Status: 501(c)3
Highest Offering: Doctorate
Accreditation: NH, MUS

01 President .... Dr. Fayneese S. MILLER
05 Provost .... Dr. John MATACHEK
10 Sr VP Business/Finance/Technology .... Ms. Margaret TUNGSETH
30 VP Development & Alumni Relations .. Mr. Tony GRUNDHAUSER
32 Dean of Students .... Dr. Alan A. SICKBERT
43 VP HR/General Counsel .... Ms. Catherine WASSBERG
13 Assoc VP/Dir IT .... Mr. Mark KONDRAK
26 Assoc VP Marketing/Communications .... Ms. JacQui GETTY
18 Assoc VP Facilities/Physical Plant .... Mr. Lowell BROMANDER
50 Dean School of Business .... Ms. Anne MCCARTHY
53 Dean School of Education .... Dr. Nancy SORENSON
49 Dean College Liberal Arts .... Ms. Marcela KOSTIHOVA
85 Ast Dn/Dir Multicult/Intl Stdt Affs .... Mr. Carlos SNEED
06 Registrar Undergrad/Grad Schools .... Ms. Gwen SHERBURNE
29 Exec Dir of Hamline Alumni Assn .... Ms. Elizabeth L. RADTKE
37 Director Financial Aid .... Ms. Lynette WAHL
07 Director Undergraduate Admission .... Ms. Mai Nhia XIONG-CHAN
15 Director Human Resources .... Ms. Julie KLINE
36 Interim Dir Career Development .... Mr. Terry MIDDENDORF
41 Athletic Director .... Mr. Jason VERDUGO
19 Director of Safety & Security .... Ms. Andrea VIRCKS
23 Director Counseling & Health Center .... Ms. Hussein RAJPUT
35 Dir Student Leadership & Activities .... Ms. Wendy BURNS
42 Chaplain & Director .... Ms. Nancy M. VICTORIN-VANGERUD
96 Director of Purchasing .... Ms. Susan BORNUS
04 Exec Assistant to the President .... Ms. Jane A. TELLEEN
09 Director of Institutional Research .... Ms. Tracy WILLIAMS
08 Head Librarian .... Mr. Terry METZ
39 Director Student Housing .... Mr. Javier GUTIERREZ

Hazelden Betty Ford Graduate School of Addiction Studies (B)

PO Box 11 (CO9), Center City MN 55012-0011
County: Chisago | FICE Identification: 040443
Unit ID: 173683
Telephone: (651) 213-4175 | Carnegie Class: Spec-4-yr-Other Health
FAX Number: (651) 213-4710 | Calendar System: Semester
URL: www.hazeldenbettyford.org
Established: 1999 | Annual Graduate Tuition & Fees: N/A
Enrollment: 103 | Coed
Affiliation or Control: Independent Non-Profit | IRS Status: 501(c)3
Highest Offering: Master's; No Undergraduates
Accreditation: NH

01 President and CEO .... Mr. Mark MISHEK
05 Chief Academic Officer & Provost .... Dr. Valerie SLAYMAKER
04 Asst to the Chief Academic Officer .... Ms. Denell BELLE ISLE
20 Dean .... Dr. Roy KAMMER
07 Mgr Enrollment & Student Services .... Ms. LeAnn BROWN
06 Registrar .... Ms. Debra MATTISON
09 Dir of Institutional Effectiveness .... Dr. Timothy SHEEHAN
06 Registrar of Administrative Service .... Ms. Twyla RAMSDELL

Herzing University (C)

5700 West Broadway, Minneapolis MN 55428
Telephone: (763) 535-3000 | FICE Identification: 011017
Accreditation: &NH, DA, DH, NURSE, OTA

† Regional accreditation is carried under the parent institution in Madison, WI.

Institute of Production and Recording (D)

300 N. 1st Avenue, Suite 500, Minneapolis MN 55401
County: Hennepin | FICE Identification: 041302
Unit ID: 454616
Telephone: (612) 244-2800 | Carnegie Class: Spec 2-yr-Tech
FAX Number: (612) 244-2801 | Calendar System: Other
URL: www.ipr.edu
Established: 2002 | Annual Undergrad Tuition & Fees: $16,560
Enrollment: 243 | Coed
Affiliation or Control: Proprietary | IRS Status: Proprietary
Highest Offering: Baccalaureate
Accreditation: ACCSC

01 Campus Director .... Stacy SEVERSON
05 Dean of Education .... Rebecca BULLER
07 Assoc Director of Admissions .... Peter YANG
36 Director of Career Services .... Sandra ROBINSON
08 Librarian .... Tina HALFMANN

Le Cordon Bleu College of Culinary Arts in Minneapolis/St Paul (E)

1315 Mendota Heights Road, Mendota Heights MN 55120-1129
Telephone: (651) 675-4700 | Identification: 666370
Accreditation: ACICS, ACFEI

† In teach-out mode through December 2017. Branch campus of Le Cordon Bleu College of Culinary Arts, Portland, OR.

Leech Lake Tribal College (F)

6945 Little Wolf Rd., NW, Cass Lake MN 56633
County: Cass | FICE Identification: 030964
Unit ID: 413626
Telephone: (218) 335-4200 | Carnegie Class: Tribal
FAX Number: (218) 335-4282 | Calendar System: Semester
URL: www.lltc.edu
Established: 1990 | Annual Undergrad Tuition & Fees: $3,916
Enrollment: 297 | Coed
Affiliation or Control: Tribal Control | IRS Status: 501(c)3
Highest Offering: Associate Degree
Accreditation: NH

01 Interim President .... Dr. Ginny CARNEY
05 Chief Academic Officer .... Vikki HOWARD
10 Chief Financial Officer .... Susan OSTLUND
32 Dean of Student Services .... Vacant
30 Director Institutional Advancement .... Amarin CHANTHORN
09 Director of Institutional Research .... Dr. Melanie WILSON

Luther Seminary (G)

2481 Como Avenue, Saint Paul MN 55108-1496
County: Ramsey | FICE Identification: 002357
Unit ID: 173896
Telephone: (651) 641-3456 | Carnegie Class: Spec-4-yr-Faith
FAX Number: (651) 641-3425 | Calendar System: Semester
URL: www.luthersem.edu
Established: 1869 | Annual Graduate Tuition & Fees: N/A
Enrollment: 622 | Coed
Affiliation or Control: Evangelical Lutheran Church In America
IRS Status: 501(c)3
Highest Offering: Doctorate; No Undergraduates
Accreditation: NH, THEOL

01 President .... Rev Dr. Robin STEINKE
05 Dean of Academic Affairs .... Dr. Craig KOESTER
10 VP Administration & Finance .... Mr. Michael MORROW
26 VP Seminary Relations .... Ms. Heidi DROEGEMUELLER
32 VP Student Affs/Enroll/Dn Students .... Ms. Carrie CARROLL
15 Director of Human Resources .... Ms. Amita WALLS
42 Seminary Pastor .... Dr. Laura THELANDER
07 Director of Admissions .... Ms. Jennifer OLSEN KRENGEL
06 Registrar .... Ms. Diane DONCITS
27 Dir of Marketing/Communications .... Ms. Diane HUMMON

Lutheran Brethren Seminary (H)

1036 Alcott Ave W, Fergus Falls MN 56537
County: Otter Tail | Identification: 666644
Telephone: (218) 739-3375 | Carnegie Class: Not Classified
FAX Number: (218) 739-1259 | Calendar System: Semester
URL: www.lbs.edu
Established: 1903 | Annual Graduate Tuition & Fees: N/A
Enrollment: N/A | Coed
Affiliation or Control: Other | IRS Status: 501(c)3
Highest Offering: Master's; No Undergraduates
Accreditation: TRACS

01 President .... Dr. David VEUM
05 Dean of the Seminary .... Dr. Eugene BOE
06 Registrar .... Dr Gaylan MATHIESEN

Macalester College (I)

1600 Grand Avenue, Saint Paul MN 55105-1801
County: Ramsey | FICE Identification: 002358
Unit ID: 173902
Telephone: (651) 696-6000 | Carnegie Class: Bac-A&S
FAX Number: (651) 696-6689 | Calendar System: Semester
URL: www.macalester.edu
Established: 1874 | Annual Undergrad Tuition & Fees: $48 887
Enrollment: 2,073 | Coed
Affiliation or Control: Presbyterian Church (U.S.A.) | IRS Status: 501(c)3
Highest Offering: Baccalaureate
Accreditation: NH

01 President .... Dr. Brian C. ROSENBERG
05 Dean of the Faculty & Provost .... Dr. Karine F. MOE
88 Chief Investment Officer .... Mr. Gary D. MARTIN
30 VP Advancement .... Mr. Andrew BROWN
32 Vice President Student Affairs .... Ms. Donna LEE
10 Vice President for Admin/Finance .... Mr. David M. WHEATON
13 Associate VP ITS/CIO .... Mr. Jerry F. SANDERS
07 Dean of Admissions/Financial Aid .... Mr. Lorne T. ROBINSON
85 Inst for Global Citizenship .... Dr. Paul OVERVOORDE
20 Director of Academic Programs .... Ms. Ann M. MINNICK
28 Dean of Multicultural Life .... Mr. Chris A. MACDONALD-DENNIS
09 Director Inst Research .... Ms. Polly A. FASSINGER

35 Dean of Students .... Ms. DeMethra BRADLEY
37 Director Student Financial Aid .... Mr. Brian LINDEMAN
06 Registrar .... Ms. Jayne L. NIEMI
36 Assoc Dean for Student Services .... Ms. Denise WARD
15 Director Human Resources .... Mr. Bob GRAF
18 Director Facilities Management .... Mr. Nathan P. LIEF
41 Athletic Director .... Ms. Kim CHANDLER
04 Assistant to the President .... Ms. Cynthia L. HENDRICKS
21 Assistant Vice President Finance .... Ms. Patricia M. LANGER
26 Asst VP Communications and PR .... Mr. David P. WARCH
29 Director Alumni Relations .... Vacant
38 Director Health and Wellness Center .... Ms. Denise WARD
96 Dir Purchasing/Accounts Payable .... Mr. Matthew D. RUMPZA
105 Director Web Services .... Ms. Sara C. SUELFLOW
84 Manager of Enrollment Systems .... Mr. Abraham NOEL
08 Head Librarian .... Ms. Teresa FISHEL
102 Dir Foundation/Corporate Relations .... Ms. Michelle EPP
103 Dean of Career Development .... Ms. Mindy J. DEARDURFF
19 Assoc Director Security/Safety .... Mr. Steve JORGENSON

Martin Luther College (J)

1995 Luther Court, New Ulm MN 56073-3300
County: Brown | FICE Identification: 002361
Unit ID: 173452
Telephone: (507) 354-8221 | Carnegie Class: Spec-4-yr-Other
FAX Number: (507) 354-8225 | Calendar System: Semester
URL: www.mlc-wels.edu
Established: 1995 | Annual Undergrad Tuition & Fees: $13,570
Enrollment: 857 | Coed
Affiliation or Control: Wisconsin Evangelical Lutheran Synod
IRS Status: 501(c)3
Highest Offering: Master's
Accreditation: NH

01 President .... Rev. Mark G. ZARLING
05 Vice President for Academics .... Dr. Jeffery P. WIECHMAN
11 Vice President for Administration .... Prof. Steven R. THIESFELDT
32 Vice President Student Life .... Prof. Jeffrey L. SCHONE
53 Academic Dean Educational Ministry .... Prof. Earl R. HEIDTKE
73 Academic Dean Pastoral Ministry .... Prof. Daniel N. BALGE
10 Director of Finance .... Mrs. Carla J. HULKE
08 Director of Library Services .... Mrs. Linda KRAMER
37 Director of Financial Aid .... Mr. Mark D. BAUER
07 Director of Admissions .... Prof. Mark A. STEIN
58 Director Graduate Studies/Cont Edu .... Prof. John E. MEYER
88 Director of Clinical Experiences .... Prof. Paul A. TESS
41 Director of Athletics .... Prof. James M. UNKE
42 Campus Pastor .... Rev. John C. BOEDER
13 Director of Technology .... Mr. James A. RATHJE
26 Director of Public Relations .... Prof. William A. PEKRUL
40 Bookstore Manager .... Mrs. Linette M. SCHARLEMANN
90 Director of Academic Computing .... Dr. James R. GRUNWALD
29 Director Alumni Relations .... Mr. Stephen J. BALZA
108 Director Institutional Assessment .... Prof. Larry W. LOTITO

McNally Smith College of Music (K)

19 Exchange Street, Saint Paul MN 55101-2220
County: Ramsey | FICE Identification: 030012
Unit ID: 367194
Telephone: (651) 291-0177 | Carnegie Class: Spec-4-yr-Arts
FAX Number: (651) 291-0366 | Calendar System: Semester
URL: www.mcnallysmith.edu
Established: 1985 | Annual Undergrad Tuition & Fees: $26,640
Enrollment: 518 | Coed
Affiliation or Control: Proprietary | IRS Status: Proprietary
Highest Offering: Baccalaureate
Accreditation: @NH, MUS

01 President .... Harry CHALMIERS
10 Chief Financial Officer .... Jakki EDWARDS
37 Financial Aid Director .... Jeffrey R. AALBERS
07 Admissions Director .... Matthew EDLUND
36 Director Career & Alumni Services .... Liz JENNINGS

Minneapolis Business College (L)

1711 W County Road B, Roseville MN 55113-4056
County: Ramsey | FICE Identification: 004645
Unit ID: 174118
Telephone: (651) 636-7406 | Carnegie Class: Assoc/HVT-High Trad
FAX Number: (651) 636-8185 | Calendar System: Semester
URL: www.minneapolisbusinesscollege.edu
Established: 1874 | Annual Undergrad Tuition & Fees: $14,680
Enrollment: 231 | Coed
Affiliation or Control: Proprietary | IRS Status: Proprietary
Highest Offering: Associate Degree
Accreditation: ACICS, MAC

01 President .... Mr. David WHITMAN
05 Director of Education .... Mr. Jon BLUMENTHAL
32 Director of Student Services .... Mrs. Marie MARTIN
36 Placement Coordinator .... Mrs. Suzanne ERICKSON

Minneapolis College of Art and Design (M)

2501 Stevens Avenue, Minneapolis MN 55404-4343
County: Hennepin | FICE Identification: 002365
Unit ID: 174127
Telephone: (612) 874-3700 | Carnegie Class: Spec-4-yr-Arts
FAX Number: (612) 874-3704 | Calendar System: Semester

URL: www.mcad.edu
Established: 1886 Annual Undergrad Tuition & Fees: $35,326
Enrollment: 783 Coed
Affiliation or Control: Independent Non-Profit IRS Status: 501(c)3
Highest Offering: Master's
Accreditation: NH, ART

01 President Mr. Jay COOGAN
04 Executive Assistant to President Ms. Sarah HARDING
05 Vice President Academic Affairs Ms. Karen WIRTH
11 Vice President Administration Ms. Pam NEWSOME
30 AVP Institutional Advancement Ms. Cindy THEIS
84 Assoc VP Enrollment Management Ms. Melissa HUYBRECHT
18 Assoc VP Facilities/Public Safety Mr. Brock RASMUSSEN
13 Assoc Vice President Technology Mr. R. Hal WELLS
32 Dean of Student Affairs Ms. Jen ZUCCOLA
06 Registrar Mr. River GORDON
51 Director of Continuing Education Ms. Lara ROY
08 Director of Library Ms. Amy BECKER
24 Director of Media Center Mr. Scott BOWMAN
36 Director of Career Services Ms. Meghana SHROFF
29 Director Alumni and Annual Giving Mr. Seth GOODSPEED
39 Director Student Housing Mr. Nate K. LUTZ
26 Director Communications Ms. Ann BENRUD
37 Director Student Financial Aid Ms. Laura LINK
40 Manager of Bookstore Ms. Allyson R. HARPER
108 Director Accreditation & Assessment Mr. Colin O'NEILL
19 Director of Public Safety Mr. Steve MCLAUGHLIN

Minneapolis Media Institute (A)

4100 West 76th Street, Edina MN 55435
Telephone: (952) 897-1111 Identification: 770578
Accreditation: ACICS

† Branch campus of Madison Media Institute-College of Media Arts, Madison, WI

Minnesota School of Business (B)

3680 Pheasant Ridge Drive NE, Blaine MN 55449
Telephone: (763) 225-8000 Identification: 770718
Accreditation: ACICS, MAAB

Minnesota School of Business (C)

5910 Shingle Creek Parkway, #200,
Brooklyn Center MN 55430-2319
Telephone: (763) 566-7777 Identification: 666453
Accreditation: ACICS, MAAB

† Branch campus of Minnesota School of Business, Richfield, MN.

Minnesota School of Business (D)

11500 193rd Avenue NW, Elk River MN 55330
Telephone: (763) 367-7000 Identification: 770719
Accreditation: ACICS, MAAB

Minnesota School of Business (E)

1455 County Road 101 North, Plymouth MN 55447
Telephone: (763) 476-2000 Identification: 770713
Accreditation: ACICS

Minnesota School of Business (F)

1401 W 76th Street, Suite 500, Richfield MN 55423-3846
County: Hennepin FICE Identification: 004646
Unit ID: 174279
Telephone: (800) 752-4223 Carnegie Class: Masters/S
FAX Number: (612) 861-5548 Calendar System: Quarter
URL: www.msbcollege.edu
Established: 1877 Annual Undergrad Tuition & Fees: $14,040
Enrollment: 763 Coed
Affiliation or Control: Proprietary IRS Status: Proprietary
Highest Offering: Master's
Accreditation: ACICS, NURSE

01 Campus Director Ms. Miriam WILLIAMS
05 Dean of Education Ms. Miriam WILLIAMS
32 Dean of Students Mr. Patrick SHAY
07 Director of Admissions Mr. Michael POSTER
36 Director of Career Services Mr. Dan WILSON
37 Director of Financial Aid Ms. Carol BARTA

Minnesota School of Business (G)

2521 Pennington Drive NW, Rochester MN 55901
Telephone: (507) 536-9500 Identification: 770716
Accreditation: ACICS, MAAB

Minnesota School of Business (H)

1201 2nd Street South, Waite Park MN 56387
Telephone: (320) 257-2000 Identification: 770715
Accreditation: ACICS

*Minnesota State Colleges and Universities System Office (I)

30 7th Street East, Suite 350, Saint Paul MN 55101-4901
County: Ramsey FICE Identification: 009346
Unit ID: 428453
Telephone: (651) 201-1800 Carnegie Class: N/A
FAX Number: (651) 297-5550
URL: www.mnscu.edu

01 Chancellor Steven J. ROSENSTONE
03 Vice Chancellor Mark CARLSON
05 Vice Chanc Academic/Student Affairs Ron ANDERSON
10 Vice Chanc Finance/CFO Laura M. KING
13 Vice Chanc Information Tech/CIO Ramon PADILLA
26 Chief Marketing/Communications Ofcr Noelle HAWTON
18 Assoc Vice Chancellor Facilities Brian D. YOLITZ
46 Assoc Vice Chanc Research/Planning Leslie K. MERCER
32 Assoc Vice Chanc Student Affairs Toyia YOUNGER
100 Chief of Staff Nancy JOYER
15 Chief Human Resource Officer Vicki DEFORD
28 Int Chief Diversity Officer Toyia YOUNGER
102 Exec Dir System/Foundation Rels Maria R. MCLEMORE
43 General Counsel Gary CUNNINGHAM
45 Program Director for Planning Todd HARMENING
21 Exec Director of Internal Auditing Vacant

*Alexandria Technical & Community College (J)

1601 Jefferson Street, Alexandria MN 56308-2796
County: Douglas FICE Identification: 005544
Unit ID: 172918
Telephone: (320) 762-0221 Carnegie Class: Assoc/MT-VT-High Non
FAX Number: (320) 762-4501 Calendar System: Semester
URL: www.alextech.edu
Established: 1961 Annual Undergrad Tuition & Fees (In-State): $5,402
Enrollment: 2,604 Coed
Affiliation or Control: State IRS Status: 501(c)3
Highest Offering: Associate Degree
Accreditation: NH, MLTAD

02 President Dr. Laura URBAN
05 Exec VP Academic/Student Affairs Dr. Ross SANTELL
41 Vice Pres/Athletic Director Vacant
51 Dean of Customized Training Mr. Robert DEFRIES
10 Chief Financial Officer Mr. David BJELLAND
20 Sr Dean Academic Affairs & Students Mr. Gregg RAISANEN
32 Dean of Student Affairs Vacant
72 Dean of Technology Mr. Steve RICHARDS
20 Associate Dean of Academic Affairs Vacant
19 Dean of Law Enforcement Mr. Scott BERGER
37 Financial Aid Director Mr. Steve RICHARDS
22 Human Rights Officer Ms. Tamzin BUKOWSKI
36 Director Student Placement Mr. Patrick RUNNING
102 Foundation Executive Director Ms. Amy ALLEN
06 Registrar Ms. Debra LEDOUX
18 Director of Facilities Mr. Joel SEELA
15 Chief Human Resources Officer Ms. Shari MALONEY
09 Director of Institutional Research Ms. Rebekah SUMMER
07 Director of Admissions Mr. William CARTER
35 Director of Student Activities Ms. Michelle AHLQUIST
38 Director of K-12 Initiatives Ms. Mary LENZ
04 Asst to Pres/Dir of Office Services Ms. Annette PAVEK
21 Director of Financial Operations Ms. Julie FENLASON
40 Bookstore Manager Ms. Karen SLACK
44 Development Officer Ms. Linda DOLAN
88 Director of Support Services Ms. Kaye MADIGAN
28 Chief Diversity Officer Ms. Debra LEDOUX

*Anoka-Ramsey Community College (K)

11200 Mississippi Boulevard NW,
Coon Rapids MN 55433-3499
County: Anoka FICE Identification: 002332
Unit ID: 172963
Telephone: (763) 433-1100 Carnegie Class: Assoc/HT-Mix Trad/Non
FAX Number: (763) 433-1121 Calendar System: Semester
URL: www.anokaramsey.edu
Established: 1965 Annual Undergrad Tuition & Fees (In-State): $5,022
Enrollment: 7,877 Coed
Affiliation or Control: State IRS Status: 501(c)3
Highest Offering: Associate Degree
Accreditation: NH, ADNUR, MUS, PTAA

02 President Dr. Kent HANSON
10 VP Finance & Administration Mr. Don LEWIS
05 VP Academic/Student Affairs Ms. Deidra PEASLEE
32 Dean of Student Affairs Ms. Lisa HARRIS
35 Dean of Student Affairs Mr. Steve CRITTENDEN
18 Physical Plant Manager Mr. Roger FREEMAN
15 Chief HR Director Mr. Jay NELSON
57 Dean of Arts & Letters Mr. Greg RATHERT
88 Dean CE/CT/Bus/Tech/Wellness Ms. Luanne KANE
35 Dean Student Life Vacant
76 Dean of Allied Health Ms. Natasha BAER
21 Director Fiscal & Auxiliary Svcs Ms. Marilyn SMITH
81 Interim Dean of STEM Ms. Melissa MILLS
09 Dean of Research & Assessment Ms. Nora MORRIS
28 Director of Multicultural Affairs Ms. Venoreen BROWNE-BOATSWAIN
102 Interim Director of Foundations Mr. Jamie BARTHEL
26 Director of Mktg/Public Relations Ms. Mary JACOBSON
19 Director of Safety & Security Mr. Cliff ANDERSON
35 Director of Student Life Ms. Joyce TRACZYK
13 Interim Director of Technology Mr. Tim ZONDLO
21 Business Manager Ms. Kim BIENFANG
37 Interim Director Financial Aid Ms. Brittany TWEED
04 Administrative Asst to President Ms. Margie SCHLUETER
06 Registrar Ms. Janine FORRER

*Anoka Technical College (L)

1355 W Highway 10, Anoka MN 55303-1590
County: Anoka FICE Identification: 007350
Unit ID: 172954
Telephone: (763) 576-4700 Carnegie Class: Assoc/HVT-High Trad
FAX Number: (763) 576-4715 Calendar System: Semester
URL: www.anokatech.edu
Established: 1967 Annual Undergrad Tuition & Fees (In-District): $5,584
Enrollment: 2,221 Coed
Affiliation or Control: State/Local IRS Status: 501(c)3
Highest Offering: Associate Degree
Accreditation: NH, CAHIIM, MAC, OTA, SURGT

02 President Dr. Kent HANSON
05 Vice Pres of Acad/Student Affs Dr. Elaina BLEIFIELD
13 Interim Chief Information Officer Richard MALOTT
10 Vice Pres Finanance & Admin Donald LEWIS
20 Academic Dean Sherry WICKSTROM
04 Assistant to the President Margie SCHLUETER
15 Chief Human Resource Officer Jay NELSON
26 Director of Marketing Mary JACOBSON
06 Director of Records Jamaica DELMAR
32 Dean of Student Affairs Sean JOHNS
37 Interim Financial Aid Director Brittany TWEED
08 Head Librarian Vacant
18 Chief Facilities/Physical Plant Roger FREEMAN
19 Director Security/Safety Clifford ANDERSON
84 Director of Enrollment Services Vacant
09 Director of Institutional Research Nora MORRIS
28 Director of Diversity Venoreen BROWNE-BOATSWAIN

*Bemidji State University (M)

1500 Birchmont Drive NE, Bemidji MN 56601-2699
County: Beltrami FICE Identification: 002336
Unit ID: 173124
Telephone: (218) 755-2001 Carnegie Class: Masters/S
FAX Number: N/A Calendar System: Semester
URL: www.bemidjistate.edu
Established: 1919 Annual Undergrad Tuition & Fees (In-State): $8,366
Enrollment: 4,986 Coed
Affiliation or Control: State IRS Status: 501(c)3
Highest Offering: Master's
Accreditation: NH, IACBE, MUS, NAIT, NURSE, SW

02 President Dr. Faith C. HENSRUD
05 Int Provst/VP Acad & Stdnt Affairs Dr. Michael ANDERSON
10 VP Finance & Administration Ms. Karen SNOREK
20 VP Innovation & Ext Learning Mr. Robert J. GRIGGS
20 Interim Asst VP Academic Affairs Dr. Randall WESTHOFF
84 Int Dean of Student Support Svcs Ms. Michelle FRENZEL
32 Interim Dean of Student Success Dr. Mary WARD
49 Dean Arts & Sciences Dr. Colleen GREER
50 Interim Dean Business Dr. Bonnie HIGGINS
76 Int Dean Health Sci/Human Ecology Dr. Troy GILBERTSON
94 Director Gender Studies Dr. Carla NORRIS-RAYNBIRD
92 Director Honors Program Vacant
06 Interim Registrar Ms. Bev HODGSON
09 Director Inst Rsrch/Effectiveness Mr. Douglas P. OLNEY
106 Director Distance Learning Ms. Lynn JOHNSON
07 Director Admissions Mr. Paul MULLER
36 Director Career Services Ms. Margie T. GIAUQUE
85 Director International Program Ctr Ms. Cherish HAGEN-SWANSON
39 Director Housing & Residential Life Dr. Jodi MONERSON
88 Director American Indian Ctr Dr. Bill BLACKWELL
37 Director Financial Aid Ms. Lesa LAWRENCE
15 Chief Human Resources Officer Ms. Megan ZOTHMAN
21 Business Manager Ms. Diane ILLIES
96 Director Procurement & Logistics Ms. Belinda S. LINDELL
19 Director Public Safety Mr. Casey J. MCCARTHY
18 Director Physical Plant Mr. Jeff A. SANDE
22 Affirmative Action & Accreditation Dr. Debra PETERSON
30 Exec Dir for University Advancement Ms. Marla PATRIAS
29 Director Alumni Relations Mr. Brett BAHR
13 Chief Information Officer Mr. Jim DILLEMUTH
26 Director Communications & Marketing Mr. Scott FAUST
41 Athletic Director Mr. Tracy DILL

*Central Lakes College (N)

501 W College Drive, Brainerd MN 56401-3900
County: Crow Wing FICE Identification: 002339
Unit ID: 173203
Telephone: (218) 855-8000 Carnegie Class: Assoc/MT-VT-High Non
FAX Number: (218) 855-8057 Calendar System: Semester
URL: www.clcmn.edu
Established: 1938 Annual Undergrad Tuition & Fees (In-State): $5,384
Enrollment: 4,333 Coed
Affiliation or Control: State IRS Status: 501(c)3
Highest Offering: Associate Degree

Accreditation: NH, DA, MAC

02 President .... Dr. Hara D. CHARLIER
05 VP Academic & Student Affairs .... Vacant
10 VP Administrative Svcs/Facilities .... Ms. Kari CHRISTIANSEN
12 Dean Technical Pgms/Staples Campus .... Ms. Rebekah KENT
32 Dean of Student Success .... Ms. Jane BIRKHOLZ
49 Dean of Liberal Arts .... Ms. Martha KUEHN
30 Director of CLC Foundation .... Ms. Jana SHOGREN
15 Director of Human Resources .... Ms. Nancy PAULSON
07 Director of Enrollment Services .... Mr. Nick HEISSERER
06 Registrar .... Ms. Michelle KANGAS
08 Librarian .... Mr. David BISSONETTE
37 Director Financial Aid .... Mr. Mike BARNABY
26 Director Marketing & PR .... Mr. Kenn DOLS
21 Director of Business Services .... Ms. Christina ANDERSON
18 Physical Plant Director .... Mr. James MCARDELL
28 Director of Diversity & Equity .... Ms. Mary SAM
04 Administrative Asst to President .... Ms. Debra K. WESP
09 Director of Institutional Research .... Ms. Wendy ADAMSON
19 Director Security/Safety .... Mr. Dave DAVIS

*Century College (A)

3300 Century Avenue N, White Bear Lake MN 55110-1894

County: Ramsey FICE Identification: 010546

Unit ID: 175315

Telephone: (651) 779-3200 Carnegie Class: Assoc/MT-VT-High Trad

FAX Number: (651) 779-3417 Calendar System: Semester

URL: www.century.edu

Established: 1967 Annual Undergrad Tuition & Fees (In-State): $5,391

Enrollment: 9,478 Coed

Affiliation or Control: State IRS Status: 501(c)3

Highest Offering: Associate Degree

Accreditation: NH, ADNUR, DA, DH, EMT, MAC, RAD

02 Interim President .... Dr. Patrick OPATZ
05 VP Academic Affairs/CAO .... Mr. Michael BERNDT
32 Int VP Enroll Mgmt/Student Svcs .... Mr. Greg MCCALLEY
10 Acting VP Finance & Administration .... Ms. Bonnie MEYERS
13 Assoc VP Information Tech/Admn Svcs .... Mr. John ROHLEDER
96 Buyer Supervisor .... Ms. Suzanne WENNEN
21 Acting Director of Finance .... Ms. Deborah MAYNE
102 Executive Director Foundation .... Ms. Jill GREENHALGH
06 Registrar .... Ms. Kirsten FABOZZI
15 Acting Director of Human Resources .... Ms. Robin LAYER
07 Assistant Director of Admissions .... Mr. Robert BEAVER
45 Director of Resource Development .... Mr. Donald LONG
37 Director of Financial Aid .... Ms. Pam ENGEBRETSON
18 Mgr of Physical Plant/Super of Bld .... Mr. Michael HOUFER
19 Director of Public Safety .... Mr. Jason PHILIPP
66 Dean Nursing/Allied Health .... Ms. Beth HEIN
75 Dean .... Ms. Jane NICHOLSON
72 Dean Science/Technology .... Dr. Iddi ADAM
81 Dean English/ESOL/Reading/Math .... Mr. Andrew NESSET
83 Dean Soc & Beh Sci/Lang/Com .... Dr. Jesse MASON
35 Dean of Student Services .... Mr. Jason CARDINAL
35 Dean of Student Services .... Ms. Andrea RYSTROM
35 Dean of Student Services .... Ms. Kristin HAGEMAN
09 Dean of Institutional Effectiveness .... Vacant
04 Executive Assistant to President .... Ms. Christine MCGING
26 Director of Marketing .... Mr. James STUMNE
28 Interim Chief Diversity Officer .... Mr. Trumanue LINDSEY

*Dakota County Technical College (B)

145th Street E, Rosemount MN 55068-2999

County: Dakota FICE Identification: 010402

Unit ID: 173416

Telephone: (651) 423-8000 Carnegie Class: Assoc/HVT-Mix Trad/Non

FAX Number: (651) 423-8775 Calendar System: Semester

URL: www.dctc.edu

Established: 1970 Annual Undergrad Tuition & Fees (In-District): $5,713

Enrollment: 2,910 Coed

Affiliation or Control: State/Local IRS Status: 501(c)3

Highest Offering: Associate Degree

Accreditation: NH, DA, MAC

02 President .... Mr. Tim WYNES
05 VP Academic & Student Affairs .... Dr. Mike OPP
09 VP Strategic Alignment .... Ms. Suzanne BRUSOE
09 Assoc VP Strategic Initiatives .... Ms. Carrie SCHNEIDER
88 Dean Transportation Indust Careers .... Mr. Chad SHEETS
49 Dean Academic Ops/Arts & Sciences .... Ms. Gayle LARSON
32 Director Student Success .... Mr. Patrick LAIR
06 Registrar/Enrollment Director .... Ms. Jodie SWEARINGEN
18 Director of Operations .... Mr. Paul DEMUTH
35 Director Student Life/Activities .... Ms. Nicole MEULEMANS
103 Dean Customized Training/Cont Educ .... Mr. Pat MCQUILLAN
07 Admissions Outreach Coordinator .... Ms. Karianne LOULA
30 Director Institutional Advancement .... Ms. Erin EDLUND
37 Director Financial Aid .... Mr. Scott ROELKE
15 Chief Human Resource Officer .... Ms. Suzanne BRUSOE

*Fond du Lac Tribal and Community College (C)

2101 14th Street, Cloquet MN 55720-2984

County: Carlton FICE Identification: 031291

Unit ID: 380368

Telephone: (218) 879-0800 Carnegie Class: Tribal

FAX Number: (218) 879-0814 Calendar System: Semester

URL: www.fdltcc.edu

Established: 1987 Annual Undergrad Tuition & Fees (In-State): $5,257

Enrollment: 2,215 Coed

Affiliation or Control: State IRS Status: 501(c)3

Highest Offering: Associate Degree

Accreditation: NH

02 President .... Mr. Larry ANDERSON
05 Vice President of Academics .... Dr. Don CARLSON
10 Chief Financial Officer .... Ms. Stephanie HAMMITT
32 Dean of Student Affairs .... Mr. Keith TURNER
26 Director of Public Information .... Mr. Tom URBANSKI
06 Registrar .... Ms. Leah TOLLEFSON
88 Disability Services/Student Service .... Ms. Shelia SUMNER
13 Information Technology Specialist .... Mr. Loran WAPPES
37 Director of Financial Aid .... Mr. David SUTHERLAND
07 Director of Admissions .... Ms. Susan BUMANN
09 Director of Institutional Research .... Dr. Anna FELLEGY
35 Dir of Student Support Services .... Ms. Peggy POITRA
62 Library Services .... Ms. Nancy BROUGHTON
30 Director of Development .... Mr. Larry ANDERSON
39 Director of Housing .... Mr. Jesse STIREWALT
15 Director of Human Resources .... Ms. Marisa HAGGY
18 Chief Facilities/Physical Plant .... Mr. Marc BERNHARDSON
40 Bookstore Coordinator .... Ms. Bonnie BERNHARDSON
04 Executive Assistant to President .... Ms. Mary SOYRING

*Hennepin Technical College (D)

9000 Brooklyn Boulevard, Brooklyn Park MN 55445-2399

County: Hennepin FICE Identification: 010491

Unit ID: 173708

Telephone: (952) 995-1300 Carnegie Class: Assoc/HVT-High Trad

FAX Number: (763) 488-2956 Calendar System: Semester

URL: www.hennepintech.edu

Established: 1972 Annual Undergrad Tuition & Fees (In-District): $5,159

Enrollment: 5,985 Coed

Affiliation or Control: State/Local IRS Status: 501(c)3

Highest Offering: Associate Degree

Accreditation: NH, ACBSP, ACFEI, DA, IFSAC, MAC

02 President .... Dr. Merrill IRVING, JR.
05 Provost .... Dr. Carmen COBALLES-VEGA
10 Vice Pres Administrative Services .... Mr. Craig ERICKSON
103 Vice Pres of Workforce Education .... Dr. Yolanda WILLIAMS
06 Registrar .... Ms. Julie HIGDEM
15 Chief Human Resources Officer .... Ms. Sharon MOHR
28 Director of Diversity .... Ms. Jean MAIERHOFER
09 Dir of Institutional Effectiveness .... Ms. Donna S. STATZELL
26 Exec Dir Inst Adv & Marketing .... Vacant
37 Director of Financial Aid .... Mr. Tim JACOBSON
84 Dean of Enrollment .... Ms. Kristine RAMOS-WALKER
88 Dean of Student Success .... Ms. Dara HAGAN
04 Administrative Asst to President .... Ms. Lisa OPEM
13 Chief Info Technology Officer (CIO) .... Mr. Jason KOPP
08 Head Librarian .... Ms. Jennie SIMNING
22 Dir Affirmative Action/EEO .... Ms. Jean MAIERHOFER
19 Director Security/Safety .... Mr. Randy ROEHRICK
32 Director Student Life .... Ms. Jessica LAURITSEN

*Hibbing Community College, A Technical and Community College (E)

1515 E 25th Street, Hibbing MN 55746-3300

County: Saint Louis FICE Identification: 002355

Unit ID: 173735

Telephone: (218) 262-7200 Carnegie Class: Assoc/MT-VT-High Trad

FAX Number: (218) 262-6717 Calendar System: Semester

URL: www.hibbing.edu

Established: 1916 Annual Undergrad Tuition & Fees (In-State): $5,310

Enrollment: 1,302 Coed

Affiliation or Control: State IRS Status: 501(c)3

Highest Offering: Associate Degree

Accreditation: NH, ADNUR, DA, MLTAD

02 President .... Mr. Bill MAKI
05 Provost .... Dr. Michael RAICH
32 Dean of Lib Arts & Student Affairs .... Ms. Lisa BESTUL
10 Chief Fiscal Officer .... Mr. Bill MANNEY
09 Institutional Research .... Ms. Tracey ROY
37 Director Student Financial Aid .... Mrs. Ann JOHNSTON
18 Plant Maintenance Engineer .... Mr. Jimmer HODGE
26 Marketing Specialist/Public Info .... Ms. Jessica MATVEY
06 Registrar .... Ms. Kari DOUCETTE
13 Chief Info Technology Officer (CIO) .... Ms. Linda RASKOVICH
39 Director Student Housing .... Vacant
41 Athletic Director .... Mr. Mike FLATEN
08 Head Librarian .... Ms. Rachel MILANI

*Inver Hills Community College (F)

2500 80th Street E, Inver Grove Heights MN 55076-3224

County: Dakota FICE Identification: 009740

Unit ID: 173799

Telephone: (651) 450-3000 Carnegie Class: Assoc/HT-Mix Trad/Non

FAX Number: (651) 450-3679 Calendar System: Semester

URL: www.inverhills.edu

Established: 1970 Annual Undergrad Tuition & Fees (In-State): $5,288

Enrollment: 5,958 Coed

Affiliation or Control: State IRS Status: 501(c)3

Highest Offering: Associate Degree

Accreditation: NH, ACBSP, ADNUR, EMT

02 President .... Mr. Timothy WYNES
05 Prov/VP Academic Affs & Student Dev .... Dr. Christina ROYAL
11 Vice Pres Administrative Services .... Ms. Dee BERNARD
32 Vice Pres Student Affairs .... Dr. Wendy ROBINSON
10 Int Chief Financial Officer .... Mr. Scott ERICKSON
45 Vice Pres Strategic Alignment .... Ms. Suzie BRUSOE
06 Registrar .... Mr. Matt TRAXLER
50 Dean of Business & Social Sci .... Vacant
76 Dean of Allied Health Sci .... Dr. Lynne HVIDSTEN
79 Dean of Liberal Arts .... Ms. Ann DEIMAN-THORNTON
81 Dean of STEM/Business/Public Policy .... Dr. Stephen L. STROM
102 Exec Dir of Foundation & Advancemnt .... Mrs. Gail MORRISON
15 Int Chief Human Resources Officer .... Ms. Laina CARLSON
103 Dean Ctr Prof/Workforce Development .... Mr. Pat MCQUILLAN
08 Librarian .... Ms. Julie BENOLKEN
84 Director of Enrollment Services .... Mr. Matt TRAXLER
88 Dir Paralegal Pgm/Ofc Sys-Legal .... Ms. Sally DAHLQUIST
90 Director Acad Tech/Computing Svcs .... Mr. Mark PETERSON
18 Director Facilities Plng/Management .... Mr. Pat BUHL
88 Interim Dir of Emer Health Svcs .... Mr. Brad WRIGHT
28 Director of Equity & Inclusion .... Vacant
37 Director of Financial Aid .... Mr. Steve YANG
09 Director of Institutional Research .... Ms. Wendy MARSON
26 Dir of Inst Advance/Mktg & PR .... Ms. Erin EDLUND
35 Director of Student Life .... Ms. Nicole MEULEMANS
20 Int Assoc Dean of Academic Affairs .... Ms. Susan DION

*Itasca Community College (G)

1851 E Highway 169, Grand Rapids MN 55744-3397

County: Itasca FICE Identification: 002356

Unit ID: 173805

Telephone: (800) 996-6422 Carnegie Class: Assoc/HT-High Trad

FAX Number: (218) 322-2332 Calendar System: Semester

URL: www.itascacc.edu

Established: 1922 Annual Undergrad Tuition & Fees (In-State): $5,325

Enrollment: 1,222 Coed

Affiliation or Control: State IRS Status: 501(c)3

Highest Offering: Associate Degree

Accreditation: NH

02 Chief Executive Officer .... Mr. William D. MAKI
03 Executive Vice President .... Ms. Karen KEDROWSKI
05 Provost .... Mr. Bart JOHNSON
20 Academic Dean .... Mr. Bart JOHNSON
10 Accounting Officer Finance .... Ms. Kristen LIND
84 Dir of Enrollment Mgmt/Admissions .... Mr. William MARSHALL
06 Registrar .... Ms. Allison GEISLER
29 Director of Alumni Relations .... Ms. Susan LYNCH
30 Director of College Development .... Vacant
37 Director of Student Financial Aid .... Mr. Nathan WRIGHT
08 Head Librarian .... Mr. Steve BEAN
18 Director of Facilities & Info Tech .... Mr. Chad HAATVEDT
40 Bookstore Manager .... Ms. Faith MCBRIDE
28 Director of Diversity .... Mr. Harold ANNETTE
09 Director of Institutional Research .... Ms. Tracey ROY
39 Director Student Housing .... Mr. Weldon BRAXTON
32 Dean of Student & Admin Services .... Mr. Richard KANGAS

*Lake Superior College (H)

2101 Trinity Road, Duluth MN 55811-3399

County: Saint Louis FICE Identification: 005757

Unit ID: 173461

Telephone: (218) 733-7600 Carnegie Class: Assoc/MT-VT-High Non

FAX Number: (218) 733-4921 Calendar System: Semester

URL: www.lsc.edu

Established: 1995 Annual Undergrad Tuition & Fees (In-State): $5,126

Enrollment: 5,101 Coed

Affiliation or Control: State IRS Status: 501(c)3

Highest Offering: Associate Degree

Accreditation: NH, ADNUR, COARC, DH, MAC, MLTAD, PNUR, PTAA, RAD, SURGT

02 President .... Dr. Patrick JOHNS
05 Vice Pres Academic/Student Affairs .... Mr. Michael SEYMOUR
10 Vice Pres Finance & Administration .... Mr. Al FINLAYSON
49 Dean of Liberal Arts & Sciences .... Ms. Hanna ERPESTAD
75 Dean of Business/Industry Division .... Ms. Jenni SWENSON
76 Dean of Allied Health & Nursing .... Ms. Laurie JENSEN
103 Exec Director of Workforce Trng .... Mr. Don NESS
09 Dir IR/Accred Assessment/Research .... Mr. Kent RICHARDS
15 Director of Human Resources .... Ms. Audra FLANAGAN
26 Dir of Public Affairs/Advancement .... Vacant
84 Director of Enrollment Mgmt .... Ms. Melissa LENO
18 Director Physical Plant .... Vacant
32 Dean of Student Services .... Mr. Wade GORDON
36 Director Career Services .... Mr. Eric BRANDT
37 Director Student Financial Aid .... Ms. LaNita ROBINSON
21 Director Business Services .... Ms. Nickoel ANDERSON
102 Foundation Director .... Vacant
13 Director Information Technology .... Mr. Steve FUDALLY
96 Purchasing Agent .... Mr. Michael FRANCISCO
04 Administrative Asst to President .... Ms. Debbie JOHNSON

*Mesabi Range College (I)

1001 Chestnut Street West, Virginia MN 55792-3401

County: Saint Louis FICE Identification: 004009

Unit ID: 173993

Telephone: (218) 741-3095 Carnegie Class: Assoc/MT-VT-High Non

FAX Number: (218) 748-2419 Calendar System: Semester

URL: www.mesabirange.edu

Established: 1963 Annual Undergrad Tuition & Fees (In-State): $5,311

Enrollment: 1,265 Coed
Affiliation or Control: State IRS Status: Exempt
Highest Offering: Associate Degree
Accreditation: NH, EMT

02 President .... Mr. William MAKI
05 Provost .... Ms. Carol HELLAND
10 Vice Pres Finance/Administration .... Ms. Karen KEDROWSKI
32 Dean of Student Services .... Mr. David DAILEY
10 Director of Finance .... Mr. Roy TROUSDELL
15 Director Human Resources .... Ms. Carmen BRADACH
37 Director Student Financial Aid .... Ms. Jodi PONTINEN
06 Registrar .... Mrs. Rebecca STEVINSON
07 Director of Admissions .... Ms. Brenda KOCHEVAR
09 Director of Institutional Research .... Ms. Tracey ROY
26 Chief Public Relations Officer .... Ms. Brenda KOCHEVAR
38 Director Student Counseling .... Ms. Kelly BAKK
36 Director Student Placement .... Ms. Shari CHRISTENSON
84 Director Enrollment Management .... Ms. Brenda KOCHEVAR
13 Chief Info Technology Officer (CIO) .... Mrs. Shelly MCCAULEY-JUGOVICH

*Metropolitan State University (A)

700 E 7th Street, Saint Paul MN 55106-5000
County: Ramsey FICE Identification: 010374
Unit ID: 174020
Telephone: (651) 793-1300 Carnegie Class: Masters/L
FAX Number: (651) 793-1235 Calendar System: Semester
URL: www.metrostate.edu
Established: 1971 Annual Undergrad Tuition & Fees (In-State): $7,566
Enrollment: 8,355 Coed
Affiliation or Control: State IRS Status: 501(c)3
Highest Offering: Doctorate
Accreditation: NH, NURSE, SW

02 President .... Ms. Virginia ARTHUR
05 Int Prov/VP Academic/Student Affs . Dr. Carol BORMANN YOUNG
11 Int Vice Pres Administrative Affs .... Mr. Bruce BISER
32 Vice Pres Student Affs/Enroll Mgmt .... Vacant
30 VP Advancement/Planning .... Vacant
84 Assoc VP Enrollment Management .... Ms. Amy DUNN
35 Dean of Students .... Mr. Herbert KING
18 Assoc Vice Pres Admin Affairs .... Vacant
13 VP Info/Telecom/Tech/CIO .... Mr. Stephen REED
10 Assoc VP Financial Management .... Mr. Anthony ROAN
15 Director Human Resources .... Ms. Deb GEHRKE
06 Registrar .... Mr. Daryl JOHNSON
37 Director Financial Aid .... Ms. Lois LARSON
26 Director Communications/Marketing .... Ms. Poh Lin KHOO
27 Publication/News Services Director .... Vacant
29 Director Alumni Relations .... Ms. Kristine HANSEN
28 Chief Diversity Officer .... Mr. Craig MORRIS
09 Director Institutional Research .... Ms. Cynthia DEVORE
07 Director of Admissions .... Mr. Julio VARGAS-ESSEX
81 Dean College of Sciences .... Dr. Thomas NELSON
58 Dean of College of Management .... Dr. Kat LUI
88 Int Dean Col Cmty Stds/Urban Affs .... Dr. Francis SCHWEIGERT
88 Dean Col Individualized Stds .... Dr. Carl POLDING
88 Dean School of Urban Education .. Dr. Rene ANTROP-GONZALEZ
49 Int Dean College of Liberal Arts .... Dr. Craig HANSEN
66 Int Dean Col of Nursing/Health Sci .... Dr. Judith GRAZIANO
08 Dean Library and Learning Center .... Ms. Christine SCHAFER

*Minneapolis Community and Technical College (B)

1501 Hennepin Avenue, Minneapolis MN 55403-9810
County: Hennepin FICE Identification: 002362
Unit ID: 174136
Telephone: (612) 659-6000 Carnegie Class: Assoc/MT-VT-High Trad
FAX Number: (612) 659-6210 Calendar System: Semester
URL: www.minneapolis.edu
Established: 1996 Annual Undergrad Tuition & Fees (In-State): $5,366
Enrollment: 9,237 Coed
Affiliation or Control: State IRS Status: 501(c)3
Highest Offering: Associate Degree
Accreditation: NH, ADNUR, DA, NDT, PNUR, POLYT

02 President .... Dr. Sharon PIERCE
05 Vice Pres Academic Affairs .... Dr. Gail O'KANE
10 Int Vice Pres Finance/Operations .... Mr. Christopher RAU
32 Int Vice President Student Affairs .... Mr. Patrick TROUP
103 Assoc VP Strategic Partnerships .... Mr. Mike CHRISTENSON
84 Dean of Enrollment Management .... Mr. Matthew CRAWFORD
49 Dean of Liberal Arts .... Mr. Derrick LINDSTROM
81 Dean of Science & Math .... Mr. Chuck PAULSON
51 Dean of Continuing Education .... Mr. Vincent THOMAS
66 Dean of Nursing & Allied Health .... Ms. Yvette TROTMAN
35 Dean of Students .... Ms. Becky NORDIN
20 Dean Academic Foundations .... Dr. Keith BROOKS
43 CHRO and Director Legal Affairs .... Ms. Dianna CUSICK
13 Chief Information Officer .... Ms. Tiffni DEEB
06 Interim Registrar .... Ms. Michele COPELAND
08 Librarian .... Mr. Tom ELAND
37 Financial Aid Director .... Ms. Angela CHRISTENSEN
09 Director of Institutional Research .... Ms. Jessica SHRAYCK
18 Director Facilities .... Mr. Roger BROZ
19 Director of Public Safety .... Mr. Curt SCHMIDT
26 Chief Public Relations Officer .... Vacant
32 Chief Student Life Officer .... Ms. Tara MARTINEZ

*Minnesota State College-Southeast Technical (C)

1250 Homer Road, Winona MN 55987-4897
County: Winona FICE Identification: 002393
Unit ID: 175263
Telephone: (507) 453-2700 Carnegie Class: Assoc/HVT-High Trad
FAX Number: (507) 453-2715 Calendar System: Semester
URL: www.southeastmn.edu
Established: 1949 Annual Undergrad Tuition & Fees (In-District): $5,618
Enrollment: 2,177 Coed
Affiliation or Control: State/Local IRS Status: 501(c)3
Highest Offering: Associate Degree
Accreditation: NH, MLTAD, PNUR, RAD

02 President .... Dr. Dorothy DURAN
05 Vice President Academic Affairs .... Dr. Leslie BLESKACHEK
32 Vice Pres Student Affairs/Life .... Mr. Nate EMERSON
10 Vice Pres Finance/Administration .... Mr. Mike KROENING
13 Chief Information Officer .... Mr. Rick NAHRGANG
49 Dean of Liberal Arts & Sciences .... Ms. Jolene PONCELET
17 Dean of Nursing & Allied Health .... Dr. Rita BERTHELSEN
20 Dean of Trade & Technology .... Mr. Travis THUL
15 Chief Human Resource Officer .... Ms. Maryellen KANZ
30 Chief Development/Advancement .... Mr. Joe KRESS
06 Registrar .... Ms. Mary JOHNSON
07 Director of Admissions .... Ms. Gale LANNING
84 Director of Recruitment .... Ms. Shannon SCHELL
37 Director Financial Aid .... Dr. Tammy VONDRASEK
18 Chief Facilities/Physical Plant .... Mr. Thomas HOFFMAN
29 Director of Alumni Relations .... Ms. Casie JOHNSON
26 Director of Marketing .... Ms. Joanne THOMPSON
103 Director of Customized Training .... Ms. Jen OLSON
08 Director of Learning Resources .... Mr. Steve ZMYEWSKI
26 Director of Communications .... Ms. Katryn CONLIN
21 Accounting Supervisor .... Ms. Lisa POZANC
16 Associate Human Resources Officer .... Ms. Nicki ADANK
19 Director of Security .... Mr. Chris CICHOSZ
04 Assistant to President .... Ms. Mary DONLIN

*Minnesota State Community and Technical College (D)

1414 College Way, Fergus Falls MN 56537-1000
County: Otter Tail FICE Identification: 005541
Unit ID: 173559
Telephone: (218) 736-1500 Carnegie Class: Assoc/MT-VT-High Trad
FAX Number: (218) 736-1510 Calendar System: Semester
URL: www.minnesota.edu
Established: 1960 Annual Undergrad Tuition & Fees (In-State): $5,338
Enrollment: 6,415 Coed
Affiliation or Control: State IRS Status: 501(c)3
Highest Offering: Associate Degree
Accreditation: NH, CAHIIM, DA, MLTAD, RAD

02 President .... Dr. Peggy KENNEDY
05 Chief Academic Officer .... Dr. Carrie BRIMHALL
15 Chief of Human Resources .... Mrs. Dacia JOHNSON
06 Registrar .... Ms. Sharlene ALLEN
13 Chief Information Officer .... Mr. Dan KNUDSON
10 Chief Finance Officer .... Mr. Pat NORDICK
32 VP of Student Devel & Marketing .... Dr. Peter WIELINSKI
84 Dean of Student Access .... Vacant
20 Assoc VP of Academic Affairs .... Dr. Jill ABBOTT
18 Director of College Facilities .... Mr. Matt SHEPPARD
35 Dean of Student Success .... Mr. Shawn ANDERSON
12 Academic Dean-Detroit Lakes .... Vacant
12 Acad Dean Lib Arts/Sci-Fergus Falls .... Dr. Gary HENRICKSON
12 Academic Dean-Wadena .... Mr. Monty JOHNSON
88 Dean of CTS/BES .... Mr. G.L TUCKER
66 Dean of Health Careers .... Mrs. Jennifer JACOBSON
09 Dean of Inst Eff/Tech Programs .... Mr. Steve ERICKSON
07 Director of Admissions .... Mr. Kyle JOHNSTON
28 Chief Diversity Officer .... Mr. Brian XIONG
30 Chief Development & Alum Officer .... Ms. Denise LAYMON
36 Career Services Director .... Ms. Sue ZURN

*Minnesota State University, Mankato (E)

309 Wigley Administration Center,
Mankato MN 56001-6062
County: Blue Earth FICE Identification: 002360
Unit ID: 173920
Telephone: (507) 389-1111 Carnegie Class: Masters/L
FAX Number: (507) 389-6200 Calendar System: Semester
URL: www.mnsu.edu
Established: 1868 Annual Undergrad Tuition & Fees (In-State): $7,836
Enrollment: 15,387 Coed
Affiliation or Control: State IRS Status: Exempt
Highest Offering: Doctorate
Accreditation: NH, AAB, ART, BUS, CAATE, CACREP, CONST, CORE, DH, DIETD, ENG, ENGT, MUS, NRPA, NURSE, SP, SPAA, SW, TED

02 President .... Dr. Richard DAVENPORT
05 Provost/Sr Vice Pres Academic Affs .... Dr. Marilyn WELLS
10 Vice Pres Finance & Administration .... Mr. Richard STRAKA
30 VP University Advancement .... Mr. Kent STANLEY
13 VP Technology/CIO .... Mr. Mark JOHNSON
88 VP Strategic/Busnss/Ed/Reg Prtrshps .... Mr. Michael GUSTAFSON
32 VP for Student Affairs .... Dr. David JONES
20 VP for Academic Affairs .... Dr. Robert FLEISCHMAN
04 Exec Assistant to the President .... Ms. Juanita MILBRETT
20 Asst VP Undergrad Studies .... Dr. Ginger ZIERDT
27 Asst VP Integrated Marketing/Comm .... Vacant
28 Dean Institutional Diversity .... Mr. Henry MORRIS
18 Facilities Service Director .... Mr. David COWAN
06 University Registrar .... Mr. Marcius BROCK
07 Director of Admissions .... Mr. Brian JONES
08 Dean Library Services .... Dr. Joan ROCA
15 Interim Director of Human Resources .... Ms. Sheri SARGENT
36 Director Career Development .... Ms. Pamela WELLER-DENGEL
26 Director Media Relations .... Mr. Daniel BENSON
41 Dir of Intercollegiate Athletics .... Mr. Kevin BUISMAN
29 Director of Alumni Relations .... Mr. Ramon PINERO
22 Director Affirmative Action .... Ms. Cyrenthia JORDAN
37 Director Student Financial Services .... Ms. Jan MARBLE
58 AVP Graduate Studies/Research .... Dr. Barry RIES
79 Interim Dean of Arts & Humanities .... Dr. Kimberly CONTAG
53 Dean of Education .... Dr. Jean HAAR
50 Dean of Business .... Dr. Brenda FLANNERY
76 Dean Allied Health/Nursing .... Dr. Kristine RETHERFORD
81 Dean Science/Engineering/Technology .... Dr. Brian MARTENSEN
83 Dean Social/Behavioral Science .... Dr. Maria BEVACQUA
38 Director Student Counseling .... Ms. Kari MUCH
09 Asst VP of Institutional Research .... Ms. Lynn AKEY
19 Director Security/Safety .... Ms. Suzanne DUGAN
39 Director Student Housing .... Ms. Cindy JANNEY

*Minnesota State University Moorhead (F)

1104 7th Avenue S, Moorhead MN 56563-2996
County: Clay FICE Identification: 002367
Unit ID: 174358
Telephone: (218) 477-4000 Carnegie Class: Masters/M
FAX Number: (218) 477-2168 Calendar System: Semester
URL: www.mnstate.edu
Established: 1887 Annual Undergrad Tuition & Fees (In-State): $8,096
Enrollment: 6,306 Coed
Affiliation or Control: State IRS Status: 501(c)3
Highest Offering: Doctorate
Accreditation: NH, ART, BUS, #CAATE, CACREP, CONST, DH, MUS, NAIT, NURSE, SP, SW, TED

02 President .... Dr. Anne BLACKHURST
05 Provost/Sr VP Academic Affairs .... Dr. Joseph BESSIE
10 VP Finance & Administration .... Ms. Jean HOLLAAR
84 VP Enrollment Mgmt/Student Affairs . Dr. Brenda AMENSON-HILL
29 VP Alumni Foundation .... Mr. Gary HAUGO
04 Assistant to the President .... Ms. Kathleen J. MCNABB
20 AVP Academic Affairs .... Dr. John (Jack) HEALY
28 Chief Diversity Officer .... Dr. Donna L. BROWN
09 Dir Institutional Effectiveness .... Mr. Kevin BROWN
41 Director of Athletics .... Mr. Doug D. PETERS
13 Chief Information Officer .... Mr. Daniel A. HECKAMAN
21 Comptroller .... Ms. Karen K. LESTER
50 Dean Business & Innovation .... Dr. Marsha L. WEBER
49 Int Dean Arts/Media/Communication .... Ms. Denise M. GORSLINE
53 Actg Dean Educ/Human Svcs/Grad Stds .... Dr. Boyd BRADBURY
83 Int Dean Sciences/Health/Environ .... Dr. Jeffrey BODWIN
79 Dean of Col Humanities/Soc Sci .... Dr. Randy L. CAGLE
15 Director Human Resources .... Ms. Ann HIEDEMAN
06 Registrar .... Ms. Heather M. SOLEIM
26 Director Marketing/Communications .... Mr. David C. WAHLBERG
19 Director of Public Safety .... Mr. James SCHUMANN
37 Dir Financial Aid & Scholarships .... Ms. Carolyn F. ZEHREN
23 Dir Health/Wellness/Counseling Ctrs .... Ms. Carol M. GRIMM
22 Director Disabilities .... Mr. Greg A. TOUTGES
36 Director of Career Development .... Mr. Troy NELLIS
07 Director of Admissions .... Vacant
32 Exec Dir Student Union .... Mr. Layne ANDERSON
39 Dir Housing & Residential Life .... Ms. Heather PHILLIPS
85 Director International Student Affs ..... Ms. Janet M. HOHENSTEIN
18 Manager Physical Plant .... Mr. Jeffrey D. GOEBEL
40 Bookstore Supervisor .... Ms. Kim M. SAMSON

*Minnesota West Community and Technical College (G)

1450 Collegeway, Worthington MN 56187
County: Nobles FICE Identification: 005263
Unit ID: 173638
Telephone: (800) 658-2330 Carnegie Class: Not Classified
FAX Number: (507) 372-5803 Calendar System: Semester
URL: www.mnwest.edu
Established: 1985 Annual Undergrad Tuition & Fees (In-State): N/A
Enrollment: N/A Coed
Affiliation or Control: State IRS Status: 501(c)3
Highest Offering: Associate Degree
Accreditation: NH, ADNUR, DA, MAC, MLTAD, RAD, SURGT

02 President .... Dr. Terry GAALSWYK
05 College Provost .... Dr. Jeff WILLIAMSON
11 Vice President of Administration .... Ms. Lori VOSS
106 Dean Technology/Distance Learning .... Ms. Kayla WESTRA
84 Director of Enrollment Management .... Vacant
37 Director of Financial Aid .... Ms. Jodi LANDGAARD
18 Chief Facilities/Physical Plant .... Vacant
06 Registrar .... Ms. Crystal STROUTH
15 Director Human Resources .... Ms. Karen MILLER
102 Foundation Director .... Mr. Michael VAN KEULEN

08 Library Director .... Mr. Kip THORSON
10 Business Manager .... Ms. Diana FLISS
26 Dir Marketing/Enrollment/Comm .... Ms. Amber LUINENBURG

*Normandale Community College (A)

9700 France Avenue S, Bloomington MN 55431-4399
County: Hennepin FICE Identification: 007954
Unit ID: 174428
Telephone: (952) 358-8200 Carnegie Class: Assoc/HT-Mix Trad/Non
FAX Number: (952) 358-8101 Calendar System: Semester
URL: www.normandale.edu
Established: 1968 Annual Undergrad Tuition & Fees (In-State): $5,736
Enrollment: 9,539 Coed
Affiliation or Control: State IRS Status: 501(c)3
Highest Offering: Associate Degree
Accreditation: NH, ACBSP, ADNUR, ART, DH, DIETT, MUS, THEA

02 President .... Dr. Joyce C. ESTER
04 Executive Assistant to President .. Mrs. Amanda RYAN-SCHMOLL
10 Vice President Finance & Operations .... Dr. Lisa WHEELER
05 Vice President of Academic Affairs .... Mrs. Julie GUELICH
32 Vice President of Student Affairs .... Dr. Orinthia MONTAGUE
15 Chief Human Resources Officer .... Mrs. Dionne DOERING
09 Dir of Research & Planning .... Dr. Mark LEWIS
50 Dean of Business & Social Sci .... Dr. Michael KIRCH
79 Dean of Humanities .... Dr. Jeffrey JUDGE
81 Dean of STEME .... Dr. Cary KOMOTO
76 Dean of Health Sciences .... Dr. Colleen BRICKLE
08 Dean of Academic Svcs & Library .... Dr. Erin DALY
21 Int Assoc VP Finance & Accounting .... Mrs. Catherine BREUER
13 Chief Information Officer .... Mr. Stephen WINCKELMAN
16 Assistant Human Resources Director .... Ms. Victoria SCHWAB
18 Assoc Vice Pres of Operations .... Mr. Patrick BUHL
102 Executive Director of Foundation .... Mrs. Colleen SIMPSON
84 Dean Outreach & Enrollment .... Mr. Torrion AMIE
35 Dean of Students .... Ms. Lynn PERKINS
26 Chief Public Relations Officer .... Mr. Steve GELLER
06 Registrar .... Ms. Tonya HANSON
07 Director of Admissions .... Ms. Nancy PATES
37 Director of Financial Aid & Scholar .... Mrs. Susan ANT
38 Assoc Director of Advising & Couns .... Ms. Kari RUSCH-CURL
19 Director of Public Safety .... Mr. Erik BENTLEY
106 Director of Online Learning .... Vacant
27 Director of Marketing Communication .... Vacant
88 Accounting Supervisor .... Mrs. Cindy LADD
40 Bookstore Assistant Manager .... Mr. Greg LYONS
25 Grant Development Director .... Mrs. Angela ARNOLD

*North Hennepin Community College (B)

7411 85th Avenue N, Brooklyn Park MN 55445-2299
County: Hennepin FICE Identification: 002370
Unit ID: 174376
Telephone: (763) 424-0702 Carnegie Class: Assoc/HT-Mix Trad/Non
FAX Number: (763) 424-0929 Calendar System: Semester
URL: www.nhcc.edu
Established: 1966 Annual Undergrad Tuition & Fees (In-State): $4,383
Enrollment: 7,384 Coed
Affiliation or Control: State IRS Status: 501(c)3
Highest Offering: Associate Degree
Accreditation: NH, ACBSP, ADNUR, HT, MLTAD

02 President .... Dr. Barbara MCDONALD
05 VP Academic & Student Affairs .... Dr. Landon PIRIUS
10 VP Finance & Facilities .... Mr. Daniel HALL
13 Int Chief Information Officer .... Mr. Najam SAEED
32 Dean Student Development .... Ms. Elena FAVELA
84 Dean of Enrollment .... Ms. Jackie OLSSON
08 Librarian .... Mr. Craig LARSON
06 Director of Admissions & Records .... Ms. Melissa LEIMBEK
15 Chief Human Resources Officer .... Mr. Michael FREER
18 Director of Plant Services .... Mr. Joseph MORAN
30 Director of Advancement .... Ms. Jennifer LAMBRECHT
28 Director Diversity/Multiculturalism .... Mr. Michael BIRCHARD
26 Dir Marketing/Communications .... Ms. Liz HOGENSON
09 Director of Institutional Research .... Ms. Sheryl OLSON
19 Director of Public Safety .... Mr. Chad HENDERSON
21 Business Manager .... Ms. Dawn BELKO
49 Dean of Liberal Arts .... Mr. Michael DUEÑES
50 Dean Business & Career Programs .... Ms. Tracey WYMAN
81 Int Dean of Math/Science .... Ms. Julie ZIEMINSKI
76 Dean of Health Sciences .... Ms. Doris HILL
60 Dean of Comm/Language & Fine Arts .... Ms. Jan MCFALL
38 Director Student Advising .... Ms. Sarah DOMAN-FLYGARE
04 Executive Assistant to President .... Ms. Nicole CARLSON
36 Director Student Placement .... Ms. Deb ATKINS
37 Director Student Financial Aid .... Mr. Steve YANG

*Northland Community and Technical College (C)

1101 Highway 1 E, Thief River Falls MN 56701-2598
County: Pennington FICE Identification: 002385
Unit ID: 174473
Telephone: (218) 683-8800 Carnegie Class: Assoc/HVT-Mix Trad/Non
FAX Number: (218) 683-8980 Calendar System: Semester
URL: www.northlandcollege.edu
Established: 1965 Annual Undergrad Tuition & Fees (In-State): $5,534
Enrollment: 3,641 Coed
Affiliation or Control: State IRS Status: 501(c)3
Highest Offering: Associate Degree
Accreditation: NH, ADNUR, COARC, EMT, OTA, PTAA, RAD, SURGT

02 President .... Dr. Dennis BONA
05 VP Academic Affairs/Student Svcs .... Mr. Carey CASTLE
10 VP of Admin Services/CFO .... Ms. Sharron JESME
04 Asst to President .... Ms. Julie FENNING
11 Campus Dean Administration .... Dr. Brian HUSCHLE
20 Dean Thief River Falls Campus .... Mr. Mike CURFMAN
32 Dean of Students East Grand Forks .... Dr. Mary FONTES
103 Dean Workforce & Econ Development .... Mr. James RETKA
66 Dean Health/Nursing & Public Svcs .... Ms. Jodi STASSEN
08 Academic Success Ctr Director .... Ms. Linnea SCHLUESSLER
38 Counselor .... Ms. Kelsy BLOWERS
38 Counselor .... Ms. Kate SCHMALENBERG
84 Dir of Enrollment Mgmt & Admission .... Ms. Nicki CARLSON
37 Director Student Financial Aid .... Mr. Gerald SCHULTE
09 Director of Institutional Research .... Dr. Mary FONTES
15 Chief Human Resource Officer .... Ms. Kristi LANE
18 Chief Facilities/Physical Plant .... Mr. Clinton CASTLE
26 Interim Director Marketing .... Mr. Chad SPERLING
44 Dir Annual Giving/Alumni Relations .... Mr. Lars DYRUD
06 Registrar .... Ms. Lisa BOTTEM
28 Diversity Coordinator .... Mr. Carey CASTLE
102 Executive Director of Foundation .... Ms. Sheila BRUHN
13 Director of Technology .... Ms. Stacey HRON
41 Dir of Student Life & Athletics .... Mr. Richard SPEAS

*Northwest Technical College (D)

905 Grant Avenue, SE, Bemidji MN 56601-4907
County: Beltrami FICE Identification: 005759
Unit ID: 173115
Telephone: (218) 333-6600 Carnegie Class: Assoc/HVT-High Non
FAX Number: (218) 333-6694 Calendar System: Semester
URL: www.ntcmn.edu
Established: 1966 Annual Undergrad Tuition & Fees (In-State): $5,480
Enrollment: 1,091 Coed
Affiliation or Control: State IRS Status: 501(c)3
Highest Offering: Associate Degree
Accreditation: NH, DA

02 President .... Dr. Richard HANSON
05 Interim Dean .... Mr. Robert GRIGGS

*Pine Technical and Community College (E)

900 Fourth Street, SE, Pine City MN 55063-2198
County: Pine FICE Identification: 005535
Unit ID: 174570
Telephone: (320) 629-5100 Carnegie Class: Assoc/HVT-High Non
FAX Number: (320) 629-5101 Calendar System: Semester
URL: www.pine.edu
Established: 1965 Annual Undergrad Tuition & Fees (In-State): $4,066
Enrollment: 1,083 Coed
Affiliation or Control: State IRS Status: 501(c)3
Highest Offering: Associate Degree
Accreditation: NH, MAC

02 President .... Mr. Joe MULFORD
05 Chief Academic Officer .... Dr. Joan BLOEMENDAAL-GRUETT
13 Chief Information Officer .... Mr. Kenneth RIES
10 Chief Financial Officer .... Ms. Janis WEGNER
32 Dean Student Affairs .... Ms. Paula HOFFMAN
51 Dean of Continuing Edu/Custom Trng .... Mr. Jason SPAETH
103 Dean of Economic/Work Devel .... Ms. Stephanie SCHROEDER
36 Exec Dir Employment/Training Ctr .... Mr. Dwayne GREEN
06 Registrar .... Ms. Darla CAVERLEY
15 Chief Human Resources Officer .... Ms. Amy KRUSE
07 Director of Admissions .... Ms. Shawnda SCHELINDER
37 Director Student Financial Aid .... Mr. Shawn REYNOLDS
18 Physical Plant Supervisor .... Mr. Steven LANGE
04 Administrative Asst to President .... Ms. Sandra CARLISLE

*Rainy River Community College (F)

1501 Highway 71, International Falls MN 56649-2187
County: Koochiching FICE Identification: 006775
Unit ID: 174604
Telephone: (218) 285-7722 Carnegie Class: Assoc/HT-Mix Trad/Non
FAX Number: (218) 285-2239 Calendar System: Semester
URL: www.rrcc.mnscu.edu
Established: 1967 Annual Undergrad Tuition & Fees (In-State): $5,325
Enrollment: 325 Coed
Affiliation or Control: State IRS Status: 501(c)3
Highest Offering: Associate Degree
Accreditation: NH

02 Provost .... Ms. Carol HELLAND
06 Registrar .... Ms. Berta HAGEN
37 Dir of Financial Aid/Housing .... Mr. Scott T. RILEY
13 Dir Information Technology .... Ms. Shelly JUGOVICH
10 Business Manager .... Mrs. Emily AHRENS

*Ridgewater College (G)

PO Box 1097, 2101 15th Ave NW, Willmar MN 56201-1097
County: Kandiyohi FICE Identification: 005252
Unit ID: 175236
Telephone: (320) 222-5200 Carnegie Class: Assoc/MT-VT-High Trad
FAX Number: (320) 222-5212 Calendar System: Semester
URL: www.ridgewater.edu
Established: 1961 Annual Undergrad Tuition & Fees (In-State): $5,406
Enrollment: 3,753 Coed
Affiliation or Control: State IRS Status: 501(c)3
Highest Offering: Associate Degree
Accreditation: NH, ADNUR, CAHIIM, EMT, MAC, PNUR

02 President .... Dr. Douglas W. ALLEN
05 Vice Pres Acad Affs/Student Svcs .... Dr. Betty J. STREHLOW
10 Vice President Finance & Operations .... Mr. Daniel F. HOLTZ
51 Dean of Cust Trng & Cont Education .... Mr. Sam BOWEN
20 Dean of Instruction/Technical Pgms .... Mr. Michael J. BOEHME
20 Dean of Instruction .... Mr. Mike KUTZKE
20 Dean Instruction/Liberal Arts/Sci .... Mr. Alan STAGE
32 Dean of Student Services .... Ms. Heidi L. OLSON
21 Director of Business Services .... Ms. Cheryl A. NORLIEN
15 Int Chief Human Resource Officer .... Mr. Keith BALASKI
66 Director of Nursing .... Ms. C. Lynn JOHNSON
37 Director of Financial Aid .... Mr. James W. RICE
07 Admissions Director .... Ms. Sally KERFELD
41 Athletic Director .... Mr. Todd M. THORSTAD
06 Registrar .... Ms. Kelli S. KIENITZ
13 Chief Information Officer .... Mr. Timothy L. FURR
26 Director of Communication/Marketing .... Ms. Liz VANDERBILL
102 Foundation Executive Director .... Ms. Kelly J. MAGNUSON
09 Director of Institutional Research .... Dr. Ellen ROSTER
28 Multicultural Outreach/Academic Adv .... Ms. Jehana KHAN
18 Physical Plant Director .... Mr. Kip R. OVESON

*Riverland Community College (H)

1900 8th Avenue, NW, Austin MN 55912-1473
County: Mower FICE Identification: 002335
Unit ID: 173063
Telephone: (507) 433-0600 Carnegie Class: Assoc/MT-VT-Mix Trad/Non
FAX Number: (507) 433-0665 Calendar System: Semester
URL: www.riverland.edu
Established: 1940 Annual Undergrad Tuition & Fees (In-State): $5,538
Enrollment: 3,243 Coed
Affiliation or Control: State IRS Status: 501(c)3
Highest Offering: Associate Degree
Accreditation: NH, ACBSP, ADNUR, RAD

02 President .... Dr. Adenuga ATEWOLOGUN
05 VP of Academic & Student Affairs .... Dr. Mary DAVENPORT
10 Chief Financial Officer .... Mr. Brad DOSS
15 VP of Employees & Tech Resources .... Ms. Celeste RUBLE
66 Director of Nursing .... Ms. Laura BEASLEY
49 Dean of Arts/Humanities/Social Sci .... Mr. Kelly MCCALLA
75 Dean of Bus Tech/Trade/Industry .... Mr. Matt BISSONETTE
32 Dean of Student Affairs .... Mr. Gary SCHINDLER
30 Dean for Institutional Advancement .... Mr. Steve BOWRON
06 Dir of Enrollment Svcs/Registrar .... Ms. Sue JECH
07 Dir of Admissions & New Student Rel .... Ms. Nel ZELLAR
26 Dir of Communications/Media & Mktg .... Mr. James DOUGLASS
37 Director of Financial Aid .... Ms. Patty HEMANN
36 Dir of College Partnerships & Trans .... Ms. Lori JENSEN
13 Director of Technology .... Mr. Dan HARBER
18 Facilities Supervisor .... Mr. Shawn O'CONNOR
96 Purchasing Agent .... Ms. Page PETERSEN
28 Regional Diversity Trainer/Investgtr .... Ms. Ricki WALTERS
08 Head Librarian .... Ms. Jeannie KEARNEY
19 Director Security/Safety .... Mr. Mike HOWE
29 Director Alumni Relations .... Ms. Laura HELLE
41 Athletic Director .... Mr. David LILLEMON

*Rochester Community and Technical College (I)

851 30th Avenue, SE, Rochester MN 55904-4999
County: Olmsted FICE Identification: 002373
Unit ID: 174738
Telephone: (507) 285-7210 Carnegie Class: Assoc/MT-VT-High Trad
FAX Number: (507) 285-7496 Calendar System: Semester
URL: www.rctc.edu
Established: 1915 Annual Undergrad Tuition & Fees (In-State): $5,638
Enrollment: 5,894 Coed
Affiliation or Control: State IRS Status: 501(c)3
Highest Offering: Associate Degree
Accreditation: NH, ACBSP, ADNUR, CAHIIM, DA, DH, PNUR, SURGT

02 Interim President .... Dr. Mary DAVENPORT
05 Vice President Academic Affairs .... Dr. Greg MOSIER
10 Vice Pres Finance and Facilities .... Mr. Steve SCHMALL
76 Dean Allied Health .... Dr. Safawo GULLO
49 Dean of Liberal Arts .... Dr. Veronica DELCOURT
75 Dean of Career/Technical .... Ms. Michelle PYFFEROEN
15 Chief Human Resources Officer .... Mrs. Renee ENGELMEYER
13 Chief Information Technology Ofcr .... Mr. Scott SAHS
32 Chief Student Affairs Officer .... Dr. Michael ANTHONY
88 Dir of Business/Econ Development .... Ms. Michelle PYFFEROEN
35 Student Life Coordinator .... Mr. Scott KROOK
06 Registrar .... Ms. Nancy SHUMAKER
07 Director Admissions .... Ms. Alicia ZEONE
37 Director Financial Aid .... Ms. Beth DIEKMANN
09 Director of Institutional Research .... Dr. Priyank SHAH
04 Assistant to President .... Mrs. Judy KINGSBURY
21 Business Office Supervisor .... Ms. Ruth SIEFERT
26 Chief Public Relations Officer .... Mr. Nate STOLTMAN
19 Security Officer .... Mr. Andrew HAMANN
40 Bookstore Coordinator .... Ms. Michelle DANIELSON
96 Purchasing Manager .... Ms. June MEITZNER
30 Foundation Executive Director .... Vacant

18 Chief Facilities/Physical Plant ....Mr. Mark FASS
38 Director Student Counseling ....Ms. Lisa MOHR
108 Dean ....Dr. Ginny BOYUM
08 Head Librarian ....Ms. Diane POLLOCK
22 Dir Affirmative Action/EEO ....Ms. Renee ENGELMEYER
41 Athletic Director ....Ms. Jean MUSGJERD

*St. Cloud State University (A)

720 4th Avenue S, Saint Cloud MN 56301-4498
County: Stearns FICE Identification: 002377
Unit ID: 174783
Telephone: (320) 308-0121 Carnegie Class: Masters/L
FAX Number: N/A Calendar System: Semester
URL: www.stcloudstate.edu
Established: 1869 Annual Undergrad Tuition & Fees (In-State): $7,814
Enrollment: 16,076 Coed
Affiliation or Control: State IRS Status: 501(c)3
Highest Offering: Doctorate
Accreditation: NH, ART, BUS, CAATE, CACREP, CORE, CS, ENG, ENGR, JOUR, MFCD, MT, MUS, NAIT, NURSE, SP, SW, TED, THEA

02 Interim President ....Dr. Ashish VAIDYA
04 Executive Asst to President ....Ms. Linda CONWAY
05 Provost/VP Academic Affairs ....Dr. Ashish VAIDYA
20 Dir of Academic Operations ....Ms. Michele MUMM
10 Vice Pres Finance/Admin ....Ms. Tammy L. MCGEE
21 Interim Assoc VP Finance/Admin ....Mr. Jeff WAGNER
88 AVP Safety/Risk Management ....Mr. Jesse CASHMAN
32 Vice Pres Student Life Development ....Dr. Wanda OVERLAND
30 Vice Pres University Advancement ....Mr. Matthew ANDREW
43 Special Advisor to the President ....Dr. Judith P. SIMINOE
22 Equity and Affirmative Action Ofc ....Ms. Ellyn BARTGES
41 Athletic Director ....Ms. Heather WEEMS
86 Dir Univ Relations/Legislative Rel ....Mr. Bernie OMANN
45 AVP/AP Strategy/Planning & Effect ....Dr. Lisa FOSS
26 Asst VP Marketing & Communications ....Mr. Loren BOONE
13 Chief Info Technology Officer (CIO) ....Mr. Henry MAY
50 Dean Herberger Business School ....Dr. David HARRIS
53 Interim Dean School of Education ....Dr. Steve HOOVER
76 Dean Health/Human Service ....Dr. Monica DEVERS
49 Dean College of Liberal Arts ....Dr. Mark SPRINGER
88 Dean School of Public Affairs ....Dr. King BANAIAN
81 Dean Science & Engineering ....Dr. Dan GREGORY
51 Interim Director Continuing Studies ....Ms. Gail RUHLAND
08 Dean Learning Resources ....Mr. Mark VARGAS
88 AP for Research/Dean ....Vacant
88 Interim AP University College ....Mr. Adam KLEPETAR
35 AP Faculty/Student Affairs ....Vacant
84 AP Undergrad Recruit & Transition ....Dr. Amber SCHULTZ
06 Registrar ....Ms. Sue BAYERL
91 Dir Information Technology Services ....Mr. Phil THORSON
29 Director of Constituent Engagement ....Ms. Terri MISCHE
36 Interim Director Career Services ....Mr. Bobbie MURPHY
37 Director of Financial Aid ....Mr. Mike T. URAN
38 Director of Counseling ....Dr. John M. EGGERS
39 Director of Student Housing ....Mr. Daniel T. PEDERSEN
09 Dir Analytics/Business Intelligence ....Mr. Brent DONNAY
15 Director Human Resources ....Ms. Holly SCHOENHERR
18 Director Facilities Management ....Mr. John FRISCHMANN
88 Director American Indian Center . Mr. Jim KNUTSON-KOLODZNE
88 Director of Atwood Services ....Vacant
88 Dir LGBT Resources ....Mr. Brandon JOHNSON
88 Director Lindgren Child Care Center ....Ms. Debra CARLSON
88 Director Multicultural Student Svcs ....Mr. Shahzad AHMED
22 Director Student Disability Service ....Mr. Owen ZIMPEL
23 Director Student Health Services ....Ms. Corie BECKERMANN
88 Director Womens Center ....Ms. Jane OLSEN
19 Director Public Safety ....Mr. Kevin WHITLOCK
88 Director of International Studies ....Mr. Shahzad AHMAD
40 Bookstore Manager ....Mr. Ted MEARS

*Saint Cloud Technical and Community College (B)

1540 Northway Drive, Saint Cloud MN 56303-1240
County: Stearns FICE Identification: 005534
Unit ID: 174756
Telephone: (320) 308-5000 Carnegie Class: Assoc/HVT-High Trad
FAX Number: (320) 308-5981 Calendar System: Semester
URL: www.sctcc.edu
Established: 1948 Annual Undergrad Tuition & Fees (In-State): $5,325
Enrollment: 4,924 Coed
Affiliation or Control: State IRS Status: 501(c)3
Highest Offering: Associate Degree
Accreditation: NH, CAHIIM, CVT, DA, DH, DMS, EMT, PNUR, SURGT

02 President ....Ms. Joyce HELENS
05 VP of Academic Affairs ....Ms. Carolyn OLSON
04 Assistant to the President ....Ms. Karen A. HIEMENZ
32 Vice President of Student Affairs ....Mr. Jonathan EICHTEN
10 Vice Pres Admin/Chief Financial Ofc ....Ms. Lori KLOOS
75 Dean Trade/Industry ....Mr. Darrin STROSAHL
81 Dean of Math/Sciences/Technology ....Ms. Tarryl CLARK
50 Dean of Business/Comm/Humanities ....Ms. Kristina KELLER
66 Dean of Nursing/Health ....Vacant
06 Registrar ....Ms. Lana L. FEDDEMA
15 Dir Personnel Svcs/Affirm Action ....Ms. Deb A. HOLSTAD
84 Dir of Enroll Management/Admissions ....Ms. Jodi M. ELNESS
08 Head Librarian ....Ms. Patricia AKERMAN
19 Security/Safety Officer ....Mr. Christopher LOOS
37 Director Student Financial Aid ....Ms. Anita G. BAUGH
36 Director Student Placement ....Ms. Jackie BAUER
40 Director Bookstore ....Mr. James SCHOLLA
38 Director Student Counseling ....Ms. Judy JACOBSON-BERG
35 Activ Dir/Chief Student Life Ofcr ....Ms. Melissa MAJERUS
18 Chief Facilities/Physical Plant ....Mr. Jason THEISEN
13 Chief Information Officer ....Ms. Viola BERGQUIST
88 Director of Academic Accountability ....Ms. Norma KONSCHAK
21 Associate Business Officer ....Mr. Duane DAHLSTROM
96 Director of Purchasing ....Ms. Susan MEYER
14 Director Library & Info Technology ....Ms. Viola BERGQUIST
22 Director Affirm Action/Equal Oppty ....Ms. Deb HOLSTAD
30 Chief Devel/Dir Annual/Planned Giv ....Ms. Lori GRESS
28 Director of Diversity ....Mr. Jonathan EICHTEN

*Saint Paul College-A Community & Technical College (C)

235 Marshall Avenue, Saint Paul MN 55102-1800
County: Ramsey FICE Identification: 005533
Unit ID: 175041
Telephone: (651) 846-1600 Carnegie Class: Assoc/HVT-Mix Trad/Non
FAX Number: (651) 846-1451 Calendar System: Semester
URL: www.saintpaul.edu
Established: 1910 Annual Undergrad Tuition & Fees (In-State): $5,480
Enrollment: 6,600 Coed
Affiliation or Control: State IRS Status: 501(c)3
Highest Offering: Associate Degree
Accreditation: NH, ACBSP, ACFEI, CAHIIM, COARC, MLTAD, PNUR

02 President ....Dr. Rassoul DASTMOZD
05 VP Academic Affs/Chief Acad Ofcr ....Dr. Kelly MURTAUGH
10 Vice President Finance & Operations ....Mr. Scott WILSON
30 Chief Development Officer ....Ms. Laura SAVIN
27 Director of TRIO ....Mr. Michael OJIBWAY
103 Dean Workforce Trng/Continuing Educ ....Ms. Tracy WILSON
84 Dean Enrollment Management ....Ms. Sarah CARRICO
90 Assoc Dean of Academic Services ....Vacant
15 Chief Human Resources Officer ....Ms. Rachelle M. SCHMIDT
06 Registrar ....Ms. Katie YEP
07 Director of Enrollment Services ....Mr. Ger VUE
09 Dean of Institutional Research ....Ms. Laura KING
29 Director of Alumni Relations ....Ms. Laura SAVIN
36 Director Student Placement ....Ms. Sheryl SAUL
38 Director Student Counseling ....Dr. Lisa HANES-GOODLANDER
96 Director of Purchasing ....Ms. Teresa SORENSEN
18 Director Facilities/Physical Plant ....Mr. Daniel KIRK
21 Business Manager ....Mr. John PALMER
28 Director of Diversity .... Mr. John PARKER-DER BOGHOSSIAN
28 Director of Diversity ....Ms. Rachelle SCHMIDT
37 Director of Student Financial Aid ....Mr. Adam JOHNSON
102 Exec Dir of Foundation/Alumni Rels ....Ms. Laura SAVIN
13 Chief Information Officer ....Mr. Najam SAEED
26 Director of Marketing ....Ms. Audrey BERGENGREN
17 Dean of Health & Services ....Mr. Brendan ASHBY
81 Dean Science/Technology/Eng & Math ....Dr. Linda KINGSTON
50 Dean Business/Career Tech Educ ....Mr. Frank BRASWELL
88 Dean Liberal & Fine Arts ....Dr. Milford MUSKETT
19 Director Security/Safety ....Mr. Thomas BERGS
108 Director Institutional Assessment ....Dr. Laura KING

*South Central College (D)

1920 Lee Boulevard, PO Box 1920,
North Mankato MN 56003
County: Nicollet FICE Identification: 005537
Unit ID: 173911
Telephone: (507) 389-7200 Carnegie Class: Assoc/MT-VT-High Non
FAX Number: (507) 388-9951 Calendar System: Semester
URL: www.southcentral.edu
Established: 1946 Annual Undergrad Tuition & Fees (In-District): $5,379
Enrollment: 3,387 Coed
Affiliation or Control: State/Local IRS Status: 501(c)3
Highest Offering: Associate Degree
Accreditation: NH, DA, EMT, MAC, MLTAD

02 President ....Dr. Annette PARKER
04 Exec Assistant to the President ....Ms. Carol FREED
05 Vice Pres Student/Academic Affs ....Dr. Susan TARNOWSKI
10 VP Finance/Facilities ....Mr. David ARMSTRONG
15 CHRO ....Ms. Dawn PEARSON
13 Vice Pres of Technology ....Dr. Mark BAAS
32 Dean of Student Affairs ....Ms. Judy ZEIGER
103 Dean of Workforce Ed/Training ....Ms. Barb EMBACHER
49 Dean of LAS ....Dr. Judy SHULTZ
47 Dean of Agriculture ....Mr. Brad SCHLOESSER
66 Dean of Allied Health & Nursing ....Ms. Michele BRIELMAIER
09 Director Rsrch/Inst Effectivenes ....Vacant
26 Public Relations/Marketing Director ....Ms. Shelly MEGAW
28 Chief Diversity Officer ....Dr. Mitzi KENNEDY
37 Director of Financial Aid ....Ms. Jayne DINSE
19 Director of Safety & Security ....Mr. Al KLUEVER
07 Director of Admissions/Advising ....Mr. Anthony RIESBERG
08 Director of Library/Media Services ....Ms. Johnna HORTON
06 Interim Registrar ....Ms. Deann SCHLOESSER

*Southwest Minnesota State University (E)

1501 State Street, Marshall MN 56258-1598
County: Lyon FICE Identification: 002375
Unit ID: 175078
Telephone: (507) 537-7678 Carnegie Class: Masters/M
FAX Number: (507) 537-7154 Calendar System: Semester
URL: www.smsu.edu
Established: 1963 Annual Undergrad Tuition & Fees (In-State): $8,326
Enrollment: 7,069 Coed
Affiliation or Control: State IRS Status: 501(c)3
Highest Offering: Master's
Accreditation: NH, MUS, NURSE, SW

02 President ....Dr. Connie J. GORES
05 Provost ....Dr. Dwight C. WATSON
10 VP Finance and Admin ....Ms. Debra KERKAERT
32 AVP Stdnt Affairs/Dean of Students ....Mr. Scott CROWELL
30 VP Advance/Foundation Ex Dir ....Mr. William MULSO
49 Dean Arts/Letters/Sciences ....Dr. Jan LOFT
50 Dean Bus/Ed/Grad/Prof Stud ....Dr. Raphael ONYEAGHALA
41 Athletic Director ....Mr. Christopher HMIELEWSKI
13 Chief Information Officer ....Mr. Dan BAUN
07 VP EMSS ....Mr. Rob FORGET
14 Director of Computer Services ....Mr. Shawn HEDMAN
06 Registrar ....Ms. Patricia CARMODY
19 Director University Public Safety ....Mr. Michael MUNFORD
28 Director Diversity & Inclusion ....Mr. Jay LEE
15 Chief Human Resources/Affirm Action ....Ms. Nancy OLSON
29 Director of Alumni ....Mr. Michael VANDREHLE
18 Facilities & Physical Plant Manager ....Ms. Cyndi HOLM
36 Director of Career Services ....Ms. Melissa SCHOLTEN
37 Director of Financial Aid ....Mr. David VIKANDER
38 Associate Professor of Counseling ....Ms. Sara FIER
96 Buyer Supervisor ....Ms. Barb BERKENPAS
21 Business Manager ....Mr. Eric RUNESTAD
26 Dir Communications/Marketing ....Mr. James TATE
04 Exec Admin Asst to President ....Ms. Chris ANDERSON
09 Director of Institutional Research ....Mr. Alan MATZNER
102 Director Development ....Ms. Stacy FROST
44 Director Annual or Planned Giving ....Mr. Erik VOGEL

*Vermilion Community College (F)

1900 E Camp Street, Ely MN 55731-1998
County: Saint Louis FICE Identification: 002350
Unit ID: 175157
Telephone: (218) 365-7200 Carnegie Class: Assoc/HT-High Trad
FAX Number: (218) 235-2173 Calendar System: Semester
URL: www.vcc.edu
Established: 1922 Annual Undergrad Tuition & Fees (In-State): $5,325
Enrollment: 712 Coed
Affiliation or Control: State IRS Status: 501(c)3
Highest Offering: Associate Degree
Accreditation: NH

02 Provost/Chief Academic Officer ....Mr. Shawn BINA
07 Director of Admissions/Student Affs ....Mr. Jeff NELSON
09 Director of Institutional Research ....Ms. Tracey ROY
10 Business Manager ....Vacant
15 Director of Human Resources ....Ms. Carmen BRADACH
32 Dir Student Life/Facil/Phy Plant ....Mr. Dave MARSHALL
36 Director of Student Placement ....Ms. Molly JOHNSTON
37 Director of Student Financial Aid ....Ms. Shannan HARDING
38 Director of Student Counseling ....Ms. Cindy ANDERSON-BINA
29 Director Alumni Relations ....Ms. Patti ZUPANCICH
28 Director of Diversity ....Ms. Patti ZUPANCICH
26 Chief Public Relations Officer ....Mr. Jeff NELSON
06 Registrar ....Ms. Chris HEGENBARTH

*Winona State University (G)

PO Box 5838, Winona MN 55987-0838
County: Winona FICE Identification: 002394
Unit ID: 175272
Telephone: (507) 457-5000 Carnegie Class: Masters/M
FAX Number: (507) 457-5586 Calendar System: Quarter
URL: www.winona.edu
Established: 1858 Annual Undergrad Tuition & Fees (In-State): $9,047
Enrollment: 8,684 Coed
Affiliation or Control: State IRS Status: 501(c)3
Highest Offering: Doctorate
Accreditation: NH, BUS, CAATE, CACREP, ENG, MT, MUS, NURSE, SW, TED, THEA

02 President ....Dr. Scott R. OLSON
05 Provost/VP Academic Affairs/CAO ....Dr. Patricia ROGERS
10 VP Finance & Administration ....Mr. Scott ELLINGHUYSEN
30 VP University Advancement ....Mr. Ron DEMPSEY
32 VP Enrollment & Student Life & Dev ....Ms. Denise MCDOWELL
13 AVP Academic Affairs/CIO ....Mr. Kenneth JANZ
26 Asst VP Marketing & Communications ....Vacant
38 Director of Counseling Svcs ....Vacant
54 Dean Col of Science/Engr ....Dr. Charla MIERTSCHIN
49 Int Assoc Dean Col of Liberal Arts ....Dr. Peter MIENE
50 Dean College of Business ....Dr. Hamid AKBARI
53 Dean College of Education ....Dr. Tarrell PORTMAN
66 Dean Col of Nursing/Health Science ....Dr. William MCBREEN
35 Dean of Students ....Ms. Karen JOHNSON
06 Sr Associate Registrar ....Ms. Tania SCHMIDT
84 Director Warrior Success Center ....Ms. Barbara OERTEL
37 Assistant Director of Financial Aid ....Ms. Charlene KREUZER
36 Associate Director Career Services ....Ms. Deanna GODDARD
07 Director of Admissions ....Mr. Carl STANGE
39 Residential College Program Coord ....Ms. Sarah OLCOTT
51 Exec Dir Outreach/Continuing Educ ....Ms. Diane DINGFELDER
29 Associate Director Alumni Relations ....Ms. Heather KOSIK
40 Bookstore Manager ....Ms. Karen KRAUSE
44 Director Development ....Ms. Debbie BLOCK

88 Director of International Svcs .... Ms. Kemale PINAR
19 Director of Security .... Mr. Don WALSKI
41 Athletic Director .... Mr. Eric SCHOH
18 Asst VP for Facilities Management .... Mr. Michael PIEPER
27 Director University Public Info .... Ms. Andrea NORTHAM
94 Director of Women's Studies .... Dr. Tamara BERG
96 Director of Purchasing .... Ms. Laura MANN
28 Director of Cultural Diversity .... Mr. Alexander HINES
15 Director of Human Resources .... Ms. Lori REED

* *Anoka-Ramsey Community College Cambridge Campus* (A)

300 Spirit River Drive South, Cambrdige MN 55008-5704
Telephone: (763) 433-1100 Identification: 770298
Accreditation: &NH

† Regional accreditation is carried under the parent institution in Coon Rapids, MN

* *Hennepin Technical College* (B)

131000 College View, Eden Prairie MN 55347
Telephone: (952) 995-1300 Identification: 770299
Accreditation: &NH, ACFEI

† Regional accreditation is carried under the parent institution in Brooklyn Park, MN

* *Mesabi Range College Eveleth* (C)

1100 Industrial Park Drive, Eveleth MN 55734
Telephone: (218) 741-3095 Identification: 770300
Accreditation: &NH

† Regional accreditation is carried under the parent institution in Virginia, MN

* *Metropolitan State University* (D)

13th Street & Harmon Place, Minneapolis MN 55403
Telephone: (651) 793-1300 Identification: 770301
Accreditation: &NH

† Regional accreditation is carried under the parent institution in Saint Paul, MN

* *Minnesota State College-Southeast Technical Red Wing Campus* (E)

308 Pioneer Road, Red Wing MN 55066
Telephone: (651) 385-6300 Identification: 770302
Accreditation: &NH

† Regional accreditation is carried under the parent institution in Winona, MN

* *Minnesota State Community and Technical College Detroit Lakes* (F)

9-- Highway 34 E, Detroit Lakes MN 56501
Telephone: (218) 846-3700 Identification: 770303
Accreditation: &NH

† Regional accreditation is carried under the parent institution in Fergus Falls, MN

* *Minnesota State Community and Technical College Moorhead* (G)

1900 28th Avenue S, Moorhead MN 56560
Telephone: (218) 299-6500 Identification: 770304
Accreditation: &NH, SURGT

† Regional accreditation is carried under the parent institution in Fergus Falls, MN

* *Minnesota State Community and Technical College Wadena* (H)

405 Colfax Avenue SW, Wadena MN 56482
Telephone: (213) 631-7800 Identification: 770305
Accreditation: &NH

† Regional accreditation is carried under the parent institution in Fergus Falls, MN

* *Minnesota West Community and Technical College Canby Campus* (I)

1011 First Street, Canby MN 56220
Telephone: (507) 223-7252 Identification: 770306
Accreditation: &NH

† Regional accreditation is carried under the parent institution in Worthington, MN

* *Minnesota West Community and Technical College Granite Falls Campus* (J)

1593 11th Avenue, Granite Falls MN 56241
Telephone: (320) 564-5000 Identification: 770307
Accreditation: &NH

† Regional accreditation is carried under the parent institution in Worthington, MN

* *Minnesota West Community and Technical College Jackson Campus* (K)

401 West Street, Jackson MN 56143
Telephone: (547) 847-7920 Identification: 770308
Accreditation: &NH

† Regional accreditation is carried under the parent institution in Worthington, MN

* *Minnesota West Community and Technical College Pipestone Campus* (L)

1314 North Hiawatha Avenue, Pipestone MN 56164
Telephone: (507) 825-6800 Identification: 770309
Accreditation: &NH

† Regional accreditation is carried under the parent institution in Worthington, MN

* *Minnesota West Community and Technical College Worthington Campus* (M)

1450 College Way, Worthington MN 56187
Telephone: (507) 372-3400 Identification: 770310
Accreditation: &NH

† Regional accreditation is carried under the parent institution in Worthington, MN

* *Northland Community and Technical College-East Grand Forks* (N)

2022 Central Avenue NE, East Grand Forks MN 56721
Telephone: (218) 793-2800 Identification: 770311
Accreditation: &NH, @DIETT

† Regional accreditation is carried under the parent institution in Thief River Falls, MN

* *Ridgewater College Hutchinson Campus* (O)

2 Century Avenue SE, Hutchinson MN 55350
Telephone: (320) 234-8500 Identification: 770312
Accreditation: &NH

† Regional accreditation is carried under the parent institution in Willmar, MN

* *Riverland Community College Albert Lea Campus* (P)

2200 Riverland Drive, Albert Lea MN 56007
Telephone: (507) 379-3300 Identification: 770313
Accreditation: &NH

† Regional accreditation is carried under the parent institution in Austin, MN

* *South Central College Faribault Campus* (Q)

1225 Third Street SW, Faribault MN 55021
Telephone: (507) 332-5800 Identification: 770314
Accreditation: &NH

† Regional accreditation is carried under the parent institution in North Mankato, MN

* *Winona State University-Rochester* (R)

859 30th Avenue SE, Rochester MN 55904
Telephone: (800) 366-5418 Identification: 770317
Accreditation: &NH

† Regional accreditation is carried under the parent institution in Winona, MN

Mitchell Hamline School of Law (S)

875 Summit Avenue, Saint Paul MN 55105-3076
County: Ramsey FICE Identification: 002391
Unit ID: 175281
Telephone: (651) 227-9171 Carnegie Class: Spec-4-yr-Law
FAX Number: (651) 290-6414 Calendar System: Semester
URL: www.mitchellhamline.edu
Established: 1900 Annual Graduate Tuition & Fees: N/A
Enrollment: 665 Coed
Affiliation or Control: Independent Non-Profit IRS Status: 501(c)3
Highest Offering: First Professional Degree; No Undergraduates
Accreditation: LAW

01 President & Dean .... Mr. Mark GORDON
04 Exec Asst to President & Board .... Ms. Lynette FRACTION
05 Assoc Dean for Academic Affairs .... Ms. Kate KRUSE
30 VP of Institutional Advancement .... Ms. Linda K. BERG
15 Director Human Resources .... Ms. Andrea BIEN
13 Director of Information Technology .... Mr. Andrew ALLEN
10 Interim Vice President Finance .... Ms. Jane GOULD
11 VP Operations/Cmty Partnerships .... Ms. Christine SZAJ
08 Director of Law Library .... Ms. Barbara KALLUSKY
28 Asst Dean/Multicultural Inclusion .... Ms. Sharon VAN LEER
36 Dean for Career Development .... Ms. Leanne FUITH
07 Dean of Admissions .... Ms. Emily DUNSWORTH

06 Registrar .... Ms. Colleen CLISH
26 Director of Marketing/Alumni Rels .... Ms. Louise COPELAND
37 Director of Financial Aid .... Ms. Patty HARRIS
96 Purchasing Manager .... Ms. Paula B. MERTH
19 Director Security .... Mr. David HELLERMANN
46 Dean of Strategic Initiatives .... Mr. Greg DUHL
32 Dean of Student Affairs .... Ms. Anne MOELK

National American University-Bloomington (T)

7801 Metro Pkwy, Suite 200, Bloomington MN 55425
Telephone: (952) 356-3600 Identification: 770397
Accreditation: &NH, MAC

† Regional accreditation is carried under the parent institution in Rapid City, SD

National American University-Brooklyn Center (U)

6200 Shingle Creek Pkwy, Suite 130, Brooklyn Center MN 55430
Telephone: (763) 852-7500 Identification: 770398
Accreditation: &NH, MAC

† Regional accreditation is carried under the parent institution in Rapid City, SD

National American University-Burnsville (V)

501 West Travelers Trail, #617, Burnsville MN 55337
Telephone: (952) 563-1250 Identification: 770399
Accreditation: &NH

† Regional accreditation is carried under the parent institution in Rapid City, SD

National American University-Rochester (W)

3906 East Frontage Highway 52 Road, Rochester MN 55901
Telephone: (866) 628-6387 Identification: 770400
Accreditation: &NH

† Regional accreditation is carried under the parent institution in Rapid City, SD

National American University-Roseville (X)

1550 W Highway 36, Roseville MN 55113
Telephone: (651) 855-6300 Identification: 770401
Accreditation: &NH, MAC

† Regional accreditation is carried under the parent institution in Rapid City, SD

North Central University (Y)

910 Elliot Avenue, Minneapolis MN 55404-1391
County: Hennepin FICE Identification: 002369
Unit ID: 174437
Telephone: (612) 343-4400 Carnegie Class: Bac-Diverse
FAX Number: (612) 343-4778 Calendar System: Semester
URL: www.northcentral.edu
Established: 1930 Annual Undergrad Tuition & Fees: $21,586
Enrollment: 1,191 Coed
Affiliation or Control: Assemblies Of God Church IRS Status: 501(c)3
Highest Offering: Master's
Accreditation: NH, SW

01 President .... Dr. Gordon L. ANDERSON
04 Executive Assistant to President .... Mrs. Bridget KNISELY
05 VP Academic Affairs/Academic Dean .... Dr. Don L. TUCKER
10 Vice President Business/Finance .... Mrs. Joy E. BRATHWAITE
32 Vice President Student Development .... Mr. Mike A. NOSSER
26 VP University Relations .... Mr. Andrew DENTON
57 Executive Director Fine Arts .... Dr. Larry C. BACH
21 Director of Accounting .... Mr. Bruce W. WHEELER
39 Dean of Residence Life .... Ms. Abigail DAVIS
31 Dean of Community Life .... Ms. Nicole PALSER
41 Director of Athletics .... Mr. Greg L. JOHNSON
37 Director of Financial Aid .... Mrs. Monica M. MUCHOW
08 Library Director .... Mrs. Judy PRUITT
13 Exec Dir Information Technology .... Vacant
06 Registrar .... Ms. Mary MURPHY
09 Dir Inst Research/Effectiveness .... Mr. Greg LEEPER
07 Director of Admissions .... Mrs. Beth HARSHBARGER
38 Director of Student Success Center .... Mr. Todd MONGER
18 Facilities/Campus Housing Manager ...... Mr. Jordon ROBERTSON

Northwestern Health Sciences University (Z)

2501 W 84th Street, Bloomington MN 55431-1599
County: Hennepin FICE Identification: 012328
Unit ID: 174507
Telephone: (952) 888-4777 Carnegie Class: Spec-4-yr-Other Health
FAX Number: (952) 888-6713 Calendar System: Trimester
URL: www.nwhealth.edu
Established: 1941 Annual Undergrad Tuition & Fees: $11,636
Enrollment: 879 Coed
Affiliation or Control: Independent Non-Profit IRS Status: 501(c)3
Highest Offering: First Professional Degree

Accreditation: NH, ACUP, CHIRO, COMTA

01 President and CEO .... Dr. Christopher CASSIRER
05 Provost and Chief Academic Officer .... Dr. Deborah BUSHWAY
10 Chief Financial Officer .... Ms. Kathy PANCIERA
32 VP Student Affs/Dean of Students .... Dr. Emily TWEED
11 Chief Operating Officer .... Ms. Leslie BRONK
07 Director of Admissions .... Ms. Alaina BERUBE
08 Director of Library Services .... Ms. Anne MACKERETH
29 Dir Alumni Relations .... Ms. Kim BAILEY
15 VP of Human Resources .... Ms. Mary GALE
51 Director Continuing Education .... Vacant
26 VP of Marketing & Institutional Adv .... Mr. Jeff RICH
13 Chief Information Officer .... Mr. Chad JOHNSON
38 University Counselor .... Ms. Becky LAWYER
18 Director Facilities Management .... Mr. Kevin WOLPERN
96 Director Bookstore & Purchasing .... Ms. Jan HALLEEN
04 Administrative Asst to President .... Ms. Nancy JOHNSON
28 Director of Diversity and Inclusion .... Dr. Alejandra DASHE
06 Director of Student Financial Svcs .... Ms. Susan NEPPL
88 Dean College of Health & Wellness .... Dr. Dale HEALEY
88 Dean College of Chiropractic .... Dr. Trevor FOSHANG

Oak Hills Christian College (A)

1600 Oak Hills Road, SW, Bemidji MN 56601-8826
County: Beltrami FICE Identification: 009992
Unit ID: 174525
Telephone: (218) 751-8670 Carnegie Class: Spec-4-yr-Faith
FAX Number: (218) 751-8825 Calendar System: Semester
URL: www.oakhills.edu
Established: 1946 Annual Undergrad Tuition & Fees: $16,165
Enrollment: 141 Coed
Affiliation or Control: Interdenominational IRS Status: 501(c)3
Highest Offering: Baccalaureate
Accreditation: BI

01 President .... Dr. Steve J. HOSTETTER
05 Dean of the College .... Dr. Steven J. WARE
30 Vice President for Advancement .... Mrs. Joan L. BERNTSON
84 VP Enrollment Management .... Mr. Mike RASCH
32 Dean of Student Life .... Mr. Brad DEJAGER
06 Registrar .... Mrs. Tammy MCCRAY
08 Library Director .... Mr. Keith BUSH
37 Director of Financial Aid .... Mr. Matt MYRICK

Presentation College Fairmont (B)

115 S Park Street, Suite 117, Fairmont MN 56031
Telephone: (507) 235-4658 Identification: 770418
Accreditation: &NH

† Regional accreditation is carried under the parent institution in Aberdeen, SD

*Rasmussen College Corporate Office (C)

8300 Norman Center Drive, Suite 300, Bloomington MN 55437
County: Washington Identification: 667034
Unit ID: 17501405
Telephone: (952) 806-3910 Carnegie Class: N/A
FAX Number: (952) 831-0624
URL: www.rasmussen.edu

01 President .... Dr. Trenda BOYUM-BREEN

*Rasmussen College - St. Cloud (D)

226 Park Avenue South, Saint Cloud MN 56301-3713
County: Stearns FICE Identification: 008694
Unit ID: 175014
Telephone: (320) 251-5600 Carnegie Class: Bac/Assoc-Mixed
FAX Number: (320) 251-3702 Calendar System: Quarter
URL: www.Rasmussen.edu
Established: 1902 Annual Undergrad Tuition & Fees: $9,360
Enrollment: 5,395 Coed
Affiliation or Control: Proprietary IRS Status: Proprietary
Highest Offering: Baccalaureate
Accreditation: NH, CAHIIM, MAAB, MLTAD, NURSE, SURGT

02 Campus Director .... Ms. Mary SWINGLE
07 Director of Admissions .... Mr. Rob RUPRECHT

† Regional accreditation carried under the parent institution in Lake Elmo, MN.

Rasmussen College - Blaine (E)

3629 95th Avenue Northeast, Blaine MN 55014
Telephone: (763) 795-4720 Identification: 667061
Accreditation: &NH, MAAB

† Regional accreditation is carried under the parent institution in Saint Cloud, MN. The tuition figure is an average, actual tuition may vary.

Rasmussen College - Bloomington (F)

4400 W 78th St, 6th Floor, Bloomington MN 55435
Telephone: (952) 545-2000 FICE Identification: 011686
Accreditation: &NH, CAHIIM, MAAB

† Regional accreditation carried under the parent institution in Saint Cloud, MN. The tuition figure is an average, actual tuition may vary.

Rasmussen College - Brooklyn Park (G)

8301 93rd Avenue North, Brooklyn Park MN 55445-1512
Telephone: (763) 493-4500 Identification: 666769
Accreditation: &NH, CAHIIM, MAAB, SURGT

† Regional accreditation carried under the parent institution in Saint Cloud, MN. The tuition figure is an average, actual tuition may vary.

Rasmussen College - Eagan (H)

3500 Federal Drive, Eagan MN 55122-1346
Telephone: (651) 687-9000 FICE Identification: 004648
Accreditation: &NH, CAHIIM, MAAB

† Regional accreditation carried under the parent institution in Saint Cloud, MN. The tuition figure is an average, actual tuition may vary.

Rasmussen College - Lake Elmo/Woodbury (I)

8565 Eagle Point Circle, Lake Elmo MN 55042
Telephone: (651) 259-6600 Identification: 770486
Accreditation: &NH, CAHIIM, MLTAD

† Regional accreditation carried under the parent institution in Saint Cloud, MN. The tuition figure is an average, actual tuition may vary.

Rasmussen College - Mankato (J)

130 Saint Andrews Drive, Mankato MN 56001
Telephone: (507) 625-6556 FICE Identification: 025033
Accreditation: &NH, CAHIIM, MAAB, MLTAD

† Regional accreditation carried under the parent institution in Saint Cloud, MN.

Rasmussen College - Moorhead Park (K)

1250 29th Avenue South, Moorhead MN 56560
Telephone: (218) 304-6200 Identification: 770487
Accreditation: &NH, MLTAD, SURGT

† Regional accreditation carried under the parent institution in Saint Cloud, MN. The tuition figure is an average, actual tuition may vary.

St. Catherine University (L)

601 25th Avenue S, Minneapolis MN 55454
Telephone: (651) 690-6000 Identification: 770315
Accreditation: &NH

† Regional accreditation is carried under the parent institution in Saint Paul, MN

St. Catherine University (M)

2004 Randolph Avenue, Saint Paul MN 55105-1789
County: Ramsey FICE Identification: 002342
Unit ID: 175005
Telephone: (651) 690-6000 Carnegie Class: Masters/L
FAX Number: (651) 690-6024 Calendar System: 4/1/4
URL: www.stkate.edu
Established: 1905 Annual Undergrad Tuition & Fees: $35,500
Enrollment: 5,055 Female
Affiliation or Control: Roman Catholic IRS Status: 501(c)3
Highest Offering: Doctorate
Accreditation: NH, ADNUR, ARCPA, CAHIIM, COARC, DIETD, DMS, EXSC, LIB, NUR, NURSE, OT, OTA, PHLEB, PTA, PTAA, RAD, SW

01 President .... Ms. ReBecca K. ROLOFF
05 Exec Vice Pres and Provost .... Dr. Colleen HEGRANES
11 Exec Vice Pres and COO .... Dr. Brian BRUESS
10 Vice Pres Finance/Administration .... Dr. Brian BRUESS
26 Vice Pres for External Relations .... Ms. Blanche ABDALLAH
04 Exec Assistant to the President .... Ms. Stacy JACOBSON
49 AVP/Dean Sch Humanities/Arts/Sci .... Dr. Alan SILVA
76 Dean/Sch of Health & Grad College .... Dr. Penelope MOYERS
50 Dean Sch Business/Professional Stds .... Dr. Joann BANGS
51 Dean Adult & Applied Learning .... Dr. Anne WEYANDT
32 Dean of Student Affairs .... Mr. Curt GALLOWAY
83 Dean School of Social Work .... Dr. Barbara SHANK
08 Library Director .... Ms. Emily ASCH
84 Dean of Enrollment Management .... Mr. Daniel THOMPSON
30 Director of Development .... Ms. Elizabeth RIEDEL CARNEY
21 Business Manager .... Ms. Tracey GRAN
13 Director of Computing Services .... Mr. John JERIES
06 Registrar .... Ms. Cynthia EGENESS
29 Director of Alumnae Relations .... Ms. Karen G. JOTHEN
27 Dir of Marketing & Communications .... Ms. Kristin CUMMINGS
07 Associate Dean of Admissions .... Ms. Cory PIPER-HAUSWIRTH
37 Associate Dean Enrollment/Fin Aid .... Ms. Elizabeth STEVENS
07 Assoc Dean Admiss/Market Devel .... Mr. Greg STEENSON
36 Director of Career Development .... Ms. Tina WAGNER
35 Associate Dean of Students .... Ms. Ellen RICHTER-NORGEL
15 Director of Human Resources .... Ms. Susan SEXTON
38 Director of Student Counseling .... Ms. Heide MALAT
92 Director of Honors Program .... Dr. Rafael CERVANTES
94 Director of Women's Studies .... Dr. Sharon DOHERTY
96 Director of Purchasing .... Ms. Gail BLIVEN
09 Dir Inst Rsrch/Plng/Assessment .... Dr. Jennifer ROBINSON KLOOS
18 Chief Facilities/Physical Plant .... Mr. James MANSHIP
28 Dir Multicultural/Intl Pgms & Svcs .... Ms. Donna HAUER

Saint John's University (N)

2850 Abbey Plaza, Box 2000, Collegeville MN 56321-2000
County: Stearns FICE Identification: 002379
Unit ID: 174792
Telephone: (320) 363-2011 Carnegie Class: Bac-A&S
FAX Number: (320) 363-2504 Calendar System: Semester
URL: www.csbsju.edu
Established: 1857 Annual Undergrad Tuition & Fees: $40,226
Enrollment: 1,895 Coordinate
Affiliation or Control: Roman Catholic IRS Status: 501(c)3
Highest Offering: Master's
Accreditation: NH, DIETD, MUS, NURSE, TED, THEOL

01 President .... Dr. Michael HEMESATH
05 Provost Academic Affairs .... Dr. Richard ICE
20 Academic Dean .... Dr. Karen ERICKSON
30 Vice President for Inst Advancement .... Mr. Rob CULLIGAN
32 Vice President Student Development .... Fr. Douglas MULLIN, OSB
10 Vice Pres Finance/Admin Services .... Mr. Richard ADAMSON
46 VP Inst Plng/Research/Communication .... Mr. Jon MCGEE
07 Vice Pres Admissions/Financial Aid .... Dr. Cal MOSLEY
73 Dean School Theology .... Fr. Dale LAUNDERVILLE, OSB
35 Dean of Students .... Mr. Michael CONNOLLY
26 Exec Director of Public Relations .... Mr. Michael HEMMESCH
08 Director of Library .... Ms. Kathleen PARKER
06 Registrar .... Ms. Julie GRUSKA
36 Director of Career Services .... Ms. Heidi HARLANDER
37 Exec Director of Financial Aid .... Mr. Stuart PERRY
13 Director of Info Technology Svcs .... Ms. Casey GORDON
29 Director of Alumni Relations .... Mr. Adam HERBST
15 Director Human Resources .... Ms. Carol ABELL
09 Assoc Director Inst Research .... Ms. Karen G. KNUTSON

Saint Mary's University of Minnesota (O)

700 Terrace Heights, Winona MN 55987-1399
County: Winona FICE Identification: 002380
Unit ID: 174817
Telephone: (507) 452-4430 Carnegie Class: Masters/L
FAX Number: (507) 457-1633 Calendar System: Semester
URL: www.smumn.edu
Established: 1912 Annual Undergrad Tuition & Fees: $31,335
Enrollment: 5,825 Coed
Affiliation or Control: Roman Catholic IRS Status: 501(c)3
Highest Offering: Doctorate
Accreditation: NH, ANEST, COPSY, IACBE, MFCD, MUS, NMT, NURSE

01 President .... Bro. William MANN, FSC
18 Vice President of Facilities .... Mr. James BEDTKE
84 Exec VP & Chief Operating Officer .... Dr. John PYLE
30 Vice Pres for Devel & Alumni Rels .... Ms. Audrey KINTZI
32 Assoc Vice President of Campus Svcs .... Mr. Chris KENDALL
10 Vice President Financial Affairs .... Mr. Ben MURRAY
43 Exec Vice Pres/General Counsel .... Ms. Ann E. MERCHLEWITZ
05 Vice President for Academic Affairs .... Vacant
58 Chief Academic Office & VP for SGPP .... Bro. Robert SMITH
26 Assistant VP of Brand Management .... Ms. Stacia VOGEL
20 Academic Dean/Assoc Vice President .... Ms. Linka HOLEY
42 Vice President for Mission .... Mr. Tim GOSSEN
04 Exec Assistant to the President .... Ms. Mary BECKER
06 Registrar .... Mr. Christopher VERCH
07 Director of Admissions .... Ms. Suzanne DERANEK
37 Director of Financial Aid .... Ms. Jayne WOBIG
88 Director of Conferencing & Camps .... Ms. Terrie LUECK
36 Dir Career Services & Internships .... Mr. Michael HAGARTY
38 Director of Counseling Center .... Dr. Ruth MATHEWS
08 Director of Library .... Ms. Laura OANES
19 Director of Campus Security .... Mr. Jason MORK
18 Director of Physical Plant .... Mr. John SCHOLLMEIER
23 Director of Health Services .... Ms. Angela WEISBROD
29 Director Alumni Relations .... Mr. Robert FISHER
41 Director of Athletics .... Ms. Nicole FENNERN
15 Director of Human Resources .... Mr. Dave MILLIOTIS
09 Institutional Researcher .... Ms. Kara WENER
53 Dean School Education .... Dr. Scott SORVAAG
79 Dean School of the Arts .... Mr. Michael CHARRON
108 Director Institutional Assessment .... Ms. Tracy LEHNERTZ
50 Dean School of Business .... Dr. Thomas MARPE
91 Director Administrative Computing .... Ms. Tianna JOHNSON

St. Olaf College (P)

1520 St. Olaf Avenue, Northfield MN 55057-1098
County: Rice FICE Identification: 002382
Unit ID: 174844
Telephone: (507) 786-2222 Carnegie Class: Bac-A&S
FAX Number: N/A Calendar System: 4/1/4
URL: wp.stolaf.edu
Established: 1874 Annual Undergrad Tuition & Fees: $42,940
Enrollment: 3,034 Coed
Affiliation or Control: Evangelical Lutheran Church In America
IRS Status: 501(c)3
Highest Offering: Baccalaureate
Accreditation: NH, ART, DANCE, MUS, NURSE, SW, THEA

01 President .... Dr. David R. ANDERSON
05 Provost & Dean of the College .... Dr. Marci J. SORTOR
10 Vice Pres & Chief Financial Officer .... Ms. Janet K. HANSON
30 Vice Pres for Advancement .... Mr. Enoch BLAZIS

32 Vice Pres of Student Life .... Mr. Greg KNESER
84 Vice Pres Enrollment/Col Relations .... Mr. Michael KYLE
88 Vice Pres for Mission .... Dr. Jo M. BELD
15 Vice Pres for Human Resources .... Mr. Michael GOODSON
43 General Counsel .... Mr. Carl CROSBY LEHMANN
18 Asst Vice President for Facilities .... Mr. Peter SANDBERG
28 Asst to the Pres for Inst Diversity .... Mr. Bruce KING
20 Associate Provost .... Dr. Dan DRESSEN
06 Asst VP/Registrar .... Dr. Steve MCKELVEY
89 Assoc Dean Interdisciplin/Gen Stds .... Dr. Dana GROSS
81 Assoc Dean Natural Sciences & Math .... Dr. Mary WALCZAK
79 Assoc Dean Humanities .... Dr. Corliss SWAIN
57 Assoc Dean Fine Arts .... Ms. Mary GRIEP
83 Assoc Dean Social Sciences .... Dr. Rebecca JUDGE
21 Asst VP/Chief Investment Officer .... Mr. Mark GELLE
109 Asst VP/Budget & Auxiliary Ops .... Ms. Angela MATHEWS
07 Dean of Admissions & Financial Aid .... Mr. Chris GEORGE
35 Dean of Students .... Dr. Rosalyn EATON-NEEB
35 Assoc Dean of Students .... Mr. Justin FLEMING
35 Assoc Dean of Students .... Mr. Timothy SCHROER
42 Campus Pastor .... Dr. Matthew MAROHL
42 Associate College Pastor .... Ms. Katherine FICK
08 Director of IT and Libraries .... Ms. Roberta LEMBKE
13 Director of IT and Libraries .... Ms. Roberta LEMBKE
19 Director of Public Safety .... Mr. Fred C. BEHR
41 Director of Athletics .... Mr. Ryan A. BOWLES
29 Dir of Engage/Alum/Parent Relations .... Mr. Brad HOFF
44 Director of Annual Giving .... Ms. Steph MCCLUSKEY
38 Director of Counseling .... Dr. Stephen O'NEILL
26 Chief Marketing Officer .... Ms. Katie WARREN
75 Dir Piper Ctr for Vocation & Career .... Ms. Leslie MOORE
36 Sr Assoc Dir Career Educ & Coaching .... Ms. Kirsten CAHOON
108 Director of Evaluation & Assessment .... Dr. Gary MUIR
09 Director of Institutional Research .... Ms. Susan CANON
39 Director of Residence Life .... Ms. Pamela MCDOWELL
40 Bookstore Director .... Ms. Victoria BEUSSMAN
37 Director of Student Financial Aid .... Ms. Carly EICHHORST
102 Dir of Govt/Fndtn & Corp Relations .... Ms. Helen WARREN
104 Dir of Intl & Off Campus Studies .... Dr. Jodi MALMGREN
85 International Student Coordinator .... Ms. Kham VANG
04 Exec Assistant to the President .... Ms. Jennifer WHITSON

Sanford-Brown College (A)

5951 Earle Brown Drive, Brooklyn Center MN 55430
Telephone: (763) 279-2400 Identification: 770733
Accreditation: ACICS

† School is in teach-out plan.

Sanford-Brown College-Mendota Heights (B)

1340 Mendota Heights Road, Mendota Heights MN 55120
County: Dakota FICE Identification: 007351
Unit ID: 174394
Telephone: (651) 905-3400 Carnegie Class: Bac-Diverse
FAX Number: (651) 905-3550 Calendar System: Other
URL: www.browncollege.edu
Established: 1946 Annual Undergrad Tuition & Fees: N/A
Enrollment: 150 Coed
Affiliation or Control: Proprietary IRS Status: Proprietary
Highest Offering: Baccalaureate
Accreditation: ACICS

01 President/Dir Brooklyn Ctr Campus .... Dr. Michelle ERNST
05 Dean of Education .... Ms. Lisa THOMAS
36 Director of Career Services .... Mr. Paul KRAIMER
13 Director of Information Technology .... Mr. John HANS
06 Registrar .... Ms. Debra NEWGARD
08 Librarian .... Mr. Philip DUDAS
10 Business Office Manager .... Ms. Jennifer BOLISH

† School is in teach-out plan through 2017.

United Theological Seminary of the Twin Cities (C)

3000 5th Street, NW, New Brighton MN 55112-2598
County: Ramsey FICE Identification: 002386
Unit ID: 175139
Telephone: (651) 633-4311 Carnegie Class: Spec-4-yr-Faith
FAX Number: (651) 633-4315 Calendar System: Semester
URL: www.unitedseminary.edu
Established: 1962 Annual Graduate Tuition & Fees: N/A
Enrollment: 129 Coed
Affiliation or Control: United Church Of Christ IRS Status: 501(c)3
Highest Offering: Doctorate; No Undergraduates
Accreditation: NH, THEOL

01 President .... Rev. Barbara A. HOLMES
05 VP for Academic Affairs/Dean .... Dr. Sharon M. TAN
10 VP for Finance and Administration .... Mr. Peter LEE
30 VP for Advancement .... Mr. Bradley O. REINERS
20 Associate Dean .... Dr. Paul CAPETZ
32 Asst Dean Students .... Ms. Margaree LEVY
107 Director of Advanced Studies .... Dr. Thorsten MORITZ
44 Director of Development .... Ms. Kit BRIEM
07 Director of Admissions .... Ms. Joelle ANDERSON
06 Registrar/Director Financial Aid .... Mr. Christian ERIKSEN
08 Director of the Library .... Mr. Dale DOBIAS
51 Community Programing Director .... Mr. Brian BRASKICH
42 Chaplain .... Rev. John LEE
18 Director Physical Plant .... Mr. Brandon KROSCH
28 Dir Diversity/Blck Chrch Leadershp .... Ms. Margaree LEVY
29 Director of Alumni Relations .... Ms. Kiely TODD ROSKA
15 Dir of Human Resources & Operations .... Ms. Vonda PEARSON
25 Dir of Church Relations & Grants .... Rev. Kathleen REMUND
26 Director of Communications .... Ms. Emily GERIS
04 Exec Assistant to the President .... Ms. Meredythe JONES ROSSI

University of Minnesota Duluth (D)

1049 University Drive, Duluth MN 55812-3011
County: Saint Louis FICE Identification: 002388
Unit ID: 174233
Telephone: (218) 726-8000 Carnegie Class: Masters/L
FAX Number: (218) 726-6254 Calendar System: Semester
URL: www.d.umn.edu
Established: 1947 Annual Undergrad Tuition & Fees (In-State): $13,082
Enrollment: 11,093 Coed
Affiliation or Control: State IRS Status: 501(c)3
Highest Offering: Doctorate
Accreditation: NH, ART, BUS, CAATE, CS, ENG, MUS, SP, SW, TED

01 Chancellor .... Dr. Lendley C. BLACK
05 Exec Vice Chanc Acad Affairs .... Dr. Fernando DELGADO
32 Vice Chanc Stdnt Life/Dean Stdnts .... Dr. Lisa ERWIN
10 Vice Chanc Finance/Operations .... Mr. Stephen W. KETO
06 Registrar .... Ms. Carla L. BOYD
08 Director of Library .... Mr. Matt ROSENDAHL
37 Director Financial Aid .... Ms. Brenda H. HERZIG
36 Director Career Services .... Ms. Julie A. WESTLUND
13 Director Info Tech Sys/Services .... Dr. Jason DAVIS
09 Director Institutional Research .... Ms. Mary KEENAN
25 Senior Grant Administrator .... Ms. Elizabeth RUMSEY
51 Director Continuing Education .... Ms. Roxanne RICHARDS
41 Athletic Director .... Mr. Josh BERLO
15 Dir Human Resources/Equal Opp .... Ms. Karna KURTZ
07 Director Admissions .... Mr. Scott SCHULZ
18 Dir Facilities/Physical Plant .... Mr. John RASHID
29 Director Alumni Relations .... Mr. Matthew DUFFY
30 Director Development .... Ms. Tricia BUNTEN
21 Director of Budget and Analysis .... Mr. Greg SATHER
86 Dir University Marketing Public Rel .... Ms. Lynne WILLIAMS
63 Associate Dean School of Med .... Dr. Paula TERMUHLEN
81 Dean College Science/Engineering .... Dr. Joshua HAMILTON
49 Dean College Liberal Arts .... Dr. Susan MAHER
53 Dean Col Education/Human Svc Prof .... Dr. Jill PINKNEY-PASTRANA
50 Dean School of Business & Economics .... Dr. Amy HIETAPELTO
57 Dean School Fine Arts .... Mr. William PAYNE
58 Director of Grad Programs .... Dr. Erik BROWN
19 Chief of Police .... Mr. Sean HULS

University of Minnesota-Crookston (E)

2900 University Avenue, Crookston MN 56716-5001
County: Polk FICE Identification: 004069
Unit ID: 174075
Telephone: (218) 281-6510 Carnegie Class: Bac-Diverse
FAX Number: (218) 281-8040 Calendar System: Semester
URL: www.crk.umn.edu
Established: 1965 Annual Undergrad Tuition & Fees (In-State): $11,646
Enrollment: 2,850 Coed
Affiliation or Control: State IRS Status: 501(c)3
Highest Offering: Baccalaureate
Accreditation: NH

01 Chancellor .... Dr. Fred WOOD
05 VC for Academic Affairs .... Dr. Barbara KEINATH
32 Assoc VC Student Affs/Enrollment .... Dr. Peter PHAIAH
18 Director Facilities/Operations .... Mr. Dave DANFORTH
10 Dir of Finance/University Services .... Ms. Tricia SANDERS
15 Director Human Resources .... Mr. Les JOHNSON
37 Director Financial Aid .... Ms. Melissa DINGMANN
26 Director of Communications .... Mr. Andrew SVEC
30 Dir Development/Alumni Relations .... Ms. Brandy CHAFFEE
08 Director Library .... Mr. Owen WILLIAMS
36 Director Career/Counseling .... Mr. Donald R. CAVALIER
49 Head of Arts/Humanities/Soc Sci ... Dr. Soo-Yin LIM-THOMPSON
47 Head Agriculture & Nat Resources .... Dr. Harouna MAIGA
72 Head Math/Science/Technology .... Dr. Joseph SHOSTELL
50 Head Business .... Dr. Kevin THOMPSON
51 Director Center for Adult Learning .... Ms. Michelle CHRISTOPHERSON
06 Registrar .... Dr. Ken MYERS
07 Director of Admissions .... Ms. Carola THORSON
28 Director of Diversity .... Ms. Lorna HOLLOWELL
85 Dir of International Programs .... Dr. Kimberly GILLETTE

University of Minnesota-Morris (F)

600 E 4th Street, Morris MN 56267-2132
County: Stevens FICE Identification: 002389
Unit ID: 174251
Telephone: (320) 589-6035 Carnegie Class: Bac-A&S
FAX Number: (320) 589-6399 Calendar System: Semester
URL: www.morris.umn.edu
Established: 1959 Annual Undergrad Tuition & Fees (In-State): $12,846
Enrollment: 1,899 Coed
Affiliation or Control: State IRS Status: 501(c)3
Highest Offering: Baccalaureate
Accreditation: NH, TED

01 Chancellor .... Dr. Jacqueline JOHNSON
05 Vice Chanc Academic Affs/Dean .... Dr. Bart FINZEL
32 Vice Chanc for Student Affairs .... Ms. Sandra OLSON-LOY
18 Vice Chanc for Finance & Facilities .... Mr. Bryan HERRMANN
10 Director for Finance .... Ms. Colleen MILLER
08 Head Librarian .... Ms. LeAnn DEAN
06 Registrar's Office .... Ms. Judy KORN
26 Director of Communications .... Ms. Melissa VANGSNESS
29 Director of Alumni Relations .... Ms. Carla RILEY
09 Director of Institutional Research .... Ms. Nancy HELSPER
36 Director Career Center .... Mr. Gary L. DONOVAN
13 Director Information Technology .... Mr. Matt SENGER
38 Director of Counseling .... Vacant
37 Director of Financial Aid .... Ms. Jill BEAUREGARD
93 Dir Multi Ethnic Student Program .... Ms. Hilda LADNER
24 Director Educational Media .... Mr. Michael CIHAK
07 Director of Admissions .... Ms. Jennifer ZYCH HERRMANN
108 Director of Institutional Effective .... Ms. Melissa BERT
53 Chair of Education Division .... Dr. Gwen RUDNEY
81 Chair of Science/Math Division .... Dr. Peh NG
79 Chair of Humanities Division .... Dr. Pieranno GARAVASO
83 Chair of Social Science Division .... Dr. Arne KILDEGAARD

University of Minnesota-Rochester Campus (G)

111 South Broadway, Suite 300, Rochester MN 55904
Telephone: (800) 947-0117 Identification: 770316
Accreditation: &NH, CT

† Regional accreditation is carried under the parent institution in Minneapolis, MN

University of Minnesota-Twin Cities (H)

100 Church Street, SE, Minneapolis MN 55455-0213
County: Hennepin FICE Identification: 003969
Unit ID: 174066
Telephone: (612) 626-1616 Carnegie Class: DU-Highest
FAX Number: (612) 625-3875 Calendar System: Semester
URL: www.umn.edu
Established: 1851 Annual Undergrad Tuition & Fees (In-State): $13,790
Enrollment: 51,147 Coed
Affiliation or Control: State IRS Status: 501(c)3
Highest Offering: Doctorate
Accreditation: NH, ANEST, AUD, BUS, CEA, CIDA, CLPSY, COARC, CONST, COPSY, DANCE, DENT, DH, DIETC, DIETD, DIETI, ENG, ENGR, FUSER, HSA, IPSY, JOUR, LAW, LSAR, MED, MFCD, MIDWF, MT, MUS, NURSE, OT, PCSAS, PH, PHAR, PLNG, PTA, RTT, SCPSY, SP, SPAA, SW, TED, THEA, VET

01 President .... Dr. Eric W. KALER
100 Chief of Staff .... Ms. Amy PHENIX
05 Exec VP Academic Affairs/Provost .... Dr. Karen HANSON
17 Vice President for Health Sciences .... Dr. R. Brooks JACKSON
10 Sr VP Finance & Operations .... Vacant
46 Vice President for Research .... Dr. Brian HERMAN
58 Vice Prov/Dean Graduate Education .... Dr. Scott LANYON
20 Vice Prov/Dean Undergrad Education .... Dr. Robert MCMASTER
15 Vice President Human Resources .... Ms. Kathryn F. BROWN
88 Vice Pres for University Services .... Ms. Pam WHEELOCK
28 Vice Pres for Equity and Diversity .... Dr. Katrice ALBERT
13 Interim VP/Chief Info Officer .... Mr. Bernard GULACHEK
43 General Counsel .... Vacant
102 President Univ Minnesota Foundation .... Ms. Katherine SCHMIDLKOFER
25 Assoc VP Sponsored Projects Admin .... Ms. Frances LAWRENZ
86 Assoc Vice Pres for Govt Relations .... Ms. Erin DADY
18 Associate VP/Chief of Facilities .... Mr. Mike BERTHELSEN
32 Vice Provost for Student Affairs .... Ms. Danita BROWN YOUNG
19 Asst VP Pub Safety/Chief of Police .... Mr. Matthew CLARK
08 University Librarian .... Dr. Wendy P. LOUGEE
06 Registrar .... Ms. Sue N. VAN VOORHIS
07 Director of Admissions .... Ms. Rachelle HERNANDEZ
09 Director of Institutional Research .... Dr. John KELLOGG
22 Director Equal Oppty/Affirm Action .. Ms. Kimberly HEWITT BOYD
37 Director of Student Finance .... Ms. Tina FALKNER
40 Director of the U of M Bookstores .... Mr. Ross ROSATI
39 Dir of Housing & Residential Life .... Ms. Laurie L. MCLAUGHLIN
48 Interim Dean College of Design .... Dr. Becky YUST
86 Director of Federal Relations .... Ms. Channing RIGGS
29 CEO Alumni Association .... Ms. Lisa LEWIS
38 Dir of Counseling & Consulting Srvc .... Dr. Glenn HIRSCH
87 Director of the Summer Session .... Ms. Michelle KOKER
21 Associate VP for Budget/Finance .... Ms. Julie A. TONNESON
96 Interim Director of Purchasing .... Mr. Tim BRAY
49 Dean of the College of Liberal Arts .... Mr. John COLEMAN
51 Dean College of Continuing Educ .... Dr. Mary L. NICHOLS
61 Dean of the Law School .... Mr. Garry JENKINS
74 Dean College of Veterinary Medicine .... Dr. Trevor R. AMES
63 Dean of the Medical School .... Dr. Brooks JACKSON
66 Dean of the School of Nursing .... Dr. Connie J. DELANEY
53 Dean College Education/Human Devel .... Dr. Jean K. QUAM
52 Dean of the School of Dentistry .... Dr. Leon ASSAEL
69 Dean of the School Public Health .... Dr. John FINNEGAN
72 Dean College of Science/Engineering .... Dr. Steven CROUCH
67 Dean of the College Pharmacy .... Dr. Marilyn K. SPEEDIE
50 Dean Carlson School of Management .... Dr. Srilata A. ZAHEER
80 Dean Humphrey Sch of Pub Aff .... Dr. Eric SCHWARTZ
81 Dean College of Biological Science .... Dr. Valery E. FORBES
47 Dean Col Food/Agric/Natural Res Sci .... Mr. Brian BUHR
41 Director Intercollegiate Athletics .... Mr. Mark COYLE
26 Deputy CoS Public Relations/URel .... Mr. Chuck TOMBARGE
26 Deputy CoS Marketing/URel .... Ms. Ann ARONSON

University of Northwestern - St. Paul (A)

3003 Snelling Avenue N, Saint Paul MN 55113-1598
County: Ramsey FICE Identification: 002371
Unit ID: 174491
Telephone: (651) 631-5100 Carnegie Class: Masters/S
FAX Number: (651) 628-3339 Calendar System: Semester
URL: www.unwsp.edu
Established: 1902 Annual Undergrad Tuition & Fees: $28,730
Enrollment: 3,427 Coed
Affiliation or Control: Independent Non-Profit IRS Status: 501(c)3
Highest Offering: Master's
Accreditation: NH, MUS, NURSE

01 President ... Dr. Alan S. CURETON
05 Senior Vice Pres Academic Affairs ... Dr. Janet B. SOMMERS
27 Senior Vice President Media ... Dr. Paul H. VIRTS
32 Vice Pres Student Life & Athletics ... Dr. Mathew B. HILL
30 Vice President Advancement ... Vacant
10 Vice President Finance/CFO ... Mr. Douglas R. SCHROEDER
15 Assoc Vice President of HR ... Mr. Timothy A. RICH
18 Assoc VP Facility Ops & Planning ... Mr. Brian L. HUMPHRIES
79 Dean College of Arts & Humanities .. Dr. Jeremy W. KOLWINSKA
83 Dean College Behave & Nat Sciences ... Dr. Daniel R. CRANE
107 Dean College Professional Studies ... Dr. Richard C. THOMAN
58 Sr Dean Col Adult & Grad Studies ... Vacant
20 Sr Dean Academic Administration ... Dr. Fengling M. JOHNSON
35 Dean of Student Life ... Mr. Paul A. BRADLEY
35 Assoc Dean Student Life ... Dr. Katie J. SMITH
39 Associate Dean for Residence Life ... Mr. Jerod L. CORNELIUS
88 Assoc Dean Commuter Life/Transition ... Mr. Jeff B. SNYDER
13 CIO ... Mr. David G. RICHERT
88 Controller ... Mr. Bryon D. KRUEGER
09 Institutional Researcher Rprt Spec ... Mr. Russell E. ERICKSON
20 Director Academic Operations ... Mr. Kevin B. MCGAUGHEY
90 Director Academic Technology ... Mr. Joel T. JOHNSON
29 Sr Dir Dev & Constituent Relations ... Mr. James K. JOHNSON
38 Director of Counseling/Student Svcs . Ms. Dannette C. WILFAHRT
88 Dir Dept of Support Servces ... Mr. David P. GOLIAS
37 Director of Financial Aid ... Mr. Richard L. BLATCHLEY
23 Director of Health Services ... Mrs. Cynthia P. REEDSTROM
08 Director of Library Services ... Mrs. Ruth A. MCGUIRE
44 Director Major Gifts ... Mr. John T. DELICH
44 Director of Planned Giving ... Mr. David D. DANIELSON
19 Director of Public Safety ... Mr. Peter L. SOLA
106 Dir Undergraduate Pathways ... Dr. Tanya L. GROSZ
96 Manager of Purchasing ... Ms. Cheryl A. GLASS
40 Manager Campus Store ... Mrs. Julienne N. ENTINGER
88 Asst to Pres for ADA Initiatives ... Dr. Yvonne R. BANKS
101 Exec Secy to Pres & Bd of Trustees ... Ms. Mona S. GRELLSON
00 President Emeritus ... Dr. Donald O. ERICKSEN
04 Administrative Asst to President ... Mrs. Rachel A. MORGAN
102 Sr Dir Advancement/VP of Foundation ... Mr. Kirby R. STOLL
103 Dir Ctr for Calling & Career ... Mrs. Diann L. LLOYD-DENNIS
26 Director Marketing & Communication ... Ms. Marita K. MEINERTS
108 Special Asst/Director of Assessment ... Dr. Barbara A. LINDMAN
28 Director/GRACE ... Dr. David E. FENRICK
41 Asst Athletic Director ... Vacant
06 Registrar ... Mr. Andy L. SIMPSON
104 Asst Dir Center for Global Programs ... Ms. Veelie P. ABBA
50 Asst Dean School of Business ... Mr. Richard F. ELLIOTT
53 Asst Dean School of Education ... Dr. Susan N. JOHNSON
84 Vice President Enrollment Mgt ... Mr. Michael R. MORONEY

† Formerly Northwestern College

University of Phoenix Minneapolis/St. Paul Campus (B)

435 Ford Road, St. Louis Park MN 55426-4915
Telephone: (952) 487-7226 Identification: 770212
Accreditation: &NH, ACBSP

† No longer accepting campus-based students.

University of Saint Thomas (C)

2115 Summit Avenue, Saint Paul MN 55105-1096
County: Ramsey FICE Identification: 002345
Unit ID: 174914
Telephone: (651) 962-5000 Carnegie Class: DU-Mod
FAX Number: (651) 962-6360 Calendar System: 4/1/4
URL: www.stthomas.edu
Established: 1885 Annual Undergrad Tuition & Fees: $38,105
Enrollment: 10,140 Coed
Affiliation or Control: Roman Catholic IRS Status: 501(c)3
Highest Offering: Doctorate
Accreditation: NH, BUS, COPSY, ENG, HSA, IPSY, LAW, MUS, SW, TED, THEOL

01 President ... Dr. Julie H. SULLIVAN
05 Provost ... Dr. Richard G. PLUMB
88 Rector/Vice Pres School of Divinity ... Msgr. Aloysius R. CALLAGHAN
32 Vice President for Student Affairs ... Dr. Karen M. LANGE
10 Vice Pres for Business Affairs/CFO ... Mr. Mark D. VANGSGARD
26 Vice President University Relations ... Mr. Doug E. HENNES
13 Int VP Information Resources & Tech ... Mr. Chris S. GREGG
20 Int Assoc Vice Pres Academic Affs ... Dr. Robert J. RILEY
84 VP Enrollment Services ... Mr. Dan MEYER
21 Assoc VP/Finance & Controller ... Mr. Gary L. THYEN
18 Associate Vice Pres Facilities ... Mr. James M. BRUMMER
109 Associate VP for Auxiliary Services ... Mr. Gerald M. ANDERLEY
49 Dean College Arts & Sciences ... Dr. Terrence G. LANGAN
50 Dean Opus College of Business ... Dr. Stefanie A. LENWAY
53 Int Dean of School of Education ... Dr. Joseph L. KREITZER
83 Dean of School of Social Work ... Dr. Barbara W. SHANK
73 Dean St Paul Seminary School of Div ... Dr. Christopher J. THOMPSON
61 Dean School of Law ... Mr. Robert VISCHER
35 Dean of Student Life ... Vacant
88 Assoc Dean Grad Prof Psychology ... Dr. Christopher VYE
58 Dir Graduate Programs/Business Comm ... Dr. Michael PORTER
88 Sr Assoc Dean College of Business ... Dr. Michael GARRISON
54 Dean School of Engineering ... Dr. Donald H. WEINKFAUF
30 Sr VP Institutional Advancement ... Ms. Kimberly J. MOTES
06 Registrar ... Mr. Paul M. SIMMONS
07 Director Admissions & Financial Aid ... Ms. Kristin ROACH
09 Director of Institutional Research ... Dr. Michael F. COGAN
35 Executive Director Campus Life ... Ms. Mary A. RYAN
36 Director of Career Services ... Ms. Diane G. CRIST
27 Director of the News Service ... Mr. James C. WINTERER
29 Exec Dir Alumni/Constituent Rels ... Ms. Rachel A. WOBSCHALL
41 Athletic Director ... Mr. Stephen J. FRITZ
40 Director Bookstore ... Mr. Tony W. ERICKSON
42 Director Campus Ministry ... Fr. Erich RUTTEN
19 Director Safety/Security ... Mr. Daniel J. MEUWISSEN
39 Director Campus Life ... Ms. Margaret D. CAHILL
38 Director Student Counseling ... Dr. Jeri M. ROCKETT
96 Director Purchasing Services ... Ms. Karen M. HARTHORN
28 Director of Diversity ... Dr. MariAnn GRAHAM

Walden University (D)

100 Washington Ave S, Suite 900, Minneapolis MN 55401
County: Hennepin FICE Identification: 025042
Unit ID: 125231
Telephone: (612) 338-7224 Carnegie Class: DU-Mod
FAX Number: (612) 338-5092 Calendar System: Other
URL: www.waldenu.edu
Established: 1970 Annual Undergrad Tuition & Fees: $12,075
Enrollment: 52,188 Coed
Affiliation or Control: Proprietary IRS Status: Proprietary
Highest Offering: Doctorate
Accreditation: NH, ACBSP, CACREP, CS, NURSE, SW, TED

01 President/Chief Executive Officer ... Mr. Jonathan A. KAPLAN
05 Chief Academic Officer ... Dr. Eric RIEDEL
76 Int VP College Health Sciences ... Dr. Shana GARRETT
83 VP College Soc & Behav Sciences ... Dr. Shana GARRETT
50 VP College of Mgmt & Tech ... Dr. L. Ward ULMER
26 VP Marketing ... Vacant
20 VP of Undergrad Programs ... Dr. L. Ward ULMER
13 CIO ... Vacant
10 CFO ... Vacant
53 Dean RWR College of Education ... Dr. Kate STEFFENS
46 Exec Dir Inst Research/Assessment ... Mr. Jim LENIO
32 Int Dean/Exec Dir Student Affairs ... Dr. Lou MILANESI
08 Exec Dir Ctr Stdnt Success/Library ... Ms. Susanna DAVIDSEN
88 Int Exec Dir Ctr for Faculty Excel ... Dr. Laurie BEDFORD
88 Exec Dir Ctr for Research Support ... Dr. Laura LYNN
104 Exec Dir International Programs ... Vacant
15 Exec Director of Human Resources ... Vacant
07 Director of Admissions ... Mr. Peter SCANLAN
21 Bursar ... Ms. Linda ANTHONY
37 Director of Financial Aid ... Ms. Melvina JOHNSON
06 Registrar ... Ms. Devon EDMUND
09 Director of Institutional Research ... Ms. Nicole HOLLAND
108 Director Institutional Assessment ... Dr. Shari JORISSEN
29 Director Alumni Relations ... Vacant

White Earth Tribal and Community College (E)

PO Box 478, Mahnomen MN 56557-0478
County: Mahnomen FICE Identification: 039214
Unit ID: 434751
Telephone: (218) 935-0417 Carnegie Class: Tribal
FAX Number: (218) 936-5814 Calendar System: Semester
URL: www.wetcc.edu
Established: 1997 Annual Undergrad Tuition & Fees: $3,285
Enrollment: 69 Coed
Affiliation or Control: Tribal Control IRS Status: 501(c)3
Highest Offering: Associate Degree
Accreditation: NH

01 Interim President ... Tracy CLARK
04 Executive Assistant ... Patty SCHULTZ
30 Special Projects/Interim Devel Dir ... Deb MCARTHUR
10 Finance Director ... Kami LHOTKA
05 Academic Dean ... Sheila MICHAELS
32 Dean of Student Services ... Melinda RUSTAD
56 Director of Extension ... Steve DAHLBERG
07 Admissions Coordinator ... Loreen STANLEY
06 Registrar ... Vacant
37 Financial Aid Coordinator ... Martha ALLEN
15 Human Resources Technician ... Denise ASKELSON
18 Facilities Manager ... Patrick SCHULTZ
13 IT Director ... Cody COAUETTE
19 Security Coordinator ... Kurt HALVORSON
26 Marketing/Communications Specialist ... Joseph ALLEN

MISSISSIPPI

Alcorn State University (F)

1000 ASU Drive, #359, Lorman MS 39096-7500
County: Claiborne FICE Identification: 002396
Unit ID: 175342
Telephone: (601) 877-6100 Carnegie Class: Masters/M
FAX Number: (601) 877-2975 Calendar System: Semester
URL: www.alcorn.edu
Established: 1871 Annual Undergrad Tuition & Fees (In-State): $6,386
Enrollment: 3,639 Coed
Affiliation or Control: State IRS Status: 501(c)3
Highest Offering: Beyond Master's But Less Than Doctorate
Accreditation: SC, AAFCS, ACBSP, ADNUR, CAEP, #DIETD, MUS, NAIT, NUR, SW

01 President ... Dr. Alfred RANKINS, JR.
05 Provost/Exec VP Academic Affairs ... Dr. Donzell LEE
11 Sr VP for Univ Operations/COO ... Vacant
04 Exec Asst to the President ... Mrs. Karen R. SHEDRICK
88 Interim Director of Internal Audit ... Ms. Tomeka MOORE
46 Chief Research Officer ... Dr. Babu P. PATLOLLA
10 VP for Finance & Administrative Svc ... Mrs. Carolyn DUPRE'
32 VP for Student Affairs ... Mr. Emanuel BARNES
10 Associate VP for Fiscal Affairs ... Mr. Bruce WILLIAMS
30 VP Institutional Advancement ... Mr. Marcus D. WARD
26 VP Marketing/Communications ... Mrs. Clara R. STAMPS
20 Vice Provost Academic Affs/GS ... Dr. John IGWEBUIKE
20 Asst VP Academic Program Support ... Dr. Martha RAVOLA
18 Assoc VP for Facilities Management ... Mr. Marlin KING
39 Director of Residence Life ... Ms. Jessica L. FOXWORTH
28 Dir of Educational Equity/Inclusion ... Mrs. Lljuna WEIR
21 Director of Accounting ... Mrs. Cassandra B. LEWIS
96 Purchasing Agent ... Ms. Mertha V. GEORGE
07 Director of Admissions/Recruiting ... Mrs. Katangela TENNER
37 Director of Financial Aid ... Mrs. Juanita RUSSELL-EDWARDS
06 Registrar ... Dr. John L. IGWEBUIKE
08 Dean University Libraries ... Dr. Blanche SANDERS
47 Interim Dean School of Agriculture ... Dr. Ivory LYLES
49 Dean School of Arts & Science ... Dr. Babu P. PATLOLLA
50 Dean School of Business ... Dr. Donna WILLIAMS
53 Dean School of Education ... Dr. Robert CARR
66 Dean School of Nursing ... Dr. Debra SPRING
88 Dean University College ... Dr. Valerie THOMPSON
13 CIO for Ctr for Info Tech Svcs ... Mrs. Donna G. HAYDEN
15 Director of Human Resources ... Mrs. Carla WILLIAMS
36 Director Career Services ... Dr. Joey MITCHELL
23 Director of Health Services ... Ms. Dorothy G. JACKSON-DAVIS
41 Director of Athletics ... Mr. Derek HORNE
40 Manager Barnes and Noble ... Mr. Domonic RABY
38 Director of Counseling & Testing ... Vacant
09 Director Institutional Res/Assess ... Dr. Ramesh MADDALI
108 Dir Institutional Effectiveness ... Dr. LaToya HART
19 Chief of Campus Police ... Mr. Douglas STEWART
88 General Manager Sodexo ... Mr. Corey D. YOUNG
102 Exec Dir ASU Foundation ... Mr. Marcus D. WARD
31 Dir Ctr Rural Life/Econ Dev ... Mr. Alfred GALTNEY
92 Director of Pre-Prof/Honors Program ... Dr. Thomas C. STURGIS
25 Grants/Contract Administrator ... Ms. Sallie GRIFFIN
88 Sp Asst to Pres Comty & Econ Dev ... Dr. Ruth R. NICHOLS
106 Director Online Educ Vicksburg ... Vacant
104 Director Study Abroad ... Dr. Dovi ALIPOE
88 AsstVP Athletic Compliance/Acad Svc ... Mr. Jason CABLE
100 Chief of Staff ... Mr. Tracy COOK

Antonelli College (G)

1500 N 31st Avenue, Hattiesburg MS 39401-3056
Telephone: (601) 583-4100 Identification: 666517
Accreditation: ACCSC

† Branch campus of Antonelli College, OH.

Antonelli College (H)

2323 Lakeland Drive, Jackson MS 39208-9549
Telephone: (601) 362-9991 Identification: 666518
Accreditation: ACCSC

† Branch campus of Antonelli College, OH.

Belhaven University (I)

1500 Peachtree Street, Jackson MS 39202-1798
County: Hinds FICE Identification: 002397
Unit ID: 175421
Telephone: (601) 968-5940 Carnegie Class: Masters/L
FAX Number: (601) 968-9998 Calendar System: Semester
URL: www.belhaven.edu
Established: 1883 Annual Undergrad Tuition & Fees: $21,816
Enrollment: 4,114 Coed
Affiliation or Control: Presbyterian Church (U.S.A.) IRS Status: 501(c)3
Highest Offering: Master's
Accreditation: SC, ART, DANCE, IACBE, MUS, SW, THEA

01 President ... Dr. Roger PARROTT
05 Exec Vice President & Provost ... Dr. Dan FREDERICKS
30 Vice Pres Institutional Advancement ... Mr. Kevin RUSSELL
88 VP of Adult & Graduate Marketing ... Dr. Audrey KELLEHER
10 Chief Financial Officer ... Mrs. Virginia HENDERSON
32 VP for Student Affairs and Athletic ... Mr. Scott LITTLE

11 Asst Vice Pres Campus Operations .... Mr. David POTVIN
51 Assistant VP for Adult Studies .... Dr. Rick UPCHURCH
20 Assoc Provost .... Dr. Dennis WATTS
12 Academic Dean/Houston Campus .... Dr. Larry RUDDELL
12 Academic Dean/Mississippi .... Dr. Ken ELLIOTT
12 Academic Dean/Memphis Tennessee .... Dr. Paul CRISS
12 Academic Dean/Chattanooga-Atlanta .... Mr. Ron PIRTLE
50 Dean of the School of Business .... Dr. Chip MASON
08 Librarian .... Mr. Chris CULLNANE
07 Asst VP Trad & Online Admissions .... Mrs. Suzanne SULLIVAN
06 Registrar .... Mrs. Donna WEEKS
26 Director of Integrated Marketing .... Mr. Bryant BUTLER
35 Director of Student Leadership .... Ms. JoBeth PETTY
13 Director Institutional Technology .... Mr. Bo MILLER
19 Director Security/Safety .... Mr. Steve FARMER
40 Bookstore Manager .... Ms. Sheila LYONS
35 Dean of Student Life .... Mr. Greg HAWKINS

Blue Mountain College (A)

201 W Main Street, PO Box 160,
Blue Mountain MS 38610-0160
County: Tippah FICE Identification: 002398
Unit ID: 175430
Telephone: (662) 685-4771 Carnegie Class: Bac-Diverse
FAX Number: (662) 685-4776 Calendar System: Semester
URL: www.bmc.edu
Established: 1873 Annual Undergrad Tuition & Fees: $10,852
Enrollment: 544 Coed
Affiliation or Control: Southern Baptist IRS Status: 501(c)3
Highest Offering: Master's
Accreditation: **SC**

01 President .... Dr. Barbara C. MCMILLIN
04 Admin Assistant to the President .... Mrs. Pam BOWMAN
05 Vice President for Academic Affairs .... Dr. Sharon B. ENZOR
58 Dean Graduate Studies .... Dr. Jenetta WADDELL
09 Director of Institutional Research .... Mr. Robert E. RUCKER
08 Director of Library Services .... Dr. Derek J. CASH
06 Registrar .... Mrs. Sheila D. FREEMAN
20 Director Teaching & Learning Center .... Dr. Delise TEAGUE
32 VP for Student Services .... Mr. Jack T. MOSER
07 Vice Pres for Enrollment Services .... Mr. Lynn GIBSON
37 Director of Financial Aid .... Mrs. Beverly HICKEY
10 Chief Financial Officer .... Mr. Steve ROBBINS
11 Chief Operating Officer .... Mrs. Joyce PETERS
40 Campus Store Manager .... Mrs. Dot M. LOCKE
41 Athletic Director .... Mr. Lavon DRISKELL
42 Director Baptist Student Union .... Mrs. Tracy S. MOSER
13 Director of Information Services .... Mr. Kevin BAREFIELD
26 Dir of PR/Publications .... Ms. Emma L. AINSWORTH
29 Director of Alumni Affairs .... Mrs. Nancy H. MCDONALD
30 Director of Development .... Mr. Jody HILL
88 Director of Church Relations .... Dr. Ronald MEEKS

Coahoma Community College (B)

3240 Friars Point Road, Clarksdale MS 38614-9700
County: Coahoma FICE Identification: 002401
Unit ID: 175519
Telephone: (662) 627-2571 Carnegie Class: Assoc/MT-VT-High Trad
FAX Number: (662) 627-9451 Calendar System: Semester
URL: www.coahomacc.edu
Established: 1949 Annual Undergrad Tuition & Fees (In-District): $2,440
Enrollment: 2,045 Coed
Affiliation or Control: State/Local IRS Status: 501(c)3
Highest Offering: Associate Degree
Accreditation: **SC**, ADNUR, #COARC, POLYT

01 President .... Dr. Valmadge T. TOWNER
05 Dean of Academics .... Dr. Rolanda BROWN
10 Chief Financial Officer .... Ms. Deborah MCNEAL
32 Dir of Enrollment & Student Svcs .... Mrs. Karen DONE
09 Dir Inst Effectiveness/SACS Liaison .... Mrs. Margaret DIXON
30 Coordinator for Federal Programs .... Mrs. Marilyn STARKS
75 Dean of Career & Technical Educ ... Mrs. Anne SHELTON-CLARK
07 Director of Admissions/Registrar .... Mrs. Delores RICHARD
08 Dir Library/Instructional Resources .... Mrs. Rose LOCKETT
13 Director Computer Services .... Mr. Matt LOGAN
19 Director of Safety/Transportation .... Vacant
26 Chief Communication Officer .... Mr. Matthew KILLEBREW
37 Director of Financial Aid .... Mr. Luke HOWARD
15 Director of Employee Services .... Mr. Michael HOUSTON
18 Chief Facilities/Physical Plant .... Mr. Jerone SHAW
51 Director of Educational Outreach .... Ms. Letha RICHARDS
29 Director Alumni Relations .... Vacant
36 Director Student Placement .... Ms. Shanelle FRAZIER
38 Director Student Counseling .... Vacant
96 Director of Purchasing .... Mrs. Deborah MCNEAL
04 Administrative Asst to President .... Ms. Yolanda D. MILLER
100 Chief of Staff .... Mr. Jerone SHAW
103 Dir Workforce/Career Development .... Mr. Steven JOSSELL
105 Director Web Services .... Mr. Ezra HOWARD
106 Dir Online Education/E-learning .... Mr. Joseph MCKEE
41 Athletic Director .... Mr. Freeman HORTON

Concorde Career College (C)

7900 Airways Boulevard, Suite 103, Southaven MS 38671
Telephone: (662) 429-9909 Identification: 770540
Accreditation: **COE**

† Branch campus of Concorde Career College, Memphis, TN

Copiah-Lincoln Community College (D)

PO Box 649, Wesson MS 39191-0649
County: Copiah FICE Identification: 002402
Unit ID: 175573
Telephone: (601) 643-5101 Carnegie Class: Assoc/MT-VT-High Trad
FAX Number: (601) 643-8212 Calendar System: Semester
URL: www.colin.edu
Established: 1928 Annual Undergrad Tuition & Fees (In-State): $2,730
Enrollment: 3,029 Coed
Affiliation or Control: State IRS Status: 501(c)3
Highest Offering: Associate Degree
Accreditation: **SC**, ADNUR, COARC, MLTAD, RAD

01 President .... Dr. Ronald E NETTLES
04 Assistant to the President .... Mrs. Brenda J. PARRETT
10 Vice President Business Affairs .... Mr. Michael TANNER
05 Vice Pres of Instructional Services .... Dr. Jane HULON
12 VP of the Simpson County Center .... Dr. Dewayne MIDDLETON
12 Vice Pres of the Natchez Campus .... Ms. Teresa BUSBY
20 Academic Dean .... Dr. Jill B. LOGAN
32 Dean of Student Services .... Mrs. Brenda SMITH
75 Dean Career & Technical Educ .... Ms. Jackie L. MARTIN
31 Dean of Community Programs .... Dr. Brenda B. ORR
41 Athletic Director .... Mr. Gwyn YOUNG
38 Director of Counseling/Recruitment .... Mrs. Lea Ann KNIGHT
35 Assistant Dean of Students .... Mr. Bryan NOBILE
37 Director Student Financial Aid .... Mrs. Leslie SMITH
40 Director Bookstore .... Mr. Charles HART
08 Director of Library Resources .... Mr. Kendall P. CHAPMAN
26 Director of Public Relations .... Mrs. Natalie DAVIS
13 Information Systems Specialist .... Ms. Deennie LETCHWORTH
19 Director of Security .... Mr. Wayne ROBERTS
09 Dir Inst Effectiv/Facilities Plng .... Dr. Jeff POSEY
07 Director of Admissions .... Mr. Chris WARREN
102 Executive Dir Foundation/Alumni .... Mr David CAMPBELL
18 Director of Physical Plant .... Mr. Daniel CASE
66 Director of Assoc Degree Nursing . Mrs. Mary Ann CANTERBURY
06 Student Records Manager .... Mrs. Gay LANGHAM
57 Chair Fine Arts Division .... Mrs. Janet SMITH
50 Chair Business Division .... Mr. Richard BAKER
68 Chair Physical Education Division .... Dr. Stephanie DUGUID
81 Chair Math/Computer Science Div .... Mr. Eddie BRITT
79 Chair Humanities Division .... Mrs. Pam REID
82 Chair Social Science Division .... Mr. David HIGGS
88 Chair Science Division .... Dr. Kevin MCKONE
96 Director of Purchasing .... Mrs. Erin LIKENS
106 Director of E-learning .... Ms. Vanessa ALEXANDER
108 QEP Director .... Ms. Glenda SILVERII
15 Human Resources Director .... Ms. Julia PARKER
39 Director Student Housing .... Mr. Allen KENT
91 Director of Technology/Info Systems .... Mr. James P MCINNIS

Delta State University (E)

1003 W. Sunflower Rd., Cleveland MS 38733
County: Bolivar FICE Identification: 002403
Unit ID: 175616
Telephone: (662) 846-3000 Carnegie Class: Masters/L
FAX Number: (662) 846-4014 Calendar System: Semester
URL: www.deltastate.edu
Established: 1924 Annual Undergrad Tuition & Fees (In-State): $6,112
Enrollment: 3,614 Coed
Affiliation or Control: State IRS Status: 501(c)3
Highest Offering: Doctorate
Accreditation: **SC**, AAB, AAFCS, ACBSP, ART, #CAATE, CACREP, DIETC, MUS, NURSE, SW, TED

01 President .... Dr. William (Bill) LAFORGE
05 Provost/VP Academic Affairs .... Dr. Charles MCADAMS
10 Vice President for Finance .... Mr. James RUTLEDGE
32 Vice President for Student Affairs .... Dr. Vernell BENNETT
100 Chief of Staff/VP Univ Relations .... Dr. Michelle A. ROBERTS
15 Director of Human Resources .... Ms. Lisa GIGER
41 Director of Athletics .... Mr. Ronnie MAYERS
84 Dean Enrollment Mgt/Director Ad Mkt .... Dr. Debbie S. HESLEP
29 Exec Dir of Alumni/Foundation .... Mr. D. Keith FULCHER
49 Dean College of Arts & Sciences .... Dr. David BREAUX
50 Dean College of Business .... Dr. Billy MOORE
53 Dean College of Education .... Dr. Leslie GRIFFIN
66 Dean School of Nursing .... Dr. Vicki L BINGHAM
08 Dean Library Services .... Mr. Jeff SLAGELL
58 Dean Grad/Cont Studies & Research .... Dr. Beverly MOON
06 Registrar .... Ms. Becky FINLEY
09 Dir of Inst Research & Planning .... Ms Emily C. DABNEY
13 Chief Information Officer .... Mr. Edwin CRAFT
30 Chief Development Officer .... Mr. Gary BOUSE
21 Comptroller/Accounting .... Ms. Beverly LINDSEY
88 Internal Auditor .... Vacant
88 Executive Director BPAC .... Ms. Laura HOWELL
88 Executive Director Student Success .... Ms. Chrissy RIDDLE
88 Director Coahoma County Higher Educ .... Ms. Jennifer WALLER
20 Coord Academic Support Services .... Ms. Tricia KILLEBREW
37 Director Student Financial Assist .... Ms. Christie ROCCONI
38 Director Counsel/Stdnt Health Svcs .... Dr. Richard HOUSTON
36 Director Career Services/Placement .... Mr. Davlon MILLER
19 Director of Police Department .... Mr N. Lynn BUFORD
39 Director of Housing .... Ms. Julie JACKSON
26 Coordinator of Communication & Mktg .... Ms. Jennifer FARISH
29 Director of Alumni Affairs .... Mr. Jeffery FARRIS
25 Director Institutional Grants .... Ms. Robin BOYLES

88 Director Student Business Svcs .... Mr. Kelvin DAVIS
88 Director Field Experiences .... Dr. Cheryl CUMMINS
106 Director of E-Learning .... Ms. Aimee KITCHING
31 Director Delta Center Culture Learn .... Dr. Rolando HERTS
88 Director of Recruiting .... Ms. Caitlyn THOMPSON
88 Director of Administrative Systems .... Mr. Chris GIGER
88 Director of Donor Relations .... Ms. Ann GIGER
88 Director of H L Nowell Union .... Vacant
88 Director of Facilities Operations .... Mr. Ted HOCHRADEL
88 Director of Post Office .... Mr. Michael MARTIN
88 Assoc Director Human Resources .... Vacant
18 Interim Dir of Facilities Mgmt .... Mr. Ted HOCHRADEL
96 Assistant Comptroller .... Vacant
35 Director Student Life .... Ms. Jeanna WILKES
40 Manager of Bookstore .... Ms. Tina GLADDEN
44 Director of Annual Giving .... Ms. Melissa PEARCE

East Central Community College (F)

PO Box 129, Decatur MS 39327-0129
County: Newton FICE Identification: 002404
Unit ID: 175643
Telephone: (601) 635-2111 Carnegie Class: Assoc/MT-VT-High Trad
FAX Number: (601) 635-4011 Calendar System: Semester
URL: www.eccc.edu
Established: 1928 Annual Undergrad Tuition & Fees (In-District): $2,190
Enrollment: 2,544 Coed
Affiliation or Control: Local IRS Status: 501(c)3
Highest Offering: Associate Degree
Accreditation: **SC**, ADNUR, EMT, SURGT

01 President .... Dr. Billy W. STEWART
05 Vice President for Instruction .... Dr. Teresa L. HOUSTON
10 Vice Pres for Business Operations .... Mr. Mickey VANCE
32 Vice President for Student Services .... Dr. Randall LEE
09 VP Institutional Research/Effective .... Mr. David CASE
26 Associate VP for Public Information .... Mr. Bill WAGNON
106 Dean of eLearning Education .... Dr. Christa WILHITE
08 Dean of Learning Resources .... Mr. Leslie HUGHES
20 Director of Academic & Cont Ed .... Ms. Misty SMITH
51 Director of ABE/GED .... Mr. Ryan CLARKE
103 Director of Workforce Education .... Mr. Wayne EASON
07 Director Admissions and Records .. Dr. Stacey HOLLINGSWORTH
15 Director of Personnel Svcs/Athletics .... Mr. Chris HARRIS
16 Director of Human Resources .... Vacant
18 Superintendent of Physical Plant .... Mr. Artie FOREMAN
13 Dean of Information Technology .... Mr. Derek PACE
14 Assoc Dir Information Technology .... Mrs. Regena BOYKIN
37 Director of Financial Aid .... Mrs. Brenda B. CARSON
19 Chief of Police .... Mr. John HARRIS
39 Director of Hous/Student Activities .... Dr. Amanda WALTON
29 Dir of Alumni Rel & the Foundation .... Mr. David LEBLANC
57 Chairperson Fine Arts Division .... Mr. Chas EVANS
83 Chairperson Social Sciences .... Mrs. Wanda HURLEY
81 Chrpn Mathematics/Computer Science .... Dr. Lisa MCMILLIN
66 Dean of Healthcare Education .... Dr. Sheryl ALLEN
81 Chairperson Science .... Mr. Curt SKIPPER
60 Chairperson Communications/
Language .... Mrs. Carol SHACKELFORD
04 Administrative Asst to President .... Ms. Carole H. GERMANY

East Mississippi Community College (G)

PO Box 158, Scooba MS 39358-0158
County: Kemper FICE Identification: 002405
Unit ID: 175652
Telephone: (662) 476-8442 Carnegie Class: Assoc/MT-VT-High Non
FAX Number: (662) 476-5058 Calendar System: Semester
URL: www.eastms.edu
Established: 1927 Annual Undergrad Tuition & Fees (In-District): $2,840
Enrollment: 4,127 Coed
Affiliation or Control: State/Local IRS Status: 501(c)3
Highest Offering: Associate Degree
Accreditation: **SC**, ADNUR, FUSER

01 President .... Dr. Thomas M. HUEBNER, JR.
05 Vice Pres for Instruction .... Dr. Thomas WARE
11 Vice President for Administration .... Dr. Paul MILLER
32 Vice President for Student Life .... Mr. Mickey STOKES
10 Chief Financial Officer .... Ms. Melissa MOSLEY
30 VP Institutional Advancement .... Mr. Nick CLARK
103 VP Workforce & Cmty Services .... Dr. Raj SHAUNAK
84 VP Enrollment Management .... Mr. James GIBSON
04 Administrative Asst to President .... Mrs. Lauren CLAY
09 Director IE/IR .... Mr. Mark ALEXANDER
08 Director of Library Services .... Ms. Donna BALLARD
13 Director of Info Technology .... Mr. Michael TVARKUNAS
18 Director of Physical Plant .... Mr. Kyle YOUNGER
37 Director of Financial Aid .... Mr. Garry JONES
07 Director Admissions/Records-SC .... Mrs. Melinda SCIPLE
07 Director Admissions/Records-GT .... Mrs. Faye MORGAN
40 Bookstore Manager .... Mrs. Ginnie CODY
26 Director of Public Information .... Ms. Suzanne MONK
35 Campus Director/Dean of Students-
SC .... Mr. Tony MONTGOMERY
35 Campus Director/Dean of Students-GT .... Mrs. Cathy KEMP
60 Athletic Director .... Dr. Randall BRADBERRY
12 Director Columbus Air Force Base .... Mrs. Jackie NEWTON
19 Chief of Police .... Mr. Archer SALLIS
91 Director Admin Comp/System Rpt .... Mr. Aaron BROOKS
15 Director Human Resources .... Ms. Theresa HARPOLE

44 Asst VP Institutional Advancement ..... Mrs. Leia HILL
20 Associate Dean of Instruction-SC ..... Mr. James RUSH
20 Associate Dean of Instruction-GT ..... Mrs. Gina THOMPSON
106 Associate Dean of E-learning ..... Mrs. Chris SQUARE
88 Associate Dean of Instruction/CT ..... Dr. Melanie SANDERS

Hinds Community College (A)

PO Box 1100, Raymond MS 39154-1100
County: Hinds FICE Identification: 002407
Unit ID: 175786
Telephone: (601) 857-5261 Carnegie Class: Assoc/MT-VT-High Trad
FAX Number: (601) 857-3518 Calendar System: Semester
URL: www.hindscc.edu
Established: 1917 Annual Undergrad Tuition & Fees (In-District): $2,600
Enrollment: 11,839 Coed
Affiliation or Control: State/Local IRS Status: 501(c)3
Highest Offering: Associate Degree
Accreditation: SC, ADNUR, CAHIIM, COARC, DA, DMS, EMT, MAC, MLTAD, PTAA, RAD, SURGT

01 President ..... Dr. Clyde MUSE
11 VP Admin Svcs/VP Utica/Vicksburg .. Dr. Debra MAYS-JACKSON
10 Vice President Business Services ..... Mr. Russell SHAW
12 VP Raymond/NSG/AH/Parallel Pgm ..... Dr. Theresa HAMILTON
12 VP Rankin/Jackson/Dir Occup Pgm ..... Dr. Norman SESSION
18 VP Physical Plant/Auxiliary Svcs ..... Mr. Thomas WASSON
30 VP Advancement ..... Ms. Jacqueline M. GRANBERRY
103 Vice Pres Workforce Development ..... Dr. Chad STOCKS
35 Assoc Vice President for Students ..... Dr. Tyrone JACKSON
84 Director of Enrollment Services ..... Ms. Kathryn B. COLE
32 District Dean of Student Affairs ..... Dr. Tyrone JACKSON
08 Dean of Learning Resources ..... Ms. Mary Beth APPLIN
05 Academic Dean ..... Dr. Benjamin G. CLOYD
15 Director of Human Resources ..... Ms. Gay Lynn CASTON
37 Dir of Financial Aid & VA Affairs ..... Mrs. Louanne LANGSTON
38 Director of Counseling Services ..... Ms. Mary Lee MCDANIEL
41 Athletic Director ..... Mr. Gene MURPHY
09 Director of Institutional Research ..... Ms. Carley DEAR
26 Public Relations Director ..... Ms. Cathy C. HAYDEN
96 Director of Purchasing ..... Mr. Samuel LEMONIS
04 Executive Secretary to President ..... Mrs. Alesia PORCH
06 Assistant Registrar ..... Mrs. Norma Jean SCRIVENER
105 Director Web Services ..... Ms. Jil WRIGHT
106 Dean Online Education/E-learning ..... Mrs. Keri COLE
13 Chief Info Technology Officer (CIO) ..... Mr. Hamp SHIVE
25 Chief Contracts/Grants Admin ..... Mr. Donald SLABACH
29 Alumni Coordinator ..... Ms. Libby POSEY
39 Director Student Housing ..... Mr. DeAndre HOUSE

Holmes Community College (B)

Hill Street, PO Box 369, Goodman MS 39079-0369
County: Holmes FICE Identification: 002408
Unit ID: 175810
Telephone: (662) 472-2312 Carnegie Class: Assoc/MT-VT-Mix Trad/Non
FAX Number: (662) 472-9152 Calendar System: Semester
URL: www.holmescc.edu
Established: 1925 Annual Undergrad Tuition & Fees (In-District): $2,360
Enrollment: 5,798 Coed
Affiliation or Control: Local IRS Status: 501(c)3
Highest Offering: Associate Degree
Accreditation: SC, ADNUR, EMT, FUSER, OTA, @PTAA, SURGT

01 President ..... Dr. Jim HAFFEY
04 Asst to President/Dir Inst Rsch ..... Dr. Lindy MCCAIN
05 Vice Pres for Academic Programs ..... Dr. Fran COX
12 Vice President Ridgeland Campus ..... Dr. Don BURNHAM
12 Vice President Grenada Center ..... Mrs. Michelle BURNEY
72 Vice Pres Career/Technical Educ ..... Mrs. Sherrie CHEEK
10 Vice Pres of Financial Services ..... Mr. Sonny SPARKS
32 Dir Goodman Campus & Athletic Dir ..... Mr. Andy WOOD
07 Director of Admissions & Records ..... Mr. Joshua GUEST
08 Librarian ..... Mrs. Joan TIERCE
26 District Director of Communications ..... Mr. Steve DIFFEY
31 Director Community/Workforce Devel ..... Mr. Mike BLANKENSHIP
37 Director Student Financial Aid ..... Mrs. Gail MUSE
15 Director Personnel Services ..... Ms. Julia BROWN
09 Director of Institutional Research ..... Mrs. Stephanie DIFFEY
18 Chief Facilities/Physical Plant ..... Vacant
96 Director of Purchasing ..... Mrs. Rosemary SELF
06 Registrar ..... Mr. Joshua GUEST
29 Director Alumni Relations ..... Mrs. Hilliary O'BRIANT
21 Business Manager ..... Mr. Matt SURRELL

Itawamba Community College (C)

602 W Hill Street, Fulton MS 38843-1022
County: Itawamba FICE Identification: 002409
Unit ID: 175829
Telephone: (662) 862-8000 Carnegie Class: Assoc/HT-High Trad
FAX Number: (662) 862-8036 Calendar System: Semester
URL: www.iccms.edu
Established: 1948 Annual Undergrad Tuition & Fees (In-District): $2,420
Enrollment: 5,654 Coed
Affiliation or Control: Local IRS Status: 501(c)3
Highest Offering: Associate Degree
Accreditation: SC, ADNUR, CAHIIM, COARC, EMT, OTA, PTAA, RAD, SURGT

01 President ..... Mr. Michael B. EATON
05 Vice President of Instruction ..... Dr. Michelle SUMEREL
10 Exec Director of Finance ..... Ms. Sandi SOUTH
32 Vice President of Student Services ..... Mr. Buddy COLLINS
30 Vice Pres Dev/Plng/Telecom/Info Svc ..... Mr. Wayne SULLIVAN
07 Dir Admission/Registration ..... Ms. Cay LOLLAR
26 Director Community Relations ..... Dr. Jan REID-BUNCH
37 Director of Financial Aid ..... Mr. Terry BLAND
24 Director of Learning Resources ..... Ms. Janet ARMOUR
08 Librarian/Tupelo ..... Ms. Holly GRAY
51 Director of Adult & Continuing Educ ..... Mr. Scott BLACKLEY
41 Athletic Director ..... Ms. Carrie BALL-WILLIAMSON
102 Director of Foundation ..... Mr. Jim INGRAM
44 Director of Development ..... Mr. Tyler CAMP
18 Chief Facilities/Physical Plant ..... Mr. Thomas BONDS
35 Director Student Affairs ..... Mr. Brad BOGGS
09 Director of Institutional Research ..... Mrs. Elizabeth EDWARDS
15 Exec Director of Human Resources ..... Mr. Timothy C. SENTER
106 Dean of eLearning ..... Ms. Denise GILLESPIE
108 Director Strategic Planning and IE ..... Mrs. Amy CAPPLEMAN
39 Director Student Housing ..... Mr. Chad CASE

Jackson State University (D)

1400 J. R. Lynch Street, Jackson MS 39217
County: Hinds FICE Identification: 002410
Unit ID: 175856
Telephone: (601) 979-2121 Carnegie Class: DU-Higher
FAX Number: (601) 979-2358 Calendar System: Semester
URL: www.jsums.edu
Established: 1877 Annual Undergrad Tuition & Fees (In-State): $6,886
Enrollment: 9,508 Coed
Affiliation or Control: State IRS Status: 501(c)3
Highest Offering: Doctorate
Accreditation: SC, ART, BUS, CACREP, CLPSY, CORE, CS, ENG, MUS, NAIT, PH, PLNG, SP, SPAA, SW, TED

01 President ..... Dr. Carolyn MEYERS
05 Sr VP/Prov Acad & Student Affairs ..... Dr. Evelyn LEGGETTE
10 Int VP for Business & Finance ..... Ms. Dana BROWN
46 VP for Rsrch/Federal Relations ..... Dr. Loretta A. MOORE
30 VP Institutional Advancement ..... Ms. Sandra HODGE
13 VP for Information Management ..... Dr. Deborah F. DENT
32 VP for Student Life ..... Vacant
84 VP Enroll Mgmt/Inst Research ..... Dr. Nicole EDWARDS-EVANS
43 General Counsel ..... Mr. Matthew A. TAYLOR
88 Internal Auditor ..... Ms. Ella HOLMES
18 Assoc VP for Facil/Construct/Mgmt ..... Mr. Wayne GOODWIN
21 Assoc VP for Business & Finance ..... Ms. Dana BROWN
20 Assoc Provost for Academic Affairs ..... Vacant
106 Executive Director JSU Online ..... Mrs. Andrea DAVIS-JONES
35 Assoc VP for Student Life/Dean Std ..... Vacant
46 Assoc VP for Research Development ..... Dr. Safiya OMARI
88 Assoc VP for Research & Admin ..... Mrs. Tracy STAPLETON
14 Assoc VP Information Tech ..... Dr. Ivory GRISKELL
19 Assoc VP for Campus Safety ..... Mr. Lindsey HORTON
53 Dean College Educ/Human Devel ..... Dr. Daniel WATKINS
58 Dean Division of Graduate Studies ..... Dr. Dorris R. ROBINSON-GARDNER
89 Int Dean Division Undergrad Studies ..... Dr. Marie O'BANNER/JACKSON
49 Dean College of Liberal Arts ..... Dr. Mario AZEVEDO
85 Int Director JSU Global ..... Ms. Shirley J. HARRISON
50 Dean College of Business ..... Dr. Raymin MAYSAMI
80 Dean College of Public Service ..... Dr. Ricardo BROWN
72 Dean College of Sci/Engr/Tech ..... Dr. Richard ALO
51 Director of Lifelong Learning ..... Dr. Carlos WILSON
08 Dean Div of Library & Info Res ..... Dr. Melissa DRUCKREY
20 Assoc Dean University College .. Dr. Marie O'BANNER-JACKSON
92 Assoc Dean of Honors College ... Dr. Loria BROWN GORDAN
88 Asst Director Testing & Assessment ..... Vacant
31 Assoc Dir Ctr Svc & Comm/Eng Lrng ..... Dr. Gisele GENTRY
29 Int Dir Alumni/Constituency Rels ..... Ms. Tabetha TERRELL-BROOKS
15 Executive Director Human Resources ... Mrs. Robin SPANN-PACK
44 Asst VP of Development ..... Mrs. Gwen CAPLES
39 Assc Director of Residence Life ..... Dr. Erin VAUGHN
37 Director of Financial Aid ..... Mrs. Betty MONCURE
21 Dir Budget & Financial Analysis ..... Mrs. Tammiko HARRISON
06 Registrar ..... Mr. Alfred B. JACKSON
23 University Physician ..... Dr. Robert SMITH
23 University Physician ..... Dr. Samuel JONES
89 Director of First Year Experience ..... Mrs. Patricia SHERIFF-TAYLOR
07 Dir Undergraduate Admissions ..... Mrs. Janieth ADAMS
07 Director Student Recruitment ..... Dr. Juanita MORRIS
41 Director of Athletics ..... Mr. Wheeler BROWN
88 Director of Title III ..... Dr. Fredrick WHITE
88 Director MS Urban Research Ctr ..... Dr. Melvin DAVIS
19 Director Public Safety ..... Mr. Thomas ALBRIGHT
26 Int Director Communications ..... Dr. Karyn HOLLINGSWORTH
22 Int Dir for ADA Services ..... Mr. Aaron RICHARDSON
109 Exec Dir Auxiliary Enterprises ..... Vacant
88 Director of Planning & Construction ..... Mr. Robert WATTS
40 Manager Bookstore ..... Mr. Mark PERSON
88 Spec Asst to the Prov for Cmty Col ..... Dr. Priscilla SLADE
108 Director Institutional Research ..... Dr. Shemeka MCCLUNG
04 Administrative Asst to President ... Mrs. Joyce JORDAN-GOODEN
36 Executive Director Career Services ..... Ms. Lashanda JORDAN
38 Director Student Counseling ..... Ms. Frances WHITE
21 Executive Director Business Office ..... Ms. Jewell HARRIS
22 Chief Diversity Officer/EEO-AA Off ..... Mr. Thomas HUDSON
105 Webmaster ..... Mr. Gerard L. HOWARD
86 Exec Director Institutions of Govt ..... Dr. Otha BURON
90 Director Academic IT ..... Ms. Emily A. BISHOP
69 Dean School of Public Health ..... Dr. Mohammad SHABAZZI
60 Dean School of Journalism ..... Dr. Elayne ANTHONY
88 Dir Research/Federal Relations ..... Dr. Loretta MOORE
104 Assoc Director Study Abroad ..... Mr. Kwame Z. SHABAZ

Jones County Junior College (E)

900 S Court Street, Ellisville MS 39437-3999
County: Jones FICE Identification: 002411
Unit ID: 175883
Telephone: (601) 477-4000 Carnegie Class: Assoc/MT-VT-High Trad
FAX Number: (601) 477-4017 Calendar System: Semester
URL: www.jcjc.edu
Established: 1927 Annual Undergrad Tuition & Fees (In-District): $2,722
Enrollment: 4,455 Coed
Affiliation or Control: State/Local IRS Status: Exempt
Highest Offering: Associate Degree
Accreditation: SC, ACBSP, ADNUR, EMT, RAD

01 President ..... Dr. Jesse R. SMITH
05 VP Instructional Affrs/Assessment ..... Ms. Candace WEAVER
10 Vice President of Business Affairs ..... Mr. Rick YOUNGBLOOD
32 Vice President of Student Affairs ..... Dr. Sam JONES
30 VP of Institutional Advancement ..... Mr. Charlie GARRETSON
13 Director of Information Technology ..... Mr. Paul SPELL
26 Vice President of Marketing ..... Ms. Finee RUFFIN
04 Assistant to the President ..... Ms. Gwen MAGEE
04 Director of Campus Operations ..... Mr. Michael BRADSHAW
35 Dean of Student Affairs ..... Mr. Mark EASLEY
75 Dean of Career & Technical Educ ..... Mr. Sandy COCHRAN
92 Dean of Arts and Honors ..... Dr. Jason DEDWYLER
103 Director of the Adv Tech Center ..... Mr. Greg BUTLER
07 Director of Admissions & Records ..... Mr. Rick HAMILTON
38 Dir of Student Success Center ..... Mr. Andrew SHARP
37 Director of Student Financial Aid ..... Ms. Jennifer SUBER
39 Director of Housing-Women ..... Ms. Michelle SHEARER
39 Director of Housing-Men ..... Mr. Joseph TUGGLE
40 Bookstore Manager ..... Mr. Kevin KUHN
41 Athletic Director ..... Ms. Katie HERRINGTON
15 Human Resources Manager ..... Mr. Luke HAMMONDS
96 Director of Purchasing ..... Ms. Daphne YEAGER
106 Dean of eLearning ..... Ms. Ashley BEARD
08 Head Librarian ..... Mr. Andrew SHARP
19 Chief Campus Police ..... Mr. Stan LIVINGSTON

Meridian Community College (F)

910 Highway 19 N, Meridian MS 39307-5890
County: Lauderdale FICE Identification: 002413
Unit ID: 175935
Telephone: (601) 483-8241 Carnegie Class: Assoc/MT-VT-High Trad
FAX Number: (601) 481-1305 Calendar System: Semester
URL: www.meridiancc.edu
Established: 1937 Annual Undergrad Tuition & Fees (In-District): $2,430
Enrollment: 3,390 Coed
Affiliation or Control: Local IRS Status: 501(c)3
Highest Offering: Associate Degree
Accreditation: SC, ADNUR, CAHIIM, COARC, DA, DH, EMT, MAC, MLTAD, PNUR, PTAA, RAD, SURGT

01 President ..... Dr. Scott D. ELLIOTT
10 Assoc Vice President for Finance ..... Mrs. Amy BRAND
03 Vice President of Operations ..... Mrs. Barbara JONES
07 Director of Admissions ..... Dr. Angela PAYNE
09 Dir Institutional Effectiveness ..... Mrs. Cathy PARKER
32 Dean of Students ..... Ms. Soraya WELDEN
05 Dean of Academic Affs/General Educ ..... Mr. Michael THOMPSON
62 Assoc Dean Learning Resources ..... Dr. Ray DENTON
30 Assoc Vice Pres for Development ..... Mrs. Kathy BROOKSHIRE
18 Director Physical Plant ..... Mr. Adam FOREMAN
37 Director Financial Aid ..... Ms. Nedra BRADLEY
15 Director Human Resources ..... Ms. Shellye ESPEY
41 Athletic Director ..... Mr. Sander ATKINSON
19 Chief of Security ..... Mr. Shane WILLIAMS
40 Bookstore Manager ..... Mrs. Cher WARREN
26 Dir Marketing/Public Relations ..... Mrs. Kay THOMAS
36 Career Center Development Director ..... Ms. Darlene MAYATT
103 Assoc Vice Pres for Workforce Educ ..... Dr. Richie MCALISTER
06 Registrar ..... Ms. Deborah OLDHAM
105 Director Web Services ..... Ms. Inga BASS
13 Chief Info Technology Officer (CIO) ..... Mr. Chris EDWARDS
39 Director Student Housing ..... Mr. Calvin BENNETT
106 Director of E-Learning ..... Mrs. Haley DUCK

Miller-Motte Technical College (G)

12121 Highway 49, Gulfport MS 39503
Telephone: (228) 273-3400 Identification: 770845
Accreditation: ACICS

† Branch campus of McCann School of Business & Technology, Pottsville, PA

Millsaps College (H)

1701 N State Street, Jackson MS 39210-0001
County: Hinds FICE Identification: 002414
Unit ID: 175980
Telephone: (601) 974-1000 Carnegie Class: Bac-A&S
FAX Number: (601) 974-1059 Calendar System: Semester
URL: www.millsaps.edu
Established: 1890 Annual Undergrad Tuition & Fees: $35,510
Enrollment: 842 Coed
Affiliation or Control: United Methodist IRS Status: 501(c)3
Highest Offering: Master's

Accreditation: SC, BUS, TED

Code	Title	Name
01	President	Dr. Rob PEARIGEN
05	VP/Dean of the College	Dr. Keith DUNN
10	Vice Pres for Planning & Assessment	Ms. Terri HUDSON
30	VP for Institutional Advancement	Vacant
32	VP Student Life/Dean Students	Dr. Brit KATZ
50	Dean of the School of Management	Dr. Kimberly G. BURKE
84	Vice Pres Enrollment/Communications	Dr. Robert ALEXANDER
79	Assoc Dean Arts & Letters	Dr. David DAVIS
81	Associate Dean Sciences Division	Dr. Timothy J. WARD
82	Assoc Dean International Education	Dr. George J. BEY
37	Director of Financial Aid	Mrs. Isabelle HIGBEE
20	Director Academic Support Services	Dr. Melissa LEA
51	Director of Continuing Education	Dr. Nola R. GIBSON
08	College Librarian	Ms. Jamie B. WILSON
36	Director of Career Center	Ms. Tonya CRAFT
41	Director of Athletics	Mr. Donnie BROOKS
15	Dir of Human Resource Services	Ms. Julie DANIELS
42	Chaplain	Vacant
21	Controller	Mrs. Whitney EMRICH
06	Registrar	Ms. Elizabeth GIDDENS
09	Director of Institutional Research	Dr. Ken THOMPSON
18	Director of Physical Plant	Mr. Michael SWITZER
29	Director Alumni Relations	Ms. Maribeth KITCHINGS
19	Director Security/Safety	Mr. John CONWAY
26	Director of Communications & Market	Mr. John SEWELL
07	Director of Admission	Mrs. Catherine P. BOX
04	Administrative Asst to President	Mrs. Penta MOORE
100	Chief of Staff	Mr. Kenneth TOWNSEND
102	Dir Foundation/Corporate Relations	Mr. Lloyd GRAY
44	Director Annual Giving	Ms. Monica DANIELS

Mississippi College (A)

200 W College Street, Clinton MS 39058-0001

County: Hinds
FICE Identification: 002415
Unit ID: 176053
Telephone: (601) 925-3000
Carnegie Class: Masters/L
FAX Number: (601) 925-3276
Calendar System: Semester
URL: www.mc.edu
Established: 1826
Annual Undergrad Tuition & Fees: $16,064
Enrollment: 4,984
Coed
Affiliation or Control: Southern Baptist
IRS Status: 501(c)3
Highest Offering: Doctorate
Accreditation: SC, ACBSP, ARCPA, CACREP, CIDA, LAW, MUS, NURSE, SW, TED

Code	Title	Name
01	President	Dr. Lee G. ROYCE
04	Sr Exec Assistant to President	Ms. Shelia CARPENTER
10	Chief Financial Officer	Ms. Donna LEWIS
05	Vice President Academic Affairs	Dr. Ronald HOWARD
32	VP Enrollment Svcs/Dean of Students	Dr. Jim TURCOTTE
45	Vice President Planning/Assessment	Dr. Debbie NORRIS
42	Vice Pres Christian Development	Dr. Eric PRATT
30	VP Inst Advan/Alum/Leg Coun to Pres	Dr. Bill TOWNSEND
11	Vice Pres Admin/Government Rels	Dr. Steve STANFORD
84	Director Enrollment Services	Mr. Mark HUGHES
06	Registrar	Ms. Megan PRITCHETT
09	Director of Institutional Research	Ms. Cassandra SESSUMS
08	Librarian	Ms. Kathleen HUTCHISON
21	Comptroller	Ms. Allison ROOKER
13	Chief Information Officer	Mr. Bill CRANFORD
38	Director Counseling/Testing Center	Dr. Morgan BRYANT
15	Director Human Resources	Ms. Donna SMITH
29	Interim Director Alumni Affairs	Ms. Lori BOBO
26	Director Public Relations	Ms. Tracey HARRISON
18	Director of Physical Plant	Mr. Billy THORNTON
39	Coordinator of Residence Life	Ms. Sharia BROCK
37	Director Student Financial Aid	Ms. Karon MCMILLAN
07	Director of Admissions	Mr. Kyle BRANTLEY
35	Assoc Dir of Student Engagement	Ms. Becca BENSON
19	Director of Public Safety	Mr. Mike WARREN
41	Director of Athletics	Mr. Mike JONES
96	Director of Purchasing	Ms. Dana ELMORE
40	Manager Bookstore	Ms. Karen BARNES
36	Asst Director of Career Services	Mr. Jim MILLER
81	Dean School of Science/Mathematics	Dr. Stan BALDWIN
50	Dean School of Business Admin	Dr. Marcelo EDUARDO
79	Dean School of Humanities	Dr. Jonathan RANDLE
53	Dean School of Education	Dr. Don LOCKE
73	Dean Sch Christian Studies/Fine Art	Dr. Wayne VAN HORN
61	Dean School of Law	Prof. Wendy SCOTT
58	Dean Grad School/Special Programs	Dr. Debbie NORRIS
66	Dean School of Nursing	Dr. Kimberly SHARP
86	Director Government Relations	Dr. Steve STANFORD

Mississippi Delta Community College (B)

PO Box 668, Moorhead MS 38761-0668

County: Sunflower
FICE Identification: 002416
Unit ID: 176008
Telephone: (662) 246-6322
Carnegie Class: Assoc/HT-Mix Trad/Non
FAX Number: (662) 246-6321
Calendar System: Semester
URL: www.msdelta.edu
Established: 1926
Annual Undergrad Tuition & Fees (In-District): $2,520
Enrollment: 2,705
Coed
Affiliation or Control: Local
IRS Status: 501(c)3
Highest Offering: Associate Degree
Accreditation: SC, ADNUR, DH, MLTAD, RAD

Code	Title	Name
01	President	Dr. Larry NABORS
03	Executive Vice President	Dr. Charles BARNETT
05	Vice President of Instruction	Mrs. Teresa WEBSTER
10	Vice President of Business Services	Mrs. Marsha LEE
32	Vice President of Student Services	Dr. Edward RICE
88	Assoc VP GHEC Operations	Dr. MaryAnne BROCATO
84	Associate Vice Pres of Enrollment	Dr. Brent GREGORY
30	Assoc VP College Advancement	Mr. Reed ABRAHAM
15	Director of Human Resources	Ms. Brenda VANLANDINGHAM
37	Director of Financial Aid	Ms. Amber KELLY
07	Director of Admissions	Dr. Brent GREGORY
13	Director Computer & Info Tech Svcs	Mr. Jim AYCOCK
08	Director of Library Services	Mrs. Krist BARIOLA
07	Director Counseling/Recruiting	Mrs. Kate FAILING
18	Director of Maintenance	Mr. Don LEE
88	Director of Special Events	Ms. Corey SMITH
09	Director of Institutional Research	Ms. Rosemary LAMB
04	Admin Asst to the President	Mrs. Debra BAKER
41	Athletic Director	Mr. Domino EELLIPANNI
19	Director Security/Safety	Mr. Henry MANUEL

Mississippi Gulf Coast Community College (C)

PO Box 609, Perkinston MS 39573-0012

County: Stone
FICE Identification: 002417
Unit ID: 176071
Telephone: (601) 928-5211
Carnegie Class: Assoc/MT-VT-High Trad
FAX Number: (601) 928-6386
Calendar System: Semester
URL: www.mgccc.edu
Established: 1911
Annual Undergrad Tuition & Fees (In-District): $3,272
Enrollment: 9,799
Coed
Affiliation or Control: Local
IRS Status: 501(c)3
Highest Offering: Associate Degree
Accreditation: SC, ACFEI, ADNUR, EMT, FUSER, MAC, MLTAD, PNUR, RAD, SURGT

Code	Title	Name
01	President	Dr. Mary S. GRAHAM
05	Exec VP Teaching/Lrng/Student Svcs	Dr. Jason PUGH
10	VP Administration/Finance	Dr. Michael J. HEINDL
12	VP Perkinston Campus (PC)	Dr. Ladd TAYLOR
12	VP Jefferson Davis Campus (JDC)	Dr. Jonathan WOODWARD
12	VP Jackson County Campus (JCC)	Dr. Tammy FRANKS
84	Exec VP Enroll Mgmt/Student Success	Dr. Carmen WALTERS
75	AVP Cmty Campus/Career Tech Educ	Mr. John SHOWS
09	Director Inst Research & Planning	Mr. Adam SWANSON
41	College Dean for Athletics	Mr. Bert PICKARD
106	Director of Distance Learning	Ms. Jennifer LEIMER
50	Director of Business Services	Mr. Wayne KUNTZ
21	Comptroller	Ms. Shelly FORD
06	Records Clerk - PC	Ms. Latrice MCDONALD
06	Records Clerk - JCC	Ms. Linda OTIS
06	Records Clerk - JDC	Ms. Mary JOYCE
20	Dean of Instruction - JCC	Dr. Cedric BRADLEY
20	Dean of Instruction - JDC	Mr. Larry MILLER
20	Dean of Instruction - PC	Dr. Jan MOODY
50	Dean of Business Services - PC	Dr. Vanessa DEDEAUX
50	Dean of Business Services - JCC	Ms. Tammy FRANKS
50	Dean of Busines Services - JDC	Ms. Stacy CARMICHAEL
66	Dean of Nursing/Allied Health	Dr. Joan HENDRIX
75	Dn Career Tech/Wrkfc/Cmty Ed - PC	Mr. Bobby GHOSAL
75	Dn Career/Tech/Wrkf/Cmty Ed - JDC	Dr. Beverly CLARK
75	Dn Career/Tech/Wrkf/Cmty Ed - JCC	Mr. Brock CLARK
08	Asst Dean LRC - PC	Dr. Brenda RIVERO
08	Asst Dean LRC - JCC	Dr. Pam LADNER
08	Asst Dean LRC - JDC	Ms. Nancy WILCOX
32	Dn Stdnt Svcs/Enroll Mgmt - PC	Dr. Jason BEVERLY
32	Dn Stdnt Svcs/Enroll Mgmt - JCC	Ms. Michelle SEKUL
32	Dn Stdnt Svcs/Enroll Mgmt - JDC	Dr. Phil BONFANTI
88	Dean George County Center	Ms. Cheryl BALIUS
07	Director of Admissions/Rec - PC	Mr. Trey ROBERTSON
07	Director of Admissions/Rec - JCC	Mr. William EVERITT
07	Director of Admissions/Rec - JDC	Mr. Christopher BAGWELL
29	Coord College Events/Special Proj	Ms. Jenifer FRERIDGE
37	Financial Aid Director - JDC	Ms. Angela BRADLEY
37	Financial Aid Director - PC	Ms. LeighAnn HUSSEY
37	Financial Aid Director - JCC	Ms. LaShanda CHAMBERLAIN
15	District Director Human Resources	Ms. Tenesha BATISTE
96	Dir Purchasing/Property Control	Ms. Lynn DEEGEN
18	Construction Manager	Mr. Jason BRELAND
44	Director Institutional Development	Ms. Brenda DAVIS
04	Exec Assistant to the President	Ms. Tracey WALTERS

Mississippi State University (D)

Lee Boulevard, Mississippi State MS 39762-5708

County: Oktibbeha
FICE Identification: 002423
Unit ID: 176080
Telephone: (662) 325-2323
Carnegie Class: DU-Higher
FAX Number: (662) 325-7455
Calendar System: Semester
URL: www.msstate.edu
Established: 1878
Annual Undergrad Tuition & Fees (In-State): $7,502
Enrollment: 20,138
Coed
Affiliation or Control: State
IRS Status: 501(c)3
Highest Offering: Doctorate
Accreditation: SC, AAFCS, ART, BUS, BUSA, CACREP, CIDA, CORE, CS, DIETD, DIETI, ENG, LSAR, MUS, SCPSY, SPAA, SW, TED, VET

Code	Title	Name
01	President	Dr. Mark E. KEENUM
05	Provost/Executive VP	Dr. Judy BONNER
46	VP Research & Economic Development	Dr. David SHAW
88	VP Agric/Forestry & Veterinary Med	Dr. Gregory BOHACH
10	VP for Budget and Planning	Mr. Don ZANT
32	VP for Student Affairs	Dr. Regina HYATT
30	VP for Development and Alumni	Mr. John P. RUSH
18	VP for Campus Services	Ms. Amy TUCK
07	Assistant VP Enrollment	Dr. John DICKERSON
41	Athletic Director	Mr. Scott STRICKLIN
43	General Counsel	Ms. Joan LUCAS
28	Interim Chief Diversity Officer	Ms. Rasheda BODDIE-FORBES
15	Director Human Resources Mgmt	Ms. Judith SPENCER
26	Exec Dir External Affairs	Mr. Kyle STEWARD
27	Director Public Affairs	Mr. Sid SALTER
86	Director Government Relations	Mr. Lee WEISKOPF
20	Assoc Provost Academic Affairs	Dr. Peter RYAN
13	Chief Information Officer	Mr. J. Mike RACKLEY
88	Exec Dir International Institute	Dr. Richard NADER
48	Dean of Architecture/Art/Design	Mr. James L. WEST
49	Interim Dean Arts & Sciences	Dr. Rick TRAVIS
50	Dean College Business	Dr. Sharon OSWALD
53	Dean of Education	Dr. Richard L. BLACKBOURN
58	Dean of Graduate Studies	Dr. Lori BRUCE
54	Dean College of Engineering	Dr. Jason KEITH
65	Dean of Forest Resources	Dr. George M. HOPPER
47	Dean College Agriculture & Life Sci	Dr. George M. HOPPER
74	Dean of Veterinary Medicine	Dr. Kent H. HOBLET
12	Admin Dir & Head of Meridian Campus	Dr. Terry CRUSE
08	Dean of Libraries	Ms. Frances N. COLEMAN
92	Dean Honors College	Dr. Christopher SNYDER
56	Dir University Extension Service	Dr. Gary JACKSON
88	Dir Agricultural Experiment Station	Dr. George M. HOPPER
06	Registrar	Dr. John R. DICKERSON
106	Int Director Distance Learning	Dr. Lynn REINSCHMIEDT
36	Director Career Services/Coop Educ	Mr. Scott MAYNARD
35	Dean of Students	Dr. Thomas BOURGEOIS
38	Director of Counseling Center	Dr. Leigh JENSEN
37	Director Student Financial Aid	Mr. Paul MCKINNEY
39	Director Housing/Residence Life	Dr. Ann BAILEY
09	Director Institutional Research	Dr. Tim CHAMBLEE
23	Director Student Health Center	Dr. Robert K. CADENHEAD
29	Director of Alumni Association	Mr. Jeffrey DAVIS
44	Director of Planned Giving	Mr. Wes GORDON
25	Director Sponsored Projects	Mrs. Jennifer EASLEY
88	Director Internal Audit	Ms. Leisa ERVIN
96	Director Procurement/Contracts	Mr. Don BUFFUM
19	Police Chief	Mr. Vance RICE

Mississippi University for Women (E)

1100 College Street, Columbus MS 39701-5800

County: Lowndes
FICE Identification: 002422
Unit ID: 176035
Telephone: (877) 462-8439
Carnegie Class: Masters/S
FAX Number: (662) 329-7297
Calendar System: Semester
URL: www.muw.edu
Established: 1884
Annual Undergrad Tuition & Fees (In-State): $5,781
Enrollment: 2,636
Coed
Affiliation or Control: State
IRS Status: 501(c)3
Highest Offering: Doctorate
Accreditation: SC, ACBSP, ADNUR, ART, MUS, NURSE, SP, TED

Code	Title	Name
01	President	Dr. Jim BORSIG
05	Interim Provost/VP Academic Affairs	Dr. Thomas RICHARDSON
10	Sr Vice Pres Administration & CFO	Ms. Nora R. MILLER
30	Exec Dir of University Relations	Ms. Maridith GEUDER
32	Vice Pres for Student Affairs	Dr. Jennifer MILES
20	Assoc Vice Pres Academic Affairs	Dr. Martin HATTON
43	University Counsel	Ms. Karen CLAY
49	Dean College Arts/Sciences	Dr. Brian ANDERSON
50	Dean Business/Professional Studies	Dr. Scott TOLLISON
53	Int Dean College Educ/Human Sci	Dr. Martin HATTON
66	Dean College Nursing/SLP	Dr. Sheila V. ADAMS
08	Dean of Library Services	Ms. Amanda C. POWERS
58	Director Graduate Studies	Dr. Martin HATTON
88	Int Director Outreach & Innovation	Ms. Melinda LOWE
06	Registrar	Ms. Lynn DOBBS
09	Director Inst Research & Assessment	Ms. Jennifer MOORE
92	Interim Director Honors College	Dr. Kim WHITEHEAD
25	Director Sponsored Programs	Mr. James DENNEY
29	Director Alumni Relations	Ms. Lyndsay CUMBERLAND
30	Exec Dir Development/Alumni Rels	Ms. Andrea N. STEVENS
44	Director Annual Giving	Ms. Brandy WILLIAMS
26	Director Public Affairs	Ms. Anika M. PERKINS
105	Dir Web Development/Univ Webmaster	Mr. Rich SOBOLEWSKI
21	Director University Accounting	Ms. Susan SOBLEY
88	Internal Auditor	Mr. Kenneth WIDNER
13	Director of Information Systems	Ms. Lisa MCDANIEL
07	Director Admissions	Ms. Shelley MCNEES MOSS
37	Director Financial Aid	Ms. Nicole PATRICK
15	Director Human Resources	Ms. Melanie H. FREEMAN
27	Chief Information Officer	Ms. Carla LOWERY
19	Chief of Police	Mr. Danny PATTON
18	Director of Facilities Management	Mr. Dewey BLANSETT
96	Director Resources Management	Ms. Angie S. ATKINS
35	Director Student Life	Ms. Jessica HARPOLE
35	Dean of Students	Ms. Sirena CANTRELL
41	Director Campus Recreation	Ms. LeAnn ALEXANDER
40	Director Bookstore	Ms. Helana ROBINSON
88	Director Student Success Center	Dr. David BROOKING
109	General Manager of MUW Dining Svcs	Mr. Alan JOHNSON
84	Enrollment Certification Officer	Ms. Laura L. BLACK
14	Director of Systems & Networks	Mr. Rodney GODFREY
104	Director Study Abroad	Dr. Kim WHITEHEAD
39	Director Housing & Residence Life	Mr. Andrew MONEYMAKER

Mississippi Valley State University (A)

14000 Highway 82 W, Itta Bena MS 38941-1400
County: Leflore FICE Identification: 002424
Unit ID: 176044
Telephone: (662) 254-9041 Carnegie Class: Masters/S
FAX Number: (662) 254-6709 Calendar System: Semester
URL: www.mvsu.edu
Established: 1950 Annual Undergrad Tuition & Fees (In-State): $5,936
Enrollment: 2,222 Coed
Affiliation or Control: State IRS Status: 501(c)3
Highest Offering: Master's
Accreditation: SC, ACBSP, ART, CS, MUS, SW, TED

01 President .... Dr. William BYNUM, JR.
05 VP Academic Affairs .... Dr. Constance BLAND
11 Exec Vice Pres/COO .... Dr. Jerryl BRIGGS, SR.
32 Vice Pres for Student Affairs .... Dr. Jacqueline GIBSON
35 Int Dean Students/Dir Res Life .... Mr. Raynaldo GILLUS
20 Assoc VP Academic Affairs .... Dr. Kathie STROMILE-GOLDEN
20 Asst VP for IRE/Strat Planning .... Dr. Sharon FREEMAN
10 VP Business & Finance/CFO .... Ms. Joyce A. DIXON
100 Chief of Staff/Legislative Liaison .... Mrs. LaShon F. BROOKS
30 Int Vice Pres for Univ Advancement .... Mr. Dameon SHAW
106 Asst VP for Distance & Online .... Dr. Kenneth DONE
58 Dean of Graduate College .... Vacant
41 Director of Athletics .... Mrs. Dianthia FORD-KEE
06 Director of Student Records .... Mr. Jeff LOGGINS
07 Director Admission/Recruitment .... Ms. Jacqueline A. WILLIAMS
08 Head Librarian .... Ms. Mantra HENDERSON
15 Director of Human Resources .... Mrs. Elizabeth HURSSEY
13 Director of Computer Center .... Mr. Steven L. PITCHFORD
37 Director of Financial Aid .... Mr. Lloyd E. DIXON
29 Manager of Alumni Relations .... Ms. Latacha DAVIS-JACKSON
26 Director of Comm/Mktg .... Mrs. Maxine GREENLEAF
19 Director University Police .... Mr. Leron WEEKS
18 Director Facilities/Physical Plant .... Mr. Tommy VERDELL
39 Asst Director Residential Life .... Ms. Glenda RANSOM
36 Director Career Development .... Ms. Tiffany WALLACE
38 Director Student Counseling .... Dr. Yolanda JONES
50 Acting Chair of Business Department .... Dr. Curressia BROWN
53 Chair of Education Dept .... Dr. Lula COLLIER
65 Chair Nat Sci/Env Health Dept .... Dr. Louis J. HALL
49 Dean College of Arts & Sciences .... Vacant
88 Chair English/Foreign Language .... Dr. John ZHENG
57 Chair Fine Arts Department .... Dr. Alphonso SANDERS
68 Chair Health/Phys Ed/Rec Dept .... Dr. Gloria ROSS
81 Chair of Math/Computer Science Dept .... Dr. Latonya GARNER
54 Acting Chair of EngineeringTech .... Mr. Antonio BROWNLOW
60 Chair Mass Communication Dept .... Dr. Samuel OSUNDE
88 Chair Criminal Justice .... Dr. Emmanual AMADI
70 Chair Social Work Department .... Dr. Catherine SINGLETON-WALKER
96 Director of Purchasing .... Mr. Billy SCOTT
04 Executive Asst to President .... Mrs. Auguster WALLACE
25 Director Sponsored Pgm/Title III .... Mr. Samuel MELTON, JR.
44 Executive Director of Development .... Mr. Dameon SHAW

Northeast Mississippi Community College (B)

101 Cunningham Boulevard, Booneville MS 38829-1731
County: Prentiss FICE Identification: 002426
Unit ID: 176169
Telephone: (662) 728-7751 Carnegie Class: Assoc/HT-High Trad
FAX Number: (662) 728-1165 Calendar System: Semester
URL: www.nemcc.edu
Established: 1948 Annual Undergrad Tuition & Fees (In-District): $2,310
Enrollment: 3,538 Coed
Affiliation or Control: State/Local IRS Status: 501(c)3
Highest Offering: Associate Degree
Accreditation: SC, ADNUR, COARC, DH, MAC, MLTAD, RAD

01 President .... Ricky G. FORD
03 Executive Vice President .... Craig-Ellis SASSSER
103 Vice Pres Wrkfrce Training/Econ Dev .... Nadara L. COLE
10 Vice President of Finance .... Chris MURPHY
26 Assoc Vice Pres of Public Info .... Tony FINCH
05 Dean of Instruction .... Rilla c. JONES
32 Dean of Students .... David ROBBINS
35 Assoc Dean of Student Activities .... Angie LANGLEY
08 Director Learning Resources .... Glenice STONE
96 Director of Purchasing .... Sheila OWENS
37 Director of Financial Aid .... Greg WINDHAM
38 Director Student Counseling .... Joey WILLIFORD
13 Director Computer Center .... Gregory SMITH
18 Director Facilities/Maintenance .... Mark HATFIELD
39 Director Residential Housing .... Rod COGGIN
75 Director of Vocational Tech Educ .... Jody PRESLEY
84 Dir of Enrollment Svcs/Registrar .... Chassie KELLY
15 Human Resources Officer .... Tammie HARDIN
04 Administrative Asst to President .... Mary A. COATS
102 Dir Foundation/Corporate Relations .... Patrick D. EATON
106 Dir Online Education/E-learning .... Kim HARRIS
19 Director Security/Safety .... Randy A. BAXTER

Northwest Mississippi Community College (C)

4975 Highway 51 N, Senatobia MS 38668-1703
County: Tate FICE Identification: 002427
Unit ID: 176178
Telephone: (662) 562-3200 Carnegie Class: Assoc/MT-VT-High Trad
FAX Number: (662) 562-3911 Calendar System: Semester
URL: www.northwestms.edu
Established: 1927 Annual Undergrad Tuition & Fees (In-State): $2,550
Enrollment: 7,559 Coed
Affiliation or Control: State IRS Status: 501(c)3
Highest Offering: Associate Degree
Accreditation: SC, ADNUR, COARC, EMT, FUSER

01 President .... Dr. Gary Lee SPEARS
10 Vice President for Fiscal Affairs .... Mr. Gary MOSLEY
32 VP Student Affairs/Chief of Staff .... Mr. Dan SMITH
05 Vice Pres for Educational Affairs .... Mr. Richie LAWSON
20 Academic Dean .... Dr. Matthew S. DOMAS
103 Dean Career Tech Ed/Wrkfce Dev Trng .... Mr. David CAMPBELL
51 Dir Division of Continuing Educ .... Ms. Pam WOOTEN
84 Dean Enrollment Mgmt & Registrar .... Mr. Larry SIMPSON
35 Director of Student Personnel .... Mr. Gerald BEARD
26 Director of Communications .... Mrs. Sarah SAPP
37 Director of Financial Aid .... Ms. Jennifer LUNA
36 Dir Student Development Center .... Ms. Meg ROSS
08 Director of Learning Resources .... Mrs. Maggie MORAN
13 Director Management Information Sys .... Mrs. Amy LATHAM
07 Director of Recruiting .... Mrs. Jere HERRINGTON
09 Director Planning/Inst Research .... Dr. Carolyn WARREN
18 Director of Physical Plant Building .... Mr. Mike ROBISON
19 Chief of Campus Security .... Mr. Zabe DAVIS
30 Director of Development/Alumni Rels .... Mrs. Sybil CANON
39 Director of Campus Life and Housing .... Mrs. Aime ANDERSON
40 Director Bookstore .... Mr. Joel BOYLES
41 Director of Athletics/Intramurals .... Mr. Don SKELTON
96 Director of Purchasing .... Mrs. Barbara YOUNG
15 Personnel Officer .... Mrs. Erica STANFORD
29 Director Alumni Relations .... Mrs. Dolores WOOTEN
21 Business Manager .... Ms. Ruthie CASTLE

Pearl River Community College (D)

101 Highway 11 N, Poplarville MS 39470-2298
County: Pearl River FICE Identification: 002430
Unit ID: 176239
Telephone: (601) 403-1000 Carnegie Class: Assoc/MT-VT-High Trad
FAX Number: (601) 403-1339 Calendar System: Semester
URL: www.prcc.edu
Established: 1909 Annual Undergrad Tuition & Fees (In-District): $2,855
Enrollment: 4,529 Coed
Affiliation or Control: State/Local IRS Status: 501(c)3
Highest Offering: Associate Degree
Accreditation: SC, ADNUR, COARC, DA, DH, MLTAD, OTA, PTAA, RAD, SURGT

01 President .... Dr. William A. LEWIS
05 VP for General Educ & Technology .... Dr. Martha L. SMITH
32 VP Poplarville Campus/Hancock Ctr .... Dr. Adam BREERWOOD
10 VP for Business/Admn Services .... Mr. Roger A. KNIGHT
08 Director of College Libraries .... Ms. Tracy SMITH
26 Director of Public Relations .... Mr. Chuck ABADIE
84 Director of Admissions and Records .... Ms. Tonia MOODY
12 VP for Forrest County Operations .... Dr. Jana CAUSEY
18 Director of Physical Plant .... Mr. Craig TYNES
30 Director Development/Alumni Rels .... Mr. Ernest L. LOVELL, JR.
37 Director Student Financial Aid .... Ms. Valerie HORNE
41 Athletic Director .... Mr. Jeff LONG
07 Director of Recruitment/Marketing .... Ms. Delana HARRIS
09 VP for Planning & Inst Research .... Dr. Jennifer SEAL
36 Dir Student Placement/Counselor .... Vacant
31 VP Econ/Comm Development .... Dr. David S. ALSOBROOKS
04 Administrative Asst to President .... Ms. Marilyn DILLARD
105 Webmaster .... Mr. Eric REID

Reformed Theological Seminary (E)

5422 Clinton Boulevard, Jackson MS 39209-3099
County: Hinds FICE Identification: 009193
Unit ID: 176284
Telephone: (601) 923-1600 Carnegie Class: Not Classified
FAX Number: (601) 923-1654 Calendar System: 4/1/4
URL: www.rts.edu
Established: 1965 Annual Graduate Tuition & Fees: N/A
Enrollment: N/A Coed
Affiliation or Control: Independent Non-Profit IRS Status: 501(c)3
Highest Offering: Doctorate; No Undergraduates
Accreditation: SC, MFCD, THEOL

00 Chancellor Emeritus .... Dr. Robert C. CANNADA, JR.
01 Chancellor/CEO .... Dr. J. Ligon DUNCAN
10 Chief Operations Financial Officer .... Mr. Bradley TISDALE
05 Provost and Chief Academic Officer .... Dr. Robert CARA
30 Chief Advancement Officer .... Rev. Lynwood C. PEREZ
12 President Charlotte Campus .... Dr. Michael J. KRUGER
12 President Orlando Campus .... Dr. Don W. SWEETING
12 President Jackson Campus .... Dr. Guy L. RICHARDSON
12 President Atlanta Campus .... Mr. John T. SOWELL
12 President Washington DC .... Dr. Scott REDD
106 Exec Dir RTS Global/Distance Educ .... Mr. David R. JOHN, III
06 Registrar Jackson Campus .... Ms. Kiama LEE
08 Library Director .... Mr. John CRABB
32 Dean of Student Affairs .... Mr. Brian C. GAULT
29 Dir Alum Rels/Dev/Supt Svcs Jackson .... Mrs. Stephanie J. HARTLEY
04 Dir Operations/Asst to Pres Jackson .... Mrs. Wanda RUSHING
88 Dir Marriage/Family Therapy Jackson .... Dr. James B. HURLEY
18 Maintenance Director Jackson Campus .... Mr. Kyle SANDIDGE
108 Chief Institutional Assessment Ofcr .... Ms. Polly STONE
15 Director Personnel Svcs Jackson .... Ms. Linda COCHRAN
07 Director Admissions .... Mr. Brian GAULT

Rust College (F)

150 Rust Avenue, Holly Springs MS 38635-2328
County: Marshall FICE Identification: 002433
Unit ID: 176318
Telephone: (662) 252-8000 Carnegie Class: Bac-Diverse
FAX Number: (662) 252-6107 Calendar System: Semester
URL: www.rustcollege.edu
Established: 1866 Annual Undergrad Tuition & Fees: $9,500
Enrollment: 963 Coed
Affiliation or Control: United Methodist IRS Status: 501(c)3
Highest Offering: Baccalaureate
Accreditation: SC, SW

01 President .... Dr. David L. BECKLEY
30 Vice President for College Relation .... Dr. Ishmell H. EDWARDS
10 Vice President for Finance .... Mr. Donald MANNING-MILLER
05 VP for Academic Affairs .... Dr. Sandra C. VAUGHN
06 Registrar .... Mr. Clarence E. SMITH
08 Library Director .... Mrs. Anita W. MOORE
13 Director Computer Center .... Ms. Barbara NAYLOR MOORE
32 Vice Pres for Student Affairs .... Mr. Carllos LASSITER
35 Director Student Activities .... Mr. Frederick TAYLOR
37 Director of Financial Aid .... Mr. Reginald B. SMITH
25 Director Contracts & Grants .... Mrs. Christine L. RATCLIFF
29 Director Alumni Development .... Ms. Jo Ann SCOTT
89 Chair First Year Experience .... Dr. Vida MAYS
26 Director of Public Relations .... Ms. Dionyale SPENCER
21 Comptroller .... Ms. Glenda KING
84 Dean of Enrollment Services .... Mr. Braque TALLEY
23 Director Student Health Services .... Dr. Dianna HUGHES-MARION
39 Director Student Housing .... Ms. Tanya K. KIRK
36 Director of Career Development .... Ms. DaShundra L. AVERY
18 Director Physical Plant .... Mr. Robert CURRY
83 Division Chair Social Science .... Dr. Alfred J. STOVALL
15 Director Personnel Services .... Ms. Patricia PEGUES
19 Chief of Security .... Mr. Eric SCOTT
30 Director of Development .... Ms. Jo Ann SCOTT
40 Bookstore Manager .... Mrs. Patricia HARRIS
42 College Chaplain .... Mr. Kelvin KOSH
96 Director of Purchasing .... Ms. Ollie BOWENS
28 Director of Diversity .... Miss Patricia PEGUES
50 Division Chair Business .... Mr. Richard FREDERICK
53 Division Chair Education .... Dr. Leon HOWARD
79 Division Chair Humanities .... Dr. Alisea MCLEOD
81 Chair Division Science & Math .... Dr. Doris WARD
70 Chair Department of Social Work .... Dr. Gemma BECKLEY
105 Director Web Services .... Mrs. Nilse F. GILLIAM
41 Athletic Director .... Dr. Ishmell H. EDWARDS
101 Secretary of the Institution/Board .... Mrs. Willa TERRY
106 Dir Online Education/E-learning .... Dr. Helen OLIVER
38 Director Student Counseling .... Mr. Carllos LASSITER
09 Director of Institutional Research .... Dr. Charles WILLIAMS
90 Director Academic Computing .... Mrs. Mollie PEGUES
91 Director Administrative Computing .... Mrs. Barbara N. MOORE

Southeastern Baptist College (G)

4229 Highway 15 N, Laurel MS 39440-1096
County: Jones FICE Identification: 002435
Unit ID: 176336
Telephone: (601) 426-6346 Carnegie Class: Spec-4-yr-Faith
FAX Number: (601) 426-6347 Calendar System: Semester
URL: www.southeasternbaptist.edu
Established: 1948 Annual Undergrad Tuition & Fees: $4,790
Enrollment: 42 Coed
Affiliation or Control: Baptist IRS Status: 501(c)3
Highest Offering: Baccalaureate
Accreditation: BI

01 President .... Mr. Danny C. PITTS
05 Academic Dean .... Dr. Scott CARSON
32 Dean of Student Services .... Dr. Daryle COATS
13 Director Information Technology .... Mr. Hubert DYESS
07 Director of Admissions .... Mr. Ronnie KITCHENS
06 Registrar .... Mrs. Emma BOND
37 Financial Aid Administrator .... Mr. Ronnie KITCHENS
08 Director of Library .... Mrs. Amy E. HINTON

Southwest Mississippi Community College (H)

1156 College Drive, Summit MS 39666-9029
County: Pike FICE Identification: 002436
Unit ID: 176354
Telephone: (601) 276-2000 Carnegie Class: Assoc/MT-VT-High Trad
FAX Number: (601) 276-3888 Calendar System: Semester
URL: www.smcc.edu
Established: 1918 Annual Undergrad Tuition & Fees (In-District): $2,720
Enrollment: 1,973 Coed
Affiliation or Control: Local IRS Status: 501(c)3
Highest Offering: Associate Degree
Accreditation: SC, ADNUR, CAHIIM

01 President .... Dr. Steve BISHOP
05 Vice President of Academic Affairs .... Ms. Alicia SHOWS
10 Vice President of Financial Affairs .... Mr. Andrew ALFORD
32 Vice President of Student Affairs .... Dr. Bill ASHLEY

75 Vice Pres Career & Tech Education ... Mr. Jeremy SMITH
06 Registrar/Vice President Admissions ... Mr. Matthew CALHOUN
37 Financial Aid Director ... Ms. Joni WILKINSON
09 Director of Institutional Research ... Ms. Lea TOUCHSTONE
08 Library Director ... Mrs. Natalie MCMAHON
39 Dir Student Activities/Housing ... Ms. Ashley GRAY

Tougaloo College (A)

500 West County Line Road, Tougaloo MS 39174-9999
County: Madison FICE Identification: 002439
Unit ID: 176406
Telephone: (601) 977-7730 Carnegie Class: Bac-A&S
FAX Number: (601) 977-7739 Calendar System: Semester
URL: www.tougaloo.edu
Established: 1869 Annual Undergrad Tuition & Fees: $10,608
Enrollment: 900 Coed
Affiliation or Control: United Church Of Christ IRS Status: 501(c)3
Highest Offering: Master's
Accreditation: SC

01 President ... Dr. Beverly W. HOGAN
05 Int Provost/VP of Academic Affairs ... Dr. Asoka SRINIVASSAN
32 Interim VP for Student Affairs ... Ms. Gladys JONES
30 Vice Pres Institutional Advance ... Dr. Delores Bolden STAMPS
10 Vice Pres Finance Administration ... Dr. Cynthia MELVIN
18 Vice Pres for Facilities Management ... Mr. Kelle MENOGAN
84 Asst VP for Enrollment Management ... Ms. Linda DANIELS
35 Asst Vice Pres for Student Affairs ... Vacant
08 Director of Library Services ... Mrs. Orthella P. MOMAN
13 Chief Information Officer ... Ms. Denese CARROLL
37 Director of Student Financial Aid ... Ms. Maria THOMAS
09 Director Inst Research/Assess/Plng ... Dr. Larry JOHNSON
06 Registrar ... Ms. Carolyn L. EVANS
15 Director Human Resources ... Ms. Doretha PRESLEY
26 Dir Communications/Public Affairs ... Mr. Kendall G. LITTLE
29 Director of Alumni Affairs ... Mrs. Doris BRIDGEMAN
07 Director of Admissions ... Ms. Junoesque JACOBS
36 Director of Career Services ... Ms. Whitney MCDOWELL
44 Director of Advancement Services ... Ms. Johnetta LINDSEY
46 Int Dir of Sponsored Pgms/Research ... Mr. Kerry THOMAS
88 Director of TRiO ... Dr. Valvia WILSON
38 Director of Counseling Services ... Dr. Rosie HARPER
96 Purchasing Agent ... Vacant
102 Dir Corporation & Foundation Rels ... Dr. Motice BRUCE
19 Director Security/Safety ... Ms. Edna DRAKE
39 Director Student Housing ... Mr. Albert GOINS
101 Secretary of the Institution/Board ... Mrs. Brenda H. WILSON
104 Director Study Abroad ... Ms. Diedra WINTER
105 Director Web Services ... Ms. Virginia VARDAMAN
41 Athletic Director ... Dr. James C. COLEMAN

University of Mississippi (B)

P.O. Box 1848, University MS 38677
County: Lafayette FICE Identification: 002440
Unit ID: 176017
Telephone: (662) 915-7211 Carnegie Class: DU-Highest
FAX Number: (662) 915-7010 Calendar System: Semester
URL: www.olemiss.edu
Established: 1844 Annual Undergrad Tuition & Fees (In-State): $7,444
Enrollment: 22,503 Coed
Affiliation or Control: State IRS Status: 501(c)3
Highest Offering: Doctorate
Accreditation: SC, ART, BUS, BUSA, CACREP, CLPSY, CS, DIETC, DIETD, ENG, FEPAC, JOUR, LAW, MUS, NRPA, PHAR, SP, SW, TED, THEA

01 Chancellor ... Dr. Jeffrey S. VITTER
05 Senior Associate Provost ... Dr. Noel E. WILKIN
10 Vice Chanc Administration & Finance ... Mr. Larry D. SPARKS
26 Int VC for University Relations ... Dr. Alice CLARK
32 Vice Chancellor for Student Affairs ... Dr. Brandi HEPHNER LABANC
46 Int VC Research/Sponsored Programs ... Dr. Josh GLADDEN
35 Asst VC Student Affs/Dean Students ... Dr. Melinda SUTTON
51 Assoc Prov/Dir Outreach/Cont Stds ... Dr. Tony AMMETER
06 Asst Provost & Registrar ... Dr. Charlotte Fant PEGUES
85 Ast Prov/Ast to Chanc Multicul Affs ... Dr. Donald R. COLE
08 Dean of Libraries ... Ms. Cecilia BOTERO
13 Chief Information Officer ... Dr. Kathryn F. GATES
30 Chief Development Officer ... Ms. Deborah S. VAUGHN
29 Exec Director of Alumni Affairs ... Mr. Kurt PURDOM
37 Director of Financial Aid ... Mrs. Laura DIVEN-BROWN
36 Director of Career Center ... Ms. Toni D. AVANT
41 Director Intercollegiate Athletics ... Mr. Ross BJORK
15 AVC/Dir of Human Res & Contr Svcs ... Mr. Clayton H. JONES
18 Director of Facilities Management ... Mr. Ashton PEARSON
19 Dir/Chief Univ Police/Campus Safety ... Mr. Tim POTTS
38 Dir of University Counseling Center ... Dr. Quinton T. EDWARDS, JR.
23 Director University Health Services ... Dr. Travis W. YATES
39 AVC Student Affs/Dir Stdnt Housing ... Mr. Lionel MATEN
09 Int Director Institutional Research ... Ms. Tiffany GREGORY
22 Dir Equal Oppty/Reg Compliance ... Ms. Rebecca B. BRESSLER
04 Assistant to the Chancellor ... Mrs. Sue T. KEISER
43 General Counsel ... Mr. Lee TYNER
96 Director of Procurement Services ... Ms. Rachel R. BOST
06 Associate Registrar ... Mrs. Denise KNIGHTON
21 Controller ... Mrs. Nina JONES
07 Director of Admissions ... Mr. Whitman SMITH
50 Dean School of Business Admin ... Dr. Kendall B. CYREE
49 Dean College of Liberal Arts ... Dr. Lee COHEN
81 Dean School of Applied Sciences ... Dr. Velmer S. BURTON, JR.
53 Dean School of Education ... Dr. David ROCK
54 Dean School of Engineering ... Dr. Alex CHENG
61 Interim Dean School of Law ... Dr. Deborah H. BELL
67 Dean of the School of Pharmacy ... Dr. David D. ALLEN
88 Dean School of Accountancy ... Dr. W. Mark WILDER
60 Dean Meek Sch Journalism/New Media ... Dr. H. Will NORTON
58 Int Dean of the Graduate School ... Dr. Christy M. WYANDT
92 Dean of SM Barksdale Honors College ... Dr. Douglass SULLIVAN-GONZALEZ
86 Spec Asst to Chanc Govt Affairs ... Mr. Perry SANSING
88 University Ombudsman ... Mrs. Brett HARRIS
88 Director of Audit ... Ms. Tanya SATTERFIELD

University of Mississippi Medical Center (C)

2500 N State Street, Jackson MS 39216-4505
County: Hinds FICE Identification: 004688
Unit ID: 176026
Telephone: (601) 984-1000 Carnegie Class: Not Classified
FAX Number: (601) 984-1013 Calendar System: Semester
URL: www.umc.edu
Established: 1955 Annual Undergrad Tuition & Fees (In-State): N/A
Enrollment: N/A Coed
Affiliation or Control: State IRS Status: 501(c)3
Highest Offering: Doctorate
Accreditation: SC, CAHIIM, DENT, DH, IPSY, MED, MT, NMT, NURSE, OT, PHAR, PTA, RAD

01 Vice Chancellor Health Affairs ... Dr. LouAnn WOODWARD
100 Chief of Staff to Vice Chancellor ... Dr. Brian RUTLEDGE
10 Chief Financial Officer ... Mr. James WENTZ
88 Chief Operating Ofcr Business Opers ... Ms. Reatha CLARK
11 Chief Administrative Officer ... Mr. Jonathan WILSON
46 Associate Vice Chanc Research ... Dr. Richard SUMMERS
05 Assoc VC for Academic Affairs ... Dr. Ralph H. DIDLAKE
23 Assoc Vice Chanc Clinical Affairs ... Dr. Charles O'MARA
17 CEO Univ Hosp & Health Systems ... Mr. Kevin COOK
88 Sr Advisor to VC for External Aff ... Dr. Claude BRUNSON
43 Chief Legal Officer ... Mr. Jeffrey WALKER
28 Chief Diversity & Inclusion Officer ... Dr. Juanyce TAYLOR
52 Vice Dean for Medical Educ SOM ... Dr. Loretta JACKSON-WILLIAMS
66 Dean School of Nursing ... Dr. Kim HOOVER
58 Dean Sch Grad Stds Health Sciences ... Dr. Joey GRANGER
76 Dean Sch Health Related Profess ... Dr. Jessica H. BAILEY
52 Dean of School of Dentistry ... Dr. David A. FELTON
66 Dean School Population Health ... Dr. Bettina BEECH
67 Assoc Dean for Clinical Affrs/SOPH ... Dr. Leigh A. ROSS

University of Phoenix Jackson Campus (D)

120 Stone Creek Blvd, Suite 200, Flowood MS 39232-8205
Telephone: (601) 664-9500 Identification: 770215
Accreditation: &NH, ACBSP

† No longer accepting campus-based students.

University of Southern Mississippi (E)

118 College Drive, #5001, Hattiesburg MS 39406-0001
County: Forrest FICE Identification: 002441
Unit ID: 176372
Telephone: (601) 266-1000 Carnegie Class: DU-Higher
FAX Number: (601) 266-5756 Calendar System: Semester
URL: www.usm.edu
Established: 1910 Annual Undergrad Tuition & Fees (In-State): $7,334
Enrollment: 14,792 Coed
Affiliation or Control: State IRS Status: 501(c)3
Highest Offering: Doctorate
Accreditation: SC, AAFCS, ANEST, ART, AUD, BUS, BUSA, CAATE, CIDA, CLPSY, CONST, CCPSY, CS, DANCE, DIETD, DIETI, ENGT, JOUR, KIN, LIB, MFCD, MT, MUS, NURSE, PH, PHLEB, SCPSY, SP, SW, TED, THEA

01 President ... Dr. Rodney D. BENNETT
04 Assistant to the President ... Ms. Chrissa MCLEOD
05 Provost & VP for Academic Affairs ... Dr. Steven MOSER
10 VP of Finance & Administration ... Dr. Douglas VINZANT
12 VP for Gulf Coast Campus ... Dr. Steven G. MILLER
32 Vice President for Student Affairs ... Dr. Thomas BURKE
30 Vice President Advancement ... Vacant
108 Assoc Prov Assessment/Accreditation ... Dr. William W. POWELL
46 Vice President Research ... Dr. Gordon CANNON
84 Assoc VP Enrollment Management ... Ms. Becky VINZANT
35 Assoc Vice President Student Affs ... Mr. Sid GONSOULIN
53 Dean College Education/Psychology ... Dr. Ann BLACKWELL
49 Dean College Arts & Letters ... Dr. Maureen RYAN
50 Dean College Business ... Dr. Faye GILBERT
66 Dean College Nursing ... Dr. Katherine NUGENT
72 Dean College Science/Technology ... Dr. David HAYHURST
92 Dean of Honors College ... Dr. Ellen WEINAUER
76 Dean College Health ... Dr. Michael FORSTER
58 Dean Graduate School ... Dr. Karen COATS
08 Dean/University Librarian ... Dr. John EYE
18 Asst VP Planning & Facilities Mgmt ... Dr. Chris CRENSHAW
13 Chief Information Officer ... Mr. David SLIMAN
41 Director Intercollegiate Athletics ... Mr. Bill MCGILLIS
06 Registrar ... Mr. Greg PIERCE
25 Asst VP for Research Administration ... Ms. Marcia LANDEN
09 Director of Institutional Research ... Dr. Michelle ARRINGTON
45 Dir of Institutional Effectiveness ... Mrs. Kathryn LOWERY
29 Alumni Activities/Exec Director ... Mr. Jerry DEFATTA
36 Director Career Services ... Mr. Russell ANDERSON
21 Asc VP for Finance & Controller ... Ms. Allyson EASTERWOOD
22 Title IX Coordinator ... Dr. Rebecca MALLEY
38 Director of Counseling Center ... Dr. Deena CRAWFORD
23 Director of Health Services ... Dr. Virginia CRAWFORD
39 Director of Residence Life ... Dr. Scott BLACKWELL
15 Associate VP of Human Resources ... Mrs. Linda RASMUSSEN
96 Director Procurement & Contracts ... Mr. Steve BALLEW
07 Interim Director of Admissions ... Ms. Susan W. SCOTT
26 Chief Communication Officer ... Mr. James P. COLL
88 Asst to Pres Military/Vet Stdnt Aff ... Gen. Jeff HAMMOND
102 Exec Dir USM Foundation ... Ms. Stace L. MERCIER
104 Assoc VP for Intl Programs ... Dr. Daniel NORTON
106 Interim Dir Learn Enhancement Ctr ... Dr. Tom HUTCHINSON
19 Chief of Police ... Mr. Bob HOPKINS
43 Dir Legal Services/General Counsel ... Mr. Robert D. GHOLSON
86 Exec Asst to Pres External Affairs ... Mr. Chad DRISKELL
37 Director Student Financial Aid ... Mr. David WILLIAMSON

Virginia College (F)

920 Cedar Lake Road, Biloxi MS 39532-2107
Telephone: (228) 546-9100 Identification: 666073
Accreditation: ACICS, MAAB, SURGT

† Branch campus of Virginia College, Birmingham, AL.

Virginia College (G)

5841 Ridgewood Road, Jackson MS 39211
Telephone: (601) 977-0960 Identification: 666032
Accreditation: ACICS, MAAB, SURGT

† Branch campus of Virginia College, Birmingham, AL.

Wesley Biblical Seminary (H)

787 E Northside Drive, Jackson MS 39206-4945
County: Hinds FICE Identification: 025162
Unit ID: 176451
Telephone: (601) 366-8880 Carnegie Class: Spec-4-yr-Faith
FAX Number: (601) 366-8832 Calendar System: Semester
URL: www.wbs.edu
Established: 1974 Annual Graduate Tuition & Fees: N/A
Enrollment: 51 Coed
Affiliation or Control: Interdenominational IRS Status: 501(c)3
Highest Offering: Master's; No Undergraduates
Accreditation: THEOL

01 President ... Dr. John E. NEIHOF, JR.
05 VP Academic Affairs/Academic Dean ... Dr. Gareth COCKERILL
10 Director Business Affairs ... Ms. Peggy PRICE
07 Exec VP Recruitment/Student Svcs ... Rev. Rob POCAI
30 Vice President Development ... Mr. John GAINEY
08 Director of Library Services ... Ms. Jane STAUBLE
18 Director of Operations ... Mr. Ken MONEY
06 Registrar/Director Financial Aid ... Mr. Karl LUMAN

William Carey University (I)

498 Tuscan Avenue, Hattiesburg MS 39401-5461
County: Forrest FICE Identification: 002447
Unit ID: 176479
Telephone: (601) 318-6051 Carnegie Class: Masters/L
FAX Number: (601) 318-6494 Calendar System: Trimester
URL: www.wmcarey.edu
Established: 1892 Annual Undergrad Tuition & Fees: $11,700
Enrollment: 3,936 Coed
Affiliation or Control: Southern Baptist IRS Status: 501(c)3
Highest Offering: Doctorate
Accreditation: SC, MUS, NURSE, OSTEO, @PTA, TED

01 President/Chief Executive Officer ... Dr. Tommy KING
03 Provost ... Dr. Scott HUMMEL
05 Vice President of Academic Affairs ... Dr. Garry M. BRELAND
10 Vice Pres Business Affs/CFO ... Mr. Grant GUTHRIE
32 Vice Pres for Student Support ... Mrs. Valerie BRIDGEFORTH
46 Vice President Inst Effectiveness ... Dr. Bennie R. CROCKETT
30 Chief Advancement Officer ... Mrs. Monica MARLOWE
63 Dean College Osteopathic Medicine ... Dr. James TURNER
12 Admin Dean Tradition Campus ... Mr. Gerald BRACEY
50 Dean School of Business ... Dr. Cheryl DALE
53 Dean School of Education ... Dr. Benjamin BURNETT
83 Dean Sch Natural/Behavioral Science ... Dr. Frank BAUGH
66 Dean School of Nursing ... Dr. Janet WILLIAMS
49 Dean School of Arts & Letters ... Dr. Myron NOONKESTER
64 Dean School of Music & Ministry ... Dr. Don ODOM
73 Chair School of Ministry Studies ... Dr. Daniel CALDWELL
84 Dean of Enrollment Management ... Mr. William N. CURRY
58 Dean of Graduate Studies ... Dr. Frank BAUGH
20 Academic Dean for Tradition ... Dr. Cassandra CONNOR
09 Director of Institutional Research ... Mrs. Susan CURRY
06 Registrar ... Mrs. Gayle KNIGHT
08 Director of Libraries ... Mr. Reese POWELL
29 Alumni Director ... Mrs. Pam SHEARER
26 Chief Public Relations Officer ... Vacant
13 Director of Information Technology ... Mr. Jeff ANDREWS
92 Director of Honors Program ... Dr. Jay RICHARDSON
21 Director of Budget Management ... Mr. Grant GUTHRIE
41 Athletic Director ... Mr. Steven H. KNIGHT
18 Dir Facilities/Grounds/Maintenance ... Mr. Robert BLEVINS

21 Dir Business Svcs Tradition Campus ....Mr. Gerald BRACEY
12 Director of Keesler Center ....Ms. Amanda KNESAL
15 Director Personnel Services ....Ms. Deidre SHOWS
19 Director Campus Security ....Mr. Bob BLEVINS
88 Coord of Instructional Technology ....Mr. David J. BROCKWAY
12 Coordinator New Orleans Campus ....Vacant
07 Director of Admissions ....Mrs. Alissa KING

MISSOURI

A. T. Still University of Health Sciences (A)

800 W Jefferson Street, Kirksville MO 63501-1497
County: Adair FICE Identification: 002477
Unit ID: 177834
Telephone: (660) 626-2391 Carnegie Class: Spec-4-yr-Med
FAX Number: (660) 626-2672 Calendar System: Semester
URL: www.atsu.edu
Established: 1892 Annual Graduate Tuition & Fees: N/A
Enrollment: 3,226 Coed
Affiliation or Control: Independent Non-Profit IRS Status: 501(c)3
Highest Offering: First Professional Degree; No Undergraduates
Accreditation: NH, DENT, OSTEO, PH

01 President ....Dr. Craig PHELPS
05 Sr VP Academic Affairs ....Dr. Norman GEVITZ
63 Dean KCOM ....Dr. Margaret WILSON
32 VP Student Affairs ....Mrs. Lori HAXTON
30 VP University Advancement ....Dr. Shaun SOMMERER
43 VP & General Counsel ....Mr. Matthew HEEREN
46 VP Inst Res Grants & Info Systems ....Dr. John HEARD
52 Dean MO Sch of Dentistry/Oral Hlth ....Dr. Dwight MCLEOD
88 Dean Col of Graduate Hlth Studies ....Dr. Don ALTMAN
52 Dean AZ Sch of Dentistry/Oral Hlth ....Dr. Jack DILLENBERG
76 Dean AZ Sch of Health Sciences ....Dr. Randy DANIELSEN
63 Dean Sch of Osteo Med in AZ ....Dr. Jeffrey MORGAN
10 Vice President Finance/CFO ....Mr. Rick RIEDER
35 Assoc VP AZ Student Affairs ....Mrs. Beth POPPRE
13 Asst VP Info Technologies/Services ....Mr. Bryan KRUSNIAK
07 Asst VP Admissions ....Dr. David KOENECKE
88 VP Strategic Univ Partnerships ....Dr. Gary CLOUD
88 Sr VP Strategic Univ Initiatives ....Dr. O.T WENDEL
25 Associate VP Sponsored Programs ....Mrs. Gaylah SUBLETTE
04 Asst to Pres & Secretary to BoT ....Mrs. Norine EITEL
06 Registrar ....Dr. Deanna HUNSAKER
08 Director Library ....Mr. Michael KRONENFIELD
15 Asst VP Human Resources ....Mrs. Donna BROWN
18 Director Facilities/Plant Operation ....Mr. Robert EHRLICH
22 Affirmative Action Officer ....Mrs. Donna BROWN
37 Dir Student Financial Assistance ....Mr. Steven JORDEN
38 Director Student Counseling ....Mr. Thomas VAN VLECK
96 Director Purchasing ....Mr. Corey LOUDER
19 Director Security ....Mr. Bob FRAIZER
28 Director of Diversity ....Mr. Clinton NORMORE
20 Associate VP/SVP Academic Affairs ....Dr. Ann BOYLE
44 Associate VP University Advancement ....Mr. Randy ROGERS
88 Assistant VP/SVP Academic Affairs ....Dr. Leonard GOLDSTEIN
21 Assistant VP for Finance ....Mrs. Tonya GRIMM
09 Director AT Still Research Insti ....Dr. Brian DEGENHARDT

† Arizona campus accreditation includes ARPCA, AUD, DENT, OSTEO, OT, PTA.

American Business & Technology University (B)

1018 West Saint Maartens Drive, Saint Joseph MO 64506
County: Buchanan FICE Identification: 041187
Unit ID: 457688
Telephone: (816) 279-7000 Carnegie Class: Bac/Assoc-Assoc Dom
FAX Number: (888) 890-8190 Calendar System: Other
URL: www.abtu.edu
Established: 2001 Annual Undergrad Tuition & Fees: N/A
Enrollment: 580 Coed
Affiliation or Control: Proprietary IRS Status: Proprietary
Highest Offering: Master's
Accreditation: DEAC

01 President ....Mr. Sam ATIEH
11 Vice President ....Mr. Lute ATIEH
45 VP of Strategic Initiatives ....Mr. Eddie COLON
37 VP of Financial Aid ....Dr. Michael CAMPBELL
13 Chief Information Officer ....Mr. Ramsey ATIEH
10 Chief Financial Officer ....Mr. Dan MARLOW
05 Director Of Education ....Dr. Luanne HAGGARD
20 Assoc Dean of Undergrad Programs ....Dr. Donald LADER
108 Director of Compliance ....Mr. Chad BREAZILE
06 Registrar ....Mrs. Kourtney DRAKE
07 Director of Admissions ....Mr. Richard LINGLE

American Trade School (C)

3925 Industrial Drive, Saint Ann MO 63074
County: Saint Louis FICE Identification: 041748
Unit ID: 461573
Telephone: (314) 423-1900 Carnegie Class: Not Classified
FAX Number: (314) 423-1911 Calendar System: Quarter
URL: www.americantradeschool.edu
Established: 2003 Annual Undergrad Tuition & Fees: N/A
Enrollment: 113 Coed
Affiliation or Control: Proprietary IRS Status: Proprietary
Highest Offering: Associate Degree
Accreditation: ACCSC

01 Campus President ....Mr. Turner BROOK

Aquinas Institute of Theology (D)

23 S Spring Avenue, Saint Louis MO 63108-3323
County: City of Saint Louis FICE Identification: 001632
Unit ID: 176600
Telephone: (314) 256-8800 Carnegie Class: Spec-4-yr-Faith
FAX Number: (314) 256-8888 Calendar System: Semester
URL: www.ai.edu
Established: 1951 Annual Graduate Tuition & Fees: N/A
Enrollment: 156 Coed
Affiliation or Control: Roman Catholic IRS Status: 501(c)3
Highest Offering: Doctorate; No Undergraduates
Accreditation: THEOL

01 President ....Rev. Sean MARTIN
05 Academic Dean ....Rev. Gregory HEILLE
10 Director of Finance ....Mr. Thomas BARBARAK
06 Registrar ....Mrs. Erin HAMMOND
30 Director of Inst Advancement ....Mrs. Stacey KRIEG
32 Director of Student Services ....Mr. Kevin SWEENEY
07 Director Admissions ....Mr. David WERTHMANN
26 Dir Communications/Financial Aid ....Mrs. Jan LINGUA

The Art Institute of St. Louis (E)

1520 South Fifth Street, Suite 107,
Saint Charles MO 63303
Telephone: (636) 688-9281 Identification: 770738
Accreditation: #ACICS

† In teach-out mode.

Assemblies of God Theological Seminary (F)

1435 N Glenstone Avenue, Springfield MO 65802-2131
County: Greene FICE Identification: 012120
Unit ID: 176619
Telephone: (417) 268-1000 Carnegie Class: Spec-4-yr-Faith
FAX Number: (417) 268-1001 Calendar System: Semester
URL: www.agts.edu
Established: 1972 Annual Graduate Tuition & Fees: N/A
Enrollment: 327 Coed
Affiliation or Control: Assemblies Of God Church IRS Status: 501(c)3
Highest Offering: Doctorate; No Undergraduates
Accreditation: THEOL

01 President ....Dr. Mark A. HAUSFELD
05 Seminary Dean ....Dr. James H. RAILEY
20 Associate Dean ....Dr. Paul W. LEWIS
58 Dir Intercultural Doctoral Studies ....Dr. DeLonn L. RANCE
58 Dir PhD Biblical Interp & Theol ....Dr. James H. RAILEY
58 Director DMin Program ....Dr. Cheryl A. TAYLOR
42 Director of Spiritual Formation ....Dr. Jay P. TAYLOR
88 Director of Veteran Center ....Mrs. Stormy M. DAVIS
26 Marketing Manager ....Mrs. Jennifer S. HALL
08 Asst Director of Library Services ....Mr. Rick E. OLIVER
06 Registrar ....Mrs. Connie S. CROSS
37 Financial Aid Coordinator ....Mr. Brian L. HAWK
29 Coord of Institutional & Alum Rels ....Ms. Deborah A. FEGLER

† The Seminary continues to offer its educational programs as a distinct unit within the consolidated Evangel University, Springfield, MO.

Avila University (G)

11901 Wornall Road, Kansas City MO 64145-9990
County: Jackson FICE Identification: 002449
Unit ID: 176628
Telephone: (816) 942-8400 Carnegie Class: Masters/M
FAX Number: (816) 942-3362 Calendar System: Semester
URL: www.avila.edu
Established: 1916 Annual Undergrad Tuition & Fees: $26,450
Enrollment: 1,907 Coed
Affiliation or Control: Roman Catholic IRS Status: 501(c)3
Highest Offering: Master's
Accreditation: NH, IACBE, NURSE, RAD, SW

01 President ....Dr. Ron SLEPITZA
05 Provost/VP of Academic Affairs ....Dr. Cathryn PRIDAL
20 VP Instl Effectiveness/Info Svcs ....Dr. Sue KING
10 Vice Pres for Finance/Admin Svcs ....Mr. Paul TOLER
26 Sr Dir Marketing/Communications ....Mr. Darren ROUBINEK
30 Chief Development Officer ....Ms. Angela HEER
32 AVP Student Development/Success ....Darby GOUGH
84 VP for Enrollment & Athletics ....Mr. Brandon JOHNSON
06 Registrar ....Ms. Michelle DRISCOLL
08 Librarian ....Ms. Kathleen FINEGAN
37 Director of Financial Aid ....Ms. Crystal BRUNTZ
42 Dir Mission Effect & Campus Ministr ....Mr. David M. ARMSTRONG
21 Controller ....Mr. Joseph H. SJUTS
29 Director Alumni ....Mrs. Bailey CARR
41 Assistant Athletic Director ....Mrs. Cristina COWAN
15 Director of Human Resources ....Ms. Janet MCMANUS
18 Chief Facilities/Physical Plant ....Mr. Mike STUCKEY
40 Bookstore Manager ....Mr. John A. TARANTO
38 Coord Counseling & Career Services ....Ms. Elizabeth MCKINLEY

Baptist Bible College (H)

628 E Kearney St, Springfield MO 65803-3498
County: Greene FICE Identification: 013208
Unit ID: 176664
Telephone: (417) 268-6000 Carnegie Class: Spec-4-yr-Faith
FAX Number: (800) 819-8330 Calendar System: Semester
URL: www.gobbc.edu
Established: 1950 Annual Undergrad Tuition & Fees: $9,894
Enrollment: 373 Coed
Affiliation or Control: Baptist IRS Status: 501(c)3
Highest Offering: First Professional Degree
Accreditation: #NH, BI

01 President ....Mr. Mark L. MILIONI
05 Vice President of Academic Affairs ....Dr. Greg T. CHRISTOPHER
10 Chief Financial Officer ....Mr. Jason L. TODD
32 Vice President of Student Affairs ....Mr. Nathaniel S. HARMON
18 Chief Facilities/Physical Plant ....Mr. Chris C. WILLIAMS
06 Registrar ....Mr. Terry A. ALLCORN
07 Dir Enrollment Services ....Mr. John DECKER
37 Director of Financial Aid ....Mr. Brian RAINS
39 Director of Resident Life ....Mr. Bill J. LEVERGOOD
15 Director of Human Resources ....Mrs. Brooke YORK
19 Director Security/Safety ....Mr. Glenn COZZENS
41 Athletic Director ....Mr. Jordan SHORT
40 Virtual Bookstore ....Mrs. Julie BECK
08 Director of Library Services ....Mr. Jon JONES
51 Dean of Continuing Education ....Ms. Cheryl PAGE

Bolivar Technical College (I)

1135 North Oakland Avenue, Bolivar MO 65613
Telephone: (417) 777-5062 Identification: 667033
Accreditation: ACICS

Brookes Bible College (J)

10257 St. Charles Rock Road, St. Ann MO 63074
County: St. Louis Identification: 667137
Telephone: (314) 773-0083 Carnegie Class: Not Classified
FAX Number: (314) 736-6293 Calendar System: Semester
URL: www.brookesbible.org
Established: 1909 Annual Undergrad Tuition & Fees: N/A
Enrollment: N/A Coed
Affiliation or Control: Independent Non-Profit IRS Status: 501(c)3
Highest Offering: Associate Degree
Accreditation: @BI

01 Interim President ....Rev. Robert D. THURMAN, JR.
05 Academic/Student Dean ....Dr. Allan HENDERSON
10 Chief Financial Officer ....Mr. Timothy SCHILLER
07 Director of Admissions ....Mr. Joshua CLUTTERHAM

Brown Mackie College-St. Louis (K)

2 Soccer Park Road, Fenton MO 63026-2564
Telephone: (636) 651-3290 Identification: 666793
Accreditation: ACICS, OTA, SURTEC

† Branch campus of Brown Mackie College, Tucson, AZ.

Bryan University (L)

3215 LeMone Industrial Boulevard, Columbia MO 65201
Telephone: (573) 777-5550 Identification: 770725
Accreditation: ACICS

† Branch campus of Bryan University, Springfield, MO.

Bryan University (M)

4255 Nature Center Way, Springfield MO 65804
County: Greene FICE Identification: 030663
Unit ID: 369516
Telephone: (417) 862-5700 Carnegie Class: Bac/Assoc-Mixed
FAX Number: (417) 865-7144 Calendar System: Other
URL: www.bryanu.edu
Established: 1982 Annual Undergrad Tuition & Fees: $15,427
Enrollment: 322 Coed
Affiliation or Control: Proprietary IRS Status: Proprietary
Highest Offering: Master's
Accreditation: ACICS

01 Executive Director ....Mr. Scott HAAR

Calvary University (N)

15800 Calvary Road, Kansas City MO 64147-1341
County: Cass FICE Identification: 002450
Unit ID: 176789
Telephone: (816) 322-0110 Carnegie Class: Spec-4-yr-Faith
FAX Number: (816) 331-4474 Calendar System: Semester
URL: www.calvary.edu
Established: 1932 Annual Undergrad Tuition & Fees: $11,320
Enrollment: 314 Coed
Affiliation or Control: Independent Non-Profit IRS Status: 501(c)3
Highest Offering: First Professional Degree
Accreditation: NH, BI

01 President/CEO ....Dr. Christopher CONE

10 Vice President of Operations ....Mr. Randy GRIMM
05 Vice President of Academics ....Dr. Teddy BITNER
30 Vice President of Development ....Dr. Skip HESSEL
32 Vice President of Student Services .....Mr. Cory D. TROWBRIDGE
34 Dean of Women ....Miss Arely PEREZ
07 Director of Admissions ....Mr. Brian MASON
08 Head Librarian ....Miss Hannah BITNER
58 Dir of Adult & Graduate Studies ....Mr. Mike PIBURN
18 Director of Maintenance ....Vacant
41 Athletic Director ....Miss Jeanette REGIER
91 Director Administrative Computing ....Mr. Aaron HEATH
38 Director Biblical Counsel/Educ Ctr ....Dr. Mark HAGER
19 Director of Security ....Mr. Glenn WILLIAMS
37 Director of Financial Aid ....Mr. Robert CRANK
26 Director of Public Relations/Market ....Mr. Jeff CAMPA
09 Institutional Research Coordinator ....Mr. Charles KURTZ
15 Human Resources Coordinator ....Mrs. Jolayne ROGERS
29 Alumni Relations Coordinator ....Mrs. Sara KLAASSEN
88 Director of The Learning Center ....Dr. Terri STRICKER
42 Director of Christian Ministries ....Mr. Joe EVERETT
109 Director of Food Service ....Mr. Joe DAPRA
04 Administrative Asst to President ....Mrs. Maryjean SPRY
105 Director Web Services ....Vacant
106 Dir Online Education/E-learning ....Mr. Mike PIBURN
44 Director Annual or Planned Giving ....Mr. Mervin WAGNER
50 Program Director Business ....Dr. Skip HESSEL
53 Dept Chair Education ....Ms. Rose HENNESS

Central Christian College of the Bible (A)

911 E Urbandale Drive, Moberly MO 65270-1997

County: Randolph FICE Identification: 022664
Unit ID: 176910
Telephone: (660) 263-3900 Carnegie Class: Spec-4-yr-Faith
FAX Number: (660) 263-3936 Calendar System: Semester
URL: www.cccb.edu
Established: 1957 Annual Undergrad Tuition & Fees: $11,900
Enrollment: 290 Coed
Affiliation or Control: Christian Churches And Churches of Christ
IRS Status: 501(c)3
Highest Offering: Baccalaureate
Accreditation: @NH, BI

01 President ....Dr. David B. FINCHER
05 Academic Dean ....Dr. Eric A. STEVENS
10 VP of Business & Finance ....Mrs. Lara LAWRENCE
07 Admissions Counselor ....Mr. Dylan HAYES
07 Executive Director of Admissions ....Mr. Rocky CHRISTENSEN
88 Director of Stewardship ....Mr. Alan G. WILSON
04 Exec Assistant to the President ....Mrs. Sherry L. WALLIS
32 Exec Dir of Student Development ....Mr. Darryl C. AMMON
34 Dean of Women ....Ms. Anne P. MENEAR
41 Athletic Director ....Mr. Jack DEFREITAS
08 Head Librarian ....Mrs. Patty A. AGEE
06 Registrar ....Vacant
37 Director of Financial Aid ....Mrs. Rhonda J. DUNHAM
13 Director of Information Technology ....Mr. Aaron MERRITT
18 Physical Plant Manager ....Mr. Mark E. DUNHAM
40 Bookstore Manager ....Mrs. Kelly HARDING
35 Director of Student Services ....Mrs. Lori PETER
39 Residence Director - Women ....Mrs. Anne MENEAR
39 Residence Director - Men ....Mr. Rocky CHRISTENSEN
21 Director of Accounting ....Mr. Matt DOUGLASS
33 Dean of Men ....Mr. Aaron P. WELCH
101 Secretary of the Institution/Board ....Mr. Ronald SELF
106 Online Education Coordinator ....Mr. James FRANKE

† Onsite students accepted into a degree or certificate program will receive Full-Tuition Scholarship which equals cost of tuition up to 18 hrs/semester. Scholarship may be reduced from deficiencies in grades, Christian service, or chapel attendance.

Central Methodist University (B)

411 Central Methodist Square, Fayette MO 65248-1198

County: Howard FICE Identification: 002453
Unit ID: 445267
Telephone: (660) 248-3391 Carnegie Class: Masters/S
FAX Number: (660) 248-2287 Calendar System: 4/1/4
URL: www.centralmethodist.edu
Established: 1854 Annual Undergrad Tuition & Fees: $5,280
Enrollment: 4,537 Coed
Affiliation or Control: United Methodist IRS Status: 501(c)3
Highest Offering: Master's
Accreditation: NH, #CAATE, MUS, NURSE, @PTAA

01 President ....Dr. Roger D. DRAKE
05 Provost ....Dr. Rita GULSTAD
13 VP Technology & Planning ....Mr. Chad GAINES
30 VP Advancement/Alumni Rels ....Dr. Joshua JACOBS
32 VP Instl Growth/Student Engagement ....Mr. Kenneth R. OLIVER
10 VP Finance & Administration ....Ms. Julee SHERMAN
20 Assoc Dean for Academics/Assessment ....Vacant
08 Director of Information Resources ....Ms. Cynthia DUDENHOFFER
37 Director of Financial Assistance ....Ms. Kristen GIBBS
29 Exec Dir Advancement & Alumni Pgm ......Mr. David HUTCHISON
44 Dir Annual Giving & Advance Opers ....Ms. Jackie JACKSON
07 Director of Admission ....Mr. Adam JENKINS
09 Institutional Research/Reporting ....Ms. Amber MONNIG
26 Exec Dir Marketing Communications ....Mr. Kent PROPST
04 Administrative Asst to President ....Ms. Catherine SHANAHAN

41 Athletic Director ....Mr. Brian SPELBAUER
15 Director of Human Resources ....Ms. Kimberly THOMSON
06 Registrar ....Ms. Kathryn WINEGARD
18 Chief Facilities/Physical Plant ....Mr. Derry WISWALL
36 Director Student Placement ....Ms. Nicolette YEVICH

Chamberlain College of Nursing-St. Louis (C)

11830 Westline Industrial, Ste 106, St. Louis MO 63146

Telephone: (314) 991-6200 Identification 770494
Accreditation: &NH, NURSE

† Regional accreditation is carried under the parent institution in Addison, IL

City Vision University (D)

3101 Troost Ave. Suite 200, Kansas City MO 64109-1845

County: United States FICE Identification: 041191
Unit ID: 457697
Telephone: (816) 960-2008 Carnegie Class: Bac-Diverse
FAX Number: (816) 256-8471 Calendar System: Other
URL: www.cityvision.edu
Established: 1998 Annual Undergrad Tuition & Fees: $6,000
Enrollment: 80 Coed
Affiliation or Control: Other IRS Status: 501(c)3
Highest Offering: Master's
Accreditation: DEAC

01 Executive Director/President ....Dr. Andrew SEARS
88 Dean Sch of Ministry & Social Svcs ....Dr. Melissa PATTON
50 Dean of School of Business ....Dr. Joy VANN-HAMILTON
10 Financial Accounting
Manager ....Mrs. AnnMarie CAMERON-THOMPSON
07 Director of Admissions ....Ms. Nancy YOUNG

† Mail address is 31 Torrey St, Dorchester, MA 02124-3543.

College of the Ozarks (E)

PO Box 17, Point Lookout MO 65726-0017

County: Taney FICE Identification: 002500
Unit ID: 178697
Telephone: (417) 334-6411 Carnegie Class: Bac-Diverse
FAX Number: (417) 335-2618 Calendar System: Semester
URL: www.cofo.edu
Established: 1906 Annual Undergrad Tuition & Fees: $18,730
Enrollment: 1,433 Coed
Affiliation or Control: Independent Non-Profit IRS Status: 501(c)3
Highest Offering: Baccalaureate
Accreditation: NH, ACFEI, DIETD, NURSE

01 President ....Dr. Jerry C. DAVIS
03 Vice President ....Dr. Howell W. KEETER
05 VP for Academic Affairs ....Dr. Eric BOLGER
30 Director of Development ....Mrs. Natalie RASNICK
10 Chief Financial Officer ....Mr. Charles F. HUGHES
11 Dean of Administration ....Dr. Marvin SCHOENECKE
103 Dean of Work Education ....Dr. Chris LARSEN
32 Dean of Student Services ....Mr. Nick SHARP
07 VP for Patriotic Activities ....Dr. Marci LINSON
42 VP of Christian Ministries ....Dr. Justin CARSWELL
88 VP Cultural Affs/Dean Character Ed ....Dr. Sue HEAD
06 Registrar ....Dr. Fran FORMAN
29 Director of Alumni Affairs ....Mrs. Angela WILLIAMSON
36 Director of Career Placement ....Mr. Jim FREEMAN
37 Director of Financial Aid ....Mr. Jeff FORD
26 Director of Public Relations ....Mrs. Valorie COLEMAN
96 Director of Purchasing ....Mr. Kurt MCDONALD
38 Student Counseling ....Mrs. Pat MCLEAN
04 Administrative Asst to President ....Ms. Elizabeth HUDSON
13 Chief Info Technology Officer ....Ms. Debbie HENDERSON
18 Chief Facilities/Physical Plant ....Mr. Jody BRASWELL
41 Athletic Director ....Mr. Steve SHEPHERD
08 Head Librarian ....Ms. Gwen SIMMONS
19 Director Security/Safety ....Mr. Robert BRIDGES

Columbia College (F)

1001 Rogers Street, Columbia MO 65216-0001

County: Boone FICE Identification: 002456
Unit ID: 177065
Telephone: (573) 875-8700 Carnegie Class: Masters/L
FAX Number: (573) 875-7209 Calendar System: Semester
URL: www.ccis.edu
Established: 1851 Annual Undergrad Tuition & Fees: $8,240
Enrollment: 16,567 Coed
Affiliation or Control: Christian Church (Disciples Of Christ)
IRS Status: 501(c)3
Highest Offering: Master's
Accreditation: NH

01 President ....Dr. Scott DALRYMPLE
04 Sr Exec Assistant to the President ....Ms. Mary BROWN
05 Provost/VP Academic Affairs ....Dr. David STARRETT
51 VP Adult Higher Education ....Dr. Jeff MUSGROVE
84 VP of Enrollment & Marketing ....Mr. Kevin PALMER
32 Dean for Student Affairs ....Ms. Faye C. BURCHARD
10 Chief Financial Officer ....Mr. Bruce E. BOYER
30 Exec Director of Advancement ....Ms. Suzanne ROTHWELL
18 Exec Director of Plant/Facilities ....Mr. Cliff JARVIS
27 Executive Director of Marketing ....Mr. Brad WUCHER

07 Director of Admissions ....Ms. Stephanie JOHNSON
06 Registrar ....Ms. Jennifer THORPE
29 Director of Alumni Relations ....Ms. Ann MERRIFIELD
26 Exec Director of Public Relations ....Ms. Suzanne ROTHWELL
37 Director of Financial Aid ....Ms. Sharon A. ABERNATHY
08 Director of Stafford Library ....Ms. Janet CARUTHERS
35 Director of Student Activities ....Ms. Kim COKE
36 Director Career Services Center ....Mr. Dan GOMEZ-PALACIO
15 Executive Director Human Resources ....Ms. Patty FISCHER
23 Director of Health Services ....Ms. Judy WOOD
13 Chief Information Officer ....Mr. Gary STANOWSKI
55 Sr Dir Adult Higher Educ Acad Spprt ......Mr. Eric CUNNINGHAM
58 Associate Dean Graduate Studies ....Vacant
41 Athletic Director ....Mr. Bob P. BURCHARD
09 Director Institutional Research ....Ms. Misty HASKAMP
19 Director of Campus Safety ....Mr. Robert KLAUSMEYER
21 Bursar ....Mr. Randal SCHENEWERK

Conception Seminary College (G)

37174 State Highway VV, PO Box 502,
Conception MO 64433-0502

County: Nodaway FICE Identification: 002467
Unit ID: 177083
Telephone: (660) 944-3105 Carnegie Class: Spec-4-yr-Faith
FAX Number: (660) 944-2829 Calendar System: Semester
URL: www.conception.edu
Established: 1883 Annual Undergrad Tuition & Fees: $20,304
Enrollment: 93 Male
Affiliation or Control: Roman Catholic IRS Status: 501(c)3
Highest Offering: Baccalaureate
Accreditation: NH

01 Rector & President ....Rev. Brendan MOSS
11 Director of Administration ....Mrs. Amy K. SCHIEBER
32 Dean of Students ....Rev. Patrick G. YORK
05 Dean of Academic Affairs ....Dr. William BROWNSBERGER
10 Business Manager/Dir Auxiliary Svcs .....Rev. Benedict T. NEENAN
30 Development Director ....Rev. Benedict T. NEENAN
07 Director of Admissions ....Bro. Luke KRAL
37 Director of Student Financial Aid ....Bro. Justin J. HERNANDEZ
06 Registrar ....Mrs. Jeanette SCHIEBER
29 Director of Alumni ....Rev. Daniel PETSCHE
08 Librarian ....Bro. Thomas SULLIVAN
26 Director of Communications ....Mrs. Jenny HUARD
13 Director of Information Technology ....Mr. Tony MEISTER
38 Director of Counseling Services ....Rev. Duane REINERT
41 Director of Wellness Program ....Mr. Skip SHEAR

Concorde Career College (H)

3239 Broadway Boulevard, Kansas City MO 64111-2407

County: Jackson FICE Identification: 023616
Unit ID: 155283
Telephone: (816) 531-5223 Carnegie Class: Spec-4-yr-Other Health
FAX Number: (816) 756-3231 Calendar System: Other
URL: www.concorde.edu
Established: 1936 Annual Undergrad Tuition & Fees: N/A
Enrollment: 590 Coed
Affiliation or Control: Proprietary IRS Status: Proprietary
Highest Offering: Baccalaureate
Accreditation: ACCSC, CCARC, DH, PTAA

01 President ....Colleen MCDERMOTT
05 Academic Dean ....April RAHE
07 Director Student Recruitment ....Jeff HARRIS

Concordia Seminary (I)

801 Seminary Place, Saint Louis MO 63105-3168

County: Saint Louis FICE Identification: 002457
Unit ID: 177092
Telephone: (314) 505-7000 Carnegie Class: Spec-4-yr-Faith
FAX Number: (314) 505-7001 Calendar System: Quarter
URL: www.csl.edu
Established: 1839 Annual Graduate Tuition & Fees: N/A
Enrollment: 583 Coed
Affiliation or Control: Lutheran Church - Missouri Synod
IRS Status: 501(c)3
Highest Offering: Doctorate; No Undergraduates
Accreditation: NH, THEOL

01 President ....Dr. Dale A. MEYER
03 Executive Vice President ....Mr. Michael LOUIS
05 Provost ....Dr. Jeffrey KLOHA
10 Sr VP for Finance/Administration ....Mr. Chad A. CATTOOR
30 Senior VP for Advancement ....Mrs. Vicki BIGGS
58 Dean of Advanced Studies ....Dr. Gerhard BODE
06 Registrar ....Mrs. Beth R. MENNEKE
08 Director of Library Services ....Rev. Benjamin HAUPT
51 Director Continuing Education ....Rev. Jason BROGE
88 Director Center for Hispanic Study ....Dr. Leopoldo A. SANCHEZ
15 Director of Human Resources ....Mr. Thomas MYERS
18 Director Facilities/Physical Plant ....Vacant
36 Director of Placement ....Rev. Wayne KNOLHOFF
37 Director of Student Financial Aid ....Mrs. Laura HEMMER
13 Chief Information Officer ....Mr. John KLINGER
29 Director of Alumni Relations ....Rev. Wayne KNOLHOFF
04 Executive Asst to President ....Vacant
07 Director of Admissions ....Rev. William WREDE
09 Director of Institutional Research ....Rev. Alan BORCHERDING

Cottey College (A)

1000 W Austin Boulevard, Nevada MO 64772-2763
County: Vernon FICE Identification: 002458
Unit ID: 177117
Telephone: (417) 667-8181 Carnegie Class: Bac/Assoc-Mixed
FAX Number: (417) 667-8103 Calendar System: Semester
URL: www.cottey.edu
Established: 1884 Annual Undergrad Tuition & Fees: $19,300
Enrollment: 269 Female
Affiliation or Control: Independent Non-Profit IRS Status: 501(c)3
Highest Offering: Baccalaureate
Accreditation: NH, MUS

01 President .... Dr. Jann WEITZEL
05 Vice President for Academic Affairs .... Dr. Chioma R. UGOCHUKWU
88 Dir Center Women's Leadership .... Ms. Denise C. HEDGES
36 Coord Career & Transfer Planning .... Ms. Renee HAMPTON
04 Assistant to the President .... Mrs. Tricia BOBBETT
10 VP for Administration & Finance .... Mrs. Amy RUETTEN
30 Int VP Institutional Advancement .... Ms. Sherri TAYLOR
32 VP for Student Life .... Dr. Mari Anne PHILLIPS
42 Dir Spiritual Life & Diversity .... Ms. Erica SIGAUKE
84 VP for Enrollment Management .... Ms. Natalie HERRING
26 Assoc VP for Marketing/Comm .... Ms. Carla FARMER
07 Director of Admissions .... Vacant
06 Registrar .... Ms. Marcia MORTON
08 Library Director .... Ms. Courtney TRAUTWEILER
18 Director Physical Plant/Security .... Mr. Neal R. SWARNES
27 Director of Public Information .... Mr. Steve E. REED
15 Director of Human Resources .... Ms. Betsy A. MCREYNOLDS
91 Director Administrative Computing .... Mr. Keith J. SPENCER
37 Director of Financial Aid .... Mrs. Sherry R. PENNINGTON
90 Director Academic Computing .... Mr. Adam S. DEAN
39 Director of Student Housing .... Ms. Helen LODGE
41 Director of Athletics .... Ms. Stephanie BEASON
40 Bookstore Manager .... Mrs. Lois J. WITTE
09 Coordinator Institutional Research .... Mrs. Nancy KERBS
29 Alumnae Relations Manager .... Ms. Tracy HASS CORDOVA
38 Coordinator of Counseling .... Ms. Jeanna BRAUER
88 Director of Food Service .... Mr. Michael RICHARDSON
88 PEO Relations Manager .... Ms. Margaret HAVERSTIC
88 Coordinator Academic Advising .... Ms. Stephanie MCGHEE
85 Coord International Student Svcs .... Ms. Jennifer CORNWELL

Court Reporting Institute of St. Louis (B)

7730 Carondelet, Clayton MO 63105
County: Saint Louis Identification: 770617
Unit ID: 481766
Telephone: (314) 290-0200 Carnegie Class: Not Classified
FAX Number: (314) 721-4085 Calendar System: Quarter
URL: www.cri.edu
Established: Annual Undergrad Tuition & Fees: $10,375
Enrollment: 247 Coed
Affiliation or Control: Proprietary IRS Status: Proprietary
Highest Offering: Associate Degree
Accreditation: ACICS

01 Campus Director .... Darrell JOY

Covenant Theological Seminary (C)

12330 Conway Road, Saint Louis MO 63141-8697
County: Saint Louis FICE Identification: 004707
Unit ID: 177126
Telephone: (314) 434-4044 Carnegie Class: Spec-4-yr-Faith
FAX Number: (314) 434-4819 Calendar System: 4/1/4
URL: www.covenantseminary.edu
Established: 1956 Annual Graduate Tuition & Fees: N/A
Enrollment: 541 Coed
Affiliation or Control: Presbyterian Church In America IRS Status: 501(c)3
Highest Offering: Doctorate; No Undergraduates
Accreditation: NH, THEOL

01 President .... Dr. Mark DALBEY
05 VP of Academic Administration .... Rev. Christopher FLORENCE
10 VP of Business and Finance .... Ms. Alice EVANS
30 VP of Advancement .... Mr. John RANHEIM
88 VP of Strategic Academic Projects .... Dr. Daniel M. DORIANI
88 Dean of Faculty .... Dr. Jay SKLAR
32 Dean of Students .... Rev. Michael HIGGINS
20 Dean of Academic Services .... Dr. Tasha CHAPMAN
18 Director of Facilities & Operations .... Mr. David BROWN
84 Sr Director of Enrollment Services .... Mr. Brian TIEMEIER
07 Int Director of Admissions .... Mr. Mark SANDVIG
08 Library Director .... Rev. James C. PAKALA
13 Director of Information Technology .... Mr. Richard HIERS
21 Controller .... Mr. Jason ROBEY
29 Alumni/Placement Services Director .... Mr. Joel HATHAWAY
37 Director of Financial Aid .... Ms. Melinda CONN
06 Registrar .... Ms. Betsy GASOSKE

Cox College (D)

1423 N Jefferson Avenue, Springfield MO 65802-1917
County: Greene FICE Identification: 020682
Unit ID: 176770
Telephone: (417) 269-3401 Carnegie Class: Spec-4-yr-Other Health
FAX Number: (417) 269-3581 Calendar System: Semester
URL: www.coxcollege.edu
Established: 1907 Annual Undergrad Tuition & Fees: $10,587
Enrollment: 807 Coed
Affiliation or Control: Independent Non-Profit IRS Status: 501(c)3
Highest Offering: Master's
Accreditation: NH, ADNUR, DIETI, DMS, NURSE, RAD

01 President .... Dr. Lance RATCLIFF
05 Vice Pres Acad Affairs/Inst Effect .... Dr. Amy DEMELO
09 Vice Pres College Svcs/Inst Rsrch .... Dr. Jim MOORE
10 Vice Pres Business/Finance .... Jayne BULLARD
97 Dean Gen Educ/Student Advancement .... Dr. Sonya HAYTER
58 Dean Interprof Graduate Studies .... Dr. Kathleen JACKSON
30 Exec Dir College Comm & Development .... Todd RUTLEDGE
37 Director of Financial Aid .... Steve NICHOLS
07 Director of Admissions .... Lindy GLOS
08 Director Library Services .... Wilma BUNCH

Crowder College (E)

601 Laclede Avenue, Neosho MO 64850-9165
County: Newton FICE Identification: 002459
Unit ID: 177135
Telephone: (417) 451-3223 Carnegie Class: Assoc/HT-High Trad
FAX Number: (417) 455-5702 Calendar System: Semester
URL: www.crowder.edu
Established: 1963 Annual Undergrad Tuition & Fees (In-District): $2,352
Enrollment: 5,710 Coed
Affiliation or Control: Local IRS Status: 501(c)3
Highest Offering: Associate Degree
Accreditation: NH, ADNUR, CAHIIM, EMT, OTA

01 President .... Dr. Jennifer METHVIN
10 Vice President of Finance .... Mrs. Amy RAND
05 Vice President of Academic Affairs .... Dr. Glenn COLTHARP
32 Vice President of Student Affairs .... Mrs. Tiffany SLINKARD
27 Assoc VP of Information Services .... Mrs. Mickie MAHAN
75 Assoc VP of Careers & Tech Educ .... Mr. Edward STEPHENS
07 Interim Director of Admissions .... Mr. JP DICKEY
09 Director of Institutional Research .... Mrs. Bobbie AUGSPURGER
08 Director of Lee Library .... Mr. Eric DEATHERAGE
26 Director of Public Information .... Mrs. Cindy BROWN
41 Athletic Director .... Mr. John SISEMORE
37 Director of Financial Aid .... Mrs. Stephanie FERGUSON
15 Director of Human Resources .... Mrs. Michelle PAUL
25 Dir of Institutional Advancement .... Mrs. Cindy BRANSCUM
40 Bookstore Manager .... Ms. Colleen HOLLAND
36 Career Services Coordinator .... Ms. Beth GANDY
13 Director of Information Technology .... Mr. Chris WOITOWITZ

Culver-Stockton College (F)

One College Hill, Canton MO 63435-1257
County: Lewis FICE Identification: 002460
Unit ID: 177144
Telephone: (573) 288-6000 Carnegie Class: Bac-Diverse
FAX Number: (573) 288-6611 Calendar System: Semester
URL: www.culver.edu
Established: 1853 Annual Undergrad Tuition & Fees: $24,900
Enrollment: 971 Coed
Affiliation or Control: Christian Church (Disciples Of Christ)
IRS Status: 501(c)3
Highest Offering: Master's
Accreditation: NH, #CAATE, IACBE, MUS

01 President .... Dr. Kelly M. THOMPSON
05 Vice Pres Academic Affs/Dean of Col .... Dr. Daniel K. SILBER
32 Dean of Student Life .... Dr. D. Christopher GILL
07 Director of Admission .... Mrs. Misty MCBEE
30 VP for Advancement .... Dr. Bill SHEEHAN
06 Registrar/Director Inst Research .... Mrs. Chris HUEBOTTER
08 Librarian .... Ms. Katherine MARNEY
26 Asst Director of Communications .... Ms. Amanda WELKER
37 Director Financial Aid .... Mrs. Tina WISEMAN
29 Director of Alumni Programs .... Mrs. Jennifer SOUSA
91 Exec Dir Admin Systems & Service .... Mr. Joseph LIESEN
10 Chief Financial Officer .... Mrs. Diane BOZARTH
15 Director of Human Resources .... Mrs. Amy BAKER
35 Coordinator of Student Activities .... Mr. Bill BOXDORFER
42 Chaplain .... Rev. Amanda SORENSON
41 Athletic Director .... Mr. Patrick ATWELL
40 Wildcat Warehouse Manager .... Mrs. Sharon FARR
04 Assistant to the President .... Ms. Cindy FREELS
19 Director Campus Security & Facil .... Mr. Michael BRINGER
49 Chair Applied Liberal Arts/ Sciences .... Dr. Lauren SCHELLENBERGER
50 Chair Business Education & Law .... Dr. Kimberly GAITHER
57 Chair Fine Applied & Literary Arts .... Mr. Kent MILLER
88 Assoc Dean of Instruction .... Dr. Dell Ann JANNEY
92 Director of Honors Program .... Dr. Haidee HEATON
93 Director of Minority Students .... Dr. Mohamed EL-BERMAWY
24 Media Coordinator .... Mrs. Julie WRIGHT
44 Director of the Annual Fund .... Mr. Steve MILLER
36 Coord of Career Services/Internship .... Ms. Kara MANDRELL
39 Director of Residential Life .... Ms. Megan CATALANO
20 Associate Dean Academic Success .... Dr. Holly ANDRESS-MARTIN
38 Dir Counseling/Student Wellness .... Ms. Susan MOON
09 Director of Institutional Research .... Mrs. Karla MCREYNOLDS
88 Director of Advancement Operations .... Mrs. Marjorie ELLISON
104 Director Study Abroad .... Dr. C. Patrick HOTLE

DeVry University - Kansas City Campus (G)

1310 E. 104th St., 2nd Floor, Kansas City MO 64131
Telephone: (816) 943-7300 FICE Identification: 002455
Accreditation: &NH, ENGT

† Regional accreditation is carried under the parent institution in Downers Grove, IL.

Drury University (H)

900 N Benton Avenue, Springfield MO 65802-3791
County: Greene FICE Identification: 002461
Unit ID: 177214
Telephone: (417) 873-7879 Carnegie Class: Bac-A&S
FAX Number: (417) 873-7529 Calendar System: Semester
URL: www.drury.edu
Established: 1873 Annual Undergrad Tuition & Fees: $24,905
Enrollment: 4,215 Coed
Affiliation or Control: Independent Non-Profit IRS Status: 501(c)3
Highest Offering: Master's
Accreditation: NH, ACBSP, BUS, MUS, TED

01 President .... Dr. Timothy CLOYD
05 Executive Vice President & Provost .... Dr. Steven COMBS
11 Vice President for Administration .... Mr. Bill SCORSE
32 Vice President for Student Services .... Dr. Tijuana S. JULIAN
30 Executive VP for Advancement .... Mr. Wayne CHIPMAN
10 Chief Financial Officer .... Mr. Rob FRIDGE
20 Assoc VP Academic Affairs Quality .... Dr. Peter K. MEIDLINGER
84 Vice President Enrollment Mgt .... Vacant
51 Assoc VP Academic Affairs - CCPS .... Mr. Aaron JONES
20 Assoc VP Academic Affairs Operation .... Dr. Bruce CALLEN
06 Registrar .... Mrs. Cindy M. JONES
26 Exec Dir Marketing/Communications .... Ms. Jann HOLLAND
37 Director of Financial Aid .... Ms. Rebecca AHRENS
88 Director of Facilities Services .... Mr. Ron CUSHMAN
08 Director of FW Olin Library .... Mr. William GARVIN
36 Dir Career Planning & Development .... Ms. Emily BUCKMASTER
15 Director of Human Resources .... Ms. Scotti SIEBERT
09 Director of Institutional Research .... Dr. Justin LEINAWEAVER
38 Dir Counseling/Disability/Testing .... Mr. Ed DERR
19 Director Safety/Security .... Ms. Sarene DEEDS
105 Associate Director Web Services .... Ms. Amanda SEAMAN
35 Director Student Affairs .... Ms. Emily GIVENS
39 Dir of Student Housing .... Ms. Holly BINDER
40 Director Univ Bookstore .... Ms. Valerie RAINS
41 Director of Athletics .... Mr. Mark FISHER
42 Chaplain .... Dr. Peter BROWNING
04 Executive Asst to President .... Ms. Donna HANLEY
101 Administrative Asst to the Board .... Ms. Bonnie WILCOX
104 Associate Dean Study Abroad .... Dr. Thomas RUSSO
106 Dir Online Education .... Mr. Steve HYNDS
50 Dean School of Business .... Dr. Robin SRONCE
53 Dean School of Education .... Dr. Lauren EDMONDSON
91 Director of Information Services .... Mr. Val SERAFIMOV

Drury University Cabool Campus (I)

620 Peabody Avenue, Cabool MO 65689
Telephone: (417) 962-5314 Identification: 770318
Accreditation: &NH

† Regional accreditation is carried under the parent institution in Springfield, MO

Drury University Ft. Leonard Wood Campus (J)

6002 Cikiradi Ave., Ft. Leonard Wood MO 65473
Telephone: (573) 329-4400 Identification: 770319
Accreditation: &NH

† Regional accreditation is carried under the parent institution in Springfield, MO

Drury University Lebanon Campus (K)

PO Box 509, Lebanon MO 65536
Telephone: (417) 532-9828 Identification: 770320
Accreditation: &NH

† Regional accreditation is carried under the parent institution in Springfield, MO

Drury University Rolla Campus (L)

1034 S. Bishop Avenue, Rolla MO 65401
Telephone: (573) 368-4959 Identification: 770321
Accreditation: &NH

† Regional accreditation is carried under the parent institution in Springfield, MO

East Central College (M)

1964 Prairie Dell Road, Union MO 63084-0529
County: Franklin FICE Identification: 008862
Unit ID: 177250
Telephone: (636) 584-6500 Carnegie Class: Assoc/HT-High Trad
FAX Number: (636) 583-1897 Calendar System: Semester
URL: www.eastcentral.edu
Established: 1968 Annual Undergrad Tuition & Fees (In-District): $2,280
Enrollment: 3,606 Coed
Affiliation or Control: Local IRS Status: 501(c)3
Highest Offering: Associate Degree

Accreditation: NH, ACFEI, ART, CAHIIM, EMT, MAC, MUS, NAIT, OTA

01 President ... Dr. C. Jon BAUER
10 Vice Pres Finance/Administration ... Mr. Phil PENA
05 Vice President Instruction ... Dr. Tia L. ROBINSON
32 Vice President Student Development ... Ms. Shelli R. ALLEN
88 VP External Relations ... Mr. Joel DOEPKER
12 Director ECC/Rolla & Sullivan ... Ms. Christina M. AYRES
30 Dir of Institutional Development ... Ms. Shannon M. GRUS
18 Director Facilities & Grounds ... Mr. Mark A. EATON
08 Director of Library Services ... Ms. Lisa M. FARRELL
96 Purchasing Manager ... Ms. Melissa D. POPP
83 Div Chair Educ/Humanities/Soc Sci ... Ms. Mary B. HUXEL
79 Div Chair Math & English ... Ms. Ann BOEHMER
81 Div Chair Science & Engineering ... Ms. Fatemeh NICHOLS
75 Division Chair Business & Industry ... Mr. Richard HUDANICK
15 Director Human Resources ... Ms. Wendy HARTMANN
66 Director of Nursing/Allied Health ... Ms. Robyn C. WALTER
37 Director Financial Aid ... Ms. Karen GRIFFIN
06 Registrar ... Ms. Marcia BAILEY
21 Director Financial Svcs/Comptroller ... Ms. Annette MOORE
09 Director of Institutional Research ... Ms. Bethany L. LOHDEN
26 Director of Public Relations ... Vacant
13 Director Information Technology ... Mr. Doug HOUSTON
40 Bookstore/Mail/Imaging Coordinator ... Mr. Doug A. AGEE
36 Coordinator Advisement Services ... Mr. Paul LAMPE
103 Executive Director Workforce Devel ... Mr. Mardy LEATHERS
51 Coordinator Adult Educ & Literacy ... Ms. Alice WHALEN
24 Coordinator Instructional Design ... Mr. R. Chad BALDWIN
35 Coordinator Student Activities ... Ms. Courtney HENRICHSEN
04 Executive Asst to President ... Ms. Bonnie S. GARDNER
41 Athletic Director ... Mr. Jay MEHRHOFF

Eden Theological Seminary (A)

475 E Lockwood Avenue,
Webster Groves MO 63119-3192

County: Saint Louis — FICE Identification: 002462
Unit ID: 177278
Telephone: (314) 961-3627 — Carnegie Class: Spec-4-yr-Faith
FAX Number: (314) 918-2626 — Calendar System: 4/1/4
URL: www.eden.edu
Established: 1850 — Annual Graduate Tuition & Fees: N/A
Enrollment: 150 — Coed
Affiliation or Control: United Church Of Christ — IRS Status: 501(c)3
Highest Offering: Doctorate; No Undergraduates
Accreditation: NH, THEOL

01 President ... Dr. David M. GREENHAW
05 Academic Dean ... Dr. Deborah KRAUSE
06 Registrar ... Ms. Michelle WOBBE
07 Director of Admissions ... Rev. Tiffany PITTMAN
04 Admin Asst to the President ... Ms. Danita CARTER
15 Director of Academic Programs ... Ms. Denise STAUFFER
101 Secretary to Board of Trustees ... Ms. Denise STAUFFER
108 Director of Assessment ... Ms. Michelle WOBBE
32 Dean of Students ... Rev. Carol SHANKS
10 Chief Financial Officer ... Ms. Tammy CRAIG
44 Director of Development ... Ms. Sandi LAFATA

Evangel University (B)

1111 N Glenstone, Springfield MO 65802-2191

County: Greene — FICE Identification: 002463
Unit ID: 177339
Telephone: (417) 865-2815 — Carnegie Class: Masters/S
FAX Number: (417) 865-9599 — Calendar System: Semester
URL: www.evangel.edu
Established: 1955 — Annual Undergrad Tuition & Fees: $21,436
Enrollment: 2,006 — Coed
Affiliation or Control: Assemblies Of God Church — IRS Status: 501(c)3
Highest Offering: Doctorate
Accreditation: NH, CAATE, MUS, SW, TED

01 President ... Dr. Carol A. TAYLOR
10 Vice Pres for Business/Finance ... Ms. Linda ALLEN
32 VP for Student Development ... Dr. Sheri PHILLIPS
30 VP for University Advancement ... Dr. Michael KOLSTAD
05 VP for Academic Affairs/Provost ... Dr. Michael MCCORCLE
84 Vice Pres Enrollment Management ... Mr. Chris BELCHER
18 Director of Physical Plant ... Mr. Brian HAUFF
41 Director of Athletics ... Dr. Dennis MCDONALD
06 Registrar ... Mrs. Cathy WILLIAMS
27 Chief Information Officer ... Mr. Gary BLACKARD
08 Librarian ... Mr. Dale JENSEN
19 Director of Public Safety ... Mr. Todd REVELL
38 Director of Counseling Services ... Mr. Brian UPTON
29 Director Alumni Relations ... Mr. Doug JENKINS
37 Dir of Student Financial Services ... Mrs. Valerie SHARP
36 Career Development/Placement ... Mrs. Tina MOORE
42 Campus Pastor ... Rev. Greg JOHNS
26 Director of Public Relations ... Mr. Paul LOGSDON
07 Executive Director of Admissions ... Ms. Patricia HANSEN
23 Director of Health Services ... Ms. Susan BRYAN
21 Controller ... Mr. Jeff HUINDA
35 Director Student Life ... Miss Gina RENTSCHLER
15 Supervisor Human Resources ... Mrs. Ocki HAAS
39 Housing Coordinator ... Mrs. Pamela SMALLWOOD
09 Director of Institutional Research ... Dr. Linda WELLBORN
04 Executive Asst to President ... Mrs. Angela DENSE
101 Secretary of the Institution/Board ... Mrs. Joanne STROM

Fontbonne University (C)

6800 Wydown Boulevard, Saint Louis MO 63105-3098

County: Saint Louis — FICE Identification: 002464
Unit ID: 177418
Telephone: (314) 862-3456 — Carnegie Class: Masters/L
FAX Number: (314) 889-1451 — Calendar System: Semester
URL: www.fontbonne.edu
Established: 1923 — Annual Undergrad Tuition & Fees: $23,790
Enrollment: 1,819 — Coed
Affiliation or Control: Roman Catholic — IRS Status: 501(c)3
Highest Offering: Master's
Accreditation: NH, ACBSP, DIETD, SP, SW, TED

01 President ... Dr. J. Michael PRESSIMONE
05 Vice President Academic Affairs ... Dr. Carey ADAMS
30 Vice President Advancement ... Mrs. Kitty LOHRUM
32 Vice President Student Affairs ... Mr. Joseph DEIGHTON
10 Vice President Finance & Admin/CFO ... Dr. Gary ZACK
84 Vice President Enrollment Mgt ... Mr. Joseph HAVIS
13 Vice Pres Information Technology ... Mr. Mark FRANZ
35 Associate Vice Pres Student Affairs ... Mrs. Carla HICKMAN
20 Associate VP Acad Affairs ... Dr. Corinne WOHLFORD
53 Dean Education ... Dr. Adam WEYHAUPT
50 Dean Global Business/Prof Studies ... Dr. Jay JOHNSON
76 Dean Educ/Allied Health Prof ... Dr. Gale RICE
88 Asst to the Pres for Mission Integ ... Dr. Mary Beth GALLAGHER
06 Registrar ... Mr. Seth CARRUTHERS
15 Director Human Resources ... Mrs. Linda PIPITONE
08 University Librarian ... Dr. Sharon MCCASLIN
45 Director Academic Resources ... Dr. Kevin PELZEL
09 Director Inst Research & Assessment ... Mrs. Meaghan ONG
26 Director Communications/Marketing ... Mr. Mark JOHNSON
106 Director Online Programs ... Ms. Joanne MATTSON
37 Director Financial Aid ... Mr. Matthew KEARNEY
88 Director Academic Advising ... Ms. Lee DELAET
85 Director International Affairs ... Mrs. Rebecca GRANT BAHAN
29 Director Alumni Relations ... Ms. Kate FLATLEY
41 Director Athletics ... Ms. Maria EFTINK
28 Director Multicultural Affairs ... Ms. Leslie DOYLE
88 Dir Ldrshp Educ & Stdnt Activities ... Dr. Janelle DENSBERGER
42 Director Campus Ministry ... Mrs. Lori HELFRICH
19 Director Public Safety ... Mr. Larry VERTREES
21 Controller ... Mr. Dennis JOHNSON
07 Associate VP Admission ... Ms. Michelle PALUMBO
18 Director Physical Plant ... Mr. Brent SPIES
04 Exec Asst to Pres/Board ... Mrs. Patricia ETTER
88 Dir Student Success/Engagement ... Ms. Amy SIMONS
36 Director Career Development ... Ms. Christine KELLER
38 Director Counseling and Wellness ... Ms. Claudia CHARLES

Global University (D)

1211 South Glenstone Avenue,
Springfield MO 65804-1894

County: Greene — Identification: 666637
Unit ID: 247296
Telephone: (800) 443-1083 — Carnegie Class: Not Classified
FAX Number: (417) 865-7167 — Calendar System: Other
URL: www.globaluniversity.edu
Established: 2000 — Annual Undergrad Tuition & Fees: N/A
Enrollment: N/A — Coed
Affiliation or Control: Assemblies Of God Church — IRS Status: 501(c)3
Highest Offering: Doctorate
Accreditation: NH

01 President ... Dr. Gary SEEVERS, JR.
03 Executive Vice President ... Rev. Keith HEERMANN
05 Provost ... Dr. John (Jack) NILL
20 Vice Provost ... Dr. Randy HUDLUN
58 Graduate School Dean ... Dr. David DEGARMO
73 UG School of Bible & Theology ... Dr. Willard TEAGUE
13 VP Info Tech/Media Dept ... Mr. Wade PETTENGER
07 Director of Enrollment Services ... Rev. Todd WAGGONER
06 Registrar ... Mrs. Lynne KROH
10 Chief Financial Officer ... Mr. Mark PERRY
15 Director of Human Resources ... Ms. Jami NEMETI
04 Administrative Asst to President ... Ms. Kristin DEGARMO
08 Head Librarian ... Rev. Russ LANGFORD
09 Director of Institutional Research ... Rev. Brad AUSBURY
18 Chief Facilities/Physical Plant ... Mr. Bruce HAVENS
30 Exec Director of Advancement ... Ms. Nicole VICARI

Goldfarb School of Nursing at Barnes-Jewish College (E)

4483 Duncan Avenue, Saint Louis MO 63110-1111

County: Saint Louis — FICE Identification: 006389
Unit ID: 177719
Telephone: (314) 454-7055 — Carnegie Class: Spec-4-yr-Other Health
FAX Number: (314) 362-9250 — Calendar System: Trimester
URL: www.barnesjewishcollege.edu
Established: 1902 — Annual Undergrad Tuition & Fees: N/A
Enrollment: 715 — Coed
Affiliation or Control: Independent Non-Profit — IRS Status: 501(c)3
Highest Offering: Doctorate
Accreditation: NH, ANEST, NURSE

01 Interim Dean ... Dr. Gretchen DRINKARD
10 Vice Dean for Finance/Admin ... Vacant
32 Vice Dean Stdnt Affairs/Diversity ... Dr. Michael WARD
46 Associate Dean for Research ... Dr. Jean DAVIS
15 Vice Dean/HR ... Ms. Rosalynn BRYANT
08 Library & Info Services Director ... Ms. Renee GORRELL
13 Information System Director ... Mr. Carlos PARDO
06 Registrar ... Ms. Terri MONTGOMERY
84 Director Enrollment Mgmnt ... Mr. Jason CROWE
04 Administrative Asst to President ... Ms. Beth HOOK
29 Director Alumni Relations ... Dr. June COWELL-OATES

Graceland University (F)

1401 West Truman Road, Independence MO 64050-3434

Telephone: (816) 833-0524 — Identification: 666262
Accreditation: &NH

† Regional accreditation is carried under the parent institution in Lamoni, IA.

Hannibal-LaGrange University (G)

2800 Palmyra Road, Hannibal MO 63401-1999

County: Marion — FICE Identification: 009089
Unit ID: 177542
Telephone: (573) 221-3675 — Carnegie Class: Bac-Diverse
FAX Number: (573) 221-6594 — Calendar System: Semester
URL: www.hlg.edu
Established: 1858 — Annual Undergrad Tuition & Fees: $21,110
Enrollment: 1,167 — Coed
Affiliation or Control: Southern Baptist — IRS Status: 501(c)3
Highest Offering: Master's
Accreditation: NH, ADNUR, NURSE

01 President ... Dr. Anthony W. ALLEN
05 VP for Academic Administration ... Dr. Miles S. MULLIN, II
45 VP for Institutional Effectiveness ... Dr. Raymond W. CARTY
10 VP for Business & Finance ... Mrs. Betty L. ANDERSON
30 VP for Institutional Advancement ... Mr. Jason GEIKEN
32 Dean of Student Development ... Dr. Jeffery BROWN
26 Director Public Relations ... Mrs. Carolyn A. CARPENTER
06 Registrar/Director of Records ... Mrs. Natasha RUSHING
37 Director of Financial Aid ... Mr. Brice D. BAUMGARDNER
29 Director Alumni Services ... Ms. Lauren YOUSE
36 Director Student Placement ... Dr. Karry D. RICHARDSON
08 Library Director ... Mrs. Julie A. ANDRESEN
18 Chief Facilities/Physical Plant ... Mr. Kevin RUSHING
19 Director Public Safety ... Mr. Kyle BRENNEMANN
39 Director of Residential Life ... Mr. Joshua PIERCE
41 Athletic Director ... Mr. Jason D. NICHOLS
40 University Bookstore Manager ... Mrs. Susan A. BOOTH
07 Director of Admissions ... Mr. Sean C. FREEMAN
102 Director of Development ... Mr. David DEXHEIMER
106 Dir Graduate and Online Division ... Dr. Jill ARNOLD

Harris-Stowe State University (H)

3026 Laclede Avenue, Saint Louis MO 63103-2199

County: Independent City — FICE Identification: 002466
Unit ID: 177551
Telephone: (314) 340-3366 — Carnegie Class: Bac-Diverse
FAX Number: (314) 340-3399 — Calendar System: Semester
URL: www.hssu.edu
Established: 1857 — Annual Undergrad Tuition & Fees (In-State): $5,220
Enrollment: 1,280 — Coed
Affiliation or Control: State — IRS Status: 501(c)3
Highest Offering: Baccalaureate
Accreditation: NH, ACBSP, IACBE, TED

01 President ... Dr. Dwaun WARMACK
05 Provost & VP Academic Affairs ... Dr. Dwayne SMITH
10 VP for Administration & Finance ... Vacant
26 Exec Dir Institutional Advancement ... Ms. Leslie HOLLOWAY
06 Registrar ... Ms. Chauvette MCELMURRY
84 Exec Dir Enrollment Management ... Vacant
08 Director Library Services ... Mrs. Barbara NOBLE
37 Director of Financial Aid ... Mr. James GREEN
15 Director Human Resources ... Vacant
38 Director Counseling Services ... Mrs. Vicki BERNARD
25 Exec Dir Title III/Sponsored Pgms ... Mrs. Heather BOSTIC
20 Dir Center for Excel & Retention ... Vacant
41 Director of Athletics ... Mr. Jamaal MAYO
18 Director of Physical Plant ... Vacant
88 Director of Business Services ... Ms. Barbara A. MORROW
13 VP Strategic Plan & IT Services ... Mr. James FOGT
36 Director of Career Services ... Mrs. Wanda MCNEIL
21 Comptroller/Grants Officer ... Mr. Brian HUGGINS
38 Dean of Student Success ... Mr. Emmanuel LALANDE
53 Dean College of Education ... Vacant
50 Dean Busch School of Business ... Ms. Fatemeh ZAKERY
49 Dean College of Arts & Sciences ... Dr. Lateef ADELANI
101 Secretary of the Institution/Board ... Mrs. Lea SUTHERLIN
19 Director Security/Safety ... Vacant
30 Chief Development/Advancement ... Ms. Leslie HOLLOWAY
32 Chief Student Affairs/Student Life ... Mr. Emmanuel LALANDE

Heartland Christian College (I)

500 New Creation Rd, Newark MO 63458

County: Knox — Identification: 667091
Telephone: (660) 284-4800 — Carnegie Class: Not Classified
FAX Number: (660) 284-4098 — Calendar System: Semester
URL: www.heartlandcollege.edu
Established: 1992 — Annual Undergrad Tuition & Fees: N/A
Enrollment: N/A — Coed
Affiliation or Control: Non-denominational — IRS Status: 501(c)3

Highest Offering: Associate Degree
Accreditation: BI

01 President Kris R. PALMER
05 Chief Academic Officer Martha PALMER
10 CFO David BARTON
06 Registrar Judi BARTON
08 Head Librarian Molly NICKERSON

Heritage College (A)

1200 E 104th Street, Suite 150,
Kansas City MO 64131-4557
Telephone: (816) 942-5474 Identification: 666155
Accreditation: ABHES

† Branch campus of Heritage College, Denver, CO.

Hickey College (B)

2700 North Lindbergh Boulevard, Saint Louis MO 63114
County: Saint Louis FICE Identification: 010279
Unit ID: 177579
Telephone: (314) 434-2212 Carnegie Class: Bac/Assoc-Mixed
FAX Number: (314) 434-1974 Calendar System: Other
URL: www.hickeycollege.edu
Established: 1933 Annual Undergrad Tuition & Fees: $13,890
Enrollment: 415 Coed
Affiliation or Control: Proprietary IRS Status: Proprietary
Highest Offering: Baccalaureate
Accreditation: ACICS, ACFEI

01 President Mr. Christopher A. GEARIN
05 Director of Education Ms. Connie L. SCOTT
32 Director of Student Services Ms. Deanna L. PECORONI
07 Director of Admissions Mr. Bill E. LEWIS

Jefferson College (C)

1000 Viking Drive, Hillsboro MO 63050-2441
County: Jefferson FICE Identification: 002468
Unit ID: 177676
Telephone: (636) 797-3000 Carnegie Class: Assoc/MT-VT-High Trad
FAX Number: (636) 789-4012 Calendar System: Semester
URL: www.jeffco.edu
Established: 1963 Annual Undergrad Tuition & Fees (In-District): $2,400
Enrollment: 4,882 Coed
Affiliation or Control: State/Local IRS Status: 501(c)3
Highest Offering: Associate Degree
Accreditation: NH, CAHIIM, OTA, PTAA, RAD

01 President Dr. Raymond V. CUMMISKEY
05 VP Instruction Dr. Caron DAUGHERTY
10 VP Finance & Administration Mr. Daryl GEHBAUER
32 VP Student Services Dr. Kimberly HARVEY
49 Dean of Arts & Science Education Ms. Shirley DAVENPORT
75 Dean Career/Technical Education Dr. Dena MCCAFFREY
15 Director of Human Resources Ms. Tasha D. WELSH
30 Executive Director of Development Ms. Patricia CHRISTEN
26 Director of PR & Marketing Mr. Roger A. BARRENTINE
21 Controller Mr. Richard H. HARDIN
13 Director Information Technology Mr. Tracy JAMES
81 Division Chair Math & Science Dr. Robert BRIELER
83 Div Chair Social Sciences/Business Dr. Terry KITE
60 Division Chair Comm/Fine Arts Dr. Michael BOOKER
76 Div Chair Health Occupation Prog Mr. Kenny WILSON
75 Div Chair Business/Technical Educ Mr. Christopher DEGEARE
90 Dir Online Lrng/Instructional Tech Mr. Allan A. WAMSLEY
12 Director Planning & Outreach Ms. Patricia AUMANN
41 Director Athletics Mr. Greg MCVEY
31 Director Business/Community Develop Mr. Bryan D. HERRICK
18 Director Buildings & Grounds Mr. Dale RICHARDSON
19 Director Public Safety Programs Ms. Diane SCANGA
66 Director of Nursing Ms. Linda BOEVINGLOH
06 Registrar Dr. Kimberly HARVEY
37 Director Student Financial Services Ms. Sarah BRIGHT
08 Director Library Services Ms. Lisa PRITCHARD
38 Director Advising & Retention Ms. Kathy JOHNSTON
35 Director Student Support Services Ms. Diane ARNZEN
74 Director Veterinary Technology Ms. Dana A. NEVOIS
84 Director Enrollment Services Ms. Holly LINCOLN
88 Director Child Care Center Ms. Stephanie CAGE
39 Director Residential & Student Life Ms. Kristen YELTON
96 Procurement Coordinator Ms. Sheree BELL
09 Research Analyst Ms. Joan WARREN
04 Admin Asst to the President & Board Ms. Lisa VINYARD

Kansas City Art Institute (D)

4415 Warwick Boulevard, Kansas City MO 64111-1874
County: Jackson FICE Identification: 002473
Unit ID: 177746
Telephone: (816) 472-4852 Carnegie Class: Spec-4-yr-Arts
FAX Number: (816) 472-3439 Calendar System: Semester
URL: www.kcai.edu
Established: 1885 Annual Undergrad Tuition & Fees: $35,270
Enrollment: 660 Coed
Affiliation or Control: Independent Non-Profit IRS Status: 501(c)3
Highest Offering: Baccalaureate
Accreditation: NH, ART

01 The Nerman Family President Mr. Tony JONES
10 EVP for Administration/CFO Ms. Laura SNOW
05 EVP for Academic Affairs Dr. Bambi BURGARD
30 Senior VP for Advancement Ms. Nicolle RATLIFF
20 VP for Academic Affairs Dr. Milton KATZ
15 Director of Human Resources Ms. Lori WOLFE
13 Vice Pres/Chief Information Officer Mr. Larry DICKERSON
32 Dean of Student Affairs Ms. Gina GOLBA
84 VP for Enrollment and Marketing Mr. Scott RAMON
07 Director of Admissions Ms. Julia WELLES
26 Director of Communications and PR Ms. Dana SAWYER
51 Dir Continuing/Professional Studies Ms. Sonja GARRETT
06 Registrar Ms. Nancy EASTMAN
35 Assistant Dean of Student Affairs Mr. Joe TIMSON
38 Psychologist and Counseling Coord Ms. Elisabeth SUNDERMEIER
18 Facilities Director/Plant Services Ms. Roxie CURTIS
29 Director of Alumni Relations Mr. Marcus CAIN
37 Director of Financial Aid Ms. Darci WEBSTER
21 Controller Ms. Suzette NAYLOR
36 Dir of Acad Advising & Career Svcs Ms. Tori SINCLAIR
08 Director of Library Ms. M.J POEHLER
24 Director of Creative Media Mr. Aldo BACCHETTA
19 Director of Safety & Security Vacant
109 Director of Auxiliary Services Mr. Ed RODRIGUEZ
88 Director of H&R Block Artspace Ms. Raechell SMITH

Kansas City University of Medicine & Biosciences (E)

1750 East Independence Avenue, Kansas City MO 64119
County: Jackson FICE Identification: 002474
Unit ID: 179812
Telephone: (816) 654-7000 Carnegie Class: Spec-4-yr-Med
FAX Number: (816) 654-7101 Calendar System: Semester
URL: www.kcumb.edu
Established: 1916 Annual Graduate Tuition & Fees: N/A
Enrollment: 1,106 Coed
Affiliation or Control: Independent Non-Profit IRS Status: 501(c)3
Highest Offering: First Professional Degree; No Undergraduates
Accreditation: NH, OSTEO

01 President & CEO Dr. Marc B. HAHN
10 EVP Finance & Ops/CFO/COO Mr. Joseph MASSMAN
31 Sr VP of Community Engagement Mr. James BARBER
46 Vice Pres for Research Dr. Jeffrey JOYCE
30 Vice Pres for Advancement Dr. Jane LAMPO
32 Vice Prov Student/Enrollment Svcs Dr. Richard P. WINSLOW
45 Assoc Prov IE/Accred/Inclusion Mr. Adrian R. CLARK
17 Vice Dean Col of Osteopathic Med Dr. Mike JOHNSTON
12 Dean Joplin Campus Dr. Paula GREGORY
81 Assistant Dean Basic Science Dr. Cheryl MCCORMICK
20 Assistant Dean Academic Affairs Dr. Schoen KRUSE
35 Asst Dean for Student Affairs Ms. LeAnn K. CARLTON
35 Asst Dean Student Svcs Joplin Dr. Nicole BROWN
100 Chief of Staff/Dir Govt Relations Dr. Brooke YODER
26 Exec Dir Marketing and Comm Ms. Angie BLEDSOE
08 Director of Library Ms. Marilyn J. DEGEUS
88 Director of Strategic Initiatives Mr. Pete STOBIE
06 Registrar Ms. Freda STRACK
18 Facilities Manager Ms. Anna GRAETHER
13 Director of Information Technology Mr. Lance HUGGINS
37 Director of Financial Aid Ms. Kristi NICHOL
88 Associate Dean of Clinical Educ Dr. John GRANETO
88 Admin Dir Clinical Education Ms. Valorie MILLICAN
19 Director Campus Operations Mr. James HERRINGTON
38 Director Counseling and Support Svc Dr. James DUGAN
29 Sr Dir Institutional Advancement Ms. Kathryn HARVEL
35 Exec Dir Community/Student Activity Ms. Sara E. SELKIRK
07 Director of Admissions Ms. Patricia HARPER
76 Dean of College of Biosciences Dr. Robert WHITE

Kenrick-Glennon Seminary, Kenrick School of Theology (F)

5200 Glennon Drive, Saint Louis MO 63119-4399
County: Saint Louis FICE Identification: 002476
Unit ID: 177816
Telephone: (314) 792-6100 Carnegie Class: Spec-4-yr-Faith
FAX Number: (314) 792-6500 Calendar System: Semester
URL: www.kenrick.edu
Established: 1893 Annual Undergrad Tuition & Fees: $20,050
Enrollment: 132 Male
Affiliation or Control: Roman Catholic IRS Status: 501(c)3
Highest Offering: Master's
Accreditation: NH, THEOL

01 President/Rector Rev. James MASON
42 Dir Pre-Theology/Vice Rector Msgr. Gregory MIKESCH
05 Academic Dean Dr. John GRESHAM
32 Dean of Seminarians Rev. Paul HOESING
08 Director of Library Ms. Mary Ann AUBIN
88 Director of Spiritual Formation Rev. Mark KRAMER, SJ
42 Director of Worship Rev. Donald ANSTOETTER
30 Director of Development Ms. Kate GUYOL
06 Registrar/Financial Aid Deacon Joseph MEIERGERD
18 Chief Facilities/Physical Plant Mr. Gerry KLAAS
04 Administrative Asst to President Vacant
10 Chief Business Officer Mr. Greg NOVAK

L'Ecole Culinaire (G)

9811 South Forty Drive, Saint Louis MO 63124
Telephone: (314) 587-2433 Identification: 666275
Accreditation: ACCSC, ACFEI

† Branch campus of Vatterott College, Des Moines, IA.

L'Ecole Culinaire Kansas City (H)

310 Ward Parkway, Kansas City MO 64112
Telephone: (816) 627-0100 Identification: 770579
Accreditation: ACCSC

† Branch campus of Vatterott College-Des Moines, Des Moines, IA

Lincoln University (I)

820 Chestnut Street, Jefferson City MO 65101-3537
County: Cole FICE Identification: 002479
Unit ID: 177940
Telephone: (573) 681-5000 Carnegie Class: Masters/S
FAX Number: (573) 681-5566 Calendar System: Semester
URL: www.lincolnu.edu
Established: 1866 Annual Undergrad Tuition & Fees (In-State): $7,042
Enrollment: 3,117 Coed
Affiliation or Control: State IRS Status: 501(c)3
Highest Offering: Beyond Master's But Less Than Doctorate
Accreditation: NH, ACBSP, ADNUR, MUS, NUR, SURGT, SW, TED

01 President Dr. Kevin D. ROME
11 Dean Administration/Student Affairs Dr. Jerome OFFORD, JR.
05 VP Academic Affairs/Provost Dr. Said SEWELL
30 Exec Director of Philanthropy Mr. Willie JUDE
83 Dean College of Arts & Sciences Vacant
107 Dean Col of Professional Studies Vacant
47 Dean of Ag/Natural Sciences Dr. Albert ESSEL
08 University Librarian Dr. Rinalda FARRAR
10 Chief Financial Officer Mrs. Sandy KOETTING
51 Director Continuing Education Mr. Brandon HILDRETH
15 Director Human Resources Mr. James MARCANTONIO
18 Director of Facilities and Planning Mrs. Sheila GASSNER
19 Director Police Department Vacant
41 Interim Director of Athletics Mr. John MOSELEY
29 Director Alumni Affairs Mrs. Sylvia WILSON
26 Director of University Relations Ms. Misty YOUNG
06 Director of Records/Registrar Ms. Liz MORROW
36 Director Career & Academic Support Mrs. Ruth CANADA
07 Director of Admissions Mr. Derocco LYNCH
09 Director Ctr Assess/Inst Rsrch Mrs. Beth NOLTE
23 Director Student Health Services Vacant
32 Director of Student Activities Mrs. Annette CROWDER
43 Director Legal Svcs/Genl Counsel Mr. Kent BROWN
37 Dir Financial Aid/Stdnt Employment Mr. Alfred L. ROBINSON
96 Director of Purchasing Ms. Debra KIDWELL
13 Chief Information Officer Vacant
39 Director of Residential Life Mr. Khalilah DOSS
12 Director Fort Leonard Wood Site Mrs. Barbara LANE
24 Dir of Center Teaching/Learning Dr. Rachel SALE
40 Manager LU Bookstore Mr. James HOWARD
101 Exec Asst to President & Curators Ms. Rose Ann ORTMEYER
85 International Student Advisor Mr. Duwon CLARK
105 Web Content Manager Mr. Derek SCHWARTZE
22 Dir Affirmative Action/EEO Mr. James MARCANTONIO

Lindenwood University (J)

209 S Kingshighway, Saint Charles MO 63301-1695
County: Saint Charles FICE Identification: 002480
Unit ID: 177968
Telephone: (636) 949-2000 Carnegie Class: DU-Mod
FAX Number: (636) 949-4910 Calendar System: Semester
URL: www.lindenwood.edu
Established: 1827 Annual Undergrad Tuition & Fees: $16,022
Enrollment: 12,151 Coed
Affiliation or Control: Independent Non-Profit IRS Status: 501(c)3
Highest Offering: Doctorate
Accreditation: NH, ACBSP, CAATE, NURSE, SW, TEAC

01 President Dr. Michael D. SHONROCK
04 Exec Asst Pres & Asst Secy to BOD Mrs. Stefani M. SCHUETTE
05 Acting Provost Dr. Marilyn ABBOTT
30 Vice Pres Development Mr. Dan GRIGG
32 Vice President Student Development Dr. Ryan GUFFEY
15 Vice Pres Human Resources Dr. Deb AYRES
84 Vice Pres for Enrollment Management Dr. Joe PARISI
12 President Belleville Campus Mr. Brett BARGER
09 Asst VP Inst Effectiveness Dr. David WILSON
06 Registrar Ms. Christine HANNAR
10 Chief Financial Officer Mr. Greg PHELPS
29 Director Alumni Relations Ms. Michelle GIESSMAN
26 Dir Community & Public Relations Mr. Scott QUEEN
13 VP Information Technology Mr. TJ RAINS
08 Dean of Library Services Ms. Elizabeth MACDONALD
37 Director of Financial Aid Ms. Lori BODE
35 Dir of Student Life & Leadership Ms. Angela ROYAL
35 Dean of Students Ms. Shane WILLIAMSON
39 Director of Student Housing Mr. Terry RUSSELL
92 Director of Honors Program Dr. Michael WHALEY
43 General Counsel Mr. Grant SHOSTAK
86 Dir of Outreach & Govt Relations Vacant
22 Director of Compliance Ms. Anna GIRDWOOD
89 Dean First Year Programs Vacant

20 Dean of Academic Services .... Mr. Barry FINNEGAN
36 Director of Career Placement .... Ms. Dana WEHRLI
41 VP Athletics .... Mr. Brad WACHLER
42 Chaplain .... Mr. Michael MASON
79 School Dean Humanities .... Dr. Michael WHALEY
81 School Dean Sciences .... Dr. Ricardo DELGADO
53 School Dean Education .... Dr. Cynthia BICE
57 Dean Fine & Performing Arts .... Mr. Joe ALSOBROOK
50 Sch Dean Business/Entrepreneurship .... Dr. Roger ELLIS
60 School Dean Communications .... Mr. Mike WALL
83 Interim Dean Human Services .... Dr. Billi PATZIUS
51 School Dean LCIE(Adult Learning) .... Dr. Gina GANAHL
68 Sch Dean Sport/Rec/Exercise Science ... Dr. Cynthia SCHROEDER
19 Director Security/Safety .... Mr. John BOWMANN
101 Secretary of the Institution/Board .... Mrs. Kimberly GERSMAN
106 Dir Online Education/E-learning .... Dr. Joe ALSOBROOK

Logan University (A)

1851 Schoettler Road, Chesterfield MO 63017

County: Saint Louis FICE Identification: 004703
Unit ID: 177986
Telephone: (636) 227-2100 Carnegie Class: Spec-4-yr-Other Health
FAX Number: N/A Calendar System: Trimester
URL: www.logan.edu
Established: 1935 Annual Undergrad Tuition & Fees: N/A
Enrollment: 899 Coed
Affiliation or Control: Independent Non-Profit IRS Status: 501(c)3
Highest Offering: First Professional Degree
Accreditation: NH, CHIRO

01 President .... Dr. Clay MCDONALD
30 VP Chiropractic/Alumni Relations .... Dr. Ralph BARRALE
84 VP Enrollment Management .... Dr. Boyd BRADSHAW
13 VP Information Technology .... Dr. Brad HOUGH
10 Chief Financial Officer .... Mr. Adil KHAN
05 VP Academic Affairs .... Dr. Kimberly PADDOCK-O'REILLY
17 Dean of Clinics .... Dr. Muriel PERILLAT

Maryville University of Saint Louis (B)

650 Maryville University Drive,
Saint Louis MO 63141-7299

County: Saint Louis FICE Identification: 002482
Unit ID: 178059
Telephone: (314) 529-9300 Carnegie Class: DU-Mod
FAX Number: (314) 529-9900 Calendar System: Semester
URL: www.maryville.edu
Established: 1872 Annual Undergrad Tuition & Fees: $26,958
Enrollment: 5,931 Coed
Affiliation or Control: Independent Non-Profit IRS Status: 501(c)3
Highest Offering: Doctorate
Accreditation: NH, ACBSP, ART, CIDA, CORE, MUS, NURSE, OT, PTA, SP, TED

01 President .... Dr. Mark LOMBARDI
05 Vice Pres Academic Affairs .... Dr. Mary Ellen FINCH
10 Vice Pres Finance & Facilities .... Mr. Steve MANDEVILLE
84 Vice President Enrollment .... Mr. Jeffrey MILLER
30 VP Inst Advancement/Chief Dev Ofcr .... Mr. Thomas ESCHEN
32 VP for Student Life .... Dr. Nina CALDWELL
20 Associate VP Academic Affairs .... Dr. Tammy GOCIAL
100 Chief of Staff .... Ms. Kathy LUNAN
50 Dean School of Business .... Dr. Melissa GRISWOLD
53 Dean School of Education .... Dr. Catherine BEAR
76 Dean School Health Professions .... Dr. Charles GULAS
49 Dean College Arts & Sciences .... Ms. Cherie FISTER
08 Dean University Library .... Dr. Eugenia MCKEE
106 Dean Adult & Online Education .... Mr. Dan VIELE
06 Exec Dir Student Svcs Ctr .... Ms. Stephanie ELFRINK
88 Dir Acad Advising & Life Coaching .... Ms. Kelly MOCK
07 Assoc VP Enrollment .... Ms. Shani LENORE-JENKINS
29 Director of Alumni Affairs .... Mr. James PAGE
41 Director of Athletics .... Mr. Marcus MANNING
42 Dir Campus Ministry & Comm Service .... Mr. Stephen DISALVO
35 Dean of Students .... Ms. Kathy QUINN
36 Director Career & Prof Development .... Ms. Leigh DEUSINGER
35 Asst Dean/Dir Student Involvement .... Mr. Brian GARDNER
21 Controller/Dir Finance .... Ms. Nikki PAYNE
102 Director of Development .... Ms. Megan HOLMES
37 Dir Student Svcs Ctr/Financial Aid .... Ms. Martha HARBAUGH
23 Director of Health & Wellness .... Ms. Pamela CULLITON
22 Asst Dean Diversity/Inclusion .... Mr. Turan MULLINS
13 Chief Technology Officer .... Mr. Doug GLAZE
09 Director Institutional Research .... Ms. Mary MERRIFIELD
90 Dir Learning Design &
Technology .... Ms. Pamela BRYAN WILLIAMS
26 VP Integrated Mktg & Communications .... Ms. Marcia SULLIVAN
18 Director of Physical Plant .... Mr. Tom BENNING
44 Director of Planned Gifts .... Mr. Mark ROCCK
102 Dir Foundation/Corp Relations .... Ms. Peggy MICHELSON
19 Director of Public Safety .... Mr. Michael PARKINSON
39 Director of Residential Life .... Ms. Amy HOWARD
88 VP for Student Success .... Dr. Jennifer MCCLUSKEY
104 Assoc VP/Dir Ctr for Global Educ .... Dr. James HARF
88 Asst Athletic Dir-Communications .... Mr. Charles YAHNG
53 Assoc Dean & Dir Teacher Education .... Dr. Mascheal SCHAPPE
21 Dir Student Svcs Ctr/Student Accts .... Ms. Elizabeth STACEY
109 Director Fresh Ideas Food Services .... Ms. Linda THACKER
38 Director Personal Counseling .... Ms. Jennifer HENRY
44 Director of Development .... Ms. Fay FETICK
88 Assoc VP Ctr for Institution Values .... Dr. Alden CRADDOCK
04 Administrative Asst to President .... Ms. Jan JOHNSTON
109 Director of Auxiliary Operations .... Ms. Laura STEVENS

Metro Business College (C)

1732 N Kingshighway, Cape Girardeau MO 63701-2122

County: Cape FICE Identification: 021802
Unit ID: 178110
Telephone: (573) 334-9181 Carnegie Class: Spec 2-yr-Health
FAX Number: (573) 334-0617 Calendar System: Other
URL: www.metrobusinesscollege.edu
Established: 1981 Annual Undergrad Tuition & Fees: $10,325
Enrollment: 118 Coed
Affiliation or Control: Proprietary IRS Status: Proprietary
Highest Offering: Associate Degree
Accreditation: ACICS

01 President .... Ms. Mary BUCKLEY
12 Campus Director .... Mrs. Jan REIMANN
05 Education Director .... Mrs. Leslie WATKINS
37 Financial Aid Director .... Mrs. Janie WARNE
36 Career Services Coordinator .... Mrs. Pamela RIEHN
07 Director of Admissions .... Mrs. Denise ACEY

Metro Business College (D)

210 El Mercado Plaza, Jefferson City MO 65109

Telephone: (573) 635-6600 Identification: 666454
Accreditation: ACICS

† Branch campus of Metro Business College, Cape Girardeau, MO.

Metro Business College (E)

1202 E Highway 72, Rolla MO 65401-3938

Telephone: (573) 364-8464 Identification: 666455
Accreditation: ACICS

† Branch campus of Metro Business College, Cape Girardeau, MO.

*Metropolitan Community College - Kansas City Administrative Center (F)

3200 Broadway, Kansas City MO 64111-2429

County: Jackson FICE Identification: 009137
Unit ID: 177995
Telephone: (816) 604-1000 Carnegie Class: N/A
FAX Number: (816) 759-1158
URL: www.mcckc.edu

01 Chancellor .... Mr. Mark S. JAMES
101 Chancellor's Asst/Board Secretary .... Ms. Cindy K. JOHNSON
05 Int Vice Chanc of Academic Affairs .... Dr. Michel HILLMAN
32 Vice Chanc Student Success/Engagmnt .... Dr. Kathrine SWANSON
10 Vice Chanc Financial & Admin
Svcs .... Mrs. Shelley TEMPLE KNEUVEAN
100 Chief of Staff/Associate VC HR .... Ms. Kathy WALTER-MACK
88 Director of Resource Dev .... Ms. Kendra EDWARDS
45 Director Budget and Planning .... Ms. Deborah BALL
13 Director Computer Services .... Mr. Gary W. SCHIEBER
102 Exec Director MCC Foundation .... Vacant
96 Manager Purchasing .... Ms. Diane PACHECO
18 Director Facility Services .... Mr. Douglas LIGHTFOOT
103 Exec Dir Workforce Dev .... Ms. Nancy RUSSELL
88 Director Educational Services .... Ms. Fran A. PADOW
106 Director Distance Education .... Dr. Leo J. HIRNER
09 Director Inst Research/Assessment .... Mrs. Melissa GIESE
35 Director of Student Dev .... Vacant
37 Director Student Financial Services .... Ms. Dena NORRIS
21 Assoc VC Fin Svcs & Admin Sys .... Ms. Patricia A. AMICK
88 Dir of Support Services PS .... Mr. Domenic R. BROUILLETTE
19 Chief of Campus Police .... Mr. Loncell JAMERSON, JR.
88 Dir of CTE Accountability & Comp .... Ms. Teresa A. LONEY
109 Director Auxiliary Services .... Mr. Scott GEORGE
36 Director Career Education .... Mr. Tristan LONDRE

*Metropolitan Community College - Blue River (G)

20301 E 78 Highway, Independence MO 64057-2053

County: Jackson FICE Identification: 032613
Unit ID: 440305
Telephone: (816) 604-1000 Carnegie Class: Not Classified
FAX Number: N/A Calendar System: Semester
URL: www.mcckc.edu
Established: 1997 Annual Undergrad Tuition & Fees (In-District): N/A
Enrollment: N/A Coed
Affiliation or Control: State/Local IRS Status: 501(c)3
Highest Offering: Associate Degree
Accreditation: &NH

02 President .... Dr. Michael BANKS
04 Assistant to the President .... Mrs. Kimberly A. MORICONI
05 Dean of Instruction .... Vacant
32 Dean of Student Development .... Dr. Jonathan L. BURKE
20 Assoc Dean of Instruction .... Mr. Steven D. JOHNSON
35 Assoc Dean of Student Development .... Mr. Basil LISTER
19 Campus Police Sergeant .... Mr. Larry MCCREA
18 Facilities Superintendent .... Mr. Tom COOLEY
26 Marketing Coordinator .... Mr. Bob K. FLORENCE

† Regional accreditation is carried under the parent institution Metropolitan Community College-Kansas City Administrative Center in Kansas City, MO.

*Metropolitan Community College - Business and Technology (H)

1775 Universal Avenue, Kansas City MO 64120-2429

County: Jackson Identification: 666295
Unit ID: 442000
Telephone: (816) 604-1000 Carnegie Class: Not Classified
FAX Number: (816) 482-5256 Calendar System: Semester
URL: www.mcckc.edu/btc
Established: 1995 Annual Undergrad Tuition & Fees (In-District): N/A
Enrollment: N/A Coed
Affiliation or Control: Local IRS Status: 501(c)3
Highest Offering: Associate Degree
Accreditation: &NH

02 President .... Dr. Jackie GILL
05 Dean of Instruction .... Vacant
32 Dean Student Development/Enrollment .... Dr. Ryan MEADOR
20 Associate Dean .... Ms. Shawn SMITH
103 Exec Dir Workforce Development .... Ms. Nancy RUSSELL
04 Admin Assistant to the President .... Ms. Jeanette JORDAN

† Regional accreditation is carried under the parent institution Metropolitan Community College-Kansas City Administrative Center in Kansas City, MO.

*Metropolitan Community College - Longview (I)

500 SW Longview Road, Lee's Summit MO 64081-2105

County: Jackson FICE Identification: 009140
Telephone: (816) 604-1000 Carnegie Class: Not Classified
FAX Number: (816) 672-2025 Calendar System: Semester
URL: www.mcckc.edu
Established: 1969 Annual Undergrad Tuition & Fees (In-District): N/A
Enrollment: N/A Coed
Affiliation or Control: Local IRS Status: 501(c)3
Highest Offering: Associate Degree
Accreditation: &NH

02 President .... Dr. Kirk A. NOOKS
05 Dean of Instruction .... Dr. Arminda MCCALLUM
32 Dean Student Devel/Enrollment
Mgmt .... Dr. Diana BOYD MCELROY
20 Associate Dean Instruction .... Mr. Gurbhushan SINGH
35 Assoc Dean Student Dev/Enroll Mgmt .... Mrs. Linda NELSON
37 Manager of Student Financial Aid .... Ms. Lisa L. FANNAN
10 Business Office Supervisor .... Ms. Dianna M. CARPENTER
18 Physical Facilities Superintendent .... Mr. Rick STANSBURY
36 Coordinator Student Employment Svcs .... Ms. Linda S. ANDERSON
38 Director Student Counseling .... Mrs. Gretchen S. BLYTHE

† Regional accreditation is carried under the parent institution Metropolitan Community College-Kansas City Administrative Center in Kansas City, MO.

*Metropolitan Community College - Maple Woods (J)

2601 NE Barry Road, Kansas City MO 64156-1299

County: Clay FICE Identification: 009139
Unit ID: 178022
Telephone: (816) 604-1000 Carnegie Class: Not Classified
FAX Number: (816) 437-3049 Calendar System: Semester
URL: www.mcckc.edu
Established: 1968 Annual Undergrad Tuition & Fees (In-District): N/A
Enrollment: N/A Coed
Affiliation or Control: Local IRS Status: 501(c)3
Highest Offering: Associate Degree
Accreditation: &NH

02 President .... Dr. Utpal K. GOSWAMI
05 Dean Instruction .... Mr. David OEHLER
32 Dean Student Devel/Enrollment .... Ms. Karen MOORE
35 Assoc Dean Student Development .... Ms. Melinda JOHNSON
20 Associate Dean .... Dr. Brian BECHTEL
08 Librarian .... Mrs. Linda CARTER
41 Athletic Director .... Dr. Brian BECHTEL
37 Manager Student Financial Aid .... Mrs. Robin STIMAC
18 Physical Facilities Superintendent .... Mr. Tom HULETT
10 Business Office Supervisor .... Ms. Emily THOMPSON
31 Community Relations Coordinator .... Mrs. Heather K. PEREZ
36 Student Employment Service Coord .... Ms. Mary Lynn MUNGER

† Regional accreditation is carried under the parent institution Metropolitan Community College-Kansas City Administrative Center in Kansas City, MO.

*Metropolitan Community College - Penn Valley (K)

3201 Southwest Trafficway, Kansas City MO 64111-2764

County: Jackson FICE Identification: 002484
Unit ID: 178785
Telephone: (816) 604-1000 Carnegie Class: Not Classified
FAX Number: (816) 759-4161 Calendar System: Semester
URL: www.mcckc.edu
Established: 1915 Annual Undergrad Tuition & Fees (In-District): N/A
Enrollment: N/A Coed
Affiliation or Control: Local IRS Status: 501(c)3
Highest Offering: Associate Degree
Accreditation: &NH, ADNUR, CAHIIM, DA, EMT, OTA, PTAA, RAD, SURGT

02 Interim President ....Dr. Tony ROSS
05 Dean of Instruction ....Dr. Cheryl CARPENTER-DAVIS
32 Dean of Student Development ....Ms. Yvette SWEENEY
84 Dean of Enrollment Services ....Ms. Yvette SWEENEY
20 Assoc Dean Instruction ....Ms. Tarana CHAPPLE
35 Assoc Dean Student Development ....Mrs. Mindy JOHNSON
23 Director of Health Sciences ....Ms. Sandy MCILNAY
08 Librarian ....Vacant
13 NUS Department Director ....Vacant
18 Facilities Services Superintendent ....Mr. Lloyd HALE
19 Campus Police Captain ....Cpt. Booker ARMSTRONG
84 Enrollment Manager ....Mr. Carlton FOWLER
41 Athletic Programs Manager ....Mr. Marcus HARVEY
37 Student Financial Aid Manager ....Ms. Rossann DOWNING
40 College Bookstore Manager ....Ms. Selin GAONA
10 Business Office Supervisor ....Ms. Michele ALLEN
26 Community & Public Relations Coord ....Ms. Kimberly RILEY
36 Career Coordinator ....Ms. Margaret STEGMAN

† Regional accreditation is carried under the parent institution Metropolitan Community College-Kansas City Administrative Center in Kansas City, MO.

Midwest Institute (A)

964 S. Highway Drive, Fenton MO 63026
County: St. Louis FICE Identification: 021211
Unit ID: 178183
Telephone: (314) 965-8363 Carnegie Class: Spec 2-yr-Tech
FAX Number: (636) 326-1059 Calendar System: Other
URL: www.midwestinstitute.com
Established: 1965 Annual Undergrad Tuition & Fees: N/A
Enrollment: 225 Coed
Affiliation or Control: Proprietary IRS Status: Proprietary
Highest Offering: Associate Degree
Accreditation: ABHES

01 Director ....Dr. Adam EPSTEIN

Midwest Institute-Earth City (B)

4260 Shoreline Drive, Earth City MO 63045
County: Saint Louis Identification: 667074
Telephone: (314) 344-4440 Carnegie Class: Not Classified
FAX Number: (314) 344-0495 Calendar System: Other
URL: www.midwestinstitute.com
Established: 1970 Annual Undergrad Tuition & Fees: N/A
Enrollment: N/A Coed
Affiliation or Control: Proprietary IRS Status: Proprietary
Highest Offering: Associate Degree
Accreditation: ABHES

01 President ....Ms. Christine SHREFFLER

Midwest University (C)

851 Parr Road, Wentzville MO 63385-0365
County: Saint Charles FICE Identification: 035283
Unit ID: 440253
Telephone: (636) 327-4645 Carnegie Class: Not Classified
FAX Number: (636) 327-4715 Calendar System: Semester
URL: www.midwest.edu
Established: 1986 Annual Undergrad Tuition & Fees: N/A
Enrollment: N/A Coed
Affiliation or Control: Non-denominational IRS Status: 501(c)3
Highest Offering: Doctorate
Accreditation: BI

01 President ....Dr. James SONG
11 Executive Assistant to President ....Ms. Taylor J. BUMILLER
05 Academic Dean ....Dr. Myeong H. OH
09 Dir of Institutional Effectiveness ....Mr. Rolfe E. KIEHNE
32 Director of Student Affairs ....Mr. Kyong S. YEOM
42 Chaplin ....Dr. Dae G. KIM
06 Registrar/Admission ....Mr. Jeoung H. HAM
08 Director of Library Services ....Mrs. Hyun Shim JUNG
106 Director of E-Learning ....Dr. Hee C. LEE
10 Director of Finance ....Mr. Kyong S. YEOM
21 Business Office Manager ....Ms. Bok H. SONG
45 Director of Planning & Marketing ....Mr. Jae P. SONG
13 Director of Information Technology ....Dr. Hee C. LEE
12 Korea Office Regional Director ....Dr. Jae M. SONG
12 Washington DC Regional Director ....Dr. Yoo K. KO
07 Admission Counselor ....Mr. Sang Bae SEO
85 International Student Officer ....Mr. Kyong S. YEOM
85 International Student Officer ....Mr. Kyoo W. SEO
104 Director of International Devel ....Dr. Hee C. LEE
50 Director of Business School ....Dr. Young S. PARK

Midwestern Baptist Theological Seminary (D)

5001 N Oak Trafficway, Kansas City MO 64118-4697
County: Clay FICE Identification: 002485
Unit ID: 178208
Telephone: (816) 414-3700 Carnegie Class: Spec-4-yr-Faith
FAX Number: (816) 414-3724 Calendar System: Semester
URL: www.mbts.edu
Established: 1957 Annual Undergrad Tuition & Fees: $6,340
Enrollment: 1,369 Coed
Affiliation or Control: Southern Baptist IRS Status: 501(c)3
Highest Offering: Doctorate
Accreditation: NH, THEOL

01 President ....Dr. Jason K. ALLEN
05 Provost ....Dr. Jason DUESING
10 VP for Inst Administration/Fin Svcs ....Mr. Gary CRUTCHER
20 Undergraduate Dean ....Dr. John Mark YEATS
58 Graduate Dean ....Dr. Thor MADSEN
09 Dean of Institutional Effectiveness ....Dr. Rodney A. HARRISON
30 VP of Institutional Relations ....Mr. Charles SMITH
13 Director of Info Technology ....Mr. David MEYER
06 Registrar ....Dr. Mike HAWKINS
08 Librarian ....Ms. Kenette HARDER
73 Director of Postgraduate Studies ....Dr. Rodney A. HARRISON
21 Director Financial Services ....Vacant
15 Director Human Resources ....Vacant
04 Exec Assistant to the President ....Mr. Patrick HUDSON
18 Director of Campus Operations ....Mr. Merv CHAPMAN
37 Financial Aid Director ....Vacant
84 Dir Student Recruitment & Admission ....Mr. Camden PULLIAM
20 Associate Dean ....Dr. Rustin UMSTATTD

Mineral Area College (E)

5270 Flat River Road, Park Hills MO 63601-2224
County: Saint Francois FICE Identification: 002486
Unit ID: 178217
Telephone: (573) 431-4593 Carnegie Class: Assoc/HT-High Trad
FAX Number: (573) 518-2164 Calendar System: Semester
URL: www.mineralarea.edu
Established: 1922 Annual Undergrad Tuition & Fees (In-District): $3,220
Enrollment: 4,632 Coed
Affiliation or Control: Local IRS Status: 501(c)3
Highest Offering: Associate Degree
Accreditation: NH, EMT, PTAA, RAD

01 President ....Dr. Steve KURTZ
03 Vice Pres/Dean Career/Tech Educ ....Mr. John (Gil) KENNON
49 Dean of Arts & Sciences ....Dr. Diana STUART
32 Dean Student Services ....Ms. Jean MERRILL-DOSS
10 Chief Financial Officer ....Ms. Shirley HOFSTETTER
13 Director of Computer Services ....Mr. Chad PIPKIN
06 Registrar ....Ms. Pam REEDER
07 Director of Admissions ....Ms. Julie SHEETS
09 Director of Institutional Research ....Ms. Lisa EDBURG
26 Chief Public Relations Officer ....Ms. Sarah HAAS
29 Director Alumni Relations ....Mr. Kevin THURMAN
15 Chief Human Resource Officer ....Ms. Kathryn NEFF
37 Director Student Financial Aid ....Ms. Denise SEBASTIAN
38 Director Student Counseling ....Mr. Michael EASTER
18 Facilities Manager ....Mr. Barry WILFONG
21 Director Payroll ....Ms. Sarah DEMENT
04 Administrative Asst to President ....Ms. Amy MCKENNA-JONES
08 Head Librarian ....Ms. Melissa HOPKINS
19 Director Security/Safety ....Mr. Jeff MCCREARY
39 Director Student Housing ....Ms. Debi BAYLESS
41 Athletic Director ....Mr. Chad MILLS

Missouri Baptist University (F)

One College Park Drive, Saint Louis MO 63141-8698
County: Saint Louis FICE Identification: 007540
Unit ID: 178244
Telephone: (314) 434-1115 Carnegie Class: Masters/L
FAX Number: (314) 434-7596 Calendar System: Semester
URL: www.mobap.edu
Established: 1964 Annual Undergrad Tuition & Fees: $23,886
Enrollment: 5,322 Coed
Affiliation or Control: Baptist IRS Status: 501(c)3
Highest Offering: Doctorate
Accreditation: NH, EXSC, MUS, TED

01 President ....Dr. R. Alton LACEY
04 Assistant to the President ....Mrs. Susan RUTLEDGE
05 Senior VP of Academic Affs/Provost ....Dr. Arlen R. DYKSTRA
30 Senior VP of Inst Advancement ....Dr. Keith ROSS
32 Senior VP of Student Development ....Dr. Andy CHAMBERS
10 Senior VP for Business Affairs ....Mr. Ken REVENAUGH
58 VP of Grad Stds/Academic Pgm Review ....Dr. Clark TRIPLETT
29 Director for Alumni Relations ....Mr. Brian KNAPP
85 Director of International Services ....Mrs. Jessica FITZGERALD
09 Director Institutional Research ....Mrs. Heather BRASE
08 Librarian ....Ms. Jeanna RYNER
37 Director Financial Services ....Mr. Zach GREENLEE
26 Director University Communications ....Mr. Bryce CHAPMAN
36 Dir Career Svcs/Assoc Dean Students ....Ms. Kimberly GREY
41 Athletic Director ....Dr. Thomas SMITH
18 Director Campus Operations ....Mr. Stu LINDLEY
06 Director of Records ....Mrs. Thea ABRAHAM
15 Director Personnel Services ....Mrs. Barb BURNS
13 Director of Information Systems ....Mr. Jerry MCKITTRICK
19 Director Public Safety ....Mr. Stephen HEIDKE
35 Director Student Activities ....Mrs. Lara HINES
21 Controller ....Mrs. Pam SAVAGE
44 Development Officer ....Mrs. Ashlee JOHNSON
07 Director of Admissions ....Mrs. Cynthia SUTTON

Missouri College (G)

1405 South Hanley Road, Brentwood MO 63144-2902
County: St. Louis FICE Identification: 009795
Unit ID: 178305
Telephone: (314) 768-7800 Carnegie Class: Spec-4-yr-Other Health
FAX Number: (314) 768-7900 Calendar System: Semester
URL: www.missouricollege.com
Established: 1963 Annual Undergrad Tuition & Fees: $12,839
Enrollment: 586 Coed
Affiliation or Control: Proprietary IRS Status: Proprietary
Highest Offering: Baccalaureate
Accreditation: ACICS, DA, DH, OTA

01 President ....Mr. Karl PETERSEN
05 Director of Education ....Mrs. Nicole GRAMLICH
07 Director of Admissions ....Ms. Heidi HOLMES
06 Registrar ....Ms. Bridget KENNEY

Missouri Southern State University (H)

3950 E Newman Road, Joplin MO 64801-1595
County: Jasper FICE Identification: 002488
Unit ID: 178341
Telephone: (417) 625-9300 Carnegie Class: Bac-Diverse
FAX Number: (417) 625-3121 Calendar System: Semester
URL: www.mssu.edu
Established: 1965 Annual Undergrad Tuition & Fees (In-State): $5,523
Enrollment: 5,613 Coed
Affiliation or Control: State IRS Status: 501(c)3
Highest Offering: Master's
Accreditation: NH, ACBSP, CAEP, COARC, DH, EMT, ENGT, NUR, NURSE, RAD, @SW

01 President ....Dr. Alan MARBLE
05 Provost/Vice Pres Academic Affairs ....Dr. Paula CARSON
32 Vice Pres Stdnt Affs/Enrollment ....Mr. Darren S. FULLERTON
10 Vice President Business Affairs ....Mr. Rob YUST
30 Exec Vice Pres for Development ....Dr. Brad HODSON
20 Prov/Vice Pres Academic Affairs ....Dr. Wendy MCGRANE
35 Dean of Students ....Dr. Ronald S. MITCHELL
06 Registrar ....Ms. Cheryl DOBSON
08 Interim Library Director ....Mr. James CAPECI
37 Director Student Financial Aid ....Ms. Becca L. DISKIN
38 Director of ACTS ....Mrs. Kelly WILSON
21 Treasurer ....Mrs. Linda EIS
15 Director Human Resources ....Mr. Evan JEWSBURY
18 Director Facilities/Physical Plant ....Mr. Robert HARRINGTON
76 Dean School Health Sciences ....Dr. Richard SCHOOLER
49 Dean School of Arts & Sciences ....Dr. Richard B. MILLER
53 Dean School of Education ....Dr. Deborah BROWN
50 Int Dean Plaster School of Business ....Dr. Chris MOOS
04 Administrative Asst to President ....Ms. Sharon ODEM
07 Director of Admissions ....Mr. Derek S. SKAGGS
103 Dir Workforce/Career Development ....Ms. Nicole R. BROWN
104 Director Study Abroad ....Dr. Chad STEBBINS
106 Director Distance Learning ....Mr. Scott SNELL
108 Dir Institutional Effectiveness ....Dr. Josie WELSH
19 Chief of Campus Police ....Mr. Kenneth KENNEDY
41 Director of Athletics ....Mr. Jared BRUGGEMAN
44 Director Annual or Planned Giving ....Ms. Elisa BRYANT
88 Dir Budget & Operations ....Mr. Jeff GIBSON
03 Executive Vice President ....Dr. Brad HODSON
101 Secretary of the Institution/Board ....Mrs. Sharon ODEM
26 Dir University Relations/Marketing ....Ms. Cassie MATHES
29 Director Alumni Relations ....Ms. Lee ELLIFF POUND
28 Director of Diversity ....Ms. Faustina ABRAHAMS
105 Director Web Services ....Mr. Peter A. BLOMGREN
13 Chief Info Technology Officer (CIO) ....Mr. Albert E. STADLER
39 Director Student Housing ....Mr. Joshua M. DOAK

Missouri State University (I)

901 S National Avenue, Springfield MO 65897-0027
County: Greene FICE Identification: 002503
Unit ID: 179566
Telephone: (417) 836-8500 Carnegie Class: Masters/L
FAX Number: (417) 836-7669 Calendar System: Semester
URL: www.missouristate.edu
Established: 1905 Annual Undergrad Tuition & Fees (In-State): $7,060
Enrollment: 21,816 Coed
Affiliation or Control: State IRS Status: 501(c)3
Highest Offering: Doctorate
Accreditation: NH, ADNUR, ANEST, ARCPA, AUD, BUS, BUSA, CAATE, CACREP, CEA, CONST, CS, DIETD, @DIETI, MUS, NRPA, NURSE, PH, PLNG, PTA, SP, SPAA, SW, TED, THEA

01 President ....Mr. Clifton M. SMART, III
05 Provost ....Dr. Frank E. EINHELLIG
12 Chancellor West Plains Campus ....Dr. Drew A. BENNETT
46 VP for Research/Economic Devel ....Dr. James P. BAKER
11 Vice Pres Administrative/Info Svcs ....Mr. Matthew MORRIS
30 Vice Pres University Advancement ....Mr. W. Brent DUNN
32 VP Student Affairs & Dean of Stdts ....Dr. Dee SISCOE
20 Deputy Provost ....Dr. Christopher J. CRAIG
20 Associate Provost ....Dr. Rachelle DARABI
20 Associate Provost ....Dr. Joye NORRIS
58 Dean of Grad College ....Dr. Julie J. MASTERSON
10 Chief Financial Officer ....Mr. Steve FOUCART
84 Associate VP Enrollment Mgmt & Svcs ....Mr. Donald E. SIMPSON
08 Dean Library Services ....Mr. Thomas A. PETERS
28 Chief Diversity Officer ....Mr. H. Wes PRATT
09 Director of Institutional Research ....Dr. Michelle D. OLSEN
29 Exec Dir of Alumni Relations ....Ms. Lori FAN
15 Director of Human Resources ....Mr. Tamaria FEW
37 Director of Student Financial Aid ....Ms. Vicki S. MATTOCKS
19 Director of Safety & Transportation ....Mr. Thomas JOHNSON
36 Director of the Career Center ....Ms. Jill WIGGINS
13 Chief Information Officer ....Mr. Jeff P. MORRISSEY
100 Chief of Staff ....Mr. Ryan DEBOEF
23 Director of Health & Wellness Svcs ....Dr. Dave MUEGGE
92 Director Honors College ....Dr. John F. CHUCHIAK

18 Director Facilities Management ....Mr. Brad B. KIELHOFNER
96 Director of Procurement .... Mr. Mike WILLS
07 Director of Admissions ....Ms. Nechell T. BONDS
06 Asst VP Enrollment Mgmt/Registrar .... Mr. Rob HORNBERGER
49 Dean College Arts & Letters ....Dr. Gloria GALANES
79 Dean Col Humanities/Public Affairs ....Dr. Victor MATTHEWS
76 Dean Col Health/Human Services ....Dr. Helen C. REID
81 Dean Col Natural/Applied Science ....Dr. Tamera S. JAHNKE
53 Dean College of Education ....Dr. David HOUGH
50 Dean College of Business ....Dr. Stephanie BRYANT
85 Associate VP International Program ... Mr. Stephen H. ROBINETTE
105 Director of Web and New Media ....Ms. Sara M. CLARK
26 VP Marketing and Communications ....Ms. Suzanne SHAW
41 Athletic Director ....Mr. Kyle MOATS
43 General Counsel ....Ms. Rachael M. DOCKERY

Missouri State University - West Plains (A)

128 Garfield, West Plains MO 65775-2715

County: Howell FICE Identification: 031060
Unit ID: 179344
Telephone: (417) 255-7255 Carnegie Class: Assoc/HT-High Trad
FAX Number: (417) 255-7962 Calendar System: Semester
URL: www.wp.missouristate.edu
Established: 1963 Annual Undergrad Tuition & Fees (In-State): $3,880
Enrollment: 2,164 Coed
Affiliation or Control: State IRS Status: 501(c)3
Highest Offering: Associate Degree
Accreditation: NH, #COARC

01 Chancellor ....Dr. Drew A. BENNETT
05 Dean of Academics .... Dr. Dennis LANCASTER
32 Dean of Student Services ....Dr. Angela TOTTY
20 Assistant Dean of Academic Affairs ....Dr. Michael ORF
10 Director of Business Services ....Mr. Scott SCHNEIDER
30 Director of Development .... Mr. Joe KAMMERER
27 Director of Univ Communications .... Mrs. Cheryl CALDWELL
31 Director of Univ/Community Pgms .... Ms. Brenda POLYARD
13 Director of Computer Services ....Mr. Paul S. MAJKUT
06 Registrar ....Mrs. Laurie WALL
07 Coord of Admissions ....Mrs. Melissa JETT
09 Coord of Institutional Research ....Ms. Carrie STEEN
26 Chief Public Relations Officer .... Mrs. Cheryl CALDWELL
36 Coord of Career Services ....Vacant
37 Coord of Student Financial Aid ....Mr. Geoffrey PING
18 Chief Facilities/Physical Plant ....Mr. Ron HENSLEY
04 Executive Asst to Chancellor ....Mrs. Debra MOSLEY
08 Head Librarian ....Mrs. Sylvia KUHLMEIER
15 Procurement/Human Resources Spec ......Mrs. Alyssa D. COLLINS
39 Coord Student Life and Development .... Mr. Jared CATES

Missouri Valley College (B)

500 E College, Marshall MO 65340-3197

County: Saline FICE Identification: 002489
Unit ID: 178369
Telephone: (660) 831-4000 Carnegie Class: Bac-Diverse
FAX Number: (660) 831-4039 Calendar System: Semester
URL: www.moval.edu
Established: 1889 Annual Undergrad Tuition & Fees: $19,000
Enrollment: 1,695 Coed
Affiliation or Control: Presbyterian Church (U.S.A.) IRS Status: 501(c)3
Highest Offering: Master's
Accreditation: NH, #CAATE, NURSE

01 President ....Dr. Bonnie HUMPHREY
00 Chancellor Emeritus ....Dr. Earl J. REEVES
10 Vice Pres Business/Finance ....Mr. Greg SILVEY
30 Vice Pres Institutional Advancement .... Mr. Eric SAPPINGTON
32 Vice Pres Student Affairs ....Mr. Heath MORGAN
05 VP Academic Affairs/Chief Acad Ofcr .Dr. Diane BARTHOLOMEW
18 Asst VP of Operations ....Mr. Tim SCHULTE
07 Dean of Admissions ....Ms. Tennille LANGDON
06 Registrar ....Ms. Marsha LASHLEY
21 Business Officer ....Mrs. Tonia BARTEL
08 Head Librarian ....Mrs. Pamela K. REEDER
41 Athletic Director/Dir of Operations ....Mr. Tom FIFER
42 Director Campus Ministry ....Rev. Pam SEBASTIAN
09 Director of Institutional Research .... Dr. Tiffany NOLAN
37 Director Student Financial Aid ....Mr. Paul GORDON
38 Director Student Counseling .... Ms. Teresa CESELSKI
13 Director of Systems Administration ....Mr. Jason RINNE
26 Dir of Marketing & Media Relations ....Ms. Danielle DURHAM
04 Administrative Asst to President .... Ms. Brandy SCHULTE

Missouri Western State University (C)

4525 Downs Drive, Saint Joseph MO 64507-2294

County: Buchanan FICE Identification: 002490
Unit ID: 178387
Telephone: (816) 271-4200 Carnegie Class: Bac-Diverse
FAX Number: N/A Calendar System: Semester
URL: www.missouriwestern.edu
Established: 1915 Annual Undergrad Tuition & Fees (In-State): $7,090
Enrollment: 5,834 Coed
Affiliation or Control: State IRS Status: 501(c)3
Highest Offering: Master's
Accreditation: NH, BUS, CAHIIM, ENGT, MUS, NURSE, PTAA, SW, TED

01 President .... Dr. Robert A. VARTABEDIAN
05 Provost/VP Academic Affairs .... Dr. Jeanne DAFFRON
30 Vice Pres University Advancement ....Mr. Jerry PICKMAN
10 VP Financial Planning and Admin ....Mr. Cale FESSLER
32 Vice Pres for Student Affairs ....Ms. Shana MEYER
20 Assoc Vice Pres Academic Affairs .... Dr. Doug DAVENPORT
21 Assoc VP Financial Plng/Admin ....Ms. Carey MCMILLIAN
84 AVP Enrollment Mgmt & Retention .... Mr. Paul ORSCHELN
107 Dean Professional Studies .... Dr. Kathleen O'CONNOR
57 Dean of Fine Arts .... Dr. Bob WILLENBRINK
49 Dean Liberal Arts & Science ....Dr. Murray NABORS
51 Dean of Western Institute ....Dr. Gordon MAPLEY
50 Dean of Business .... Dr. Mike LANE
35 Dean of Students ....Dr. Judith GRIMES
06 Registrar ....Ms. Susan BRACCIANO
07 Director of Admissions ....Vacant
08 Director of Library .... Ms. Sally GIBSON
37 Director Student Financial Aid ....Ms. Marilyn BAKER
13 Director of Information Technology .... Mr. Mark MABE
38 Director Student Counsel & Testing ....Mr. H. David BROWN
18 Director Physical Plant .... Mr. Jerry GENTRY
41 Director of Athletics ....Mr. Kurt MCGUFFIN
15 Director of Human Resources ....Ms. Sally SANDERS
86 Director of External Relations ....Mr. Brandt SHIELDS
26 Dir of Public Relations & Marketing ....Ms. Jomel NICHOLS
29 Director of Alumni Services ....Ms. Colleen KOWICH
96 Director of Purchasing ....Ms. Letha NOLD
04 Executive Associate to President ....Ms. Corrie BROCK
103 Dir Workforce/Career Development ....Ms. Kay-lynne TAYLOR
39 Director Student Housing ....Mr. Nathan ROBERTS
19 Chief of University Police ....Ms. Yvonne MEYER

Moberly Area Community College (D)

101 College Avenue, Moberly MO 65270-1304

County: Randolph FICE Identification: 002491
Unit ID: 178448
Telephone: (660) 263-4100 Carnegie Class: Assoc/HT-Mix Trad/Non
FAX Number: (660) 263-6252 Calendar System: Semester
URL: www.macc.edu
Established: 1927 Annual Undergrad Tuition & Fees (In-District): $3,060
Enrollment: 5,431 Coed
Affiliation or Control: State/Local IRS Status: 501(c)3
Highest Offering: Associate Degree
Accreditation: NH, MLTAD, OTA

01 President ....Dr. Jeffery LASHLEY
10 Vice President for Finance ....Mr. Gary STEFFES
05 Vice President for Instruction ....Dr. Paula GLOVER
75 Dean of Career/Technical Educ ....Ms. Jo FEY
32 Dean of Student Affairs & Enroll .... Ms. Michele MCCALL
20 Dean of Academic Affairs ....Ms. Jacqueline FISCHER
09 Director Inst Effectiveness/Plng .... Ms. Meghan HOLLERAN
21 Director Business Services .... Ms. Sandra MAREK
26 Dir of Mktg and Public Relations .... Mr. Paul ZACHARIAS
18 Director of Plant Operations ....Mr. Eric ROSS
13 Chief Information Officer ....Mr. Lloyd MARCHANT
08 Director of Library & Academic Reso .... Ms. Valerie DARST
15 Director of Human Resources ....Ms. Ann PARKS
40 Director of Inst Svcs/Bookstore Mgr ....Ms. Virginia GEBHARDT
37 Director of Financial Aid ....Ms. Amy HAGER
06 Registrar .... Ms. Julie PERKINS
29 Dir of Inst Dev & Alumni Svc ....Ms. Susan ARMENT
36 Dir of Career and Technical Pgms .... Ms. Suzi MCGARVEY
88 Dir of Academic Services ....Ms. Katelyn BRANDKAMP

National American University-Independence (E)

3620 Arrowhead Avenue, Independence MO 64057

Telephone: (816) 418-7700 Identification: 770402
Accreditation: &NH, MAC, OTA

† Regional accreditation is carried under the parent institution in Rapid City, SD

National American University-Lee's Summit (F)

401 NW Murray Road, Lee's Summit MO 64081

Telephone: (816) 600-3900 Identification: 770404
Accreditation: &NH

† Regional accreditation is carried under the parent institution in Rapid City, SD

National American University-Zona Rosa (G)

7490 NW 87th Street, Kansas City MO 64153

Telephone: (816) 412-5500 Identification: 770403
Accreditation: &NH, ADNUR, MAC, MLTAD

† Regional accreditation is carried under the parent institution in Rapid City, SD

Nazarene Theological Seminary (H)

1700 E Meyer Boulevard, Kansas City MO 64131-1263

County: Jackson FICE Identification: 002494
Unit ID: 178518
Telephone: (816) 268-5400 Carnegie Class: Spec-4-yr-Faith
FAX Number: (816) 268-5500 Calendar System: Semester
URL: www.nts.edu
Established: 1945 Annual Graduate Tuition & Fees: N/A
Enrollment: 239 Coed
Affiliation or Control: Church Of The Nazarene IRS Status: 501(c)3
Highest Offering: Doctorate; No Undergraduates
Accreditation: THEOL

01 President ....Dr. Carla SUNBERG
05 Dean of the Faculty ....Dr. Josh SWEEDEN
11 Dean for Administration .... Rev. Chet DECKER
08 Director Library Service ....Mrs. Debra BRADSHAW
06 Registrar/Director of Admissions ....Mrs. Pamela ASHER
37 Financial Aid Coordinator .... Mr. Jeremy SHUNK
26 Director of Communications ....Ms. Marsha SAILORS

North Central Missouri College (I)

1301 Main Street, Trenton MO 64683-1824

County: Grundy FICE Identification: 002514
Unit ID: 179715
Telephone: (660) 359-3948 Carnegie Class: Assoc/MT-VT-Mix Trad/Non
FAX Number: (660) 359-2211 Calendar System: Semester
URL: www.ncmissouri.edu
Established: 1925 Annual Undergrad Tuition & Fees (In-District): $3,180
Enrollment: 1,746 Coed
Affiliation or Control: Local IRS Status: 501(c)3
Highest Offering: Associate Degree
Accreditation: NH, DH, OTA

01 President ....Dr. Lenny KLAVER
10 Chief Financial Officer ....Mr. Tyson OTTO
32 Dean of Student Services ....Dr. Kristen ALLEY
05 Dean of Instruction ....Dr. Sharon WEISER
76 Dean Allied Health Sciences ....Ms. Brooke MCATEE
06 Registrar ....Ms. Linda BROWN
13 Chief Information Officer ....Mr. Alan BARNETT
08 Librarian ....Ms. Beth CALDARELLO
37 Director of Financial Aid ....Ms. Kimberly MEEKER
30 Director Development ....Ms. Teresa CROSS
40 Director Bookstore ....Ms. Cecilia MARSH
39 Director Student Housing .... Mr. Donnie HILLERMAN
41 Athletic Director .... Mr. Steve RICHMAN
18 Director of Facilities ....Mr. Randy YOUNG
105 Director Web Services ....Mr. Anthony ALEXANDER
09 Director of Institutional Research ....Ms. Tara NOAH
04 Administrative Asst to President ....Ms. Kristi HARRIS
07 Director of Admissions .... Ms. Kristie CROSS

Northwest Missouri State University (J)

800 University Drive, Maryville MO 64468-6015

County: Nodaway FICE Identification: 002496
Unit ID: 178624
Telephone: (660) 562-1212 Carnegie Class: Masters/L
FAX Number: (660) 562-1900 Calendar System: Trimester
URL: www.nwmissouri.edu
Established: 1905 Annual Undergrad Tuition & Fees (In-State): $6,767
Enrollment: 6,720 Coed
Affiliation or Control: State IRS Status: 501(c)3
Highest Offering: Beyond Master's But Less Than Doctorate
Accreditation: NH, ACBSP, DIETD, MUS, NRPA, TED

01 President ....Dr. John JASINSKI
05 Provost ....Dr. Timothy MOTTET
10 Vice Pres for Finance ....Ms. Stacy CARRICK
32 VP Student Affairs/Dean of Students ....Dr. Matt BAKER
13 Vice Pres for Information Systems ....Vacant
26 Vice President University Relations ....Mr. Brandon STANLEY
15 Vice Pres of Strategy and Operation ....Ms. Nola BOND
30 VP University Advancement .... Mr. Michael JOHNSON
84 Dean Enrollment Management .... Ms. Beverly S. SCHENKEL
09 Assoc Dir Institutional Research ....Ms. Mary Ann PENNISTON
08 Dir of Library Services and Opers ....Ms. Kathy HART
06 Registrar ....Ms. Terri VOGEL
37 Director Financial Assistance ....Mr. Charles MAYFIELD
36 Director of Career Services .... Ms. Joan SCHNEIDER
29 Director Alumni Relations ....Mr. Robert MACHOVSKY
19 Chief University Police Department .... Mr. Clarence GREEN
41 Director Athletics/HPERD .... Mr. Mel TJEERDSMA
23 Director Wellness Services ....Dr. Gerald WILMES
96 Director of Purchasing .... Ms. Ann MARTIN
18 Director Facility Services ....Mr. Allen MAYS
58 Assoc Prov for Grad Studies & Spec ....Dr. Gregory HADDOCK
53 Dean School of Education .... Dr. Timothy WALL
49 Dean Col of Arts & Sciences .... Dr. Michael STEINER
50 Dean Col of Business/Prof Stds ....Vacant
38 Director Student Counseling Center ....Vacant
07 Associate Director of Admissions ....Ms. Tamara J. GROW
04 Administrative Asst to President .... Ms. Lynne GILBERT

Ozark Christian College (K)

1111 N Main Street, Joplin MO 64801-4804

County: Jasper FICE Identification: 022027
Unit ID: 178679
Telephone: (417) 626-1234 Carnegie Class: Spec-4-yr-Faith
FAX Number: (417) 624-0090 Calendar System: Semester
URL: www.occ.edu
Established: 1942 Annual Undergrad Tuition & Fees: $11,800
Enrollment: 733 Coed
Affiliation or Control: Independent Non-Profit IRS Status: 501(c)3
Highest Offering: Baccalaureate
Accreditation: BI

01 President ....Matt PROCTOR
03 Executive Vice President .... Damien SPIKEREIT

04 Executive Asst to the President .... Kathy BOWERS
05 Exec VP Academic Affairs/Dean .... Doug ALDRIDGE
06 Registrar .... Jennifer MCMILLIN
32 Vice Pres of Student Life .... Monte SHOEMAKE
10 Vice Pres of Campus Operations .... David MCMILLIN
84 Vice Pres of Enrollment Management .... Troy NELSON
43 General Counsel .... Doug MILLER
29 Vice Pres of Alumni Relations .... Dru ASHWELL
30 VP of Development & Diversity .... Travis HURLEY
88 Assoc Dir of Development .... Sergio RIZO
28 Assoc Director of Diversity .... Matthew MCBIRTH
09 VP Institutional Research & Effecti .... Teresa WELCH
20 Assistant Academic Dean .... Chad RAGSDALE
26 Vice Pres of College Relations .... Jim DALRYMPLE
37 Director of Student Financial Aid .... Kim BALENTINE
90 LMS Administrator .... David FISH
07 Director of Recruitment .... Marley BUTLER
08 Director of Library Services .... John HUNTER
106 Dean of Online Learning .... Shawn LINDSAY
88 Director of Worship Arts Dept .... Matt STAFFORD
38 Student Counselor .... Sharon ENGELBRECHT
109 Director of Food Services .... Teresa BAKER
23 Campus Nurse .... Sara WOOD
34 Dean of Women .... Lisa WHITE
42 Director Campus Ministry .... Kevin GREER
88 Director of Ministry Center .... Bob WITTE
40 Director of Bookstore .... Bob HEATH
41 Director of Athletics .... Chris LAHM
18 Director Physical Plant .... Tim RUNYON
13 Director of IT Dept .... Mitchell PIERCY
07 Director of Enrollment Services .... Ashley NEGRON
105 Web Developer/Network Admin .... Matt DICKEY
14 Coordinator of Data Processing .... Gary WHEAT

Ozarks Technical Community College (A)

1001 E Chestnut Expressway, Springfield MO 65802-3625
County: Greene FICE Identification: 030830
Unit ID: 177472
Telephone: (417) 447-7500 Carnegie Class: Assoc/MT-VT-High Trad
FAX Number: N/A Calendar System: Semester
URL: www.otc.edu
Established: 1990 Annual Undergrad Tuition & Fees (In-District): $2,930
Enrollment: 14,396 Coed
Affiliation or Control: State/Local IRS Status: 501(c)3
Highest Offering: Associate Degree
Accreditation: NH, ACFEI, ADNUR, CAHIIM, COARC, DA, DH, EMT, IFSAC, MLTAD, OTA, PTAA, SURGT

01 Chancellor .... Dr. Hal L. HIGDON
100 Chief of Staff .... Ms. Stephanie SUMNERS
101 Secretary to the Chancellor .... Ms. Janel GRASSI
05 Vice Chancellor Academic Affairs .... Dr. Steve BISHOP
11 Vice Chancellor Admin Services .... Mr. Rob RECTOR
32 Vice Chancellor Student Affairs .... Ms. Joan BARRETT
10 Vice Chancellor Finance .... Ms. Marla MOODY
12 President Table Rock Campus .... Mr. Cliff DAVIS
12 President Richwood Valley Campus .... Dr. Jeff JOCHEMS
13 Chief Technology Officer .... Mr. David ESPING
15 Assoc VC Human Resources/Workforce .... Mr. Tim BALTES
20 Dean of Academic Services .... Dr. Vivian ELDER
76 Dean of Allied Health Programs .... Dr. Sherry TAYLOR
97 Dean of General Education .... Mr. Lance RENNER
72 Dean of Technical Education .... Dr. Matthew HUDSON
103 Exec Dir Workforce Development .... Mr. James ABRAMOVITZ
88 Director Business Development .... Ms. Sherry COKER
06 Asst Registrar Records/Registration .... Ms. Katie MOORE
38 Director of Counseling Services .... Ms. Joyce BATEMAN
26 College Dir Comm & Marketing .... Mr. Mark MILLER
18 College Director Facilities/Grounds .... Mr. Rickie TAYLOR
28 College Director Equity & Complianc .... Ms. Julie EDWARDS
37 College Director of Financial Aid .... Ms. Kim CARY
08 Director College Library .... Vacant
88 Director College Library RVC/TRC .... Ms. Angela SWIFT
36 Director of Career Employment Svcs .... Ms. Kathy CHRISTY
102 Exec Director of OTC Foundation .... Ms. Stephanie SUMNERS
44 College Director of Development .... Ms. Amy BACON
09 College Dir Research/Strategic Plng .... Mr. Matthew SIMPSON
19 College Director Safety & Security .... Mr. Scott LEVEN
35 Dean of Students .... Ms. Karla GREGG
88 Director Dual Credit/HS Admissions .... Ms. Piper WILSON
105 Director Web Services .... Mr. George LAMELZA
106 Dir Online Education/E-learning .... Mr. Matthew HARRIS
25 Chief Contracts/Grants Admin .... Vacant
96 Director of Procurement .... Ms. J'Neal MCCOY
07 Director of Admissions .... Ms. Lacey MATTHEIS

Ozarks Technical Community College Richwood Valley (B)

3369 W Jackson Street, Nixa MO 65714
Telephone: (417) 447-7700 Identification: 770324
Accreditation: &NH

† Regional accreditation is carried under the parent institution in Springfield, MO

Ozarks Technical Community College Table Rock Campus (C)

10698 Historic Highway 165, Hollister MO 65672
Telephone: (417) 336-6239 Identification: 770325
Accreditation: &NH

† Regional accreditation is carried under the parent institution in Springfield, MO

Park University (D)

8700 River Park Drive, Parkville MO 64152-3795
County: Platte FICE Identification: 002498
Unit ID: 178721
Telephone: (816) 741-2000 Carnegie Class: Masters/M
FAX Number: (816) 746-6423 Calendar System: Semester
URL: www.park.edu
Established: 1875 Annual Undergrad Tuition & Fees: $11,470
Enrollment: 10,792 Coed
Affiliation or Control: Independent Non-Profit IRS Status: 501(c)3
Highest Offering: Master's
Accreditation: NH, ACBSP, ADNUR, #CAATE, NUR, SW

01 President .... Dr. Greg GUNDERSON
05 Provost & VP for Academic Affairs .... Dr. Doug FIORE
10 Interim Chief Financial Officer .... Mr. Brian BODE
30 Assoc VP of Advancement .... Mr. Nathan MARTICKE
84 VP Enrollment & Student Services .... Mr. Shane SMEED
43 Vice President & General Counsel .... Ms. Courtney GODDARD
20 Associate VP for Academic Affairs .... Dr. Rebekkah STUTEVILLE
29 Assoc VP for External Relations .... Mr. Erik BERGRUD
32 Dean of Student Life .... Dr. Jayme UDEN
58 Dean School of Grad & Prof Studies .... Dr. Laurie DIPADOVA-STOCKS
06 Registrar .... Ms. Melissa GEIER
37 Director Student Financial Service .... Ms. Brynn BOLOGNA
08 Interim Director of Library Systems .... Ms. Ann SCHULTIS
07 Exec Dir of Enrollment Services .... Mr. Eric BLAIR
44 Director Advancement Services .... Ms. Jessica GREASON
15 Assoc VP for Human Resources .... Mr. Roger DUSING
41 Director of Athletics .... Mr. Claude ENGLISH
66 Director of Nursing Program .... Ms. Gerry WALKER
85 Senior Dir Intl Students .... Mr. Kevin VICKER
13 Chief Information Officer .... Mr. David WHITTAKER
108 Director Academic Assessment .... Vacant
19 Interim Director of Campus Safety .... Ms. Kathryn HWANG
50 MBA Gen Concentration Coordinator .... Dr. Nick KOUDOU
04 Executive Asst to the President .... Ms. Ami WISDOM
50 Dean School of Business/Mgmt .... Dr. Brad KLEINDL
106 Director of Online Operations .... Dr. Gregory ROSE
49 Dean Liberal Arts & Sciences .... Dr. Emily DONNELLI-SALLEE
53 Dean School for Education .... Dr. Michelle MYERS
101 Asst Secretary to Board of Trustees .... Ms. Ami WISDOM
100 Chief of Staff .... Ms. Laure CHRISTENSEN
104 Director Global Educ/Study Abroad .... Ms. Angela PETERSON
105 Web Services Manager .... Ms. Gariela SA TELES
18 Manager Facilities Maintenance .... Mr. Kevin MARTINEAU
26 Dir of Comm & Public Relations .... Mr. Brad BILES
36 Director of Career Development .... Ms. Leah FLETCHER
38 Director of Counseling Center .... Mr. Dustin WALL
39 Director Student Housing .... Ms. Karie SCHAEFER
96 Budget & Procurement Manager .... Ms. Robin MATNEY

Pinnacle Career Institute (E)

10301 Hickman Mills Drive, Kansas City MO 64137
County: Jackson FICE Identification: 010405
Unit ID: 177302
Telephone: (816) 331-5700 Carnegie Class: Spec 2-yr-Health
FAX Number: (816) 331-2026 Calendar System: Quarter
URL: www.pcitraining.edu
Established: 1953 Annual Undergrad Tuition & Fees: N/A
Enrollment: 580 Coed
Affiliation or Control: Proprietary IRS Status: Proprietary
Highest Offering: Associate Degree
Accreditation: ACICS

01 Executive Director .... Matt KILLDAY
05 Director of Education .... Guy COGNET
36 Director Student and Career Service .... Nick FOLEY

Pinnacle Career Institute (F)

11500 Ambassador Road, Suite 221, Kansas City MO 64153
Telephone: (816) 270-5300 Identification: 770737
Accreditation: ACICS

Ranken Technical College (G)

4431 Finney Avenue, Saint Louis MO 63113-2898
County: Saint Louis FICE Identification: 012500
Unit ID: 178891
Telephone: (314) 371-0236 Carnegie Class: Bac/Assoc-Mixed
FAX Number: (314) 371-0241 Calendar System: Semester
URL: www.ranken.edu
Established: 1907 Annual Undergrad Tuition & Fees: $14,457
Enrollment: 1,851 Coed
Affiliation or Control: Independent Non-Profit IRS Status: 501(c)3
Highest Offering: Baccalaureate
Accreditation: NH

01 President .... Mr. Stan SHOUN
10 Vice President for Finance & Admin .... Mr. Peter T. MURTAUGH
03 Executive Vice President .... Mr. Don POHL
51 Dean of Continuing Education .... Mr. Keyvan GERAMI
05 Dean Academic Affairs .... Ms. Crystal HERRON
07 Admissions Director .... Mr. Michael E. HAWLEY
06 Registrar .... Ms. Carol J. WINKLER
18 Director Buildings & Grounds .... Mr. David CADLE
29 Director of Alumni Relations .... Ms. Kathy T. FERN
37 Director Financial Aid .... Ms. Michelle L. WILLIAMS
21 Business Office Manager .... Ms. Sara M. DAMINSKI
36 Career Services Coordinator .... Ms. Janie K. SUMMERS
15 Human Resources Coordinator .... Ms. Janice A. BOLLMANN
04 Administrative Asst to President .... Ms. Patricia CAPPS

Research College of Nursing (H)

2525 E Meyer Boulevard, Kansas City MO 64132-1133
County: Jackson FICE Identification: 006392
Unit ID: 178989
Telephone: (816) 995-2800 Carnegie Class: Spec-4-yr-Other Health
FAX Number: (816) 995-2817 Calendar System: Semester
URL: www.researchcollege.edu
Established: 1980 Annual Undergrad Tuition & Fees: N/A
Enrollment: 415 Coed
Affiliation or Control: Proprietary IRS Status: Proprietary
Highest Offering: Master's
Accreditation: NH, NURSE

01 President .... Dr. Nancy O. DEBASIO
05 Dean .... Dr. Julie NAUSER
07 Director Admissions .... Ms. Leslie BURRY
32 Director Student Affairs .... Ms. Amanda GRAY
37 Director Financial Aid .... Ms. Stacie WITHERS
24 Director LRC .... Ms. Tobey STOSBERG
105 Director Web Based Education .... Ms. Sheryl MAX
09 Senior Technology Analyst .... Mr. Bill HAMPSON
04 Administrative Asst to President .... Mrs. Sherry L. OWEN
06 Registrar .... Ms. Camelia WILLIAMS
08 Head Librarian .... Ms. Kitty SERLING

Rockbridge Seminary (I)

3111 East Battlefield Street, Springfield MO 65804
County: Greene Identification: 667151
Telephone: (866) 931-4300 Carnegie Class: Not Classified
FAX Number: (866) 931-4300 Calendar System: Semester
URL: www.rockbridge.edu
Established: 2002 Annual Graduate Tuition & Fees: N/A
Enrollment: N/A Coed
Affiliation or Control: Independent Non-Profit IRS Status: 501(c)3
Highest Offering: Doctorate; No Undergraduates
Accreditation: DEAC

01 President .... Dr. Daryl ELDRIDGE
05 Chief Learning Officer .... Dr. Sam SIMMONS
08 Head Librarian .... Seth ALLEN
04 Administrative Asst to President .... Heather WILLIAMSON
29 Director Alumni Relations .... Linda GRABER

Rockhurst University (J)

1100 Rockhurst Road, Kansas City MO 64110-2561
County: Jackson FICE Identification: 002499
Unit ID: 179043
Telephone: (816) 501-4000 Carnegie Class: Masters/L
FAX Number: (816) 501-4588 Calendar System: Semester
URL: www.rockhurst.edu
Established: 1910 Annual Undergrad Tuition & Fees: $34,790
Enrollment: 3,002 Coed
Affiliation or Control: Roman Catholic IRS Status: 501(c)3
Highest Offering: Doctorate
Accreditation: NH, BUS, OT, PTA, SP, TEAC

01 President .... Rev. Thomas B. CURRAN
30 Vice Pres University Advancement .... Mr. Robert GRANT
10 Chief Financial Officer .... Mr. Gerald MOENCH
05 Vice Pres for Academic Affairs .... Dr. Douglas N. DUNHAM
88 Asst to Pres for Mission & Ministry .... Dr. Ellen SPAKE
32 VP Student Development/Athletics .... Dr. Matthew D. QUICK
18 Assoc VP Facilities & Technology .... Mr. Matt W. HEINRICH
84 Associate Vice Pres Enrollment .... Mr. Lane RAMEY
20 Assoc VP Academic Affairs/Planning .... Dr. Paula SHORTER
35 Director of Student Life .... Ms. Angie CARR ROBINETT
88 Assistant Dean of Students .... Mrs. Sandy WADDELL
39 Associate Dean of Students .... Mr. Mark HETZLER
04 Assistant to the President .... Ms. Decla TYLER-SIMPSON
50 Dean Helzberg Sch of Management .... Dr. Cheryl M. MCCONNELL
49 Dean Arts & Sciences .... Dr. Pedro MALIGO
58 Int Dean Sch Graduate/Prof Studies .... Dr. Michael CLUMP
66 Pres Research College of Nursing .... Dr. Nancy DEBASIO
08 Director Library .... Ms. Laurie E. HATHMAN
06 Registrar .... Ms. Minda THROWER
37 Director Student Financial Aid .... Ms. Maureen MCKINNON
41 Director of Athletics .... Mr. Gary BURNS
15 Director of Human Resources .... Ms. Barbra UPTON-GARVIN
13 Director of Infrastructure Services .... Mr. Michael CRAIG
36 Director of Career Center .... Mr. Michael J. THEOBALD
102 Director Foundation/Corp Relations .... Ms. Amy DROUIN
26 Director of Public Relations .... Ms. Katherine FROHOFF
29 Director of University Engagement .... Ms. Mary MOONEY BURNS
88 Director of Marketing .... Ms. Jennifer KNOBEL
42 Director of Campus Ministry .... Ms. Cindy SCHMERSAL
19 Director Security/Safety .... Mr. Randy HOPKINS
38 Director of Student Counseling .... Dr. Elbert DARDEN
31 Director Community Relations .... Ms. Alicia R. DOUGLAS

07	Director of Operations-Admission	Ms. Annie LEHWALD
40	Director Bookstore	Ms. Jami CADE
92	Director Honors Program	Dr. Mindy WALKER
108	Assessment Coordinator	Ms. Annalisa GRAMLICH
09	Institutional Research Coordinator	Ms. Wendy PICKEL
28	Area & Diversity Coordinator	Ms. Emily J. KEMPF
14	Support Manager - Computer Services	Mr. Darnell JONES
88	Controller	Ms. Kris PACE
88	Dean Research College of Nursing	Ms. Julie NAUSER
105	Web Development Director	Mr. Jeremiah BARBER
104	Study Abroad Advisor	Ms. Paivi GIANNIOS

St. Charles Community College (A)

4601 Mid Rivers Mall Drive, Cottleville MO 63376-2865

County: Saint Charles — FICE Identification: 025306
Unit ID: 262031
Telephone: (636) 922-8000 — Carnegie Class: Assoc/HT-High Trad
FAX Number: (636) 922-8352 — Calendar System: Semester
URL: www.stchas.edu
Established: 1986 — Annual Undergrad Tuition & Fees (In-District): $2,472
Enrollment: 7,153 — Coed
Affiliation or Control: State/Local — IRS Status: 501(c)3
Highest Offering: Associate Degree
Accreditation: NH, ADNUR, CAHIIM, EMT, OTA

01	Interim President	Mr. Todd GALBIERZ
04	Exec Assistant to the President	Ms. Julie PARCEL
05	Int VP Academic/Student Affairs	Dr. John BOOKSTAVER
30	VP College Advancement/Planning	Ms. Kasey MCKEE
10	VP Administrative Services	Mr. Todd GALBIERZ
15	VP Human Resources	Ms. Donna DAVIS
26	VP Marketing/Enrollment Services	Ms. Heather MCDORMAN
18	Director of Facilities	Mr. Al KOEHLER
20	AVP for Academic/Student Affairs	Dr. Michael B. DOMPIERRE
62	Dean Learning Resources & Acad Sup	Dr. Stephanie TOLSON
09	Director Grants and Research	Dr. Chris JACKSON
13	AVP Technology/Online Learning	Mr. William STRECKER
84	Dean Enrollment Services	Ms. Kathy BROCKGREITENS
19	Director Public Safety	Mr. Bob RONKOSKI
90	Director Technology Support	Ms. Lisa MOUSER
32	Dean of Student Success	Mr. Boyd COPELAND
51	Assoc Dean Continuing Education	Ms. Tina SIEKER
50	Dean Bus/Sci/Educ/Math & Comp Sci	Dr. John BOOKSTAVER
57	Dean Arts/Humanities & Soc Sci	Ms. Karen JONES
40	Director Bookstore and Food Service	Ms. Patricia A. HAYNES
41	Athletic Director	Mr. Chris G. GOBER
96	Director Purchasing	Ms. Christine E. ROMER
91	Director Administrative Computing	Mr. David SCHULTE
06	Registrar	Ms. Kathy BROCKGREITENS
21	Director Financial Services	Ms. Susan RUBEMEYER
36	Job Placement Coordinator	Ms. Martha A. TOEBBEN
51	Dean Corporate & Community Dev	Ms. Amanda SIZEMORE
88	Assoc Dean Student Success	Ms. Kelley PFEIFFER

Saint Louis Christian College (B)

1360 Grandview Drive, Florissant MO 63033-6499

County: Saint Louis — FICE Identification: 012580
Unit ID: 179256
Telephone: (314) 837-6777 — Carnegie Class: Spec-4-yr-Faith
FAX Number: (314) 837-8291 — Calendar System: Semester
URL: https://stlchristian.edu/
Established: 1956 — Annual Undergrad Tuition & Fees: $10,075
Enrollment: 179 — Coed
Affiliation or Control: Other Protestant — IRS Status: 501(c)3
Highest Offering: Baccalaureate
Accreditation: BI

00	Chancellor	Mr. Thomas W. MCGEE
01	President	Dr. Guthrie VEECH
05	Academic Dean	Dr. Eddy SANDERS
10	Vice Pres of Finance/Operations	Dr. Judy LINCOLN
32	Dean of Students	Ms. Christine CABLE
08	Library Manager	Dr. Michael PABARCUS
41	Athletic Director	Mr. Scott WOMBLE
06	Registrar	Ms. Cindy BINGAMON
37	Financial Aid Director	Ms. Pam RALLS
40	Bookstore Manager	Ms. Jeri Ann JERALDS
07	Admissions Counselor	Ms. Haley WOMBLE

Saint Louis College of Health Careers-Fenton Campus (C)

1297 N Highway Drive, Fenton MO 63026-1909

Telephone: (636) 529-0000 — Identification: 666274
Accreditation: ABHES, COARC, OTA, PTAA

† Branch campus of Saint Louis College of Health Careers-South Taylor, Saint Louis, MO.

Saint Louis College of Health Careers-South Taylor (D)

909 S Taylor Avenue, Saint Louis MO 63110-1511

County: Saint Louis — FICE Identification: 023405
Unit ID: 179511
Telephone: (314) 652-0300 — Carnegie Class: Spec 2-yr-Health
FAX Number: (314) 652-2125 — Calendar System: Semester
URL: www.slchc.com
Established: 1981 — Annual Undergrad Tuition & Fees: N/A
Enrollment: 305 — Coed
Affiliation or Control: Proprietary — IRS Status: Proprietary
Highest Offering: Associate Degree
Accreditation: ABHES

32	Student Services Coordinator	Ms. Teresa JACKSON
07	Director of Admissions	Ms. Joanna FINCH
11	Chief of Administration	Dr. Rush ROBINSON
36	Director Student Placement	Ms. Melissa BROWN
53	Director of Education	Ms. Melissa BROWN

St. Louis College of Pharmacy (E)

4588 Parkview Place, Saint Louis MO 63110-1088

County: Independent City — FICE Identification: 002504
Unit ID: 179265
Telephone: (314) 367-8700 — Carnegie Class: Spec-4-yr-Other Health
FAX Number: (314) 446-8304 — Calendar System: Semester
URL: www.stlcop.edu
Established: 1864 — Annual Undergrad Tuition & Fees: $27,847
Enrollment: 1,361 — Coed
Affiliation or Control: Independent Non-Profit — IRS Status: 501(c)3
Highest Offering: First Professional Degree
Accreditation: NH, PHAR

01	President	Dr. John A. PIEPER
30	Vice Pres Devel/Alumni Relations	Mr. Brett T. SCHOTT
10	VP Finance/Administration/CFO	Ms. Heather FLABIANO
84	VP Enrollment Services/Marketing	Ms. Beth KESERAUSKIS
90	Vice Pres Info Technology & CIO	Mr. Chad SHEPHERD
18	AVP College Services	Mr. Eric KNOLL
49	Dean Arts & Science/Student Affairs	Dr. Kimberly J. KILGORE
67	Dean of Pharmacy	Dr. Bruce CANADAY
15	Director of Human Resources	Ms. Daniel C. BAUER
30	Senior Development Officer	Ms. Colleen WATERMON
06	Registrar	Ms. Laura KLOS
08	Library Director	Ms. Jill NISSEN
37	Director of Financial Aid	Mr. Daniel J. STIFFLER
41	Director of Athletics	Ms. Jill HARTER
88	Special Assistant to the President	Sr. Mary Louise DEGENHART
88	Special Assistant to the President	Mr. Michael SASS
07	Director of Admissions	Mr. Chase DAVIS
108	AVP Institutional Effectiveness	Mr. George VINEYARD
19	Director Security/Safety	Mr. Scott PATTERSON
29	Director Alumni Relations	Ms. Stephanie HOFFMANN
38	Director Counseling Center	Ms. Michelle HASTINGS
43	General Counsel	Mr. Kenneth FLEISCHMANN
44	Annual Giving Officer	Mr. Kevin LISTER

*Saint Louis Community College Center (F)

300 S Broadway, Saint Louis MO 63102-2820

County: Saint Louis — FICE Identification: 002471
Unit ID: 179283
Telephone: (314) 539-5000 — Carnegie Class: N/A
FAX Number: (314) 539-5170
URL: www.stlcc.edu

01	Chancellor	Dr. Jeff PITTMAN
05	Vice Chanc Academic Affairs	Vacant
10	Vice Chanc Finance/Administration	Mr. Kent KAY
103	Assoc VC Workforce & Cmty Develop	Mr. Stephen LONG
102	Executive Director Foundation	Ms. Jo-Ann DIGMAN
84	Director Enrollment Management	Vacant
15	Assoc Vice Chanc HR	Mr. Bill MILLER
26	Director Public Info/Marketing	Mr. Dan KIMACK
09	Director of Institutional Research	Ms. Kelli BURNS
20	Director Instructional Resources	Ms. Sheila OUELLETTE
30	Director of Grants	Ms. Gina BENESH
06	Sr Mgr/Enrollment Processing	Ms. Karla GABLE
04	Administrative Asst to Chancellor	Ms. Yvonne HELBERG
101	Secretary of the Board	Ms. Rebecca GARRISON
106	Director Online Education	Ms. Robin E. GREBING
37	Dir Dist Financial Aid/Scholarships	Ms. Regina G. BLACKSHEAR
96	Assistant Controller	Ms. Cindy GREEN
19	Director Security/Safety	Mr. Mark POTRATZ
41	Athletic Director	Mr. Shawn SUMME
43	Dir Legal Services/General Counsel	Ms. Mary NELSON

**Saint Louis Community College at Forest Park* (G)

5600 Oakland Avenue, Saint Louis MO 63110-1393

Telephone: (314) 644-9100 — Identification: 770946
Accreditation: NH, ACFEI, ADNUR, CAHIIM, COARC, DA, DH, DMS, EMT, FUSER, MLTAD, RAD, SURGT

**Saint Louis Community College at Florissant Valley* (H)

3400 Pershall Road, Saint Louis MO 63135-1499

Telephone: (314) 513-4200 — FICE Identification: 002470
Accreditation: &NH, ADNUR, ART, DIETT, ENGT

† Regional accreditation is carried under the parent institution in Saint Louis, MO

**Saint Louis Community College at Meramec* (I)

11333 Big Bend Road, Kirkwood MO 63122-5799

Telephone: (314) 984-7500 — FICE Identification: 002472
Accreditation: &NH, ADNUR, ART, OTA, PTAA

† Regional accreditation is carried under the parent institution in Saint Louis, MO

**Saint Louis Community College at Wildwood* (J)

2645 Generations Drive, Wildwood MO 63040-1168

Telephone: (636) 422-2000 — Identification: 667084
Accreditation: &NH

† Regional accreditation is carried under the parent institution in Saint Louis, MO

Saint Louis University (K)

One Grand Boulevard, Saint Louis MO 63103-2097

County: Independent City — FICE Identification: 002506
Unit ID: 179159
Telephone: (314) 977-2500 — Carnegie Class: DU-Higher
FAX Number: (314) 977-3874 — Calendar System: Semester
URL: www.slu.edu
Established: 1818 — Annual Undergrad Tuition & Fees: $39,226
Enrollment: 17,052 — Coed
Affiliation or Control: Roman Catholic — IRS Status: 501(c)3
Highest Offering: Doctorate
Accreditation: NH, AAB, ARCPA, ART, BUS, BUSA, CAATE, CAHIIM, CLPSY, CYTO, DENT, DIETD, DIETI, ENG, HSA, LAW, MED, MFCD, MT, NMT, NURSE, OT, PH, PTA, RTT, SP, SW, TED

01	President	Dr. Fred P. PESTELLO
05	Provost	Dr. Nancy BRICKHOUSE
10	Vice Pres/Chief Financial Officer	Mr. David HEIMBURGER
18	Assoc VP Facilities Management	Mr. Michael LUCIDO
84	VP Enrollment & Ret Management	Mr. Jay GOFF
12	Director Madrid Campus	Dr. Paul VITA
15	VP Human Resources	Mr. Mickey LUNA
26	VP Marketing and Communications	Mr. Jeffrey FOWLER
43	Vice President/General Counsel	Mr. William R. KAUFFMAN
32	Vice President Student Development	Dr. Kent PORTERFIELD
30	VP Development	Ms. Sheila M. MANION
42	Spcl Asst to Pres Mission/Identity	Fr. Christopher COLLINS, SJ
13	Vice Pres Information Tech Svcs/CIO	Mr. David HAKANSON
23	Vice President for Medical Affairs	Dr. Philip O. ALDERSON
27	Asst VP for Marketing & Creat Svcs	Ms. Laura GEISER
29	Exec Development Director	Ms. Meg CONNOLLY
21	Assistant VP & Controller	Mr. David GRABE
35	Associate VP and Dean of Students	Dr. Ramona HICKS
54	Dean Parks Col Engr/Aviation	Dr. Michelle SABICK
76	Dean Doisy College of Health Scis	Dr. Mardell WILSON
49	Dean Arts & Sciences	Dr. Christopher DUNCAN
50	Dean Cook School of Business	Dr. Mark HIGGINS
61	Dean of Law	Mr. Michael A. WOLFF
63	Dean of Medical School	Dr. Philip O. ALDERSON
79	Dean Philosophy & Letters	Bro. William REHG, SJ
69	Dean Col Pub Health & Soc Justice	Dr. Collins AIRHIHENBUWA
53	Dean Col of Educ & Public Svc	Dr. Anne RULE
08	University Librarian	Mr. David CASSENS
88	Exec Dir Ctr for Health Care Ethics	Dr. Jeffrey BISHOP
52	Exec Dir Ctr Advanced Dental Educ	Dr. John HATTON
46	Vice President for Research	Dr. Kenneth OLLIFF
19	Asst VP Pub Safety & Emergency Prep	Mr. James MORAN
06	University Registrar	Mr. Jay HAUGEN
07	Dean of Undergraduate Admission	Ms. Jean GILMAN
37	Director Financial Aid	Ms. Cari S. WICKLIFFE
39	Director Housing & Res Life	Ms. Melinda CARLSON
41	Athletics Director	Mr. Christopher V. MAY
36	Director Career Services	Ms. Kim REITTER
85	Director International Center	Vacant
92	Director Honors Program	Dr. Jessica PEROLIO
23	Director Student Health Center	Ms. Deborah M. SCHEFF
31	Pgm Mgr Leadership Community Svcs	Dr. Bryan SOKOL
100	Director of the Pres Office	Ms. Barb SAPIENZA
88	Director Univ Museums/Galleries	Dr. Petruta LIPAN
44	Exec Development Dir Planned Giving	Mr. Kent G. LEVAN
40	Manager Bookstore	Ms. Debbie SCHNEIDER
20	Asst Academic Vice President	Dr. Steven SANCHEZ
96	Director of Business Services	Mr. Jeff HOVEY
22	Dir Ofc of Inst Equity & Diversity	Ms. Michelle LEWIS
86	Director Government Relations	Mr. Marc SCHEESSELE
28	Spcl Asst to Pres Diversity/Com Eng	Dr. Jonathan C. SMITH
103	Executive Dir Workforce Development	Ms. Katherine CAIN
105	Director Web Services	Mr. Mark RIMAR
38	Director Student Counseling	Dr. Steve BYRNES

Saint Luke's College of Health Sciences (L)

624 Westport Road, Kansas City MO 64111

County: Jackson — FICE Identification: 009782
Unit ID: 179450
Telephone: (816) 936-8700 — Carnegie Class: Spec-4-yr-Other Health
FAX Number: N/A — Calendar System: Semester
URL: www.saintlukescollege.edu
Established: 1903 — Annual Undergrad Tuition & Fees: N/A
Enrollment: 453 — Coed
Affiliation or Control: Independent Non-Profit — IRS Status: 501(c)3
Highest Offering: Master's
Accreditation: NH, NURSE

01	President	Dr. Hubert BENITEZ
05	Academic Dean	Dr. Victoria GRANDO
10	Chief Financial Officer	Ms. Rebecca PECK
32	Dean of Students	Ms. Marcia LADAGE
88	Director Accreditation/Quality Mgmt	Ms. Tere NAYLOR
30	Director of Development	Dr. Melody MESSNER

06 Registrar/Dir Records Mgmt ... Ms. Jean SUMMERS
26 Communications/Alumni Rels Mgr ... Ms. Laurie DELONG
84 Director Enrollment Management ... Mr. Josh RICHARDS

Southeast Missouri Hospital College of Nursing and Health Sciences (A)

2001 William Street, 2nd Floor,
Cape Girardeau MO 63703-5815
County: Cape Girardeau FICE Identification: 030709
Unit ID: 417734
Telephone: (573) 334-6825 Carnegie Class: Spec 2-yr-Health
FAX Number: (573) 339-7805 Calendar System: Semester
URL: www.sehcollege.edu
Established: 1990 Annual Undergrad Tuition & Fees: $17,580
Enrollment: 233 Coed
Affiliation or Control: Independent Non-Profit IRS Status: 501(c)3
Highest Offering: Baccalaureate
Accreditation: NH, ADNUR, MT, RAD, SURGT

01 President ... Dr. Tonya BUTTRY
05 Dean for General Education ... Dr. Leon BOOK
66 Dean of Nursing ... Dr. Rebecca WHIFFEN
06 Registrar ... Ms. Debbie HOWEY
37 Financial Aid Coordinator ... Ms. Margie SCHWENT
07 Admissions/Instl Research Officer ... Ms. Rhonda VANDERGRIFF
10 Business Officer ... Ms. Deanna SELLS

Southeast Missouri State University (B)

One University Plaza, Cape Girardeau MO 63701-4799
County: Cape Girardeau FICE Identification: 002501
Unit ID: 179557
Telephone: (573) 651-2000 Carnegie Class: Masters/L
FAX Number: (573) 651-2200 Calendar System: Semester
URL: www.semo.edu
Established: 1873 Annual Undergrad Tuition & Fees (In-State): $6,990
Enrollment: 12,087 Coed
Affiliation or Control: State IRS Status: 501(c)3
Highest Offering: Beyond Master's But Less Than Doctorate
Accreditation: NH, BUS, CAATE, CACREP, CEA, CS, DIETD, DIETI, ENG, ENGT, JOUR, MUS, NAIT, NRPA, NURSE, SP, SW, TED, THEA

01 President ... Dr. Carlos VARGAS
05 Provost/Chief Academic Ofcr ... Dr. Karl KUNKEL
10 VP Finance & Administration ... Mrs. Kathy M. MANGELS
84 VP Enrollment Mgmt/Student Success ... Dr. Debbie BELOW
30 Vice Pres University Advancement ... Mr. Bill HOLLAND
20 Vice Provost ... Dr. Charles MCALLISTER
108 Asst Provost for Inst Rsch & Assess ... Dr. Kang BAI
04 Associate to the President ... Ms. Diane O. SIDES
100 Sr Assoc to the President/Board Sec ... Vacant
22 Coord of Inst Equity & Diversity ... Ms. Sonia RUCKER
13 Asst Vice Pres Information Tech ... Mr. Floyd DAVENPORT
106 Dean Online Lrng ... Dr. Allen GATHMAN
58 Dean Sch of Grad Studies ... Dr. Charles MCALLISTER
89 Dean of University Studies ... Dr. Francisco BARRIOS
50 Dean DL Harrison Col of Business ... Dr. Gerald MCDOUGALL
53 Dean College of Education ... Dr. Diana ROGERS-ADKINSON
76 Dean College Health & Human Svc ... Dr. Morris JENKINS
79 Dean College of Liberal Arts ... Dr. Francisco BARRIOS
72 Dean College of Science/Tech & Ag ... Dr. Chris MCGOWAN
32 Dean of Students ... Dr. Debbie BELOW
08 Dean of Kent Library ... Ms. Barbara GLACKIN
07 Director of Admissions ... Ms. Lenell HAHN
109 AVP Stdnt Success & Auxiliary Svcs ... Dr. Bruce SKINNER
35 Director of Campus Life & Event Svc ... Ms. Michele IRBY
26 Exec Dir Univ Comm & Mktg ... Mr. Jeff HARMON
41 Director of Athletics ... Mr. Brady L. BARKE
29 Director Alumni Services ... Mr. Jay WOLZ
85 Exec Dir Intl Education & Svcs ... Mr. Kevin TIMLIN
51 Dir Extended & Continuing Education ... Vacant
12 Director Malden Campus ... Dr. Nicholas THIELE
12 Director Kennett Campus ... Ms. Marsha L. BLANCHARD
12 Director Sikeston Campus ... Mr. Stephen BORGSMILLER
18 Director of Facilities Management ... Ms. Angela MEYER
37 Director of Financial Aid ... Ms. Karen WALKER
27 Director of News Bureau ... Ms. Ann K. HAYES
15 Director of Human Resources ... Mr. Jim COOK
19 Interim Dir of Public Safety/Trans ... Ms. Beth GLAUS
06 Registrar ... Ms. Sandy L. HINKLE
88 Director of Show Me Center ... Mr. Wil GORMAN
92 Director Jane Stephens Honors Pgm ... Dr. Kevin DICKSON
38 Dir Counseling & Disability Svcs ... Ms. Torie GROGRAN
96 Purchasing Manager ... Ms. Sarah STEINNERD
102 Director of Corporate Relations ... Mr. Chris MARTIN
39 Director of Residence Life ... Dr. Kendra SKINNER

Southwest Baptist University (C)

1600 University Avenue, Bolivar MO 65613-2597
County: Polk FICE Identification: 002502
Unit ID: 179326
Telephone: (417) 328-5281 Carnegie Class: Masters/M
FAX Number: (417) 328-1514 Calendar System: Semester
URL: www.sbuniv.edu
Established: 1878 Annual Undergrad Tuition & Fees: $21,908
Enrollment: 3,696 Coed
Affiliation or Control: Southern Baptist IRS Status: 501(c)3
Highest Offering: Doctorate
Accreditation: NH, ACBSP, ADNUR, #CAATE, CS, MUS, NUR, PTA, RAD, SW

01 President ... Dr. Pat TAYLOR
05 Provost ... Dr. Lee SKINKLE
11 Vice President Administration ... Mrs. Tara PARSON
30 Vice President University Relations ... Dr. Brad JOHNSON
84 Dean of Enrollment Management ... Mr. Darren CROWDER
32 Vice Pres for Student Development ... Dr. Rob HARRIS
88 Vice Pres Oper Mercy Col Nurs & HS ... Dr. Robert MCGLASSON
20 Associate Provost ... Dr. Allison LANGFORD
10 Controller ... Ms. Terri ROGERS
29 Director of Alumni Engagement ... Mrs. Holly BRIDGE
07 Director Admissions ... Mrs. Becky VAN STAVERN
41 Athletic Director ... Mr. Mike PITTS
06 Registrar ... Mr. John CREDILLE
35 Director Student Activities ... Mr. Nathan PENLAND
39 Director Residence Life ... Ms. Landee NEVILLS
42 Director University Ministries ... Mr. Kurt CADDY
15 Director of Human Resources ... Mrs. Carolyn O'KELLEY
18 Director Physical Plant ... Mr. Bob GLIDWELL
19 Director Campus Security ... Mr. Mark GRABOWSKI
08 Director of Library Services ... Dr. Ed WALTON
50 Dean College Business/Computer Sci ... Dr. Troy BETHARDS
73 Dean College Theology/Ministry ... Dr. Rodney REEVES
53 Dean Education/Social Sciences ... Dr. Kevin SCHRIVER
57 Dean Music/Arts/Letters ... Dr. Jeff WATERS
81 Dean Science/Math ... Dr. Perry TOMPKINS
36 Director of Career Services ... Mrs. Suzanne POWERS
13 Network Administrator ... Mr. Kevin KELLEY
90 Director Instructional Technology ... Mr. Neal CROSS
91 Chief Technology Officer ... Mr. David BOLTON
38 Director Counseling Services ... Mrs. Debbie WALKER
37 Director Student Financial Planning ... Mr. Brad GAMBLE
56 Director Extended Learning ... Mr. Scott MCNEAL
26 Chief Public Relations Officer ... Mrs. Charlotte MARSCH
09 Director of Institutional Research ... Dr. Duke JONES
96 Director of Purchasing ... Vacant
40 Book Store Manager ... Ms. Carol SHOEMAKER
04 Administrative Asst to President ... Mrs. Ashley DINWIDDIE

Southwest Baptist University Mountain View Center (D)

209 W First Street, Mountain View MO 65548
Telephone: (417) 934-2999 Identification: 770326
Accreditation: &NH

† Regional accreditation is carried under the parent institution in Bolivar, MO

Southwest Baptist University Salem Center (E)

501 S Grand, Salem MO 65560
Telephone: (573) 729-7071 Identification: 770327
Accreditation: &NH

† Regional accreditation is carried under the parent institution in Bolivar, MO

Southwest Baptist University Springfield Center (F)

4431 S Fremont, Springfield MO 65804
Telephone: (417) 820-5049 Identification: 770328
Accreditation: &NH

† Regional accreditation is carried under the parent institution in Bolivar, MO

State Fair Community College (G)

3201 W 16th Street, Sedalia MO 65301-2199
County: Pettis FICE Identification: 008080
Unit ID: 179539
Telephone: (660) 596-7222 Carnegie Class: Assoc/HT-Mix Trad/Non
FAX Number: (660) 596-7335 Calendar System: Semester
URL: www.sfccmo.edu
Established: 1966 Annual Undergrad Tuition & Fees (In-District): $2,640
Enrollment: 4,983 Coed
Affiliation or Control: Local IRS Status: 501(c)3
Highest Offering: Associate Degree
Accreditation: NH, CAHIIM, CONST, DH, OTA, RAD

01 President ... Dr. Joanna ANDERSON
05 VP for Educ/Student Support Svcs ... Dr. Brent BATES
10 VP for Finance/Administration & HR ... Mr. Garry SORRELL
13 Chief Information Officer ... Mr. Mark HAVERLY
20 Dean of Academic Affairs ... Mr. Jim CUNNINGHAM
75 Dean Vocational/Technical Studies ... Mr. Mark KELCHNER
38 Dean Student Support ... Dr. Joe GILGOUR
102 Exec Director SFCC Foundation ... Ms. Mary TEURNER
06 Registrar ... Mrs. Jennifer WILBANKS
37 Director of Financial Aid ... Ms. Lana DEJAYNES
18 Chief Facilities/Physical Plant ... Mr. Justin O'NEAL
21 Controller Business Officer ... Mrs. Diane BROCKMAN
26 Director of Marketing/Communication ... Mrs. Dana KELCHNER
07 Director of Admissions ... Mrs. Amanda STOECKLEIN
04 Administrative Asst to President ... Ms. Toni WALTER
41 Athletic Director ... Mr. Darren PAMMIER
15 Director Human Resources ... Ms. Linda CHURCH

State Technical College of Missouri (H)

One Technology Drive, Linn MO 65051-0479
County: Osage FICE Identification: 004711
Unit ID: 177977
Telephone: (573) 897-5000 Carnegie Class: Assoc/HVT-High Trad
FAX Number: (573) 897-4656 Calendar System: Semester
URL: www.statetechmo.edu
Established: 1961 Annual Undergrad Tuition & Fees (In-State): $5,873
Enrollment: 1,259 Coed
Affiliation or Control: State IRS Status: 501(c)3
Highest Offering: Associate Degree
Accreditation: NH, DA, NAIT, PTAA, RAD

01 President ... Dr. Shawn D. STRONG
05 Dean Academic Affairs/Student Svcs ... Victoria SCHWINKE
13 Dean Information Technology ... Don LLOYD
09 Dean Institutional Research/Plng ... Dr. Rick MIHALEVICH
30 Executive Director Development ... Scott PETERS
08 Int College Librarian ... Christina PRUCHA
37 Director Student Financial Aid ... Becky WHITHAUS
06 Registrar ... Elaine BRANDT
07 Director Admissions ... Kathy SCHEULEN
10 Director of Finance ... Jennifer JACOBS
20 Associate Academic Officer ... Janet CLANTON
21 Controller ... Lisa BUTLER
29 Dir Alumni Relations/Chief PR Ofcr ... Scott PETERS
32 Director Student Affairs ... Richard PEMBERTON
36 Director Student Placement ... Glenda WHITNEY
28 Director of Diversity ... Richard PEMBERTON
15 Director Personnel Services ... Jennifer JACOBS
84 Director Enrollment Management ... Kathy SCHEULEN
18 Chief Facilities/Physical Plant ... Don LLOYD
38 Student Counselor ... Rebecca MEHMERT
101 Secretary of the Institution/Board ... Sue GOVE
86 Director Government Relations ... Becky DUNN

Stephens College (I)

1200 E Broadway, Columbia MO 65215-0001
County: Boone FICE Identification: 002512
Unit ID: 179548
Telephone: (573) 442-2211 Carnegie Class: Masters/S
FAX Number: (573) 876-7248 Calendar System: Semester
URL: www.stephens.edu
Established: 1833 Annual Undergrad Tuition & Fees: $29,176
Enrollment: 862 Female
Affiliation or Control: Independent Non-Profit IRS Status: 501(c)3
Highest Offering: Master's
Accreditation: NH, #ARCPA, CAHIIM

01 President ... Dr. Dianne LYNCH
10 Vice Pres Finance/Business/CFO ... Dr. Lindi OVERTON
05 Vice Pres Academic Affairs ... Dr. Leslie WILLEY
30 Vice Pres Institutional Advancement ... Ms. Meichele FOSTER
32 Vice Pres Student Development ... Dr. Vicky OWLES
26 VP of Marketing/Public Relations ... Ms. Rebecca KLINE
06 Registrar ... Ms. Linda SHARP
13 IT Director ... Mr. Mark BRUNNER
41 Athletic Director ... Mr. Adam SAMSON
21 Director of Accounting ... Mr. Josh HENGGLER
37 Director of Financial Aid ... Ms. Kimberly STONECIPHER-FISHER
04 Executive Asst to President ... Ms. Lita PISTONO
07 Director of Admissions ... Ms. Tiffany GOALDER
08 Head Librarian ... Mr. Dan KAMMER
18 Director of Facilities Mgmt ... Mr. Gregory MANKEY
19 Director Security/Safety ... Mr. Ken HAMMOND
39 Director of Residence Life ... Ms. Alissa PEI

Stevens Institute of Business & Arts (J)

1521 Washington Avenue, Saint Louis MO 63103
County: Saint Louis FICE Identification: 008552
Unit ID: 178767
Telephone: (314) 421-0949 Carnegie Class: Spec-4-yr-Bus
FAX Number: (314) 421-0304 Calendar System: Quarter
URL: www.siba.edu
Established: 1947 Annual Undergrad Tuition & Fees: $13,230
Enrollment: 143 Coed
Affiliation or Control: Proprietary IRS Status: Proprietary
Highest Offering: Baccalaureate
Accreditation: ACICS

01 President ... Ms. Cynthia A. MUSTERMAN
05 Academic Dean & Registrar ... Ms. Emilee SCHNEFKE
37 Financial Aid Director ... Ms. Christa SIAMPOS
07 Director of Admissions ... Ms. Sara DORN
36 Career Services Director ... Ms. Emily HUEY

Texas County Technical College (K)

6915 S Highway 63 PO Box 314, Houston MO 65483
County: Texas FICE Identification: 035793
Unit ID: 441487
Telephone: (417) 967-5466 Carnegie Class: Spec 2-yr-Health
FAX Number: (417) 967-4604 Calendar System: Semester
URL: www.texascountytech.edu
Established: 1986 Annual Undergrad Tuition & Fees: $15,292
Enrollment: 125 Coed
Affiliation or Control: Independent Non-Profit IRS Status: 501(c)3

Highest Offering: Associate Degree
Accreditation: ACICS

01 President .... Ms. Charlotte GRAY
07 Director of Admissions/Registrar .... Ms. Clarice CASEBEER
37 Financial Aid Liaison .... Ms. Clarice CASEBEER

Three Rivers Community College (A)

2080 Three Rivers Boulevard,
Poplar Bluff MO 63901-2350
County: Butler FICE Identification: 004713
Unit ID: 179645
Telephone: (573) 840-9600 Carnegie Class: Assoc/HT-Mix Trad/Non
FAX Number: (573) 840-9604 Calendar System: Semester
URL: www.trcc.edu
Established: 1966 Annual Undergrad Tuition & Fees (In-State): $4,104
Enrollment: 4,201 Coed
Affiliation or Control: State IRS Status: 501(c)3
Highest Offering: Associate Degree
Accreditation: NH, ACBSP, ADNUR, EMT, MLTAD, OTA

01 President .... Dr. Wesley A. PAYNE
10 Chief Financial Officer .... Ms. Charlotte EUBANK
05 VP for Academic and Student Service .... Dr. Mary Lou BROWN
08 Director Library Services .... Ms. Kathy SANDERS
37 Director Financial Aid .... Ms. Regina MORRIS
06 Registrar .... Ms. Melanie HAMANN
32 Dean of Student Services .... Ms. Ann MATTHEWS
09 Dean of Institutional Effectiveness .... Dr. Maribeth PAYNE
09 Director of Institutional Research .... Ms. Bridgett BARNHILL
18 Chief Facilities/Physical Plant .... Mr. Rob TOMLINSON
15 Director Human Resources .... Ms. Kristina D. MCDANIEL
26 Chief Public Relations Officer .... Ms. Teresa JOHNSON
30 Chief Development/Dir Alumni Rels ...... Ms. Michelle REYNOLDS
84 Director Enrollment Management .... Mr. Chris ADAMS
96 Dir Procurement/Risk Management .... Ms. Cambrea HALCUMB
04 Administrative Asst to President .... Ms. Janine HEATH
103 Dir Workforce/Career Development .... Mr. Kevin SWAN
13 Chief Info Technology Officer (CIO) .... Mr. Steve ATWOOD
22 Dir Affirmative Action/EEO .... Ms. Kristina D. MCDANIEL
39 Director Student Housing .... Ms. Laura MILLIGAN

Truman State University (B)

100 E Normal, Kirksville MO 63501-4221
County: Adair FICE Identification: 002495
Unit ID: 178615
Telephone: (660) 785-4000 Carnegie Class: Masters/M
FAX Number: (660) 785-4030 Calendar System: Semester
URL: www.truman.edu
Established: 1867 Annual Undergrad Tuition & Fees (In-State): $7,456
Enrollment: 6,248 Coed
Affiliation or Control: State IRS Status: 501(c)3
Highest Offering: Master's
Accreditation: NH, BUS, BUSA, CAATE, MUS, NURSE, SP

01 Interim President .... Dr. Susan L. THOMAS
05 Int Exec VP Acad Affairs & Provost .... Mr. Richard COUGHLIN
30 Int Co-Director Univ Advancement .... Mr. Charles HUNSAKER
30 Int Co-Director Univ Advancement .... Mrs. Denise L. SMITH
10 VP for Admin Finance & Planning .... Mr. David RECTOR
84 VP for Enrollment Management .... Mrs. Regina MORIN
32 VP for Student Affairs .... Dr. Lou Ann GILCHRIST
43 General Counsel .... Mr. Warren WELLS
21 Comptroller .... Mrs. Judy MULLINS
41 Athletic Director .... Mr. Jerry WOLLMERING
15 Executive Dir of Human Resources .... Ms. Sally HERLETH
07 Director of Admissions .... Mrs. Melody CHAMBERS
37 Financial Aid Director .... Mrs. Kathy ELSEA
06 Registrar .... Mrs. Margaret HERRON
13 Director Information Technology .... Mrs. Donna LISS
26 Director of Public Relations .... Mrs. Heidi TEMPLETON
88 Dir of Institute for Acad Outreach .... Dr. Kevin MINCH
38 Dir Student Health/Counseling Svcs .... Dr. Brenda HIGGINS
83 Dean Sch Social & Cultural Studies .... Dr. Elizabeth CLARK
49 Dean School of Arts & Letters .... Dr. James O'DONNELL
50 Dean School of Business .... Dr. Debra KERBY
53 Dean Sch of Health Sciences & Educ .... Dr. Janet GOOCH
81 Int Dean Sch Science & Mathematics .... Dr. Janet GOOCH

University of Central Missouri (C)

Administration Building, room 101,
Warrensburg MO 64093-5299
County: Johnson FICE Identification: 002454
Unit ID: 176965
Telephone: (660) 543-4255 Carnegie Class: Masters/L
FAX Number: (660) 543-4200 Calendar System: Semester
URL: www.ucmo.edu
Established: 1871 Annual Undergrad Tuition & Fees (In-State): $7,322
Enrollment: 13,379 Coed
Affiliation or Control: State IRS Status: 501(c)3
Highest Offering: Beyond Master's But Less Than Doctorate
Accreditation: NH, AAB, AAFCS, ART, BUS, BUSA, CAATE, CACREP, CEA, CIDA, CONST, CS, DIETD, ENGR, MUS, NAIT, NURSE, SP, SW, TED, THEA

01 President .... Dr. Charles M. AMBROSE
101 Exec Asst to Pres/Asst Sec to Board ..... Ms. Monica R. HUFFMAN
05 Provost/Chief Learning Officer .... Dr. Deborah J. CURTIS
32 Vice Prov Student Experience/Engage .Dr. Sharlene GARBER BAX
20 Vice Prov Academic Program/Services .... Dr. Kim ANDREWS
35 Assoc Vice Prov Student Services .... Dr. Corey L. BOWMAN
84 Vice Prov Recruitment/Outreach .... Dr. Mike GODARD
30 Vice Pres Univ Development .... Mr. Jason S. DRUMMOND
08 Dean of Library Services .... Dr. Gail STAINES
49 Dean College of Arts/Humanities/Sci .... Dr. Gersham NELSON
72 Dean College of Health/Science/Tech .... Dr. Alice L. GREIFE
50 Dean Harmon Col Business/Prof Stds .... Dr. Roger J. BEST
92 Dean Honors College & Intl
Affairs .... Dr. Joseph D. LEWANDOWSKI
53 Dean of College of Education .... Dr. Michael D. WRIGHT
10 Vice Pres Finance/Chief Ops Ofcr .... Vacant
13 Vice Provost for Technology & CIO .... Dr. James F. GRAHAM
41 Athletic Director .... Mr. Jerry M. HUGHES
06 Director of Registrar .... Ms. Teri A. BOWMAN
26 Interim Chief Comm Officer .... Mr. Dennis CRYDER
09 Director Testing Services .... Ms. Carole NIMMER
36 Dir Career Development Services .... Mr. Kenneth SCHUELLER
37 Dir Student Financial Assistance .... Ms. Angela L. KARLIN
19 Director of Public Safety .... Mr. Scott RHOAD
109 AVP Student Auxiliary Services .... Mr. Patrick J. BRADLEY
21 Controller .... Ms. Toni L. KREKE
18 Dir Facilities & Planning Op .... Mr. Chris BAMMAN
96 Director Purchasing .... Ms. Lisa BUTLER
15 Employee Relations Specialist .... Mr. Rick L. DIXON
40 Director of Univ Store & Textbooks .... Mr. Charles D. RUTT
56 Vice Provost of Extended Studies .... Ms. Laurel HOGUE
07 Director Admissions .... Ms. Ann A. NORDYKE
16 Asst Director of Human Resources .... Ms. Cheryl D. TRELOW
29 Asst VP Resources Development ...Ms. Jennifer L. VANDERBOUT
38 Director Counseling Center .... Dr. Paul D. POLYCHRONIS
24 Director CentralNET .... Mr. Michael JEFFRIES

*University of Missouri System Administration (D)

321 University Hall, Columbia MO 65211-3020
County: Boone FICE Identification: 002515
Unit ID: 178439
Telephone: (573) 882-2011 Carnegie Class: N/A
FAX Number: (573) 882-2721
URL: www.umsystem.edu

01 Interim President .... Mr. Michael A. MIDDLETON
100 Chief of Staff .... Ms. Zora Z. MULLIGAN
10 Vice President Finance .... Dr. Brian D. BURNETT
28 Chief Diversity/Equity/Incl Ofcr .... Dr. Kevin G. MCDONALD
05 Int VP Acad Affairs/Rsrch/Econ Dev .....Dr. Robert W. SCHWARTZ
13 Vice President Info Technology .... Dr. Gary K. ALLEN
86 Vice President University Relations .... Mr. Stephen C. KNORR
15 Int Vice Pres Human Resource Svcs .... Ms. Kelley STUCK
20 Sr Assoc Vice Pres Academic Affairs ....Dr. Steven W. GRAHAM
43 General Counsel .... Mr. Stephen J. OWENS
26 Chief Communications Officer .... Mr. John FOUGERE
17 CEO/COO UM Health Care .... Mr. Mitch WASDEN
21 Treasurer .... Mr. Tom F. RICHARDS
21 Controller .... Mr. Ryan RAPP
04 Executive Asst to President .... Ms. Regina A. MAY
101 Secretary of the Board of Curators .... Ms. Cindy S. HARMON

*University of Missouri - Columbia (E)

Columbia MO 65211-0001
County: Boone FICE Identification: 002516
Unit ID: 178396
Telephone: (573) 882-2121 Carnegie Class: DU-Highest
FAX Number: (573) 882-9907 Calendar System: Semester
URL: www.missouri.edu
Established: 1839 Annual Undergrad Tuition & Fees (In-State): $9,509
Enrollment: 35,425 Coed
Affiliation or Control: State IRS Status: 501(c)3
Highest Offering: Doctorate
Accreditation: NH, BUS, BUSA, CAATE, CIDA, CLPSY, COARC, COPSY, CS, DIETC, DMS, ENG, HSA, IPSY, JOUR, LAW, LIB, MED, MUS, NMT, NRPA, NURSE, OT, PCSAS, PH, PHAR, PTA, RAD, SCPSY, SP, SFAA, SW, TEAC, VET

02 Interim Chancellor .... Dr. Henry (Hank) C. FOLEY
05 Exec Vice Chanc Acad Affs/Provost .... Dr. Garnett STOKES
20 Senior Associate Provost .... Mr. Kenneth D. DEAN
20 Senior Associate Provost .... Dr. Patricia OKKER
32 Vice Chancellor Student Affairs .... Dr. Catherine C. SCROGGS
10 Vice Chancellor for Finance & CFO .... Ms. Rhonda GIBLER
28 Int VC Inclusion/Diversity/Equity .... Mr. Chuck HENSON
58 Assc VC Grad Stds/Assc VP Acad Affs .... Dr. Leona RUBIN
30 Vice Chancellor Univ Advancement .... Dr. Tom HILES
29 Assoc VC Alumni Relations .... Mr. Todd A. MCCUBBIN
17 Interim Exec VC Health Affairs .. Dr. Harold A. WILLIAMSON, JR.
57 Director School of Music .... Dr. Robert SHAY
84 Interim VProv Enrollment Mgmt .... Ms. Kim HUMPHREY
56 Vice Provost for Extension .... Dr. Marshall STEWART
85 Interim VProv International Pgms .... James SCOTT
46 Interim VC Research & Grad Studies .... Dr. Mark MCINTOSH
13 Chief Information Officer .... Dr. Gary K. ALLEN
15 Interim AVP Human Resources .... Ms. Jatha SADOWSKI
88 Asst Deputy Chancellor Diversity .... Ms. Noor AZIZAN-GARDNER
18 Chief Operations Officer .... Mr. Gary L. WARD
35 Asst Vice Chanc Student Affairs .... Dr. Jeffrey ZEILENGA
06 University Registrar .... Ms. Brenda V. SELMAN
09 VProv Inst Research & Quality Impr .... Dr. Mardy T. EIMERS
08 Acting Director of Libraries .... Ms. Ann C. RILEY
37 Director Student Financial Aid .... Mr. Nick PREWETT
47 Vice Chanc/Dean Agric/Food/Nat Res .... Dr. Thomas L. PAYNE
49 Dean Arts & Science .... Vacant
50 Interim Dean of Business .... Dr. Stephen P. FERRIS
88 Director School of Accountancy .... Dr. Vairam ARUNACHALAM
53 Dean of Education .... Dr. Kathryn B. CHVAL
54 Dean of Engineering .... Dr. Elizabeth G. LOBOA
65 Dir School of Natural Resources .... Dr. Mark R. RYAN
76 Dean School of Health Professions .... Dr. Kristofer HAGGLUND
59 Interim Dean Human Environ
Science .... Dr. James (Sandy) S. RIKOON
60 Dean of Journalism .... Dr. David D. KURPIUS
61 Dean of Law .... Dr. Gary MYERS
63 Dean of Medicine .... Dr. Patrice DELAFONTAINE
66 Dean of Nursing .... Dr. Judith FITZGERALD MILLER
70 Director School of Social Work .... Dr. Marjorie SABLE
74 Dean of Veterinary Medicine .... Dr. Neil OLSON
19 Director of University Police .... Mr. Doug SCHWANDT
26 Interim VC Marketing & Comm ....Dr. Jennifer HOLLINGSHEAD
41 Athletic Director .... Mr. Mack RHOADES
39 Director Residential Life .... Mr. Frankie D. MINOR
25 Director Sponsored Program Admin .... Mr. David CRAIG
40 Regional Director Retail Operations .... Ms. Sherry POLLARD
38 Director Counseling Services .... Dr. David WALLACE
88 Director International Center .... Dr. James K. SCOTT
36 Director Career Center .... Dr. Rob MCDANIELS
23 Director Student Health Services .... Dr. Susan E. EVEN
92 Director Honors College .... Dr. J. D. BOWERS
94 Director Women's/Gender Studies .... Dr. Jacquelyn S. LITT
88 Director Info Science Learning Tech .... Dr. John WEDMAN
80 Director Truman Schl Public Affairs ...... Dr. Barton J. WECHSLER
07 Director of Admissions .... Mr. Charles A. MAY
35 Director Student Life .... Dr. Mark L. LUCAS
104 Director Study Abroad .... Ms. Barbara LINDEMAN
105 Director Web Services .... Ms. Lori CROY
106 Dir Online Education/E-learning .... Ms. Kim SIEGENTHALER
108 Director Institutional Assessment .... Dr. Gera C. BURTON

*University of Missouri - Kansas City (F)

5100 Rockhill Road, Kansas City MO 64110-2499
County: Jackson FICE Identification: 002518
Unit ID: 178402
Telephone: (816) 235-1000 Carnegie Class: DU-Higher
FAX Number: (816) 235-1717 Calendar System: Semester
URL: www.umkc.edu
Established: 1929 Annual Undergrad Tuition & Fees (In-State): $7,837
Enrollment: 16,146 Coed
Affiliation or Control: State IRS Status: 501(c)3
Highest Offering: Doctorate
Accreditation: NH, AA, #ARCPA, BUS, CEA, CLPSY, COPSY, CS, DANCE, DENT, DH, EMT, ENG, IPSY, LAW, MED, MUS, NURSE, OTA, PHAR, SPAA, SW, TED, THEA

02 Chancellor .... Mr. Leo E. MORTON
28 Vice Chanc Diversity & Inclusion .... Dr. Susan WILSON
05 Provost .... Dr. Barbara BICHELMEYER
32 Vice Chanc Stdnt Affs/Enroll Mgmt .... Mr. Melvin C. TYLER
10 Vice Chanc Finance/Administration ..... Ms. Sharon LINDENBAUM
21 Director Budgeting and Planning .... Ms. Karen D. WILKERSON
102 Pres UMKC Foundation .... Mr. Steven NORRIS
30 Vice Chanc for Univ Advancement .... Mr. Curt J. CRESPINO
41 Athletic Director .... Ms. Carla WILSON
13 CIO & Senior Vice Prov .... Dr. Mary Lou A. FRITTS
20 Deputy Prov for Academic Affairs ...... Dr. Cynthia L. PEMBERTON
20 Vice Prov for Faculty Affairs .... Dr. Denis M. MEDEIROS
49 Dean College of Arts & Sciences .... Dr. Wayne VAUGHT
50 Dean Bloch School of Management .... Dr. David DONNELLY
81 Dean Sch of Biological Sciences .... Dr. Theodore WHITE
64 Dean Conservatory of Music & Dance .... Mr. Peter T. WITTE
52 Dean School of Dentistry .... Dr. Marsha A. PYLE
53 Dean School of Education .... Dr. Justin PERRY
54 Dean Sch of Computing/Engineering .... Dr. Kevin Z. TRUMAN
61 Dean School of Law .... Ms. Ellen Y. SUNI
63 Dean School of Medicine .... Dr. Steven KANTER
66 Dean Sch of Nursing & Health Stds .... Dr. Ann CARY
67 Dean School of Pharmacy .... Dr. Russell B. MELCHERT
62 Dean University Libraries .... Dr. Bonnie POSTLETHWAITE
58 Dean School of Graduate Studies .... Dr. Denis M. MEDEIROS
108 Director of Assessment .... Dr. Ruth CAIN
09 Int Dir Institutional Research .... Ms. Amy PRETTEJOHN
15 Vice Chanc Human Resources .... Ms. Carol HINTZ
84 Assoc Vice Chanc Enrollment Mgmt ... Ms. Jennifer DEHAEMERS
35 Assistant Vice Chanc Student Affs .... Dr. Jeff TRAIGER
35 Assistant Vice Chanc Student Affs .... Ms. Tiffany S. WILLIAMS
88 Director Student Involvement .... Dr. Angela COTTRELL
88 Vice Chan Strategic Market & Comm .... Ms. Anne SPENNER
26 Director Media Relations .... Mr. John MARTELLARO
29 Asst VC Alumni/Constituent Relations .... Ms. Lisen TAMMEUS
86 Asst Vice Chanc External Relations .... Mr. Troy LILLEBO
22 Title IX Coordinator .... Dr. Mikah THOMPSON
88 Int Dir Acad Support and Mentoring .... Dr. Rodney SMITH
07 Director of Admissions .... Ms. Tamara C. BYLAND
85 Director Internatl Student Affairs .... Ms. Sandra GAULT
37 Director Student Financial Aid .... Mr. Scott YOUNG
06 Registrar .... Mr. Doug SWINK
19 Chief Campus Police .... Mr. Michael BONGARTZ
40 Director Bookstore .... Mr. Pete EISENTRAGER
38 Dir Counseling/Health/Disability .... Dr. Arnold ABELS
88 Director Women's Center .... Dr. Brenda BETHMAN
36 Director Career Services .... Mr. Greg HAYES
39 Director Residential Life .... Mr. Sean GRUBE
88 Dir Multicultural Student Affairs . Ms. Keichanda DEES-BURNETT
96 Manager Campus Procurement .... Ms. Catherine A. SIMONDS
25 Business Manager for Admin Services .... Mr. Jeffery ROSS

18 Assoc Vice Chanc Campus Facilities ..... Mr. Robert A. SIMMONS
104 Director International Acad Pgms .... Dr. Linna F. PLACE
106 Vice Provost Online Education .... Dr. Devon CANCILLA

*University of Missouri - Saint Louis (A)

One University Boulevard, Saint Louis MO 63121-4400
County: Saint Louis FICE Identification: 002519
Unit ID: 178420
Telephone: (314) 516-5000 Carnegie Class: DU-Higher
FAX Number: (314) 516-5378 Calendar System: Semester
URL: www.umsl.edu
Established: 1963 Annual Undergrad Tuition & Fees (In-State): $9,394
Enrollment: 17,072 Coed
Affiliation or Control: State IRS Status: 501(c)3
Highest Offering: Doctorate
Accreditation: NH, BUS, BUSA, CACREP, CLPSY, ENG, IPSY, MUS, NURSE, OPT, OPTR, SPAA, SW, TED

02 Chancellor .... Dr. Thomas F. GEORGE
05 Int Provost/Vice Chanc Acad Affairs ...... Dr. Christopher SPILLING
10 Vice Chanc Finance/Admn & CFO .... Mr. Rick BANIAK
30 Vice Chancellor Univ Advancement .... Mr. Martin F. LEIFELD
26 Sr Assoc VC Univ Marketing/Comm .... Mr. Ronald H. GOSSEN
27 Assoc Vice Chanc Communications .... Mr. Robert D. SAMPLES
22 Dir of Equal Opportunity/Diversity .... Ms. Deborah J. BURRIS
46 Int Vice Provost Research Admin .... Dr. Wesley HARRIS
32 Vice Provost Student Affairs .... Dr. Curtis C. COONROD
58 Dean Graduate School .... Dr. Wesley HARRIS
13 Executive Director Info Technology .... Vacant
88 Dir Center for Teaching & Learning .... Mr. J. Andy GOODMAN
85 Director International Studies .... Dr. Joel N. GLASSMAN
49 Dean College Arts & Sciences .... Dr. Ronald YASBIN
50 Dean College Business Admin .... Mr. Charles E. HOFFMAN
53 Int Dean College of Education .... Dr. Ann TAYLOR
79 Assoc Dean Arts/Humanities .... Dr. Barbara HARBACH
66 Dean College of Nursing .... Dr. Susan DEAN-BAAR
92 Int Dean Honors College .... Dr. Daniel GERTH
88 Dean College of Optometry .... Dr. Larry J. DAVIS
08 Dean of Libraries .... Mr. Christopher DAMES
54 Dean Engineering Program .... Dr. Joseph O'SULLIVAN
88 Special Asst to the Chancellor .... Ms. Elizabeth VAN UUM
23 Asst Vice Provost Hlth/Wellness .... Dr. Nancy M. MAGNUSON
88 Asst Dean of Students/Stdnt Conduct .... Dr. D'Andre BRADDIX
93 Asst Dean of Stdnts/MultiCultural .... Ms. Natissia SMALL
35 Asst Dean of Students/Student Life .... Ms. Miriam I. ROCCIA
41 Director of Athletics .... Ms. Lori FLANAGAN
07 Dean of Enrollment .... Mr. Alan BYRD
40 Manager Bookstore .... Ms. Stephanie EATON
36 Director Career Services .... Ms. Teresa A. BALESTRERI
06 Acting Registrar .... Ms. Theresa KEUSS
39 Director Residential Life .... Mr. Jonathan A. LIDGUS
37 Director Student Financial Aid .... Dr. Anthony C. GEORGES
88 Director Ctr Nanoscience .... Dr. George W. GOKEL
88 Director Center Neurodynamics .... Dr. Sonya BAHAR
88 Dir Scientific & Computing/ITE .... Mr. William J. LEMON
88 Dir MO Inst of Mental Health .... Dr. Robert H. PAUL
25 Manager Bus/Fiscal/Research Admin .... Ms. Karen O. BOYD
18 Asst Vice Chancellor Facilities Mgt .... Mr. Larry A. EISENBERG
88 Director Budget Services .... Ms. Joann F. WIILKINSON
88 Director of Finance & Accounting .... Mr. Randall VOGAN
88 Director Cashiers/Student Accounts .... Mr. Mitchell R. HESS
15 Executive Director Human Resources .... Mr. James W. HERTEL
19 Director Institutional Safety .... Mr. Forrest L. VAN NESS
09 Director Institutional Research .... Mr. Lawrence W. WESTERMEYER
102 Assoc VC Development .... Ms. Beth KRUMM
88 Director St Louis Public Radio .... Mr. Tim J. EBY
29 Assoc VC Engagemen/Annual Giving .... Ms. Jennifer JEZEK-TAUSSIG
94 Director Women's & Gender Studies .... Dr. Kathy J. GENTILE
70 Director Social Work .... Dr. Sharon JOHNSON
44 Sr Director Planned Giving .... Mr. Lyle W. BRIZENDINE
88 Dir Public Policy Administration .... Dr. Deborah B. BALSER
88 Director Public Policy Research Ctr .... Dr. Mark TRANEL
88 Dir Sue Shear Institute for Women .... Ms. Vivian EVELOFF
31 Director Community College Relation .... Ms. Krystal P. LANG
88 Managing Dir Performing Arts Center ... Mr. John R. CATTANACH
88 Dir Des Lee Collaborative Vision .... Ms. Patricia ZAHN
108 Assoc Provost Planning/ Assessment .... Dr. Paulette E. ISAAC-SAVAGE
88 Center for Ethics in Public Life .... Dr. Walter M. STEWART

*Missouri University of Science & Technology (B)

300 W 13th Street, Rolla MO 65409-0001
County: Phelps FICE Identification: 002517
Unit ID: 178411
Telephone: (573) 341-4111 Carnegie Class: DU-Higher
FAX Number: (573) 341-4307 Calendar System: Semester
URL: www.mst.edu
Established: 1870 Annual Undergrad Tuition & Fees (In-State): $9,048
Enrollment: 8,640 Coed
Affiliation or Control: State IRS Status: 501(c)3
Highest Offering: Doctorate
Accreditation: NH, BUS, CEA, CS, ENG

02 Chancellor .... Dr. Cheryl B. SCHRADER
05 Provost/Exec Vice Chanc Acad Affs .... Dr. Robert MARLEY
10 Vice Chanc Finance/Admin Services .... Mr. Walter J. BRANSON
30 Vice Chanc University Advancement .... Ms. Joan M. NESBITT
32 Vice Chancellor Student Affairs .... Dr. Debra A G. ROBINSON
88 Vice Chanc Global/Strat Partnershp .... Dr. Warren K. WRAY
15 Vice Chanc HR/Equity & Inclusion .... Ms. Shenethia MANUEL
35 Assoc VC Student Affairs .... Dr. James H. MURPHY
46 Vice Provost for Research Services .... Dr. Mariesa L. CROW
20 Vice Provost Undergrad Studies .... Dr. Jeffrey CAWLFIELD
58 Vice Provost Graduate Studies .... Dr. Venkata ALLADA
56 Asst Vice Chanc Global Learning .... Dr. Anthony R. PETROY
84 Vice Prov & Dean Enrollment Mgmt .... Ms. Laura K. STOLL
54 Int VP/Dean Col Engr & Computing .... Dr. John MYERS
49 VP/Dean Col of Arts/Sci & Business .... Dr. Stephen ROBERTS
45 Exec Dir Strategy/Planning/Assess .... Ms. Rose HORTON
08 Director of Library .... Ms. Tracy PRIMICH
102 Executive Dir Corporate Relations .... Mr. John EASH
13 Interim Chief Information Officer .... Mr. Dan UETRECHT
06 Registrar .... Ms. Deanne JACKSON
38 AVC Student Affairs/Support Svcs .... Dr. Carl F. BURNS
41 Director of Athletics .... Mr. Mark E. MULLIN
23 Senior Dir Student Health Services .... Dr. Dennis S. GOODMAN
36 Dir Career Opportunities Center .... Dr. Edna GROVER-BISKER
85 AVC International/Cultural Affairs .... Dr. Jeanie H. HOFER
35 Director Student Life .... Mr. John GALLAGHER
39 Director Residential Life .... Dr. Dorie PAINE
09 Asst Vice Prov Inst Research/Assess ...... Dr. Oyebanjo LAJUBUTU
07 Director of Admissions .... Ms. Lynn STICHNOTE
29 Asst Vice Chanc Advancement Svcs .... Ms. Darlene RAMSAY
37 Director Student Financial Aid .... Ms. Bridgette K. BETZ
26 Executive Director Communications .... Mr. Andrew P. CAREAGA
18 Director of Physical Facilities .... Mr. James PACKARD
93 Dir Student Div/Outreach/Women .... Ms. Cecilia ELMORE
40 Manager of University Bookstore .... Mr. Mark GALLARDO
19 Director University Police .... Mr. Douglas P. ROBERTS
100 Chief of Staff .... Ms. Elizabeth SMITH
11 Associate Provost of Administration .... Dr. Caprice MOORE
88 Assoc Dir Stategic Communications .... Ms. Cheryl A. MCKAY

*Missouri University of Science & Technology Engineering Education Center (C)

12837 Flushing Meadows Drive, St. Louis MO 63131
Telephone: (314) 835-9822 Identification: 770323
Accreditation: &NH

† Regional accreditation is carried under the parent institution in Rolla, MO

University of Phoenix Kansas City Campus (D)

1310 E 104th Street, Kansas City MO 64131-4504
Telephone: (816) 943-9600 Identification: 770213
Accreditation: &NH, ACBSP

† No longer accepting campus-based students.

University of Phoenix St. Louis Campus (E)

13801 Riverport Drive, St. Louis MO 63043
Telephone: (314) 298-9755 Identification: 770214
Accreditation: &NH, ACBSP

† No longer accepting campus-based students.

Urshan Graduate School of Theology (F)

704 Howdershell Road, Florissant MO 63031-7526
County: St. Louis FICE Identification: 041461
Unit ID: 455099
Telephone: (314) 921-9290 Carnegie Class: Spec-4-yr-Faith
FAX Number: (314) 921-9203 Calendar System: Semester
URL: www.ugst.edu
Established: 2001 Annual Undergrad Tuition & Fees: N/A
Enrollment: 55 Coed
Affiliation or Control: Other Protestant IRS Status: 501(c)3
Highest Offering: Master's
Accreditation: THEOL

01 President .... Dr. David K. BERNARD
03 Executive Vice President .... Mrs. Jennie RUSSELL
05 Academic Dean .... Dr. Chris PARIS
32 Dean of Students .... Mr. David REID
06 Registrar .... Dr. Jeanie BLAND
08 Head Librarian .... Dr. Gary ERICKSON

Vatterott College-Joplin (G)

809 Illinois, Joplin MO 64801-9538
Telephone: (417) 781-5633 Identification: 666060
Accreditation: ACCSC

† Branch campus of Vatterott College-North Park, Berkeley, MO.

Vatterott College-Kansas City (H)

4131 N. Corrington Avenue, Kansas City MO 64117-1681
Telephone: (816) 861-1000 Identification: 666519
Accreditation: ACCSC

† Branch campus of Vatterott College-North Park, Berkeley, MO.

Vatterott College-NorthPark (I)

8580 Evans Avenue, Berkeley MO 63134-2900
County: Saint Louis FICE Identification: 025997
Unit ID: 245342
Telephone: (314) 264-1000 Carnegie Class: Bac/Assoc-Assoc Dom
FAX Number: (314) 522-6174 Calendar System: Other
URL: www.vatterott-college.edu
Established: 1969 Annual Undergrad Tuition & Fees: $12,724
Enrollment: 1,287 Coed
Affiliation or Control: Proprietary IRS Status: Proprietary
Highest Offering: Baccalaureate
Accreditation: ACCSC

01 Campus Director .... Mr. Robert DONNELL
05 Director of Education .... Ms. Brenetta UNDERWOOD
06 Head Registrar .... Ms. Denise DAVIS
07 Director of Admissions .... Ms. Sherri MEDLIN

Vatterott College-St. Charles (J)

3550 West Clay Street, St. Charles MO 63301
Telephone: (636) 940-4100 Identification: 666584
Accreditation: ACCSC

† Branch campus of Vatterott College-North Park, Berkeley, MO.

Vatterott College-Saint Joseph (K)

3709 N. Belt Highway, Saint Joseph MO 64506-1364
Telephone: (816) 558-7500 Identification: 666520
Accreditation: ACCSC

† Branch campus of Vatterott College-Des Moines, Des Moines, IA.

Vatterott College-Springfield (L)

3850 S Campbell Avenue, Springfield MO 65807-5340
Telephone: (417) 831-8116 Identification: 666521
Accreditation: ACCSC

† Branch campus of Vatterott College-North Park, Berkeley, MO.

Vatterott College-Sunset Hills (M)

12900 Maurer Industrial Drive, Sunset Hills MO 63127
Telephone: (314) 843-4200 Identification: 666522
Accreditation: ACCSC

† Branch campus of Vatterott College-North Park, Berkeley, MO.

Washington University in St. Louis (N)

One Brookings Drive, Saint Louis MO 63130-4899
County: Saint Louis FICE Identification: 002520
Unit ID: 179867
Telephone: (314) 935-5000 Carnegie Class: DU-Highest
FAX Number: N/A Calendar System: Semester
URL: www.wustl.edu
Established: 1853 Annual Undergrad Tuition & Fees: $48,093
Enrollment: 14,348 Coed
Affiliation or Control: Independent Non-Profit IRS Status: 501(c)3
Highest Offering: Doctorate
Accreditation: NH, ACAE, ART, AUD, BUS, CLPSY, ENG, LAW, LSAR, MED, OT, PCSAS, PH, PTA, SW

01 Chancellor .... Dr. Mark S. WRIGHTON
05 Provost/Exec VC Academic Affairs .... Dr. Herbert Holden THORP
11 Exec VC Administration .... Mr. Henry S. WEBBER
63 Exec Vice Chanc/Dean of Medicine ... Dr. David H. PERLMUTTER
43 Exec Vice Chanc/General Counsel .... Mr. Michael R. CANNON
30 Exec VC Alumni & Development .... Mr. David T. BLASINGAME
10 Vice Chancellor for Finance/CFO .... Ms. Amy B. KWESKIN
46 Vice Chancellor for Research .... Dr. Jennifer K. LODGE
15 Vice Chanc for Human Resources .... Ms. Legail P. CHANDLER
13 Vice Chanc & Chief Info Officer .... Mr. John L. GOHSMAN, JR.
32 Vice Chancellor for Students .... Dr. Lori S. WHITE
26 Vice Chanc for Public Affairs .... Ms. Jill D. FRIEDMAN
86 VC Government & Community Relations . Ms. Pamela S. LOKKEN
88 Chief Investment Officer .... Ms. Kimberly G. WALKER
21 Assoc VC for Finance and Treasurer .... Vacant
49 Dean Faculty of Arts & Sciences .... Dr. Barbara A. SCHAAL
61 Dean School of Law .... Dr. Nancy STAUDT
54 Dean Engineering & Applied Sciences .... Dr. Aaron F. BOBICK
57 Dean Sam Fox Sch Design/Visual Arts .... Prof. Carmon COLANGELO
58 Dir College & Grad Sch of Art .... Prof. Heather A. CORCORAN
50 Dean Olin School of Business .... Prof. Mahendra R. GUPTA
58 Dean Graduate School of A & S .... Prof. William F. TATE
70 Dean Brown School of Social Work .... Prof. Edward F. LAWLOR
55 Interim Dean University College .... Dr. Steven M. EHRLICH
48 Dean Architecture .... Prof. Bruce M. LINDSEY
100 Assoc Vice Chanc/Chief of Staff .... Mr. Steven J. GIVENS
101 Secretary to the Board of Trustees .... Ms. Ida H. EARLY
07 Vice Chancellor for Admissions .... Mr. John A. BERG
20 Vice Provost/Assoc VC Academic Affs .... Prof. Gerhild S. WILLIAMS
88 Assoc VC for Development .... Mr. William S. STOLL
29 Assoc VC Alumni & Development Pgm .. Ms. Pamella A. HENSON
26 Assoc VC Medical Public Affairs ...... Ms. Joni L. WESTERHOUSE
28 Vice Provost .... Prof. Adrienne D. DAVIS
85 VC for International Affairs .... Prof. James V. WERTSCH
08 University Librarian .... Mr. Jeffrey G. TRZECIAK
39 Assoc VC Students/Dean Students .... Mr. Justin X. CARROLL
35 Assoc Vice Chanc for Students .... Dr. Robert M. WILD
92 Assoc VC & Dean Ervin Scholars Pgm ...... Ms. Robyn S. HADLEY
13 Assoc VC Info Services & Tech .... Vacant
27 Asst VC for Campus Communications .... Ms. Julie A. FLORY

85 Asst VC/Dir International Students ...... Ms. Kathy STEINER-LANG
96 Asst Vice Chanc Resource Management ..... Mr. Alan S. KUEBLER
36 Assoc VC/Director Career Center .... Mr. Mark W. SMITH
18 Assoc VC Facilities Planning/Mgmt ... Mr. Arthur J. ACKERMANN
88 Asst VC Environ Health & Safety .... Mr. Bruce D. BACKUS
88 Assoc VC Real Estate .... Ms. Mary B. CAMPBELL
72 Interim Asst VC/Tech Management .... Ms. Nichole R. MERCIER
14 Asst VC Univ Admin/Acad Computing .... Ms. Denise R. HIRSCHBECK
23 Asst VC/Dir Stdnt Hlth Counslng Svc .... Dr. Alan I. GLASS
37 Director Student Financial Services .... Mr. Michael J. RUNIEWICZ
41 Director of Athletics .... Mr. Joshua H. WHITMAN
19 Interim Director of Campus Police .... Mr. Mark R. GLENN
07 Director of Admissions .... Ms. Julie SHIMABUKURO
06 University Registrar .... Ms. Susan E. HOSACK
38 Director of Mental Health Services .... Dr. Thomas M. BROUNK

Washington University in St. Louis-School of Medicine (A)

660 Euclid Avenue, Saint Louis MO 63110

Telephone: (314) 360-5000 Identification: 770329

Accreditation: &NH

† Regional accreditation is carried under the parent institution in Saint Louis, MO

Webster University (B)

470 E Lockwood, Webster Groves MO 63119-3141

County: Saint Louis FICE Identification: 002521

Unit ID: 179894

Telephone: (800) 981-9801 Carnegie Class: Masters/L

FAX Number: N/A Calendar System: Semester

URL: www.webster.edu

Established: 1915 Annual Undergrad Tuition & Fees: $25,500

Enrollment: 16,769 Coed

Affiliation or Control: Independent Non-Profit IRS Status: 501(c)3

Highest Offering: Doctorate

Accreditation: NH, ACBSP, ANEST, CACREP, MUS, NUR, TED

01 President .... Dr. Elizabeth J. STROBLE
05 Provost .... Dr. Julian Z. SCHUSTER
30 Vice Pres Advancement .... Mr. Charles HAHN
84 Interim Vice Pres Enrollment .... Mr. Robert PARRENT
10 Int VP & Chief Financial Officer .... Mr. Douglas ANDERSON
13 VP & Chief Information Officer .... Mr. Kenneth FREEMAN
101 University Secretary .... Ms. Jeanelle WILEY
20 Vice Provost .... Ms. Nancy HELLERUD
58 Asst Provost for Graduate Studies .... Dr. Elizabeth RUSSELL
04 Executive Assistant to President .... Ms. Shari SKRABACZ
50 Int Dean School Business/Technology .... Dr. Thomas JOHNSON
53 Dean School of Education .... Dr. Brenda S. FYFE
57 Dean Leigh Gerdine Col of Fine Arts .... Mr. Peter E. SARGENT
49 Int Co-Dean Col of Arts & Sciences .... Dr. Jennifer BROEDER
49 Int Co-Dean Col of Arts & Sciences .... Mr. Joseph STIMPFL
60 Dean School of Communications .... Mr. Eric ROTHENBUHLER
08 Dean of University Library .... Ms. Laura REIN
32 Associate VP/Dean of Students .... Dr. Ted HOEF
12 Dean of Extended Education .... Ms. Thao DANG-WILLIAMS
39 Assoc Dean Stdts/Housing/Res Life .... Dr. John BUCK
106 AVP/Dir OnLine Learning Center .... Mr. Michael COTTAM
82 Int AVP Academic Affairs Intl Pgms .... Dr. Peter MAHER
15 AVP & Chief Human Resources Officer .... Ms. Betsy SCHMUTZ
88 AVP Military & Government Programs .... Mr. Sean COLEMAN
27 Int AVP & Chief Comm Officer .... Mr. Rick ROCKWELL
12 AVP Extended US Campuses .... Dr. Donavan OUTTEN
37 AVP UG Admiss/Dir Financial Aid .... Mr. James MYERS
28 AVP Diversity & Inclusion .... Ms. Nicole ROACH
06 Registrar .... Mr. Don MORRIS
20 Director of Academic Advising .... Mr. Kim KLEINMAN
21 Dir Resource Plng & Budget .... Ms. Kathleen PARDO
19 Director Public Safety .... Mr. Rick GERGER
26 Dir Public Relations/Global Mktg .... Mr. Patrick GIBLIN
24 Dir of Media & Acad Tech Services .... Mr. Dewey MARTIN
36 Dir Career Planning & Dev Center . Ms. Tamara GEGG-LAPLUME
88 Director of Alumni Programs .... Ms. Lara TUREK
41 Director Athletics .... Mr. Scott KILGALLON
88 Director International Recruitment .... Mr. Calvin SMITH
23 Director Student Health Svcs .... Ms. Ann BROPHY
35 Director Student Engagement .... Ms. Jennifer STEWART
38 Director Counsel & Life Development .... Dr. Patrick STACK
96 Director of Procurement Services .... Ms. Maria HEIN
09 Int Director of Inst Effectiveness .... Mr. Justin BITNER
18 Director Facilities Planning .... Mr. Craig MILLER
104 Dir Study Abroad & Intl Projects .... Mr. Guillermo RODRIGUEZ
44 Director Annual or Planned Giving .... Mr. Kenneth NICKLESS
07 Director of UG Admissions/Int GR .... Mr. John MASSENA

WellSpring School of Allied Health-Kansas City (C)

9140 Ward Pkwy Ste 100, Kansas City MO 64114

County: Jackson FICE Identification: 039704

Unit ID: 447999

Telephone: (816) 523-9140 Carnegie Class: Spec 2-yr-Health

FAX Number: (816) 523-0741 Calendar System: Other

URL: www.wellspring.edu

Established: 1988 Annual Undergrad Tuition & Fees: N/A

Enrollment: 133 Coed

Affiliation or Control: Proprietary IRS Status: Proprietary

Highest Offering: Associate Degree

Accreditation: ABHES

01 President .... Donald FARQUHARSON

Wentworth Military Academy and College (D)

1880 Washington Avenue, Lexington MO 64067-1799

County: Lafayette FICE Identification: 002522

Unit ID: 179919

Telephone: (800) 962-7682 Carnegie Class: Assoc/-T-High Non

FAX Number: (660) 259-2677 Calendar System: Semester

URL: www.wma.edu

Established: 1880 Annual Undergrad Tuition & Fees: $19,000

Enrollment: 780 Coed

Affiliation or Control: Independent Non-Profit IRS Status: 501(c)3

Highest Offering: Associate Degree

Accreditation: #NH

01 President/Superintendent .... Col. Michael LIERMAN
05 Chief Academic Officer .... Col. Timothy CASEY
30 Vice Pres for Advancement & Alumni ...... LtCol. Marnie MORGAN
32 Commandant of Cadets .... LtCol. Darren FITZGERALD
84 Vice Pres for Enrollment Management .... Col. Rick COTTRELL
41 Athletic Director .... LtCol. Tom GANG
10 CFO .... LtCol. Glenn MILLER
81 Professor of Military Science .... LtCol. Grant MONTGOMERY
29 Director of Alumni Relations .... LtCol. Marnie MORGAN
04 Executive Assistant .... Capt. Sheri ALLRED
06 Registrar .... Capt. Beth SCHLESSELMAN
08 Librarian .... Maj. Linda CHRISTIAN
37 Director Student Financial Aid .... Maj. Cindy HOWARD
85 Director Foreign Students .... Maj. Christhina STARKE
23 Director Health Services .... Capt. Barb PIERCE
35 Director Student Affairs .... LtCol. Darren FITZGERALD
09 Director of Institutional Research .... Col. Rick COTTRELL
15 Director Personal Services .... Capt. Cindy MIKOYCHIK
18 Chief Facilities/Physical Plant .... Mr. Wally RATLIFFE
40 Director Bookstore .... Capt. Jerry MAGGERT

Westminster College (E)

501 Westminster Avenue, Fulton MO 65251-1230

County: Callaway FICE Identification: 002523

Unit ID: 179946

Telephone: (573) 642-3361 Carnegie Class: Bac-A&S

FAX Number: (573) 592-5227 Calendar System: Semester

URL: www.westminster-mo.edu

Established: 1851 Annual Undergrad Tuition & Fees: $23,480

Enrollment: 954 Coed

Affiliation or Control: Independent Non-Profit IRS Status: 501(c)3

Highest Offering: Baccalaureate

Accreditation: NH, ACBSP

01 President .... Dr. Benjamin AKANDE
05 Sr Vice President/Dean of Faculty .... Dr. Carolyn J. PERRY
30 VP for Advancement .... Vacant
10 Interim VP for Business and CFO .... Mr. Joe STONER
84 VP/Dean of Enrollment Management .... Mr. Robert ANDREWS
26 VP & Chief Communications Officer .... Ms. Lana POOLE
27 Director Media & Public Relations .... Mr. Robert CROUSE
32 Interim VP & Dean of Student Life .... Mr. Daniel HASLAG
20 Associate Academic Dean .... Dr. David JONES
08 Director of Library Services .... Ms. Angela GROGAN
06 Registrar .... Ms. Phyllis J. MASEK
13 IT Technical Services Manager .... Mr. Glen KEHL
37 Director of Financial Aid .... Ms. Aimee BRISTOW
15 Assoc VP/Chief HR Officer .... Ms. Lisa OTTO
39 Director of Residential/Greek Life .... Ms. Jacqueline J. WEBER
41 Athletic Director .... Ms. Tracey BRADEN
23 Exec Director Wellness Center .... Dr. Kasi LACEY
29 Dir Alumni Engagement .... Ms. Sarah MUNNS
36 Director of Career Services .... Ms. Meg LANGLAND
18 Interim Exec Dir Plant Operations .... Mr. Jack BENKE
07 Director of Admissions .... Ms. Amy MAREK
09 Director of Institutional Research .... Dr. Ray BROWN
19 Dir Campus Safety & Security .... Vacant
42 Chaplain .... Rev. Jamie HASKINS
100 Chief of Staff .... Mr. Gary STOCKER

William Jewell College (F)

500 College Hill, Liberty MO 64068-1896

County: Clay FICE Identification: 002524

Unit ID: 179955

Telephone: (816) 781-7700 Carnegie Class: Bac-A&S

FAX Number: (816) 415-5027 Calendar System: Semester

URL: www.jewell.edu

Established: 1849 Annual Undergrad Tuition & Fees: $32,330

Enrollment: 1,060 Coed

Affiliation or Control: Independent Non-Profit IRS Status: 501(c)3

Highest Offering: Master's

Accreditation: NH, MUS, NURSE

01 President .... Dr. Elizabeth MACLEOD WALLS
05 Provost .... Dr. Anne C. DEMA
10 Vice Pres for Finance & Operations .... Mr. Brian CLEMONS
30 Vice Pres Institutional Advancement .... Mr. Clark MORRIS
88 Vice Pres for Social Responsibility .... Dr. Andrew L. PRATT
32 Dean of Student Life .... Ms. Shelly KING
07 Dean of Admission .... Dr. Cory SCHEER
06 Registrar .... Dr. Edwin H. LANE
08 Director of Library Services .... Ms. Rebecca HAMLETT
21 Controller .... Mr. Ron DEMPSEY
13 Director of Information Technology .... Ms. Lan GUO
97 Assoc Dean Core Curriculum .... Dr. Gary ARMSTRONG
37 Director of Financial Aid .... Mr. Daniel HOLT
15 Director of Human Resources .... Ms. Cherie SMITH
18 Director of Facilities Management .... Mr. Randy ALEWINE
57 Executive Director Harriman-Jewell .... Mr. Clark W. MORRIS
41 Director of Athletics .... Dr. Darlene BAILEY
36 Director of Career Development .... Ms. Marissa BLAND
38 Director of Counseling Services .... Ms. Tricia HAGER
29 Director of Alumni Relations .... Ms. Andrea MELOAN
104 Director of Global Studies .... Ms. Sara ROUND
04 Executive Asst to President .... Ms. Dayna BEINKE
19 Director of Campus Safety .... Mr. Landon JONES
26 Director of Communications .... Ms. Cara DAHLOR
39 Director of Residence Life .... Mr. Ernie STUFFLEBEAN
44 Director of Annual Giving .... Ms. Laura HANAVAN
90 Director of Teaching/Learning Tech .... Ms. Elise FISHER

William Woods University (G)

One University Avenue, Fulton MO 65251-1098

County: Callaway FICE Identification: 002525

Unit ID: 179964

Telephone: (800) 995-3159 Carnegie Class: Masters/L

FAX Number: (573) 592-1146 Calendar System: Semester

URL: www.williamwoods.edu

Established: 1870 Annual Undergrad Tuition & Fees: $22,160

Enrollment: 2,031 Coed

Affiliation or Control: Christian Church (Disciples Of Christ)

IRS Status: 501(c)3

Highest Offering: Doctorate

Accreditation: NH, ACBSP, #CAATE, SW, TEAC

01 President .... Dr. Jahnae H. BARNETT
03 University Vice President .... Scott GALLAGHER
84 Vice President Enrollment & Mktg .... Kathy GROVES
32 Vice President/Dean of Student Life .... Dr. Venita MITCHELL
05 Executive Vice President Acad Affs .... Dr. Michael W. WESTERFIELD
04 Executive Assistant to President .... Kenda E G. SHINDLER
20 Academic Dean .... Dr. Aimee SAPP
58 Vice President of Graduate College .... Dr. Betsy TUTT
53 Dean of Education .... Dr. E. Douglas EBERSOLD
50 Dean of Business .... Lee BAILEY
41 Director of Athletics .... Jason VITTONE
20 Assoc Dean Academic Services .... Dr. Tom FRANKMAN
09 Director of Institutional Research .... Dr. Paul STURGIS
30 Director of Advancement .... Dr. Shawn HULL
108 Assoc Dean Assessment .... Dr. Carrie MCCRAY
08 Director Libraries .... Erlene DUDLEY
26 Director of University Relations .... Mary Ann BEAHON
27 Director of Marketing .... Vacant
18 Director of Buildings & Grounds .... Mike DILLON
13 Director of Technology .... Jim LONG
06 Director of Records/Registrar .... Tara EMERSON
10 Chief Financial Officer .... Julie HOUSEWORTH
37 Director Student Financial Services .... Deana READY
36 Dir Career Svcs/Student Success .... Amy DITTMER
39 Dir Residential Life/Campus Safety .... Mike WILLS
29 Director of Alumni Activities .... Becky STINSON
53 Chair Education Division .... Dr. Tim HANRAHAN
49 Chair Arts and Humanities .... Dr. Caroline BOYER FERHAT
88 Chair Equestrian Studies Division .... Jennifer PETTERSON
88 Chair Undergraduate Business .... Dr. Linda DAVIS
88 Chair Human Performance Division .... Raymond HUNE
83 Chair Behavioral/Soc Sciences Div .... Vacant
35 Coord Greek Life/Student Involvement .... Lacy SWEETEN
42 Chaplain/Faith & Service Director .... Rev. Travis TAMERIUS
88 ADA Coordinator/Interpreter .... Margie COATNEY
28 Coordinator Multicultural Affairs .... Cyndi KOONSE
38 Counselor .... Rebecca SEITZ
15 Director Personnel Services .... Margie BRAMON

MONTANA

Aaniiih Nakoda College (H)

PO Box 159, Harlem MT 59526-0159

County: Blaine FICE Identification: 025175

Unit ID: 180203

Telephone: (406) 353-2607 Carnegie Class: Tribal

FAX Number: (406) 353-2898 Calendar System: Semester

URL: www.ancollege.edu

Established: 1984 Annual Undergrad Tuition & Fees: $2,410

Enrollment: 291 Coed

Affiliation or Control: Tribal Control IRS Status: 501(c)3

Highest Offering: Associate Degree

Accreditation: NW

01 President .... Dr. Carole FALCON-CHANDLER
05 Dean of Academic Affairs .... Ms. Carmen CORNELIUS TAYLOR
32 Dean of Student Affairs .... Ms. Clarena BROCKIE
10 Comptroller .... Ms. Debra EVE
06 Registrar/Admissions Officer .... Mrs. Dixie BROCKIE
37 Financial Aid Director .... Ms. Toma CAMPBELL-HOOPS
08 Library Director .... Ms. Eva ENGLISH
25 Sponsored Programs Director .... Mr. Scott FRISKICS
13 Information Systems Manager .... Mr. Harold H. HEPPNER
40 Bookstore Manager .... Ms. Kimberly BROCKIE
04 Assistant to the President .... Ms. Michele BROCKIE
09 Institutional Research Assistant .... Ms. Danielle JACKSON

Blackfeet Community College (A)

Box 819, Browning MT 59417-0819
County: Glacier FICE Identification: 025106
Unit ID: 180054
Telephone: (406) 338-5441 Carnegie Class: Tribal
FAX Number: (406) 338-3272 Calendar System: Semester
URL: www.bfcc.edu
Established: 1976 Annual Undergrad Tuition & Fees: $2,890
Enrollment: 495 Coed
Affiliation or Control: Independent Non-Profit IRS Status: 501(c)3
Highest Offering: Associate Degree
Accreditation: NW

01 President ....Dr. Billie Jo KIPP
05 Dean Academic Affairs ....Mrs. Carol MURRAY
32 Dean Student Services ....Mrs. Anne RACINE
10 Chief Financial Officer ....Mr. James LORAN
37 Director of Financial Aid ....Mrs. Gaylene DUCHARME
06 Registrar ....Ms. Deana M. MCNABB
15 Director Human Resources ....Mr. Lyle W. MACDONALD
07 Director of Admissions ....Ms. Deana M. MCNABB
09 Director of Institutional Research ....Mr. Brad R. HALL
18 Chief Facilities/Physical Plant ....Mr. Curtis HENRIKSEN

Carroll College (B)

1601 N Benton Avenue, Helena MT 59625-0002
County: Lewis And Clark FICE Identification: 002526
Unit ID: 180106
Telephone: (406) 447-4300 Carnegie Class: Bac-Diverse
FAX Number: (406) 447-4533 Calendar System: Semester
URL: www.carroll.edu
Established: 1909 Annual Undergrad Tuition & Fees: $30,754
Enrollment: 1,440 Coed
Affiliation or Control: Roman Catholic IRS Status: 501(c)3
Highest Offering: Baccalaureate
Accreditation: NW, ENG, IACBE, NURSE

01 President ....Dr. Thomas EVANS
05 Vice President Academic Affairs ....Dr. Colin IRVINE
10 VP for Finance & Administration ....Ms. Lori PETERSON
31 VP Community Relations ....Mr. Thomas J. MCCARVEL
32 Vice President for Student Life ....Dr. James D. HARDWICK
30 VP of Philanthropy ....Ms. Karin OLSEN
84 Vice Pres of Enrollment Management ....Ms. Nina LOCOCO
42 Chaplain/Director ....Rev. Marc LENNEMAN
26 Director of Public Relations ....Ms. Sarah LAWLOR
27 Dir of Marketing/Communications ....Ms. Patty WHITE
06 Registrar ....Ms. Cassie HALL
08 Director of Library ....Mr. Christian FRAZZA
37 Financial Aid Director ....Ms. Janet RIIS
36 Dir of Career Services/Testing ....Ms. Rosalie K. WALSH
07 Director Admissions/Enrollment Ops ....Ms. Cynthia J. THORNQUIST
15 Dir Human Resources & Admin Svcs ..Ms. Renee M. MCMAHON
18 Director of Facilities ....Mr. Walter H. BISKUPIAK
39 Director of Community Living ....Ms. Maureen WARD
35 Dir Student Activities/Leadership ....Mr. Patrick HARRIS
38 Director of Counseling ....Dr. James ROGERS
21 Controller ....Ms. Kari BRUSTKERN
13 Director Information Technology ....Ms. Loretta ANDREWS
29 Director Alumni Relations ....Ms. Kathy RAMIREZ
09 Dir Research/Planning/Assessment ....Dr. Dawn GALLINGER
41 Athletic Director ....Mr. Curt APSEY

Chief Dull Knife College (C)

One College Drive, PO Box 98, Lame Deer MT 59043
County: Rosebud FICE Identification: 025452
Unit ID: 180160
Telephone: (406) 477-6215 Carnegie Class: Tribal
FAX Number: (406) 477-6219 Calendar System: Semester
URL: www.cdkc.edu
Established: 1975 Annual Undergrad Tuition & Fees: $2,260
Enrollment: 192 Coed
Affiliation or Control: Independent Non-Profit IRS Status: 501(c)3
Highest Offering: Associate Degree
Accreditation: NW

01 President/Int Dean Cultural Affairs ....Dr. Richard LITTLEBEAR
03 Vice President ....Mr. William WERTMAN
05 Dean Academic Affairs ....Dr. John TUTHILL
32 Dean Student Affairs ....Mr. Zane SPANG
37 Director Financial Aid ....Mr. Devin WERTMAN
08 Head Librarian ....Mrs. Joan HANTZ

Dawson Community College (D)

Box 421, Glendive MT 59330-0421
County: Dawson FICE Identification: 002529
Unit ID: 180151
Telephone: (406) 377-3396 Carnegie Class: Assoc/HT-High Non
FAX Number: (406) 377-8132 Calendar System: Semester
URL: www.dawson.edu
Established: 1940 Annual Undergrad Tuition & Fees (In-District): $3,570
Enrollment: 305 Coed
Affiliation or Control: State/Local IRS Status: 501(c)3
Highest Offering: Associate Degree
Accreditation: NW

01 President ....Dr. Scott R. MICKELSEN
05 Vice President of Academic Affairs ....Vacant
11 Vice President of Administration ....Ms. Kathleen ZANDER
32 Vice President of Student Affairs ....Mr. John BOLE
06 Registrar ....Ms. Virginia BOYSUN
08 Library Director ....Vacant
37 Director of Financial Aid ....Ms. Danielle DINGES
13 Director of Information Technology ....Mr. Frank ROJAS
15 Interim Human Resources Director ....Ms. Leslie WELDON

Flathead Valley Community College (E)

777 Grandview Drive, Kalispell MT 59901
County: Flathead FICE Identification: 006777
Unit ID: 180197
Telephone: (406) 756-3822 Carnegie Class: Assoc/MT-VT-High Non
FAX Number: (406) 756-3815 Calendar System: Semester
URL: www.fvcc.edu
Established: 1967 Annual Undergrad Tuition & Fees (In-District): $3,964
Enrollment: 2,161 Coed
Affiliation or Control: Local IRS Status: 501(c)3
Highest Offering: Associate Degree
Accreditation: NW, EMT, MAC, PTAA, SURGT

01 President ....Dr. Jane A. KARAS
05 Vice President Academic Affairs ....Dr. Brad ELDREDGE
10 Vice Pres Administration & Finance ....Mr. Kirk ZANDER
12 Director Lincoln County Campus ....Mr. Chad SHILLING
32 Dean of Students ....Ms. Brenda HANSON
51 Exec Dir Economic Dev/Cont Educ ....Ms. Susan BURCH
30 Exec Dir Institutional Advancement ....Ms. Colleen UNTERREINER
13 Exec Dir Mgmt Information Services ....Mr. Bill E. BOND
15 Exec Director of Human Resources ....Ms. Karen GLASSER
06 Registrar/Coord/Admissions/Records ....Ms. Marlene STOLTZ
37 Director Student Financial Aid ....Ms. Cindy KIEFER
88 Director of Adult Basic Education ....Ms. Margaret L. GIRKINS
18 Director Maintenance Service ....Mr. David EVANS
21 Controller ....Vacant
26 Director Marketing and Communicati ....Ms. Diane SKYLAND
96 Director of Purchasing ....Mr. Steve LARSON
24 Coord Instructional Media Services ....Ms. Malinda CRAWFORD
36 Coord Career Development ....Ms. Karen DARROW
04 Administrative Asst to President ....Ms. Monica SETTLES

Fort Peck Community College (F)

PO Box 398, Poplar MT 59255-0398
County: Roosevelt FICE Identification: 023430
Unit ID: 180212
Telephone: (406) 768-6300 Carnegie Class: Tribal
FAX Number: (406) 768-6301 Calendar System: Semester
URL: www.fpcc.edu
Established: 1978 Annual Undergrad Tuition & Fees: $2,250
Enrollment: 346 Coed
Affiliation or Control: Tribal Control IRS Status: 501(c)3
Highest Offering: Associate Degree
Accreditation: NW

01 President ....Ms. Haven GOURNEAU
05 Vice President Academic Affairs ....Mr. Wayne TWO BULLS
32 Vice President Student Services ....Mr. Elijah HOPKINS
30 Director Institutional Development ....Mr. Craig SMITH
10 Business Manager ....Ms. Rose ATKINSON
06 Registrar ....Ms. Linda L. HANSEN
37 Financial Aid Officer ....Ms. Lanette CLARK
40 Bookstore Manager ....Ms. Jackie AZURE
08 Head Librarian ....Mrs. Anita A. SCHEETZ

Little Big Horn College (G)

PO Box 370, Crow Agency MT 59022-0370
County: Big Horn FICE Identification: 022866
Unit ID: 180328
Telephone: (406) 638-3104 Carnegie Class: Tribal
FAX Number: (406) 638-3169 Calendar System: Semester
URL: www.lbhc.edu
Established: 1980 Annual Undergrad Tuition & Fees: $3,200
Enrollment: 263 Coed
Affiliation or Control: Tribal Control IRS Status: 501(c)3
Highest Offering: Associate Degree
Accreditation: NW

01 President ....Dr. David YARLOTT, JR.
05 Academic Dean ....Miss Frederica LEFT HAND
32 Dean of Student Services ....Miss Te-Atta OLD BEAR
11 Dean of Administration ....Mr. David SMALL
06 Registrar ....Mr. William OLD CROW
08 Director of Library ....Mr. Tim BERNARDIS
13 Chief Information Officer ....Mr. Franklin COOPER
10 Chief Finance Officer ....Ms. Aldean GOOD LUCK
15 Director Human Resources ....Ms. Shaleen OLD COYOTE
07 Admissions Officer ....Ms. Arlene DAWES
97 Dept Head/General Stds/Crow Stds ....Dr. Tim MCCLEARY
81 Dept Head/Math/Science/Technology ....Vacant
25 Chief Contracts/Grants Admin ....Mr. Curtis RIDES HORSE

Miles Community College (H)

2715 Dickinson, Miles City MT 59301-4799
County: Custer FICE Identification: 002528
Unit ID: 180373
Telephone: (406) 874-6100 Carnegie Class: Assoc/HT-Mix Trad/Non
FAX Number: (406) 874-6282 Calendar System: Semester
URL: www.milescc.edu
Established: 1939 Annual Undergrad Tuition & Fees (In-District): $3,945
Enrollment: 420 Coed
Affiliation or Control: State/Local IRS Status: 501(c)3
Highest Offering: Associate Degree
Accreditation: NW, ADNUR, PHLEB

01 President ....Dr. Stacy KLIPPENSTEIN
10 VP Administration & Finance ....Ms. Lisa SMITH
05 Vice Pres of Academic Affairs ....Dr. Rita KRATKY
32 VP Student Success/Inst Research ....Ms. Jessie DUFNER
08 Director of Library ....Ms. Paula DEMARS
13 Director Information Technology ....Mr. Donald D. WARNER
37 Director Student Financial Aid ....Mr. Loren LANCASTER
18 Chief Facilities/Physical Plant ....Mr. Ross LAWRENCE
21 Business Services Director ....Ms. Nancy AABERGE
06 Registrar ....Ms. Lisa BLUNT
15 Director Human Resources ....Ms. Kylene PHIPPS
66 Director Nursing ....Ms. Karla LUND
20 Associate Academic Officer ....Mr. Garth SLEIGHT
40 Manager Bookstore ....Ms. Karmalee YOUNG
04 Administrative Asst to President ....Ms. Candy LANEY

Montana Bible College (I)

3625 South 19th Avenue, Bozeman MT 59718-9108
County: Gallatin FICE Identification: 041403
Unit ID: 262165
Telephone: (406) 586-3585 Carnegie Class: Spec-4-yr-Faith
FAX Number: (406) 586-3585 Calendar System: Semester
URL: www.montanabiblecollege.edu
Established: 1987 Annual Undergrad Tuition & Fees: $7,220
Enrollment: 81 Coed
Affiliation or Control: Independent Non-Profit IRS Status: 501(c)3
Highest Offering: Baccalaureate
Accreditation: BI

01 President ....Mr. Jim CARLSON
05 Academic Dean ....Dr. Gale HEIDE
06 Registrar ....Mrs. Louise TURNER
07 Admissions Director ....Mrs. Susan JACKSON
08 Library Director ....Mrs. Jessica CARLSON
32 Dean of Students ....Mr. Scott MORNINGSTAR
10 Business Manager ....Mrs. Leota FRED
21 Office Manager ....Mrs. Tasha OARD
18 Facilities Manager ....Mr. Danny JOHNSON
84 Director of Enrollment Management ....Mr. Dan HOVESTOL
29 Alumni Director ....Ms. Jenni O'BRIAN
42 Director Church Relations ....Mr. Ryan WARD
13 Information Technology Director ....Mr. Austin RUHL

*Montana University System Office (J)

2500 Broadway, Helena MT 59601-3201
County: Lewis And Clark FICE Identification: 029072
Unit ID: 180470
Telephone: (406) 444-6570 Carnegie Class: N/A
FAX Number: (406) 444-1469
URL: www.mus.edu

01 Commissioner Higher Education ....Mr. Clayton T. CHRISTIAN
05 Deputy Comm Academic/Student Affs ....Dr. John CECH
10 Dpty Comm Fiscal Affs/Chf of Staff ....Mr. Chuck JENSEN
45 Deputy Comm for Plng/Public Policy ....Mr. Tyler TREVOR
15 Deputy Comm Communications/HR ....Mr. Kevin MCRAE
43 Chief Legal Counsel/Deputy Comm ....Ms. Viv HAMMILL
103 Deputy Comm Two-Year Educ ....Mr. John CECH
88 Director of Benefits ....Mrs. Connie WELSH
21 Chief Financial Officer ....Ms. Robin GRAHAM
21 Director Accounting & Budget ....Ms. Frieda HOUSER
88 Director of Work Comp Risk Mgmt ....Ms. Leah Jo TIETZ
93 Dir Minority/Amer Ind Achievement ....Ms. Angela MCLEAN
13 OCHE IT Manager ....Ms. Edwina MORRISON

*University of Montana - Missoula (K)

32 Campus Drive, Missoula MT 59812-0001
County: Missoula FICE Identification: 002536
Unit ID: 180489
Telephone: (406) 243-2311 Carnegie Class: DU-Higher
FAX Number: (406) 243-2797 Calendar System: Semester
URL: www.umt.edu
Established: 1893 Annual Undergrad Tuition & Fees (In-State): $6,158
Enrollment: 13,952 Coed
Affiliation or Control: State IRS Status: 501(c)3
Highest Offering: Doctorate
Accreditation: NW, ART, BUS, BUSA, CAATE, CACREP, CLPSY, COARC, CS, JOUR, LAW, MUS, PH, PHAR, PTA, SCPSY, SP, SW, TED, THEA

02 President ....Dr. Royce C. ENGSTROM
05 Interim Provost/VP Academic Affairs ....Dr. Beverly EDMOND
10 Vice President Finance/Admin ....Mr. Michael REID
84 VP for Enrollment/Student Affairs ....Dr. Thomas CRADY
46 Vice Pres Research/Development ....Dr. Scott WHITTENBURG
88 AVP for Student Success ....Ms. Sharon O'HARE
26 AVP for Integrated Communications ....Mr. Mario SCHULZKE
45 AVP for Plng/Budget Analysis ....Ms. Dawn RESSEL
15 AVP Human Resource Services ....Ms. Terri PHILLIPS
20 Associate Provost ....Dr. Nathan LINDSAY
32 Dean of Students ....Ms. Rhondie VOORHEES
43 Legal Counsel ....Ms. Lucy FRANCE

12 Director Mansfield Center .... Mr. Abraham KIM
104 Assoc Provost Global Century Educ ..... Mr. Paulo ZAGALO-MELO
88 Interim Dir Broadcast Media Center .... Ms. Linda TALBOTT
22 Dir Equal Opportunity/Affirm Action .... Ms. Jessica WELTMAN
06 Registrar .... Mr. Joseph HICKMAN
18 Director Facilities Svcs .... Mr. Kevin KREBSBACH
13 CIO .... Mr. Matt RILEY
38 Director Counseling .... Mr. Mike FROST
36 Director Career Services .... Ms. Laurie FISHER
37 Director of Financial Aid .... Mr. Kent MCGOWAN
29 Director of Alumni Relations .... Mr. William S. JOHNSTON
102 President & CEO/UM Foundation .... Mr. Shane GIESE
19 Director of Public Safety .... Mr. Martin LUDEMANN
23 Director Curry Health Center .... Dr. Rick CURTIS
39 Director Residence Life .... Ms. Sandra SCHOONOVER
41 Athletic Director .... Mr. Kent HASLAM
85 Dir Foreign Student & Scholar Svcs .... Ms. Effie F. KOEHN
21 Director Business Services .... Mr. John MCCORMICK
88 Exec Director Student Success .... Mr. Brian FRENCH
08 Dean Mansfield Library .... Dr. Sha Li ZHANG
51 Dean Continuing Education .... Dr. Roger MACLEAN
49 Dean College Humanities & Sciences ...... Dr. Christopher COMER
61 Dean School of Law .... Mr. Paul KIRGIS
65 Dean College Forestry/Conservation .... Dr. Thomas DELUCA
50 Dean School of Business Admin .... Dr. Christopher SHOOK
76 Dean Col Health Prof & Biomed Sci .... Dr. Reed HUMPHREY
60 Dean School of Journalism .... Mr. Larry ABRAMSON
53 Dean College of Educ & Human Svcs .... Dr. Roberta EVANS
57 Dean College Visual/Performing Arts .... Mr. Stephen KALM
75 Dean Missoula College .... Dr. Shannon O'BRIEN
92 Dean Honors College .... Dr. Brock TESSMAN

*The University of Montana Western (A)

710 S Atlantic St, Dillon MT 59725-3598
County: Beaverhead　　FICE Identification: 002537
Unit ID: 180692
Telephone: (406) 683-7011　　Carnegie Class: Bac-Diverse
FAX Number: (406) 683-7493　　Calendar System: Other
URL: www.umwestern.edu
Established: 1893　　Annual Undergrad Tuition & Fees (In-State): $4,835
Enrollment: 1,375　　Coed
Affiliation or Control: State　　IRS Status: 501(c)3
Highest Offering: Baccalaureate
Accreditation: NW, CAEP, IACBE

02 Chancellor .... Dr. Beth WEATHERBY
05 Provost .... Dr. Deborah HEDEEN
10 Vice Chanc Administration/Finance .... Ms. Susan BRIGGS
26 Director Marketing/Univ Relations .... Mr. Kent J. ORD
20 Dean of Outreach .... Ms. Anneliese RIPLEY
06 Registrar .... Ms. Charity WALTERS
07 Director of Admissions .... Mr. Matt ALLEN
08 Librarian .... Mr. Michael SCHULZ
36 Director of Field Learning .... Mr. Adam MASTANDREA
27 Public Relations Manager .... Mr. Rainier BUTLER
41 Director of Athletics .... Mr. Russ RICHARDSON
13 Director of Information Technology .... Mr. Chad BAVER
32 Dean of Students .... Ms. Nicole HAZELBAKER
30 Director of Devel/Alumni Relations .... Ms. Roxanne ENGELLANT
37 Int Dir of Student Fin Aid .... Ms. Arlene WILLIAMS
38 Director Student Counseling .... Mr. Jerry GIRARD
15 Human Resources .... Ms. Patti LAKE
04 Administrative Asst to Chancellor .... Ms. Hillary LOWELL
22 Dir Affirmative Action/EEO .... Ms. Liane FORRESTER

*Helena College University of Montana (B)

1115 N Roberts, Helena MT 59601-3098
County: Lewis and Clark　　FICE Identification: 007570
Unit ID: 180276
Telephone: (406) 447-6900　　Carnegie Class: Assoc/HVT-Mix Trad/Non
FAX Number: (406) 447-6397　　Calendar System: Semester
URL: www.umhelena.edu
Established: 1939　　Annual Undergrad Tuition & Fees (In-State): $3,085
Enrollment: 1,564　　Coed
Affiliation or Control: State　　IRS Status: 501(c)3
Highest Offering: Associate Degree
Accreditation: NW, ADNUR, IFSAC

02 Dean/CEO .... Dr. Daniel J. BINGHAM
04 Administrative Assoc to Dean/CEO ..... Ms. Summer S. MARSTON
05 Assoc Dean of Academic Affairs/VP .... Dr. Chad HICKOX
07 Director of Admissions and Records .... Ms. Sarah DELLWO
08 Director of Library Services .... Ms. Della DUBBE
51 Director of Continuing Education .... Ms. Mary LANNERT
18 Assistant Dean of Fiscal & Plant .... Mr. Russ FILLNER
13 Director of IT Services .... Mr. Jeff BLOCK
40 Bookstore Manager .... Mr. Josh BENNETT
32 Assistant Dean of Student Services .... Ms. Elizabeth STEARNS-SIMS
26 Director of Marketing .... Ms. Barb MCALMOND
37 Director Financial Aid .... Ms. Valerie CURTIN
88 Director of Student Success .... Mr. Rick CARON
15 Director of Human Resources .... Mr. Matthew RICHARDS
36 Career Services Coordinator .... Mr. Alan THOMPSON
09 Director of Institutional Research .... Mr. Michael BROWN

*Montana State University (C)

PO Box 172190, Bozeman MT 59717-2190
County: Gallatin　　FICE Identification: 002532
Unit ID: 180461
Telephone: (406) 994-2452　　Carnegie Class: DU-Higher
FAX Number: (406) 994-1923　　Calendar System: Semester
URL: www.montana.edu
Established: 1893　　Annual Undergrad Tuition & Fees (In-State): $6,849
Enrollment: 14,982　　Coed
Affiliation or Control: State　　IRS Status: 501(c)3
Highest Offering: Doctorate
Accreditation: NW, ART, BUS, CACREP, CAEP, CS, DIETC, DIETI, ENG, ENGT, IPSY, MT, MUS, NURSE

02 President .... Dr. Waded CRUZADO
05 Interim Provost/VP Acad Affairs .... Dr. Robert MOKWA
20 Assoc Provost .... Dr. David SINGEL
88 Assoc Provost Accreditation .... Dr. Ron LARSEN
10 Vice Pres Admin/Finance .... Mr. Terry LEIST
32 Vice Pres Student Success .... Dr. Chris KEARNS
56 Director Extension .... Dr. Jeff BADER
46 VP Research/Creat/Tech Transf .... Dr. Renee REIJO PERA
04 Special Assistant to the President .... Vacant
18 Assoc Vice Pres University Services .... Mr. Daniel STEVENSON
88 Assoc VP Res/Creativity/Tch Trnsfer .... Dr. Mark YOUNG
15 Chief Human Resources Officer .... Ms. Cathy HASENPFLUG
21 Assoc Vice Pres Financial Services .... Ms. Laura HUMBERGER
102 President/CEO MSU Foundation .... Mr. Christopher C. MURRAY
104 Assoc Prov International Programs .... Dr. David DI MARIA
26 Exec Director Univ Communications .... Mr. Tracy ELLIG
88 Exec Director Museum of the Rockies ...... Mr. Sheldon MCKAMEY
50 Dean Business .... Dr. Kregg AYTES
53 Dean Education/Health/Human Dev .... Dr. Alison HARMON
54 Dean Engineering .... Dr. Brett GUNNINK
49 Dean Letters & Science .... Dr. Nicol RAE
66 Dean Nursing .... Dr. Helen MELLAND
08 Dean Libraries .... Mr. Kenning ARLITSCH
35 Dean Students .... Dr. Matthew CAIRES
58 Dean Graduate School .... Dr. Karlene HOO
92 Dean Honors College .... Dr. Ilse-Mari LEE
47 VP and Dean Agriculture .... Dr. Charles BOYER
48 Dean Arts/Architecture .... Dr. Royce SMITH
70 Dean Gallatin College Programs .... Mr. Robert HIETALA
07 Director Admissions .... Ms. Ronda RUSSELL
22 Director Institutional Equity .... Ms. Jyl SHAFFER
29 Pres/CEO Alumni Foundation .... Mr. Christopher D. MURRAY
41 Director Athletics .... Mr. Leon COSTELLO
109 Director Auxiliary Services .... Mr. Tom STUMP
36 Dir Allen Yarnell Center .... Dr. Carina BECK
38 Int Dir Counseling/Psych Services .... Dr. Elizabeth ASSERSON
22 Dir Disability/Re-ent/Veteran Svcs .... Ms. Brenda YORK
56 Exec Director Extended University .... Dr. Kim OBBINK
37 Director Financial Aid .... Ms. Brandi PAYNE
43 Legal Counsel .... Ms. Kellie PETERSON
45 Director Planning & Analysis .... Dr. Chris FASTNOW
96 Director Procurement .... Mr. Brian O'CONNOR
06 Registrar .... Mr. Tony CAMPEAU
27 Director Marketing/Creative Service .... Ms. Julie KIPFER
19 Director University Police .... Mr. Robert PUTZKE
100 Asst to the President .... Ms. Maggie HAMMETT
105 Dir Web Communications .... Mr. Brett DAVIS
13 Chief Information Officer .... Mr. Jerry SHEEHAN
25 Asst Vice Pres for Research .... Ms. Leslie SCHMIDT
39 Chief Housing Officer .... Mr. Jeff BONDY
14 Asst CEO IT .... Mr. Adam EDELMAN

*Montana State University - Billings (D)

1500 University Drive, Billings MT 59101-0245
County: Yellowstone　　FICE Identification: 002530
Unit ID: 180179
Telephone: (406) 657-2011　　Carnegie Class: Masters/M
FAX Number: (406) 657-2302　　Calendar System: Semester
URL: www.msubillings.edu
Established: 1927　　Annual Undergrad Tuition & Fees (In-State): $5,808
Enrollment: 4,768　　Coed
Affiliation or Control: State　　IRS Status: 501(c)3
Highest Offering: Master's
Accreditation: NW, ART, BUS, CAATE, CORE, EMT, MUS, TED

02 Chancellor .... Dr. Mark NOOK
10 Administrative Vice Chancellor .... Ms. Terrie IVERSON
05 Academic Vice Chancellor & Provost .... Dr. Robert HOAR
32 Vice Chancellor for Student Affairs .... Dr. Joseph ORAVECZ
20 Vice Provost Academic Affairs .... Dr. Matthew FEDINGER
102 President/CEO Foundation .... Mr. Bill KENNEDY
08 Director Library Services .... Mr. Brent ROBERTS
07 Director Admiss/Records/Registrar .... Dr. Cheri JOHANNES
15 Director Human Resources/EEO AA .... Ms. Janet SIMON
36 Director Advising/Career Services .... Dr. Becky LYONS
13 Chief Information Officer .... Dr. Michael J. BARBER
56 Director Extended Campus .... Mr. Kevin NEMETH
25 Dir Grants & Sponsored Pgms .... Dr. David MCGINNIS
26 Director University Relations .... Mr. Aaron CLINGINGSMITH
09 Director Institutional Research .... Ms. Joann STRYKER
18 Director Facility Services .... Mr. Jason MCGIMPSEY
58 Int Director Graduate Programs .... Dr. Diane DUIN
41 Athletic Director .... Ms. Krista MONTAGUE
19 Chief of Campus Police .... Mr. Scott FORSHEE
29 Director Alumni Relations .... Ms. Sarah BROCKEL
37 Director Student Financial Aid .... Ms. Emily WILLIAMSON
40 Director Bookstore .... Mr. Chad SCHREIER
39 Int Dean Student Life & Auxiliaries .... Ms. Kathy KOTECKI
31 Coordinator Community Involvement .... Ms. Jennifer RANDALL
21 University Budget Director .... Ms. Trudy COLLINS
96 Director of Business Services .... Ms. Barb SHAFER
20 Dir Academic Support Center .... Mr. John GILLETTE
28 Dir Montana Ctr for Inclusive Educ .... Ms. Marsha SAMPSON
89 Dir New Student/Retention Services .... Ms. Tammi WATSON
88 Director American Indian Outreach .... Ms. Reno CHARETTE
85 Exec Dir Intl Studies/Outreach .... Dr. Paul FOSTER
106 Director e-Learning .... Dr. Susan BALTER-REITZ
92 Dir of University Honors Program .... Dr. David CRAIG
104 Specialist Int Marketing/Outreach .... Mr. Neil BEYER
49 Dean of Arts & Sciences .... Dr. Christine SHEARER
53 Dean of Education .... Dr. Mary Susan FISHBAUGH
50 Dean College of Business .... Dr. Barbara WHEELING
12 Dean City College MSU Billings .... Dr. Clifford COPPERSMITH
76 Dean College of Allied Health Prof .... Dr. Diane DUIN
88 Asc Dean City College MSU Billings .... Dr. Florence GARCIA

*Montana State University - Northern (E)

PO Box 7751, Havre MT 59501-7751
County: Hill　　FICE Identification: 002533
Unit ID: 180522
Telephone: (406) 265-3700　　Carnegie Class: Bac-Diverse
FAX Number: N/A　　Calendar System: Semester
URL: www.msun.edu
Established: 1929　　Annual Undergrad Tuition & Fees (In-State): $5,329
Enrollment: 1,230　　Coed
Affiliation or Control: State　　IRS Status: 501(c)3
Highest Offering: Master's
Accreditation: NW, ADNUR, ENGT, NUR

02 Chancellor .... Mr. Gregory D. KEGEL
05 Provost/Vice Chanc Academic Affairs .... Dr. William RUGG
10 VC Finance & Administration .... Mr. Brian SIMONSON
102 Executive Director of Foundation .... Mr. Jim BENNETT
72 Dean College Technical Sciences .... Dr. Larry STRIZICH
32 Dean of Students .... Vacant
53 Dean Col Educ/Arts & Sci/Nursing .... Dr. Carol REIFSCHNEIDER
06 Registrar .... Ms. Alisha SCHROEDER
66 Director of Nursing .... Dr. Janice STARR
21 Controller .... Mr. Chris WENDLAND
41 Athletic Director .... Mr. Christian OBERQUELL
36 Director Career Center .... Ms. Mary HELLER
13 Interim Chief Info Tech Officer .... Ms. Marianne HOPPE
37 Director of Financial Aid .... Ms. Cindy SMALL
26 Director of University Relations .... Mr. James POTTER
08 Director of Library .... Ms. Vicki GIST
38 Director Student Support Services .... Mr. John A. DONALDSON
07 Director of Admissions .... Ms. Kristi PETERSON
15 Director Human Resources .... Ms. Kathy JAYNES
35 Sr Director Student Success .... Ms. Tracey JETTE
18 Facilities Manager .... Mr. Dan ULMEN
29 Alumni Associate .... Ms. Becka STONE

*Great Falls College Montana State University (F)

2100 16th Avenue South, Great Falls MT 59405-4909
County: Cascade　　FICE Identification: 009314
Unit ID: 180249
Telephone: (406) 771-4300　　Carnegie Class: Assoc/MT-VT-Mix Trad/Non
FAX Number: (406) 771-4317　　Calendar System: Semester
URL: gfcmsu.edu
Established: 1969　　Annual Undergrad Tuition & Fees (In-State): $3,130
Enrollment: 1,772　　Coed
Affiliation or Control: State　　IRS Status: 501(c)3
Highest Offering: Associate Degree
Accreditation: NW, CAHIIM, COARC, DA, DH, EMT, MAC, PTAA, SURGT

02 CEO/Dean .... Dr. Susan J. WOLFF
04 Executive Assistant to the CEO/Dean .... Ms. Lorene JAYNES
10 Chief Financial Officer .... Dr. Darryl STEVENS
05 Chief Academic Officer .... Dr. Heidi PASEK
32 Chief Student Affairs & HR Officer .... Ms. Mary Kay BONILLA
26 Exec Dir Development/Comm & Mktg .... Mr. Lewis CARD
13 Director IT Services-Interim .... Mr. David BONILLA
18 Director of Facilities Services .... Mr. Dennis DEVINE
36 Director Advising & Career Center .... Mr. Troy STODDARD
37 Director Student Financial Aid .... Ms. Leah HABEL
40 Bookstore Manager .... Mr. Steve HALSTED
96 Budget & Purchasing Analyst .... Ms. Carmen ROBERTS
09 Research Analyst .... Dr. Grace ANDERSON
08 Director of eLearning & Library .... Ms. Laura WIGHT
88 Trades Division Director .... Mr. Joel SIMS
97 Dir of Gen Educ/Bus/Tech & Transfer .... Ms. Leanne FROST
76 Director of Health Sciences .... Dr. Frankie LYONS
06 Registrar .... Ms. Dena WAGNER-FOSSEN
07 Director of Admissions .... Mr. Joe SIMONSEN

*Montana Tech of The University of Montana (G)

1300 W Park Street, Butte MT 59701-8997
County: Silver Bow　　FICE Identification: 002531
Unit ID: 180416
Telephone: (800) 445-8324　　Carnegie Class: Bac-Diverse
FAX Number: (406) 496-4710　　Calendar System: Semester
URL: www.mtech.edu
Established: 1893　　Annual Undergrad Tuition & Fees (In-State): $6,539

Enrollment: 2,085 Coed
Affiliation or Control: State IRS Status: 501(c)3
Highest Offering: Master's
Accreditation: NW, CS, ENG, ENGR, NURSE

02 Chancellor .... Dr. Donald M. BLACKKETTER
05 Provost .... Dr. Douglas M. ABBOTT
10 Business Officer/Controller .... Mr. John C. BADOVINAC
11 VC for Administration & Finance .... Ms. Maggie PETERSON
30 VC for Development & Univ Relations .... Mr. Joseph MCCLAFFERTY
32 Assoc VC for Student Affairs .... Mr. Paul V. BEATTY
46 VC Research & Dean Grad Sch .... Dr. Beverly HARTLINE
65 Director Bureau of Mines & Geology .... Dr. John J. METESH
84 Director of Enrollment Management .... Ms. Leslie DICKERSON
31 Dir Inst of Educational Opportunity .... Ms. Amy VERLANIC
36 Director Career Services .... Ms. Sarah RAYMOND
08 Director Library .... Mr. Scott JUSKIEWICZ
37 Director of Financial Aid .... Mr. Michael W. RICHARDSON
18 Director of Physical Facilities .... Mr. Michael ALLEN
29 Director Alumni Affairs .... Ms. Peggy S. MCCOY
41 Athletic Director .... Mr. Chuck MORRELL
72 Dean College of Technology .... Mr. John GARIC
81 Dean Col Letters/Sci/Prof Studies .... Dr. Douglas A. COE
54 Dean School of Mines & Engineering .... Dr. H. Peter KNUDSEN
44 Director of Development .... Mr. Michael BARTH
39 Director Residence Life .... Mr. Scott FORTHOFER
26 Director Public Relations .... Ms. Amanda BADOVINAC
40 Bookstore Director .... Ms. Laurie VANDEL
09 Director Institutional Research .... Ms. Melissa KUMP
06 Interim Registrar .... Ms. Leslie DICKERSON
07 Director of Recruiting .... Ms. Stephanie CROWE
105 Webmaster .... Mr. David NOLT
106 Director of Distance Learning .... Mr. David BENTZ
13 Director of Network Services .... Mr. Mike KUKAY
91 Director of Information Services .... Ms. Jennifer SIMON
96 Dir Purchasing & Budgets .... Ms. Marissa BENTLEY
15 Dir Human Resources .... Ms. Vanessa VAN DYK
04 Assistant to the Chancellor .... Ms. Carmen NELSON
22 Dir of Human Resources .... Ms. Vanessa VAN DYK
25 Dir of Sponsored Programs .... Ms. Carleen CASSIDY

† Granted candidacy at the Doctorate level.

* *City College at Montana State University Billings* (A)

3803 Central Avenue, Billings MT 59102-4398
Telephone: (406) 247-3000 FICE Identification: 010166
Accreditation: &NW

† Regional accreditation is carried under the parent institution Montana State University-Billings, Billings, MT.

* *Highlands College of Montana Tech* (B)

25 Basin Creek Road, Butte MT 59701-9704
Telephone: (406) 496-3701 FICE Identification: 009282
Accreditation: &NW

† Regional accreditation is carried under the parent institution Montana Tech of The University of Montanna, Butte, MT.

* *The University of Montana - Missoula College* (C)

909 South Avenue West, Missoula MT 59801
Telephone: (406) 243-7811 FICE Identification: 007561
Accreditation: &NW, ACFEI, ADNUR, SURGT

† Regional accreditation is carried under the parent institution The University of Montana-Missoula, Missoula, MT.

Rocky Mountain College (D)

1511 Poly Drive, Billings MT 59102-1796
County: Yellowstone FICE Identification: 002534
Unit ID: 180595
Telephone: (406) 657-1000 Carnegie Class: Bac-Diverse
FAX Number: (406) 259-9751 Calendar System: Semester
URL: www.rocky.edu
Established: 1878 Annual Undergrad Tuition & Fees: $25,742
Enrollment: 1,007 Coed
Affiliation or Control: Interdenominational IRS Status: 501(c)3
Highest Offering: Master's
Accreditation: NW, AAB, ARCPA

01 President .... Dr. Robert WILMOUTH
05 Academic Vice President .... Dr. Stephen A. GERMIC
32 Vice President for Student Life .... Mr. Bradley A. NASON
30 Vice President of Advancement .... Ms. Kelly EDWARDS
10 Chief Financial Officer .... Ms. Melodie CHARETTE
88 Director of Educational Leadership .... Dr. Stevie SCHMITZ
08 Director of the Library .... Ms. Bobbi OTTE
44 Director of Major Gifts .... Mr. Peter BOLENBAUGH
26 Director of Communications .... Mr. Andrew KEATING
13 Director of Information Technology .... Mr. Daniel WOLTERS
18 Director of Campus Facilities .... Vacant
41 Director of Athletics .... Mr. Bruce PARKER
30 Director of Annual Fund .... Ms. Della GARDNER
09 Institutional Research Analyst .... Miss Erica WALL
06 Registrar .... Mr. Erik WILLBORG
37 Director of Financial Assistance .... Ms. Jessica FRANCISCHETTI
39 Director of Residence Life .... Ms. Shaydean SAYE
04 Executive Assistant to the Pres .... Ms. Tracy DAVIDSON
29 Director of Alumni Relations .... Mr. Daniel PAROD
84 Dean of Enrollment Services .... Mr. Austin MAPSTON
19 Director Security/Safety .... Mr. Theodore MANAZIR
91 Director Administrative Computing .... Ms. Kellee PIERCE

Salish Kootenai College (E)

PO Box 70, Pablo MT 59855-0070
County: Lake FICE Identification: 021434
Unit ID: 180647
Telephone: (406) 275-4800 Carnegie Class: Tribal
FAX Number: (406) 275-4801 Calendar System: Quarter
URL: www.skc.edu
Established: 1977 Annual Undergrad Tuition & Fees: $4,191
Enrollment: 859 Coed
Affiliation or Control: Independent Non-Profit IRS Status: 501(c)3
Highest Offering: Baccalaureate
Accreditation: NW, ADNUR, DA, NUR, SW

01 President .... Dr. Sandra BOHAM
05 Vice President of Academic Affairs .... Vacant
10 Vice Pres Business Affairs .... Ms. Audrew PLOUFFE
32 Vice Pres Student Affairs .... Mr. Dan DURGLO
06 Registrar .... Ms. Cleo KENMILLE
37 Financial Aid Director .... Ms. Jackie SWAIN
09 Dir Institutional Effectiveness .... Dr. Stacey SHERWIN
15 Director Personnel Services .... Mrs. Dawn BENSON
30 Development Director .... Ms. Angelique ALBERT
35 Dean of Students .... Ms. Tracie MCDONALD
13 Director of Information Technology .... Mr. Al ANDERSON
18 Facilities/Physical Plant Manager .... Mr. Michael BIGCRANE
04 Exec Admin Assistant to President .... Mr. Victor MONTOYA

Stone Child College (F)

8294 Upper Box Elder Road, Box Elder MT 59521-9796
County: Hill FICE Identification: 026109
Unit ID: 366340
Telephone: (406) 395-4875 Carnegie Class: Tribal
FAX Number: (406) 395-4836 Calendar System: Semester
URL: www.stonechild.edu/
Established: 1984 Annual Undergrad Tuition & Fees: $2,645
Enrollment: 458 Coed
Affiliation or Control: Tribal Control IRS Status: 501(c)3
Highest Offering: Associate Degree
Accreditation: NW

01 President .... Dr. Nathaniel ST. PIERRE
05 Dean of Academics .... Ms. Cory SANGREY-BILLY
32 Dean of Student Services .... Ms. Aimee MONTES
10 Business Office/Finance Manager .... Ms. Jewel L. WHITFORD
04 Admin Asst to the President .... Ms. Wanda ST. MARKS
06 Registrar .... Ms. Gaile TORRES
13 Network Administator .... Mr. Tony WOODS
40 Bookstore Manager .... Ms. Sue HAY
37 Financial Aid Officer .... Ms. Tiffany GALBAVY
18 Facilities/Maintenance Supervisor .... Mr. Gus BACON
08 Head Librarian .... Ms. Joy BRIDWELL

University of Great Falls (G)

1301 Twentieth Street S, Great Falls MT 59405-4996
County: Cascade FICE Identification: 002527
Unit ID: 180258
Telephone: (800) 856-9544 Carnegie Class: Bac-Diverse
FAX Number: (406) 791-5209 Calendar System: Semester
URL: www.ugf.edu
Established: 1932 Annual Undergrad Tuition & Fees: $22,170
Enrollment: 1,117 Coed
Affiliation or Control: Roman Catholic IRS Status: 501(c)3
Highest Offering: Master's
Accreditation: NW, NURSE

01 President .... Dr. Anthony ARETZ
05 VP for Academic Affairs .... Dr. Timothy LAURENT
10 Vice President for Finance .... Ms. Stacey EVE
84 VP for Enrollment Management .... Ms. Julie EDSTROM
32 VP for Student Development .... Ms. Sherrie AREY
41 Athletic Director .... Mr. Dave GANTT
20 Academic Dean .... Dr. Gregory MADSON
37 Director Financial Aid .... Ms. Kelli ENGELHARDT
06 Registrar .... Ms. Brittany BUDESKI
14 Director Administrative Computing .... Ms. Kathryn CARBIS
26 Director of Marketing and PR .... Vacant
18 Director Physical Plant .... Mr. Chet PIETRYKOWSKI
38 Director Student Counseling .... Ms. Linda FAGENSTROM
21 Director of the Business Office .... Ms. Amber HERIGON
106 Director of Distance Learning .... Mr. Jim GRETCH
15 VP for Human Resources .... Ms. Stacey EVE
09 Director of Institutional Research .... Dr. Gregory MADSON
40 Campus Store Manger .... Mr. Lance LOHNSON
13 Chief Technology Officer .... Mr. John KOEHLER
88 Director Student Support Services .... Mr. Matthew HAUK
39 Director of Residential Life .... Ms. Barbara PALACIOS

Yellowstone Christian College (H)

1515 S. Shiloh Road, Billings MT 59106
County: Yellowstone Identification: 667254
Telephone: (406) 656-9950 Carnegie Class: Not Classified
FAX Number: N/A Calendar System: Semester
URL: www.yellowstonechristian.edu
Established: 1880 Annual Undergrad Tuition & Fees: N/A
Enrollment: N/A Coed
Affiliation or Control: Independent Non-Profit IRS Status: 501(c)3
Highest Offering: Baccalaureate
Accreditation: @BI

01 President .... Bruce CANNON
32 Dean of Students .... Remigio RAMOS

NEBRASKA

Bellevue University (I)

1000 Galvin Road S, Bellevue NE 68005-3098
County: Sarpy FICE Identification: 009743
Unit ID: 180814
Telephone: (402) 293-2000 Carnegie Class: Masters/L
FAX Number: (402) 293-2020 Calendar System: Other
URL: www.bellevue.edu
Established: 1966 Annual Undergrad Tuition & Fees: $7,050
Enrollment: 9,879 Coed
Affiliation or Control: Independent Non-Profit IRS Status: 501(c)3
Highest Offering: Doctorate
Accreditation: NH, IACBE

01 President .... Dr. Mary B. HAWKINS
03 Vice President Administration .... Mr. Jerry A. BLASIG
10 Exec VP University Affairs .... Ms. Donna BARNES
05 Chief Academic Officer .... Mr. Rod HEWLETT
11 Chief Operating Officer .... Mr. Matthew DAVIS
72 Dean of College of Science & Tech .... Ms. Mary DOBRANSKY
50 Dean College of Business .... Dr. Rebecca MURDOCK
49 Dean College of Arts & Sciences .... Dr. Clif MASON
51 Dean of Continuing and Profess Educ .... Dr. Michelle EPPLER
13 Asst VP of Information Technology .... Mr. James S. VEREBELY
04 Exec Assistant to the President .... Ms. Christine HOW
32 VP Community & Student Affairs .... Mr. Russ LANE
37 Director Student Financial Svcs .... Ms. Janet YALE
08 Sr Dir Library Services .... Ms. Robin BERNSTEIN
102 Foundation CEO .... Mr. Russ RUPIPER
41 Director of Athletics .... Mr. Ed LEHOTAK
40 Director Bookstore .... Mr. Mark RIGGERT
18 Director of Facilities .... Mr. Ralph (Sam) J. BORER
30 VP Development Programs .... Ms. Dorothy MORROW
21 Controller .... Ms. Lori PIRSCH
15 VP Performance Management .... Mr. Tim DORN
19 Director of Security/Safety .... Mr. Greg ALLEN
88 Quality Assurance Programs Director .... Mr. Pete HEINEMAN
26 Associate Dir Public Relations .... Mr. Jim MAXWELL
26 Sr Dir Marketing Operations .... Ms. Geri MASON
06 Registrar .... Ms. Liz BRADLEY

Bryan College of Health Sciences (J)

5035 Everett Street, Lincoln NE 68506-1315
County: Lancaster FICE Identification: 006399
Unit ID: 180878
Telephone: (402) 481-8697 Carnegie Class: Spec-4-yr-Other Health
FAX Number: N/A Calendar System: Semester
URL: www.bryanhealthcollege.edu
Established: 2001 Annual Undergrad Tuition & Fees: $14,169
Enrollment: 691 Coed
Affiliation or Control: Independent Non-Profit IRS Status: 501(c)3
Highest Offering: Doctorate
Accreditation: NH, ANEST, CVT, DMS, NUR

01 President .... Dr. Marilyn MOORE
05 Provost .... Dr. Kay MAIZE
97 Dean General Studies/Acad Avance .... Dr. Kristy PLANDER
11 Dean of Operations .... Dr. June SMITH
66 Dean of Undergraduate Nursing .... Dr. Theresa DELAHOYDE
76 Dean of Health Professions .... Dr. Kay CRABTREE
58 Dean of Graduate Studies .... Dr. Sharon HADENFELDT
32 Dean of Students .... Ms. Debra BORDER
08 Director of Library Services .... Ms. Anne HEIMANN
07 Director of Admissions .... Ms. Kelli BACKMAN
06 Registrar .... Ms. Pam MCMASTER

Central Community College (K)

PO Box 4903, Grand Island NE 68802-4903
County: Hall FICE Identification: 020995
Unit ID: 180902
Telephone: (308) 398-4222 Carnegie Class: Assoc/HVT-High Non
FAX Number: (308) 398-7398 Calendar System: Semester
URL: www.cccneb.edu
Established: 1966 Annual Undergrad Tuition & Fees (In-District): $2,820
Enrollment: 6,377 Coed
Affiliation or Control: Local IRS Status: 501(c)3
Highest Offering: Associate Degree
Accreditation: NH, ADNUR, CAHIIM, DA, DH, EMT, MAC, MLTAD, OTA

01 College President .... Dr. Greg P. SMITH
05 Executive Vice President .... Dr. Deb BRENNAN
12 Columbus Campus President .... Dr. Matt R. GOTSCHALL
12 Grand Island Campus President .... Dr. Thomas A. WALKER
12 Hastings Campus President .... Mr. Bill HITESMAN
26 Public Relations/Marketing Director .... Mr. Scott MILLER
10 College Business Officer .... Mr. Joel KING
13 Dir Information Technology Services .... Mr. Tom PETERS
102 Foundation Director .... Mr. Dean MOORS

15 Human Resource Executive Director ....Dr. Chris WADDLE
06 Registrar ....Ms. Barb LARSON
29 Director Alumni Relations ....Ms. Cheri BEDA
37 Director Student Financial Aid ....Ms. Victoria KUCERA
84 Director Enrollment Management ....Mr. Jerry RACIOPPI
09 Director Institutional Research ....Mr. Brian MCDERMOTT
28 Director Diversity ....Dr. Chris WADDLE
32 Director Student Affairs ....Mr. Jerry RACIOPPI
96 Director of Purchasing ....Ms. Marilyn BOTTRELL
29 Alumni Coordinator ....Ms. Pat STANGE
07 Director of Admissions Columbus ....Ms. Kristin HOESING
07 Director of Admissions Grand Island ....Ms. Erin LESIAK
07 Director of Admissions Hastings ....Mr. Robert GLENN
41 Athletic Director ....Mr. Jack GUTIERREZ

Central Community College Columbus Campus (A)

PO Box 1027, 4500 63rd Street,
Columbus NE 68602-1027
Telephone: (402) 564-7132 Identification: 770331
Accreditation: &NH

† Regional accreditation is carried under the parent institution in Grand Island, NE

Central Community College Hastings Campus (B)

550 S Technical Blvd, PO Box 1024,
Hastings NE 68902-1024
Telephone: (402) 463-9811 Identification: 770332
Accreditation: &NH

† Regional accreditation is carried under the parent institution in Grand Island, NE

CHI Health School of Radiologic Technology (C)

6901 North 72nd Street, Omaha NE 68122
County: Douglas FICE Identification: 008492
Unit ID: 181145
Telephone: (402) 572-3650 Carnegie Class: Spec 2-yr-Health
FAX Number: (402) 398-6650 Calendar System: Semester
URL: www.chihealth.com/school-of-radiologic-technology
Established: 1953 Annual Undergrad Tuition & Fees: N/A
Enrollment: 22 Coed
Affiliation or Control: Independent Non-Profit IRS Status: 501(c)3
Highest Offering: Associate Degree
Accreditation: RAD

01 Program Director ....Robert A. HUGHES
10 Chief Financial Officer ....Jeanette WOJTALEWICZ

Clarkson College (D)

101 S 42nd Street, Omaha NE 68131-2739
County: Douglas FICE Identification: 009862
Unit ID: 180332
Telephone: (402) 552-3100 Carnegie Class: Spec-4-yr-Other Health
FAX Number: (402) 552-3369 Calendar System: Semester
URL: www.clarksoncollege.edu
Established: 1888 Annual Undergrad Tuition & Fees: $13,904
Enrollment: 1,221 Coed
Affiliation or Control: Independent Non-Profit IRS Status: 501(c)3
Highest Offering: Doctorate
Accreditation: NH, ANEST, CAHIIM, NUR, PTAA, RAD

11 President ....Dr. Tony M. DAMEWOOD
00 President Emeritus ....Dr. Louis W. BURGHER
05 VP of Academic Affairs ....Dr. Andriea NEBEL
10 Controller ....Megan WICKLESS
06 Registrar ....Michele D. STIRTZ
15 Director Human Resources .... Deb TOMEK
13 Director Technology ....Ryan SCHURMAN
26 Director of Marketing ....Jina PAUL
28 Director Diversity Services ....Aubray D. ORDUNA
37 Director Student Financial Services .... Dale BROWN
08 Director Library Services ....Nancy M. RALSTON
38 Director Success Center ....Chuck C. MACDONELL
97 Director General Education ....Lori BACHLE
66 Dean Nursing/Dir BS & Grad Nursing .... Dr. Aubray ORDUNA
50 Dir of Business & HIM ....Carla DIRKSCHNEIDER
76 Dir Medical Imaging/Radiologic Tech ....Ellen COLLINS
76 Dir Physical Therapist Asst Pgm ....Andreia NEBEL
07 Director Admissions .... Denise WORK
51 Director of Professional Dev ....Judi B. DUNN
29 Director Alumni Relations ....Rita VANFLEET
106 Coordinator Online Education ....Vacant
09 Coord Inst Effect/Quality Assurance ....Chris SWANSON

College of Saint Mary (E)

7000 Mercy Road, Omaha NE 68106-2606
County: Douglas FICE Identification: 002540
Unit ID: 181604
Telephone: (402) 399-2400 Carnegie Class: Masters/S
FAX Number: (402) 399-2647 Calendar System: Semester
URL: www.csm.edu
Established: 1923 Annual Undergrad Tuition & Fees: $28,964
Enrollment: 1,018 Female
Affiliation or Control: Roman Catholic IRS Status: 501(c)3
Highest Offering: Doctorate
Accreditation: NH, #ARCPA, NUR, OT

01 President ....Dr. Maryanne STEVENS, RSM
32 Vice President Student Development ....Dr. Tara KNUDSON-CARL
05 Vice Pres Academic Affairs ....Dr William MANGAN
07 Vice President Marketing ....Mr. Greg FRITZ
10 Vice Pres Financial Services/CFO ....Ms. Sarah KOTTICH
04 Executive Asst to the President ....Ms. Brenda ELLIOTT
84 Vice President Enrollment ....Ms. Sara HANSON
06 Registrar ....Mrs. Deb NUGEN
08 Director of Library ....Ms. Sara WILLIAMS
13 Vice President IT ....Mrs. Victoria HOSKOVEC
29 Vice Pres Alumnae/Donor Relations ....Dr. Christine PHARR
37 Director Student Financial Aid ....Ms. Beth S SK
26 Public Relations Director ....Mr. Brittney LONG
35 Assoc Dean Student Affairs ....Mrs. Katty PETAK
39 Director Student Housing ....Ms. Erittany STEGEMAN
40 Director Bookstore ....Mr. Steve WESTENBROEK
41 Athletic Director ....Mr. Peter HARING
42 Director Campus Ministry ....Ms. Julie CHRISTENSEN
42 Director Mission Integration ....Ms. Marian STANDEVEN
18 Director Physical Plant ....Mr. Dan SPARGEN
44 Director Annual Giving ....Ms. Janelle DOMEYER
21 Associate Business Officer ....Ms. Bridgette RENBARGER
15 Director Human Resources ....Ms. Sarah M. LIVINGSTON
11 Chief of Administration ....Mrs. Kim SAVICKY
19 Director Security/Safety ....Mr. David FERBER

Concordia University (F)

800 N Columbia Avenue, Seward NE 68434-1599
County: Seward FICE Identification: 002541
Unit ID: 180984
Telephone: (402) 643-3651 Carnegie Class: Masters/L
FAX Number: (402) 643-4073 Calendar System: Other
URL: www.cune.edu
Established: 1894 Annual Undergrad Tuition & Fees: $27,110
Enrollment: 2,332 Coed
Affiliation or Control: Lutheran Church - Missouri Synod
IRS Status: 501(c)3
Highest Offering: Master's
Accreditation: NH, IACBE, MUS, NURSE, TED

01 President ....Rev Dr. Brian L. FRIEDRICH
05 Provost ....Dr. Jenny MUELLER-ROEBKE
30 Vice President Inst Advancement ....Mr. Kurth BRASHEAR
84 VP Enroll Mgt/Stdnt Svcs/Athletics ....Mr. Scott SEEVERS
32 VP for Student Affairs & Athletics ....Mr. Gene BROOKS
10 Chief Financial Officer ....Mr. David KUMM
53 Dean of Educ/Health & Human Svcs ....Dr. Nancy ELWELL
49 Dean of Arts & Sciences ....Dr. Brent ROYUK
13 Chief Information Officer ....Dr. Kent EINSPAHR
58 Dean College Grad Studies/Adult Ed ....Mr. Jonathon MOBERLY
08 Director of Library Services ....Mr. Philip HENDRICKSON
36 Synodical & Education Placement Dir ....Mr. William SCHRANZ
29 Director Alumni/University Rels ....Mrs. Jennifer FURR
36 Career Counselor ....Mr. Corey GRAY
41 Athletic Director ....Mr. Devin SMITH
42 Campus Pastor ....Rev. Ryan MATTHIAS
37 Director of Financial Aid ....Mrs. Gloria HENNIG
18 Chief Facilities/Physical Plant ....Mr. Rick IHDE
15 Director of Human Resources ....Mrs. Connie BUTLER
07 Director Undergraduate Admissions ....Mr. Aaron ROBERTS
26 Director of Marketing ....Mr. Seth MERANDA
21 Dir Invest/Student Admin Svcs ....Mr. Curt SHERMAN
44 Coord of Resource Devel Ops ....Vacant
38 Director of Counseling ....Ms. Cara KROEKER
106 Dir Classroom Innov & Online Educ ....Ms. Angie WASSENMILLER

Creative Center (G)

10850 Emmet Street, Omaha NE 68164-2911
County: Douglas FICE Identification: 031643
Unit ID: 430485
Telephone: (402) 898-1000 Carnegie Class: Spec-4-yr-Arts
FAX Number: (402) 898-1301 Calendar System: Semester
URL: www.creativecenter.edu
Established: 1993 Annual Undergrad Tuition & Fees: $27,700
Enrollment: 78 Coed
Affiliation or Control: Proprietary IRS Status: Proprietary
Highest Offering: Baccalaureate
Accreditation: ACCSC

01 President ....Mr. Ray DOTZLER
05 Director ....Ms. Kim GUYER
07 Director of Admissions ....Mr. Richard CALDWELL
10 Chief Business Officer ....Ms. Beth CONNOR
37 Director Student Financial Aid ....Ms. Sandy LAROCCA

Creighton University (H)

2500 California Plaza, Omaha NE 68178-0001
County: Douglas FICE Identification: 002542
Unit ID: 181002
Telephone: (402) 280-2700 Carnegie Class: Masters/L
FAX Number: N/A Calendar System: Semester
URL: www.creighton.edu
Established: 1878 Annual Undergrad Tuition & Fees: $36,422
Enrollment: 8,236 Coed
Affiliation or Control: Roman Catholic IRS Status: 501(c)3
Highest Offering: Doctorate
Accreditation: NH, BJS, BUSA, DENT, EMT, LAW, MED, NURSE, OT, PHAR, PTA, SW, TED

00 Chairman Creighton University Board ....Mr. Michael R. MCCARTHY
01 President ....Rev. Daniel S. HENDRICKSON, SJ
05 Interim Provost ....Dr. Thomas F. MURRAY
100 AVP/Chief of Staff ....Ms. Colette O'MEARA-MCKINNEY
04 Sr Exec Assistant President Office ....Ms. Terri L. KILGARIN
101 Corporate Secretary ....Mr. James S. JANSEN
04 Asst to the President for Mission .....Rev. Richard J. HAUSER, SJ
03 Sr Vice President Operations ....Mr. Daniel E. BURKEY
42 Vice Provost Mission & Ministry ....Dr. Eileen C. BURKE-SULLIVAN
30 Vice President University Relations ....Mr. Richard P. VIRGIN
45 Director Strategic Planning .....Ms. Colette O'MEARA-MCKINNEY
108 Assoc VP Acad Excel & Assessment ... Dr. Mary Ann DANIELSON
08 University Librarian ....Mr. James BOTHMER
106 Exec Dir Ctr for Acad Innovation ....Dr. Tracy A. CHAPMAN
09 Director Institutional Research ......Dr. Somchan VUTHIPADADON
06 Registrar ....Ms. Melinda STONER
88 Dir Military/Veterans Liaison Svcs ....Mr. Mark P. TURNER
22 Director Disability Accommodations ....Ms. Denise Y. LE CLAIR
36 Interim Director Career Center ....Mr. Jeremy M. FISHER
103 Assoc Director Career Development ....Ms. Lisa L. BROCKHOFF FITZSIMMONS
43 General Counsel ....Mr. James S. JANSEN
17 Sr Vice Provost Clinical Affairs ....Dr. Donald R. FREY
31 Assoc VP Multicultr & Comm Affairs . Dr. Sade KOSOKO-LASAKI
51 Assoc VP Continuing Education ....Dr. Sally C. O'NEIL
88 Dir Ctr for Hlth Policy & Ethics ....Dr. Amy M. HADDAD
32 Vice Provost Student Life ....Dr. Tanya C. WINEGARD
39 Assoc VP Resident Life ....Dr. Richard E. ROSSI
35 Assoc VP Student Life ....Dr. Wayne YOUNG
35 Assoc VP Student Life ....Dr. Michele K. BOGARD
41 Athletic Director ....Mr. Bruce D. RASMUSSEN
46 Assoc VP Research & Scholarship ....Dr. Thomas F. MURRAY
88 AVP Health Science Mission/Identity . Rev. James F. CLIFTON, SJ
46 Dir Ctr UG Research & Scholarship ....Dr. Juliane K. STRAUSS-SOUKUP
84 Vice Provost Enrollment Management ....Dr. Mary E. CHASE
84 Director Enrollment Services ....Dr. Lori K. GIGLIOTTI
07 Director Admissions/Scholarships .... Ms. Sarah D. RICHARDSON
37 Director Student Financial Aid ....Ms. Paula S. KOHLES
88 Director Academic Success ....Dr. Joe ECKLUND
49 Dean Arts & Sciences ....Dr. Bridget M. KEEGAN
50 Dean Heider College of Business ....Dr. Anthony R. HENDRICKSON
107 Dean College of Prof Studies ....Dr. Gail M. JENSEN
52 Dean Dentistry ....Dr. Mark A. LATTA
58 Dean Graduate School ....Dr. Gail M. JENSEN
61 Dean Law ....Mr. Paul E. MCGREAL
63 Dean Medicine ....Dr. Robert W. DUNLAY
66 Dean Nursing ....Dr. Catherine M. TODERO
67 Dean Pharmacy & Health Professions ...Dr. J. Chris BRADBERRY
26 Chief Marketing & Comm Officer .... Mr. Jim BERSCHEIDT
27 Director Public Relations ....Ms. Cindy R. WORKMAN
11 Vice President Administration ....Mr. John L. WILHELM
18 Asst VP Facility Mgmt & Planning ....Mr. Timothy P. NORTON
19 Director Public Safety ....Mr. Richard J. MCAULIFFE
10 Vice President Finance ....Vacant
21 Assoc VP Finance ....Mr. John J. JESSE, III
96 Director Purchasing ....Mr. Joseph J. ZABOROWSKI
15 Assoc VP Human Resources ....Mr. Jeffrey C. BRANSTETTER
13 Vice Pres Information Technology .... Mr. Tim BROOKS
14 Asst VP Information Technology ....Mr. Mark J. MONGAR
90 Executive Director IT ....Mr. Ryan M. CAMERON
91 Director IT Service & Support .... Mr. J. D. RUMMEL
88 Site Dir Alegent/CU Hlth Systems .... Mr. Thomas HALEY
22 Exec Director Equity & Inclusion ....Ms. Allison S. TAYLOR
88 Sr Philanthropic Advisor ....Mr. Steven A. SCHOLER
44 Asst VP Office of Development ....Mr. Matthew C. GERARD
44 Asst VP Office of Development ....Ms. Kelly K. PTACEK
29 Asst VP Alumni Relations ....Ms. Anna NUBEL
102 Dir Corp & Foundation Relations ....Mr. Jeremy J. BOUMAN
23 Sr Director Student Health Services ....Ms. Debra C. SAURE
24 Director Learning Environment ....Mr. Charles A. LENOSKY
25 Director Sponsored Programs Admin ....Ms. Beth J. HERR
28 Director Multicultural Affairs ....Mr. Ricardo M. ARIZA
38 Sr Director Counseling Services ....Dr. Michael KELLEY
40 Bookstore Manager ....Mr. Calvin PETERSEN
85 Exec Dir Global Engagement Office ....Dr. Rene PADILLA
86 Director Cmty & Govt Relationships ....Mr. Chris T. RODGERS
87 Director Summer Session ....Ms. Christine BILLINGS
92 Director Honors Program ....Dr. Jeffrey P. HAUSE
94 Director Women's & Gender Studies ....Dr. Susan A. CALEF
104 Global Programs Coordinator ....Ms. Lizzy E. CURRAN
20 Vice Provost Learning & Assessment ....Dr. Gail M. JENSEN
88 Assoc Provost Academic Admin ....Ms. Tricia A. BRUNDO-SHARRAR
88 Assoc Provost Academic Finance ....Ms. Jessica M. GRANER
89 Director Advising and Operation ....Ms. Sandy V. CIRIACO

Doane College (I)

3180 W U.S. Highway 34, Grand Island NE 68801
Telephone: (308) 398-0800 Identification: 770333
Accreditation: &NH

† Regional accreditation is carried under the parent institution in Crete, NE

Doane College **(A)**

303 North 52nd Street, Lincoln NE 68504
Telephone: (402) 466-4774 Identification: 770334
Accreditation: &NH

† Regional accreditation is carried under the parent institution in Crete, NE

Doane University (B)

1014 Boswell Avenue, Crete NE 68333
County: Saline FICE Identification: 002544
Unit ID: 181020
Telephone: (402) 826-2161 Carnegie Class: Bac-A&S
FAX Number: (402) 826-8600 Calendar System: 4/1/4
URL: www.doane.edu
Established: 1872 Annual Undergrad Tuition & Fees: $28,790
Enrollment: 1,065 Coed
Affiliation or Control: United Church Of Christ IRS Status: 501(c)3
Highest Offering: Doctorate
Accreditation: NH, NURSE, TED

01 President .... Dr. Jacque CARTER
05 Vice President Academic Affairs .... Dr. John BURNEY
10 Vice President Financial Affairs .... Ms. Julie SCHMIDT
30 Executive Director of Advancement .... Ms. Amy JURGENS
32 Vice President Student Affairs .... Ms. Carrie LOVELACE PETR
13 VP for Information Technology .... Mr. Mike CARPENTER
07 VP for Enrollment Svcs & Marketing .... Mr. Joel WEYAND
88 Dean of Educational Leadership .... Dr. Jed JOHNSTON
20 Dean of Curriculum & Instruction .... Dr. Lyn FORESTER
58 Dean of Grad Studies in Mgmt .... Ms. Janice M. HADFIELD
51 Dean Adult Undergraduate Studies .... Ms. Janice M. HADFIELD
35 Asst Dean for Student Affairs .... Vacant
06 Registrar .... Ms. Denise ELLIS
37 Director of Financial Aid .... Ms. Peggy TVRDY
08 Director of the Library .... Ms. Julie PINNELL
21 Controller .... Mr. Ned TUCKER
36 Director College to Career Center .... Ms. Sarah BARG
26 Sr Director of Strategic Comm .... Mr. Mike LEFLER
29 Director of Alumni Relation .... Ms. Anne ZIOLA
44 Exec Dir of Campgns/Chief Dev Ofcr .... Mr. Marty FYE
15 Director of Human Resources .... Ms. Laura SEARS
18 Dir of Facilities & Constr Proj .... Mr. Brian FLESNER
88 Interim Director Master of Couns .... Ms. Jean KILNOSKI
12 Director of Omaha Campus .... Ms. Dena STEVENSON
12 Director of Grand Island Campus ... Ms. Jennifer WORTHINGTON
41 Athletic Director .... Ms. Jill MCCARTNEY
42 Chaplain .... Ms. Karla COOPER
40 Bookstore Manager .... Ms. Lynette NEWTON
28 Director of Multicultural Pgm & Edu .... Ms. Wilma JACKSON
23 Director of Health and Wellness .... Ms. Kelly JIROVEC
35 Director of Student Support Service .... Ms. Sherri HANIGAN
09 Director of Institutional Research .... Dr. Raja TAYEH
19 Dir of Campus Safety/Assoc Dean .... Mr. Russ HEWITT

Grace University (C)

1311 S 9th Street, Omaha NE 68108-3629
County: Douglas FICE Identification: 002547
Unit ID: 181093
Telephone: (402) 449-2800 Carnegie Class: Bac-Diverse
FAX Number: (402) 449-2999 Calendar System: Semester
URL: www.graceuniversity.edu
Established: 1943 Annual Undergrad Tuition & Fees: $20,548
Enrollment: 469 Coed
Affiliation or Control: Independent Non-Profit IRS Status: 501(c)3
Highest Offering: Master's
Accreditation: NH, BI

00 CEO .... Mr. Bill BAUHARD
01 Interim President .... Dr. John D. HOLMES
05 VP of Academic Affairs .... Dr. Karl PAGENKEMPER
84 VP of Enrollment .... Mr. Chris PRUITT
30 VP of Advancement .... Vacant
21 Director of Finance .... Ms. Anita RODRIGUEZ
06 Registrar .... Dr. Kris J. UDD
58 Dean Professional & Graduate Stds .... Mr. C. James SANTORO
09 Dir of Assessment & Inst Research .... Vacant
37 Director of Financial Aid .... Mrs. Mackenzie DEHMER
15 Director Human Resources .... Ms. Deb OSMANSON
08 Librarian .... Vacant
04 Admin Assistant to the President .... Ms. Joanne R. FAST
33 Dean of Men .... Mr. Jeff BANKS
34 Dean of Women .... Dr. Tara RYE
41 Athletic Director .... Mr. Willie WILLIAMS
11 Asst VP Administration .... Ms. Deb OSMANSON

Hastings College (D)

710 N Turner Avenue, Box 269, Hastings NE 68902-0269
County: Adams FICE Identification: 002548
Unit ID: 181127
Telephone: (402) 463-2402 Carnegie Class: Bac-Diverse
FAX Number: (402) 461-7490 Calendar System: 4/1/4
URL: www.hastings.edu
Established: 1882 Annual Undergrad Tuition & Fees: $27,300
Enrollment: 1,212 Coed
Affiliation or Control: Presbyterian Church (U.S.A.) IRS Status: 501(c)3
Highest Offering: Master's
Accreditation: NH, MUS, TED

01 President .... Mr. Donald JACKSON
00 Chairman of the Board .... Mr. Harold (Hal) E. DITTMER
30 Exec VP for External Relations .... Mr. Gary FREEMAN
10 VP for Finance .... Mr. Tony BEATA
84 VP for Enrollment and Marketing .... Ms. Susan MEESKE
05 Exec VP of Acad Affairs and Provost .... Dr. Gary C. JOHNSON
32 Vice President for Student Affairs .... Vacant
20 Assoc VP for Academic Affairs .... Dr. Liz FROMBGEN
100 Chief of Staff .... Ms. Alicia O'DONNELL
41 Athletic Director .... Ms. Patty SITORIUS
35 Assoc VP for Student Affairs .... Mr. Dan PETERS
44 Assoc VP for Planned & Major Gifts .... Mr. Michael KARLOFF
88 Assoc VP of Scholarship Development .... Vacant
102 Assoc VP for Development .... Ms. Judee L. KONEN
06 Registrar .... Mr. Jim BOEVE
37 Director of Financial Aid .... Ms. Traci BOEVE
39 Director of Housing .... Vacant
15 Director of Human Resources .... Ms. Kari FLUCKEY
26 Director of Marketing .... Mr. Michael HOWIE
08 Director of Libraries .... Ms. Susan FRANKLIN
29 Director of Alumni Relations .... Mr. Matt FONG
13 Chief Info and Compliance Officer .... Mr. Steve HUTCHINSON
14 Network Administrator .... Mr. Jim MACKIN
90 Acad Computer Support Specialist .... Mr. Erik NIELSEN
18 Director Physical Plant Services .... Mr. James RUZICKA
93 Minority Students .... Dr. Moses DOGBEVIA
28 International Studies/Diversity Pgm .... Dr. Liz FROMBGEN
36 Director of Career Services .... Ms. Kimberly K. GRAVIETTE
23 Director Campus Health Services .... Ms. Beth LITTRELL
42 Chaplain .... Rev. Damen HEITMANN
21 Director of Accounting .... Ms. Susan TEUTSCHMANN
35 Director of Student Engagement .... Mr. Colt KRAUS
19 Director of Security/Safety .... Mr. John SILVESTER
38 Director of Counseling Services .... Mr. Jon LOETTERLE
40 Bookstore Manager .... Ms. Nancy GLEASON
88 Graphic Designer/Publisher .... Mrs. Camille KASTL
85 Foreign Students/Student Life .... Dr. Antje ANDERSON
04 Executive Asst to President .... Ms. Marin SUHR
07 Director of Admissions .... Ms. Chris SCHUKEI

Kaplan University **(E)**

1821 K Street, PO Box 82826, Lincoln NE 68501-2826
Telephone: (402) 474-5315 FICE Identification: 004721
Accreditation: &NH, ACBSP, MAC

† Regional accreditation is carried under the parent institution in Davenport, IA.

Kaplan University **(F)**

5425 N. 103rd Street, Omaha NE 68134-1002
Telephone: (402) 431-6100 FICE Identification: 008491
Accreditation: &NH, ACBSP, DA

† Regional accreditation is carried under the parent institution in Davenport, IA.

Little Priest Tribal College (G)

601 East College Drive, PO Box 270, Winnebago NE 68071-0270
County: Thurston FICE Identification: 033233
Unit ID: 434016
Telephone: (402) 878-2380 Carnegie Class: Tribal
FAX Number: (402) 878-2355 Calendar System: Semester
URL: www.littlepriest.edu
Established: 1996 Annual Undergrad Tuition & Fees: $5,085
Enrollment: 127 Coed
Affiliation or Control: Independent Non-Profit IRS Status: 501(c)3
Highest Offering: Associate Degree
Accreditation: NH

01 President .... Mr. Maunka MORGAN
05 Academic Dean .... Ms. Betty REDLEAF
10 Controller .... Mr. David MUELLER
37 Director of Financial Aid .... Ms. Yatty MOHAMMAD
13 IT Director .... Mr. Morrie CONWAY
09 Dir Inst Research/Stdnt Records .... Vacant
06 Registrar .... Ms. Cherie HEISE

Mary Lanning Healthcare School of Radiology (H)

715 North St. Joseph Avenue, Hastings NE 68901
County: Adams FICE Identification: 004431
Unit ID: 181251
Telephone: (402) 461-5177 Carnegie Class: Not Classified
FAX Number: (402) 460-5059 Calendar System: Other
URL: www.marylanning.org
Established: 1952 Annual Undergrad Tuition & Fees: N/A
Enrollment: N/A Coed
Affiliation or Control: Independent Non-Profit IRS Status: 501(c)3
Highest Offering: Associate Degree
Accreditation: RAD

01 Program Director .... Cristi L. ENGEL
10 Chief Financial Officer .... Shawn NORDBY
26 Dir of Public Rels/Marketing Svcs .... Lisa BRANDT

McCook Community College **(I)**

1205 East Third Street, McCook NE 69001
Telephone: (308) 345-8100 Identification: 770337
Accreditation: &NH, EMT

† Regional accreditation is carried under the parent institution in North Platte, NE

Metropolitan Community College (J)

PO Box 3777, Omaha NE 68103-0777
County: Douglas FICE Identification: 012586
Unit ID: 181303
Telephone: (402) 457-2400 Carnegie Class: Assoc/MT-VT-High Non
FAX Number: (402) 457-2395 Calendar System: Quarter
URL: www.mccneb.edu
Established: 1974 Annual Undergrad Tuition & Fees (In-District): $2,745
Enrollment: 14,675 Coed
Affiliation or Control: Local IRS Status: 501(c)3
Highest Offering: Associate Degree
Accreditation: NH, ACBSP, ACFEI, ADNUR, CAHIIM, COARC, CSHSE, DA, EMT, MAC

01 President .... Mr. Randy SCHMAILZL
03 Executive Vice President .... Mr. James GROTRIAN
05 Vice President Academic Affairs .... Dr. Tom MCDONNELL
11 VP Technology/Administrative Svcs .... Dr. Mary K. WISE
32 VP of Campuses/Student Affairs .... Dr. Arthur RICH
28 Assoc Vice Pres Equity/Diversity .... Dr. Cynthia GOOCH
15 Assoc Vice Pres of Human Resources .... Ms. Maureen MOEGLIN
30 Assoc Vice Pres of Development .... Ms. Pat CRISLER
20 Associate VP for Effect & Engag .... Mr. William OWEN
84 Asst Vice Pres for Student Affairs .... Ms. Marie VAZQUEZ
10 Executive College Business Officer .... Mr. Dave KOEBEL
26 Exec Director of Public Affairs .... Ms. Sheila O'CONNOR
18 Director Facilities Management .... Mr. Bernard SEDLACEK
37 Director of Financial Aid .... Ms. Wilma HJELLUM
96 Director Administrative Management .... Mr. Richard HANNEMAN
19 Chief of Police/Dir Emergency Mgmt .... Mr. David FRIEND
84 Dean of Enrollment Management .... Ms. Ingrid BERLIN
27 Chief Information Officer .... Mr. Mick GAHAN
06 Registrar .... Ms. Albertha SCHMID
43 Dir Legal Services/General Counsel .... Mr. Jim THIBODEAU
44 Director of Development .... Ms. Jacqueline ALMQUIST
91 Director Administrative Computing .... Ms. Jodie SNIDER

Metropolitan Community College Elkhorn Valley Campus **(K)**

204th & Way Dodge Road, Omaha NE 68022
Telephone: (402) 289-1200 Identification: 770335
Accreditation: &NH

† Regional accreditation is carried under the parent institution in Omaha, NE

Metropolitan Community College South Omaha Campus **(L)**

2909 Edward Babe Gomez Avenue, Omaha NE 68107
Telephone: (402) 738-4500 Identification: 770336
Accreditation: &NH

† Regional accreditation is carried under the parent institution in Omaha, NE

Mid-Plains Community College (M)

601 W State Farm Road, North Platte NE 69101-9491
County: Lincoln FICE Identification: 002557
Unit ID: 181312
Telephone: (800) 658-4308 Carnegie Class: Assoc/MT-VT-High Non
FAX Number: (308) 535-3794 Calendar System: Semester
URL: www.mpcc.edu
Established: 1926 Annual Undergrad Tuition & Fees (In-District): $2,880
Enrollment: 2,143 Coed
Affiliation or Control: State/Local IRS Status: 501(c)3
Highest Offering: Associate Degree
Accreditation: NH, ADNUR, DA, EMT, MLTAD

01 President .... Mr. Ryan PURDY
12 VP North Platte Community College .... Dr. Jody TOMANEK
12 Vice Pres McCook Community College .... Mr. Andrew LONG
10 Area Business Officer .... Mr. Michael STEELE
05 Area VP for Academic Affairs .... Dr. Jody TOMANEK
09 Area Dir Instl Effectiveness .... Mr. Tad PFEIFER
32 Area Dean of Student Life .... Dr. Brian OBERT
56 Area Director of Outreach .... Ms. Gail KNOTT
36 Area Dean of Career Services .... Mr. Bill EAKINS
84 Area Dean of Enrollment Management .... Ms. Kelly RIPPEN
06 Area Registrar .... Ms. Mari Jo WIDGER
26 Area Dir Public Inform/Marketing .... Mr. Charles SALESTROM
15 Area Director of Human Resources .... Ms. Rebecca WRAGE
13 Area Director Information Services .... Mr. Tim HALL
37 Area Dir of Student Financial Aid .... Ms. Erinn BRAUER

Midland University (N)

900 N Clarkson, Fremont NE 68025-4395
County: Dodge FICE Identification: 002553
Unit ID: 181330
Telephone: (402) 721-5480 Carnegie Class: Bac-Diverse
FAX Number: (402) 721-0250 Calendar System: 4/1/4

URL: www.midlandu.edu
Established: 1883 Annual Undergrad Tuition & Fees: $29,400
Enrollment: 1,362 Coed
Affiliation or Control: Evangelical Lutheran Church In America
IRS Status: 501(c)3
Highest Offering: Master's
Accreditation: NH, COARC, NUR

01 President ... Ms. Jody HORNER
05 Vice Pres Academic Affairs ... Ms. Susan KRUMI
32 Vice Pres Student Affairs ... Mr. Merritt NELSON
10 Vice Pres Finance & Administration ... Ms. Jodi BENJAMIN
30 Vice Pres for Development ... Ms. Jessica JANSSEN
84 VP Admissions/Enrollment Management ... Ms. Eliza FERZELY
15 Vice Pres Human Resources ... Ms. Stephanie GOULD
26 Vice Pres Communications ... Mr. Nate NEUFIND
06 Registrar ... Mr. Eric MACZKA
07 Director of Admissions ... Mr. Nick BOONE
37 Director of Financial Aid ... Mr. Douglas WATSON
21 Controller ... Ms. Denise PRATT
41 Athletic Director ... Mr. Dave GILLESPIE
66 Director of Nursing ... Dr. Linda QUINN
13 Chief Information Officer ... Mr. Shane PERRIEN
18 Director Facilities Management ... Mr. Shawn NELSON
44 Director of Annual Giving ... Mr. Brad EBERSPACHER

Myotherapy Institute (A)

4001 Pioneer Woods Drive, Lincoln NE 68506-7547
County: Lancaster FICE Identification: 032793
Unit ID: 434432
Telephone: (402) 421-7410 Carnegie Class: Spec 2-yr-Health
FAX Number: (402) 421-6736 Calendar System: Other
URL: www.myotherapy.edu
Established: 1992 Annual Undergrad Tuition & Fees: $16,800
Enrollment: 15 Coed
Affiliation or Control: Proprietary IRS Status: Proprietary
Highest Offering: Associate Degree
Accreditation: ACCSC

01 Director ... Ms. Sue KOZISEK

National American University-Bellevue (B)

3604 Summit Plaza Drive, Bellevue NE 68123
Telephone: (402) 972-4250 Identification: 770406
Accreditation: &NH, MAC

† Regional accreditation is carried under the parent institution in Rapid City, SD

Nebraska Indian Community College (C)

1111 Hwy 75 - PO Box 428, Macy NE 68039-0428
County: Thurston FICE Identification: 025508
Unit ID: 181419
Telephone: (402) 494-2311 Carnegie Class: Tribal
FAX Number: (402) 837-4183 Calendar System: Semester
URL: www.thenicc.edu
Established: 1973 Annual Undergrad Tuition & Fees: $4,080
Enrollment: 120 Coed
Affiliation or Control: Tribal Control IRS Status: Exempt
Highest Offering: Associate Degree
Accreditation: NH

01 President ... Dr. Michael OLTROGGE
05 Academic Dean ... Mary JOHNSON
32 Dean Student Services ... Dawne PRICE
13 Chief Information Officer ... Justin KOCIAN
06 Registrar ... Troy MUNHOFEN
15 Human Resource Director ... Cheryl HANSEN

Nebraska Indian Community College-Santee (D)

415 North River Road, Santee NE 68760
Telephone: (402) 494-2311 Identification: 770339
Accreditation: &NH

† Regional accreditation is carried under the parent institution in Macy, NE

Nebraska Indian Community College-South Sioux City (E)

2605 1/2 Dakota Avenue, South Sioux City NE 68776
Telephone: (402) 494-2311 Identification: 770340
Accreditation: &NH

† Regional accreditation is carried under the parent institution in Macy, NE

Nebraska Methodist College (F)

720 N 87th Street, Omaha NE 68114-2852
County: Douglas FICE Identification: 006404
Unit ID: 181297
Telephone: (402) 354-7000 Carnegie Class: Spec-4-yr-Other Health
FAX Number: (402) 354-7090 Calendar System: Semester
URL: www.methodistcollege.edu
Established: 1891 Annual Undergrad Tuition & Fees: $13,418
Enrollment: 1,000 Coed
Affiliation or Control: Independent Non-Profit IRS Status: 501(c)3
Highest Offering: Doctorate
Accreditation: NH, COARC, DMS, MAC, NURSE, PTAA, RAD, SURGT

01 President ... Dr. Dennis A. JOSLIN
05 Vice President Academic Affairs ... Dr. Jody WOODWORTH
10 VP Bus Ops & Strategic Initiatives ... Dr. Deborah CARLSON
84 VP Enrollment & Student Success ... Dr. Brian SAJKO
66 Dean Nursing ... Dr. Linda HUGHES
58 Program Director Master's Nursing ... Dr. Linda FOLEY
66 Pgm Director Undergrad Nursing ... Dr. Karen JOHNSON
88 Director of Special Pgms Nursing ... Dr. Susie WARD
76 Dean Health Professions ... Vacant
97 Dean General Education ... Dr. Dean MANTERNACH
76 Pgm Director Phys Therapist Asst ... Ms. Shannon STRUBY
76 Program Director Respiratory Care ... Dr. John JAROSZ
88 Program Director Radiography ... Ms. Amy BOYD
88 Program Director Sonography ... Ms. Rebecca MATHIASEN
88 Pgm Director Surgical Technology ... Ms. Christy GRANT
08 Director of Library Services ... Ms. Beverly SEDLACEK
42 Dir Spiritual Dev/Campus Ministry ... Vacant
29 Alumni Engagement Director ... Ms. Angela HEESACKER-SMITH
07 Director Enrollment Services ... Ms. Megan MARYOTT
06 Director Registration & Records ... Ms. Melinda STONER
37 Director Financial Aid ... Ms. Penny JAMES
107 Exec Dir Professional Development ... Ms. Jillian PLYMESSER
88 Educational Compliance Officer ... Mr. Ryan PORTWOOD
04 Administrative Asst to President ... Ms. Cathy BECK
18 Chief Facilities/Physical Plant ... Ms. Pam EDGERTON
53 Director of Education ... Ms. Lisa NASSER

*Nebraska State College System (G)

1327 H Street, Suite 200, Lincoln NE 6850[illegible]
County: Lancaster FICE Identification: 033441
Telephone: (402) 471-2505 Carnegie Class: N/A
FAX Number: (402) 471-2669
URL: www.nscs.edu

01 Chancellor ... Mr. Stan CARPENTER
43 General Counsel & VC for Emp Rel ... Ms. Kristin PETERSEN
10 Vice Chancellor Finance/Admin ... Ms. Carolyn MURPHY
32 VC Stdnt Affs/Mktg/Enrol/Pub Info ... Dr. Korinne TANDE
18 Vice Chanc Facilities & Info Tech ... Mr. Steve HOTOVY
05 VC Acad Planning/Partnerships ... Dr. Jodi KUPPER
11 Operations Director ... Ms. Becky KOHRS
88 Director of Systemwide Accounting ... Ms. Amy HOCK
13 System Data Analyst/Reports Develop ... Mr. Mike DUNKLE
88 Director of Risk Mgmt & Compliance ... Ms. Angela MELTON

*Chadron State College (H)

1000 Main Street, Chadron NE 69337-2690
County: Dawes FICE Identification: 002539
Unit ID: 180948
Telephone: (308) 432-6000 Carnegie Class: Masters/M
FAX Number: (308) 432-6464 Calendar System: Semester
URL: www.csc.edu
Established: 1911 Annual Undergrad Tuition & Fees (In-State): $6,220
Enrollment: 3,033 Coed
Affiliation or Control: State IRS Status: 501(c)3
Highest Offering: Master's
Accreditation: NH, ACBSP, SW, TED

02 President ... Dr. Randy RHINE
05 Vice President Academic Affairs ... Dr. Charles SNARE
10 Vice Pres Administration & Finance ... Mr. Dale E. GRANT
84 Vice Pres Enrollment Mgmt & Mktg ... Mr. Jon HANSEN
20 Assoc VP Teaching & Learning Tech ... Vacant
13 Chief Information Officer ... Ms. Ann M. BURK
58 Dean Graduate Studies/BEAMS ... Dr. Joel HYER
49 Dean Essential Studies/Liberal Art ... Dr. James MARGETTS
108 Dean Assessment & Accreditation ... Dr. James POWELL
21 Comptroller ... Ms. Kari GASWICK
09 Director Institutional Research ... Vacant
102 Executive Director CS Foundation ... Ms. Connie A. RASMUSSEN
06 Director of Records ... Ms. Melissa MITCHELL
32 Sr Director Student Services ... Dr. Pat BEU
32 Assoc VP Student Services ... Ms. Sherry L. DOUGLAS
07 Director of Admissions ... Ms. Lisa STEIN
15 Assoc VP Human Resources ... Ms. Anne DEMERSSEMAN
39 Director of Housing ... Ms. Sherri J. SIMONS
41 Athletics Director ... Mr. Joel SMITH
36 Director of Internships/Career Svcs ... Ms. Deena KENNELL
21 Budget Director ... Ms. Melany HUGHES
26 Director College Relations ... Mr. Alex HELMBRECHT
18 Coordinator of Physical Facilities ... Mr. Blair BRENNAN
108 Director Inst Assessment ... Dr. Bob ADEBAYO

*Peru State College (I)

PO Box 10, Peru NE 68421-0010
County: Nemaha FICE Identification: 002559
Unit ID: 181534
Telephone: (402) 872-3815 Carnegie Class: Masters/S
FAX Number: (402) 872-2375 Calendar System: Semester
URL: www.peru.edu
Established: 1867 Annual Undergrad Tuition & Fees (In-State): $6,816
Enrollment: 2,499 Coed
Affiliation or Control: State IRS Status: 501(c)3
Highest Offering: Master's
Accreditation: NH, TED

02 President ... Dr. Daniel HANSON
05 Vice Pres Academic Affairs ... Dr. Tim BORCHERS
10 Vice Pres Administration & Finance ... Ms. Kathy CARROLL
32 VP Enrollment Mgmt/Student Services ... Dr. Michaela WILLIS
35 Dean of Student Life ... Mr. Jesse DORMAN
102 Exec Director PSC Foundations ... Mr. Todd SIMPSON
41 Director of Athletics ... Mr. Steve SCHNEIDER
26 Dir of Marketing & Communications ... Mr. Jason HOGUE
06 Dir Student Records/Coll Registrar ... Ms. Deann BAYNE
37 Director of Financial Aid ... Ms. Cheryl REID
08 Director of Library ... Ms. Veronica MCASEY
15 Director of Human Resources ... Ms. Eulanda CADE
18 Director Campus Services ... Ms. Jill MCCORMICK
21 Director of Business Services ... Ms. Kathy TYNON
07 Director of Admissions ... Mr. Heath CHRISTIANSEN
38 Licensed Student Counselor ... Ms. Jamie EBERLY
108 Director Institutional Assessment ... Ms. Kristin BUSCHER
13 Chief Info Technology Officer (CIO) ... Mr. Gene BEARDSLEE
19 Director Security/Safety ... Mr. Tim ROBERTSON

*Wayne State College (J)

1111 Main Street, Wayne NE 68787-1172
County: Wayne FICE Identification: 002566
Unit ID: 181783
Telephone: (402) 375-7000 Carnegie Class: Masters/M
FAX Number: (402) 375-7204 Calendar System: Semester
URL: www.wsc.edu
Established: 1909 Annual Undergrad Tuition & Fees (In-State): $5,898
Enrollment: 3,470 Coed
Affiliation or Control: State IRS Status: 501(c)3
Highest Offering: Beyond Master's But Less Than Doctorate
Accreditation: NH, ART, CACREP, CSHSE, IACBE, MUS, TED

02 President ... Dr. Marysz RAMES
05 Vice President Academic Affairs ... Mr. Steven ELLIOTT
10 Vice Pres Admin/Finance ... Ms. Angela FREDRICKSON
30 CEC Foundation Office ... Mr. Kevin ARMSTRONG
32 Vice President & Dean Students ... Dr. Jeffrey CARSTENS
37 Director Financial Aid ... Ms. Annette KAUS
07 Director of Admissions ... Mr. Kevin HALLE
38 Director of Counseling ... Ms. Lin BRUMMELS
39 Director of Residence Life ... Ms. Quinneka LEE
36 Director of Career Services ... Mr. Jason BARELMAN
13 Chief Information Officer ... Mr. John DUNNING
26 Director College Relations ... Mr. Jay COLLIER
41 Director of Athletics ... Mr. Mike POWICKI
18 Director of Facility Services ... Mr. Chad ALTWINE
08 Director of Library Services ... Mr. David GRABER
06 Registrar ... Ms. Cheri PARRAMORE
29 Dir Development & Alumni Relations ... Ms. Deb LUNDAHL
15 Director of Human Resources ... Ms. Candace TIMMERMAN
79 Dean School of Arts & Hum ... Vacant
50 Dean Sch of Business & Technology ... Dr. Vaughn BENSON
53 Dean Sch of Educ & Couns ... Dr. David HARYCKI
83 Dean Sch of Natural/Social Sci ... Dr. Tammy EVETOVICH
28 Director of Multicultural Affairs ... Dr. Leah KEINO
09 Research Analyst ... Ms. Jeannette BARRY
108 Director of Assessment ... Ms. Sue SYDOW
91 Director Administrative Computing ... Ms. Janell SCARDINO
04 Administrative Asst to President ... Ms. Joni BACKER
106 Extended Campus Program Coordinator ... Ms. Lisa REYNOLDS
19 Campus Security Manager ... Mr. Jason MRSNY

Nebraska Wesleyan University (K)

5000 St. Paul Avenue, Lincoln NE 68504-2794
County: Lancaster FICE Identification: 002555
Unit ID: 181446
Telephone: (402) 466-2371 Carnegie Class: Masters/M
FAX Number: (402) 465-2179 Calendar System: Semester
URL: www.nebrwesleyan.edu
Established: 1887 Annual Undergrad Tuition & Fees: $29,800
Enrollment: 2,083 Coed
Affiliation or Control: United Methodist IRS Status: 501(c)3
Highest Offering: Master's
Accreditation: NH, CAATE, MUS, NURSE, SW, TED

01 President ... Dr. Frederik OHLES
05 Provost ... Dr. Judy A. MUYSKENS
10 Vice Pres Finance/Administration ... Ms. Tish GADE-JONES
84 Vice President Enrollment Mgmt ... Mr. Bill MOTZER
30 Vice President Advancement ... Mr. John GREVING
58 Dean of University College ... Vacant
28 Associate VP ... Mr. T. J. MCDOWELL, JR.
32 Dean of Students ... Mr. Peter ARMSTRONG
42 University Minister/Church Relation ... Rev. Eduardo BOUSSON
49 Dean College of Lib Arts & Sciences ... Dr. Sarah A. KELEN
88 Asst Provost Integr/Exper Learning ... Dr. Patrick HAYDEN-ROY
21 Asst VP & Controller ... Mr. Greg D. MASCHMAN
06 Vice Provost for Academic Systems ... Ms. Patty HALL
15 Asst VP Human Resources ... Vacant
18 Asst VP Physical Plant ... Mr. Matthew T. KADAVY
07 Director of Admissions ... Mr. Gordie COFFIN
27 Director of Public Relations ... Ms. Sara M. OLSON
88 Director Student Success Retention ... Ms. Candice HOWELL
08 University Librarian ... Ms. Martha TANNER
37 Director of Financial Aid ... Mr. Tom J. OCHSNER
29 Director of Alumni Relations ... Ms. Shelley MCHUGH
41 Athletic Director ... Dr. Ira A. ZEFF
13 Director of Computer Services ... Mr. Steven R. DOW
90 Director Instructional Technology ... Mr. Jay L. KAHLER
14 Director Administrative Systems ... Mr. Mark MURPHY
26 Director of Marketing ... Ms. Peggy S. HAIN

36 Director Career Center Ms. Janelle S. ANDREINI
39 Director Residential Education Ms. Brandi SESTAK
104 Director of Global Engagement Ms. Sarah BARR
92 Director Wesleyan Honors Academy Dr. Marian BORGMANN-INGWERSEN
35 Dir Student Involvement & Ldrship Ms. Karri SANDERSON
102 Director of Foundation Relations Ms. Nancy WEHRBEIN
23 Director Student Health Services Ms. Nancy J. NEWMAN
04 Special Asst to President Ms. P. J. RABEL
44 Director Archway Fund Ms. Erika PASCHOLD
09 Assoc Director Inst Research Ms. Brooke GLENN
91 Director Administrative Computing Mr. Gredon TURNER
38 Director Counseling Services Dr. Kimberly CORNER

North Platte Community College-North Campus (A)

1101 Halligan Drive, North Platte NE 69101
Telephone: (308) 535-3600 Identification: 770338
Accreditation: &NH

† Regional accreditation is carried under the parent institution in North Platte, NE

Northeast Community College (B)

801 E Benjamin, PO Box 469, Norfolk NE 68702-0469
County: Madison FICE Identification: 011667
Unit ID: 181491
Telephone: (402) 371-2020 Carnegie Class: Assoc/MT-VT-High Non
FAX Number: (402) 844-7400 Calendar System: Semester
URL: www.northeast.edu
Established: 1973 Annual Undergrad Tuition & Fees (In-District): $3,165
Enrollment: 5,061 Coed
Affiliation or Control: Local IRS Status: 501(c)3
Highest Offering: Associate Degree
Accreditation: NH, ADNUR, EMT, PTAA

01 President Dr. Michael R. CHIPPS
03 Executive Vice President Mrs. Mary J. HONKE
05 Vice President Educational Services Mr. John V. BLAYLOCK
10 Vice Pres of Administrative Svcs Ms. Lynne D. KOSKI
32 Vice President of Student Services Dr. Karen J. SEVERSON
13 Vice President of Technology Mr. Derek BIERMAN
88 Associate VP of Ctr for Enterprise Mr. Eric JOHNSON
30 Assoc VP of Devel/External Affairs Dr. Tracy L. KRUSE
15 Associate VP of Human Resources Mr. Craig GARRETT
75 Dean of Applied Technology Mr. Lyle J. KATHOL
47 Dean Ag/Health/Sciences Mrs. Corinne MORRIS
49 Dean Humanities/Arts/Social Sci Mrs. Faye KILDAY
50 Dean of Business/Math/Tech Dr. Wade HERLEY
76 Dean of Health/Wellness Dr. Michele GILL
11 Dean of Administrative Services Mrs. Coleen BRESSLER
21 Director of Business Services Mrs. Mary J. MEYER
44 Dean of Institutional Advancement . Ms. Michela KEELER-STROM
84 Dean of Enrollment Management Mrs. Amanda NIPP
18 Director of Physical Plant Mr. Brandon MCLEAN
06 Registrar Mrs. Kathy J. STOVER
37 Financial Aid Director Ms. Stacy DIECKMAN
36 Director of Career Services Mrs. Terri HEGGEMEYER
66 Director of Nursing Programs Mrs. Karen K. WEIDNER
21 Director of Accounting Services Mr. John ROBERTSON
16 Human Resources Coordinator Mrs. Jennifer HAPPOLD
96 Director of Purchasing Mr. Chris RUTTEN
41 Director of Athletics Mr. Jacob RIPPLE
39 Director Residence Life & Food Svcs Mr. Pete RIZZO
105 Director of Web System Services Mr. Mike AUTEN
08 Director of Library Services Mrs. Mary Louise FOSTER
26 Director of Public Relations Mr. James CURRY
40 College Store Manager Mrs. Julie CARLSON
35 Director of Student Conduct Mrs. Maureen BAKER
09 Director of Institutional Research Ms. Julie MELNICK
35 Student Activities Coordinator Ms. Carissa KOLLATH
27 Director of Marketing Ms. Jennifer GREVE
07 Director of Admissions Mr. Bradley RANSLEM
04 Administrative Asst to President Ms. Diane REIKOFSKI
28 Director of Diversity Mr. Ted MYERS
38 Director Student Counseling Ms. Stephanie BRUNDIECK
104 Director Study Abroad Ms. Pam SAALFELD

Omaha School of Massage and Healthcare of Herzing University (C)

9478 Park Drive, Omaha NE 68127
Telephone: (402) 331-3694 Identification: 770432
Accreditation: &NH

† Regional accreditation is carried under the parent institution in Madison, WI

Saint Gregory the Great Seminary (D)

800 Fletcher Road, Seward NE 68434-8145
County: Seward Identification: 667027
Telephone: (402) 643-4052 Carnegie Class: Not Classified
FAX Number: (402) 643-6964 Calendar System: Semester
URL: www.stgregoryseminary.edu
Established: 1998 Annual Undergrad Tuition & Fees: N/A
Enrollment: N/A Male
Affiliation or Control: Roman Catholic IRS Status: 501(c)3
Highest Offering: Baccalaureate
Accreditation: NH

01 Rector/President Father. Jeffrey EICKHOFF

Southeast Community College (E)

4771 West Scott Road, Beatrice NE 68310-7042
Telephone: (402) 228-3468 Identification: 770341
Accreditation: &NH

† Regional accreditation is carried under the parent institution in Lincoln, NE

Southeast Community College (F)

301 S 68 Street Place, Lincoln NE 68510-2449
County: Lancaster FICE Identification: 025083
Unit ID: 181640
Telephone: (402) 323-3400 Carnegie Class: Assoc/HVT-High Non
FAX Number: (402) 323-3420 Calendar System: Quarter
URL: www.southeast.edu
Established: 1973 Annual Undergrad Tuition & Fees (In-District): $3,218
Enrollment: 9,392 Coed
Affiliation or Control: State/Local IRS Status: 501(c)3
Highest Offering: Associate Degree
Accreditation: NH, ACBSP, ACFEI, ADNUR, COARC, CSHSE, DA, DIETT, EMT, MAC, MLTAD, PNUR, POLYT, PTAA, RAD, SURGT

01 President Dr. Paul ILLICH
05 Vice President Instruction Dr. Dennis HEADRICK
22 Vice Pres Access/Equity/Diversity Mr. Jose SOTO
11 VP Administrative Svcs/Res Devel Ms. Amy G. JORGENS
12 VP Student Svcs/Campus Director Ms. Bev HARVEY
12 VP Technology/Campus Director Mr. Ed KOSTER
15 Vice Pres Human Resources Mr. Bruce TANGEMAN
12 Dean of Virtual Learning/Campus Dir Mr. Robert MORGAN
37 Director of Financial Aid Ms. Melissa TROYER
32 Dean Student Svcs/Dir Stdnt Support Dr. Thomas CARDWELL
84 Dean Student Svcs/Dir Enrollment Mr. Mike PEGRAM
26 Dir of Public Information/Marketing Mr. Stu OSTERTHUN
90 Information Services Manager Mr. Alan BRUNKOW
09 Director of Institutional Research Ms. Robin MOORE

Southeast Community College (G)

600 State Street, Milford NE 68405-8498
Telephone: (402) 761-2131 Identification: 770342
Accreditation: &NH

† Regional accreditation is carried under the parent institution in Lincoln, NE

Summit Christian College (H)

2025 21st Street, Gering NE 69341
County: Scotts Bluff Identification: 667209
Unit ID: 181543
Telephone: (308) 632-6933 Carnegie Class: Not Classified
FAX Number: (308) 632-8599 Calendar System: Semester
URL: www.summitcc.net
Established: 1951 Annual Undergrad Tuition & Fees: $5,912
Enrollment: 40 Coed
Affiliation or Control: Independent Non-Profit IRS Status: 501(c)3
Highest Offering: Baccalaureate
Accreditation: @BI

01 President David K. PARRISH
05 Academic Dean Scott GRIBBLE
06 Registrar Andi GRANT

Union College (I)

3800 S 48th, Lincoln NE 68506-4300
County: Lancaster FICE Identification: 002563
Unit ID: 181738
Telephone: (402) 486-2600 Carnegie Class: Bac-Diverse
FAX Number: (402) 486-2895 Calendar System: Semester
URL: www.ucollege.edu
Established: 1891 Annual Undergrad Tuition & Fees: $21,970
Enrollment: 887 Coed
Affiliation or Control: Seventh-day Adventist IRS Status: 501(c)3
Highest Offering: Master's
Accreditation: NH, ARCPA, NURSE, SW, TED

01 President Dr. Vinita SAUDER
05 Vice President for Academic Admin Dr. Malcolm RUSSELL
10 Vice President for Financial Admin Mr. Jeff LEEPER
32 Vice President Student Services Dr. Linda BECKER
30 Vice President for Advancement Ms. LuAnn DAVIS
84 Vice President Enrollment Services Ms. Nadine NELSON
42 Vice President for Spiritual Life Dr. Rich CARLSON
08 Library Director Ms. Sabrina RILEY
13 Director of Information Systems Mr. Richard HENRIQUES
33 Dean of Men Mr. Doug TALLMAN
06 Dir Records/Registrar Ms. Michelle YOUNKIN
26 Director of Public Relations Mr. Ryan TELLER
29 Director Alumni Relations Ms. Kenna Lee CARLSON
37 Director Student Financial Aid Ms. Taryn ROUSE
15 Director for Human Resources Mr. Jonathan SHIELDS
36 Career Center Coordinator Ms. Teresa EDGERTON

Universal College of Healing Arts (J)

8702 N 30th Street, Omaha NE 68112-1810
County: Douglas FICE Identification: 038214
Unit ID: 446598
Telephone: (402) 556-4456 Carnegie Class: Spec 2-yr-Health
FAX Number: (402) 561-0635 Calendar System: Semester
URL: www.ucha.edu
Established: 1995 Annual Undergrad Tuition & Fees: $15,390
Enrollment: 14 Coed
Affiliation or Control: Proprietary IRS Status: Proprietary
Highest Offering: Associate Degree
Accreditation: ABHES

01 Executive Director Ms. Paulette GENTHON

*University of Nebraska Central Administration (K)

3835 Holdrege, Lincoln NE 68583-0745
County: Lancaster FICE Identification: 008025
Unit ID: 181747
Telephone: (402) 472-8636 Carnegie Class: N/A
FAX Number: (402) 472-1237
URL: www.nebraska.edu

01 President Dr. Hank BOUNDS
05 Exec Vice President & Provost Dr. Susan M. FRITZ
10 Sr Vice Pres Business & Finance Mr. David E. LECHNER
43 Vice President & General Counsel Mr. Joel D. PEDERSEN
47 Int VP Agriculture/Natural Res Dr. Ronald (Ron) YODER
100 Chief of Staff Vacant
13 Chief Information Officer Mr. Walter G. WEIR
101 Corporation Secretary Ms. Carmen K. MAURER
86 Sr Assoc VP/Director Govt Relations Mr. Ron E. WITHEM
18 Asst VP/Dir Facility Plng/Mgmt Ms. Rebecca H. KOLLER
09 Asst VP/Dir Inst Research/Planning Dr. Kristin YATES
88 Asst VP P-16 Initiatives Dr. Gabrielle A. BANICK
88 Asst VP Global Strategy/Intl Init Dr. Steven T. DUKE
26 Asst VP Univ Affs/Dir Comm & Mktg Ms. Jacqueline M. OSTROWICKI

*University of Nebraska at Kearney (L)

905 W 25th Street, Kearney NE 68849
County: Buffalo FICE Identification: 002551
Unit ID: 181215
Telephone: (308) 865-8208 Carnegie Class: Masters/L
FAX Number: (308) 865-8665 Calendar System: Semester
URL: www.unk.edu
Established: 1903 Annual Undergrad Tuition & Fees (In-State): $6,711
Enrollment: 6,902 Coed
Affiliation or Control: State IRS Status: 501(c)3
Highest Offering: Beyond Master's But Less Than Doctorate
Accreditation: NH, BUS, CAATE, CACREP, CIDA, MUS, NAIT, SP, SW, TED

02 Chancellor Dr. Douglas A. KRISTENSEN
05 Sr VC Academic & Student Affairs Dr. Charles J. BICAK
10 Vice Chanc Business & Finance Mr. Jon C. WATTS
26 Asst VC Comm/Community Relations Ms. Kelly H. BARTLING
30 Vice President Development Mr. Lucas DART
13 Asst Vice Chanc Info Technology Ms. Debbie SCHROEDER
21 Asst Vice Chanc Business & Finance Ms. Jane SHELDON
81 Dean Natural/Social Science Dr. John C. LA DUKE
50 Dean Business/Technology Dr. Timothy J. BURKINK
53 Dean of Education Dr. Sheryl J. FEINSTEIN
57 Dean Fine Arts & Humanities Dr. William JURMA
58 Dean Graduate Studies & Research Dr. Kenya S. TAYLOR
32 Dean of Student Affairs Dr. Gilbert HINGA
04 Exec Assistant to the Chancellor Mr. Neal H. SCHNOOR
06 Registrar Ms. Kim SCHIPPOREIT
08 Dean of the Library Ms. Janet S. WILKE
36 Director Academic & Career Services .. Ms. Amy L. RUNDSTROM
07 Dir UG Recruitment/Admissions Mr. Dusty NEWTON
18 Dir Facilities Mgmt & Planning Mr. Lee MCQUEEN
19 Director Police & Parking Services Mr. James F. DAVIS
22 Dir Affirm Action/Equal Opportunity Ms. Mary J. CHINNOCK PETROSKI
09 Director Institutional Research Ms. Kathy LIVINGSTON
27 Dir News/Internal Commununication Mr. Todd GOTTULA
29 Director Alumni Services Mr. Lucas DART
88 Director Student Life Ms. Sharon PELC
23 Director Counseling & Health Care Ms. Wendy L. SCHARDT
39 Director Residence Life Mr. George HOLMAN
40 Director Bookstore Mr. Len J. FANGMEYER
41 Athletic Director Mr. Paul M. PLINSKE
21 Director Finance Ms. Jill PURDY
108 Director Assessment Vacant
25 Director Sponsored Programs Mr. Richard A. MOCARSKI
85 Asst Vice Chanc for Intl Affairs Mr. Michael J. STOPFORD
21 Budget Director Ms. Jean MATTSON
96 Director Bus Svcs & Accts Payable Mr. Scott A. BENSON
37 Director Financial Aid Ms. Mary SOMMERS
93 Director Multicultural Affairs Mr. Juan GUZMAN
92 Director Honors Program Dr. John FALCONER
84 Assoc VC Acad Svcs/Enroll Mgmt .Dr. Edgar (Ed) L. SCANTLING

*University of Nebraska - Lincoln (M)

14th and R Streets, Lincoln NE 68588-0002
County: Lancaster FICE Identification: 002565
Unit ID: 181464
Telephone: (402) 472-7211 Carnegie Class: DU-Highest
FAX Number: (402) 472-2410 Calendar System: Semester
URL: www.unl.edu
Established: 1869 Annual Undergrad Tuition & Fees (In-State): $8,367
Enrollment: 25,006 Coed
Affiliation or Control: State IRS Status: 501(c)3
Highest Offering: Doctorate

Accreditation: NH, ART, AUD, BUS, BUSA, CAATE, CIDA, CLPSY, CONST, COPSY, CS, DANCE, DIETD, DIETI, ENG, IPSY, JOUR, LAW, LSAR, MFCD, MUS, PLNG, SCPSY, SP, TEAC, THEA

02 Chancellor .....Dr. Ronnie D. GREEN
05 Int Sr Vice Chanc Academic Affairs .....Dr. Marjorie KOSTELNIK
10 Vice Chanc Business & Finance .....Ms. Christine JACKSON
32 Vice Chancellor Student Affairs .....Dr. Juan FRANCO
65 Int Vice Chanc Agric/Nat Resources .....Dr. Ron YODER
46 VC Research & Economic Development .....Dr. Prem S. PAUL
13 VC Information Technology & CIO .....Mr. Mark ASKREN
04 Associate to Chancellor .....Mr. William NUNEZ
31 Asst to Chanc Community Relations .....Ms. Michelle WAITE
15 Asst Vice Chanc for Human Resources .....Mr. Bruce A. CURRIN
20 Assoc Vice Chanc ASEM .....Dr. Amy GOODBURN
18 Executive Director .....Mr. Mark MILLER
07 Director Admissions .....Ms. Amber S. WILLIAMS
08 Dean University Libraries .....Dr. Nancy BUSCH
58 Dean Graduate Studies .....Dr. Lance C. PEREZ
49 Dean Arts & Sciences .....Dr. Joseph FRANCISCO
54 Dean Engineering .....Dr. Timothy WEI
61 Interim Dean of Law .....Dr. Richard MOBERLY
47 Dean Agric Scienc/Nat Resources .....Dr. Steven WALLER
50 Dean Business Administration .....Dr. Donde PLOWMAN
60 Dean Journ/Mass Communications .....Dr. Maria MARRON
53 Int Dean Education & Human Sciences .....Dr. Beth DOLL
48 Dean College Architecture .....Dr. Katherine ANKERSON
47 Dean Agricultural Research Division .....Dr. Archie CLUTTER
56 Dean & Dir Cooperative Extens .....Dr. Charles HIBBERD
93 Director Educ Access & TRIO Pgms .. Ms. Catherine YAMAMOTO
57 Dean Fine & Performing Arts .....Dr. Charles D. O'CONNOR
37 Actg Dir Scholarships/Financial Aid .....Mr. James VOLKMER
09 Director Inst Research & Planning .....Dr. William J. NUNEZ
84 Dir Enrollment Strategy/Analytics .....Mr. James VOLKMER
92 Director Honors Program .....Dr. Patrice BERGER
94 Director Women's Studies .....Dr. Marie-Chantal KALISA
06 University Registrar .....Dr. Richard MORRELL
36 Director Career Services Center .....Dr. Larry R. ROUTH
19 Chief University Police Services .....Mr. Owen YARDLEY
22 Director Inst Equity & Compliance .....Ms. Susan FOSTER
23 Director University Health Center .....Dr. James GUEST
39 Director Housing Office .....Ms. Susan M. GILDERSLEEVE
41 Director of Athletics .....Mr. Shawn EICHORST
55 Dir Distance Education Services .....Dr. Nancy ADEN-FOX
29 Exec Director Alumni Association .....Ms. Shelley ZABOROWSKI
26 Director University Communications .....Dr. Meg LAUERMAN
20 Associate Academic Officer .....Dr. Lance C. PEREZ
30 Chief Development .....Mr. Brian HASTINGS
38 Director Student Counseling .....Dr. Robert N. PORTNOY
96 Director of Purchasing .....Mr. Gary L. KRAFT

*University of Nebraska Medical Center (A)

987020 Nebraska Medical Center, Omaha NE 68198-7020
County: Douglas FICE Identification: 006895
Unit ID: 181428
Telephone: (402) 559-4000 Carnegie Class: Spec-4-yr-Med
FAX Number: (402) 559-4396 Calendar System: Semester
URL: www.unmc.edu
Established: 1869 Annual Undergrad Tuition & Fees (In-State): N/A
Enrollment: 3,696 Coed
Affiliation or Control: State IRS Status: 501(c)3
Highest Offering: Doctorate
Accreditation: NH, ARCPA, CYTO, DENT, DH, DIETI, DMS, MED, MT, NMT, NURSE, PERF, PH, PHAR, PTA, RAD, RADMAG, RTT

02 Chancellor .....Dr. Jeffery P. GOLD
05 Vice Chancellor Acad Affairs .....Dr. H. Dele O. DAVIES
10 Int Vice Chanc Business & Finance .....Ms. Deborah THOMAS
46 Vice Chancellor Research .....Dr. Jennifer LARSEN
86 Vice Chancellor External Affairs .....Mr. Robert BARTEE
20 Assoc Vice Chanc Academic Affairs .....Dr. James TURPEN
20 Asst Vice Chanc Acad Affairs .....Dr. Jilian ZHENG
20 Assoc Vice Chanc Acad Affs/Reg Comp ..Dr. Ernest D. PRENTICE
45 Assoc Vice Chanc Basic Sci Rsch .....Dr. Kenneth BAYLES
45 Assoc Vice Chancellor Clinical Rsch .....Dr. Christopher KRATOCHVIL
21 Sr Assoc Vice Chan Business/Finance .....Ms. Deborah THOMAS
13 Assoc Vice Chanc Bus Dev/CTO .....Dr. Rodney MARKIN
18 Asst Vice Chanc Facilities/Mgt/Plng .....Mr. Kenneth HANSEN
14 Asst Vice Chancellor ITS .....Ms. Yvette A. HOLLY
58 Dean Graduate Studies .....Dr. H. Dele O. DAVIES
52 Dean College of Dentistry .....Dr. Janet GUTHMILLER
63 Dean College of Medicine .....Dr. Bradley E. BRITIGAN
66 Dean College of Nursing .....Dr. Juliann SEBASTIAN
67 Dean College of Pharmacy .....Dr. Courtney FLETCHER
69 Dean College of Public Health .....Dr. Ali KHAN
76 Dean College of Allied Health Prof .....Dr. Kyle P. MEYER
88 Dir Eppley Cancer Research Inst .....Dr. Kenneth H. COWAN
88 Director Munroe-Meyer Institute .....Dr. Karoly MIRNICS
08 Director Library of Med .....Ms. Emily J. MCELROY
37 Dir Financial Aid Office .....Ms. Judith D. WALKER
26 Director of Public Relations .....Mr. William O'NEILL
15 Asst Vice Chanc for Human Resources .....Ms. Aileen WARREN
29 Director Alumni Affairs .....Ms. Roxana JOKELA
38 Director Student Counseling .....Dr. David S. CARVER
28 Director of Diversity .....Ms. Linda CUNNINGHAM
96 Director Procurement & Mtrls Mgt .....Mr. Jeffrey ELLIOTT
09 Director Institutional Research .....Ms. Jeanne FERBRACHE
19 Director Campus Security .....Mr. Gary SVANDA

*University of Nebraska at Omaha (B)

6001 Dodge Street, Omaha NE 68182-0001
County: Douglas FICE Identification: 002554
Unit ID: 181394
Telephone: (402) 554-2200 Carnegie Class: DU-Mod
FAX Number: (402) 554-3555 Calendar System: Semester
URL: www.unomaha.edu
Established: 1908 Annual Undergrad Tuition & Fees (In-State): $6,898
Enrollment: 15,227 Coed
Affiliation or Control: State IRS Status: 501(c)3
Highest Offering: Doctorate
Accreditation: NH, AAB, ART, BUS, BUSA, #CAATE, CACREP, CS, MUS, SP, SPAA, SW, TED

02 Chancellor .....Dr. John E. CHRISTENSEN
05 Sr Vice Chanc Acad/Student Affs .....Dr. Burton J. REED
10 Vice Chanc Business & Finance .....Mr. Bill CONLEY
13 Chief Information Officer .....Mr. Bret BLACKMAN
21 Assoc Vice Chanc Business & Finance .....Ms. Carol KIRCHNER
32 Assoc Vice Chanc Student Affairs .....Dr. Daniel SHIPP
84 Assoc Vice Chanc Enroll Mgmt Svcs .....Mr. Omar CORREA
58 Dean Graduate Studies .....Dr. Deb SMITH-HOWELL
57 Dean Fine Arts/Communication/Media .....Dr. Gail BAKER
53 Dean of Education .....Dr. Nancy EDICK
50 Dean of Business Administration .....Dr. Lou POL
49 Dean of Arts & Sciences .....Dr. David J. BOOCKER
82 Dean of International Studies/Pgms .....Mr. Patrick MCNAMARA
72 Dean Info Science/Technology .....Dr. Hesham ALI
80 Dean Public Affairs/Community .....Dr. John F. BARTLE
62 Dean of Library Services .....Mr. David E. RICHARDS
09 Dir Institutional Effectiveness .....Dr. T Hank ROBINSON
35 Chief Student Life Officer .....Ms. Rita HENRY
15 Director Human Resources .....Mr. Cecil HICKS, JR.
18 Director Facilities Mgmt/Planning .....Mr. John AMEND
06 Registrar .....Mr. Mark GOLDSBERRY
07 Director of Admissions .....Mr. Chris LIEWER
37 Director Financial Aid .....Mr. Marty HABROCK
88 Director Student Testing Center .....Ms. Marion FORTIN-WAVRA
41 Vice Chanc Athletic Leadership/Mgmt .....Mr. Trev ALBERTS
29 President/CEO Alumni Association .....Mr. Lee DENKER
26 Exec Dir University Communications .....Ms. Erin OWEN
96 Procurement Systems Coordinator .....Ms. Lynn MCALPINE
40 Manager Book Store .....Vacant
19 Director of Public Safety .....Ms. Charlotte EVANS

*University of Nebraska - Nebraska College of Technical Agriculture (C)

404 E 7th Street, Curtis NE 69025-9502
County: Frontier FICE Identification: 007358
Unit ID: 181765
Telephone: (308) 367-4124 Carnegie Class: Spec 2-yr-Other
FAX Number: (308) 367-5203 Calendar System: Semester
URL: www.ncta.unl.edu
Established: 1912 Annual Undergrad Tuition & Fees (In-State): $4,602
Enrollment: 384 Coed
Affiliation or Control: State IRS Status: 501(c)3
Highest Offering: Associate Degree
Accreditation: NH

02 Dean .....Dr. Ron ROSATI
10 Asst Dean Finance/Ops/Student Svcs .....Ms. Jennie A. MCCONVILLE
21 Business Manager/Human Resources .....Ms. Jan GILBERT

Western Nebraska Community College (D)

1601 E 27th Street, Scottsbluff NE 69361-1315
County: Scotts Bluff FICE Identification: 002560
Unit ID: 181817
Telephone: (308) 635-3606 Carnegie Class: Assoc/MT-VT-High Non
FAX Number: (308) 635-6100 Calendar System: Semester
URL: www.wncc.edu
Established: 1926 Annual Undergrad Tuition & Fees (In-District): $2,616
Enrollment: 1,836 Coed
Affiliation or Control: State/Local IRS Status: 501(c)3
Highest Offering: Associate Degree
Accreditation: NH, CA, CAHIIM, PHLEB, PNUR

01 President .....Dr. Todd R. HOLCOMB
05 Executive Vice President .....Dr. Kim KUSTER-DALE
15 VP Human Resources/Inst Development .....Mr. David E. GROSHANS
32 Vice President Student Services .....Ms. Nina GRANT
10 Vice Pres Administrative Services .....Mr. William D. KNAPPER
20 Interim Dean of Instruction .....Ms. Hallie FEIL
103 Dean of Instruction/Workforce Dev .....Mr. Jason L. STRATMAN
50 Harms Adv Tech Ctr Exec Director .....Ms. Judith L. AMOO
35 Dean Student Services .....Dr. Michael HOUDYSHELL
12 Sidney Campus Director .....Ms. Paula J. ABBOTT
88 Assoc Dean Instruct Support Svcs .....Ms. Ellen M. DILLON
102 Foundation Executive Director .....Ms. Jennifer ROGERS
06 Registrar .....Mr. Roger S. HOVEY
37 Financial Aid Director .....Ms. Sheila R. JOHNS
26 Public Relations & Marketing Dir .....Ms. Allison JUDY
38 Counseling Director .....Mr. Norman J. STEPHENSON
62 Library Services Director .....Vacant
21 Accounting Services Director .....Mr. David KOEHLER
41 Athletic Director .....Mr. Ryan C. BURGNER

51 Lifelong Learning Director .....Ms. Lori S. STROMBERG
07 Admissions Director .....Ms. Gretchen K. FOSTER
39 Residence Life Director .....Mr. Norman COLEY
13 Information Technology Director .....Mr. Joe W. DEER
40 Bookstore Operations Director .....Mr. Rich RIDDICK
19 Safety/Environmental Mgmt Director .....Ms. Katrina TYLEE
09 Institutional Research Director .....Ms. Mary E. BARKELOO
88 Academic Testing & Tutoring Coord .....Ms. Tammie KLEICH
39 Student Life Assistant Director .....Ms. Megan WESCOAT
39 Student Life Assistant Director .....Ms. Molly A. BONUCHI
50 Div Chair Business/Applied Tech .....Ms. Aletia NORWOOD
79 Div Chair Acad Enrich/Lang/Fine Art ...Ms. Jennifer L. PEDERSEN
66 Nursing Program Director .....Ms. Rebecca KAUTZ
81 Division Chair Math & Science .....Ms. Laurie ALKIRE
83 Div Chair Social Sci/Human Perf .....Ms. Maria L. WINN-RATLIFF
88 Health Info Technology Program Dir .....Ms. Peg A. WOLFF
76 Division Chair Health Sciences .....Dr. Ronda KINSEY
29 Director Alumni Relations/Steward .....Ms. Jennifer R. SIBAL
106 Instructional Tech Coordinator .....Ms. Heidi JACKSON

Western Nebraska Community College Alliance Campus (E)

1750 Sweetwater Avenue, Alliance NE 69301
Telephone: (308) 763-2000 Identification: 770343
Accreditation: &NH

† Regional accreditation is carried under the parent institution in Scottsbluff, NE

Western Nebraska Community College Sidney Campus (F)

371 College Drive, Sidney NE 69162
Telephone: (308) 254-5450 Identification: 770344
Accreditation: &NH

† Regional accreditation is carried under the parent institution in Scottsbluff, NE

York College (G)

1125 E 8th Street, York NE 68467-2699
County: York FICE Identification: 002567
Unit ID: 181853
Telephone: (402) 363-5600 Carnegie Class: Bac-Diverse
FAX Number: (402) 363-5667 Calendar System: Semester
URL: www.york.edu
Established: 1890 Annual Undergrad Tuition & Fees: $17,200
Enrollment: 408 Coed
Affiliation or Control: Churches Of Christ IRS Status: 501(c)3
Highest Offering: Master's
Accreditation: NH, TED

01 President .....Dr. Steven W. ECKMAN
05 Provost .....Dr. Shane MOUNTJOY
10 Vice President Finance & Operations .....Mr. Todd SHELDON
30 Vice Pres Advancement .....Mr. Brent MAGNER
41 VP for Athletics and Enrollment .....Mr. Jared STARK
32 Dean of Student Development .....Mrs. Catherine SEUFFERLEIN
21 Business Manager .....Mr. Dan COLE
06 Registrar .....Mr. Jared LEINEN
35 Dean of Students .....Mr. Jeff FINCH
08 Director of Library .....Mrs. Ruth CARLOCK
26 Director of Publications .....Mr. Steddon L. SIKES
37 Financial Aid Director .....Mr. Brien ALLEY
40 Campus Store Manager .....Mrs. Janet RUSH
18 Supervisor Buildings & Grounds .....Mr. Bob GAVER
42 Campus Minister .....Dr. Sam GARNER
50 Chair Business .....Vacant
53 Chair Education .....Vacant
73 Chair Bible .....Dr. Frank E. WHEELER
88 Chair History .....Mr. Tim D. MCNEESE
50 Chair English .....Dr. Jennifer DUTCH
81 Chair Math/Sciences .....Dr. Alex WILLIAMS
57 Chair Performing Arts/Communication .....Dr. Clark A. ROUSH
29 Dir Alumni & Community Relations .....Mrs. Chrystal HOUSTON
04 Executive Asst to President .....Mrs. Gayle A. GOOD
44 Director Annual or Planned Giving .....Mr. Brent N. MAGNER
13 Chief Info Technology Officer (CIO) .....Mr. Joel COEHOORN
39 Director Student Housing .....Mr. Larry GOOD
106 Dir Online Education/E-learning .....Dr. Kirk MALLETTE
07 Director of Admissions .....Mr. David ODOM

NEVADA

The Art Institute of Las Vegas (H)

2350 Corporate Circle, Henderson NV 89074-7737
Telephone: (702) 369-9944 FICE Identification: 030846
Accreditation: #ACICS, ACFEI, CIDA

† Branch campus of The Art Institute of Phoenix, AZ.

Brightwood College (I)

3535 West Sahara Ave, Las Vegas NV 89102
County: Clark FICE Identification: 030432
Unit ID: 374875
Telephone: (702) 368-2338 Carnegie Class: Spec 2-yr-Health
FAX Number: (702) 368-3853 Calendar System: Other
URL: www.kaplancollege.com
Established: 1991 Annual Undergrad Tuition & Fees: N/A

Enrollment: 944 Coed
Affiliation or Control: Proprietary IRS Status: Proprietary
Highest Offering: Associate Degree
Accreditation: **ACICS**, CAHIIM, PNUR

01 Campus President .... Ms. Lisia MOORE
05 Academic Dean .... Ms. Shanel OLIVER
07 Director of Admissions .... Ms. Kristie CHILES
10 Director of Finance .... Mr. Dean RILING
67 Dept Chair Pharmacy Technician .... Mr. Mark BRUNTON
36 Director of Career Services .... Ms. Hanna LIND
66 Director of Nursing/PN .... Ms. Julia MILLARD

Career College of Northern Nevada (A)

1421 Pullman Drive, Sparks NV 89434
County: Washoe FICE Identification: 026215
Unit ID: 181941
Telephone: (775) 856-2266 Carnegie Class: Spec 2-yr-Health
FAX Number: (775) 856-0935 Calendar System: Quarter
URL: www.ccnn.edu
Established: 1984 Annual Undergrad Tuition & Fees: N/A
Enrollment: 581 Coed
Affiliation or Control: Proprietary IRS Status: Proprietary
Highest Offering: Associate Degree
Accreditation: **ACCSC**

01 President .... Mr. L. Nathan N. CLARK

Carrington College - Las Vegas (B)

5740 S Eastern Avenue, Suite 140, Las Vegas NV 89119
Telephone: (702) 688-4300 Identification: 770742
Accreditation: **&WJ**, COARC, PTAA

† Regional accreditation is carried under the parent institution in Sacramento, CA.

Carrington College - Reno (C)

5580 Kietzke Lane, Reno NV 89511
Telephone: (775) 335-2900 Identification: 770743
Accreditation: **&WJ**, ADNUR

† Regional accreditation is carried under the parent institution in Sacramento, CA.

Chamberlain College of Nursing-Las Vegas (D)

9901 Covington Cross Dr, Las Vegas NV 89144
Telephone: (702) 786-1660 Identification: 770852
Accreditation: **&NH**, NURSE

† Regional accreditation is carried under the parent institution in Addison, IL

Everest College (E)

170 North Stephanie Street, Henderson NV 89074
County: Clark FICE Identification: 022375
Unit ID: 182148
Telephone: (702) 567-1920 Carnegie Class: Assoc/HVT-Mix Trad/Non
FAX Number: (702) 566-9725 Calendar System: Semester
URL: www.everest.edu
Established: 2004 Annual Undergrad Tuition & Fees: $12,864
Enrollment: 800 Coed
Affiliation or Control: Proprietary IRS Status: Proprietary
Highest Offering: Associate Degree
Accreditation: **ACICS**, ADNUR

01 President .... Dr. Peter PERHAC
03 Vice President .... Vacant

Le Cordon Bleu College of Culinary Arts in Las Vegas (F)

1451 Center Crossing Road, Las Vegas NV 89144-7047
Telephone: (702) 365-7690 Identification: 666303
Accreditation: **ACCSC**, ACFEI, ACICS

† In teach-out mode through December 2017. Branch campus of Le Cordon Bleu Institute of Culinary Arts, Scottsdale, AZ.

*Nevada System of Higher Education (G)

2601 Enterprise Road, Reno NV 89512-1666
County: Washoe FICE Identification: 008026
Unit ID: 182519
Telephone: (775) 784-4901 Carnegie Class: N/A
FAX Number: (775) 784-1127
URL: www.nevada.edu

01 Chancellor .... Mr. John WHITE
05 VC Academic & Student Affairs .... Ms. Crystal ABBA
10 Vice Chanc for Finance .... Mr. Vic REDDING
101 Chief Exec Ofcr Board of Regents .... Mr. Dean J. GOULD
43 Vice Chanc for Legal Affairs .... Ms. Brooke NIELSEN
86 VC Govt and Community Affairs .... Ms. Constance BROOKS
13 Vice Chanc for Info Tech .... Mr. Bob MOULTON
88 Vice Chanc for Health Sci Sys .... Dr. Marcia TURNER

*College of Southern Nevada (H)

6375 W Charleston Boulevard, Las Vegas NV 89146-1139
County: Clark FICE Identification: 010362
Unit ID: 182005
Telephone: (702) 651-5000 Carnegie Class: Bac/Assoc-Assoc Dom
FAX Number: (702) 651-4835 Calendar System: Semester
URL: www.csn.edu
Established: 1971 Annual Undergrad Tuition & Fees (In-State): $2,805
Enrollment: 35,943 Coed
Affiliation or Control: State IRS Status: 501(c)3
Highest Offering: Baccalaureate
Accreditation: **NW**, ACBSP, ACFEI, ADNUR, CAHIIM, CEA, COARC, DA, DH, DMS, EMT, ENGT, MAC, MLTAD, OPD, PNUR, PTAA, SURGT

02 President .... Dr. Michael D. RICHARDS
04 Exec Assistant to the President .... Ms. Annette LORD
03 Sr VP Strategic Initiatives .... Ms. Patricia A. CHARLTON
05 Interim Vice Pres Academic Affairs .... Dr. Hyla D. WINTERS
32 Vice President of Student Affairs ..... Ms. Juanita CHRYSANTHOU
10 Vice President of Finance .... Ms. Mary Kaye BAILEY
18 Assoc VP Facilities/Oper/Maint .... Ms. Sherri PAYNE
43 Legal Counsel .... Mr. Richard HINCKLEY
06 Registrar .... Ms. Pat ZOZAYA
88 Exec Director Foundation Ops .... Mr. Dan MORRIS
103 Int Dir Workforce Education .... Ms. Melissa SCHROEDER
102 Exec Dir CSN Foundation .... Mr. Alan DISKIN
72 Dean Adv & Applied Technologies .... Dr. Michael SPANGLER
81 Dean Science & Mathematics .... Dr. John ADLISH
83 Dean Social Sciences & Education .... Dr. Charles OKEKE
88 Interim Dean Arts & Letters .... Mr. Lester TANAKA
76 Dean Health Sciences .... Dr. Josh HAMILTON
50 Dean of Business .... Dr. Marcus JOHNSON
96 Associate VP of Purchasing .... Mr. Rolando MOSQUEDA
41 Director of Athletics .... Mr. L. Dexter IRVIN
26 Director of Communications .... Ms. Kathryn C. BREKKEN
86 Director Government Relations .... Mr. Michael FLORES
88 Director of Budget Services .... Ms. Lisa BAKKE
09 Director of Institutional Research .... Mr. John BEARCE
62 Director Library Services .... Ms. Clarissa ERWIN
37 Director Student Financial Aid .... Ms. Victoria GOEKE
19 Chief of Police .... Mr. Darryl CARABALLO
85 Dir International Student Ctr .... Ms. Mary SASSO
13 Technology CIO .... Mr. Mugunth VAITHYLINGAM
15 Sr Director of Personnel Services .... Mr. John SCARBOROUGH
28 Executive Director of Diversity .... Ms. Maria MARINCH
106 Dir Online Education/E-learning .... Mr. Terry NORRIS
22 Dir Affirmative Action/EEO .... Vacant

*Great Basin College (I)

1500 College Parkway, Elko NV 89801-5032
County: Elko FICE Identification: 006977
Unit ID: 182306
Telephone: (775) 738-8493 Carnegie Class: Bac/Assoc-Mixed
FAX Number: (775) 738-8771 Calendar System: Semester
URL: www.gbcnv.edu
Established: 1967 Annual Undergrad Tuition & Fees (In-State): $2,805
Enrollment: 3,024 Coed
Affiliation or Control: State IRS Status: 501(c)3
Highest Offering: Baccalaureate
Accreditation: **NW**, ADNUR, CSHSE, NUR, RAD

02 President .... Dr. Mark CURTIS
32 Vice Pres Academic/Student Affairs .... Mrs. Lynn M. MAHLBERG
10 Vice President for Business Affairs .... Ms. Sonja SIBERT
106 Associate VP for Distance Education .... Ms. Lisa FRAZIER
04 Assistant to the President .... Ms. Mardell WILKINS
07 Director of Admissions .... Ms. Janice KING
09 Dir Institutional Rsrch/Effective .... Dr. Cathy FULKERSON
37 Dir Student Financial Svcs & VA .... Mr. Scott NIELSEN
84 Director Enrollment Management .... Ms. Julie BYRNES
74 Dean of Arts and Letters .... Mr. Thomas REAGAN
75 Dean of Applied Science .... Mr. Bret MURPHY
76 Dir of Health Sciences & Human Svcs .... Dr. Amber DONNELLI
12 Director Ely Center .... Ms. Veronica NELSON
12 Director Winnemucca Center .... Ms. Lisa CAMPBELL
12 Manager Pahrump Valley Center .... Ms. Diane WRIGHTMAN
51 Director Continuing Education .... Mrs. Angie DEBRAGA
102 Director Foundation .... Mr. Gregory BRORBY
19 Director Safety and Security .... Ms. Patricia ANDERSON
25 Director Grants .... Ms. Jeannie BAILEY
43 General Counsel .... Mr. John ALBRECHT

*Nevada State College (J)

1125 Nevada State Drive, Henderson NV 89002-9455
County: Clark FICE Identification: 041143
Unit ID: 441900
Telephone: (702) 992-2000 Carnegie Class: Bac-Diverse
FAX Number: (702) 992-2226 Calendar System: Semester
URL: www.nsc.edu
Established: 2002 Annual Undergrad Tuition & Fees (In-District): $4,738
Enrollment: 3,555 Coed
Affiliation or Control: State/Local IRS Status: 501(c)3
Highest Offering: Baccalaureate
Accreditation: **NW**, NURSE

02 President .... Bart PATTERSON
03 Executive Vice President .... Dr. Erika BECK
08 Head Librarian .... Nathaniel KING
09 Director of Institutional Research .... Dr. Sandip THANKI
28 Director of Diversity .... Dr. Edith FERNANDEZ
32 Chief Student Affairs/Student Life .... Dr. Richard YAO
37 Director Student Financial Aid .... Anthony MORRONE
53 Dean of Education .... Dr. Dennis POTTHOFF
06 Registrar .... Adelfa SULLIVAN
10 Chief Business Officer .... Kevin BUTLER

*Truckee Meadows Community College (K)

7000 Dandini Boulevard, Reno NV 89512-3999
County: Washoe FICE Identification: 021077
Unit ID: 182500
Telephone: (775) 673-7000 Carnegie Class: Assoc/MT-VT-Mix Trad/Non
FAX Number: (775) 673-7108 Calendar System: Semester
URL: www.tmcc.edu
Established: 1971 Annual Undergrad Tuition & Fees (In-State): $2,805
Enrollment: 11,106 Coed
Affiliation or Control: State IRS Status: 501(c)3
Highest Offering: Associate Degree
Accreditation: **NW**, ACFEI, ADNUR, DA, DH, DIETT, EMT

02 Acting President .... Dr. Kyle C. DALPE
04 Executive Assistant to President .... Ms. Lisa D. FARMER
05 Vice President Academic Affairs .... Dr. Barbara BUCHANAN
10 Vice Pres Finance & Admin Services ...... Dr. Rachel SOLEMSAAS
32 VP of Student Services .... Ms. Estela LEVARIO GUTIERREZ
81 Dean Division of Sciences .... Dr. Lance BOWEN
49 Dean Division of Liberal Arts .... Dr. Armida FRUZZETTI
50 Dean Division of Business .... Dr. Marie MURGOLO-POORE
72 Dean Division of Tech Sciences .... Mr. Jim NEW
20 Assoc Dean Office of the President .... Dr. Kyle DALPE
30 Exec Dir Institutional Advancement .... Mrs. Gretchen SAWYER
07 Director Admissions & Records .... Mr. Andrew HUGHES
21 Program Director Accounting Svcs .... Mr. Rich WILLIAMS
37 Director Financial Aid .... Ms. Sharon WURM
22 Director Disability Resource Center .... Ms. Joan STEINMAN
15 Chief Human Resources Officer .... Mr. Rich OLSON
18 Exec Director Facilities Services .... Mr. Dave ROBERTS
103 Dir Workforce Devel/Cont Education .... Ms. Deb O'GORMAN
38 Director Counseling .... Vacant
13 Chief Info Tech Officer .... Mr. Thomas DOBBERT
19 Chief of Police/Campus Police .... Mr. Randy FLOCCHINI
09 Exec Dir Institutional Research .... Ms. Elena BUBNOVA
28 Director of Equity & Inclusion .... Ms. Jill ATKINSON
29 Alumni Coordinator .... Vacant
08 Head Librarian .... Mr. Ken SULLIVAN

† Granted candidacy at the Baccalaureate level.

*University of Nevada, Las Vegas (L)

4505 S Maryland Parkway, Las Vegas NV 89154-1001
County: Clark FICE Identification: 002569
Unit ID: 182281
Telephone: (702) 895-3201 Carnegie Class: DU-Higher
FAX Number: (702) 895-1088 Calendar System: Semester
URL: www.unlv.edu
Established: 1957 Annual Undergrad Tuition & Fees (In-State): $6,943
Enrollment: 28,515 Coed
Affiliation or Control: State IRS Status: 501(c)3
Highest Offering: Doctorate
Accreditation: **NW**, ART, BUS, BUSA, CAATE, CACREP, CIDA, CLPSY, CONST, CS, DENT, DIETD, DIETI, ENG, ENGR, LAW, LSAR, MFCD, MUS, NURSE, PH, PTA, RAD, SPAA, SW

02 President .... Dr. Len JESSUP
100 Chief of Staff .... Dr. Fred TREDUP
05 Executive Vice President & Provost .... Dr. Diane CHASE
88 Special Counsel to the President .... Mrs. Nancy B. RAPOPORT
10 Senior Vice Pres Finance & Business .... Mr. Gerry BOMOTTI
41 Director of Athletics .... Ms. Tina KUNZER-MURPHY
32 Vice President for Student Affairs .... Dr. Juanita FAIN
58 Int VP Research & Graduate Studies .... Dr. Thomas C. PIECHOTA
30 Int VP Philanthropy & Alumni .... Mr. Scott ROBERTS
86 VP Diversity & Govt Relations .... Mr. Luis VALERA
26 Sr Assoc VP Integrated Marketing .... Mr. Vince ALBERTA
43 General Counsel .... Mrs. Elda SIDHU
07 AVP Enrollment & Student Services .... Dr. Mike SAUER
35 Assoc VP for Student Affairs .... Ms. Karen STRONG
29 Sr Assoc VP Alumni Relations .... Mr. Jim RATIGAN
31 Int Exec Dir of Community Relations .... Mrs. Sue DIBELLA
15 Chief Human Resources Officer .... Mr. Larry HAMILTON
87 Int Vice Prov Educational Outreach .... Dr. Margaret REES
13 Vice Provost Info Technology .... Dr. Lori TEMPLE
50 Dean Business .... Dr. Brent A. HATHAWAY
49 Dean Liberal Arts .... Dr. Chris HEAVEY
53 Dean of Education .... Dr. Kim K. METCALF
54 Dean of Engineering .... Dr. Rama VENKAT
63 Dean School of Medicine .... Dr. Barbara ATKINSON
52 Dean School of Dental Medicine .... Dr. Karen P. WEST
61 Dean School of Law .... Mr. Daniel W. HAMILTON
81 Dean of Sciences .... Dr. Stan SMITH
88 Dean College of Hotel Admin .... Dr. Stowe SHOEMAKER
57 Dean Fine Arts .... Dr. Nancy USCHER
08 Dean of Libraries .... Ms. Patricia IANNUZZI
88 Dean Urban Affairs .... Dr. Robert R. ULMER
92 Dean Honors College .... Dr. Marta MEANA
88 Dean Academic Success Ctr .... Dr. Ann MCDONOUGH
88 Dean Community Health Sciences . Dr. Shawn GERSTENBERGER
76 Dean Sch Allied Health Sciences .... Dr. Ronald T. BROWN
06 Registrar .... Ms. Katie HUMPHREYS

84 Assoc VP for Enrollment Management ....Dr. Michael L. SAUER
37 Dir Financial Aid & Scholarships .... Mr. Norm BEDFORD
27 Assoc VP Univ Communications ....Vacant
19 Director Public Safety .... Mr. Jose ELIQUE
09 Director Inst Analysis/Planning ....Mrs. Kari C. COBURN
39 Exec Dir Residential Life .... Mr. Richard CLARK
38 AVP Student Wellness ....Dr Jamie DAVIDSON
23 Director Student Health ....Ms. Kathy A. UNDERWOOD
96 Director Purchasing ....Ms. Sharrie MAYDEN
85 Director Intl Students & Scholars ....Ms. Kristen YOUNG
25 Director Sponsored Programs ....Ms. Rochelle ATHEY
46 AVP for Research ....Dr. Stan SMITH

*University of Nevada, Reno (A)

1664 N. Virginia Street, Reno NV 89557
County: Washoe FICE Identification: 002568
Unit ID: 182290
Telephone: (775) 784-1110 Carnegie Class: DU-Higher
FAX Number: (775) 784-1300 Calendar System: Semester
URL: www.unr.edu
Established: 1874 Annual Undergrad Tuition & Fees (In-State): $6,902
Enrollment: 19,934 Coed
Affiliation or Control: State IRS Status: 501(c)3
Highest Offering: Doctorate
Accreditation: **NW**, BUS, BUSA, CACREP, CEA, CLPSY, CS, DIETD, DIETI, ENG, JOUR, MED, MUS, NURSE, PH, SP, SW

02 President .... Dr. Marc JOHNSON
05 Exec Vice Pres & Provost .... Dr. Kevin CARMAN
11 Vice Pres Administration & Finance ....Mr. Ronald M. ZUREK
63 VP Health Sci/Dean Sch of Medicine ....Dr. Thomas L. SCHWENK
30 Vice President Devel/Alumni Rels .... Mr. John CAROTHERS
32 Vice President for Student Services ....Dr. Shannon ELLIS
46 Vice President for Research ....Dr. Mridul GAUTAM
08 Dean of Libraries ....Dr. Kathlin D. RAY
20 Vice Prov Instr/Undergrad Programs ....Dr. Joseph CLINE
20 Vice Provost Faculty Affairs .... Dr. Stacy BURTON
58 Vice Provost/Dean Grad School ....Dr. David ZEH
51 Vice Provost for Extended Studies ....Dr. Fred B. HOLMAN
10 Assoc VP Business & Finance ....Vacant
84 Assoc VP Enrollment Services .... Dr. Melisa N. CHOROSZY
38 Assoc VP Student Success Services ....Dr. Jerry MARCZYNSKI
45 Assoc VP Planning/Budget/Analysis ....Mr. Bruce L. SHIVELY
18 Asst Vice Pres Facilities Svcs ....Mr. Sean MCGOLDRICK
21 Controller ....Ms. Sheri MENDEZ
41 Director Athletics ....Mr. Doug KNUTH
96 Director Purchasing ....Mr. Raymond MORAN
19 Director University Police Svcs ....Mr. Adam GARCIA
22 Dir Equal Opportunity & Title IX .... Ms. Denise CORDOVA
37 Director Student Financial Svcs .... Mr. Timothy WOLFE
39 Director Resident Life & Housing . Mr. Rodney L. AESCHLIMANN
23 Director Student Health Svcs .... Dr. Cheryl HUG-ENGLISH
09 Director Institutional Analysis .... Dr. Serge HERZOG
86 Spec Asst to Pres External Affairs .... Ms. Heidi GANSERT
65 Dir Mackay Sch Mines/Earth Science .... Dr. Russell FIELDS
66 Director of Nursing ....Dr. Patsy L. RUCHALA
57 Director School of the Arts .... Dr. Larry ENGSTROM
25 Director Sponsored Projects ....Ms. Charlene HART
40 Director Wolf Shop ....Mr. Steve DUBEY
49 Acting Dean Liberal Arts .... Dr. Larry ENGSTROM
47 Dean Agriculture/Biotech/Nat Res .... Dr. William PAYNE
50 Dean Business Administration .... Dr. Gregory MOSIER
53 Dean of Education .... Dr. Kenneth COLL
54 Dean Engineering .... Dr. Emmanuel MARAGAKIS
60 Dean School of Journalism .... Mr. Alan STAVITSKY
81 Dean College of Science .... Dr. Jeffrey S. THOMPSON
07 Director of Admissions .... Dr. Stephen MAPLES
29 Director Alumni Relations .... Ms. Amy CAROTHERS
06 Associate Registrar .... Ms. Heather TURK FIECOAT
26 Exec Dir Marketing & Commun .... Mr. Thomas WHITE
04 Executive Asst to President ....Ms. Janet SANDERSON
100 Chief of Staff .... Ms. Patricia RICHARD
104 Dir/CEO Univ Study Abroad Consort .... Dr. Carmelo URZA
13 Chief Info Technology Officer (CIO) .... Mr. Steven SMITH
28 Acting Director of Diversity .... Ms. Patricia RICHARD
43 General Counsel ....Ms. Mary DUGAN
44 Director of Planned Giving ....Ms. Lisa RILEY

*Western Nevada College (B)

2201 W College Parkway, Carson City NV 89703-7316
County: Carson FICE Identification: 010363
Unit ID: 182564
Telephone: (775) 445-3000 Carnegie Class: Bac/Assoc-Assoc Dom
FAX Number: (775) 445-3051 Calendar System: Semester
URL: www.wnc.edu
Established: 1971 Annual Undergrad Tuition & Fees (In-State): $2,805
Enrollment: 3,951 Coed
Affiliation or Control: State IRS Status: 501(c)3
Highest Offering: Baccalaureate
Accreditation: **NW**, ADNUR

02 President .... Mr. Chet BURTON
04 Assistant to the President .... Ms. Deb CONRAD
05 Vice Pres Academic/Student Affairs .... Dr. Robert WYNEGAR
11 Vice Pres Admin/Legal Svcs .... Mr. Mark GHAN
20 Dean of Instruction ....Vacant
32 Dean Student Services ....Mr. John KINKELLA
10 Controller ....Ms. Coral LOPEZ
88 Director Child Development Center ....Ms. Andrea DORAN
38 Director of Counseling/Advising .... Ms. Piper MCCARTHHY
18 Director Facilities Mgmt/Planning ....Mr. Kevin GAFFNEY
37 Director Financial Aid ....Mr. John (JW) LAZZARI
26 Director Information & Marketing .... Ms. Anne P. HANSEN
08 Director Library & Media Services ....Mr. Kenneth A. SULLIVAN
06 Registrar/Director of Admissions ....Ms. Dianne HILLIARD
30 Director of Development ....Ms. Niki GLADYS
09 Director of Institutional Research .... Ms. Cathy FULKERSON
13 Director of Computing Services .... Ms. Susan HOWLAND
21 Budget Officer ....Ms. Carla DODGE
15 Asst Director Human Resources ....Ms. Irene TUCKER
35 Student Life Coordinator ....Ms. Lilly LEON-VICKS
49 Academic Director Liberal Arts .... Mr. Scott MORRISON
72 Academic Director Career & Tech Div .... Dr. Georgia WHITE
66 Academic Dir Nursing/Allied Health ....Dr. Judith CORDIA
19 Director Security/Safety ....Mr. Jack PIIRAINEN
41 Athletic Director ....Mr. John KINKELLA

Northwest Career College (C)

7398 Smoke Ranch Road, Las Vegas NV 89128
County: Clark FICE Identification: 038385
Unit ID: 445948
Telephone: (702) 254-7577 Carnegie Class: Spec 2-yr-Other
FAX Number: (702) 256-9181 Calendar System: Other
URL: www.northwestcareercollege.edu
Established: 1997 Annual Undergrad Tuition & Fees: N/A
Enrollment: 189 Coed
Affiliation or Control: Proprietary IRS Status: Proprietary
Highest Offering: Associate Degree
Accreditation: **ABHES**

01 Director .... Dr. John KENNY
11 COO .... Patrick KENNY
10 CFO ....Stephanie KENNY
37 Director of Financial Aid ....Austen DUNN
36 Director of Career Services ....Jillian LOPEZ
09 Director of Compliance ....Thomas KENNY
07 Director of Admissions ....Derrick PERRY
13 Director of Technology ....Michael KENNY
06 Registrar ....Cheryl DADEY

Pima Medical Institute-Las Vegas (D)

3333 E Flamingo Road, Las Vegas NV 89121-4329
Telephone: (702) 458-9650 Identification: 666273
Accreditation: **ABHES**, COARC, PTAA, RAD

† Branch campus of Pima Medical Institute, Tucson, AZ.

Roseman University of Health Sciences (E)

11 Sunset Way, Henderson NV 89014-2333
County: Clark FICE Identification: 040653
Unit ID: 445735
Telephone: (702) 990-4433 Carnegie Class: Spec-4-yr-Other Health
FAX Number: (702) 990-4435 Calendar System: Other
URL: www.roseman.edu
Established: 1999 Annual Undergrad Tuition & Fees: N/A
Enrollment: 1,404 Coed
Affiliation or Control: Independent Non-Profit IRS Status: 501(c)3
Highest Offering: Doctorate
Accreditation: **NW** DENT, IACBE, NUR, PHAR

01 President ....Dr. Renee COFFMAN
12 Chancellor Summerlin Campus .... Dr. Mark A. PENN
12 Chancellor Henderson Campus ....Dr. Eucharia E. NNADI
10 VP Business & Finance ....Mr. Ken WILKINS
11 VP of Operations ....Mr. Terrell SPARKS
03 Vice President Executive Affairs ....Dr. Charles F. LACY
26 Vice President Communications & PR .... Mr. Jason ROTH
09 VP Qual Assurance/Intercampus Cons .... Dr. Thomas METZGER
32 VP for Student Services ....Dr. Michael DEYOUNG
67 Dean College of Pharmacy ....Dr. Scott STOLTE
67 Campus Dean College of Pharmacy UT ....Dr. Larry FANNIN
66 Dean College of Nursing ....Dr. Mable H. SMITH
52 Dean College of Dental Medicine ....Dr. Frank LICARI
52 Dean College of Dental Medicine Hen .....Dr. Jaleh POURHAMIDI
50 Director MBA Program ....Dr. Okeleke NZEOGWU
37 Director of Financial Aid .... Ms. Sally MICKELSON
51 Director of Continuing Education .... Dr. Katherine SMITH
52 Assoc Dean Clinical Affairs ....Dr. Kenneth KING
07 Assoc Dean Admissions/Student Svcs ....Dr William HARMAN
15 Director of Human Resources .... Ms. Saralyn BARNES
62 Director of Library Services .... Ms. Karen CANEPI
06 Registrar/Director of Student Svcs .... Ms. Angela D. BIGBY

Sanford-Brown College (F)

2495 Village View Drive, Henderson NV 89074
Telephone: (702) 990-0150 Identification: 770744
Accreditation: **ACICS**

† School is in teach-out plan.

Sierra Nevada College (G)

999 Tahoe Boulevard, Incline Village NV 89451-9500
County: Washoe FICE Identification: 009192
Unit ID: 182458
Telephone: (775) 831-1314 Carnegie Class: Masters/M
FAX Number: (775) 832-1696 Calendar System: Semester
URL: www.sierranevada.edu
Established: 1969 Annual Undergrad Tuition & Fees: $29,994
Enrollment: 1,039 Coed
Affiliation or Control: Independent Non-Profit IRS Status: 501(c)3
Highest Offering: Masters
Accreditation: **NW**

00 Chairman Board of Trustees ....Dr. Atam LALCHANDANI
01 President ....Dr. Alan G. WALKER
05 Executive Vice President/Provost ....Ms. Shannon BEETS
30 Interim Vice President Development .... Ms. Dianne SEVERANCE
32 Dean of Students ....Mr. Will HOIDA
84 Interim Director of UG Admissions ....Mr. Jake YALE
20 Associate Provost ....Dr. Dan O'BRYAN
10 Chief Financial Officer ....Ms. Susan JOHNSON
37 Director of Financial Aid ....Ms. Nicole FERGUSON
26 Director of Marketing ....Mr. Jim SCRIPPS
09 Director of Institutional Research .... Ms. Annamarie JONES
18 Chief Facilities/Physical Plant ....Mr. Layne SESSIONS
08 Director of Library ....Dr. Elizabeth MARKLE
06 Registrar ....Ms. Rose WEHBY
53 Statewide Dir Teacher Education .... Ms. Beth TALIAFERRO
13 Director Information Technology ....Ms. Nicole FERGERSON
15 Human Resources Coordinator .... Ms. Dana HOFFELT
21 Controller ....Ms. Lynda ODELL
04 Executive Asst to the President .... Ms. Kristine YOUNG

Touro University Nevada (H)

874 American Pacific Drive, Henderson NV 89014
Telephone: (702) 777-8637 Identification: 770966
Accreditation: **&WC** ARCPA, NURSE, OSTEO, OT

† Regional accreditation is carried under the parent institution in Vallejo, CA

University of Phoenix Las Vegas Campus (I)

3755 Breakthrough Way, Las Vegas NV 89135-3047
Telephone: (702) 638-7279 Identification: 770220
Accreditation: **&NH**, ACBSP

† Regional accreditation is carried under the parent institution in Tempe, AZ

Wongu University of Oriental Medicine (J)

8620 S Eastern Avenue Ste 5, Las Vegas NV 89123
County: Clark Identification: 667262
Telephone: (702) 463-2122 Carnegie Class: Not Classified
FAX Number: (702) 946-5050 Calendar System: Quarter
URL: www.wongu.org
Established: 2012 Annual Graduate Tuition & Fees: N/A
Enrollment: N/A Coed
Affiliation or Control: Independent Non-Profit IRS Status: 501(c)3
Highest Offering: Master's; No Undergraduates
Accreditation: **@ACUP**

01 President ....Dr. Daniel DAVIES
05 Chief Academic Officer ....Dr. Yeaji SUH
10 Chief Financial Officer .... Carolyn YANAI
20 Dean of Academic & Clinical Affs ....Dr. Vim OSATHANUGRAH
06 Registrar ....Chau NGUYEN
07 Admissions Coordinator .... Deborah FIALA

NEW HAMPSHIRE

Antioch University New England (K)

40 Avon Street, Keene NH 03431-3516
Telephone: (800) 553-8920 Identification: 666992
Accreditation: **&NH**, CACFEP, CLPSY, MFCD

† Regional accreditation is carried under the parent institution in Yellow Springs, OH.

Colby-Sawyer College (L)

541 Main Street, New London NH 03257-7835
County: Merrimack FICE Identification: 002572
Unit ID: 182634
Telephone: (603) 526-3000 Carnegie Class: Bac-Diverse
FAX Number: (603) 526-2135 Calendar System: Semester
URL: www.colby-sawyer.edu
Established: 1837 Annual Undergrad Tuition & Fees: $38,860
Enrollment: 1,369 Coed
Affiliation or Control: Independent Non-Profit IRS Status: 501(c)3
Highest Offering: Baccalaureate
Accreditation: **EH**, ACBSP, #CAATE, NURSE

01 President .... Dr. Susan D. STUEBNER
05 Interim Academic Vice Pres ....Dr. Laura A. ALEXANDER
15 Vice President for Human Resources .... Mr. Douglas G. ATKINS
10 Vice Pres for Finance & Treasurer .... Mr. Todd C. EMMONS
32 Interim VP Studen: Dev .... Ms. Robin BURROUGHS DAVIS
30 Vice President Advancement .... Ms. Kathleen BONAVIST
84 Vice Pres Enrollment Management ....Mr. David L. PLACEY
101 Secretary of the College ....Ms. Linda J. VARNUM
100 Chief of Staff/Dir Strategic Plng ....Ms. Lisa F. TEDESCHI
21 Controller ....Ms. Karen I. BONEWALD
09 Director Institutional Research ....Dr. Yi NI
20 Academic Dean ....Dr. J. Burton KIRKWOOD

39 Director Residential Education .... Ms. Mary MCLAUGHLIN
37 Director of Financial Aid .... Ms. Beth W. RENZULLI
30 Director of Development .... Vacant
08 College Librarian .... Ms. Carrie THOMAS
06 Registrar .... Ms. Diane H. DRISCOLL
07 Director of Admission .... Ms. Anna G. MINER
13 Director Information Resources .... Mr. Kenneth G. KOCHIEN
41 Director of Athletics .... Mr. Bill FOTI
41 Director of Athletics .... Mr. George MARTIN
88 Dir Student Lrng Collaborative .... Ms. Caren BALDWIN-DIMEO
44 Dir Annual Giving .... Mr. Luke GORMAN
29 Dir Alumni Relations .... Ms. Tracey M. AUSTIN
19 Director of Campus Safety .... Mr. Peter L. BERTHIAUME
18 Senior Dir of Facilities .... Mr. Robert VACHON
40 Bookstore Manager .... Ms. Alison SEWARD
23 Dir of Baird Health & Counsel Ctr .... Ms. Pamela SPEAR
92 Coordinator of the Honors Program .... Ms. Ann Page STECKER

*Community College System of New Hampshire (A)

26 College Drive, Concord NH 03301-7407

County: Merrimack Identification: 666462
Telephone: (603) 230-3500 Carnegie Class: N/A
FAX Number: (603) 271-2725
URL: www.ccsnh.edu

01 Chancellor .... Dr. Ross GITTELL
03 Vice Chancellor .... Vacant
10 Assoc Vice Chanc Fin/Strategic Plng .... Kristyn VAN OSTERN
15 Assoc Vice Chanc Human Res Plng/Dev ...... Richard COLADARCI
26 Director of Communications .... Shannon REID
13 Chief Info Technology Officer (CIO) .... Susan BROUILLET

*Great Bay Community College (B)

320 Corporate Drive, Portsmouth NH 03801-2879

County: Rockingham FICE Identification: 002583
Unit ID: 183150
Telephone: (603) 427-7600 Carnegie Class: Assoc/HT-Mix Trad/Non
FAX Number: (603) 334-6308 Calendar System: Semester
URL: www.greatbay.edu
Established: 1945 Annual Undergrad Tuition & Fees (In-State): $7,104
Enrollment: 2,079 Coed
Affiliation or Control: State IRS Status: 501(c)3
Highest Offering: Associate Degree
Accreditation: EH, ACBSP, ADNUR, SURGT

02 President .... Mr. Wildolfo ARVELO
05 Vice President Academic Affairs .... Mr. Paul PETRITIS
32 Vice Pres Student Affairs .... Dr. Sarah BEDINGFIELD
10 Chief Financial Officer .... Ms. Joanne BERRY
06 Registrar .... Ms. Sandra HO
07 Director Admissions .... Ms. Carey WALKER
09 Director Institutional Research .... Ms. Fran CHICKERING

*Lakes Region Community College (C)

379 Belmont Road, Laconia NH 03246-1364

County: Belknap FICE Identification: 007555
Unit ID: 183123
Telephone: (603) 524-3207 Carnegie Class: Assoc/MT-VT-High Non
FAX Number: (603) 527-2042 Calendar System: Semester
URL: www.lrcc.edu
Established: 1967 Annual Undergrad Tuition & Fees (In-District): $6,642
Enrollment: 1,183 Coed
Affiliation or Control: State/Local IRS Status: 501(c)3
Highest Offering: Associate Degree
Accreditation: EH

02 President .... Dr. Scott KALICKI
05 VP of Academic & Community Affairs .... Vacant
32 VP of Student Services & Enrollment .... Dr. Larissa BAIA
10 Chief Financial Officer .... Ms. Sunshine FISK
04 Administrative Asst to President .... Mrs. Julia L. VELIE
06 Registrar .... Ms. Laura LEMIEN
07 Director of Admissions .... Mr. Wayne FRASER
37 Director Student Financial Aid .... Ms. Kristen PURRINGTON
26 Public Information Officer .... Mr. Max BROWN

*Manchester Community College (D)

1066 Front Street, Manchester NH 03102-8518

County: Hillsborough FICE Identification: 002582
Unit ID: 183132
Telephone: (603) 206-8000 Carnegie Class: Assoc/MT-VT-Mix Trad/Non
FAX Number: (603) 668-5354 Calendar System: Semester
URL: www.mccnh.edu
Established: 1945 Annual Undergrad Tuition & Fees (In-State): $6,880
Enrollment: 3,455 Coed
Affiliation or Control: State IRS Status: 501(c)3
Highest Offering: Associate Degree
Accreditation: EH, ACBSP, ADNUR, MAC

02 President .... Dr. Susan D. HUARD
05 Vice President Academic Affairs .... Dr. John B. COOK
32 VP Students/Community Development .... Kim KEEGAN
20 Associate VP Academic Affairs .... Vacant
07 Director of Admissions .... Miho BEAN
26 Director of Marketing .... Victoria JAFFE
37 Financial Aid Officer .... Stephanie J. WELDON

06 Registrar .... Evelyn R. PERRON
08 Library Director .... Vandana DHAKAR
09 Director Institutional Research .... Dr. Jere TURNER
10 Business Affairs Officer .... Kelly CHISHOLM
22 Human Resources Officer .... Jeannette DIBELLA
40 Bookstore Manager .... Vacant
66 Nursing Director .... Charlene WOLFE-STEPRO
21 Accountant I .... Carol DESPATHY
13 Director Information Technology .... George WAGGONER
35 Director Student Life .... Aileen CLAY
88 Bursar .... Amy WHEELER
04 Administrative Asst to President .... Karen KEELER
103 Dir Workforce/Career Development .... Vacant
106 Dir Online Education/E-learning .... Brian CHICK
18 Chief Facilities/Physical Plant .... Joshua MURPHY
19 Director Security/Safety .... Jeff NYHAN
29 Director Alumni Relations .... Vacant

*Nashua Community College (E)

505 Amherst Street, Nashua NH 03063-1092

County: Hillsborough FICE Identification: 009236
Unit ID: 183141
Telephone: (603) 882-6923 Carnegie Class: Assoc/HT-Mix Trad/Non
FAX Number: (603) 882-8690 Calendar System: Semester
URL: www.nashuacc.edu
Established: 1967 Annual Undergrad Tuition & Fees (In-State): $6,912
Enrollment: 2,184 Coed
Affiliation or Control: State IRS Status: 501(c)3
Highest Offering: Associate Degree
Accreditation: EH, ACBSP, ADNUR, ENGT

02 President .... Ms. Lucille A. JORDAN
05 Vice Pres Academic Affairs .... Mr. William A. MCINTYRE
32 Vice Pres Student & Community Affs .... Ms. Lizbeth GONZALEZ
10 Business Affairs Officer .... Ms. Esther GEOFFROY
09 Assoc VP Inst Research/Acad Affs .... Mr. Phil FRANKLAND
06 Registrar-Nashua .... Ms. Jennifer LEITNER
37 Financial Aid Officer .... Ms. Ann EULE
15 Human Resources .... Ms. Catherine BARRY
18 Plant Maintenance Engineer .... Mr. Scott BIENVENUE
26 Director Marketing/Public Relations .... Mr. Barry MEEHAN
04 Administrative Asst to President .... Ms. Lucy JENKINS

*NHTI-Concord's Community College (F)

31 College Drive, Concord NH 03301-7412

County: Merrimack FICE Identification: 002581
Unit ID: 183099
Telephone: (603) 271-6484 Carnegie Class: Assoc/HT-High Trad
FAX Number: (603) 230-9311 Calendar System: Semester
URL: www.nhti.edu
Established: 1965 Annual Undergrad Tuition & Fees (In-State): $7,104
Enrollment: 4,284 Coed
Affiliation or Control: State IRS Status: 501(c)3
Highest Offering: Associate Degree
Accreditation: EH, ACBSP, ADNUR, DA, DH, DMS, EMT, ENGT, RAD, RTT

02 President .... Dr. Susan B. DUNTON
32 VP Student Affairs .... Mr. Stephen P. CACCIA
35 Associate VP Student Affairs .... Dr. Charles LLOYD
05 Vice President Academic Affairs .... Dr. Pamela LANGLEY
20 Assoc Vice Pres of Academic Affairs .... Dr. Denis NORMANDIN
10 Chief Financial Officer .... Ms. Melanie KIRBY
08 Director Learning Resources .... Mr. Stephen AMBRA
07 Director of Admissions .... Vacant
06 Registrar .... Ms. Michele KARWOCKI
13 Director of Computer Services .... Mr. Thomas TOWLE
18 Director of Facilities Maintenance .... Vacant
26 Director of Communications .... Mr. Alan BLAKE
36 Dir Residence Life/Career Counsel .... Ms. Trish LORING
38 Director Student Counseling .... Ms. Donna DOOLEY
37 Financial Aid Director .... Ms. Sheri GONTHIER
19 Chief of Campus Safety .... Mr. Jason BISHOP
41 Athletic Director .... Mr. Paul HOGAN
15 Director Human Resources .... Ms. Alyssa LABELLE
28 Dir Cross-Cultural Education/ESOL .... Ms. Dawn HIGGINS
96 Director of Purchasing .... Ms. Barbara ANSTEY
105 Website Coordinator .... Ms. Christine METCALF
106 Dir Online Learning .... Ms. Trisha DIONNE

*River Valley Community College (G)

1 College Place, Claremont NH 03743-9707

County: Sullivan FICE Identification: 007560
Unit ID: 183114
Telephone: (603) 542-7744 Carnegie Class: Assoc/HVT-High Non
FAX Number: (603) 543-1844 Calendar System: Semester
URL: www.rivervalley.edu
Established: 1968 Annual Undergrad Tuition & Fees (In-State): $6,855
Enrollment: 1,009 Coed
Affiliation or Control: State IRS Status: 501(c)3
Highest Offering: Associate Degree
Accreditation: EH, ACBSP, ADNUR, COARC, MAC, MLTAD, OTA, PTAA, RAD

02 President .... Dr. Alicia B. HARVEY-SMITH
05 Vice President of Academic Affairs .... Dr. Ali RAFIEYMEHR
32 VP of Student & Community Affairs .... Dr. Alex HERZOG
35 Associate VP of Student Services .... Mrs. Kathleen ODELL-CARLSON

12 AVP of AA/Dir RVCC at Keene .... Ms. Linda RICHELSON
12 AVP of AA/Dir RVCC at Lebanon .... Ms. Kristen MCKENNA
37 Financial Aid Officer .... Ms. Julia DOWER
06 Registrar .... Ms. Sharon GILBERT
26 Chief Public Relations/Marketing .... Mrs. Lynne BIRMINGHAM
10 Business Affairs Officer .... Ms. Andrea PINEAU ALLBEE

*White Mountains Community College (H)

2020 Riverside Drive, Berlin NH 03570-3799

County: Coos FICE Identification: 005291
Unit ID: 183105
Telephone: (603) 752-1113 Carnegie Class: Assoc/MT-VT-High Non
FAX Number: (603) 752-6335 Calendar System: Semester
URL: www.wmcc.edu
Established: 1966 Annual Undergrad Tuition & Fees (In-State): $7,344
Enrollment: 845 Coed
Affiliation or Control: State IRS Status: 501(c)3
Highest Offering: Associate Degree
Accreditation: EH, MAC

02 President .... Matthew WOOD
05 Vice Pres Academic Affairs .... Fran RANCOURT
32 Vice President Student Affairs .... Martha LAFLAMME
10 Chief Financial Officer .... Lynn MOORE
06 Registrar .... Laurie CARRIER
08 Director Learning Resources .... Meagan CARR
18 Chief Facilities/Physical Plant .... Stephen DEROSIER
13 Director Computer Center .... Vacant
91 Director Administrative Computing .... Donald WEEKS
22 Dir Affirmative Action/Equal Oppty .... Donna BRIERE
40 Director Bookstore .... Karen SEVIER
07 Director of Admissions .... Vacant
09 Director of Institutional Research .... Suzanne WASILESKI
37 Director Student Financial Aid .... Kathryn DUCHESNE
105 Director Web Services .... Milton CAMILLE
15 Director Personnel Services .... Gretchen TAILLON

Daniel Webster College (I)

20 University Drive, Nashua NH 03063-1300

County: Hillsborough FICE Identification: 004731
Unit ID: 182661
Telephone: (603) 577-6000 Carnegie Class: Masters/S
FAX Number: (603) 577-6001 Calendar System: Semester
URL: www.dwc.edu
Established: 1965 Annual Undergrad Tuition & Fees: $15,630
Enrollment: 732 Coed
Affiliation or Control: Proprietary IRS Status: Proprietary
Highest Offering: Master's
Accreditation: EH, ENG

01 President .... Dr. Michael E. DIFFILY
05 Provost .... Dr. Jeremy OWENS
10 Sr Director of Finance & Operations .... Ms. Darla AMMIDOWN
09 Director of Institutional Research .... Ms. Heidi CROWELL
84 Director of Enrollment Management .... Ms. Cynthia SYLVESTER
04 Exec Assistant to the President .... Mrs. Dee KOUMARIANOS
49 Dean Arts and Sciences .... Dr. Kathleen HIPP
88 Dean Aviation Sciences .... Mr. Glenn CARTER
50 Dean Business Management .... Dr. Deborah JAMESON
54 Dean Engineering & Computer Sci .... Dr. Bo-Kyoung KIM
07 Manager of Recruitment .... Ms. Jennifer O'NEILL
08 Librarian .... Ms. Kristin HAYS
08 Librarian .... Ms. Elyse WOLF
06 Registrar .... Ms. Laura CLEAVES
32 Dean of Students .... Ms. Susan ELSASS
36 Director of Career Services .... Ms. Karen SOLIMINI
41 Director of Athletics .... Mr. Chris GILMORE
19 Director of Campus Safety .... Mr. Kevin MOORE
15 Human Resources Generalist .... Ms. Donna BAILEY

† In teach-out through June 2017

Dartmouth College (J)

Hanover NH 03755-4030

County: Grafton FICE Identification: 002573
Unit ID: 182670
Telephone: (603) 646-1110 Carnegie Class: DU-Higher
FAX Number: N/A Calendar System: Quarter
URL: www.dartmouth.edu
Established: 1769 Annual Undergrad Tuition & Fees: $49,506
Enrollment: 6,298 Coed
Affiliation or Control: Independent Non-Profit IRS Status: 501(c)3
Highest Offering: Doctorate
Accreditation: EH, BUS, ENG, IPSY, MED, PAST, PH

01 President .... Dr. Philip J. HANLON
03 Executive Vice President .... Mr. Richard G. MILLS
101 Secretary to Board of Trustees .... Ms. Marcia J. KELLY
05 Provost .... Dr. Carolyn M. DEVER
30 Sr Vice President for Advancement .... Mr. Robert W. LASHER
46 Vice Provost for Research .... Dr. Martin N. WYBOURNE
10 CFO and Vice Pres Finance .... Mr. Michael F. WAGNER
26 VP Communications .... Mr. Justin ANDERSON
28 Vice Pres for Inst Diversity/Equity .... Dr. Evelynn ELLIS
15 Chief Human Resources Officer .... Mr. Scot R. BEMIS
29 Vice President Alumni Relations .... Ms. Martha J. BEATTIE
63 Interim Dean Geisel Sch of Med .... Dr. Duane A. COMPTON
18 VP of Campus Services .... Ms. Lisa HOGARTY

43 General Counsel .... Mr. Robert B. DONIN
20 Dean of the College .... Dr. Rebecca E. BIRON
06 Registrar .... Ms. Meredith BRAZ
07 VProv Enroll/Dean Admiss & Fin Aid .... Mr. Lee COFFIN
37 Director of Financial Aid .... Mr. Gordon D. KOFF
13 Int VP for Information Technology .... Mr. Joseph R. DOUCET
08 Dean of Libraries/Librarian of Col .... Vacant
49 Dean of Faculty of Arts & Sciences .. Dr. Michael MASTANDUNO
50 Dean of Amos Tuck School .... Dr. Matthew J. SLAUGHTER
54 Dean of the Thayer School .... Dr. Joseph HELBLE
58 Dean of Graduate Studies .... Dr. F. Jon KULL
102 Dean of Tucker Foundation .... Rabbi Daveen H. LITWIN
41 Director of Athletics .... Mr. Harry SHEEHY
88 Dir Risk/Internal Control Svcs .... Ms. Catherine LARK
23 Director of the Health Services .... Dr. Mark REED
36 Director Center for Prof Dev .... Mr. Roger W. WOOLSEY
25 Dir Office of Sponsored Projects .... Ms. Jill M. MORTALI
32 Vice Provost for Student Affairs .... Dr. Inge-Lise AMEER
19 Director Safety & Security .... Mr. Harry C. KINNE, III
09 Director of Institutional Research .... Ms. Alicia M. BETSINGER
38 Dir Counseling/Human Development .... Dr. Heather A. EARLE
22 Dir Equal Opportunity/Affirm Action .... Ms. Beatriz CANTADA
96 Director of Procurement .... Ms. Tammy L. MOFFATT
44 Chief Investment Officer .... Ms. Pamela L. PEEDIN
35 Sr Assoc Dean for Student Affairs .... Ms. Elilzabeth L. AGOSTO
21 Controller .... Ms. Gail C. GOODNESS
04 Senior Executive Asst to President .... Ms. Jennifer A. SHEPHERD
100 Chief of Staff .... Ms. Laura H. HERCOD

Franklin Pierce University (A)

40 University Drive, Rindge NH 03461-5046
County: Cheshire — FICE Identification: 002575
Unit ID: 182795
Telephone: (603) 899-4000 — Carnegie Class: Masters/M
FAX Number: (603) 899-6448 — Calendar System: Semester
URL: www.franklinpierce.edu
Established: 1962 — Annual Undergrad Tuition & Fees: $33,320
Enrollment: 2,275 — Coed
Affiliation or Control: Independent Non-Profit — IRS Status: 501(c)3
Highest Offering: Doctorate
Accreditation: EH, ARCPA, IACBE, NUR, PTA

01 President .... Dr. Kim MOONEY
05 VP Academic Affairs/Provost .... Vacant
11 VP & COO .... Dr. Nathaniel PEIRCE
10 Vice Pres Finance & Administration .... Ms. Sandra QUAYE
32 Vice President for Student Affairs .... Dr. James P. EARLE
30 Vice Pres for Institutional Advance .... Vacant
29 VP Alumni & Comm Rels .... Mr. Lawrence LEACH
84 Asst Vice Pres Enrollment Mgmt .... Ms. Linda QUIMBY
58 Dean Grad/Professional Studies .... Dr. Maria R. ALTOBELLO
35 Asst Dean Student Affairs .... Ms. Jill BASSETT
41 Athletic Director .... Mr. Bruce M. KIRSH
15 Director of Human Resources .... Ms. Roberta DELLHIME
06 Registrar .... Ms. Tonya B. LABROSSE
08 Director of Library Resource Center .... Vacant
37 Asst Vice Pres Financial Services .... Mr. Kenneth FERREIRA
29 Director of Alumni & Parent Rel .... Ms. Julie ZAHN
12 Academic Dean Rindge Campus .... Dr. Kerry MCKEEVER
26 Dir of Marketing & Communication .... Mr. James WOLKEN
36 Director of Career Development .... Ms. Rosemary NICHOLS
20 Dir Center for Academic Excellence .... Dr. Karen J. BROWN
42 Chaplain .... Vacant
19 Director Campus Safety .... Ms. Maureen STURGIS
39 Director Residential Life .... Ms. Kathleen DOUGHERTY
18 Chief Facilities/Physical Plant .... Mr. Doug LEAR
21 Accountant & Payroll Mgr .... Ms. Kathleen MAHONEY
96 Director of Purchasing .... Ms. Chere HALLETT-ADAMS
104 Director Study Abroad .... Ms. Patti VORFELD
13 Chief Info Technology Officer (CIO) .... Mr. Thomas MANLEY
04 Executive Asst to the President .... Ms. Heather RINGWALD

MCPHS-Manchester Campus (B)

1260 Elm Street, Manchester NH 03101
Telephone: (603) 314-0210 — Identification: 770113
Accreditation: &EH, #ARCPA, PHAR

† Regional accreditation is carried under the parent institution in Boston, MA

New England College (C)

98 Bridge Street, Henniker NH 03242-3244
County: Merrimack — FICE Identification: 002579
Unit ID: 182980
Telephone: (603) 428-2211 — Carnegie Class: Masters/L
FAX Number: (603) 428-7230 — Calendar System: Semester
URL: www.nec.edu
Established: 1946 — Annual Undergrad Tuition & Fees: $34,306
Enrollment: 2,399 — Coed
Affiliation or Control: Independent Non-Profit — IRS Status: 501(c)3
Highest Offering: Doctorate
Accreditation: EH

01 President .... Dr. Michele D. PERKINS
05 Interim VP of Academic Affairs .... Mr. John O'CONNOR
84 VP of Enrollment .... Mr. Brad POZNANSKI
10 Sr Vice President/CEO .... Dr. Paula A. AMATO
30 Vice Pres Advancement/Communication .... Vacant
08 Library Director .... Ms. Chelsea HANRAHAN
20 Assoc VP of Academic Effectiveness .... Dr. Nelly LEJTER
07 Director SGPS Admissions Operation .... Ms. Laura TREMBLAY
04 Admin Assistant to President .... Ms. Betsy MEDVETZ
13 VP for Information Technology .... Ms. Carol THOMAS
06 Registrar .... Ms. Beth DOWLING
37 Director Student Financial Svcs .... Ms. Kristen BLASE
21 Controller .... Ms. Carolyn MADDEN
36 Director Career/Life Planning .... Mr. Gene DURKEE
30 Director of Development .... Ms. Meghan HALLOCK
26 Dir of Public Rels/Communications .... Mr. David DEZIEL
15 Human Resources Manager .... Ms. Julie GENDRON
102 Dir Corp & Foundation Relations .... Mr. Gregory PALMER
106 Dir Online & Custom Education .... Ms. Sarah WHITE
18 AVP of Capital and Facilities Mgmt .... Mr. Dan GEARAN
19 Director Campus Safety .... Mr. Bill CHRISTIANO
28 Director of Diversity and Inclusion .... Ms. Lai-Monte HUNTER
39 Director Res Life & Student Housing .... Ms. Doreen LONG
41 Athletic Director .... Mr. Lou IZZI

New Hampshire Institute of Art (D)

148 Concord Street, Manchester NH 03104-4858
County: Hillsborough — FICE Identification: 031823
Unit ID: 430810
Telephone: (603) 623-0313 — Carnegie Class: Spec-4-yr-Arts
FAX Number: (603) 641-1832 — Calendar System: Semester
URL: www.nhia.edu
Established: 1898 — Annual Undergrad Tuition & Fees: $24,690
Enrollment: 508 — Coed
Affiliation or Control: Independent Non-Profit — IRS Status: 501(c)3
Highest Offering: Master's
Accreditation: EH, ART

01 President .... Mr. Kent DEVEREAUX
10 Vice President of Finance .... Ms. Leanne FLEMING
30 Vice President of Development .... Vacant
84 Vice President of Enrollment .... Mr. Jonathan LINDSAY
12 Sharon Arts Campus Director .... Ms. Camellia SOUSA
04 Executive Assistant to President .... Ms. Sara DADIAN PEREZ
05 Interim Dean of Undergrad Studies .... Mr. Patrick MCCAY
58 Dean of Graduate Studies .... Ms. Lucinda BLISS
08 Library Director .... Ms. Betsy HOLMES
88 Director of Advising .... Ms. Tricia GIBBS
06 Registrar .... Ms. Karen GOSSELIN
20 Academic Affairs Administrator .... Ms. Claire SHEA
88 Bursar .... Vacant
32 Director of Student Affairs .... Ms. Michele TRACIA
37 Assistant Director Financial Aid .... Ms. Audrey KAY
31 Community Education Director .... Mr. Chris ARCHER
15 Director of Human Resources .... Ms. Katrina KRAMER
21 Accounting Manager .... Ms. Nancy JORDAN
18 Facilities Manager .... Mr. Paul GYMZIAK
13 Manager of Information Technologies .... Mr. John FALLAVOLLITA
88 IT Specialist .... Mr. Bob MASTERTON
38 Counselor .... Ms. Tanya POPOLOSKI
88 Academic Support Center Coordinator .... Ms. Kristen DRONEY

Northeast Catholic College (E)

511 Kearsarge Mountain Road, Warner NH 03278-4012
County: Merrimack — FICE Identification: 022233
Unit ID: 182917
Telephone: (603) 456-2656 — Carnegie Class: Bac/Assoc-Mixed
FAX Number: (603) 456-2660 — Calendar System: Semester
URL: www.NortheastCatholic.edu
Established: 1973 — Annual Undergrad Tuition & Fees: $21,200
Enrollment: 61 — Coed
Affiliation or Control: Roman Catholic — IRS Status: 501(c)3
Highest Offering: Baccalaureate
Accreditation: @EH

01 President .... Dr. George A. HARNE
05 Academic Dean .... Dr. Joe FORTE
10 CFO .... Mr. Daniel PETERSON
32 Dean of Students .... Miss Katherine PAGOR
07 Director of Admissions .... Ms. Katie MOFFETT
37 Director Financial Aid/Librarian .... Mrs. Marie LASHER

Rivier University (F)

420 S Main Street, Nashua NH 03060-5086
County: Hillsborough — FICE Identification: 002586
Unit ID: 183211
Telephone: (603) 888-1311 — Carnegie Class: Masters/L
FAX Number: (603) 897-8811 — Calendar System: Semester
URL: www.rivier.edu
Established: 1933 — Annual Undergrad Tuition & Fees: $29,700
Enrollment: 2,349 — Coed
Affiliation or Control: Roman Catholic — IRS Status: 501(c)3
Highest Offering: Doctorate
Accreditation: EH, ADNUR, NUR

01 President .... Sr. Paula Marie BULEY
05 Vice President for Academic Affairs .... Dr. Douglas HOWARD
10 Vice Pres Finance & Administration .... Mr. Scott FIELDS
32 Vice President Student Affairs .... Mr. Kurt STIMELING
84 Vice Pres Enrollment Management .... Ms. Karen SCHEDIN
30 Vice Pres University Advancement .... Ms. Karen COOPER
35 Asst Vice Pres Student Affairs .... Ms. Paula FANDAZZA
13 Chief Information Officer .... Mr. Toby SINGER
21 Controller .... Ms. Jennifer YEOMANS
06 Registrar .... Mr. Kevin GATELY
08 Library Director .... Mr. Daniel SPEIDEL
36 Dir Career Development Center .... Ms. Marie SULLIVAN
37 Director Student Financial Aid .... Ms. Valerie PATNAUDE
15 Director Human Resources .... Ms. Cheryl BAGTAZ
18 Director Facilities Management .... Mr. Richard PERRINE
14 Director Instructional Computing .... Sr. Martha VILLENEUVE
41 Athletic Director .... Ms. Joanne MERRILL
42 Chaplain Campus Ministry .... Bro. Paul DEMERS
28 Director Multicultural Affairs .... Ms. Sharron ROWLETT
29 Dir Alumni Relations/Special Events .... Ms. Mary BOLLINGER
26 Director Marketing/Communication .... Ms. Patricia GARRITY

Saint Anselm College (G)

100 Saint Anselm Drive, Manchester NH 03102-1310
County: Hillsborough — FICE Identification: 002587
Unit ID: 183239
Telephone: (603) 641-7000 — Carnegie Class: Bac-A&S
FAX Number: (603) 641-7116 — Calendar System: Semester
URL: www.anselm.edu
Established: 1889 — Annual Undergrad Tuition & Fees: $37,904
Enrollment: 1,968 — Coed
Affiliation or Control: Roman Catholic — IRS Status: 501(c)3
Highest Offering: Baccalaureate
Accreditation: EH, NURSE

01 President .... Dr. Steven R. DISALVO
05 Vice Pres Academic Affairs .... Br. Isaac MURPHY, OSB
30 Sr VP College Advancement .... Mr. James P. FLANAGAN
11 Vice President for Administration .... Ms. Patricia SHUSTER
32 Vice President Student Affairs .... Dr. Joseph M. HORTON
26 Exec Dir Col Comm & Mktg .... Ms. Michelle ADAMS O'REGAN
10 Chief Financial Ofcr/Sr VP Finance .... Dr. Harry E. DUMAY
06 Registrar .... Fr. Benet PHILLIPS
07 Dean of Admissions/VP Enrollment .... Mr. Eric NICHOLS
08 Librarian .... Mr. Charles M. GETCHELL, JR.
37 Director of Financial Aid .... Ms. Elizabeth KEUFFEL
35 Dean of Students .... Dr. Alicia A. FINN
20 Dean of Freshmen .... Dr. Anne E. HARRINGTON
66 Exec Director of Nursing .... Dr. Maureen A. O'REILLY
04 Assistant to the President .... Ms. Janet L. POIRIER
18 Director of Physical Plant .... Mr. Donald MOREAU
23 Director of Health Services .... Ms. Maura MARSHALL
29 Asst VP of Alum/Advanc Programming .... Ms. Patrice RUSSELL
41 Director of Athletics .... Mr. Daron MONTGOMERY
42 Director of Campus Ministry .... Ms. Susan S. GABERT
09 Director of Institutional Research .... Dr. Hui-Ling CHEN
13 Chief Information Officer .... Mr. Adam R. ALBINA
15 Director Human Resources .... Mr. David HARRINGTON
19 Director Security/Safety .... Mr. Donald DAVIDSON
53 Director Education Planning .... Dr. Laura WASIELEWSKI
28 Director Multicultural Center .... Vacant
39 Director Student Housing .... Ms. Susan WEINTRAUB
96 Director of Purchasing .... Mr. Jacques PLANTE
104 Assoc Dir Study Abroad .... Ms. Sarah GOOLKASIAN
25 Dir Sponsored Programs & Research .... Dr. William PLLOG
44 Asst VP Individual Giving .... Vacant
101 Secretary of the Institution/Board .... Ms. Janet L. POIRIER
86 Director Government Relations .... Mr. Neil LEVESQUE

St. Joseph School of Nursing (H)

5 Woodward Avenue, Nashua NH 03060
County: Hillsborough — FICE Identification: 021404
Unit ID: 183248
Telephone: (603) 594-2567 — Carnegie Class: Spec 2-yr-Health
FAX Number: (603) 578-5028 — Calendar System: Semester
URL: www.sjson.edu
Established: 1908 — Annual Undergrad Tuition & Fees: $17,272
Enrollment: 144 — Coed
Affiliation or Control: Independent Non-Profit — IRS Status: 501(c)3
Highest Offering: Associate Degree
Accreditation: ACCSC, ADNUR

01 Dean .... Vickie K. FIELER

Southern New Hampshire University (I)

2500 North River Road, Manchester NH 03106-1045
County: Hillsborough — FICE Identification: 002580
Unit ID: 183026
Telephone: (603) 626-9100 — Carnegie Class: Masters/L
FAX Number: (603) 645-9665 — Calendar System: Semester
URL: www.snhu.edu
Established: 1932 — Annual Undergrad Tuition & Fees: $30,386
Enrollment: 43,274 — Coed
Affiliation or Control: Independent Non-Profit — IRS Status: 501(c)3
Highest Offering: Doctorate
Accreditation: EH, ACBSF, NURSE

01 President .... Dr. Paul LEBLANC
04 Director/Assistant to President .... Ms. Lisa JENNINGS
100 SVP/University Chief of Staff .... Mr. William ZEMP
05 EVP/University College Provost .... Dr. Patricia LYNOTT
15 Sr VP Human Resources .... Ms. Danielle STANTON
51 EVP COCE .... Ms. Amelia MANNING
88 SVP College for America .... Ms. Kris CLERKIN
10 CFO Finance & Administration .... Mr. Joseph SERGI
13 SVP Technology & Transformation .... Mr. Thomas DIONISIO
43 General Counsel/Secretary to Board .... Ms. Yvette CLARK
30 SVP Institutional Advancement .... Mr. Donald BREZINSKI

26 VP UCMarketing & Student Recruiting ... Mr. Gregg MAZZOLA
18 VP Facilities/Physical Plant ... Ms. Patricia WHITNEY
20 VP Academic Affairs ... Mr. Michael EVANS
09 AVP Research & Planning ... Mr. Thomas BERALDI, JR.
06 University Registrar ... Ms. Deanna BECHARD
49 Dean School of Arts & Sciences ... Vacant
50 Dean School of Business ... Vacant
53 Dean School of Education ... Mr. Raymond MCNULTY
08 Dean of the Library ... Vacant
32 Dean of Students ... Ms. Heather LORENZ
20 Dean of Student Success ... Ms. Carey GLINES
19 Assoc Dean/Dir of Public Safety ... Mr. James WINN
27 SVP External Affairs/Communications ... Ms. Libby MAY
07 Director Freshman Admissions ... Mr. Timothy WHITTUM
07 Director of Transfer Admissions ... Ms. Julie CALLAHAN
31 Dir Community Engaged Learning ... Ms. Elizabeth RICHARDS
29 Director of Alumni Relations ... Ms. Kristi DURETTE
26 Director Community Relations ... Ms. Helen DAVIES
23 Director Wellness Center ... Ms. Sheila LAMBERT
36 Exec Dir Career Development Ctr ... Ms. Beth PRIETO
39 Director of Residence Life ... Ms. Shannon BROWN
41 Director of Athletics ... Mr. Anthony FALLACARO
42 Director of Campus Ministry ... Rev. Bruce COLLARD
92 Director of Univ Honors Program ... Dr. Andrew MARTINO
85 Dir International Student Services ... Ms. Dawn SEDUTTO
96 Sr Dir of Procurement/Contracts ... Ms. Mary DUKAKIS
25 Director of Grants ... Ms. Audrey MCLAUGHLIN
14 Chief Operating Officer ITS ... Mr. Daryl DREFFS
105 Director of Web Services ... Mr. Curtis KIMBALL
88 Director of Academic Advising ... Ms. Leah RICHARDS
88 Director of the Learning Center ... Ms. Lori DECONINCK
22 Director of Disability Services ... Mr. Dennis GREEN
104 Director Study Abroad ... Mr. Stefano PARENTI
108 Director of Learning Assessment ... Dr. Randall CASE
90 Assoc Dir of Academic Computing ... Mr. Aaron FLINT
24 AV Services Manager ... Mr. Thomas HELM

The Thomas More College of Liberal Arts (A)

6 Manchester Street, Merrimack NH 03054-4805

County: Hillsborough — FICE Identification: 030431
Unit ID: 183275
Telephone: (603) 880-8308 — Carnegie Class: Bac-A&S
FAX Number: (603) 880-9280 — Calendar System: Semester
URL: www.thomasmorecollege.edu
Established: 1978 — Annual Undergrad Tuition & Fees: $20,400
Enrollment: 93 — Coed
Affiliation or Control: Independent Non-Profit — IRS Status: 501(c)3
Highest Offering: Baccalaureate
Accreditation: EH

01 President ... Dr. William E. FAHEY
30 Vice Pres Institutional Advancement ... Mr. Paul JACKSON
05 Academic Dean ... Dr. Walter THOMPSON
32 Dean of Students ... Mr. Denis KITZINGER
44 Director Institutional Advancement ... Mr. Paul JACKSON
10 Director of Business ... Ms. Pamela BERNSTEIN
35 Director of Student Life ... Dr. Sara KITZINGER
04 Executive Asst President's Office ... Ms. Valerie BURGESS
06 Registrar ... Ms. Pamela BERNSTEIN
07 Director of Admissions ... Mr. Paul JACKSON

*University System of New Hampshire (B)

5 Chenell Drive, Suite 301, Concord NH 03301

County: Merrimack — FICE Identification: 008027
Unit ID: 183327
Telephone: (603) 862-1800 — Carnegie Class: N/A
FAX Number: (603) 862-0908
URL: usnh.edu

01 Chancellor ... Dr. Todd J. LEACH
03 Vice Chancellor & Treasurer ... Ms. Catherine A. PROVENCHER
43 General Counsel ... Mr. Ronald F. RODGERS
86 Assoc Vice Chanc Government Affs ... Vacant
05 Assoc Vice Chanc Academic & Student ... Vacant
09 Dir of Institutional Research ... Ms. Heidi HEDEGARD
15 Chief Human Resource Officer ... Mr. James MCGRAIL

*University of New Hampshire (C)

105 Main Street, Durham NH 03824

County: Strafford — FICE Identification: 002589
Unit ID: 183044
Telephone: (603) 862-1234 — Carnegie Class: DU-Higher
FAX Number: N/A — Calendar System: Semester
URL: www.unh.edu
Established: 1866 — Annual Undergrad Tuition & Fees (In-State): $16,986
Enrollment: 15,117 — Coed
Affiliation or Control: State — IRS Status: 501(c)3
Highest Offering: Doctorate
Accreditation: EH, ACFEI, BUS, CAATE, CAEP, CARTE, CS, DIETD, DIETI, DIETT, ENG, ENGT, IPSY, LAW, MFCD, MT, MUS, NRPA, NURSE, OT, PH, SP, SW, TEAC

02 President ... Dr. Mark W. HUDDLESTON
100 Chief of Staff ... Ms. Megan W. DAVIS
05 Int Prov & VP Academic Affairs ... Dr. Palligarnai T. VASUDEVAN
10 VP Finance/Administration ... Mr. Christopher D. CLEMENT
84 VP Enrollment Management ... Ms. Victoria DUTCHER
46 Sr Vice Provost Research ... Dr. Jane A. NISBET
26 Assoc VP Univ Communications ... Mr. Joel SELIGMAN
43 General Counsel ... Mr. Ronald F. RODGERS
88 Assoc Prov Academic Administration ... Ms. Leigh Anne MELANSON
28 Assoc VP Cmty/Equity/Diversity ... Ms. Jamie NOLAN
20 Int Sr Vice Prov Academic Affairs ... Dr. Mary RHIEL
15 Assoc VP/Chief HR Officer ... Ms. Kathleen A. NEILS
20 Asst Prov Acad Adm/MPA Program Dir ... Mr. James S. VARN
88 Sr VProv Engagement & Acad Outreach ... Dr. Julie E. WILLIAMS
21 Assoc VP for Finance ... Ms. Kerry SCALA
13 Asst VP Enterprise Computing ... Mr. William HALL
40 Manager of UNH Bookstore ... Ms. Karen MCLAUGHLIN
16 Asst VP Human Resources ... Ms. Sari M. BENNETT
21 Assoc VP Business Affairs ... Mr. David J. MAY
18 Assoc VP Facilities ... Mr. William P. JANELLE
32 Dean of Students ... Dr. John T. KIRKPATRICK
35 Director Residential Life ... Mr. Scott CHESNEY
23 Director Health Services ... Dr. Kevin E. CHARLES
36 Assoc Prov Acad Achievement/Support ... Dr. Judith SPILLER
25 Dir Sponsored Programs ... Mr. Victor SOSA
30 VP Advancement ... Ms. Deborah DUTTON COX
47 Dean Life Sciences/Agriculture ... Dr. Jon M. WRAITH
49 Dean Liberal Arts ... Dr. Kenneth FULD
50 Dean Paul College of Business ... Dr. Deborah MERRILL-SANDS
58 Dean Graduate School ... Dr. Harry J. RICHARDS
76 Dean Health & Human Services ... Dr. Michael FERRARA
54 Dean Engineering/Physical Sciences ... Dr. Samuel MUKASA
12 Dean UNH at Manchester ... Dr. Michael P. DECELLE
08 Dean University Library ... Dr. Tara Lynn FULTON
56 Dean/Dir Cooperative Extension ... Dr. Ken LAVALLEY
88 Dir Thompson School Appl Science ... Dr. Regina A. SMICK-ATTISANO
22 Dir Affirmative Action & Equity ... Ms. Donna Marie SORRENTINO
07 Director Admissions ... Mr. Robert P H. MCGANN
06 Registrar ... Mr. Andrew COLBY
37 Dir Financial Aid ... Ms. Susan K. ALLEN
41 Dir Intercollegiate Athletics ... Mr. Martin SCARANO
38 Dir Counseling Center ... Dr. David CROSS
102 Dir Finance & Operations UNH Found ... Mr. Erik GROSS
39 Dir Housing/Conf Services ... Ms. Kathy IRLA-CHESNEY
19 Asst VP Public Safety & Risk Mgt ... Chief Paul M. DEAN
85 Dir Intl Students & Scholars ... Ms. Leila L. PAJE-MANALO
42 University Chaplain ... Pastor Larry BRICKNER-WOOD
96 Dir Purchasing & Contract Svcs ... Ms. Denise M. SMITH
92 Dir Honors Program ... Dr. Jerry MARX
09 Dir Inst Research & Assessment ... Dr. Yun XIANG
88 Dir Writing Program ... Dr. Edward A. MUELLER
104 Dir Center International Education ... Dr. Claire L. MALARTE-FELDMAN
94 Coord Women's Studies Program ... Dr. Marla B. BRETTSCHNEIDER
88 Asst VP Public Relations ... Mr. Mica STARK
106 UNH Online Director ... Ms. Terri WINTERS
04 Sr Admin Asst to President ... Ms. Annie JONES

*Granite State College (D)

25 Hall Street, Concord NH 03301-7317

County: Merrimack — FICE Identification: 031013
Unit ID: 183257
Telephone: (603) 228-3000 — Carnegie Class: Bac-Diverse
FAX Number: (603) 513-1389 — Calendar System: Quarter
URL: www.granite.edu
Established: 1972 — Annual Undergrad Tuition & Fees (In-State): $7,257
Enrollment: 2,209 — Coed
Affiliation or Control: State — IRS Status: 501(c)3
Highest Offering: Master's
Accreditation: EH, NURSE

02 President ... Dr. Mark RUBINSTEIN
05 Provost/VP Academic Affairs ... Dr. Scott A. STANLEY
13 Chief Information Officer ... Mr. Kenneth WHITELAW
10 VP Finance/Technology/Infrastruct ... Ms. Lisa L. SHAWNEY
53 Interim Dean of School of Education ... Mr. Nick MARKS
20 Vice Provost for Academic Affairs ... Dr. Johnna A. HERRICK-PHELPS
20 Vice Provost for Academic Affairs ... Dr. Carole BEAUCHEMIN
84 Assoc VP of Enrollment Management ... Ms. Tara PAYNE
06 Registrar ... Ms. Kristin MULLANEY
24 Director of Educational Technology ... Ms. Reta CHAFFEE
15 VP of Student/Administrative Svcs ... Ms. Beth DOLAN
09 Director of Institutional Research ... Mr. Jim MILLER
18 Dir of Facilities/Safety/Sustain ... Mr. Peter CONKLIN
08 Assistant Dean of Library Services ... Ms. Patricia ERWIN-PLOOG
21 Director of Financial Operations ... Mr. Steve PERROTTA
21 Bursar ... Ms. Jodi WOLBERT
04 Administrative Asst to President ... Ms. Susan L. ORR
37 Director Student Financial Aid ... Mr. Mac BRODERICK

*Keene State College (E)

229 Main Street, Keene NH 03435-0001

County: Cheshire — FICE Identification: 002590
Unit ID: 183062
Telephone: (603) 352-1909 — Carnegie Class: Masters/S
FAX Number: (603) 358-2257 — Calendar System: Semester
URL: www.keene.edu
Established: 1909 — Annual Undergrad Tuition & Fees (In-State): $13,228
Enrollment: 4,957 — Coed
Affiliation or Control: State — IRS Status: 501(c)3
Highest Offering: Master's
Accreditation: EH, #CAATE, DIETD, DIETI, MUS, NURSE, TED

02 President ... Dr. Anne E. HUOT
05 Provost/VP Academic Affairs ... Mr. William SEIGH
32 VP Student Affairs & Enroll Mgmt ... Dr. Kemal ATKINS
10 Interim VP Finance & Planning ... Dr. Dan PETREE
100 Chief of Staff ... Ms. Kathleen WILLIAMS
04 Executive Assoc to the President ... Ms. Cindy KRAUTWURST
35 Dean of Students ... Dr. Gail ZIMMERMAN
08 Dean of Library ... Dr. Celia E. RABINOWITZ
07 Director of Admissions ... Ms. Margaret RICHMOND
06 Registrar ... Mr. Thomas RICHARD
13 Chief Information Officer ... Ms. Laura SERAICHICK
15 Special Asst to President for HR ... Ms. Carol CORCORAN
26 Director of Marketing & Comm ... Ms. Kathleen WILLIAMS
84 AVP for Enrollment Management ... Mr. Steven A. GOETSCH
18 Director Physical Plant ... Mr. Frank MAZZOLA
39 Director of Residential Life ... Mr. Kent DRAKE-DEESE
09 Director of Institutional Research ... Dr. Cathryn TURRENTINE
29 Alumni & Parent Relations Director ... Vacant
38 Director Student Counseling ... Dr. Brian QUIGLEY
96 Purchasing Agent ... Vacant
81 Dean of Sciences ... Dr. Gordon LEVERSEE
58 Dean Prof/Graduate Studies ... Vacant
79 Dean Arts & Humanities ... Dr. Sara HOTTINGER
28 Chief Officer Diversity/Multicult ... Dr. Dottie MORRIS

*Plymouth State University (F)

17 High Street, Plymouth NH 03264-1595

County: Grafton — FICE Identification: 002591
Unit ID: 183080
Telephone: (603) 535-5000 — Carnegie Class: Masters/L
FAX Number: (603) 535-2654 — Calendar System: Semester
URL: www.plymouth.edu
Established: 1871 — Annual Undergrad Tuition & Fees (In-State): $13,128
Enrollment: 4,855 — Coed
Affiliation or Control: State — IRS Status: 501(c)3
Highest Offering: Doctorate
Accreditation: EH, ACBSP, ART, CAATE, CACREP, NURSE, SW, TED

02 President ... Dr. Donald L. BIRX
05 Vice Pres Academic Affairs/Provost ... Vacant
10 VP for Finance & Administration ... Vacant
32 Interim VP Student Affairs ... Mr. Mark J. FISCHLER
88 University Ombuds Officer ... Dr. David ZEHR
30 VP for University Advancement ... Ms. Paula L. HOBSON
13 AVP Info Tech Svcs/Chief Info Ofcr ... Mr. Richard G. GROSSMAN
84 Dean Enroll Mgmt/Dir Admissions ... Mr. Jason MORAN
39 Dir Res Life/Housing/Conf Svcs ... Mr. Thomas B. WEEKS
35 Dean of Students ... Mr. Jeffrey C. FURLONE
09 Dir Institutional Research ... Ms. Joyce LARSON
06 Registrar ... Dr. Stacey L. CURDIE
08 Int Dean Library/Academic Support ... Ms. Elaine ALLARD
29 Director of Alumni Relations ... Mr. Rodney EKSTROM
37 Director of Financial Aid ... Ms. Crystal GAFF
15 Director of Human Resources ... Ms. Caryn L. INES
19 Chief of Campus Police ... Mr. Steven H. TEMPERINO
41 Interim Athletic Director ... Ms. Kim M. BOWNES
18 Director of Physical Plant ... Ms. Ellen SHIPPEE
38 Director of Counseling ... Mr. Robert G. HLASNY
40 Bookstore Manager ... Mr. Steve RHEAUME

NEW JERSEY

Assumption College for Sisters (G)

200A Morris Avenue, Denville NJ 07834

County: Morris — FICE Identification: 002595
Unit ID: 183600
Telephone: (973) 957-0188 — Carnegie Class: Assoc/HT-High Trad
FAX Number: (973) 957-0190 — Calendar System: Semester
URL: www.acs350.org
Established: 1953 — Annual Undergrad Tuition & Fees: $5,383
Enrollment: 39 — Female
Affiliation or Control: Roman Catholic — IRS Status: 501(c)3
Highest Offering: Associate Degree
Accreditation: M

01 President/Chief of Development ... Sr. Joseph SPRING, SCC
05 Academic Dean ... Sr. Teresa BRUNO, SC
10 Treasurer/Institutional Advancement ... Mrs. Patricia MCGRADY
32 Chief Student Life Officer ... Sr. Marie Cecelia LANDIS, SCC
06 Registrar ... Mrs. Barbara KELLY-VERGONA

Atlantic Cape Community College (H)

5100 Black Horse Pike, Mays Landing NJ 08330-2699

County: Atlantic — FICE Identification: 002596
Unit ID: 183655
Telephone: (609) 343-4900 — Carnegie Class: Assoc/HT-High Trad
FAX Number: (609) 343-4917 — Calendar System: Semester
URL: www.atlantic.edu
Established: 1964 — Annual Undergrad Tuition & Fees (In-District): $4,266
Enrollment: 6,845 — Coed
Affiliation or Control: State/Local — IRS Status: 501(c)3
Highest Offering: Associate Degree
Accreditation: M, ACFEI, ADNUR

01 President ... Dr. Peter L. MORA
03 Executive Vice President ... Dr. Richard PERNICIARO

15 Dean Human Resources & Compliance ... Ms. Eileen CURRISTINE
11 Dean Administration and Business .... Mr. August DAQUILA
100 Dean Res Dev/Pres & BOT Operations .... Ms. Jean MCALISTER
13 Dean Information Tech Services ....Mr. Douglas HEDGES
05 Vice President Academic Affairs .... Dr. Otto HERNANDEZ
10 Dean Finance ....Ms. Leslie JAMISON
32 Vice President Student Affairs ....Dr. Mitchell LEVY
84 Dean Enrollment Management ....Mr. Andre RICHBURG
08 Assoc Dean Academic Support Svcs .... Ms. Janet MARLER
49 Interim Dean Liberal Studies .... Dr. Denise COULTER
88 Dean Academy of Culinary Arts ....Ms. Kelly MCCLAY
75 Dean Career Education .... Ms. Donna VASSALLO
81 Dean STEM ....Dr. Richard PAGAN
26 Director College Relations ....Ms. Stacey CLAPP
38 Director Student Counseling .... Ms. Paula DAVIS
37 Director Financial Aid ....Ms. Linda DESANTIS
07 Director Admissions ....Ms. Kristin JACKSON
96 Director Business Services .... Ms. Dorie KEENER
102 Sr Director Res Dev/Alumni Outreach .... Ms. Maria KELLETT
09 Director Inst Research Plng/Assess .... Mr. Luis MONTEFUSCO
06 Registrar .... Ms. Heather PETERSON
35 Dir Student Dev & Judicial Officer .... Ms. Nancy PORFIDO
18 Director Facilities Management .... Mr. Russell WAUGH

Bais Medrash Mayan Hatorah (A)

101 Milton Street, Lakewood NJ 08701

County: Ocean — Identification: 667280
Telephone: (732) 367-9900 — Carnegie Class: Not Classified
FAX Number: N/A — Calendar System: Other
Established: — Annual Undergrad Tuition & Fees: N/A
Enrollment: N/A — Male
Affiliation or Control: Independent Non-Profit — IRS Status: 501(c)3
Highest Offering: First Talmudic Degree
Accreditation: AIJS

Bais Medrash Toras Chesed (B)

910 Monmouth Avenue, Lakewood NJ 08701-1921

County: Ocean — FICE Identification: 040813
Unit ID: 449558
Telephone: (732) 364-1220 — Carnegie Class: Spec-4-yr-Faith
FAX Number: (732) 886-2323 — Calendar System: Semester
Established: 1999 — Annual Undergrad Tuition & Fees: $9,100
Enrollment: 111 — Male
Affiliation or Control: Independent Non-Profit — IRS Status: 501(c)3
Highest Offering: Baccalaureate
Accreditation: RABN

01 Dean ....Rabbi N. STEIN
37 Director of Financial Aid ....Mrs. H. WEISS
19 Campus Security Officer ....Rabbi M. GELFAND

Bais Medrash Zicron Meir (C)

1500 Vermont Ave, Lakewood NJ 08701

County: Ocean — Identification: 667259
Telephone: (732) 370-1560 — Carnegie Class: Not Classified
FAX Number: (732) 363-7864 — Calendar System: Semester
Established: 2013 — Annual Undergrad Tuition & Fees: N/A
Enrollment: N/A — Male
Affiliation or Control: Independent Non-Profit — IRS Status: 501(c)3
Highest Offering: First Talmudic Degree
Accreditation: @RABN

01 CEO ....Zev MINTZ
10 CFO ....Nissim BASALA
37 Dir Student Financial Aid/Registrar ....Shimshon AMSEL

Bard High School Early College Newark (D)

321 Bergen Street, Newark NJ 07103

Telephone: (973) 733-8363 — Identification: 770980
Accreditation: &EH

† Regional accreditation is carried under the parent institution in Great Barrington, MA

Bergen Community College (E)

400 Paramus Road, Paramus NJ 07652-1595

County: Bergen — FICE Identification: 004736
Unit ID: 183743
Telephone: (201) 447-7100 — Carnegie Class: Assoc/HT-High Trad
FAX Number: (201) 447-9042 — Calendar System: Semester
URL: www.bergen.edu
Established: 1965 — Annual Undergrad Tuition & Fees (In-District): $4,278
Enrollment: 15,651 — Coed
Affiliation or Control: State/Local — IRS Status: 501(c)3
Highest Offering: Associate Degree
Accreditation: M, ADNUR, COARC, DH, DMS, MAC, RAD, RTT, SURGT

01 President ....Dr. B. Kaye WALTER
05 Vice President of Academic Affairs ....Dr. William MULLANEY
32 Vice President Student Services .... Dr. Naydeen GONZALEZ-DE JESUS
09 Vice Pres of Inst Effectiveness ....Dr. Yun KIM
50 Int Dean Business/Arts & Social Sc ....Dr. Laura OCHOA
79 Dean Humanities/English & Language ....Vacant
76 Dean Health Professions ....Dr. Susan BARNARD
81 Dean Science/Math & Technology ....Dr. Pascal J. RICATTO
51 Dean of Continuing Education ....Ms. Christine GILLESPIE
08 Dean Library Services ....Vacant
35 Dean of Student Affairs at Ciarco .Ms. Denise JERMAN LIGUORI
35 Dean of Student Support Services ....Ms. Jennifer REYES
15 Executive Director Human Resources ....Mr. James MILLER
18 Actg Mnging Director Physical Plant ....Mr. Samuel JOHN
19 VP Facil Opers/Plng & Pub Safety ....Mr. William CORCORAN
13 Executive Dir of Info Technology ....Mr. Stephen VALKENBURG
06 Mnging Dir Registration & Records ....Ms. Jacqueline OTTEY
88 Director of Community/Cultural Affs .... Mr. Peter LEDONNE
101 Exec Asst Board of Trustees/Pre ....Ms. Maria FERRARA
29 Managing Director of Alumni Affairs ....Vacant
37 Mnging Dir Fin Ops/Stdnt Assistance .... Ms. Caroline OFODILE
102 Exec Dir Foundation/Development ....Ms. Lindsay MAURER
25 Dir Grants Admin/Inst Effectiveness ....Dr William YAKOWICZ
96 Director of Purchasing & Services .... Ms. Barbara HAMILTON-GOLDEN
26 Managing Dir of Public Relations .... Mr. Lawrence HLAVENKA
04 Exec Assistant to the President .... Dr. Ursula DANIELS

Berkeley College (F)

44 Rifle Camp Road, Woodland Park NJ 07424-3367

County: Passaic — FICE Identification: 007502
Unit ID: 183789
Telephone: (973) 278-5400 — Carnegie Class: Spec-4-yr-Bus
FAX Number: (973) 278-0282 — Calendar System: Semester
URL: www.berkeleycollege.edu
Established: 1931 — Annual Undergrad Tuition & Fees: $24,300
Enrollment: 3,659 — Coed
Affiliation or Control: Proprietary — IRS Status: Proprietary
Highest Offering: Master's
Accreditation: M, MAC, SURGT

00 Chairman of the Board ....Mr. Kevin L. LUING
01 President ....Mr. Michael J. SMITH
04 Special Assistant to the President ....Dr. Rose Mary HEALY
05 Provost ....Dr. Beth CASTIGLIA
84 SVP Enrollment Management ....Ms. Diane RECINOS
10 Vice Pres Finance & Administration ....Mr. Dino KASAMIS
45 VP Planning & Chief of Staff ....Vacant
43 VP & Chief Compliance Officer ....Mr. William BRANDT
26 Chief Marketing Officer ....Mr. William DIMASI
13 Chief Information Officer ....Mr. Leonard DE BOTTON
86 SVP Government Relations NJ ....Ms. Teri DUDA
86 VP Government Relations NY ....Mr. Gbubemi OKOTIEURO
88 VP Academic Advisement ....Ms. Liz BARRETT
08 VP Library Services ....Ms. Marlene DOTY
32 VP Student Development/Campus Life ....Dr. Dallas REED
36 VP Career Services ....Mr. Brian MAHER
37 VP Financial Aid ....Mr. Howard LESLIE
21 VP Budget & Student Accounts .... Ms. Eileen LOFTUS-BERLIN
85 VP International Division .... Ms. Cynthia C. MARCHESE
18 VP Operations ....Mr. Mark WAGENER
50 Dean School of Business ....Dr. Beth CASTIGLIA
76 Interim Dean School Health Studies ... Ms. Elizabeth FITZGERALD
49 Dean School of Liberal Arts ....Dr. Don KIEFFER
107 Dean School of Professional Studies ....Ms. Lenore MOLEE
20 Associate Provost Academic Affairs ....Dr. Judith KORNBERG
06 Associate Provost & Registrar ....Ms. Gail OKUN
106 Assistant Provost Online ....Ms. Carol SMITH
88 Dean Academic Support ....Dr. Gerald IACULLO
108 AVP Institutional Effectiveness ....Dr. Rachel FESTER
31 AVP Communications & Ext Relations .... Ms. Angela HARRINGTON
19 AVP Public Safety ....Mr. William ORTMAN
27 Director Media Relations ....Ms. Ilene GREENFIELD
41 Director Athletics ....Mr. Andrew DESTEPHANO
29 Director Alumni Relations ....Ms. Jennifer PORTER
09 Director of Institutional Research ....Ms. Rebecca J. DRENNEN

Beth Medrash Govoha (G)

617 Sixth Street, Lakewood NJ 08701-2797

County: Ocean — FICE Identification: 007947
Unit ID: 183804
Telephone: (732) 367-1060 — Carnegie Class: Spec-4-yr-Faith
FAX Number: (732) 367-7487 — Calendar System: Semester
URL: www.bmg.edu
Established: 1943 — Annual Undergrad Tuition & Fees: N/A
Enrollment: 6,721 — Male
Affiliation or Control: Independent Non-Profit — IRS Status: 501(c)3
Highest Offering: Beyond Master's But Less Than Doctorate
Accreditation: RABN

01 President/Chief Executive Officer ....Rabbi Aaron KOTLER
05 Chairman Academic Council ....Rabbi A. Malkiel KOTLER
10 VP Finance/Technology Compliance ....Mr. Isaac LEVINE
43 VP Finance/Corporate/Legal Affairs ....Rabbi Eli KUPERMAN
11 Vice President Admin/Campus Life ....Rabbi Yitzchok S. KOTLER
33 Dean of Students ....Rabbi Mattisyahu SALOMON
58 Dean of Graduate Studies ....Rabbi Yisroel NEUMAN
30 Vice President of Fundraising ......Rabbi Mordechai HERSKOWITZ
88 Senior Executive Director ....Rabbi Yaakov APPLEGRAD
86 Director Government Affairs ....Mrs. Chanie JACOBOWITZ
06 Registrar ....Rabbi Jacob BURSZTYN
07 Director of Admissions ....Rabbi Avraham FEUER
08 Director Library/Research Programs ....Rabbi Benjamin SPIEGEL
36 Director of Field Services ....Rabbi Jacob SHULMAN
39 Director of Residence Halls ....Rabbi Avrohom COLMAN

Bloomfield College (H)

467 Franklin Street, Bloomfield NJ 07003-3425

County: Essex — FICE Identification: 002597
Unit ID: 183822
Telephone: (973) 748-9000 — Carnegie Class: Bac-A&S
FAX Number: (973) 743-3998 — Calendar System: Semester
URL: www.bloomfield.edu
Established: 1868 — Annual Undergrad Tuition & Fees: $27,800
Enrollment: 2,004 — Coed
Affiliation or Control: Presbyterian Church (U.S.A.) — IRS Status: 501(c)3
Highest Offering: Master's
Accreditation: M, NURSE TEAC

01 President ....Richard A. LEVAO
10 Vice Pres of Finance/Admin ....Howard BUXBAUM
04 Administrative Asst to President ....Christina NOLAN
05 Vice President Academic Affairs ....Tresmaine GRIMES
07 VP Enrollment Management/Admission ....Adam CASTRO
32 VP Student Affairs/Dean of Students ....Patrick J. LAMY
30 VP for Advancement ....Jacqueline BARTLEY
88 VP Inst Intl Training/Prof Studies ....Peter JEONG
21 AVP for Finance and Administration .... William A. MCDONALD
06 Registrar and Director of Advising ....Annette RAYMOND
09 Director Instl Research/Assessment ....Eugene W. MULLER
20 Associate Dean for Faculty ....Carolyn I. SPIES
79 Chair Div of Humanities ....Angela CONRAD
83 Chair Div Social/Behavioral Science ....Daniel SKINNER
66 Chair Div of Nursing ....Neddie SERRA
81 Chair Div of Natural Science/Math ....Jim MURPHY
57 Chair Div Creative Arts Technology ....Yuichiro NISHIZAWA
50 Chair Div Accounting/Business/CIS ....Robert COLLMIER
53 Chair Div of Education ....Amy EGUCHI
88 Assoc Dean Inst Educ Support Svcs ....Leonard ROBERTS
08 Library Director ....Danilo H. FIGUEREDO
13 Director of Information Services ....Erzsebet FELSOVALYI
36 Director of Career Services ....Rachel M. JACKIEWICZ
37 Director of Financial Aid ....Breanne SIMKIN
35 Associate Dean Student Development ....Rose MITCHELL
15 Assoc Director Human Resources ....Susan DACEY
18 Supervisor of Buildings & Grounds ....Jack V. MCGRANE
07 Coord Intl Admissions/Student Svcs ....Jamilah MOUDIAB
44 Dir Annual Fund/Alumni Innovation ....Vacant
38 Director Personal Counseling ....Nicole PALAGANO
26 Director Public Rels/Advancemnt Mkt ....Alicia COOK
42 Int Dir Spirtual Life/Col Chaplain ....Rev. Terri OFORI
88 Director Teacher Education ....Mary PORCELLI
41 Director of Athletics ....Sheila WOOTEN
88 Director Center Academic Develop ....Heather SHPIRO
19 Director of Security ....Jack CORTEZ
39 Director Res Educ & Housing ....Nicole FAISON
105 Webmaster ....Miguel RODRIGUEZ
24 Director of Media Center ....Barbara ISACSON
88 Director Institutional Technology ....Yifeng BAI
40 Store Manager ....Elizabeth MCLEOD

Brookdale Community College (I)

Newman Springs Road, Lincroft NJ 07738-1597

County: Monmouth — FICE Identification: 008404
Unit ID: 183859
Telephone: (732) 842-1900 — Carnegie Class: Assoc/HT-Mix Trad/Non
FAX Number: (732) 224-2242 — Calendar System: Other
URL: www.brookdalecc.edu
Established: 1967 — Annual Undergrad Tuition & Fees (In-District): $3,653
Enrollment: 14,144 — Coed
Affiliation or Control: State/Local — IRS Status: 501(c)3
Highest Offering: Associate Degree
Accreditation: M, ACFEI, ADNUR, CAHIIM, COARC, MLTAD, #RAD

01 President ....Dr. Maureen MURPHY
03 Executive Vice President ....Dr. Matthew REED
10 Vice Pres Finance/Operations ....Ms. Maureen LAWRENCE
46 Vice Pres Plng/Dev/Govt & Comm Rels ....Vacant
84 Dean Enrollment Dev/Student Affairs ....Dr. David STOUT
15 Dean Human Resources ....Ms. Patricia SENSI
08 Executive Director Library ....Dr. William BURNS
45 Dean Plng & Institutional Effective ....Dr. Nancy KEGELMAN
27 Dir Communications & Public Rels ....Ms. Avis MCMILLON
102 Exec Dir Foundation/Alumni Affs ....Mr. Timothy ZEISS
32 Dir Student Affairs/Support Svcs ....Dr. David STOUT
37 Director of Financial Aid ....Ms. Stephanie FITZSIMMONS
25 Director Grants & Institutional Dev .....Ms. Laura V. QAISSAUNEE
38 Director Student Services ....Dr. Stephen A. CURTO
06 Registrar ....Ms. Kimberly HEUSER
09 Dir of Institutional Research/Evalu ....Dr. Laura LONGO
26 Dir of Marketing/Creative Services ....Ms. Laurie BENDER
28 Mgr Diversity/Inclusion/Compliance ....Ms. Sondra CANNON
101 Secretary of the Institution/Board ....Ms. Cynthia GRUSKOS
103 Dir Workforce/Career Development ....Mr. Dominic LATORRACA
104 Director Study Abroad ....Ms. Janice THOMAS
13 Chief Info Technology Officer (CIO) ....Ms. Camille SHELLEY
19 Director Security/Safety ....Mr. Robert KIMLER
41 Athletic Director ....Mr. Shawn NOEL
50 Dean Business & Social Science ....Ms. Patricia GALLO
81 Dean of STEM ....Dr. Anoop AHLUWALIA

Brookdale Community College Western Monmouth Branch Campus (J)

3680 US Highway 9 South, Freehold NJ 07728

Telephone: (732) 780-0020 — Identification: 770125
Accreditation: &M

† Regional accreditation is carried under the parent institution in Lincroft, NJ

Caldwell University (A)

120 Bloomfield Avenue, Caldwell NJ 07006-5310
County: Essex FICE Identification: 002598
Unit ID: 183910
Telephone: (973) 618-3000 Carnegie Class: Masters/M
FAX Number: (973) 618-3300 Calendar System: Semester
URL: www.caldwell.edu
Established: 1939 Annual Undergrad Tuition & Fees: $31,200
Enrollment: 2,184 Coed
Affiliation or Control: Roman Catholic IRS Status: 501(c)3
Highest Offering: Doctorate
Accreditation: M, ACBSP, CACREP, NURSE, TEAC

01 President .... Dr. Nancy BLATTNER
05 Vice President for Academic Affairs .... Dr. Barbara CHESLER
10 Vice President for Finance & Admin .... Mr. Jack T. RAINEY
15 VP Institutional Effectiveness .... Mrs. Sheila N. O'ROURKE
32 Vice President for Student Affairs .... Sr. Kathleen TUITE
84 Vice President for Enrollment/Comm .... Mr. Joseph J. POSILLICO
30 Vice Pres Development/Alumni Affs .... Mr. Kevin BOYLE
50 Associate Dean Business Division .... Dr. Bernard C. O'ROURKE
53 Associate Dean Education Division .... Dr. Joan MORIARTY
35 Director International Student Svcs .... Mr. Maulin JOSHI
44 Director Development .... Ms. Beth GORAB
29 Director of Gift Planning .... Ms. Kathleen BUSE
06 Registrar & Director Inst Research .... Mr. Ian K. WHITE
08 Executive Director of Library .... Dr. Nancy BECKER
07 Asst Vice President Enrollment .... Mr. Stephen QUINN
58 Director Graduate Studies .... Dr. Ellina CHERNOBILSKY
88 Assoc Dean External Partnerships .... Vacant
38 Director of Counseling .... Ms. Robin DAVENPORT
39 Director Residence LIfe .... Ms. Crystal LOPEZ
13 Exec Director Information Techn .... Mr. Donald O'HAGAN
36 Dir Career Plng & Development .... Ms. Geraldine PERRET
37 Director Financial Aid .... Ms. Eileen FELSKE
42 Chaplain .... Fr. Thomas F. BLIND
41 Executive Director of Athletics .... Mr. Mark A. CORINO
88 Director Technical Support Services .... Vacant
26 Dir Media Relations and Advertising .... Ms. Colette LIDDY
19 Director Campus Safety .... Mr. Glenn GATES
91 Director Administrative Technology .... Mr. David BOHNY
16 Director of Human Resources .... Mrs. Michelle STAUSS
35 Director Student Engagement .... Mr. Timothy KESSLER-CLEARY
20 Associate Academic Officer .... Vacant
106 Dir Online Education/E-learning .... Ms. Soheila KOBLER
108 Director Assessment .... Mrs. Susan HAYES

Camden County College (B)

PO Box 200, Blackwood NJ 08012-0200
County: Camden FICE Identification: 006865
Unit ID: 183938
Telephone: (856) 227-7200 Carnegie Class: Assoc/HT-Mix Trad/Non
FAX Number: (856) 374-4894 Calendar System: Semester
URL: www.camdencc.edu
Established: 1967 Annual Undergrad Tuition & Fees (In-District): $4,320
Enrollment: 12,051 Coed
Affiliation or Control: State/Local IRS Status: 501(c)3
Highest Offering: Associate Degree
Accreditation: M, CAHIIM, DA, DH, DIETT, OPD

01 President .... Mr. Donald BORDEN
05 Vice Pres Academic Affairs .... Dr. Margaret HAMILTON
84 Exec Dean Enrollment/Student Svcs .... Dr. James CANONICA
10 Exec Dir Finance & Planning .... Ms. Helen ANTONAKAKIS
11 Exec Dir Financial Admin Svcs .... Mr. Maris KUKAINIS
15 Executive Director Human Resources .... Ms. Rose COSTON-MCHUGH
06 Dir Student System Records .... Ms. Bunny KOHL
08 Asst Director Library Services .... Ms. Isabel GRAY
37 Director of Financial Aid .... Ms. Felicia BRYANT
88 Director of Testing .... Mr. Daniel MCMASTERS
09 Ex Dir Institutional Effectiveness .... Dr. Vanessa O'BRIEN-MCMASTERS
09 Dean Inst Research/Plng/ Grants .... Dr. Rebecca FIDLER-SHEPPARD
07 Dir Admissions/Registration Svcs .... Mr. Steve D'AMBROSIO
12 Exec Dean William G Rohrer Center ... Dr. Robert KACZOROWSKI
81 Dean Arts/Humanities/Soc Science .... Dr. Judith ROWLANDS
66 Int Dean Math/Science/Health Career .... Dr. William LOVELL
50 Dean Div Business/Comptr/Tech Stds .... Dr. Robert KACZOROWSKI
51 Dean School & Comm Academic Pgm .... Ms. Margo VENABLE
12 Exec Dean Camden City Campus .... Mr. Gary DIVENS
41 Athletic Director .... Mr. William BANKS
13 Chief Info Technology Officer (CIO) .... Vacant
19 Director Public Safety .... Mr. Stephen HETHERINGTON
29 External Resources Develop Assoc .... Ms. Melissa DALY
43 Dir Legal Services/General Counsel .... Mr. Karl MCCONNELL

Camden County College Camden City Campus (C)

200 N Broadway, Camden NJ 08102-1185
Telephone: (856) 338-1817 Identification: 770126
Accreditation: &M

† Regional accreditation is carried under the parent institution in Blackwood, NJ

Centenary College (D)

400 Jefferson Street, Hackettstown NJ 07840-2100
County: Warren FICE Identification: 002599
Unit ID: 183974
Telephone: (908) 852-1400 Carnegie Class: Masters/M
FAX Number: (908) 850-9508 Calendar System: Semester
URL: www.centenarycollege.edu
Established: 1867 Annual Undergrad Tuition & Fees: $31,754
Enrollment: 2,318 Coed
Affiliation or Control: Independent Non-Profit IRS Status: 501(c)3
Highest Offering: Doctorate
Accreditation: M, IACBE, SW, TEAC

01 President .... Dr. David HANEY
05 Provost & Chief Academic Officer .... Dr. James PATTERSON
10 Chief Operating Officer .... Mr. Roger ANDERSON
26 VP for College Relations .... Mr. John CARNO
84 VP of Enrollment Management .... Dr. Robert L. MILLER, JR.
18 Director of Facilities .... Mr. Len TEMPEST
31 Dean Community & College Affairs .... Ms. Nancy PAFFENDORF
09 Dean of Inst Research/Assessment .... Dr. Jeremy A. HOUSKA
35 Sr Dir Student Engagement .... Ms. Tiffany KUSHNER
32 Dean of Students .... Ms. Kerry MULLINS
06 Registrar/Academic Dean .... Dr. Thomas BRUNNER
08 Director Taylor Memorial Library .... Mr. Timothy DOMICK
36 Director Career Development Center .... Mr. Joshua D. WALKER
15 Chief Human Resources Officer .... Ms. Virginia GALDIERI
41 Director of Athletics .... Mr. Keith O'CONNOR
19 Assistant Dean for Campus Safety .... Mr. Leonard KUNZ
38 Director of Counseling Center .... Ms. Lorna FARMER
29 Exec Dir of Alumni Engagement .... Ms. Deana CYNAR
13 Chief Information Officer .... Mr. Terry T. BAZYLEWICZ
40 Manager of the Bookstore .... Vacant

Chamberlain College of Nursing-North Brunswick (E)

630 US Highway One, North Brunswick NJ 08902
Telephone: (732) 875-1300 Identification: 770850
Accreditation: &NH, NURSE

† Regional accreditation is carried under the parent institution in Addison, IL

The College of New Jersey (F)

2000 Pennington Road, Ewing NJ 08628-1104
County: Mercer FICE Identification: 002642
Unit ID: 187134
Telephone: (609) 771-1855 Carnegie Class: Masters/L
FAX Number: (609) 637-5191 Calendar System: Semester
URL: www.tcnj.edu
Established: 1855 Annual Undergrad Tuition & Fees (In-State): $15,466
Enrollment: 7,409 Coed
Affiliation or Control: State IRS Status: 501(c)3
Highest Offering: Master's
Accreditation: M, ART, BUS, CACREP, CS, ENG, MUS, NURSE, TED

01 President .... Dr. R. Barbara GITENSTEIN
05 Provost/VP Academic Affairs .... Dr. Jacqueline TAYLOR
11 Vice Pres for Administration .... Mr. Curt HEURING
10 Treasurer .... Mr. Lloyd RICKETTS
43 General Counsel .... Mr. Thomas MAHONEY
30 Vice Pres Advancement .... Mr. John DONOHUE
32 Vice President Student Affairs .... Dr. Amy HECHT
15 Vice Pres Human Resources .... Dr. Gregory POGUE
84 Vice Pres Enrollment Management .... Ms. Lisa ANGELONI
13 CIO & VP for Info Technology .... Dr. Sharon BLANTON
100 Chief of Staff/Secy to Board .... Ms. Heather FEHN
18 Assoc VP Facilities & Admin Svcs .... Ms. Kathryn LEVERTON
44 Assoc Vice President of Development .... Mr. Charles WRIGHT
35 Asst VP for Student Affairs/Engage .... Ms. Elizabeth BAPASOLA
35 Asst Vice Pres Student Affairs .... Ms. Angela CHONG
26 Assoc VP for College Relations .... Ms. Stacy SCHUSTER
20 Vice Provost .... Dr. Ieva ZAKE
57 Dean School of The Arts & Comm .... Dr. John LAUGHTON
50 Dean School of Business .... Dr. William KEEP
79 Dean Sch Humanities/Soc Sci .... Dr. Jane WONG
53 Dean School of Education .... Dr. Jeffrey PASSE
54 Dean School of Engineering .... Dr. Steven SCHREINER
66 Dean Nursing/Health/Exercise Scienc .... Dr. Carole KENNER
81 Dean School of Science .... Dr. Jeffrey OSBORN
58 Dir Grad & Intersession Programs .... Dr. Susan HYDRO
37 Exec Dir of Student Fin Assistance .... Mr. Wil CASAINE
09 Asst Provost Ctr for Inst Effective .... Dr. Mosen AURYAN
41 Director of Athletics .... Vacant
29 Director Alumni Affairs .... Mr. John CASTALDO
102 Assoc VP Comm/Mktg/Brand Mgmt .... Mr. David MUHA
18 Director of Campus Construction .... Mr. William RUDEAU
23 Assoc Director for Health Services .... Ms. Janice VERMEYCHUK
06 Exec Director Records/Registration .... Mr. Frank COOPER
19 Chief of Police/Dir Campus Police .... Chief John COLLINS
21 Exec Dir Procurement Services .... Mr. Anup KAPUR
28 Assoc VP/Chief Diversity Officer .... Ms. Kerry TILLETT
07 Director of Admissions .... Ms. Grecia MONTERO
36 Director Career Center .... Ms. Debra KELLY
38 Director of Counseling & Psych Svcs .... Dr. Mark FOREST
96 Asst Director of Purchasing .... Ms. Kristine D'APOLITO

College of Saint Elizabeth (G)

2 Convent Road, Morristown NJ 07960-6989
County: Morris FICE Identification: 002600
Unit ID: 186618
Telephone: (973) 290-4000 Carnegie Class: Masters/M
FAX Number: (973) 290-4488 Calendar System: Semester
URL: www.cse.edu
Established: 1899 Annual Undergrad Tuition & Fees: $31,688
Enrollment: 1,411 Coed
Affiliation or Control: Roman Catholic IRS Status: 501(c)3
Highest Offering: Doctorate
Accreditation: M, DIETD, DIETI, NUR, TEAC

01 President .... Dr. Helen J. STREUBERT
05 VP for Academic Affairs .... Dr. Monique GUILLORY
32 VP Student Life .... Ms. Katherine BUCK
10 VP Finance Admin/Treasurer .... Mr. Michael FESCOE
30 Vice Pres Institutional Advancement .... Ms. Sally CLEARY
84 VP Enrollment Management .... Mr. Alexander SCOTT
21 Controller .... Mr. Greg TONDI
06 Registrar .... Ms. Marybeth OBRYCKI
09 Director Institutional Research .... Dr. Louise MURRAY
08 Director of Library .... Ms. Amira UNVER
42 Campus Minister .... Ms. Abigail CIMORELLI
18 Director of Facilities & Security .... Mr. James GERRISH
37 Director of Financial Aid .... Ms. Jacqueline WEISKOPFF
26 Director Marketing/Communications .... Ms. Maryann MATLOCK
22 Director EOF Program .... Mr. Clifford WOODWARD
36 Dir Experiential Lrng & Career Svcs .... Ms. Teri CORSO
38 Director of Counseling .... Ms. Zsuzsanna NAGY
88 Dir Volunteerism & Svc Learning .... Vacant
35 Director of Student Engagement .... Ms. Naima K. RICKS
41 Director of Athletics .... Ms. Juliene SIMPSON
44 Director of Annual Fund .... Ms. Tanya SORCE
24 Director Media Services .... Mr. Ronald LONEKER
29 Exec Director Alumni Relations .... Ms. Debbie MARTIN
15 Director Human Resources .... Ms. Rochelle DICKERSON
85 Director Intl/Multicultural Affairs .... Ms. Lenee WOODSON
40 College Store Manager .... Vacant
102 Dir Corp Foundation/Corp Relations .... Ms. Janice HILL
105 Webmaster .... Mr. David B. RABINOWITZ
108 Asst Dean of Assessment .... Ms. Michele YURECKO
04 Administrative Asst to President .... Ms. MaryAnn RICCIOTTI
13 Chief Info Technology Officer .... Ms. Margie ROHR
28 Director of Diversity .... Ms. Lenee WOODSON
107 Dean of Professional Studies .... Dr. Patricia HEINDEL
49 Dean of Arts and Sciences .... Dr. Anthony SANTAMARIA
104 Coord Acad Internships & StudyAway .... Ms. Lindsey ROMES
19 Director Security/Safety .... Mr. Richard WALL
39 Director Residence Life .... Ms. Trisha D. FUENTES
90 Director Academic Computing .... Ms. Sook May ONG
91 Director Administrative Computing .... Ms. Angela IANNELLI

County College of Morris (H)

214 Center Grove Road, Randolph NJ 07869-2086
County: Morris FICE Identification: 007729
Unit ID: 184180
Telephone: (973) 328-5000 Carnegie Class: Assoc/HT-High Trad
FAX Number: (973) 328-1282 Calendar System: Semester
URL: www.ccm.edu
Established: 1965 Annual Undergrad Tuition & Fees (In-District): $4,570
Enrollment: 8,096 Coed
Affiliation or Control: State/Local IRS Status: 501(c)3
Highest Offering: Associate Degree
Accreditation: M, ACBSP, ADNUR, COARC, ENGT, RAD

01 President .... Dr. Anthony J. IACONO
05 Vice President of Academic Affairs .... Dr. Dwight L. SMITH
10 Vice President of Business/Finance .... Ms. Karen VANDERHOOF
32 VP of Student Development .... Dr. Bette M. SIMMONS
30 Exec Dir Col Advancement/Planning .... Mr. Joseph VITALE
15 Dir Human Resources & Labor Rels .... Mr. Thomas BURK
09 Director Inst Research & Planning .... Ms. Phebe LACAY
21 Director Budget & Business Services .... Mr. John YOUNG
25 Director Resource Development .... Dr. Kevin KEEFE
07 Admissions Officer .... Mr. Eugene SOLTYS
37 Director Financial Aid .... Mr. Harvey WILLIS
06 Registrar .... Ms. Laura Lee BOWENS
26 Chief Public Relations Officer .... Ms. Kathleen BRUNET EAGAN
29 Director Alumni Office .... Ms. Barbara CAPSOURAS
13 Director Information Systems .... Mr. Roger FLAHIVE
08 Director of Library Services .... Ms. Heather CRAVEN
36 Director Career Svcs/Coop Education .... Ms. Denise SCHMIDT
38 Counseling Services Coordinator .... Ms. Janique CAFFIE
79 Dean Liberal Arts .... Dr. Bruce DUTRA
76 Dean Health/Natural Sciences .... Ms. Monica MARASKA
81 Dean Business/Math/Engr/Technology .... Mr. Patrick ENRIGHT
19 Director Security & Safety .... Mr. Harvey JACKSON
41 Director Athletics .... Mr. Jack SULLIVAN
23 Health Services Coordinator .... Ms. Elizabeth HOBAN
18 Director of Plant & Maintenance .... Mr. Joseph PONTURO
96 Director of Purchasing .... Ms. Joanne KEARNS
40 Bookstore Manager .... Mr. Jeff LUBNOW

Cumberland County College (I)

3322 College Drive, PO Box 1500,
Vineland NJ 08362-1500
County: Cumberland FICE Identification: 002601
Unit ID: 184205
Telephone: (856) 691-8600 Carnegie Class: Assoc/HT-High Trad
FAX Number: (856) 690-0812 Calendar System: Semester

URL: www.cccnj.edu
Established: 1963 Annual Undergrad Tuition & Fees (In-District): $4,290
Enrollment: 3,844 Coed
Affiliation or Control: State/Local IRS Status: 501(c)3
Highest Offering: Associate Degree
Accreditation: M, ADNUR, RAD

01 President ... Dr. Yves SALOMON-FERNANDEZ
05 VP Academic Affairs/Student Svcs ... Dr. Jacqueline GALBIATI
10 Executive Director Finance/Budget ... Ms. Sherri L. WELCH
30 Exec Dir Grant Develop/Trustee Rels ... Ms. Anne M. BERGAMO
07 Executive Director Enrollment Svcs ... Ms. Anne M. DALY EIMER
08 Director Library Services ... Ms. Patti A. SCHMID
20 Exec Dir Ctr Acad & Student Success ... Ms. Kellie W. SLADE
26 Director Communications & Marketing ... Mr. Keith WASSERMAN
29 Exec Dir Foundation & Alumni ... Ms. Sue A. PERRY
37 Director Student Financial Aid ... Mr. Maurice THOMAS
50 Dean Business/Educ/Soc Sci ... Dr. Lynn LICHTENBERGER
103 Exec Dir Workforce & Cmty Educ ... Ms. Wendy ARDAGNA
81 Dean STEM ... Vacant
57 Dean Arts & Humanities ... Mr. James PICCONE
100 Assistant to the President ... Ms. Anne M. BERGAMO
15 Executive Director Human Resources ... Ms. Rosemarie FISCUS
72 Executive Director IT Services ... Mr. Bernie CASTRO
18 Director Facilities & Grounds ... Mr. Brian EWAN
96 Purchasing Agent ... Ms. Melissa FALANCE
09 Director IR/Planning ... Ms. Dorothy ABRUZZO-KLUMPP
108 Director Assessment ... Vacant
19 Director Security/Safety ... Mr. Philip CECOLA
41 Athletic Director ... Mr. Keith GORMAN
04 Administrative Asst to President ... Ms. Jennifer L. SWEENEY
32 Director Student Life & Athletics ... Mr. Keith GORMAN

DeVry University - North Brunswick Campus (A)

630 US Highway One, North Brunswick NJ 08902-3362
Telephone: (732) 729-3960 FICE Identification: 009228
Accreditation: &NH, CAHIIM, ENGT, NDT

† Regional accreditation is carried under the parent institution in Downers Grove, IL.

Drew University (B)

36 Madison Avenue, Madison NJ 07940-1493
County: Morris FICE Identification: 002603
Unit ID: 184348
Telephone: (973) 408-3000 Carnegie Class: DU-Mod
FAX Number: N/A Calendar System: 4/1/4
URL: www.drew.edu
Established: 1866 Annual Undergrad Tuition & Fees: $46,684
Enrollment: 2,113 Coed
Affiliation or Control: Independent Non-Profit IRS Status: 501(c)3
Highest Offering: Doctorate
Accreditation: M, TEAC, THEOL

01 President ... Dr. MaryAnn BAENNINGER
05 Chief Academic Officer ... Dr. Christopher TAYLOR
30 Vice Pres Advanc/Alumni Affairs ... Dr. Kenneth ALEXO
10 Vice Pres Finance/Business Affairs ... Mr. John VITALI
49 Dean of College of Liberal Arts ... Dr. Christopher TAYLOR
73 Dean Theological School ... Dr. Javier VIERA
08 Associate Dean of Libraries ... Dr. Chris ANDERSON
32 Vice President Student Life ... Dr. Sara WALDRON
26 VP Communications & Marketing ... Ms. Kira POPLOWSKI
15 Director of Human Resources ... Vacant
22 Title IX Coordinator ... Ms. Emily RALPH
90 Dir Instructional Technology Svcs ... Dr. Gamin BARTLE
21 Controller ... Ms. Renee LISCHIN
96 Director Purchasing ... Mr. Mark MEHLER
18 Director Facilities Operations ... Mr. Michael KOPAS
37 Director Finan Assistance ... Ms. Colby MCCARTHY
19 Director Public Safety ... Mr. William ORTMAN
23 Director Health Services ... Ms. Joyce MAGLIONE
35 Director Student Activities ... Ms. Michelle BRISSON
38 Director Counseling Services ... Dr. Jim MANDALA
07 Director Theological Admissions ... Mr. Kevin D. MILLER
07 Director Graduate Admissions ... Ms. Corinn MCBRIDE
09 Dir Institutional Research ... Mr. Alex MCCLUNG
84 Director Enrollment Management ... Mr. Robert MASSA
41 Director Athletics ... Mr. Jason FEIN
06 Registrar ... Mr. Daniel OSTIN
40 Manager Bookstore ... Ms. Liz GALLO
04 Administrative Asst to President ... Ms. Kathleen SUTHERLAND
100 Chief of Staff ... Ms. Marti WINER
104 Director Study Abroad ... Ms. Stacy FISCHER
105 Webmaster ... Mr. Justin JACKSON
13 Chief Info Technology Officer (CIO) ... Mr. E. Axel LARSSON
25 Chief Contracts/Grants Admin ... Ms. Linda DETITTA
29 Director Alumni Relations ... Mr. John HOLDEN
36 Director Student Placement ... Ms. Suzanne CERAVOLO
43 Dir Legal Services/General Counsel ... Mr. William BROWN

Eastern International College (C)

684 Newark Avenue, Jersey City NJ 07306
County: Hudson FICE Identification: 031226
Unit ID: 421878
Telephone: (201) 216-9901 Carnegie Class: Spec-4-yr-Other Health
FAX Number: (201) 533-1027 Calendar System: Semester
URL: www.eicollege.edu
Established: 1990 Annual Undergrad Tuition & Fees: $21,225
Enrollment: 217 Coed
Affiliation or Control: Proprietary IRS Status: Proprietary
Highest Offering: Baccalaureate
Accreditation: ACCSC, CVT, DH

01 President ... Mr. Bashir MOHSEN
05 Vice President of Academic Affairs ... Dr. Mustafa MUSTAFA
06 Registrar ... Mrs. Soha ELSHICK
10 Chief Business Officer ... Ms. Agnieszka DRUPKA
36 Corporate Director of Career Svcs ... Ms. Jennifer BATE
37 Director Student Financial Aid ... Ms. Kinga GIZYNSKA
53 Dean of Education ... Mrs. Kimberly MCDONALD
04 Administrative Asst to President ... Ms. Soha ELSHICK
07 Director of Admissions ... Ms. Ruth ZAYAS
13 Chief Info Technology Officer (CIO) ... Mr. Marc JEAN
32 Student Life Coordinator/Counselor ... Ms. Donna NUCERA

Eastern International College- Belleville Campus (D)

251 Washington Avenue, Belleville NJ 07109
Telephone: (973) 751-9051 Identification: 770580
Accreditation: ACCSC

Eastwick College (E)

250 Moore Street, Hackensack NJ 07601
County: Bergen Identification: 667131
Unit ID: 183488
Telephone: (201) 488-9400 Carnegie Class: Spec 2-yr-Health
FAX Number: (201) 488-1007 Calendar System: Quarter
URL: www.eastwick.edu
Established: 1985 Annual Undergrad Tuition & Fees: $15,609
Enrollment: 375 Coed
Affiliation or Control: Proprietary IRS Status: Proprietary
Highest Offering: Associate Degree
Accreditation: ACICS, FUSER

01 President ... Thomas M. EASTWICK

Eastwick College (F)

103 Park Avenue, Nutley NJ 07110
County: Essex FICE Identification: 020923
Unit ID: 185721
Telephone: (973) 661-0600 Carnegie Class: Not Classified
FAX Number: (973) 661-2954 Calendar System: Quarter
URL: www.eastwick.edu
Established: 2014 Annual Undergrad Tuition & Fees: $15,189
Enrollment: 321 Coed
Affiliation or Control: Proprietary IRS Status: Proprietary
Highest Offering: Associate Degree
Accreditation: ACICS

01 President ... Thomas EASTWICK
11 Vice Pres of Operations ... Bhavna TAILOR
05 Dean of Academics ... Sameh FARAGALLA

Eastwick College (G)

10 South Franklin Turnpike, Ramsey NJ 07446
County: Bergen FICE Identification: 020537
Unit ID: 184959
Telephone: (201) 327-8877 Carnegie Class: Spec 2-yr-Health
FAX Number: (201) 327-9054 Calendar System: Other
URL: www.eastwick.edu
Established: 1968 Annual Undergrad Tuition & Fees: $16,793
Enrollment: 865 Coed
Affiliation or Control: Proprietary IRS Status: Proprietary
Highest Offering: Associate Degree
Accreditation: ACICS, CVT, #OTA, SURGT

01 Corporate Systems Administrator ... Mike MARQUES
03 Executive Vice President ... Rafael CASTILLA
05 Vice President Academic Affairs ... Joyce TRAINA
07 Vice President Admissions ... Vacant
32 Dean of Students ... Bobby DAVIES
37 Director of Financial Aid ... Christy DELAGUERRA

Essex County College (H)

303 University Avenue, Newark NJ 07102-1798
County: Essex FICE Identification: 007107
Unit ID: 184481
Telephone: (973) 877-3000 Carnegie Class: Assoc/HT-High Trad
FAX Number: (973) 877-3044 Calendar System: Other
URL: www.essex.edu
Established: 1966 Annual Undergrad Tuition & Fees (In-District): $4,213
Enrollment: 11,468 Coed
Affiliation or Control: State/Local IRS Status: 501(c)3
Highest Offering: Associate Degree
Accreditation: M, ACBSP, ADNUR, ENGT, OPD, PTAA, RAD

01 Acting President ... Dr. A. Zachary YAMBA
05 Vice Pres/Chief Academic Officer ... Dr. Jeffrey LEE
100 Exec Dir/Pres Initiatives ... Vacant
04 Exec Asst to the President ... Vacant
10 VP Administration & Finance ... Dr. Joyce W. HARLEY
49 Dean Liberal Arts ... Dr. S. Aisha STEPLIGHT JOHNSON
21 Comptroller ... Vacant
15 VP Human Resources/Gen Counsel ... Vacant
108 VP Planning Research & Assessment ... Vacant
13 Exec Dean/CIO Admin & Learning Tech ... Mr. Mohamed SEDDIKI
106 Assoc Dean Online Learning Resource ... Dr. Leigh BELLO-DECASTRO
25 Assoc Director Grants ... Ms. Cynthia ROBERSON
09 Director Institutional Research ... Dr. Jinsoo PARK
88 Asst Dean Retention/Acad Advisement ... Ms. Marva MACK
51 Acting Dean Comm & Cont Educ/WEC ... Dr. Elvira VIEIRA
08 Director MLK Library ... Mrs. Gwendolyn SLATON
32 Assoc Dean Student Life/Development ... Ms. Patricia SLADE
18 Director Facilities Mgmt ... Mr. Jeff SHAPIRO
19 Director Public Safety ... Mr. Anthony CROMARTIE
29 Resource Specialist ... Vacant
96 Director Purchasing ... Mrs. Marylyn RUTHERFORD
37 Director Financial Aid ... Mrs. Mildred COFER
06 Registrar/Asst Dean Stdnt Affairs ... Ms. Zewdnesh KASSA
21 Director Bursar's Office ... Ms. Darlene MILLER
36 Director Student Development ... Ms. Pamela MAYNARD
88 Director Child Development Center ... Ms. Deloris GRIMSLEY
41 Director Athletics ... Mr. Melvin KNIGHT
24 Director Media Prod Tech ... Mrs. Nadine ABRAM
88 Director College Information Ctr ... Mr. Ronald ROSS
00 President Emeritus ... Dr. A. Zachary YAMBA

Essex County College-West Essex Branch Campus (I)

730 West Bloomfield Avenue, West Caldwell NJ 07006
Telephone: (973) 877-6590 Identification: 770127
Accreditation: &M

† Regional accreditation is carried under the parent institution in Newark, NJ

Fairleigh Dickinson University (J)

1000 River Road, Teaneck NJ 07666-1996
County: Bergen FICE Identification: 002607
Unit ID: 184603
Telephone: (201) 692-2000 Carnegie Class: DU-Mod
FAX Number: N/A Calendar System: Semester
URL: www.fdu.edu
Established: 1942 Annual Undergrad Tuition & Fees: $36,910
Enrollment: 8,777 Coed
Affiliation or Control: Independent Non-Profit IRS Status: 501(c)3
Highest Offering: Doctorate
Accreditation: M, BUS, CACREP, CLPSY, CS, ENG, ENGT, NURSE, PHAR, TEAC

51 Dean Petrocelli Col of Cont Stds ... Dr. Lisa BRAVERMAN
01 President ... Dr. Christopher CAPUANO
43 University Counsel/Secretary ... Mr. John CODD
05 University Provost/VPAA ... Dr. Gillian SMALL
30 Sr Vice Pres University Advancement ... Mr. Richard REISS
03 Senior Vice President & CEO ... Vacant
10 Senior VP for Finance & COO ... Ms. Hania FERRARA
11 Vice President for Administration ... Mr. Richard A. FRICK
84 AVP Admissions/Fin Aid/Enrollment ... Ms. Traci BANKS
13 VP/Chief Information Officer ... Mr. Neal M. STURM
26 Associate VP Communications ... Mr. Angelo CARFAGNA
15 Associate VP Human Resources ... Ms. Rose D'AMBROSIO
29 Director Alumni Affairs ... Mr. Okang MCBRIDE
49 Dean Becton Col of Arts & Sci ... Dr. Geoffrey WEINMAN
50 Interim Dean College Business Admin ... Dr. James ALMEIDA
20 Dean University College ... Dr. Patti MILLS
32 Dean of Students-Teaneck Campus ... Ms. Michelle MCCROY-HEINS
32 Dean of Students-Madison Campus ... Dr. Jas VEREM
08 Assoc University Librarian-Florham ... Vacant
08 Associate University Librarian-Met ... Ms. Kathy STEIN-SMITH
51 Director Continuing Education ... Dr. Thomas SWANZEY
88 Dir Public Administration Institute ... Dr. William ROBERTS
38 Director Psychology ... Dr. Ronald DUMONT
21 Director Internal Audit ... Vacant
53 Director School of Education ... Dr. Vicki COHEN
66 Director Sch of Nurs/Allied Health ... Dr. Minerva GUTTMAN
41 Director of Athletics-Teaneck ... Mr. David LANGFORD
41 Director of Athletics-Madison ... Mr. William KLIKA
07 Univ Dir of Undergrad Admissions ... Mr. Andrew IPPOLITO
09 Director of Institutional Research ... Ms. Indira GOVINDAN
37 University Director Financial Aid ... Ms. Renee VOLAK
19 Campus Dir Public Safety/F/M Campus ... Ms. Willie THORNTON
20 Provost Metropolitan Campus ... Dr. Robert VODDE
12 Provost Florham/Madison Campus ... Dr. Peter WOOLLEY
19 Univ Dir Public Safety/T/H Campus ... Mr. David A. MILES
96 Director of Purchasing ... Ms. Juliette BROOKS

Felician University (K)

262 S Main Street, Lodi NJ 07644-2198
County: Bergen FICE Identification: 002610
Unit ID: 184612
Telephone: (201) 559-6000 Carnegie Class: Masters/S
FAX Number: (201) 559-6188 Calendar System: Semester
URL: www.felician.edu
Established: 1942 Annual Undergrad Tuition & Fees: $31,235
Enrollment: 1,953 Coed
Affiliation or Control: Roman Catholic IRS Status: 501(c)3
Highest Offering: Doctorate
Accreditation: M, IACBE, NURSE, TEAC

01 President ... Dr. Anne PRISCO
03 Senior Exec Vice President ... Vacant
05 Provost/Vice Pres Acad Affairs ... Dr. Edward OGLE

20 Asst VP Academic Support Services ... Dr. Ann V. GUILLORY
30 Vice Pres Institutional Advancement ... Mr. Edward EICHHORN
10 Vice Pres for Business/Finance ... Ms. Heidi SZYMANSKI
84 VP Enroll Mgmt & Student Affairs ... Ms. Francine ANDREA
04 Admin Assistant to the President ... Ms. Meggan O'NEILL
06 Registrar ... Ms. Priscilla KLYMENKO
07 Assoc Vice Pres Grad & Intl Enroll ... Mr. Michael SZAREK
07 Director Undergraduate Admissions ... Ms. Colleen FULLER
08 Director of the Library ... Mrs. Susan WENGLER
09 Director Institutional Research ... Ms. Reema NEGI
15 Director of Human Resources ... Ms. Virginia TOPOLSKI
88 Director Conferences and Event Plng ... Ms. Maria MALLIA
37 Director Student Financial Aid ... Ms. Cynthia MONTALVO
29 Director of Alumni Relations ... Ms. Patricia MALIZIA
42 Director Campus Ministry/Chaplain ... Fr. Richard KELLY
39 Director of Residence Life ... Ms. Laura PIEROTTI
36 Director of Career Counseling ... Ms. Melissa FAULKNER
13 Asst VP of Information Technology ... Mr. Christopher FINCH
24 Director A-V Center ... Mr. Anthony KLYMENKO
88 Assoc Director Center for Learning ... Mr. Hamdi SHAHIN
26 Dir Inst Marketing & Publications . Ms. Barbara PURDUE-LYNCH
40 Manager College Bookstore ... Ms. Beth LIGNOWSKI
76 Dean School of Nursing ... Dr. Muriel SHORE
53 Dean School of Education ... Dr. Rose RUDNITSKI
49 Dean School of Arts/Science ... Dr. George E. ABAUNZA
50 Dean School of Business ... Dr. Beth CASTIGLIA
108 Dean Assessment/Fac Excellence ... Dr. Dolores HENCHY
88 Director EOF Program ... Ms. Dinelia GARDNER
104 Director Study Abroad Program ... Mr. Carlo COLECCHIA
51 Dir of Cont/Professional Studies ... Dr. Geraldine KOCH
23 Director Health Services ... Ms. Carolyn LEWIS
41 Director of Athletics ... Mr. Benjamin DINALLO, JR.
92 Director Honors Program ... Dr. Maria VECCHIO
91 Director Administrative Computing ... Mr. John PANNEGGIANTE
14 Director of Information Systems ... Mr. Wisam SHAHIN

Georgian Court University (A)

900 Lakewood Avenue, Lakewood NJ 08701-2697
County: Ocean FICE Identification: 002608
Unit ID: 184773
Telephone: (732) 987-2200 Carnegie Class: Masters/M
FAX Number: N/A Calendar System: Semester
URL: www.georgian.edu
Established: 1908 Annual Undergrad Tuition & Fees: $31,618
Enrollment: 2,308 Coed
Affiliation or Control: Roman Catholic IRS Status: 501(c)3
Highest Offering: Master's
Accreditation: M, ACBSP, CACREP, NURSE, SW, TEAC

01 President ... Dr. Joseph R. MARBACH
05 Provost ... Dr. William BEHRE
10 Chief Financial Officer/VP Finance ... Mr. John SOMMER
30 Vice Pres Institutional Advancement ... Vacant
20 Assoc Provost Academic Pgm Devel ... Dr. Michael GROSS
07 Dean of Admissions ... Mr. Justin ROY
32 Dean of Students ... Vacant
42 Director of Campus Ministry ... Mr. Jeff SCHAFFER
41 Director Athletics/Recreation ... Ms. Laura LIESMAN
50 Dean School of Business ... Dr. Janice WARNER
53 Dean of School of Education ... Dr. Lynn DECAPUA
49 Dean School of Arts & Sciences ... Dr. Mary CHINERY
09 Director of Institutional Research ... Mr. Wayne ARNDT
08 Interim Director of Library Svcs ... Mr. Jeffrey DONNELLY
06 Registrar ... Ms. Christina REEVES
21 Controller ... Ms. Maureen RYAN-HOFFMAN
15 Director of Human Resources ... Ms. Tracey OWENS
13 Chief Information Officer ... Mr. Steve CAROL
07 Director Undergraduate Admissions ... Mr. Steven LAMBERT
37 Director of Financial Aid ... Mr. Randy BROWN
26 Exec Dir of Marketing & Comm ... Ms. Gail TOWNS
31 Dir Conferences & Special Events ... Ms. Mary CRANWELL
29 Dir of Alumni & Donor Engagement ... Ms. Jennifer SHUFRAN
36 Exec Dir of Career Svc & Corp Engag ... Ms. Kathleen BRADY
38 Director of Counseling ... Dr. Robin SOLBACH
23 Director of Health Services ... Ms. Cynthia MATTIA
22 Affirmative Action Officer ... Ms. Tracey OWENS
18 Director of Facilities ... Mr. Mark BIANCHI
19 Director of Security ... Mr. Thomas ZAMBRANO
07 Director Graduate Admissions ... Mr. Patrick GIVENS
39 Director of Residence Life ... Mr. Gary MILLER
04 Executive Asst to President ... Ms. Kathy SMITH
105 Web Administrator ... Mr. Richard BERARDI
108 Director of Assessment ... Sr. Janet THIEL
96 Purchasing Coordinator ... Ms. Julie PARLACOSKI

Hudson County Community College (B)

70 Sip Avenue, Jersey City NJ 07306
County: Hudson FICE Identification: 012954
Unit ID: 184995
Telephone: (201) 714-7100 Carnegie Class: Assoc/HT-High Trad
FAX Number: (201) 656-1799 Calendar System: Semester
URL: www.hccc.edu
Established: 1974 Annual Undergrad Tuition & Fees (In-District): $5,083
Enrollment: 9,203 Coed
Affiliation or Control: State/Local IRS Status: 501(c)3
Highest Offering: Associate Degree
Accreditation: M, ACFEI

01 President ... Dr. Glen E. GABERT
05 Senior Vice Pres Academic Affairs ... Dr. Eric FRIEDMAN
30 VP Development/Asst to President ... Mr. Joseph SANSONE
12 Senior VP North Hudson Campus ... Dr. Paula PANDO
88 Dean for Non Traditional Programs ... Ms. Ana CHAPMAN
32 Assoc Dean Student Services ... Mr. Michael REIMER
09 Assoc Dean Institutional Rsrch/Plng ... Dr. Jerry TROMBELLA
84 Assoc Dean Enrollment Services ... Vacant
50 Assoc Dean Business and Science ... Ms. Catherine SIRANGELO-ELBADAWY
37 Assoc Dean Student Financial Asst ... Ms. Sylvia F. MENDOZA
88 Assoc Dean ESL/Bilingual & Dev Educ ... Mr. Chris WAHL
06 Registrar ... Ms. Victoria ORELLANA
13 Chief Information Officer ... Mr. Vincent SALAMONE
10 Chief Fiscal Officer ... Ms. Veronica ZEICHNER
07 Director of Admissions ... Mr. Jose OLIVARES
49 Dean of Arts and Sciences ... Mr. Chris WAHL
88 Director Testing & Assessment ... Ms. Darlery FRANCO
88 Director EOF ... Ms. Joy SMITH
88 Executive Director Culinary Arts ... Mr. Paul DILLON
88 Ex Dir Ctr Bus/Industry/Cntrct Trng ... Ms. Ana CHAPMAN
45 Director Academic Foundations ... Ms. Elizabeth NESIUS
21 Controller ... Mr. Geoffrey SIMS
25 Director of Grants ... Mr. Ryan MARTIN
08 Librarian ... Ms. Carol VAN HOUTEN
35 Director Student Activities ... Ms. Veronica ZEROSIMO
26 Director of Communications ... Ms. Jennifer CHRISTOPHER
29 Director Alumni Relationsl ... Mr. Joseph SANSONE
15 Executive Director Human Resources ... Ms. Vivyen RAY
38 Director Advisement & Counseling ... Ms. Sabrina MAGLIULO
40 Manager HCCC Bookstore ... Ms. Tom COLBAN
96 Manager Purchasing ... Mr. Marvin SMITH
36 Coordinator Career & Transfer Svc ... Ms. Jennie NESENJUK
19 Director Security/Safety ... Mr. Rafael NIVAR
04 Administrative Asst to President ... Ms. Jennifer OAKLEY
101 Secretary of the Institution/Board ... Ms. Jennifer OAKLEY
18 Exec Dir Engineering Operations ... Mr. Ilya ASHMYAN

Kean University (C)

1000 Morris Avenue, Union NJ 07083-0411
County: Union FICE Identification: 002622
Unit ID: 185262
Telephone: (908) 737-5326 Carnegie Class: Masters/L
FAX Number: (908) 737-4636 Calendar System: Semester
URL: www.kean.edu
Established: 1855 Annual Undergrad Tuition & Fees (In-State): $11,581
Enrollment: 14,359 Coed
Affiliation or Control: State IRS Status: 501(c)3
Highest Offering: Doctorate
Accreditation: M, ART, #CAATE, CACREP, CIDA, CS, MUS, NUR, OT, PSPSY, @PTA, SP, SPAA, SW, TED, THEA

01 President ... Dr. Dawood FARAHI
10 Exec VP of Operations ... Mr. Philip CONNELLY
05 Provost/VP Academic Affairs ... Dr. Jeffrey TONEY
32 VP for Student Affairs ... Ms. Janice MURRAY-LAURY
30 VP Institutional Advancement ... Ms. Carla WILLIS
26 VP University Relations ... Ms. Susan KAYNE
100 Chief of Staff ... Ms. Audrey KELLY
43 Assoc VP/Chief University Counsel ... Ms. Geri BENEDETTO
88 Assoc VP for SIS & SP Counsel ... Ms. Felice VAZQUEZ
20 Assoc VP for Learning Support ... Dr. Sophia HOWLETT
12 Assoc VP/Dean Kean Ocean ... Dr. Stephen KUBOW
12 Assoc VPAA Kean Wenzhou ... Dr. Holger HENKE
84 Assoc VP Enrollment Management ... Ms. Marsha MCCARTHY
20 Asst VP Academic Affairs ... Ms. Joy MOSKOVITZ
39 Asst VP Residential Stdnt Services ... Ms. Maximina RIVERA
18 Asst VP for Operations ... Ms. Phyllis DUKE
58 Dean Nathan Weiss Grad Col ... Dr. Jeffrey BECK
53 Dean Col Education ... Dr. Anthony PITTMAN
79 Dean Col Humanities/Social Sci ... Dr. Suzanne BOUSQUET
81 Dean Col Nat & Appl Hlth Sci ... Dr. George CHANG
50 Dean Col Business & Public Mgt ... Dr. Michael COOPER
48 Dean Michael Graves Col ... Dr. David MOHNEY
57 Dean Col Visual & Performing Arts ... Vacant
15 Dir Human Resources ... Mr. Faruque CHOWDHURY
06 Registrar ... Mr. Ken WOLPIN
09 Dir Institutional Research ... Dr. Shiji SHEN
108 Assoc Dir Accredit & Assessment ... Ms. Susan DEMATTEO
84 Exec Dir Enroll Mgt Operations ... Mr. Chad AUSTEIN
37 Dir Financial Aid ... Ms. Sherrell WATSON-HALL
07 Dir of Admissions ... Ms. Jennifer KANELLIS
13 Dir Office for Computer/Inform Svcs ... Mr. Anthony SANTORA
21 Dir General Accounting ... Mr. Joseph ANTONOWICZ
08 Acting Dir University Librarian ... Ms. Kimberly FRAONE
25 Dir Research & Sponsored Pgms ... Ms. Susan GANNON
106 Dir Online Learning ... Mr. Corey VIGDOR
96 Dir for Purchasing ... Mr. George THORN
27 Dir Media Relations ... Ms. Margaret MCCORRY
29 Dir Alumni Relations ... Ms. Stella MAHER
22 Dir Affirmative Action ... Dr. Charlie WILLIAMS
38 Dir Counseling & Disability Servs ... Ms. Sharon MCNULTY
65 Dir for Sustainability ... Dr. Feng QI
104 Dir Center International Studies ... Ms. Yaruby PETIT-FRERE
41 Dir for Athletics ... Mr. Jack MCKIERNAN
35 Dir Ctr for Student Lead & Svcs ... Mr. Scott SNOWDEN
19 Acting Dir of Campus Police ... Ms. Ana ZSAK
23 Dir for Health Services ... Ms. Robin MANSFIELD
88 Veterans Affairs ... Ms. Lilliam BANNER
42 Chaplain for Campus Ministry ... Ms. Jackie OESMANN

Mercer County Community College (D)

1200 Old Trenton Road, PO Box 17202, West Windsor NJ 08550
County: Mercer FICE Identification: 004740
Unit ID: 185509
Telephone: (609) 586-4800 Carnegie Class: Assoc/HT-High Trad
FAX Number: (609) 570-3870 Calendar System: Semester
URL: www.mccc.edu
Established: 1966 Annual Undergrad Tuition & Fees (In-District): $3,648
Enrollment: 7,839 Coed
Affiliation or Control: State/Local IRS Status: 501(c)3
Highest Offering: Associate Degree
Accreditation: M, AAB, ADNUR, FUSER, MACTE, MLTAD, PTAA, RAD

01 President ... Dr. Jianping WANG
30 Vice President College Advancement ... Mr. Edward GWAZDA
05 Vice President Academic Affairs ... Dr. David EDWARDS
10 VP for Admin & Finance ... Dr. Mark HARRIS
32 Exec Dean for Student Affairs ... Dr. Diane CAMPBELL
76 Dean Health Professions ... Dr. Robert SCHREYER
49 Dean Liberal Arts ... Dr. Robert KLEINSCHMIDT
50 Dean Business/Technology and STEM ... Mr. Winston MADDOX
31 Dean and Provost JKC ... Ms. Monica WEAVER
21 Exec Dir of Finance ... Mr. Brian MCCLOSKEY
26 Dir Marketing/Public Information ... Ms. Lynn HOLL
15 Exec Dir for Compliance & Human Res ... Vacant
06 Registrar ... Ms. Joan GUGGENHEIM
37 Director of Financial Aid ... Mr. Jason TAYLOR
09 Director Institutional Research ... Ms. Nina MAY
18 Chief Facilities/Physical Plant ... Mr. Bryon MARSHALL
96 Director of Purchasing ... Mr. Stephen GREGOROWICZ
07 Director of Admissions & Outreach ... Ms. Savita BAMBHROLIA
84 Asst Dean Enrollment Management ... Ms. Savita BAMBHROLIA
08 Director of Library Services ... Ms. Pam PRICE
101 Secretary of the Institution/Board ... Ms. Diane BADESSA
103 Dean Workforce/Career Development ... Dr. Lynn COOPERSMITH
104 Coord of Global Education ... Prof. Andrea LYNCH
106 Dir Online Education/E-learning ... Dr. Alexandra SALAS
25 Chief Contracts/Grants Admin ... Ms. Kami ABDALA
36 Director Transfer & Career Services ... Ms. Laurene JONES
41 Athletic Director ... Mr. John SIMONE
108 Dean Inst Assessment ... Vacant
19 Director Security/Safety ... Mr. Bryon MARSHALL

Middlesex County College (E)

2600 Woodbridge Avenue, Edison NJ 08818-3050
County: Middlesex FICE Identification: 002615
Unit ID: 185536
Telephone: (732) 548-6000 Carnegie Class: Assoc/HT-Mix Trad/Non
FAX Number: (732) 494-8244 Calendar System: Semester
URL: www.middlesexcc.edu
Established: 1964 Annual Undergrad Tuition & Fees (In-District): $3,372
Enrollment: 12,059 Coed
Affiliation or Control: State/Local IRS Status: 501(c)3
Highest Offering: Associate Degree
Accreditation: M, ADNUR, DH, DIETT, ENGT, MLTAD, RAD

01 President ... Dr. Joann LA PERLA-MORALES
05 VP Academic & Student Affairs ... Dr. Mark MCCORMICK
10 VP Finance & Administration ... Ms. Susan K. PERKINS
30 VP for Institutional Advancement ... Mr. Patrick MADAMA
32 Dean Student Affairs ... Ms. Marla BRINSON
84 Dean Enrollment Management ... Mr. Brian CLEMMONS
107 Dean Professional Studies ... Mr. Jeffrey HERRON
51 Dean Continuing Education ... Dr. Roseann BUCCIARELLI
18 Exec Director Facilities Management ... Mr. Donald DROST
13 Exec Director Information Tech ... Mr. Bradley MORTON
21 Controller ... Ms. Lori PATTON
07 Acting Director of Admissions . Ms. Lisa RODRIGUEZ-GREGORY
06 Registrar ... Mr. Richard COLE
37 Financial Aid Director ... Ms. Lujia ZHANG
26 Chief Public Relations Officer ... Mr. Thomas PETERSON
96 Director of Purchasing ... Mr. David FRICKE
09 Director of Institutional Research ... Ms. Meghan ALAI
25 Director Grants Development ... Mr. Til DALLAVALLE
29 Dir Development & Alumni Relations ... Ms. Veronica CLINTON
41 Athletic Director ... Mr. Robert WISNIEWSKI

Monmouth University (F)

400 Cedar Avenue, West Long Branch NJ 07764-1898
County: Monmouth FICE Identification: 002616
Unit ID: 185572
Telephone: (732) 571-3400 Carnegie Class: Masters/L
FAX Number: (732) 571-3629 Calendar System: Semester
URL: www.monmouth.edu
Established: 1933 Annual Undergrad Tuition & Fees: $33,729
Enrollment: 6,395 Coed
Affiliation or Control: Independent Non-Profit IRS Status: 501(c)3
Highest Offering: Doctorate
Accreditation: M, #ARCPA, BUS, CACREP, CS, ENG, NURSE, @SP, SW, TED

01 President ... Dr. Paul R. BROWN
04 Executive Assistant to President ... Ms. Annette GOUGH
101 Special Asst Board of Trustees ... Ms. Janet FELL
05 Provost/VP Academic Affairs ... Dr. Laura MORIARTY
58 Vice Provost for Graduate Studies ... Dr. Michael PALLADINO
20 Vice Provost for Global Educ ... Dr. Jon STAUFF

20 Vice Provost for Transform Lrng .... Dr. Kathryn KLOBY
20 Vice Provost for Plng & Dec Support ....Ms. Christine BENOL
20 Vice Provost for Acad & Fac Affs .... Dr. Nicolle PARSONS-POLLARD
06 Registrar ....Mrs. Lynn REYNOLDS
49 Dean Sch Humanities/Social Science .... Dr. Kenneth WOMACK
50 Dean Leon Hess Business Sch .... Dr. Donald MOLIVER
53 Dean School of Education ....Dr. John HENNING
81 Dean Sch of Science .... Dr. Steven BACHRACH
66 Dean School of Nursing/Health Stds .... Dr. Janet MAHONEY
70 Dean School of Social Work ....Dr. Robin MAMA
92 Interim Dean Honors School ....Dr. Stanley BLAIR
08 University Librarian ....Mr. Kurt WAGNER
10 Vice President Finance .... Mr. William G. CRAIG
21 Assoc VP for Finance/Budgets .... Mr. Jack GAVIN
96 Director of Purchasing ....Mr. Mark MIRANDA
43 Vice President & General Counsel .... Mr. John J. CHRISTOPHER
88 Dir of Compliance/Risk Mgr .... Mr. Michael WUNSCH
22 Director Equity and Diversity .... Ms. Nina ANDERSON
11 Vice President Administrative Svcs ....Mrs. Patricia SWANNACK
18 Assoc VP Campus Plng/Construction .... Mr. Robert CORNERO
19 Director/Chief of Police .... Capt. William MCELRATH
15 Director of Human Resources ....Ms. Robyn SALVO
32 VP Student Life & Ldrshp Engagement ...... Mrs. Mary Anne NAGY
35 Assoc VP for Student Life .... Mr. James PILLAR
35 Dir Student Activities/Student Ctr ....Ms. Amy BELLINA
27 Chief Univ Editor/Dir Exec Com .... Mr. Michael MAIDEN
30 Vice Pres External Affairs .... Mr. Jason KROLL
26 Assoc VP Univ Mktg/Communications .... Ms. Tara PETERS
29 Asst VP for University Engagement ....Ms. Yasmin NIELSEN
84 Vice Pres Enrollment Management ....Dr. Robert MC CAIG
37 Assoc VP Enr Mgmt/Dir Fin Aid .... Ms. Claire ALASIO
07 Assoc VP for UG & GR Admission ... Ms. Lauren VENTO-CIFELLI
41 Vice Pres & Director of Athletics .... Dr. Marilyn MCNEIL
13 Vice Pres Information Management .....Dr. Edward CHRISTENSEN
97 Assoc Vice Prov/Acad Found/Gen Ed ....Dr. Judith NYE
09 Director Plng & Decision Support .... Dr. Eleanor SWANSON
36 Assistant Dean for Career Services ....Mr. William HILL
86 Dir of Government & Community Rels .... Mr. Paul DEMENT
25 Director of Grants & Contracts ....Mr. Tony LAZROE

Montclair State University (A)

1 Normal Avenue, Montclair NJ 07043-9987
County: Essex and Passaic FICE Identification: 002617
Unit ID: 185590
Telephone: (973) 655-4000 Carnegie Class: DU-Mod
FAX Number: N/A Calendar System: Semester
URL: www.montclair.edu
Established: 1908 Annual Undergrad Tuition & Fees (In-State): $11,773
Enrollment: 20,022 Coed
Affiliation or Control: State IRS Status: 501(c)3
Highest Offering: Doctorate
Accreditation: M, ART, AUD, BUS, CAATE, CACREP, CS, DANCE, DIETD, DIETI, MUS, PH, SP, TED, THEA

01 President ....Dr. Susan A. COLE
05 Provost/Vice Pres Academic Affairs ......Dr. Willard P. GINGERICH
10 Vice Pres Finance & Treasurer ....Mr. Jonathan ROSENHEIN
32 Vice Pres Student Devel/Campus Life .Dr. Karen L. PENNINGTON
30 Vice Pres University Advancement ....Mr. John T. SHANNON
15 Vice Pres Human Resources ....Mr. Jerry M. CUTLER
18 Vice Pres Univ Facilities .... Mr. Shawn M. CONNOLLY
13 Vice Pres Info Technology .... Ms. Candace C. FLEMING
88 Executive Director Enterprise Systems ....Mr. Samir BAKANE
43 University Counsel ....Mr. Mark FLEMING
86 Director Government Relations ....Ms. Shivaun P. GAINES
45 Exec Director Budget and Planning .... Mr. David JOSEPHSON
79 Dean Col Humanities & Soc Sciences ... Dr. Robert S. FRIEDMAN
81 Dean Col Science & Mathematics ....Dr. Robert S. PREZANT
53 Dean Col Educ & Human Services .... Dr. Tamara F. LUCAS
57 Dean Col of the Arts .... Mr. Daniel A. GURSKIS
50 Dean School of Business ....Dr. Alan G. CANT
66 Dean School of Nursing .... Dr. Janice SMOLOWITZ
08 Dean Library Services .... Dr. Judith L. HUNT
58 Dean of the Graduate School ....Dr. Joan C. FICKE
35 Dean of Students ....Ms. Margaree COLEMAN-CARTER
20 Assoc Provost for Academic Affairs ....Dr. Frederick BONATO
108 Assoc Provost Acad Pgm/ Assessment ....Dr. Joanne F. COTE-BONANNO
20 Assoc Provost Undergrad Educ .... Dr. James D. GERMAN
21 Assoc VP Finance .... Ms. Katharine BROPHY
91 Assoc VP Enterprise App Services ....Ms. Donna SADLON
35 Assoc VP Student Dev/Campus Life .... Ms. Kathleen E. RAGAN
16 Assoc VP for Human Resources .... Mr. Gilbert RIVERA
16 Asst VP for HR Operations ....Ms. Catherine N. BONGO
88 Asst VP Talent Management .... Ms. Keesha CHAVIS
64 Director School of Music .... Dr. J. Robert CART
09 Director Institutional Research ....Dr. Steven L. JOHNSON
06 Registrar .... Ms. Leslie SUTTON-SMITH
07 Director Undergraduate Admissions .... Mr. Jeffrey D. INDIVERI-GANT
26 Asst VP Communications & Marketing .... Ms. Ellen GRIFFIN
31 Exec Director Community Relations .... Ms. Julie ADAMS
29 Asst VP Annual Giving & Alumni Eng ....Ms. Jeanne MARANO
19 Chief of University Police .... Mr. Paul M. CELL
22 Dir EO/Affirmative Action/Diversity ....Ms. Barbara J. MILTON
38 Dir Counseling & Psych Services .... Dr. Jaclyn J. FRIEDMAN-LOMBARDO
39 Exec Director Residence Life ....Mr. John DELATE
40 Gen Manager University Bookstore ....Ms. Diane PELLEGRINO
41 Dir Intercollegiate Athletics .... Ms. Holly P. GERA
37 Director Financial Aid ....Mr. James T. ANDERSON

96 Acting Dir Procurement/Goods Svcs ....Ms. Christine G. PALMA
88 Exec Dir Ctr Advising/Stdnt Trans ....Dr. Michele CAMPAGNA
92 Director Honors Program ....Dr. Gregory L. WATERS
21 Controller ....Mr. Michael GALVIN
21 Director of Student Accounts .... Ms. Marion CAGGIANO
23 Director University Health Center ....Ms. Donna M. BARRY
104 Exec Director International Affairs ....Vacant
28 Director Equity & Diversity .... Dr. Sidney GARDNER
25 Dir Research & Sponsored Programs ....Mr. Frederic J. RUSSO
88 Asst Dean of Students ....Vacant
105 Director Web Services .... Ms. Katherine TASHEFF
04 Exec Assistant to the President .... Ms. Phyllis L. WOOSTER
42 Chaplain .... Fr. James CHERN
88 Dir Construction Procurement .... Mr. Daniel ROCHE
88 Dir Tech Training and Integration ....Dr. Yanling SUN
88 Dir Environmental Health and Safety ...... Ms. Amy V. FERDINAND
27 Director Media Relations ....Vacant
100 Chief of Staff .... Mr. Keith D. BARRACK
106 Exec Dir Online Extended Learning ....Dr. Peter MCALINEY

New Brunswick Theological Seminary (B)

35 Seminary Place, New Brunswick NJ 08901
County: Middlesex FICE Identification: 002619
Unit ID: 185758
Telephone: (732) 247-5241 Carnegie Class: Spec-4-yr-Faith
FAX Number: (732) 249-5412 Calendar System: Semester
URL: www.nbts.edu
Established: 1784 Annual Graduate Tuition & Fees: N/A
Enrollment: 178 Coed
Affiliation or Control: Reformed Church In America IRS Status: 501(c)3
Highest Offering: Doctorate; No Undergraduates
Accreditation: THEOL

01 President ....Dr. Gregg A. MAST
04 Assistant to the President ....Ms. Michelle SANDERS
05 Dean of the Seminary ....Dr. Willard W.C ASHLEY, SR.
10 Chief Financial Officer .... Mr. Kenneth TERMOTT
21 Accounting Manager .... Ms. Tara HAMILL
30 Director of Development .... Ms. Catherine PROCTOR
08 Director of the Library ....Tracy HUNTER HAYES
06 Registrar ....Ms. Yasha PEOPLE
32 Dean of Students/Title IX Coord ....Ms. Joan MARSHALL
07 Admissions Committee Chair .... Dr. Beth L. TANNER
18 Facilities Manager .... Mr. Paul KUHN
13 Network Technician .... Mr. Thomas SCHLATTER
108 Director of Assessment .... Dr. Terry SMITH
36 Director of Field Education .... Dr. Faye TAYLOR

New Jersey City University (C)

2039 Kennedy Boulevard, Jersey City NJ 07305-1597
County: Hudson FICE Identification: 002613
Unit ID: 185129
Telephone: (201) 200-2000 Carnegie Class: Masters/L
FAX Number: (201) 200-2352 Calendar System: Semester
URL: www.njcu.edu
Established: 1927 Annual Undergrad Tuition & Fees (In-State): $11,180
Enrollment: 8,136 Coed
Affiliation or Control: State IRS Status: 501(c)3
Highest Offering: Doctorate
Accreditation: M, ACBSP, ART, CACREP, MUS, NUR, TEAC

01 President ....Dr. Sue HENDERSON
05 Provost/Sr VP Academic Affairs .... Dr. Daniel J. JULIUS
32 Vice Pres for Student Affairs .... Dr. Jimmy JUNG
10 Vice Pres Administration/Finance .... Dr. Aaron ASKA
30 Vice Pres University Advancement ..... Mr. Daniel P. ELWELL, SR.
21 Controller .... Ms. Colleen O'KEEFE
13 Assoc VP Computer Info Systems .... Mr. Robert MCBRIDE
18 Interim AVP Facil/Construction Mgmt ....Mr. Michael D'AQUILA
07 Assoc VP Admissions/Enrollment Mgmt .... Mr. Benjamin ROHDIN
26 Assoc VP of Communications .... Dr. Sherrie MADIA
20 Assoc VP Academic Affairs .... Dr. Guillermo DE VEYGA
15 Assoc VP Human Resources .... Ms. Natalie THOMPSON
20 Assistant Provost .... Dr. Nurcan AYDIN
20 Assistant Provost .... Dr. Karen MORGAN
27 Asst VP Pub Info/Community Rels .... Ms. Ellen WAYMAN-GORDON
14 Asst VP Information Technology .... Ms. Phyllis SZANI
30 Asst VP of Development .... Ms. Lori FUNICELLO
88 Asst VP Univ Advancement .... Mr. Michael PERNA
35 Asst Vice Pres Student Affairs .... Dr. Demond HARGROVE
45 Executive Asst to the President .... Ms. Maria COBARRUBIAS
88 Asst VP for Global Initiatives ....Ms. Tamara CUNNINGHAM
49 Dean Arts & Sciences .... Dr. Joao SEDYCIAS
53 Dean Education & Prof Studies .... Dr. Allan DE FINA
50 Dean School of Business .... Dr. Bernard MCSHERRY
35 Dean of Students .... Dr. Lyn HAMLIN
108 Asst VP Institutional Effectivenes ....Dr. Sue GERBER
08 Director of the University Library .... Mr. Frederick SMITH
06 Registrar ....Ms. Miriam LARIA
36 Director Career Planning/Placement .... Dr. Jennifer JONES
16 Director Human Resources .... Mr. Robert PIASKOWSKY
19 Director Public Safety .... Dr. Ronald HURLEY
41 Director Athletics/Recreation .... Ms. Alice DE FAZIO
22 Dir Affirmative Action/Equal Oppty .... Ms. Lisa NORCIA
29 Director Alumni Relations .... Ms. Jane MCCLELLAN
38 Director Student Counseling .... Dr. Abisola GALLAGHER
96 Director of Purchasing .... Ms. Edie DELVECCHIO
43 University Counsel .... Mr. Alfred E. RAMEY, JR.

85 Director of International Programs ....Mr. Craig KATZ
37 Director Student Financial Aid ....Mr. Frank CUOZZO
88 Director Student Fin Svcs/Risk Mgr .... Mr. Jeffrey BRUNETTO
16 Labor Relations Assoc for Academic ....Mr. Matthew STIEGLITZ
39 Director Student Housing ....Ms. Jodi BAILEY

New Jersey Institute of Technology (D)

University Heights, Newark NJ 07102-1982
County: Essex FICE Identification: 002621
Unit ID: 185828
Telephone: (973) 596-3000 Carnegie Class: DU-Higher
FAX Number: (973) 642-4380 Calendar System: Semester
URL: www.njit.edu
Established: 1881 Annual Undergrad Tuition & Fees (In-State): $16,108
Enrollment: 10,646 Coed
Affiliation or Control: State IRS Status: 501(c)3
Highest Offering: Doctorate
Accreditation: M, ART, BUS, CIDA, CS, ENG, ENGT, PH

01 President ....Dr. Joel S. BLOOM
05 Provost and Senior Executive VP ....Dr. Fadi P. DEEK
10 Senior Vice Pres Admin & Treasurer ....Mr. Henry A. MAUERMEYER
30 Vice Pres University Advancement ....Dr. Charles DEES
46 Sr VP Tech & Bus Dev/Pres NJII .... Dr. Donald H. SEBASTIAN
88 VP for Real Estate & Capital Dev ....Mr. Andrew P. CHRIST
15 Vice President Human Resources ....Ms. Kay CLARKE-TURNER
32 VP Academic Support & Stdnt Affairs ....Dr. Charles J. FEY
20 Vice Provost for Academic Affairs .... Dr. Basil BALTZIS
54 Dean Newark College of Engineering ....Dr. Moshe KAM
48 Dean of CoAD ....Mr. Urs P. GAUCHAT
49 Dean Col Sci/Liberal Arts ....Dr. Kevin D. BELFIELD
50 Dean School of Management ....Dr. Reggie J. CAUDILL
92 Dean A Dorman Honors College ....Dr. Katia PASSERINI
77 Dean College of Computing Science ....Dr. Marek E. RUSINKIEWICZ
88 Vice Provost for Research ....Dr. Atam P. DHAWAN
21 Assoc Vice Pres Finance & Controlle ....Mr. William GARCIA
18 Assoc VP Design & Construction .... Mr. Joseph F. TARTAGLIA
58 Assoc Provost Grad Studies .... Dr. Sotirios G. ZIAVRAS
13 Assoc Provost Information Svcs Tech ....Mr. David F. ULLMAN
45 Assoc VP for Business & Econ Devel ...Dr. Timothy V. FRANKLIN
51 Assoc VP Cont/Distance Education .... Dr. Gale T. SPAK
84 Assoc VP Enroll Mgmt & Acad ....Dr. Wendy LIN-COOK
44 Assoc VP for Development ....Ms. Jacqueline G. RHODES
88 Exec Dir Pre-College Program .... Dr. Jacqueline L. CUSACK
35 Assoc VP Stdnt Engag/Dean of Stdnts .... Dr. Laura VALENTE
89 Assoc Dean Ctr First Year Students ....Dr. Sharon E. MORGAN
26 Assoc VP Comm/Marketing & Branding ....Ms. Lauren D. UGORJI
29 Sr Exec Dir for Constituent Rels .... Mr. Michael A. WALL
04 Sr Assistant to President ....Ms. Mary Jane POHERO
36 Exec Director Career Devel Svcs .... Mr. Gregory MASS
27 Asst VP for Communications ....Dr. Denise ANDERSON
09 Director Inst Research/Planning ....Dr. Eugene P. DEESS
08 University Librarian .... Mr. Richard T. SWEENEY
06 Registrar .... Mr. Michael E. MAYSILLES
37 Dir Student Financial Aid Services ....Ms. Ivon NUNEZ
88 Executive Director EOP ....Mr. Laurence A. HOWELL
38 Dir Counseling & Psych Services ....Dr. Phyllis BOLLING
19 Chief of Police ....Mr. Joseph S. MARSWILLO
24 Dir Instructional Tech/Media Svcs ....Mr. William F. REYNOLDS
41 Asst VP & Dir Athletics/Phys Educ ....Mr. Leonard I. KAPLAN
85 Director International Students/Fac ....Mr. Jeffrey W. GRUNDY
88 Interim Director Campus Center ....Mr. Albert M. MARTINEZ
96 Director Purchasing/Office Services ....Ms. Eugenia REGENCIO
43 Office of General Counsel ....Ms. Holly C. STERN
100 Special Asst to Pres Pol/Govt Rels ...Ms. Angela R. GARRETSON
105 Director Web Services ....Mr. Aslam ERSAL
108 Director Academic Assessment .... Dr. Charles R. BROOKS
07 Dir of Univ Admissions .... Mr. Stephen M. ECK

Ocean County College (E)

PO Box 2001, Toms River NJ 08754-2001
County: Ocean FICE Identification: 002624
Unit ID: 185873
Telephone: (732) 255-0400 Carnegie Class: Assoc/HT-Mix Trad/Non
FAX Number: (732) 255-0444 Calendar System: Semester
URL: www.ocean.edu
Established: 1964 Annual Undergrad Tuition & Fees (In-District): $4,255
Enrollment: 9,296 Coed
Affiliation or Control: State/Local IRS Status: 501(c)3
Highest Offering: Associate Degree
Accreditation: M, ADNUR, EMT

01 President ....Dr. Jon H. LARSON
10 Exec VP of Finance & Administration ..... Ms. Sara WINCHESTER
32 VP Student Affairs ....Dr. Norma BETZ
05 VP of Academic Affairs ....Vacant
15 Asst VP Human Resources .... Ms. Tracey DONALDSON
20 Asst VP for Academic Affairs ....Dr. Antoinette M. CLAY
18 Asst VP Facilities ....Mr. Matthew KENNEDY
04 Senior Asst to the President ....Vacant
20 Assoc VP of Academic Affairs ....Dr. Lisa DIBISCEGLIE
57 Dean Language and the Arts .... Dr. Amy GILLEY
81 Dean Math/Science & Tech .... Mr. Paul SILBERQUIT
66 Dean of Nursing ....Ms. Teresa WALSH
83 Dean of Social Science ....Ms. Rosann BAR
88 Dean of Instructional Outreach ....Dr. Maysa HAYWARD
12 Director of Off-Campus Programs ....Ms. Sabrina MATHUES

102 Exec Dir OCC Foundation .... Ms. Heather BARBERI
103 Asst VP CPE/Workforce Devel .... Ms. Patricia FENN
106 Assoc VP of e-Learning .... Mr. Jeff S. HARMON
106 Dean of e-Learning Faculty .... Mr. Jack KELNHOFER
08 Director of Library Services .... Ms. Donna ROSINSKI-KAUS
13 Chief Information Officer .... Mr. Hatem AKL
37 Director of Financial Aid .... Ms. Eileen BUCKLE
06 Registrar .... Mr. Eric DANIELS
88 Dir of Academic Advising Services .... Ms. Anna REGAN
19 Director of College Security .... Mr. Frank IANNONE
26 Exec Director of College Relations .... Ms. Jan KIRSTEN
07 Director of Admissions .... Ms. Lisa KASPER
93 Director of EOF & OMS .... Ms. Laura RICKARDS
18 Director of Facilities .... Mr. James CALAMIA
41 Exec Dir of Judicial Aff & Athletic .... Ms. Ilene COHEN
45 Exec Dir of Institutional Planning .... Ms. Alexa BESHARA
21 Exec Dir of Strategic Projects .. Ms. Karen PAPAKONSTANTINOU
20 Dean of Academic Services .... Ms. Maureen REUSTLE
35 Director of Student Life .... Ms. Jennifer FAZIO
29 Director Alumni Relations .... Vacant

Passaic County Community College (A)

1 College Boulevard, Paterson NJ 07509-1179
County: Passaic FICE Identification: 009994
Unit ID: 186034
Telephone: (973) 684-6868 Carnegie Class: Assoc/HT-High Trad
FAX Number: (973) 684-5843 Calendar System: Semester
URL: www.pccc.edu
Established: 1968 Annual Undergrad Tuition & Fees (In-District): $4,410
Enrollment: 8,968 Coed
Affiliation or Control: State/Local IRS Status: 501(c)3
Highest Offering: Associate Degree
Accreditation: M, ADNUR, CAHIIM, ENGT, RAD

01 President .... Dr. Steven ROSE
05 Vice Pres Academic/Student Affairs .... Dr. Jacqueline KINEAVY
10 Vice Pres Finance/Administration .... Mr. Steven HARDY
12 Vice Pres Passaic Academic Center . Ms. Josephine HERNANDEZ
13 Vice Pres Information Technology .... Mr. Robert MONDELLI
15 Associate Vice Pres Human Resources ...... Mr. Jose FERNANDEZ
20 Dean Academic Affairs .... Dr. Bassel STASSIS
08 Associate Dean Learning Resources .... Mr. Greg FALLON
66 Assoc Dean Nurse Educ/Health Scis ... Ms. Donna STANKIEWICZ
88 Asst Dean for Testing & Tutoring .... Mr. Peter HYNES
09 Dir Institutional Research .... Mr. Justin HULL
88 Ex Dir Cultural Affs/The Poetry Ctr .... Ms. Maria GILLAN
30 Exec Dir of Institutional Devel .... Mr. Todd SORBER
84 Exec Dir of Enrollment Management .... Ms. Betsy MARINACE
18 Exec Dir Facilities Mgmt/Planning .... Mr. Brian EGAN
37 Director Financial Aid .... Ms. Linda GAYTON
06 Registrar .... Ms. Donna FISCHER
19 Director Security .... Mr. Glenn BROWN
35 Director Student Activities .... Ms. Maria MARTE
41 Athletic Director .... Mr. Wayne MARTIN
07 Director of Admissions .... Ms. Stephanie DECKER
29 Director Alumni Relations .... Mr. William MORRISON
32 Chief Student Life Officer .... Dr. Sharon GOLDSTEIN
26 Chief Public Relations Officer .... Ms. Betsy MARINACE
96 Director of Purchasing .... Mr. Michael D'AGATI
101 Dir Board Affairs/Asst to President .... Ms. Evelyn DEFEIS
103 Dir Workforce/Career Development .... Mr. Michael POWELL

Pillar College (B)

60 Park Place, Suite 701, Newark NJ 07102
County: Essex FICE Identification: 036663
Unit ID: 440794
Telephone: (973) 803-5000 Carnegie Class: Spec-4-yr-Faith
FAX Number: (973) 242-3282 Calendar System: Semester
URL: www.pillar.edu
Established: 1908 Annual Undergrad Tuition & Fees: $19,440
Enrollment: 478 Coed
Affiliation or Control: Other IRS Status: 501(c)3
Highest Offering: Baccalaureate
Accreditation: M, BI

01 President .... Dr. David E. SCHROEDER
05 Provost/Int Chief Academic Officer .... Mr. Daniel W. WRIGHT
20 VP Academic Affairs .... Dr. Alford H. OTTLEY
11 VP Operations/Public Affairs .... Dr. Ralph T. GRANT
32 VP Student Life .... Ms. Linda SCHMITT
100 Chief of Staff .... Ms. Keyla PAVIA
51 VP Strategic Alliances .... Dr. Wayne R. DYER
10 Assistant VP of Financial Services .... Mr. Joel DAVIS
20 Assistant VP of Academics .... Mrs. Amy HUBER
06 Registrar .... Mr. Brian SCHROEDER
37 Assistant Director of Financial Aid .... Ms. Eboni CRAWFORD
07 Director of Admissions .... Mr. Dominic DIGIOACCHINO
42 Coordinator of Spiritual Formation .... Mr. Nishanth THOMAS
04 Administrative Asst to President .... Ms. Ivette MUNIZ
08 Director of Library .... Ms. Lorraine HODGES
26 Director of Marketing .... Mr. Kelvin THOMAS

Princeton Theological Seminary (C)

PO Box 821, Princeton NJ 08542-0803
County: Mercer FICE Identification: 002626
Unit ID: 186122
Telephone: (609) 921-8300 Carnegie Class: Spec-4-yr-Faith
FAX Number: (609) 924-2973 Calendar System: Semester
URL: www.ptsem.edu
Established: 1812 Annual Graduate Tuition & Fees: N/A
Enrollment: 523 Coed
Affiliation or Control: Presbyterian Church (U.S.A.) IRS Status: 501(c)3
Highest Offering: Doctorate; No Undergraduates
Accreditation: M, THEOL

01 President .... Dr. M. Craig BARNES
10 Sr Vice Pres/Chief Oper Ofcr/Treas .... Mr. John W. GILMORE
30 VP for Advancement .... Ms. Jaime ZAMPARELLI
26 VP for Communication & External Rel .... Dr. Shane A. BERG
05 Dean and VP of Academic Affairs .... Dr. James F. KAY
32 Dean Student Life & VP Stdnt Rels .... Rev. John E. WHITE
45 Assoc Dean of Planning & Assessmen .... Dr. Shawn OLIVER
35 Assoc Dean Stdnt Life/Dir Sr Plcmnt .. RevDr. Catherine C. DAVIS
51 Assoc Dean of Continuing Educ .... Rev. Dayle G. ROUNDS
21 Assoc VP for Finance and Admin .... Mr. Kurt A. GABBARD
21 Controller .... Mr. Victor DEMEO
88 Director of Church Relations .... Rev. Larissa KWONG ABAZIA
06 Registrar .... Ms. Brenda D. WILLIAMS
07 Director Admissions/Financial Aid .... Mr. Matthew R. SPINA
08 Interim Librarian .... Ms. Melody MAZUK
88 Assoc VP for Advancement .... Rev. J. Thomas KORT
15 Director of Human Resources .... Ms. Barbara MECCIA
13 Chief Technology Officer .... Mr. William FRENCH
18 Director of Facilities .... Mr. German MARTINEZ
88 Director of Campus Relations ..... Rev. Joicy BECKER-RICHARDS
39 Director of Housing/Auxiliary Svcs .... Mr. Stephen CARDONE
20 Assoc Dean for Academic Admin .... Dr. Rose Ellen DUNN
38 Director of Student Counseling .... Rev. Nancy L. SCHONGALLA-BOWMAN
42 Minister of the Chapel .... Rev. Janice S. AMMON
28 Director Multicultural Relations .... Rev. Victor ALOYO, JR.
04 Executive Asst to the President .... Vacant
37 Assoc Director Financial Aid .... Mr. Michael D. LIVIO
44 Director of Annual Giving .... Ms. Cheryl ALI
44 Director of Planned Giving ..... Mr. Murray LOPDELL-LAWRENCE
106 Director of Digital Learning .... Mr. Reno LAURO

Princeton University (D)

Princeton NJ 08544-1098
County: Mercer FICE Identification: 002627
Unit ID: 186131
Telephone: (609) 258-3000 Carnegie Class: DU-Highest
FAX Number: N/A Calendar System: Semester
URL: www.princeton.edu
Established: 1746 Annual Undergrad Tuition & Fees: $43,450
Enrollment: 8,088 Coed
Affiliation or Control: Independent Non-Profit IRS Status: 501(c)3
Highest Offering: Doctorate
Accreditation: M, ENG, TEAC

01 President .... Cristopher L. EISGRUBER
03 Executive Vice President .... Treby WILLIAMS
05 Provost .... David S. LEE
04 Vice President & Secretary .... Robert K. DURKEE
10 Vice Pres for Finance & Treasurer .... Carolyn N. AINSLIE
30 Vice President for Development .... Elizabeth B. WOOD
26 Vice President for Public Affairs .... Robert K. DURKEE
32 Vice President of Campus Life .... Rochelle CALHOUN
18 Vice President for Facilities .... Michael E. MCKAY
13 Vice President Info Technology/CIO .... Jay DOMINICK
15 Vice President for Human Resources .... Lianne C. SULLIVAN-CROWLEY
11 VP for University Services .... Chad L. KLAUS
20 Vice Provost Academic Affairs .... Katherine ROHRER
22 Vice Provost Instl Equity/Diversity .... Michelle MINTER
09 Vice Provost Institutional Research .... Jed MARSH
25 Vice Prov Space Programming/Plan .... Paul LAMARCHE
21 Budget Dir/Vice Provost Finance .... Steven GILL
20 Vice Provost Intl Initiatives .... Anastasia T. VRACHNOS
27 Asst Vice President Communications .... Daniel A. DAY
29 Asst Vice President Alumni Affairs .... Margaret M. MILLER
44 Asst Vice President Annual Giving .... William M. HARDT
88 Asst VP for University Services .... Amy CAMPBELL
88 AVP Facilities Design/Construction .... Anne ST. MAURO
18 Asst Vice Pres University Services .... Andrew KANE
46 Chair Univ Rsrch Bd/Dean Research .... Pablo DEBENEDETTI
43 General Counsel .... Ramona E. ROMERO
88 President PRINCO .... Andrew K. GOLDEN
88 Dean of the Faculty .... Deborah PRENTICE
58 Dean of Graduate School .... Sanjeev KULKARNI
49 Dean of the College .... Jill S. DOLAN
54 Dean of School of Engineering .... H. Vincent POOR
82 Dean of WW Sch of Public/Intl Affs .... Cecilia ROUSE
48 Dean of School of Architecture .... Monica PONCE DE LEON
42 Dean of Religious Life .... Alison BODEN
35 Dean of Undergraduate Students .... Kathleen DEIGNAN
07 Dean of Admission .... Janet L. RAPELYE
17 Exec Director Health Services .... John KOLLIGIAN
08 University Librarian .... Karin TRAINER
06 Registrar .... Polly WINFREY GRIFFIN
37 Dir Undergraduate Financial Aid .... Robin A. MOSCATO
86 Director Government Affairs .... Joyce A. RECHTSCHAFFEN
31 Dir Community & Regional Affairs .... Kristin APPELGET
41 Director of Athletics .... Mollie D. MARCOUX
96 Director of Purchasing .... Donald E. WESTON, JR.
38 Dir of Counseling & Psych Services .... Anita MCLEAN
16 Director Human Resources .... Claire JACOBS ELSON
85 Director Davis International Center .... Jackie LEIGHTON
36 Executive Director Career Services .... Pulin SANGHVI
90 Assoc CIO/Dir Academic Services OIT .... Serge J. GOLDSTEIN
14 Assoc CIO/Dir Support Services OIT .... Steven M. SATHER
91 Dir Enterprise Infrastructure OIT .... Donna E. TATRO
44 AVP for Development .... Kerstin LARSEN
104 Sr Asc Dn of Col/Dir Ofc Intl Pgms .... Nancy A. KANACH
39 Director Housing .... Andrew KANE
19 Executive Director Public Safety .... Paul OMINSKY

Rabbi Jacob Joseph School (E)

1 Plainfield Avenue, Edison NJ 08817-4494
County: Middlesex FICE Identification: 030775
Unit ID: 384421
Telephone: (732) 985-6533 Carnegie Class: Spec-4-yr-Faith
FAX Number: (732) 985-6553 Calendar System: Semester
URL: www.jfgmc.org/rjjy/htm
Established: 1982 Annual Undergrad Tuition & Fees: $11,400
Enrollment: 84 Male
Affiliation or Control: Independent Non-Profit IRS Status: 501(c)3
Highest Offering: Baccalaureate
Accreditation: @RABN

01 President .... Dr. Marvin SCHICK
03 Rosh Yeshiva .... Rabbi Yaakov BUSEL
05 Rosh Yeshiva .... Rabbi Joseph EICHENSTEIN
37 Financial Aid Director .... Rabbi Yitzchok WEINTRAUB

Rabbinical College of America (F)

226 Sussex Avenue, Morristown NJ 07960-3600
County: Morris FICE Identification: 008609
Unit ID: 186186
Telephone: (973) 267-9404 Carnegie Class: Spec-4-yr-Faith
FAX Number: (973) 267-5208 Calendar System: Trimester
URL: www.rca.edu
Established: 1956 Annual Undergrad Tuition & Fees: $11,000
Enrollment: 212 Male
Affiliation or Control: Independent Non-Profit IRS Status: 501(c)3
Highest Offering: Baccalaureate
Accreditation: RABN

01 Dean .... Rabbi Moshe HERSON
04 Admin Assistant to the Dean .... Rabbi Mendy HERSON
26 Public Relations Officer .... Rabbi Mendel SOLOMON
06 Registrar .... Mrs. Shoshana SOLOMON
88 Director New Direction Program .... Rabbi Zalman DUBINSKY
10 Chief Business Officer .... Vacant
37 Director Student Financial Aid .... Rabbi Yisroel GOLDBERG
08 Chief Librarian .... Rabbi Sholom SPALTER
51 Dir Continuing Educ/Alumni Rels .... Rabbi Boruch HECHT
88 Director Semicha Program .... Rabbi Chaim SCHAPIRO
18 Director Building and Grounds .... Rabbi Hershel LIPSKIER

Ramapo College of New Jersey (G)

505 Ramapo Valley Road, Mahwah NJ 07430-1680
County: Bergen FICE Identification: 009344
Unit ID: 186201
Telephone: (201) 684-7500 Carnegie Class: Masters/M
FAX Number: (201) 684-7508 Calendar System: Semester
URL: www.ramapo.edu
Established: 1969 Annual Undergrad Tuition & Fees (In-State): $13,698
Enrollment: 6,003 Coed
Affiliation or Control: State IRS Status: 501(c)3
Highest Offering: Master's
Accreditation: M, BUS, NUR, SW, TEAC

01 President .... Dr. Peter P. MERCER
05 Provost/VP Academic Affairs .... Dr. Beth BARNETT
10 VP Administration & Finance .... Ms. Kirsten DASILVA
43 VP and General Counsel .... Mr. Michael A. TRIPODI
102 VP Inst Advance/Dir Fdtn/Chief Dev .... Ms. Cathleen DAVEY
84 Assoc VP of Enrollment Mgmt .... Mr. Christopher ROMANO
46 Chief Planning Officer .... Dr. Dorothy ECHOLS TOBE
100 Chief of Staff .... Ms. Brittany A. WILLIAMS-GOLDSTEIN
88 Director of Internal Audit .... Ms. Patricia CHAVEZ
20 Vice Provost for Academic Affairs .... Dr. Eric DAFFRON
21 Assoc Vice Pres Admin/Finance .... Mr. Richard ROBERTS
13 Assoc VP/Chief Information Officer .... Mr. George TABBACK
86 Asst Vice Pres Government Rels .... Ms. Anna FARNESKI
105 Asst VP Mktg & Web Administrator .... Ms. Melissa HORVATH-PLYMAN
26 Asst VP of Comm & Public Relations .... Vacant
08 College Librarian/Dean .... Ms. Elizabeth SIECKE
06 Registrar .... Ms. Michele DUNN
07 Director of Admissions .... Mr. Peter RICE
37 Director of Financial Aid .... Mr. F. Shawn O'NEILL
21 Controller .... Mr. Lawrence FERRIER
15 Director of Human Resources .... Mr. David VERNON
78 Dir Exper Learning/Career Svcs .... Ms. Beth RICCA
32 Dean of Students .... Ms. Melissa VAN DER WALL
41 Director of Athletics .... Mr. Harold CROCKER
18 Interim Director of Facilities .... Mr. Michael CUNNINGHAM
19 Director Security & Safety .... Mr. Vincent MARKOWSKI
88 Director Educ Opportunity Program .... Ms. Barbara HARMON-FRANCIS
50 Dean Anisfield School of Business .... Dr. Edward PETKUS
82 Dean Salameno Sch Amer Intl Studies .... Dr. Stephen RICE
57 Dean Sch of Contemporary Arts .... Mr. Steven PERRY
83 Dean Sch Soc Science & Human Svc .... Dr. Aaron R S. LORENZ
81 Dean Sch Theoretical/Applied Sci .... Dr. Edward SAIFF
53 Asst Dean for Teacher Education .... Dr. Rexton LYNN
38 Director Ctr for Health/Counseling .... Dr. Judith GREEN
29 Dir Alumni Relations/Dev Info Svcs .... Ms. Purvi PAREKH

24 Asst Manager Academic Media Svcs ...... Mr. Michael SAVIANESO
04 Executive Assistant to President .... Ms. Sara GAZZILLO
23 Coordinator Health Services .... Ms. Debbie LUKACSKO
09 Director of Institutional Research .... Dr. Gurvinder KHANEJA
22 Dir Affirmative Action/EEO .... Ms. Katherine MCGEE
40 Bookstore Manager .... Ms. Theresa KING
85 Exec Director of Intl Education .... Mr. Ben LEVY
36 Asst Dir Career Dev & Placement .... Ms. Debra STARK
96 Director of Purchasing .... Mr. Stephen SONDEY

Raritan Valley Community College (A)

118 Lamington Road, Branchburg NJ 08876
County: Somerset FICE Identification: 007731
Unit ID: 186645
Telephone: (908) 526-1200 Carnegie Class: Assoc/HT-Mix Trad/Non
FAX Number: (908) 526-0253 Calendar System: Semester
URL: www.raritanval.edu
Established: 1966 Annual Undergrad Tuition & Fees (In-District): $4,048
Enrollment: 8,214 Coed
Affiliation or Control: State/Local IRS Status: 501(c)3
Highest Offering: Associate Degree
Accreditation: M, ADNUR, CAHIIM, MAC, OPD

01 President .... Dr. Michael MCDONOUGH
05 Sr Vice Pres Academic Affairs .... Vacant
10 Vice President Finance/Facilities .... Mr. John TROJAN
13 Vice Pres Technology/Assess/Plng .... Mr. Charles E. CHULVICK
15 VP Human Resources/Labor Relations .... Ms. Nancy MOORE
30 VP of Strategic Programs & Develop .... Ms. Jackie BELIN
20 Dean Academic Affairs .... Dr. Patrice MARKS
32 Dean Student Services .... Ms. Diane LEMCOE
85 Dean Multicultural Affairs .... Ms. Richeleen DASHIELD
18 Exec Director Facilities/Grounds .... Mr. Brian O'ROURKE
38 Dir of Student Advising & Couns .... Mr. Greg DESANCTIS
24 Director Media Relations .... Ms. Donna STOLZER
88 Conference Services Director .... Ms. Karen VAUGHAN
72 Executive Director Inst Technology .... Mr. Michael E. MACHNIK
102 Executive Director Foundation .... Ms. Ronnie WEYL
14 Information Technology Director .... Mr. Robert PESCINSKI
21 Controller/Exec Dir of Finance .... Ms. Violet J. WILLENSKY
57 Director of Theatre .... Mr. Alan C. LIDDELL
09 Dir of Inst Research/Assessment .... Mr. Faxian YANG
88 Director of Planetarium .... Ms. Amy GALLAGHER
88 Director of Child Care Center .... Ms. Cathy GRIFFIN
37 Director of Financial Aid .... Mr. Lenny MESONAS
08 Library Director .... Vacant
06 Registrar .... Mr. Dan PALUBNIAK
96 Executive Director Business Service .... Mr. Lester MILLER
35 Director of Student Life .... Mr. Russell BAREFOOT
36 Director Transfer/Career Services .... Mr. Paul MICHAUD
26 Executive Director Marketing .... Ms. Janet THOMPSON
07 Director of Admissions .... Ms. Jache WILLIAMS
103 Exec Dir Workforce Development .... Ms. Michele BORONKAS
19 Director Security/Safety .... Mr. Robert SZKODNEY
41 Athletic Director .... Ms. Amanda DEMARTINO

Rider University (B)

2083 Lawrenceville Road, Lawrenceville NJ 08648-3099
County: Mercer FICE Identification: 002628
Unit ID: 186283
Telephone: (609) 896-5000 Carnegie Class: Masters/L
FAX Number: (609) 896-8029 Calendar System: Semester
URL: www.rider.edu
Established: 1865 Annual Undergrad Tuition & Fees: $38,360
Enrollment: 5,294 Coed
Affiliation or Control: Independent Non-Profit IRS Status: 501(c)3
Highest Offering: Master's
Accreditation: M, BUS, BUSA, CACREP, MUS, NURSE, TED

01 President .... Dr. Gregory DELL'OMO
05 Provost/Vice Pres Academic Affairs .... Dr. DonnaJean A. FREDEEN
10 Vice President Finance/Treasurer .... Ms. Julie A. KARNS
30 Vice Pres University Advancement .... Mr. Jonathan D. MEER
32 VP Student Affairs/Dean of Students .... Dr. Anthony CAMPBELL
84 Vice Pres Enrollment Management .... Mr. James P. O'HARA
13 Assoc VP Information Technology .... Ms. Carol S. KONDRACH
21 Associate Vice President/Controller .... Ms. Jennifer M. POTTER
09 Assoc Vice Pres Institutional Rsrch .... Mr. Ronald WALKER
18 AVP Facilities/Auxiliary Services .... Mr. Michael F. RECA
45 Associate Vice President Planning .... Ms. Debbie STASOLLA
26 Asst VP for Univ Comm/Marketing .... Vacant
20 Associate Provost .... Dr. James O. CASTAGNERA
12 Dean Westminster .... Dr. Matthew R. SHAFTEL
07 Dean of Enrollment .... Ms. Susan C. CHRISTIAN
51 Dean College of Cont Studies .... Mr. Boris VILIC
49 Dean Liberal Arts & Science .... Dr. Jonathan MILLEN
53 Dean School of Education .... Dr. Sharon SHERMAN
50 Dean Business Administration .... Vacant
06 Registrar .... Ms. Susan A. STEFANICK
08 Dean of Library Services .... Mr. F. William CHICKERING
15 Dir Human Resources/Affirm Action .... Mr. Robert STOTO
19 Director of Public Safety .... Ms. Vickie L. WEAVER
29 Director of Alumni Relations .... Ms. Natalie M. POLLARD
41 Director of Athletics .... Mr. Donald P. HARNUM
37 Director Student Financial Svcs .... Mr. Drew C. AROMANDO
40 Manager College Store .... Vacant
04 Director of Office of the President .... Ms. Christine ZELENAK
27 Communications Director .... Vacant
36 Director of Career Placement .... Vacant

Rowan College at Burlington County (C)

601 Pemberton Browns Mills Road,
Pemberton NJ 08068-1599
County: Burlington FICE Identification: 007730
Unit ID: 183877
Telephone: (609) 894-9311 Carnegie Class: Assoc/HT-High Non
FAX Number: (609) 894-0183 Calendar System: Semester
URL: www.rcbc.edu
Established: 1966 Annual Undergrad Tuition & Fees (In-District): $4,065
Enrollment: 9,438 Coed
Affiliation or Control: State/Local IRS Status: 501(c)3
Highest Offering: Associate Degree
Accreditation: M, ADNUR, CAHIIM, DH, DMS, ENGT, RAD

01 President .... Mr. Paul DRAYTON
04 Exec Asst to the President .... Ms. Lynne Marie DEVERICKS
05 Sr Vice President/Provost .... Dr. David SPANG
84 VP Enroll Mgmt and Student Success .... Mr. Michael CIOCE
103 VP WDI and Lifelong Learning ...... Ms. Anna FAYANZO COTTON
13 Chief Information Officer .... Mr. Mark MEARA
10 Chief Financial/Admin Officer .... Ms. Jaclyn ANGERMEIER
11 Chief Operations Officer .... Mr. Matthew FARR
102 Exec Director Foundation .... Ms. Anika RAGINS-RILEY
26 Exec Dir Marketing/Communications .... Mr. Greg VOLPE
15 Exec Director of HR/Admin Svcs .... Ms. Stacy JANKIEWICZ
49 Dean of Liberal Arts .... Ms. Donna VANDERGRIFT
81 Dean of STEM .... Dr. Edem TETTEH
66 Dean of Nursing/Allied Health .... Dr. Karen MONTALTO
106 Dean of Learning Resources .... Mr. Martin A. HOFFMAN, SR.
32 Dean of Student Success .... Dr. Catherine R. BRIGGS
20 Dean of Enrollment Management .... Dr. Karen L. ARCHAMBAULT
06 Registrar .... Ms. LacyJane RYMAN-MESCAL
41 Director of Athletics .... Ms. Heather CONGER
36 Manager of Career Services .... Mr. Anthony PHILLIPS
88 Int Dir Cultural Arts/Hosp & Tour .... Mr. James BRUDNICKI
88 Director of EOF Program .... Ms. Edith CORBIN
25 Director of Educ Pgm & Grant Dev .... Dr. Nicole SCOTT
19 Director of Public Safety .... Ms. Linda SCHMIDT
88 Director of Transfer Center .... Ms. Anne EDWARDS

Rowan College at Gloucester County (D)

1400 Tanyard Road, Sewell NJ 08080-9518
County: Gloucester FICE Identification: 006901
Unit ID: 184791
Telephone: (856) 468-5000 Carnegie Class: Assoc/HT-High Trad
FAX Number: N/A Calendar System: 4/1/4
URL: www.rcgc.edu
Established: 1966 Annual Undergrad Tuition & Fees (In-District): $4,325
Enrollment: 7,130 Coed
Affiliation or Control: State/Local IRS Status: 501(c)3
Highest Offering: Associate Degree
Accreditation: M, ADNUR, DMS, NMT

01 President .... Dr. Frederick KEATING
05 VP Academic Services .... Dr. Linda HURLBURT
03 Vice President & COO .... Mr. Dominick BURZICHELLI
32 Vice President Student Svcs .... Ms. Judith ATKINSON
13 Vice President/CIO .... Mr. Josh R. PIDDINGTON
10 Exec Director Financial Services .... Mrs. Elizabeth HALL
15 Exec Director Human Resource .... Mrs. Marlene LOGLISCI
04 Sr Exec Assistant to the President .... Mrs. Karen SITARSKI
22 Exec Dir Diversity and Equity .... Mrs. Almarie JONES
09 Dean Inst Research & Assessment .... Ms. Karen DURKIN
66 Dean Nursing & Allied Health .... Dr. Susan HALL
49 Dean Liberal Arts .... Dr. Paul RUFINO
81 Dean STEM .... Dr. Brenden RICKARDS
20 Dean Academic Compliance .... Ms. Yvonne GREENBAUM
88 Dean Public Safety & Security .... Mr. Fred H. MADDEN
50 Dean Business Studies .... Ms. Patricia CLAGHORN
07 Director Admissions/Registrar .... Ms. Sandra HOFFMAN
36 Director Career & Academic Planning .... Mr. John ORTIZ
35 Exec Director Student Engagement .... Ms. Samantha VAN KOOY
08 Director Library Services .... Mrs. Jane S. CROCKER
30 Director Institutional Advancement .... Ms. Randee DAVIDSON
19 Director Security/Safety .... Mr. Joseph GETSINGER
37 Exec Dir Financial Aid & Admission .... Mr. Michael CHANDO
96 Director of Purchasing .... Mr. Mark ZORZI

Rowan University (E)

201 Mullica Hill Road, Glassboro NJ 08028-1700
County: Gloucester FICE Identification: 002609
Unit ID: 184782
Telephone: (856) 256-4000 Carnegie Class: Masters/L
FAX Number: (856) 256-4929 Calendar System: Semester
URL: www.rowan.edu
Established: 1923 Annual Undergrad Tuition & Fees (In-State): $12,864
Enrollment: 14,778 Coed
Affiliation or Control: State IRS Status: 501(c)3
Highest Offering: Doctorate
Accreditation: M, ART, BUS, CAATE, CACREP, CS, ENG, MED, MUS, NURSE, OSTEO, TED, THEA

01 President .... Dr. Ali A. HOUSHMAND
03 Executive VP .... Mr. Carl OXHOLM, III
05 Provost .... Dr. James NEWELL
10 Senior Vice Pres of Finance/CFO .... Mr. Joseph F. SCULLY
30 Senior VP University Advancement .... Mr. John ZABINSKI
32 VP Student Life/Dean of Students .... Mr. Richard JONES
86 EVP Policy/External Relationships .... Mr. Steve WEINSTEIN
18 Senior VP for Facilities & Opers .... Mr. Donald MOORE
44 VP Advance/Deputy Exec Dir Fndn .... Mr. Ronald J. TALLARIDA
20 VP Academic Affairs .... Dr. Roberta HARVEY
103 SVP Cmty/Economic Development .... Mr. Robert ZAZZALI
46 VP Research .... Dr. Shreekanth MANDAYAM
13 VP Information Resources/CIO .... Dr. Mira LALOVIC-HAND
26 VP for University Relations .... Dr. Jose CARDONA
84 VP Strategic Enrollment Management .... Dr. Jeffrey HAND
88 Asst VP Campus Rec/Stdnt Ctr/CES .... Ms. Tina M. PINOCCI
19 Asst VP Public Safety/Emerg Mgmt .... Mr. Michael KANTNER
15 Asst VP Labor Relations .... Mr. Kenneth KUERZI
38 Sr Dir Counseling/Psych Services .... Dr. David RUBENSTEIN
91 Asst VP of EIS .... Mr. James HENDERSON
63 Dean of Cooper Medical School of RU .... Dr. Paul KATZ
08 Assoc Provost Library Info Services .... Mr. Scott MUIR
50 Dean Rohrer College of Business .... Dr. Susan LEHRMAN
81 Dean College of Science/Mathematics .. Dr. Karen MAGEE-SAUER
53 Dean of Education .... Dr. Monika SHEALEY
57 Dean of Performing Arts .... Dr. John R. PASTIN
58 VP Global Learning & Partnerships .... Dr. Horacio SOSA
54 Dean of Engineering .... Dr. Tony LOWMAN
60 Dean Communication & Creative Arts .... Vacant
83 Dean Humanities & Social Sciences .... Vacant
88 Dean School of Osteopathic Medicine ...... Dr. Thomas CAVALIERI
88 AVP Global Learning & Partnerships .... Ms. Lorraine RICCHEZZA
16 Assoc VP Employment/Labor Relations .... Ms. Eileen SCOTT
22 Asst VP for Equity and Diversity .... Dr. Johanna VELEZ-YELIN
41 Director of Athletics .... Mr. Dan GILMORE
88 Dir Distinguished Events/Spec Proj .... Ms. Kathy ROZANSKI
07 Director of Admissions .... Dr. Albert BETTS
36 Asst Dir Ofc Career Advancement .... Dr. Alicia MONROE
96 Sr Dir Contracting & Procurement ...... Ms. Christina BRASTETER
27 Asst VP University Relations .... Ms. Lori MARSHALL
105 Director University Web Services .... Ms. Jennifer BELL
85 Assoc Director International Center .... Ms. Ghina NAJJAR
28 Asst VP Acad Enrich/EOF/MAP Dir .... Dr. Penny MCPHERSON
100 Chief of Staff/BOT Liaison .... Dr. Joanne M. CONNOR

*Rutgers the State University of New Jersey Central Office (F)

83 Somerset Street New Brunswick NJ 08901-1281
County: Middlesex FICE Identification: 002629
Unit ID: 186362
Telephone: (848) 445-4636 Carnegie Class: N/A
FAX Number: (732) 932-8060
URL: www.rutgers.edu

01 President .... Dr. Robert L. BARCHI
10 VP Finance & Assoc Treasurer .... Mr. Richard M. AKS
05 Sr VP Academic Affairs .... Dr. Barbara A. LEE
102 Pres Rutgers Found/EVP Dev & Alum .... Mr. Nevin E. KESSLER
11 Senior VP for Finance & Admin .... Mr. John M. GOWER
21 Vice President Budgeting .... Dr. Nancy S. WINTERBAUER
13 Vice President Info Tech .... Ms. Michele NARIN
26 VP Univ Communications & Mktg ..... Ms. Kimberly M. MANNING
45 Vice Pres Inst Planning & Operation .... Mr. Antonio CALCADO
88 Vice Chanc Interprofessional Educ .... Dr. Denise RODGERS
43 Senior VP & General Counsel .... Mr. John J. HOFFMAN
30 Sr VP Campaign & Development Oper .... Ms. Julie SHADLE
04 Exec Assistant to the President .... Ms. Jessica OTERO
20 VP Academic Affairs & Admin .... Dr. Karen R. STUBAUS
15 VP HR and Org Effectiveness .... Ms. Vivian FERNANDEZ
08 VP Info Services & Univ Librarian .... Ms. Krisellen MALONEY
101 Interim Secretary of the University .... Ms. Kimberlee M. PASTVA
19 Exec Director Police Services .... Mr. Kenneth B. COP
23 Asst Vice Chancellor Health Svcs .... Dr. Melodee S. LASKY
06 Executive University Registrar .... Mr. Kenneth J. IUSO
37 University Dir Financial Aid .... Ms. Jean MCDONALD-RASH
41 Director Intercollegiate Athletics .... Mr. Patrick HOBBS
22 Assoc VP Labor Relations .... Mr. Harry M. AGNOSTAK
36 Director Career Services .... Ms. Jennifer BROYLES
09 VP Inst Research & Planning .... Dr. Robert J. HEFFERNAN
86 Senior VP External Affairs .... Mr. Peter J. MCDONOUGH, JR.
84 VP Enrollment Management .... Dr. Courtney MCANUFF
29 VP Alumni Relations & Annual Giving ..... Ms. Donna THORNTON
86 Asst VP Federal Relations .... Ms. Francine PFEIFFER
86 VP State Government Affairs .... Mr. David A. WEINSTEIN
88 Assc VP Promtg Women Sci Eng Math ...... Dr. Joan W. BENNETT
88 VP Health Science Partnerships .... Dr. Kenneth J. BRESLAUER
12 Chancellor Rutgers-New Brunswick .... Dr. Richard EDWARDS
12 Chancellor Rutgers-Camden .... Dr. Phoebe A. HADDON
12 Chancellor RU Newark .... Dr. Nancy E. CANTOR
88 Chancellor Biomed & Health Sci .... Dr. Brian L. STROM
88 Interim Dir Cancer Institute NJ .... Dr. Bruce HAFFTY
88 Senior VP Research & Econ Dev .... Dr. Christopher J. MOLLOY
88 VP Physical Sci & Eng Partnership .... Dr. Leonard C. FELDMAN
88 Sr Vice Chancellor Pub Affairs .... Dr. Peter T. ENGLOT
11 Vice Chancellor Admin & Finance .... Dr. Larry R. GAINES, JR.
20 Vice Chancellor Acad Pgms & Svcs .... Dr. John GUNKEL
88 University Controller .... Mr. Stephen J. DIPAOLO
21 VP Finance & Assoc Treasurer .... Ms. Delanie S. MOLER
88 VP International & Global Affairs .... Dr. Eric L. GARFUNKEL
106 VP Cont Stdnt & Dist Educ .... Dr. Richard J. NOVAK
28 VP Intl Diversity & Inclusion .... Dr. Jorge R. SCHEMENT
88 Interim Sr VP/Chief Enterprise Risk .... Dr. Frances V. BOUCHOUX
18 VP University Facilities .... Mr. John SHULACK
88 Vice President Business Services .... Mr. Henry X. VELEZ
88 Vice Chancellor UG Academic Affairs .... Dr. Ben SIFUENTES-JAUREGUI
88 Senior Vice Chanc Clinic Affairs .... Dr. Vincente H. GRACIAS

*Rutgers the State University of New Jersey Camden Campus (A)

303 Cooper Street, Camden NJ 08102-1461
County: Camden FICE Identification: 004741
Unit ID: 186371
Telephone: (856) 225-6026 Carnegie Class: Masters/L
FAX Number: (856) 225-6495 Calendar System: Semester
URL: www.camden.rutgers.edu
Established: 1927 Annual Undergrad Tuition & Fees (In-State): $14,000
Enrollment: 6,321 Coed
Affiliation or Control: State IRS Status: 501(c)3
Highest Offering: Doctorate
Accreditation: &M, BUS, LAW, NURSE, PTA, SPAA, TEAC

02 Chancellor .... Dr. Phoebe A. HADDON
05 Provost .... Dr. Michael PALIS
11 Sr Vice Chancellor Admin & Finance .....Dr. Larry R. GAINES, JR.
32 Vice Chancellor Student Life .... Dr. Mary Beth B. DAISEY
20 Vice Chancellor for UG Education .... Dr. Julie AMON
84 Vice Chancellor Enroll Mgmt .... Dr. Craig WESTMAN
88 Assoc Chancellor Civic Engage .... Ms. Nyemma WATSON
88 Director Economic Development .... Mr. Gregory GAMBLE
61 Co-Dean School of Law .... Dr. Michael T. CAHILL
58 Dean Grad School .... Dr. Kriste LINDENMEYER
50 Dean School of Business .... Dr. Jaishankar GANESH
49 Dean Fac Arts & Sci/Univ Col .... Dr. Kriste LINDENMEYER
66 Dean School of Nursing .... Dr. Joanne P. ROBINSON
26 Assoc Chancellor for Ext Relations .... Mr. Michael J. SEPANIC
06 Registrar .... Ms. Theresa R. CRISTOFARO
37 Director Financial Aid .... Ms. Linda J. TAYLOR-BURCH
10 Director Campus Financial Services .... Ms. Rosa M. RIVERA
19 Chief Campus Police .... Chief Guy M. STILL
29 Director Alumni Relations .... Mr. Scott D. OWENS
15 Human Resources Manager .... Mr. Gregory M. O'SHEA
18 Assoc Director Facilities Services .... Ms. Rona LEHTONEN
21 Business Manager FAS Camden .... Ms. Marlene DRUDING
41 Dir Athletics & Rec Services .... Mr. Jeffrey L. DEAN
36 Asst Dean Career Center .... Ms. Cheryl A. HALLMAN
23 Health Center Director .... Dr. Neuza M. SERRA
30 Director of Development .... Ms. Akua ASIAMAH-ANDRADE
08 Director Paul Robeson Library .... Dr. Gary A. GOLDEN
39 Director Housing .... Mr. Brandon CHANDLER
87 Summer Coord/Sr Program Coordinator .... Dr. Paul C. BUTLER
46 Director Sponsored Research .... Ms. Carberta A. MORRISON
13 Director Information Technology .... Mr. Joseph R. SANDERS
30 Acting Assoc Chancellor Development .... Ms. Kate BRENNAN
07 Director of Admissions .... Ms. Victoria E. TOOMER
85 Asst Dean International Students .... Ms. Elizabeth A. ATKINS
35 Dean of Students .... Dr. Thomas J. DIVALERIO
96 Senior Buyer .... Mr. Christian AHA
100 Chief of Staff .... Dr. Loree D. JONES

† Regional accreditation is carried under Rutgers the State University of New Jersey New Brunswick.

*Rutgers the State University of New Jersey New Brunswick Campus (B)

85 Somerset Street, New Brunswick NJ 08901-1281
County: Middlesex FICE Identification: 006964
Unit ID: 186380
Telephone: (848) 932-4636 Carnegie Class: DU-Highest
FAX Number: (732) 932-8060 Calendar System: Semester
URL: www.rutgers.edu
Established: 1766 Annual Undergrad Tuition & Fees (In-State): $14,131
Enrollment: 46,378 Coed
Affiliation or Control: State IRS Status: 501(c)3
Highest Offering: Doctorate
Accreditation: M, CACREP, CEA, CLPSY, DANCE, DIETD, ENG, LIB, LSAR, MUS, PCSAS, PH, PHAR, PLNG, SCPSY, SPAA, SW, TEAC

02 Chancellor Rutgers New Brunswick .... Dr. Richard EDWARDS
32 Vice Chancellor Student Affairs .... Ms. Felicia E. MCGINTY
10 Vice Chancellor Finance & Admin .... Ms. Mary Lou ORTIZ
05 Provost New Brunswick .... Dr. Lily Y. YOUNG
84 VP Enrollment Management .... Dr. Courtney O. MCANUFF
11 VP Acad Affairs & Administration .... Dr. Karen R. STUBAUS
28 VP Inst Diversity & Inclusion .... Dr. Jorge R. SCHEMENT
08 Interim VP Info Svcs/U Librarian .... Ms. Jeanne E. BOYLE
58 Dean Graduate School-NB .... Dr. Jerome J. KUKOR
80 Dean EJB School Plng/Public Policy .... Dr. James W. HUGHES
81 Exec Dean Sch Enviro/Biological Sci .... Dr. Robert M. GOODMAN
12 Dean Douglass Residential College .... Dr. Jacquelyn S. LITT
12 Dean Livingston Campus .... Dr. Lea P. STEWART
12 Dean Busch Campus .... Dr. Thomas V. PAPATHOMAS
49 Executive Dean SAS .... Dr. Peter MARCH
92 Honors College Admin Dean .... Dr. Paul GILMORE
12 Dean Cook Campus .... Dr. Judith STORCH
88 Acting Dean Univ College Community .... Dr. Dona SCHNEIDER
54 Dean School of Engineering .... Dr. Thomas N. FARRIS
67 Dean Ernest Mario Sch Pharm .... Dr. Joseph BARONE
57 Dean Mason Gross School of Art .... Dr. George B. STAUFFER
62 Dean Sch Communication & Info .... Dr. Jonathan POTTER
83 Dean Grad School Applied/Prof Psych .... Dr. Francine CONWAY
53 Dean Grad School of Education .... Dr. Wanda J. BLANCHETT
66 Dean School of Nursing .... Dr. William L. HOLZEMER
70 Dean School of Social Work .... Dr. Cathryn C. POTTER
50 Dean Sch of Business Newark/NB .... Dr. Lei LEI
88 Dean Sch Mgmt Labor Relations .... Dr. James C. HAYTON
06 Executive University Registrar .... Mr. Kenneth J. IUSO
104 Director Rutgers Study Abroad .... Dr. Giorgio G. DIMAURO
07 Director Graduate Admissions .... Ms. Linda J. COSTA
37 University Dir Financial Aid .... Ms. Jean MCDONALD-RASH
36 Director Career Services .... Ms. Jennifer BROYLES
26 Sr VP & Chief Information Officer .... Ms. Michele NORIN
09 VP Institutional Rsrch & Plng .... Dr. Robert J. HEFFERNAN
39 Director Residence Life .... Mr. Michael TOLBERT
19 Exec Dir Police Services/Chief .... Mr. Kenneth B. COP
88 Dean College Avenue Campus .... Dr. Matthew K. MATSUDA
12 Director Rutgers China Office .... Dr. Jeff (Jianfeng) WANG
41 Director Intecollegiate Athletics .... Mr. Patrick E. HOBBS

*Rutgers the State University of New Jersey Newark Campus (C)

249 University Avenue, Newark NJ 07102-1897
County: Essex FICE Identification: 002631
Unit ID: 186399
Telephone: (973) 353-5568 Carnegie Class: DU-Higher
FAX Number: (973) 353-1048 Calendar System: Semester
URL: www.newark.rutgers.edu
Established: 1892 Annual Undergrad Tuition & Fees (In-State): $13,597
Enrollment: 11,314 Coed
Affiliation or Control: State IRS Status: 501(c)3
Highest Offering: Doctorate
Accreditation: &M, ANEST, BUS, LAW, NURSE, SPAA, SW, TEAC

02 Chancellor .... Dr. Nancy E. CANTOR
05 Provost & Exec Vice Chancellor .... Dr. Jerome D. WILLIAMS
11 Exec Vice Chanc & Chief Oper Ofcr .... Dr. Shirley M. COLLADO
100 Senior Vice Chanc & Chief of Staff .... Dr. Peter T. ENGLOT
10 Vice Chancellor Admin & CFO .... Dr. Arcelio APONTE
86 Vice Chanc External & Govt Rels .... Dr. Marcia W. BROWN
15 Asst Vice Chanc Human Resources .... Dr. Bil LEIPOLD
18 Assoc Vice Chancellor Facilities .... Dr. Christopher PYE
30 Vice Chancellor for Development .... Dr. Irene O'BRIEN
20 Vice Chancellor Acad Pgms & Svcs .... Dr. John GUNKEL
46 Vice Chancellor Research .... Dr. Nabil ADAM
84 Asst Chanc Enrollment Management .... Dr. Ben ROHDIN
45 Asst Provost for Budget .... Dr. Mary TAMASCO
32 Vice Chancellor for Student Affairs .... Dr. Corlisse THOMAS
31 Asst Chancellor Comm Partner .... Dr. Diane HILL
06 Registrar .... Dr. Marie DIAZ-TORRES
21 Exec Dir Business & Financial Svcs .... Dr. Sanjana RIMAL
13 Interim Dir Information Technology .... Mr. Galen J. WORK
07 Asst Prov & Dean of Admissions .... Ms. LaToya BATTLE-BROWN
19 Director Public Safety Newark .... Mr. Carmelo V. HUERTAS
26 Acting Director of Communications .... Ms. Ferlanda F. NIXON
37 Director Financial Aid .... Ms. Natalie L. MORISSEAU
49 Dean Faculty Arts & Science .... Dr. Jan Ellen LEWIS
61 Co-Dean of School of Law .... Dr. Ronald K. CHEN, JR.
50 Dean Business Newark/New Bruns .... Dr. Lei LEI
66 Dean School of Nursing .... Dr. William L. HOLZEMER
88 Dean School Criminal Justice .... Dr. Rod BRUNSON
38 Director Student Counseling .... Dr. Anice THOMAS
96 Senior Buyer .... Ms. Ida ANGELONE
80 Interim Dean Sch Pub Aff & Admin .... Dr. Gregg G. VAN RYZIN
39 Director Housing & Residence Life .... Dr. Angelita BONILLA
23 Director Health Services .... Dr. Sandra SAMUELS
41 Director of Athletics & Recreation .... Mr. Mark GRIFFIN
82 Director of Global Affairs .... Dr. Jean-Marc COICAUD
58 Dean Graduate School Newark .... Dr. Kyle W. FARMBRY
87 Manager Summer Session .... Ms. Carmen L. PARDO
88 Assoc Dean/Dir Robeson Campus Ctr .... Dr. Clayton WALTON
04 Sr Exec Assoc to the Chancellor .... Ms. Sharon MACKLIN

† Regional accreditation is carried under Rutgers the State University of New Jersey New Brunswick.

*Rutgers Graduate School of Biomedical Sciences (D)

185 South Orange Avenue, MSB C-696, Newark NJ 07107-1709
Telephone: (973) 972-5332 FICE Identification: 011174
Accreditation: &M

† Regional accreditation is carried under the parent institution in New Brunswick, NJ

*Rutgers-New Jersey Medical School (E)

185 S Orange Avenue, Newark NJ 07101-1709
Telephone: (973) 972-4538 FICE Identification: 002620
Accreditation: &M, MED

† Regional accreditation is carried under the parent institution in New Brunswick, NJ

*Rutgers - Robert Wood Johnson Medical School (F)

675 Hoes Lane, Piscataway NJ 08854-5635
Telephone: (732) 235-6300 FICE Identification: 024549
Accreditation: &M, IPSY, MED, PAST

† Regional accreditation is carried under the parent institution in New Brunswick, NJ

*Rutgers School of Dental Medicine (G)

110 Bergen Street, Room B-830, Newark NJ 07101-1709
Telephone: (973) 972-4633 FICE Identification: 024635
Accreditation: &M, DENT

† Regional accreditation is carried under the parent institution in New Brunswick, NJ

*Rutgers School of Health Professions (H)

65 Bergen Street, Room 149, Newark NJ 07101-1709
Telephone: (973) 972-5454 FICE Identification: 020668
Accreditation: &M, ARCPA, CACREP, CAHIIM, COARC, CORE, CVT, CYTO, DA, DH, DIETC, DIETI, DMS, MT, NMT, OTA, PHLEB, PTA

† Regional accreditation is carried under the parent institution in New Brunswick, NJ

*Rutgers School of Nursing (I)

180 University Avenue, Newark NJ 07102
Telephone: (973) 353-5293 Identification: 666970
Accreditation: &M, MIDWF, NURSE

† Regional accreditation is carried under the parent institution in New Brunswick, NJ

*Rutgers School of Public Health (J)

683 Hoes Lane West, Room 235, Piscataway NJ 08854-8021
Telephone: (732) 235-9700 Identification: 666991
Accreditation: &M, PH

† Regional accreditation is carried under the parent institution in New Brunswick, NJ

Saint Peter's University (K)

2641 Kennedy Boulevard, Jersey City NJ 07306-5997
County: Hudson FICE Identification: 002638
Unit ID: 186432
Telephone: (201) 761-6000 Carnegie Class: Masters/L
FAX Number: (201) 761-7801 Calendar System: Semester
URL: www.saintpeters.edu
Established: 1872 Annual Undergrad Tuition & Fees: $34,198
Enrollment: 3,302 Coed
Affiliation or Control: Roman Catholic IRS Status: 501(c)3
Highest Offering: Doctorate
Accreditation: M, IACBE, NURSE, TEAC

01 President .... Dr. Eugene J. CORNACCHIA
05 Provost/VP Academic Affairs .... Dr. Gerard P. O'SULLIVAN
10 Vice Pres of Finance & Business .... Mr. Denton L. STARGEL
30 Vice President Advancement .... Ms. Leah LETO
32 Assc VP Stdnt Life & Dev/Dean Stdnt .... Mr. Anthony SKEVAKIS
42 Vice Pres for Mission & Ministry .... Fr. Rocco DANZI, SJ
84 VP Enrollment Mgmt & Marketing .... Mr. Jeffrey HANDLER
45 Spec Asst to President for Planning .... Dr. Virginia BENDER
51 Dean & Director of JC SPCS .... Ms. Elizabeth KANE
78 Exec Dir of Experiential Lrng .... Ms. Laura PAKHMANOV
20 Associate Dean of Undergraduates .... Dr. Anna CICIRELLI
26 Director University Communications .... Ms. Sarah MALINOWSKI-FERRARY
84 Director Enrollment/Research/Tech .... Mr. Ben SCHOLZ
07 Assoc VP and Dean of Admissions .... Ms. Elizabeth SULLIVAN
08 Director of the Libraries .... Ms. Daisy DECOSTER
37 Director of Student Fin Aid .... Ms. Jennifer RAGSDALE
06 Registrar .... Ms. Kamla SINGH
13 VP & Chief Information Officer .... Mr. Milos TOPIC
09 Director of Institutional Research .... Mr. Lamberto C. NIEVES
66 Dean of Nursing .... Dr. Lauren O'HARE
19 Director of Campus Safety .... Mr. Scott TORRE
15 Director of Human Resources .... Ms. Elena SERRA
29 Exec Director Alumni Engagement .... Ms. Gloria MERCURIO
30 Director of Gift/Planning .... Ms. Ana M. CRAVO
38 Director Personal Development .... Mr. Ron BECKER
39 Director of Residence Life .... Ms. Victoria FARRIS
41 Director of Athletics .... Ms. Belinda PEARMAN
42 Director of Campus Ministry .... Ms. Christine BOYLE
14 Director of Network Services .... Mr. Bert VABRE
85 Foreign Studies Adviser .... Mr. Tushar TRIVEDI
18 Manager of College Services .... Ms. Anna DE PAULA
102 Dir Foundation/Corp & Govt Rels .... Mr. Emory EDWARDS
104 Director Study Abroad .... Mr. Scott KELLER
105 Director Web Services .... Mr. Kyle RIVERS
50 Dean School of Business .... Mr. Bruce ROSENTHAL
53 Dean School of Education .... Dr. Joseph DORIA
96 Director of Purchasing .... Mr. John MATTHEWS
04 Administrative Asst to President .... Ms. Janice P. VIZZACCHERO
101 Secretary of the Institution/Board .... Dr. Virginia A. BENDER

Salem Community College (L)

460 Hollywood Avenue, Carneys Point NJ 08069-2799
County: Salem FICE Identification: 005461
Unit ID: 186469
Telephone: (856) 299-2100 Carnegie Class: Assoc/MT-VT-High Trad
FAX Number: (856) 351-2634 Calendar System: Semester
URL: www.salemcc.edu
Established: 1972 Annual Undergrad Tuition & Fees (In-District): $4,104
Enrollment: 1,173 Coed
Affiliation or Control: State/Local IRS Status: 501(c)3
Highest Offering: Associate Degree
Accreditation: M, ADNUR

01 President ... Dr. Michael GORMAN
05 VP of Academic Affairs/CAO ... Dr. Eric PELLEGRINO
04 Admin Asst Office to the President ... Ms. Maria FANTINI
20 Associate Dean of Academic Affairs ... Mr. John STEINER
88 Assistant Dean of Academic Affairs ... Mr. Kenneth ROBEL
07 Dean of Enrollment/Admissions ... Mr. Kevin CATALFAMO
10 Chief Financial/Business Ofcr ... Mr. Kevin KUTCHER
06 Registrar ... Ms. Jill JAMES
88 Dir of Institutional Effectiveness ... Mr. Marc ROY
19 Director of Security/Safety ... Mr. John MORRISON
103 Director of Workforce/Career Dev ... Ms. Mary Ellen HASSLER
15 Director of Human Resources ... Ms. Caroline COULET DUGARD
88 Director of Retention & Admissions ... Ms. Jasmine LYNCH
09 Director Inst Rsrch/Planning/Devel ... Ms. Denise DERSCH
30 Dir of Inst Advancement/Alumni ... Mr. William CLARK
37 Dir Student Financial Services ... Mr. Ronald BURKHARDT
66 Director of Nursing ... Mr. Charles MCGLADE
88 Director of Academic & Info Svcs ... Ms. Jennifer PIERCE
13 Director of Information Technology ... Mr. Larry MCKEE
102 Chief Foundation Officer ... Ms. Ceil SMITH
21 Manager of Finance ... Ms. Catherine PRIEST
96 Manager of Purchasing ... Vacant
88 Accounts Manager ... Ms. Maureen DOUGHERTY

Seton Hall University (A)

400 S Orange Avenue, South Orange NJ 07079-2697
County: Essex — FICE Identification: 002632
Unit ID: 186584
Telephone: (973) 761-9000 — Carnegie Class: DU-Mod
FAX Number: N/A — Calendar System: Semester
URL: www.shu.edu
Established: 1856 — Annual Undergrad Tuition & Fees: $38,072
Enrollment: 9,627 — Coed
Affiliation or Control: Roman Catholic — IRS Status: 501(c)3
Highest Offering: Doctorate
Accreditation: M, ARCPA, BUS, BUSA, CAATE, COPSY, HSA, LAW, MFCD, NURSE, OT, PTA, SP, SPAA, SW, TED, THEOL

01 President ... Dr. A. Gabriel ESTEBAN
05 Provost & Executive Vice President ... Dr. Larry A. ROBINSON
20 Senior Associate Provost ... Dr. Joan GUETTI
20 Associate Vice Provost ... Msgr. Robert COLEMAN
10 Vice Pres for Finance/CFO ... Mr. Stephen A. GRAHAM
11 Vice President for Administration ... Mr. Dennis J. GARBINI
43 Vice President & General Counsel ... Ms. Catherine A. KIERNAN
30 Vice Pres Univ Advancement ... Mr. David BOHAN
32 Vice President Student Affairs ... Dr. Tracy T. GOTTLIEB
84 Vice President of Enrollment Mgmt ... Dr. Alyssa MCCLOUD
42 Vice Pres for Mission & Ministry ... Msgr. C. Anthony ZICCARDI
15 Assoc Vice Pres Human Resources ... Mr. Michael SILVESTRO
29 Assoc VP Alumni/Government Rels ... Mr. Matthew BOROWICK
44 Assoc Vice Pres Univ Advance ... Mr. Joseph GUASCONI
26 Assoc VP Public Relations & Mktg ... Mr. Dan P. KALMANSON
18 Assoc VP for Facilities & Operation ... Mr. John SIGNORELLO
35 Asst VP Student Affs/Dir Pub Safety ... Mr. Patrick LINFANTE
31 Asc VP/Dean of Students/Cmty Dev ... Ms. Karen VAN NORMAN
88 Assoc Prov Finance/Administration ... Ms. Mary Ann HART
45 Assoc Provost/Dean Rsrch/Grad Stds ... Dr. Gregory A. BURTON
88 Assoc Provost for Academic Projects ... Mr. Erik LILLQUIST
49 Dean of Arts & Sciences ... Dr. Peter SHOEMAKER
50 Dean School of Business ... Dr. Joyce A. STRAWSER
60 Dean Communication & the Arts ... Ms. Deirdre YATES
66 Dean of Nursing ... Dr. Marie FOLEY
53 Dean College Education Svcs ... Dr. Maureen GILLETTE
73 Dean School of Theology ... Msgr. Joseph R. REILLY
63 Dean School of Health & Med Science ... Dr. Brian SHULMAN
82 Dean Diplomacy/Intl Relations ... Dr. Andrea BARTOLI
63 Dean Medical School ... Dr. Bonita STANTON
61 Dean of Law School ... Ms. Kathleen BOOZANG
08 Dean of University Libraries ... Dr. John E. BUSCHMAN
51 Dean Cont Educ/Professional Studies ... Ms. Karen PASSARO
88 Assoc Dean/Director of EOP ... Dr. Majid WHITNEY
88 Assoc Dean/Exec Dir of Special Pgms ... Ms. Cassandra E. DAVIS
21 Director of Business Affairs ... Mr. Michael GARCIA
13 Chief Information Officer ... Dr. Stephen LANDRY
28 Director Compliance & Risk Mgmt ... Ms. Lori A. BROWN
37 Director for Financial Aid ... Ms. Javonda ASANTE
39 Director of Housing/Residence Life ... Ms. Tara HART
06 University Registrar ... Ms. Mary Ellen FARRELL
36 Director of the Career Center ... Ms. Reesa GREENWALD
41 Dir Athletics/Recreational Services ... Mr. Patrick G. LYONS
18 Director of Physical Plant ... Mr. Steve KURTYKA
38 Director of Counseling ... Dr. Katherine EVANS
42 Director of Campus Ministry ... Rev. Robert P. MCLAUGHLIN
88 Minister to Priest Community ... Msgr. Robert M. COLEMAN
09 Dir Plng Inst Research & Assessment ... Ms. Connie L. BEALE
07 Dir of Undergraduate Admissions ... Ms. Mary Clare CULLUM
96 Director of Procurement ... Mr. Martin E. KOELLER
23 Director Health Services ... Ms. Mary Elizabeth COSTELLO
88 Director Core Curriculum ... Dr. Anthony C. SCIGLITANO, JR.
102 Dir Foundation/Corporate Relations ... Ms. Lily M. CABRERA
104 Director Study Abroad ... Ms. Maria BOUZAS
108 Director Institutional Assessment ... Ms. Agata WOLFE
88 Asst Provost for Academic Affairs ... Dr. Christopher CUCCIA
86 Director Government Relations ... Mr. Matthew BOROWICK

Stevens Institute of Technology (B)

Castle Point on Hudson, Hoboken NJ 07030-5991
County: Hudson — FICE Identification: 002639
Unit ID: 186867
Telephone: (201) 216-5000 — Carnegie Class: DU-Higher
FAX Number: (201) 216-8341 — Calendar System: Semester
URL: www.stevens.edu
Established: 1870 — Annual Undergrad Tuition & Fees: $47,190
Enrollment: 6,125 — Coed
Affiliation or Control: Independent Non-Profit — IRS Status: 501(c)3
Highest Offering: Doctorate
Accreditation: M, BUS, CS, ENG

01 President ... Dr. Nariman FARVARDIN
04 Exec Assistant to the President ... Ms. Karen CUOZZO
05 Provost/University Vice President ... Dr. George P. KORFIATIS
30 Vice President for Development ... Mr. Brodie REMINGTON
10 CFO/VP for Finance/Treasurer ... Mr. Louis MAYER
84 VP Enrollment Mgt/Student Affairs ... Ms. Marybeth MURPHY
15 Vice President Human Resources ... Vacant
43 Vice President General Counsel ... Ms. Kathy L. SCHULZ
13 VP for Information Technology & CIO ... Mr. David DODD
26 VP Communications & Marketing ... Mr. Edward STUKANE
18 VP for Facilities/Campus Operations ... Mr. Robert MAFFIA
32 Assistant VP Student Affairs ... Ms. Sara KLEIN
21 AVP for Financial Planning/Budget ... Mr. Justin OATES
20 Dean Undergraduate Academics ... Dr. Larry RUSS
35 Dean of Student Life ... Mr. Kenneth NILSEN
39 Dean for Residence Life ... Ms. Trina BALLANTYNE
20 Assoc Dean Undergraduate Academics ... Dr. Erol CESMEBASI
29 AVP Alumni Engagement & ED/SAA ... Ms. Melissa FUEST
36 Exec Director of Career Services ... Ms. Lynn INSLEY
19 Chief & Director of Campus Safety ... Mr. Timothy GRIFFIN
41 Athletic Director ... Mr. Russell ROGERS
85 Dir of Intl Student/Scholar Svcs ... Ms. Doris CLAUSEN
38 Director of Student Counseling ... Dr. Joel STREICH
40 Manager Campus Bookstore ... Ms. Teresa TRIDENTE
25 Exec Director Sponsored Research ... Ms. Barbara DEHAVEN
58 Dean of Graduate Academics ... Dr. Charles SUFFEL
54 Interim Dean School of Engr & Sci ... Dr. Keith SHEPPARD
50 Dean School of Business ... Dr. Gregory PRASTACOS
49 Dean College of Arts & Letters ... Dr. Kellarc THOMAS
88 Dean School of Systems & Enterprise ... Dr. Dinesh VERMA
09 Director of Institutional Research ... Ms. Minghui WANG
100 Chief of Staff/Director ... Ms. Elisabeth MCGRATH
28 Exec Director Diversity & Inclusion ... Ms. Susan METZ
88 Vice Provost Strategic Initiatives ... Mr. Ralph G. GIFFIN
20 Vice Provost of Academics ... Dr. Constantin CHASSAPIS
46 Vice Provost of Research ... Dr. Mo DEHGHANI
06 Registrar ... Vacant
08 Director of Library & Info Svcs ... Ms. Linda BENINGHOVE
104 Director International Programs ... Ms. Susan RACHOUH
105 Director Enterprise Web Services ... Mr. Aaron GARY
106 Assistant Dean Web Campus ... Mr. Robert ZOTTI
37 Director Student Financial Aid ... Ms. Susan GROSS
96 Director of Procurement ... Mr. Jeff HADLEY

Stockton University (C)

101 Vera King Farris Drive, Galloway NJ 08205-9441
County: Atlantic — FICE Identification: 009345
Unit ID: 186876
Telephone: (609) 652-1776 — Carnegie Class: Masters/L
FAX Number: (609) 652-0275 — Calendar System: Semester
URL: www.stockton.edu
Established: 1969 — Annual Undergrad Tuition & Fees (In-State): $12,820
Enrollment: 8,570 — Coed
Affiliation or Control: State — IRS Status: 501(c)3
Highest Offering: Doctorate
Accreditation: M, BUS, NURSE, OT, PTA, SP, SW, TEAC

01 President ... Dr. Harvey KESSELMAN
05 Provost & VP for Academic Affairs ... Dr. Lori VERMEULEN
100 Exec VP and Chief of Staff ... Dr. Susan C. DAVENPORT
10 Vice Pres Administration & Finance ... Mr. Charles E. INGRAM
32 Vice President Student Affairs ... Dr. Thomasa GONZALEZ
20 Asst Provost Programs & Planning ... Dr. Carra HOOD
96 Director of Purchasing ... Ms. Margaret QUINN
13 Chief Information Officer ... Mr. Robert R. HEINRICH
21 AVP Business Svcs/Chief Bdgt Ofcr ... Mr. James TIERNEY
18 Assoc VP Facilities/Construction ... Mr. Donald M. HUDSON
22 Chief Ofcr Inst Diversity/Equity ... Dr. Valerie HAYES
26 Chief Univ Relations/Marketing Ofcr ... Ms. Sharon SCHULMAN
30 Chief Dev Ofcr/Exec Dir Foundation ... Dr. Philip T. ELLMORE
84 Dean of Enrollment Management ... Mr. John IACOVELLI
07 Associate Dean of Admissions ... Ms. Alison HENRY
35 Dean of Students ... Dr. Pedro SANTANA
06 Assoc Dean Records/Registration ... Mr. Joseph LOSASSO
53 Dean School of Education ... Dr. Claudine KEENAN
97 Dean School of General Studies ... Dr. Robert S. GREGG
79 Dean School Arts & Humanities ... Dr. Lisa HONAKER
50 Dean School of Business ... Dr. Janet M. WAGNER
84 Dean of Graduate Enrollment Mgmt ... Ms. AmyBeth GLASS
81 Dean School of Natural Sci/Math ... Dr. Peter STRAUB
83 Dean Sch Social/Behavioral Sciences ... Dr. Cheryl KAUS
76 Dean School of Health Sciences ... Dr. Theresa BARTOLOTTA
15 Director Human Resource Management ... Mr. Thomas P. CHESTER
09 Director Institutional Research ... Dr. Xiangping KONG
08 Director of Library Services ... Mr. Joseph TOTH
88 Director South Regional ETTC ... Ms. Patricia WEEKS
37 Director of Financial Aid ... Ms. Jeanne LEWIS
19 Interim Chief of Police ... Ms. Cynthia Ann PARKER
88 Manager Performing Arts Center ... Ms. Suze DI PIETRO-STEWART
41 Dir of Athletics and Recreations ... Mr. Lonnie FOLKS
39 Director of Residential Life ... Dr. Denise O'NEILL
36 Director of Career Services ... Mr. Walter L. TARVER, III
43 General Counsel ... Mr. Michael ANGULO
38 Director of Counseling ... Dr. Donald CASSIDY
88 Dir Center for Academic Advising ... Dr. Peter HAGEN
21 Director Budget & Fiscal Planning ... Mr. Michael WOOD
29 Director Alumni Relations ... Ms. Sara FAUROT
44 Assoc Chf Devel Ofcr/Campaign Mgr ... Ms. Cindy CRAGER
12 COO Atlantic City Campus ... Mr. Brian K. JACKSON

Sussex County Community College (D)

One College Hill Road, Newton NJ 07860-1146
County: Sussex — FICE Identification: 025688
Unit ID: 247603
Telephone: (973) 300-2100 — Carnegie Class: Assoc/HT-High Trad
FAX Number: (973) 579-3351 — Calendar System: Semester
URL: www.sussex.edu
Established: 1982 — Annual Undergrad Tuition & Fees (In-District): $6,000
Enrollment: 3,064 — Coed
Affiliation or Control: State/Local — IRS Status: 501(c)3
Highest Offering: Associate Degree
Accreditation: M, MAC, SURGT

01 President ... Dr. Jon H. CONNOLLY
04 Asst to President/Board of Trustees ... Wendy FULLEM
05 Int VP of Academic Affairs/CAO ... Dr. James BAKER
10 Exec VP of Finance/Operations/CFO ... Frank NOCELLA
49 Int Asst VP Acad Affs/Dean of Fac ... Dr. Kathleen OKAY
32 Int Dean Student Services/Affairs ... Curtis BIGGS
15 Exec Dir of Human Resources ... Michael GALLEGLY
26 Dir of Marketing/Public Info ... Kathleen PETERSON
30 VP Institutional Advancement ... Karen DIMARIA
24 Assoc Dean of Learning Resources ... Jan TENSEN
41 Dir of Athletics/Dean Student Affs ... John KUNTZ
21 Director of Accounting ... Manal MESCHA
19 Interim Director Safety & Security ... William FICHTER
13 Int Director Information Technology ... David LITTERAL
88 Dir of Bursar/Financial Services ... Tatsiana SHUMSKAYA
106 Dir of Media Services/Distance Educ ... Tony SELIMO
08 Director of College Library ... Stephanie COOPER
07 Director of Admissions ... Todd POLTERSDORF
37 Director of Financial Aid ... Diane PIENTA-LETTA
09 Dir of Inst Research & Assessment ... Cory HOMER
06 Registrar ... Solweig DIMINO
108 Director Institutional Assessment ... Cory HOMER

Talmudical Academy of New Jersey (E)

Route 524, Adelphia NJ 07710-9999
County: Monmouth — FICE Identification: 011989
Unit ID: 186900
Telephone: (732) 431-1600 — Carnegie Class: Spec-4-yr-Faith
FAX Number: (732) 431-3951 — Calendar System: Semester
URL: taofnj@gmail.com
Established: 1971 — Annual Undergrad Tuition & Fees: $12,000
Enrollment: 69 — Male
Affiliation or Control: Independent Non-Profit — IRS Status: 501(c)3
Highest Offering: Baccalaureate
Accreditation: RABN

01 President ... Mr. Charles SEMAH
05 Dean ... Rabbi Yeruchim SHAIN

Thomas Edison State University (F)

111 W State Street, Trenton NJ 08608-1176
County: Mercer — FICE Identification: 021922
Unit ID: 187046
Telephone: (609) 984-1100 — Carnegie Class: Masters/M
FAX Number: (609) 292-9000 — Calendar System: Other
URL: www.tesu.edu
Established: 1972 — Annual Undergrad Tuition & Fees (In-State): $6,135
Enrollment: 21,495 — Coed
Affiliation or Control: State — IRS Status: 501(c)3
Highest Offering: Doctorate
Accreditation: M, ENGT, NUR, NURSE, POLYT, TEAC

01 President ... Dr. George A. PRUITT
05 Vice President & Provost ... Mr. William J. SEATON
10 Vice Pres Administration & Finance ... Mr. Christopher STRINGER
26 Vice President Public Affairs ... Mr. John P. THURBER
31 Vice Pres Cmty & Govt Affairs ... Ms. Robin WALTON
45 VP Institutional Planning/Research ... Dr. Dennis DEVERY
84 VP Enrollment Mgmt/Learner Services ... Dr. Mary Ellen CARO
58 Vice Prov Acad Admin/Dean Grad Pgms ... Dr. Henry VAN ZYL
51 Vice Prov/Dean Watson Sch Cont Stds ... Dr. Joseph YOUNGBLOOD
88 Vice Prov Ctr Assessment of Lrng ... Mr. Marc SINGER
88 Assoc VP Enrollment Management ... Ms. Sylvia HAMILTON
88 Assoc VP Military/Veteran Education ... Mr. Louis MARTINI
32 Assoc VP and Dean of Learner Svcs ... Dr. Raymond YOUNG
09 Assoc VP for Planning & Research ... Dr. Ann Marie SENIOR
27 Assoc VP/Director of Communications ... Mr. Joseph GUZZARDO
88 Assoc Provost Learning Technology ... Mr. Matthew COOPER
21 Treasurer ... Mr. Stephen D. ALBANO
100 Chief of Staff ... Ms. Linda M. MEEHAN
27 Director Market Research/Assessment ... Ms. Marie R. POWER-BARNES
43 General Counsel ... Ms. Barbara KLEVA
66 Dean School of Nursing ... Dr. Phyllis MARSHALL
49 Dean Heavin Sch of Arts & Sciences ... Dr. John WOZNICKI
50 Dean School of Business & Mgmt ... Dr. Michael WILLIAMS
06 Registrar ... Ms. Catharine PUNCHELLO-COBOS

72 Dean School of Applied Sci/Tech .... Dr. John AJE
21 Acting Controller .... Ms. Nancy BROGLIE
13 Chief Information Officer .... Mr. Drew W. HOPKINS
07 Director Admissions .... Mr. David HOFTIEZER
29 Director of Alumni Affairs .... Ms. Roxanne GLOBIS
37 Director of Financial Aid .... Mr. James OWENS
18 Director Facilities & Operations .... Ms. Mary C. HACK
21 Admin of Student Fees & Revenues .... Mr. Philip SANDERS
30 Associate VP for Development .... Ms. Misty ISAK
102 Director Corporate Relations .... Mr. Frederick BRAND
08 State Librarian .... Ms. Mary CHUTE
105 Director Website & Multimedia Produ .... Mr. Jeffery LUSHBAUGH
88 Director of Advancement Services .... Ms. Erica SPIZZIRRRI
44 Dir Annual Fund/Donor Relations .... Ms. Jennifer GUERRERO
88 Executive Director Watson Institute .... Ms. Barbara JOHNSON
88 Dir Learning Outcomes Assessment ..... Ms. Cynthia MACMILLAN
88 ADA Coordinator .... Ms. Laura BRENNER-SCOTTI
04 Assistant to the President .... Ms. Melissa A. MASZCZAK

Union County College (A)

1033 Springfield Avenue, Cranford NJ 07016-1598

County: Union FICE Identification: 002643
Unit ID: 187198
Telephone: (908) 709-7000 Carnegie Class: Assoc/HT-High Trad
FAX Number: (908) 709-0527 Calendar System: Semester
URL: www.ucc.edu
Established: 1933 Annual Undergrad Tuition & Fees (In-District): $4,450
Enrollment: 11,781 Coed
Affiliation or Control: State/Local IRS Status: 501(c)3
Highest Offering: Associate Degree
Accreditation: M, PNUR, PTAA

01 President .... Dr. Margaret M. MCMENAMIN
05 Vice President Academic Affairs .... Dr. Maris LOWN
10 Vice Pres Financial Affs/Treasurer .... Mr. Bernard LENIHAN
32 Vice President Student Development .... Ms. Helen BREWER
11 Vice Pres Administrative Services .... Dr. Stephen NACCO
12 Provost Elizabeth Campus .... Dr. Barbara GABA
12 Interim Dean Plainfield Campus .... Dr. Patricia CASTALDI
26 Exec Director College Relations .... Ms. Ellen DOTTO
13 Director of IT Operations .... Mr. Thomas CHERUBINO
06 Dir Admissions/Records/Registrar .... Ms. Nina HERNANDEZ
08 Director of Libraries .... Ms. Dena LEITER
38 Director of Counseling .... Ms. Heather KEITH
37 Director of Financial Aid .... Mr. Dayne CHANCE
21 Director of Student Accounts .... Mr. Larry GOLDMAN
51 Dean Continuing Educ & Prof Educ .... Dr. Lisa HISCANO
108 Exec Dir of Institutional Research .... Ms. Elizabeth COONER
15 Director of Human Resources .... Mr. Vincent LOTANO
18 Director Facilities .... Mr. Henry KEY
45 Director of Grants .... Ms. Cheryl SHIBER
102 Exec Director Foundation .... Mr. Douglas ROUSE
20 Director Student Assessment Center .... Dr. Susan METTLEN
28 Director EOF .... Mr. Ruben MELENDEZ
41 Dean of College Life .... Ms. Tamalea SMITH
19 Director Public Safety .... Mr. Joseph HINES
27 Director Media Services .... Mr. Stephen KATO
88 Asst Dir Acad Learning Center .... Mr. Jose PAEZ-FIGUEROA
21 Controller .... Ms. Lynne WELCH
96 Director of Purchasing .... Ms. Sandra AULD
40 Manager Bookstore .... Ms. Christine SALZMAN
88 AVP/Dean of American Honors .... Dr. Negar FARAKISH
84 Director Enrollment Services .... Ms. Beatriz RODRIGUEZ

Union County College Elizabeth Campus (B)

40 W Jersey Street, Elizabeth NJ 07202-2314

Telephone: (908) 965-6000 Identification: 770134
Accreditation: &M, EMT

† Regional accreditation is carried under the parent institution in Cranford, NJ

Union County College Plainfield Campus (C)

232 E 2nd Street, Plainfield NJ 07060

Telephone: (908) 412-3599 Identification: 770135
Accreditation: &M

† Regional accreditation is carried under the parent institution in Cranford, NJ

University of Phoenix Jersey City Campus (D)

100 Town Square Place, Jersey City NJ 07310-1756

Telephone: (201) 610-1408 Identification: 770218
Accreditation: &NH, ACBSP

† Regional accreditation is carried under the parent institution in Tempe, AZ

Warren County Community College (E)

475 Route 57 W, Washington NJ 07882-4343

County: Warren FICE Identification: 025039
Unit ID: 245625
Telephone: (908) 835-9222 Carnegie Class: Assoc/HT-High Trad
FAX Number: (908) 689-9262 Calendar System: Semester
URL: www.warren.edu
Established: 1981 Annual Undergrad Tuition & Fees (In-District): $4,410
Enrollment: 2,573 Coed
Affiliation or Control: State/Local IRS Status: 501(c)3
Highest Offering: Associate Degree
Accreditation: M, ADNUR, MAC

01 President .... Dr. William AUSTIN
10 Vice Pres Finance & Operations .... Ms. Barbara PRATT
51 Vice Pres Corporate/Continuing Educ .... Ms. Eve AZAR
11 Dean of Administration .... Mr. Dennis FLORENTINE
05 Acting VP of Academics .... Mr. Jeremy BEELER
37 Director of Financial Aid .... Ms. Debra WULFF
15 Director Human Resources .... Ms. Sharon HINTZ
32 Director Student Activities .... Ms. Rose LYNCH
21 Director Business Services .... Mr. Jay ALEXANDER
04 Administrative Asst to President .... Ms. Genevieve VASKO
07 Director of Admissions .... Ms. Shannon HORWATH
08 Head Librarian .... Ms. Lisa STOLL
09 Director of Institutional Research .... Ms. Nikki DADARRIA
102 Dir Foundation/Corporate Relations .... Ms. Samir ELBASSIOUNY
106 Dir Online Education/E-learning .... Ms. Marianne VANDEURSEN

Westminster Choir College (F)

101 Walnut Lane, Princeton NJ 08540

Telephone: (609) 921-7100 Identification: 770128
Accreditation: &M

† Regional accreditation is carried under the parent institution in Lawrenceville, NJ

William Paterson University of New Jersey (G)

300 Pompton Road, Wayne NJ 07470-2152

County: Passaic FICE Identification: 002625
Unit ID: 187444
Telephone: (973) 720-2000 Carnegie Class: Masters/L
FAX Number: N/A Calendar System: Semester
URL: www.wpunj.edu
Established: 1855 Annual Undergrad Tuition & Fees (In-State): $12,365
Enrollment: 11,048 Coed
Affiliation or Control: State IRS Status: 501(c)3
Highest Offering: Doctorate
Accreditation: M, ART, BUS, CAATE, CACREP, CS, MUS, NURSE, SP, TED

01 President .... Dr. Kathleen WALDRON
05 Senior Vice President/Provost .... Dr. Warren SANDMANN
100 Chf of Staff to Pres/Board of Trust .... Dr. Robert SEAL
10 Vice Pres Administration/Finance .... Mr. Stephen BOLYAI
30 Vice Pres Institutional Advancement .... Ms. Pamela FERGUSON
32 Vice President Student Development .... Dr. Miki CAMMARATA
84 VP of Enrollment Management .... Dr. Reginald ROSS
88 Assoc Provost Academic Development .... Ms. Danielle LIAUTAUD
12 Assoc VP Finance Budget/Fiscal Plng .... Ms. Pamela WINSLOW
11 Assoc VP for Administration .... Mr. Richard STOMBER
26 VP Mktg & Public Relations .... Mr. Stuart GOLDSTEIN
15 Associate Vice Pres Human Resources .... Mr. John POLDING
08 Assoc VP Library Services/Info Tech .... Vacant
19 Dir Public Safety & Univ Police .... Vacant
35 Associate VP for Campus Life .... Mr. Francisco DIAZ
35 Assoc VP/Dean Student Development .... Dr. Glen SHERMAN
60 Dean Col Arts/Comm .... Mr. Daryl MOORE
53 Dean College of Education .... Dr. Candace BURNS
66 Dean College of Science & Health .... Dr. Kenneth WOLF
79 Dean Human & Social Science .... Dr. Kara M. RABBITT
50 Dean College of Business .... Dr. Siamack SHOJAI
08 Dean D & L Cheng Library .... Dr. Edward OWUSU-ANSAH
21 Assoc VP Finance & Comptroller .... Ms. Samantha GREEN
28 Dir Employment Equity & Diversity .... Ms. Michele JOHNSON
46 Exec Director Academic Development ... Ms. Janet DAVIS-DUKES
51 Exec Dir Cont Educ/Distance Lrng .... Dr. Bernadette TIERNAN
20 Associate Provost Academic Affairs .... Dr. Stephen HAHN
20 Assoc Prov for Curriculum & Intl Ed .... Dr. Jonathan LINCOLN
86 Assoc VP Govt & External Relations .... Mr. Patrick DEDEO
27 Director Public Information .... Ms. Mary Beth ZEMAN
29 Executive Director Alumni .... Ms. Janis SCHWARTZ
45 Director Inst Research & Assessment .... Dr. Jane ZEFF
13 Chief Information Officer .... Mr. Eric ROSENBERG
43 General Counsel .... Mr. Glenn JONES
16 Director of Human Resources ...... Ms. Denise ROBINSON-LEWIS
07 Director of Undergrad Admissions . Mr. Michael DIBARTOLOMEO
37 Director Financial Aid .... Mr. Michael CORSO
06 Registrar .... Ms. Nina TRELISKY
41 Director Athletics .... Ms. Sabrina GRANT
36 Director of Career Dev & Advisement ... Ms. Sharon ROSENGART
39 Director of Residence Life .... Mr. Joseph CAFFARELLI
23 Dir Counseling/Health & Wellness .... Dr. Eileen LUBECK
90 Deputy Chief CIO .... Dr. Sandra MILLER
09 Dir Institutional Research/Assess .... Dr. Jane ZEFF
40 Director Bookstore .... Mr. Scott DUNLAP
24 Head Audio Visual-Library .... Vacant
18 Director Capital Plng/Design/Constr .... Vacant
85 Director International Student Svcs .... Ms. Cinzia RICHARDSON
94 Director of Women's Center .... Ms. Librada SANCHEZ
96 Director of Purchasing .... Mr. Lirse JONES
89 Director of Freshmen Studies .... Dr. Kim DANIEL-ROBINSON
92 Director of Honors College .... Dr. Barbara ANDREW
35 Dir Campus Activ/Svc & Leadership .... Ms. Donna MINNICH SPUHLER
88 Assoc Dir Instruction/Research Tech .... Mr. Patrick RYAN
04 Administrative Asst to President .... Ms. Sherin FAVOCCI

Yeshiva Bais Aharon (H)

905 Park Avenue, Lakewood NJ 08701

County: Ocean Identification: 667291
Telephone: (732) 367-7604 Carnegie Class: Not Classified
FAX Number: (732) 367-1777 Calendar System: Semester
Established: 2012 Annual Undergrad Tuition & Fees: N/A
Enrollment: N/A Male
Affiliation or Control: Independent Non-Profit IRS Status: 501(c)3
Highest Offering: First Talmudic Degree
Accreditation: RABN

01 CEO .... Binyomin SCHULGASSER
06 Registrar .... Nosson SCHULGASSER
36 Financial Aid Administrator .... Aharon FISCHER

Yeshiva Chemdas Hatorah (I)

950 Massachusetts Avenue, Lakewood NJ 08701

County: Ocean Identification: 667281
Telephone: N/A Carnegie Class: Not Classified
FAX Number: N/A Calendar System: Other
Established: Annual Undergrad Tuition & Fees: N/A
Enrollment: N/A Male
Affiliation or Control: Independent Non-Profit IRS Status: 501(c)3
Highest Offering: First Talmudic Degree
Accreditation: AIJS

Yeshiva Gedolah Keren Hatorah (J)

1083 Brook Road, Lakewood NJ 08701

County: Ocean Identification: 667282
Telephone: N/A Carnegie Class: Not Classified
FAX Number: N/A Calendar System: Other
Established: Annual Undergrad Tuition & Fees: N/A
Enrollment: N/A Male
Affiliation or Control: Independent Non-Profit IRS Status: 501(c)3
Highest Offering: First Talmudic Degree
Accreditation: AIJS

Yeshiva Gedolah Shaarei Schmuel (K)

511 Ocean Ave, Lakewood NJ 08701

County: Ocean Identification: 667260
Telephone: (732) 363-2164 Carnegie Class: Not Classified
FAX Number: (732) 364-3331 Calendar System: Other
Established: 2008 Annual Undergrad Tuition & Fees: N/A
Enrollment: N/A Male
Affiliation or Control: Independent Non-Profit IRS Status: 501(c)3
Highest Offering: First Talmudic Degree
Accreditation: @RABN

Yeshiva Gedolah Tiferes Boruch (L)

21 Rockview Avenue, North Plainfield NJ 07060

County: Union Identification: 667283
Telephone: N/A Carnegie Class: Not Classified
FAX Number: N/A Calendar System: Other
Established: Annual Undergrad Tuition & Fees: N/A
Enrollment: N/A Male
Affiliation or Control: Independent Non-Profit IRS Status: 501(c)3
Highest Offering: First Talmudic Degree
Accreditation: AIJS

Yeshiva Gedolah Zichron Leyma (M)

2035 Vauxhall Road, Union NJ 07083

County: Union FICE Identification: 041924
Unit ID: 476692
Telephone: (908) 587-0502 Carnegie Class: Spec-4-yr-Faith
FAX Number: N/A Calendar System: Semester
Established: 1999 Annual Undergrad Tuition & Fees: $11,500
Enrollment: 28 Male
Affiliation or Control: Independent Non-Profit IRS Status: 501(c)3
Highest Offering: First Talmudic Degree
Accreditation: RABN

Yeshiva Toras Chaim (N)

999 Ridge Avenue, Lakewood NJ 08701-2120

County: Ocean FICE Identification: 041311
Unit ID: 451398
Telephone: (732) 414-2834 Carnegie Class: Spec-4-yr-Faith
FAX Number: (732) 414-2838 Calendar System: Semester
Established: 2000 Annual Undergrad Tuition & Fees: $11,950
Enrollment: 215 Male
Affiliation or Control: Independent Non-Profit IRS Status: 501(c)3
Highest Offering: Baccalaureate
Accreditation: RABN

05 Chief Academic Officer .... Rabbi Mendel SLOMOVITS
06 Registrar .... Mrs. Devoiry DURST
10 Bookkeeper .... Mrs. Ruth GROSSMAN

Yeshiva Yesodei Hatorah (O)

2 Yesodei Court, Lakewood NJ 08701

County: Ocean Identification: 667109
Unit ID: 481438
Telephone: (732) 370-3360 Carnegie Class: Spec-4-yr-Faith
FAX Number: (732) 886-2659 Calendar System: Semester
Established: 1995 Annual Undergrad Tuition & Fees: $11,000
Enrollment: 69 Male
Affiliation or Control: Independent Non-Profit IRS Status: 501(c)3
Highest Offering: First Talmudic Degree

Accreditation: **RABN**

05 Dean .... Rabbi Shaya TREFF
10 Chief Financial/Business Officer .... Rabbi Shaya UNGAR
20 Associate Academic Officer .... Rabbi Yisroel Meir TREFF

Yeshivas Be'er Yitzchok (A)

1391 North Avenue, Elizabeth NJ 07208-2480
County: Union FICE Identification: 041234
Unit ID: 451370
Telephone: (908) 354-6057 Carnegie Class: Spec-4-yr-Faith
FAX Number: (908) 820-0431 Calendar System: Semester
Established: 1999 Annual Undergrad Tuition & Fees: $10,200
Enrollment: 49 Male
Affiliation or Control: Independent Non-Profit IRS Status: 501(c)3
Highest Offering: Baccalaureate
Accreditation: **RABN**

01 Chief Executive Officer .... Rabbi Avrohom SCHULMAN
37 Director of Student Financial Aid .... Chani MILLER
11 Chief of Administration .... Chani MILLER

NEW MEXICO

Brookline College (B)

4201 Central Avenue NW Ste J,
Albuquerque NM 87105-1649
Telephone: (505) 880-2877 Identification: 666724
Accreditation: **ACICS**, NUR

† Branch campus of Brookline College, Phoenix, AZ

Brown Mackie College - Albuquerque (C)

10500 Cooper Avenue NE, Albuquerque NM 87123
Telephone: (505) 559-5200 Identification: 770741
Accreditation: **ACICS**, OTA, SURTEC

† Branch campus of The Art Institute of Phoenix, Phoenix, AZ

Burrell College of Osteopathic Medicine (D)

3501 Arrowhead Drive, Las Cruces NM 88001
County: Dona Ana Identification: 667248
Telephone: (575) 647-2266 Carnegie Class: Not Classified
FAX Number: (575) 647-2267 Calendar System: Semester
URL: www.bcomnm.org
Established: 2013 Annual Graduate Tuition & Fees: N/A
Enrollment: N/A Coed
Affiliation or Control: Independent Non-Profit IRS Status: 501(c)3
Highest Offering: Doctorate; No Undergraduates
Accreditation: **@OSTEO**

01 Dean .... George MYCHASKIW

Carrington College - Albuquerque (E)

1001 Menaul Boulevard NE, Albuquerque NM 87107-1642
Telephone: (505) 254-7777 Identification: 666014
Accreditation: **&WJ**, PTAA

† Regional accreditation is carried under the parent institution in Sacramento, CA.

Central New Mexico Community College (F)

525 Buena Vista, SE, Albuquerque NM 87106-4096
County: Bernalillo FICE Identification: 004742
Unit ID: 187532
Telephone: (505) 224-4412 Carnegie Class: Assoc/MT-VT-Mix Trad/Non
FAX Number: (505) 224-4417 Calendar System: Semester
URL: www.cnm.edu
Established: 1965 Annual Undergrad Tuition & Fees (In-District): $1,448
Enrollment: 26,771 Coed
Affiliation or Control: State/Local IRS Status: 501(c)3
Highest Offering: Associate Degree
Accreditation: **NH**, ACBSP, ACFEI, ADNUR, CAHIIM, COARC, CONST, DA, DMS, EMT, MLTAD, @PTAA, SURGT

01 President .... Dr. Katharine W. WINOGRAD
05 Vice President for Academic Affairs ... Dr. Sydney D. GUNTHORPE
35 Vice President for Student Services .... Mr. Phillip BUSTOS
10 Vice Pres for Finance & Operations ...... Mrs. Katherine ULIBARRI
84 Assoc Vice Pres Enrollment Mgmt .... Mr. Eugene PADILLA
08 Director Learning Resources ...... Ms. Poppy JOHNSON RENVALL
13 Director Info Technology Services .... Mr. Joe GIERI
103 Assoc Dir Workforce Training Ctr .... Ms. Evelyn DOW
36 Academic Advisement Job Connection .... Ms. Stacey COOLEY
30 Exec Director of Development .... Mr. Clinton WELLS
07 Director Enrollment Services .... Mr. Glenn DAMIANI
26 Dir Marketing & Public Relations .... Mrs. Jennifer BROWER
27 Dir Communications & Media Relation .... Mr. Brad MOORE
37 Director Student Financial Aid .... Mr. Lee CARRILLO
15 Executive Director Human Resources .... Mr. Thomas MANNING
81 Dean Sch of Math/Sci/Engr .... Mr. John CORNISH
50 Dean School of Bus/Info Technology .... Ms. Donna DILLER
72 Dean School of Applied Technologies .... Mr. John BRONISZ
97 Dean Sch of Adult & Gen Educ .... Ms. LouAnne LUNDGREN
83 Dean Comm/Humanities/Soc Sci .... Ms. Erica VOLKERS
76 Dean Health/Well/Pub Safety .... Ms. Tamra MASON
06 Registrar .... Ms. Yvonne MARTINEZ
18 Interim Sr Dir Physical Plant .... Ms. Myrna MARQUEZ
21 Exec Dir Fiscal Ops/Comptroller .... Ms. Wanda HELMS
32 Dean of Student Services .... Mr. Rudy GARCIA
96 Director of Purchasing .... Ms. Wanda HELMS
19 Chief of Safety & Security .... Mr. John CORVINO
04 Administrative Asst to President .... Ms. Erin BRADSHAW
09 Sr Dir Outcomes And Assessment .... Ms. Ursula WALN

Clovis Community College (G)

417 Schepps Boulevard, Clovis NM 88101 8381
County: Curry FICE Identification: 004743
Unit ID: 187639
Telephone: (575) 769-2811 Carnegie Class: Assoc/HVT-High Non
FAX Number: (575) 769-4190 Calendar System: Semester
URL: www.clovis.edu
Established: 1971 Annual Undergrad Tuition & Fees (In-State): $1,176
Enrollment: 3,745 Coed
Affiliation or Control: State IRS Status: 501(c)3
Highest Offering: Associate Degree
Accreditation: **NH**, ADNUR, @PTAA, RAD

01 President .... Dr. Becky ROWLEY
03 Executive Vice President .... Dr. Robin JONES
10 Chief Financial Officer .... Mr. John RUSH
05 Chief Academic Officer .... Dr. Robin JONES
13 Chief Information Officer .... Mr. Norman KIA
11 VP Administration/Govt Relations .... Mr. Tom DRAKE
21 Director of Business Affairs .... Ms. Jayne CRAIG
07 Dir Admissions/Records/Registrar .... Ms. Rosie CORRIE
37 Director of Financial Aid .... Ms. April CHAVEZ
08 Director Library/Learning Resources .... Ms. Kelly GRAY
32 Dir Center for Student Success .... Mrs. Mona Lee NORMAN-ARMSTRONG
38 Dir of Counseling/Testing/Advisemnt .... Mr. Marcus SMITH
15 Director of Human Resource Services .... Mrs. Rhonda JESKO
88 Director Small Business Development .... Mrs. Sandra TAYLOR-SAWYER
91 Director of Administrative Info Sys .... Ms. Teresa WHITEHEAD
56 Director Extended Learning .... Ms. Robin KUYKENDALL
36 Director Student Placement .... Vacant
30 Dir of Institutional Advancement .... Ms. Natalie DAGGETT
18 Director of Physical Plant .... Mr. Paul ARAGON
26 Director of Marketing/Cmty Rels .... Ms. Lisa SPENCER
76 Div Chair Allied Health Programs .... Ms. Shawna MCGILL
83 Div Chair Liberal Arts/Dev Studies .... Ms. Shelley DENTON
50 Div Chair of Business Admin & Tech . Mrs. Becky CARRUTHERS
81 Division Chair of Math/Science .... Mr. Todd KUYKENDALL

Dine College Shiprock Branch (H)

1228 Yucca St., PO Box 580, Shiprock NM 87420
Telephone: (505) 368-3500 Identification: 770007
Accreditation: **&NH**

† Regional accreditation is carried under the parent institution in Tsaile, AZ

Eastern New Mexico University Main Campus (I)

1500 S Avenue K, Portales NM 88130-7400
County: Roosevelt FICE Identification: 002651
Unit ID: 187648
Telephone: (575) 562-1011 Carnegie Class: Masters/M
FAX Number: (575) 562-2980 Calendar System: Semester
URL: www.enmu.edu
Established: 1927 Annual Undergrad Tuition & Fees (In-State): $4,858
Enrollment: 5,879 Coed
Affiliation or Control: State IRS Status: 501(c)3
Highest Offering: Master's
Accreditation: **NH**, ACBSP, MUS, NUR, SP, SW, TED

01 President .... Dr. Steven GAMBLE
05 Vice President Academic Affairs .... Dr. Jamie LAURENZ
10 Vice President Business Affairs .... Mr. Scott SMART
32 Vice President for Student Affairs .... Dr. Jeff LONG
13 Vice President of Technology .... Mr. Clark ELSWICK
04 Special Assistant to the President .... Ms. Bonnie BIRDSONG
45 Exec Dir Planning/Analysis/Inst Ren .... Dr. Patrice CALDWELL
20 Asst Vice Pres for Academic Affairs .... Dr. Renee NEELY
20 Asst Vice Pres Academic Affairs .... Dr. John MONTGOMERY
21 Comptroller .... Mrs. Carol FLETCHER
53 Dean Education/Technology .... Dr. Penny A. GARCIA
50 Dean Business .... Dr. Janet BUZZARD
57 Interim Dean Fine Arts .... Dr. John OLSEN
49 Dean Liberal Arts & Science .... Dr. Mary AYALA
58 Dean Graduate School .... Dr. Linda WEEMS
22 Affirmative Action Officer .... Vacant
08 Director of Library .... Ms. Melveta WALKER
06 Interim Registrar .... Ms. DeLynn BARGAS
37 Director Student Financial Aid .... Mr. Brent SMALL
07 Director Enrollment Services .... Mr. Cody SPITZ
30 Director Development .... Ms. Noelle BARTL
15 Director of Human Resources .... Mr. Benito GONZALES
88 Director of Broadcasting .... Mr. Duane RYAN
18 Director Physical Plant .... Mr. Ted FARES
41 Athletic Director .... Dr. Greg WAGGONER
19 Chief of University Police .... Mr. Brad MAULDIN
36 Dir Counseling Ctr/Career Svcs .... Ms. Susan LARSEN
39 Director Student Housing .... Mr. Steven ESTOCK
09 Dir Institutional Research .... Vacant
96 Director of Purchasing .... Mr. Brad KEMPER
26 Director of Publications .... Mr. John HOUSER
29 Coordinator of Alumni .... Mr. Robert GRAHAM
56 Dir of Distance Learning/Outreach .... Ms. Trish MAGUIRE
35 Director Campus Life .... Mr. Ron WILLIAMS

Eastern New Mexico University-Roswell (J)

PO Box 6000, Roswell NM 88202-6000
County: Chaves FICE Identification: 002661
Unit ID: 187666
Telephone: (575) 624-7000 Carnegie Class: Assoc/HVT-High Non
FAX Number: (575) 624-7342 Calendar System: Semester
URL: www.roswell.enmu.edu
Established: 1958 Annual Undergrad Tuition & Fees (In-State): $1,824
Enrollment: 3,303 Coed
Affiliation or Control: State IRS Status: 501(c)3
Highest Offering: Associate Degree
Accreditation: **NH**, ADNUR, COARC, EMT, MAC, OTA

01 President .... Dr. John MADDEN
05 VP for Academic Affairs .... Mr. Ken MAGUIRE
10 VP for Business Affairs .... Mr. Eric JOHNSTON-ORTIZ
32 VP for Student Affairs .... Mr. Mike MARTINEZ
21 Controller .... Ms. Karen FRANKLIN
35 Asst VP for Student Affairs .... Vacant
08 Director Learning Resource Center .... Mr. Rollah ASTON
37 Director Financial Aid .... Ms. Jessie SJUE
30 Director College Development .... Ms. Donna ORACION
07 Director Admissions and Records .... Ms. Linda NEEL
13 Director of Computer Services .... Vacant
15 Director of Human Resources .... Dr. Steve CHAMBERS
18 Director of Physical Plant .... Mr. Derek DUBIEL
19 Director of Security .... Mr. Robert NEWBERRY
96 Director of Purchasing .... Mr. Stephen WATTERS
09 Institutional Research Professional .... Ms. Rhonda CROCKER
04 Administrative Asst to President .... Ms. Lorinda WILKINS
49 Dean of Liberal Arts .... Ms. Joan ARNOLD
76 Dean of Health Services .... Ms. Susan GOLDEN
103 Dean of Career & Technical Educ .... Dr. Kenneth MAGUIRE

EC-Council University (K)

101C Sun Avenue NE, Albuquerque NM 87109
County: Bernalillo Identification: 667232
Telephone: (505) 922-2886 Carnegie Class: Not Classified
FAX Number: (505) 341-0050 Calendar System: Other
URL: www.eccuni.us
Established: 2003 Annual Undergrad Tuition & Fees: N/A
Enrollment: N/A Coed
Affiliation or Control: Proprietary IRS Status: Proprietary
Highest Offering: Master's
Accreditation: **DEAC**

01 CEO/President .... Sanjay BAVISI
05 Dean .... Randy PLUNKETT
84 Mgr Enrollment/Student Services .... Gregoria A. CAVAZOS
07 Mgr Outreach/Recruitment .... Roxann CURRIER
24 Moodle Admin/Faculty Coordd .... Amber BLEA

Institute of American Indian Arts (L)

83 Avan Nu Po Road, Santa Fe NM 87508-1300
County: Santa Fe FICE Identification: 021464
Unit ID: 187745
Telephone: (505) 424-2300 Carnegie Class: Tribal
FAX Number: (505) 424-4500 Calendar System: Semester
URL: www.iaia.edu
Established: 1962 Annual Undergrad Tuition & Fees: $4,440
Enrollment: 486 Coed
Affiliation or Control: Federal IRS Status: Exempt
Highest Offering: Master's
Accreditation: **NH**, ART

01 President .... Dr. Robert MARTIN
05 Academic Dean .... Ms. Charlene TETERS
10 Chief Financial Officer .... Mr. Larry MIRABAL
32 Dean of Student Life .... Ms. Carmen HENAN
84 Chief Enrollment & Retention Ofcr .... Ms. Nena ANAYA
30 Dir of Institutional Advancement .... Mr. Alex SHAPIRO
26 Dir of Marketing and Communication .... Mr. Eric DAVIS
88 Director of Land Grant Programs .... Ms. Charlene CARR
88 Dir of IAIA Museum .... Ms. Patsy PHILLIPS
102 Dir of Sponsored Programs .... Ms. Laurie BRAYSHAW
09 Dir of Institutional Research .... Dr. William SAYRE

Luna Community College (M)

366 Luna Drive, Las Vegas NM 87701-1510
County: San Miguel FICE Identification: 009962
Unit ID: 363633
Telephone: (505) 454-2500 Carnegie Class: Assoc/MT-VT-High Non
FAX Number: (505) 454-2519 Calendar System: Semester
URL: www.luna.edu
Established: 1970 Annual Undergrad Tuition & Fees (In-District): $886
Enrollment: 1,440 Coed
Affiliation or Control: State/Local IRS Status: 501(c)3

Highest Offering: Associate Degree
Accreditation: NH, ACBSP, ADNUR, DA

01 President .... Dr. Leroy (Huero) SANCHEZ
05 Vice Pres of Instruction .... Dr. Sharon LALLA
10 Vice Pres of Finance/ Administration .... Ms. Donna FLORES-MEDINA
09 Exec Dir Inst Research/Development .... Vacant
07 Director of Admissions .... Mr. Moses MARQUEZ
06 Registrar .... Ms. Henrietta MAESTAS
18 Manager Physical Plant .... Mr. Matthew CORDOVA
37 Director Financial Aid .... Mr. Michael MONTOYA
15 Director Human Resources .... Ms. Leticia ARCHULETA
30 Chief Development .... Ms. Mary WARD
13 Director of Computer Services .... Ms. Denise MONTOYA

Mesalands Community College (A)

911 S 10th Street, Tucumcari NM 88401-3352
County: Quay FICE Identification: 032063
Unit ID: 188261
Telephone: (505) 461-4413 Carnegie Class: Assoc/HVT-High Trad
FAX Number: (505) 461-1901 Calendar System: Semester
URL: www.mesalands.edu
Established: 1980 Annual Undergrad Tuition & Fees (In-District): $1,608
Enrollment: 793 Coed
Affiliation or Control: State/Local IRS Status: 501(c)3
Highest Offering: Associate Degree
Accreditation: NH

01 President .... Dr. Thomas W. NEWSOM
04 Executive Asst to President .... Ms. Consuelo E. CHAVEZ
32 Vice President Student Affairs .... Dr. Aaron KENNEDY
05 Vice President of Academic Affairs .... Ms. Natalie GILLARD
10 Dir Business/Auxiliary Services .... Ms. Amanda HAMMER
37 Director Financial Aid .... Ms. Jessica ELEBARIO
26 Director Public Relations .... Ms. Kimberly HANNA
72 Director of NAWRTC .... Mr. Jim MORGAN
84 Director of Enrollment Management .... Ms. Amber MCCLURE
13 Director of Inst Technology .... Mr. James JONES
09 Dir Inst Research and Development .... Dr. Forrest KAATZ
15 Director of Human Resources .... Ms. Kacee BENFORD
20 Director of Academic Affairs .... Ms. Donna GARCIA
102 Foundation Chair .... Ms. Laurie BIDEGAIN
21 Business Manager .... Vacant
08 Library Director .... Mr. Todd MORRIS

National American University-Albuquerque (B)

4775 Indian School Road NE, Ste 200, Albuquerque NM 87110
Telephone: (505) 348-3700 Identification: 770407
Accreditation: &NH, MAC

† Regional accreditation is carried under the parent institution in Rapid City, SD

National American University-Albuquerque West (C)

10131 Coors Blvd NW, Suite I-01, Albuquerque NM 87114
Telephone: (505) 348-3750 Identification: 770408
Accreditation: &NH

† Regional accreditation is carried under the parent institution in Rapid City, SD

National College of Midwifery (D)

1041 Reed Street, Suite C, Taos NM 87571
County: Taos Identification: 666251
Telephone: (575) 758-8914 Carnegie Class: Not Classified
FAX Number: N/A Calendar System: Other
URL: www.midwiferycollege.edu
Established: 1989 Annual Undergrad Tuition & Fees: N/A
Enrollment: N/A Coed
Affiliation or Control: Independent Non-Profit IRS Status: 501(c)3
Highest Offering: Doctorate
Accreditation: #MEAC

01 CEO/President .... Martha ANDREW
11 COO .... Anna KHAMSAMRAN
30 Chief Development Officer .... Cassaundra JAH

Navajo Technical College (E)

PO Box 849, Crownpoint NM 87313-0849
County: McKinley FICE Identification: 023576
Unit ID: 187596
Telephone: (505) 786-4100 Carnegie Class: Tribal
FAX Number: (505) 786-5644 Calendar System: Semester
URL: www.navajotech.edu
Established: 1979 Annual Undergrad Tuition & Fees: $4,170
Enrollment: 2,075 Coed
Affiliation or Control: Tribal Control IRS Status: 501(c)3
Highest Offering: Baccalaureate
Accreditation: NH, ACFEI

01 President .... Dr. Elmer GUY
05 Provost .... Vacant
32 Dean of Student Services .... Ms. Delores BECENTI
10 Chief Financial Officer .... Mr. Anthony W. MAJOR, JR.
06 Registrar/Director of Admissions .... Ms. Jerlynn HENRY
09 Data Assessment Director .... Ms. Shawnia GAMBLE
25 Contracts & Grant Officer .... Ms. Thomasina GREY
37 Student Financial Aid Officer .... Mr. Tyrrell HARDY
15 Interim Human Resources Director .... Mr. Anthony MAJOR
18 Director of Operations .... Mr. Hank NEWMAN
20 Associate Academic Officer .... Dr. Casmir AGBARAJI
08 Head Librarian .... Mr. Darwin C. HENDERSON
04 Executive Assistant .... Ms. Tonilee BECENTI
13 IT Director .... Mr. Jason ARVISO
36 Job Placement Coordinator .... Vacant
41 Athletic Director .... Mr. George LAFRANCE

† Tuition figure is for a student enrolled in a federally recognized Indian tribe.

New Mexico Highlands University (F)

PO Box 9000, Las Vegas NM 87701-9000
County: San Miguel FICE Identification: 002653
Unit ID: 187897
Telephone: (505) 425-7511 Carnegie Class: Masters/L
FAX Number: N/A Calendar System: Semester
URL: www.nmhu.edu
Established: 1893 Annual Undergrad Tuition & Fees (In-State): $4,800
Enrollment: 3,546 Coed
Affiliation or Control: State IRS Status: 501(c)3
Highest Offering: Master's
Accreditation: #NH, ACBSP, CORE, NURSE, SW, TED

01 President .... Dr. Sam MINNER
05 Interim VP for Academic Affairs .... Dr. Carol LINDER
10 Interim VP Finance & Admin .... Mr. Max BACA
84 VP for Strategic Enroll Mgmt .... Dr. Edward MARTINEZ
32 Dean of Students .... Ms. Kimberly BLEA
07 Dir of Student Recruitment/Admiss .... Ms. Jessica JARAMILLO
06 Registrar .... Mr. Michael RAINE
08 Library Director .... Mr. Ruben ARAGON
09 Dir Inst Effectiveness & Research .... Dr. Jean HILL
13 Director of Information Technology .... Vacant
15 Director Human Resources .... Vacant
18 Interim Dir of Facilities Mgmt .... Ms. Sylvia BACA
19 Chief Police/Security .... Mr. Donato SENA
21 Comptroller .... Mr. Jesus BAQUERA
26 Director of University Relations .... Mr. Sean WEAVER
29 Coordinator of Alumni Affairs .... Ms. Juli SALMAN
30 Vice President for Advancement .... Ms. Theresa LAW
36 Director of Career Services .... Mr. Ron GARCIA
37 Director of Financial Aid .... Ms. Eileen SEDILLO
40 Bookstore Manager .... Mr. Justin RICE
41 Athletic Director .... M. Bob CLIFFORD
49 Dean College of Arts & Sci .... Dr. Kenneth STOKES
50 Dean School of Business .... Dr. William TAYLOR
70 Dean School of Social Work .... Dr. Andrew ISRAEL
53 Dean School of Education .... Dr. Lora BAILEY
96 Director of Purchasing .... Vacant
04 Administrative Asst to President .... Ms. Carolina MARTINEZ
39 Director Student Housing .... Ms. Yvette WILKES

New Mexico Institute of Mining and Technology (G)

801 Leroy Place, Socorro NM 87801-4796
County: Socorro FICE Identification: 002654
Unit ID: 187967
Telephone: (575) 835-5434 Carnegie Class: Masters/S
FAX Number: (575) 835-6329 Calendar System: Semester
URL: www.nmt.edu
Established: 1889 Annual Undergrad Tuition & Fees (In-State): $6,613
Enrollment: 2,127 Coed
Affiliation or Control: State IRS Status: 501(c)3
Highest Offering: Doctorate
Accreditation: NH, CS, ENG

01 President .... Dr. Stephen G. WELLS
10 Vice Pres Administration & Finance .... Mr. Richard CERVANTES
05 Int Vice President Academic Affairs .... Dr. Peter MOZLEY
32 VP Student & Univ Rels/Dean Stdnt .... Ms. Melissa JARAMILLO FLEMING
46 Vice Pres Research/Economic Devel .... Dr. Van D. ROMERO
20 Assoc Vice Pres Academic Affairs .... Dr. Peter MOZLEY
45 Assoc VP Research/Econ Development .... Mr. Carlos REY ROMERO
58 Dean of Graduate Studies .... Dr. Lorie LIEBROCK
08 Librarian .... Ms. Lisa BEINHOFF
15 Director of Human Resources .... Ms. Joann SALOME
06 Registrar .... Ms. Sara GRIJALVA
07 Director of Admission .... Mr. Anthony ORTIZ
37 Director of Financial Aid .... Ms. Marliss MONETTE
30 Director Office for Advancement .... Ms. Colleen GUENGERICH
22 Director Affirm Action & Compliance .... Mr. Randy SAAVEDRA
14 Director Computer Center .... Vacant
13 Director of Information Services .... Mr. Joseph FRANKLIN
65 Director Bur Geology & Mineral Res .... Dr. Matthew RHOADES
12 Director Petro Recovery Res Ctr .... Dr. Robert L. LEE
18 Director Facilities Management .. Ms. Yvonne MANZANO-BROWN
21 Director of Finance .... Ms. Arleen VALLES
31 Dir Community Education/Outreach .... Ms. Lillian ARMIJO
38 Dir Counseling/Disabilities Svcs .... Ms. Janet WARD
96 Chief Procurement Officer .... Ms. Kimela MILLER
09 Institutional Researcher .... Ms. Stephany MOORE

New Mexico Junior College (H)

1 Thunderbird Circle, Hobbs NM 88240-9123
County: Lea FICE Identification: 002655
Unit ID: 187903
Telephone: (575) 392-4510 Carnegie Class: Assoc/HT-High Non
FAX Number: (575) 492-2732 Calendar System: Semester
URL: www.nmjc.edu
Established: 1965 Annual Undergrad Tuition & Fees (In-District): $1,248
Enrollment: 3,332 Coed
Affiliation or Control: Local IRS Status: 501(c)3
Highest Offering: Associate Degree
Accreditation: NH, ADNUR

01 President .... Dr. Kelvin SHARP
05 Vice President Instruction .... Dr. Dennis ATHERTON
10 Vice President Finance .... Dan HARDIN
32 Vice President Student Services .... Phillip ROYBAL
103 Vice President Training & Outreach .... Jeff MCCOOL
84 Dean Enrollment Management .... Dr. Michele CLINGMAN
13 Dir Computer Information System .... Bill KUNKO
26 Director of Communications .... Susan FINE
04 Executive Asst to the President .... Norma FAUGHT
37 Director Financial Aid .... Kerrie MITCHELL
09 Director of Inst Effectiveness .... Dr. Larry SANDERSON
66 Director of Nursing .... Delores THOMPSON
18 Chief Facilities/Physical Plant .... Dr. Charley CARROLL
81 Dean Business/Math & Sciences .... Kelly HOLLADAY
79 Dean Arts & Humanities .... Dianne MARQUEZ
40 Director of Bookstore Services .... Robert ADAMS
75 Dean of Public Safety .... Dr. August FONS
08 Director of Library Services .... James BRITSCH
96 Coordinator of Purchasing .... Regina CHOATE
41 Director of Athletics .... Jeremy CAPO
102 Acct/Controller-NMJC Foundation .... Christina KUNKO
11 Director of Administrative Services .... Bill MORRILL
88 Controller .... Joshua MORGAN
39 Director Student Housing .... Sandy HARDIN
88 Executive Director WHM/LCCHF .... Dr. Darrell BEAUCHAMP
88 Exec Dir NMJC Research Foundation .... Dale GANNAWAY
06 Associate Registrar .... Rebecca WHITLEY
19 Director of Public Safety .... Dennis KELLEY
106 Dean Distance Lrng & Prof Studies .... Dr. Steve HILL

New Mexico Military Institute (I)

101 W College, Roswell NM 88201-5173
County: Chaves FICE Identification: 002656
Unit ID: 187912
Telephone: (575) 622-6250 Carnegie Class: Assoc/HT-High Trad
FAX Number: (575) 624-8058 Calendar System: Semester
URL: www.nmmi.edu
Established: 1891 Annual Undergrad Tuition & Fees (In-State): $4,677
Enrollment: 459 Coed
Affiliation or Control: State IRS Status: 501(c)3
Highest Offering: Associate Degree
Accreditation: NH

01 Superintendent/President .... MGen. Jerry W. GRIZZLE
32 Commandant .... LtCol. Jonathan K. GRAFF
100 Chief of Staff .... Col. David WEST
10 Chief Financial Officer .... Col. Judy SCHARMER
05 Dean .... BGen. Douglas J. MURRAY
41 Athletic Director/Dir Physical Educ .... Col. Jose BARRON
30 Development and Advancement Officer .... Maj. Kris WARD
21 Internal Auditor .... Col. David GRAY
88 Professor of Military Science .... LtCol. Hubert STEPHENS
20 Vice Dean & High School Princ .... Col. George BRICK
15 Assistant Human Resources Director .... Ms. Carmen BELL
50 Assoc Dean Social Science/Business .... LtCol. Philip BACA
81 Assoc Dean Science/Mathematics .... Col. John R. MCVAY
79 Associate Dean Humanities .... Maj. Joel DYKSTRA
64 Director of Music .... LtCol. Stephen M. THORP
08 Director of the Library .... Col. Jerome J. KLOPFER
26 Marketing & Communication Director .... LtCol. Colleen COLE-VELASQUEZ
18 Chief Facilities/Physical Plant .... Mr. Kent TAYLOR
06 Registrar .... Maj. Chris WRIGHT
37 Director of Financial Aid .... Maj. Sonya F. RODRIGUEZ
88 Mil Services Academies Prep Dir .... LtCol. Jonathan GRAFF
19 Chief of Campus Police .... Mr. Jerrold LONOWSKI
38 Director of Cadet Counseling Center .... Maj. Chance MACE
29 Director Alumni Association .... LtCol. Danny ARMIJO
04 Executive Secretary to President .... Ms. Bernadette BEATTY
09 Director of Institutional Research .... Ms. Michele BATES
102 Dir Foundation/Corporate Relations .... Mr. Jimmy BARNES
13 Chief Info Technology Officer .... Mr. Duane ELMS

New Mexico State University Main Campus (J)

Box 30001, Las Cruces NM 88003-8001
County: Dona Ana FICE Identification: 002657
Unit ID: 188030
Telephone: (575) 646-2035 Carnegie Class: DU-Higher
FAX Number: (575) 646-6334 Calendar System: Semester
URL: www.nmsu.edu
Established: 1888 Annual Undergrad Tuition & Fees (In-State): $6,094
Enrollment: 15,829 Coed
Affiliation or Control: State IRS Status: 501(c)3
Highest Offering: Doctorate

Accreditation: NH, BUS, BUSA, CAATE, CACREP, COPSY, CS, DIETD, @DIETI, ENG, ENGT, IPSY, MUS, NURSE, PH, SP, SPAA, SW, TED

01 President ... Dr. Garrey E. CARRUTHERS
05 Provost & Exec VP ... Dr. Dan HOWARD
10 Sr VP Administration/Finance ... Ms. Angela THRONEBERRY
30 VP Univ Advance/Pres NMSU Found ... Ms. Andrea S. TAWNEY
32 VP Student Affairs/Enroll Mgmt ... Dr. Bernadette MONTOYA
85 Assoc Provost Intl & Border Program ... Dr. Cornell MENKING
26 Assoc VP Univ Comm/Marketing ... Ms. Maureen HOWARD
21 Assoc VP Admin & Finance ... Ms. D'Anne STUART
15 Assoc VP Human Resources Svcs ... Dr. Andrew M. PENA
20 Assoc VP/Deputy Provost ... Dr. Greg FANT
09 Asst VP Institutional Analysis ... Ms. Judy BOSLAND
86 Asst VP Government Relations ... Mr. Ricardo REL
49 Dean College of Arts & Sciences ... Dr. Enrico PONTELLI
50 Dean Business College ... Dr. James HOFFMAN
53 Dean College of Education ... Dr. Don POPE-DAVIS
54 Interim Dean College of Engineering ... Mr. Steven STOCHAJ
58 Dean Graduate School ... Dr. Loui REYES
76 Dean Col Health & Social Svcs ... Dr. Donna WAGNER
35 Dean of Students ... Dr. Michael D. JASEK
13 Chief Information Officer ... Ms. Norma GRIJALVA
06 Interim University Registrar ... Ms. Dacia SEDILLO
43 General Counsel ... Ms. Liz ELLIS
08 Dean University Library ... Dr. Elizabeth TITUS
29 AVP Alumni Engagement/Participation ... Ms. Leslie CERVANTES
25 Assoc Controller Sponsored Projects ... Ms. Norma NOEL
39 Director Student Housing ... Mr. Matt CROUSE
23 Director Student Health Center ... Ms. Lori MCKEE
38 Director Counseling Center ... Dr. Karen D. SCHAEFER
41 Director Athletics ... Mr. Mario MOCCIA
35 Director Student Affairs ... Dr. Anthony S. MARIN
96 Dir Procurement Services ... Mr. Bill HARTY
28 Dir Institutional Equity/EEO ... Mr. Gerard NEVAREZ
07 Director Admissions ... Ms. Delia DELEON
18 Assoc VP Facilities/Services ... Mr. Glen HAUBOLD
27 Dir of Marketing/Creative Svcs ... Ms. Ellen J. CASTELLO
47 Dean College of Agric ... Dr. Jim LIBBIN
92 Dean Honors College ... Dr. Miriam CHAIKEN
12 President NMSU-DACC ... Dr. Renay SCOTT
12 President NMSU Alamogordo ... Dr. Ken VAN WINKLE
12 President NMSU-Carlsbad ... Dr. John GRATTON
12 Interim President NMSU-Grants ... Dr. Harry SHESKI
100 Chief of Staff ... Ms. Sharon JONES

New Mexico State University at Alamogordo (A)

2400 N Scenic Drive, Alamogordo NM 88310-4239
County: Otero FICE Identification: 002658
Unit ID: 187994
Telephone: (575) 439-3600 Carnegie Class: Assoc/HT-High Non
FAX Number: (575) 439-3643 Calendar System: Semester
URL: www.nmsua.edu
Established: 1958 Annual Undergrad Tuition & Fees (In-State): $1,968
Enrollment: 2,095 Coed
Affiliation or Control: State IRS Status: 501(c)3
Highest Offering: Associate Degree
Accreditation: NH

01 President ... Dr. Ken VAN WINKLE
05 Vice President for Academic Affairs ... Dr. Mark CAL
32 Vice President for Student Services ... Dr. Vandeen MCKENZIE
10 Vice President for Business/Finance ... Mr. Antonio SALINAS
56 Assoc Vice Pres Extended Programs ... Mrs. Donna L. COOK
26 Marketing Representative ... Ms. Catherine PACELLI
13 Chief Info Technology Officer (CIO) ... Mr. David SANDERS
08 Librarian ... Dr. Sharon JENKINS
07 Director of Admissions/Registrar ... Ms. Rose PENA
37 Director Student Financial Aid ... Dr. Vandeen MCKENZIE
09 Director of Institutional Research ... Mr. Greg HILLIS
15 Director Human Resources ... Mrs. Brenda W. GARCIA
18 Director Facilities/Physical Plant ... Ms. Nancy WILKSON
96 Buyer Sr ... Mr. Lee M. KINNEY
04 Administrative Asst to President ... Ms. Mary FECHNER
106 Dir Online Education/E-learning ... Mrs. Sherrell WHEELER

New Mexico State University at Carlsbad (B)

1500 University Drive, Carlsbad NM 88220-3598
County: Eddy FICE Identification: 002659
Unit ID: 188003
Telephone: (575) 234-9200 Carnegie Class: Assoc/HT-High Non
FAX Number: (575) 885-4951 Calendar System: Semester
URL: www.carlsbad.nmsu.edu
Established: 1950 Annual Undergrad Tuition & Fees (In-State): $1,108
Enrollment: 1,852 Coed
Affiliation or Control: State IRS Status: 501(c)3
Highest Offering: Associate Degree
Accreditation: NH, ADNUR

01 Campus President ... Dr. John GRATTON
05 Chief Academic Officer/Provost ... Dr. Andrew I. NWANNE
32 Vice Pres Student Services ... Ms. Jeannie BACA
10 VP Business & Finance ... Ms. Gaylyn YANKE
37 Director Financial Aid ... Ms. Diana CAMPOS
15 Human Resources Specialist ... Ms. Rebecca SILVA
26 Director Marketing & Publications ... Mr. Khushroo GHADIALI
09 Director of Institutional Research ... Mr. William FINLEY

New Mexico State University Dona Ana Community College (C)

Box 30001, MSC 3DA, Las Cruces NM 88003-8001
County: Dona Ana Identification: 666649
Unit ID: 187620
Telephone: (575) 527-7500 Carnegie Class: Assoc/HT-Mix Trad/Non
FAX Number: (575) 527-7515 Calendar System: Semester
URL: dacc.nmsu.edu
Established: 1973 Annual Undergrad Tuition & Fees (In-State): $1,632
Enrollment: 8,448 Coed
Affiliation or Control: State IRS Status: 501(c)3
Highest Offering: Associate Degree
Accreditation: NH, ACBSP, ADNUR, COARC, DA, DH, DMS, EMT, IFSAC

01 President/CEO ... Dr. Renay M. SCOTT
05 VP for Academic Affairs ... Dr. Monica TORRES
10 VP for Business & Finance ... Ms. Kelly BROCKS
32 VP for Student Services ... Mr. Amadeo LEDESMA
20 Assoc VP for Academic Affairs ... Dr. John WALKER
50 Division Dean Business/Public Svcs ... Ms. Lydia BAGWELL
97 Division Dean General Studies ... Dr. Bernard PINA
76 Div Dean Health/Public Services ... Mr. Douglas SCRIBNER
72 Division Dean Technical Studies ... Ms. Saundra CASTILLO
103 Exec Director Workforce Dev/Trng ... Mr. Fred OWENSKY
62 Director Library Services ... Ms. Tammy POWERS
36 Dir Career Development/ Placement ... Ms. Rosa DE LA TORRE-BURMEISTER
09 Campus Inst Effectiveness/Plng Ofcr ... Dr. Fred LILLIBRIDGE
26 Dir Public Relations/Development ... Mr. Arthur BINDER
27 Director of Marketing/Publications ... Mr. John PAULMAN
31 Director Community Education ... Ms. Vickie GALINDO
40 Bookstore Manager ... Mr. Roman CORONADO
21 Manager Business Office ... Ms. Nancy RITTER
15 Human Resources Operation Manager ... Mr. Mack ADAMS
90 Director Computer Support ... Ms. Lori ALLEN
18 Manager Facilities Services ... Ms. Kathleen REDDINGTON
07 Director Admissions ... Ms. Geraldine MARTINEZ
37 Assoc Director Financial Aid ... Ms. Michelle LUKESH
22 Director Disabled Student Services ... Mr. Jesse HAAS

New Mexico State University Dona Ana Community College East Mesa Campus (D)

2800 N Sonoma Ranch Boulevard, Las Cruses NM 88011
Telephone: (575) 528-7250 Identification: 770346
Accreditation: &NH

† Regional accreditation is carried under the parent institution in Las Cruces, NM

New Mexico State University Grants (E)

1500 Third Street, Grants NM 87020-2025
Telephone: (505) 287-6678 FICE Identification: 008854
Accreditation: &NH

† Regional accreditation is carried under the parent institution in Las Cruces, NM.

Northern New Mexico College (F)

921 N Paseo de Onate, Espanola NM 87532-2649
County: Rio Arriba FICE Identification: 020839
Unit ID: 188058
Telephone: (505) 747-2100 Carnegie Class: Bac/Assoc-Mixed
FAX Number: (505) 747-2170 Calendar System: Semester
URL: www.nnmc.edu
Established: 1909 Annual Undergrad Tuition & Fees (In-State): $4,367
Enrollment: 1,371 Coed
Affiliation or Control: State IRS Status: 501(c)3
Highest Offering: Baccalaureate
Accreditation: NH, ACBSP, ENGT, NURSE

53 Dean College of Teacher Education ... Dr. Joaquin VILA
01 Interim President ... Mr. Domingo SANCHEZ
10 Vice Pres Finance & Administration ... Mr. Domingo SANCHEZ
30 Vice Pres Institutional Advancement ... Vacant
05 Provost/VP Academic Affairs ... Dr. Pedro L. MARTINEZ
32 Dean of Student Services ... Dr. Pedro MARTINEZ
12 Director El Rito Campus ... Vacant
06 Registrar ... Ms. Kathleen SENA
08 Head Librarian ... Ms. Amy ORTIZ
84 Director of Recruitment ... Mr. Frank ORONA
37 Director of Financial Aid ... Mr. Jacob PACHECO
13 Director of IT ... Mr. Jimi MONTOYA
15 Director of Human Resources ... Ms. Henrietta TRUJILLO
18 Director of Facilities ... Mr. Andy ROMERO
09 Director of Institutional Research ... Ms. Carmella SANCHEZ
21 Director of Business Operations ... Ms. Henrietta TRUJILLO
108 Dir Inst Advise/Coord Stdnt Advise ... Mr. Tobe BOTT-LYONS
41 Athletic Director/Coach ... Mr. Ryan CORDOVA
51 Coordinator Continuing Education ... Ms. Cecilia ROMERO
49 Dean College of Arts and Sciences ... Vacant
76 Dean of College of Health Sciences ... Ms. Ellen TRABKA
04 Administrative Asst to President ... Ms. Amy PENA
07 Director of Admissions ... Mr. Frank ORONA
102 Dir Foundation/Corporate Relations ... Mr. Terry MULERT
28 Director of Equity & Diversity ... Dr. Patricia TRUJILLO
50 Dean Business Administration ... Dr. Lori BACA
54 Dean Engineering & Technology ... Dr. Ivan LOPEZ

Pima Medical Institute-Albuquerque (G)

4400 Cutler Avenue NE, Albuquerque NM 87110-3935
Telephone: (505) 881-1234 FICE Identification: 036783
Accreditation: ABHES, COARC, DH, PTAA, RAD

† Branch campus of Pima Medical Institute-Tucson, Tucson, AZ

Ruidoso Branch Community College (H)

709 Mechem Drive, Ruidoso NM 88345
Telephone: (575) 257-2120 Identification: 770345
Accreditation: &NH

† Regional accreditation is carried under the parent institution in Portales, NM

St. John's College (I)

1160 Camino de la Cruz Blanca, Santa Fe NM 87505-4599
County: Santa Fe FICE Identification: 002093
Unit ID: 245652
Telephone: (505) 984-6000 Carnegie Class: Bac-A&S
FAX Number: (505) 984-6003 Calendar System: Semester
URL: www.sjc.edu
Established: 1964 Annual Undergrad Tuition & Fees: $49,644
Enrollment: 397 Coed
Affiliation or Control: Independent Non-Profit IRS Status: 501(c)3
Highest Offering: Master's
Accreditation: NH

01 President ... Mr. Mark ROOSEVELT
05 Dean ... Mr. Matt DAVIS
30 Vice President for Development ... Ms. Phelosha COLLAROS
10 Treasurer ... Mr. Bryan VALENTINE
06 Registrar ... Mrs. Marline MARQUEZ-SCALLY
08 Library Director ... Ms. Jennifer SPRAGUE
07 Director of Admissions ... Mr. Yvette SHAFFER
58 Director of Graduate Institute ... Mr. David MCDONALD
09 Director of Institutional Research ... Mr. Brian CONNOLLY
15 Director of Human Resources ... Mr. Aaron YOUNG
18 Chief Facilities/Physical Plant ... Mr. Pat HOLMAN
26 Dir of Communications/External Rels ... Mr. Gabe GOMEZ
29 Director of Alumni Relations ... Ms. Sarah PALACIOS
36 Director Student Placement ... Ms. Margaret ODELL
37 Director Student Financial Aid ... Mr. Mike RODRIQUEZ

† Affiliated with St. John's College, Maryland.

San Juan College (J)

4601 College Boulevard, Farmington NM 87402-4699
County: San Juan FICE Identification: 002660
Unit ID: 188100
Telephone: (505) 326-3311 Carnegie Class: Assoc/MT-VT-Mix Trad/Non
FAX Number: (505) 566-3385 Calendar System: Semester
URL: www.sanjuancollege.edu
Established: 1956 Annual Undergrad Tuition & Fees (In-District): $1,474
Enrollment: 8,323 Coed
Affiliation or Control: Local IRS Status: 501(c)3
Highest Offering: Associate Degree
Accreditation: NH, ADNUR, CAHIIM, #COARC, DH, EMT, MLTAD, OTA, PTAA, SURGT

01 President ... Dr. Toni PENDERGRASS
05 Vice Pres for Learning ... Dr. Barbara AKE
10 Vice Pres Administrative Services ... Mr. Edward DESPLAS
32 Vice Pres for Student Services ... Mr. David EPPICH
04 Executive Asst to President ... Ms. Jeanne NOTSON
20 Assoc VP Learning/Strategic Init ... Ms. Adrienne FORGETTE
102 Executive Director Foundation ... Ms. Gayle DEAN
31 Chief Community Relations Officer ... Ms. Nancy SHEPHERD
21 Controller ... Mr. Kristie ELLIS
26 Director Marketing/Public Relations ... Ms. Rhonda SCHAEFER
88 Dir Ctr for Student Engagement ... Dr. Michaele BRANDON
84 Sr Dir Enrollment Management ... Mr. Jon BETZ
50 Dean Sch Business & Workforce Dev ... Mr. Brad PURDY
79 Dean School of Humanities ... Mr. Allan NASS
76 Interim Dean Sch of Health Sciences ... Ms. Nisa BRUCE
65 Interim Dean School of Energy ... Mr. Ken JOHNSON
72 Dean School Trades & Technology ... Mr. Bill LEWIS
81 Dean Math/Science & Engineering ... Mr. Michael OTTINGER
22 Director Affirmative Action/EO ... Ms. Stacey ALLEN
88 Director Native American Programs ... Ms. Michele PETERSON
08 Director Library Services ... Mr. Chris SCHIPPER
37 Director of Financial Aid ... Ms. Mindi-Kim SCHRUM
18 Director Physical Plant ... Mr. Chris HARRELSON
19 Director Security/Safety ... Mr. Kelly ANDERSON
35 Director Student Activities ... Ms. Marcia STERLING
96 Director Purchasing ... Mr. Frank COLE
38 Director Student Advising Center ... Ms. Christy FERRATO
74 Director Vet-Tech Program ... Dr. David WRIGHT
06 Registrar ... Ms. Sherri GAUGH
09 Dir of Institutional Research ... Mr. Ron JERNIGAN
15 Senior Director Human Resources ... Ms. Kerri LANGONI
13 Chief Info Technology Officer (CIO) ... Ms. Shelley AMATOR

Santa Fe Community College (K)

6401 Richards Avenue, Santa Fe NM 87508-4887
County: Santa Fe FICE Identification: 022781
Unit ID: 188137
Telephone: (505) 428-1000 Carnegie Class: Assoc/MT-VT-High Non

FAX Number: (505) 428-1296 Calendar System: Semester
URL: www.sfcc.edu
Established: 1983 Annual Undergrad Tuition & Fees (In-State): $1,494
Enrollment: 5,475 Coed
Affiliation or Control: State IRS Status: 501(c)3
Highest Offering: Associate Degree
Accreditation: NH, ADNUR, COARC, DA, MAC

01 President ... Mr. Randy W. GRISSOM
05 Vice Pres Academic Affairs ... Ms. Margaret PETERS
10 Vice Pres Finance ... Mr. Nick TELLES
09 VP Planning & Inst Effectiveness ... Mr. Yash MORIMOTO
21 Associate Vice President Finance ... Vacant
84 Assoc VP Enrollment & Student Svcs ... Dr. Cheryl FIELDS
51 Director Cont Educ/Workforce Dev ... Mr. Gordon FLUKE
26 Exec Dir Marketing/Public Rels ... Ms. Janet WISE
102 Exec Dir SFCC Foundation ... Ms. Deborah BOLDT
06 Registrar ... Ms. Barbara TUCCI
13 Interim Chief Information Officer ... Mr. Jeremy LOVATO
37 Financial Aid Director ... Mr. Scott WHITAKER
66 Director of Nursing ... Vacant
08 Library Director ... Ms. Peg JOHNSON
15 Exec Director of Human Resources ... Mr. Daniel GUTIERREZ
88 Director Small Business Development ... Mr. Brian DUBOFF
18 Director Plant & Operations Mgmt ... Mr. Henry MIGNARDOT
12 Executive Director HEC ... Ms. Rebecca ESTRADA
49 Dean School of Liberal Arts ... Dr. Bernadette JACOBS
54 Dean Sch Health/Engineering & Math ... Dr. Jenny LANDEN
76 Dean School of Fitness Education ... Dr. Jenny LANDEN
57 Dean Sch Arts/Design & Media Arts ... Dr. Bernadette JACOBS
75 Dean Trds/Tech/Sustn & Prof Stds ... Dr. Camilla BUSTAMANTE
50 Dean School of Business & Educ ... Dr. Camilla BUSTAMANTE
101 Executive Asst to the President ... Ms. Rosemarie M. GARCIA
96 Director of Purchasing ... Vacant
25 Chief Contracts/Grants Admin ... Ms. Ann BLACK

Santa Fe University of Art and Design (A)

1600 St. Michael's Drive, Santa Fe NM 87505-7634
County: Santa Fe FICE Identification: 002649
Unit ID: 188146
Telephone: (505) 473-6011 Carnegie Class: Spec-4-yr-Arts
FAX Number: (505) 473-6127 Calendar System: Semester
URL: www.santafeuniversity.edu
Established: 1947 Annual Undergrad Tuition & Fees: $32,346
Enrollment: 950 Coed
Affiliation or Control: Proprietary IRS Status: Proprietary
Highest Offering: Master's
Accreditation: NH

01 President ... Mr. Laurence A. HINZ
03 Interim Provost ... Ms. Debra TERVALA
32 Exec Dir Student Affairs/Operations ... Ms. Melissa LEWIS
35 Asst Dir Student Affs/Operations ... Mr. Jeremy HADLEY
07 Director of Enrollment ... Ms. Christine GUEVARA
10 Director of Finance ... Mr. Steven POSEY
18 Dir Facilities & Security ... Mr. Peter ROMERO
13 Dir Campus Technology Services ... Mr. Jeff PEARCE
37 Director of Financial Aid ... Ms. Celeste FRANKLIN
36 Director of Career Services ... Ms. Joanie SPAIN
15 Manager of Human Resources ... Ms. Yolanda SMITH MORA
06 Registrar ... Ms. Mary ANGELL
88 Executive Director of Marketing ... Ms. Betty CESARANO
26 External & Public Relations Manager ... Ms. Lauren MCDANIEL

† Annual tuition for Graphic Design, Creative Writing, Digital Arts and Arts Management programs is $19,646.

Southwest Acupuncture College (B)

1622 Galisteo Street, Santa Fe NM 87505-6351
County: Santa Fe FICE Identification: 026220
Unit ID: 366605
Telephone: (505) 438-8884 Carnegie Class: Spec-4-yr-Other Health
FAX Number: (505) 438-8883 Calendar System: Semester
URL: www.acupuncturecollege.edu
Established: 1980 Annual Undergrad Tuition & Fees: N/A
Enrollment: 48 Coed
Affiliation or Control: Proprietary IRS Status: Proprietary
Highest Offering: Master's; No Lower Division
Accreditation: ACUP

01 CEO ... Dr. Anthony ABBATE
03 Executive Director ... Dr. Skya ABBATE
10 Chief Fiscal Officer ... Mr. Charles ROUNTREE
12 Campus Director Santa Fe ... Dr. Paul ROSSIGNOL
17 Clinical Director Santa Fe ... Dr. Melanie RICHARDSON
05 Academic Dean Santa Fe ... Ms. Susan CHANEY
37 Director of Financial Aid ... Ms. Angela ANAYA
07 Director of Admissions ... Ms. Cecily MARTIN

Southwest University of Visual Arts (C)

5000 Marble Avenue, NE, Albuquerque NM 87110-6344
Telephone: (505) 254-7575 Identification: 666524
Accreditation: &NH, CIDA

† Regional accreditation is carried under the parent institution in Tucson, AZ.

Southwestern College (D)

3960 San Filipe Road, Santa Fe NM 87507
County: Santa Fe FICE Identification: 030761
Unit ID: 188207
Telephone: (505) 471-5756 Carnegie Class: Masters/S
FAX Number: (505) 471-4071 Calendar System: Quarter
URL: www.swc.edu
Established: 1979 Annual Graduate Tuition & Fees: N/A
Enrollment: 162 Coed
Affiliation or Control: Independent Non-Profit IRS Status: 501(c)3
Highest Offering: Master's; No Undergraduates
Accreditation: NH

01 President ... Dr. Jim NOLAN
03 Exec VP/Dir New Earth Institute SWC ... Ms. Katherine NINOS
05 Vice Pres Academic Affairs/Dean ... Dr. Ann FILEMYR
07 Director of Admissions ... Ms. Dru PHOENIX
06 Registrar ... Ms. Andrea PACHECO
10 Finance Manager ... Ms. Rhonda CHASE
13 Chief Technology Officer ... Ms. Donna HARRINGTON

Southwestern Indian Polytechnic Institute (E)

9169 Coors Blvd., NW, Albuquerque NM 87120
County: Bernalillo FICE Identification: 025110
Unit ID: 188216
Telephone: (505) 346-2348 Carnegie Class: Tribal
FAX Number: (505) 346-2343 Calendar System: Trimester
URL: www.sipi.edu
Established: 1971 Annual Undergrad Tuition & Fees: $1,095
Enrollment: 481 Coed
Affiliation or Control: Federal IRS Status: 501(c)3
Highest Offering: Associate Degree
Accreditation: NH, OPD, OPLT

01 President ... Dr. Sherry ALLISON
10 Vice Pres College Operations ... Mr. Eric CHRISTENSEN
05 Vice President Academic Programs ... Ms. Valerie MONTOYA
09 Dir Institutional Rsch/Effect/Plng ... Mr. Edward HUMMINGBIRD
32 Director of Student Services ... Mr. Allen (Ray) GACHUPIN
07 Director Admissions/Registrar ... Mr. Joseph CARPIO
15 Human Resources Specialist ... Ms. Dawn AMI
18 Facilities Director ... Ms. Renee ALLEN
37 Director Student Financial Aid ... Mr. Joseph CARPIO

University of New Mexico Main Campus (F)

1 University of New Mexico, Albuquerque NM 87131-0001
County: Bernalillo FICE Identification: 002663
Unit ID: 187985
Telephone: (505) 277-0111 Carnegie Class: DU-Highest
FAX Number: (505) 277-6019 Calendar System: Semester
URL: www.unm.edu
Established: 1889 Annual Undergrad Tuition & Fees (In-State): $7,071
Enrollment: 27,844 Coed
Affiliation or Control: State IRS Status: 501(c)3
Highest Offering: Doctorate
Accreditation: NH, ARCPA, BUS, BUSA, CAATE, CACREP, CLPSY, CONST, CS, DANCE, DENT, DH, DIETD, DIETI, EMT, ENG, IPSY, JOUR, LAW, LSAR, MED, MIDWF, MT, MUS, NMT, NURSE, OT, PH, PHAR, PLNG, PTA, SP, SPAA, TED, THEA

01 President ... Dr. Robert G. FRANK
05 Provost/Exec VP Academic Affs ... Dr. Chaouki T. ABDALLAH
17 Chancellor of Health Sciences Ctr ... Dr. Paul B. ROTH
10 Exec Vice Pres Administration ... Dr. David W. HARRIS
100 Chief of Staff ... Dr. Amy WOHLERT
12 Special Asst for Branch Affairs ... Dr. Wynn M. GOERING
20 Sr Vice Provost Academic Affairs ... Carol PARKER
106 Vice Provost Extended Learning ... Dr. Monica OROZCO
46 Vice President Research ... Dr. Gabriel J. LOPEZ
25 AVP Research Administration ... Patricia HENNING
20 Assoc Provost Faculty Development ... Dr. Virginia SCHARFF
20 Assoc Provost Curriculum ... Dr. Gregory HEILEMAN
32 Vice President Student Affairs ... Dr. Eliseo S. TORRES
28 Vice President Equity & Inclusion ... Dr. Josephine DE LEON
28 Vice Chancellor HSC Diversity ... Dr. Valerie ROMERO-LEGGOTT
84 AVP Enrollment Management ... Dr. Terry BABBITT
15 Vice President Human Resources ... Dorothy ANDERSON
41 Vice President for Athletics ... Paul R. KREBS
21 University Controller ... Elizabeth METZGER
13 Interim Chief Information Officer ... Duane ARRUTTI
14 Int Deputy Chief Information Ofcr ... Brian PIETREWICZ
43 University Counsel ... Elsa KIRCHER COLE
29 AVP Alumni Relations ... Dana ALLEN
20 AVP Academic Administration ... Curtis R. PORTER
21 AVP Planning/Budget & Analysis ... Vacant
35 AVP Student Life ... Dr. Walter C. MILLER
35 AVP Student Services ... Dr. Tim GUTIERREZ
50 Interim Dean ASM ... Dr. Craig WHITE
48 Dean Sch of Architecture & Planning ... Dr. Geraldine FORBES ISAIS
49 Dean College of Arts & Sciences ... Dr. Mark PECENY
53 Dean College of Education ... Dr. Hector OCHOA
54 Interim Dean School of Engineering ... Dr. Joseph CECCHI
57 Dean College of Fine Arts ... Dr. Kymberly PINDER
61 Dean School of Law ... Alfred MATHEWSON
63 Exec Vice Dean School of Medicine ... Dr. Martha MCGREW
66 Dean College of Nursing ... Dr. Nancy A. RIDENOUR
67 Dean College of Pharmacy ... Dr. Lynda S. WELAGE
80 Interim Dir School of Public Admin ... Dr. Philip GONZALES
92 Dean Honors & University Colleges ... Dr. Kate KRAUSE
58 Dean Office of Graduate Studies ... Dr. Julie COONROD
51 Assoc Dean Continuing Education ... Joseph MIERA
08 Dean University Libraries ... Dr. Richard CLEMENT
26 Chief Univ Marketing & Comm Officer ... Cinnamon BLAIR
27 HSC Exec Dir Comm & Marketing ... William O. SPARKS
27 Director University Communications ... Dianne ANDERSON
105 Mgr University Web Communications ... Matt CARTER
86 Interim Director Government Affairs ... Connie BEIMER
09 Director Institutional Analytics ... Paige BRIGGS
18 University Architect ... Amy COBURN
18 Director Physical Plant ... Jeff ZUMWALT
19 Chief of Police ... Kevin MCCABE
96 Chief Procurement Officer ... Bruce E. CHERRIN
23 Director Student Health Center ... Dr. Beverly KLOEPPEL
22 Director Equal Opportunity ... Francie CORDOVA
24 Dir New Media & Extended Learning ... Debby KNOTTS
35 Dean of Students ... Nasha TORREZ
07 Director Admissions and Recruitment ... Matt HULETT
06 Registrar ... Alex GONZALEZ
37 Director Student Financial Aid ... Brian MALONE
36 Director Career Services ... Jenna S. CRABB
39 Director Student Housing & Res Life ... Wayne SULLIVAN
40 Director Bookstore ... Carrie MITCHELL
108 Director of Assessment ... Neke MITCHELL
102 UNM Foundation President and CEO ... Henry NEMCIK
30 VP University Development ... Larry RYAN
30 VP Development Health Sciences Ctr ... Bill UHER
88 CEO UNM Hospital ... Steve MCKERNAN
04 Administrative Asst to President ... Mitch GARRITY
101 Secretary of the Institution/Board ... Mallory REVIERE

University of New Mexico-Gallup (G)

705 Gurley Avenue, Gallup NM 87301
Telephone: (505) 863-7500 FICE Identification: 006881
Accreditation: &NH, ADNUR, CAHIIM, DA, MLTAD

† Regional accreditation is carried under the parent institution in Albuquerque, NM.

University of New Mexico-Los Alamos (H)

4000 University Drive, Los Alamos NM 87544-2233
Telephone: (505) 662-5919 Identification: 666742
Accreditation: &NH

† Regional accreditation is carried under the parent institution in Albuquerque, NM.

University of New Mexico-Taos (I)

1157 Country Road 110, Ranchos de Taos NM 87557
Telephone: (575) 737-6200 Identification: 666743
Accreditation: &NH, ADNUR

† Regional accreditation is carried under the parent institution in Albuquerque, NM.

University of New Mexico-Valencia (J)

280 La Entrada Road, Los Lunas NM 87031-7633
Telephone: (505) 925-8500 Identification: 666741
Accreditation: &NH

† Regional accreditation is carried under the parent institution in Albuquerque, NM.

University of Phoenix New Mexico Campus (K)

5700 Pasadena Avenue, NE,
Albuquerque NM 87113-1570
Telephone: (505) 821-4800 Identification: 770219
Accreditation: &NH, ACBSP

† Regional accreditation is carried under the parent institution in Tempe, AZ

University of St. Francis (L)

1500 N. Renaissance Blvd, NE, Ste C,
Albuquerque NM 87107
Telephone: (505) 266-5565 Identification: 770099
Accreditation: &NH, ARCPA

† Regional accreditation is carried under the parent institution in Joliet, IL

University of the Southwest (M)

6610 Lovington Highway, Hobbs NM 88240-9129
County: Lea FICE Identification: 002650
Unit ID: 188182
Telephone: (575) 392-6561 Carnegie Class: Masters/M
FAX Number: (575) 392-6006 Calendar System: Semester
URL: www.usw.edu
Established: 1962 Annual Undergrad Tuition & Fees: $14,616
Enrollment: 1,009 Coed
Affiliation or Control: Independent Non-Profit IRS Status: 501(c)3
Highest Offering: Master's
Accreditation: NH

01 President .... Dr. Quint THURMAN
05 Provost .... Dr. Larry GUERRERO
10 VP for Financial Services/CFO .... Mr. Ronald MCBEE
84 VP for Enrollment Management .... Mrs. Michele GOAR
30 VP for Institutional Advancement .... Mr. William J. WEIDNER
18 Campus Steward .... Dr. David ARNOLD
15 Asst VP HR & Regulatory Compliance ...... Mrs. Veronica TORREZ
49 Dean School of Arts & Sciences .... Dr. Elyn PALMER
50 Dean School of Business .... Dr. Ryan TIPTON
53 Dean School of Education .... Dr. Mary R. HARRIS
08 Dean Library Services .... Mr. John MCCANCE
41 Dir of Intercollegiate Athletics .... Mr. William J. WEIDNER
42 Campus Pastor .... Dr. Danny KIRKPATRICK
06 University Registrar .... Ms. Caitlin ODOM
37 Financial Aid Director .... Mrs. Dawny KRINGEL
108 Director Institutional Assessment .... Dr. Stephanie FERGUSON
07 Director of Admissions .... Ms. Lissete TERRAZAS
29 Director Alumni Relations .... Mrs. Kathryn EADES
26 Development & External Relations .... Mrs. Kathryn EADES
32 Director of Student Life .... Ms. Melissa MIRELES
39 Director Student Housing .... Mr. Ryan MORGAN
105 Director Web Services .... Mr. David BARRETT
101 Secretary of the Institution/Board .... Mrs. Linda WOODFIN
04 Administrative Asst to President .... Mrs. Linda WOODFIN
88 Maintenance Supervisor .... Mr. Lonnie HARRISON

Western New Mexico University (A)

PO Box 680, Silver City NM 88062-0680

County: Grant — FICE Identification: 002664
Unit ID: 188304
Telephone: (505) 538-6011 — Carnegie Class: Masters/M
FAX Number: (505) 538-6364 — Calendar System: Semester
URL: www.wnmu.edu
Established: 1893 — Annual Undergrad Tuition & Fees (In-State): $5,704
Enrollment: 3,557 — Coed
Affiliation or Control: State — IRS Status: 501(c)3
Highest Offering: Beyond Master's But Less Than Doctorate
Accreditation: NH, ACBSP, ADNUR, NURSE, #OT, #OTA, SW, TED

01 President .... Dr. Joseph SHEPARD
05 Provost/Vice Pres Academic Affairs .... Dr. Jack CROCKER
32 VP Student Affairs/Enrollment Mgmt .... Dr. Isaac BRUNDAGE
10 Vice President Business Affairs .... Dr. Brenda FINDLEY
30 VP External Affairs .... Dr. Magdaleno MANZANARES
20 Assoc Vice Pres Academic Affairs .... Dr. Linda HOY
06 Registrar .... Ms. Betsy MILLER
08 University Librarian .... Ms. Gilda BAEZA-ORTEGO
37 Director Student Financial Aid .... Vacant
07 Interim Director Admissions .... Mr. Matthew LARA
09 Director of Institutional Research .... Vacant
15 Director of Human Resources .... Ms. Maura GONSIOR
18 Chief Facilities/Physical Plant .... Vacant
26 Chief Public Relations Officer .... Mr. Abe VILLARREAL
29 Int Director of Alumni Relations .... Ms. Cari LEMON
36 Career Services Coord .... Vacant
28 Dir Multi-Cultural Affs/Student Act .... Ms. Jessica MORALES
96 Director of Purchasing .... Ms. Amy BACA
100 Chief of Staff .... Ms. Julie MORALES
19 Director Security/Safety .... Mr. Eddie FLORES
41 Athletic Director .... Mr. Mark COLEMAN
49 Dean of College of Arts and Science .... Dr. Jose HERRERA
53 Interim Dean of Education .... Dr. Barbara TAYLOR

NEW YORK

Adelphi University (B)

1 South Avenue, PO Box 701,
Garden City NY 11530-0701

County: Nassau — FICE Identification: 002666
Unit ID: 188429
Telephone: (516) 877-3000 — Carnegie Class: DU-Mod
FAX Number: (516) 877-3545 — Calendar System: Semester
URL: www.adelphi.edu
Established: 1896 — Annual Undergrad Tuition & Fees: $34,034
Enrollment: 7,610 — Coed
Affiliation or Control: Independent Non-Profit — IRS Status: 501(c)3
Highest Offering: Doctorate
Accreditation: M, BUS, CLPSY, NURSE, SP, SW, TED

01 President .... Dr. Christine M. RIORDAN
05 Interim Provost/Exec VP .... Dr. Sam L. GROGG
10 Executive VP of Finance & Admin .... Mr. Timothy P. BURTON
28 VP of Diversity and Inclusion .... Dr. Perry GREENE
30 VP of University Advancement .... Dr. Christian VAUPEL
26 VP for Communications .... Ms. Lori DUGGAN-GOLD
20 Deputy Provost .... Dr. Audrey S. BLUMBERG
20 Sr Assoc Provost for UG Programs ...... Dr. Lester B. BALTIMORE
07 Assoc VP of Admissions .... Ms. Kristen CAPEZZA
32 Assoc VP of Student Affairs .... Ms. Esther GOODCUFF
18 Asst VP of Facilities .... Mr. Robert J. SHIPLEY
21 Assoc VP for Finance & Co-Treasurer ...... Mr. Robert L. DECARLO
15 Assoc VP Human Resource/Labor Rel .... Ms. Lisa ARAUJO
16 Director Employee & Labor Relations .... Ms. Jane FISHER
49 Acting Dean of Arts & Sciences .... Dr. Susan BRIZIARELLI
53 Dean RS Ammon School of Education .... Dr. Jane ASHDOWN
66 Dean Col of Nursing & Public Hlth .... Dr. Patrick R. COONAN
70 Dean School of Social Work .... Dr. Andrew SAFYER
58 Dean Derner Inst Advanc Psych Std .... Dr. Jacques BARBER
50 Dean RB Willumstad Sch of Business .... Dr. Rajib N. SANYAL
92 Dean of Honors College .... Dr. Richard GARNER
88 Dean of University College .... Dr. Shawn O'RILEY
08 Dean University Libraries .... Mr. Brian LYM
35 Dean Student Affairs/Asst VP .... Mr. Jeffrey A. KESSLER
13 Chief Information Officer/CIO .... Mr. Jack CHEN
14 Deputy CIO .... Ms. Carol Ann BOYLE
41 Director of Athletics .... Mr. Daniel MCCABE
19 Asst VP for Public Safety .... Mr. Eugene PALMA
09 Assistant Provost for IR .... Dr. Nava LERER
37 Asst VP Student Financial Aid .... Ms. Sheryl L. MICHOPULOS
36 Exec Dir Career Plng & Placement .... Mr. Thomas J. WARD
06 Registrar .... Ms. Jill GLATTER
104 Director International Education .... Ms. Shannon HARRISON
23 Director Health Services .... Ms. Jacqueline CARTABUKE
38 Director Counseling & Support Svcs .... Dr. Carol A. LUCAS
39 Director Residential Life/Housing .... Mr. Guy SENEQUE
29 Exec Director Alumni Relations .... Ms. Polly SCHMITZ
21 Assoc Treasurer/Budget Director .... Mr. Michael J. MCLEOD
21 Director Business Affairs .... Mr. Russell A. PALMER
96 Purchasing Manager .... Ms. Elizabeth F. KASH
108 Director Institutional Assessment .... Dr. Lori HOEFFNER
100 Chief of Staff .... Ms. Maggie GRAFER

Albany College of Pharmacy and Health Sciences (C)

106 New Scotland Avenue, Albany NY 12208-3492

County: Albany — FICE Identification: 002885
Unit ID: 188526
Telephone: (518) 694-7200 — Carnegie Class: Spec-4-yr-Other Health
FAX Number: (518) 694-7202 — Calendar System: Semester
URL: www.acphs.edu
Established: 1881 — Annual Undergrad Tuition & Fees: $31,081
Enrollment: 1,563 — Coed
Affiliation or Control: Independent Non-Profit — IRS Status: 501(c)3
Highest Offering: Doctorate
Accreditation: M, CYTO, MT, PHAR

01 President .... Greg DEWEY
05 Provost .... Tarun PATEL
46 Vice Provost for Research .... Shaker MOUSA
88 Vice Provost Innovative Learning .... Jennifer MCVAY-DYCHE
49 Dean School of Arts and Sciences .... David CLARKE
67 Interim Dean of the School of Pharm .... Robert HAMILTON
45 Associate Vice President Inst Effec .... Angela DOMINELLI
58 Dean School of Graduate Studies .... Martha HASS
12 Associate Dean for Vermont Campus .... Robert HAMILTON
32 Dean of Students .... Wendy NEIFELD WHEELER
43 General Counsel .... Vacant
10 VP of Finance .... Michele VIEN
30 VP of Institutional Advancement .... Vicki DILORENZO
84 VP of Enrollment Management .... Tiffany GUTIERREZ
13 Chief Technology Officer .... Joshua SINGLETARY
11 AVP of Administrative Operations .... Packy MCGRAW
07 Director of Admissions .... Nicholas BALK
06 Registrar .... Jeff DUFOUR
08 Director of Library Services .... Sue IWANOWICZ
26 Exec Director of Marketing/Comm .... Gil CHORBAJIAN
41 Interim Director of Athletics & Rec .... Christine KANAWADA
15 Director of Human Resources .... Susan KARAVOLAS
09 Director of Prospect Research .... Deanna ENNELLO-BUTLER

Albany Law School (D)

80 New Scotland Avenue, Albany NY 12208-3494

County: Albany — FICE Identification: 002886
Unit ID: 188535
Telephone: (518) 445-2311 — Carnegie Class: Spec-4-yr-Law
FAX Number: (518) 445-2315 — Calendar System: Semester
URL: www.albanylaw.edu
Established: 1851 — Annual Undergrad Tuition & Fees: N/A
Enrollment: 475 — Coed
Affiliation or Control: Independent Non-Profit — IRS Status: 501(c)3
Highest Offering: First Professional Degree
Accreditation: LAW

01 President & Dean .... Dean Alicia OUELLETTE
05 Assoc Dean Acad Affairs .... Dean Connie MAYER
10 Vice President Finance & Business .... Mr. Victor E. RAUSCHER
08 Director of Library .... Ms. Colleen SMITH
30 Asst Dean Inst Advancement .... Ms Anne Marie JUDGE
32 Associate Dean for Student Affairs .... Prof. Rosemary QUEENAN
06 Assistant Dean and Registrar .... Ms. Joanne FITZSIMMONS
36 Asst Dean Career Center .... Ms. Mary WALSH FITZPATRICK
26 Director Communications .... Mr. David SINGER
04 Executive Assistant to the Dean ...... Ms. Barbara JORDAN-SMITH
07 Assistant Dean of Admissions .... Ms. Nadia CASTRIOTA
88 Director Clinical Program .... Prof. Sarah ROGERSON
13 Director Enterprise Tech Services .... Vacant
29 Director Alumni Affairs .... Ms. Tammy WEINMAN
15 Director Human Resources .... Ms. Sherri DONNELLY
37 Director Student Financial Aid .... Ms. Andrea WEDLER
18 Facilities Manager .... Mr. Brian LAPLANTE
36 Director of Career Services .... Ms. Joanne CASEY

Albany Medical College (E)

47 New Scotland Avenue, Mail #34,
Albany NY 12208-3479

County: Albany — FICE Identification: 002887
Unit ID: 188580
Telephone: (518) 262-6008 — Carnegie Class: Spec-4-yr-Med
FAX Number: (518) 262-6515 — Calendar System: Other
URL: www.amc.edu
Established: 1839 — Annual Graduate Tuition & Fees: N/A
Enrollment: 823 — Coed
Affiliation or Control: Independent Non-Profit — IRS Status: 501(c)3
Highest Offering: Doctorate; No Undergraduates
Accreditation: M, ANEST ARCPA, IPSY, MED, PAST

01 Dean/Exec VP Health Affairs .... Dr. Vincent P. VERDILE
10 EVP/Chief Financial Officer .... Ms. Frances SPREER-ALBERT
05 Vice Dean for Academic Admin .... Dr. Henry S. POHL
17 Vice Dean Clinical Affairs .... Dr. Ferdinand VENDITTI
32 Assoc Dean for Acad & Student Affs .... Dr. Kimberly KILBY
63 Assoc Dean Graduate Medical Educ .... Dr. Joel BARTFIELD
90 Assoc Dean Info Resources & Tech .... Ms. Enid GEYER
22 Assoc Dean Cmty Outreach/Medical Ed ...... Dr. Ingrid M. ALLARD
08 Asc Dn Info Resrcs/Tech/Dir Library .... Ms. Enid GEYER
88 Asst Dean Medical Education .... Dr. Rebecca KELLER
58 Assoc Dean for Graduate Studies .... Dr. Richard KELLER
06 Registrar .... Mr. Len SCHLEGEL
63 Director Graduate Medical Education .... Ms. Catherine RIDDLE
76 Director Physician Asst Program .... Dr. David IRVINE
07 Asst Dean Admiss & Student Records ..... Mr. Donald PRITCHETT
29 Executive Director Alumni Relations .... Ms. Maura MACK-HISGEN
26 Director Public Relations .... Mr. Jeffrey GORDON
30 Chief Development .... Ms. Molly NICHOL
51 Director Cont Medical Education .... Ms. Jennifer PRICE
15 Director Human Resources .... Ms. Cathy HALAKAN
37 Director Student Financial Aid .... Ms. Ann LOUGHMAN
96 Director of Purchasing .... Ms. Ann CRISLIP
27 Marketing Specialist .... Ms. Nicolette VISCUSI
03 Executive Assoc Dean .... Mr. John DEPAOLA
09 Director of Institutional Research .... Dr. Paul FEUSTEL
85 Director Foreign Students .... Ms. Marianne R. WILLIAMS
13 Chief Info Technology Officer (CIO) .... Mr. George HICKMAN
18 Chief Facilities Physical Plant .... Mr. Donald STICHTER
19 Director Security/Safety .... Mr. John HERRITAGE
88 Assoc Dean Medical Education .... Dr. Jonathan ROSEN
38 Director Student Counseling .... Dr. Jeffrey WINSEMAN
43 Dir Legal Services/General Counsel .... Mr. Lee HESSBERG
45 Chief Institutional Planning .... Ms. Courtney BURKE
88 Director Nurse Anesthesia Pgm .... Dr. Jodi DELLA ROCCA

Alfred University (F)

One Saxon Drive, Alfred NY 14802-1205

County: Allegany — FICE Identification: 002668
Unit ID: 188641
Telephone: (607) 871-2111 — Carnegie Class: Bac-A&S
FAX Number: (607) 871-2339 — Calendar System: Semester
URL: www.alfred.edu
Established: 1836 — Annual Undergrad Tuition & Fees: $26,261
Enrollment: 2,310 — Coed
Affiliation or Control: Independent Non-Profit — IRS Status: 501(c)3
Highest Offering: Doctorate
Accreditation: M, ART, BUS, #CAATE, CACREP, ENG, SCPSY, TEAC

01 President .... Dr. Mark A. ZUPON
05 Provost/VP for Academic Affairs .... Dr. Rick STEPHENS
10 VP for Business & Finance/Treasurer .... Ms. Giovina LLOYD
30 Acting VP for University Relations ... Mrs. Susan C. GOETSCHIUS
84 VP for Enrollment Management .... Mr. Earl E. PIERCE, JR.
32 VP for Student Affairs .... Mrs. Kathy WOUGHTER
57 Int Dean School of Art & Design .... Mr. Gerar EDIZEL
49 Dean Col of Lib Arts & Sciences .... Dr. Louis J. LICHTMAN
107 Dean College of Prof Studies .... Dr. Nancy EVANGELISTA
54 Dean School of Engineering .... Dr. Doreen EDWARDS
35 Dean of Students .... Mr. Norm POLLARD
29 Exec Dir Annual Giv/Alum Relations .... Vacant
37 Director of Student Financial Aid .... Ms. Diana M. MULKIN
07 Director of Admissions .... Mr. Jamie MARCUS
06 Registrar .... Mr. Lawrence J. CASEY
19 Chief of Public Safety .... Mr. John M. DOUGHERTY
26 Acting Director of Communications .... Mrs. Deborah E. CLARK
39 Director of Residence Life .... Ms. Vicky GEBEL
13 Director Information Tech Svcs .... Mr. Gary O. ROBERTS
36 Director Career Development Ctr .... Mr. Mark MCFADDEN
41 Athletic Director .... Mr. Paul VECCHIO
23 Dir Counseling & Wellness Center .... Dr. Stanley TAM
18 Director of Physical Plant .... Mr. Brian R. DODGE
08 Dir Herrick Lib/Dean of Libraries .... Mr. Stephen S. CRANDALL
08 Director of Scholes Library .... Mr. Mark SMITH
15 Director of Human Resources .... Mr. Mark A. GUINAN
21 Controller .... Ms. Jodi L. HOWE
92 Director of the Honors Program .... Dr. Gordan ATLAS
94 Coord of Women's Leadership Center .... Ms. Ana M. GAUTHIER
35 Director of Student Activities .... Mr. Daniel NAPOLITANO
43 Dir Capital Operations/Leg Affairs .. Mr. Michael A. NEIDERBACH
101 Secretary to the Corporation .... Ms. Mary C. MCALLISTER
104 Dir Intl Programs/Writing Ctr .... Dr. Vicky WESTACOTT
40 Bookstore Manager .... Mrs. Marcy K. BRADLEY
87 Dir of Summer/Parent Programs .... Mrs. Bonnie J. DUNGAN

AMDA College and Conservatory of the Performing Arts (G)

211 West 61st Street, New York NY 10023-7832

County: New York — FICE Identification: 007572
Unit ID: 188854
Telephone: (212) 787-5300 — Carnegie Class: Spec-4-yr-Arts
FAX Number: (212) 247-0488 — Calendar System: Semester
URL: www.amda.edu
Established: 1964 — Annual Undergrad Tuition & Fees: $33,920
Enrollment: 1,735 — Coed
Affiliation or Control: Independent Non-Profit — IRS Status: 501(c)3

Highest Offering: Baccalaureate
Accreditation: THEA

01 President/Artistic Director .... Mr. David MARTIN
03 President/Executive Director .... Ms. Jan MARTIN
32 Director of Student Affairs .... Mr. Robert MANGANARO
07 Director of Admissions .... Ms. Karen JACKSON
37 Assoc Dir Financial Aid/Cont Stdnt .... Ms. Gloria LITTLE

American Academy of Dramatic Arts (A)

120 Madison Avenue, New York NY 10016-7089
County: New York FICE Identification: 007465
Unit ID: 188678
Telephone: (212) 686-9244 Carnegie Class: Spec 2-yr-A&S
FAX Number: (212) 545-7934 Calendar System: Other
URL: www.aada.edu
Established: 1884 Annual Undergrad Tuition & Fees: $30,650
Enrollment: 253 Coed
Affiliation or Control: Independent Non-Profit IRS Status: 501(c)3
Highest Offering: Associate Degree
Accreditation: M, THEA

01 President .... Ms. Susan ZECH
10 Chief Financial Officer .... Mr. Joel BLOCK
05 Director of Instruction .... Mr. Constantine SCOPAS
07 Director of Admissions .... Ms. Kerin REILLY
27 Director of Marketing .... Mr. Lance STICKSEL
37 Director Financial Aid .... Mr. Roberto LOPEZ
08 Librarian .... Ms. Deborah PICONE
21 Controller .... Ms. Linda VIALA
11 Director of Operations .... Mr. Peter TUFEL
26 Director External Affairs .... Mrs. Elizabeth LAWSON
04 Assistant to the President .... Ms. Jackie REINKING

American Academy McAllister Institute of Funeral Service (B)

619 W 54th Street, 2nd Floor, New York NY 10019
County: New York FICE Identification: 010813
Unit ID: 188687
Telephone: (212) 757-1190 Carnegie Class: Spec 2-yr-A&S
FAX Number: (212) 765-5923 Calendar System: Semester
URL: www.funeraleducation.org
Established: 1926 Annual Undergrad Tuition & Fees: $15,878
Enrollment: 424 Coed
Affiliation or Control: Independent Non-Profit IRS Status: 501(c)3
Highest Offering: Associate Degree
Accreditation: FUSER

01 President/CEO .... Ms. Meg DUNN
03 Executive Vice President .... Dr. George CONNICK
10 Bursar .... Mr. Jay TSO
37 Financial Aid Officer .... Ms. Natalie GIVAN
05 Dir Student Svcs/CH General Educ .... Ms. Regina SMITH
69 Div Chair Public Health/Technical .... Dr. Elissa DEBENEDICTS
50 Division Chair Business/Law/Ethics .... Mr. Brian KASLER
06 Registrar .... Mr. Andre RAMPAUL
07 Dir of Admissions/Enrollment Mgmt .... Mr. Alan LOVEDER
08 Librarian .... Ms. Mary MOON
20 Academic Advisor .... Ms. Charlotte RERRICK
20 Academic Advisor .... Ms. Karen CARR
04 Exec Assistant to the President .... Ms. Stephanie HELSTON
43 Legal Counsel .... Mr. Charles MAURER

The Art Institute of New York City (C)

218-232 W. 40th Street, New York NY 10018
County: New York FICE Identification: 025256
Unit ID: 365055
Telephone: (212) 226-5500 Carnegie Class: Spec 2-yr-A&S
FAX Number: (212) 226-5644 Calendar System: Quarter
URL: www.ainyc.aii.edu
Established: 1980 Annual Undergrad Tuition & Fees: $19,752
Enrollment: 898 Coed
Affiliation or Control: Proprietary IRS Status: Proprietary
Highest Offering: Associate Degree
Accreditation: #ACICS

† School is in teach-out plan.

ASA College (D)

81 Willoughby Street, Brooklyn NY 11201
County: Kings FICE Identification: 030955
Unit ID: 404994
Telephone: (718) 522-9073 Carnegie Class: Assoc/MT-VT-Mix Trad/Non
FAX Number: (718) 532-1433 Calendar System: Semester
URL: www.asa.edu
Established: 1985 Annual Undergrad Tuition & Fees: $12,898
Enrollment: 4,624 Coed
Affiliation or Control: Proprietary IRS Status: Proprietary
Highest Offering: Baccalaureate
Accreditation: M, ACICS, MAC

01 President .... Mr. Alex SHCHEGOL
05 Vice President Academic Affairs .... Dr. Shanthi KONKOTH
14 Vice President for Facilities & IT .... Ms. Alla SHCHEGOL
07 Vice President Marketing/Admissions .. Ms. Victoria KOSTYUKOV
36 Vice Pres Placement/Alumni Svcs .... Ms. Lesia WILLIS
86 Vice Pres Govt & Community Rels .... Mr. Roberto DUMAUAL
37 Vice President Financial Aid Svcs .... Ms. Victoriya SHTAMLER
06 Registrar .... Ms. Mariana ZINDER
08 Head Librarian .... Mr. Brook STOWE
10 Chief Business Officer .... Mr. Jose VALENCIA
13 Chief Info Technology Officer .... Mr. David ESTRIN
04 Administrative Asst to President .... Ms. Ksenia KASIMOVA
09 Director of Institutional Research .... Ms. Anna BOUKHMAN
15 Director Personnel Services ..... Ms. Austria Jazmin GREENBLATT
18 Chief Facilities/Physical Plant .... Mr. Walter KRUMER
32 Chief Student Affairs/Student Life .... Mr. Marcus BROWNE
41 Athletic Director .... Mr. Kenneth WILCOX
50 Dean of Business .... Dr. Edward KUFUOR
76 Dean of Health Disciplines .... Vacant
88 Dean of Legal Studies .... Dr. Oscar ODOM, III
49 Dean of Arts and Sciences .... Mr. Lizhi (Frank) ZHU
106 Dir Online Education/E-learning .... Mr. Gabriel NUNEZ
108 Director Institutional Assessment .... Vacant
38 Director Student Counseling ..... Ms. Tatyana KRYZHANOVSKAYA
39 Director Student Housing .... Mr. Carlyle HICKS

† Bachelor degrees are only offered at the additional location in North Miami Beach, FL.

Bank Street College of Education (E)

610 W 112 Street, New York NY 10025-1898
County: New York FICE Identification: 002669
Unit ID: 189015
Telephone: (212) 875-4400 Carnegie Class: Spec-4-yr-Other
FAX Number: (212) 875-4759 Calendar System: Semester
URL: www.bankstreet.edu
Established: 1916 Annual Graduate Tuition & Fees: N/A
Enrollment: 747 Coed
Affiliation or Control: Independent Non-Profit IRS Status: 501(c)3
Highest Offering: Master's; No Undergraduates
Accreditation: M, TED

01 President .... Shael POLAKOW-SURANSKY
100 Chief of Staff .... Katherine CONNELLY
10 Chief Financial Officer .... Marion KOWALSKI
11 Chief Operating Officer .... Justin TYACK
30 VP Development/External Relations .... Sonja CARTER
86 VP Governance/Community Engagement .... Akilah ROSADO
05 Dean of Innov/Policy & Research .... Josh THOMASES
58 Dean of the Graduate School .... Cecelia TRAUGH
88 Dean of Children's Programs .... Jed LIPPARD
11 Associate Dean of Administration .... Barbara COLEMAN
20 Associate Dean of Academic Affairs .... Wendi WILLIAMS
07 Interim Director of Admissions .... Jesse NGUYEN
06 Registrar .... Ann COX
37 Director of Student Financial Aid .... Emmett COOPER
29 Director of Alumni Relations .... Linda REING
15 Chief Human Resources Officer .... Elyse MATTHEWS
13 Chief Information Officer .... Judith JOHNSON
18 Director of Facilities .... Daniel BENCHIMOL
08 Director of Library Services .... Kristin FREDA
36 Director of Student Placement .... Susan LEVINE
09 Director of Institutional Research .... Amy KLINE
19 Director of Security/Safety .... Daniel BENCHIMOL
04 Executive Assistant to President .... Regina WRIGHT

Bard College (F)

PO Box 5000, Annandale-On-Hudson NY 12504-5000
County: Dutchess FICE Identification: 002671
Unit ID: 189088
Telephone: (845) 758-6822 Carnegie Class: Bac-A&S
FAX Number: (845) 758-4294 Calendar System: Semester
URL: www.bard.edu
Established: 1860 Annual Undergrad Tuition & Fees: $49,906
Enrollment: 2,469 Coed
Affiliation or Control: Independent Non-Profit IRS Status: 501(c)3
Highest Offering: Doctorate
Accreditation: M

01 President .... Dr. Leon BOTSTEIN
03 Executive Vice President of College .... Dr. Dimitri B. PAPADIMITRIOU
100 Vice President/Chief of Staff .... Mr. Taun TOAY
30 Vice Pres Alumni/ae Affairs/Devel .... Ms. Debra PEMSTEIN
10 VP for Admin & Finance/CFO .... Dr. James BRUDVIG
11 Vice President for Administration .... Ms. Coleen MURPHY ALEXANDER
05 Vice President/Dean of the College .... Ms. Rebecca THOMAS
32 VP Student Affairs/Dir Admissions .... Ms. Mary I. BACKLUND
20 VP Acad Affairs/Dir Civic Engagmt .... Dr. Jonathan BECKER
20 Associate VP for Academic Affairs .... Dr. David SHEIN
08 VP/Dean Info Svcs/Dir Libraries .... Mr. Jeffrey KATZ
32 VP for Student Affairs .... Ms. Erin CANNAN
09 VP for Institutional Research .... Dr. Mark D. HALSEY
35 Dean of Student Affairs .... Ms. Bethany NOHLGREN
57 Dir Milton Avery Grad Sch of Arts .... Mr. Arthur GIBBONS
88 Dir Bard Grad Ctr Decorative Arts .... Dr. Susan WEBER
88 Exec Dir Ctr Curatorial Studies .... Mr. Tom ECCLES
88 Director of Institutional Support .... Ms. Karen UNGER
88 Director Ctr Environmental Policy .... Dr. Eban GOODSTEIN
37 Director Financial Aid .... Ms. Denise ACKERMAN
06 Registrar .... Mr. Peter GADSBY
26 Associate VP of Communications .... Mr. Mark PRIMOFF
15 Director of Human Resources .... Ms. Kimberly ALEXANDER
21 Associate VP for Finance .... Mr. Kevin PARKER
88 Director Inst Writing/Thinking .... Ms. Peg PEOPLES
18 Director of Buildings & Grounds .... Mr. Randy CLUM
13 Director Mgmt Info Systems .... Mr. Michael TOMPKINS
29 Director Alumni/ae Affairs .... Ms. Jane BRIEN
36 Director Career Development .... Ms. Elizabeth GIGLIO
19 Director Safety & Security .... Mr. Kenneth COOPER
09 Director of Institutional Research .... Mr. Joseph F. AHERN
24 Director of Audio/Video Services .... Mr. Paul LABARBERA
28 Director of Multicultural Affairs .... Dr. Ann SEATON
41 Director of Athletics .... Ms. Kristin E. HALL
40 Bookstore Manager .... Ms. Merry MEYER
23 Director Student Health Services .... Ms. Marsha DAVIS
38 Director Student Counseling .... Ms. Tamara TELBERG
96 Director of Purchasing .... Ms. Theresa VANETTEN

Bard High School Early College Manhattan (G)

525 East Houston Street, New York NY 10002
Telephone: (212) 995-8479 Identification: 770114
Accreditation: &EH

† Regional accreditation is carried under the parent institution in Great Barrington, MA

Bard High School Early College Queens (H)

30-20 Thomson Avenue, Long Island City NY 11101
Telephone: (718) 361-3133 Identification: 770115
Accreditation: &EH

† Regional accreditation is carried under the parent institution in Great Barrington, MA

Barnard College (I)

3009 Broadway, New York NY 10027-6598
County: New York FICE Identification: 002708
Unit ID: 189097
Telephone: (212) 854-5262 Carnegie Class: Bac-A&S
FAX Number: (212) 854-6220 Calendar System: Semester
URL: www.barnard.edu
Established: 1889 Annual Undergrad Tuition & Fees: $47,631
Enrollment: 2,573 Female
Affiliation or Control: Independent Non-Profit IRS Status: 501(c)3
Highest Offering: Baccalaureate
Accreditation: M, DANCE, TEAC

01 President .... Debora L. SPAR
43 Chief of Staff to Pres/Gen Counsel .... Jomysha STEPHEN
05 Provost & Dean of Faculty .... Linda BELL
03 Chief Operating Officer .... Robert GOLDBERG
20 Dean of the College .... Avis HINKSON
30 Vice President for Development .... Bret SILVER
26 Vice Pres Comm/Counsel to Pres .... Joanne KWONG
10 Vice President for Finance .... Eileen M. DIBENEDETTO
11 Vice Pres Campus Services .... Gail BELTRONE
13 Vice Pres Information Technology .... Carol KATZMAN
15 Vice President of Human Resources .... Catherine GEDDIS
88 Dean of Studies .... Natalie FRIEDMAN
84 Dean of Enrollment Management .... Jennifer FONDILLER
06 Registrar .... Constance BROWN
37 Director of Financial Aid .... Nanette DILAURO
32 Associate Dean for Student Life .... Alina WONG
39 Exec Dir Res Life and Housing .... Alicia LAWRENCE
23 Exec Director of Student Health Svc .... Mary Joan MURPHY
36 Director of Career Development .... Robert EARL
29 Exec Director of Alumnae Relations .... Caitlin TRAMEL
08 Dean of the Library .... Vacant
101 Secretary to the Board of Trustees .... Alyssa SCHIFFMAN
19 Director of Safety/Security .... Dianna PENNETTI
109 Director of Business Operations .... Douglas MAGET
18 Director Facilities Services .... Daniel DAVIS
09 Dir Institutional Research & Assess .... Rebecca FRIEDKIN

† Affiliated with Columbia University in the City of New York.

Be'er Yaakov Talmudic Seminary (J)

12 Jefferson Avenue, Spring Valley NY 10977
County: Rockland FICE Identification: 041928
Unit ID: 476717
Telephone: (845) 362-3053 Carnegie Class: Spec-4-yr-Faith
FAX Number: (845) 406-9699 Calendar System: Semester
Established: 1995 Annual Undergrad Tuition & Fees: $8,750
Enrollment: 382 Male
Affiliation or Control: Independent Non-Profit IRS Status: 501(c)3
Highest Offering: First Talmudic Degree
Accreditation: RABN

01 CEO .... Mr. Jacob UNGAR
05 Dean .... Rabbi Israel EISENBERGER
06 Registrar/Administrator .... Rabbi Yitzchok SOIFER
37 Financial Aid Administrator .... Mrs. Chana NOTIS

Beis Medrash Heichal Dovid (K)

211 Beach 17th Street, Far Rockaway NY 11691-4433
County: Queens FICE Identification: 037133
Unit ID: 444413
Telephone: (718) 868-2300 Carnegie Class: Spec-4-yr-Faith
FAX Number: (718) 868-0517 Calendar System: Semester
Established: 1999 Annual Undergrad Tuition & Fees: $9,200
Enrollment: 111 Male
Affiliation or Control: Independent Non-Profit IRS Status: 501(c)3

Highest Offering: Second Talmudic Degree
Accreditation: **RABN**

01 Dean .... Rabbi Yaakov BENDER
05 Rosh Yeshiva .... Rabbi Shlomo Avidgor ALTUSKY
37 Financial Aid Officer .... Rabbi Aaron STEINBERG

The Belanger School of Nursing (A)

650 McClellan Street, Schenectady NY 12304
County: Schenectady — FICE Identification: 006448
Unit ID: 190956
Telephone: (518) 243-4471 — Carnegie Class: Spec 2-yr-Health
FAX Number: (518) 243-4470 — Calendar System: Other
URL: www.ellisbelangerschoolofnursing.org
Established: 1903 — Annual Undergrad Tuition & Fees: $9,632
Enrollment: 127 — Coed
Affiliation or Control: Independent Non-Profit — IRS Status: 501(c)3
Highest Offering: Associate Degree
Accreditation: **ADNUR**

01 Director .... Dr. Marilyn STAPLETON
37 Student Financial Aid Coordinator .... Mr. Michael DAGGETT
03 Associate Director .... Ms. Michele HEWITT
88 ADA Coordinator .... Ms. Amy TESSITORE

Berkeley College (B)

3 East 43rd Street, New York NY 10017-4604
County: New York — FICE Identification: 007394
Unit ID: 189228
Telephone: (212) 986-4343 — Carnegie Class: Spec-4-yr-Bus
FAX Number: (212) 818-1169 — Calendar System: Semester
URL: www.berkeleycollege.edu
Established: 1931 — Annual Undergrad Tuition & Fees: $24,300
Enrollment: 4,479 — Coed
Affiliation or Control: Proprietary — IRS Status: Proprietary
Highest Offering: Baccalaureate
Accreditation: **M**

00 Chairman of the Board .... Mr. Kevin L. LUING
01 President .... Mr. Michael J. SMITH
04 Special Assistant to the President .... Dr. Rose Mary HEALY
04 Special Assistant to the President .... Vacant
05 Provost .... Dr. Beth CASTIGLIA
84 SVP Enrollment Management .... Ms. Diane RECINOS
10 Vice Pres Finance & Administration .... Mr. Dino KASAMIS
45 VP Planning & Chief of Staff .... Vacant
43 VP & Chief Compliance Officer .... Mr. William BRANDT
26 Chief Marketing Officer .... Mr. William DIMASI
13 Chief Information Officer .... Mr. Leonard DE BOTTON
86 SVP Government Relations NJ .... Ms. Teri DUDA
86 VP Government Relations NY .... Mr. Gbubemi OKOTIEURO
20 VP Academic Advisement .... Ms. Liz BARRETT
08 VP Library Services .... Ms. Marlene DOTY
32 VP Student Development/Campus Life .... Dr. Dallas REED
36 VP Career Services .... Mr. Brian MAHER
37 VP Financial Aid .... Mr. Howard LESLIE
21 VP Budget & Student Accounts .... Ms. Eileen LOFTUS-BERLIN
85 VP International Division .... Ms. Cynthia C. MARCHESE
18 VP Operations .... Mr. Mark WAGENER
50 Dean School of Business .... Dr. Beth CASTIGLIA
76 Interim Dean School Health Studies .... Ms. Elizabeth FITZGERALD
49 Dean School of Liberal Arts .... Dr. Don KIEFFER
107 Dean School of Professional Studies .... Ms. Lenore MOLEE
20 Associate Provost Academic Affairs .... Dr. Judith KORNBERG
06 Registrar .... Ms. Deborah PALICIA
106 Assistant Provost Online .... Ms. Carol SMITH
88 Dean Academic Support .... Dr. Gerald IACULLO
108 AVP Institutional Effectiveness .... Dr. Rachel FESTER
31 AVP Communications & Ext Relations .... Ms. Angela HARRINGTON
19 AVP Public Safety .... Mr. William ORTMAN
27 Director Media Relations .... Ms. Ilene GREENFIELD
41 Director Athletics .... Mr. Andrew DESTEPHANO
29 Director Alumni Relations .... Ms. Jennifer PORTER
09 Director Institutional Research .... Ms. Rebecca J. DRENNEN

Bet Medrash Gadol Ateret Torah (C)

901 Quentin Road, Brooklyn NY 11223
County: Kings — Identification: 667146
Telephone: (347) 394-1036 — Carnegie Class: Not Classified
FAX Number: (347) 394-1096 — Calendar System: Semester
Established: 1992 — Annual Undergrad Tuition & Fees: N/A
Enrollment: N/A — Male
Affiliation or Control: Independent Non-Profit — IRS Status: 501(c)3
Highest Offering: Second Talmudic Degree
Accreditation: **@RABN**

01 President/CEO .... Rabbi Joseph HARARI-RAFUL
10 Chief Financial/Business Officer .... Irwin SHAMAH
06 Registrar .... Mrs. Ruchana MANSOUR
11 Chief of Operations/Administration .... Zev KLEINER

Beth Benjamin Academy of Connecticut (D)

51 Carlton Road, Monsey NY 10952
FICE Identification: 029120
Unit ID: 414975
Telephone: (845) 207-0330 — Carnegie Class: Not Classified
FAX Number: N/A — Calendar System: Trimester
Established: 1976 — Annual Undergrad Tuition & Fees: N/A
Enrollment: N/A — Male
Affiliation or Control: Independent Non-Profit — IRS Status: 501(c)3
Highest Offering: First Talmudic Degree
Accreditation: **RABN**

01 Rosh Hayeshiva .... Rabbi M. HERSHKOWITZ
04 Associate Rosh Hayeshiva .... Rabbi Yeruchom ZEILBERGER
05 Dean .... Rabbi Michael BENDER

Beth Hamedrash Shaarei Yosher Institute (E)

4102-10 16th Avenue, Brooklyn NY 11204-1099
County: Kings — FICE Identification: 011192
Unit ID: 189273
Telephone: (718) 854-2290 — Carnegie Class: Spec-4-yr-Faith
FAX Number: (718) 436-9045 — Calendar System: Semester
Established: 1962 — Annual Undergrad Tuition & Fees: $8,250
Enrollment: 48 — Male
Affiliation or Control: Independent Non-Profit — IRS Status: 501(c)3
Highest Offering: Second Talmudic Degree
Accreditation: **RABN**

05 Chief Academic Officer .... Rabbi Yosef ROSENBLUM
10 Chief Business Officer .... Rabbi Pinches KAFF
29 Director Alumni Association .... Rabbi Chaim ROSENBERG
15 Director Personnel Services .... Rabbi Mordechai MARGULIES
37 Director Student Financial Aid .... Rabbi Aaron ROTTENBERG
06 Registrar .... Rabbi Sol ROSENBERG

Beth Hatalmud Rabbinical College (F)

2127 82nd Street, Brooklyn NY 11214-2594
County: Kings — FICE Identification: 011922
Unit ID: 189264
Telephone: (718) 259-2525 — Carnegie Class: Spec-4-yr-Faith
FAX Number: (718) 256-5592 — Calendar System: Semester
Established: 1950 — Annual Undergrad Tuition & Fees: $7,700
Enrollment: 29 — Male
Affiliation or Control: Independent Non-Profit — IRS Status: 501(c)3
Highest Offering: Second Talmudic Degree
Accreditation: **RABN**

01 President .... Rabbi Chaim STEFANSKY
10 Fiscal Officer .... Rabbi C. L. PERKOWSKI
08 Librarian .... Mr. Shimon HESS

Beth Medrash Meor Yitzchok (G)

65 Dykstra's Way East, Monsey NY 10952
County: Rockland — Identification: 667111
Telephone: (845) 426-3488 — Carnegie Class: Not Classified
FAX Number: (845) 425-5415 — Calendar System: Semester
Established: 2007 — Annual Undergrad Tuition & Fees: N/A
Enrollment: N/A — Male
Affiliation or Control: Independent Non-Profit — IRS Status: 501(c)3
Highest Offering: First Talmudic Degree
Accreditation: **RABN**

Bill and Sandra Pomeroy College of Nursing at Crouse Hospital (H)

736 Irving Avenue, Syracuse NY 13210
County: Onondaga — FICE Identification: 006445
Unit ID: 190451
Telephone: (315) 470-7481 — Carnegie Class: Spec 2-yr-Health
FAX Number: (315) 470-7774 — Calendar System: Semester
URL: www.crouse.org/nursing
Established: 1913 — Annual Undergrad Tuition & Fees: $11,078
Enrollment: 345 — Coed
Affiliation or Control: Independent Non-Profit — IRS Status: 501(c)3
Highest Offering: Associate Degree
Accreditation: **ADNUR**

01 Dean .... Rhonda READER
06 Registrar .... Cari MCLAUGHLIN
07 Director of Admissions .... Amy GRAHAM
08 Head Librarian .... Kristine DELANEY
37 Director Student Financial Aid .... Kenny KENDALL

Boricua College (I)

3755 Broadway, New York NY 10032-1599
County: New York — FICE Identification: 013029
Unit ID: 189413
Telephone: (212) 694-1000 — Carnegie Class: Bac/Assoc-Mixed
FAX Number: (212) 694-1015 — Calendar System: Semester
URL: www.boricuacollege.edu
Established: 1974 — Annual Undergrad Tuition & Fees: $10,625
Enrollment: 1,163 — Coed
Affiliation or Control: Independent Non-Profit — IRS Status: 501(c)3
Highest Offering: Master's
Accreditation: **M, TEAC**

01 President .... Dr. Victor G. ALICEA
04 Exec Assistant to the President .... Ms. Sandra BELLAMY
03 Sr Vice President .... Dr. Maria MONTES-MORALES
05 VP Academic Affairs .... Dr. Shivaji SENGUPTA
13 VP Information & Tech/Facil Mgmt .... Mr. Irving RAMIREZ
20 VP Academic Planning & Programming .... Dr. John GUZMAN
43 Legal Counsel .... Mr. Jorge BATISTA
10 Director Finance .... Mr. Elias OYOLA
07 Director Admissions Bronx Campus .... Ms. Brenda RODRIGUEZ
07 Director Admissions Manhattan Ctr .... Mr. Ismael SANCHEZ
07 Director Admissions Graham Ctr .... Ms. Aurea MORALES
06 Director Registration & Assessments .... Ms. Beatriz AHORRIO
37 Director Financial Aid .... Ms. Rosalia CRUZ
15 Director Personnel/Human Resources .... Ms. Francia L. CASTRO
08 Director Library/Learning Resources .... Ms. Liza RIVERA
18 Director Environmental Services .... Mr. Elias RIVERA
41 Director of Athletics .... Vacant
30 Director of Development .... Vacant
20 Dean Academic Affairs Manhattan Ctr .... Mr. Moises PEREYRA
20 Dean of Academic Affairs Bronx Ctr .... Mr. Jose Israel LOPEZ

Bramson ORT College (J)

69-30 Austin Street, Forest Hills NY 11375-4239
County: Queens — FICE Identification: 021068
Unit ID: 189422
Telephone: (718) 261-5800 — Carnegie Class: Assoc/HVT-High Non
FAX Number: (718) 575-5119 — Calendar System: Semester
URL: www.bramsonort.edu
Established: 1977 — Annual Undergrad Tuition & Fees: $11,330
Enrollment: 641 — Coed
Affiliation or Control: Independent Non-Profit — IRS Status: 501(c)3
Highest Offering: Associate Degree
Accreditation: **NY**

01 President .... Dr. David KANANI
05 Actg Dean of Academic Services .... Mr. David YURMAN
07 Director of Admissions .... Ms. Julie DABOIN
08 Librarian .... Ms. Shelly SANTOS
21 Bursar .... Ms. Mazzie DOUSTAR
37 Financial Aid Coordinator .... Ms. Angelina MARRA
49 Arts/Science Coordinator .... Ms. Helen POLYNSKY
36 Job Development Advisor .... Ms. Angela NASIMOVA
50 Actg Chair Business Tech/Accounting .... Ms. Shery DENG
88 Paralegal Program Coordinator .... Ms. Aisha CESAR
56 Computer Tech/Distance Learn Coord .... Mr. Damindra PERSAUD
56 Director Brooklyn Extension Site .... Mr. Yair ROSENRAUCH
76 Medical Assistant Program Coord .... Dr. Emil ASDURIAN
96 Director of Purchasing .... Mr. Mark MIRENBERG
06 Registrar .... Ms. Aleksandra KAGAN
10 Controller .... Mr. Mark MIRENBERG
32 Director of Student Services .... Ms. Angela NASIMOVA

Briarcliffe College (K)

1055 Stewart Avenue, Bethpage NY 11714-3545
County: Nassau — FICE Identification: 020757
Unit ID: 189459
Telephone: (516) 918-3600 — Carnegie Class: Bac/Assoc-Mixed
FAX Number: (516) 470-6020 — Calendar System: Semester
URL: www.briarcliffe.edu
Established: 1966 — Annual Undergrad Tuition & Fees: $14,349
Enrollment: 1,719 — Coed
Affiliation or Control: Proprietary — IRS Status: Proprietary
Highest Offering: Baccalaureate
Accreditation: **M, DH**

01 Campus Dir/VP Operations .... Mr. Louis COMMISSO
07 Vice Pres Admissions .... Mr. C. Gabriel CASTANO
32 Vice President Student Affairs .... Ms. Kathy GENUA
10 VP Finance/CFO .... Mr. Louis COMMISSO
13 Director of Information Systems .... Mr. Hoober ZULUAGA
21 Business Office Manager .... Ms. Cindy ROYS
06 Registrar .... Ms. Christy LAW
36 Director of Career Services .... Mr. Tony EMERSON
08 Librarian .... Mr. Jeremy LAUBER

† Currently in teach-out mode. Closing December 2018.

Brooklyn Law School (L)

250 Joralemon Street, Brooklyn NY 11201-3798
County: Kings — FICE Identification: 002677
Unit ID: 189501
Telephone: (718) 625-2200 — Carnegie Class: Spec-4-yr-Law
FAX Number: (718) 780-0393 — Calendar System: Semester
URL: www.brooklaw.edu
Established: 1901 — Annual Graduate Tuition & Fees: N/A
Enrollment: 1,141 — Coed
Affiliation or Control: Independent Non-Profit — IRS Status: 501(c)3
Highest Offering: First Professional Degree; No Undergraduates
Accreditation: **LAW**

00 Dean and President Emerita .... Dean Joan G. WEXLER
01 President/Dean .... Dean Nicholas W. ALLARD
05 Vice Dean of Academic Affairs .... Dean William ARAIZA
20 Assoc Dean for Profess Legal Educ .... Dean Stacy CAPLOW
20 Vice Dean .... Dean Suzanne DENNIS
32 Dean of Students .... Dean Jennifer R. LANG
10 Chief Financial Officer .... Ms. Laurie H. NEWITZ
21 Treasurer .... Ms. Shoshanna M. CAMPBELL
07 Dean of Admissions .... Dean Eulas BOYD, JR.
08 Director of Library & Assoc Prof .... Prof. Janet SINDER
30 Director of Development .... Ms. Kamille JAMES
29 Asst Director of Alumni Relations .... Ms. Andrea POLCI
36 Asst Dean of Career Development .... Ms. Karen EISEN

06 Registrar .... Mr. Christian BESTER
37 Director of Financial Aid .... Ms. Nancy L. ZAHZAM
11 Chief Operating Ofcr/Chief of Staff .... Ms. Linda HARVEY
18 Facilities Manager .... Mr. Salvatore DECANDIA
15 Human Resources Manager .... Ms. Christina WALLACE
13 Chief Info Technology Officer (CIO) .... Mr. Steven MARKS
19 Director of Public Safety .... Ms. Mercedes RAVELO
43 Gen Counsel/Chf Compliance Officer .... Ms. Stephanie VULLO

*Bryant & Stratton College System Office (A)

2410 N. Forest Road, Suite 101, Getzville NY 14068-1224
County: Erie | Identification: 666828
Telephone: (716) 250-7500 | Carnegie Class: N/A
FAX Number: (716) 250-7510
URL: www.bryantstratton.edu

01 President & CEO .... Dr. Francis J. FELSER
11 VP/Chief Operating Officer .... Mr. David VADEN
05 VP/Chief Academic Officer .... Ms. Beth A. TARQUINO
10 VP/Chief Financial Officer .... Mr. Christopher GERACE
13 VP/Online Division and CIO .... Ms. Doreen JUSTINGER
07 VP/Marketing and Admissions .... Ms. Tracy NANNERY
108 Exec Dir Strat Plng & Assessment .... Ms. Anne LORIA

*Bryant & Stratton College (B)

465 Main Street, Suite 400, Buffalo NY 14203-1795
County: Erie | FICE Identification: 002678
Unit ID: 189583
Telephone: (716) 884-9120 | Carnegie Class: Bac/Assoc-Assoc Dom
FAX Number: (716) 884-0091 | Calendar System: Semester
URL: www.bryantstratton.edu
Established: 1854 | Annual Undergrad Tuition & Fees: $16,404
Enrollment: 800 | Coed
Affiliation or Control: Proprietary | IRS Status: Proprietary
Highest Offering: Baccalaureate
Accreditation: M, MAC

02 Campus Director .... Dr. Marvel E. ROSS-JONES
05 Dean of Instruction .... Dr. Adiam TSEGAI
07 Director of Admissions .... Vacant
36 Director of Career Services .... Ms. Diane WESTBROOK
10 WNY Business Office Director .... Ms. Kathleen OWCZARCZAK

*Bryant & Stratton College (C)

1259 Central Avenue, Albany NY 12205-5230
Telephone: (518) 437-1802 | FICE Identification: 004749
Accreditation: &M, MAC

† Regional accreditation is carried under the parent institution in Buffalo, NY

*Bryant & Stratton College (D)

854 Long Pond Road, Rochester NY 14612-3049
Telephone: (585) 720-0660 | FICE Identification: 012470
Accreditation: &M, MAC

† Regional accreditation is carried under the parent institution in Buffalo, NY

*Bryant & Stratton College (E)

953 James Street, Syracuse NY 13203-2502
Telephone: (315) 472-6603 | FICE Identification: 008276
Accreditation: &M, MAC, OTA, @PTAA

† Regional accreditation is carried under the parent institution in Buffalo, NY

Canisius College (F)

2001 Main Street, Buffalo NY 14208-1098
County: Erie | FICE Identification: 002681
Unit ID: 189705
Telephone: (716) 883-7000 | Carnegie Class: Masters/L
FAX Number: (716) 888-2525 | Calendar System: Semester
URL: www.canisius.edu
Established: 1870 | Annual Undergrad Tuition & Fees: $34,690
Enrollment: 4,181 | Coed
Affiliation or Control: Roman Catholic | IRS Status: 501(c)3
Highest Offering: Master's
Accreditation: M, BUS, #CAATE, CACREP, TED

01 President .... Mr. John J. HURLEY
05 VP Academic Affairs .... Dr. Margaret MCCARTHY
10 Vice President Business & Finance .... Mr. Marco F. BENEDETTI
32 VP Student Affs & Dean of Students .... Dr. Terri L. MANGIONE
30 VP Institutional Advancement .... Mr. William COLLINS, II
84 VP Enrollment Management .... Ms. Kathleen B. DAVIS
20 Assoc VP for Academic Affairs .... Dr. Sara MORRIS
88 Asst VP/Dir Stdnt Rec & Fin Svcs .... Mr. Kevin M. SMITH
08 Director of Library .... Ms. Kristine E. KASBOHM
07 Director Undergrad Admissions .... Mr. Justin P. ROGERS
44 Director of Principal Gifts .... Mr. J. Patrick GREENWALD
21 Controller .... Mr. Ronald J. HABERER
49 Int Dean Col of Arts & Sciences .... Dr. Elizabeth A. GILL
50 Dean School of Business .... Dr. Daniel J. BORGIA
37 Assoc Dir of Stdnt Records/Fin Svcs .... Ms. Mary A. KOEHNEKE
06 Registrar/Asst Dir Stdnt Rec & FA .... Ms. Deborah W. PROHN
26 Director of Public Relations .... Ms. Eileen C. HERBERT
15 Director of Human Resources .... Ms. Linda M. WALLESHAUSER
88 Director of the Canisius Fund .... Ms. Erin HARTNETT
53 Assc Dean School Ed/Human Svcs .... Dr. Shawn O'ROURKE
25 Director of Sponsored Programs .... Ms. Mary Ann LANGLOIS
18 Director Facilities Management .... Mr. Thomas E. CIMINELLI
19 Director of Public Safety .... Mr. H. Wilson JOHNSON
23 Director Student Health Center .... Ms. Patricia H. CREAHAN
38 Director Counseling Center .... Ms. Eileen A. NILAND
39 Assoc Dean of Stdnts/Dir Resid Life .... Mr. Matthew H. MULVILLE
104 Director Study Abroad .... Mr. Brian SMITH
40 Course Materials Manager/Bookstore .... Mr. Andrew J. THOMAS
41 Director Athletics .... Mr. William J. MAHER
42 Director Campus Ministry .... Mr. Michael F. HAYES, JR.
88 Director of Creative Services .... Ms. Andalyn M. COURTNEY
90 Int Director of User Services .... Mr. Scott D. CLARK
94 Dir of Women's Business Center .... Ms. Sara L. VESCIO
92 Director of All College Honors Pgm .... Dr. Bruce J. DIERENFIELD
09 Sr Analyst Research & Inst Effect .... Mr. Michael W. TAMPIO
88 Director of Multi Cultural Programs .... Mr. Sababu C. NORRIS
13 Interim Chief Information Officer .... Mr. Lawrence DENI
24 Director Media Center .... Mr. Daniel J. DREW
96 Director of Purchasing .... Mr. Gary B. LEW
105 Web Development Specialist .... Mr. Kevin M. BLAKE
04 Assistant to the President .... Ms. Erica C. SAMMARCO
102 Asst Director Canisius Fund .... Ms. Summer L. HANDY
91 Director Administrative Computing .... Ms. Michele FOLSOM

Cayuga Community College (G)

197 Franklin Street, Auburn NY 13021-3099
County: Cayuga | FICE Identification: 002861
Unit ID: 189839
Telephone: (315) 255-1743 | Carnegie Class: Assoc/HT-High Non
FAX Number: (315) 255-2117 | Calendar System: Semester
URL: www.cayuga-cc.edu
Established: 1953 | Annual Undergrad Tuition & Fees (In-District): $4,742
Enrollment: 4,290 | Coed
Affiliation or Control: State/Local | IRS Status: 501(c)3
Highest Offering: Associate Degree
Accreditation: M, ADNUR

01 President .... Mr. Brian M. DURANT
04 Assistant to President/Board .... Ms. Carolyn L. GUARIGLIA
05 Provost/Vice Pres Academic Affairs .... Dr. Anne J. HERRON
32 Vice President Student Affairs .... Mr. Jeffrey E. ROSENTHAL
10 Vice Pres Administration/Treasurer .... Ms. Diane L. HUTCHINSON
102 Executive Director Foundation .... Mr. Jeffrey L. HOFFMAN
84 Dean Enrollment Management .... Ms. Cheryl A. LINDSAY
13 Dean Information Technology .... Mr. John KAFTAN
07 Director of Admissions .... Mr. Bruce M. BLODGETT
09 Director Institutional Research .... Ms. Carol E. RUNGE
41 Director Athletics .... Mr. Peter E. LIDDELL
15 Director HR & Affirmative Action .... Mr. Scott M. WHALEN
06 Interim Asst Registrar .... Mr. John W. CALLAN
35 Director Student Activities .... Mr. Norman LEE

Cazenovia College (H)

22 Sullivan Street, Cazenovia NY 13035
County: Madison | FICE Identification: 002685
Unit ID: 189848
Telephone: (800) 654-3210 | Carnegie Class: Bac-Diverse
FAX Number: (315) 655-4143 | Calendar System: Semester
URL: www.cazenovia.edu
Established: 1824 | Annual Undergrad Tuition & Fees: $31,754
Enrollment: 1,091 | Coed
Affiliation or Control: Independent Non-Profit | IRS Status: 501(c)3
Highest Offering: Baccalaureate
Accreditation: M, IACBE, TEAC

01 President .... Dr. Ronald D. CHESBROUGH
05 VP Academic Affs/Dean of Faculty .... Dr. Sharon A. DETTMER
10 VP Financial Affs/Chief Fin Officer .... Mr. Mark H. EDWARDS
84 VP Enrol Mgmt/Dean Admiss/Fin Aid .... Vacant
30 VP for Institutional Advancement .... Ms. Carol SATCHWELL
32 Dean for Student Life .... Ms. Katie O'BRIEN
89 Dean First Year Program .... Mr. Jesse LOTT
08 Director of Library Services .... Ms. Heather C. WHALEN-SMITH
37 Assoc Dean Financial Aid/Registrar .... Ms. Christine MANDEL
26 Director Marketing/Communications .... Mr. Timothy D. GREENE
15 Director Human Resources .... Ms. Janice ROMAGNOLI
23 Director Health Services .... Ms. Deborah FRANK
36 Dir Career/Extended Learning Svcs .... Ms. Christine RICHARDSON
41 Director Intercollegiate Athletics .... Vacant
13 Director of Technology Development .... Mr. David PALMER
06 Registrar .... Ms. Christine MANDEL
09 Dir Institutional Rsrch/Assessment .... Dr. Sara S. PHILLIPS
18 Dir of Physical Plant Operations .... Mr. Jeff SLOCUM
29 Director Alumni Relations .... Ms. Shari WHITAKER
42 Chaplain .... Ms. Elizabeth BURLEW
07 Sr Assistant Director of Admissions .... Mr. Brett M. CARGUELLO

Central Yeshiva Beth Joseph (I)

1502 Avenue N, Brooklyn NY 11230
County: Kings | Identification: 667157
Telephone: (718) 530-6934 | Carnegie Class: Not Classified
FAX Number: (347) 228-3677 | Calendar System: Semester
Established: 1942 | Annual Undergrad Tuition & Fees: N/A
Enrollment: N/A | Male
Affiliation or Control: Independent Non-Profit | IRS Status: 501(c)3
Highest Offering: First Talmudic Degree
Accreditation: RABN

01 Chief Executive Officer .... Rabbi Mordechai JOFEN
37 Director Student Financial Aid .... Rabbi Baruch MILLER
06 Registrar .... Rabbi Avraham JOFEN

Central Yeshiva Tomchei Tmimim Lubavitch America (J)

841-853 Ocean Parkway, Brooklyn NY 11230-2798
County: Kings | FICE Identification: 004776
Unit ID: 189857
Telephone: (718) 434-0784 | Carnegie Class: Spec-4-yr-Faith
FAX Number: (718) 434-1519 | Calendar System: Semester
Established: 1941 | Annual Undergrad Tuition & Fees: $6,700
Enrollment: 726 | Male
Affiliation or Control: Independent Non-Profit | IRS Status: 501(c)3
Highest Offering: Second Talmudic Degree
Accreditation: RABN

01 President .... Rabbi Shloime ZARCHI
05 Dean .... Rabbi Zalman LABKOWSKI
06 Registrar .... Rabbi Joseph WILMOWSKY
37 Financial Aid Director .... Rabbi Moshe M. GLUCKOWSKY
26 Director Public Relations .... Mr. Shaya BOYMELGREEN
10 Treasurer .... Rabbi Moshe BOGOMILSKY

Christ the King Seminary (K)

711 Knox Road, P.O. Box 607,
East Aurora NY 14052-0607
County: Erie | FICE Identification: 002822
Unit ID: 189981
Telephone: (716) 652-8900 | Carnegie Class: Spec-4-yr-Faith
FAX Number: (716) 652-8903 | Calendar System: Semester
URL: www.cks.edu
Established: 1974 | Annual Graduate Tuition & Fees: N/A
Enrollment: 101 | Coed
Affiliation or Control: Roman Catholic | IRS Status: 501(c)3
Highest Offering: Master's; No Undergraduates
Accreditation: M, THEOL

01 Rector/President .... Rev. Joseph C. GATTO
03 Vice Rector .... Rev. Robert A. WOZNIAK
05 Academic Dean .... Mr. Michael SHERRY
10 Comptroller .... Mrs. Nancy M. EHLERS
30 Director Institutional Advancement .... Mrs. Susan LANKES
18 Director of Facilities .... Rev. John M. STAAK, OMI
08 Library Director .... Ms. Teresa LUBIENECKI
06 Registrar .... Mrs. Julie GALEY
04 Administrative Asst to President .... Ms. Nadine OATES
15 Director Personnel Svcs/Fin Aid .... Mrs. Nancy M. EHLERS

Christie's Education, New York (L)

1230 Avenue of the Americas, Fl 20, New York NY 10020
County: New York | FICE Identification: 036654
Unit ID: 475510
Telephone: (212) 355-1501 | Carnegie Class: Spec-4-yr-Arts
FAX Number: (212) 355-7370 | Calendar System: Quarter
URL: www.christies.edu
Established: 1993 | Annual Graduate Tuition & Fees: N/A
Enrollment: 65 | Coed
Affiliation or Control: Proprietary | IRS Status: Proprietary
Highest Offering: Master's; No Undergraduates
Accreditation: NY

01 Academic Director .... Dr. Veronique CHAGNON-BURKE
08 Learning Resources Manager .... Ms. Karen MAGUIRE
07 Recruitment and Admissions Officer .... Ms. Hilary SMITH
21 Admissions and Business Coordinator .... Ms. Mackenzie WELLS
10 Business Manager .... Ms. Margaret CONKLIN
37 Academic/Financial Aid Administator .... Ms. Catherine WARDEN
26 Senior Marketing Officer .... Ms. Jillian SCOTT

*City University of New York (M)

205 E. 42nd Street, New York NY 10017
County: New York | FICE Identification: 025061
Unit ID: 190035
Telephone: (646) 664-9100 | Carnegie Class: N/A
FAX Number: (646) 664-3868
URL: www2.cuny.edu

01 Chancellor .... Mr. James B. MILLIKEN
05 Exec VC/University Provost .... Dr. Vita RABINOWITZ
26 Sr Vice Chanc University Relations .... Mr. Jay HERSHENSON
43 Sr Vice Chancellor Legal Affairs .... Mr. Frederick P. SCHAFFER
10 Sr Advisor for Fiscal Policy .... Mr. Marc SHAW
18 VC Facility Plng/Constr Mgt .... Ms. Judy BERGTRAUM
13 VC/Chief Information Officer .... Mr. Brian COHEN
32 Interim VC Student Affairs .... Dr. Chris ROSA
21 Vice Chancellor Budget/Finance .... Mr. Matthew SAPIENZA
88 Vice Chancellor for Labor Relations .... Ms. Pamela S. SILVERBLATT
09 Vice Chancellor for Research .... Vacant
15 Vice Chanc for Human Resources Mgmt .... Ms. Gloriana WATERS
102 Ass VC for Corporate Foundation .... Ms. Andrea SHAPIRO DAVIS
88 Sr Dean and Special Counsel .... Mr. Dave FIELDS
20 Sr Dean for Academic Affairs .... Mr. John MOGULESCU
06 Registrar .... Vacant

84 Sr University Dean for Enrollment ....Mr. Robert A. PTACHIK
27 Dean of Communications/Marketing ....Mr. Michael ARENA
09 Dean Institutional Research ....Mr. David CROOK
88 Senior Advisor for Communications ....Mr. James STERNGOLD
88 Sr Advisor Strategic Partnerships .... Dr. Ann KIRSCHNER
07 Director of Admissions ....Ms. Clare NORTON
100 Chief of Staff ....Ms. Doris L. SUAREZ

*Baruch College/City University of New York (A)

One Bernard Baruch Way, New York NY 10010-5526

County: New York FICE Identification: 007273
Unit ID: 190512
Telephone: (646) 312-1000 Carnegie Class: Masters/L
FAX Number: N/A Calendar System: Semester
URL: www.baruch.cuny.edu
Established: 1968 Annual Undergrad Tuition & Fees (In-District): $6,810
Enrollment: 18,090 Coed
Affiliation or Control: State/Local IRS Status: 501(c)3
Highest Offering: Doctorate
Accreditation: M, BUS, BUSA, HSA, IPSY, SPAA

02 President ....Dr. Mitchel B. WALLERSTEIN
05 Provost/SVP Academic Affairs ....Dr. David CHRISTY
10 Vice Pres Administration/Finance .... Ms. Katharine COBB
84 Int VP Enroll Mgmt/Strategic Init .... Ms. Mary GORMAN
30 VP for College Advancement ....Mr. David SHANTON
13 VP for Information Services ....Mr. Arthur DOWNING
26 VP for Cmty/Ext Rels & Econ Dev ....Ms. Christina LATOUF
32 VP Student Affairs/Dean of Students ....Dr. Art KING
18 Asst VP Campus Facilities ....Ms. Lisa EDWARDS
21 Asst Vice President Finance ....Ms. Mary FINNEN
102 President Baruch College Fund .... Mr. Joel J. COHEN
50 Dean Zicklin School of Business .... Dr. Fenwick HUSS
49 Dean of the Weissman School .... Dr. Aldemaro ROMEO, JR.
80 Dean School Public/Intl Affairs .... Dr. David BIRDSELL
08 Dean of Library ....Mr. Arthur DOWNING
20 Associate Provost ....Dr. Erec KOCH
20 Associate Provost ....Dr. Dennis SLAVIN
43 Executive Legal Counsel ....Ms. Olga DAIS
58 Executive Officer Doctoral Program .... Dr. Joseph WEINTROP
100 Interim Chief of Staff .... Ms. Kenya N. LEE
25 Director of Sponsored Programs ....Mr. Dominic ESPOSITO
15 Exec Dir of Human Resources ....Ms. Monique GEORGE
36 Director Career Development Center ....Dr. Patricia IMBIMBO
90 Asst Dir Client Svcs/Fac Liaison .... Mr. Frank WERBER
85 Director Intl Student Office ....Ms. Rosa KELLEY
19 Director Public Safety .... Mr. Henry J. MCLAUGHLIN
09 Dir Institutional Rsrch/Pgm Assess .... Mr. John CHOONDO
29 Director Alumni Relations .... Ms. Janet ROSSBACH
96 Director of Purchasing .... Dr. Diane OQUENDO
22 Chief Diversity Officer .... Ms. Kieran MORROW
41 Athletic Director .... Ms. Heather MACCULLOCH
86 Dir of Govt and Community Relations ....Mr. Eric LUGO
06 Registrar .... Mr. Edward ADAMS
104 Director Study Abroad .... Dr. Richard MITTEN
37 Director of Financial Aid Services ....Ms. Elizabeth RIQUEZ
07 Dir of Undergraduate Admissions ....Ms. Marisa DELACRUZ

*City University of New York Borough of Manhattan Community College (B)

199 Chambers Street, New York NY 10007-1047

County: New York FICE Identification: 002691
Unit ID: 190521
Telephone: (212) 220-1230 Carnegie Class: Assoc/HT-High Trad
FAX Number: (212) 220-1244 Calendar System: Semester
URL: www.bmcc.cuny.edu
Established: 1963 Annual Undergrad Tuition & Fees (In-District): $5,170
Enrollment: 26,606 Coed
Affiliation or Control: State/Local IRS Status: 501(c)3
Highest Offering: Associate Degree
Accreditation: M, ADNUR, CAHIIM, COARC, EMT

02 President ....Dr. Antonio PEREZ
05 Provost/Senior VP Academic Affairs .... Dr. Karrin WILKS
11 Vice President Administration/Plng ....Mr. G. Scott ANDERSON
43 VP Legal Affs/Faculty & Staff Rels ....Mr. Robert DIAZ
32 Vice President of Student Affairs .... Dr. Marva CRAIG
30 Vice Pres of Development ....Ms. Doris HOLZ
10 Asst Vice Pres of Finance ....Ms. Elena SAMUELS
51 Dean Ctr for Cont Ed/Workforce Dev ....Dr. Sunil GUPTA
25 Dean Grants & Development .... Mr. John MONTANEZ
20 Dean for Instruction/Curriculum .... Dr. Erwin WONG
88 Assoc Dean Academic Support Svcs .... Dr. James BERG
37 Director Financial Aid ....Mr. Ralph W. BUXTON
15 Deputy Director Human Resources .... Ms. Gloria CHAO
07 Assoc Director of Admissions .... Ms. Antoinette MIDDLETON
84 Director Enrollment Management ....Dr. Eugenio BARRIOS
06 Senior Registrar .... Mr. Mohammad ALAM
08 Act Dir Learning Resource Center ....Mr. Gregory FARRELL
09 Dean Institutional Research .... Dr. Christopher SHULTS
28 Chief Diversity Officer ....Ms. Odelia LEVY
18 Campus Facilities Officer ....Vacant
26 Public Relations Officer ....Mr. Manuel ROMERO
41 Director of Athletics ....Mr. Stephen KELLY
102 Dir Foundation/Corporate Relations ....Mr. Bryan HALLER
36 Act Dir Acad Advise/Transfer Ctr ....Ms. Carei THOMAS
38 Director Counseling Center .... Dr. Cicely Horsham BRATHWAITE
96 Director of Procurement ....Mr. Robert COX

*City University of New York Bronx Community College (C)

2155 University Avenue, Bronx NY 10453-2895

County: Bronx FICE Identification: 002692
Unit ID: 190530
Telephone: (718) 289-5100 Carnegie Class: Assoc/HT-High Trad
FAX Number: (718) 289-6011 Calendar System: Semester
URL: www.bcc.cuny.edu
Established: 1957 Annual Undergrad Tuition & Fees (In-District): $5,206
Enrollment: 11,506 Coed
Affiliation or Control: State/Local IRS Status: 501(c)3
Highest Offering: Associate Degree
Accreditation: M, ACBSP, ADNUR, ENGT, NMT, RAD

02 President ....Dr. Thomas ISEKENEGBE
05 VP of Academic Affairs & Provost .... Dr. Claudia V. SCHRADER
86 Government Rels and Ext Affairs Dir ....Mr. David W. LEVERS
71 Director of Special Projects ....Ms. Carmen VÁSQUEZ
32 VP for Student Affairs ....Vacant
30 VP for Advance/Comm & Ext Rels .... Dr. Eddy BAYARDELLE
26 Asst VP Comm & Marketing .... Ms. Diane WEATHERS
35 Dean of Student Services ....Mr. Bernard GANTT
11 AVP for Administrative Affairs .... Mr. David A. TAYLOR
44 Asst VP for Development ....Ms. Angela WAMBUGU COBB
103 Asst VP Workforce Dev & Cont Educ ....Vacant
45 Dean for Research/Plng & Assessment .... Dr. Nancy RITZE
20 Assoc Dean AA for Curr & Fac Dev ....Dr. Alexander OTT
10 Dir for Financial & Business Svcs ....Ms. Gina GALLIGAN
06 Registrar/Dir Enrollment .... Mr. Sanjay RAMDATH
13 Chief Information Officer .... Mr. Loïc AUDUSSEAU
37 Financial Aid Director ....Mr. Sinu JACOB
07 Admissions Officer .... Ms. Patricia A. RAMOS
15 Human Resources Director .... Mrs. Shelley LEVY
08 Chief Librarian ....Prof. Michael J. MILLER
19 Public Safety Director ....Mr. James VERDICCHIO
41 Student Athletics Manager ....Vacant
18 Chief Super Phys Plant Svcs ....Mr. Lamont WATSON
29 Alum Rel/Plan Giv/Indiv Donors Mgr ....Mr. Robert WHELAN
35 Assoc Dean Stdnt Engagement/Success ....Vacant
88 Mgr of College Discovery ....Ms. Cynthia SUAREZ-ESPINAL
43 Exe Counsel & Deputy to President ....Ms. Earla R. WILLIAMS
96 Director of Purchasing ....Ms. Anjanette ANTONIO
28 Chief Diversity/Affirm Act Ofcr ... Mrs. Jesenia MINIER-DELGADO
14 Deputy Chief Technology Officer ....Ms. Luisa MARTICH
108 Academic Assessment Manager ....Dr. Richard LAMANNA
20 Dean for Academic Affairs .... Dr. Luis MONTENEGRO
90 Dir for Academic Comp Svcs Desk .... Ms. Wanda SANTIAGO
91 Manager of Admin Systems & Svcs ....Mr. Rolly WILTSHIRE
51 Mgr Continuing/Prof Education ....Mr. Wendell JOYNER
25 Dir of Grants Development ....Ms. Carin SAVAGE
22 Affirmative Action Specialist .... Mr. Raymond GONZALEZ
102 Dev Corp and Foundation Rel Mgmt ....Ms. Julia OLIVA
104 Dir Intl Educ and Study Aboard Pgm ....Vacant
09 DIR Inst Research Specialist ....Mrs. Chelsea RAMOS
46 Director of Research & Testing ....Mr. Chris EFTHIMIOU
101 Conf Exec Assistant to the
Pres ....Mrs. Amirah COUSINS MELENDEZ
106 Dir IT Academic App/CTLT ....Mr. Mark LENNERTON
36 Dir Transfer and Job Placement ....Mr. Alán FUENTES

*City University of New York Brooklyn College (D)

2900 Bedford Avenue, Brooklyn NY 11210-2889

County: Kings FICE Identification: 002687
Unit ID: 190549
Telephone: (718) 951-5000 Carnegie Class: Masters/L
FAX Number: N/A Calendar System: Semester
URL: www.brooklyn.cuny.edu
Established: 1930 Annual Undergrad Tuition & Fees (In-District): $6,838
Enrollment: 17,390 Coed
Affiliation or Control: State/Local IRS Status: 501(c)3
Highest Offering: Master's
Accreditation: M, AJD, CACREP, DIETD, DIETI, PH, SP, TED

02 President ....Dr. Michael J. ANDERSON
05 Provost/Sr Vice Pres Acad Affairs . Dr. William A. TRAMONTANO
10 Sr VP for Finance & Administration .... Mr. Joseph GICVANNELLI
30 Vice Pres Institutional Advancement ....Dr. Andrew SILLEN
32 Interim VP for Student Affairs .... Ronald JACKSON
26 AVP of Communications/Marketing .... Mr. Jason CAREY
84 Interim AVP Enrollment Management .... Dr. Lillian O'REILLY
100 Chief of Staff to President .... Ms. Nicole HAAS
86 Exec Dir Govt & External Affairs ....Mr. Steven SCHECHTER
20 Assoc Provost for Academic Pgms .... Dr. Terrence CHENG
20 Assoc Provost for Faculty & Admin ....Dr. Stuart MACLELLAND
53 Dean School of Education .... Dr. April BEDFORD
57 Dean Schl Visual Media & Perf Arts ....Dr. Maria A. CONELLI
50 Dean School of Business ....Dr. Willie HOPKINS
83 Dean Schl Humanities & Social Sci ....Dr. Richard GREENWALD
81 Dean Schl Natural & Behav Sciences .... Dr. Peanthis PSARRIS
35 Dean of Students .... Mr. Ronald C. JACKSON
21 Assoc VP Budget & Planning/CFO ....Mr. Alan GILBERT
18 Asst VP Facilities Plng/Operations .....Mr. Francis X. FITZGERALD
13 Asst VP Info Technology Svcs/CIO ....Mr. Mark GOLD
88 Asst Dean Grad Center for Worker Ed ....Dr. Lucas RUBIN
08 Act Chief Librar/Dir Acad Info Tech ....Ms. Jane CRAMER
09 Sen Dir Inst Plan Research & Assess .... Dr. Michael AYERS
25 Dir Research & Sponsored Programs ....Ms. Sabrina CERERZO
37 Director Financial Aid ....Mr. Ahad FARHANG
06 Registrar ....Mr. Richard FELTMAN

41 Dir Rec Intramurals/Intercol Athl ....Mr. Bruce FILOSA
36 Dir Magner Ctr Career Dev/Interns .... Ms. Natalia GUARIN-KLEIN
29 Acting Director of Alumni Relations ....Mr. Michael IADAROLA
30 Assoc Exec Director of Development ....Ms. Beth F. LEVINE
22 Dir Diversity & Equity Programs . Ms. Natalie L. MASON-KINSEY
43 Legal Counsel to the President ....Ms. Pamela POLLACK
92 Dir Scholars Pgm & Honors Academy .... Dr. Lisa SCHWEBEL
15 AVP Human Resource Services ....Mr. Michael T. HEWITT
07 Dir Undergrad Admiss & Recruitment ....Ms. Penelope TERRY
88 Dir Feirstein Grad School of Cinema ....Mr. Jonathan WACKS
19 Director Safety & Security ....Mr. Donald A. WENZ
108 Director Academic Assessment ....Vacant

*City University of New York The City College (E)

160 Convent Avenue, New York NY 10031-9198

County: New York FICE Identification: 002688
Unit ID: 190567
Telephone: (212) 650-7000 Carnegie Class: Masters/L
FAX Number: (212) 650-7680 Calendar System: Semester
URL: www.ccny.cuny.edu
Established: 1847 Annual Undergrad Tuition & Fees (In-District): $6,689
Enrollment: 15,579 Coed
Affiliation or Control: State/Local IRS Status: 501(c)3
Highest Offering: Doctorate
Accreditation: M, ARCPA, CLPSY, CS, ENG, LSAR, #MED, TED

02 Interim President ....Dr. Mary E. DRISCOLL
05 Int Provost/Sr VP Academic Affairs .... Dr. Mary E. DRISCOLL
26 Vice Pres Communication/Marketing .... Dr. Deidra W. HILL
30 VP Development/Inst Advancement .... Mr. Jeffrey MACHI
29 Executive Director Alumni Affairs ....Mr. Donald K. JORDAN
10 Vice Pres Finance & CFO ....Mr. Felix LAM
84 Asst Vice Pres Enrollment Mgmt .... Ms. Celia P. LLOYD
18 AVP Facilities Mgmt ....Mr. David ROBINSON
31 VP Governmental/Community Affairs .. Ms. Karen WITHERSPOON
32 Vice Pres for Student Affairs ....Ms. Juana REINA
13 AVP Information Technology/CIO ....Mr. Kenneth IHRER
100 Sr Advisor to Pres/Chief of Staff .... Ms. Deborah HARTNETT
63 Dean Sophie Davis Sch of BioMed Ed ..... Dr. Maurizio TREVISAN
54 Dean of Engineering .... Dr. Gilda BARABINO
53 Dean of the School of Education .... Dr. Mary Erina DRISCOLL
47 Acting Dean School of Architecture ....Mr. Gordon GEBERT
88 Dean of CWE-Div of Interdiscip Stds . Dr. Juan Carlos MERCADO
81 Dean of Science ....Dr. Tony LISS
83 Dean Sch Civic & Global Leadership ....Dr. Vincent BOUDREAU
79 Acting Dean Humanities & The Arts .... Dr. Doris CINTRON
43 Counsel to President ....Mr. Paul F. OCCHIOGROSSO
15 Asst Vice Pres of Human Resources ....Mr. John SIDERAKIS
35 Director Student Support Resources .... Ms. Teresa WALKER
06 Senior Registrar ....Vacant
35 Exec Dir of Student Affairs at CWE ....Ms. Sophia DEMETRIOU
08 Acting Chief Librarian .... Dr. Charles STEWART
46 Director Research Administration ....Dr. Alan SHIH
09 Director of Institutional Research .... Mr. Edward SILVERMAN
37 Director of Financial Aid ....Ms. Arshaw RAMKARAN
27 Assoc Director of Public Relations .... Mr. Sydney STEINHARDT
28 Chf Diversity Ofcr/Dean Faculty Rel ....Ms. Michele BAPTISTE
90 Dir Messaging/General Support Svcs ....Mr. Curtis RIAS
36 Director of Career Services ....Ms. Katie NAILLER
19 Exec Dir Public Safety/Security ....Mr. Pat MORENA
11 Administrative Superintendent ....Mr. Kyle MANLEY
24 Director of Instructional Media ....Mr. Nana ABEYIE
07 Exec Director of Admissions ....Mr. Joseph FANTOZZI
38 Director Student Counseling ....Vacant
21 Director of Business & Finance ....Vacant
96 Director of Purchasing .... Mr. Mario CRESCENZO

*College of Staten Island CUNY (F)

2800 Victory Boulevard, Staten Island NY 10314-6600

County: Richmond FICE Identification: 002698
Unit ID: 190558
Telephone: (718) 982-2000 Carnegie Class: Masters/L
FAX Number: N/A Calendar System: Semester
URL: www.csi.cuny.edu
Established: 1976 Annual Undergrad Tuition & Fees (In-District): $6,890
Enrollment: 14,346 Coed
Affiliation or Control: State/Local IRS Status: 501(c)3
Highest Offering: Doctorate
Accreditation: M, ADNUR, CS, ENG, ENGT, MT, NUR, PTA, SW, TED

02 President ....Dr. William J. FRITZ
05 Sr VP Acad Affairs/Provost .... Dr. Gary W. REICHARD
10 VP for Finance and Administration ....Mr. Ira PERSKY
32 VP Student & Enrollment Services ....Ms. Jennifer S. BORRERO
30 VP Inst Advance/External
Affairs ....Ms. Khatmeh OSSEIRAN-HANNA
13 VP Info Tech & Economic Devel ....Dr. Michael KRESS
21 AVP for Finance & Budget .... Mr. Carlos SERRANO
100 Deputy to President/Chief of Staff ....Mr. Kenichi IWAMA
35 AVP Student Services Dean Students . Dr. Christopher GIORDANO
20 Int Assoc Provost Undergrad Studies .... Dr. Ralf PEETZ
18 AVP Campus Planning/Facilities Mgmt ....Vacant
90 AVP Technology Systems .... Dr. Patricia KAHN
26 AVP Inst Advance/External Affairs ....Vacant
81 Acting Dean of Science & Tech ....Dr. Alfred LEVINE
79 Dean Humanities & Social Sci ....Dr. Nan M. SUSSMAN
08 Assoc Dean/Chief Librarian ....Dr. Wilma JONES
43 Special Counsel ....Ms. Meryl KAYNARD
28 Director of Diversity & Compliance ..... Ms. Danielle E. DIMITROV

50 Dean of School of Business .... Dr. Susan L. HOLAK
76 Interim Dean School of Health Sci .... Dr. Maureen BECKER
53 Dean School of Education .... Dr. Kenneth GOLD

*City University of New York Graduate Center (A)

365 Fifth Avenue, New York NY 10016-4309
County: New York FICE Identification: 004765
Unit ID: 190576
Telephone: (212) 817-7000 Carnegie Class: DU-Highest
FAX Number: N/A Calendar System: Semester
URL: www.gc.cuny.edu
Established: 1961 Annual Undergrad Tuition & Fees (In-District): N/A
Enrollment: 7,013 Coed
Affiliation or Control: State/Local IRS Status: 501(c)3
Highest Offering: Doctorate
Accreditation: M, AUD, CAHIIM, JOUR, NURSE, PH, SCPSY

02 President .... Dr. Chase F. ROBINSON
05 Provost and Sr VP .... Dr. Joy CONNOLLY
10 Sr VP Finance and Administration .... Dr. Sebastian T. PERSICO
13 VP Information Technology .... Mr. Robert D. CAMPBELL
30 VP Institutional Advancement .... Mr. Jay GOLAN
26 VP Communications .... Ms. Rebecca KORNFELD
32 VP Student Affairs .... Mr. Matthew G. SCHOENGOOD
21 Asst Vice President Finance .... Mr. Stuart B. SHOR
81 Dean for the Sciences .... Dr. Joshua BRUMBERG
20 Int Assoc Provost & Dean Acad Aff .... Dr. David OLAN
08 Chief Librarian .... Ms. Polly THISTLETHWAITE
100 Chief of Staff .... Ms. Jane HERBERT
19 Exec Dir Security & Public Safety .... Mr. John FLAHERTY
15 Exec Director of Human Resources .... Ms. Ella KISELYUK
46 Exec Dir Research & Sponsored Pgm .... Dr. Edith GONZALEZ
37 Exec Dir Fellowships/Financial Aid .... Ms. Phyllis SCHULZ
20 Exec Director of Academic Affairs .... Ms. Stacie TIONGSON
06 Dir Stdnt Services/Senior Registrar .... Mr. Vincent J. DELUCA
88 Director of Special Events .... Ms. Harlisha HAMM
85 Director International Students .... Mr. Douglas EWING
09 Dir Institutional Research & Effect .... Ms. Jennifer KOBRIN
43 Legal Counsel & Labor Designee .... Ms. Lynette M. PHILLIPS
18 Director Facilities .... Mr. Charles SCOTT
22 Chief Diversity Officer .... Ms. Edith RIVERA
07 Director Admissions .... Mr. Les GRIBBEN
25 Director Sponsored Research .... Ms. Hilry FISHER
88 Director Building Design/Exhibits .... Mr. Ray RING
28 Executive Officer Educ Opp/Div Pgm .... Dr. Herman BENNETT
88 Dir Well Ctr/Psy Coun Svc/Adult Dev .... Dr. Robert HATCHER
35 Director Student Affairs .... Ms. Sharon LERNER
23 Director Student Health Services .... Ms. Adraenne BOWE
96 Director of Purchasing .... Mr. Ronald PAYNTER
04 Administrative Asst to President .... Ms. Alexandra ROBINSON

*City University of New York Herbert H. Lehman College (B)

250 Bedford Park Boulevard W, Bronx NY 10468-1589
County: Bronx FICE Identification: 007022
Unit ID: 190637
Telephone: (718) 960-8000 Carnegie Class: Masters/L
FAX Number: N/A Calendar System: Semester
URL: www.lehman.cuny.edu
Established: 1968 Annual Undergrad Tuition & Fees (In-District): $6,760
Enrollment: 12,398 Coed
Affiliation or Control: State/Local IRS Status: 501(c)3
Highest Offering: Master's
Accreditation: M, CACREP, DIETD, DIETI, NURSE, PH, SP, SW, TED

02 President .... Dr. Jose L. CRUZ
100 Chief of Staff/Chief Diversity Ofcr .... Ms. Dawn EWING-MORGAN
43 Sp Coun to Pres Legal Affs/Lab Rels .... Ms. Mary T. ROGAN
05 Provost/SVP Academic Affairs .... Vacant
10 Vice Pres Administration/Finance .... Mr. Vincent W. CLARK
32 Vice President Student Affairs .... Mr. Jose MAGDALENO
30 Vice Pres Institutional Advancement .... Mr. Mario DELLAPINA
13 Vice Pres/Chief Info Officer .... Mr. Ronald BERGMANN
103 VP Workforce/Global Partnerships .... Dr. Milton SANTIAGO
84 Assoc Provost/VP Enroll Mgmt .... Ms. Reine SARMIENTO
20 Vice Provost Academic Personnel .... Dr. Davina POROCK
20 Vice Provost Academic Programs .... Dr. Stefan BECKER
18 Asst VP Campus Planning/Facilities .... Ms. Rene M. ROTOLO
88 Exec Asst to Vice Pres Student Affs .... Mr. Vincent ZUCCHETTO
14 Asst VP Information Technology .... Mr. Ediltrudys RUIZ
79 Dean School of Arts/Humanities .... Dr. Deirdre PENNIPIECE
53 Dean School of Education .... Dr. Harriet FAYNE
83 Dean School of Nat & Soc Sci .... Dr. Gautam SEN
76 Dean Sch Heath Sci/Hum Svc & Nurs .... Dr. William LATIMER
35 Dean of Student Affairs .... Mr. John HOLLOWAY
21 Asst VP for Financial Operations .... Ms. Gina HARWOOD
08 Chief Librarian .... Dr. Kenneth SCHLESINGER
06 Senior Registrar .... Ms. Yvette ROSARIO
07 Director of Admissions .... Ms. Laurie AUSTIN
29 Director of Alumni Relations .... Ms. Maria-Cristina NECULA
88 Director of the Art Gallery .... Mr. Bartholomew F. BLAND
36 Director Career Services .... Ms. Nancy A. CINTRON
38 Director Counseling Center .... Dr. Norma COFRESI
37 Director Financial Aid .... Ms. Alvira SENESE
89 Director Freshman Year Initiative .... Dr. Steven WYCKOFF
46 Dir Research & Sponsored Programs .... Ms. Saeedah HICKMAN
92 Director of Honors College Program .... Dr. Gary SCHWARTZ
15 Director of Human Resources .... Mr. Eric WASHINGTON
14 Director Info Tech Resources .... Vacant

09 Director of Institutional Research .... Dr. Susanne M. TUMELTY
38 Dir Instruct Support Services Pgm .... Ms. Althea FORDE
26 Dir Media Relations & Publications .... Mr. Joseph TIRELLA
88 Director Performing Arts Center .... Ms. Eva BORNSTEIN
19 Director of Public Safety .... Mr. Fausto RAMIREZ
96 Director of Purchasing .... Ms. Andrea PINNOCK
41 Athletic Director .... Dr. Martin ZWIREN
40 Bookstore Manager .... Ms. Caitlin NEWSOME

*Hostos Community College-City University of New York (C)

500 Grand Concourse, Bronx NY 10451-5323
County: Bronx FICE Identification: 008611
Unit ID: 190585
Telephone: (718) 518-4300 Carnegie Class: Assoc/HT-High Trad
FAX Number: (718) 518-4294 Calendar System: Semester
URL: www.hostos.cuny.edu
Established: 1970 Annual Undergrad Tuition & Fees (In-District): $5,208
Enrollment: 6,985 Coed
Affiliation or Control: State/Local IRS Status: 501(c)3
Highest Offering: Associate Degree
Accreditation: M, DH, RAD

02 President .... Dr. David GOMEZ
05 Provost/VP for Academic Affairs .... Dr. Christine MANGINO
10 Senior Vice Pres for Admin/Finance .... Ms. Esther RODRIGUEZ-CHARDAVOYNE
32 VP Student Development/Enroll Mgmt .... Mr. Nathaniel CRUZ
100 Deputy to President .... Ms. Dolly MARTINEZ
30 Vice Pres Institutional Advancement .... Ms. Ana M. CARRION-SILVA
103 VP for Cont Educ & Workforce Dev .... Dr. Carlos MOLINA
13 Asst Vice Pres Info Technology .... Mr. Varun SEHGAL
21 Finance/Budget Director .... Ms. Fanny DUMANCELA
18 Exec Dir Facil Plng Des Mgmt .... Ms. Elizabeth FRIEDMAN
04 Associate Dean for Community Rels .... Ms. Ana I. GARCIA-REYES
20 Asst Dean of Academic Affairs .... Mr. Felix CARDONA
35 Assistant Dean of Student Life .... Ms. Johanna GOMEZ
43 Actg Exec Counsel & Labor Designee .... Mr. Eugene SOHN
26 Dir of Publications Development .... Vacant
38 Director of Counseling .... Ms. Linda ALEXANDER-WALLACE
15 Director Human Resources .... Ms. Shirley SHEVACH
86 Dir Government/External Affairs .... Mr. Joshua RIVERA
06 Registrar .... Ms. Nelida PASTORIZA
07 Director of Admissions .... Mr. Roland VELEZ
37 Director of Financial Aid .... Mr. Joseph ALICEA
19 Director of Campus Security .... Mr. Arnaldo BERNABE
25 Director Grants & Contracts .... Ms. Lourdes TORRES
09 Director Institutional Research .... Mr. Piotr KOCIK
08 Head Librarian .... Ms. Madeline FORD
22 Int Chief Diversity Officer .... Ms. Michele DICKINSON
29 Dir Development/Alumni Relations .... Ms. Nydia EDGECOMBE
36 Director Student Career Programs .... Ms. Lisanette ROSARIO
35 Director Student Activities .... Mr. Jerry ROSA
96 Director of Procurement .... Mr. Kevin CARMINE

*City University of New York Hunter College (D)

695 Park Avenue, New York NY 10065
County: New York FICE Identification: 002689
Unit ID: 190594
Telephone: (212) 772-4000 Carnegie Class: Masters/L
FAX Number: N/A Calendar System: Semester
URL: www.hunter.cuny.edu
Established: 1870 Annual Undergrad Tuition & Fees (In-District): $6,782
Enrollment: 23,112 Coed
Affiliation or Control: State/Local IRS Status: 501(c)3
Highest Offering: Doctorate
Accreditation: M, AUD, CACREP, CORE, CYTO, DIETD, DIETI, ENGR, NURSE, PH, PLNG, PTA, SP, SW, TED

02 President .... Ms. Jennifer J. RAAB
100 Chief of Staff/Exec Asst to Pres .... Ms. Anne LYTLE
10 Vice Pres/Chief Operating Officer .... Mr. Robert PIGNATELLO
05 Provost/Vice Pres Academic Affairs .... Mr. Lon KAUFMAN
32 VP Student Affs/Dean of Stdnts .... Ms. Eija AYRAVAINEN
43 Counsel to the President .... Ms. Laura HERTZOG
30 Asst VP Institutional Advancement .... Mr. John WIELK
26 Asst VP & Dir Communication .... Vacant
13 Asst Vice Pres Information Tech .... Mr. Mitch AHLBAUM
21 Executive Director Business Svcs .... Ms. Livia CANGEMI
21 Asst Vice Pres Business Services .... Ms. Patricia KETTERER
35 Asst Vice Pres of Student Affairs .... Ms. Madlyn STOKELY
18 Asst Vice Pres of Facilities .... Mr. James GLEBA
28 Dean Diversity and Compliance .... Mr. John ROSE
49 Dean School of Arts & Sciences .... Dr. Andrew POLSKY
70 Acting Dean School of Social Work .... Ms. Mary CAVANAUGH
53 Acting Dean School of Education .... Ms. Jennifer TUTEN
66 Dean School of Nursing .... Dr. Gail C. MCCAIN
08 Chief Librarian .... Mr. Daniel CHERUBIN
06 Registrar .... Ms. Marilyn DALEY-WESTON
09 Director of Institutional Research .... Ms. Joan LAMBE
15 Director of Human Resources .... Ms. Galia GALANSKY
35 Director Student Advising .... Mr. Bryan MAASJO
36 Director Student Placement .... Ms. Susan MCCARTY
37 Director Student Financial Aid .... Ms. Aristalia RODRIGUEZ
29 Director Alumni Relations .... Mr. Jorge DEJESUS
19 College Security Director .... Mr. Joseph FOELSCH
07 Director of Admissions .... Ms. Lori JANOWSKI
104 Director Study Abroad .... Ms. Elizabeth SACHS

108 Dir Institutional Assessment .... Dr. Meredith REITMAN
41 Athletic Director .... Ms. Terry WANSART
84 Dir Enrollment Mgmt/Recruit .... Ms. Sarah FARSAD

*City University of New York John Jay College of Criminal Justice (E)

524 West 59th Street, New York NY 10019-1093
County: New York FICE Identification: 002693
Unit ID: 190600
Telephone: (212) 237-8000 Carnegie Class: Masters/L
FAX Number: (212) 237-8607 Calendar System: Semester
URL: www.jjay.cuny.edu
Established: 1964 Annual Undergrad Tuition & Fees (In-District): $6,810
Enrollment: 15,045 Coed
Affiliation or Control: State/Local IRS Status: 501(c)3
Highest Offering: Master's
Accreditation: M, CLPSY, FEPAC, SPAA

02 President .... Mr. Jeremy TRAVIS
05 Prov/Sr Vice Pres Academic Affairs .... Dr. Jane BOWERS
32 Vice Pres Student Affairs .... Ms. Lynette COOK-FRANCIS
30 Vice Pres Marketing/Dev .... Ms. Jayne ROSENGARTEN
84 Vice Pres Enrollment Management .... Dr. Robert TROY
45 Assoc Provost for Effect/Assessment .... Dr. James LLANA
04 Interim Exec Assoc to President .... Ms. Raeanne DAVIS
100 Chief of Staff .... Ms. Rulisa GALLOWAY-PERRY
58 Assoc Prov & Dean of Grad Studies .... Dr. Anne LOPES
46 Associate Provost/Dean of Research .... Dr. Anthony CARPI
32 Asst VP and Dean of Students .... Vacant
11 Interim Asst VP for Administration .... Mr. Raj SINGH
20 Assoc Prov & Dean of Undergrad Stds .... Dr. Dara BRYNE
10 Interim Assoc VP for Finance .... Mr. Mark FLOWER
08 Chief Librarian .... Dr. Lawrence SULLIVAN
37 Director of Financial Aid .... Ms. Sylvia CRESPO-LOPEZ
44 Director of Development .... Ms. Kathryn COUSINS
35 Director Student Activities .... Ms. Danielle OFFICER
25 Director of Funded Research .... Ms. Susy MENDES
09 Director of Institutional Research .... Mr. Ricardo ANZALDUA
89 Director of First Year Experience .... Ms. Katalin SZUR
06 Interim Registrar .... Dr. Robert TROY
88 Director of CRJ Research & Eval .... Dr. Jeffrey BUTTS
07 Interim Director of Admissions .... Dr. Robert TROY
13 Chief Information Officer .... Mr. Joe LAUB
19 Director of Public Safety .... Mr. Kevin CASSIDY
90 Director Technology Services .... Vacant
24 Director of Media Services .... Vacant
26 Chief Communications Officer .... Ms. Rama SUDHAKAR
36 Director of Career Development Svcs .... Mr. Will SIMPKINS
38 Director of Counseling .... Dr. Gerard BRYANT
41 Athletic Director .... Ms. Carol KASHOW
21 Associate Business Officer .... Ms. Emily KARP
29 Director Alumni Relations .... Ms. Jerylle KEMP
96 Director of Purchasing .... Mr. Daniel DOLAN
04 Senior International Officer .... Ms. Mayra NIEVES
18 Director Facilities/Physical Plant .... Vacant
43 Assistant Vice President & Counsel .... Ms. Marjorie SINGER
86 Exec Dir of External Relations .... Ms. Mindy BOCKSTEIN
88 Director of Academic Advisement .... Dr. Sumaya VILLANUEVA
22 Int Dir of Accessibility Services .... Ms. Malanie CLARKE
104 Director Study Abroad .... Mr. Kenneth YANES
28 Director of Diversity .... Ms. Silvia MONTALBAN
39 Director Student Housing .... Ms. Jessica CARSON

† The Clinical Psychology PhD is awarded through the CUNY Graduate Center.

*City University of New York Kingsborough Community College (F)

2001 Oriental Boulevard, Brooklyn NY 11235-2333
County: Kings FICE Identification: 002694
Unit ID: 190619
Telephone: (718) 368-5109 Carnegie Class: Assoc/HT-Mix Trad/Non
FAX Number: (718) 368-5003 Calendar System: Other
URL: www.kbcc.cuny.edu
Established: 1963 Annual Undergrad Tuition & Fees (In-District): $5,202
Enrollment: 17,758 Coed
Affiliation or Control: State/Local IRS Status: 501(c)3
Highest Offering: Associate Degree
Accreditation: M, ADNUR, PTAA, SURGT

02 President .... Mr. Farley HERZEK
05 Vice Pres Academic Affs/Provost .... Dr. Joanne RUSSELL
10 Vice Pres Finance/Administration .... Mr. Eduardo RIOS
100 Executive Chief of Staff .... Dr. Tasheka SUTTON-YOUNG
32 Vice Pres of Student Affairs .... Mr. Peter COHEN
51 Dean Continuing Education .... Ms. Christine BECKNER
35 Director of Student Life .... Ms. Maria PATESTAS
20 Vice Pres Academic Administration .... Vacant
84 Vice Pres Enrollment Management .... Mr. Thomas FRIEBEL
09 Vice Pres Inst Effectiveness .... Dr. Richard FOX
30 Vice Pres Institutional Advancement .... Dr. Elizabeth BASILE
15 Director of Human Resources .... Ms. Micheline DRISCOLL
22 Dir Affirmative Action/EO Officer .... Ms. Victoria AJIBADE
19 Director of Security & Safety .... Vacant
08 Chief Librarian .... Ms. Josephine MURPHY
06 Registrar .... Mr. Michael KLEIN
18 Campus Facilities Officer .... Mr. Anthony CORAZZA
37 Financial Aid Officer .... Mr. Wayne H. HAREWOOD
13 Chief Information Officer .... Mr. Asif HUSSAIN
36 Dir Career Couns/Placement/Transfer .... Vacant

24 Director of Educational Media .... Mr. Michael ROSSON
41 Director of Athletics .... Mr. Damani THOMAS
26 AVP Public Relations .... Ms. Dawn WALKER
96 Director of Purchasing .... Ms. Lynn RELAY
07 Director of Admissions .... Ms. Rosalie FAYAD
29 Director Alumni Relations .... Ms. Laura GLAZIER-SMITH
38 Director Student Counseling .... Ms. Dasha GORINSHTEYN
21 Business Manager .... Vacant
88 Deputy Business Officer .... Mr. Bill CORRENTI

*LaGuardia Community College/ City University of New York (A)

31-10 Thomson Avenue, Long Island City NY 11101-3083
County: Queens FICE Identification: 010051
Unit ID: 190628
Telephone: (718) 482-7200 Carnegie Class: Assoc/HT-High Trad
FAX Number: (718) 609-2000 Calendar System: Semester
URL: www.lagcc.cuny.edu
Established: 1971 Annual Undergrad Tuition & Fees (In-District): $5,218
Enrollment: 20,231 Coed
Affiliation or Control: State/Local IRS Status: 501(c)3
Highest Offering: Associate Degree
Accreditation: M, ADNUR, DIETT, EMT, OTA, PTAA

02 President .... Dr. Gail O. MELLOW
05 Provost and Senior Vice President .... Dr. Paul ARCARIO
04 Executive Associate to President .... Ms. Rosemary TALMADGE
11 Vice President of Administration .... Mr. Shahir ERFAN
30 VP of Institutional Advancement .... Ms. Susan LYDDON
13 Vice Pres Information Technology .... Mr. Henry SALTIEL
32 Vice President Student Affairs .... Dr. Michael BASTON
51 Vice Pres Adult/Continuing Educ .... Ms. Jane SCHULMAN
20 Assoc Dean for Academic Affairs .... Mr. Bret EYNON
84 Asst Dean Enrollment Services .... Ms. Nireata SEALS
18 Exec Dir Facilities Mgmt/Planning .... Mr. Kenneth CAMPANELLI
15 Exec Director of Human Resources .... Vacant
10 Exec Director Finance & Business .... Mr. Thomas HLADEK
86 Government Relations Manager .... Ms. Claudia CHAN
08 Chief Librarian .... Ms. Scott WHITE
37 Director Student Financial Services .... Ms. Gail BAKSH-JARRETT
36 Assoc Dean Acad & Career Develop .... Ms. Jane MACKILLOP
103 Asst Dean of Workforce Development .... Ms. Francesca FIORE
07 Director of Admissions .... Ms. LaVora DESVIGNE
26 Dir Marketing/Communications .... Mr. Charles ELIAS
43 Legal & Labor Relations Officer .. Ms. Jemma ROBAIN LACAILLE
22 Affirmative Action Specialist .... Vacant
09 Director of Institutional Research .... Mr. Nathan DICKMEYER
21 Associate Business Manager .... Ms. Carmen LUONG
36 Director Employment/Career Svc Ctr .... Ms. Claudia BALDONEDO
96 Director Procurement & Contracts .... Mr. Mitchell HENDERSON
20 Assoc Dean for Academic Affairs .... Ms. Ann FEIBEL
88 Asst Dean Ctr for Teaching & Lrng .... Mr. Howard WACH

*City University of New York Medgar Evers College (B)

1650 Bedford Avenue, Brooklyn NY 11225-2010
County: Kings FICE Identification: 010097
Unit ID: 190646
Telephone: (718) 270-4900 Carnegie Class: Bac-Diverse
FAX Number: (718) 270-5126 Calendar System: Semester
URL: www.mec.cuny.edu
Established: 1970 Annual Undergrad Tuition & Fees (In-District): $6,680
Enrollment: 6,701 Coed
Affiliation or Control: State/Local IRS Status: 501(c)3
Highest Offering: Baccalaureate
Accreditation: M, ACBSP, ADNUR, NUR, SW, TED

02 President .... Dr. Rudolph F. CREW
11 Chief Operating Officer .... Mr. Jerald POSMAN
05 Provost/Senior Vice President .... Dr. Augustine OKEREKE
10 VP Finance & Administration .... Ms. Jacqueline CLARK
32 VP of Student Affairs/Enroll Mgmt .... Dr. Evelyn CASTRO
51 Interim Dean Sch Prof & Comm Dev .... Dr. Simone RODRIGUEZ-DORESTANT
50 Dean of the School of Business .... Dr. Jo-Ann ROLLE
49 Interim Dean Sch of Lib Arts & Educ .... Dr. J. A. George IRISH
72 Dean School of Science/Health/Tech .... Dr. Mohsin PATWARY
100 Chief of Staff .... Ms. Lakisha MURRAY
43 Counsel to President .... Mr. Gary JOHNSON
04 Exec Assistant to the President .... Mrs. Lisa ANDERSON
22 Director of Affirmative Action .... Ms. Sylvia KINARD
06 Registrar .... Ms. Tatiana MEJIC
13 Chief Information Officer .... Mr. Praveen PANCHAL
37 Director of Financial Aid .... Mr. Nigel THOMPSON
38 Director of Counseling .... Dr. JoAnn JOYNER-GRAHAM
19 Director of Security .... Mr. Victor STEVENS
41 Director of Athletics .... Ms. Renee BOSTIC
25 Grants Officer .... Mr. Chi KOON
89 Dir Freshman Year Program .... Dr. Zulema BLAIR
55 Director Evening/Weekend Programs .... Ms. Yvette WALL
36 Sr Director of Career Development .... Vacant
30 Exec Director of Development .... Vacant
18 Supt of Buildings & Grounds .... Vacant
07 Director of Admissions .... Mrs. Shannon CLARKE-ANDERSON
29 Director of Alumni Relations ...... Mrs. Tara REGIST-TOMLINSON
84 Director Enrollment .... Mr. Jeffrey SIGLER
09 Director of Institutional Research .... Dr. Eva CHAN
08 Chief Librarian .... Dr. David ORENSTEIN
66 Interim Chair Dept of Nursing .... Dr. Georgia MCDUFFIE
50 Chair Dept of Business Admin .... Ms. Evelyn MAGGIO
53 Chair Department of Education .... Dr. Sheilah PAUL
60 Interim Chair Dept of Mass Comm .... Dr. Clinton CRAWFORD
88 Chair Department Accounting .... Dr. Rosemary WILLIAMS
81 Chair Department of Mathematics .... Dr. Terrance BLACKMAN
77 Chair Dept Physical/Computer Sci .... Dr. Wilbert HOPE
81 Chair Department of Biology .... Dr. Anthony UDEOGALANYA
83 Chair Dept of Social/Behavioral Sci .... Dr. Owen BROWN
88 Chair Department of Psychology .... Dr. Ethan GOLOGOR
88 Chair Dept of Public Administration .... Dr. Wallace FORD
13 Chair Computer Info Systems .... Dr. Adesina FADARIO
88 Chair Department Economics/Finance .... Dr. Emmanuel EGBE
88 Chair Department of English .... Ms. Brenda GREENE
88 Chair Dept of Philosophy & Religion .... Dr. Gary SEAY
88 Chair Dept of Foreign Languages .... Dr. Maria-Luisa RUIZ
35 Director of Student Life .... Mr. Larry MARTIN
15 Executive Dir of Human Resources .... Ms. Tanya ISAACS
88 Director of Bursar .... Ms. Thais PILIERI
28 Chief Diversity Officer .... Dr. Sylvia E. KINARD
104 Director Study Abroad .... Mr. Eugene PURSOO
86 Director Government Relations .... Ms. Jennifer JAMES

*New York City College of Technology/City University of New York (C)

300 Jay Street, Brooklyn NY 11201-1909
County: Kings FICE Identification: 002696
Unit ID: 190655
Telephone: (718) 260-5000 Carnegie Class: Bac-Diverse
FAX Number: (718) 260-5198 Calendar System: Semester
URL: www.citytech.cuny.edu
Established: 1946 Annual Undergrad Tuition & Fees (In-District): $6,669
Enrollment: 17,374 Coed
Affiliation or Control: State/Local IRS Status: 501(c)3
Highest Offering: Baccalaureate
Accreditation: M, ADNUR, CSHSE, DH, DT, ENGT, NUR, OPD, RAD, TED

02 President .... Dr. Russell K. HOTZLER
05 Provost .... Dr. Bonne AUGUST
10 Vice Pres Finance/Administration .... Dr. Miguel CAIROL
84 VP Enrollment/Student Affairs .... Dr. Marcela ARMOZA
20 Associate Provost Academic Affairs .... Dr. Pamela BROWN
22 Counsel/Affirmative Action Officer .... Ms. Gilen CHAN
07 Director of Admissions .... Ms. Alexis CHACONIS
06 Registrar .... Ms. Tasha RHODES
37 Director of Financial Aid .... Ms. Sandra HIGGINS
08 Librarian .... Ms. Maura SMALE
13 Director of Computer Center .... Ms. Fita UDDIN
107 Int Dean of Professional Studies .... Mr. David SMITH
54 Interim Dean of Technology .... Mr. Kevin HOM
49 Dean of Arts & Science .... Mr. Justin VASQUEZ-PORITZ
51 Dean Continuing Education .... Dr. Carol SONNENBLICK
55 Director Evening Session .... Mr. James LAP
15 Director of Human Resources .... Ms. Sandra GORDON
25 Grants Officer .... Ms. Barbara BURKE
24 Director of Inst Tech/Media Svcs .... Ms. Karen LUNDSTREM
09 Director of Assessment .... Dr. Tammie CUMMING
26 Interim Exec Dir Public Relations .... Ms. Faith CORBETT
29 Director Alumni Relations .... Ms. Jessica MALAVEZ
36 Director Student Placement .... Mr. Adrian GRIFFIN
38 Director Student Counseling .... Ms. Cynthia BINK
96 Director of Purchasing .... Mr. Wayne ROBINSON
18 Chief Facilities/Physical Plant .... Mr. James VASQUEZ
30 Chief Development/Spec Asst to Pres .... Dr. Stephen SOIFFER
32 Administrator Student Affairs .... Vacant
21 Business Manager .... Mr. Wayne ROBINSON

*City University of New York Queens College (D)

65-30 Kissena Boulevard, Flushing NY 11367-1597
County: Queens FICE Identification: 002690
Unit ID: 190664
Telephone: (718) 997-5000 Carnegie Class: Masters/L
FAX Number: (718) 997-5598 Calendar System: Semester
URL: www.qc.cuny.edu
Established: 1937 Annual Undergrad Tuition & Fees (In-District): $6,938
Enrollment: 19,310 Coed
Affiliation or Control: State/Local IRS Status: 501(c)3
Highest Offering: Master's
Accreditation: M, AAFCS, CAEP, CLPSY, DIETD, DIETI, LAW, LIB, SP, TED

02 President .... Dr. Felix V. MATOS RODRIGUEZ
05 Provost .... Dr. Elizabeth HENDREY
10 Vice Pres Finance/Administration .... Mr. William KELLER
32 Vice President for Student Affairs .... Dr. Adam ROCKMAN
91 Asst Vice Pres Converging Tech .... Ms. Claudia COLBERT
84 VP Enrollment & Retention .... Mr. Richard ALVAREZ
20 Assoc Provost Academic Plng/Pgms .... Dr. Steven SCHWARZ
43 AVP General Counsel/Chief of Staff .... Ms. Glenda GRACE
27 Director of Communications .... Ms. Leanna YIP
21 Assistant VP Business Affairs .... Mr. Brian MURPHY
30 VP Institutional Advancement .... Ms. Laurie DORF
88 Assistant Provost .... Dr. June BOBB
57 Dean Arts & Humanities .... Dr. William MCCLURE
81 Dean Math & Natural Sciences .... Dr. Robert ENGEL
53 Dean Education .... Dr. Craig MICHAELS
58 Dean of Research/Grad Studies .... Dr. Richard BODNAR
83 Dean Social Sciences .... Dr. Dean SAVAGE
15 Director Human Resources/Payroll .... Ms. Reinalica MEDINA
41 Assistant Vice President Athletics .... Ms. China JUDE
88 Director of Events .... Vacant
18 Asst VP Facilities .... Mr. Zeco KRCIC
07 Executive Director Admissions .... Mr. Vincent ANGRISANI
38 Dir of Counseling and Advisement .... Dr. Barbara MOORE
06 Director Registrar's Office .... Mr. Matthew CASANOVA
09 Director of Institutional Research .... Dr. Margaret MCAULIFFE
08 Chief Librarian .... Dr. Rolf SWENSEN
37 Director Financial Aid Services .... Mr. Clifford COULOTTE
29 Manager Alumni Affairs .... Mr. Christopher GREAVES
19 Director Security/Safety .... Mr. Pedro PINEIRO
22 Dir Affirmative Action/Diversity .... Ms. Cynthia ROUNTREE
96 Director of Purchasing .... Mr. Surinder VIRK
86 Director Government Relations .... Mr. Jeffrey ROSENSTOCK
26 Director of Marketing .... Vacant
100 Deputy Chief of Staff .... Dr. Odalys DIAZPINEIRO

† The Clinical Psychology PhD is awarded through the CUNY Graduate Center.

*City University of New York Queensborough Community College (E)

222-05 56th Avenue, Bayside NY 11364-1497
County: Queens FICE Identification: 002697
Unit ID: 190673
Telephone: (718) 631-6262 Carnegie Class: Assoc/HT-High Trad
FAX Number: N/A Calendar System: Semester
URL: www.qcc.cuny.edu
Established: 1958 Annual Undergrad Tuition & Fees (In-District): $5,210
Enrollment: 16,182 Coed
Affiliation or Control: State/Local IRS Status: 501(c)3
Highest Offering: Associate Degree
Accreditation: M, ACBSP, ADNUR, ENGT, THEA

02 President .... Dr. Diane CALL
11 Sr Vice Pres/Chief Operating Ofcr .... Ms. Sherri NEWCOMB
05 Interim Vice Pres Academic Affairs .... Dr. Sandra PALMER
10 Vice Pres Finance & Admin .... Mr. William FAULKNER
30 Vice Pres Institutional Advancement .... Ms. Rosemary S. ZINS
32 Vice President Student Affairs .... Mr. Michel HODGE
15 Dean Human Resource/Labor Rels .... Ms. Liza LARIOS
51 VP Continuing Ed/Workforce Dev .... Ms. Denise WARD
108 VP Strategic Plng/Assessment .... Dr. Karen B. STEELE
88 Dean Accred Assessment .... Dr. Arthur CORRADETTI
13 Chief Information Technology Ofcr .... Mr. George SHERMAN
08 Chief Librarian .... Ms. Jeanne GALVIN
06 Registrar .... Ms. Ann TULLIO
37 Financial Aid Exec Director .... Ms. Veronica LUKAS
07 Asst Dean Admissions & Recruitment .... Ms. Laura BRUNO
09 Director of Institutional Research .... Ms. Elisabeth LACKNER
16 Personnel Officer .... Ms. Ellen ADAMS
26 Exec Dir Communications/Marketing .... Mr. Stephen DI DIO
19 Director of Safety & Security .... Mr. John WARD
22 Chief Diversity Officer .... Ms. Josephine PANTALEO
04 Executive Assistant to President .... Ms. Millie CONTE
104 Dir Ctr for Intl Stds/Study Abroad .... Ms. Lampeto (Betty) EFTHYMIOU
18 Chief Admin Superintendent .... Mr. Joseph CARTOLANO
36 Director of Career Services .... Ms. Constance PELUSO
44 Development Officer .... Ms. Saji SHEERAZI
21 Exec Dir Finance & Admin Services .... Mr. David WASSERMAN
45 Exec Dir Budget/Resource Planning .... Mr. Mark CARPENTIER
20 Dean for Academic Operations .... Mr. Glenn BURDI
35 Asst Dean of Student Development .... Dr. Brian KERR

*City University of New York Stella and Charles Guttman Community College (F)

50 West 40th Street, New York NY 10018
County: New York Identification: 667126
Unit ID: 475565
Telephone: (646) 313-8000 Carnegie Class: Not Classified
FAX Number: N/A Calendar System: Semester
URL: www.guttman.cuny.edu
Established: 2011 Annual Undergrad Tuition & Fees (In-District): $5,194
Enrollment: 691 Coed
Affiliation or Control: State/Local IRS Status: 501(c)3
Highest Offering: Associate Degree
Accreditation: ⊕M, HY

02 President .... Scott EVENBECK
05 Provost and Vice President .... Joan M. LUCARIELLO
10 Vice Pres Admin & Finance .... Mary COLEMAN
45 Dean Strategic Plng & Effectiveness .... Stuart COCHRAN
09 Director of Institutional Research .... Elisa HERTZ
100 Chief of Staff .... Linda MERIANS
13 Chief Info Technology Officer (CIO) .... John STROUD
15 Director Human Resources .... Nila BHAUMIK
18 Director Facilities Planning .... Shirley LAW
19 Director Public Safety .... Anastasia KOUTSIDIS
37 Director Student Financial Aid .... Vera SENESE
06 Registrar .... Cortes MARISOL
07 Director of Admissions .... So SOPHEA
86 Director Government Relations .... Manny LOPEZ
04 Administrative Asst to President .... Nina CONROY
102 Dir Foundation/Corporate Relations .... Bruce LYONS
29 Director Alumni Relations .... LaToya JACKSON
43 Dir Legal Services/General Counsel .... Lynette PHILLIPS

*City University of New York York College (A)

94-20 Guy Brewer Boulevard, Jamaica NY 11451-0001
County: Queens FICE Identification: 004759
Unit ID: 190691
Telephone: (718) 262-2000 Carnegie Class: Bac-Diverse
FAX Number: (718) 262-2730 Calendar System: Semester
URL: www.york.cuny.edu
Established: 1966 Annual Undergrad Tuition & Fees (In-District): $6,748
Enrollment: 8,493 Coed
Affiliation or Control: State/Local IRS Status: 501(c)3
Highest Offering: Master's
Accreditation: M, ARCPA, MT, NUR, OT, SW, TED

02 President Dr. Marcia V. KEIZS
05 Provost/Sr VP for Academic Affs Dr. Panayiotis MELETIES
10 VP of Administration & Finance/COO Mr. Ronald C. THOMAS
32 Vice Pres for Student Development Vacant
100 Dean for the Executive Office Dr. William V. DINELLO
49 Dean School of Arts & Sciences Dr. Donna CHIRICO
83 Dean Sch of Health & Behavioral Sci Dr. Lynne CLARK
50 Dean Sch of Business & Info Systems Dr. Charles GENGLER
43 Labor & Legal Affairs Russell PLATZEK
15 Assoc Exec Director HR Ms. Barbara MANUEL
13 Chief Information Officer Mr. Peter TIGHE
09 Director Institutional Research Dr. Aghajan MOHAMMADI
06 Registrar Ms. Sharon DAVIDSON
08 Chief Librarian Ms. Njoki KINYATTI
90 Director of Academic Computing Dr. Che-Tsao HUANG
86 Dir of Govt and Community Relations Dr. Earl G. SIMONS
19 Director of Security Chief Rufus MASSIAH
37 Director of Financial Aid Ms. Beverly BROWN
18 Director Campus Planning Mr. Noel GAMBOA
35 Director Student Activities Dr. Jean PHELPS
36 Director Career Services Ms. Linda H. CHESNEY
25 Dir Research/Sponsored Programs Ms. Dawn HEWITT
38 Interim Director of Counseling Dr. Jayoung CHOI
41 Athletic Director Vacant
04 Executive Asst to the President Ms. Sandra BELL ADAMS
07 Director of Admissions Dr. Latoro YATES
29 Director Alumni Relations Ms. Mondell SEALY
30 Chief Development/Advancement Ms. Dolores SWIRIN-YAO
28 Interim Director of Diversity Ms. Alicia FRANQUI
96 Director of Purchasing Ms. Rashmi MALESH
108 Director Institutional Assessment Dr. Mary OSBORNE

Clarkson University (B)

8 Clarkson Ave, Potsdam NY 13699
County: St. Lawrence FICE Identification: 002699
Unit ID: 190044
Telephone: (315) 268-6400 Carnegie Class: DU-Mod
FAX Number: (315) 268-7647 Calendar System: Semester
URL: www.clarkson.edu
Established: 1896 Annual Undergrad Tuition & Fees: $44,630
Enrollment: 3,873 Coed
Affiliation or Control: Independent Non-Profit IRS Status: 501(c)3
Highest Offering: Doctorate
Accreditation: M, ARCPA, BUS, ENG, HSA, PTA, TEAC

01 President Dr. Anthony G. COLLINS
05 Senior Vice President & Provost Dr. Charles E. THORPE
26 Vice Pres External Relations Mrs. Kelly O. CHEZUM
32 VP Student Affairs & Intl Relations Ms. Kathryn B. JOHNSON
30 Vice Pres Devel & Alumni Relations Mr. Patrick ROCHE
07 VP Enrollment Mgmt & Stdnt Advance Mr. Brian T. GRANT
28 Assoc VP Stdnt Succ/Diversity/Incl Mrs. Catherine MCNAMARA
10 Chief Financial Officer Mr. James D. FISH
28 Chief Inclusion & Human Res Officer Ms. Suong IVES
13 Chief Information Officer Mr. Joshua A. FISKE
50 Dean of School of Business Dr. Dayle M. SMITH
54 Dean of Engineering Dr. William JEMISON
49 Dean of Arts & Sciences Dr. Peter TURNER
35 Dean of Stdnt & Lifetime Engagement Mr. Stephen NEWKOFSKY
21 Controller Mr. Christopher ALGER
38 Exec Dir Counseling & Health Svcs Mr. James PITTMAN
44 Sr Dir of Devel & Alumni Relations Mr. Andrew BREWER
29 Director Alumni Relations Ms. Teresa PLANTY
41 Director Athletics & Recreation Mr. Steven J. YIANOUKOS
45 Director Budget & Planning Mrs. Allison S. ALDRICH
19 Director Campus Safety & Security Mr. David W. DELISLE
36 Director Career Center Mr. Jeffrey D. TAYLOR
18 Director Facilities & Services Mr. Ian HAZEN
37 Director Financial Aid Mrs. Pamela NICHOLS
92 Director Honors Program Mr. Jonathan D. GOSS
15 Director Human Resources Operations Mrs. Amy MCGAHERAN
85 Director Intl Students & Scholars Mrs. Tess C. CASLER
08 Director Libraries Ms. Michelle L. YOUNG
96 Dir Payroll/Purchasing/Risk Mgmt Mr. George GIORDANO
46 Director Research & Tech Transfer Mr. Gregory C. SLACK
88 Dir Student Administrative Services Mrs. Suzanne E. DAVIS
23 Director Student Health Services Mrs. Susan KNOWLES
105 Director Web Development Mrs. Julie DAVIS
102 Dir Corp & Foundation Rels Mrs. Elizabeth COLELLO
91 Director Administrative Computing Mr. Chris CUTLER
15 Director Academic Policies & Practi Mrs. Amanda PICKERING
06 Registrar Mrs. Karen J. BURKUM
39 Assoc Dean for Residence Life Mr. Mark DERITIS
09 Assoc Director Institutional Rsrch Mrs. Jenna STONE
25 Contract & Grant Administrator Ms. Anna Marie DAWLEY
40 Bookstore Manager Ms. Sara JOHNSON
106 Distance Learning Coordinator Mrs. Laura PERRY
04 Assistant to the President Mrs. Barbara PARKER

Clinton Community College (C)

136 Clinton Point Drive, Plattsburgh NY 12901-9573
County: Clinton FICE Identification: 006787
Unit ID: 190053
Telephone: (518) 562-4200 Carnegie Class: Assoc/HT-High Trad
FAX Number: (518) 561-4890 Calendar System: Semester
URL: www.clinton.edu
Established: 1966 Annual Undergrad Tuition & Fees (In-District): $4,670
Enrollment: 1,870 Coed
Affiliation or Control: State/Local IRS Status: 501(c)3
Highest Offering: Associate Degree
Accreditation: M, ADNUR

01 President Vacant
05 Vice President for Academic Affairs Dr. Cheryl A. LESSER
10 Vice Pres for Admin/Business Affs Mrs. Lisa SHOVAN
32 Vice President for Student Affairs Vacant
30 Vice Pres InstitutionalAdvancement Mr. Steven G. FREDERICK
08 Dean Learning Resource Center Vacant
84 Assoc Dean Student Retention Svcs Vacant
09 Assoc Dean Inst Research/Planning Vacant
20 Assoc Vice Pres Academic Affairs Ms. Michele SNYDER
37 Director of Financial Aid Ms. Mary LA PIERRE
07 Director Admissions Vacant
06 Registrar Ms. Lauren CURRIE
13 Mgmt Information Systems Director Mr. Rick BATCHELDER
15 Human Resource/Affirm Act Officer Ms. Sarah POTTER
26 Director of College Relations Vacant
18 Chief Facilities/Physical Plant Mr. John CONLEY

Cochran School of Nursing (D)

967 North Broadway, Yonkers NY 10701-1399
County: Westchester FICE Identification: 006443
Unit ID: 190071
Telephone: (914) 964-4282 Carnegie Class: Spec 2-yr-Health
FAX Number: (914) 964-4266 Calendar System: Semester
URL: www.cochranschoolofnursing.us
Established: 1894 Annual Undergrad Tuition & Fees: N/A
Enrollment: 93 Coed
Affiliation or Control: Independent Non-Profit IRS Status: 501(c)3
Highest Offering: Associate Degree
Accreditation: ADNUR

01 Dean Dr. Annemarie MCALLISTER
08 Learning Resources Director Ms. Paula GRAHAM
06 Registrar Ms. Janee MCCOY
32 Dir Student Services/Finances Ms. Mirna PANTOJA

Cold Spring Harbor Laboratory/ Watson School of Biological Sciences (E)

PO Box 100, One Bungtown Road,
Cold Spring Harbor NY 11724-0100
County: Suffolk FICE Identification: 034563
Unit ID: 436377
Telephone: (516) 367-6890 Carnegie Class: Not Classified
FAX Number: (516) 367-6919 Calendar System: Other
URL: www.cshl.edu
Established: 1890 Annual Graduate Tuition & Fees: N/A
Enrollment: N/A Coed
Affiliation or Control: Independent Non-Profit IRS Status: 501(c)3
Highest Offering: Doctorate; No Undergraduates
Accreditation: NY

00 Chancellor Emeritis Dr. James D. WATSON
01 President Dr. Bruce STILLMAN
05 Dean Dr. Alexander GANN

Colgate Rochester Crozer Divinity School (F)

1100 S Goodman Street, Rochester NY 14620-2589
County: Monroe FICE Identification: 002700
Unit ID: 190080
Telephone: (585) 271-1320 Carnegie Class: Spec-4-yr-Faith
FAX Number: (585) 271-8013 Calendar System: Semester
URL: www.crcds.edu
Established: 1817 Annual Graduate Tuition & Fees: N/A
Enrollment: 80 Coed
Affiliation or Control: Independent Non-Profit IRS Status: 501(c)3
Highest Offering: Doctorate; No Undergraduates
Accreditation: THEOL

01 President Dr. Marvin A. MCMICKLE
05 VP Academic Life & Dean of Faculty Prof. Stephanie L. SAUVE
10 Chief Financial Officer Mr. Gerald E. VANSTRYDONCK
84 Vice Pres of Enrollment Services Ms. Melissa MORRAL
30 VP Institutional Advancement Mr. W. Thomas MCDADE-CLAY
94 Dean of Women & Gender Studies Dr. Barbara MOORE
06 Registrar Ms. Andrea MASON
18 Director of Facilities Mr. Mark DEVINCENTIS
08 Director of Library Services Ms. Margaret A. NEAD
40 Director Bookstore Ms. Margaret A. NEAD
37 Director of Financial Aid Ms. Andrea MASON
26 Communications Coordinator Ms. Michele KAIDER-KOROL
07 Admissions Coordinator Ms. Polly BUSH
29 Director of Alumni Relations Mr. W. Thomas MCDADE-CLAY
60 Dir of Learning Comm/Online Pgms Dr. Rachel A. MCGUIRE

Colgate University (G)

13 Oak Drive, Hamilton NY 13346-1386
County: Madison FICE Identification: 002701
Unit ID: 190099
Telephone: (315) 228-1000 Carnegie Class: Bac-A&S
FAX Number: (315) 228-7798 Calendar System: Semester
URL: www.colgate.edu
Established: 1819 Annual Undergrad Tuition & Fees: $49,970
Enrollment: 2,888 Coed
Affiliation or Control: Independent Non-Profit IRS Status: 501(c)3
Highest Offering: Master's
Accreditation: M, TEAC

01 President Brian W. CASEY
101 VP/Sr Advisor/Sec Board of Trustees Robert L. TYBURSKI
05 Interim Dean of Faculty & Provost Constance HARSH
10 VP for Finance & Admin Brian HUTZLEY
30 Sr VP External Rels/Advancement Murray DECOCK
07 VP & Dean of Admiss/Financial Aid Gary L. ROSS
32 Interim VP & Dean of the College Mark THOMPSON
21 Associate Vice Pres/Controller Thomas O'NEILL
18 Assoc VP for Buildings Stephen HUGHES
15 Interim VP for Human Resources Judith DORSEY
20 Associate Dean of the Faculty Kenneth BELANGER
28 Assoc Provost Equity & Diversity Marilyn RUGG
06 Interim Registrar Tori CARHART
08 University Librarian Joanne SCHNEIDER
13 VP & Chief Information Officer Steve FABIANI
29 AVP Inst Advancement/Alumni Affairs Tim MANSFIELD
37 Director of Financial Aid Gina M. SOLIZ
109 AVP Cmty Affairs/Auxiliary Services Joanne BORFITZ
19 Director of Campus Safety William FERGUSON
36 AVP of Adv & Dir of Career Services Michael SCIOLA
41 VP & Director of Athletics Victoria CHUN
40 Dir Off-Campus Retail Operations Leslie PASCO
42 University Chaplain Mark SHINER
44 AVP Inst Advancement/Planned Giving Andrew CODDINGTON
38 Director Counseling/Psych Services Dawn LAFRANCE
96 Director of Purchasing Alan LEONARD
23 Director Student Health Services Merrill MILLER
94 Director Women's Studies Meika LOE
44 Director Annual Fund Operations Sara GROH
39 Director of Residential Housing Stacey MILLARD
09 Dir Institutional Planning/Research Neil ALBERT
04 Assistant to the President Claudia CARAHER
22 Dir EEO & Affirmative Action Tamala FLACK
102 Dir of Corp Foundation & Govt Rels Helen KEBABIAN
104 Director of Off-Campus Study Joanna HOLVEY BOWLES

College of Mount Saint Vincent (H)

6301 Riverdale Avenue, Riverdale NY 10471-1093
County: Bronx FICE Identification: 002703
Unit ID: 193399
Telephone: (718) 405-3200 Carnegie Class: Masters/S
FAX Number: (718) 601-6392 Calendar System: Semester
URL: www.mountsaintvincent.edu
Established: 1847 Annual Undergrad Tuition & Fees: $22,490
Enrollment: 1,915 Coed
Affiliation or Control: Independent Non-Profit IRS Status: 501(c)3
Highest Offering: Master's
Accreditation: M, ACBSP, NURSE, TEAC

01 President Dr. Charles L. FLYNN, JR.
05 Provost/Dean of Faculty Dr. Sarah STEVENSON
20 Dean Undergraduate College Dr. Patrick VALDEZ
07 Sr VP for Admission/External Rels Ms. Madeleine MELKONIAN
10 Executive VP/Treasurer/CFO Mr. Abed ELKESHK
11 VP for Operations Mr. Kevin DEGROAT
32 Dean of Students Ms. Kelli BODRATO
88 Executive Director Mission Vacant
30 Assoc VP Institutional Advancement Sr. Kathleen TRACEY, SC
51 Dean School Professional/Cont Stds Dr. Mitchell SAKOFS
06 Registrar Mrs. Jeannette PICHARDO
08 Director of Library Mr. Sebastian DERRY
13 VP Information Technology/CIO Mr. Adam WICHERN
09 Director of Institutional Research Sr. Carol M. FINEGAN, SC
36 Director Internships/Career Devel Vacant
37 Director of Financial Aid Ms. Lorena MATOS
42 Dir Campus Ministry/Act Dir Mission Mr. Mathew SHIELDS
35 Dir of Student Affairs/Assoc Dean Dr. Gabrielle OCCHIOGROSSO
41 Acting Dir Athletics & Recreation Mr. Barima YEBOAH
38 Director Counseling Services Ms. Vicki HALLAS
23 Director of Health Services Mrs. Eileen MCCABE
29 Dir Alumnae Relations/Annual Giving Mr. Michael QUINN
26 Assoc Director of College Relations Ms. Leah MUNCH
19 Dir Campus Safety/Security Mr. Paul RUNG
66 Director of Nursing Dr. Susan SALADINO
44 Assoc Dir Alumnae Rels/Annual Giv Mr. Michael SIN
15 Director of Human Resources Mr. Joseph BEHAN
21 Controller Mr. Ping XIE
04 Assistant to the President Ms. Catherine MCKENNA
18 Director of Facilities & Operations Mr. Ryan ANDERSON
07 Director of Admissions Ms. Jackie WILLIAMS
92 Director of Honors Program Dr. Heather ALUMBAUGH
97 Director of Core Curriculum Dr. Robert JACKLOSKY

The College of New Rochelle (A)

29 Castle Place, New Rochelle NY 10805-2338
County: Westchester FICE Identification: 002704
Unit ID: 193645
Telephone: (914) 654-5000 Carnegie Class: Masters/L
FAX Number: (914) 654-5554 Calendar System: Semester
URL: www.cnr.edu
Established: 1904 Annual Undergrad Tuition & Fees: $33,600
Enrollment: 3,740 Coed
Affiliation or Control: Independent Non-Profit IRS Status: 501(c)3
Highest Offering: Master's
Accreditation: M, NURSE, SW, TEAC

01 President ....Mrs. Judith A. HUNTINGTON
05 Sr Vice Pres Acad Affairs & Provost ..Dr. Dorothy A. ESCRIBANO
10 Vice President Financial Affairs ....Dr. Betty ROBERTS
32 Vice President Student Services ....Ms. Elaine T. WHITE
84 VP for Enrollment Management ....Mr. Kevin CAVANAGH
30 Vice President College Advancement ....Ms. Brenna S. MAYER
49 Interim Dean School of Arts & Sci ....Dr. David DONNELLY
58 Dean of the Graduate School ....Dr. David DONNELLY
51 Dean School of New Resources ....Dr. Kristine SOUTHARD
66 Dean School of Nursing ....Dr. H. Michael DREHER
06 Registrar ....Ms. Tania QUINN
08 Dean of the Library ....Ms. Ana FONTOURA
37 Director of Financial Aid ....Ms. Anne C. PELAK
36 Director of Career Development ....Ms. Mariela TORRES
15 Director of Human Resources ....Ms. JoEllen L. VAVASOUR
18 Director of Facilities Management ....Mr. Fred SULLO
09 Interim Director of Inst Research ....Mr. Damien GERMINO
21 Assistant VP for Finance/Controller ... Mr. Thomas CUNNINGHAM
13 Chief Info Technology Officer (CIO) ....Mr. Warren ANDREWS
19 Director Security/Safety ....Mr. Rodney SAMUELS

The College of Saint Rose (B)

432 Western Avenue, Albany NY 12203-1490
County: Albany FICE Identification: 002705
Unit ID: 195234
Telephone: (518) 454-5111 Carnegie Class: Masters/L
FAX Number: (518) 438-3293 Calendar System: Semester
URL: www.strose.edu
Established: 1920 Annual Undergrad Tuition & Fees: $29,826
Enrollment: 4,499 Coed
Affiliation or Control: Independent Non-Profit IRS Status: 501(c)3
Highest Offering: Master's
Accreditation: M, ACBSP, ART, MUS, SP, SW, TED

01 President ....Dr. Carolyn J. STEFANCO
100 Chief of Staff ....Ms. Lisa HALEY-THOMSON
05 Int Provost/VP Academic Affairs ....Dr. Barbara SCHIRMER
10 Vice Pres Finance/Administration ....Mr. Al SKUDZINSKAS
32 Vice President Student Affairs ....Dr. Dennis CHAMBERLAIN
84 Vice Pres of Enrollment Mgmt ....Mrs. Mary M. GRONDAHL
30 Vice Pres Institutional Advancement ....Ms. Rhonda TOON
15 Assoc Vice Pres Human Res/Risk Mgt ....Mr. Jeffrey KNAPP
07 Asst VP of Undergrad Admissions ....Mr. Jeremy BOGAN
07 Asst VP of Graduate Admissions ....Ms. Susan PATTERSON
37 Asst VP of Financial Aid ....Mr. Steven W. DWIRE
26 VP of PR and Strategic Comm ....Mrs. Lisa HALEY-THOMSON
35 Asst VP Student Affairs ....Ms. Mary R. MCLAUGHLIN
18 AVP for Facilities ....Vacant
42 Dean of Spiritual Life ....Vacant
86 Exec Dir of Govt Community Affairs ....Mr. Michael D'ATTILIO
90 Exec Dir of Info Technology Service ....Mr. John ELLIS
29 Director Alumni Relations ....Ms. Lorrie PIZZOLA
21 Assoc VP for Finance & Comptroller ....Ms. Debra Lee POLLEY
06 Registrar ....Mr. Craig TYNAN
08 Director of Library ....Mr. Andrew URBANEK
39 Director Residence Life ....Ms. Jennifer RICHARDSON
36 Director Career Development Center ....Ms. Michelle OSBORNE
38 Clinical Dir Counseling/Psych Svcs ....Mr. Ronald J. HAMER
41 Director Athletics & Recreation ....Ms. Catherine A. HAKER
91 Director Administrative Info Sys ....Mr. William TRAVER
44 Director Annual Giving ....Mr. Jason MANNING
31 Director Community Services ....Mr. Kenneth SCOTT
42 Director of Campus Ministry ....Ms. Joan HORGAN
23 Director of Health Services ....Ms. Sandra FREHSE
19 Director of Safety/Security ....Mr. Steven STELLA
28 Director of Diversity ....Ms. Shai BUTLER
38 Director of Advisement ....Dr. Kelly MEYER
88 Art Gallery Director ....Ms. Jeanne FLANAGAN
23 Director of Clinical Services ....Ms. Jacqueline KLEIN
96 Director Purchasing/Auxiliary Svcs ....Ms. Patricia BUCKLEY
27 Assoc Dir Media Relations ....Mr. Benjamin MARVIN
18 Dir of Facilities Planning & Mgmt ....Ms. Nancy MACDONALD
09 Director of Institutional Research ....Ms. Lisa KEATING
40 Manager of Campus Store ....Mr. Chris WILSON
24 Dir of Computer/Media Services ....Mr. Michael STRATTON
04 Exec Admin Asst to the President ....Mrs. Julie KOCHAN

The College of Westchester (C)

PO Box 710, White Plains NY 10602-0710
County: Westchester FICE Identification: 005208
Unit ID: 197285
Telephone: (914) 948-4442 Carnegie Class: Bac/Assoc-Mixed
FAX Number: (914) 948-5441 Calendar System: Semester
URL: www.cw.edu
Established: 1915 Annual Undergrad Tuition & Fees: $21,015
Enrollment: 1,125 Coed
Affiliation or Control: Proprietary IRS Status: Proprietary
Highest Offering: Baccalaureate
Accreditation: M

00 Chairman Emeritus ....Mr. Ernest H. SUTKOWSKI
01 President & CEO ....Mrs. Mary Beth DEL BALZO
05 Provost/VP Academic Affairs ....Dr. Warren ROSENBERG
88 Vice President Special Projects ....Mr. Dale T. SMITH
20 Dean Academic Services ....Dr. Daphne GALKIN
84 Sr Director Enrollment Management ....Mr. Matt CURTIS
36 Director of Career Services ....Ms. Joann SONDEY
88 Dir of Student Success/Retention ....Dr. Judith LILLESTON
37 Dir of Student Financial Services ....Mrs. Dianne PEPITONE

Columbia-Greene Community College (D)

4400 Route 23, Hudson NY 12534-9543
County: Columbia FICE Identification: 006789
Unit ID: 190169
Telephone: (518) 828-4181 Carnegie Class: Assoc/HT-Mix Trad/Non
FAX Number: (518) 828-8543 Calendar System: Semester
URL: www.sunycgcc.edu
Established: 1966 Annual Undergrad Tuition & Fees (In-District): $4,552
Enrollment: 2,047 Coed
Affiliation or Control: State/Local IRS Status: 501(c)3
Highest Offering: Associate Degree
Accreditation: M, ADNUR

01 President ....Mr. James R. CAMPION
05 VP & Dean of Academic Affairs ....Ms. Phyllis CARITO
10 Vice Pres & Dean of Administration ....Mr. F. Joseph MATTIES
32 VP/Dean of Students/Enrollment Mgmt ....Dr. Joseph WATSON
38 Counselor ....Ms. Diane JOHNSON
18 Director Building & Grounds ....Mr. James FOLZ
26 Director Public Information ....Mr. Allen KOVLER
37 Dir Stndt Fin Aid/Asst Dean Stdnts ....Ms. Joel PHELPS
21 Assistant Dean of Administration ....Ms. Dianne TOPPLE
06 Registrar ....Ms. Gail SHADER
13 Director Information Systems ....Mr. Gino RIZZI
15 Director of Human Resources ....Ms. Melissa FANDOZZI
22 Affirmative Action Officer ....Ms. Melissa FANDOZZI
09 Dir of Institutional Effectiveness ....Mr. Casey O'BRIEN
31 Director of Community Services ....Mr. Robert BODRATTI
41 Acting Athletic Director ....Ms. Richanna LINDO
88 Director Academic Support Center ....Dr. Mary-Teresa HEATH
103 Director of Workforce Development ....Ms. Mary Alane WILTSE
07 Acting Director of Admissions ....Ms. Rachel KAPPEL
30 Dir of Development & Alumni Svcs ....Ms. Joan KOWEEK
20 Assistant Dean of Academic Affairs ....Ms. Carol DOERFER
21 Bursar ....Ms. Christy DECKER
19 Director of Security ....Mr. John LEONE
96 Purchasing Officer ....Ms. Patricia DAY
62 Department Chair Library Services ....Ms. Geralynn DEMAREST
83 Div Chair Behavioral/Social Science ....Mr. Ted HILSCHER
81 Div Chair Math & Science ....Ms. Dawn HOLSAPPLE
57 Division Chair Arts & Humanities ....Mr. Michael ALLARD
66 Division Chair Nursing ....Ms. Dawn WRIGLEY
72 Division Chair Technology ....Ms. Marcia FITZGERALD

Columbia University in the City of New York (E)

615 West 131st Street, New York NY 10027-6902
County: New York FICE Identification: 002707
Unit ID: 190150
Telephone: (212) 854-1754 Carnegie Class: DU-Highest
FAX Number: (212) 851-7022 Calendar System: Semester
URL: www.columbia.edu
Established: 1754 Annual Undergrad Tuition & Fees: $53,000
Enrollment: 27,589 Coed
Affiliation or Control: Independent Non-Profit IRS Status: 501(c)3
Highest Offering: Doctorate
Accreditation: M, ANEST, BUS, CEA, DENT, ENG, HSA, IPSY, JOUR, LAW, MED, MIDWF, NURSE, OT, PH, PLNG, PTA, SPAA, SW

01 President ....Mr. Lee C. BOLLINGER
05 Provost ....Dr. John COATSWORTH
49 Exec Vice Pres Arts & Sciences ....Mr. David MADIGAN
76 Exec VP Health/Biomed Sciences ....Dr. Lee GOLDMAN
09 Exec Vice President Research ....Dr. G. Michael PURDY
86 Exec Vice Pres Govt & Cmty Affairs ....Ms. Maxine F. GRIFFITH
43 General Counsel ....Ms. Jane E. BOOTH
26 Exec Vice Pres Communications ....Mr. David M. STONE
101 Secretary of the University ....Mr. Jerome DAVIS
10 Exec Vice President for Finance ....Ms. Anne R. SULLIVAN
18 Exec Vice President Facilities ....Mr. David GREENBERG
88 Exec Vice President Global ....Mr. Safwan M. MASRI
30 Exec Vice Pres Development & Alumni ....Ms. Amelia J. ALVERSON
88 Special Advisor to the President ....Ms. Susan K. FEAGIN
32 Exec Vice President University Life ....Ms. Suzanne B. GOLDBERG
41 Athletic Director ....Mr. Peter E. PILLING
88 Ombuds Officer ....Ms. Joan WATERS
100 Chief of Staff to President ....Ms. Susan K. GLANCY
88 CEO IMC Ofc of Univ Investments ....Mr. Nirmal P. NARVEKAR
20 Vice Provost Academic Programs ....Dr. Melissa D. BEGG
20 Vice Provost Faculty Affairs ....Mr. Christopher L. BROWN
11 Vice Provost Administration ....Mr. Troy EGGERS
88 Vice Provost Teaching & Learning ....Soulaymane KACHANI
28 Vice Provost Diversity & Inclusion ....Dr. Dennis MITCHELL
08 Vice Provost & Univ Librarian ....Ms. Ann D. THORNTON
48 Dean Grad School Arch/Plng/Preserv ....Ms. Amale ANDRAOS
57 Dean School of the Arts ....Dr. Carol BECKER
58 Dean Grad School of Arts & Science ....Dr. Carlos J. ALONSO
50 Dean Graduate School of Business ....Dr. R. Glenn HUBBARD
49 Dean Columbia College ....Dr. James J. VALENTINI
51 Dean School Continuing Education ....Mr. Jason M. WINGARD
54 Dean Sch Engr/Applied Science ....Dr. Mary C. BOYCE
82 Dean School Intl/Public Affairs ....Ms. Merit E. JANOW
97 Dean School General Studies ....Dr. Peter AWN
60 Dean Graduate School Journalism ....Mr. Stephen W. COLL
61 Dean School of Law ....Ms. Gillian LESTER
70 Dean School of Social Work ....Dr. Jeanette C. TAKAMURA
63 Dean Faculty of Medicine ....Dr. Lee GOLDMAN
52 Dean Sch Dental & Oral Surgery ....Dr. Christian S. STOHLER
66 Dean School of Nursing ....Dr. Bobbie BERKOWITZ
69 Dean School of Public Health ....Dr. Linda P. FRIED
38 Exec Director Student Counseling ....Dr. Richard EICHLER
37 Assoc VP Student Financial Svcs ....Ms. Jane HOJAN-CLARK
06 Assoc Vice Pres & Registrar ....Mr. Barry S. KANE
07 Dean of Undergraduate Admissions ....Ms. Jessica MARINACCIO

† Parent institution of Barnard College and Teachers College, Columbia University.

Concordia College (F)

171 White Plains Road, Bronxville NY 10708-1923
County: Westchester FICE Identification: 002709
Unit ID: 190248
Telephone: (914) 337-9300 Carnegie Class: Bac-Diverse
FAX Number: (914) 395-4500 Calendar System: Semester
URL: www.concordia-ny.edu
Established: 1881 Annual Undergrad Tuition & Fees: $29,700
Enrollment: 1,037 Coed
Affiliation or Control: Lutheran Church - Missouri Synod
IRS Status: 501(c)3
Highest Offering: Master's
Accreditation: M, IACBE, NURSE, SW, TED

01 President ....Rev.Dr. John A. NUNES
05 Provost ....Dr. Sherry J. FRASER
10 Chief Financial Officer ....Mr. Theodore FRANCAVILLA
11 Vice Pres Administration ....Mr. Lloyd WARDLEY
32 VP of Student Development ....Dr. Lisa DECKER
26 Chief Marketing Officer ....Mr. James BUNN
84 VP of Enrollment Management ....Mr. Donald VOS
43 Director of Legal Affairs ....Ms. Arlene TORRES
20 Vice Prov Undergraduate Acad Affs ....Dr. Mandana NAKHAI
106 Vice Prov Graduate/Online Educ ....Dr. James BURKEE
66 Dean Division of Nursing ....Dr. Kathleen FLAHERTY
88 Dean of Adult Education & Business ....Dr. William M. SALVA
42 Campus Chaplain ....Rev Dr. Joshua HOLLMANN
32 Dean of Students ....Mr. Michael KUSH
06 Registrar ....Mr. Mark E. BLANCO
08 Library Director ....Mr. William L. PERRENOD
38 Director of Counseling ....Ms. Marilyn AMES
41 Athletic Director ....Mr. Ivan MARQUEZ
23 Director Health Services ....Ms. Susan CRANE
88 Assoc Dean Academic Operations ....Mr. Christopher D'AMBROSIO
18 Director Support Services ....Mr. Paul A. SCHULZ
26 Senior Director of Marketing ....Mr. North CALLAHAN
42 Director of Church Relations ....Ms. Kathy DRESSER
31 Dir of Cmty Life & Judicial Affairs ....Vacant
92 Director of Honors Program ....Dr. Kate E. BEHR
15 Director of Human Resources ....Ms. Terry VIDAL
13 Director of Information Services ....Mr. Aaron J. MEYER
21 Controller ....Mr. Edward J. MCPARTLAN
44 Director of Development ....Vacant
35 Director of Student Success ....Ms. Johanna L. PERRY
36 Director of Career Development ....Ms. Laura GREVI
88 Dean of Teacher Education ....Ms. Christine ROWE
85 Dir of Intl Stdn Recruitment/Advis ....Ms. Claire ZHOU
29 Dir of Alumni/Donor Relations ....Mr. William DEITTE
09 Director of Institutional Research ....Ms. Kimberly GARGIULO
102 Dir Foundation/Corporate Relations ....Ms. Joyce KENNEDY
103 Director Career Development ....Ms. Laura GREVI
19 Director of Campus Safety ....Mr. Stephen BONURA
106 Dir Online Education/E-learning ....Dr. Michael SCHLABRA
108 Director Institutional Assessment ....Ms. Kimberly GARGIULO

Cooper Union (G)

30 Cooper Square, New York NY 10003-7120
County: New York FICE Identification: 002710
Unit ID: 190372
Telephone: (212) 353-4100 Carnegie Class: Bac-Diverse
FAX Number: (212) 353-4244 Calendar System: Semester
URL: www.cooper.edu
Established: 1859 Annual Undergrad Tuition & Fees: $42,650
Enrollment: 966 Coed
Affiliation or Control: Independent Non-Profit IRS Status: 501(c)3
Highest Offering: Master's
Accreditation: M, ART, ENG

01 Acting President ....William E. MEA
10 Vice President Finance and Admin ....William MEA
26 Vice President of External Affairs ....Vacant
30 Int VP of Alumni Affs/Development ....Chris CLOUD
100 Chf of Staff/Secy Board of Trustees ....Lawrence CACCIATORE
07 VP Enrollment Svcs/Dean Admissions ....Mitchell LIPTON
32 VP Student Affs/Community Relation ....Vacant
57 Acting Dean School of Art ....Mike ESSL
48 Dean School of Architecture ....Nader TEHRANI
79 Dean Humanities/Social Sciences ....William GERMANO
08 Director of the Library ....Carol SALOMON

21 Dir Budget/Personnel/Inst Research ... Steven GLEIMER
44 Director of Gift Planning ... Peter CONGLETON
27 Vice President of Communications ... Justin HARMON
13 Chief Technology Officer ... Robert P. HOPKINS
09 Director Assessment & Innovation ... Gerardo DEL CERRO
88 Director of Off Campus Programming ... Margaret MORTON
18 Director of Facilities Mgmt ... Carmelo PIZZUTO
51 Director of Continuing Education ... David GREENSTEIN
36 Director of Career Services ... Robert THILL
24 Director of Audiovisual/Media ... Paul TUMMOLO
35 Dean of Students ... Christopher CHAMBERLIN
91 Director of Administrative Database ... Sue MCCOY

† Every student receives a full-tuition scholarship.

Cornell University (A)

Day Hall Lobby, Ithaca NY 14850
County: Tompkins FICE Identification: 002711
Unit ID: 190415
Telephone: (607) 255-2000 Carnegie Class: DU-Highest
FAX Number: (607) 255-5396 Calendar System: Semester
URL: www.cornell.edu
Established: 1865 Annual Undergrad Tuition & Fees: $49,116
Enrollment: 21,679 Coed
Affiliation or Control: Independent Non-Profit IRS Status: 501(c)3
Highest Offering: Doctorate
Accreditation: M, BUS, CIDA, DIETD, DIETI, ENG, HSA, LAW, LSAR, PLNG, VET

01 Interim President ... Hunter R. RAWLINGS, III
05 Provost ... Michael I. KOTLIKOFF
63 Prov Medical Affairs/Dean Med Col ... Laurie GLIMCHER
20 Sr Vice Provost Academic Affairs ... John A. SILICIANO
46 Senior Vice Provost Research ... Robert A. BUHRMAN
58 Senior Vice Prov & Dean Grad School ... Barbara A. KNUTH
88 Vice Prov for International Affairs ... Laura M. SPITZ
88 Vice Provost ... Judith A. APPLETON
45 Vice Pres Planning & Budget ... Paul STREETER
30 Interim VP Alumni Affairs & Develop ... Jeffrey M. MCCARTHY
15 Vice President Human Resources ... Mary George G. OPPERMAN
32 VP Student & Campus Life ... Ryan T. LOMBARDI
26 Vice Pres for University Relations ... Joel M. MALINA
27 Vice President Univ Communications ... Tracy VOSBURGH
86 Associate VP for Govt Relations ... Charles KRUZANSKY
88 Vice Provost Cornell NYC Tech ... Daniel S. HUTTENLOCHER
43 University Counsel & Secretary Corp ... James J. MINGLE
10 VP Financial Affairs/CFO ... Joanne M. DESTEFANO
13 CIO and VP for Info Technology ... Thomas E. DODDS
18 Vice President Facilities/Services ... Kyu-Jung WHANG
84 Assoc Vice Provost Enrollment ... Jason LOCKE
21 University Controller ... Aimee L. TURNER
21 Assoc Vice President/Treasurer ... Harper WATTERS
21 University Auditor ... Glen C. MULLER
20 Dean of Faculty ... Joseph A. BURNS
47 Dean Col Agriculture/Life Sciences ... Kathryn J. BOOR
48 Dean College Arch/Art/Planning ... Kent KLEINMAN
49 Dean College Arts & Science ... Gretchen RITTER
54 Dean College of Engineering ... Lance R. COLLINS
88 Dean School Hotel Administration ... Michael D. JOHNSON
59 Dean College Human Ecology ... Alan D. MATHIOS
50 Dean Johnson Graduate School Mgmt ... Soumitra DUTTA
50 Dean Industrial/Labor Rels ... Kevin F. HALLOCK
61 Dean Law School ... Eduardo M. PEÑALVER
74 Dean College Veterinary Medicine ... Lorin D. WARNICK
77 Dean of Computing and Info Science ... Greg MORRISETT
51 Dean Cont Education/Summer Session ... Glenn C. ALTSCHULER
08 University Librarian ... Anne R. KENNEY
88 Director Africana Studies/Research ... Gerard L. ACHING
07 Dir Undergraduate Admissions ... Shawn FELTON
37 Director Financial Aid ... Susan HITCHCOCK
35 Dean of Students ... Kent L. HUBBELL
06 University Registrar ... Cassandra C. DEMBOSKY
41 Director Athletics/Physical Educ ... J. Andrew NOEL, JR.
36 Director of Cornell Career Services ... Rebecca M. SPARROW
22 Assoc VP Wrkfrce Dvrsty & Inclusion ... Lynette CHAPPELL-WILLIAMS
23 Assoc Vice Pres Campus Health ... Janet L. CORSON-RIKERT
93 Dean of Students ... Renee T. ALEXANDER
28 Assoc Vice Provost Acad Diversity ... Andrew T. MILLER
28 Assoc Vice Provost Facult Diversity ... Yael LEVITTE
42 Dir Cornell United Religious Works ... Kenneth I. CLARKE
25 Assoc Vice Pres Research Admin ... Catherine E. LONG
25 Sr Director Sponsored Fin Svcs ... Jeffrey A. SILBER
19 Chief Cornell Police ... Kathy R. ZONER
96 Sr Dir Procurement and Bus Svcs ... Thomas W. ROMANTIC
29 Assoc Vice Pres Alumni Affairs ... James A. MAZZA
09 Director Inst Research/Planning ... Marin E. CLARKBERG

† Parent institution of Weill Medical College of Cornell University.

Corning Community College (B)

One Academic Drive, Corning NY 14830-3297
County: Steuben FICE Identification: 002863
Unit ID: 190442
Telephone: (607) 962-9011 Carnegie Class: Assoc/HT-Mix Trad/Non
FAX Number: (607) 962-9456 Calendar System: Semester
URL: www.corning-cc.edu
Established: 1956 Annual Undergrad Tuition & Fees (In-District): $4,774
Enrollment: 4,520 Coed
Affiliation or Control: State/Local IRS Status: 501(c)3
Highest Offering: Associate Degree
Accreditation: M, ADNUR

01 President ... Dr. Katherine P. DOUGLAS
05 Vice President Academic Affairs ... Dr. Marian EBERLY
11 Vice President Administrative Svcs ... Mr. Thomas F. CARR
32 Interim VP & Dean of Student Devel ... Ms. E. Joseph LEE
30 Exec Dir Institutional Advancement ... Mr. William LITTLE
08 Director Learning Resources Center ... Ms. Sarah WEISMAN
06 Registrar ... Ms. Karen BOULAS
07 Director of Admissions ... Ms. Tyre BUSH
15 Director Human Resources ... Ms. Nannette NICHOLAS
10 Chief Business Officer ... Mr. Thomas F. CARR
18 Chief Facilities/Physical Plant ... Mr. Calvin WILLIAMS
37 Director Student Financial Aid ... Ms. Nancy JOHNSON
09 Research Analyst ... Ms. Virginia RUDNICK

The Culinary Institute of America (C)

1946 Campus Drive, Hyde Park NY 12538-1499
County: Dutchess FICE Identification: 007304
Unit ID: 190503
Telephone: (845) 905-4288 Carnegie Class: Spec-4-yr-Other
FAX Number: (845) 452-0165 Calendar System: Semester
URL: www.ciachef.edu
Established: 1946 Annual Undergrad Tuition & Fees: $29,250
Enrollment: 2,778 Coed
Affiliation or Control: Independent Non-Profit IRS Status: 501(c)3
Highest Offering: Baccalaureate
Accreditation: M

01 President ... Dr. Tim RYAN
10 Senior VP Finance/Administration ... Ms. Maria KRUPIN
30 VP Advancement & Business Develop ... Dr. Victor GIELISSE
05 Provost ... Mr. Mark ERICKSON
11 VP Administration & Shared Svcs ... Mr. Richard MIGNAULT
20 Vice Pres Academic Affairs ... Dr. Michael SPERLING
84 VP Enrollment Management ... Dr. Jackie NEALON
32 Assoc VP & Dean of Student Affairs ... Dr. Kathleen MERGET
35 Assoc Dean Student Activities ... Mr. David WHALEN
38 Director Counseling Services ... Dr. Daria PAPALIA
09 Director Assessment & Inst Research ... Ms. Elizabeth CARROLL
26 Director of Communications ... Mr. Stephen HENGST
23 Director Health Services ... Ms. Katherine MILLER
21 Director Finance & Accounting ... Mr. Steven STROM
96 Director Purchasing & Storeroom ... Mr. Brad MATTHEWS
88 Dir Student Financial & Reg Svcs ... Ms. Linda TERWILLIGER
18 Director Facilities ... Mr. Thomas M. HIRST
19 Director Safety ... Mr. William CAREY
37 Director Financial Aid ... Ms. Kathleen GAILOR
44 Senior Advancement Officer ... Ms. Denise ZANCHELLI
88 Dean Academic Engagement & Admin ... Ms. Carolyn TRAGNI
12 Assoc VP Branch Campuses ... Ms. Susan CUSSEN
88 Dean Culinary Arts ... Mr. Brendan WALSH
88 Dean Baking & Pastry Arts ... Mr. Thomas VACCARO
49 Dean of Liberal Arts ... Ms. Denise BAUER
108 Dir Inst Liaison & Accreditation ... Ms. Sharon ZRALY
06 Registrar ... Mr. Chester KOULIK
36 Director Career Services & Advising ... Ms. Crystal DECAROLIS
08 Director Library & Information Sys ... Mr. Jon GRENNAN
13 Chief of Staff/CIO ... Mr. Rick TIETJEN
88 Director Compliance ... Ms. Maura KING
15 Director HR Administration ... Ms. Shaynan GARRIOCH
04 Administrative Asst to President ... Ms. Shannon CAMPER
102 Senior Advancement Officer ... Ms. Elly ERICKSON
50 Dean of Business Management ... Ms. Annette GRAHAM

Daemen College (D)

4380 Main Street, Amherst NY 14226-3592
County: Erie FICE Identification: 002808
Unit ID: 190725
Telephone: (716) 839-3600 Carnegie Class: Masters/L
FAX Number: (716) 839-8516 Calendar System: Semester
URL: www.daemen.edu
Established: 1947 Annual Undergrad Tuition & Fees: $25,995
Enrollment: 2,800 Coed
Affiliation or Control: Independent Non-Profit IRS Status: 501(c)3
Highest Offering: Doctorate
Accreditation: M, ARCPA, CAATE, IACBE, NUR, PTA, SW, TEAC

01 President ... Dr. Gary A. OLSON
05 VP Academic Affairs/Dean ... Dr. Michael S. BROGAN
10 VP for Business Affairs & Treasurer ... Mr. Richard G. SCHOTT
30 VP Institutional Advancement ... Mr. Craig HARRIS
84 VP for Enrollment Management ... Dr. Patricia R. BROWN
32 VP Student Affairs ... Dr. Greg J. NAYOR
20 Assoc VP Academic Affairs ... Dr. Kathleen C. BOONE
07 Dean of Admissions/Assoc VP Enroll ... Mr. Frank S. WILLIAMS
21 Controller & VP for Business Affs ... Ms. Lisa A. ARIDA
13 Chief Information Technology Ofcr ... Ms. Kelly DURAN
09 Director of Institutional Research ... Dr. Patricia L. BEAMAN
108 Assoc VP of Inst Effectivness ... Dr. Mimi H. STEADMAN
08 Director of RIC and Library Service ... Ms. Melissa PETERSON
06 Registrar ... Ms. Irene HOLOHAN-MOYER
100 Exec Director President's Office ... Ms. Sherrie A. GUSTAS
88 Dir for Academic Advisement ... Ms. Sabrina FENNELL
37 Director of Financial Aid ... Mr. Jeffrey M. PAGANO
15 Director of Human Resources ... Mrs. Pamela R. NEUMANN
26 Dir of Institutional Communication ... Ms. Paula WITHERELL
44 Director of Development and Gifts ... Mr. Justin JOHNSTON
78 Director of Career Services ... Dr. Maureen MILLANE
39 Dir of Housing & Residence Life ... Ms. Danielle WEAVER
35 Director of Student Activities ... Mr. Christopher P. MALIK
18 Director of Facilities ... Mr. Don PHILLIPS
19 Director Security & Fire Safety ... Mr. Ken BAKER
42 Director Campus Ministry ... Rev. Cassandra L. SALTER-SMITH
41 Director of Athletics ... Ms. Bridget NILAND
96 Dir of Purchasing/Central Services ... Ms. Gwendolyn M. WALKER
92 Director of Honors Program ... Dr. Matthew WARD
29 Director Alumni Relations ... Ms. Katie M. GRAF
40 Bookstore Manager ... Ms. Jaclyn HERNE
88 Dir of New Program Development ... Ms. Susan M. MARCHIONE
04 Admin Asst Office of the President ... Ms. Emily R. HOFFMAN
104 Director Study Abroad ... Ms. Ann ROBINSON
106 Dir Online Education/E-learning ... Mr. Thomas WOJCIECHOWSKI
28 Director of Diversity ... Mr. Alvin ROBERTS, III
38 Director Student Counseling ... Ms. Shannon RADDER

Davis College (E)

400 Riverside Drive, Johnson City NY 13790-2714
County: Broome FICE Identification: 021691
Unit ID: 194569
Telephone: (607) 729-1581 Carnegie Class: Spec-4-yr-Faith
FAX Number: (607) 729-2962 Calendar System: Semester
URL: www.davisny.edu
Established: 1900 Annual Undergrad Tuition & Fees: $13,540
Enrollment: 396 Coed
Affiliation or Control: Independent Non-Profit IRS Status: 501(c)3
Highest Offering: Baccalaureate
Accreditation: M, BI

01 Chief Executive Officer ... Dr. Dino J. PEDRONE
03 Provost ... Dr. Keith MARLETT
05 Academic Dean ... Vacant
84 Enrollment Management Officer ... Mr. Charles DRESSER
32 Student Development Officer ... Mrs. Nichole POST
11 Operating Officer ... Vacant
10 Financial Officer ... Mr. Larry ELLIS
04 Assistant to the President ... Mr. Corey ADAMS
06 Registrar ... Mrs. Susan VANDEVENTER
08 Library Manager ... Mrs. Shelley BYRON
37 Director Financial Aid ... Mr. William REICHEL
88 Assistant to the Provost ... Miss Naomi SARAVANAPAVAN

Dominican College of Blauvelt (F)

470 Western Highway, Orangeburg NY 10962-1210
County: Rockland FICE Identification: 002713
Unit ID: 190761
Telephone: (845) 848-7800 Carnegie Class: Masters/S
FAX Number: (845) 359-2313 Calendar System: Semester
URL: www.dc.edu
Established: 1952 Annual Undergrad Tuition & Fees: $26,450
Enrollment: 1,980 Coed
Affiliation or Control: Independent Non-Profit IRS Status: 501(c)3
Highest Offering: Doctorate
Accreditation: M, #CAATE, IACBE, NURSE, OT, PTA, SW, TEAC

01 President ... Sr Dr. Mary Eileen O'BRIEN
00 Chancellor ... Sr. Kathleen SULLIVAN
05 Vice Pres/Dean Academic Affairs ... Dr. Thomas S. NOWAK
84 Vice Pres of Enrollment Management ... Mr. Brian FERNANDES
32 Dean of Students ... Mr. John BURKE
10 Director of Fiscal Affairs ... Mr. Anthony CIPOLLA
06 Registrar ... Ms. Mary MCFADDEN
07 Director of Admissions ... Vacant
08 Librarian ... Ms. Jennifer SHELTON
30 Director of Inst Advancement ... Ms. Dorothy FILORAMO
15 Director Human Resources ... Ms. Marybeth BRODERICK
26 Chief Public Relations Officer ... Mr. Brett BEKRITSKY
29 Director Alumni Relations ... Ms. Mary MCHUGH
35 Director Student Activities ... Ms. Katrina REDMOND
09 Inst Research/Plng/Assessment Ofcr ... Dr. Shao-Wei WU
37 Director Student Financial Aid ... Ms. Stacy SALINAS
36 Director Student Placement ... Ms. Evelyn FISKAA
38 Director Student Counseling ... Ms. Alise COHEN
21 Controller ... Vacant
13 Director Information Technology ... Mr. Russell DIAZ
18 Chief Facilities/Physical Plant ... Mr. Michael DEMPSEY
20 Associate Academic Officer ... Ms. Ann VAVOLIZZA
39 Director Student Housing ... Mr. Ryan O'GORMAN
41 Athletic Director ... Mr. Joseph CLINTON
42 Director Campus Ministry ... Sr. Barbara MCENEANY
96 Director of Purchasing ... Ms. Amy BIANCO
28 Director of Diversity ... Vacant
19 Director of Security/Safety ... Mr. John LENNON
42 Chaplain ... Vacant
31 Dir Cmty Engagemt/Ldrship Develop ... Ms. Melissa GRAU

Dutchess Community College (G)

53 Pendell Road, Poughkeepsie NY 12601-1595
County: Dutchess FICE Identification: 002864
Unit ID: 190840
Telephone: (845) 431-8000 Carnegie Class: Assoc/HT-Mix Trad/Non
FAX Number: (845) 431-8984 Calendar System: Semester
URL: www.sunydutchess.edu
Established: 1957 Annual Undergrad Tuition & Fees (In-District): $3,866
Enrollment: 9,905 Coed
Affiliation or Control: State/Local IRS Status: 501(c)3
Highest Offering: Associate Degree
Accreditation: M, ADNUR, EMT, MLTAD

01 President ... Dr. Pamela R. EDINGTON
05 VP of Academic Affairs ... Dr. Ellen M. GAMBINO
32 VP & Dean of Student Services ... Dr. Carol STEVENS

10 VP & Dean of Administration ....Mr. William ANDERSON
20 Associate Dean of Academic Affairs ....Ms. Colleen TROGISCH
20 Associate Dean of Academic Affairs ....Mr. Michael BODEN
20 Associate Dean of Academic Affairs ....Dr. Holly MOLELLA
31 Dean Community Svcs/Special Pgms ....Ms. Virginia STOEFFEL
21 Associate Dean Administration ....Ms. Donna ROCAP
06 Interim Registrar ....Mr. William BENEDETTO
84 Associate Dean of Enrollment Mgmt ....Mr. Michael ROE
08 Director of the Library ....Ms. Cathy CARL
14 Director Information Systems ....Mr. Patrick GRIFFIN
30 Director Institutional Advancement ....Ms. Diana POLLARD
09 Director Planning/Inst Research ....Ms. Donna JOHNSON
37 Director Financial Aid ....Ms. Susan MEAD
36 Director Counseling/Career Svcs ....Mr. Mark BALABAN
15 Director Human Resources Mgmt ....Ms. Esther COURET
18 Assoc Dean of Admin Facilities Mgmt . Ms. Bridgette ANDERSON
19 Director Campus Security ....Mr. Ed COX
13 Assoc Dean Admin Info Technology ....Mr. Klaus GESSLER
35 Director of Student Activities ....Mr. Michael WEIDA
26 Chief Public Relations Officer ....Ms. Judi STOKES
88 Assoc Dir Teaching Learning Center ....Ms. Chrisie MITCHELL
88 Director of Scheduling ....Ms. Virginia POZNACK
12 Director DCC South Branch ....Mr. Timothy DECKER
04 Assistant to the President ....Ms. AnneMarie ANDREWS
101 Secretary to the Board of Trustees ....Ms. Linda M. BEASIMER
22 Dir Affirmative Action/EEO ....Ms. Esther COURET
39 Director Residence Life ....Ms. Christina LANDETA

D'Youville College (A)

320 Porter Avenue, Buffalo NY 14201-1084

County: Erie FICE Identification: 002712
Unit ID: 190716
Telephone: (716) 829-8000 Carnegie Class: Masters/L
FAX Number: (716) 829-7820 Calendar System: Semester
URL: www.dyc.edu
Established: 1908 Annual Undergrad Tuition & Fees: $24,370
Enrollment: 3,067 Coed
Affiliation or Control: Independent Non-Profit IRS Status: 501(c)3
Highest Offering: Doctorate
Accreditation: M, CHIRO, ARCPA, DIETC, IACBE, NURSE, OT, PHAR, PTA

01 President ....Dr. William MARIANI
05 Vice President for Academic Affairs ....Dr. Arup SEN
10 Vice President Financal Affairs ....Mr. John GARFOOT
32 VP Student Affairs & Enroll Mgmt ....Mr. Robert P. MURPHY
30 Vice Pres Institutional Advancement ....Ms. Kathleen CHRISTY
11 Associate Vice Pres of Operations ....Mr. Nathan MARTON
88 VP Admin Svcs & External Relations ....Dr. William MARIANI
06 Registrar ....Mr. Daryl SMITH
66 Dean School of Nursing ....Dr. Judith LEWIS
49 Dean Sch of Arts/Sciences & Educ ....Dr. Jason ADSIT
67 Dean School of Pharmacy ....Dr. Canio MARASCO
76 Dean School of Health Professions ....Dr. Maureen FINNEY
88 Artistic Director Kavinoky Theater ....Mr. David LAMB
35 Associate VP for Student Affairs ....Mr. Jeffrey PLATT
35 Assistant VP for Student Affairs ....Mr. Anthony SPINA
21 Bursar ....Mrs. Lisa HIGGINS
21 Controller ....Ms. Laurie HALL
09 Dir Inst Rsrch & Assessment Support ....Mr. Mark ECKSTEIN
91 Director Administrative Computing ....Mr. Robert HALL
29 Director Alumni Relations ....Ms. Meg RITTLING
44 Director Annual Giving ....Mrs. Aimee PEARSON
41 Director Athletics ....Mr. Brian CAVANAUGH
42 Director Campus Ministry ....Fr. Patrick O'KEEFE
36 Director Career Services Center ....Ms. Christine DEMCIE
88 Director College Center ....Ms. Deborah E. OWENS
14 Director Computer & Network Svcs ....Ms. Mary SPENCE
102 Director Foundation Relations ....Mr. William P. MCKEEVER
25 Director Government Grants ....Mrs. Laurie Ann STAHL
23 Director Health Center ....Mrs. Nicole CONROE
15 Director Human Resources ....Ms. Linda MORETTI
85 Director International Stdnt Svcs ....Mrs. Laryssa PETRYSHYN
88 Director Learning Center ....Mrs. Christina SPINK-FORMANSKI
08 Director Library Services ....Mr. Rand BELLAVIA
44 Director Major & Planned Gifts ....Dr. David CRISTANTELLO
28 Director Multicultural Affairs ....Mrs. Yolanda WOOD
38 Director Personal Counseling ....Ms. Kimberly ZITTEL
26 Director Public Relations ....Mr. D. John BRAY
19 Director of Security ....Mr. Jeremy SMITH
37 Director Student Financial Aid ....Mr. Matthew METZ
07 Director Undergraduate Admissions ....Dr. Steve SMITH
07 Director Graduate Admissions ....Mr. Mark PAVONE
07 Director Intl Admiss & Marketing ....Mr. Ronald DANNECKER
88 Director Veterans Affairs Office ....Mr. Benjamin RANDLE
13 Chief Information Officer ....Mr. Roozbeh TAVAKOLI
51 Director Prof Development Center ....Vacant

Elim Bible Institute (B)

7245 College Street, Lima NY 14485

County: Livingston Identification: 667245
Telephone: (800) 670-3546 Carnegie Class: Not Classified
FAX Number: (585) 582-8130 Calendar System: Semester
URL: www.elim.edu
Established: 1924 Annual Undergrad Tuition & Fees: N/A
Enrollment: N/A Coed
Affiliation or Control: Independent Non-Profit IRS Status: 501(c)3
Highest Offering: Associate Degree
Accreditation: @TRACS

01 President ....Mike CAVANAUGH
05 VP of Academic Affairs ....Danuta CASE
33 Dean of Students ....Stacy CLINE
04 Administration Director ....Chris LAMPSON
07 Director of Admissions ....Wayne HEDLUND

The Elmezzi Graduate School of Molecular Medicine (C)

350 Community Drive, Manhasset NY 11030-3826

County: Nassau Identification: 666671
Telephone: (516) 562-3405 Carnegie Class: Not Classified
FAX Number: (516) 562-1022 Calendar System: Other
URL: www.elmezzigraduateschool.org
Established: 1999 Annual Graduate Tuition & Fees: N/A
Enrollment: N/A Coed
Affiliation or Control: Independent Non-Profit IRS Status: 501(c)3
Highest Offering: Doctorate; No Undergraduates
Accreditation: NY

01 President ....Dr. Kevin J. TRACEY
03 Provost ....Dr. Bettie M. STEINBERG
05 Dean ....Dr. Annette LEE
20 Associate Dean ....Dr. Christine METZ
10 Chief Business Officer ....Ms. Cynthia HAHN
101 Secretary of the Institution/Board ....Mr. Laurence KRAEMER
11 Chief of Administration ....Ms. Emilia HRISTIS
19 Director Security/Safety ....Mr. Robert KIKEL
25 Director Contracts/Grants Admin ....Ms. Diane MARBURY

Elmira Business Institute (D)

Langdon Plaza, 303 N Main Street, Elmira NY 14901-3086

County: Chemung FICE Identification: 009043
Unit ID: 190974
Telephone: (888) 986-6561 Carnegie Class: Spec 2-yr-Health
FAX Number: (607) 733-7178 Calendar System: Semester
URL: www.ebi-college.com
Established: 1858 Annual Undergrad Tuition & Fees: $20,780
Enrollment: 400 Coed
Affiliation or Control: Proprietary IRS Status: Proprietary
Highest Offering: Associate Degree
Accreditation: ACICS, MAC

01 President ....Mr. Brad C. PHILLIPS
11 Vice President of Administration ......Mrs. Kathleen M. HAMILTON
05 Chief Academic Officer ....Vacant
32 Dean of Students ....Dr. Brian MCCONNELL
35 Director of Student Services ....Ms. Lindsay N. DULL
15 Director Human Resources ....Ms. Erin MCCANN
07 Regional Director of Admissions ....Mr. Scott GALELEI
26 Regional Director of PR & Grad Svc ....Mr. Josh PATTON

Elmira Business Institute (E)

4100 Old Vestal Road, Vestal NY 13850

Telephone: (607) 729-8915 Identification: 770745
Accreditation: ACICS

Elmira College (F)

One Park Place, Elmira NY 14901-2099

County: Chemung FICE Identification: 002718
Unit ID: 190983
Telephone: (607) 735-1800 Carnegie Class: Bac-A&S
FAX Number: (607) 735-1758 Calendar System: Other
URL: www.elmira.edu
Established: 1855 Annual Undergrad Tuition & Fees: $39,950
Enrollment: 1,482 Coed
Affiliation or Control: Independent Non-Profit IRS Status: 501(c)3
Highest Offering: Master's
Accreditation: M, NUR, TEAC

01 President ....Dr. Norman R. SMITH
10 VP of Finance and Administration ....Mr. Robert J. CAMPE
05 Provost ....Dr. Charles W. LINDSAY
30 Vice Pres of External Relations ....Mr. Michael B. ROGERS
84 Vice Pres of Enrollment Management ...Mr. Christopher R. COONS
41 Vice President of Athletics ....Ms. Patricia A. THOMPSON
32 Dean of Students ....Mr. Brandon T. DAWSON
51 Interim Dean of Continuing Educ ....Ms. Joann KOWALSKI
37 Dean of Financial Aid ....Ms. Kathleen L. COHEN
06 Registrar ....Mr. Michael HALPERIN
08 Dean of Library ....Ms. Elizabeth M. WAVLE-BROWN
36 Director of Career Development ....Ms. Julie FIELDING
88 Director of Experiential Education ....Mr. Michael BLASIC
50 Dept Chair of Business/Economics ....Dr. Mariam KHAWAR
57 Dept Chair of Creative Arts ....Prof. John J. KELLY
79 Dept Chair of Humanities ....Dr. Mitchell R. LEWIS
81 Dept Chair of Math/Natural Sciences ....Dr. Corey E. STILTS
83 Dept Chair of Soc/Behavior Science ....Dr. Jim TWOMBLY
107 Dept Chair of Professional Programs ....Dr. Deborah OWENS
29 Director of Alumni Relations ....Ms. Ellen HIMMELREICH
66 Dean of Health Sciences ....Dr. Kathy T. LUCKE
18 Director of Facilities Management ....Ms. Tessa MOORE
105 Dir of Web Comm & Digital Media ....Mrs. Kiersten TARKETT
39 Director of Residence Life ....Ms. Erin HUNTER
40 Dir of Bookstore & Special Projects ....Ms. Shannon MOYLAN
15 Director of Human Resources ....Ms. Jessica CARPENTER
09 Director of Institutional Research ....Ms. Karen L. JOHNSON
20 Dean of Academic Affairs ....Dr. Charles E. MITCHELL
13 Chief Information Officer ....Mr. Brian CORNELL
19 Director of Campus Security ....Mr. Gary D. MILLER
44 Director of Annual Giving ....Mr. Kyle A. SMITH
102 Director of Grants ....Ms. Valerie R. ROSPLOCK
23 Director of Health Services ....Ms. Wendy BELL
04 Exec Assistant to the President ....Mrs. Mary C. BARRETT
38 Director of Counseling ....Dr. Kevin MURPHY

Elyon College (G)

1400 West 6th Street, Brooklyn NY 11204

County: Kings Identification: 667290
Telephone: (718) 259-5600 Carnegie Class: Not Classified
FAX Number: (218) 259-8024 Calendar System: Trimester
URL: elyoncollege.org
Established: Annual Undergrad Tuition & Fees: N/A
Enrollment: N/A Coed
Affiliation or Control: Independent Non-Profit IRS Status: 501(c)3
Highest Offering: Associate Degree
Accreditation: CNCE

01 President ....Chaim A. WALDMAN

Erie Community College (H)

121 Ellicott Street, Buffalo NY 14203-2698

County: Erie FICE Identification: 010684
Unit ID: 191083
Telephone: (716) 842-2770 Carnegie Class: Assoc/HT-Mix Trad/Non
FAX Number: (716) 851-1129 Calendar System: Semester
URL: www.ecc.edu
Established: 1971 Annual Undergrad Tuition & Fees (In-District): $5,189
Enrollment: 12,733 Coed
Affiliation or Control: State/Local IRS Status: 501(c)3
Highest Offering: Associate Degree
Accreditation: M, ACFEI, ADNUR, CAHIIM, COARC, DH, DIETT, DT, EMT, ENGT, MAC, MLTAD, OPD, OTA, PTA

01 President ....Mr. Jack F. QUINN
11 Sr Vice Pres for Operations ....Mr. Michael PIETKIEWICZ
05 Exec Vice Pres Academic Affairs .... Mr. Richard C. WASHOUSKY
20 Associate Vice President Academics ....Dr. Edward J. HOLMES
32 Exec Vice President Student Affairs ....Vacant
35 Associate VP Student Success ....Dr. Nuriyah CLARK
35 Dean of Students City ....Ms. Petrina HILL-CHEATOM
35 Dean of Students North ....Vacant
35 Dean of Students South ....Ms. Heather A. CRUZ
43 Exec Vice Pres Legal Affairs ....Vacant
23 Associate Vice Pres Health Sciences ....Mr. Patrick J. WILES
13 AVP Data Analytics/Sys Integration ....Mr. Rob ELNICKY
14 Director of ERP Sys & Info Svcs ....Mr. David L. ARLINGTON
19 Assoc Vice President Security ....Mr. Tracy GAST
102 Associate Vice Pres Foundation ....Mr. Jeffrey BAGEL
10 Chief Admin & Financial Officer ....Mr. William D. REUTER
109 Coordinator Institutional Services ....Mr. Joel J. DAMIANI
15 Human Resources Director ....Ms. Tracey CLEVELAND
16 Assistant Director Human Resources ....Ms. Maria CARROLL
103 Exec Dean Workforce Dev/Cmty Svcs ....Ms. Carrie W. KAHN
49 Asst Acad Dean Liberal Arts City ....Vacant
49 Asst Acad Dean Liberal Arts North ....Ms. Mary A. BEARD
49 Asst Acad Dean Liberal Arts South ....Vacant
50 Asst Academic Dean Business ....Dr. Kenneth J. BARNES
56 Director Dist Learning/Altern Pgm ....Mr. Patrick RYAN
72 Assistant Academic Dean Technology ....Mr. Mark S. HOEBER
78 Coordinator Internships/Coop ....Vacant
28 Director of Equity & Diversity ....Ms. Darley WILLIS
06 Director of Registration ....Mr. Paul A. LAMANA
06 Registrar City ....Ms. Rochelle WEBBER
06 Registrar South ....Ms. Cynthia LUDLOW
07 Director of Admissions ....Mr. Philip STRUEBEL
84 Asst VP Enrollment Mgmt/Marketing ....Dr. Erik D'AQUINO
08 Librarian City ....Ms. Kathleen POWERS
08 Librarian North ....Mr. Matthew BEST
08 Librarian South ....Ms. Taheera SHAHEED-SONUBI
40 Bookstore Manager City ....Ms. Susan SCHMITTENDORF
40 Bookstore Manager North ....Ms. Teresa KALINOWSKI
40 Bookstore Manager South ....Mr. Michael FOX
88 Health Services Nurse South ....Ms. Frances WILLIAMS
88 Health Services Nurse North ....Ms. Maryetta DUBOIS
88 Health Services Nurse City ....Ms. Kelly ROCKWELL
36 Career Resource Center Director ....Vacant
36 Career Resource Center Coord City ....Ms. Katherine MARSHALL
36 Career Resource Center Coord North ....Mr. Joseph P. ABBARNO
26 Director Marketing & Communications ....Mr. Lance R. KONKLE
09 Director Institutional Research ....Ms. Marlene ARNO
45 Interim Assoc VP IRAAP ....Dr. Fabio ESCOBAR
27 Public Information Officer ....Mr. Michael FARRELL
41 Director of Athletics ....Mr. Peter J. JEREBKO
88 Assistant Director Athletics ....Mr. Steve L. MULLEN
18 Director Buildings & Grounds ....Mr. Anthony NESCI
37 Director of Financial Aid ....Mr. Scott WELTJEN
37 Financial Aid Coordinator City ....Ms. Charlotte M. COSTON
88 Financial Aid Asst Coordinator ....Ms. Robin FILIPPONE
21 Business Manager ....Mr. Paul F. DANIEU
24 Audio Visual Coordinator City ....Vacant
24 Audio Visual Coordinator North ....Mr. Ryan NOGLE
24 Audio Visual Coordinator North ....Mr. Nicholas SONRICKER
24 Audio Visual Coordinator South ....Mr. David G. MALLORY
92 Coordinator Honors Program ....Vacant
88 Coordinator of Corporate Training ....Mr. John P. SLISZ
25 Grants Coordinator ....Mr. Michael J. BIGGANE
29 Director of Alumni Affairs ....Ms. Stephanie KING
04 Assistant to the President ....Mr. John FOLEY
85 Foreign Student Advisor ....Mr. John DANNA
88 Director of Student Access ....Dr. Marilou C. BLAIR

88 Advanced Studies Coordinator .... Ms. Deborah F. SCHMITT
88 Project Dir Transition Programs .... Ms. Joanne COLMERAUER

Excelsior College (A)

7 Columbia Circle, Albany NY 12203-5156
County: Albany FICE Identification: 002834
Unit ID: 196680
Telephone: (518) 464-8500 Carnegie Class: Masters/L
FAX Number: (518) 464-8777 Calendar System: Other
URL: www.excelsior.edu
Established: 1971 Annual Undergrad Tuition & Fees: N/A
Enrollment: 41,527 Coed
Affiliation or Control: Independent Non-Profit IRS Status: 501(c)3
Highest Offering: Master's
Accreditation: M, ADNUR, CS, ENGT, IACBE, NUR

01 President .... Dr. John F. EBERSOLE
03 Acting President .... Dr. James BALDWIN
43 General Counsel .... Ms. Karen HALACO
84 VP Enrollment Management .... Mr. Craig MASLOWSKY
05 Chief Academic Officer/Provost .... Dr. Mary Beth HANNER
20 Vice Provost .... Dr. Patrick JONES
88 Associate Provost .... Dr. George TIMMONS
88 Associate Provost .... Ms. Telaekah BROOKS
32 Assoc Provost Student & Fac Svcs .... Dr. Joan MIKALSON
13 VP Information Technology & CIO .... Dr. Wayne BROWN
15 VP HR & Facilities .... Mr. Mark HOWE
10 VP Finance & Administration .... Mr. John M. PONTIUS, JR.
44 VP Institutional Advancement .... Mr. Keith BARROWS
56 VP for Extended Education .... Ms. Chris MONTAGNINO
45 VP Strategy & IE .... Ms. Susan O'HERN
88 AVP for Analytics .... Dr. Lisa DANIELS
88 AVP for Academic Operations .... Ms. Emilsen HOLGUIN
86 AVP for Government Relations .... Dr. Paul SHIFFMAN
88 AVP for Enrollment Management .... Mr. Thomas DALTON
21 AVP Budgets & Financial Analysis .... Mr. Todd S. THOMAS
14 AVP Information Technology .... Mr. Ronald MARZITELLI
16 AVP for Human Resources .... Ms. Anita BURNS
88 AVP Center for Military Education .... Ms. Susan DEWAN
88 AVP COELAS .... Dr. Jennifer MCVAY-DYCHE
56 CEO Extended Education .... Dr. Susan KRYCZKA
88 AVP ESE .... Mr. Christopher GILMORE
108 AVP of SIE .... Dr. Mohua BOSE
21 Controller .... Ms. Hillary HARDING
49 Dean of Liberal Arts .... Dr. George TIMMONS
50 Dean of Business & Technology .... Dr. Karl LAWRENCE
66 Dean of Nursing .... Dr. Mary Lee POLLARD
76 Dean of Health Sciences .... Dr. Debbie SOPCZYK
97 Dean of Public Service .... Dr. Robert WATERS
88 Ombudsperson .... Ms. Kathy MORAN
88 Exec Director of CAPITAL .... Ms. Tina GRANT
88 Director Leadership Academy .... Dr. Murray BLOCK
88 Exec Dir of Outreach .... Ms. Lynda HOLT
06 Registrar .... Ms. Lori MORANO
07 Exec Director of Admissions .... Ms. Shannon EASTON
88 Exec Director of Outreach/Access .... Ms. Lisa LAVIGNA
88 Exec Dir Professional Dev .... Ms. Jennifer HUMMER
88 General Manager CEM .... Ms. Nurit SONNENSCHEIN
26 Exec Director of Marketing .... Ms. JoAnne LATHAM
30 Director of Development .... Ms. Marcy STRYKER
102 Director of Grants and Research .... Ms. Patricia CROOP
88 Director of Digital Engagement .... Mr. Donn AIKEN
88 Director of Technical Services .... Ms. Mare DONOHUE
88 Director of Business Intelligence .... Ms. Sophia BRAGA
88 Director of Applications Dev .... Mr. James SUN
19 Dir of Infrastructure and Security .... Mr. Scott GILREATH
88 Exec Dir Enrollment Mgmt Ops .... Mr. Dan MERKT
88 Director of Publications .... Ms. Maria SPARKS
29 Alumni Affairs Manager .... Ms. Renee KELLY
18 Chief Facilities/Physical Plant .... Mr. Robert RANALLI
88 Director of Hudson Whitman Press .... Ms. Susan PETRIE
27 Director of Communications .... Ms. Alicia JACOBS
88 Chief Communications Officer .... Mr. Michael LESCZINSKI
28 Diversity Coordinator .... Ms. Toby HAMLIN
04 Asst to Pres for Trustee .... Ms. Laurie KEENAN
09 Exec Director of IR .... Dr. Georgia BROOKE
37 Exec Dir Financial Aid .... Ms. Susan MERCHANT

Fashion Institute of Technology (B)

Seventh Avenue at 27 Street, New York NY 10001-5992
County: New York FICE Identification: 002866
Unit ID: 191126
Telephone: (212) 217-7999 Carnegie Class: Bac/Assoc-Mixed
FAX Number: N/A Calendar System: Semester
URL: www.fitnyc.edu
Established: 1944 Annual Undergrad Tuition & Fees (In-District): $5,230
Enrollment: 9,764 Coed
Affiliation or Control: State/Local IRS Status: 501(c)3
Highest Offering: Master's
Accreditation: M, ART, CIDA

01 President .... Dr. Joyce F. BROWN
10 Treasurer/VP Finance/Administration .... Ms. Sherry F. BRABHAM
101 Secy of College/General Counsel .... Dr. Stephen TUTTLE
05 Vice President Academic Affairs .... Dr. Giacomo OLIVA
26 Vice Pres Comm/External Rels .... Ms. Loretta LAWRENCE KEANE
84 Vice Pres Enrollment Mgmt/Student .... Dr. Kelly BRENNAN
15 Int VP Human Res Mgmt/Labor Rels .... Ms. Brenda J. SMITH
13 VP for Information Technology/CIO .... Mr. Gregg CHOTTINER
30 VP Devel & Exec Dir Foundation .... Mr. Robert FERGUSON
20 Assoc Vice Pres Academic Affairs .... Dr. Ronald MILON
88 Asst Vice Pres Human Res/Labor Rels .... Ms. Karen YUEN
21 Asst Vice Pres Finance .... Mr. Mark BLAIFEDER
21 Assistant VP of Administration .... Ms. Rebecca CORRADO
88 Asst VP Software Svcs/Info Access .... Mr. Van Buren WINSTON
27 Asst Vice Pres for Communications .... Ms. Carol LEVEN
88 VP Inst Effect/Deputy to the Pres .... Ms. Shari PRUSSIN
20 Asst VP/Faculty & Academic Pgm Supp .... Dr. Yasemin JONES
51 Dean Continuing & Prof Studies .... Vacant
57 Dean Art & Design .... Ms. Joanne ARBUCKLE
58 Dean School of Graduate Studies .... Dr. Mary DAVIS
49 Dean Liberal Arts .... Dr. Patrick KNISLEY
50 Dean Business & Technology .... Mr. Steven FRUMKIN
07 Dir of Admissions/Strat Recruiting .... Ms. Magda FRANCOIS
88 Director Special Events .... Ms. Vicki GURANOWSKI
11 Director Operational Services .... Mr. John WILSON
18 Executive Director of Facilities .... Mr. George JEFREMOW
22 Affirm Action Ofcr/Dir Compliance .... Ms. Griselda GONZALEZ
38 Director of the Counseling Center .... Ms. Terry GINDER
37 Director of Financial Aid .... Ms. Mina FRIEDMANN
08 Dir of the Gladys Marcus Library .... Mr. NJ BRADEEN
06 Director of Registration & Records .... Ms. Rita CAMMARATA
39 Director of Residental Life .... Ms. Ann Marie GRAPPO
36 Director Career & Internship .... Vacant
32 Director of Student Life .... Ms. Michelle VAN-ESS
23 Director of Health Services .... Ms. Anne MILLER
19 Director of Campus Safety .... Mr. Mario CABRERA
88 Director of The Museum at FIT .... Dr. Valerie STEELE
09 Asst Dean Inst Research & Effect .... Mr. Darrell GLENN
86 Dir Government/Community Relations .... Ms. Lisa WAGER
27 Exec Director of Public & Media Rel .... Ms. Cheri FEIN
104 Dean of International Programs .... Dr. Deirdre SATO
41 Director of Athletics & Recreation .... Ms. Kerri-Ann MCTIERNAN
96 Director of Budget .... Ms. Nancy SU
88 Dir of Education Opportunity Pgms .... Ms. Taur D. ORANGE
21 Controller/Assistant Treas .... Mr. John JOHNSTON
88 Int Dir Env Health/Sfty Compliance .... Mr. Paul DEBIASE
92 Coord Presidential Scholars Pgm .... Dr. Irene BUCHMAN
105 Manager Digital Strategies .... Ms. Taryn REJHOLEC
55 Dir Evening/Weekend/Pre-College .... Ms. Michele NAGEL
29 Manager Alumni Engagement & Giving .... Vacant
28 Chair of Diversity Council .... Ms. Griselda GONZALEZ
28 Chair of Diversity Council .... Mr. Michael COKKINOS

Fei Tian College (C)

140 Galley Hill Road, Cuddebackville NY 12729
County: Orange Identification: 667205
Telephone: (845) 672-0550 Carnegie Class: Not Classified
FAX Number: (845) 977-0481 Calendar System: Semester
URL: www.feitian.edu
Established: Annual Undergrad Tuition & Fees: N/A
Enrollment: N/A Coed
Affiliation or Control: Independent Non-Profit IRS Status: 501(c)3
Highest Offering: Baccalaureate
Accreditation: NY

01 President .... Ms. Vina LEE

Finger Lakes Community College (D)

3325 Marvin Sands Drive, Canandaigua NY 14424-8405
County: Ontario FICE Identification: 007532
Unit ID: 191199
Telephone: (585) 394-3522 Carnegie Class: Assoc/HT-High Non
FAX Number: (585) 394-5005 Calendar System: Semester
URL: www.flcc.edu
Established: 1965 Annual Undergrad Tuition & Fees (In-District): $4,704
Enrollment: 6,793 Coed
Affiliation or Control: State/Local IRS Status: 501(c)3
Highest Offering: Associate Degree
Accreditation: M, ADNUR

01 President .... Dr. Robert NYE
05 Provost .... Ms. Kristen M. FRAGNOLI
10 Sr Vice President of Admin/Finance .... Mr. James R. FISHER
84 Vice Pres Enrollment Management .... Ms. Carol S. URBAITIS
32 Assoc Vice Pres of Student Affairs .... Ms. Sarah E. WHIFFEN
20 Assoc VP Instruction & Assessment .... Dr. Cathryn KENT
20 Assoc VP Academic Affairs .... Mr. Jacob E. AMIDON
15 Director of Human Resources .... Ms. Grace H. LOOMIS
30 Chief Advancement Officer .... Mr. Joseph NAIRN
19 Dir of Campus Security Operations .... Mr. Jason R. MAITLAND
21 Controller .... Mr. Joseph L. DELFORTE
18 Director of Facilities & Grounds .... Ms. Catherine AHERN
07 Director of Admissions .... Ms. Bonnie B. RITTS
06 Registrar .... Mr. Michael FISHER
25 Director of Grants Development .... Ms. Karen A. VAN KEUREN
37 Director of Financial Aid .... Ms. Susan M. ROMANO
35 Director of Student Life .... Ms. Jennie ERDLE
13 Chief Information Officer .... Mr. John TAYLOR
38 Dir Educ Planning/Career Services .... Ms. Corrine M. CANOUGH
36 Career Services Coordinator .... Ms. Tammie WOODY
08 Director Library Learning Resources .... Ms. Sarah MOON
26 Director of Marketing .... Ms. Heidi C. MARCIN
23 Director of Student Health Services .... Ms. Karen P Z. STEIN
24 Dir Instructional Technology .... Mr. Daniel P. FARSACI
09 Director Institutional Effectivenes .... Ms. Mary MCLEAN-SCANLON
29 Director of Alumni Relations .... Ms. Lisa L. SCOTT
96 Director of Business Services .... Ms. Andrea BARBER
72 Chair Science & Technology .... Dr. Melissa A. MILLER
50 Chair Business .... Ms. Mary M. WILSEY
65 Chair Environment Conservation Hort .... Mr. Ann B. SCHNELL
57 Chair Visual/Performing Arts .... Mr. Richard D. COOK
66 Chair Nursing .... Ms. Nancy E. CLARKSON
68 Chair Physical Education .... Mr. Dennis T. MOORE
81 Chair Computer Science .... Ms. April A. DEVAUX
79 Chair Humanities .... Mr. Jon A. PALZER
83 Chair Social Science .... Mr. Joshua W. HELLER
81 Chair Mathematics .... Ms. Theresa GAUTHIER

Finger Lakes Health College of Nursing (E)

196 North Street, Geneva NY 14456
County: Ontario Identification: 667154
Unit ID: 475422
Telephone: (315) 787-4000 Carnegie Class: Spec 2-yr-Health
FAX Number: (313) 787-4770 Calendar System: Semester
URL: www.flhealth.org/nursingeducation
Established: 2008 Annual Undergrad Tuition & Fees: $11,540
Enrollment: 135 Coed
Affiliation or Control: Independent Non-Profit IRS Status: 501(c)3
Highest Offering: Associate Degree
Accreditation: ABHES, ADNUR, SURGT, SURTEC

01 Dean .... Victoria RECORD
32 Student Services Coordinator .... Ann DRAKE

Five Towns College (F)

305 North Service Road, Dix Hills NY 11746-6055
County: Suffolk FICE Identification: 012561
Unit ID: 191205
Telephone: (631) 656-2157 Carnegie Class: Bac-Diverse
FAX Number: (631) 656-2172 Calendar System: Semester
URL: www.ftc.edu
Established: 1972 Annual Undergrad Tuition & Fees: $21,500
Enrollment: 687 Coed
Affiliation or Control: Proprietary IRS Status: Proprietary
Highest Offering: Doctorate
Accreditation: M, TED

01 Acting President .... Mr. David COHEN
05 Provost .... Ms. Carolann MILLER
10 Vice President of Finance .... Mr. Robert DANIELS
32 Dean of Students .... Dr. Jennifer ALBERT
06 Registrar .... Ms. Mara MALTZ
106 Director of Online Education .... Vacant
37 Director of Financial Aid .... Mr. Jason LABONTE
08 Library Director .... Mr. John VANSTEEN
38 College Counselor .... Ms. Carolyn NEWMAN
64 Chair of Music Division .... Prof. Jill MILLER-THORN
50 Deputy Chair of Business Division .... Ms. Mary LOBIONDO
49 Chair of Liberal Arts Division .... Vacant
53 Chair of Education Division .... Mr. William FORTGANG
88 Chair of Film/Video .... Dr. Kathy CURTISS
88 Chair of Theatre Arts .... Mr. James BENEDUCE
36 Director Student Placement .... Ms. Krysti O'ROURKE
18 Chief Facilities/Physical Plant .... Mr. Mark SHAUGHNESSY
19 Director of Security .... Mr. Len DEVLIN
39 Director of Residential Life .... Mr. Thomas O'BOYLE
07 Director of Admissions .... Ms. Terry DONOHUE
09 Director of Institutional Research .... Vacant

Fordham University (G)

441 East Fordham Road, Bronx NY 10458-9993
County: Bronx FICE Identification: 002722
Unit ID: 191241
Telephone: (718) 817-1000 Carnegie Class: DU-Higher
FAX Number: (718) 817-4925 Calendar System: Semester
URL: www.fordham.edu
Established: 1841 Annual Undergrad Tuition & Fees: $47,317
Enrollment: 15,231 Coed
Affiliation or Control: Independent Non-Profit IRS Status: 501(c)3
Highest Offering: Doctorate
Accreditation: M, BUS, CLPSY, COPSY, DANCE, LAW, SCPSY, SW, TED

01 President .... Rev. Joseph M. MCSHANE, SJ
04 Exec Assistant to the President .... Ms. Dorothy MARINUCCI
04 Asst Univ Sec/Spec Asst to Pres .... Mr. Michael R. TREROTOLA
05 Provost .... Dr. Stephen FREEDMAN
10 SVP/CFO and Treasurer .... Ms. Martha K. HIRST
32 Sr Vice President Student Affairs .... Mr. Jeffrey L. GRAY
21 Vice President for Finance .... Mr. Nicholas B. MILOWSKI
13 VP for Information Technology/CIO .... Dr. Frank SIRIANNI
84 Vice President for Enrollment .... Dr. Peter A. STACE
12 Vice President for Lincoln Center .... Dr. Brian J. BYRNE
30 Vice President for Development .... Mr. Roger A. MILICI, JR.
88 Vice President for Mission .... Rev. Michael C. MCCARTHY, SJ
18 VP for Facilities Management .... Mr. Marco VALERA
11 Vice President for Administration .... Mr. Thomas A. DUNNE
101 Secretary of the University .... Ms. Margaret T. BALL
20 Assoc Vice Pres Academic Affairs .... Dr. Benjamin CROOKER
20 Assoc Vice Pres Academic Affairs .... Dr. Jonathan CRYSTAL
20 Assoc Vice Pres Academic Affairs .... Dr. Ron JACOBSON
26 AVP Univ Marketing Communications .... Ms. Catherine SPENCER
29 AVP/Director of Alumni Relations .... Mr. Michael GRIFFIN
07 Assoc Vice Pres Undgrad Enrollment .... Mr. John W. BUCKLEY
06 Asst Vice Pres Enrollment/Registrar .... Dr. Gene FEIN
37 Assoc VP Student Financial Services .... Ms. Angela VAN DEKKER
86 Assoc Vice Pres for Government Rels .... Mr. Joseph P. MURIANA
86 Assoc Vice Pres for Government Rels .... Ms. Lesley A. MASSIAH-ARTHUR

43 General Counsel ... Ms. Elaine CROSSON
35 Asst VP and Dean of Students ... Mr. Christopher RODGERS
35 Asst VP & Dean of Student Services ... Mr. Gregory J. PAPPAS
49 Dean/AVP Arts & Sciences Education ... Dr. John HARRINGTON
12 Dean Fordham College at Rose Hill ... Dr. Maura B. MAST
58 Dean Graduate Arts & Science ... Dr. Eva BADOWSKA
73 Dean Graduate Religious Education ... Dr. C. Colt ANDERSON
50 Dean Gabelli Schools of Business ... Dr. Donna RAPACCIOLI
107 Dean Sch of Prof and Cont Studies ... Dr. Anthony R. DAVIDSON
12 Dean Fordham College Lincoln Center ... Rev. Robert GRIMES, SJ
53 Dean Graduate Education LC ... Dr. Virginia ROACH
61 Dean School of Law LC ... Mr. Matthew DILLER
70 Dean Graduate Social Service LC ... Dr. Debra MCPHEE
15 Exec Director of Human Resources ... Mr. Michael MINEO
09 Director Institutional Research ... Dr. Peter FEIGENBAUM
42 Executive Director Campus Ministry ... Rev. Jose-Luis SALAZAR, SJ
21 Controller ... Mr. Anthony GRONO
19 AVP Public Safety ... Mr. John CARROLL
22 Director of Institutional Equity ... Ms. Anastasia COLEMAN
46 Chief Research Officer/AVP ... Dr. Z. George HONG
08 Director of University Libraries ... Ms. Linda LOSCHIAVO
24 Director Media Center ... Mr. Jerry GREEN
23 Director of Health Center ... Ms. Kathleen MALARA
35 Asst Dean Student Involvement ... Vacant
41 AVP of Athletic Alumni Relations ... Mr. Francis X. MCLAUGHLIN
96 Director of Procurement ... Mr. Frank A. DEORIO
38 Director of Psychological Svcs ... Dr. Jeffrey NG
28 Asst Dean/Dir Multicultural Affairs ... Mr. Juan Carlos MATOS
36 Director Career Services ... Ms. Stefany FATTOR
39 Asst Dean/Dir of Residential Life ... Ms. Kimberly RUSSELL

Fulton-Montgomery Community College (A)

2805 State Highway 67, Johnstown NY 12095-3790

County: Montgomery — FICE Identification: 002867 — Unit ID: 191302
Telephone: (518) 736-3622 — Carnegie Class: Assoc/HT-High Trad
FAX Number: (518) 762-5693 — Calendar System: Semester
URL: www.fmcc.edu
Established: 1963 — Annual Undergrad Tuition & Fees (In-District): $4,440
Enrollment: 2,589 — Coed
Affiliation or Control: State/Local — IRS Status: 501(c)3
Highest Offering: Associate Degree
Accreditation: M, ADNUR, RAD

01 President ... Dr. Dustin SWANGER
05 Provost/Vice Pres Academic Affairs ... Dr. Greg TRUCKENMILLER
10 Vice Pres Finance & Administration ... Mr. David M. MORROW
32 Vice President of Student Affairs ... Ms. Jane KELLEY
20 Dean of Academic Affairs ... Ms. Diana PUTNAM
20 Assistant Dean of Academic Affairs ... Ms. Ronalyn WILSON
21 Director of Business Affairs ... Mr. Gregg WILBUR
13 Director of Information Technology ... Mr. Gregg ROTH
18 Director of Facilities ... Mr. Joshua FLEMING
07 Director of Admissions ... Ms. Laura LAPORTE
06 Registrar ... Mr. Scott COLLINS
08 Librarian ... Ms. Mary DONOHUE
36 Director of Career Planning ... Ms. Andrea SCRIBNER
38 Director Advisement/Counseling/Test ... Ms. Mary-Jo FERRAUILO-DAVIS
30 Chief Development ... Ms. Lesley LANZI
09 Director of Institutional Research ... Mr. Eric KIMMELMAN
37 Coordinator Financial Aid ... Ms. Rebecca COZZOCREA
04 Administrative Asst to President ... Ms. Paula WEAVER
108 Director Institutional Assessment ... Ms. Jacqueline SNYDER
15 Director of Human Resources ... Mr. Jason RAUCH
19 Director of Public Safety ... Mr. Mark PIERCE
25 Director of Grants ... Ms. Jean KARUTIS
26 Coordinator Public Relations ... Ms. Amy RADIK
39 Director Student Housing ... Ms. Christine SMITH
41 Athletic Director ... Mr. Kevin JONES
90 IT Infrastructure Administrator ... Mr. William BONNER
91 Associate Director of IT ... Mr. Paul PUTMAN

General Theological Seminary (B)

440 West 21st Street, New York NY 10011-2981

County: New York — FICE Identification: 002726 — Unit ID: 191320
Telephone: (212) 243-5150 — Carnegie Class: Spec-4-yr-Faith
FAX Number: (212) 727-3907 — Calendar System: Semester
URL: www.gts.edu
Established: 1817 — Annual Graduate Tuition & Fees: N/A
Enrollment: 76 — Coed
Affiliation or Control: Protestant Episcopal — IRS Status: 501(c)3
Highest Offering: Doctorate; No Undergraduates
Accreditation: THEOL

01 President and Dean ... Rev. Kurt DUNKLE
11 Vice President of Operations ... Mr. Anthony KHANI
30 VP for Institutional Advancement ... Ms. Donna ASHLEY
05 VP & Dean of Academic Affairs ... Dr. Michael DELASHMUTT
08 Head Librarian ... Vacant
26 Director of Communications ... Mr. Chad RANCOURT
06 Registrar ... Ms. Stacie WARING
04 Exec Asst to the President & Dean ... Ms. Kim ROBEY
15 Director of HR ... Ms. Trecia O'SULLIVAN
10 Controller ... Mr. Robert ELLIOT
30 Director of Development ... Mr. Jonathan SILVER

Genesee Community College (C)

One College Road, Batavia NY 14020-9704

County: Genesee — FICE Identification: 006782 — Unit ID: 191339
Telephone: (585) 343-0055 — Carnegie Class: Assoc/HT-Mix Trad/Non
FAX Number: (585) 343-4541 — Calendar System: Semester
URL: www.genesee.edu
Established: 1966 — Annual Undergrad Tuition & Fees (In-District): $4,410
Enrollment: 6,876 — Coed
Affiliation or Control: State/Local — IRS Status: 501(c)3
Highest Offering: Associate Degree
Accreditation: M, ADNUR, COARC, POLYT, PTAA

01 President ... Dr. James SUNSER
05 Provost/Exec VP Academic Affairs ... Dr. Kathleen SCHIEFEN
81 Dean Math/Science/Career Education ... Dr. Rafael ALICEA-MALDONADO
83 Dean Human Communication/Behavior ... Dr. Katharina E. KOVACH-ALLEN
56 Dean of Distributed Learning ... Dr. Craig LAMB
20 Asc Dean Accelerated Col Enrol Pgms ... Mr. Edward LEVINSTEIN
06 Registrar ... Mr. Terrence REDING
57 Director Fine & Performing Arts ... Ms. Maryanne ARENA
68 Director of Health & Physical Educ ... Ms. Rebecca DZIEKAN
45 Exec VP for Planning/Inst Effectiv ... Mr. William T. EMM
09 Assoc VP Inst Rsrch & Assessment ... Ms. Carol MARRIOTT
15 Assoc VP for Human Resources ... Ms. Gina WEAVER
25 Director of Grants Services ... Mr. James DONSBACH
103 Exec Dir for Workforce Development ... Mr. Reid SMALLEY
88 Director Business Skills Training ... Mr. John MCGOWAN
10 Vice Pres for Finance & Operations ... Mr. Kevin HAMILTON
21 Controller ... Ms. Kristin L. YUNKER
13 Director of Computer Services ... Ms. Cindy DELMAR
18 Director of Buildings & Grounds ... Mr. Timothy M. LANDERS
32 VP for Student & Enrollment Svcs ... Dr. Virginia TAYLOR
35 Assoc Dean for Student Development ... Dr. Margaret HEATER
35 Dean of Students ... Ms. Jennifer M. NEWELL
07 Director of Admissions ... Ms. Tanya LANE-MARTIN
37 Director of Financial Aid ... Mr. Joseph A. BAILEY
88 Director of Student Activities ... Mr. Clifford M. SCUTELLA
41 Director of Athletics ... Ms. Kristen SCHUTH
30 Director Devel & External Affairs ... Mr. Richard G. ENSMAN, JR.
90 Manager of Academic Computing ... Mrs. Mary Jane HEIDER
04 Administrative Asst to President ... Ms. Cathy COSTELLO

Hamilton College (D)

198 College Hill Road, Clinton NY 13323-1218

County: Oneida — FICE Identification: 002728 — Unit ID: 191515
Telephone: (315) 859-4011 — Carnegie Class: Bac-A&S
FAX Number: (315) 859-4991 — Calendar System: Semester
URL: www.hamilton.edu
Established: 1812 — Annual Undergrad Tuition & Fees: $49,500
Enrollment: 1,904 — Coed
Affiliation or Control: Independent Non-Profit — IRS Status: 501(c)3
Highest Offering: Baccalaureate
Accreditation: M

01 President ... David WIPPMAN
05 VPAA/Dean of Faculty ... Margaret GENTRY
11 Vice Pres Administration/Finance ... Karen L. LEACH
30 Vice Pres Communication/Development ... Lori R. DENNISON
13 Vice Pres Information Technology ... David L. SMALLEN
07 VP/Dean Admission & Financial Aid ... Monica C. INZER
32 Vice Pres/Dean of Students ... Nancy R. THOMPSON
20 Associate Dean of Faculty ... Samuel PELLMAN
41 Athletic Director ... Jonathan T. HIND
39 Director Residential Life ... Travis R. HILL
10 Controller ... Shari K. WHITING
08 Dir of Library/Info Technology ... David L. SMALLEN
27 Director Strategic Communications ... Stacey J. HIMMELBERGER
37 Director of Financial Aid ... K. Cameron FEIST
36 Int Exec Director Career Center ... Sam WELCH
06 Registrar ... Kristin M. FRIEDEL
15 Director of Human Resources ... Stephen STEMKOSKI
23 Medical Dir Student Health Services ... Vacant
18 Director Physical Plant ... Steven J. BELLONA
19 Director of Campus Safety ... Francis A. MANFREDO
38 Director Counseling/Psych Services ... David WALDEN
42 Newman Chaplain ... John CROGHAN
24 Director Audiovisual Services ... Timothy J. HICKS
09 Director of Institutional Research ... Gordon J. HEWITT
26 Exec Director of Communications ... Michael J. DEBRAGGIO
28 Chief Diversity Officer ... Phyllis BRELAND
29 Director Alumni Relations ... Sharon T. RIPPEY
96 Director of Purchasing ... Irene K. CORNISH
40 Manager College Store ... Jennifer PHILLIPS

Hartwick College (E)

One Hartwick Drive, Oneonta NY 13820-4020

County: Otsego — FICE Identification: 002729 — Unit ID: 191533
Telephone: (607) 431-4000 — Carnegie Class: Bac-A&S
FAX Number: (607) 431-4206 — Calendar System: 4/1/4
URL: www.hartwick.edu
Established: 1797 — Annual Undergrad Tuition & Fees: $41,440
Enrollment: 1,540 — Coed
Affiliation or Control: Independent Non-Profit — IRS Status: 501(c)3
Highest Offering: Baccalaureate
Accreditation: M, ART, MUS, NURSE, TEAC

01 President ... Dr. Margaret L. DRUGOVICH
05 Executive Vice President & Provost ... Dr. Michael TANNENBAUM
10 Vice President Finance/CFO ... Mr. George J. ELSBECK
30 Vice Pres Institutional Advancement ... Mr. Gregg FORT
32 Vice President for Student Life ... Dr. Meg NOWAK
84 Vice Pres for Enrollment Management ... Ms. Karen MCGRATH
04 Senior Assistant to the President ... Ms. Kerri GREEN
15 Director Human Resources ... Ms. Suzanne JANITZ
39 Director Residence Life ... Mr. Zachary BROWN
06 Registrar ... Mr. Matthew SANFORD
20 Dean of Academic Affairs ... Dr. Kellie BEAN
37 Director of Financial Aid ... Ms. Melissa ALLEN
08 Director of Libraries ... Mr. F. Paul COLEMAN
85 Director International Pgms ... Dr. Godlove FONJWENG
13 Director Inst Info Systems Services ... Ms. Deb B. HILTS
91 Director Technologies Services ... Ms. Suzanne GAYNOR
18 Director of Facilities Services ... Mr. Joseph MACK
41 Director of Athletics ... Dr. Kimberly FIERKE
38 Director of Counseling Services ... Mr. Gary ROBINSON
23 Director of Student Health Center ... Vacant
27 Marketing Communications Manager ... Mr. Christopher LOTT
26 Exec Dir of Donor & Alumni Rels ... Ms. Alicia FISH
07 Director Admissions ... Ms. Lisa STARKEY-WOODS
12 Interim Director Pine Lake Campus ... Ms. Erin TOAL
21 Director Financial Svcs/Controller ... Ms. Karen ZUILL
09 Director of Institutional Research ... Ms. Amanda Kay MOSKE
29 Director of Alumni Engagement ... Vacant
19 Director of Campus Safety ... Mr. Thomas KELLY
40 Manager of B&N Bookstore ... Mr. Frank WERDANN
96 Manager of Purchasing ... Vacant
102 Dir Foundation/Corporate Relations ... Ms. Margaret ARTHURS
105 Director Web Services ... Ms. Stephanie BRUNETTA
108 Dean of Assessment ... Dr. Kimberly YOUSNEY-ELSENER

Hebrew Union College-Jewish Institute of Religion (F)

1 West 4th Street, New York NY 10012-1186

County: New York — FICE Identification: 004054 — Unit ID: 203067
Telephone: (212) 674-5300 — Carnegie Class: Spec-4-yr-Faith
FAX Number: (212) 388-1720 — Calendar System: Semester
URL: www.huc.edu
Established: 1875 — Annual Graduate Tuition & Fees: N/A
Enrollment: 346 — Coed
Affiliation or Control: Jewish — IRS Status: 501(c)3
Highest Offering: Doctorate; No Undergraduates
Accreditation: M

01 President ... Rabbi Aaron PANKEN
30 Vice President Inst Advancement ... Dr. Lissie DIRINGER
10 Chief Financial Officer ... Ms. Sandra M. MILLS
05 Vice Pres Academic Affairs/Provost ... Rabbi Michael MARMUR
101 Admin Exec to Board of Governors ... Ms. Sylvia POSNER
26 AVP National Dir Public Affs/Comm ... Ms. Jean B. ROSENSAFT
44 Natl Dir of Institutional Giving ... Dr. Andrew GRANT
08 Director of Libraries ... Dr. David GILNER
79 Director American Jewish Archives ... Dr. Gary ZOLA
09 Manager Institutional Research ... Mr. Bobby COVITZ
06 Assistant Registrar ... Rabbi Andrew GOODMAN
13 Director of Information Systems ... Mr. John H. BRUGGEMAN
15 Director of Legal Affairs & HR ... Mr. Jeremy PERLIN
07 Director of Admissions ... Rabbi Rachel SABATH BEIT-HALACHMI
37 Director of Financial Aid ... Ms. Roseanne ACKERLEY

Helene Fuld College of Nursing (G)

24 East 120th Street, New York NY 10035

County: New York — FICE Identification: 010153 — Unit ID: 191597
Telephone: (212) 616-7200 — Carnegie Class: Spec-4-yr-Other Health
FAX Number: (212) 616-7299 — Calendar System: Quarter
URL: www.helenefuld.edu
Established: 1945 — Annual Undergrad Tuition & Fees: $18,764
Enrollment: 444 — Coed
Affiliation or Control: Independent Non-Profit — IRS Status: 501(c)3
Highest Offering: Baccalaureate
Accreditation: M, ADNUR, NURSE

01 President ... Dr. Wendy ROBINSON
05 Vice President for Academic Affairs ... Dr. Cynthia HUGHES
10 Head of Finance ... Mrs. Galina VILKINA
11 Director of Administration ... Ms. Celeste WALLIN
32 Director of Student Services ... Mrs. Sandra SENIOR
08 Director of Library & IT ... Mr. Indrajeet SINGH CHAUHAN
35 Assoc Director of Student Services ... Ms. Gladys PINEDA
26 Director of External Affairs ... Ms. Michelle HERNANDEZ
30 Development Officer ... Ms. Barbara PAXON
88 Director of BSN program ... Dr. Wendy ROBINSON
20 Director of Associate Program ... Ms. Heather LASHLEY
37 Financial Aid Counselor ... Ms. Andrine THOMAS
15 Human Resources Generalist ... Ms. Kimberly LIPSCOMB
09 Institutional Researcher ... Mr. Robert RAWLINS
38 College Counselor ... Ms. Dana GOLIN
88 Executive Assistant ... Ms. Kadia DARBY
13 Information Technology/Library Asst ... Mr. Eickel ORTIZ
07 College Recruiter ... Ms. Alphonsa ITTOOP
29 Director Alumni Relations ... Ms. Barbara PAXTON

Herkimer County Community College (A)

100 Reservoir Road, Herkimer NY 13350-1598

County: Herkimer FICE Identification: 004788
Unit ID: 191612
Telephone: (315) 574-3997 Carnegie Class: Assoc/HT-High Non
FAX Number: (315) 866-7253 Calendar System: Semester
URL: www.herkimer.edu
Established: 1966 Annual Undergrad Tuition & Fees (In-District): $4,590
Enrollment: 3,259 Coed
Affiliation or Control: State/Local IRS Status: 501(c)3
Highest Offering: Associate Degree
Accreditation: M, EMT, PTAA

01 President ..... Dr. Cathleen C. MCCOLGIN
10 Sr VP for Admin & Finance ..... Mr. Nicholas LAINO
05 Provost ..... Mr. Michael ORIOLO
32 Dean of Students ..... Dr. Matthew HAWES
20 Associate Dean Academic Affairs BH ..... Mr. Alan CRONAUER
13 Exec Director Information Services ..... Mrs. AnneMarie AMBROSE
07 Sr Admissions Asst ..... Ms. Rebecca KOHLER
83 Assoc Dean Academic Affairs Soc Sci ..... Dr. Robin VOETTERL RIECKER
20 Assoc Dean of Academic Affairs ..... Mrs. Linda LAMB
15 Director of Human Resources ..... Mr. James SALAMY
41 Director of Athletics ..... Mr. Donald DUTCHER
08 Director of Library Services ..... Mr. Alfred BEROWSKI
09 Director Institutional Research ..... Ms. Karen AYOUCH
100 Assistant to the President ..... Mr. Daniel SARGENT
18 Director Facilities Operations ..... Mr. Robert WOUDENBERG
37 Director Student Financial Aid ..... Mrs. Susan TRIPP
26 Director of Public Relations ..... Ms. Rebecca RUFFING
06 Asst Dean of Academic Affairs ..... Mr. Eric VERNOLD
36 Career Services Counselor ..... Mrs. Suzanne PADDOCK
40 Bookstore Manager ..... Ms. Krista MEZIK
96 Purchasing Agent ..... Mr. Robert NEARY
102 Dir Foundation/Corporate Relations ..... Mr. Robert FOWLER
19 Director of Campus Safety ..... Mr. Timothy ROGERS
39 Director Residence Life ..... Mr. Jason RATHBUN
84 Dean of Enrollment Management ..... Ms. Erin CRAIG

Hilbert College (B)

5200 S Park Avenue, Hamburg NY 14075-1597

County: Erie FICE Identification: 002735
Unit ID: 191621
Telephone: (716) 649-7900 Carnegie Class: Bac-Diverse
FAX Number: (716) 649-0702 Calendar System: Semester
URL: www.hilbert.edu
Established: 1957 Annual Undergrad Tuition & Fees: $20,700
Enrollment: 1,012 Coed
Affiliation or Control: Independent Non-Profit IRS Status: 501(c)3
Highest Offering: Master's
Accreditation: M

01 President ..... Dr. Cynthia A. ZANE
05 Int Provost/Vice Pres Academic Affs ..... Dr. Kristina LANTZKY-EATON
30 Vice Pres Inst Advancement ..... Ms. Kelly SMITH
10 Vice President Business/ Finance ..... Mr. Richard J. PINKOWSKI, JR.
27 Vice President Information Services ..... Mr. Michael MURRIN
84 Int VP Enrollment Mgmt/Retention ..... Mr. Larry LESICK
88 Vice Prov for Student Engagement ..... Ms. Denise HARRIS
32 VProv Leadership Dev/Dean of Stdnts ..... Mr. James P. STURM
49 Chair Arts & Sciences ..... Dr. Amy E. SMITH
26 Director Public Relations ..... Mr. Matthew HEIDT
92 Director Honors Program ..... Dr. Amy E. SMITH
39 Dir Residence Life/Judicial Affairs ..... Ms. Jill COLE
41 Athletic Director ..... Mr. John CZARNECKI
19 Director Security/Safety ..... Mr. Matthew SCHAMANN
29 Engagement Ofcr Alumni & Spec Event ..... Vacant
42 Dir Mission Intgrtn/Campus Ministry ..... Mr. Jeffrey PAPIA
08 Director of McGrath Library ..... Mr. Wilson PROUT
07 Director of Admissions ..... Mr. Jacob YALE
36 Director Placement/Career Services ..... Ms. Katie MARTOCHE
37 Director Financial Aid ..... Ms. Beverly CHUDY-SZCZUR
06 Director of Student Records ..... Ms. Caprice ARABIA
38 Director Student Counseling ..... Ms. Phyllis K. DEWEY
09 Director of Institutional Research ..... Dr. Ron ESKEW
15 Director of Human Resources ..... Ms. Maura FLYNN
28 Director of Multicultural Affairs ..... Ms. Ahyana KING
35 Director of Student Activities ..... Mr. Thomas VANE
96 Director of Purchasing ..... Mr. Gary DILLSWORTH
21 Asst Vice Pres Business/Finance ..... Mr. Anthony WIERTEL
18 Chief Facilities/Physical Plant ..... Mr. Gary DILLSWORTH
04 Administrative Asst to President ..... Ms. Kathleen FAIRBANKS

Hobart and William Smith Colleges (C)

300 Pulteney Street, Geneva NY 14456-3397

County: Ontario FICE Identification: 002731
Unit ID: 191630
Telephone: (315) 781-3000 Carnegie Class: Bac-A&S
FAX Number: (315) 781-3654 Calendar System: Semester
URL: www.hws.edu
Established: 1822 Annual Undergrad Tuition & Fees: $49,677
Enrollment: 2,425 Coordinate
Affiliation or Control: Independent Non-Profit IRS Status: 501(c)3
Highest Offering: Master's
Accreditation: M, TEAC

01 President ..... Mr. Mark D. GEARAN
05 Provost and Dean of Faculty ..... Dr. Titilayo UFOMATA
84 VP for Enrollment/Dean of Admission ..... Mr. Robert MURPHY
32 Vice President for Student Affairs ..... Mr. Robert FLOWERS
30 Vice President for Advancement ..... Mr. Robert O'CONNOR
10 Vice President for Finance/CFO ..... Ms. Carolee WHITE
13 VP for Strategic Initiatives/CIO ..... Mr. Fred DAMIANO
15 Associate VP for Human Resources ..... Ms. Sonya WILLIAMS
26 Vice President for Communications ..... Ms. Cathy WILLIAMS
33 Dean of Hobart College ..... Dr. Eugen BAER
34 Dean of William Smith College ..... Dr. Catherine GALLOUET
42 Chaplain ..... Rev. D. Maurice CHARLES
100 Chief of Staff and Council ..... Mr. Louis GUARD
04 Exec Assistant to the President ..... Ms. Valerie VISTOCCO
20 Associate Dean of Faculty ..... Dr. Dwayne LUCAS
20 Associate Provost ..... Dr. Virgina MANSFIELD-RICHARDSON
104 Associate Dean Global Education ..... Dr. Thomas D'AGOSTINO
108 Assoc Dean Teach/Learn & Assessment ..... Dr. Susan PLINER
48 Director Finger Lakes Institute ..... Dr. Lisa CLECKNER
08 Director of the Library ..... Mr. Vincent BOISSELLE
06 Registrar ..... Mr. Peter SARRATORI
09 Assoc Dean Inst Research/Retent ..... Mr. Don EMMONS
31 Dir Community Engagement ..... Ms. Kathleen FLOWERS
88 Director Academic Opportunity Pgm ..... Mr. James BURRUTO
37 Director of Financial Aid ..... Ms. Beth NEPA
07 Director of Admissions ..... Mr. John YOUNG
36 Director Center for Career Services ..... Ms. Brandi FERRARA
35 Assistant VP for Student Affairs ..... Dr. Montrose STREETER
41 Director of Hobart Athletics ..... Mr. Michael HANNA
41 Director of William Smith Athletics ..... Ms. Deborah STEWARD
38 Dir Counseling Ctr/Student Wellness ..... Dr. Shelly LEAR
23 Coordinator Health Services/NP ..... Ms. Betti GREEN
19 Director of Campus Safety ..... Mr. Martin CORBETT
88 Director of Intercultural Affairs ..... Dr. Alejandra MOLINA
85 Director of International Students ..... Mr. David GAGE
44 Associate VP for Advancement ..... Ms. Leila RICE
29 Assistant VP for Alumni Relations ..... Mr. Jared WEEDEN
29 Assistant VP for Alumnae Relations ..... Ms. Kathleen REGAN
102 Director Corp/Foundation Relations ..... Ms. Martha BOND
88 Director Advancement Services ..... Ms. Karen REUSCHER
21 Associate Controller ..... Ms. Angela FREEMAN
88 Director Conferences/Events ..... Ms. Erica COONEY-CONNOR
40 Director of the College Store ..... Ms. Lucille SMART
16 Associate Director Human Resources ..... Ms. Peggy FERRAN
88 Director of Communications ..... Ms. Mary LECLAIR
88 Director of Publications ..... Ms. Margaret KOWALIK
105 Director Web Development ..... Mr. Michael DIMAURO
88 Director Athletic Communications ..... Mr. Ken DEBOLT
88 Director Enterprise Solutions ..... Mr. Jeremy TRUMBLE
88 Director Operations & Tech Services ..... Ms. Kelly Anne MCLAUGHLIN
14 Dir Network/Systems Infrastructure ..... Mr. Derek LUSTIG
106 Director of Digital Learning ..... Ms. Juliet BOISSELLE
88 Associate Hobart Dean ..... Mr. Chip CAPRARO
88 Assistant Hobart Dean ..... Mr. David MAPSTONE
88 Associate William Smith Dean ..... Ms. Lisa KAENZIG
88 Assistant William Smith Dean ..... Ms. Valerie GUNTER
39 Asst Dean of Students/Dir Resid Edu ..... Mr. Brandon BARILE

Hofstra University (D)

Hempstead NY 11549-1000

County: Nassau FICE Identification: 002732
Unit ID: 191649
Telephone: (516) 463-6600 Carnegie Class: DU-Mod
FAX Number: (516) 463-4848 Calendar System: Semester
URL: www.hofstra.edu
Established: 1935 Annual Undergrad Tuition & Fees: $40,460
Enrollment: 10,953 Coed
Affiliation or Control: Independent Non-Profit IRS Status: 501(c)3
Highest Offering: Doctorate
Accreditation: M, ARCPA, AUD, BUS, BUSA, CAATE, CACREP, CLPSY, CORE, ENG, JOUR, LAW, MED, SCPSY, SP, TEAC

01 President ..... Mr. Stuart RABINOWITZ
05 Provost/Sr VP for Academic Affairs ..... Dr. Gail M. SIMMONS
45 Sr VP for Planning and Admin ..... Ms. M. Patricia ADAMSKI
10 VP Financial Affairs/Treasurer ..... Ms. Catherine HENNESSY
32 Vice President for Student Affairs ..... Mr. W. Houston DOUGHARTY
30 Vice President for Development ..... Mr. Alan J. KELLY
26 Vice President University Relations ..... Ms. Melissa A. CONNOLLY
43 VP Legal Affairs & General Counsel ..... Ms. Dolores FREDRICH
13 Vice Pres Information Technology ..... Mr. Robert W. JUCKIEWICZ
18 VP for Facilities and Operations ..... Mr. Joseph BARKWILL
84 Vice Pres Enrollment Management ..... Ms. Jessica L. EADS
91 Asst VP for Information Technology ..... Ms. Linda J. HANTZSCHEL
09 VP Inst Research/Admin Assess ..... Dr. Stephanie BUSHEY
20 Vice Provost for Academic Affairs ..... Dr. Cliff JERNIGAN
21 Assoc Provost Budget & Planning ..... Mr. Richard M. APOLLO
25 Assoc Provost Rsrch/Sponsored Pgms ..... Ms. Sofia KAKOULIDIS
07 VP Admissions & Financial Aid ..... Ms. Jessica L. EADS
50 Dean Zarb Sch of Business ..... Dr. Herman A. BERLINER
54 Dean School of Engineering ..... Dr. Sina Y. RABBANY
60 Dean School of Communication ..... Dr. Evan W. CORNOG
53 Dean School of Education ..... Dr. Sean A. FANELLI
49 Dean College Liberal Arts/Science ..... Dr. Bernard J. FIRESTONE
08 Acting Dean Library & Info Services ..... Dr. Bernard J. FIRESTONE
88 Dean for University Advisement ..... Ms. Anne M. MONGILLO
61 Dean of Maurice Deane School of Law ..... Mr. Eric LANE
63 Dean Medical School ..... Dr. Lawrence SMITH
66 Dean Sch/Grad Nursing & Health Prof ..... Dr. Kathleen GALLO
35 Dean of Students ..... Ms. Sofia B. PERTUZ
29 Senior Director Alumni Affairs ..... Ms. Amy R. REICH
39 Assoc Director Residential Programs ..... Ms. Novia P. WHYTE
38 Dir Student Counseling Services ..... Dr. John C. GUTHMAN
22 Equal Rights/Opportunity Ofcr ..... Ms. Jennifer MONE
23 Director Health & Wellness Center ..... Dr. Maureen B. HOUCK
41 Director Intercollegiate Athletics ..... Mr. Jeffrey HATHAWAY
15 Director of Human Resources ..... Ms. Evelyn V. MILLER-SUBER
90 Director Faculty Computing Services ..... Ms. Judith L. TABRON
40 Manager Bookstore ..... Mr. Steven BABBITT
19 Director Public Safety ..... Ms. Karen O'CALLAGHAN
96 Director of Procurement Services ..... Mr. John JAGARD
92 Dean Honors College ..... Dr. Warren FRISINA
06 Registrar ..... Ms. Lynne DOUGHERTY
04 Admin Assistant to the President ..... Ms. Isabel D. FREY
37 Director Student Financial Aid ..... Ms. Sandra MERVIUS

Holy Trinity Orthodox Seminary (E)

PO Box 36, Jordanville NY 13361-0036

County: Herkimer FICE Identification: 002733
Unit ID: 191658
Telephone: (315) 858-0945 Carnegie Class: Not Classified
FAX Number: (315) 858-0945 Calendar System: Semester
URL: www.hts.edu
Established: 1948 Annual Undergrad Tuition & Fees: N/A
Enrollment: N/A Male
Affiliation or Control: Russian Orthodox IRS Status: 501(c)3
Highest Offering: Baccalaureate
Accreditation: NY

01 Rector and Dean ..... V.Rev. Luke MURIANKA
20 Assistant Dean ..... Rev. Ephraim WILLMARTH
32 Dean of Students ..... Rev. Cyprian ALEXANDROU
06 Registrar ..... V.Rev. Theophylact CLAPPER-DEWELL
07 Director of Admissions ..... Rev. Ephraim WILLMARTH
08 Librarian ..... Mr. Michael PEREKRESTOV

Houghton College (F)

One Willard Avenue, Houghton NY 14744-0128

County: Allegany FICE Identification: 002734
Unit ID: 191676
Telephone: (585) 567-9200 Carnegie Class: Bac-A&S
FAX Number: (585) 567-9572 Calendar System: Semester
URL: www.houghton.edu
Established: 1883 Annual Undergrad Tuition & Fees: $29,458
Enrollment: 1,073 Coed
Affiliation or Control: Wesleyan Church IRS Status: 501(c)3
Highest Offering: Master's
Accreditation: M, MUS, TEAC

01 President ..... Dr. Shirley A. MULLEN
05 Vice President for Academic Affairs ..... Dr. Jack CONNELL
32 Vice President for Student Life ..... Mr. Robert POOL
10 Vice President for Finance and Plng ..... Mr. David SMITH
30 Vice President for Advancement ..... Mr. Karl SISSON
84 Vice President for Enrollment ..... Vacant
04 Dir of Operations Ofc of the Pres ..... Ms. Cindy LASTORIA
06 Registrar ..... Mr. Kevin KETTINGER
37 Director of Financial Aid ..... Ms. Marianne LOPER
08 Director of the Library ..... Mr. David STEVICK
29 Dir Alumni & Community Relations ..... Ms. Phyllis GAERTE
42 Dean of the Chapel ..... Dr. Michael JORDAN
09 Assoc Dean Institutional Research ..... Dr. John WISE
36 Director of VOCA ..... Ms. Kim POOL
15 Director of Human Resources ..... Mr. Dale F. WRIGHT
26 Dir Marketing & Communications ..... Mr. Jeff BABBITT
13 Director of Technology ..... Mr. Donald HAINGRAY
18 Director of Facilities ..... Mr. Chad PLYMALE
19 Chief Security Officer ..... Mr. Ray M. PARLETT
23 Director of Health Services ..... Dr. David BRUBAKER
41 Executive Director of Athletics ..... Mr. Harold W. LORD
21 Controller ..... Ms. Danae FORREST
39 Director Residence Life ..... Mr. Marc SMITHERS
38 Director Counseling Services ..... Dr. William BURRICHTER
92 Director of Honors Program ..... Dr. Benjamin LIPSCOMB

Hudson Valley Community College (G)

80 Vandenburgh Avenue, Troy NY 12180-6096

County: Rensselaer FICE Identification: 002868
Unit ID: 191719
Telephone: (518) 629-4822 Carnegie Class: Assoc/MT-VT-Mix Trad/Non
FAX Number: (518) 629-4576 Calendar System: Semester
URL: www.hvcc.edu
Established: 1953 Annual Undergrad Tuition & Fees (In-District): $5,188
Enrollment: 12,177 Coed
Affiliation or Control: State/Local IRS Status: 501(c)3
Highest Offering: Associate Degree
Accreditation: M, ADNUR, COARC, DH, DMS, EMT, ENGT, FUSER, POLYT

01 President ..... Dr. Andrew J. MATONAK
14 VP Technology/Inst Assess/Planning ..... Dr. Michael S. GREEN
04 Assistant to the President ..... Ms. Suzanne K. KALKBRENNER
11 VP for Administration ..... Mr. James J. LAGATTA
05 Vice President for Academic Affairs ..... Dr. Carolyn G. CURTIS
32 VP Enroll Mgmt/Student Development ..... Dr. Alexander J. POPOVICS
10 Vice President for Finance ..... Mr. Joel R. FATATO
49 Dean School of Liberal Arts ..... Vacant
72 Dean Engr/Indus Tech/Business ..... Mr. P. Phillip WHITE

107 Dean Cmty/Professional Pgms ....Ms. Christine A. HELWIG
76 Int Dean School of Health Sciences ....Dr. Carol BOSCO
08 Dir of Learning Resources Center ....Vacant
07 Director of Admissions ....Ms. Mary Claire BAUER
06 Registrar ....Ms. Kathleen PETLEY
13 Chief Information Officer ....Mr. Jonathan BRENNAN
18 Director Physical Plant ....Mr. Richard EDWARDS
38 Exec Dir Student Development ....Dr. Kathleen SWEENER
37 Director of Financial Aid ....Ms. Lisa VAN WIE
36 Dir Center For Careers & Transfer ....Ms. Gayle HEALY
15 Director of Human Resources ....Mr. John TIBBETTS
19 Director of Public Safety ....Mr. Fred ALIBERTI
23 Coordinator Health Services ....Ms. Claudine POTVIN-GIORDANO
22 Director of Disability Resources ....Ms. Deanne MARTOCCI
09 Director Planning & Research ....Mr. James F. MACKLIN
35 Director of Student Life ....Mr. Louis COPLIN
85 International Student Advisor ....Dr. Jay DEITCHMAN
40 Director of Bookstore ....Mr. Stephen J. STEGMAN
41 Director of Athletics ....Ms. Kristan M. PELLETIER
72 Interim Asst to VP of Academics ....Dr. David C. CLICKNER
88 Assoc Dean Instruct SuppSvcs/Reten .Ms. Karen FERRER-MUNIZ
96 Dir Business Services/Purchasing ....Ms. Patricia GASTON
21 Comptroller ....Mr. John BRAUNGARD
26 Exec Dir Communications/Marketing ....Mr. Dennis KENNEDY
102 Interim Exec Director Foundation ....Ms. Regina LAGATTA
103 Assoc Dean Workforce Development . Mr. Richard E. BENNETT, II
25 Director of Grants ....Ms. Cheryl L. BEAUCHAMP
29 Dir of Development/Donor Relations ....Mr. Geoffrey N. MILLER
88 Scholarship & Operations Coord ....Ms. Kimberly G. BERRY
106 Director of Distance Learning ....Ms. Susan P. GALLAGHER
108 Dean Institutional Assessment ....Dr. Margaret GEEHAN

Icahn School of Medicine at Mount Sinai (A)

One Gustave L. Levy Place, New York NY 10029-6500
County: New York FICE Identification: 007026
Unit ID: 193405
Telephone: (212) 241-6500 Carnegie Class: Spec-4-yr-Med
FAX Number: (212) 241-7146 Calendar System: Other
URL: www.icahn.mssm.edu
Established: 1963 Annual Graduate Tuition & Fees: N/A
Enrollment: 1,074 Coed
Affiliation or Control: Independent Non-Profit IRS Status: 501(c)3
Highest Offering: Doctorate; No Undergraduates
Accreditation: M, DENT, IPSY, MED, PH

01 President & CEO ....Dr. Kenneth L. DAVIS
05 Exec Vice Pres/Dean Sch of Medicine ....Dr. Dennis S. CHARNEY
63 Dean for Medical Education ....Dr. David MULLER
11 Dean for Operations ....Mr. Jeffrey SILBERSTEIN
04 Administrative Asst to President ....Ms. JoAnn L. FINK
10 Chief Business Officer ....Mr. Stephen HARVEY
28 Director of Diversity ....Dr. Gary BUTTS
90 Director Academic Computing ....Mr. Paul LAWRENCE

Iona College (B)

715 North Avenue, New Rochelle NY 10801-1890
County: Westchester FICE Identification: 002737
Unit ID: 191931
Telephone: (914) 633-2000 Carnegie Class: Masters/L
FAX Number: (914) 633-2642 Calendar System: Semester
URL: www.iona.edu
Established: 1940 Annual Undergrad Tuition & Fees: $35,324
Enrollment: 3,909 Coed
Affiliation or Control: Independent Non-Profit IRS Status: 501(c)3
Highest Offering: Master's
Accreditation: M, BUS, CS, JOUR, MFCD, @SP, SW, TED

01 President ....Dr. Joseph E. NYRE
05 Provost/Sr VP Academic Affairs ....Dr. Vincent CALLUZZO
10 Sr Vice President Finance & Admin ....Ms. Anne Marie SCHETTINI-LYNCH
30 Sr VP Advance/External Affairs ....Mr. Paul J. SUTERA
100 Chief of Staff and Board Secretary ....Ms. MaryEllen CALLAGHAN
84 VP Enrollment Management ....Ms. Mary Beth CAREY
13 Vice Provost Info Technology/CIO ....Ms. Joanne STEELE
32 Vice Provost Student Life ....Ms. Denise HOPKINS-POSELLE
37 Asst VP Student Financial Services ....Ms. Eileen DOYLE
91 Asst Vice Provost for Info Tech ....Mr. Dimitris HALARIS
20 Assistant VP Academic Affairs ....Dr. Michael JORDAN
35 Asst Vice Provost Student Devel ....Ms. Elizabeth OLIVIERI-LENAHAN
49 Dean School Arts & Sciences ....Dr. Sibdas GHOSH
50 Dean Hagan School of Business ....Vacant
43 General Counsel ....Ms. Kathleen MCELROY
18 Director of Facilities Management ....Mr. Richard MURRAY
39 Director Residential Life ....Mr. Michael LABELLA
15 Director of Human Resources ....Ms. Tracey WILMOT
38 Director of Counseling Center ....Dr. Brielle STARK-ADLER
36 Director of Career Development ....Ms. F. Phyllis BLAKE
08 Director of Libraries ....Mr. Richard PALLADINO
42 Director of Campus Ministries ....Mr. Carl PROCARIO-FOLEY
06 Registrar ....Ms. Brooke ANDERSEN
41 Director of Athletics ....Mr. Richard COLE, JR.
86 Director of Govt Relations/Grants ....Mr. Daniel KONOPKA
12 Co-Director of Rockland Campus ....Ms. Mary Beth CAREY
12 Co-Director of Rockland Campus ....Dr. Vincent CALLUZZO
09 Dir of Inst Effectiveness/Planning ....Mr. Jason DIFFENDERFER
21 Director of Business Services ....Ms. Nancy MORANO
26 Director of Public Relations ....Ms. Dawn INSANALLI

19 Dir Campus Safety and Security ....Mr. Dominic LOCATELLI
23 Director of Health Services . Ms. Jacqueline AGNELLO-VAZQUEZ
44 Director of Annual Giving ....Ms. Kara BRENNAN
96 Purchasing Coordinator ....Ms. Kimberly MONTEMURRO
92 Director of Honors Program ....Dr. Kim PAFFENROTH
07 Director of Graduate Admissions ....Vacant
04 Administrative Asst to President ....Ms. Rochelle PATRICK

Island Drafting and Technical Institute (C)

128 Broadway, Amityville NY 11701-2704
County: Suffolk FICE Identification: 007375
Unit ID: 191959
Telephone: (631) 691-8733 Carnegie Class: Spec 2-yr-Tech
FAX Number: (631) 691-8738 Calendar System: Semester
URL: www.idti.edu
Established: 1957 Annual Undergrad Tuition & Fees: $16,200
Enrollment: 110 Coed
Affiliation or Control: Proprietary IRS Status: Proprietary
Highest Offering: Associate Degree
Accreditation: ACCSC

01 President ....Mr. James G. DI LIBERTO
03 Vice President ....Mr. John G. DI LIBERTO
05 Dean ....Ms. Patricia HAUSFELD

Ithaca College (D)

953 Danby Road, Ithaca NY 14850-7001
County: Tompkins FICE Identification: 002739
Unit ID: 191968
Telephone: (607) 274-3011 Carnegie Class: Masters/L
FAX Number: N/A Calendar System: Semester
URL: www.ithaca.edu
Established: 1892 Annual Undergrad Tuition & Fees: $40,658
Enrollment: 6,587 Coed
Affiliation or Control: Independent Non-Profit IRS Status: 501(c)3
Highest Offering: Doctorate
Accreditation: M, BUS, CAATE, MUS, NRPA, OT, PTA, SP, TED, THEA

01 President ....Dr. Thomas R. ROCHON
04 Exec Assistant to President ....Ms. Amanda L. LIPPINCOTT
05 Provost/Vice Pres Education Affairs ....Dr. Benjamin RIFKIN
10 VP of Finance & Administration ....Mr. Gerald HECTOR
43 Senior VP & General Counsel ....Ms. Nancy E. PRINGLE
84 VP Enrollment Management ....Mr. Gerard TURBIDE
30 VP Institutional Advancement & Comm .....Mr. Christopher BIEHN
20 Asst Prov/Dean Interdis/Intl Stds ....Dr. Tanya R. SAUNDERS
26 Assoc VP Marketing/Communications .....Ms. Jennifer CAMPBELL
13 Assoc VP for Info Tech Svcs ....Mr. Keith MCINTOSH
15 VP for Human Resources ....Dr. Brian DICKENS
18 Assoc VP for Facilities Management ....Mr. Tim CAREY
32 Assoc Prov Diversity/Inclusion/Eng ....Dr. Roger RICHARDSON
20 Vice Provost ....Ms. Danette JOHNSON
49 Dean School Humanities/Sci ....Dr. Vincent WANG
64 Dean of School of Music ....Dr. Karl PAULNACK
76 Dean Sch Health Sciences/Human Perf .....Ms. Linda PETROSINO
50 Dean School of Business ....Mr. Sean REID
60 Dean School of Communications ....Ms. Diane GAYESKI
29 Executive Director Alumni Relations ....Ms. Carrie BROWN
06 Registrar ....Ms. Vikki LEVINE
09 Dir Institutional Research ....Vacant
07 Director of Admission ....Ms. Nicole EVERSLEY BRADWELL
12 Director London Center ....Ms. Thorunn LONSDALE
36 Director Career Services ....Vacant
38 Director Counseling/Health/Wellness ....Dr. Deborah HARPER
37 Dir of Student Financial Services ....Mrs. Lisa HOSKEY
39 Dir Res Life/Judicial Affairs ....Ms. Bonnie S. PRUNTY
08 College Librarian ....Ms. Lisabeth CHABOT
41 Dir Intercol Athletics/Rec Sports ....Ms. Susan BASSETT
21 Director of Budget ....Ms. Sally DIETZ
19 Director Public Safety ....Ms. Terri STEWART
27 Senior Assoc Dir for Campus Comm ....Mr. David C. MALEY
40 Manager of College Stores ....Mr. Rick WATSON
42 Coordinator of Chaplains ....Fr. Carsten P. MARTENSEN
89 Director of First Year Experience ....Ms. Erica SHOCKLEY
28 Director of Mulitcultural Affairs ....Ms. Malinda SMITH
85 Dir International Student Services ....Ms. Diana DIMITROVA
104 Director of Study Abroad ....Ms. Rachel CULLENEN
88 Dir Center for Faculty Excellence ....Mr. Wade PICKREN

Jamestown Business College (E)

7 Fairmount Avenue, Box 429, Jamestown NY 14702-0429
County: Chautauqua FICE Identification: 008495
Unit ID: 192004
Telephone: (716) 664-5100 Carnegie Class: Spec-4-yr-Bus
FAX Number: (716) 664-3144 Calendar System: Quarter
URL: www.jamestownbusinesscollege.edu
Established: 1886 Annual Undergrad Tuition & Fees: $12,300
Enrollment: 318 Coed
Affiliation or Control: Proprietary IRS Status: Proprietary
Highest Offering: Baccalaureate
Accreditation: M

01 President ....Mr. David CONKLIN
05 Dean ....Ms. Pamela REESE
06 Registrar & Assistant to the Dean ......Ms. Cynthia CARTWRIGHT
07 Director Admissions ....Ms. Brenda SALEMME
37 Director of Financial Aid ....Mrs. Diane STURZENBECKER
26 Communications ....Ms. Lauren JOHNSON

Jamestown Community College (F)

525 Falconer Street, Jamestown NY 14701
County: Chautauqua FICE Identification: 002869
Unit ID: 191986
Telephone: (716) 338-1000 Carnegie Class: Assoc/HT-Mix Trad/Non
FAX Number: (716) 338-1466 Calendar System: Semester
URL: www.sunyjcc.edu
Established: 1950 Annual Undergrad Tuition & Fees (In-District): $5,360
Enrollment: 5,065 Coed
Affiliation or Control: State/Local IRS Status: 501(c)3
Highest Offering: Associate Degree
Accreditation: M, ADNUR, OTA

01 President ....Dr. Cory L. DUCKWORTH
05 Vice Pres of Academic Affairs ....Dr. Marilyn A. ZAGORA
32 Vice Pres of Student Development ....Dr. Eileen J. GOODLING
84 VP Enrollment Mgmt/Advancement ....Mr. Kirk YOUNG
12 VP of Catt County Campus/Cont Educ ....Mr. John J. SAYEGH
11 Int Vice Pres of Administration ....Mr. Michael MARTELLO
09 Dean Research & Planning ....Ms. Barbara RUSSELL
06 Interim Registrar ....Ms. Tracy KELLY
07 Director Admission ....Ms. Wendy PRESENT
08 Library Director ....Mr. Timothy ARNOLD
37 Exec Dir Student Finance/Records ....Ms. Laurie A. VORP
15 Exec Director Human Resources ....Ms. Susan BRONSTEIN
41 Athletic Director ....Mr. Keith MARTIN
43 Legal Counsel ....Mr. Stephen ABDELLA
18 Director Facilities/Physical Plant ....Mr. David JOHNSON
04 Administrative Asst to President ....Ms. Marsha L. HERN
19 Director Security/Safety ....Ms. Denise BURBEY
30 Chief Development/Advancement ....Ms. Kristen JOHNSON
39 Director Student Housing ....Ms. Amy HADLEY

Jamestown Community College Cattaraugus County Campus (G)

260 North Union Street, PO Box 5901,
Olean NY 14760-5901
Telephone: (716) 376-7500 Identification: 770138
Accreditation: &M

† Regional accreditation is carried under the parent institution in Jamestown, NY

Jefferson Community College (H)

1220 Coffeen Street, Watertown NY 13601-1897
County: Jefferson FICE Identification: 002870
Unit ID: 192022
Telephone: (315) 786-2200 Carnegie Class: Assoc/HT-Mix Trad/Non
FAX Number: (315) 786-0158 Calendar System: Semester
URL: www.sunyjefferson.edu
Established: 1961 Annual Undergrad Tuition & Fees (In-District): $4,835
Enrollment: 3,880 Coed
Affiliation or Control: State/Local IRS Status: 501(c)3
Highest Offering: Associate Degree
Accreditation: M, ADNUR

01 President ....Dr. Carole A. MCCOY
05 Vice President Academic Affairs ....Mr. Thomas FINCH
10 Vice President Admin/Finance ....Mr. Daniel DUPEE
32 Vice Pres of Students/Enrollment ....Ms. Betsy S. PENROSE
49 Associate VP for Liberal Arts ....Ms. Jerilyn FAIRMAN
81 Associate VP for Math/Science ....Ms. Linda DITTRICH
20 Dean for Instructional Support ....Vacant
51 Dean for Continuing Education ....Mr. Terrence HARRIS
32 Dean of Students ....Vacant
04 Assistant to the President ....Ms. Karen FREEMAN
08 Library Director ....Ms. Connie HOLBERG
07 Director of Admissions ....Ms. Roseanne N. WEIR
37 Director Financial Aid ....Mr. James AMBROSE
06 Registrar ....Ms. Deborah M. ELLIOTT
88 Director Small Business Center ....Mr. Eric F. CONSTANCE
09 Director of Institutional Research ....Ms. Mary A. PERRINE
18 Chief Facilities/Physical Plant ....Mr. Bruce ALEXANDER
29 Director Alumni Relations ....Ms. Edie ROGGIE
35 Director Student Devel/Activities ....Mr. Frank DOLDO
36 Director Student Placement ....Ms. Michele D. GEFELL
38 Director Student Counseling ....Mr. Matthew LAMBERT
26 Chief Public Relations Officer ....Ms. Karen J. FREEMAN
15 Exec Dir Finance/Human Resources ....Ms. Kerry A. YOUNG
30 College Development Officer ....Vacant
31 Coordinator Community Services ....Ms. Andrea PEDRICK
13 Chief Information Officer ....Mr. James BUYEA
19 Director Security/Safety ....Mr. Wesley HISSONG
41 Athletic Director ....Mr. Jeffrey WILEY

Jewish Theological Seminary of America (I)

3080 Broadway, New York NY 10027-4649
County: New York FICE Identification: 002740
Unit ID: 192040
Telephone: (212) 678-8023 Carnegie Class: Spec-4-yr-Faith
FAX Number: (212) 678-8947 Calendar System: Semester
URL: www.jtsa.edu
Established: 1886 Annual Undergrad Tuition & Fees: $20,340
Enrollment: 405 Coed
Affiliation or Control: Independent Non-Profit IRS Status: 501(c)3
Highest Offering: Doctorate
Accreditation: M, PAST

Code	Title	Name
01	Chancellor	Dr. Arnold M. EISEN
03	Exec VC/Chief Operating Officer	Mr. Marc GARY
30	Vice Chanc/Chief Development Office	Ms. Bonnie EPSTEIN
05	Provost	Dr. Alan COOPER
10	Chief Financial Officer	Mr. Fred SCHNUR
43	General Counsel	Mr. Martin OPPENHEIMER
49	Dean List College Jewish Studies	Dr. Shuly SCHWARTZ
53	Dean Davidson School of Education	Dr. Bill ROBINSON
58	Dean The Graduate School	Dr. Shuly SCHWARTZ
64	Director Miller Cantorial School	Cantor Nancy ABRAMSON
73	Dean of Religious Leadership	Rabbi Daniel NEVINS
32	Dean of Student Life	Ms. Sara HOROWITZ
08	Librarian	Dr. David KRAEMER
15	Director of Human Resources	Ms. Diana TORRES-PETRILLI
18	Director of Operations	Mr. James ESPOSITO
13	Director Information Technology	Mr. Hal POLLENZ
26	Chief Communications Officer	Ms. Elise DOWELL
06	Registrar/Director Financial Aid	Ms. Amy HERSH
39	Director of Residence Life	Mr. Bradley MOOT
84	Director of Enrollment Management	Ms. Melissa PRESENT
35	Director of Student Life	Ms. Ruth DECALO
38	Director Student Counseling	Dr. David DAVAR
29	Director of Alumni Affairs	Mrs. Melissa FRIEDMAN
20	Associate Provost	Dr. Stephen GARFINKEL
37	Director of Financial Aid	Ms. Amy HERSH
88	Director of Community Engagement	Rabbi Julia ANDELMAN
04	Executive Asst to Chancellor	Ms. Michelle GIOVANELLO
19	Director Security/Safety	Chief Anthony VAUGHAN

The Juilliard School (A)

60 Lincoln Center Plaza, New York NY 10023-6588

County: New York — FICE Identification: 002742

Unit ID: 192110

Telephone: (212) 799-5000 — Carnegie Class: Spec-4-yr-Arts

FAX Number: (212) 724-0263 — Calendar System: Semester

URL: www.juilliard.edu

Established: 1905 — Annual Undergrad Tuition & Fees: $39,720

Enrollment: 926 — Coed

Affiliation or Control: Independent Non-Profit — IRS Status: 501(c)3

Highest Offering: Doctorate

Accreditation: M

Code	Title	Name
01	President	Dr. Joseph W. POLISI
05	Provost & Dean	Mr. Ara GUZELIMIAN
10	Vice Pres/Chief Financial Officer	Ms. Christine TODD
30	Vice Pres for Dev/Public Affairs	Ms. Elizabeth HURLEY
08	VP for Library/Info Resources	Ms. Jane GOTTLIEB
18	Vice Pres for Facilities Management	Mr. Joseph MASTRANGELO
84	Vice Pres for Enroll Mgmt/Stdnt Dev	Ms. Joan D. WARREN
88	Vice Pres for Global Initiatives	Mr. Christopher MOSSEY
43	Vice Pres Admin/General Counsel	Mr. Maurice F. EDELSON
100	Chief of Staff	Ms. Jacqueline SCHMIDT
26	Assoc VP Marketing/Communications	Ms. Alexandra DAY
88	Assoc VP for Special Projects	Ms. Tricia ROSS
32	Dean of Student Affairs	Ms. Jennifer AWE
20	Associate Dean Academic Affairs	Mr. Jose GARCIA-LEON
64	Assoc Dean/Director Music Division	Mr. Adam MEYER
64	Asst Dean/Dir of Chamber Music	Ms. Barli NUGENT
35	Asst Dean for Student Affairs	Ms. Sabrina TANBARA
57	Director Richard Rodgers Drama Div	Mr. James HOUGHTON
57	Artistic Director of Dance Division	Mr. Lawrence RHODES
88	Artistic Director of Vocal Arts	Mr. Brian ZEGER
88	Artist in Residence/Artistic Advise	Ms. Monica HUGGETT
88	Director of Performance Activities	Ms. Monica THAKKAR
88	Artistic Dir Pre-College Division	Ms. Yoheved KAPLINSKY
06	Registrar	Ms. Katherine GERTSON
07	Director Admissions/Academic Affs	Ms. Ekaterina LAWSON
15	Director of Human Resources	Ms. Caryn G. DOKTOR
38	Director of Counseling Services	Mr. William BUSE
37	Director Student Financial Aid	Ms. Tina GONZALEZ
88	Director of Juilliard Jazz	Mr. Wynton MARSALIS
96	Director of Office Services	Mr. Scott A. HOLDEN
36	Director Career Services	Mr. Barrett HIPES
13	Chief Technology Officer	Mr. Tunde GIWA

Kehilath Yakov Rabbinical Seminary (B)

638 Bedford Avenue, Brooklyn NY 11211-8007

County: Kings — FICE Identification: 010549

Unit ID: 192165

Telephone: (718) 963-1212 — Carnegie Class: Spec-4-yr-Faith

FAX Number: (718) 387-8586 — Calendar System: Semester

Established: 1948 — Annual Undergrad Tuition & Fees: $9,400

Enrollment: 125 — Male

Affiliation or Control: Independent Non-Profit — IRS Status: 501(c)3

Highest Offering: First Talmudic Degree

Accreditation: RABN

Code	Title	Name
01	President	Mr. Sandor SCHWARTZ

Keuka College (C)

141 Central Avenue, Keuka Park NY 14478

County: Yates — FICE Identification: 002744

Unit ID: 192192

Telephone: (315) 279-5000 — Carnegie Class: Masters/M

FAX Number: (315) 279-5216 — Calendar System: Semester

URL: www.keuka.edu

Established: 1890 — Annual Undergrad Tuition & Fees: $28,917

Enrollment: 1,997 — Coed

Affiliation or Control: Independent Non-Profit — IRS Status: 501(c)3

Highest Offering: Master's

Accreditation: M, IACBE, NURSE, OT, SW, TEAC

Code	Title	Name
01	President	Dr. Jorge L. DIAZ-HERRERA
05	Provost/VP for Academic Affairs	Dr. Paul FORESTELL
10	VP for Finance/Administration	Mr. Jerry HILLER
30	VP for Advancement/External Affs	Ms. Amy STOREY
84	VP for Enroll Mgmt/Student Devel	Mr. Mark PETRIE
20	Assoc Provost for Acad Innovation	Dr. Timothy SELLERS
36	Dean Student Engagement/Success	Ms. Elizabeth LAMBERT
08	Director of Library	Ms. Linda PARK
29	Director of Alumni/Family Relations	Ms. Kathy WAYE
20	AVP for Program Development	Dr. Vicki SMITH
37	Exec Director Financial Aid	Ms. Jennifer BATES
108	Dir of Institutional Assessment	Ms. Dorothy SCHRAMM
13	Chief Information Officer	Ms. Andrea CAMPBELL
18	Director of Facilities	Mr. Tony TUFANO
21	Controller	Ms. Carol N. GROVER
19	Director of Campus Safety	Mr. James CUNNINGHAM
23	Coordinator of Health Services	Ms. Cindy CHRISTIE
38	Director of Counseling Services	Ms. Mary MARTINI-HAUSNER
32	AVP for Student Devel/Dean Stdnts	Dr. Tracy MCFARLAND
07	Director of Admissions on Campus	Ms. Megan PERKINS
41	Director of Athletics	Mr. David M. SWEET
107	AVP Center for Professional Studies	Dr. Anne KILLEN
42	College Chaplain	Mr. Eric DETAR
06	Registrar	Mr. Carl DICKINSON
44	Sr Director of Advancement	Ms. Ann TURNER
26	Sr Dir of Marketing/Communications	Mr. Pete BEKISZ
96	Purchasing Liaison	Ms. Brenda DEUCK
15	Director of Human Resources	Ms. Michelle POLOWCHAK
76	Div Chair Occupational Therapy	Dr. Dianne TRICKEY-ROKENBROD
83	Div Chair Basic Soc & Applied Sci	Dr. Tom TREMER
50	Div Chair Business & Management	Ms. Ann TUTTLE
53	Div Chair Ed & Dir Ed Grad Studies	Dr. Patricia PULVER
79	Div Chair Humanities/Fine Arts	Dr. Jennie JOINER
81	Div Chair Natural Sciences/Math	Dr. Mark SUGALSKI
66	Div Chair Nursing	Dr. Debra GATES
70	Div Chair Social Work	Dr. Ed SILVERMAN

The King's College (D)

56 Broadway, New York NY 10004-1613

County: New York — FICE Identification: 040953

Unit ID: 454184

Telephone: (212) 659-7200 — Carnegie Class: Bac-A&S

FAX Number: (212) 659-7210 — Calendar System: Semester

URL: www.tkc.edu

Established: 1938 — Annual Undergrad Tuition & Fees: $33,270

Enrollment: 487 — Coed

Affiliation or Control: Independent Non-Profit — IRS Status: 501(c)3

Highest Offering: Baccalaureate

Accreditation: M

Code	Title	Name
00	Chairman of the Board of Trustees	Mr. William Lee HANLEY
01	President	Dr. Gregory A. THORNBURY
07	Vice Pres Admissions/Advancement	Dr. Kimberly THORNBURY
32	Vice President Student Development	Mr. Eric BENNETT
05	Vice President for Academic Affairs	Dr. Mark HIJLEH
35	Dean of Students	Mr. David LEEDY
10	Vice President Finance/CFO	Mr. Frank TORINO
21	Controller	Ms. Judy BARRINGER
06	Registrar	Mr. Paul MIDDLEKAUFF
37	Director of Financial Services	Ms. Anna PETERS
04	Exectutive Asst to President	Ms. Bre DUFFY
09	Director of Institutional Research	Dr. Kimberly THORNBURY
11	Chief Administration Officer	Mr. Kevin BROWN
15	Director Personnel Services	Ms. Melody GARCIA
18	Chief Facilities/Physical Plant	Mr. Rich SWITZER
26	Chief Public Relations Officer	Ms. Natalie NAKAMURA
29	Acting Director of Alumni Relations	Dr. Kimberly THORNBURY
36	Director Student Placement	Ms. Bethany JENKINS
38	Director Student Counseling	Ms. Eileen HAWKINS
84	Director Enrollment Management	Mr. Luke SMITH
08	Head Librarian	Ms. Christina ROGERS
39	Director Student Housing	Mr. Nick SWEDICK
41	Athletic Director	Mr. Sean HORAN

Le Moyne College (E)

1419 Salt Springs Road, Syracuse NY 13214-1301

County: Onondaga — FICE Identification: 002748

Unit ID: 192323

Telephone: (315) 445-4100 — Carnegie Class: Masters/L

FAX Number: (315) 445-4540 — Calendar System: Semester

URL: www.lemoyne.edu

Established: 1946 — Annual Undergrad Tuition & Fees: $32,250

Enrollment: 3,381 — Coed

Affiliation or Control: Independent Non-Profit — IRS Status: 501(c)3

Highest Offering: Master's

Accreditation: M, ARCPA, BUS, NURSE, TEAC

Code	Title	Name
01	President	Dr. Linda M. LEMURA
05	Provost & VP Acad Affairs	Rev. Joseph MARINA
10	Senior VP Fin & Admin & Treasurer	Mr. Roger W. STACKPOOLE
30	Vice Pres Inst Advancement	Mr. Bill BROWER
32	Vice Pres Student Development	Dr. Deborah M. CADY MELZER
88	Special Asst for Mission & Identity	Rev. David C. MCCALLUM, SJ
88	Rector of the Jesuit Community	Rev. John P. BUCKI, SJ
49	Dean of Arts & Sciences	Dr. Kathleen P. COSTELLO-SULLIVAN
50	Dean School of Business	Mr. James E. JOSEPH
58	Dean of Graduate & Prof Studies	Dr. Dennis R. DEPERRO
20	Assoc Provost	Dr. Mary K. COLLINS
21	Assoc VP for Finance & Controller	Mr. Brian M. LOUCY
15	Asst VP for HR and Org Dev	Ms. Karin BOTTO
41	Asst VP & Director of Athletics	Mr. Matthew D. BASSETT
18	Asst VP Facilities Mgmt & Planning	Mr. Jed S. SCHNEIDER
26	Assoc VP for Marketing	Mr. Peter S. KILLIAN
37	Int Asst VP for Enrollment Mngt	Mr. William C. CHEETHAM
35	Dean of Students	Ms. Anne E. KEARNEY
35	Asst Dean for Student Development	Mr. Mark G. GODLESKI
88	Asst Dean for Academic Advising	Ms. Allison FARRELL
88	Asst Dean/Dir CSTEP & STEP	Ms. Darshini ROOPNARINE
88	Sr Dir Enrollment Management	Ms. Kristen P. TRAPASSO
07	Senior Director of Admission	Ms. Mary CHANDLER
51	Director of Continuing Education	Ms. Patricia J. BLISS
84	Chief Enrollment Strategist	Mr. Don SALEH
88	Dir of Transfer Admission	Mr. Scott SETEK
16	Director of Human Resources	Mr. Tim BARRETT
13	Director of Info Technology	Mr. Shaun C. BLACK
09	Director of Institutional Research	Dr. Daniel L. SKIDMORE
22	EEO/Affirmative Action Officer	Mr. Tim BARRETT
06	Registrar/Sr Director Enrollment	Ms. Cynthia A. ALIBRANDI
08	Director of the Library	Dr. Robert C. JOHNSTON
42	Director of Campus Ministry	Rev. John P. BUCKI, SJ
27	Director of Communications	Mr. Joseph B. DELLA POSTA
88	Director Campus Life & Leadership	Mr. John R. HALEY
19	Director of Security	Mr. Mark J. PETTERELLI
88	Senior Dir Leadership Giving	Ms. Kimberly B. MCAULIFF
39	Dir of Campus Life & Leadership	Mr. John HALEY
36	Director Career Advising/Devpment	Vacant
04	Assistant to the President	Ms. Carly J. COLBERT
28	Asst to the Provost for Diversity	Mr. Ludger VIEFHUES-BAILEY
44	Sr Dir Annual Giving/Stewardship	Ms. Katherine COGSWELL
86	Director Govt/Foundation Relations	Mr. Steven W. KULICK
88	Senior Philanthropic Advisor	Mr. Philip J. GEORGE
88	Director of Advancement Services	Mr. Paul F. LYNCH
29	Dir of Alumni Engagement	Ms. Kasha GODLESKI
23	Dir Wellness Ctr for Health & Couns	Ms. Maria RANDAZZO
88	Int Director of HEOP and AHANA	Ms. Lynnell CABEZAS
40	Bookstore Manager	Ms. Jessica L. MANNINO

LIM College (F)

12 E 53rd Street, New York NY 10022-5268

County: New York — FICE Identification: 007466

Unit ID: 192271

Telephone: (212) 752-1530 — Carnegie Class: Spec-4-yr-Bus

FAX Number: (212) 832-6109 — Calendar System: Semester

URL: www.limcollege.edu

Established: 1939 — Annual Undergrad Tuition & Fees: $24,825

Enrollment: 1,737 — Coed

Affiliation or Control: Proprietary — IRS Status: Proprietary

Highest Offering: Master's

Accreditation: M, ACBSP

Code	Title	Name
01	President	Elizabeth S. MARCUSE
03	Provost & Executive Vice President	Christopher J. CYPHERS
10	Exec VP Finance & Operations/Treas	Michael T. DONOHUE
00	President Emeritus	Adrian G. MARCUSE
04	Special Assistant to the President	Linda HARRIS PAOLILLO
88	Special Asst to the Provost & EVP	Thomas MCDONALD
04	Assistant to the President	Ann M. GONG
05	Dean of Academic Affairs	Michael P. LONDRIGAN
58	Dean of Graduate Studies	Jacqueline M. JENKINS
20	Assoc Dean of Academic Affairs	Patricia FITZMAURICE
08	Director of Library Services	Lou ACIERNO
06	College Registrar	Carolyn DISNEW
36	Sr Dir Exper Educ & Career Mgmt	Susan L. BAUER
32	VP for Student Development	Michael H. FERRY
35	Dean of Student Affairs	Michael RICHARDS
35	Assistant Dean of Student Life	Christopher CONZEN
38	Sr Dir Counseling & Wellness Svcs	Jodi N. LICHT
39	Dir of Housing & Residence Life	Jennifer K. LUCIANO
07	Dean of Admissions	Kristina ORTIZ
07	Sr Associate Director of Admissions	Anthony M. URMEY
88	Director of Online Admissions	Michael VILLANELLA
88	Asst VP for Student Success	William IMBRIALE
09	Director of Institutional Research	Nikisha WILLIAMS
21	Accounting Manager	Svetlana KANEVSKAYA
96	Purchasing Director	Eric MARTIN
88	VP Student Finance/Chief Compl Ofcr	Christopher E. BARTO
37	Sr Dir of Student Financial Svcs	Vacant
30	VP for Institutional Advancement	Gail NARDIN
88	VP for Strategic Initiatives	Pamela LINTON
26	Director of Communications	Meredith FINNIN
88	Director of College Marketing	Laura CIOFFI
105	Web Application Developer	Joshua J. HELLER
13	Chief Technology Officer	Maurice MORENCY
14	Director of Information Technology	Nelson LEON
90	Director of Instructional Tech	Joseph THOMAS
15	Dir of HR & Title IX Coordinator	Andrea L. GRANVILLE
18	Manager of Facilities	Jonathan ABREU
108	VP for Planning & Assessment	Jacqueline LEBLANC

Long Island Business Institute (G)

6500 Jericho Turnpike, Commack NY 11725

Telephone: (631) 499-7100 — Identification: 770746

Accreditation: ACICS

Long Island Business Institute (A)

136-18 39th Avenue, Flushing NY 11354
County: Queens FICE Identification: 020937
Unit ID: 192509
Telephone: (718) 939-5100 Carnegie Class: Spec 2-yr-Other
FAX Number: (718) 939-9235 Calendar System: Semester
URL: www.libi.edu
Established: 1968 Annual Undergrad Tuition & Fees: $14,279
Enrollment: 397 Coed
Affiliation or Control: Proprietary IRS Status: Proprietary
Highest Offering: Associate Degree
Accreditation: ACICS

01 President ....Ms. Monica W. FOOTE
05 Provost ....Ms. Stacey JOHNSON
12 Asst Campus Program Director ....Mr. Jonathan ABAR
11 Dean of Administration ....Vacant
37 Financial Aid Director ....Mr. Li HU
08 Librarian Commack Campus ....Ms. Terry CANAVAN
08 Librarian Flushing Campus ....Ms. Adrianna ARGUELLES

*Long Island University (B)

700 Northern Boulevard, Brookville NY 11548-1327
County: Nassau FICE Identification: 002751
Unit ID: 192457
Telephone: (516) 299-2501 Carnegie Class: N/A
FAX Number: N/A
URL: www.liu.edu

01 President ....Dr. Kimberly R. CLINE
11 COO & University Counsel ....Ms. Gale STEVENS HAYNES
30 Chief of Strategic Partnerships/Adv ....Mr. Michael GLICKMAN
05 Vice President Academic Affairs ....Dr. Jeffrey KANE
10 Vice President Finance & Treasurer ....Mr. Christopher N. FEVOLA
88 Sr Advisor & Treasurer Emerita ....Mrs. Mary M. LAI
13 VP for Information Technology & CIO ....Mr. George BAROUDI
20 Deputy VP Academic Affairs ....Dr. Lori KNAPP
32 Chief of Admin & Student Affairs ....Mr. Joseph SCHAEFER
09 Chief of IR & Effectiveness ....Mr. Andy PERSON
21 Assoc Vice Pres/Controller ....Mr. Mark SCHMOTZER
37 Assoc VP Financial Svcs/Compliance ....Mr. David MAINENTI
21 Assoc VP Finance and Budget Dir ....Mr. Kirk LENGA
14 Deputy CIO Information Systems ....Mr. Gavi NARRA
18 Assoc VP for Capital Projects ....Mr. Peter TYMUS
26 Dir Marketing/Advancement Ops ....Ms. Jennifer CARPENTER LOW
84 Assoc Dean Enrollment/Registrar ....Ms. Beth WILKOW
15 Interim Exec Dir Human Resources ....Dr. Lee KELLY
25 Executive Director of Grants ....Mr. Alan EVELYN
102 Dir Foundation Relations ....Ms. Suzanne FARRELL
105 Assistant VP of Creative Services ....Mr. Stephen HAUSLER
62 Dean of University Libraries ....Ms. Valeda DENT
96 Dir Sourcing/Procurement Svcs ....Mr. Allan HOWELL

*LIU Post (C)

720 Northern Boulevard, Brookville NY 11548-1300
County: Nassau FICE Identification: 002754
Unit ID: 192448
Telephone: (516) 299-2900 Carnegie Class: Masters/L
FAX Number: (516) 299-2137 Calendar System: Semester
URL: www.liu.edu/post
Established: 1954 Annual Undergrad Tuition & Fees: $35,546
Enrollment: 9,486 Coed
Affiliation or Control: Independent Non-Profit IRS Status: 501(c)3
Highest Offering: Doctorate
Accreditation: M, BUS, CACR

02 President ....Dr. Kimberly R. CLINE
11 Exec Dir Operations/Partnerships ....Ms. Rita LANGDON
07 Director of Freshman Admissions ....Ms. Marcelle HICKS
37 Exec Dir of Student Financial Svcs ....Ms. Joanne GRAZIANO
49 Acting Dean College Lib Arts Scienc ....Dr. Jeffrey BELNAP
66 Dean Sch Health Prof/Nursing ....Dr. Stacy GROPACK
50 Dean College of Management ....Dr. Robert VALLI
57 Actg Dean Col Arts/Comm & Design ....Dr. Christine KERR
51 Dir Hutton House Continuing Educ ....Dr. Kay SATO
32 Dean of Students/LIU Promise ....Ms. Abagail VAN VLERAH
41 Director of Athletics ....Mr. Bryan COLLINS
35 Associate Dean of Students ....Mr. Adam GROHMAN
88 Director of Campus Life ....Mr. Michael BERTHEL
18 Director of Facilities ....Mr. William KIRKER
19 Director of Public Safety ....Mr. Paul RAPESS

*LIU Brentwood (D)

Grant Campus, 1001 Crooked Hill Rd.,
Brentwood NY 11717
Telephone: (631) 287-8500 Identification: 666076
Accreditation: &M

† Regional accreditation is carried under the parent institution in Brookville, NY

*LIU Brooklyn (E)

1 University Plaza, Brooklyn NY 11201-5372
Telephone: (718) 488-1011 FICE Identification: 004779
Accreditation: &M, ARCPA, #CAATE, CLPSY, COARC, DMS, NURSE, OT, PHAR, PTA, SP, SPAA, SURGT, SW, TEAC

† Regional accreditation is carried under the parent institution in Brookville, NY

*LIU Hudson at Rockland (F)

70 Route 340, Orangeburg NY 10962
Telephone: (845) 359-7200 Identification: 666077
Accreditation: &M

† Regional accreditation is carried under the parent institution in Brookville, NY

*LIU Hudson at Westchester (G)

735 Anderson Hill Road, Purchase NY 10577
Telephone: (914) 831-2700 Identification: 666078
Accreditation: &M, TEAC

† Regional accreditation is carried under the parent institution in Brookville, NY

*LIU Riverhead (H)

121 Speonk-Riverhead Road - LIU Bld,
Riverhead NY 11901-3499
Telephone: (631) 287-8010 Identification: 666174
Accreditation: &M, TEAC

† Regional accreditation is carried under the parent institution in Brookville, NY

Louis V. Gerstner Jr. Graduate School of Biomedical Sciences, Memorial Sloan Kettering Cancer Center (I)

1275 York Avenue, P.O. Box 441, New York NY 10065
County: New York Identification: 666643
Unit ID: 458511
Telephone: (646) 888-6639 Carnegie Class: Not Classified
FAX Number: N/A Calendar System: Semester
URL: www.sloankettering.edu
Established: 2004 Annual Graduate Tuition & Fees: N/A
Enrollment: N/A Coed
Affiliation or Control: Independent Non-Profit IRS Status: 501(c)3
Highest Offering: Doctorate; No Undergraduates
Accreditation: NY

01 President ....Dr. Craig B. THOMPSON
05 Provost ....Dr. Joan MASSAGUE
20 Dean ....Dr. Kenneth J. MARIANS
88 Associate Dean ....Mrs. Linda BURNLEY
06 Registrar ....Vacant
08 Director of Library Services ....Ms. Donna S. GIBSON

Machzikei Hadath Rabbinical College (J)

5407 16th Avenue, Brooklyn NY 11204-1305
County: Kings FICE Identification: 013026
Unit ID: 192624
Telephone: (718) 854-8777 Carnegie Class: Spec-4-yr-Faith
FAX Number: (718) 851-1265 Calendar System: Semester
Established: 1956 Annual Undergrad Tuition & Fees: $11,050
Enrollment: 147 Male
Affiliation or Control: Independent Non-Profit IRS Status: 501(c)3
Highest Offering: First Talmudic Degree
Accreditation: RABN

01 President ....Mr. Alexander SCHAECHTER

Mandl School - The College of Allied Health (K)

254 W 54th Street, 9th Floor, New York NY 10019
County: New York FICE Identification: 007401
Unit ID: 192688
Telephone: (212) 247-3434 Carnegie Class: Spec 2-yr-Health
FAX Number: (212) 247-3617 Calendar System: Semester
URL: www.mandl.edu
Established: 1924 Annual Undergrad Tuition & Fees: $13,095
Enrollment: 707 Coed
Affiliation or Control: Proprietary IRS Status: Proprietary
Highest Offering: Associate Degree
Accreditation: ABHES, #COARC, SURTEC

01 President ....Mr. Melvyn P. WEINER
05 Vice President of Academic Affairs ....Dr. Orsete DIAS
37 EVP/Director of Financial Aid ....Mr. Stuart WEINER
36 Vice President of Career Services ....Mr. James FLANAGAN
06 Dean of Records & Registration ....Mr. Marc WEINER
84 Director of Enrollment Management ....Ms. Rancie SENSER
06 Registrar ....Ms. Tina PAPULI
07 Director of Recruitment ....Ms. Racquel GARCIA
08 Head Librarian ....Ms. Clover STEELE
32 Assistant Dean Student Support Svcs ....Dr. Karlene RICHARDSON
10 Chief Business Officer ....Mrs. Nettie WEINER
100 Chief of Staff ....Ms. Maritza E. MERCADO

Manhattan College (L)

Manhattan College Parkway, Bronx NY 10471-4099
County: Bronx FICE Identification: 002758
Unit ID: 192703
Telephone: (718) 862-8000 Carnegie Class: Masters/M
FAX Number: (718) 862-8014 Calendar System: Semester
URL: www.manhattan.edu
Established: 1853 Annual Undergrad Tuition & Fees: $38,580
Enrollment: 3,970 Coed
Affiliation or Control: Independent Non-Profit IRS Status: 501(c)3
Highest Offering: Master's
Accreditation: M, BUS, ENG, TEAC

01 President ....Dr. Brennan O'DONNELL
05 Executive Vice President & Provost ....Dr. William CLYDE
10 VP for Finance & CFO ....Mr. Matthew S. MCMANNESS
32 Vice President Student Life ....Dr. Richard SATTERLEE
30 Vice President College Advancement ....Mr. Thomas MAURIELLO
15 Vice President for Human Resources ....Ms. Barbara A. FABE
18 Vice President for Facilities ....Mr. Andrew RYAN
84 Vice President Enrollment Mgmt ....Dr. William J. BISSET
88 Vice President for Mission ....Br. Jack CURRAN
20 Assoc Prov Res/Fac/Computer System ....Mr. Walter F. MATYSTIK
35 Assistant VP of Student Life ....Dr. Emmanuel AGO
35 Dean of Students ....Dr. Michael CAREY
06 Registrar ....Ms. Susan ASTARITA
07 Director of Admissions ....Ms. Caitlin READ
08 Director of Libraries ....Dr. William WALTERS
13 Director of Information Tech Svcs ....Mr. Jake HOLMQUIST
19 Director of Public Safety ....Mr. Juan E. CEREZO
29 Director of Alumni Relations ....Mr. Thomas MCCARTHY
26 Director of Mktg & Communications ....Mrs. Lydia E. GRAY
36 Director Ctr Career Development ....Vacant
36 Director Ctr Career Development ....Ms. Rachel CIRELLI
38 Dir of Counseling & Health Services ....Dr. Terence HANNIGAN
39 Director of Residence Life ....Mr. Andrew WEINGARTEN
41 Director of Athletics ....Ms. Marianne REILLY
42 Director of Campus Ministry ....Ms. Lois HARR
44 Director of Development/Advancement ....Mr. Stephen WHITE
78 Director Academic Support Services ....Ms. Marilyn CARTER-STEVENS
40 Director of Campus Bookstore ....Mr. Henry CASTILLO
22 Dir of Personnel/Affirm Action Ofcr ....Ms. Vickie M. COWAN
09 Dir Inst Research/Assessment ....Dr. David MAHAN
21 Controller ....Mr. Dennis LONERGAN
21 Business Manager ....Mr. Kenneth WALDHOF
85 International Student Advisor ....Ms. Debra L. DAMICO
37 Director of Student Financial Svcs ....Vacant
49 Dean of Liberal Arts ....Dr. Keith BROWER
50 Dean of Business ....Dr. Salwa AMMAR
53 Dean of Education & Health ....Dr. Karen NICHOLSON
54 Dean of Engineering ....Dr. Tim WARD
51 Exec Dir Sch Cont & Prof Studies ....Dr. Cheryl HARRISON
88 Director Ctr for Academic Success ....Ms. Marisa PASSAFIUME
81 Dean of Science ....Dr. Constantine THEODOSIOU
88 Dir of Specialized Resource Center ....Ms. Anne VACCARO
88 Dir Grad & Fellowship Advisement ....Dr. Rani R. ROY

Manhattan School of Music (M)

120 Claremont Avenue, New York NY 10027-4698
County: New York FICE Identification: 002759
Unit ID: 192712
Telephone: (212) 749-2802 Carnegie Class: Spec-4-yr-Arts
FAX Number: (212) 749-5471 Calendar System: Semester
URL: www.msmnyc.edu
Established: 1917 Annual Undergrad Tuition & Fees: $42,600
Enrollment: 957 Coed
Affiliation or Control: Independent Non-Profit IRS Status: 501(c)3
Highest Offering: Doctorate
Accreditation: M

01 President ....Dr. James GANDRE
05 Provost and Senior Vice President ....Dr. Marjorie MERRYMAN
10 VP for Business and Finance ....Mr. Gary MEYER
30 Int Vice President for Advancement ....Mr. Brian DAILEY
26 VP for Media and Communications ....Mr. Jeff BREITHAUPT
84 Dean of Enrollment Management ....Ms. Amy A. ANDERSON
32 Dean of Students ....Dr. Monica CHRISTENSEN
15 Sr Director Admin & Human Relations ....Ms. Carol MATOS
106 Dean of Dist Learning & Rec Arts ....Ms. Christianne ORTO
101 Liaison to the Board of Trustees ....Mr. Marc DAY
20 Assistant Dean of Academics ....Dr. Marjean OLSON
06 Registrar ....Mr. David MCDONAGH
13 Transition Chief Information Ofcr ....Ms. Kathy BURTON JONES
14 Assistant IT Director ....Mr. Luis MOREL
37 Director of Financial Aid ....Mr. Adam GHILONI
35 Director of Student Engagement ....Ms. Melanie DORSEY
39 Director of Residence Life ....Mr. Jim LOVE
31 Director of Educational Outreach ....Ms. Rebecca CHARNOW
29 Alumni Manager ....Ms. Lauren FRANKOVICH
08 Director of Library Services ....Mr. Peter CALEB
102 Director of Foundation Relations ....Ms. Ronnie BORISKIN
40 Campus Store Manager ....Ms. Katherine COPLAND
85 Director Intl Student Services ....Mr. Michael LOCKHART
88 Dir Ctr for Music Entrepreneurship ....Dr. Angela BEECHING
88 Dean of Instrumental Performance ....Mr. David GEBER
21 Director of Accounting & Controller ....Ms. Susan FINK
18 Dir of Facilities & Campus Safety ....Mr. Luis PLAZA
07 Director of Admissions ....Ms. Christan CASSIDY
100 Chief of Staff ....Mr. Bryan GREANEY

Manhattanville College (N)

2900 Purchase Street, Purchase NY 10577-2132
County: Westchester FICE Identification: 002760
Unit ID: 192749
Telephone: (914) 694-2200 Carnegie Class: Bac-A&S
FAX Number: (914) 694-2386 Calendar System: Semester

URL: www.mville.edu
Established: 1841 Annual Undergrad Tuition & Fees: $36,220
Enrollment: 2,865 Coed
Affiliation or Control: Independent Non-Profit IRS Status: 501(c)3
Highest Offering: Doctorate
Accreditation: M, IACBE, TED

01 President Dr. Michael E. GEISLER
04 Exec Admin Asst to the President Ms. Deborah A. FALLONE
05 Provost/VP of Academic Affairs Dr. Lisa DOLLING
10 VP Finance/Administration Ms. Marina VASARHELYI
84 Vice Pres Enrollment Management Mr. Nikhil KUMAR
30 Vice Pres Inst Advance/Alum Rels Ms. Teresa WEBER
11 Vice President of Operations Mr. Gregory PALMER
32 Int Vice Pres of Student Affairs Mr. John BALOG
58 Dean School of Business Dr. Anthony DAVIDSON
53 Dean School of Education Dr. Shelley WEPNER
26 Managing Dir Media/PR/Comm Ms. Jennifer JAMES PRYOR
06 Registrar Mr. Thomas MURASSO
85 Director of English Lang Institute Ms. Marisa ANNUNZIATA
08 Director of the Library Mr. Jeff ROSEDALE
37 Director of Financial Aid Mr. Robert GILMORE
38 Director of Counseling Center Dr. Glenn POLLACK
35 Dean of Students Ms. Sharlise SMITH-RODRIGUEZ
41 Director of Athletics Mr. Keith LEVINTHAL
42 Int Catholic Chpln/Interfaith Coord Fr. Wil TYRRELL
36 Director Center for Career Devel Ms. Shannon HARGROVE
19 Director of Security Mr. Anthony HERRMANN
07 Director of Admissions Mr. Joseph COSENTINO
15 Director of Human Resources Mr. Don DEAN
35 Asst Director of Student Activities Mr. Andrew FULTON
96 Director of Purchasing Ms. Cheryl DOBSON
104 Director Study Abroad Mr. Wil TYRRELL
22 Dir Affirmative Action/EEO Mr. Donald DEAN
23 Director Health Center Ms. Kristen DONOHUE-GONZALEZ

Maria College of Albany (A)

700 New Scotland Avenue, Albany NY 12208-1798
County: Albany FICE Identification: 002763
Unit ID: 192785
Telephone: (518) 438-3111 Carnegie Class: Spec-4-yr-Other Health
FAX Number: (518) 438-7170 Calendar System: 4/1/4
URL: www.mariacollege.edu
Established: 1958 Annual Undergrad Tuition & Fees: $13,340
Enrollment: 859 Coed
Affiliation or Control: Independent Non-Profit IRS Status: 501(c)3
Highest Offering: Baccalaureate
Accreditation: M, ADNUR, NUR, OTA

01 President Dr. Thomas J. GAMBLE
05 Dean/Vice Pres Academic Affairs Dr. John KOWAL
10 Chief Financial Officer Mr. John BECKVOLD
30 Director Development Ms. Helen ADAMS-KEANE
37 Director Financial Aid Ms. Donna MYERS
84 Dean of Enrollment Management Mr. Thomas D. IWANKOW
21 Director of Business Affairs Mrs. Frances BERNARD
06 Registrar Ms. Kari BENNETT
07 Director of Admissions Mr. John RAMOSKA
08 Director Library Vacant
32 AVP Student Life/Mission Integr Ms. Victoria L. BATTELL
13 Director of Information Technology Mr. Mark HATLEE
18 Superintendent Physical Plant Mr. Andrew PEREZ
26 Director Marketing/Communications Ms. Beth WALES
42 Campus Minister Mrs. Michelle THIVIERGE
36 Career Services Coordinator Mr. David COVEY

Marist College (B)

3399 North Road, Poughkeepsie NY 12601-1387
County: Dutchess FICE Identification: 002765
Unit ID: 192819
Telephone: (845) 575-3000 Carnegie Class: Masters/L
FAX Number: (845) 471-6213 Calendar System: Semester
URL: www.marist.edu
Established: 1929 Annual Undergrad Tuition & Fees: $33,840
Enrollment: 6,356 Coed
Affiliation or Control: Independent Non-Profit IRS Status: 501(c)3
Highest Offering: Doctorate
Accreditation: M, #ARCPA, BUS, CAATE, MT, SPAA, SW, TED

01 President Dr. David YELLEN
03 Executive Vice President Dr. Geoffrey L. BRACKETT
05 Vice President for Academic Affairs Dr. Thomas S. WERMUTH
84 VP Admission & Enrollment Planning Mr. Sean P. KAYLOR
30 Vice President College Advancement Mr. Christopher M. DELGIORNO
13 VP Information Technology/CIO Mr. William T. THIRSK
32 VP/Dean of Student Affairs Mrs. Deborah A. DICAPRIO
10 Vice President Business Affairs/CFO Mr. John P. PECCHIA
20 Assoc VP/Dean Academic Affairs Dr. John RITSCHDORFF
07 Asst VP Enroll Mgmt/Dean UG Admiss Mr. Kenton W. RINEHART
35 Assoc Dean of Student Affairs Mr. Steve SANSOLA
29 Executive Director Alumni Relations Ms. Amy K. WOODS
09 Director Inst Research & Planning Dr. Judith STODDARD
20 Assoc Dean of Academic Affairs Mrs. Judith IVANKOVIC
37 Exec Dir Student Financial Services Mr. Joseph R. WEGLARZ
08 Director Library Vacant
90 Director Academic Technology Vacant
18 Director of Physical Plant Mr. Justin BUTWELL
26 Chief Public Affairs Officer Mr. Gregory CANNON
15 Assoc VP for Human Resources Mrs. Deborah RAIKES-COLBERT
96 Director of Purchasing Mr. Stephen J. KOCHIS
36 Director Career Services Vacant
19 Director of Safety & Security Vacant
39 Director of Housing & Resident Life Mrs. Sarah H. ENGLISH
41 Director of Athletics Mr. Timothy S. MURRAY
04 Exec Assistant to the President Ms. Eileen SICO
24 Director of Media & Instruct Tech Ms. Joey WALL
23 Director of Health Services Vacant
38 Director of Counseling Dr. Naomi A. FERLEGER
43 Director Campus Ministry Bro. Francis E. KELLY
44 Director of Annual Giving Ms. Jeanine M. THOMPSON
105 Director Web Services Mr. Antoni SOUSA

Marymount Manhattan College (C)

221 E 71st Street, New York NY 10021-4597
County: New York FICE Identification: 002769
Unit ID: 192864
Telephone: (212) 517-0400 Carnegie Class: Bac-A&S
FAX Number: (212) 517-0541 Calendar System: Semester
URL: www.mmm.edu
Established: 1936 Annual Undergrad Tuition & Fees: $28,700
Enrollment: 1,858 Coed
Affiliation or Control: Independent Non-Profit IRS Status: 501(c)3
Highest Offering: Baccalaureate
Accreditation: M

01 President Dr. Kerry WALK
05 Interim VP Acad Aff/Dean of Faculty Dr. Kathleen LEBESCO
10 Exec Vice Pres Admin & Finance Mr. Paul CIRAULO
30 VP Institutional Advancement Ms. Marilyn L. WILKIE
32 VP Student Affairs/Dean of Students Dr. Carol JACKSON
21 Associate Vice Pres & Controller Mr. Wayne SANTUCCI
07 Dean of Admissions Mr. James ROGERS
20 Acting Assoc Dean for Acad Affairs Dr. Peter NACCARATO
06 Registrar Ms. Regina CHAN
15 Assistant VP of Human Resources Ms. Bree BULLINGHAM
08 Librarian Mr. Brian ROCCO
13 Chief Information Officer Ms. Dale HOCHSTEIN
37 Asst VP of Fin & Registration Svcs Ms. Maria DEINNOCENTIIS
38 Dir Counseling & Psychological Svcs Dr. Paul GRAYSON
18 Director of Facilities Mr. Pete ROMAIN
36 Director Career Svcs & Internships Vacant
96 Director of Administrative Services Ms. Maria MARZANO
88 Asst Controller Ms. Cassie GOULD
44 Director of Development Vacant
09 Dir Institutional Research Ms. Cheryl GOLDSTEIN
19 Director of Campus Safety Mr. James CAMBRIA
26 Dir Public Relations/ Communications Ms. Stephanie POLICASTRO
28 Asst VP Str Init/Diversity/Title IX Ms. Christine GREGORY
39 Asst Dean Stdnt Aff/Dir of Res Life Ms. Emmalyn YAMRICK

Medaille College (D)

18 Agassiz Circle, Buffalo NY 14214-2695
County: Erie FICE Identification: 002777
Unit ID: 192925
Telephone: (716) 880-2000 Carnegie Class: Masters/L
FAX Number: (716) 884-0291 Calendar System: Semester
URL: www.medaille.edu
Established: 1875 Annual Undergrad Tuition & Fees: $26,252
Enrollment: 2,479 Coed
Affiliation or Control: Independent Non-Profit IRS Status: 501(c)3
Highest Offering: Doctorate
Accreditation: M, CACREP, CAHIIM, IACBE, TEAC

01 President Dr. Kenneth M. MACUR
05 Vice President Academic Affairs Dr. Lori QUIGLEY
10 Vice President Business/Finance Mr. Matthew J. CARVER
30 Vice Pres for College Relations Mr. John P. CRAWFORD
07 VP Enroll Mgmt/Marketing/Admiss Mr. Christopher LARUSSO
09 Asst Vice Pres Institutional Rsrch Mr. Patrick S. MCDONALD
32 VP for Student Development Ms. Amy M. DEKAY
44 Dir of Major Gifts & Planned Giving Ms. Jeanine PURCELL
41 Athletic Director Ms. Amy DEKAY
36 Director Career Planning/Placement Ms. Carol CULLINAN
13 Chief Information Officer Mr. Robert D. CHYKA
06 Registrar Mrs. Kathleen LAZAR
08 Library Director Mr. Andrew YEAGER
37 Director Financial Aid Ms. Catherine BUZANSKI
15 Director of Human Resources Ms. Barbara J. BILOTTA
35 Director of Student Involvement Ms. Kayla A. BETACCHINI
38 Director Counseling Services Ms. Rosalina B. RIZZO
19 Director of Campus Public Safety Mr. Earl WELLS
29 Coordinator of Alumni Relations Mr. Nicholas J. KOZIOL
26 Director of Marketing Ms. Melissa D. HARRIS

Medaille College Rochester Branch Campus (E)

1880 S Winston Road, Rochester NY 14618
Telephone: (585) 272-0030 Identification: 770140
Accreditation: &M

† Regional accreditation is carried under the parent institution in Buffalo, NY

Memorial School of Nursing (F)

600 Northern Boulevard, Albany NY 12204-1004
County: Albany FICE Identification: 012203
Unit ID: 192961
Telephone: (518) 471-3260 Carnegie Class: Spec 2-yr-Health
FAX Number: (518) 447-3559 Calendar System: Semester
URL: www.nehealth.com
Established: Annual Undergrad Tuition & Fees: $11,288
Enrollment: 131 Coed
Affiliation or Control: Independent Non-Profit IRS Status: 501(c)3
Highest Offering: Associate Degree
Accreditation: NY, ADNUR

01 Director Ms. Mary-Jane S. ARALDI

Mercy College (G)

555 Broadway, Dobbs Ferry NY 10522-1189
County: Westchester FICE Identification: 002772
Unit ID: 193016
Telephone: (800) 637-2969 Carnegie Class: Masters/L
FAX Number: (914) 674-5978 Calendar System: Semester
URL: www.mercy.edu
Established: 1950 Annual Undergrad Tuition & Fees: $18,076
Enrollment: 11,272 Coed
Affiliation or Control: Independent Non-Profit IRS Status: 501(c)3
Highest Offering: Doctorate
Accreditation: M, ARCPA, CAEP, NURSE, OT, OTA, PTA, SP, SW, TED

01 President Mr. Timothy HALL
05 Provost & Vice Pres Acad Affairs Dr. Concetta STEWART
20 Associate Provost for Acad Affairs Dr. Lucretia MANN
50 Dean School of Business Dr. Ed WEIS
53 Interim Dean School of Education Mr. Andrew PEISER
83 Dean School Soc/Behavioral Sci Dr. Karol DEAN
76 Dean School Health/Natural Sci Dr. Joan TOGLIA
49 Dean School Liberal Arts Dr. Tamara JHASHI
15 Exec Dir of Human Resources/Safety Ms. Anne GILMARTIN
11 VP Operations & Facilities Mr. Thomas SIMMONDS
84 Vice Pres for Enrollment Management Ms. Deirdre WHITMAN
10 VP & Chief Financial/Plng Officer Mr. Donald AUNGST
32 VP of Student Services Ms. Margaret MCGRAIL
30 Chief Advancement Officer Ms. Bernadette WADE
100 Chief of Staff Ms. Irene BUCKLEY
04 Staff Assistant Ms. Grace CREIGHTON
108 Director of Educational Assessment Ms. Victoria FERRARA
43 General Counsel Ms. Kristen BOWES
07 Executive Director of Admissions Ms. Tara FAY-REILLY
09 Dir Institutional Research/Planning Ms. Victoria TYLER
39 Assistant Dean of Student Affairs Ms. Patricia CHRISTIANO
35 Dean of Student Affairs Mr. Kevin JOYCE
13 Director of Information Technology Mr. Todd PRATTELLA
06 Exec Director of Sys Mgmt/Registrar Ms. Debra KENNEY
45 Asst VP of Inst Assess/Plng/Analy Ms. Jessica HABER
21 Director of Student Accounts Ms. Felicia BRANDON
21 Controller Ms. Narda ROMERO
45 Director of Budgets & Planning Mr. Bernard COSTELLO
96 Director of Purchasing Ms. Patricia SABATINO
08 Director of Mercy College Libraries Mr. Mustafa SAKARYA
41 Director of Athletics Mr. Matt KILCULLEN
27 Director of Communications Ms. Jessica BAILY
29 Director of Alumni Relations Ms. Alexis MCGRATH
25 Dir Sponsored Programs Ms. Janet PARTENZA
104 Director Center Global Engagement Dr. Sheila GERSH
106 Director Online Learning Dr. Mary LOZINA
103 Senior Director of Career Services Ms. Jill HART
101 Secretary of the Institution/Board Ms. Irene BUCKLEY
26 Exec Dir Marketing Ms. Alexis D'AGOSTINO
37 VP Enrollment Services Ms. Margaret MCGRAIL
44 Director Annual or Planned Giving Mr. Phil KEEFE

Mesivta of Eastern Parkway Rabbinical Seminary (H)

510 Dahill Road, Brooklyn NY 11218-5559
County: Kings FICE Identification: 009335
Unit ID: 193061
Telephone: (718) 438-1002 Carnegie Class: Spec-4-yr-Faith
FAX Number: (718) 438-2591 Calendar System: Semester
Established: 1947 Annual Undergrad Tuition & Fees: $8,600
Enrollment: 35 Male
Affiliation or Control: Independent Non-Profit IRS Status: 501(c)3
Highest Offering: Second Talmudic Degree
Accreditation: RABN

01 President Rabbi Issac HEIMOVITZ
32 Dean of Students Rabbi Shlomo Z. EPSTEIN
37 Director of Student Financial Aid Rabbi Ira LIBERMAN
46 Director of Research Rabbi Hersch BASCH
10 Chief Fiscal Officer Rabbi Joseph HALBERSTADT

Mesivta Tifereth Jerusalem of America (I)

145 E Broadway, New York NY 10002-6301
County: New York FICE Identification: 003974
Unit ID: 193070
Telephone: (212) 964-2830 Carnegie Class: Spec-4-yr-Faith
FAX Number: (212) 349-5213 Calendar System: Semester
Established: 1907 Annual Undergrad Tuition & Fees: $10,250
Enrollment: 72 Male
Affiliation or Control: Independent Non-Profit IRS Status: 501(c)3
Highest Offering: Second Talmudic Degree
Accreditation: RABN

01 President & Dean Faculties .... Rabbi David FEINSTEIN
06 Registrar .... Chana YAMPOLSKY

Mesivta Torah Vodaath Seminary (A)

425 E Ninth Street, Brooklyn NY 11218-5299
County: Kings FICE Identification: 007264
Unit ID: 193052
Telephone: (718) 941-8000 Carnegie Class: Spec-4-yr-Faith
FAX Number: (718) 941-8032 Calendar System: Semester
Established: 1918 Annual Undergrad Tuition & Fees: $11,010
Enrollment: 344 Male
Affiliation or Control: Independent Non-Profit IRS Status: 501(c)3
Highest Offering: Second Talmudic Degree
Accreditation: **RABN**

01 Dean .... Rabbi Yisroel BELSKY
03 Executive Director .... Rabbi Yitzchok GOTTDIENER
06 Registrar .... Rabbi Yaakov EHRENREICH
33 Dean of Men .... Rabbi Elya KATZ
31 Director Community Services .... Mr. Shraga WERNER

Metropolitan College of New York (B)

60 West Street, New York NY 10006
County: New York FICE Identification: 009769
Unit ID: 190114
Telephone: (212) 343-1234 Carnegie Class: Masters/L
FAX Number: (212) 343-7399 Calendar System: Semester
URL: www.metropolitan.edu
Established: 1964 Annual Undergrad Tuition & Fees: $18,030
Enrollment: 1,228 Coed
Affiliation or Control: Independent Non-Profit IRS Status: 501(c)3
Highest Offering: Master's
Accreditation: **M, ACBSP, TED**

01 President .... Dr. Vinton THOMPSON
10 VP Finance & Administration/CFO .... Mr. Thomas BURKE
05 Chief Academic Officer .... Dr. Tilokie DEPOO
84 Vice Pres for Enrollment Management .... Dr. Collette GARRITY
07 Director of Admissions .... Mr. Stephen OSTENDORFF
58 Dean School Public Affairs & Admin .... Dr. Humphrey CROOKENDALE
50 Dean School for Business .... Dr. Tilokie DEPOO
88 Dean ACSHSE .... Dr. Adele WEINER
32 Dean of Students .... Ms. Dona SOSA
37 Acting Director of Financial Aid .... Mr. Douane CAMPBELL
06 Registrar .... Ms. Noreen SMITH
08 Co-Director of Library Services .... Ms. Kate ADLER
08 Co-Director of Library Services .... Ms. Emma MOORE
09 Dir Institutional Rsrch/Assessment .... Mr. Anthony WILLIAMS
15 Director Human Resources .... Ms. Judith SANTIAGO
18 Chief Facilities/Physical Plant .... Ms. Mercedes MELENDEZ
30 Chief Development Officer .... Ms. Beth DUNPHE
26 Chief Public Relations Officer .... Ms. Tina GEORGIOU
13 Director of Technology .... Mr. Adrian SMITH
21 Bursar .... Mr. Taurean KENNEDY
88 Director Academic Support Services .... Ms. Parker PRACJEK
04 Exec Assistant to the President .... Ms. Isabel CABRERA
29 Director Alumni Relations .... Ms. Tina GEORGIOU

Mildred Elley (C)

855 Central Avenue, Albany NY 12206
County: Albany FICE Identification: 022195
Unit ID: 193201
Telephone: (518) 786-0855 Carnegie Class: Assoc/HVT-High Non
FAX Number: (518) 786-0898 Calendar System: Other
URL: www.mildred-elley.edu
Established: 1917 Annual Undergrad Tuition & Fees: $11,205
Enrollment: 748 Coed
Affiliation or Control: Proprietary IRS Status: Proprietary
Highest Offering: Associate Degree
Accreditation: **ACICS**

01 President .... Ms. Faith A. TAKES

Mildred Elley-New York City (D)

25 Broadway, 16th Floor, New York NY 10004
Telephone: (212) 380-9004 Identification: 770747
Accreditation: **ACICS**

Mirrer Yeshiva Central Institute (E)

1795 Ocean Parkway, Brooklyn NY 11223-2010
County: Kings FICE Identification: 004798
Unit ID: 193247
Telephone: (718) 645-0536 Carnegie Class: Spec-4-yr-Faith
FAX Number: (718) 645-9251 Calendar System: Semester
Established: 1947 Annual Undergrad Tuition & Fees: $6,650
Enrollment: 197 Male
Affiliation or Control: Independent Non-Profit IRS Status: 501(c)3
Highest Offering: Second Talmudic Degree
Accreditation: **RABN**

00 Chancellor .... Rabbi Avrohom Yaakov NELKENBAUM
01 President and Dean .... Rabbi Osher KALMANOWITZ
05 Vice President & Dean .... Rabbi Osher BERENBAUM
33 Dean of Men .... Rabbi Esrael ERLANGER
03 Executive Director .... Rabbi Pinchas HECHT
06 Registrar-Administrator .... Mrs. Devorah BERENBAUM
08 Director of the Library .... Rabbi Jacob FELDMANN
38 Director of Guidance .... Rabbi Yisroel FISHMAN
37 Financial Aid Director .... Mrs. Rachel BERENBAUM

Mohawk Valley Community College (F)

1101 Floyd Avenue, Rome NY 13440
Telephone: (315) 339-3470 Identification: 770141
Accreditation: **&M**

† Regional accreditation is carried under the parent institution in Utica, NY

Mohawk Valley Community College (G)

1101 Sherman Drive, Utica NY 13501-5394
County: Oneida FICE Identification: 002871
Unit ID: 193283
Telephone: (315) 792-5400 Carnegie Class: Assoc/HT-Mix Trad/Non
FAX Number: (315) 792-5666 Calendar System: Semester
URL: www.mvcc.edu
Established: 1946 Annual Undergrad Tuition & Fees (In-District): $4,616
Enrollment: 7,149 Coed
Affiliation or Control: State/Local IRS Status: 501(c)3
Highest Offering: Associate Degree
Accreditation: **M, ADNUR, CAHIIM, COARC, ENGT, RAD, SURTEC**

01 President .... Dr. Randall I. VAN WAGONER
04 Assistant to the President .... Ms. Jill HEINTZ
88 Exec Dir Organizational Development .... Mr. David KATZ
09 Dir Institutional Research/Analysis .... Mr. Mark E. RADLOWSKI
05 Vice Pres Learning/Academic Affairs .... Dr. Maryrose EANNACE
20 Director of Academic Systems .... Mr. Richard PUCINE
88 Asst Vice Pres Bus/Educ/Lib Arts .... Mr. Lewis KAHLER
53 Assoc Dean Educ & Lang Studies .... Ms. Julie DEWAN
88 Asst Vice Pres STEM/Health/Soc Sci .... Dr. Kathleen LINAKER
54 Assoc Dean Phys Sci/Engr/App Tech .... Mr. Timothy THOMAS
57 Assoc Dean Art .... Mr. Todd EEHRENDT
77 Assoc Dean Bus/Cyber/Comp Sci .... Mr. Jake MIHEVC
81 Assoc Dean Math & Natural Sci .... Dr. Robert WOODROW
79 Assoc Dean Humanities .... Vacant
76 Assoc Dean Health Professions .... Vacant
83 Assoc Dean Soc Sci & Public Svc .... Vacant
88 Dean of Emer Prep & Public Svc .... Ms. Marianne BUTTENSCHON
08 Director College Libraries .... Mr. Stephen FRISBEE
88 Exec Dean Academic Dev & Innovation .... Mr. James LYNCH
10 Vice Pres Administrative Services .... Mr. Thomas SQUIRES
32 Vice Pres Student Affairs .... Ms. Stephanie C. REYNOLDS
84 Assoc Dean Enrollment & Advisement .... Mrs. Jennifer DEWEERTH
36 Assoc Dean Development & Transition .... Mr. James MAIO
39 Assoc Dean Student & Residence Life .... Mr. Dennis GIBBONS
31 Assoc VP of Workforce Development .... Ms. Franca ARMSTRONG
30 Exec Dir Institutional Advancement .... Mr. Frank DUROSS
44 Dir of Donor & Resource Development .... Ms. Deanna FERRO
96 Coord Expend/Fixed Asset Procure .... Ms. Joyce PALMER
13 Exec Dir of Information Technology .... Mr. Paul KATCHMAR
103 Dir Ctr Community/Economic Dev .... Ms. Kristen SKOBLA
15 Exec Director of Human Resources .... Mrs. Kimberly EVANS-DAME
26 Director Marketing/Communications .... Mr. Matthew SNYDER
07 Director of Admissions .... Mr. Daniel IANNO
37 Director of Financial Aid .... Mr. Michael PEDE
06 Dir of Student Records/Registrar .... Mrs. Rosemary V. SPETKA
18 Dir of Facilities and Operations .... Mr. Michael MCHARRIS
19 Exec Dir Public Safety & Emerg Mgmt .... Mr. David AMICO
21 Business Office Controller .... Mr. Brian MOLINARO
29 Coord Annual Funds/Alumni Relations .... Ms. Marie KOHL
41 Athletic Director .... Mr. Gary BROADHURST

Molloy College (H)

1000 Hempstead Avenue, PO Box 5002,
Rockville Centre NY 11571-5002
County: Nassau FICE Identification: 002775
Unit ID: 193292
Telephone: (516) 323-3000 Carnegie Class: Masters/L
FAX Number: N/A Calendar System: 4/1/4
URL: www.molloy.edu
Established: 1955 Annual Undergrad Tuition & Fees: $28,030
Enrollment: 4,497 Coed
Affiliation or Control: Independent Non-Profit IRS Status: 501(c)3
Highest Offering: Doctorate
Accreditation: **M, COARC, CVT, MUS, NMT, NURSE, SP, SW, TED**

01 President .... Dr. Drew BOGNER
05 VP Academic Affairs/Dean of Faculty .... Dr. Ann Z. BRANCHINI
10 Vice Pres for Finance & Treasurer .... Mr. Michael MC GOVERN
84 Vice Pres Enrollment Management .... Ms. Linda ALBANESE
30 VP for Mission & Advancement .... Mr. Edward J. THOMPSON
32 Vice President Student Affairs .... Mr. Robert HOULIHAN
45 VP Tech & Inst Effectiveness .... Mr. Michael TORRES
42 Director of Campus Ministries .... Mr. Scott SALVATO
37 Director Student Financial Services .... Ms. Debra OCONNOR
36 Director of Career Development .... Ms. Mary BROSNAN
41 Director of Athletics .... Ms. Susan CASSIDY
07 Dean of Admissions .... Ms. Marguerite LANE
37 Director of Financial Aid .... Mrs. Ana C. LOCKWARD
21 Assistant Treasurer .... Ms. Barbara CALISSI
44 Asst VP Mission Int & Development .... Ms. Catherine MUSCENTE
06 Registrar .... Ms. Susan FORTMAN
09 Dir of Institutional Effectiveness .... Ms. Christina D'AMATO
15 Director of Human Resources .... Ms. Lisa MILLER
18 Director of Facilities .... Mr. James MULTARI
26 Director Public Relations .... Mr. Ken YOUNG
96 Director Purchasing & Admin Service .... Ms. Lorraine JACKSON
35 Dean of Students .... Dr. Janine PAYTON
29 Director of Alumni Relations .... Ms. Mary Jane REILLY
19 Director of Public Safety .... Mr. Harry HERMAN
85 Director of International Education .... Ms. Kathleen REBA
105 Director Web Technologies .... Mr. Keith REDO
24 Director of Special Projects .... Mr. Nick SIMONE
20 Director Academic Support Services .... Ms. Nicolette CEO
13 Director of MIS & Operations .... Mr. Michael OLIVO
88 Director of Network Technology .... Mr. Sean LAURIE
08 Head Librarian .... Ms. Judith BRINK-DRESCHER
100 Chief of Staff .... Ms. Diane K. FORNIERI
106 Dean Innovative Delivery Methods .... Ms. Amy GAIMARO

Monroe College (I)

2501 Jerome Avenue, Bronx NY 10468-5407
County: Bronx FICE Identification: 004799
Unit ID: 193308
Telephone: (718) 933-6700 Carnegie Class: Bac/Assoc-Mixed
FAX Number: (718) 295-5861 Calendar System: Semester
URL: www.monroecollege.edu
Established: 1933 Annual Undergrad Tuition & Fees: $14,148
Enrollment: 7,002 Coed
Affiliation or Control: Proprietary IRS Status: Proprietary
Highest Offering: Master's
Accreditation: **M, ACBSP, ACFEI**

01 President .... Stephen J. JEROME
03 Exec VP/Director of Branch Campus .... Marc M. JEROME
05 Vice President for Academics .... Dr. Karenann CARTY
11 Vice President Administration .... David DIMOND
10 Vice President for Finance .... Michael ANASTASIO
84 Vice Pres Enroll Mgmt/Campus Dean .... Anthony ALLEN
32 Vice President Student Affairs .... Roberta GREENBERG
58 Dean of Graduate Programs .... Alex CANALS
12 Assoc Vice Pres New Rochelle Camp .... Carol GENESE
86 Asst Vice Pres Governmental Affairs .... Dr. Donald E. SIMON
108 Asst VP Institutional Effectiveness .... Dr. Edward S. SCHNEIDERMAN
55 Director of Evening Division .... Allen JENKINS
26 Director of Marketing .... Shane SEAMAN
06 Registrar .... Abigail THORPE
09 Dir Institutional Research .... Peter NWAKEZE
21 Bursar/Branch Campus .... Michael NIEDZWIECKI
21 Director Student Financial Services .... Daniel SHARON
21 Bursar .... Villan CRUZ
35 Dean for Student Services .... Mark SONNENSTEIN
109 Director Auxiliary Services .... Nivia CAMARA
07 Dean of Admissions Branch .... Gersom LOPEZ
07 Vice President Admissions .... Craig PATRICK
37 Dir Student Financial Aid Services .... Vacant
36 Exec Dir Ofc of Career Services .... Pamela DELLAPORTA
08 Director of Library Services .... Christine ARTIS
08 Director of Library Services/Branch .... Angela LAURETANO
39 Exec Director of Residential Life .... Mark GOODMAN
29 Director of Alumni Relations .... Leslie JEROME
13 Chief Info Technology Officer (CIO) .... Terrance MCGOWAN

Monroe Community College (J)

1000 E Henrietta Road, Rochester NY 14623-5780
County: Monroe FICE Identification: 002872
Unit ID: 193326
Telephone: (585) 292-2000 Carnegie Class: Assoc/HT-High Non
FAX Number: (585) 427-2749 Calendar System: Semester
URL: www.monroecc.edu
Established: 1961 Annual Undergrad Tuition & Fees (In-District): $4,554
Enrollment: 15,335 Coed
Affiliation or Control: State/Local IRS Status: 501(c)3
Highest Offering: Associate Degree
Accreditation: **M, ADNUR, CAHIIM, DA, DH, EMT, ENGT, MLTAD, RAD**

01 President .... Dr. Anne M. KRESS
05 Provost & VP Academic Svcs .... Dr. Andrea C. WADE
84 Int AVP Enrollment Mgmt .... Ms. Christine CASALINUOVO-ADAMS
32 Vice President Student Services .... Dr. Lloyd A. HOLMES
10 CFO and VP Administrative Svcs .... Mr. Hezekiah N. SIMMONS
103 VP Econ Dev/Workforce Svc .... Mr. Todd M. OLDHAM
102 Exec Director MCC Foundation .... Ms. Diane L. SHOGER
12 Exec Dean Damon City Campus .... Dr. Joel L. FRATER
26 Asst to the Pres Mktg & Comm Rels .... Ms. Cynthia L. COOPER
35 Asst Vice Pres Student Services .... Dr. Susan D. BAKER
88 Int Asst VP Educational Tech Svcs .... Mr. David J. LANE
18 Assistant Vice President Facilities .... Mr. Paul E. WURSTER
88 Asst Vice Pres ETS .... Mr. Terrance KEYS
20 Asst Vice Pres Academic Services .... Ms. Kimberley COLLINS
20 Interim Dean Curriculum/Pgm Devel .... Ms. MaryJo A. WITZ
37 Director Financial Aid .... Mr. Jerome S. ST. CROIX
09 Director Institutional Research .... Mr. Angel E. ANDREU
08 Director ETS Libraries .... Mr. Mark F. MCBRIDE
36 Interim Director Career Center .... Ms. Michelle P. MAYO
21 Asst Vice President Admin Svcs .... Mr. Darrell K. JACHIM-MOORE
06 Director Registrar & Records .... Ms. Elizabeth R. RIPTON
30 Director of Development .... Mr. Mark J. PASTORELLA
38 Dir Counseling Center & Vet Svcs .... Ms. Peggy A. HARVEY-LEE
19 Director Public Safety .... Mr. Salvatore J. SIMONETTI
41 Director Athletics .... Mr. Dudley (Skip) L. BAILEY
25 Director Grants .... Ms. Patricia R. WILLIAMS
35 Director of Student Life .... Ms. Elizabeth J. STEWART

23 Director of Health Services ... Ms. Donna G. MUELLER
21 Controller ... Mr. Michael G. QUINN
79 Interim Dean Liberal Arts ... Ms. Nayda PARES-KANE
50 Dean Science/Health/Business ... Ms. Laurel T. SANGER
88 Dean Academic Foundations ... Ms. Catherine E. SMITH
19 Dean Public Safety Training Ctr ... Mr. Michael S. KARNES
32 Dean Student Services-DCC ... Dr. Ann V. TOPPING
35 Director Student Svcs-DCC ... Ms. Shelitha WILLIAMS
20 Interim Dean Acad Svcs DCC ... Dr. Kimberly MCKINSEY-MABRY
15 Asst to President HR/Affirm Act Ofc ... Ms. Melissa A. FINGAR
40 Manager Bookstore ... Ms. Carol M. MCKEOWN
88 Director Educ Opportunity Program ... Ms. Brenda A. SMITH
78 Director Adult/Experiential Lrng ... Mr. William D. SIGISMOND
43 Legal Counsel ... Vacant
88 Assoc Dir Master Scheduling ... Mr. Rick F. SADWICK
96 Director of Purchasing ... Mr. Patrick M. BATES
39 Director Housing/Residence Life ... Ms. Amy GREER
28 Chief Diversity Officer ... Dr. Lloyd A. HOLMES
04 Executive Asst to President ... Ms. Sheila M. STRONG
07 Director of Admissions ... Ms. Christine CASALINUOVO-ADAMS
101 Secy to the Board of Trustees/Pres ... Ms. Linda M. HALL
108 Asst Director Assess and Curriculum ... Mr. Michael A. HEEL
29 Coord Alumni & Annual Giving ... Ms. Karen A. SHAW
45 Director Planning ... Ms. Valarie L. AVALONE
90 Director Comm and Network Services ... Ms. Donna J. POGROSZEWSKI

Montefiore School of Nursing (A)

53 Valentine Street, Mount Vernon NY 10550

County: Westchester — FICE Identification: 022178
Unit ID: 193380
Telephone: (914) 361-6221 — Carnegie Class: Not Classified
FAX Number: (914) 665-7047 — Calendar System: Semester
URL: www.montefioreschoolofnursing.org
Established: 2014 — Annual Undergrad Tuition & Fees: N/A
Enrollment: N/A — Coed
Affiliation or Control: Independent Non-Profit — IRS Status: 501(c)3
Highest Offering: Associate Degree
Accreditation: **ADNUR**

01 Dean ... Rebecca GREER
06 Registrar ... Sandra FARRIOR
07 Director of Admissions ... Sandra FARRIOR

Mount Saint Mary College (B)

330 Powell Avenue, Newburgh NY 12550-3412

County: Orange — FICE Identification: 002778
Unit ID: 193353
Telephone: (845) 561-0800 — Carnegie Class: Masters/M
FAX Number: (845) 562-6762 — Calendar System: Semester
URL: www.msmc.edu
Established: 1959 — Annual Undergrad Tuition & Fees: $28,233
Enrollment: 2,479 — Coed
Affiliation or Control: Independent Non-Profit — IRS Status: 501(c)3
Highest Offering: Master's
Accreditation: **M**, IACBE, NURSE, TED

01 Acting President ... Mr. James RAIMO
05 Vice President Academic Affairs ... Dr. Ilona MCGUINESS
10 Vice Pres Finance & Admin/Treasurer ... Mr. Art GLASS
30 Vice Pres for College Advancement ... Mr. Joseph VALENTI
32 Vice President for Students ... Mrs. Elaine O'GRADY
18 Vice Pres Facilities & Operations ... Mr. James RAIMO
07 Interim Dean of Admissions ... Mr. John MAHON
35 Dean of Students ... Ms. Kelly YOUGH
38 Asst Dean of Support Services ... Dr. Orin STRAUCHLER
20 Asst Vice Pres Academic Affairs ... Mr. Michael OLIVETTE
06 Registrar ... Mr. Carlos TONCHE, JR.
07 Director of Admissions ... Mrs. Nancy SCAFFIDI CLARKE
08 Director of the Library ... Mrs. Barbara W. PETRUZZELLI
37 Director of Financial Aid ... Ms. Barbara WINCHELL
09 Director of Planning and Research ... Mr. Ryan WILLIAMS
15 Director of Human Resources ... Mr. Lee ZAWISTOWSKI
42 Chaplain ... Fr. Francis AMODIO
35 Dean of Campus Life ... Ms. Sandra HENDERSON
39 Exec Dir of Operations and Housing ... Mr. Michael O'KEEFE
29 Director of Alumni Affairs ... Ms. Michelle A. IACUESSA
41 Director of Athletics & Recreation ... Mr. Dan TWOMEY
36 Exec Director of the Career Center ... Mrs. Janet ZEMAN
13 Chief Information Officer ... Mr. Dennis RUSH
96 Purchasing Manager ... Mr. Brian MOORE
106 Director of Online Learning ... Ms. Kristen DELLASALA
39 Director of Residence Life ... Ms. Maxine MONROE
18 Exec Director of Facilities & Space ... Ms. Maryann PILON
26 Director of Marketing & Advertising ... Mr. Dean DIMARZO
04 Administrative Asst to President ... Ms. Barbara CONNOLLY
104 Director Study Abroad ... Vacant
19 Director Security/Safety ... Mr. Matthew BYRNE
44 Director Annual Giving ... Ms. Natalie MCKINSTRIE

Nassau Community College (C)

1 Education Drive, Garden City NY 11530-6793

County: Nassau — FICE Identification: 002873
Unit ID: 193478
Telephone: (516) 572-7501 — Carnegie Class: Assoc/HT-High Trad
FAX Number: (516) 572-7750 — Calendar System: Semester
URL: www.ncc.edu
Established: 1959 — Annual Undergrad Tuition & Fees (In-District): $4,854
Enrollment: 22,374 — Coed
Affiliation or Control: State/Local — IRS Status: 501(c)3
Highest Offering: Associate Degree
Accreditation: **#M**, ADNUR, COARC, ENGT, FUSER, MLTAD, MUS, PTAA, RTT, SURGT

01 Interim President ... Dr. Thomas P. DOLAN
03 Executive Vice President ... Dr. Kenneth K. SAUNDERS
05 Vice Pres Academic Affairs ... Vacant
11 Vice Pres Facilities Management ... Dr. Joseph V. MUSCARELLA
10 Vice President Finance ... Ms. Inna REZNIK
32 Vice Pres Academic/Student Svcs ... Ms. Maria P. CONZATTI
22 AVP Equity & Inclusion/AA Officer ... Mr. Craig J. WRIGHT
43 Spec Asst to Pres/College Counsel ... Ms. Donna M. HAUGEN
103 Asst Vice Pres Workforce Devel ... Dr. Janet CARUSO
21 Treasurer ... Ms. Lisa HAHN
13 Dean Management Info Svcs ... Vacant
18 Asst VP Maintenance/Operations ... Mr. Masoom ALI
15 Assoc Vice Pres Human Resources ... Ms. Dorlena DUNBAR
96 Director Procurement ... Mr. Phillip CAPPELLO
35 Dean of Students ... Ms. Charmian SMITH
09 Dean Institutional Effectiveness ... Dr. Dean KEVLIN
37 Dean Financial Aid ... Ms. Patricia NOREN
07 Dean of Admissions ... Mr. David FOLLICK
25 Resource Devel/Grants Fiscal Mgr ... Mr. Edmund KOEPPEL
86 General Counsel for Govt Relations ... Ms. Kate MURRAY
26 Director Marketing/Communications ... Ms. Alicia STEGER
08 Director of Library ... Ms. Nancy WILLIAMSON
41 Director Special Pgm Athletics/PED ... Ms. Kerri-Ann MCTIERNAN
06 Registrar ... Mr. Chester BARKAN
19 Director of Public Safety ... Mr. Martin RODDINI
23 Director Health Services ... Ms. Margaret MCGOVERN
36 Director of Placement Testing ... Ms. Noreen WADE
38 Acting Director Academic Advisement ... Ms. Amanda FOX
14 Chief Information Officer ... Mr. Richard LAWLESS
102 Exec Dir Nassau CC Foundation ... Ms. Joy DEDONATO
04 Administrative Asst to President ... Ms. Anne E. BRANDI

Nazareth College of Rochester (D)

4245 East Avenue, Rochester NY 14618-3790

County: Monroe — FICE Identification: 002779
Unit ID: 193584
Telephone: (585) 389-2525 — Carnegie Class: Masters/L
FAX Number: (585) 586-2452 — Calendar System: Semester
URL: www.naz.edu
Established: 1924 — Annual Undergrad Tuition & Fees: $31,745
Enrollment: 2,818 — Coed
Affiliation or Control: Independent Non-Profit — IRS Status: 501(c)3
Highest Offering: Doctorate
Accreditation: **M**, IACBE, MUS, NURSE, OT, PTA, SP, SW, TEAC

01 President ... Mr. Daan BRAVEMAN
04 Assistant to President ... Ms. Patricia GENTHNER
04 Executive Assistant to President ... Ms. Cathleen M. STEVENS
05 Vice President Academic Affairs ... Dr. Sara VARHUS
30 Vice Pres Institutional Advancement ... Ms. Kelly GAGAN
10 Vice President Finance & Admin ... Mr. Patrick RICHEY
32 Vice President Student Development ... Mr. Kevin WORTHEN
84 Vice Pres Enrollment Management ... Mr. Ian MORTIMER
29 Director of Alumni Relations ... Ms. Donna BORGUS
15 Assoc VP Human Resources ... Mrs. JoEllen PINKHAM
20 Asst VP Academic Affairs ... Dr. James DOUTHIT
06 Registrar ... Ms. Alison TEETER
37 Director Student Financial Aid ... Ms. Janice SCHEUTZOW
26 Director Marketing & Communications ... Ms. Elizabeth ZAPATA
13 Director Information Tech Svcs ... Ms. Karen KUPPINGER
08 Director of Library ... Ms. Catherine DOYLE
19 Director of Security ... Mr. Timothy YOUNG
39 Director of Campus Life ... Ms. Carey BACKMAN
41 Director of Athletics ... Mr. Peter G. BOTHNER
42 Director Center for Spirituality ... Mr. Jamie FAZIO
36 Director of Career Services ... Mr. Michael D. KAHL
18 Director Buildings/Grounds ... Mr. Peter LANA
09 Director of Institutional Research ... Mr. Nicholas LAMENDOLA
23 Director of Health Services ... Ms. Susan QUINN
20 Director of Academic Advisement ... Ms. Linda SEARING
88 Director of the Arts Center ... Vacant
21 Bursar ... Mr. John GARBE
92 Director Honors Program ... Dr. Marjorie ROTH
49 Dean of Col of Arts and Sciences ... Dr. Diane OLIVER
76 Dean School of Health & Human Svcs ... Dr. Brigid NOONAN
53 Dean School of Education ... Dr. Kathleen DABOLL-LAVOIE
88 Dean School of Management ... Mr. Gerard ZAPPIA
88 Exec Dir of Ctr International Educ ... Dr. Nevan FISHER
88 Dir of Center for Service Learning ... Dr. Brian BAILEY
89 Dir Stdnt Transition/First Year Ctr ... Mr. Thomas CHEW
96 Director of Purchasing ... Ms. Joanne FITZGERALD
88 Exec Dir Center 4 Civic Engagement ... Ms. Nuala BOYLE
07 Dir Graduate Admissions/Transfer ... Ms. Judith G. BAKER
86 Director Government Relations ... Ms. Mary Kay BISHOP

The New School (E)

66 W 12th Street, New York NY 10011-8603

County: New York — FICE Identification: 020662
Unit ID: 193654
Telephone: (212) 229-5600 — Carnegie Class: DU-Higher
FAX Number: N/A — Calendar System: Semester
URL: www.newschool.edu
Established: 1919 — Annual Undergrad Tuition & Fees: $43,813
Enrollment: 10,477 — Coed
Affiliation or Control: Independent Non-Profit — IRS Status: 501(c)3
Highest Offering: Doctorate
Accreditation: **M**, ART, CLPSY, SPAA

01 President ... Dr. David VAN ZANDT
04 Executive Assistant to President ... Ms. Lindsey WARFORD
05 Provost and Chief Academic Officer ... Mr. Tim MARSHALL
88 Exec Asst and Comm Mgr to Prov ... Ms. Heather O'BRIEN
48 Exec Dean Parsons School for Design ... Mr. Joel TOWERS
88 Exec Dean School for Public Engage ... Dr. Mary WATSON
64 Exec Dean Perf Arts and Dean Mannes ... Mr. Richard KESSLER
83 Dean New School for Social Research ... Dr. William MILBERG
49 Dean Eugene Lang College ... Ms. Stephanie BROWNER
84 Chief Enrollment & Success Officer ... Mr. Donald RESNICK
11 Chief Operating Officer ... Mr. Tokumbo SHOBOWALE
30 Chief Development Officer ... Mr. Mark GIBBEL
26 Chief Marketing Officer ... Ms. Anne ADRIANCE
43 Chief Legal Officer & Sec of Corp ... Mr. Roy P. MOSKOWITZ
13 Sr VP & Chief Information Officer ... Mr. Anand PADMANABHAN
15 Sr VP for HR & Labor Relations ... Ms. Carol CANTRELL
10 VP Finance/Business & Treasurer ... Mr. Steve STABILE
32 VP for Student Success ... Ms. Michelle RELYEA
88 Int VP Distributed & Global Educ ... Ms. Cynthia LAWSON
88 VP Design/Construction & Facilities ... Ms. Lia GARTNER
100 Chief of Staff ... Ms. Deborah BOGOSIAN
20 Dep Provost & Sr VP Academic Affs ... Dr. Bryna SANGER
20 Vice Provost Acad Planning Admin ... Ms. Pat BAXTER
20 Vice Provost Curriculum & Learning ... Ms. Stefania DEKENESSEY
07 VP Strat Enrollment Mgmt ... Dr. Carol KIM
88 Assoc Dean/Dean Fashion ... Mr. Burak CAKMAK
88 Assoc Dean/Dean Milano School ... Ms. Michelle DEPASS
88 Assc Dn/Dean Art/Design Hist/Theory ... Dr. Sarah LAWRENCE
88 Assoc Dean/Dean Art/Media & Tech ... Ms. Anne GAINES
48 Assoc Dean/Dean Constructed Envir ... Mr. Robert KIRKBRIDE
88 Assoc Dean/Dean Media Studies ... Dr. Carol WILDER
48 Assoc Dean/Dean Design Strategies ... Ms. Jane PIRONE
88 Assoc Dean/Dean Undergrad Stds ... Dr. Melissa FRIEDLING
88 Assoc Dean/Dean School of Drama ... Mr. Pippin PARKER
64 Assoc Dean/Dean School of Jazz ... Mr. Martin MUELLER
20 Assoc Provost Faculty Affairs ... Dr. Eleni LITT
09 Assoc Provost Inst Rsrch/Effectiv ... Dr. Paula MAAS
108 Assoc Provost for Assessment ... Dr. Michaela ROME
46 Assoc Provost Research ... Dr. Michael SCHOBER
20 Assoc Provost Acad Budget & Plan ... Vacant
27 Assoc VP Strategic Marketing ... Ms. Lisa PRESTON
35 Asst VP for Student Equity & Access ... Ms. Jennifer FRANCONE
21 Asst VP & Controller ... Ms. Natalie PRESSEY
21 Asst VP Budget & Planning ... Ms. Loretta FERRARI
06 Interim Associate Registrar ... Ms. Alina BABOOLAL
16 Asst VP Human Resources ... Mr. Irwin KROOT
91 Asst VP IT Enterprise Applications ... Mr. Chris BREZIL
90 Asst VP IT Educational Services ... Ms. Lillian SARTORI
91 Asst VP IT Enterprise Applications ... Mr. Marcus LONGMUIR
102 Asst VP Development ... Ms. Marie-Noel APPEL
88 Asst VP Design & Constuction ... Ms. Marla APPELBAUM
88 Asst VP Capital Infrastructure ... Mr. Silviu HERSCHER
88 Asst VP Process Improvement ... Ms. Lisa BONNER
08 University Librarian ... Mr. Ed SCARCELLE
27 Director of Communications (PR) ... Ms. Josephine PARR
23 LCSW/Asst VP Student Health ... Ms. Tracy ROBIN
19 Director Security ... Mr. Thomas ILICETO
37 Senior Director Financial Aid ... Ms. Lisa SHAHEEN
18 Asst VP Facilities Management ... Mr. Thomas WHALEN
96 Sr Director of Business Operations ... Mr. Ed VERDI
85 Int Dir International Student Svcs ... Ms. Linda ASARO
38 Director Counseling Services ... Dr. Jerry FINKELSTEIN
36 Director of Career Success ... Ms. Kelly AHN
28 Director Social Justice Initiatives ... Ms. Gail DRAKES
28 Director Intercultural Support ... Ms. Keisha DAVENPORT-RAMIREZ
29 Director Alumni Engagement ... Ms. Amy GARAWITZ
22 Director Student Disability Svcs ... Mr. Jason LUCHS
25 Director Research Support ... Vacant
24 Director Media Services ... Mr. Mark FITZPATRICK
41 Director Athletics and Recreation ... Ms. Diane YEE
101 Asst Secretary to the Corporation ... Ms. Lori SINGER

New York Academy of Art (F)

111 Franklin Street, New York NY 10013

County: New York — FICE Identification: 026001
Unit ID: 366368
Telephone: (212) 966-0300 — Carnegie Class: Spec-4-yr-Arts
FAX Number: N/A — Calendar System: Semester
URL: www.nyaa.edu
Established: 1982 — Annual Graduate Tuition & Fees: N/A
Enrollment: 108 — Coed
Affiliation or Control: Independent Non-Profit — IRS Status: 501(c)3
Highest Offering: Master's; No Undergraduates
Accreditation: **M**, NY, ART

01 President ... Mr. David KRATZ
05 Dean of Academic Affairs ... Mr. Peter DRAKE
10 Chief Financial Officer ... Mr. Stephan KORSAKOV
11 Director of Operations ... Mr. Michael SMITH
06 Registrar ... Ms. Katie HEMMER
08 Director of Libraries ... Ms. Holly FRISBEE
30 Director of Development ... Ms. Lisa KIRK

New York Career Institute (G)

11 Park Place, 4th Floor, New York NY 10007

County: New York — FICE Identification: 021634
Unit ID: 195845
Telephone: (212) 962-0002 — Carnegie Class: Spec 2-yr-Other
FAX Number: (212) 385-7574 — Calendar System: Trimester
URL: www.nyci.edu
Established: 1941 — Annual Undergrad Tuition & Fees: $13,650
Enrollment: 545 — Coed

Affiliation or Control: Proprietary IRS Status: Proprietary
Highest Offering: Associate Degree
Accreditation: **NY**

01 CEO ... Ivan LONDA
05 Chief Academic Officer ... Lisa Therese FOWLER
32 Director of Student Services ... Cindy MCMAHON
37 Director Financial Aid ... Brenda SORIANO

New York Chiropractic College (A)

2360 State Route 89, Seneca Falls NY 13148-0800
County: Seneca FICE Identification: 012277
Unit ID: 193751
Telephone: (315) 568-3000 Carnegie Class: Spec-4-yr-Other Health
FAX Number: (315) 568-3012 Calendar System: Trimester
URL: www.nycc.edu
Established: 1919 Annual Undergrad Tuition & Fees: N/A
Enrollment: 965 Coed
Affiliation or Control: Independent Non-Profit IRS Status: 501(c)3
Highest Offering: First Professional Degree
Accreditation: **M, ACUP, CHIRO**

01 President ... Dr. Frank J. NICCHI
05 Exec Vice President & Provost ... Dr. Michael A. MESTAN
10 Vice Pres of Finance/Admin Svcs ... Mr. Sean ANGLIM
30 VP Inst Advance/Spec Asst to Pres ... Dr. David R. ODIORNE
84 Vice Pres Enrollment Management ... Ms. Magdalen KELLOGG
96 Assoc VP Admin Svcs/Dir Purchasing ... Mr. Richard B. WORDEN
20 Assoc VP Acad Affairs & Inst Effect ... Ms. Jennifer VONHAHMANN
13 Assoc VP Informational Tech ... Mr. Christophe MCQUEENEY
58 Dean Academic Programs & Services ... Dr. Nicolas POIRIER
88 Dean of Chiropractic ... Dr. Karen A. BOBAK
06 Registrar ... Mr. Kevin MCCARTHY
07 Director of Admissions ... Mr. Michael LYNCH
37 Director Financial Aid ... Mr. Darrin ROOKER
88 Director of Bachelor Prof Studies ... Dr. John DEMETROS
46 Dean of Research ... Dr. Jeanmarie R. BURKE
12 Depew Health Center Administrator ... Dr. Michael FLYNN
12 Levittown Health Ctr Chief of Staff ... Ms. Melissa MURPHY
17 Seneca Falls Hlth Ctr Chf of Staff ... Dr. Wendy L. MANERI
51 Dean Post Grad & Cont Educ ... Dr. Thomas VENTIMIGLIA
08 Director of the Library ... Ms. Bethyn BONI
88 Dir Academy Admc Excl Stdnt Success ... Mr. Peter THOMPSON
39 Secretary Housing ... Ms. Janette ELSTER
41 Dir Health & Fitness Education ... Mr. Rhett TICCONI
32 Director Student Life ... Ms. Holly Anne WAYE
36 Dir Ctr Career Dev Prof Success ... Ms. Susan D. PITTENGER
29 Director of Alumni Relations ... Ms. Diane ZINK
45 Director Accreditation ... Dr. Beth DONOHUE
09 Quality Engineer ... Ms. Patricia MERKLE
15 Human Resources Manager ... Ms. Christine MCDERMOTT
91 Information Tech Administrator ... Mr. Shane SHOWERS
19 Director Facilities/Security ... Mr. William WAYNE
40 Bookstore Manager ... Ms. Helen STUCK
58 Dir MS Clinical Anatomy Pgm ... Dr. Jennette BALL
76 Dir Applied Clinical Nutrition Pgm ... Dr. Peter NICKLESS
88 Dean of FL Sch Acup/Oriental Med ... Mr. Jason WRIGHT
88 Dir MS Diagnostic Imaging Program ... Dr. Chad WARSHEL
88 Dir Academy for Teaching Excellence ... Ms. Amy SIMOLO
12 Campus Health Ctr Chief of Staff ... Dr. Jonathon EGAN
12 Rochester Hlth Ctr Chf of Staff ... Dr. Ryan NADEAU
90 Systems Administrator ... Ms. Shelly STUCK
24 Educational Tech Administrator ... Mr. Bernard CECCHINI
23 Director Health Center Operations ... Mrs. Melissa BAXTER
21 Controller ... Ms. Karen QUEST
88 Dir MS Hum Anat Phys Instructn Pgm ... Dr. William GERMANO

New York College of Health Professions (B)

6801 Jericho Turnpike, Syosset NY 11791-4413
County: Nassau FICE Identification: 025994
Unit ID: 418126
Telephone: (516) 364-0808 Carnegie Class: Spec-4-yr-Other Health
FAX Number: (516) 364-6645 Calendar System: Trimester
URL: www.nycollege.edu
Established: 1981 Annual Undergrad Tuition & Fees: $14,226
Enrollment: 732 Coed
Affiliation or Control: Independent Non-Profit IRS Status: 501(c)3
Highest Offering: Master's
Accreditation: **NY, ACUP**

01 President ... Ms. Lisa PAMINTUAN
10 Chief Financial Officer ... Mr. Errol VIRASAWMI
63 Dean Grad Sch Oriental Medicine ... Dr. A. Li SONG
05 Acting Dean of Academic Affairs ... Ms. Moftia AUJERO
06 Registrar ... Ms. Cory WALTER
88 Senior Admissions Counselor ... Ms. Mary RODAS
08 Dir Library/Information Services ... Ms. Cynthia CAYEA
09 Director of Institutional Research ... Mr. Ross GRIFFITH
21 Bursar ... Ms. Jacqueline MCINTYRE
13 Manager Information Technology ... Mr. Brian ALVAREZ
32 Director of Student Services ... Ms. Mary RODAS
88 Dean Sch of Massage Therapy NYC ... Vacant

New York College of Podiatric Medicine (C)

53 E 124th Street, New York NY 10035-1815
County: New York FICE Identification: 002749
Unit ID: 194073
Telephone: (212) 410-8000 Carnegie Class: Spec-4-yr-Other Health
FAX Number: (212) 876-7670 Calendar System: Semester
URL: www.nycpm.edu
Established: 1911 Annual Undergrad Tuition & Fees: N/A
Enrollment: 381 Coed
Affiliation or Control: Independent Non-Profit IRS Status: 501(c)3
Highest Offering: First Professional Degree
Accreditation: **POD**

01 President ... Mr. Louis L. LEVINE
05 Vice Pres Academic Affairs/Dean ... Dr. Michael J. TREPAL
11 Chief Operating Ofcr/VP Admin ... Mr. Joel STURM
10 Chief Financial Officer ... Mr. Greg ONAIFO
13 Vice Pres Info Systems & Technology ... Mr. Aman SAFAEI
63 VP Medical Education/Medical Dir ... Dr. Mark SWARTZ
30 VP of Development & Operations ... Mr. Desander MAS
32 Dean Student Affairs ... Ms. Lisa LEE
20 Dean Clinical Educ/Dir Res Pgms ... Dr. Robert ECKLES
09 Dean Institutional Research ... Dr. Eileen CHUSID
07 Assoc Dean Admissions/Student Svcs ... Ms. Lili YOUNG
26 Director Public Affairs/Development ... Ms. Ellen LUBELL
08 Director of Library ... Mr. Paul TREMBLAY
37 Director Financial Aid ... Ms. Eve TRAUBE
06 Registrar ... Ms. Kristy DIPALMA
19 Director Security/Safety ... Mr. James WARREN, JR.

New York College of Traditional Chinese Medicine (D)

200 Old Country Road, Suite 500, Mineola NY 11501-4204
County: Nassau FICE Identification: 034433
Unit ID: 439783
Telephone: (516) 739-1545 Carnegie Class: Spec-4-yr-Other Health
FAX Number: (516) 873-9622 Calendar System: Trimester
URL: www.nyctcm.edu
Established: 1996 Annual Undergrad Tuition & Fees: N/A
Enrollment: 155 Coed
Affiliation or Control: Independent Non-Profit IRS Status: 501(c)3
Highest Offering: Master's
Accreditation: **ACUP**

01 President ... Dr. Yemeng CHEN
10 Administrative Dean ... Dr. James S. BARE
05 Academic Dean ... Dr. Sunny SHEN
07 Admissions Manager ... Ms. Jinglin BAI
23 Clinic Director ... Mr. Martin SILBER
88 Clinic Manager ... Ms. Yibing ZHAO
06 Records Manager ... Ms. Susan SU
37 Financial Aid/Admin Coordinator ... Ms. Elise MA
21 Financial Manager ... Ms. Lily ZOU
08 Operations Manager ... Ms. Ling Ling CHANG

The New York Conservatory for Dramatic Arts (E)

39 West 19th Street, New York NY 10011
County: New York FICE Identification: 031207
Unit ID: 421841
Telephone: (212) 645-0030 Carnegie Class: Spec 2-yr-A&S
FAX Number: (212) 645-0039 Calendar System: Semester
URL: www.nycda.edu
Established: 1980 Annual Undergrad Tuition & Fees: $31,200
Enrollment: 237 Coed
Affiliation or Control: Proprietary IRS Status: Proprietary
Highest Offering: Associate Degree
Accreditation: **THEA**

00 Artistic Director ... Joan SEE
01 CEO ... David PALMER
05 Director of Education ... Richard OMAR
20 Assoc Director of Education ... Jay R. GOLDENBERG
06 Registrar ... Stefon SIMMONS
08 Head Librarian ... Martha REPETTO

New York Graduate School of Psychoanalysis (F)

16 West Tenth Street, New York NY 10011
Telephone: (212) 260-7050 Identification: 770116
Accreditation: **&EH**

† Regional accreditation is carried under the parent institution in Brookline, MA

New York Institute of Technology (G)

Northern Boulevard, Old Westbury NY 11568-8000
County: Nassau FICE Identification: 004804
Unit ID: 194091
Telephone: (516) 686-7516 Carnegie Class: Masters/L
FAX Number: (516) 686-7613 Calendar System: Semester
URL: www.nyit.edu
Established: 1955 Annual Undergrad Tuition & Fees: $33,480
Enrollment: 7,872 Coed
Affiliation or Control: Independent Non-Profit IRS Status: 501(c)3
Highest Offering: Doctorate
Accreditation: **M, ARCPA, BUS, CACREP, CIDA, ENG, ENGT, NURSE, OSTEO, OT, PTA, TED**

01 President ... Dr. Edward GUILIANO
05 Provost/Vice Pres Academic Affairs ... Dr. Rahmat SHOURESHI
100 Chief of Staff ... Mr. Peter KINNEY
45 Vice Pres for Planning/Assessment ... Dr. Harriet ARNONE
30 Vice President for Development ... Mr. John ELIZANDRO
17 Vice President Health Affairs ... Dr. Barbara ROSS-LEE
32 VP Stdnt Affs/Chief Stdnt Affs Ofcr ... Dr. Patrick LOVE
13 Vice Pres of IT & Infrastructure ... Dr. Niyazi BODUR
84 Vice President Enrollment ... Mr. Ronald MAGGIORE
26 Vice Pres Comm & Mktg ... Ms. Nancy DONNER
10 CFO & Treasurer ... Mr. Leonard AUBREY
21 Controller ... Ms. Barbara HOLAHAN
43 General Counsel ... Ms. Catherine FLICKINGER
06 Registrar ... Ms. Kristen SMITH
76 Dean School of Health Professions ... Dr. Patricia CHUTE
48 Dean Sch Architecture & Design ... Ms. Judith DIMAIO
53 Dean School of Education ... Vacant
54 Dean School of Engr & Comp Sciences ... Dr. Nada ANID
49 Dean School Arts & Sciences ... Dr. James SIMON
50 Dean School of Management ... Dr. Jess BORONICO
108 Dean Operations/Assessments & Acc ... Dr. Patricia BURLAUD
35 Dean for Campus Life ... Ms. Gabrielle ST. LEGER
36 Dean of Career Services ... Mr. John HYDE
75 Dean Voc Independence Program ... Dr. Ernst VANBERGEIJK
09 Director Inst Research & Assessment ... Mr. Michael LANE
07 Dean Admissions & Financial Aid ... Ms. Karen VAHEY
27 Director Publications & Advertising ... Vacant
27 Director of Communications ... Ms. Bobbie DELL'AQUILO
29 Director of Alumni Relations ... Ms. Jennifer KELLY
18 Director of Facilities Operations ... Mr. William MARCHAND
37 Associate Dean of Financial Aid ... Ms. Rosemary FERRUCCI
19 Director Security ... Mr. Anthony REPALONE
41 Director Athletics & Recreation ... Mr. Duane BAILEY
25 Asst Provost Spnsrd Pgms & Research ... Dr. Allison ANDORS
88 Director Plng & Business Affairs ... Ms. Ajisa DERVISEVIC
96 Director Procurement Services ... Ms. Gina ARMS
88 Director of Internal Audit ... Ms. Rachel BERTHOUMIEUX
38 Director Counseling & Wellness Svcs ... Ms. Alice HERON-BURKE
88 Assistant Dean Academic Enrichment ... Ms. Monika SCHUEREN
15 Director of Human Resources ... Ms. Carol JABLONSKY
90 Director Client Services ... Ms. Laurie HARVEY
91 Director Systems & Network ... Mr. Brian MAROLDO
35 Assoc Dean Student Development ... Ms. Zennabelle SEWELL
88 Dir Events Planning & Hospitality ... Mr. Jerry LIMONCELLI
63 Vice President Med Affs/Global Hlth ... Dr. Jerry BALENTINE

New York Law School (H)

185 West Broadway, New York NY 10013-2959
County: New York FICE Identification: 002783
Unit ID: 193821
Telephone: (212) 431-2100 Carnegie Class: Spec-4-yr-Law
FAX Number: (212) 965-8838 Calendar System: Semester
URL: www.nyls.edu
Established: 1891 Annual Graduate Tuition & Fees: N/A
Enrollment: 1,029 Coed
Affiliation or Control: Independent Non-Profit IRS Status: 501(c)3
Highest Offering: Doctorate; No Undergraduates
Accreditation: **LAW**

01 Dean and President ... Dean Anthony CROWELL
05 Assoc Dean Academic & Student Engag ... Dean William P. LAPIANA
03 Executive VP & Chief Strategy Ofcr ... Ms. Carole POST
10 Senior Vice President & CFO ... Mr. Stuart KLEIN
11 Assoc Dean for Inst Accountability ... Dean Joan R. FISHMAN
26 VP of Marketing & Communications ... Ms. Silvia ALVAREZ
30 VP of Institutional Advancement ... Mr. Elliot BERGER
08 Director of Law Library/Assoc Dean ... Prof. Camille BROUSSARD
84 Assoc Dean Admissions & Prof Dev ... Mr. Jeffery BECHERER
07 Asst Dean of Admissions & Finan Aid ... Ms. Ella Mae ESTRADA
36 Asst Dean of Advising & Prof Dev ... Ms. Courtney FITZGIBBONS
21 Asst VP Financial Planning & Mgmt ... Ms. Susan REDLER
18 Chief Maintenance/Operations/Secur ... Mr. Paul REPETTO
15 Asst Vice President Human Resources ... Ms. Jody PARIANTE
09 Asst VP Institutional Research ... Dr. Joanne INGHAM
32 Assistant Dean for Student Engagemt ... Ms. Helena PRIGAL
21 Asst Vice Pres Business Operations ... Mr. George HAYES
44 Director of Development ... Ms. Anna FERBER
20 Asst Dean Academic Program Develop ... Ms. Erin BOND
06 Assistant Dean and Registrar ... Mr. Oral HOPE
13 Chief Information Officer ... Mr. Thomas SOCASH
35 Sr Director of Student Life ... Ms. Sally HARDING
20 Assoc Director Academic Planning ... Ms. Kiera FLAD
96 Purchasing Coordinator ... Mr. Norman DAWKINS
39 Admissions Counselor/Housing Coord ... Ms. Lauren MAJCHROWSKI
04 Admin Assistant to the President ... Ms. Mary Sue DANIELS
104 Director Study Abroad ... Mr. Michael RHEE
86 Director Government Relations ... Mr. Ariel DVORKIN

New York Medical College (I)

40 Sunshine Cottage Road, Valhalla NY 10595-1690
County: Westchester FICE Identification: 002784
Unit ID: 193830
Telephone: (914) 594-4900 Carnegie Class: Spec-4-yr-Med
FAX Number: (914) 594-4145 Calendar System: Other
URL: www.nymc.edu
Established: 1860 Annual Graduate Tuition & Fees: N/A
Enrollment: 1,482 Coed
Affiliation or Control: Jewish IRS Status: 501(c)3
Highest Offering: Doctorate; No Undergraduates
Accreditation: **M, DENT, MED, PAST, PH, PTA, SP**

01 President ....Dr. Alan H. KADISH
03 Administrator ....Ms. Vilma BORDONARO
05 Vice Prov/Sr Assoc Dean Acad Admin ....Mr. William A. STEADMAN, II
17 CEO/Exec Dean/Chanc Health Affairs ....Dr. Edward C. HALPERIN
10 Vice Pres Financial Operations ....Mr. Adam D. HAMMERMAN
63 Dean School of Medicine ....Dr. D. Douglas MILLER
58 Dean Grad Sch Basic Medical Science .....Dr. Francis L. BELLONI
43 Vice President/General Counsel ....Mr. Waldemar A. COMAS
30 Vice Pres Devel/Alumni Affairs ....Ms. Amy S. KAHN
86 Vice President Government Affairs ....Dr. Robert W. AMLER
11 Vice President Operations ....Mr. Michael ROGOVIN
21 Assoc Vice Pres/Controller ....Mr. George NESTLER
43 Assoc Vice Pres Legal Affairs ....Ms. Dana LEE
20 Assoc Dean Academic Administration ...Mr. Randi D. SCHWARTZ
26 Director Communications ....Ms. Jennifer RIEKERT
13 Sr Dir Information Tech Services ....Mr. Luis MONTES
76 Dean Sch Health Sciences & Practice ....Dr. Robert W. AMLER
63 Vice Dean Grad Med Ed/Affiliations ..Dr. Richard G. MCCARRICK
09 Assoc Dean Research Administration .Mr. Charles B. HATHAWAY
32 Sr Assoc Dean Student Affairs ....Dr. Gladys M. AYALA
37 Asc Dn Stdnt Affs/Dir Finan Plng ....Mr. Anthony M. SOZZO
07 Sr Associate Dean Admissions ....Dr. Fern R. JUSTER
51 Assoc Dean Continuing Med Education ....Dr. Joseph F. DURSI
08 Assoc Dean/Dir Health Sci Library ....Ms. Marie ASCHER
07 Director of Admissions ....Ms. Robin BAUM
06 University Registrar ....Ms. Jennifer SIMMONS
39 Director Student Housing ....Ms. Katherine E. DILLON
18 Dir Capital Planning/Facilities ....Mr. Thomas ALLEN
19 Director of Security ....Mr. William ALLISON
85 Intl Student/Scholar Advisor ....Ms. Elizabeth WARD
51 Director of Continuing Medical Educ .....Ms. Kathy J. KAVANAGH
23 Director Health Services ....Dr. Joseph F. DURSI
38 Director Student Counseling ....Dr. Mark SINGER
105 Director Web Services ....Mr. Kevin R. CUMMINGS
40 Director Bookstore ....Ms. Liz REYNOLDS
24 Head Educational Media ....Mr. Michael COTTER
14 Coord of Instruct Computing Tech ....Mr. Jason DI NARDI
04 Administrative Asst to President ....Ms. Vera ROSARIO

New York School of Interior Design (A)

170 East 70th Street, New York NY 10021-5110
County: New York FICE Identification: 020690
Unit ID: 194116
Telephone: (212) 472-1500 Carnegie Class: Spec-4-yr-Arts
FAX Number: (212) 472-3800 Calendar System: 4/1/4
URL: www.nysid.edu
Established: 1916 Annual Undergrad Tuition & Fees: $22,670
Enrollment: 539 Coed
Affiliation or Control: Independent Non-Profit IRS Status: 501(c)3
Highest Offering: Master's
Accreditation: M, ART, CIDA

01 President ....Mr. David SPROULS
05 VP Academic Affairs/Dean ....Dr. Ellen FISHER
10 VP for Finance & Administration ....Ms. Jane CHEN
32 Dean of Students ....Ms. Karen HIGGINBOTHAM
04 Assistant to the President ....Ms. Jeanne KO
06 Registrar ....Ms. Jennifer MELENDEZ
08 Director of the Library ....Mr. Billy KWAN
07 Director of Admissions ....Ms. Celeste COLLINS
37 Financial Aid Coordinator ....Ms. Audrey ZAHOR
15 Director of Personnel Services ....Ms. Yvonne MORAY
18 Chief Facilities/Physical Plant ....Mr. Zeke KOLENOVIC
26 Director of External Relations ....Ms. Samantha HOOVER
20 Associate Dean ....Ms. Barbara LOWENTHAL
13 Dir Computing/Information Mgmt ....Mr. Tomasz SOWINSKI
90 Director Academic Computing ....Mr. Richard T. CLASS
38 Director Student Counseling ....Dr. Penny MORGANSTEIN
09 Director of Institutional Research ....Mr. Christopher VINGER
30 Director Development ....Ms. Elizabeth GRAY KOGEN

New York Theological Seminary (B)

475 Riverside Drive, Suite 500, New York NY 10115-0083
County: New York FICE Identification: 002674
Unit ID: 193894
Telephone: (212) 870-1211 Carnegie Class: Spec-4-yr-Faith
FAX Number: (212) 870-1236 Calendar System: Semester
URL: www.nyts.edu
Established: 1900 Annual Graduate Tuition & Fees: N/A
Enrollment: 396 Coed
Affiliation or Control: Independent Non-Profit IRS Status: 501(c)3
Highest Offering: Doctorate; No Undergraduates
Accreditation: THEOL

01 President ....Dr. Dale T. IRVIN
30 VP Development/Inst Advancement ....Dr. Courtney WILEY-HARRIS
05 Academic Dean ....Dr. Kirkpatrick G. COHALL
10 Chief Financial Officer/Controller ....Mr. Craig KING
08 Librarian ....Dr. Jerry REISIG
06 Registrar ....Ms. Lydia R. BUMGARDNER
37 Director Financial Aid ....Ms. Tamisia WHITE
26 Coordinator Publications/Marketing ....Ms. Cathy A. MORALES
105 Director Web Services ....Ms. Angelica C. MORALES
106 Dir Online Education/E-learning ....Ms. Ava CARROLL
108 Director Institutional Assessment ....Dr. Elaine PADILLA
29 Director Alumni Relations ....Ms. Cynthia GARDNER-BRIM
38 Director Student Counseling ....Dr. Edward L. HUNT

New York University (C)

70 Washington Square S, New York NY 10012-1092
County: New York FICE Identification: 002785
Unit ID: 193900
Telephone: (212) 998-1212 Carnegie Class: DU-Highest
FAX Number: N/A Calendar System: Semester
URL: www.nyu.edu
Established: 1831 Annual Undergrad Tuition & Fees: $47,750
Enrollment: 49,274 Coed
Affiliation or Control: Independent Non-Profit IRS Status: 501(c)3
Highest Offering: Doctorate
Accreditation: M, BUS, COPSY, DENT, DH, DIETD, DIETI, ENG, HSA, IPSY, JOUR, LAW, MED, MIDWF, NURSE, OT, PAST, PH, PLNG, PTA, SP, SPAA, SURGT, SW, TEAC

01 President ....Dr. Andrew HAMILTON
05 Provost ....Dr. Katherine FLEMING
10 Executive VP for Finance/IT ....Dr. Martin DORPH
11 Executive VP for Operations ....Vacant
17 Executive VP for Health ....Dr. Robert BERNE
03 Chief of Staff to the President ....Mr. Richard BAUM
20 Deputy Provost & VC Europe ....Vacant
26 Sr VP for Univ Rels/Pub Affairs ....Dr. Lynne BROWN
30 Sr VP Development/Alumni Relations ......Ms. Debra A. LAMORTE
32 Sr Vice Pres for Student Affairs ....Dr. Marc L. WAIS
43 General Counsel & Secretary ....Mr. Terrance NOLAN
28 VProv Faculty/Arts/Human/Diversity ....Dr. Ulrich C. BAER
46 Sr Vice Provost for Research ....Dr. Paul M. HORN
03 Senior Presidential Fellow ....Ms. Ellen SCHALL
88 Sr VProv Global Fac Dev NYUAD/NYUSH ....Dr. Ron ROBIN
20 Sr Vice Provost Academic Affairs ... Dr. Matthew S. SANTIROCCO
45 Vice Chancellor Strategic Planning ....Vacant
35 VC Global Pgms/Univ Life at NYU ....Dr. Linda G. MILLS
54 Exec VProv Engineering/Applied Sci ....Dr. Katepalli R. SREENIVASAN
18 VP Facilities & Construction Mgmt ....Mr. David ALONSO
26 Vice Pres for Public Affairs ....Mr. John H. BECKMAN
45 VP Public Resource Admin & Develop ....Dr. Richard N. BING
84 Vice Pres Enrollment ....Ms. MJ KNOLL-FINN
88 VP Univ Enterprise Initiatives ....Vacant
44 VP Development and Campaigns ....Vacant
15 Vice Pres Human Resources ....Ms. Sabrina ELLIS
13 VP for Global Technology & CGTO ....Mr. Thomas DELANEY
86 VP Govt Affs/Community Engagement ....Vacant
21 VP Budget & Planning ....Mr. Anthony JIGA
88 VP of Global Campus Services ....Vacant
21 VP Finance Operations/Treasurer ....Ms. Stephanie PIANKA
19 VP Global Campus Safety ....Vacant
105 VP Info Technology & CITO ....Vacant
06 University Registrar ....Ms. Elizabeth A. KIENLE-GRANZO
54 Vice Prov Science/Engineering Devel ..Mr. Gerard A. BEN AROUS
45 VProv & Assoc VC Strategic Planning .....Mr. Joseph P. JULIANO
88 Vice Prov Research/Faculty Affairs ....Dr. C. Cybele RAVER
88 Vice Prov Global Stdnt Ldrshp Init ....Ms. Melody C. BARNES
21 Assoc VP Facilities Finance & Tech ....Mr. Chris TANG
27 Assoc VP for Univ Rels & Pub Affs .....Ms. Deborah BRODERICK
29 Assoc VP for Alumni Relations ....Mr. Brian PERILLO
88 Assoc VProv Rsrch Compliance/Admin ....Dr. Martha L. DUNNE
96 Assoc VP Purchasing & Logistics ....Vacant
88 Assoc VP Fac Housing/Resid Svcs ....Vacant
88 VP for Global Programs ....Dr. Nancy J. MORRISON
20 Sr Assoc Prov/Chf of Staff to Prov ....Dr. Carol K. MORROW
07 Asst VP for Undergrad Admissions ....Mr. Shawn L. ABBOTT
20 Asst Provost Academic Pgm Review ....Mr. Barnett W. HAMBERGER
31 Asst VP Cmty Outreach/Engagement ... Mr. Allen M. MCFARLANE
21 Assoc Vice Pres Fin Ops/Controller ....Ms. Kerri J. TRICARICO
41 Asst VP Stdnt Affairs/Dir Athletics ....Mr. Christopher BLEDSOE
23 Assoc VP Stdnt Hlth/Exec Dir SHC ....Dr. Carlo CIOTOLI
37 Asst VP Financial Aid ....Ms. Lynn E. HIGINBOTHAM
102 Dir Office of Sponsored Programs ....Ms. Nancy S. DANEAU
88 Asst VP Internal Audit ....Ms. Jasmine DE NULLY
22 Exec Dir Ofc of Equal Opportunity ....Ms. Mary SIGNOR
36 Asst VP Student Affairs ....Ms. Trudy G. STEINFELD
08 Dean of Libraries ....Ms. Carol A. MANDEL
38 Sr Director SHC ....Ms. Patricia DELORENZO
39 Sr Director Housing Services ....Mr. Neil S. HANRAHAN
50 Dean Business ....Dr. Peter B. HENRY
53 Dean Education ....Dr. Dominic BREWER
04 Counselor to the President ....Mr. Norman DORSEN
104 Vice Chancellor for Global Programs ....Dr. Linda MILLS
108 Asst V Prov Acad Pgm Review/Assess ....Dr. Diana KARAFIN

Niagara County Community College (D)

3111 Saunders Settlement Road, Sanborn NY 14132-9460
County: Niagara FICE Identification: 002874
Unit ID: 193946
Telephone: (716) 614-6200 Carnegie Class: Assoc/MT-VT-High Trad
FAX Number: (716) 614-6700 Calendar System: Semester
URL: www.niagaracc.suny.edu
Established: 1962 Annual Undergrad Tuition & Fees (In-District): $4,370
Enrollment: 6,478 Coed
Affiliation or Control: State/Local IRS Status: 501(c)3
Highest Offering: Associate Degree
Accreditation: M, ACFEI, ADNUR, MAC, PTAA, RAD, SURGT

01 President ....Dr. James KLYCZEK
05 Vice President Academic Affairs ....Dr. Luba CHLIWNIAK
103 Asst VP Workforce Development ....Ms. Phyllis ULETT
10 Vice President of Finance/Info Tech ......Mr. William SCHICKLING
32 Vice President of Student Services ....Mrs. Julia PITMAN
11 Vice President of Operations ....Mr. Michael DOMBROWSKI
09 Director Planning and Research ....Dr. Mary Jane FELDMAN
15 Director of Human Resources ....Ms. Catherine BROWN
07 Interim Director of Admissions ....Mr. James TRIMBOLI
21 Director of Business Services ....Ms. Theresa DIGREGORIO
04 Assistant to President ....Ms. Barbara WALCK
06 Registrar ....Ms. Julie SCHUCKER
35 Director of Student Development ....Mrs. Allison ARMUSEWICZ
30 Chief Development Officer ....Ms. Deborah BREWER
37 Director of Financial Aid ....Mr. James TRIMBOLI
26 Director Public Relations ....Ms. Gina BEAM
18 Assistant Director of Facilities ....Mr. Dennis GASBARRO
28 Asst Director of HR/Compliance ....Mr. William SABIO
08 Head Librarian ....Ms. Nancy KENNEDY
105 Director Web Services ....Mr. Cory WRIGHT
106 Dir Online Education/E-learning ....Ms. Lisa DUBUC
13 Chief Info Technology Officer ....Mr. Dennis MICHAELS
19 Director Security/Safety ....Ms. Lisa BABCOCK
102 Foundation Director ....Ms. Deborah BREWER
39 Interim Director Student Housing ....Ms. Kathleen SAUNDERS
41 Athletic Director ....Mr. Robert MCKEOWN
91 Dir User & Administrative Tech ....Ms. Cindy MACK

Niagara University (E)

Niagara University NY 14109-9999
County: Niagara FICE Identification: 002788
Unit ID: 193973
Telephone: (716) 285-1212 Carnegie Class: Masters/L
FAX Number: (716) 286-8710 Calendar System: Semester
URL: www.niagara.edu
Established: 1856 Annual Undergrad Tuition & Fees: $29,900
Enrollment: 4,015 Coed
Affiliation or Control: Independent Non-Profit IRS Status: 501(c)3
Highest Offering: Doctorate
Accreditation: M, BUS, CACREP, NURSE, SW, TED

01 President ....Rev. James MAHER, CM
03 Exec Vice President ....Dr. Debra COLLEY
05 Interim Provost/VP for Acad Affairs ....Dr. Timothy IRELAND
10 Senior VP Operations & Finance ....Ms. Mary E. BORGOGNONI
11 VP for Administration ....Mr. Michael S. JASZKA
32 VP for Enrollment Management and St ....Dr. Kevin HEARN
88 Interim VP for Intl Relations ....Rev. Kevin CREAGH, CM
30 VP for Institutional Advancement ....Dr. Derek M. WESLEY
42 VP Univ Mission and Ministry ....Rev. Kevin CREAGH, CM
20 Assoc VP Acad Affs/Pgms & Policy ....Vacant
26 Assoc VP of Comm/Public Relations ....Mr. Thomas BURNS
44 Assoc VP for Institutional Advance ....Mr. Benjamin D. MARCHIONE
84 Asst VP Enrollment Management ....Ms. Cathleen ANDERSON
45 Exec Dir Univ Planning & Assessment ....Mr. Christopher R. SHEFFIELD
43 General Counsel ....Ms. Stephanie A. COLE
35 Dean of Student Affairs ....Mr. Jason JAKUBOWSKI
49 Interim Dean Col of Arts & Sci ....Dr. Peter BUTERA
50 Interim Dean Col of Business Admin ....Dr. Tenpao LEE
53 Dean College of Education ....Dr. Chandra FOOTE
88 Dean Col Hospit/Tourism Mgtality ....Dr. Kurt A. STAHURA
09 Director of Institutional Research ....Dr. Vennessa L. WALKER
88 Facility Planner ....Mr. Daniel MCMANN
07 Director of Admissions Operations ....Mr. Harry S. GONG
07 Director of Admissions ....Mr. Mark E. WOJNOWSKI
08 Director of Libraries ....Mr. David SCHOEN
19 Director of Campus Safety ....Mr. John F. BARKER
37 Director of Financial Aid ....Ms. Katie L. KOCSIS
39 Director of Residence Life ....Ms. Kimberly FENTON
35 Director of Campus Activities ....Mrs. Mati ORTIZ
29 Exec Director Alumni Engagement ....Ms. Christine S. O'HARA
13 Director Information Technology ....Mr. Richard P. KERNIN
57 Director of Art Museum ....Ms. Kate KOPERSKI
15 Director of Human Resources ....Ms. Donna MOSTILLER
23 Director of Health Services ....Ms. Cheryl LYON
41 Director of Athletics ....Mr. Simon GRAY
18 Director of Facility Services ....Mr. Daniel M. GUARIGLIA
88 Exec Dir Division of Academic Svcs ....Ms. Antonia KNIGHT
88 Director of Academic Support ....Mrs. Diane STOELTING
51 Dir Continuing/Community Education ....Mr. Jon Jay STOCKSLADER
31 Dir Institute for Civic Engagement ....Dr. David B. TAYLOR
88 Dir Rec & Intramurals/Kiernan Ctr ....Mr. John K. SPANBAUER
38 Director Counseling Services ....Ms. Jeannine D. SUK
21 Controller ....Mr. Donald E. SMITH
96 Dir of Contract Services & Risk Mgt ....Ms. Christy FERGUSON
88 Assoc Dean for Graduate Recruitment ....Mr. Evan F. PIERCE
92 Honors Program Coordinator ....Dr. Michael BARNWELL
85 Dir Multicultural & Intl Stdnt Affs ....Ms. Averl HARBIN
06 University Registrar ....Mr. R. Ryan KENDRICK
88 Director of Student Accounts ....Ms. Martie HOWELL
25 Director Grants & Sponsored Program ....Ms. Valerie NOLAN
36 Director of Career Services ....Mr. Robert P. SWANSON
88 Director of Academic Exploration .... Mrs. Stephanie CHESEBRO
104 Director of International Relations .... Ms. Bernadette BRENNEN
31 Director of Learn and Serve ....Ms. Fran BOLTZ
88 Veterans Services Coordinator ....Mr. Robert HEALY
29 Assoc Dir Alumni & Volunteer Engmt ... Mr. Howard M. MORGAN
44 Assoc Dir Leadership Giving ....Ms. Jaclyn R. ROSSI
44 Director of Planned Giving ....Ms. Leslie K. WISE
04 Administrative Asst to President ....Ms. Jesenia RIVERA

North Country Community College (A)

23 Santanoni Avenue, PO Box 89,
Saranac Lake NY 12983-0089
County: Essex FICE Identification: 007111
Unit ID: 194028
Telephone: (518) 891-2915 Carnegie Class: Assoc/MT-VT-Mix Trad/Non
FAX Number: (518) 891-2915 Calendar System: Semester
URL: www.nccc.edu
Established: 1967 Annual Undergrad Tuition & Fees (In-District): $5,303
Enrollment: 1,962 Coed
Affiliation or Control: State/Local IRS Status: 501(c)3
Highest Offering: Associate Degree
Accreditation: M

01 President .... Dr. Steve J. TYRELL
05 Int Vice Pres of Academic Affairs .... Mr. Joe KEEGAN
10 Vice Pres for Administration/CFO .... Mr. Robert FARMER
07 Dean of Admissions .... Mr. Christopher TACEA
06 Int Registrar/Records Officer .... Ms. Shelly ST. LOUIS
09 Asst Dean Inst Research/Support .... Mr. Scott HARWOOD
32 Director of Campus & Student Life .... Vacant
29 Director Alumni Relations .... Ms. Diana FORTUNE
04 Administrative Asst to President .... Ms. Jan M. BRHEL
37 Director Student Financial Aid .... Mr. Matthew SANCHEZ
41 Athletic Director .... Mr. Chad LADUE

Northeastern Seminary (B)

2265 Westside Drive, Rochester NY 14624-1932
County: Monroe FICE Identification: 034194
Unit ID: 439817
Telephone: (585) 594-6800 Carnegie Class: Spec-4-yr-Faith
FAX Number: (585) 594-6801 Calendar System: Semester
URL: www.nes.edu
Established: 1998 Annual Graduate Tuition & Fees: N/A
Enrollment: 154 Coed
Affiliation or Control: Independent Non-Profit IRS Status: 501(c)3
Highest Offering: Doctorate; No Undergraduates
Accreditation: M, THEOL

01 President .... Dr. Deana L. PORTERFIELD
05 Academic Vice President and Dean .... Dr. Douglas CULLUM
26 AVP for Communications/Enrollment .... Ms. Lisa BENNETT
07 Director of Admissions .... Mr. Caleb MATTHEWS
04 Administrative Asst to President .... Mrs. Patti RADEL
06 Registrar .... Vacant
10 Chief Business Officer .... Mrs. Laurie LEO
11 Vice President for Administration .... Mrs. Ruth LOGAN
30 VP for Institutional Advancement .... Mr. Darrell BELL

† The Seminary is affiliated with Roberts Wesleyan College.

Nyack College (C)

1 South Boulevard, Nyack NY 10960-3698
County: Rockland FICE Identification: 002790
Unit ID: 194161
Telephone: (845) 675-4400 Carnegie Class: Masters/L
FAX Number: (845) 358-1751 Calendar System: Semester
URL: www.nyack.edu
Established: 1882 Annual Undergrad Tuition & Fees: $24,300
Enrollment: 2,896 Coed
Affiliation or Control: The Christian And Missionary Alliance
IRS Status: 501(c)3
Highest Offering: Doctorate
Accreditation: M, MUS, NURSE, SW, TED, THEOL

01 President .... Dr. Michael G. SCALES
04 Assistant to the President .... Mrs. Carol Ann FREEMAN
10 Exec Vice President & Treasurer .... Mr. David C. JENNINGS
05 Provost/VP for Academic Affairs .... Dr. David F. TURK
84 Vice President for Enrollment .... Mr. Bill VOLTMER
30 Vice President of Advancement .... Rev. Jeffery QUINN
20 Assistant Provost .... Dr. Bennett SCHEPENS
20 Assoc Dean Faculty Development .... Dr. Leonard KAGELER
73 Dean Seminary .... Dr. Ronald WALBORN
50 Dean School of Business & Ldrshp .... Dr. Anita UNDERWOOD
64 Dean School of Music .... Dr. Glenn KOPONEN
53 Dean School of Education .... Dr. JoAnn LOONEY
66 Dean School of Nursing .... Mrs. Elizabeth SIMON
49 Dean College of Arts & Sciences .... Dr. Fernando ARZOLA
08 Dean of Library Services .... Mrs. Linda K. POSTON
89 Assoc Dean Student Success .... Dr. Gwen PARKER AMES
73 Assoc Dean Seminary (NYC) .... Dr. Luis CARLO
73 Asst Dean Seminary (Puerto Rico) .... Dr. Julio APONTE
32 Assoc Dean of Students .... Mrs. Wanda VELEZ
32 Assoc Dean of Students (NYC) .... Mr. Charles HAMMOND
06 Undergraduate Registrar .... Ms. Evangeline COUCHEY
06 Graduate Registrar .... Ms. Rebecca NOSS
07 Dir of Admissions Undergrad .... Mr. Dan BAILEY
07 Dir of Graduate Admissions .... Vacant
21 Assistant Treasurer .... Mrs. Dona P. SCHEPENS
37 Dir of Fin Svcs Undergrad .... Mr. Steve PHILLIPS
37 Dir of Fin Svcs Undergrad (NYC) .... Mr. Isaac FOSTER
31 Executive Director of Community Rel .... Mr. Earl MILLER
41 Director of Athletics .... Mr. Keith A. DAVIE
36 Director of Career Services .... Mrs. Tiffany AUSTIN
15 Director of Human Resources .... Mrs. Karen DAVIE
13 Director of Information Technology .... Mr. Kevin A. BUEL
09 Director of Institutional Research .... Mr. Greg BEEMAN
18 Director of Operations/Aramark .... Mr. Doug WALKER
26 Dir of Public & Media Relations .... Mrs. Deborah WALKER
42 Director of Spiritual Formation .... Mrs. Wanda F. WALBORN
38 Director of Wellness Services .... Mrs. Drusila F. NIEVES
29 Coordinator of Alumni Services .... Mrs. Melissa HICKEY
105 Webmaster .... Mr. Joshua WAY

Nyack College Manhattan Center (D)

2 Washington Street, New York NY 10004
Telephone: (212) 625-0500 Identification: 770143
Accreditation: &M

† Regional accreditation is carried under the parent institution in Nyack, NY

Ohr Hameir Theological Seminary (E)

141 Furnace Woods Road,
Cortlandt Manor NY 10567-6112
County: Westchester FICE Identification: 011984
Unit ID: 194189
Telephone: (914) 736-1500 Carnegie Class: Spec-4-yr-Faith
FAX Number: (914) 736-1055 Calendar System: Semester
Established: 1962 Annual Undergrad Tuition & Fees: $10,000
Enrollment: 96 Male
Affiliation or Control: Independent Non-Profit IRS Status: 501(c)3
Highest Offering: Second Talmudic Degree
Accreditation: RABN

01 President .... Rabbi E. KANAREK
30 Chief Devel Ofcr/Dir Financial Aid .... Rabbi Jacob ROTHBERG
06 Registrar .... Rabbi Berel KANAREK

Ohr Somayach Tanenbaum Educational Center (F)

244 Route 306, Monsey NY 10952-0334
County: Rockland FICE Identification: 023201
Unit ID: 243805
Telephone: (845) 425-1370 Carnegie Class: Not Classified
FAX Number: (845) 425-8865 Calendar System: Trimester
URL: www.os.edu
Established: 1979 Annual Undergrad Tuition & Fees: N/A
Enrollment: N/A Coordinate
Affiliation or Control: Independent Non-Profit IRS Status: 501(c)3
Highest Offering: First Professional Degree
Accreditation: RABN

01 Director .... Rabbi Abraham BRAUN
05 Dean .... Rabbi Israel ROKOWSKY
06 Registrar .... Mrs. Miriam GROSSMAN
10 Chief Business Officer .... Rabbi Eli ROKOWSKY

Onondaga Community College (G)

4585 West Seneca Turnpike, Syracuse NY 13215-4585
County: Onondaga FICE Identification: 002875
Unit ID: 194222
Telephone: (315) 498-2622 Carnegie Class: Assoc/HT-High Non
FAX Number: (315) 492-9208 Calendar System: Semester
URL: www.sunyocc.edu
Established: 1962 Annual Undergrad Tuition & Fees (In-District): $5,014
Enrollment: 12,271 Coed
Affiliation or Control: State/Local IRS Status: 501(c)3
Highest Offering: Associate Degree
Accreditation: M, ADNUR, CAHIIM, PTAA, SURGT

01 President .... Dr. Casey CRABILL
05 Provost and SVP Educational Svcs .... Vacant
10 SVP College-affltd Ent & Asset Mgmt .... Mr. David W. MURPHY
88 VP Student Engmnt & Learning Supp .... Dr. Julie WHITE
03 VP College-affiliated Enterprises .... Mr. Seth TUCKER
03 VP College-affiliated Enterprises .... Ms. Anastasia URTZ
30 Vice President Development .... Ms. Lisa MOORE
15 VP HR & External Affairs .... Ms. Amy KREMENEK
09 VP Inst Planning/Assess/Research .... Dr. Agatha AWUAH
13 Chief Information Officer .... Ms. Andrea VENUTI
21 Chief Financial Officer .... Mr. Mark MANNING
20 AVP Student Engagement .... Ms. Rebecca HODA-KEARSE
20 Asst VP Academic & Support Svcs .... Ms. Kathleen D'APRIX
28 VP/Chief Diversity Officer .... Ms. Eunice WILLIAMS
18 VP Property Management .... Mr. John PADDOCK
84 AVP Enrollment Development .... Ms. Shannon PATRIE
37 Director Financial Aid .... Ms. Rebecca ROSE
41 Athletic Director .... Mr. Michael BORSZ
08 Chair Library .... Ms. Pauline SHOSTACK
38 Chair Counseling Department .... Mr. Timothy SINGER
19 VP Campus Safety & Security .... Vacant
22 Director Disability Services .... Ms. Nancy CARR
06 Registrar .... Ms. Tracey GREEN
21 Assistant Director Student Accounts .... Ms. Sally LUTON
96 Assistant VP Management Services .... Mr. Michael MCMULLEN
39 Exec Dir Housing & Campus Services .... Ms. Cathy DOTTERER
32 Coordinator Student Leadership Dev .... Ms. Sarah COLLINS
07 Associate VP Enrollment Management .... Mr. Denny NICHOLSON
38 Director Advising & Counseling .... Ms. Jeanine ECKENRODE
18 Director of Sustainability .... Mr. Sean VORMWALD
04 Assistant to the President .... Ms. Julie HART
103 AVP Economic & Workforce Dev .... Mr. Michael METZGAR
25 AVP Research & Grants .... Ms. Nicole SCHLATER
29 Assistant Director Alumni Comm .... Mr. Russ CORBIN
45 AVP Inst Effectiveness & Planning .... Ms. Wendy TARBY
26 AVP Advancement Communications .... Ms. Susan TORMEY
43 Interim General Counsel .... Dr. Kevin MOORE

Orange County Community College (H)

115 South Street, Middletown NY 10940-6437
County: Orange FICE Identification: 002876
Unit ID: 194240
Telephone: (845) 344-6222 Carnegie Class: Assoc/HT-High Trad
FAX Number: (845) 343-1228 Calendar System: Semester
URL: www.sunyorange.edu
Established: 1950 Annual Undergrad Tuition & Fees (In-District): $5,122
Enrollment: 6,951 Coed
Affiliation or Control: State/Local IRS Status: 501(c)3
Highest Offering: Associate Degree
Accreditation: M, ACBSP, ADNUR, DH, MLTAD, OTA, PHLEB, PTAA, RAD

01 President .... Dr. Kristine M. YOUNG
05 Int Vice Pres Academic Affairs .... Ms. Stacey MOEGENBURG
32 Int Vice Pres Student Services .... Ms. Gerianne BRUSATI
10 Int VP Administration/Finance .... Ms. Jo Ann HAMBURG
30 Vice Pres Institutional Advancement .... Mr. Vinnie CAZZETTA
13 Chief Information Ofcr .... Mr. Brian MCDONALD
20 Sr Assoc Vice Pres Newburgh Campus .... Dr. Peter SOSCIA
84 Assoc VP for Enrollment Management .... Vacant
76 Assoc VP Health Professions .... Dr. Michael GAWRONSKI, JR.
88 Assoc Vice Pres Resource Devel .... Dr. Russell HAMMOND
50 Int Assoc VP Business/Math/Sci/Tech .... Ms. Anne PRIAL
35 Assoc Vice Pres Stdnt Engagemt/ Comp .... Ms. Madeline TORRES-DIAZ
15 Assoc Vice Pres Human Resources .... Ms. Wendy HOLMES
08 Director Learning Resource .... Ms. Susan PARRY
51 Dir Continuing/Professional Educ .... Mr. David KOHN
19 Director Campus Security/Safety .... Mr. Ed KIELY
09 Inst Plng/Assessment/Research Ofcr .... Ms. Christine WORK
18 Director Administrative Services .... Mr. Michael WORDEN
37 Director of Financial Aid .... Mr. John IVANKOVIC
06 Registrar .... Vacant
26 Communications Officer .... Mr. Mike ALBRIGHT
88 Director Academic Advising .... Ms. Talia LLOSA
07 Director of Admissions .... Mr. Maynard SCHMIDT
35 Director Student Activities .... Mr. Steve HARPST
37 Assoc Director of Financial Aid .... Ms. Rosemary BARRETT
04 Administrative Asst to President .... Ms. Carol MURRAY
41 Athletic Director .... Mr. Wayne SMITH

Orange County Community College Newburgh Branch Campus (I)

1 Washington Center, Newburgh NY 12550
Telephone: (845) 562-2454 Identification: 770144
Accreditation: &M

† Regional accreditation is carried under the parent institution in Middletown, NY

Pace University (J)

1 Pace Plaza, New York NY 10038-1598
County: New York FICE Identification: 002791
Unit ID: 194310
Telephone: (212) 346-1200 Carnegie Class: DU-Mod
FAX Number: (212) 346-1933 Calendar System: Semester
URL: www.pace.edu
Established: 1906 Annual Undergrad Tuition & Fees: $41,333
Enrollment: 12,857 Coed
Affiliation or Control: Independent Non-Profit IRS Status: 501(c)3
Highest Offering: Doctorate
Accreditation: M, ARCPA, BUS, BUSA, CS, IPSY, LAW, NURSE, PSPSY, TED

01 President .... Mr. Stephen J. FRIEDMAN
10 Exec Vice President/CFO .... Mr. Robert C. ALMON
05 Provost/Exec VP Academic Affairs .... Dr. Uday SUKHATME
11 Sr Vice Pres/Chief Admin Ofcr .... Mr. William MCGRATH
84 Vice Pres Enrollment/Placement .... Ms. Robina C. SCHEPP
30 VP Development/Alumni Relations .... Ms. Spiridoula K. ASGARIAN
13 Int VP Information Tech/CIO .... Mr. Christopher ELARDE
26 VP/Chief Marketing Ofcr Univ Rels .... Ms. Frederica N. WALD
15 Assoc Vice Pres Human Resources .... Mr. Matt RENNA
09 Asst Vice Pres Plng/Assess/Inst Res .... Ms. Barbara S. PENNIPEDE
86 Asst Vice Pres Govt/Community Rels .... Ms. Vanessa J. HERMAN
32 AVP Ofc Student Assistance .... Vacant
27 Assoc VP Marketing/Communications .... Mr. Peter R. SIKOWITZ
21 Asst Vice Pres Academic Finance .... Mr. Dominick BUMBACO
19 Associate VP General Services .... Mr. Frank MCDONALD
35 Assoc Vice Pres/Dean of Students .... Dr. Mark Allen POISEL
20 Assoc Provost for Academic Affairs .... Dr. Adelia WILLIAMS
50 Dean Lubin School of Business .... Mr. Neil S. BRAUN
49 Dean Dyson College Arts/Sci .... Dr. Nira HERRMANN
53 Dean School of Education .... Dr. Andrea M. SPENCER
76 Dean College Health Professions .... Dr. Harriet R. FELDMAN
77 Dean School of CSIS .... Dr. Amar GUPTA
32 Dean of Students New York .... Dr. Edith N. ARENAS-RIVERA
32 Dean of Students Westchester .... Dr. Lisa BARDILL MOSCARITOLO
61 Dean School of Law .... Mr. David YASSKY
06 Assoc VP Sdnt Svcs/Univ Registrar .... Vacant
06 Graduate Registrar .... Ms. Margaret JONES
06 Registrar Pleasantville .... Ms. Annmarie MCGRAIL
06 Law School Registrar .... Ms. Nilda RODRIGUEZ

88 Associate University Registrar .... Ms. Barbara MCCARTHY
36 Exec Director Career Svcs/Coop Educ .... Ms. Jody QUEEN-HUBERT
88 Asst Director Adult Education NY .... Ms. Nicola FOSTER
21 Interim Comptroller .... Mr. William VOLL
44 Manager Annual Fund .... Ms. Nicole L. SOUZA
29 Director of Alumni Relations .... Ms. Sheri GIBSON
43 University Counsel .... Mr. Stephen BRODSKY
08 Associate Director Library .... Mr. Melvin ISAACSON
21 University Bursar .... Ms. Susan WEYGANT
37 Director Financial Aid .... Mr. Steven JOHNSON
07 Dir of Admissions NY/Westchester .... Ms. Joanna BRODA
45 Director Budget/Planning/Analysis .... Mr. Len CERTA
22 Affirmative Action Officer .... Ms. Arletha MILES
14 Univ Director Computer Systems .... Mr. Gerard TARPEY
24 Univ Director Educational Media Svc .... Mr. Frank MANNLE
84 Director Adult Enroll Svcs/New York .... Ms. Janet KIRTMAN
23 Assoc Director Health Care Unit .... Ms. Jamesetta NEWLAND
27 Director of Media Relations .... Mr. Christopher CORY
88 Director Pace Adult Resource Center .... Ms. Tamra PLOTNICK
35 Director of Student Devel New York .... Dr. David CLARK
38 Director Counseling Services .... Dr. Richard SHADICK
39 Director of Residential Life .... Mr. A. Patrick ROGER-GORDON
40 Executive Director Bookstore .... Ms. Mary LIETO
85 Assoc Dir Intl Pgms & Services .... Mr. Kraig WALKUP
96 Director of Purchasing - Contracts .... Ms. Alice SEIFERT
18 Director Facilities/Physical Plant .... Mr. Abdul JABAR
28 Director of Diversity .... Ms. Shanelle HENRY ROBINSON

Pacific College of Oriental Medicine (A)

110 William Street, 19th Floor, New York NY 10038
Telephone: (212) 982-3456 Identification: 666139
Accreditation: &WC, ACUP, NUR

† Branch campus of Pacific College of Oriental Medicine, San Diego CA.

Paul Smith's College (B)

PO Box 265, Paul Smiths NY 12970-0265
County: Franklin FICE Identification: 002795
Unit ID: 194392
Telephone: (518) 327-6000 Carnegie Class: Bac-Diverse
FAX Number: N/A Calendar System: Trimester
URL: www.paulsmiths.edu
Established: 1937 Annual Undergrad Tuition & Fees: $27,130
Enrollment: 892 Coed
Affiliation or Control: Independent Non-Profit IRS Status: 501(c)3
Highest Offering: Baccalaureate
Accreditation: M, ACFEI, ENGT

01 President .... Dr. Cathy S. DOVE
04 Assistant to the President .... Ms. Kathleen A. KECK
05 Provost .... Dr. Nicholas HUNT-BULL
10 Vice Pres Finance/Administration .... Mr. Martin HANIFIN
30 Vice President Inst Advancement .... Mr. F. Raymond AGNEW
84 Vice Pres Enrollment Management .... Mr. Peter BURNS
18 VP Facilities Mgmt/Capital Project ... Mr. Steven W. MCFARLAND
13 Director Information Services .... Mr. Jeffrey WALTON
29 Director of Alumni Relations .... Ms. Heather TUTTLE
38 Director of Student Development .... Ms. Ellen GOOCH
37 Director of Financial Aid .... Ms. Mary Ellen M. CHAMBERLAIN
23 Director of Health Services .... Ms. Reiko REXILIUS-TUTHILL
24 Director Education Support Services .... Mr. Michael BECCARIA
26 Director of Communications .... Mr. Robert BENNETT
06 Registrar .... Ms. Kristin EATON
07 Director of Admissions .... Mr. Keith BRAUN
19 Lead Campus Safety Officer .... Ms. Holly PARKER
09 Director Institutional Research .... Dr. Jeffrey WALTON
22 Director HEOP .... Ms. Kate MULLEN
41 Dir of Athletics/Physical Educ .... Mr. James TUCKER
21 Comptroller .... Ms. Laura ROZELL
32 VP Student Affairs/Campus Life .... Mr. Terry LINDSAY
40 Manager of College Store .... Ms. Diana L. LYNG-GLIDDI
15 Human Resources Director .... Ms. Sharon VAN AUKEN
96 Purchasing Coordinator .... Ms. Cynthia LEMERY
36 Career Coordinator .... Ms. Debra DUTCHER
49 Int Dean Commercial/Appl/Lib Arts .... Dr. Eric HOLMLUND
65 Int Dean Natural Res Mgmt/Ecology .... Dr. Dan KELTING
20 Assoc Academic Officer/Provost .... Vacant

Phillips Beth Israel School of Nursing (C)

776 Sixth Avenue, 4th Floor, New York NY 10001-6354
County: New York FICE Identification: 006438
Unit ID: 189282
Telephone: (212) 614-6110 Carnegie Class: Spec-4-yr-Other Health
FAX Number: (212) 614-6109 Calendar System: Semester
URL: www.pbisn.edu
Established: 1904 Annual Undergrad Tuition & Fees: $22,545
Enrollment: 278 Coed
Affiliation or Control: Independent Non-Profit IRS Status: 501(c)3
Highest Offering: Baccalaureate
Accreditation: NY, ADNUR

01 Dean .... Dr. Todd AMBROSIA
05 Assistant Dean .... Mrs. Bernice PASS-STERN
32 Director Student Services .... Ms. Linda FABRIZIO

Plaza College (D)

118-33 Queens Boulevard, Forest Hills NY 11375
County: Queens FICE Identification: 012358
Unit ID: 194499
Telephone: (718) 779-1430 Carnegie Class: Bac/Assoc-Mixed
FAX Number: (718) 779-7423 Calendar System: Semester
URL: www.plazacollege.edu
Established: 1916 Annual Undergrad Tuition & Fees: $11,350
Enrollment: 716 Coed
Affiliation or Control: Proprietary IRS Status: Proprietary
Highest Offering: Baccalaureate
Accreditation: M, MAC

01 President .... Charles E. CALLAHAN, SR.
05 Provost .... Charles E. CALLAHAN, III
10 Vice Pres of Financial Services .... Vacant
11 Chief Operating Officer .... Charles E. CALLAHAN, IV
20 Dean of Academic Affairs .... Marie DOLLA
06 Registrar .... Carol GARCIA
21 Comptroller .... Linda ROCKHILL
07 Dean of Admissions .... Vanessa LOPEZ
20 Dean Curriculum Development .... Marianne C. ZIPF
08 College Librarian .... Eva BABALIS
23 Director Health Services .... Candice CALLAHAN
37 Director Financial Aid .... Peggy CHUNG
35 Dean Student Activities .... Jonathan HOWLE
100 Chief of Staff/HR Officer/Placement .... Correne CAVALIERI
09 Assoc Dean Institutional Research .... Edward DEE
13 Director Information Technology .... David COLUCCI
32 Dean of Students .... Dawn VETRANO
88 Director of ARC/Library .... Michelle RULLO
14 Manager Information Technology .... Norman ALVARADO
76 Program Director Medical Assisting .... Daryl ANDERSON
26 Director of Communications .... Brittany TRAVIS
38 Freshman Counseling .... Caroline CALLAHAN
103 Dir Career Services & Alumni Dev .... Anita LUCKETT

Pratt Institute (E)

200 Willoughby Avenue, Brooklyn NY 11205-3899
County: Kings FICE Identification: 002798
Unit ID: 194578
Telephone: (718) 636-3600 Carnegie Class: Spec-4-yr-Arts
FAX Number: (718) 636-3670 Calendar System: Semester
URL: www.pratt.edu
Established: 1887 Annual Undergrad Tuition & Fees: $46,586
Enrollment: 4,690 Coed
Affiliation or Control: Independent Non-Profit IRS Status: 501(c)3
Highest Offering: Master's
Accreditation: M, ART, CIDA, #LIB, PLNG, TEAC

01 President .... Dr. Thomas F. SCHUTTE
05 Provost .... Mr. Kirk PILLOW
32 Vice President for Student Life .... Dr. Helen MATUSOW-AYRES
10 Vice Pres Finance/Administration .... Ms. Cathleen KENNY
30 VP Institutional Advancement .... Ms. Joan BARRY MCCORMICK
84 Vice President for Enrollment .... Ms. Judith AARON
20 Associate Provost Academic Affairs .... Ms. Donna HEILAND
11 Assistant to Pres Administration .... Ms. Josie CAPORUSCIO
06 Registrar .... Mr. Lisle HENDERSON
08 Director of the Library .... Mr. Russ ABELL
15 Director Human Resources .... Mr. Tom GREENE
51 Dean Continuing Education .... Ms. Maira SEARA
26 Executive Director Public Relations .... Ms. Mara MCGINNIS
36 Director of Career Services .... Ms. Rhonda SCHALLER
37 Director Student Financial Aid .... Mr. Nedzad GOGA
09 Exec Dir Institutional Research .... Mr. Vladimir BRILLER
07 Director of Undergraduate Admission .... Mr. William SWAN
96 Director of Purchasing .... Ms. Mitzi BRYAN
57 Dean of Art .... Mr. Gerry SNYDER
49 Dean Liberal Arts/Science .... Dr. Andrew BARNES
48 Dean School of Architecture .... Mr. Thomas HANRAHAN
62 Dean Information/Library Sci .... Dr. Tula GIANNINI
88 Dean of Design .... Ms. Anita COONEY
13 Chief Info Technology Officer (CIO) .... Mr. Joseph HEMWAY
19 Director Security/Safety .... Mr. William SCHMITZ
39 Director Student Housing .... Mr. Christopher KASIK
41 Athletic Director .... Mr. Walter RICKARD

Rabbinical Academy Mesivta Rabbi Chaim Berlin (F)

1605 Coney Island Avenue, Brooklyn NY 11230-4715
County: Kings FICE Identification: 003976
Unit ID: 194657
Telephone: (718) 377-0777 Carnegie Class: Spec-4-yr-Faith
FAX Number: (718) 338-5578 Calendar System: Semester
Established: 1939 Annual Undergrad Tuition & Fees: $12,250
Enrollment: 249 Male
Affiliation or Control: Independent Non-Profit IRS Status: 501(c)3
Highest Offering: Second Talmudic Degree
Accreditation: RABN

01 Provost .... Rabbi Abraham H. FRUCHTHANDLER
05 President of the Faculty .... Rabbi Aaron M. SCHECHTER
03 Executive Director .... Rabbi Y. Mayer LASKER
29 Director of Alumni Association .... Mendel SCHECHTER
45 Chief Planning Officer .... Rabbi Tuvia M. OBERMEISTER
20 Associate Director .... Eli RABINOWITZ
37 Financial Aid Administrator .... Michael A. REISS

Rabbinical College Beth Shraga (G)

28 Saddle River Road, Monsey NY 10952-3035
County: Rockland FICE Identification: 010943
Unit ID: 194693
Telephone: (845) 356-1980 Carnegie Class: Spec-4-yr-Faith
FAX Number: (845) 425-2604 Calendar System: Semester
Established: 1965 Annual Undergrad Tuition & Fees: $12,050
Enrollment: 41 Male
Affiliation or Control: Independent Non-Profit IRS Status: 501(c)3
Highest Offering: Second Talmudic Degree
Accreditation: RABN

01 President .... Rabbi Emanuel SCHIFF

Rabbinical College Bobover Yeshiva B'nei Zion (H)

1577 48th Street, Brooklyn NY 11219-3293
County: Kings FICE Identification: 008614
Unit ID: 194666
Telephone: (718) 438-2018 Carnegie Class: Spec-4-yr-Faith
FAX Number: (718) 871-9031 Calendar System: Semester
Established: 1947 Annual Undergrad Tuition & Fees: $7,750
Enrollment: 321 Male
Affiliation or Control: Independent Non-Profit IRS Status: 501(c)3
Highest Offering: Second Talmudic Degree
Accreditation: RABN

01 President .... Rabbi Boruch Avrohom HOROWITZ

Rabbinical College of Long Island (I)

205 W Beech Street, Long Beach NY 11561-0630
County: Nassau FICE Identification: 010378
Unit ID: 194736
Telephone: (516) 255-4700 Carnegie Class: Spec-4-yr-Faith
FAX Number: (516) 255-4701 Calendar System: Semester
Established: 1965 Annual Undergrad Tuition & Fees: $8,800
Enrollment: 115 Male
Affiliation or Control: Independent Non-Profit IRS Status: 501(c)3
Highest Offering: First Talmudic Degree
Accreditation: RABN

01 President .... Rabbi Yitzchok FEIGELSTOCK
06 Registrar .... Rabbi Dovid N. ROTHSCHILD
32 Dean of Students .... Rabbi Yeruchem PITTER
07 CEO and Director of Admissions .... Rabbi Chaim HOBERMAN
37 Financial Aid Administrator .... Rabbi Shlomo TEICHMAN

Rabbinical College Ohr Shimon Yisroel (J)

215-217 Hewes Street, Brooklyn NY 11211-8102
County: Kings FICE Identification: 031292
Unit ID: 405854
Telephone: (718) 855-4092 Carnegie Class: Spec-4-yr-Faith
FAX Number: (718) 855-8479 Calendar System: Semester
Established: Annual Undergrad Tuition & Fees: $11,600
Enrollment: 164 Male
Affiliation or Control: Independent Non-Profit IRS Status: 501(c)3
Highest Offering: First Talmudic Degree
Accreditation: @RABN

01 President .... Rabbi Shulem WALTER

Rabbinical College Ohr Yisroel (K)

8800 Seaview Avenue, Brooklyn NY 11236
County: Kings Identification: 667145
Unit ID: 484871
Telephone: (718) 633-4715 Carnegie Class: Not Classified
FAX Number: (347) 702-5436 Calendar System: Semester
Established: 2009 Annual Undergrad Tuition & Fees: $9,000
Enrollment: 104 Male
Affiliation or Control: Independent Non-Profit IRS Status: 501(c)3
Highest Offering: First Talmudic Degree
Accreditation: @RABN

01 President .... Rabbi Daniel GELDZAHLER

Rabbinical Seminary of America (L)

76-01 147th Street, Flushing NY 11367-3148
County: Queens FICE Identification: 003978
Unit ID: 194763
Telephone: (718) 268-4700 Carnegie Class: Spec-4-yr-Faith
FAX Number: (718) 268-4684 Calendar System: Semester
Established: 1933 Annual Undergrad Tuition & Fees: $9,600
Enrollment: 500 Male
Affiliation or Control: Independent Non-Profit IRS Status: 501(c)3
Highest Offering: Second Talmudic Degree
Accreditation: RABN

01 President .... Rabbi David HARRIS
01 President .... Rabbi Akiva GRUNBLATT
03 Executive Vice President .... Rabbi Hayim SCHWARTZ
11 Director of Operation .... Rabbi Meir GLAZER
06 Registrar .... Rabbi Abraham SEMMEL

30 Director Development .... Rabbi Yossi SINGER
37 Director of Financial Aid .... Mrs. Laya EISENSTEIN
18 Chief Physical Plant .... Mr. Ariel WOLFARTH
88 Director of Special Projects .... Vacant
91 Director of Admin Computing .... Mr. Jonathan PLATOVSKY
39 Director Student Housing .... Rabbi Elisha FEINBERG
46 Director Research & Development .... Vacant

Relay Graduate School of Education (A)

40 West 20th Street, 7th Floor, New York NY 10011
County: New York Identification: 667117
Unit ID: 475033
Telephone: (212) 228-1888 Carnegie Class: Spec-4-yr-Other
FAX Number: (212) 228-1855 Calendar System: Other
URL: www.relayschool.org
Established: 2011 Annual Graduate Tuition & Fees: N/A
Enrollment: 958 Coed
Affiliation or Control: Independent Non-Profit IRS Status: 501(c)3
Highest Offering: Master's; No Undergraduates
Accreditation: M, TED

01 Co-Founder/President .... Mr. Norman ATKINS
05 Provost .... Dr. Brent MADDIN
10 Chief Financial Officer .... Ms. Piper EVANS
11 Chief Operating Officer .... Mr. Tim SAINTSING
13 Chief Technology Officer .... Mr. Rob UNDERWOOD
20 Dean .... Ms. Mayme HOSTELLER

Rensselaer Polytechnic Institute (B)

110 8th Street, Troy NY 12180-3590
County: Rensselaer FICE Identification: 002803
Unit ID: 194824
Telephone: (518) 276-6000 Carnegie Class: DU-Higher
FAX Number: N/A Calendar System: Semester
URL: www.rpi.edu
Established: 1824 Annual Undergrad Tuition & Fees: $49,341
Enrollment: 6,835 Coed
Affiliation or Control: Independent Non-Profit IRS Status: 501(c)3
Highest Offering: Doctorate
Accreditation: M, BUS, ENG

01 President .... Dr. Shirley Ann JACKSON
05 Provost .... Dr. Prabhat HAJELA
11 Vice President for Administration .... Mr. Claude ROUNDS
26 VP Strategic Comm/External Rels .... Ms. Richie C. HUNTER
10 Vice President for Finance/CFO .... Ms. Virginia GREGG
45 Vice Pres for Research .... Mr. Jonathan S. DORDICK
30 Vice Pres Institutional Advancement .... Mr. Graig R. EASTIN
32 Vice President Student Life .... Dr. Frank ROSS, III
15 Vice Pres Human Resources .... Mr. Curtis N. POWELL
13 Vice Pres for Info Services & CIO .... Mr. John E. KOLB
84 Vice Pres Enrollment Management .... Dr. Jonathan D. WEXLER
43 Secretary of Inst/General Counsel .... Mr. Charles F. CARLETTA
100 Chief of Staff .... Ms. Elisha MOZERSKY
21 Asst Vice Pres for Administration .... Mr. Paul MARTIN
86 Asst VP for Govt & Ext Relations .... Ms. Allison NEWMAN
29 Asst Vice Pres Alumni Relations .... Mr. Jeff SCHANZ
54 Dean School of Engineering .... Dr. Shekhar GARDE
81 Dean School of Science .... Dr. Curt BRENEMAN
79 Dean Sch of Humanities/Social Sci .... Dr. Mary SIMONI
50 Dean Lally School of Mgmt/Tech .... Dr. Thomas BEGLEY
48 Dean School of Architecture .... Mr. Evan DOUGLIS
20 Associate Dean for Information Tech .... Mr. David SPOONER
35 Dean of Students .... Mr. Mark SMITH
06 Dir Stdnt Records/Fin Svcs/Registr .... Ms. Sharon L. KUNKEL
37 Director Financial Aid .... Mr. Larry CHAMBERS
09 Director of Institutional Research .... Mr. Jack MAHONEY
08 Director of Libraries .... Vacant
25 Director Office Contracts & Grants .... Mr. Richard E. SCAMMELL
36 Director Career Development Center .... Mr. Thomas L. TARANTELLI
07 Director Undergrad Admissions .... Ms. Karen S. LONG
18 Director Physical Plant .... Mr. Mark FROST
86 Director of Federal Relations .... Ms. Deborah E. ALTENBURG
23 Director Student Health Center .... Dr. Leslie LAWRENCE
38 Director Student Counseling .... Dr. Benjamin MARTE
96 Manager Purchasing Systems .... Mr Craig MCINTOSH

Richard Gilder Graduate School at the American Museum of Natural History (C)

Central Park West at 79th Street, New York NY 10024
County: New York Identification: 667003
Unit ID: 458548
Telephone: (212) 769-5055 Carnegie Class: Not Classified
FAX Number: (212) 769-5257 Calendar System: Other
URL: www.amnh.org/our-research/richard-gilder-graduate-school
Established: 2006 Annual Graduate Tuition & Fees: N/A
Enrollment: N/A Coed
Affiliation or Control: Independent Non-Profit IRS Status: 501(c)3
Highest Offering: Doctorate; No Undergraduates
Accreditation: NY

01 Dean .... Dr. John J. FLYNN

Roberts Wesleyan College (D)

2301 Westside Drive, Rochester NY 14624-1997
County: Monroe FICE Identification: 002805
Unit ID: 194958
Telephone: (585) 594-6000 Carnegie Class: Masters/L
FAX Number: (585) 594-6371 Calendar System: Semester
URL: www.roberts.edu
Established: 1866 Annual Undergrad Tuition & Fees: $28,630
Enrollment: 1,762 Coed
Affiliation or Control: Independent Non-Profit IRS Status: 501(c)3
Highest Offering: Doctorate
Accreditation: M, ART, IACBE, MUS, NURSE, SW, TEAC

01 President .... Dr. Deana L. PORTERFIELD
05 Sr VP & Chief Academic Officer .... Dr. David BASINGER
10 Sr Vice President & Treasurer .... Ms. Laurie LEO
32 VP for Student Development .... Dr. Nelson W. HILL
11 Vice President for Administration .... Mrs. Ruth LOGAN
30 VP Institutional Advancement .... Mr. Darrell BELL
84 VP for Enrollment Management .... Mrs. Kimberley WIEDEFELD
07 Assoc VP for UG Admissions .... Mr. JP ANDERSON
44 Assoc VP for Major Gifts .... Mr. Maurice (Max) MCGINNIS
26 AVP for Brand/Marketing Comm .... Ms. Donna MCLAREN
13 Assoc VP for Information Technology .... Mr. Pradeep SAXENA
40 Director of Bookstore Services .... Mr. Darren WALTON
41 Director of Athletics .... Mr. Robert SEGAVE
37 Director of Student Financial Svcs .... Mr. Stephen G. FIELD
09 Dir Institutional Research/Assess .... Dr. Paul W. KENNEDY
42 Chaplain .... Rev. Jonathan BRATT
06 Registrar .... Mrs. Lesa J. KOHR
04 Administrative Asst to President .... Mrs. Patti RADEL
15 Director Personnel Services .... Mrs. Amy PORPILIA
18 Chief Facilities/Physical Plant .... Mr. T. Richard GREER
19 Director Security/Safety .... Mr. Rick BILLITIER
25 Chief Contracts/Grants Admin .... Mrs. Lisa TIFFIN
29 Director Alumni Relations .... Mr. Kirk KETTINGER

† Parent institution of Northeastern Seminary.

Rochester Institute of Technology (E)

1 Lomb Memorial Drive, Rochester NY 14623-5604
County: Monroe FICE Identification: 002806
Unit ID: 195003
Telephone: (585) 475-2411 Carnegie Class: DU-Mod
FAX Number: (585) 475-7049 Calendar System: Quarter
URL: www.rit.edu
Established: 1829 Annual Undergrad Tuition & Fees: $37,124
Enrollment: 16,310 Coed
Affiliation or Control: Independent Non-Profit IRS Status: 501(c)3
Highest Offering: Doctorate
Accreditation: M, ARCPA, ART, BUS, CIDA, CS, DIETD, DMS, ENG, ENGT, TEAC

01 President .... Dr. William W. DESTLER
05 Provost & Sr VP for Acad Affs .... Dr. Jeremy A. HAEFNER
100 Chief of Staff .... Mrs. Karen A. BARROWS
10 Sr Vice Pres Finance/Administration .... Dr. James H. WATTERS
84 Sr VP Enroll Mgmt/Career Svcs .... Dr. James G. MILLER
32 Sr Vice President Student Affairs .... Dr. Sandra S. JOHNSON
46 President NTID/RIT Vice Pres & Dean .... Dr. Gerard J. BUCKLEY
12 President RIT Dubai .... Dr. Yousef AL-ASSAF
30 VP for Development & Alumni Rels .... Dr. Lisa CAUDA
86 Vice President Govt/Cmty Relations .... Ms. Deborah M. STENDARDI
46 Vice President Research .... Dr. Ryne RAFFAELLE
28 Int VP for Diversity & Inclusion .... Dr. Keith JENKINS
12 VP AUK/Academic Dir RIT Pgms Kosovo .... Dr. Daniel COSENTINO
76 VP/Dean Coll Health Sciences/Tech .... Dr. Daniel B. ORNT
46 Senior Assoc Provost .... Dr. Christine M. LICATA
36 Sr AVP/Dir Coop Educ/Career Svcs .... Dr. Emanuel CONTOMANOLIS
26 Chief Communications Officer .... Mr. Robert FINNERTY
20 Asst Provost and Director CIMS .... Dr. Nabil NASR
08 Director of RIT Libraries .... Vacant
88 Assoc Provost Fac Dev Wallace Ctr .... Dr. Lynn A. WILD
12 President-RIT Croatia .... Mr. Donald HUDSPETH
29 Assoc VP Alumni/Parent & Annual Giv .... Ms. Kimberly SLUSSER
21 Asst VP/Controller/Asst Treasurer .... Ms. Lyn KELLY
18 Asst VP Facilities Management Svs .... Mr. John MOORE
06 Assoc VP/Registrar .... Mr. Joe LOFFREDO
07 Assoc VP/Exec Dir of Admissions .... Mr. Daniel SHELLEY
37 Asst VP & Dir Fin Aid & Scholarship .... Vacant
84 Assoc VP & Dir Grad/PT Enroll Svc .... Ms. Diane ELLISON
44 Assoc VP for Campaigns & Const Dev .... Ms. Heather ENGEL
09 Asst VP Inst Rsrch/Policy Studies .... Dr. Joan E. GRAHAM
15 Asst VP/Director Human Resources .... Ms. Judy BENDER
44 Exec Dir Fund for RIT .... Ms. Marisa PSAILA
35 Assoc VP for Student Affairs .... Dr. Dawn SOUFLERIS
35 Assoc VP Student Affairs .... Dr. Heath BOICE-PARDEE
85 Director International Student Svcs .... Mr. Jeffrey W. COX
96 Exec Director Procurement Services .... Ms. Debra KUSSE
102 Sr Director Foundation Relations .... Ms. Bonnie BUTKUS
102 Exec Dir Corp/Foundation Relations .... Mr. Paul HARRIS
101 Secretary of the Institute .... Mrs. Karen A. BARROWS
50 Dean of Business .... Dr. Jacqueline MOZRALL
54 Dean of Engineering .... Dr. Doreen EDWARDS
72 Int Dean Applied Science/Technology .... Dr. S. Manian RAMKUMAR
49 Dean of Liberal Arts .... Dr. James J. WINEBRAKE
81 Dean of Science .... Dr. Sophia MAGGELAKIS
57 Dean College Imaging Arts/Sci .... Dr. Lorraine JUSTICE
77 Dean Col Computer/Info Science .... Dr. Anne HAAKE
58 Dean Graduate Studies .... Dr. Twyla CUMMINGS
04 Exec Admin Asst to President .... Ms. Sonia RODRIGUEZ
11 Chief of Administration .... Ms. Karen A. BARROWS
13 Chief Info Technology Officer (CIO) .... Ms. Jeanne CASARES
41 Exec Dir Intercollegiate Athletics .... Mr. Louis SPIOTTI
26 Chief Marketing Officer .... Mr. John K. TRIERWEILER

Rockefeller University (F)

1230 York Avenue, New York NY 10065-6399
County: New York FICE Identification: 002807
Unit ID: 195049
Telephone: (212) 327-8000 Carnegie Class: DU-Higher
FAX Number: (212) 327-8699 Calendar System: Other
URL: www.rockefeller.edu
Established: 1901 Annual Graduate Tuition & Fees: N/A
Enrollment: 209 Coed
Affiliation or Control: Independent Non-Profit IRS Status: 501(c)3
Highest Offering: Doctorate; No Undergraduates
Accreditation: NY

01 President .... Dr. Marc TESSIER-LAVIGNE
03 Executive Vice President .... Dr. Timothy O'CONNOR
43 Vice President & General Counsel .... Ms. Harriet RABB
05 Vice President Academic Affairs .... Mr. Michael W. YOUNG
10 Vice President Finance .... Mr. James H. LAPPLE
30 Sr Vice President Development .... Ms. Maren E. IMHOFF
17 Vice President for Medical Affairs .... Dr. Barry S. COLLER
20 Dean & Vice Pres of Educ Affairs .... Dr. Sidney STRICKLAND
15 Vice President Human Resources .... Ms. Virginia A. HUFFMAN
18 Assoc Vice Pres Plant Operations .... Mr. Alexander KOGAN
45 Assoc Vice Pres Plng & Constr .... Mr. George B. CANDLER
13 Chief Information Officer .... Mr. Anthony CARVALLOZA
25 Dir Pgm Dev & Sponsored Research .... Ms. Collette L. RYDER
08 University Librarian .... Ms. Carol FELTES
19 Director Security .... Mr. James ROGERS

Rockland Community College (G)

145 College Road, Suffern NY 10901-3699
County: Rockland FICE Identification: 002877
Unit ID: 195058
Telephone: (845) 574-4000 Carnegie Class: Assoc/HT-High Trad
FAX Number: (845) 574-4463 Calendar System: Semester
URL: www.sunyrockland.edu
Established: 1959 Annual Undergrad Tuition & Fees (In-District): $4,654
Enrollment: 7,520 Coed
Affiliation or Control: State/Local IRS Status: 501(c)3
Highest Offering: Associate Degree
Accreditation: M, ADNUR, OTA

01 President .... Dr. Cliff L. WOOD
10 VP Finance/Administration .... Dr. Nayyer HUSSAIN
05 Provost/VP Academic & Student Affs .... Dr. Susan DEER
21 Assoc VP Finance/Administration .... Mr. Joseph MARRA
88 AVP Academic/Community Partnership .... Mr. Thomas DELLA TORRE
32 AVP Student Development .... Vacant
84 AVP of Enrollment Management .... Ms. Dana STILLEY
37 Director Financial Aid .... Ms. Debra BOUABIDI
06 Registrar .... Ms. Robin CONKLIN
13 Director of Information Services .... Dr. Steven FERRES
08 Director of Library/Learning Res .... Dr. Jingfeng XIA
18 Chief Facilities/Physical Plant .... Mr. Douglas SCHMIDT
28 Dir Equity/Compliance/Affirm Act .... Ms. Melissa ROY
09 Director of Institutional Research .... Dr. Jim ROBERTSON
20 Asst to Vice Pres Academic Affairs .... Ms. Patricia KOBES
26 Chief Public Relations Officer .... Ms. Tzipora REITMAN
04 Administrative Asst to President .... Mr. Ben NAYLOR
07 Director of Admissions .... Mr. Jude FLEURISMOND
101 Secretary of the Board .... Mr. Ben NAYLOR
106 Dir Online Education/E-learning .... Ms. Lilia JUELE
11 Chief of Administration .... Mr. Dennis CALLINAN
15 Director Human Resources .... Vacant
19 Director Public Safety .... Mr. William MURPHY
25 Assoc VP for Resource Development .... Ms. Elizabeth KENDALL
41 Athletic Director .... Mr. Dan KEELEY
90 Director Academic Computing .... Ms. Lilia JUELE

The Sage Colleges (H)

65 First Street, Troy NY 12180-4199
County: Rensselaer FICE Identification: 002810
Unit ID: 195128
Telephone: (518) 244-2000 Carnegie Class: Masters/L
FAX Number: (518) 244-2460 Calendar System: Semester
URL: www.sage.edu
Established: 1916 Annual Undergrad Tuition & Fees: $28,400
Enrollment: 2,878 Coed
Affiliation or Control: Independent Non-Profit IRS Status: 501(c)3
Highest Offering: Doctorate
Accreditation: M, ART, DIETD, DIETI, IACBE, NURSE, OT, PTA, TED

01 President .... Dr. Susan C. SCRIMSHAW
05 Provost .... Dr. Susan W. BEATTY
30 VP for Institutional Advancement .... Ms. Melissa KOMORA
12 Dean Sage College of Albany .... Ms. Jean DAHLGREN
12 Dean Russell Sage College .... Dr. Deborah LAWRENCE
51 Dean Prof & Continuing Education .... Dr. Albert ORBINATI
10 VP for Finance & Treasurer .... Mr. Patrick JACOBSON-SCHULTE
32 Vice Pres for Campus Life .... Ms. Patricia CELLEMME

11 VP Administration & Planning .... Ms. Deirdre ZARRILLO
35 Assoc VP for Student Life-RSC ...... Mr. Michael BAUMGARDNER
35 Assoc VP for Student Life-SCA .... Ms. Sharon MURRAY
76 Dean of Health Sciences .... Dr. Theresa HAND
06 Registrar .... Ms. Marah JACOBSON-SCHULTE
07 Senior Director of UG Admission .... Mr. Thomas BREEN
88 Assoc Dean School of Management .... Dr. Kimberly FREDERICKS
53 Interim Dean School of Education .... Dr. John PELIZZA
29 Dir of Alumni Relations SCA/SGS .... Ms. Katherine GENOVESE
29 Director Alumnae Relations RSC .... Ms. Joan CLIFFORD
07 Dir of Graduate & Adult Admissions ..... Ms. Wendy DIEFENDORF
37 Director of Financial Aid .... Ms. Kelley ROBINSON
15 Director of Human Resources .... Ms. Carla MASTRIANO
09 Director of Institutional Research .... Ms. Lori PIZER
18 Director Facilities Management .... Mr. John ZAJACESKOWSKI
36 Associate Dean of Academic Advising .... Ms. Karen SCHELL
36 Associate Dean of Academic Advising .... Ms. Stacy GONZALEZ
26 Dir of Communications & Marketing .... Ms. Shannon BALLARD GORMAN
92 Director of Honors Programs .... Dr. Tonya MOUTRAY
21 Director of Finance .... Ms. Kristina L. PRILL
96 Dir of Purchasing/Accts Payable .... Ms. Paula SELMER
04 Administrative Asst to President .... Ms. Rosemary L. GRIGNON
08 Head Librarian .... Ms. Lisa C. BRAINARD
105 Webmaster .... Mr. Kurt EYE
108 Director Institutional Assessment .... Dr. Donna HEALD
19 Director Security/Safety .... Mr. Robert GREBERT
39 Director of Residence Life .... Mr. Christopher OERTEL
41 Athletic Director .... Ms. Dani DREWS
44 Sr Director of Annual Giving .... Ms. Kathleen DANICA
86 Assoc Director Government Relations ...... Mr. Nicholas DECAPRIO
91 Director of IT/Network Services .... Mr. John HARRIS
106 Dir Online Education/E-learning .... Dr. Albert ORBINATI

Saint Bernard's School of Theology & Ministry (A)

120 French Road, Rochester NY 14618-3822
County: Monroe FICE Identification: 002815
Unit ID: 195155
Telephone: (585) 271-3657 Carnegie Class: Spec-4-yr-Faith
FAX Number: (585) 271-2045 Calendar System: Semester
URL: www.stbernards.edu
Established: 1893 Annual Graduate Tuition & Fees: N/A
Enrollment: 93 Coed
Affiliation or Control: Roman Catholic IRS Status: 501(c)3
Highest Offering: Master's; No Undergraduates
Accreditation: THEOL

01 President .... Rev. George P. HEYMAN
05 Academic Dean .... Dr. Devadasan N. PREMNATH
06 Registrar .... Ms. Ellen MORNINGSTAR
10 Controller .... Ms. Mary MUGGLETON
07 Admiss Director/Dir Stdnt Fin Aid .... Mr. Jonathan SCHOTT
51 Dir Certification/Professional Dev .... Rev. George HEYMAN
08 Librarian .... Ms. Katherine WAHL

St. Bonaventure University (B)

P.O. Box 2450, St. Bonaventure NY 14778
County: Cattaraugus FICE Identification: 002817
Unit ID: 195164
Telephone: (716) 375-2000 Carnegie Class: Masters/M
FAX Number: N/A Calendar System: Semester
URL: www.sbu.edu
Established: 1858 Annual Undergrad Tuition & Fees: $31,389
Enrollment: 2,150 Coed
Affiliation or Control: Roman Catholic IRS Status: 501(c)3
Highest Offering: Master's
Accreditation: M, BUS, CACREP

01 President .... Dr. Andrew ROTH
05 Provost and VP for Academic Affairs .... Dr. Joseph ZIMMER
32 Vice President for Student Affairs .. Mr. Richard C. TRIETLEY, JR.
10 Senior VP Finance & Administration .... Ms. Nancy K. TAYLOR
26 Vice Pres University Relations .... Mr. Thomas MISSEL
42 Exec Director of Faith Formation .. Fr. Francis J. DISPIGNO, OFM
88 Vice Pres for Franciscan Mission .... Vacant
30 Assoc VP Development .... Mr. Bernard VALENTO
57 Exec Dir of Q Arts Center .... Mr. Ludwig BRUNNER
20 Assoc Provost Academic Affairs .... Vacant
11 Director of Operations Ofc of Pres .... Mr. Thomas BUTTAFARRO, JR.
15 Director Human Resources .... Mr. Erik SEASTEDT
07 Director of Recruitment .... Mr. Douglas BRADY
37 Director of Financial Aid .... Mr. Troy MARTIN
06 Registrar .... Mr. George B. SWINDOLL
39 Exec Dir Res Living/Chief Judicial .... Ms. Nichole GONZALEZ
13 Exec Director Technology Services .... Dr. Michael HOFFMAN
08 Director of Friedsam Mem Library .... Mr. Paul J. SPAETH
38 Director Counseling .... Vacant
41 Director of Athletics .... Mr. Tim KENNEY
09 Director of Inst Research .... Vacant
29 Director of Alumni Services .... Ms. Monica MATTIOLI
36 Director of Career Services .... Ms. Connie F. WHITCOMB
43 University Counsel .... Mr. Jeff REISNER
23 Director Wellness Center .... Mr. Christopher ANDERSON
18 Director Physical Plant .... Mr. Philip G. WINGER
21 Controller .... Mr. Karl STRAUSS
19 Director of Safety and Security .... Mr. Gary SEGRUE
40 Manager Bookstore .... Ms. Annette DONAVON
44 Director Annual Giving Program .... Vacant
92 Director of Honors Program .... Dr. Darryl MAYEAUX
96 Director of Budget & Purchasing .... Ms. Lorraine SMITH
73 Dean SFS/Dir Franciscan Institute ... Fr. David COUTURIER, OFM
49 Dean School of Arts & Sci .... Dr. David HILMEY
50 Dean School of Business .... Dr. Matricia JAMES
58 Assc Provost/Dean Sch Graduate Stds .... Vacant
53 Dean School of Education .... Dr. Nancy CASEY
60 Dean Jandoli Sch Journ/Mass Comm ...... Dr. Pauline HOFFMANN
104 Director of International Studies .... Vacant
26 Director Marketing and Promotions .... Mr. Seth JOHNSON

St. Elizabeth College of Nursing (C)

2215 Genesee Street, Utica NY 13501-5998
County: Oneida FICE Identification: 006461
Unit ID: 195702
Telephone: (315) 798-8144 Carnegie Class: Not Classified
FAX Number: (315) 798-8271 Calendar System: Semester
URL: www.secon.edu
Established: 1904 Annual Undergrad Tuition & Fees: $14,864
Enrollment: 209 Coed
Affiliation or Control: Independent Non-Profit IRS Status: 501(c)3
Highest Offering: Associate Degree
Accreditation: M, ADNUR

01 President .... Mrs. Varinya SHEPPARD
32 Dean of Students/Faculty Devel .... Mrs. Beverly PLANTE
32 Dean of Students/Faculty Devel .... Mrs. Shannon HOLTSLAG
06 Registrar & Bursar .... Ms. Eileen MUHLIG
84 Director of Finance & Enrollment .... Ms. Sherry WOJNAS

St. Francis College (D)

180 Remsen Street, Brooklyn NY 11201-4398
County: Kings FICE Identification: 002820
Unit ID: 195173
Telephone: (718) 522-2300 Carnegie Class: Bac-Diverse
FAX Number: (718) 522-1274 Calendar System: Semester
URL: www.sfc.edu
Established: 1859 Annual Undergrad Tuition & Fees: $23,800
Enrollment: 2,749 Coed
Affiliation or Control: Independent Non-Profit IRS Status: 501(c)3
Highest Offering: Master's
Accreditation: M, NURSE, TEAC

01 President .... Mr. Brendan J. DUGAN
10 Exec Vice President for Finance .... Ms. June MCGRISKEN
05 Provost/Vice Pres for Academic Affs .... Dr. Timothy J. HOULIHAN
26 Vice Pres Govt/Community Relations .... Ms. Linda WERBEL DASHEFSKY
30 Vice President of Development .... Mr. Thomas FLOOD
84 Asst Vice Pres Enrollment Mgmt .... Mr. Joseph CUMMINGS
18 Asst Vice Pres Facilities Mgmt .... Mr. Kevin O'ROURKE
21 Asst Vice President for Finance .... Mr. John RAGNO
88 Dean Academic Program Development ...... Dr. Allen BURDOWSKI
20 Asst Dean of Academic Affairs .... Dr. Michele HIRSCH
89 Asst Dean of Freshmen Studies .... Ms. Monica MICHALSKI
15 Exec Director Human Resources .... Mr. Richard GRASSO
13 Director of IT Operations .... Mr. Matthew HOGAN
06 Registrar .... Ms. Susan E. WEISMAN
32 Dean of Students .... Dr. Jose RODRIGUEZ
08 Director Library Services .... Dr. James SMITH
36 Director of Career Development .... Ms. Naomi KINLEY
29 Director of Alumni Relations .... Mr. Dennis MCDERMOTT
41 Director of Athletics .... Ms. Irma GARCIA
42 Director Campus Ministry .... Fr. Brian JORDAN
09 Director of Institutional Research .... Mr. Steven CATALANO
07 Senior Admissions Counselor .... Ms. Cortney ROBERT

St. John Fisher College (E)

3690 East Avenue, Rochester NY 14618-3597
County: Monroe FICE Identification: 002821
Unit ID: 195720
Telephone: (585) 385-8000 Carnegie Class: DU-Mod
FAX Number: (585) 899-3870 Calendar System: Semester
URL: www.sjfc.edu
Established: 1948 Annual Undergrad Tuition & Fees: $30,690
Enrollment: 3,856 Coed
Affiliation or Control: Independent Non-Profit IRS Status: 501(c)3
Highest Offering: Doctorate
Accreditation: M, BUS, CACREP, NURSE, PHAR, TED

01 President .... Dr. Gerard J. ROONEY
04 Exec Asst to Pres/Secy to Board .... Ms. Joan R. BENULIS
05 Provost .... Dr. Kevin RAILEY
84 Interim VP Enrollment Management .... Mr. Jose J. PERALES
10 Vice President for Finance/CFO ..... Ms. Jacqueline S. DISTEFANO
32 VP Student Affairs & Diversity .... Dr. Richard DEJESUS-RUEFF
49 Int Dean School of Arts/Sciences .... Dr. James R. BOWERS
50 Dean School of Business .... Dr. Rama YELKUR
53 Dean School of Education .... Dr. Michael WISCHNOWSKI
66 Dean School of Nursing .... Dr. Dianne C. COONEY MINER
67 Interim Dean School of Pharmacy .... Dr. Christine R. BIRNIE
28 Director Multicultural Affairs .... Mr. Yantee SLOBERT
06 Registrar .... Ms. Julia M. THOMAS
15 Asst Vice Pres Human Resources .... Ms. Elizabeth SKRAINER
26 Director Marketing & Communications .... Ms. Kate M. TOROK
06 Associate Registrar .... Ms. Cheryl O. EVANS
08 Director of the Library .... Ms. Melissa JADLOS
13 Chief Information/Computing Officer .... Mr. Stacy S. SLOCUM
16 Director of Payroll & Benefits .... Ms. Mary R. POWLEY
29 Director Alumni Relations .... Mr. Christopher B. SULLIVAN
37 Director Student Financial Aid .... Mrs. Angela B. MONNAT
42 Director Campus Ministry .... Vacant
19 Director of Safety & Security .... Mr. David DICARO
41 Athletic Director .... Mr. Robert A. WARD
18 Director of Physical Plant .... Mr. Larry P. JACOBSON
21 Controller .... Ms. Linda M. STEINKIRCHNER
23 Int Director of Wellness Center .... Ms. Terri L. TRAVAGLINI
31 Director of Community Service .... Mrs. Sally J. VAUGHAN
07 Director of Freshman Admissions .... Ms. Stacy A. LEDERMANN
07 Dir of Transfer/Graduate Admissions .... Vacant
09 Director of Institutional Research .... Ms. Elizabeth A. LACHANCE
35 Director Student Affairs .... Ms. Teah M. TERRANCE
36 Director Career Services .... Mr. Matt CARDIN
105 Webmaster .... Ms. Jody C. BENEDICT
108 Director Institutional Assessment .... Ms. Liz LACHANCE

St. John's University (F)

8000 Utopia Parkway, Queens NY 11439-0001
County: Queens FICE Identification: 002823
Unit ID: 195809
Telephone: (718) 990-6161 Carnegie Class: DU-Mod
FAX Number: (718) 990-5723 Calendar System: Semester
URL: www.stjohns.edu
Established: 1870 Annual Undergrad Tuition & Fees: $38,680
Enrollment: 20,445 Coed
Affiliation or Control: Roman Catholic IRS Status: 501(c)3
Highest Offering: Doctorate
Accreditation: M, ARCPA, ART, AUD, BUS, BUSA, CACREP, CLPSY, EMT, LAW, LIB, MT, PHAR, RAD, SCPSY, SP, TEAC

01 President .... Dr. Conrado M. GEMPESAW
03 Executive VP Mission .... Rev. Bernard M. TRACEY, CM
05 Provost .... Dr. Robert A. MANGIONE
10 VP Business Affairs/CFO/ Treasurer .... Ms. Sharon HEWITT WATKINS
30 Interim VP University Advancement .... Rev. Bernard M. TRACEY, CM
43 Gen Counsel/Univ Secy/HR/Pub Safety .... Mr. Joseph E. OLIVA
32 VP Student Affairs .... Dr. Kathryn T. HUTCHINSON
84 Vice Provost & Chief Enroll Officer .... Mr. Jorge RODRIGUEZ
20 Senior Vice Provost .... Dr. Simon MOLLER
13 VP Information Technology/CIO .... Mr. Joseph J. TUFANO
19 VP Public Safety .... Mr. Thomas J. LAWRENCE
31 VP Community Relations .... Mr. Joseph A. SCIAME
20 Vice Provost Acad Support Services .... Dr. Andre A. MCKENZIE
106 Vice Provost Online Learning .... Dr. Elizabeth CIABOCCHI
12 Vice Provost - SI .... Dr. James O'KEEFE
49 Dean St John's College .... Dr. Jeffrey W. FAGEN
53 Dean The School of Education .... Dr. Michael SAMPSON
61 Dean School of Law .... Mr. Michael A. SIMONS
67 Dean Pharmacy/Health Sciences .... Dr. Russell J. DIGATE
50 Dean Tobin College of Business .... Dr. Norean R. SHARPE
107 Dean College Prof Studies .... Dr. Katia PASSERINI
08 Dean University Libraries .... Dr. Valeda F. DENT
30 Assoc VP Advancement .... Ms. Jeanne M. UMLAND
41 Assoc VP Athletic/Int Athletic Dir .... Ms. Kathleen F. MEEHAN
21 Assoc VP Business Affairs .... Mr. Anthony MACALUSO
15 Assoc VP Human Resources .... Mr. Thomas A. GALARD
18 Assoc VP Campus Facilities/Services .... Mr. Brian BAUMER
26 Assoc VP External Relations .... Mr. Dominic SCIANNA
91 Assoc VP Information Technology .... Ms. Maura A. WOODS
42 Assoc VP University Ministry .... Ms. Victoria R. SANTANGELO
27 Assoc VP Marketing & Communications .... Ms. Caren BATZER
20 Assoc Provost Administration .... Ms. Linda A. SHANNON
20 Assoc Provost Global Programs .... Mr. Matthew PUCCIARELLI
20 Assoc Provost Student Success .... Dr. Jacqueline H. GROGAN
20 Assoc Provost Academic - SI .... Dr. Robert FANUZZI
86 Asst VP Government Relations .... Mr. Brian BROWNE
31 Asst VP University Events .... Ms. Nunziatina A. MANULI
20 Asst Provost Acad Res & Mmgt Plng .... Ms. Judy CHEN
06 University Registrar .... Ms. Joanne A. LLERANDI
88 Exec Director Vincentian Center .... Rev. Patrick J. GRIFFIN, CM
14 Exec Director Enterprise Infrastruc .... Ms. Anne L. ROCCO
90 Exec Director User Services .... Mr. Kenneth J. MAHLMEISTER
36 Senior Director Employer Relations ..... Ms. Paulette B. GONZALEZ
29 Director Alumni Relations .... Mr. Mark A. ANDREWS
88 Director Ctr for Teaching/Learning .... Dr. Maura C. FLANNERY
07 Director Admissions .... Mrs. Samantha R. WRIGHT
105 Director Digital Communications .... Ms. Luci GERACI
92 Director Honors Program .... Dr. Robert J. FORMAN
16 Director Human Resources Services ...... Ms. Cynthia F. SIMPSON
25 Director Grants & Research .... Mr. Jared E. LITTMAN
88 Director Internal Audit .... Mr. Alex J. HOEHN
37 Director Int Financial Aid/Research ..... Ms. Maryanne H. TWOMEY
44 Director Planned Giving .... Ms. Susan M. DAMIANI
88 Dir Pre-Admin/Asst to VP & OP .... Mrs. Cecelia M. RUSSO
96 Director Purchasing .... Mr. Jeffery I. WEISS
39 Director Residence Life .... Mr. Eric M. FINKELSTEIN
23 Director Queens Health Services .... Mrs. Pauline TUMMINO
09 Acting Dir Institutional Research .... Ms. Christine M. GOODWIN
37 Assoc Director Financial Aid .... Ms. Nemaris C. RODRGUEZ
38 Assoc Director Counseling Center .... Ms. Dorothy M. SCHMITT
85 Asst Dir Int Students/Scholar Svcs .... Ms. Amy HARVEY
07 Asst Director Admissions-SI .... Mr. Daniel WU
39 Asst Dir Student & Res Life-SI .... Mr. Jason T. BARTLETT
40 Manager of Bookstore .... Mrs. Denise SERVIDIO

Saint Joseph's College, New York (G)

245 Clinton Avenue, Brooklyn NY 11205-3688
County: Kings FICE Identification: 002825
Unit ID: 195544
Telephone: (718) 940-5300 Carnegie Class: Masters/L

FAX Number: (718) 636-7245 Calendar System: Semester
URL: www.sjcny.edu
Established: 1916 Annual Undergrad Tuition & Fees: $24,113
Enrollment: 4,979 Coed
Affiliation or Control: Independent Non-Profit IRS Status: 501(c)3
Highest Offering: Master's
Accreditation: M, ADNUR, NRPA, NUR, TEAC

01 President .... Dr. Jack P. CALARESO
30 VP for Institutional Advancement .... Ms. Carrie BHADA
84 VP for Enrollment Management - BK .... Ms. Christine MURPHY
05 VP for Academic Affairs - BK .... Dr. Barb GARII
32 VP for Student Life - BK .... Ms. Sherrie VAN ARNAM
10 Chief Financial Officer .... Mr. John C. ROTH
13 VP IT and Chief Information Officer .... Ms. Michelle PAPAJOHN
06 College Registrar .... Mr. Robert PERGOLIS
08 Director of Library .... Dr. Elizabeth POLLICINO MURPHY
37 Director of Financial Aid .... Ms. Amy THOMPSON
36 Exec Director Career Development .... Ms. Ellen BURTI
41 AVP and Senior Athletics Director .... Ms. Shantey HILL
29 AVP Alumni Relations/Stewardship .... Ms. Mary Jo B. CHIARA
21 Controller .... Mr. Matthew BRELLIS
88 Director of Child Study Center .... Dr. Susan SHAPIRO
18 Director Physical Plant .... Mr. Fred FORAN
15 Exec Director of Human Resources .... Ms. D'adra CRUMP
28 Coordinator of Diversity .... Ms. Christy BANKS
26 VP of Marketing and Communications .... Ms. Jessica MCALEER
88 Director of Public Affairs .... Mr. Michael BANACH
14 Exec Director Network Operations .... Mr. Ted DEC
90 Exec Director Client Services .... Ms. Lichele ABEAR
04 Executive Admin Asst to President .... Ms. Ann PAIVA
04 Executive Admin Asst to President .... Ms. Linda RYAN
09 Director of Institutional Research .... Ms. Allison LIST
19 Director Security/Safety .... Mr. Michael MCGRANN

Saint Joseph's College, New York - Suffolk Campus (A)

155 W Roe Boulevard, Patchogue NY 11772-2399
Telephone: (631) 687-5100 FICE Identification: 029081
Accreditation: &M, NRPA

† Regional accreditation is carried under the parent institution in Brooklyn, NY.

St. Joseph's College of Nursing (B)

206 Prospect Avenue, Syracuse NY 13203-1806
County: Onondaga FICE Identification: 006467
Unit ID: 195191
Telephone: (315) 448-5040 Carnegie Class: Spec 2-yr-Health
FAX Number: (315) 448-5745 Calendar System: Semester
URL: www.sjhcon.org
Established: 1898 Annual Undergrad Tuition & Fees: $18,600
Enrollment: 317 Coed
Affiliation or Control: Independent Non-Profit IRS Status: 501(c)3
Highest Offering: Associate Degree
Accreditation: M

01 Dean .... Mrs. Marianne MARKOWITZ

Saint Joseph's Seminary (C)

Dunwoodie, #201 Seminary Avenue, Yonkers NY 10704-1852
County: Westchester FICE Identification: 002826
Unit ID: 195571
Telephone: (914) 968-6200 Carnegie Class: Not Classified
FAX Number: (914) 376-2019 Calendar System: Semester
URL: www.dunwoodie.edu
Established: 1896 Annual Graduate Tuition & Fees: N/A
Enrollment: N/A Coed
Affiliation or Control: Roman Catholic IRS Status: 501(c)3
Highest Offering: Master's; No Undergraduates
Accreditation: M, THEOL

01 Rector .... Msgr. Peter I. VACCARI
05 Academic Dean .... Rev. Kevin P. O'REILLY
32 Dean of Students/Admissions .... Rev. Nicholas A. ZIENTARSKI
08 Director Library Services .... Vacant
10 Director Finance .... Mr. Ronald TUTTLE
30 Director of Development .... Vacant
06 Registrar .... Ms. Kathleen M. RUSSELL
38 Director of Psychological Services .... Dr. Richard GALLAGHER
18 Director of Buildings & Grounds .... Mr. Joseph DI LELLO
26 Director of Communications .... Ms. Cynthia F. HARRISON
07 Director of Admissions .... Fr. Thomas BERG
04 Administrative Asst to President .... Mrs. Mary C. BROGLIE
108 Director Institutional Assessment .... Msgr. Michael CURRAN

St. Lawrence University (D)

23 Romoda Drive, Canton NY 13617-1423
County: St. Lawrence FICE Identification: 002829
Unit ID: 195216
Telephone: (315) 229-5011 Carnegie Class: Bac-A&S
FAX Number: (315) 229-5502 Calendar System: Other
URL: www.stlawu.edu
Established: 1856 Annual Undergrad Tuition & Fees: $49,420
Enrollment: 2,419 Coed
Affiliation or Control: Independent Non-Profit IRS Status: 501(c)3
Highest Offering: Master's
Accreditation: M, TEAC

01 President .... Dr. William FOX
05 Vice Pres/Dean Academic Affairs .... Dr. Karl K. SCHONBERG
30 Vice Pres University Advancement .... Mr. Thomas PYNCHON
10 Vice President Finance & Treasurer .... Mr. Joseph MANORY
32 Vice Pres/Dean Student Life .... Dr. Joseph TOLLIVER
07 Vice Pres/Dean Admissions/Fin Aid .... Mr. Jeffrey RICKEY
31 VP for Employee/Community Relations .... Mrs. Lisa M. CANIA
21 Assoc Vice President for Finance .... Ms. Carol GABLE
89 Associate Dean of the First-Year .... Dr. Jennifer HANSEN
35 Associate Dean of Student Life .... Mr. Rance DAVIS
06 Registrar .... Ms. Lorie MACKENZIE
37 Director of Financial Aid .... Mrs. Patricia J. E. FARMER
08 VP Libraries & Information Tech .... Mr. Justin SIPHER
36 Director of Career Planning .... Dr. Carol BATE
09 Director of Institutional Research .... Ms. Christine ZIMMERMAN
18 Chief Facilities/Physical Plant .... Mr. Daniel B. SEAMAN
20 Asst Dean of Academic Affairs .... Ms. Lorie MACKENZIE
29 Director Alumni Relations .... Ms. Kimberly HISSONG
35 Director Residence Life .... Mr. Christopher MARQUARDT
23 Director of Health & Counseling .... Ms. Pat ELLIS
84 Director Enrollment Management .... Mr. Jeffrey RICKEY
96 Director of Purchasing .... Ms. Ruta OZOLS
15 Director Personnel Services .... Mrs. Colleen MANLEY
38 Director Student Counseling .... Mr. Timothy CORBITT
26 Communications Coordinator .... Ms. Bev GAUTHIER

St. Paul's School of Nursing (E)

97-77 Queens Blvd, Rego Park NY 11374
County: Queens FICE Identification: 012364
Unit ID: 189811
Telephone: (718) 357-0500 Carnegie Class: Spec 2-yr-Health
FAX Number: (718) 357-4683 Calendar System: Semester
URL: www.stpaulsschoolofnursing.edu
Established: 1969 Annual Undergrad Tuition & Fees: $21,946
Enrollment: 504 Coed
Affiliation or Control: Proprietary IRS Status: Proprietary
Highest Offering: Associate Degree
Accreditation: ABHES

01 President .... Dr. Eric RICIOPPO
66 Regional Dean of Nursing Schools .... Genevieve M. JENSEN
37 Financial Aid Director .... Andrea HICKS
07 Asst Director of Admissions .... Jafet BREMER-LOPEZ
08 Head Librarian .... Kevin SAW
10 Chief Financial/Business Officer .... Martin FOKUSORGEOR
06 Registrar .... Claudia MENJIVAR

Saint Paul's School of Nursing-Staten Island (F)

2 Teleport Dr Ste 203, Corp Comm 2, Staten Island NY 10311
County: Richmond FICE Identification: 009479
Unit ID: 195784
Telephone: (718) 818-6470 Carnegie Class: Spec 2-yr-Health
FAX Number: (718) 818-6020 Calendar System: Semester
URL: www.stpaulsschoolofnursing.edu
Established: 1904 Annual Undergrad Tuition & Fees: $21,769
Enrollment: 694 Coed
Affiliation or Control: Proprietary IRS Status: Proprietary
Highest Offering: Associate Degree
Accreditation: ABHES

01 Interim President .... Mr. Eric JACOBS
05 Director of Education .... Dr. Ann LUBRANO
66 Dean of Nursing .... Dr. Colleen KUMAR
06 Registrar .... Ms. Pamela HORVATH
10 Business Office Manager .... Ms. Olga FORINA
07 Director of Admissions .... Ms. Nickeshia BULLOCK
32 Director of Career Services .... Ms. Lynn SALVAGE
37 Director of Financial Aid .... Ms. Nayanka WARD
88 LRC Manager .... Ms. Judy LEE

St. Thomas Aquinas College (G)

125 Route 340, Sparkill NY 10976-1050
County: Rockland FICE Identification: 002832
Unit ID: 195243
Telephone: (845) 398-4000 Carnegie Class: Masters/S
FAX Number: (845) 359-8136 Calendar System: 4/1/4
URL: www.stac.edu
Established: 1952 Annual Undergrad Tuition & Fees: $28,740
Enrollment: 1,942 Coed
Affiliation or Control: Independent Non-Profit IRS Status: 501(c)3
Highest Offering: Master's
Accreditation: M, ACBE

01 President .... Dr. Margaret M. FITZPATRICK, SC
03 Senior Vice President .... Mr. Vincent CRAPANZANO
10 Vice Pres Administration & Finance .... Mr. Joseph DONINI
05 Provost/Vice Pres Academic Affairs .... Dr. Robert MURRAY
32 Vice Pres/Dean Student Development .... Dr. Kirk MANNING
30 Vice Pres Institutional Advancement .... Mr. Kevin DUIGNAN
15 Director Human Resources .... Mrs. Maria COUPE
07 Director Admissions .... Ms. Samantha BAZILE
09 Dir Inst Research/Program Develop .... Dr. Renee QUINTYNE
21 Controller .... Ms. Jennifer MAZZA
44 Dir Annual Giving & Alumni Affairs .... Mrs. Joanne FAVATA
35 Director Student Activities .... Mr. Dave ENG
38 Director Student Counseling .... Dr. Louis MUGGEO
06 Registrar .... Ms. Eileen MURPHY
36 Director Placement Services .... Mrs. Maureen MULHERN
37 Director Financial Aid .... Mrs. Jean Marie MOHR
13 Director of Computing Services .... Mr. Sunny ANTHWAL
18 Dir Facilities & Construction .... Mr. Patrick LAMBERT
26 Director Communications .... Mrs. Danielle KOBRYN
50 Dean School of Business .... Mr. Michael MURPHY
53 Dean School of Education .... Dr. Meenakshi GAJRIA
49 Dean School of Arts & Sciences .... Dr. Steven BURNS
04 Administrative Asst to President .... Ms. Lee TAUSSI

Saint Vladimir's Orthodox Theological Seminary (H)

575 Scarsdale Road, Yonkers NY 10707
County: Westchester FICE Identification: 002833
Unit ID: 195580
Telephone: (914) 961-8313 Carnegie Class: Spec-4-yr-Faith
FAX Number: (914) 961-4507 Calendar System: Semester
URL: www.svots.edu
Established: 1938 Annual Graduate Tuition & Fees: N/A
Enrollment: 88 Coed
Affiliation or Control: Independent Non-Profit IRS Status: 501(c)3
Highest Offering: Doctorate; No Undergraduates
Accreditation: THEOL

01 Chancellor/CEO .... V.Rev. Chad HATFIELD
05 Dean .... V.Rev. John BEHR
10 Assoc Chanc for Finance .... Ms. Melanie RINGA
13 Chief Technology Officer .... Mr. Georgios KOKONAS
20 Assoc Dean Academic Affairs .... Dr. John BARNET
32 Assoc Dean for Student Affairs .... RevDr. David MEZYNSKI
06 Registrar .... Dr. John BARNET
08 Librarian .... Ms. Eleana SILK
35 Student Affairs Administrator .... Ms. Nina MATUSIAK
09 Dir Institutional Assessment .... Dr. Peter BOUTENEFF
07 Director Admissions/Financial Aid .... Pdn. Joseph MATUSIAK
30 Sr Advisor Advancement .... Mr. Ted BAZIL
26 Director Marketing/Operations .... Rev Dn. Gregory HATRAK

Salvation Army College for Officer Training (I)

201 Lafayette Avenue, Suffern NY 10901-4707
County: Rockland Identification: 666020
Telephone: (845) 368-7200 Carnegie Class: Not Classified
FAX Number: (845) 357-6644 Calendar System: Other
URL: www.use.salvationarmy.org
Established: 1905 Annual Undergrad Tuition & Fees: N/A
Enrollment: N/A Coed
Affiliation or Control: Independent Non-Profit IRS Status: 501(c)3
Highest Offering: Associate Degree
Accreditation: NY

01 Principal .... Col. Janet A. MUNN
03 Associate Principal .... Major William F. FURMAN
11 Asst Principal for Administration .... Major Jongwoo KIM
05 Director of Curriculum .... Major James H. GUEST
06 Registrar .... Ms. Allyssa COMPTON
09 Coord Inst Research/Accred Liaison . Dr. Dennis VANDER WEELE
10 Chief Business Officer .... Major Ronald STARNES
15 Director Personnel Services .... Major Sherry PELLETIER
20 Associate Academic Officer .... Major Lois A. GUEST
21 Associate Business Officer .... Mrs. Robin FRASER
32 Director Student Affairs .... Vacant

Samaritan Hospital School of Nursing (J)

1300 Massachusetts Avenue, Troy NY 12180
County: Rensselaer FICE Identification: 009248
Unit ID: 195289
Telephone: (518) 268-5010 Carnegie Class: Spec 2-yr-Health
FAX Number: (518) 268-5040 Calendar System: Semester
URL: www.nehealth.com
Established: 1903 Annual Undergrad Tuition & Fees: $12,142
Enrollment: 164 Coed
Affiliation or Control: Independent Non-Profit IRS Status: 501(c)3
Highest Offering: Associate Degree
Accreditation: NY, ADNUR, PNUR

01 Director .... Ms. Susan BIRKHEAD

Sarah Lawrence College (K)

1 Meadway, Bronxville NY 10708-5999
County: Westchester FICE Identification: 002813
Unit ID: 195304
Telephone: (914) 337-0700 Carnegie Class: Bac-A&S
FAX Number: (914) 395-2668 Calendar System: Semester
URL: www.slc.edu
Established: 1926 Annual Undergrad Tuition & Fees: $51,038
Enrollment: 1,761 Coed
Affiliation or Control: Independent Non-Profit IRS Status: 501(c)3
Highest Offering: Master's
Accreditation: M, TEAC

01 President .... Dr. Karen R. LAWRENCE

05 Dean of the College ... Dr. Kanwal SINGH
10 Vice Pres Finance/Operations ... Stephen SCHAFER
30 Interim VP for Advancement ... Ellen REYNOLDS
26 Vice Pres Communication & Marketing ... Lyn CHAMBERLIN
11 Vice President for Administration ... Thomas L. BLUM
20 Associate Dean of the College ... Cameron AFZAL
32 Dean of Studies & Student Life ... Daniel TRUJILLO
22 Dean of Equity and Inclusion ... Dr. Allen GREEN
35 Dean of Student Affairs ... Dr. Paige CRANDALL
07 Dean of Enrollment ... Kevin MCKENNA
58 Dean Graduate/Professional Studies ... Dr. Judith BABBITTS
06 Registrar ... Daniel LICHT
08 Director of Libraries ... Bobbie SMOLOW
13 Chief Technology Officer ... Sean JAMESON
29 Director of Alumni ... Dania ABU-SHAHEEN
36 Director Career Counseling ... Angela CHERUBINI
44 Individual Giving Officer ... Elisa BALESTRA
28 Director of Diversity ... Natalie GROSS
18 Asst Vice President of Facilities ... Maureen GALLAGHER
19 AVP of Public Safety/Purchasing ... Larry HOFFMAN
04 Executive Asst to President ... Rosemary DAHILL
100 Chief of Staff ... Thomas BLUM
104 Asst Dean Study Abroad ... Prema SAMUEL
37 Director Student Financial Aid ... Nick SALINAS

SBI Campus-An Affiliate of Sanford-Brown (A)

320 S Service Road, Melville NY 11747-3201
County: Suffolk FICE Identification: 011647
Unit ID: 192156
Telephone: (631) 370-3300 Carnegie Class: Spec 2-yr-Health
FAX Number: (631) 293-5872 Calendar System: Quarter
URL: www.sbmelville.edu
Established: 2008 Annual Undergrad Tuition & Fees: N/A
Enrollment: 240 Coed
Affiliation or Control: Proprietary IRS Status: Proprietary
Highest Offering: Associate Degree
Accreditation: ACICS

01 President ... Mr. James SWIFT
05 Director of Education ... Dr. Bindu PILLAI
06 Registrar ... Ms. Andreia GONCALVES

† School is in teach-out plan through November 2016.

Schenectady County Community College (B)

78 Washington Avenue, Schenectady NY 12305
County: Schenectady FICE Identification: 006785
Unit ID: 195322
Telephone: (518) 381-1200 Carnegie Class: Assoc/HT-Mix Trad/Non
FAX Number: (518) 346-0379 Calendar System: Semester
URL: www.sunysccc.edu
Established: 1967 Annual Undergrad Tuition & Fees (In-District): $4,054
Enrollment: 6,497 Coed
Affiliation or Control: State/Local IRS Status: 501(c)3
Highest Offering: Associate Degree
Accreditation: M, ACFEI, MUS

01 President ... Dr. Steady MOONO
05 Vice President of Academic Affairs ... Dr. Penny A. HAYNES
10 Vice President of Administration ... Mr. Charles J. RICHARDSON
32 Vice President Student Affairs ... Dr. Martha J. ASSELIN
30 VP Development/External Affairs ... Ms. Marcia STEINER
103 VP Workforce Development/Cmty Educ ... Ms. Denise ZIESKE
13 Chief Information Officer ... Mr. Antione HARRISON
20 Assistant VP Academic Affairs ... Dr. Carlos PENALOZA
11 Assoc VP for Business Development ... Ms. Susan BEAUDOIN
35 Dean Enrollment Mgt/Student Success ... Mr. Stephen FRAGALE
108 Act Asst Dean for Assessment & Int ... Mr. Odo BUTLER
45 Asst Dean for Planning/Acct/Effect ... Mr. Darren JOHNSON
37 Director of Financial Aid ... Ms. Cynthia ASTEMBORSKI-DECKER
06 Registrar ... Ms. Pamela ENSER
07 Dir Admiss/Matriculated Enrollment ... Mr. David G. SAMPSON
08 Director Library Services ... Ms. Lynne O. KING
90 Director of Academic Computing ... Vacant
18 Director of Facilities ... Mr. Alan J. YAUNEY
91 Manager of Administrative Computing ... Vacant
36 Exec Dir SUNY Col/Career Coun Ctr ... Dr. DeShawn MCGARRITY
15 Human Resources Specialist ... Ms. Carianne TROTTA
88 Recruitment Specialist ... Ms. Sandra TROIANO
09 Coordinator Institutional Research ... Ms. Brandie DINGMAN
28 Dir Educ Opportunity Pgms/Access ... Ms. Angela WEST-DAVIS
21 Controller ... Ms. Aimee S. WARFIELD
100 Chief of Staff ... Ms. Paula OHLHOUS
26 Director Marketing/Public Relations ... Mr. David REGAN WHITE
27 Public Rels/Publications Specialist ... Ms. Heather L. MEANEY

School of Visual Arts (C)

209 E 23rd Street, New York NY 10010-3994
County: New York FICE Identification: 007468
Unit ID: 197151
Telephone: (212) 592-2000 Carnegie Class: Spec-4-yr-Arts
FAX Number: (212) 725-3587 Calendar System: Semester
URL: www.sva.edu
Established: 1947 Annual Undergrad Tuition & Fees: $35,000
Enrollment: 4,397 Coed
Affiliation or Control: Proprietary IRS Status: Proprietary
Highest Offering: Master's
Accreditation: M, ART, CIDA, TED

01 President ... David J. RHODES
03 Executive Vice President ... Anthony P. RHODES
05 Provost ... Jeffrey NESIN
10 Chief Financial Officer ... Gary SHILLET
32 Exec Dir of Student Affairs/Admiss ... Javier VEGA
26 Exec Director of External Relations ... Susan MODENSTEIN
13 Chief Information Officer ... Cosmin TOMESCU
06 Registrar ... Jason KOTH
07 Exec Director Admission ... Javier VEGA
35 Director of Student Affairs ... Bill MARTINO
08 Director Visual Arts Library ... Robert LOBE
37 Director Financial Aid ... William BERRIOS
36 Director Career Development ... Angie WOJAK
30 Director Development/Alumni Affairs ... Jane NUZZO
19 Director Security ... Nick AGJMURATI
15 Exec Director of Human Resources ... Frank AGOSTA
09 Director of Institutional Research ... Jerold DAVIS
27 Director of Communications ... Vacant

Sh'or Yoshuv Rabbinical College (D)

1 Cedar Lawn Avenue, Lawrence NY 11559-1714
County: Nassau FICE Identification: 025059
Unit ID: 195438
Telephone: (516) 239-9002 Carnegie Class: Spec-4-yr-Faith
FAX Number: (516) 239-9003 Calendar System: Semester
URL: www.shoryoshuv.org
Established: 1963 Annual Undergrad Tuition & Fees: $9,460
Enrollment: 153 Male
Affiliation or Control: Independent Non-Profit IRS Status: 501(c)3
Highest Offering: Second Talmudic Degree
Accreditation: RABN

01 Dean ... Rabbi Naftalie JAEGER
05 Executive Director ... Mr. Moshe RUBIN
32 Director of Student Affairs ... Rabbi Elysha SANDLER
06 Registrar ... Mrs. Sheila FLEISCHER
37 Director SFA ... Rabbi Chaim MAJEROVIC

Siena College (E)

515 Loudon Road, Loudonville NY 12211-1462
County: Albany FICE Identification: 002816
Unit ID: 195474
Telephone: (518) 783-2300 Carnegie Class: Bac-A&S
FAX Number: (518) 783-4293 Calendar System: Semester
URL: www.siena.edu
Established: 1937 Annual Undergrad Tuition & Fees: $33,415
Enrollment: 3,179 Coed
Affiliation or Control: Independent Non-Profit IRS Status: 501(c)3
Highest Offering: Master's
Accreditation: M, BUS, SW, TED

01 President ... Bro. F. Edward COUGHLIN, OFM
05 Vice President for Academic Affairs ... Dr. Margaret MADDEN
32 Vice President for Student Life ... Dr. Maryellen GILROY
10 Vice President for Finance & Admin ... Mr. Paul T. STEC
84 VP for Enrollment Management ... Mr. Ned J. JONES
30 VP for Development & External Affs ... Mr. David B. SMITH
100 VP & Chief of Staff ... Mr. Michael J. HICKEY
13 Chief Information Officer ... Mr. Mark A. BERMAN
49 Int Dean of Liberal Arts ... Mr. James C. HARRISON
50 Dean of Business ... Dr. Charles SEIFERT
81 Dean of Science ... Vacant
88 Assoc VP Stdnt Retention & Success ... Dr. Peter C. ELLARD
45 Assoc VP Acad Affs/Inst Effectivns ... Dr. Mary Lou D'ALLEGRO
15 Asst VP for Human Resources ... Ms. Cynthia B. KING-LEROY
07 Assoc VP Enrollment Management ... Vacant
21 Asst VP for Finance & Admin ... Ms. Mary C. STRUNK
18 Asst VP for Facilities Management ... Mr. Mark FROST
19 Asst VP Stdnt Aff/Dir Public Safety ... Mr. Michael PAPADOPOULOS
88 Assoc VP Acad Affs Mgmt/Compliance ... Vacant
06 Registrar ... Mr. James SERBALIK
37 Assoc Vice Pres Financial Aid ... Ms. Mary K. LAWYER
08 Dir of Library/Audio Visual Svcs ... Mr. Gary THOMPSON
92 Director of Honors Program ... Dr. Lois K. DALY
35 Dean of Students ... Mr. John R. FELIO
39 Director of Community Living ... Mr. Adam CASLER
41 VP & Director of Athletics ... Mr. John D'ARGENIO
36 Director of Career Center ... Ms. Debra DELBELSO
26 Deputy Chief Information Officer ... Ms. Mary W. PARLETT-SWEENEY
42 Chaplain of the College ... Fr. Lawrence ANDERSON, OFM
38 Director of Counseling Center ... Dr. Wally B. BZBELL
29 Director of Alumni Relations ... Ms. Mary Beth FINNERTY
09 Dir of Institutional Research ... Mr. Lee ALLARD
88 Dir of Risk Analysis/Project Mgmt ... Ms. Sandy SERBALIK
94 Dir Sr Thea Bowman Ctr for Women ... Dr. Shannon O'NEILL
23 Director of Health Services ... Ms. Carrie HOGAN
40 Bookstore Manager ... Mr. Richard IVES
44 Director of Development ... Mr. Brad R. BODMER
28 Dir of Damietta Cross-Cultural Ctr ... Ms. Christa J. GRANT
104 Director of Study Abroad/Intl Pgms ... Bro. Brian C. BELANGER, OFM
96 Dir of Auxiliary Svcs & Procurement ... Ms. Laura S. PARRY
88 Institutional Research Analyst ... Ms. Kai ZHOU
43 Legal Services/General Counsel ... Ms. Rose SEGGOS

Skidmore College (F)

815 N Broadway, Saratoga Springs NY 12866-1632
County: Saratoga FICE Identification: 002814
Unit ID: 195526
Telephone: (518) 580-5000 Carnegie Class: Bac-A&S
FAX Number: (518) 580-5936 Calendar System: Semester
URL: www.skidmore.edu
Established: 1911 Annual Undergrad Tuition & Fees: $49,120
Enrollment: 2,646 Coed
Affiliation or Control: Independent Non-Profit IRS Status: 501(c)3
Highest Offering: Master's
Accreditation: M, ART, SW, TEAC

01 President ... Dr. Philip A. GLOTZBACH
05 VP Academic Affairs/Dean of Faculty ... Dr. Beau BRESLIN
10 Vice President Finance/Treasurer ... Mr. Michael D. WEST
30 Vice President for Advancement ... Mr. Michael T. CASEY
15 Assoc VP Fin & Admin/Dir of HR ... Ms. Barbara E. BECK
32 Dean of Students and Vice President ... Ms. Cerri A. BANKS
07 VP & Dean of Admiss & Fin Aid ... Ms. Mary Lou W. BATES
71 Dean of Special Programs ... Mr. Paul CALHOUN
06 Registrar ... Mr. David DECONNO
20 Assoc Dean for Student Academics ... Dr. Corey FREEMAN-GALLANT
28 Assoc Dn for Diversity/Faculty Affs ... Dr. Crystal D. MOORE
89 Dir of First Year Experience ... Ms. Janet CASEY
35 Assoc Dean Student Affs/Campus Life ... Ms. Mariel MARTIN
39 Director of Residential Life ... Ms. Ann Marie PRZYWARA
45 VP Strategic Plng & Inst Diversity ... Dr. Joshua C. WOODFORK
26 Interim VP Communications & Mktg ... Ms. Debra TOWNSEND
09 Director of Institutional Research ... Mr. Joseph STANKOVICH
102 Dir Foundation & Corporate Rels ... Mr. Barry PRITZKER
46 Director of Sponsored Research ... Mr. Bill TOMLINSON
13 Dir Network & Technical Services ... Mr. Mark BAUER
105 Director Web Communications ... Mr. Andy CAMP
87 Director of Summer Acad Pgm & Resid ... Dr. Auden THOMAS
88 Director for Intercultural Studies ... Dr. Kristie A. FORD
22 Asst Dir EEO & Workforce Diversity ... Mr. Herb CROSSMAN
91 Director IT-Enterprise Systems ... Mr. Jeffrey A. CLARK
104 Dir of Off-Campus Study & Exchanges ... Ms. Cori FILSON
44 Senior Director Donor Relations ... Ms. Mary L. SOLOMONS
30 Director of Development ... Ms. Lori EASTMAN
29 Executive Dir Alumni Aff & Col Eve ... Mr. Michael SPOSILI
36 Director Career Development Center ... Ms. Kim CRABBE
37 Director of Financial Aid ... Ms. Beth POST-LUNDQUIST
38 Director Counseling Center ... Dr. Julia C. ROUTBORT
21 Director of Business Services ... Ms. Christine KACZMAREK
23 Director of Clinical Services ... Ms. Patricia BOSEN
18 Director of Facilities Services ... Mr. Daniel RODECKER
19 Director of Campus Safety ... Mr. Dennis S. CONWAY
08 College Librarian ... Ms. Marta BRUNNER
96 Director of Purchasing ... Mrs. Carol N. SCHNITZER
42 Int Dir Religious & Spiritual Life ... Ms. Parker DIGGORY
24 Director of Media Services ... Mr. T. Hunt CONARD
40 Director Skidmore Shop ... Mr. Jon NEIL
88 Special Assistant to the President ... Ms. Jeanne M. SISSON
101 Board Coordinator ... Ms. Susan W. KOPPI

Sotheby's Institute of Art (G)

570 Lexington Ave, 6th Floor, New York NY 10022
County: New York Identification: 667007
Unit ID: 481094
Telephone: (212) 517-3929 Carnegie Class: Spec-4-yr-Arts
FAX Number: (212) 517-6568 Calendar System: Semester
URL: www.sothebysinstitute.com
Established: 2006 Annual Graduate Tuition & Fees: N/A
Enrollment: 153 Coed
Affiliation or Control: Proprietary IRS Status: Proprietary
Highest Offering: First Professional Degree; No Undergraduates
Accreditation: ART

01 Director ... Ms. Christine KUAN
06 Registrar ... Ms. Tammy PARKS
07 Director of Admissions ... Ms. Melba REMICE
08 Head Librarian ... Ms. Erin ELLIOTT
10 Chief Business Officer ... Ms. Lilly KOGAN
15 Director Personnel Services ... Ms. Christine KUAN
32 Chief Student Affairs/Student Life ... Ms. Sara MOORE

*State University of New York System Office (H)

State University Plaza, Albany NY 12246-0001
County: Albany FICE Identification: 008788
Unit ID: 195827
Telephone: (518) 320-1100 Carnegie Class: N/A
FAX Number: (518) 320-1561
URL: www.suny.edu

01 Chancellor ... Dr. Nancy L. ZIMPHER
03 Provost & Executive Vice Chancellor ... Dr. Alexander CARTWRIGHT
10 Vice Chancellor for Finance and CFO ... Ms. Eileen MCLOUGHLIN
05 Vice Provost & VC for Acad Affairs ... Dr. Elizabeth BRINGSJORD
43 VC for Legal Affairs & General Coun ... Mr. Joseph PORTER
100 Chief of Staff ... Ms. Stacey HENGSTERMAN
88 Assoc VC for External Affairs ... Ms. Jennifer LOTURCO
26 Director of Communications ... Ms. Casey VATTIMO
88 Sr VC for Cmty Col & Educ Pipeline ... Ms. Johanna DUNCAN-POITIER

11 Assistant VC for Operations .... Ms. Kellie J. DUPUIS
88 Pres Faculty Council of Cmty Col .... Ms. Nina TAMROWSKI
18 VC for Cap Facil/GM Constr Fund .... Mr. Robert HAELEN
88 University Faculty Senate President .... Mr. Peter KNUEPFER
20 Sr Assoc VC and Vice Prov Acad Affs .... Mr. Jason LANE
15 Vice Chancellor for Human Resources .... Mr. Curtis LLOYD
84 Assoc VC for Enrollment Management .... Mr. Paul MARTHERS

*University at Albany, SUNY (A)

1400 Washington Avenue, Albany NY 12222-1000

County: Albany FICE Identification: 002835
Unit ID: 196060
Telephone: (518) 442-3300 Carnegie Class: DU-Highest
FAX Number: N/A Calendar System: Semester
URL: www.albany.edu
Established: 1844 Annual Undergrad Tuition & Fees (In-State): $8,996
Enrollment: 17,273 Coed
Affiliation or Control: State IRS Status: 501(c)3
Highest Offering: Doctorate
Accreditation: M, BUS, BUSA, CLPSY, COPSY, IPSY, LIB, PH, PLNG, SCPSY, SPAA, SW, TEAC

02 President .... Robert J. JONES
05 Sr VP for Academic Affs & Provost .... James R. STELLER
46 Vice President for Research .... James DIAS
10 Vice Pres Finance & Business .... James VAN VOORST
30 VP Univ Dev & Exec Dir UA Found .... Fardin SANAI
26 VP Communications and Marketing .... Joseph A. BRENNAN
41 Director of Athletics .... Mark BENSON
21 Assoc Vice President & Controller .... Kevin WILCOX
32 Assoc VP Student Success .... Ed ENGELBRIDE
11 Vice Provost for Administration .... Bruce SZELEST
18 Associate VP Facilities .... John GIARRUSSO
20 VP & Assoc VP for Academic Affairs .... Sandra STARKE
88 Vice Provost Acad Resource Plng .... Jack D. MAHONEY
28 Asst VP Diversity/Inclusion .... Tamra MINOR
84 AVP for Enrollment Management .... Robert K. ANDREA, JR.
97 Vice Prov Undergrad Educ/Dean Psych .... Jeanette ALTARRIBA
49 Dean of College of Arts & Sciences .... Edelgard WULFERT
53 Dean School of Education .... Robert BANGERT-DROWNS
50 Dean School of Business .... Donald S. SIEGEL
69 Dean School of Public Health .... Philip NASCA
61 Dean of Criminal Justice .... William A. PRIDEMORE
80 Dean Rockefeller Col of Pub Affs .... R. Karl RETHEMEYER
70 Dean of School of Social Welfare .. Katharine H. BRIAR-LAWSON
77 Dean Col of Computing & Info .... Sue R. FAERMAN
54 Dean Engineering & Applied Sci .... Kim L. BOYER
58 Dean of Graduate Studies .... Kevin WILLIAMS
08 Dean/Director of Libraries .... Mary F. CASSERLY
13 VP Chief Information Officer .... Simeon ANANOU
06 Registrar .... Karen CHICO HURST
29 Exec Director Alumni Association .... Lee SERRAVILLO, JR.
90 Dir Academic Computing Center .... Felix WU
100 Chief of Staff .... Leanne WIRKKULA
20 Asst Vice Prov/Dir Advisement Ctr .... Suzanne K. FREED
43 Senior Counsel .... John H. REILLY
38 Director of Counseling & Psych Svcs .... Estela RIVERO
36 Director Career Services .... Philippe ABRAHAM
07 Director of Admissions .... Timothy LEE
105 Director Web Services .... Fred DOYLE
32 Vice President Student Affairs .... Michael N. CHRISTAKIS

*State University of New York at Binghamton (B)

Vestal Parkway E, Box 6000, Binghamton NY 13902-6000

County: Broome FICE Identification: 002836
Unit ID: 196079
Telephone: (607) 777-2000 Carnegie Class: DU-Higher
FAX Number: (607) 777-4000 Calendar System: Semester
URL: www.binghamton.edu
Established: 1946 Annual Undergrad Tuition & Fees (In-State): $9,053
Enrollment: 16,695 Coed
Affiliation or Control: State IRS Status: 501(c)3
Highest Offering: Doctorate
Accreditation: M, BUS, CLPSY, CS, ENG, MUS, NURSE, SPAA, SW, TEAC

02 President .... Dr. Harvey G. STENGER, JR.
100 Chief of Staff .... Mr. Terrence KANE
05 Exec VP for Academic Affs/Provost .... Dr. Donald NIEMAN
10 Vice President Operations .... Ms. JoAnn NAVARRO
32 Vice Pres Student Affairs .... Mr. Brian T. ROSE
09 Vice President for Research .... Dr. Bahgat SAMMAKIA
104 Exec Vice Prov Intl Initiatives .... Dr. Hari SRIHARI
45 Senior Vice Provost .... Dr. Michael F. MCGOFF
58 Vice Prov/Dean of Graduate School .... Dr. Susan STREHLE
18 Assoc VP Facilities Management .... Mr. Lawrence J. ROMA
35 Dean of Students .... Dr. April THOMPSON
102 Exec Dir of Bing Foundation .... Ms. Sheila DOYLE
26 Assoc Vice Pres Univ Comm/Mktg .... Mr. Gregory DELVISCIO
27 Chief Information Officer .... Ms. Sharon PITT
04 Exec Assistant to the President .... Ms. Laura L. O'NEIL
15 Asst Vice Pres for Human Resources .... Mr. Joseph P. SCHULTZ
07 Asst Vice Prov & Dir of Admissions .... Mr. Randall EDOUARD
08 Dean of Libraries .... Dr. Curtis KENDRICK
85 Director Intl Students/Scholar Svcs .... Ms. Patricia MARRAPESE
86 Director of State Relations .... Mr. Terrence KANE
37 Dir Financial Aid/Stdnt Records .... Mr. Dennis J. CHAVEZ
06 University Registrar .... Vacant
38 Director Health & Counseling .... Ms. Johann FIORE CONTE
36 Director Career Development Center .... Ms. Kelli SMITH
19 Director Public Safety .... Mr. Timothy FAUGHANAN
41 Director Athletics .... Mr. Patrick ELLIOTT
71 Director Educ Opportunities Prog .... Mr. Calvin GANTT
22 Dir Diversity/Equity & Inclusive .... Ms. Valerie J. HAMPTON
28 Director Multi-Cultural Res Ctr .... Ms. Nicole SIRJU-JOHNSON
92 Director Binghamton Univ Scholars .... Dr. William ZIEGLER
94 Exec Director of Women's Studies .... Ms. Dara J. SILBERSTEIN
96 Director of Purchasing .... Mr. Kenneth G. WASKIE
09 Asst Provost Institutional Research .... Ms. Nasrin FATIMA
49 Int Dean Arts & Science Harpur Col .... Dr. Terrence DEAK
53 Interim Dean School of Education .... Dr. Susan STREHLE
50 Dean School of Management .... Dr. Upinder S. DHILLON
54 Dn Watson Sch Engr/Applied Science .... Dr. Hari SRIHARI
66 Dean Decker School of Nursing .... Dr. Mario ORTIZ
31 Dean Community & Public Affairs .... Dr. Laura BRONSTEIN
106 Dir Center for Innov/Cont Educ .... Mr. Thomas KOWALIK
29 Sr Director Alumni Relations .... Ms. Rose FRIERMAN
43 Campus Atty/General Counsel .... Ms. Barbara SCARLETT

*University at Buffalo-SUNY (C)

3435 Main Street, Buffalo NY 14214

County: Erie FICE Identification: 002837
Unit ID: 196088
Telephone: (716) 645-2000 Carnegie Class: DU-Highest
FAX Number: N/A Calendar System: Semester
URL: www.buffalo.edu
Established: 1846 Annual Undergrad Tuition & Fees (In-State): $9,381
Enrollment: 29,995 Coed
Affiliation or Control: State IRS Status: 501(c)3
Highest Offering: Doctorate
Accreditation: M, ANEST, AUD, BUS, BUSA, CEA, CLPSY, CORE, CS, DA, DENT, DIETI, ENG, IPSY, LAW, LIB, MED, MT, NMT, NURSE, OT, PH, PHAR, PLNG, PSPSY, PTA, SP, SW, TEAC

53 Dean Graduate Sch of Education .... Dr. Jaekyung LEE
02 President .... Dr. Satish K. TRIPATHI
05 Provost/Exec VP Academic Affs .... Dr. Charles F. ZUKOSKI
10 Vice Pres Finance & Administration .... Ms. Laura E. HUBBARD
32 Vice President Student Affairs .... Vacant
17 Vice President Health Sciences .... Dr. Michael CAIN
30 Vice Pres Philanthropy & Alumni Eng .... Ms. Nancy L. WELLS
46 Vice President for Research/EcoDev .... Dr. Venu GOVINDARAJU
84 Vice Provost of Enrollment .... Dr. Lee H. MELVIN
15 Assoc VP Human Resources .... Mr. Mark COLDREN
58 Vice Provost Graduate Education .... Dr. Graham L. HAMMILL
20 Sr Vice Provost Acad Affairs .... Dr. A. Scott WEBER
20 Vice Provost for Faculty Affairs .... Prof. Robert GRANFIELD
104 Vice Provost for International Educ .... Dr. Stephen C. DUNNETT
45 Vice Provost Academic Plng & Budget .... Vacant
08 Assoc VP for Univ Libraries .... Mr. H. Austin BOOTH
13 VP & Chief Information Officer .... Mr. Brice BIBLE
37 Director Financial Aid .... Mr. John GOTTARDY
09 Assoc V Provost/Dir Inst Research .... Mr. Craig W. ABBEY
96 Asst Vice Pres Procurement Services .... Mr. Daniel VIVIAN
26 VP Univ Communications .... Ms. Nancy E. PATON
22 Vice Provost Equity & Inclusion .... Ms. Teresa A. MILLER
28 Dir Equity/Diversity/Inclusion .... Ms. Sharon E. NOLAN-WEISS
41 Director of Athletics .... Mr. Allen GREENE
91 Director Enterprise Application Svc .... Ms. Susan A. HUSTON
07 Director of UG Admissions .... Mr. Jose AVILES
19 Chief of Police .... Mr. Gerald W. SCHOENLE, JR.
39 Director of Campus Living .... Ms. Andrea COSTANTINO
38 Director of Counseling Services .... Dr. Sharon L. MITCHELL
23 Director Health Services .... Ms. Susan M. SNYDER
36 Director Career Services .... Ms. Arlene F. KAUKUS
85 Director Intl Students/Scholar Svc .... Ms. Ellen A. DUSSOURD
40 Director University Bookstores .... Mr. Gregory NEUMANN
92 Admin Dir Univ Honors College .... Ms. Krista L. HANYPSIAK
29 Sr Director Dev & Alumni Events .... Mr. Jay R. FRIEDMAN
27 Director of Marketing .... Mr. David WEDEKINDT
20 Dean of Undergraduate Educ .... Dr. Andrew M. STOTT
48 Dean School Arch & Planning .... Dr. Robert SHIBLEY
49 Dean College of Arts/Sciences .... Dr. Robin G. SCHULZE
52 Dean School Dental Medicine .... Dr. Joseph ZAMBON
54 Dean School Engr/Applied Sci .... Dr. Liesl FOLKS
61 Interim Dean School of Law .... Prof. James A. GARDNER
50 Dean School of Management .... Prof. Paul E. TESLUK
63 Dean School Medicine/Biomed Sci .... Dr. Michael E. CAIN
66 Dean School of Nursing .... Dr. Marsha L. LEWIS
67 Dean School Pharmacy/Pharm Sciences .... Dr. James O'DONNELL
76 Dean Sch Public Hlth/Hlth Prof .... Dr. Jean WACTAWSKI-WENDE
70 Dean School of Social Work .... Dr. Nancy J. SMYTH
06 Registrar .... Dr. Kara C. SAUNDERS

*State University of New York at Fredonia (D)

138 Fenton Hall, Fredonia NY 14063-1136

County: Chautauqua FICE Identification: 002844
Unit ID: 196158
Telephone: (716) 673-3111 Carnegie Class: Masters/M
FAX Number: N/A Calendar System: Semester
URL: www.fredonia.edu
Established: 1826 Annual Undergrad Tuition & Fees (In-State): $8,074
Enrollment: 5,215 Coed
Affiliation or Control: State IRS Status: 501(c)3
Highest Offering: Master's
Accreditation: M, ART, CAEP, MUS, SP, SW, TED, THEA

02 President .... Dr. Virginia S. HORVATH
05 Provost & VP for Acad Affairs .... Dr. Terry BROWN
10 Interim VP for Finance and Admin .... Dr. Kevin SEITZ
32 Vice President for Student Affairs .... Dr. Cedric B. HOWARD
35 Assoc Vice Pres for Student Affairs .... Ms. Monica J. WHITE
30 Interim VP for Univ Advancement .... Ms. Betty GOSSETT
20 Assoc VP Curriculum/Assessment/Ac .... Dr. Lisa HUNTER
49 Dean College of Liberal Arts & Sci .... Dr. Roger A. BYRNE
88 VP Engagement & Economic Dev .... Dr. Kevin KEARNS
57 Dean College of Visual & Perf Arts .... Dr. Ralph BLASTING
58 Assoc Provost for Graduate Studies .... Dr. Judy HOROWITZ
50 Dean School of Business .... Dr. Russell P. BOISJOLY
53 Dean College of Education .... Dr. Christine E. GIVNER
102 Interim Director Corp/Univ Advance .... Ms. Betty GOSSETT
18 Director Facilities Services .... Mr. Kevin P. CLOOS
06 Registrar .... Mr. Scott D. SAUNDERS
07 Director of Admissions .... Mr. Cory M. BEZEK
37 Director Financial Aid .... Mr. Daniel M. TRAMUTA
08 Director Library Services .... Mr. Randolph Lee GADIKIAN
09 Dir Institutional Research/Planning .... Dr. Xiao Y. ZHANG
36 Director of Career Development .... Ms. Tracy COLLINGWOOD
84 Assoc Vice Pres for Enrollment Mgmt .... Mr. Daniel M. TRAMUTA
19 Chief University Police .... Ms. Ann K. BURNS
39 Director Residence Life .... Mrs. Kathy FORSTER
41 Athletic Director .... Mr. Gregory D. PRECHTL
23 Director of Health Services .... Ms. Deborah A. DIBBLE
38 Director Counseling Center .... Dr. Tracy L. STENGER
90 Academic Information Technology .... Mr. Stephen J. RIEKS
15 Director of Human Resources .... Mr. Michael D. DALEY
26 Director of Public Relations .... Vacant
85 Director of Multicultural Affairs .... Ms. Jellema STEWART
92 Director of Honors Program .... Dr. David KINKELA
94 Coordinator of Women's Studies .... Mr. Jeffry J. IOVANNONE
96 Director of Purchasing .... Mrs. Shari K. MILLER
28 Chief Diversity Officer .... Dr. William BOERNER
29 Director Alumni Affairs .... Ms. Patricia A. FERALDI
04 Administrative Asst to President .... Mrs. Denise M. SZALKOWSKI

*State University of New York at New Paltz (E)

1 Hawk Drive, New Paltz NY 12561-2443

County: Ulster FICE Identification: 002846
Unit ID: 196176
Telephone: (845) 257-7869 Carnegie Class: Masters/L
FAX Number: (845) 257-3009 Calendar System: Semester
URL: www.newpaltz.edu
Established: 1823 Annual Undergrad Tuition & Fees (In-State): $7,737
Enrollment: 7,692 Coed
Affiliation or Control: State IRS Status: 501(c)3
Highest Offering: Beyond Master's But Less Than Doctorate
Accreditation: M, AFT, BUS, ENG, MUS, SP, TED, THEA

02 President .... Dr. Donald P. CHRISTIAN
100 Chief of Staff/VP Communication .... Ms. Shelly A. WRIGHT
05 Interim Provost .... Dr. Stella DEEN
10 Vice Pres Administration & Finance .... Ms. Michele HALSTEAD
30 VP Development/Alumni Relations .... Ms. Erica MARKS
32 Student Affairs Vice President .... Dr. L. David ROONEY
84 Vice Pres Enrollment Management .... Mr. L. David EATON
58 Assoc Provost/Dean Graduate School .... Dr. Laurel GARRICK DUHANEY
13 Asst Vice Pres Tech/Info Systems .... Mr. Jonathan D. LEWIT
21 Asst Vice President Administration .... Ms. Julieta MAJAK
88 Asst VP Budget .... Ms. Julie WALSH
09 Asst VP Inst Research/Planning .... Ms. Lucy WALKER
18 Asst VP Facilities Management .... Mr. John SHUPE
53 Dean of Education .... Dr. Michael ROSENBERG
57 Dean Fine & Performing Arts .... Dr. Jennifer MOKREN
49 Dean Liberal Arts & Sciences .... Dr. Laura BARRETT
50 Dean School of Business .... Dr. Kristin BACKHAUS
54 Dean Science and Engineering .... Dr. Daniel FREEDMAN
07 Dean of Admissions .... Ms. Lisa JONES
08 Dean Sojourner Truth Library .... Mr. W. Mark COLVSON
86 Ex Dir Compliance/Camp Clm/Title IX .... Ms. Tanhena PACHECO DUNN
07 Assoc Dean/Dir Freshmen Admissions .... Ms. Kimberly STRANO
15 Director Human Resources .... Ms. Dawn BLADES
37 Director of Financial Aid .... Ms. Maureen LOHAN-BREMER
06 Registrar .... Ms. Laura SCHULTZ
29 Director Alumni Relations .... Vacant
38 Director Student Counseling .... Dr. Gweneth LLOYD
26 Media Relations Manager .... Ms. Melissa KACZMAREK
96 Director of Purchasing/Procurement .... Mr. David FARBANIEC
19 Director Security/Safety .... Mr. David DUGATKIN
41 Athletic Director .... Mr. Stuart ROBINSON

*State University of New York at Oneonta (F)

108 Ravine Parkway, Oneonta NY 13820-4015

County: Otsego FICE Identification: 002847
Unit ID: 196185
Telephone: (607) 436-3500 Carnegie Class: Masters/S
FAX Number: N/A Calendar System: Semester
URL: www.oneonta.edu
Established: 1889 Annual Undergrad Tuition & Fees (In-State): $7,870
Enrollment: 6,101 Coed
Affiliation or Control: State IRS Status: 501(c)3
Highest Offering: Master's
Accreditation: M, AAFCS, BUS, DIETD, DIETI, MUS, TED, THEA

02 President .... Dr. Nancy KLENIEWSKI
04 Exec Assistant to the President .... Ms. Colleen E. BRANNAN

05 Provost/Vice Pres Academic Affairs Dr. James MACKIN
10 Vice Pres Finance/Administration Mr. Todd D. FOREMAN
32 Vice President Student Development Dr. Franklin D. CHAMBERS
30 Vice President College Advancement Mr. Paul J. ADAMO
09 Assoc Prov Inst Assessment & Eff Dr. Wade THOMAS
20 Assoc Provost Academic Programs Dr. Eileen MORGAN-ZAYACHEK
83 Dean School of Arts and Humanities Dr. Joao SEDYCIAS
50 Dean School of Econ & Business Dr. David YEN
53 Dean School of Educ & Human Ecology Dr. Jan BOWERS
81 Dean School of Nat/Math Sciences Dr. Venkat SHARMA
83 Dean School of Social Science Dr. Susan TURELL
58 Director of Graduate Studies Mr. Patrick J. MENTE
84 Chief Enrollment Services Officer Mr. Kevin JENSEN
35 Assoc Vice Pres Student Life Vacant
18 Assoc Vice Pres Facilities/Safety Mr. Thomas M. RATHBONE
19 Chief of Police Mr. Daniel P. CHAMBERS
15 Sr Exec Employee Services Officer Ms. Lisa M. WENCK
26 Exec Director of Communications Mr. Hal S. LEGG
07 Director of Admissions Ms. Karen A. BROWN
29 Director of Alumni Engagement Ms. Laura MADELONE LINCOLN
88 Director Advancement Services Mr. Michael SULLIVAN
44 Director Fund for Oneonta Ms. Kim NOSTROM
41 Athletic Director Ms. Tracey M. RANIERI
21 Budget Control Officer/Budget Dir Ms. Julie PISCITELLO
25 Director Business Services Ms. Betty M. TIRADO
36 Dir Career Dev/Student Emp Svcs Dr. Amy BENEDICT
13 Dir Computing Ctr/Chief Info Ofcr Dr. Karlis KAUGARS
90 Director IT Customer Support Mr. Steven J. MANISCALCO
23 Dir Health & Counseling Services Dr. Melissa A. FALLON-KORB
24 Director Creative Media Services Mr. David W. GEASEY
37 Director Financial Aid Mr. Bill GOODHUE
09 Dir Institutional Research Mr. Ernesto HENRIQUEZ
85 Director of International Education Dr. Vernon C. LARSON
89 Director Orientation/First Year Exp Ms. Monica C. GRAU
96 Procurement/Travel Office Manager Ms. Terri THOMAS
06 College Registrar Ms. Maureen P. ARTALE
39 Director Residential Community Life Ms. Michele LUETTGER
93 Director Special Programs/EOP Ms. Lynda D. BASSETTE-FARONE
28 Chief Diversity Officer Dr. Terrence MITCHELL
22 Affirmative Action Officer Mr. Andrew STAMMEL

*Stony Brook University (A)

310 Administration Building, Stony Brook NY 11794-0701
County: Suffolk FICE Identification: 002838
Unit ID: 196097
Telephone: (631) 632-6265 Carnegie Class: DU-Highest
FAX Number: (631) 632-6621 Calendar System: Semester
URL: www.stonybrook.edu
Established: 1957 Annual Undergrad Tuition & Fees (In-State): $8,855
Enrollment: 24,607 Coed
Affiliation or Control: State IRS Status: 501(c)3
Highest Offering: Doctorate
Accreditation: M, ARCPA, CAATE, CLPSY, COARC, COARCP, CS, DENT, DIETI, ENG, IPSY, JOUR, MED, MIDWF, MT, NURSE, OT, PCSAS, PH, POLYT, PTA, RADDOS, SW, TED

02 President/CEO Dr. Samuel L. STANLEY
05 Interim Provost Dr. Charles TABER
63 Sr VP HSC/Dean School of Medicine Dr. Kenneth KAUSHANSKY
46 Vice President Research Dr. David CONOVER
32 Vice President Student Affairs Dr. Peter M. BAIGENT
10 VP Finance Mr. Lyle GOMES
30 Sr VP University Advancement Mr. Dexter BAILEY
54 VP Econ Dev/Dean Engr/Applied Sci Dr. Yacov SHAMASH
100 Chief Deputy to President Ms. Judith GREIMAN
21 Associate VP for Budget Mr. Mark MACIULAITIS
11 Sr VP for Administration Vacant
26 VP Comm & Mktg/Chief Comm Officer Mr. Nicholas SCIBETTA
39 Asst Vice Pres Campus Residences Dr. Dallas BAUMAN
17 CEO University Hospital Dr. Reuven PASTERNAK
84 Assoc Prov Enrollment/Retent Mgmt Mr. Rodney MORRISON
13 CIO Mr. Michael OSPITALE
45 Vice President Strategic Initiatves Dr. Matthew WHELAN
43 Senior Counsel in Charge Ms. Susan BLUM
49 Dean College Arts & Sciences Dr. Sacha KOPP
88 Dean School of Marine & Atmos Sci Dr. Minghua ZHANG
52 Dean School of Dental Medicine Dr. Mary R. TRUHLAR
68 Dean Div Physical Educ & Athletics Mr. Shawn R. HEILBRON
58 Dean Grad Sch & Sch of Prof Develop Dr. Charles TABER
76 Dean School Health Technology Mgmt Dr. Craig LEHMANN
35 Dean of Students Dr. Timothy ECKLUND
66 Dean School of Nursing Dr. Lee XIPPOLITOS
70 Dean School of Social Welfare Dr. Frances L. BRISBANE
08 Dean of Libraries Dr. Constantia CONSTANINOU
86 VP Government & Community Relations Vacant
88 Exec Dir LI State Vets Home Mr. Fred SGANGA
19 Chief of Police Mr. Robert LENAHAN
15 VP Human Resource Svcs Ms. Lynn JOHNSON
28 Dir Diversity/AA/Equal Employ Oppty Ms. Marjolie LEONARD
09 AVP Inst Rsrch/Plng/Effectiveness Dr. Braden J. HOSCH
85 Interim Dean International Programs Dr. Imin KAO
102 Exec Dir of Stony Brook Foundation Mr. Dexter A. BAILEY
29 Director Alumni Relations Mr. Matthew COLSON
23 Director University Health Services Dr. Rachel BERGESON
38 Int Dir Counseling/Psych Services Dr. Julian PESSIER
36 Director Career Placement Center Ms. Marianna SAVOCA
06 Registrar Ms. Diane BELLO
37 Financial Aid/Scholarships Ms. Jacqueline PASCARIELLO

50 Dean College of Business Dr. Manuel LONDON
27 University Media Relations Officer Ms. Lauren SHEPROW
96 Director of Purchasing/Procurement Mr. James FABIAN
60 Dean School of Journalism Mr. Howard SCHNEIDER
04 Executive Asst to President Ms. Carol LONDOIRO

*SUNY Downstate Medical Center (B)

450 Clarkson Avenue, Brooklyn NY 11203-2098
County: Kings FICE Identification: 002839
Unit ID: 196255
Telephone: (718) 270-1000 Carnegie Class: Spec-4-yr-Med
FAX Number: (718) 270-4092 Calendar System: Semester
URL: www.downstate.edu
Established: 1860 Annual Undergrad Tuition & Fees (In-State): N/A
Enrollment: 1,865 Coed
Affiliation or Control: State IRS Status: 501(c)3
Highest Offering: Doctorate
Accreditation: M, ANEST, ARCPA, DMS, MED, MIDWF, NURSE, OT, PH, PTA

02 Officer in Charge Dr. Michael LUCCHESI
10 Chief Financial Officer Ms. Melanie GEHEN
11 COO/Exec Vice Pres Administration Ms. Astra BAIN-DOWELL
05 VP Acad Affs/SVP Inst Dev/Philthrpy Dr. JoAnn BRADLEY
32 Assoc VP Student Aff/Dean of Stdnts Dr. Jeffrey PUTMAN
30 AVP Institutional Advancement Ms. Ellen WATSON
13 Chief Information Officer Vacant
07 Director of Admissions Ms. Shushawna DEOLIVEIRA
06 Registrar Ms. Anne SHONBRUN
37 Director Student Financial Aid Mr. James NEWELL
26 Chief Public Relations Officer Ms. Ellen WATSON
04 Administrative Asst to President Linda CORBY
08 Head Librarian Dr. Richard WINANT
09 Director of Institutional Research Charis NG
15 Director Personnel Services Anthony PARKER
18 Chief Facilities/Physical Plant Tim HERZOG
19 Director Security/Safety Vincent CARDOZO
22 Dir Affirm Action/EEO/Diversity Kevin ANTOINE
25 Chief Contracts/Grants Admin Maureen CRYSTAL
29 Director Alumni Relations Eric SHOEN
39 Director Student Housing Margaret O'SULLIVAN
43 Dir Legal Services/General Counsel Kevin O'MARA
45 Chief Institutional Planning Dorothy FYFE
53 Dean College of Nursing Dr. Daisy CRUZ-RICHMAN
86 Director Government Relations Michael HARRELL
90 Director Academic Computing Gregory CONYERS
96 Director of Purchasing Martin DEANE

*State University of New York Upstate Medical University (C)

750 E Adams Street, Syracuse NY 13210-2375
County: Onondaga FICE Identification: 002840
Unit ID: 196307
Telephone: (315) 464-5540 Carnegie Class: Spec-4-yr-Med
FAX Number: (315) 464-8823 Calendar System: Semester
URL: www.upstate.edu
Established: 1834 Annual Undergrad Tuition & Fees (In-State): N/A
Enrollment: 1,516 Coed
Affiliation or Control: State IRS Status: 501(c)3
Highest Offering: Doctorate
Accreditation: M, ARCPA, COARC, DENT, DMOLS, IPSY, MED, MT, NURSE, PAST, PERF, PH, PTA, RAD, RTT

02 President Dr. Danielle L. LARAQUE-ARENA
63 Dean College of Medicine Dr. David B. DUGGAN
17 CEO University Hospital Dr. John MCCABE
10 Vice President Finance & Management Mr. Eric SMITH
05 Vice President Academic Affairs Dr. Lynn CLEARY
46 Dean College Graduate Studies Dr. Mark SCHMITT
32 Dean Student Affairs Dr. Julie R. WHITE
102 Exec Director HSC Foundation Ms. Eileen PEZZI
66 Dean College of Nursing Dr. Joyce GRIFFIIN-SOBEL
76 Dean College Health Profession Dr. Hugh W. BONNER
06 Registrar/Dir Inst Research Ms. Jennifer MARTIN TSE
25 Vice President for Research Dr. Rosemary ROCHFORD
29 Director of Medical Alumni Affairs Mr. Paul W. NORCROSS
15 Assoc VP Human Resources Mr. Eric FROST
13 Chief Information Officer Ms. Teresa J. WAGNER
08 Director of Libraries Ms. Christina POPE
28 Dir Diversity & Affirmative Action Ms. Maxine THOMPSON
07 Assoc Dean Admissions/Financial Aid Ms. Jennifer C. WELCH
18 Chief Facilities/Physical Plant Mr. Bob LOTKOWICTZ
21 Assistant Vice President Finance Mr. David ANTHONY
37 Director Student Financial Aid Mr. Michael ALSHEIMER

*SUNY Broome Community College (D)

PO Box 1017, Binghamton NY 13902-1017
County: Broome FICE Identification: 002862
Unit ID: 189547
Telephone: (607) 778-5000 Carnegie Class: Assoc/HT-High Trad
FAX Number: (607) 778-5310 Calendar System: Semester
URL: www.sunybroome.edu
Established: 1946 Annual Undergrad Tuition & Fees (In-District): $4,721
Enrollment: 5,944 Coed
Affiliation or Control: State/Local IRS Status: 501(c)3
Highest Offering: Associate Degree
Accreditation: M, ADNUR, CAHIIM, DH, ENGT, MAC, MLTAD, PTAA, RAD

02 President Dr. Kevin DRUMM
05 Exec VP/Chief Academic Officer Dr. Francis BATTISTI
11 Vice Pres Admin/Financial Affairs Ms. Regina LOSINGER
32 VP Student and Economic Development Ms. Debra MORELLO
10 Associate Vice Pres & Controller Ms. Jeanette TILLOTSON
50 Assoc VP & Dean Bus/Public Svcs Ms. Elizabeth MOLLEN
76 Assoc VP & Dean of Health Sciences Dr. Amy BRANDT
49 Assoc VP & Dean of Liberal Arts Dr. Michael KINNEY
51 Dir Continuing Educ & Workforce Dev Ms. Janet HERTZOG
81 Assoc Vice Pres & Dean STEM Dr. Kelli LIGEIKIS
35 Dean of Students Mr. Scott SCHUHERT
102 Executive Director BCC Foundation Ms. Catherine R. WILLIAMS
08 Director Learning Resource Center Ms. Robin PETRUS
07 Director of Admissions Mr. Jesse WELLS
15 Human Resources Officer Ms. Lynn FEDORCHAK
06 Registrar Mr. Martin GUZZI
36 Director of Placement Services Vacant
09 Dean Institutional Effectiveness Dr. Sesime ADANU
18 Campus Operations Director Mr. Phil TESTA
37 Director of Financial Aid Ms. Laura HODEL
13 Dir Information Technology Services Mr. John PETKASH
23 Director of Health Services Mr. Joseph O'CONNOR
25 Director of Sponsored Programs Ms. Shelli CORDISCO
41 Director of Athletics Mr. Brett CARTER
19 Dir of Campus Safety & Security Mr. Joseph O'CONNOR
29 Director Alumni Affairs Ms. Regina ALFIERI
40 Bookstore Manager Mr. Ryan SNYDER
88 Dir Educational Opportunity Pgm Ms. Claudia CLARKE
96 Director of Purchasing Mr. Randy CAMPBELL
26 Dir of Marketing/Communications Mr. Jesse WELLS
85 Ast Dir Intl Admiss/Intl Stdnt Stds Ms. Susan WELLINGTON
104 Coordinator Study Abroad Program Ms. Maria BASUALDO
38 Student Counseling Ms. Mary MCCARTHY
101 Secretary of the Institution/Board Ms. Patricia G. O'DAY
22 Dir Affirmative Action/EEO Ms. Paige SEDLACEK
39 Director Student Housing Ms. Amy ZIEZIULA
04 Administrative Asst to President Ms. Patricia O'DAY
84 Exec Enrollment Management Officer Mr. Jesse WELLS

*State University of New York, The College at Brockport (E)

350 New Campus Drive, Brockport NY 14420-2914
County: Monroe FICE Identification: 002841
Unit ID: 196121
Telephone: (585) 395-2211 Carnegie Class: Masters/L
FAX Number: (585) 395-2401 Calendar System: Semester
URL: www.brockport.edu
Established: 1867 Annual Undergrad Tuition & Fees (In-State): $7,904
Enrollment: 8,106 Coed
Affiliation or Control: State IRS Status: 501(c)3
Highest Offering: Master's
Accreditation: M, BUS, CAATE, CACREP, CS, DANCE, EXSC, NRPA, NURSE, SPAA, SW, TED, THEA

02 President Dr. Heidi R. MACPHERSON
05 Int Provost & VP Academic Affairs Dr. James HAYNES
10 VP Administration & Finance Dr. James A. WILLIS
32 VP Enrollment Mgmt/Student Affairs Dr. Kathryn WILSON
30 VP Advancement Mr. Michael ANDRIATCH
20 Vice Provost Dr. P. Michael FOX
58 Asst Provost Research/Dean Grad Sch Dr. James SPILLER
28 Interim Asst Provost for Diversity Dr. Faith PRATHER
18 Asst VP Facilities & Planning Mr. Robert HENRY
21 Asst VP Finance & Management Ms. Karen M. RIOTTO
88 Asst VP Enroll Mgmt Mr. Randall LANGSTON
13 Assoc Provost & CIO Mr. Jeff SMITH
49 Dean Arts/Humanities & Social Sci Dr. Darwin PRIOLEAU
50 Interim Dean Business Dr. Susan STITES-DOE
53 Dean Education & Human Services Dr. Thomas J. HERNANDEZ
68 Dean Health & Human Performance Dr. Mark KITTLESON
81 Dean Science & Mathematics Dr. Jose MALIEKAL
14 Director of Info Tech System Mr. David R. STRASENBURGH
07 Int Dir of Undergrad Admissions Mr. Randall LANGSTON
56 Exec Dir Brockport Metro Center Dr. Celia WATT
51 Exec Dir Continuing Prof Education Ms. Kathleen H. GROVES
104 Exec Dir International Education Dr. Ralph R. TRECARTIN
26 Chief Communications Officer Mr. David MIHALYOV
37 Dir Financial Aid & Enrollment Svcs Mr. J. Scott ATKINSON
36 Director of Career Services Ms. Jill WESLEY
19 Chief of University Police Mr. Robert J. KEHOE
06 College Registrar Mr. Peter DOWE
15 Director of Human Resources Ms. Wendy CRANMER
22 Affirmative Action Officer Mr. Ryan REYNOLDS
23 Director Student Health/Counseling Ms. Elizabeth S. CARUSO
39 Dir Res Life/Learning Comm Dr. Sara KELLY
41 Director of Athletics Mr. Erick HART
25 Director of Grants Development Ms. Patricia WILLIAMS
92 Director of Honors Program Dr. Donna M. KOWAL
09 Director of Inst Effectiveness Dr. Jeffrey T. LASHBROOK
96 Director of Procurement & Payment Mr. Mark W. STACY
94 Dir of Women and Gender Studies Dr. Barbara LESAVOY
29 Director Alumni Relations Mr. Kerry GOTHAM
04 Assistant to the President Ms. Julie A. PRUSS
08 Directory of Library Services Dr. Mary Jo ORZECH
108 Director Institutional Assessment Dr. Jeffrey LASHBROOK
86 Director Government Relations Mr. David MIHALYOV
88 Title IX & College Compliance Ofcr Ms. Denine CARR

*State University of New York College at Buffalo (F)

1300 Elmwood Avenue, Buffalo NY 14222-1091
County: Erie FICE Identification: 002842
Unit ID: 196130

Telephone: (716) 878-4000 Carnegie Class: Masters/L
FAX Number: (716) 878-3039 Calendar System: Semester
URL: www.buffalostate.edu
Established: 1871 Annual Undergrad Tuition & Fees (In-State): $7,669
Enrollment: 11,083 Coed
Affiliation or Control: State IRS Status: 501(c)3
Highest Offering: Master's
Accreditation: M, ART, CIDA, DIETC, DIETD, ENGT, FEPAC JOUR, MUS, NAIT, SP, SW, TED, THEA

02 President ....Dr. Katherine S. CONWAY-TURNER
100 Chief of Staff/Secretary to Board ....Dr. Bonita R. DURAND
27 Asst to the Pres for Communications ....Vacant
05 Provost ....Dr. Melanie L. PERREAULT
10 Vice President Finance & Management ......Mr. Michael F. LEVINE
32 Vice President Student Affairs ....Dr. Hal D. PAYNE
30 Vice Pres Inst Advancement & Devel ....Dr. Susanne P. BAIR
28 Chief Diversity Officer ....Dr. Karen A. CLINTON JONES
13 Chief Information Officer ....Dr. David M. DEMERS
19 Chief University Police ....Mr. Peter M. CAREY
84 Associate Vice Pres Enrollment Mgmt ....Ms. Erin R. ALONZO
21 Assoc Vice President & Comptroller ....Mr. James A. THOR
88 AVP for Student Success ....Dr. Daniel C. VELEZ
15 Assoc VP Human Resource Management .Ms. Susan J. EARSHEN
20 Special Adv to Provost for Educ ....Dr. John F. SISKAR
35 Assoc VP Student Affs/Dean of Stdnt ....Dr. Charles B. KENYON
14 Assoc Vice Pres Computing Services ......Ms. Judith B. BASINSKI
108 Assoc VP Curriculum/Assessment ....Dr. Rosalyn A. LINDNER
26 Assoc VP College Relations ....Mr. Timothy J. WALSH
08 Assoc VP ISAS ....Ms. Maryruth F. GLOGOWSKI
44 Interim Assoc VP Development ....Mr. J. Patrick HULSMAN
86 AVP Govt Relations/Alumni Director ....Mr. William J. BENFANTI
51 Assoc VP Continuing Prof Studies ....Dr. Margaret A. SHAW-BURNETT
20 Dean/AVP Ungrad & Intl Education ....Dr. Scott L. JOHNSON
53 Dean School of Education ....Dr. Wendy A. PATERSON
49 Dean School of Arts & Humanities ....Mr. Benjamin C. CHRISTY
83 Dean Natural & Social Sciences ....Dr. Mark W. SEVERSON
107 Dean Professions ....Dr. James MAYROSE
58 Interim Dean Graduate School ....Dr. Kevin J. MILLER
88 Resident Manager Chartwells ....Vacant
88 Exec Director Child Care Center ....Ms. Jennifer J. MINET
88 Director Liberty Partnership ....Ms. Patrice A. CATHEY
88 Director STEP ....Mr. Darryl CARTER
88 Director Upward Bound ....Mr. Donald A. PATTERSON
36 Director of Career Development ....Ms. Stephanie B. ZUCKERMAN-AVILES
27 Director Public Relations ....Mr. Jerod T. DAHLGREN
07 Director Admissions ....Dr. Carmela THOMPSON
06 Registrar ....Dr. Nigel R. MARRINER
37 Director of Financial Aid ....Ms. Connie F. COOKE
39 Director Residence Life ....Mr. Michael A. HEFLIN
88 Director of Student Accounts ....Ms. Susan F. WRIGHT
38 Director Counseling Center ....Dr. Joan L. MCCOOL
41 Director Intercollegiate Athletics ....Mr. Jerry S. BOYES
39 Director of Housing ....Mr. Kris A. KAUFMAN
88 Director Orientation & New Student ....Mr. David W. COX
23 Director Student Health Center ..Dr. Theresa R. STEPHAN HAINS
35 Director Student Life ....Ms. Sarah M. YOUNG
85 Director Intl Student Affairs ....Dr. Jean F. GOUNARD
88 Director Accounts Payable & Travel ....Mr. Robert L. BAUMET
25 AVP for Sponsored Program Operation ......Mrs. Donna L. SCUTO
88 Director Special Events & Protocol ....Ms. Kathyrn C. NEESON
18 Director Campus Services ....Mr. Terry M. HARDING
88 Director Budget & Internal Controls ....Ms. Rebecca J. SCHENK
09 Director Institutional Research ....Mr. Yves M. GACHETTE
29 Director of Alumni Affairs ....Ms. Mary-Jo JAGORD
88 Director Parking Services ....Ms. Jayme S. RITER
96 Asst to Comptroller for Procurement ....Mr. Steven M. OLSEN
40 Manager BSC Bookstore ....Ms. Lynn M. PUMA
88 Director Campbell Student Union ....Mrs. Sarah M. VELEZ
22 Director Disability Service ....Ms. Lisa T. MORRISON-FRONCKOWIAK
88 Director Judicial Affairs ....Dr. Latonia D. MARSH
88 Manager Design & Construction ....Mr. Steven E. SHAFFER

*State University of New York College at Cortland (A)

PO Box 2000, Cortland NY 13045-0900
County: Cortland FICE Identification: 002843
Unit ID: 196149
Telephone: (607) 753-2011 Carnegie Class: Masters/L
FAX Number: (607) 753-5999 Calendar System: Semester
URL: www.cortland.edu
Established: 1868 Annual Undergrad Tuition & Fees (In-State): $8,050
Enrollment: 6,958 Coed
Affiliation or Control: State IRS Status: 501(c)3
Highest Offering: Master's
Accreditation: M, CAATE, NRPA, @SP, TED

02 President ....Dr. Erik J. BITTERBAUM
05 Provost ....Dr. Mark PRUS
32 Vice Pres Student Affairs ....Mr. C. Gregory SHARER
30 Vice Pres Inst Advancement ....Mr. Peter PERKINS
10 Vice Pres for Finance & Admin ....Mr. David DURYEA
21 Assoc VP for Finance ....Ms. Mary K. MURPHY
13 Assoc Provost for Info Resources ....Ms. Amy BERG
18 Assoc VP Facilities Management ....Ms. Nasrin PARVIZI
20 Assoc Prov for Academic Affairs ....Dr. Carol VAN DER KARR
84 Asst Vice Pres Enrollment Mgmt ....Mr. Mark YACAVONE
27 Assoc Vice Pres Communications ....Vacant
04 Exec Assistant to the President ....Dr. Virginia LEVINE
09 Assoc Dir Inst Rsrch/Assessment ....Dr. Stephen CHEMSAK
08 Director of Libraries ....Ms. Gail WOOD
06 Registrar ....Mr. Thomas HANFORD
36 Director of Career Services ....Mr. John SHIRLEY
15 Asst VP Human Resources ....Mr. Gary EVANS
29 Director Alumni Affairs ....Mr. Michael SGRO
38 Dir Counseling/Student Devel ....Dr. Carolyn BERSHAD
37 Dir of Student Financial Aid ....Ms. Karen GALLAGHER
19 Chief of University Police ....Mr. Steven DANGLER
91 Director Admin Computing Svcs ....Mr. Daniel SIDEBOTTOM
90 Director Campus Technology Services ....Ms. Lisa KAHLE
107 Dean Professional Studies ....Dr. John COTTONE
49 Dean Arts & Sciences ....Dr. Bruce MATTINGLY
26 Chief Public Relations Officer ....Mr. Frederic PIERCE
53 Dean of Education ....Dr. Andrea LACHANCE
93 Director Educational Oppty Program .... Dr. Lewis ROSENGARTEN
92 Director of Honors Program ....Dr. Frank ROSSI
94 Director of Women's Studies ....Dr. Caroline KALTEFLEITER
96 Director of Purchasing ....Mr. Samuel COLOMBO
22 Affirmative Action Officer ....Ms. Dawn NORCROSS
28 Int Dir Multicult Life/Diversity ....Ms. AnnaMaria CIFRINCIONE
41 Athletic Director ....Mr. Mike URTZ
104 Director International Programs ....Dr. Mary SCHLARB
25 Asst VP Research & Sponsored Pgms ....Ms. Amy HENDERSON-HARR
39 Director Student Housing ....Mr. Ralph CARRASQUILLO
07 Director of Admissions ....Mr. Mark YACAVONE

*State University of New York College at Geneseo (B)

1 College Circle, Geneseo NY 14454-1401
County: Livingston FICE Identification: 002845
Unit ID: 196167
Telephone: (585) 245-5000 Carnegie Class: Masters/S
FAX Number: (585) 245-5005 Calendar System: Semester
URL: www.geneseo.edu
Established: 1871 Annual Undergrad Tuition & Fees (In-State): $8,113
Enrollment: 5,658 Coed
Affiliation or Control: State IRS Status: 501(c)3
Highest Offering: Master's
Accreditation: M, BUS, TED

02 President ....Dr. Denise A. BATTLES
05 Provost ....Dr. Carol S. LONG
20 Interim Associate Provost ....Dr. Kenneth KALLIO
11 Vice President Administration ....Dr. James B. MILROY
32 Vice Pres for Student & Campus Life ....Dr. Robert A. BONFIGLIO
30 Interim VP of College Advancement ....Mr. Jon HYSELL
84 Vice Pres Enrollment Mgmt ....Dr. Meaghan ARENA
10 Assoc VP Administration/Controller ....Mr. Brice M. WEIGMAN
26 Chief Comm & Marketing Officer ....Ms. Gai GLOVER
86 Asst Prov of International Affairs ....Dr. Rebecca LEWIS
15 Asst Vice Pres Human Resources ....Ms. Julie A. BRIGGS
44 Asst VP for College Advancement ....Ms. Kim FABER
29 Director of Alumni & Parent Rels ....Ms. Ronna BOSKO
20 Asst Provost Curriculum & Assess ....Dr. Savithri V. IYER
35 Dean of Students ....Dr. Leonard SANCILIO
07 Director of Admissions ....Mr. Kevin REED
08 Interim Library Director ....Ms. Katherine PITCHER
13 Director Computing/Info Technology ..Ms. Susan E. CHICHESTER
37 Director of Financial Aid ....Vacant
25 Director of Sponsored Research ....Dr. Anne E. BALDWIN
09 Director of Institutional Research ....Dr. Julie M. RAO
06 Registrar ....Ms. Kimberley WILLIS
36 Director of Career Development ....Ms. Stacey WILEY
22 Affirmative Action Officer ....Ms. Adrienne COLLIER
88 Asst Dean of Stdnt for Multicul Pgm .....Ms. Fatima R. JOHNSON
19 Chief of University Police ....Mr. Thomas KILCULLEN
18 Chief Facilities/Physical Plant ....Mr. George F. STOOKS
21 Dir of Acct & Budgeting Services ....Mr. Jeffrey NORDLAND
38 Clinical Dir Counseling Services ....Dr. Beth K. CHOLETTE
96 Director of Purchasing ....Ms. Rebecca E. ANCHOR
04 Administrative Asst to President ....Ms. Gayle DYCKMAN
100 Senior Associate to the President ....Vacant
88 Dean of Acad Planning & Advising ....Dr. Celia A. EASTON
41 Dir of Intercollegiate Athletics ....Mr. Michael C. MOONEY
50 Dean of School of Business ....Dr. Denise ROTONDO
53 Dean of the School of Education ....Dr. Anjoo SIKKA
90 Asst Director & Manager Sys Net ....Mr. Kirk ANNE
91 Asst Director & Manager Info Sys ....Mr. Paul JACKSON

*State University of New York College at Old Westbury (C)

P.O. Box 210, 223 Store Hill Road, Old Westbury NY 11568-0210
County: Nassau FICE Identification: 007109
Unit ID: 196237
Telephone: (516) 876-3000 Carnegie Class: Masters/S
FAX Number: (516) 876-3209 Calendar System: Semester
URL: www.oldwestbury.edu
Established: 1965 Annual Undergrad Tuition & Fees (In-State): $7,643
Enrollment: 4,504 Coed
Affiliation or Control: State IRS Status: 501(c)3
Highest Offering: Master's
Accreditation: M, TED

02 President ....Dr. Calvin O. BUTTS, III
100 Chief of Staff ....Ms. Mona G. RANKIN
05 Provost/Sr VP Academic Affairs ....Dr. Patrick O'SULLIVAN
84 VP for Enrollment Services ....Ms. Mary MARQUEZ BELL
32 VP Student Affs/Chf Diversity Ofcr ....Dr. Wayne EDWARDS
10 Sr VP Div Business & Finance/CFO ....Mr. Len L. DAVIS
15 Asst to Pres for Admin/Dir HR ....Mr. William P. KIMMINS
30 Asst to President for Advancement ....Mr. Michael G. KINANE
21 Assoc VP Bus Affairs/Controller ....Mr. Pat LETTINI
21 Assoc VP of Business Compliance ....Mr. Arthur H. ANGST, JR.
20 Asst Vice Pres Academic Affairs ....Mr. Anthony BARBERA
35 Asst Vice Pres Student Affairs ....Mr. Usama SHAIKH
49 Dean School of Arts & Sciences ....Dr. Barbara HILLERY
50 Interim Dean School of Business ....Dr. Jishan ZHU
53 Dean School of Education ....Dr. Nancy BROWN
35 Dean of Students ....Mr. Omar ESTRADA TORRES
19 Chief of Police ....Mr. Steven SIENA
26 Director Public & Media Relations ....Mr. Michael G. KINANE
13 Chief Information Officer ....Mr. Evan KOBOLAKIS
06 Registrar ....Ms. Patricia A. SMITH
96 Director of Purchasing ....Mr. Patrick ADAMS
89 Director First-Year Experience ....Dr. Laura M. ANKER
31 Director of Community Relations ....Ms. Carolyn BENNETT
38 Dir Counseling/Psych Wellness Svcs ....Dr. Trisha BILLARD
88 Environmental Health & Safety Ofcr ..Mr. Douglas BRODMERKEL
29 Director of Alumni Affairs ....Ms. Penny J. CHIN
71 Dir Special Student Programs ....Ms. Stacey DEFELICE
92 Director Honors College ....Dr. Anthony L. DELUCA
23 Interim Dir Student Health Svcs ....Ms. Kate EADEROSO
88 Dir Commuter Program & Svcs ....Ms. Veronica GEROSIMO
88 Coordinator of Scholarships ....Ms. Pritpal KAINTH
09 Director of Institutional Research ....Ms. Sandra KAUFMANN
109 Exec Dir Auxiliary Svc Corp ....Ms. Carol KAUNITZ
08 Library Director ....Mr. Stephen KIRKPATRICK
88 Director of Capital Planning ....Mr. Ray MAGGIORE
71 Dir Spec Programs Acad Affairs ....Mr. Yves M. MAGLOIRE
36 Dir Career Plng & Development ....Ms. Jerilyn MARINAN
88 Dir Educational Opportunity Program ..Mr. Alonzo L. MCCOLLUM
18 Director of Facilities ....Mr. Timothy MCGARRY
35 Director of Student Activities ....Ms. Suzanne MCLOUGHLIN
25 Director of Sponsored Programs ....Mr. Thomas MURPHY
37 Director Financial Aid ....Ms. Mildred O'KEEFE
07 Director of Admissions ....Mr. Frank PIZZARDI
88 Dir Ofc of Student Conduct ....Mr. Brian SCHWIRZBIN
39 Director Residential Life ....Mr. Gareth SHUMACK
88 Dir Orientation & Special Events ....Ms. Jaclyn VENTO
41 Director of Athletics ....Ms. Lenore J. WALSH

*State University of New York College at Oswego (D)

7060 State Route 104, Oswego NY 13126-3501
County: Oswego FICE Identification: 002848
Unit ID: 196194
Telephone: (315) 312-2500 Carnegie Class: Masters/L
FAX Number: (315) 312-5799 Calendar System: Semester
URL: www.oswego.edu
Established: 1861 Annual Undergrad Tuition & Fees (In-State): $7,934
Enrollment: 8,034 Coed
Affiliation or Control: State IRS Status: 501(c)3
Highest Offering: Master's
Accreditation: M, ART, BUS, MUS, TED, THEA

02 President ....Dr. Deborah F. STANLEY
05 Acting VP Academic Affairs/Provost ....Dr. Walter B. ROETTGER
10 Vice President Admin/Finance ....Mr. Nicholas A. LYONS
84 Vice Pres Student Affs/Enroll Mgmt ....Dr. Jerald WOOLFOLK
30 Vice Pres Devel/Alumni Relations ....Ms. Kerry DORSEY
100 Chief of Staff ....Ms. Kristi ECK
88 Dep to the Pres Ext Prtnr Econ Dev ......Ms. Pamela CARACCIOLI
32 Assoc VP/Dean of Students Affs ....Dr. Jerri DRUMMOND
18 Asst VP for Facilities Services ....Mr. Mitch FIELDS
21 Actg Asst VP for Finance & Budget ....Ms. Vicki FURLONG
20 Associate Provost ....Dr. Rameen MOHAMMADI
04 Ex Asst to Pres/Int Affrm Act Ofcr ....Mr. Howard GORDON
26 Chief Communication Officer ....Vacant
25 Dir Research/Sponsored Pgms ....Mr. William BOWERS
94 Director Gender & Women's Studies ....Dr. Mary MCCUNE
06 Registrar ....Mr. Jerret LEMAY
08 Director of Libraries ....Ms. Sarah CONRAD WEISMAN
91 Assoc Dir Campus Tech Services ....Mr. Michael C. PISA
37 Director of Financial Aid ....Mr. Mark HUMBERT
09 Director Inst Research & Assessment ....Dr. Mehran NOJAN
36 Director Career Services ....Mr. Gary MORRIS
38 Director Counseling Services Center ....Ms. Katherine WOLFE-LYGA
15 Director Human Resources ....Ms. Amy PLOTNER
19 University Police Chief ....Mr. John ROSSI
23 Director of Student Health Center ....Ms. Angela BROWN
11 Asst Provost for Operations ....Dr. Michael AMEIGH
28 Assoc Prov Multicltrl Pgms & Opps ....Ms. Catherine SANTOS
39 Dir Residence Life/Housing ....Dr. Richard KOLENDA
41 Director of Athletics ....Ms. Susan VISCOMI
96 Director Purchasing ....Mr. Mark COLE
13 Chief Technology Officer ....Mr. Sean MORIARTY
29 Director Alumni Relations ....Ms. Laura KELLY
07 Director of Admissions ....Mr. Daniel GRIFFIN
40 College Store Manager ....Ms. Susan RABY
49 Dean Col Lib Arts & Science ....Dr. Adrienne MCCORMICK
53 Dean School of Education ....Dr. Pamela MICHEL
58 Interim Dean Grad Studies ....Dr. Brad KORBESMEYER
50 Dean School of Business ....Dr. Richard J. SKOLNIK
51 Dean of Extended Learning ....Ms. Jill PIPPIN
88 Dean of Comm/Media & the Arts ....Dr. Julie PRETZAT
35 Asst VP Student Affairs ....Ms. Kathleen EVANS

109 Director of Auxiliary Services ... Mr. Michael FLAHERTY
44 Director Annual or Planned Giving ... Ms. Joy KNOPP

*State University of New York College at Plattsburgh (A)

101 Broad Street, Plattsburgh NY 12901-2637
County: Clinton FICE Identification: 002849
Unit ID: 196246
Telephone: (518) 564-2000 Carnegie Class: Masters/L
FAX Number: (518) 564-7827 Calendar System: Semester
URL: www.plattsburgh.edu
Established: 1889 Annual Undergrad Tuition & Fees (In-State): $7,850
Enrollment: 5,968 Coed
Affiliation or Control: State IRS Status: 501(c)3
Highest Offering: Master's
Accreditation: M, BUS, CACREP, DIETD, NURSE, SP, SW, TEAC

02 President ... Dr. John ETTLING
04 Exec Assistant to the President ... Mr. Keith D. TYO
05 Provost/Vice Pres Academic Affairs ... Dr. James A. LISZKA
10 Vice President for Administration ... Mr. John R. HOMBURGER
30 Vice Pres Institutional Advancement ... Ms. Anne W. HANSEN
32 Vice President for Student Affairs ... Mr. Bryan G. HARTMAN
49 Dean of Arts & Sciences ... Dr. Andrew S. BUCKSER
53 Dean Educ/Health/Human Services ... Dr. Michael D. MORGAN
50 Dean of Business/Economics ... Dr. Rowena ORTIZ-WALTERS
12 Dean Branch Campus at Queensbury ... Mr. Stephen DANNA
08 Dean Library/Info Services ... Ms. Holly B. HELLER-ROSS
22 Director of Affirmative Action ... Dr. Lynda J. AMES
88 Title IX Coordinator ... Ms. Butterfly L. BLAISE
07 Assoc VP Enroll Mgmt/Admissions ... Mr. Richard J. HIGGINS
20 Assistant Provost ... Ms. Diane K. MERKEL
21 Asst to Vice Pres Administration ... Mr. Sean B. DERMODY
15 Asst VP for Human Resources ... Ms. Susan T. WELCH
88 Asst VP for Institutional Advanc ... Mr. David P. GREGOIRE
06 Registrar ... Ms. Denise M. PHILO
11 Assoc VP for Admin & Finance ... Mr. Clark M. FOSTER
22 Budget Officer ... Ms. Magen M. RENADETTE
19 Chief University Police ... Mr. Jerry W. LOTTIE
109 Exec Dir College Auxiliary Services ... Mr. Wayne A. DUPREY
26 Exec Dir Marketing & Comm ... Mr. Kennith KNELLY
88 Director of Academic Advising ... Ms. Suzanne L. DALEY
29 Director of Alumni Relations ... Ms. Joanne E. NELSON
44 Director of Annual Giving ... Vacant
41 Director of Athletics ... Mr. Michael P. HOWARD
36 Director of Career Development Ctr .. Ms. Julia OVERTON-HEALY
40 Director of College Store ... Mr. Jerry L. DECELLE
30 Director of Development ... Ms. Faith M. LONG
18 Director of Facilities ... Mr. Kevin W. ROBERTS
37 Director of Financial Aid ... Mr. Todd A. MORAVEC
39 Director of Housing ... Mr. Stephen P. MATTHEWS
09 Dir of Institutional Effectiveness ... Mr. Robert M. KARP
28 Dir of Institutional Marketing ... Vacant
96 Director of Purchasing ... Mr. Christopher J. JACKSON
46 Dir Sponsored Research/Programs ... Mr. Michael E. SIMPSON
88 Director of Student Conduct ... Mr. Larry K. ALLEN
23 Dir Ctr for Stdnt Hlth & Psych Svcs ... Dr. Kathleen M. CAMELO
91 Programming Manager ... Mr. Thomas J. HIGGINS

*State University of New York College at Potsdam (B)

44 Pierrepont Avenue, Potsdam NY 13676-2294
County: Saint Lawrence FICE Identification: 002850
Unit ID: 196200
Telephone: (315) 267-2000 Carnegie Class: Bac-A&S
FAX Number: (315) 267-2496 Calendar System: Semester
URL: www.potsdam.edu
Established: 1816 Annual Undergrad Tuition & Fees (In-State): $7,923
Enrollment: 3,979 Coed
Affiliation or Control: State IRS Status: 501(c)3
Highest Offering: Master's
Accreditation: M, IACBE, MUS, TED, THEA

02 President ... Dr. Kristin G. ESTERBERG
03 Executive Vice President ... Dr. Enrico A. MILLER
05 Provost ... Dr. Bette S. BERGERON
10 Vice President for Business Affairs ... Mr. Gerhard O. VOGGEL
32 Vice President for Student Affairs ... Vacant
30 Vice President College Advancement ... Ms. Vicki L. TEMPLETON-CORNELL
84 Assoc VP Enroll Mgmt/Inst Effect ... Vacant
04 Assistant to the President ... Ms. Carol M. ROURKE
20 Interim Associate Provost ... Dr. Jill R. PEARON
18 Asst Vice Pres for Facilities ... Mr. James A. DITULLIO
27 Chief Information Officer ... Mr. Kyle A. BROWN
53 Interim Dean Educ & Prof Studies ... Dr. Robyn L. HOSLEY
49 Dean of Arts and Sciences ... Dr. Steven J. MARQUSEE
64 Dean of Music ... Dr. Michael R. SITTON
15 Asst VP for Human Resources ... Ms. Mary K. DOLAN
08 Director of Libraries ... Ms. Jenica P. ROGERS
06 Interim Registrar ... Ms. Stephanie L. CLAXTON
07 Director of Admissions ... Mr. Thomas W. NESBITT
37 Director of Financial Aid ... Ms. Susan E. GODREAU
36 Interim Director of Career Planning ... Ms. Margaret M. BAIN
38 Director of Counseling Center ... Mrs. Gena C. NELSON
19 Chief of University Police ... Mr. Tim M. ASHLEY
29 Director of Alumni Relations ... Ms. Mona O. VROMAN
31 Executive Dir of Auxiliary Corp ... Mr. Daniel J. HAYES
23 Director of Health Services ... Mrs. Gena C. NELSON
39 Interim Assoc Dean Students ... Mr. Eric D. DUCHSCHERER

40 Director of College Bookstore ... Mr. Lyndon J. LAKE
41 Athletic Director ... Mr. James A. ZALACCA
25 Director Research & Sponsored Pgms ... Dr. Nancy M. DODGE-REYOME
92 Director of Honors Program ... Dr. Thomas N. BAKER
94 Director of Women's Studies ... Dr. Christine M. DORAN
26 Asst VP Marketing/Communications ... Vacant
86 Community/Govt Rels Associate ... Mrs. Alexandra M. JACOBS-WILKE
58 Director of Graduate and Cont Ed ... Mr. Joshua J. LAFAVE
28 Chief Diversity Officer ... Dr. Bernadette S. TIAPO

*Purchase College, State University of New York (C)

735 Anderson Hill Road, Purchase NY 10577-1402
County: Westchester FICE Identification: 006791
Unit ID: 196219
Telephone: (914) 251-6000 Carnegie Class: Bac-A&S
FAX Number: (914) 251-6014 Calendar System: Semester
URL: www.purchase.edu
Established: 1967 Annual Undergrad Tuition & Fees (In-State): $8,267
Enrollment: 4,225 Coed
Affiliation or Control: State IRS Status: 501(c)3
Highest Offering: Master's
Accreditation: M, ART

02 President ... Mr. Thomas J. SCHWARZ
19 Chief of University Police ... Mr. Dayton TUCKER
10 CFO/VP Operations ... Ms. Judy NOLAN
05 Provost/VP Academic Affairs ... Dr. Barry PEARSON
32 Int Vice President Student Affairs ... Dr. Jean KIM
84 VP Enroll Mgmt/Integrated Mktg ... Mr. Dennis CRAIG
30 Int VP of Institutional Advance ... Ms. Catherine BROD
57 Director Conservatory Theatre Arts ... Dr. Rebecca RUGG
51 Exec Dir Liberal Stds/Cont Educ ... Ms. Trudy MILBURN
81 Dean Sch Natural/Social Sciences ... Dr. Suzanne KESSLER
79 Chair School of Humanities ... Dr. Ross DALY
20 Associate Provost ... Dr. Peggy DECOOKE
88 Interim Dir Performing Arts Center ... Mr. Seth SOLOWAY
88 Director Neuberger Museum of Art ... Dr. Tracy FITZPATRICK
08 Director of the Library ... Mr. Patrick F. CALLAHAN
64 Director Conservatory of Music ... Dr. James UNDERCOFLER
57 Dean School of Arts ... Mr. Ravi RAJAN
13 Director Campus Technology Services ... Mr. Bill JUNOR
37 Director Student Financial Services ... Corey YORK
38 Director of Counseling Center ... Dr. Cathie CHESTER
36 Director Career Development ... Ms. Wendy MOROSOFF
15 Director of Human Resources ... Ms. Kathleen FARRELL
41 Athletic Director ... Mr. Chris BISIGNANO
39 Director Community Engagement ... Mr. Mario RAPETTI
96 Director of Purchasing ... Mr. Nikolaus LENTNER
06 Exec Dir Enroll Svcs/Assoc Dean Ac ... Ms. Patricia BICE
09 Director of Institutional Research ... Ms. Barbara MOORE
18 Int Dir Capital Facilities Planning ... Mr. Steve DORSO
22 Affirmative Action Officer ... Mr. Joel AURE
88 Environmental Health/Safety Officer ... Mr. Edward MUSAL
44 Director Annual Giving ... Ms. Carla WEILAND-ZALEZNAK
26 Dir Communications/Creative Svcs ... Ms. Sandy DYLAK
86 Director of Govt Relations/Sp Proj ... Ms. Elizabeth C. ROBERTSON
04 Assistant to President ... Ms. Carrie K. BIANCHI
104 Director Study Abroad ... Ms. Suzanne NEARY

*State University of New York College of Agriculture and Technology at Cobleskill (D)

Route 7, Knapp Hall, Cobleskill NY 12043
County: Schoharie FICE Identification: 002856
Unit ID: 196033
Telephone: (518) 255-5011 Carnegie Class: Bac/Assoc-Mixed
FAX Number: (518) 255-5333 Calendar System: Semester
URL: www.cobleskill.edu
Established: 1911 Annual Undergrad Tuition & Fees (In-State): $7,719
Enrollment: 2,535 Coed
Affiliation or Control: State IRS Status: 501(c)3
Highest Offering: Baccalaureate
Accreditation: M, ACFEI, EMT, HT

02 President ... Dr. Marion TERENZIO
05 Provost & Vice Pres Academic Affs ... Dr. Susan ZIMMERMANN
100 Chief of Staff ... Ms. Amy HEALY
32 VP for Student Affairs ... Dr. Anne HOPKINS-GROSS
10 Vice Pres Business & Finance ... Ms. Wendy GILMAN
11 Vice Pres Operations ... Ms. Bonnie MARTIN
30 Chief Advancement Officer ... Ms. Lois GOBLET
47 Dean Agriculture/Natural Res ... Mr. Timothy MOORE
49 Dean Liberal Arts & Sciences ... Dr. Jeffrey ANDERSON
08 Dean Library/Information Svcs ... Ms. Elizabeth ORGERON
26 Director of Communications ... Mr. James FELDMAN
16 Director Employee Relations ... Ms. Lynn BERGER
06 Registrar ... Ms. Christine JOHANNESEN
21 Chief Business Officer ... Ms. Carol VOSATKA
84 Chief Enrollment Officer ... Dr. Tara WINTER
29 Director Alumni Relations ... Mr. Matthew S. BARNEY
07 Assistant Director of Admissions ... Mr. Caleb GRANT
39 Director of Residential Life ... Mr. Edward E. ASSELIN
36 Director of Student Success Ctr ... Ms. Donna PESTA
23 Co-Director Wellness Center ... Ms. Mary RADLIFF
23 Co-Director Wellness Center ... Ms. Lynn ONTL

37 Director of Financial Aid ... Ms. Louise BIRON
35 Director Student Life Center ... Mr. Jeffrey C. FOOTE
41 Director of Athletics ... Mr. Kevin MCCARTHY
13 Director Information Tech Services ... Mr. James DUTCHER
19 Chief University Police Dept ... Mr. Frank LAWRENCE
09 Director of Institutional Research ... Vacant
15 Human Resources Operations Manager ... Ms. Jan ELWELL
18 Director Facilities/Physical Plant ... Mr. Joseph BATCHELDER
40 Manager Bookstore ... Ms. Jeri USATCH
85 Director of International Programs ... Dr. Susan JAGENDORF
96 Director of Purchasing ... Ms. Laura GROSS
25 Dir of Grants and Sponsored Program ... Mr. Barry GELL
22 Director of EOP ... Mr. Derwin BENNETT
88 Dir of Student Accounts ... Ms. Sarah LEDERMANN
105 Webmaster ... Ms. Naomi MEKEEL

*State University of New York College of Environmental Science and Forestry (E)

1 Forestry Drive, Syracuse NY 13210-2778
County: Onondaga FICE Identification: 002851
Unit ID: 196103
Telephone: (315) 470-6500 Carnegie Class: DU-Mod
FAX Number: (315) 470-6779 Calendar System: Semester
URL: www.esf.edu
Established: 1911 Annual Undergrad Tuition & Fees (In-State): $7,848
Enrollment: 2,200 Coed
Affiliation or Control: State IRS Status: 501(c)3
Highest Offering: Doctorate
Accreditation: M, ENG, ENGT, LSAR

02 President ... Dr. Quentin D. WHEELER
05 Interim Provost/EVP Acad Affairs ... Dr. Valerie LUZADIS
11 Vice President for Administration ... Mr. Joseph RUFO
100 Chief of Staff ... Mr. Mark LICHTENSTEIN
04 Asst to the President ... Ms. Ragan A. SQUIER
86 VP for Govt & External Relations ... Dr. Maureen O. FELLOWS
30 Asst VP for Development ... Ms. Brenda T. GREENFIELD
46 Vice Provost for Research ... Dr. Neil H. RINGLER
58 Assoc Prov & Dean Grad School ... Mr. Scott S. SHANNON
84 Chief Enrollment Management Officer ... Vacant
32 Vice Provost/Dean Student Affairs ... Dr. Anne E. LOMBARD
10 Director of Business Affairs ... Mr. David R. DZWONKOWSKI
13 Director of Information Technology ... Vacant
15 Director Human Resources ... Ms. Marcia A. BARBER
26 Director of Communications ... Mrs. Claire B. DUNN
19 Chief of University Police ... Mr. Thomas LEROY
08 Director of College Libraries ... Vacant
07 Director of Admissions ... Mrs. Susan H. SANFORD
06 Registrar ... Ms. Leslie RUTKOWSI
37 Director of Financial Aid ... Mr. Mark J. HILL
29 Director of Alumni Affairs ... Ms. Debbie J. CAVINESS
28 Director of Multicultural Affairs ... Dr. Raydora S. DRUMMER FRANCIS
18 Dir of Facilities/Physical Plant ... Mr. Gary S. PEDEN
36 Dir of Career Services ... Mr. John TURBEVILLE
38 Dir of Counseling Services ... Ms. Ruth LARSON
35 Director Student Activities ... Mrs. Laura CRANDALL
51 Asst to President for Outreach ... Dr. Charles M. SPUCHES
41 Coordinator of College Athletics ... Mr. Daniel RAMIN
43 Associate Counsel ... Mr. Kevin HAYDEN
104 Coordinator International Education ... Mr. Thomas E. CARTER

*State University of New York College of Optometry (F)

33 W 42nd Street, New York NY 10036-8003
County: New York FICE Identification: 009929
Unit ID: 196228
Telephone: (212) 938-4000 Carnegie Class: Spec-4-yr-Other Health
FAX Number: (212) 938-5696 Calendar System: Semester
URL: www.sunyopt.edu
Established: 1971 Annual Graduate Tuition & Fees: N/A
Enrollment: 363 Coed
Affiliation or Control: State IRS Status: 501(c)3
Highest Offering: Doctorate; No Undergraduates
Accreditation: M, OPT, OPTR

02 President ... Dr. David A. HEATH
05 Dean/VP Academic Affairs ... Dr. David TROILO
10 VP For Administration and Finance ... Mr. David A. BOWERS
32 Vice Pres Student Affairs ... Dr. Guilherme ALBIERI
17 Vice Pres for Clinical Admin ... Ms. Liduvina MARTINEZ-GONZALEZ
30 Vice Pres Institutional Advancement ... Ms. Ann WARWICK
04 Assistant to the President ... Ms. Karen DEGAZON
09 Dir Institutional Research/Planning ... Dr. Steven SCHWARTZ
08 Director Library Services ... Ms. Elaine WELLS
15 Director of Human Resources ... Mr. Douglas SCHADING
37 Financial Aid Officer ... Mr. Vito CAVALLARO
06 Registrar ... Ms. Jacqueline MARTINEZ
58 Assoc Dean Rsrch/Graduate Studies ... Dr. Stewart BLOOMFIELD
26 Director of Communications ... Vacant
13 Chief Info Technology Officer (CIO) ... Mr. Robert PELLOT
84 Director Enrollment Management ... Dr. Guilherme ALBIERI
96 Director of Purchasing ... Mr. Roger CRUTTENDEN

*Alfred State College (G)

10 Upper College Drive, Alfred NY 14802-1196
County: Allegany FICE Identification: 002854
Unit ID: 196006

Telephone: (607) 587-4010 Carnegie Class: Bac/Assoc-Mixed
FAX Number: N/A Calendar System: Semester
URL: www.alfredstate.edu
Established: 1908 Annual Undergrad Tuition & Fees (In-State): $8,057
Enrollment: 3,661 Coed
Affiliation or Control: State IRS Status: 501(c)3
Highest Offering: Baccalaureate
Accreditation: M, ADNUR, CAHIIM, CONST, ENGT, FEPAC, NURSE

02 President .... Dr. Irby (Skip) SULLIVAN
05 Vice Pres Academic Affairs .... Ms. Kristin POPPO
32 Vice President Student Affairs .... Mr. Gregory S. SAMMONS
11 Exec VP Administration/Enrollment .... Ms. Valerie NIXON
30 Sr Dir Institutional Advancement .... Ms. Danielle M. WHITE
20 Assoc Vice Pres Academic Affairs .... Mr. Charles V. NEAL
09 Institutional Research Analyst .... Mr. Daniel D. JARDINE
84 Assoc VP for Enrollment Mgmt .... Ms. Deborah J. GOODRICH
13 Director Computer Services .... Mr. Michael A. CASE
15 Director Human Res/Affirm Action .... Ms. Wendy DRESSER-RECKTENWALD
37 Sr Dir Student Financial Services .... Mrs. Jane A. GILLILAND
29 Director Alumni Relations .... Ms. Colleen ARGENTIERI
18 Director of Physical Plant .... Mr. Glenn R. BRUBAKER
14 Asst Director of Computing Services .... Mr. Carl H. RAHR, JR.
23 Sr Director Health Svcs/Wellness .... Ms. Hollie M. HALL
38 Director Learning Center .... Ms. Janette B. THOMAS
19 Lieutenant University Police .... Mr. Matthew D. HELLER
96 Director of Purchasing .... Mr. Glen E. CLINE
10 Controller .... Mr. Joseph T. GREENTHAL
36 Director of Career Services .... Ms. Elaine MORSMAN
49 Dean School of Arts & Sciences .... Dr. Robert CURRY
54 Dean School of Mgmt & Engr Tech .... Dr. John WILLIAMS
75 Dean Sch Applied Technology .... Ms. Ana MCCLANAHAN

*SUNY Adirondack (A)

640 Bay Road, Queensbury NY 12804-1498
County: Warren FICE Identification: 002860
Unit ID: 188438
Telephone: (518) 743-2200 Carnegie Class: Assoc/HT-High Trad
FAX Number: (518) 745-1433 Calendar System: Semester
URL: www.sunyacc.edu
Established: 1960 Annual Undergrad Tuition & Fees (In-District): $4,423
Enrollment: 4,247 Coed
Affiliation or Control: State/Local IRS Status: 501(c)3
Highest Offering: Associate Degree
Accreditation: M, ADNUR

02 President .... Dr. Kristine DUFFY
04 Assistant to the President .... Ms. Tressie LAFAY
05 Vice Pres Academic Affairs .... Mr. John JABLONSKI
10 Vice Pres Admin Services/Treasurer .... Ms. Ann Marie SOMMA
30 Exec Dir Dev/Alumni Rels/ACC Fndtn .... Ms. Rachael HUNSINGER PATTEN
20 Dean for Academic Initiatives .... Ms. Diane WILDEY
32 Dean for Student Affairs .... Mr. Jason ENSER
26 Dean of Enrollment Mgt and Mktg .... Mr. Rob PALMIERI
09 Director of Inst Research/Planning .... Ms. Carol RUNGE
13 Chief Information Officer .... Ms. Mary HAND
15 Director of Human Resources .... Ms. Mindy WILSON
51 Asst Dean Cont Educ & Workforce .... Mrs. Caelynn PRYLO
40 Director Bookstore .... Mr. Tom KENT
21 Director of Business Affairs .... Ms. Lisa DESTER
18 Director Facilities .... Mr. Anthony PALANGI
37 Director Financial Aid .... Ms. Colleen WISE
06 Registrar .... Ms. Cindy ZIELASKOWSKI
84 Director of Admissions .... Ms. Sarah J. LINEHAN
90 Director of Educational Technology .... Ms. Roseann ANZALONE
08 Director of Library Services .... Ms. Teresa RONNING
35 Director of Student Activities .... Ms. Heather WHITNEY
41 Athletic Director .... Mr. John QUATTROCCHI
101 Secretary of the Institution/Board .... Ms. Kathy DRISLANE
102 Dir Foundation/Corporate Relations .... Ms. Rachael HUNSINGER PATTEN
19 Asst Director of Public Safety .... Mr. Richard CONINE
39 Director of Residence Life .... Ms. Mary ALDOUS

*SUNY Canton-College of Technology (B)

34 Cornell Drive, Canton NY 13617-1098
County: Saint Lawrence FICE Identification: 002855
Unit ID: 196015
Telephone: (315) 386-7011 Carnegie Class: Bac/Assoc-Mixed
FAX Number: (315) 386-7930 Calendar System: Semester
URL: www.canton.edu
Established: 1906 Annual Undergrad Tuition & Fees (In-State): $7,855
Enrollment: 3,278 Coed
Affiliation or Control: State IRS Status: 501(c)3
Highest Offering: Baccalaureate
Accreditation: M, ADNUR, DH, ENGT, FUSER, NUR, PTAA

02 President .... Dr. Zvi SZAFRAN
05 Provost .... Dr. Douglas SCHEIDT
11 Vice Pres for Administration .... Ms. Shawn MILLER
10 Chief Financial Officer .... Ms. Shawn MILLER
30 Vice Pres for Advancement .... Ms. Anne SIBLEY
32 Vice President for Student Affairs .... Ms. Courtney D. BISH
35 Dean of Students .... Ms. Courtney D. BISH
72 Dean Canino Sch Eng Tech .... Mr. Michael J. NEWTOWN
76 Dean Sch Sci/Health/Crim Justice .... Dr. Kenneth M. ERICKSON
50 Dean Sch Business/Liberal Arts .... Mr. Jondavid S. DELONG
88 Dean Acad Support Svcs/Instr Tech .... Dr. Molly A. MOTT
41 Director of Athletics .... Mr. Randy B. SIEMINSKI
100 Exec Dir for University Relations .... Ms. Lenore VANDERZEE
101 College Council Secretary .... Ms. Michaela J. YOUNG
04 Assistant to the President .... Ms. Michaela J. YOUNG
35 Director Student Activities .... Ms. Priscilla LEGGETTE
28 Director of Diversity .... Ms. Lashawanda T. INGRAM
96 Director of Purchasing .... Ms. Bethany A. MARTIN
37 Director of Financial Aid .... Ms. Kerrie L. COOPER
88 College Accountant .... Mr. Colin MACKEY
15 Director of Human Resources .... Mr. David M. ROURKE
36 Director of Career Services .... Ms. Julie PARKMAN
06 Registrar .... Ms. Memorie L. SHAMPINE
08 Director of Library Services .... Ms. Michelle L. CURRIER
18 Director of Physical Plant .... Mr. Patrick J. HANSS
18 Plant Superintendent .... Mr. Martin D. AVERY
19 Chief of University Police .... Mr. Alan MULKIN
23 Director of Health Services .... Ms. Patricia A. TODD
26 Acting Dir Public Rels/Web Coord .... Mr. Travis SMITH
40 Manager Campus Store .... Mr. Corey JORDAN
39 Director of Residence Life .... Mr. John M. KENNEDY
09 Dir of Inst Research/Assessment .... Ms. Sarah E. TODD
13 Assistant VP IT/CIO .... Mr. Kyle BROWN
22 Director of Affirmative Action .... Ms. Amanda C. ROWLEY
29 Director of Alumni Affairs .... Ms. Peggy S. LEVATO
38 Director of Counseling .... Ms. Melinda A. MILLER
07 Director of Admissions .... Ms. Melissa EVANS
88 Director of Facilities .... Mr. Michael R. MCCORMICK
44 Director of Development .... Ms. Peggy S. LEVATO
90 Int Help Desk Coordinator .... Mr. Thomas PEARSON
104 Coord Intl Student Initiatives .... Ms. Erin LASSIAL
103 Dir of Workforce Development .... Mr. Art GARNO
25 Grants Coordinator .... Ms. JoAnne M. FASSINGER
109 Exec Dir of College Association .... Vacant

*State University of New York College of Technology at Delhi (C)

454 Delhi Drive, Delhi NY 13753-4454
County: Delaware FICE Identification: 002857
Unit ID: 196024
Telephone: (607) 746-4000 Carnegie Class: Bac/Assoc-Mixed
FAX Number: (607) 746-4208 Calendar System: Semester
URL: www.delhi.edu
Established: 1913 Annual Undergrad Tuition & Fees (In-State): $7,855
Enrollment: 3,598 Coed
Affiliation or Control: State IRS Status: 501(c)3
Highest Offering: Master's
Accreditation: M, ACFEI, ADNUR, CONST, NUR

02 President .... Dr. Michael R. LALIBERTE
05 Interim Provost .... Dr. David C. BROWER
32 VP for Student Life .... Ms. Barbara E. JONES
10 VP for Business & Finance .... Ms. Carol M. BISHOP
11 VP for Operations .... Ms. Bonnie G. MARTIN
30 VP for College Relations & Advance .... Mr. Joel M. SMITH
36 Coordinator Career & Transfer Svcs .... Ms. Kristin A. DEFOREST
07 Director of Admissions .... Mr. Robert C. PIJUROWSKI
13 Chief Information Officer .... Mr. Shawn P. BRISLIN
19 Chief of University Police .... Mr. Martin A. PETTIT
39 Director of Residence Life .... Mr. John J. FADOVANI
08 Director of the Resnick Library .... Ms. Virginia M. TROW
36 Dir Career & Business Development .... Ms. Glenda V. ROBERTS
28 Chief Diversity Officer .... Ms. Michele T. DEFREECE
18 Director of Physical Plant .... Mr. David A. LOVELAND
41 Director of Athletics .... Mr. Robert H. BACKUS
06 Registrar .... Ms. Nancy L. SMITH
37 Director of Financial Aid .... Ms. Nancy B. HUGHES
38 Director Counseling & Health Svcs .... Ms. Lori B. OSTERHOUDT
29 Alumni/Annual Giving Coordinator .... Ms. Lucinda C. BRYDON
21 Controller .... Ms. Amy L. BROWN
26 Dir of Communications & News Media .... Ms. Kimberly M. MACLEOD
09 Asst for Institutional Research .... Ms. JoAnna M. BROSNAN
04 Administrative Asst to President .... Vacant
102 Exec Dir College Foundation .... Mr. Joel M. SMITH
15 Mgr of Human Resource Operations .... Ms. Jan A. ELWELL
22 Dir Affirmative Action & Empl Rels .... Ms. Lynn A. BERGER
25 Grants Specialist .... Ms. Ellen A. L. BERATORI
96 Accts Payable/Purchasing Manager .... Ms. Cheryl L. DIETZMAN

*State University of New York Empire State College (D)

2 Union Avenue, Saratoga Springs NY 12866-4390
County: Saratoga FICE Identification: 010286
Unit ID: 196264
Telephone: (518) 587-2100 Carnegie Class: Masters/M
FAX Number: (518) 587-2886 Calendar System: Other
URL: www.esc.edu
Established: 1971 Annual Undergrad Tuition & Fees (In-State): $6,985
Enrollment: 11,952 Coed
Affiliation or Control: State IRS Status: 501(c)3
Highest Offering: Master's
Accreditation: M, IACBE, NURSE, TEAC

02 President .... Dr. Merodie HANCOCK
100 Chief of Staff .... Mr. Michael MANCINI
05 Provost/Vice Pres AA .... Dr. Alfred NTOKO
86 VP for Communications & Govt Rels .... Ms. Mary Caroline VAN DER VEER
30 VP of Advancement .... Mr. Walter WILLIAMS
13 Int Executive VP for ITS & Admin .... Dr. Samuel CONN
84 VP for Enrollment Management .... Dr. Clayton STEEN
09 VP for Decision Support .... Dr. Mitchell S. NESLER
20 Interim VP Academic Administration .... Dr. Tai ARNOLD
10 Assoc Vice Pres for Administration .. Mr. Frederick BARTHELMAS
97 Dean Undergrad Studies .... Dr. Nikki SHRIMPTON
20 Dean Academic/Instructional Svcs .... Dr. Lisa D'ADAMO-WEINSTEIN
88 Dean HVA Center for Labor Studies .... Vacant
16 Associate Dean Human Services .... Dr. John LAWLESS
70 Associate Dean Social Science .... Dr. Frank VANDER VALK
81 Assoc Dean Science/Math/Technology .... Dr. Brian HAGENBUCH
50 Associate Dean Business .... Dr. Julie GEDRO
79 Associate Dean Humanities .... Dr. Megan MULLEN
58 Assoc Dean School for Grad Studies .... Dr. Nathan GONYEA
66 Dean School of Nursing .... Dr. Bridget NETTLETON
20 Vice Provost for Academic Affairs .... Dr. Thomas MACKEY
14 Executive Director ITT .... Mr. AJ LACOMBA
12 Executive Director Western Region .... Ms. Cathleen SHEILS
12 Co-Int Exec Director Metro Center .... Dr. Christopher WHANN
12 Co-Int Exec Director Metro Center .... Dr. Catherine LEAKER
91 Director Admin Applications .... Mr. Mark CLAVERIE
88 Director Advancement Services .... Ms. Vicki SCHAAKE
29 Dir Alumni and Student Relations .... Ms. Maureen WINNEY
44 Director of the Fund .... Ms. Stephanie CORP
21 Director Business Office .... Ms. Becky PALMIERI
20 Dir Collegewide Academic Review .... Dr. Nan TRAVERS
32 Dir Collegewide Student Services .... Ms. Patricia MYERS
26 Director of Communications .... Mr. David HENAHAN
88 Director of Academic Development .... Mr. Brian GOODALE
88 Dir Compliance/Environment Sustain .... Ms. Sadie ROSS
18 Senior Director of Operations .... Mr. Rick REIMANN
37 Director Financial Aid .... Ms. Kristina DELBRIDGE
30 Director of Development .... Mr. Toby TOBROCKE
15 Assoc VP for Human Resources .... Ms. Mary Ellen R. KEENEY
88 Director College Project Management .... Mr. Walter LEWIS
96 Director Procurement .... Mr. Charley SUMMERSELL
24 Director Publications .... Mr. Kirk STARCZEWSKI
19 Director of Safety & Security .... Mr. Mark JANKOWSKI
21 Director Student Accounts .... Ms. Pamela MALONE
88 Int Dir Veteran & Military Educ .... Ms. Desiree DRINDAK
22 Affirmative Action Officer .... Ms. Mary MORTON
06 Registrar .... Vacant
07 Director Admissions .... Ms. Jennifer D'AGOSTINO

*Farmingdale State College (E)

2350 Broadhollow Road, Farmingdale NY 11735-1021
County: Suffolk FICE Identification: 002858
Unit ID: 196042
Telephone: (631) 420-2000 Carnegie Class: Bac-Diverse
FAX Number: N/A Calendar System: Semester
URL: www.farmingdale.edu
Established: 1912 Annual Undergrad Tuition & Fees (In-State): $7,808
Enrollment: 8,394 Coed
Affiliation or Control: State IRS Status: 501(c)3
Highest Offering: Baccalaureate
Accreditation: M, DH, ENGT, MLTAD, MT, NAIT, NURSE

02 President .... Dr. John S. NADER
05 Provost/Vice Pres for Academic Affs .... Dr. Laura JOSEPH
10 Senior Vice President & CFO .... Mr. George P. LAROSA
32 Vice Pres Student Affairs .... Dr. Tom CORTI
84 VP Inst Advancement/Enrollment Mgmt .... Mr. Patrick CALABRIA
30 Chief Development Officer .... Dr. Henry SIKORSKI
20 Acting Associate Provost .... Dr. Michael GOODSTONE
11 Director of Admin Services .... Ms. Dorothy HUGHES
35 Dean of Students .... Ms. Terry ESNES-JOHNSON
07 Dir Admissions/Enrollment Planning .... Mr. Jim HALL
19 Chief University Police .... Mr. Marvin J. FISCHER
18 Director of Physical Plant .... Mr. John S. DZINANKA
26 Sr Director of Communications .... Ms. Kathryn S. COLEY
06 Registrar .... Ms. Cindy MCCUE
08 Head Librarian .... Mr. Michael KNAUTH
15 Director Human Resources .... Ms. Marybeth INCANDELA
90 Director of Admin Technology .... Mr. Jeffrey BORAH
36 Director Career Development .... Ms. Dolores CIACCIO
37 Director Student Financial Services .... Ms. Diane KAZANECKI-KEMPTER
09 Chief Inst Research Officer .... Ms. Patricia LIND-GONZALEZ
23 Director Student Health Services .... Ms. Audrey KRAPF
41 Dir Athletics Admin & Ext Affairs .... Mr. Michael HARRINGTON
40 Dir of Athletics Comp & Operations .... Mr. Tom AZZARA
39 Director of Residence Life .... Ms. Angela JASUR
102 President Farmingdale Foundation .... Mr. John MOLLOY
24 Director Media Resources .... Mr. Martin BRANDT
29 Director Alumni Relations .... Ms. Michelle JOHNSON
28 Chief Diversity Officer .... Dr. Veronica HENRY
40 Manager Bookstore .... Ms. Roberta MIRRO
21 Controller .... Ms. Ellen WEBER
96 Purchasing Associate .... Ms. Lisa BRUNS
75 Interim Dir LI Ed Oppty Center .... Dr. Karen COUTRIER
50 Dean School of Business .... Dr. Richard VOGEL
76 Dean School Health Sciences .... Dr. Denny RYMAN
49 Acting Dean Sch of Arts & Sciences .... Dr. Charles ADAIR
54 Dean Sch Engineer Technology .... Dr. Kamal SHAHRABI
104 Director Study Abroad .... Ms. Jessica ZUNIGA
105 Director Web Services .... Ms. Sylvia NAVARRO-NICOSIA
53 Dean International Education .... Dr. Lorraine GREENWALD
04 Administrative Asst to President .... Ms. Claire LISI

*State University of New York Maritime College (A)

6 Pennyfield Avenue, Throggs Neck NY 10465-4198
County: Bronx FICE Identification: 002853
Unit ID: 196291
Telephone: (718) 409-7200 Carnegie Class: Masters/S
FAX Number: (718) 409-7392 Calendar System: Semester
URL: www.sunymaritime.edu
Established: 1874 Annual Undergrad Tuition & Fees (In-State): $7,809
Enrollment: 1,799 Coed
Affiliation or Control: State IRS Status: 501(c)3
Highest Offering: Master's
Accreditation: M, ENG

02 President ... RADM. Michael A. ALFULTIS
04 Executive Assistant to President ... Ms. Claudine TAVIN
05 Provost/Vice Pres Academic Affairs ... Dr. Timothy LYNCH
10 Vice Pres Finance/Admin ... Mr. Scott DIETERICH
26 Vice President University Relations ... Ms. Aimee BERNSTEIN
32 Commandant of Cadets/Master TSES ... CAPT. Richard S. SMITH
20 Academic Dean ... Dr. Gilbert TRAUB
100 Chief of Staff ... CAPT. Mark WOOLLEY
07 Dean of Admissions ... Ms. Yamiley SAINTVIL
35 Assoc Provost/Dean of Students ... Dr. Irene R. DELGADO
21 Director of Business Affairs ... Mr. Keith MURPHY
27 Exec Director of External Affairs ... Ms. Mary MUECKE
15 Director Human Resources ... Ms. LuAnn AUGUSTINE-PLAISANCE
19 University Police Chief ... Mr. Myron PRYJMAK
84 Exec Dir Enroll Svcs/Financial Aid ... Mr. Paul BAMONTE
41 Int Director of Athletics ... Mr. Chris MONASCH
06 Registrar ... Ms. Sarah GRADY
09 Dir Inst Research/Assessment ... CAPT. Mark WOOLLEY
08 Library Director ... Mr. Shafeek FAZAL
88 Dean of Maritime Educ/Training ... CAPT. Ernest FINK

*Morrisville State College (B)

PO Box 901, Morrisville NY 13408-0901
County: Madison FICE Identification: 002859
Unit ID: 196051
Telephone: (315) 684-6000 Carnegie Class: Bac/Assoc-Mixed
FAX Number: (315) 684-6116 Calendar System: Semester
URL: www.morrisville.edu
Established: 1908 Annual Undergrad Tuition & Fees (In-State): $7,970
Enrollment: 2,910 Coed
Affiliation or Control: State IRS Status: 501(c)3
Highest Offering: Baccalaureate
Accreditation: M, ACBSP, ADNUR, DIETT, ENGT

02 President ... Dr. David E. ROGERS
05 Provost ... Dr. Barry A. SPRIGGS
10 Vice Pres for Administration ... Ms. Mary Ellen BURDICK
32 Dean of Students ... Mr. Geoffrey S. ISABELLE
47 Dean School Agriculture & Business . Dr. Christopher L. NYBERG
81 Dean School Sci/Tech & Health ... Dr. Joseph H. BULARZIK
49 Dean School of Liberal Arts ... Dr. Paul F. GRIFFIN
97 Dean School of General Studies ... Ms. Jeannette H. EVANS
30 Exec Dir Advancement & PR ... Ms. Lisa A. IANELLO
07 Dean of Admission ... Mr. Robert C. BLANCHET
37 Director of Financial Aid ... Ms. Dacia L. BANKS
09 Director of Institutional Research ... Ms. Marian D. WHITNEY
08 Director of Library ... Ms. Christine A. RUDECOFF
23 Director Student Health Center ... Ms. Debra P. BABOWICZ
15 Dir HR/Affirmative Action ... Ms. Sarah G. STEELE
29 Coordinator of Alumni Relations ... Ms. Anastasia BRENCHER
26 Exec Director Communication Mktg ... Mr. Graham GARNER
06 Associate Registrar ... Ms. Tashana M. CURTIS
13 Chief Info Technology Officer (CIO) ... Vacant
18 Chief Facilities/Physical Plant ... Mr. Mark P. GRISI
19 Director Security/Safety ... Mr. Enrico L. D'ALESSANDRO
36 Career Planning/Development Ofcr ... Ms. Barbara A. ROBACK
39 Director Student Housing ... Ms. Ursula M. HERZ
41 Athletic Director ... Mr. Gregory M. CARROLL
14 Asst Dir of Technology Services ... Mr. Jeff GAY

*SUNY Polytechnic Institute (C)

100 Seymour Road, Utica NY 13502
County: Oneida FICE Identification: 011678
Unit ID: 196112
Telephone: (315) 792-7100 Carnegie Class: Masters/M
FAX Number: (315) 792-7222 Calendar System: Semester
URL: www.sunypoly.edu
Established: 1966 Annual Undergrad Tuition & Fees (In-State): $7,759
Enrollment: 2,740 Coed
Affiliation or Control: State IRS Status: 501(c)3
Highest Offering: Master's
Accreditation: M, BUS, CAHIIM, ENG, ENGT, NURSE

02 President ... Dr. Alain KALOYEROS
03 Senior Vice President & COO ... Dr. Robert E. GEER
46 Executive VP of Innovation & Tech ... Dr. Michael LIEHR
04 Executive Assistant ... Ms. Stephanie LEE
101 Executive Assistant ... Ms. Laurie HARTMAN
05 Provost/Vice Pres Academic Affairs ... Dr. William DURGIN
84 VP for Enrollment Management ... Mr. Richard FULLER
26 VP for Strategic Communications ... Mr. Jerry GRETZINGER
30 VP for Advancement ... Vacant
15 Associate VP for Human Resources ... Ms. Rhonda HAINES
32 Assoc Provost for Student Affairs ... Ms. Marybeth LYONS
19 VP for Security & Safety Mgmt ... Mr. Tom LOUIS
49 Dean Arts & Sciences ... Dr. Andrew RUSSELL
76 Int Dean Health Sciences & Mgmt ... Dr. Robert YEH
54 Interim Dean Engineering ... Dr. Andrew WOLFE
72 Int Dean NanoEngr & Tech Innovation ... Dr. Pradeep HALDER
81 Int Dean Nanoscale Science ... Dr. Alain DIEBOLD
46 Associate VP for Research ... Dr. John MARSH
18 Vice President of Facilities ... Mr. Jonathan HOLDER
25 Assoc VP of Sponsored Programs ... Ms. Christine WALLER
41 Director Athletics ... Mr. Kevin M. GRIMMER
10 Associate VP for Finance ... Mr. Scott BATEMAN
21 Associate VP of Business Affairs ... Ms. Susan HEAD
88 Director of Student Conduct ... Ms. Megan WYETT
36 Director Career Services ... Mr. Sim COVINGTON
23 Director Health & Wellness Center ... Ms. Jo RUFFRAGE
09 Assistant VP Institutional Research ... Ms. Valerie FUSCO
39 Director of College Housing ... Mrs. Jennifer ADAMS
37 Director Student Financial Aid ... Ms. Melissa ROSE
06 Registrar ... Mrs. Meghan GETMAN
58 Coordinator Graduate Center ... Ms. Maryrose RAAB
102 Interim Director Foundation ... Mr. Anthony LAPOLLA
43 Associate Counsel ... Mr. Mark LEMIRE
88 VP Business Dev & Economic Outreach ... Mr. Michael FANCHER
108 Director Institutional Assessment ... Dr. Joanne JOSEPH
13 Chief Information Officer ... Mr. Andrew BELLINGER
07 Director of Admissions ... Ms. Gina LISCIO
08 Director of Library Services ... Mr. Shannon PRITTING
106 Dir Online Education/E-learning ... Mr. Rick SHELTON
29 Director Alumni Relations ... Ms. Courtney KERWIN
86 Vice President Government Relations ... Mr. David DOYLE
96 Director of Purchasing ... Mr. David MANORE

*Suffolk County Community College Central Administration (D)

533 College Road, Selden NY 11784-2899
County: Suffolk Identification: 666658
Unit ID: 366395
Telephone: (631) 451-4000 Carnegie Class: N/A
FAX Number: (631) 451-4715
URL: www.sunysuffolk.edu

01 President ... Dr. Shaun L. MCKAY
27 College Communications Director ... Mr. Drew BIONDO
43 College General Counsel ... Mr. Louis S. PETRIZZO
05 VP Academic Affairs ... Dr. Suzanne JOHNSON
10 VP Business Financial Affairs ... Ms. Gail VIZZINI
30 Vice Pres Institutional Advancement ... Ms. Mary Lou ARANEO
45 VP Planning/Inst Effectiveness ... Dr. Jeffrey M. PEDERSEN
20 Assoc VP Academic Affairs ... Dr. Maria DELONGORIA
32 VP of Student Affairs ... Dr. Christopher J. ADAMS
13 VP Information Technology ... Vacant
103 Assoc VP Workforce/Econ Development ... Mr. John LOMBARDO
15 Assistant VP Human Resources ... Mr. Jeffrey L. TEMPERA
84 College Dean Enrollment Management ... Ms. Joanne E. BRAXTON
06 Assoc Dean Master Sched/Registrar ... Ms. Anna FLACK
35 Campus Assoc Dean Student Serv ... Mr. Charles BARTOLOTTA
37 College Director of Financial Aid ... Ms. Rose BANCROFT
28 Col Coord Multicultural Affairs ... Mr. James W. BANKS
100 Assistant to the President ... Ms. Sandra O'HARA
102 Exec Dir Development/Foundation ... Ms. Sylvia DIAZ
30 Col Assoc Dean Inst Advancement ... Mr. Andrew FAWCETT
104 Col Assoc Dean Spec Prog & Ext Part ... Ms. Iavoslava BABENCHUK
106 Assoc Dean Instructional Technology ... Mr. Troy J. HAHN
14 Assoc Dean Computer Info Systems ... Mr. Gary RIS
19 Director Security/Safety ... Mr. Baycan FIDELI
22 Affirmative Action Officer/Title IX ... Ms. Christina VARGAS
25 Chief Contracts/Grants Admin ... Mr. William T. TUCKER
26 Chief Public Relations/Marketing ... Ms. Mary M. FEDER
29 Director Alumni Relations ... Mr. Russell MALBROUGH
41 Athletic Director ... Mr. Kevin FOLEY
86 Col Director Legislative Affairs ... Mr. Benjamin ZWIRN
96 Director of Purchasing ... Vacant
36 Dir Career Services/Coop Educ ... Ms. Sylvia E. CAMACHO
04 Executive Asst to President ... Ms. Carol WICKLIFFE-CAMPBELL
18 Chief Facilities/Physical Plant ... Mr. Paul COOPER

*Suffolk County Community College Ammerman Campus (E)

533 College Road, Selden NY 11784-2899
County: Suffolk FICE Identification: 002878
Unit ID: 195951
Telephone: (631) 451-4000 Carnegie Class: Not Classified
FAX Number: (631) 451-4015 Calendar System: Semester
URL: www.sunysuffolk.edu
Established: 1959 Annual Undergrad Tuition & Fees (In-District): N/A
Enrollment: N/A Coed
Affiliation or Control: State/Local IRS Status: 501(c)3
Highest Offering: Associate Degree
Accreditation: M, ADNUR, EMT, PTAA

02 Executive Dean/Campus CEO ... Mr. P. Wesley LUNDBURG
05 Assoc Dean Academic Affairs ... Dr. Sandra SPROWS
32 Assoc Dean of Student Services ... Mr. Charles BARTOLOTTA
37 Director of Financial Aid ... Ms. Nancy BREWER
07 Director of Admissions ... Ms. Katherine AGUIRRE
08 Head Librarian ... Ms. Susan LIEBERTHAL
13 Asst Dir of Application Development ... Mr. Christopher T. BLAKE
18 Chief Facilities/Physical Plant ... Mr. Edward BENZ
36 Dir Career Svcs/Cooperative Educ ... Ms. Sylvia E. CAMACHO
92 Coordinator Honors Program ... Mr. Albin COFONE
10 Director of Business Affairs ... Mr. John P. CIENSKI
90 ETU Coordinator ... Mr. Paul BASILEO
91 Data Control Supervisor ... Mr. Paul MATUS

*Suffolk County Community College Eastern Campus (F)

121 Speonk-Riverhead Road, Riverhead NY 11901-3499
Telephone: (631) 548-2500 FICE Identification: 004816
Accreditation: &M, DIETT, PNUR

† Regional accreditation is carried under the parent institution in Selden, NY

*Suffolk County Community College Grant Campus (G)

1001 Crooked Hill Road, Brentwood NY 11717-1091
Telephone: (631) 851-6700 FICE Identification: 013204
Accreditation: &M, ADNUR, CAHIIM, OTA

† Regional accreditation is carried under the parent institution in Selden, NY

Sullivan County Community College (H)

112 College Road, Loch Sheldrake NY 12759-5721
County: Sullivan FICE Identification: 002879
Unit ID: 195988
Telephone: (845) 434-5750 Carnegie Class: Assoc/HT-Mix Trad/Non
FAX Number: (845) 434-4806 Calendar System: Semester
URL: www.sunysullivan.edu
Established: 1962 Annual Undergrad Tuition & Fees (In-District): $5,500
Enrollment: 1,643 Coed
Affiliation or Control: State/Local IRS Status: 501(c)3
Highest Offering: Associate Degree
Accreditation: M, ACBSP, #COARC

01 Interim President ... Mr. John (Jay) QUAINTANCE
05 Vice Pres Academic & Student Affs ... Dr. Robert SCHULTZ
10 Chief Financial Officer/Controller ... Ms. Susan HORTON
45 Assoc VP for Planning/HR & Facil ... Mr. Stephen MITCHELL
20 Asst VP Academic/Student Affairs ... Vacant
32 Interim Dean Student Services ... Mr. Chris DEPEW
45 Dean of Community Outreach ... Ms. Cindy KASHAN
39 Asst Dean Student Life & Housing ... Vacant
04 Exective Assistant to the President ... Ms. Linda ROFFEL
18 Chief Facilities/Physical Plant ... Mr. Tracy HALL
07 Director Admissions/Registration ... Vacant
37 Director of Financial Aid ... Mr. James WINDERL
08 Director of Library Services ... Ms. Evangela OATS
35 Director Student Activities ... Vacant
41 Director of Athletics ... Mr. Chris DEPEW
15 Asst Director of Human Resources ... Ms. Stephanie SMART
09 Director Institutional Research ... Ms. Janet HALPRIN
38 Director Student Counseling ... Ms. Rose HANOFEE
96 Purchasing Agent ... Ms. Lorry IRWIN
13 Director Institutional Computing ... Ms. Cheryl WELSCH
06 Coord of Registration Services ... Ms. Anne MARCHAL
26 Coord of Public & Alumni Relations ... Vacant
50 Chair Business/Information Tech ... Ms. Mary SUDOL
79 Chair Liberal Arts & Humanities ... Dr. Paul REIFENHEISER
83 Chair Health/Social/Behavioral Sci ... Dr. Susan ROGERS
81 Chair Mathematics/Natural Sciences ... Ms. Debra LEWKIEWICZ
19 Director Security/Safety ... Mr. David SEIGERMAN

Swedish Institute-College of Health Sciences (I)

226 W 26th Street, New York NY 10001-6700
County: New York FICE Identification: 021700
Unit ID: 196389
Telephone: (212) 924-5900 Carnegie Class: Spec 2-yr-Health
FAX Number: (212) 924-7600 Calendar System: Semester
URL: www.swedishinstitute.edu
Established: 1916 Annual Undergrad Tuition & Fees: $13,750
Enrollment: 792 Coed
Affiliation or Control: Proprietary IRS Status: Proprietary
Highest Offering: Associate Degree
Accreditation: ACCSC, ADNUR, SURGT

01 President ... Mr. Peter NEIGLER
03 Executive Vice President ... Ms. Stacey JAMESON
05 Director of Education ... Dr. Joseph BALATBAT
10 Chief Financial Officer ... Mr. Bill BERNARD
29 Dean of Alumni/Career Services ... Ms. Meg DARNELL
07 Director of Admissions ... Vacant
88 VP for Program Development ... Mr. John KATOMSKI
88 Dean of Advanced Personal Training ... Mr. Vincent METZO
88 Dean for Massage Therapy ... Ms. Ericka CLINTON
66 Dean of Nursing ... Dr. Maxinee BLACK-ARIAS
13 Director of Information Technology ... Mr. Rob SIEFKEN
32 Director of Student Services ... Ms. Theresa ROBBINSON
26 Director of Public Relations ... Vacant
37 Financial Aid Director ... Ms. Desire DEJESUS-AVILES
08 Director of Library Services ... Mr. Matthew FORTINO
06 Registrar ... Mr. Jeff NAMIAN

21 Bursar .... Ms. Beatriz ACEVEDO
51 Director of Continuing Education .... Ms. Tania OGULLUKIAN
40 Bookstore Manager .... Mr. Dan YUEN
36 Director of Career Services .... Mr. Richard GARDNER

Syracuse University Main Campus (A)

900 South Crouse Avenue, Syracuse NY 13244

County: Onondaga　FICE Identification: 002882
Unit ID: 196413
Telephone: (315) 443-1870　Carnegie Class: DU-Highest
FAX Number: (315) 443-3503　Calendar System: Semester
URL: www.syr.edu
Established: 1870　Annual Undergrad Tuition & Fees: $43,318
Enrollment: 21,492　Coed
Affiliation or Control: Independent Non-Profit　IRS Status: 501(c)3
Highest Offering: Doctorate
Accreditation: M, ART, AUD, BUS, CACREP, CIDA, CLPSY, CS, DIETD, DIETI, ENG, JOUR, LAW, LIB, MFCD, MUS, PH, SCPSY, SP, SPAA, SW, TED

01 Chancellor & President .... Mr. Kent SYVERUD
05 Vice Chanc/Prov Academic Affs .... Dr. Michele WHEATLY
10 Executive Vice President & CFO .... Dr. Louis G. MARCOCCIA
43 Interim Sr VP University Counsel .... Mr. Daniel J. FRENCH
30 Chief Advancement Ofcr/Senior VP .... Mr. Matthew TER MOLEN
32 Sr Vice Pres/Dean Student Affairs .... Ms. Rebecca REED KANTROWITZ
46 Interim Vice Pres Research .... Dr. Peter VANABLE
41 Interim Athletic Director .... Mr. Daniel J. FRENCH
26 Sr Vice Pres Public Affairs .... Mr. Kevin C. QUINN
21 Comptroller .... Ms. Jean B. GALLIPEAU
104 Assoc Prov International Education .... Dr. Margaret R. HIMLEY
08 Dean of University Libraries .... Mr. David SEAMAN
15 Chief Human Resources Officer .... Mr. Andrew GORDON
20 Assoc Provost Academic Programs .... Ms. Andria COSTELLO STANIEC
48 Dean School of Architecture .... Dr. Michael A. SPEAKS
49 Dean College of Arts & Sciences .... Dr. Karin RUHLANDT
53 Dean School of Education .... Dr. Joanna O. MASINGILA
76 Dean Col of Sport & Human Dynamics .... Dr. Diane Lyden MURPHY
54 Dean Col Engineering/Computer Sci .... Dr. Teresa DAHLBERG
62 Dean School of Info Studies .... Dr. Elizabeth D. LIDDY
61 Dean College of Law .... Dr. Craig M. BOISE
50 Dean Whitman School of Management .... Dr. Kenneth A. KAVAJECZ
80 Dean Maxwell Sch of Citizenship .... Vacant
60 Dean Newhouse School of Public Comm .... Ms. Lorraine BRANHAM
57 Dean Col Visual & Performing Arts .... Ms. Ann CLARKE
58 Int Dean Graduate Studies .... Dr. Peter VANABLE
51 Dean University College .... Ms. Bethaida GONZALEZ
101 Secretary Board of Trustees .... Ms. Lisa A. DOLAK
07 Dean of Admissions .... Dr. Maurice A. HARRIS

Talmudical Institute of Upstate New York (B)

769 Park Avenue, Rochester NY 14607-3046

County: Monroe　FICE Identification: 025506
Unit ID: 196440
Telephone: (585) 473-2810　Carnegie Class: Spec-4-yr-Faith
FAX Number: (585) 442-0417　Calendar System: Semester
Established: 1974　Annual Undergrad Tuition & Fees: $5,100
Enrollment: 21　Male
Affiliation or Control: Independent Non-Profit　IRS Status: 501(c)3
Highest Offering: Second Talmudic Degree
Accreditation: RABN

01 Dean .... Rabbi Menachem DAVIDOWITZ
03 Executive Vice President .... Rabbi Shlomo NOBLE

Talmudical Seminary of Bobov (C)

5120 New Utrecht Avenue, Brooklyn NY 11204-1108

County: Kings　FICE Identification: 041155
Unit ID: 451404
Telephone: (718) 854-8700　Carnegie Class: Spec-4-yr-Faith
FAX Number: (718) 854-8707　Calendar System: Semester
Established: 2005　Annual Undergrad Tuition & Fees: $7,500
Enrollment: 327　Male
Affiliation or Control: Independent Non-Profit　IRS Status: 501(c)3
Highest Offering: First Talmudic Degree
Accreditation: RABN

01 Dean .... Rabbi Joshua RUBIN
37 Director Student Financial Aid .... Josef DEUTSCH

Talmudical Seminary Oholei Torah (D)

667 Eastern Parkway, Brooklyn NY 11213-3397

County: Kings　FICE Identification: 012011
Unit ID: 196431
Telephone: (718) 774-5050　Carnegie Class: Spec-4-yr-Faith
FAX Number: (718) 778-0784　Calendar System: Semester
Established: 1956　Annual Undergrad Tuition & Fees: $9,300
Enrollment: 330　Male
Affiliation or Control: Independent Non-Profit　IRS Status: 501(c)3
Highest Offering: First Talmudic Degree
Accreditation: RABN

01 Chief Executive Officer .... Mende MARSOW
05 Dean .... Elchonon LESCHES
10 Business Officer .... Gary SUSSKIND
37 Financial Aid Officer .... Sholom ROSENFELD

Teachers College, Columbia University (E)

525 West 120th Street, New York NY 10027

County: New York　FICE Identification: 003979
Unit ID: 196468
Telephone: (212) 678-3000　Carnegie Class: DU-Higher
FAX Number: (212) 678-4048　Calendar System: Semester
URL: www.tc.columbia.edu
Established: 1887　Annual Graduate Tuition & Fees: N/A
Enrollment: 5,011　Coed
Affiliation or Control: Independent Non-Profit　IRS Status: 501(c)3
Highest Offering: Doctorate; No Undergraduates
Accreditation: M, CLPSY, COPSY, DIETI, SCPSY, SP, TED

01 President .... Dr. Susan H. FUHRMAN
05 Provost & VP for Academic Affairs .... Dr. Thomas JAMES
100 Secretary to College/Chief of Staff .... Dr. Katie CONWAY
10 Vice Pres Finance & Administration .... Mr. Harvey SPECTOR
30 Vice Pres Devel/External Affairs .... Ms. Suzanne MURPHY
22 Vice Pres/Dir Diversity/Cmty Affs .... Ms. Janice S. ROBINSON
88 VP/Sch/Cmty Partnshp/Spec Advis .... Dr. Nancy STREIM
21 Assoc Vice Pres/Controller .... Mr. Henry PERKOWSKI
18 Asst VP Facilities .... Mr. Suzanne JABLONSKI
84 Vice Provost Enrollment Services .... Dr. Thomas ROCK
06 Registrar .... Mr. Sam FUGAZZOTTO
13 Chief Information Officer .... Mr. Naveed HUSAIN
08 Library Director .... Dr. Gary NATRIELLO
15 Director Human Resources .... Mr. Randy GLAZER
19 Director Public Safety .... Mr. John DE ANGELIS
43 General Counsel .... Ms. Lori E. FOX

† Affiliated with Columbia University in the City of New York.

Technical Career Institutes (F)

320 W 31st Street, New York NY 10001-2789

County: New York　FICE Identification: 011031
Unit ID: 196477
Telephone: (212) 594-4000　Carnegie Class: Assoc/HVT-Mix Trad/Non
FAX Number: (212) 330-0898　Calendar System: Semester
URL: www.tcicollege.edu
Established: 1909　Annual Undergrad Tuition & Fees: $13,700
Enrollment: 2,762　Coed
Affiliation or Control: Proprietary　IRS Status: Proprietary
Highest Offering: Associate Degree
Accreditation: M, NY, ENGT, OPD

00 Chief Executive Officer .... Dr. John MCGRATH
01 President .... Mr. William TALBOT
05 Provost & VP for Academic Affairs .... Dr. Clotilda DILLON
11 Exec Vice Pres Administration .... Mr. Felix PRETTO
84 Exec VP Enrollment Management .... Mr. Michael GALL
37 Vice Pres Student Financial Svcs .... Ms. Cynthia FEKARIS
09 Vice Pres for Research and Planning .... Ms. Susanna KUNG
10 Chief Financial Officer .... Mr. Thomas BICKART
07 Assoc Vice Pres for Admissions .... Ms. Iveth ZUNIGA
20 Dean of Academic Administration .... Ms. Patsy JAMES
49 Dean of Arts & Sciences .... Dr. John LUUKKONEN
88 Dean of Facilities Technologies .... Ms. Regina CAHILL
50 Dean of Business and New Media Tech .... Ms. Clotilde DILLON
72 Dean of Technology .... Mr. Seyed AKHAVI
76 Dean of Health Sciences and Tech .... Dr. Michael MEIR

Tompkins Cortland Community College (G)

170 North Street, PO Box 139, Dryden NY 13053-8504

County: Tompkins　FICE Identification: 006788
Unit ID: 196565
Telephone: (607) 844-8211　Carnegie Class: Assoc/HT-High Non
FAX Number: (607) 844-9665　Calendar System: Semester
URL: www.TompkinsCortland.edu
Established: 1968　Annual Undergrad Tuition & Fees (In-District): $5,666
Enrollment: 5,559　Coed
Affiliation or Control: State/Local　IRS Status: 501(c)3
Highest Offering: Associate Degree
Accreditation: M, ADNUR

01 President .... Dr. Carl E. HAYNES
03 Provost and VP of College .... Dr. John R. CONNERS
32 Dean of Student Life .... Mr. John BRADAC
05 Dean of Instruction .... Mr. Carl PENZIUL
08 Library Director .... Mr. Gregg KIEHL
84 Dean Operations & Enrollment Mgmt .... Ms. Bixy K. TAETZSCH
20 Assoc Dean Curriculum & Acad Record .... Ms. Jane F. HAMMOND
14 Director of Technology Support .... Mr. Brian ACKLEY
88 Dean Org Success & Learning .... Ms. Kathryn WUNDERLICH
09 Assoc Dean IR and Org Learning .... Dr. Kristine ALTUCHER
37 Director of Financial Aid .... Ms. LaSonya GRIGGS
26 Dean of External Relations .... Dr. Bruce RYAN
15 Human Resources Administrator .... Ms. Sharon DOVI
07 Director of Admissions .... Mr. Sandy DRUMLUK
10 Director of Budget & Finance .... Ms. Susan DEWEY
13 Chief Information Officer .... Mr. Timothy DENSMORE
19 Director of Safety & Security .... Mr. J. Beau SAUL
41 Athletic Director .... Mr. Mick R. MCDANIEL
39 Director Residence Life .... Ms. Darese DOSKAL
36 Coordinator Counseling/Career Svcs .... Ms. Joan DONOVAN
18 Director of Facilities .... Mr. James TURNER
23 Director of Health Services .... Ms. Shari SHAPLEIGH
28 Director of Multicultural Services .... Mr. Seth THOMPSON
101 Asst to President/Clerk of Board .... Ms. Cathy NORTHROP

Torah Temimah Talmudical Seminary (H)

507 Ocean Parkway, Brooklyn NY 11218-5913

County: Kings　FICE Identification: 021916
Unit ID: 196583
Telephone: (713) 853-8500　Carnegie Class: Spec-4-yr-Faith
FAX Number: (718) 438-5779　Calendar System: Semester
Established: 1978　Annual Undergrad Tuition & Fees: $10,750
Enrollment: 102　Male
Affiliation or Control: Independent Non-Profit　IRS Status: 501(c)3
Highest Offering: Second Talmudic Degree
Accreditation: RABN

01 President & Dean .... Rabbi L. MARGULIES
03 Executive Director .... Rabbi L. MARGULIES
05 Chief Academic Officer .... Rabbi Lipa GELDWORTH
37 Financial Aid Administrator .... Mr. Mendel ROCHLITZ
38 Director of Guidance .... Rabbi Yirmiya GUGENHEIMER
11 Administrator .... Rabbi Yisroel KLEINMAN

Touro College (I)

500 7th Avenue, New York NY 10018

County: New York　FICE Identification: 010142
Unit ID: 196592
Telephone: (646) 565-6000　Carnegie Class: Masters/L
FAX Number: N/A　Calendar System: Semester
URL: www.touro.edu
Established: 1970　Annual Undergrad Tuition & Fees: $16,700
Enrollment: 12,381　Coordinate
Affiliation or Control: Independent Non-Profit　IRS Status: 501(c)3
Highest Offering: Doctorate
Accreditation: M, ARCPA, LAW, NURSE, OSTEO, OT, #OTA, PHAR, PTA, SP, SW, TEAC

01 President/Chief Executive Officer .... Dr. Alan KADISH
03 Executive Vice President .... Mr. David RAAB
03 Executive Vice President .... Mr. Moshe KRUPKA
10 Senior Vice President & CFO .... Mr. Melvin M. NESS
11 Sr Vice Pres/Chief Admin Officer .... Mr. Jeffrey ROSENGARDEN
30 Vice Pres Institutional Advancement .... Mr. Henry RUBIN
05 VP Undergrad Acad Affs/Dean of Fac .... Dr. Stanley L. BOYLAN
58 Vice Pres of Grad Studies .... Dr. Nadja GRAFF
45 VP Plng & Assessment/Dean of Stdnts .... Dr. Robert GOLDSCHMIDT
13 VP of Operations & Info Systems .... Dr. Franklin STEEN
84 VP Student Administrative Services .... Mr. Matthew BONILLA
53 Dean Grad School Education .... Dean Arnold SPINNER
56 Vice President Com Ed/Ex Dn NYSCAS .... Ms. Eva SPINELLI-SEXTER
106 VP Online Edu/Dean Women's Division .... Dr. Marian STOLTZ-LOIKE
09 Director Institutional Research .... Mr. Michael LIPKIN
43 Senior VP of Legal Affairs .... Mr. Michael NEWMAN
58 Provost Graduate/Professional Div .... Dr. Patricia SALKIN
63 Dean Col of Osteopathic Medicine .... Dr. Robert GOLDBERG
67 Dean College of Pharmacy .... Dr. Katherine KNAPP
70 Dean School of Social Work .... Dr. Steven HUBERMAN
76 Dean of School of Health Sciences .... Dr. Louis H. PRIMAVERA
58 Dean Grad School Jewish Studies .... Dr. Michael A. SHMIDMAN
90 Dn Grad Sch of Tech/Dir Acad Comp .... Dr. Issac HERSKOWITZ
12 Dean Lander College for Men .... Dr. Moshe Z. SOKOL
50 Acting Dean Grad School of Business .... Dr. Sabra BROCK
38 Dean of Advising & Counseling .... Dr. Avery HOROWITZ
51 Asst Dean School Lifelong Education .... Dr. Briendy STERN
06 University Registrar .... Ms. Lidia MEINDL
37 Int Dir Financial Aid/Compliance .... Ms. Margherite POWELL
08 Director of Libraries .... Ms. Bashe SIMON
07 Director of Admissions .... Mr. Arthur WIGFALL
76 Director Physician Asst Program .... Dr. Joseph TOMMASINO
75 Director of Occupational Therapy .... Dr. Stephanie DAPICE-WONG
76 Director of Physical Therapy .... Ms. Jill HORBACEWICZ
88 Pgm Dir Speech Lang Path/Grad Pgm .... Ms. Hindy LUBINSKY
44 Director Annual or Planned Giving .... Ms. Adrienne GRUSKIN
14 Director of OIT .... Mr. Len NIEBO
91 Chief Info Security Officer .... Ms. Patricia CIUFFO
19 Director of Security .... Ms. Lydia PEREZ
19 Dir of Emergency Preparedness .... Ms. Shoshana YEHUDAH
15 Director of Human Resources .... Ms. Roberta ROSENBLATT
96 Director of Purchasing .... Ms. Wanda HERNANDEZ
18 Dir of Facilities/Real Estate .... Mr. Kenneth DAVID
21 Controller .... Mr. Stuart LIPPMAN
26 Dir of Communication/External Rels .... Ms. Elisheva SCHLAM
29 Director Alumni Relations .... Vacant
36 Director Student Placement .... Mr. Stuart ANSEL
108 Director of Assessment & Evaluation .... Dr. Eric LINDEN
25 Director Office Sponsored Pgm .... Mr. Glenn DAVIS
04 Administrative Asst to President .... Ms. Elaine GOLDBERG
104 Director Study Abroad .... Dr. Chana SOSEVSKY
105 Director Web Services .... Ms. Lisa HALBERSTAM
41 Athletic Director .... Mr. Irv BADER
45 Director of Budget & Planning .... Mr. David BELL

Touro College Bay Shore (A)

1700 Union Boulevard, Bay Shore NY 11706
Telephone: (631) 665-1600 Identification: 770145
Accreditation: &M, ARCPA, OT

† Regional accreditation is carried under the parent institution in New York, NY

Touro College Flatbush (B)

1602 Avenue J, Brooklyn NY 11230
Telephone: (718) 252-7800 Identification: 770146
Accreditation: &M

† Regional accreditation is carried under the parent institution in New York, NY

Touro Law School (C)

225 Eastview Drive, Central Islip NY 11722
Telephone: (631) 761-7000 Identification: 770148
Accreditation: &M

† Regional accreditation is carried under the parent institution in New York, NY

Tri-State College of Acupuncture (D)

80 Eighth Avenue, #400, New York NY 10011-0890
County: New York FICE Identification: 025460
Unit ID: 130581
Telephone: (212) 242-2255 Carnegie Class: Spec-4-yr-Other Health
FAX Number: (212) 242-2920 Calendar System: Semester
URL: www.tsca.edu
Established: 1982 Annual Graduate Tuition & Fees: N/A
Enrollment: 110 Coed
Affiliation or Control: Proprietary IRS Status: Proprietary
Highest Offering: Master's; No Undergraduates
Accreditation: ACUP

01	President	Dr. Dennis MOSEMAN
06	Registrar	Sandra TURNER

Trocaire College (E)

360 Choate Avenue, Buffalo NY 14220-2094
County: Erie FICE Identification: 002812
Unit ID: 196653
Telephone: (716) 826-1200 Carnegie Class: Spec-4-yr-Other Health
FAX Number: (716) 828-6107 Calendar System: Semester
URL: www.trocaire.edu
Established: 1958 Annual Undergrad Tuition & Fees: $16,290
Enrollment: 1,467 Coed
Affiliation or Control: Independent Non-Profit IRS Status: 501(c)3
Highest Offering: Baccalaureate
Accreditation: M, ADNUR, CAHIIM, DIETT, MAC, NUR, PHLEB, PNUR, RAD, SURGT

01	President	Dr. Bassam M. DEEB
05	Vice President of Academic Affairs	Dr. Richard T. LINN
10	VP for Finance	Mr. John J. HUDACK
30	VP Development & Cmty Engagement	Ms. Pamela WITTER
21	Associate VP for Finance	Mr. Edward JOHNSON
32	Chief Student Affairs Officer	Mr. Tony FUNIGIELLO
84	Chief Enrollment Officer	Ms. Jacqueline MATHENY
66	Dean Catherine McAuley Sch Nursing	Dr. Catherine GRISWOLD
15	Chief Human Resources Officer	Ms. Janet PETERS
37	Director of Financial Aid	Mr. Jeffrey LUCAS
25	Director of Grants/Govt Relations	Ms. Sandra MILLER
26	Director of Public Relations	Ms. Emily Burns PERRYMAN
06	Registrar	Mrs. Theresa HORNER
36	Director Career Center	Mrs. Maureen PERNICK HUBER
18	Facilities Director	Mr. Robert GARUS
44	Director of Development	Ms. Lindsey DOTSON
07	Dean of Admissions & Workforce Dev	Mrs. Mollie A. BALLARO
38	Director Academic Support & Retent	Ms. Kristin NESBITT
40	Manager Bookstore	Ms. Debbie CAMMARATA
49	Dean of Arts/Sciences & Prof Stds	Dr. Jennifer Higgins MCCORMICK
76	Dean Division of Health Prof	Dr. Linda KERWIN
108	Director of Assessment & Research	Dr. Nicole TOMASELLO
88	Director of Mission & Service	Sr. Margaret Mary GORMAN

Ulster County Community College (F)

491 Cottekill Road, PO Box 557, Stone Ridge NY 12484
County: Ulster FICE Identification: 002880
Unit ID: 196699
Telephone: (845) 687-5000 Carnegie Class: Assoc/HT-High Non
FAX Number: (845) 687-5083 Calendar System: Semester
URL: www.sunyulster.edu
Established: 1961 Annual Undergrad Tuition & Fees (In-District): $4,942
Enrollment: 3,594 Coed
Affiliation or Control: State/Local IRS Status: 501(c)3
Highest Offering: Associate Degree
Accreditation: M, ADNUR

01	President	Dr. Alan P. ROBERTS
84	Sr Vice Pres Enrollment Mgmt	Ms. Ann MARROTT
05	VP for Academic Affairs	Mr. Kevin STONER
51	Dean of Continuing & Prof Educ	Mr. Christopher MARX
10	VP Admin Svcs/Chief Business Ofcr	Mr. Christopher NGUYEN
30	Exec Dir of Inst Advance & Ext Rels	Ms. Lorraine SALMON
04	Assistant to President	Ms. Jennifer ZELL
08	Director of Library Services	Ms. Kari MACK
37	Director of Financial Aid	Mr. Christopher CHANG
06	Registrar	Ms. Debra MILLER
41	Athletic Director	Mr. Matthew BRENNIE
19	Director of Safety & Security	Mr. Wayne FREER
07	Asst Dean Enrollment & Dir Admiss	Mr. Matthew GREEN
26	Chief Public Relations Officer	Ms. Ann MARROTT
36	Dir Student Place/Acad Support Svcs	Ms. Jane KITHCART
32	Director Student Affairs	Ms. Ann MARROTT
18	Director of Plant Operations	Vacant
09	Director of Institutional Research	Mr. Clarence (Hank) MILLER
103	Workforce Development	Mr. Christopher MARX
15	Coordinator of Personnel Services	Mrs. Debra DELANOY
21	Asst Dean of Admin Services	Ms. Amy WINTERS
96	Coord Procurement/General Services	Mr. Stephen GALLART
101	Secretary of the Institution/Board	Ms. Jennifer ZELL
38	Assistant Dean of Student Success	Ms. Wendy MCCORRY

Unification Theological Seminary (G)

30 Seminary Drive, Barrytown NY 12507-5021
County: Dutchess FICE Identification: 032163
Unit ID: 246789
Telephone: (845) 752-3000 Carnegie Class: Spec-4-yr-Faith
FAX Number: (845) 758-2156 Calendar System: Semester
URL: www.uts.edu
Established: 1975 Annual Undergrad Tuition & Fees: N/A
Enrollment: 122 Coed
Affiliation or Control: Unification Church IRS Status: 501(c)3
Highest Offering: Doctorate
Accreditation: M

01	President	Dr. Hugh SPURGIN
05	Vice President for Academic Affairs	Dr. Kathy WININGS
11	VP for Administration	Dr. Michael MICKLER
88	Director of Field Education	Dr. Jacob DAVID
10	Director of Finances	Mr. Frank ZOCHOL
06	Registrar	Mrs. Ute DELANEY
08	Library Technician	Mr. Robert WAGNER
37	Student Financial Aid Director	Mr. Henry CHRISTOPHER
18	Plant Director	Mr. Carl VERDERBER
07	Director of Admissions	Mr. Henry CHRISTOPHER
30	Dir for Development & Alumni Rels	Mr. Robin GRAHAM
108	Director Institutional Assessment	Dr. Keisuke NODA
32	Chief Student Affairs/Student Life	Dr. Drissa KONE

Union College (H)

807 Union Street, Schenectady NY 12308-3181
County: Schenectady FICE Identification: 002889
Unit ID: 196866
Telephone: (518) 388-6000 Carnegie Class: Bac-A&S
FAX Number: (518) 388-6800 Calendar System: Trimester
URL: www.union.edu
Established: 1795 Annual Undergrad Tuition & Fees: $50,013
Enrollment: 2,242 Coed
Affiliation or Control: Independent Non-Profit IRS Status: 501(c)3
Highest Offering: Baccalaureate
Accreditation: M, ENG

01	President	Dr. Stephen C. AINLAY
05	VP Academic Affs/Dean Faculty	Dr. Strom THACKER
30	Vice President College Relations	Ms. Terri A. CERVENY
10	Vice President for Finance & Admin	Ms. Diane T. BLAKE
07	VP Admissions/Fin Aid/Enrollment	Mr. Matthew J. MALATESTA
100	Chief of Staff	Dr. Robert D. KELLY
22	Chief Diversity Officer	Dr. Gretchel L. HATHAWAY
32	VP Student Affairs/Dean of Students	Dr. Stephen C. LEAVITT
20	Dean of Studies	Dr. Mark E. WUNDERLICH
13	Chief Information Officer	Ms. Ellen Y. BORKOWSKI
06	Registrar	Ms. Penelope S. ADEY
30	Sr Director of Development	Mr. Dominick F. FAMULARE
08	College Librarian	Ms. Frances J. MALOY
26	Director of Media and Public Rels	Mr. Phillip J. WAJDA
37	Director of Financial Aid	Ms. Linda M. PARKER
38	Director of Student Counseling	Mr. Marcus S. HOTALING
36	Director of Career Center	Mr. Robert C. SOULES
15	Director of Human Resources	Mr. Eric NOLL
41	Director of Athletics	Mr. James MCLAUGHLIN
19	Director Campus Safety	Mr. Christopher HAYEN
39	Director Residence Life	Ms. Amanda BINGEL

† Tuition figure is a comprehensive fees figure.

Union Theological Seminary (I)

3041 Broadway, New York NY 10027-5792
County: New York FICE Identification: 002890
Unit ID: 196884
Telephone: (212) 662-7100 Carnegie Class: Spec-4-yr-Faith
FAX Number: (212) 280-1416 Calendar System: Semester
URL: www.utsnyc.edu
Established: 1836 Annual Graduate Tuition & Fees: N/A
Enrollment: 233 Coed
Affiliation or Control: Independent Non-Profit IRS Status: 501(c)3
Highest Offering: Doctorate; No Undergraduates
Accreditation: M, THEOL

01	President	Dr. Serene JONES
03	Executive Vice President	Mr. Fred DAVIE
10	Int VP Finance & Operations	Mr. Brent DICKMAN
30	VP for Development	Mr. Martin DUUS
05	Dean of Academic Affairs	Dr. Mary C. BOYS
32	Associate Dean Student Affairs	Dr. Yvette WILSON-BARNES
08	Associate Academic Dean	Dr. Beth BIDLACK
88	Senior Director of Integrative Educ	Dr. Su Y. PAK
06	Registrar/Asst Dir Financial Aid	Mr. Rafael ORTIZ
18	Deputy Vice Pres Building/Grounds	Mr. Michael MALONEY
88	Sr Director Special Initiatives	Rev. Richard LANDERS
39	Director Housing/Campus Services	Mr. Michael ORZECHOWSKI
07	Assoc Dean Admissions/Financial Aid	Ms. Nichelle JENKINS
15	Director Personnel Services	Ms. Diana TORRES-PETRILLI

United Talmudical Seminary (J)

191 Rodney Street, Brooklyn NY 11211-7900
County: Kings FICE Identification: 011189
Unit ID: 197018
Telephone: (718) 963-9770 Carnegie Class: Spec-4-yr-Faith
FAX Number: (718) 963-9775 Calendar System: Semester
Established: 1949 Annual Undergrad Tuition & Fees: $13,575
Enrollment: 2,421 Male
Affiliation or Control: Independent Non-Profit IRS Status: 501(c)3
Highest Offering: Second Talmudic Degree
Accreditation: RABN

01	Dean	Rabbi Zalman TEITLBAUM
05	Assoc Dean Scholastic Services	Rabbi Yeruchem DEUTSCH
37	Financial Aid Administrator	Mr. Bernard KATZ
10	Business Officer	Mr. Shia GREENFELD

University of Rochester (K)

500 Joseph C. Wilson Boulevard, Rochester NY 14627
County: Monroe FICE Identification: 002894
Unit ID: 195030
Telephone: (585) 275-2121 Carnegie Class: DU-Highest
FAX Number: (585) 275-0359 Calendar System: Semester
URL: www.rochester.edu
Established: 1850 Annual Undergrad Tuition & Fees: $48,280
Enrollment: 11,060 Coed
Affiliation or Control: Independent Non-Profit IRS Status: 501(c)3
Highest Offering: Doctorate
Accreditation: M, BUS, CACREP, CLPSY, DENT, ENG, IPSY, MED, MFCD, MUS, NURSE, PAST, PDPSY, PH, TED

01	President and CEO	Mr. Joel SELIGMAN
05	Provost and Sr VP for Research	Mr. Rob CLARK
88	Dean of Faculty of Arts/Sci & Engr	Mr. Peter LENNIE
10	Sr VP Administration & Fin/CFO	Ms. Holly CRAWFORD
88	VP and University Dean	Mr. Paul J. BURGETT
17	Sr VP Health Sciences/Med Ctr CEO	Dr. Mark B. TAUBMAN
45	Sr VP for Institutional Resources	Mr. Douglas PHILLIPS
30	Sr VP and Chief Advanc Officer	Mr. Thomas FARRELL
43	VP and General Counsel	Ms. Gail NORRIS
26	VP for Communications	Ms. Elizabeth STAUDERMAN
13	VP and CIO for the University	Mr. David E. LEWIS
15	Assoc VP Human Resources	Mr. Tony KINSLOW
58	Vice Provost/Univ Dean Grad Studies	Ms. Margaret KEARNEY
100	General Secy/Pres Chief of Staff	Ms. Lamar R. MURPHY
28	Vice Provost Fac Devel & Diversity	Dr. Vivian LEWIS
08	Dean River Campus Libraries	Ms. Mary Ann MAVRINAC
88	Vice President/Laser Lab Director	Mr. Robert L. MCCRORY
49	Dean of School of Arts & Sciences	Ms. Gloria CULVER
54	Dean of Hajim Engineering School	Ms. Wendi HEINZELMAN
84	Dean AS&E Undergrad Admis & Fin Aid	Mr. Jonathan BURDICK
37	Director of Financial Aid	Ms. Samantha VEEDER
108	Asst Provost for Academic Admin	Ms. Jane Marie SOUZA
21	Sr Assoc VP for Budgets & Planning	Mr. Michael ANDREWS
32	Dean of Students Arts/Sci & Engr	Mr. Matthew BURNS
63	Dean of School of Medicine & Dent	Dr. Mark B. TAUBMAN
64	Dean of Eastman School of Music	Mr. Jamal ROSSI
66	Dean of School of Nursing	Ms. Kathy RIDEOUT
50	Dean of Simon Business School	Mr. Andrew AINSLIE
53	Dean Warner Grad Sch Educ & Hum Dev	Ms. Raffaella BORASI
89	Dean of Freshmen Arts/Sci & Engr	Ms. Marcy KRAUS
88	Dean of Sophmores Arts/Sci & Engr	Mr. Sean HANNA
35	Assoc Dean Students Arts/Sci & Engr	Ms. Anne-Marie ALGIER
23	Strong Health Chief Medical Officer	Dr. Raymond MAYEWSKI
52	Dir Eastman Institute Oral Health	Dr. Eli ELIAV
25	Assoc VP Research & Project Admin	Ms. Gunta LIDERS
18	Assoc VP Facilities & Services	Mr. Bruce BASHWINER
86	Executive Director Govt Relations	Mr. Peter J. ROBINSON
96	Assoc VP Purchasing & Supply	Mr. Carl TIETJEN
04	Executive Asst to the President	Ms. Susan NIGGLI
06	University Registrar	Ms. Nancy SPECHT
19	Director of Public Safety	Mr. Mark T. FISCHER
57	Dir of the Memorial Art Gallery	Mr. Jonathan BINSTOCK
41	Director of Athletics & Recreation	Mr. George VANDERZWAAG
39	Exec Dir Res Life & Housing Svcs	Ms. Laurel CONTOMANOLIS
36	Exec Dir Career & Internship Center	Mr. Joe TESTANI
101	Administrator to Board of Trustees	Ms. Jackie E. KING
42	Director Religious & Spiritual Life	Rev. Denise YARBROUGH
104	Director Study Abroad	Ms. Tynelle STEWART
22	Equal Opp Dir and Title IX Coord	Ms. Morgan LEVY

USC The Business College (L)

201 Bleecker Street, Utica NY 13501-2200
County: Oneida FICE Identification: 009077
Unit ID: 197081
Telephone: (315) 733-2307 Carnegie Class: Spec 2-yr-Other
FAX Number: (315) 733-9281 Calendar System: Semester

URL: www.uscny.edu
Established: 1896 Annual Undergrad Tuition & Fees: $13,500
Enrollment: 282 Coed
Affiliation or Control: Proprietary IRS Status: Proprietary
Highest Offering: Associate Degree
Accreditation: NY

01 President & Treasurer .... Mr. Philip M. WILLIAMS
05 Exec Vice President for Academics .... Dr. Mark MONTGOMERY
32 Exec Vice Pres Student Affairs .... Mr. Scott K. WILLIAMS
11 Exec Vice President Administration .... Mr. John L. CROSSLEY
103 VP Corp/Workforce Develop .... Mr. Donald G. REESE
10 Vice President of Finance .... Mr. Richard H. HILTON
43 General Counsel .... Mr. John H. STORY, JR.
12 Director Canastota Branch .... Mrs. Wendy M. CARY
06 Registrar/Bursar .... Mrs. Marian J. NIELSON
30 Director of Development .... Mr. John CROSSLEY
08 Head Librarian .... Ms. Anne K. NASSAR
37 Financial Aid Consultant .... Mr. Fred P. ZUCALLA
12 Director Oneonta Campus .... Ms. Deborah E. HADDOW
07 Director of Admissions .... Mr. Tom VERDOW
13 Director Information Technology ... Mr. Joseph M. CHEVRETTE, II
36 Dir of Career Svc/Human Resources .... Ms. Emily TRACY
18 Facilities Manager Physical Plant .... Mr. Dave DUTCHER

U.T.A. Mesivta of Kiryas Joel (A)

PO Box 2009, Monroe NY 10949-8509
County: Orange FICE Identification: 038023
Unit ID: 446604
Telephone: (845) 783-9901 Carnegie Class: Spec-4-yr-Faith
FAX Number: (845) 782-3620 Calendar System: Semester
Established: 1999 Annual Undergrad Tuition & Fees: $9,800
Enrollment: 1,634 Male
Affiliation or Control: Independent Non-Profit IRS Status: 501(c)3
Highest Offering: First Talmudic Degree
Accreditation: RABN

00 Chief Executive Officer .... David GOLDBERGER
01 President .... Elias HOROWITZ
05 Rosh Yeshiva .... Rabbi Aharon TEITELBAUM
37 Financial Aid Director .... David SCHWARTZ

Utica College (B)

1600 Burrstone Road, Utica NY 13502-4892
County: Oneida FICE Identification: 002883
Unit ID: 197045
Telephone: (315) 792-3111 Carnegie Class: Masters/L
FAX Number: (315) 792-3292 Calendar System: Semester
URL: www.utica.edu
Established: 1946 Annual Undergrad Tuition & Fees: $34,466
Enrollment: 4,249 Coed
Affiliation or Control: Independent Non-Profit IRS Status: 501(c)3
Highest Offering: Doctorate
Accreditation: M, CONST, NURSE, OT, PTA, TEAC

01 President .... Dr. Laura CASAMENTO
05 Provost & Vice Pres Academic Aff .... Dr. John JOHNSEN
10 Vice Pres Financial Affs/Treasurer .... Ms. Pamela SALMON
32 Vice Pres Student Affairs .... Mr. Jeffrey GATES
04 Executive Assistant to President .... Ms. Kim D. LAMBERT
30 VP of Advancement .... Vacant
84 Vice President for Enrollment Mgmt .... Mr. Jeffrey GATES
20 Associate Provost .... Dr. Robert M. HALLIDAY
26 Asst VP Marketing/Communication .... Mr. Kelly L. ADAMS
76 Dean for Health Professions/Educ .... Dr. Harry SLIFE
49 Dean for Arts & Sciences .... Dr. Sharon H. WISE
50 Dean for Business & Justice Studies .... Mr. James NORRIE
53 Dean for Education .... Dr. Patrice HALLOCK
35 Dean of Students .... Ms. Alane P. VARGA
21 Director of Student Acct Operation .... Ms. Gail TUTTLE
29 Director Alumni & Parent Relations .... Mr. Mark C. KOVACS
36 Director Career Services .... Ms. Halina LOTYCZEWSKI
37 Exec Dir of Student Financial Svcs .... Ms. Laura BEDFORD
06 Registrar .... Mr. Craig DEWAN
44 Director of Development .... Mr. Athony VILLANTI
41 Director of Physical Educ/Athletics .... Mr. David FONTAINE
39 Director of Residence Life .... Mr. Scott NONEMAKER
13 Dir College Info & Application Svcs .... Mr. Scott HUMPHREY
15 Director of Human Resources .... Ms. Lisa GREEN
24 Dir Computer User Svcs .... Mr. Daniel SLOAN
31 Exec Dir Corp/Professional Pgms .... Ms. Joni L. PULLIAM
51 Director of Credit Programs .... Ms. Evelyn FAZEKAS
85 Dean of International Education .... Mr. Christopher JOHNSON
18 Director Facilities Management .... Mr. Donald L. HARTER
19 Director of Campus Safety .... Mr. Wayne SULLIVAN
92 Director Honors Program .... Dr. Lawrence DAY
28 Dir Office of Opportunity Programs .... Ms. Johnni F. MAHDI
96 Manager of Purchasing .... Ms. Bobbie H. SMOROL
09 Assoc VP IT & Inst Research .... Mr. Matthew S. CARR
101 Secretary of the Institution/Board .... Ms. Jacqueline LYNCH
108 Director Institutional Assessment .... Ms. Marie MIKNAVICH
38 Director Student Counseling .... Ms. Alison FRANKLIN
07 Asst VP UG Admissions .... Ms. Donna SHAFFNER
08 Head Librarian .... Mr. James K. TELIHA
106 Assoc Prov/VP E-learning .... Dr. Polly SMITH
43 Dir Legal Services/General Counsel ..... Mr. Andrew W. BEAKMAN

† Utica College maintains an academic tie with Syracuse University that allows undergraduates to receive a Syracuse University degree.

Vassar College (C)

124 Raymond Avenue, Poughkeepsie NY 12604-0001
County: Dutchess FICE Identification: 002895
Unit ID: 197133
Telephone: (845) 437-7000 Carnegie Class: Bac-A&S
FAX Number: (845) 437-7187 Calendar System: Semester
URL: www.vassar.edu
Established: 1861 Annual Undergrad Tuition & Fees: $51,250
Enrollment: 2,421 Coed
Affiliation or Control: Independent Non-Profit IRS Status: 501(c)3
Highest Offering: Master's
Accreditation: M, TEAC

01 Interim President .... Dr. Jonathan CHENETTE
05 Acting Dean of the Faculty .... Dr. Stephen ROCK
20 Dean of the College .... Dr. Christopher ROELLKE
10 Actg Vice Pres for Finance & Admin .... Mr. Stephen DAHNERT
30 VP Alumnae/i Affairs/Development .... Ms. Catherine E. BAER
26 Vice Pres for Communications .... Ms. Susan DEKREY
13 Chief Information Officer .... Mr. Michael CATO
32 Dean of Students .... Dr. Adriana DIBARTOLO
07 Dean Admission/Financial Aid .... Mr. Art D. RODRIGUEZ
49 Dean of Studies .... Dr. Benjamin LOTTO
20 Associate Dean College .... Mr. Edward L. PITTMAN
35 Assoc Dean Col/Dir Campus Activit .... Ms. Teresa QUINN
06 Registrar .... Ms. Colleen MALLET
08 Director of the Libraries .... Mr. Andrew ASHTON
37 Director of Financial Aid .... Ms. Jessica BERNIER
36 Director Career Development Center .... Ms. Stacy Lee SCHNEIDER BINGHAM
87 Director Conferences/Summer Pgms .... Ms. Katherine BUSH
39 Director Residential Life .... Mr. Luis INOA
09 Director of Institutional Research ..... Mr. David DAVIS-VAN ATTA
15 Director Human Resources .... Ms. Ruth SPENCER
18 Exec Dir of Facilities Operations .... Mr. William PEABODY
38 Director of Psychological Services .... Dr. Wendy A. FREEDMAN
96 Director of Purchasing .... Ms. Rosaleen CARDILLO
04 Administrative Asst to President .... Ms. Ilene COOKE
100 Chief of Staff .... Ms. Kathy KNAUSS
101 Secretary of the Institution/Board .... Dr. Christopher SMART
104 Director Study Abroad .... Dr. Tracey HOLLAND
108 Director Institutional Assessment ...... Dr. David DAVIS-VAN ATTA
19 Director Security/Safety .... Ms. Arlene SABO
29 Director Alumni Relations .... Ms. Lisa TESSLER
41 Athletic Director .... Ms. Michelle WALSH

Vaughn College of Aeronautics and Technology (D)

86-01 23rd Avenue, Flushing NY 11369
County: Queens FICE Identification: 002665
Unit ID: 188340
Telephone: (718) 429-6600 Carnegie Class: Bac/Assoc-Mixed
FAX Number: (718) 429-0256 Calendar System: Semester
URL: www.vaughn.edu
Established: 1932 Annual Undergrad Tuition & Fees: $22,680
Enrollment: 1,614 Coed
Affiliation or Control: Independent Non-Profit IRS Status: 501(c)3
Highest Offering: Master's
Accreditation: M, ENG, ENGT, IACBE

01 President .... Dr. Sharon B. DEVIVO
05 Sr Vice Pres Academic/Student Affs .... Vacant
10 Vice Pres for Business & Finance ...... Mr. Robert G. WALDMANN
84 Vice President Enrollment Services .... Mr. Ernie SHEPELSKY
11 Assoc VP College Services/Human Res .... Ms. Mary DURKIN
20 Vice Pres of Academic Affairs .... Dr. Paul LAVERGNE
32 VP Student Affairs & Svcs .... Mr. Said LAMHAOUAR
35 Assoc VP/Dean Student Affairs .... Vacant
88 VP Inst Rels/New Initiatives .... Vacant
37 Director of Financial Aid .... Vacant
06 Registrar/Assoc VP Enrollment .... Mrs. Beatriz CRUZ
08 Librarian .... Ms. Joann JAYNE
102 Asst VP of Planning/Assessments .... Ms. Calli KOUTSOUTIS
26 Director of Public Affairs .... Ms. Maureen KIGGINS
96 Coordinator of Purchasing .... Mr. Ernie MARSHALL
09 Asst Director of Inst Effectiveness .... Mr. Tipton RUSSELL
07 Acting Director of Admissions .... Mr. David SOOKDEO
18 Associate VP/College Services .... Mr. Michael DALY
38 Dir Student Counseling/Wellness .... Dr. Dinely HOLDER
13 Asst Director Computer Operations ..... Mr. Harnwant (Neil) SINGH
88 Vice Pres Training .... Mr. Domenic PROSCIA

Villa Maria College of Buffalo (E)

240 Pine Ridge Road, Buffalo NY 14225-3999
County: Erie FICE Identification: 002896
Unit ID: 197142
Telephone: (716) 896-0700 Carnegie Class: Bac/Assoc-Mixed
FAX Number: (716) 896-0705 Calendar System: Semester
URL: www.villa.edu
Established: 1960 Annual Undergrad Tuition & Fees: $20,260
Enrollment: 477 Coed
Affiliation or Control: Independent Non-Profit IRS Status: 501(c)3
Highest Offering: Baccalaureate
Accreditation: M, CIDA, MUS, PTAA

01 President .... Sr. Marcella Marie GARUS
05 Vice President for Academic Affairs .... Dr. Matthew GIORDANO
10 Vice President for Business Affairs .... Mr. Michael EADIE
30 Vice President for Development .... Mrs. Mary ROBINSON
32 VP for Enroll Mgmt & Student Svcs .... Mr. Brian EMERSON
06 Registrar .... Ms. Melany SHIELDS
07 Director of Admissions .... Mr. Kevin DONOVAN
08 Director of Library .... Ms. Lucy BUNGO
37 Director of Financial Aid .... Ms. Aimee MURCH
09 Director of Institutional Research .... Sr. Mary Albertine STACHOWSKI
38 Director Student Counseling .... Ms. Palma M. ZANGHI
13 Director of Computer Services ...... Ms. Christine E. PALCZEWSKI
88 Systems Analyst .... Ms. Francis MONTGOMERY
18 Plant & Grounds Manager .... Mr. David WISNER
23 Director of Health Services .... Mrs. Minerva MONTIJO
25 Director of Grants .... Vacant
88 Instructional Design & Program Dev .... Dr. Ryan HARTNETT
36 Director of Career Services .... Ms. Blythe KACZMARCZYK
42 Director of Campus Ministry .... Ms. Joan MULLIN
85 Director of Foreign Students .... Ms. Palma ZANGHI
26 Communications Specialist .... Ms. Kristen SCHOBER
35 Director of Student Life .... Mr. DJ SCHIER
88 Archivist .... Sr. Mary Mark JANIK
22 Affirmative Action Officer .... Ms. Diane M. HANDZLIK
29 Director of Alumni Relations .... Ms. Katheryn ROSS-WINNIE
88 Director Student Success Center .... Ms. Agnes ZAK-MOSKAL
57 Art Department Chair .... Mr. Robert GRIZANTI
64 Music Department Chair .... Dr. Sylvia GRMELA
49 LiberalArts/Prof Studies Chair .... Ms. Joyce KESSEL
108 Director Institutional Assessment .... Dr. Janice HERCHMER
04 Administrative Asst to President .... Mrs. Kathy IVES
103 Dir Workforce/Career Development .... Dr. Ryan HARTNETT
41 Athletic Director .... Mr. Don SILVERI

Wagner College (F)

1 Campus Road, Staten Island NY 10301-4479
County: Richmond FICE Identification: 002899
Unit ID: 197197
Telephone: (718) 390-3100 Carnegie Class: Masters/M
FAX Number: (718) 390-3467 Calendar System: Semester
URL: www.wagner.edu
Established: 1883 Annual Undergrad Tuition & Fees: $42,480
Enrollment: 2,231 Coed
Affiliation or Control: Independent Non-Profit IRS Status: 501(c)3
Highest Offering: Master's
Accreditation: M, ACBSP, ARCPA, NUR, TED

01 President .... Dr. Richard GUARASCI
05 Provost/SVP Academic Affairs .... Dr. Lily D. MCNAIR
84 Sr VP for Planning & Enrollment .... Mr. Angelo G. ARAIMO
30 VP Instititutional Advancement .... Vacant
11 VP Administration .... Mr. Joseph ROMANO
04 Assistant to the President .... Ms. Pat FITZPATRICK
88 VP Internationalization .... Ms. Ruta SHAH-GORDON
10 CFO and VP for Finance & Business .... Mr. John CARRESCIA
108 Assoc Provost for Assessment .... Dr. Anne LOVE
20 Vice Provost for Academic Affairs .... Dr. Jeffrey KRAUS
06 Registrar .... Dr. Anne LOVE
13 Chief Information Officer .... Mr. Frank CAFASSO
42 Chaplain .... Rev. Martin MALZAHN
29 Director Alumni Relations .... Mr. Christopher FOURMAN
39 Director Residential Educ .... Ms. Angelica CONCEPCION
30 Chief Development Officer .... Mr. Patrick MINSON
18 Director of Campus Operations .... Mr. Christian MILLER
41 Director of Athletics .... Mr. Walter HAMELINE
23 Assistant Dean Health & Wellness .... Ms. Kathleen OBERFELDT
19 Director of Public Safety .... Mr. Edwin MOSS
15 Director of Human Resources ..... Ms. Jazzmine CLARKE-GLOVER
37 Director of Financial Aid .... Ms. Theresa WEIMER
58 Dean of Graduate Studies .... Dr. Jeffrey KRAUS
07 Dean of Enrollment .... Mr. Robert HERR
88 Asst Dean of Enrollment .... Ms. Patricia CLANCY
32 Dean of Campus Life and Leadership .... Mr. Curtis WRIGHT
35 Dean of Campus Life and Engagement .... Dr. Sara KLEIN
36 Senior Assoc Dean & Director CACE .... Mr. Geoffrey HEMPILL
08 Head Librarian .... Ms. Dorothy DAVISON
100 Chief of Staff .... Vacant
101 Secretary to the Board of Trustees .... Mr. David MARTIN

Webb Institute (G)

298 Crescent Beach Road, Glen Cove NY 11542-1398
County: Nassau FICE Identification: 002900
Unit ID: 197221
Telephone: (516) 671-2213 Carnegie Class: Spec-4-yr-Eng
FAX Number: (516) 674-9838 Calendar System: Semester
URL: www.webb.edu
Established: 1889 Annual Undergrad Tuition & Fees: $46,000
Enrollment: 90 Coed
Affiliation or Control: Independent Non-Profit IRS Status: 501(c)3
Highest Offering: Baccalaureate
Accreditation: M, ENG

01 President .... Mr. R. Keith MICHEL
05 Dean .... Prof. Matthew R. WERNER
20 Assistant Dean .... Prof. Richard C. HARRIS
08 Librarian .... Ms. Patricia M. PRESCOTT
30 Chief Development .... Mr. Anthony ZIC
10 Director of Financial Affairs .... Ms. Rhonda LIGHTCAP
09 Director of Institutional Research .... Prof. Richard A. ROYCE
32 Director of Student Affairs .... Vacant
18 Director of Facilities .... Mr. John FERRANTE
84 Director of Enrollment Management .... Ms. Lauren CARBALLO
29 Director of Alumni Relations .... Ms. Gailmarie SUJECKI

26 Chief Public Relations Officer .... Ms. Kerri ALLEGRETTA
13 Director of Communications and IT .... Mr. Peter MILLER
06 Registrar .... Ms. Jocelyn M. WILSON
37 Director of Financial Aid .... Ms. Jocelyn M. WILSON
04 Administrative Asst to President .... Ms. Gailmarie SUJECKI
15 Director Personnel Services .... Ms. Svetlana MILLER
07 Asst Dir Student Svcs/Admissions .... Vacant

Weill Cornell Medical College (A)

1300 York Avenue, F-113, New York NY 10065-4805
Telephone: (212) 746-5900 FICE Identification: 004762
Accreditation: &M, ARCPA, DENT, IPSY, MED

† Regional accreditation is carried under the parent institution Cornell University, Ithaca, NY.

Wells College (B)

170 Main Street, Aurora NY 13026-0500
County: Cayuga FICE Identification: 002901
Unit ID: 197230
Telephone: (315) 364-3266 Carnegie Class: Bac-A&S
FAX Number: (315) 364-3227 Calendar System: Semester
URL: www.wells.edu
Established: 1868 Annual Undergrad Tuition & Fees: $37,500
Enrollment: 550 Coed
Affiliation or Control: Independent Non-Profit IRS Status: 501(c)3
Highest Offering: Baccalaureate
Accreditation: M, TEAC

01 President .... Dr. Jonathan GIBRALTER
05 Provost and Dean of the College .... Dr. Cindy SPEAKER
10 Chief Financial Officer .... Mr. Robert A. CREE
21 Treasurer and Controller .... Ms. Susan WEATHERBY
30 Vice President for Advancement .... Dr. Craig S. EVANS
32 Dean of Students .... Ms. Jennifer MICHAEL
07 Dir of Admissions/Financial Aid .... Ms. Susan SLOAN
06 Registrar .... Ms. Nicole PELLEGRINO
08 Library Director .... Ms. Carol HENDERSON
37 Director Financial Aid .... Ms. Laura BURNS
44 Director of Annual Giving .... Ms. Pamela SHERADIN
26 Dir of Communications/Marketing .... Ms. Ann ROLLO
29 Director Alumni Relations .... Ms. Pamela SHERADIN
19 Director of Security .... Mr. Dennis FAIRCHILD
18 Dir of Facilities/Physical Plant .... Mr. Brian BROWN
15 Manager of Human Resources .... Ms. Kit VAN ORMAN

Westchester Community College (C)

75 Grasslands Road, Valhalla NY 10595-1636
County: Westchester FICE Identification: 002881
Unit ID: 197294
Telephone: (914) 606-6600 Carnegie Class: Assoc/HT-Mix Trad/Non
FAX Number: (914) 606-6780 Calendar System: Semester
URL: www.sunywcc.edu
Established: 1946 Annual Undergrad Tuition & Fees (In-District): $4,723
Enrollment: 13,916 Coed
Affiliation or Control: State/Local IRS Status: 501(c)3
Highest Offering: Associate Degree
Accreditation: M, COARC, DIETT, RAD

01 President .... Dr. Belinda S. MILES
05 Acting VP Academic Affairs .... Dr. Peggy BRADFORD
32 Act VP Stdnt Access/Involve/ Success .... Ms. Sara THOMPSON-SWEEDY
10 Vice Pres Administrative Services .... Mr. Pat D'IMPERIO
102 VP Ext Affs/Exec Dir Found for WCC .... Mrs. Eve LARNER
51 VP & Dean Community/Adult/Cont Educ ...... Ms. Teresita WISELL
81 Assoc Dean Math/Phys Engr/Tech .... Dr. Kwesi AMOA
76 Assoc Dean Natural/Health Sciences .... Dr. Ronald BLOOM
83 Assoc Dean Bus/Behav/Soc Sci Svcs .... Dr. Carmen Leonor MARTINEZ-LOPEZ
79 Assoc Dean Arts/Humanities/Lrng Res .... Dr. Jessica SEESSEL
22 Associate Dean & Director of EOC .... Ms. Gina GAINES
35 Assoc Dean Student Personnel Svcs .... Ms. Ellen ZENDMAN
08 Asc Dn Lrng Res/Dist Lrng/Inst Tech .... Ms. Pamela POLLARD
26 Director of College/Cmty Relations .... Mr. Patrick HENNESSEY
06 Registrar .... Mr. John CAPOCCI
37 Dir of Student Financial Assistance .... Ms. Anita COOK
13 Vice President of IT .... Mr. Anthony SCORDINO
07 Director of Admissions .... Ms. Gloria LEON
38 Acting Director of Counseling .... Mr. Ruben BARATO
15 Director Human Resources .... Ms. Sabrina J. CHANDLER
88 Director Faculty Student Assoc .... Mr. David SKLAR
09 Director Inst Research & Planning .... Vacant
19 Director of Security .... Mr. Brian P. DOLANSKY
24 Director Media Services .... Mr. Gennaro MASELLI
41 Athletic Director .... Mr. Larry MASSARONI
21 Assoc Business Officer/Controller .... Ms. Dawn GILLIS
18 Director Physical Plant .... Mr. Robert CIRILLO
96 Deputy Purchasing Agent .... Mr. Richard CASHMAN
27 Publications Manager .... Mr. Craig FISCHER
23 Coordinator Student Health Services .... Ms. Janice GILROY
75 Coord of Transfer & Career Service ..... Dr. Gwen D. ROUNDTREE
04 Administrative Asst to President .... Ms. Yolanda M. HOWELL

Wood Tobé-Coburn School (D)

Eight E 40th Street, New York NY 10016
County: New York FICE Identification: 007405
Unit ID: 197522
Telephone: (212) 686-9040 Carnegie Class: Assoc/MT-VT-High Trad
FAX Number: (212) 686-9171 Calendar System: Semester
URL: www.woodtobecoburn.edu
Established: 1879 Annual Undergrad Tuition & Fees: $16,860
Enrollment: 411 Coed
Affiliation or Control: Proprietary IRS Status: Proprietary
Highest Offering: Associate Degree
Accreditation: NY, MAC

01 President .... Ms. Sandra GRUNINGER
05 Director of Education .... Mr. James INDELICATO
07 Director of Admissions .... Ms. Sandra ANDUJAR-WENDLAND
32 Student Services Director .... Ms. Celeste GRIFFITH
37 Financial Aid Administrator .... Ms. Celeste GRIFFITH
36 Placement Director .... Mr. Christopher MASSEY

Yeshiva Derech Chaim (E)

1573 39th Street, Brooklyn NY 11218-4413
County: Kings FICE Identification: 022651
Unit ID: 197647
Telephone: (718) 438-5476 Carnegie Class: Spec-4-yr-Faith
FAX Number: (718) 435-9285 Calendar System: Semester
Established: 1975 Annual Undergrad Tuition & Fees: $11,300
Enrollment: 151 Male
Affiliation or Control: Independent Non-Profit IRS Status: 501(c)3
Highest Offering: Second Talmudic Degree
Accreditation: RABN

01 President .... Rabbi Chaim RENNERT
01 President .... Rabbi Yisroel PLUTCHOK

Yeshiva D'Monsey Rabbinical College (F)

2 Roman Boulevard, Monsey NY 10952-3106
County: Rockland FICE Identification: 031473
Unit ID: 420325
Telephone: (845) 426-3276 Carnegie Class: Spec-4-yr-Faith
FAX Number: (845) 352-1119 Calendar System: Semester
Established: 1984 Annual Undergrad Tuition & Fees: $6,000
Enrollment: 60 Male
Affiliation or Control: Independent Non-Profit IRS Status: 501(c)3
Highest Offering: Second Talmudic Degree
Accreditation: RABN

01 Rosh Yeshiva .... Rabbi Moishe GREEN
05 Rosh Yeshiva .... Rabbi Ruvain GREEN
37 Financial Aid Director .... Rabbi Aron BERGER

Yeshiva of Far Rockaway (G)

802 Hicksville Road, Far Rockaway NY 11691-5219
County: Queens FICE Identification: 041196
Unit ID: 190752
Telephone: (718) 327-7600 Carnegie Class: Spec-4-yr-Faith
FAX Number: (718) 327-1430 Calendar System: Semester
Established: 1969 Annual Undergrad Tuition & Fees: $10,500
Enrollment: 38 Male
Affiliation or Control: Independent Non-Profit IRS Status: 501(c)3
Highest Offering: First Talmudic Degree
Accreditation: RABN

01 President .... Rabbi Yechiel I. PERR
03 Executive Director .... Rabbi Shayeh KOHN
32 Dean of Students .... Rabbi Dovid KLEINKAUFMAN
06 Registrar .... Mrs. Tamara MASLOW

Yeshiva Gedolah Imrei Yosef D'Spinka (H)

1466 56th Street, Brooklyn NY 11219-4696
County: Kings FICE Identification: 030001
Unit ID: 375230
Telephone: (718) 851-8721 Carnegie Class: Spec-4-yr-Faith
FAX Number: (718) 686-8849 Calendar System: Semester
Established: 1987 Annual Undergrad Tuition & Fees: $8,000
Enrollment: 122 Male
Affiliation or Control: Independent Non-Profit IRS Status: 501(c)3
Highest Offering: First Talmudic Degree
Accreditation: @RABN

01 President .... Joseph SOLOMON

Yeshiva Gedolah Kesser Torah (I)

28 Cedar Lane, Monsey NY 10952
County: Rockland Identification: 667112
Unit ID: 481410
Telephone: (845) 406-4308 Carnegie Class: Spec-4-yr-Faith
FAX Number: (845) 406-4199 Calendar System: Semester
Established: 2004 Annual Undergrad Tuition & Fees: $10,200
Enrollment: 67 Male
Affiliation or Control: Independent Non-Profit IRS Status: 501(c)3
Highest Offering: First Talmudic Degree
Accreditation: RABN

00 CEO .... Rabbi David FISHMAN
01 President .... David BERNSTEIN

Yeshiva Gedolah Ohr Yisrael (J)

2899 Nostrand Avenue, Brooklyn NY 11229
County: Kings Identification: 667077
Telephone: (718) 382-8702 Carnegie Class: Not Classified
FAX Number: (718) 382-8703 Calendar System: Semester
Established: 1999 Annual Undergrad Tuition & Fees: N/A
Enrollment: N/A Male
Affiliation or Control: Independent Non-Profit IRS Status: 501(c)3
Highest Offering: First Talmudic Degree
Accreditation: RABN

01 Rosh Yeshiva .... Avraham ZUCKER
10 Treasurer .... Avi KAHN

Yeshiva Karlin Stolin Beth Aaron V'Israel Rabbinical Institute (K)

1818 54th Street, Brooklyn NY 11204-1545
County: Kings FICE Identification: 025058
Unit ID: 197601
Telephone: (718) 232-7800 Carnegie Class: Spec-4-yr-Faith
FAX Number: (718) 331-4833 Calendar System: Semester
Established: 1948 Annual Undergrad Tuition & Fees: $9,650
Enrollment: 113 Male
Affiliation or Control: Independent Non-Profit IRS Status: 501(c)3
Highest Offering: Second Talmudic Degree
Accreditation: RABN

01 Chief Executive Officer .... Rabbi Yochanan PILCHICK
05 Dean Theology/Chief Acad Officer .... Rabbi Chaim WOLPIN
06 Registrar .... Rabbi Aryeh WOLPIN
08 Librarian .... Rabbi Yochanan GOLDHABER
10 Fiscal Officer .... Rabbi Irving PERRES
37 Financial Aid Director .... Rabbi David STEIN
33 Dean of Men .... Rabbi Gedelyah MACHLIS

Yeshiva and Kolel Bais Medrash Elyon (L)

73 Main Street, Monsey NY 10952-3013
County: Rockland Identification: 666707
Unit ID: 245777
Telephone: (845) 371-2481 Carnegie Class: Spec-4-yr-Faith
FAX Number: (845) 356-7065 Calendar System: Semester
Established: 1945 Annual Undergrad Tuition & Fees: N/A
Enrollment: 97 Male
Affiliation or Control: Independent Non-Profit IRS Status: 501(c)3
Highest Offering: Second Talmudic Degree
Accreditation: @RABN

01 President .... Rabbi Yerachmiel CENSOR
05 Dean .... Rabbi Israel FALK

Yeshiva and Kollel Harbotzas Torah (M)

1049 E 15th Street, Brooklyn NY 11230-4462
County: Kings FICE Identification: 023506
Unit ID: 245731
Telephone: (718) 692-0208 Carnegie Class: Spec-4-yr-Faith
FAX Number: (718) 692-0363 Calendar System: Semester
Established: 1969 Annual Undergrad Tuition & Fees: N/A
Enrollment: 52 Male
Affiliation or Control: Independent Non-Profit IRS Status: 501(c)3
Highest Offering: Second Talmudic Degree
Accreditation: @RABN

01 President .... Rabbi Y. BITTERSFELD

Yeshiva of Machzikai Hadas (N)

1301 47th Street, Brooklyn NY 11219
County: Kings FICE Identification: 041381
Unit ID: 455257
Telephone: (718) 853-2442 Carnegie Class: Spec-4-yr-Faith
FAX Number: (718) 853-2504 Calendar System: Semester
Established: 2001 Annual Undergrad Tuition & Fees: $8,000
Enrollment: 373 Male
Affiliation or Control: Independent Non-Profit IRS Status: 501(c)3
Highest Offering: First Talmudic Degree
Accreditation: RABN

01 Rosh Yeshiva .... Rabbi Yidel MONHEIT

Yeshiva Mikdash Melech (O)

1326 Ocean Parkway, Brooklyn NY 11230-5655
County: Kings FICE Identification: 025068
Unit ID: 197610
Telephone: (718) 339-1090 Carnegie Class: Spec-4-yr-Faith
FAX Number: (718) 998-9321 Calendar System: Semester
Established: 1972 Annual Undergrad Tuition & Fees: $8,100
Enrollment: 140 Male
Affiliation or Control: Independent Non-Profit IRS Status: 501(c)3
Highest Offering: Second Talmudic Degree
Accreditation: RABN

01 Dean .... Rabbi Haim BENOLIEL

05 Dean of Faculty .... Rabbi David LOPIAN
06 Registrar .... Rabbi Josh SANANES
10 Chief Business Officer .... Rabbi Amram SANANES
11 Administrator .... Rabbi Abraham BENOLIEL

Yeshiva of Nitra Rabbinical College (A)

194 Division Avenue, Brooklyn NY 11211-7199
County: Kings FICE Identification: 011670
Unit ID: 197674
Telephone: (718) 387-0422 Carnegie Class: Spec-4-yr-Faith
FAX Number: (718) 387-9400 Calendar System: Semester
Established: 1946 Annual Undergrad Tuition & Fees: $8,200
Enrollment: 267 Male
Affiliation or Control: Independent Non-Profit IRS Status: 501(c)3
Highest Offering: Second Talmudic Degree
Accreditation: **RABN**

01 President .... Mr. Alfred SCHOENBERGER
03 Vice President .... Mr. Mendel KLEIN
05 Dean .... Rabbi Samuel D. UNGAR
11 Administrative Officer .... Mr. Ernest SCHWARTZ

Yeshiva Ohr Naftoli (B)

701 Blooming Grove Turnpike, New Windsor NY 12553
County: Orange Identification: 667284
Telephone: (845) 784-4020 Carnegie Class: Not Classified
FAX Number: N/A Calendar System: Other
Established: Annual Undergrad Tuition & Fees: N/A
Enrollment: N/A Male
Affiliation or Control: Independent Non-Profit IRS Status: 501(c)3
Highest Offering: First Talmudic Degree
Accreditation: **AIJS**

Yeshiva Shaar HaTorah-Grodno (C)

83-96 117th Street, Kew Gardens NY 11415
County: Queens FICE Identification: 021520
Unit ID: 197692
Telephone: (718) 846-1940 Carnegie Class: Spec-4-yr-Faith
FAX Number: (718) 850-7916 Calendar System: Semester
Established: 1976 Annual Undergrad Tuition & Fees: $14,960
Enrollment: 76 Male
Affiliation or Control: Independent Non-Profit IRS Status: 501(c)3
Highest Offering: Second Talmudic Degree
Accreditation: **RABN**

01 Administrator .... Rabbi Yoel YANKELEWITZ

Yeshiva Shaarei Torah of Rockland (D)

91 W Carlton Road, Suffern NY 10901-4013
County: Rockland FICE Identification: 034963
Unit ID: 441609
Telephone: (845) 352-3431 Carnegie Class: Spec-4-yr-Faith
FAX Number: (845) 352-3433 Calendar System: Semester
Established: 1977 Annual Undergrad Tuition & Fees: $11,600
Enrollment: 98 Male
Affiliation or Control: Independent Non-Profit IRS Status: 501(c)3
Highest Offering: First Talmudic Degree
Accreditation: **RABN**

01 President .... Rabbi Eli ABRAHAM
37 Financial Aid Administrator .... Mrs. Teri SCHILLER
06 Registrar .... Mrs. Rachel CELNIK

Yeshiva Sholom Shachna (E)

401 Elmwood Avenue, Brooklyn NY 11230
County: Kings Identification: 667147
Telephone: (718) 252-6333 Carnegie Class: Not Classified
FAX Number: (718) 338-2536 Calendar System: Semester
Established: 2005 Annual Undergrad Tuition & Fees: N/A
Enrollment: N/A Male
Affiliation or Control: Independent Non-Profit IRS Status: 501(c)3
Highest Offering: First Talmudic Degree
Accreditation: **@RABN**

01 Chief Executive Officer .... Rabbi Meir Chaim GUTFREUND
10 Chief Financial/Business Officer .... Mrs. Dina GUTFREUND
05 Chief Academic Officer/Registrar .... Rabbi Simcha OLEN
37 Director Student Financial Aid .... Mrs. Malka Bracha KRUPNIK

Yeshiva of the Telshe Alumni (F)

4904 Independence Avenue, Riverdale NY 10471
County: Bronx FICE Identification: 025463
Unit ID: 431983
Telephone: (718) 601-3523 Carnegie Class: Spec-4-yr-Faith
FAX Number: (718) 601-2141 Calendar System: Semester
Established: 1981 Annual Undergrad Tuition & Fees: $9,100
Enrollment: 116 Male
Affiliation or Control: Independent Non-Profit IRS Status: 501(c)3
Highest Offering: First Talmudic Degree
Accreditation: **RABN**

01 President .... Rabbi Avrohom AUSBAND
03 Executive Director .... Rabbi Noson JOSEPH
29 Director Alumni Relations .... Rabbi Moshe FERBER

Yeshiva University (G)

500 W 185th Street, New York NY 10033-3201
County: New York FICE Identification: 002903
Unit ID: 197708
Telephone: (212) 960-5400 Carnegie Class: DU-Higher
FAX Number: (212) 960-0055 Calendar System: Semester
URL: www.yu.edu
Established: 1886 Annual Undergrad Tuition & Fees: $39,530
Enrollment: 6,348 Coordinate
Affiliation or Control: Independent Non-Profit IRS Status: 501(c)3
Highest Offering: Doctorate
Accreditation: **M, BUS, CLPSY, DENT, IPSY, LAW, MED, PSPSY, @SP, SW, TEAC**

01 President .... Mr. Richard M. JOEL
05 Provost/Sr VP Academic Affairs .... Dr. Selma BOTMAN
100 Sr Vice Pres/Chief of Staff .... Mr. Josh JOSEPH
17 Vice President Medical Affairs .... Dr. Allen M. SPIEGEL
10 Vice Pres/Chief Financial Officer .... Mr. Jacob HARMAN
30 Vice Pres Institutional Advancement .... Mr. Seth MOSKOWITZ
11 Vice President University Affairs .... Dr. Herbert C. DOBRINSKY
13 VP Information Technology/CIO .... Vacant
43 VP Legal Afts/Secretary/Gen Counsel .... Mr. Andrew J. LAUER
32 Vice Pres Univ & Cmty Life .... Rabbi Kenneth BRANDER
26 Exec Dir Communications/Public Affs .... Dr. Paul OESTREICHER
18 Vice Pres Administrative Services .... Mr. Jeffrey ROSENGARTEN
04 Exec Assistant to President .... Ms. Linda DOS SANTOS
08 Dean of University Libraries .... Mrs. Pearl BERGER
35 Dean of Students .... Mr. David HIMBER
49 Dean Yeshiva College .... Dr. Barry EICHLER
49 Dn Undergrad Jewish Stds/Mazer Sch .... Rabbi Yona REISS
49 Dean Stern College for Women .... Dr. Karen BACON
50 Dean Sy Syms School of Business .... Dr. Moses PAVA
63 Dean Albert Einstein Col Medicine .... Dr. Allen M. SPIEGEL
58 Dean Ferkauf Graduate School Psych .... Dr. Lawrence J. SIEGEL
58 Dean Bernard Revel Graduate School .... Dr. David BERGER
58 Dean Azrieli Grad Sch Jewish Educ .... Dr. David J. SCHNALL
70 Dean Wurzweiler School Social Work .... Dr. Carmen ORTIZ HENDRICKS
58 Director Sue Golding Grad Program .... Dr. Victoria FREEDMAN
84 Director Enrollment Management .... Ms. Diana BENMERGUI
37 Director of Student Finances .... Mr. Robert FRIEDMAN
07 Director Undergraduate Admissions .... Mr. Michael KRANZLER
29 Director University Alumni Affairs .... Ms. Barbara BIRCH
06 University Registrar .... Ms. Diana CHADI
09 Director of Institutional Research .... Dr. Ariel FISHMAN
96 Director of Purchasing .... Mr. Jack ZENCHECK
15 Chief Human Resources Officer .... Ms. Yvonne RAMIREZ
38 Director Student Counseling .... Dr. Chaim NISSEL

Yeshiva Zichron Aryeh (H)

1213 Bay 25th Street, Far Rockaway NY 11691
County: Queens Identification: 667110
Telephone: (347) 619-9074 Carnegie Class: Not Classified
FAX Number: (516) 295-5737 Calendar System: Semester
Established: 1992 Annual Undergrad Tuition & Fees: N/A
Enrollment: N/A Male
Affiliation or Control: Independent Non-Profit IRS Status: 501(c)3
Highest Offering: Second Talmudic Degree
Accreditation: **RABN**

03 Executive Vice President .... Rabbi Shaya COHEN
06 Registrar .... Rabbi Yosef AMSTER
07 Director of Admissions .... Rabbi Yehuda COHEN
10 Controller/Financial Aid Admin .... Mr. Yaakov JAFFE
18 Chief Facilities .... Mr. Danny SCHUSTER

Yeshivas Maharit Dsatmar (I)

475 County Rt. 105, Monroe NY 10950
County: Orange Identification: 667204
Telephone: (845) 782-1380 Carnegie Class: Not Classified
FAX Number: (845) 782-5169 Calendar System: Semester
Established: 2011 Annual Undergrad Tuition & Fees: N/A
Enrollment: N/A Male
Affiliation or Control: Independent Non-Profit IRS Status: 501(c)3
Highest Offering: First Talmudic Degree
Accreditation: **RABN**

01 CEO .... Abraham LIEBERMAN
06 Registrar .... Yitzchok TYRNAUER
37 Director of Financial Aid .... Joel BRAVER
10 Associate Business Officer .... Moses JACOBOWITZ

Yeshivas Novominsk (J)

1690 60th Street, Brooklyn NY 11204-2138
County: Kings FICE Identification: 031271
Unit ID: 405058
Telephone: (718) 438-2727 Carnegie Class: Spec-4-yr-Faith
FAX Number: (718) 438-2472 Calendar System: Semester
Established: 1988 Annual Undergrad Tuition & Fees: $9,700
Enrollment: 129 Male
Affiliation or Control: Independent Non-Profit IRS Status: 501(c)3
Highest Offering: First Talmudic Degree
Accreditation: **RABN**

01 Executive Director .... Rabbi Lipa BRENNAN
32 Dean of Students .... Rabbi Yaakov PERLOW
11 Administrator .... Rabbi Boruch TWERSKI

Yeshivath Viznitz (K)

PO Box 446, Monsey NY 10952-0446
County: Rockland FICE Identification: 013027
Unit ID: 197735
Telephone: (845) 731-3700 Carnegie Class: Spec-4-yr-Faith
FAX Number: (845) 356-7359 Calendar System: Semester
Established: 1946 Annual Undergrad Tuition & Fees: $8,600
Enrollment: 631 Male
Affiliation or Control: Independent Non-Profit IRS Status: 501(c)3
Highest Offering: Second Talmudic Degree
Accreditation: **RABN**

01 President .... Gershon NEIMAN
10 Chief Fiscal Officer .... Rabbi J. LURIA

Yeshivath Zichron Moshe (L)

PO Box 580, South Fallsburg NY 12779-0580
County: Sullivan FICE Identification: 011821
Unit ID: 197744
Telephone: (845) 434-5240 Carnegie Class: Spec-4-yr-Faith
FAX Number: (845) 434-1009 Calendar System: Semester
Established: 1969 Annual Undergrad Tuition & Fees: $11,600
Enrollment: 194 Male
Affiliation or Control: Independent Non-Profit IRS Status: 501(c)3
Highest Offering: Second Talmudic Degree
Accreditation: **RABN**

01 President .... Rabbi Ephraim Y. SHER
37 Director Student Financial Aid .... Rabbi Dov PERECMAN
06 Registrar .... Mrs. Miryom R. MILLER

NORTH CAROLINA

Apex School of Theology (M)

1701 T. W. Alexander Drive, Durham NC 27703-8024
County: Durham FICE Identification: 035134
Unit ID: 441511
Telephone: (919) 572-1625 Carnegie Class: Spec-4-yr-Faith
FAX Number: (919) 572-1762 Calendar System: Other
URL: www.apexsot.edu
Established: 1995 Annual Undergrad Tuition & Fees: $5,000
Enrollment: 770 Coed
Affiliation or Control: Independent Non-Profit IRS Status: 501(c)3
Highest Offering: Doctorate
Accreditation: **TRACS**

01 President .... Dr. Joseph E. PERKINS
03 Executive Vice President .... Dr. Herbert R. DAVIS
05 Academic Dean/Graduate Dean .... Dr. Lafayette MAXWELL
06 Registrar .... Mr. Joseph A. PERKINS
08 Head Librarian .... Ms. Cynthia RUFFIN
10 Director of Finance .... Mrs. Carolyn PEEBLES
20 Undergraduate Dean .... Dr. Gladys LONG
88 Dean Master of Arts Christian Couns .... Dr. Tonya ARMSTRONG
73 Dean Doctor of Ministry .... Dr. Lafayette MAXWELL
32 Director Student Affairs .... Rev. George T. DANIELS
09 Dir of Institutional Effectiveness .... Dr. Henry D. WELLS, JR.
04 Executive Admin Asst to President .... Ms. Rolanda J. HOLLAND
07 Admissions Coordinator .... Ms. Sandra J. MANNING
13 Dir of Educational Technology .... Dr. Clarence BURKE
18 Chief Facilities/Physical Plant .... Mr. Anthony PATTERSON
26 Director of Recruiting .... Rev. M. Andrew DAVIS
37 Director Student Financial Aid .... Ms. Floya COTTEN-BROWN

The Art Institute of Charlotte (N)

2110 Water Ridge Parkway, Charlotte NC 28217-4536
Telephone: (704) 357-8020 FICE Identification: 021105
Accreditation: **&SC, ACFEI**

† Regional accreditation is carried under the parent institution in Savannah GA.

The Art Institute of Raleigh-Durham (O)

410 Blackwell Street, Suite 200, Durham NC 27701
Telephone: (919) 317-3050 Identification: 770843
Accreditation: **&SC, ACFEI**

† Regional accreditation is carried under the parent institution in Savannah GA

Barton College (P)

704-A College Street, PO Box 5000, Wilson NC 27893
County: Wilson FICE Identification: 002908
Unit ID: 197911
Telephone: (252) 399-6300 Carnegie Class: Bac-Diverse
FAX Number: (252) 399-6374 Calendar System: Semester
URL: www.barton.edu
Established: 1902 Annual Undergrad Tuition & Fees: $27,941
Enrollment: 1,035 Coed
Affiliation or Control: Christian Church (Disciples Of Christ)
IRS Status: 501(c)3
Highest Offering: Master's

Accreditation: SC, NURSE, SW, TED

01 President ... Dr. Douglas N. SEARCY
05 Vice President Academic Affairs ... Dr. Gary DAYNES
10 Vice Pres Finance & Aministration ... Mr. David A. BROWNING
30 Vice President Inst Advancement ... Ms. Jan Y. MERIWETHER
32 Vice President Student Life ... Mr. George SOLAN
100 Senior Advisor to President ... Mrs. Carolyn L. HARMON
20 Associate Provost ... Dr. Jill FEGLEY
07 Asst VP of Admissions ... Ms. Amanda METTS
30 Asst VP for Development ... Mr. Tom MAZE
50 Dean School of Business ... Mr. Ron EGGERS
66 Dean School of Nursing ... Dr. Sharon SARVEY
53 Dean School of Education ... Dr. Jackie ENNIS
79 Dean School of Humanities ... Dr. James CLARK
81 Dean School of Sciences ... Dr. Kevin PENNINGTON
76 Dean Allied Health & Sport Studies ... Dr. Claudia DUNCAN
88 Dean School of Social Work ... Dr. Barbara CONKLIN
57 Dean Visual/Performing & Comm Arts ... Ms. Susan FECHO
41 Athletic Director ... Mr. Todd WILKINSON
09 VP Institutional Effectiveness ... Dr. Jill FEGLEY
106 Dir Online Education/E-learning ... Ms. Lorraine RAPER
38 Asst Dean of Student Success ... Ms. Angie WALSTON
06 Registrar ... Ms. Sheila MILNE
21 Controller ... Mr. Larry GRIFFIN
37 Director Student Financial Aid ... Ms. Bridget ELLIS
26 Director of Public Relations ... Mrs. Kathy DAUGHETY
08 Director of the Library ... Mr. George LOVELAND
15 Director Human Resources ... Mrs. Linda TYSON
23 Director of Health Services ... Mrs. Amy BRIDGERS
29 Director of Alumni Affairs ... Ms. Summer BROCK
14 Director Technology ... Vacant
13 Director of Information Resources ... Mrs. Susan WEEKLEY
35 Dean of Students ... Mr. Jared TICE
28 Director of Diversity and Inclusion ... Ms. Holly ZACHARIAS
18 Director of Physical Plant ... Mr. Sean WOODARD
42 Chaplain ... Rev. Jamie EUBANKS
40 Bookstore Manager ... Ms. Candice MOORE
04 Executive Asst to President ... Mrs. Sheila WILSON
39 Director of Housing/Res Life ... Mr. Joseph DLUGOS
43 Legal Counsel ... Mrs. Shannon RUSSELL
88 Director of Publications ... Mr. Keith TEW
105 Director Web Services ... Mr. Ken DOZIER
44 Director Annual Giving ... Mr. Brent GODWIN
91 Director Administrative Computing ... Ms. Linda MERCER

Belmont Abbey College (A)

100 Belmont Mount Holly Road, Belmont NC 28012-1802
County: Gaston FICE Identification: 002910
Unit ID: 197984
Telephone: (704) 461-6701 Carnegie Class: Bac-Diverse
FAX Number: (704) 461-6670 Calendar System: Semester
URL: belmontabbeycollege.edu/
Established: 1876 Annual Undergrad Tuition & Fees: $18,500
Enrollment: 1,560 Coed
Affiliation or Control: Roman Catholic IRS Status: 501(c)3
Highest Offering: Baccalaureate
Accreditation: SC

01 President ... Dr. William K. THIERFELDER
10 Chief Financial Officer ... Mr. Allan MARK
05 VP for Academic Affairs ... Dr. David WILLIAMS
26 VP College Relations ... Mr. Gregory SWANSON
20 Assoc Dean for Academic Affairs ... Dr. Stephen SHIVONE
30 Director of Development ... Vacant
29 Alumni & Community Relations Dir ... Ms. Chris Goff PEELER
08 Director of the Library ... Mr. Donald BEAGLE
06 Registrar ... Ms. Margot RHOADES
09 Director of Institutional Research ... Ms. Sharell CANNADY
36 Director Career Counseling/Placemnt ... Ms. Stephannie MILES
27 Director Marketing ... Mr. Rolando RIVAS
37 Director of Financial Aid ... Mrs. Anne A. STEVENS
38 Wellness Center Counselor ... Mrs. Melanie ECKSTEIN
41 Athletic Director ... Mr. Stephen MISS
21 Staff Accountant ... Ms. Patti PIZZANO
19 Chief of Campus Police ... Mr. Makiem MILLER
42 Director of Campus Ministry ... Mr. Patrick FORD
15 Director of Human Resources ... Ms. Cheryl TROTTER
18 Chief Facilities/Physical Plant ... Mr. J. R. MARR
07 Executive Director of Admissions ... Ms. Nicole FOCARETO
13 Chief Info Technology Officer (CIO) ... Ms. Nancy OLIVER
32 Dean of Student Life ... Mr. Tom MACALESTER
04 Sr Executive Assistant ... Ms. Ashley MCCALLISTER

Bennett College (B)

900 E Washington Street, Greensboro NC 27401-3239
County: Guilford FICE Identification: 002911
Unit ID: 197993
Telephone: (336) 273-4431 Carnegie Class: Bac-Diverse
FAX Number: (336) 370-8688 Calendar System: Semester
URL: www.bennett.edu
Established: 1873 Annual Undergrad Tuition & Fees: $18,150
Enrollment: 633 Female
Affiliation or Control: United Methodist IRS Status: 501(c)3
Highest Offering: Baccalaureate
Accreditation: SC, SW, TED

01 President ... Dr. Rosalind FUSE-HALL
05 Provost/Academic VP ... Dr. Phyllis DAWKINS
100 Chief of Staff ... Dr. Rolanda BURNEY
10 Interim VP Admin & Finance ... Mr. Jeffrey CAUSEY
30 Vice Pres Inst Advancement ... Ms. Evelyn LEATHERS
26 Dir Public Relations & Publication ... Ms. Sharon SAUNDERS
09 Dir Institutional Rsrch & Testing ... Ms. Karen JAMES
20 Assoc Provost of Academic Affairs ... Vacant
06 Registrar ... Ms. Gisele ABRON
08 Director of Holgate Library ... Ms. Joan WILLIAMS
07 Director of Admissions ... Ms. Jocelyn BIGGS
37 Director of Financial Aid ... Mr. Shawn GUY
29 Director Alumnae Affairs ... Ms. Audrey FRANKLIN
36 Director Career Services ... Mr. Darryl JOHNSON
38 Dir Coun Svcs/Supervisor Health Svc ... Ms. Robin CAMPBELL
23 Director of Health Services ... Vacant
15 Director of Human Resources ... Ms. Linda DIAMOND
42 Chaplain/Director Campus Ministry ... Rev Dr. Natalie MCLEAN
88 Chair Curriculum & Instruction ... Dr. Henry JOHNSON
79 Int Chair Humanities ... Ms. Keri PETERSEN
81 Chair Natural & Behavioral Sciences ... Dr. Michael COTTON

Brevard College (C)

One Brevard College Drive, Brevard NC 28712-3306
County: Transylvania FICE Identification: 002912
Unit ID: 198066
Telephone: (828) 883-8292 Carnegie Class: Bac-Diverse
FAX Number: (828) 884-3790 Calendar System: Semester
URL: www.brevard.edu
Established: 1853 Annual Undergrad Tuition & Fees: $26,980
Enrollment: 705 Coed
Affiliation or Control: United Methodist IRS Status: 501(c)3
Highest Offering: Baccalaureate
Accreditation: SC, MUS

01 President ... Dr. David C. JOYCE
05 VP Academic Affairs/Dean of Faculty ... Dr. Roy S. SHEFFIELD
10 Vice President for Business/Finance ... Ms. Deborah P. HALL
30 Vice Pres Institutional Advancement ... Ms. Kathryn HOLTEN
07 Vice Pres Admissions/Financial Aid ... Mr. Ryan C. HOLT
04 Assistant to the President ... Mrs. Mary WALDROFF
32 Dean of Students ... Mrs. Debora D'ANNA
13 Int Dir of Information Technology ... Mr. Jay TRUSSELL
06 Registrar ... Mrs. Amy HERTZ
37 Director of Financial Aid ... Mrs. Caron SURRETT
08 Director of Library ... Dr. Marie JONES
29 Director of Alumni Affairs ... Vacant
19 Dir of Safety/Security/Risk Mgmt ... Mr. Stan JACOBSEN
41 Director of Athletics ... Mr. Juan MASCARO
18 Director of Facilities/Grounds ... Mr. Burke ULREY
24 Director Academic Enrichment Ctr ... Ms. Shirley E. ARNOLD
36 Director of Career Exploration/Dev ... Ms. Nacole POTTS
92 Director of Honors Program ... Dr. Robert J. CABIN
21 Controller ... Mr. Thomas Ove ANDERSEN
38 Assoc Dean/Dir of Counseling ... Ms. Deanne DASBURG
57 Chair Division of Fine Arts ... Dr. Laura P. MCDOWELL
79 Chair Division of Humanities ... Dr. Tom J. BELL
83 Chair Div of Social Sciences ... Dr. Barbara B. BOERNER
81 Chair Div Env Stds/Math/Nat Science ... Dr. Jennifer E. FRICK-RUPPERT
88 Chair Division of WLEE ... Dr. Jennifer L. KAFSKY
09 Director of Institutional Research ... Ms. Sherry DOWNING

Brightwood College (D)

6070 East Independence Boulevard, Charlotte NC 28212
Telephone: (704) 567-3700 Identification: 770543
Accreditation: ACICS

† Branch campus of Brightwood College, Nashville, TN

Cabarrus College of Health Sciences (E)

401 Medical Park Drive, Concord NC 28025-3959
County: Cabarrus FICE Identification: 006477
Unit ID: 198109
Telephone: (704) 403-1555 Carnegie Class: Spec-4-yr-Other Health
FAX Number: (704) 403-1764 Calendar System: Semester
URL: www.cabarruscollege.edu
Established: 1942 Annual Undergrad Tuition & Fees: $11,976
Enrollment: 448 Coed
Affiliation or Control: Independent Non-Profit IRS Status: 501(c)3
Highest Offering: Master's
Accreditation: SC, ADNUR, MAC, NURSE, OT, OTA, SURGT

01 President ... Dr. Dianne O. SNYDER
05 Provost ... Dr. Margaret B. PATCHETT
32 Dean of Student Aff/Enrollment Mgt ... Ms. Christine L. CORSELLO
10 Chief Financial Officer ... Mrs. Kim BRADSHAW
66 ADN Program Chair ... Mrs. Kim PLEMMONS
66 BSN Program Chair ... Dr. Colleen BURGESS
88 OT Assistant Program Chair ... Ms. Nancy GREEN
88 Master OT Program Chair ... Dr. Carol FAIN
88 Medical Assisting Program Chair ... Ms. Rachel HOUSTON
88 Surgical Technology Program Chair ... Mrs. Michelle GAY
88 Medical Imagining Program Chair ... Mrs. Rhonda WEAVER
88 Associate in Science Program Chair ... Mrs. Zinat HASSANPOUR
88 Pharmacy Technology Program Chair ... Mrs. Annette SIMMONS
88 General Education Program Chair ... Mrs. Stacey WILSON
88 Coord Campus & Community Outreach ... Mrs. Cara LURSEN
26 Coord of Marketing & Graduate Educ ... Mrs. Melanie GASS
37 Director of Financial Aid ... Mrs. Valerie RICHARD
06 Dir Student Records & Info Mgmt ... Mr. Todd DEESE
07 Director of Recruitment & Retention ... Mrs. Lorri B. CONNOR
04 Administrative Asst to President ... Mrs. Donna HARLESS
08 Head Librarian ... Ms. Emily PATRIDGE

Campbell University (F)

PO Box 97, Buies Creek NC 27506-0097
County: Harnett FICE Identification: 002913
Unit ID: 198136
Telephone: (910) 893-1200 Carnegie Class: Masters/L
FAX Number: (910) 893-1424 Calendar System: Semester
URL: www.campbell.edu
Established: 1887 Annual Undergrad Tuition & Fees: $28,820
Enrollment: 6,101 Coed
Affiliation or Control: Baptist IRS Status: 501(c)3
Highest Offering: Doctorate
Accreditation: SC, ACBSP, ARCPA, CAATE, LAW, @OSTEO, PHAR, @PTA, SW, THEOL

00 Chancellor ... Dr. Jerry WALLACE
01 President ... Dr. J. Bradley CREED
05 Vice Pres Academic Affs & Provost ... Dr. Mark HAMMOND
10 Vice President Business/Treasurer ... Mr. Jim O. ROBERTS
30 Vice President for Advancement ... Mr. Britt DAVIS
32 Vice President for Student Life ... Dr. Dennis BAZEMORE
84 Vice Pres Enrollment Management ... Vacant
07 Asst Vice Pres of Admissions ... Mr. Jason HALL
49 Dean of College of Arts & Science ... Dr. Michael WELLS
61 Dean of the Law School ... Mr. J. Rich LEONARD
50 Dean Lundy-Fetterman Sch Business ... Mr. Kevin O'MARA
53 Dean School of Education ... Dr. Karen NERY
67 Acting VP of Health Sciences & Dean ... Dr. Michael ADAMS
63 Dean of Osteopathic Medical School ... Dr. John M. KAUFFMAN, JR.
35 Dean of Students ... Vacant
06 Registrar ... Mr. David MCGIRT
21 Assistant VP for Business ... Mr. Al HARDISON
29 Director of Alumni Relations ... Ms. Sarah SWAIN
89 Director of Freshman Experience ... Dr. Jennifer A. LATINO
08 Dean of Library ... Mrs. Borree KWOK
37 Director of Financial Aid ... Ms. Mary KOSIN
13 Director of Computing Services ... Mr. Chris BUCKLEY
26 Director of Public Information ... Ms. Haven HOTTEL
15 Human Resources Director ... Mr. Bob COGSWELL
18 Chief Facilities/Physical Plant ... Mr. J. Scot PHILLIPS
38 Director Student Counseling ... Mrs. Laura RICH
96 Director of Purchasing ... Mr. Win QUAKENBUSH
92 Director of Honors Program ... Dr. Ann ORTIZ
09 Asst Provost for Inst Effectivness ... Mrs. Maren HESS
106 Dean of Adult & Online Education ... Dr. John ROBERSON
04 Executive Asst to the President ... Dr. John ROBERSON
108 Director of Assessment ... Ms. Jessica WRENN
41 Athletic Director ... Mr. Robert ROLLER
43 Dir Legal Services/General Counsel ... Mr. Bob COGSWELL

Carolina Christian College (G)

PO Box 777, Winston-Salem NC 27102
County: Forsyth FICE Identification: 035703
Unit ID: 199971
Telephone: (336) 744-0900 Carnegie Class: Spec-4-yr-Faith
FAX Number: (336) 744-0901 Calendar System: Semester
URL: www.carolina.edu
Established: 1945 Annual Undergrad Tuition & Fees: $4,025
Enrollment: 53 Coed
Affiliation or Control: Independent Non-Profit IRS Status: 501(c)3
Highest Offering: Master's
Accreditation: BI

01 President ... Ms. LaTanya V. TYSON
05 VP of Academics ... Ms. Derrick THORPE
32 Dean of Students ... Mr. Thayer TYSON
10 Chief Business Officer ... Ms. Amy BARNHART
08 Library Director ... Ms. Laura RHODEN
37 Financial Aid Director ... Vacant
06 Registrar ... Vacant
26 Chief Public Relations Officer ... Mr. MacArthur DAVIS
09 Director of Institutional Research ... Vacant

Carolina College of Biblical Studies (H)

817 S. McPherson Church Road, Fayetteville NC 28303
County: Cumberland FICE Identification: 041542
Unit ID: 461032
Telephone: (910) 323-5614 Carnegie Class: Spec-4-yr-Faith
FAX Number: (910) 323-0425 Calendar System: Quarter
URL: www.ccbs.edu
Established: 1973 Annual Undergrad Tuition & Fees: $4,941
Enrollment: 111 Coed
Affiliation or Control: Non-denominational IRS Status: 501(c)3
Highest Offering: Baccalaureate
Accreditation: BI

01 President ... Dr. Bill KORVER
05 Academic Dean ... Dr. Harry GHEE
30 Vice Pres Strategic Development ... Dr. Bill BOYD
06 Financial Aid Officer/Registrar ... Ms. Kathy SCHULTINGKEMPER
07 Admissions Director ... Ms. Marcia KORVER

Carolinas College of Health Sciences (A)

1200 Blythe Boulevard, Charlotte NC 28203

County: Mecklenburg FICE Identification: 031042
Unit ID: 433174
Telephone: (704) 355-5043 Carnegie Class: Spec 2-yr-Health
FAX Number: (704) 355-9336 Calendar System: Semester
URL: www.CarolinasCollege.edu
Established: 1990 Annual Undergrad Tuition & Fees (In-District): $13,900
Enrollment: 486 Coed
Affiliation or Control: State/Local IRS Status: 501(c)3
Highest Offering: Associate Degree
Accreditation: SC, ADNUR, HT, MT, PHLEB, RAD, RTT, SURGT

01 President .... Dr. Ellen SHEPPARD
05 Provost .... Dr. Lori BEQUETTE
10 Dean of Business/Finance/Technology .... Ms. Kim BRADSHAW
32 Dean Student Svcs/Enrollment Mgmt .... Dr. T. Hampton HOPKINS
66 Dean of Nursing .... Dr. Deborah BLACKWELL
06 Registrar .... Ms. Sue ROUX
51 Director Continuing Education .... Ms. Susan THOMASSON
29 Director Alumni Relations .... Ms. Ruthie MIHAL
07 Admissions Coordinator .... Ms. Rhoda RILLORTA
37 Financial Aid Coordinator .... Ms. Jill POWELL
90 Instructional Tech Coordinator .... Mr. Larry TURNER
09 Institutional Research Coordinator .... Ms. Cheryl PULLIAM
04 Administrative Asst to President .... Ms. Pat LEWIS

Catawba College (B)

2300 W Innes Street, Salisbury NC 28144-2488

County: Rowan FICE Identification: 002914
Unit ID: 198215
Telephone: (704) 637-4111 Carnegie Class: Bac-Diverse
FAX Number: (704) 637-4444 Calendar System: Semester
URL: www.catawba.edu
Established: 1851 Annual Undergrad Tuition & Fees: $28,730
Enrollment: 1,300 Coed
Affiliation or Control: United Church Of Christ IRS Status: 501(c)3
Highest Offering: Master's
Accreditation: SC, CAATE, TED

01 President .... Mr. Brien LEWIS
03 Senior Vice President/Chaplain .... Dr. Kenneth W. CLAPP
05 Provost .... Dr. Michael BITZER
30 Vice President of Development .... Vacant
84 Vice Pres of Enrollment Management .... Mrs. Cindy BARR
04 Assistant to President .... Mrs. Amy H. WILLIAMS
09 Dir Institutional Research .... Mr. Timothy KENNEDY
10 Chief Financial Officer .... Mr. Nelson MURPHY
15 Chief Human Resources Officer .... Mr. Larry G. FARMER
26 Chief Public Relations Officer .... Mrs. Tonia BLACK-GOLD
32 Interim Dean of Students .... Dr. Michael BITZER
39 Associate Dean of Residence Life .... Ms. Kara OSTLUND
08 Head Librarian .... Dr. Steve MCKINZIE
06 Registrar .... Ms. Susan AGNER
07 Sr Director of Admissions .... Mrs. Elaine P. HOLDEN
37 Director of Financial Assistance .... Ms. Kelli HAND
36 Director of Placement .... Ms. Robin PERRY
88 Director Sports Info & Promotion .... Mr. Jim D. LEWIS
40 Director Bookstore .... Mrs. Stephanie TAYLOR
41 Athletic Director .... Mr. Larry W. LECKONBY
18 Chief Facilities/Physical Plant .... Vacant
29 Director Alumni Relations .... Vacant
38 Director Student Counseling .... Dr. Nancy ZIMMERMAN

Chamberlain College of Nursing-Charlotte (C)

2015 Ayrsley Town Blvd, Ste 204, Charlotte NC 28273

Telephone: (980) 939-6241 Identification: 770979
Accreditation: &NH, NURSE

† Regional accreditation is carried under the parent institution in Addison, IL

Charlotte Christian College and Theological Seminary (D)

PO Box 790106, Charlotte NC 28206-7901

County: Mecklenburg FICE Identification: 038273
Unit ID: 444778
Telephone: (704) 334-6882 Carnegie Class: Spec-4-yr-Faith
FAX Number: (704) 334-6885 Calendar System: Semester
URL: www.charlottechristian.edu
Established: 1996 Annual Undergrad Tuition & Fees: $9,320
Enrollment: 130 Coed
Affiliation or Control: Independent Non-Profit IRS Status: 501(c)3
Highest Offering: Doctorate
Accreditation: TRACS

01 President .... Dr. Eddie G. GRIGG
04 Executive Asst to the President .... Mr. Heith PICKLESIMER
05 Vice President of Academic Affairs .... Dr. James GIFFORD
32 Vice President of Student Affairs .... Vacant
30 Director of Advancement .... Vacant
06 Registrar/Dir International Student .... Ms. Nancy MCNAMARA
08 Head Librarian .... Mr. Robert MCINNES
07 Director of Admissions .... Mr. George SHEARS, III
10 Chief Financial Officer .... Mr. Craig M. MAZZUCCA
37 Financial Aid Officer .... Mr. Kenneth ROACH

Charlotte School of Law (E)

201 South College Street, Charlotte NC 28244

County: Mecklenburg FICE Identification: 041435
Unit ID: 455169
Telephone: (704) 971-8500 Carnegie Class: Spec-4-yr-Law
FAX Number: (704) 971-8599 Calendar System: Semester
URL: www.charlottelaw.edu
Established: 2008 Annual Graduate Tuition & Fees: N/A
Enrollment: 1,267 Coed
Affiliation or Control: Proprietary IRS Status: Proprietary
Highest Offering: First Professional Degree; No Undergraduates
Accreditation: LAW

01 President .... Mr. Chidi OGENE
05 Dean .... Mr. Jay CONISON
10 CFO .... Mr. Chris SCHMITZ
26 Sr Dir Mktg & Admissions Outcomes .... Mr. Dallas BRAGG
13 Director of Information Technology .... Mr. Clark MACIAG
20 Assoc Dean for Acad Svcs & Faculty .... Ms. Camille DAVIDSON
88 Assc Dean Practice Ready Education .... Mr. Jason HUBER
84 Assoc Dean of Enrollment Management .... Mr. Michael FARLEY
20 Asst Dean for Academic Affairs .... Ms. Beth KOBACK
36 Director of Center for Prof Dev .... Ms. Aithyn RUCKER
32 Asst Dean for Student Success .... Ms. Odessa ALM
08 Associate Dean for Library Services .... Ms. Katie BROWN
21 Assistant Dir of Fiscal Affairs .... Ms. Tamika JACKSON
88 Asst Dean for Academic Services .... Ms. Traci FLEURY
35 Director of Student Engagement .... Mr. Branden NICHOLSON
18 Facilities Manager .... Mr. Jay BEAM
19 Director of Security .... Mr. William HARPER
06 Registrar .... Ms. Jessica PRIMERANO
07 Director of Admissions Operations .... Mr. Steve JONES

The Chef's Academy (F)

2001 Carrington Mill Boulevard, Morrisville NC 27560

Telephone: (919) 246-9394 Identification: 770101
Accreditation: ACICS

† Branch campus of Harrison College - Indianapolis Downtown Campus, Indianapolis, IN

Chowan University (G)

One University Place, Murfreesboro NC 27855-1844

County: Hertford FICE Identification: 002916
Unit ID: 198303
Telephone: (252) 398-6500 Carnegie Class: Bac-Diverse
FAX Number: (252) 398-1190 Calendar System: Semester
URL: www.chowan.edu
Established: 1848 Annual Undergrad Tuition & Fees: $23,400
Enrollment: 1,484 Coed
Affiliation or Control: Baptist IRS Status: 501(c)3
Highest Offering: Master's
Accreditation: SC, MUS, TED

01 President .... Dr. M. Chrisopher WHITE
05 Vice President Academic Affairs .... Dr. Danny B. MOORE
10 Vice President Business Affairs .... Mr. Donnie O. CLARY
32 Vice President Student Affairs .... Mr. F. Randy HARRELL
30 Vice President Advancement .... Mr. John TAYLOE
15 Vice President Human Resources .... Mr. John A. HINTON
07 Vice President Admissions .... Mr. F. Randy HARRELL
13 Exec Dir Info Tech/Network Svcs .... Mr. James R. HOWELL
06 Registrar .... Ms. Donna ROBBINS
26 Director of Public Relations .... Mrs. Brooke REICH
08 Head Librarian .... Mrs. Georgia E. WILLIAMS
37 Director of Financial Aid .... Mrs. Sharon ROSE
42 Campus Minister .... Ms. Mary E. WILES
18 Director Physical Plant .... Mr. Rex HARRELL
19 Chief of Security .... Mr. Derek A. BURKE
35 Director Student Life .... Ms. Leah LAMBSON
38 Director Counseling/Career Services .... Ms. Yolanda MAJETTE
39 Director Housing & Residence Life .... Ms. Danielle COLEMAN
41 Athletics Director .... Mr. F. Ozzie MCFARLAND
09 Director Institutional Research .... Mrs. Lori HARDERS
88 Director Upward Bound .... Mr. E. Frank STEPHENSON
21 Director Business Services .... Mrs. Julie W. EMORY
29 Director Alumni Services .... Mrs. Kay M. THOMAS
49 Dean Liberal Arts .... Dr. John DILUSTRO
50 Dean Business .... Dr. Linda MILES
53 Dean Education .... Dr. Ella BENSON
40 Bookstore Manager .... Vacant

Daoist Traditions College of Chinese Medical Arts (H)

382 Montford Avenue, Asheville NC 28801

County: Buncombe FICE Identification: 041464
Unit ID: 455178
Telephone: (828) 225-3993 Carnegie Class: Spec-4-yr-Other Health
FAX Number: (828) 255-3306 Calendar System: Semester
URL: www.daoisttraditions.edu
Established: 2003 Annual Graduate Tuition & Fees: N/A
Enrollment: 76 Coed
Affiliation or Control: Proprietary IRS Status: Proprietary
Highest Offering: Master's; No Undergraduates
Accreditation: ACUP

01 President .... Dr. Mary Cissy MAJEBE

Davidson College (I)

PO Box 5000, Davidson NC 28035-5000

County: Mecklenburg FICE Identification: 002918
Unit ID: 198385
Telephone: (704) 894-2000 Carnegie Class: Bac-A&S
FAX Number: (704) 894-2005 Calendar System: Semester
URL: www.davidson.edu
Established: 1837 Annual Undergrad Tuition & Fees: $46,966
Enrollment: 1,770 Coed
Affiliation or Control: Presbyterian Church (U.S.A.) IRS Status: 501(c)3
Highest Offering: Baccalaureate
Accreditation: SC

01 President .... Dr. Carol E. QUILLEN
05 Vice Pres Acad Affs/Dean of Faculty .... Dr. Wendy E. RAYMOND
26 Vice President College Relations .... Ms. Eileen M. KEELEY
10 Vice Pres Finance & Administration .... Mr. Edward A. KANIA
32 VP Student Life/Dean of Students .... Dr. Thomas C. SHANDLEY
07 VP & Dean Admissions/Financial Aid .... Mr. Christopher J. GRUBER
09 VP Planning/Institutional Research .... Ms. Linda M. LEFAUVE
43 VP and General Counsel .... Mrs. Sarah L. PHILLIPS
30 Assoc VP of Advancement Operations .... Ms. Cat S. NIEKRO
20 Assoc Dean Academic Administration .... Ms. Leslie M. MARSICANO
45 VP for Strategic Initiatives .... Dr. Patrick J. SELLERS
20 Assoc Dean Teaching/Lrng/Rsrch .... Dr. Verna M. CASE
06 Registrar .... Ms. Angela B. DEWBERRY
13 Chief Information Officer .... Ms. Raechelle CLEMMONS
37 Director Financial Aid .... Mr. David GELINAS
15 Director of Human Resources .... Dr. Kim BALL
41 Director of Athletics .... Mr. James E. MURPHY, III
08 Director of the Library .... Ms. Gillian (Jill) S. GREMMELS
29 Director Alumni Relations .... Ms. Marya L. HOWELL
21 Controller/Director Business Svcs .... Ms. Lori GASTON
18 Director Facilities & Engineering .... Mr. David M. HOLTHOUSER
19 Chief of Campus Police .... Mr. Todd D. SIGLER
36 Executive Director Career Services .... Mrs. Jeanne-Marie C. RYAN
35 Director of College Union .... Mr. William H. BROWN
39 Dir Resid Life/Assoc Dean Students .... Mr. Jason S. SHAFFER
42 College Chaplain .... Dr. Robert C. SPACH
71 Dir Cntr for Interdisciplinary Stds .... Dr. Peter M. KRENTZ
82 Assoc Dean Int'l Programs/Studies .... Dr. M. Christopher ALEXANDER
25 Director of Grants & Contracts .... Dr. Mary W. MUCHANE
24 Director Instructional Support .... Ms. Diane S. STIRLING
38 Director Student Counseling Center .... Dr. Trish MURRAY
44 Director of Annual Giving .... Ms. Lisa H. COMBS
96 Director of Purchasing .... Ms. Elizabeth S. CHRISTENBURY
40 College Store General Manager .... Mr. William T. REILLY
04 Executive Asst to President .... Mrs. Traci L. RUSS-WILSON

Duke University (J)

Durham NC 27706-8001

County: Durham FICE Identification: 002920
Unit ID: 198419
Telephone: (919) 684-8111 Carnegie Class: DU-Highest
FAX Number: (919) 684-3200 Calendar System: Semester
URL: www.duke.edu
Established: 1838 Annual Undergrad Tuition & Fees: $49,241
Enrollment: 15,856 Coed
Affiliation or Control: Independent Non-Profit IRS Status: 501(c)3
Highest Offering: Doctorate
Accreditation: SC, ANEST, ARCPA, BUS, CLPSY, @DIETI, ENG, IPSY, LAW, MED, NURSE, PA, PAST, PCSAS, PTA, TED, THEOL

01 President .... Richard H. BRODHEAD
05 Provost .... Sally KORNBLUTH
17 Chancellor for Health Affairs .... A. Eugene WASHINGTON
03 Exec Vice Pres for Administration .... Tallman TRASK, III
10 Vice President Financial Services .... Timothy WALSH
15 Vice President for Administration .... Kyle CAVANAUGH
07 Dean Undergraduate Admissions .... Christoph O. GUTTENTAG
21 Exec Vice Provost Finance & Admin .... James S. ROBERTS
13 Vice Prov Information Technology .... Tracy FUTHEY
88 Vice Provost Interdisciplin Studies .... Edward BALLEISEN
20 Vice Provost for Academic Affairs .... Vacant
88 Vice Prov Faculty Diversity & Dev .... Vacant
88 Vice Provost for the Arts .... Scott A. LINDTORTH
46 Vice Provost for Research .... Lawrence CARIN
88 Vice Prov Innov/Entrepreneurship .... Eric TOONE
08 Librarian/Vice Prov Library Affairs .... Deborah JAKUBS
37 Asst Vice Provost/Dir Financial Aid .... Alison RABIL
65 Vice Provost Sch of the Environment .... Alan TOWNSEND
61 Dean of Law School .... David F. LEVI
63 Dn Sch Med/Sr Vice Chanc Acad Affs .... Nancy ANDREWS
50 Dean Fuqua School of Business .... William BOULDING
73 Dean of the Divinity School .... Richard HAYS
58 Dean Grad Sch/Vice Prov Grad Educ .... Paula D. MCCLAIN
49 Dean Faculty Arts/Science .... Valerie ASHBY
66 Dean School of Nursing .... Marion BROOME
54 Dean of Engineering .... George TRUSKEY
88 Director Duke University Press .... Stephen A. COHN
18 Vice President for Facilities .... John NOONAN
88 Vice Pres/Vice Prov Global Strategy .... Michael H. MERSON
06 Registrar .... Frank BLALARK
09 Director of Institutional Research .... David JAMIESON-DRAKE
04 Executive Asst to the President .... Lisa JORDAN
101 VP and University Secretary .... Richard RIDDELL
102 Asst VP Foundation Relations .... Beth EASTLICK
104 Director Study Abroad .... Amanda KELSOE

Code	Title	Name
105	Senior Manager Web Services	Ryn NASSER
22	Vice President Institutional Equity	Benjamin REESE, JR.
26	Chief Public Relations/Marketing	Michael SCHOENFELD
29	Director Alumni Relations	Sterly WILDER
30	Vice President Development	Robert SHEPARD
32	Vice President Student Affairs	Larry MONETA
36	Director Career Center	William WRIGHT-SWADEL
38	Director Student Counseling	Wanda COLLINS
39	Director Student Housing	Rick JOHNSON
41	VP and Director Athletics	Kevin WHITE
43	Vice President and General Counsel	Pamela BERNARD
44	Asst VP Annual Giving	Jennifer SPISAK-CAMERON
53	Vice Provost Undergraduate Educ	Stephen NOWICKI
86	Assoc VP Federal Relations	Christopher SIMMONS
96	Assoc VP Procurement	Jane PLEASANTS

ECPI University-Charlotte (A)

4800 Airport Center Pkwy #100, Charlotte NC 28208

Telephone: (704) 399-1010 Identification: 770951

Accreditation: &SC, MAAB

† Regional accreditation is carried under the parent institution in Virginia Beach, VA

ECPI University-Greensboro (B)

7802 Airport Center Drive, Greensboro NC 27409

Telephone: (336) 665-1400 Identification: 770952

Accreditation: &SC, MAAB

† Regional accreditation is carried under the parent institution in Virginia Beach, VA

ECPI University-Raleigh (C)

4101 Coie Cope Road, Raleigh NC 27613

Telephone: (919) 571-0057 Identification: 770953

Accreditation: &SC, MAAB

† Regional accreditation is carried under the parent institution in Virginia Beach, VA

Elon University (D)

2700 Campus Box, Elon NC 27244-2010

County: Alamance FICE Identification: 002927

Unit ID: 198516

Telephone: (336) 278-2000 Carnegie Class: Masters/M

FAX Number: N/A Calendar System: 4/1/4

URL: www.elon.edu

Established: 1889 Annual Undergrad Tuition & Fees: $32,172

Enrollment: 6,483 Coed

Affiliation or Control: Independent Non-Profit IRS Status: 501(c)3

Highest Offering: Doctorate

Accreditation: SC, #ARCPA, BUS, JOUR, LAW, PTA, TED

Code	Title	Name
01	President	Dr. Leo M. LAMBERT
05	Provost/Exec VP Academic Affairs	Dr. Steven D. HOUSE
100	Chief of Staff/Sec to the Board	Mr. Jeff STEIN
07	VP of Admissions/Financial Planning	Mr. Greg ZAISER
10	Senior VP for Business/Finance/ Tech	Mr. Gerald O. WHITTINGTON
30	Vice Pres Institutional Advancement	Mr. James B. PIATT
32	Vice Pres/Dean of Student Life	Dr. G. Smith JACKSON
26	Vice Pres University Communications	Mr. Daniel J. ANDERSON
108	Associate Provost for Assessment	Dr. Maurice LEVESQUE
88	Asst Provost for Comm & Operations	Dr. Paul MILLER
20	Interim Assoc Provost for Inclusion	Dr. Brooke BARNETT
88	Associate Provost for Faculty Affs	Dr. Tim PEEPLES
21	Asst VP for Business and Finance	Ms. Susan M. KIRKLAND
49	Interim Dean College of Arts & Sci	Dr. Gabie SMITH
50	Dean Love School of Business	Dr. Raghu TADEPALLI
60	Dean of School of Communications	Dr. Paul F. PARSONS
53	Interim Dean of School of Education	Dr. Deborah LONG
61	Dean of School of Law	Mr. Luke BIERMAN
76	Dean of School of Health Sciences	Dr. Elizabeth A. ROGERS
85	Dean of Global Studies	Mr. Woody PELTON
35	Associate VP of Student Life	Mrs. Jana Lynn F. PATTERSON
08	Dean and University Librarian	Ms. Joan RUELLE
41	Director of Athletics	Mr. Dave L. BLANK
06	Registrar	Dr. Rodney PARKS
42	University Chaplain	Dr. Janet FULLER
37	Director of Financial Planning	Dr. M. Patrick MURPHY
29	Dir of Alumni Engagement	Mr. Brian FEELEY
88	Assoc Dean of Academic Support	Dr. Becky OLIVE-TAYLOR
36	Exec Director of Career Services	Vacant
88	Dir of Planning/Design/Construction	Mr. Brad D. MOORE
18	Assoc VP for Facilities Management	Mr. Robert BUCHHOLZ
15	Exec Director of Human Resources	Mr. John LEW
109	Director of Auxiliary Services	Ms. Carrie RYAN
19	Director of Campus Safety & Police	Mr. Dennis FRANKS
23	Director of Health Services	Dr. Ginette ARCHINAL
38	Director Counseling Services	Mr. Bruce F. NELSON
11	Assistant VP for Admin Svcs	Mr. Christopher D. FULKERSON
09	Exec Director Institutional Rsch	Dr. Robert I. SPRINGER
13	Assistant VP for Technology and CIO	Mr. Christopher C. WATERS
25	Director of Sponsored Programs	Ms. Bonnie BRUNO
88	Associate VP for Campus Engagement	Dr. Randy WILLIAMS
92	Director of Honors Program	Dr. Tom MOULD
94	Director Women's Stds/Gender Stds	Dr. Kim EPTING
96	Director of Purchasing	Mr. Jeff HENDRICKS
88	Director of Sustainability	Ms. Elaine DURR

Gardner-Webb University (E)

PO Box 897 (110 South Main Street), Boiling Springs NC 28017-0897

County: Cleveland FICE Identification: 002929

Unit ID: 198561

Telephone: (704) 406-2361 Carnegie Class: DU-Mod

FAX Number: (704) 406-4329 Calendar System: Semester

URL: www.gardner-webb.edu

Established: 1905 Annual Undergrad Tuition & Fees: $28,280

Enrollment: 4,470 Coed

Affiliation or Control: Baptist IRS Status: 501(c)3

Highest Offering: Doctorate

Accreditation: SC, ACBSP, ADNUR, #ARCPA, CAATE, CACREP, MUS, NUR, TED, THEOL

Code	Title	Name
01	President	Dr. A. Frank BONNER
05	Provost & Executive Vice President	Dr. Benjamin C. LESLIE
04	Sr Assistant to the President	Mrs. Stephanie L. STEARNS
10	Vice President for Administration	Mr. Mike W. HARDIN
27	VP of Marketing	Mr. Richard K. MCDEVITT
26	VP for External Affairs	Mr. H. Woodrow FISH
30	Vice President for Advancement	Mr. Patrick W. WAGNER
32	Vice Pres Student Development	Dr. Delores HUNT
84	Vice Pres Enrollment Management	Mr. David HAWSEY
41	Vice President for Athletics	Mr. Chuck S. BURCH
09	VP Planning & Inst Effectiveness	Dr. Jeffrey L. TUBBS
18	Assoc Vice Pres for Operations	Mr. Wayne E. JOHNSON
91	Assoc VP for Technology Services	Mr. Gregory G. HUMPHRIES
20	Assoc Provost Prof/Graduate Studies	Dr. Franki BURCH
49	Assoc Provost for Arts & Sciences	Dr. Earl LEININGER
21	Assoc VP for Business & Finance	Ms. Robin G. HAMRICK
51	Asst Provost for Distance Education	Dr. Bobbie COX
07	Assoc VP for Undergrad Admissions	Ms. Gretchen G. TUCKER
37	Asst VP for Financial Planning	Ms. Summer NANCE
06	Registrar	Mrs. LouAnn P. SCATES
35	Assoc Provost Academic Development	Dr. Doug BRYAN
19	Chief of University Police	Mr. Barry JOHNSON
27	Assoc VP for Marketing/Comm	Mr. Noel T. MANNING
08	Director of the Library	Ms. Mary ROBY
38	Director of Counseling Services	Ms. Cindy WALLACE
89	Director of Freshmen Programs	Ms. Jessica HERRNDON
58	Dean of Graduate School	Dr. Jeffrey ROGERS
73	Dean of Divinity School	Dr. Robert W. CANOY
66	Dean of Nursing School	Dr. Sharon STARR
50	Director of School Management	Dr. Sue C. CAMP
92	Director of Honors Program	Dr. Thomas H. JONES
88	Director Program for Blind/Deaf	Mrs. Cheryl J. POTTER
21	Comptroller	Ms. Haley KENDRICK
35	Director Student Activities	Ms. Karissa L. WEIR
42	Minister to the University	Dr. Tracy C. JESSUP
39	Director of Residence Life	Mr. John R. JOHNSON, JR.
50	Dean of Business School	Dr. Anthony I. NEGBENEBOR
15	Director Human Resources	Mr. W. Scott WHITE
09	Director of Institutional Research	Mr. Garry MCSWAIN
29	Director Alumni Relations	Mrs. Leah CLEVENGER
44	Director of Annual Campaign	Ms. Sara MCCALL
24	Asst Dir University Media Relations	Ms. Kathy MARTIN
40	Bookstore Manager	Ms. Cary CALDWELL
109	Director of Operations Support	Mr. Brian SPEER

Grace College of Divinity (F)

5117 Cliffdale Road, Fayetteville NC 28314

County: Cumberland FICE Identification: 041737

Unit ID: 461528

Telephone: (910) 221-2224 Carnegie Class: Spec-4-yr-Faith

FAX Number: (910) 221-2226 Calendar System: Semester

URL: www.gcd.edu

Established: 2000 Annual Undergrad Tuition & Fees: $4,240

Enrollment: 122 Coed

Affiliation or Control: Other Protestant IRS Status: 501(c)3

Highest Offering: Baccalaureate

Accreditation: BI

Code	Title	Name
01	President	Dr. Steven CROWTHER
11	Vice President of Administration	Ms. Cathy LUCAS
05	Academic Dean	Mr. Ron MCBRIDE
84	Dean of Enrollment Management	Mr. Jason CROWTHER
32	Dean of Students	Mrs. Stefanie ERTEL
106	Dean of Online Education/E-Learning	Mr. Tom JOHNSON
10	Chief Financial Officer	Ms. Omayra COON
08	Librarian	Mr. David ASPINALL
108	Director of Assessment & Planning	Ms. Sharyn J. TEAGUE
06	Registrar	Mr. Kevin ORTIZ

Greensboro College (G)

815 W Market Street, Greensboro NC 27401-1875

County: Guilford FICE Identification: 002930

Unit ID: 198598

Telephone: (336) 272-7102 Carnegie Class: Bac-Diverse

FAX Number: (336) 217-6634 Calendar System: Semester

URL: www.greensboro.edu

Established: 1838 Annual Undergrad Tuition & Fees: $26,900

Enrollment: 905 Coed

Affiliation or Control: United Methodist IRS Status: 501(c)3

Highest Offering: Master's

Accreditation: SC, ACBSP, #CAATE, MUS

Code	Title	Name
01	President	Dr. Lawrence D. CZARDA
04	Exec Asst to President/Clerk to BoT	Ms. Susan J. BARRINGER
05	Senior VP Chief Academic Officer	Dr. Paul L. LESLIE
11	Exec VP Chief Operating Officer	Dr. Robin L. DANIEL
10	VP Chief Financial Officer	Mr. Chris ELMORE
30	VP Chief Advancement Officer	Ms. Anne J. HURD
20	Assoc VP Academic Admin	Ms. Martha M. BUNCH
20	Dean of the Faculty	Dr. Richard A. MAYES
57	Dean School of Arts	Dr. David SCHRAM
50	Dean School of Business	Dr. William K. MACREYNOLDS
53	Dean School of Soc Sci & Education	Dr. Rebecca BLOMGREN
79	Dean School of Humanities	Dr. Daniel MALOTKY
81	Dean School of Science & Mathematic	Dr. Jessica G. SHARPE
07	Dean of Admissions	Ms. Julianne SCHATZ
13	Asst VP Information Technology	Dr. Larry BURTON
37	Financial Aid Director	Ms. Lindsay S. LATHEM
26	Communications Director	Mr. Lex ALEXANDER
27	Marketing Director	Mr. Tom SAITTA
06	Registrar	Mr. Travis MICKEY
32	Dean of Students	Dr. Matthew LONG
39	Residence Life Director	Ms. Shana PLASTERS
36	Career Services Director	Ms. Caryn ATWATER
09	Institutional Research Director	Ms. Patricia ALBERT
35	Academic Success Director	Ms. Tica D. GREEN
15	Human Resources Director	Ms. Sonia HOFFMAN
18	Facilities Director	Mr. Justin LISZKA
19	Security Director	Mr. Calvin L. GILMORE
23	Student Health Director	Ms. Lauren T. CHILDREY
38	Counseling Services Director	Ms. Emily HOLMES
92	George Ctr/Honors Studies Director	Mr. Neill CLEGG
44	Asst VP Development	Ms. Ellie YEARNS
29	Alumni Engagement Director	Ms. Kristen C. BROWN
85	International Programs Director	Ms. Cathryn BENNETT
08	Library Director	Mr. Will RITTER
41	Athletic Director	Mr. Bryan GALUSKI
42	Campus Chaplain	Rev. Robert W. BREWER
40	Bookstore Manager	Mr. Cliff BRALY, JR.
21	Controller	Ms. Melissa HOFF

Guilford College (H)

5800 W Friendly Avenue, Greensboro NC 27410-4173

County: Guilford FICE Identification: 002931

Unit ID: 198613

Telephone: (336) 316-2000 Carnegie Class: Bac-A&S

FAX Number: (336) 316-2950 Calendar System: Semester

URL: www.guilford.edu

Established: 1837 Annual Undergrad Tuition & Fees: $34,090

Enrollment: 2,137 Coed

Affiliation or Control: Friends IRS Status: 501(c)3

Highest Offering: Baccalaureate

Accreditation: SC, ACBSP

Code	Title	Name
01	President	Dr. Jane K. FERNANDES
05	Vice President & Academic Dean	Dr. Beth RUSHING
04	Executive Assoc to the President	Mrs. Joyce A. EATON
10	Vice Pres Finance/Administration	Mr. Len SIPPEL
26	Vice President for Marketing	Mr. Roger DEGERMAN
30	Vice Pres Institutional Advancement	Ms. Ava SERJOIE
32	Vice President Student Affairs	Dr. Todd A. CLARK
27	Assoc VP Communications & Marketing	Mr. R. Ty BUCKNER
29	Assoc Vice Pres Alumni Relations	Mr. Jerry W. HARRELSON
51	Asst Dean Continuing Education	Mr. Martee HOLT
07	Vice President of Enrollment	Dr. Arlene W. CASH
31	Asst Dean of Career/Community Lrng	Mr. Alan C. MUELLER
20	Assistant Academic Dean	Dr. Barbara LAWRENCE
20	Assistant Academic Dean	Dr. Barbara G. BOYETTE
37	Director Student Financial Svcs	Mr. Brian DE YOUNG
06	Registrar	Mrs. Norma L. MIDDLETON
08	Director of the Library	Ms. Suzanne M. BARTELS
41	Director of Athletics	Mr. Tom J. PALOMBO
19	Director of Public Safety	Mr. William ANDERSON
15	Director Human Resources	Mr. Rick WILLIAMS
09	Dir Institutional Research/Assess	Ms. Stephanie HARGRAVE
90	Director Info Technology & Services	Mr. Chuck CURRY, JR.
42	Campus Ministry Coordinator	Rev. C. Wess DANIELS
38	Director Student Counseling	Ms. Gaither M. TERRELL
92	Director Honors Program	Dr. Heather HAYTON
89	Director of First Year Program	Dr. Barbara G. BOYETTE
96	Director of Purchasing	Ms. Tracy A. HALL
104	Director Study Abroad	Mr. Daniel DIAZ
25	Chief Contracts/Grants Admin	Vacant

Heritage Bible College (I)

PO Box 1628, Dunn NC 28335-1628

County: Harnett FICE Identification: 030893

Unit ID: 198677

Telephone: (910) 892-3178 Carnegie Class: Spec-4-yr-Faith

FAX Number: (910) 891-1809 Calendar System: Semester

URL: www.heritagebiblecollege.edu

Established: 1971 Annual Undergrad Tuition & Fees: $9,168

Enrollment: 68 Coed

Affiliation or Control: Other IRS Status: 501(c)3

Highest Offering: Baccalaureate

Accreditation: TRACS

Code	Title	Name
01	President	Dr. Elvin BUTTS
05	Academic Dean	Mr. Stephen RZONCA
32	Dean Student Services	Mr. Randy BARKER
06	Registrar/Director of Financial Aid	Ms. Kayla SUTTON-COLLIER
07	Admissions	Ms. Kayla SUTTON-COLLIER
10	Business Administrator	Ms. LeAnne PAGE
29	Director Alumni Rels/Inst Effectiv	Mr. Sterling THARRINGTON
30	Director of Advancement	Ms. Iris PRINCE

13 Chief Info Technology Officer (CIO) ....Mr. James SHEARON
26 Chief Public Relations/Marketing ....Ms. Iris PRINCE

High Point University (A)

One University Parkway, High Point NC 27268-0001
County: Guilford FICE Identification: 002933
Unit ID: 198695
Telephone: (336) 841-9000 Carnegie Class: Bac-Diverse
FAX Number: (336) 841-4599 Calendar System: Semester
URL: www.highpoint.edu
Established: 1924 Annual Undergrad Tuition & Fees: $32,430
Enrollment: 4,399 Coed
Affiliation or Control: United Methodist IRS Status: 501(c)3
Highest Offering: Doctorate
Accreditation: SC, #ARCPA, CAATE, CIDA, @PHAR, @PTA TED

01 President ....Dr. Nido R. QUBEIN
05 Provost ....Dr. Dennis G. CARROLL
03 Executive Vice President ....Dr. Denny G. BOLTON
46 VP for Research and Planning ....Dr. Jeffrey M. ADAMS
84 Sr VP for Enrollment .... Mr. Andy BILLS
26 Sr VP for Communications .... Mr. Roger D. CLODFELTER, JR.
32 Sr VP for Student Life ....Mrs. Gail C. TUTTLE
44 Sr VP for Development .... Mr. Christopher H. DUDLEY
18 VP for Facilities & Auxillary Svcs ....Mr. Stephen L. POTTER
41 Director for Athletics ....Mr. Dan HAUSER
07 Assoc VP of Graduate Admissions ....Mr. Andy MODLIN
07 Assoc VP of Undergrad Admissions ....Mr. Kerr C. RAMSAY
76 Dean of School of Health Sciences .... Dr. Daniel E. ERB
49 Dean of College of Arts & Science ......Dr. Carole B. STONEKING
57 Dean of School of Art and Design ....Dr John C. TURPIN
50 Dean of School of Business ....Dr. James B. WEHRLEY
63 Dean of School of Education ....Dr. Mariann W. TILLERY
67 Dean of School of Pharmacy ....Dr. Ronald E. RAGAN
35 Asst VP for Student Life & Dean .... Dr. Paul KITTLE
20 Assistant Dean Academic Services ....Ms. Karen C. NAYLON
89 Assoc Dean of Student Success ....Dr. Beth HOLDER
08 Director of Library Services ....Mr. David L. BRYDEN
23 Medical Director ....Dr. Marnie S. MARLETTE
88 Bishop in Residence ....Bishop Thomas B. STOCKTON
19 Chief of Security ....Mr. Jeff A. KARPOVICH
06 Registrar ....Mr. Danny K. BROOKS
10 VP for Financial Affairs ....Ms. Debi S. BUTT
13 Chief Information Officer ....Mr. John E. CHAMPION
29 Director of Alumni Engagement ....Ms. Kim M. BLAIR
37 Dir of Student Financial Planning .... Mr. Ronald ELMORE
25 Director of Sponsored Programs ....Mr. Timothy L. LINKER
15 Director of Human Resources ....Mrs. Kathy S. SMITH
88 Director of Student Accounts ....Ms. Janice A. FOLEY
38 Director of Counseling Services ....Ms. Lynda D. NOFFSINGER
88 Sr Director of Interactive Media ....Ms. Hillary C. KOKAJKO
88 Director of University Events ....Ms. Melissa L. ANDERSON
108 Dir of Inst Research & Assessment ....Ms. Andrea KENNEDY
88 Director of Campus Enhancement ....Mr. Troy J. THOMPSON
88 Asst AD/Facilities/Operations ....Mr. Sam PHIPPS
40 Manager Bookstore ....Mr. William HOLSTON
85 Director of International Students ....Ms. Marjorie R. CHURCH
36 Director of Career Services ....Ms. Bridget HOLCOMBE
104 Director of Study Abroad ....Ms. Heidi FISCHER
88 Director of Service Learning ....Dr. Joseph D. BLOSSER
88 Director of Undergraduate Research ....Dr. Joanne D. ALTMAN
27 Media Relations Coordinator ....Ms. Pamela J. HAYNES
04 Admin Assistant to President ....Ms. Judy K. RAY
88 Manager of University Mail Center ....Mr. Michael R. HALL
96 Mgr Contracts & Procurement ....Mr. Gene BUNTING

Hood Theological Seminary (B)

1810 Lutheran Synod Drive, Salisbury NC 28144-5768
County: Rowan FICE Identification: 036633
Unit ID: 443076
Telephone: (704) 636-7611 Carnegie Class: Spec-4-yr-Faith
FAX Number: (704) 636-7699 Calendar System: Semester
URL: www.hoodseminary.edu
Established: 1904 Annual Undergrad Tuition & Fees: N/A
Enrollment: 188 Coed
Affiliation or Control: African Methodist Episcopal Zion Church
IRS Status: 501(c)3
Highest Offering: Doctorate
Accreditation: THEOL

01 President-Elect ....Dr. Vergel L. LATTIMORE
05 Academic Dean ....Dr. Trevor EPPEHIMER
32 Dean of Students .... Dr. Dora R. MBUWAYESANGO
10 Chief Financial Ofcr/Dir Human Res .... Dr. Regina M. DANCY
26 Dir Communication/Info/Pub ....Ms. Carol PALMER
30 Institutional Advancement Officer ....Vacant
06 Registrar ....Ms. Nancy BAKER

John Wesley University (C)

1215 Eastchester Drive, High Point NC 27265-3115
County: Guilford FICE Identification: 002935
Unit ID: 198747
Telephone: (336) 887-3000 Carnegie Class: Spec-4-yr-Faith
FAX Number: (336) 889-2261 Calendar System: Semester
URL: www.johnwesley.edu
Established: 1903 Annual Undergrad Tuition & Fees: $10,570
Enrollment: 199 Coed
Affiliation or Control: Independent Non-Profit IRS Status: 501(c)3
Highest Offering: Doctorate
Accreditation: BI

01 President ....Dr. Stephen M. CONDON
10 Vice Pres for Finance & Instruction ....Vacant
05 Academic Dean .... Dr. Ron SELLECK
73 Dean School of Ministry ....Dr. John LINDSEY
06 Registrar ....Mr Greg WORKMAN
32 Exec Dir Stdt Svcs/Spiritual Life .... Rev. Kim MILLER
37 Director of Financial Aid ....Ms. Kady HILL
09 Dir Institutional Effectiveness ....Vacant
08 Director of Library Services ....Mrs. April LINDSEY
15 Exec Director of Human Resources ....Mrs. Kathy CUTRELL
21 Asst Director of Business Services ....Ms. Kady HILL
50 Acad Advisor School of Management ....Dr. Dennis RENFROE
29 Alumni Coordinator ....Ms. Kathy CUTRELL

Johnson & Wales University-Charlotte (D)

801 W Trade Street, Charlotte NC 28202-1122
Telephone: (980) 598-1000 Identification: 666375
Accreditation: &EH

† Regional accreditation is carried under the parent institution in Providence, RI.

Johnson C. Smith University (E)

100 Beatties Ford Road, Charlotte NC 28216-5398
County: Mecklenburg FICE Identification: 002936
Unit ID: 198756
Telephone: (704) 378-1000 Carnegie Class: Bac-A&S
FAX Number: (704) 372-1242 Calendar System: Semester
URL: www.jcsu.edu
Established: 1867 Annual Undergrad Tuition & Fees: $18,236
Enrollment: 1,402 Coed
Affiliation or Control: Independent Non-Profit IRS Status: 501(c)3
Highest Offering: Master's
Accreditation: SC, SW

01 President ....Dr Ronald L. CARTER
05 VP for Academic/Student Services ....Dr. Kelli RAINEY
10 Vice Pres for Finance .... Mr. Greg PETZKE
30 Vice President for Inst Advancement .... Ms. Joy PAIGE-SPRINGS
86 VP Government Sponsored Pgms ....Dr. Diane BOWLES
15 Asst VP for Human Resources .... Ms. Latrelle P. MCALLISTER
18 Asst VP for Business Operations ....Mr. Anayo EZEIGBO
30 Asst VP for Institutional Advancmnt ....Vacant
20 Dean of STEM ....Dr. Hang CHEN
49 Dean of Arts and Letters ....Dr. Brian JONES
107 Dean of Professional Studies ....Dr. Helen CALDWELL
84 Dean of Enrollment Services ....Ms. Cathy HURD
89 Associate Dean of First-Year Exper ....Dr. Cathy JONES
88 Dean of the University College ....Dr. Antonio HENLEY
51 Dean Metro College ....Dr. Laura MCLEAN
88 Dean of Academic Support Services ....Mr. John NORRIS
08 Director of the Library ....Ms. Monika RHUE
07 Director of Admissions ....Mr James BURRELL
13 Director Information Technology ....Mr. John NORRIS
09 Dir Plng/Assess/Effect/Rsrch ....Mrs. Harriet HOBBS
26 Director of Comm and Marketing .... Ms. Sherri BELFIELD
29 Director Alumni Affairs ....Mr Ron MATTHEWS
37 Director Financial Aid ....Vacant
38 Director Counseling ....Mr. Frederick MURPHY
19 Director of Campus Police ....Vacant
32 Director of Student Activities .... Mr. Alexander WHITFIELD
41 Athletic Director .... Mr. Stephen JOYNER, SR.
06 Registrar ....Mrs. Keisha WILSON
44 Major Gift Officer .... Mr. Alvin AUSTIN
96 Director of Procurement ....Ms. Angela MAULDIN
39 Director Residence Life ....Mr. Terry MCPHERSON
40 Manager of Bookstore ....Ms. Robin SORENSEN
16 Manager Risk Management .... Mrs. Debra HOLLIS
23 Health Center Coordinator .... Ms. Marian JONES

King's College (F)

322 Lamar Avenue, Charlotte NC 28204-2493
County: Mecklenburg FICE Identification: 002937
Unit ID: 382504
Telephone: (704) 372-0266 Carnegie Class: Assoc/HVT-High Trad
FAX Number: (704) 348-2029 Calendar System: Semester
URL: www.kingscollegecharlotte.edu
Established: 1901 Annual Undergrad Tuition & Fees: $14,280
Enrollment: 395 Coed
Affiliation or Control: Proprietary IRS Status: Proprietary
Highest Offering: Associate Degree
Accreditation: ACICS, MAC

01 School Director ....Mrs. Diane RYON
05 Chief Academic Officer .... Ms. Barbara ROCKECHARLIE

Lees-McRae College (G)

191 Main Street, Banner Elk NC 28604-0128
County: Avery FICE Identification: 002939
Unit ID: 198808
Telephone: (828) 898-5241 Carnegie Class: Bac-Diverse
FAX Number: (828) 898-8814 Calendar System: Semester
URL: www.lmc.edu
Established: 1900 Annual Undergrad Tuition & Fees: $25,404
Enrollment: 940 Coed
Affiliation or Control: Presbyterian Church (U.S.A.) IRS Status: 501(c)3
Highest Offering: Baccalaureate
Accreditation: SC, #CAATE, NURSE, TEAC

01 President ....Dr. Barry M. BUXTON
04 Secretary to the President ....Ms. Darcy VASILAS
05 Provost & Dean of Faculty ....Dr. Todd LIDH
10 VP Finance/Business Affairs ....Ms. Suzette FRONK
32 VP Stdnt Dev & Dean of Students ....Mr. Jon DRIGGERS
45 VP Strategic Planning/Effectiveness ....Mr. Blaine J. HANSEN
106 VP Extended Campus/Online Learning ....Dr. Bo BENNETT
30 VP Advancement ....Mr. Brent THOMAS
18 Director Facilities ....Mr. Paul BRAESE
41 VP Athletics/Club Sports ....Mr. Craig MCPHAIL
20 Associate Provost ....Dr. Kacy CRABTREE
13 Director Technology ....Mr. Tom BURNE
26 Director of Marketing & Design ....Ms. Lauren FOSTER
08 Director Libraries ....Ms. Peuler MOLLIE
66 Dean Nursing/Health Sciences ....Dr. Laura FERO
71 Director of Burton Center for Lrng ....Ms. Keri MAGANA
50 Dean of Business ....Ms. Amy ANDERSON
53 Director of Education ....Ms. Pamela VESELY
57 Assistant Dean of Arts/Humanities ....Ms. Danielle CURTIS
79 Dean Arts/Humanities/Education ....Dr. Ken CRAIG
81 Dean Natural & Behavioral Sciences ....Mr. Billy CARVER
83 Assistant Dean Natural & Behavioral ....Mr. Sean COLLINS
19 Director Security/Safety ....Mr. H.D STEWART
07 Director of Admissions ....Ms. Candace SILVER
06 Registrar ....Ms. Lynn HINSHAW
37 Director Financial Aid ....Ms. Cathy SHELL
15 Director Human Resources ....Mrs. Carolyn WARD

Lenoir-Rhyne University (H)

625 7th Avenue NE, Hickory NC 28601-3984
County: Catawba FICE Identification: 002941
Unit ID: 198835
Telephone: (828) 328-1741 Carnegie Class: Masters/S
FAX Number: (828) 328-7368 Calendar System: Semester
URL: www.lr.edu
Established: 1891 Annual Undergrad Tuition & Fees: $32,140
Enrollment: 2,050 Coed
Affiliation or Control: Evangelical Lutheran Church In America
IRS Status: 501(c)3
Highest Offering: Master's
Accreditation: SC, ACBSP, #ARCPA, CAATE, CACREP, @DIETI, NURSE, OT, TED, THEOL

01 President ....Dr. Wayne POWELL
05 Provost ....Dr. Larry HALL
10 Sr Vice President Finance/Admin ....Mr. Peter KENDALL
30 Vice Pres Institutional Advancement ....Dr. Drew VAN HORN
84 Vice President for Enrollment Mgmt .... Ms. Rachel NICHOLS
32 Asst Provost/Dean of Students ....Dr. Katie FISHER
104 Assoc Dean Global Learning ....Ms. Charlotte WILLIAMS
58 Dean Grad Studies/Lifelong Learning ....Dr. Amy WOOD
06 Registrar ....Mr. Stacey BRACKETT
08 Librarian ....Ms. Rita JOHNSON
15 Director of Human Resources ....Mr. Rick NICHOLS
40 Director of Bookstore ....Ms. Lucy MANZANARES
18 Director of Facilities/Plant ....Mr. Otis PITTS
41 Athletic Director ....Ms. Kim PATE
42 Campus Pastor ....Rev. Andrew WEISNER
19 Director of Security ....Mr. Norris YODER
92 Director of Honors Program ....Dr. Joshua RING
13 Interim CIO ....Mr. James BLAKESLEE
26 Dir of Marketing/Communication ....Ms. Angela REITER
88 Director of Conferences & Events .... Ms. Janet MATTHEWS
29 Director of Alumni Relations ....Vacant
07 Director of Enrollment Services ....Mr. Eric BRANDON
09 Director of Institutional Research ....Dr. Debra TEMPLETON
37 Director Student Financial Aid ....Mr. Nick JENKINS
38 Dir Student Counseling/Placement ....Ms. Jenny SMITH
88 Dir Liberal Arts/Visiting Writers ....Dr. Rand BRANDES
28 Director Multicultural Affairs ....Ms. Emma SELLERS
88 Dir of Deaf/Hard-of-Hearing Svcs ....Ms. Shawn FRANK
88 Institute on Obesity ....Ms. Kimberly PENNINGTON
65 Institute on Conservation ....Dr. John BRZORAD
85 Dir of International Programs ....Dr. Laura DOBSON
53 College of Education/Human Services .....Dr. Hank WEDDINGTON
76 College of Health Sciences ....Dr. Michael MCGEE
49 College of Arts & Sciences ....Dr. Dan KISER
81 Col of Professional/Math Studies ....Dr. Mary LESSER
04 Administrative Asst to President ....Ms. Sherry ERIKSON
36 Director Student Placement ....Ms. Katie WOHLMAN
39 Director Student Housing ....Mr. Jonathan RINK
43 Dir of Compliance/Title IX ....Ms. Dawn FLOYD

Living Arts College @ School of Communication Arts (I)

3000 Wakefield Crossing Drive, Raleigh NC 27614-7076
County: Wake FICE Identification: 031090
Unit ID: 421832
Telephone: (919) 488-8500 Carnegie Class: Bac-Diverse
FAX Number: (919) 488-8490 Calendar System: Quarter
URL: www.living-arts-college.edu
Established: 1992 Annual Undergrad Tuition & Fees: $16,780
Enrollment: 413 Coed
Affiliation or Control: Proprietary IRS Status: Proprietary
Highest Offering: Baccalaureate
Accreditation: ACICS, MAC

01 Director ....Ms. Debra A. HOOPER

Livingstone College (A)

701 W Monroe Street, Salisbury NC 28144-5298
County: Rowan FICE Identification: 002942
Unit ID: 198862
Telephone: (704) 216-6000 Carnegie Class: Bac-Diverse
FAX Number: (704) 216-6217 Calendar System: Semester
URL: www.livingstone.edu
Established: 1879 Annual Undergrad Tuition & Fees: $17,244
Enrollment: 1,301 Coed
Affiliation or Control: African Methodist Episcopal Zion Church
IRS Status: 501(c)3
Highest Offering: Baccalaureate
Accreditation: **SC**, SW, TED

01 President .... Dr. Jimmy R. **JENKINS, SR.**
04 Exec Asst to the President .... Dr. State **ALEXANDER**
05 Vice Pres Academic Affairs .... Dr. Carolyn W. **DUNCAN**
10 Vice Pres Business & Finance/Ops .... Mr. Reginald **DICKENS**
32 Vice President Student Affairs .... Dr. Orlando **LEWIS**
30 Vice Pres Inst Advance/College Rels .... Dr. Herman **FELTON**
35 Assoc Vice Pres of Student Affairs .... Mr. Tony **BALDWIN**
20 Asst Vice Pres Academic Affairs .... Dr. Alexander **ERWIN**
38 Dean of Counseling Services . Mrs. Elizabeth **ALSTON-PINCKNEY**
06 Registrar .... Mrs. Wendy **JACKSON**
08 Director Library Services .... Ms. Laura **JOHNSON**
26 Vice Pres Communications & PR .... Dr. State W. **ALEXANDER**
37 Director of Financial Aid .... Ms. Stephanie **MCNEIL**
36 Director of Career Services .... Ms. Sophia **GAITHER**
13 Director of Computer Info Systems .... Mr. Chong **DAN**
15 Director of Human Resources .... Mr. Mark **SANDERS**
29 Director Alumni Affairs .... Ms. Carmen C. **WILDER**
09 Director of Institutional Research .... Mr. Robert L. **MCINNIS**
84 Dir Enrollment Mgmt & Admissions .... Vacant
07 Director of Admissions .... Ms. Katrina **JARRETT**
40 Bookstore Director .... Mr. Keith **ANDERSON**
41 Athletic Director .... Mr. Andre **SPRINGS**
96 Director of Purchasing .... Ms. Debra **WOOD**
18 Director of Physical Plant .... Ms. Jean **GRIFFIN**
23 Health Services Manager .... Ms. Ethel **PEEBLES**

Louisburg College (B)

501 N. Main Street, Louisburg NC 27549-7705
County: Franklin FICE Identification: 002943
Unit ID: 198871
Telephone: (919) 496-2521 Carnegie Class: Assoc/HT-High Trad
FAX Number: (919) 496-7141 Calendar System: Semester
URL: www.louisburg.edu
Established: 1787 Annual Undergrad Tuition & Fees: $17,346
Enrollment: 701 Coed
Affiliation or Control: United Methodist IRS Status: 501(c)3
Highest Offering: Associate Degree
Accreditation: **SC**

01 President .... Rev Dr. Mark D. **LA BRANCHE**
05 Provost .... Dr. James C. **ECK**
11 VP of Administration/Inst Effect .... Vacant
30 VP of Institutional Advancement .... Mr. Chad **BAREFOOT**
32 VP of Student Life .... Mr. Jason E. **MODLIN**
10 VP of Finance .... Ms. Dawn **ROBINSON**
84 Senior VP of Enrollment Management .... Ms. Stephanie B. **TOLBERT**
29 Alumni Director .... Ms. Jamie **PATRICK**
06 Registrar .... Dr. Michelle **AHERON**
08 Librarian .... Ms. Pat **HINTON**
38 Director of Counseling Services .... Ms. Fonda **PORTER**
37 Director of Financial Aid .... Mr. Thomas **WELCH**
26 Director of College Communications .... Ms. Candy **GREGOR**
18 Associate VP of Facilities .... Mr. Nathan **BIEGENZAHN**
04 Executive Asst to President ... Ms. Jennifer **MITCHELL WHEELER**
07 Director of Admissions .... Ms. Maura **BUDUSKY**
09 Director of Institutional Research .... Ms. Brittany **HUNT**
19 Campus Police Chief .... Vacant
39 Director of Housing .... Mr. Christopher **REID**
41 Athletic Director .... Mr. Mike **HOLLOMAN**
13 Chief Technology Officer .... Mr. Mark **JOYNER**
15 Director of Human Resources .... Ms. Terry **WRIGHT**

Mars Hill University (C)

PO Box 370, Mars Hill NC 28754-0370
County: Madison FICE Identification: 002944
Unit ID: 198899
Telephone: (828) 689-1307 Carnegie Class: Bac-Diverse
FAX Number: (828) 689-1478 Calendar System: Semester
URL: www.mhu.edu
Established: 1856 Annual Undergrad Tuition & Fees: $29,382
Enrollment: 1,435 Coed
Affiliation or Control: Independent Non-Profit IRS Status: 501(c)3
Highest Offering: Master's
Accreditation: **SC**, #CAATE, MUS, SW, TED, THEA

01 President .... Dr. Dan G. **LUNSFORD**
30 Vice President for Inst Advancement .... Mr. Harold (Bud) G. **CHRISTMAN**
05 Int Vice Pres for Academic Affairs .... Dr. Jason A. **PIERCE**
10 Vice Pres Finance/Facilities Mgmt .... Mr. Neil **TILLEY**
32 Assoc Vice Pres for Student Devel ...... Dr. Laura **WHITAKER-LEA**
20 Asst Vice Pres for Academic Admin .... Dr. Jim **BROWN**
07 Director of Admissions .... Ms. Kristie **VANCE**
06 Dean Academic Records/Registrar .... Ms. Marie **NICHOLSON**
08 Director of Library Services .... Ms. Beverly **ROBERTSON**
26 Sr Director of Marketing .... Ms. Samantha **FENDER**
42 Campus Chaplain .... Rev. Stephanie **MCLESKEY**
41 Director of Athletics .... Mr. David W. **RIGGINS**
37 Director of Financial Aid .... Ms. Nichole **BUCKNER**
29 Director of Alumni & Donor Rels .... Mr. John **CHASTAIN**
85 Director International Education .... Mr. Gordon **HINNERS**
09 Director Institutional Research .... Dr. Suzanne C. **KLONIS**
38 Director Student Counseling .... Ms. Cassandra **PAVONE**
15 AVP Human Resources/Strategic Init .... Dr. Joy **KISH**
13 Director Information Technology Svc .... Mr. Gerald D. **BALL**
18 Director of Facilities .... Mr. Donald **EDWARDS**
40 Director of Bookstore .... Mr. Darryl R. **NORTON**
51 Dean of Adult & Graduate Studies .... Vacant
97 Chair of General Studies .... Ms. Cathy L. **ADKINS**

Meredith College (D)

3800 Hillsborough Street, Raleigh NC 27607-5298
County: Wake FICE Identification: 002945
Unit ID: 198950
Telephone: (919) 760-8600 Carnegie Class: Bac-A&S
FAX Number: (919) 760-2828 Calendar System: Semester
URL: www.meredith.edu
Established: 1891 Annual Undergrad Tuition & Fees: $33,730
Enrollment: 1,886 Female
Affiliation or Control: Independent Non-Profit IRS Status: 501(c)3
Highest Offering: Master's
Accreditation: **SC**, BUS, CIDA, DIETD, DIETI, MUS, SW, TED

01 President .... Dr. Jo **ALLEN**
05 Sr Vice Pres and Provost .... Dr. Matthew **POSLUSNY**
30 Vice Pres Institutional Advancement .... Dr. Charles (Lennie) **BARTON**
10 Vice Pres for Business & Finance .... Mr. Craig **BARFIELD**
32 Vice President for College Programs .... Dr. Jean **JACKSON**
35 Dean of Students .... Ms. Ann C. **GLEASON**
58 Director of Graduate Programs .... Dr. Monica **MCKINNEY**
06 Registrar .... Ms. Evie **ODOM**
09 Dir Research/Planning & Assessment .... Dr. C. Dianne **RAUBENHEIMER**
08 Director Library Info Services .... Ms. Laura **DAVIDSON**
07 Director of Admissions .... Ms. Shery **BOYLES**
37 Director of Financial Assistance .... Mr. Kevin **MICHAELSEN**
26 Executive Director of Marketing ... Ms. Kristi **EAVES-MCLENNAN**
35 Dir Student Activ/Leadership Devel .... Ms. Cheryl S. **JENKINS**
28 Assistant Dean of Students .... Ms. Tomecca **SLOANE**
36 Director Office of Career Planning .... Ms. Dana **SUMNER**
29 Dir of Alumnae & Parent Relations .... Ms. Hilary **ALLEN**
38 Director of Counseling Center .... Ms. Beth A. **MEIER**
39 Director Resident Life/Housing .... Ms. Heidi **LECOUNT**
20 Director of Academic Advising .... Mr. Alex **DAVIS**
31 Director Campus Events .... Mr. Bill **BROWN**
23 Director Health Services .... Dr. Mary **JOHNSON**
42 Campus Minister .... Rev. Donna **COLTRANE BATTLE**
13 Chief Information Officer .... Mr. Jeffrey **HOWLETT**
19 Chief Campus Police .... Mr. Al **WHITE**
15 Director of Human Resources .... Ms. Pamela **DAVIS**
18 Chief Facilities/Physical Plant .... Ms. Sharon **CAMPBELL**
21 Director of Accounting .... Ms. Susan **WILLIAMS**
88 Director of Learning Center .... Dr. Carmen **CHRISTOPHER**
104 Director of International Programs .... Dr. Brooke **SHURER**
88 Dir Retention & Student Success .... Mr. Brandon **STOKES**
88 Director of Strong Points .... Ms. Candice **WEBB**

Methodist University (E)

5400 Ramsey Street, Fayetteville NC 28311-1498
County: Cumberland FICE Identification: 002946
Unit ID: 198969
Telephone: (910) 630-7000 Carnegie Class: Masters/S
FAX Number: (910) 630-7317 Calendar System: Semester
URL: www.methodist.edu
Established: 1956 Annual Undergrad Tuition & Fees: $30,530
Enrollment: 2,461 Coed
Affiliation or Control: United Methodist IRS Status: 501(c)3
Highest Offering: Doctorate
Accreditation: **SC**, ACBSP, ARCPA, CAATE, NURSE, @PTA, SW

01 President .... Dr. Ben E. **HANCOCK, JR.**
05 Exec Vice Pres & Academic Dean .... Dr. Delmas S. **CRISP, JR.**
10 VP Business Affairs/Controller .... Ms. Dawn **AUSBORN**
32 Vice President for Student Affairs .... Mr. William **WALKER**
30 VP Univ Relations & Advancement .... Ms. Sandy **AMMONS**
09 VP Planning & Evaluation .... Dr. Donald L. **LASSITER**
84 Vice Pres Enrollment Management .... Mr. Rick D. **LOWE**
20 Associate VP for Academic Affairs .... Ms. Beth **CARTER**
35 Assoc Dean Student Services .... Mr. Todd D. **HARRIS**
42 VP Campus Ministry/Cmty Engagement .... Rev. Kelli **TAYLOR**
26 Director of Public Relations .... Mrs. Sandy **AMMONS**
41 VP/Director of Athletics .... Mr. Robert T. **MCEVOY**
29 Director of Alumni Affairs .... Ms. Kirbie **DOCKERY**
07 Dean of Admissions .... Mr. Jamie W. **LEGG**
37 Director of Financial Aid .... Ms. Bonnie J. **ADAMSON**
06 Registrar .... Ms. Jasmin K. **BROWN**
08 Head Librarian .... Ms. Tracey **PEARSON**
104 Dir Intl Programs/Study Abroad .... Mr. Lyle **SHEPPARD**
19 Director Police/Public Safety .... Mr. Mark **BREWINGTON**
15 Director Personnel Services .... Mrs. Debra **YEATTS**
18 Director of Facilities .... Mr. Charles **GOURLAY**
36 Director Career Services .... Ms. Antoinette P. **BELLAMY**
38 Director Student Counseling .... Ms. Darlene **HOPKINS**
96 Director of Purchasing .... Ms. Deborah **DEMBOSKY**

Mid-Atlantic Christian University (F)

715 N Poindexter, Elizabeth City NC 27909-4054
County: Pasquotank FICE Identification: 022809
Unit ID: 199458
Telephone: (252) 334-2000 Carnegie Class: Spec-4-yr-Faith
FAX Number: (252) 334-2071 Calendar System: Semester
URL: www.macuniversity.edu
Established: 1948 Annual Undergrad Tuition & Fees: $13,440
Enrollment: 196 Coed
Affiliation or Control: Churches Of Christ IRS Status: 501(c)3
Highest Offering: Baccalaureate
Accreditation: **SC**

01 President .... Dr. D. Clay **PERKINS**
05 Vice President Academic Affairs .... Dr. Kevin W. **LARSEN**
32 Vice President Student Services .... Dr. Ken S. **GREENE**
30 Vice President Institutional Advanc .... Mr. John **MAURICE**
10 Vice President Finance .... Mrs. Carol M. **STUART**
09 Director of Institutional Research .... Dr. Kevin W. **LARSEN**
06 Registrar .... Miss Yolanda K. **TESKE**
08 Director of Library .... Mr. Ken D. **GUNSELMAN**
38 Counselor .... Mr. Donald W. **MCKINNEY**
37 Financial Aid Administrator .... Mrs. Jenny **ROWLAND**
42 Campus Minister .... Mr. Drew **BROMM**
49 Chair of Arts and Sciences .... Dr. Robert W. **SMITH**
73 Chair of Biblical Studies .... Dr. Lee M. **FIELDS**
42 Chair of Christian Ministry .... Dr. Claudio F. **DIVINO**
88 Chair of Marketplace Ministry .... Mr. Donald W. **MCKINNEY**
35 Student Life Administrator .... Miss Andrea A. **STRAWDERMAN**
07 Enrollment Director .... Mr. Daniel C. **SMITH**

Miller-Motte College (G)

2205 Walnut Street, Cary NC 27518
Telephone: (919) 532-7171 Identification: 770726
Accreditation: **ACICS**, MAC, SURGT

† Branch campus of Miller-Motte Technical College, Lynchburg, VA

Miller-Motte College (H)

3725 Ramsey Street, Fayetteville NC 28311
Telephone: (910) 354-1900 Identification: 770728
Accreditation: **ACICS**

† Branch campus of Miller-Motte Technical College, Lynchburg, VA

Miller-Motte College (I)

1021 W.H. Smith Blvd, Suite 102, Greenville NC 27834
Telephone: (252) 215-2000 Identification: 770730
Accreditation: **ACICS**

† Branch campus of Miller-Motte Technical College, Clarksville, TN

Miller-Motte College (J)

1291 Hargett Street, Jacksonville NC 28540
Telephone: (910) 478-4300 Identification: 770729
Accreditation: **ACICS**

† Branch campus of Miller-Motte Technical College, Lynchburg, VA

Miller-Motte College (K)

3901 Capital Boulevard, Suite 151, Raleigh NC 27604
Telephone: (919) 723-2820 Identification: 770727
Accreditation: **ACICS**, DA, MAC

† Branch campus of Miller-Motte Technical College, Lynchburg, VA

Miller-Motte Technical College (L)

5000 Market Street, Wilmington NC 28405-3430
Telephone: (910) 392-4660 FICE Identification: 030632
Accreditation: **ACICS**, DA, MAC, SURGT

† Branch campus of Miller-Motte Technical College, TN.

Montreat College (M)

PO Box 1267, 310 Gaither Circle,
Montreat NC 28757-1267
County: Buncombe FICE Identification: 002948
Unit ID: 199032
Telephone: (828) 669-8012 Carnegie Class: Masters/S
FAX Number: (828) 669-9554 Calendar System: Semester
URL: www.montreat.edu
Established: 1916 Annual Undergrad Tuition & Fees: $24,220
Enrollment: 933 Coed
Affiliation or Control: Non-denominational IRS Status: 501(c)3
Highest Offering: Master's
Accreditation: **SC**

01 President .... Dr. Paul J. **MAURER**
10 VP for Finance and Administration .... Mr. Jack **HEINEN**
30 VP of Advancement .... Mr. Alex **MILLER**
58 VP and Dean for Adult/Grad Studies .... Mrs. Susan **DEWOODY**
05 VP and Dean for Academic Affairs .... Dr. Greg **KERR**
84 VP for Enrollment and Management .... Ms. Kristin **JANES**
32 VP and Dean for Student Services .... Dr. Daniel **BENNETT**
88 Counselor to the President .... Mr. Joe **KIRKLAND**

26 Exec Dir Marketing/Communications .... Mrs. Annie CARLSON
09 Assoc Dean of Academics & Inst Eff .... Vacant
20 Associate Dean of Academic Affairs .... Mr. Tom OXENREIDER
41 Athletic Director .... Mr. Jose LARIOS
29 Director Alumni Relations .... Mr. David WALTERS
37 Director of Financial Aid .... Ms. Beth POCOCK
38 Director of Counseling .... Mrs. Holleigh WOODWARD
88 Director for Advancement Services .... Ms. Kristine BUCKWALTER
08 Library Director .... Ms. Elizabeth R. PEARSON
21 Controller .... Mrs. Patti GUFFEY
04 Executive Assistant to President .... Ms. Hope DEIFELL
42 Dean of Spiritual Formation .... Rev. David TAYLOR
06 Registrar .... Ms. Keri BOER
40 Bookstore Manager .... Mr. Robert WALKER
19 Interim Chief of Campus Police .... Ms. Phyllis COMRIE
18 Chief Facilities/Physical Plant .... Mr. Jim LEENHOUTS

Native American Bible College (A)

PO Box 248, Shannon NC 28386

County: Robeson Identification: 667092
Telephone: (910) 843-5304 Carnegie Class: Not Classified
FAX Number: N/A Calendar System: Semester
URL: nativeamericanbiblecollege.org
Established: 1968 Annual Undergrad Tuition & Fees: N/A
Enrollment: N/A Coed
Affiliation or Control: Assemblies Of God Church IRS Status: 501(c)3
Highest Offering: Baccalaureate
Accreditation: @BI

01 President .... James A. KEYS
05 Chief Academic Officer .... Dossie MORRIS WOOD, JR.
32 Chief Student Development Officer .... John DAVIS
08 Chief Librarian .... T. Liisa KELLY
07 Director of Admissions/Registrar .... April LOCKLEAR

*North Carolina Community College System (B)

200 W Jones Street, 5001 MSC, Raleigh NC 27699-5001

County: Wake FICE Identification: 033445
Unit ID: 199166
Telephone: (919) 807-7100 Carnegie Class: N/A
FAX Number: (919) 807-7166
URL: www.nccommunitycolleges.edu

01 President .... Dr. James WILLIAMSON
05 Senior VP Programs/Chief Acad Ofcr .... Dr. Lisa CHAPMAN
10 Exec VP Operation/Chief Fin Ofcr .... Ms. Jennifer HAYGOOD
13 VP Technology Solutions .... Ms. Julie BATCHELOR
46 Assoc VP for STEM Innovation .... Dr. Matthew MEYER
101 Exec Director State Board Affairs .... Mr. Bryan JENKINS
04 Special Assistant to the President .... Ms. Pia MCKENZIE

*Alamance Community College (C)

1247 Jimmie Kerr Road/PO Box 8000,
Graham NC 27253-8000

County: Alamance FICE Identification: 005463
Unit ID: 199786
Telephone: (336) 578-2002 Carnegie Class: Assoc/MT-VT-Mix Trad/Non
FAX Number: (336) 578-1987 Calendar System: Semester
URL: www.alamancecc.edu
Established: 1958 Annual Undergrad Tuition & Fees (In-District): $2,190
Enrollment: 4,437 Coed
Affiliation or Control: State/Local IRS Status: 501(c)3
Highest Offering: Associate Degree
Accreditation: SC, ACFEI, DA, MAC, MLTAD

02 President .... Dr. Algie C. GATEWOOD
05 Executive Vice President .... Mr. Scott QUEEN
10 VP Admin & Fiscal Svcs .... Ms. Cynthia COLLIE
30 VP Institutional Advancement .... Ms. Carolyn RHODE
49 VP of Instruction .... Ms. Catherine W. JOHNSON
103 VP Workforce Development .... Mr. Gary SAUNDERS
32 VP Student Success .... Dr. Carol DISQUE
50 Dean Business/Arts & Sciences .... Ms. Sonya MCCOOK
72 Dean Industrial Technologies .... Mr. Wally M. SHEARIN
69 Dean Health & Public Svcs .... Mr. David FRAZEE
21 Controller .... Mr. Matthew BANKO
06 Registrar .... Mr. Kenneth DOBBINS
11 Director Administrative Services .... Vacant
15 Director Human Resources .... Ms. Lorri ALLISON
13 Director Information Services .... Mr. Winfield HENRY
08 Director Learning Resources Center .... Ms. Sheila STREET
26 Director Public Information/Mktg .... Mr. Edward WILLIAMS
56 Director Occupational Ext Program .... Mr. David PARKER
84 Director Enrollment Management .... Ms. Elizabeth BREHLER
37 Director Financial Aid .... Ms. Sabrina DEGAIN
36 Director Counseling & Career Svcs .... Ms. Ilona OWENS
38 Special Needs/Counseling Svcs Coord .... Ms. Monica ISBELL
88 Academic Support Specialist .... Ms. Jennifer BROWNELL
09 Institutional Researcher .... Dr. Jessica HARRELL
19 Director Security/Safety .... Mr. David PREVATTE

*Asheville - Buncombe Technical Community College (D)

340 Victoria Road, Asheville NC 28801-4897

County: Buncombe FICE Identification: 004033
Unit ID: 197887
Telephone: (828) 254-1921 Carnegie Class: Assoc/MT-VT-Mix Trad/Non
FAX Number: (828) 251-6355 Calendar System: Semester
URL: www.abtech.edu
Established: 1959 Annual Undergrad Tuition & Fees (In-District): $2,419
Enrollment: 7,507 Coed
Affiliation or Control: State/Local IRS Status: 501(c)3
Highest Offering: Associate Degree
Accreditation: SC, ACFEI, DA, DH, DMS, EMT, MAC, MLTAD, PHLEB, RAD, SURGT

02 President .... Dr. Dennis KING
10 VP Business & Finance/CFO .... Dr. Dirk WILMOTH
13 Vice Pres Information Technology .... Mr. Brian WILLIS
05 VP Instructional Services .... Ms. Melissa QUINLEY
20 Associate VP Instructional Services .... Dr. Gene LOFLIN
32 VP Student Services .... Dr. Terry BRASIER
15 Vice President Human Resources & OD .... Ms. Kaye SCHMIDT
103 VP Econ Workforce Dev/Cont Educ .... Ms. Shelley WHITE
04 Executive Administrative Assistant .... Ms. Martha SHANKS
49 Dean Arts & Sciences .... Dr. Beth STEWART
50 Dean Business & Hospitality Educ .... Mr. RJ CORMAN
54 Dean Engineering & Applied Tech .... Mr. Vernon D. DAUGHERTY
91 Director Info Systems Technology .... Mr. David C. MCKINNEY
30 Int Exec Dir College Advancement .... Ms. Susan HALDANE
35 Director Student Life/Development .... Ms. Michele HATHCOCK
61 Director Law Enforcement Academy .... Vacant
21 Director Business Services .... Vacant
37 Director of Financial Aid .... Ms. Cynthia ANDERSON
06 Registrar .... Ms. LaCandance SPEIGHT
84 Director Enrollment Services .... Ms. Lisa F. BUSH
24 Director Library Services .... Mr. Russell TAYLOR
12 Director Madison County Campus .... Ms. Sherri DAVIS
18 Director Plant Operations .... Mr. Benny R. SMITH
19 Chief of Police/Security .... Ms. Kara WALKER
31 Director Community Services Program .... Ms. Brenda W. CALDWELL
08 Librarian .... Ms. Margaret HIGGINS
09 Exec Director Research & Planning .... Mr. David B. WHITE
26 Exec Dir Community Rels/Marketing .... Ms. Kerr GLOVER
28 Director of Diversity .... Vacant
40 Bookstore Manager .... Mr. Kevin MILLS
96 Purchasing Agent .... Ms. Rebecca R. WATKINS
72 Dir Cust Rels/Technology Services .... Mr. Cris HARSHMAN

*Beaufort County Community College (E)

5337 US Hwy 264 East, Washington NC 27889-7989

County: Beaufort FICE Identification: 008558
Unit ID: 197966
Telephone: (252) 946-6194 Carnegie Class: Assoc/MT-VT-Mix Trad/Non
FAX Number: (252) 946-0271 Calendar System: Semester
URL: www.beaufortccc.edu
Established: 1967 Annual Undergrad Tuition & Fees (In-District): $2,368
Enrollment: 2,035 Coed
Affiliation or Control: State/Local IRS Status: 501(c)3
Highest Offering: Associate Degree
Accreditation: SC, MLTAD

02 President .... Dr. Barbara TANSEY
05 VP of Academics .... Dr. Crystal ANGE
10 VP of Administrative Services .... Mr. Mark NELSON
32 VP of Student Services .... Mr. Rick ANDERSON
51 VP of Continuing Education .... Ms. Stacey GERARD
45 VP of Research & Inst Effectiveness .... Dr. Jay SULLIVAN
26 Public Relations Coordinator .... Ms. Betty GRAY
31 Dir of Community Partnerships .... Mr. Clay CARTER
76 Dean Allied Health/Profess Services .. Mrs. Erica S. CARACOGLIA
49 Dean Arts & Sciences .... Mrs. Lisa HILL
50 Dean of Business & Industrial Tech .... Mr. Ben MORRIS
08 Dir Learning Resources Center .... Mrs. Penny SERMONS
14 Network Administrator .... Mr. Whiting TOLER
91 System Administrator .... Mr. Randy BURNETTE
15 Director of Human Resources .... Mrs. Emily WOOLARD
19 Chief of Campus Police .... Mr. Christopher HARRISON
88 Systems Administrator Assistant .... Mr. Brandon BUNCH
37 Director of Financial Aid .... Ms. Jo WOOLARD
06 Registrar .... Ms. Melissa A. FRANCIS
07 Director of Admissions .... Mrs. Michele MAYO
103 Dir of Business & Industry Svcs .... Mr. Lentz STOWE
04 Administrative Asst to President .... Mrs. Jennie SINGLETON
96 Purchasing Coordinator .... Ms. Rebecca ADAMS
38 Director of Counseling .... Mrs. Kimberly JACKSON
102 Executive Dir of Foundation .... Ms. Serena SULLIVAN
105 Webmaster .... Mr. Keith SULLIVAN
18 Dir Campus Operations .... Mr. Wesley ADAMS
13 Director of Information Technology .... Mr. Arthur RICHARD
21 Director of Accounting .... Ms. Cecelia SCOTT

*Bladen Community College (F)

PO Box 266, Dublin NC 28332-0266

County: Bladen FICE Identification: 007987
Unit ID: 198011
Telephone: (910) 879-5500 Carnegie Class: Assoc/MT-VT-High Non
FAX Number: (910) 879-5564 Calendar System: Semester
URL: www.bladencc.edu
Established: 1967 Annual Undergrad Tuition & Fees (In-State): $2,397
Enrollment: 1,334 Coed
Affiliation or Control: State IRS Status: 501(c)3
Highest Offering: Associate Degree
Accreditation: SC

02 President .... Dr. William FINDT

04 Exec Admin Asst to the President .... Ms. Missi HESTER
05 Executive VP and Chief Acad Officer .... Mr. Jeffrey KORNEGAY
51 VP for Continuing Education .... Ms. Sondra GUYTON
20 Assoc VP for Academic Services .... Ms. Cynthia MCKOY
32 Vice President for Student Services .... Mr. Barry PRIEST
10 Vice President for Finance .... Mr. Jay STANLEY
88 Assoc VP for Program Services .... Mr. Lynn KING
21 Director of Budgeting .... Ms. Sheila DOCKERY
08 Director Student Resource Center .... Ms. Sherwin RICE
09 Dir Institutional Effect & Planning .... Ms. Twyla DAVIS
37 Director of Financial Aid .... Ms. Samantha BENSON
106 Director of Distance Learning .... Mr. Ray SHEPPARD
15 Human Resources Officer .... Ms. Tiina MUNDY
18 Director of Facilities .... Mr. Bradley TAYLOR
26 Public Information Specialist .... Ms. Cathy KINLAW
102 Foundation Specialist .... Ms. Linda BURNEY

*Blue Ridge Community College (G)

180 W Campus Drive, Flat Rock NC 28731-4728

County: Henderson FICE Identification: 009684
Unit ID: 198039
Telephone: (828) 694-1700 Carnegie Class: Assoc/MT-VT-High Trad
FAX Number: (828) 694-1690 Calendar System: Semester
URL: www.blueridge.edu
Established: 1969 Annual Undergrad Tuition & Fees (In-District): $2,389
Enrollment: 2,215 Coed
Affiliation or Control: State/Local IRS Status: 501(c)3
Highest Offering: Associate Degree
Accreditation: SC, EMT, SURGT

02 President .... Dr. Molly PARKHILL
05 VP for Instruction .... Dr. Alan H. STEPHENSON
32 VP for Student Services .... Ms. Marcia L. STONEMAN
13 VP for Technology-CIO .... Vacant
103 VP Workforce Dev/Cont Education .... Ms. Julie G. THOMPSON
10 AVP for Finance/CFO .... Ms. Carolyn W. ALLEY
11 Vice Pres General Administration .... Dr. Chad MERRILL
49 Dean for Arts and Sciences .... Mr. David H. DAVIS
72 Dean for Applied Technology .... Mr. Chris ENGLISH
76 Dean for Allied Health Programs .... Ms. Rita D. CONNER
97 Dean for Basic Skills .... Ms. Robin NORRIS-PAULISON
50 Dean for Business/Service Careers .... Ms. Kathy ALLEN
102 Executive Director Foundation .... Ms. Ann F. GREEN
44 Institutional Advance/Rsrch Coord .... Ms. Carol Ann LYDON
06 Registrar .... Ms. Kirsten H. BUNCH
08 Director for Library Services .... Ms. Susan D. WILLIAMS
37 Director Financial Aid .... Ms. Lisanne MASTERSON
38 Director for Counseling .... Vacant
14 Director Information Technologies .... Mr. Steve YOUNG
18 Director of Facilities .... Mr. Peter HEMANS
26 Dir of Marketing & Communications .... Ms. Lee Anna HANEY
35 Student Activities Coordinator .... Ms. Cathy STEPHENSON
84 Director of Enrollment Management .... Ms. Cathy STEPHENSON
15 Director of Human Resources .... Mr. Tommy OAKMAN

*Brunswick Community College (H)

50 College Road, Bolivia NC 28422

County: Brunswick FICE Identification: 021707
Unit ID: 198084
Telephone: (910) 755-7300 Carnegie Class: Assoc/HT-High Trad
FAX Number: (910) 754-9609 Calendar System: Semester
URL: www.brunswickcc.edu
Established: 1979 Annual Undergrad Tuition & Fees (In-State): $2,404
Enrollment: 1,814 Coed
Affiliation or Control: State IRS Status: 501(c)3
Highest Offering: Associate Degree
Accreditation: SC, CAHIIM, PHLEB

02 President .... Dr. Susanne H. ADAMS
05 VP Academic & Student Affairs .... Vacant
10 Vice President Budget and Finance .... Ms. Sheila GALLOWAY
32 Dean Student Services/Enroll Mgmt .... Ms. Lori GRAHAM
11 Vice President Operations .... Mr. Donald BASSINGER
09 Director of Institutional Planning .... Mr. Michael COBB
08 Director Library .... Ms. Carmen BLANTON
06 Registrar .... Ms. Christine DYE
15 Director Human Resources .... Ms. Nicole WILLIAMS
19 Public Safety/Police Director .... Mr. Lindsay WALTON
18 Physical Plant Director .... Mr. Jack LUCIANO
102 Director Resource Development .... Ms. Elina DICOSTANZO
26 Director of Marketing & Public Info .... Ms. London SCHMIDT
37 Financial Aid/Veterans Affs Coord .... Ms. Tracy SOMERLAD
72 Dean Professional Technical Service .... Ms. Gina ROBINSON
49 Dean Arts & Sciences .... Dr. John GRAY
04 Sr Executive Asst to President .... Ms. Bea PALAZZI
13 Chief Info Officer .... Mr. Ronnie BRYANT
41 Athletic Director .... Mr. Robert ALLEN
36 Director Student Placement .... Mrs. Christen COX

*Caldwell Community College and Technical Institute (I)

2855 Hickory Boulevard, Hudson NC 28638-1399

County: Caldwell FICE Identification: 004835
Unit ID: 198118
Telephone: (828) 726-2200 Carnegie Class: Assoc/HT-High Trad
FAX Number: (828) 726-2216 Calendar System: Semester
URL: www.cccti.edu
Established: 1964 Annual Undergrad Tuition & Fees (In-District): $2,444
Enrollment: 3,876 Coed
Affiliation or Control: State/Local IRS Status: 501(c)3

Highest Offering: Associate Degree
Accreditation: SC, DMS, NMT, PTAA, RAD

02 President ... Dr. Kenneth A. BOHAM
03 Executive Vice President ... Dr. Mark POARCH
18 Director Facility Services ... Mr. Jeff HERMAN
32 Vice President Student Services ... Mrs. Dena HOLMAN
103 VP Continuing Educ/Workforce Dev ... Mrs. Elaine LOCKHART
12 Executive Director Watauga Campus ... Mr. Steve MELTON
05 Director Academic Support ... Vacant
84 Dir Enrollment Mgmt Services ... Mr. Dennis SEAGLE
08 Director Learning Resources Center ... Ms. Alison BEARD
37 Director Financial Aid/Veterans Aff ... Mrs. Shanna KIRBY
36 Dir Career Planning/Job Placement ... Mr. Rick SHEW
15 Director Human Resources ... Mrs. Kathy SEITZ
26 Director Marketing & Communications ... Mrs. Sherry WILSON
10 Controller ... Mr. Scott ROGERS
09 Dir Inst Effectiveness/Research ... Mrs. Kim GANT
27 Public Relations Officer ... Mr. Edward TERRY
102 Director Foundation Office ... Ms. Marla CHRISTIE
28 Director of Diversity ... Mr. Jimmie GRIFFITH
38 Director Student Counseling ... Mr. Shannon BROWN
96 Director of Purchasing ... Mrs. Marcia POTTS
40 Manager Bookstore ... Mrs. Trina CURTIS
04 Executive Assistant ... Mrs. Donna CHURCH
19 Director Security/Safety ... Mr. Dennis HOPKINS
06 Registrar ... Mrs. Debra YOUNT
13 Chief Info Technology Officer (CIO) ... Ms. Susan WOOTEN

*Cape Fear Community College (A)

411 N Front Street, Wilmington NC 28401-3993
County: New Hanover FICE Identification: 005320
Unit ID: 198154
Telephone: (910) 362-7000 Carnegie Class: Assoc/MT-VT-Mix Trad/Non
FAX Number: (910) 763-2279 Calendar System: Semester
URL: www.cfcc.edu
Established: 1958 Annual Undergrad Tuition & Fees (In-District): $2,654
Enrollment: 9,062 Coed
Affiliation or Control: State/Local IRS Status: 501(c)3
Highest Offering: Associate Degree
Accreditation: SC, ADNUR, DA, DH, DMS, OTA, PHLEB, RAD, SURGT

02 President ... Dr. Amanda LEE
05 VP Academic Affairs & Workforce Dev ... Ms. Melissa SINGLER
10 VP Business & Financial Services ... Mr. Jim MORTON
32 VP Student Svcs & Enrollment Mgmt ... Mr. Daryl MINUS
09 Exec Dir Inst Effective/Planning ... Mr. Pat HOGAN
06 Registrar ... Vacant
102 Exec Dir of the Foundation ... Ms. Margaret ROBISON
31 Exec Dir Community Relations ... Ms. Rachel NADEAU
84 Director of Enrollment Management ... Ms. Linda KASYAN
08 Dean Learning Resources Center ... Ms. Catherine LEE
37 Director of Financial Aid ... Ms. Rachel CAVANUAGH
36 Director of Career & Testing ... Mr. Patrick PITTMAN
26 Dir of Marketing/Creative Services ... Mr. David M. HARDIN
15 Chief Human Resources Officer ... Ms. Elaine DOELL
35 Dean of Student Affairs ... Mr. Robert MCGEE
96 Director of Purchasing & Inventory ... Mr. Wade QUINN
38 Director Student Counseling ... Ms. Jacqueline FOSTER
21 Controller ... Ms. Christina GREENE
28 Director of Diversity ... Mr. David HARDIN
07 Director of Admissions ... Ms. Linda KASYAN
44 Annual Giving Director ... Vacant
51 Dean of Continuing Education ... Mr. Robert TURNER
75 Dean Vocational/Technical Education ... Mr. Mark COUNCIL
49 Dean Arts & Sciences ... Ms. Orangel J. DANIELS
105 Web Services Analyst ... Ms. Christina HEIKKILA
04 Exec Assistant to the President ... Ms. Michelle LEE
19 Director Security/Safety ... Chief Dan WILCOX
89 First Year Student Success Init ... Dr. Jennifer MCBRIDE
79 Dir Humanities & Fine Arts Center ... Mr. Shane FERNANDO
25 Director of Grant Development ... Ms. Val CLEMMONS
22 Dir of Disability Support Services ... Ms. Aimee HELMUS
41 Dir Student Activities/Athletics ... Mr. Ryan MANTLO
88 Dir of Capital Projects Mgmt/Reno ... Mr. David KANOY
106 Online Learning Coordinator ... Dr. Chantae CALHOUN
13 Chief Info Technology Officer (CIO) ... Mr. Wellington DE SOUZA

*Carteret Community College (B)

3505 Arendell Street, Morehead City NC 28557-2989
County: Carteret FICE Identification: 008081
Unit ID: 198206
Telephone: (252) 222-6000 Carnegie Class: Assoc/MT-VT-High Trad
FAX Number: (252) 222-2514 Calendar System: Semester
URL: www.carteret.edu
Established: 1963 Annual Undergrad Tuition & Fees (In-District): $2,704
Enrollment: 1,659 Coed
Affiliation or Control: State/Local IRS Status: 501(c)3
Highest Offering: Associate Degree
Accreditation: SC, ADNUR, COARC, MAC, RAD

02 President ... Dr. Kerry L. YOUNGBLOOD
05 VP for Instruction/Student Support ... Ms. Tracy MANCINI
10 VP Finance/Administrative Services ... Ms. Kary PORTER
31 Vice Pres Corp/Community Education ... Mr. Perry L. HARKER
04 Exec Dir Office of the President ... Ms. Logan L. OKUN
08 Director LRC ... Ms. Elizabeth BAKER
32 Dean of Student Services ... Ms. Robie MCFARLAND
35 Director of Student Success ... Mr. Rick HILL
13 Director Information Technology ... Mr. John GREEN
15 Director of Human Resources ... Ms. Barbara I. COOPER
30 Director of Development ... Ms. Brenda REASH
49 Dean Arts & Sciences ... Ms. Doree HILL
76 Dean of Health Sciences ... Ms. Laurie A. FRESHWATER
88 Dean of Applied Science ... Ms. Susan H. MCINTYRE
37 Financial Aid Officer ... Ms. Brenda J. LONG
06 Registrar ... Ms. Tammi COBLE
07 Admissions Officer ... Mr. Martin NICHOLS
09 Dir of Institutional Effectiveness ... Ms. Mary CLARK
18 Dir Operations/Facil Maintenance ... Mr. Steve SPARKS
26 Director of Public Affairs ... Ms. Alize PROISY
96 Purchasing/Accts Payable Manager ... Ms. Donna L. CUMBIE
106 Director Distance Learning ... Ms. Mary WALTON

*Catawba Valley Community College (C)

2550 Highway 70, SE, Hickory NC 28602-9699
County: Catawba FICE Identification: 005318
Unit ID: 198233
Telephone: (828) 327-7000 Carnegie Class: Assoc/HT-Mix Trad/Non
FAX Number: (828) 327-7276 Calendar System: Semester
URL: www.cvcc.edu
Established: 1960 Annual Undergrad Tuition & Fees (In-District): $2,195
Enrollment: 4,742 Coed
Affiliation or Control: State/Local IRS Status: 501(c)3
Highest Offering: Associate Degree
Accreditation: SC, ADNUR, CAHIIM, COARC, DH, EMT, IFSAC, NDT, POLYT, RAD, SURGT

02 President ... Dr. Garrett D. HINSHAW
05 Exec Vice President of Instruction ... Dr. Keith MACKIE
10 Sr VP Business Affairs-Operations ... Mr. Wes BUNCH
32 Dean of Student Access/Development ... Mrs. Cindy COULTER
15 Director Human Resources ... Mr. Roger IRVIN
07 Director of Admissions/Records ... Ms. Kelly PLUMLEY
21 Controller ... Ms. Jennifer HAMM
37 Director Scholarships/Financial Aid ... Ms. RaChele SUMMERS
09 Ofc Accountability/Efficienc/Effect ... Mr. Kevin ROUSE
88 Director Industrial Training ... Ms. Crystal GLENN
88 Director Small Business Center ... Mr. Jeff NEUVILLE
50 Director Business/Technology Ext ... Ms. Susan KILLIAN
88 Director Hosiery Technology Center ... Mr. Daniel C. ST. LOUIS
13 Director Information Technologies ... Mr. Ken ELLIOTT
19 Director Campus Safety/Security ... Mr. Steve HUNT
31 Director Community Education ... Ms. Chanell MORELLO
36 Counselor/Job Placement Svcs Coord ... Ms. Teresa RAY
16 Coordinator Health/Human Services ... Ms. Robin ROSS
04 Administrative Asst to President ... Ms. Sherry WILLIAMS
29 Director Alumni Relations ... Ms. Mary REYNOLDS
41 Athletic Director ... Mr. Nick SCHROEDER

*Central Carolina Community College (D)

1105 Kelly Drive, Sanford NC 27330-9000
County: Lee FICE Identification: 005449
Unit ID: 198251
Telephone: (919) 775-5401 Carnegie Class: Assoc/MT-VT-Mix Trad/Non
FAX Number: (919) 718-7380 Calendar System: Semester
URL: www.cccc.edu
Established: 1958 Annual Undergrad Tuition & Fees (In-District): $2,412
Enrollment: 4,776 Coed
Affiliation or Control: State/Local IRS Status: 501(c)3
Highest Offering: Associate Degree
Accreditation: SC, DA, DH, MAC, POLYT

02 President ... Dr. T. Eston MARCHANT
05 Vice President of Student Learning ... Dr. Brian MERRITT
11 Vice Pres of Administrative Svcs ... Mr. Philip PRICE
32 Vice President Student Services ... Mr. Ken R. HOYLE
51 VP Economic & Community Development ... Ms. Pamela SENEGAL
26 Assoc VP of Marketing/HR ... Ms. Marcie DISHMAN
12 Provost Chatham Campus ... Mr. Mark HALL
12 Provost Harnett Campus ... Mr. William R. TYSON
20 Dean of Student Learning ... Mr. Mike BECK
08 Director of Library Services ... Ms. Tara LUCAS
15 Assoc Director of Human Resources ... Ms. Valerie BENN
102 Exec Director of CCCC Foundation ... Ms. Emily HARE
06 Dean of Enrollment/Registrar ... Ms. Jamie CHILDRESS
07 Director of Admissions ... Ms. Jamee STIFFLER
37 Director Financial Aid ... Ms. Zilma LOPES
96 Purchasing Director ... Mrs. Starlene JACKSON
18 Physical Plant Manager ... Mr. Ronnie MEASAMER
75 Dean Vocational/Technical Programs ... Dr. Stephan ATHANS
36 Dean of College & Career Readiness ... Ms. Dawn TUCKER
76 Dean of Health Sciences ... Ms. Lisa GODFREY

*Central Piedmont Community College (E)

PO Box 35009, Charlotte NC 28235-5009
County: Mecklenburg FICE Identification: 002915
Unit ID: 198260
Telephone: (704) 330-2722 Carnegie Class: Assoc/HT-Mix Trad/Non
FAX Number: (704) 330-5045 Calendar System: Semester
URL: www.cpcc.edu
Established: 1963 Annual Undergrad Tuition & Fees (In-District): $2,664
Enrollment: 19,957 Coed
Affiliation or Control: State/Local IRS Status: 501(c)3
Highest Offering: Associate Degree
Accreditation: SC, ACFEI, ADNUR, CAHIIM, COARC, CVT, CYTO, DA, DH, EMT, ENGT, MAC, MLTAD, OTA, PTAA, SURGT

02 President ... Dr. P. Anthony ZEISS
05 VP for Learning and Workforce Devel ... Mr. Richard ZOLLINGER
84 VP Enrollment & Student Services ... Dr. Marcia CONSTON
10 VP Finance/Administrative Services ... Mr. Michael MOSS
13 VP for Technology and CIO ... Mr. David KIM
30 VP for Institutional Advancement ... Dr. Kevin MCCARTHY
04 Exec Assistant to the President ... Dr. Tracie CLARK
26 PIO & Asst to Pres Cmty Rels/Mktg ... Mr. Jeffrey LOWRANCE
103 Assoc VP Learning and Workforce Dev ... Dr. Deborah BOUTON
11 Assoc VP Financial Services ... Mr. Michael WHITEMAN
18 Assoc VP Facilities & Construction ... Ms. Vicki SAVILLE
09 Assoc VP Institutional Research ... Dr. Terri MANNING
88 Assoc VP Compliance and Audit ... Dr. Brenda LEONARD
15 Assoc VP of Human Resources ... Mr. Paul SANTOS
25 Assoc VP Government Rels & Grants ... Mr. Michael HORN
88 Assoc VP Services Corporation ... Ms. Quincy FOIL WHITE
35 Assoc VP Student Success ... Ms. Rita DAWKINS
12 Dean Levine Campus ... Dr. Edith MCELROY
12 Dean Merancas Campus ... Ms. Tamara WILLIAMS
12 Dean Central Campus ... Dr. Paul KOEHNKE
12 Dean Cato Campus ... Mr. George HENDERSON
12 Dean Harris Campus/AVP Corp Dev ... Ms. Mary VICKERS-KOCH
12 Dean Harper Campus ... Dr. Kelly TRAINOR
54 Dean STEM-S ... Mr. Chris PAYNTER
88 Dean Retention Services ... Dr. Clint MCELROY
32 Dean Student Life/Service Learning ... Mr. Mark HELMS
84 Dean Enrollment Management ... Dr. Daniel (JJ) MCEACHERN
08 Dean Libraries ... Ms. Gloria KELLEY
88 Dean College & Career Readiness ... Ms. Kathi MCLENDON
07 Dean Enrollment Services ... Dr. April JONES
106 Dean Profess Development/eLearning ... Ms. Karen MERRIMAN
88 Dir/Gen Station Manager WTVI PBS ... Ms. Amy BURKETT
22 Dir Affirmative Action/EEO ... Mr. Leon MATTHEWS
88 Dean Center for Global Engagement ... Ms. Janet MALKEMES

*Cleveland Community College (F)

137 S Post Road, Shelby NC 28152-6296
County: Cleveland FICE Identification: 008082
Unit ID: 198321
Telephone: (704) 669-6000 Carnegie Class: Assoc/MT-VT-Mix Trad/Non
FAX Number: (704) 669-4202 Calendar System: Semester
URL: www.clevelandcc.edu
Established: 1965 Annual Undergrad Tuition & Fees (In-District): $2,398
Enrollment: 2,990 Coed
Affiliation or Control: State/Local IRS Status: 501(c)3
Highest Offering: Associate Degree
Accreditation: SC, EMT, RAD, SURGT

02 President ... Dr. L. Steve THORNBURG
05 Vice President of Academic Programs ... Dr. Becky SAIN
32 Vice President of Student Services ... Dr. Andy GARDNER
03 Executive Vice President ... Dr. Shannon KENNEDY
51 Vice Pres of Continuing Education ... Mr. Ken MOONEY
30 Sr Dean Devel/Governmental Rels ... Mr. Eddie HOLBROOK
102 Executive Director CCC Foundation ... Mr. U. L. PATTERSON, III
09 Dean of Plng & Institutional Effect ... Mrs. Laura BOWEN
88 Director CECHS Relations ... Ms. Nedra MADDOX
37 Financial Aid Coordinator ... Ms. Emily HURDT
08 Dean of Learning Resources ... Mrs. Barbara MCKIBBIN
96 Purchasing Officer ... Mrs. Kathy EVERETT
18 Director of Physical Plant ... Mr. Mark FOX
19 Director of Security ... Mr. Richard FIELDS
15 Human Resources & Safety Manager ... Mr. Allen KNICELEY
13 Chief Information Officer ... Mr. Adam SWEEZY
14 Network Administrator ... Mr. Robin DYER
24 Audiovisual Coordinator ... Mr. Rodger PERRY
26 Public Info/Marketing Coordinator ... Mrs. Paula VESS
07 Admissions/Records Coordinator ... Ms. Emily AREY
49 Dean Arts & Sciences ... Vacant
50 Dean Business & Allied Health ... Dr. John LATTIMORE
75 Dean Vocational/Engrng/Public Svcs ... Mr. Bruce MACK
88 Dean Learning Center ... Dr. Chris NANNEY

*Coastal Carolina Community College (G)

444 Western Boulevard, Jacksonville NC 28546-6816
County: Onslow FICE Identification: 005316
Unit ID: 198330
Telephone: (910) 455-1221 Carnegie Class: Assoc/HVT-Mix Trad/Non
FAX Number: (910) 455-7027 Calendar System: Semester
URL: www.coastalcarolina.edu
Established: 1963 Annual Undergrad Tuition & Fees (In-District): $2,334
Enrollment: 4,355 Coed
Affiliation or Control: State/Local IRS Status: 501(c)3
Highest Offering: Associate Degree
Accreditation: SC, DA, DH, MLTAD, SURGT

02 President ... Dr. Ronald K. LINGLE
11 Executive Vice President ... Mr. David L. HEATHERLY
05 VP for Instruction ... Ms. Ginger TUTON
09 VP Inst Eff/Research/Innovation ... Ms. Sharon R. MCGINNIS
32 Division Chair for Student Services ... Dr. Donald R. HERRING
15 Personnel Officer ... Ms. Cindy B. WOOLRIDGE
26 Pub Info Ofcr/Ex Dir Col Foundation ... Ms. Krystal PHILLIPS
07 Director of Admissions ... Dr. Jessica RANERO-RAMIREZ
18 Dir Physical Plant/Auxiliary Svcs ... Ms. Carol PHILLIPS
37 Director for Financial Aid Services ... Ms. Tammy LYON

88 Director for Veterans Services ... Mr. Christopher P. SABIN
88 Director Economic Development ... Ms. Anne C. SHAW
84 Coordinator for Enrollment Services ... Mr. Timothy TOLFREE
04 Exec Assistant to the President ... Ms. Tonya L. MORTON

*College of the Albemarle (A)

1208 North Road Street, Elizabeth City NC 27906-2327
County: Pasquotank — FICE Identification: 002917
Unit ID: 197814
Telephone: (252) 335-0821 — Carnegie Class: Assoc/HT-Mix Trad/Non
FAX Number: (252) 335-2011 — Calendar System: Semester
URL: www.albemarle.edu
Established: 1960 — Annual Undergrad Tuition & Fees (In-District): $2,211
Enrollment: 2,408 — Coed
Affiliation or Control: State/Local — IRS Status: 501(c)3
Highest Offering: Associate Degree
Accreditation: SC, ADNUR, MAC, MLTAD, SURGT

02 President ... Dr. Kandi W. DEITEMEYER
10 Chief Financial Officer ... Mrs. Susan GENTRY
05 Vice President for Learning ... Dr. Evonne CARTER
32 VP for Student Suc & Enr Mgnt ... Ms. Lynn HURDLE-WINSLOW
12 Dean Dare County Campus ... Mr. Timothy SWEENEY
35 Assistant Dean SSEM ... Ms. Martha JOHNSON
30 Executive Director Foundation & Dev ... Mrs. Lisa A. JOHNSON
07 Director Admissions & Testing ... Vacant
37 Director Admissions & Financial Aid ... Ms. Angela R. GODFREY-DAWSON
88 Director Student Life & Leadership ... Ms. Brooke DOVE
06 Registrar ... Ms. Andrea DANCE
88 Director Small Business Center ... Ms. Ginger H. O'NEAL
78 Work-Based Learning Liaison ... Mrs. Lynn JENNINGS
04 Exec Assistant to the President ... Mrs. Jenna HATFIELD
08 Director Library ... Mr. Rodney WOOTEN
12 Dean Edenton-Chowan Campus ... Mr. Charles PURSER
13 Director Mgmt Information Services ... Mr. Wayman WHITE
15 Director Human Resources ... Ms. Wendy W. BRICKHOUSE
18 Director Physical Facilities ... Mr. Patrick CUTHRELL
11 Chief Operations Officer ... Mr. Joseph TURNER
40 Administrative Services Manager ... Ms. Lisa JONES
36 Director Counseling & Career Devel ... Vacant
09 Director of Inst Effectiveness ... Ms. Pamela FEDERLINE
88 Coord Prison Education Programs ... Mr. Andre WILLIAMS
88 Coordinator Secondary Education ... Mr. Derek MEREDITH
49 Dean Arts and Sciences ... Mr. Dean ROUGHTON
50 Dean Business & Applied Tech ... Mrs. Michelle WATERS
76 Dean Health & Wellness ... Ms. Robin HARRIS
83 Department Chair Social Sciences ... Mr. Rodger ROSSMAN
60 Dept Chair English & Comm ... Mrs. Laura MORRISON
81 Dept Chair Math and Science ... Ms. Rhonda WATTS
75 Dept Chair Design Manuf & Ind Tech ... Mr. Charles PURSER
77 Dept Chair Bus & Computer Sys Tech ... Ms. Sharon BROWN
57 Department Chair Human & Fine Arts ... Ms. Gale FLAX
88 Department Chair Public Services ... Mrs. Robin ZINSMEISTER
19 Director Public Safety & Preparedns ... Mr. Dennis SMITH
88 Dir Basic Skills/Workforce Reading ... Mrs. Wanda FLETCHER

*Craven Community College (B)

800 College Court, New Bern NC 28562-4984
County: Craven — FICE Identification: 006799
Unit ID: 198367
Telephone: (252) 638-7200 — Carnegie Class: Assoc/HT-Mix Trad/Non
FAX Number: (252) 638-4232 — Calendar System: Semester
URL: www.cravencc.edu
Established: 1965 — Annual Undergrad Tuition & Fees (In-District): $1,927
Enrollment: 2,991 — Coed
Affiliation or Control: State/Local — IRS Status: 501(c)3
Highest Offering: Associate Degree
Accreditation: SC, ACBSP, CAHIIM, MAC, PTAA

02 President ... Dr. Ray STAATS
05 VP for Instruction ... Ms. Kathleen GALLMAN
11 Vice Pres of Administrative Svcs ... Dr. Karla (Page) JONES-VARNELL
32 VP for Students ... Mr. Gery BAUCHER
49 Dean Liberal Arts & Univ Transfer ... Dr. Betty K. HATCHER
36 Dean Career Programs ... Mr. James R. MILLARD
09 Exec Dir of Institutional Effective ... Dr. Cynthia M. BELLACERO
06 Registrar ... Mr. John A. FONVILLE
30 Int Exec Dir Inst Advancement ... Mr. Charles WETHINGTON
12 Dean Havelock-Cherry Point Campus ... Mr. Walter CALABRESE
37 Director Financial Aid ... Ms. Kathryn M. BANKS
103 Dir Workforce Readiness & Spec Pgms ... Mr. Mark W. BEST
88 Director Basic Skills Programs ... Ms. Zeledith BLAKELY
08 Director Library Services ... Mrs. Catherine C. CAMPBELL
10 Exec Dir Financial Svcs/Purchasing ... Mrs. Cynthia A. PATTERSON
88 Director TRIO Student Support Svcs ... Ms. Jennifer BUMGARNER
15 Exec Dir HR/Chief Diversity Officer ... Mrs. Vickie MOSELEY-JONES
103 Dean Workforce Development ... Mr. Robin MATTHEWS
18 Director of Facilities ... Mr. John MELVILLE
13 Dean Technology Services/Facilities ... Ms. Bambi EDWARDS
96 Procurement & Fixed Assets Officer ... Mr. Hiram Todd MURPHREY
84 Dean Enrollment Management ... Ms. Zomar PETER
25 Dir Strategic Partnerships/Grants ... Ms. Monica MINUS
04 Exec Asst to Pres/Board of Trustees ... Ms. Cynthia ENSLEY
19 Dir of Security & Emergency Mgmt ... Mr. Paul DAMICO

*Davidson County Community College (C)

PO Box 1287, Lexington NC 27293-1287
County: Davidson — FICE Identification: 002919
Unit ID: 198376
Telephone: (336) 249-8186 — Carnegie Class: Assoc/MT-VT-High Trad
FAX Number: (336) 249-0379 — Calendar System: Semester
URL: www.davidsonccc.edu
Established: 1958 — Annual Undergrad Tuition & Fees (In-District): $2,460
Enrollment: 4,102 — Coed
Affiliation or Control: State/Local — IRS Status: 501(c)3
Highest Offering: Associate Degree
Accreditation: SC, ADNUR, CAHIIM, MAC, MLTAD

02 President ... Dr. Mary E. RITTLING
05 VP Academic Programs & Services ... Ms. Jeannine H. WOODY
32 VP Student Affairs ... Dr. Rhonda Q. COATS
10 VP Financial/Administrative Svcs ... Dr. Rusty HUNT
102 VP Ext Affairs/Exec Dir Foundation ... Ms. Jenny M. VARNER
76 Dean Health/Wellness/Pub Safety ... Ms. Rose MCDANIEL
97 Dean Gen Studies & Acad Support ... Dr. Christy FORREST
50 Dean Business Engineering Technical ... Mr. Rodney JACKSON
12 Dean Davie Campus ... Ms. Teresa KINES
35 Dean Student Services ... Mr. Kevin LINEBERRY
21 Dean Financial/Admin Svcs ... Ms. Laura L. YARBROUGH
27 VP Student Success & Communications ... Ms. Susan BURLESON
26 Sen Dir Marketing & Communications ... Ms. Terri SMITH
06 Dir Student Records/Registration ... Mr. Bryan MCCULLOUGH
36 Director Career Development ... Mr. Charles MAYER
18 Director Physical Plant Services ... Mr. Keith RAKER
15 Director Personnel Services ... Ms. Denise BARNHARDT
04 Administrative Asst to President ... Ms. Carleen TERRELL
08 Head Librarian ... Mr. Jason SETZER
37 Director Student Financial Aid ... Ms. Lori BLEVINS
41 Athletic Director ... Mr. Kenneth KIRK
07 Director of Admissions ... Mr. Antonio JORDAN
09 Director of Institutional Research ... Mr. Mark PUTERBAUGH
19 Director Security/Safety ... Ms. Rita MATHEWS
30 Chief Development/Advancement ... Ms. Kristin BRIGGS

*Durham Technical Community College (D)

1637 Lawson Street, Durham NC 27703-5023
County: Durham — FICE Identification: 005448
Unit ID: 198455
Telephone: (919) 536-7200 — Carnegie Class: Assoc/HT-Mix Trad/Non
FAX Number: (919) 686-3601 — Calendar System: Semester
URL: www.durhamtech.edu
Established: 1961 — Annual Undergrad Tuition & Fees (In-District): $1,840
Enrollment: 5,035 — Coed
Affiliation or Control: State/Local — IRS Status: 501(c)3
Highest Offering: Associate Degree
Accreditation: SC, ADNUR, CAHIIM, COARC, DT, EMT, MAC, OPD, OTA, PNUR, SURGT

02 President ... Dr. William G. INGRAM
30 Sr Vice Pres Institutional Advance ... Mr. Tom JAYNES
05 VP Stdnt Learning/Instruction Svcs ... Ms. Susan PARIS
10 VP Finance and Administration ... Mr. Matt WILLIAMS
51 VP Corp/Continuing Education ... Dr. Peter WOOLDRIDGE
32 VP Student Engage Dev Support ... Dr. Christine KELLY KLEESE
04 Executive Secy to the President ... Ms. Gloria GAY
09 Director Institutional Research ... Dr. Teri L. KAASA
35 Dean Student Services ... Ms. Lisa INMAN
13 Executive Director Info Tech Svcs ... Mr. Patrick HINES
15 Director Human Resources ... Ms. Kathy MCKINLEY
08 Director Library & Assoc Dean ... Ms. Irene H. LAUBE
37 Director Financial Aid ... Ms. Kevi DIXON
109 Director Auxiliary Services ... Ms. Yolanda V. MOORE-JONES
06 Director Student Records ... Ms. Castine WILLIAMS
84 Exec Dir Enrollment Management ... Vacant

*Edgecombe Community College (E)

2009 W Wilson Street, Tarboro NC 27886-9399
County: Edgecombe — FICE Identification: 008855
Unit ID: 198491
Telephone: (252) 823-5166 — Carnegie Class: Assoc/HVT-Mix Trad/Non
FAX Number: (252) 823-6817 — Calendar System: Semester
URL: www.edgecombe.edu
Established: 1967 — Annual Undergrad Tuition & Fees (In-District): $2,376
Enrollment: 2,552 — Coed
Affiliation or Control: State/Local — IRS Status: 501(c)3
Highest Offering: Associate Degree
Accreditation: SC, ADNUR, CAHIIM, COARC, MAC, PNUR, RAD, SURGT

02 President ... Dr. Deborah L. LAMM
05 Vice President of Instruction ... Dr. John D. ENAMAIT
11 Vice Pres Administrative Services ... Mr. Charlie R. HARRELL
32 Vice President Student Services ... Mr. Michael L. JORDAN
20 AVP Instruc/Curriculum/Cont Educ ... Mr. Lynn CALE
84 Dean Enrollment Management ... Mr. Tony ROOK
35 Dean of Students ... Ms. Samantha PHILLIPS
45 Director of Inst Effectiveness ... Ms. Sheila HOSKINS
26 Director of Public Information ... Ms. Mary T. BASS
08 Director of Library Services ... Ms. Deborah PARISHER
06 Registrar ... Ms. Cathy F. DUPREE
15 Director Personnel Services ... Ms. Susan BARKALOW
18 Chief Facilities/Physical Plant ... Mr. John BUTZ
37 Director Student Financial Aid ... Mr. Sherlock MCDOUGALD
04 Administrative Asst to President ... Ms. Julie B. THOMAS
13 Chief Info Technology Officer ... Mr. Neil BAKER
43 Dir Legal Services/General Counsel ... Ms. Carmen NUNALEE

*Fayetteville Technical Community College (F)

PO Box 35236, 2201 Hull Road, Fayetteville NC 28303-0236
County: Cumberland — FICE Identification: 007640
Unit ID: 198534
Telephone: (910) 678-8400 — Carnegie Class: Assoc/HT-Mix Trad/Non
FAX Number: (910) 678-8269 — Calendar System: Semester
URL: www.faytechcc.edu
Established: 1961 — Annual Undergrad Tuition & Fees (In-State): $2,394
Enrollment: 12,103 — Coed
Affiliation or Control: State — IRS Status: 501(c)3
Highest Offering: Associate Degree
Accreditation: SC, ADNUR, COARC, DA, DH, EMT, FUSER, NMT, PTAA, RAD, SURGT

02 President ... Dr. Larry KEEN
11 Vice Pres for Administrative Svcs ... Mr. Joseph W. LEVISTER, JR.
05 Sr Vice Pres Academic/Student Svcs ... Dr. David BRAND
15 VP Human Res/Inst Effect/Assessment ... Mr. Carl MITCHELL
10 Sr Vice Pres Business and Finance ... Mrs. Betty J. SMITH
26 Exec Dir Marketing/Public Relations ... Mr. Brent MICHAELS
72 Vice Pres Learning Technologies ... Mr. Bob J. ERVIN
51 Assoc Vice Pres for Cont Educ ... Dr. Jolee MARSH
32 Assoc Vice Pres Student Services ... Dr. Rosemary KELLY
88 Assoc Vice Pres Curriculum Programs ... Vacant
84 Dean Enrollment Mgmt/Financial Aid ... Mr. Harper SHACKELFORD
06 Registrar ... Ms. Melissa A. JONES
21 Assoc Vice Pres Business & Finance ... Mrs. Robin DEAVER
07 Director of Admissions ... Dr. Louanna CASTLEMAN
13 Director Management Information Svc ... Mrs. Pamela SCULLY
12 Dean of Spring Lake Campus ... Ms. DeSandra WASHINGTON
18 Director of Facility Services ... Mr. Harold WYCKOFF
96 Procurement Manager Business/Financ ... Ms. Amy SAMPERTON
50 Dean of Business Programs ... Mrs. Cindy BURNS
49 Dean of Arts/Humanities ... Mr. Antonio JACKSON
76 Dean of Health Programs ... Mrs. Susan ELLIS
54 Dean Engr/Applied Tech Pgms ... Mrs. Pamela GIBSON
81 Dean of Sciences & Mathematics ... Mr. Chris DIORIETES
88 Dean of Public Service ... Mrs. Linda NOVAK
77 Dean of Computer Technologies ... Mrs. Darlene WOOD

*Forsyth Technical Community College (G)

2100 Silas Creek Parkway, Winston-Salem NC 27103-5197
County: Forsyth — FICE Identification: 005317
Unit ID: 198552
Telephone: (336) 723-0371 — Carnegie Class: Assoc/MT-VT-High Trad
FAX Number: (336) 761-2399 — Calendar System: Semester
URL: www.forsythtech.edu
Established: 1960 — Annual Undergrad Tuition & Fees (In-State): $2,025
Enrollment: 9,148 — Coed
Affiliation or Control: State — IRS Status: 501(c)3
Highest Offering: Associate Degree
Accreditation: SC, COARC, CVT, DA, DH, DMS, ENGT, MAC, NMT, RAD, RTT

02 President ... Dr. Gary M. GREEN
03 Executive Vice President ... Dr. Rachel M. DESMARAIS
05 Vice Pres Instructional Svcs ... Dr. Joel WELCH
13 Vice Pres of Planning & Info Svcs ... Vacant
32 Vice President Student Services ... Dr. Jewel B. CHERRY
30 VP Inst Advancement/Exec Dir Found ... Vacant
10 Vice President Business Services ... Ms. Wendy R. EMERSON
103 Vice Pres Economic & Workforce Dev ... Mr. Alan K. MURDOCK
100 Director Office of the President ... Ms. Sherri W. BOWEN
50 Dean Business Info Tech Div ... Ms. Pamela SHORTT
79 Dean of Humanities/Social Sci Div ... Vacant
81 Dean Math/Science & Technologies ... Mr. Michael V. AYERS
54 Dean of Engineering Tech Div ... Mr. Leonard R. KISER
17 Int Dean of Health Technologies ... Ms. Jean E. MIDDLESWARTH
31 Dean Community/Economic Development ... Ms. Sharon D. ANDERSON
08 Dean Learning Resources ... Mr. J. Randel CANDELARIA
88 Dean Adult Literacy ... Mr. Michael E. HARRIS
66 Director Nursing ... Ms. Linda H. LATHAM
76 Director Imaging ... Ms. Tamara BECK
76 Director Health Services ... Ms. Jean E. MIDDLESWARTH
84 Dean Enrollment & Student Svcs ... Vacant
21 Dean Financial Services ... Ms. Melanie L. NUCKOLS
38 Dir Student Success Ctr/Counseling ... Mr. Joe E. MCINTOSH
15 Director Human Resources ... Mr. Gregory M. CHASE
09 Dir Institutional Effectiveness ... Ms. Dana L. DALTON
14 Director Information Systems ... Mr. Chris PEARCE
88 Dir Recruiting/Student Support Svcs ... Mr. Edwin B. WADDELL
37 Director Student Financial Services ... Mr. Ricky C. HODGES
06 Director Records/Registrar ... Ms. Gwen D. WHITAKER
07 Director of Admissions ... Ms. Jean M. GROOME
18 Director Physical Plant Services ... Mr. Scott BOOTH
19 Director Campus Police ... Mr. Renarde D. EARL
88 Director Small Business Center ... Mr. Allan YOUNGER
35 Director Student Activities ... Ms. Beverly N. LEWIS
96 Director Purchasing/Equipment ... Mr. Philip L. MCCLUNG
40 Director Auxiliary Svcs/Bookstore ... Mr. Brian A. HICKS

12 Director Grady Swisher Center ... Ms. Mary B. KING
12 Director Mazie Woodruff Center ... Mr. TerCraig D. EDWARDS
12 Director Northwest Forsyth Center ... Ms. Kristie F. HENDRIX
12 Sr Dir Off-Campus/Stokes Cty Op ... Ms. Ann B. WATTS
88 Director Educational Partnerships ... Ms. Kimberly BRYANT
88 Dean Business and Industry ... Ms. Jennifer B. COULOMBE
88 Dean Health and Emergency Programs ... Mr. Wesley D. HUTCHINS
88 Dir Transportation Technology Ctr ... Ms. S. Lynn GARWOOD
88 Dean Learning Technologies ... Mr. James COOK
44 Dir Major Gifts & Planned Giving ... Ms. Edyce ELWORTH
44 Dir Annual Giving & Special Events ... Ms. Angela BRYANT
04 Senior Administrative Associate ... Ms. Dawn P. MITCHELL
25 Director Grants and Contracts ... Mr. Mike MASSOGLIA

*Gaston College (A)

201 Highway 321 South, Dallas NC 28034-1499
County: Gaston FICE Identification: 002973
Unit ID: 198570
Telephone: (704) 922-6200 Carnegie Class: Assoc/MT-VT-High Trad
FAX Number: (704) 922-2323 Calendar System: Semester
URL: www.gaston.edu
Established: 1964 Annual Undergrad Tuition & Fees (In-District): $2,562
Enrollment: 5,777 Coed
Affiliation or Control: State/Local IRS Status: 501(c)3
Highest Offering: Associate Degree
Accreditation: SC, ACBSP, ADNUR, DIETT, EMT, ENGT, IFSAC, MAC, PNUR

02 President ... Dr. Patricia A. SKINNER
05 VP Academic Affairs ... Dr. Don AMMONS
103 VP Economic & Workforce Develop ... Dr. Dennis MCELHOE
10 VP Finance/Facilities/Operations ... Ms. Cynthia MCCRORY
32 VP Student Affairs/Enrollment Mgmt ... Dr. Silvia Patricia RIOS-HUSAIN
11 Chief Administrative Officer ... Mr. Todd BANEY
30 Chief Development Officer ... Ms. Julia ALLEN
04 Exec Admin Assistant to Pres ... Ms. Mary Ellen DILLON
20 Assoc VP Academic Affairs ... Dr. Dewey DELLINGER
21 Assoc VP Fin/Oper/Fac & Controller ... Mr. Bruce COLE
35 Asst VP Student Affairs ... Ms. Audrey SHERRILL
12 Dean Kimbrell Campus/Textile Ctr ... Dr. Joe KEITH
12 Dean Lincoln Campus ... Dr. John MCHUGH
50 Dean Business & Information Tech ... Vacant
72 Dean Engr/Industrial Technologies ... Mr. Virgil COX
66 Dean Health & Human Services ... Ms. Juanita GUNNELL
49 Dean Liberal Arts & Sciences ... Ms. Heather WOODSON
07 Dir Admissions/Counseling ... Ms. Jennifer NICHOLS
40 Dir Bookstore/Vending Services ... Mr. Charles WILSON
78 Dir Educational Partnerships ... Ms. Kimberly WYONT
18 Dir Facilities Management ... Mr. Russell SMYRE
37 Dir Financial Aid/Veteran Affs ... Mr. Everett JETER
25 Dir Grants/Special Projects ... Mr. Luke UPCHURCH
09 Dir Institutional Effectiveness ... Dr. Rex CLAY
88 Dir Learn/Persist/Retent/Completion ... Mr. John ERICKSON
08 Dir Libraries ... Dr. Harry COOKE
26 Dir Marketing/PR ... Ms. Stephanie MICHAEL-PICKETT
96 Dir Purchasing/Receiving/Shipping ... Vacant
06 Dir Registration/Records ... Ms. Alisa ROY
75 Dir Textile Technology Ctr ... Mr. Sam BUFF
19 Chief Campus Police & Security ... Mr. Billy LYTTON
13 Chief Technology Services Officer ... Ms. Savonne MCNEILL
15 Mgr HR/Envir/Health/Safety/Prof Dev ... Ms. Carol DENTON

*Guilford Technical Community College (B)

PO Box 309, Jamestown NC 27282-0309
County: Guilford FICE Identification: 004838
Unit ID: 198622
Telephone: (336) 334-4822 Carnegie Class: Assoc/HVT-High Trad
FAX Number: (336) 454-2745 Calendar System: Semester
URL: www.gtcc.edu
Established: 1958 Annual Undergrad Tuition & Fees (In-State): $2,064
Enrollment: 12,430 Coed
Affiliation or Control: State IRS Status: 501(c)3
Highest Offering: Associate Degree
Accreditation: SC, ACFEI, DA, DH, EMT, MAC, PTAA, RAD, SURGT

02 President ... Dr. Randy PARKER
03 Executive Vice President ... Vacant
05 Vice President of Instruction ... Dr. Beth PITONZO
32 Vice Pres Student Support Services ... Dr. Quentin JOHNSON
11 Assoc Vice Pres Administrative Svcs ... Mr. Mitchell JOHNSON
10 Assoc VP of Business & Finance ... Ms. Nancy B. SOLLOSI
20 Assoc VP Student Support Services ... Dr. Alison WIERS
51 VP Corp & Continuing Educ ... Dr. Ralph SONEY
30 Exec Dir Institutional Advancement ... Mr. Alan PIKE
12 Dean Greensboro Campus ... Dr. Manuel DUDLEY
12 Dean High Point Campus ... Mr. Mark HARRIS
50 Dir Business & Industry Training ... Mr. Stephen CASTELLOE
30 Director of Development ... Mr. Harry STILLERMAN
15 Director of Human Resources ... Ms. Gwendolyn BURSTON
13 Chief Information Officer ... Mr. Rob RAMEY
18 Director of Construction ... Mr. Charles YOUNG
09 Director of Institutional Research ... Mr. Rod FOTH
07 Director of Admissions ... Mr. Jesse CROSS
35 Director of Student Life ... Ms. Berri V. CROSS
37 Director Financial Aid ... Ms. Lisa A. KORETOFF
19 Chief of Campus Police ... Mr. James PHILLIPS
06 Registrar ... Mr. Kirby MOORE
21 Controller ... Ms. Angela M. CARTER
40 Bookstore Manager ... Mr. Shawn G. DEE
36 Coordinator Career Services ... Mr. Daniel J. GRIGG
38 Director Counseling & Assessment ... Mr. Chris CHAFIN
29 Asst Director of Development ... Ms. Nancy GRIFFIN CALKINS
08 Dir of Library Services ... Ms. Monica YOUNG
41 Athletic Director ... Mr. Kirk CHANDLER
96 Director of Purchasing ... Mr. Michael STOUT

*Halifax Community College (C)

PO Drawer 809, Weldon NC 27890-0809
County: Halifax FICE Identification: 007986
Unit ID: 198640
Telephone: (252) 536-4221 Carnegie Class: Assoc/HVT-Mix Trad/Non
FAX Number: (252) 536-4144 Calendar System: Semester
URL: www.halifaxcc.edu
Established: 1967 Annual Undergrad Tuition & Fees (In-District): $2,436
Enrollment: 1,293 Coed
Affiliation or Control: State/Local IRS Status: 501(c)3
Highest Offering: Associate Degree
Accreditation: SC, DH, MLTAD, PHLEB

02 President ... Dr. Ervin V. GRIFFIN, SR.
04 Exec Assistant to the President ... Ms. Kimberly J. MACK
05 Vice Pres Academic Affairs ... Dr. Deryl FULMER
10 Vice President Admin Services ... Ms. Debra SMITH
30 Vice Pres Institutional Advancement ... Dr. Dianne RHOADES
32 Dean Student Svcs & Enrollment Mgmt ... Dr. Barbara BRADLEY-HASTY
20 Dean of Curriculum Programs ... Ms. B. T. BROWN
06 Registrar ... Ms. Dawn VELIKY
07 Director of Admissions ... Mr. James Bernard WASHINGTON
08 Director Learning Resources ... Mr. Marc FINNEY
09 Dir of Institutional Effectiveness ... Dr. Adriane LECHE
26 Dir Public Relations & Marketing ... Ms. Molly WALLACE
40 Bookstore Manager ... Mrs. Doris GARNER
38 Director Counseling Services ... Ms. Teresa MAYLE
18 Facilities/Physical Plant ... Ms. Debra SMITH
36 Coord of Testing & Job Placement ... Ms. Angela RANDOLPH
37 Director of Financial Aid ... Mrs. Tara KEETER
96 Purchasing Agent ... Ms. Darlene PERRY
15 Personnel Officer ... Mrs. Margaret MURGA
13 Computer Network Manager ... Mr. Jerry THOMPSON
49 Div Chair Arts & Sciences/Business ... Mr. Calvin STANSBURY
76 Div Chair Health Sciences & Humanit ... Mr. Michael EARL
75 Div Chair Vocation/Industrial Tech ... Mr. Hunter TAYLOR
106 Dir Online Education/E-learning ... Mrs. Beth GRAY-ROBERTSON
19 Director Security/Safety ... Mr. Emmett SMITH
25 Chief Contracts/Grants Admin ... Mr. Daniel LOVETT
44 Director Annual or Planned Giving ... Dr. Dianne BARNES-RHOADES

*Haywood Community College (D)

185 Freedlander Drive, Clyde NC 28721-9453
County: Haywood FICE Identification: 008083
Unit ID: 198668
Telephone: (828) 627-2821 Carnegie Class: Assoc/MT-VT-High Trad
FAX Number: (828) 627-3606 Calendar System: Semester
URL: www.haywood.edu
Established: 1965 Annual Undergrad Tuition & Fees (In-State): $2,410
Enrollment: 2,069 Coed
Affiliation or Control: State IRS Status: 501(c)3
Highest Offering: Associate Degree
Accreditation: SC, MAC

02 President ... Dr. Barbara PARKER
05 Vice President of Instruction ... Mrs. Wendy HINES
32 Vice President Student Services ... Dr. Laura LEATHERWOOD
10 Vice President Business Operations ... Mrs. Karen DENNEY
18 Director of Campus Development ... Mr. Brek LANNING
30 Dir Institutional Advancement ... Mrs. Pam HARDIN
26 Director Marketing & Communications ... Mr. Aaron MABRY
15 Director of Human Resources ... Mrs. Marsha STINES
84 Director of Enrollment Management ... Mrs. Jennifer HERRERA
37 Director of Financial Aid ... Mrs. Tracy RAPP
36 Career Devel Specialist/Recruiter ... Ms. Sharon CHILDERS
09 Data Analyst/SACSCOC Liaison ... Mr. David ONDER
103 Dean of Workforce Dev/Cont Educ ... Mr. Doug BURCHFIELD

*Isothermal Community College (E)

PO Box 804, Spindale NC 28160-0804
County: Rutherford FICE Identification: 002934
Unit ID: 198710
Telephone: (828) 286-3636 Carnegie Class: Assoc/HVT-High Non
FAX Number: (828) 286-1120 Calendar System: Semester
URL: www.isothermal.edu
Established: 1964 Annual Undergrad Tuition & Fees (In-District): $2,358
Enrollment: 2,057 Coed
Affiliation or Control: State/Local IRS Status: 501(c)3
Highest Offering: Associate Degree
Accreditation: SC

02 President ... Mr. Walter H. DALTON
11 Vice Pres Administrative Services ... Mr. Stephen MATHENY
05 Executive Vice President ... Dr. Kim GOLD
103 Vice Pres Cmty/Workforce Educ ... Mr. Thad HARRILL
30 VP for Institutional Advancement ... Mr. Thad HARRILL
32 Dean of Student Affairs ... Vacant
50 Dean of Business Sciences ... Ms. Kim ALEXANDER
49 Dean of Arts & Sciences ... Dr. Kathy ACKERMAN
75 Dean of Applied Science & Engr ... Mr. Joe LOONEY
51 Dean of Continuing Education ... Mrs. Donna HOOD
12 Director of Polk Campus ... Mrs. Kate BARKSCHAT
20 Director Academic Development ... Mrs. Debbie PUETT
08 Director Library Services ... Mr. Charles WIGGINS
10 Controller ... Mrs. Amy M. PENSON
37 Financial Aid Officer ... Mrs. Pamela ELLIS
26 Dir Marketing/Community Relations ... Mr. Mike GAVIN
18 Dir Plant Operations/Maintenance ... Mr. Rick EDWARDS
38 Director of Retention & Support ... Mrs. Kimberly SNYDER
84 Director of Enrollment Management ... Ms. Alice MCCLUNEY
06 Registrar ... Ms. Vanessa CAPPS
96 Director of Purchasing ... Ms. Trish HUNTSINGER
13 Director of Information Technology ... Mr. Robby WALTERS
40 Bookstore Manager ... Mrs. Danielle ALEY
04 Administrative Asst to President ... Mrs. DeeDee BARNARD

*James Sprunt Community College (F)

PO Box 398, Kenansville NC 28349-0398
County: Duplin FICE Identification: 007687
Unit ID: 198729
Telephone: (910) 296-2400 Carnegie Class: Assoc/HT-High Non
FAX Number: (910) 296-1636 Calendar System: Semester
URL: www.jamessprunt.edu
Established: 1964 Annual Undergrad Tuition & Fees (In-State): $2,374
Enrollment: 1,213 Coed
Affiliation or Control: State IRS Status: 501(c)3
Highest Offering: Associate Degree
Accreditation: SC, MAC

02 Chief Executive Officer/President ... Dr. Lawrence L. ROUSE
05 VP of Curriculum Services ... Ms. June DAVIS
51 VP of Continuing Education ... Vacant
10 VP of Admin & Fiscal Services ... Mr. John HARDISON
32 VP of Student Services ... Vacant
30 VP Col Advance/Inst Effectiveness ... Mr. Jimmy T. TATE
06 Registrar ... Ms. Patricia NORRIS
07 Admissions Specialist ... Ms. Wanda EDWARDS
37 Director Financial Aid/Vet Affairs ... Ms. Tracy WARD
38 Director of Student Counseling ... Ms. Amber FERRELL
08 Director Library Services ... Ms. Christine VASICA
15 Dir Human Resources/Campus Safety ... Ms. Debbie MARTIN
97 Director of General Education ... Mr. Andy CAVENAUGH
09 Dir Research/Plng/Instl Effective ... Mr. William (Bill) CANUETTE, JR.
26 Dir of Public Info/Print Media ... Vacant
18 Chief Facilities/Physical Plant ... Mr. Dennis SUTTON
96 Director of Purchasing ... Ms. Toni HENDERSON
55 Instr/Coord Evening/Weekend Svcs ... Mr. James THOMAS
13 Chief Info Technology Officer (CIO) ... Vacant
19 Director Security/Safety ... Mr. Richard WHITMAN

*Johnston Community College (G)

PO Box 2350, 245 College Road,
Smithfield NC 27577-2350
County: Johnston FICE Identification: 009336
Unit ID: 198774
Telephone: (919) 934-3051 Carnegie Class: Assoc/HVT-High Trad
FAX Number: (919) 209-2142 Calendar System: Semester
URL: www.johnstoncc.edu
Established: 1969 Annual Undergrad Tuition & Fees (In-District): $2,401
Enrollment: 4,021 Coed
Affiliation or Control: State/Local IRS Status: 501(c)3
Highest Offering: Associate Degree
Accreditation: SC, DMS, MAC, NMT, RAD

02 President ... Dr. David N. JOHNSON
10 VP Admin/Financial & IT Resourc ... Dr. Darryl MCGRAW
05 Vice Pres of Instruction ... Mrs. Dee Dee D. DAUGHTRY
32 Vice Pres of Student Services ... Dr. Pamela J. HARRELL
09 Dir of Research and IE ... Dr. Terri S. LEE
30 Executive Director of Foundation ... Dr. Twyla C. WELLS
13 Executive Director Info Technology ... Mr. Hal MURY
08 Library Administrator ... Ms. Jaxie BRYAN
105 Internet Info Systems Coordinator ... Ms. Lisa H. MCLAURIN
06 Registrar ... Ms. Deena H. HENRY
37 Director Financial Aid ... Mrs. Betty C. WOODALL
109 Assoc VP of Auxiliary Enterprises ... Mr. Ken H. MITCHELL
15 Director of Human Resources ... Ms. Bernadette CARTER-DOVE
07 Dir of Enrollment & Student Success ... Mrs. Megan L. SHANER
103 Dean of Economic and Community Dev ... Mrs. Joy T. CALLAHAN
76 Dean Health/Wellness & Human Svcs ... Dr. Linda D. SMITH
49 Dean Arts/Sciences & Learning Res ... Mrs. Dawn S. DIXON
71 Dean of Found Studies and Acad Supp ... Dr. Pam J. EARP
26 Senior Director of Communications ... Mrs. Traci D. ASHLEY
18 Maintenance Director ... Mr. Michael MASSEY
96 Purchasing and Equipment Director ... Ms. Cassandra HAIRE
88 Secy and Emer Preparedness Coord ... Ms. Sarah GIBBS
25 Grants Director ... Ms. Leslie VANHOY
04 Exec Asst to the President ... Ms. Sandy MILLARD

*Lenoir Community College (H)

231 Highway 58 South, Kinston NC 28502-0188
County: Lenoir FICE Identification: 002940
Unit ID: 198817
Telephone: (252) 527-6223 Carnegie Class: Assoc/MT-VT-High Non
FAX Number: (252) 233-6879 Calendar System: Semester
URL: www.lenoircc.edu
Established: 1958 Annual Undergrad Tuition & Fees (In-District): $2,423
Enrollment: 2,959 Coed
Affiliation or Control: State/Local IRS Status: 501(c)3

Highest Offering: Associate Degree
Accreditation: SC, ACFEI, EMT, MAC, POLYT, RAD, SURGT

02 President .... Dr. Brantley BRILEY
51 VP Continuing Education .... Dr. Jay CARRAWAY
11 Senior VP Administrative Services .... Ms. Deborah SUTTON
05 Sr VP Instruc & Student Services .... Dr. Deborah GRIMES
10 Chief Financial Officer .... Ms. Deborah S. SUTTON
06 Registrar .... Ms. Shelia WIGGINS
84 Director Enrollment Mgmt/Admissions .... Vacant
32 Dean of Student Services .... Dr. John Paul BLACK
37 Director of Student Financial Aid .... Mr. J. D GIBBS
13 Chief Information Officer .... Mr. Lee WETHERINGTON
09 Director Inst Effectiveness .... Mrs. Jo WILSON
15 Director Human Resources .... Mrs. Tasha JOHNSON
18 Director of Maintenance .... Mr. Reed LOVICK
41 Athletic Director .... Mrs. Shelly BARNES
21 Director of Financial Services .... Ms. Jessica MCMAHON
96 Purchasing Agent .... Ms. Rhonda DEAVER
26 Director of Mktg/Recruiting/Comm .... Mrs. Richy HUNEYCUTT
30 Director Institutional Advancement .... Mrs. Jeanne KENNEDY
103 Work-Based Lrng Coord .... Mrs. Sherry IRSIK
08 Director of Learning Resources .... Mr. Rich GARAFOLO
50 Dean of Business/Industrial/Technol .... Mr. Gary CLEMENTS
49 Dean of Arts & Sciences .... Dr. Levy BROWN
76 Dean of Health Sciences & Nursing .... Dr. Alexis WELCH
92 Dean/Director of Honors Program .... Dr. John Paul BLACK
94 Dean/Director of Women's Studies .... Dr. Deborah GRIMES
35 Director Student Activities .... Mrs. Shelly BARNES

*Martin Community College (A)

1161 Kehukee Park Road, Williamston NC 27892-9988
County: Martin FICE Identification: 007988
Unit ID: 198905
Telephone: (252) 792-1521 Carnegie Class: Assoc/HVT-Mix Trad/Non
FAX Number: (252) 792-0826 Calendar System: Semester
URL: www.martincc.edu
Established: 1967 Annual Undergrad Tuition & Fees (In-State): $1,838
Enrollment: 477 Coed
Affiliation or Control: State IRS Status: 501(c)3
Highest Offering: Associate Degree
Accreditation: SC, DA, MAC, PTAA

02 President .... Dr. Ann BRITT
05 Dean Academic Affairs/Student Svcs .... Dr. Jennifer BURRUSS
11 Dean of Administrative Services .... Mr. Steve TAYLOR
10 Business Services Director .... Ms. Cynthia JERNIGAN
20 Assoc Dean Acad Affs/Student Svcs .... Dr. Brian BUSCH
04 Asst to Pres for Business/Industry .... Mr. Billy BARBER
37 Financial Aid Director .... Vacant
38 Counselor and Admissions .... Ms. Crystal PUGH
06 Registrar .... Vacant
51 Exec Dir Continuing Education .... Mr. AJ TYSON
13 Systems Administrator .... Ms. Donna ROGERS
18 Director of Facilities .... Mr. Walter WHEELER
15 Human Resource Director .... Mr. Harland FRYE
14 Telecommunication/Network Manager .... Mr. Elijah T. FREEMAN
09 Director of Institutional Research .... Vacant
96 Director of Purchasing .... Ms. Jennifer CHERRY
12 Director of Bertie Campus .... Mr. Norman CHERRY
08 Library Director .... Ms. Mary Anne CAUDLE
101 Exec Asst to President and BOT .... Ms. Kismet MATTHEWS
13 Director of IT .... Mr. Jeff PICKERING
26 Dir Public Affairs/Inst Advancement .... Ms. Judy JENNETTE
07 Counselor and Admissions .... Mr. John WELLS

*Mayland Community College (B)

PO Box 547, Spruce Pine NC 28777-0547
County: Avery FICE Identification: 011197
Unit ID: 198914
Telephone: (828) 765-7351 Carnegie Class: Assoc/MT-VT-High Non
FAX Number: (828) 765-0728 Calendar System: Semester
URL: www.mayland.edu
Established: 1971 Annual Undergrad Tuition & Fees (In-District): $2,430
Enrollment: 973 Coed
Affiliation or Control: State/Local IRS Status: 501(c)3
Highest Offering: Associate Degree
Accreditation: SC, MAC

02 President .... Dr. John C. BOYD
04 Assistant to the President .... Ms. Brooke BURLESON
05 VP Academics & Student Development .... Mr. Randy LEDFORD
10 Vice President Administrative Svcs .... Mr. Gerald HYDE
103 Vice Pres Economic/Workforce Devel .... Mrs. Rita EARLEY
32 Dean of Students .... Ms. Michelle MUSICH
76 Dean of Health Sciences Programs .... Mrs. Kim BURR
49 Acting Dean of Arts & Sciences .... Mr. Scott EVANS
72 Dean of Career Technologies .... Ms. Brenda MCFEE
08 Director Learning Resources Center .... Mr. Jon WILMESHERR
09 Director Institutional Effectivness .... Mrs. Liz SILVERS
06 Registrar .... Vacant
88 Dean of Basic Skills Programs .... Mr. Steve GUNTER
12 Dean Avery County EWD .... Mrs. Melissa C. PHILLIPS
12 Dean Mitchell County EWD .... Mr. Chris HELMS
12 Dean Yancey County EWD .... Dr. Monica S. CARPENTER
37 Director Student Financial Aid .... Mrs. Cassie FORBES
18 Director Facilities/Physical Plant .... Mr. Lee WHITTINGTON
13 Dir Management Information Systems .... Mr. Tommy R. LEDFORD
15 Director Personnel Services .... Mr. Judy MCCLURE
26 Chief Public Relations Officer .... Mrs. Beth MORRIS
96 Coordinator of Purchasing/Equipment .... Mr. Eddie BUCHANAN

*McDowell Technical Community College (C)

54 College Drive, Marion NC 28752-8728
County: McDowell FICE Identification: 008085
Unit ID: 198923
Telephone: (828) 652-6021 Carnegie Class: Assoc/MT-VT-High Non
FAX Number: (828) 652-1014 Calendar System: Semester
URL: www.mcdowelltech.edu
Established: 1964 Annual Undergrad Tuition & Fees (In-District): $1,776
Enrollment: 1,056 Coed
Affiliation or Control: State/Local IRS Status: 501(c)3
Highest Offering: Associate Degree
Accreditation: SC, CAHIIM

02 President .... Dr. Bryan W WILSON
05 Vice Pres for Learning/Student Svcs .... Dr. John GOSSETT
10 Vice Pres Finance/Administration .... Mr Ryan GARRISON
20 Dean Academic Programs .... Dr. James BENTON
09 Director of Inst Effectiveness .... Mr Ladelle HARMON
26 Director of External Relations .... Mr. Michael K. LAVENDER
13 Director of Technology/Info Systems .... Mr. Elmer R. MACOPSON
08 Director of Library Services .... Ms Sharon P. SMITH
88 Director of Correctional Programs .... Mr. Frank D. SILVER
88 Director of Industrial Training .... Mr. Eddie SHUFORD
76 Director of Health Sciences .... Mrs. Penny CROSS
06 Registrar .... Ms. Kelly HAMLIN
37 Director Student Financial Aid .... Ms. Kim M. LEDBETTER
36 Director of Student Enrichment Ctr .... Mrs. Donna SHORT
88 Director Adult Basic Skills .... Mrs. Teresa VALENTINO
88 Counselor/VA Director .... Mrs. Donna SHORT
51 Director of Continuing Education .... Mr. Brad LEDBETTER
88 Director Basic Law Enforcement Trng .... Mr. Stacy BUFF
07 Director of Admissions .... Mr. Wingate CAIN
15 Director of Human Resources Devel .... Mrs. Mary L. LEDBETTER
30 Foundation Resource Devel Officer .... Ms. Susan BERLEY
106 Coordinator of Distance Education .... Mrs. Joan WEILER
18 Coord Maintenance/Custodial Svcs .... Mr. Carl COSTNER
88 Coord of Small Business Center .... Mr. H. Dean KANIPE
04 Exec Assistant to the President .... Ms. Rhonda SILVER

*Mitchell Community College (D)

500 W Broad Street, Statesville NC 28677-5293
County: Iredell FICE Identification: 002947
Unit ID: 198987
Telephone: (704) 878-3200 Carnegie Class: Assoc/HT-High Trad
FAX Number: (704) 878-0872 Calendar System: Semester
URL: www.mitchellcc.edu
Established: 1852 Annual Undergrad Tuition & Fees (In-State): $2,407
Enrollment: 3,106 Coed
Affiliation or Control: State IRS Status: 501(c)3
Highest Offering: Associate Degree
Accreditation: SC, ADNUR, MAC

02 President .... Dr. Tim BREWER
05 Vice President of Instruction .... Dr. Camille REESE
10 Vice Pres of Finance/Administration .... Mr. John WILKINSON
103 Vice Pres Workforce Development/CEC .... Ms. Carol JOHNSON
32 Vice Pres Student Services .... Vacant
09 Director of Research & Planning .... Ms. Eva EISNAUGLE
08 Director of Learning Resources .... Vacant
37 Director of Financial Aid .... Ms. Candace COOPER
18 Facilities Supervisor II .... Mr. Chad LACKEY
26 Public Relations/Marketing .... Ms. Megan SUBER
30 Dir Development/College Relations .... Ms. Celeste GRUNER

*Montgomery Community College (E)

1011 Page Street, Troy NC 27371-0787
County: Montgomery FICE Identification: 008087
Unit ID: 199023
Telephone: (910) 576-6222 Carnegie Class: Assoc/HVT-Mix Trad/Non
FAX Number: (910) 576-2176 Calendar System: Semester
URL: www.montgomery.edu
Established: 1967 Annual Undergrad Tuition & Fees (In-District): $2,409
Enrollment: 863 Coed
Affiliation or Control: State/Local IRS Status: 501(c)3
Highest Offering: Associate Degree
Accreditation: SC, CSHSE, DA, MAC

02 President .... Dr. Chad A. BLEDSOE
05 Vice Pres of Instruction .... Lee PROCTOR
11 VP of Administrative Services .... Jeanette MCBRIDE
32 VP of Student Services .... Beth SMITH
51 Dean of Continuing Education .... Jonathan THILL
102 Executive Director Foundation/Grant .... Gay ROATCH
26 Public Information Officer .... Michele HAYWOOD
09 Dir Institutional Effectiveness .... Carol HOLTON
13 Dir of Information Technology .... Mitch WALKER
04 Assistant to the President .... Korrie ERVIN
38 Counseling Services .... Natalie WINFREE
07 Admissions Officer .... Karen FRYE
37 Director of Financial Aid .... Doni S. CODY
15 Coordinator Of Human Resources .... Melisa BOND
10 Acccuntant .... Cathy BIBY
18 Director of Facilities .... Wanda FRICK
35 Student Activities Coordinator .... Riley BEAMAN

*Nash Community College (F)

522 N Old Carriage Road, Rocky Mount NC 27804-0488
County: Nash FICE Identification: 008557
Unit ID: 199087
Telephone: (252) 443-4011 Carnegie Class: Assoc/MT-VT-Mix Trad/Non
FAX Number: (252) 451-8201 Calendar System: Semester
URL: www.nashcc.edu
Established: 1967 Annual Undergrad Tuition & Fees (In-District): $2,504
Enrollment: 3,537 Coed
Affiliation or Control: State/Local IRS Status: 501(c)3
Highest Offering: Associate Degree
Accreditation: SC, MAC, PHLEB, PTAA

02 President .... Dr. William S. CARVER, II
05 Vice President for Instruction .... Dr. Trent L. MOHRBUTTER
10 Vice President of Finance .... Ms. Adrienne COVINGTON
88 Dean of Transfer .... Ms. Deana GUIDO
88 Director Small Business Center .... Mr. Fred BROOKS
86 Assoc VP Community & Govt Affairs .... Dr. Keith SMITH
32 Dean Student & Enrollment Svcs .... Mr. Michael COLEMAN
20 Assoc VP Curriculum .... Mr. Mike LATHAM
09 Assoc Dean Institutional Effective .... Ms. Farley PHILLIPS
13 Chief Information Officer .... Mr. Jonathan VESTER
07 Director of Admissions .... Ms. Stephanie BROWN
06 Registrar .... Ms. Kathy S. ADCOX
37 Director of Financial Aid .... Ms. Tammy LESTER
15 Director Human Resources .... Ms. Michelle NOYES
04 Administrative Asst to President .... Ms. Faye CAHOON
24 Dir Instructional Publ/Printing .... Mr. James M. QUIGLEY
18 Director of Facilities .... Mr. Greg DEANS
26 Sr Dir Marketing/Communication .... Ms. Kelley DEAL

*Pamlico Community College (G)

PO Box 185, Grantsboro NC 28529-0185
County: Pamlico FICE Identification: 007031
Unit ID: 199263
Telephone: (252) 249-1851 Carnegie Class: Assoc/HVT-High Non
FAX Number: (252) 249-2377 Calendar System: Semester
URL: www.pamlicocc.edu
Established: 1962 Annual Undergrad Tuition & Fees (In-District): $2,347
Enrollment: 410 Coed
Affiliation or Control: State/Local IRS Status: 501(c)3
Highest Offering: Associate Degree
Accreditation: SC, MAC, NDT

02 President .... Dr. Jim ROSS
11 Vice Pres Administrative Svcs .... Mr. Mark PULLIAM
05 Vice Pres Instructional Svcs .... Dr. Maria FRASER-MOLINA
32 Vice Pres of Student Services .... Mr. Jamie GIBBS
09 Director of Planning & Research .... Ms. Brandi MCCULLOUGH
06 Registrar .... Ms. Tammy SPAIN
37 Director of Financial Aid .... Ms. Melissa WHITMAN
10 Controller .... Ms. Sherry RABY
26 Director of Public Affairs .... Ms. Townley CHEEK

*Piedmont Community College (H)

1715 College Dr, Roxboro NC 27573-1197
County: Person FICE Identification: 009646
Unit ID: 199324
Telephone: (336) 599-1181 Carnegie Class: Assoc/MT-VT-Mix Trad/Non
FAX Number: (336) 597-3817 Calendar System: Semester
URL: www.piedmontcc.edu
Established: 1970 Annual Undergrad Tuition & Fees (In-District): $2,419
Enrollment: 1,475 Coed
Affiliation or Control: State/Local IRS Status: 501(c)3
Highest Offering: Associate Degree
Accreditation: SC, EMT, MAC

02 President .... Dr. Walter C. BARTLETT
05 Vice Pres Instruction/Student Devel .... Dr. Joyce B. JOHNSON
31 Vice Pres Continuing Education .... Dr. Doris W. CARVER
11 Vice Pres Administrative Services .... Mr. Richard B. SELF
12 Provost Caswell County Campus .... Ms. Shelly T. STONE
106 Spec Asst to VP/Distance Educ .... Dr. Libbie M. MOORE
51 Dean Adult Basic Skills .... Ms. Debra B. HARLOW
103 Dean Occupational Ext & Corr Ed .... Ms. Tracey P. BRANDON
76 Dean Health Sciences and Human Svcs .... Ms. Alisa L. MONTGOMERY
79 Dean Humanities and Social Sciences .... Mr. Wayne L. COHAN
08 Dean LRC .... Ms. Vanessa L. BASS
88 Early College High School Liaison .... Mr. Walter C. MONTGOMERY
105 Webmaster/Graphics Designer .... Mr. Kevin R. TYBURSKI
88 Director TRiO Programs .... Ms. Carolyn W. FUNDERBURK
103 Dean Workforce Development .... Ms. Angela P. WEBB
06 Registrar .... Ms. Susan L. GREINER
37 Dir Financial Aid/Veterans Affairs .... Ms. Paulita N. WILLIAMS
18 Director Buildings and Grounds .... Mr. Bruce T. CHISHOLM
25 Director Grants .... Mr. Ricky FARMER
15 Director Personnel/Payroll .... Ms. Pamelia C. HOBBS
88 Director QEP .... Ms. Lisa K. COOLEY
26 Director Public Information .... Ms. Elizabeth R. TOWNSEND
09 Dir Research/Inst Effectiveness .... Dr. Jeff PATON
13 Chief Information Officer .... Mr. Kumar LAKHAVANI
19 Deputy Director College Safety .... Mr. Adam W. IRBY
29 Fin Coord Foundation/Alumni Rels .... Ms. Patricia I. CLAYTON
96 Purchasing Officer/Accountant .... Ms. Jovana AMARO
40 Manager Bookstore .... Ms. Tammy H. MORRIS
04 Administrative Asst to President .... Ms. Cindy W. FOX
10 Controller .... Ms. Beverly J. MURPHY

*Pitt Community College (A)

PO Drawer 7007, Greenville NC 27835-7007
County: Pitt FICE Identification: 004062
Unit ID: 199333
Telephone: (252) 493-7200 Carnegie Class: Assoc/MT-VT-Mix Trad/Non
FAX Number: (252) 321-4458 Calendar System: Semester
URL: www.pittcc.edu
Established: 1961 Annual Undergrad Tuition & Fees (In-State): $2,317
Enrollment: 8,872 Coed
Affiliation or Control: State IRS Status: 501(c)3
Highest Offering: Associate Degree
Accreditation: SC, ADNUR, CAHIIM, COARC, CSHSE, DMS, MAC, OTA, POLYT, RAD, RADDOS, RTT

02 President ....Dr. Dennis MASSEY
05 Vice President Academic Affairs ....Dr. Thomas GOULD
11 Vice Pres Administrative Services ....Mr. Rick OWENS
32 Vice President Student Development ....Dr. Donald R. SPELL
30 Vice Pres Institutional Advancement ....Mrs. Susan Q. NOBLES
20 Asst Vice Pres Academic Affairs ....Ms. Lori PREAST
13 AVP Information Technology/Services ....Mr. Ernest SIMONS
10 Chief Financial Officer ....Mr. Ricky BROWN
04 Administrative Asst to President ....Mrs. Kathy M. CARNES
31 Dean Economic & Cmty Development ....Vacant
08 Director Library ....Ms. Leigh RUSSELL
09 Dean of Planning & Research ....Vacant
46 Resource Development Director ....Vacant
15 Director of Human Resources ....Vacant
91 Director of Admin Computing ....Mrs. Janet MINTERN
06 Registrar ....Ms. Angela CLINE
38 Director of Counseling ....Dr. Kimberly WILLIAMSON
88 Director Basic Skills Program ....Vacant
18 Director of Facilities ....Mr. Timothy STRICKLAND
103 Director of JobLink Career Center ....Vacant
84 Dean Student Svcs/Enrollment Mgmt ....Ms. Joanne T. CERES
41 Athletic Director ....Mr. William BAILEY
29 Director of Alumni Relations ....Mrs. Ashley SMITH
36 Director of Student Placement ....Mrs. Sharon CERES
96 Director of Purchasing ....Ms. Jane ALLIGOOD
19 Chief Public Safety/Campus Police ....Mr. Jay SHINGLETON
88 Director Business & Industry Svcs ....Vacant
104 Director Study Abroad ....Mrs. Darlene SMITH-WORTHINGTON
09 Director Planning & Analysis ....Dr. Brian MILLER
37 Director Financial Aid ....Ms. Tamara GLASPIE
40 Manager of College Store ....Vacant
106 Coord Instructional Tech/Dist Educ ....Mr. Mike CLENDENEN
55 Coord/Counselor Evening Programs ....Mr. Kendrick PRICE
50 Division Dean of Business ....Ms. Katherine CLYDE
76 Division Dean Health Sciences ....Ms. Donna V. NEAL
49 Division Dean of Art & Sciences ....Dr. Stephanie MANLEY-ROOK
75 Div Dean Construct/Indus Tech ....Mr. Mark FAITHFUL
61 Div Dean Legal Sci/Public Svc ....Dr. Dan MAYO

*Randolph Community College (B)

629 Industrial Park Avenue, Asheboro NC 27205
County: Randolph FICE Identification: 005447
Unit ID: 199421
Telephone: (336) 633-0200 Carnegie Class: Assoc/MT-VT-High Trad
FAX Number: (336) 629-4695 Calendar System: Semester
URL: www.randolph.edu
Established: 1962 Annual Undergrad Tuition & Fees (In-District): $1,912
Enrollment: 2,771 Coed
Affiliation or Control: State/Local IRS Status: 501(c)3
Highest Offering: Associate Degree
Accreditation: SC, MAC, RAD

02 President ....Dr. Robert S. SHACKLEFORD, JR.
10 Vice Pres Administrative Services ....Ms. Daffie H. GARRIS
05 Vice Pres Instructional Services ....Ms. Suzanne Y. ROHRBAUGH
32 Vice President Student Services ....Mr. James W. KELLEY
51 VP Workforce Development/Cont Educ ....Mr. Elbert J. LASSITER
30 Assoc VP Institutional Advancement ....Ms. Shelley W. GREENE
62 Dean Library Services ....Ms. Deborah S. LUCK
12 Director Archdale Center ....Ms. Wanda H. BECK
21 Dir Financial Svcs/Controller ....Ms. Susan I. RICE
26 Director Marketing ....Mr. Kris N. JULIAN
18 Director Facilities Operations ....Ms. Cindi J. GOODWIN
13 Director Information Tech Svcs ....Ms. Tara A. WILLIAMS
09 Planning & Assessment Specialist ....Ms. Stacy C. SCHMITT
15 Director of Human Resources ....Ms. Melanie AVELINO
37 Director Student Support Services ....Mr. Chad WILLIAMS
06 Director Enrollment Mgmt/Registrar ....Ms. Brandi F. HAGERMAN
106 Director Distance Education ....Mr. Devin A. SOVA
88 Director of ABE and AHS ....Ms. Sandra J. HARTZ
88 Director Public Safety Programs ....Ms. Regina L. BREWER
96 Purchasing Agent ....Ms. Sharon P. REYNOLDS
27 Asst Dir Public Information ....Ms. Cathy D. HEFFERIN
04 Exec Asst to Pres/Board of Trustees ....Ms. Heather O. CLOUSTON
102 Dir Foundation/Corporate Relations ....Ms. Lorie L. MCCROSKEY
19 Dir Safety/Emergency Preparedness ....Mr. Matthew R. NEEDHAM

*Richmond Community College (C)

Box 1189, Hamlet NC 28345-1189
County: Richmond FICE Identification: 005464
Unit ID: 199449
Telephone: (910) 410-1700 Carnegie Class: Assoc/MT-VT-High Trad
FAX Number: (910) 582-7028 Calendar System: Semester
URL: www.richmondcc.edu
Established: 1964 Annual Undergrad Tuition & Fees (In-District): $2,446
Enrollment: 2,531 Coed
Affiliation or Control: State/Local IRS Status: 501(c)3
Highest Offering: Associate Degree
Accreditation: SC, MAC

02 President ....Dr. W. Dale MCINNIS
32 Vice President for Student Services ....Ms. Sharon GOODMAN
05 Vice President for Instruction/CAO ....Mr. Kevin PARSONS
10 Executive VP and CFO ....Mr. Brent BARBEE
103 VP for Workforce & Economic Develop ....Dr. Robbie TAYLOR
08 Dean of Learning Resources ....Ms. Carolyn BITTLE
88 Director of Basic Skills ....Mr. John KESTER
108 Dean of Inst Effectiveness & Improv ....Ms. Sheri DUNN-RAMSAY
09 Director of Institutional Research ....Ms. Chihoko TERRY
15 Director of Human Resources ....Ms. Gaye CLARK
26 Dir of Marketing & Communications ....Ms. Wylie BELL
21 Controller ....Ms. Debbie CASHWELL
36 Director of Career and Transfer Ser ....Ms. Patsy STANLEY
37 Director Student Financial Aid ....Mr. Andrea DANIELS
96 Purchasing Officer ....Mr. Martin BRIDGES
18 Director of Facility Services ....Mr. Scotty MABE
38 Director Student Counseling ....Mr. Chris GARDNER
04 Executive Asst to President ....Ms. Teena PARSONS
06 Registrar ....Ms. Cayce HOLMES
106 Director of Distance Learning ....Mr. Alan QUESTELL
13 Chief Information Officer ....Mr. Lee MONTROSE

*Roanoke-Chowan Community College (D)

109 Community College Road, Ahoskie NC 27910
County: Hertford FICE Identification: 008613
Unit ID: 199467
Telephone: (252) 862-1200 Carnegie Class: Assoc/MT-VT-High Trad
FAX Number: (252) 862-1358 Calendar System: Semester
URL: www.roanokechowan.edu
Established: 1967 Annual Undergrad Tuition & Fees (In-District): $2,478
Enrollment: 1,007 Coed
Affiliation or Control: State/Local IRS Status: 501(c)3
Highest Offering: Associate Degree
Accreditation: SC

02 Interim President ....Dr. W. Eric THOMAS
05 Sr Dean Instruction/Student Success ....Ms. Myra POOLE
76 Director Allied Health Programs ....Ms. Jamie BURNS
32 Dean of Student Services ....Mrs. Wendy VANN
10 Controller ....Ms. Sheena SUGGS
08 Dean Learning Res/Info Systems ....Mrs. Monique MITCHELL
18 Director Facilities ....Mr. Charles STRICKLAND
106 Director Distance Learning ....Ms. Melanie TEMPLE
37 Director Financial Aid ....Mrs. Crystal HARRIS
13 Director of Information Systems ....Dr. Mary LEARY
84 Director Enrollment Svcs/Curric Reg ....Mrs. Amy F. WIGGINS
35 Director Student Support Services ....Ms. Lorraine C. MITCHELL
15 Director Human Resources ....Ms. Kathleen TOURE
06 Registrar/Continuing Educ/Workforce ....Ms. Shirley GAY
102 Director R-CCC Foundation ....Ms. Tarsha DUDLEY
19 Chief Campus Security & Safety ....Mr. Johnny JOYNER

*Robeson Community College (E)

PO Box 1420, Lumberton NC 28359-1420
County: Robeson FICE Identification: 008612
Unit ID: 199476
Telephone: (910) 272-3700 Carnegie Class: Assoc/MT-VT-Mix Trad/Non
FAX Number: (910) 272-3328 Calendar System: Semester
URL: www.robeson.edu
Established: 1965 Annual Undergrad Tuition & Fees (In-District): $2,401
Enrollment: 1,988 Coed
Affiliation or Control: State/Local IRS Status: 501(c)3
Highest Offering: Associate Degree
Accreditation: SC, COARC, RAD, SURGT

02 Interim President ....Dr. William AIKEN
05 VP Instruction/Sppt Svcs/CAO ....Mr. Bill MAUNEY
51 Vice Pres Adult & Continuing Educ ....Mr. R. Channing JONES
10 Vice President Business Services ....Mrs. Tami B. GEORGE
11 VP for Institutional Services ....Mr. Alphonzo MCRAE
55 Asst VP Public Svc/Appl Tech Pgms ....Mr. William L. LOCKLEAR
88 Asst VP Univ Transfer/Bus/Hlth Pgms ....Ms. Sheila A. REGAN
32 Asst Vice Pres Student Services ....Mr. Billy L. MAUNEY
13 Asst VP/Chief Information Officer ....Mr. Dustin LONG
07 Director of Admissions/Enroll Svcs ....Mr. Ronnie LOCKLEAR
22 Director Affirm Action/Equal Oppty ....Mr. Alphonzo MCRAE
08 Director of Learning Resource Svcs ....Mrs. Maryellen O'BRIEN
38 Director Counseling & Testing ....Mr. Danford F. GROVES
06 Dir Records/Registration/Registrar ....Mrs. Beth CARMICAL
37 Financial Aid Director ....Ms. Teresa TUBBS
25 Director of Grants and Sponsored ....Mrs. Lisa O. HUNT
18 Chief Facilities/Physical Plant ....Mr. Alphonzo MCRAE
102 Director Foundation/Development ....Ms. Rebekah R. LOWRY
29 Director Alumni Relations ....Ms. Rebekah LOWRY
36 Counseling & Career Services ....Ms. Bonita BELL
15 Personnel Services Specialist ....Ms. Pam ROMANO
96 Purchasing Officer ....Mr. Jason O. LEVISTER

*Rockingham Community College (F)

PO Box 38, Wentworth NC 27375-0038
County: Rockingham FICE Identification: 002958
Unit ID: 199485
Telephone: (336) 342-4261 Carnegie Class: Assoc/MT-VT-Mix Trad/Non
FAX Number: (336) 349-9986 Calendar System: Semester
URL: www.rockinghamcc.edu
Established: 1963 Annual Undergrad Tuition & Fees (In-District): $1,844
Enrollment: 1,597 Coed
Affiliation or Control: State/Local IRS Status: 501(c)3
Highest Offering: Associate Degree
Accreditation: SC, COARC, PHLEB, SURGT

02 President ....Dr. Mark O. KINLAW
05 Vice President for Academic Affairs ....Ms. Suzanne Y. ROHRBAUGH
11 VP of Administrative Services ....Mr. Steven W. WOODRUFF
32 Vice Pres for Student Development ....Dr. Robert S. LOWDERMILK
88 Assoc VP Administrative Services ....Dr. E. Anthony GUNN
103 Dean of Workforce Development ....Ms. Laura F. COFFEE
49 Dean of Arts & Sciences ....Ms. Celeste H. ALLIS
76 Dean of Health & Public Safety ....Dr. Kimberly M. CLARK
88 Assoc Dean Learning Resources ....Ms. Kimberly SHIREMAN
45 Assoc VP Inst Effectiveness ....Mr. Kevin OSBORNE
06 Registrar ....Ms. Carla MOORE
08 Director Library/Archivist ....Ms. Mary GOMEZ
30 Director Development/Foundation ....Ms. Gaye B. CLIFTON
13 Dir Technology Support Services ....Ms. Gretchen PARRISH
37 Director of Financial Aid ....Ms. Sarah EVANS
84 Director of Enrollment Services ....Mr. Derick SATTERFIELD
35 Director Student Life ....Mr. Stewart MCCLINTOCK
40 Bookstore Manager ....Ms. Della J. GASTON
15 Director Human Resources ....Ms. Joy G. CHAPPELL
26 Director Public Information ....Ms. Kim A. PRYOR
96 Director of Purchasing ....Mr. John PARRISH

*Rowan-Cabarrus Community College (G)

1333 Jake Alexander Blvd., South, Salisbury NC 28145
County: Rowan FICE Identification: 005754
Unit ID: 199494
Telephone: (704) 216-7222 Carnegie Class: Assoc/HVT-Mix Trad/Non
FAX Number: N/A Calendar System: Semester
URL: www.rccc.edu
Established: 1963 Annual Undergrad Tuition & Fees (In-State): $2,506
Enrollment: 6,420 Coed
Affiliation or Control: State IRS Status: 501(c)3
Highest Offering: Associate Degree
Accreditation: SC, ADNUR, DA, PNUR, RAD

02 President ....Dr. Carol SPALDING
05 Academic Vice President ....Dr. Michael D. QUILLEN
10 Chief Financial Officer ....Ms. Janet SPRIGGS
32 Vice President Student Services ....Ms. Gaye MCCONNELL
51 Vice President of Corp & Cont Educ ....Mr. Craig LAMB
13 Chief Information Officer ....Mr. Kenneth G. INGLE, III
15 CO Human Resource/Org Effectiveness ....Ms. Tina HAYNES
18 Chief Facilities Officer ....Mr. Jonathan CHAMBERLAIN
102 CO Governance/Foundation & Pub Rels ....Ms. Carla HOWELL
20 Assoc Academic Vice President ....Mr. Angelo MARKANTONAKIS
21 Assoc VP & Controller ....Ms. Kizzy LEA
35 Assoc VP Student Services ....Mr. Mark EBERSOLE
103 Assoc VP Corporate/Continuing Educ ....Mrs. Ann MORRIS
76 Dean Health Programs ....Mrs. Wendy BARNHARDT
50 Dean Science Bus Math & Info Tech ....Ms. Carol SCHERCZINGER
49 Dean Liberal Arts & General Educ ....Vacant
71 Dean Public Services ....Vacant
54 Dean Engineering & Bus Technologies ....Mr. Van MADRAY
106 Dean Eductional Resource Services ....Ms. Debra NEESMITH
88 Exec Dir Pre-College Studies ....Mr. Gary CONNOR
08 Director Learning Resource Ctr ....Mr. Rodney LIPPARD
25 Director Grants Development ....Ms. Rebecca HOOKS
37 Director Fin Aid & VA Benefit ....Mrs. Lisa LEDBETTER
96 Director of Purchasing ....Ms. Kathy PIPER
07 Director Admissions & Recruitment ....Vacant
06 Director Enrollment & Records ....Mrs. Joan CREEGER
35 Director Student Life & Leadership ....Ms. Natasha LIPSCOMB
38 Director Counseling and Career Svs ....Ms. Marcia MILLER
16 Director of Human Resources ....Mrs. Nekita EUBANKS
09 Dir Research/Plng/Inst Effectiv ....Vacant
19 Director of Campus Security ....Mr. Tim BOST
102 Director RCCC Foundation ....Mr. Marty RICHARDS
26 Dir College Relations Mktg & Comm ....Ms. Paula DIBLEY

*Sampson Community College (H)

PO Box 318, Clinton NC 28329-0318
County: Sampson FICE Identification: 007892
Unit ID: 199625
Telephone: (910) 592-8081 Carnegie Class: Assoc/MT-VT-High Trad
FAX Number: (910) 592-8048 Calendar System: Semester
URL: www.sampsoncc.edu
Established: 1967 Annual Undergrad Tuition & Fees (In-District): $2,381
Enrollment: 1,551 Coed
Affiliation or Control: State/Local IRS Status: 501(c)3
Highest Offering: Associate Degree
Accreditation: SC, ADNUR, PNUR

02 President ....Dr. Paul C. HUTCHINS
05 Vice Pres Academic Affairs/Admin ....Dr. William STARLING
10 Vice Pres Finance/Auxiliary Svcs ....Mrs. Virginia S. LUCAS
32 Dean of Student Services ....Ms. Blair HAIRR
51 Dean of Continuing Education ....Mrs. Ann BUTLER
07 Director of Admissions ....Ms. Holly BREWINGTON
06 Registrar ....Mrs. Delsey BREWINGTON
26 Public Information Office ....Mr. Dan GRUBB
37 Dir Financial Aid/Veteran Services ....Ms. Maureen POWELL
08 Director Library Services ....Vacant
102 Foundation Director ....Mrs. Lisa TURLINGTON
15 Personnel Ofcr/Exec Asst to Pres ....Mrs. Frankie K. SUTTER

*Sandhills Community College (A)

3395 Airport Road, Pinehurst NC 28374-8283

County: Moore — FICE Identification: 002961
Unit ID: 199634
Telephone: (910) 692-6185 — Carnegie Class: Assoc/MT-VT-Mix Trad/Non
FAX Number: (910) 695-1823 — Calendar System: Semester
URL: www.sandhills.edu
Established: 1963 — Annual Undergrad Tuition & Fees (In-State): $2,401
Enrollment: 4,016 — Coed
Affiliation or Control: State — IRS Status: 501(c)3
Highest Offering: Associate Degree
Accreditation: SC, COARC, MLTAD, POLYT, RAD, SURGT

02 President .... Dr. John R. DEMPSEY
11 Exec Vice President Administration .... Ms. Brenda JACKSON
05 VP of Academic Affairs .... Dr. Rebecca ROUSH
32 VP of Student Services .... Mrs. Kellie SHOEMAKE
51 VP of Continuing Education .... Ms. Andi KORTE
35 Dean of Student LIfe .... Mr. David FARMER
04 Exec Assistant to the President .... Ms. Heather LYONS
10 Chief Financial Officer .... Ms. Elizabeth THOMAS
20 Dean of Instruction .... Ms. Linda CHANDLER
09 Dean of Institutional Plng/Rsrch .... Dr. Kristie SULLIVAN
102 Exec Director of SCC Foundation .... Ms. Germaine ELKINS
08 Dean of Learning Resources .... Dr. John STACEY
06 Director of Records & Registration .... Ms. Jean BLUE
37 Financial Aid Officer .... Ms. Lindsey FARMER
106 Director of Distance Learning .... Ms. Wendy KAUFFMAN
13 Director Information Services/CIO .... Mr. Roderick BROWER
19 Director of Security/Safety .... Mr. Dwight THREET
18 Physical Plant Manager .... Mr. Doug SMITH
15 Director Human Resources .... Ms. Wendy B. DODSON
21 Dir Finance & Student Accounts .... Mr. Joseph BROWN
26 Director of Marketing and PR .... Ms. Karen MANNING
40 Bookstore Manager .... Ms. Sandra DALES
07 Director of Admissions .... Ms. Cary GREENE

*South Piedmont Community College (B)

PO Box 126, Polkton NC 28135-0126

County: Anson/Union — FICE Identification: 007985
Unit ID: 197850
Telephone: (704) 272-5300 — Carnegie Class: Assoc/MT-VT-High Non
FAX Number: (704) 272-5350 — Calendar System: Semester
URL: www.spcc.edu
Established: 1999 — Annual Undergrad Tuition & Fees (In-District): $1,873
Enrollment: 2,658 — Coed
Affiliation or Control: State/Local — IRS Status: 501(c)3
Highest Offering: Associate Degree
Accreditation: SC, DMS, MAC

02 Interim President .... Dr. Jerry MCGEE
03 Exec Vice President .... Mr. John DEVITTO
05 Vice Pres Academic Affairs/CAO .... Ms. Joyce LONG
10 VP Finance/Administrative Svcs/CFO .... Ms. Michelle BROCK
32 Vice Pres Student Services .... Mrs. Elaine CLODFELTER
31 Vice Pres Community/Corporate Rels .... Mr. Dan MERLE
30 VP Inst Advancement/SPCC Foundation .... Ms. Hayne WHITE
04 Exec Assistant to President .... Ms. Sara NICHOLS
15 Assoc VP Human Res/Payroll/Org Dev .... Ms. Lauren SELLERS
21 Asst Vice Pres Finance/Admin Svcs .... Mr. Richard ASHLEY
13 Int Asst VP Info Tech Svcs/CIO .... Ms. Natisha GIVENS
18 Asst VP of Facilities .... Mr. William M. TRUETT
108 Assoc VP Planning/IE .... Ms. Jill MILLARD
49 Dean School of Arts & Science .... Mr. Carl BISHOP
76 Dean Allied Health .... Ms. Alice BRADLEY
66 Dean Nursing .... Ms. Alice BRADLEY
72 Dean Applied Science & Technology .... Dr. Maria LANDER
84 Dean of Enrollment Services .... Mr. John RATLIFF
35 Dean of Student Development .... Ms. Makena STEWART
06 Registrar .... Ms. Cathy HORNE
102 Executive Director SPCC Foundation .... Ms. Laura BYRD
08 Director Library Services .... Mr. Grant LEFOE
88 Director of Basic Skills .... Ms. Denise WILSON
16 Director Human Resources .... Ms. Linda KAPPAUF
107 Director Professional Programs .... Ms. Geri DUNCAN
38 Director of Counseling .... Vacant
36 Director of Advising/QEP .... Dr. Malinda DANIEL
35 Director Student Engagement .... Mr. Michael MAFFUCCI
44 Development Officer .... Ms. Gina RHODES
25 Dir Corporate/Community Development .... Mr. Scott COLLIER
26 Dir Marketing/Public Info Ofcr .... Mr. Michael MCALLISTER
09 Dir Institutional Research/Effect .... Ms. Marci JACKSON

*Southeastern Community College (C)

4564 Chadbourn Highway, PO Box 151, Whiteville NC 28472-0151

County: Columbus — FICE Identification: 002964
Unit ID: 199722
Telephone: (910) 642-7141 — Carnegie Class: Assoc/HVT-High Non
FAX Number: (910) 642-5658 — Calendar System: Semester
URL: www.sccnc.edu
Established: 1964 — Annual Undergrad Tuition & Fees (In-State): $2,457
Enrollment: 1,348 — Coed
Affiliation or Control: State — IRS Status: 501(c)3
Highest Offering: Associate Degree
Accreditation: SC, MLTAD

02 President .... Dr. Anthony CLARKE
10 Vice President Administrative Svcs .... Ms. Betty Jo RAMSEY
05 Acting Vice Pres Academic Affairs .... Ms. Lauren G. COLE
103 VP Workforce & Cmty Development .... Ms. Beverlee S. NANCE
32 Exec Dean Student Services .... Ms. Sylvia COX
76 Dean Allied Hlth/Sci/Fine Arts/Math .... Dr. James HUTCHERSON
103 Dn Workforce/Community Development .... Ms. Teresa TRIPLETT
08 Librarian .... Ms. Kay HOUSER
30 Director Institutional Advancement .... Ms. Lisa CLARK
15 Human Resources Director .... Mr. Bill MAULTSBY
21 Controller/Operations/Finance .... Ms. Donna TURBEVILLE
26 Director Marketing & Outreach .... Ms. Liz MCLEAN
13 Director of Information Technology .... Mr. Jason STRICKLAND
51 Director of Continuing Education .... Ms. Brenda ORDERS
37 Director of Financial Aid .... Mr. Justin CRISTELLO
06 Dir of Student Records/Registrar .... Ms. Sylvia MCQUEEN
36 Director of Counseling .... Ms. Julia ROBERTS
09 Research & Reporting Coordinator .... Mr. Don WHITE

*Southwestern Community College (D)

447 College Drive, Sylva NC 28779-8581

County: Jackson — FICE Identification: 008466
Unit ID: 199731
Telephone: (828) 339-4000 — Carnegie Class: Assoc/MT-VT-High Non
FAX Number: (828) 586-3129 — Calendar System: Semester
URL: www.southwesterncc.edu
Established: 1964 — Annual Undergrad Tuition & Fees (In-District): $2,100
Enrollment: 2,528 — Coed
Affiliation or Control: State/Local — IRS Status: 501(c)3
Highest Offering: Associate Degree
Accreditation: SC, CAHIIM, COARC, DMS, EMT, MAC, MLTAD, OTA, PHLEB, PTAA, RAD

02 President .... Dr. Don L. TOMAS
05 Exec VP Instructional/Student Svcs .... Dr. Thom R. BROOKS
10 VP for Financial & Admin Services .... Mr. Clifford STALTER
13 VP Information Technology .... Mr. Scott BAKER
30 Exec Dir Institutional Development .... Ms. Lynda W. PARLETT
103 Dean of Workforce/Economic Devel .... Mr. Jason LAMBERT
12 Dean Macon Campus .... Dr. Cheryl DAVIDS
32 Dean of Students .... Ms. Cheryl CONTINE-CONNER
06 Dir Student Records/Registrar .... Ms. Clyanne HYDE
08 Library Director .... Mrs. Dianne LINDGREN
09 Director Inst Research & Planning .... Mr. Jonathan E. DEAN
37 Financial Aid Director .... Ms. Melody L. LAWRENCE
26 Director of Public Relations .... Mr. Tyler GOODE
102 Director of SCC Foundation .... Mr. Bret WOODS
84 Director of Enrollment Management .... Mr. Marin AUCOIN
18 Chief Facilities/Physical Plant .... Ms. Lisa SIZEMORE

*Stanly Community College (E)

141 College Drive, Albemarle NC 28001-7458

County: Stanly — FICE Identification: 011194
Unit ID: 199740
Telephone: (704) 982-0121 — Carnegie Class: Assoc/MT-VT-High Non
FAX Number: (704) 982-0819 — Calendar System: Semester
URL: www.stanly.edu
Established: 1971 — Annual Undergrad Tuition & Fees (In-District): $2,523
Enrollment: 2,745 — Coed
Affiliation or Control: State/Local — IRS Status: 501(c)3
Highest Offering: Associate Degree
Accreditation: SC, COARC, MAC, MLTAD, RAD

02 President .... Dr. John ENAMAIT
05 Exec VP of Educational Services .... Mrs. Robin MCCREE
32 VP Student Success/Dean of Students .... Dr. Myra FARR
10 VP Administrative Services/CFO .... Ms. Stephanie FISHER
76 Assoc VP Health & Public Svcs .... Dr. Tammy CRUMP
50 Assoc VP Business & Technology .... Mrs. Merlin AMIRTHARAJ
04 Exec Aide to Pres/Governmental Affs .... Mrs. Ashley SMITH
37 Dean Financial Aid Management .... Ms. Petra FIELDS
84 Dean of Enrollment Management .... Mr. Patrick HOLYFIED
36 Asst Dean Students/Career Placement .... Mr. Marcus PRYOR
06 Dir Registration/Stdnt Information .... Ms. Michelle POPLIN
26 Director Marketing & Communication .... Mrs. Michele PEIFER
07 Director of Admissions .... Ms. Jearia MARTIN
21 Controller .... Mrs. Debra HARWOOD
18 Director of Facilities Services .... Mr. Blake BOSTIC
102 Exec Director of SCC Foundation .... Ms. Christy BOGLE
15 Human Resources Officer .... Vacant
08 Director Library Services .... Mrs. Erin ALLEN
24 Media Specialist Services .... Mr. Mark SAMPLE
96 Purchasing Agent .... Mrs. Shelley OSBORNE

*Surry Community College (F)

630 S Main Street, Dobson NC 27017-0304

County: Surry — FICE Identification: 002970
Unit ID: 199768
Telephone: (336) 386-8121 — Carnegie Class: Assoc/MT-VT-Mix Trad/Non
FAX Number: (336) 386-8951 — Calendar System: Semester
URL: www.surry.edu
Established: 1964 — Annual Undergrad Tuition & Fees (In-State): $2,476
Enrollment: 3,294 — Coed
Affiliation or Control: State — IRS Status: 501(c)3
Highest Offering: Associate Degree
Accreditation: SC, MAC, PTAA

02 President .... Dr. David R. SHOCKLEY
05 Vice Pres Curriculum Programs .... Dr. Jami WOODS
10 Vice President for Finance .... Mr. Tony L. MARTIN
45 Vice Pres Institutional Effective .... Dr. Anne R. HENNIS
51 VP Corporate & Cont Education .... Dr. George O. SAPPENFIELD
13 Vice President Technology Services .... Dr. Candace HOLDER
15 Director Personnel Services .... Ms. Melonie WEATHERS
18 Chief Facilities/Physical Plant .... Mr. Randy ROGERS
19 Director Security/Safety .... Mr. Marty SHROPSHIRE
26 Chief Public Relations/Marketing .... Ms. Julie PHARR
41 Athletic Director .... Mr. Mark TUCKER

*Tri-County Community College (G)

21 Campus Circle, Murphy NC 28906-7919

County: Cherokee — FICE Identification: 009430
Unit ID: 199795
Telephone: (828) 837-6810 — Carnegie Class: Assoc/HT-High Non
FAX Number: (828) 837-0028 — Calendar System: Semester
URL: www.tricountycc.edu
Established: 1964 — Annual Undergrad Tuition & Fees (In-State): $2,363
Enrollment: 1,273 — Coed
Affiliation or Control: State — IRS Status: 501(c)3
Highest Offering: Associate Degree
Accreditation: SC

02 President .... Dr. Donna TIPTON-ROGERS
09 VP Instruction/Institution Effect .... Dr. Steve WOOD
13 Dir of Computing & Information Mgt .... Mr. Jason OUTEN
88 Coordinator Recruitment/Retention .... Ms. Samantha MAJOR
103 Dir of Economic & Workforce Develop .... Mr. Paul WORLEY
45 VP College & Community Initiatives .... Mr. Bo GRAY
12 Asst to Pres Graham Cty Operations .... Ms. Charlene WOOD
88 Dean Research & Planning/EC Liaison .... Dr. Jason CHAMBERS
10 VP for Business & Finance .... Mr. Bill VESPASIAN
15 Director of Human Resources .... Ms. Sallie BAKER
91 Systems Administrator/Data Base Mgr .... Mr. Randy GUYETTE
08 Dean Learning Resources .... Ms. Linda KRESSAL
106 Learning Mgt Systems Administrator .... Mr. Cody ANDERSON
30 Coordinator Institutional Advancemt .... Mr. Roarke ARROWOOD
06 Registrar Curriculum .... Ms. Holly HYDE
37 Director of Financial Aid .... Ms. Diane OWL
96 Purchasing Agent .... Ms. Judy OWENBY
84 Director of Enrollment Management .... Ms. Lee BEAL
18 Coordinator of Facility Services .... Mr. Tim NICHOLSON

*Vance-Granville Community College (H)

PO Box 917, Henderson NC 27536-0917

County: Vance — FICE Identification: 009903
Unit ID: 199838
Telephone: (252) 492-2061 — Carnegie Class: Assoc/MT-VT-High Trad
FAX Number: (252) 430-0460 — Calendar System: Semester
URL: www.vgcc.edu
Established: 1969 — Annual Undergrad Tuition & Fees (In-State): $1,891
Enrollment: 4,025 — Coed
Affiliation or Control: State Related — IRS Status: 501(c)3
Highest Offering: Associate Degree
Accreditation: SC, CSHSE, MAC, RAD

02 President .... Dr. Stelfanie WILLIAMS
05 Vice Pres of Acad & Stdnt Affairs .... Dr. Angela BALLENTINE
10 Vice Pres for Finance & Operations .... Mr. Steve GRAHAM
09 VP of Institutional Research & Tech .... Dr. Kenneth A. LEWIS, JR.
26 VP of Employee & Public Relations .... Ms. Stacey CARTER-COLEY
12 Dean South Campus .... Ms. Cecilia B. WHEELER
12 Dean Franklin County Campus .... Ms. Bobbie Jo C. MAY
12 Dean Warren County Campus .... Mr. Lyndon HALL
08 Director Learning Resources Center .... Ms. Elaine STEM
06 Registrar .... Ms. Kathy KTUL
15 Director of Human Resources .... Ms. Audrey PARKER
37 Director of Financial Aid .... Ms. Kali BROWN
18 Director of Plant Operations .... Mr. Jack PUCKETT
27 Director of Communications .... Mr. James EDWARDS
38 Dir of Student Success .... Ms. Amy O'GEARY
84 Dean of Enrollment and Outreach .... Mr. Jeff ALLEN
09 Director of Planning & Research .... Ms. Julie HICKS
40 Bookstore Manager .... Ms. Sandra NEWTON

*Wake Technical Community College (I)

9101 Fayetteville Road, Raleigh NC 27603-5696

County: Wake — FICE Identification: 004844
Unit ID: 199856
Telephone: (919) 866-5000 — Carnegie Class: Assoc/HT-Mix Trad/Non
FAX Number: (919) 779-3360 — Calendar System: Semester
URL: www.waketech.edu
Established: 1958 — Annual Undergrad Tuition & Fees (In-District): $2,768
Enrollment: 21,384 — Coed
Affiliation or Control: State/Local — IRS Status: 501(c)3
Highest Offering: Associate Degree
Accreditation: SC, ACFEI, ADNUR, DA, DH, MAC, MLTAD, PHLEB, RAD, SURGT

02 President .... Dr. Stephen C. SCOTT
03 Executive Vice President .... Mrs. Gayle GREENE
102 Executive Director of Foundation .... Mr. Matthew B. SMITH
43 General Counsel/VP Legal Services .... Clay T. HINES
05 VP Curriculum Education Svcs .... Mrs. Sandra L. DIETRICH
32 SVP Enrollment & Student Services .... Mrs. Rita H. JERMAN
103 VP Workforce Continuing Education .... Mr. Anthony CAISON
10 AVP of Financial & Business Svcs .... Mrs. Marla L. TART

18 Facility Engineering Officer .... Mr. Wendell B. GOODWIN
26 VP Communications/Public Relations ...Mrs. Laurie C. CLOWERS
20 AVP Arts and Sciences .... Ms. Tonya FORBES
20 AVP Career Programs .... Ms. Sandra DIETRICH
84 AVP Enrollment Services .... Mr. John W. SAPARILAS
15 AVP Human Res and Title IX Coord .... Ms. Benita I. CLARK
19 Chief of Police .... Mr. Michael A. PENRY
21 AVP Accounting Officer .... Ms. Marla L. TART
10 AVP Business Services .... Mrs. Debra S. WALLACE
46 Dean IE/Accreditation & Research .... Dr. John B. BOONE
30 Sr Dir Foundation Rels/Admin .... Mrs. Stephanie S. LAKE
25 Dean Sponsored Programs .... Mr. Richard W. SULLINS
06 Senior Associate Registrar for Spec .... Ms. Salanna D. HOLMES
06 Dean/Curriculum Registrar .... Ms. Holly Elaine SWART
35 Dean Student Dev/Stdnt Conduct Ofcr .... Mr. Mark T. GIBSON
72 Dean Educ Svcs & Technology .... Mr. Ray L. TIMS
37 Dean Financial Aid/Veterans Affairs ...... Mrs. Regina M. HUGGINS
35 Sr Dean Strat Innovations Sp Proj .... Mrs. Karen B. PHINAZEE
88 Dean BioNetwork Capstone Center .... Ms. Ana M. MCCLANAHAN
20 AVP Student Services .... Mr. Kevin A. BROWN
07 Dean Admissions/Outreach Services .Ms. Susan R. BLOOMFIELD
08 Interim Dean Library Services .... Ms. Julia MIELISH
12 Dean Public Safety Education Campus ......Ms. Angela J. MIZELLE
27 Dir Communications Ops/Brand Mgmt .... Mrs. Francie W. SANDERSON
36 Assoc Dean Career & Empl Resources .....Mrs. Lynn E. KAVCSAK
76 Dean Health Sciences Campus .... Dr. Molly CURRY
81 Dean Mathematics/Sciences Div .... Ms. Sharon L. WELKER
79 Dean Arts/Humanities/Soc Sci Div .... Dr. Rebecca NEAGLE
50 Dean Business & Public Svcs Tech .... Mr. Walter MARTIN
75 Dean Applied Engr & Technologies ....Ms. Patricia A. GODIN
88 Sr Dean Instructional Support .... Mr. James A. ROBERSON
55 Director Career Dev & Pers Enrich ....Mr. Larry M. BUIE
77 Dean Computer Technologies .... Ms. Angela L. BEQUETTE
88 AVP CE Open Enrollment .... Mrs. Monica P. GEMPERLEIN

*Wayne Community College (A)

3000 Wayne Memorial Drive Box 8002,
Goldsboro NC 27533-8002

County: Wayne FICE Identification: 002980
Unit ID: 199892
Telephone: (919) 735-5151 Carnegie Class: Assoc/MT-VT-Mix Trad/Non
FAX Number: (919) 736-9425 Calendar System: Semester
URL: www.waynecc.edu
Established: 1957 Annual Undergrad Tuition & Fees (In-District): $2,396
Enrollment: 3,351 Coed
Affiliation or Control: State/Local IRS Status: 501(c)3
Highest Offering: Associate Degree
Accreditation: SC, ADNUR, DA, DH, MAC, PNUR

02 President .... Dr. Kay H. ALBERTSON
05 VP Academic and Student Services .... Mr. Gene SMITH
10 VP Finance/Chief Financial Officer .... Mrs. Joy KORNEGAY
11 Vice Pres Administrative Services .... Mr. Don MAGOON
45 VP Inst Effectiveness/Innovation .... Dr. Tracey IVEY
32 AVP Academic and Student Services ...Ms. Joanna MORRISETTE
51 AVP Continuing Education Services ....Ms. Renita DAWSON
15 AVP Human Res/Safety/Compliance .... Mr. Charles GAYLOR, IV
72 Division Chair Applied Technologies ....Mr. Ernie WHITE
49 Division Chair Arts & Sciences .... Dr. Brandon JENKINS
50 Div Chair Business & Computer Tech .... Mrs. Beth HOOKS
76 Division Chair Allied Health ....Mrs. Pattie PFEIFFER
88 Division Chair Public Safety .... Ms. Beverly DEANS
08 Director Library Services ....Dr. Ruth Aletha ANDREW
12 Coordinator Seymour Johnson AFB ....Mrs. Dori FRASER
92 Honors Program Coordinator .... Mr. Brandon JENKINS
106 Distance Education Specialist .... Mr. Randall SHEARON
105 Coord Educ Tech Services/Webmaster .... Mr. Brent HOOD
13 Director Information Technology .... Mr. Matt BAUER
18 Facility Operations Superintendent .... Mr. Edward E. FARRIS
19 Chief Campus Police & Security ....Chief Willie L. BRINSON
40 Director Bookstore .... Mrs. Trellie HERRING
88 Ex Dir Wayne Bus/Indus Ctr & WORKS ....Mrs. Diane IVEY
07 Director Admissions & Records .... Ms. Jennifer MAYO
37 Director Student Financial Aid .... Mrs. Brenda D. MERCER
84 Dir Student Devel/Enrollment Mgmt ... Mrs. Joanna MORRISETTE
36 Coord Coop Educ and Career Services ....Mrs. Lorie WALLER
78 Director Cooperative Programs .... Mrs. Lorie WALLER
35 Student Activities Coordinator .... Ms. Paige HAM
96 Accountant/Equipment Coordinator .... Mr. Mark R. JOHNSON
102 Executive Director of Foundation .... Mr. Jack KANNAN
26 Public Information Officer .... Ms. Tara HUMPHRIES
16 Director Human Resources .... Mrs. Ina R. RAWLINSON
55 Evening Coord/Security Services .... Mr. James BYNUM

*Western Piedmont Community College (B)

1001 Burkemont Avenue, Morganton NC 28655-4504

County: Burke FICE Identification: 002982
Unit ID: 199908
Telephone: (828) 438-6000 Carnegie Class: Assoc/MT-VT-Mix Trad/Non
FAX Number: (828) 438-6015 Calendar System: Semester
URL: www.wpcc.edu
Established: 1964 Annual Undergrad Tuition & Fees (In-State): $2,513
Enrollment: 2,056 Coed
Affiliation or Control: State IRS Status: 501(c)3
Highest Offering: Associate Degree
Accreditation: SC, ADNUR, DA, MAC, MLTAD

02 President .... Dr. Michael S. HELMICK
05 VP Academic & Student Services .... Ms. Rhia M. CRAWFORD
10 VP Admin Svcs/Chief Financial Ofcr ...... Ms. Sandra K. HOILMAN
26 VP External Affairs & Workforce Dev ...... Mr. Atticus J. SIMPSON
103 Dean Workforce Dev & Cont Educ .... Mr. Lee KISER
32 Dean of Student Services .... Ms. Susan WILLIAMS
08 Library Director .... Ms. Nancy DANIEL
54 Dean HEAT .... Mr. Michael DANIELS
49 Dean Arts & Sciences .... Ms. Ann Marie MCNEELY
50 Dean Business/PS/Academic Support .... Ms. Leslie MCKESSON
21 Controller .... Mr. Michael BINGHAM
06 Director Records & Registration .... Mrs. Joan P. HOGAN
15 Director Human Resources .... Ms. Lisa H. SESSIONS
84 Director Enrollment Management .... Mrs. Jennifer PROPST
37 Director Student Financial Aid .... Ms. Dori BARRON
13 Director Management Info Systems .... Ms. Nancy E. NORRIS
09 Director Inst Research/Eval .... Ms. Susan A. BERLEY
96 Director of Purchasing .... Ms. Linda CARSWELL
18 Director of Maintenance .... Vacant
04 Exec Admin Asst to President .... Ms. Kathy F. DURHAM

*Wilkes Community College (C)

1328 S Collegiate Drive, Wilkesboro NC 28697-0120

County: Wilkes FICE Identification: 002983
Unit ID: 199926
Telephone: (336) 838-6100 Carnegie Class: Assoc/HT-Mix Trad/Non
FAX Number: (336) 903-3219 Calendar System: Semester
URL: www.wilkescc.edu
Established: 1965 Annual Undergrad Tuition & Fees (In-State): $2,508
Enrollment: 2,718 Coed
Affiliation or Control: State IRS Status: 501(c)3
Highest Offering: Associate Degree
Accreditation: SC, COARC, DA, MAC, RAD

02 President .... Dr. Jeff A. COX
05 VP of Instruction .... Ms. Blair HANCOCK
10 Senior VP of Administration .... Mr. D. Morgan FRANCIS, JR.
20 VP of Instr Support/Student Svcs .... Ms. Kim E. FAW
103 VP of IWD-Alleghany Center .... Dr. John HAUSER
13 Assoc VP Information Technology .... Mr. Mike WINGLER
51 VP of CE/Ashe Campus .... Mr. Christopher D. ROBINSON
12 Director Alleghany Center .... Ms. Jayne PHIPPS-BOGER
09 Inst Effectiveness Exec Director .... Mr. J. Kelly PIPES, III
50 Dean Business/Public Svc Tech Div .... Mrs. Robin PHILLIPS-HAUSER
76 Dean Health Sciences Division .... Mr. Billy WOODS
18 Exec Director/Facilities Services .... Mr. Ronald DOLLYHITE
30 Exec Director/Endowment .... Ms. Allison PHILLIPS
15 Director of Human Resources .... Ms. Sherry P. COX
06 Registrar .... Ms. Melonie KILBY
07 Director of Admissions .... Mr. Scott JOHNSON
37 Director of Financial Aid .... Ms. Vickie G. CALL
38 Director Counseling & Career Svcs .... Dr. Lynda K. BLACK
32 Director Enrollment Mgmt/Stdnt Life .... Mr. Curt MILLER
08 Director Learning Resources .... Ms. Christy EARP
38 Director Student Support Services .... Mr. John CANTY
40 Bookstore Manager .... Ms. Holly EDWARDS
26 PIO & Relations Officer .... Ms. Amber HERMAN
19 Safety & Security Manager .... Mr. Jamie MCGUIRE
04 Executive Asst to President .... Ms. Cynthia ALFORD
96 Director of Purchasing .... Ms. Kim BARFIELD

*Wilson Community College (D)

PO Box 4305, Wilson NC 27893-0305

County: Wilson FICE Identification: 004845
Unit ID: 199953
Telephone: (252) 291-1195 Carnegie Class: Assoc/MT-VT-High Non
FAX Number: (252) 243-7148 Calendar System: Semester
URL: www.wilsoncc.edu
Established: 1958 Annual Undergrad Tuition & Fees (In-State): $2,393
Enrollment: 1,777 Coed
Affiliation or Control: State IRS Status: 501(c)3
Highest Offering: Associate Degree
Accreditation: SC, SURGT

02 President .... Dr. Tim WRIGHT
05 Int Vice Pres for Academic Affairs .... Mr. Robert HOLSTEN
10 Vice Pres for Finance & Admin Svcs .... Mr. Hadie C. HORNE
09 Director of Institutional Effective .... Mr. Andrew WALKER
51 Exec Dean of Cont Educ/Ind Tech .... Mr. Robert D. HOLSTEN
32 Exec Dean of Student Development .... Ms. Amy NOEL
76 Dean of Allied Health & Sciences .... Ms. Glenda P. BONDURANT
50 Dean Business/Applied Tech/Ed Part .... Mr. Wes HILL
15 Director of Human Resources .... Ms. Kathy WILLIAMSON
08 Head Librarian .... Mr. Gerry J. O'NEILL
21 Controller .... Ms. Jessica S. JONES
06 Registrar .... Ms. Jennifer DAVIS
07 Assoc Dean of Enrollment .... Ms. Sandra LACKNER
18 Director of Facilities .... Mr. Ray OWEN
37 Dir of Financial Aid/Vet Affairs .... Ms. Lisa SHEARIN
30 Director of Institutional Advance .... Ms. Renee WATKEVICH
13 Director of IT .... Ms. Molly ARMSTRONG
96 Purchasing & Capital Projects Mgr .... Ms. Donna A. TURNER
40 Bookstore Manager .... Ms. Kaschia SPELLS

North Carolina Wesleyan College (E)

3400 N Wesleyan Boulevard,
Rocky Mount NC 27804-8630

County: Nash FICE Identification: 002951
Unit ID: 199209
Telephone: (252) 985-5100 Carnegie Class: Bac-Diverse
FAX Number: (252) 985-5231 Calendar System: 4/1/4
URL: www.ncwc.edu
Established: 1956 Annual Undergrad Tuition & Fees: $28,150
Enrollment: 1,872 Coed
Affiliation or Control: United Methodist IRS Status: 501(c)3
Highest Offering: Baccalaureate
Accreditation: SC, TED

01 President .... Dr. Dewey CLARK
05 Interim Provost/VP Academic Affairs .... Dr. Evan DUFF
10 Vice President of Finance .... Mr. Jason EDWARDS
30 Interim VP of Advancement .... Mr. Eddie COATS
84 Vice President of Enrollment .... Mrs. Judy ROLLINS
32 VP Student Affairs/Dean of Students .... Mr. Edward NAYLOR
09 Chief Planning & Research Officer .... Dr. Larry H. KELLEY
06 Registrar .... Mrs. Candace CASHWELL
08 Director of Library .... Mrs. Kathy WINSLOW
26 Director of Communications .... Mrs. Susan BEST
23 Director Health Services .... Ms. Jessica BRYS-WILSON
36 Director Internship & Career Center .... Vacant
19 Director of Campus Security .... Mr. J. W. SEARS
41 Director of Athletics .... Mr. John THOMPSON
29 Director Alumni Rels/Annual Fund .... Ms. Tammy HARRELL
21 Controller .... Ms. Suzanne BRACKETT
37 Director of Financial Aid .... Ms. Leah HILL
15 Director of Human Resources .... Mr. Darrell S. WHITLEY
18 Director of Facilities .... Mr. Raymond THOMPSON
07 Assistant Director of Admissions .... Mr. Ben LILLEY
38 Director Student Counseling .... Vacant
40 Manager College Store .... Mr. Marcus RICH
20 Associate Academic Officer .... Dr. Molly WYATT
108 Director Institutional Assessment .... Dr. Larry H. KELLEY
13 Chief Info Technology Officer (CIO) .... Mr. Gregory BOYKIN
39 Director Student Housing .... Ms. Jesse LANGLEY
50 Chair Business .... Dr. Jackie LEWIS

Pfeiffer University (F)

48380 US Highway 52 N / PO Box 960,
Misenheimer NC 28109-0960

County: Stanly FICE Identification: 002955
Unit ID: 199306
Telephone: (704) 463-1360 Carnegie Class: Masters/L
FAX Number: (704) 463-1363 Calendar System: Semester
URL: www.pfeiffer.edu
Established: 1885 Annual Undergrad Tuition & Fees: $27,125
Enrollment: 1,784 Coed
Affiliation or Control: United Methodist IRS Status: 501(c)3
Highest Offering: Master's
Accreditation: SC, MFCD, MUS, NURSE, TED

01 President .... Dr. Colleen PERRY KEITH
04 Executive Assistant to President .... Ms. Teena P. MAULDIN
11 Chief Operations Officer .... Vacant
10 Vice President for Finance/CFO .... Mr. Jeffrey B. PLYLER
05 Provost/VP Academic Affairs .... Dr. Tracy Y. ESPY
32 VP Student Affairs/Dean of Students .... Mr. Ron LAFFITTE
30 Vice Pres Inst Advancement .... Mr. Robert FUZY
84 Vice Pres for Enrollment .... Mr. Christopher PARKER
41 Vice Pres Athletics .... Mr. Bob REASSO
06 Registrar .... Ms. Stacy ATKINSON
84 Director of Enrollment Operations .... Vacant
15 Director of Human Resources .... Ms. Twyla KIDD
09 Exec Director IR/Plng & Research .....Ms. Mary Ellen GOLDSTEIN
26 Director Inst Communications .... Ms. Susan G. MESSINA
38 Int Director Counseling .... Mr. Tony OETTINGER
08 Director of the Library .... Ms. Lara LITTLE
37 Exec Director of Financial Aid .... Ms. Frances KING
13 Director Information Technology .... Mr. William SEWARD, II
07 Director of Undergrad Admissions .... Ms. Emily CARELLA
20 Dir of Academic Support Services .... Dr. Jim E. GULLEDGE
19 Dir of Campus Safety & Security .... Mr. Erik MCGINNIS
23 Director of Health Services .... Vacant
18 Director of Facilities .... Ms. Sharon K. BARD
42 Minister to the University .... Rev. Dana MCKIM
36 Director of Career Development .... Mr. Jay LAURENS
39 Director of Residence Life .... Ms. Regina SIMMONS
58 Director of MCE Program .... Rev. Kathleen KILBOURNE
31 Director of Community Relations .... Ms. Carol MAY
29 Director of Alumni Affairs .... Ms. Amy BUNTING
12 Director of Triangle Campus .... Vacant
44 Advisor Planned Giving .... Mr. John LELFER
39 Asst Director of Residence Life .... Ms. Jill ROGERS
40 Bookstore Manager .... Ms. Dechelle ELLIS
104 Coord of Intl Studies/Study Abroad .... Ms. Rebecca HRACZO
50 Int Dean Division of Business .... Dr. Dawn LUCAS
53 Dean Division of Education .... Dr. Dawn LUCAS
79 Dean Division of Humanities .... Dr. David HECKEL
49 Dean Division of Liberal Arts .... Dr. Marilyn SUTTON-HAYWOOD
83 Dean Div of Social & Behav Sciences .... Dr. Donald POE, JR.
51 Dean of Cont Educ & Adult Prof Stds .... Dr. Paulita BROOKER
76 Dean Div of Applied Health Science .... Ms. Vernease MILLER

Piedmont International University (G)

420 S Broad Street, Winston-Salem NC 27101-5197

County: Forsyth FICE Identification: 002956
Unit ID: 199315
Telephone: (336) 725-8344 Carnegie Class: Spec-4-yr-Faith
FAX Number: (336) 725-5522 Calendar System: Semester
URL: www.piedmontu.edu
Established: 1945 Annual Undergrad Tuition & Fees: $9,580
Enrollment: 388 Coed
Affiliation or Control: Independent Non-Profit IRS Status: 501(c)3
Highest Offering: Doctorate

Accreditation: TRACS

00 Chancellor ... Dr. Howard L. WILBURN
01 President ... Dr. Charles W. PETITT
05 Provost ... Dr. Beth D. ASHBURN
11 Vice President of Operations ... Mr. Chris RONK
73 Vice Pres Temple Baptist Seminary ... Dr. Barkev TRACHIAN
20 VP of Academic Initiatives ... Dr. Byron EDENS
06 Registrar ... Mr. Jeremy PATTISALL
08 Librarian ... Dr. Catherine CHATMON
32 Director of Student Services ... Mr. Paul SMELTZER
34 Dean of Women ... Mrs. Rebecca BOTTOMS
42 Director of Church Relations ... Mr. Tony WILSON

Queens University of Charlotte (A)

1900 Selwyn Avenue, Charlotte NC 28274-0001
County: Mecklenburg FICE Identification: 002957
Unit ID: 199412
Telephone: (704) 337-2200 Carnegie Class: Masters/M
FAX Number: (704) 337-2517 Calendar System: Semester
URL: www.queens.edu
Established: 1857 Annual Undergrad Tuition & Fees: $32,560
Enrollment: 2,248 Coed
Affiliation or Control: Presbyterian Church (U.S.A.) IRS Status: 501(c)3
Highest Offering: Master's
Accreditation: SC, BUS, MUS, NURSE, TED

01 President ... Dr. Pamela L. DAVIES
05 VP Academic Affairs & Provost ... Dr. Lynn MORTON
30 VP University Advancement ... Mr. James BULLOCK
26 VP Marketing & Community Relations . Mrs. Rebecca ANDERSON
45 VP Campus Planning and Services ... Mr. Bill NICHOLS
10 CFO & VP for Administration ... Mr. Matthew PACKEY
49 Dean Col Arts & Sci & Cato Sch Educ ... Dr. John SISKO
50 Dean of McColl School of Business ... Dr. Richard MATHIEU
60 Dean Knight School of Communication ... Vacant
76 Dean Blair College of Health ... Dr. Tama MORRIS
20 Assoc Provost/Dean Univ Programs ... Dr. Sarah FATHERLY
06 Registrar ... Ms. Linda FLEISCHMAN
15 Director of Human Resources ... Ms. Teri ORSINI, SPHR

Reformed Theological Seminary (B)

2101 Carmel Road, Charlotte NC 28226-6399
Telephone: (704) 366-5066 Identification: 666785
Accreditation: &SC, THEOL

† Regional accreditation is carried under the parent institution in Jackson, MS.

St. Andrews University (C)

1700 Dogwood Mile, Laurinburg NC 28352-5598
Telephone: (910) 277-5000 FICE Identification: 002967
Accreditation: &SC

† Regional accreditation is carried under the parent institution, Webber International University, Babson Park, FL.

Saint Augustine's University (D)

1315 Oakwood Avenue, Raleigh NC 27610-2298
County: Wake FICE Identification: 002968
Unit ID: 199582
Telephone: (919) 516-4000 Carnegie Class: Bac-Diverse
FAX Number: (919) 828-0817 Calendar System: Semester
URL: www.st-aug.edu
Established: 1867 Annual Undergrad Tuition & Fees: $17,890
Enrollment: 1,016 Coed
Affiliation or Control: Protestant Episcopal IRS Status: 501(c)3
Highest Offering: Baccalaureate
Accreditation: SC

01 President ... Dr. Everett B. WARD
04 Exec Assistant to the President ... Ms. Audrey IVORY
30 VP Inst Advance & Chief Oper Ofcr ... Dr. Steven E. HAIRSTON
05 Provost and VP of Academic Affairs ... Dr. Yvonne COSTON
10 VP for Business & Finance ... Mr. Walter C. DAVENPORT
32 VP Enrollment Mgmt & Student Svcs ... Dr. Gaddis J. FAULCON
26 VP Marketing & Communications Ofcr ... Mrs. Shelley M. WILLINGHAM-HINTON
11 VP for Administration ... Ms. Sharon M. LIPSCOMB
09 Assoc Provost/Inst Eff & Planning ... Dr. Orlando E. HANKINS
21 Assoc VP/Comptroller ... Ms. Pamela E. TWITTY
20 Assoc Provost/ADA Coordinator ... Dr. Linda H. CURTIS
15 Acting Director Human Resources ... Ms. Lottie FERRELL
89 Dean of First Year Experience ... Mr. Paul A. NORMAN
34 Dean of Women/Director Student Act ... Ms. Ann BROWN
42 Chaplain ... Rev. Nita BYRD
13 Chief Information Officer ... Mr. Harod C. DEMBY
41 Director Athletics ... Mr. George D. WILLIAMS
06 Associate Registrar ... Ms. Martarash M. TORAIN
50 Dean Business/Mgmt & Technology ... Dr. Kanton REYNOLDS
83 Dean Social and Behavioral Sciences ... Dr. Zaphon WILSON
81 Dean Sciences/Math/Public Health ... Dr. Mark A. MELTON
49 Dean Liberal Arts & Educ ... Dr. Lynne T. JEFFERSON
97 Executive Director General College ... Dr. Sevealyn V. SMITH
07 Dean of Enrollment ... Mr. Christopher J. WITHERS
37 Director Financial Aid/ Scholarships ... Ms. Carrmela D. COHEN-PERRY
08 Director of Library Service ... Ms. Tiawanna S. NEVELS
36 Director of Professional Management ... Ms. Cindy LOVE

19 Chief of Police ... Mr. George H. BOYKIN, III
18 Director Physical Plant ... Mr. Hector F. GALLEGO
29 Director Alumni Affairs ... Ms. Sheryl H. XIMINES
88 Dir of Cmty Develop/Corp Program ... Ms. Bernadine WALDEN

Salem College (E)

601 South Church Street, Winston-Salem NC 27101
County: Forsyth FICE Identification: 002960
Unit ID: 199607
Telephone: (336) 721-2600 Carnegie Class: Bac-A&S
FAX Number: (336) 917-5339 Calendar System: 4/1/4
URL: www.salem.edu
Established: 1772 Annual Undergrad Tuition & Fees: $26,236
Enrollment: 1,118 Female
Affiliation or Control: Moravian Church IRS Status: 501(c)3
Highest Offering: Master's
Accreditation: SC, MUS, TED

01 President ... Dr. D. E. Lorraine STERRITT
05 VP Acad & Stdnt Affs/Dn of College ... Dr. Susan CALOVINI
30 VP for Institutional Advancement ... Vacant
07 VP for Enrollment/Fin Aid/Comm ... Ms. Katherine K. WATTS
32 Dean of Students ... Ms. Krispin W. BARR
58 Dean of Graduate Studies ... Dr. Sheryl LONG
51 Dean of Continuing Studies ... Dr. Sydney RICHARDSON
20 Dean Undergraduate Studies ... Dr. Richard VINSON
11 VP for Admin/Special Asst to Pres ... Ms. Anna GALLIMORE
08 Director of Libraries ... Ms. Elizabeth NOVICKI
44 Director Annual Giving ... Vacant
13 Director Information Technology ... Mr. Paul BENNINGER
15 Director of Payroll & Benefits ... Ms. Cheryl HAMILTON
10 Chief Financial Officer ... Vacant
38 Director Counseling Services ... Dr. Jack LOCICERO
37 Director Student Financial Aid ... Mr. Paul COSCIA
36 Director Career Devel/Internships ... Ms. Monica BOYD
06 Registrar/Dir Inst Research ... Ms. Jeannette RORK
18 Chief Facilities/Physical Plant ... Mr. George MORALES
29 Director Alumnae Relations ... Ms. Jerry STOKES
21 Accounts Receivable Manager ... Ms. Nikki BROCK
21 Accounts Payable Manager ... Ms. Judy SIGMON
19 Coordinator Institutional Services ... Mr. Tommy WILLIAMSON
04 Executive Asst to President ... Ms. Rosemary L. WHEELER
102 Dir Foundation/Corporate Relations ... Ms. Lynne STEWART
41 Athletic Director ... Ms. Melissa BARRETT

Shaw University (F)

118 E South Street, Raleigh NC 27601
County: Wake FICE Identification: 002962
Unit ID: 199643
Telephone: (919) 546-8300 Carnegie Class: Bac-Diverse
FAX Number: (919) 546-8301 Calendar System: Semester
URL: www.shawu.edu
Established: 1865 Annual Undergrad Tuition & Fees: $16,580
Enrollment: 1,802 Coed
Affiliation or Control: Baptist IRS Status: 501(c)3
Highest Offering: Master's
Accreditation: SC, #CAATE, KIN, SW, TED, THEOL

01 President ... Dr. Tashni-Ann DUBROY
05 Vice Pres for Academic Affairs ... Dr. Paulette DILLARD
10 Vice Pres for Finance & Admin ... Ms. Gwen WEBB
30 Vice Pres Institutional Advancement ... Ms. Clarenda STANLEY-ANDERSON
32 Vice Pres for Student Affairs ... Dr. Stanley ELLIOTT
84 Chief Enrollment Management Officer ... Mr. Anthony BROOKS
13 Chief Information Officer ... Mr. Peter NOWAK
20 Assoc VP for Academic Affairs ... Dr. Renata DUSENBURY
44 Assoc VP Institutional Advancement ... Ms. Sonya BENNETT-BELLAMY
35 Asst VP for Student Affairs ... Dr. Keith POWELL
15 Director of Human Resources ... Mr. Lee WOOD
84 Director of Financial Aid ... Ms. Marlyn Kevi DIXON
07 Director of Admissions/Recruitment ... Ms. Stacey SOWELL
06 Registrar ... Ms. Jody HAMILTON
88 Executive Director of CAPE ... Dr. Michael WEST
26 Dir Memberships(WSHA) & Public Rel ... Ms. Odessa HINES
08 Int Director of Library Services ... Mr. Thomas CLARK
45 Director of OSPIRE ... Dr. Stefanie RACHIS
41 Director of Athletics ... Dr. Alfonza CARTER
38 Director of Counseling Center ... Ms. Jerelene CARVER
88 Director of Judicial Affairs ... Ms. Agnes BAXTER
88 Director of Academic Success ... Ms. Richard WEDDERBURN
36 Dir Exper Learning/Career Develop ... Ms. Nikesha ROLLACK
50 Div Head Business & Prof Studies ... Dr. Mma KALU
53 Div Head Education & Social Work ... Dr. Paula MOTEN-TOLSON
81 Div Head Science & Technology ... Dr. Doreen CUNNINGHAM
76 Div Head Health & Human Sciences ... Dr Vanessa RAYNOR
60 Div Head Communications&Humanities ... Dr. Cassandra MITCHELL
83 Interim Div Head Social Sciences ... Dr Cynthia GRAHAM
89 Div Head Gen Ed/First Yr Experience ... Dr. James KIRKLEY
19 Chief of Campus Police & Security ... Mr. Martin MCCOY
18 Facility Manager ... Mr. Donald PEARSALL

Shepherds Theological Seminary (G)

6051 Tryon Road, Cary NC 27518-9316
County: Wake FICE Identification: 041730
Unit ID: 461485
Telephone: (919) 573-5350 Carnegie Class: Spec-4-yr-Faith
FAX Number: (919) 573-1433 Calendar System: Semester
URL: www.shepherds.edu
Established: 2003 Annual Graduate Tuition & Fees: N/A
Enrollment: 75 Coed
Affiliation or Control: Independent Non-Profit IRS Status: 501(c)3
Highest Offering: Master's; No Undergraduates
Accreditation: @THEOL, TRACS

01 President ... Dr. Stephen DAVEY
05 Provost/Dean ... Dr. Larry PETTEGREW
20 Vice President of Academic Affairs ... Mr. Edward HERRELKO
30 Vice President of Advancement ... Dr. Alan POTTER
10 Chief Financial Officer ... Mr. Ewart HODGINS
07 Director of Recruitment ... Dr. Douglas BOOKMAN
18 Chief Facilities/Physical Plant ... Dr. Samuel WINCHESTER
06 Registrar/Financial Aid Officer ... Mrs. Lucy BURGGRAFF

South University (H)

3975 Premier Drive, High Point NC 27265
Telephone: (336) 812-7200 Identification: 770915
Accreditation: &SC, ACBSP, NURSE, @PTAA

† Regional accreditation is carried under the parent institution in Savannah, GA

Southeastern Baptist Theological Seminary (I)

Box 1889, Wake Forest NC 27588-1889
County: Wake FICE Identification: 002963
Unit ID: 199759
Telephone: (919) 761-2100 Carnegie Class: Masters/L
FAX Number: N/A Calendar System: Semester
URL: www.sebts.edu
Established: 1950 Annual Undergrad Tuition & Fees: $8,124
Enrollment: 2,748 Coed
Affiliation or Control: Southern Baptist IRS Status: 501(c)3
Highest Offering: Doctorate
Accreditation: SC, THEOL

01 President ... Dr. Daniel L. AKIN
05 Provost/Dean of Faculty ... Dr. Bruce R. ASHFORD
10 Executive VP for Operations ... Mr. Ryan HUTCHINSON
20 VP Academic Administration ... Dr. Keith WHITFIELD
30 Vice Pres Institutional Advancement ... Mr. Art RAINER
32 VP Student Services/Dean Students ... Mr. Mark LIEDERBACH
04 Administrative Asst to President ... Mrs. Kim HUMPHREY
06 Registrar ... Mr. Cody OLDARCE
07 Director of Admissions ... Mr. Larry LYON
29 Dir Financial/Alumni Development ... Mr. Jonathan SIX
37 Director of Financial Aid ... Dr. Don ALLARD
08 Director Library Services ... Mr. Jason FOWLER
106 Dir Online Education ... Mr. Jerry LASSETTER
108 Coord Institutional Research ... Mr. Andrew J. SPENCER
13 Director Information Technologies ... Mr. Wayne JENKS
15 Director Human Resources ... Mrs. Dawn SATTERWHITE
28 Spec Asst Pres for Diversity ... Mr. Walter STRICKLAND
39 Director Student Housing ... Mr. Doug NALLEY
43 General Counsel ... Mr. George HARVEY

Southern Evangelical Seminary (J)

3000 Tilley Morris Road, Matthews NC 28105-8635
County: Union FICE Identification: 036115
Unit ID: 438522
Telephone: (704) 847-5600 Carnegie Class: Not Classified
FAX Number: (704) 845-1747 Calendar System: Semester
URL: www.ses.edu
Established: 1992 Annual Undergrad Tuition & Fees: N/A
Enrollment: N/A Coed
Affiliation or Control: Independent Non-Profit IRS Status: 501(c)3
Highest Offering: Doctorate
Accreditation: #TRACS

01 President & COO ... Dr. Richard D. LAND
05 Academic Dean ... Dr. J. Thomas BRIDGES
07 Director of Admissions ... Ms. Dianna NEWMAN
10 Business Manager ... Mr. Christian DRAKE
08 Librarian ... Mr. Ronald I. JORDAHL
06 Registrar ... Dr. Douglas E. POTTER
32 Director Student Services ... Mrs. Jill JOYNER
13 Dir of Information Technology ... Mr. Timothy BURKETT
26 Dir Communications/Special Events ... Mr. Eric T. GUSTAFSON
04 Executive Asst to President ... Mrs. Christina S. WOODSIDE
33 Dean of Men ... Dr. Brian HUFFLING
88 Director Missions ... Mr. Adam TUCKER
106 Dir Online Education/E-learning ... Mr. Jeff LENHART
30 Dir of Institutional Advancement ... Mr. Robert ANDREWS
12 Director of Bible College ... Dr. Floyd ELMORE

University of Mount Olive (K)

634 Henderson Street, Mount Olive NC 28365-1263
County: Wayne FICE Identification: 002949
Unit ID: 199069
Telephone: (919) 658-2502 Carnegie Class: Bac-Diverse
FAX Number: (919) 658-7180 Calendar System: Semester
URL: www.umo.edu
Established: 1951 Annual Undergrad Tuition & Fees: $18,400
Enrollment: 3,456 Coed
Affiliation or Control: Original Free Will Baptist Church IRS Status: 501(c)3
Highest Offering: Master's
Accreditation: SC, ACBSP, NURSE

01 President Dr. Philip P. KERSTETTER
03 Executive Vice President Dr. Carol G. CARRERE
05 VP for Academic Affairs Dr. Kenneth D. HINES
10 VP for Finance & Administration Mr. John KUNST
84 VP for Enrollment Dr. Barbara R. KORNEGAY
32 VP for Student Affairs Mr. Dan SULLIVAN
30 VP for Institutional Advancement Ms. Teresa HINES
49 Dean School of Arts and Sciences Dr. Burt LEWIS
50 Dean Tillman School of Business Dr. Kathy BEST
56 Dean of Extended Education Ms. Lisa M. NUESELL
08 Director of Library Services Ms. Pamela R. WOOD
12 Director of UMO New Bern Mr. Luis MIRANDA
12 Director of UMO Jacksonville Vacant
12 Director of UMO Goldsboro Dr. John P. RUTTER
12 Director of UMO Evening College Dr. John P. RUTTER
12 Director of UMO Wilmington Dr. Marna R. MCMURRY
12 Director UMO Research Triangle Park Mr. Oscar RODRIGUEZ
09 Director Inst Research & Planning Dr. Juliane SANTIAGO
108 Director of Assessment Dr. Ron STEVENS
07 Director of Admissions Mr. Timothy E. WOODARD
06 Registrar Mr. David L. BOURGEOIS
35 Director of Campus Life Ms. Nicole L. GARRETT
36 Director of Career Center Ms. Laurica YANCEY
39 Director of Housing/Resident Life Mr. Ian FOLEY
26 Director of Public Relations Ms. Rhonda E. JESSUP
102 Dir Foundations & Sponsored Program Ms. Kari SANDER
29 Director of Alumni Relations .Ms. Hope S. MCPHERSON FIELDS
44 Director of Annual Fund Ms. Melinda HOLLAND
37 Director of Financial Aid Ms. Katrina K. LEE
15 Director of Human Resources Ms. Cordelia A. WILCOX
23 Student Health Services Ms. Joanne L. MORGAN
42 Campus Chaplain Ms. Carla WILLIAMSON
04 Assistant to the President Ms. Katherine B. GARDNER
18 Director Building & Grounds Mr. Jeff D. BROGDEN
13 Director Technology Support Mr. Robert R. PRUETT
88 Director Technology Services Mr. Kenneth M. DAVIS, JR.
92 Director Honors Program Dr. Brenda B. CATES
41 VP for Athletics Mr. Jeffrey M. EISEN
20 AVP Acad Affairs/Dean Grad Studies Dr. David DOMMER

*University of North Carolina General Administration (A)

Box 2688, 910 Raleigh Road, Chapel Hill NC 27515-2688
County: Orange FICE Identification: 002971
Unit ID: 199175
Telephone: (919) 962-1000 Carnegie Class: N/A
FAX Number: (919) 962-2751
URL: www.northcarolina.edu

01 President Dr. Margaret SPELLINGS
11 Sr Vice Pres/Chief Operating Ofcr Mr. Charles E. PERUSSE
100 Chief of Staff Ms. Meredith DIDIER
05 Sr Vice Pres Academic Affairs Dr. Junius GONZALES
10 Sr Vice President Finance/Budget Mr. Jonathan PRUITT
88 VP Academic & University Programs Dr. Alisa CHAPMAN
13 Vice Pres Information Resources/CIO Mr. John LEYDON
43 VP Legal Affs/General Counsel Mr. Thomas SHANAHAN
46 VP Academic Pgms/Faculty/Research Ms. Kim VAN NOORT
101 Sr Assoc VP/Sec of the University Ms. Andrea POOLE
86 Vice President for Govt Relations Mr. Drew MORETZ
86 Actg Vice Pres Federal Relations Mr. Jonathan KAPPLER
26 Vice President for Communications Ms. Joni WORTHINGTON
15 Vice Pres for Human Resources Mr. Matthew BRODY
88 VP for Intl/Community/Econ Engagmnt Mr. Leslie BONEY

*Appalachian State University (B)

287 Rivers Street, Boone NC 28608-0001
County: Watauga FICE Identification: 002906
Unit ID: 197869
Telephone: (828) 262-2000 Carnegie Class: Masters/L
FAX Number: (828) 262-2347 Calendar System: Semester
URL: www.appstate.edu
Established: 1899 Annual Undergrad Tuition & Fees (In-State): $6,852
Enrollment: 18,026 Coed
Affiliation or Control: State IRS Status: 501(c)3
Highest Offering: Doctorate
Accreditation: SC, ART, BUS, CAATE, CACREP, CIDA, CS, DANCE, DIETD, DIETI, IPSY, MFCD, MUS, NRPA, NURSE, SP, SPAA, SW, TED, THEA

02 Chancellor Dr. Sheri N. EVERTS
100 Vice Chanc/Actg Chief of Staff Ms. Debra F. COVINGTON
05 Provost/Exec Vice Chancellor Dr. Darrell P. KRUGER
10 Int Vice Chanc Business Affairs Mr. Timothy H. BURWELL
32 Int Vice Chanc Student Development Mr. Leroy WRIGHT
30 Int Vice Chanc Univ Advancement Dr. Randy EDWARDS
20 Vice Provost for Undergrad Educ Dr. Mike W. MAYFIELD
46 Vice Provost for Research Dr. Alan UTTER
26 Sr Assc VC Advance/Chief Comm Ofcr Mr. Hank T. FOREMAN
84 Assoc VC for Enrollment Services Mrs. Susan DAVIES
22 AVC Equity/Diversity/Compliance Ms. Bindu K. JAYNE
29 Exec Director of Alumni Affairs Mr. Patrick K. SETZER
43 General Counsel Mr. Dayton T. COLE
13 Chief Information Officer Mrs. Cathy J. BATES
06 University Registrar Ms. Debbie RACE
38 Dir Counseling/Psychological Svcs Dr. Dan L. JONES
37 Director of Financial Aid Ms. Lori A. TOWNSEND
15 Director of Human Resources Mr. Mark BACHMEIER
09 Int Director Inst Research/Planning Mrs. Heather H. LANGDON
51 Exec Director of Distance Education Dr. Terry RAWLS
41 Director of Athletics Mr. Douglas P. GILLIN
49 Dean for College of Arts & Sciences Dr. Anthony G. CALAMAI
50 Dean for College of Business Dr. Heather NORRIS
53 Int Dean for College of Education Dr. Robin GROCE
57 Dean for College Fine/Applied Arts Dr. Glenda J. TREADAWAY
64 Dean for the School of Music Dr. William L. PELTO
58 Dean of Research/Graduate Studies Dr. Max C. POOLE
08 Dean of Libraries Ms. Joyce L. OGBURN
18 Director of the Physical Plant Mr. Mike J. O'CONNOR
21 Budget Director Mr. Ken W. SMITH
35 Dean of Students/Assoc VC Stdnt Dev Mr. J.J BROWN
96 Director of Materials Management Mr. Dwayne E. ODVODY
28 Dir Multicultural Student Devel Ms. Traci D. ROYSTER

*East Carolina University (C)

1000 East Fifth Street, Greenville NC 27858-4353
County: Pitt FICE Identification: 002923
Unit ID: 198464
Telephone: (252) 328-6212 Carnegie Class: DU-Higher
FAX Number: (252) 328-4155 Calendar System: Semester
URL: www.ecu.edu
Established: 1907 Annual Undergrad Tuition & Fees (In-State): $6,580
Enrollment: 27,511 Coed
Affiliation or Control: State IRS Status: 501(c)3
Highest Offering: Doctorate
Accreditation: SC, AAFCS, ANEST, ARCPA, ART, AUD, BUS, CAATE, CACREP, CAHIIM, CARTE, CEA, CIDA, CLPSY, CONST, CORE, DENT, DIETD, DIETI, ENG, ENGR, LIB, MED, MFCD, MIDWF, MT, MUS, NAIT, NRPA, NURSE, OT, PH, PLNG, PTA, SCPSY, SP, SPAA, SW, TED, THEA

02 Chancellor Dr. Cecil P. STATON
100 Chief of Staff Mr. Chris LOCKLEAR
05 Provost & Sr VC Academic Affairs Dr. Ron MITCHELSON
32 Vice Chancellor for Student Affairs Dr. Virginia HARDY
17 Vice Chanc Health Sciences Dr. Phyllis N. HORNS
10 Vice Chanc Administration & Finance .Dr. Frederick NISWANDER
30 Vice Chanc Univ Advancement Mr. Christopher DYBA
46 Int VC Research/Graduate Studies Dr. Michael VAN SCOTT
29 VC for Alumni Relations Mr. Heath BOWMAN
39 Assoc VC Camp Liv/Dining Mr. William L. MCCARTNEY, JR.
38 Assoc Vice Chanc & Dean of Stdnts Dr. Lynn M. ROEDER
35 Assoc Dean of Students Dr. Lathan E. TURNER
22 Assoc Provost Equity/Diversity Ms. Lakesha ALSTON FORBES
43 Vice Chancellor for Legal Affairs Ms. Donna G. PAYNE
09 Associate Provost IPAR Dr. Ying ZHOU
41 Athletic Director Mr. Jeff COMPHER
13 CIO and Assoc Vice Chanc ITCS Mr. Don SWEET
15 Assoc Vice Chanc Human Resources Ms. Melissa BARD
18 Assoc VC for Campus Opers Mr. William BAGNELL
21 Assoc VC for Business Services Mr. A. Scott BUCK
88 Assoc VC Environ Health & Safety Mr. Bill KOCH
88 Int Exec Dir of Global Affairs Dr. Ravi PAUL
88 Assoc VC for Emerging Acad Init Dr. Elmer POE
20 Int Dir Acad Pgm Planning & Develop Ms. Rita REAVES
88 Dir of Campus Rec & Wellness Mr. William EHLING
84 Assoc Provost for Enrollment Svcs Dr. John FLETCHER
26 Ex Dir Communication/Pub Affs/Mktg Ms. Mary C. SHULKEN
07 Director of Admissions Dr. Dave MEREDITH
06 Registrar Ms. Angela R. ANDERSON
08 Director JY Joyner Library Ms. Jan LEWIS
88 Int Dir Health Sciences Library Ms. Beth KETTERMAN
101 Asst Secretary to Board of Trustees Dr. Steve DUNCAN
37 Director of Financial Aid Ms. Julie POORMAN
19 Interim Chief of Police Mr. Jason SUGG
51 Director of Continuing Studies Mr. Anthony BRITT
27 Director of University Marketing Mr. Clint BAILEY
27 Director of Publications Mr. Jimmy ROSTAR
88 Director of Military Programs Mr. Tim WISEMAN
96 Director of Purchasing Mr. Kevin CARRAWAY
36 Director Career Center Ms. Leslie ROGERS
88 Director of Internal Audit Ms. Stacie TRONTO
21 Interim AVC for Financial Services Ms. Dee BOWLING
49 Dean College of Arts & Sciences Dr. William DOWNS
76 Dean College of Allied Health Dr. Greg HASSLER
68 Dean Col Health/Human Performance Dr. Glen G. GILBERT
59 Dean College of Human Ecology Dr. Judy SIGUAW
66 Dean College of Nursing Dr. Sylvia BROWN
50 Dean College of Business Dr. Stanley G. EAKINS
57 Dean Col Fine Arts/Comm Dr. Christopher BUDDO
53 Dean College of Education Dr. B. Grant HAYES
72 Dean Col of Engineering and Tech Dr. David WHITE
58 Dean Graduate School Dr. Paul GEMPERLINE
92 Dean Honors College Dr. David WHITE
63 Dean Brody School of Medicine Dr. Paul R G. CUNNINGHAM
52 Dean School of Dental Medicine Dr. Gregory CHADWICK
04 Assistant to Chancellor Ms. Christy DANIELS
85 Dir of Grants and Contracts Mr. Steve AYERS
86 Director of Strategic Initiatives Ms. Michelle BROOKS
102 President/CEO ECU Foundation Mr. Chris DYBA
54 Chairperson Engineering Dr. Hayden GRIFFIN

*Elizabeth City State University (D)

1704 Weeksville Road, Elizabeth City NC 27909-7806
County: Pasquotank FICE Identification: 002926
Unit ID: 198507
Telephone: (252) 335-3400 Carnegie Class: Masters/S
FAX Number: (252) 335-3731 Calendar System: Semester
URL: www.ecsu.edu
Established: 1891 Annual Undergrad Tuition & Fees (In-State): $4,657
Enrollment: 1,867 Coed
Affiliation or Control: State IRS Status: 501(c)3
Highest Offering: Master's
Accreditation: SC, BUS, ENGT, MUS, SW, TED

02 Interim Chancellor Dr. Thomas CONWAY
05 VC Academic Affairs Dr. Vann NEWKIRK
20 Interim Assoc VC Academic Affairs Dr. Harry BASS
10 VC for Business & Finance/CFO Mr. Joshua LASSITER
30 VC for Institutional Advancement Mr. Cliff VANTERPOOL
43 General Counsel Mr. Alyn GOODSON
32 Chief Student Affairs Officer Mr. Nolan DAVIS
13 Chief Information Officer Mr. Suresh MARUGAN
15 Director Human Resources Mr. Rafeal BONES
41 Athletic Director Mr. Derrick JOHNSON
84 Asst VC Enrollment Mgmt Mr. Andre FARLEY
09 Int Dir Institutional Effectiveness Mr. Brian JORDAN
06 Registrar Ms. Althea L. RIDDICK
35 Asst VC/Dean of Students Mr. Kelvin BROWN
08 Director of Library Services Dr. Juanita MIDGETTE
07 Director of Admissions Vacant
38 Dir Counsel/Test Student Affairs Ms. Felicia BROWN
36 Director of Career Services Ms. Makitta WHITEHURST-MCLEAN
37 Director Student Financial Aid Ms. Jill GABLE
29 Director of Alumni Relations Ms. Barbara B. SUTTON
18 Director of Facilities/Planning Mr. Charles HALL
26 Director Univ Relation/Marketing Dr. Linita SHANNON
87 Director of Summer School Mr. Derrick WILKINS
92 Director of Honors Program Dr. Kenneth JONES
96 Director of Purchasing Ms. Rachel HAINES
58 Director of Graduate Education Dr. Harry BASS
04 Administrative Asst to President Ms. Lucretia BANKS
101 Secretary of the Institution/Board Ms. Gwendolyn SANDERS
104 Director Study Abroad Dr. Glen BOWMAN
105 Director Web Services Ms. Dana COBB
106 Dir Online Education/E-learning Dr. Kim STEVENSON
100 Chief of Staff Ms. Theresa TIBBS
19 Director Security/Safety Mr. John MANLEY
39 Interim Director Student Housing Ms. Sabrina WILLIAMS
86 Director Government Relations Mrs. Kathryn UNDERWOOD

*Fayetteville State University (E)

1200 Murchison Road, Fayetteville NC 28301-4298
County: Cumberland FICE Identification: 002928
Unit ID: 198543
Telephone: (910) 672-1111 Carnegie Class: Masters/M
FAX Number: (910) 672-1769 Calendar System: Semester
URL: www.uncfsu.edu
Established: 1867 Annual Undergrad Tuition & Fees (In-State): $4,885
Enrollment: 5,899 Coed
Affiliation or Control: State IRS Status: 501(c)3
Highest Offering: Doctorate
Accreditation: SC, ART, BUS, CS, MUS, NURSE, SW, TED

02 Chancellor Dr. James A. ANDERSON
100 Vice Chancellor and Chief of Staff Vacant
05 Provost & Vice Chanc Academic Affs Dr. Jon YOUNG
10 Vice Chancellor Business/Finance Mr. Kenneth CRAIG
32 Vice Chancellor Student Affairs Dr. Janice HAYNIE
30 Vice Chancellor Inst Advancement Mr. Getchel CALDWELL
13 Vice Chanc Info Technology/CIO Mr. Arasu GANESAN
44 Asst Vice Chanc for Advancement Vacant
35 Assoc Vice Chanc Student Affairs Dr. Juanette COUNCIL
18 Assoc Vice Chanc Facilities Mgmt Mr. Rudolph CARDENAS
21 Asst VC Business/Financ/Controller Ms. Christine M. JUMALON
15 Assoc Vice Chanc Human Resources Ms. Terri TIBBS
85 Asst VC Acad Affs/Interntl Studies Dr. Chen YUNKAI
88 Senior Assoc Vice Chancellor Dr. Perry A. MASSEY
45 Assoc VC Pgms/Plng/Assessment Vacant
36 Director Career Svcs & Bus Mgr SA Dr. Curtis STREET
92 Acting Program Director Honors Dr. Erin WHITE
06 Registrar Ms. Sarah BAKER
29 Director of Alumni Affairs Ms. YaKima RHINEHART
26 Director Public Relations Mr. Jeff WOMBLE
08 Director of Library Services Mr. Bobby C. WYNN
07 Director of Admissions Ms. Ulisa BOWLES
90 Director of IT Operations Ms. Michelle WHITAKER
09 Director Institutional Research Vacant
39 Director of Residence Life Mr. Greg MOYD
37 Director Student Financial Aid Ms. Kamesia EWING
43 General Counsel Mrs. Wanda LESSANE JENKINS
41 Athletic Director Mr. Anthony T. BENNETT
96 Director of Purchasing Ms. Willie MCINTYRE
38 Dir Center Personal Development Mr. Fred SAPP
28 Director of Diversity Vacant
88 Dean University College Dr. John I. BROOKS
66 Department Chair Nursing Dr. Afua ARHIN
50 Dean School Business/Economics Dr. Pamela JACKSON
53 Dean School of Education Dr. Marion GILLIS-OLION
49 Actg Dean College Arts and Sciences Dr. Samuel ADU-MIREKU
101 Secretary of Univ/Board Liaison Ms. Suzetta M. PERKINS
19 Asst VC Police & Public Safety Mr. Charles F. KIMBLE
04 Administrative Asst to President Mrs. Ann ZOMERFELD
86 Director Government Relations Mr. Wesley FOUNTAIN
25 Chief Contracts/Grants Admin Ms. Chrystal COOPER

*North Carolina Agricultural and Technical State University (F)

1601 East Market Street, Greensboro NC 27411-0001
County: Guilford FICE Identification: 002905
Unit ID: 199102
Telephone: (336) 334-7500 Carnegie Class: DU-Higher
FAX Number: (336) 334-7136 Calendar System: Semester
URL: www.ncat.edu
Established: 1891 Annual Undergrad Tuition & Fees (In-State): $5,972
Enrollment: 10,725 Coed

Affiliation or Control: State IRS Status: 501(c)3
Highest Offering: Doctorate
Accreditation: **SC**, AAFCS, BUS, BUSA, CACREP, CONST, CORE, CS, #DIETD, ENG, #JOUR, LSAR, MUS, NAIT, NUR, SW, TED, THEA

02 Chancellor .... Dr. Harold L. MARTIN, SR.
05 Provost/Vice Chanc Academic Affairs .... Dr. Joe B. WHITEHEAD, JR.
10 Vice Chanc Business & Finance .... Mr. Robert POMPEY, JR.
100 Chief of Staff .... Ms. Nicole PRIDE
46 Vice Chanc Research/Economic Dev .... Dr. Barry L. BURKS
32 Vice Chancellor of Student Affairs .... Dr. Melody C. PIERCE
15 Vice Chancellor for Human Resources .... Dr. Ericka M. SMITH
13 Interim VC Info Tech Services/CIO .... Mr. H. Thomas JACKSON
43 General Counsel for Legal Affairs .... Dr. J. Charles WALDRUP
20 Vice Prov for Acad Affs/UG Programs .... Dr. G. Scott JENKINS
26 Associate VC for Univ Relations .... Vacant
45 Asst VC for Budget & Planning .... Mrs. Chartarra JOYNER
88 Vice Prov Rsrch Grad Pgm/Extnd Lrng .... Dr. Sanjiv SARIN
18 Asst VC for Bus/Finance/Facilities .. Mr. Andrew M. PERKINS, JR.
19 Asst VC Police/Public Safety .... Mr. Charles E. WILSON, JR.
08 Dean of Library Services .... Ms. Vicki COLEMAN
47 Dean Agric/Environmental Sci .... Dr. Shirley HYMON-PARKER
49 Dean Arts & Sciences .... Dr. Goldie S. BYRD
53 Dean of Education .... Dr. Anthony GRAHAM
54 Dean of Engineering .... Dr. Robin N. COGER
58 Dean of Graduate School .... Dr. Sanjiv SARIN
66 Interim Dean of Nursing .... Dr. Terry WARD
50 Dean of Business & Economics .... Dr. Beryl MCEWEN
72 Dean School of Technology .... Dr. Benjamin O. UWAKWEH
88 Dean Joint Sch Nanoscience/Nanoengr .... Dr. James G. RYAN
09 Asst VC for Inst Research/Planning .... Vacant
06 Interim University Registrar .... Dr. Dawn FORBES MURPHY
84 AVC for Enroll Management .... Mrs. Erin HILL HART
37 Director Financial Aid .... Mrs. Sherri M. AVENT
36 Director Career Services .... Ms. Joyce P. EDWARDS
91 Asst VC for Info Syst/Data Ctr Ops .... Vacant
29 Interim Assoc VC for Alumni Affairs .... Ms. Teresa DAVIS
85 Dir International Student Affairs .... Ms. Loreatha D. GRAVES
88 Dir Multicultural Student Center .... Mr. Gerald SPATES
41 Director of Athletics .... Mr. Earl M. HILTON, III
39 Dir Student Housing/Residence Life .... Ms. Linda D. INMAN
23 Phys/Dir Student Health Services .... Dr. David H. WAGNER
38 Director of Counseling Service .... Dr. Vivian D. BARNETTE
25 Director of Contracts/Grants .... Ms. Natalie TEAGLE
92 Director of Honors Program .... Dr. Michael CUNDALL, JR.
96 Interim Director of Purchasing .... Ms. Martinique WILLIAMS
27 Director of Media Relations .... Vacant
40 Bookstore Manager .... Ms. Michaele WIGGINS
102 Dir Foundation/Corporate Relations .... Mr. Stephone WHITE
88 Ctr for Leadership & Org Excellence .... Vacant
104 Asst Director for Study Abroad .... Mr. Christopher M. BROWN
106 Dir of ITS/Distance Education .... Dr. Tracie O. LEWIS
108 AVC Institutional Research .... Dr. William B. ZHANG
22 Dir Affirmative Action/EEO .... Ms. Linda MANGUM
44 Director of Annual Giving .... Vacant
88 Senior Director of Development .... Ms. Carletta SIMMONS
86 Director External Affairs .... Mr. Michael A. BROWN, II

*North Carolina Central University (A)

1801 Fayetteville Street, Durham NC 27707-3129
County: Durham FICE Identification: 002950
Unit ID: 199157
Telephone: (919) 530-6100 Carnegie Class: Masters/L
FAX Number: (919) 530-5014 Calendar System: Semester
URL: www.nccu.edu
Established: 1910 Annual Undergrad Tuition & Fees (In-State): $5,755
Enrollment: 7,687 Coed
Affiliation or Control: State IRS Status: 501(c)3
Highest Offering: Doctorate
Accreditation: **SC**, BUS, #CAATE, CACREP, DIETD, DIETI, LAW, LIB, NRPA, NUR, SP, SW, TED, THEA

02 Chancellor .... Dr. Debra SAUNDERS-WHITE
05 Provost/VC Academic Affairs .... Dr. Johnson AKINLEYE
100 Chief of Staff .... Mr. Wendell F. PHILLIPS
43 General Counsel .... Ms. Hope TYEHIMBA
46 Interim VC Res/Economic Devel .... Dr. Undi N. HOFFLER
11 Vice Chanc Admin & Finance .... Mr. Benjamin DURANT
32 Vice Chancellor Student Affairs .... Dr. Miron P. BILLINGSLEY
30 Vice Chanc Inst Advancement .... Dr. Harriet F. DAVIS
20 Assoc Provost for Academic Programs .... Dr. Tau KADHI
10 Assoc VC Administration/ Finance .... Ms. Yolanda E. BANKS-DEAVER
20 Assoc VC Faculty Develop .... Dr. Yolanda B. ANDERSON
15 Interim Chief Human Resources .... Ms. Sylvia ANDERSON
88 Assoc VC Innovat/Engaged & Global .... Dr. Ontario S. WOODEN
88 Director Student Union .... Dr. Toya CORBETT
45 Director Strategic Planning .... Mr. Johnnie SOUTHERLAND
35 Assistant VC of Student Affairs .... Mr. Gary L. BROWN
13 Chief Information Officer .... Ms. Leah KRAUS
07 Director Undgraduate Admissions .... Dr. Nicole GIBBS
31 Director of External Affairs .... Ms. Pamela THORPE-YOUNG
88 Dir Bio Rsch Inst/Tech Ent .... Vacant
06 Registrar .... Dr. Jerome GOODWIN
91 Interim Dir Enterprise Info System .... Ms. Billie HANES
29 Director of Alumni Relations .... Ms. Chatonda COVINGTON
26 Assoc VC for Public Relations .... Ms. Ayana D. HERNANDEZ
37 Director of Financial Aid .... Ms. Sharon J. OLIVER
08 Director Library Services .... Dr. Theodosia T. SHIELDS
19 Chief of University Police .... Ms. Odetta JOHNSON
88 Assoc Dean Univ Clge/Acad Advising .... Dr. Jennifer SCHUM
88 Director Art Museum .... Dr. Kenneth G. RODGERS
18 Director Facilities Services .... Mr. Phillip POWELL
39 Director Residential Life .... Mr. Ronnie DAVIS
41 Director Athletics .... Dr. Ingrid L. WICKER-MCCREE
09 Interim VC Inst Research/Eval/Plng .... Dr. Jeanette BARKER
96 Interim Director of Purchasing .... Ms. Constance G. MALLETTE
92 Director of Honors Program .... Dr. Ansel E. BROWN
38 Exec Director of Counseling Center . Dr. Ruth GILLIAM PHILLIPS
22 Director of EEO & Employee Relation .. Ms. Sylvia C. ANDERSON
84 Assoc VC Enrollment Management .... Dr. Monica T. LEACH
21 Dir Auxiliaries/Business Services .... Mr. Timothy J. MOORE
40 Manager Bookstore .... Ms. Stephanie L. GETCHELL
58 Dean Sch Grad Stds/Asc VC Grad Rsch .... Dr. Jaleh REZAIE
61 Dean of the Law School .... Ms. Phyliss J. CRAIG-TAYLOR
62 Dean School of Library/Info Science .... Dr. Irene OWENS
50 Interim Dean School of Business .... Dr. Wanda LESTER
88 Dean of University College .... Dr. Ontario S. WOODEN
49 Dean College of Arts and Sciences .... Dr. Carlton E. WILSON
83 Dean College Behavioral/Social Scis .... Dr. Debra O. PARKER
53 Interim Dean School of Education .... Dr. Audrey W. BEARD
04 Executive Asst to Chancellor .... Ms. Zelda STANFIELD
101 Secretary of the Board of Trustees .... Mr. Wendell F. PHILLIPS
102 Executive Director NCCU Foundation .... Mr. Ernest JENKINS
104 Asst Director International Affairs .... Dr. Olivia JONES
105 Director Web Services .... Mr. Damond NOLLAN
106 Director Division Extended Studies .... Ms. Kimberly C. PHIFER-MCGHEE
108 Director of Assessment .... Ms. Tia M. DOXEY
25 Director Contracts/Grants Admin .... Ms. Denise Y. WYNN
36 Director Career Services .... Ms. Donna Y. HEMBRICK

*North Carolina State University (B)

20 Watauga Club Drive, Raleigh NC 27695-0001
County: Wake FICE Identification: 002972
Unit ID: 199193
Telephone: (919) 515-2191 Carnegie Class: DU-Highest
FAX Number: (919) 515-7740 Calendar System: Semester
URL: www.ncsu.edu
Established: 1887 Annual Undergrad Tuition & Fees (In-State): $8,581
Enrollment: 33,989 Coed
Affiliation or Control: State IRS Status: 501(c)3
Highest Offering: Doctorate
Accreditation: **SC**, ART, BUS, BUSA, CACREP, CAEP, CS, ENG, LSAR, NRPA, SCPSY, SPAA, SW, TED, VET

02 Chancellor .... Dr. William Randy WOODSON
05 Provost/Exec Vice Chancellor .... Dr. Warwick A. ARDEN
43 Vice Chanc & General Counsel .... Ms. Eileen GOLDGEIER
10 Vice Chanc Finance & Admin .... Mr. Scott R. DOUGLASS
46 Vice Chanc Research & Innovation .... Dr. Alan REBAR
32 Vice Chan/Dean Div Acad & Stdnt Aff .... Dr. Michael D. MULLEN
30 Vice Chanc Univ Advancement .... Mr. Brian C. SISCHO
13 Vice Chanc Information Technology .... Dr. Marc I. HOIT
101 Secretary of the University .... Ms. P. J. TEAL
86 Int Asst to Chanc External Affairs .... Ms. Sarah STONE
88 Sr Vice Provost for Acad Strategy .... Dr. Duane K. LARICK
106 Sr Vice Prov Acad Outreach/Entrepre .... Dr. Thomas K. MILLER
08 Vice Provost/Director of Libraries .... Ms. Susan K. NUTTER
22 Vice Pres Inst Equity & Diversity .... Ms. Linda MCCABE SMITH
21 Assoc Vice Chanc Finance/Res Mgt .... Mr. Stephen W. KETO
18 Assoc Vice Chanc Facilities .... Mr. Steve A. ARNDT
39 Vice Provost for Residential Life .... Dr. Timothy R. LUCKADOO
26 AVC/Chief Communications Officer .... Mr. Brad BOHLANDER
29 Assoc Vice Chanc Alumni Relations .... Mr. Benny SUGGS
15 Assoc Vice Chanc Human Resources .... Ms. Marie WILLIAMS
19 Director Public Safety .... Mr. Jack W. MOORMAN
09 Sr Vice Prov Inst Rsrch & Planning .... Ms. Mary K. LELIK
07 Director Undergrad Admissions .... Mr. Thomas H. GRIFFIN
06 Registrar & Vice Provost .... Dr. Louis D. HUNT
25 Director Contracts & Grants .... Ms. Julie A. BRASFIELD
27 Director News Services .... Mr. Fred W. HARTMAN
37 Director of Financial Aid .... Ms. Krista F. DOMNICK
38 Director of Counseling Center .... Dr. Monica OSBURN
41 Director Athletics .... Ms. Deborah YOW
84 Asst Director of Enrollment Plng .... Mr. Trey STANDISH
21 Treasurer .... Ms. Mary T. PELOQUIN-DODD
88 Director of Materials Management .... Ms. Sharon LOOSMAN
79 Dean Humanities/Social Sciences .... Dr. Jeffery P. BRADEN
48 Dean of Design .... Dr. Marvin J. MALECHA
54 Dean of Engineering .... Dr. Louis A. MARTIN-VEGA
47 Dean Agriculture/Life Sciences .... Dr. Richard H. LINTON
65 Dean of Natural Resources .... Dr. Mary WATZIN
53 Interim Dean of Education .... Dr. Mary Ann DANOWITZ
50 Dean of Management .... Dr. Ira R. WEISS
81 Dean College of Sciences .... Dr. Daniel L. SOLOMON
88 Interim Dean of Textiles .... Dr. David HINKS
74 Dean of Veterinary Medicine .... Dr. D. Paul LUNN
58 Dean of Graduate School .... Dr. Maureen G. GRASSO

*University of North Carolina at Asheville (C)

1 University Heights, Asheville NC 28804-8503
County: Buncombe FICE Identification: 002907
Unit ID: 199111
Telephone: (828) 251-6600 Carnegie Class: Bac-A&S
FAX Number: (828) 251-6495 Calendar System: Semester
URL: www.unca.edu
Established: 1927 Annual Undergrad Tuition & Fees (In-State): $6,605
Enrollment: 3,845 Coed
Affiliation or Control: State IRS Status: 501(c)3
Highest Offering: Master's
Accreditation: **SC**, BUS, ENG, TED

02 Chancellor .... Dr. Mary K. GRANT
100 Chief of Staff .... Ms. Shannon C. EARLE
05 Provost/VC Academic Affairs .... Dr. Joseph URGO
10 Vice Chancellor Admin & Finance .... Mr. John PIERCE
30 Vice Chancellor Advancement .... Ms. Elizabeth BAGWELL
32 Vice Chanc for Student Affairs .... Dr. Bill HAGGARD
41 Director of Athletics .... Ms. Janet R. CONE
43 University General Counsel .... Vacant
15 Dir Human Res/Affirmative Action .... Ms. Nicole NORIAN
09 Dir Inst Research/Effect/Plng .... Dr. Michael GASS
20 Asst Provost Academic Admin .... Ms. Patricia MCCLELLAN
81 Dean Natural Science .... Dr. Keith KRUMPE
79 Dean Humanities .... Dr. Wiebke STREHL
83 Dean Social Science .... Dr. Jeff KONZ
88 Asst Provost/Dean Univ Programs .... Dr. Edward J. KATZ
08 University Librarian .... Ms. Leah DUNN
13 Chief Information Officer .... Mr. Jeff BROWN
07 Asst Provost for Admiss/Fin Aid .... Vacant
58 Dir Graduate Studies/Continuing Ed .... Dr. Gerard VOOS
06 Registrar .... Ms. Lynne HORGAN
21 Assoc Vice Chancellor of Finance .... Ms. Suzanne BRYSON
21 Controller .... Ms. Mary HALL
19 Asst VC for Public Safety .... Mr. Eric BOYCE
96 Purchasing Officer .... Ms. Darlene BERGER
26 Chief Communication & Mktg Ofc .... Mr. Luke BUKOSKI
27 Public Communication Spec .... Mr. Steve PLEVER
23 Dir Student Health/Counseling .... Mr. John CUTSPEC
88 Assoc Dean of Students .... Ms. Melanie FOX
39 Dir of Housing/Student Life Opers .... Mr. Vollie BARNWELL
36 Dir Ctr for Career Development .... Ms. Marlane MOWITZ
35 Dean of Students .... Ms. Jackie MCHARGUE
04 Exec Asst to Chancellor .... Ms. Chelsey BURKE

*University of North Carolina at Chapel Hill (D)

Chapel Hill NC 27599-0001
County: Orange FICE Identification: 002974
Unit ID: 199120
Telephone: (919) 962-2211 Carnegie Class: DU-Highest
FAX Number: (919) 962-5604 Calendar System: Semester
URL: www.unc.edu
Established: 1789 Annual Undergrad Tuition & Fees (In-State): $8,591
Enrollment: 29,135 Coed
Affiliation or Control: State IRS Status: 501(c)3
Highest Offering: Doctorate
Accreditation: **SC**, ACAE, #ARCPA, AUD, BUS, CAATE, CACREP, CLPSY, CORE, DA, DENT, DH, DIETC, DMOLS, HSA, IPSY, JOUR, LAW, LIB, MED, MT, NMT, NURSE, OT, PAST, PH, PHAR, PLNG, PTA, RAD, RADDOS, RTT, SCPSY, SP, SPAA, SW

02 Chancellor .... Dr. Carol L. FOLT
05 Exec Vice Provost/Chief Intl Ofcr .... Dr. Ronald STRAUSS
10 Vice Chancellor Finance & Admin .... Mr. Matthew W. FAJACK
32 Vice Chancellor Student Affairs .... Mr. Winston B. CRISP
13 VC Info Technology/Chief Info Ofcr .... Mr. Chris KIELT
46 Vice Chancellor for Research .... Dr. Terry MAGNUSON
26 Assoc Vice Chanc Univ Relations .... Vacant
90 Asst VC Rsch Computing/Learng Tech .... Dr. Michael BARKER
08 Assoc Prov/University Librarian .... Ms. Sarah MICHALAK
21 Vice Prov Finance & Acad Planning .... Dr. Dwayne PINKNEY
20 Vice Provost Academic Initiatives .... Dr. Carol TRESOLINI
18 Assoc Vice Chanc Facilities Plng .... Ms. Anna WU
31 Director Community Relations .... Ms. Linda DOUGLAS
28 Vice Prov Diversity/Multicultural .... Vacant
11 Provost Administration .... Dr. Lynn E. WILLIFORD
39 Dir Housing & Residential Education .... Mr. Alan BLATTNER
41 Director of Athletics .... Mr. Lawrence (Bubba) R. CUNNINGHAM
06 Asst Prov/University Registrar .... Mr. Christopher DERICKSON
07 Vice Prov Enrollment & Ugrad Admiss ... Dr. Stephen M. FARMER
29 Pres/Director General Alumni Assoc .... Mr. Douglas S. DIBBERT
37 Assoc Prov/Dir Scholar/Student Aid .... Ms. Shirley A. ORT
36 Director University Career Services .... Mr. Ray ANGLE
38 Dir Counseling & Psychological Svcs .... Dr. Allen H. O'BARR
44 Director of Annual Giving .... Vacant
19 Dir Public Safety/Chief of Police .... Chief Jeff B. MCCRACKEN
51 Director Center for Cont Education .... Mr. Rob BRUCE
27 Director University Relations .... Mr. Mike MCFARLAND
96 Director Procurement Services .... Ms. Martha PENDERGRASS
35 Assoc Vice Chanc Student Affairs .... Dr. Bettina SHUFORD
87 Dean of the Summer School .... Ms. Jan YOPP
49 Dean College Arts & Sciences .... Dr. Kevin GUSKIEWICZ
61 Dean School of Law .... Mr. Martin BRINKLEY
17 V Chanc Med Affs/CEO UNC HlthCare .... Dr. William L. ROPER
52 Interim Dean School of Dentistry .... Dr. Ken MAY
58 Dean of Graduate School .... Dr. Steven W. MATSON
50 Dean Kenan-Flagler Business School .... Mr. Douglas SHACKLEFORD
70 Dean School of Social Work .... Dr. Jack M. RICHMAN
67 Dean School of Pharmacy .... Dr. Robert A. BLOUIN
60 Dean School of Journalism/Mass Comm .... Ms. Susan R. KING
62 Dean School of Info/Library Science .... Dr. Gary MARCHIONINI
69 Dean School of Public Health .... Dr. Barbara K. RIMER
53 Dean School of Education .... Dr. Fouad ABD-EL-KHALICK
80 Dean School of Government .... Dr. Michael R. SMITH
23 Exec Dir Campus Health Services .... Dr. Mary COVINGTON
92 Associate Dean for Honors .... Dr. James L. LELOUDIS

*University of North Carolina at Charlotte (A)

9201 University City Boulevard, Charlotte NC 28223-0001
County: Mecklenburg FICE Identification: 002975
Unit ID: 199139
Telephone: (704) 687-8622 Carnegie Class: DU-Higher
FAX Number: N/A Calendar System: Semester
URL: www.uncc.edu
Established: 1946 Annual Undergrad Tuition & Fees (In-State): $6,532
Enrollment: 27,238 Coed
Affiliation or Control: State IRS Status: 501(c)3
Highest Offering: Doctorate
Accreditation: SC, ANEST, BUS, BUSA, CAATE, CACREP, CLPSY, DANCE, ENG, ENGT, EXSC, HSA, IPSY, MUS, NURSE, PH, POLYT, SPAA, SW, TED

02 Chancellor Dr. Philip L. DUBOIS
100 Chief of Staff Vacant
05 Provost/Vice Chanc Acad Affairs Dr. Joan F. LORDEN
20 Senior Associate Provost Dr. Jay RAJA
88 Int Assc Prov Met Stds/Ext Acad Pgm Mr. Curt WALTON
10 Vice Chancellor Business Affairs Ms. Elizabeth A. HARDIN
30 Vice Chancellor Univ Advancement Mr. Niles F. SORENSEN
86 Spec Asst for Constituent Relations Ms. Betty DOSTER
32 Vice Chancellor Student Affairs Dr. Arthur R. JACKSON
46 Vice Chanc Research/Econ Dev Dr. Robert W. WILHELM
13 Vice Chanc Info Tech Svcs/CIO Dr. Michael CARLIN
18 Assoc Vice Chanc Facilities Mgmt Mr. Philip M. JONES, JR.
08 Dean Atkins Library Dr. Anne C. MOORE
88 Assoc Prov Budget & Personnel Ms. Lori MCMAHON
82 Asst Provost for Intl Programs Mr. Joel A. GALLEGOS
88 Assistant Provost Dr. Leslie ZENK
26 Exec Dir Univ Communications Mr. Stephen P. WARD
106 Dir Distance Educ/Summer School Mr. Jody CEBINA
51 Dir Continuing Education Mr. Asher HAINES
27 Director of Public Relations Mr. John D. BLAND
31 Director Community Affairs Ms. Jeanette SIMS
39 Assoc Vice Chanc/Dir Residence Life Ms. Jacklyn A. SIMPSON
21 Assoc Vice Chancellor for Finance Vacant
21 Assoc Vice Chanc Business Svcs Mr. Keith N. WASSUM
58 Assoc Provost/Dean Graduate School Dr. Thomas L. REYNOLDS
84 Assoc Provost for Enrollment Mgmt Ms. Tina M. MCENTIRE
43 General Counsel Mr. James E. HUMPHREY, IV
07 Director Undergraduate Admissions Ms. Claire J. KIRBY
35 Dean of Students/Assoc VC Stdnt Aff Ms. Christine REED DAVIS
37 Director of Financial Aid Mr. Bruce BLACKMON
38 Assoc VC Health Programs & Services Dr. David B. SPANO
36 Director University Career Center Dr. Patrick MADSEN
40 Bookstore and Licensing Manager Mr. Greg MCCAMBRIDGE
29 Exec Director Alumni Affairs Ms. Jenny JONES
88 Assoc VC Risk Mgmt/Safety/Security Mr. Henry D. JAMES
19 Chief/Dir Police & Public Safety Mr. Jeffrey A. BAKER
09 Asst Provost Institutional Research Mr. Stephen A. COPPOLA
41 Director of Athletics Ms. Judy W. ROSE
96 Director of Purchasing Mr. Randy DUNCAN
93 Dir Multicultural Academic Services Dr. Sam T. LOPEZ
23 Admin Director Student Health Svcs Mr. David ROUSMANIERE
15 Assoc Vice Chanc Human Res/Aff Act Mr. Gary W. STINNETT
16 Exec Dir HR/EPA/Emp Rel/Complianc Ms. Jeanne L. MADORIN
85 Dir Intl Student/Scholar Svcs Mr. Tarek A. ELSHAYEB
104 Director Study Abroad Mr. Brad SEKULICH
48 Dean College of Arts/Architecture Mr. Kenneth A. LAMBLA
50 Dean College of Business Dr. Steven H. OTT
54 Dean College of Engineering Dr. Robert E. JOHNSON
53 Dean College of Education Dr. Ellen C. MCINTYRE
49 Dean Col of Liberal Arts & Sciences Dr. Nancy A. GUTIERREZ
88 Dean College Health & Human Svcs Dr. Nancy FEY-YENSAN
72 Dean College Computing/Informatics Dr. Yi DENG
97 Dean University College Dr. John SMAIL
92 Exec Director of Honors College Dr. Malin PEREIRA
06 University Registrar Mr. Christopher B. KNAUER
44 Director of Planning Giving Mr. John W. CULLUM
44 Director of Annual Giving Ms. Stacie G. YOUNG
04 Executive Asst to President Ms. Shari DUNN
108 Exec Dir Assessment & Accreditation Dr. Christine ROBINSON
25 Exec Dir Contracts/Grants Admin Mr. Lou HARRELL
28 Director Faculty Affairs/Diversity Dr. Yvette HUET

*University of North Carolina at Greensboro (B)

PO Box 26170,1000 Spring Garden St, Greensboro NC 27402-6170
County: Guilford FICE Identification: 002976
Unit ID: 199148
Telephone: (336) 334-5000 Carnegie Class: DU-Higher
FAX Number: (336) 256-0408 Calendar System: Semester
URL: www.uncg.edu
Established: 1891 Annual Undergrad Tuition & Fees (In-State): $6,745
Enrollment: 18,647 Coed
Affiliation or Control: State IRS Status: 501(c)3
Highest Offering: Doctorate
Accreditation: SC, ANEST, BUS, BUSA, CAATE, CACREP, CIDA, CLPSY, CS, DANCE, DIETD, DIETI, LIB, MUS, NRPA, NUR, NURSE, PH, SP, SPAA, SW, TED, THEA

02 Chancellor Dr. Franklin D. GILLIAM
100 Chief of Staff Ms. Waiyi TSE
05 Provost Exec VC Academic Affairs Dr. Dana L. DUNN
10 Vice Chancellor Business Affairs Mr. Charles A. MAIMONE
11 Int Vice Chanc Info Tech Services Ms. Donna R. HEATH
32 Vice Chanc for Student Affairs Dr. Cheryl M. CALLAHAN
84 Vice Chancellor Enrollment Mgmt Dr. Bryan J. TERRY
30 VC University Advancement Ms. Janis I. ZINK
43 Interim University Counsel Mr. Michael R. JUNG
20 Senior Vice Provost Dr. Alan J. BOYETTE
97 Dir Univ Teaching/Learning Commons Dr. David J. TEACHOUT
46 Vice Chanc Research & Econ Devel Dr. Terri L. SHELTON
104 Assoc Provost Intl Programs Dr. Penelope J. PYNES
15 Assoc VC Human Resource Services Vacant
21 Associate VC Financial Services Mr. Steven W. RHEW
18 Associate Vice Chanc for Facilities Mr. Jorge QUINTAL
09 Assoc Vice Prov/Director Research Dr. Larry D. MAYES
88 Director of External Reporting Dr. Sarah D. CARRIGAN
26 Vice Chanc University Relations Mr. James L. THORNTON
35 Associate VC for Student Affairs Dr. Jim S. SETTLE
91 Assoc VC for Admin Systems Mr. Lee NORRIS
58 Vice Provost Graduate Education Dr. Kelly J. BURKE
49 Dean of Arts & Sciences Dr. John Z. KISS
50 Dean of Business & Economics Dr. McRae BANKS
53 Dean of Education Dr. Randall D. PENFIELD
68 Dean of Health & Human Sciences Dr. Celia R. HOOPER
64 Dean of Music/Theatre & Dance Dr. Peter ALEXANDER
66 Dean of Nursing Dr. Robin E. REMSBURG
54 Dean Joint Sch NanoScience/Engineer Dr. James G. RYAN
08 Int Dean of University Libraries Ms. Kathryn M. CROWE
06 University Registrar Ms. Deb B. HURLEY
108 Dir Assessment and Accreditation Dr. Jodi E. PETTAZZONI
07 Director of Admissions Mr. Christopher J. KELLER
29 Dir Alumni Assoc & Annual Giving Ms. Mary G. LANDERS
88 Director of Campus Recreation Ms. Jill BEVILLE
23 Director Student Health Services Vacant
36 Int Director Career Services Ctr Dr. Margaret J. MCKEON
51 Dean Division of Continual Lrng Dr. James M. EDDY
25 Dir Contracts and Grants Mr. William D. WALTERS
37 Director of Financial Aid Ms. Deborah TOLLEFSON
39 Director Housing & Residence Life Mr. Timothy JOHNSON
41 Director Intercollegiate Athletics Ms. Kim RECORD
88 Director New Student Transitions Dr. Kim SOUSA-PEOPLES
19 Assoc VC for Safety/Emergency Mgmt Mr. Rollin DONELSON
28 Director Multicultural Affairs Vacant
96 Director Purchasing Mr. Michael F. LOGAN
40 University Bookstore Manager Mr. Brad LIGHT

*University of North Carolina at Pembroke (C)

One University Drive, PO Box 1510, Pembroke NC 28372-1510
County: Robeson FICE Identification: 002954
Unit ID: 199281
Telephone: (910) 521-6000 Carnegie Class: Masters/L
FAX Number: (910) 521-6176 Calendar System: Semester
URL: www.uncp.edu
Established: 1887 Annual Undergrad Tuition & Fees (In-State): $5,564
Enrollment: 6,269 Coed
Affiliation or Control: State IRS Status: 501(c)3
Highest Offering: Master's
Accreditation: SC, ART, BUS, CAATE, CACREP, MUS, NURSE, SW, TED

02 Chancellor Dr. Robin G. CUMMINGS
43 General Counsel Mr. Joshua MALCOLM
100 Chief of Staff Mr. Daniel KENNEY
26 Dir University Communications/Mktg Ms. Jodi PHELPS
88 Chief Audit Officer Ms. Kelley R. HORTON
10 Vice Chanc Finance & Administration Dr. Steven E. ARNDT
41 Director of Athletics Mr. Dick CHRISTY
30 Vice Chancellor for Advancement Ms. Wendy LOWERY
32 Interim Vice Chanc Student Affairs Dr. Lisa L. SCHAEFFER
88 Director Title IX and Clery Act Co Ms. Ronette SUTTON GERBER
46 Asst to the Chancellor Rsrch/Comm Mr. Justin S. SMITH
04 Executive Asst to the Chancellor Ms. Marla LOCKLEAR
05 Provost/VC Academic Affairs Dr. Zoe W. LOCKLEAR
20 Assoc Vice Chanc Planning and Acred Dr. Elizabeth NORMANDY
84 Assoc Vice Chanc for Enrollment Mgt Vacant
09 Director Inst Research Dr. Chunmei YAO
58 Dean of Grad Studies & Research Dr. Irene AIKEN
92 Dean of Honors College Dr. Mark MILEWICZ
53 Dean of School of Education Dr. Alfred BRYANT, JR.
49 Dean of Arts & Sciences Dr. Jeff FREDERICK
50 Dean of School of Business Dr. Barry O'BRIEN
45 Assoc Vice Chanc for Startegic Plng Dr. Glen BURNETTE, JR.
25 Assoc VC Research and Sponsored Dr. Rebecca BULLARD-DILLARD
08 Dean of Library Services Dr. Dennis SWANSON
88 Assco Vice Chanc for Outreach Dr. Cammie HUNT
88 Director for Academic Resources Ms. Leslie T. BELL
21 Asst Vice Chancellor for Finance Mr. Carlton SPELLMAN
35 Assoc Vice Chanc Student Affairs Vacant
13 Assoc VC Information Resources/CIO Ms. Nancy CROUCH
15 Asst Vice Chanc for Human Resources Ms. Angela REVELS-BULLARD
88 Faculty Senate Chair Dr. Sara SAMMONS
06 Registrar Ms. Lourdes SILVA
85 Director of International Programs Ms. Jessica HALL
07 Director of Admissions Ms. Lela CLARK
37 Director Financial Aid Ms. Jenelle HANDCOX
88 Dir Center for Student Success Dr. Derek OXENDINE
106 Dir Online/Distance Education Vacant
39 Director Housing and Resident Life Mr. R. Preston SWINEY
38 Director Counseling/Testing Center Vacant
36 Director Career Services Center Ms. Dawn A. WHEELER
29 Director Alumni Relations Ms. Morgan HUNT
40 Interim Director of Bookstore Mr. Keats L. ELLIS
28 Dir Multicultural/Minority Affairs Mr. Robert L. CANIDA, II
22 Acting Dir Accessibility Resource Dr. Nicolette CAMPOS
96 Director of Business Services Ms. Karen SWINEY
104 Director Study Abroad Vacant
23 Director of Student Health Services Ms. Cora BULLARD
88 Director Public Administration Pgm Dr. Michael PENNINGTON
44 Assistant Director of Annual Fund Vacant
88 Sports Information Director Mr. Todd ANDERSON
88 Dir Fac Plng/Construction/Univ Engr Mr. Michael CLARK
19 Director Security/Safety Mr. McDuffie CUMMINGS, JR.
18 Director of Physical Plant Vacant

*University of North Carolina Wilmington (D)

601 S College Road, Wilmington NC 28403-5931
County: New Hanover FICE Identification: 002984
Unit ID: 199218
Telephone: (910) 962-3030 Carnegie Class: Masters/L
FAX Number: (910) 962-4050 Calendar System: Semester
URL: www.uncw.edu
Established: 1947 Annual Undergrad Tuition & Fees (In-State): $6,691
Enrollment: 14,570 Coed
Affiliation or Control: State IRS Status: 501(c)3
Highest Offering: Doctorate
Accreditation: SC, BUS, CAATE, CEA, CS, MUS, NURSE, PH, SPAA, SW, TED

02 Chancellor Dr. Jose V. SARTARELLI
05 Provost/Vice Chanc Academic Affairs Dr. Marilyn SHEERER
10 Vice Chancellor Business Affairs Dr. Rick WHITFIELD
32 Vice Chanc for Student Affairs Ms. Patricia L. LEONARD
30 Vice Chanc University Advancement Mr. Eddie STUART
21 Vice Chancellor Business Affairs Mr. Rick N. WHITFIELD
44 Assoc Vice Chanc Univ Advancement Vacant
20 Interim VP SA/VC Academic Affairs Dr. Cathy C. BARLOW
21 Assoc Vice Chanc Business Services Ms. Sharon H. BOYD
21 Assoc VC Business Affs/Facilities Mr. Mark D. MORGAN
28 Chief Diversity Officer Dr. Kent GUION
26 Exec Dir of University Relations Ms. Janine IAMUNNO
09 Assoc Prov Inst Research/ Assessment Dr. Rigoberto J. RINCONES-GOMEZ
35 Assoc VC/Dean of Students Dr. Michael A. WALKER
84 Assoc Provost for Enrollment Mgmt Dr. Terrence M. CURRAN
85 Assoc VC International Programs Dr. Michael WILHEIM
15 Assoc VC for Human Resources Dr. Rosalynn MARTIN
100 Chief of Staff Mr. Bradley BALLOU
06 Registrar Mr. Jonathan REECE
08 University Librarian Ms. Sarah WATSTEIN
37 Interim Director Financial Aid Mr. Frederick HOLDING
18 Interim Director of Physical Plant Mr. David OLSON
19 Director Envir Health & Safety Mr. Stanley H. HARTS
23 Dir Student Health/Wellness Center Ms. Katrin WESNER
109 Director of Auxiliary Services Mr. Brian DAILEY
41 Director of Athletics Mr. Jimmy BASS
36 Director Career Services Mr. Thomas D. RAKES
29 Director of Alumni Relations Mrs. Lindsay LEROY
96 Director of Purchasing Ms. Mary E. FORSYTHE
38 Director Student Counseling Center Dr. Lynne REEDER
40 Manager Bookstore Mr. Nick CARROLL
49 Dean Col Arts & Sciences Dr. Aswani VOLETY
50 Dean Cameron School of Business Dr. Robert BURRUS
53 Dean Watson School of Education Dr. Van O. DEMPSEY
66 Director School of Nursing Dr. Laurie BADZEK
58 Assoc Prov/Dean of Graduate School Dr. Ron VETTER
76 Dean Col Health & Human Svcs Dr. Charles HARDY

*University of North Carolina School of the Arts (E)

1533 S Main Street, Winston-Salem NC 27127-2738
County: Forsyth FICE Identification: 003981
Unit ID: 199184
Telephone: (336) 770-3399 Carnegie Class: Spec-4-yr-Arts
FAX Number: (336) 770-3375 Calendar System: Semester
URL: www.uncsa.edu
Established: 1963 Annual Undergrad Tuition & Fees (In-State): $8,983
Enrollment: 958 Coed
Affiliation or Control: State IRS Status: 501(c)3
Highest Offering: Master's
Accreditation: SC

02 Chancellor Mr. Lindsay BIERMAN
05 Interim Provost Dr. David ENGLISH
10 Senior Director of Business Affairs Ms. Carin IOANNOU
11 Chief Operating Officer Mr. George BURNETTE
18 Assoc VC Facilities/Services Mr. Chrispher BOYD
09 Director of Institutional Research Dr. Xiaoyun YANG
07 Director of Admissions Ms. Sheeler LAWSON
08 Librarian Ms. Vicki WEAVIL
26 Director of Communications Ms. Marla CARPENTER
27 Chief Marketing Officer Ms. Katharine LAIDLAW
06 Registrar Ms. Erin MORIN
15 Director Human Resources Mr. James LUCAS
37 Director Financial Aid Mrs. Jane KAMIAB
49 Dean of Liberal Arts & Grad Studies Mr. Dean WILCOX
64 Dean School of Music Mr. Brian COLE
57 Dean School of Dance Ms. Susan JAFFE
88 Dean Sch of Design/Production Mr. Michael KELLEY
88 Dean School of Drama Mr. Carl FORSMAN

13 Chief Information Officer ... Ms. Lisa HARDEN SMITH
19 Chief of Police ... Mr. Gregory HARRIS
38 Dir of Counseling & Testing Svcs ... Dr. Thomas MURRAY
20 Interim Vice Provost & Dean AA ... Ms. Karen BERES
30 Chief Advancement Officer ... Mr. Edward LEWIS
32 Vice Provost & Dean Student Affairs ... Mr. Ward CALDWELL
96 Director of Purchasing ... Mr. Allen CARNES
88 Dir Ctr for Design Innovation ... Dr. Pamela JENNINGS
88 Ex Dir Kenan Inst for the Arts ... Ms. Corey MADDEN
88 Dean School of Filmmaking ... Ms. Susan RUSKIN
88 Interim Dean HS Academic Program ... Ms. Elaine PRUITT
88 Director of Student Engagement ... Mr. Steve GALLAGHER
87 Dir Educ Outreach & Summer Programs .. Ms. Suzanna WATKINS
39 Assistant Dean & Dir of RLPH ... Mr. Joseph RICK
23 Interim Dir of Health Services ... Mr. Joseph RICK
100 Chief of Staff ... Mr. James DECRISTO
43 General Counsel ... Mr. David HARRISON
102 Foundation Executive Dir ... Ms. Cindy LIBERTY
24 Director of Digitial Media ... Ms. Claire MACHAMER

*Western Carolina University (A)

65 West University Way, HFR 501,
Cullowhee NC 28723-9646
County: Jackson FICE Identification: 002981
Unit ID: 200004
Telephone: (828) 227-7211 Carnegie Class: Masters/L
FAX Number: (828) 227-7202 Calendar System: Semester
URL: www.wcu.edu
Established: 1889 Annual Undergrad Tuition & Fees (In-State): $6,623
Enrollment: 10,382 Coed
Affiliation or Control: State IRS Status: 501(c)3
Highest Offering: Doctorate
Accreditation: SC, ANEST, ART, BUS, CAATE, CACREP, CARTE, CIDA, CONST, DIETD, DIETI, EMT, ENG, ENGT, MUS, NURSE, PTA, SP, SPAA, SW, TED, THEA

02 Chancellor ... Dr. David O. BELCHER
05 Provost ... Dr. Alison MORRISON-SHETLAR
10 Vice Chanc Admin & Finance ... Mr. Mike BYERS
32 Vice Chancellor/Student Affairs ... Dr. H. Samuel MILLER
35 Asst Vice Chanc Student Affairs .... Mrs. Jane ADAMS-DUNFORD
35 Asst Vice Chanc Student Success ... Dr. Lowell K. DAVIS
35 Asst Vice Chanc/Student Affairs ... Ms. Kellie MONTEITH
30 Assoc Vice Chancellor Development ... Mrs. Lori LEWIS
44 Assoc Provost Academic Affairs ... Dr. Brandon SCHWAB
20 Assoc Provost Undergraduate Studies ... Dr. Carol BURTON
18 Assoc VC for Facilities Management ... Mr. Joe WALKER
100 Chief of Staff ... Dr. Melissa WARGO
04 Assistant to the Chancellor ... Ms. Terry WELCH
43 Legal Counsel ... Ms. Mary Ann LOCHNER
38 Director of Counseling Services ... Dr. Kimberly GORMAN
06 Registrar ... Mr. Larry HAMMER
07 Director of Student Recruitment ... Mr. Phil CAULEY
09 Asst Vice Chancellor of OIPE ... Mr. Tim METZ
37 Director of Financial Aid ... Ms. Trina ORR
15 Assoc VC of Human Resources ... Dr. Cory CAUSBY
13 Chief Information Officer ... Mr. Craig FOWLER
29 Director of Alumni Affairs ... Mr. Marty RAMSEY
08 Dean of Library Services ... Dr. Farzaneh RAZZAGHI
19 Director University Police ... Mr. Earnest HUDSON
88 Exec Director Education Outreach ... Dr. Susan FOUTS
31 Director Campus Services ... Mr. Bryant BARNETT
41 Athletic Director ... Mr. Randy EATON
23 Director University Health Services ... Ms. Pamela BUCHANAN
28 Asst Director Intercultural Affairs ... Ms. Niki PAGANELLI
96 Director of Purchasing ... Ms. Cindy NICHOLSON
40 Director Book & Supply Store ... Ms. Pamela DEGRAFFENREID
88 Director of Orientation ... Ms. Tammy HASKETT
38 Director of Advising Center ... Mr. Travis BULLUCK
36 Director of Career Services ... Ms. Theresa CRUZ PAUL
26 Sr Director Comm & Public Relations ... Mr. Bill STUDENC
57 Dean of Fine & Performing Arts ... Mr. George H. BROWN
58 Dean Grad School & Research ... Dr. Brian KLOEPPEL
49 Dean Arts & Sciences ... Dr. Richard STARNES
72 Dean Kimmel School Constr Mgmt/Tech ... Dr. Jeffrey RAY
50 Dean College of Business ... Dr. Darrell PARKER
53 Dean Educ & Allied Professions ... Dr. Dale CARPENTER
76 Dean Health & Human Sciences ... Dr. Douglas R. KESKULA
92 Dean of Honors College ... Dr. Jill GRANGER
88 Director of Marketing ... Ms. Robin C. OLIVER
86 Director of External Relations ... Ms. Meredith WHITFIELD
25 Director of Sponsored Research ... Ms. Andrea MOSHIER
39 Director of Residence Life ... Ms. Mistie BIBBEE

*Winston-Salem State University (B)

601 MLK Jr. Drive, 200 Blair Hall,
Winston-Salem NC 27110-0001
County: Forsyth FICE Identification: 002986
Unit ID: 199999
Telephone: (336) 750-2000 Carnegie Class: Masters/M
FAX Number: (336) 750-2049 Calendar System: Semester
URL: www.wssu.edu
Established: 1892 Annual Undergrad Tuition & Fees (In-State): $5,707
Enrollment: 5,220 Coed
Affiliation or Control: State IRS Status: 501(c)3
Highest Offering: Doctorate
Accreditation: SC, BUS, CORE, CS, MT, MUS, NRPA, NURSE, OT, PTA, SW, TED

02 Chancellor ... Dr. Elwood L. ROBINSON
05 Provost/VC Academic Affairs ... Dr. Brenda ALLEN
32 Vice Chancellor Student Affairs ... Dr. Trae COTTON
09 Associate Provost ... Dr. Carolynn BERRY
45 Asst Prov Administration/Plng ... Mrs. Letitia C. WALL
10 Vice Chanc Finance & Admin ... Dr. Randy W. MILLS
30 Vice Chanc University Advance ... Mrs. Michelle COOK
18 Assoc Vice Chanc Facilities Mgmt ... Ms. Rosabla LEDEZMA
13 Assoc Prov/Chief Information Ofcr ... Dr. Derrick MURRAY
88 Director Internal Audit/Compliance ... Ms. Shannon B. HENRY
19 Chief of Campus Police ... Mrs. Patricia D. NORRIS
08 Director of Library Services ... Ms. Wanda BROWN
39 Director Hous/Residence Life ... Ms. Chantal BOUCHEREAU
37 Director of Financial Aid ... Mr. Robert MUHAMMED
15 Asst Vice Chanc Human Resources ... Mr. Lester ARNOLD
36 Asst Director of Career Services ... Ms. LaMonica SLOAN
26 Director Marketing/Communications ... Ms. Jamie HUNT
88 Dir Enrollment Communications ... Ms. Cathy HOOTS
29 Director of Alumni Affairs ... Mr. Gregory G. HAIRSTON
44 Director Annual Fund ... Mrs. Kimberly REESE
35 Assoc Director Student Activities ... Ms. Heather DAVIS
23 Dir of Student Health Center ... Dr. Philadelphia ANTHONY
41 Athletic Director ... Mrs. Toria WALKER
101 VIce Chancellor/Sec of Univ ... Mrs. Camille KLUTTZ-LEACH
07 Director of Admissions ... Dr. Kerwin GRAHAM
43 Int General Legal Counsel ... Mr. Ivey BROWN
96 Director Purchasing ... Mr. Alan IRELAND
90 Director Academic Computer Center ... Mr. Cuthrell JOHNSON
88 Dean University College LLL ... Dr. Doria K. STITTS
49 Dean College Arts/Sci/Business/Educ ... Dr. Corey D. WALKER
76 Dean School of Health Sciences ... Dr. Peggy VALENTINE
88 Director of Title III ... Dr. Everette L. WITHERSPOON
06 Registrar ... Ms. Sharon STODDARD
108 Director Institutional Assessment . Dr. Becky MUSSAT-WHITLOW
22 Dir Affirmative Action/EEO ... Mrs. Sylvia RAMOS

University of Phoenix Charlotte Campus (C)

3800 Arco Corporate Drive, Charlotte NC 28273-3409
Telephone: (704) 504-5409 Identification: 770216
Accreditation: &NH, ACBSP

† Regional accreditation is carried under the parent institution in Tempe, AZ

Virginia College (D)

3740 South Holden Road, Greensboro NC 27406
Telephone: (336) 398-5400 Identification: 770619
Accreditation: ACICS, MAAB

† Branch campus of Virginia College, Birmingham, AL

Wake Forest University (E)

1834 Wake Forest Road, Winston-Salem NC 27109-8758
County: Forsyth FICE Identification: 002978
Unit ID: 199847
Telephone: (336) 758-5000 Carnegie Class: DU-Higher
FAX Number: (336) 758-6074 Calendar System: Semester
URL: www.wfu.edu
Established: 1834 Annual Undergrad Tuition & Fees: $47,682
Enrollment: 7,788 Coed
Affiliation or Control: Independent Non-Profit IRS Status: 501(c)3
Highest Offering: Doctorate
Accreditation: SC, ANEST, ARCPA, BUS, BUSA, CACREP, DENT, LAW, MED, TED, THEOL

01 President ... Dr. Nathan O. HATCH
43 VP Gen Counsel/Sec Board of Trust ... Mr. J. Reid MORGAN
10 Sr Vice Pres/Chief Financial Ofcr ... Mr. B. Hofler MILAM
05 Provost ... Mr. Rogan KERSH
17 CEO Wake Forest Baptist Med Ctr ... Dr. John D. MCCONNELL
11 Vice President for Administration ... Vacant
30 Vice Pres University Advancement ... Mr. Mark A. PETERSEN
32 Vice Pres Campus Life ... Dr. Penny RUE
88 Vice Pres/Chief Investment Officer ... Mr. James J. DUNN
100 Chief of Staff ... Ms. Mary E. PUGEL
35 Assoc VP/Dean of Student Services ... Mr. Adam GOLDSTEIN
44 Ast VP/Dir Parent/Donor Relations ... Ms. Minta A. MCNALLY
30 Asst VP/Director of Development ... Mr. Robert T. BAKER
13 CIC/Assoc Provost for Tech/IS ... Mr. Mur MUCHANE
46 Assoc Provost for Research ... Dr. S. Bruce KING
49 Dean of the College ... Dr. Michele K. GILLESPIE
63 Dean School Med/Int Health Sci Pres ... Dr. Edward ABRAHAM
61 Dean School of Law ... Mr. Suzanne REYNOLDS
50 Dean of Business ... Mr. Charles IACOVOU
73 Dean of Divinity ... Dr. Gail R. O'DAY
09 Dir Inst Research/Academic Admin ... Mr. Phil HANDWERK
08 Dir of the Z Smith Reynolds Library ... Dr. Lynn SUTTON
85 Director of International Studies ... Mr. Steven DUKE
07 Director of Admissions ... Ms. Martha B. ALLMAN
37 Director of Financial Aid ... Mr. William T. WELLS
36 VP/Office of Personal & Career Dev ... Mr. Andy CHAN
06 Registrar ... Mr. Harold PACE
41 Director of Athletics ... Mr. Ronald D. WELLMAN
15 Chief Human Resources Officer ... Ms. Carmen I. CANALES
18 Director Facilities Management ... Mr. John SHENETTE
38 Dir University Counseling Center ... Dr. Marianne A. SCHUBERT
23 Director Student Health Service ... Dr. Cecil D. PRICE
39 Dean Residence Life & Housing ... Ms. Donna MCGALLIARD
42 Chaplain ... Rev. Timothy L. AUMAN
19 Chief University Police ... Ms. Regina G. LAWSON
22 EEO Mgr/Diversity & Compliance Dir ... Ms. Angela CULLER
94 Director Women's & Gender Studies ... Dr. Wanda BALZANO

26 Chief Public Relations Officer ... Mr. Brett EATON
28 Director of Diversity & Inclusion ... Dr. Barbee OAKES
102 Dir Foundation/Corporate Relations ... Ms. Linda LUVAAS
104 Director Study Abroad ... Mr. David F. TAYLOR
29 Director Alumni Engagement ... Mrs. Kelly MCCONNICO

Warren Wilson College (F)

PO Box 9000, Asheville NC 28815-9000
County: Buncombe FICE Identification: 002979
Unit ID: 199865
Telephone: (828) 298-3325 Carnegie Class: Bac-A&S
FAX Number: (828) 771-7097 Calendar System: Semester
URL: www.warren-wilson.edu
Established: 1894 Annual Undergrad Tuition & Fees: $32,560
Enrollment: 890 Coed
Affiliation or Control: Presbyterian Church (U.S.A.) IRS Status: 501(c)3
Highest Offering: Master's
Accreditation: SC, SW

01 President ... Dr. Steven L. SOLNICK
05 VP Academic Affairs/Dean of College ... Dr. Paula K. GARRETT
10 VP for Administration & Finance ... Mr. Scott MCKINNEY
30 Acting Vice Pres for Advancement ... Mr. Zanne GARLAND
84 VP Enrollment Management ... Ms. Janelle HOLMBOE
32 Dean of Students ... Mr. Paul C. PERRINE
88 Dean of Work ... Mr. Ian ROBERTSON
88 Dean of Service ... Ms. Cathy KRAMER
06 Registrar ... Miss Christa L. BRIDGMAN
09 Director Institutional Research ... Ms. Allyson HETTRICK
37 Assoc Director Financial Aid ... Ms. Eleanor WILL
21 Controller ... Ms. Mary DAVIS
29 Director Alumni Relations ... Mr. Rodney LYTLE
26 Director of Media Relations ... Mr. Benjamin J. ANDERSON
31 Director Community Relations ... Ms. Ally WILSON
20 Director Academic Support Service ... Ms. Lyn O'HARE
88 Director of Service Leaning ... Ms. Brooke MILLSAPS
35 Director of Student Activities ... Mr. Daniel SEEGER
38 Director of Counseling ... Mr. Arthur SHUSTER
36 Director Career Services ... Ms. Wendy SELIGMANN
42 Dir of Spiritual Life & Chaplain ... Rev. Brian AMMONS
41 Athletic Director ... Ms. Stacey ENOS
91 Dir Admin Data Processing ... Ms. Omega HODGES
15 Director Human Resources ... Ms. Gail BAYLOR
18 Acting Dir Facil Mgmt/Tech Svcs ... Ms. Deborah ANSTROM
19 Director Public Safety ... Mr. Terry PAYNE
88 Int Dir Environment Leadership Ctr ... Mr. Stan CROSS
88 Director Swannanoa Gathering ... Mr. Jim MAGILL
104 Director of International Programs ... Ms. Naomi OTTERNESS
28 Inclusion/Diversity/Equity Director ... Mr. Obie FORD, III
96 Director of Purchasing ... Ms. Deborah ANSTROM
13 Manager Computing Services ... Mr. David HARPER

William Peace University (G)

15 E Peace Street, Raleigh NC 27604-1194
County: Wake FICE Identification: 002953
Unit ID: 199272
Telephone: (919) 508-2000 Carnegie Class: Bac-A&S
FAX Number: (919) 508-2326 Calendar System: Semester
URL: www.peace.edu
Established: 1857 Annual Undergrad Tuition & Fees: $25,850
Enrollment: 1,077 Coed
Affiliation or Control: Presbyterian Church (U.S.A.) IRS Status: 501(c)3
Highest Offering: Baccalaureate
Accreditation: SC

01 President ... Dr. Brian C. RALPH
04 Executive Assistant to President ... Ms. Patricia L. LUKASZEWSKI
05 Vice President for Academic Affairs ... Dr. Charles DUNCAN
32 Vice President for Student Services ... Mr. Frank RIZZO
30 Vice President for Advancement ... Ms. Jodi S. PEELER
06 Registrar ... Ms. Sharon KISSICK
09 Director of Institutional Research ... Ms. Ying LIU
10 Vice Pres Finance & Administration ... Mr. George A. YEARWOOD
84 Vice Pres Enrollment Mgmt/Marketing ... Dr. Kristin E. COHEN
15 Assoc Vice Pres for Human Resources ... Ms. Amber M. KIMBALL
13 Chief Information Technology Office ... Mr. Josh FRANK
18 Asst VP for Buildings and Grounds ... Mr. John B. CRANHAM
37 Director of Financial Aid ... Ms. Michelle HEMMER
41 Director of Athletics ... Mr. Philip ROWE

Wingate University (H)

220 N. Camden Street, Wingate NC 28174-0159
County: Union FICE Identification: 002985
Unit ID: 199962
Telephone: (704) 233-8000 Carnegie Class: Masters/M
FAX Number: (704) 233-8014 Calendar System: Semester
URL: www.wingate.edu
Established: 1896 Annual Undergrad Tuition & Fees: $27,930
Enrollment: 3,034 Coed
Affiliation or Control: Southern Baptist IRS Status: 501(c)3
Highest Offering: Doctorate
Accreditation: SC, ACBSP, ARCPA, #CAATE, MUS, NUR, PHAR, @PTA

01 President ... Dr. T. Rhett BROWN
05 Provost ... Dr. Helen TATE
107 Sr Vice Provost for Prof Studies ... Dr. Martha S. ASTI
10 VP Business/Chief Financial Ofcr ... Mr. William H. DURHAM
30 VP Resource Development ... Mr. E. Vincent TILSON
41 VP & Director of Athletics ... Mr. R. Stephen POSTON

84 VP for Enrollment and Planning ... Dr. Heather C. MILLER
76 Vice Provost Health Sciences ... Dr. Robert B. SUPERNAW
11 VP for Business Operations ... Mr. Scott E. HUNSUCKER
88 Assoc VP Resource Development ... Mr. Roy Lee RAGSDALE, JR.
88 Asst VP/Director of Development ... Ms. Hannah DICKERSON
88 AVP for Proj Mgmt & Sustainability ... Mr. Cameron JACKSON
32 Dean of Academic Support ... Mrs. Glenda H. BEBBER
49 Dean School Arts & Sciences ... Dr. H. Donald MERRILL
50 Dean School of Business ... Dr. Peter FRANK
53 Dean School of Education ... Dr. Sarah H. BURNS
08 Director of Library ... Mrs. Amee M. ODOM
39 Assoc Dean Res Life & Involvement ... Ms. Brandy SHOTT
37 Director Student Financial Planning ... Ms. Teresa G. WILLIAMS
12 Asst VP Ballantyne Campus ... Mr. Jeffrey ATKINSON
91 Director Administrative Computing ... Mr. Timothy D. HERRIN
29 Director of Alumni Development ... Vacant
42 Minstr to Stdnts/Asst Dn Stdnt Affs ... Rev. A. Dane JORDAN
40 Director of Campus Store ... Mrs. Sherri SHANK
19 Campus Safety Chief ... Mr. Mike EASLEY
44 Director of Annual Giving ... Ms. Candice KANE
44 Director of Gift Planning ... Mr. J. Theodore JOHNSON
38 Director of Counseling Services ... Ms. Lori HINNANT
13 Director of Information Technology ... Ms. Jeanette K. BUJAK
36 Dir of Internships and Career Svcs ... Ms. Sharon ROBINSON
15 Human Resources Coordinator ... Mrs. Lisa B. RAGSDALE
39 Dir Resid Life/Asst Dn Stdnt Affs ... Mr. Michael REYNOLDS
35 Dir of Retention/Asst Dn Stdnt Affs ... Ms. Kristin WHARTON
06 Registrar ... Ms. Maria TAYLOR
07 Director of Admissions ... Mr. Gabe HOLLINGSWORTH
04 Executive Assistant to President ... Ms. Tammy T. BRITT

NORTH DAKOTA

Cankdeska Cikana Community College (A)

PO Box 269, 214 First Avenue,
Fort Totten ND 58335-0269
County: Benson — FICE Identification: 022365
Unit ID: 200208
Telephone: (701) 766-4415 — Carnegie Class: Tribal
FAX Number: (701) 766-4077 — Calendar System: Semester
URL: www.littlehoop.edu
Established: 1974 — Annual Undergrad Tuition & Fees: $3,300
Enrollment: 185 — Coed
Affiliation or Control: Independent Non-Profit — IRS Status: 501(c)3
Highest Offering: Associate Degree
Accreditation: #NH

01 President ... Dr. Cynthia A. LINDQUIST
05 Academic Dean ... Mrs. Teresa HARDING
10 CFO ... Mrs. Chelly VEER
11 Dean of Administration ... Mr. Stuart YOUNG
06 Registrar ... Mr. Ermen BROWN, JR.

*North Dakota University System Office (B)

600 E Boulevard Avenue, Dept 215,
Bismarck ND 58505-0230
County: Burleigh — FICE Identification: 033434
Telephone: (701) 328-2960 — Carnegie Class: N/A
FAX Number: (701) 328-2961
URL: www.ndus.edu

01 Chancellor ... Mark HAGEROTT
05 Int Vice Chanc Acad/Student Affairs ... Richard ROTHAUS
10 Chief Financial Officer ... Tammy DOLAN
45 VC of Strategic Engagement ... Linda DONLIN
13 VC for IT & Institutional Research ... Lisa FELDNER
37 Director Financial Aid ... Brenda ZASTOUPIL
20 Dir Acad Pgm Rsrch & Accreditation ... Richard M. ROTHAUS
21 Director of Finance ... Cathy MCDONALD
88 Research Analyst ... Jennifer WEBER
100 Interim Chief of Staff ... Lisa FELDNER
26 Dir of Communications & Media Rels ... Billie Jo LORIUS
88 Director Financial Reporting ... Robin PUTNAM
106 Exec Dir Acad Tech/Dist Educ/K-12 ... Tanya SPILOVOY
88 Dir Student Entry Trans & Retention ... Lisa JOHNSON
32 Director of Student Affairs ... Vacant
18 Director Facility Planning ... Rick TONDER

*University of North Dakota (C)

264 Centennial Drive, Grand Forks ND 58202
County: Grand Forks — FICE Identification: 003005
Unit ID: 200280
Telephone: (701) 777-2011 — Carnegie Class: DU-Higher
FAX Number: (701) 777-2696 — Calendar System: Semester
URL: www.und.edu
Established: 1883 — Annual Undergrad Tuition & Fees (In-State): $7,965
Enrollment: 14,906 — Coed
Affiliation or Control: State — IRS Status: 501(c)3
Highest Offering: Doctorate
Accreditation: NH, AAB, ANEST, ARCPA, ART, BUS, CAATE, CLPSY, COPSY, CS, DIETC, ENG, HT, IPSY, LAW, MED, MT, MUS, NAIT, NURSE, OT, PH, PTA, #SP, SPAA, SW, TED, THEA

02 President ... Mr. Mark KENNEDY
29 CEO Alumni Assoc & Foundation ... Ms. Deanna CARLSON ZINK
05 Vice Pres Academic Affairs/Provost ... Dr. Thomas DILORENZO
10 Vice President Operations/Finance ... Ms. Alice BREKKE
32 Int Vice Pres Student Affairs ... Dr. Laurie BETTING
17 Vice President Health Affairs ... Dr. Joshua WYNNE
46 VP Research/Economic Devel ... Dr. Grant MCGIMPSEY
26 Int VP for University/Public Affs ... Mr. Peter B. JOHNSON
27 Exec Assoc VP University Rels ... Mr. Peter B. JOHNSON
30 Chief Development Officer ... Mr. Dan MUUS
35 Associate VP & Dean of Students ... Dr. Cara HALGREN
21 Assoc VP Finance ... Ms. Karla MONGEON-STEWART
18 Assoc VP Facilities ... Vacant
45 Assoc VP Research/Econ Dev/RDC ... Dr. Barry MILAVETZ
88 Assoc VP Research/Capacity Building ... Dr. Mark HOFFMANN
25 AVP Intellectual Prop Comm/Econ Dev ... Mr. Michael MOORE
25 AVP Res & Econ Dev/Grants/Contracts ... Mr. David O. SCHMIDT
20 Asst VP Student Academic Services ... Ms. Lisa BURGER
07 Asst VP Enrollment Services ... Mr. Sol JENSEN
88 Vice Prov & Chief Strategy Officer ... Dr. Joshua RIEDY
20 Assoc VP for Academic Affairs ... Dr. Steven LIGHT
28 Assoc VP Diversity & Inclusion ... Ms. Sandra MITCHELL
27 Director Branding ... Ms. Susan CARAHER
08 Dean of Libraries & Info Res ... Ms. Stephanie WALKER
06 Registrar ... Mr. Scott CORRELL
15 Dir Human Resources/Payroll Svcs ... Ms. Patricia HANSON
19 AVP Public Safety/Police Chief ... Mr. Eric PLUMMER
38 Director Counseling Center ... Dr. Kenneth CARLSON
36 Director Career Services ... Ms. Ilene ODEGARD
20 Director Instructional Development ... Dr. Anne KELSCH
22 Director EEO/Affirmative Action ... Ms. Donna SMITH
37 Director Student Financial Aid ... Ms. Janelle KILGORE
39 Exec Director Housing & Dining ... Ms. Connie FRAZIER
23 Director of Student Health ... Ms. Michelle D. ESLINGER-SCHNEIDER
43 General Counsel ... Ms. Heather WAGES
41 Director Athletics ... Mr. Brian FAISON
85 Director International Programs ... Ms. Katie DAVIDSON
21 Controller ... Ms. Sharon LOILAND
88 Director Judicial Affs/Crisis Pgm ... Mr. Alex POKORNOWSKI
09 Director of Institutional Research ... Ms. Carmen WILLIAMS
94 Director Women's Center ... Ms. Kay MENDICK
96 Director Purchasing ... Ms. Jana THOMPSON
92 Director Honors Program ... Dr. Amanda BOYD
28 Dir Multicultural Student Services ... Vacant
21 Budget Manager ... Ms. Cindy FETSCH
40 Manager University Bookstore ... Mr. Griffin GILLESPIE
49 Dean of Arts & Sciences ... Dr. Debbie STORRS
58 Dean School of Graduate Studies ... Dr. Grant MCGIMPSEY
61 Dean School of Law ... Ms. Kathryn RAND
66 Dean Col Nursing/Profess Discip ... Dr. Gayle ROUX
50 Dean Business/Public Administration ... Dr. Margaret WILLIAMS
54 Dean College of Engr/Mines ... Dr. Hesham EL-REWINI
53 Int Dean Col Education/Human Devel ... Dr. Cindy JUNTUNEN
88 Dean of Aerospace Sciences ... Dr. Paul LINDSETH
63 Dean Sch Medicine/Health Science ... Dr. Joshua WYNNE
88 Dir American Indian Student Svcs ... Dr. Leigh JEANOTTE
35 Asst Dean of Students ... Dr. Cassie GERHARDT
88 Director Memorial Union ... Ms. Cheryl GREW-GILLEN
88 Director Wellness Center ... Ms. Jenn PUHL WINKLER
88 Dir Health & Wellness Promotions ... Ms. Jane CROEKER
109 Director Dining Services ... Mr. Orlynn ROSAASEN
88 Dir Children's Learning Center ... Ms. Dawnita NILLES
13 Dir Admin Service Technology ... Ms. Sherry LAWDERMILT
22 Dir Disability Svcs for Students ... Ms. Debrah GLENNEN
88 Director TRIO Programs ... Mr. Derek SPORBERT
27 Director Student Affairs Marketing ... Ms. Sarah NISSEN
88 Dir One Stop Student Serv ... Mr. Matt LUKACH
07 Director Admissions ... Mr. Jason TRAINER

*Dickinson State University (D)

291 Campus Drive, Dickinson ND 58601-4896
County: Stark — FICE Identification: 002989
Unit ID: 200059
Telephone: (701) 483-2507 — Carnegie Class: Bac-Diverse
FAX Number: (701) 483-2006 — Calendar System: Semester
URL: www.dickinsonstate.edu
Established: 1918 — Annual Undergrad Tuition & Fees (In-State): $6,172
Enrollment: 1,479 — Coed
Affiliation or Control: State — IRS Status: 501(c)3
Highest Offering: Baccalaureate
Accreditation: NH, IACBE, MUS, NUR, PNUR, TED

02 President ... Dr. Thomas MITZEL
05 Provost/Vice Pres Academic Affairs ... Dr. Carmen WILSON
10 Int VP for Finance & Administration ... Mr. Scott HANSON
32 VP for Student Affairs & Enrollment ... Ms. Melanie TUCKER
20 Dean of Instruction ... Dr. Kenneth HAUGHT
29 Exec Dir Alumni Assoc/Foundation ... Mr. Ty ORTON
84 Exec Dir Communications/Public Aff ... Ms. Marie MOE
41 Director of Intercollege Athletics ... Mr. Tim DANIEL
56 Asst Director of Extended Learning ... Mr. Anthony WILLER
12 Director of DSU Bismarck/Williston ... Ms. Annette MARTEL
06 Director of Academic Records ... Ms. Kathy MEYER
08 Director of Library Services ... Ms. Mary SHEAHAN
13 Director of Information Technology ... Mr. Todd HAUF
37 Int Director of Financial Aid ... Mr. Dale GEHRING
88 Asst Director Academic Success Ctr ... Ms. Jennifer WITHERS
109 Director of Food Service ... Mr. Jason BENSON
40 Manager University Store ... Ms. Loretta A. HEIDT
21 Controller ... Ms. Janet REISENAUER
36 Director of Career Services ... Ms. Amanda BENEDICT-BARBIAN
09 Coordinator of Institutional Rsrch ... Dr. Chris P. BELCHER
85 Assoc Dir International Program ... Ms. Perzen POLISHWALLA
39 Housing Coordinator ... Vacant
15 Coordinator of Human Resources ... Ms. Gail EBELTOFT
04 Administrative Asst to President ... Ms. Kari HANSTAD
18 Chief Facilities/Physical Plant ... Mr. Mick RIESINGER
19 Director Security/Safety ... Mr. Jack SCHULZ
22 Dir Affirmative Action/EEO ... Dr. Christopher BELCHER
26 Chief Public Relations/Marketing ... Ms. Marie MOE

*Mayville State University (E)

330 3rd Street, NE, Mayville ND 58257-1299
County: Traill — FICE Identification: 002993
Unit ID: 200226
Telephone: (701) 788-2301 — Carnegie Class: Bac-Diverse
FAX Number: (701) 788-4748 — Calendar System: Semester
URL: www.mayvillestate.edu
Established: 1889 — Annual Undergrad Tuition & Fees (In-State): $6,380
Enrollment: 1,081 — Coed
Affiliation or Control: State — IRS Status: 501(c)3
Highest Offering: Master's
Accreditation: NH, NURSE, TED

02 President ... Dr. Gary D. HAGEN
05 Vice President for Academic Affairs ... Dr. Keith A. STENEHJEM
10 Vice President for Business Affairs ... Mr. Steven P. BENSEN
32 Vice President for Student Affairs ... Dr. Andrew J. PFLIPSEN
102 Executive Foundation Director ... Mr. John J. KLOCKE
09 Exec Dir Institution Effectiveness ... Ms. Maren A. JOHNSON
41 Athletic Director ... Mr. Mike K. MOORE
04 Exec Assistant to the President ... Ms. Mary L. TRUDEAU
26 Assoc Dir Found/Dir Marketing ... Ms. Beth I. SWENSON
07 Director of Admissions ... Mr. James R. MOROWSKI
06 Dir Academic Records/Registrar ... Ms. Pamela K. BRAATEN
106 Director of Extended Learning ... Ms. Misti L. WUORI
37 Director of Financial Aid ... Ms. Shirley M. HANSON
08 Director of Library Services ... Ms. Kelly J. KORNKVEN
35 Director of Student Life ... Dr. Jeffry A. POWELL
40 Director of Bookstore ... Ms. Pam B. SOHOLT
18 Director of Physical Plant ... Mr. Dan P. LORENZ
18 Director of Facilities Services ... Mr. Bob J. KOZOJED
15 Director of Human Resources ... Ms. Crystal BEGGS
13 Chief Information Officer ... Mr. Patrick W. STEELE
21 Controller ... Ms. Laura M. NELSON
38 Dir Counseling/Freshmen Retention ... Ms. Kristi L. LENTZ
88 Dir Student Success/Disability Svc ... Ms. Katie J. RICHARDS
108 Dir Acad Assess/Instruct Design ... Ms. Chris GONNELLA
28 Dir Cultural Diversity/Inclusion ... Ms. Dina ZAVALA-PETHERBRIDGE
36 Director of Career Services ... Mr. Jay A. HENRICKSON
27 Dir Strategic Student Communication ... Mr. Catlin E. SOLUM
50 Director of Business ... Ms. Rhonda L. NELSON
53 Dean of Education ... Dr. Andi L. DULSKI-BUCHOLZ
88 Director of Physical Education ... Dr. Jeremiah T. MOEN
81 Director of Mathematics/Science ... Dr. Bob D. MIESS
66 Director of Nursing ... Ms. Tami L. SUCH
83 Dir of Social/Behavioral Science ... Dr. Dalton MCMAHON

*Minot State University (F)

500 University Avenue W, Minot ND 58707-0001
County: Ward — FICE Identification: 002994
Unit ID: 200253
Telephone: (701) 858-3000 — Carnegie Class: Masters/M
FAX Number: (701) 839-6933 — Calendar System: Semester
URL: www.minotstateu.edu
Established: 1913 — Annual Undergrad Tuition & Fees (In-State): $6,390
Enrollment: 3,410 — Coed
Affiliation or Control: State — IRS Status: 501(c)3
Highest Offering: Beyond Master's But Less Than Doctorate
Accreditation: NH, CAATE, IACBE, MUS, NUR, SP, SW, TED

02 President ... Dr. Steven SHIRLEY
05 VP for Academic Affairs ... Dr. Laurie GELLER
10 Vice President for Finance/Admin ... Mr. Brent WINIGER
30 Vice President for Advancement ... Mr. Rick HEDBERG
32 Vice President for Student Affairs ... Mr. Kevin HARMON
21 AVP Business Services/Controller ... Ms. Jonelle WATSON
07 Admissions ... Ms. Katie TYLER
18 Facilities Management ... Mr. Brian SMITH
06 Registrar ... Ms. Rebecca RINGHAM
08 Director of the Library ... Mr. Stephen BANISTER
35 Director of Student Wellness ... Ms. Lisa ERIKSMOEN
37 Director of Financial Aid ... Ms. Laurie WEBER
58 Asst Dean of Graduate School ... Dr. Lorraine WILLOUGHBY
50 Dean College of Business ... Dr. Jacek MROZIK
49 Dean College Arts & Science ... Dr. Conrad DAVIDSON
53 Dean Col Education/Health Sci ... Dr. Cheryl NILSEN
51 Dean Continuing Education ... Dr. Kristin WARMOTH
29 Director Alumni Relations ... Ms. Janna MCKECHNIE
13 Director Computer Services ... Mr. George WITHUS
40 Director Bookstore ... Ms. Gerri KUNA
41 Athletic Director ... Mr. Andy CARTER
26 Director of Public Information ... Ms. Alysia HUCK
15 Director of Human Resources ... Dr. Marc WACHTFOGEL
12 Dean of Dakota College at Bottineau ... Dr. Jerry MIGLER
36 Director of Campus Career Services ... Ms. Lynda BERTSCH
25 Grants & Contracts Accountant ... Ms. Sheila LATHAM
09 Director of Institutional Research ... Ms. Cari OLSON
04 Administrative Asst to President ... Ms. Deb WENTZ
39 Director Student Housing ... Mr. Devin MCCALL
27 Director of Marketing ... Ms. Teresa LOFTESNES
104 Director International Programs ... Ms. Libby CLAERBOUT
19 Director Security/Safety ... Mr. Gary ORLUCK

88 Director of Veterans Services .... Mr. Andrew HEITKAMP
88 Title IX Coordinator .... Ms. Lisa DOOLEY

*North Dakota State University Main Campus (A)

P.O. Box 6050, Fargo ND 58108-6050
County: Cass FICE Identification: 002997
Unit ID: 200332
Telephone: (701) 231-8011 Carnegie Class: DU-Higher
FAX Number: (701) 231-8722 Calendar System: Semester
URL: www.ndsu.edu
Established: 1890 Annual Undergrad Tuition & Fees (In-State): $8,098
Enrollment: 14,747 Coed
Affiliation or Control: State IRS Status: 501(c)3
Highest Offering: Doctorate
Accreditation: NH, ART, BUS, CAATE, CACREP, CIDA, CCARC, CONST, DIETC, DIETD, ENG, EXSC, LSAR, MFCD, MUS, NURSE, PHAR, TED, THEA

02 President .... Dr. Dean BRESCIANI
05 Provost/Vice Pres Academic Affairs .... Dr. Beth INGRAM
10 Vice President Business & Finance .... Mr. Bruce BOLLINGER
32 Vice President for Student Affairs .... Dr. Timothy ALVAREZ
46 Vice Pres Research Crea Act & Tech .... Dr. Kelly RUSCH
88 Vice Presdent Ag/Univ Extension .... Dr. Ken GRAFTON
30 Int Pres/CEO Dev/Fdn/Alum Assn .... Mr. Keith BJERKE
13 VP Information Technology .... Mr. Marc WALLMAN
22 VP Equity/Diversity/Global Outreach .... Mrs. Eveadean MYERS
84 Dean of Enrollment Management .... Ms. Laura OSTER-AALAND
88 Assoc VP Sponsored Programs Admin .... Ms. Valrey V. KETTNER
06 University Registrar .... Ms. Rhonda KITCH
88 Director Student Affairs Admin Sys .... Mr. Viet DOAN
08 Dean of Libraries .... Ms. Bridget BURKE
35 Dean Student Life .... Ms. Janna M. STOSKOPF
51 Int Dir Distance/Continuing Educ .... Mr. Paul KELTER
37 Director Student Financial Services .... Mr. Jeff JACOBS
36 Director Career Center .... Ms. Jill J. WILKEY
26 Communication Coordinator .... Ms. Ann ROBINSON-PAUL
88 Assoc VP University Relations .... Ms. Laura MCDANIEL
56 Director Extension Service .... Mr. Chris BOERBOOM
50 Interim Dean Business .... Dr. Jane SCHUH
54 Dean Engineering/Architecture .... Dr. Gary R. SMITH
59 Dean Human Development & Education .... Dr. Virginia L. CLARK JOHNSON
49 Dean Arts/Humanities/Social Science .... Dr. Kent SANDSTROM
81 Dean of Science & Math .... Dr. Scott WOOD
67 Dean of Pharmacy/Nursing/Allied Sci .... Dr. Charles D. PETERSON
58 Dean Graduate School .... Dr. David A. WITTROCK
89 Assoc Dean University Studies .... Dr. Carolyn A. SCHNELL
21 Director of Budget .... Ms. Cynthia ROTT
25 Manager Grant & Contract Accounting .... Ms. Karen HENDRICKSON
18 Director Facilities Management .... Mr. Mike ELLINGSON
19 Dir of Univ Police/Safety Officer .... Mr. Mike BORR
38 Director Counseling/Disability Svcs .... Dr. William BURNS
23 Director Wellness Center .... Mr. Jobey LICHTBLAU
39 Director of Residence Life .... Mr. Rian NOSTRUM
40 Director Bookstore .... Ms. Carol J. MILLER
41 Director of Athletics .... Mr. Matt LARSEN
57 Director Fine Arts .... Dr. E. John MILLER
09 Int Dir Inst Research/Analysis .... Ms. Emily BERG
96 Director of Purchasing .... Ms. Stacey O. WINTER
07 Interim Director of Admissions .... Ms. Merideth SHERLIN
04 Executive Asst to President .... Ms. Barb PEDERSON
108 Dir Accred/Assessment/Acad Advising .... Dr. Larry PETERSON
15 Director HR/Payroll .... Ms. Colette ERICKSON

*Valley City State University (B)

101 College Street, SW, Valley City ND 58072-4098
County: Barnes FICE Identification: 003008
Unit ID: 200572
Telephone: (701) 845-7122 Carnegie Class: Bac-Diverse
FAX Number: (701) 845-7104 Calendar System: Semester
URL: www.vcsu.edu
Established: 1889 Annual Undergrad Tuition & Fees (In-State): $6,800
Enrollment: 1,378 Coed
Affiliation or Control: State IRS Status: 501(c)3
Highest Offering: Master's
Accreditation: NH, CAATE, MUS, TED

02 President .... Dr. Tisa MASON
05 Vice Pres Academic Affairs .... Dr. Margaret DAHLBERG
10 Vice President Business Affairs .... Mr. Wesley WINTCH
32 Vice President Student Affairs .... Mr. Pete SMITHHISLER
53 Dean Sch of Educ/Graduate Stds .... Dr. Gary THOMPSON
08 Library Director .... Ms. Donna JAMES
20 Director Student Academic Services .... Mr. John ANDRICK
37 Director Student Financial Aid .... Ms. Betty A. SCHUMACHER
13 Chief Information Officer .... Mr. Joseph TYKWINSKI
41 Athletic Director .... Mr. Nathan STEWART
84 Director of Enrollment Services .... Ms. Charlene STENSON
30 Director of University Advancement .... Mr. Larry J. ROBINSON
18 Director of Facilities Services .... Mr. Ron POMMERER
15 Human Resources Director .... Ms. Jennifer LARSON
44 Asst Dir Univ Advance/Alumni Rels .... Ms. Kim HESCH
38 Director of Student Counseling .... Ms. Erin KLINGENBERG
26 Director Marketing/Communications .... Mr. Greg VANNEY
40 Director Bookstore .... Mr. Todd ROGELSTAD
06 Registrar .... Ms. Jody KLIER
09 Dir Institutional Rsch/Assessment .... Mr. Gregory CARLSON
36 Career Services Coordinator .... Ms. Kari BODINE
28 Coord of Diversity & Stdnt Success .... Ms. Amy FUGLESTAD

*Bismarck State College (C)

PO Box 5587, Bismarck ND 58506-5587
County: Burleigh FICE Identification: 002988
Unit ID: 200022
Telephone: (701) 224-5400 Carnegie Class: Bac/Assoc-Assoc Dom
FAX Number: (701) 224-5550 Calendar System: Semester
URL: bismarckstate.edu
Established: 1939 Annual Undergrad Tuition & Fees (In-State): $3,604
Enrollment: 4,002 Coed
Affiliation or Control: State IRS Status: 501(c)3
Highest Offering: Baccalaureate
Accreditation: NH ADNUR, EMT, ENGT, MLTAD, PHLEB, SURGT

02 President .... Dr. Larry C. SKOGEN
03 Executive Vice President .... Mr. Dave CLARK
05 Interim Provost/VP Academic Affairs .... Dr. Larry SKOGEN
30 VP College Advance/Exec Dir Found .... Ms. Kari KNUDSON
10 Assoc VP Finance/Operations .... Ms. Tamara BARBER
32 Dean Student Affairs .... Dr. Donna FISHBECK
88 Dean Nat Energy Ctr of Excell .... Mr. Bruce EMMIL
49 Dean Humanities/Arts & Science .... Mr. Dan LEINGANG
88 Dean Current & Emerging Technology .... Ms. Carla HIXON
13 Chief Information Officer .... Mr. Elmer WEIGEL
15 Chief Human Resources Officer .... Ms. Rita LINDGREN
09 Chief Inst Effect/Strat Plan Office .... Dr. Stacie IKEN
106 Chief Dist Learning/Military Affs .... Mr. Lane HUBER
51 Director Cont Educ/Training & Innov .... Ms. Sara VOLLMER
08 Director of Library Services .... Ms. Marlene ANDERSON
26 Director of College Relations .... Ms. Marnie PIEHL
18 Chief Buildings/Grounds Officer .... Mr. Don ROETHLER
41 Director of Athletics .... Mr. Buster GILLISS
37 Director of Financial Aid .... Mr. Scott LINGEN
07 Dir Admissions/Enrollment Services .... Ms. Karen ERICKSON
88 Dir Great Plains Energy Corridor .... Ms. Emily CASH
35 Director Student & Residence Life .... Ms. Heather SHEEHAN
06 Director Academic Records/Registrar .... Mr. Tom LENO
35 Associate Dean of Student Affairs .... Mr. Jay MEIER
36 Dir Counseling & Advising Services .... Vacant
88 Program Manager NECE .... Mr. Dan SCHMIDT
88 Project Manager NECE .... Mr. Zachery ALLEN
88 Program Manager NECE .... Mr. Ryan CAYA
88 Program Manager NECE .... Mr. Kyran MILLER
88 Training & Program Manager NECE .... Ms. Alicia UHDE
46 Resource Development Manager .... Ms. Janet DIXON
29 Alumni Coordinator .... Ms. Rita NODLAND
40 Bookstore Manager/Purchasing Coord .... Ms. Debra SANDNESS
04 Executive Assistant to President .... Ms. Janell CAMPBELL
19 Campus Safety & Security Manager .... Mr. Duane JOHNSON

*Dakota College at Bottineau (D)

105 Simrall Boulevard, Bottineau ND 58318-1198
County: Bottineau FICE Identification: 002995
Unit ID: 200314
Telephone: (701) 228-2277 Carnegie Class: Assoc/MT-VT-Mix Trad/Non
FAX Number: (701) 228-5468 Calendar System: Semester
URL: www.dakotacollege.edu
Established: 1906 Annual Undergrad Tuition & Fees (In-State): $4,181
Enrollment: 753 Coed
Affiliation or Control: State IRS Status: 501(c)3
Highest Offering: Associate Degree
Accreditation: NH, EMT

02 Campus Dean .... Dr. Ken GROSZ
10 Director of Business Affairs .... Ms. Laura PFEIFER
32 Assoc Dean for Student Affairs .... Mr. Dan DAVIS
05 Assoc Dean for Academic Affairs .... Mr. Larry BROOKS
08 Librarian .... Ms. Hattie ALBERTSON
07 Director of Admissions .... Vacant
06 Registrar .... Mr. Dan DAVIS
37 Director Financial Aid .... Ms. Valerie HEILMAN
41 Athletic Director .... Mr. Brandon COLVIN
29 Director Alumni Relations .... Ms. Courtney VANDAL
39 Housing Director .... Ms. Michelle DAVIS
28 Director of Diversity .... Mr. Marcus JOHNSON
40 Bookstore Manager .... Ms. Janeen POLLMAN
18 Chief Facilities/Physical Plant .... Mr. Darrell WATERS
38 Director Student Counseling .... Ms. Corey GORDER

*Lake Region State College (E)

1801 College Drive N, Devils Lake ND 58301-1598
County: Ramsey FICE Identification: 002991
Unit ID: 200192
Telephone: (701) 662-1600 Carnegie Class: Assoc/HT-High Non
FAX Number: (701) 662-1570 Calendar System: Semester
URL: www.lrsc.edu
Established: 1941 Annual Undergrad Tuition & Fees (In-State): $4,138
Enrollment: 1,988 Coed
Affiliation or Control: State IRS Status: 501(c)3
Highest Offering: Associate Degree
Accreditation: NH, ADNUR

02 President .... Dr. Douglas G. DARLING
05 VP Academic/Student Affairs .... Mr. Lloyd HALVORSON
10 VP Administrative Affairs .... Mr. Corry G. KENNER
12 Director of Branch Campus .... Mr. John COWGER
30 Vice Pres Advancement/Foundation .... Ms. Laurel GOULDING
84 Director of Enrollment Management .... Ms. Stephanie SHOCK
37 Dir Student Finan Aid/Placemnt Svcs .... Ms. Katie NETTELL
109 Director Food Service .... Ms. Rosalie SEIBEL
18 Director Physical Plant .... Mr. Chad ESTENSON
08 Librarian .... Ms. Celeste ERTELT
41 Director Athletics .... Mr. Daniel MERTENS
13 Chief Information Officer .... Ms. Toofawn SIMHAI
15 HR Risk Mgmt/Placement Svcs .... Mrs. Sandi LILLEHAUGEN
40 Director of Bookstore .... Ms. Melissa STOTTS
06 Registrar .... Mr. Daniel JOHNSON
26 Director of Public Relations/Mktg .... Ms. Erin WOOD
31 Director Community Education .... Mr. Daniel DRIESSEN
09 Director of Institutional Research .... Ms. Brandi NELSON
28 Director of Diversity .... Mrs. Kristi HERNANDEZ
38 Director Counseling Services .... Mrs. Brigitte GREYWATER
07 Director of Admissions .... Ms. Stephanie SHOCK
21 Controller .... Ms. Joann KITCHENS
04 Administrative Asst to President .... Ms. Bobbi J. LUNDAY
29 Director Alumni Relations .... Mrs. Laurel GOULDING
39 Director Student Housing .... Dr. Randall FIXEN

*North Dakota State College of Science (F)

800 N Sixth Street, Wahpeton ND 58076-0002
County: Richland FICE Identification: 002996
Unit ID: 200305
Telephone: (800) 342-4325 Carnegie Class: Assoc/HVT-High Trad
FAX Number: (701) 671-2145 Calendar System: Semester
URL: www.ndscs.edu
Established: 1903 Annual Undergrad Tuition & Fees (In-State): $4,571
Enrollment: 3,033 Coed
Affiliation or Control: State IRS Status: 501(c)3
Highest Offering: Associate Degree
Accreditation: NH, CAHIIM, DA, DH, EMT, OTA, PNUR

02 President .... Dr. John RICHMAN
05 VP Academic & Student Affairs .... Mr. Harvey LINK
10 Vice Pres Administrative Affairs .... Mr. Dennis GLADEN
32 Vice Pres Student Affairs .... Mrs. Jane VANGSNESS FRISCH
37 Director Financial Aid .... Mrs. Shelley BLOME
08 Director Library .... Ms. Tina GRENIER
26 Dir Marketing/Communications/PR .... Mrs. Barbara SPAETH-BAUM
29 Exec Dir of Alumni Foundation .... Mrs. Kim NELSON
41 Athletic Director .... Mr. Stuart ENGEN
15 Exec Dir Human Resources .... Mrs. Sandi GILBERTSON
18 Director Facilities/Physical Plant .... Mr. Dallas FOSSUM
20 Academic Services Director .... Ms. Maria KADUC
39 Director of Residence Life .... Mrs. Melissa JOHNSON
07 Director of Admissions & Records .... Mrs. Barb MUND
21 Business Manager .... Mr. Keith JOHNSON
24 Instructional Technology Coord .... Mr. Tom HICKMAN
06 Asst Director Admissions & Records .... Mr. Justin GRAMS
38 Counseling Center .... Mr. Vince PLUMMER
49 Dean Arts Sciences/Business .... Mr. Ken KOMPELIEN
72 Dean Technology Services Division .... Mrs. Barbara BANG
64 Director of Music .... Vacant
56 Dean of Extended Learning .... Vacant
88 Dean of College Outreach .... Mrs. Patricia KLINE

*Williston State College (G)

1410 University Avenue, Williston ND 58801-1326
County: Williams FICE Identification: 003007
Unit ID: 200341
Telephone: (701) 774-4200 Carnegie Class: Assoc/HT-Mix Trad/Non
FAX Number: (701) 774-4211 Calendar System: Semester
URL: www.willistonstate.edu
Established: 1961 Annual Undergrad Tuition & Fees (In-State): $5,233
Enrollment: 863 Coed
Affiliation or Control: State IRS Status: 501(c)3
Highest Offering: Associate Degree
Accreditation: NH

02 Acting President .... Dr. John MILLER
05 Vice President Academic Affairs .... Dr. John MILLER
26 VP College Advancement .... Vacant
32 Vice President Student Affairs .... Kaylyn BONDY
10 Chief Financial Officer .... Laurie FURUSETH
103 CEO of Workforce Education Train .... Deanette PIESIK
37 Director Student Financial Aid .... Heather FINK

Nueta Hidatsa Sahnish College (H)

PO Box 490, New Town ND 58763-0490
County: Mountrail FICE Identification: 025537
Unit ID: 200086
Telephone: (701) 627-4738 Carnegie Class: Tribal
FAX Number: (701) 627-3609 Calendar System: Semester
URL: www.nhsc.edu
Established: 1973 Annual Undergrad Tuition & Fees: $4,210
Enrollment: 158 Coed
Affiliation or Control: Independent Non-Profit IRS Status: 501(c)3
Highest Offering: Baccalaureate
Accreditation: NH

01 President .... Dr. Twyla BAKER-DEMARAY
05 Vice President of Academics .... Dr. Waylon BAKER
32 Vice Pres Student Services .... Dr. Constance FRANKBERRY
10 Chief Finance Ofcr/VP Support Svcs .... Mr. Philip LEWIS
37 Financial Aid Assistant .... Mr. Tim OLSON
06 Registrar .... Vacant
08 Director Library Services .... Ms. Amy SOLIS
38 Guidance Counselor .... Ms. Deanna RAINBOW
40 Bookstore Manager .... Ms. Iona LITTLE WHITEMAN

Rasmussen College - Fargo/Moorhead (A)

4012 19th Avenue, SW, Fargo ND 58103-7196
Telephone: (701) 277-3889 FICE Identification: 004846
Accreditation: &NH

† Regional acrreditation is carried under parent institution in Saint Cloud, MN. The tuition figure is an average, actual tuition may vary.

Sitting Bull College (B)

9299 Highway 24, Fort Yates ND 58538-9706
County: Sioux FICE Identification: 021882
Unit ID: 200466
Telephone: (701) 854-8000 Carnegie Class: Tribal
FAX Number: (701) 854-8197 Calendar System: Semester
URL: www.sittingbull.edu
Established: 1971 Annual Undergrad Tuition & Fees: $3,910
Enrollment: 289 Coed
Affiliation or Control: Tribal Control IRS Status: 501(c)3
Highest Offering: Master's
Accreditation: NH

01 President .... Dr. Laurel VERMILLION
05 Vice President of Academic Affairs .... Dr. Koreen RESSLER
37 Director Financial Student Aid .... Ms. Donna SEABOY
06 Registrar .... Ms. Melody AZURE
08 Head Librarian .... Mr. Mark HOLMAN
40 Director of Bookstore .... Mrs. Tracy MAHER

Trinity Bible College & Graduate School (C)

50 S 6th Avenue, Ellendale ND 58436-7150
County: Dickey FICE Identification: 012059
Unit ID: 200484
Telephone: (701) 349-3621 Carnegie Class: Spec-4-yr-Faith
FAX Number: (701) 349-5786 Calendar System: Semester
URL: www.trinitybiblecollege.edu
Established: 1948 Annual Undergrad Tuition & Fees: $15,506
Enrollment: 230 Coed
Affiliation or Control: Assemblies Of God Church IRS Status: 501(c)3
Highest Offering: Master's
Accreditation: BI

01 President .... Dr. Paul ALEXANDER
03 Executive Vice President .... Rev. Ian O'BRIEN
05 Vice President of Academic Affairs .... Rev. Rick WADHOLM
32 Vice President of Student Affairs .... Ms. Twyla KUNTZ
07 Director Enrollment Management .... Rev. Jordy H. NUNEZ
58 Director of Graduate School .... Dr. Carol ALEXANDER
106 Director of Distance Education .... Mr. Daryel ERICKSON
06 Academic Registrar .... Ms. Sara BEST
08 Librarian .... Mrs. Phyllis KUNO
13 Director of Computer Services .... Mr. Matthew JOHNSON
18 Director of Facility Services .... Mr. Bryan JACOBSON
41 Athletic Director .... Mr. Jordan NOWELL
29 Director Alumni Relations .... Vacant

Turtle Mountain Community College (D)

Box 340, Belcourt ND 58316-0340
County: Rolette FICE Identification: 023011
Unit ID: 200527
Telephone: (701) 477-7862 Carnegie Class: Tribal
FAX Number: (701) 477-7870 Calendar System: Semester
URL: www.tm.edu
Established: 1972 Annual Undergrad Tuition & Fees: $2,250
Enrollment: 520 Coed
Affiliation or Control: Independent Non-Profit IRS Status: 501(c)3
Highest Offering: Baccalaureate
Accreditation: NH, MLTAD, PHLEB

01 President .... Jim L. DAVIS
05 Academic Dean/Dean of Student Affs .... Wanda LADUCER
10 Comptroller .... Tracy AZURE
75 Director Vocational/Education .... Sheila TROTTIER
06 Registrar .... Angel GLADUE
36 Career Ladder Coordinator .... Vacant
31 Dir of Community/Adult Education .... Sandra LAROCQUE
07 Director of Admissions .... Joni LAFONTAINE
15 Director Personnel Services .... Holly CAHILL
37 Financial Aid Officer .... Alexsis MARCELLAIS
40 Director of Bookstore .... Laisee ALLERY
18 Chief Facilities/Physical Plant .... Wesley DAVIS
30 Chief Development .... Dave RIPLEY
13 Chief Informational Officer .... Vacant
32 Student Support Services Coord .... Vacant
04 Administrative Asst to President .... Judy A. BELGARDE
101 Secretary of the Institution/Board .... Candace LONGIE
38 Director Student Counseling .... Tammy MORIN
41 Athletic Director .... Vacant
09 Director of Institutional Research .... Terri MARTIN-PARISIEN
19 Director Security/Safety .... Wesley DAVIS
108 Director Institutional Assessment .... Kellie HALL
25 Chief Contracts/Grants Admin .... Lyle POITRA

United Tribes Technical College (E)

3315 University Drive, Bismarck ND 58504-7596
County: Burleigh FICE Identification: 022429
Unit ID: 200554
Telephone: (701) 255-3285 Carnegie Class: Tribal
FAX Number: (701) 530-0605 Calendar System: Semester
URL: www.uttc.edu
Established: 1969 Annual Undergrad Tuition & Fees: $5,400
Enrollment: 434 Coed
Affiliation or Control: Independent Non-Profit IRS Status: 501(c)3
Highest Offering: Baccalaureate
Accreditation: NH, PNUR

01 President .... Dr. Leander MCDONALD
05 Vice Pres Academic Affairs .... Dr. Lisa AZURE
32 Vice Pres Student Services .... Vacant
11 Vice Pres Campus Services .... Dr. William GOURNEAU
10 Finance Director .... Mrs. Katina DECOTEAU
07 Admissions Director .... Mr. Donovan LAMBERT
06 Registrar .... Mr. Charles GITTER
15 Human Resources Director .... Mrs. Rae GUNN
41 Athletic Director .... Mr. Hunter BERG
13 IT Director .... Mr. Christopher BAILLIE
19 Safety and Security Director .... Mr. Joely HEAVY RUNNER
04 Exec Assistant to the President .... Mrs. Charisse FANDRICH
08 Librarian .... Mrs. Charlene WEIS
30 Institutional Resources Director .... Mrs. Larretta HALL
37 Financial Aid Director .... Mr. Scott SKARRO
106 Dir Online Education/E-learning .... Ms. Leah HAMANN
108 Director Institutional Assessment .... Mr. Monte SCHAFF
39 Director Student Housing .... Ms. Jolene DECOUTEAU

University of Jamestown (F)

6000 College Lane, Jamestown ND 58405-0001
County: Stutsman FICE Identification: 002990
Unit ID: 200156
Telephone: (701) 252-3467 Carnegie Class: Bac-Diverse
FAX Number: (701) 253-4318 Calendar System: Semester
URL: www.uj.edu
Established: 1883 Annual Undergrad Tuition & Fees: $19,870
Enrollment: 970 Coed
Affiliation or Control: Presbyterian Church (U.S.A.) IRS Status: 501(c)3
Highest Offering: Doctorate
Accreditation: NH, IACBE, NUR, PTA

01 President .... Dr. Robert S. BADAL
05 Vice Pres/Dean Academic Affairs .... Dr. Paul OLSON
32 Dean of Students .... Mr. Gary VAN ZINDEREN
11 VP Planning/Administrative Services .... Mr. Thomas R. HECK
03 Executive Vice President .... Ms. Polly J. PETERSON
84 Vice President of Enrollment Mgmt .... Mr. Mike HEITKAMP
26 VP for Marketing/Public Relations .... Ms. Tena LAWRENCE
101 Asst to Pres/Secy to Bd of Trustees .... Ms. Erin KLEIN
06 Registrar .... Mr. Michael P. WOODLEY
37 Director of Financial Aid .... Ms. Judy HAGER
08 Librarian .... Mrs. Phyllis K. BRATTON
36 Director Experiential Education .... Ms. Heidi LARSON
27 Director Information Office .... Ms. Donna SCHMITZ
41 Athletic Director .... Mr. Sean JOHNSON
13 Director Computer Center .... Mr. Chris HOKE
18 Chief Facilities/Physical Plant .... Mr. Mark KOEPKE
105 Director Web Services .... Mr. Dallas ROSIN
19 Director Security/Safety .... Mr. Gary VAN ZINDEREN
22 Dir Affirmative Action/EEO .... Ms. Becky KNODEL
39 Director Student Housing .... Mr. Eric THORSON

University of Mary (G)

7500 University Drive, Bismarck ND 58504-9652
County: Burleigh FICE Identification: 002992
Unit ID: 200217
Telephone: (701) 255-7500 Carnegie Class: Masters/L
FAX Number: (701) 255-7687 Calendar System: Other
URL: www.umary.edu
Established: 1959 Annual Undergrad Tuition & Fees: $16,685
Enrollment: 2,809 Coed
Affiliation or Control: Roman Catholic IRS Status: 501(c)3
Highest Offering: Doctorate
Accreditation: NH, CAATE, COARC, EXSC, IACBE, MUS, NURSE, OT, PTA, SW

01 President .... Msgr. James P. SHEA
03 Executive Vice President .... Mr. Gregory A. VETTER
05 Vice President for Academic Affairs .... Dr. Diane FLADELAND
10 Vice President Financial Affairs .... Vacant
32 Vice President Student Development .... Dr. Timothy SEAWORTH
26 Vice President for Public Affairs .... Mr. Jerome J. RICHTER
30 Director of Mission Advancement .... Vacant
06 Registrar .... Ms. Melissa MCDOWALL
08 Librarian .... Mr. David GRAY
37 Director of Financial Aid .... Mrs. Janell D. THOMAS
07 Director of Admissions .... Mr. Michael MCMAHON
09 Director of Institutional Research .... Mr. Phil REESE
15 Director Human Resources .... Mrs. Bonnie L. DAHL
18 Chief Facilities/Physical Plant .... Mr. Mark R. STEPHENS

OHIO

AIC College of Design (H)

1171 East Kemper Road, Cincinnati OH 45246-3322
County: Hamilton FICE Identification: 021286
Unit ID: 200624
Telephone: (513) 751-1206 Carnegie Class: Spec-4-yr-Arts
FAX Number: (513) 751-1209 Calendar System: Semester
URL: www.aic-arts.edu
Established: 1976 Annual Undergrad Tuition & Fees: $23,341
Enrollment: 36 Coed
Affiliation or Control: Proprietary IRS Status: Proprietary
Highest Offering: Baccalaureate
Accreditation: ACCSC

00 CEO .... Ms. Marion K. ALLMAN
01 President .... Mr. Sean M. MENDELL
07 Director of Admissions .... Ms. Cyndi MENDELL
08 Head Librarian .... Ms. Donna WAKEFIELD
10 Chief Business Officer .... Ms. Laura LEWIS
36 Director Student Placement .... Mr. Dennis GATES
37 Director Student Financial Aid .... Ms. Rita SCHRAND

Allegheny Wesleyan College (I)

2161 Woodsdale Road, Salem OH 44460-8920
County: Columbiana FICE Identification: 034573
Unit ID: 200873
Telephone: (330) 337-6403 Carnegie Class: Spec-4-yr-Faith
FAX Number: (424) 228-3006 Calendar System: Semester
URL: www.awc.edu
Established: 1956 Annual Undergrad Tuition & Fees: $5,000
Enrollment: 62 Coed
Affiliation or Control: Wesleyan Church IRS Status: 501(c)3
Highest Offering: Baccalaureate
Accreditation: BI

01 President .... Rev. Daniel R. HARDY, SR.
05 Academic Dean .... Dr. Tony BUCHANAN
10 Business Manager .... Mr. Troy MUIR
32 Dean of Students .... Rev. Timothy FORRIDER
30 Director of Development .... Mr. Tom SANDERS
06 Registrar & Director Admissions .... Mrs. Jeanne ZVARITCH
08 Head Librarian .... Mrs. Alice WEINGARD
37 Financial Aid Administrator .... Mrs. Esther PHELPS
09 Dir of Institutional Effectiveness .... Mrs. Jeanne ZVARITCH
40 Bookstore Manager .... Rev. Daniel R. HARDY
33 Dean of Men .... Mr. Stefan LETONEK
34 Dean of Women .... Mrs. Holly FORRIDER
07 Director of Admissions .... Mrs. Jeanne ZVARITCH
18 Chief Facilities/Physical Plant .... Mr. Darrin PATTERSON
21 Associate Business Officer .... Vacant
29 Director Alumni Relations .... Rev. Rocky NEWMAN
35 Director Student Affairs .... Rev. Timothy FORRIDER
38 Director Student Counseling .... Mrs. Kimberly FORD

American Institute of Alternative Medicine (J)

6685 Doubletree Avenue, Columbus OH 43229-1113
County: Franklin FICE Identification: 035344
Unit ID: 441636
Telephone: (614) 825-6255 Carnegie Class: Spec 2-yr-Health
FAX Number: (614) 825-6279 Calendar System: Quarter
URL: www.aiam.edu
Established: 1994 Annual Undergrad Tuition & Fees: N/A
Enrollment: 337 Coed
Affiliation or Control: Proprietary IRS Status: Proprietary
Highest Offering: Master's
Accreditation: ACCSC, ACUP

01 Campus President .... Mark SULLIVAN
05 Academic Dean .... Dr. Elaine HIATT
10 Chief Financial Officer .... Helen YEE
32 Dir of Student & Graduate Services .... Linda FLEMING-WILLIS
06 Registrar .... Emily MINNEMA
37 Financial Aid Officer .... Ulrike ROSSER
07 Director of Admissions .... Bonnie SHACKELFORD

American National University (K)

4736 Dressler Road NW, Canton OH 44718
Telephone: (330) 492-5300 Identification: 770698
Accreditation: ACICS, MAC

† Branch campus of American National University, Salem, VA

American National University (L)

6871 Steger Drive, Cincinnati OH 45237
Telephone: (513) 761-1291 Identification: 770699
Accreditation: ACICS, MAC, SURGT

† Branch campus of American National University, Salem, VA

American National University (M)

5665 Forest Hills Boulevard, Columbus OH 43231
Telephone: (614) 212-2800 Identification: 770700
Accreditation: ACICS, CAHIIM, MAC

† Branch campus of American National University, Salem, VA

American National University (N)

1837 Woodman Center Drive, Kettering OH 45420
Telephone: (937) 299-9450 Identification: 770697
Accreditation: ACICS, CAHIIM, MAC, SURGT

† Branch campus of American National University, Salem, VA

American National University (A)

3855 Fishcreek Road, Stow OH 44224
Telephone: (330) 676-1351 Identification: 770702
Accreditation: ACICS, MAC, SURGT

† Branch campus of American National University, Salem, VA

American National University (B)

27557 Chardon Road, Willoughby Hills OH 44092
Telephone: (440) 944-0825 Identification: 770703
Accreditation: ACICS, MAC

† Campus in teach-out, not enrolling new students.

American National University (C)

3487 Belmont Avenue, Youngstown OH 44505
Telephone: (330) 759-0205 Identification: 770701
Accreditation: ACICS, CAHIIM, MAC, SURGT

† Branch campus of American National University, Salem, VA

Antioch College (D)

One Morgan Place, Yellow Springs OH 45387
County: Greene Identification: 667214
Unit ID: 483018
Telephone: (937) 767-1286 Carnegie Class: Not Classified
FAX Number: N/A Calendar System: Quarter
URL: www.antiochcollege.org
Established: 1853 Annual Undergrad Tuition & Fees: $34 004
Enrollment: 238 Coed
Affiliation or Control: Independent Non-Profit IRS Status: 501(c)3
Highest Offering: Baccalaureate
Accreditation: NH

01 President .... Dr. Thomas MANLEY
05 Provost/Vice Pres Acad Affairs .... Dr. Lori COLLINS-HALL
10 VP Finance/Operations .... Ms. Andi ADKINS
30 Vice Pres Advancement .... Ms Susanne HASHIM
07 Dean of Admission .... Vacant
06 Registrar .... Mr. Ron NAPOLI
09 Dir Institutional Research .... Ms. Hannah SPIRRISON
04 Administrative Asst to President .... Ms. Nancy WUEBBEN

*Antioch University (E)

900 Dayton Street, Yellow Springs OH 45387-1635
County: Greene FICE Identification: 003010
Unit ID: 442392
Telephone: (937) 769-1351 Carnegie Class: N/A
FAX Number: (937) 769-1350
URL: www.antioch.edu

01 Interim Chancellor .... Mr. William GROVES
10 Vice Chancellor/CFO .... Dr. Allan GOZUM
05 Vice Chancellor Academic Affairs .... Dr. Iris WEISMAN
30 Vice Chancellor Inst Advancement .... Mr. Tim FORBESS
26 Vice Chancellor for Marketing .... Dr. MB LUFKIN
13 Chief Operations Officer .... Dr. Bob DEWITT
15 Chief Human Resources Officer .... Ms. Suzette CASTONGUAY
88 Chief Global Officer .... Ms. Felice NUDELMAN
91 Dir Administrative Info Systems .... Ms. Candice SANTELL
04 Executive Asst Chancellor's Office .... Ms. Jeannie SPINNATI
06 Registrar .... Ms. Maureen HEACOCK
08 Head Librarian .... Mr. Steve SHAW
101 Secretary to the Board .... Ms. Leslie JOHNSON
29 Director Alumni Relations .... Mr. Brice THOMAS
37 Director Student Financial Aid .... Ms. Susan HOWARD
86 Director Government Relations .... Mr. Paul BRADLEY

† Parent institution of Antioch University Midwest in OH; Antioch University Seattle in WA; Antioch University New England in NH; and Antioch University Los Angeles and Antioch University Santa Barbara in CA.

*Antioch University Midwest (F)

900 Dayton Street, Yellow Springs OH 45387-1745
County: Greene Identification: 666811
Unit ID: 245892
Telephone: (937) 769-1800 Carnegie Class: Masters/S
FAX Number: (937) 769-1806 Calendar System: Semester
URL: www.antiochmidwest.edu
Established: 1988 Annual Undergrad Tuition & Fees: N/A
Enrollment: 256 Coed
Affiliation or Control: Independent Non-Profit IRS Status: 501(c)3
Highest Offering: Doctorate
Accreditation: NH, TED

02 President .... Dr. Karen SCHUSTER WEBB
05 Chief Academic Officer .... Dr. Marian GLANCY
10 Regional CFO .... Ms. Barbara STEWART
04 Executive Assistant to President .... Ms. Jennifer MAYNARD
84 Enrollment Services Director .... Vacant
37 Assoc Director Financial Aid .... Ms. Tina BUNCH
26 Campus Marketing Manager .... Mr Michael METCALF
15 Director Personnel Services .... Ms. Suzette CASTONGUAY
21 Associate Business Officer .... Ms. Kyle FUCHS
62 Library Director .... Dr. Stephen SHAW
06 Registrar .... Dr. Maureen HEACOCK
18 Director Facility Management .... Mr. Ray SIMONELLI
30 Director Institutional Advancement .... Mr. Paul BRADLEY
53 Dir Division of Education .... Dr. Michele NOBEL
43 Dir Legal Services/General Counsel .... Mr. William GROVES
101 Secretary of the Institution/Board .... Ms. Jennifer MAYNARD
09 Institutional Research Analyst .... Ms. Sarah WALLIS
19 Director Security/Safety .... Mr. Ray SIMONELLI

Antonelli College (G)

124 E Seventh Street, Cincinnati OH 45202-2592
County: Hamilton FICE Identification: 012891
Unit ID: 201016
Telephone: (800) 505-4338 Carnegie Class: Assoc/HT-High Non
FAX Number: (513) 241-9396 Calendar System: Semester
URL: www.antonellicollege.edu
Established: 1947 Annual Undergrad Tuition & Fees: $15,980
Enrollment: 173 Coed
Affiliation or Control: Proprietary IRS Status: Proprietary
Highest Offering: Associate Degree
Accreditation: ACCSC

01 Campus President .... Ms. Leah ELKINS
05 Director Of Education .... Ms. Andrea MILLETTE
32 Associate Campus Director .... Mr. Corey EJARNSON
06 Registrar .... Ms. Tasnena REED
36 Career Services Coordinator .... Ms. Charlene SMITH

Art Academy of Cincinnati (H)

1212 Jackson Street, Cincinnati OH 45202-7106
County: Hamilton FICE Identification: 003011
Unit ID: 201061
Telephone: (513) 562-6262 Carnegie Class: Spec-4-yr-Arts
FAX Number: (513) 562-8778 Calendar System: Semester
URL: www.artacademy.edu
Established: 1869 Annual Undergrad Tuition & Fees: $27 788
Enrollment: 209 Coed
Affiliation or Control: Independent Non-Profit IRS Status: 501(c)3
Highest Offering: Master's
Accreditation: NH, ART

01 President .... Mr. John M. SULLIVAN
05 VP for Academic Affairs/CAO .... Mr. Kimberly G. KRAUSE
10 VP for Finance & Operations/CFO .... Mr. Thomas J. PACK
30 VP of Institutional Advancement .... Ms. Joan KAUP
07 Director of Admissions .... Vacant
37 Director of Financial Aid .... Ms. Dawn RECK
06 Registrar .... Mr. Alex SIEBERT
21 Director of Finance .... Ms. Jean SPOHR
84 Dir of Enrollment Management .... Ms. Jamie OWENS
18 Director of Facilities and Security .... Mr. Jack HENNEN
32 Director of Student Services .... Mr. Mae MAYNARD
04 Executive Assistant to President .... Ms. Kelly ENWRIGHT
105 Digital Media Specialist .... Mr. Jimmy BAKER
13 Lead Systems Engineer .... Mr. Kyle GRIZZELL
26 Marketing/Communications Specialist .... Ms. Marcelina ROBLEDO

The Art Institute of Ohio-Cincinnati (I)

8845 Governors Hill Drive, Cincinnati OH 45249
Telephone: (513) 833-2400 Identification: 666693
Accreditation: &NH, ACFEI

† In teach-out mode. Regional accreditation is carried under the parent institution The Illinois Institute of Art, Chicago, IL. School is in teach-out plan.

Ashland University (J)

401 College Avenue, Ashland OH 44805
County: Ashland FICE Identification: 003012
Unit ID: 201104
Telephone: (800) 882-1548 Carnegie Class: DU-Mod
FAX Number: N/A Calendar System: Semester
URL: www.ashland.edu
Established: 1878 Annual Undergrad Tuition & Fees: $20,242
Enrollment: 5,428 Coed
Affiliation or Control: Brethren Church IRS Status: 501(c)3
Highest Offering: Doctorate
Accreditation: NH, ACBSP, CAATE, CACREP, CEA, DIETD, MUS, NURSE, SW, TED, THEOL

01 President .... Dr. Carlos CAMPO
73 President Theological Seminary .... Dr. Mark HARDEN
11 VP of Admin & Strategic Planning .... Dr. Scott D. VAN LOO
05 Provost .... Dr. Eun-Woo CHANG
32 Vice President Student Affairs .... Dr. Hannah CLAYBORNE
30 Vice Pres Development & Inst Advanc .... Mrs. Margaret POMFRET
18 Vice Pres Facilities/Mgmt & Plng .... Mr. Rick M. EWING, II
10 Vice President/CFO .... Dr. Stephen STORCK
13 Exec Director of IT .... Mr. Bob MATNEY
42 Director of Religious Life .... Mr. Jason BARNHART
06 Registrar .... Ms. Dorothy COLLURA
37 Director Student Financial Aid .... Mr. Stephen C. HOWELL
29 Director Alumni/Parent Relations .... Mr. Jeff ALIX
15 Director of Human Resources/Legal .... Mr. Joshua A. HUGHES
36 Executive Director Career Services .... Ms. Karen HAGANS
26 Director of Public Relations .... Mr. Steven M. HANNAN
41 Director of Athletics .... Mr. Albert KING
88 Exec Dir Ashbrook Ctr .... Mr. Roger BECKETT
09 Director Inst Research & Assessment .... Dr. Larry BUNCE
07 Director of Admissions .... Mr. W.C VANCE
49 Dean College of Arts & Sciences .... Dr. Dawn WEBER
50 Dean College Business/Econ .... Dr. Elad GRANOT
53 Dean College of Education .... Dr. Donna BREAULT
66 Dean Col Nursing & Health Sci .... Dr. Faye GRUND
51 Dir Founders School of Cont Educ .... Dr. Eugene LINTON
28 Dir Multicultural Stdnt Svcs & Stds .... Mr. Jonathan E. LOCUST, JR.
19 Director Security/Safety .... Mr. David B. MCLAUGHLIN
38 Director of Counseling .... Dr. Oscar MCKNIGHT
44 Director Planned Giving .... Vacant
39 Director Student Housing .... Ms. Kimberly LAMMERS

Athenaeum of Ohio (K)

6616 Beechmont Avenue, Cincinnati OH 45230-5900
County: Hamilton FICE Identification: 003013
Unit ID: 201140
Telephone: (513) 231-2223 Carnegie Class: Spec-4-yr-Faith
FAX Number: (513) 231-3254 Calendar System: Semester
URL: www.athenaeum.edu
Established: 1829 Annual Graduate Tuition & Fees: N/A
Enrollment: 235 Coed
Affiliation or Control: Roman Catholic IRS Status: 501(c)3
Highest Offering: Master's; No Undergraduates
Accreditation: NH, THEOL

01 President & Rector .... Rev. Benedict O'CINNSEALAIGH
10 Vice President for Finance .... Mr. Dennis K. EAGAN
30 Vice President for Advancement .... Mr. Kyle ISAACK
05 Dean of Athenaeum .... Rev. David ENDRES
08 Librarian .... Mrs. Connie SONG
06 Registrar .... Mr. Nicholas JOBE
42 Dir Lay Pastoral Ministry Program .... Dr. Susan MCGURGAN
108 Director of Assessment .... Mr. Nicholas JOBE

Aultman College of Nursing and Health Sciences (L)

2600 Sixth Street SW, Canton OH 44710-1799
County: Stark FICE Identification: 006487
Unit ID: 201177
Telephone: (330) 363-6347 Carnegie Class: Spec-4-yr-Other Health
FAX Number: (330) 580-6654 Calendar System: Semester
URL: www.aultmancollege.edu
Established: 2004 Annual Undergrad Tuition & Fees: $16,340
Enrollment: 358 Coed
Affiliation or Control: Independent Non-Profit IRS Status: 501(c)3
Highest Offering: Baccalaureate
Accreditation: NH, ADNUR, NURSE, RAD

01 President .... Ms. Rebecca R. CROWL
10 VP Business & Student Affairs .... Ms. Jeannine SHAMBAUGH
05 VP Academic Affairs .... Dr. Jean PADDOCK
30 VP Community Engagement .... Ms. Vi LEGGETT
09 Director IE and Compliance .... Ms. Lyn SABINO

Baldwin Wallace University (M)

275 Eastland Road, Berea OH 44017-2088
County: Cuyahoga FICE Identification: 003014
Unit ID: 201195
Telephone: (440) 826-2900 Carnegie Class: Masters/L
FAX Number: (440) 826-2329 Calendar System: Semester
URL: www.bw.edu/
Established: 1845 Annual Undergrad Tuition & Fees: $29,908
Enrollment: 3,979 Coed
Affiliation or Control: United Methodist IRS Status: 501(c)3
Highest Offering: Masters
Accreditation: NH, #ARCPA, CAATE, MUS, NURSE, @SP, TED

01 President .... Dr. Robert C. HELMER
03 Senior Vice President .... Mr. Richard L. FLETCHER
05 Provost .... Dr. Stephen D. STAHL
10 Vice President for Finance & Admin .... Mr. William M. RENIFF
32 VP Student Affairs/Dean of Students .... Dr. Trina DOBBERSTEIN
84 Vice Pres of Enrollment Management .... Dr. Scott SCHULZ
26 Asst VP/Director College Relations .... Mr. Dan KARP
20 Associate Provost .... Dr. Guy E. FARISH
35 Director of Student Success .... Mr. Marc ADKINS
51 Director of Adult Learning .... Ms. Nancy JIROUSEK
08 Director of Ritter Library .... Mr. John DIGENNARO
13 Chief Information Officer .... Mr. Greg G. FLANIK
44 Director Annual Giving .... Ms. Christina ALDRICH
29 Director Alumni Relations .... Mr. Terry J. KURTZ
30 Senior Advancement Officer .... Ms. Deborah S. MILLER
37 Director of Financial Aid .... Dr. George ROLLESTON
15 Asst VP for Human Resources .... Mr. Sam RAMIREZ
38 Director of Counseling Services .... Ms. Joy D. WYATT
36 Director of Academic Advising .... Ms. Margaret STINER
06 Registrar .... Ms. Linda L. YOUNG
07 Interim Dir Undergraduate Admission .... Ms. Winifred W. GERHARDT
88 Dir of Adult/Cont Educ Admission .... Ms. Winifred GERHARDT
18 Director of Buildings & Grounds .... Mr. William KERBUSCH
88 Director of Intercultural Education .... Dr. Judith B. KRUTKY
96 Director of Purchasing .... Ms. Karen STENGER
28 Director Campus Diversity Affairs .... Mr. Charles HARKNESS
04 Administrative Asst to President .... Ms. Kimberlee A. KUHAJDA
09 Director of Institutional Research .... Ms. Susan T. WARNER
104 Director Study Abroad .... Ms. Christy L. SHREFLER
39 Director Student Housing .... Mr. Robin W. GAGNOW

102 Dir Foundation/Corporate Relations ......Ms. Annie HEIDERSBACH
19 Director Security/Safety .... Mr. Gary BLACK
41 Athletic Director .... Mr. Kris DIAZ

Beckfield College (A)

225 Pictoria Drive Suite 200, Cincinnati OH 45246
Telephone: (513) 671-1920 Identification: 666673
Accreditation: ACICS

† Branch campus of Beckfield College, Florence, KY.

Belmont College (B)

68094 Hammond Road, Saint Clairsville OH 43950-9766
County: Belmont FICE Identification: 009941
Unit ID: 201283
Telephone: (740) 695-9500 Carnegie Class: Assoc/HVT-Mix Trad/Non
FAX Number: (740) 695-2247 Calendar System: Semester
URL: www.belmontcollege.edu
Established: 1969 Annual Undergrad Tuition & Fees (In-State): $3,596
Enrollment: 1,042 Coed
Affiliation or Control: State IRS Status: 501(c)3
Highest Offering: Associate Degree
Accreditation: NH, MAC

01 President .... Dr. Paul GASPARRO
05 VP of Learning & Student Success .... Dr. Rebecca KURTZ
11 Vice Pres of Administrative Affairs ..Mr. John S. KOUCOUMARIS
32 Dean of Student Services .... Mr. Tim HOUSTON
18 Director of Facilities Management .... Mr. Steve MORGAN
06 Registrar .... Ms. Jennifer NIPPERT
15 Vice President of HR & Org Dev .... Mr. Matt KENDALL
37 Assoc Dean of Financial Aid .... Ms. Alicia FREY
88 Dir Teaching and Learning .... Mrs. Amy LEONI
36 Transfer/Articulat/Academic Advisor .... Ms. Jane BLACK
13 Exec Dir of Information Services .... Mr. Troy CALDWELL
30 Vice President of Advancement & Mkt .... Mr. RJ KONKOLESKI
04 Asst to President .... Ms. Kristy KOSKY
19 Director Security/Safety .... Mr. Glenn TRUDO
26 Public Relations Coordinator .... Ms. Julie MAMIE

Bexley Seabury (C)

583 Sheridan Avenue, Columbus OH 43209
County: Franklin FICE Identification: 037473
Unit ID: 443702
Telephone: (614) 231-3095 Carnegie Class: Spec-4-yr-Faith
FAX Number: (614) 231-3236 Calendar System: Semester
URL: www.bexleyseabury.edu
Established: 1824 Annual Graduate Tuition & Fees: N/A
Enrollment: 12 Coed
Affiliation or Control: Independent Non-Profit IRS Status: 501(c)3
Highest Offering: Master's; No Undergraduates
Accreditation: THEOL

01 President .... Rev. Roger A. FERLO
05 VP Academic Affairs/Academic Dean .Rev. Thomas C. FERGUSON
10 Director of Finance .... Mr. Robert DOAK

Bluffton University (D)

1 University Drive, Bluffton OH 45817-2104
County: Allen FICE Identification: 003016
Unit ID: 201371
Telephone: (419) 358-3000 Carnegie Class: Bac-Diverse
FAX Number: (419) 358-3323 Calendar System: Semester
URL: www.bluffton.edu
Established: 1899 Annual Undergrad Tuition & Fees: $30,168
Enrollment: 1,094 Coed
Affiliation or Control: Mennonite Church IRS Status: 501(c)3
Highest Offering: Master's
Accreditation: NH, DIETD, MUS, SW, TED

01 President .... Dr. James M. HARDER
10 Vice President for Fiscal Affairs .... Mr. Kevin A. NICKEL
30 Vice President for Inst Advancement .... Dr. Hans HOUSHOWER
05 Vice Pres & Dean Academic Affairs .... Dr. Sally W. SOMMER
84 VP for Enrollment Management/Mktg .... Mr. Ronald HEADINGS
32 VP for Student Life/Dean of Stdnts .... Dr. Julie DEGRAW
21 Chief Business Officer .... Mr. Richard LICHTLE
08 Director of Libraries .... Ms. Mary Jean JOHNSON
06 Registrar .... Ms. Iris NEUFELD
26 Chief Public Relations Officer .... Mrs. Robin BOWLUS
29 Dir of Alumni Relations/Annual Giv .... Mrs. Julia SZABO
07 Director of UG Admissions .... Mrs. Robin HOPKINS
18 Director Building/Grounds .... Mr. Mustaq AHMED
15 Director Human Resources .... Mr. Scott A. SHARIK
04 Administrative Asst to President .... Ms. Sally L. SIFERD
13 Chief Info Technology Officer (CIO) .... Ms. Deb TURNER
36 Director Student Placement .... Ms. Shari AYERS
38 Director Student Counseling .... Ms. Rae STATON
39 Director Student Housing .... Mr. Caleb FARMER
41 Athletic Director .... Mr. Phillip TALAVINIA
44 Director Annual or Planned Giving .... Ms. Julia SZABO
105 Director Web Services .... Ms. Sara KISSEBERTH
37 Director of Financial Aid .... Mr. Christopher FOWLER

Bowling Green State University (E)

220 McFall Center, Bowling Green OH 43403-0001
County: Wood FICE Identification: 003018
Unit ID: 201441
Telephone: (419) 372-2211 Carnegie Class: DU-Higher
FAX Number: (419) 372-8446 Calendar System: Semester
URL: www.bgsu.edu
Established: 1910 Annual Undergrad Tuition & Fees (In-State): $10,796
Enrollment: 16,554 Coed
Affiliation or Control: State IRS Status: 501(c)3
Highest Offering: Doctorate
Accreditation: NH, ART, BUS, BUSA, #CAATE, CACREP, CLPSY, CONST, DIETD, DIETI, ENGT, EXSC, IPSY, #JOUR, MT, MUS, NAIT, NRPA, NURSE, PH, SP, SPAA, SW, TED, THEA

01 President .... Dr. Mary Ellen MAZEY
05 Sr VP Academic Affairs/Provost .... Dr. Rodney K. ROGERS
10 CFO/VP Finance & Admin .... Ms. Sherideen S. STOLL
100 Chief of Staff .... Ms. Lisa C. MATTIACE
32 Vice President Student Affairs .... Dr. Tom GIBSON
04 Asst to President .... Ms. Laurel E. ZAWODNY
30 VP Univ Advancement .... Mr. Shea MCGREW
84 VP Strategic Enrollment Planning .... Ms. Cecilia CASTELLANO
20 Vice Provost Undergraduate Educ .... Dr. John FISCHER
35 Dean of Students .... Ms. Jodi WEBB
11 Assoc VP for Campus Operations .... Mr. Bruce MEYER
26 Chief Marketing & Comm Officer .... Mr. David KIELMEYER
29 Director Alumni Affairs .... Ms. Becky KOCHER
46 VP Research & Econ Dev .... Dr. Michael Y. OGAWA
41 Asst VP Student Affs/Dir Rec Sports .... Dr. Stephen KAMPF
41 Director of Athletics .... Mr. Bob MOOSBRUGGER
15 Chief Human Resources Officer .... Ms. Viva MCCARVER
39 Director of Residence Life .... Ms. Sarah WATERS
45 VP Capital Planning & Design .... Mr. Steve P. KRAKOFF
13 Chief Information Officer .... Mr. John M. ELLINGER
43 Vice President & General Counsel .... Mr. Sean P. FITZGERALD
28 Director Equity & Diversity .... Ms. Barbara WADDELL
58 Dean Graduate College .... Dr. Michael OGAWA
49 Dean College Arts/Sciences .... Dr. Raymond CRAIG
50 Dean College Business Admin .... Mr. Raymond BRAUN
51 Exec Director University Outreach .... Dr. Marcia SALAZAR-VALENTINE
53 Dean Col of Educ & Human Dev .... Dr. Dawn SHINEW
12 Dean Firelands College .... Dr. Andrew KURTZ
69 Dean College Hlth/Human Svcs .... Dr. Marie HUFF
08 Dean University Libraries .... Ms. Sara BUSHONG
64 Dean College of Musical Arts .... Dr. Jeffrey A. SHOWELL
72 Interim Dean College of TAAE .... Dr. Venu DASIGI
57 Interim Director of School of Art .... Dr. Charlie KANWISCHER
60 Dir Sch of Media & Communication .... Dr. Laura STAFFORD
88 Dir Sch Human Move/Sport/ Leisure .... Dr. Stephen J. LANGENDORGER
88 Dir Sch Family & Consumer Sciences .... Dr. Deborah G. WOOLDRIDGE
53 Dir Dir Sch Educ Fnds/Leadership/Policy .... Dr. Patrick PAUKEN
53 Int Dir Sch of Teaching & Learning .... Dr. Tim MURNEN
92 Dean Honors College .... Dr. Simon MORGAN-RUSSELL
106 Exec Director On-line Programs .... Dr. Marcia SALAZAR-VALENTINE
85 Exec Dir International Student Svcs .... Dr. Marcia SALAZAR-VALENTINE
21 Exec Dir of Business Operations .... Mr. Bradley K. LEIGH
07 Director Admissions .... Ms. Adrea SPOON
21 Dir Budgeting & Resource Planning .... Mr. Geofrey L. TRACY
06 University Registrar .... Mr. Christopher P. COX
40 Director Bookstore .... Mr. Jeffrey D. NELSON
19 Director Public Safety .... Ms. Monica M. MOLL
36 Director Career Center .... Mr. Jeff JACKSON
23 Exec Director Center for Health .... Mr. Richard G. SIPP
38 Director Counseling Center .... Dr. Garrett GILMER
37 Dir Student Financial Aid .... Ms. Betsy JOHNSON
23 Asst Director Center for Health .... Ms. Marlene REYNOLDS
44 Director of Annual Giving .... Ms. Jenny WENSINK
101 Secretary to the Board .... Dr. Patrick PAUKEN
88 Co-Gen Manager WBGU Public Media .... Mr. Anthony E. SHORT
88 Co-Gen Manager WBGU Public Media .... Ms. Tina L. SIMON
35 Director TRIO Collegiate Services .... Mr. Sidney CHILDS
21 Internal Auditing & Adv Svcs .... Mr. James LAMBERT
88 Director Women's Center .... Dr. Mary M. KRUEGER
22 Assoc Director Disability Services .... Ms. Peggy DENNIS
88 Dir President's Leadership Acad .... Dr. Julie A. SNYDER
109 Director Dining Services .... Mr. Michael L. PAULUS
96 Director of Business Operations .... Mr. Andrew D. GRANT
88 Director Student Employment .... Ms. Dawn CHONG
88 Director Learning Commons .... Mr. Mark NELSON
88 Director Advising Services .... Mr. Dermot M. FORDE
88 Asst VP Non-Trad & Transfer Svcs .... Dr. Barbara L. HENRY
09 Assoc VP for Inst Effectiveness .... Dr. Julia MATUGA
65 Dir Sch Earth/Environ & Society .... Dr. Charles ONASCH
88 Asst VP Development .... Ms. Cynthia ANDERSON
102 Dir Foundation/Corporate Relations .... Ms. Paula DAVIS

Bowling Green State University Firelands College (F)

One University Drive, Huron OH 44839-9719
Telephone: (419) 433-5560 FICE Identification: 007856
Accreditation: &NH, CAHIIM, COARC, DMS

† Regional accreditation is carried under the parent institution in Bowling Green, OH.

Bradford School (G)

2469 Stelzer Road, Columbus OH 43219-3129
County: Franklin FICE Identification: 004853
Unit ID: 202161
Telephone: (614) 416-6200 Carnegie Class: Assoc/HVT-Mix Trad/Non
FAX Number: (614) 416-6210 Calendar System: Semester
URL: www.bradfordschoolcolumbus.edu
Established: 1985 Annual Undergrad Tuition & Fees: $13,980
Enrollment: 443 Coed
Affiliation or Control: Proprietary IRS Status: Proprietary
Highest Offering: Associate Degree
Accreditation: ACICS, ACFEI, MAC, PTAA

01 President .... Mr. Dennis BARTELS
05 Director of Education .... Ms. Beth WOOD
07 Director of Admissions .... Ms. Raeann LEE

Brightwood College (H)

2800 East River Road, Dayton OH 45439
County: Montgomery FICE Identification: 020520
Unit ID: 204626
Telephone: (937) 294-6155 Carnegie Class: Spec 2-yr-Health
FAX Number: (937) 294-2259 Calendar System: Quarter
URL: brightwood.edu
Established: 1971 Annual Undergrad Tuition & Fees: N/A
Enrollment: 317 Coed
Affiliation or Control: Proprietary IRS Status: Proprietary
Highest Offering: Associate Degree
Accreditation: ACICS, MAC

01 President .... Mr. Greg SHIELDS
05 Director of Education .... Ms. Melissa CURRY

Brown Mackie College-Akron (I)

755 White Pond Drive, Suite 101, Akron OH 44320-4221
Telephone: (330) 869-3600 Identification: 666470
Accreditation: ACICS, OTA

† Branch campus of Brown Mackie College-Cincinnati, Cincinnati, OH.

Brown Mackie College-Cincinnati (J)

1011 Glendale-Milford Road, Cincinnati OH 45215-1107
Telephone: (513) 771-2424 FICE Identification: 005127
Accreditation: ACICS

† Branch campus of The Art Institute of Phoenix, Phoenix, AZ

Brown Mackie College-Findlay (K)

1700 Fostoria Avenue, Suite 100, Findlay OH 45840-6857
Telephone: (419) 423-2211 FICE Identification: 026162
Accreditation: ACICS, OTA, SURTEC

† Branch campus of The Art Institute of Phoenix, Phoenix, AZ

Brown Mackie College-North Canton (L)

4300 Munson Street, NW, Canton OH 44718-3674
Telephone: (330) 494-1214 FICE Identification: 030778
Accreditation: ACICS, SURTEC

† Branch campus of Brown Mackie College-Tucson, Tucson, AZ.

Bryant & Stratton College (M)

12955 Snow Road, Parma OH 44130-1013
Telephone: (216) 265-3151 FICE Identification: 022744
Accreditation: &M, MAC, NURSE, @PTAA

† Regional accreditation is carried under the parent institution (corporate office) in Buffalo, NY.

Capital University (N)

1 College and Main Street, Columbus OH 43209-2394
County: Franklin FICE Identification: 003023
Unit ID: 201548
Telephone: (614) 236-6011 Carnegie Class: Masters/M
FAX Number: (614) 236-6820 Calendar System: Semester
URL: www.capital.edu
Established: 1850 Annual Undergrad Tuition & Fees: $32,830
Enrollment: 3,494 Coed
Affiliation or Control: Evangelical Lutheran Church In America
IRS Status: 501(c)3
Highest Offering: First Professional Degree
Accreditation: NH, ACBSP, CAATE, LAW, MUS, NURSE, SW, TED

01 President .... Dr. Elizabeth L. PAUL
05 Interim VP Academic/Student Affairs .... Dr. Terry D. LAHM
10 Vice President Business & Finance .... Dr. Michael D. HORAN
20 Assoc Provost Academic/Student Aff .... Dr. Jody FOURNIER
30 Interim Vice Pres Advancement .... Ms. Jennifer PATTERSON
84 Interim VP Enrollment Services .... Dr. Amy ADAMS
21 Director Business Services .... Ms. Mary Ellen BORCHERS
44 Asst Vice President Major Gifts .... Ms. April NOVOTNY
43 University Counsel .... Dr. Tanya J. POTEET
101 Dir Pres Ofc/Liaison to Board Trust .... Ms. Nona S. MCGUIRE
27 Exec Director Integrated Mktg/Comm ... Ms. D. Nichole JOHNSON
26 Director Public Relations .... Ms. Denise RUSSELL
09 Director of Institutional Research .... Dr. Larry T. HUNTER
06 Registrar .... Mr. Brent KOERBER
37 Director of Financial Aid .... Ms. Susan E. KANNENWISCHER
07 Director of Admissions .... Ms. Amanda SOHL
29 Director Alumni/Parent Relations .... Ms. Diane LOESER
36 Director of Career Services .... Mr. Eric R. ANDERSON
08 University Librarian/Director IMC .... Vacant
88 Academic Service Coordinator .... Mr. Bruce EPPS

41 Athletic Director .... Dr. Steve BRUNING
13 Assoc Dir Information Technology .... Ms. Annette SHORT
85 Director Intl Education & ESL Pgm .... Ms. Jennifer ADAMS
32 Director Student Engagement .... Ms. Deanna WAGNER
18 Director Facilities Management .... Ms. Beth Anne CARMAN
15 Director of Human Resources .... Ms. Theresa FELDMEIER
38 Dir Univ Counseling/Health Svcs .... Dr. Cathy MCDANIELS WILSON
28 Dir Diversity and Inclusion .... Mr. Almar WALTERS
92 Honors Program .... Dr. Stephanie GRAY WILSON
40 Manager Bookstore .... Mr. Joseph AMBUSKE
42 Dean of the Chapel .... Mr. Gary SANDBERG
61 Interim Dean of Law School .... Ms. Rachel JANUTIS
64 Assoc Dean of the College .... Dr. Lynn ROSEBERRY
102 Dir Foundation/Corporate Relations .... Ms. Ashley STRIGLE
108 Assoc Provost Inst Effectiveness .... Dr. Jens HEMMINGSEN

Capital University Law School (A)

303 East Broad Street, Columbus OH 43215
Telephone: (614) 236-6500 Identification: 770347
Accreditation: &NH

† Regional accreditation is carried under the parent institution in Columbus, OH

Case Western Reserve University (B)

10900 Euclid Avenue, Cleveland OH 44106-7001
County: Cuyahoga FICE Identification: 003024
Unit ID: 201645
Telephone: (216) 368-2000 Carnegie Class: DU-Highest
FAX Number: N/A Calendar System: Semester
URL: www.case.edu
Established: 1826 Annual Undergrad Tuition & Fees: $44,560
Enrollment: 10,771 Coed
Affiliation or Control: Independent Non-Profit IRS Status: 501(c)3
Highest Offering: Doctorate
Accreditation: NH, AA, ANEST, #ARCPA, BUS, BUSA, CLPSY, CS, DENT, DIETD, DIETI, ENG, LAW, MED, MIDWF, MUS, NURSE, PH, SP, SW, TEAC

01 President .... Ms. Barbara R. SNYDER
05 Provost/Executive Vice President .... Dr. William A. BAESLACK, III
20 Deputy Provost/VP Academic Affairs .... Dr. Lynn T. SINGER
10 Senior Vice Pres for Finance & CFO .... Mr. John F. SIDERAS
11 Senior Vice Pres for Administration .... Ms. Elizabeth J. KEEFER
30 Sr VP for Univ Rels & Development .... Mr. Bruce A. LOESSIN
17 Sr VP Medical Affairs/Dean Medicine .... Dr. Pamela B. DAVIS
46 Vice President for Research .... Vacant
13 VP for Information Services/CIO .... Ms. Sue B. WORKMAN
32 Vice President for Student Affairs .... Mr. Louis W. STARK
18 VP Campus Planning/Facilities Mgmt .... Mr. Stephen CAMPBELL
15 Vice President for Human Resources .... Ms. Carolyn GREGORY
43 Sr Vice Pres/Gen Counsel/Secretary .... Ms. Elizabeth KEEFER
19 Vice President for Campus Services .... Mr. Richard J. JAMIESON
26 Vice Pres for University Relations .... Ms. Lara A. KALAFATIS
86 Assoc VP Govt/Foundation Relations .... Dr. Julie M. REHM
86 Exec Director Government Relations .... Ms. Jennifer RUGGLES
31 Sr Director Local Govt and Comm Rel .... Ms. Latisha JAMES
45 Vice Pres for University Planning .... Ms. Christine A. ASH
84 Vice Pres for Enrollment Management .... Mr. Richard W. BISCHOFF
28 VP Inclusion/Diversity/Equal Opptny .... Dr. Marilyn S. MOBLEY
27 Vice Pres Marketing/Communications .... Ms. Chris SHERIDAN
88 Treasurer .... Mr. Robert C. BROWN
45 Chief Investment Officer .... Ms. Sally STALEY
20 Vice Provost Undergrad Education .... Dr. Donald L. FEKE
82 Vice Prov International Affairs .... Mr. David FLESHLER
88 Dean of Undergraduate Studies .... Mr. Jeffrey WOLCOWITZ
21 Interim Controller .... Ms. Patricia L. KOST
06 Registrar .... Ms. Amy S. HAMMETT
37 Director of Financial Aid .... Ms. Venus PULIAFICO
07 Director Undergraduate Admissions .... Mr. Robert R. MCCULLOUGH
08 University Librarian .... Mr. Arnold HIRSHON
36 Director Career Center .... Dr. Thomas MATTHEWS
85 Dir International Student Svcs .... Ms. Marielena MAGGIO
38 Director University Counseling Svcs .... Dr. James E. SELLERS
09 Director of Institutional Research .... Ms. Jean E. GUBBINS
96 Int Dir Procurement/Distrib Svcs .... Ms. Mandy CARTE
41 Athletic Director .... Ms. Amy BACKUS
61 Co-Dean of Law .... Mr. Michael P. SCHARF
61 Co-Dean of Law .... Ms. Jessica W. BERG
49 Dean of Arts & Sciences .... Dr. Cyrus C. TAYLOR
63 Dean of Medicine .... Dr. Pamela B. DAVIS
66 Dean of Nursing .... Dr. Mary E. KERR
52 Dean of Dental Medicine .... Dr. Kenneth B. CHANCE
50 Dean of Management .... Dr. Robert E. WIDING, II
70 Dean Applied Social Science .... Dr. Grover C. GILMORE
54 Dean of Engineering .... Dr. Jeffrey DUERK
58 Dean of Graduate Studies .... Dr. Charles E. ROZEK
04 Executive Asst to President .... Ms. Jane M. VONDRAK
102 Senior Exec Director Corporate Rels .... Ms. Anne M. BORCHERT

Cedarville University (C)

251 N Main Street, Cedarville OH 45314-0601
County: Greene FICE Identification: 003025
Unit ID: 201654
Telephone: (937) 766-2211 Carnegie Class: Bac-Diverse
FAX Number: (937) 766-2760 Calendar System: Semester
URL: www.cedarville.edu
Established: 1887 Annual Undergrad Tuition & Fees: $27,206
Enrollment: 3,585 Coed
Affiliation or Control: Baptist IRS Status: 501(c)3
Highest Offering: Doctorate
Accreditation: NH, ACBSP, CAATE, CS, ENG, MUS, NURSE, PHAR, SW, TED

01 President .... Dr. Jerry T. WHITE
05 Vice President for Academics .... LtGen. Loren RENO, RET.
10 Vice President for Business .... Mr. Christopher SOHN
30 Vice President for Advancement .... Dr. Rick MELSON
32 VP Stdt Life/Christian Ministries .... Mr. Jon WOOD
84 Vice Pres Enrollment Mgmt/Marketing .... Dr. Janice SUPPLEE
43 General Counsel .... Mr. John HART
11 Assoc VP for Operations .... Mr. Rodney JOHNSON
06 University Registrar .... Mrs. Fran CAMPBELL
15 Assoc VP of Human Resources .... Mrs. Lydia GADDIS
13 Assoc VP Information Technology/CIO .... Dr. David L. ROTMAN
69 Dean of Undergraduate Programs .... Dr. Pamela D. JOHNSON
58 Dean of Graduate Programs .... Dr. Mark MCCLAIN
08 Dean of Library Services .... Mr. Lynn A. BROCK
67 Dean School of Pharmacy .... Dr. Marc SWEENEY
34 Assoc Dean Women .... Miss Rebecca STOWERS
35 Associate Dean Campus Life .... Mr. Brad D. SMITH
37 Executive Director of Financial Aid .... Mr. Kim JENERETTE
38 Director of Counseling Services .... Miss Mindy MAY
29 Director of Alumni Relations .... Ms. Stephanie CARROLL
36 Director Career Services .... Mr. Jeff REEP
92 Director Honors Program .... Dr. Thomas MACH
96 Director of Purchasing/Inventory .... Mr. Tim P. JOHNSON
04 Executive Asst to the President .... Mr. Zach BOWDEN
41 Athletic Director .... Dr. Alan GEIST
26 Exec Director of Public Relations .... Mr. Mark WEINSTEIN
19 Director of Campus Safety .... Mr. Douglas W. CHISHOLM
40 Manager of Retail Services .... Mrs. Tammy L. SLONE

Central Ohio Technical College (D)

1179 University Drive, Newark OH 43055-1767
County: Licking FICE Identification: 011046
Unit ID: 201672
Telephone: (740) 366-1351 Carnegie Class: Assoc/HT-High Non
FAX Number: (740) 366-5047 Calendar System: Semester
URL: www.cotc.edu
Established: 1971 Annual Undergrad Tuition & Fees (In-State): $4,296
Enrollment: 3,567 Coed
Affiliation or Control: State IRS Status: 501(c)3
Highest Offering: Associate Degree
Accreditation: NH, ADNUR, CSHSE, DMS, EMT, ENGT, RAD, SURGT

01 President .... Dr. Bonnie L. COE
10 Vice President Business & Finance .... Mr. David BRILLHART
32 Director of Student Life .... Ms. Holly MASON
15 VP for Instl Planning & HR Develop .... Ms. Jacqueline PARRILL
08 Director of Library .... Ms. Katie BLOCKSIDGE
06 Records Manager/Registrar .... Ms. Veronica RINE
84 Director of Enrollment Management .... Mr. Brad PULCINI
26 Director Marketing/Public Relations .... Ms. Cheri RUSSO
37 Director Financial Aid/Veteran Affs .... Ms. Faith PHILLIPS
19 Director Public Safety .... Mr. Denny HOLLERN
29 Dir Alumni Rels/Development Officer .... Mr. Matthew KELLY
35 Asst Director of Student Affairs .... Vacant
13 Chief Information Officer .... Mr. Howard IMHOF
22 Program Mgr Learn Asst Ctr Disabled .... Ms. Connie ZANG
05 Director of Academic Operations .... Mr. Chad WEIRICK
96 Manager of Purchasing .... Ms. Kimberley SIBERT
18 Manager Facilities .... Mr. Brian BOEHMER
51 Coord of Community Svc/Learning .... Ms. Vorley TAYLOR
36 Dir Career Dev & Experiential Lrng .... Mr. Derek THATCHER
04 Assistant to the President .... Ms. Jan TOMLINSON
09 Director of Institutional Research .... Ms. Misty MCKEE
50 Dean for Business/Engineering/IT .... Vacant
07 Gateway Manager/Admission .... Mr. Dustin DUNLAVY
101 Secretary of the Institution/Board .... Ms. Jan TOMLINSON
103 Manager Workforce Development .... Ms. Vicki MAPLE

Central Ohio Technical College Coshocton Campus (E)

200 North Whitewoman Street, Coshocton OH 43812
Telephone: (740) 622-1408 Identification: 770348
Accreditation: &NH

† Regional accreditation is carried under the parent institution in Newark, OH

Central Ohio Technical College Knox Campus (F)

236 South Main Street, Mount Vernon OH 43050
Telephone: (740) 392-2526 Identification: 770350
Accreditation: &NH

† Regional accreditation is carried under the parent institution in Newark, OH

Central Ohio Technical College Pataskala Campus (G)

8660 East Broad Street, Reynoldsburg OH 43068
Telephone: (740) 755-7090 Identification: 770351
Accreditation: &NH

† Regional accreditation is carried under the parent institution in Newark, OH

Central State University (H)

PO Box 1004, 1400 Brush Row Road, Wilberforce OH 45384-1004
County: Greene FICE Identification: 003026
Unit ID: 201690
Telephone: (937) 376-6332 Carnegie Class: Bac-Diverse
FAX Number: (937) 376-6138 Calendar System: Semester
URL: www.centralstate.edu
Established: 1887 Annual Undergrad Tuition & Fees (In-State): $6,246
Enrollment: 1,751 Coed
Affiliation or Control: State IRS Status: 501(c)3
Highest Offering: Master's
Accreditation: NH, ACBSP, ART, ENG, MUS, @SW

01 President .... Dr. Cynthia JACKSON-HAMMOND
100 Chief of Staff .... Mrs. Wendy HAYES
05 Provost/VP Academic Affairs .... Dr. Pedro L. MARTINEZ
10 Vice President Admin & Finance .... Mr. Curtis PETTIS
30 Vice Pres Institutional Advancement .... Mr. Anthony FAIRBANKS
11 Asst VP Administration & Finance .... Vacant
32 Vice President Student Affairs .... Ms. Stephanie KRAH
13 Vice Pres/Chief Information Officer .... Mr. Keith MATTHEWS
20 Assoc Vice Pres Academic Affairs .... Dr. Lovette CHINWAH
06 University Registrar .... Mrs. LaTonya BRANHAM
07 Asst Director of Admissions .... Vacant
08 Director of Hallie Q Brown Library .... Ms. Carolin STERLING
89 Assoc Dean of University College .... Dr. Dwedor FORD
12 Dean CSU Dayton Campus .... Dr. Lovette CHINWAH
09 Director Assessment/Inst Research .... Mr. Mohammad ALI
19 Chief of Police .... Capt. Mark MACHAN
26 Director Public Relations .... Dr. Edwina BLACKWELL-CLARK
23 Medical Director .... Dr. Karen MATHEWS
29 Director Alumni Relations .... Mr. Keith PERKINS
36 Director Career Services .... Ms. Karla HARPER
37 Director Student Financial Aid .... Ms. Sonia SLOMBIA
39 Director Residence Life .... Mr. Dillon BECKFORD
41 Athletic Director .... Mr. Jahan CULBREATH
42 Director Campus Ministry .... Rev. Kima CUNNINGHAM
46 Director Sponsored Pgms/Research .... Mr. Morakinyo KUTI
49 Dean Coll Humanities/Arts & Sci .... Dr. James SMITH
50 Dean College of Business .... Dr. Fidelis M. IKEM
53 Dean College of Education .... Dr. Charles HODGE
15 Int Director of Human Resources .... Dr. Evelyn GORDON
21 Director Business Svcs/Capital Dev .... Ms. Cynthia MICHAEL
25 Director Grants Accounting .... Vacant
92 Director Honors Program .... Dr. Geoffrey J. GIDDINGS
21 Interim Controller .... Ms. Terri LEWIS-CHAMBERS
21 Budget Director .... Ms. Sheila BROWN
38 Director Student Counseling .... Mr. NseAbasi EKPO
84 Enrollment Specialist .... Mr. William RANDOLPH

Chamberlain College of Nursing-Cleveland (I)

6700 Euclid Avenue, Suite 201, Cleveland OH 44103
Telephone: (216) 361-6005 Identification: 770505
Accreditation: &NH, NURSE

† Regional accreditation is carried under the parent institution in Addison, IL

Chamberlain College of Nursing-Columbus Campus (J)

1350 Alum Creek Drive, Columbus OH 43209
Telephone: (614) 252-8890 Identification: 770499
Accreditation: &NH, ADNUR, NURSE

† Regional accreditation is carried under the parent institution in Addison, IL

Chatfield College (K)

20918 State Route 251, Saint Martin OH 45118-9059
County: Brown FICE Identification: 010880
Unit ID: 201751
Telephone: (513) 875-3344 Carnegie Class: Assoc/HT-High Trad
FAX Number: (513) 875-3912 Calendar System: Semester
URL: www.chatfield.edu
Established: 1971 Annual Undergrad Tuition & Fees: $9,695
Enrollment: 408 Coed
Affiliation or Control: Independent Non-Profit IRS Status: 501(c)3
Highest Offering: Associate Degree
Accreditation: NH

01 President .... Mr. John P. TAFARO
03 Vice President/CEO .... Mr. Robert ELMORE
05 Chief Academic Officer/Dean .... Mr. Kenneth SPENCER
10 Director of Finance .... Ms. Mary R. JACOBS
30 Director of Advancement .... Mr. James LUDWIG
07 Director of Admissions .... Mr. John PENROSE
20 Associate Dean/Site Director .... Sr. Patricia HOMAN
26 Director of Marketing Communication .... Ms. Pamela SPENCER
04 Administrative Asst to President .... Ms. Cheryl A. KERN
06 Registrar .... Mr. Gordon GILES
08 Head Librarian .... Ms. Dolores BERISH
13 Chief Info Technology Officer .... Mr. Nathan SCHULER
29 Director Alumni Relations .... Mr. James LUDWIG
37 Director Student Financial Aid .... Ms. Dawn HUNDLEY
09 Inst Research/Assessment .... Ms. Mary Fran HEINSCH
101 Secretary of the Institution/Board .... Ms. Cheryl A. KERN
44 Director Annual or Planned Giving .... Mr. James P. LUDWIG

The Christ College of Nursing and Health Sciences (A)

2139 Auburn Avenue, Cincinnati OH 45219
County: Hamilton FICE Identification: 006489
Unit ID: 201821
Telephone: (513) 585-2401 Carnegie Class: Spec-4-yr-Other Health
FAX Number: (513) 585-3540 Calendar System: Semester
URL: www.thechristcollege.edu
Established: 2006 Annual Undergrad Tuition & Fees: $14,667
Enrollment: 712 Coed
Affiliation or Control: Independent Non-Profit IRS Status: 501(c)3
Highest Offering: Baccalaureate
Accreditation: NH, ADNUR, NURSE

01 President .... Dr. W. Gary PACK
05 Dean of Academics .... Dr. Kelly M. SIMMONS
20 Dean of College Support Services .... Dr. Meghan E. HOLLOWELL
11 Dn Operations/Presidential Liaison .... Ms. Carolyn A. HUNTER
84 Dean of Enrollment Management .... Mr. Bradley A. JACKSON
04 Assistant to the President .... Ms. Cheryl A. BOONE

Cincinnati Christian University (B)

2700 Glenway Avenue, Cincinnati OH 45204-3200
County: Hamilton FICE Identification: 003029
Unit ID: 201858
Telephone: (513) 244-8100 Carnegie Class: Spec-4-yr-Faith
FAX Number: (513) 244-8140 Calendar System: Semester
URL: www.ccuniversity.edu
Established: 1924 Annual Undergrad Tuition & Fees: $15,966
Enrollment: 835 Coed
Affiliation or Control: Christian Churches And Churches of Christ
IRS Status: 501(c)3
Highest Offering: First Professional Degree
Accreditation: NH, BI, CACREP, MUS, TEAC, THEOL

01 Interim President .... Dr. David H. RAY
05 Chief Academic Officer .... Dr. Tom THATCHER
44 Director Annual or Planned Giving .... Mr. Dick DEVINE
10 Director of Financial Services .... Mr. Randy KOEHLER
30 Dir of Advancement & Development .... Vacant
51 Dir of College of Adult Learning .... Mr. Byron WILLIAMS
84 Director of Adult Enrollment .... Mr. Mark TUCKER
73 Dean of Russell School of Ministry .... Dr. David H. RAY
49 Dean Biblical Studies/Arts & Sci .... Mr. Paul FRISKNEY
83 Dean Education/Behavioral Sciences .... Dr. Marlene ESTENSON
50 Dean of School of Business .... Dr. Daryl SMITH
108 Dean of Institutional Effectiveness .... Dr. Sara FUDGE
20 Director of Faculty Development .... Dr. James A. SMITH
21 Bursar .... Mrs. Linda WAUGH
06 Registrar .... Mrs. Amanda DERICO
08 Director of Library Services .... Mr. Scott LLOYD
32 Director of Student Life .... Mr. Ray HORTON
33 Dean of Men/Campus Minister .... Vacant
37 Associate Director of Financial Aid .... Ms. Marcella FARMER
07 Director of Undergrad Admissions .... Ms. Sarah BEVARD
106 Director of Online Learning .... Vacant
29 Manager of Alumni Relations .... Vacant
41 Director of Athletics .... Mr. Kellen ZAWADZKI
18 Director of Operations .... Mr. Rich ELLISON
15 Director of Human Resources .... Ms. Leticia CRENSHAW
13 Director of Information Technology .... Vacant
19 Director of Security .... Mr. Dan JACKSON
40 Manager of Bookstore .... Vacant
04 Exec Assistant to the President .... Mrs. Wendy SPALDING
104 Director Study Abroad .... Vacant
89 First Year Programs Coordinator .... Ms. Kaci DURHAM

Cincinnati College of Mortuary Science (C)

645 W North Bend Road, Cincinnati OH 45224-1462
County: Hamilton FICE Identification: 010906
Unit ID: 201867
Telephone: (513) 761-2020 Carnegie Class: Spec-4-yr-Other
FAX Number: (513) 761-3333 Calendar System: Semester
URL: www.ccms.edu
Established: 1882 Annual Undergrad Tuition & Fees: N/A
Enrollment: 85 Coed
Affiliation or Control: Independent Non-Profit IRS Status: 501(c)3
Highest Offering: Baccalaureate
Accreditation: NH, FUSER

01 President .... Mr. Jack E. LECHNER, JR.
07 Admissions Director .... Dr. Blanche KABENGELE
37 Financial Aid Director .... Mr. Russ ROMANDINI
04 Administrative Asst to President .... Mrs. Beth WILLIAMS
05 Chief Academic Officer .... Ms. Teresa DUTKO
08 Head Librarian .... Ms. Molly JONES
10 Chief Business Officer .... Mrs. Leslie BOEHM

Cincinnati State Technical and Community College (D)

3520 Central Parkway, Cincinnati OH 45223-2690
County: Hamilton FICE Identification: 010345
Unit ID: 201928
Telephone: (513) 569-1500 Carnegie Class: Assoc/MT-VT-Mix Trad/Non
FAX Number: (513) 569-1495 Calendar System: Other
URL: www.cincinnatistate.edu
Established: 1966 Annual Undergrad Tuition & Fees (In-State): $3,825
Enrollment: 10,707 Coed
Affiliation or Control: State IRS Status: 501(c)3
Highest Offering: Associate Degree
Accreditation: NH, ACFEI, ADNUR, CAHIIM, COARC, CONST, DIETT, DMS, EMT, ENGT, IFSAC, MAC, MLTAD, OTA, SURGT

01 Interim President .... Dr. Monica POSEY
03 Executive Vice President .... Ms. Carla CHANCE
05 Interim Provost .... Ms. Robbin HOOPES
13 Vice President for Technology .... Dr. David HICKEY
10 Int VP College Administration .... Mr. Michael SCHWEINFEST
26 Vice Pres Marketing/Communications .... Ms. Jean MANNING
103 Vice Pres Workforce Development .... Ms. Amy WALDBILLIG
84 VP Enrollment/Student Development .... Dr. Soni HILL
72 Dean of Engineering Technology .... Mr. Doug BOWLING
50 Dean of Business Technologies .... Dr. Linda SCHAFFELD
76 Dean Health/Public Safety .... Dr. Jean CHAPPELL
81 Dean Humanities/Sciences .... Ms. Robbin HOOPES
06 Registrar .... Vacant
08 Library Director .... Mrs. Cindy SEFTON
41 Dir Athletics/Student Activities .... Mr. Tom HATHAWAY
18 Director of Facilities .... Mr. Rob EPLING
09 Director of Institutional Research .... Ms. Anne FOSTER
07 Director of Admissions .... Ms. Gabriele BOECKERMANN
15 Director of Human Resources .... Ms. Lisa EVANS
32 Chief Student Life Officer .... Vacant
30 Chief of Development .... Mr. Elliott RUTHER
35 Director of Student Affairs .... Mrs. Sharon DAVIS
96 Director of Purchasing .... Mr. Jeffrey COOK
92 Coordinator Honors Program .... Dr. Andrea LESLIE
86 Director of Government Affairs .... Ms. Nan KOHNEN-CAHALL
04 Executive Administrative Associate .... Mrs. Lachanna JACKSON
19 Director of Public Safety .... Mr. Michael WYLIE
37 Director of Financial Aid .... Mrs. La Saundra CRAIG
101 Secretary to the Board of Trustees .... Mrs. Nancy STUBBEMAN
88 Director of Student Success .... Mr. Martino HARMON
25 Contract Administrator .... Mrs. Ann JAMES

Clark State Community College (E)

570 E Leffel Lane, PO Box 570,
Springfield OH 45501-0570
County: Clark FICE Identification: 004852
Unit ID: 201973
Telephone: (937) 325-0691 Carnegie Class: Assoc/MT-VT-Mix Trad/Non
FAX Number: (937) 328-6142 Calendar System: Quarter
URL: www.clarkstate.edu
Established: 1966 Annual Undergrad Tuition & Fees (In-State): $3,359
Enrollment: 5,969 Coed
Affiliation or Control: State IRS Status: 501(c)3
Highest Offering: Associate Degree
Accreditation: NH, ADNUR, EMT, MAC, MLTAD, PTAA

01 President .... Dr. Jo A. BLONDIN
05 Provost/Vice Pres Academic Affairs .... Dr. Amit SINGH
10 Vice President Business Affairs .... Joseph R. JACKSON
30 Foundation Director .... Catie STIPE
21 Controller .... Dixie A. DEPEW
32 Dean Student Support Services .... Dr. Edward J. BUSHER
08 Director Library Services .... Dr. Sterling J. COLEMAN, JR.
84 Dean Enrollment Services .... Nina WILEY
49 Dean Arts & Sciences .... Naomi LOUIS
50 Dean Business/Applied Technologies .... Aimee BELANGER-HAAS
76 Dean Health and Human Services .... Kathleen J. WILCOX
37 Financial Aid Director .... Kathy A. KLAY
06 Registrar .... Diane SEAMAN
31 Director of Community Outreach .... Corey HOLLIDAY
13 Chief Information Officer .... Matt FRANZ
15 Chief Human Resources Officer .... Marvin NEPHEW
57 Exec Dir Performing Arts Center .... Adele ADKINS
18 Interim Dir Facilities/Oper/Maint .... Daniel AYARS
41 Dir Athletics/Act & Evening Svcs .... Vacant
103 Director Workforce Development .... Duane HODGE
09 Institutional Research Technician .... Kelly NERIANI
04 Assistant to the President .... Mellanie TOLES
26 Marketing Director .... Laurie MEANS

Clark State Community College Greene Center (F)

3775 Pentagon Boulevard, Beavercreek OH 45431
Telephone: (937) 429-8819 Identification: 770352
Accreditation: &NH

† Regional accreditation is carried under the parent institution in Springfield, OH

Cleveland Institute of Art (G)

11610 Euclid Avenue, Cleveland OH 44106-1710
County: Cuyahoga FICE Identification: 003982
Unit ID: 202046
Telephone: (216) 421-7000 Carnegie Class: Spec-4-yr-Arts
FAX Number: (216) 421-7438 Calendar System: Semester
URL: www.cia.edu
Established: 1882 Annual Undergrad Tuition & Fees: $38,487
Enrollment: 559 Coed
Affiliation or Control: Independent Non-Profit IRS Status: 501(c)3
Highest Offering: Baccalaureate
Accreditation: NH, ART

01 President & CEO .... Mr. Grafton J. NUNES
05 Sr VP Faculty Affairs & CAO .... Mr. Chris WHITTEY
30 Vice President Inst Advancement .... Ms. Malou MONAGO
10 Sr VP Business Affairs/CFO .... Mrs. Almut ZVOSEC
26 Vice President Mktg & Communication .... Mr. Mark INGLIS
84 VP Enrollment/Dean Admissions & Fin ..... Mr. Jonathan WEHNER
37 Asst Director of Financial Aid .... Ms. Delores HALL
06 Registrar .... Mrs. Karen HUDY
08 Library Director .... Ms. Laura PONIKVAR
07 Assoc Director of Admissions .... Mr. Tom GREEN
13 VP Support Service & CIO .... Mr. Mat FELTHOUSEN
29 Director Annual Giving/Alumni Rels .... Ms. Liz HUFF
20 Director of Academic Services .... Ms. Anne GATES
44 Dir Leadership/Planned Giving .... Ms. Sarah OTT-HANSEN
15 Exec Dir of HR & Inclusion .... Mr. Raymond SCRAGG
32 Dean of Student Affairs .... Ms. Nancy NEVILLE
37 Director of Financial Aid .... Mr. Martin CARNEY
27 Director of Mktg & Communications ...... Ms. Karen SANDSTROM
57 Art Director .... Mr. Richard SARIAN
21 Assoc VP of Business Affairs .... Ms. Julie MELVIN
25 Director of Grants/Special Projects .... Ms. Jennifer GRASSO

Cleveland Institute of Music (H)

11021 East Boulevard, Cleveland OH 44106-1776
County: Cuyahoga FICE Identification: 003031
Unit ID: 202073
Telephone: (216) 791-5000 Carnegie Class: Spec-4-yr-Arts
FAX Number: (216) 791-3063 Calendar System: Semester
URL: www.cim.edu
Established: 1920 Annual Undergrad Tuition & Fees: $47,565
Enrollment: 450 Coed
Affiliation or Control: Independent Non-Profit IRS Status: 501(c)3
Highest Offering: Doctorate
Accreditation: NH, MUS

01 President/CEO .... Mr. Paul HOGLE
03 Vice President/COO/Asst Treasurer .... Mr. Eric BOWER
45 VP for Strategic Initiatives .... Ms. Karin STONE
05 Interim Sr Assoc Dean .... Mr. Brian SWEIGART
64 Interim Dean of Conservatory .... Ms. Joyce GRIGGS
26 Director Marketing & Communications .... Ms. Susan ILER
13 Director Systems Management .... Mr. Daniel BETTING
07 Director Admission & Enrollment Mgt .... Ms. Lynn JOHNSON
32 Associate Dean of Student Affairs .... Mr. David GILSON
37 Director Financial Aid .... Ms. Kristine GRIPP
10 Chief Financial Officer .... Ms. Kristen KOLLAR
06 Assoc Dean Stdnt Acad Affs/Registr .... Ms. Hallie MOORE
15 Director Human Resources .... Mrs. Megan SWERBINSKY
08 Director of the Library .... Ms. Jean TOOMBS
88 Director of Concerts & Events .... Ms. Lori WRIGHT
40 Bookstore Manager .... Ms. Antoinette MILLER
106 Director of Distance Learning .... Mr. Gregory HOWE
04 Executive Admin Asst to President .... Ms. Nancy SNELL
09 Institutional Research Analyst .... Mrs. Caryn REYNOLDS

Cleveland State University (I)

2121 Euclid Avenue, Cleveland OH 44115-2214
County: Cuyahoga FICE Identification: 003032
Unit ID: 202134
Telephone: (216) 687-2000 Carnegie Class: DU-Higher
FAX Number: (216) 687-9366 Calendar System: Semester
URL: www.csuohio.edu
Established: 1964 Annual Undergrad Tuition & Fees (In-State): $9,696
Enrollment: 16,936 Coed
Affiliation or Control: State IRS Status: 501(c)3
Highest Offering: Doctorate
Accreditation: NH, ARCPA, BUS, BUSA, CACREP, CEA, COPSY, ENG, ENGT, LAW, MUS, NURSE, OT, PH, PLNG, PTA, SP, SPAA, SW, TED

01 President .... Dr. Ronald M. BERKMAN
100 Chief of Staff/Spec Advisor to Pres .... Mr. James BENNETT
05 Int Provost/Sr VP Academic Affairs .... Dr. Jianping ZHU
10 VP Business Affairs/Finance .... Ms. Stephanie MCHENRY
84 VP Enrollment Services .... Dr. Cindy SKARUPPA
46 VP Research .... Dr. Jerzy SAWICKI
28 VP Univ Engagement/Chief Diversity .... Dr. Byron WHITE
30 VP Univ Advancement/Exec Dir Found .... Ms. Berinthia LEVINE
32 VP Student Affairs .... Dr. Ernest YARBROUGH
20 Vice Provost for Academic Planning .... Dr. Teresa LAGRANGE
26 Assoc VP University Mktg .... Mr. Robert SPADEMAN
15 Asst VP Human Resources .... Mr. Jesse DRUCKER
88 Assoc VP Student Affairs .... Ms. Clare RAHM
21 Controller/Asst VP Finance .... Ms. Kathleen MURPHY
49 Dean Col Liberal Arts/Soc Sci .... Dr. Gregory M. SADLEK
81 Dean College of Science .... Dr. Meredith R. BOND
50 Dean College of Business .... Dr. Richard REED
53 Dean College Education & Human Svcs ...... Dr. Sajit ZACHARIAH
54 Dean Fenn College of Engineering .... Dr. Anette KARLSSON
58 Dean College Graduate Studies .... Dr. Donna SCHULTHEISS
61 Int Dean of College of Law .... Mr. Lee FISHER
80 Dean College Urban Affairs .... Dr. Roland ANGLIN
92 Dean Honors College .... Dr. Elizabeth LEHFELDT
43 General Counsel .... Ms. Sonali B. WILSON
101 Sr Advisor to Pres/Sec Bd Trustees .... Dr. William NAPIER
08 Director of Libraries .... Dr. Glenda THORNTON
22 Dir Office of Institutional Equity .... Ms. Yulanda MCCARTY-HARRIS
07 Director Undergraduate Admissions .... Ms. Lee FURBECK
09 Director Institutional Research .... Mr. Tom GEAGHAN
85 Director International Programs .... Mr. Harlan SMITH
36 Director Talent Development Career ... Ms. Mitzi VAZQUEZ-LONG

38 Director Counseling Center ... Dr. Katharine HAHN
19 Assoc VP Administration/Operations ... Dr. Joseph HAN
37 Director Student Financial Aid ... Ms. Rachel SCHMIDT
06 Asst Vice President/Registrar ... Ms. Janet STIMPLE
41 Director of Athletics ... Mr. John PARRY
29 Director Alumni Affairs ... Mr. Brian BREITHOLZ
18 Director Facilities Management ... Mr. Shehadeh ABDELKARIM
96 Director of Purchasing ... Ms. Laurie MCCOMBS
92 Director Honors Program ... Dr. Peter MEIKSINS
04 Administrative Asst to President ... Ms. Shane CONNOR
13 Chief Info Technology Officer (CIO) ... Mr. William WILSON

The College of Wooster (A)

1189 Beall Avenue, Wooster OH 44691-2363
County: Wayne FICE Identification: 003037
Unit ID: 206589
Telephone: (330) 263-2000 Carnegie Class: Bac-A&S
FAX Number: (330) 263-2427 Calendar System: Semester
URL: www.wooster.edu
Established: 1866 Annual Undergrad Tuition & Fees: $44,950
Enrollment: 2,049 Coed
Affiliation or Control: Independent Non-Profit IRS Status: 501(c)3
Highest Offering: Baccalaureate
Accreditation: NH, MUS, TED

01 President ... Dr. Sarah BOLTON
05 Provost ... Dr. Carolyn NEWTON
10 Vice Pres Finance/Bus/Treasurer ... Ms. Dee MCCORMICK
30 Vice President for Development ... Ms. Laurie HOUCK
84 Vice Pres Enrollment/College Rels ... Dr. Scott FRIEDHOFF
32 VP Stdnt Affairs/Dean of Students ... Mr. Scott C. BROWN
04 Administrative Asst to President ... Mrs. Lynette ARNER
26 Assoc VP College Rels & Marketing ... Mr. John HOPKINS
109 Assoc VP Facilities & Auxiliaries ... Ms. Jacqueline MIDDLETON
15 Assoc VP of Human Resources ... Ms. Marcia BEASLEY
20 Dean Curriculum/Academic Engagement ... Dr. Henry B. KREUZMAN
20 Dean for Faculty Development ... Dr. Heather M. FITZGIBBON
07 Dean of Admissions ... Ms. Jennifer D. WINGE
35 Assoc Dean of Students ... Ms. Robyn LADITKA
85 Dir Office of Intl Student Affairs ... Mr. Yorgun MARCEL
09 Chief Information Planning Officer ... Dr. Ellen FALDUTO
06 Registrar ... Ms. Suzanne BATES
08 Director of Libraries ... Mr. Mark A. CHRISTEL
37 Director of Financial Aid ... Mr. Joseph WINGE
27 Director Office Public Information ... Mr. John FINN
29 Dir of Alumni Rels & Wooster Fund ... Ms. Heidi A. MCCORMICK
36 Director Career Services ... Ms. Lisa KASTOR
41 Dir Phys Educ/Athletics/Recreat ... Dr. Keith BECKETT
18 Director Physical Plant Operations ... Mr. Doug LADITKA
19 Director Security/Protective Svcs ... Mr. Steven GLICK
42 Camp Chaplain/Dir Intfth Camp Mins ... Rev. Linda MORGAN-CLEMENT
101 Secretary of College/Chief Staff ... Ms. Angela JOHNSTON

Columbus College of Art & Design (B)

60 Cleveland Avenue, Columbus OH 43215-1758
County: Franklin FICE Identification: 003039
Unit ID: 202170
Telephone: (614) 224-9101 Carnegie Class: Spec-4-yr-Arts
FAX Number: (614) 222-4040 Calendar System: Semester
URL: www.ccad.edu
Established: 1879 Annual Undergrad Tuition & Fees: $32,710
Enrollment: 1,288 Coed
Affiliation or Control: Independent Non-Profit IRS Status: 501(c)3
Highest Offering: Master's
Accreditation: NH, ART

01 President ... Dr. Melanie CORN
04 Exec Assistant to the President ... Ms. Sheri LUCAS
05 Provost ... Mr. Kevin J. CONLON
10 Senior Vice President/CFO ... Mr. Jeffrey A. FISHER
30 Vice President for Advancement ... Ms. Lindsey DUNLEAVY
26 Assoc VP Communications & Marketing ... Vacant
07 Assoc VP for Enrollment Operations ... Mr. Densil R. PORTEOUS
32 Int VP Student Affairs/Dn Students ... Mr. Chris MUNDELL
60 Dean School of Design Arts ... Mr. Tom GATTIS
57 Dean School of Studio Arts ... Ms. Julie TAGGART
58 Director Graduate Studies ... Mr. Ric PETRY
06 Registrar ... Ms. Michele KIBLER
13 Chief Information Officer ... Mr. Jeffrey BROTHERTON
15 Director of Human Resources ... Ms. Barbara DAVIS
08 Director of Library Services ... Ms. Leslie JANKOWSKI NIEMCZURA
19 Director of Safety & Security ... Mr. Wallace TANKSLEY
18 Director of Facilities ... Mr. Joseph SPYBEY
38 Director of Counseling & Wellness ... Ms. Erin VLACH
37 Director Student Financial Aid ... Ms. Anna M. SCHOFIELD
36 Director Career Resources ... Ms. Tiffany SPERRING
21 Controller ... Mr. Roger ESCOLAS
35 Dir of Student Involvement ... Ms. Heather BRAY
51 Dir Continuing/Professional Study ... Ms. Dorothy KEIL
39 Director of Residence Life ... Mr. Mickey HART
88 Director of Special Projects ... Mr. Dave STOCKWELL
40 Supply Store Manager ... Mr. Danny HINTY

Columbus State Community College (C)

Box 1609, Columbus OH 43216-1609
County: Franklin FICE Identification: 006867
Unit ID: 202222
Telephone: (614) 287-5353 Carnegie Class: Assoc/MT-VT-High Non
FAX Number: (614) 287-5113 Calendar System: Semester
URL: www.cscc.edu
Established: 1963 Annual Undergrad Tuition & Fees (In-State): $3,808
Enrollment: 24,448 Coed
Affiliation or Control: State IRS Status: 501(c)3
Highest Offering: Associate Degree
Accreditation: NH, ACBSP, ACFEI, ADNUR, CAHIIM, CCARC, CONST, CSHSE, DH, DIETT, EMT, ENGT, MAC, MLTAD, PHLEB, RAD, SURGT

01 President ... Dr. David T. HARRISON
05 Senior Vice Pres Academic Affairs ... Dr. John COOLEY
10 VP Business Svcs/CFO/Treasurer ... Ms. Aletha SHIPLEY
26 Vice Pres Marketing/Communications ... Mr. Allen KRAUS
13 Vice Pres Information Technology ... Vacant
43 Vice President and General Counsel ... Ms. Kimberly HALL
32 Vice Pres Student Svcs/Enroll Mgmt ... Vacant
84 Dean of Enrollment Services ... Dr. Martin MALIWESKY
12 Dean of Delaware Campus ... Dr. Stacia EDWARDS
49 Dean of Arts & Sciences ... Dr. Allysen TODD
76 Dean Health and Human Services ... Dr. Thomas HABEGGER
50 Dean Business & Engineering Tech ... Mr. Angelo FROLE
35 Dean Student Life ... Ms. Renee HILL
102 Executive Director Foundation ... Ms. Pamela BISHOP
91 Director IT Budget/Planning ... Mr. Etienne MARTIN
21 Director Business/College Services ... Ms. Aletha SHIPLEY
06 Director of Records & Registration ... Dr. Regina RANDALL
37 Director Financial Aid ... Mr. David METZ
19 Chief of Police ... Chief Sean ASBURY
18 Director of Facilities Management ... Mr. Mark FRENCH
28 Dir of Global Diversity/Inclusion ... Mr. Brett WELSH
09 Dir Institutional Effectiveness ... Ms. Jennifer ANDERSON
08 Director Library ... Mr. Bruce MASSIS
07 Director of Admissions ... Ms. Gina GILES-HISER
40 Director of Operations/Bookstore ... Ms. Stacy MULINEX
96 Director Procurement/College Svcs ... Mr. Bradley FARMER
14 Chief Technology Officer ... Mr. James BEIDLER

Columbus State Community College-Delaware (D)

5100 Cornerstone Drive, Delaware OH 43015
Telephone: (740) 203-8000 Identification: 770353
Accreditation: &NH

† Regional accreditation is carried under the parent institution in Columbus, OH

Cuyahoga Community College (E)

700 Carnegie Avenue, Cleveland OH 44115-2878
County: Cuyahoga FICE Identification: 003040
Unit ID: 202356
Telephone: (216) 987-4000 Carnegie Class: Assoc/HT-High Non
FAX Number: (216) 566-5977 Calendar System: Semester
URL: www.tri-c.edu
Established: 1963 Annual Undergrad Tuition & Fees (In-District): $3,136
Enrollment: 27,084 Coed
Affiliation or Control: State/Local IRS Status: 501(c)3
Highest Offering: Associate Degree
Accreditation: NH, ACFEI, ADNUR, ARCPA, CAHIIM, COARC, DH, DIETT, DMS, EMT, ENGT, MAC, MLTAD, NDT, NMT, OTA, POLYT, PTAA, RAD, SURGT

01 President ... Dr. Alex JOHNSON
05 Provost/Chief Academic Officer ... Dr. Craig FOLTIN
10 Exec Vice Pres Admin & Finance/CFO ... Mr. David KUNTZ
103 Exec Vice Pres Workforce & Econ Dev ... Mr. William GARY
12 Campus President/VP East Campus ... Dr. J. Michael THOMSON
12 Corporate College President ... Mr. Robert PETERSON
12 Campus President/VP Metro Campus ... Dr. Michael SCHOOP
12 Campus President/VP WestshoreCampus ... Dr. Terri POPE
12 Campus Pres West Campus ... Dr. Donna IMHOFF
21 Vice Pres Finance & Business Svcs ... Mr. Mike ABOUSERHAL
15 Vice Pres/Chief Human Res Officer ... Ms. Judith MCMULLEN
30 Vice Pres Development/Foundation ... Ms. Megan O'BRYAB
27 Vice Pres/Chief Information Officer ... Mr. Gerard HOURIGAN
09 Vice Pres Evidence & Inquiry ... Vacant
86 Vice Pres Govt Affair/Comm Outreach ... Ms. Claire ROSACCO
84 Vice President Access & Completion ... Dr. Karen MILLER
26 Vice Pres Integrated Communications ... Mr. David HOOVLER
43 Vice Pres Legal Svcs/Gen Counsel ... Ms. Renee RICHARD
20 Vice Pres Learning & Engagement ... Ms. Lisa WILLIAMS
17 VP Health Care Educ Initiatives ... Ms. Patricia REID
19 Vice Pres Public Safety & Security ... Chief Clayton HARRIS
18 Vice President Ops & Mfg ... Ms. Alicia BOOKER
32 Assoc VP Access & Comm Engagement ... Dr. JaNice MARSHALL
88 Exec Dir Access Learning & Success ... Ms. Sandra MCKNIGHT
88 Exec Dir Business Continuity ... Mr. Marvin RICHARDS
88 Exec Director Media Engineering ... Mr. Robert BRYAN
13 Exec Director EIS ... Mr. Jon DOLINAR
07 Executive Director Enrollment Opers ... Ms. Angela JOHNSON
88 Exec Director Plant Operations ... Mr. Blair BOSWORTH
88 Exec Dir Veteran Services/Programs ... Mr. Richard DE CHANT
88 Exec Dir College Svcs & Retail ... Mr. Chris MOIR
88 Exec Dir College Pathway Programs ... Mr. Kenneth HALE
96 Executive Dir Supplier Managed Svcs ... Ms. Cynthia LEITSON
88 Exec Dir/GM Hospitality Mgmt ... Mr. Brandt EVANS
88 Exec Dir Organizational Development ... Mr. Barry ROYKO
20 Dean Learning & Engagement East ... Dr. John W. MARR, JR.
20 Dean Learning & Engagement West ... Dr. Janice TAYLOR HEARD
20 Dean Learning & Engagement Metro ... Mr. Lindsay ENGLISH
20 Dean Lrng & Engagement Westshore ... Mr. Robert SEARSON
35 Dean Access & Completion Metro ... Ms. Denise MCCORY
35 Dean Access & Completion West ... Ms. Diana DEL ROSARIO
35 Dean Access & Completion East ... Dr. Mel A. MAY
35 Dean Access & Completion Westshore ... Dr. Ann PROUDFIT
66 Dean Nursing ... Dr. Vivian M. YATES
79 Dean for Humanities ... Dr. Lauren ONKEY
88 Assoc Dean Creative Arts Metro ... Ms. Amy PARKS
76 Assoc Dean Health Careers & Science ... Ms. Barbara MIKUSZEWSKI
76 Assoc Dean Health Careers & Science ... Ms. Lisa DIONISI
81 Interim Assoc Dean Math West ... Mr. Paul ROKICKY
83 Assoc Dean Social Sciences West ... Vacant
49 Assoc Dean Liberal Arts East ... Dr. William CUNION
49 Assoc Dean Liberal Arts Metro ... Dr. Jocelyn LADNER-MATHIS
49 Assoc Dean Liberal Arts West ... Ms. Delia BOBER
50 Assoc Dean Bus/Math & Tech Metro ... Dr. Pamela ELLISON
50 Assoc Dean Bus/Math & Tech East ... Dr. Lorraine HARTLEY
72 Assoc Dean Bus IT Applied Tech West ... Mr. Scott HALM
54 Assoc Dean Engineering Metro ... Mr. Lam WONG
88 Interim Assoc Dean Hospitality Mgmt ... Dr. John MARR
76 Assoc Dean Health Careers West ... Mr. David FRAZEE
66 Assoc Dean Nursing Metro ... Ms. Irene MEYER
100 Chief of Staff/Exec Asst to Pres ... Ms. Ronna MCNAIR
23 Dir Healthcare Industry Solutions ... Dr. John SCHMIDT
28 Director of Diversity & Inclusion ... Dr. Deborale RICHARDSON-PHILLIPS
37 District Dir Student Financial Aid ... Ms. Kimberly NASH-YORE
29 Director Alumni Relations ... Mr. John NOLAN
105 Director Info Technology Svcs ... Mr. Dana WALTERS
108 Director Institutional Research ... Mr. G. Rob STUART
38 Assistant Dean Counseling-Metro ... Mrs. Ralonda ELLIS-HILL
38 Assistant Dean Counseling-East ... Ms. Johanna BACIK
38 Assistant Dean Counseling-West ... Mr. Marcos RIVERA
04 Admin Associate to President ... Ms. Barbara BELL
102 Exec Dir Foundation/Corporate Rel ... Ms. Kate MCDADE
41 Athletic Director West ... Mr. Mark RODRIGUEZ
41 Athletic Director East ... Ms. Rita MCKINLEY
41 Athletic Director Metro ... Ms. Jennifer ELLIS

Cuyahoga Community College Eastern Campus (F)

4250 Richmond Road, Highland Hills OH 44122
Telephone: (800) 954-8742 Identification: 770355
Accreditation: &NH

† Regional accreditation is carried under the parent institution in Cleveland, OH

Cuyahoga Community College Metropolitan Campus (G)

2900 Community College Avenue, Cleveland OH 44115
Telephone: (800) 954-8742 Identification: 770354
Accreditation: &NH, PHLEB

† Regional accreditation is carried under the parent institution in Cleveland, OH

Cuyahoga Community College Western Campus (H)

11000 Pleasant Valley Road, Parma OH 44130
Telephone: (800) 954-8742 Identification: 770356
Accreditation: &NH

† Regional accreditation is carried under the parent institution in Cleveland, OH

Cuyahoga Community College Westshore (I)

31001 Clemens Road, Westlake OH 44145
Telephone: (800) 954-8742 Identification: 770357
Accreditation: &NH

† Regional accreditation is carried under the parent institution in Cleveland, OH

Davis College (J)

4747 Monroe Street, Toledo OH 43623-4389
County: Lucas FICE Identification: 004855
Unit ID: 202435
Telephone: (419) 473-2700 Carnegie Class: Assoc/HVT-High Non
FAX Number: (419) 473-2472 Calendar System: Quarter
URL: www.daviscollege.edu
Established: 1858 Annual Undergrad Tuition & Fees: $14,130
Enrollment: 170 Coed
Affiliation or Control: Proprietary IRS Status: Proprietary
Highest Offering: Associate Degree
Accreditation: NH, MAC

01 President ... Diane BRUNNER
32 VP of Student & Academic Services ... Mary RYAN BULONE
06 Registrar ... Terry DIPPMAN
37 Director Student Financial Aid ... Marilyn BOVIA
07 Director of Admissions ... Timothy BRUNNER
36 Director of Student Placement ... Nick NIGRO
04 Assistant to the President ... Jane MULLIKIN
30 VP of Institutional Advancement ... Tim BRUNNER
18 Chief Facilities/Physical Plant ... Greg RIPPKE
08 Librarian ... Peggy PETERSON-SENIUK
13 Director of Information Technology ... Brian FROST
108 Director Institutional Assessment ... Vacant

50 Program Director Business & IT ..... Mary DELOE
57 Program Director Design ..... Janet WEBER
97 Program Director General Education ..... Jane PFEIFER
76 Prog Director Admin & Allied Health ..... Terry DIPPMAN

The Defiance College (A)

701 N Clinton Street, Defiance OH 43512-1695
County: Defiance FICE Identification: 003041
Unit ID: 202514
Telephone: (419) 784-4010 Carnegie Class: Bac-Diverse
FAX Number: (419) 784-4101 Calendar System: Semester
URL: www.defiance.edu
Established: 1850 Annual Undergrad Tuition & Fees: $31,082
Enrollment: 920 Coed
Affiliation or Control: United Church Of Christ IRS Status: 501(c)3
Highest Offering: Master's
Accreditation: NH, #CAATE, IACBE, NURSE, SW, TED

01 President ..... Dr. Richanne C. MANKEY
05 Interim VP for Academic Affairs ..... Dr. Timothy RICKABAUGH
10 Vice Pres for Finance & Management ..... Mrs. Lois N. MCCULLOUGH
84 VP Enrollment Mgmt/Dean of Stdnts ..... Mrs. Lisa MARSALEK
88 Dean McMaster Sch Adv Hum ..... Mrs. Mary Ann STUDER
07 Director of Admissions & Fin Aid ..... Mr. Brad HARSHA
15 Director of Human Resources ..... Mrs. Mary E. BURKHOLDER
08 Dir of Library and Instr Resource ..... Mrs. Michelle BLANK
26 Director Public Relations/Marketing ..... Mrs. Kathy M. PUNCHES
13 Director of Computer Services ..... Mr. Jeremy KENNEDY
06 Registrar ..... Mrs. Mariah ORZOLEK
37 Director of Financial Aid ..... Mrs. Amy FRANCIS
41 Athletic Director ..... Mr. Rudy YOVICH
28 Director Intercultural Relations ..... Ms. Mercedes CLAY
39 Director of Residence Life ..... Ms. Jennifer WALTON
18 Director of Physical Plant ..... Mr. James CORESSEL
21 Director of Accounting ..... Mrs. Kristine BOLAND
04 Administrative Asst to President ..... Mrs. Judy LYMANSTALL
103 Dir Workforce/Career Development ..... Ms. Sally BISSELL
50 Dean of Business ..... Dr. Patricia GALDEEN
53 Dean of Education ..... Dr. Carla HIGGINS

Denison University (B)

100 W College Street, Granville OH 43023-1359
County: Licking FICE Identification: 003042
Unit ID: 202523
Telephone: (740) 587-0810 Carnegie Class: Bac-A&S
FAX Number: (740) 587-6417 Calendar System: Semester
URL: www.denison.edu
Established: 1831 Annual Undergrad Tuition & Fees: $47,290
Enrollment: 2,278 Coed
Affiliation or Control: Independent Non-Profit IRS Status: 501(c)3
Highest Offering: Baccalaureate
Accreditation: NH, #CAATE

01 President ..... Dr. Adam S. WEINBERG
05 Provost ..... Dr. Kimberly A. COPLIN
20 Associate Provost Faculty Affairs ..... Dr. Catherine L. DOLLARD
20 Associate Provost Academic Admin ..... Dr. James R. PLETCHER
28 Associate Provost Diversity ..... Dr. Alison P. WILLIAMS
10 VP Finance & Management ..... Mr. David A. ENGLISH
30 VP Institutional Advancement ..... Ms. Julia BEYER HOUPT
32 VP Student Development ..... Dr. Laurel B. KENNEDY
84 VP Enrollment Management ..... Mr. Gregory W. SNEED
07 Director of Admissions ..... Mr. Michael S. HILLS
89 Dean of First-Year Students ..... Dr. Mark MOLLER
35 Dean of Students ..... Mr. William A. FOX
06 Registrar ..... Ms. Yadigar COLLINS
08 Director of Libraries ..... Ms. BethAnn ZAMBELLA
37 Dir of Financial Aid & Student Empl ..... Ms. Laura E. MEEK
13 Dir Information Technology Services ..... Ms. Dena L. SPERANZA
15 Director of Human Resources ..... Mr. Jim ABLES
18 Director of Facilities Services ..... Mr. Arthur J. CHONKO
19 Director of Campus Safety ..... Mr. Daniel HECT
26 Dir of Univ Communications ..... Mr. Jack HIRE
88 Dir of Strategic Communications ..... Ms. Barbara STAMBAUGH
29 Interim Dir of Alumni Relations ..... Ms. Mary FRAZELL
36 Dir Career Exploration & Dev ..... Mr. Richard T. BERMAN
38 Dir of Health & Counseling Svc ..... Ms. Amanda L. LEFELD
42 Chaplain/Director of Religious Life ..... Vacant
100 Special Asst to Pres/Chief of Staff ..... Dr. Joyce MEREDITH
93 Dir Multicultural Stdnt Affs/Ast Dn ..... Mr. Erik S. FARLEY
11 Director of Administrative Services ..... Ms. Jenna MCDEVITT
09 Director of Institutional Research ..... Dr. Todd M. JAMISON
41 Director of Athletics ..... Ms. Nan CARNEY-DEBORD
88 Chief Investment Officer ..... Ms. Adele N. GORRILLA
04 Sr Executive Asst to President ..... Ms. Trish RUESS
102 Dir Foundation/Corporate Relations ..... Vacant
104 Director Study Abroad ..... Dr. Sue F. DAVIS
39 Director Student Housing ..... Ms. Kristan R. HAUSMAN
44 Assoc VP Inst Advancement ..... Mr. Greg R. BADER
22 Dir Affirmative Action/EEO ..... Ms. Barbara A. LAY

DeVry University - Columbus Campus (C)

1350 Alum Creek Drive, Columbus OH 43209-2705
Telephone: (614) 253-1525 FICE Identification: 003099
Accreditation: &NH, ENGT

† Regional accreditation is carried under the parent institution in Downers Grove, IL.

Eastern Gateway Community College - Jefferson County Campus (D)

4000 Sunset Boulevard, Steubenville OH 43952-3594
County: Jefferson FICE Identification: 007275
Unit ID: 203331
Telephone: (740) 264-5591 Carnegie Class: Assoc/MT-VT-Mix Trad/Non
FAX Number: (740) 264-1338 Calendar System: Semester
URL: www.egcc.edu
Established: 1966 Annual Undergrad Tuition & Fees (In-District): $3,405
Enrollment: 3,182 Coed
Affiliation or Control: State/Local IRS Status: 501(c)3
Highest Offering: Associate Degree
Accreditation: NH, CAHIIM, COARC, DA, EMT, MAC, MLTAD, RAD

01 President ..... Dr. Jimmie D. BRUCE
05 Int Vice Pres Academic Affairs ..... Dr. Ken KNOX
10 Vice Pres Business Services ..... Mr. James J. MCGRAIL, III
11 Vice Pres Administrative Services ..... Ms. Sherri VAN TASSEL
32 Int Vice Pres Student Affairs ..... Ms. Christina WANAT
46 Vice Pres Strategic Initiatives ..... Vacant
84 Dean Enrollment Management ..... Ms. Patty J. STURCH
76 Dean Health & Biological Sciences ..... Dr. Robin FLOHR
81 Dean Student Learning/Humanities ..... Ms. Christina WANAT
35 Dean TRIO/Student Svcs & Retention ..... Dr. Dorothy COLLINS
50 Dean Business/Engineering & Info ..... Mr. Jerry KLINESMITH
21 Controller ..... Ms. Joanna FLANIGAN
07 Dean of Admissions ..... Mr. Ryan OGRODNIK
26 Dir Public Information/Web Coord ..... Vacant
37 Exec Director Student/Financial Aid ..... Ms. Kelly WILSON
102 Exec Director EGCC Foundation ..... Dr. James BABER
103 Workforce/Community Outreach Coord ..... Mr. Jerry KLINESMITH
13 Int Director Technology Services ..... Mr. David SMITH
36 Director Career Services/Alumni ..... Vacant
40 Director of Bookstore ..... Mrs. Judith LUDE
21 Director Student Billing/Payroll ..... Ms. Tonya LOGAN
18 Director Building & Grounds ..... Mr. Julius J. DZIEWATKOSKI
08 Director of Library Services ..... Mrs. Lois T. REKOWSKI
06 Registrar ..... Ms. Patty J. STURCH
29 Director of Alumni Relations ..... Vacant

Edison State Community College (E)

1973 Edison Drive, Piqua OH 45356-9239
County: Miami FICE Identification: 012750
Unit ID: 202648
Telephone: (937) 778-8600 Carnegie Class: Assoc/MT-VT-Mix Trad/Non
FAX Number: (937) 778-1920 Calendar System: Semester
URL: www.edisonohio.edu
Established: 1973 Annual Undergrad Tuition & Fees (In-State): $4,219
Enrollment: 3,042 Coed
Affiliation or Control: State IRS Status: 501(c)3
Highest Offering: Associate Degree
Accreditation: NH, ADNUR, MAC, MLTAD, PHLEB, PTAA

01 President ..... Dr. Doreen LARSON
04 Executive Asst to the President ..... Ms. Heather LANHAM
05 Provost ..... Mr. Chris SPRADLIN
10 VP of Administration & Finance ..... Mr. John W. SHISHOFF
30 VP for Institutional Advancement ..... Ms. Kimberly HORTON
32 Vice President of Student Affairs ..... Mr. Scott M. BURNAM
31 VP Business/Cmty Partnerships ..... Mr. Rick HANES
13 Chief Information Officer ..... Mr. Harry LAWHORN
15 Exec Director Human Resources ..... Mrs. Linda M. PELTIER
35 Director of Student Services ..... Mr. Nathan COLE
49 Dean of Arts and Science ..... Ms. Naomi LOUIS
50 Dean of Business/IT & Engineering ..... Ms. Shirley MOORE
66 Dean of Nursing & Health Sciences ..... Ms. Gwendolyn A. STEVENSON
09 Dean Inst Planning/Effectiveness ..... Ms. Mona WALTERS
88 Director of Student Success ..... Ms. Pamela GIBELLINO
21 Controller ..... Mr. James LEHMKKUHL
41 Director Athletics ..... Mr. Nathan COLE
37 Director of Financial Aid ..... Ms. Kathi S. RICHARDS
26 Dir of Marketing & Communications ..... Mr. Bruce MCKENZIE
84 Enrollment Manager ..... Ms. Stacey BEAN
06 Registrar ..... Ms. Mary BORNHORST
08 Director of Library/Learning Center ..... Ms. Lisa HOOPS
18 Dir of Physical Plant/Facilities ..... Mr. Douglas RIEHLE

Edison State Community College Darke County Campus (F)

601 Wagner Avenue, Greenville OH 45331
Telephone: (937) 548-5546 Identification: 770358
Accreditation: &NH

† Regional accreditation is carried under the parent institution in Piqua, OH

ETI Technical College of Niles (G)

2076-86 Youngstown-Warren Road, Niles OH 44446-4398
County: Trumbull FICE Identification: 030790
Unit ID: 200590
Telephone: (330) 652-9919 Carnegie Class: Assoc/HVT-High Non
FAX Number: (330) 652-4399 Calendar System: Semester
URL: www.eticollege.edu
Established: 1989 Annual Undergrad Tuition & Fees: $10,032
Enrollment: 152 Coed
Affiliation or Control: Proprietary IRS Status: Proprietary
Highest Offering: Associate Degree
Accreditation: ACCSC

01 Director ..... Mrs. Renee ZUZOLO
07 Director of Admissions ..... Mrs. Diane MARSTELLER
37 Director Financial Aid ..... Ms. Kay MADIGAN

Fortis College (H)

555 E Alex-Bell Road, Centerville OH 45459-6120
County: Montgomery FICE Identification: 021907
Unit ID: 205179
Telephone: (937) 433-3410 Carnegie Class: Bac/Assoc-Assoc Dom
FAX Number: (937) 435-6516 Calendar System: Semester
URL: www.fortiscollege.edu
Established: 1970 Annual Undergrad Tuition & Fees: $18,122
Enrollment: 1,645 Coed
Affiliation or Control: Proprietary IRS Status: Proprietary
Highest Offering: Baccalaureate
Accreditation: ACCSC, ADNUR, MAC, NURSE

01 President ..... Richard MALLOW
05 VP/Chief Academic Officer ..... Diana LAWRENCE
09 Dir Inst Effectiveness/Compliance ..... LaRee PINGATORE
20 Director Education ..... Diana LAWRENCE
07 Director Admissions ..... Mike MONTGOMERY
37 Director Financial Aid ..... Rachel KARMON

Fortis College (I)

2545 Bailey Road, Cuyahoga Falls OH 44221-2949
County: Summit FICE Identification: 009412
Unit ID: 204307
Telephone: (330) 923-9959 Carnegie Class: Spec 2-yr-Health
FAX Number: (330) 923-0886 Calendar System: Other
URL: www.fortis.edu
Established: 1922 Annual Undergrad Tuition & Fees: N/A
Enrollment: 526 Coed
Affiliation or Control: Proprietary IRS Status: Proprietary
Highest Offering: Associate Degree
Accreditation: ACCSC, DA

01 President ..... Ms. Carson BURKE

Fortis College (J)

653 Enterprise Parkway, Ravenna OH 44266-8058
Telephone: (330) 297-7319 FICE Identification: 023036
Accreditation: ACICS, CAHIIM

† Branch campus of Fortis College, Norfolk, VA

Fortis College (K)

4151 Executive Parkway, Suite 120, Westerville OH 43081-3860
County: Franklin Identification: 666602
Unit ID: 450058
Telephone: (614) 882-2551 Carnegie Class: Spec 2-yr-Health
FAX Number: (614) 882-2914 Calendar System: Other
URL: www.fortis.edu
Established: 2010 Annual Undergrad Tuition & Fees: $14,477
Enrollment: 694 Coed
Affiliation or Control: Proprietary IRS Status: Proprietary
Highest Offering: Associate Degree
Accreditation: ABHES, RAD, SURGT, SURTEC

01 President ..... Mr. Peter MARTINELLO

Franciscan University of Steubenville (L)

1235 University Boulevard, Steubenville OH 43952-1763
County: Jefferson FICE Identification: 003036
Unit ID: 205957
Telephone: (740) 283-3771 Carnegie Class: Masters/M
FAX Number: (740) 283-6472 Calendar System: Semester
URL: www.franciscan.edu
Established: 1946 Annual Undergrad Tuition & Fees: $24,780
Enrollment: 2,714 Coed
Affiliation or Control: Roman Catholic IRS Status: 501(c)3
Highest Offering: Master's
Accreditation: NH, CACREP, NUR, SW, TED

01 President ..... Rev. Sean SHERIDAN, TOR
88 Vice Pres of Pastoral Care & Evange ..... Rev. Nathan MALAVOLTI, TOR
10 VP of Finance & Admin Operations ..... Mr. David M. SKIVIAT
05 Vice President of Academic Affairs ..... Dr. Daniel KEMPTON
30 Vice President of Advancement ..... Mr. Michael HERNON
31 Vice Pres of Community Relations ..... Vacant
46 Vice Pres for Mission Effectiveness ..... Vacant
15 Vice Pres of Human Resources ..... Mr. Brenan PERGI
32 Vice President of Student Life ..... Mr. David A. SCHMIESING
84 Vice Pres of Enrollment Management ..... Mr. Joel S. RECZNIK
88 Religious Administrator ..... Rev. John SHANAHAN, TOR
42 University Chaplain ..... Rev. Shawn ROBERSON, TOR
20 Dir of Advising & Acad Operations ..... Ms. Ann DULANY
13 Exec Dir of Information Technology ..... Mr. Kevin G. SEBOLT
35 Asst Vice Pres of Student Life ..... Ms. Catherine J. HECK
08 Director of Library ..... Mr. William JAKUB
88 Exec Director Christian Outreach ..... Mr. Mark JOSEPH

44 Director of Planned Giving ... Dr. Mark E. RECZNIK
30 Director of Development ... Mr. Mark NEHRBAS
29 Director of Alumni Relations ... Mr. Timothy J. DELANEY
26 Director of Public Relations ... Miss Lisa M. FERGUSON
07 Director of Admissions ... Mrs. Margaret WEBER
07 Director of Graduate Enrollment ... Mr. Mark T. MCGUIRE
06 Registrar ... Mr. Cody SCHMITZ
84 Exec Dir of Enrollment Services ... Mr. John L. HERRMANN
09 Director of Institutional Research ... Dcn. Mark A. ERSTE, SR.
21 Controller ... Mr. John A. STEITZ
96 Director of Business Services ... Ms. Marlene K. TERPENNING
40 Bookstore Manager ... Mr. John RECZNIK
91 Director of Administrative Systems ... Mrs. Pam SHANE
16 Director of Human Resources ... Vacant
18 Director Physical Plant Services ... Mr. Joseph P. MCGURN
88 Director of Missionary Outreach ... Mr. Rhett YOUNG
88 Director of Chapel Ministries ... Mr. Robert PALLADINO
88 Director of JCW Center/Planning ... Mrs. Kathy L. MATTIOLI
104 Director of Study Abroad ... Mr. Mark HANRAHAN
38 Director of Counseling ... Mr. Joseph A. LOIZZO
41 Director of Athletics ... Mr. Christopher L. LEDYARD
36 Director Career Planning/Placement ... Mrs. Nancy S. RONEVICH
73 Director MA Theology Program ... Dr. Michael SIRILLA
50 Director MBA Program ... Mr. Joseph ZORIC
83 Director MA Counseling Program ... Dr. Christin JUNGERS
53 Director MS Education Program ... Dr. Mark FURDA
88 Director MA Philosophy Program ... Dr. John CROSBY
90 Coord Academic Computer Services ... Ms. Sandy M. RADVANSKY
28 Director of Diversity ... Vacant
66 Director MS Nursing ... Dr. Carolyn MILLER
19 Director Security/Safety ... Mr. Michael CONN
106 Dir Online Education/E-learning ... Dr. Cory MALONEY
108 Director Institutional Assessment ... Vacant
04 Executive Asst to President ... Mr. Daniel MILES
37 Director Student Financial Aid ... Ms. Jody PEELER
45 Exec Dir Institutional Effectivenes ... Dr. James MELLO
26 Exec Dir Marketing & Communication ... Ms. Kimberly SPONSELLER

Franklin University (A)

201 S Grant Avenue, Columbus OH 43215-5399

County: Franklin — FICE Identification: 003046 — Unit ID: 202806
Telephone: (614) 797-4700 — Carnegie Class: Spec-4-yr-Bus
FAX Number: N/A — Calendar System: Trimester
URL: www.franklin.edu
Established: 1902 — Annual Undergrad Tuition & Fees: $11,641
Enrollment: 5,732 — Coed
Affiliation or Control: Independent Non-Profit — IRS Status: 501(c)3
Highest Offering: Doctorate
Accreditation: NH, IACBE, NURSE

01 President ... Dr. David R. DECKER
11 Sr VP Administration/Chief of Staff ... Ms. Christi L. CABUNGCAL
05 Provost/Sr VP for Academic Affairs ... Dr. Christopher L. WASHINGTON
07 VP Enrollment & Student Affairs ... Ms. Linda M. STEELE
30 Vice Pres University Advancement ... Ms. Bonnie SMITH QUIST
15 VP of Human Resources & Campus Svcs ... Ms. Christi CABUNGCAL
09 VP Accred/Institutional Effective ... Dr. Pamela SHAY
22 VP Planning & University Services ... Ms. Evelyn LEVINO
20 Associate Provost Academic Quality ... Dr. Karen MINER ROMANOFF
04 Executive Assistant to President ... Ms. Bonnie MCCANN
32 Dean of Students ... Dr. Lynne HULL
108 Dean/Exec Dir of AIE ... Vacant
10 Chief Financial Officer ... Mr. Marvin BRISKEY
13 Chief Information Officer ... Mr. Rick SUNDERMAN
20 Dir of Academic Support Services ... Ms. Susanne SMITH
06 Registrar ... Mr. Frank YANCHAK
08 Director of Library Services ... Ms. Alyssa DARDEN
37 Director of Financial Aid ... Ms. Goldie LANGLEY
46 Director of Strategic Relations ... Ms. Jody NOREEN
35 Dir Student Development ... Ms. Wendi ROBINSON
88 VP Franklin Learning Systems ... Mr. Patrick BENNETT
84 Exec Director of Marketing & Enroll ... Vacant
12 Exec Dir Domestic Expan/Reg Cmps ... Mr. Bill CHAN
18 Director of Facilities ... Mr. Carl BROWN
26 Director of Public Relations ... Ms. Sherry MERCURIO
29 Director of Alumni Engagement & Dev ... Mr. Kevin GREENWOOD
96 Director of Purchasing ... Mr. Bob DONAHUE
28 Director of Benefits ... Ms. Brenda LISTON
24 Director of Student Learning Center ... Vacant
88 Director of Teaching Effectiveness ... Dr. Fawn WINTERWOOD
49 Dean Arts/Science & Technology ... Dr. Keith GROFF
50 Dean College of Business ... Dr. Tom SEILER
69 Dean College of Health & Public Adm ... Dr. Leslie KING
88 Dean Global Programs ... Dr. Godfrey MENDES
16 Director of Human Resources ... Ms. Randi QUINN
88 Director of Accounting ... Mr. Jeffrey GERBERRY
88 Exec Dir of Financial Services ... Mr. Randolph SNYDER

Galen College of Nursing (B)

100 E Business Way, Suite 200, Cincinnati OH 45241
Telephone: (513) 475-3600 — Identification: 770537
Accreditation: &SC, ADNUR

† Regional accreditation is carried under the parent institution in Louisville, KY

Gallipolis Career College (C)

1176 Jackson Pike, Suite 312, Gallipolis OH 45631-2600

County: Gallia — FICE Identification: 030079 — Unit ID: 205513
Telephone: (740) 446-4367 — Carnegie Class: Assoc/MT-VT-Mix Trad/Non
FAX Number: (740) 446-4124 — Calendar System: Quarter
URL: www.gallipoliscareercollege.edu
Established: 1962 — Annual Undergrad Tuition & Fees: $12,050
Enrollment: 96 — Coed
Affiliation or Control: Proprietary — IRS Status: Proprietary
Highest Offering: Associate Degree
Accreditation: ACICS

01 President ... Mr. Robert L. SHIREY, JR.
05 Director of Education ... Mr. John T. DANICKI
07 Director of Admissions ... Mr. Jason BUSH
10 Director of Finance ... Mrs. Jeanette SHIREY
37 Director Student Financial Aid ... Ms. Christina SHOCKEY

God's Bible School and College (D)

1810 Young Street, Cincinnati OH 45202-6838

County: Hamilton — FICE Identification: 022205 — Unit ID: 202903
Telephone: (513) 721-7944 — Carnegie Class: Spec-4-yr-Faith
FAX Number: (513) 763-6649 — Calendar System: Semester
URL: www.gbs.edu
Established: 1900 — Annual Undergrad Tuition & Fees: $7,040
Enrollment: 310 — Coed
Affiliation or Control: Interdenominational — IRS Status: 501(c)3
Highest Offering: Master's
Accreditation: NH, BI

01 President ... Dr. Michael R. AVERY
05 Vice President Academic Affairs ... Dr. Aaron PROFITT
32 Vice President Student Development ... Mr. Richard MILES
30 Director Institutional Advancement ... Ms. Maria STETLER
06 Registrar ... Mr. Christopher LAMBETH
08 Head Librarian ... Mr. Joshua AVERY
10 Director of Finance ... Mr. David FREDERICK
11 Campus Administrator ... Mr. Richard MILES
26 Director of Public Relations ... Mr. Dor DAVISON
13 Dir of UX and Digital Strategies ... Mr. Jason WEED
07 Student Recruiter ... Mr. Kent STETLER
37 Financial Aid Coordinator ... Ms. Sharnee POUZAR
84 Director Enrollment Services ... Mr. Nathan DAHLER

Good Samaritan College of Nursing and Health Science (E)

375 Dixmyth Avenue, Cincinnati OH 45220-2489

County: Hamilton — FICE Identification: 006494 — Unit ID: 202912
Telephone: (513) 862-2743 — Carnegie Class: Spec-4-yr-Other Health
FAX Number: (513) 862-3572 — Calendar System: Semester
URL: www.gscollege.edu
Established: 2001 — Annual Undergrad Tuition & Fees: $15,054
Enrollment: 353 — Coed
Affiliation or Control: Independent Non-Profit — IRS Status: 501(c)3
Highest Offering: Baccalaureate
Accreditation: NH, ADNUR, NUR

01 President ... Mr. Morris COHEN
05 Dean of Academic Affairs ... Ms. Patricia MCMAHON
32 Dean of Students/Alumni ... Ms. Mary Jo KATHMAN
09 Dir of Inst Assessment/Planning ... Dr. Terri PULLEN
84 Dean of Enrollment Management ... Dr. Linda HAYES
13 IT Administrator ... Mr. Larry WEBER

Harrison College-Columbus Ohio Campus (F)

3880 Jackpot Road, Grove City OH 43123
Telephone: (614) 539-8800 — Identification: 770748
Accreditation: ACICS, MAC

† Branch campus of Harrison College - Indianapolis Downtown Campus, Indianapolis, IN

Heidelberg University (G)

310 E Market Street, Tiffin OH 44883-2462

County: Seneca — FICE Identification: 003048 — Unit ID: 203085
Telephone: (419) 448-2000 — Carnegie Class: Bac-A&S
FAX Number: (419) 448-2124 — Calendar System: Semester
URL: www.heidelberg.edu
Established: 1850 — Annual Undergrad Tuition & Fees: $28,500
Enrollment: 1,230 — Coed
Affiliation or Control: United Church Of Christ — IRS Status: 501(c)3
Highest Offering: Master's
Accreditation: NH, ACBSP, CAATE, CACREP, MUS, TED

01 President ... Dr. Robert HUNTINGTON
05 VP for Academic Affairs & Provost ... Dr. Beth SCHWARTZ
10 VP for Admin & Business Affairs ... Mr. Hoa NGUYEN
84 VP for Enrollment Mgmt ... Mr. Doug KELLAR
26 VP Univ Advancement & Marketing ... Vacant
20 Assoc VP Acad Affs/Dean Undergr Fac ... Dr. Vicki OHL
29 Exec Dir of Alumni Eng & Major Gift ... Ms. Ashley HELMSTETTER
13 Assoc VP for Information Resources ... Mr. Kurt HUENEMANN
18 Assoc VP for Facilities & Engrng ... Mr. Rodney MORRISON
50 Dean of the School of Business ... Dr. Haseeb AHMED
06 Registrar ... Ms. Cindy SUTER
88 Director MA in Counseling Pgm ... Dr. Jo-Ann SANDERS
53 Director of School of Education ... Dr. Karen JONES
64 Director of School of Music ... Dr. Carol DUSDIEKER
92 Assoc Dean for Honors Program ... Dr. Emily ISAACSON
104 Director Intl Affairs & Studies ... Ms. Julie ARNOLD
27 Dir of Marketing & Communications ... Ms. Audrey BURKHOLDER
36 Dir of Career Develop & Placemenet ... Mr. Mark MCKEE
58 Dir Graduate Studies in Business ... Mr. Allen UNDERWOOD
88 Dir of Graduation Support Services ... Dr. Ellen NAGY
08 Director of Library ... Dr. Nainsi HOUSTON
41 Athletic Director ... Mr. Matt PALM
21 Business Officer ... Ms. Barb GABEL
37 Director Student Financial Aid ... Mrs. Juli WEININGER
30 Exec Dir for Development ... Mr. James MINEHART
32 Dean of Student Affairs ... Mr. Dustin BRENTLINGER
39 Asst Dn Stdnt Affs for Campus Life ... Mr. Mark ZENO
88 Dir Student Engagement ... Ms. Jacqueline SIRONEN
15 Director of Human Resources ... Ms. Margaret RUDOLPH
21 Controller ... Ms. Kelly WARNKE
04 Exec Assistant to President ... Ms. Monica VERHOFF
40 Director of University Bookstore ... Ms. Gail ROBERTS
42 Director of Campus Ministry ... Rev. Paul STARK
19 Director Security/Safety ... Mr. Jeff RHOADES

Herzing University-Akron (H)

1600 S Arlington Street, Akron OH 44306-3958
Telephone: (330) 724-1600 — FICE Identification: 020695
Accreditation: &NH, ADNUR, DA, MAC, MLTAD

† Regional accreditation is carried under the parent institution in Madison, WI.

Herzing University Toledo Campus (I)

5212 Hill Avenue, Toledo OH 43615
Telephone: (419) 776-0030 — Identification: 770434
Accreditation: &NH, MAAB, SURTEC

† Regional accreditation is carried under the parent institution in Madison, WI

Hiram College (J)

Box 67, Hiram OH 44234-0067

County: Portage — FICE Identification: 003049 — Unit ID: 203128
Telephone: (330) 569-3211 — Carnegie Class: Bac-A&S
FAX Number: (330) 569-5494 — Calendar System: Other
URL: www.hiram.edu
Established: 1850 — Annual Undergrad Tuition & Fees: $31,530
Enrollment: 1,259 — Coed
Affiliation or Control: Independent Non-Profit — IRS Status: 501(c)3
Highest Offering: Master's
Accreditation: NH, MUS, NURSE, TED

01 President ... Dr. Lori E. VARLOTTA
05 Vice President & Dean of College ... Dr. Robert HAAK
10 Interim CFO ... Mr. Richard BARTREM
30 Chief Development Officer ... Ms. Jennifer SCHULLER
32 Vice President & Dean of Students ... Ms. Elizabeth M. OKUMA
07 VP of Enrollment ... Ms. Lindajean H. WESTERN
20 Associate Dean of the College ... Ms. Ellen L. WALKER
107 Director Professional/Grad Studies ... Ms. Jennifer L. MILLER
06 Registrar ... Ms. Lisa N. DELANEY
08 Head Librarian ... Mr. David D. EVERETT
29 Director Alumni Relations ... Mr. John B. COYNE
37 Interim Director Financial Services ... Ms. Linda SHIREY NELSON
36 Director of Career Services ... Ms. Heather M. BALAS
13 Director of Computer Center ... Mr. Frank J. VENTURA
09 Director of Institutional Research ... Ms. Maria A. O'CONNOR
41 Director of Athletics ... Ms. Ellen E. DEMPSEY
15 Director of Human Resources ... Ms. Lynn M. KOSTRAB
18 Director of the Physical Plant ... Vacant
21 Controller ... Vacant
35 Int Director of Campus Involvement ... Ms. Sarah DOWD
38 Director Student Counseling ... Dr. Kevin P. FEISTHAMEL
28 Director Ethnic Diversity Affairs ... Ms. Detra E. WEST
96 Director of Purchasing ... Ms. Martha A. SCHETTLER
26 Chief Public Affairs Officer ... Ms. Cristine D. BOYD
04 Executive Asst to President ... Mr. Phil J. EAVES
25 Dir Institutional Grants ... Ms. Jenna CARIGLIO-DORRIS
104 Study Away Coordinator ... Ms. Brittany JACKSON
19 Director Security/Safety ... Mr. Steve J. CHAPMAN
39 Director Student Housing ... Vacant
44 Exec Dir Annual Giving ... Ms. Aimee BELL

Hocking College (K)

3301 Hocking Parkway, Nelsonville OH 45764-9704

County: Athens — FICE Identification: 007598 — Unit ID: 203155
Telephone: (740) 753-3591 — Carnegie Class: Assoc/HVT-Mix Trad/Non
FAX Number: (740) 753-7005 — Calendar System: Semester
URL: www.hocking.edu
Established: 1968 — Annual Undergrad Tuition & Fees (In-State): $4,390
Enrollment: 3,474 — Coed
Affiliation or Control: State — IRS Status: 501(c)3
Highest Offering: Associate Degree

Accreditation: NH, ACBSP, ACFEI, ADNUR, CAHIIM, MAC, PNUR, PTAA

01 President ....Dr. Betty YOUNG
10 Vice President & Treasurer ....Ms. Gina FETTY
05 Provost/VP Acad & Student Affairs ....Dr. Myriah DAVIS
11 Vice Pres/COO/Assoc Chief Fin Ofcr .. Ms. Jacqueline HAGEROTT
15 AVP HR/Diversity/Campus Relations ....Mr. Jeffrey WHITE
20 Assoc VP Student Affairs ....Mr. Joe WAKEMAN
04 Executive Assistant to President ....Ms. Sheree CUNNINGHAM
66 Dean School Nursing/Allied Health ....Ms. Bonnie ALLEN-SMITH
13 Chief Technology Officer ....Mr. Ben DALTON
37 Exec Director Financial Aid ....Ms. Deneene MERCHANT
19 Commander Public Safety Services ....Dr. Penny PAYNE
08 Dir Learning Resource Ctr/Librarian ....Mr. Jeff GRAFFIUS
26 Exec Dir Marketing/Public Relations ....Vacant
19 Director Campus Safety ....Mr. Al MATTHEWS
06 Registrar ....Vacant
18 Director Building/Grounds ....Mr. Andrew FREEMAN
29 Dir Alumni Relations/Foundation ....Vacant
09 Director of Institutional Research ....Ms. Kensey LOVE
21 Controller/Assistant Treasurer ....Mrs. Anna JOHNSON
101 Development Coordinator Foundation ....Ms. Jestinah MCDONALD

Hocking College Perry Campus (A)

5454 State Route 37, New Lexington OH 43764
Telephone: (740) 342-3337 Identification: 770359
Accreditation: &NH

† Regional accreditation is carried under the parent institution in Nelsonville, OH

Hondros College (B)

1810 Successful Drive, Fairborn OH 45324
Telephone: (937) 879-1940 Identification: 770751
Accreditation: ACICS

Hondros College (C)

4100 Rockside Road, Second Floor,
Independence OH 44131
Telephone: (216) 524-1143 Identification: 770750
Accreditation: ACICS

Hondros College (D)

7600 Tyler's Place Boulevard, West Chester OH 45069
Telephone: (513) 508-3005 Identification: 770749
Accreditation: ACICS

Hondros College (E)

4140 Executive Parkway, Westerville OH 43081-3855
County: Franklin FICE Identification: 040743
Unit ID: 203386
Telephone: (614) 508-7277 Carnegie Class: Spec-4-yr-Other Health
FAX Number: (614) 508-7280 Calendar System: Quarter
URL: www.hondros.edu
Established: 1981 Annual Undergrad Tuition & Fees: $18,725
Enrollment: 1,924 Coed
Affiliation or Control: Proprietary IRS Status: Proprietary
Highest Offering: Baccalaureate
Accreditation: ACICS, NURSE

01 CEO ....Mr. Harry T. WILKINS
66 President Nursing Programs ....Ms. Carol THOMAS
07 Director of Admission ....Ms. Tenique DENNIS
06 Registrar ....Ms. Michelle HARDEN

International College of Broadcasting (F)

6 S Smithville Road, Dayton OH 45431-1898
County: Montgomery FICE Identification: 013132
Unit ID: 203289
Telephone: (937) 258-8251 Carnegie Class: Spec 2-yr-A&S
FAX Number: (937) 258-8714 Calendar System: Semester
URL: www.icb.edu
Established: 1968 Annual Undergrad Tuition & Fees: $12,569
Enrollment: 74 Coed
Affiliation or Control: Proprietary IRS Status: Proprietary
Highest Offering: Associate Degree
Accreditation: ACCSC

01 President ....J. Michael LEMASTER
05 School Director ....Eric CLARK

James A. Rhodes State College (G)

4240 Campus Drive, Lima OH 45804-3597
County: Allen FICE Identification: 010027
Unit ID: 203678
Telephone: (419) 995-8200 Carnegie Class: Assoc/MT-VT-Mix Trad/Non
FAX Number: (419) 221-0450 Calendar System: Semester
URL: www.rhodesstate.edu
Established: 1971 Annual Undergrad Tuition & Fees (In-State): $4,045
Enrollment: 3,657 Coed
Affiliation or Control: State IRS Status: 501(c)3
Highest Offering: Associate Degree
Accreditation: NH, ACBSP, ADNUR, COARC, COARCP, CSHSE, DH, EMT, ENGT, MAC, OTA, PTAA, RAD

01 President ....Dr. Debra L. MCCURDY
10 Vice President Business & Treasurer ....Vacant
05 VP Academic Affairs ....Dr. Chris BOYETT
32 Vice President Student Affairs ....Dr. John BERRY
45 VP Institutional Effect/Planning ....Ms. Becky BURRELL
35 Associate Dean for Student Services ....Ms. Judi MAZZARELLLI
06 Assoc VP Student Affairs/Registrar ....Dr. Rose REINHART
30 Executive Director of Development ....Mr. Kevin L. REEKS
20 Associate VP of Academic Affairs ....Dr. Antoinette BALDIN
07 Director of Admissions ....Ms. Traci R. COX
37 Director Student Financial Aid ....Ms. Cathy L. KOHLI
09 Director Institutional Research ....Vacant
36 Director of Career Services ....Ms. Krista RICHARDSON
08 Head Librarian ....Ms. Tina SCHNEIDER
103 Exec Dir for Workforce & Econ Dev ....Vacant
15 Director Human Resources ....Vacant
54 Dean Business/Tech & Public Svcs ....Mr. Ken BAKER
49 Interim Dean Div of Arts & Sciences ....Ms. Andrea FABER
76 Dean of Health Sciences ....Dr. Paula BOLEY
18 Chief Facilities/Physical Plant ....Vacant
21 Assoc VP Fin/Controller/Asst Treas ....Ms. Beverly REX-COOK
26 Asst Dir Mktg & College Relations . Ms. Anne COBURN-GRIFFIS
38 Director Advising & Counseling ....Ms. Andrea ANDERSON

John Carroll University (H)

1 John Carroll Boulevard,
University Heights OH 44118-4581
County: Cuyahoga FICE Identification: 003050
Unit ID: 203368
Telephone: (216) 397-1886 Carnegie Class: Bac-A&S
FAX Number: (216) 397-4256 Calendar System: Semester
URL: www.jcu.edu
Established: 1886 Annual Undergrad Tuition & Fees: $37,180
Enrollment: 3,688 Coed
Affiliation or Control: Roman Catholic IRS Status: 501(c)3
Highest Offering: Beyond Master's But Less Than Doctorate
Accreditation: NH, BUS, BUSA, CACREP, TED

01 President ....Rev. Robert L. NIEHOFF, SJ
88 Title IX Investigator ....Ms. Kendra E. SVILAR
88 Title IX Coordinator ....Mr. David J. SIPUSIC
04 Assistant to the President ....Ms. Bridget RINI
11 Vice President for Administration ....Mr. Richard F. MAUSSER
88 Asst to Pres External Affairs ....Mr. James P. CROSBY
43 General Counsel ....Ms. Colleen TREML
88 VP for Univ Mission & Identity ....Dr. Edward J. PECK
05 Provost & Academic Vice President ....Dr. Jeanne COLLERAN
30 Vice Pres University Advancement ....Ms. Doreen K. RILEY
84 Vice President for Enrollment ....Dr. Brian G. WILLIAMS
10 Chief Financial Officer ....Mr. Dennis F. HAREZA
32 Vice President for Student Affairs ....Dr. Mark D. MCCARTHY
20 Assoc Academic Vice President ....Dr. James H. KRUKONES
21 Director Academic Budget ....Mr. David W. WONG
09 Assoc Provost for Accred & IE ....Dr. Nicholas R. SANTILLI
108 Dir Office of Academic Assessment ....Dr. Robert (Todd) BRUCE
49 Dean College of Arts & Sciences ....Dr. Margaret E. FARRAR
50 Dean Boler School of Business ....Dr. Alan R. MICIAK
79 Assoc Dean Humanities/GR Programs ....Dr. Anne KUGLER
81 Assoc Dean Science and Health ....Dr. Graciela LACUEVA
83 Assoc Dean Soc Sci/Global/Ed ....Dr. Pamela MASON
35 Dean of Students ....Dr. Sherri A. CRAHEN
13 Chief Information Officer ....Mr. Michael J. BESTUL
18 Assoc Vice Pres for Facilities ....Ms. Carol P. DIETZ
26 Int Exec Director of Communications ....Ms. Tonya STRONG CHARLES
15 Asst Vice Pres Human Resources ....Mr. Alex J. TEODOSIO
08 Director of the Library ....Ms. Michelle MILLET
86 Assoc VP & Dir of Govt & Cmty Rels ....Ms. Dora J. PRUCE
36 Int Director Center for Career Svcs ....Dr. Cynthia D. MARCO SCANLON
28 Asst Prov Diversity & Inclus Excel ....Dr. Terry L. MILLS
22 Affirmative Action Officer/EEO ....Dr. James H. KRUKONES
06 Registrar ....Ms. Martha C. MONDELLO-HENDREN
21 Controller ....Mr. John P. CLIFFORD
88 Bursar & Dir of Student Accounts ....Ms. Diane M. WARD
39 Director of Residence Life ....Ms. Lisa M. BROWN
92 Director Honors Program ....Dr. Angela C. JONES
07 Executive Director of Enrollment ....Mr. Steven P. VITATOE
88 Sr Dir Major Gifts/Liaison to A&S ....Ms. Mary RYCYNA
14 Associate CIO ....Mr. James A. BURKE
37 Director of Financial Aid ....Ms. Claudia A. WENZEL
88 Director Budget/Financial Analysis ....Ms. Jennifer A. DILLON
31 Dir Ctr Service and Social Action ....Ms. Katherine FEELY, SND
42 Director of Campus Ministry ....Mr. John B. SCARANO
38 Director Univ Counseling Center ....Dr. Mark ONUSKO
23 Director Student Health Center ....Ms. Janet M. KREVH
41 Sr Director Athletics & Recreation ....Ms. Laurie J. MASSA
29 Director Alumni Relations ....Mr. David A. VITATOE
44 Sr Director Philanthropic Relations ....Mr. Peter R. BERNARDO
102 Dir Corporate Giving/Liaison Bus ....Ms. Christina BEG
102 Director Foundation Relations/Grant ....Ms. Pamela L. GEORGE
96 Director Purchasing/Auxiliary Svcs ....Mr. Andrew F. FRONCZEK
25 Director Sponsored Research ....Ms. Catherine T. ANSON
19 Director & Chief JCUPD ....Mr. Brian K. HURD
91 Director Enterprise Applications ....Mr. John M. SULLY
88 Exec Dir Mktg/Creative Svcs ....Mr. Michael J. RICHWALSKY
88 Center Digital Media Fac Liaison ....Dr. Jay TARBY
104 Asst Dir Center for Global Studies ....Dr. David M. KLEINBERG

Kent State University Main Campus (I)

PO Box 5190, Kent OH 44242-0001
County: Portage FICE Identification: 003051
Unit ID: 203517
Telephone: (330) 672-3000 Carnegie Class: DU-Higher
FAX Number: (330) 672-2190 Calendar System: Semester
URL: www.kent.edu
Established: 1910 Annual Undergrad Tuition & Fees (In-State): $10,012
Enrollment: 29,477 Coed
Affiliation or Control: State IRS Status: 501(c)3
Highest Offering: Doctorate
Accreditation: NH, AAB, ART, BUS, BUSA, CAATE, CACREP, CIDA, CLPSY, CORE, DANCE, DIETD, DIETI, ENGT, EXSC, JOUR, LIB, MUS, NAIT, NRPA, NURSE, PH, POD, SCPSY, SP, SPAA, TED, THEA

01 President ....Dr. Beverly J. WARREN
05 Provost/Sr VP Academic Affairs ....Dr. Todd DIACON
10 Vice Pres Finance & Administration ....Mr. Mark M. POLATAJKO
15 Interim Vice Pres Human Resources ....Mr. Willis WALKER
30 Vice Pres Institutional Advancement ....Mr. Jeff L. MCLAIN
32 Vice Pres Student Affairs ....Dr. Shay DAVIS LITTLE
26 Interim Vice Pres Univ Relations ....Ms. Rebecca MURPHY
46 Vice President Research ....Dr. Paul E. DICORLETO
13 Vice Pres Information Services/CIO ....Mr. Edward G. MAHON
22 VP Diversity/Equity/Inclusion ....Dr. Alfreda BROWN
20 Dean Undergraduate Studies ....Ms. Eboni PRINGLE
35 Interim Student Ombuds ....Ms. Patricia DENNISON
45 Sr Assoc Provost ....Dr. Melody TANKERSLEY
20 Assoc Provost Faculty Affairs ....Ms. Sue AVERILL
84 Sr Assoc Vice Pres Enrollment Svcs ....Mr. David GARCIA
29 Asst Vice Pres Alumni Affairs ....Mrs. Lori RANDORF
07 Director of Admissions ....Ms. Nancy J. DELLAVECCHIA
16 Human Resources Director-CPM ....Mr. David DIXON
06 Registrar ....Ms. Gail REBETA
43 Vice Pres University Counsel ....Mr. Willis WALKER
100 VP and University Secretary ....Ms. Charlene K. REED
41 Director Intercollegiate Athletics ....Mr. Joel NIELSON
22 Director of Compliance & Benefits ....Ms. Loretta SHIELDS
37 Director Student Financial Aid ....Mr. Mark EVANS
19 Director of Public Safety ....Vacant
12 Dean Trumbull Campus ....Dr. Lance GRAHN
96 Director of Procurement ....Mr. Timothy J. KONCZAL
49 Dean Arts & Sciences ....Dr. James BLANK
50 Dean of Business Administration ....Dr. Deborah F. SPAKE
53 Interim Dean EHHS ....Dr. Mark KRETOVICS
57 Dean of the Arts ....Dr. John CRAWFORD
66 Dean College of Nursing ....Dr. Barbara BROOME
51 Exec Director Continuing Studies ....Ms. Deborah C. HUNTSMAN
92 Interim Dean Honors College ....Dr. Donald F. PALMER
08 Dean Library & Media Services ....Dr. James BRACKEN
48 Dean Architect/Environ Design ....Mr. Douglas STEIDL
60 Dean Col of Comm & Information ....Dr. Amy REYNOLDS
72 Interim Dean Applied Engr/Sust/Tech ....Dr. Robert G. SINES
58 Interim Dean of Graduate Studies ....Dr. Melody TANKERSLEY
88 Dean College of Podiatric Medicine ....Dr. Allan BOIKE
20 Sr Assoc Dean-CPM ....Dr. Vincent J. HETHERINGTON
21 Sr Business Manager-CPM ....Mr. Mark M. MATEJCIK
08 Librarian-CPM ....Mrs. Donna M. PERZESKI
18 Director of Facilities Planning-CPM ....Mr. Dan RIDGWAY
84 Director of Enrollment Mgmt-CPM ....Vacant

Kent State University at Ashtabula (J)

3300 Lake Road W, Ashtabula OH 44004-2299
Telephone: (440) 964-3322 FICE Identification: 003052
Accreditation: &NH, ADNUR, COARC, OTA, PTAA, RAD

† Regional accreditation is carried under the parent institution in Kent, OH.

Kent State University East Liverpool Campus (K)

400 E Fourth Street, East Liverpool OH 43920-3497
Telephone: (330) 385-3805 FICE Identification: 003056
Accreditation: &NH, ADNUR, OTA

† Regional accreditation is carried under the parent institution in Kent, OH.

Kent State University Geauga Campus (L)

14111 Claridon-Troy Road,
Burton Township OH 44021-9500
Telephone: (440) 834-4187 FICE Identification: 003059
Accreditation: &NH, ADNUR

† Regional accreditation is carried under the parent institution in Kent, OH.

Kent State University Salem Campus (M)

2491 State Road 45 South, Salem OH 44460-9412
Telephone: (330) 332-0361 FICE Identification: 003061
Accreditation: &NH, RAD, RTT

† Regional accreditation is carried under the parent institution in Kent, OH.

Kent State University Stark Campus (N)

6000 Frank Avenue NW, North Canton OH 44720-9988
Telephone: (330) 499-9600 FICE Identification: 003054
Accreditation: &NH

† Regional accreditation is carried under the parent institution in Kent, OH.

Kent State University Trumbull Campus (A)

4314 Mahoning Avenue, NW, Warren OH 44483-1998
Telephone: (330) 847-0571 FICE Identification: 003064
Accreditation: &NH

† Regional accreditation is carried under the parent institution in Kent, OH.

Kent State University Tuscarawas Campus (B)

330 University Drive, NE,
New Philadelphia OH 44663-9403
Telephone: (330) 339-3391 FICE Identification: 003062
Accreditation: &NH, ADNUR, ENGT

† Regional accreditation is carried under the parent institution in Kent, OH.

Kenyon College (C)

106 College-Park Street, Gambier OH 43022-9623
County: Knox FICE Identification: 003065
Unit ID: 203535
Telephone: (740) 427-5000 Carnegie Class: Bac-A&S
FAX Number: (740) 427-3077 Calendar System: Semester
URL: www.kenyon.edu
Established: 1824 Annual Undergrad Tuition & Fees: $49,140
Enrollment: 1,662 Coed
Affiliation or Control: Independent Non-Profit IRS Status: 501(c)3
Highest Offering: Baccalaureate
Accreditation: NH

01 President .... Dr. Sean DECATUR
05 Provost .... Dr. Joe L. KLESNER
30 Vice President College Relations .... Ms. Heidi H. MCCRORY
10 Vice President for Finance .... Mr. Todd E. BURSON
08 Vice Pres Library & Info Svcs .... Mr. Ronald K. GRIGGS
100 Chief of Staff .... Ms. Susan MORSE
21 Assoc Vice President for Finance .... Vacant
44 Assoc VP College Relations .... Mr. Kyle W. HENDERSON
32 Dean of Students .... Vacant
07 Dean of Admissions/Fin Aid .... Ms. Diane ANCI
20 Associate Provost .... Dr. Jan THOMAS
20 Associate Provost .... Dr. Ivonne GARCIA
08 Director of Information Resources .... Mr. Joseph M. MURPHY
06 Registrar/Dean Academic Support .... Ms. Ellen K. HARBOURT
26 Director of Public Affairs .... Vacant
13 Director Systems Design/Consulting .... Vacant
29 Dir Alumni/Parent Rels .... Mr. Scott R. BAKER
37 Director of Financial Aid .... Mr. Craig A. DAUGHERTY
38 Director of Counseling Services .... Vacant
15 Director of Human Resources .... Ms. Jennifer G. CABRAL
42 Director of Religious/Spiritual .... Rabbi Marc BRAGIN
21 Chief Business Officer .... Mr. Mark KOHLMAN
22 Civil Rights/Title IX Coordinator .... Ms. Samantha HUGHES
19 Director of Campus Safety .... Mr. Robert D. HOOPER
09 Director of Institutional Research .... Ms. Erika M. FARFAN
21 Manager of Business Services .... Mr. Frederick S. LINGER
28 Director of Multicultural Affairs .... Mr. A. Chris KENNERLY
101 Director of Board Relations .... Ms. Kathryn LAKE

Kettering College (D)

3737 Southern Boulevard, Kettering OH 45429-1299
County: Montgomery FICE Identification: 007035
Unit ID: 203544
Telephone: (937) 395-8601 Carnegie Class: Spec-4-yr-Other Health
FAX Number: (937) 395-8106 Calendar System: Semester
URL: www.kc.edu
Established: 1967 Annual Undergrad Tuition & Fees: $10,944
Enrollment: 760 Coed
Affiliation or Control: Seventh-day Adventist IRS Status: 501(c)3
Highest Offering: Doctorate
Accreditation: NH, ADNUR, ARCPA, COARC, DMS, NUR, PAST, RAD

00 Chairman of the Board .... Mr. Jarrod MCNAUGHTON
01 President .... Dr. Nate BRANDSTATER
15 Vice President Human Resources .... Mr. Timothy DUTTON
05 Dean for Academic Affairs .... Dr. Ruth ABBOTT
05 Dean for Academic Affiars .... Dr. Loren AGREY
102 President Foundation .... Mrs. Susan BARCUS
84 Dean Enrollment Mgmt/Student Affs .... Mr. Victor BROWN
10 Chief Business Officer .... Mr. Terry BURNS
21 Director of Finance/Administration .... Mr. Nicholas HENSON
06 Registrar .... Mrs. Robin VANDERBILT
88 Dean Assessment & Learning Support .... Vacant
37 Director Student Financial Aid .... Mrs. Kim SNELL
40 Manager Bookstore .... Mrs. Jessica HILL
42 Chaplain Director Campus Ministry .... Mr. Steve CARLSON
32 Director Student Life .... Mr. Kris HARTER
26 Public Relations Officer .... Ms. Jessica BEANS
08 Director of Library .... Mr. John KISSINGER
29 Director Alumni Relations .... Mrs. Teresa SIMMONS
07 Director of Admissions .... Mrs. Katrina HILL
13 Senior Information Officer .... Mr. Jim NESBIT

Lake Erie College (E)

391 W Washington Street, Painesville OH 44077-3389
County: Lake FICE Identification: 003066
Unit ID: 203580
Telephone: (440) 375-7000 Carnegie Class: Masters/S
FAX Number: (440) 375-7005 Calendar System: Semester
URL: www.lec.edu
Established: 1856 Annual Undergrad Tuition & Fees: $29,162
Enrollment: 1,155 Coed
Affiliation or Control: Independent Non-Profit IRS Status: 501(c)3
Highest Offering: Master's
Accreditation: NH, #ARCPA, IACBE, TEAC

01 President .... Dr. Brian POSLER
05 Vice Pres for Academic Affairs/CAO .... Bryan DEPOY
10 Vice Pres Administration & Finance .... Brian DIRK
30 VP for Institutional Advancement .... Scott EVANS
20 Assoc VP for Academic Admin .... Dr. Jennifer COLLIS
53 Dean School of Educ & Prof Studies .... Dr Katharine DELAVAN
50 Dean School of Business .... Dr. Robert TREBAR
88 Dean School of Equine Studies .... Dr Pam HESS
88 Interim Dean Sch of Arts/Human & SS .... Dr. Jennine SWARTZ-LEVINE
81 Dean School of Nat Sci & Math .... Dr. Jonathan TEDESCO
06 Registrar .... Barbara ARILSON
107 Director Prof Development .... Lisa STRAUSBAUGH
58 Director Parker MBA Program .... Donna BARES
88 Director Physician Assistant Pgm .... Joe WEBER
36 Director Career Services .... Sarah KOSTIHA-SMITH
13 Director of Information Technology .... Brad LUHTA
38 Director Student Success Center .... Dr. John SPIESMAN
15 Director Human Resources .... Andrea MYERS
32 VP Student Affairs .... Billie DUNN
84 VP for Enrollment & Fin Aid .... Terry FINEFROCK
18 Director Physical Plant .... Herb DILL
29 Director Alumni & Community Rels .... Debra FEMINGTON
41 Director Athletics .... Reid GUARNIERI
08 Director Lincoln Library .... Christopher BENNETT
19 Director Security .... Richard KLINE
39 Director Residence Life .... Megan MCKENNA
40 Bookstore Manager .... Natalie SCALA
04 Executive Asst to President & BOD .... Julie HERBERT
26 Director of PR/Mktg and Comm Relati .... Rura GREINER
44 Director of Development .... Pamela PALERMO
07 Director of Admissions .... Liz SELLERS
37 Director Student Financial Aid .... Tricia PANGONIS

Lakeland Community College (F)

7700 Clocktower Drive, Kirtland OH 44094-5198
County: Lake FICE Identification: 006804
Unit ID: 203599
Telephone: (440) 525-7000 Carnegie Class: Assoc/HT-Mix Trad/Non
FAX Number: (440) 525-7651 Calendar System: Semester
URL: www.lakelandcc.edu
Established: 1967 Annual Undergrad Tuition & Fees (In-District): $3,316
Enrollment: 8,250 Coed
Affiliation or Control: State/Local IRS Status: 501(c)3
Highest Offering: Associate Degree
Accreditation: NH, ADNUR, CAHIIM, COARC, DH, ENGT, HT, IFSAC, MAC, MLTAD, RAD, SURGT

01 President .... Dr. Morris W. BEVERAGE, JR.
05 Exec VP & Provost .... Dr. Laura BARNARD
10 Exec Vice Pres Admin Svcs/Treasurer .... Mr. Michael E. MAYHER
100 Chief of Staff/Sr VP Inst Effectiv .... Ms. Catherine BUSH
26 Chief Commun Ofcr/VP College Rels .... Ms. Dawn M. PLANTE
20 Assoc Provost Teach & Learn .... Dr. Deborah L. HARDY
84 Assoc Provost for Enrollment Mgmt .... Mr. William KRAUS
20 Assoc VP Student Development .... Mr. Richard L. NOVOTNY
81 Dean of Arts and Sciences .... Dr. Steven OLUIC
76 Dean of Health Technologies .... Dr. Deborah L. HARDY
50 Dean of Applied Studies .... Mr. William KRAUS
88 Chief Academic Technologies Officer .... Mr. William KNAPP
21 Assoc VP Bus Svcs/Deputy Treasurer .... Mr. Brian COOK
13 Dir Administrative Technologies .... Mr. Rick PENNY
21 Controller .... Mr. Michael GRAFF
15 Director Human Resources .... Ms. Cathy BUSH
18 Director for Facilities Management .... Mr. Bert DIEHL
19 Chief of Police/Director of Safety .... Mr. Ronald MORENZ
07 Director for Admissions/Registrar .... Ms. Tracey L. COOPER
37 Dir Financial Aid/Enroll Support .... Ms. Melissa A. AMSPAUGH
32 Director of Student Activities .... Mr. Mario PETITTI
30 Dir Development/Alumni Relations .... Dr. Robert CAHEN
96 Director of Purchasing .... Mr. Tom A. KIRCHNER
09 Director of Institutional Research .... Mrs. Lisa DURST

Lakewood College (G)

2231 North Taylor Road, Cleveland Heights OH 44112
County: Cuyahoga Identification: 666715
Telephone: (800) 517-0857 Carnegie Class: Not Classified
FAX Number: (216) 803-9899 Calendar System: Other
URL: www.lakewoodcollege.edu
Established: 1998 Annual Undergrad Tuition & Fees: N/A
Enrollment: N/A Coed
Affiliation or Control: Independent Non-Profit IRS Status: 501(c)3
Highest Offering: Associate Degree
Accreditation: DEAC

01 CEO and Founder .... Ms. Tanya HAGGINS
11 Vice President of Operations .... Ms. Aleia EVANS
10 Vice President of Administration .... Ms. Summer HAGGINS
30 Vice President of Business Develop .... Mr. Isaac HAGGINS

Lorain County Community College (H)

1005 N Abbe Road, Elyria OH 44035-1691
County: Lorain FICE Identification: 003068
Unit ID: 203748
Telephone: (440) 365-5222 Carnegie Class: Assoc/HT-High Trad
FAX Number: (440) 365-6519 Calendar System: Semester
URL: www.lorainccc.edu
Established: 1963 Annual Undergrad Tuition & Fees (In-District): $3,077
Enrollment: 11,569 Coed
Affiliation or Control: State/Local IRS Status: 501(c)3
Highest Offering: Associate Degree
Accreditation: NH, ADNUR, ART, DH, DMS, EMT, ENGT, MAC, MLTAD, OTA, PHLEB, PNUR, PTAA, RAD, SURGT

01 President .... Dr. Marcia J. BALLINGER
46 VP Strategic & Institutional Devel .... Ms. Tracy A. GREEN
05 Provost/VP for Acad & Learner Svcs .... Dr. Jonathan N. DRYDEN
10 Vice President Admin Svcs/Treasurer .... Mr. David CUMMINS
88 Assoc Prov University Partnership .... Dr. John R. CROOKS
08 Int Dean Library/Instruction Media .... Ms. Susan PAUL
84 Dean Enroll Svcs/Fin Aid/Registrar .... Ms. Stephanie SUTTON
09 Dean Rsch/Inst Effect/Public Svcs .... Ms. Shara DAVIS
13 Director Information Systems .... Mr. Lou KOMPARE
15 Director Human Resources/Campus Sec .... Mr. Keith BROWN
88 Dir Entrepreneurship Innov Inst .... Ms. Terri B. SANDU
18 Director of Physical Plant .... Mr. Robert FLYER
51 Director Public Services .... Ms. Shara DAVIS
57 Dir Stocker Humanit/Fine Arts Ctr .... Ms. Janet HERMAN-BARLOW
96 Dir Purchasing/Facilities Planning .... Ms. Laura K. CARISSIMI
54 Dean Engineering & Information Tech .... Ms. Kelly ZELESNIK
76 Int Dean Allied Health & Nursing .... Dr. Hope MOON
79 Dean Arts/Humanities .... Dr. Robert A. BECKSTROM
81 Dean Science/Math .... Dr. Rosa HAINAJ
83 Dean Social Science/Human Svc .... Vacant
06 Registrar .... Ms. Sun Kyong JAMERSON
101 Secretary of the Institution/Board .... Ms. Karen BUESCHER
19 Director Security/Safety .... Mr. Ken COLLINS
26 Chief Public Relations/Marketing .... Ms. Cynthia KUSHNER

Lourdes University (I)

6832 Convent Boulevard, Sylvania OH 43560-2898
County: Lucas FICE Identification: 003069
Unit ID: 203757
Telephone: (419) 885-3211 Carnegie Class: Masters/M
FAX Number: (419) 882-3987 Calendar System: Semester
URL: www.lourdes.edu
Established: 1958 Annual Undergrad Tuition & Fees: $19,370
Enrollment: 1,780 Coed
Affiliation or Control: Roman Catholic IRS Status: 501(c)3
Highest Offering: Master's
Accreditation: NH, ANEST, IACBE, NURSE, SW, TEAC

01 President .... Dr. Mary Ann GAWELEK
00 President Emerita .... Sr. Ann Francis KLIMKOWSKI
05 Provost .... Dr. Geoffrey J. GRUBB
32 Vice Pres for Student Life .... Vacant
10 Vice Pres Finance & Administration .... Dr. Robert ROOD
42 Vice Pres for Mission & Ministry .... Sr. Ann Carmen BARONE, OSF
30 Vice President for Inst Advancement .... Ms. Mary ARQUETTE
84 Vice President of Enrollment .... Dr. Dean LUDWIG
45 Asst Vice Pres for Inst Planning .... Ms. Michelle RABLE
49 Dean College of Arts & Sciences .... Dr. Holly L. BAUMGARTNER
53 Int Dean Col Education/Human Svcs .... Mr. Terry KELLER
66 Int Dean College of Nursing .... Dr. Hollis HAMILTON
50 Dean College Business & Leadership .... Ryan BUTT
58 Int Dean of Graduate School .... Mr. Robert ARQUETTE
35 Dean of Student Life .... Ms. Rachel DUFF-ANDERSON
39 Director of Residence Life .... Mr. Andy HAM
37 Dir of Student Financial Services .... Ms. Deb LAJEUNESSE
26 Director of University Relations .... Ms. Helene SHEETS
08 Director of Library Services .... Sr. Sandra RUTKOWSKI
06 Registrar .... Ms. Michelle A. RABLE
13 Asst VP for Technology & CIO .... Mr. Scott CROW
15 Director of Human Resources .... Mr. Scott SIMON
85 Director Foreign Students .... Vacant
36 Director of Career Counseling .... Ms. Andrea DOMACHOWSKI
21 Director of Finance .... Ms. Kimberly MCGILL
88 Director Academic Advising .... Vacant
30 Director of Development .... Mr. Michael GEORGE
18 Director of Facilities & Grounds .... Mr. Michael CRAVENS
19 Title IX Coord & Dir Public Safety .... Ms. Michelle MCDEVITT
07 Director of Admissions .... Mr. Shawn BUSSELL
07 Director of Graduate Admissions .... Ms. Tara HANNA
88 Dir Campus Ministry/Svc Learning .... Sr. Barbara VANO, OSF
29 Alumni Relations Officer .... Vacant
40 Manager of Bookstore .... Ms. Ann MORRIS

Malone University (J)

2600 Cleveland Avenue NW, Canton OH 44709-3308
County: Stark FICE Identification: 003072
Unit ID: 203775
Telephone: (330) 471-8100 Carnegie Class: Masters/M
FAX Number: (330) 471-8478 Calendar System: Semester
URL: www.malone.edu
Established: 1892 Annual Undergrad Tuition & Fees: $27,960
Enrollment: 1,962 Coed
Affiliation or Control: Friends IRS Status: 501(c)3
Highest Offering: Master's
Accreditation: NH, ACBSP, CACREP, MUS, NURSE, SW, TED

01 President .... Dr. David A. KING
10 Vice Pres for Finance/CFO .... Mrs. Elaine C. ARICK
05 Provost .... Dr. D. Nathan PHINNEY
32 Vice Pres for Student Development .... Dr. Christopher T. ABRAMS
30 Vice Pres for Univ Advancement .... Mr. Stephen T. WEINGART
26 Vice Pres for Marketing & Comm .... Mr. Timothy A. BRYAN

84 Vice Pres for Enrollment Management .... Mr. Mark SEYMOUR
49 Int Dean Col of Theol/Arts & Sci .... Dr. James H. BROWNLEE
53 Dean Sch of Education & Human Devel .... Vacant
66 Dean Sch of Nursing & Health Sci .... Dr. Debra A. LEE
44 Associate VP for Development ....Ms. Sharon L. SIRPILLA
21 Finance Manager .... Mr. Tracy L. MILLER
06 Registrar .... Mr. Gary L. PHELPS
07 Director of Admissions ....Mrs. Linda A. KURTZ HOFFMAN
29 Dir of Alumni & Parent Relations .... Mrs. Deborah M. ROBINSON
44 Director of Annual Giving ....Mrs. Paula M. CALHOUN
108 Dir Inst Effectiveness/Assessment ....Dr. Charles R. LARTEY
37 Director of Financial Aid ....Mrs. Pamela S. PUSTAY
15 Director of Human Resources .... Mr. Michael J. FAIRLESS
41 Athletic Director ....Mr. Charles R. GRIMES
08 Director of Library .... Ms. Rebecca L. FORT
106 Dir Online Education/E-learning ..... Mr. John W. KOSHMIDER, III
93 Director of Multicultural Services .... Mrs. Brenda D. STEVENS
104 Dir Ctr/Cross-Cultural Engagement .... Mr. Ryan J. DONALD
19 Director Security/Safety ....Mr. David W. BURNIP
24 Support and Infrastructure Manager ....Mr. M. Adam KLEMANN
90 Senior Systems Engineer .... Mr. Alexander YU
42 Director of Spiritual Formation ....Rev Dr. Linda J. LEON
105 Content Mgr for Publications/Web ....Mrs. Amber L. BALASH
40 Bookstore Manager ....Mrs. Kathy L. SECREST
04 Exec Asst to Pres/Asst to Board ....Mrs. Teresa L. PITTINGER
09 Assistant to the Provost ....Ms. Karen R. WARNER
92 Director of Honors Program ....Dr. Steven M. JENSEN
89 Dir of the College Experience Pgm ....Dr. Marcia K. EVERETT
38 Director of Counseling Center .... Mr. Timothy T. MORBER
23 Health Center Nurse ....Mrs. Janet A. PERKO

Marietta College (A)

215 Fifth Street, Marietta OH 45750-4033
County: Washington FICE Identification: 003073
Unit ID: 203845
Telephone: (740) 376-4000 Carnegie Class: Bac-Diverse
FAX Number: (740) 376-4896 Calendar System: Semester
URL: www.marietta.edu
Established: 1835 Annual Undergrad Tuition & Fees: $34,300
Enrollment: 1,500 Coed
Affiliation or Control: Independent Non-Profit IRS Status: 501(c)3
Highest Offering: Master's
Accreditation: NH, ARCPA, CAATE, ENG, MUS, TED

01 President ....Dr. William N. RUUD
05 Provost/Dean of Faculty .... Dr. Janet L. BLAND
10 VP for Administration & Finance ....Mr. Daniel C. BRYANT
30 VP for Advancement ....Ms. Angela B. ANDERSON
32 VP Student Life/Chf Diversity Ofcr ....Dr. Richard K. DANFORD
84 Interim VP for Enrollment Mgmt .... Mr. Thomas WEEDE
88 Dean McDonough Ctr for Leadership ....Dr. Gamaliel (Gama) PERRUCI
101 Secretary to the Board of Trustees ......Mr. William H. DONNELLY
08 Director of Library ....Dr. N. Douglas ANDERSON
21 Assistant VP for Finance ....Ms. Michele MARRA
07 Assistant VP for Enrollment Mgmt .... Ms. Emily G. SCHUCK
18 Director of Physical Plant ....Mr. Fred R. SMITH
06 Registrar .... Ms. Tina K. PERDUE
15 Director of Human Resources .... Ms. Debra C. WAYLAND
19 Chief of Campus Police .... Mr. James S. WEAVER
26 Exec Dir of Strategic Comm & Mktg .... Mr. Thomas D. PERRY
09 Director of Institutional Research ...Dr. Gregory J. DELEMEESTER
36 Career Center Director .... Ms. B. Hilles HUGHES
41 Director of Athletics ....Mr. Larry R. HISER
13 Director of Information Technology .... Mr. Aaron COWDERY
63 PA Program Director .... Ms. Miranda COLLINS
104 Director of Education Abroad .... Ms. Christy BURKE
25 Grants Officer ....Ms. Robin STEWART
51 Continuing Education ....Ms. Tina K. PERDUE
35 Dean of Students ....Dr. Lisa PHILLIPS

Marion Technical College (B)

1467 Mount Vernon Avenue, Marion OH 43302-5694
County: Marion FICE Identification: 010736
Unit ID: 203881
Telephone: (740) 389-4636 Carnegie Class: Assoc/HT-Mix Trad/Non
FAX Number: (740) 389-6136 Calendar System: Semester
URL: www.mtc.edu
Established: 1971 Annual Undergrad Tuition & Fees (In-State): $4,480
Enrollment: 2,468 Coed
Affiliation or Control: State IRS Status: 501(c)3
Highest Offering: Associate Degree
Accreditation: NH, ADNUR, CAHIIM, DMS, MAC, MLTAD, OTA, PTAA, RAD

01 President .... Dr. Ryan MCCALL
05 Chief Academic Officer ....Dr. Vicky WOOD
32 Dean of Student Services ....Mr. Mike STUCKEY
84 Dean of Enrollment Services ....Mr. Joel O. LILES
06 Registrar ....Mr. Jim LAVERY
13 Executive Director IT Operations .... Mr. Steve DUVALL
26 Director of Public Relations .... Vacant
66 Director of Nursing Technology .... Ms. Cynthia HARTMAN
103 Director Ctr Workforce Development .... Ms. Tami GALLOWAY
15 Director Human Resources ....Ms. Brenda FEASEL
88 Dir Physical Therapist Asst Pgm ....Mr. Chad HENSEL
88 Dir Occupational Therapy ....Mr. Chad SCHNEIDER
100 Chief of Staff ....Ms. Teresa PARKER
18 Coord Facil Improvements/Operations ....Ms. Leeann GRAU
37 Director Student Financial Aid ....Ms. Deb LANGDON
54 Director of Engineering Technology .... Mr. Matthew FARSON
50 Dean of Business/Information Tech ....Ms. Debbie STARK

49 Dean of Arts and Sciences .... Vacant
76 Dean of Allied Health ....Mr. Chris GASE
10 Chief Financial Officer ....Mr. Jeff NUTTER
108 Dean Institutional Effectiveness .... Dr. Bob HAAS
07 Director of Admissions .... Mr. Brandon MOONEY

Mercy College of Ohio (C)

2221 Madison Avenue, Toledo OH 43604
County: Lucas FICE Identification: 030970
Unit ID: 203960
Telephone: (419) 251-1313 Carnegie Class: Spec-4-yr-Other Health
FAX Number: (419) 251-1570 Calendar System: Semester
URL: www.mercycollege.edu
Established: 1993 Annual Undergrad Tuition & Fees: $12,530
Enrollment: 1,196 Coed
Affiliation or Control: Roman Catholic IRS Status: 501(c)3
Highest Offering: Baccalaureate
Accreditation: NH, ADNUR, CAHIIM, CVT, EMT, NURSE, POLYT, RAD

01 President ....Dr. Susan WAJERT
05 Int VP Acad Affs/Dean of Faculty ....Ms. Patricia REID
32 Int VP Student Affs/Dean of Student ....Ms. Leslie ERWIN
66 Interim Dean Nursing ....Dr. Elizabeth SPRUNK
76 Dean of Science & Allied Hlth Prof ....Dr. Barbara STOOS
97 Dean of Gen Ed & Acad Resource Ctr .... Dr. Jeremy ECCLES
88 Dir of Compliance/Risk Mgmt ....Mr. Christopher BAUER
13 Dir of College Info Tech Services .... Mr. David BURGIN
10 Director College Finances/Res Plng ..Ms. Joan M. RUTHERFORD
30 Director College Advancement .... Mr. Michael WHALEN
84 VP of Strategic Plng & Enroll Mgmt ....Ms. Lori EDGEWORTH
08 Director Library/Resource Services ....Ms. Deborah JOHNSON
09 Dir Inst Research/Registrar ....Vacant
37 Financial Aid Director ....Ms. Julie LESLIE
26 Director of Communication ....Ms. Denise HUDGIN
42 Dir Campus Ministry & Svcs Learning ....Sr. Sally BOHNETT
21 Business Manager ....Ms. Diane RAHN
18 Facilities Manager ....Ms. Sherri BOGGS
29 Director Alumni Relations ....Vacant
38 Director of Counseling & Wellness .... Ms. Lisa SANCRANT
36 Director of Career Services ....Vacant
106 Dir of Distance Education ....Vacant
28 Dir of Diversity/Inclusion & Reten ..Dr. Shelly MCCOY GRISSOM
04 Administrative Asst to President ....Ms. Jane STUNTZ
07 Director of Admissions ....Ms. Amy MERGEN

Methodist Theological School in Ohio (D)

3081 Columbus Pike, Delaware OH 43015-3211
County: Delaware FICE Identification: 003075
Unit ID: 203997
Telephone: (740) 363-1146 Carnegie Class: Spec-4-yr-Faith
FAX Number: (740) 362-3135 Calendar System: 4/1/4
URL: www.mtso.edu
Established: 1958 Annual Graduate Tuition & Fees: N/A
Enrollment: 175 Coed
Affiliation or Control: United Methodist IRS Status: 501(c)3
Highest Offering: Doctorate; No Undergraduates
Accreditation: NH, THEOL

01 President ....Rev. Jay A. RUNDELL
05 Dean and VP for Academic Affairs ....Dr. Lisa WITHROW
30 VP of Institutional Advancement .... Ms. April CASPERSON
04 Executive Asst to the President ....Ms. Leigh PRECISE
26 Director of Communications ....Mr. Danny RUSSELL
07 Director of Admissions ....Rev. Benjamin HALL
06 Registrar ....Ms. Sue LAMPHERE
08 Director of the Library .... Mr. Paul BURNAM
10 Controller ....Rev. Jim SUMMERS
18 Facilities Manager ....Mr. Keith HUFFMAN
32 Director of Student Services .... Ms. Kristin LOFRUMENTO
13 Director Information Technology ....Mr. Matthew REHM
37 Director of Financial Aid .... Ms. Molly HOFFMAN
44 Director of Annual Giving .... Rev. Claudine LEARY

Miami-Jacobs Career College (E)

150 E Gay Street, 1st Floor, Columbus OH 43215-3227
Telephone: (614) 221-7770 Identification: 666465
Accreditation: ACICS, MAC, #SURGT

† Branch campus of McCann School of Business & Technology, Pottsville, PA

Miami-Jacobs Career College (F)

401 E. Third Street, Dayton OH 45402
Telephone: (937) 552-4006 FICE Identification: 003076
Accreditation: ACICS, MAC, #SURGT

† Branch campus of McCann School of Business & Technology, Pottsville, PA

Miami-Jacobs Career College (G)

6400 Rockside Road, Independence OH 44131
Telephone: (216) 834-1400 FICE Identification: 021521
Accreditation: ACICS

† Branch campus of McCann School of Business & Technology, Pottsville, PA

Miami-Jacobs Career College (H)

2 Crowne Point Court, Suite 100, Sharonville OH 45241
Telephone: (513) 693-4400 Identification: 770755
Accreditation: ACICS, #SURGT

† Branch campus of McCann School of Business & Technology, Pottsville, PA

Miami-Jacobs Career College (I)

875 Central Avenue, Springboro OH 45066
Telephone: (937) 746-1830 Identification: 770757
Accreditation: ACICS, DA

† Branch campus of McCann School of Business & Technology, Pottsville, PA

Miami-Jacobs Career College (J)

865 West Market Street, Troy OH 45373
Telephone: (937) 332-8585 Identification: 770756
Accreditation: ACICS

† Branch campus of McCann School of Business & Technology, Pottsville, PA

Miami University (K)

501 E High Street, Oxford OH 45056-1846
County: Butler FICE Identification: 003077
Unit ID: 204024
Telephone: (513) 529-1809 Carnegie Class: DU-Higher
FAX Number: (513) 529-3841 Calendar System: Semester
URL: www.miamioh.edu
Established: 1809 Annual Undergrad Tuition & Fees (In-State): $14,287
Enrollment: 18,620 Coed
Affiliation or Control: State IRS Status: 501(c)3
Highest Offering: Doctorate
Accreditation: NH, ART, BUS, BUSA, #CAATE, CIDA, CLPSY, CS, DIETD, ENG, ENGT, IPSY, MUS, NURSE, SP, SW, TED, THEA

01 President ....Dr. Gregory CRAWFORD
05 Provost ....Dr. Phyllis CALLAHAN
10 VP Finance & Bus Svcs/Treasurer .... Dr. David CREAMER
32 Vice President Student Affairs ....Dr. Jayne E. BROWNELL
30 VP University Advancement ....Mr. Tom HERBERT
13 VP Information Technology .... Mr. J. Peter NATALE
15 Ast Prov Personnel/Dir Acad Per Svc .... Dr. Janet L. COX
21 Assoc VP Finance/Business Svcs ....Dr. David A. ELLIS
20 Assoc Provost for Undergrad Studies ....Dr. Carolyn A. HAYNES
35 Dean of Students .... Dr. Michael A. CURME
26 Assoc VP Comm/Marketing ....Ms. Deedie Kay DOWDLE
18 Assoc VP Facilities Planning & Op ....Mr. Cody J. POWELL
84 VP Enrollment Management ....Mr. Michael S. KABBAZ
28 Assoc VP Inst Diversity ....Dr. Ronald B. SCOTT
29 Asst Vice Pres Alumni Relations ....Mr. Raymond F. MOCK
27 Director Institutional Relations ....Mr. Randi Malcolm THOMAS
27 Assoc Dir Univ Communications ....Ms. Claire M. WAGNER
100 Secy Board/Exec Asst to President ....Mr. Ted O. PICKERILL
49 Dean College Arts & Science ....Dr. Christopher A. MAKAROFF, JR.
53 Dean Education/Health & Society .... Dr. Michael DANTLEY
50 Dean Farmer Sch of Business .... Dr. Matthew B. MYERS
57 Dean College of Creative Arts ....Dr. Elizabeth R. MULLENIX
54 Dean College of Engr & Computing ....Dr. Marek DOLLAR
08 Dean University Libraries .... Mr. Jerome CONLEY
58 Dean Graduate School .... Dr. James T. ORIS
107 Dean College of Prof Studies/App Sc .... Dr. G. Michael PRATT
07 Director of Admissions ....Ms. Susan SCHAURER
88 Asst Provost Global Initiatives ....Ms. Cheryl D. YOUNG
108 Univ Dir Ctr for Teaching Excellenc ....Dr. Rose Marie WARD
88 Univ Dir Liberal Educ/Assessment ....Dr. Richard TAYLOR
92 Univ Dir Honors & Scholars Program .... Dr. Linda MARCHANT
16 Int Assoc VP Human Resources .... Ms. Kate STOSS
88 Dir Center American/World Cultures ....Dr. Mary Jane BERMAN
23 Medical Director Student Health Svc ....Dr. Gregory CALKINS
104 Director Intl Education Services ....Dr. David KEITGES
06 University Registrar .... Mr. David M. SAUTER
36 Director Career Services .... Mr. Michael GOLDMAN
38 Director Student Counseling Service .... Dr. Kip C. ALISHIO
09 Director Institutional Research ....Ms. Denise A. KRALLMAN
19 Chief of Police/Dir Public Safety .... Mr. John MCCANDLESS
96 Sr Director Purchasing/Central Svcs .... Mr. William G. SHAWVER
43 University General Counsel ....Ms. Robin L. PARKER
22 Director Equity & Equal Opportunity .... Ms. Kenya D. ASH
41 Director Intercollegiate Athletics ....Mr. David A. SAYLER
17 Asst VP Student Health & Wellness ....Ms. Gail A. WALENGA
04 Assistant to the President ....Ms. Deborah P. MASON
106 Asst Provost for E-learning ....Dr. Beth RUBIN
37 Director Student Financial Aid ....Mr. Brent L. SHOCK
102 Dir Corporate/Found Relations ....Mr. Whitney RILEY
109 Assoc VP Auxiliaries ....Mrs. Kim K. KINSEL
44 Sr Director Annual Giving ....Ms. Emily BERRY
45 Assoc VP Budgeting & Analysis ....Dr. David A. ELLIS
105 Univ Web Content Manager ....Ms. Jeri MOORE
25 Dir Research & Sponsored Pgms ....Ms. Anne P. SCHAUER
39 Int Dir Residential Services ....Ms. Stacy GEORGE

Miami University Hamilton Campus (L)

1601 University Boulevard, Hamilton OH 45011-3399
Telephone: (513) 785-3000 FICE Identification: 003079
Accreditation: &NH

† Regional accreditation is carried under the parent institution in Oxford, OH.

Miami University Middletown **(A)**

4200 N University Boulevard, Middletown OH 45042-3497

Telephone: (513) 727-3200 FICE Identification: 003080

Accreditation: &NH

† Regional accreditation is carried under the parent institution in Oxford, OH.

Mount Carmel College of Nursing (B)

127 S Davis Avenue, Columbus OH 43222-1504

County: Franklin FICE Identification: 030719

Unit ID: 204176

Telephone: (614) 234-5800 Carnegie Class: Spec-4-yr-Other Health

FAX Number: (614) 234-2875 Calendar System: Semester

URL: www.mccn.edu

Established: 1990 Annual Undergrad Tuition & Fees: $12,180

Enrollment: 1,084 Coed

Affiliation or Control: Roman Catholic IRS Status: 501(c)3

Highest Offering: Doctorate

Accreditation: NH, NURSE

01 President ... Dr. Christine A. WYND
05 Academic Dean ... Dr. Tara SPALLA
66 Int Asc Dean Undergrad Nursing Pgm ... Dr. Scott DOLAN
58 Associate Dean Graduate Nursing Pgm ... Dr. Jill KILANOWSKI
106 Associate Dean Distance Education ... Dr. Tara SPALLA
06 Director of Records & Registration ... Ms. Karen L. GREENE
10 Director Business Affairs ... Ms. Kathy SMITH
84 Director Enrollment Management ... Ms. Kim CAMPBELL
13 Systems Administrator ... Mr. Tim TABOL
37 Director Financial Aid ... Ms. Mary CANNON
32 Director Student Life ... Ms. Colleen CIPRIANI
28 Director Diversity/Comm Initiative ... Ms. Kathlynne D. ESPY
29 Director Alumni Relations ... Ms. Debbie DUNN BOGGS
26 Dir Marketing/College Relations ... Ms. Robin HUTCHINSON BELL
08 Regional Director Library Services ... Mr. Stevo ROKSANDIC

Mount St. Joseph University (C)

5701 Delhi Road, Cincinnati OH 45233-1670

County: Hamilton FICE Identification: 003033

Unit ID: 204200

Telephone: (513) 244-4200 Carnegie Class: Masters/M

FAX Number: (513) 244-4654 Calendar System: Semester

URL: www.msj.edu

Established: 1920 Annual Undergrad Tuition & Fees: $27,500

Enrollment: 2,219 Coed

Affiliation or Control: Roman Catholic IRS Status: 501(c)3

Highest Offering: Doctorate

Accreditation: NH, CAATE, NURSE, PTA, SW, TEAC

01 President ... Dr. H. James WILLIAMS
30 Vice Pres Institutional Advancement ... Vacant
84 Vice Pres Enrollment Management ... Vacant
05 Provost ... Dr. Joel THIERSTEIN
10 Chief Financial Officer ... Ms. Anne Marie WAGNER
43 Chief Compliance and Risk Officer ... Ms. Linda PANZECA
20 Associate Academic Dean ... Ms. Maggie DAVIS
15 Director of Human Resources ... Ms. Lisa KOBMAN
32 Dean of Students ... Ms. Janet COX
06 Registrar ... Ms. Irene RICHARDSON
29 Director of Alumni Relations ... Ms. Gina BATH
37 Director Student Admin Services ... Ms. Kathy KELLY
36 Director Career/Experi Educ ... Ms. Linda POHLGEERS
102 Director Corporate & Found Rels ... Ms. Linda B. LIEBAU
18 Director Buildings & Grounds ... Mr. Michael DITTMER
09 Director Institutional Rsrch ... Ms. Erin MULLIGAN-NGUYEN
07 Director of Admission ... Ms. Peggy MINNICH
21 Controller Fiscal Operations ... Mr. Ronald KUKER
38 Director Wellness Center ... Ms. Patsy SCHWAIGER
08 Director Library ... Mr. Paul JENKINS
13 Director Instructional Technology ... Ms. Kim HUNTER
19 Director of Campus Police ... Mr. John KRAFT
41 Director of Athletics ... Mr. Steve RADCLIFFE
88 Director Learning Center ... Ms. Meghann LITTRELL
42 Director of Campus Ministry ... Sr. Nancy BRAMLAGE, SC
44 Director of Development ... Ms. Lisa ODENBECK
40 Manager of Bookstore ... Ms. Lori HATTENDORF
76 Dean Div of Health Sciences ... Dr. Darla VALE
79 Dean of Div of Arts & Hum ... Dr. Michael SONTAG
50 Dean of Business ... Dr. Jamal RASHED
53 Interim Dean of Education ... Dr. Darla VALE
83 Interim Dean Behav/Natural Sci ... Dr. Michael SONTAG
26 Director of Marketing ... Ms. Kathleen CARDWELL
91 Director Administrative Computing ... Mr. Dan LUKAC
105 Webmaster ... Ms. Carolyn BOLAND
88 Director Individual & Campaign Giv ... Mr. Joe CORNELY
88 Exec Dir Ethical Leadership Devel ... Dr. Tim BRYANT
44 Coord Annual Giv & Young Alum Pgm ... Mr. Mark OSBORNE
23 Coordinator Health Services ... Ms. Amy DEMKO
39 Coordinator of Residence Life ... Mr. Warren GROVE
04 Admin Asst to the President ... Ms. Tina MERSMANN
108 Academic Assessment Coordinator ... Dr. Mary Kay FLEMING
28 Director of Diversity ... Dr. Terri HURDLE

Mount Vernon Nazarene University (D)

800 Martinsburg Road, Mount Vernon OH 43050-9500

County: Knox FICE Identification: 007085

Unit ID: 204194

Telephone: (740) 392-6868 Carnegie Class: Masters/L

FAX Number: (740) 397-2769 Calendar System: Semester

URL: www.mvnu.edu

Established: 1968 Annual Undergrad Tuition & Fees: $25,748

Enrollment: 2,137 Coed

Affiliation or Control: Church Of The Nazarene IRS Status: 501(c)3

Highest Offering: Master's

Accreditation: NH, ACBSP, MUS, NURSE, SW, TED

01 President/CEO ... Dr. Henry W. SPAULDING, II
10 Vice Pres for Finance/CFO ... Dr. Robert P. HAMILL
05 Vice Pres for Academic Affairs/CAO ... Dr. B.Barnett COCHRAN
32 Vice President Student Life ... Rev. Joe NOONEN
42 University Chaplain ... Rev. Joe NOONEN
26 VP for University Relations ... Rev. Scott PETERSON
30 Managing Dir of Advancement ... Mrs. Laura M. SHORT
21 Director of Business Services ... Mr. Steven JENKINS
07 Asst VP for Traditional Admission ... Mr. James SMITH
58 Director of Faculty Services GPS ... Mr. Kevin CHANEY
06 University Registrar ... Mr. Mel SEVERNS
15 Director of Human Resources ... Mr. Alan SHAFFER
38 Director Counseling and Wellness ... Dr. Eric BROWNING
13 Director of Information Tech ... Mr. John WALCHLE
19 Director of Campus Safety ... Mr. Denny TAYLOR
29 Director of Alumni Relations ... Mr. Travis KELLER
40 Director of the Bookstore ... Mrs. Gina A. BLANCHARD
41 Athletic Director ... Mr. Keith VEALE
27 Coord Communications & Pub Rels ... Ms. Emily ROGERS
53 Dir Teacher Education/Certification ... Dr. Sharon METCALFE
37 Dir of Student Fin Services ... Mr. Jared SPONSELLER
18 Director of Facilities Management ... Mr. Dennis D. TAYLOR
21 Controller ... Ms. Debra DEVORE
35 Director of Campus Life ... Ms. Rochel FURNISS
35 Dean of Students ... Mr. Aaron M. QUINN
28 Director Intercultural Affairs ... Mr. James M. SINGLETARY
108 Director Assessment & Reporting ... Mrs. Kathy GRIFFITH
04 Assistant to President ... Mrs. Pamela K. SNOW
08 Director of the Library ... Mr. Paul NIXON
105 Director Web Services ... Mr. Carlos SERRAO
106 Dir Online Education/E-learning ... Dr. Dean GOON
50 Dean of the School of Business ... Dr. Melanie TIMMERMAN
81 Dean School of Natural & Social Sci ... Dr. Richard SUTHERLAND

Muskingum University (E)

163 Stormont Street, New Concord OH 43762-1199

County: Muskingum FICE Identification: 003084

Unit ID: 204264

Telephone: (740) 826-8211 Carnegie Class: Masters/M

FAX Number: (740) 826-8404 Calendar System: Semester

URL: www.muskingum.edu

Established: 1837 Annual Undergrad Tuition & Fees: $25,776

Enrollment: 2,074 Coed

Affiliation or Control: Presbyterian Church (U.S.A.) IRS Status: 501(c)3

Highest Offering: Beyond Master's But Less Than Doctorate

Accreditation: NH, ENG, MUS, NURSE, TED

01 President ... Dr. Susan SCHNEIDER HASSELER
05 Vice President Academic Affairs ... Dr. James E. CALLAGHAN
10 Vice President Business & Finance ... Mr. Philip LAUBE
30 Int Vice Pres of Inst Advancement ... Ms. Janet HEETER-BASS
32 Vice President of Student Life ... Mrs. Janet A. HEETER-BASS
84 Vice President of Enrollment ... Mr. Jeff N. ZELLERS
20 Associate Academic Dean ... Vacant
08 Director of Library ... Dr. Sheila J. ELLENBERGER
06 Registrar ... Mr. Daniel B. WILSON
36 Assistant Director Career Services ... Mrs. Jacquelyn L. VASCURA
13 Director of Computing Services ... Mr. Ryan D. HARVEY
26 Director Public Relations ... Ms. Janice L. TUCKER-MCCLOUD
29 Director Alumni Relations ... Ms. Jennifer L. BRONNER
07 Director of Admissions ... Mrs. Beth A. DALONZO
19 Director of Public Safety ... Mr. Danny E. VINCENT
42 College Minister ... Rev. William E. MULLINS
18 Supt of Building & Grounds ... Mr. Kevin L. WAGNER
41 Director of Athletics ... Mr. Larry L. SHANK
21 Associate Business Officer ... Mr. Timothy CROSS
35 Director of Student Affairs ... Ms. Susan H. WARYCK
37 Director of Student Financial Aid ... Mrs. Beth A. DALONZO
38 Director of Student Counseling ... Mrs. Tracy F. BUGGLIN
40 Manager of Bookstore ... Ms. Jessica M. MILLER
15 Coordinator of Human Resources ... Ms. Kathy J. MOORE

National Institute of Massotherapy (F)

3681 Manchester Road, Suite 304, Akron OH 44319

County: Summit FICE Identification: 034684

Unit ID: 412003

Telephone: (330) 867-1996 Carnegie Class: Spec 2-yr-Health

FAX Number: (330) 867-6422 Calendar System: Other

URL: www.nim.edu

Established: 1991 Annual Undergrad Tuition & Fees: N/A

Enrollment: 48 Coed

Affiliation or Control: Proprietary IRS Status: Proprietary

Highest Offering: Associate Degree

Accreditation: CNCE

01 President ... Mr. Stephen PERKINSON
32 Dean of Students ... Ms. Ewa PERKINSON
37 Director Financial Aid ... Mr. Dan BILICH

North Central State College (G)

2441 Kenwood Circle, Mansfield OH 44906

County: Richland FICE Identification: 005313

Unit ID: 204422

Telephone: (419) 755-4800 Carnegie Class: Assoc/MT-VT-High Trad

FAX Number: (419) 755-4750 Calendar System: Semester

URL: www.ncstatecollege.edu

Established: 1961 Annual Undergrad Tuition & Fees (In-State): $3,591

Enrollment: 2,937 Coed

Affiliation or Control: State IRS Status: 501(c)3

Highest Offering: Associate Degree

Accreditation: NH, ACBSP, ADNUR, COARC, OTA, PTAA, RAD

01 President ... Dr. Dorey DIAB
04 Exec Assistant to the President ... Mr. Stephen R. WILLIAMS
10 VP Business Services ... Mr. Koffi AKAKPO
05 Vice President Academic Services ... Dr. Karen A. REED
26 Chief Public Affairs Officer ... Mr. Keith STONER
32 Interim Dean of Student Services ... Mr. Thomas MANSPERGER
15 Director of Human Resources ... Mr. R. Douglas HANUSCIN
37 Director of Financial Aid ... Mr. James PHINNEY
08 Head Librarian ... Ms. Pamela BENJAMIN
22 Coord Disability Services ... Mr. Doug HESTAND
49 Dean of Lib Arts/Ed/Prof & Pub Svcs ... Mr. Gregory BUSCH
88 Asst Dean Liberal Arts ... Ms. Deborah HYSELL
53 Asst Dean Education/Prof/Pub Svcs ... Mr. Craig ALI
50 Dean of Business Ind & Technology ... Dr. Gregory TIMBERLAKE
88 Asst Dean Business Ind & Technology ... Mr. Daniel WAGNER
76 Dean Health & Public Services ... Mr. James L. HULL
66 Asst Dean Health Sci/Dir Nursing ... Ms. Kelly GRAY
13 Interim Director IT ... Mr. Major PRICE, JR.
06 Registrar ... Mr. Mark J. MONNES
18 Chief Facilities/Physical Plant ... Mr. Dean SCHAAD
96 Purchasing Specialist ... Ms. Renee NUSSBAUM
102 Foundation Director ... Mr. Scott HEIMANN
09 Director of Institutional Research ... Mr. Thomas M. PRENDERGAST
84 Dir of Student Success & Retention ... Mr. Troy SHUTLER
88 Director of Title III ... Ms. Beverly WALKER
88 Phi Theta Kappa Advisor ... Ms. Barb KEENER
40 Campus Bookstore Manager ... Ms. Carla BUTDORFF
21 Controller ... Ms. Lori MCKEE
105 Web Master ... Mr. Mark HUPP
88 Director of Tech Prep ... Mr. Tom KLUDING
51 Continuing Education Director ... Ms. Gina KAMWITHI
35 Int Coord Student Life Activities ... Mr. Mike LACROIX
41 Dir Athletics & Student Engagement ... Mr. Mike LACROIX
29 Coord of Alumni/Employer Relations ... Ms. Mary J. RODRIGUEZ
36 Career Development Counselor ... Ms. Caitlyn RETHORST
07 Dir of Admissions/Recruitment ... Mr. Thomas MANSPERGER

Northeast Ohio Medical University (H)

4209 State Route 44, PO Box 95,
Rootstown OH 44272-0095

County: Portage FICE Identification: 024544

Unit ID: 204477

Telephone: (330) 325-2511 Carnegie Class: Spec-4-yr-Med

FAX Number: (330) 325-7943 Calendar System: Other

URL: www.neomed.edu

Established: 1973 Annual Graduate Tuition & Fees: N/A

Enrollment: 893 Coed

Affiliation or Control: State IRS Status: 501(c)3

Highest Offering: First Professional Degree; No Undergraduates

Accreditation: NH, MED, PH, PHAR

01 President ... Dr. Jay A. GERSHEN
100 Chief of Staff/VP Div Equity & Incl ... Ms. Carolyn D. LANIER
26 VP External Affairs ... Mr. Richard W. LEWIS
86 Secretary to the Board of Trustees ... Mr. Richard W. LEWIS
46 VP Research ... Vacant
05 VP for Academic Affairs ... Dr. Charles T. TAYLOR
17 VP Health Affairs & Cmty Health ... Dr. Jeffrey L. SUSMAN
10 VP Administration/Finance ... Mr. John W. WRAY
30 VP Advancement ... Mr. Daniel S. BLAIN
63 Dean College of Medicine ... Dr. Jeffrey L. SUSMAN
58 Dean College of Graduate Studies ... Vacant
67 Dean College of Pharmacy ... Dr. Charles T. TAYLOR
43 General Counsel ... Ms. Maria R. SCHIMER
04 Exec Assistant to the President ... Ms. Michelle M. MULHERN
32 Chief Student Affairs Officer ... Ms. Sandra M. EMERICK
88 Exec Dir Interprofess Education ... Ms. Holly A. GERZINA
88 Executive Director Research ... Ms. Elizabeth W. CLINE
09 Exec Dir Institutional Research ... Dr. Margarita D. KOKINOVA
84 Exec Dir Enrollment Services ... Ms. Heidi L. TERRY
88 Exec Dir Academic Services ... Ms. Penny R. SMITH
88 Director Comparative Medicine Unit ... Dr. Stanley D. DANNEMILLER
29 Director Alumni Relations ... Mr. Craig S. EYNON
38 Director Counseling Services ... Ms. Theresa C. NOVAK
11 Chief Operating Officer ... Ms. Carrie L. BAST
109 Dir Operations & Auxiliary Services ... Mr. Chris J. METTEE
13 Director Information Technology ... Mr. Ronald L. MCGRADY
15 Director Human Resources ... Ms. Barbara A. TOBIAS
18 Director Campus Operations ... Mr. James W. RANKIN
24 Dir Academic Technology Services ... Mr. Rey T. NOTARESCHI
26 Director Public Relations ... Mr. Roderick L. INGRAM, SR.
88 Director Learning Center ... Mr. Craig THEISSEN
19 Director Public Safety/Police Chief ... Ms. Kali A. MEONSKE
35 Dir Career Development & Advising ... Ms. Anita R. POKORNY
07 Director of Admissions ... Mr. James F. BARRETT
96 Accounting Purchasing Controller ... Ms. Kathy L. CHUDAKOFF
40 Supervisor Bookstore ... Ms. Christine L. KOVACICH
06 Registrar ... Ms. Mary Beth SEITH
37 Assoc Dir Financial Aid ... Mr. Michael A. KEMPE

Northwest State Community College (A)

22-600 State Route 34, Archbold OH 43502-9542
County: Henry FICE Identification: 008677
Unit ID: 204440
Telephone: (419) 267-5511 Carnegie Class: Assoc/HVT-High Non
FAX Number: (419) 267-3688 Calendar System: Semester
URL: www.northweststate.edu
Established: 1968 Annual Undergrad Tuition & Fees (In-State): $3,989
Enrollment: 3,612 Coed
Affiliation or Control: State IRS Status: 501(c)3
Highest Offering: Associate Degree
Accreditation: NH, ACBSP, ADNUR, MAC

01 President .... Dr. Thomas L. STUCKEY
05 VP for Academics .... Dr. Cindy KRUEGER
30 VP for Institutional Advancement .... Ms. Mari YODER
88 VP for Innovation .... Mr. Todd HERNANDEZ
32 Dean of Student Services .... Mr. Michael BLACK
50 Dean of Business Technologies .... Dr. Michael WOLFE
69 Dean of Allied Health & Public Svcs .... Mrs. Lori ROBISON
49 Dean of Arts & Science .... Ms. Lana SNIDER
66 Dean of Nursing .... Mrs. Lori BIRD
06 Registrar .... Ms. Connie KLINGSHIRN
18 Director of Plant Operations .... Mr. Timothy NELSON
15 Human Resource Officer .... Ms. Kathryn MCKELVEY
21 Director of Business Services .... Ms. Lynn SPEISER
07 Director of Admissions .... Ms. Amanda POTTS
10 Chief Fiscal Officer .... Ms. Kathy SOARDS
44 Chief Development .... Ms. Robbin WILCOX
37 Director Student Financial Aid .... Ms. Amber YOCOM
35 Coordinator Student Activities .... Mr. Michael JACOBS
26 Coordinator Communications .... Ms. Dawn HAUTER
40 Bookstore Manager .... Mr. Kemp STAPLETON

Notre Dame College (B)

4545 College Road, South Euclid OH 44121-4293
County: Cuyahoga FICE Identification: 003085
Unit ID: 204468
Telephone: (216) 381-1680 Carnegie Class: Masters/S
FAX Number: (216) 381-3802 Calendar System: Semester
URL: www.notredamecollege.edu
Established: 1922 Annual Undergrad Tuition & Fees: $27,520
Enrollment: 2,281 Coed
Affiliation or Control: Roman Catholic IRS Status: 501(c)3
Highest Offering: Master's
Accreditation: NH, NURSE, TED

01 President .... Mr. Thomas KRUCZEK
05 Int Vice Pres Student/Academic Affs .... Dr. Vincent PALOMBO
10 Sr Vice Pres Finance/Administration .... Mr. John TORTELLI
45 Vice Pres for Assessment Planning .... Vacant
30 Dir of Institutional Advancement .... Ms. Shawna WHITLOCK
31 Vice Pres for Board/Community Rels .... Ms. Karen L. POELKING
20 Assoc Dean of Academic Affairs .... Vacant
66 Nursing Division Chair .... Dr. Patrice MCCARTHY
53 Education Division Chair .... Dr. Yvonne ALLEN
81 Math & Science Division Chair .... Dr. Sharon BALCHAK
50 Business Division Chair .... Mr. Vince PALOMBO
57 Fine Arts Division Chair .... Ms. Lynn ZIMMERMAN
27 Director of Public Relations .... Vacant
84 Dean of Enrollment .... Ms. Beth FORD
07 Director of Admissions .... Mr. David HILBORN
88 Int Dir of the Finn Center (Adult) .... Dr. Carol ZIEGLER
32 Dean for Student Affairs .... Dr. Karl RISHE
06 Registrar .... Ms. Jameka WINDHAM
37 Dir Student Financial Assistance .... Ms. Mary MCCRYSTAL
88 Director of Student Accounts .... Ms. Annette SZALAY
19 Director Security/Safety .... Mr. Jeff SCOTT
18 Director Physical Plant .... Mr. Tom MEEKS
13 Director Information Technology .... Mr. Michael KIEC
15 Director Personnel Services .... Ms. Susan ANDERSON
08 Director of Library .... Ms. Karen ZOLLER
42 Director Ctr Campus Theol/Ministry .... Mr. Ted STEINER
78 Director Coop Educ & Career Devel .... Ms. Sarah HYDE-PINNER
38 Director of Counseling Center .... Mr. Jerry HAYES
39 Director of Residence Life .... Mr. Nick AYLWARD
29 Dir Alumni Rels/Asc Dir Development .... Ms. Heather COONTZ
04 Admin Assistant to the President .... Ms. April KENNEDY
14 Chief Information Officer .... Vacant
26 Chief Communications Officer .... Mr. Brian JOHNSTON
106 Online Education/E-learning .... Dr. Carol ZIEGLER

Oberlin College (C)

173 West Lorain Street, Oberlin OH 44074-1057
County: Lorain FICE Identification: 003086
Unit ID: 204501
Telephone: (440) 775-8121 Carnegie Class: Bac-A&S
FAX Number: (440) 775-8886 Calendar System: 4/1/4
URL: www.oberlin.edu
Established: 1833 Annual Undergrad Tuition & Fees: $50,582
Enrollment: 2,978 Coed
Affiliation or Control: Independent Non-Profit IRS Status: 501(c)3
Highest Offering: Master's
Accreditation: NH

01 President .... Mr. Marvin KRISLOV
10 Vice President for Finance .... Dr. Michael FRANDSEN
30 VP Development/Alumni Affair .... Mr. William BARLOW
26 Vice President College Relations .... Mr. Ben JONES
05 Dean of Studies .... Dr. Joyce BABYAK
49 Dean of Arts & Sciences .... Dr. Timothy ELGREN
64 Dean Conservatory Music .... Ms. Andrea KALYN
32 Dean of Student Life .... Dr. Eric ESTES
45 VP for Strategic Initiatives .... Dr. Kathryn STUART
07 Dean Admissions/Financial Aid .... Mrs. Debra J. CHERMONTE
43 VP/General Counsel and Secretary .... Ms. Sandhya SUBRAMANIAN
86 Spec Asst Community/Govt Relations .... Ms. Tita REED
21 Assoc Vice Pres Finance/Controller .... Mr. Mark R. BATES
29 Exec Director Alumni Assoc .... Ms. Danielle YOUNG
88 Sr Assoc Dean of College Arts & Sci .... Dr. Steve WOJTAL
88 Assoc Dean of College of Arts & Sci .... Dr. Pablo MITCHELL
13 Chief Tech Ofcr/Dir Computing Ctr .... Dr. John E. BUCHER
08 Interim Director of Libraries .... Dr. Alan BOYD
07 Director Admissions Conservatory .... Mr. Michael C. MANDEREN
38 Director of Counseling Center .... Mr. John HARSHBARGER
57 Director of Allen Art Museums .... Dr. Andria DERSTINE
06 Registrar .... Ms. Elizabeth CLERKIN
37 Director of Financial Aid .... Mr. Robert A. REDDY, JR.
09 Director of Institutional Research .... Mr. Ross PEACOCK
18 Asst VP for Facilities .... Mr. Tom PICCORELLI
36 Director Career Devel/Placement .... Vacant
42 Director Religious and Spiritual Li .... Rev. David F. DORSEY
39 Dir Residential/Dining Services .... Mr. Adrian BATISTA
41 Director of Physical Educ/Athletics .... Ms. Natalie WINKELFOOS
19 Director of Safety & Security .... Ms. Marjorie BURTON
28 Director Multicultural Affairs .... Vacant
96 Director of Purchasing .... Mr. James S. KLAIBER
15 Chief Human Resources Officer .... Mr. Joseph VITALE, JR.
04 Administrative Asst to President .... Mrs. Jennifer S. BRADFIELD
104 Assoc Dean & Dir of Intl Studies .... Ms. Ellen SAYLES
100 Chief of Staff .... Ms. Jane MATHISON
102 Exec Dir Office of Foundations .... Ms. Pamela SNYDER
44 Sr Philanthropic Advisor .... Ms. Catherine GLETHEROW

Ohio Business College (D)

4525 Trueman Boulevard, Hilliard OH 43026
Telephone: (614) 891-5030 FICE Identification: 030658
Accreditation: ACICS, MAC

Ohio Business College (E)

5202 Timber Commons Drive, Sandusky OH 44870-5894
Telephone: (419) 627-8345 Identification: 666467
Accreditation: ACICS, MAC

† Branch campus of Ohio Business College, Sheffield Village, OH.

Ohio Business College, Lorain Branch (F)

5095 Waterford Drive, Sheffield Village OH 44035-0701
County: Lorain FICE Identification: 021585
Unit ID: 203720
Telephone: (440) 934-3101 Carnegie Class: Assoc/HVT-High Non
FAX Number: (440) 934-3105 Calendar System: Quarter
URL: www.ohiobusinesscollege.edu
Established: 1903 Annual Undergrad Tuition & Fees: $8,672
Enrollment: 420 Coed
Affiliation or Control: Proprietary IRS Status: Proprietary
Highest Offering: Associate Degree
Accreditation: ACICS, MAC

01 Executive Director .... Mrs. Rosanne CATELLA
07 Admissions Director .... Mrs. Rosemerry NICKELS
10 Financial Manager .... Mrs. Christine TODD
36 Career Services .... Ms. Cheryl JANKOWSKI

Ohio Christian University (G)

1476 Lancaster Pike, Circleville OH 43113-0458
County: Pickaway FICE Identification: 003030
Unit ID: 201964
Telephone: (740) 474-8896 Carnegie Class: Bac-Diverse
FAX Number: (740) 477-7755 Calendar System: Semester
URL: www.ohiochristian.edu
Established: 1948 Annual Undergrad Tuition & Fees: $18,840
Enrollment: 4,058 Coed
Affiliation or Control: Other Protestant IRS Status: 501(c)3
Highest Offering: Master's
Accreditation: NH, BI, NURSE, TEAC

01 President .... Dr. Mark A. SMITH
05 Provost .... Dr. Hank KELLY
10 Vice President of Finance .... Mr. Robert HARTMAN
30 Vice President for Advancement .... Mr. Craig BROWN
32 Vice President Student Development .... Dr. Rick CHRISTMAN
11 Vice President of Operations .... Mr. Mike FRACASSA
13 Vice President for IT .... Mr. Ryan WHISLER
09 Asst VP for Institutional Research .... Dr. Cynthia TWEEDELL
06 Registrar .... Dr. Rodney SONES
84 Vice President of Enrollment .... Mr. Michael EGENREIDER
55 VP College of Adult & Graduate Stds .... Dr. Bradford SAMPLE
84 VP of AGS Enrollment Mgmt .... Ms. Sylvia LACASCHI-DECKER
35 Asst VP of Student Developement .... Ms. Rebecca WAKEMAN
08 Director of Library Services .... Mrs. Barbara MEISTER
37 Director Student Financial Services .... Mr. Wes BROTHERS
41 Athletic Director .... Mr. Ben BELLEMAN
29 Alumni Relations Coordinator .... Mr. Jonathan FAULKS
50 Dean/Director of Business .... Mr. Monty LOBB
50 Director of Business AGS .... Dr. Debra GRIMM
53 Director of Education .... Ms. Valerie JONES
04 Administrative Asst to President .... Mrs. Ronda BALDWIN
07 Director of Admissions .... Mr. Kevin EDWARDS
105 Director Web Services/Social Media .... Mr. Jeremy DAVIS
106 PSEO Director .... Mrs. Beth ASH
19 Director of Security .... Mr. Tyler PAYNE
26 Communications & Marketing Coord .... Ms. Sarah COX
43 Legal Services .... Mr. Jeremy DAVITZ

Ohio College of Massotherapy (H)

225 Heritage Woods Drive, Akron OH 44321-1363
County: Summit FICE Identification: 031163
Unit ID: 204592
Telephone: (330) 665-1084 Carnegie Class: Spec 2-yr-Health
FAX Number: (330) 319-7733 Calendar System: Semester
URL: www.ocm.edu
Established: 1973 Annual Undergrad Tuition & Fees: $8,475
Enrollment: 72 Coed
Affiliation or Control: Proprietary IRS Status: Proprietary
Highest Offering: Associate Degree
Accreditation: ACCSC

01 President .... Mr. Jeffrey S. MORROW
11 Director of Administration .... Mrs. Debra M. SMITH

Ohio Dominican University (I)

1216 Sunbury Road, Columbus OH 43219-2099
County: Franklin FICE Identification: 003035
Unit ID: 204617
Telephone: (614) 251-4500 Carnegie Class: Masters/M
FAX Number: (614) 251-4634 Calendar System: Semester
URL: www.ohiodominican.edu
Established: 1911 Annual Undergrad Tuition & Fees: $30,270
Enrollment: 2,707 Coed
Affiliation or Control: Roman Catholic IRS Status: 501(c)3
Highest Offering: Master's
Accreditation: NH, ACBSP, #ARCPA, SW, TED

01 President .... Dr. Peter CIMBOLIC
05 Vice President Academic Affairs .... Dr. Theresa HOLLERAN
32 Vice Pres Stdnt Dev/Dean Retention .... Dr. James A. CARIDI
10 Vice Pres Finance & Admin/CFO .... Mr. Clair KNAPP
30 Vice President for Advancement .... Mr. Adam NEAL
26 Vice Pres Marketing & Public Rels .... Mr. Mark COOPER
04 Executive Asst to the President .... Ms. Amy THOMAS
35 Asst Vice Pres Student Development .... Ms. Sharon REED
20 Assoc Vice Pres Academic Affairs .... Dr. Linda WOLF
58 Dean Graduate/Professional Studies .... Vacant
51 Exec Dir of Adult/Continuing Educ .... Ms. Karen GRAY
09 Dir of Inst Research/Assessment .... Dr. Linda WOLF
06 Registrar .... Mrs. Christine GROVES
07 Director of Admissions .... Ms. Michelle HOUCK
08 Director of the Library .... Ms. Michelle SARFF
37 Director of Financial Aid .... Ms. Tara SCHNEIDER
36 Director Career Services .... Ms. Mandy POWELL
38 Director of Counseling Services .... Mr. Michael LEWIS
85 Director of International Education .... Ms. Deanna SHINE
42 Director of Campus Ministry .... Sr. Margie DAVIS
13 Chief Information Officer .... Ms. Christine KURTH
15 Director of Human Resources .... Ms. Krystina LAMB
18 Director of Physical Facilities .... Mr. Rick HENDERSON
29 Dir of Alumni Rels/Annual Giving .... Ms. Christie FLOOD-WEINER
39 Director of Resident Life .... Ms. Lara CONRAD
41 Athletic Director .... Mr. Jeff BLAIR
96 Director of Purchasing .... Vacant
19 Director of Safety & Security .... Ms. Lisa SPRAGUE
92 Director of Honors Program .... Mr. John MARAZITA

Ohio Northern University (J)

525 S Main Street, Ada OH 45810-1599
County: Hardin FICE Identification: 003089
Unit ID: 204635
Telephone: (419) 772-2000 Carnegie Class: Bac-Diverse
FAX Number: (419) 772-1932 Calendar System: Semester
URL: www.onu.edu
Established: 1871 Annual Undergrad Tuition & Fees: $28,810
Enrollment: 3,695 Coed
Affiliation or Control: United Methodist IRS Status: 501(c)3
Highest Offering: First Professional Degree
Accreditation: NH, BUS, CAATE, CEA, CS, ENG, EXSC, LAW, MT, MUS, NAIT, NURSE, PHAR, TED

01 President .... Dr. Daniel A. DIBIASIO
05 Provost/Vice Pres Academic Affairs .... Dr. David C. CRAGO
10 Vice President Financial Affairs .... Mr. William H. BALLARD
30 Vice Pres of University Advancement .... Ms. Shannon SPENCER
84 Vice Pres Enrollment Management .... Dr. William T. EIOLA
32 VP Student Affairs/Dean of Students .... Dr. Adriane THOMPSON-BRADSHAW
49 Interim Dean of Arts & Sciences .... Dr. Tena ROEPKE
54 Dean of Engineering .... Dr. Eric T. BAUMGARTNER
67 Dean of Pharmacy .... Dr. Steven J. MARTIN
50 Dean Business Administration .... Dr. James W. FENTON
61 Dean of Law .... Mr. Richard C. BALES
30 Senior Director of Development .... Mr. Scott D. WILLS
08 Director of Heterick Library .... Ms. Kathleen BARIL
39 Dir of Res Life/Int Dir Career Svcs .... Mr. Justin COURTNEY

38 Director of Counseling ... Dr. Michael SCHAFER
29 Int Director of Alumni Relations . Mrs. Annmarie BAUMGARTNER
08 Law Librarian ... Dr. Nancy A. ARMSTRONG
42 University Chaplain ... Dr Rev. David MACDONALD
18 Director of Physical Plant ... Mr. Marc STALEY
13 Director of Technology ... Mr. Jeff RIEMAN
09 Director of Institutional Research ... Dr. Omer MINHAS
15 Director of Human Resources ... Ms. Tonya PAUL
20 Associate Academic Officer ... Dr. Juliet K. HURTIG
37 Director of Student Financial Aid ... Mrs. Melanie WEAVER
92 Director of Honors Program ... Dr. Patrick T. CROSKERY
21 Controller ... Mr. Mark RUSSELL
26 Dir of Communications & Marketing ... Mrs. Amy PRIGGE
07 Director of Admissions ... Ms. Deborah MILLER
06 Registrar ... Ms. Melanie HOUGH
28 Director Multicultural Development ... Ms. LaShonda GURLEY
41 Athletic Director ... Mr. Thomas SIMMONS
44 Director of Annual Giving ... Ms. Kelly ANDERSON
96 Manager of Purchasing ... Ms. Vicki J. NIESE
04 Executive Assistant to President ... Ms. Ann DONNELLY HAMILTON
101 Secretary of the Institution/ Board ... Ms. Sharon A. STECHSCHULTE
19 Director Security/Safety ... Mr. George SLEESMAN
25 Chief Contracts/Grants Admin ... Ms. Beckie WATERCUTTER

The Ohio State University Main Campus (A)

281 W. Lane Ave., Columbus OH 43210-1358
County: Franklin FICE Identification: 003090
Unit ID: 204796
Telephone: (614) 292-6446 Carnegie Class: DU-Highest
FAX Number: (614) 292-9180 Calendar System: Semester
URL: www.osu.edu
Established: 1870 Annual Undergrad Tuition & Fees (In-State): $10,037
Enrollment: 58,322 Coed
Affiliation or Control: State IRS Status: 501(c)3
Highest Offering: Doctorate
Accreditation: NH, ACAE, ART, AUD, BUS, BUSA, CAATE, CACREP, CAHIIM, CIDA, CLPSY, COARC, CONST, CS, DANCE, DENT, DH, DIETC, DIETD, DIETI, DMS, ENG, HSA, IPSY, LAW, LSAR, MED, #MFCD, MIDWF, MT, MUS, NMT, NURSE, OPT, OPTR, OT, PCSAS, PH, PHAR, PLNG, PTA, FTT, SP, SPAA, SW, TED, THEA, VET

01 President ... Dr. Michael V. DRAKE
05 Executive Vice Pres/Provost ... Dr. Bruce MCPHERON
10 Senior VP Business & Finance/CFO ... Mr. Geoffrey CHATAS
43 Sr VP & General Counsel ... Mr. Christopher M. CULLEY
32 Sr Vice President for Student Life . Dr. Javaune ADAMS-GASTON
20 Vice Provost for Academic Planning ... Mr. Michael J. BOEHM
26 VP University Communications ... Ms. Ann HAMILTON
15 Sr VP Talent/Cult & Human Resources .. Ms. Andreaa DOUGLASS
46 Sr Vice Pres for Research ... Dr. Caroline WHITACRE
86 Vice Pres of Govt Affairs ... Mr. Blake THOMPSON
23 Exec Vice Pres Health Sciences ... Dr. Sheldon M. RETCHIN
47 Vice Pres Ag Admin & Dean FAES ... Dr. Bruce MCPHERON
30 Sr VP for Advance/Pres OSU Found ... Mr. Michael EICHER
28 Vice Prov Diversity & Inclusion ... Dr. Sharon DAVIES
20 Vice Prov UG Studies & Dean UG Educ .. Dr. Wayne E. CARLSON
58 Int Vice Provost/Dean Grad School ... Dr. Scott HERNESS
41 Vice President/Director Athletics ... Mr. Gene D. SMITH
44 Vice President of Development ... Mr. David RIPPLE
18 Assoc VP Facilities Op/Dev ... Ms. Mary L. READEY
07 Assoc VP Enrol Svcs & Dir of Admiss ... Mr. Vern GRANGER
13 Vice President and CIO ... Mr. Michael HOFHERR
08 Director of Libraries ... Ms. Carol P. DIEDRCHS
100 Chief of Staff ... Ms. Katie HALL
101 Secretary Board of Trustees ... Mr. Blake THOMPSON
17 COO Medical Center ... Dr. Peter E. GEIER
85 Vice Prov Global Strat/Intl Affs ... Dr. William I. BRUSTEIN
90 Exec Dir Ohio Supercomputr Ctr ... Mr. Pankaj SHAW
29 SVP Alumni Rels/CEO Alumni Assoc ... Mr. James E. SMITH
12 Exec Dean of Reg Campuses ... Dr. William L. MACDONALD
49 Vice Prov & Exec Dean Arts & Sci ... Dr. David C. MANDERSCHEID
50 Dean Fisher Col of Business ... Dr. Anil K. MAKHIJA
52 Dean College of Dentistry ... Dr. Patrick M. LLOYD
53 Dean College of Educ & Hum Ecology ... Dr. Cheryl L. ACHTERBERG
54 Dean College of Engineering ... Dr. David B. WILLIAMS
61 Dean College of Law ... Dr. Alan C. MICHAELS
63 Dean College of Medicine ... Dr. E. Christopher ELLISON
88 Dean College of Optometry ... Dr. Karla S. ZADNIK
67 Dean College of Pharmacy ... Dr. Henry J. MANN
69 Dean College of Public Health ... Dr. William J. MARTIN
70 Dean College of Social Work ... Dr. Tom GREGOIRE
74 Dean Col Veterinary Medicine ... Dr. Lonnie KING
66 Dean College of Nursing ... Dr. Bernadette MELNYK
84 VP Strategic Enrollment Planning ... Mr. Dolan EVANOVICH
09 Asst VP Inst Research/Planning .... Ms. Julie CARPENTER-HUBIN
37 Exec Dir Student Financial Aid ... Ms. Diane CORBETT
06 University Registrar ... Mr. Brad MYERS
88 Director of OES Analysis & Reportng ... Ms. Gail C. STEPHENOFF
35 Sr Assoc VP Student Life ... Dr. Gretchen METZELAARS
96 Director of Purchasing ... Mr. Russell CHUNG
11 Sr Vice Pres Admin & Planning ... Mr. Jay D. KASEY
40 General Manager OSU Bookstores ... Ms. Kathy SMITH
19 Asst VP Public Safety ... Mr. Vernon L. BAISDEN
39 Director Housing Administration . Ms. Toni GREENSLADE-SMITH
88 Dean JG College of Public Affairs ... Dr. Trevor L. BROWN

The Ohio State University Agricultural Technical Institute (B)

1328 Dover Road, Wooster OH 44691-4000
County: Wayne FICE Identification: 010687
Unit ID: 204662
Telephone: (330) 264-3911 Carnegie Class: Spec 2-yr-Other
FAX Number: (330) 287-1333 Calendar System: Semester
URL: ati.osu.edu/
Established: 1971 Annual Undergrad Tuition & Fees (In-State): $7,203
Enrollment: 702 Coed
Affiliation or Control: State IRS Status: 501(c)3
Highest Offering: Associate Degree
Accreditation: NH

01 Interim Director ... Dr. Thom JANINI
05 Assoc Director Academic Affairs ... Ms Jeanne OSBORNE
26 Mrktng & Communications Coordinator ... Ms. Frances P. WHITED
03 Assistant Director ... Vacant
37 Coordinator Student Financial Aid ... Ms. Barbara LAMOREAUX
07 Manager of Enrollment ... Mr. David DIETRICH
10 Business Manager ... Ms. Lisa SIMPSON
32 Coordinator Student Programs ... Ms. Kathy E. MAKSYMICZ
40 Bookstore Manager ... Vacant
08 ATI Head Librarian ... Ms. Kathy YODER
19 Police Seargent ... Mr. Chad K. STANTON
13 Systems Manager ... Mr. Rick L. MITCHELL
50 Director Business Trng & Educ Svcs ... Ms. Kimberly J. SAYERS
39 Housing Coordinator ... Mr. Michael STEINER
88 Licensed Psych/Disability Svcs ... Dr. Jaqueline BELANGER
88 Program Director Program EXCEL ... Ms Dee Dee SNYDER
06 Academic Records Manager ... Ms Peggy E. LAMBERT
35 Coordinator Student Services ... Ms. Ruth MONTZ

The Ohio State University at Lima Campus (C)

4240 Campus Drive, Lima OH 45804-3597
Telephone: (419) 995-8600 FICE Identification: 003092
Accreditation: &NH

† Regional accreditation is carried under the parent institution in Columbus, OH.

The Ohio State University Mansfield Campus (D)

1760 University Drive, Mansfield OH 44906-1599
Telephone: (419) 755-4011 FICE Identification: 003093
Accreditation: &NH

† Regional accreditation is carried under the parent institution in Columbus, OH.

The Ohio State University at Marion (E)

1465 Mount Vernon Avenue, Marion OH 43302-5628
Telephone: (740) 389-6786 FICE Identification: 003094
Accreditation: &NH

† Regional accreditation is carried under the parent institution in Columbus, OH.

The Ohio State University Newark Campus (F)

1179 University Drive, Newark OH 43055-1990
Telephone: (740) 366-3321 FICE Identification: 003095
Accreditation: &NH

† Regional accreditation is carried under the parent institution in Columbus, OH.

Ohio Technical College (G)

1374 E 51st Street, Cleveland OH 44103-1269
County: Cuyahoga FICE Identification: 011745
Unit ID: 204608
Telephone: (216) 881-1700 Carnegie Class: Spec 2-yr-Tech
FAX Number: (216) 881-9145 Calendar System: Quarter
URL: www.ohiotech.edu
Established: 1969 Annual Undergrad Tuition & Fees: N/A
Enrollment: 1,073 Coed
Affiliation or Control: Proprietary IRS Status: Proprietary
Highest Offering: Associate Degree
Accreditation: ACCSC

01 President ... Mr. Bill HANTL
07 Director of Admissions ... Mr. Greg KOZARIK

Ohio University Main Campus (H)

1 Ohio University, Athens OH 45701-2979
County: Athens FICE Identification: 003100
Unit ID: 204857
Telephone: (740) 593-1000 Carnegie Class: DU-Higher
FAX Number: N/A Calendar System: Semester
URL: www.ohio.edu
Established: 1804 Annual Undergrad Tuition & Fees (In-State): $11,548
Enrollment: 29,217 Coed
Affiliation or Control: State IRS Status: 501(c)3
Highest Offering: Doctorate
Accreditation: NH, AAFCS, ADNUR, #ARCPA, AUD, BUS, BUSA, CAATE, CACREP, CIDA, CLPSY, CORE, CS, DANCE, DIETD, @DIETI, ENG, FEPAC, JOUR, MUS, NAIT, NFPA, NURSE, OSTEO, PH, PTA, SP, SW, TED, THEA

01 President ... Dr. Roderick J. MCDAVIS
100 Chief of Staff President's Ofc ... Ms. Jennifer KIRKSEY
05 Executive Vice President & Provost ... Dr. Pam BENOIT
10 VP for Finance & Administration ... Ms. Deborah SHAFFER
32 VP for Student Affairs ... Dr. Jason PINA
30 VP Univ Advance/Pres/CEO OU Fdn ... Mr. Bryan BENCHOFF
13 Chief Information Officer ... Mr. Craig BANTZ
46 VP Research & Dean Grad College ... Dr. Joseph SHIELDS
84 Vice Provost Enrollment Management ... Mr. Craig CORNELL
43 General Counsel ... Mr. John J. BIANCAMANO
26 Exec Dir Comm/Marketing ... Ms. Renea MORRIS
88 Interim Dean University College ... Dr. Peter MATHER
45 Sr Vice Pres Strategic Initiatives ... Mr. Stephen GOLDING
49 Dean College of Arts & Sciences ... Dr. Robert FRANK
50 Dean College of Business ... Dr. Hugh SHERMAN
60 Dean Scripps Col Communication ... Dr. Scott TITSWORTH
53 Dean Patton College of Education ... Dr. Renee A. MIDDLETON
54 Dean Russ Col Engineering/Tech ... Dr. Dennis IRWIN
57 Interim Dean College of Fine Arts ... Dr. Elizabeth SAYRS
69 Dean Col Health/Human Services ... Dr. Randy LEITE
92 Dean Honors Tutorial College ... Dr. Jeremy WEBSTER
63 Dean Heritage Col Osteopathic Med ... Dr. Kenneth JOHNSON
62 Dean University Libraries ... Mr. Scott H. SEAMAN
35 Dean of Students ... Dr. Jenny HALL-JONES
12 Exec Dean Regional Campuses ... Dr. William WILLAN
12 Dean Eastern Campus ... Dr. Paul ABRAHAM
12 Dean Southern Campus ... Dr. Nicole PENNINGTON
12 Dean Chillicothe Campus ... Dr. Martin TUCK
12 Dean Lancaster Campus ... Dr. James SMITH
12 Dean Zanesville Campus ... Dr. Jenifer CUSHMAN
20 Associate Provost Academic Affairs ... Dr. Howard DEWALD
58 Director Graduate Student Services ... Dr. Katherine TADLOCK
88 Vice Provost Global Affairs ... Dr. Lorna Jean EDMONDS
28 Vice Prov Diversity & Inclusion ... Dr. Shari CLARKE
09 Assoc Prov Inst Rsrch/Effectiveness ... Dr. Barbara WHARTON
41 Director of Athletics ... Mr. Jim SCHAUS
06 University Registrar ... Mrs. Debra M. BENTON
15 Chief Human Resources Officer ... Ms. Colleen BENDEL
29 Asst Vice Pres Alumni Relations ... Ms. Jennifer NEUBAUER
36 Asst Dean for Career Services ... Mr. Imants JAUNARAJS
07 Asst Vice Provost/Dir Ungrad Admiss .. Ms. Candace BOENINGER
38 Director Counseling Services ... Dr. Alfred B. WEINER
44 Exec Dir of Develop Planned Giving ... Ms. Kelli KOTOWSKI
37 Director Student Financial Aid ... Ms. Valerie MILLER
23 Medical Dir of Campus Care ... Dr. John J. KEMERER
106 Senior Vice Provost for Instruction ... Mr. Brad COHEN
96 Director of Procurement Services ... Ms. Laura NOWICKI
19 Chief of Police/Dir Campus Safety ... Chief Andrew POWERS
85 Assoc Dir Intl Students/Fac Svcs ... Dr. Krista MCCALLUM-BEATTY
39 Exec Director of Residential Hous ... Mr. Peter TRENTACOSTE
109 Asst Vice Pres Auxiliary Services ... Ms. Christine SHEETS
24 Media Library Manager ... Ms. Robin KRIVESTI
88 Bursar ... Ms. Sherry DOWNS
101 Secretary to Board of Trustees ... Dr. David MOORE
11 Sr Assoc VP of Tech/Admin Svcs ... Mr. Joseph LALLEY
86 Director of Government Relations ... Mr. Eric BURCHARD
88 Ombudsman ... Mr. Mac STRICKLEN
04 Administrative Asst to President ... Ms. Kelli TACKETT

Ohio University Chillicothe Campus (I)

PO Box 629, 101 University Drive,
Chillicothe OH 45601-0629
Telephone: (740) 774-7200 FICE Identification: 003102
Accreditation: &NH

† Regional accreditation is carried under the parent institution in Athens, OH.

Ohio University Eastern Campus (J)

45425 National Road, Saint Clairsville OH 43950-9724
Telephone: (740) 695-1720 FICE Identification: 003101
Accreditation: &NH

† Regional accreditation is carried under the parent institution in Athens, OH.

Ohio University Lancaster Campus (K)

1570 Granville Pike, Lancaster OH 43130-1097
Telephone: (740) 654-6711 FICE Identification: 003104
Accreditation: &NH, MAC

† Regional accreditation is carried under the parent institution in Athens, OH.

Ohio University Southern Campus (L)

1804 Liberty Avenue, Ironton OH 45638-2279
Telephone: (740) 533-4600 Identification: 666000
Accreditation: &NH

† Regional accreditation is carried under the parent institution in Athens, OH.

Ohio University Zanesville Branch (M)

1425 Newark Road, Zanesville OH 43701-2695
Telephone: (740) 453-0762 FICE Identification: 003108

Accreditation: &NH

† Regional accreditation is carried under the parent institution in Athens, OH.

Ohio Valley College of Technology (A)

15258 State Route 170, East Liverpool OH 43920
County: Columbiana FICE Identification: 023014
Unit ID: 204884
Telephone: (330) 385-1070 Carnegie Class: Spec 2-yr-Health
FAX Number: (330) 385-4606 Calendar System: Semester
URL: www.ovct.edu
Established: 1886 Annual Undergrad Tuition & Fees: $11,698
Enrollment: 146 Coed
Affiliation or Control: Proprietary IRS Status: Proprietary
Highest Offering: Associate Degree
Accreditation: ACICS, MAAB

01 President .... Mr. Scott S. ROGERS
05 Director of Academic Operations ..... Ms. Angel BROCK-MURPHY
37 Director of Financial Aid .... Ms. Rebecca STECKMAN

Ohio Wesleyan University (B)

61 S Sandusky Street, Delaware OH 43015-2398
County: Delaware FICE Identification: 003109
Unit ID: 204909
Telephone: (740) 368-2000 Carnegie Class: Bac-A&S
FAX Number: (740) 368-3299 Calendar System: Semester
URL: www.owu.edu
Established: 1842 Annual Undergrad Tuition & Fees: $43,230
Enrollment: 1,734 Coed
Affiliation or Control: United Methodist IRS Status: 501(c)3
Highest Offering: Baccalaureate
Accreditation: NH, MUS, TED

01 President .... Dr. Rockwell F. JONES
05 Provost .... Dr. Charles L. STINEMETZ
10 Int VP for Finance/Admin/Treasurer .... Dr. Alan NORTON
44 VP for University Advancement .... Ms. Colleen C. GARLAND
84 Vice President for Enrollment .... Ms. Susan R. DILENO
32 Vice President for Student Affairs .... Dr. Dwayne K. TODD
30 Asst VP for University Advancement .... Ms. Jodi L. BOPP
20 Dean of Academic Affairs .... Vacant
09 Assoc Provost for Inst Research .... Dr. Dale E. SWARTZENTRUBER
108 Asst Provost Assmt/Accreditation .... Dr. Barbara S. ANDERECK
37 Director Student Financial Aid .... Mr. Kevin F. PASKVAN
36 Director of Career Services .... Ms. Leslie J. MELTON
08 Chief Info Officer/Dir of Libraries .... Vacant
06 Registrar .... Ms. Shelly A. MCMAHON
14 Director of Computer Center .... Mr. Brian RELLINGER
13 Exec Director Information Tech .... Mr. Brian A. RELLINGER
19 Director of Public Safety .... Mr. Robert A. WOOD
29 Director Alumni Relations .... Ms. Katie P. WEBSTER
26 Director Marketing/Communications .... Mr. Will E. KOPP
85 Director International Student Svcs .... Mr. Darrell J. ALBON
18 Director Physical Plant .... Mr. Peter K. SCHANTZ
15 Interim Director Human Resources .... Mr. John A. SANDERS
31 Director Community Svc Learning .... Ms. Sally S. LEBER
04 Asst to President/Board Secy .... Ms. Shelly J. NUTTER
23 Director Wellness Center .... Ms. Marsha A. TILDEN
35 Dean of Students .... Vacant
39 Director Residential Life .... Ms. Wendy L. PIPER
41 Director of Athletics .... Mr. Roger D. INGLES
42 Chaplain .... Rev. Jon R. POWERS
89 Dean First Year Students .... Vacant
92 Honors Program Director .... Dr. Amy MCCLURE
93 Dir Multicultural Student Affairs .... Ms. Terree L. STEVENSON
102 Dir Foundation/Corp/Govt Relations .... Ms. Karen CROSMAN
07 Associate Director of Admissions .... Ms. Alisha M. COUCH
40 Bookstore Manager .... Ms. Lisa K. TACKETT
38 Coord Counseling/Mental Health Svcs .... Dr. Doug L. BENNETT
96 Purchasing Coordinator .... Ms. Melanie T. KALB

Otterbein University (C)

1 South Grove Street, Westerville OH 43081-2006
County: Franklin FICE Identification: 003110
Unit ID: 204936
Telephone: (614) 890-3000 Carnegie Class: Masters/M
FAX Number: (614) 823-3114 Calendar System: Semester
URL: www.otterbein.edu
Established: 1847 Annual Undergrad Tuition & Fees: $31,624
Enrollment: 2,791 Coed
Affiliation or Control: United Methodist IRS Status: 501(c)3
Highest Offering: Doctorate
Accreditation: NH, ANEST, CAATE, MUS, NURSE, TED, THEA

01 President .... Dr. Kathy A. KRENDL
100 Chief of Staff .... Ms. Kristine ROBBINS
05 Provost/VPAA .... Dr. Miguel MARTINEZ-SAENZ
32 Vice President Student Affairs .... Mr. Robert M. GATTI
10 Vice President for Business Affairs .... Mrs. Rebecca D. VAZQUEZ-SKILLINGS
30 VP Institutional Advancement .... Mr. Michael MCGREEVEY
84 Vice President for Enrollment .... Mr. Jefferson BLACKBURN-SMITH
20 Assoc VP AA/Dean Academic Services .... Dr. Wendy SHERMAN-HECKLER
91 Exec Director of Information Tech .... Mr. Dave BENDER
08 Director of the Library .... Ms. Tiffany LIPSTREU
06 Registrar .... Mr. David SCHNEIDER
26 Exec Dir Marketing/Communications .... Mrs. Jennifer PEARCE
36 Director Career Planning/Placement .... Mr. Ryan BRECHBILL
37 Director of Financial Aid .... Mr. Thomas V. YARNELL
41 Athletic Director .... Ms. Dawn STEWART
42 Chaplain .... Dr. Judy GUION-UTSLER
107 Dean School of Prof Studies .... Dr. Barbara H. SCHAFFNER
49 Dean School of Arts/Sciences .... Dr. Paul EISENSTEIN
85 Exec Director Intl Programs .... Vacant
07 Director of Admissions .... Mr. Mark MOFFETT
15 Director Human Resources .... Mr. Scott FITZGERALD
18 Director/Physical Plant .... Mr. David D. BELL
29 Director Alumni Relations .... Ms. Rebecca F. SMITH
28 Director of Diversity .... Mr. James PRYSOCK
21 Inst Rsrch Spec/Financial Analyst .... Mr. Christopher A. HAYTER
09 Director of Institutional Research .... Dr. Sean M. MCLAUGHLIN
19 Director of Security .... Mr. Larry BANASZAK
04 Executive Assistant to President .... Mrs. Tamara LOWKS
39 Director Student Housing .... Ms. Tracy BENNER
38 Director Student Counseling .... Dr. Kathleen RYAN
44 Director Annual or Planned Giving .... Mr. Matthew D'OYLY

Owens Community College (D)

30335 Oregon, PO Box 10000, Toledo OH 43699-1947
County: Wood FICE Identification: 005753
Unit ID: 204945
Telephone: (567) 661-7000 Carnegie Class: Assoc/MT-VT-Mix Trad/Non
FAX Number: N/A Calendar System: Semester
URL: www.owens.edu
Established: 1965 Annual Undergrad Tuition & Fees (In-State): $4,233
Enrollment: 12,561 Coed
Affiliation or Control: State IRS Status: 501(c)3
Highest Offering: Associate Degree
Accreditation: NH, ACBSP, ACFEI, ADNUR, CAHIIM, DH, DIETT, DMS, EMT, MAC, NAIT, OTA, PTAA, RAD, RADMAG, SURGT

01 President .... Dr. Mike BOWER
101 Secretary to the Board of Trustees .... Ms. Patricia JEZAK
04 Executive Assistant to President .... Ms. Vicki DUPKE
05 VP Academic Affairs/Provost .... Dr. Steve ROBINSON
10 Treasurer .... Mr. David CANNON
15 VP Human Resources .... Mr. Jack WITT
84 Int VP Enroll Mgmt/Stdnt Svcs .... Ms. Amy GIORDANO
20 Assoc VP Academic Services .... Ms. Denise SMITH
103 Executive Dir Wrkfrce/Comm Service .... Dr. Brian PASKVAN
12 Associate VP Findlay Campus .... Dr. Melissa GREEN
21 Controller .... Mr. Jeffrey GANUES
13 Chief Information Officer .... Dr. Connie SCHAFFER
19 Chief of Police .... Mr. Scott STEINKE
37 Director Financial Aid .... Ms. Andrea MORROW
26 Director Mktg & Communications .... Mr. Jason GRIFFIN
18 Executive Director Operations .... Mr. Michael MCDONALD
09 Director Inst Research .... Ms. Debra RATHKE
81 Dean School of STEM .... Mr. Glenn RETTIG
66 Dean School of Nursing/Health Prof .... Ms. Cathy FORD
50 Dean School Business/Info/Publc Svc .... Dr. Ann THEIS
57 Dean School of Liberal Arts .... Ms. Michele JOHNSON
62 Dean Library .... Mr. Tom SINK
106 Director eLearning .... Mr. Mark KARAMOL
43 Legal Services Coordinator .... Ms. Linda WIRICK
06 Registrar .... Mr. David SHAFFER
86 Exec Dir Govt/Comm Relations .... Ms. Jennifer FEHNRICH
29 Director Alumni Affairs .... Ms. Laura MOORE
32 Director Student Life/Stdnt Conduct .... Ms. Danielle FILIPCHUK
109 Director Auxiliary Services .... Ms. Danielle TRACY
85 Manager Intl Stdnt Services .... Ms. Annette SWANSON
41 Director Athletics .... Mr. JD ETTORE

Owens Community College Findlay Campus (E)

3200 Bright Road, Findlay OH 45840
Telephone: (567) 429-3500 Identification: 770360
Accreditation: &NH

† Regional accreditation is carried under the parent institution in Toledo, OH

Payne Theological Seminary (F)

PO Box 474, Wilberforce OH 45384-0474
County: Greene FICE Identification: 010017
Unit ID: 204990
Telephone: (937) 376-2946 Carnegie Class: Spec-4-yr-Faith
FAX Number: (937) 376-3330 Calendar System: 4/1/4
URL: www.payne.edu
Established: 1844 Annual Graduate Tuition & Fees: N/A
Enrollment: 125 Coed
Affiliation or Control: African Methodist Episcopal IRS Status: 501(c)3
Highest Offering: Master's; No Undergraduates
Accreditation: THEOL

01 Interim President .... Dr. Michael BROWN
05 Academic Dean .... Dr. Michael BROWN
100 Chief of Staff .... Rev. Brandon STEWART
20 Associate Dean .... Dr. Michael MILLER
30 Director of Development .... Rev. Jules DUNHAM HOWIE
10 Controller .... Ms. Elise PEYROUX
37 Financial Aid Officer .... Ms. Pat COPELY
06 Registrar .... Ms. Maryjo LEWIS

Pontifical College Josephinum (G)

7625 N High Street, Columbus OH 43235-1498
County: Franklin FICE Identification: 003113
Unit ID: 205027
Telephone: (614) 885-5585 Carnegie Class: Spec-4-yr-Faith
FAX Number: (614) 885-2307 Calendar System: Semester
URL: www.pcj.edu
Established: 1888 Annual Undergrad Tuition & Fees: $21,748
Enrollment: 226 Male
Affiliation or Control: Roman Catholic IRS Status: 501(c)3
Highest Offering: Beyond Master's But Less Than Doctorate
Accreditation: NH, THEOL

01 Rector/President .... R.Msgr. Christopher J. SCHRECK
10 VP for Administration/Treasurer .... Mr. John O. ERWIN
05 Vice Rec Sch Theology/Dn Cmty Life .... Rev. Raymond N. ENZWEILER
30 Vice President for Advancement .... Rev. John A. ALLEN
49 Vice Rector College Liberal Arts .... Rev. John ROZEMBAJGIER
73 Academic Dean School of Theology .... Dr. Perry J. CAHALL
49 Academic Dean College Liberal Arts .... Dr. David J. DE LEONARDIS
06 Registrar .... Mr. Samuel J. DEAN
08 Librarian .... Mr. Peter G. VERACKA
31 Dean of Community Life .... Rev. John S. BAKER
07 Director of Admissions .... Rev. Joseph A. MURPHY
37 Director Financial Aid .... Mrs. Marky LEICHTNAM
108 Dir of Inst Plng/Assessment/Accred .... Mr. Eric S. GRAFF
26 Director of Communications .... Ms. Carolyn DINOVO

PowerSport Institute (H)

21210 Emery Road, North Randall OH 44128
Telephone: (216) 587-5000 Identification: 770582
Accreditation: ACCSC

Professional Skills Institute (I)

1505 Holland Road, Maumee OH 43537
County: Lucas FICE Identification: 023377
Unit ID: 205054
Telephone: (419) 720-6670 Carnegie Class: Spec 2-yr-Health
FAX Number: (419) 720-6674 Calendar System: Quarter
URL: www.proskills.edu
Established: 1984 Annual Undergrad Tuition & Fees: $16,321
Enrollment: 286 Coed
Affiliation or Control: Proprietary IRS Status: Proprietary
Highest Offering: Associate Degree
Accreditation: ABHES, PTAA

01 CEO .... Mr. Daniel FINCH
07 Admissions Director .... Mr. Joe GRAHAM

Rabbinical College of Telshe (J)

28400 Euclid Avenue, Wickliffe OH 44092-2584
County: Lake FICE Identification: 003115
Unit ID: 205124
Telephone: (440) 943-5300 Carnegie Class: Spec-4-yr-Faith
FAX Number: (440) 943-5303 Calendar System: Quarter
Established: 1941 Annual Undergrad Tuition & Fees: $10,300
Enrollment: 88 Male
Affiliation or Control: Independent Non-Profit IRS Status: 501(c)3
Highest Offering: Doctorate
Accreditation: RABN

01 President .... Rabbi David GOLDBERG
06 Registrar .... Rabbi Abraham MATITIA

Remington College Cleveland Campus (K)

14445 Broadway Avenue, Cleveland OH 44125-1900
County: Cuyahoga FICE Identification: 007777
Unit ID: 375416
Telephone: (216) 475-7520 Carnegie Class: Spec 2-yr-Other
FAX Number: (216) 475-6055 Calendar System: Other
URL: www.remingtoncollege.edu
Established: 1990 Annual Undergrad Tuition & Fees: $15,933
Enrollment: 510 Coed
Affiliation or Control: Independent Non-Profit IRS Status: 501(c)3
Highest Offering: Associate Degree
Accreditation: ACCSC, PTAA

01 Campus President .... Mr. Todd ZVAIGZNE

Rosedale Bible College (L)

2270 Rosedale Road, Irwin OH 43029-9517
County: Madison FICE Identification: 034253
Unit ID: 439899
Telephone: (740) 857-1311 Carnegie Class: Spec 2-yr-Other
FAX Number: (877) 857-1312 Calendar System: Semester
URL: www.rosedale.edu
Established: 1952 Annual Undergrad Tuition & Fees: $8,336
Enrollment: 57 Coed
Affiliation or Control: Mennonite Church IRS Status: 501(c)3
Highest Offering: Associate Degree
Accreditation: BI

01 President .... Mr. Jonathan SHOWALTER
05 Academic Dean .... Mr. Phil WEBER
32 Dean of Students .... Mr. Matthew SHOWALTER
84 Director of Enrollment Services .... Mr. Hans SHENK
08 Director of Library Services .... Mr. Reuben SAIRS
06 Registrar .... Ms. Bethany GEIB
10 Chief Financial Officer .... Mr. Lynford SCHROCK
26 Chief Public Relations Officer .... Mr. Kenneth MILLER
04 Administrative Asst to President .... Mrs. Twila WEBER
18 Chief Facilities/Physical Plant .... Mr. Darnell BRENNEMAN

Saint Mary Seminary and Graduate School of Theology (A)

28700 Euclid Avenue, Wickliffe OH 44092-2585
County: Lake FICE Identification: 004061
Unit ID: 205319
Telephone: (440) 943-7600 Carnegie Class: Not Classified
FAX Number: (440) 943-7577 Calendar System: Semester
URL: www.stmarysem.edu
Established: 1848 Annual Graduate Tuition & Fees: N/A
Enrollment: N/A Coed
Affiliation or Control: Roman Catholic IRS Status: 501(c)3
Highest Offering: Doctorate; No Undergraduates
Accreditation: NH, THEOL

01 President/Rector .... Rev. Mark A. LATCOVICH
03 Vice President/Vice Rector .... Rev. Gerald J. BEDAR
05 Academic Dean .... Sr. Mary MCCORMICK, OSU
33 Student Dean .... Rev. Michael G. WOOST
42 Spiritual Director .... Rev. Mark HOLLIS
06 Registrar/Assistant Dean .... Sr. Brendon ZAJAC, SND
08 Librarian .... Mr. Alan K. ROME
10 Treasurer .... Mr. Philip GUBAN
04 Administrative Asst to President .... Ms. Kathryn C. SIMMONS
90 Director Academic Computing .... Sr. Brendon ZAJAC
18 Chief Facilities/Physical Plant .... Mr. Philip GUBAN
108 Director Institutional Assessment .... Dr. Edward KACZUK
13 Chief Info Technology Officer (CIO) .... Mr. Alan K. ROME
19 Director Security/Safety .... Mr. Philip GUBAN

School of Advertising Art (B)

1725 E David Road, Dayton OH 45440-1612
County: Montgomery FICE Identification: 025530
Unit ID: 205391
Telephone: (877) 300-9866 Carnegie Class: Spec 2-yr-A&S
FAX Number: (937) 294-5869 Calendar System: Semester
URL: www.saa.edu
Established: 1983 Annual Undergrad Tuition & Fees: $25,442
Enrollment: 139 Coed
Affiliation or Control: Proprietary IRS Status: Proprietary
Highest Offering: Associate Degree
Accreditation: ACCSC

01 Owner/President/Creative Director .... Ms. Jessica BARRY
03 Vice President .... Mr. Matt FLICK
06 Vice President/HR/Registrar .... Mr. Nathan SUMMERS
05 Director of Education .... Ms. Karen ABNEY KORN
36 Director of Career Services .... Ms. Roxann PATRICK
37 Director of Financial Aid .... Ms. Tracy GARDNER
26 Director of Communications .... Ms. Betsy WOODS
07 Director of Admissions .... Ms. Mariesa BLOOM

Shawnee State University (C)

940 Second Street, Portsmouth OH 45662-4344
County: Scioto FICE Identification: 009942
Unit ID: 205443
Telephone: (740) 351-3205 Carnegie Class: Bac-Diverse
FAX Number: (740) 351-3470 Calendar System: Semester
URL: www.shawnee.edu
Established: 1975 Annual Undergrad Tuition & Fees (In-State): $7,364
Enrollment: 4,247 Coed
Affiliation or Control: State IRS Status: 501(c)3
Highest Offering: Master's
Accreditation: NH, ADNUR, #CAATE, COARC, DH, EMT, MLTAD, NUR, OT, OTA, PTAA, RAD, TED

01 President .... Dr. Rick KURTZ
05 Provost/VP Academic Affairs .... Dr. Jeff BAUER
10 Vice President for Finance & Admin .... Dr. Elinda BOYLES
44 VP for Advancement & External Affs .... Mr. Eric BRAUN
84 VP for Enrollment Mgmt & Stdnt Affs .. Dr. Anne Marie GILLESPIE
43 General Counsel/Asst to the Pres .... Ms. Cheryl HACKER
26 Director Communications .... Ms. Elizabeth BLEVINS
107 Dean College Professional Studies .... Dr. Paul MADDEN
49 Dean College Arts & Sciences .... Dr. Roberta MILLIKEN
62 Dean Library Services .... Mr. Bob TRUSZ
13 Director Univ Information Systems .... Mr. Charles WARNER
30 Executive Director of Development .... Mr. Eric BRAUN
07 Interim Director of Admission .... Mr. Rick MERB
06 Registrar .... Mr. Mark MOORE
32 Dean of Students .... Ms. Marcie SIMMS
15 Director of Human Resources .... Ms. Malonda JOHNSON
41 Athletic Director .... Mr. Jeff HAMILTON
37 Director of Financial Aid .... Dr. Nicole NEAL
36 Director Student Career Development .... Ms. Nikki KARABINIS
38 Director of Counseling & Psych Svcs .... Dr. Linda KOENIG
58 Acting Dean of Graduate Studies .... Dr. Becky THIEL
88 Dean University College .... Dr. Brenda HAAS

85 Director for International Pgms .... Mr. Ryan WARNER
96 Dir of Procurement Services .... Ms. Fat CARSON
18 Director of Facilities .... Mr. Butch KOTCAMP
97 Director General Education Program .... Dr. Phil BLAU
09 Dir of Institutional Effectiveness .... Mr. Christopher SHAFFER
21 Controller .... Mr. Greg BALLENGEE
19 Chief of Police .... Mr. David THOROUGHMAN

Sinclair Community College (D)

444 W Third Street, Dayton OH 45402-1460
County: Montgomery FICE Identification: 003119
Unit ID: 205470
Telephone: (937) 512-3000 Carnegie Class: Assoc/MT-VT-High Non
FAX Number: (937) 512-4596 Calendar System: Semester
URL: www.sinclair.edu
Established: 1887 Annual Undergrad Tuition & Fees (In-District): $2,476
Enrollment: 19,093 Coed
Affiliation or Control: State/Local IRS Status: 501(c)3
Highest Offering: Associate Degree
Accreditation: NH, ACBSP, ACFEI, ADNUR, ART, CAHIIM, COARC, CSHSE, DH, DIETT, EMT, ENGT, MAC, MUS, OTA, PTAA, RAD, SURGT, THEA

00 President Emeritus .... Dr. Ned J. SIFFERLEN
01 President .... Dr. Steven L. JOHNSON
05 Provost .... Dr. Dave COLLINS
103 VP for Workforce Development .... Ms. Deb NORRIS
100 Chief of Staff .... Mr. Mitchell BAILEY
30 VP for Advancement .... Ms. Madeline ISELI
10 Sr VP and CFO .... Mr. Jeff BOUDOURIS
21 VP for Business Operations .... Dr. Ty STONE
88 VP for School & Community Partners .... Dr. Annesa CHEEK
45 VP for Organizational Development .... Dr. Mary GAIER
84 VP Enroll Mgmt & Student Affairs .... Vacant
12 VP for Regional Centers .... Dr. Scott MARKLAND
20 Associate Provost Stdnt Completion .... Dr. Kathleen CLEARY
81 Dean of Science/Math/Engineering .... Mr. Anthony PONDER
76 Dean Health Sciences .... Ms. Reni SHUCHAT
105 Dean Distance Learning/Inst Support .... Dr. Nancy THIBEAULT
20 Associate Provost .... Dr. Lori ZAKEL
50 Dean Business & Public Services .... Dr. Sue MERRELL
26 Director of Public Affairs .... Mr. Adam MURKA
83 Dean Arts/Commun & Social Science .... Ms. Shari RETHMAN
13 Chief Information Officer .... Mr. Scott MCCOLLUM
43 General Counsel .... Ms. Lauren ROSS
06 Registrar .... Ms. Tina HUMMONS
37 Director Financial Aid .... Mr. Matthew MOORE
104 Director International Education .... Ms. Deborah GAVLIK
88 Chief Academic Advising Officer .... Mr. Andy RUNYAN

South University (E)

4743 Richmond Road, Cleveland OH 44128
Telephone: (216) 755-5000 Identification: 770916
Accreditation: &SC, ACBSP, CACREP, NURSE, PTAA

† Regional accreditation is carried under the parent institution in Savannah, GA

Southern State Community College (F)

100 Hobart Drive, Hillsboro OH 45133-9488
County: Highland FICE Identification: 012870
Unit ID: 205966
Telephone: (937) 393-3431 Carnegie Class: Assoc/MT-VT-High Trad
FAX Number: (937) 393-9370 Calendar System: Semester
URL: www.sscc.edu
Established: 1975 Annual Undergrad Tuition & Fees (In-State): $4,352
Enrollment: 2,462 Coed
Affiliation or Control: State IRS Status: 501(c)3
Highest Offering: Associate Degree
Accreditation: NH, ADNUR, MAC

01 President .... Dr. Kevin S. BOYS
05 Vice President Academic Affairs .... Dr. Nicole ROADES
10 Vice President Business & Finance .... Mr. James E. BUCK
32 Vice Pres Student Svcs/Enroll Mgmt .... Mr. James BLAND
12 Director of Fayette Campus .... Dr. Jessica WISE
12 Director of Brown Co Campus .... Dr. J.R ROUSH
12 Director of Central Campus .... Mr. Jeff MONTGOMERY
103 Dean Workforce Dev/Community Svcs .... Mr. John JOY
15 Director of Human Resources .... Ms. Mindy MARKEY-GRABILL
88 Dean of Adult Opportunity Center .... Ms. Karyn EVANS
91 Computer System/Communication Mgr .... Ms. Shirley A. CORNWELL
26 Director of Public Relations .... Ms. Chris CROSS
06 Registrar .... Ms. Amanda THOMPSON
66 Director of Nursing .... Dr. Julianne KREBS
08 Librarian .... Ms. Angel MOOTISPAW
37 Director Financial Aid .... Ms. Linda MYERS
07 Director of Admissions .... Ms. Lisa HORD
41 Athletic Director .... Mr. Matt WELLS
13 Executive Director of IT Services .... Mr. Brian RICE
04 Executive Asst to President .... Ms. Robin THOLEN

† Enrollment figure emcompasses all 4 campuses

Southern State Community College Brown County Campus (G)

351 Brooks-Malott Rd, Mt Orab OH 45154
Telephone: (937) 444-7722 Identification: 770361
Accreditation: &NH

† Regional accreditation is carried under the parent institution in Hillsboro, OH

Southern State Community College Fayette Campus (H)

1270 US Route 62 SW, Washington Court House OH 43160
Telephone: (740) 333-5115 Identification: 770362
Accreditation: &NH, COARC

† Regional accreditation is carried under the parent institution in Hillsboro, OH

Southern State Community College North Campus (I)

1850 Davids Drive, Wilmington OH 45177
Telephone: (937) 382-6645 Identification: 770363
Accreditation: &NH

† Regional accreditation is carried under the parent institution in Hillsboro, OH

Stark State College (J)

6200 Frank Avenue, NW, North Canton OH 44720-7299
County: Stark FICE Identification: 010881
Unit ID: 205841
Telephone: (330) 494-6170 Carnegie Class: Assoc/MT-VT-High Trad
FAX Number: (330) 497-6313 Calendar System: Semester
URL: www.starkstate.edu
Established: 1960 Annual Undergrad Tuition & Fees (In-District): $3,686
Enrollment: 14,097 Coed
Affiliation or Control: State/Local IRS Status: 501(c)3
Highest Offering: Associate Degree
Accreditation: NH, ACBSP, ADNUR, CAHIIM, COARC, DH, @DIETT, ENGT, MAC, MLTAD, OTA, PTAA

01 President .... Dr. Para M. JONES
05 Provost and Chief Academic Officer .. Dr. Lada GIBSON-SHREVE
10 VP for Business and Finance .... Mr. Thomas A. CHIAPPINI
11 VP for EM/SS and Administration .... Mr. Michael DRONEY
15 Director of Human Resources .... Ms. Melissa A. GLANZ
53 Dean Ed/Liberal Arts/Math/Science .... Mr. Andrew STEPHAN
76 Dean Health and Human Services .... Vacant
21 Controller .... Mr. Scott ANDREANI
36 Director of Career Development .... Ms. Kristin HANNON
37 Dean Financial Aid and Registration .... Ms. Amy WELTY
18 Director of Physical Plant and Cons .... Mr. Steve SPRADLING
40 Bookstore Manager .... Ms. Kathryn FEICHTER
06 Registrar .... Ms. Pam ARRINGTON
26 Exec Dir Mktg & SSC Foundation .... Ms. Marisa ROHN
21 Director of Budget .... Mr. Bruce WYDER
09 Director of Institutional Research .... Mr. Peter TRUMPOWER
54 Dean Eng Tech/Info Tech .... Mr. Don BALL
106 Director eStarkState .... Ms. Linda MOROSKO
08 Head Librarian .... Ms. Marcia ADDISON
04 Exec Admin Asst to President .... Ms. Catherine D. SPINO
103 Exec Dir Workforce and Econ Devel .... Dr. Daryl REVOLDT
07 Exec Director of Admissions .... Mr. J.P COONEY

Stautzenberger College (K)

8001 Katherine Boulevard, Brecksville OH 44141
Telephone: (440) 838-1999 Identification: 770760
Accreditation: ACICS, CVT

Stautzenberger College (L)

1796 Indian Wood Circle, Maumee OH 43537-4007
County: Lucas FICE Identification: 004866
Unit ID: 205887
Telephone: (419) 866-0261 Carnegie Class: Assoc/HVT-Mix Trad/Non
FAX Number: (419) 867-9821 Calendar System: Quarter
URL: www.sctoday.edu
Established: 1926 Annual Undergrad Tuition & Fees: $11,610
Enrollment: 708 Coed
Affiliation or Control: Proprietary IRS Status: Proprietary
Highest Offering: Associate Degree
Accreditation: ACICS, MAC

01 Campus President .... Mr. Steven R. ALLEN
09 Compliance Officer .... Mr. Brian E. NIEDZWIECKI
07 Director of Admissions .... Ms. Amanda L. BOYD
05 Dean of Academics .... Ms. Susan M. LIPPENS
37 Financial Aid Director .... Mrs. Mari L. HUFFMAN
36 Career Services Director .... Mr. Robert A. GARVER
06 Registrar .... Ms. Victoria MEYERS
08 Head Librarian .... Ms. Lori VAN LIERE

Terra State Community College (M)

2830 Napoleon Road, Fremont OH 43420-9670
County: Sandusky FICE Identification: 008278
Unit ID: 206011
Telephone: (419) 334-8400 Carnegie Class: Assoc/MT-VT-High Trad
FAX Number: (419) 334-3719 Calendar System: Semester
URL: www.terra.edu
Established: 1968 Annual Undergrad Tuition & Fees (In-State): $4,284
Enrollment: 2,603 Coed

Affiliation or Control: State IRS Status: 501(c)3
Highest Offering: Associate Degree
Accreditation: NH, ADNUR, CAHIIM, PTAA

01 President Dr. Jerome WEBSTER
10 VP for Financial Affairs Mr. Randy MCCULLOUGH
84 Dean of Enroll & Student Services Mr. Heath MARTIN
15 Director of Human Resources Ms. Nanci KOSANKA
05 Vice President Academic Affairs Dr. Cindy KRUEGER
50 Dean Business/Communication/Arts Ms. Jolene MEYERS
81 Dean STEM and Workforce Mr. Andrew G. CARROLL
76 Dean Allied Health/Nursing/Pub Ser Ms. Amy ANWAY
30 VP Inst Advancement Dr. Cory STINE
09 Dean Planning & Inst Effect Vacant
09 Interim Shared Registrar Ms. Connie KLINGSHIRN
37 Interim Director Financial Aid Ms. Marla MOHR
19 Director Campus Safety/Evening Svcs Mr. Jeffery HUFFMAN
21 Coordinator of Financial Services Ms. Renee D. BROWN
13 Manager Information Technology Mr. Wayne YERDON
08 Librarian Ms. Clare KEATING
88 Coordinator of Global Partnerships Dr. Julianna G. BORDERS
04 Administrative Asst to President Ms. Holly HOFFMAN
106 Instructional Technologist Ms. Melinda YERDON
32 Associate Dean of Students Ms. Elizabeth SABEL
38 Director ASC & Student Counseling Ms. Dori DALTON

Tiffin University (A)

155 Miami Street, Tiffin OH 44883-2161
County: Seneca FICE Identification: 003121
Unit ID: 206048
Telephone: (419) 447-6442 Carnegie Class: Masters/L
FAX Number: N/A Calendar System: Semester
URL: www.tiffin.edu
Established: 1888 Annual Undergrad Tuition & Fees: $22,165
Enrollment: 4,100 Coed
Affiliation or Control: Independent Non-Profit IRS Status: 501(c)3
Highest Offering: Master's
Accreditation: NH, ACBSP

01 President Dr. Lillian SCHUMACHER
05 Interim VP Academic Affairs Dr. Teresa SHAFER
30 Interim VP University Advancement Mr. David FERGUSON
10 VP Finance/Administration Ms. Donna FRANK
15 VP Human Resources/Campus Services Ms. Lori HALL
84 VP for Enrollment Management Dr. Jeremy MARINIS
04 Exec Assistant to the President Ms. Nancy GILBERT
32 Dean of Students Mr. Mike HERDLICK
13 Chief Information Officer Mr. Scott FERGUSON
07 Director Undergrad Admissions Ms. Sarah JOHNSON
26 Exec Dir Media Rels/Publications Ms. Lisa WILLIAMS
06 Registrar Ms. Melissa WEININGER
41 Director Athletics Mr. Lonny ALLEN
21 Controller Mr. Robert WATSON
08 Head Librarian Ms. Frances FLEET
29 Director Alumni Relations Ms. Vickie WILKINS
36 Director of Career Development Ms. Celinda SCHERGER
18 Director of Facilities Mr. Harold KINN
22 Equal Opportunity Officer Ms. Lori HALL
39 Director of Residence Life Ms. Mandi HUMMEL
44 Director of Annual Fund Mr. Joe BORICH
28 Asst VP for Diversity & Equity Dr. Sharon PERRY-FANTINI
37 Director Student Financial Aid Ms. Andrea FABER
49 Dean of Arts & Sciences Dr. Joyce HALL-YATES
50 Dean of Business Dr. Maneesh SHARMA
83 Dean Criminal Justice/Social Sci Mr. Kevin CASHEN
09 Director of Institutional Research Mr. Mondrail MYRICK
104 Director Study Abroad Ms. Tiffanie GOFF
106 Dir Online Education/E-learning Dr. John NWORIE
19 Director Security/Safety Ms. Jennifer BOUCHER

Tri-State Bible College (B)

506 Margaret Street, PO Box 445,
South Point OH 45680-8402
County: Lawrence FICE Identification: 034754
Unit ID: 206154
Telephone: (740) 377-2520 Carnegie Class: Spec-4-yr-Faith
FAX Number: (740) 377-0001 Calendar System: Semester
URL: www.tsbc.edu
Established: 1970 Annual Undergrad Tuition & Fees: $7,800
Enrollment: 67 Coed
Affiliation or Control: Independent Non-Profit IRS Status: 501(c)3
Highest Offering: Baccalaureate
Accreditation: BI

00 Chancellor Dr. Clifford L. MARQUARDT
01 President Dr. Jack R. FINCH
05 Vice President Academic Affairs Mr. John DUNCAN
10 Vice President Finance Mr. Brian TRIPPETT
11 Vice President Administrative Affs Ms. Roberta (Bobby) MERCER
32 Vice Pres Student Affairs Mr. Leroy FULFORD
18 Vice President Operations Dr. Manfred LANGER

Trinity Lutheran Seminary (C)

2199 E Main Street, Columbus OH 43209-2334
County: Franklin FICE Identification: 003044
Unit ID: 206215
Telephone: (614) 235-4136 Carnegie Class: Spec-4-yr-Faith
FAX Number: (614) 238-0263 Calendar System: Semester
URL: www.TLSohio.edu
Established: 1830 Annual Graduate Tuition & Fees: N/A
Enrollment: 111 Coed
Affiliation or Control: Evangelical Lutheran Church In America
IRS Status: 501(c)3
Highest Offering: Doctorate; No Undergraduates
Accreditation: NH, THEOL

01 President Rev. Robert C. BARGER
30 Vice President for Advancement Mr. Bradley A. GEE
11 Vice President for Operations Mr. Ronald W. BENEDICK
88 Vice Pres Leadership Formation Ms. Denise SAGER
05 Academic Dean Dr. Brad A. BINAU
20 Associate Academic Dean Dr. Diane J. HYMANS
88 Dean of Leadership Formation Rev. Emlyn A. OTT
07 Director of Recruiting/Admissions Mr. Seth BRIDGER
06 Registrar Mr. Lee RICHARDS
08 Director Hamma Library Mr. Ray A. OLSON
26 Director Communications/Marketing Ms. Margaret L. FARNHAM
37 Director Financial Aid Mrs. Melissa CURTIS POWELL
88 Director Contextual Education Sister Becky SWANSON
88 Director MA in Church Music Program Ms. May L. SCHWARZ
58 Director Graduate Studies Dr. Walter F. TAYLOR, JR.
88 Director MACE/MAYFM Programs Dr. Diane J. HYMANS
10 Controller Mrs. Patricia A. FORK
18 Director Facilities Management Ms. Laura K. STARKEY

Trumbull Business College (D)

3200 Ridge Road, Warren OH 44484-3272
County: Trumbull FICE Identification: 020543
Unit ID: 206224
Telephone: (330) 369-3200 Carnegie Class: Assoc/HVT-Mix Trad/Non
FAX Number: (330) 369-6792 Calendar System: Quarter
URL: www.trumbull.edu
Established: 1972 Annual Undergrad Tuition & Fees: $12,389
Enrollment: 192 Coed
Affiliation or Control: Proprietary IRS Status: Proprietary
Highest Offering: Associate Degree
Accreditation: ACICS

01 President Mr. Dennis J. GRIFFITH
37 Director of Financial Aid Ms. Sarah PALMER
36 Director of Student Placement Ms. Kimberly STRANIAK
12 Director of Branch Campus Ms. Kimberly STRANIAK
06 Registrar Ms. Teresa SHAMBACH

Union Institute & University (E)

440 E McMillan Street, Cincinnati OH 45206-1947
County: Hamilton FICE Identification: 010923
Unit ID: 206279
Telephone: (513) 861-6400 Carnegie Class: DU-Mod
FAX Number: (513) 861-0779 Calendar System: Semester
URL: www.myunion.edu
Established: 1964 Annual Undergrad Tuition & Fees: $12,144
Enrollment: 1,567 Coed
Affiliation or Control: Independent Non-Profit IRS Status: 501(c)3
Highest Offering: Doctorate
Accreditation: NH, SW

01 President Dr. Roger H. SUBLETT
05 VP Academic Affairs Dr. Nelson SOTO
04 Executive Assistant to President Ms. Carolyn KRAUSE
10 Chief Fiscal Officer Mr. Tom CUNNINGHAM
15 Vice President Human Resources Ms. Deborah EAMOE
84 VP Enrollment Management Ms. Kimbrea BROWNING
30 Vice President Advancement Ms. Carolyn KRAUSE
46 Assoc VP Inst Effectiveness Dr. Elizabeth PRUDEN
58 Assoc VP Grad Programs Dr. Arlene SACKS
58 Dean PsyD Program Dr. William LAX
06 Registrar Ms. Lew Rita MOORE
09 Director Institutional Research Ms. Millie MILLER
13 Director Information Technology Dr. Bob COTTER
18 Director Facilities Management Mr. Ken LAMB
12 Regional Dean Florida Center Vacant
12 Regional Dean LA Center Dr. Elizabeth PASTORRES-PALFFY
12 National Dean Undergrad Programs Dr. Peter CACCAVERI
12 Regional Dean Sacramento Center Ms. Julie CRANDALL
08 Library Director Mr. Matthew PAPPATHAN
37 Interim Director Financial Aid Ms. Jean POHLMAN
29 Director Alumni Relations Dr. Neal MEIER
32 Director Student Success Dr. Jay KEEHN
106 Dir Center for Teaching & Learning Dr. Bob COTTER

United Theological Seminary (F)

4501 Denlinger Road, Dayton OH 45426-2308
County: Montgomery FICE Identification: 003122
Unit ID: 206288
Telephone: (937) 529-2201 Carnegie Class: Spec-4-yr-Faith
FAX Number: (866) 433-8235 Calendar System: Semester
URL: www.united.edu
Established: 1871 Annual Graduate Tuition & Fees: N/A
Enrollment: 638 Coed
Affiliation or Control: United Methodist IRS Status: 501(c)3
Highest Offering: Doctorate; No Undergraduates
Accreditation: NH, THEOL

01 Interim President & CEO Dr. Kent MILLARD
05 Vice Pres Academic Affairs & Dean Dr. David WATSON
10 Vice Pres Finance/Treasurer Mr. Steven SWALLOW
07 Vice Pres Enrollmnt/Assoc Dean DMin Dr. Harold HUDSON
101 Sr Asst to the President/Corp Secy Ms. Laura WEBER
20 Assoc Dean Academic Affairs Dr. Vivian JOHNSON
06 Registrar Ms. Courtney WARD
13 Director of Information Technology Mr. Rick MOHR
106 Dir Distance Learning/Educ Tech Ms. Phyllis ENNIST
08 Librarian Ms. Sarah D. BROOKS BLAIR
42 Director of Contextual Ministries Rev. Dan GILDNER
26 Coordinator of Communications Ms. Rachel HURLEY
37 Director Financial Aid Ms. Marcia BYRD
29 Coordinator of Alumni/ae Relations Rev. Tesia MALLORY
18 Facility Manager Mr. Max FULLER
108 Chf Strategy/Admin/Assessment Ofcr Ms. Karen E. PAYNE
84 Senior Dir Enrollment Mgmt Rev. Trent HAYES
36 Director of Student Success Rev. R. Dean BLIMLINE
30 Sr Dir of Development Operations Ms. Calle PICARDO

The University of Akron, Main Campus (G)

302 Buchtel Common, Akron OH 44325
County: Summit FICE Identification: 003123
Unit ID: 200800
Telephone: (330) 972-7111 Carnegie Class: DU-Higher
FAX Number: (330) 972-6990 Calendar System: Semester
URL: www.uakron.edu
Established: 1870 Annual Undergrad Tuition & Fees (In-State): $10,509
Enrollment: 23,962 Coed
Affiliation or Control: State IRS Status: 501(c)3
Highest Offering: Doctorate
Accreditation: NH, ACBSP, ANEST, ART, BUS, BUSA, CAATE, CACREP, CIDA, COARC, COPSY, DANCE, DIETC, DIETD, ENG, ENGR, ENGT, IFSAC, IPSY, LAW, MAC, MFCD, MUS, NURSE, PH, RAD, SP, SURGT, SW, TED

01 President Mr. Matthew J. WILSON
05 Senior Vice Pres & Provost Dr. Rex RAMSIER
45 VP Innovation & Economic Dev Dr. William M. SHERMAN
10 VP Finance & Administration/CFO Mr. Nathan J. MORTIMER
43 Vice President & General Counsel Mr. Ted A. MALLO
13 Chief Information Officer Mr. Godfrey OVWIGHO
18 Vice Pres Capital Plng/Facil Mgmt Vacant
101 Secretary Board of Trustees Mr. Ted A. MALLO
32 Dean of Students Mr. Mike STRONG
30 Assoc Vice Pres Development Mrs. Kimberly M. COLE
88 Dir of Presidential Communication Mr. David NYPAVER
21 Assc VP Treasury/Financial Planning Mr. Brian E. DAVIS
46 Assoc Vice President for Research Mr. Kenneth G. PRESTON
22 Interim Chief Diversity Officer Dr. Lakeesha K. RANSOM
15 Assoc VP Talent Dev/Human Resources Mr. Bill J. VIAU
26 Assoc VP/Chief Marketing Officer Mr. Wayne R. HILL
35 Assoc VP of Student Affairs Dr. John A. MESSINA
19 Ast VP Camp Safety/Chf Univ Police Major Jim P. WEBER
43 Asst VP & Assoc General Counsel Mr. Sidney C. FOSTER, JR.
06 Registrar Mr. Ronald L. BOWMAN, JR.
07 Director of Admissions Ms. Diane R. RAYBUCK
09 Int Director Institutional Research Ms. Lynn LUCAS
14 Director Technology Transfer Mr. Kenneth G. PRESTON
08 Interim Dean University Libraries Dr. Aimee L. DECHAMBEAU
49 Int Dean Buchtel College Arts & Sci Dr. John C. GREEN
54 Interim Dean College of Engineering Dr. Donald P. VISCO, JR.
53 Interim Dean College of Education Dr. Susan G. CLARK
50 Dean College of Business Admin Dr. Ravi KROVI
76 Dean College Health Professions Vacant
72 Int Dean Col of Appl Sci & Tech Dr. Elizabeth A. KENNEDY
61 Interim Co-Dean School of Law Ms. Sarah CRAVENS
61 Interim Co-Dean School of Law Mr. Ryan G. VACCA
54 Dean of Polymer Science/Engineering Dr. Eric J. AMIS
12 Dean Wayne College Dr. jarrod TUDOR
37 Director Student Financial Aid Mrs. Jennifer E. HARPHAM
29 Director of Alumni Relations Mr. Willy KOLLMAN
96 Director of Purchasing Mr. Andrew W. ROTH
88 Senior Director Integrated Comm Mr. Robert KROPFF
105 Director of Web Services Mr. Eric W. KRIEDER
92 Dean Honors College Dr. Lakeesha K. RANSOM
88 Director UA Adult Focus Mrs. Laura H. CONLEY
41 Director Athletics Mr. Lawrence R. WILLIAMS
36 Ex Dir Counseling/Test/Career Ctr Dr. Juanita K. MARTIN
39 Asst VP & Chief Housing Officer Mr. John A. MESSINA
25 Asst VP Office Research Admin Ms. Katie WATKINS-WENDELL
85 Director International Programs Vacant
23 Director Health Services Ms. Alma E. OLSON
86 Dir Government Relations Dr. Matthew P. AKERS
88 Asst VP Computer Operations Mrs. Deborah WHITE
88 Director of Media Relations Mr. Dan MINNICH
102 Asst VP Corp Fund Relations Mrs. Ellen PERDUYN
84 Assoc VP Enrollment Management Ms. Lauri S. THORPE

The University of Akron-Wayne College (H)

1901 Smucker Road, Orrville OH 44667-9758
County: Wayne FICE Identification: 010818
Unit ID: 200846
Telephone: (330) 683-2010 Carnegie Class: Assoc/HT-High Non
FAX Number: (330) 684-8989 Calendar System: Semester
URL: www.wayne.uakron.edu
Established: 1972 Annual Undergrad Tuition & Fees (In-State): $6,116
Enrollment: 1,779 Coed
Affiliation or Control: State IRS Status: 501(c)3
Highest Offering: Associate Degree
Accreditation: NH

01 Dean Dr. Jarrod TUDOR
04 Senior Admin Assistant to Dean Ms. Ann MARTIN

05 Associate Dean of Instruction ... Vacant
10 Director Business/Finance ... Vacant
32 Asst Dean Student Services ... Mr. Gordon K. HOLLY
18 Chief Facilities/Physical Plant ... Mr. Shon ENOS
26 Chief Public Relations Officer ... Mrs. Debby MUNIAK
08 Director Library Services ... Mrs. Maureen T. LERCH
06 Registrar/Manager Student Services ... Mrs. Barb CAILLET
07 Director of Admissions ... Mrs. Alicia BROADUS
09 Director of Institutional Research ... Mr. William CLARK
15 Director Personnel Services ... Ms. Kathy BATCHELDER
20 Associate Academic Officer ... Mr. Garth D. SCHOFFMAN
30 Director of Development ... Mr. Kevin E. ENGLE
35 Student Activities Coordinator ... Ms. Jackie E. ASHBAUGH
36 Coord Career and Assessment Svcs ... Ms. Carol J. PLEUSS
37 Manager Student Svcs/Financial Aid ... Ms. Barb CAILLET
38 Coordinator of Academic Advising ... Ms. Wendy CUNDIFF
96 Assistant Director Business/Finance ... Ms. Amy M. HAYNES
13 Manager Technical Support Services ... Ms. Cher DEEDS
19 University Police ... Lt. Chad CUNNINGHAM
40 Director Bookstore ... Ms. Pat PAXTON
41 Athletic Director ... Mr. Dave RUBENS

University of Cincinnati Main Campus (A)

2624 Clifton Avenue, Cincinnati OH 45221-0001
County: Hamilton | FICE Identification: 003125
Unit ID: 201885
Telephone: (513) 556-6000 | Carnegie Class: DU-Highest
FAX Number: (513) 556-3237 | Calendar System: Quarter
URL: www.uc.edu
Established: 1819 | Annual Undergrad Tuition & Fees (In-State): $11,000
Enrollment: 35,313 | Coed
Affiliation or Control: State | IRS Status: 501(c)3
Highest Offering: Doctorate
Accreditation: NH, ANEST, ART, AUD, BUS, CAATE, CACREP, CAEP, CAHIIM, CIDA, CLPSY, CONST, CS, DANCE, DENT, DIETC, DIETD, ENG, ENGR, ENGT, LAW, MED, MIDWF, MT, MUS, NMT, NURSE, PH, PHAR, PLNG, PTA, SP, SURGA, SW, TED, THEA

01 Interim President ... Dr. Beverly J. DAVENPORT
05 Sr VP/Provost Academic Affairs ... Peter E. LANDGREN
11 Sr VP for Administration & Finance ... Mr. Robert AMBACH
03 Executive VP ... Dr. Ryan HAYS
46 Vice President for Research ... Dr. Patrick A. LIMBACH
63 Dean Medicine/Sr VP Health Affairs ... Dr. Williams S. BALL
30 VP Development/Alumni Rels ... Mr. Rod M. GRABOWSKI
86 Vice Pres Govt Rels/University Comm ... Mr. Gregory J. VEHR
32 Vice Pres Student Affairs & Svcs ... Ms. Debra S. MERCHANT
10 Vice President for Finance ... Mr. Patrick A. KOWALSKI
13 VP & CIO for Information Technology ... Dr. Nelson C. VINCENT
20 Sr Vice Provost Academic Affairs ... Dr. Eileen L. STREMPEL
43 Interim General Counsel ... Ms. Karen S. KOVACH
15 Sr Assoc VP/Chief HR Officer ... Ms. Tamie L. GRUNOW
84 Sr Assoc Vice President Enrollment ... Dr. Caroline B. MILLER
21 Assoc VP Community Development ... Mr. Gerald A. SIEGERT
26 Director Media Relations ... Ms. MB REILLY
07 Assoc Vice Pres for Admissions ... Dr. Thomas CANEPA
44 Assoc Vice Pres for Principal Gifts ... Mr. E.R. (Jay) BROWNING
76 Dean Allied Health Sciences ... Dr. Tina WHALEN
49 Dean Arts & Sciences ... Dr. Kenneth PETREN
50 Dean Business Administration ... Dr. David M. SZYMANSKI
64 In Dn College-Conservatory of Music ... Dr. Bruce d. MCCLUNG
48 Dean Design/Architecture/Art & Plng ... Dr. Robert PROBST
53 Dean Education/Crim Justice & HS ... Dr. Lawrence J. JOHNSON
54 Dean Engineering & Applied Sci ... Dr. Teik C. LIM
61 Dean Law ... Dr. Jennifer S. BARD
66 Dean Nursing ... Dr. Greer L. GLAZER
67 Dean Pharmacy ... Dr. Neil J. MACKINNON
70 Director School Social Work ... Mr. James CLARK
08 Dean Library ... Mr. Xuemao WANG
29 VP Alumni Affairs ... Ms. Jennifer HEISEY
28 VP Equity & Inclusion ... Dr. Bleuzette MARSHALL
41 Director Athletics ... Mr. Michael BOHN
40 Director Bookstore ... Ms. Linda K. GINDELE
36 Director Career Development ... Ms. Kathleen GRANT
38 Director Counseling Center ... Dr. Tow Y. YAU
22 Exec Director Equal Opportunity ... Mr. Matthew J. OLOVSON
39 Asst VP Housing/Food Service ... Mr. Todd DUNCAN
37 Director Student Financial Aid ... Mr. Randy ULSES
09 Director Institutional Research ... Mrs. Suzana H. LUZURIAGA
19 Director Public Safety ... Mr. James L. WHALEN
06 Registrar ... Dr. Douglas BURGESS
96 Assoc VP Purchasing ... Mr. Thomas B. GUERIN
45 Co-Dir Institute for Policy Rsrch ... Dr. Eric RADEMACHER
45 Co-Dir Institute for Policy Rsrch ... Dr. Kimberly DOWNING
104 Vice Provost International Programs ... Dr. Raj MEHTA
18 Chief Facilities/Physical Plant ... Mr. Joseph H. HARRELL
101 Secretary of the Institution/Board ... Ms. Nicole BLOUNT
102 Dir Foundation/Corporate Relations ... Mr. Tom I. SEDDON
105 Asst VP Digital Comm ... Ms. Nicola ZIADY
25 Assoc VP Sponsored Research ... Ms. Deborah J. GALLOWAY
90 Director Academic Computing ... Mr. Christopher J. EDWARDS
04 Administrative Asst to President ... Mr. Lawrence P. LAMPE
100 Chief of Staff ... Dr. Ryan HAYS
106 Asst VP Online Educ/E-learning ... Mr. Christopher J. EDWARDS

University of Cincinnati Blue Ash College (B)

9555 Plainfield Road, Blue Ash OH 45236-1096
County: Hamilton | FICE Identification: 004868
Unit ID: 201955
Telephone: (513) 745-5600 | Carnegie Class: Bac/Assoc-Assoc Dom
FAX Number: (513) 745-5780 | Calendar System: Semester
URL: www.ucblueash.edu
Established: 1967 | Annual Undergrad Tuition & Fees (In-State): $6,746
Enrollment: 5,024 | Coed
Affiliation or Control: State | IRS Status: 501(c)3
Highest Offering: Baccalaureate
Accreditation: NH, ADNUR, ART, DH, EMT, MAC, RAD

01 Dean ... Dr. Cady SHORT-THOMPSON
05 Assoc Dean Academic Affairs ... Dr. Robin LIGHTNER
10 Director Business Affairs ... Mr. Marc WATSON
20 Asst Dean Academic Affairs ... Dr. Gregory METZ
18 Director Facilities & Campus Plan ... Mr. Rob KNARR
13 Director Information Technology ... Mr. Dale HOFSTETTER
07 Director Admissions ... Mr. Brad TATE
09 Director Institutional Research ... Mr. Steve MILLER
30 Director Development ... Ms. Meredith DELANEY
08 Library Director ... Ms. Heather MALONEY
26 Director Communication ... Mr. Peter GEMMER
32 Director Student Engagement ... Mr. Marcus LANGFORD
88 Director Acad/Student Advising ... Mr. Mark MILLER
35 Director One Stop Student Service ... Ms. Martha GEIGER
15 HR Manager ... Ms. Amy SMITH

University of Cincinnati-Clermont College (C)

4200 Clermont College Drive, Batavia OH 45103-1785
County: Clermont | FICE Identification: 010805
Unit ID: 201946
Telephone: (513) 732-5200 | Carnegie Class: Bac/Assoc-Mixed
FAX Number: (513) 732-5275 | Calendar System: Quarter
URL: www.ucclermont.edu
Established: 1972 | Annual Undergrad Tuition & Fees (In-State): $6,052
Enrollment: 3,246 | Coed
Affiliation or Control: State | IRS Status: 501(c)3
Highest Offering: Baccalaureate
Accreditation: NH, CAHIIM, COARC, MAC, PTAA, SURGT

01 Dean ... Dr. Jeffrey C. BAUER
05 Int Assoc Dean Academic Affairs ... Ms. Kim JACOBS-BECK
20 Sr Assistant Dean Academic Affairs ... Ms. Mary F. STEARNS
08 Director Library ... Ms. Katie FORHAN-MULCAHY
24 Dir Learning Center ... Ms. Amy ABAFO
09 Director of Institutional Research ... Ms. Susan RILEY
10 Director Business Affairs ... Ms. Maria KERI
32 Sr Dir Retention & Student Success ... Ms. Jennifer RADT
07 Sr Director Recruitment ... Mr. John STILES
06 Asst Dir Registration & Scheduling ... Ms. Kristine LOUGHRAN
88 Director Disability Services ... Vacant
35 Director of Student Life ... Ms. Kimberly ELLISON
41 Program Coord/Athletic Director ... Mr. Brian SULLIVAN
18 Asst Dean Facilities & Tech Svcs ... Mr. Stephen W. YOUNG
30 Director of Development ... Ms. Dara PARKER
26 Asst Dean Communications & Mktg ... Ms. Mae HANNA

University of Dayton (D)

300 College Park, Dayton OH 45469-0001
County: Montgomery | FICE Identification: 003127
Unit ID: 202480
Telephone: (937) 229-1000 | Carnegie Class: DU-Higher
FAX Number: (937) 229-4000 | Calendar System: Semester
URL: www.udayton.edu
Established: 1850 | Annual Undergrad Tuition & Fees: $39,090
Enrollment: 11,343 | Coed
Affiliation or Control: Roman Catholic | IRS Status: 501(c)3
Highest Offering: Doctorate
Accreditation: NH, #ARCPA, ART, BUS, BUSA, CACREP, CEA, CS, DIETD, ENG, ENGT, LAW, MUS, PTA, SPAA, TED

01 President ... Dr. Eric F. SPINA
05 Provost ... Dr. Paul H. BENSON
32 VP Student Development ... Mr. William M. FISCHER
10 VP Finance & Admin Services ... Mr. Andrew E. HORNER
30 VP Univ Advancement ... Ms. Jennifer L. HOWE
41 VP/Director of Athletics ... Mr. Neil G. SULLIVAN
15 VP Human Resources ... Mr. Troy W. WASHINGTON
84 VP for Enrollment Mgmt ... Dr. Jason K. REINOEHL
46 VP of Research/Exec Dir UDRI ... Dr. John E. LELAND
44 Sr Development Officer ... Mr. James F. BROTHERS
42 Director Campus Ministry ... Ms. Crystal C. SULLIVAN
88 VP for Mission and Rector ... Rev. James F. FITZ, SM
31 Dir Ctr for Ldrshp in Cmty ... Ms. Hunter P. GOODMAN
20 Assoc Provost Faculty & Admin Affs ... Dr. Carolyn ROECKER-PHELPS
88 Asc Prov Lrng Spprt/Dir Rch Tch Ctr ... Dr. Deborah J. BICKFORD
06 Registrar ... Ms. Jennifer M. CREECH
07 Asst VP/Dean of Admission ... Mr. Robert F. DURKLE
19 Exec Director/Chief of Police ... Mr. Rodney CHATMAN
09 Director Institutional Studies ... Ms. Susan K. SEXTON
21 Comptroller ... Ms. Angela K. BUECHELE
88 Assoc VP/Dean of Students ... Ms. Christine M. SCHRAMM
36 Director Career Services ... Mr. Jason C. ECKERT
38 Asst VP Student Dev/Dir Counseling ... Dr. Steven D. MUELLER
18 VP for Facilities/Campus Opers ... Ms. Beth H. KEYES
23 Medical Director Univ Health Ctr ... Dr. Mary P. BUCHWALDER
08 Dean University Libraries ... Ms. Kathleen M. WEBB
49 Dean College A&S ... Dr. Jason L. PIERCE
61 Dean School of Law ... Mr. Andrew L. STRAUSS
50 Interim Dean Sch of Business Admin ... Dr. James E. DUNNE
58 Assoc Prov Graduate Acad Affairs ... Dr. Paul M. VANDERBURGH
53 Dean School of Educ & Allied Prof ... Dr. Kevin R. KELLY
54 Dean School of Engineering ... Dr. Eddy M. ROJAS
29 Sr Development Officer ... Mr. Todd W. IMWALLE
35 Dir Student Life & Kennedy Union ... Ms. Amy L. LOPEZ-MATTHEWS
37 Exec Dir Flyers First/Dir Fin Aid ... Ms. Catherine MIX
39 Asst Dean Students & Dir Res Life ... Mr. Steven T. HERNDON
40 Manager UD Bookstore ... Ms. Julie M. BANKS
43 Univ Counsel/Dir Legal Affairs ... Ms. Mary A. RECKER
96 Dir Univ Purchases/Business Service ... Mr. Ken R. SOUCY
92 Dir University Honors/Scholars Pgm ... Dr. David W. DARROW
94 Women's and Gender Studies Program ... Dr. Rebecca S. WHISNANT
22 Dir Affirmative Action & Compliance ... Ms. Patricia BERNAL-OLSON
86 Government/Regional Relations Dir ... Mr. S. Ted BUCARO
28 VP Diversity & Inclusion ... Dr. Lawrence A. BURNLEY
26 Dir Marketing & Creative Services ... Ms. Kim B. LALLY
04 Exec Asst to President ... Ms. Jane PERRICH
100 Executive Director/Chief of Staff ... Mr. Thomas U. WECKESSER
101 Assoc Sec of the Board of Trustees ... Ms. Lisa S. RISMILLER
13 Chief Info Technology Officer (CIO) ... Dr. Thomas D. SKILL

The University of Findlay (E)

1000 North Main Street, Findlay OH 45840-3653
County: Hancock | FICE Identification: 003045
Unit ID: 202763
Telephone: (419) 422-8313 | Carnegie Class: Masters/L
FAX Number: (419) 434-4822 | Calendar System: Semester
URL: www.findlay.edu
Established: 1882 | Annual Undergrad Tuition & Fees: $31,508
Enrollment: 5,172 | Coed
Affiliation or Control: Church Of God | IRS Status: 501(c)3
Highest Offering: Doctorate
Accreditation: NH, ACBSP, ARCPA, CAATE, CEA, DMS, ENGR, NMT, OT, PHAR, PTA, SW, TED

01 President ... Dr. Katherine R. FELL
05 Vice President for Academic Affairs ... Dr. Darin FIELDS
10 Vice President for Business Affairs ... Mr. Leon WYDEN, JR.
84 Vice President Enrollment Mgmt ... Ms. Rebecca A. BUTLER
20 Assoc VPAA/Inst Effectiveness ... Dr. John OSAE-KWAPONG
30 Vice Pres University Advancement ... Dr. Marcia SLOAN LATTA
32 Vice President for Student Affairs ... Mr. David W. EMSWELLER
04 Assistant to the President ... Ms. Liz DITTO
81 Dean College of Sciences ... Dr. Jeffrey FRYE
50 Dean College of Business ... Dr. E. Kevin RENSHLER
49 Dean College of Liberal Art ... Dr. Ronald TULLEY
76 Dean College of Health Professions ... Dr. Andrea KOEPKE
67 Dean College of Pharmacy ... Dr. Debra PARKER
53 Dean College of Education ... Dr. Julie MCINTOSH
18 Director of Physical Plant ... Mr. Myreon K. COBB
09 Director of Institutional Research ... Mr. Tony G. GOEDDE
06 Registrar ... Mr. Tony G. GOEDDE
41 Athletic Director ... Ms. Brandi LAURITA
08 Director of Shafer Library ... Mr. Andrew WHITIS
37 Director of Financial Aid ... Mr. Edward R. RECKER
13 Chief Information Officer ... Dr. Raymond MCCANDLESS
29 Director of Alumni Affairs ... Ms. Deanna SPRAW
26 Dir Public Relations/Media Rels ... Ms. Rebecca JENKINS
36 Director of Career Placement ... Mr. Bradley C. HAMMER
15 Director of Human Resources ... Mr. Robert LINK
23 Director of Health Services ... Ms. Julie R. YINGLING
38 Director Counseling Services ... Ms. Karyn J. WESTRICK
40 Manager of Bookstore ... Mr. Jay CANTERBURY
42 Director Christian Ministries ... Mr. Matthew GINTER
19 Chief of Police/Dir of Security ... Mr. William SPRAW
21 Business Manager ... Mr. Robert LINK
28 Asst Dean International Education ... Mr. Christopher SIPPEL
85 Dir Intl Student Adm & Svcs ... Mr. Martin BENNETT
101 Secretary to the Board of Trustees ... Ms. C. Sue PIRSCHEL
25 Grants Manager ... Ms. Tricia VALASEK
07 Director of Admissions ... Mr. Christopher HARRIS
21 Associate Business Officer ... Mr. Dane ERFORD
22 Director Affirmative Action/Equal ... Mr. Robert LINK
35 Asst Dean of Students ... Vacant
39 Director Student Housing ... Ms. Rachel WALTER
44 Director Annual Giving ... Mr. Todd LACOMBA

University of Mount Union (F)

1972 Clark Avenue, Alliance OH 44601-3993
County: Stark | FICE Identification: 003083
Unit ID: 204185
Telephone: (330) 821-5320 | Carnegie Class: Bac-Diverse
FAX Number: (330) 823-3457 | Calendar System: Semester
URL: www.mountunion.edu
Established: 1846 | Annual Undergrad Tuition & Fees: $28,550
Enrollment: 2,262 | Coed
Affiliation or Control: United Methodist | IRS Status: 501(c)3
Highest Offering: Doctorate
Accreditation: NH, ARCPA, #CAATE, ENG, MUS, NURSE, @PTA, TED

01 President ... Dr. W. R. MERRIMAN
05 Vice Pres Acad Affs/Dean of Univ ... Dr. Patricia H. DRAVES
10 Vice Pres Business Affs/Treasurer ... Mr. Patrick D. HEDDLESTON
30 Vice President Univ Advancement ... Mr. Gregory KING
32 Vice Pres Student Affs/Dean Stdnts ... Mr. John FRAZIER
84 Vice President for Enrollment Mgmt ... Ms. Michelle SUNDSTROM
26 Vice President for Marketing ... Ms. Melissa GARDNER
08 Librarian ... Mr. Robert R. GARLAND

06 Registrar ..... Ms. Wendy LEWIS
07 Director of Admission ..... Ms. Jessie CANAVAN
44 Director of Planned Giving ..... Ms. Sherrie WALLACE
13 Director of Information Technology ..... Ms. Tina STUCHELL
88 Director of Advancement ..... Mr. Joseph D. MONTGOMERY
29 Director Alumni/College Activities ..... Ms. Tiffany HOGYA
85 Director Center for Global Educ ..... Dr. Jennifer HALL
18 Director of Physical Plant ..... Mr. Blaine D. LEWIS
15 Director of Human Resources ..... Ms. Pamela NEWBOLD
39 Director of Residence Life ..... Ms. Sara SHERER
42 Chaplain ..... Rev. Martha D. CASHBURLESS
36 Exec Director of Career Services ..... Ms. Jessica CUNION
37 Director of Student Financial Svcs ..... Ms. Emily MATTISON
40 Manager of College Bookstore ..... Ms. Aimee SCHULLER
41 Athletic Director ..... Mr. Larry T. KEHRES
04 Exec Assistant to the President ..... Ms. Audra YOUNGEN
21 Assoc VP for Business Affairs ..... Mr. Ronald CROWL
35 Associate Dean of Students ..... Ms. Michelle GAFFNEY
96 Purchasing Agent ..... Mr. Shawn BAGLEY
19 Director Security/Safety ..... Mr. William KETJEN
28 Director of Diversity ..... Mr. Ronald HOLDEN

University of Northwestern Ohio (A)

1441 N Cable Road, Lima OH 45805-1498

County: Allen — FICE Identification: 004861
Unit ID: 204486
Telephone: (419) 227-3141 — Carnegie Class: Bac/Assoc-Mixed
FAX Number: (419) 229-6926 — Calendar System: Quarter
URL: www.unoh.edu
Established: 1920 — Annual Undergrad Tuition & Fees: $9,930
Enrollment: 4,111 — Coed
Affiliation or Control: Independent Non-Profit — IRS Status: 501(c)3
Highest Offering: Master's
Accreditation: NH, ACBSP, CAHIIM, MAC

01 President ..... Dr. Jeffrey A. JARVIS
05 Vice Provost/Dean Col Business ..... Dr. Dean HOBLER
10 Vice President Finance ..... Mrs. Marcia EICKHOLT
84 Vice Pres Enrollment Management ..... Mr. Tony AZZARELLO
18 Vice Pres of Property Management ..... Mr. Don RICKER
26 VP Public Rels/Mktg/Special Events ..... Mrs. Cheryl STEINWEDEL
30 Vice President Development ..... Mr. Steve FARMER
15 Exec Director of Human Resources ..... Ms. Geri MORRIS
21 Controller ..... Mr. James S. BRONDER
37 Director of Financial Aid ..... Mr. Wendell SCHICK
04 Executive Assistant to President ..... Mrs. Jennifer BENDELE
72 Dean College of Technologies ..... Mr. Andy O'NEAL

University of Phoenix Cleveland Main Campus (B)

3401 Enterprise Parkway, Suite 115,
Beachwood OH 44122-7343

Telephone: (216) 378-0473 — Identification: 770238
Accreditation: &NH, ACBSP

† No longer accepting campus-based students.

University of Rio Grande (C)

218 N College Avenue, PO BOX 500,
Rio Grande OH 45674-3100

County: Gallia — FICE Identification: 003116
Unit ID: 205203
Telephone: (740) 245-5353 — Carnegie Class: Bac/Assoc-Mixed
FAX Number: (740) 245-5266 — Calendar System: Semester
URL: www.rio.edu
Established: 1876 — Annual Undergrad Tuition & Fees: $23,860
Enrollment: 2,202 — Coed
Affiliation or Control: Independent Non-Profit — IRS Status: 501(c)3
Highest Offering: Master's
Accreditation: NH, ADNUR, COARC, DMS, IACBE, NUR, RAD, SW, TED

01 President ..... Dr. Michelle R. JOHNSTON
05 Provost/VP of Academic Affairs ..... Dr. Richard SAX
26 VP Marketing & Enrollment Mgmt ..... Mr. James BESSETTE
10 Chief Financial Officer ..... Mr. Tim PRUETT
32 VP Student & Administrative Affairs ..... Mrs. Rebecca LONG
15 Director of Human Resources ..... Mr. Chris NOURSE
28 Chief Compliance Officer ..... Mr. Russell HENCHEY
49 Dean Col of Arts & Sciences ..... Dr. David LAWRENCE
76 Dean College Prof/Tech Studies ..... Dr. Donna MITCHELL
06 Registrar ..... Mrs. Tami SHEETS
07 Director Admissions ..... Ms. Kristie RUSSELL
30 Director of Development ..... Mrs. Kara WILLIS
32 Dean of Students ..... Vacant
41 Athletics Director ..... Mr. Jeff LANHAM
08 Director of the Library ..... Ms. Amy R. WILSON
14 Dir Campus Computing & Networking ..... Mr. Kingsley MEYER
13 Acting MIS Director ..... Mr. Scott COLLEY
29 Director of Alumni Relations ..... Mrs. Annette P. WARD
04 Exec Assistant to the President ..... Mrs. Lori TAYLOR

University of Toledo (D)

2801 W Bancroft, Toledo OH 43606-3390

County: Lucas — FICE Identification: 003131
Unit ID: 206084
Telephone: (419) 530-4636 — Carnegie Class: DU-Higher
FAX Number: (419) 530-4984 — Calendar System: Semester
URL: www.utoledo.edu
Established: 1872 — Annual Undergrad Tuition & Fees (In-State): $9,547
Enrollment: 20,626 — Coed
Affiliation or Control: State — IRS Status: 501(c)3
Highest Offering: Doctorate
Accreditation: NH, ARCPA, ART, BUS, BUSA, CAATE, CACREP, CAHIIM, CLPSY, COARC, CS, DENT, ENG, ENGR, ENGT, LAW, MED, MT, MUS, NRPA, NURSE, OT, PH, PHAR, PTA, SP, SPAA, SW, TED

01 President ..... Dr. Sharon L. GABER
100 Chief of Staff ..... Mr. Matt J. SCHROEDER
05 EVP Academic Affairs/Provost ..... Dr. Andrew HSU
63 EVP for Clin Affs/Dean COMLS ..... Dr. Christopher COOPER
10 EVP Finance & Admin/CFO ..... Mr. Lawrence KELLEY
43 Vice President/General Counsel ..... Mr. Peter J. PAPADIMOS
32 Sr VP for Student Affairs ..... Dr. Kaye PATTEN
30 Vice President for Advancement ..... Vacant
84 Int VP Enrollment Management ..... Ms. Stephanie SANDERS
46 Vice President Research ..... Dr. Frank J. CALZONETTI
13 Vice President CIO/CTO ..... Mr. William MCCREARY
41 Vice Pres and Director of Athletics ..... Mr. Michael E. O'BRIEN
17 Int CEO Univ Toledo Med Ctr ..... Mr. Dan BARBEE
09 Exec Dir Inst Research ..... Mr. Ying LIU
86 AVP Government Relations ..... Ms. Diane MILLER
06 Interim University Registrar ..... Ms. Julie R. QUINONEZ
58 Dean College of Graduate Studies ..... Dr. Amanda BRYANT-FRIEDRICH
50 Dean Business & Innovation ..... Dr. Gary INSCH
53 Int Dean J Herb College of Educ ..... Dr. Virginia KEIL
54 Dean Engineering ..... Dr. Nagi NAGANATHAN
76 Dean Health & Human Services ..... Dr. Christopher INGERSOLL
83 Dean Arts & Letters ..... Dr. Jamie BARLOWE
61 Dean Law ..... Mr. Ben BARROSS
81 Dean Natural Sciences & Mathematics ..... Dr. Karen BJORKMAN
66 Int Dean Nursing ..... Dr. Kelly PHILLIPS
67 Dean Pharmacy & Pharm Sciences ..... Dr. Johnnie EARLY
92 Dean Jesup Scott Honors College ..... Dr. Heidi APPEL
88 Dean University College ..... Dr. Barbara KOPP-MILLER
35 Dean of Students ..... Mr. Phillip COCKRELL
39 AVP Residence Life ..... Ms. Virginia SPEIGHT
37 AVP Financial Aid/Enrollment Svcs ..... Mr. Stephen SCHISSLER
15 Sr Director Faculty Labor Relations ..... Mr. Kevin WEST
102 President Foundation ..... Ms. Brenda LEE
29 Assoc Vice Pres Alumni Relations ..... Mr. Daniel J. SAEVIG
36 Dir Exp Lrng and Career Svcs ..... Ms. Shelly DROUILLARD
85 Asst Provost Ctr for Intl Studies ..... Mr. Sammy SPANN
21 Director Internal Audit ..... Mr. David CUTRI
19 Chief of Police ..... Mr. Jeff NEWTON
40 General Manager Bookstore SU ..... Ms. Colleen STRAYER
18 AVP Facilities/Physical Plant ..... Mr. Jason TOTH
08 Int Director University Libraries ..... Ms. Barbara FLOYD

Urbana University (E)

579 College Way, Urbana OH 43078-2091

County: Champaign — FICE Identification: 003133
Unit ID: 206330
Telephone: (937) 484-1400 — Carnegie Class: Bac-Diverse
FAX Number: (937) 484-1322 — Calendar System: Semester
URL: www.urbana.edu
Established: 1850 — Annual Undergrad Tuition & Fees: $22,012
Enrollment: 1,922 — Coed
Affiliation or Control: Independent Non-Profit — IRS Status: 501(c)3
Highest Offering: Master's
Accreditation: #NH, IACBE, NURSE

01 President ..... Dr. George LUCAS, JR.
05 Vice President for Academic Affairs ..... Dr. Shah HASAN
30 Int Vice Pres Inst Advancement ..... Mr. David ORMSBEE
100 Chief of Staff ..... Ms. Evelyn LEVINO
44 Exec Director of Development ..... Mr. David ORMSBEE
06 Assistant Registrar ..... Ms. Cassie NEWCOMER
37 Director of Financial Aid ..... Ms. Goldie LANGLEY
09 Dean of Institutional Research ..... Dr. Denise BOLDMAN
32 Dean of Students ..... Mr. John GORE
08 Director Library Services ..... Mrs. Julie MCDANIEL
35 Assoc Dean Students/Campus Life ..... Mr. Mitch JOSEPH
13 Director Computer Center ..... Mrs. Monica KRAMER
07 Director of Admissions ..... Mr. Donnell WIGGINS
26 Director Communications ..... Ms. Cherie MOORE
41 Athletic Director ..... Mr. Larry COX
40 Bookstore Manager ..... Ms. Karen ENGLE
15 Human Resources Generalist ..... Ms. Mitali RAI
19 Campus Safety Coordinator ..... Mr. David FLEECE

Ursuline College (F)

2550 Lander Road, Cleveland OH 44124-4398

County: Cuyahoga — FICE Identification: 003134
Unit ID: 206349
Telephone: (440) 449-4200 — Carnegie Class: Masters/L
FAX Number: (440) 646-8318 — Calendar System: Semester
URL: www.ursuline.edu
Established: 1871 — Annual Undergrad Tuition & Fees: $28,520
Enrollment: 1,236 — Female
Affiliation or Control: Roman Catholic — IRS Status: 501(c)3
Highest Offering: Doctorate
Accreditation: NH, CAEP, IACBE, NURSE, SW, TED

01 President ..... Sr. Christine DEVINNE
05 Interim Vice Pres Academic Affairs ..... Dr. Elizabeth KAVRAN
10 Vice Pres & Chief Financial Officer ..... Mr. Timothy REARDON
30 Vice Pres Institutional Advancement ..... Mr. Richard KONISIEWICZ
18 Vice Pres of Facility Management ..... Ms. June GRACYK
32 Vice President of Student Affairs ..... Ms. Deanne HURLEY
84 Vice Pres of Enrollment Management ..... Ms. Deanne HURLEY
58 Interim Dean of Graduate Studies ..... Dr. Joseph LAGUARDIA
49 Interim Dean of Arts & Sciences ..... Dr. Sarah PRESTON
66 Dean Division of Nursing ..... Dr. Patricia SHARPNACK
88 Exec Director Accelerated Program ..... Ms. Brooke SCHARLOTT
08 Director of Library ..... Ms. Betsey BELKIN
06 Registrar ..... Ms. Leah SULLIVAN
21 Accounting Manager ..... Ms. Susan VALITSKY
44 Director of Development ..... Dr. Patrick RILEY
07 Director of Admissions ..... Ms. Carolyn NOLL SORG
37 Director of Financial Aid ..... Ms. Mary Lynn PERRI
29 Dir Alumae Relations/Dev Specialist ..... Ms. Tiffany MUSHRUSH-MENTZER
26 Dir of Marketing/Communications ..... Ms. Angela DELPRETE
38 Director Counseling & Career Svcs ..... Ms. Geraldine M. JENKINS
15 Director of Personnel ..... Ms. Kelli KNAUS
13 Dir of Computer Information Svcs ..... Mr. Tim FARRIS
09 Director of Institutional Research ..... Vacant
102 Dir of Corp & Foundation Relations ..... Vacant
39 Director of Residence Life ..... Ms. Gina DEMART-KRAUS
42 Director Campus Ministry ..... Dr. Joann PIOTRKOWSKI
28 Asst Dean of Inclusion ..... Ms. Tina LINING
93 Director of Wellness Program ..... Vacant
24 Library Electronic & Media Services ..... Ms. Marylouise DEEHR
40 Manager Bookstore ..... Ms. Kendra CORENO
41 Athletic Director ..... Ms. Cynthia MCKNIGHT
43 Dir Legal Services/General Counsel ..... Mr. Terry BILLUPS
09 Institutional Research Analyst ..... Ms. Marilyn VALENCIA

Valor Christian College (G)

PO Box 800, Columbus OH 43216

County: Franklin — Identification: 667093
Telephone: (614) 837-4088 — Carnegie Class: Not Classified
FAX Number: (614) 837-6904 — Calendar System: Semester
URL: www.valorcollege.com
Established: 1990 — Annual Undergrad Tuition & Fees: N/A
Enrollment: N/A — Coed
Affiliation or Control: Independent Non-Profit — IRS Status: 501(c)3
Highest Offering: Associate Degree
Accreditation: BI

01 President ..... Randy TURPIN
05 Vice Pres Academic Affairs ..... Laquetta CORTNER
32 Dean of Students ..... Edward RAMIREZ
84 VP for Institutional Advancement ..... Tim HOUSTON
35 Director of Student Life ..... Ashton PARSLEY
04 Admin Asst to Pres/Office Mgr ..... Holly BARNETT
37 Director of Financial Aid ..... Norm STOPPENBRINK

Vatterott College-Cleveland (H)

5025 E Royalton Road,
Broadview Heights OH 44147-3502

Telephone: (440) 526-1660 — Identification: 666156
Accreditation: ACCSC, MAAB

† Branch campus of Vatterott College-North Park, Berkeley, MO.

Virginia Marti College of Art & Design (I)

11724 Detroit Avenue, Lakewood OH 44107-3002

County: Cuyahoga — FICE Identification: 012896
Unit ID: 206394
Telephone: (216) 221-8584 — Carnegie Class: Assoc/HT-High Trad
FAX Number: (216) 221-2311 — Calendar System: Quarter
URL: www.vmcad.edu
Established: 1966 — Annual Undergrad Tuition & Fees: $17,419
Enrollment: 166 — Coed
Affiliation or Control: Proprietary — IRS Status: Proprietary
Highest Offering: Associate Degree
Accreditation: ACCSC

01 Director of Operations ..... Mr. Dennis MARTI
11 Assistant Director ..... Vacant
05 Dean of Academic Affairs ..... Mr. Patrick MELNICK
37 Financial Aid Administrator ..... Ms. Martha SNODGRASS
06 Registrar ..... Ms. Lisa ALESSANDRO
07 Director of Admissions ..... Ms. Robin BROADHURST
36 Director of Career Services ..... Mr. Matt DODD

Walsh University (J)

2020 East Maple Street, North Canton OH 44720

County: Stark — FICE Identification: 003135
Unit ID: 206437
Telephone: (330) 490-7090 — Carnegie Class: Masters/M
FAX Number: (330) 499-7165 — Calendar System: Semester
URL: www.walsh.edu
Established: 1958 — Annual Undergrad Tuition & Fees: $27,710
Enrollment: 2,919 — Coed
Affiliation or Control: Roman Catholic — IRS Status: 501(c)3
Highest Offering: Doctorate
Accreditation: NH, CACREP, NURSE, PTA, TED

01 President ..... Mr. Richard JUSSEAUME
10 Vice Pres Finance/Business Affairs ..... Ms. Shelley BROWN
32 VP Student Affairs/Dean of Students ..... Ms. Amy MALASKA
05 Vice Pres Academic Affairs ..... Dr. Douglas PALMER

30 Vice Pres of Advancement/Univ Rels ... Mr. Eric BELDEN
41 Vice Pres for Athletics ... Mr. Dale S. HOWARD
88 VP Acad Proj/Coord Cultural Events ... Ms. Nancy BLACKFORD
26 VP for Marketing/Communications ... Ms. Teresa FOX
13 VP of Administration/CIO ... Mr. Brian GREENWELL
20 Dean for Academic Services ... Ms. Edna MCCULLOH
09 Dean Inst Effectiveness ... Dr. Ute LAHAIE
18 Director of Facilities & Grounds ... Mr. John SCHISSLER
91 Database Administrator ... Ms. Hope STANCIU
22 Director of Compliance ... Mr. Jason FAUTAS
36 Director of Career Services ... Mr. Andy WEYAND
42 Chaplain ... Fr. Thomas CEBULA
38 Director Counseling Services ... Ms. Frances MORROW
42 Director of Campus Ministry ... Mr. Miguel CHAVEZ
31 Dir Campus & Community Programs ... Ms. Jacqueline M. MANSER
37 Director Financial Aid ... Mrs. Holly VAN GILDER
15 Director of Human Resources ... Mr. Frank MCKNIGHT
29 Director of Alumni Relations ... Ms. Sarah TRESCOTT
25 Director of Grants ... Ms. Rachel HAMMEL
19 Chief of Campus Police ... Mr. Louis DARROW
08 Director of Library Services ... Ms. Heidi BEKE-HARRIGAN
83 Dean School of Behav/Health Science ... Dr. Pamela RITZLINE
49 Dean School of Arts & Sciences ... Dr. Michael DUNPHY
66 Dean Byers School of Nursing ... Dr. Linda LINC
73 Chair Div of Philosophy/Theology ... Dr. Bradley BEACH
81 Chair Division of Math & Sciences ... Dr. Jackie NOVAK
92 Director Honors Program ... Dr. Koop BERRY
04 Administrative Asst to President ... Ms. Christine SCHEETZ
06 Registrar ... Ms. Stacie HERMAN
50 Dean DeVille School of Business ... Dr. Carole MOUNT
53 Chair Div of Education ... Dr. Jeannie DEFAZIO

Washington State Community College (A)

710 Colegate Drive, Marietta OH 45750-9225

County: Washington FICE Identification: 010453
Unit ID: 206446
Telephone: (740) 374-8716 Carnegie Class: Assoc/MT-VT-High Non
FAX Number: (740) 374-9562 Calendar System: Semester
URL: www.wscc.edu
Established: 1971 Annual Undergrad Tuition & Fees (In-State): $4,490
Enrollment: 1,623 Coed
Affiliation or Control: State IRS Status: 501(c)3
Highest Offering: Associate Degree
Accreditation: NH, COARC, MLTAD, PTAA

01 President ... Dr. Bradley J. EBERSOLE
10 VP of Finance and Operations/Treas ... Mr. Jess N. RAINES
84 VP of Enrollment & Student Success ... Ms. Amanda K. HERB
05 Vice President for Academic Affairs ... Dr. Mark NUTTER
27 Chief Information Officer ... Mr. Terry RATAICZAK
15 Executive Director Human Resources ... Mr. Jeff FARLEY
102 Exec Dir Foundation & Grants Dev ... Vacant
76 Dean of Health Sciences ... Dr. Heather KINCAID
49 Dean of Arts and Sciences ... Mr. Allen SHORE
50 Dean of Bus/Engr/Industrial Tech ... Ms. Brenda L. KORNMILLER
36 Director of Advising & Transfer ... Vacant
06 Registrar ... Ms. Sarah ALLAN
07 Director of Admissions ... Ms. Carrie THRASH
26 Dir of Marketing & Communications ... Ms. Amanda HERB
37 Director of Financial Aid ... Ms. Shannon VENEZIA
08 Director Library Services ... Ms. Mary Lou MOEGLING
37 Assistant Director of Financial Aid ... Ms. Reba BARTRUG
88 Director of College Access and ETS ... Ms. Donna MUNTZ

Wilberforce University (B)

PO Box 1001, Wilberforce OH 45384-1001

County: Greene FICE Identification: 003141
Unit ID: 206491
Telephone: (937) 376-2911 Carnegie Class: Bac-Diverse
FAX Number: (937) 376-2627 Calendar System: Semester
URL: www.wilberforce.edu
Established: 1856 Annual Undergrad Tuition & Fees: $13,475
Enrollment: 387 Coed
Affiliation or Control: African Methodist Episcopal IRS Status: 501(c)3
Highest Offering: Master's
Accreditation: NH, CORE

01 President ... Dr. Algeania W. FREEMAN
45 Provost/VP of Institutional Effect ... Dr. Delbert BUFFINGER
05 Vice Pres Academic Affairs ... Dr. Robin MOORE-COOPER
10 Sr VP of Administration & Finance ... Mr. William WOODSON
84 VP of Enrollment Management ... Mrs. Terry JEFFRIES
30 VP of Institutional Advancement ... Ms. Annie PRICE
32 VP of Student Services ... Mr. Dana MERCK
31 VP of Church & Community Relations ... Rev. John E. FREEMAN
09 AVP Institutional Effectiveness ... Ms. Dadra DRISCOLL
20 AVP Academic Affairs/Support Svcs ... Ms. Brittany MOTLEY
11 AVP Admin and Finance/Controller ... Mr. Kevin HOWARD
15 Senior Director of Human Resources ... Ms. Anita GOMEZ
78 Dir Cooperative Ed & Career Service ... Mr. Victor JONES
41 Athletic Director ... Ms. Dorianne JOHNSON
13 Deputy Director of IT ... Mr. Mayhew CUTHBERTSON
107 Dean of Professional Studies ... Mr. Michael SIMMONS
49 Dean of Arts & Sciences ... Dr. Sharon TIPPINS
06 Registrar ... Mrs. Rudell MOORE
25 Director Title III/Sponsored Pgms ... Mrs. Lisa TURNER
51 AVP Academic Affairs CLIMB Pgms ... Ms. Virginia DAVENPORT
07 Director of Admissions ... Ms. Kenielle E. MORRIS

35 Director of Student Activities ... Ms. Angela WILSON
08 Chief Librarian ... Mr. Colin DUBE
21 Assistant Bursar ... Ms. Debra OLIVER

Wilmington College (C)

1870 Quaker Way, Wilmington OH 45177-2499

County: Clinton FICE Identification: 003142
Unit ID: 206507
Telephone: (937) 382-6661 Carnegie Class: Bac-Diverse
FAX Number: (937) 383-8574 Calendar System: Semester
URL: www.wilmington.edu
Established: 1870 Annual Undergrad Tuition & Fees: $24,500
Enrollment: 1,200 Coed
Affiliation or Control: Friends IRS Status: 501(c)3
Highest Offering: Master's
Accreditation: NH, CAATE, TEAC

01 President ... Dr. James M. REYNOLDS
04 Assistant to the President ... Mrs. Leslie A. NICHOLS
05 Vice President Academic Affairs ... Dr. Erika A. GOODWIN
10 Vice President Business/Finance ... Mr. Bradley J. MITCHELL
30 Vice President College Advancement ... Mr. Matt WAHRHAFTIG
88 Vice President External Programs ... Ms. Sylvia STEVENS
32 Vice President Student Affairs ... Ms. Sigrid B. SOLOMON
41 Vice President Athletic Admin ... Dr. Terry A. RUPERT
84 Chief Enrollment Officer ... Mr. Dennis KELLY
20 Assoc Vice Pres Academic Affairs ... Dr. Mei Mei BURR
35 Assoc Vice Pres Student Affairs ... Mr. Kenneth A. LYDY
09 AVP Acad Affs/Institutional Effect ... Ms. Katie BONTRAGER
26 Director of Public Relations ... Mr. Randall F. SARVIS
06 Registrar ... Ms. Sue HUTCHENS
08 Director of Watson Library ... Mr. Brian HICKAM
15 Director of Human Resources ... Ms. Libby HAYES
36 Director of Career Services ... Ms. Tammy FRASER
18 Director of Physical Plant ... Mr. Terry L. JOHNSON
29 Dir Alumni/Parent Rels/Advancement ... Ms. Kathy L. MILAM
37 Dir Financial Aid/One Stop Center ... Ms. Cheryl LOUALLEN
07 Director of Admission ... Mr. Adam LOHREY
96 Purchasing Manager ... Ms. Laura BAESSLER

Wilmington College Blue Ash Branch (D)

9987 Carver Road, Blue Ash OH 45242

Telephone: (513) 793-1337 Identification: 770364
Accreditation: &NH

† Regional accreditation is carried under the parent institution in Wilmington, OH

Winebrenner Theological Seminary (E)

950 N Main Street, Findlay OH 45840-3652

County: Hancock FICE Identification: 004060
Unit ID: 206516
Telephone: (419) 434-4200 Carnegie Class: Spec-4-yr-Faith
FAX Number: (419) 434-4267 Calendar System: Trimester
URL: www.winebrenner.edu
Established: 1942 Annual Graduate Tuition & Fees: N/A
Enrollment: 64 Coed
Affiliation or Control: Independent Non-Profit IRS Status: 501(c)3
Highest Offering: Doctorate; No Undergraduates
Accreditation: #NH, THEOL

01 President/CEO ... Dr. Brent C. SLEASMAN
30 VP of Institutional Advancement ... Dr. Jim ALLEN
05 VP of Academic Advancement ... Dr. Joel COCKLIN
84 Director of Enrollment Management ... Mr. James SMARKEL
08 Director of Library Services ... Mrs. Margaret HIRSCHY
06 Registrar ... Ms. Shari BUIS
04 Assistant to the President ... Vacant
108 Director Institutional Assessment ... Dr. Kathryn HELLEMAN

Wittenberg University (F)

PO Box 720, Springfield OH 45501-0720

County: Clark FICE Identification: 003143
Unit ID: 206525
Telephone: (937) 327-6231 Carnegie Class: Bac-A&S
FAX Number: (937) 327-6340 Calendar System: Semester
URL: www.wittenberg.edu
Established: 1845 Annual Undergrad Tuition & Fees: $38,090
Enrollment: 1,964 Coed
Affiliation or Control: Evangelical Lutheran Church In America
IRS Status: 501(c)3
Highest Offering: Master's
Accreditation: NH, MUS, TED

01 Interim President ... Dr. Richard HETTON
05 Interim Provost ... Dr. Mary Jo ZEMBAR
10 Vice Pres Finance/Administration ... Mr. Randal FREEBOURN
32 Vice Pres Student Development ... Vacant
46 Vice Pres Strategic Initiatives ... Dr. Ty BUCKMAN
30 Interim Vice Pres Advancement ... Ms. Wendy KOBLER
20 Asst Provost Academic Services ... Dr. Mary Jo ZEMBAR
31 Dean School Community Education ... Dr. Thomas KAPLAN
35 Dean of Students ... Ms. Casey GILL
88 Assoc Dean Student Success/Retent ... Mr. Jonathan DURAJ
85 Director International Education ... Ms. JoAnn BENNETT
42 Pastor to the University ... Rev. Rachel SANDUM TUNE

08 Director of the Library ... Mr. Douglas K. LEHMAN
13 Chief Information Officer ... Mr. Richard MICKOOL
26 Vice Pres Marketing/Communications ... Ms. Karen GERBOTH
31 Director Community Service ... Ms. Kristen L. COLLIER
06 Registrar ... Mr. Jack M. CAMPBELL
41 Director Athletics/Recreation ... Dr. Gary WILLIAMS
58 Director Graduate Studies in Educ ... Dr. Roberta LINDER
94 Director of Women's Studies ... Dr. Heather H. WRIGHT
09 Asst Prov Acad Affs/Inst Research ... Dr. Darby L. HILLER-FREUND
29 Director of Alumni Relations ... Ms. Linda M. BEALS
27 Sports Information Director ... Mr. Kuris DUGGAN
105 Webmaster ... Mr. Ryan MAURER
39 Associate Dean for Residence Life ... Vacant
38 Director Student Counseling ... Ms. Linda M. LAUFFENBURGER
88 Director Fraternity & Sorority Life ... Ms. Carol NICKOSON
28 Assoc Dean Multicultural Affairs ... Mr. John YOUNG
07 Exec Director of Admission ... Ms. Karen HUNT
37 Exec Director of Financial Aid ... Mr. Jonathan RANDY GREEN
18 Asst VP Plant/Safety & Environment ... Vacant
15 Director Human Resources ... Vacant
19 Chief of Police ... Mr. Jim HUTCHINS
40 Manager of Bookstore ... Ms. Amy DALTON

Wright State University Lake Campus (G)

7600 Lake Campus Drive, Celina OH 45822-2952

Telephone: (419) 586-0300 FICE Identification: 009169
Accreditation: &NH

† Regional accreditation is carried under the parent institution in Dayton, OH.

Wright State University Main Campus (H)

3640 Colonel Glenn Highway, Dayton OH 45435-0001

County: Greene FICE Identification: 003078
Unit ID: 206604
Telephone: (937) 775-3333 Carnegie Class: DU-Mod
FAX Number: (937) 775-3301 Calendar System: Semester
URL: www.wright.edu
Established: 1964 Annual Undergrad Tuition & Fees (In-State): $8,730
Enrollment: 16,342 Coed
Affiliation or Control: State IRS Status: 501(c)3
Highest Offering: Doctorate
Accreditation: NH, BUS, BUSA, CAATE, CACREP, CEA, CLPSY, CORE, CS, ENG, EXSC, IPSY, MED, MT, MUS, NURSE, PH, SPAA, SW, TED

53 Dean Education/Human Services ... Dr. Joseph E. KEFERL
01 President ... Dr. David R. HOPKINS
05 Provost ... Dr. Thomas A. SUDKAMP
10 Vice Pres Business and Finance ... Mr. Jeff ULLIMAN
32 Vice President Student Affairs ... Dr. Dan ABRAHAMOWICZ
46 Vice Pres Research/Graduate Studies ... Dr. Robert FYFFE
30 Vice Pres University Advancement ... Ms. Rebecca S. COLE
84 Vice Pres Enrollment Management ... Ms. Mary Ellen ASHLEY
20 VP Instruction & Curriculum ... Vacant
58 Dean Sch Graduate Studies ... Dr. Robert FYFFE
45 Exec Vice President for Planning ... Dr. Robert J. SWEENEY
08 University Librarian ... Mrs. Sheila G. SHELLABARGER
26 Executive Director of Marketing ... Ms. Denise ROBINOW
15 Assoc Vice Pres for Human Resources ... Ms. Shari MICKEY-BOGGS
18 Assoc VP Facilities Mgmt & Svcs ... Mr. Dan PAPAY
35 Associate Vice Pres Student Affairs ... Ms. Katherine W. MORRIS
50 Dean Raj Soin College of Business ... Dr. Joanne LI
54 Dean Engineering/Computer Science ... Dr. Nathan W. KLINGBEIL
12 Dean WSU Lake Campus ... Dr. Jay ALBAYYARI
49 Dean Liberal Arts ... Dr. Kristin SOBOLIK
66 Dean College of Nursing & Health ... Dr. Rosalie O'DELL MAINOUS
63 Dean Boonshaft School of Medicine ... Dr. Margaret DUNN
83 Dean Sch of Prof Psychology ... Dr. LaPearl Logan WINFREY
81 Interim Dean Science/Mathematics ... Dr. Kathrin ENGISCH
06 Registrar ... Ms. Amanda STEELE-MIDDLETON
07 AVP Undergraduate Admissions ... Ms. Cathleen M. DAVIS
13 Chief Information Officer ... Mr. Craig WOOLLEY
46 Asst VP Research/Sponsored Pgms ... Ms. Ellen REINSCH FRIESE
36 Director Career Services ... Ms. Cheryl STUART
37 Director of Financial Aid ... Ms. Amy BARNHART
38 Director Counsel/Wellness Svcs ... Dr. Robert A. RANDO
29 Exec Director Alumni Relations ... Mr. Gregory SCHARER
22 Director Equity and Inclusion ... Mr. Matt BOAZ
22 Director Disability Services ... Mr. Tom WEBB
86 Assoc VP Public Affairs ... Mr. Robert E. HICKEY, JR.
41 Director of Athletics ... Mr. Bob GRANT
43 General Counsel ... Mr. Larry CHAN
40 Store Manager ... Ms. Jennifer L. GEBHART
85 Director Intl Student/Scholar Svcs ... Mr. Steven J. LYONS
39 Director Residence Services ... Mr. Daniel BERTSOS
19 Chief Police Department ... Mr. David A. FINNIE
96 Dir Strategic Procurement & Contr ... Vacant
92 Director Honors Program ... Dr. Susan CARRAFIELLO
94 Director Womens Studies Program ... Dr. Hope JENNINGS
09 Asst VP Institutional Research ... Mr. Craig THIS
28 VP Multicultural Affairs & Comm Eng ... Dr. Kimberly BARRETT
04 Executive Asst to President ... Ms. Teresa M. BEDWELL
102 CFO WSU Foundation ... Mr. Robert BATSON
44 Director Annual or Planned Giving ... Ms. Jennifer M. FOSTER

Xavier University (I)

3800 Victory Parkway, Cincinnati OH 45207-1096

County: Hamilton FICE Identification: 003144
Unit ID: 206622

Telephone: (513) 745-3000 Carnegie Class: Masters/L
FAX Number: (513) 745-4223 Calendar System: Semester
URL: www.xavier.edu
Established: 1831 Annual Undergrad Tuition & Fees: $35,080
Enrollment: 6,508 Coed
Affiliation or Control: Roman Catholic IRS Status: 501(c)3
Highest Offering: Doctorate
Accreditation: NH, BUS, CAATE, CACREP, CEA, CLPSY, HSA, MACTE, MUS, NURSE, OT, #RAD, SW, TEAC

01 President .... Rev. Michael J. GRAHAM, SJ
11 Administrative Vice President .... Dr. John F. KUCIA
05 Int Provost/Chief Academic Officer .... Dr. Brian LEVIN-STANKEVICH
10 Exec VP Financial Admin/CFO .... Ms. Maribeth AMYOT
26 Vice Pres for University Relations .... Mr. Gary R. MASSA
88 Asst to Pres for Mission & Identity .... Dr. Debra MOONEY
13 Exec Dir Information Technologies .... Mr. Mark BROCKMAN
28 Chief Diversity/Inclusion Officer .... Dr. Janice WALKER
27 Director Strategic Communications .... Ms. Kelly LEON
30 Assoc VP for University Relations .... Ms. Susan ABEL
32 Assoc Provost for Student Affairs .... Mr. David J. JOHNSON
18 Vice President for Facilities .... Mr. Robert M. SHEERAN
41 Director Athletics .... Mr. Greg CHRISTOPHER
15 Assoc Vice Pres for Human Resources .... Mrs. Connie PERME
84 Vice Pres Enrollment Management .... Mr. Aaron MEIS
44 Exec Dir Gifts & Estate Planning .... Mr. Mark MCLAUGHLIN
42 Dir Center for Mission/Identity .... Mr. Joseph SHADLE
06 Registrar .... Dr. Andrea WAWRZUSIN
85 Exec Dir Center for Intl Education .... Ms. Lea MINNITI
105 Exec Dir University Communications .... Mr. Doug RUSCHMAN
39 Sr Dir Student Affairs/Ofc Res Life .... Ms. Lori A. LAMBERT
40 Director of Bookstore .... Mr. Michael HUBBARD
86 Director of Government Relations .... Mr. Sean COMER
83 Dean Col of Professional Sciences .... Dr. Paul GORE
07 Dean of Admission/Undergrad Admiss .... Ms. Lauren COBBLE
35 Senior Director Student Affairs .... Ms. Leah BUSAM
23 Director for Health Services .... Ms. Mary ROSENFELDT
49 Dean College Arts & Sciences .... Dr. David MENGEL
19 Dir Public Safety/Chief of Police .... Chief Joseph MILEK
37 Director of Scholarships .... Ms. Donna SALAK
43 General Counsel/Sec of the Board .... Mr. Joseph H. FELDHAUS
29 Dir Alumni Rels/Ex Dir Athletic Dev .... Mr. Brian MALEY
09 Dir Office Institutional Research .... Mrs. Emily SHIPLEY
50 Dean Williams College of Business .... Dr. Thomas HAYES
51 Director Weekend Degree Program .... Ms. Patricia MEYER
96 Dir Purchasing & Supply Management .... Mr. John MERCER
88 Dir TRIO Student Support Services .... Dr. Daniel MCSPADDEN

Youngstown State University (A)

One University Plaza, Youngstown OH 44555-0001
County: Mahoning FICE Identification: 003145
Unit ID: 206695
Telephone: (330) 941-3001 Carnegie Class: Masters/L
FAX Number: (330) 941-7169 Calendar System: Semester
URL: www.ysu.edu
Established: 1908 Annual Undergrad Tuition & Fees (In-State): $8,317
Enrollment: 12,503 Coed
Affiliation or Control: State IRS Status: 501(c)3
Highest Offering: Doctorate
Accreditation: NH, AAFCS, ANEST, ART, BUS, CACREP, COARC, COARCP, DH, DIETC, DIETD, DIETT, EMT, ENG, ENGT, MAC, MLTAD, MUS, NUR, PH, PTA, SW, TED, THEA

01 President .... Mr. James P. TRESSEL
05 Provost & VP for Academic Affairs .... Dr. Martin ABRAHAM
10 Vice Pres Finance & Business Op .... Mr. Neal P. MCNALLY
26 Assoc VP for University Relations .... Mrs. Shannon TIRONE
32 Assoc VP for Student Experience .... Dr. Eddie HOWARD, JR.
84 Assoc Vice Pres Enrollment Mgmt .... Mr. Gary D. SWEGAN
43 Vice President and General Counsel .... Ms. Holly A. JACOBS
49 Dean Liberal Arts/Soc Science .... Dr. Kristine BLAIR
50 Dean of Business Administration .... Dr. Betty Jo LICATA
53 Dean of Education .... Dr. Charles HOWELL
81 Dean of Science/Tech/Eng/Math .... Dr. Wim F. STEELANT
57 Dean Creative Arts & Communication .... Dr. Phyllis M. PAUL
76 Dean Health & Human Services .... Dr. Joseph L. MOSCA
58 Dean College of Graduate Studies .... Dr. Salvatore A. SANDERS
45 Assoc Provost Acad Pgms/Planning .... Dr. Kevin BALL
20 Senior Associate Provost .... Vacant
15 Chief Human Resources Officer .... Mr. Kevin W. REYNOLDS
13 Director Computer Services .... Mr. Richard J. MARSICO
41 Exec Director of Athletics .... Mr. Ronald A. STROLLO
35 Assoc VP for Student Success .... Dr. Michael REAGLE
08 Manager Library Operations .... Ms. Anna TORRES
88 Director Special Projects .... Mr. Jack FAHEY
29 Dir University Events & Protocol .... Ms. Jacquelyn LEVISEUR
28 Ex Director Multicultural Affairs .... Dr. Sylvia J. IMLER
07 Director Undergrad Recruit/Admiss .... Ms. Sue E. DAVIS
06 Registrar .... Ms. Jeanne HERMAN
19 Chief of University Police .... Mr. Shawn V. VARSO
18 Executive Director Facilities .... Mr. John P. HYDEN
21 Director Student Accts/Receivables .... Ms. Gloria KOBUS
23 Dir Environ/Occup Health & Safety .... Mr. Daniel SAHLI
37 Director Financial/Scholarships .... Ms. Elaine RUSE
21 Director General Accounting .... Ms. Katrena J. DAVIDSON
21 Cash Management Officer .... Mr. David EDWARDS
25 Director Grants & Sponsored Pgms .... Mr. Andrew P. SHEPARD-SMITH
39 Director Housing Services .... Ms. Danielle MEYER
85 AVP for International & Global Init .... Dr. Nathan R. MYERS
30 Director of Development .... Ms. Catherine CALA
28 Director Student Diversity Programs .... Mr. William J. BLAKE
88 Dir Assoc Degree/Tech Prep Pgms .... Ms. Arlene FLOYD
40 Director of Bookstore .... Mr. Charles A. SABATINO
88 Director Support Services .... Mr. Danny J. O'CONNELL
88 Dir Electronic Maintenance Svcs .... Mr. Michael REPETSKI
90 Director Media/Acad Computing .... Mr. Michael S. HRISHENKO
92 Director Univ Scholars/Honors Pgm .... Dr. Ronald SHAKLEE
96 Director Procurement Services .... Vacant
91 Manager IT Operations .... Mr. Troy CROSS
35 Dir Campus Rec/Intramural Sports ... Ms. Joy POLKABLA-BYERS
88 Director WYSU-FM .... Mr. Gary SEXTON
04 Exec Assistant to President .... Ms. Cynthia M. BELL
106 Dir Online Education/E-learning .... Ms. Millie RODRIGUEZ
86 Director Government Relations .... Dr. William C. BINNING

Zane State College (B)

9900 Brick Church Road, Cambridge OH 43725
Telephone: (740) 432-6568 Identification: 770365
Accreditation: &NH

† Regional accreditation is carried under the parent institution in Zanesville, OH

Zane State College (C)

1555 Newark Road, Zanesville OH 43701-2626
County: Muskingum FICE Identification: 008133
Unit ID: 204255
Telephone: (740) 454-2501 Carnegie Class: Assoc/MT-VT-Mix Trad/Non
FAX Number: (740) 454-0035 Calendar System: Semester
URL: www.zanestate.edu
Established: 1969 Annual Undergrad Tuition & Fees (In-State): $4,646
Enrollment: 4,009 Coed
Affiliation or Control: State IRS Status: 501(c)3
Highest Offering: Associate Degree
Accreditation: NH, ACBSP, ACFEI, CAHIIM, ENGT, MAC, MLTAD, OTA, PTAA, RAD

01 President .... Dr. Chad M. BROWN
102 Exec Dir Inst Advancemnt/Foundation .. Mr. Anthony ADORNETTO
05 Provost/Executive Vice President .... Dr. Richard WOODFIELD
10 Vice Pres for Business Services .... Ms. Terri M. BALDWIN
32 Vice Pres for Student Success .... Dr. Tricia LEGGETT
54 Acad Dean Business & Engineering .... Mr. Randy WHARTON
103 Assoc Dean Workforce Development .... Ms. Tracey TONNOUS
15 Vice Pres for CHRO .... Dr. James KEMPER
13 Exec Chief Info Officer .... Dr. Terry HERMAN
08 Library Director .... Ms. Janelle HUBBLE
09 Dir of Inst Effectiveness & Plng .... Dr. Tricia LEGGETT
25 Director of Grants & Contracts .... Vacant
07 Director of Admissions .... Mrs. Jody BURCHETT
37 Director Student Financial Aid .... Ms. Amanda B. REISINGER
36 Director Career/Employment Services .... Ms. Jamie K. CLARK
26 Director Marketing & Communications .... Mr. Nick WELCH
38 Dir of One Stop .... Mrs. Jamie K. CLARK
21 Comptroller .... Ms. Tammy S. HUFFMAN
40 Director of Bookstore Operations .... Ms. Linda D. METZ
19 Director of Safety and Security .... Mr. Joseph KEATING
76 Dean Health/Liberal Arts/Public Svc .... Dr. Barbara SHELBY
06 Asst Dean Curriculum/Registrar .... Ms. Theresa KOLK-CONNER
18 Director Facilities Management .... Mr. Joseph KEATING
04 Administrative Asst to President .... Mrs. Julie A. MACLAINE

OKLAHOMA

Bacone College (D)

2299 Old Bacone Road, Muskogee OK 74403-1568
County: Muskogee FICE Identification: 003147
Unit ID: 206817
Telephone: (918) 683-4581 Carnegie Class: Bac/Assoc-Mixed
FAX Number: (918) 781-7422 Calendar System: Semester
URL: www.bacone.edu
Established: 1880 Annual Undergrad Tuition & Fees: $14,500
Enrollment: 968 Coed
Affiliation or Control: American Baptist IRS Status: 501(c)3
Highest Offering: Baccalaureate
Accreditation: NH, IACBE, NURSE, RAD

01 President .... Mr. Franklin K. WILLIS
05 Provost .... Dr. Robert K. BROWN
20 Interim Dean of Faculty .... Dr. Jonathan THOMASON
88 Director Center for American Indian .... Dr. Patricia J. KING
30 Exec Director of Development .... Vacant
84 Director of Enrollment Management .... Mr. Kindle HOLDERBY
42 Chair Christian Ministry .... Rev Dr. Leroy THOMPSON
10 VP Finance .... Mr. Mustafa YUNDEM
32 Director of Student Life/Housing .... Mr. Kindle HOLDERBY
06 Registrar .... Mrs. Virginia THOMPSON
40 Bookstore Manager .... Ms. Dawn OSBORNE
41 Asst VP Athletics .... Mr. Alan FOSTER
37 Asst Director Financial Aid .... Ms. Misty OLESON
15 Asst Director Human Resources .... Ms. Jeanetta RAINWATER
07 Director of Admissions .... Vacant
108 Coord Institutional Assessment Data .... Ms. Linda MILAM
36 Director of Career Services .... Vacant
08 Dir Betts Library/Head Librarian .... Ms. Faye DAVIS
13 Director of Network Systems .... Mr. Chris EHLERS
04 Assistant to President .... Ms. Marcia TAYLOR
19 Chief of Campus Police .... Mr. Brad BEESLEY

Brown Mackie College-Oklahoma City (E)

7101 Northwest Expy, Suite 800, Oklahoma City OK 73132
Telephone: (405) 261-8000 Identification: 770252
Accreditation: &NH, OTA

† Regional accreditation is carried under the parent institution in Salina, KS

Brown Mackie College-Tulsa (F)

4608 South Garnett Road, Ste. 110, Tulsa OK 74146
Telephone: (918) 628-3700 Identification: 666783
Accreditation: ACICS, OTA, SURGT, SURTEC

† Branch campus of Brown Mackie College, South Bend, IN. No longer enrolling new students.

Cameron University (G)

2800 W Gore Boulevard, Lawton OK 73505-6377
County: Comanche FICE Identification: 003150
Unit ID: 206914
Telephone: (580) 581-2200 Carnegie Class: Masters/M
FAX Number: (580) 581-2867 Calendar System: Semester
URL: www.cameron.edu
Established: 1908 Annual Undergrad Tuition & Fees (In-State): $5,580
Enrollment: 5,537 Coed
Affiliation or Control: State IRS Status: 501(c)3
Highest Offering: Master's
Accreditation: NH, ACBSP, COARC, MUS, TED

01 President .... Dr. John M. MCARTHUR
05 Vice President for Academic Affairs .. Dr. Ronna J. VANDERSLICE
10 Vice Pres for Business & Finance .... Ms. Ninette CARTER
30 Vice Pres University Advancement ... Mr. Albert D. JOHNSON, JR.
84 VP for Enroll Mgmt & Stdnt Success .... Mr. Jon HORINEK
20 Assoc Vice Pres Academic Affairs .... Dr. Sylvia BURGESS
20 Asst Vice Pres Academic Affairs .... Dr. Margery KINGSLEY
49 Dean School of Arts and Sciences .... Dr. Von E. UNDERWOOD
58 Dean Sch of Grad and Prof Studies .... Dr. Lisa HUFFMAN
12 Director Duncan Campus .... Ms. Susan CAMP
21 Controller .... Mr. Donald HALL
26 Senior Director of Public Affairs .... Mr. Keith MITCHELL
29 Director Develop & Alumni Relations .. Ms. Maurissa BUCHWALD
41 Director Athletic Administration .... Mr. Jim C. JACKSON
07 Director of Admissions .... Vacant
06 Registrar .... Mrs. Linda PHILLIPS
09 Dir Inst Rsrch/Assess/Accountabity .... Dr. Karla OTY
37 Director of Financial Assistance .... Mr. Gary GAROFFOLO
13 Director Information Tech Services .... Mr. Kelly MCCLURE
15 Director of Human Resources .... Mr. Gordon SHAW
38 Director of Student Development .... Dr. Jennifer PRUCHNICKI
32 Dean of Students .... Mr. Zeak NAIFEH
19 Director Public Safety .... Mr. John DEBOARD
18 Director Physical Facilities .... Mr. Robert HANEFIELD
96 Purchasing Agent .... Mr. Richard MCCOMAS
22 EEO Officer/Title IX Coordinator .... Mr. Thomas RUSSELL

Career Point College (H)

3138 South Garnett Road, Tulsa OK 74146-1933
Telephone: (918) 627-8074 Identification: 770761
Accreditation: ACICS

† Branch campus of Career Point College, San Antonio, TX

Carl Albert State College (I)

1507 S McKenna, Poteau OK 74953-5208
County: Le Flore FICE Identification: 003176
Unit ID: 206923
Telephone: (918) 647-1200 Carnegie Class: Assoc/HT-High Trad
FAX Number: (918) 647-1201 Calendar System: Semester
URL: www.carlalbert.edu
Established: 1933 Annual Undergrad Tuition & Fees (In-State): $3,011
Enrollment: 2,241 Coed
Affiliation or Control: State IRS Status: 501(c)3
Highest Offering: Associate Degree
Accreditation: NH, ACBSP, ADNUR, PTAA

01 President .... Mr. Jay FAULKNER
32 Vice President for Student Affairs .... Vacant
05 Vice President of Academic Affairs .... Dr. Jason MORRISON
10 Vice Pres for Business Operations .... Mr. Tony CROUCH
32 Assoc Vice Pres Student Affairs .... Mr. Randy GRAVES
84 Director Enrollment Mgmt .... Ms. Jennifer HUMPHREYS
13 Director Information Technology .... Mr. Michael MARTIN
04 Assistant to the President .... Vacant
26 Dir Public Relations/Marketing .... Ms. Judi WHITE
06 Registrar/Director Admissions .... Ms. Dee Ann DICKERSON
37 Director of Financial Aid .... Ms. Robin BENSON
86 Director Federal Programs .... Ms. Michelle WHITE
08 Head Librarian .... Ms. Terri CARROLL
18 Director of Physical Plant .... Mr. Chuck LEWIS
15 Director Personnel Services .... Ms. Vicki SULLIVAN
21 Business Office Manager .... Ms. Rena BROOKS
108 Institutional Effectiveness Officer .... Dr. Kathy HARRELL
101 Secretary of the Institution/Board .... Ms. Jean Ann BARLOW
102 Dir Foundation/Corporate Relations .... Ms. Mandy ROBERTS
106 Dir Online Education/E-learning .... Ms. Sarah BROWN
19 Directory Security/Safety .... Mr. Chad BROWN

Carl Albert State College (A)
1601 S. Opdyke St, Sallisaw OK 74955
Telephone: (918) 775-6977 Identification: 770366
Accreditation: &NH

† Regional accreditation is carried under the parent institution in Poteau, OK

Clary Sage College (B)
3131 South Sheridan Road, Tulsa OK 74145-1102
Telephone: (918) 298-8200 Identification: 666368
Accreditation: ACICS

† Branch campus of Community Care College, Tulsa, OK.

College of the Muscogee Nation (C)
PO Box 917, 2170 Raven Circle, Okmulgee OK 74447
County: Okmulgee Identification: 667122
Unit ID: 480967
Telephone: (918) 549-2800 Carnegie Class: Tribal
FAX Number: (918) 549-2880 Calendar System: Semester
URL: www.mvsktc.org
Established: 1994 Annual Undergrad Tuition & Fees: $6,600
Enrollment: 188 Coed
Affiliation or Control: Tribal Control IRS Status: 501(c)3
Highest Offering: Associate Degree
Accreditation: @NH

01 President .... Mr. Robert BIBLE
05 Dean of Academic Affairs .... Mr. Monte RANDALL

Comanche Nation College (D)
1608 SW 9th Street, Lawton OK 73501
County: Comanche Identification: 667123
Unit ID: 483522
Telephone: (580) 591-0203 Carnegie Class: Not Classified
FAX Number: (580) 591-0643 Calendar System: Semester
URL: www.cnc.cc.ok.us
Established: 2002 Annual Undergrad Tuition & Fees: $3,750
Enrollment: 50 Coed
Affiliation or Control: Tribal Control IRS Status: 501(c)3
Highest Offering: Associate Degree
Accreditation: @NH

01 President .... Dr. Robbie WAHNEE
05 Vice Pres Student/Academic Affairs .... Johnny POOLAW
06 Registrar .... Sarah GODSAVE
108 Dir Institutional Effectiveness .... Dr. Kurtis KOLL
32 Director Student Services .... Natalie YOUNGBULL

Community Care College (E)
4242 S Sheridan Road, Tulsa OK 74145-1119
County: Tulsa FICE Identification: 033674
Unit ID: 439570
Telephone: (918) 610-0027 Carnegie Class: Spec 2-yr-Health
FAX Number: (918) 610-0029 Calendar System: Other
URL: www.communitycarecollege.edu
Established: 1995 Annual Undergrad Tuition & Fees: N/A
Enrollment: 626 Coed
Affiliation or Control: Independent Non-Profit IRS Status: 501(c)3
Highest Offering: Associate Degree
Accreditation: ACICS, MAAB, SURGT

00 CEO .... Ms. Teresa L. KNOX
01 President .... Dr. Kevin L. KIRK

Connors State College (F)
700 College Road, Warner OK 74469-9700
County: Muskogee FICE Identification: 003153
Unit ID: 206996
Telephone: (918) 463-2931 Carnegie Class: Assoc/HT-High Trad
FAX Number: (918) 463-2233 Calendar System: Semester
URL: www.connorsstate.edu
Established: 1908 Annual Undergrad Tuition & Fees (In-State): $2,990
Enrollment: 2,278 Coed
Affiliation or Control: State IRS Status: 501(c)3
Highest Offering: Associate Degree
Accreditation: NH, ADNUR

01 Interim President .... Dr. Ron RAMMING
05 Interim VP for Academic Affairs .... Dr. Julie DINGER
10 VP for Fiscal Services .... Mr. Mike LEWIS
21 Assoc VP for Fiscal Services .... Vacant
30 Assoc VP for External Affairs .... Dr. Ryan BLANTON
37 Director of Financial Aid .... Mr. Baxter STEWART
08 Director of Learning Center .... Ms. Ona BRITTON-SPEARS
13 Director of Information Technology .... Mr. Heath HODGES
06 Registrar .... Ms. Kwanna KING
07 Director of Recruitment .... Ms. Logan KNAPPER
26 Director of Public Information .... Vacant
15 Director of Human Resources .... Mr. Nate WALKER
09 Director of Institutional Research .... Mr. Heath HODGES
41 Athletic Director .... Mr. Bill MUSE
32 Dean of Students .... Mr. Mike JACKSON
19 Chief of Police .... Mr. James MENDENHALL
04 Executive Asst to the President .... Ms. Cindy ANDERSON
04 Executive Asst to the President .... Ms. Jocy BUTLER
108 Asst VP Acad/Stdt Affs/Assessment .... Vacant
20 Asst VP Acad/Stdt Affs/Acad Support .... Ms. Robin O'QUINN

Connors State College Muskogee Port Branch Campus (G)
2501 N 41st Street East, Muskogee OK 74403
Telephone: (918) 687-6747 Identification: 770367
Accreditation: &NH

† Regional accreditation is carried under the parent institution in Warner, OK

East Central University (H)
1100 E 14th Street, Ada OK 74820-6899
County: Pontotoc FICE Identification: 003154
Unit ID: 207041
Telephone: (580) 332-8000 Carnegie Class: Masters/L
FAX Number: (580) 332-1623 Calendar System: Semester
URL: www.ecok.edu
Established: 1909 Annual Undergrad Tuition & Fees (In-State): $5,874
Enrollment: 4,428 Coed
Affiliation or Control: State IRS Status: 501(c)3
Highest Offering: Master's
Accreditation: NH, ACBSP, #CAATE, CACREP, CORE, MUS, NUR, SW, TED

01 President .... Dr. John R. HARGRAVE
05 Provost/VP Academic Affairs .... Dr. Katricia PIERSON
10 Exec VP Administration/Finance .... Ms. Jessica BOLES
32 VP Student Development .... Dr. Gerald FORBES
20 Asst VP Academic Affairs .... Dr. Adrianna LANCASTER
35 AVP Stdnt Devel/Dean of Stdnts .... Dr. Boomer APPLEMAN
53 Dean College of Educ & Psych .... Dr. Brenda SHERBOURNE
50 Dean School of Business .... Mr. Wendell GODWIN
81 Dean College of Health & Sciences .... Dr. Carl GILBERT
49 Dean College of Lib Arts & Soc Sci .... Dr. Brad JESSOP
58 Dean College of Grad Studies .... Dr. Adrianna LANCASTER
06 Registrar .... Ms. Deidra SIMMONS
13 Director Information Technology .... Mr. Jeremy BENNETT
09 Director Institutional Research .... Ms. Meredith JONES
26 Director Mktg & Communication .... Ms. Amy FORD
41 Director Athletics .... Dr. Jeff WILLIAMS
18 Director Facilities Mgmt .... Mr. Darryl OVERSTREET
15 Director Employment Services .... Mr. Lynn LOFTON
29 Director Alumni Relations .... Ms. Katie WELLINGTON
84 Director Enrollment Mgmt .... Mr. B. J. ECHARD
96 Director Purchasing .... Ms. Jo Ann JOHNSON
37 Director Financial Aid .... Ms. Becky ISAACS
08 Director Library .... Ms. Dana BELCHER
23 Director Stdnt Health Services .... Ms. Lisa YOUNG
39 Director Housing & Resid Life .... Ms. Debbie CHALMERS
38 Director Stdnt Counseling Ctr .... Ms. Jennifer COX
85 Director Intl Student Pgms & Svcs .... Ms. Jessika BAILEY
108 Director Assessment .... Dr. Robin ROBERSON
103 Director Career Development .... Ms. Peggy SAUNKEAH
25 Director Grants & Research .... Ms. Leah LYON
20 Director Academic Services .... Ms. Holly SEWELL
88 Coordinator Disability Services .... Ms. Kim ROGERS
21 Controller .... Ms. Susie SHOCKEY
21 Bursar .... Mr. Ty ANDERSON
19 Chief of University Police .... Mr. Bert MILLER

Eastern Oklahoma State College (I)
1301 W Main Street, Wilburton OK 74578-4999
County: Latimer FICE Identification: 003155
Unit ID: 207050
Telephone: (918) 465-2361 Carnegie Class: Assoc/HT-High Trad
FAX Number: (918) 465-2431 Calendar System: Semester
URL: www.eosc.edu
Established: 1909 Annual Undergrad Tuition & Fees (In-State): $3,947
Enrollment: 1,673 Coed
Affiliation or Control: State IRS Status: 501(c)3
Highest Offering: Associate Degree
Accreditation: NH, ADNUR, MLTAD

01 President .... Dr. Stephen E. SMITH
05 Vice President of Academic Affairs .... Dr. Janet WANSICK
10 Vice Pres of Business Affairs .... Ms. La Donna HOWELL
32 Vice Pres for Student Affairs .... Dr. Steve G. GLAZIER
12 Director of McAlester Campus .... Ms. Ann BROOKS
35 Director of Student Life .... Ms. Cindy SHERO
41 Athletic Director .... Mr. Kirk KELLEY
30 Exec Dir Development/Alumni Rels .... Ms. Treva KENNEDY
26 Dir Marketing/Communications .... Ms. Trish MCBEATH
09 Director of Institutional Research .... Dr. Janet WANSICK
20 Associate Academic Officer .... Dr. Janet WANSICK
84 Dir Enrollment Mgmt/Financial Aid .... Dr. Steve GLAZIER
13 Chief Technical Officer .... Mr. Jeff WEEMS
08 Director Library & Media Services .... Ms. Maria MARTINEZ
15 Director Human Resources .... Mrs. Joyce BILLS
06 Registrar .... Mrs. Jennifer LABOR
18 Int Dir Physical Plant Operations .... Mr. Alan MOSS
44 Dir of Institutional Advancement .... Ms. Treva KENNEDY
37 Financial Aid Director .... Ms. Mimi KELLEY
19 Campus Police Chief .... Mr. Bryan DENNY

Eastern Oklahoma State College McAlester Campus (J)
1802 E College Avenue, McAlester OK 74501
Telephone: (918) 426-5272 Identification: 770368
Accreditation: &NH

† Regional accreditation is carried under the parent institution in Wilburton, OK

Family of Faith College (K)
PO Box 1805, Shawnee OK 74802-1805
County: Pottawatomie FICE Identification: 036763
Unit ID: 443058
Telephone: (405) 273-5331 Carnegie Class: Spec-4-yr-Faith
FAX Number: (405) 273-8535 Calendar System: Semester
URL: www.familyoffaithcollege.edu
Established: 1992 Annual Undergrad Tuition & Fees: $6,070
Enrollment: 24 Coed
Affiliation or Control: Independent Non-Profit IRS Status: 501(c)3
Highest Offering: Baccalaureate
Accreditation: BI

01 President .... Dr. Samuel W. MATTHEWS
05 Vice President Academic Affairs .... Mrs. Elaine W. PHILLIPS
10 Actg Vice Pres Operations/Finance .... Mr. Daniel MATTHEWS
32 Vice Pres Student Affs/Dir Fin Aid .... Mrs. Dara GILLIAM
46 Director of Resource Development .... Vacant
42 Director of Spiritual Life .... Mr. Daniel J. MATTHEWS
108 Dir of Accreditation/Assessment .... Mrs. Elaine W. PHILLIPS
104 Director of International Studies .... Mrs. Dara GILLIAM

Heritage College (L)
7202 I-35 Services Road, Oklahoma City OK 73149-2740
County: Oklahoma FICE Identification: 031151
Unit ID: 410070
Telephone: (405) 631-3399 Carnegie Class: Spec 2-yr-Health
FAX Number: (405) 631-6711 Calendar System: Quarter
URL: www.heritage-education.com
Established: 2002 Annual Undergrad Tuition & Fees: N/A
Enrollment: 715 Coed
Affiliation or Control: Proprietary IRS Status: Proprietary
Highest Offering: Associate Degree
Accreditation: ABHES, SURTEC

01 Director .... Ms. Marilyn LONG

Langston University (M)
PO Box 1500, Langston OK 73050
County: Logan FICE Identification: 003157
Unit ID: 207209
Telephone: (405) 466-2231 Carnegie Class: Masters/M
FAX Number: N/A Calendar System: Semester
URL: www.langston.edu
Established: 1897 Annual Undergrad Tuition & Fees (In-State): $5,042
Enrollment: 2,482 Coed
Affiliation or Control: State IRS Status: 501(c)3
Highest Offering: Doctorate
Accreditation: NH, ACBSP, CORE, NUR, PTA, TED

01 President .... Dr. Kent J. SMITH, JR.
05 Vice President Academic Affairs .... Dr. Clyde MONTGOMERY, JR.
10 VP Fiscal/Admin Affairs .... Dr. Sharron T. BURNETT
32 VP Student Affairs .... Dr. Raphael X. MOFFETT
30 VP Inst Development/External Affs .... Mrs. Mautra JONES
100 Chief of Staff .... Ms. Theresa D. GRAVES
13 Chief Information Officer .... Mr. Pritchard MONCRIFFE
20 Assoc VP Academic Affairs LU/ CKC .... Mrs. Alice STRONG-SIMMONS
20 COO/Assoc VP Academic Affs LU/Tulsa .... Dr. Lisa K. WEIS
21 Asst VP of Accounting/Budgeting .... Ms. Helen RAMBO
35 Interim Dean of Students .... Ms. Helen M. ALATORRE
29 Director Alumni Affairs .... Mrs. Vonnie W. ROBERTS
36 Dir Assessment/Career Placement .... Mr. James A. WALLACE
26 Director Public Relations .... Mrs. Cynthia BUCKLEY
07 Director of Admissions .... Mr. Jeremy LANE
37 Director Financial Aid .... Ms. Shelia R. MCGILL
15 Director of Human Resources .... Mrs. Cynthia S. BUCKLEY
18 Director Facilities .... Mr. Jason KINDER
38 Acting Director of Counseling Svcs .... Dr. Jason K. WHITE
09 Director Inst Research & Planning .... Dr. Carol S. CAWYER
08 Director of Libraries .... Ms. Bettye R. BLACK
06 Registrar .... Mrs. Kathy SIMMONS
41 Athletic Director .... Mrs. Donnita ROGERS
58 Director of Graduate Programs .... Dr. Alex O. LEWIS
19 Chief of Police .... Mr. Demario HOLLAND
96 Purchasing Manager .... Mrs. Charlotte BROWN
49 Dean School of Arts & Sciences .... Dr. Alonzo PETERSON
50 Acting Dean School of Business .... Dr. Joshua M. SNAVELY
46 Dean School Agric/Applied Science .... Dr. Marvin BURNS
66 Dean School of Nursing/Hlth Profess .... Dr. Teressa HUNTER
53 Dean School of Education/Behav Sci .... Dr. Ruth R. JACKSON
08 Dean School of Physical Therapy .... Dr. Aliya CHAUDRY
88 Director Entrepreneurial Studies .... Dr. Sharron HUNTER-RAINEY
84 Exec Director Enrollment Mgmt .... Mr. Chauncey J. JACKSON

Langston University Oklahoma City Campus (N)
4205 N Lincoln, Oklahoma City OK 73105
Telephone: (405) 962-1620 Identification: 770370

Accreditation: &NH

† Regional accreditation is carried under the parent institution in Langston, OK

Langston University Tulsa Campus (A)

914 North Greenwood, Tulsa OK 74106
Telephone: (918) 877-8100 Identification: 770371
Accreditation: &NH

† Regional accreditation is carried under the parent institution in Langston, OK

McCurtain County Higher Education Center (B)

2805 NE Lincoln Road, Idabel OK 74745
Telephone: (580) 286-9431 Identification: 770369
Accreditation: &NH

† Regional accreditation is carried under the parent institution in Wilburton, OK

Mid-America Christian University (C)

3500 SW 119th Street, Oklahoma City OK 73170-4500
County: Cleveland FICE Identification: 006942
Unit ID: 245953
Telephone: (405) 691-3800 Carnegie Class: Masters/M
FAX Number: (405) 692-3165 Calendar System: Semester
URL: www.macu.edu
Established: 1953 Annual Undergrad Tuition & Fees: $16,798
Enrollment: 2,688 Coed
Affiliation or Control: Church Of God IRS Status: 501(c)3
Highest Offering: Master's
Accreditation: NH

01 President ... Dr. John D. FOZARD
05 Vice Pres for Academic Affairs ... Dr. Sharon LEASE
30 Vice Pres Strategic Initiatives ... Mr. Eric JOSEPH
84 VP Student Engagement/Success ... Mrs. Jessica RIMMER
26 Vice Pres Strategic Initiatives ... Mr. Eric JOSEPH
13 Chief Information Officer ... Mr. Jody ALLEN
15 Chief Administration Officer (HR) ... Mr. Owen SEVIER
20 Exec Dir Academic Assessment/Accred ... Mr. Saeed SARANI
42 Exec Director of Church Relations ... Rev. Morgan ALSIP
06 Registrar ... Ms. Stephanie DAVIDSON
37 Director Student Financial Services ... Ms. Emily LYNCH
07 Director of Admissions ... Mr. Mike WILKINSON
18 Director of Facilities ... Ms. Connie GALL
29 Director Alumni Relations ... Vacant

Murray State College (D)

One Murray Campus, Tishomingo OK 73460-3130
County: Johnston FICE Identification: 003158
Unit ID: 207236
Telephone: (580) 371-2371 Carnegie Class: Assoc/HT-High Trad
FAX Number: (580) 371-9844 Calendar System: Semester
URL: www.mscok.edu
Established: 1908 Annual Undergrad Tuition & Fees (In-State): $4,340
Enrollment: 2,473 Coed
Affiliation or Control: State IRS Status: 501(c)3
Highest Offering: Associate Degree
Accreditation: NH, ADNUR, OTA, PTAA

01 President ... Ms. Joy MCDANIEL
05 VP Acad Affs/Institutional Effect ... Ms. Becky HENTHORN
04 Exec Assistant to President/Board ... Mrs. Malynda COBB
10 VP Finance/Administration/CFO ... Mr. Dennis WESTMAN
32 Vice Pres for Student Affairs ... Ms. Michaelle GRAY
20 Dean of Instruction ... Ms. Ginger COTHRAN
18 Exec Director Campus Facilities ... Mr. Sam HOLT
102 Exec Director MSC Foundation ... Dr. Brenda STACY
84 Exec Dir Enrollment Services ... ms. Marilyn SCHWARZ
37 Dir Financial Aid/Acad Advisement ... Ms. Machelle ELLIS
08 Director of Library ... Ms. Mary RIXEN
74 Veterinary Tech Program Director ... Dr. Carey FLOYD
66 Director of Nursing ... Ms. Robin COPPEDGE
88 Director of Academic Advisement ... Ms. Amanda BALDRIDGE
07 Registrar ... Ms. Pam WARD
15 Director of Human Resources ... Ms. Michelle GRAY
35 Director Student Support Services ... Ms. Linda TAYLOR
21 Comptroller ... Ms. Sherry GRAY-DEVINE

National American University-Tulsa (E)

8040 S Sheridan Road, Tulsa OK 74133
Telephone: (918) 879-8400 Identification: 770409
Accreditation: &NH, MAC

† Regional accreditation is carried under the parent institution in Rapid City, SD

Northeastern Oklahoma Agricultural and Mechanical College (F)

200 I Street, NE, Miami OK 74354-6434
County: Ottawa FICE Identification: 003160
Unit ID: 207290
Telephone: (918) 542-8441 Carnegie Class: Assoc/HT-High Trad
FAX Number: (918) 542-9759 Calendar System: Semester
URL: www.neo.edu
Established: 1919 Annual Undergrad Tuition & Fees (In-State): $3,832
Enrollment: 2,274 Coed
Affiliation or Control: State IRS Status: 501(c)3
Highest Offering: Associate Degree
Accreditation: NH, ADNUR, MLTAD, PTAA

01 President ... Dr. Jeffery L. HALE
05 Vice President Academic Affairs ... Dr. Bethene FAHNESTOCK
10 Vice President for Fiscal Affairs ... Mr. Mark RASOR
32 VP Student Affairs/Enrollment Svcs ... Mrs. Amy ISHMAEL
20 Asst VP for Academic Affairs ... Dr. Shannon CUNNINGHAM
37 Director of Financial Aid ... Mr. David FISHER
26 Chief Public Relations Officer ... Mr. Jordan ADAMS
15 Director Human Resources ... Vacant
18 Director Facilities/Physical Plant ... Mr. Steve GRIMES
13 Coord InstructionalTechnology ... Mr. Matt WESTPHAL
30 Exec Dir Development Foundation ... Ms. Jennifer HESSEE
38 Director Academic Advising Center ... Mrs. Rachel LLOYD
41 Athletic Director ... Mr. Dale PATTERSON
88 Economic Development Coordinator ... Vacant
105 Webmaster ... Mr. David FRAZIER
06 Registrar ... Mrs. Melanie STEGEMAN
21 AVP for Fiscal Affairs/Controller ... Mr. Michael ALLGOOD
40 Bookstore Manager ... Mrs. Kathryn VANOVER
36 Dir Ctr for Academic Success & Adv ... Ms. Rachel LLOYD
08 Director Library Services ... Ms. Sloane ARANA
47 Department Chair Agriculture ... Vacant
83 Department Chair Social Science ... Dr. Jeff BIRDSONG
57 Dept Chair Commun/Performing Arts ... Vacant
81 Dept Chair Mathematics/Science ... Dr. Mark GRIGSBY
66 Dept Chr Nurs/Allied Hlth/Phys Educ ... Mrs. Deborah MORGAN
50 Dept Chair Business and Technology ... Mrs. Pat CREECH
04 Executive Asst to President ... Ms. Cindy BIGBY
19 Director Security/Safety ... Mr. Mark WALL
39 Director Student Housing ... Mr. Jim ROWLAND
90 Dir Academic/Admin Computing ... Ms. Kimberly BUNCH
96 Coord of Purchasing ... Ms. Kendra CUMMINS

Northeastern State University (G)

600 N Grand Avenue, Tahlequah OK 74464-2399
County: Cherokee FICE Identification: 003161
Unit ID: 207263
Telephone: (918) 456-5511 Carnegie Class: Masters/L
FAX Number: (918) 458-2015 Calendar System: Semester
URL: www.nsuok.edu
Established: 1909 Annual Undergrad Tuition & Fees (In-State): $5,547
Enrollment: 8,310 Coed
Affiliation or Control: State IRS Status: 501(c)3
Highest Offering: First Professional Degree
Accreditation: NH, ACBSP, CACREP, DIETD, MT, MUS, NUR, OPT, OPTR, SP, SW, TED

01 President ... Dr. Steve TURNER
05 Provost & Vice Pres Academic Affs ... Dr. Mark ARANT
11 Vice President for Administration ... Mr. Darren BURGESS
86 Dir Community/Government Relations ... Mr. Jerry COOK
26 VP University Relations ... Mr. Ben HARDCASTLE
32 Vice President Student Affairs ... Dr. Jerrid FREEMAN
58 Asst VP Acad Affs/Research ... Dr. Tom JACKSON
30 Asst VP Educ Foundation Leadership ... Dr. Pam FLY
12 Dean Broken Arrow Campus ... Dr. Roy WOOD
12 Dean Muskogee Campus ... Dr. Tim MCELROY
49 Dean College of Liberal Arts ... Dr. Phillip BRIDGMON
50 Dean College of Business/Technology ... Dr. Roger COLLIER
53 Dean College of Education ... Dr. Debbie LANDRY
81 Dean Science & Health Professions ... Dr. Pamela HATHORN
88 Dean Optometry ... Dr. Douglas PENISTEN
10 Asst Vice Pres Business Finance ... Ms. Christy LANDSAW
08 Exec Director of NSU Libraries ... Mr. Steven EDSCORN
06 Exec Dir Inst Effectiveness ... Dr. Julie SAWYER
21 Director of Budget ... Vacant
30 Director of Development ... Ms. Peggy GLENN-SUMMITT
15 Director of Human Resources ... Ms. Alisa HAMETT
37 Director Student Financial Services ... Dr. Teri COCHRAN
06 Registrar ... Ms. Janet KELLEY
07 Director Admissions/Recruitment ... Ms. Jennifer MCCLENDON
84 Director Enrollment Management ... Mr. Olaf STANDLEY
18 Assistant VP Facilities ... Mr. Jonathan ASBILL
41 Director of Athletics ... Mr. Tony DUCKWORTH
27 Director of Communications ... Mr. David JOPLIN
19 Director of Campus Police ... Ms. Patti BUHL
29 Director Alumni Services ... Mr. Daniel JOHNSON
07 Asst Director of Admission/Rec ... Ms. Damita CUNNINGHAM
109 Director of Auxiliary Services ... Mr. Chris ADNEY
39 Director of Housing ... Mr. Craig REINEHR
38 Director Student Counseling ... Ms. Sheila SELF
96 Purchasing Agent ... Mr. Thad TURMAN
44 Stewards/Annual Giving Coordinator ... Ms. Cami HIGHERS
04 Administrative Asst to President ... Ms. Robin HUTCHINS
13 Chief Info Technology Officer (CIO) ... Dr. Richard REIF

Northeastern State University (H)

3100 East New Orleans St, Broken Arrow OK 74014
Telephone: (918) 449-6000 Identification: 770372
Accreditation: &NH

† Regional accreditation is carried under the parent institution in Tahlequah, OK

Northeastern State University at Muskogee (I)

2400 W Shawnee, Muskogee OK 74401
Telephone: (918) 683-0040 Identification: 770373
Accreditation: &NH, OT

† Regional accreditation is carried under the parent institution in Tahlequah, OK

Northern Oklahoma College (J)

PO Box 2300, Enid OK 73702
Telephone: (580) 242-6300 Identification: 770374
Accreditation: &NH

† Regional accreditation is carried under the parent institution in Tonkawa, OK

Northern Oklahoma College (K)

PO Box 1869, Stillwater OK 74076
Telephone: (405) 744-2246 Identification: 770375
Accreditation: &NH

† Regional accreditation is carried under the parent institution in Tonkawa, OK

Northern Oklahoma College (L)

1220 E Grand Avenue, PO Box 310,
Tonkawa OK 74653-0310
County: Kay FICE Identification: 003162
Unit ID: 207281
Telephone: (580) 628-6200 Carnegie Class: Assoc/HT-Mix Trad/Non
FAX Number: (580) 628-6209 Calendar System: Semester
URL: www.noc.edu
Established: 1901 Annual Undergrad Tuition & Fees (In-State): $3,454
Enrollment: 4,766 Coed
Affiliation or Control: State IRS Status: 501(c)3
Highest Offering: Associate Degree
Accreditation: NH, ACBSP, ADNUR, COARC

01 President ... Dr. Cheryl EVANS
05 Vice President for Academic Affairs ... Dr. Pam STINSON
10 Vice President Financial Affairs ... Mrs. Anita SIMPSON
12 Vice President for NOC Enid ... Dr. Ed VINEYARD
12 Vice President for NOC Stillwater ... Dr. Shannon CUNNINGHAM
32 Vice President for Student Affairs ... Mr. Jason JOHNSON
30 Vice President for Devel/Cmty Rels ... Mrs. Sheri SNYDER
13 Director Information Technology ... Mr. Michael MACHIA
15 Director Human Resources ... Ms. Shannon CRANFORD
84 Vice Pres Enroll Mgmt/Registrar ... Dr. Rick EDGINGTON
08 Director of Library Services ... Mr. Benjamin HAINLINE
18 Assoc Vice Pres of Physical Plant ... Mr. Larry DYE
41 Athletic Director ... Mr. Jeremy HISE
37 Director Student Financial Aid ... Ms. Holly LEE
40 Manager Student Bookstore ... Mrs. Jimilea JANSSON

Northwestern Oklahoma State University (M)

709 Oklahoma Boulevard, Alva OK 73717-2799
County: Woods FICE Identification: 003163
Unit ID: 207306
Telephone: (580) 327-1700 Carnegie Class: Masters/S
FAX Number: (580) 327-1881 Calendar System: Semester
URL: www.nwosu.edu
Established: 1897 Annual Undergrad Tuition & Fees (In-State): $6,112
Enrollment: 2,166 Coed
Affiliation or Control: State IRS Status: 501(c)3
Highest Offering: Master's
Accreditation: NH, ACBSP, NUR, SW, TED

01 President ... Dr. Janet L. CUNNINGHAM
10 Vice President for Administration ... Dr. David M. PECHA
05 Vice President for Academics ... Dr. Bo S. HANNAFORD
20 Assoc VP for Academics ... Dr. James L. BELL
26 Assoc VP for University Relations ... Mr. Steven J. VALENCIA
32 Dean of Student Affairs ... Mr. Calleb N. MOSBURG
41 Athletic Director ... Vacant
06 Registrar ... Mrs. Sheri K. LAHR
37 Director Financial Aid ... Ms. Rita J. CASTLEBERRY
21 Bursar ... Mrs. Fawn M. KINGCADE
07 Director of Recruitment ... Ms. Paige L. FISCHER
18 Chief Facilities/Physical Plant ... Mr. Jim DETGEN
15 Human Resource Director ... Mr. Tim J. LAUDERDALE
39 Director of Students/Housing ... Mrs. Kaylyn L. HANSEN
29 Director Alumni Relations ... Mr. John W. ALLEN
58 Assoc Dean of Graduate Studies ... Dr. Shawn P. HOLLIDAY
08 Director of Libraries ... Mrs. Susan K. JEFFRIES
09 Institutional Research Specialist ... Ms. Kylea C. AMERIN

Northwestern Oklahoma State University (N)

2929 E Randolph, Enid OK 73701
Telephone: (580) 237-0334 Identification: 770376
Accreditation: &NH

† Regional accreditation is carried under the parent institution in Alva, OK

Northwestern Oklahoma State University (A)

2007 34th Street, Woodward OK 73801
Telephone: (580) 256-0049 Identification: 770377
Accreditation: &NH

† Regional accreditation is carried under the parent institution in Alva, OK

Oklahoma Baptist University (B)

500 W University, Shawnee OK 74804-2590
County: Pottawatomie FICE Identification: 003164
Unit ID: 207403
Telephone: (405) 585-4000 Carnegie Class: Bac-Diverse
FAX Number: N/A Calendar System: Semester
URL: www.okbu.edu
Established: 1910 Annual Undergrad Tuition & Fees: $24,000
Enrollment: 1,979 Coed
Affiliation or Control: Southern Baptist IRS Status: 501(c)3
Highest Offering: Master's
Accreditation: NH, ACBSP, MUS, NURSE, TED

01 President ... Dr. David W. WHITLOCK
05 Provost/Exec Vice Pres Campus Life ... Dr. Robert S. NORMAN
10 Exec VP Business Affs/Admin Svcs ... Mr. Randy L. SMITH
30 Sr VP for Advancement & Univ Rels ... Mr. Will SMALLWOOD
13 VP Info Int & CIO/Dean Library Svc ... Mr. Paul ROBERTS
42 Dean of Spiritual Life ... Mr. Dale M. GRIFFIN
26 Assoc VP Marketing & Communication ... Mrs. Paula GOWER
79 Assc Provost/Dn Humanities/Soc Sci ... Dr. Pam ROBINSON
14 Asst Vice Pres Info Sys/Services ... Mr. Gary NICKERSON
32 Dean of Students ... Vacant
29 Exec Director OBU Alumni Assn ... Mrs. Lori R. HAGANS
11 Director of Executive Offices ... Mrs. Tonia KELLOGG
37 Director Student Financial Services ... Mrs. Jonna G. RANEY
88 Dir of Events/Conf & Camps ... Ms. Cynthia K. GATES
06 Dir Academic Records/Registrar ... Ms. Marcia MCQUERRY
21 Asst VP Finance/Admin Svcs ... Mrs. Lauri A. FLUKE
21 Controller ... Mr. Steven FLOYD
15 Director of Human Resources ... Mr. Mike JOHNSON
35 Director of Campus Services ... Mr. Larry A. WALKER
19 Chief of University Police ... Mr. David SHANNON
41 Athletic Director ... Mr. Robert DAVENPORT
18 Dir Facilities Mgt & Services ... Mr. George HAINES
96 Director of Purchasing ... Mr. Larry WALKER
84 Assoc VP for Enrollment Management ... Mr. Bruce PERKINS
58 Dean College of Grad & Prof Stds ... Dr. Rhonda RICHARDS
36 Director of Career Development ... Ms. Marissa LIGHTSEY
57 Dean College of Fine Arts ... Dr. Chris MATHEWS
81 Dean College of Math and Science ... Dr. Chris JONES
73 Dean College Christian Service ... Vacant
50 Dean College of Business ... Dr. David C. HOUGHTON
66 Dean College of Nursing ... Mrs. Lepaine MCHENRY
108 Director of Assessment ... Mr. Andrew SPENCER
07 Director of Admissions ... Mr. Will BRANTLEY
04 Exec Secretary to the President ... Mrs. Angela WILLIAMS
39 Director Student Housing ... Vacant

Oklahoma Christian University (C)

PO Box 11000, Oklahoma City OK 73136-1100
County: Oklahoma FICE Identification: 003165
Unit ID: 207324
Telephone: (405) 425-5000 Carnegie Class: Masters/L
FAX Number: (405) 425-5090 Calendar System: Semester
URL: www.oc.edu
Established: 1950 Annual Undergrad Tuition & Fees: $19,890
Enrollment: 2,475 Coed
Affiliation or Control: Independent Non-Profit IRS Status: 501(c)3
Highest Offering: Master's
Accreditation: NH, ACBSP, CIDA, ENG, MUS, NURSE, TED

01 President ... Mr. John DESTEIGUER
03 Executive Vice President ... Dr. William GOAD
05 Vice Pres for Academic Affairs ... Dr. Scott LAMASCUS
11 Exec Dir of University Services ... Mr. Kinney BRYANT
26 Vice Pres for Marketing ... Mrs. Risa FORRESTER
29 Exec Dir for Alumni Relations ... Mr. Bob LASHLEY
44 Vice Pres Estate/Planned Giving ... Mr. Stephen ECK
32 Vice Pres and Dean of Student Life ... Mr. Neil ARTER
84 Vice President for Admissions ... Mrs. Risa FORRESTER
13 Vice President for Information Tech ... Mr. John HERMES
43 Vice President & General Counsel ... Mr. Stephen ECK
30 Vice President for Advancement ... Mr. Kent ALLEN
50 Dean Col of Business Administration ... Dr. Jeff SIMMONS
73 Dean College of Biblical Studies ... Dr. Charles RIX
49 Dean College of Liberal Arts ... Dr. David LOWRY
54 Dean Col of Engineering & Comp Sci ... Dr. Byron NEWBERRY
81 Dean Col of Nat & Health Sciences ... Dr. Jeff MCCORMACK
06 Registrar ... Dr. Stephanie BAIRD
08 Library Director ... Mrs. Tamie L. WILLIS
19 Chief of Police Dept ... Mr. Greg GILTNER
41 Athletic Director ... Mr. Curtis JANZ
18 Director of Physical Plant Services ... Mr. Cary FALLING
27 Director Communications Marketing ... Mr. Wes MCKINZIE
37 Exec Dir Financial Svcs & Budgets ... Mr. Clint LARUE
104 Director of International Programs ... Mr. John OSBORNE
15 Vice Pres and Chief HR Officer ... Mr. Terry WINN
42 Dean for Spiritual Life ... Mr. Jeff MCMILLON
89 Dir of Freshman Experience ... Ms. Kirby KILLEN
88 Director of Creative Services ... Mr. Judson COPELAND
36 Director of Career Services ... Mrs. Candace OWENS
85 International Student Adviser ... Mrs. Joslyn HILL
38 Director of Counseling Services ... Mr. Sheldon ADKINS
35 Director of Student Services ... Mrs. Amy JANZEN
28 Multicultural & Service Learning ... Mr. Gary JONES
04 Administrative Asst to President ... Mrs. Brooke TALLON
09 Institutional Effectiveness Analyst ... Mr. Phil DREW
39 Director Student Housing ... Mr. Curtis SMITH

Oklahoma City Community College (D)

7777 S May Avenue, Oklahoma City OK 73159-4444
County: Oklahoma FICE Identification: 010391
Unit ID: 207449
Telephone: (405) 682-1611 Carnegie Class: Assoc/HT-Mix Trad/Non
FAX Number: (405) 682-7585 Calendar System: Other
URL: www.occc.edu
Established: 1972 Annual Undergrad Tuition & Fees (In-District): $3,391
Enrollment: 13,444 Coed
Affiliation or Control: State/Local IRS Status: 501(c)3
Highest Offering: Associate Degree
Accreditation: NH, ACBSP, ADNUR, COARC, EMT, OTA, PTAA

01 President ... Dr. Jerry L. STEWARD
100 Chief of Staff ... Dr. Marlene SHUGART
04 Exec Assistant to the President ... Ms. Gina QUINN
101 Exec Asst to the Board of Regents ... Ms. Paige LANDRETH
03 Executive Vice President ... Mr. Steven BLOOMBERG
05 Acting VP for Academic Affairs ... Mr. Greg GARDNER
45 Executive Dir Planning & Research ... Mr. Stu HARVEY
84 VP Enrollment/Student Svcs ... Dr. Lisa FISHER
10 Chief Financial Officer ... Dr. John BOYD
31 VP Community/Workforce Development ... Mr. Lemuel BARDEGUEZ
15 Vice Pres Human Resources ... Dr. Angie CHRISTOPHER
13 VP for Info/Instructional Tech Svcs ... Mr. David ANDERSON
20 Associate VP Academic Affairs ... Mr. Greg GARDNER
18 Exec Dir of Facilities Management ... Mr. Chris SNOW
32 Assoc VP Enrollment/Student Svcs ... Vacant
49 Dean of Arts ... Ms. Ruth CHARNAY
79 Dean of English/Humanities ... Ms. Kim JAMESON
76 Dean of Health Professions ... Mr. Thomas KRAFT
81 Dean Math/Engineering/Phys Science ... Dr. Max SIMMONS
83 Dean of Social Sciences ... Dr. Susan TABOR
88 Dean Chemistry/Biological Sciences ... Dr Sonya WILLIAMS
50 Act Dean of Bus & Information Tech ... Dr. John BOYD
44 Director of Development ... Ms. Jennifer HARRISON
26 Exec Director of Marketing & PR ... Mr. Cordell JORDAN
25 Director of Grants & Contracts ... Mr. Joe SWALWELL
09 Dir Institutional Effectiveness ... Dr. Janet PERRY
37 Director of Student Financial Aid ... Ms. Sonya GORE
35 Director of Student Life ... Ms. Erin LOGAN
88 Dir Child Development/Lab School ... Ms. Bonita SPINNER
106 Director of E-Student Services ... Ms. EJ WARREN
21 Director of Financial Accounting ... Ms. Brenda CARPENTER
21 Dir of Budgeting/Fiscal Planning ... Mr. David CHURCHILL
19 Chief of Police ... Mr. Daniel PIAZZA
21 Bursar ... Ms. Cynthia GARY
40 Director of Bookstore ... Ms. Brenda REINKE
88 Act Dir Emerg Planning/Risk Mgmt ... Ms. Erin LOGAN
96 Director of Purchasing ... Mr. Craig SISCO
88 Director of Cultural Programs ... Mr. Richard CHARNAY
88 Dir Recreation and Fitness ... Mr. Michael SHUGART
31 Actg Dir Community Outreach & Educ ... Ms. Gloria TORRES
103 Director Career Transitions Program ... Ms. Lisa BROWN
88 Director of Prof Development Inst ... Mr. John CLAYBON
16 Dir Employment & Employee Relations ... Dr. Jana LEGAKO
16 Dir of Compensation & HR Systems ... Mr. Larry ROBERTSON
22 Director of Equal Opportunity ... Dr. Regina SWITZER
14 Dir Enterprise Resource Planning ... Ms. Connie DRUMMOND
14 Dir Info Technology Infrastructure ... Mr. Rod GREGGS
14 Dir of Info Systems and Services ... Mr. Tim WHISENHUNT
08 Director of Library Services ... Ms. Barbara KING
88 Dir of Curriculum and Assessment ... Ms. Catherine KINYON
88 Director Cooperative Alliances ... Ms. Alexa MASHLAN
90 Dir of Cntr for Learning/Teaching ... Dr. Glenne WHISENHUNT
07 Dir of Recruitment & Admissions ... Ms. Mary BODINE AL-SHARIF
88 Director of Academic Advising ... Ms. Tamara MADDEN
06 Registrar ... Mr. Alan STRINGFELLOW

Oklahoma City University (E)

2501 N Blackwelder, Oklahoma City OK 73106-1493
County: Oklahoma FICE Identification: 003166
Unit ID: 207458
Telephone: (405) 208-5000 Carnegie Class: Masters/L
FAX Number: (405) 208-5916 Calendar System: Semester
URL: www.okcu.edu
Established: 1904 Annual Undergrad Tuition & Fees: $30,726
Enrollment: 3,035 Coed
Affiliation or Control: United Methodist IRS Status: 501(c)3
Highest Offering: First Professional Degree
Accreditation: NH, #ARCPA, BUS, LAW, MACTE, MUS, NUR, TED

01 President ... Mr. Robert H. HENRY
05 Interim Provost/VPAA ... Dr. Kent L. BUCHANAN
30 Vice Pres University Advancement ... Mr. Marty O'GWYNN
26 Vice Pres Univ/Church Relations ... Rev. Charles NEFF
10 CFO/VP Finance & Business Opers ... Ms. Catherine MANINGER
32 VP Student Affairs/Dean of Students ... Dr. Amy AYRES
84 Asst VP/Dean Enrollment Services ... Mr. Kevin WINDHOLZ
06 Registrar ... Mr. Charles MONNOT
09 Director of Institutional Research ... Dr. Kelly MEREDITH
08 Director Dulaney-Browne Library ... Dr. Victoria SWINNEY
37 Director of Financial Aid ... Ms. Denise FLIS
27 Director of Communications ... Ms. Leslie BERGER
15 Chief Human Resources Officer ... Ms. Joey CROSLIN
92 Director of Honors Program ... Dr. Karen YOUMANS
07 Director of Undergrad Admissions ... Ms. Michelle COOK
18 Chief Facilities/Physical Plant ... Mr. Mark CLOUSE
29 Director Alumni Relations ... Mr. Cary PIRRONG
36 Director of Career Services ... Ms. Amelia HURT
49 Interim Dean of Arts & Sciences ... Dr. Amy E. CATALDI
50 Dean School of Business ... Dr. Steve AGEE
61 Dean School of Law ... Dr. Valerie COUCH
64 Dean School of Music ... Mr. Mark PARKER
66 Dean of School of Nursing ... Dr. Lois SALMERON
73 Dean School of Religion ... Dr. Mark DAVIES
88 Dean School of Amer Dance/Arts Mgt ... Mr. John BEDFORD
88 Associate Dean School of Theatre ... Mr. Brian PARSONS
104 Director Study Abroad ... Ms. Mary BENNER
108 Director Institutional Assessment ... Dr. Jo Lynn DIGRANES
13 Chief Info Officer (CIO) ... Mr. Gerry HUNT
19 Chief of Police ... Mr. Bradd BROWN
38 Director of Counseling Services ... Ms. Mindy WINDHOLZ
39 Director University Housing ... Mr. Michael BURNS
41 Director of Athletics ... Mr. Jim ABBOTT
43 University General Counsel ... Ms. Casey ROSS-PETHERICK
44 Assistant Director Annual Giving ... Ms. Carrie SAUER
106 Instructional Technologist ... Ms. Amanda DILLS
04 Administrative Asst to President ... Ms. Emily ALLEN
28 Dir Stdnt Engage/Incl/Multicult Pgm ... Mr. Russ TALL CHIEF

Oklahoma Panhandle State University (F)

Box 430, Goodwell OK 73939-0430
County: Texas FICE Identification: 003174
Unit ID: 207351
Telephone: (580) 349-2611 Carnegie Class: Bac-Diverse
FAX Number: (580) 349-2302 Calendar System: Semester
URL: www.opsu.edu
Established: 1909 Annual Undergrad Tuition & Fees (In-State): $7,461
Enrollment: 1,298 Coed
Affiliation or Control: State IRS Status: 501(c)3
Highest Offering: Baccalaureate
Accreditation: NH, NUR

01 President ... Dr. David A. BRYANT
05 Vice Pres Academic Affairs/Outreach ... Ms. Diane MURPHEY
10 Vice Pres Business & Fiscal Affairs ... Mr. Benny DAIN
47 Dean Agriculture ... Dr. Peter CAMFIELD
50 Dean Business & Technology ... Mr. Joe BREEDEN
53 Dean Education ... Dr. R. Wayne STEWART
57 Dean Liberal Arts ... Dr. Sara RICHTER
66 Dean Science/Mathematics/Nursing ... Dr. Justin COLLINS
32 Directorof Student Services ... Mr. Rantz TRAYLER
06 Registrar/Director of Admissions ... Mr. Bobby JENKINS
37 Director Student Financial Aid ... Ms. Lori FERGUSON
09 Director Institutional Research ... Mr. Nick TUTTLE
13 Director of Technology ... Mr. Howard HENDERSON
15 Director Personne Services ... Ms. Dana COLLINS
08 Director of Library ... Ms. Alton (Tony) HARDMAN
21 Comptroller ... Ms. Elizabeth MCMURPHY
38 Director Counseling/Career Services ... Ms. Deanna Rene RAMON
26 Campus Communications Director ... Ms. Danae MOORE
41 Athletic Officer ... Dr. R. Wayne STEWART
40 Bookstore Manager ... Ms. Mandy BATENHORST
18 Director Physical Plant ... Mr. Bob SCOTT
29 Director Alumni Relations ... Mr. Nick TUTTLE
96 Director of Purchasing ... Ms. Elizabeth MCMURPHY
04 Administrative Asst to President ... Ms. Jill OLSON

Oklahoma State University (G)

Stillwater OK 74078
County: Payne FICE Identification: 003170
Unit ID: 207388
Telephone: (405) 744-5000 Carnegie Class: DU-Higher
FAX Number: N/A Calendar System: Semester
URL: osu.okstate.edu/
Established: 1890 Annual Undergrad Tuition & Fees (In-State): $7,778
Enrollment: 25,962 Coed
Affiliation or Control: State IRS Status: 501(c)3
Highest Offering: Doctorate
Accreditation: NH, AAB, BUS, BUSA, CAATE, CACREP, CARTE, CIDA, CLPSY, COPSY, DIETD, DIETI, ENG, ENGT, JOUR, LSAR, MFCD, MUS, SCPSY, SP, TED, THEA, VET

01 President ... Dr. V. Burns HARGIS
04 Exec Assistant to the President ... Ms. Deborah LANE
29 President & CEO OSU Alumni Assoc ... Mr. Chris BATCHELDER
102 President & CEO OSU Foundation ... Mr. Kirk JEWELL
88 President OSU Research Foundation ... Dr. David WAITS
03 Sr Vice President & General Counsel ... Mr. Gary C. CLARK
05 Provost & Sr Vice President ... Dr. Gary SANDEFUR
10 Sr Vice Pres Admin & Finance ... Mr. Joseph B. WEAVER, JR.
47 VP/Dean/Director Ag Sci & Nat Res ... Dr. Thomas COON
41 Vice President Athletic Programs ... Mr. Mike HOLDER
26 Vice Pres Enroll Mgmt/Univ Mktg ... Mr. Kyle WRAY
46 Vice President for Research ... Dr. Kenneth SEWELL
32 Vice President Student Affairs ... Dr. Lee E. BIRD
09 Assoc VP/Dir Inst Res/Info Mgmt ... Dr. Christie HAWKINS
20 Assoc Prov/Assoc VP Undergrad Educ ... Dr. Pamela FRY
58 Assoc Provost/Dean Graduate College ... Dr. Sheryl TUCKER
21 Assoc Vice President & Controller ... Ms. Kathy ELLIOTT

28 Assoc VP Institutional Diversity .... Dr. Jason KIRKSEY
15 Asst Vice Pres Human Resources .... Ms. Jamie A. PAYNE
24 Asst Prov/Dir Inst Tch/Lrng Excel .... Dr. Christine ORMSBEE
88 Asst VP/Director Student Union .... Mr. Mitch KILCREASE
13 Chief Information Officer .... Ms. Darlene HIGHTOWER
18 Chief Facilities Officer .... Mr. Richard KRYSIAK
96 Chief Procurement Officer ....Mr. Scott SCHLOTTHAUER
19 Chief Public Safety Officer .... Mr. Michael ROBINSON
36 Director Career Services ....Dr. Pam EHLERS
27 Director Communication Services .... Mr. Gary SHUTT
22 Director EEO/Title IX/ADA ....Dr. Rosalyn GREEN
25 Dir Grants/Contracts/Financial Admn ....Dr. Robert DIXON
37 Director Scholarships/Financial Aid .... Mr. Chad BLEW
39 Director of University Housing .... Dr. Leon MCCLINTON
07 Director Undergraduate Admissions .... Ms. Christine CRENSHAW
108 Director Univ Assessment & Testing .... Dr. Sarah GORDON
38 Director University Counseling Svcs ....Dr. Suzanne M. BURKS
23 Director University Health Services .... Mr. Christopher BARLOW
88 Assoc Dir Institutional Research ....Mr. Doug REED
40 Asst Dir Student Union Bookstore .... Mr. Lance HINKLE
39 Asst Director Resident Life .... Ms. Tanya MASSEY
85 Asst Dir Intl Students & Scholars .... Mr. Tim T. HUFF
49 Dean Arts & Sciences .... Dr. Bret DANILOWICZ
53 Dean College of Education .... Dr. John ROMANS
54 Dean Engineering .... Dr. Paul J. TIKALSKY
92 Dean Honors College .... Dr. Keith GARBUTT
59 Dean Human Sciences .... Dr. Stephan M. WILSON
08 Dean Library ....Dr. Sheila G. JOHNSON
50 Dean Spears School of Business .... Dr. Ken EASTMAN
74 Dean Veterinary Medicine ....Dr. Jean E. SANDER
43 Board of Regents General Counsel ....Mr. Steve STEPHENS
06 Registrar .... Dr. K. Celeste TABER

Oklahoma State University Center for Health Sciences College of Osteopathic Medicine (A)

1111 W 17th Street, Tulsa OK 74107-1898

Telephone: (918) 582-1972 FICE Identification: 011282

Accreditation: &NH, FEPAC, OSTEO

† Regional accreditation is carried under the parent institution in Stillwater, OK.

Oklahoma State University Institute of Technology-Okmulgee (B)

1801 E Fourth Street, Okmulgee OK 74447-3901

County: Okmulgee FICE Identification: 003172

Unit ID: 207564

Telephone: (918) 293-4678 Carnegie Class: Bac/Assoc-Mixed

FAX Number: (918) 293-4644 Calendar System: Trimester

URL: www.osuit.edu

Established: 1946 Annual Undergrad Tuition & Fees (In-State): $4,860

Enrollment: 3,379 Coed

Affiliation or Control: State IRS Status: 501(c)3

Highest Offering: Baccalaureate

Accreditation: NH, ADNUR, ENGT

01 President ....Dr. Bill PATH
10 VP Fiscal Services .... Mr. Jim SMITH
05 VP Academic Affairs .... Dr. Scott NEWMAN
32 VP Student Services .... Dr. Ina AGNEW
20 Associate VP Academic Affairs .... Ms. Jody GRAMMER
66 Nursing & Health Sciences .... Ms. Jana MARTIN
49 Arts & Sciences .... Dr. Mark ALLEN
72 Automotive Technologies .... Mr. Leo VAN DELFT
72 Construction Technologies .... Mr. Steve OLMSTEAD
88 Culinary Arts .... Mr. Rene JUNGO
54 Engineering Technologies .... Dr. Abul HASAN
88 Diesel & Heavy Equipment Tech .... Mr. Terryl LINDSEY
88 Energy Technologies .... Mr. Roy ACHEMIRE
77 Information Technologies .... Mr. Randy RITCHEY
88 Watchmaking .... Mr. Jason CHAMPION
57 Visual Communications .... Mr. James MCCULLOUGH
37 Dir Student Financial Services .... Ms. Diana SANDERS
13 Associate VP Technology Services .... Mr. Kevin HULETT
06 Registrar .... Ms. Crystal BOWLES
07 Director of Admissions .... Mr. Kyle GREGORIO
106 Director of Distance Learning .... Mr. David FILES
103 Associate VP Workforce & Econ Dev .... Ms. Sheryl HALE
15 Director of Human Resources .... Ms. Paula NORTH
09 Director of Institutional Research .... Ms. Michelle CANAN
18 Dir Physical Plant Services .... Mr. Mark PITCHER
35 Dean of Students .... Mr. Devin DEBOCK
109 Dir Student Union & Auxiliary Svcs .... Mr. James BYRD
35 Director of Student Life .... Mr. Bruce FORCE
39 Director of Residential Life .... Mr. Bo HUDSON
08 Director of Library .... Ms. Jenny DUNCAN
96 Director of Purchasing .... Mrs. Chandra MILLER
12 Dir MAIP-Pryor Campus .... Mr. Mani KARUPIAH
38 Counselor .... Ms. Kathy AVERY
40 Manager Bookstore .... Ms. Alison WARD
26 Director of Marketing .... Ms. Shari ERWIN
19 Campus Police Chief .... Mr. Matt WOOLIVER
04 Admin Asst to President .... Ms. Claudette BUTCHER
88 Dir Tutoring Ctr/Acad Accommodation .... Mr. Chad SPURLOCK
29 Director Alumni Relations .... Mr. Bruce FORCE
30 Director Development .... Mr. Glenn ZANNOTTI

Oklahoma State University - Oklahoma City (C)

900 N Portland Ave, Oklahoma City OK 73107-6195

County: Oklahoma FICE Identification: 009647

Unit ID: 207397

Telephone: (405) 947-4421 Carnegie Class: Bac/Assoc-Assoc Dom

FAX Number: (405) 945-3289 Calendar System: Semester

URL: www.osuokc.edu

Established: 1961 Annual Undergrad Tuition & Fees (In-State): $2,859

Enrollment: 6,712 Coed

Affiliation or Control: State IRS Status: 501(c)3

Highest Offering: Baccalaureate

Accreditation: NH, ADNUR, DIETT, DMS, EMT, IFSAC

01 President .... Ms. Natalie SHIRLEY
05 Vice President Academic Affairs .... Dr. Joey FRONHEISER
10 Vice President Budget & Finance .... Ms. Ronda REECE
32 Vice President Student Services .... Mr. Brad WILLIAMS
50 Vice Pres for Business and Industry ....Ms. Robin ROBERTS KRIEGER
20 Associate VP Academic Affairs .... Mr. Tracy EDWARDS
84 Sr Dir Enrollment Management .... Mr. Kyle WILLIAMS
30 Associate Dir Development .... Mr. Donovan WOODS
11 Vice Pres of Operations .... Mr. Mike WIDELL
08 Director Library Services .... Ms. Elaine REGIER
37 Director Financial Aid .... Ms. Bessie CARTER
15 Director Human Resources .... Ms. Melissa HERREN
18 Dir of Building Maint/Energy Mgr .... Mr. Mickey FULLER
26 Sr Dir Marketing/Communications .... Ms. Sandy PANTLIK
07 Dir of Recruitiment & Admissions .... Mr. Jason ROCKWELL
96 Director of Purchasing .... Ms. Sharon FITZPATRICK
06 Registrar .... Ms. Lyndsay PITTMAN
25 Sr Dir Institutional Grants .... Ms. Amber COLE
19 Director Security/Safety .... Mr. Sam COX
108 Sr Dir Institutional Effectiveness .... Ms. Lisa DILLON

Oklahoma State University - Tulsa (D)

700 N Greenwood Avenue, Tulsa OK 74106-0702

Telephone: (918) 594-8000 Identification: 666053

Accreditation: &NH

† Regional accreditation is carried under the parent institution in Stillwater, OK.

Oklahoma Technical College (E)

4444 South Sheridan, Tulsa OK 74145-1122

Telephone: (918) 895-7500 Identification: 666718

Accreditation: ACICS

Oklahoma Wesleyan University (F)

2201 Silver Lake Road, Bartlesville OK 74006-6299

County: Washington FICE Identification: 003151

Unit ID: 206835

Telephone: (918) 333-6151 Carnegie Class: Masters/S

FAX Number: (918) 335-6228 Calendar System: Semester

URL: www.okwu.edu

Established: 1910 Annual Undergrad Tuition & Fees: $24,108

Enrollment: 1,345 Coed

Affiliation or Control: Wesleyan Church IRS Status: 501(c)3

Highest Offering: Master's

Accreditation: NH, IACBE, NURSE

01 President .... Dr. Everett G. PIPER
05 Provost/Exec VP for Acad Affairs .... Dr. Robert HERRON
07 Executive Vice President .... Mr. John MEANS
10 Vice President for Business Affairs .... Mrs. Andrea ZEPEDA
32 Vice President for Student Life .... Mr. Kyle WHITE
20 Assoc VP for Academic Affairs .... Dr. Mark WEETER
42 Assoc VP for Student Dev .... Rev. Ben ROTZ
07 Assoc VP for Admissions .... Mrs. Samantha PETERSON
53 Dean of School of Education .... Dr. Jeffrey KEENEY
73 Dean of School of Religion & Phil .... Dr. Mark WEETER
49 Dean of School of Arts & Sciences .... Dr. Gentry SUTTON
50 Dean of School of Business .... Dr. Brian EPPERSON
66 Dean School of Nursing .... Mrs. Jessica JOHNSON
106 Director of Online Learning .... Dr. Bryan EASLEY
108 Dir Academic Effectiveness .... Mrs. Elizabeth SMITH
21 Director of Accounting .... Mrs. Betty-Jo ANDERSON
06 Registrar .... Mr. Jeff LEBERT
13 Director of Computer Services .... Mr. Eric GOINGS
08 Head Librarian .... Mr. Gavin WOLTJERS
37 Director of Financial Aid .... Mrs. Kandi MOLDER
88 Exec Dir Oper Innovation .... Ms. Julia CROUCH
41 Athletic Director .... Mr. Mark MOLDER
29 Director of University Relations .... Mrs. Marci PIPER
15 Human Resources Administrator .... Mrs. Jessica MORROW
04 Executive Assistant to President .... Mrs. Kathy LINDQUIST
39 Dir of Residential Life .... Mr. Chris BREILAND
34 Women's RD/Campus Care .... Mrs. Whitney BREILAND
88 FYE/SYE Director .... Mr. Aaron BUNKER
23 Director Student Health .... Mrs. Debra COOK
18 Director of Buildings and Grounds .... Mr. Dalton HIGGINS
19 Dir of Security/Educ Counselor .... Mr. Stevan DJUKIC
101 Secretary of the Institution/Board .... Mr. Francisco GONZALEZ
40 Bookstore Manager .... Mrs. Melissa HECK

Oklahoma Wesleyan University (G)

10810 E 45th Street, Tulsa OK 74146

Telephone: (918) 728-6143 Identification: 770378

Accreditation: &NH

† Regional accreditation is carried under the parent institution in Bartlesville, OK

Oral Roberts University (H)

7777 S Lewis Avenue, Tulsa OK 74171-0003

County: Tulsa FICE Identification: 003985

Unit ID: 207582

Telephone: (918) 495-6161 Carnegie Class: Masters/M

FAX Number: (918) 495-6033 Calendar System: Semester

URL: www.oru.edu

Established: 1965 Annual Undergrad Tuition & Fees: $24,792

Enrollment: 3,481 Coed

Affiliation or Control: Independent Non-Profit IRS Status: 501(c)3

Highest Offering: Doctorate

Accreditation: NH, ACBSP, ENG, MUS, NURSE, SW, TED, THEOL

01 President .... Dr. William M. WILSON
05 Provost .... Dr. Kathaleen REID-MARTINEZ
10 Chief Financial Officer .... Mr. Neal STENZEL
11 Chief Operations Officer .... Mr. Tim PHILLEY
30 VP for Development/Alumni Relations .... Mrs. Laura BISHOP
84 VP for Enrollment Management .... Dr. Nancy BRAINARD
43 University Counsel .... Mr. Terry KOLLMORGEN
32 Vice President Student Life .... Dr. Dan GUAJARDO
26 VP Comm/Mktg/Exec Dir Empowered .... Mr. Ossie MILLS
13 Chief Information Officer .... Mr. Michael MATHEWS
21 Controller .... Ms. Michelle MCMILLAN
42 Dean of Spiritual Formation .... Dr. Clarence BOYD
08 Dean of the University Library .... Dr. William JERNIGAN
54 Dean Col of Science & Engineering .... Dr. Kenneth WEED
49 Dean Col of Arts & Cultural Studies .... Dr. Mark HALL
73 Dean College Theology/Ministry .... Dr. Thomson MATHEW
50 Dean College of Business .... Dr. Julie HUNTLEY
66 Dean & Chairman College of Nursing .... Dr. Kenda JEZEK
53 Dean College of Education .... Dr. Kim BOYD
32 Dean of Student Development .... Ms. Lori COOK
88 Dean of Student Success/Retention .... Dr. Matthew OLSEN
09 Dir of Institutional Effectiveness .... Dr. Cal EASTERLING
41 Director for Athletics .... Mr. Mike CARTER
25 Director of Sponsored Programs .... Ms. Kim FALCON
38 Director of Student Counseling .... Ms. Michelle TAYLOR
35 Director of Student Resources .... Mr. Tom BELLATTI
92 Director of Honors Program .... Dr. John KORSTAD
88 Director Student Accounts .... Ms. Karen JOHNSON
96 Director of Purchasing .... Mr. Mark PEPIN
06 Registrar .... Mr. David FULMER
07 Director of Admissions Operations .... Mr. Jordan CRANDALL
84 Dir of Admiss/Marketing/Enrol Mgmt .... Ms. Wendy MORTON
84 Exec Dir of Online Enrollment .... Mr. Nathan SOLTICE
37 Director of Financial Aid .... Mr. William WOMACK
29 Director of Alumni Relations .... Mr. Robert BEARD
19 Director of Security/Safety .... Mr. Jerry ISAACS
15 Director Human Resources/Risk Mgmt .... Dr. Karen ADAMS
04 Executive Asst to President .... Mrs. Lisa BOWMAN
101 Secretary of the Institution/Board .....Ms. Marian BAUMGARDNER

Phillips Theological Seminary (I)

901 N Mingo Road, Tulsa OK 74116-5612

County: Tulsa FICE Identification: 025602

Unit ID: 414966

Telephone: (918) 610-8303 Carnegie Class: Spec-4-yr-Faith

FAX Number: (918) 610-8404 Calendar System: Semester

URL: www.ptstulsa.edu

Established: 1906 Annual Graduate Tuition & Fees: N/A

Enrollment: 110 Coed

Affiliation or Control: Christian Church (Disciples Of Christ) IRS Status: 501(c)3

Highest Offering: Doctorate; No Undergraduates

Accreditation: NH, THEOL

01 President .... Gary PELUSO-VERDEND
05 Vice Pres Academic Affairs & Dean .... Nancy Claire PITTMAN
10 Vice Pres Finance & Admin .... Karen MCMILLAN
108 Assoc Dn Assessment & Faculty .... Joseph A. BESSLER
20 Assoc Dn Contextual Ed/Church Rels .... John THOMAS, JR.
88 Doctor of Ministry Program Director .... Kathleen D. MCCALLIE
37 Financial Aid Officer .... John FOREST
08 Library Director .... Sandy SHAPOVAL
29 Sr Director Stewardship .... Geoffrey BREWSTER
44 Stewardship Director .... Malisa PIERCE
26 Sr Director Seminary Relations .... Kurt GWARTNEY
06 Registrar .... Toni WINE IMBLER
15 Human Resources Manager .... Gwen DERRICK
04 Executive Assistant to President .... Mary E. MCGILVRAY

Platt College (J)

111 SW C Avenue, Lawton OK 73501

Telephone: (580) 215-7050 Identification: 770971

Accreditation: ACCSC

Platt College (K)

201 N Eastern Avenue, Moore OK 73160

Telephone: (405) 912-3260 Identification: 770585

Accreditation: ACCSC, ACFEI, COARC

Platt College (A)

2727 W Memorial Road, Oklahoma City OK 73134
Telephone: (405) 749-2433 Identification: 770584
Accreditation: ACCSC

Platt College (B)

3801 S Sheridan, Tulsa OK 74145-1132
County: Tulsa FICE Identification: 023068
Unit ID: 245962
Telephone: (918) 663-9000 Carnegie Class: Bac/Assoc-Assoc Dom
FAX Number: (918) 622-1240 Calendar System: Other
URL: www.plattcolleges.edu
Established: 1979 Annual Undergrad Tuition & Fees: N/A
Enrollment: 276 Coed
Affiliation or Control: Proprietary IRS Status: Proprietary
Highest Offering: Baccalaureate
Accreditation: ACCSC, ACFEI

01 Director of Campus .... Mr. David STEVENSON
07 Director of Admission & Marketing .... Ms. Dawn BONEBREAK

Platt College-OKC Central (C)

309 South Ann Arbor Avenue,
Oklahoma City OK 73128-1112
Telephone: (405) 946-7799 Identification: 666341
Accreditation: ACCSC, ACFEI, SURGT

† Branch campus of Platt College, Tulsa, OK.

Randall University (D)

PO Box 7208, Moore OK 73153-1208
County: Cleveland FICE Identification: 010266
Unit ID: 207157
Telephone: (405) 912-9000 Carnegie Class: Spec-4-yr-Faith
FAX Number: (405) 912-9050 Calendar System: Semester
URL: www.hc.edu
Established: 1959 Annual Undergrad Tuition & Fees: $12,340
Enrollment: 234 Coed
Affiliation or Control: Free Will Baptist IRS Status: 501(c)3
Highest Offering: Master's
Accreditation: TRACS

01 President .... Dr. Timothy W. EATON
05 Chief Academic Officer .... Dr. Mark H. BRAISHER
10 Chief Business Officer .... Ms. Pat MILLER
30 Director Institutional Advancement .... Mr. Bob THOMPSON
07 Admissions Coordinator .... Ms. Lyndsey BRAISHER
37 Financial Aid Coordinator .... Ms. Denise CONKLIN
08 LRC Director .... Ms. Nancy J. DRAPER
13 Director of MIS .... Mr. Quentin C. LOOP
06 Registrar .... Ms. Patti ASHBY
58 Dean of Graduate Studies .... Dr. Mark H. BRAISHER
39 Resident Life Coordinator .... Ms. Jody BLACKWELL
41 Athletic Director .... Mr. Mark BEROKOFF
32 Dean of Students .... Ms. Jody BLACKWELL
40 Bookstore Manager .... Mr. Lee BAUDER
106 Director of Online Learning .... Dr. Paulette JONES

Redlands Community College (E)

1300 S Country Club Road, El Reno OK 73036-5304
County: Canadian FICE Identification: 003156
Unit ID: 207069
Telephone: (405) 262-2552 Carnegie Class: Assoc/HT-High Non
FAX Number: (405) 422-1200 Calendar System: Semester
URL: www.redlandscc.edu
Established: 1938 Annual Undergrad Tuition & Fees (In-District): $3,882
Enrollment: 2,661 Coed
Affiliation or Control: State/Local IRS Status: 501(c)3
Highest Offering: Associate Degree
Accreditation: NH, ADNUR, EMT

01 President .... Mr. Jack BRYANT
10 Vice Pres Finance/Campus Services .... Ms. Jena MARR
32 Dean of Student Services .... Vacant
46 Assoc VP Communications/Research .... Vacant
05 Dean of Academic & Inst Dev .... Ms. Reonna SLAGELL-GOSSEN
18 Director Physical Plant .... Mr. Richard BUCHHOLZ
66 Dean of Service Dev/Allied Health .... Ms. Rose Marie SMITH
81 Dir Math/Science/Developmental Stds .... Ms. Barbara KNOP-COX
08 Director Learning Resource Center .... Mrs. Christine DETTLAFF
06 Registrar/Director Student Records .... Mr. Dennis HARRIS
37 Director Financial Aid .... Ms. Paris PRZEKURAT
41 Athletic Director .... Mr. Eli ZUCKSWORTH
13 Director Administrative Computing .... Mr. Troy MILLIGAN
22 Director of Upward Bound .... Mrs. Linda MCDOWN
09 Director of Institutional Research .... Mr. Troy MILLIGAN
84 Dean of Enrollment Management .... Mrs. Tricia HOBSON
21 Associate Business Officer .... Mrs. Maxine CALVERT
36 Coordinator Career Services .... Vacant
15 Coordinator Personnel/Payroll .... Mrs. Kim ANDRADE
26 Communication Liaison .... Mrs. Marcia SHOTTENKIRK
29 Coord Alumni Rels/Alternative Educ .... Vacant
39 Coordinator of Resident Life .... Ms. Tina JACOBS

Rogers State University (F)

1701 W Will Rogers Boulevard,
Claremore OK 74017-3252
County: Rogers FICE Identification: 003168
Unit ID: 207661
Telephone: (918) 343-7777 Carnegie Class: Bac-Diverse
FAX Number: (918) 343-7898 Calendar System: Semester
URL: www.rsu.edu
Established: 1909 Annual Undergrad Tuition & Fees (In-State): $6,009
Enrollment: 4,030 Coed
Affiliation or Control: State IRS Status: 501(c)3
Highest Offering: Master's
Accreditation: NH, ADNUR, EMT, NUR

01 President .... Dr. Larry RICE
05 Vice President for Academic Affairs .... Dr. Richard BECK
10 Exec VP for Admin & Finance .... Mr. Tom VOLTURO
30 Vice President for Development .... Dr. Maynard PHILLIPS
32 Vice Pres for Student Affairs .... Dr. Brent MARSH
84 Vice President Enrollment Mgmt .... Ms. Heidi HOSKINSON
09 Asst VP Accountability & Academics .... Dr. Mary MILLIKIN
21 Comptroller/Asst Vice Pres Bus Affs .... Mr. Mark MEADORS
12 Director Pryor Campus .... Ms. Sherry ALEXANDER
12 Director Bartlesville Campus .... Vacant
107 Dean School of Professional Studies .... Dr. Susan WILLIS
49 Dean School of Arts and Sciences .... Dr. Keith MARTIN
35 Director of Student Development .... Ms. Katy LAUNIUS
08 Director of the Library .... Mr. J. Alan LAWLESS
07 Director of Admissions .... Ms. Joy Lin HALL
29 Director of Alumni .... Ms. Katelyn TITTLE
04 Exec Assistant to the President .... Ms. Rhonda SPURLOCK
18 Director Physical Plant .... Mr. Karl REYNOLDS
19 Director Campus Police .... Mr. Gary BOERGERMANN
26 Director Public Relations .... Mr. David HAMBY
37 Director of Financial Aid .... Ms. Kelly HICKS
91 Director Administrative Computing .... Ms. Cathy BURNS
13 Director Information Technology .... Mr. Brian REEVES
15 Director Employment & Benefits .... Vacant
41 Director of Athletics .... Mr. Ryan ERWIN
39 Director Residential Life .... Ms. Kyla SHORT
23 Director Student Health Clinic .... Ms. Lisa MARTIN
25 Director Research & Sponsored Pgm .... Mr. Daniel MARANGONI

Rogers State University-Bartlesville (G)

401 South Dewey Avenue, Bartlesville OK 74003
Telephone: (918) 338-8000 Identification: 770379
Accreditation: &NH

† Regional accreditation is carried under the parent institution in Claremore, OK

Rogers State University-Pryor (H)

2155 Highway 69A, Pryor Creek OK 74361
Telephone: (918) 825-6117 Identification: 770380
Accreditation: &NH

† Regional accreditation is carried under the parent institution in Claremore, OK

Rose State College (I)

6420 SE 15th, Midwest City OK 73110-2799
County: Oklahoma FICE Identification: 009185
Unit ID: 207670
Telephone: (405) 733-7311 Carnegie Class: Assoc/HT-Mix Trad/Non
FAX Number: (405) 733-7399 Calendar System: Semester
URL: www.rose.edu
Established: 1970 Annual Undergrad Tuition & Fees (In-District): $3,375
Enrollment: 6,891 Coed
Affiliation or Control: State/Local IRS Status: 501(c)3
Highest Offering: Associate Degree
Accreditation: NH, ADNUR, CAHIIM, COARC, DA, DH, MLTAD, RAD

01 President .... Dr. Jeanie WEBB
10 Exec Vice President and CFO .... Dr. Kent LASHLEY
05 Vice President for Academic Affairs .... Dr. Frances HENDRIX
32 VP for Student Affairs & Marketing .... Ms. Tamara PRATT
13 Vice President for Info Technology .... Mr. John PRIMO
103 Vice President for Workforce Devel .... Mr. Stan GREIL
41 Exec Dir Athletic Programs .... Mr. Joey DAVAULT
102 Exec Dir Foundation & Resource Dev .... Ms. Cindy MIKEMAN
20 Associate VP Academic Affairs .... Dr. Jeff CALDWELL
09 Assoc VP Inst Effectiveness .... Ms. Isabelle BILLEN
31 Assoc VP Workforce and Comm Dev .... Dr. Bret WOOD
21 Sr Dir Fiscal Operations .... Mr. Raymond BLANKE
15 Sr Dir Human Res/Affirm Act Ofcr .... Ms. Alberta NUTTER
109 Sr Dir Campus Operation .... Mr. Richard ANDREWS
06 Registrar/Dir Admissions &
Records .... Ms. Mechelle ATSON-FOESSLER
37 Director Financial Aid .... Mr. Steve DAFFER
26 Director Marketing .... Ms. Ali SEXTON
18 Director Operations .... Mr. Ardie RODGERS
41 Dir Health & Wellness Activities .... Mr. Chris LELAND
36 Director Spec Svcs/Student Outreach .... Dr. Joanne STAFFORD
08 Dean Learning Resources Center .... Mr. Chris MEYER
50 Dean Business & Info Tech Division .... Dr. Mark TIPPIN
54 Dean Engineering & Science Division .... Dr. Wayne JONES
79 Dean Humanities Division .... Ms. Claudia BUCKMASTER
76 Dean Health Sciences Division .... Mr. Dan POINTS
83 Dean Social Sciences Division .... Dr. Juanita ORTIZ

St. Gregory's University (J)

1900 W MacArthur, Shawnee OK 74804-2499
County: Pottawatomie FICE Identification: 003183
Unit ID: 207689
Telephone: (405) 878-5100 Carnegie Class: Bac-Diverse
FAX Number: (405) 878-5198 Calendar System: Semester
URL: www.stgregorys.edu
Established: 1875 Annual Undergrad Tuition & Fees: $20,280
Enrollment: 649 Coed
Affiliation or Control: Roman Catholic IRS Status: 501(c)3
Highest Offering: Master's
Accreditation: NH, ACBSP, NURSE

01 President .... Dr. Michael SCAPERLANDA
04 Executive Asst to President .... Mrs. Debra CARLILE
11 Interim VP Finance & Administration .... Dr. Ron DIGGS
05 Interim VP Academic Affairs .... Dr. Richard MELOCHE
66 Dean of Nursing .... Dr. Susan BARNES
10 Chief Financial Officer .... Mr. Joe FLECKINGER
30 Vice President for Development .... Mr. James YORK
108 Director of Compliance & Accred .... Dr. Anita POOLE-ENDSLEY
32 Dean of Students .... Ms. Emilia (Lilly) BERMUDEZ
06 Registrar .... Mrs. Ramah NATION
84 Interim Director of Admissions .... Mr. Marvin BENNETT
08 Library Director .... Mrs. Anita SEMTNER
37 Associate Director Financial Aid .... Mrs. Lori DEARDORFF
26 Director of Marketing .... Mrs. Amber THEINERT
41 Athletic Director .... Mr. John MARTIN
15 Director of Human Resources .... Ms. Sherri CONATSER
18 Director of Operations .... Mr. Mark SAUNDERS
13 Director of Information Systems .... Mr. Chris FLY
19 Director Security .... Mr. Darvin GORE
39 Director Student Life .... Mr. Stephen ZABOROWSKI

St. Gregory's University Tulsa Campus (K)

5801 E 41st Street, Suite 900, Tulsa OK 74135
Telephone: (405) 878-5200 Identification: 770381
Accreditation: &NH

† Regional accreditation is carried under the parent institution in Shawnee, OK

Seminole State College (L)

PO Box 351, Seminole OK 74818-0351
County: Seminole FICE Identification: 003178
Unit ID: 207740
Telephone: (405) 382-9950 Carnegie Class: Assoc/HT-Mix Trad/Non
FAX Number: (405) 382-9122 Calendar System: Semester
URL: www.sscok.edu
Established: 1931 Annual Undergrad Tuition & Fees (In-District): $3,808
Enrollment: 1,895 Coed
Affiliation or Control: State/Local IRS Status: 501(c)3
Highest Offering: Associate Degree
Accreditation: NH, ADNUR, MLTAD

01 President .... Dr. Jim W. UTTERBACK
05 Vice President Academic Affairs .... Dr. Tom MILLS
10 Vice President Fiscal Affairs .... Mr. Braden BROWN
30 Exec VP Institutional Advancement .... Ms. Lana REYNOLDS
32 Vice President of Student Affairs .... Mr. Bill KNOWLES
13 Director Mgmt Information Systems .... Mr. Marc HUNTER
66 Director of Nursing .... Vacant
06 Registrar .... Mrs. Corey QUIETT
15 Director Personnel Services .... Mrs. Courtney JONES
26 Coordinator of Media Relations .... Ms. Kristin DUNN
04 Administrative Asst to President .... Ms. Mechell DOWNEY
22 Dir Affirmative Action/EEO .... Mr. Sam RIVERA
37 Director Student Financial Aid .... Ms. Melanie RINEHART
39 Director Student Housing .... Ms. Melinda SIMS
41 Athletic Director .... Mr. Mike ST. JOHN

Southeastern Oklahoma State University (M)

1405 N 4th Avenue, Durant OK 74701-3330
County: Bryan FICE Identification: 003179
Unit ID: 207847
Telephone: (580) 745-2000 Carnegie Class: Masters/M
FAX Number: N/A Calendar System: Semester
URL: www.se.edu
Established: 1909 Annual Undergrad Tuition & Fees (In-State): $5,975
Enrollment: 3,878 Coed
Affiliation or Control: State IRS Status: 501(c)3
Highest Offering: Master's
Accreditation: NH, AAB, BUS, CACREP, MUS, TED

01 President .... Mr. Sean BURRAGE
05 Vice Pres Acad Affairs .... Dr. Bryon CLARK
10 Vice President Business Affairs .... Mr. Dennis WESTMAN
32 Dean of Student Affairs .... Ms. Liz MCCRAW
07 Assoc Dean Admissions/Registrar .... Ms. Kristie LUKE
58 Dean Graduate School .... Mr. Tim BOATMUN
13 Exec Dir of Information Technology .... Mr. Dan MOORE
30 Vice President of Univ Advancement .... Mr. Kyle STAFFORD
37 Director Student Financial Aid .... Mr. Tony LEHRLING
08 Library Director .... Ms. Sharon MORRISON
41 Director of Athletics .... Mr. Keith BAXTER
26 Dir Univ Comm/Spec Asst Pres .... Mr. Alan BURTON

21 Director Finance/Controller Ms. Kay Lynn ROBERTS
18 Director Facilities/Physical Plant Mr. Dan SIMMONS
28 Director of Compliance and Safety Mr. Mike DAVIS
96 Purchasing Agent Mrs. Carol COATS
40 Book Store Manager Ms. Jackie CODNER
29 Director Alumni Relations Ms. Stephanie SHADE-DAVISON
106 Dir Online Education/E-learning Ms. Christala SMITH
19 Director Security/Safety Mr. Stacy BALLEW
39 Director Student Housing Dr. Kelly D'ARCY
04 Exec Admin Asst to President Ms. Terri ROGERS

Southern Nazarene University (A)

6729 NW 39 Expressway, Bethany OK 73008-2694
County: Oklahoma FICE Identification: 003149
Unit ID: 206862
Telephone: (405) 789-6400 Carnegie Class: Masters/L
FAX Number: (405) 491-6381 Calendar System: Semester
URL: www.snu.edu
Established: 1899 Annual Undergrad Tuition & Fees: $23,320
Enrollment: 2,254 Coed
Affiliation or Control: Church Of The Nazarene IRS Status: 501(c)3
Highest Offering: Master's
Accreditation: NH, ACBSP, #CAATE, MUS, NURSE, TED

01 President Dr. Loren P. GRESHAM
05 Provost & VP Academic Affairs Dr. Melany KYZER
10 Vice President Financial Affairs Dr. Scott STRAWN
30 VP of Univ Advance & Church Rels Dr. Terry TOLER
32 Vice President Student Development Dr. Mike REDWINE
42 University Pastor Dr. Blair SPINDLE
84 Vice Pres of Enrollment Management Dr. Linda CANTWELL
79 Dean College of Humanities Dr. Steve BETTS
81 Dean College of Sci & Health Dr. Mark WINSLOW
06 Registrar Mr. Charles CHITWOOD
37 Director Student Financial Aid Vacant
35 Director Student Affairs Mrs. Marian REDWINE
38 Director Student Counseling Mrs. Kimberly CAMPBELL
36 Director Career Planning/Placement Mrs. Angela RHODES
08 Director Learning Resources Center Prof. Katie KING
29 Director Alumni Relations Mrs. Marcia MOSSHART
13 Director Information Technology Vacant
88 Director Academic Services Mr. Wes LEE
09 Director Institutional Research Dr. Randy ZABEL
58 Dean Col of Grad & Prof Study Dr. Davis BERRYMAN
66 Director of Nursing Dr. Mary HIBBERT
15 Director Human Resources Mr. Chris PETERSON
18 Director of Physical Plant Mr. Ron LESTER
24 Director Network Mrs. Chichi FREELANDER
26 Director Communications & Marketing Mr. Bill MCCLOUD
40 Bookstore Manager Mr. Reggie COLEMAN
41 Athletic Director Mr. Bobby MARTIN
88 Dean College of Teach & Learn Dr. Dennis WILLIAMS
04 Administrative Asst to President Mrs. Rita MCCLAIN
19 Director Security/Safety Mr. Glen HOLCOMB
25 Chief Contracts/Grants Admin Dr. Gwen HACKLER
39 Director Student Housing Mrs. Maia O'BANNON
44 Director Annual/Planned Giving Mr. Todd BRANT

Southwestern Christian University (B)

PO Box 340, 7210 NW 39th Expressway,
Bethany OK 73008-0340
County: Oklahoma FICE Identification: 003180
Unit ID: 207856
Telephone: (405) 789-7661 Carnegie Class: Bac-Diverse
FAX Number: (405) 495-0078 Calendar System: Semester
URL: www.swcu.edu
Established: 1946 Annual Undergrad Tuition & Fees: $12,830
Enrollment: 813 Coed
Affiliation or Control: Pentecostal Holiness Church IRS Status: 501(c)3
Highest Offering: Master's
Accreditation: NH

01 President Dr. Reggies WENYIKA
05 VP Academic Affairs Dr. Dana DELONG
10 Vice President for Fiscal Affairs Mr. Wallace O. HAMILTON
32 Vice President for Student Life Mr. Brad DAVIS
41 Vice President of Athletics Mr. Mark ARTHUR
37 Director of Financial Aid Mrs. Kellye JOHNSON
07 Director of Admissions & Enrollment Mrs. Jesse BURPO
08 Director of Library Services Mr. Michael LOWDER
06 Registrar Mrs. Sherri HENDRIX
107 Dean of Professional Studies & Grad Dr. Adrian HINKLE
49 Dean of Arts & Sciences Dr. Gayle KEARNS
18 Director of Plant/Property Mgmt Vacant
26 Director of Sports Information/PR Mr. Matthew STEPHENS
13 Director of Information Technology Mr. Daniel DRESSLER
106 Dean of Online Educ/Adult Studies Vacant
108 Dean of Institutional Effectiveness Dr. Dana OWENS-DELONG
15 Director of Employee Relations Ms. Rita PALMER
30 Chief Development Officer Mr. Joe BLACKWELL
84 Director Enrollment Management Dr. Amara SCHOOK
04 Administrative Asst to President Ms. Erin BROWN
09 Director of Institutional Research Mr. George WASHINGTON
19 Director Security/Safety Mr. Da'juan HAWKINS
39 Director Student Housing Mr. Zach SHERRILL

Southwestern Oklahoma State University (C)

100 Campus Drive, Weatherford OK 73096-3098
County: Custer FICE Identification: 003181
Unit ID: 207865
Telephone: (580) 772-6611 Carnegie Class: Masters/L
FAX Number: (580) 774-3795 Calendar System: Semester
URL: www.swosu.edu
Established: 1901 Annual Undergrad Tuition & Fees (In-State): $6,090
Enrollment: 4,994 Coed
Affiliation or Control: State IRS Status: 501(c)3
Highest Offering: First Professional Degree
Accreditation: NH, #CAATE, CAHIIM, ENGT, IACBE, MUS, NAIT, NUR, OTA, PHAR, PTAA, TED

01 President Dr. Randy L. BEUTLER
10 Exec Vice Pres Business and Finance Mr. Thomas W. FAGAN
05 VP for Academic Affairs/Provost Dr. James D. SOUTH
32 VP Student Affairs/Assoc Provost Dr. Ruth BOYD
20 Assoc Provost Acad Affairs Dr. Monica VARNER
26 VP for Marketing/Public Relations Mr. Brian D. ADLER
30 Asst to Pres for Inst Advancement Mr. Garrett KING
96 Dir Business Affairs/Comptroller Ms. Brenda K. BURGESS
35 Dean of Students/Dir Student Act Ms. Cynthia R. DOUGHERTY
13 Dir Information Technology Services Ms. Karen KLEIN
06 Registrar Mr. Shamus MOORE
08 Library Director Mr. Jason M. DUPREE
37 Director Student Financial Services Mr. Jerome L. WICHERT
15 Dir Human Resources/Affirm Action Mr. David MISAK
84 Dir Enrollment Mgmt/Career Svcs Mr. Todd T. BOYD
41 Athletic Director Mr. Todd A. THURMAN
06 Registrar Sayre Campus Ms. Terry L. BILLEY
38 Director Counseling Services Ms. Kim K. LIEBSCHER
18 Director Physical Plant Mr. Rick SKINNER
57 Manager Fine Arts Center Mr. Kyle J. BARTEL
36 Career Services Coordinator Ms. Savannath SCHONES
58 Dean College of Prof/Grad Studies Dr. Ken G. ROSE
49 Dean College of Arts/Sciences Dr. Peter GRANT
67 Dean College of Pharmacy Dr. David RALPH
12 Dean College of Assoc/Applied Prog Ms. Sherron K. MANNING
53 Assoc Dean Sch of Behavioral Sci Dr. L. Chad KINDER
50 Assoc Dean School of Business/Tech Dr. Patsy PARKER
66 Assoc Dn Sch Nursing/Allied Health Dr. Marcy TANNER

† Campus at Sayre offers a two-year degree and is regionally accredited (NH) under parent institution.

Southwestern Oklahoma State University-Sayre (D)

409 E Mississippi, Sayre OK 73662
Telephone: (580) 928-5533 Identification: 770382
Accreditation: &NH, MLTAB, RAD

† Regional accreditation is carried under the parent institution in Weatherford, OK

Spartan College of Aeronautics and Technology (E)

8820 E Pine Street, Tulsa OK 74115
County: Tulsa FICE Identification: 007678
Unit ID: 207254
Telephone: (918) 836-6886 Carnegie Class: Spec-4-yr-Other Tech
FAX Number: (918) 831-5287 Calendar System: Other
URL: www.spartan.edu
Established: 1928 Annual Undergrad Tuition & Fees: $16,395
Enrollment: 849 Coed
Affiliation or Control: Proprietary IRS Status: Proprietary
Highest Offering: Baccalaureate
Accreditation: ACCSC

00 CEO Mr. Peter H. HARRIS
01 President Mr. Lamar HAYNES
10 CFO Mr. Neil D. AMARI
32 VP Student Services Mr. Damon BOWLING

Tulsa Community College (F)

6111 E Skelly Drive, Tulsa OK 74135-6198
County: Tulsa FICE Identification: 009763
Unit ID: 207935
Telephone: (918) 595-7000 Carnegie Class: Assoc/HT-Mix Trad/Non
FAX Number: (918) 595-7910 Calendar System: Semester
URL: www.tulsacc.edu
Established: 1968 Annual Undergrad Tuition & Fees (In-State): $2,900
Enrollment: 17,861 Coed
Affiliation or Control: State IRS Status: 501(c)3
Highest Offering: Associate Degree
Accreditation: NH, ADNUR, CAHIIM, COARC, CVT, DH, MLTAD, OTA, PHLEB, PTAA, RAD

01 President/CEO Dr. Leigh GOODSON
05 Sr VP and Chief Academic Officer Dr. Cynthia HESS
100 Sr Advisor to the President Dr. Bill IVEY
30 VP Ext Affairs & Foundation Pres Ms. Lauren F. BROOKEY
11 VP Administration Mr. Sean A. WEINS
10 Chief Financial Officer Vacant
32 Sr Student Affairs Officer Dr. Jan L. CLAYTON
12 Provost NE Campus & VP Wrkfrc Dev Dr. Brett S. CAMPBELL
12 Provost West Campus & Assoc VP IE Dr. Kevin M. DAVID
12 Provost Metro Campus Dr. Greg STONE
12 Provost Southeast Campus Dr. John GIBSON
84 Asst VP Enrollment Mgmt Ms. Eileen KENNEY
28 Asst VP Diversity/Inclusion Ms. Eunice TARVER
13 Chief Technology Officer Mr. Michael SIFTAR
15 Chief Human Resources Officer Ms. Sandy COOPER
102 President of TCC Foundation Ms. Lauren BROOKEY
12 Dean Community Campuses Dr. Paula WILLYARD
08 Dean Libraries Ms. Paula SETTOON
51 Dir Continuing Education Vacant
06 Dir Compl Repting/Col Registrar Ms. Traci HECK
26 Sr Dir Marketing/Communications Ms. Kari CULP
18 Dir Physical Facilities Mr. Steven COX
37 Dir Financial Aid Ms. Karen JEFFERS
96 Dir Purch & Inventory Control Mr. Bill CREECH
09 Dir Institutional Research/Assess Dr. Jennifer IVIE
19 Dir Campus Public Safety Mr. Gene WIDEMAN
92 Honors Program Coord Ms. Susan ONEAL
25 Dir Sponsored Programs Vacant
104 Dir Global Learning Dr. Douglas PRICE
106 Dir Online Learning Mr. Randy G. DOMINGUEZ
105 Web Manager Mr. Steven RHOM
04 Exec Asst to President Ms. Carrie BATESON
07 Dir Admissions/Prosp Stdnt Svcs Mr. Michael HARRIS
44 Director Development Ms. Rachel HUTCHINGS
36 Director Career and Retention Ms. Kristie COLEMAN

Tulsa Community College Metro Campus (G)

909 South Boston Avenue, Tulsa OK 74119
Telephone: (918) 595-7224 Identification: 770383
Accreditation: &NH, DMS

† Regional accreditation is carried under the parent institution in Tulsa, OK

Tulsa Community College Northeast Campus (H)

3727 East Apache Street, Tulsa OK 74115
Telephone: (918) 595-7524 Identification: 770384
Accreditation: &NH

† Regional accreditation is carried under the parent institution in Tulsa, OK

Tulsa Community College Southeast Campus (I)

10300 East 81st Street, Tulsa OK 74133
Telephone: (918) 595-7724 Identification: 770385
Accreditation: &NH

† Regional accreditation is carried under the parent institution in Tulsa, OK

Tulsa Community College West Campus (J)

7505 W 41st Street South, Tulsa OK 74102
Telephone: (918) 595-8100 Identification: 770386
Accreditation: &NH

† Regional accreditation is carried under the parent institution in Tulsa, OK

Tulsa Welding School (K)

2545 E 11th Street, Tulsa OK 74104-3909
County: Tulsa FICE Identification: 009618
Unit ID: 207962
Telephone: (918) 587-6789 Carnegie Class: Spec 2-yr-Tech
FAX Number: (918) 587-8170 Calendar System: Other
URL: www.weldingschool.com
Established: 1949 Annual Undergrad Tuition & Fees: N/A
Enrollment: 1,054 Coed
Affiliation or Control: Proprietary IRS Status: Proprietary
Highest Offering: Associate Degree
Accreditation: ACCSC

01 Campus President Susan KUHL
05 Academic Dean Mr. David GILLIAM
07 Senior Director of Admissions Mr. Joe MCKINNEY
37 Director of Financial Aid Richelle DIORIO
36 Regional Director of Career Service Mr. Charles HARBIN

University of Central Oklahoma (L)

100 N University Drive, Edmond OK 73034-5209
County: Oklahoma FICE Identification: 003152
Unit ID: 206941
Telephone: (405) 974-2000 Carnegie Class: Masters/L
FAX Number: (405) 359-5841 Calendar System: Semester
URL: www.uco.edu
Established: 1890 Annual Undergrad Tuition & Fees (In-State): $6,096
Enrollment: 16,840 Coed
Affiliation or Control: State IRS Status: 501(c)3
Highest Offering: Master's
Accreditation: NH, ACBSP, ART, CAATE, CIDA, CS, DIETD, DIETI, ENG, EXSC, FEPAC, FUSER, MUS, NUR, NURSE, SP, TED

01 President Dr. Don BETZ
03 Vice President of Administration Dr. Don CHRUSCIEL
05 Provost/Vice Pres Academic Affairs Dr. John BARTHELL
32 Vice President Student Affairs Dr. Myron POPE
13 Vice President Information Tech Dr. Cynthia ROLFE
26 Vice Pres University Relations Mr. Charlie JOHNSON
88 Vice Pres Public Affairs Dr. Mark KINDERS
102 Vice Pres Development/Foundation Mrs. Anne HOLZBERLEIN
11 Assoc VP Planning & Budget Ms. Patti NEUHOLD

06 Associate Vice President/Registrar .... Dr. Adam JOHNSON
20 Assoc VP Academic Affairs .... Dr. Charlotte SIMMONS
20 Assoc VP Inst Effectiveness .... Dr. Gary STEWARD
10 Asst VP Financial Operations .... Ms. Lisa HARPER
18 Asst Vice Pres Facilities Mgt .... Mr. Mark RODOLF
35 Asst Vice Pres Student Affairs .... Mr. Cole STANLEY
23 Asst VP Wellness/Sports .... Mr. Mark HERRIN
21 Asst VP Business Enterprises .... Mr. Kevin FREEMAN
88 Operations Manager Student Affairs .... Ms. Amy ROGALSKY
41 Athletic Director .... Mr. Joe MULLER
09 Exec Dir Institutional Research .... Ms. Cindy BOLING
08 Exec Director University Libraries .... Dr. Habib TABATABAI
37 Director Student Financial Services .... Ms. Susan PRATER
29 Director Alumni Relations .... Mr. David LEWIS
85 Exec Dir Global Affairs .... Dr. Dennis DUNHAM
39 Exec Dir Business Enterprises .... Dr. Josh OVEROCKER
19 Exec Dir Public Safety/Trans .... Mr. Jeff HARP
15 Asst VP Human Resources .... Ms. Diane FEINBERG
88 Exec Director Leadership Central .... Dr. Jarrett JOBE
07 Dir of Undergraduate Admissions .... Mr. Dallas CALDWELL
28 Director of Diversity & Inclusion .... Ms. MeShawn CONLEY
96 Director of Purchasing .... Mr. David YOUNG
43 Senior Legal Counsel .... Dr. Brad MORELLI
50 Dean of Business Administration .... Dr. Mickey HEPNER
53 Dean College Education .... Dr. James MACHELL
49 int Dean College of Liberal Arts .... Dr. Joan LUXENBURG
81 Int Dean College Math/Science .... Dr. Wei CHEN
58 Dean Graduate Studies .... Dr. Richard BERNARD
57 Dean College Fine Arts & Design .... Dr. Pamela WASHINGTON

University of Oklahoma Health Sciences Center (A)

1100 N. Lindsay, Oklahoma City OK 73104
Telephone: (405) 271-4000 FICE Identification: 005889
Accreditation: &NH, #ARCPA, AUD, DENT, DH, DIETC, DIETD, DIETI, DMS, ENGR, HSA, IPSY, MED, NMT, NUR, NURSE, OT, PDPSY, PH, PHAR, PTA, RAD, RADDOS, RTT, SP

† Regional accreditation is carried under the parent institution in Norman, OK.

University of Oklahoma Norman Campus (B)

660 Parrington Oval, Norman OK 73019-3070
County: Cleveland FICE Identification: 003184
Unit ID: 207500
Telephone: (405) 325-0311 Carnegie Class: DU-Highest
FAX Number: (405) 325-7605 Calendar System: Semester
URL: www.ou.edu
Established: 1890 Annual Undergrad Tuition & Fees (In-State): $10,090
Enrollment: 27,261 Coed
Affiliation or Control: State IRS Status: 501(c)3
Highest Offering: Doctorate
Accreditation: NH, AAB, BUS, BUSA, CIDA, CONST, COPSY, CS, ENG, JOUR, LAW, LIB, LSAR, MUS, PLNG, SW, TED

01 President .... Mr. David L. BOREN
10 VP Administration & Finance .... Mr. Nicholas S. HATHAWAY
88 VP for Univ Governance .... Dr. Chris A. PURCELL
05 Senior Vice President/Provost .... Dr. Kyle HARPER
43 VP of Univ/General Counsel .... Mr. Anil V. GOLLAHALLI
32 Vice President for Student Affairs .... Mr. Clarke A. STROUD
30 Vice Pres for University Devel .... Mr. Jim HALL, III
51 VP Univ Outreach/Dn Col Lib Std .... Dr. James P. PAPPAS
58 Interim Dean Graduate College .... Dr. Randy HEWES
46 Vice President for Research .... Dr. Kelvin K. DROEGEMEIER
26 Vice President for Public Affairs .... Ms. Catherine F. BISHOP
13 Assoc VP/Chief Information Ofcr .... Ms. Loretta M. EARLY
86 Vice Pres for Governmental Relation .... Mr. W. Scott MASON, IV
20 Associate Provost/Dir of Acad Integ .... Dr. Gregory M. HEISER
20 Assoc Prov for Acad Advising .... Dr. Kathleen S. SMITH
09 Assoc Provost/Dir Inst Research .... Ms. Susannah B. LIVINGOOD
06 Registrar/VP Enroll/Stdnt Fin Svcs .... Mr. Matthew W. HAMILTON
35 Dir Student Life/Asst Dean of Stdnt .... Ms. Kristen N. PARTRIDGE
21 Assoc VP Administration & Finance .... Mr. B. Burr MILLSAP
21 Assoc VP Admin & Finance/CFO .... Mr. Chris KUWITZKY
29 Assoc VP Alum & Dev/Ex Dir Alum Asn .... Mr. Jean Paul AUDAS
18 Director Facilities Management .... Mr. Brian F. ELLIS
39 Director of Housing & Food Services .... Mr. David L. ANNIS
41 Director of Athletics .... Mr. Joseph R. CASTIGLIONE
21 Asst VP for Admin & Fin/Controller .... Ms. Terri B. PINKSTON
23 Asst VP/Dir Goddard Health Center .... Dr. William R. WAYNE
36 Director Career Services .... Ms. Robin E. HUSTON
19 Chief of Police .... Ms. Elizabeth G. WOOLLEN
15 Interim Assoc VP/Chief HR Officer .... Ms. Cynthia B. CLEGG
22 Equal Opportunity Officer .... Mr. Bobby J. MASON
07 Director of Admissions/Recruitment .... Mr. Jeffrey J. BLAHNIK
25 Assoc VP for Research Services .... Ms. Andrea D. DEATON
85 Dir International Student Services .... Ms. Robyn D. ROJAS
104 Director Education Abroad .... Dr. Laura R. BRUNSON
37 Director of Financial Aid .... Ms. Caryn L. PACHECO
48 Interim Dean Col of Architecture .... Mr. Hans W. BUTZER
49 Dean College Arts & Sciences .... Dr. Kelly R. DAMPHOUSSE
53 Dean Jeannine Rainbolt Col of Educ .... Dr. Gregg A. GARN
54 Dean Gallogly Col of Engineering .... Dr. Thomas L. LANDERS
57 Dean Weitzenhoffer Col Fine Arts .... Ms. Mary Margaret HOLT
61 VP/Dean College of Law .... Mr. Joseph HARROZ, JR.
62 Dean University Libraries .... Mr. Richard E. LUCE
65 VP/Dn Col Atmospheric/Geographic Sc .... Dr. Berrien MOORE, III
50 Dean Price Col of Business .... Mr. Daniel W. PULLIN
92 Dean McClendon Honors College .... Dr. David H. RAY
60 Dean Gaylord Col Journ/Mass Comm .... Mr. Ed KELLEY
89 Dean University College .... Dr. Nicole J. CAMPBELL
65 Dean Mewborne Col of Earth & Energy .... Dr. J. Michael STICE
82 Vice Provost/Dean Col Intl Studies .... Dr. Suzette R. GRILLOT
28 VP for the University Community .... Mr. Jabar SHUMATE
84 Assoc VP Enrollment/Stdnt Fin Svcs .... Mr. Bradley T. BURNETT
04 Administrative Asst to President .... Ms. Sherry L. EVANS
102 Dir Foundation/Corporate Relations .... Mr. Guy L. PATTON
103 Dir Workforce/Career Development .... Ms. Cynthia B. CLEGG
105 Assoc VP/Director Web Services .... Ms. Erin A. YARBROUGH
106 Asst VP/Dir Online Educ/E-learning .... Mr. Shad B. SATTERTHWAITE
38 Director Student Counseling .... Dr. William R. WAYNE
96 Director of Purchasing .... Mr. Byron E. MILLSAP

† Tuition is based on 30 credit hour per year.

University of Oklahoma Schusterman Center (C)

4502 E 41st Street, Tulsa OK 74135-2512
Telephone: (918) 660-3000 Identification: 770387
Accreditation: &NH, ARCPA, OT

† Regional accreditation is carried under the parent institution in Norman, OK

University of Science and Arts of Oklahoma (D)

1727 W Alabama, Chickasha OK 73018-5322
County: Grady FICE Identification: 003167
Unit ID: 207722
Telephone: (405) 224-3140 Carnegie Class: Bac-A&S
FAX Number: (405) 574-1220 Calendar System: Trimester
URL: www.usao.edu
Established: 1908 Annual Undergrad Tuition & Fees (In-State): $6,270
Enrollment: 904 Coed
Affiliation or Control: State IRS Status: 501(c)3
Highest Offering: Baccalaureate
Accreditation: NH, MUS

53 Chair Division of Education .... Dr. Vicki FERGUSON
01 President .... Dr. John H. FEAVER
05 VP for Academic Affairs .... Dr. Krista MAXSON
10 Vice Pres for Business & Finance .... Mr. Mike D. COPONITI
84 Vice Pres for Enrollment Management .... Ms. Monica TREVINO
30 Vice Pres University Advancement .... Mr. Sic HUDSON
13 VP for Information Services & Tech .... Ms. Lynn BOYCE
06 Registrar/Dir of Enrollment/Records .... Ms. Chelsea PHILLIPS
08 Director of Nash Library .... Ms. Kelly BROWN
26 Dir of Communications/Marketing .... Ms. Amy GODDARD
37 Director of Financial Aid .... Ms. Laura L. COPONITI
32 Dean of Students/Dir Student Svcs .... Ms. Nancy HUGHES
27 Director Media/Community Relations .... Vacant
29 Director of Alumni Development .... Mr. Eric FEUERBORN
18 Director of Physical Plant .... Mr. Mike COPONITI
14 Director of Data Processing .... Ms. Lynn BOYCE
09 Director of Institutional Research .... Vacant
15 Director Personnel Services .... Mr. Mike COPONITI
07 Acting Director of Admissions .... Ms. Monica TREVINO
38 Director Student Counseling .... Ms. Misty STEELE
49 Chair Div of Arts & Humanities .... Dr. Stephen WEBER
50 Chair Div of Business & Social Sci .... Dr. James WELCH
81 Chair Div of Science/Physical Educ .... Dr. J.C. SANDERS
88 Chair Interdisciplinary Studies .... Dr. Jennifer LONG
19 Director Security/Safety .... Mr. Chris BASCO
41 Athletic Director .... Mr. Brisco MCPHERSON

University of Tulsa (E)

800 S Tucker, Tulsa OK 74104
County: Tulsa FICE Identification: 003185
Unit ID: 207971
Telephone: (918) 631-2000 Carnegie Class: DU-Higher
FAX Number: (918) 631-2033 Calendar System: Semester
URL: www.utulsa.edu
Established: 1894 Annual Undergrad Tuition & Fees: $39,521
Enrollment: 4,682 Coed
Affiliation or Control: Independent Non-Profit IRS Status: 501(c)3
Highest Offering: Doctorate
Accreditation: NH, BUS, CAATE, CEA, CLPSY, CS, ENG, LAW, MUS, NUR, SP, TEAC

01 President .... Dr. Steadman UPHAM
10 Exec Vice President & Treasurer .... Mr. Kevan C. BUCK
05 Provost/Vice Pres Academic Affairs .... Dr. Roger N. BLAIS
45 Vice Pres Institutional Advancement .... Dr. Kayla ACEBO
84 VP Enrollment Mgmt/Student Services .... Mr. Earl JOHNSON
41 VP & Athletic Director .... Dr. Derrick GRAGG
13 VP Info Services & CIO .... Mr. Richard KEARNS
28 VP Diversity & Engagement .... Ms. Jacqueline H. CALDWELL
86 VP Public Affairs/COO Gilcrease .... Ms. Susan NEAL
20 Sr Vice Provost/Assoc VP Acad Affs .... Ms. Winona M. TANAKA
46 Vice Prov Research/Dean Grad School .... Dr. Janet A. HAGGERTY
104 Vice Provost Global Education .... Dr. Cheryl MATHERLY
09 Assoc VP Institutional Research .... Mr. John BURY
42 University Chaplain .... Dr. Jeffrey FRANCIS
49 Dean Arts & Sciences .... Dr. Kalpana MISRA
50 Dean Business Administration .... Dr. A. Gale SULLENBERGER
54 Dean Engineering/Natural Sciences .... Dr. James R. SOREM, JR.
61 Dean Law .... Ms. Lyn ENTZEROTH
08 RM & Ida McFarlin Dean of Library .... Mr. Adrian W. ALEXANDER
30 Assoc VP Institutional Advancement .... Ms. Amy ENGLAND
06 Registrar .... Ms. Ginna V. LANGSTON
15 Associate VP Human Resources .... Mr. Wayne PAULISON
22 Dir Acad Support/504 Coordinator .... Dr. Tawny TAYLOR
18 Assoc VP Operations/Physical Plant .... Mr. Robert SHIPLEY
21 Assoc VP & Controller .... Mr. Michael D. THESENVITZ
07 Assoc VP Enrollment Dean Admission .... Ms. Barbara ADKINS
32 Assoc VP Enrollment Dean Students .... Ms. Yolanda D. TAYLOR
39 Assoc VP Director Housing .... Ms. Melissa H. FRANCE
85 Dean International Students .... Ms. Pamela A. SMITH
51 Dean Lifelong Learning .... Dr. J. Phillip APPLEGATE
62 Assoc Dean McFarlin Library .... Ms. Francine J. FISK
23 Director Health Center .... Ms. Stephanie FELL
88 Director Helmerich Center .... Dr. Duane KING
38 Director Counseling & Psych Svcs .... Dr. Thomas J. BRIAN
19 Director Campus Security .... Mr. Joseph F. TIMMONS
29 Exec Director Alumni Relations .... Ms. Amy M. FREIBERGER
36 Director Career Services .... Ms. Shelly HOLLY
37 Director Student Financial Svcs .... Ms. Vicki A. HENDRICKSON
96 Director Purchasing .... Mr. Jerry R. HOLLOWAY
90 Dir Academic Tech Services .... Ms. Janet CAIRNS
91 Dir ERP Operations .... Mr. Martin PAGE
31 Assoc Dean Community Relations .... Mr. Michael MILLS
26 Dir Marketing & Communications .... Ms. Mona CHAMBERLIN
105 Exec Dir Digital Communication .... Mr. Matt CASTEEL
101 Secretary Board of Trustees .... Ms. June E. BROWN
04 Sr Admin Associate to President .... Ms. Susan LAYMAN

Vatterott College-Oklahoma City (F)

5537 NW Expressway, Warr Acres OK 73132-5230
Telephone: (405) 945-0088 Identification: 666061
Accreditation: ACCSC

† Branch campus of Vatterott College, Quincy, IL.

Vatterott College-Tulsa (G)

4343 S 118th E Avenue, Ste A, Tulsa OK 74146-4406
Telephone: (918) 835-8288 Identification: 666102
Accreditation: ACCSC

† Branch campus of Vatterott College-NorthPark, Berkeley, MO.

Virginia College (H)

5124 South Peoria Avenue, Tulsa OK 74105
Telephone: (918) 960-5400 Identification: 770825
Accreditation: ACICS

† Branch campus of Virginia College, Birmingham, AL

Western Oklahoma State College (I)

2801 N Main Street, Altus OK 73521-1397
County: Jackson FICE Identification: 003146
Unit ID: 208035
Telephone: (580) 477-2000 Carnegie Class: Assoc/HT-Mix Trad/Non
FAX Number: (580) 477-7777 Calendar System: Semester
URL: www.wosc.edu
Established: 1926 Annual Undergrad Tuition & Fees (In-State): $3,196
Enrollment: 1,460 Coed
Affiliation or Control: State IRS Status: 501(c)3
Highest Offering: Associate Degree
Accreditation: NH, ADNUR, RAD

01 President .... Dr. Phil BIRDINE
04 Admin Secretary to the President .... Ms. Briar JENKINS
05 VP for Academic Affairs .... Ms. Lisa GREENLEE
10 Vice President for Business Affairs .... Ms. Tricia LATHAM
32 Vice Pres Student Support Services .... Mr. Chad WIGINTON
49 Dean Arts & Sciences .... Ms. Jeri DULANEY
72 Dean of Technical Education .... Ms. Chrystal OVERTON
09 Dir of Institutional Effectiveness .... Mr. Justin SMITH
13 Chief Info Technology Officer .... Mr. Steve PRATER
26 Dir Public Information/Marketing .... Ms. Judith MEYER
07 Director of Admissions & Registrar .... Ms. Lana SCOTT
37 Director of Financial Aid .... Ms. Myrna J. CROSS
29 Dir Development/Alumni Relations .... Ms. Lora Lea PICKERING
41 Director Athletics .... Mr. Bob PEARSON
62 Director of Learning Resources .... Ms. Suzanne ROOKER
15 Director Personnel Services .... Ms. April NELSON
18 Director Physical Plant .... Mr. Doyle JENCKS
40 Bookstore Manager .... Ms. Kass DEWEESE
38 Counselor .... Ms. April DILL
81 Science Instructor .... Mr. Don SCROGGINS
88 History Instructor .... Mr. Mickey GRAHAM

OREGON

American College of Healthcare Sciences (J)

5005 SW Macadam, Portland OR 97239
County: Multnomah FICE Identification: 041944
Unit ID: 443599
Telephone: (503) 244-0726 Carnegie Class: Spec-4-yr-Other Health
FAX Number: (503) 244-0727 Calendar System: Semester
URL: www.achs.edu
Established: 1978 Annual Undergrad Tuition & Fees: $10,800
Enrollment: 603 Coed
Affiliation or Control: Proprietary IRS Status: Proprietary

Highest Offering: Master's
Accreditation: DEAC

01 President/CEO ... Dorene PETERSEN
11 Chief Operating Officer ... Tracey ABELL
45 Chief Strategy Officer ... Erika YIGZAW
10 Chief Financial Officer ... Debbie PARIGIAN
88 Director of Operations ... Heather BALEY
07 Dean of Admissions ... Amy SWINEHART
06 Registrar ... Jennifer MORRISON
26 Chief Marketing Officer ... Kate HARMON

The Art Institute of Portland (A)

1122 NW Davis Street, Portland OR 97209-2911
County: Multnomah FICE Identification: 007819
Unit ID: 208239
Telephone: (503) 228-6528 Carnegie Class: Spec-4-yr-Arts
FAX Number: (503) 228-4227 Calendar System: Quarter
URL: www.artinstitutes.edu/portland
Established: 1963 Annual Undergrad Tuition & Fees: $17,412
Enrollment: 1,111 Coed
Affiliation or Control: Proprietary IRS Status: Proprietary
Highest Offering: Baccalaureate
Accreditation: NW, CIDA

01 President ... Dr. Gregg CROWE
05 Dean of Academic Affairs ... Dr. Robert RIDEL
32 Dean of Student Affairs ... Mr. Jason CLARY
06 Registrar ... Ms. Yvonne PETERSON
07 Director of Admission ... Ms. Tami BELLENGHI
08 Head Librarian ... Ms. Jennifer COX
37 Financial Aid Director ... Ms. Lauren PATTERSON

† Granted candidacy at the Master's level.

Birthingway College of Midwifery (B)

12113 SE Foster Road, Portland OR 97266-4042
County: Multnomah FICE Identification: 036683
Unit ID: 442949
Telephone: (503) 760-3131 Carnegie Class: Spec-4-yr-Other Health
FAX Number: (503) 760-3332 Calendar System: Quarter
URL: www.birthingway.edu
Established: 1993 Annual Undergrad Tuition & Fees: N/A
Enrollment: 76 Coed
Affiliation or Control: Independent Non-Profit IRS Status: 501(c)3
Highest Offering: Baccalaureate
Accreditation: MEAC

01 President ... Ms. Holly SCHOLLES
05 Academic Coordinator ... Ms. Nichole REDING
10 Finance Coordinator ... Ms. Elizabeth BRAGG
20 Faculty Coordinator ... Ms. Natalie HUTCHINSON
37 Financial Aid Officer ... Ms. Stace MAURER
06 Registrar ... Ms. Sadie JULIN
88 Midwifery Program Coordinator ... Ms. Rhonda RAY
88 Lactation Program Coordinator ... Ms. Sarah LONGWELL
88 Administrative Programs Coordinator ... Ms. Amari FAUNA
08 Head Librarian ... Ms. Kathryn CONSTANT

Blue Mountain Community College (C)

PO Box 100, Pendleton OR 97801-0100
County: Umatilla/Morrow/Baker FICE Identification: 003186
Unit ID: 208275
Telephone: (541) 276-1260 Carnegie Class: Assoc/HT-High Non
FAX Number: (541) 278-5886 Calendar System: Quarter
URL: www.bluecc.edu
Established: 1962 Annual Undergrad Tuition & Fees (In-District): $4,443
Enrollment: 1,731 Coed
Affiliation or Control: State/Local IRS Status: 501(c)3
Highest Offering: Associate Degree
Accreditation: NW, DA

01 President ... Ms. Camille PREUS
05 Vice President of Instruction ... Vacant
32 Vice Pres Student Affairs ... Ms. Diane DREBIN
11 Vice Pres Admin Services ... Ms. Tammie PARKER
08 Director of Library & Media Svcs ... Ms. Jacqueline RAY
102 Executive Director Foundation ... Ms. Margaret GIANOTTI
29 Director Alumni Relations ... Vacant
25 Director of Grants ... Vacant
37 Director of Student Financial Aid ... Ms. Yadira GONZALEZ
04 Administrative Asst to President ... Ms. Shannon FRANKLIN
10 AVP Finance & Business Operations ... Ms. Celeste INSKO
106 Dir Online Education/E-learning ... Mr. Bruce KAUSS
13 Chief Info Technology Officer (CIO) ... Mr. Brad HOLDEN
38 Director Student Counseling ... Ms. Cindy WOMACK
15 Director Human Resources ... Vacant
41 Athletic Director ... Mr. Brett BRYAN
09 Director of Institutional Research ... Mr. Toshihiko MURATA
26 Chief Public Relations/Marketing ... Ms. Casey WHITE-ZOLLMAN
75 Dean CTE/Community Ed ... Mr. Carl MELLE
36 Director Student Placement ... Mr. Wade MULLER
84 Director Enrollment Svcs/Registrar ... Ms. Theresa BOSWORTH

Central Oregon Community College (D)

2600 NW College Way, Bend OR 97703
County: Deschutes FICE Identification: 003188
Unit ID: 208318
Telephone: (541) 383-7700 Carnegie Class: Assoc/MT-VT-Mix Trad/Non
FAX Number: (541) 383-7506 Calendar System: Quarter
URL: www.cocc.edu
Established: 1949 Annual Undergrad Tuition & Fees (In-District): $3,555
Enrollment: 6,312 Coed
Affiliation or Control: Local IRS Status: 501(c)3
Highest Offering: Associate Degree
Accreditation: NW, ACFEI, CAHIIM, COMTA, DA, EMT, IFSAC, MAC

01 President ... Dr. Shirley I. METCALF
05 Vice President for Instruction ... Dr. Betsy JULIAN
11 Vice Pres for Administration ... Mr. Matthew J. MCCOY
10 Chief Financial Officer ... Mr. David DONA
51 Dean of Extended Learning ... Mr. Jerry SCHULZ
20 Instructional Dean ... Dr. Michael FISHER
20 Instructional Dean ... Dr. Chad HARRIS
20 Instructional Dean ... Dr. Jennifer NEWBY
84 Dean of Student/Enrollment Svcs ... Dr. Alicia MOORE
07 Director of Admissions & Records ... Ms. Courtney WHETSTINE
08 Director of Library Services ... Dr. Tina HOVEKAMP
26 Director College Relations ... Mr. Ronald S. PARADIS
13 Director Information Technology ... Mr. Dan CECCHINI
18 Director Campus Services ... Mr. Joe VIOLA
15 Director Human Resources ... Vacant
22 Affirmative Action Officer ... Ms. Diane ROSS
37 Director Student Financial Aid ... Mr. Kevin MULTOP
28 Dir of Multicultural Activities ... Ms. Karen ROTH
32 Director of Student Life ... Mr. Andrew DAVIS
09 Dir Institutional Effectiveness ... Ms. Brynn PIERCE
38 Director Student Counseling ... Ms. Seana BARRY
40 Director Bookstore/Auxiliary Svcs ... Ms. Lori BENEFIEL
108 Director Curriculum & Assessment ... Ms. Vickery VILES
19 Director Security/Safety ... Mr. Jim BENNETT
25 Director Contracts/Risk Management ... Ms. Sharla ANDRESEN
39 Director Student Housing ... Mr. Paul WHEELER
102 Director Foundation ... Mr. Zak BOONE
51 Director of Continuing Education ... Ms. Glenda LANTIS

Chemeketa Community College (E)

PO Box 14007, Salem OR 97309-7070
County: Marion FICE Identification: 003218
Unit ID: 208390
Telephone: (503) 399-5000 Carnegie Class: Assoc/HT-High Non
FAX Number: (503) 399-5214 Calendar System: Quarter
URL: www.chemeketa.edu
Established: 1962 Annual Undergrad Tuition & Fees (In-District): $4,230
Enrollment: 11,101 Coed
Affiliation or Control: Local IRS Status: 501(c)3
Highest Offering: Associate Degree
Accreditation: NW, ADNUR, DA, EMT, IFSAC

01 President/Chief Executive Officer ... Ms. Julie HUCKESTEIN
05 VP/Chief Academic Officer ... Mr. Jim EUSTROM
12 Campus President Yamhill Valley ... Mr. Jim EUSTROM
20 Exec Dean Career/Tech Education ... Mr. Johnny MACK
32 Exec Dean Student Dev/Learning Res ... Dr. Claire OLIVEROS
88 Exec Dean Acad Progress/Reg Ed Svcs ... Dr. Susan MURRAY
88 Dean Emergency Services ... Mr. Marshall ROACHE
83 Dean Liberal Arts & Social Sciences ... Mr. Don BRASE
76 Dean Health Services ... Ms. Sandi KELLOGG
37 Dean Financial Aid/Enrollment Svcs ... Ms. Kathy CAMPBELL
38 Dean Counseling/Career Services ... Vacant
72 Dean Applied Technologies ... Mr. Larry CHEYNE
81 Dean Science/Engineering/Math ... Mr. Michael MILHAUSEN
50 Dean Bus/Tech/Early Childhood Educ ... Ms. R. TAYLOR
84 Dean Marketing/Student Recruitment ... Mr. Greg HARRIS
53 Dean Teaching and Learning ... Dr. Deborah SIPE
47 Director Wine Studies ... Ms. Jessica SANDROCK
11 VP Governance & Administration ... Mr. Andrew BONE
08 Director Learning Resource Center ... Ms. Natalie BEACH
88 Director Enterprise Services ... Mr. Brian RADER
10 Assoc VP Financial Management ... Ms. Miriam SCHARER
18 Director Facilities & Operations ... Mr. Phil WRIGHT
15 Director Human Resources ... Ms. Alice SPRAGUE
19 Director Public Safety ... Mr. Bill KOHLMEYER
109 Director Auxiliary Services ... Ms. Meredith SCHREIBER
41 Athletic Director ... Ms. Cassie BELMODIS
50 Dir Chemeketa Ctr for Bus/Industry ... Ms. Diane MCLARAN
88 Coordinator Prof Tech Educ ... Mr. Ed WOODS
28 Diversity & Equity Officer ... Ms. Linda HERRERA
35 Director Student Life/Retention ... Mr. Manuel GUERRA
07 Registrar/Director of Admissions ... Ms. Melissa FREY
26 Assoc VP/Chief Information Officer ... Mr. Tim ROGERS
102 Executive Director Foundation ... Ms. Nancy DUNCAN
25 Grants Coordinator ... Ms. Peggy GREENE
09 Director of Institutional Research ... Mr. Fauzi NAAS
43 General Counsel ... Ms. Rebecca HILLYER

Clackamas Community College (F)

19600 Molalla Avenue, Oregon City OR 97045-7998
County: Clackamas FICE Identification: 004878
Unit ID: 208406
Telephone: (503) 594-6000 Carnegie Class: Assoc/HT-High Non
FAX Number: N/A Calendar System: Quarter
URL: www.clackamas.edu
Established: 1966 Annual Undergrad Tuition & Fees (In-District): $4,268
Enrollment: 7,302 Coed
Affiliation or Control: Local IRS Status: 501(c)3
Highest Offering: Associate Degree
Accreditation: NW, CA, MAC

01 President ... Dr. Joanne TRUESDELL
05 VP Instruct & Stdnt Svcs/Provost ... Dr. David PLOTKIN
11 Vice Pres College Services ... Mr. Jim HUCKESTEIN
04 Executive Asst to the President ... Ms. Denice BAILEY
30 Assoc VP Govt/Cmty/Bus ... Ms. Shelly PARINI
102 Executive Director Foundation ... Mr. Greg FITZGERALD
26 Public Information Officer ... Ms. Lori HALL
88 Dean Acad Found/Connections Div ... Mr. Phillip KING
06 Registrar ... Mr. Chris SWEET
32 Assoc Dean Acad Found/Connect Div ... Ms. Tara SPREHE
13 Dean/CIO Information Technology ... Mr. Dion BAIRD
49 Dean Arts & Sciences ... Ms. Sue GOFF
46 Dean Curriculum/Planning/Research ... Mr. Bill WATERS
72 Dean Tech/Hlth Occup/Workforce Div ... Ms. Cynthia RISAN
15 Dean Human Resources ... Ms. Patricia ANDERSON WIECK
88 Director Educational Partnerships ... Ms. Jaime CLARKE
10 Director Business Services ... Ms. Chris ROBUCK
11 Dean Campus Services ... Mr. Bob COCHRAN
18 Director Campus Services ... Mr. Lloyd HELM
41 Director Athletics/Health/PE ... Mr. Jim MARTINEAU

Clatsop Community College (G)

1651 Lexington Avenue, Astoria OR 97103
County: Clatsop FICE Identification: 003189
Unit ID: 208415
Telephone: (503) 325-0910 Carnegie Class: Assoc/MT-VT-High Non
FAX Number: (503) 325-5738 Calendar System: Quarter
URL: www.clatsopcc.edu
Established: 1958 Annual Undergrad Tuition & Fees (In-District): $4,014
Enrollment: 857 Coed
Affiliation or Control: State/Local IRS Status: 501(c)3
Highest Offering: Associate Degree
Accreditation: NW

01 President ... Mr. Chris BREITMEYER
05 VP Academic & Student Affairs ... Vacant
10 Vice President Finance & Operations ... Ms. JoAnn ZAHN
84 Dean Students & Enrollment Mngt ... Dr. Chris OUSLEY
06 Registrar ... Dr. Chris OUSLEY
26 Director Marketing & Communication ... Ms. Julie HRUBES
78 Dir Co-op Educ & Special Project ... Ms. Christine RIEHL
51 Director Distance Education ... Mrs. Kirsten HORNING
15 Director Personnel Services ... Ms. Leslie LIPE
37 Director Student Financial Aid ... Mr. Lloyd MUELLER
09 Director of Institutional Research ... Mr. Tom GILL
18 Chief Facilities/Physical Plant ... Mr. Greg DORCHEUS
21 Associate Business Officer ... Ms. Margaret ANTILLA
102 Foundation Director ... Ms. Sunny KLEVER
04 Administrative Asst to President ... Ms. Stephanie DORCHEUS

College of Emergency Services (H)

9800 SE McBrod Ave, Ste 200, Milwaukie OR 97222
County: Clackamas Identification: 667128
Telephone: (971) 236-9231 Carnegie Class: Not Classified
FAX Number: (971) 653-9239 Calendar System: Semester
URL: www.collegeofems.com
Established: 1995 Annual Undergrad Tuition & Fees: N/A
Enrollment: N/A Coed
Affiliation or Control: Proprietary IRS Status: Proprietary
Highest Offering: Associate Degree
Accreditation: ABHES, EMT

01 Program Director ... Mr. William THRASHER

Columbia Gorge Community College (I)

400 East Scenic Drive, The Dalles OR 97058
County: Wasco FICE Identification: 041519
Unit ID: 420556
Telephone: (541) 506-6000 Carnegie Class: Assoc/MT-VT-High Non
FAX Number: N/A Calendar System: Quarter
URL: www.cgcc.edu
Established: 1977 Annual Undergrad Tuition & Fees (In-District): $3,816
Enrollment: 991 Coed
Affiliation or Control: State/Local IRS Status: 501(c)3
Highest Offering: Associate Degree
Accreditation: NW, MAC

01 President ... Dr. Frank TODA
05 Chief Academic/Student Affairs Ofcr ... Lori UFFORD
10 Chief Financial Officer ... Will NORRIS
11 Chief Operating Officer ... Robb VAN CLEAVE
30 Chief Inst Advancement Officer ... Dan SPATZ
13 Chief Technology/Planning Officer ... Bill BOHN
101 Dir of Board/Executive Services ... Tria BULLARD
06 Registrar ... Dawn SALLEE-JUSTESEN
07 Director of Admissions ... Vacant
08 Director of Library Services ... John SCHOPPERT
09 Institutional Researcher ... Matt BYRNE
15 Director Human Resources ... Vacant
18 Director of Facilities Services ... Jim AUSTIN
37 Director Financial Aid ... Sara VIEMEISTER

Concorde Career College (J)

1425 NE Irving Street, Suite 300, Portland OR 97232
County: Multnomah FICE Identification: 008887
Unit ID: 208479
Telephone: (503) 281-4181 Carnegie Class: Spec 2-yr-Health
FAX Number: (503) 281-6739 Calendar System: Other

URL: www.concorde.edu/campus/portland
Established: 1996 Annual Undergrad Tuition & Fees: N/A
Enrollment: 804 Coed
Affiliation or Control: Proprietary IRS Status: Proprietary
Highest Offering: Associate Degree
Accreditation: ACCSC, COARC, MAC, SURGT

01 Campus President ... Kim IERIEN

Concordia University (A)

2811 NE Holman Ave, Portland OR 97211-6099
County: Multnomah FICE Identification: 003191
Unit ID: 208488
Telephone: (503) 288-9371 Carnegie Class: Spec-4-yr-Other
FAX Number: (503) 280-8518 Calendar System: Semester
URL: www.cu-portland.edu
Established: 1905 Annual Undergrad Tuition & Fees: $28,510
Enrollment: 7,435 Coed
Affiliation or Control: Lutheran Church - Missouri Synod
IRS Status: 501(c)3
Highest Offering: Doctorate
Accreditation: NW, ACBSP, #LAW, NURSE, SW

01 President ... Dr. Charles E. SCHLIMPERT
26 Exec Vice Pres External Affairs ... Dr. Gary WITHERS
102 Exec Vice Pres Strategic Planning ... Mr. Johnnie DRIESSNER
05 Provost/Chief Academic Officer ... Dr. Mark E. WAHLERS
10 Chief Financial Officer ... Mr. Dennis J. STOECKLIN
11 Chief Operating Officer ... Ms. Jilma MENESES
32 VP Student Svcs/Enrollment Mgmt ... Dr. Glenn C. SMITH
04 Executive Administrator ... Ms. Brenna THOMAS
30 Chief Development Officer ... Mr. Kevin MATHENY
06 Registrar ... Ms. Danielle AMBROSE
07 Vice President Enrollment ... Ms. Bobi SWAN
09 Director of Institutional Research ... Mr. Ron FONGER
15 Vice President of Human Resources ... Ms. Heyke KIRKENDALL-BAKER
18 Chief Facilities/Physical Plant ... Mr. Doug MEYER
20 Associate Academic Officer ... Vacant
88 Chief Public Relations Officer ... Ms. Madeline TURNOCK
29 Director Alumni & Parent Engagement ... Ms. Becky SPRECHER
35 Dean of Students ... Mr. Steve DEKLOTZ
08 Librarian ... Mr. Brent MAI
37 Senior Director of Financial Aid ... Mr. Robert CLARKE
41 Athletic Director ... Mr. Brian JAMROS
38 Director Student Counseling ... Ms. Jaklin PEAKE
85 Director of International Studies ... Ms. Linda ROUNTREE
42 Campus Pastor ... Rev. Bo BAUMEISTER
13 Chief Information Officer ... Dr. Joe MANNION
50 Dean School of Management ... Dr. Michelle COWING
53 Interim Dean College of Education ... Dr. Sheryl REINISCH
49 Dean Theol Studies/Arts/Sciences ... Dr. David KLUTH
76 Dean Col of Health/Human Service ... Dr. Sarah SWEITZER
61 Dean School of Law ... Ms. Cathy SILAK
19 Director Security/Safety ... Mr. Todd TAYLOR

Corban University (B)

5000 Deer Park Drive SE, Salem OR 97317
County: Marion FICE Identification: 001339
Unit ID: 210331
Telephone: (503) 581-8600 Carnegie Class: Masters/S
FAX Number: (503) 585-4316 Calendar System: Semester
URL: www.corban.edu
Established: 1935 Annual Undergrad Tuition & Fees: $29,640
Enrollment: 1,125 Coed
Affiliation or Control: Independent Non-Profit IRS Status: 501(c)3
Highest Offering: Master's
Accreditation: NW

01 President ... Dr. Sheldon NORD
05 Provost/Executive Vice President ... Dr. Matthew LUCAS
10 Vice President For Business ... Mr. Kevin BRUBAKER
32 Vice President For Student Life ... Dr. Brenda ROTH
26 Vice President for Mktg & Comm ... Mr. Steve SAMMONS
30 Vice President for Advancement ... Vacant
35 Dean of Students ... Mr. Nathan GEER
88 Director of DMin Program ... Dr. Leroy GOERTZEN
88 Associate Provost Global Engagement ... Dr. Janine ALLEN
20 Associate Provost for Academics ... Dr. Pam TESCHNER
50 Dean Hoff School of Business ... Mr. P. Griffith LINDELL
53 Dean of Education and Counseling ... Dr. Kristin DIXON
13 Chief Information Officer ... Mr. Brian SCHMIDT
18 Campus Care Project Manager ... Mr. Troy CROFF
06 Assoc Provost/Enrollment Management ... Dr. Chris VETTER
08 Librarian ... Mr. Garrett TROTT
07 Director of Admissions ... Vacant
39 Director of Community Life ... Mr. Eugene EDWARDS
42 Dean School of Ministry ... Dr. Gregory TRULL
41 Athletic Director ... Mr. Greg EIDE
36 Director of Student Support ... Mr. Daren MILIONIS
37 Director of Financial Aid ... Mrs. Ellen ZARFAS
29 Director of Alumni Services ... Vacant
21 Associate Business Officer ... Mr. Brian ELLIOTT
40 Bookstore Manager ... Mr. Larry HULTBERG
88 Asst Dir Grad/Online Admissions ... Ms. Allison SMALL
04 Executive Asst to President ... Ms. Jodi CARLSON
09 Director of Assessment & Inst Rsrch ... Dr. Felicia SQUIRES
104 Director Study Abroad ... Mr. Sam PEARSON
105 Director of Institutional Marketing ... Mr. David SANFORD
106 Online Support Coordinator ... Ms. Sue ROTH

15 Director of Human Resources ... Ms. Nancy MARSHALL
19 Chief of Security ... Mr. Mike ROTH
38 Clinical Director ... Dr. Mary AGUILERA

Eastern Oregon University (C)

One University Boulevard, La Grande OR 97850-2807
County: Union FICE Identification: 003193
Unit ID: 208646
Telephone: (541) 962-3672 Carnegie Class: Masters/S
FAX Number: (541) 962-3493 Calendar System: Quarter
URL: www.eou.edu
Established: 1929 Annual Undergrad Tuition & Fees (In-State): $7,764
Enrollment: 3,653 Coed
Affiliation or Control: State IRS Status: 501(c)3
Highest Offering: Master's
Accreditation: NW, IACBE

01 President ... Mr. Thomas INSKO
05 Provost/Sr VP Academic Affairs ... Dr. Sarah WITTE
32 Vice President for Student Services ... Vacant
10 Vice President Finance & Admin ... Ms. Lara MOORE
30 Vice Pres UA ... Mr. Tim SEYDEL
49 Int Dean College Arts & Science ... Dr. Regina BRAKER
50 Int Dean College of Business & Educ ... Dr. Dan MIELKE
37 Director of Financial Aid ... Ms. Lara MOORE
08 Director of Pierce Library ... Ms. Karen CLAY
07 Director of Admissions ... Ms. Gina GALAVIZ
06 Interim Registrar ... Ms. Emily SHARRATT
15 Director of Human Resources ... Mr. Chris MCLAUGHLIN
29 Dir of Alumni Relations ... Ms. Jessie BRETT
41 Director of Athletics ... Ms. Anji WEISSENFLUH
39 Director of Residence Life ... Mr. Jeremy JONES
18 Director of Facilities & Planning ... Mr. David LAGESON
38 Director Counseling Center ... Dr. Marianne WEAVER
04 Exec Assistant to the President ... Ms. Heather CASHELL
21 Director of Business Affairs ... Ms. Cora BEACH
20 Int Vice Provost Academic Affairs ... Dr. Donald WOLFF
88 Learning Center Operations Manager ... Ms. Kathryn SHORTS
35 Director of Student Relations ... Ms. Colleen DUNNE-CASCIO
19 Campus Security/Public Safety Ofcr ... Mr. Bill BENSON

George Fox University (D)

414 N Meridian, Newberg OR 97132-2697
County: Yamhill FICE Identification: 003194
Unit ID: 208822
Telephone: (503) 538-8383 Carnegie Class: Masters/L
FAX Number: (503) 554-3834 Calendar System: Semester
URL: www.georgefox.edu
Established: 1891 Annual Undergrad Tuition & Fees: $33,142
Enrollment: 3,786 Coed
Affiliation or Control: Friends IRS Status: 501(c)3
Highest Offering: Doctorate
Accreditation: NW, ACBSP, CAATE, CACREP, CLPSY, ENG, IPSY, MUS, NURSE, PTA, SW, TED, THEOL

01 President ... Dr. Robin E. BAKER
03 Vice President/Dean of Seminary ... Dr. Charles J. CONNIRY, JR.
05 Provost ... Dr. Linda SAMEK
10 Exec VP Finance/Business Operations ... Mr. Ted ALLEN
30 Vice President Advancement ... Dr. Lynn ANDREWS
32 Vice President Student Life ... Dr. Bradley A. LAU
26 Exec VP Marketing/Enrollment Svcs ... Mr. Robert K. WESTERVELT
04 Executive Assistant to President ... Ms. Missy D. TERRY
28 AVP Intercultural Engagement ... Dr. Rebecca HERNANDEZ
21 Asst VP of Finance/Controller ... Ms. Cris BANTON
08 Dean of Libraries ... Mr. Merrill L. JOHNSON
07 Director of Undergrad Admissions ... Ms. Lindsay KNOX
06 Registrar ... Ms. Melissa THOMAS
29 Director University Events ... Ms. Jill DOWNING
36 Dir of Career Services/IDEA Center ... Ms. Deb MUMM-HILL
18 Director of Plant Services ... Mr. Clyde G. THOMAS
37 Director of Financial Aid ... Ms. Johanna SCHWEITZER
96 Director Purchasing/Admin Services ... Vacant
41 Director of Athletics ... Mr. Craig B. TAYLOR
105 Director of Web Development ... Mr. Peter CRACKENBERG
15 Director Human Resources ... Mr. Andrew JACOBS
42 Univ Pastor/Dean of Spiritual Life ... Ms. Jamie NOLLING-AUTH
27 Dir Pub Info/Mrkting/Communications ... Mr. Rob FELTON
13 Chief Information Officer ... Mr. Tim GOODFELLOW
19 Director Security Services ... Mr. Ed GIEROK
35 Dean Stdnt Svcs/Dir Hlth/Counseling ... Dr. William C. BUHROW
49 Dean School of Arts & Sciences ... Ms. Laura HARTLEY
83 Dean Sch Behavioral/Health Sci ... Dr. James E. FOSTER
53 Dean School of Education ... Dr. Scot HEADLEY
50 Dean School of Business ... Vacant

Gutenberg College (E)

1883 University Street, Eugene OR 97403-1368
County: Lane FICE Identification: 039324
Unit ID: 420510
Telephone: (541) 683-5141 Carnegie Class: Not Classified
FAX Number: (541) 683-6997 Calendar System: Quarter
URL: www.gutenberg.edu
Established: 1994 Annual Undergrad Tuition & Fees: N/A
Enrollment: N/A Coed
Affiliation or Control: Independent Non-Profit IRS Status: 501(c)3
Highest Offering: Baccalaureate
Accreditation: TRACS

01 President ... David CRABTREE
03 Vice President ... Richard BOOSTER
05 Dean ... Thomas DEWBERRY
07 Admissions Director ... Tim MCINTOSH
06 Registrar ... Chris SWANSON

Klamath Community College (F)

7390 S 6th Street, Klamath Falls OR 97603-7121
County: Klamath FICE Identification: 034283
Unit ID: 428392
Telephone: (541) 882-3521 Carnegie Class: Assoc/MT-VT-High Non
FAX Number: (541) 885-7758 Calendar System: Quarter
URL: www.klamathcc.edu
Established: 1996 Annual Undergrad Tuition & Fees (In-District): $3,687
Enrollment: 1,343 Coed
Affiliation or Control: State/Local IRS Status: 501(c)3
Highest Offering: Associate Degree
Accreditation: NW

01 President ... Dr. Roberto GUTIERREZ
11 Vice Pres Administrative Svcs ... Ms. Allison BRYSON
05 Vice Pres Academic Affairs ... Ms. Jamie JENNINGS
07 Vice Pres Enroll & External Affairs ... Ms. Julie MURRAY-JENSEN
15 VP Human Res & Legal Counsel ... Dr. Anthony ROSILEZ
20 Dean of Instruction ... Dr. Ronda WERY
20 Dean of Instruction ... Mr. Christopher STICKLES
103 Director of Workforce ... Mr. Charles MASSIE
102 Exec Director of Foundation KCC ... Ms. Julie MURRAY-JENSEN
13 Director Information Services ... Mr. Paul BREEDLOVE
06 Registrar/Dean of Enrollment ... Dr. Elizabeth WHITE-HURST
26 Chief Public Information Officer ... Ms. Lacey JARRELL
18 Facilities Director ... Mr. Mike HOMFELDT
10 Director Business Services ... Mr. Melissa LINDSAY
37 Financial Aid Director ... Ms. Robin SUNDSETH
04 Administrative Asst to President ... Ms. Shannon CHILDS
09 Institutional Researcher ... Mr. Bill JENNINGS
101 Secretary to the Board ... Ms. Shannon CHILDS
25 Grants Program Manager ... Ms. Paula PENCE

Lane Community College (G)

4000 E 30th Avenue, Eugene OR 97405-0640
County: Lane FICE Identification: 003196
Unit ID: 209038
Telephone: (541) 463-3000 Carnegie Class: Assoc/MT-VT-Mix Trad/Non
FAX Number: (541) 463-5201 Calendar System: Quarter
URL: www.lanecc.edu
Established: 1964 Annual Undergrad Tuition & Fees (In-District): $4,047
Enrollment: 9,236 Coed
Affiliation or Control: Local IRS Status: 501(c)3
Highest Offering: Associate Degree
Accreditation: NW, ACFEI, COARC, DA, DH, EMT, MAC, PTAA

01 President ... Dr. Mary SPILDE
05 Int Exec Vice President/CAO ... Ms. Dawn DEWOLF
11 Vice President College Operations ... Mr. Brian KELLY
32 Exec Dean Student/Academic Affairs ... Ms. Kerry LEVETT
20 Exec Dean Academic Affs/Career Tech ... Ms. Mary Jeanne KUHART
20 Exec Dean Academic Affs/Transfer ... Dr. Jennifer FREI
35 Div Dean Student Life/Leadership ... Vacant
68 Div Dean Health/Physical Education ... Mr. Chris HAWKIN
28 Chief Diversity Officer ... Vacant
13 Chief Information Officer ... Mr. Bill SCHUETZ
10 Chief Financial Officer ... Mr. Greg HOLMES
15 Chief Human Resources Officer ... Mr. Dennis CARR
09 Dir Inst Research/Assess/Planning ... Dr. Craig TAYLOR
18 Interim Director Facilities & PM ... Mr. Todd SMITH
19 Director Public Safety ... Mr. Jace SMITH
08 Interim Library Director ... Ms. Lori WAMSLEY
38 Dir Counseling/Student Placement ... Mr. Jerry DELEON
37 Director of Financial Aid ... Ms. Helen FAITH
21 Budget Director ... Ms. Rose ELLIS
26 Public Information Officer ... Ms. Joan ASCHIM
102 Foundation Director ... Ms. Wendy JETT
04 Administrative Asst to President ... Ms. Donna ZMOLEK
30 Development Director ... Ms. Tiana MARRONE-CREECH
44 Annual Gifts Officer ... Mr. Philip HUDSPETH

Le Cordon Bleu College of Culinary Arts in Portland (H)

600 SW 10th Avenue, Suite 500, Portland OR 97205-2793
County: Multnomah FICE Identification: 030226
Unit ID: 375841
Telephone: (503) 223-2245 Carnegie Class: Spec 2-yr-A&S
FAX Number: (503) 223-0126 Calendar System: Other
URL: www.chefs.edu/portland
Established: 1983 Annual Undergrad Tuition & Fees: $13,875
Enrollment: 452 Coed
Affiliation or Control: Proprietary IRS Status: Proprietary
Highest Offering: Associate Degree
Accreditation: ACICS, ACFEI

01 Campus President/CAO ... Brian WILLIAMS
05 Campus Director ... Adam THOMPSON
07 Director of Admissions ... Richard BUNCH, III
32 Director Student Services ... Marsha PARMER
10 Business Operations Manager ... Lizza NOVO
06 Associate Registrar ... John ELIASSEN

† In teach-out mode through September 2017.

Lewis and Clark College (A)

0615 SW Palatine Hill, Portland OR 97219-7899
County: Multnomah FICE Identification: 003197
Unit ID: 209056
Telephone: (503) 768-7000 Carnegie Class: Bac-A&S
FAX Number: (503) 768-7055 Calendar System: Semester
URL: www.lclark.edu
Established: 1867 Annual Undergrad Tuition & Fees: $45,104
Enrollment: 3,504 Coed
Affiliation or Control: Independent Non-Profit IRS Status: 501(c)3
Highest Offering: Doctorate
Accreditation: NW, CACREP, LAW, MFCD, TED

01 President ... Dr. Barry GLASSNER
03 Vice President & Provost ... Dr. Jane M. ATKINSON
43 VP General Counsel/Secy of College ... Mr. David ELLIS
53 Dean Grad Sch Education/Counseling ... Dr. Scott FLETCHER
49 Dean College of Arts & Sciences ... Dr. Catherine KODAT
61 Dean of the Law School ... Ms. Jennifer JOHNSON
10 Vice Pres Business/Finance/Treas ... Mr. Alan FINN
30 Vice Pres Institutional Advancement ... Mr. Kenneth WALTER
32 Dean of Students ... Dr. Anna GONZALEZ
09 Assoc Provost Research & Planning ... Dr. Mark FIGUEROA
26 Exec Dir of Public Affairs & Comm ... Mr. Joe BECKER
07 Dean for Enrollment & Communication ... Ms. Lisa MEYER
13 Assoc Vice Pres & Chief Info Ofcr ... Mr. Adam BUCHWALD
15 Assoc VP/Director Human Resources ... Mr. Isaac DIXON
18 Assoc Vice Pres Facilities ... Mr. Michel GEORGE
49 Assoc Dean College of Arts/Science ... Dr. John KRUSSEL
49 Assoc Dean College of Arts/Science ... Dr. Bruce SUTTMEIER
06 Registrar College of Arts/Sciences ... Ms. Judy FINCH
06 Registrar Law School ... Mr. Seneca GRAY
06 Registrar Graduate School ... Ms. River MONTIJO
37 Director of Financial Aid ... Ms. Anastacia DILLON
08 Director of Watzek Library ... Mr. Mark DAHL
35 Assoc Dean of Student Engagement ... Ms. Cathy BUSHA
85 Assoc Dean Intl Stdnts & Scholars ... Mr. Brian WHITE
44 Assoc VP & Director of Development ... Mr. Aaron WHITEFORD
29 Senior Director Alumni/Parent Pgms ... Mr. Andrew MCPHEETERS
19 Director of Campus Safety ... Mr. Timothy O'DWYER
42 Dean of Religious & Spiritual Life ... Dr. Mark DUNTLEY
41 Director of Athletics ... Ms. Shana LEVINE
39 Director of Housing & Orientation ... Ms. Sandi BOTTEMILLER
24 Director of IT Ops/Instr Media Svc ... Mr. Patrick RYALL
17 Assoc Dean Stdnt Health & Wellness ... Dr. John HANCOCK
04 Executive Asst Board Relations ... Ms. Tina BLACKWELL
04 Special Assistant to the President ... Ms. Annette LANIER
102 Dir Corporate/Foundation Relations ... Mr. Erik FAST
104 Actg Dir Overseas & Off Campus Pgms ... Ms. Blythe KNOTT

Linfield College (B)

900 SE Baker Street, McMinnville OR 97128-6894
County: Yamhill FICE Identification: 003198
Unit ID: 209065
Telephone: (503) 883-2200 Carnegie Class: Bac-A&S
FAX Number: (503) 883-2472 Calendar System: 4/1/4
URL: www.linfield.edu
Established: 1858 Annual Undergrad Tuition & Fees: $38,754
Enrollment: 1,683 Coed
Affiliation or Control: American Baptist IRS Status: 501(c)3
Highest Offering: Baccalaureate
Accreditation: NW, CAATE, MUS, NURSE

01 President ... Dr. Thomas HELLIE
05 Vice Pres Acad Affs/Dean of Faculty ... Ms. Susan AGRE-KIPPENHAN
10 Vice Pres Finance/Admin/CFO ... Ms. Mary Ann RODRIGUEZ
30 Vice Pres Institutional Advancement ... Mr. David OSTRANDER
84 Vice Pres for Enrollment Management ... Mr. Daniel PRESTON
32 VP Student Svcs/Dean of Students ... Ms. Susan HOPP
43 Vice President & General Counsel ... Mr. John MCKEEGAN
66 Dean of Nursing ... Dr. Mallie KOZY
20 Associate Dean of Faculty ... Dr. J. Christopher GAISER
35 Associate Dean of Students ... Mr. Jeff MACKAY
15 Interim Director of Human Resources ... Ms. Betty HENNINGER
18 Director Facilities & Auxiliary Svc ... Ms. Allison HORN
28 Director Multicultural Programs ... Mr. Jason RODRIQUEZ
06 Registrar ... Ms. Diane CRABTREE
07 Director of Admission ... Ms. Lisa KNODLE-BRAGIEL
08 Library Director ... Ms. Susan BARNES WHYTE
09 Director of Institutional Research ... Ms. Jennifer BALLARD
37 Director of Financial Aid ... Ms. Keri BURKE
13 Chief Technology Officer ... Ms. Virginia TOMLINSON
91 Assoc Director Integrated Tech Svcs ... Mr. Michael BLANCO
105 Webmaster ... Mr. Jonathan PIERCE
85 Director of International Programs ... Dr. Shaik ISMAIL
51 Director of Continuing Education ... Dr. Laura BRENER
19 Director of Security ... Mr. Ronald NOBLE
38 Director of Counseling Services ... Ms. Patricia HADDELAND
26 Director of Public Relations ... Ms. Mardi MILEHAM
44 Director of Annual Giving ... Ms. Lisa GOODWIN
44 Director of Philanthropic Planning ... Mr. Craig HAISCH
102 Dir Corp & Foundation Relations ... Ms. Catherine JARMIN MILLER
29 Director of Alumni/Parent Relations ... Ms. Debbie HARMON
36 Director Career & Development ... Mr. Michael HAMPTON
42 Chaplain ... Dr. David MASSEY
41 Athletic Director ... Mr. Scott CARNAHAN
40 Bookstore Manager ... Mr. Chad COTTRILL
04 Exec Assistant to the President ... Ms. Jolene SMITH

Linn-Benton Community College (C)

6500 Pacific Boulevard, SW, Albany OR 97321-3774
County: Linn FICE Identification: 006938
Unit ID: 209074
Telephone: (541) 917-4999 Carnegie Class: Assoc/MT-VT-High Non
FAX Number: (541) 917-4445 Calendar System: Quarter
URL: www.linnbenton.edu
Established: 1966 Annual Undergrad Tuition & Fees (In-District): $4,265
Enrollment: 5,314 Coed
Affiliation or Control: State/Local IRS Status: 501(c)3
Highest Offering: Associate Degree
Accreditation: NW, DA, MAC, OTA, POLYT

01 President ... Dr. Gregory J. HAMANN
05 Vice Pres Academic Affs/Wrkfce Dev ... Ms. Ann BUCHELE
10 Vice Pres Finance & Operations ... Mr. Dave HENDERSON
32 Vice President Student Affairs ... Dr. Bruce CLEMETSEN
35 Assoc Dean Student Affairs ... Ms. Lynne COX
12 Regional Director Linn County ... Mr. Gary PRICE
12 Regional Director Benton County ... Mr. Jeff DAVIS
15 Dir Human Resources/Affirm Act Ofcr ... Mr. Scott ROLEN
41 Director of Athletics ... Mr. Randy FALK
81 Dean Science/Engr & Tech ... Mr. Andrew FELDMAN
49 Dean Arts/Soc Sci/Humanities Div ... Ms. Katie WINDER
20 Dean Instruction ... Ms. Sally WIDENMANN
30 Exec Dir Institutional Advancement ... Mr. Dale STOWELL

Marylhurst University (D)

PO Box 261, 17600 Pacific Highway,
Marylhurst OR 97036-0261
County: Clackamas FICE Identification: 003199
Unit ID: 209108
Telephone: (503) 636-8141 Carnegie Class: Masters/L
FAX Number: (503) 636-9526 Calendar System: Quarter
URL: www.marylhurst.edu
Established: 1893 Annual Undergrad Tuition & Fees: $20,835
Enrollment: 1,273 Coed
Affiliation or Control: Independent Non-Profit IRS Status: 501(c)3
Highest Offering: Master's
Accreditation: NW, CIDA, IACBE, MUS

01 President ... Dr. Melody ROSE
05 Provost ... Dr. Ann Marie FALLON
10 VP Finance/Administration ... Mr. Rich RUBSAMEN
30 Vice Pres Institutional Advancement ... Ms. Nicola SYSYN
88 Vice Pres Mission Integration ... Ms. Joan SAALFELD
84 VP Enrollment Mgmt/Student Services ... Ms. Beth WOODWARD
04 Chief Assistant to the President ... Mr. Rod JOHNSON
07 Director of Admissions ... Mr. Ryan CLARK
06 Registrar ... Ms. Gwen HYATT
08 University Librarian ... Ms. Nancy HOOVER
26 Director Marketing & Communications ... Ms. Simona BEATTIE
37 Director of Financial Aid ... Ms. Tracy REISINGER
88 Director Art Therapy Graduate Pgm ... Ms. Christine TURNER
72 Director Center for Learning Tech ... Mr. Nathan PHILLIPS
13 Director of Infrastructure Services ... Mr. Keelan CLEARY
18 Director of Facilities ... Mr. Mark STRULOEFF
49 Chair Sci/Religion/Interdisc Stds ... Dr. Jan DABROWSKI
88 Chair Art/Music/Creative Therapies ... Dr. Laura BEER
64 Director of Choral Activities ... Dr. Justin SMITH
57 Art Dept/Dir Interior Design Dept ... Ms. Nancy HISS
73 Religious Studies & Philosophy ... Dr. Jeroid ROUSSELL
88 Interdisciplinary Studies ... Mr. Simeon DREYFUSS
79 Chrpsn Culture & Media ... Dr. David DENNY
81 Science & Math ... Mr. Greg DARDIS
83 Chairperson Human Sciences ... Dr. Jennifer SASSER
88 Real Estate Studies ... Mr. Sunny LISTON
88 Chrpsn English Literature/Writing ... Dr. Meg ROLAND
60 Communication Studies ... Vacant
50 Acting Director of Business ... Mr. Paul VENTURA
109 Chair Food Systems & Society ... Dr. Patricia ALLEN

Mount Angel Seminary (E)

1 Abbey Drive, St. Benedict OR 97373-0505
County: Marion FICE Identification: 003203
Unit ID: 209241
Telephone: (503) 845-3951 Carnegie Class: Spec-4-yr-Faith
FAX Number: (503) 845-3128 Calendar System: Semester
URL: www.mountangelabbey.org
Established: 1887 Annual Undergrad Tuition & Fees: $20,176
Enrollment: 152 Coed
Affiliation or Control: Roman Catholic IRS Status: 501(c)3
Highest Offering: Master's
Accreditation: NW, THEOL

01 President/Rector ... Msgr. Joseph V. BETSCHART
05 Vice President/Academic Dean ... Dr. Owen CUMMINGS
11 VP of Admin/Dir Pastoral Formation ... Rev. Stephen CLOVIS
08 Librarian ... Ms. Victoria ERTELT
10 Business Manager ... Fr. Martin GRASSEL, OSB
06 Registrar & Student Financial Aid ... Ms. Marina KEYS
32 Dean of Students Theology ... Abbot Peter EBERLE, OSB
32 Dean of Students College ... Rev. Terrence TOMPKINS
20 Academic Dean College ... Dr. Andrew CUMMINGS
85 Director of Foreign Students ... Ms. Tamara SWANSON-ORR
07 Director of Admissions ... Fr. Ralph RECKER, OSB
04 Admin Asst to the President/Rector ... Mrs. Carol MARTIN
13 Information Technology Manager ... Mr. Steve PATTERSON
40 Bookstore Manager ... Mrs. Beth WELLS
20 Academic Dean Theology ... Dr. Seymour HOUSE
29 Director Alumni Relations ... Vacant

† Granted candidacy at the Doctorate level.

Mt. Hood Community College (F)

26000 SE Stark, Gresham OR 97030-3300
County: Multnomah FICE Identification: 003204
Unit ID: 209250
Telephone: (503) 491-6422 Carnegie Class: Assoc/HT-High Non
FAX Number: (503) 491-7389 Calendar System: Quarter
URL: www.mhcc.edu
Established: 1965 Annual Undergrad Tuition & Fees (In-District): $4,841
Enrollment: 9,276 Coed
Affiliation or Control: Local IRS Status: 501(c)3
Highest Offering: Associate Degree
Accreditation: NW, COARC, DH, FUSER, PTAA, SURGT

01 President ... Dr. Debra DERR
11 VP of Administrative Services ... Mr. Richard DOUGHTY
05 Vice Pres Instruction ... Ms. Christie PLINSKI
32 Vice Pres of Student Development ... Dr. Waldon HAGAN
15 Director Human Resources ... Ms. Gale BLESSING
88 Dir Child Dev/Family Support Pgms ... Ms. Jean WAGNER
18 Director Facilities Management ... Mr. Charles GEORGE
10 Director of Finance ... Ms. Jennifer DEMENT
09 Director of Institutional Research ... Mr. Sergey SHEPELOV
37 Director Student Financial Aid ... Ms. Christi HART
07 Director of Admissions ... Mr. John HAMBLIN
13 Chief Information Officer ... Ms. Linda VIGESAA
28 Director of Diversity ... Mr. David SUSSMAN
29 Exec Dir Foundation/Alumni Rels ... Mr. Al SIGALA
76 Dean Allied Health & Nursing ... Ms. Janie GRIFFIN
81 Dean Perf/Visual Arts/Integ Media ... Ms. Janet MCINTYRE
79 Dean Humanities ... Ms. Sara RIVARA
72 Dean Sciences ... Vacant
50 Dean Business and Info Systems ... Mr. Rod BARKER
103 Exec Dean WF Dev & Industrial Tech ... Mr. Jarrod HOGUE
26 Chief Public Relations Officer ... Mr. Bruce BATTLE
84 Director Enrollment Management ... Mr. John HAMBLIN

Multnomah University (G)

8435 NE Glisan Street, Portland OR 97220-5898
County: Multnomah FICE Identification: 003206
Unit ID: 209287
Telephone: (503) 255-0332 Carnegie Class: Spec-4-yr-Faith
FAX Number: (503) 254-1268 Calendar System: Semester
URL: www.multnomah.edu
Established: 1936 Annual Undergrad Tuition & Fees: $22,760
Enrollment: 753 Coed
Affiliation or Control: Independent Non-Profit IRS Status: 501(c)3
Highest Offering: Doctorate
Accreditation: NW, THEOL

01 President ... Dr. G. Craig WILLIFORD
05 VP Academic Initiatives ... Dr. Wayne G. STRICKLAND
84 VP Enrollment Management/IT ... Ms. Gina BERQUIST
10 CFO and VP Administration ... Mr. W. Chandler WILSON
49 Dean School of Arts and Sciences ... Dr. Daniel SCALBERG
73 Dean School of Bible & Theology ... Dr. Roy ANDREWS
107 Dean Adult & Professional Studies ... Dr. Steve HOLLER
32 Director/Dean of Students ... Ms. Kim STAVE
35 Associate Dean of Students ... Mr. Richard WARD
35 Associate Dean of Students ... Dr. Karen FANCHER
12 Executive Director of MU Reno ... Mr. John MCKENDRICKS
108 Dir of Institutional Effectiveness ... Dr. David FUNK
06 Registrar ... Ms. Amy M. STEPHENS
21 Controller ... Mrs. Debbie WHITEHEAD
08 Librarian ... Dr. Philip M. JOHNSON
37 Director Student Financial Aid ... Mrs. Stephanie POLLARD
36 Seminary Director of Placement ... Dr. Roger TRAUTMANN
13 Director Information Technology ... Mrs. Brenda GIBSON
15 Director of Human Resources ... Ms. Tracy L. MORESCHI
41 Athletic Director ... Ms. Lois VOS
26 Director of Marketing ... Mr. Tom MORLAN
07 Director of Admissions ... Mrs. Mindy-Kate RAWLINS
18 Director of Campus Facilities ... Mr. Eric LINMAN
29 Director Alumni Relations ... Mrs. Michelle UNDERWOOD
04 Assistant to the President ... Mrs. Denise STONE
19 Director of Campus Safety ... Mr. Josh HARPER
38 Director Student Counseling ... Ms. Lisa WOLD
39 Assistant Director of Housing ... Mrs. Christy MARTIN
106 Dir Online Education/E-learning ... Mr. Levi MARTIN
30 Vice President of Advancement ... Mr. Steve CUMMINGS
50 Dean of Business ... Mr. Lee SELLERS
53 Dean of Education ... Ms. Susan BOE

National University of Natural Medicine (H)

049 SW Porter Street, Portland OR 97201-4878
County: Multnomah FICE Identification: 025340
Unit ID: 209296
Telephone: (503) 552-1555 Carnegie Class: Spec-4-yr-Other Health
FAX Number: (503) 499-0022 Calendar System: Quarter
URL: nunm.edu
Established: 1956 Annual Undergrad Tuition & Fees: N/A
Enrollment: 613 Coed
Affiliation or Control: Independent Non-Profit IRS Status: 501(c)3
Highest Offering: Doctorate

Accreditation: NW, ACUP, NATUR

01 President — Dr. David J. SCHLEICH
05 Provost/VP Academic Affairs — Dr. Sandra SNYDER
10 Chief Financial Officer/EVP Finance — Mr. Gerald BORES
30 VP of Advancement — Ms. Susan HUNTER
09 VP of Inst Research & Compliance — Dr. Andrea C. SMITH
15 VP of Human Resources — Ms. Kathy STANFORD
32 AVP of Student Affairs — Ms. Cheryl MILLER
84 AVP of Enrollment Management — Mr. Brandon HAMILTON
04 Executive Asst to the President — Ms. Colleen CORDER
63 Dean of Naturopathic Medicine — Dr. Melanie HENRIKSEN
63 Dean Classical Chinese Medicine — Dr. Laurie REGAN
46 Dean of Research & Graduate Studies — Dr. Heather ZWICKEY
20 Assoc Dean of Undergraduate Studies — Dr. Denise DALLMANN
17 Dean of Clinics/Chief Medical Offic — Dr. Regina DEHEN
06 Registrar — Ms. Kelly GAREY
26 Director PR & Communications — Ms. Marilynn S. CONSIDINE
07 Assoc Director of Admissions — Ms. Danielle LAW
37 Director of Financial Aid — Ms. Laurie RADFORD
23 Executive Director of Clinics — Mr. Michael SORENSEN
13 Manager of IT — Mr. Steve FONG
08 College Librarian — Ms. Noelle STELLO
108 Dir of Inst Research & Compliance — Ms. Laurie MCGRATH
18 Director Campus Development — Mr. Keith NORTH
35 Director of Student Life & Conduct — Mr. Christopher POTTS
19 Director of Campus Security — Mr. Spencer BRAZES
36 Manager of Career Services — Ms. Tafflyn WILLIAMS-THOMAS
109 Director Ancillary Services — Ms. Nicole WRIGHT
51 Assoc Director Continuing Education — Mr. Justin FOWLER
105 Webmaster — Ms. Ellen YARNELL
38 Director Student Counseling — Dr. Adrienne WOLMARK
28 Manager of Intercultural Engagemen& — Ms. Ayasha SAHMSUD-DIN

New Hope Christian College (A)

2155 Bailey Hill Road, Eugene OR 97405-1194
County: Lane — FICE Identification: 021597
Unit ID: 208725
Telephone: (541) 485-1780 — Carnegie Class: Spec-4-yr-Faith
FAX Number: (541) 343-5801 — Calendar System: Semester
URL: www.newhope.edu
Established: 1925 — Annual Undergrad Tuition & Fees: $14,230
Enrollment: 162 — Coed
Affiliation or Control: Other — IRS Status: 501(c)3
Highest Offering: Baccalaureate
Accreditation: BI

00 Chancellor — Mr. Wayne CORDEIRO
01 President/Dir College Advancement — Dr. Mark KELLY
04 Executive Assistant to President — Mrs. Lori HIGASHI
05 Academic Dean — Dr. Mark L. KELLEY
32 Dean of Student Services — Mr. Gary MATSDORF
29 Director of Alumni Relations — Ms. Karen BOBST
10 Business Administrator — Dale SORENSEN
06 Registrar — Ms. Mary Ellen PEREIRA
84 Enrollment Management — Ms. Crystie RIOS
37 Director of Financial Aid — Mr. Casey CRAIGIE
08 Head Librarian — Ms. Janet L. KELLEY
38 Director of Christian Counseling — Ms. Fay DEMEYER

Northwest Christian University (B)

828 E. 11th Ave., Eugene OR 97401-3745
County: Lane — FICE Identification: 003208
Unit ID: 209409
Telephone: (541) 343-1641 — Carnegie Class: Masters/S
FAX Number: (541) 343-9159 — Calendar System: Semester
URL: www.nwcu.edu
Established: 1895 — Annual Undergrad Tuition & Fees: $27,270
Enrollment: 705 — Coed
Affiliation or Control: Christian Church (Disciples Of Christ) — IRS Status: 501(c)3
Highest Offering: Master's
Accreditation: NW, IACBE

01 President — Dr. Joseph WOMACK
05 VP Academic Affairs/Dean of Faculty — Dr. Dennis LINDSAY
10 Vice Pres Finance/Administration — Mr. Gene DE YOUNG
30 Vice President Advancement — Mr. Keith POTTER
32 VP Student Development/Enrollment — Mr. Michael FULLER
26 Director Marketing & Communication — Mr. Patrick WALSH
39 Director Residence Life & Student Svcs — Mr. Greg BROCK
08 Director Kellenberger Library — Mr. Steve SILVER
06 Registrar — Mr. Aaron PRUITT
42 Campus Pastor Dir Church Relations — Mr. Troy DEAN
37 Director Financial Aid — Ms. Jocelyn HUBBS
07 Executive Director Admissions — Ms. Kacie GERDRUM
35 Director Student Programs — Ms. Princess FOX
18 Plant Manager — Mr. Oskar BUCHER
41 Athletic Director — Mr. Corey ANDERSON
36 Dir Academic Svc & Career Develop — Ms. Angela DOTY
04 Exec Administrative Assistant — Ms. Carla AYDELOTT
44 Director of Annual Fund — Ms Glenda GORDON
108 Director of Assessment — Mr. Brian MILLS
29 Director of Alumni Relations — Ms Corynn GILBERT
88 Asst Dean Adult Studies — Ms. Melanie TOWNE
88 Asst Dean Business — Mr. Pete DIFFENDERFER
88 Dean of Counseling & Education — Mr. Gene JAMES

Oregon College of Art and Craft (C)

8245 SW Barnes Road, Portland OR 97225-6349
County: Washington — FICE Identification: 030073
Unit ID: 209533
Telephone: (503) 297-5554 — Carnegie Class: Spec-4-yr-Arts
FAX Number: (503) 297-3155 — Calendar System: Semester
URL: www.ocac.edu
Established: 1907 — Annual Undergrad Tuition & Fees: $29,580
Enrollment: 174 — Coed
Affiliation or Control: Independent Non-Profit — IRS Status: 501(c)3
Highest Offering: Baccalaureate
Accreditation: NW, ART

01 President — Ms. Denise MULLEN
10 Chief Financial Officer — Mr. Michael LAMMERS
05 Dean of Academic Affairs — Ms. Jiseon LEE ISBARA
30 Chief Advancement Officer — Mr. Joe PEACOCK
07 Chief Enroll Officer/Dir of Admiss — Ms. Anne BOERNER
06 Registrar — Ms. Anna VARGAS
08 Head of Library Services — Ms. Elsa LOFTIS
32 Director of Student Services — Mr. Eric GOODWIN
31 Community Programs Coordinator — Ms. Katie WISDOM WEINSTEIN
37 Director of Financial Aid — Ms. Linda ANDERSON
29 Dir of Exhibitions/Alumni Affairs — Vacant
04 Exec Assistant to the President — Ms. Kris KEBISEK

† Granted candidacy at the Master's level.

Oregon College of Oriental Medicine (D)

75 NW Couch Street, Portland OR 97209-4018
County: Multnomah — FICE Identification: 026037
Unit ID: 369659
Telephone: (503) 253-3443 — Carnegie Class: Spec-4-yr-Other Health
FAX Number: (503) 253-2701 — Calendar System: Quarter
URL: www.ocom.edu
Established: 1983 — Annual Graduate Tuition & Fees: N/A
Enrollment: 272 — Coed
Affiliation or Control: Independent Non-Profit — IRS Status: 501(c)3
Highest Offering: Doctorate; No Undergraduates
Accreditation: ACUP

01 President — Dr. Deborah HOWE
10 Chief Finance Officer — Bill MCCRAE
11 Vice Pres Planning & Operations — Vacant
05 Vice Pres Comm & Academic Services — Beth HOWLETT
58 Dean of Master's Studies — Dr. Martin KIDWELL
88 Dean of Doctoral Studies — Dr. Beth BURCH
32 Dean of Students — Nancy GROTTON
30 Chief Development Officer — Dave ESHBAUGH
17 Assoc Dean of Clinical Education — Dr. Debra MULROONEY
46 Interim Director of Research — Ben MARX
15 Chief Human Resources Officer — Joyce GATES
06 Registrar — Carol ACHESON

Oregon Culinary Institute (E)

1701 SW Jefferson Street, Portland OR 97201-2571
Telephone: (503) 961-6200 — Identification: 666177
Accreditation: ACICS

† Branch campus of Pioneer Pacific College, Wilsonville, OR

Oregon Health & Science University (F)

3181 SW Sam Jackson Park Road, Portland OR 97239-3098
County: Multnomah — FICE Identification: 004882
Unit ID: 209490
Telephone: (503) 494-8311 — Carnegie Class: Spec-4-yr-Med
FAX Number: (503) 494-5738 — Calendar System: Quarter
URL: www.ohsu.edu
Established: 1974 — Annual Undergrad Tuition & Fees (In-State): N/A
Enrollment: 2,861 — Coed
Affiliation or Control: State — IRS Status: 501(c)3
Highest Offering: Doctorate
Accreditation: NW, ANEST, ARCPA, CAHIIM, DENT, DIETI, EMT, IPSY, MED, MIDWF, MT, NURSE, PH, RTT

01 President — Dr. Joseph E. ROBERTSON
03 Executive Vice Provost — Dr. David W. ROBINSON
05 Provost Education & Research — Dr. Jeanette MLADENOVIC
18 Assoc VP Facilities/Physical Plant — Mr. Scott PAGE
84 Vice Prov Enroll & Academic Program — Ms. Cherie HONNELL
63 Dean School of Medicine — Dr. Mark RICHARDSON
52 Dean School of Dentistry — Dr. Phillip T. MARUCHA
66 Dean School of Nursing — Dr. Susan BAKEWELL-SACHS
06 Registrar — Mrs. Mickie BUSH
17 Director University Hospital — Mr. Peter RAPP
88 Director Vollum Inst Adv Biomed Res — Dr. Richard H. GOODMAN
15 Vice Provost of Human Resources — Mr. Dan FORBES
08 Director Health Sciences Libraries — Mr. Chris SHAFFER
46 Senior Vice Pres for Research — Dr. Daniel DORSA
26 VP and Chief Marketing Officer — Ms. Kimberly OVITT
88 Director Child Devel/Rehab Center — Dr. Brian ROGERS
37 Director Student Financial Aid — Ms. Rachel DURBIN
28 Vice Pres for Equity & Inclusion — Dr. Brian GIBBS

Oregon Institute of Technology (G)

3201 Campus Drive, Klamath Falls OR 97601-8801
County: Klamath — FICE Identification: 003211
Unit ID: 209506
Telephone: (541) 885-1000 — Carnegie Class: Bac-Diverse
FAX Number: (541) 885-1101 — Calendar System: Quarter
URL: www.oit.edu
Established: 1947 — Annual Undergrad Tuition & Fees (In-State): $8,838
Enrollment: 4,260 — Coed
Affiliation or Control: State — IRS Status: 501(c)3
Highest Offering: Master's
Accreditation: NW, COARC, DH, DMS, ENG, ENGR, ENGT, IACBE, MT, POLYT

01 Interim President — Dr. Jay KENTON
05 Provost/Vice Pres Academic Affairs — Vacant
10 VP Finance/Administration — Vacant
32 VP Student Affairs/Dean of Students — Dr. Erin FOLEY
35 Dean of Students — Dr. Erin FOLEY
37 Director of Financial Aid — Ms. Tracey A. LEHMAN
15 Director of Human Resources — Vacant
07 Director of Admissions — Mr. Carl THOMAS
06 Registrar — Ms. Wendy IVIE
21 Director of Business Affairs — Ms. Michelle MEYER
13 Assoc VP/Chief Information Officer — Mr. Paul ROWAN
23 Director Student Health Services — Mrs. Gaylyn MAURER
18 Director Facilities Services — Mr. Brian ADAIR
41 Athletic Director — Mr. Michael J. SCHELL
35 Director Campus Life — Vacant
36 Director of Career Services — Vacant
09 Institutional Research Analyst — Mr. Farooq SULTAN
30 Assoc VP Devel/Alumni Relations — Mrs. Tracy RICKETTS

Oregon State University (H)

Corvallis OR 97331-8507
County: Benton — FICE Identification: 003210
Unit ID: 209542
Telephone: (541) 737-0123 — Carnegie Class: DU-Highest
FAX Number: N/A — Calendar System: Quarter
URL: www.oregonstate.edu
Established: 1868 — Annual Undergrad Tuition & Fees (In-State): $10,107
Enrollment: 28,886 — Coed
Affiliation or Control: State — IRS Status: 501(c)3
Highest Offering: Doctorate
Accreditation: NW, BUS, BUSA, CAATE, CACREP, CEA, CONST, CS, DIETD, DIETI, ENG, ENGR, IPSY, PH, PHAR, SPAA, TED, VET

01 President — Dr. Edward J. RAY
05 Int Provost/Exec Vice President — Dr. Ron ADAMS
10 Int Vice Pres Finance/Admin — Mr. Mike GREEN
30 Vice Pres University Advancement — Mr. Steve CLARK
46 Vice President for Research — Ms. Cynthia SAGERS
20 Vice Prov Academic Affs/Intl Pgms — Vacant
13 Vice Prov for Information Svcs/CIO — Ms. Lois BROOKS
32 Vice Prov for Student Affairs — Dr. Susie BRUBAKER-COLE
56 Vice Prov Univ Outreach/Engagement — Dr. Scott REED
12 V Prov/Campus Ex Ofcr OSU-Cascades — Dr. Rebecca JOHNSON
84 Asst Provost Enrollment Management — Ms. Kate M. PETERSON
102 President & CEO OSU Foundation — Mr. Mike GOODWIN
47 Dean of Agricultural Sciences — Dr. Dan ARP
50 Dean of Business — Dr. Mitzi MONTOYA
54 Dean of Engineering — Dr. Scott ASHFORD
65 Dean of Forestry — Dr. Thomas MANESS
68 Dean of Health & Human Sciences — Dr. Javier NIETO
49 Interim Dean of Liberal Arts — Dr. Larry RODGERS
65 Dean of Earth/Ocean & Atmos Science — Vacant
67 Dean of Pharmacy — Dr. Mark ZABRISKIE
81 Dean of Science — Dr. Sastry PANTULA
74 Interim Dean of Veterinary Medicine — Dr. Susan TORNQUIST
51 Assoc Provost Extended Campus — Dr. David A. KING
58 Dean of Graduate School — Dr. Jennifer DENNIS
35 Interim Dean of Student Life — Ms. Tracy BENTLEY-TOWNLIN
92 Dean University Honors College — Dr. Toni DOOLEN
53 Dean of Education — Dr. Larry FLICK
08 University Librarian — Ms. Faye CHADWELL
22 Director Equity and Inclusion — Vacant
43 General Counsel — Ms. Becca GOSE
41 Director Intercollegiate Athletics — Mr. Todd STANSBURY
36 Director of Career Services — Mr. Douglas COCHRAN
37 Dir of Financial Aid/Scholarship — Mr. Doug SEVERS
31 Director Memorial Union — Vacant
23 Int Dir Student Health Services — Dr. Jeff MULL
38 Dir Univ Counseling/Psych Svcs — Dr. Jackie ALVAREZ
39 Director Univ Housing/Dining Svcs — Mr. Dan LARSON
06 Registrar — Ms. Rebecca MATHERN
07 Director of Admissions — Mr. Noah BUCKLEY
24 Director Media & Outreach Services — Mr. John GREYDANUS
14 Dir of Enterprise Computing Service — Mr. Kent KUO
21 AVP Finance & Administration — Mr. Mike GREEN
15 Director of Human Resources — Ms. Donna CHASTAIN
18 Assoc Vice Pres Facilities — Ms. Anita AZAREKNO
19 Director Public Safety — Mr. Denson CHATFIELD
29 Exec Dir of Alumni Association — Ms. Kathy BICKEL
86 Director Government Relations — Mr. Jock S. MILLS
44 Director of Annual Giving — Ms. Lacie LA RUE
27 Dir News/Comm Svcs/Asst Vice Pres — Ms. Annie HECK
26 Director of University Marketing — Ms. Melody K. OLDFIELD
105 Asst Director Web Communications — Mr. David A. BAKER
28 Interim Chief Diversity Officer — Ms. Angela BATISTA
09 Director of Institutional Research — Mr. Salvador CASTILLO
40 General Mgr & CEO OSU Bookstores — Mr. Steve E. ECKRICH
96 Manager Procurement/Contract Svcs — Ms. Kelly L. KOZISEK

Pacific Bible College (A)

409 N. Front Street, Medford OR 97501

County: Jackson | Identification: 667252
Telephone: (541) 776-9942 | Carnegie Class: Not Classified
FAX Number: (541) 770-9065 | Calendar System: Semester
URL: www.pacificbible.com
Established: 1991 | Annual Undergrad Tuition & Fees: N/A
Enrollment: N/A | Coed
Affiliation or Control: Non-denominational | IRS Status: 501(c)3
Highest Offering: Associate Degree
Accreditation: @BI

01 President Mr. Mike ROBINSON
11 Vice President Administration Mr. Dennis ALLEN
05 Chief Academic Officer Mr. John OSBOURN
32 Dean of Men & Women Mr. Daniel NICHOLAS

Pacific Northwest College of Art (B)

511 NW Broadway, Portland OR 97209-3023

County: Multnomah | FICE Identification: 003207
Unit ID: 209603
Telephone: (503) 226-4391 | Carnegie Class: Spec-4-yr-Arts
FAX Number: (503) 226-3587 | Calendar System: Semester
URL: www.pnca.edu
Established: 1909 | Annual Undergrad Tuition & Fees: $33,070
Enrollment: 519 | Coed
Affiliation or Control: Independent Non-Profit | IRS Status: 501(c)3
Highest Offering: Master's
Accreditation: NW, ART

01 President Mr. Don TUSKI
05 Dean of Academic Affairs Ms. Tracey COCKRELL
10 Chief Financial Officer/HR Director Mr. Mark MORELAND
84 Vice Pres Enrollment Services Mr. Kavin BUCK
04 Executive Administrative Assistant Vacant
51 Director of Continuing Education Mr. Patrick FORSTER
37 Director Financial Aid Ms. Heidi LOCKE
26 Director of Communications Ms. Gillian FLOREN
06 Registrar Mr. Ron RUTTER
08 Interim Dir of Library Services Ms. Serenity IBSEN
07 Director of Admissions Ms. D. Jean HESTER
15 HR Director Mr. Sean WOODARD
100 Chief of Staff Ms. Gillian FLOREN
18 Facilities Manager Mr. Charles VAWTER
32 Director of Student Services Ms. Rachael ALLEN
39 Assoc Director of Residence Life Mr. Jordan BERMINGHAM
45 Major Gifts Officer Ms. Sharon JOHNSON

Pacific University (C)

2043 College Way, Forest Grove OR 97116-1797

County: Washington | FICE Identification: 003212
Unit ID: 209612
Telephone: (503) 357-6151 | Carnegie Class: Masters/L
FAX Number: (503) 352-2242 | Calendar System: Semester
URL: www.pacificu.edu
Established: 1849 | Annual Undergrad Tuition & Fees: $39,858
Enrollment: 3,640 | Coed
Affiliation or Control: Independent Non-Profit | IRS Status: 501(c)3
Highest Offering: Doctorate
Accreditation: NW, ARCPA, @AUD, CAATE, CLPSY, DH, IPSY, MUS, OPT, OPTR, OT, PHAR, PTA, @SP, SW, TED

01 President Dr. Lesley M. HALLICK
05 Vice Pres Academic Affairs/Provost Dr. John MILLER
10 Vice Pres Finance & Administration Mr. Mike MALLERY
30 Vice Pres University Advancement Ms. Cassie WARMAN
32 Vice Pres Enrollment/Student Affs Dr. Mark ANKENY
35 Assoc Vice Pres Student Affairs Mr. Will PERKINS
21 Assistant Vice Pres for Finance Mr. William RAY
26 Assoc VP for University Relations Ms. Jan STRICKLIN
18 Director of Facilities Ms. Cindy SCHUPPERT
07 Executive Director of Admissions Ms. Karen DUNSTON
06 Registrar Ms. Anne HERMAN
37 Director Financial Aid Ms. Leslie LIMPER
13 Chief Information Officer Mr. James FLEMING
88 Director of Conference Services Ms. Lois HORNBERGER
88 Director University Events Ms. Paula THATCHER
76 Exec Dean Col of Health Professions Dr. Ann BARR-GILLESPIE
49 Dean of Arts & Sciences Dr. Lisa CARSTENS
63 Dean of Optometry Dr. Jennifer COYLE
67 Dean of Pharmacy Dr. Reza KARIMIGEVARI
53 Dean College of Education Dr. Leif GUSTAVSON
83 Dean Sch Professional Psychology Dr. Christiane BREMS
41 Athletic Director Mr. Kenneth SCHUMANN
76 Director School Physical Therapy Dr. Kevin CHUI
76 Dir School Occupational Therapy Dr. Gregory WINTZ
15 Director of Human Resources Mr. Kris KOSIK
23 Director of Health Services Ms. Kathryn L. EISENBARTH
88 Acad Coord/English Language Inst Ms. Monique GRINDELL
44 Director of Annual Giving Ms. Kristin STORFA
07 Exec Director of Grad/Prof Admiss Mr. Jon-Erik LARSEN
76 Director Physician Asst Studies Dr. Mary VON
29 Director Alumni Relations Ms. Martha CALUS-MCLAIN
88 Dir External Relations Optometry Ms. Jeanne OLIVER
08 Interim Library Director Mr. Isaac GILMAN
88 Senior Editor/Writer Ms. Jenni LUCKETT
32 Dir Univ Center/Student Activities Mr. Steve KLEIN
36 Director Career Development Mr. Brian O'DRISCOLL
52 Program Director-Dental Ms. Lisa ROWLEY
40 Manager Bookstore Ms. Stacie BLANKENHORN
38 Director Counseling Center Ms. Robin KEILLOR
09 Director of Institutional Research Mr. William O'SHEA
04 Executive Asst to President Ms. Sue WEINBENDER
100 Chief of Staff Ms. Mic HOWE
43 Dir Legal Services/General Counsel Mr. Scott SHUMAN

Pioneer Pacific College (D)

27501 SW Parkway Avenue, Wilsonville OR 97070-9296

County: Clackamas | FICE Identification: 023301
Unit ID: 210076
Telephone: (503) 682-3903 | Carnegie Class: Bac/Assoc-Assoc Dom
FAX Number: (503) 682-1514 | Calendar System: Other
URL: www.pioneerpacific.edu
Established: 1981 | Annual Undergrad Tuition & Fees: $13,972
Enrollment: 1,195 | Coed
Affiliation or Control: Proprietary | IRS Status: Proprietary
Highest Offering: Baccalaureate
Accreditation: ACICS, RAD

01 President Mr. Don MOUTOS
05 Vice President of Academic Affairs Mr. Fred OSBORN
10 Controller Ms. Wendy HUTCHISONS

Pioneer Pacific College-Eugene Branch (E)

3800 Sports way, Springfield OR 97447

Telephone: (541) 684-4644 | Identification: 770764
Accreditation: ACICS

Portland Community College (F)

PO Box 19000, Portland OR 97280-0990

County: Multnomah | FICE Identification: 003213
Unit ID: 209746
Telephone: (971) 722-6111 | Carnegie Class: Assoc/MT-VT-Mix Trad/Non
FAX Number: (971) 722-4960 | Calendar System: Quarter
URL: www.pcc.edu/
Established: 1961 | Annual Undergrad Tuition & Fees (In-District): $3,766
Enrollment: 30,929 | Coed
Affiliation or Control: Local | IRS Status: 501(c)3
Highest Offering: Associate Degree
Accreditation: NW, ADNUR, CAHIIM, DA, DH, DT, EMT, IFSAC, MAC, MLTAD, RAD

01 College President Mr. Mark MITSUI
100 Chief of Staff Dr. Traci FORDHAM
05 Interim VP Academic Affairs Ms. Elizabeth LUNDY
32 Interim VP Student Affairs Mr. Jim PEREZ
11 Vice Pres Finance/Administration Mr. Jim LANGSTRAAT
10 Assoc VP Financial Services Mr. Eric BLUMENTHAL
13 Chief Information Officer Mr. Michael NORTHOVER
44 Assoc VP College Advancement Mr. Robert A. WAGNER
12 Campus President Sylvania Dr. Lisa AVERY
12 Campus President Cascade Dr. Karin EDWARDS
12 Campus President Rock Creek Dr. Sandra FOWLER-HILL
12 Campus President Southeast Dr. Jessica HOWARD
20 Int Dean Instruction Sylvania Dr. Karen PAEZ
20 Dean Instruction Cascade Campus Mr. Kurt SIMONDS
20 Int Dean Instr Rock Creek Campus Dr. Cheryl SCOTT
20 Dean Instruction Southeast Campus Dr. Craig KOLINS
32 Dean Student Dev Sylvania Campus Ms. Heather LANG
32 Dean Stdnt Dev Rock Creek Campus Ms. Narce RODRIGUEZ
32 Dean Student Dev Cascade Campus Ms. Michele CRUSE
35 Dean Student Affairs Ms. Tammy N. BILLICK
15 Associate VP Human Resources Ms. Lisa BLEDSOE
18 Director Facilities Management Mr. Tony ICHSAN
08 Interim Director Libraries Ms. Maria WAGNER
09 Dir Institutional Effectiveness Ms. Laura MASSEY
19 Director Public Safety Mr. Derrick FOXWORTH
37 Acting Director Financial Aid Mr. Elijah HERR
22 Chief Diversity Officer Ms. Kim BAKER-FLOWERS
30 Director of Development Ms. Ann PRATER
84 Dir of Enrollment Services Vacant

Portland State University (G)

PO Box 751, Portland OR 97207-0751

County: Multnomah | FICE Identification: 003216
Unit ID: 209807
Telephone: (503) 725-3000 | Carnegie Class: DU-Higher
FAX Number: (503) 725-4882 | Calendar System: Quarter
URL: www.pdx.edu
Established: 1946 | Annual Undergrad Tuition & Fees (In-State): $8,034
Enrollment: 27,696 | Coed
Affiliation or Control: State | IRS Status: 501(c)3
Highest Offering: Doctorate
Accreditation: NW, BUS, BUSA, CACREP, CAEP, CEA, CORE, CS, ENG, HSA, MUS, PH, PLNG, SP, SPAA, SW, TED, THEA

01 President Dr. Wim WIEWEL
43 General Counsel Mr. David REESE
05 Provost & VP Academic Affairs Dr. Sona ANDREWS
10 Vice President Finance/Admin Dr. Kevin REYNOLDS
102 CEO PSU Foundation Mr. Bill BOLDT
100 Chief of Staff & VP Public Affairs Ms. Lois DAVIS
32 VP Enroll Mgmt & Student Affairs Dr. John FRAIRE
46 VP Rsrch & Strategic Partnerships Vacant
22 VP Global Diversity & Inclusion Dr. Carmen SUAREZ
45 Vice Prov Academic/Fiscal Planning Mr. Scott MARSHALL
20 Vice Provost Acad Pers Ldrshp & Dev Dr. Shelly CHABON
26 Assoc VP Communications Mr. Christopher BRODERICK
09 Director Inst Research/Planning Dr. Kathi A. KETCHESON
19 Director Campus Public Safety Mr. Phil ZERZAN
14 AVP Strategic Plng/Prtnrshps/Tech Mr. Erin FLYNN
08 Dean University Librarian Dr. Marilyn MOODY
41 Athletics Director Mr. Mark ROUNTREE
88 Vice Prov Acad Innov/Stdnt Success Mr. Sukhwant S. JHAJ
49 Dean of CLAS Dr. Karen MARRONGELLE
50 Dean of SBA Mr. Clifford ALLEN
53 Dean Graduate Sch of Education Dr. Randy HITZ
54 Dean Col Engr/Computer Science Dr. Ren Jeng SU
57 Dean College of the Arts Dr. Robert BUCKER
70 Dean School of Social Work Dr. Laura NISSEN
80 Dean College Urban/Public Affairs Dr. Stephen PERCY
35 Dean Student Life Ms. Michele TOPPE
13 AVP/Chief Information Officer Mr. Kirk KELLY
85 Dir Diversity & Mult Student Svcs Ms. Cece RIDDER
06 AVP & University Registrar Ms. Cindy BACCAR
86 Asst Director Government Relations Ms. Alyson KRAUS
86 Dir State Govt Relations Ms. Debbie KORESKI
23 Exec Dir Stdnt Health & Counseling Dr. Dana TASSON
58 AVP & Dean Graduate Studies Ms. Margaret EVERETT
46 AVP Research Ms. Lisa ZURK

Process Work Institute (H)

2049 NW Hoyt St, Portland OR 97209

County: Multnomah | Identification: 667297
Telephone: (503) 223-8188 | Carnegie Class: Not Classified
FAX Number: (503) 227-7003 | Calendar System: Quarter
URL: www.processwork.org
Established: | Annual Graduate Tuition & Fees: N/A
Enrollment: N/A | Coed
Affiliation or Control: Independent Non-Profit | IRS Status: 501(c)3
Highest Offering: Master's; No Undergraduates
Accreditation: ACICS

01 President Dr. Chris ALLEN

Reed College (I)

3203 SE Woodstock Boulevard, Portland OR 97202-8199

County: Multnomah | FICE Identification: 003217
Unit ID: 209922
Telephone: (503) 771-1112 | Carnegie Class: Bac-A&S
FAX Number: (503) 777-7769 | Calendar System: Semester
URL: www.reed.edu
Established: 1908 | Annual Undergrad Tuition & Fees: $49,940
Enrollment: 1,394 | Coed
Affiliation or Control: Independent Non-Profit | IRS Status: 501(c)3
Highest Offering: Master's
Accreditation: NW

01 President Mr. John KROGER
05 Dean of the Faculty Dr. Nigel J. NICHOLSON
26 Vice President College Relations Dr. Hugh E. PORTER
10 Vice President & Treasurer Ms. Lorraine ARVIN
32 Vice President for Student Services Dr. Michael BRODY
04 Exec Asst to the President Ms. Dawn G. THOMPSON
28 Dean for Institutional Diversity Dr. Mary B. JAMES
35 Dean of Students Mr. Bruce SMITH
23 Director Health & Counseling Ms. Kathryn A. SMITH
07 Vice Pres/Dean Admission & Fin Aid Mr. Milyon TRULOVE
06 Registrar Ms. Nora MCLAUGHLIN
08 College Librarian Ms. Dena HUTTO
30 Director of Development Ms. Jan KURTZ
37 Director of Financial Aid Ms. Sandy SUNDSTROM
09 Director of Institutional Research Mr. Mike TAMADA
27 Exec Dir Comm & Public Affairs Ms. Mandy HEATON
29 Director of Alumni Programs Ms. Katie RAMSEY
13 Chief Information Officer Dr. Martin D. RINGLE
105 Director of Web Support Services Ms. Marianne M. COLGROVE
91 Director Administrative Computing Mr. Gabriel LEAVITT
21 Controller Ms. Tracy L. FRANTEL
15 Director of Human Resources Ms. Michelle VALINTIS
44 Dir Alumni Programs & Annual Fund Ms. Mary M. ASKELSON
102 Dir Corporate/Foundation Support Ms. Diane B. GUMZ
104 Director International Programs Dr. Paul D. DEYOUNG
36 Dean of Stdnts/Dir Life Beyond Reed Ms. Alice HARRA
88 Director of Special Programs Ms. Barbara A. AMEN
18 Director Facilities Operations Mr. Townsend ANGELL
19 Director Community Safety Mr. Gary GRANGER
68 Director of Physical Education Mr. Michael LOMBARDO
40 Manager of the Bookstore Mr. Ueli STADLER
39 Asst Dean of Students for Res Life Ms. Amy SCHUCKMAN

Rogue Community College (J)

3345 Redwood Highway, Grants Pass OR 97527-9298

County: Josephine | FICE Identification: 010182
Unit ID: 209940
Telephone: (541) 956-7500 | Carnegie Class: Assoc/MT-VT-High Non
FAX Number: (541) 471-3591 | Calendar System: Quarter
URL: www.roguecc.edu
Established: 1970 | Annual Undergrad Tuition & Fees (In-District): $4,005
Enrollment: 5,099 | Coed
Affiliation or Control: Local | IRS Status: 501(c)3
Highest Offering: Associate Degree
Accreditation: NW, EMT

01 College President Dr. Cathy KEMPER-PELLE

05 VP of Instruction/CAO .... Mr. Kirk GIBSON
13 VP of College Services/CIO .... Mr. Curtis SOMMERFELD
32 Vice President Student Services .... Ms. Kori EBENHACK
103 Dean School of Workforce/Col Prep .... Ms. Theresa RIVENES
72 Dean Sch Arts/Tech/Health/Pub Svc .... Mr. Kevin HOFF
88 Director SBDC .... Mr. Ronald GOSS
81 Dean School of Science and Tech .... Mr. Steve SCHILLING
08 Head Librarian .... Mr. Robert FELTHOUSEN
102 Executive Director Foundation .... Ms. Judith BASKER
15 Dir HR and Risk Mgmt .... Ms. Sara MOYE
24 Director Instructional Media .... Mr. Josh OGLE
109 Director Auxiliary Services .... Ms. Laura HAGA-DUFFY
26 Dir Marketing & Recruitment .... Mr. Grant WALKER
37 Director Student Financial Aid .... Ms. Anna MANLEY
14 Director I/T Network & User Support .... Mr. Mike MCCLURE
71 Director TRiO-EOC .... Mr. Jason FIANO
71 Director TRiO-SSS .... Ms. Colletta YOUNG
51 Apprenticeship Coordinator .... Ms. Cathy PIERSON
96 Contract and Procurement Manager .... Ms. Jodie FULTON
25 Grants and Planning Coordinator .... Ms. Mary O'KIEF
91 Director of IT Programming .... Mr. Al SHELDON
18 Director of Facilities/Operations .... Mr. Grant LAGORIO
20 Dir Curriculum and Scheduling .... Ms. Laura BENNETT
88 Director of Student Programs .... Ms. Rene MCKENZIE
07 Director Enrollment Services .... Mr. John DUARTE
04 Asst to President and Board .... Ms. Denise NELSON
35 Dean of Student Success .... Vacant
10 Chief Financial Officer .... Ms. Lisa STANTON
41 Vice President of Student Services .... Ms. Kori EBENHACK
108 Outcomes & Assessment Strategist .... Ms. Lori SOURS
28 Asst to VP SS and Diversity Coord .... Ms. Sharon SMITH
38 Faculty/Chair Student Counseling .... Ms. Gaia LAYSER
50 Faculty/Dept Chair Bus Tech .... Dr. Randy WADE

Southern Oregon University (A)

1250 Siskiyou Boulevard, Ashland OR 97520-5001

County: Jackson FICE Identification: 003219
Unit ID: 210146
Telephone: (541) 552-7672 Carnegie Class: Masters/L
FAX Number: (541) 552-6329 Calendar System: Quarter
URL: www.sou.edu
Established: 1872 Annual Undergrad Tuition & Fees (In-State): $8,145
Enrollment: 5,954 Coed
Affiliation or Control: State IRS Status: 501(c)3
Highest Offering: Master's
Accreditation: NW, ACBSP, CACREP, MUS

01 Interim President .... Dr. Roy H. SAIGO
05 Int Prov/VP Acad & Student Affairs .... Dr. Susan WALSH
10 VP for Finance & Administration .... Mr. Craig MORRIS
30 Int Vice President Development .... Ms. Janet FRATELLA
15 Director for Human Resource Svcs .... Vacant
100 Chief of Staff/Dir Government Rels .... Ms. Liz SHELBY
84 Assoc VP Enrollment & Retention .... Ms. Lisa GARCIA-HANSON
26 Ex Dir Interactive Mktg/Media Rels .... Ms. Nicolle ALEMAN
18 Dir for Facilities Mgmt & Planning .... Mr. Drew GILLILAND
58 Assoc Provost/Director Grad Stds .... Dr. Jody WATERS
21 Director of Business Services .... Mr. Steve LARVICK
08 University Librarian .... Mr. Jeffrey GAYTON
32 Director for Student Life .... Ms. Jennifer FOUNTAIN
51 Exec Dir Division of Continuing Edu .... Ms. Jeanne STALLMAN
19 Co-Director of Campus Public Safety .... Mr. Frederick CREEK
19 Co-Director of Campus Public Safety .... Mr. Randall SCHOEN
13 Director of Information Technology .... Mr. Brad CHRIST
29 Director of Alumni Affairs .... Mr. Mike BEAGLE
21 Assoc Director of Business Services .... Ms. Debbie MICHAELS
106 Director of Distance Education .... Dr. Vicki SUTER
88 Director of Schneider Museum of Art .... Ms. Erika LEPPMANN
88 Dir of Accelerated Baccalureate Pgm .... Mr. Curt BACON
28 Director of Diversity and Inclusion .... Ms. Marjorie TRUEBLOOD-GAMBLE
44 Annual Fund Coordinator .... Ms. Chava FLORENDO
57 Director Performing Arts .... Dr. David HUMPHREY
83 Director Social Sciences .... Dr. Dan DENEUI
97 Director Undergraduate Studies .... Dr. Lee AYERS
81 Director STEM .... Dr. Sherry ETTLICH
50 Director Business Comm & Environmt .... Dr. Greg JONES
79 Director Humanities & Culture .... Dr. Scott REX
88 Director Educ Health & Leadership .... Dr. John KING
06 Registrar .... Dr. Matt STILLMAN
07 Director of Admissions .... Ms. Kelly MOUTSATSON
37 Director of Financial Aid .... Ms. Patricia MCAULEY
09 Director of Institutional Research .... Mr. Chris STANEK
25 Chief Contracts/Grants Admin .... Ms. Joanne PRESTON
41 Athletic Director .... Mr. Matt SAYRE

Southwestern Oregon Community College (B)

1988 Newmark Avenue, Coos Bay OR 97420-2911

County: Coos FICE Identification: 003220
Unit ID: 210155
Telephone: (541) 888-2525 Carnegie Class: Assoc/MT-VT-High Trad
FAX Number: (541) 888-7285 Calendar System: Quarter
URL: www.socc.edu
Established: 1961 Annual Undergrad Tuition & Fees (In-District): $5,625
Enrollment: 2,316 Coed
Affiliation or Control: Local IRS Status: 501(c)3
Highest Offering: Associate Degree
Accreditation: NW, ACFEI, EMT

01 President .... Dr. Patty SCOTT
11 VP Administrative Services .... Mr. Eric STASAK
05 VP Instructional Services .... Dr. Ross TOMLIN
12 Dean Curry County .... Ms. Janet PRETTI
72 Dean of Career and Technical Educ .... Ms. Cody YEAGER
56 Dean of Extended Learning .... Ms. Karen DOMINE
32 Dean of Student Services .... Mr. Tim DAILEY
84 Exec Director Enrollment Management .... Mr. Tom NICHOLLS
13 Director Integrated Technology .... Mr. Rocky LAVOIE
88 Exec Director OCCI (Culinary) .... Mr. Shawn HANLIN
20 Assoc Dean of LDC & Devel Education .... Mr. Rod KELLER
41 Director Athletics .... Mr. Mike HERBERT
07 Director of Admissions .... Mr. Tom NICHOLLS
19 Director Campus Safety .... Mr. Joe THOMAS
30 Dir College Advancement/Alumni Rels .... Ms. Elise HAMNER
18 Director Facilities Services .... Ms. Emerald BRUNETT
06 Registrar .... Vacant
37 Director Financial Aid .... Ms. Avena SINGH
15 Exec Director Human Resources .... Mr. Matt GILROY
08 Manager of Learning Resources .... Ms. Alicia MUELLER
66 Director Nursing .... Ms. Susan WALKER
39 Director Residence Life .... Mr. Jeff WHITEY
88 Director SOCC Business Dev Center .... Ms. Arlene SOTO
38 Director Student Support Srvcs .... Ms. Michele BENOIT
40 Manager Bookstore .... Ms. Shawna STEPHENS
09 Institutional Researcher .... Ms. Robin BUNNELL
35 Coordinator Student Life and Events .... Mr. Kyle CROY
04 Exec Asst to the Pres/Board of Educ .... Ms. Deb NICHOLLS
10 Chief Business Officer .... Ms. Kathy DIXON
26 Chief Public Relations/Marketing .... Ms. Anne MATTHEWS

Sumner College (C)

15115 SW Sequoia Parkway, Ste 200,
Tigard OR 97224-7157

County: Multnomah FICE Identification: 021049
Unit ID: 208512
Telephone: (503) 223-5100 Carnegie Class: Spec 2-yr-Other
FAX Number: (503) 952-0010 Calendar System: Other
URL: www.sumnercollege.edu
Established: 1974 Annual Undergrad Tuition & Fees: N/A
Enrollment: 262 Coed
Affiliation or Control: Proprietary IRS Status: Proprietary
Highest Offering: Associate Degree
Accreditation: ACICS

01 President .... Jeanna S. RUSSELL

Tillamook Bay Community College (D)

4301 3rd Street, Tillamook OR 97141

County: Tillamook Identification: 666647
Unit ID: 420723
Telephone: (503) 842-8222 Carnegie Class: Assoc/HT-High Non
FAX Number: (503) 842-8336 Calendar System: Quarter
URL: www.tillamookbaycc.edu
Established: 1981 Annual Undergrad Tuition & Fees (In-District): $4,725
Enrollment: 473 Coed
Affiliation or Control: State/Local IRS Status: 501(c)3
Highest Offering: Associate Degree
Accreditation: NW

01 President .... Dr. Constance C. GREEN
05 Chief Academic Officer .... Dr. Ann HOVEY
10 Comptroller/Budget Officer .... Ms. Kyra WILLIAMS
30 Chief Development .... Mrs. Heidi LUQUETTE
32 Dir Student Services & Registrar .... Ms. Rhoda HANSON
15 Dir Human Resources/Facilities .... Mr. Pat RYAN
09 Coordinator Institutional Research .... Vacant

Treasure Valley Community College (E)

650 College Boulevard, Ontario OR 97914-3423

County: Malheur FICE Identification: 003221
Unit ID: 210234
Telephone: (541) 881-8822 Carnegie Class: Assoc/MT-VT-High Non
FAX Number: (541) 881-5525 Calendar System: Quarter
URL: www.tvcc.cc
Established: 1961 Annual Undergrad Tuition & Fees (In-District): $5,310
Enrollment: 2,396 Coed
Affiliation or Control: Local IRS Status: 501(c)3
Highest Offering: Associate Degree
Accreditation: NW, ADNUR

01 President .... Ms. Dana YOUNG
05 Vice President of Academic Affairs .... Mr. Eddie ALVES
11 Int Vice Pres Admin Services .... Mr. Kevin KIMBALL
08 Librarian .... Mr. Dennis GILL
32 Interim Vice President Student Svcs .... Ms. Michelle MCKAY
26 Assoc VP College/Public Relations .... Ms. Abby LEE
10 Comptroller .... Ms. Shirley HAIDLE
37 Financial Aid Director .... Ms. Diahann DERRICK
13 Director Information Technology .... Mr. Scott CARPENTER
07 Director of Admissions .... Ms. Stephanie OESTER
15 Director of Human Resources .... Mr. Brad VERIGAN
51 Director of Continuing Education .... Ms. Andrea TESTI
18 Dir of Housing/Building & Grounds .... Mr. Bernie BABCOCK
41 Athletic Director .... Mr. Ed ARONSON
88 Corrections Education Director .... Mr. Jeremy YRAGUEN
06 Registrar .... Vacant
09 Director of Institutional Effective .... Mr. David KOEHLER
28 Director of Diversity .... Ms. Michelle MCKAY
102 TVCC Foundation Exec Dir .... Ms. Cathy YASUDA
40 Bookstore Manager .... Mr. Kjetil ROM
04 Executive Asst to President .... Ms. Gina ROPER
84 Director Enrollment Management .... Mr. Sage MWIINGA

Umpqua Community College (F)

1140 Umpqua College Road, Roseburg OR 97470

County: Douglas FICE Identification: 003222
Unit ID: 210270
Telephone: (541) 440-4600 Carnegie Class: Assoc/MT-VT-High Non
FAX Number: (541) 440-4637 Calendar System: Quarter
URL: www.umpqua.edu
Established: 1964 Annual Undergrad Tuition & Fees (In-District): $4,678
Enrollment: 2,045 Coed
Affiliation or Control: Local IRS Status: 501(c)3
Highest Offering: Associate Degree
Accreditation: NW, ADNUR, DA, EMT

01 President .... Dr. Debra THATCHER
05 Vice President for Instruction .... Dr. Roxanne KELLY
10 Vice President/CFO .... Ms. Rebecca REDELL
32 Interim VP Student Services .... Mr. David FARRINGTON
37 Director of Financial Aid .... Ms. Michelle BERGMANN
13 Director Informational Technology .... Mr. Dan YODER
08 Director of Library Services .... Ms. Carol MCGEEHON
103 Director of Community/Workforce .... Ms. Robin VAN WINKLE
09 Director Institutional Research .... Ms. Xiana SMITHHART
15 Director of Human Resources .... Ms. Lynn JOHNSON
04 Administrative Asst to President .... Ms. Robynne WILGUS
06 Registrar .... Mr. David FARRINGTON
30 Chief Development/Advancement .... Ms. Susan TAYLOR

University of Oregon (G)

1585 E. 13th Avenue, Eugene OR 97403

County: Lane FICE Identification: 003223
Unit ID: 209551
Telephone: (541) 346-1000 Carnegie Class: DU-Highest
FAX Number: (541) 346-3017 Calendar System: Quarter
URL: www.uoregon.edu
Established: 1876 Annual Undergrad Tuition & Fees (In-State): $10,289
Enrollment: 24,396 Coed
Affiliation or Control: State IRS Status: 501(c)3
Highest Offering: Doctorate
Accreditation: NW, ART, BUS, BUSA, CAATE, CEA, CIDA, CLPSY, COPSY, CSHSE, IPSY, JOUR, LAW, LSAR, MFCD, MUS, PCSAS, PLNG, SCPSY, SP, SPAA

01 President .... Mr. Michael H. SCHILL
100 Senior Advisor/Chief of Staff .... Mr. Greg J. STRIPP
05 Senior Vice President & Provost .... Dr. Scott L. COLTRANE
10 VP Finance & Admin & CFO .... Ms. Jamie H. MOFFITT
32 Vice President for Student Life .... Dr. Robin H. HOLMES
30 Vice Pres University Advancement .... Mr. Michael C. ANDREASEN
46 VP Research/Dean Graduate School .... Vacant
26 VP University Communications .... Mr. Kyle HENLEY
43 Vice President and General Counsel .... Mr. Kevin REED
20 Vice Provost Undergraduate Studies .... Dr. Lisa FREINKEL
28 Vice Pres Inst Equity/Diversity .... Dr. Yvette M. ALEX-ASSENSOH
13 Vice Prov Information Services/CIO .... Vacant
85 Vice Provost International Affairs .... Dr. Dennis C. GALVAN
86 Assoc Vice Pres Federal Affairs .... Ms. Betsy A. BOYD
29 AVP Alumni Affairs/Exec Dir UOAA .... Ms. Kelly MENACHEMSON
43 Actg General Counsel to University .... Mr. Doug Y. PARK
102 Chief Investment Officer Foundation .... Mr. Jay NAMYET
06 University Registrar .... Ms. Susan M. EVELAND
07 Director of Admissions .... Mr. Jim H. RAWLINS
08 Philip H Knight Dean of Libraries .... Dr. Adriene I. LIM
21 Dir Business Affairs and Controller .... Mr. Kelly B. WOLF
37 Director Student Financial Aid .... Mr. Jim J. BROOKS
36 Director of Career Center .... Dr. Daniel PASCOE AGUILAR
15 Chief Human Resources Officer .... Ms. Nancy E. RESNICK
18 Assoc VP Campus Operations .... Mr. George E. HECHT
22 Director Affirmative Action .... Ms. Penny J. DAUGHERTY
41 Director Intercollegiate Athletics .... Mr. Rob A. MULLENS
56 Executive Dir UO Academic Extension .... Ms. Sandra K. GLADNEY
49 Int Dean College Arts & Sciences .... Dr. W. Andrew MARCUS
48 Actg Dean Architecture/Allied Arts .... Mr. Brook W. MULLER
50 Dean College of Business .... Dr. Cornelis A. DE KLUYVER
53 Dean College of Education .... Dr. Randy W. KAMPHAUS
60 Actg Dean School of Journ & Comm .... Ms. Julianne H. NEWTON
58 Dean of Graduate School .... Dr. Scott L. PRATT
61 Dean School of Law .... Mr. Michael L. MOFFITT
64 Dean School of Music & Dance .... Dr. Brad FOLEY
92 Dean Clark Honors College .... Dr. Terry L. HUNT
09 Director of Institutional Research .... Dr. JP MONROE
35 Associate VP for Student Life .... Mr. Michael E. EYSTER
38 Dir Counseling & Testing Center .... Dr. Shelly K. KERR
84 VP for Enrollment Management .... Mr. Roger J. THOMPSON
96 Dir Purchasing & Contracting Svcs .... Ms. Catherine D. SUSMAN
101 Secretary of the Institution/Board .... Ms. Angela WILHELMS
19 Chief of Police .... Vacant
39 Director Student Housing .... Mr. Michael M. GRIFFEL
44 Director Annual Giving Program .... Mr. Rick F. ERICSON
45 Vice Provost Budget & Planning .... Dr. Brad SHELTON
90 Director Academic Technology .... Ms. Helen Y. CHU

University of Phoenix Oregon Campus (A)

13221 SW 68th Parkway, Tigard OR 97223-8328
Telephone: (503) 403-2900 Identification: 770222
Accreditation: &NH, ACBSP

† No longer accepting campus-based students.

University of Portland (B)

5000 N Willamette Boulevard, Portland OR 97203-5798
County: Multnomah FICE Identification: 003224
Unit ID: 209825
Telephone: (503) 943-8000 Carnegie Class: Masters/M
FAX Number: (503) 943-7491 Calendar System: Semester
URL: www.up.edu
Established: 1901 Annual Undergrad Tuition & Fees: $42,288
Enrollment: 4,143 Coed
Affiliation or Control: Independent Non-Profit IRS Status: 501(c)3
Highest Offering: Doctorate
Accreditation: NW, BUS, CS, ENG, MUS, NURSE, SW, TED, THEA

01 President ... Rev. Mark L. POORMAN, CSC
05 Provost ... Dr. Thomas G. GREENE
26 Vice Pres for University Relations . Rev. Gerard J. OLINGER, CSC
11 Vice Pres for University Operations ... Mr. James B. RAVELLI
10 Vice Pres for Financial Affairs ... Mr. Alan P. TIMMINS
32 Vice President for Student Affairs ... Rev. John J. DONATO, CSC
43 Gen Couns & Specia Asst to the Pres ... Ms. Danielle E. HERMANNY
07 Dean of Admissions ... Mr. Jason S. MCDONALD
21 Controller ... Mr. Eric C. BARGER
06 Registrar ... Ms. Roberta D. LINDAHL
08 Head Librarian ... Ms. Xan ARCH
30 Sr Assoc Vice President Development ... Mr. Bryce B. STRANG
36 Director Career Services ... Ms. Amy CAVANAUGH
15 Assoc VP for Human Resources ... Ms. Sandy CHUNG
37 Director Student Financial Aid ... Ms. Janet K. TURNER
27 Director of Marketing ... Ms. Rachel E. BARRY-ARQUIT
49 Dean of Arts & Sciences ... Dr. Michael F. ANDREWS
50 Dean of the Business School ... Dr. Robin D. ANDERSON
66 Dean of Nursing ... Dr. Joane T. MOCERI
54 Dean of Engineering ... Dr. Sharon A. JONES
53 Dean of Education ... Dr. John L. WATZKE
23 Director University Health Services ... Ms. Margaret TROUT
19 Director of Public Safety ... Mr. Gerald A. GREGG
29 Director Alumni Relations ... Mr. Craig SWINYARD
39 Director Residence Life ... Mr. Christopher HAUG
41 Athletic Director ... Mr. Scott LEYKAM
42 Director Campus Ministry ... Rev. James T. GALLAGHER, CSC
102 Director Foundation Relations ... Mr. Tim FOLEY
18 Director Facilities Planning Constr ... Mr. Paul J. LUTY
18 Director Physical Plant ... Mr. Andre HUTCHINSON
40 Director Bookstore ... Ms. Erin L. BRIGHT
88 Director University Events ... Mr. William O. REED
09 Director of Institutional Research ... Vacant
35 Director Student Activities ... Mr. Jeromy A. KOFFLER
04 Administrative Asst to President ... Ms. Kathy M. SIMEK
104 Director Study Abroad ... Mr. Eduardo CONTRERAS
13 Chief Info Technology Officer ... Mr. Curtis PEDERSON
44 Director Annual or Planned Giving ... Ms. Sharon HOGAN

University of Western States (C)

2900 NE 132nd Avenue, Portland OR 97230-3099
County: Multnomah FICE Identification: 012309
Unit ID: 210438
Telephone: (503) 256-3180 Carnegie Class: Spec-4-yr-Other Health
FAX Number: (503) 251-5723 Calendar System: Quarter
URL: www.uws.edu
Established: 1904 Annual Undergrad Tuition & Fees: N/A
Enrollment: 690 Coed
Affiliation or Control: Independent Non-Profit IRS Status: 501(c)3
Highest Offering: Doctorate
Accreditation: NW, CHIRO, COMTA

01 President ... Dr. Joseph BRIMHALL
10 Chief Business Officer ... Ms. Lisa LOPEZ
05 Provost/VP Academic Affairs ... Dr. Bernadette HOWLETT
88 Special Assistant to the President ... Dr. Patrick BROWNE
23 Vice President of Clinic Affairs ... Dr. Joseph PFEIFER
09 Ex Dir Institutional Effectiveness ... Dr. Rebekah ANDERSON
86 VP for University Affairs ... Ms. Rosalia MESSINA
109 Assoc VP for University Operations ... Ms. Sara MATHOV
46 Assoc Vice President of Research ... Dr. Mitch HAAS
23 Assoc VP of Clinical Internships ... Dr. Stanley EWALD
13 Director of Information Technology ... Mr. Erick RUIZ
84 Dean of Enrollment & Student Svcs ... Dr. Colman JOYCE
26 Dir of PR/Marketing/Communications ... Ms. Megan NUGENT
15 Director Human Resources ... Ms. Kathleen CANNON
06 Registrar ... Ms. Michelle DODGE
08 University Librarian ... Ms. Janet TAPPER
108 Exec Director Academic Assessment ... Mr. Jim MASCENIK
07 Director of Admissions ... Ms. Mary STAFFORD
18 Director Campus Facilities ... Mr. Terry COWDIN
37 Director Financial Aid ... Mr. Peter GROSS
31 Director of Community Relations/CE ... Ms. Alisa FAIRWEATHER
21 Controller ... Ms. Olga KLOCHKOVA
30 Development Officer ... Ms. Kelli RULE

Warner Pacific College (D)

2219 SE 68th Avenue, Portland OR 97215
County: Multnomah FICE Identification: 003225
Unit ID: 210304
Telephone: (503) 517-1000 Carnegie Class: Bac-Diverse
FAX Number: (503) 517-1350 Calendar System: Semester
URL: www.warnerpacific.edu
Established: 1937 Annual Undergrad Tuition & Fees: $21,460
Enrollment: 554 Coed
Affiliation or Control: Church Of God IRS Status: 501(c)3
Highest Offering: Master's
Accreditation: NW, @SW

01 President ... Dr. Andrea P. COOK
05 Vice Pres Acad Affs/Dean of Faculty ... Dr. Reginald NICHOLS
10 Vice Pres of Operations ... Mr. Steve STENBERG
30 Vice President for Inst Advancement ... Mr. Aaron MCMURRAY
32 Dean of Students ... Mr. Jon SAMPSON
20 Assoc VP for Acad Affairs/Dean ADP ... Dr. Lori K. JASS
84 VP for Enrollment and Marketing ... Mr. Dale SEIPP
37 Dir of Student Financial Services ... Mrs. Cindy POLLARD
07 Director of Admissions ... Mr. Geraldo CIFUENTES
41 Director of Athletics ... Vacant
08 Director of Library Services ... Vacant
06 Registrar ... Ms. Victoria R. CUMINGS
13 Director of Information Technology ... Ms. Linda RUDAWITZ
29 Director of Alumni/Church Relations ... Ms. Serena CLINE
88 Dir of Contextualized Ministries ... Dr. Jess BIELMAN
42 Associate Dir Campus Ministries ... Ms. Michelle LANG
39 Dir of Res Life & Judicial Affairs ... Mr. Jared VALENTINE
18 Director of Facilities ... Mr. Dean JENKS
15 Dir of Human Resources/Prof Devel ... Mrs. Bev FITTS
09 Dir of Institutional Effectiveness ... Vacant
40 Director Bookstore ... Mrs. Mimi FONSECA
26 Marketing/College Relations ... Ms. Melody BURTON
38 Director Student Counseling ... Dr. Carol DELLOLIVER
21 Associate Business Officer ... Mr. Nathan DUNBAR
36 Director of Academic Success ... Mr. Rod JOHANSON

Western Oregon University (E)

345 N Monmouth Avenue, Monmouth OR 97361-1394
County: Polk FICE Identification: 003209
Unit ID: 210429
Telephone: (503) 838-8000 Carnegie Class: Masters/M
FAX Number: (503) 838-8474 Calendar System: Quarter
URL: www.wou.edu
Established: 1856 Annual Undergrad Tuition & Fees (In-State): $9,369
Enrollment: 6,049 Coed
Affiliation or Control: State IRS Status: 501(c)3
Highest Offering: Beyond Master's But Less Than Doctorate
Accreditation: NW, CORE, MUS, TED

01 President ... Dr. Rex FULLER
03 Vice President & General Counsel ... Mr. Ryan HAGEMANN
05 Provost/Vice Pres Academic Affairs ... Dr. Stephen SCHECK
32 Vice President Student Affairs ... Dr. Gary DUKES
10 Vice Pres Finance & Administration ... Mr. Eric YAHNKE
35 Dean of Students ... Ms. Tina M. FUCHS
49 Dean Col Liberal Arts & Sciences ... Dr. Susanne MONAHAN
53 Dean College of Education ... Dr. Mark GIROD
20 Associate Provost ... Mr. David MCDONALD
56 Director Division Extended Progams ... Mr. Dan CLARK
06 Registrar ... Ms. Amy CLARK
30 Director of Development ... Mr. Tommy LOVE
08 Dean Hamersly Library ... Dr. Allen MCKIEL
13 Director University Computing Svcs ... Mr. William KERNAN
15 Director Human Resources ... Ms. Judy J. VANDERBURG
18 Director Physical Plant ... Mr. Tom NEAL
19 Director University Public Safety ... Ms. Rebecca CHILES
23 Dir Student Health/Counseling Ctr ... Mr. Jaime SILVA
26 Dir Public Relations/Communications ... Ms. Denise VISUANO
32 Dir Student Leadership & Activities ... Mr. Patrick MOSER
37 Director Financial Aid ... Ms. Kella HELYER
41 Athletic Director ... Ms. Barbara DEARING
46 Dir of Teaching Research Institute ... Dr. Ella TAYLOR
85 Dir Intl Students/Scholars Affairs ... Mr. Neng YANG
88 Dir Multicultural Student Svcs/ Pgms ... Ms. Anna HERNANDEZ-HUNTER
22 Director AAEO ... Ms. Judy J. VANDERBURG
29 Dir Leadership Giving/Athletic Dev ... Mr. Michael FEULING
04 Executive Asst to President ... Mrs. LouAnn VICKERS
21 Director of Business Services ... Mr. Darin SILBERNAGEL
07 Director of Admissions ... Mr. Rob FINDTNER

Western Seminary (F)

5511 SE Hawthorne Boulevard, Portland OR 97215-3399
County: Multnomah FICE Identification: 007178
Unit ID: 210368
Telephone: (503) 517-1800 Carnegie Class: Spec-4-yr-Faith
FAX Number: (503) 517-1801 Calendar System: Semester
URL: www.westernseminary.edu
Established: 1927 Annual Graduate Tuition & Fees: N/A
Enrollment: 743 Coed
Affiliation or Control: Independent Non-Profit IRS Status: 501(c)3
Highest Offering: Doctorate; No Undergraduates
Accreditation: NW, CACREP, THEOL

01 President ... Dr. Randal R. ROBERTS
10 Administrative Vice President/CFO ... Mr. Wing-Kit CHUNG
05 Academic Dean ... Dr. Rob WIGGINS
88 VP of Educ Innovation/Global Outrea ... Andy PETERSON
30 VP for Advancement/Dir Alumni Rels ... Mr. Greg MOON
20 Associate Academic Dean ... Vacant
06 Dean Student Devel/Registrar ... Dr. Reid KISLING
21 Controller ... Ms. Patricia A. PRICHARD
32 Dean of Students ... Mr. Andy PELOQUIN
36 Director of Student Placement ... Dr. Larry MCCRACKEN
13 Director of Information Services ... Mr. Doug MABRY
37 Financial Aid Director ... Ms. Shelle RIEHL
56 Asst Director of Distance Education ... Mr. Jon RAIBLEY
88 Assistant Registrar ... Ms. Hannah HAYES
15 Human Resources Director ... Ms. Julia EIDENBERG
08 Library Director ... Dr. Robert A. KRUPP
84 Director Enrollment Services/Mktg ... Mr. P.J OSWALD
18 Chief Facilities/Physical Plant ... Mr. Cliff STEIN
106 Director of Distance Education ... Mr. James STEWART
07 Director of Admissions ... Mr. Demetrius ROGERS

Willamette University (G)

900 State Street, Salem OR 97301-3930
County: Marion FICE Identification: 003227
Unit ID: 210401
Telephone: (503) 370-6300 Carnegie Class: Bac-A&S
FAX Number: (503) 370-6148 Calendar System: Semester
URL: www.willamette.edu
Established: 1842 Annual Undergrad Tuition & Fees: $45,617
Enrollment: 2,780 Coed
Affiliation or Control: Independent Non-Profit IRS Status: 501(c)3
Highest Offering: Doctorate
Accreditation: NW, BUS, CEA, LAW, MUS, SPAA

01 President ... Dr. Stephen THORSETT
10 Senior VP Finance & Administration ... Ms. Monica RIMAI
05 Vice Pres Academic Affs/Dean ... Dr. Carol LONG
30 Vice President for Advancement ... Ms. Shelby RADCLIFFE
07 Vice President Enrollment/Registrar ... Mr. Michael BESEDA
13 Chief Information Officer ... Ms. Jacqueline BARRETTA
18 VP Capital Planning & Facilities ... Mr. James R. BAUER
32 Vice President for Campus Life ... Dr. Edward G. WHIPPLE
49 Dean of the College Liberal Arts ... Dr. Ruth P. FEINGOLD
61 Dean of Law ... Mr. Curtis BRIDGEMAN
50 Dean Graduate School Management ... Ms. Debra RINGOLD
42 Chaplain ... Dr. Karen WOOD
23 Director of Bishop Wellness Center ... Mr. Donald A. THOMSON
88 Director Center Dispute Resolution ... Dr. Richard BIRKE
91 Director Administrative Computing .. Mr. Harvey J. PRUDHOMME
37 Director Student Financial Aid ... Ms. Patricia K. HOBAN
09 Director of Institutional Research ... Dr. Michael J. MOON
06 University Registrar ... Ms. Laura JACOBS ANDERSON
08 University Librarian ... Mr. Craig MILBERG
21 Controller ... Mr. Kenneth PIFER
40 Bookstore Director ... Mr. Donald C. BECKMAN
104 Director of International Education ... Mr. Kris LOU
41 Athletic Director ... Ms. Valerie A. CLEARY
29 Assistant VP Alumni Relations ... Mr. James LIPPINCOTT
44 Senior Director Gift Planning & Dev ... Ms. Lori L. HOBY
15 Associate VP Human Resources ... Ms. Shana SECHRIST
35 Director of Student Activities ... Ms. Lisa C. HOLLIDAY
36 Director Career Services ... Vacant
28 Director of Multicultural Affairs ... Mr. Gordon K. TOYAMA
18 Manager Operations/Energy ... Mr. Gary GRIMM
96 Purchasing Coordinator ... Ms. Kindra K. JORDAY
26 Int Dir Marketing Communications ... Mr. Adam TORGERSON
19 Director Security/Safety ... Mr. Ross STOUT

PENNSYLVANIA

Albright College (H)

13th & Bern Streets, PO Box 15234,
Reading PA 19612-5234
County: Berks FICE Identification: 003229
Unit ID: 210571
Telephone: (610) 921-2381 Carnegie Class: Bac-A&S
FAX Number: (610) 921-7530 Calendar System: 4/1/4
URL: www.albright.edu
Established: 1856 Annual Undergrad Tuition & Fees: $39,850
Enrollment: 2,393 Coed
Affiliation or Control: United Methodist IRS Status: 501(c)3
Highest Offering: Master's
Accreditation: M

01 President ... Dr. Lex O. MCMILLAN, III
05 Provost & VP Academic Affairs ... Dr. Mary MCGEE
10 Vice President Finance & Admin ... Mr. Gregory L. FULMER
30 Vice President Advancement ... Ms. Deborah M. MCCREERY
84 VP Enrollment Mgt/Dean Admission ... Mr. Gregory E. EICHHORN
32 VP Student Affairs/Dean of Students ... Dr. Gina-Lyn CRANCE
26 Assoc VP College Relations/Mktg ... Mr. Thomas W. DURSO
13 Chief Information Officer ... Ms. Rashmi RADHAKRISHNAN
04 Executive Assistant to President ... Mrs. Kathy L. CAFONCELLI
20 Dean of Undergraduate Studies ... Dr. Joseph THOMAS
08 Interim Library Director ... Ms. Sandra STUMP
44 Asst VP for Development ... Mr. Jud CRIHFIELD
14 Sr Dir of Information Tech Svcs ... Mr. Hoerr U. JASON
21 Controller ... Mr. Rick W. MELCHER
37 Director of Financial Aid ... Mr. Christopher HANLON
58 Chair of Education Graduate Program ... Dr. Rodney E. WARFIELD
35 Assistant Dean of Students ... Ms. Amanda HANINCIK

06 Registrar ...... Mr. David C. BALLABAN
36 Director Career Development Center ...... Ms. Karen V. EVANS
39 Director of Residential Life ...... Mr. Timothy R. MORAN
38 Director of Counseling Center ...... Dr. Brenda J. INGRAM-WALLACE
29 Dir of Alumni Relations ...... Mrs. Karen MORAN
18 Director Facilities/Operations/Svcs ...... Mr. Timothy RISSEL
41 Co-Athletic Director ...... Mr. Richard E. FERRY
41 Co-Athletic Director ...... Ms. Janice J. LUCK
19 Director of Safety & Security ...... Mr. Michael L. GROSS
40 Book Store Manager ...... Ms. Coreen MCCAFFERTY
23 Director of Gable Health Center ...... Ms. Samantha WESNER
42 Chaplain ...... Rev. Paul E. CLARK
22 Affirmative Action Coord/Dir HR ...... Ms. Kimberly A. HUBRIC
85 Asst Dir Multi-Ethnic Student Affs ...... Ms. Tiffany CLAYTON
88 Dir of Accelerated & Grad Program ...... Mr. Kevin EZZELL
09 Director of Institutional Research ...... Mr. Jack LAFAYETTE
35 Director of Student Involvement ...... Mr. Bradley A. SMITH
25 Dir of Corp & Foundation Relations ...... Ms. Charlene WYSOCKI
92 Director Honors Program ...... Dr. Julia F. HEBERLE
07 Director of Admission ...... Ms. Jennifer WILLIAMSON
88 Director of Conferences ...... Ms. Lois A. KUBINAK

Allegheny College (A)

520 N Main Street, Meadville PA 16335-3902
County: Crawford | FICE Identification: 003230
Unit ID: 210669
Telephone: (814) 332-3100 | Carnegie Class: Bac-A&S
FAX Number: (814) 332-2796 | Calendar System: Semester
URL: www.allegheny.edu
Established: 1815 | Annual Undergrad Tuition & Fees: $42,470
Enrollment: 2,023 | Coed
Affiliation or Control: United Methodist | IRS Status: 501(c)3
Highest Offering: Baccalaureate
Accreditation: M

01 President ...... Dr. James H. MULLEN
03 Exec Vice President and COO ...... Vacant
30 Vice Pres Devel & Alumni Affairs ...... Ms. Marjorie S. KLEIN
84 VP for Enrollment & Dean of Admiss ...... Mr. Cornell LESANE, II
04 Assistant to the President ...... Ms. Pamela S. HIGHAM
28 AVP for Diversity & Org Development ...... Dr. Andrea D AZ
10 Sr Assoc Vice President of Finance ...... Vacant
45 Assoc Vice Pres for Advancement ...... Vacant
29 AVP Development & Alumni Affairs ...... Mr. Philip R. FOXMAN
26 Vice President College Relations ...... Ms. Susan SALTON
05 Provost & Dean of the College ...... Dr. Ronald B. COLE
32 VP & Dean of Students ...... Dr. Kimberly FERGUSON
28 Assoc Dean/Dir CIASS ...... Mr. Justin ADKINS
20 Associate Provost ...... Dr. Terry BENSEL
37 Director Financial Aid ...... Mr. Jonathan BOLERATZ
108 VP for Info Svcs & Assessment ...... Dr. Richard A. HOLMGREN
06 Registrar ...... Dr. Ian BINNINGTON
08 Director of the Library ...... Ms. Linda G. BILLS
15 Director of Human Resources ...... Ms. Patricia A. FERREY
19 Director Campus Safety & Security ...... Vacant
44 Director of Annual Giving ...... Ms. Sara PINEO
18 Director Physical Plant ...... Mr. Cliff K. WILLIS
91 Associate Director of Info Tech Svc ...... Mr. Richard A. METZGER
41 Director of Athletics ...... Ms. Portia HOEG
31 Director of Civic Engagement ...... Dr. David RONCOLATO
13 Dir Tech Computer & Networking Svcs ...... Mr. Tim W. HUNTER
100 Chief of Staff ...... Vacant
38 Director of Counseling Center ...... Ms. Theresa PALASKI
102 AVP of Development ...... Dr. Ann H. ARESON
09 Director of Institutional Research ...... Ms. Marian D. SHERWOOD
36 Director Career Education ...... Mr. James FITCH
35 Associate Dean of Students ...... Ms. Jacquelyn KONDROT
21 CFO & Treasurer ...... Ms. Linda S. WETSELL
42 Chaplain ...... Dr. Jane Ellen NICKELL
88 Dir Center Political Participation ...... Dr. Brian HARWARD
22 Director of Disability Services ...... Mr. John J. MANGINE
57 Art Director ...... Ms. Penny M. DREXEL
07 Sr Asst Director of Admissions ...... Mr. Jason ANDRACKI
40 Manager of Bookstore ...... Mr. Peter M. LEBAR
96 Purchasing & Student Services Coord ...... Ms. Kathleen M. CONAWAY
88 Int Assoc Dir Student Involvement ...... Ms. Jayne PISKORIK

Allegany College of Maryland Bedford County Campus (B)

18 North River Lane, Everett PA 15337-1410
Telephone: (814) 652-9528 | Identification: 770124
Accreditation: &M

† Regional accreditation is carried under the parent institution in Cumberland, MD

Allegany College of Maryland Somerset County Campus (C)

6022 Glades Pike, Suite 100, Somerset PA 15501-4300
Telephone: (814) 445-9848 | Identification: 770123
Accreditation: &M

† Regional accreditation is carried under the parent institution in Cumberland, MD

Alvernia University (D)

400 Saint Bernardine Street, Reading PA 19607-1799
County: Berks | FICE Identification: 003233
Unit ID: 210775
Telephone: (610) 796-8200 | Carnegie Class: Masters/M
FAX Number: (610) 777-6632 | Calendar System: Semester
URL: www.alvernia.edu
Established: 1958 | Annual Undergrad Tuition & Fees: $31,100
Enrollment: 2,917 | Coed
Affiliation or Control: Roman Catholic | IRS Status: 501(c)3
Highest Offering: Doctorate
Accreditation: M, ACBSP, CAATE, NURSE, OT, @PTA, SW

01 President ...... Dr. Thomas F. FLYNN
05 Provost ...... Dr. Shirley J. WILLIAMS
10 VP for Finance & Administration ...... Mr. Douglas F. SMITH
30 Vice Pres for Advancement ...... Mr. Tony DEMARCO
32 Vice Pres Univ Life/Dean of Stdnts ...... Dr. Joseph J. CICALA, RSM
84 Vice Pres for Enrollment Management ...... Mr. John F. MCCLOSKEY, JR.
42 Asst to the President For Mission ...... Sr. Roberta MCKELVIE, OSF
26 VP Mktg & Comms/Chief PR Ofcr ...... Mr. Brad DREXLER
35 Director of Student Activities ...... Ms. Abby SWATCHICK
39 Director Residence Life ...... Ms. Karolina DREHER
06 Registrar ...... Ms. Beki STEIN
21 Controller ...... Mr. Larry SHAUB
29 Assoc VP of Advancement ...... Mr. Thomas MINICK
92 Director Honors Program ...... Dr. Victoria WILLIAMS
41 Director Athletics & Recreation ...... Mr. Bill STILES
07 Dean of UG Admissions ...... Ms. Rebecca FINNKENNEY
09 Director of Institutional Research ...... Dr. Evelina PANAYOTOVA
15 Director Human Resources ...... Ms. Laurel CLINE
18 Dir of Facilities Planning ...... Mr. David REPPERT
36 Director of Career Services ...... Mrs. Megan ADUKAITIS
27 Dir of Marketing/Communications ...... Ms. Tricia SZURGOT
37 Dir of Student Financial Planning ...... Ms. Christine SAADI
96 Procurement Manager ...... Ms. Ann NAWROCKI
28 Dir of Multicultural Initiatives ...... Ms. Wanda COPELAND
21 Director of Student Billing ...... Ms. Gwynne KOLODZIEJSKI
31 Dir Ctr for Community Engagement ...... Mr. Jay WORRALL
58 Dean of Graduate & Cont Studies ...... Ms. Daria LATORRE
49 Dean of Arts & Sciences ...... Dr. Beth ROTH
76 Dean of Professional Programs ...... Ms. Karen S. THACKER
04 Assistant to the President ...... Ms. Karen SCHRODER
13 Chief Info Technology Officer (CIO) ...... Ms. Robin ALLEN
19 Director of Public Safety ...... Mr. Edward HEIM
08 Director of Library ...... Ms. Sharon NEAL
25 Director of Grants ...... Ms. Mary RIZZO

The American College of Financial Services (E)

270 S Bryn Mawr Avenue, Bryn Mawr PA 19010-2196
County: Delaware | FICE Identification: 033173
Unit ID: 210809
Telephone: (610) 526-1000 | Carnegie Class: Spec-4-yr-Bus
FAX Number: (610) 526-1310 | Calendar System: Quarter
URL: www.theamericancollege.edu
Established: 1927 | Annual Graduate Tuition & Fees: N/A
Enrollment: 20,911 | Coed
Affiliation or Control: Independent Non-Profit | IRS Status: 501(c)3
Highest Offering: Doctorate; No Undergraduates
Accreditation: M

01 President & CEO ...... Dr. Robert R. JOHNSON
11 Executive Vice President & COO ...... Mr. Keith E. HICKERSON
05 Dean & Chief Academic Office ...... Dr. Michael FINKE
30 Sr Vice President Advancement ...... Mr. Charles CRONIN
15 VP Admin & Chief HR Officer ...... Ms. Debra GLENN
45 VP Organizational Effectiveness ...... Mr. Bryan JOHNSON
32 VP Student Experience ...... Mr. Brian KAIN
04 Assistant to the President ...... Ms. Mary C. VARNER
10 Chief Financial and Risk Officer ...... Mr. Gary TANG
26 Chief Marketing Officer ...... Mr. Jack HONDROS
13 Chief Technology Officer ...... Mr. Ed M. MCEVOY
108 AVP Institutional Assessment ...... Mr. Thomas ARMINGTON
06 Registrar ...... Ms. Antoinette CHRISTALDI
08 Head of Library Services ...... Mr. John H. WHITHAM
88 Director Exam Systems ...... Ms. Diane M. HAMMONDS
88 Chief Product & Innovation Officer ...... Mr. David EURICH

Antonelli Institute (F)

300 Montgomery Avenue, Erdenheim PA 19038-8242
County: Montgomery | FICE Identification: 007430
Unit ID: 210890
Telephone: (215) 836-2222 | Carnegie Class: Spec 2-yr-A&S
FAX Number: (215) 836-2794 | Calendar System: Semester
URL: www.antonelli.edu
Established: 1938 | Annual Undergrad Tuition & Fees: $19,830
Enrollment: 188 | Coed
Affiliation or Control: Proprietary | IRS Status: Proprietary
Highest Offering: Associate Degree
Accreditation: ACCSC

01 President ...... Mr. John E. HAYDEN
05 Director of Education/Student Svcs ...... Ms. Trish FLEMING
37 Financial Aid Officer ...... Ms. Stephanie BROCKLEHURST

Arcadia University (G)

450 S Easton Road, Glenside PA 19038-3295
County: Montgomery | FICE Identification: 003235
Unit ID: 211088
Telephone: (215) 572-2900 | Carnegie Class: Bac-A&S
FAX Number: (215) 572-0240 | Calendar System: Semester
URL: www.arcadia.edu
Established: 1853 | Annual Undergrad Tuition & Fees: $39,560
Enrollment: 3,939 | Coed
Affiliation or Control: Independent Non-Profit | IRS Status: 501(c)3
Highest Offering: Doctorate
Accreditation: M, ACBSP, ARCPA, ART, FEPAC, PH, PTA

01 President ...... Dr. Nicolette D. CHRISTENSEN
05 Provost & VP Academic Affairs ...... Dr. John HOFFMAN
84 VP Enrollment Management ...... Mr. Mark LAPREZIOSA
10 VP Finance & Treasurer ...... Mr. Eric R. NELSON
26 VP University Relations ...... Dr. Matthew GOLDEN
43 General Counsel ...... Mr. Michael KOROLISHIN
13 Chief Information Officer ...... Vacant
30 VP University Advancement ...... Ms. Mary MCRAE
88 VP/Exec Dir Col of Global Studies ...... Ms. Lorna STERN
32 Dean of Students ...... Mr. Andrew GORETSKY
18 Assoc VP Facilities/Capital Plng ...... Mr. Thomas J. MACCHI
21 Assoc VP Finance & COO TCGS ...... Ms. Colleen BURKE
15 Assoc VP Human Resources ...... Ms. Rhonda HOSPEDALES
20 Deputy Provost ...... Dr. Thomas EGAN
06 Registrar ...... Mr. William ELNICK
06 Associate Registrar ...... Mrs. Nicole M. ZUCKER
49 Int Dean College Arts & Sciences ...... Dr. Sandra CRENSHAW
76 Dean College of Health Sciences ...... Dr. Rebecca L. CRAIK
51 Coord Office of Continuing Studies ...... Ms. Kathryn PHILLIPS
50 Dean School of Global Business ...... Dr. Alla WILSON
58 Dean Graduate & Undergrad Studies ...... Ms. Nancy ROSOFF
82 Dean International Affairs ...... Dr. Warren HAFFAR
53 Dean School of Education ...... Dr. Graciela SLESARANSKY-POE
28 Assoc Dean Institutional Diversity ...... Ms. Judith DALTON
35 Assoc Dean of Students ...... Ms. Dian TAYLOR-ALLEYNE
20 Assoc Dean Undergraduate Studies ...... Mr. Bruce KELLER
88 Asst Dean Graduate Studies ...... Ms. Mary Kate MCNULTY
37 Exec Dir Federal Aid Pgms & FA ...... Ms. Elizabeth RIHL-LEWINSKY
14 Deputy CIO Operations & Plans ...... Mr. Eric MCCLOY
109 Director Auxiliary Services ...... Ms. Mimi BASSETTI
29 Director Alumni Relations ...... Mr. Jeffery SPENCE
88 Director University Art Gallery ...... Mr. Richard TORCHIA
41 Director Athletics & Recreation ...... Mr. Brian GRANATA
88 Director Campus Visits and EM ...... Ms. Kathleen BEARDSLEY
36 Director Career Education ...... Ms. Marissa DEITCH
38 Director Counseling Services ...... Ms. Amy HENNING
37 Exec Director EM & Financial Aid ...... Ms. Holly R. KIRKPATRICK
91 Director Enterprise Applications ...... Mr. Scott GRABUS
25 Director Sponsored Research ...... Ms. Nataliia SHABLIA
09 Director Institutional Research ...... Mr. Will PADDOCK
88 Director of Academic Administration ...... Ms. Kristin O. JUDGE
88 Assoc Dean Instr Tech & Lib Res ...... Dr. Jeanne BUCKLEY
96 Purchasing Coordinator ...... Ms. Jennifer SUDLOW
88 Payroll Manager ...... Ms. Sharon ANTHONY
19 Director of Public Safety ...... Ms. Joanna GALLAGHER
39 Asst Dean of Students ...... Mr. James POOLE
88 Title IX Coordinator ...... Ms. Nora NELLE
101 Executive Dir Board of Trustees ...... Mr. Kevin MULDOON
104 Assoc Dean International Affairs ...... Ms. Janice FINN
04 Administrative Manager Pres Office ...... Ms. Joemille SANTIAGO

Art Institute of Philadelphia (H)

1622 Chestnut Street, Philadelphia PA 19103-5198
County: Philadelphia | FICE Identification: 008350
Unit ID: 210942
Telephone: (215) 567-7080 | Carnegie Class: Spec-4-yr-Arts
FAX Number: (215) 405-6398 | Calendar System: Quarter
URL: www.artinstitutes.edu/philadelphia
Established: 1971 | Annual Undergrad Tuition & Fees: $17,916
Enrollment: 1,953 | Coed
Affiliation or Control: Proprietary | IRS Status: Proprietary
Highest Offering: Baccalaureate
Accreditation: M, ACFEI, CIDA

01 President ...... Mr. Bob JAMES
05 Dean of Academic Affairs ...... Dr. Harry COSTIGAN
10 Regional Director of Finance ...... Mr. Norman BEASLEY
07 Director of Admissions ...... Ms. Amanda HOSKING
36 Director of Career Services ...... Ms. Kimberly BURNS
20 Assoc Dean of Academic Affairs ...... Mr. Harry COSTIGAN
32 Dean of Students ...... Mr. John ROBINSON
37 Director Student Financial Services ...... Ms. Tanya YOUNG
06 Registrar ...... Ms. Adriane MEDFORD
08 Library Director ...... Ms. Marie DENNIS
38 Counselor/Disability Coordinator ...... Ms. Lisa STANKIEWICZ
40 Manager Supply Store ...... Ms. Sharon MASULLO

Art Institute of Pittsburgh (I)

420 Boulevard of the Allies, Pittsburgh PA 15219-1301
County: Allegheny | FICE Identification: 007470
Unit ID: 210960
Telephone: (412) 263-6600 | Carnegie Class: Spec-4-yr-Arts
FAX Number: (412) 263-3715 | Calendar System: Quarter
URL: www.artinstitutes.edu/pittsburgh
Established: 1921 | Annual Undergrad Tuition & Fees: $17,628
Enrollment: 1,280 | Coed
Affiliation or Control: Proprietary | IRS Status: Proprietary
Highest Offering: Baccalaureate
Accreditation: M, ACFEI, CIDA

01 President ...... Mr. George W. SEBOLT
10 Vice Pres/Dir Admin/Financial Svcs ...... Mr. Kevin KOLESZAR
05 VP/Dean Academic Affairs ...... Mr. Daniel GARLAND
32 Vice Pres/Director Student Affairs ...... Ms. Nadine W. JOSEPHS

36 VP/Director Career Services .... Ms. Dana MELVIN
07 Director of Admissions .... Ms. Jennifer O"BRIEN
37 Director Student Financial Aid .... Ms. Lara HEMWALL
15 Director Human Resources .... Ms. Bobbi Jo GRAHAM
97 Director General Education .... Ms. Katie TALERICO
105 Dir Graphic/Dig Design/Web Design .... Ms. Patricia HUETTEL
72 Director of Technology .... Mr. Ryan SLATER
88 Dir Indust Dsgn Tech/Entertnmt Dsgn .... Ms. Kelly SPEWOCK
88 Dir Media Animation/Game Design .... Mr. Hans WESTMAN
88 Dir of Photography/Video Production .... Mr. Andrew ENGLISH
06 Registrar .... Ms. Diane E. CARNEY
84 Enrollment Management Supervisor .... Ms. Lara HEMWALL
88 Director Culinary .... Mr. Shawn CULP
88 Dir Fashion/Retail Mktng/Fashn Dsgn .... Ms. Stephanie TAYLOR
88 College Affiliate/HS Articulation .... Mr. Daniel GARLAND
29 Director Alumni Relations .... Ms. Janey CINK

The Art Institute of York - Pennsylvania (A)

1409 Williams Road, York PA 17402-9012
County: York FICE Identification: 025578
Unit ID: 210906
Telephone: (717) 755-2300 Carnegie Class: Bac-Diverse
FAX Number: (717) 757-5552 Calendar System: Other
URL: www.artinstitutes.edu/york
Established: 1952 Annual Undergrad Tuition & Fees: $17,340
Enrollment: 369 Coed
Affiliation or Control: Proprietary IRS Status: Proprietary
Highest Offering: Baccalaureate
Accreditation: #ACICS

01 President .... Mr. Tim HOWARD
05 Dean of Academic Affairs .... Ms. Marla PRICE

† School is in teach-out plan.

Berks Technical Institute (B)

2205 Ridgewood Road, Wyomissing PA 19610-1168
County: Berks FICE Identification: 022539
Unit ID: 213534
Telephone: (610) 372-1722 Carnegie Class: Assoc/HVT-Mix Trad/Non
FAX Number: (610) 376-4684 Calendar System: Other
URL: www.berks.edu
Established: 1974 Annual Undergrad Tuition & Fees: $10,120
Enrollment: 985 Coed
Affiliation or Control: Proprietary IRS Status: Proprietary
Highest Offering: Associate Degree
Accreditation: ACICS, MAC

01 Campus Director .... Mr. Joseph F. REICHARD
05 Dean .... Mr. Elizabeth VLASTOS

Biblical Theological Seminary (C)

200 N Main Street, Hatfield PA 19440-2499
County: Montgomery FICE Identification: 023230
Unit ID: 211130
Telephone: (215) 368-5000 Carnegie Class: Spec-4-yr-Faith
FAX Number: (215) 368-2301 Calendar System: Semester
URL: www.biblical.edu
Established: 1971 Annual Graduate Tuition & Fees: N/A
Enrollment: 282 Coed
Affiliation or Control: Independent Non-Profit IRS Status: 501(c)3
Highest Offering: Doctorate; No Undergraduates
Accreditation: M, THEOL

01 President .... Dr. Frank JAMES, III
30 VP for Advancement .... Mr. Thomas SKINNER
05 Academic Dean .... Dr. R. Todd MANGUM
10 Special Advisor to the President .... Mr. David VIEHMAN
04 Executive Assistant to the Pres .... Mrs. Beatrice L. BARKLEY
21 Accounting Manager .... Ms. Cynthia DAYMON
88 Director of DMin Program .... Dr. Kyuboem LEE
88 Director of Urban Initiatives .... Dr. Dan WILLIAMS
20 Director of Academic Services .... Mr. Rick HOUSEKNECHT
13 Director of Information Technology .... Mr. Kelly PFLEIGER
18 Director of Physical Plant .... Mr. Anthony W. PLETSCHER
06 Registrar .... Mr. Rick HOUSEKNECHT
101 Secretary of the Institution/Board .... Mrs. Patricia MILLEN
37 Director Student Financial Aid .... Mrs. Virginia HARTMAN
44 Director Annual or Planned Giving .... Mr. Thomas CAULEY

Bidwell Training Center (D)

1815 Metropolitan Street, Pittsburgh PA 15233-2200
County: Allegheny FICE Identification: 031015
Unit ID: 211149
Telephone: (412) 323-4000 Carnegie Class: Spec 2-yr-Tech
FAX Number: (412) 325-7378 Calendar System: Quarter
URL: www.bidwell-training.org
Established: 1968 Annual Undergrad Tuition & Fees: N/A
Enrollment: 169 Coed
Affiliation or Control: Independent Non-Profit IRS Status: 501(c)3
Highest Offering: Associate Degree
Accreditation: ACCSC

01 Exec Director/Sr Vice President .... Ms. Valerie NJIE
11 Senior Director/Operations .... Mr. Ken HUSELTON

Bradford School (E)

125 W Station Square Drive, Ste 129, Pittsburgh PA 15219-2602
County: Allegheny FICE Identification: 009721
Unit ID: 211200
Telephone: (412) 391-6710 Carnegie Class: Assoc/HVT-High Trad
FAX Number: (412) 471-6714 Calendar System: Semester
URL: www.bradfordpittsburgh.edu
Established: 1968 Annual Undergrad Tuition & Fees: $15,340
Enrollment: 413 Coed
Affiliation or Control: Proprietary IRS Status: Proprietary
Highest Offering: Associate Degree
Accreditation: ACICS, DA, MAC

01 President .... Mr. Vincent S. GRAZIANO

Brightwood Career Institute (F)

5650 Derry Street, Harrisburg PA 17111-4112
County: Dauphin FICE Identification: 004910
Unit ID: 251075
Telephone: (717) 564-4112 Carnegie Class: Assoc/HVT-High Non
FAX Number: (717) 564-3779 Calendar System: Quarter
URL: www.brightwoodcareer.edu
Established: 1918 Annual Undergrad Tuition & Fees: N/A
Enrollment: 217 Coed
Affiliation or Control: Proprietary IRS Status: Proprietary
Highest Offering: Associate Degree
Accreditation: ACICS, MAC

01 Executive Director .... Susan LYNCH
07 Director Admissions .... Jamie EARLEY
36 Director Student Placement .... Jennifer RIORDAN
05 Director of Education .... Jenny PIPER
37 Director Student Financial Aid .... Sarah BROOKER

Brightwood Career Institute (G)

177 Franklin Mills Boulevard, Philadelphia PA 19154-3140
County: Bucks FICE Identification: 022898
Unit ID: 211617
Telephone: (215) 612-6600 Carnegie Class: Assoc/HVT-Mix Trad/Non
FAX Number: (215) 612-6695 Calendar System: Quarter
URL: www.brightwoodcareer.edu
Established: 1982 Annual Undergrad Tuition & Fees: N/A
Enrollment: 640 Coed
Affiliation or Control: Proprietary IRS Status: Proprietary
Highest Offering: Associate Degree
Accreditation: ACICS, COARC

01 President .... Ms. Karen SPRINGER
07 Director of Admissions .... Mr. Dan WATKINS
05 Education Department Head .... Mrs. Diane DARLING
36 Director of Placement .... Ms. Cheryl BRAIDES
37 Director Financial Aid .... Ms. India FLOYD

Brightwood Career Institute (H)

933 Penn Avenue, Pittsburgh PA 15222-3802
County: Allegheny FICE Identification: 007436
Unit ID: 213002
Telephone: (412) 338-4770 Carnegie Class: Assoc/HVT-Mix Trad/Non
FAX Number: (412) 261-0998 Calendar System: Quarter
URL: www.brightwoodcareer.edu
Established: 1963 Annual Undergrad Tuition & Fees: N/A
Enrollment: 444 Coed
Affiliation or Control: Proprietary IRS Status: Proprietary
Highest Offering: Associate Degree
Accreditation: ACICS, MAC, OTA

01 Interim President .... Ms. Deana SOUTHERLAND
05 Director of Education .... Ms. Jacqueline KELLY
37 Director of Financial Aid .... Mr. Chris FOX
07 Director of Admissions .... Mr. Justin PAPARIELLA
36 Director of Career Services .... Ms. Jennifer KELLY

Brightwood Career Institute - Broomall Campus (I)

1991 Sproul Road, Suite 42, Broomall PA 19008-3516
County: Delaware FICE Identification: 007781
Unit ID: 215646
Telephone: (610) 353-7630 Carnegie Class: Spec 2-yr-Health
FAX Number: (610) 359-1370 Calendar System: Quarter
URL: www.brightwoodcareer.edu
Established: 1958 Annual Undergrad Tuition & Fees: N/A
Enrollment: 337 Coed
Affiliation or Control: Proprietary IRS Status: Proprietary
Highest Offering: Associate Degree
Accreditation: ACICS

01 President .... Mr. William SCHNELL
05 Academic Dean .... Ms. Amy BERRIOS
36 Career Development Director .... Mr. James LINCKE
07 Director of Admissions .... Mr. Mark GARNER

Bryn Athyn College of the New Church (J)

PO Box 717, Bryn Athyn PA 19009-0717
County: Montgomery FICE Identification: 003228
Unit ID: 210492
Telephone: (267) 502-2400 Carnegie Class: Bac-A&S
FAX Number: (215) 938-2658 Calendar System: Trimester
URL: www.brynathyn.edu
Established: 1876 Annual Undergrad Tuition & Fees: $19,353
Enrollment: 281 Coed
Affiliation or Control: Church of New Jerusalem IRS Status: 501(c)3
Highest Offering: Master's
Accreditation: M

01 President .... Mr. Brian BLAIR
10 Chief Finance Officer .... Mr. Daniel T. ALLEN
05 Dean of Academic Affairs .... Dr. Allen BEDFORD
73 Dean of Theological School .... Rev. Andrew M T. DIBB
32 Dean of Student Affairs .... Ms. Kiri ROGERS
07 Director of Admissions .... Ms. Roberta NOLAN
08 Director of Swedenborg Library .... Mrs. Carroll C. ODHNER
41 Director of Athletics .... Mr. Matthew KENNEDY
13 Director of Information Technology .... Ms. Lelia HOWARD
15 Director of Human Resources .... Ms. Renee ROSENFELD
19 Director of Security & Safety .... Mr. R. Scott COOPER
42 Chaplain .... Rev. Thane GLENN
04 Administrative Asst to President .... Ms. Melodie GREER
37 Director of Financial Aid .... Mr. Brian KEISTER

Bryn Mawr College (K)

101 N Merion Avenue, Bryn Mawr PA 19010-2899
County: Montgomery FICE Identification: 003237
Unit ID: 211273
Telephone: (610) 526-5000 Carnegie Class: Bac-A&S
FAX Number: (610) 526-7450 Calendar System: Semester
URL: www.brynmawr.edu
Established: 1885 Annual Undergrad Tuition & Fees: $47,140
Enrollment: 1,709 Female
Affiliation or Control: Independent Non-Profit IRS Status: 501(c)3
Highest Offering: Doctorate
Accreditation: M, SW

01 President .... Kimberly CASSIDY
05 Provost .... Mary J. OSIRIM
49 Interim Dean Undergraduate College .... Judith BALTHAZAR
10 Chief Financial Officer .... Kari FAZIO
30 Chief Development Officer .... Bob MILLER
07 Chief Enrollment Officer .... Pelema I. MORRICE
08 Director Libraries/Chief Info Ofcr .... Gina SIESING
58 Dean of Graduate Studies .... Sharon BURGMAYER
28 Asst Dean Col of Access/Cmty Devel .... Vanessa CHRISTMAN
06 Registrar .... Kirsten O'BEIRNE
37 Director of Financial Aid .... Ethel M. DESMARAIS
19 Director of Public Safety .... Tom KING
68 Dir Athletics & Physical Education .... Kathleen TIERNEY
21 Controller .... Betsy STEWART
09 Director of Institutional Research .... Richard BARRY
18 Director of Facilities .... Nina BISBEE

Bucknell University (L)

1 Dent Drive, Lewisburg PA 17837
County: Union FICE Identification: 003238
Unit ID: 211291
Telephone: (570) 577-2000 Carnegie Class: Bac-A&S
FAX Number: (570) 577-3760 Calendar System: Semester
URL: www.bucknell.edu
Established: 1846 Annual Undergrad Tuition & Fees: $50,152
Enrollment: 3,624 Coed
Affiliation or Control: Independent Non-Profit IRS Status: 501(c)3
Highest Offering: Master's
Accreditation: M, BUS, CS, ENG, MUS

01 President .... Dr. John C. BRAVMAN
05 Provost .... Dr. Barbara ALTMAN
10 VP Finance & Administration .... Mr. David J. SURGALA
30 VP Development & Alumni Rels .... Dr. Scott G. ROSEVEAR
43 General Counsel .... Ms. Amy C. FOERSTER
84 VP Enrollment Management .... Mr. William T. CONLEY
41 Director Athletics & Recreation .... Mr. John P. HARDT
08 VP Library & Information Technology .... Mr. Param S. BEDI
26 VP Communications & Cmty Rels .... Mr. Andrew HIRSCH
49 Dean of Arts & Sciences .... Dr. Karl VOSS
54 Dean of Engineering .... Dr. Patrick MATHER
15 Assoc VP Human Resources .... Mr. Pierre D. JOANIS
32 Acting Dean of Students .... Ms. Amy A. BADAL
21 Associate VP Finance .... Mr. Dennis W. SWANK
21 Treasurer and Controller .... Mr. Michael S. COVER
29 Assoc VP Development & Alumni Rels .... Ms. Kathleen GRAHAM
06 AProv/Regis/Dn Grad Std & Summ Sess .... Dr. Robert M. MIDKIFF, JR.
20 Assoc Provost .... Dr. Karen M. MORIN
50 Director School of Management .... Dr. Michael E. JOHNSON-CRAMER
18 Associate VP Facilities .... Mr. Kenneth OGAWA
45 Director Business Planning .... Mr. Edward J. LOFTUS
28 Assoc Provost for Diversity .... Vacant
04 Dir President Ofc & Univ Secretary .... Ms. Carol M. KENNEDY
46 Assistant Provost for Research .... Vacant

88 Director of Internal Audit .... Mr. Robert L. HOSTER
88 Executive Dir Leadership Gifts .... Mr. Mark SHARER
29 Exec Dir Alumni Relations .... Mr. Joshua L. GRILL
88 Exec Dir Advancement Services .... Ms. Cindy BELKNAP
44 Executive Director of Annual Fund .... Ms. Lucille M. TARIN
102 Dir Corporate & Foundation Rels .... Vacant
88 Director Parents Fund .... Ms. Ann L. DISTEFANO
44 Director of Gift Planning .... Ms. Melissa M. DIEHL
14 Asst Chief Information Officer .... Mr. Mark E. YERGER
14 Director of Enterprise Systems .... Mr. Kevin WILLEY
13 Chief Info Sec Officer .... Mr. Christopher BERNARD
27 Asst VP of Communications .... Mr. Andrew H. HIRSCH
88 Dir of Construction & Design .... Vacant
88 Dir of Facility Services .... Mr. Michael J. PATTERSON
84 Asst VP Enroll Mgmt/Dir Partnershps .... Mr. Mark D. DAVIES
07 Dean of Admissions .... Mr. Robert G. SPRINGALL
37 Director Financial Aid .... Ms. Andrea C. LEITHNER STAUFFER
38 Dir Counseling & Stdnt Dev Ctr .... Dr. Kelly KETTLEWELL
88 Dir of Investments .... Mr. John R. LUTHI
36 Exec Director Career Services .... Ms. Pamela G. KEISER
16 Dir of Recruitment & Compensation .... Ms. Marcia J. COONEY
16 Director of HRIS & Benefits .... Ms. Cindy L. BILGER
09 Asst Provost Inst Research/Assess .... Mr. Kevork T. HORISSIAN
109 Director of Business Services .... Ms. Lori J. WILSON
88 Exec Dir Events Management Office .... Ms. Dana M. MIMS
88 Assoc Controller Financial Services .... Mr. Ronald E. STAUFFER, II
88 Assoc Controller Accounting Svcs .... Mr. William D. GEORGE
88 Asst Controller .... Ms. Michelle M. HENDRICKS
104 Dir Global & Off-Campus Education .... Mr. Stephen K. APPIAH-PADI
88 Dir Risk Management & Insurance .... Mr. Clint D. WEVODAU
19 Chief of Public Safety .... Mr. Stephen J. BARILAR
35 Associate Dean of Students .... Ms. Kari M. CONRAD
35 Associate Dean of Students .... Mr. Daniel C. REMLEY
88 Exec Dir Weis Center Perform Arts .... Ms. Kathryn L. MAGUET
88 Title IX Coord Clery Act Comp .... Ms. Kathleen GRIMES
88 Dir of Instructional Technology .... Mr. Matthew K. GARDZINA
88 Dir Advancement Campaign Mgmt .... Ms. Barbara A. HARTMAN
88 Dir Dev Research & Prospect Mgmt .... Ms. Cynthia D. JANESCH
42 University Chaplain .... Mr. John P. COLATCH
109 Dir Publications/Print & Mail .... Ms. Lisa D. HOOVER
105 Interim Dir Digital Communications .... Mr. Ryan LEBRETON
88 Dir Provost Business Operations .... Ms. Pamela A. BENFER
88 Director of Disbursement Services .... Mr. Jody D. GRAYBILL
105 Dir University Marketing & Web .... Ms. Molly E. O'BRIEN-FOELSCH
88 Dir Small Business Development Ctr .... Mr. Steven V. STUMBRIS
88 Dir Card Svcs & Student Transit .... Mr. Glenn R. FISHER
88 Dir of Civic Engagement .... Ms. Janice R. BUTLER
96 Director of Procurement Services .... Mr. Donald A. KRECH
88 Dir Financial Information Systems .... Ms. Pamela K. NOONE
22 Dir of Disability Services .... Ms. Heather L. FOWLER
85 Dir International Student Services .... Ms. Jennifer E. FIGUEROA
88 Director Office of LGBTQ Resources .... Mr. William K. MCCOY
92 Honors Council Chair .... Ms. Sharon GARTHWAITE
88 Director of Writing Center .... Ms. Deirdre M. O'CONNOR
39 Dir of Housing Services .... Mr. Stephen J. APANEL

Bucks County Community College (A)

275 Swamp Road, Newtown PA 18940-4106
County: Bucks FICE Identification: 003239
Unit ID: 211307
Telephone: (215) 968-8000 Carnegie Class: Assoc/HT-Mix Trad/Non
FAX Number: (215) 968-8129 Calendar System: Semester
URL: www.bucks.edu
Established: 1964 Annual Undergrad Tuition & Fees (In-District): $4,178
Enrollment: 8,979 Coed
Affiliation or Control: Local IRS Status: 501(c)3
Highest Offering: Associate Degree
Accreditation: M, ACBSP, ADNUR, ART, MUS, RAD

01 President .... Dr. Stephanie SHANBLATT
05 Provost .... Vacant
10 VP for Administrative Affairs & CFO .... Mr. Dennis W. MATTHEWS
32 VP Student Affairs/Dean of Students .... Ms. Barbara H. YETMAN
13 Vice Pres/Chief Info Technology .... Vacant
30 Vice Pres Advancement .... Dr. Tobias BRUHN
20 Assoc Provost Academic Svcs .... Ms. Catherine C. MCELROY
84 Dean Enrollment Services .... Dr. Eric HILTON
38 Dean Advising & Student Planning .... Dr. Christine HAGEDORN
21 Exec Dir Budget & Internal Audit .... Ms. Loren HERBERT
09 Exec Dir Inst Research & Assessment .... Dr. Jenell BRAMLAGE
12 Exec Dir Upper Bucks Campus .... Dr. Rodney H. ALTEMOSE
88 Exec Dir Public Safety Training .... Mr. Rob FREESE
103 Exec Dir Workforce Development .... Ms. Lauren LOEFFLER
18 Exec Director Physical Plant .... Mr. Martin SNYDER
26 Exec Dir Marketing/Public Relations .... Ms. Marta KAUFMANN
04 Exec Assistant to President .... Ms. Kathleen C. FEDORKO
15 Exec Director Human Resources .... Dr. Patricia BRINING
96 Director of Purchasing .... Mr. James F. LOUGHERY
106 Director Online Learning .... Ms. Georglyn L. DAVIDSON
37 Director Financial Aid .... Ms. Donna M. WILKOSKI
36 Director Career Services .... Ms. Sharon STEPHENS
35 Director Student Life & Athletics .... Mr. Matt J. CIPRIANO
19 Exec Dir Security & Safety .... Mr. Dennis MCCAULEY
08 Director Library Services .... Ms. Linda MCCANN
20 Executive Assistant to Provost .... Dr. Charlie GROTH
07 Director of Admissions .... Ms. Marlene T. BARLOW
06 Registrar .... Mr. Robert MALEY
29 Alumni Relations Manager .... Ms. Jackie GEAR
68 Dean Kinesiology & Sport Studies .... Dr. Priscilla RICE
81 Dean STEM .... Ms. Lisa ANGELO
50 Dean Business Studies .... Ms. Tracy TIMBY
57 Dean Arts .... Mr. John MATHEWS
88 Dean Language & Literature .... Dr. Kelly KELLEWAY
83 Dean Social & Behavioral Sci .... Dr. Lynn DELLAPIETRA
107 Dean Professional Studies .... Dr. Maria TOTH
88 Dean Learning Res/Online .... Mr. Bill HEMMIG
45 Liaison Pres Strategies/Initiatives .... Mr. Jason MAYLAND
102 Asst Dir Foundation/Alumni .... Ms. Jennifer SALISBURY

Butler County Community College (B)

107 College Drive, Butler PA 16002
County: Butler FICE Identification: 003240
Unit ID: 211343
Telephone: (724) 287-8711 Carnegie Class: Assoc/HT-High Trad
FAX Number: (724) 285-6047 Calendar System: Semester
URL: www.bc3.edu
Established: 1965 Annual Undergrad Tuition & Fees (In-District): $4,230
Enrollment: 3,570 Coed
Affiliation or Control: Local IRS Status: 501(c)3
Highest Offering: Associate Degree
Accreditation: M, ACBSP, ADNUR, MAC, PTAA

01 President .... Dr. Nicholas C. NEUPAUER
05 Interim VP for Academic Affairs .... Dr. Bruce RUSSELL
11 VP for Administration & Finance .... Mr. James A. HRABOSKY
32 VP Student Affairs/Enrollment Mgt .... Dr. G. Case WILLOUGHBY
51 VP Continuing Ed Off-Campus Centers .... Mr. William T. O'BRIEN
10 Chief Business Officer .... Mr. Wm. Jake FRIEL
50 Interim Dean of Business .... Ms. Ann MCCANDLESS
83 Dean of Social Science/Humanities .... Mr. William L. MILLER
66 Dean of Nursing/Allied Health .... Ms. Patricia T. ANNEAR
72 Dean of Nat Science/Tech .... Mr. Matt KOVAC
106 Dean of Education Technology .... Ms. Ann MCCANDLESS
08 Dean of Library Services .... Mr. Stephen M. JOSEPH
35 Dean of Students .... Mr. Joshua NOVAK
103 Exec Dir Workforce Dev Training .... Dr. Stephen R. CATT
15 Exec Director Human Resources .... Ms. Linda M. DODD
26 Interim Director of Comm & Mktg .... Ms. Jessica M. MATONAK
51 Director Adult/Continuing Education .... Mr. Paul M. LUCAS
06 Director of Records & Registration .... Ms. Amy DOUBLE FIGNATORE
13 Dir Telecommunications & MIS .... Ms. Kathleen C. SOMMERS
32 Director of Student Life .... Mr. Rob A. SNYDER
09 Dir Instl Research/Strategic Plng .... Ms. Shara M. ANKE
18 Exec Director of Operations .... Mr. Brian R. OPITZ
07 Director of Admissions .... Mr. Robert MORRIS
12 Director of EC3 @ Lawrence Crossing .... Mr. Sean M. CARROLL
12 Director of EC3 @ Cranberry .... Mr. Alex J. GLADIS
12 Director of EC3 @ LindenPointe .... Mr. John P. SUESSER
12 Director of EC3 @ Brockway .... Ms. Jill MARTIN-REND
37 Financial Aid Director .... Ms. Julianne E. LOUTTIT
41 Athletic Director .... Mr. Rob A. SNYDER
50 Director of Business/Industry Trng .... Ms. Lisa M. CAMPBELL
38 Director Student Counseling .... Vacant
29 Director Alumni Relations .... Ms. Michelle E. JAMIESON
30 Exec Director of Advancement .... Ms. Ruth PURCELL
19 Int Dir of Campus Police/Security .... Mr. K. Scott RICHARDSON
88 Director of Cultural Center .... Mr. Lawrence E. STOCK
88 Director of Children's Center .... Ms. Judith A. ZUZACK
88 Associate Director Admissions .... Ms. Morgan M. RIZZARDI
40 Bookstore Manager .... Ms. Donna L. PALLONE
96 Director of Purchasing .... Ms. Nicole BARNES
105 Director Web Services .... Mr. R. Dennis BIRKES
108 Director Institutional Assessment .... Dr. Sunday O. FASEYITAN
44 Director Annual or Planned Giving .... Ms. Michelle E. JAMIESON

Byzantine Catholic Seminary of Ss. Cyril and Methodius (C)

3605 Perrysville Avenue, Pittsburgh PA 15214-2229
County: Allegheny FICE Identification: 041180
Unit ID: 444103
Telephone: (412) 321-8383 Carnegie Class: Spec-4-yr-Faith
FAX Number: (412) 321-9936 Calendar System: Semester
URL: www.bcs.edu
Established: 1950 Annual Graduate Tuition & Fees: N/A
Enrollment: 22 Coed
Affiliation or Control: Other IRS Status: 501(c)3
Highest Offering: Master's; No Undergraduates
Accreditation: THEOL

01 Rector .... Rev. Robert M. PIPTA
05 Academic Dean .... Rev. Christiaan KAPPES
06 Registrar .... Ms. Carol PRZYBOROKI

Cabrini University (D)

610 King of Prussia Road, Radnor PA 19087-3698
County: Delaware FICE Identification: 003241
Unit ID: 211352
Telephone: (610) 902-8200 Carnegie Class: Masters/L
FAX Number: (610) 902-8204 Calendar System: Semester
URL: www.cabrini.edu
Established: 1957 Annual Undergrad Tuition & Fees: $29,842
Enrollment: 2,203 Coed
Affiliation or Control: Roman Catholic IRS Status: 501(c)3
Highest Offering: Doctorate
Accreditation: M, SW

01 President .... Dr. Donald TAYLOR
05 Provost/VP Academic Affairs .... Dr. Jeffrey GINGERICH
10 VP Finance & Treasurer .... Mr. Eric OLSON
30 VP Institutional Advancement .... Mr. Stephen HIGHSMITH
32 VP of Student Life .... Dr. Christine LYSIONEK
84 VP of Enrollment Management .... Mr. Robert REESE
35 Asst VP Student Life/Dean of Studen .... Dr. George STROUD
50 Dean School Business/Arts & Media .... Dr. Mary VAN BRUNT
53 Dean School of Education .... Dr. Beverly BRYDE
04 Executive Asst to the President .... Ms. Joan KLECKNER
06 Registrar .... Ms. M. Frances HARKNESS
08 Library Director .... Dr. Roberta JACQUET
13 Interim Dir Info Tech & Resources .... Mr. Chris SHIELDS
19 Director Public Safety .... Mr. Joseph FUSCO
18 Director of Facilities .... Ms. Dawn BARNETT
29 Interim Dir of Alumni Engagement .... Ms. Jackie MARCIANO
37 Director of Financial Aid .... Ms. Elizabeth GINGERICH
36 Dir of Career & Professional Dev .... Ms. Nancy HUTCHISON
41 Director of Athletics & Recreation .... Mr. Bradley KOCH
15 Director of Human Resources .... Ms. Susan ROHANNA
21 Controller .... Ms. Diane SCUTTI
24 Coord of Education Resources Center .... Ms. Mary BUDZILOWICZ
40 Bookstore Manager .... Mr. Bill BRIDDES
105 Digital Designer .... Mr. Matthew HOLMES
09 Director of Institutional Research .... Vacant
35 Dir Student Engagement & Leadership .... Ms. Anne FILIPPONE
92 Co-Director of the Honors Program .... Dr. Paul WRIGHT
92 Co-Director of the Honors Program .... Dr. Leonard PRIMIANO
28 Dir Student Diversity Initiatives .... Ms. Stephanie REED
38 Director Counseling/Psych Service .... Dr. Sara MAGGITTI
39 Director of Residence Life .... Ms. Sue KRAMER
07 Director of Admissions .... Ms. Shannon ZOTTOLA
101 Exec Governance Admin Sec Board .... Mrs. Nancy OLLINGER
102 Dir Sponsored Pgms & Foundation Rel .... Ms. Jean JACOBSON
108 Asst to Provost Assess/Accred .... Dr. Maliha ZAMAN
88 Creative Director .... Mr. Kevin HAUGH
44 Director Annual Giving .... Mr. William GUSLER
86 VP Community Dev & Ext Relations .... Mr. Brian EURY
91 Director Administrative Computing .... Mr. Rob GETZ

Cairn University (E)

200 Manor Avenue, Langhorne Manor PA 19047-2990
County: Bucks FICE Identification: 003351
Unit ID: 215114
Telephone: (215) 752-5800 Carnegie Class: Masters/S
FAX Number: (215) 702-4341 Calendar System: Semester
URL: www.cairn.edu
Established: 1913 Annual Undergrad Tuition & Fees: $23,920
Enrollment: 1,058 Coed
Affiliation or Control: Independent Non-Profit IRS Status: 501(c)3
Highest Offering: Master's
Accreditation: M, BI, IACBE, MUS, SW

01 President .... Dr. Todd J. WILLIAMS
05 Provost .... Dr. Brian G. TOEWS
32 Sr VP Student Affairs .... Mr. J. Scott CAWOOD
10 Sr VP Finance & Administration .... Vacant
30 Sr VP Univ Advancement .... Mr. Russell T. NIXON
26 Sr VP Marketing & Enrollment .... Mr. Paul NEAL
15 VP Human Resources .... Ms. Mary BOYER
108 Vice Provost .... Dr. Jean MINTO
06 Registrar .... Dr. Steven SCHLENKER
08 Dean Educational Resources .... Dr. Timothy K. HUI
35 Dean Student Life .... Mr. Tom SHERF
73 Dean School of Divinity .... Dr. Jonathan L. MASTER
49 Dean School of Liberal Arts & Sci .... Dr. Brenda MELLEN
50 Dean School of Business .... Mr. Yunn K. KANG
53 Dean School of Education .... Ms. Paula GOSSARD
64 Dean School of Music .... Dr. Benjamin HARDING
70 Dean School of Social Work .... Dr. Llloyd GESTOSO
07 Director Admissions .... Ms. Rebecca LIPPERT
29 Director Alumni Relations .... Mr. Nathan WAMBOLD
18 Director Campus Services .... Mr. Andrew NORTON
40 Campus Store Manager .... Ms. Emily BRUNNER
36 Director Career Center .... Ms. Teri T. CANTANIO
37 Director Financial Aid .... Mr. Stephen CASSEL
23 Director Health Services .... Ms. Alison KIKENDALL
09 Director Institutional Research .... Dr. Lynn WALLACE
39 Director Resident Life .... Mr. Evan CURRY
19 Director Safety & Security .... Mr. Chris LLOYD
38 Director Student Counseling .... Vacant
13 Director Technology Services .... Mr. Curt D. WINTERS
106 Dir Online Education/E-learning .... Mr. Sali KACELI
11 Controller .... Mr. Jeff EUBANK
21 Asst Director Business Services .... Dr. Andrew HUI
04 Administrative Asst to President .... Ms. Lori MILLER
41 Athletic Director .... Ms. Laura BEHNKE

Career Training Academy (F)

179 Hillcrest Shopping Center, Lower Burrell PA 15068
County: Westmoreland FICE Identification: 026095
Unit ID: 210951
Telephone: (724) 337-1000 Carnegie Class: Spec 2-yr-Health
FAX Number: N/A Calendar System: Other
URL: www.careerta.edu
Established: 1986 Annual Undergrad Tuition & Fees: N/A
Enrollment: 171 Coed
Affiliation or Control: Proprietary IRS Status: Proprietary
Highest Offering: Associate Degree
Accreditation: ACCSC

01 Campus Director .... Mr. Michael DISCELLO

Career Training Academy (A)

4314 Old William Penn Hwy, Ste 103,
Monroeville PA 15146-1455
Telephone: (412) 372-3900 Identification: 666051
Accreditation: ACCSC

† Branch campus of Career Training Academy, New Kensington, PA.

Career Training Academy (B)

1014 West View Park Drive, Pittsburgh PA 15229
Telephone: (412) 367-4000 Identification: 666100
Accreditation: ACCSC

† Branch campus of Career Training Academy, New Kensington, PA.

Carlow University (C)

3333 Fifth Avenue, Pittsburgh PA 15213-3165
County: Allegheny FICE Identification: 003303
Unit ID: 211431
Telephone: (800) 333-2275 Carnegie Class: Masters/L
FAX Number: (412) 578-6668 Calendar System: Semester
URL: www.carlow.edu
Established: 1929 Annual Undergrad Tuition & Fees: $26,832
Enrollment: 2,201 Coed
Affiliation or Control: Roman Catholic IRS Status: 501(c)3
Highest Offering: Doctorate
Accreditation: M, #COARC, COPSY, NURSE, SW

01 President ... Dr. Suzanne K. MELLON
05 Provost/VP Academic Affairs ... Deanne H. D'EMILIO
10 CFO/VP Finance ... Mr. David J. MEADOWS
30 VP Advancement ... Vacant
84 VP Enrollment Management ... Ms. Carol A. DESCAK
13 Chief Information Officer ... Mr. Jeffrey P. DEVLIN
26 VP Marketing & Communications ... Dr. Jeanne A. HARTIG
88 Special Asst to Pres/Mercy Heritage ... Sr. Sheila A. CARNEY
32 VP Student Engagement ... Dr. Jennifer A. CARLO
09 AVP Inst Rsrch/Effect & Planning ... Ms. Anne M. CANDREVA
04 Asst to the President ... Ms. Barbara L. GILLES
15 Director Human Resources ... Ms. Bridgette N. COFIELD
42 Campus Minister ... Ms. Siobhan K. DEWITT
06 Registrar ... Mr. Jason KRALL
88 Exec Dir & Principal Campus School ... Ms. Michelle A. PEDUTO
07 Director Undergraduate Admissions ... Ms. Wivinia A. CHMURA
36 Director Career Development ... Vacant
58 Dir Student Accounts ... Mr. James V. SHANKEL
08 Director Library Services ... Vacant
85 Coordinator Center for Global Lrng ... Mr. Benjamin J. PILCHER
35 Director Campus Life ... Mr. Charlie N. JUDGE
39 Asst Director Campus Life ... Ms. Gwendolyn M. STEVENS
23 Director Health Services ... Vacant
41 Director Athletics ... Mr. George S. SLIMAN
88 Director Wellness & Fitness Svcs ... Ms. Julie M. GAUL
28 Dir Inclusion & Intercultural Init ... Ms. Barbara G. JOHNSON
21 Controller ... Vacant
18 Director Facilities ... Mr. Timothy D. CARNEY
19 Chief of Police ... Vacant
37 Director Financial Aid ... Ms. Natalie L. WILSON
44 Exec Director Philanthropy ... Ms. Anita S. DACAL
29 Director Alumni Relations ... Ms. Rose M. WOOLLEY
44 Senior Director Philanthropy ... Ms. Marcia M. WALLANDER
102 Director of Corp & Found Relations ... Ms. Marjorie P. BERNARD
27 Director Media & Public Rels ... Mr. Andrew G. WILSON
105 Director Digital Comm/Mktg/Comm ... Mr. Carl R. ZAPPA
108 Director of Assessment ... Mr. August C. DELBERT
106 Int Dir Online Educ/E-learning ... Ms. Rachael O. AFOLABI

Carnegie Mellon University (D)

5000 Forbes Avenue, Pittsburgh PA 15213-3890
County: Allegheny FICE Identification: 003242
Unit ID: 211440
Telephone: (412) 268-2000 Carnegie Class: DU-Highest
FAX Number: (412) 268-2330 Calendar System: Semester
URL: www.cmu.edu
Established: 1900 Annual Undergrad Tuition & Fees: $50,665
Enrollment: 12,587 Coed
Affiliation or Control: Independent Non-Profit IRS Status: 501(c)3
Highest Offering: Doctorate
Accreditation: M, BUS, ENG, MUS, SPAA

01 President ... Dr. Subra SURESH
05 Provost ... Dr. Farnam JAHANIAN
10 Interim Vice President and CFO ... Ms. Angela BLANTON
30 VP for University Advancement ... Mr. Scott MORY
46 Vice Provost for Research ... Dr. Gary FEDDER
43 Vice President/General Counsel ... Ms. Mary Jo DIVELY
26 VP Marketing & Communications ... Mr. Steven KLOEHN
101 Interim Secretary Board of Trustee ... Ms. Cathy A. LIGHT
04 Exec Asst to President ... Ms. Caryn MAKER
20 Vice Provost for Education ... Dr. Amy L. BURKERT
11 Vice President for Operations ... Dr. Rodney P. MCCLENDON
13 Vice Provost for Computer Svcs/CIO ... Mr. Steven K. HUTH
15 Interim VP HR & Chief HR Officer ... Mr. Dan MCNULTY
29 Exec Director Alumni Relations ... Ms. Nancy MERRITT
18 Asc VP Campus Design/Facility Devel ... Mr. Ralph R. HORGAN
27 Exec Dir For Media Relations ... Mr. Kenneth WALTERS
28 Asst Vice Pres for Diversity & EOS ... Mr. Everett L. TADAMY
41 Dir Athletics & Physical Education ... Mr. Josh CENTOR
19 Director Security/Chief Univ Police ... Mr. Thomas A. OGDEN
32 VP Student Affairs/Dean of Students ... Ms. Gina CASALEGNO
84 AVP & Dir of Enrollment Services ... Ms. Lisa M. KRIEG
14 Director Software Engr Inst ... Dr. Paul D. NIELSEN
07 Director of Admission ... Mr. Michael STEIDEL
08 Dean of University Libraries ... Mr. Keith WEBSTER
06 Registrar ... Mr. John R. PAPINCHAK
09 Director of Institutional Research ... Ms. Janel SUTKUS
36 Assoc Dean for Career/Prof Dev ... Mr. Kevin MONAHAN
38 Dir Counseling & Psychological Svcs ... Dr. Kurt KUMLER
54 Dean Carnegie Inst of Technology ... Dr. James GARRETT
57 Dean College Fine Arts ... Dr. Dan J. MARTIN
49 Dean Dietrich College ... Dr. Richard SCHEINES
50 Dean Tepper School of Business ... Dr. Robert DAMMON
81 Dean Mellon College of Science ... Dr. Frederick J. GILMAN
80 Dean Heinz Sch Publ Policy/Mgmt ... Dr. Ramayya KRISHNAN
77 Dean School of Computer Science ... Dr. Andrew MOORE
35 Asst Dean of Student Affairs ... Ms. Anne WITCHNER
100 Director Office of President ... Ms. Cathy LIGHT
102 Dir Foundation Relations ... Ms. Lauren WARD
104 Director of International Education ... Ms. Linda GENTILE
25 Chief Contracts/Grants Admin ... Mr. Matthew D'EMILIO
37 Director Student Financial Aid ... Mr. Brian HILL
39 Director Housing Services ... Mr. Thomas COOLEY
44 Sr Assoc Vice Pres for Development ... Ms. Pamela EAGER
86 Assoc VP Government Relations ... Mr. Timothy MCNULTY

Cedar Crest College (E)

100 College Drive, Allentown PA 18104-6196
County: Lehigh FICE Identification: 003243
Unit ID: 211468
Telephone: (610) 437-4471 Carnegie Class: Bac-Diverse
FAX Number: (610) 437-5955 Calendar System: Semester
URL: www.cedarcrest.edu
Established: 1867 Annual Undergrad Tuition & Fees: $35,600
Enrollment: 1,531 Female
Affiliation or Control: Non-denominational IRS Status: 501(c)3
Highest Offering: Master's
Accreditation: M, ACBSP, DIETD, DIETI, FEPAC, NUR, SW

01 President ... Ms. Carmen T. AMBAR
05 Provost ... Dr. Elizabeth MEADE
10 Chief Financial Officer/Treasurer ... Ms. Audra J. KAHR
30 VP of Advancement ... Ms. Susan ARNOLD
32 VP Student Affairs/Trad Enrollment ... Ms. Mary-Alice OZECHOSKI
06 Registrar ... Ms. Janet BAKER
29 Exec Director for Alumnae Affairs ... Ms. Susan S. COX
19 Chief of Campus Safety and Security ... Mr. Mark VITALOS
18 Director of Facilities ... Mr. Matthew YENCHA
08 Library Director ... Ms. Mary Beth FREEH
91 Director Administrative Technology ... Mrs. Kathleen CUNNINGHAM
09 Dir of Institutional Research ... Ms. Lyn WILLIAMS
04 Assistant to the President ... Ms. Meghan GRADY
37 Dir Student Financial Services ... Ms. Valerie KREISER
22 Director Health/Counseling Services ... Ms. Nancy ROBERTS
26 Chief Marketing Officer ... Mr. Gaetan GIANNINI
96 Purchasing Coordinator ... Ms. Karen KHATTARI
40 Manager Bookstore ... Ms. Maureen YOACHIM

Central Penn College (F)

College Hill Road, Summerdale PA 17093-0309
County: Cumberland FICE Identification: 004890
Unit ID: 211477
Telephone: (800) 759-2727 Carnegie Class: Bac-Diverse
FAX Number: (717) 732-5254 Calendar System: Quarter
URL: www.centralpenn.edu
Established: 1881 Annual Undergrad Tuition & Fees: $17,151
Enrollment: 1,330 Coed
Affiliation or Control: Proprietary IRS Status: Proprietary
Highest Offering: Master's
Accreditation: M, MAC, OTA, PTAA

01 President ... Dr. Karen SCOLFORO
03 Provost ... Dr. Linda FEDRIZZI-WILLIAMS
07 Vice President Enrollment ... Ms. Stacey OBI
10 Chief Financial Officer ... Mr. Richard VARMECKY
29 Director Alumni Relations ... Ms. Sarah BLUMENSCHEIN
06 Director Records & Registration ... Mr. Jen CORRELL
88 Director of Compliance ... Ms. Kathy ANDERSEN
18 Facilities Director ... Mr. Robert WHITCOMB III
26 Marketing Services Manager ... Mrs. Mary E. WETZEL
37 Financial Aid Director ... Ms. Kathy J. SHEPARD
41 Athletic Director ... Mr. Dave BAKER
36 Career Services Director ... Mr. Steven HASSINGER
15 Director Personnel Services ... Ms. Maggie LEBO
39 Director Student Housing ... Ms. Megan PETERSON

Chatham University (G)

Woodland Road, Pittsburgh PA 15232-2826
County: Allegheny FICE Identification: 003244
Unit ID: 211556
Telephone: (412) 365-1100 Carnegie Class: Masters/L
FAX Number: (412) 365-1505 Calendar System: Other
URL: www.chatham.edu
Established: 1869 Annual Undergrad Tuition & Fees: $34,440
Enrollment: 2,134 Coed
Affiliation or Control: Independent Non-Profit IRS Status: 501(c)3
Highest Offering: Doctorate
Accreditation: M, ARCPA, CIDA, COPSY, IACBE, LSAR, NURSE, OT, PTA, SW

01 President ... Dr. David FINEGOLD
10 Vice Pres Finance/Administration ... Mr. Walter B. FOWLER
05 Vice President Academic Affairs ... Dr. Jenna TEMPLETON
84 Vice Pres Enrollment Management ... Ms. Amy BECHER
32 VP Student Affairs/Dean of Stdnts ... Dr. Zauyah WAITE
26 Vice Pres for Mktg & Communications ... Mr. Bill CAMPBELL
30 Vice Pres University Advancement ... Mr. Kevin FORTWENDEL
106 Director Chatham Online ... Mr. Mark KASSEL
88 Dn Falk Sch Sustainability/Environ ... Dr. Peter WALKER
21 Asst VP Finance/Administration ... Ms. Jennifer LUNDY
45 VP of Planning/Sec to the Board ... Mr. Sean COLEMAN
09 Director of Institutional Research ... Dr. Robert ZHANG
06 Registrar ... Ms. Maria KRONISER
37 Director of Financial Aid ... Ms. Jennifer A. BURNS
08 Director of Library ... Ms. Jill AUSEL
29 Exec Director Alumni Relations ... Ms. Catherine LUNN
44 Director of Annual Giving ... Mr. Dominick OLIVER
102 Director of Foundation/Corp Support ... Ms. Leah PICKER
15 Director of Human Resources ... Mr. Frank M. GRECO
18 Director of Facilities Management ... Mr. Robert R. DUBRAY
19 Director of Safety & Security ... Mr. Don AUBRECHT
41 Director of Athletics ... Mr. Leonard TREVINO
36 Asst Dean for Career Development ... Vacant
38 Director of Student Counseling ... Dr. Elsa M. ARCE
35 Dir Student Affs/Residence Life ... Ms. Heather BLACK
49 Dean School Arts/Science/Business ... Dr. Darlene MOTTLEY
76 Dean School of Health Sciences ... Dr. Patricia DOWNEY

Chestnut Hill College (H)

9601 Germantown Avenue, Philadelphia PA 19118-2693
County: Philadelphia FICE Identification: 003245
Unit ID: 211583
Telephone: (215) 248-7000 Carnegie Class: Masters/L
FAX Number: (215) 248-7155 Calendar System: Semester
URL: www.chc.edu
Established: 1924 Annual Undergrad Tuition & Fees: $33,130
Enrollment: 2,063 Coed
Affiliation or Control: Roman Catholic IRS Status: 501(c)3
Highest Offering: Doctorate
Accreditation: M, CLPSY, IPSY, MACTE

01 President ... Sr. Carol Jean VALE, SSJ
05 Vice Pres for Academic Affairs ... Dr. Wolfgang NATTER
10 Sr Vice Pres for Financial Affairs ... Ms. Lauri STRIMKOVSKY
30 Vice President for Inst Advancement ... Ms. Susannah COLEMAN
32 Vice President for Student Life ... Dr. Lynn ORTALE
11 Asst to Pres for Administration ... Sr. Kathryn MILLER, SSJ
42 Asst to Pres for Mission & Ministry ... Sr. Roseann QUINN, SSJ
58 Dean School of Graduate Studies ... Dr. Barbara HOGAN
97 Dean School of Undergrad Studies ... Sr. Cecelia CAVANAUGH, SSJ
51 Dean of Continuing Studies ... Dr. Elaine GREEN
08 Dean Library/Information Resources ... Sr. Mary Josephine LARKIN, SSJ
07 Vice President for Admissions ... Ms. Jodie KING
20 Assoc Dir Student Success ... Ms. Clare DOYLE
06 Registrar ... Mr. Michael REIG
35 Director of Student Activities ... Ms. Emily SCHADEMAN
38 Director Counseling Center ... Sr. Sheila KENNEDY, SSJ
85 Foreign Student Advisor ... Ms. Trachanda BROWN
28 Dir Cultural Diversity Initiatives ... Vacant
92 Director of Honors Programs ... Vacant
23 Director Health Services ... Ms. Barbara DOUGHERTY
36 Director of Career Services ... Ms. Nancy DACHILLE
07 Dir Admission/Sch Graduate Studies ... Vacant
07 Director Accelerated Admissions ... Sr. Mary Esther LEE, SSJ
21 Controller ... Ms. Ellen MCGUINN
37 Director Financial Aid ... Ms. Dawn SNOOK
09 Director of Institutional Research ... Sr. Patricia O'DONNELL, SSJ
102 Dir Corporate/Found/Govt Relations ... Ms. Charles BLACHFORD
29 Director of Alumnae/i Affairs ... Ms. Maureen MCLAUGHLIN
41 Director of Athletics ... Ms. Lynn TUBMAN
15 Director Human Resources ... Ms. Sharon DOUGHERTY
19 Dir Security/Safety/Bldgs/Grounds ... Ms. Polly TETI
18 Director of Physical Plant ... Mr. Mark MCGRATH
91 Administrative Software Manager ... Ms. Darlene BROWN
26 Director of Communications ... Ms. Kathleen SPIGELMYER
40 Manager of Campus Store ... Ms. Christina WEBSTER
04 Administrative Asst to President ... Ms. Regina BERNHARDT
39 Director Student Housing ... Ms. Jenn THORPE

The Commonwealth Medical College (I)

525 Pine Street, Scranton PA 18509
County: Lackawanna FICE Identification: 041672
Unit ID: 456542
Telephone: (570) 504-7000 Carnegie Class: Masters/S
FAX Number: (570) 504-9660 Calendar System: Semester
URL: www.tcmc.edu
Established: 2009 Annual Graduate Tuition & Fees: N/A
Enrollment: 409 Coed
Affiliation or Control: Independent Non-Profit IRS Status: 501(c)3
Highest Offering: Doctorate; No Undergraduates
Accreditation: M, MED

01 President and Dean ... Dr. Steven J. SCHEINMAN
10 VP for Finance & Admin/CFO ... Ms. Anna RUSNAK NOON
30 VP Institutional Advancement ... Ms. Marise GAROFALO
31 VP Cmty & Government Relations ... Ms. Ida L. CASTRO
05 VP Acad & Clin Affairs/Vice Dean ... Dr. William IOBST

45 VP Strategic Initiatives/Planning .... Mr. V. Scott KOERWER
32 Director of Student Affairs .... Ms. Julia KOLCHARNO
20 Assoc Dean of Fac Affairs/Fac Devel .... Ms. Andrea DIMATTIA
07 Assoc Dean Admission/Enrol/Fin Aid ...... Ms. Michelle SCHMUDE
20 Assoc Dean of Curriculum .... Ms. Carien WILLIAMS
15 Assoc VP & Chief HR Officer .... Mr. Joseph CORTESE
21 Dir Budgeting & Financial Services .... Mr. Sam DIAZ
13 Chief Information Technology Ofcr .... Mr. James MICHAELS
35 Asst Dean of Students .... Ms. Jacquelyn GHORMOZ
06 Registrar .... Mr. Edward LAHART
37 Director of Financial Aid .... Ms. Ellen MCGUIRE
29 Dir Alumni Relations/Annual Giving .... Ms. Chris CARROLL

Commonwealth Technical Institute at the Hiram G. Andrews Center (A)

727 Goucher Street, Johnstown PA 15905-3092
County: Cambria FICE Identification: 025366
Unit ID: 212975
Telephone: (814) 255-8200 Carnegie Class: Assoc/HVT-High Non
FAX Number: (814) 255-5709 Calendar System: Semester
URL: www.hgac.org
Established: 1959 Annual Undergrad Tuition & Fees: $16,836
Enrollment: 222 Coed
Affiliation or Control: Proprietary IRS Status: Proprietary
Highest Offering: Associate Degree
Accreditation: ACCSC

01 President .... Vacant
12 Center Director .... Jill MORICONI
12 Center Deputy Director .... James MARKER
05 Director of Education .... Karen BILCHAK
07 Director of Admissions .... Jason GIES
32 Chief Student Life Officer .... Stacie ANDREWS
37 Director Student Financial Aid .... Vacant

Community College of Allegheny County (B)

800 Allegheny Avenue, Pittsburgh PA 15233-1895
County: Allegheny FICE Identification: 003231
Unit ID: 210605
Telephone: (412) 323-2323 Carnegie Class: Assoc/MT-VT-Mix Trad/Non
FAX Number: (412) 237-4420 Calendar System: Semester
URL: www.ccac.edu
Established: 1966 Annual Undergrad Tuition & Fees (In-District): $3,999
Enrollment: 17,153 Coed
Affiliation or Control: State/Local IRS Status: 501(c)3
Highest Offering: Associate Degree
Accreditation: M, ADNUR, CA, CAHIIM, COARC, DIETT, DMS, EMT, MAC, MLTAD, NMT, OTA, PTAA, RAD, RTT, SURGT

01 President .... Dr. Quintin B. BULLOCK
05 Provost/Exec Vice Pres Acad Affairs .... Dr. Stuart BLACKLAW
10 Vice President Finance .... Ms. Joyce BRECKENRIDGE
43 Vice President and General Counsel .... Mr. Anthony DITOMASSO
12 Campus President Allegheny .... Dr. Evon WALTERS
12 Campus President Boyce .... Hon. Charles MARTONI
12 Campus President North .... Dr. Gretchen SAWICKI
12 Campus President South .... Dr. Charlene NEWKIRK
86 Executive Director Govt Affairs .... Ms. Nancilee BURZACHECHI
103 VP Workforce Development .... Ms. Theresa BRYANT
15 VP Human Resources .... Ms. Kimberly MANIGAULT
102 CEO Educational Foundation .... Ms. Rose Ann DICOLA
13 Interim Chief Information Officer .... Dr. Diane JACOBS
06 Registrar .... Dr. Diane JACOBS
51 Dir Center Professional Dev .... Mr. Reginald OVERTON
45 AVP Strategic Plng/Inst Researc .... Mr. Kevin SMAY
18 Director of Facilities Management .... Mr. James MESSER
21 Controller .... Vacant
25 Director Contracts & Grants .... Dr. Carol YOANNONE
96 Director Purchasing/Contracts Admin .... Mr. Mike CVETIC
28 Special Asst to Pres for Diversity .... Mr. Clyde PICKETT
100 Assistant to the President .... Ms. Bonita L. RICHARDSON
29 Dir Alumni Affairs .... Mr. Rocco PALELLA
26 Executive Director Public Relations .... Ms. Elizabeth JOHNSTON

Community College of Allegheny County Boyce Campus (C)

595 Beatty Road, Monroeville PA 15146-1348
Telephone: (724) 325-6614 Identification: 770150
Accreditation: &M

† Regional accreditation is carried under the parent institution in Pittsburgh, PA

Community College of Allegheny County North Campus (D)

8701 Perry Highway, Pittsburgh PA 15237-5353
Telephone: (412) 366-7000 Identification: 770151
Accreditation: &M

† Regional accreditation is carried under the parent institution in Pittsburgh, PA

Community College of Allegheny County, South Campus (E)

1750 Clairton Road, West Mifflin PA 15122-3029
Telephone: (412) 469-1100 Identification: 770152
Accreditation: &M

† Regional accreditation is carried under the parent institution in Pittsburgh, PA

Community College of Beaver County (F)

1 Campus Drive, Monaca PA 15061-2588
County: Beaver FICE Identification: 006807
Unit ID: 211079
Telephone: (724) 480-2222 Carnegie Class: Assoc/MT-VT-High Trad
FAX Number: (724) 480-3573 Calendar System: Semester
URL: www.ccbc.edu
Established: 1966 Annual Undergrad Tuition & Fees (In-District): $5,460
Enrollment: 2,255 Coed
Affiliation or Control: State/Local IRS Status: 501(c)3
Highest Offering: Associate Degree
Accreditation: M, ADNUR, PHLEB

01 President .... Dr. Christopher M. REBER
05 Executive Vice President & Provost .... Dr. Roger W. DAVIS
10 VP Finance & Operations .... Mr. Glenn NATALI
15 VP Human Resources .... Ms. Sally MERCER
26 Exec Dir Mktg/Comm Rels & Advance ..... Ms. Leslie A. TENNANT
13 VP Information Technology .... Mr. Walter P. LUKHAUP
38 VP Student Affairs & Enrollment .... Ms. Janice M. KAMINSKI
18 Assoc VP & Dir Facilities & Ground .... Mr. Scott MONIT
84 Director Enrollment Services .... Ms. Angela M. HAMILTON
103 Dean Workforce & Continuing Educ .... Mr. John S. GOBERISH
09 Exec Dir Inst Research/Engagement .... Mr. Brian J. HAYDEN
37 Director Student Financial Services .... Ms. Janet DAVIDSON
04 Assistant to the President & Board .... Ms. Leanne CONDRON
76 Dean Nursing & Allied Health .... Dr. Shelly MOORE
49 Dean Business/Arts/Sciences & Tech .... Dr. John HIGGS
88 Dean Aviation Sciences .... Ms. Dara DONATI
41 Athletic Director .... Mr. John ASHAOLU
88 Dean HS Academies & Dual Enroll .... Col. Bill PINTER

Community College of Philadelphia (G)

1700 Spring Garden Street, Philadelphia PA 19130-3991
County: Philadelphia FICE Identification: 003249
Unit ID: 215239
Telephone: (215) 751-8000 Carnegie Class: Assoc/HT-High Trad
FAX Number: (215) 751-8762 Calendar System: Semester
URL: www.ccp.edu
Established: 1965 Annual Undergrad Tuition & Fees (In-District): $4,920
Enrollment: 19,119 Coed
Affiliation or Control: State/Local IRS Status: 501(c)3
Highest Offering: Associate Degree
Accreditation: M, ACFEI, ADNUR, COARC, DH, MLTAD, PHLEB, RAD

01 President .... Dr. Donald GENERALS
10 Vice President Business & Finance .... Mr. Jacob EAPEN
45 VP Strategic Initiatives and COS .... Dr. Judith GAY
30 Vice Pres Institutional Advancement .... Mr. Gregory MURPHY
05 VP Academic and Student Success .... Dr. Samuel HIRSCH
86 Vice Pres Marketing/Government Rels .... Ms. Lynette BROWN-SOW
103 VP Workforce Dev & Economic Innova .... Ms. Carol DE FRIES
43 General Counsel .... Ms. Victoria ZELLERS
13 Chief Information Officer .... Ms. Jody BAUER
32 Dean of Students .... Dr. Donovan MCCARGO
84 Interim Dean of Enrollment Services .... Dr. Donna RICHEMOND
49 Dean Liberal Studies .... Dr. Chae SWEET
51 Dean Div Adult/Community Education .... Dr. David E. THOMAS
72 Div Dean of Business/Technology .... Dr. Pam CARTER
09 Director Institutional Research .... Dr. Dawn SINNOT
06 Director Stdnt Records/Registration ..... Ms. Bonnie HARRINGTON
18 Chief Facilities/Physical Plant .... Mr. Harry MOORE
28 Affirmative Action Director .... Mr. Simon BROWN
07 Director of Recruitment/Admissions .... Ms. Jen DRAPER
37 Director Financial Aid .... Mr. Gim LIM
96 Director of Purchasing .... Ms. Marsia HENLEY
38 Dept Head Student Counseling .... Mr. Todd JONES
36 Coord Career Info/Placement Svcs .... Ms. Tarsha SCOVENS
29 Coord Alumni Rels/Annual Giving .... Ms. Lyvette BROOKS
25 Coord Grants/Prospect Research .... Ms. Anne GRECO

Consolidated School of Business (H)

2124 Ambassador Circle, Lancaster PA 17603-2389
County: Lancaster FICE Identification: 030299
Unit ID: 260354
Telephone: (717) 394-6211 Carnegie Class: Assoc/HVT-High Trad
FAX Number: (717) 394-6213 Calendar System: Other
URL: www.csb.edu
Established: 1981 Annual Undergrad Tuition & Fees: N/A
Enrollment: 99 Coed
Affiliation or Control: Proprietary IRS Status: Proprietary
Highest Offering: Associate Degree
Accreditation: ACICS

01 CEO/President .... Mr. Robert L. SAFRAN
11 Vice President for Administration .... Mr. William HOYT
10 Vice President for Finance .... Mr. Craig D. ELLIS
05 School Director .... Dr. Andrea STEPHENSON
37 Financial Aid Director .... Ms. Gail DOUGHERTY
36 Placement Director .... Ms. Kelly SWIGERT
13 Data Systems Director .... Mr. Gholamereza SALARI
21 Bursar .... Mrs. Diane GRANT

Consolidated School of Business (I)

1605 Clugston Road, York PA 17404-1798
County: York FICE Identification: 022896
Unit ID: 211820
Telephone: (717) 764-9550 Carnegie Class: Assoc/HVT-High Trad
FAX Number: (717) 764-9469 Calendar System: Other
URL: www.csb.edu
Established: 1981 Annual Undergrad Tuition & Fees: N/A
Enrollment: 107 Coed
Affiliation or Control: Proprietary IRS Status: Proprietary
Highest Offering: Associate Degree
Accreditation: ACICS

01 CEO/President .... Mr. Robert L. SAFRAN
11 Vice President .... Mr. Bill HOYT
37 Financial Aid Director .... Mrs. Gail E. DOUGHERTY
05 School Director .... Ms. Debra MARTINEZ

Curtis Institute of Music (J)

1726 Locust Street, Philadelphia PA 19103-6187
County: Philadelphia FICE Identification: 003251
Unit ID: 211893
Telephone: (215) 893-5252 Carnegie Class: Spec-4-yr-Arts
FAX Number: (215) 893-9065 Calendar System: Semester
URL: www.curtis.edu
Established: 1924 Annual Undergrad Tuition & Fees: $2,525
Enrollment: 176 Coed
Affiliation or Control: Independent Non-Profit IRS Status: 501(c)3
Highest Offering: Master's
Accreditation: M, MUS

01 President & Chief Executive Officer .... Mr. Roberto DIAZ
10 Sr VP Admin/Chief Financial Officer .... Mr. Rauli GARCIA
30 Sr VP Advancement .... Ms. Kristin B. LODEN
05 Dean of Faculty/Students .... Mr. Paul BRYAN
06 Registrar .... Mr. Darin KELLY
07 Admissions Officer .... Mr. Christopher HODGES
08 Library Director .... Ms. Michelle OSWELL

Dean Institute of Technology (K)

1501 W Liberty Avenue, Pittsburgh PA 15226-1197
County: Allegheny FICE Identification: 009186
Unit ID: 211909
Telephone: (412) 531-4433 Carnegie Class: Assoc/HVT-High Trad
FAX Number: (412) 531-4435 Calendar System: Quarter
URL: www.deantech.edu
Established: 1947 Annual Undergrad Tuition & Fees: $13,550
Enrollment: 166 Coed
Affiliation or Control: Proprietary IRS Status: Proprietary
Highest Offering: Associate Degree
Accreditation: ACCSC

01 President/Director .... Mr. James S. DEAN
05 Director of Education/Asst Director .... Mr. Richard D. ALI
07 Director of Admissions .... Mr. Nicholas D. ALI
37 Director Student Financial Aid .... Ms. Valerie L. VELTRI
36 Placement Director .... Ms. Valerie A. HAGEDORN
26 Director Information Office .... Mr. Stephen FALAVOLITO

Delaware County Community College (L)

901 S Media Line Road, Media PA 19063-1094
County: Delaware FICE Identification: 007110
Unit ID: 211927
Telephone: (610) 359-5000 Carnegie Class: Assoc/HT-High Trad
FAX Number: (610) 359-5343 Calendar System: Semester
URL: www.dccc.edu
Established: 1967 Annual Undergrad Tuition & Fees (In-District): $4,760
Enrollment: 12,459 Coed
Affiliation or Control: State/Local IRS Status: 501(c)3
Highest Offering: Associate Degree
Accreditation: M, ADNUR, COARC, EMT, MAC, SURGT

01 President .... Dr. Jerome S. PARKER
10 Vice Pres Administration/Treasurer .... Mr. John A. GLAVIN, JR.
05 Acting Provost .... Dr. Eric R. WELLINGTON
30 Vice President for Advancement .... Ms. Kathleen A. BRESLIN
12 Vice Provost & Vice Pres Chester Co .... Dr. Mary Jo BOYER
15 Vice President of Human Resources .... Ms. Connie L. MCCALLA
84 Vice President of Enrollment Mgmt . Ms. Frances M. CUBBERLEY
13 VP & CIO Information Technology .... Mr. George J. SULLIVAN
32 Vice Provost Student/Instr Support .... Dr. Grant S. SNYDER
96 Assoc VP Admin & Facilities Plng .... Mr. Jeffrey S. BAUN
88 Director Learning Commons .... Ms. Dawn M. MOSCARIELLO
88 Director Municipal Police Academy .... Mr. William DAVIS
106 Director Distance Learning Services ..... Mr. Alexander PLUCHUTA
37 Director of Financial Aid .... Mr. Raymond L. TOOLE
07 Asst VP Enrollment Svcs & Registrar .... Ms. Hope L. DIEHL
36 Director Career/Counseling Center .... Vacant
09 Assoc Vice Prov Inst Effectiveness .... Dr. Christopher TOKPAH
21 Associate VP Finance .... Vacant
103 Director Workforce Entry Center .... Ms. Susan E. BOND
85 Director International Student Svcs .... Ms. Kathryn A. LOZIER
16 Director Human Resources .... Mr. Christopher M. DICKERMAN

14 Assoc CIO OIT/Technical Services ... Ms. Bianca VALENTE
91 Director Admin Computing ... Mr. Bob HARDCASTLE
29 Director Alumni Programs ... Mr. Douglas J. FERGUSON
25 Director Grants Management ... Ms. Susan M. SHISLER-RAPP
31 Director Community Education ... Ms. Patricia S. SCEPANSKY
35 Director Campus Life ... Ms. Allison GLEESON
19 Director Safety & Security ... Mr. Raymond VISCUSI
88 Dir Dual Enrollment HS Initiatives ... Ms. Katherine DIAMOND-ROTHSTEIN
12 Director Southeast & UD Centers ... Ms. Jane SCHURMAN
89 Director First Year Experiences ... Dr. Kendrick MICKENS
88 Director Assessment Center ... Ms. Carol MULLIN
96 Director Purchasing ... Ms. Jenny M. RARIG
18 Dir Plant Oper/Construction Svcs ... Mr. Tony DELUCA
103 Dean Workforce Dev & Cmty Educ ... Ms. Karen KOZACHYN
81 Acting Dean STEM ... Dr. Mark SCHWARTZ
88 Dean Educational Support Svcs ... Ms. Tonya M. BRIGGS
50 Dean Business & Social Science ... Dr. Marian MCGORRY
79 Dean Comm/Arts & Humanities ... Vacant
76 Dean Health/Nursing/EMS ... Dr. Faye A. MELOY
40 Manager Bookstore ... Mr. Kris STACHOWIAK
04 Executive Assistant to President ... Ms. Loretta BEVILACQUA
26 Director of Marketing ... Mr. Daniel KANAK
45 Asst to President for Planning ... Mr. Craig R. FITZ
86 Asst to President for Communication ... Mr. Anthony TWYMAN

Delaware Valley University (A)

700 E Butler Avenue, Doylestown PA 18901-2697

County: Bucks | FICE Identification: 003252 | Unit ID: 211981
Telephone: (215) 345-1500 | Carnegie Class: Masters/S
FAX Number: (215) 345-5277 | Calendar System: Semester
URL: www.delval.edu
Established: 1896 | Annual Undergrad Tuition & Fees: $35,256
Enrollment: 2,137 | Coed
Affiliation or Control: Independent Non-Profit | IRS Status: 501(c)3
Highest Offering: Doctorate
Accreditation: M

01 President ... Dr. Maria GALLO
100 Administrative Director ... Ms. Angela T. RECKNER
05 VP Acad Affairs/Dean of the Faculty ... Dr. Bashar W. HANNA
32 VP Student Affairs/Dean of Students ... Dr. April VARI
10 VP for Finance & Administration ... Ms. Jenni SAUER
30 Vice President for Inst Advancement ... Mr. Joseph ERCKERT
09 AVP Rsrch/Plng/Accr & Dir I&R ... Ms. Deborah DAILEY
84 VP for Enrollment Mgmt ... Mr. Arthur GOON
81 Dean of Life & Physical Sciences ... Dr. Benjamin RUSILOSKI
47 Interim Dean of Agric & Environ Sci ... Dr. Christopher TIPPING
50 Dean of Business & Humanities ... Vacant
58 Dean of Grad/Prof & Entr ... Dr. James MORYAN
06 Registrar ... Mr. James SLIZEWSKI
41 Athletic Director ... Mr. Steve CANTRELL
26 Chief Marketing Officer ... Ms. Laurie WARD
07 Director of Admissions ... Mr. Dwayne WALKER
13 Exec Dir of Technology Services ... Mr. Mike DAVIS
36 Exec Dir Ctr for Student Prof Dev ... Dr. Benjamin RUSILOSKI
08 Librarian ... Mr. Peter A. KUPERSMITH
37 Director Student Financial Aid ... Mrs. Joan HOCK
58 Director Graduate & Prof Studies ... Ms. Yolonda UDVARDY
38 Director Counseling/Learn Support ... Ms. Sharon DONNELLY
23 Director Health Services ... Ms. Miriam TORRES
14 Assoc Dir of Help Desk Operations ... Mr. Darren MOSES
39 Director of Residence Life ... Mr. Derek SMITH
19 Director Security/Public Safety ... Vacant
15 Director Human Resources ... Ms. Barbara HLADIK
18 Director Physical Plant ... Mr. Joseph GUCKAVAN
44 Director Annual Fund ... Ms. Jennifer ROCK
96 Director of Purchasing ... Mr. William LYLE
102 Dir Foundation/Corporate Relations ... Ms. Wendy CONNUCK
103 Dir Workforce/Career Development ... Ms. Deanna PARKTON
104 Director Study Abroad ... Vacant
106 Dir Online Education/E-learning ... Ms. Cynthia RENNER
29 Director Alumni Engagement ... Ms. Lynn CARROLL
04 Admin Asst to the President ... Ms. Kristen OLSZEWSKI

DeSales University (B)

2755 Station Avenue, Center Valley PA 18034-9568

County: Lehigh | FICE Identification: 003986 | Unit ID: 210739
Telephone: (610) 282-1100 | Carnegie Class: Masters/L
FAX Number: (610) 282-2254 | Calendar System: Semester
URL: www.desales.edu
Established: 1965 | Annual Undergrad Tuition & Fees: $33,350
Enrollment: 3,190 | Coed
Affiliation or Control: Roman Catholic | IRS Status: 501(c)3
Highest Offering: Doctorate
Accreditation: M, ACBSP, ARCPA, NURSE, @PTA

01 President ... Dr. Bernard F. O'CONNOR, OSFS
04 Admin Assistant to the President ... Ms. Mary A. GOTZON
05 Provost/Vice Pres Academic Affairs ... Dr. Karen WALTON
06 Registrar ... Mr. Thomas MANTONI
08 Librarian ... Ms. Deborah MALONE
51 Dean of Lifelong Learning ... Ms. Deborah BOOROS
88 Dean of Undergraduate Education ... Dr. Robert BLUMENSTEIN
36 Director of Career Development ... Ms. Kristin EICHOLTZ
30 Vice Pres Institutional Advancement ... Mr. Thomas L. CAMPBELL
86 Director of Government Relations ... Dr. Bernard F. O'CONNOR, OSFS
102 Director Corp/Foundation Relations ... Mrs. Kathy DIAMANDOPOULOS
26 Executive Director of Communication ... Mr. Thomas MCNAMARA
44 Executive Director of Annual Giving ... Ms. Lina BARBIERI
29 Director of Alumni Relations ... Ms. Nicole GINGRICH
10 VP for Admin/Finance & Campus Env ... Mr. Robert J. SNYDER
45 Assoc VP for Admin & Planning ... Mr. Peter RAUTZHAN
21 Director of Finance/Treasurer ... Mr. Michael SWEETANA
19 Chief of Police ... Chief Steven MARSHALL
09 Dir of Institutional Rsrch/Analysis ... Ms. Lisa PLUMMER
88 Assoc VP of Campus Environment ... Mr. Marc ALBANESE
18 Director of Facilities ... Mr. Jim MOLCHANY
40 Campus Store Manager ... Ms. Bridget SCOGNA
15 Director of Human Resources ... Mrs. Margie GRANDINETTI
16 Employment Benefits Coord/HR Gen ... Ms. Lisa LIGHTCAP
13 Director of Information Technology ... Ms. Patricia CLAY
32 Vice President Student Life ... Dr. Gerard JOYCE
84 Dean of Enrollment Mgmt ... Mrs. Mary BIRKHEAD
35 Dean of Students ... Mrs. Linda ZERBE
39 Director of Residence Life ... Ms. Melinda QUINONES
07 Director of Admissions ... Mr. Derrick WETZEL
37 Director of Student Financial Aid ... Mrs. Joyce FARMER
42 Chaplain ... Fr. Timothy MCINTIRE, OSFS
38 Director of Counseling Center ... Ms. Wendy KRISAK
41 Athletic Director ... Mr. Scott COVAL
28 Director Multicultural/Intl Affairs ... Vacant
58 Dean of Graduate Education ... Dr. Peter LEONARD, OSFS
96 Campus Environment/Dir Purchasing ... Mr. Michael DUFFY
103 Dir Workforce/Career Development ... Ms. Kristin EICHOLTZ
104 Director of International Learning ... Mr. Brian MACDONALD
50 Division Head of Business ... Mr. Christopher R. COCOZZA
53 Dean of Education ... Dr. Judith RANCE-RONEY
105 Director Web Services ... Ms. Kristin LAUDENSLAGER
106 Dir Online Education/E-learning ... Dr. Eric HAGAN

DeVry University - Fort Washington Campus (C)

1140 Virginia Drive, Fort Washington PA 19034-3204

Telephone: (215) 591-5700 | Identification: 666218
Accreditation: &NH, ENGT

† Regional accreditation is carried under the parent institution in Downers Grove, IL.

Dickinson College (D)

Box 1773, College & Louther Street, Carlisle PA 17013-2896

County: Cumberland | FICE Identification: 003253 | Unit ID: 212009
Telephone: (717) 243-5121 | Carnegie Class: Bac-A&S
FAX Number: N/A | Calendar System: Semester
URL: www.dickinson.edu
Established: 1783 | Annual Undergrad Tuition & Fees: $49,489
Enrollment: 2,364 | Coed
Affiliation or Control: Independent Non-Profit | IRS Status: 501(c)3
Highest Offering: Baccalaureate
Accreditation: M

01 Interim President ... Dr. Neil B. WEISSMAN
05 Interim Provost/Dean of the College ... Dr. Robert P. WINSTON
84 VP Enrollment Marketing and Comm ... Dr. Stefanie D. NILES
10 VP Finance & Administration ... Dr. Bronté BURLEIGH-JONES
30 VP College Advancement ... Mr. Kirk I. SWENSON
32 VP Student Life ... Ms. Joyce A. BYLANDER
13 VP & Chief Information Officer ... Mr. Robert E. RENAUD
09 VP Institutional Initiatives ... Mr. Michael E. REED
07 Dean of Admissions ... Ms. Catherine M. DAVENPORT
15 Assoc VP Human Resource Services ... Ms. Debra HARGROVE
43 General Counsel ... Ms. Dana E. SCADUTO
101 Chief of Staff/Secretary of College ... Ms. Karen N. FARYNIAK
18 Assoc VP Sustain & Facilities Plng ... Mr. Kenneth E. SHULTES
20 Sr Assoc Provost Academic Affairs ... Dr. John H. HENSON
20 Sr Assoc Provost Academic Affairs ... Dr. Brenda K. BRETZ
44 Assoc VP College Advance ... Mr. Brian G. FALCK
109 Assoc VP Auxil Svcs & Budget Mgmt ... Mr. Stephen C. HIETSCH
26 Exec Dir Marketing & Communications ... Ms. Connie MCNAMARA
06 Registrar ... Ms. Karen A. WEIKEL
41 Director Athletics ... Mr. Joe GIUNTA
09 Director Institutional Research ... Dr. Jason E. RIVERA
37 Director of Financial Aid ... Mr. Richard A. HECKMAN
104 Exec Dir Ctr Global Stdy & Engagmnt ... Ms. Samantha C. BRANDAUER
36 Dean Career Dev/Asst VP Student Dev ... Mr. Philip JONES
88 Executive Director Wellness Center ... Dr. Alecia D. SUNDSMO
35 Assoc VP Stdnt Ldrshp/Campus Engage ... Ms. Rebecca J. HAMMELL
90 Director Academic Computing ... Ms. Patricia A. PEHLMAN
88 Director of Media Relations ... Ms. Christine BAKSI
29 Asst VP Engagement/Annual Fund ... Ms. Coco MINARDI
08 Director Library Services ... Ms. Eleanor MITCHELL
40 Dir College Bookstore/Central Svcs ... Mr. David A. NELSON
19 Asst VP Compliance/Campus Safety ... Ms. Dolores A. DANSER
91 Assoc VP Enterprise Systems ... Ms. Jill M. FORRESTER
102 Dir Academic & Foundation Relations ... Ms. Cheryl E. KREMER
39 Assoc Dean Stdnts/Dir Res Life ... Ms. Angie HARRIS
102 Executive Director Donor Relations ... Ms. Tara C. RENAULT
105 Director Online Marketing ... Ms. Sarah M. SHERIFF
42 Director Cmty Svcs/Religious Life ... Rev. Donna D. HUGHES
100 Asst Chief of Staff ... Ms. Ashley M. PERZYNA

Dickinson Law (E)

150 South College Street, Carlisle PA 17013

Telephone: (717) 240-5000 | FICE Identification: 003254
Accreditation: &M, LAW

† Part of Penn State University. Regional accreditation is carried under the parent institution in University Park, PA.

Douglas Education Center (F)

130 Seventh Street, Monessen PA 15062-1097

County: Westmoreland | FICE Identification: 020683 | Unit ID: 212045
Telephone: (724) 684-3684 | Carnegie Class: Spec 2-yr-A&S
FAX Number: (724) 684-7463 | Calendar System: Semester
URL: www.dec.edu
Established: 1904 | Annual Undergrad Tuition & Fees: $18,737
Enrollment: 267 | Coed
Affiliation or Control: Proprietary | IRS Status: Proprietary
Highest Offering: Associate Degree
Accreditation: ACICS

01 President ... Mr. Jeffrey D. IMBRESCIA
05 Executive Director of Education ... Mr. Julian IMBRESCIA
10 Chief Financial Officer ... Mr. Jay B. CLAYTON
20 Senior Academic Affairs Coordinator ... Ms. N. Renee MCDOWELL
06 Registrar/Academic Affairs ... Ms. Cynthia V. YOUNG
07 Director of Admissions ... Mr. Tony BAEZ MILAN
37 Executive Director of Financial Aid ... Ms. Amanda PHILLIPS
26 Chief Marketing Officer ... Mr. Kevin G. FEAR
88 Supervisor of Cosmetology ... Ms. Carrie HOLMAN
36 Director of Career Services ... Ms. Lauri ASTON
32 Student Life/Social Media ... Ms. Janelle IMBRESCIA
13 Director of Information Technology ... Mr. John SECHRIST

Drexel University (G)

3141 Chestnut Street, Philadelphia PA 19104-2875

County: Philadelphia | FICE Identification: 003256 | Unit ID: 212054
Telephone: (215) 895-2000 | Carnegie Class: DU-Higher
FAX Number: (215) 895-1414 | Calendar System: Quarter
URL: www.drexel.edu
Established: 1891 | Annual Undergrad Tuition & Fees: $48,791
Enrollment: 26,359 | Coed
Affiliation or Control: Independent Non-Profit | IRS Status: 501(c)3
Highest Offering: Doctorate
Accreditation: M, ANEST, ARCPA, ART, BUS, CEA, CIDA, CLPSY, CONST, CS, DENT, DIETD, ENG, ENGT, HT, LAW, LIB, MED, MFCD, NURSE, PA, PH, PTA

01 President ... Mr. John A. FRY
05 Provost/Executive Vice President ... Dr. Brian BLAKE
30 SVP Inst Advancement ... Mr. David L. UNRUH
11 Exec Vice Pres/Treasurer/COO ... Mrs. Helen Y. BOWMAN
84 SVP Enrollment Mgmt/Student Success ... Dr. Randall C. DEIKE
26 Sr VP University Communications ... Ms. Lori N. DOYLE
43 Sr VP & General Counsel ... Mr. Michael J. EXLER
86 Sr VP Govt & Community Relations ... Mr. Brian T. KEECH
20 Sr Vice Provost Undergrad Ed ... Dr. N. John DINARDO
13 Vice Pres IRT & CIO ... Mr. Thomas DECHIARO
10 Vice Pres/CFO & Assoc Treasurer ... Mr. Jeffrey A. EBERLY
88 Exec Dir & Vice Prov Cultural Partn ... Dr. Rosalind REMER
07 Int Vice Pres/Dean of Admissions ... Ms. Evelyn THIMBA
102 Sr VP Corp Relations & Economic Dev ... Mr. Keith A. ORRIS
46 Sr Vice Provost for Research ... Dr. Aleister SAUNDERS
32 Vice Pres and Dean of Student Life ... Dr. Subir SAHU
09 Vice Provost Institutional Research ... Dr. Mark FREEMAN
100 VP & Exec Dir Office of President ... Mr. Gregory P. MONTANARO
108 VP Compliance/Privacy & IA ... Mr. Edward G. LONGAZEL
88 Vice President Investments ... Ms. Catherine B. ULOZAS
88 Sr Vice Provost Partnerships ... Dr. Lucy E. KERMAN
18 Vice Pres Univ Facilities ... Dr. Robert A. FRANCIS
15 Vice Pres Human Resources & PMOE ... Ms. Megan E. WEYLER
49 Dean College Arts & Sciences ... Dr. Donna MURASKO
50 Dean LeBow College of Business ... Dr. Francis LINNEHAN
54 Dean College of Engineering ... Dr. Joseph B. HUGHES
77 Dean Col of Computing & Informatics ... Dr. Yi DENG
92 Dean of Pennoni Honors College ... Dr. Paula COHEN
88 Dean Grad Sch of Biomed Science ... Dr. Elisabeth VANBOCKSTAELE
62 Dean of Libraries ... Dr. Danuta A. NITECKI
88 Dean of Close School ... Dr. Donna M. DECAROLIS
58 Exec Vice Prov & Dean Grad Studies ... Dr. James D. HERBERT
61 Dean Kline School of Law ... Mr. Roger J. DENNIS
60 Dean Col of Media Arts & Design ... Mr. Allen C. SABINSON
53 Dean School of Education ... Dr. Nancy B. SONGER
63 Sr VP & Dean College of Medicine ... Dr. Daniel V. SCHIDLOW
66 Int Dean Col Nursing/Health Prof ... Dr. Susan S. SMITH
69 Dean Urban Health Collaborative ... Dr. Ana V. DIEZ ROUX
88 Pres Academy of Natural Sciences ... Mr. George W. GEPHART, JR.
88 Int Dean School Biomed Engineering ... Dr. Kenneth A. BARBEE
19 Vice President Public Safety ... Ms. Eileen W. BEHR
109 Vice President Campus Services ... Ms. Rita E. LARUE
41 Athletic Director ... Dr. Eric A. ZILLMER
36 Vice Prov Career Development Ctr ... Mr. Peter J. FRANKS
22 Assoc VP Equality & Diversity ... Ms. Michele M. ROVINSKY-MAYER
106 SVP of Drexel & President of DEL ... Dr. Susan C. ALDRIDGE
85 Sr Vice Provost Global Initatives ... Dr. Julie MOSTOV
88 Vice Chair Faculty Senate ... Dr. Michael KENNEDY
88 Director AJ Drexel Autism Institute ... Dr. Craig J. NEWSCHAFFER
96 Assoc Vice Pres Procurement Svcs ... Mr. Stephen G. MACK

Duquesne University (A)

600 Forbes Avenue, Pittsburgh PA 15282-0001
County: Allegheny — FICE Identification: 003258
Unit ID: 212106
Telephone: (412) 396-6000 — Carnegie Class: DU-Higher
FAX Number: (412) 396-4186 — Calendar System: Semester
URL: www.duq.edu
Established: 1878 — Annual Undergrad Tuition & Fees: $33,778
Enrollment: 9,648 — Coed
Affiliation or Control: Roman Catholic — IRS Status: 501(c)3
Highest Offering: Doctorate
Accreditation: M, ARCPA, BUS, CAATE, CACREP, CEA, CLPSY, FEPAC, LAW, MUS, NURSE, OT, PHAR, PTA, SCPSY, SP, TED

01	President	Mr. Kenneth G. GORMLEY
04	Assistant to the President	Ms. Margaret EISEMAN
05	Provost/Academic Vice President	Dr. Timothy R. AUSTIN
10	Vice Pres for Management Business	Dr. Matthew J. FRIST
32	Vice Pres for Student Life	Dr. Douglas FRIZZELL
30	VP for University Advancement	Mr. John J. PLANTE
88	Vice President Mission & Identity	Rev. Raymond FRENCH, CSSP
43	VP Legal Affairs & General Counsel	Ms. Madelyn REILLY
20	Assoc Academic Vice Pres Research	Dr. Alan W. SEADLER
20	Assoc Academic Vice President	Dr. Jeffrey A. MILLER
13	Asst Vice President/CIO	Dr. Charles R. BARTEL
109	Director Auxiliary Services	Mr. Scott RICHARDS
85	Exec Dir International Programs	Dr. Roberta C. ARONSON
84	Assoc Vice Pres Enrollment Mgmt	Mr. Paul-James CUKANNA
06	Registrar	Ms. Kim HOERTZ
08	Librarian	Dr. Sara BARON
29	Director Alumni Relations	Ms. Sarah SPERRY
09	Director of Institutional Research	Mr. Matthew NORTH
37	Director Financial Aid	Mr. Richard C. ESPOSITO
15	Asst Vice Pres/CHRO	Mr. John G. GREENO
19	Director of Security	Mr. Thomas HART
88	Dir Environmental Health/Safety	Ms. Paula D. SWEITZER
18	Asst VP/Chief Facilities Officer	Mr. Rodney W. DOBISH
36	Director of Career Services	Ms. Nicole FELDHUES
41	Director of Athletics	Mr. David HARPER
26	Assoc Vice Pres of Public Affairs	Ms. Bridget M. FARE
22	Director of Anti-discrimination	Mr. Sean F. WEAVER
23	Director Health Service	Ms. Dessa MRVOS
38	Dir University Counseling Center	Dr. Ian C. EDWARDS
39	Director Residence Life	Mrs. Sharon G. OELSCHLAGER
42	Director Campus Ministry	Rev. Daniel WALSH, CSSP
28	Director of Multicultural Affairs	Mr. Jeff MALLORY
50	Dean Business & Administration	Dr. Dean B. MCFARLIN
66	Dean of Nursing	Dr. Mary Ellen S. GLASGOW
67	Dean of Pharmacy	Dr. J. Douglas BRICKER
64	Dean of Music	Dr. Seth BECKMAN
53	Dean of Education	Dr. Cindy M. WALKER
76	Interim Dean of Health Sciences	Dr. Paula S. TUROCY
61	Interim Dean of Law	Ms. Maureen LALLY-GREEN
49	Dean of Liberal Arts/Graduate	Dr. James SWINDAL
65	Dean of Natural/Environment Sci	Dr. Philip P. REEDER
40	Bookstore Manager	Mr. John KACHUR
07	Director of Admissions	Ms. Debra A. ZUGATES
88	Asst VP for Executive Affairs	Ms. Mary Ellen SOLOMON
88	Asst VP for External Relations	Ms. Mary Beth FORD
106	Dir Online Education/E-learning	Dr. Michael W. BRIDGES

Eastern University (B)

1300 Eagle Road, Saint Davids PA 19087-3696
County: Delaware — FICE Identification: 003259
Unit ID: 212133
Telephone: (610) 341-5800 — Carnegie Class: Masters/L
FAX Number: (610) 341-1377 — Calendar System: Semester
URL: www.eastern.edu
Established: 1925 — Annual Undergrad Tuition & Fees: $30,640
Enrollment: 3,762 — Coed
Affiliation or Control: American Baptist — IRS Status: 501(c)3
Highest Offering: Doctorate
Accreditation: M, CAATE, EXSC, NURSE, SW

01	President	Dr. Robert DUFFETT
10	Vice Pres for Finance/Operations	Mr. J. Pernell JONES
21	Associate VP Finance	Ms. Polly BEROL
03	Executive Vice President	Dr. M. Thomas RIDINGTON
05	Provost	Dr. R. Keith IDDINGS
06	Registrar	Ms. Sara ROCHE
32	Vice Provost Student Development	Dr. Bettie Ann BRIGHAM
45	Vice Pres Inst Plng Research Assess	Dr. Christine P. MAHAN
30	Vice President Advancement	Ms. Lisa TITUS
84	Vice Pres Enrollment/Marketing	Dr. Kenton SPARKS
07	Exec Director Enrollment	Mr. Michael DZIEDZIAK
07	Sr Admissions Couns Palmer Sem	Ms. Tiffany MURPHY
15	Senior Director of Human Resources	Ms. Kacey BERNARD
04	Exec Asst to the President	Ms. Heather NORCINI
35	Dean of Students	Mr. Daryl HAWKINS
49	Vice Provost Acad Affairs/Dean CAS	Dr. John PAULEY, II
12	Academic Dean Esperanza College	Dr. Elizabeth CONDE-FRAZIER
83	Dean College of Health/Soc Sciences	Dr. Patricia REGER
73	Dean College of Theology/Ministry	Dr. F. David BRONKEMA
50	Dean College of Business	Dr. Douglas CLARK
92	Dean Templeton Honors College	Dr. Jonathan YONAN
53	Dean College of Education	Dr. Harry GUTELIUS
66	Chair Department of Nursing	Dr. Dianne DELONG
18	Exec Director Campus Services	Mr. Jeffrey GROMIS
105	Dir Web and User Services	Mr. Mark HOFFMAN
09	Director Institutional Research	Mr. Thomas A. DAHLSTROM
108	Director of Assessment	Vacant
26	Director of Communications	Ms. Denise MCMILLAN
88	Senior Director Student Accounts	Ms. Lisa WELLER
08	Library Director	Dr. James L. SAUER
42	University Chaplain	Rev Dr. Joseph E. MODICA
37	Director of Financial Aid	Ms. Christal JENNINGS
13	Interim Exec Director Tech Services	Mr. Philip MUGRIDGE
36	Director of Talent & Career Dev	Ms. Sarah TODD
29	Dir Alumni/Parent Relations	Ms. Mary GARDNER
25	Dir Foundations/Grants/Govt Rel	Ms. Ingrid COOPER
41	Interim Director of Athletics	Ms. Heidi BIRTWISTLE
19	Director of Public Safety	Mr. Jim MAGEE
88	Director of Conferences/Spec Events	Ms. Meggin CAPERS
38	Dir Counseling/Academic Support	Dr. Lisa M. HEMLICK
23	Director University Health Center	Ms. Bridget MCGUIGAN
85	Dir Intl Student & Scholar Services	Ms. Augusta ALLEN
39	Coordinator of Housing	Mr. Kyle SULLIVANAHARRIS8@EASTERN.
40	Follett Bookstore Manager	Ms. Helen RICOTTA
88	Chair Urban Studies	Dr. Kimberlee JOHNSON
28	Asst Dean Stdnts for Multicultural	Ms. Jacqueline IRVING
88	Asst Dean Students/Dir of Advising	Mr. David SCHLOSSER
109	Director Auxiliary Services	Mr. Byron MCMILLAN
88	Dir Faculty Development	Dr. Michael THOMAS
101	Assistant to the President - Board	Ms. Beth RUTLEDGE
44	Director Annual Giving	Mr. Joseph TREMOGLIE

† Parent institution of Palmer Theological Seminary.

Elizabethtown College (C)

1 Alpha Drive, Elizabethtown PA 17022-2298
County: Lancaster — FICE Identification: 003262
Unit ID: 212197
Telephone: (717) 361-1000 — Carnegie Class: Bac-A&S
FAX Number: (717) 361-1207 — Calendar System: Semester
URL: www.etown.edu
Established: 1899 — Annual Undergrad Tuition & Fees: $41,710
Enrollment: 1,822 — Coed
Affiliation or Control: Church Of The Brethren — IRS Status: 501(c)3
Highest Offering: Master's
Accreditation: M, ACBSP, ENG, MUS, OT, SW

01	President	Dr. Carl J. STRIKWERDA
05	Sr Vice Pres Acad Affs/Dn Faculty	Dr. Elizabeth (Betty) RIDER
10	Vice Pres Administration/Finance	Mr. Robert M. WALLET
30	Vice President Advancement/Cmty Rel	Mr. David C. BEIDLEMAN
84	Int Vice Pres Enrollment Mgmt	Mr. Peter NACY
32	VP Student Affairs/Dean of Students	Ms. Marianne CALENDA
51	Dean Ctr Continuing Educ/Dist Lrng	Mr. John KOKOLUS
07	Director Admissions	Ms. Lauren C DEIBLER
35	Asst Dean of Students & Dir of CSS	Ms. Stephanie A. RANKIN
26	Exec Dir Marketing/Communications	Ms. Elizabeth (Liz) A. BRAUNGARD
13	Exec Director Information/Tech Svcs	Mr. Ronald F. HEASLEY
102	Exec Dir Foundation/Govt Relations	Ms. Lesley M. FINNEY
46	Director Research & Planning	Dr. Richard BASOM
37	Director of Financial Aid	Ms. Melodie R. JACKSON
08	Director The High Library	Ms. Sarah PENNIMAN
29	Director Alumni Devel & Programs	Mr. Mark A. CLAPPER
19	Director of Campus Security	Mr. Andrew L. POWELL
41	Director of Athletics	Mr. Chris MORGAN
42	Chaplain/Director Religious Life	Dr. Tracy SADD

Erie Institute of Technology (D)

940 Millcreek Mall, Erie PA 16565-1002
County: Erie — FICE Identification: 022039
Unit ID: 212434
Telephone: (814) 868-9900 — Carnegie Class: Spec 2-yr-Tech
FAX Number: (814) 868-9977 — Calendar System: Semester
URL: www.erieit.edu
Established: 1958 — Annual Undergrad Tuition & Fees: $13,770
Enrollment: 232 — Coed
Affiliation or Control: Proprietary — IRS Status: Proprietary
Highest Offering: Associate Degree
Accreditation: ACCSC

01	Director	Mr. Paul FITZGERALD
05	Director of Education	Ms. Kate HUSHON
37	Financial Aid Officer	Ms. Kelly SCHULTZ
07	Admissions Director	Ms. Barb BOLT
36	Placement Director	Mr. Quentin TARASZEWSKI

Esperanza College (E)

4261 North 5th Street, Philadelphia PA 19140
Telephone: (215) 324-0746 — Identification: 770153
Accreditation: &M

† Regional accreditation is carried under the parent institution in Saint Davids, PA

Evangelical Theological Seminary (F)

121 S College Street, Myerstown PA 17067-1222
County: Lebanon — FICE Identification: 003263
Unit ID: 212443
Telephone: (717) 866-5775 — Carnegie Class: Spec-4-yr-Faith
FAX Number: (717) 866-4667 — Calendar System: 4/1/4
URL: www.evangelical.edu
Established: 1953 — Annual Graduate Tuition & Fees: N/A
Enrollment: 123 — Coed
Affiliation or Control: Evangelical Congregational Church — IRS Status: 501(c)3
Highest Offering: Master's; No Undergraduates
Accreditation: M, MFCD, THEOL

01	President	Dr. Anthony L. BLAIR
30	Vice Pres Institutional Advancement	Rev. Ann E. STEEL
10	Vice President Finance & Operations	Mr. Kevin C. HENRY
26	VP of Marketing/Communications	Mr. George DAVIS
05	Dean of Academic Programs	Dr. Laurie A. MELLINGER
08	Head Librarian	Dr. Mark DRAPER
18	Director of Buildings & Grounds	Mr. William J. ROBERTSON
88	Database Manager	Mrs. Marsha A. CONLEY
06	Registrar/Financial Aid Admin	Mr. Ellis I. KIRK
07	Director of Admissions	Ms. Gwen SCHEIRER

Fortis Institute (G)

5757 West Ridge Road, Erie PA 16506-1013
County: Erie — FICE Identification: 030108
Unit ID: 216418
Telephone: (814) 838-7673 — Carnegie Class: Assoc/HVT-High Trad
FAX Number: (814) 838-8642 — Calendar System: Quarter
URL: www.fortis.edu
Established: 1984 — Annual Undergrad Tuition & Fees: $13,062
Enrollment: 652 — Coed
Affiliation or Control: Proprietary — IRS Status: Proprietary
Highest Offering: Associate Degree
Accreditation: ACICS, DH

01	President	Mr. Peter CORREA
05	Director of Education	Mr. Michael CARR
10	Business Officer	Ms. Shelley FAYTAK
07	Admissions	Mr. Michael MURRAY
06	Registrar	Ms. Margo DEVERS
37	Financial Aid	Mr. Marc GRUTKOWSKI
36	Placement	Mr. John ZACZYK

Fortis Institute (H)

166 Slocum Street, Forty Fort PA 18704-2347
County: Luzerne — FICE Identification: 030115
Unit ID: 249609
Telephone: (570) 288-8400 — Carnegie Class: Spec 2-yr-Health
FAX Number: (570) 287-7936 — Calendar System: Other
URL: www.fortis.edu
Established: 1984 — Annual Undergrad Tuition & Fees: $15,214
Enrollment: 186 — Coed
Affiliation or Control: Proprietary — IRS Status: Proprietary
Highest Offering: Associate Degree
Accreditation: ACCSC

01	Campus President	Ruth BRUMAGIN
05	Director of Education	Ruth BRUMAGIN
07	Director of Admissions	Jane AUSTIN

Fortis Institute (I)

517 Ash Street, Scranton PA 18509
County: Lackawanna — FICE Identification: 030116
Unit ID: 385503
Telephone: (570) 558-1818 — Carnegie Class: Spec 2-yr-Health
FAX Number: (570) 342-4537 — Calendar System: Other
URL: www.fortis.edu/scranton-pennsylvania.php
Established: 1986 — Annual Undergrad Tuition & Fees: $26,756
Enrollment: 385 — Coed
Affiliation or Control: Proprietary — IRS Status: Proprietary
Highest Offering: Associate Degree
Accreditation: ACCSC, DH

01	Campus President	Ms. Madeline LEVY CRUZ
06	Registrar	Mr. Jacy HOBBS
07	Director of Admissions	Mr. Timothy PARSONS
36	Director Student Placement	Mr. Kyle ROBBINS
37	Director Student Financial Aid	Ms. Stacie TAROLI

† Tuition varies by degree program.

Franklin & Marshall College (J)

PO Box 3003, Lancaster PA 17604-3003
County: Lancaster — FICE Identification: 003265
Unit ID: 212577
Telephone: (717) 358-3971 — Carnegie Class: Bac-A&S
FAX Number: (717) 358-4183 — Calendar System: Semester
URL: www.fandm.edu
Established: 1787 — Annual Undergrad Tuition & Fees: $50,400
Enrollment: 2,209 — Coed
Affiliation or Control: Independent Non-Profit — IRS Status: 501(c)3
Highest Offering: Baccalaureate
Accreditation: M

01	President	Dr. Daniel R. PORTERFIELD
10	Vice Pres for Finance and Treasurer	Mr. David R. PROULX
30	Vice Pres for College Advancement	Mr. Matthew EYNON
84	VP/Dean of Admission/Financial Aid	Mr. Eric G. MAGUIRE
26	Vice Pres for College Communication	Mr. Kevin BURKE
05	Provost/Dean of Faculty	Dr. Joel MARTIN
20	Dean of the College	Ms. Margaret HAZLETT
88	Assoc Dean of Col & Dir Klehr Ctr	Dr. Ralph TABER
21	Assoc Vice President for Finance	Ms. Wendy S. STARNER

Code	Title	Name
11	Associate VP for Administration	Mr. Barry BOSLEY
45	VP for Planning	Dr. Alan S. CANIGLIA
100	Chief of Staff	Ms. Robyn PIGGOTT
08	College Librarian	Mr. Scott VINE
44	Major Gifts Officer	Ms. Catherine T. FERRY
85	Assoc Dean International Programs	Ms. Sue MENNICKE
20	Associate Dean of Faculty	Dr. Ken KREBS
20	Associate Dean of Faculty	Dr. Kimberly ARMSTRONG
32	Assoc Dean of Multicultural Affairs	Dr. Marion A. COLEMAN
88	Associate Dean/House Dean	Ms. Katharine J. SNIDER
88	Associate Dean/House Dean	Dr. Suzanna L. RICHTER
88	Associate Dean/House Dean	Dr. Beth PROFFITT
88	Associate Dean/House Dean	Dr. Amy R. MORENO
21	Controller	Mr. Sean GALLOWAY
15	Director Human Resources	Ms. Laura FIORE
18	Associate VP/Facilities Management	Mr. Mike WETZEL
19	Director Public Safety	Mr. William MCHALE, JR.
23	Director Health Services	Dr. Amy A. MYERS
13	Assoc VP/Chief Information Officer	Ms. Carrie RAMPP
37	Director Financial Aid	Mr. Clarke C. PAINE
38	Clinical Dir Counseling Services	Dr. Christine G. CONWAY
90	Dir Instruct/Emerging Technology	Mr. Teb LOCKE
06	Registrar & Assoc Director Inst Res	Ms. Christine D. ALEXANDER
29	Executive Dir of Alumni Relations	Ms. Mary MAZZUCA
07	Director of Admission	Ms. Julie A. KERICH
41	Athletic Director	Ms. Patricia EPPS
43	General Counsel	Mr. Pierce BULLER

Gannon University (A)

University Square, Erie PA 16541-0001

County: Erie — FICE Identification: 003266 — Unit ID: 212601

Telephone: (814) 871-7000 — Carnegie Class: Masters/L
FAX Number: (814) 871-7338 — Calendar System: Other
URL: www.gannon.edu
Established: 1925 — Annual Undergrad Tuition & Fees: $29,258
Enrollment: 4,410 — Coed
Affiliation or Control: Roman Catholic — IRS Status: 501(c)3
Highest Offering: Doctorate
Accreditation: M, ACBSP, ANEST, ARCPA, CAATE, CACREP, COARC, COARCP, CS, ENG, NURSE, OT, PTA, RAD, SW

Code	Title	Name
01	President	Dr. Keith TAYLOR
05	VP Academic Affairs	Dr. Walter IWANENKO, JR.
10	Vice President Finance/Admin	Mrs. Linda L. WAGNER
30	Vice Pres University Advancement	Mr. R. Scott RASH
88	Assoc Vice President for Mission	Rev. Michael KESICKI
84	Vice President for Enrollment	Mr. William EDMONDSON
32	VP Student Development & Engagement	Mr. Brian NICHOLS
20	VP Academic Administration	Dr. Steven A. MAURO
04	Assistant to the President	Mrs. Darlene A. THEISEN
79	Dean Col Humanities/Educ/Soc Sci	Dr. Linda FLEMING
54	Dean College Engineering/Business	Dr. William L. SCHELLER
76	Dean Morosky Col Health Profess/Sci	Dr. Carolynn B. MASTERS
49	Director of Liberal Studies	Dr. Penny L. SMITH
08	Director Nash Library	Mr. Ken BRUNDAGE
37	Director of Financial Aid	Ms. Sharon A. KRAHE
06	Registrar	Ms. Kara A. MORGAN
36	Dir Career Develop/Employment Svcs	Mr. Brian COLLINGWOOD
39	Director of Residence Life	Ms. Denise GOLDEN
23	Head Nurse	Vacant
88	Dir Student Organiz/Leadership Dev	Ms. Beth Ann SCHICK
44	Director Development	Ms. Cathy FRESCH
26	Dir Marketing & Communications	Ms. Melanie A. WHALEY
102	Dir of Research/Foundation Rels	Ms. Anita L. MILLER
21	Controller	Mr. Jeffrey S. TAYLOR
45	Director of Budgeting	Ms. Mary Kathleen LEONARD
15	Director of Human Resources	Mr. Robert J. CLINE
41	Director of Athletics	Ms. Lisa GODDARD MCGUIRK
19	Director Campus Police & Safety	Mr. Ted MARNEN
13	Director of Computing/Telecomm	Mr. Mark JORDANO
42	University Chaplain	Vacant
07	Director of Admissions	Mr. Thomas P. CAMILLO
09	Director of Institutional Research	Ms. Margaret JAMES
18	Chief Facilities/Physical Plant	Mr. Gary G. GARNIC
27	Chief Media Relations Officer	Vacant
38	Director Student Counseling	Mr. Brian COLLINGWOOD
86	Dir Community/Government Relations	Ms. Erika A. RAMALHO
96	Director of Purchasing	Mr. Andrew TEETS
40	Bookstore Manager	Ms. Amber COOK

Geneva College (B)

3200 College Avenue, Beaver Falls PA 15010-3557

County: Beaver — FICE Identification: 003267 — Unit ID: 212656

Telephone: (724) 846-5100 — Carnegie Class: Masters/M
FAX Number: (724) 847-6687 — Calendar System: Semester
URL: www.geneva.edu
Established: 1848 — Annual Undergrad Tuition & Fees: $25,450
Enrollment: 1,717 — Coed
Affiliation or Control: Reformed Presbyterian Church — IRS Status: 501(c)3
Highest Offering: Master's
Accreditation: M, ACBSP, CACREP, ENG

Code	Title	Name
01	President	Dr. William J. EDGAR
03	Executive Vice President	Mr. Larry K. GRIFFITH
05	Chief Academic Officer	Dr. Melinda R. STEPHENS
30	Vice Pres of Advancement	Vacant
10	Assoc Vice Pres & Controller	Mr. Stephen C. ROSS
15	Assoc Vice Pres & Director of HR	Mr. Timothy R. BAIRD
32	Dean of Students	Mr. Brian C. JENSEN
20	Dean of Undergraduate Programs	Dr. Melinda R. STEPHENS
84	Assoc VP for Enrollment	Mr. David B. LAYTON
35	Director of Student Programs	Mr. Ryan J. HOLT
58	Dean Grad/Adult & Online Programs	Mr. John D. GALLO
06	Registrar	Mrs. Jennifer L. CARTER
37	Director of Financial Aid	Mr. Steven K. BELL
08	Librarian	Dr. John G. DONCEVIC
26	Director Public Relations	Mrs. Cheryl L. JOHNSTON
29	Director of Alumni Relations	Ms. Laura A. DEPIETRO
88	Assoc Dir Parent & Church Relations	Vacant
13	CIO & AVP Information Technology	Mr. Scott F. BARNES
41	Director of Athletics	Mr. Van G. ZANIC
18	Director of Physical Plant	Mr. Robert M. SKOFF
36	Director of Career Development	Mrs. Joy E. DOYLE
85	International Admissions Counselor	Ms. Jillian MOOMAW
88	Director International Student Svcs	Vacant
40	Campus Store Manager	Ms. Rachael E. VAN DERVEER
19	Director of Security	Mr. Dennis E. DAMAZO
44	Director of Planned Giving	Vacant
93	Interim Coordinator of Diversity	Mrs. Kristie A. MARTEL
92	Director of Honors Program	Dr. Eric MILLER
39	Director of Residence Life	Mr. Neil A. BEST
23	Health Services Director	Mrs. Connie I. ERWIN
96	Director of Purchasing	Mrs. Nancy D. GRAHAM
21	Accounting and Payroll Manager	Ms. Ruth Ann HARTZEL
38	ACCESS Director	Mr. Thomas C. PYLE
04	Administrative Asst to President	Miss Barbara J. MCKENZIE
09	Director of Institutional Research	Mr. Jordan BOUSCHER
50	Business Dept Chair	Dr. Gordon RICHARDS
53	Education Dept Chair	Mrs. Adel G. AIKEN
54	Engineering Dept Chair	Dr. James S. GIDLEY
90	Director of Technology Services	Dr. Joseph D. HINES
07	Assoc Director of Admissions	Mr. Joel A. BRUBAKER
104	Dir Crossroads/Ctr Special Progrm	Dr. Jeffrey S. COLE
105	Online Marketing/Webmaster	Mr. Michael W. DUNCAN
28	Dir of Multicultural Student Svcs	Vacant

Gettysburg College (C)

300 N Washington Street, Gettysburg PA 17325-1486

County: Adams — FICE Identification: 003268 — Unit ID: 212674

Telephone: (717) 337-6000 — Carnegie Class: Bac-A&S
FAX Number: (717) 337-6008 — Calendar System: Semester
URL: www.gettysburg.edu
Established: 1832 — Annual Undergrad Tuition & Fees: $49,140
Enrollment: 2,447 — Coed
Affiliation or Control: Evangelical Lutheran Church In America — IRS Status: 501(c)3
Highest Offering: Baccalaureate
Accreditation: M, MUS

Code	Title	Name
01	President	Dr. Janet MORGAN RIGGS
03	Executive Vice President	Ms. Jane D. NORTH
05	Provost	Dr. Christopher ZAPPE
30	Vice Pres Dev & Alumni/Parent Rels	Mr. Robert KALLIN
10	Vice President Finance/Treasurer	Mr. Daniel T. KONSTALID
32	Vice President for College Life	Dr. Julie L. RAMSEY
84	Vice Pres Enrollment/Education Svcs	Ms. Barbara B. FRITZE
13	Vice President Information Tech	Dr. Rod TOSTEN
45	Assoc Provost for Planning	Mrs. Rhonda GOOD
28	Chief Diversity Officer	Ms. Jeanne ARNOLD
20	Assoc Provost for Faculty Dev	Mr. Robert E. BOHRER
21	Associate Vice President/Treasurer	Mr. Christopher DELANEY
26	Exec Dir of Comm & Marketing	Mr. Paul W. REDFERN
35	Associate Dean of College Life	Mr. James P. DUFFY
30	Associate Vice Pres for Development	Ms. Susan PYRON
93	Dean Intercultural Resource Ctr	Mr. H. Pete CURRY, JR.
06	Registrar	Mr. Brian REESE
37	Director of Financial Aid	Ms. Christina L. GORMLEY
07	Director Admissions	Ms. Gail M. SWEEZEY
42	Chaplain	Rev. Joseph A. DONNELLA, II
09	Director for Institutional Analysis	Ms. Suhua DONG
38	Exec Dir of Health & Counseling	Ms. Kathy BRADLEY
36	Exec Director of Career Services	Ms. Kathleen L. WILLIAMS
08	Dean of the Library	Ms. Robin WAGNER
29	Exec Director of Alumni Relations	Mr. Joe LYNCH
41	Asst VP for Athletics	Mr. David W. WRIGHT
19	Exec Dir of Campus Safety/Security	Mr. William J. LAFFERTY
18	Director Facilities Planning & Mgmt	Mr. James BIESECKER
21	Dir of Financial Svs/Controller	Ms. Sharon S. DAYHOFF
80	Director Center for Public Service	Ms. Gretchen NATTER
39	Director Residence Life	Ms. Danielle PHILLIPS
20	Dean of Academic Advising	Ms. Gail Ann RICKERT
23	Director Health Services	Ms. Susan S. REYNOLDS
35	Director Student Activities	Mr. Joseph GURRERI
40	Director of College Bookstore	Mr. Michael J. KOTLINSKI
94	Dir Women's Center	Ms. Jennifer Q. MCCARY
96	Asst Director of Procurement	Ms. Patricia K. VERDEROSA
15	Co-Director Human Resources	Ms. Jennifer R. LUCAS
15	Co-Director Human Resources	Ms. Regina Z. CAMPO
25	Asst Dir of Found/Govt Grants	Ms. Laura RUNYAN
27	Dir of Comm & Media Relations	Ms. Jamie YATES
104	Director of Off-Campus Studies	Ms. Rebecca A. BERGREN
04	Administrative Asst to President	Ms. Pamela EISENHART
109	Dir of Auxiliary/Life Sfty Manger	Mr. Peter C. NORTH

Gratz College (D)

7605 Old York Road, Melrose Park PA 19027-3010

County: Montgomery — FICE Identification: 004058 — Unit ID: 212771

Telephone: (215) 635-7300 — Carnegie Class: Spec-4-yr-Other
FAX Number: (215) 635-1046 — Calendar System: Trimester
URL: www.gratz.edu
Established: 1895 — Annual Undergrad Tuition & Fees: N/A
Enrollment: 612 — Coed
Affiliation or Control: Independent Non-Profit — IRS Status: 501(c)3
Highest Offering: Doctorate
Accreditation: M

Code	Title	Name
01	President	Ms. Joy W. GOLDSTEIN
05	Dean and Vice Pres for Acad Affairs	Dr. Rosalie GUZOFSKY
26	Chief Public Relations Officer	Ms. Dodi KLIMOFF
08	Librarian	Ms. Nancy NITZBERG
10	Director of Finance	Mr. Michael FOLENSBEE
06	Director of Student Records	Ms. Lovisa WOODSON
15	Director Personnel Services	Ms. Yaffa HOWARD
30	Dir of Institutional Advancement	Mr. Len ZIMMERMAN
09	Director of Institutional Research	Vacant
07	Director Admissions	Ms. Ann SABOL
88	Dir Jewish Community High Sch	Rabbi Erin HIRSH
37	Student Financial Services Advisor	Ms. Michelle TAYLOR
105	Director Web Services	Ms. Rose ACTOR-ENGEL
106	Dir Online Education/E-learning	Ms. Deborah ARON
13	Chief Info Technology Officer	Ms. Suzette MARTINEZ-QUILES
53	Director of Jewish Education Prog	Dr. Saul WACHS
03	Executive Vice President	Dr. Rosalie GUZOFSKY
18	Chief Facilities/Physical Plant	Ernest COLLINS
04	Administrative Asst to President	Ms. Dodi KLIMOFF

Great Lakes Institute of Technology (E)

5100 Peach Street, Erie PA 16509

County: Erie — FICE Identification: 021122 — Unit ID: 213181

Telephone: (814) 864-6666 — Carnegie Class: Spec 2-yr-Health
FAX Number: (814) 868-1717 — Calendar System: Other
URL: www.glit.edu
Established: 1965 — Annual Undergrad Tuition & Fees: N/A
Enrollment: 427 — Coed
Affiliation or Control: Proprietary — IRS Status: Proprietary
Highest Offering: Associate Degree
Accreditation: ACCSC, DMS, SURGT

Code	Title	Name
01	Executive Director	Tony PICCIRILLO
07	Director of Admissions	Barbara BOLT
37	Director Student Financial Aid	Erin POULLIOTT
05	Director of Education	Vickie CLEMENTS

Grove City College (F)

100 Campus Drive, Grove City PA 16127-2104

County: Mercer — FICE Identification: 003269 — Unit ID: 212805

Telephone: (724) 458-2000 — Carnegie Class: Bac-A&S
FAX Number: (724) 458-2190 — Calendar System: Semester
URL: www.gcc.edu
Established: 1876 — Annual Undergrad Tuition & Fees: $16,154
Enrollment: 2,509 — Coed
Affiliation or Control: Non-denominational — IRS Status: 501(c)3
Highest Offering: Baccalaureate
Accreditation: M, ACBSP, CS, ENG, EXSC

Code	Title	Name
01	President	Mr. Paul J. MCNULTY
05	Provost & VP for Academic Affairs	Dr. Robert J. GRAHAM
10	Vice Pres for Financial Affairs	Mr. Roger K. TOWLE
32	Vice Pres For Student Life/Learning	Mr. Larry E. HARDESTY
30	Vice President for Inst Advancement	Mr. Jeffrey D. PROKOVICH
11	Vice President for Operations	Mr. James M. LOPRESTI
13	Vice Pres/Chief Information Officer	Dr. Vincent F. DISTASI
84	VP of Enrollment Svcs & Registrar	Dr. John G. INMAN
20	Assistant Provost	Dr. P. Jesse RINE
04	Assistant to the President	Ms. Betty L. TALLERICO
49	Dean of School of Arts/Letters	Dr. David J. AYERS
81	Dean of School of Sci/Engr/Math	Dr. Stacy G. BIRMINGHAM
21	Director of Financial Services	Mrs. Michelle M. WILLIAMS
15	Dir of HR & Business Operations	Mrs. Marci K. WAGNER
35	Assistant Dean of Students	Mr. John M. COYNE
07	Director of Admissions	Mrs. Sarah E. GIBBS
88	Admn Dir For Ctr For Vision/Values	Mr. Lee S. WISHING, III
36	Director of Career Services	Dr. James T. THRASHER
08	Librarian	Mrs. Barbra M. MUNNELL
37	Director of Financial Aid	Mr. Thomas G. BALL
88	Dir Std Rec/Club Sports/Frat Life	Mr. Andrew A. TONCIC, JR.
35	Director Stdnt Activities/Programs	Mr. T. Scott GORDON
19	Director of Campus Safety	Mr. Seth J. VAN TIL
23	Director of Health & Wellness Ctr	Mrs. Amy E. PAGANO
40	Bookstore Manager	Mrs. Carrie J. ROSE
41	Athletic Director	Mr. Todd D. GIBSON
42	Dean of the Chapel	Rev. F. Stanley KEEHLWETTER
29	Sr Dir Alumni & College Relations	Ms. Melissa A. MACLEOD
88	Sr Director of Development	Mr. Brian M. POWELL
26	Sr Dir Marketing & Communications	Mrs. Jacquelyn P. MULLER
38	Director of College Counseling	Dr. Suzanne N. HOUK
39	Director of Residence Life	Mrs. Lyndsay L. GRIMM

Gwynedd Mercy University (G)

1325 Sumneytown Pike, PO Box 901,
Gwynedd Valley PA 19437-0901

County: Montgomery — FICE Identification: 003270 — Unit ID: 212832

Telephone: (215) 646-7300 — Carnegie Class: Masters/M

FAX Number: (215) 641-5596 Calendar System: Semester
URL: www.gmercyu.edu
Established: 1948 Annual Undergrad Tuition & Fees: $31,360
Enrollment: 2,459 Coed
Affiliation or Control: Roman Catholic IRS Status: 501(c)3
Highest Offering: Doctorate
Accreditation: M, ADNUR, COARC, IACBE, NUR, RTT

01 President .... Dr. Kathleen C. OWENS
05 VP Academic Affairs .... Dr. Frank E. SCULLY, JR.
10 Vice President Finance & Admin .... Mr. Kevin O'FLAHERTY
30 Vice Pres Institutional Advancement ..... Mr. Gerald MCLAUGHLIN
26 Chief Communications Officer .... Ms. Kelly STATMORE
84 Vice Pres for Enrollment & SS .... Dr. Cheryl L. HORSEY
101 Secretary of the Institution/Board .... Ms. Barbara MCHALE
108 AVP for Assessment & Compliance .... Dr. Dawn HAYWARD
06 Registrar .... Ms. Joanna VACCHIANO
08 Director of Library .... Mr. Daniel SCHABERT
37 Director of Student Financial Aid .... Ms. Elizabeth HOWARD
13 Chief Information Officer .... Vacant
32 Dean of Students .... Dr. Carol GRUBER
29 Director Alumni Relations .... Ms. Gianna QUINN
35 Director Student Activities ... Ms. Rouseline EMMANUEL-FRENEL
09 Director of Institutional Research .... Dr. Jing GAO
15 Director Human Resources .... Ms. Donna HAWKINS
18 Director of Physical Plant .... Mr. Kevin WALDRON
21 Controller .... Ms. Jennifer GINNETTI
38 Director Counseling .... Ms. Pamela MOORE
07 Director of Undergrad Admissions .... Ms. Michele DIEHL
96 Director of Purchasing/Payables .... Ms. Joyce SCHARLE
102 Dir Foundation/Corporate Relations .... Ms. Bernadette WALSH
19 Director Campus Safety/Security .... Mr. James MCNESBY
41 Athletic Director .... Mr. Keith MONDILLO
39 Director Student Housing .... Mr. Bryan DUNPHY-CULP

Gwynedd Mercy University at East Norriton (A)

480 East Germantown Pike, East Norriton PA 19401
Telephone: (215) 643-8458 Identification: 770155
Accreditation: &M

† Tuition varies by degree program. Additional sites include Gwynedd Mercy University Philadelphia and Gwynedd Mercy University Bensalem.

Harcum College (B)

750 Montgomery Avenue, Bryn Mawr PA 19010-3476
County: Montgomery FICE Identification: 003272
Unit ID: 212869
Telephone: (610) 525-4100 Carnegie Class: Assoc/MT-VT-High Trad
FAX Number: (610) 526-6009 Calendar System: Semester
URL: www.harcum.edu
Established: 1915 Annual Undergrad Tuition & Fees: $22,060
Enrollment: 1,588 Coed
Affiliation or Control: Independent Non-Profit IRS Status: 501(c)3
Highest Offering: Associate Degree
Accreditation: M, ADNUR, DA, DH, HT, MLTAD, OTA, PTAA, RAD

01 President .... Dr. Jon Jay DETEMPLE
05 VP of Academic & Legal Affairs .... Ms. Julia INGERSOLL
10 Vice Pres of Finance & Operations .... Ms. Patricia BENSON
32 Dean of Student Life .... Mr. Urick LEWIS
07 Exec Dir Enrollment Management .... Ms. Rachel BOWEN
30 VP of College Advancement .... Dr. Susan BARRETT
20 Asst VP Academic Support Services .... Ms. Koyuki YIP
51 Exec Dir of Partnership Sites .... Ms. Evelyn SANTANA
18 Facilities Manager .... Mr. Nikolay KARPALO
15 Exec Dir of Human Resources .... Ms. Claudine VITA
06 Registrar .... Ms. Karen GREEN
08 Director of Library Services .... Ms. Katie MCGOWAN
85 Director of International Programs .... Mr. Daniel STABB
26 Dir of Communications & Marketing .... Ms. Gale MARTIN
29 Director of Alumni Relations .... Ms. Melissa SAMANGO
38 Director of Counseling Services .... Ms. Kathy ANTHONY
36 Dir of Career & Transfer Services .... Ms. Danyele DOVE
37 Director of Financial Aid .... Ms. Melissa WALSH
39 Director of Residence Life .... Mr. Jameel TUCKER
35 Director of Campus Activities .... Ms. Laurie PLAZA
21 Director of Business Services .... Mr. Stephen KLEPONIS
19 Director of Campus Safety .... Mr. Rick SANFILIPPO
41 Director of Athletics .... Mr. Drew KELLY
04 Executive Assistant to President .... Ms. Margaret WALLACE
13 Director of IT Services .... Mr. Joseph DONAHUE
09 Director of Institutional Research .... Mr. Tim ELY
101 Secretary of the Institution/Board .... Ms. Margaret T. WALLACE
106 Dir Online Education/E-learning .... Mr. Stephen PIPITONE
108 Director Institutional Assessment .... Mr. Tim ELY
50 Director of Business Mgmt Program .... Mr. Mike PRUSHAN
86 Director External Affairs .... Dr. Edward D'ALESSIO

Harrisburg Area Community College (C)

1 HACC Drive, Harrisburg PA 17110-2999
County: Dauphin FICE Identification: 003273
Unit ID: 212878
Telephone: (717) 780-2300 Carnegie Class: Assoc/HT-High Trad
FAX Number: (717) 780-2551 Calendar System: Semester
URL: www.hacc.edu
Established: 1964 Annual Undergrad Tuition & Fees (In-District): $6,015
Enrollment: 20,230 Coed
Affiliation or Control: State/Local IRS Status: 501(c)3
Highest Offering: Associate Degree
Accreditation: M, ACBSP, ACFEI, ADNUR, ART, COARC, CSHSE, CVT, DA, DH, DMS, EMT, MAC, MLTAD, PNUR, RAD, SURGT

01 President/CEO .... Dr. John J. SYGIELSKI
05 Provost/VP Academic Affairs .... Dr. Cynthia A. DOHERTY
32 VP Student Affairs/Enrollment Mgmt .... Dr. Rob R. STEINMETZ
10 Vice Pres Finance/CFO .... Mr. Timothy SANDOE
30 VP College Advancement .... Dr. Linnie S. CARTER
20 Assoc Provost Academic Affairs .... Dr. Kathleen T. DOHERTY
103 Assoc Provost Workforce Development .... Mr. Victor RODGERS
15 Chief HR Officer .... Ms. Aimee B. BROUGH
12 Campus VP Harrisburg Campus .... Dr. Irvin CLARK, III
12 Campus VP Lancaster/Lebanon .... Mr. Victor E. RAMOS
12 Exec Dir Lebanon Campus .... Ms. Laurie A. BOWERSOX
12 Campus VP Gettysburg .... Ms. Shannon S. HARVEY
12 Interim Campus VP York .... Dr. Marjorie A. MATTIS
106 Exec Dir Virtual Learning Outreach .... Ms. Amy S. WITHROW
08 Executive Director HACC Libraries .... Ms. Beth A. EVITTS
35 Dean Student/Acad Success .... Ms. Christine M. NOWIK
06 Registrar .... Ms. Cenita D. MANGUM
26 Chief Information Officer .... Mr. Robert H. MESSNER
96 Director Procurement .... Vacant
19 Director Safety and Security .... Mr. Ivan A. QUINONES
29 Director Alumni Relations .... Vacant
40 Director College Bookstores .... Mr. Kyle J. DIBRITO
21 Controller .... Vacant
104 Director Global Education .... Ms. Christine M. NOWIK
09 Dir Institutional Effectiveness .... Mr. Lynold K. MCGHEE
37 Director Financial Aid .... Ms. Leanne C. FRECH
84 Int Dean Student Affs/Enroll Mgmt .... Ms. Jennifer PRICE
102 Executive Director HACC Foundation .... Dr. Linnie S. CARTER

Harrisburg Area Community College Gettysburg Campus (D)

731 Old Harrisburg Road, Gettysburg PA 17325
Telephone: (717) 337-3855 Identification: 770156
Accreditation: &M

† Regional accreditation is carried under the parent institution in Harrisburg, PA

Harrisburg Area Community College Lancaster Campus (E)

1641 Old Philadelphia Pike, Lancaster PA 17602
Telephone: (717) 293-5000 Identification: 770157
Accreditation: &M

† Regional accreditation is carried under the parent institution in Harrisburg, PA

Harrisburg Area Community College Lebanon Campus (F)

735 Cumberland Street, Lebanon PA 17042
Telephone: (717) 270-4222 Identification: 770158
Accreditation: &M

† Regional accreditation is carried under the parent institution in Harrisburg, PA

Harrisburg Area Community College York Campus (G)

2010 Pennsylvania Avenue, York PA 17404
Telephone: (717) 718-0328 Identification: 770159
Accreditation: &M

† Regional accreditation is carried under the parent institution in Harrisburg, PA

Harrisburg University of Science and Technology (H)

326 Market Street, Harrisburg PA 17101-2116
County: Dauphin FICE Identification: 039483
Unit ID: 446640
Telephone: (717) 901-5100 Carnegie Class: Masters/S
FAX Number: (717) 901-3152 Calendar System: Trimester
URL: www.harrisburgu.edu
Established: 2001 Annual Undergrad Tuition & Fees: $23,900
Enrollment: 892 Coed
Affiliation or Control: Independent Non-Profit IRS Status: 501(c)3
Highest Offering: Master's
Accreditation: M

01 President .... Dr. Eric D. DARR
05 Provost/Chief Academic Officer .... Dr. Bili S. MATTES
10 Vice Pres Finance & Chief Fin Ofcr .... Mr. Duane F. MAUN
103 VP Strategic Workforce Devel .... Ms. Kelly POWELL LOGAN
26 Assoc VP Comm/Marketing/Alum Rels ..... Mr. Steven M. INFANTI
88 Assoc VP for University Centers .... Mr. Dale HAMBY
15 Dir Human Resources/Administration .... Vacant
13 Director of Technology Services .... Mr. Alex C. PITZNER
09 Dir Institutional & Grant Research .... Mr. Frank FERNANDEZ
30 Director of Advancement .... Ms. Amy SCHREIBER
37 Director Financial Aid .... Mr. Vincent P. FRANK
06 Director Records & Registration .... Ms. Jeanne A. WAGNER
84 Director Enrollment Mgmt/Admissions .... Mr. Timothy DAWSON
08 University Librarian .... Mr. David RUNYON
32 Asst Director of Student Affairs .... Ms. Kimberly BOWMAN

Haverford College (I)

370 Lancaster Avenue, Haverford PA 19041-1392
County: Delaware & Montgomery FICE Identification: 003274
Unit ID: 212911
Telephone: (610) 896-1000 Carnegie Class: Bac-A&S
FAX Number: (610) 896-4202 Calendar System: Semester
URL: www.haverford.edu
Established: 1833 Annual Undergrad Tuition & Fees: $49,098
Enrollment: 1,194 Coed
Affiliation or Control: Independent Non-Profit IRS Status: 501(c)3
Highest Offering: Master's
Accreditation: M

01 President .... Dr. Kimberly BENSTON
05 Provost .... Dr. Frances BLASE
10 Vice Pres Finance & Administration .... Mitchell L. WEIN
30 VP of Advancement .... Ann W. FIGUEREDO
20 Dean of the College .... Dr. Martha DENNEY
07 Dean of Admission .... Jess LORD
104 Dean of Intl Academic Programs .... Dr. Donna MANCINI
89 Dean of Freshmen Students .... Michael MARTINEZ
21 Asst VP for Budgeting and Finance .... Michael CASEL
88 Assistant VP of Inst Advancement .... Diane WILDER
100 Chief of Staff .... Dr. Jesse LYTLE
41 Director of Athletics .... Wendall SMITH
26 VP College Communications .... Chris MILLS
09 Director of Institutional Research .... Catherine FENNELL
08 Librarian .... Dr. Terry SNYDER
15 Director of Human Resources .... T. Muriel BRISBON
21 Senior Controller .... Karen PEDANO
96 Director of Purchasing .... Nikoletta MILLAS
18 Director of Physical Plant .... Donald CAMPBELL
19 Director of Safety & Security .... Thomas KING
88 Director Conferences/Dir Campus Ctr .... Geoffey LABE
109 Director of Dining Services .... Bernie CHUNG
40 Bookstore Manager .... Lydia WHITELAW
39 Director of Student Housing .... Marianne SMITH
34 Director of Women's Center .... Vacant
23 Director of Health Services .... Catherine SHARBAUGH
38 Director Counseling/Disability Svcs .... Dr. Philip ROSENBAUM
36 Dean for Career and Prof Develop .... Kelly CLEARY
06 Registrar .... James KEANE
37 Director of Financial Aid .... Michael COLAHAN
29 Director of Alumni & Parent Rels .... Lauren NASH
44 Director of Individual Giving .... Deborah STRECKER
88 Director of Gift Planning .... Steven KAVANAUGH
102 Dir Foundation/Corporate Relations .... Dr. John MOSTELLER
28 Director of Multicultural Affairs .... Dr. Theresa TENSUAN
32 Coordinator of Student Activities .... Lilly LAVNER
13 Chief Information Officer .... Megan FITCH
04 Administrative Asst to President .... Joan WANKMILLER

Holy Family University (J)

9801 Frankford Avenue, Philadelphia PA 19114-2009
County: Philadelphia FICE Identification: 003275
Unit ID: 212984
Telephone: (215) 637-7700 Carnegie Class: Masters/L
FAX Number: (215) 637-3787 Calendar System: Semester
URL: www.holyfamily.edu
Established: 1954 Annual Undergrad Tuition & Fees: $29,168
Enrollment: 2,658 Coed
Affiliation or Control: Roman Catholic IRS Status: 501(c)3
Highest Offering: Doctorate
Accreditation: M, ACBSP, IFSAC, NURSE, RAD

01 President .... Sr. Maureen MCGARRITY
10 Vice Pres Finance & Administration .... Mr. James TRUSDELL
42 Vice President for Mission .... Ms. Margaret S. KELLY
13 Vice Pres Information Technology .... Mr. Mark GALGANO
32 Vice President for Student Life .... Sr. Marcella BINKOWSKI
30 Interim VP for Development .... Mr. John RICHERT
84 VP for Enrollment Services .... Vacant
06 Assoc VP Academic Svcs/Registrar .... Ms. Ann Marie VICKERY
45 Assoc VP for Planning & Pgm Dev .... Ms. Karen GALARDI
37 Director of Student Financial Aid .... Mrs. Janice HETRICK
21 Associate VP/Controller & Treas .... Ms. Judy KLEIN
15 Asst VP for Human Resources .... Ms. Jennifer LULING
08 Director of Library Services .... Ms. Shannon BROWN
36 Director of the Career Center .... Mr. Don BROM
26 Dir Marketing/Communications .... Ms. Heather DOTCHEL
38 Director Counseling Center .... Ms. Tara GUTGESELL
42 Chaplain/Campus Minister .... Rev. James MACNEW
07 Executive Director of Admissions .... Ms. Lauren CAMPBELL
41 Assoc VP/Dir Athletics .... Mrs. Sandra MICHAEL
53 Dean of the School of Education .... Dr. Kevin ZOOK
66 Dean Nursing/Allied Health Prof .... Dr. Cynthia RUSSELL
49 Dean of School of Arts & Sciences .... Dr. Rochelle ROBBINS
50 Dean of School of Business Admin .... Dr. J. Barry DICKINSON
29 Director Alumni & Parent Giving .... Ms. Kathy WARCHOL
09 Dir of Inst Research & Assessment .... Mr. Chad L. MAY
18 Mgr Maintenance & Operations & Fac .... Mr. Joseph GLASSON
96 Director of Purchasing .... Mrs. Marie MELNICK
28 Coordinator Diversity .... Dr. Gloria KERSEY-MATUSIAK
39 Director of Residence Life .... Mr. Brett BUCKRIDGE
102 Dir Foundation/Corporate Relations .... Mrs. Suzanne LEWIS
05 Chief Academic Officer .... Dr. Michael MARKOWITZ
100 Chief of Staff .... Ms. Kate CHAAR
105 Web Specialist .... Mr. Robert TOEPPNER
19 Director Security/Safety .... Mr. Joseph MCBRIDE

Hussian School of Art (A)

111 S Independence Mall East, #300,
Philadelphia PA 19106-2521
County: Philadelphia FICE Identification: 007469
Unit ID: 212993
Telephone: (215) 574-9600 Carnegie Class: Spec-4-yr-Arts
FAX Number: (215) 574-9800 Calendar System: Semester
URL: www.hussianart.edu
Established: 1946 Annual Undergrad Tuition & Fees: $18,550
Enrollment: 79 Coed
Affiliation or Control: Proprietary IRS Status: Proprietary
Highest Offering: Baccalaureate
Accreditation: ACCSC

01 President ... Ms. Melissa MORGAN
06 Dir of Student Services/Registrar ... Ms. Maureen P. FLANAGAN
37 Director Financial Aid ... Ms. Susan J. COHEN
07 Admissions Representative ... Mr. Mark CERNERO
10 Director of Finance ... Mr. Eric STRUBEL
11 Administrative Coordinator ... Ms. Jodi BRABAZON

Immaculata University (B)

1145 King Road, Immaculata PA 19345-0654
County: Chester FICE Identification: 003276
Unit ID: 213011
Telephone: (610) 647-4400 Carnegie Class: DU-Mod
FAX Number: (610) 251-1668 Calendar System: Semester
URL: www.immaculata.edu
Established: 1920 Annual Undergrad Tuition & Fees: $33,280
Enrollment: 3,299 Coed
Affiliation or Control: Roman Catholic IRS Status: 501(c)3
Highest Offering: Doctorate
Accreditation: M, ACBSP, CAATE, CACREP, CLPSY, DIETD, DIETI, IPSY, MUS, NURSE

01 President ... Sr. R. Patricia FADDEN
05 Vice President Academic Affairs ... Dr. Maria GREEN COWLES
10 Vice Pres Finance/Administration ... Vacant
30 Vice Pres University Advancement ... Mr. Kevin QUINN
32 Vice Pres Student Development ... Dr. John STAFFORD
26 Vice Pres of Univ Communications ... Mr. Kevin QUINN
84 Vice President Enrollment Mgmt ... Mr. Gerald WARGO
20 Assistant VP of Academic Affairs ... Dr. Angela TEKELY
06 Registrar ... Ms. Janice BATES
09 Dir Inst Res/Planning/Effectiveness ... Dr. Erin EBERSOLE
08 Executive Director of Library ... Dr. Jeffrey ROLLISON
37 Director Student Financial Aid ... Mr. Robert FOREST
44 Director Planned Giving ... Sr. Rita O'LEARY
91 Director Administrative Computing ... Mr. Grant DAVIS
102 Dir Corp/Foundation and Government ... Ms. Laura CHISHOLM
29 Director Alumni Relations ... Ms. Karen MATWEYCHUK
36 Director Career Development ... Ms. Kathleen MCCAULEY
41 Athletic Director ... Ms. Patricia CANTERINO
85 International Student Advisor ... Sr. Catarin CONJAR
90 Director Academic Technology ... Ms. Sharon AINSLEY
42 Chaplain ... Rev. Samuel VERRUNI
58 Dean Graduate Division ... Dr. Thomas O'BRIEN
34 Dean College of Undergrad Studies ... Sr. Joseph CARTER
51 Dean College of Lifelong Learning ... Dr. Angela TEKELY
19 Director Campus Safety ... Mr. Dennis DOUGHERTY
15 Director of Human Resources ... Ms. Geri LARSEN
18 Director of Administrative Services ... Mr. Dennis SHORES
44 Director of the Annual Fund ... Ms. Melissa HENRY
42 Vice Pres of Mission and Ministry ... Sr. Mary HENRICH
07 Exec Director of Admissions ... Dr. Nicola DIFRONZO-HEITZER
20 Dean of Academic Affairs ... Ms. Mary Kate BOLAND
25 Assoc Director Academic Assessment ... Ms. Bobbijo PINNELLI
38 Director Counseling Services ... Dr. Jamie HAGENBAUGH
13 Chief Info Technology Officer (CIO) ... Mr. Mike SALEM
39 Director Student Housing ... Ms. Rhonda FIORESI
04 Administrative Asst to President ... Ms. Leslie BOKOSKI
104 Director Study Abroad ... Sr. Elaine GLANZ
106 Dir Online Education/E-learning ... Mr. Dean JULIAN
84 Senior Enrollment Counselor ... Mr. Dan BERADI
101 Secretary of the Institution/Board ... Sr. Marie Hubert KEALY, IHM

International Institute for Restorative Practices (C)

P.O. Box 229, Bethlehem PA 18016-0229
County: Northampton FICE Identification: 042061
Unit ID: 448691
Telephone: (610) 807-9221 Carnegie Class: Spec-4-yr-Other
FAX Number: (610) 807-0423 Calendar System: Trimester
URL: www.iirp.edu
Established: 2005 Annual Graduate Tuition & Fees: N/A
Enrollment: 50 Coed
Affiliation or Control: Independent Non-Profit IRS Status: 501(c)3
Highest Offering: Master's; No Undergraduates
Accreditation: M

01 President ... Dr. John BAILIE
05 Provost ... Dr. Craig ADAMSON
11 Vice President for Administration ... Ms. Judy B. HAPP
30 Vice President for Advancement ... Ms. Linda KLIGMAN

JNA Institute of Culinary Arts (D)

1212 S Broad Street, Philadelphia PA 19146-3119
County: Philadelphia FICE Identification: 031033
Unit ID: 419341
Telephone: (215) 468-8800 Carnegie Class: Spec 2-yr-A&S
FAX Number: (215) 468-8838 Calendar System: Quarter
URL: www.culinaryarts.edu
Established: 1988 Annual Undergrad Tuition & Fees: $12,725
Enrollment: 59 Coed
Affiliation or Control: Proprietary IRS Status: Proprietary
Highest Offering: Associate Degree
Accreditation: ACCSC

01 Director ... Mr. Joseph DIGIRONIMO
07 Director of Admission ... Ms. Cheryl FREEDMAN

Johnson College (E)

3427 North Main Avenue, Scranton PA 18508-1495
County: Lackawanna FICE Identification: 021142
Unit ID: 213233
Telephone: (570) 342-6404 Carnegie Class: Assoc/HVT-High Trad
FAX Number: (570) 348-2181 Calendar System: Semester
URL: www.johnson.edu
Established: 1912 Annual Undergrad Tuition & Fees: $17,614
Enrollment: 455 Coed
Affiliation or Control: Independent Non-Profit IRS Status: 501(c)3
Highest Offering: Associate Degree
Accreditation: ACCSC, PTAA, RAD

01 President & CEO ... Dr. Ann L. PIPINSKI
10 Chief Financial Officer ... Mr. Jeffrey NOVAK
30 Sr VP of Institutional Advancement ... Ms. Katie LEONARD
09 Dir of Program & Research ... Ms. Shirley HELBING

Juniata College (F)

1700 Moore Street, Huntingdon PA 16652-2119
County: Huntingdon FICE Identification: 003279
Unit ID: 213251
Telephone: (814) 641-3000 Carnegie Class: Bac-A&S
FAX Number: (814) 641-3199 Calendar System: Semester
URL: www.juniata.edu
Established: 1876 Annual Undergrad Tuition & Fees: $40,600
Enrollment: 1,632 Coed
Affiliation or Control: Independent Non-Profit IRS Status: 501(c)3
Highest Offering: Master's
Accreditation: M, SW

01 President ... Dr. James A. TROHA
05 Provost ... Dr. Lauren BOWEN
84 VP Enrollment and Retention ... Mr. Robert E. YELNOSKY
10 Vice President Finance/Operations ... Mr. John WILKIN
26 Vice President Advancement/Mkt ... Mr. Gabriel WELSCH
13 Asst VP/Chief Information Officer ... Ms. Anne WOOD
27 Exec Director of Marketing ... Ms. Rosann BROWN
07 Dean of Enrollment ... Ms. Michelle M. BARTOL
85 Dean of International Education ... Ms. Kati R. CSOMAN
06 Registrar ... Ms. Athena D. FREDERICK
36 Director Career Services ... Dr. Darwin V. KYSOR
37 Enrollment Mgr/Dir Student Fin Plng ... Mr. Shane D. HIMES
08 Library Director ... Vacant
91 Director Admin Information Svcs ... Mr. Rick BROWN
15 Director of Human Resources ... Ms. Gail L. ULRICH
32 VP Student Life & Dean of Students ... Dr. Matthew DAMSCHRODER
09 Dir Institutional Planning/Research ... Ms. Carlee K. RANALLI
18 Director of Facilities Services ... Mr. Tristan S. DEL GIUDICE
19 Director Public Safety ... Mr. Jesse W. LEONARD
41 Athletic Director ... Mr. Greg M. CURLEY
90 Dir Technology Solutions Center ... Mr. Joel C. PHEASANT
21 Bursar ... Ms. Lauren A. PEROW
21 Budget Director ... Ms. Susan F. SHONTZ
21 Controller ... Ms. Karla D. WISER
44 Executive Director of Development ... Mr. Joseph M. SCIALABBA
35 Assistant Dean of Students ... Ms. Ellen CAMPBELL
42 College Chaplain ... Mr. Lowell D. WITKOVSKY
20 Director of Academic Support Svcs ... Vacant
88 Director of Student Engagement ... Ms. Erin PASCHAL
88 Director of Conferences & Events ... Ms. Lorri P. SHIDELER
07 Senior Associate Dean of Admission ... Ms. Terri L. BOLLMAN-DALANSKY
38 College Counselor ... Ms. Kerry HARPER
28 Asst to Pres Diversity & Inclusion ... Dr. Grace FALA
29 Director Alumni Relations ... Mr. David D. MEADOWS
39 Director of Residential Life ... Ms. Tasia Y. WHITE
04 Executive Asst to President ... Mrs. Bethany D. SHEFFIELD

Kaplan Career Institute (G)

3010 Market Street, Philadelphia PA 19104
Telephone: (215) 594-4000 Identification: 770766
Accreditation: ACICS

Keystone College (H)

One College Green, P.O. Box 50,
La Plume PA 18440-0200
County: Lackawanna FICE Identification: 003280
Unit ID: 213303
Telephone: (570) 945-8000 Carnegie Class: Bac-Diverse
FAX Number: (570) 945-8962 Calendar System: Semester
URL: www.keystone.edu
Established: 1868 Annual Undergrad Tuition & Fees: $24,300
Enrollment: 1,484 Coed
Affiliation or Control: Independent Non-Profit IRS Status: 501(c)3
Highest Offering: Baccalaureate
Accreditation: M, IACBE

01 President ... Dr. David L. COPPOLA
03 Executive Vice President ... Dr. Marie GEORGE
05 Vice President for Academic Affairs ... Dr. Karen YARRISH
10 Vice Pres Finance & Administration ... Mr. Kevin WILSON
30 Vice President for Advancement ... Ms. Charlotte RAVAIOLI
84 Dean of Enrollment ... Dr. Janine BECKER
32 Interim Dean of Student Life ... Ms. Nicole LANGAN
08 Director Miller Library ... Ms. Mari FLYNN
07 Director of Admissions ... Ms. Jennifer SEKOL
06 Registrar ... Ms. Kate OWENS
37 Dir Financial Assistance & Planning ... Ms. Delaina JAYNE
13 Director Information Technology ... Mr. Charles L. PROTHERO
15 Director of Human Resources ... Ms. Alberta GRUSHINSKI
26 Senior Director College Relations ... Mr. Fran CALPIN
29 Director of Alumni Outreach ... Ms. Mariellen WALSH
36 Director Career Development ... Ms. Kourtney SHICK
09 Director Institutional Research ... Mr. Curtis BAUMAN
41 Director of Athletics ... Dr. Matthew GRIMALDI

Keystone Technical Institute (I)

2301 Academy Drive, Harrisburg PA 17112-1012
County: Dauphin FICE Identification: 022342
Unit ID: 210483
Telephone: (717) 545-4747 Carnegie Class: Assoc/HVT-Mix Trad/Non
FAX Number: (717) 901-9090 Calendar System: Semester
URL: www.kti.edu
Established: 1980 Annual Undergrad Tuition & Fees: N/A
Enrollment: 341 Coed
Affiliation or Control: Proprietary IRS Status: Proprietary
Highest Offering: Associate Degree
Accreditation: ACCSC, ACFEI, MAC

01 President ... Mr. David W. SNYDER
03 Vice President ... Mrs. Andrea SNYDER
05 Dean of Education ... Mr. Jason KARMANN
07 Admissions Officer ... Ms. Donna STIRBER-GAMELIN
10 Chief Business Officer ... Mr. Dennis FIELDS
37 Director Student Financial Aid ... Ms. Tracy STEWART

King's College (J)

133 N River Street, Wilkes-Barre PA 18711-0801
County: Luzerne FICE Identification: 003282
Unit ID: 213321
Telephone: (570) 208-5900 Carnegie Class: Masters/S
FAX Number: (570) 825-9049 Calendar System: Semester
URL: www.kings.edu
Established: 1946 Annual Undergrad Tuition & Fees: $33,090
Enrollment: 2,308 Coed
Affiliation or Control: Roman Catholic IRS Status: 501(c)3
Highest Offering: Master's
Accreditation: M, ARCPA, BUS, CAATE, TED

01 President ... Rev. John RYAN, CSC
05 Provost & VP for Academic Affairs ... Dr. Joseph EVAN
10 Executive VP for Business Affairs ... Mr. John LOYACK
30 Vice President for Inst Advancement ... Mr. Frederick PETTIT
32 Vice President for Student Affairs ... Ms. Janet E. MERCINCAVAGE
84 Vice President for Enrollment Mgmt ... Mr. Corry UNIS
04 Exec Assistant to the President ... Mrs. Anne NOONE
13 Associate VP/Chief Info Officer ... Mr. Paul J. MORAN
08 Director of Library ... Dr. Terrence F. MECH
88 Assoc VP Stdnt Success & Retention ... Ms. Teresa M. PECK
35 Assoc Vice Pres Student Affairs ... Mr. Robert B. MCGONIGLE
07 Director of Admissions ... Mr. James ANDERSON
50 Dean Wm G McGowan Sch Business ... Dr. Barry WILLIAMS
06 Registrar ... Mr. Daniel T. CEBRICK
37 Director of Financial Aid ... Ms. Donna CERZA
42 Chaplain/Director Campus Ministry ... Rev. Thomas LOONEY, CSC
36 Director Career Planning & Placemnt ... Mr. Christopher SUTZKO
15 Director of Human Resources ... Ms. Lita PIEKARA
26 Director of Public Relations ... Mr. John MCANDREW
29 Director of Alumni Relations ... Ms. Patrice PERSICO
18 Executive Director of Facilities ... Mr. Thomas BUTCHKO
19 Director of Security/Safety ... Mr. Gerard DESSOYE
41 Dir of Intercollegiate Athletics ... Ms. Cheryl J. ISH
21 Associate VP/Controller & CAO ... Mr. Thomas GRABER
39 Director of Residence Life ... Ms. Megan SELLICK
09 Director of Institutional Research ... Ms. Marian K. PALMERI
28 Director of College Diversity ... Ms. Jasmine TABRON
90 Managing Dir of User Services ... Mr. Raymond G. PRYOR
91 Managing Director for MIS ... Mr. William M. CORCORAN
44 Dir Major Gifts & Planned Giving ... Mr. William LYNN
104 Director Study Abroad ... Ms. Margaret KOWALSKY

La Roche College (K)

9000 Babcock Boulevard, Pittsburgh PA 15237-5898
County: Allegheny FICE Identification: 003987
Unit ID: 213358
Telephone: (412) 367-9300 Carnegie Class: Bac-Diverse
FAX Number: (412) 536-1062 Calendar System: Semester
URL: www.laroche.edu
Established: 1963 Annual Undergrad Tuition & Fees: $26,250
Enrollment: 1,412 Coed
Affiliation or Control: Roman Catholic IRS Status: 501(c)3
Highest Offering: Doctorate
Accreditation: M, ACBSP, ADNUR, ANEST, ART, CIDA, NUR

01 President .... Sr. Candace INTROCASO, CDP
04 Exec Admin Asst to the President .... Ms. Karen P. WILLOUGHBY
05 VP for Acad Affairs & Acad Dean .... Dr. Howard J. ISHIYAMA
84 VP for Enrollment Mgmt .... Dr. James (Chip) E. WEISGERBER
10 VP for Business & Finance .... Mr. Robert VOGEL
32 VP for Student Life/Dean Stdnts .... Ms. Colleen RUEFLE
30 VP for Institutional Advancement .... Mr. Michael ANDREOLA
20 Assoc VP Academic Affairs .... Dr. Rosemary MCCARTHY
20 Assoc VP Academic Affairs .... Dr. Thomas G. SCHAEFER
36 Assoc Dean Academic/Student Support .... Ms. Marie DEEM
35 Director of Student Development .... Mr. David DAY
83 Div Chair Natural & Behavioral Sci .... Ms. Jane ARNOLD
79 Div Chair Humanities .... Sr. Michele BISBEY, CDP
50 Div Co-Chair Business .... Dr. Lynn ARCHER
50 Div Co-Chair Business .... Ms. Shelia MUELLER
57 Div Chair Design .... Ms. Lisa KAMPHAUS
53 Div Co-Chair Education & Nursing .... Dr. Kathryn SILVIS
53 Div Co-Chair Education & Nursing .... Dr. Terri LIBERTO
06 Registrar .... Ms. Joan CUTONE
08 Director Library/Learning Center .... Ms. Laverne COLLINS
07 Director of Admissions .... Mr. Terrance KIZINA
26 Director of Mktg & Media Relations .... Mr. Brady BUTLER
37 Director of Financial Aid .... Ms. Sharon PLATT
41 Director of Athletics .... Mr. Jim TINKEY
42 Director of Mission & Ministry .... Sr. Elena ALMENDAREZ
07 Director Grad Studies/Adult Educ .... Ms. Hope SCHIFFGENS
39 Director Residence Life .... Mr. Christopher WILLIS
13 Director Information Technology .... Ms. Terri BALLARD
85 Director International Student Svcs .... Dr. Natasha GARRETT
29 Director Alumni Relations .... Ms. Gina MILLER
21 Director of Finance .... Ms. Cathleen JACOBS
09 Director of Institutional Research .... Ms. Patricia A. CONNOLLY
18 Assoc VP of Facilities Management .... Mr. J.R YOUNG
38 Director Counseling Services .... Ms. Lori AREND
19 Director Public Safety .... Mr. Mark WILCOX
15 Assoc VP of Human Resources .... Ms. Eileen PETRONE
40 Bookstore Manager .... Mr. Tim JONES
88 Director of Student Accounts .... Ms. Danya TINKEY
101 Secretary of the Institution/Board .... Ms. Kathy KOZDEMBA
104 Coordinator Study Abroad .... Ms. Nicole GABLE
44 Director Annual or Planned Giving .... Mr. Craig BRUNO
86 Director Government Relations .... Mr. Michael ANDREOLA

La Salle University (A)

1900 W Olney Avenue, Philadelphia PA 19141-1199

County: Philadelphia　FICE Identification: 003287
Unit ID: 213367
Telephone: (215) 951-1000　Carnegie Class: Masters/L
FAX Number: N/A　Calendar System: Semester
URL: www.lasalle.edu
Established: 1863　Annual Undergrad Tuition & Fees: $41,100
Enrollment: 6,242　Coed
Affiliation or Control: Roman Catholic　IRS Status: 501(c)3
Highest Offering: Doctorate
Accreditation: M, ANEST, BUS, CACREP, CLPSY, DIETC, DIETD, MFCD, NURSE, SP, SW

01 President .... Dr. Colleen M. HANYCZ
05 Provost/VP Academic Affairs .... Dr. Brian A. GOLDSTEIN
04 Exec Assistant to the President .... Bro. Joseph WILLARD
30 VP University Advancement ..... Ms. Cathleen PARSONS-NIKOLIC
10 VP Finance and Admin and Treasurer .... Mrs. Amy BOSIO
32 VP Student Affairs/Dean of Students .... Dr. James E. MOORE
84 VP for Enrollment .... Mr. Thomas F. DELAHUNT, III
43 Vice President and General Counsel .... Mr. Kevin DOLAN
20 Assistant Provost .... Bro. John MCGOLDRICK
07 Asst VP Enrollment Services .... Ms. Kathryn PAYNE
88 Asst VP Development .... Mr. Richard VAN FOSSEN, JR.
49 Dean School of Arts & Sciences .... Dr. Thomas A. KEAGY
50 Dean School of Business Admin .... Dr. Gary A. GIAMARTINO
66 Dean School of Nursing/Health Sci .... Dr. Kathleen CZEKANSKI
22 Affirmative Action Officer/Title IX .... Ms. Rose Lee PAULINE
26 Chief Mktg and Chief Comm Officer .... Ms. Jaine LUCAS
29 Asst VP Alumni Relations .... Mr. Trey P. ULRICH
88 Exec Dir Constituent Rel & Oper .... Mr. Nikolas G. KOZEL
82 Dir Grad Ctr/East Eur Studies .... Vacant
77 Director Grad Computer Info Science .... Ms. Margaret MCCOEY
53 Director Grad Education Program .... Dr. Greer RICHARDSON
83 Dir Grad Counseling & Family Therap .... Dr. Donna A. TONREY
73 Director Grad Pgms of Theology .... Fr. Francis J. BERNA
60 Dir Grad Prof Bus Communication .... Dr. Pamela LANNUTTI
66 Director Undergraduate Nursing .... Dr. Jane KURZ
66 Dir Grad Nursing RN-MSN Pgm .... Dr. Patricia DILLON
69 Dir Master Public Health Program .... Dr. Jillian BAKER
88 Dir Grad Econ Crime Forensics .... Ms. Margaret MCCOEY
88 Dir Grad Pgm Human Capital Develop .... Ms. Kathleen BAGNELL FINNEGAN
58 Dir Grad Pgm Nonprofit Leadership .... Dr. Laura OTTEN
35 Senior Assoc Dean of Students .... Mr. Alan B. WENDELL
35 Associate Dean of Students .... Dr. Lane B. NEUBAUER
35 Associate Dean of Students .... Ms. Anna M. ALLEN
42 Director Univ Ministry & Service .... Bro. Robert J. KINZLER
92 Dir University Honors Program .... Bro. Michael MCGINNISS
13 Chief Information Officer .... Vacant
08 Director of the Library .... Mr. John S. BAKY
18 Asst VP Facilities Mgmt/Capital Dev .... Mr. Robert C. KROH, JR.
19 Interim Dir for Safety & Security .... Mr. Dennis GRAEBER
15 Exec Director of Human Resources .... Mrs. Tara MILLARD
41 Int Dir Intercollegiate Athletics .... Mr. William BRADSHAW
44 Senior Director of Major Gifts .... Mr. Daniel JOYCE
102 Director of The La Salle Fund .... Ms. Helene HOLMES BACZKOWSKI
88 Director Prospect Research .... Mr. Patrick LIENHARD
07 Executive Director of Admission .... Mr. James C. PLUNKETT
37 Director Financial Aid .... Mr. Joseph ALAIMO
06 Registrar .... Ms. Jean W. LANDIS
09 Exec Dir Inst Eff and Spons Rsrch .... Mr. Eric DAVENPORT
88 Dir Doctorate in Psych Program .... Dr. Randy FINGERHUT
88 Dir Graduate English Studies .... Dr. Elizabeth LANGEMAK
88 Grad Director Instr Tech Mgt .... Ms. Margaret MCCOEY
88 Director Part-time MBA Program .... Vacant
88 Director Full-time MBA Program .... Ms. Elizabeth A. SCOFIELD
40 Manager Campus Store .... Mr. Mark ALLAN
28 Multicultural Education Coordinator .... Ms. Cheryn L. RUSH
105 Director of Web Communication .... Mr. Gregory FALA
88 Dir Doctor of Nursing Practice Pgm .... Vacant
88 Director Graduate History .... Dr. George B. STOW
58 Associate Provost .... Dr. Holly HARNER
88 Dir Prof Clinical Counseling Psych .... Dr. John J. ROONEY
44 Senior Director of Major Gifts ... Ms. Felicia GORDON-RIEHMAN
88 Sr Dir Development for Athletics .... Mr. Brian QUINN
88 Sr Dir of Brand Marketing .... Ms. Amy CRANSTON
100 Chief of Staff/Dir of Gov Affairs .... Mr. Joseph MEADE
104 Director Study Abroad .... Ms. Melinda INGERSOLL
96 Procurement Manager .... Mr. Christopher KANE

Lackawanna College (B)

501 Vine Street, Scranton PA 18509-3206

County: Lackawanna　FICE Identification: 003283
Unit ID: 213376
Telephone: (570) 961-7810　Carnegie Class: Assoc/HT-High Non
FAX Number: (570) 961-7858　Calendar System: 4/1/4
URL: www.lackawanna.edu
Established: 1894　Annual Undergrad Tuition & Fees: $14,110
Enrollment: 1,490　Coed
Affiliation or Control: Independent Non-Profit　IRS Status: 501(c)3
Highest Offering: Baccalaureate
Accreditation: M, DMS, EMT, PTAA, SURGT

01 President .... Mr. Mark VOLK
03 Exec Vice President/CAO .... Dr. Jill MURRAY
10 Vice Pres Finance/Administration .... Ms. Alycia SCHWARTZ
05 Vice President Academic Affairs .... Dr. Erica PRICCI
32 VP for Student Affairs .... Mrs. Suellen MUSEWICZ
35 Dean of Students .... Mr. Dan LAMAGNA
84 VP for Enrollment Management .... Mr. Brian COSTANZO
20 Dean of Faculty .... Mrs. Suzanne CERCONE
29 Director Alumni Relations .... Vacant
88 Dir Programming & Special Events .... Mr. Jim CULLEN
31 Director of External Relations .... Ms. Wendy HINTON
41 Director of Athletics .... Mrs. Kim MECCA
88 Director of Advising & Transfer Svc . Mrs. Barbara NOWOGORSKI
06 Registrar .... Mrs. Theresa SCOPELLITI
19 Director of Public Safety .... Mr. Gary SHOENER
12 Director of Hazleton Center .... Mrs. April HARRIS-SNYDER
12 Director of Center Operations .... Mr. Jeffery GREGORY
12 Exec Director School of PNGT .... Mr. Richard MARQUARDT
91 Director Admin Computing Svcs .... Vacant
08 Library Director .... Mrs. Mary Beth ROCHE
102 Director of Grant Support Services .... Ms. Michele MCGLOIN
39 Director Housing & Residence Life .... Mr. Stephen DUDA
15 Director of Human Resources .... Mrs. Sharon EBERT
18 Director of Facilities .... Mr. Derek GREGORY
37 Director of Financial Aid .... Mr. Matthew PETERS
12 Director Towanda Center .... Ms. Kim MAPES
13 Director of MIS .... Mrs. Melanie KOWALSKI
35 Director of Student Life .... Ms. Karen LEGGE
07 Assistant Director of Admissions .... Mrs. Michele KETTEN
88 Service Learning Coordinator .... Ms. Jo-Ann ORCUTT

Lafayette College (C)

730 High Street, Easton PA 18042-1798

County: Northampton　FICE Identification: 003284
Unit ID: 213385
Telephone: (610) 330-5000　Carnegie Class: Bac-A&S
FAX Number: (610) 330-5127　Calendar System: Semester
URL: www.lafayette.edu
Established: 1826　Annual Undergrad Tuition & Fees: $47,760
Enrollment: 2,503　Coed
Affiliation or Control: Independent Non-Profit　IRS Status: 501(c)3
Highest Offering: Baccalaureate
Accreditation: M, CS, ENG

01 President .... Dr. Alison R. BYERLY
05 Provost .... Dr. S. Abu Turab RIZVI
30 Vice Pres Dev/College Relations .... Ms. Kimberly SPANG
32 VP Campus Life .... Dr. Annette DIORIO
15 Vice President Human Resources ..... Ms. Leslie F. MUHLFELDER
26 Interim VP Marketing/Communications .... Mr. John L. O'KEEFE
13 VP and Chief Information Officer .... Mr. John L. O'KEEFE
10 VP Finance & Administration .... Mr. Roger DEMARESKI
54 Director of Engineering .... Dr. Scott R. HUMMEL
100 VP & Liaison to Board of Trustees .... Dr. James F. KRIVOSKI
84 Vice Pres for Enrollment Management .... Mr. Gregory MACDONALD
88 Dean Advising & Co-Curricular Pgms .... Dr. Erica D'AGOSTINO
08 Acting Dean of Libraries .... Ms. Terese A. HEIDENWOLF
35 Dean of Students .... Dr. Paul J. MCLOUGHLIN, II
07 Dean of Admissions .... Mr. Matthew HYDE
37 Director of Student Financial Aid .... Ms. Ashley BIANCHI
09 Director of Institutional Research .... Dr. James P. SCHAFFER
06 Registrar .... Mr. Francis A. BENGINIA
41 Director of Athletics .... Dr. Bruce E. MCCUTCHEON
36 Int Exec Director Career Services .... Ms. Nanette COOLEY
23 Director Health Services .... Dr. Jeffrey E. GOLDSTEIN
38 Director Counseling Center .... Dr. Karen J. FORBES
19 Director of Public Safety .... Mr. Jeffrey E. TROXELL
18 Dir Physical Planning & Plant Oper .... Mr. Bruce S. FERRETTI
29 Executive Director Alumni Relations .... Ms. Rachel NELSON MOELLER
16 Director of HR/Employment .... Ms. Lisa Youngkin REX
96 Manager of Procurement .... Ms. Linda L. JROSKI
88 Title IX Coordinator .... Ms. Amy A. O'NEILL
20 Dean of Faculty/Chf Diversity Ofcr .... Dr. Robin C. RINEHART
21 Chief Investment Officer .... Mr. Joseph S. BOHRER
04 Executive Assistant to President .... Ms. Marie L. ENEA

Lake Erie College of Osteopathic Medicine (D)

1858 W Grandview Boulevard, Erie PA 16509-1025

County: Erie　FICE Identification: 030908
Unit ID: 407629
Telephone: (814) 866-6641　Carnegie Class: Spec-4-yr-Med
FAX Number: (814) 866-3123　Calendar System: Semester
URL: www.lecom.edu
Established: 1993　Annual Graduate Tuition & Fees: N/A
Enrollment: 3,772　Coed
Affiliation or Control: Independent Non-Profit　IRS Status: 501(c)3
Highest Offering: First Professional Degree; No Undergraduates
Accreditation: M, OSTEO, PHAR

01 President/CEO .... Dr. John M. FERRETTI
05 Provost/Sr Vice Pres/Dean Acad Affs .... Dr. Silvia M. FERRETTI
10 Vice Pres of Fiscal Affairs/CFO .... Mr. Richard P. OLINGER
20 VP Acad Affs/Dn LECOM Sch Pharmacy .... Dr. Hershey BELL
12 Vice Pres for LECOM at Seton Hill .... Dr. Irving FREEMAN
52 Dean School of Dental Medicine .... Dr. Mathew BATEMAN
58 Assoc Dean Students/Grad Studies .... Dr. Mark KAUFFMAN
20 Assoc Dean Acad Affairs Bradenton .... Dr. Robert GEORGE
63 Assoc Dean Clinical Educ Bradenton ..... Dr. Anthony J. FERRETTI
63 Assoc Dean of Preclinical Educ .... Dr. Christine KELL
63 Asst Dean of Clinical Education .... Dr. Regan SHABLOSKI
63 Asst Dean Preclinical Ed Bradenton .... Dr. Mark COTY
63 Asst Dean Preclinical Educ Erie .... Dr. Jon KALMEY
63 Asst Dean of Biomed Sci .... Dr. Randy KULESZA
20 Asst Dean Acad Affairs Bradenton .... Dr. Ronald BEREZNIAK
67 Assoc Dean of Accelerated Pathway .... Dr. Rachel OGDEN
67 Assoc Dean for Traditional Pathway .... Dr. Julie WILKINSON
67 Assistant Dean for Assessment .... Dr. Nina PAVULURI
52 Asst Dean Preclinical Dental .... Dr. Mark ROMER
88 Asst Dean Clinical Dental Med .... Dr. Francis CURD
32 Director of Student Affairs .... Dr. David FRIED
09 Inst Dir Plng/Assess/Accred/Rsrch .... Dr. Mathew BATEMAN
26 Inst Dir Communications/Marketing .... Mr. Pierre A. BELLICINI
08 Inst Dir of Learning Resources .... Mr. Dan WELCH
13 Director of Information Technology .... Mr. Randy HARRIS
46 Director of Research .... Dr. Bertalan DUDAS
15 Inst Dir of Human Resources .... Mr. Aaron SUSMARSKI
19 Acting Dir of Security .... Mr. Kevin GOODE
38 Director Behavioral Health .... Dr. Richard HAHN
88 Inst Dir of Faculty Development .... Dr. Mark TERRELL
27 Asst Dir Communications/Marketing .... Vacant
18 Building Operations Supervisor .... Mr. Brian KING
37 Inst Director of Financial Aid .... Ms. Bonnie CRILLEY
06 Registrar .... Mr. Jeremy SIVILLO
07 Admissions Coordinator .... Ms. Amy W. ROWE
40 Bookstore Manager .... Ms. Naz KROL

Lancaster Bible College (E)

901 Eden Road, Lancaster PA 17601-5036

County: Lancaster　FICE Identification: 003285
Unit ID: 213400
Telephone: (717) 569-7071　Carnegie Class: Spec-4-yr-Faith
FAX Number: (717) 560-8260　Calendar System: Semester
URL: www.lbc.edu
Established: 1933　Annual Undergrad Tuition & Fees: $19,980
Enrollment: 2,011　Coed
Affiliation or Control: Independent Non-Profit　IRS Status: 501(c)3
Highest Offering: Doctorate
Accreditation: M, BI, SW

01 President .... Dr. Peter W. TEAGUE
04 Assistant to the President .... Mrs. Judith M. HECKAMAN
03 Executive Vice President .... Mr. John ZESWITZ
05 Provost .... Dr. Philip E. DEARBORN
84 VP for Student Experience .... Mr. Josh BEERS
30 VP of Advancement .... Mr. Ron KUBEK
13 Vice President Information Systems .... Mr. Vince JOHNSON
10 VP of Finance .... Mr. Matthew MASON
09 AVP of Institutional Effectiveness .... Dr. Dale MORT
20 VP of Strategic Initiatives .... Vacant
06 Registrar .... Mr. Jeffrey HOOVER
32 Dean of Students .... Mr. Scott BOYER
38 Director of Student Development .... Mrs. Kathleen CLARK
08 Director of Library Services .... Mr. Clint BANZ
37 Director of Financial Aid .... Mrs. Karen L. FOX
21 Controller .... Mr. Ethan MCNAUGHTON
18 Director of Plant Operations .... Mr. Paul MUTCHLER
23 Director of Health Services .... Vacant
29 Dir of Alumni & Career Services .... Mr. Rodney CARTER, JR.
41 Athletic Director .... Mr. Peter BEERS
15 Director of People Development & HR .... Mrs. Paula POOLE
07 Director of Admissions .... Mr. David BURGE

19 Director Security/Safety .... Mr. Robert WEGMAN
26 Chief Public Relations/Marketing .... Mr. Keith BAUM
39 Director Student Housing .... Mrs. Monique BURGE

Lancaster County Career and Technology Center (A)

1730 Hans Herr Drive, P.O. Box 527,
Willow Street PA 17584
County: Lancaster FICE Identification: 023108
Unit ID: 418533
Telephone: (717) 464-7050 Carnegie Class: Spec 2-yr-Health
FAX Number: (717) 464-9518 Calendar System: Semester
URL: www.lancasterctc.edu
Established: 1970 Annual Undergrad Tuition & Fees (In-District): N/A
Enrollment: 462 Coed
Affiliation or Control: State/Local IRS Status: 501(c)3
Highest Offering: Associate Degree
Accreditation: COE

01 Executive Director .... David WARREN

Lancaster Theological Seminary (B)

555 W James Street, Lancaster PA 17603-2812
County: Lancaster FICE Identification: 003286
Unit ID: 213446
Telephone: (717) 393-0654 Carnegie Class: Spec-4-yr-Faith
FAX Number: (717) 393-4254 Calendar System: Semester
URL: www.lancasterseminary.edu
Established: 1825 Annual Graduate Tuition & Fees: N/A
Enrollment: 118 Coed
Affiliation or Control: United Church Of Christ IRS Status: 501(c)3
Highest Offering: Doctorate; No Undergraduates
Accreditation: M, THEOL

01 President .... Dr. Carol E. LYTCH
10 Vice President Business & Finance .... Ms. Elizabeth P. BENNETT
05 Vice Pres Academic Affairs & Dean .... Dr. David M. MELLOTT
07 Dean of Admissions .... Rev. Ruth-Aimée BELONNI-ROSARIO
08 Seminary Librarian .... Mrs. Myka K. STEPHENS
06 Registrar .... Mrs. Teresa BENNEIAN
29 Director Alumni/ae Relations .... Rev. Paul EYER
13 Director Computing/Information Mgmt .... Mr. Augustine APPREY
30 Executive Director of Development .... Vacant
04 Exec Assistant to the President .... Ms. Carter FARMER

Lansdale School of Business (C)

290 Wissahickon Ave, North Wales PA 19454-4114
County: Montgomery FICE Identification: 007779
Unit ID: 213473
Telephone: (215) 699-5700 Carnegie Class: Assoc/HVT-Mix Trad/Non
FAX Number: (215) 699-8770 Calendar System: Semester
URL: www.LSB.edu
Established: 1918 Annual Undergrad Tuition & Fees: $10,140
Enrollment: 344 Coed
Affiliation or Control: Proprietary IRS Status: Proprietary
Highest Offering: Associate Degree
Accreditation: ACICS

01 President .... Mr. Marlon D. KELLER
03 Executive Director .... Mrs. Marianne H. JOHNSON
05 Academic Dean .... Mr. David P. HEFFLEY
32 Student Services Coordinator .... Ms. Jacklyn G. WHEELER
08 Librarian .... Mrs. Marie B. WALCROFT
37 Financial Aid Coordinator .... Mr. David E. SOUZA
36 Career Services Coordinator .... Ms. Susan M. SCARPIELLO

Laurel Business Institute (D)

11 East Penn Street, Uniontown PA 15401-3453
County: Fayette FICE Identification: 025462
Unit ID: 250027
Telephone: (724) 439-4900 Carnegie Class: Assoc/HVT-Mix Trad/Non
FAX Number: (724) 439-3607 Calendar System: Semester
URL: www.laurel.edu
Established: 1985 Annual Undergrad Tuition & Fees: $9,744
Enrollment: 233 Coed
Affiliation or Control: Proprietary IRS Status: Proprietary
Highest Offering: Associate Degree
Accreditation: ACICS, COARC, MLTAD

01 President .... Mrs. Nancy M. DECKER
11 Executive Director .... Mrs. Bonnie MARSH
10 Vice President of Finance .... Ms. Vicki M. JOLLIFFE
15 Vice President of Human Resources .... Mr. Chuck SANTORE, JR.
05 Director of Education .... Mrs. Toni R. HARTLEY
13 Director of IT .... Mr. Ken LAPIKAS
37 Vice President of Financial Aid .... Ms. Stephanie M. MIGYANKO
07 Executive VP of Operations .... Mr. Douglas S. DECKER

Laurel Technical Institute (E)

200 Sterling Avenue, Sharon PA 16146
County: Mercer FICE Identification: 020925
Unit ID: 215992
Telephone: (724) 983-0700 Carnegie Class: Assoc/HVT-High Trad
FAX Number: (724) 983-8355 Calendar System: Semester
URL: www.laurel.edu
Established: 1925 Annual Undergrad Tuition & Fees: $9,744
Enrollment: 157 Coed
Affiliation or Control: Proprietary IRS Status: Proprietary
Highest Offering: Associate Degree
Accreditation: ACICS, COARC, MLTAD

01 President .... Ms. Nancy DECKER
05 Director/Exec VP of Operations .... Mr. Douglas DECKER
07 Director of Admission .... Mr. Douglas DECKER

Lebanon Valley College (F)

101 N College Avenue, Annville PA 17003-1400
County: Lebanon FICE Identification: 003288
Unit ID: 213507
Telephone: (717) 867-6161 Carnegie Class: Masters/S
FAX Number: (717) 867-6124 Calendar System: Semester
URL: www.lvc.edu
Established: 1866 Annual Undergrad Tuition & Fees: $39,030
Enrollment: 1,901 Coed
Affiliation or Control: United Methodist IRS Status: 501(c)3
Highest Offering: Doctorate
Accreditation: M, ACBSP, MUS, PTA

01 President .... Dr. Lewis E. THAYNE
05 Vice Pres Acad Affs/Dean of Faculty .... Dr. Michael R. GREEN
30 Vice President of Advancement .... Mr. Daniel HELWIG
10 Vice Pres Finance/Administration .... Mr. Shawn P. CURTIN
84 Vice President of Enrollment .... Mr. Edwin R. WRIGHT
32 VP Student Affairs/Dean of Students . Mr. Gregory H. KRIKORIAN
101 VP for Strategic Initiatives & Secy .... Mr. Steven P. O'DAY
26 Exec Dir Marketing/Communications .... Mr. Martin J. PARKES
13 Director of Information Technology .... Mr. David W. SHAPIRO
15 Director of HR/Title IX Coordinator .... Mrs. Ann C. HAYES
20 Associate Dean of Academic Affairs .... Dr. Ann E. DAMIANO
09 Director of Institutional Research .... Mrs. Jessica L. ICKES
58 Assoc Dean of Grad Stds/Cont Educ .... Vacant
06 Registrar .... Mr. Jeremy A. MAISTO
41 Director of Athletics .... Mr. Richard L. BEARD
88 Dir of Finance and Budget .... Ms. Wendy ALBERT
21 Controller .... Mr. Gabriel PAZ
37 Director of Financial Aid .... Mrs. Kendra M. FEIGERT
36 Director of Career Development .... Vacant
28 Director of Multicultural Affairs .... Vacant
19 Director of Public Safety .... Mr. Brent OBERHOLTZER
104 Director of Global Education .... Mrs. Jill T. RUSSELL
39 Director of Residential Life .... Dr. Michael R. DIESNER
22 Director of Disability Services .... Ms. Dawn R. SHOWERS
50 Director of the MBA Program .... Dr. David M. SETLEY
107 Director of Professional Studies .... Ms. Beth E. ROMANSKI
08 Director of the Bishop Library .... Ms. Sarah E. GREENE
105 Director of Communications .... Mrs. Jasmine A. BUCHER
102 Director of Development .... Mr. Matthew WEAVER
18 Sr Director Facilities Management ... Mr. Donald SANTOSTEFANO
35 Assoc Dean Student Affairs .... Dr. Robert L. MIKUS
42 Chaplain .... Rev. Paul FULLMER
07 Director of Admission .... Vacant
27 Dir Editorial Standards/Brand Msgng .... Dr. Thomas M. HANRAHAN
91 Dir Enterprise Information Systems .... Mr. Robert J. DILLANE
90 Director Technology/User Support .... Mr. Michael C. ZEIGLER
24 Director of Audiovisual Technology .... Mr. Andrew S. GREENE
38 Director of Counseling .... Dr. Stephanie A. FALK
88 Director of Student Activities .... Mrs. Jennifer M. EVANS
23 Director of Health Services .... Ms. Valerie G. ANGELI
88 Assistant Controller .... Mr. Todd M. LATSHAW
04 Executive Asst to President .... Ms. Amy LINTZ

Lehigh Carbon Community College (G)

4525 Education Park Drive, Schnecksville PA 18078-2598
County: Lehigh FICE Identification: 006810
Unit ID: 213525
Telephone: (610) 799-2121 Carnegie Class: Assoc/MT-VT-Mix Trad/Non
FAX Number: (610) 799-1527 Calendar System: Semester
URL: www.lccc.edu
Established: 1966 Annual Undergrad Tuition & Fees (In-District): $3,800
Enrollment: 6,779 Coed
Affiliation or Control: Local IRS Status: 501(c)3
Highest Offering: Associate Degree
Accreditation: M, ACBSP, ADNUR, CAHIIM, CSHSE, MAC, OTA, PNUR, PTAA

01 President .... Dr. Ann D. BIEBER
05 VP Academic/Student Development .... Dr. Thomas W. MEYER
10 VP Finance & Admin Svcs .... Mr. Brian KAHLER
84 VP Enrollment Management .... Ms. Cindy M. HANEY
04 Exec Asst to President and Board .... Mrs. Cindy L. BROOKS
32 Dean of Student Development .... Ms. Peggy M. HEIM
72 Int Dean Commun Arts/Computers/Tech .... Dr. Richard W. WILT
81 Interim Dean Sci/Eng/Math .... Dr. Barry L. SPRIGGS
13 Exec Dir Information Technology .... Mr. Ervin J. MEASE
106 Assoc Dean Distance Education .... Mr. Dominic CHRISTISON
79 Interim Dean Humanities & Soc Sci .... Dr. Andra M. BASU
76 Interim Dean Healthcare Sciences .... Ms. Larissa M. VERTA
103 Dean Employer Engage & Cmty Educ .... Ms. Terri K. KEEFE
26 Exec Dir College Relations .... Ms. Linda BAKER
09 Assoc Dean Inst Research & Effectiv .... Dr. Glynis A. DANIELS
50 Interim Dean Bus/Educ/Legal/Soc Svc .... Dr. Cecelia A. CONNELLY-WEIDA
21 Dir Budgets & Purchasing .... Ms. Shannon HELMER
102 Executive Director Foundation .... Vacant
38 Dir Advising .... Ms. Susan J. FREAD
07 Dir Recruitment & Admissions .... Vacant
88 Dir Application Services .... Mr. Robert F. GARVEY
36 Dir Career Development .... Ms. Christina L. MOYER
88 Assoc Dean Prof Accred/Curriculum .... Mr. Scott W. AQUILA
88 Dir High School Connections .... Ms. Jennifer K. AQUILA
15 Dir HR/Title IX/Equity Coord .... Ms. Donna M. WILLIAMS
88 Dir Infrastructure Svcs/Client Sol .... Mr. Frank D. MROZ
88 Dir Fac Dev/Student Retention .... Ms. Cheryl A. DOLL
66 Director Nursing Programs .... Ms. Barbara H. LUPOLE
35 Dir Student Life .... Ms. Gene F. EDEN
14 Dir IT Support Services .... Mr. George C. HEGEDUS
18 Dir Facilities Management .... Mr. Carl S. PECKITT, JR.
37 Dir of Financial Aid .... Ms. Marian L. SNYDER
25 Dir Academic Grants .... Ms. Linda L. MESICS
41 Director Athletics .... Mr. Andrew JOHNSON
88 Dir Early Learning Center .... Ms. Mary G. SALINGER
12 Dir of Community Outreach/Strategic .... Dr. David LAPINSKY
88 Dir of Literacy and Job Training .... Ms. Mary KOVALCHICK
88 Dir Audits & Reporting .... Ms. Stefanie E. NESTER
25 Dir Institutional Advance Grants .... Mr. Thomas J. MULDERICK
74 Co-Dir Veterinary Tech Program .... Ms. Lisa A. MARTINI-JOHNSON
27 Dir Marketing and Publications .... Ms. Holly YACYNYCH
06 Dir Registration/Student Records .... Mr. Gregory J. GOLETZ, JR.
40 Bookstore Manager .... Ms. Jennifer L. ERB
88 Assoc Dean Student Success .... Mr. Brian C. DELONG
19 Dir Public Safety .... Mr. James W. SURGEONER
88 Dir Student Accounts .... Ms. Stacey A. BETZ

Lehigh University (H)

27 Memorial Drive W, Bethlehem PA 18015-3094
County: Northampton FICE Identification: 003289
Unit ID: 213543
Telephone: (610) 758-3000 Carnegie Class: DU-Higher
FAX Number: (610) 691-5420 Calendar System: Semester
URL: www.lehigh.edu
Established: 1865 Annual Undergrad Tuition & Fees: $46,230
Enrollment: 7,119 Coed
Affiliation or Control: Independent Non-Profit IRS Status: 501(c)3
Highest Offering: Doctorate
Accreditation: M, BUS, BUSA, COPSY, CS, ENG, IPSY, SCPSY, THEA

01 President .... Dr. John D. SIMON
05 Provost & VP for Academic Affairs .... Dr. Patrick V. FARRELL
10 Vice Pres Finance & Administration .... Ms. Patricia A. JOHNSON
88 VP for International Affairs .... Dr. Cheryl A. MATHERLY
30 Interim Vice President Advancement .... Mr. John W. WELTY
46 VP & Assoc Prov Research/Graduate .... Dr. Alan J. SNYDER
26 VP Communications & Public Affairs ... Mr. Frederick J. MCGRAIL
44 Chief Investment Officer .... Vacant
09 Vice Provost Institutional Research .... Dr. Henry Y. ZHENG
32 Vice Provost Student Affairs .... Dr. John W. SMEATON
13 Vice Provost Library & Tech Svcs .... Dr. Bruce M. TAGGART
86 Assoc VP for Govt Relations .... Mr. William D. MICHALERYA
21 Assoc VP Finance/Asst Secy Board .... Ms. Denise M. BLEW
15 Assoc VP for Human Resource .... Mr. Chris HALLADAY
18 Assoc Vice Pres Facilities Services .... Vacant
20 Deputy Provost Academic Affairs .... Ms. Jennifer M. JENSEN
35 Assoc Vice Provost Dean of Students .... Ms. Sharon K. BASSO
29 Asst VP of Alumni Engagement .... Ms. Jennifer L. CUNNINGHAM
31 Asst VP Community & Regional Affs .... Ms. Adrienne J. WASHINGTON
54 Interim Dean Engr & Applied Science .... Dr. John P. COULTER
49 Dean Arts & Sciences .... Dr. Donald E. HALL
50 Dean of Business/Economics .... Dr. Georgette C. PHILLIPS
53 Dean of Education .... Dr. Gary M. SASSO
07 Dean of Admissions/Financial Aid .... Mr. J. Leon WASHINGTON
41 Murray H Goodman Dean of Athletics ... Mr. Joseph D. STERRETT
06 Registrar .... Mr. Emil A. GNASSO
37 Director Financial Aid .... Ms. Jennifer L. MERTZ
106 Director Distance Education .... Ms. Margaret A. PORTZ
36 Director Career Services .... Ms. Lori B. KENNEDY
23 Director Health Center .... Dr. Susan C. KITEI
39 Director Residential Services .... Mr. Ozzie BREINER
40 Director Bookstore .... Mr. Brian ADLER
19 Chief University Police .... Mr. Edward K. SHUPP
38 Director of Counseling Services .... Dr. Ian T. BIRKY
42 Chaplain .... Rev. Lloyd H. STEFFEN
43 General Counsel .... Mr. Frank A. ROTH
21 Director of Budget .... Mr. Stephen J. GUTTMAN
28 Vice Provost for Academic Diversity .... Mr. Henry U. ODI
96 Manager Strategic Sourcing .... Ms. Jane ALTEMOSE
84 Director Enrollment Management .... Ms. Jennifer E. O'BRIEN-KNOTTS
100 Chief of Staff .... Mr. Erik J. WALKER

Lincoln Technical Institute (I)

5151 Tilghman Street, Allentown PA 18104-3298
County: Lehigh FICE Identification: 007759
Unit ID: 213570
Telephone: (610) 398-5300 Carnegie Class: Assoc/HVT-High Non
FAX Number: (610) 395-2706 Calendar System: Semester
URL: www.lincolnedu.com
Established: 1946 Annual Undergrad Tuition & Fees: N/A
Enrollment: 540 Coed
Affiliation or Control: Proprietary IRS Status: Proprietary
Highest Offering: Associate Degree
Accreditation: ACCSC

01 Campus President .... Mrs. Lisa M. KUNTZ
05 Director of Education .... Ms. Anne CONNELY
11 Director of Administration .... Mrs. Angela REPPERT

07 Director of Admissions ....Mr. Vincent SALVANTORIELLO
36 Director of Career Services ....Mrs. Charmain BRODY
37 Financial Aid Manager ....Ms. Erica BRANDI

Lincoln Technical Institute (A)

9191 Torresdale Avenue, Philadelphia PA 19136-1595
County: Philadelphia FICE Identification: 007832
Unit ID: 213589
Telephone: (215) 335-0800 Carnegie Class: Spec 2-yr-Tech
FAX Number: (215) 335-1443 Calendar System: Other
URL: www.lincolntech.com
Established: 1946 Annual Undergrad Tuition & Fees: N/A
Enrollment: 360 Coed
Affiliation or Control: Proprietary IRS Status: Proprietary
Highest Offering: Associate Degree
Accreditation: ACCSC

01 Campus President ....Mr. John WILLIE
07 Dir Admiss High School/Adult Educ ....Ms. Nicole ZUCCHERI
32 Student Services Coordinator ....Ms. Tijania GOODWIN
05 Director of Education ....Mr. Michael CONCILIO
11 Director Administration ....Ms. Gina ALTSHULER
36 Director of Career Services ....Ms. TaJuan BUSH

Lincoln University (B)

PO Box 179, 1570 Baltimore Pike,
Lincoln University PA 19352-0999
County: Chester FICE Identification: 003290
Unit ID: 213598
Telephone: (484) 365-8000 Carnegie Class: Masters/M
FAX Number: (484) 365-7316 Calendar System: Semester
URL: www.lincoln.edu
Established: 1854 Annual Undergrad Tuition & Fees (In-State): $10,878
Enrollment: 1,819 Coed
Affiliation or Control: State Related IRS Status: 501(c)3
Highest Offering: Master's
Accreditation: M, NURSE

01 Interim President ....Dr. Richard GREEN
30 Interim VP for Institutional Advanc ....Mr. Kevan TURMAN
100 Chief of Staf/Mgr Board of Trustees ....Ms. Diane M. BROWN
05 Provost and VP for Academic Affairs ....Dr. Patricia RAMSEY
10 Vice Pres Fiscal Affairs/Treasurer ....Mr. Charles GRADOWSKI
32 Vice Pres for Student Affairs ....Dr. Juliana M. MOSLEY
13 Asst VP for Information Technology ....Mr. Andre WARNER
43 General Counsel ....Vacant
09 Asst Dir Institutional Research ....Ms. Nancy SMITH
108 Dir of Assessment & Accreditation ....Vacant
39 Dean Students and Campus Life ....Dr. Lenetta LEE
84 Assoc VP of Enrollment
Management ....Ms. Kimberly TAYLOR-BENNS
08 Director of Library ....Vacant
26 Assoc VP External Relations/Mktg ....Ms. Maureen STOKES
27 Director of Communications ....Mr. Eric C. WEBB
29 Acting Dir of Alumni Relations ....Mr. Richard LANCASTER
06 Registrar ....Ms. Catherine RUTLEDGE
30 Director Development & Major Gifts ....Vacant
36 Director Counseling/Career Svcs Ctr ....Mr. Ralph SIMPSON
41 Director of Athletics ....Dr. Darryl POPE
42 Chaplain ....Mr. Frederick FAISON
21 Controller ....Ms. Cynthia GORTON
85 Director International Services ....Ms. Constance L. LUNDY
23 Director Health Services ....Ms. Velva GREENE-RAINEY
58 Dir Graduate Student Svcs/Admission ....Ms. Jernice LEA
35 Director of Student Life & Develop ....Ms. Ihsan R. MUJAHID
37 Director Financial Aid ....Ms. Kim ANDERSON
96 Director of Purchasing ....Ms. Sue REED
81 Dean College of Science & Tech ....Dr. Patricia JOSEPH
83 Dean Col Professional/Grad/Ext Stds ....Dr. Virginia SMITH
79 Dean Col of Arts/Humanities/Soc Sci .....Dr. Cheryl Renee GOOCH

Lutheran Theological Seminary at Gettysburg (C)

61 Seminary Ridge, Gettysburg PA 17325-1795
County: Adams FICE Identification: 003291
Unit ID: 213631
Telephone: (717) 334-6286 Carnegie Class: Spec-4-yr-Faith
FAX Number: (717) 334-3469 Calendar System: 4/1/4
URL: www.ltsg.edu
Established: 1826 Annual Graduate Tuition & Fees: N/A
Enrollment: 178 Coed
Affiliation or Control: Evangelical Lutheran Church In America
IRS Status: 501(c)3
Highest Offering: Doctorate; No Undergraduates
Accreditation: M, THEOL

01 President ....Rev. Michael L. COOPER-WHITE
30 Chief Advancement Officer ....Rev. Glenn LUDWIG
10 Chief Financial Officer ....Mrs. Jennifer BYERS
05 Dean of the Seminary ....Dr. Kristin LARGEN
08 Library Director and Archivist ....Dr. Briant BOHLEKE
06 Registrar ....Dr. Marty STEVENS
26 Exec Asst to Pres for Comm/Plng ....Rev. John R. SPANGLER
91 Director of Info Systems/Ed Tech ....Mr. Donald L. REDMAN
15 Asst to the Pres/Personnel Officer ......Mrs. Elizabeth A. MEIGHAN
07 Director of Admissions ....Rev. Lauren MURATORE

Lutheran Theological Seminary at Philadelphia (D)

7301 Germantown Avenue, Philadelphia PA 19119-1794
County: Philadelphia FICE Identification: 003292
Unit ID: 213640
Telephone: (215) 248-4616 Carnegie Class: Spec-4-yr-Faith
FAX Number: (215) 248-4577 Calendar System: Other
URL: www.ltsp.edu
Established: 1864 Annual Graduate Tuition & Fees: N/A
Enrollment: 200 Coed
Affiliation or Control: Evangelical Lutheran Church In America
IRS Status: 501(c)3
Highest Offering: Doctorate; No Undergraduates
Accreditation: M, THEOL

01 President ....Dr. David J. LOSE
05 Dean ....Dr. J. Jayakiran SEBASTIAN
10 Chief Financial Officer ....Mr. John HEIDGERD
30 Vice President of Advancement ....Dr. Dennis TROTTER
58 Director of Graduate Studies ....Dr. J. Jayakiran SEBASTIAN
08 Director of the Library ....Dr. Karl KRUEGER
88 Vice President for Student Vocation .....Rev. Christina JOHNSTEN
21 Director of Finance ....Ms. Mariam NOWAR
15 Human Resources ....Ms. Yvonne CURTIS
32 Director of Student Services ....Rev. Heidi RODRICK-SCHNAATH
06 Registrar ....Ms. Renee DIEMER
37 Financial Aid Associate ....Mrs Susan KOWALSKI
19 Director of Security/Safety ....Mr Vincent FERGUSON
13 Director of Information and LDL ....Mr. Kyle BARGER
26 Director of Communications ....Ms. Merri BROWN
42 Chaplain ....Dr. Michael KRENTZ
108 VP Planning/Assessment and Admin ....Dr. David GRAFTON
04 Executive Assistant to President ....Ms. Diana DOWNEY
18 Director of Operations ....Mr. Craig E SENHARD
44 Director of Donor Services ....Ms. Kathie AFFLERBACH
07 Director of Admissions ....Rev. Nate PRIESENGER
88 Director of Contextual Education ....Dr. Charles LEONARD
88 Director of Urban Theological Inst ....Dr. Quintin ROBERTSON

Luzerne County Community College (E)

1333 S Prospect Street, Nanticoke PA 18634-3899
County: Luzerne FICE Identification: 006811
Unit ID: 213659
Telephone: (570) 740-0200 Carnegie Class: Assoc/MT-VT-High Trad
FAX Number: (570) 740-0386 Calendar System: Semester
URL: www.luzerne.edu
Established: 1966 Annual Undergrad Tuition & Fees (In-District): $4,770
Enrollment: 6,049 Coed
Affiliation or Control: Local IRS Status: 501(c)3
Highest Offering: Associate Degree
Accreditation: M, ACBSP, ADNUR, COARC, DA, DH, EMT, SURGT

01 President ....Mr. Thomas P. LEARY
101 Admin Asst to President/BOT ....Ms. Paula LABENSKI
05 Vice Pres Academic Affairs/Provost ....Dr. Dana CLARK
32 Dean Enrollment Mgmt/Student Dev ....Ms. Rosana REYES
103 VP Workforce/Community Development ....Ms. Susan SPRY
15 Dean Human Resources ....Mr. John SEDLAK
66 Dean of Nursing/Health Sciences .....Ms. Deborah VILEGI PAYNE
50 Dean of Business/Technologies ....Ms. Bonita MOYER
49 Dean of Arts & Sciences ....Vacant
10 Dean Finance ....Mr. Joseph GASPER
13 Chief Technology Office ....Mr. Don NELSON
07 Assistant Director Admissions ....Mr. Ed HENNIGAN
37 Director of Student Financial Aid ....Mr. Mark CARPENTIER
08 Director of Library ....Mrs. Mia W. BASSHAM
38 Dir Counseling/Stdnt Support Svcs ....Ms. Linda WALTERS
35 Dir Student Life/Athletics ....Ms. Mary SULLIVAN
09 Director Inst Research/Planning ....Ms. Graceann PLATUKUS
36 Director Career Services ....Ms. Mary GHILANI
18 Director of Physical Plant ....Mr. Keith GRAHAM
30 Exec Dir of Institutional Advance ....Ms Sandra NICHOLAS
84 Director Enrollment Management ....Mr. Jim DOMZALSKI
26 Chief Public Relations Officer ....Ms. Lisa NELSON
29 Director Alumni Relations ....Ms. Bonnie LAUER
96 Director of Purchasing ....Mr. Len OLZINSKI
28 Diversity Coordinator ....Ms. Judi MYERS
19 Director of Safety/Security ....Mr. William BARRETT

Lycoming College (F)

700 College Place, Williamsport PA 17701-5192
County: Lycoming FICE Identification: 003293
Unit ID: 213668
Telephone: (570) 321-4000 Carnegie Class: Bac-A&S
FAX Number: (570) 321-4337 Calendar System: Semester
URL: www.lycoming.edu
Established: 1812 Annual Undergrad Tuition & Fees: $35,900
Enrollment: 1,353 Coed
Affiliation or Control: United Methodist IRS Status: 501(c)3
Highest Offering: Baccalaureate
Accreditation: M

01 President ....Dr. Kent C. TRACHTE
05 Provost and Dean of the College ....Dr. Philip W. SPRUNGER
10 VP for Finance and Admin/Treasurer ....Mr. Jeffrey L. BENNETT
30 Vice President for Advancement ....Mr. Charles W. EDMONDS
84 VP for Enrollment Management ....Mr. Michael J. KONOPSKI
21 Controller ....Ms. Dawn HENDRICKS
32 Vice President for Student Life ....Dr. Daniel P. MILLER
44 Associate VP for Development ....Ms. Loni KLINE
20 Assoc Provost for Experiential Lrng ....Dr. Susan ROSS
89 Dean for First Year Students ....Mr. Andrew W. KILPATRICK
08 Director of Snowden Library ....Ms. Alison GREGORY
06 Registrar ....Ms. Whitney A. MERINAR
26 Exec Dir Marketing & Communications ....Mr. Patrick MARTY
37 Director of Financial Aid ....Mr. James LAKIS
13 Chief Information Officer ....Mr. Robert L. DUNKLEBERGER
29 Director Alumni Relations ....Ms. Amy S. REYES
44 Planned Giving Officer ....Ms. Karen M. SHEAFFER
35 Director of Student Programs ... Mr. Lawrence P. MANNOLINI, III
39 Director Residence Life ....Ms. Kate HUMMEL
41 Director of Athletics ....Mr. Michael CLARK
30 Senior Major Gift Officer ....Mr. Gregory J. BELL
44 Director of Annual Giving ....Ms. Lesley LARSON
42 Campus Minister ....Rev. Jeffrey L. LECRONE
15 Director of Human Resources ....Ms. Jackie BILGER
18 Chief Facilities/Physical Plant ....Mr. F. Douglas KUNTZ
23 Director of Health Services ....Ms. Sondra L. STIPCAK
38 Director Student Counseling ....Mr. Townsend VELKOFF
40 Campus Store Manager ....Ms. Patricia E. BAUSINGER
92 Lycoming Scholars ....Dr. Cullen J. CHANDLER
94 Women's Studies ....Dr. Kerry RICHMOND
16 Human Resources Coordinator ....Mrs. Cathleen A. LUTZ
04 Assistant to the President ....Ms. Diane CARL
09 Director of Institutional Research ....Dr. Chiaki KOTORI
108 Associate Provost ....Dr. Eileen PELUSO
90 Dir Instructional & Emerging Tech ....Mr. Steve CARAVAGGIO
91 Director Administrative Computing ....Ms. Janet PAYNE
07 Director of Admissions ....Ms. Jessica A. QUINTANA HESS
102 Foundations Relations Officer ....Ms. Melanie TAORMINA
104 Coordinator of Study Abroad ....Mr. Philip WITHERUP
105 Director Web Services ....Mr. Robert BROWN

Manor College (G)

700 Fox Chase Road, Jenkintown PA 19046-3399
County: Montgomery FICE Identification: 003294
Unit ID: 213774
Telephone: (215) 885-2360 Carnegie Class: Assoc/MT-VT-High Trad
FAX Number: (215) 576-6564 Calendar System: Semester
URL: www.manor.edu
Established: 1947 Annual Undergrad Tuition & Fees: $16,550
Enrollment: 780 Coed
Affiliation or Control: Independent Non-Profit IRS Status: 501(c)3
Highest Offering: Associate Degree
Accreditation: M, ACBSP, DA, DH

01 President ....Dr. Jonathan PERI
05 Exec VP/Dean of Academic Affairs ....Dr. Stephen GRIECO
06 Registrar ....Ms. Dianne I. SARIDAKIS
10 Director Finance & Physical Plant ....Mr. John W. WINICKI
13 Director Information Technology ....Mr. Paul VAN RIJN
15 Human Resource Generalist ....Ms. Christine COLELLA
18 Director Finance & Physical Plant ....Mr. John W. WINICKI
19 Manager of Security Information ....Ofcr. William PEPITONE
30 Interim Director of Development ....Ms. Christine LINVILL
26 Associate Director Marketing ....Ms. Kelly PEIFFER
32 Director of Student Engagement ....Ms. Allison C. MOOTZ
37 Director Financial Aid ....Mr. Chris T. HARTMAN
38 Director Counseling ....Ms. Christine B. PRINCE
39 Residence Hall Coordinator ....Ms. Lynn WALES
41 Director Athletics ....Mr. Robert F. REEVES
49 Lib Arts Chair/Dir of Psychology ....Ms. Christine ERDNER
08 Head Librarian ....Ms. Donna GUERIN
09 Director of Institutional Research ....Mr. John T. KREBS
07 Director of Admissions ....Ms. Stephanie WALKER

Marywood University (H)

2300 Adams Avenue, Scranton PA 18509-1598
County: Lackawanna FICE Identification: 003296
Unit ID: 213826
Telephone: (570) 348-6211 Carnegie Class: Masters/L
FAX Number: (570) 961-4769 Calendar System: Semester
URL: www.marywood.edu
Established: 1915 Annual Undergrad Tuition & Fees: $32,692
Enrollment: 3,056 Coed
Affiliation or Control: Roman Catholic IRS Status: 501(c)3
Highest Offering: Doctorate
Accreditation: M, ACBSP, ARCPA, ART, #CAATE, CACREP, CLPSY, DIETC, DIETD, DIETI, MUS, NUR, NURSE, SP, SW, TED

01 President ....Sr. Mary PERSICO, IHM
05 Int Vice Pres Academic Affairs ....Dr. Alan M. LEVINE
10 VP Business Affairs/Treasurer ....Vacant
30 Vice Pres University Advancement ....Ms. Renee G. ZEHEL
84 VP Enrollment Svcs/Student Success ...Ms. Ann BOLAND-CHASE
101 Secretary Univ & General
Counsel ....Atty. Mary T. GARDIER PATERSON
15 Assoc Vice Pres for Human
Resources ....Dr. Patricia E. DUNLEAVY
26 Assoc VP Marketing/Communication ....Mr. Peter KILCULLEN
18 Asst VP for Buildings & Grounds ....Mrs. Wendy YANKELITIS
32 Asst VP for Student Life ....Dr. Amy PACIEJ-WOODRUFF
49 Dn Munley College Liberal Arts/Sci ......Dr. Frances M. ZAUHAR
53 Int Dean Reap College Ed/Human Dev ....Dr. Teresa A. PETERS
76 Dean Col of Health/Human Svcs ....Dr. Mark E. RODGERS
88 Dn Col of Creative/Performing Arts ....Mr. Collier B. PARKER
48 Dean School of Architecture ....Mr. James SULLIVAN

90 Director User Support Services .... Dr. Michael MIRABITO
70 Director School of Social Work .... Dr. Diane W. KELLER
08 Director of Library Services .... Mr. David G. SCHAPPERT
06 Registrar .... Ms. Rosemary BURGER
07 Sr Dir of University Admissions ... Mr. Christian M. DIGREGORIO
21 Controller/Asst Treasurer .... Mr. Patrick E. CASTELLANI
21 Asst Controller .... Ms. Melissa A. SADDLEMIRE
13 Director of Enterprise Systems .... Mr. Michael P. GIBBONS
88 Asst Director Buildings & Grounds .... Mr. Myron MARCINEK
37 Director of Financial Aid .... Ms. Barbara L. SCHMITT
102 Corporate Foundation Relations Ofcr .... Ms. Tina L. MCGOVERN
44 Director of Planned Giving .... Ms. Elizabeth A. CONNERY
27 Public Relations Director .... Ms. Juneann GRECO
42 Chaplain/Asst Dir Campus Ministry .... Rev. Joseph P. ELSTON
39 Sr Dir Student Conduct/Res Life .... Mr. Ross NOVAK
41 Director Athletics/Recreation .... Dr. Mary Jo GUNNING
36 Director of Career Services .... Dr. Carole R. GUSTITUS
42 Director of Campus Ministry .... Sr. Catherine LUXNER
88 Resident District Manager .... Mr. Thomas K. NOTCHICK
13 Chief Information Officer .... Mr. Anthony SPINILLO
19 Chief Campus Safety .... Mr. Michael J. FINEGAN
23 Director of Student Health Services .... Ms. Linda MCDADE
38 Director Counseling & Student Devel .... Dr. Robert S. SHAW
40 Bookstore Manager .... Ms. Joan DIEHL
104 Assoc Dir International Affairs .... Vacant
14 Director of Operations .... Mr. John B. PORTER
44 Dir Advancement Services .... Ms. Elizabeth M. STIRES
29 Director of Alumni Engagement .... Ms. Ann L. WILLIAMS
35 Dir of Student Act/Leadership Devel .... Ms. Callie FRIELER
28 Director of Diversity .... Dr. Lia Richards PALMITER
88 Director Human Physiology Lab .... Vacant
09 Sr Director Institutional Research .... Dr. Ellen BOYLAN
45 Assoc VP Plng/Inst Effectiveness ..... Dr. Kathleen O. RUTHKOSKY
90 Asst Director of User Support .... Ms. Katherine P. LEWIS

McCann School of Business & Technology (A)

2200 North Irving Street, Allentown PA 18109
Telephone: (484) 223-4601 Identification: 770768
Accreditation: ACICS, MAC, MLTAD, SURGT

McCann School of Business & Technology (B)

346 York Road, Carlisle PA 17013
Telephone: (714) 218-3400 Identification: 770767
Accreditation: ACICS, SURGT

McCann School of Business & Technology (C)

2227 Scranton Carbondale Highway,
Dickson City PA 18519
Telephone: (570) 969-4330 Identification: 770769
Accreditation: ACICS, MAC

McCann School of Business & Technology (D)

370 Maplewood Drive, Humbolt Ind Pk,
Hazleton PA 18202-9790
Telephone: (570) 454-6172 Identification: 666484
Accreditation: ACICS, MAC, SURGT

† Branch campus of McCann School of Business & Technology, Pottsville, PA.

McCann School of Business & Technology (E)

7495 Westbranch Highway, Lewisburg PA 17837
Telephone: (570) 497-8014 Identification: 666485
Accreditation: ACICS, MAC, MLTAD, SURGT

† Branch campus of McCann School of Business & Technology, Pottsville, PA.

McCann School of Business & Technology (F)

2650 Woodglen Road, Pottsville PA 17901-1335
County: Schuylkill FICE Identification: 004898
Unit ID: 438212
Telephone: (570) 622-7622 Carnegie Class: Assoc/HVT-Mix Trad/Non
FAX Number: (570) 622-7770 Calendar System: Quarter
URL: www.mccann.edu
Established: 1897 Annual Undergrad Tuition & Fees: $9,948
Enrollment: 3,346 Coed
Affiliation or Control: Proprietary IRS Status: Proprietary
Highest Offering: Associate Degree
Accreditation: ACICS, MAC, MLTAD

01 Campus Director Hazleton .... Mr. William BURKE
05 Director of Education .... Mrs. Barbara REESE
36 Director of Career Services .... Mr. Matthew ADAMS

McCann School of Business & Technology (G)

264 Highland Park Boulevard, Wilkes Barre PA 18702
Telephone: (570) 235-2200 Identification: 770770
Accreditation: ACICS

Mercyhurst University (H)

501 E 38th Street, Erie PA 16546-0001
County: Erie FICE Identification: 003297
Unit ID: 213987
Telephone: (814) 824-2000 Carnegie Class: Masters/M
FAX Number: (814) 824-2438 Calendar System: Semester
URL: www.mercyhurst.edu
Established: 1926 Annual Undergrad Tuition & Fees: $33,314
Enrollment: 2,871 Coed
Affiliation or Control: Roman Catholic IRS Status: 501(c)3
Highest Offering: Doctorate
Accreditation: M, #ARCPA, CAATE, DANCE, IACBE, MUS, PTAA, SW

01 President .... Mr. Michael T. VICTOR
05 Provost & VP Academic Affairs .... Dr. David DAUSEY
10 Vice Pres Finance & Administration .... Mr. David P. MYRON
12 Exec VP Mercyhurst - NE .... Dr. Gary BROWN
30 Vice Pres University Development .... Mr. Caleb M. PIFER
32 Vice Pres of Student Life .... Dr. Laura ZIRKEL
84 VP for Enrollment .... Mr. Joe HOWARD
13 Chief Information Officer .... Ms. Jeanette BRITT
18 Director Facilities/Physical Plant .... Mr. Forrest DAVIS
38 Director Student Counseling Service .... Ms. Judy SMITH
07 Director Undergraduate Admissions .... Mr. Christian BEYER
06 Registrar .... Ms. Michele WHEATON
08 Dir Univ Libraries/Online Learning .... Ms. Darci JONES
39 Dir Residential Life/Stdnt Conduct .... Ms. Megan MCKENNA
19 Director of Public Safety Programs ..... Mr. Donald J. FUHRMANN
29 Dir Alumni Rels & Annual Giving .... Ms. Tamara WALTERS
42 Director of Campus Ministry .... Fr. James PISZKER
37 Director of Student Financial Svcs .... Ms. Carrie NEWMAN
41 Director of Athletics .... Mr. Joseph KIMBALL
09 Director of Institutional Research .... Mrs. Sheila W. RICHTER
15 Director Human Resources .... Mr. Jim TOMETSKO
28 Director Multicultural Affairs .... Ms. Petrina MARRERO
04 Administrative Asst to President .... Ms. Stacey WILEY
104 Director Study Abroad .... Dr. Heidi HOSEY
26 Chief Public Relations/Marketing .... Mrs. Dionne VEITCH
43 Dir Legal Services/General Counsel .Mrs. Meredith BOLLHEIMER

Mercyhurst University Northeast (I)

16 W Division Street, North East PA 16428
Telephone: (814) 725-6100 Identification: 770161
Accreditation: &M, ADNUR, COARC, MLTAD, NUR, OTA

† Regional accreditation is carried under the parent institution in Erie, PA

Messiah College (J)

One College Avenue, Mechanicsburg PA 17055
County: Cumberland FICE Identification: 003298
Unit ID: 213996
Telephone: (717) 766-2511 Carnegie Class: Bac-Diverse
FAX Number: (717) 691-6025 Calendar System: Semester
URL: www.messiah.edu
Established: 1909 Annual Undergrad Tuition & Fees: $32,240
Enrollment: 3,234 Coed
Affiliation or Control: Interdenominational IRS Status: 501(c)3
Highest Offering: Doctorate
Accreditation: M, ACBSP, ART, CAATE, CACREP, DIETD, @DIETI, ENG, MUS, NURSE, SW, THEA

01 President .... Dr. Kim S. PHIPPS
05 Provost .... Dr. Randall G. BASINGER
30 Vice President for Advancement .... Mr. Barry G. GOODLING
84 Vice Pres for Enrollment Management .... Mr. John A. CHOPKA
10 Vice Pres for Finance & Planning .... Mr. David S. WALKER
15 VP for Human Res & Compliance .... Ms. Amanda A. COFFEY
13 VP Info Technology/Assoc
Provost .... Dr. William G. STRAUSBAUGH
11 Vice President for Operations .... Mrs. Kathrynne G. SHAFER
32 Vice Provost & Dean of
Students .... Dr. Kristin M. HANSEN-KIEFFER
58 Int Asst Prov Grad & Nontrad Pgms .... Dr. Robert PEPPER
57 Dean School of the Arts .... Dr. Richard E. ROBERSON
53 Dean Sch Bus/Educ/Soc Sci .... Dr. Carolyn MAURER
79 Dean School of Humanities .... Dr. Peter K. POWERS
81 Int Dean School of Sci/Engr/Health .... Dr. Angela HARE
35 Associate Dean of Students .... Mr. Douglas M. WOOD
88 Dir of Intercultural Office .... Mrs. Faith MINNICH KJESBO
88 Dir Stdnt Involvemnt Leadership Pgm .... Mr. Kevin J. VILLEGAS
07 Director of Admissions .... Mrs. Dana J. BRITTON
37 Director of Financial Aid .... Mr. Gregory L. GEARHART
39 Asst Dir of Residence Life/Housing .... Mrs. Rhonda KING
21 Dir Financial Operations/Controller .... Mrs. Christine HARTMAN
06 Registrar .... Mr. James J. SOTHERDEN
08 Director of the Murray Library .... Mr. Jonathan D. LAUER
41 Director Information Services .... Mr. John P. LUFT
90 Dir Learning Technology Services .... Mrs. Susan K. SHANNON
09 Director of Institutional Research .... Ms. Laura M. MILLER
42 College Pastor .... Dr. Donald OPITZ
30 Director of Development .... Dr. Jon C. STUCKEY
26 Exec Dir Marketing & Communications .... Mrs. Carla E. GROSS
29 Director Alumni & Parent Relations ...... Mr. Jay W. MCCLYMONT
44 Director of Annual Giving .... Ms. Beth TROTT CLARK
38 Director of the Engle Center .... Ms. Eleanor M. ADDLEMAN
23 Coordinator of Health Services .... Mrs. Michelle LUCAS
41 Director of Athletics .... Mr. Jack T. COLE
92 Dir of the College Honors Program .... Dr. Dean C. CURRY
18 Director of Facility Services .... Mr. Bradley A. MARKLEY
36 Director of Career Development .... Mrs. Christina R. HANSON
40 Campus Store Manager .... Ms. Candice TRITLE
19 Director Safety/Dispatch Services .... Ms. Cindy L. BURGER
04 Executive Asst to President .... Ms. Melissa COHEN
96 Purchasing Manager .... Mrs. Daisy ANDERSON

Misericordia University (K)

301 Lake Street, Dallas PA 18612-1098
County: Luzerne FICE Identification: 003247
Unit ID: 214069
Telephone: (570) 674-6400 Carnegie Class: Masters/M
FAX Number: (570) 675-2441 Calendar System: Semester
URL: www.misericordia.edu
Established: 1924 Annual Undergrad Tuition & Fees: $29,840
Enrollment: 3,054 Coed
Affiliation or Control: Roman Catholic IRS Status: 501(c)3
Highest Offering: Doctorate
Accreditation: M, #ARCPA, DMS, IACBE, NURSE, OT, PTA, RAD, SP, SW

01 President .... Dr. Thomas J. BOTZMAN
10 Vice Pres Finance & Administration .... Ms. Beatrice FEVRY
05 Vice President Academic Affairs .... Dr. Charles J. BRODY
30 VP of Institutional Advancement .... Ms. Susan M. HELWIG
88 Vice Pres of Mission Integration .... Sr. Jean MESSAROS
45 Sec to BOT/VP Plng/External Rels .Dr. Barbara SAMUEL LOFTUS
32 Vice President of Student Life .... Ms. Kathleen FOLEY
21 Controller .... Mr. Ronald S. HROMISIN
06 Registrar .... Mr. Joseph REDINGTON
84 Director Enrollment Management .... Ms. Jane F. DESSOYE
29 Director Alumni Relations .... Ms. Denise MISCAVAGE
08 Librarian .... Ms. Jennifer LUKSA
04 Exec Assistant to the President .... Ms. Michelle DONATO
96 Director of Purchasing .... Mr. Thomas F. KANE
38 Exec Dir Learning Resource Ctr .... Ms. Jennifer RANDALL
42 Director Campus Ministry .... Ms. Christine SOMERS
41 Director of Athletics .... Mr. David MARTIN
39 Director of Residents .... Ms. Donna ELLIS
13 Manager Applications Development .... Mr. Matt MIHAL
14 Director of Information Technology .... Mr. Val APANOVICH
35 Director of Student Life .... Ms. Darcy BRODMERKEL
36 Dir Insalaco Ctr Career Development ... Ms. Bernadette RUSHMER
102 Dir Foundation/Government Relations .... Mr. Larry PELLEGRINI
51 Director of Adult Education/CACE .... Mr. Paul NARDONE
15 Director of Human Resources .... Ms. Pamela PARSNIK
07 Director of Admissions .... Mr. Glenn BOZINSKI
04 Special Assistant to President .... Mr. James ROBERTS
37 Director of Financial Aid .... Ms. Susan FRONZONI
28 Dir Multicultural/Student Outreach .... Dr. Charmaine AGUILAR
19 Assoc Director Security/Safety .... Mr. Robert ZAVADA
18 Director of Facilities .... Mr. Mark VAN ETTEN
09 Asst Dir of Institutional Research .... Ms. Sharon HUDAK
90 Manager of User Services .... Mr. David A. JOHNDROW

Montgomery County Community College (L)

340 Dekalb Pike, Blue Bell PA 19422-1400
County: Montgomery FICE Identification: 004452
Unit ID: 214111
Telephone: (215) 641-6300 Carnegie Class: Assoc/HT-Mix Trad/Non
FAX Number: (215) 461-1460 Calendar System: Semester
URL: www.mc3.edu
Established: 1964 Annual Undergrad Tuition & Fees (In-District): $4,920
Enrollment: 12,805 Coed
Affiliation or Control: State/Local IRS Status: 501(c)3
Highest Offering: Associate Degree
Accreditation: M, ADNUR, CSHSE, DH, IFSAC, MAC, MLTAD, PHLEB, RAD, SURGT

01 President .... Dr. Kevin POLLOCK
04 Exec Assistant to the President .... Vacant
101 Exec Asst to the Board of Trustees .... Ms. Deborah ROGERS
05 VP for Academic Affairs &
Provost .... Dr. Victoria BASTECKI-PEREZ
12 VP of the West Campus .... Dr. David DIMATTIO
13 VP for Information Technology .... Ms. Celeste M. SCHWARTZ
10 VP for Finance & Administration .... Vacant
30 Vice Pres of Devel & External Rels .... Ms. Arline STEPHAN
84 VP for Stdnt Affs & Enroll Mgmt .... Mr. Philip NEEDLES
06 Registrar .... Ms. Sherry PHILLIPS
15 Executive Director Human Resources .... Ms. Diane O'CONNOR
21 Controller .... Vacant
44 Senior Director of Development .... Ms. Leslie BLUESTONE
19 Director of Campus Safety .... Mr. Joseph MCGURIMAN
37 Director of Financial Aid .... Ms. Tracey RICHARDS
09 Exec Dir of Inst Research .... Mr. David KOWALSKI
28 Dir Equity & Diversity Initiatives .... Ms. Rose MAKOFSKE
29 Dir of Alumni Rel & Major Gifts .... Mr. Bradley SMITH
26 Director Media/Public Relations .... Vacant
103 Dean Workforce Development & CE ...... Ms. Suzanne HOLLOMAN
41 Dir of Athletics & Campus Rec .... Mr. Bruce BACH
07 Director of Student Recruitment .... Ms. Joyce WHEATLEY
08 Dean of Libraries & Acad Support .... Ms. Jenifer BLADWIN
18 Director of Facilities Mgmt .... Mr. Charles SCANDONE
25 Dir of Corp & Found Rels & Grants .... Ms. Susan FRIEDLAND
32 Dean of Student Affairs .... Ms. Nicole HENDERSON
96 Director of Procurement & Aux Svcs .... Ms. Vicki GIAMMARCO

Montgomery County Community College West Campus (M)

101 College Drive, Pottstown PA 19464
Telephone: (610) 718-1800 Identification: 770162
Accreditation: &M

† Regional accreditation is carried under the parent institution in Blue Bell, PA

Moore College of Art and Design (A)

20th and The Parkway, Philadelphia PA 19103-1179
County: Philadelphia　FICE Identification: 003300
Unit ID: 214148
Telephone: (215) 965-4000　Carnegie Class: Spec-4-yr-Arts
FAX Number: (215) 568-8017　Calendar System: Semester
URL: www.moore.edu
Established: 1848　Annual Undergrad Tuition & Fees: $36,828
Enrollment: 453　Female
Affiliation or Control: Independent Non-Profit　IRS Status: 501(c)3
Highest Offering: Master's
Accreditation: M, ART, CIDA

01 President .... Ms. Cecelia FITZGIBBON
10 SVP Finance & Administration .... Mr. William L. HILL, II
05 Academic Dean .... Ms. Patti PHILLIPS
32 Dean of Students .... Ms. Ruth ROBBINS
20 Assoc Dean Educational Support Svcs ...... Ms. Claudine THOMAS
39 Director Residence Life/Housing .... Mr. Matthew POINT
88 Interim Director of Galleries .... Ms. Gabrielle LAVIN
51 Director of Continuing Education .... Ms. Judith WOODWORTH
26 Dir of Marketing/Communications .... Mr. Roy A. WILEUR
30 Assoc Director of Development .... Vacant
29 Dir Alumnae Affairs/Annual Fund .... Ms. Kathryn MYERS
08 Library Director .... Vacant
07 Exec Director of Admissions .... Ms. Elizabeth MATHIS
37 Director of Financial Aid .... Ms. Devon WEAVER
06 Registrar .... Vacant
18 Director of Operations .... Mr. Kenneth M. FERRETTI
15 Director Human Resources .... Ms. Rachel PHILLIPS
36 Director Career Center .... Ms. Belena CHAPP
58 Director of Graduate Studies .. Ms. Michelle GARRIGAN-DURANT
38 Director Student Counseling .... Ms. Ruth R. GAYLE
90 Academic Computing Manager .... Mr. Dennis DAWTON

Moravian College (B)

1200 Main St., Bethlehem PA 18018-6650
County: Northampton　FICE Identification: 003301
Unit ID: 214157
Telephone: (610) 861-1300　Carnegie Class: Bac-A&S
FAX Number: (610) 625-7918　Calendar System: Semester
URL: www.moravian.edu
Established: 1742　Annual Undergrad Tuition & Fees: $38 832
Enrollment: 1,970　Coed
Affiliation or Control: Moravian Church　IRS Status: 501(c)3
Highest Offering: Master's
Accreditation: M, ACBSP, MUS, NURSE, THEOL

01 President .... Dr. Bryon L. GRIGSBY
05 Provost .... Dr. Cynthia KOSSO
10 Vice President Finance & Admin .... Mr. Mark F. REED
30 Vice Pres Institutional Advancement .... Mr. Gary CARNEY
32 Vice President Student Affairs .... Dr. Nicole L. LOYD
73 Vice Pres/Dean of the Seminary .... Dr. Frank CROUCH
84 Vice President for Enrollment .... Mr. Steven SOBA
13 Chief Information Officer .... Mr. Scott HUGHES
09 VP Planning and Research .... Ms. Carole A. REESE
15 Chief Human Resources Officer .... Mr. Jon B. CONRAD
35 Dean of Students .... Dr. Nicole L. LOYD
36 Assoc Dean of Stdnts/Dir Career Dev .... Ms. Amy SAUL
20 Dean of Curriculum .... Dr. Carol TRAUPMAN-CARR
28 Assoc Dean Intercultural Advance .... Mr. Chris HUNT
39 Asst Dean for Residence Life .... Ms. Liz YATES
59 Asst Dean of Continuing/Graduate .... Ms. LaKeisha THORPE
88 Asst Dean for Academic Advising .... Dr. James SKALNIK
21 Treasurer .... Ms. Anne M. REID
88 Bursar .... Ms. Susan O'HARE
06 Institutional Registrar .... Ms. Alexandra SMITH
88 Director of Event Management .... Mrs. Ann E. CLAUSSEN
21 Dir Business/Financial Operations .... Ms. Amy JOHNSON
22 Dir Academic & Disability Support .... Ms. Laurie ROTH
44 Director of Leadership Giving .... Ms. Bertie KNISELY
18 Dir Facilities Mgt Plng/Construct .... Mr. Douglas J. PLOTTS
19 Director of Campus Safety .... Mr. George BOKSAN
26 Dir of Marketing & Communications .... Vacant
08 Library Director .... Ms. Janet OHLES
37 Director of Financial Aid .... Dr. Dennis P. LEVY
38 Director of Counseling .... Dr. Ronald J. KLINE
40 Bookstore Manager .... Mr. Robert RUSH, III
41 Director of Athletics .... Mr. George L. BRIGHT
42 College Chaplain .... Rev. Jennika BORGER
88 Director of the Payne Gallery .... Dr. Diane RADYCKI
101 Asst to Pres Projects & Board Suppt .... Mrs. Elaine C. DEITCH
23 Nurse Coordinator .... Mrs. Stephanie C. DILLMAN
104 Director of International Studies .... Mr. Christian SINCLAIR
24 Media Center Manager .... Mr. Craig UNDERWOOD
04 Executive Secretary to President .... Ms. Monique HANEY
07 Executive Director of Admissions .... Mr. Scott DAMS
29 Director Alumni Relations .... Ms. Patricia HANNA

Mount Aloysius College (C)

7373 Admiral Peary Highway, Cresson PA 16630-1999
County: Cambria　FICE Identification: 003302
Unit ID: 214166
Telephone: (814) 886-6300　Carnegie Class: Bac/Assoc-Mixed
FAX Number: (814) 886-2978　Calendar System: Semester
URL: www.mtaloy.edu
Established: 1853　Annual Undergrad Tuition & Fees: $21,360
Enrollment: 1,867　Coed
Affiliation or Control: Independent Non-Profit　IRS Status: 501(c)3
Highest Offering: Master's
Accreditation: M, ADNUR, DMS, MAC, MLTAD, NUR, PTAA, SURGT

01 President .... Dr. Thomas P. FOLEY
05 Sr VP Academic Affs/Dean of Faculty .... Dr. Stephen PUGLIESE
11 Sr VP Administrative Services .... Vacant
32 VP Student Affs/Dean Students .... Dr. Jane M. GRASSADONIA
84 VP Enrollment Mgmt/Dean Admissions .... Mr. Francis C. CROUSE, JR.
07 Director of Freshmen Admissions .... Mr. Andrew D. CLOUSE
07 Director of Transfer Admissions .... Mr. Richard MISHLER
30 VP Institutional Advancement .... Ms. Jennifer DUBUQUE
10 VP Finance & Administration .... Ms. Donna K. YODER
06 Registrar .... Dr. Christopher M. LOVETT
08 Director of Library .... Dr. Michael JONES
37 Director of Financial Aid .... Ms. Stacy L. SCHENK
15 Director of Human Resources .... Ms. Tonia J. GORDON
26 Director of Communications .... Mr. John COYLE
13 Director of Information Technology .... Mr. Rich J. SHEA
23 Director of Health Services .... Ms. Shannon D. GROVE
40 Director of Bookstore .... Ms. Christine M. CLINTON
41 Director of Athletics .... Mr. Ryan M. SMITH
19 Director of Safety & Security .... Mr. William H. TREXLER
18 Director of Physical Plant .... Mr. Gerald RUBRITZ
09 Institutional Researcher .... Mr. Bryan J. PEARSON
36 Career Development Coordinator .... Ms. Kristy MAGEE
38 Dir Student Counseling/Disabilities .... Ms. Marisa L. EVANS
39 Director of Residence Life .... Mr. Matthew LOVELL
88 Exec Dir of Mission Integration .... Ms. Christina KOREN
42 Director Campus Ministry .... Ms. Andrea T. CECILLI
44 Manager of Annual Giving .... Ms. Sally GORDON
04 Administrative Asst to President .... Ms. Carla NELEN

Muhlenberg College (D)

2400 West Chew Street, Allentown PA 18104-5586
County: Lehigh　FICE Identification: 003304
Unit ID: 214175
Telephone: (484) 664-3100　Carnegie Class: Bac-A&S
FAX Number: (484) 664-3234　Calendar System: Semester
URL: www.muhlenberg.edu
Established: 1848　Annual Undergrad Tuition & Fees: $45,875
Enrollment: 2,440　Coed
Affiliation or Control: Evangelical Lutheran Church In America
IRS Status: 501(c)3
Highest Offering: Baccalaureate
Accreditation: M

01 President .... Mr. John I. WILLIAMS, JR.
05 Interim Provost .... Dr. Kathleen HARRING
10 Treasurer & Vice Pres for Finance .... Mr. Kent DYER
26 Vice President of Public Relations ...... Mr. Michael S. BRUCKNER
30 VP of Advancement .... Ms. Rebekkah L. BROWN
15 Vice President of Human Resources .... Ms. Anne SPECK
32 Vice Pres Student Affairs .... Ms. Allison GULATI
04 Exec Assistant to the President .... Mr. Ken BUTLER
102 Asst VP Corporate/Found & Govt Rels .... Ms. Deborah J. KIPP
35 Dean of Students .... Ms. Karen GREEN
20 Dean of College for Academic Life .... Dr. Michael HUBER
108 VP/Dn Institutional Effectiveness .... Dr. Kathleen E. HARRING
86 Assoc Dean International Programs .... Dr. Donna V. KISH-GOODLING
37 Associate Dean Financial Aid .... Mr. Gregory S. MITTON
22 Asst Dean Acad Res/Disability Svcs .... Mr. David HALLOWELL
29 Alumni Relations Director .... Ms. Natalie HAND
55 Dean Wescoe Sch Muhlenberg College .... Ms. Jane E. HUDAK
84 VP of Enrollment Management .... Mr. Christopher HOOKER-HARING
08 Director of Trexler Library .... Ms. Tina L. HERTEL
06 Registrar .... Ms. Deborah TAMTE-HORAN
13 Chief Information Officer .... Mr. Allan CHEN
19 Director of Campus Safety/Security .... Mr. Brian FIDATI
39 Director of Residence Life .... Ms. Janette SCHUMACHER
36 Director of the Career Center .... Ms. Alana M. ALBUS
21 Assistant Treasurer .... Mr. Jason FEIERTAG
23 Director of Student Health Services .... Ms. Erynnmarie DORSEY
38 Director Counseling Services .... Ms. Anita KELLY
42 Chaplain .... Rev. Callista S. ISABELLE
09 Director of Institutional Research .... Ms. Nicole HAMMEL
18 Chief Facilities/Physical Plant .... Mr. Michael H. BREWER
96 Director of Purchasing .... Ms. Elizabeth M. LEES
40 Bookstore Manager .... Ms. Karen R. NORMANN

Neumann University (E)

One Neumann Drive, Aston PA 19014-1298
County: Delaware　FICE Identification: 003988
Unit ID: 214272
Telephone: (610) 459-0905　Carnegie Class: Masters/M
FAX Number: (610) 459-1370　Calendar System: Semester
URL: www.neumann.edu
Established: 1965　Annual Undergrad Tuition & Fees: $26,918
Enrollment: 3,047　Coed
Affiliation or Control: Roman Catholic　IRS Status: 501(c)3
Highest Offering: Doctorate
Accreditation: M, ACBSP, #CAATE, CACREP, MT, NUR, PTA, @SW

01 President .... Dr. Rosalie M. MIRENDA
05 Vice President Academic Affairs .... Dr. Lawrence DIPAOLO
43 General Counsel .... Ms. Danielle MCNICHOL
10 Vice Pres Finance/Administration .... Mr. Gene MCWILLIAMS
42 Vice President Mission/Ministry .... Sr. Marguerite O'BEIRNE, OSF
30 Vice Pres Inst Advance/Univ Rels .... Mr. Henry A. SUMNER
32 Vice Pres Student Affairs & Enroll .... Dr. Dianna C. DALE
15 Vice President HR & Risk Management .... Mr. David W. BROWNLEE
49 Dean Division of Arts & Science .... Dr. Alfred G. MUELLER, II
50 Dean Div of Business/Info Mgmt .... Dr. Lawrence E. BURGEE
53 Dean Div of Educ/Human Svcs .... Dr. Barbara HANES
51 Interim Dean Cont Adult/Prof Stds .... Dr. Jilian DONNELLY
66 Dean Div Nursing/Health Sciences .... Dr. Kathleen HOOVER
04 Assistant to President .... Ms. Danielle WAGNER
06 Registrar .... Mr. Joel A. NATALE
18 Facilities Director .... Mr. William LEONARD
19 Director Safety & Security .... Mr. Leon FRANCIS
08 Director Library .... Ms. Tiffany MCGREGOR
26 Exec Director Mktg/Communications .... Mr. Stephen BELL
09 Dir of IR and Assessment .... Ms. Melissa THORPE
42 Chaplain .... Fr. Stephen D. THORNE
44 Director Annual Giving/Prospect Mgt .... Ms. Christina FARRELL
29 Dir Alumni Rels/Special Programs .... Ms. Judi STANAITIS
88 Director Inst Gifts/Donor Rels .... Ms. Josephina E. BANNER
38 Director Counseling .... Mr. Fritz HAAS
39 Director Housing & Residence Life .... Mr. Michael WEBSTER
13 Exec Director University Computing .... Mr. David O'LEARY
24 Director Academic Resource Center .... Ms. Theresa HUKE
41 Director Athletics .... Mr. Chuck SACK
36 Dir Career & Personal Development .... Ms. Mary MCCAFFREY
88 Dean Academic Support Services .... Mr. Michael MULLEN
88 Director Child Development Center .... Ms. Mary Ann MELISI
21 Controller .... Mr. John YOUHOUSE
37 Director Financial Assistance .... Ms. Andrea DEL VACCHIO
23 Director Health Services .... Ms. Janet GEDDIS
96 Coordinator for Purchasing .... Ms. Elena BARRAR
88 Director Physical Therapy Program .... Dr. Robert POST
07 Director of Admissions .... Mr. Christopher MAYERSKI
88 Dir Ctr for Sprt/Spir/Char Dev .... Ms. Lee M. DELLEMONACHE
90 Director Instructional Technology .... Mr. Scott BEADENKOPF
88 Director Conference/Scheduling Svcs .... Ms. Melissa HAINES
40 Director University Bookstore .... Ms. Natalie VAN WYK
88 Director Transitional Education .... Ms. Lori BLOUNT
104 Coord International Studies Educ .... Ms. Jen MINTZER
88 Director of Student Success .... Ms. Coleen NEDBALSKI
105 Director Web Services .... Ms. Lisa CADORETTE
106 Dir Online Education/E-learning .... Dr. Jilian DONNELLY
84 Assoc Dean of Enrollment Management . Mr. Kevin MACCARELLA
88 Program Director Athletic Training .... Dr. Hubert LEE

New Castle School of Trades (F)

4117 Pulaski Road, New Castle PA 16101
County: Lawrence　FICE Identification: 007780
Unit ID: 214290
Telephone: (724) 964-8811　Carnegie Class: Assoc/HVT-Mix Trad/Non
FAX Number: (724) 202-6147　Calendar System: Other
URL: www.ncstrades.edu
Established: 1945　Annual Undergrad Tuition & Fees: N/A
Enrollment: 825　Coed
Affiliation or Control: Proprietary　IRS Status: Proprietary
Highest Offering: Associate Degree
Accreditation: ACCSC

01 Director .... Mr. Jim BUTTERMORE
05 Director of Education .... Mr. Tony GIOVANNELLI
07 Director of Admissions .... Mr. Joe BLAZAK
88 Veteran Affairs Director .... Mr. Jim CATHELINE
10 Fiscal Director .... Mrs. JoAnn MELNIK
36 Director Student Placement .... Ms. Carrie KRAYNAK
37 Director Student Financial Aid .... Miss Trudy SOTTER

Northampton Community College (G)

3835 Green Pond Road, Bethlehem PA 18020-7599
County: Northampton　FICE Identification: 007191
Unit ID: 214379
Telephone: (610) 861-5300　Carnegie Class: Assoc/MT-VT-High Trad
FAX Number: (610) 861-5070　Calendar System: Semester
URL: www.northampton.edu
Established: 1966　Annual Undergrad Tuition & Fees (In-District): $3,990
Enrollment: 10,531　Coed
Affiliation or Control: State/Local　IRS Status: 170(c)1
Highest Offering: Associate Degree
Accreditation: M, ACBSP, ADNUR, DH, DMS, FUSER, PNUR, RAD

01 President .... Dr. Mark H. ERICKSON
05 Vice President Academic Affairs .... Dr. Carolyn BORTZ
11 Vice Pres Administrative Affairs .... Ms. Helene M. WHITAKER
10 Vice President Finance & Operations .... Mr. James F. DUNLEAVY
30 Vice Pres Institutional Advancement .... Ms. Sharon BEALES
32 Vice Pres Enroll/Student Affairs .... Vacant
31 Vice President Community Education .... Dr. Paul E. PIERPOINT
12 Dean Monroe Campus .... Dr. Matthew J. CONNELL
79 Dean Humanities & Social Sciences .... Dr. Christine PENSE
53 Dean Education/Academic Success .... Dr. Elizabeth BUGAIGHIS
50 Dean Business & Technology .... Dr. Denise FRANCOIS-SEENY
76 Dean Allied Health & Sciences .... Dr. Judith REX
13 Assoc VP/Chief Information Officer .... Dr. Deborah BURAK
26 Director Public Info/Community Rels .... Ms. Heidi BUTLER
06 Registrar .... Ms. Kara HOWE
07 Director Admissions .... Mr. James MCCARTHY
37 Director Financial Aid .... Ms. Cynthia L. KING
108 Director of Assessment .... Dr. E. Jill HIRT
15 Exec Director of Human Resources .... Mr. Brett I. LAST
09 Director of Institutional Research .... Ms. Kathy KAPCSOS
18 Director Buildings & Grounds .... Mr. Mark K. CULP
29 Dir Alumni Engagement/Annual Fund .... Ms. Karen GLOSE
36 Director Career Services .... Ms. Karen VERES

35 Dean of Students ... Dr. Gloria LOPEZ
84 Senior Assoc Dir of Enrollment Svcs ... Ms. Mary S. MANCINO

Northampton Community College Monroe County Branch Campus (A)

205 Old Mill Road, Tannersville PA 18372
Telephone: (570) 620-9221 Identification: 770164
Accreditation: &M

† Regional accreditation is carried under the parent institution in Bethlehem, PA

Orleans Technical College (B)

2770 Red Lion Road, Philadelphia PA 19114-1014
County: Philadelphia FICE Identification: 021830
Unit ID: 214528
Telephone: (215) 728-4700 Carnegie Class: Spec 2-yr-Other
FAX Number: (215) 745-1689 Calendar System: Semester
URL: www.orleanstech.edu
Established: 1974 Annual Undergrad Tuition & Fees: N/A
Enrollment: 332 Coed
Affiliation or Control: Independent Non-Profit IRS Status: Exempt
Highest Offering: Associate Degree
Accreditation: ACCSC

01 Campus President ... Ms. Jayne SINIARI
72 Technology Program Director ... Mr. Bruce WARTMAN
05 Director of Academic Affairs ... Ms. Anna BOGDANOV
11 Associate Director ... Mr. William LYNCH
07 Director of Admissions ... Ms. Debbie BELLO
36 Director Career Services ... Ms. Tawana SKIPPER
37 Director Student Financial Services ... Ms. Latanya BYRD

Palmer Theological Seminary of Eastern University (C)

1300 Eagle Road, St. Davids PA 19087
County: Montgomery FICE Identification: 003260
Unit ID: 212124
Telephone: (610) 896-5000 Carnegie Class: Not Classified
FAX Number: (610) 649-3834 Calendar System: 4/1/4
URL: www.palmerseminary.edu
Established: 1925 Annual Graduate Tuition & Fees: N/A
Enrollment: N/A Coed
Affiliation or Control: American Baptist IRS Status: 501(c)3
Highest Offering: Doctorate; No Undergraduates
Accreditation: THEOL

01 University President ... Dr. Robert G. DUFFETT
05 Int Dean Palmer Seminary ... Dr. F. David BRONKEMA
10 Vice President of Finance ... Mr. Pernell JONES
04 President's Executive Assistant ... Ms. Heather NORCINI
15 Director of Human Resources ... Ms. Kacey BERNARD
29 Director Alumni & Church Relations ... Ms. Mary GARDNER
42 University Chaplain ... Dr. Joseph MODICA
08 Director University Libraries ... Mr. James SAUER
09 Director of Institutional Research ... Dr. Thomas DAHLSTROM

† Affiliated with Eastern University, Saint Davids, PA.

Peirce College (D)

1420 Pine Street, Philadelphia PA 19102-4699
County: Philadelphia FICE Identification: 003309
Unit ID: 214883
Telephone: (215) 545-6400 Carnegie Class: Bac-Diverse
FAX Number: (215) 670-9366 Calendar System: Semester
URL: www.peirce.edu
Established: 1865 Annual Undergrad Tuition & Fees: $14,184
Enrollment: 1,833 Coed
Affiliation or Control: Independent Non-Profit IRS Status: 501(c)3
Highest Offering: Master's
Accreditation: M, ACBSP, CAHIIM

01 President & CEO ... Mr. James J. MERGIOTTI
10 VP Finance/Administration ... Ms. Elizabeth M. KNAPP
05 VP Academic Advancement ... Dr. Rita J. TOLIVER-ROBERTS
30 VP Institutional Advancement ... Ms. Uva C. COLES
26 VP Marketing & Admissions ... Ms. Lisa PARIS
32 VP Student Services/Retention Mgmt ... Mr. Brad K. HODGE
15 VP Human Res/Chief Diversity Ofcr ... Ms. Harriet S. GOLEN
108 Asst VP Institutional Assessment ... Ms. Debra S. SCHRAMMEL
13 Chief Information Officer ... Mr. James T. BURNS
109 Chief Auxiliary Services Officer ... Mr. Vito R. CHIMENTI
20 Assoc Dean Academic Ops/Faculty Sup ... Mr. Jon LENROW

Penn Commercial Business/ Technical School (E)

242 Oak Spring Road, Washington PA 15301-6822
County: Washington FICE Identification: 004902
Unit ID: 214892
Telephone: (724) 222-5330 Carnegie Class: Assoc/HVT-High Trad
FAX Number: (724) 222-4722 Calendar System: Quarter
URL: www.penncommercial.edu
Established: 1929 Annual Undergrad Tuition & Fees: $22,500
Enrollment: 335 Coed
Affiliation or Control: Proprietary IRS Status: Proprietary
Highest Offering: Associate Degree
Accreditation: ACICS

01 Director ... Mr. Robert S. BAZANT
11 Vice President of Operations ... Ms. Marianne ALBERT
04 Assistant to the President ... Ms. Barbara KENNEDY
07 Director of Admissions ... Mr. Ron ZUBATY
32 Director of Student Affairs ... Ms. Sandy PHILLIPS
37 Director of Financial Aid ... Ms. Cyndi GALLOWAY
88 Director of Education ... Ms. Pat DECONCILLIS
05 Director of Academic Affairs ... Ms. Sandy PHILLIPS
09 Dir of Reports & Statistics ... Mrs. Melissa PAPSON
36 Director of Career Services ... Mrs. Kristin WISSINGER

Penn State University Park (F)

201 Old Main, University Park PA 16802
County: Centre FICE Identification: 003329
Unit ID: 214777
Telephone: (814) 865-4700 Carnegie Class: DU-Highest
FAX Number: (814) 863-7590 Calendar System: Semester
URL: www.psu.edu
Established: 1855 Annual Undergrad Tuition & Fees (In-State): $17,514
Enrollment: 47,040 Coed
Affiliation or Control: State Related IRS Status: 501(c)3
Highest Offering: Doctorate
Accreditation: M, ADNUR, ART, BUS, CACREP, CEA, CLPSY, COPSY, CORE, DIETD, DIETI, ENG, FEPAC, HSA, IPSY, JOUR, LAW, LSAR, MUS, NURSE, SCPSY, SP, TED, THEA

01 President ... Dr. Eric J. BARRON
05 Executive Vice President & Provost ... Dr. Nicholas P. JONES
46 Vice President Research ... Dr. Neil A. SHARKEY
32 Vice President Student Affairs ... Dr. Damon R. SIMS
26 Vice Pres Strategic Communications ... Mr. Lawrence H. LOKMAN
30 Sr Vice Pres Devel/Alumni Relations ... Mr. Rodney P. KIRSCH
10 Sr Vice Pres Finance & Bus/Treas ... Mr. David J. GRAY
106 VP Outreach/Vice Prov Online Educ ... Dr. Craig D. WEIDEMANN
11 Vice President for Administration ... Dr. Thomas G. POOLE
104 Vice Provost for Global Programs ... Dr. Michael A. ADEWUMI
43 Vice President & General Counsel ... Dr. Stephen S. DUNHAM
49 Vice Pres & Dean Undergrad Educ ... Dr. Robert N. PANGBORN
20 Vice Provost Academic Affairs ... Dr. Blannie E. BOWEN
28 Vice Provost Educ Equity ... Dr. Marcus A. WHITEHURST
12 Vice Pres Commonwealth Campuses ... Dr. Madlyn L. HANES
13 Interim VP Information Technology ... Mr. Matthew E. DECKER
45 Vice Provost Plng and Assessment ... Dr. Lance C. KENNEDY-PHILLIPS
09 Assoc VP Plng/Inst Research ... Dr. Betty J. HARPER
108 Assoc VP Lng Outcomes Assessment ... Dr. Barbara A. MASI
22 Vice Provost for Affirmative Action . Dr. Kenneth F. LEHRMAN, III
88 University Budget Officer ... Ms. Rachel E. SMITH
21 Assoc Vice Pres Finance/Corp Cont ... Mr. Joseph J. DONCSECZ
21 Interim Asst VP Finance/Business ... Ms. Lisa A. BERKEY
15 Vice President Human Resources ... Ms. Susan M. BASSO
18 Assoc Vice President Physical Plant ... Mr. H. Ford STRYKER
21 Assoc VP Auxiliary & Business Svcs ... Ms. Gail A. HURLEY
106 Associate Vice Prov Online Programs ... Dr. Renata S. ENGEL
27 Director News/Media Relations ... Ms. Lisa M. POWERS
39 Asst VP HFS & Residence Life ... Ms. Diane L. ANDREWS
37 Asst VP UG Ed/Exec Dir Stdnt Aid ... Ms. Anna M. GRISWOLD
29 Assoc VP Alum Rel/CEO PS Alum Assoc ... Mr. Paul J. CLIFFORD
88 Exec Director Office of Investment ... Mr. David E. BRANIGAN
07 Exec Director Undergrad Admissions ... Mr. Clark V. BRIGGER
38 Director Counseling/Psych Services ... Dr. Dennis E. HEITZMANN
41 Athletic Director ... Ms. A. Sandy BARBOUR
86 Vice President for Govt Affairs ... Mr. Michael J. DIRAIMO
06 University Registrar ... Mr. Robert A. KUBAT
36 Senior Director Career Services ... Dr. Robert M. ORNDORFF
17 Sr Vice Pres Hlth Affs/CEO & Dean ... Dr. A. Craig HILLEMEIER
08 Dean Univ Libraries/Scholar Comm ... Ms. Barbara I. DEWEY
47 Dean Agricultural Sciences ... Dr. Richard T. ROUSH
48 Dean Arts & Architecture ... Dr. Barbara O. KORNER
50 Dean Business ... Dr. Charles H. WHITEMAN
60 Dean Communications ... Dr. Marie HARDIN
65 Dean Earth & Mineral Sciences .. Dr. William E. EASTERLING, III
53 Dean Education ... Dr. David H. MONK
54 Dean Engineering ... Dr. Amr S. ELNASHAI
58 V Prov Grad Educ/Dean Grad School ... Dr. Regina VASILATOS-YOUNKEN
76 Dean Health & Human Development ... Dr. Ann C. CROUTER
66 Dean School of Nursing ... Dr. Paula F. MILONE-NUZZO
56 Assoc Dean/Dir Cooperative Exten ... Dr. Dennis D. CALVIN
83 Dean Liberal Arts ... Dr. Susan WELCH
81 Dean Science ... Dr. Douglas R. CAVENER
72 Dean Info Sciences and Technology ... Dr. Andrew L. SEARS
92 Dean Honors College ... Dr. Christian M. BRADY
61 Interim Dean Penn State Law ... Dr. James W. HOUCK
63 Dean College of Medicine ... Dr. A. Craig HILLEMEIER
75 Chief Penn College of Technology ... Dr. Davie J. GILMOUR
44 Executive Director Annual Giving ... Ms. Jennifer D. BENOIT
25 Assoc Vice President for Research ... Dr. John W. HANOLD
19 Interim Dir/Chief of Police/Pub Saf ... Mr. Michael D. LOWERY
23 Director University Health Services ... Dr. Robin E. OLIVER-VERONESI
96 Director Procurement Services ... Ms. Joyce A. HANEY
31 Director Campus & Comm Affairs ... Ms. Barbara ETTARO
102 Exec Dir Corp/Foundation Relations ... Mr. Mark S. ARMAGOST
04 Exec Admin Assistant to President ... Ms. Carmella MULROY-DEGENHART
40 General Manager Bookstore ... Mr. Steve J. FALKE
25 Contract Coordinator ... Ms. Cristene N. BOOB
16 Senior Director Employee Relations ... Ms. Susan RUTAN
21 Director of Internal Audit ... Mr. Daniel P. HEIST

† The legal name of Penn State and all its campuses is The Pennsylvania State University. For communication purposes, the name is shortened to Penn State followed by the name of the campus.

Penn State Abington (G)

1600 Woodland Road, Abington PA 19001
Telephone: (215) 881-7300 FICE Identification: 003342
Accreditation: &M, ENG

† Regional accreditation is carried under the parent institution in University Park, PA.

Penn State Altoona (H)

3000 Ivyside Park, Altoona PA 16601
Telephone: (814) 949-5000 FICE Identification: 003331
Accreditation: &M, ENGT

† Regional accreditation is carried under the parent institution in University Park, PA.

Penn State Beaver (I)

100 University Drive, Monaca PA 15061
Telephone: (724) 773-3800 FICE Identification: 003332
Accreditation: &M

† Regional accreditation is carried under the parent institution in University Park, PA.

Penn State Berks (J)

Tulpehocken Road, PO Box 7009, Reading PA 19610
Telephone: (610) 396-6000 FICE Identification: 003334
Accreditation: &M, ENG, ENGT, OTA

† Regional accreditation is carried under the parent institution in University Park, PA.

Penn State Brandywine (K)

25 Yearsley Mill Road, Media PA 19063
Telephone: (610) 892-1200 FICE Identification: 006922
Accreditation: &M, ENG

† Regional accreditation is carried under the parent institution in University Park, PA.

Penn State DuBois (L)

One College Place, DuBois PA 15801
Telephone: (814) 375-4700 FICE Identification: 003335
Accreditation: &M, ENG, ENGT, OTA, PTAA

† Regional accreditation is carried under the parent institution in University Park, PA.

Penn State Erie, The Behrend College (M)

4701 College Drive, Erie PA 16563
Telephone: (814) 898-6000 FICE Identification: 003333
Accreditation: &M, BUS, ENG, ENGT

† Regional accreditation is carried under the parent institution in University Park, PA.

Penn State Fayette, The Eberly Campus (N)

2201 University Drive, Lemont Furnace PA 15456
Telephone: (724) 430-4100 FICE Identification: 003336
Accreditation: &M, ENGT, PTAA

† Regional accreditation is carried under the parent institution in University Park, PA.

Penn State Great Valley School of Graduate Professional Studies (O)

30 E Swedesford Road, Malvern PA 19355
Telephone: (610) 648-3200 FICE Identification: 003348
Accreditation: &M, BUS

† Regional accreditation is carried under the parent institution in University Park, PA.

Penn State Greater Allegheny (P)

4000 University Drive, McKeesport PA 15132
Telephone: (412) 675-9000 FICE Identification: 003339
Accreditation: &M

† Regional accreditation is carried under the parent institution in University Park, PA.

Penn State Harrisburg (Q)

777 West Harrisburg Pike, Middletown PA 17057
Telephone: (717) 948-6250 FICE Identification: 006814
Accreditation: &M, BUS, ENG, ENGT, SPAA, TED

† Regional accreditation is carried under the parent institution in University Park, PA.

Penn State Hazleton (A)

76 University Drive, Hazleton PA 18202
Telephone: (570) 450-3000 FICE Identification: 003338
Accreditation: &M, ENG, MLTAD, PTAA

† Regional accreditation is carried under the parent institution in University Park, PA.

Penn State Lehigh Valley (B)

2809 Saucon Valley Road, Center Valley PA 18034
Telephone: (610) 285-5000 FICE Identification: 003330
Accreditation: &M

† Regional accreditation is carried under the parent institution in University Park, PA.

Penn State Milton S. Hershey Medical Center College of Medicine (C)

500 University Drive, Hershey PA 17033
Telephone: (717) 531-8563 FICE Identification: 006813
Accreditation: &M, #ARCPA, IPSY, MED, PAST, PH

† Regional accreditation is carried under the parent institution in University Park, PA.

Penn State Mont Alto (D)

One Campus Drive, Mont Alto PA 17237
Telephone: (717) 749-6000 FICE Identification: 003340
Accreditation: &M, OTA, PTAA

† Regional accreditation is carried under the parent institution in University Park, PA.

Penn State New Kensington (E)

3550 Seventh Street Road, Route 780,
New Kensington PA 15068
Telephone: (724) 334-5466 FICE Identification: 003341
Accreditation: &M, ENGT, RAD

† Regional accreditation is carried under the parent institution in University Park, PA.

Penn State Schuylkill (F)

200 University Drive, Schuylkill Haven PA 17972
Telephone: (570) 385-6000 FICE Identification: 003343
Accreditation: &M, RAD

† Regional accreditation is carried under the parent institution in University Park, PA.

Penn State Shenango (G)

147 Shenango Avenue, Sharon PA 16146
Telephone: (724) 983-2803 FICE Identification: 003345
Accreditation: &M, OTA, PTAA

† Regional accreditation is carried under the parent institution in University Park, PA.

Penn State Wilkes-Barre (H)

Old Route 115, PO Box PSU, Lehman PA 18627
Telephone: (570) 675-2171 FICE Identification: 003346
Accreditation: &M, ENG, ENGT

† Regional accreditation is carried under the parent institution in University Park, PA.

Penn State Worthington-Scranton (I)

120 Ridge View Drive, Dunmore PA 18512
Telephone: (570) 963-2500 FICE Identification: 003344
Accreditation: &M

† Regional accreditation is carried under the parent institution in University Park, PA.

Penn State York (J)

1031 Edgecomb Avenue, York PA 17403
Telephone: (717) 771-4000 FICE Identification: 003347
Accreditation: &M, ENGT

† Regional accreditation is carried under the parent institution in University Park, PA.

Pennco Tech (K)

3815 Otter Street, Bristol PA 19007-3696
County: Bucks FICE Identification: 009449
Unit ID: 214944
Telephone: (215) 785-0111 Carnegie Class: Spec 2-yr-Tech
FAX Number: (215) 785-1945 Calendar System: Other
URL: www.penncotech.edu
Established: 1973 Annual Undergrad Tuition & Fees: N/A
Enrollment: 500 Coed
Affiliation or Control: Proprietary IRS Status: Proprietary
Highest Offering: Associate Degree
Accreditation: ACCSC

01 CEO .... Michael E. HOBYAK
03 School Director .... Scott SIMPSON
05 Director of Education .... Steve CAIMI
07 Director of Admissions .... Vacant
06 Registrar .... Sandra KOOB
32 Director Student Services .... Haiden COLES
37 Director Student Financial Aid .... Keena FITZHUGH
36 Director Student Placement .... Teresa SCHEERER

Pennsylvania Academy of the Fine Arts (L)

128 N Broad St, Philadelphia PA 19102-1424
County: Philadelphia FICE Identification: 021073
Unit ID: 214971
Telephone: (215) 972-7600 Carnegie Class: Spec-4-yr-Arts
FAX Number: (215) 569-0153 Calendar System: Semester
URL: www.pafa.edu
Established: 1805 Annual Undergrad Tuition & Fees: $34,410
Enrollment: 258 Coed
Affiliation or Control: Independent Non-Profit IRS Status: 501(c)3
Highest Offering: Master's
Accreditation: M, ART

01 President & CEO .... Dr. David R. BRIGHAM
30 Exec Vice President Development .... Ms. Melissa D. KAISER
26 Exec Vice President of Marketing .... Ms. Heike RASS
10 Chief Financial Officer .... Mr. Anthony DECOCINIS
07 Dean of Admissions .... Vacant
57 Dean of the School of Fine Arts .... Mr. Clint A. JUKKALA
32 Dean of Students .... Ms. Anne K. STASSEN
37 Director of Financial Aid .... Ms. Dana MOORE
36 Director of Career Services .... Mr. Gregory MARTINO
08 Director of Library Services .... Mr. Brian DUFFY
06 Registrar .... Mr. Peter MEDWICK
18 Director of Facilities Management .... Mr. Ed POLETTI
19 Director of Security and Safety .... Mr. Jimmie GREENO
13 Director of Information Technology .... Mr. Kevin MARTIN
05 Director of Academic Affairs .... Mr. Nathanael T. BROUHARD
04 Exec Assistant to President and CEO .... Ms. Shery KESSLER
58 Director of Grad Program Services .... Mr. Steven CONNELL
20 Academic Services Coordinator .... Mr. CJ STAHL

Pennsylvania College of Art & Design (M)

204 N Prince Street, Box 59, Lancaster PA 17608-0059
County: Lancaster FICE Identification: 022699
Unit ID: 215053
Telephone: (717) 396-7833 Carnegie Class: Spec-4-yr-Arts
FAX Number: (717) 396-1339 Calendar System: Semester
URL: www.pcad.edu
Established: 1982 Annual Undergrad Tuition & Fees: $22,800
Enrollment: 200 Coed
Affiliation or Control: Independent Non-Profit IRS Status: 501(c)3
Highest Offering: Baccalaureate
Accreditation: M, ART

01 President .... Ms. Mary Colleen HEIL
05 Academic Dean .... Mr. Marc TORICK
32 Dean of Student Services .... Ms. Jessica EDONICK
26 Director of Communications .... Ms. Kathleen TROY SMYSER
10 VP for Finance & Operations .... Ms. Patricia ERNST
07 Dir of Admiss/Mktg & Recruitment .... Ms. Natalie LASCEK-SPEAKMAN
84 Director of Enrollment Planning .... Ms. Barbara ELLIOTT
37 Director Financial Aid .... Mr. J. David HERSHEY
08 Library Director .... Ms. Karen HUTCHISON
30 Director of Development .... Ms. Megan GALLAGHER
51 Director of Continuing Education .... Mr. Nick MOHLER
18 Director of Facilities .... Mr. Dan FREILER
06 Registrar .... Ms. Katie MYERS
13 Director of Information Technology .... Mr. Derrick GUTIERREZ

Pennsylvania College of Health Sciences (N)

850 Greenfield Road, Lancaster PA 17601
County: Lancaster FICE Identification: 009863
Unit ID: 442356
Telephone: (800) 622-5443 Carnegie Class: Spec-4-yr-Other Health
FAX Number: (717) 947-6250 Calendar System: Semester
URL: www.pacollege.edu
Established: 1903 Annual Undergrad Tuition & Fees: $24,453
Enrollment: 1,447 Coed
Affiliation or Control: Independent Non-Profit IRS Status: 501(c)3
Highest Offering: Master's
Accreditation: M, ADNUR, COARC, CVT, DMS, EMT, MT, NMT, NURSE, RAD, SURGT

01 President .... Dr. Mary Grace SIMCOX
05 Vice Pres of Academic Affairs .... Dr. Fenni LONGENECKER
10 Vice President of Finance & Admin .... Mr. Thomas HULSTINE
30 Vice President of Advancement .... Ms. Ellen WILEY
84 VP of Strategic Enrollment Mgmt .... Ms. Anne HAMILL
15 VP of Human Resources .... Ms. Nancy FLOREY

Pennsylvania College of Technology (O)

One College Avenue, Williamsport PA 17701-5799
County: Lycoming FICE Identification: 003395
Unit ID: 366252
Telephone: (570) 326-3761 Carnegie Class: Bac/Assoc-Mixed
FAX Number: (570) 327-4503 Calendar System: Semester
URL: www.pct.edu
Established: 1989 Annual Undergrad Tuition & Fees (In-State): $15,810
Enrollment: 5,623 Coed
Affiliation or Control: State IRS Status: 501(c)3
Highest Offering: Baccalaureate
Accreditation: M, ACBSP, ACFEI, ADNUR, ARCPA, CAHIIM, CONST, CSHSE, DH, EMT, ENGT, NAIT, NUR, OTA, PNUR, @PTAA, RAD, SURGT

01 President .... Dr. Davie Jane GILMOUR
05 VP for Academic Affairs/Provost .... Dr. Paul L. STARKEY
10 VP for Finance/CFO .... Ms. Suzanne T. STOPPER
30 Vice Pres Institutional Advancement .... Ms. Debra M. MILLER
13 Vice Pres for Info Tech/CIO .... Mr. Michael M. CUNNINGHAM
15 VP for College Services .... Mr. R. David KAY
84 VP Enrollment Mgmt & Assoc Provost .... Dr. Carolyn R. STRICKLAND
20 Director for Academic Services .... Ms. Wendy A. MILLER
20 Associate VP for Instruction .... Mr. Tom F. GREGORY
04 Administrative Asst to President .... Mrs. Valerie A. BAIER
32 Chief Student Affairs Officer .... Mr. Elliott STRICKLAND, JR.
103 VP for Workforce Development .... Dr. Tracy L. BRUNDAGE
76 Dean of Health Sciences .... Dr. Edward A. HENNINGER
88 Dean Construction & Design Tech .... Mr. Marc E. BRIDGENS
54 Dean Industrial/Comp/Engineering .... Mr. Dave R. COTNER
81 Dean of Sciences/Human/Visual Comm .... Dr. Michael J. REED
65 Dean Transportation/Natl Resources .... Mr. Brett A. REASNER
50 Dean of Business/Hospitality .... Dr. Gerri F. LUKE
37 Assoc Dean of Admissions & Fin Aid .... Mr. Dennis L. CORRELL
102 Exec Dir of Penn College Foundation .... Mr. Robert C. DIETRICH
08 Director of the Madigan Library .... Ms. Tracey AMEY
56 Director Instructional Technology .... Mr. Walter J. SHULTZ, JR.
18 Director of Facilities Operations .... Mr. Don J. LUKE
09 Exec Dir Assessment/Research/Plng .... Dr. Brian L. CYGAN
06 Registrar .... Ms. Heather A. SWIMLEY
35 Associate Dean of Student Affairs .... Dr. Jennifer MCLEAN
39 Dir Residence Life/Judicial Affairs .... Mr. Jon D. WESCOTT
19 Chief of Police .... Mr. Chris E. MILLER
26 VP Public Relations & Marketing .... Mr. Joseph S. YODER
29 Director Alumni Relations .... Vacant
44 Director of Corporate Relations .... Ms. Elizabeth A. BIDDLE
88 Director Children Learning Center .... Ms. Barbara J. ALBERT
40 Director of College Store .... Mr. Matthew P. BRANCA
41 Director of Athletics .... Mr. Scott E. KENNELL
90 Director Network Services .... Mr. Mike E. RAE
91 Director Administrative Info Sys .... Mr. Randall L. MONROE
23 Director College Health Services .... Mr. Carl L. SHANER
28 Dir of Diversity & Cultural Life .... Vacant
22 Coordinator of Disability Services .... Ms. Kay E. DUNKLEBERGER
85 International Programs Specialist .... Ms. Shanin L. DOUGHERTY
96 Director/Procurement Services .... Ms. Karen P. FESSLER
07 Director of Admissions .... Ms. Ashley R. MURPHY
89 Dean Acad Svcs/First Year Programs .... Mr. Paul R. WATSON, II

† Affiliate of Pennsylvania State University.

Pennsylvania Highlands Community College (P)

101 Community College Way, Johnstown PA 15904-2949
County: Cambria FICE Identification: 031804
Unit ID: 414911
Telephone: (814) 262-6400 Carnegie Class: Assoc/MT-VT-High Non
FAX Number: (814) 269-9700 Calendar System: Semester
URL: www.pennhighlands.edu
Established: 1994 Annual Undergrad Tuition & Fees (In-District): $5,670
Enrollment: 2,470 Coed
Affiliation or Control: State/Local IRS Status: 501(c)3
Highest Offering: Associate Degree
Accreditation: M, MAC

01 President .... Dr. Walter J. ASONEVICH
05 VP of Academic Affairs .... Dr. Edward NICHOLS
32 VP of Student Services .... Trish CORLE
10 VP of Finance/Administration .... Lorraine DONAHUE
30 Assoc VP of External Affairs .... Dr. Melissa MURRAY
15 Assistant VP of Human Resources .... Susan FISHER
12 Director Blair Center .... Julie PATOSKY
12 Director Huntingdon Center .... Marissa GRACEY
12 Director Somerset Center .... Adam BOWSER
12 Director Ebensburg Center .... Robert SEKERAK
84 Dean Enrollment Services/Registrar .... Michelle STUMPF
20 Dean of Faculty .... Erica REIGHARD
13 Chief Information Officer .... Danielle GERKO
08 Dean for Learning Resources .... Dr. Barbara ZABOROWSKI
09 Assoc Dean Inst Research/Assessment .... Gary BOAST
103 Assoc Dean Career Svcs/Workforce Ed .... Larry BRUGH
51 Assoc Dn Curriculum/Cont Educ .... Cynthia MCCABE
88 Associate Dean for Adjunct Faculty .... Christine ZERNICK
07 Director of Admissions .... Jeffrey MAUL
18 Director of Facilities Operation .... Reb BROWNLEE
21 Director of Finance/Administration .... Christopher PRIBULSKY
37 Interim Director of Financial Aid .... Judy EBBERTS
26 Director of Marketing .... Raymond WEIBLE, JR.
19 Director of Security and Safety .... Gregg DIBERT

35 Dir of Student Activities/Athletics .... Suzanne BRUGH
88 Director of Student Success Center .... Mindy NITCH
04 Exec Asst to the President's Office .... Michelle MAKSYMIK

Pennsylvania Institute of Health and Technology (A)

PO Box 278, Mount Braddock PA 15465-0278
Telephone: (724) 437-4600 Identification: 666035
Accreditation: ACICS

† Branch campus of West Virginia Junior College, Morgantown, WV.

Pennsylvania Institute of Technology (B)

800 Manchester Avenue, Media PA 19063-4098
County: Delaware FICE Identification: 010998
Unit ID: 214582
Telephone: (610) 892-1500 Carnegie Class: Assoc/HVT-High Non
FAX Number: (610) 892-1510 Calendar System: Semester
URL: www.pit.edu
Established: 1953 Annual Undergrad Tuition & Fees: $13,200
Enrollment: 661 Coed
Affiliation or Control: Independent Non-Profit IRS Status: 501(c)3
Highest Offering: Associate Degree
Accreditation: M, PTAA

01 President .... Mr. Walter R. GARRISON
11 Chief Operating Officer .... Ms. Jayne B. GARRISON
03 Vice President .... Mr. Jack BACON
05 Provost .... Dr. Robert E. HANCOX
10 Chief Financial Officer .... Ms. Annamarie CASSIDY
32 Dean of Student Services .... Dr. Dona M. FABRIZIO
06 Dir of Inst Research/Registrar .... Mr. Craig M. JACOBS
07 Director of Admissions .... Mr. Matthew MYERS
37 Financial Aid Director .... Ms. Laura BLOMGREN
18 Director of Facilities .... Mr. Frederick FIVECOAT
13 Dir of Information Technology .... Mr. Michael TESTA
36 Coordinator Job Placement/Transfer .... Ms. Heather DILALLA
08 Director of the Library .... Ms. Lynea ANDERMAN
20 Asst Dean of Academic Affairs .... Ms. Rachelle CHAYKIN
04 Executive Asst to President .... Ms. Kathryn DIGIORGIO

*Pennsylvania State System of Higher Education, Office of the Chancellor (C)

Dixon University Ctr, 2986 N 2nd St,
Harrisburg PA 17110-1201
County: Dauphin FICE Identification: 029371
Unit ID: 214661
Telephone: (717) 720-4000 Carnegie Class: N/A
FAX Number: (717) 720-4011
URL: www.passhe.edu

01 Chancellor .... Mr. Frank T. BROGAN
03 Executive Vice Chancellor .... Dr. Peter H. GARLAND
10 Vice Chancellor Admin/Finance .... Mr. James S. DILLON
05 Dpty Vice Chanc Acad/Stdnt Affairs .... Dr. Kathleen HOWLEY
21 Assoc Vice Chancellor Admin/Finance ...... Ms. Lois M. JOHNSON
100 Chief of Staff .... Mr. Randy GOIN, JR.
18 Asst Vice Chancellor Facilities .... Mr. Steven DUPES
43 Chief Legal Counsel .... Mr. Andrew LEHMAN

*Bloomsburg University of Pennsylvania (D)

400 E Second Street, Bloomsburg PA 17815-1399
County: Columbia FICE Identification: 003315
Unit ID: 211158
Telephone: (570) 389-4000 Carnegie Class: Masters/L
FAX Number: (570) 389-3700 Calendar System: Semester
URL: www.bloomu.edu
Established: 1839 Annual Undergrad Tuition & Fees (In-State): $9,326
Enrollment: 9,998 Coed
Affiliation or Control: State IRS Status: 501(c)3
Highest Offering: Doctorate
Accreditation: M, ANEST, ART, AUD, BUS, CAATE, CS, ENGT, EXSC, MUS, NURSE, SP, SW, TED, THEA

02 President .... Dr. David L. SOLTZ
05 Sr VP/Provost Academic Affairs .... Dr. Ira BLAKE
10 Vice Pres Finance/Administration .... Mr. John F. LOONAN
32 Vice Pres Student Affairs .... Dr. Dionne D. SOMERVILLE
30 Vice Pres University Advancement .... Mr. Erik EVANS
84 VP Strategic Enrol Mgt/Dean Ext Pgm ..... Mr. Thomas FLETCHER
22 Deputy to Pres for Equity .... Dr. Robert WISLOCK
86 Director External & Govt Relations .... Mr. Dan KNORR
04 Exec Asst to the President .... Ms. Brenda CROMLEY
58 Assoc VP/Dean Grad Studies .... Dr. Robert GATES
13 Assoc VP Technology & Library Serv .... Mr. Wayne C. MOHR
108 Asst VP Planning & Assessment .... Dr. Sheila Dove JONES
18 Asst VP for Facilities Management .... Mr. Eric NESS
21 Asst VP Finance/Budget & Bus Svcs .... Ms. Claudia THRUSH
35 Asst VP Student Affairs .... Mr. Thomas KRESCH
26 AVP Marketing/Communications .... Ms. Rosalee RUSH
29 AVP Alumni/Professional Engagement .... Ms. Lynda MICHAELS
49 Dean College of Liberal Arts .... Dr. James BROWN
50 Dean College of Business .... Dr. Jeffrey KRUG
81 Dean College of Science/Tech .... Dr. Robert S. ARONSTAM
53 Dean College of Education .... Dr. Elizabeth MAUCH
88 Sp Asst to Provost Acad Achievement .... Dr. Patricia J. BEYER
15 Director Human Resources/Labor Rel .... Mr. Jerry REED
46 Interim Dir Research/Sponsored Pgms .... Dr. John M. HRANITZ
06 Registrar/Dir Enroll Services .... Mr. Joseph KISSELL
07 Director of Admissions .... Mr. Christopher LAPOS
09 Director of Institutional Research .... Ms. Karen L. SLUSSER
104 Director Global & Multicultural Ed .... Ms. Nawal BONOMO
37 Interim Director Financial Aid .... Ms. Amanda KISHBAUGH
36 Dir Career/Professional Development .... Dr. Wren FRITSKY
38 Director of Counsel & Human Devel .... Dr. William R. HARRAR
90 Manager Technology Support Services .... Mr. David S. CELLI
40 Manager University Store .... Mr. Carl SODERGREN
41 Director of Athletics .... Mr. Michael S. MCFARLAND
85 Director International Educ Svcs .... Dr. Madhav P. SHARMA
42 Director Protestant Campus Ministry .... Rev. Jill YOUNG
42 Director Catholic Campus Ministry .... Fr. David HERESHKO
19 Dir Univ Safety & Police .... Mr. Tom PHILLIPS
92 Director Univ Honors Pgm .... Dr. Julie VANDIVERE
96 Director Procurement & Operations .... Mr. Jeffrey MANDEL
08 Director Library Services .... Ms. Charlotte DROLL
91 Dir Applications Develop/Operations .... Mr. James C. GESSNER
102 Exec Dir BU Foundation .... Mr. Jerome DVORAK

*California University of Pennsylvania (E)

250 University Avenue, California PA 15419-1394
County: Washington FICE Identification: 003316
Unit ID: 211361
Telephone: (724) 938-4000 Carnegie Class: Masters/L
FAX Number: (724) 938-4138 Calendar System: Semester
URL: www.calu.edu
Established: 1852 Annual Undergrad Tuition & Fees (In-State): $9,936
Enrollment: 7,978 Coed
Affiliation or Control: State IRS Status: 501(c)3
Highest Offering: Doctorate
Accreditation: M, ART, #CAATE, CACREP, CS, ENGT, NAIT, NRPA, NURSE, PTAA, SP, SW, THEA

02 President .... Ms. Geraldine JONES
05 Provost/Vice Pres Academic Affairs .... Dr. Bruce BARNHART
10 VP Administration & Finance .... Mr. Robert THORN
09 Director Institutional Research .... Dr. Wei ZHOU
58 Dean of Graduate Studies .... Dr. Stan KOMACEK
20 Assoc Provost/Student Retent Ofcr .... Dr. Dan M. ENGSTROM
30 Assoc VP for Development & Alumni ...... Mr. Anthony F. MAURO
72 Dean of Science/Technology .... Dr. John A. KALLIS
49 Dean of Liberal Arts .... Dr. Mohamed YAMBA
53 Dean Col Education/Human Svcs .... Dr. Kevin A. KOURY
62 Dean of Library Services .... Mr. Douglas HOOVER
07 Dean of Admissions .... Ms. Tracey SHEETZ
37 Director of Financial Aid .... Mrs. Jill FERNANDES
37 Sr Assoc Director of Financial Aid .... Mr. Jeff DERUBBO
06 Registrar .... Ms. Heidi WILLIAMS
36 Director of Career Services .... Ms. Rhonda GIFFORD
92 Director Honors Program .... Mr. Mark AUNE
29 Director of Alumni Relations .... Ms. Leslie FLEENOR
38 Assoc VP Student Development & Svcs .... Dr. Timothy SUSICK
13 Assoc VP for University Technology .... Mr. Brian KRAUS
39 Director of University Housing .... Ms. Jackie THORN
94 Director Women's Studies .... Dr. Marta MCCLINTOCK
85 International Student Advisor .... Mr. John WATKINS
41 Athletic Director .... Dr. Karen HJERPE
15 Interim Director of Personnel .... Mr. Eric GUISER
22 Director of Social Equity .... Dr. John BURNETT
19 Chief of Police .... Mr. Ed MCSHEFFERY
18 Director of Physical Plant .... Mr. Michael PEPLINSKI
26 Director of Communications & PR .... Mrs. Christine KINDL
27 Director of Publications .... Mr. Greg SOFRANKO
40 Book Store Manager .... Ms. Amy NASH
96 Director of Purchasing .... Ms. Joyce SHEPPICK
106 Dir Online Education/E-learning .... Ms. Stephanie L. FRANKS-HELWICH

*Cheyney University of Pennsylvania (F)

1837 University Circle PO Box 200,
Cheyney PA 19319-0200
County: Delaware FICE Identification: 003317
Unit ID: 211608
Telephone: (610) 399-2000 Carnegie Class: Bac-A&S
FAX Number: (610) 399-2415 Calendar System: Semester
URL: www.cheyney.edu
Established: 1837 Annual Undergrad Tuition & Fees (In-State): $9,344
Enrollment: 1,022 Coed
Affiliation or Control: State IRS Status: 501(c)3
Highest Offering: Master's
Accreditation: #M

02 Interim President .... Dr. Frank POGUE
05 Interim Provost .... Dr. Robert M. DIXON
10 Vice Pres Finance & Administration .... Vacant
21 Asst VP of Finance/Controller .... Ms. Layna HOLMES-BUTLER
38 Chairperson Guidance & Counseling .... Ms. Jolly RAMAKRISHNAN
06 Registrar .... Ms. Brenda SHIELDS
37 Director Financial Aid .... Mr. Lawrence BRITTON
09 Director Institutional Research .... Dr. Erika SHEHATA
18 Facilities Manager .... Mr. Charlie BERKHEIMER
19 Director Public Safety .... Mr. Lawrence RICHARDS
36 Director Career Services .... Vacant
41 Athletic Director .... Ms. Sue KILIAN
17 College Physician .... Dr. Pamela HADLEY
43 University Legal Counsel .... Ms. Anne ST. LEDGER
32 Director Student Affairs .... Ms. Sharon THORN
29 Director Alumni Relations .... Mr. Gregory BENJAMIN
39 Manager Housing Ops/Auxiliary Svcs .... Ms. Elizabeth BURTON
103 Dir Economic/Workforce Devel .... Ms. Sharon CANNON
88 Bursar .... Ms. Lauronda FLETCHER
92 Dean of Keystone Honors Academy .... Dr. Tara KENT
84 Interim Dir of Enrollment Mgmt .... Ms. Christina M. DENNIS

*Clarion University of Pennsylvania (G)

840 Wood Street, Clarion PA 16214-1232
County: Clarion FICE Identification: 003318
Unit ID: 211644
Telephone: (814) 393-2000 Carnegie Class: Masters/L
FAX Number: (814) 393-1826 Calendar System: Semester
URL: www.clarion.edu
Established: 1867 Annual Undergrad Tuition & Fees (In-State): $10,190
Enrollment: 5,712 Coed
Affiliation or Control: State IRS Status: 501(c)3
Highest Offering: Master's
Accreditation: M, ART, BUS, CORE, CSHSE, LIB, SP, TED

02 President .... Dr. Karen M. WHITNEY
05 Int Provost/AVP .... Dr. Todd PFANNESTIEL
32 Vice Pres Student & University Affs .... Dr. Susanne FENSKE
10 Vice Pres Finance/Administration .... Mr. Len CULLO
102 Chief Exec Officer Foundation .... Mr. Michael R. KEEFER
30 Vice President Univ Advancement .... Mr. James GEIGER
21 Assoc VP for Administration .... Mr. Timothy P. FOGARTY
22 Int Director of Social Equity .... Ms. Amy SALSGIVER
12 Executive Dean Venango College .... Dr. Roxanne GONZALES
84 Int Dean of Enrollment Management .... Ms. Merrilynn DUNLAP
08 Dean of Libraries .... Dr. Terry S. LATOUR
49 Int Dean of Arts & Sciences .... Dr. Bruce SMITH
50 Dean of Business Administration .... Dr. Philip FRESE
06 Registrar .... Ms. Lisa L. HEPLER
21 Comptroller .... Ms. Tamara B. VARSEK
13 Assoc VP for Information Technology .... Mr. Samuel T. PULEIO
46 Director Faculty Research .... Ms. Kristen GEIGER
26 Dir of Marketing & Communications .... Mr. David LOVE
37 Director of Student Financial Svcs .... Mr. David HOGUE
18 Director of Facilities Mgmt .... Mr. Eric MARTIN
29 Director of Alumni Relations .... Ms. Laura C. KING
36 Director Career Services .... Mr. William BAILEY
39 Director of Residence Life .... Vacant
19 Director of Public Safety .... Mr. Jason HENDERSHOT
41 Interim Athletic Director .... Ms. Wendy SNODGRASS
96 Director of Purchasing .... Mr. Rein A. POLD

*East Stroudsburg University of Pennsylvania (H)

200 Prospect Street, East Stroudsburg PA 18301-2999
County: Monroe FICE Identification: 003320
Unit ID: 212115
Telephone: (570) 422-3211 Carnegie Class: Masters/M
FAX Number: (570) 422-3777 Calendar System: Semester
URL: www.esu.edu
Established: 1893 Annual Undergrad Tuition & Fees (In-State): $9,684
Enrollment: 6,819 Coed
Affiliation or Control: State IRS Status: 501(c)3
Highest Offering: Doctorate
Accreditation: M, CAATE, CS, EXSC, NRPA, NUR, PH, SP, SW, TED

02 President .... Dr. Marcia G. WELSH
05 Provost & Vice Pres Academic Affair .... Ms. Joanne Z. BRUNO
32 Vice President Student Affairs .... Dr. Doreen TOBIN
10 Vice Pres Administration & Finance .... Mr. Kenneth A. LONG
46 Vice Pres Research & Econ Dev .. Ms. Mary Frances POSTUPACK
84 Vice Pres Enrollment Management .... Mr. David BOUSQUET
58 Dean of Graduate College .... Vacant
49 Dean of Arts & Sciences .... Dr. Peter HAWKES
76 Dean of Health Sciences .... Dr. Alberto CARDELLE
53 Dean of Education .... Dr. Terry BARRY
50 Dean of Business & Management .... Dr. Tribhuvan PURI
08 Dean of Library & Univ Collections .... Dr. Jingfeng XIA
20 Assoc Provost & Dean Univ College .... Dr. Thomas TAUER
35 Asst Vice President Student Affairs .... Mr. Michael SACHS
100 Chief of Staff .... Mr. Miguel BARBOSA
88 Asst Vice Pres Instruct Supp & Outr .... Mr. Michael SOUTHWELL
07 Director of Admissions .... Mr. Jeff JONES
06 Registrar/Dir Enrollment Services .... Ms. Kizzy MORRIS
37 Sr Assoc Director Financial Aid .... Vacant
36 Director of Career Services .... Ms. Daria WIELEBINSKI
38 Director Counseling Center .... Dr. Linda L. VAN METER
41 Director Intercollegiate Athletics .... Mr. Joshua LOONEY
39 Director of Residence Life .... Mr. Robert M. MOSES
88 Dir of Student Activity Association .... Mr. Joe AKOB
21 Controller .... Ms. Donna R. BULZONI
13 Chief Information Officer .... Mr. Robert D'AVERSA
15 Director of Human Resources .... Ms. Teresa FRITSCHE
18 Int Director Facilities Management .... Mr. John BLOSHINSKI
96 Director of Procurement/Contracting .... Ms. Patricia REICH
29 Director of Alumni Engagement .... Mr. Leon S. JOHN, JR.
26 Director University Relations .... Dr. Brenda FRIDAY
09 Director Inst Research & Assessment .... Vacant

*Edinboro University (A)

219 Meadville Street, Edinboro PA 16444-0001
County: Erie FICE Identification: 003321
Unit ID: 212160
Telephone: (814) 732-2000 Carnegie Class: Masters/L
FAX Number: (814) 732-2880 Calendar System: Semester
URL: www.edinboro.edu
Established: 1857 Annual Undergrad Tuition & Fees (In-State): $9,536
Enrollment: 6,837 Coed
Affiliation or Control: State IRS Status: 501(c)3
Highest Offering: Doctorate
Accreditation: M, ART, ACBSP, CACREP, CORE, CS, MUS, NUR, NURSE, SP, SW, TED

02 President .... Dr. H. Fred WALKER
05 Provost/VP Academic Affairs .... Dr. Michael HANNAN
10 VP Finance & Administration .... Mr. Guilbert BROWN
32 Vice President for Student Affairs .... Dr. Kahan SABLO
30 Vice Pres University Advancement .... Ms. Tina MENGINE
15 Assoc VP Human Res/Fac Rels .... Mr. Sid BOOKER
08 Assoc VP University Libraries .... Dr. Donald H. DILMORE
84 Assoc VP for Enrollment Services .... Mr. William EDMONDS
09 Dir Inst Research & Assessment .... Mr. Matthew CETTIN
20 Sr Exec Associate to the Provost .... Ms. Judy KUBEJA
18 Dir Facilities Management/Planning .... Mr. Michael HILBERT
27 Director of Communications .... Mr. Jeffrey HILEMAN
26 Director of Marketing .... Mr. William BERGER
37 Int Director of Financial Aid .... Ms. Kelly VITELLI
92 Director Honors Program .... Dr. Jean JONES
22 Dir of Social Equity/Ombudsperson .... Ms. Valerie O. HAYES
79 Int Dn Col Arts/Humanities/Soc Sci .... Dr. Scott MILLER
81 Dean Col Science & Health Prof .... Dr. Nathan RITCHEY
58 Dean of Graduate Studies/Research .... Dr. Alan BIEL
53 Dean School of Education .... Dr. Alan BIEL
50 Dean School of Business .... Dr. Scott MILLER
06 Registrar .... Mr. Tim W. PILEWSKI
36 Dir Office of Career Development .... Dr. Jody GALLAGHER
29 Dir Alumni Relations/Fund Devel .... Mr. Jon PULICE
41 Athletic Director .... Mr. Bruce BAUMGARTNER
38 Dir Counseling/Psychological Svcs .... Dr. Michael BUCELL
19 Chief of Police .... Ms. Angela VINCENT
22 Dir Ofc Students with Disabilities .... Ms. Kim KENNEDY
12 Dir & Outreach Coord EUP in Erie .... Ms. Janet L. BOWKER
23 Medical Dir Student Health Services .... Dr. Ronald C. MARTIN
109 Director Auxiliary Operations .... Mr. Paul B. KIGHTLINGER
85 Dir International Student Services .... Ms. Linda KIGHTLINGER
25 Int Dir Grant & Sponsored Programs .... Ms. Kristina HUBER
14 Dir Networks & Telecommunications .... Ms. Karen MURDZAK
90 Director Client Support Services .... Mr. Dennis J. BRADLEY
13 Director of Information Services .... Ms. Sallie A. TERPACK
96 Director Purchasing & Contracts .... Ms. Darla SPAID
30 Director of Development .... Ms. Julie A. CHACONA
44 Major Gifts Officer .... Ms. Marilyn GOELLNER
88 Director of Budget and Payroll .... Ms. Theresa VILLELLA
21 Controller .... Mr. Wayne T. OCHS
88 Bursar .... Mr. Mark MATLOCK
35 Dir Campus Life/Leadership Dev .... Ms. Michelle BARBICH
17 Director of Health & Wellness Ctr .... Ms. Darla ELDER
106 Manager of Online Programs .... Dr. James BOULDER
24 Learning Technology Svcs Manager .... Mr. Randall MCCASLIN
88 Coordinator Non-Credit Programs .... Ms. Beth ZEWE

*Indiana University of Pennsylvania (B)

1011 South Drive, Indiana PA 15705-0001
County: Indiana FICE Identification: 003277
Unit ID: 213020
Telephone: (724) 357-2100 Carnegie Class: DU-Mod
FAX Number: (724) 357-6213 Calendar System: Semester
URL: www.iup.edu
Established: 1875 Annual Undergrad Tuition & Fees (In-State): $9,936
Enrollment: 14,534 Coed
Affiliation or Control: State IRS Status: 501(c)3
Highest Offering: Doctorate
Accreditation: M, ACFEI, ART, BUS, #CAATE, CACREP, CLPSY, COARC, CS, DIETD, DIETI, ENGR, EXSC, MUS, NURSE, PLNG, SP, TED, THEA

02 President .... Dr. Michael DRISCOLL
05 Provost & VP Academic Affairs .... Dr. Timothy S. MOERLAND
11 Vice Pres Administration/Finance .... Dr. Cornelius WOOTEN
32 Vice President Student Affairs .... Dr. Rhonda H. LUCKEY
30 Vice Pres University Advancement .... Mr. William SPEIDEL, III
20 Assoc VP Academic Administration .... Dr. John N. KILMARX
58 Dean Graduate Studies & Research .... Dr. Randy MARTIN
15 Assoc Vice Pres Human Resources .... Mr. Craig BICKLEY
79 Dean College Humanities & Soc Sci .... Dr. Yaw A. ASAMOAH
50 Dean Eberly Col Bus/Inform Tech .... Dr. Robert C. CAMP
53 Dean College Educ/Educ Tech .... Dr. Lara LUETKEHANS
81 Dean Col Natural Science & Math .... Dr. Deanne SNAVELY
57 Dean College of Fine Arts .... Mr. Michael J. HOOD
66 Dean College Health & Human Svcs .... Dr. Mary E. WILLIAMS
84 VP Enrollment Mgmt & Communications .... Mr. James BEGANY
08 Dean of Libraries .... Dr. Luis GONZALEZ
06 Registrar .... Mr. Robert SIMON
13 Chief Information Officer .... Mr. Bill BALINT
09 Inst Research Planning & Assessment .... Mrs. Barbe MOORE
14 Exec Dir of Technology Services Ctr .... Mr. Todd CUNNINGHAM
28 Dir Social Equity/Civic Engagement .... Mr. Pablo MENDOZA
19 Director of Public Safety .... Mr. Kevin THELEN
36 Director Career Development Ctr .... Dr. Tammy MANKO
29 Exec Director Alumni Association .... Mrs. Mary MORGAN
44 Director Annual Giving .... Ms. Emily SMELTZ
85 Asst VP Intl Education & Global .... Dr. Michele PETRUCCI
46 Assistant Dean for Research .... Dr. Hilliary CREELY
39 Exec Director Housing/Resid Living .... Ms. Sondra R. DENNISON
40 Bookstore Director .... Mr. Tim SHARBAUGH
41 Director Athletics .... Mr. Steve ROACH
23 Director Health Services .... Ms. Melissa DICK
12 Dean Northpointe Campus .... Mr. Richard MUTH
12 Dean Punxsutawney Campus .... Dr. Terry APPOLONIA
43 Staff Attorney .... Ms. Suzanne WILLIAMSON
26 Exec Dir Commun & Media Relations .... Ms. Michelle FRYLING
96 Director of Purchasing .... Mr. Terry BRESLAWSKI
10 Assoc Vice President for Finance .... Mrs. Susanna C. SINK
86 Exec Asst to Pres for Govt Relation .... Ms. Robin GORMAN
37 Director of Financial Aid .... Ms. Ragan GRIFFIN
35 Assoc VP Student Affairs/Well-Being .... Mr. Michael LEMASTERS
88 Dir Admin Services Culinary Arts .... Ms. Enid RESENIC
07 Director of Admissions .... Ms. Stacy HOPKINS
105 Director Web Services .... Mr. Michael POWERS
18 Chief Facilities/Physical Plant .... Mr. R. Michael BROWN
31 Assoc VP Univ & Community Rels .... Dr. Kate LINDER

*Kutztown University of Pennsylvania (C)

15200 Kutztown Road, Kutztown PA 19530-0730
County: Berks FICE Identification: 003322
Unit ID: 213349
Telephone: (610) 683-4000 Carnegie Class: Masters/L
FAX Number: (610) 683-4693 Calendar System: Semester
URL: www.kutztown.edu
Established: 1866 Annual Undergrad Tuition & Fees (In-State): $9,411
Enrollment: 9,218 Coed
Affiliation or Control: State IRS Status: 501(c)3
Highest Offering: Doctorate
Accreditation: M, ART, BUS, CACREP, MUS, SW, TED

02 President .... Dr. Kenneth S. HAWKINSON
05 Provost/VP Academic Affairs .... Dr. Anne ZAYAITZ
10 VP Administration & Finance .... Mr. Gerald L. SILBERMAN
84 Vice Presiden Enrollment Management .... Dr. Warren HILTON
22 Deputy to Pres Compliance/Equity .... Mr. Jesus PENA
102 Executive Director KU Foundation .... Ms. Tracey THOMPSON
30 Assoc Vice Pres Comm/Mktg & Ext Aff .... Mr. John C. GREEN
20 Vice Prov Acad Affs/Dean Grad Stds .... Dr. Carole WELLS
21 Acting Asst VP Admin & Finance .... Mr. Matthew DELANEY
32 Assoc Provost/Dean of Students .... Mr. Robert WATROUS
13 Asst Vice Pres/Info Technology .... Mr. Mitchell FREED
15 Executive Director Human Resources .... Ms. Sharon M. PICUS
18 Asst Vice President for Facilities .... Mr. Terry BROWN
27 AVP Communications & Marketing .... Mr. John GREEN
88 Dean College Visual/Performing Arts .... Dr. William J. MOWDER
49 Actg Dean College Liberal Arts/Sci .... Dr. David BEOUGHER
50 Dean College of Business .... Dr. Martha GEANEY
53 Dean College Education .... Dr. Kenneth TEITELBAUM
62 Director of Library Services .... Ms. Martha STEVENSON
26 Director of University Relations .... Mr. Matthew SANTOS
09 Director Institutional Research .... Ms. Natalie SNOW
06 Registrar .... Mr. Ted WITRYK
37 Director of Financial Aid .... Mr. Bernard L. MCCREE
39 Director Housing/Residential Svcs .... Mr. Kent R. DAHLQUIST
41 Director of Athletics .... Mr. Gregory BAMBERGER
38 Director Counseling & Psych Svcs .... Dr. Lisa COULTER
96 Purchasing Manager .... Ms. Barbara REITZ
07 Director of Admissions .... Ms. Nancy WUNDERLY
19 Acting Chief of Police .... Mr. John DILLON
36 Director Career/Community Services .... Ms. Kerri GARDI
29 Director Dev & Alumni Engagement .... Mr. Alex OGEKA
04 Executive Asst to President .... Ms. Toyia HEYWARD
108 Asst Vice Provost/Assessment .... Mr. Ernest CLARY
106 Dir Online Education/E-learning .... Mr. Douglas SCOTT

*Lock Haven University (D)

401 N Fairview Street, Lock Haven PA 17745-2390
County: Clinton FICE Identification: 003323
Unit ID: 213613
Telephone: (570) 484-2001 Carnegie Class: Masters/M
FAX Number: (570) 484-2432 Calendar System: Semester
URL: www.lhup.edu
Established: 1870 Annual Undergrad Tuition & Fees (In-State): $9,380
Enrollment: 4,917 Coed
Affiliation or Control: State IRS Status: 170(c)1
Highest Offering: Master's
Accreditation: M, ACBSP, ADNUR, ARCPA, CAATE, CACREP, NRPA, NUR, SW, TED

02 President .... Dr. Michael FIORENTINO, JR.
05 Provost & Executive Vice President .... Dr. Donna WILSON
11 COO & Senior Vice President .... Mr. William HANELLY
32 Dean of Student Affairs .... Dr. Dwayne ALLISON
84 Vice President for Enrollment Mgmt .... Ms. Tyana LANGE
49 Dean of Liberal Arts & Education .... Dr. Susan RIMBY
83 Dean Natural/Behavioral/Health Sci .... Dr. Scott CARNICOM
50 Dean Business/Info Sys/Human Svcs .... Dr. Stephen NEUN
12 Director Clearfield Branch Campus .... Dr. William CURLEY
85 Director of International Studies .... Ms. Rosana CAMPBELL
09 Director Institutional Research .... Mr. Mike ABPLANALP
15 Associate VP of Human Resources .... Ms. Deana HILL
07 Director of Admissions .... Ms. Donna TATARKA
06 Registrar .... Mrs. Jill MITCHLEY
22 Dir Affirm Action/Equal Opportunity .... Ms. Jamie PENN
37 Director of Financial Aid .... Mr. Robert FRYER
36 Director of Career Services .... Ms. Maryjo CAMPANA
26 Vice President for University Rels .... Mr. Rodney JENKINS
19 Director of Public Safety .... Mr. Paul ALTIERI
18 Director of Facilities .... Mr. Keith ROUSH
41 Director of Athletics .... Dr. Tom GIOGLIO
66 Director of Nursing Program .... Ms. Kimberly OWENS
38 Director of Counseling .... Dr. Dan E. TESS
90 Dir Computing/Instructional Tech .... Mr. Donald W. PATTERSON
88 Director of Physician Asst Program .... Mr. Walt EISENHAUER
92 Director Honors Program .... Dr. Jacqueline WHITLING
94 Director Women's Studies .... Dr. Kimberly ALEXANDER
93 Director Minority Students .... Mr. Kenneth L. HALL
40 Manager University Bookstore .... Mr. James KOWNACKI
29 Director Alumni Relations .... Ms. Ashley KOSER
102 Dir Foundation/Corporate Relations .... Mr. Troy MILLER
103 Dir Workforce Development & CE .... Ms. Shannon TYSON

*Mansfield University of Pennsylvania (E)

Academy Street, Mansfield PA 16933-1697
County: Tioga FICE Identification: 003324
Unit ID: 213783
Telephone: (570) 662-4000 Carnegie Class: Masters/S
FAX Number: (570) 662-4995 Calendar System: Semester
URL: www.mansfield.edu
Established: 1857 Annual Undergrad Tuition & Fees (In-State): $9,806
Enrollment: 2,752 Coed
Affiliation or Control: State IRS Status: 501(c)3
Highest Offering: Master's
Accreditation: M, ACBSP, COARC, DIETD, MUS, NUR, RAD, SW

02 President .... Gen. Francis L. HENDRICKS
10 VP Finance/Administration .... Vacant
30 AVP for University Advancement .... Ms. Rita DIBBLE
32 VP for Student Affairs .... Vacant
39 Assoc Vice Pres Residence Life .... Mr. Chuck COLBY
05 Provost/Sr Vice Pres Acad Affs .... Dr. Steven SICONOLFI
15 Exec Dir Employee & Leadership Svcs .... Ms. Kacy HAGAN
08 Director Library/Info Resource Svcs .... Mr. Scott R. DIMARCO
18 Int Director Facilities .... Mr. Jim WELCH
84 Exec Director Enrollment Management .... Vacant
35 Interim Dean of Students .... Mr. Nigel LONG
26 Assoc Dir Public & Media Relations .... Ms. Terry DAY
27 Director of Marketing .... Ms. Casey WOOD
37 Director of Student Financial Aid .... Mr. Charles SCHEETZ
19 Director University Police & Safety .... Ms. Christine SHEGAN
41 Director of Athletics .... Ms. Deb SOLFARO
85 Social Equity/Multicultural Affairs .... Vacant
09 Dir Institutional Rsrch/Assess Data .... Dr. John COSGROVE
29 Director of Alumni/Govt Relations .... Ms. Lindsey SIKORSKI
06 Registrar .... Ms. Lori CASS
38 Director Counseling Center .... Ms. Jolene MEISNER
07 Dir of Admissions Tactical/Enroll .... Ms. Rachel GREEN
13 Chief Info Technology Officer .... Mr. Nicholas ANDRE

*Millersville University of Pennsylvania (F)

PO Box 1002, Millersville PA 17551-0302
County: Lancaster FICE Identification: 003325
Unit ID: 214041
Telephone: (717) 871-4636 Carnegie Class: Masters/L
FAX Number: (717) 871-7930 Calendar System: 4/1/4
URL: www.millersville.edu
Established: 1855 Annual Undergrad Tuition & Fees (In-State): $10,918
Enrollment: 8,047 Coed
Affiliation or Control: State IRS Status: 501(c)3
Highest Offering: Doctorate
Accreditation: M, ACBSP, ART, COARC, CS, ENGR, MUS, NAIT, NUR, SW, TED

02 President .... Dr. John M. ANDERSON
05 Vice Pres Academic Affs/Provost .... Dr. Vilas A. PRABHU
10 Vice Pres Finance & Administration .... Mr. Roger BRUSZEWSKI
30 Vice Pres for Advancement .... Dr. Aminta HAWKINS BREAUX
32 VP Student Affs & Enrollment Mgmt .... Mr. Brian HAZLETT
22 Int Dir Diversity & Social Justice .... Ms. Janice BECHTEL
20 Associate Provost Academic Admin .... Dr. Jeffrey R. ADAMS
20 Asst VP for Student Success and Ret .... Dr. Candice BALDWIN
108 Asst VP Inst Assessment & Planning .... Dr. Lisa R. SHIBLEY
21 Chief Information Officer .... Ms. Nancy PRUSKOWSKI
39 Assoc Vice President .... Dr. Michelle PEREZ
15 Exec Director of Human Resources .... Mrs. Melanie A. DESANTIS
37 Asst VP Enrollment Mgmt/Dir Fin Aid .... Mr. Dwight G. HORSEY
35 Assoc VP/Dean of Students .... Mr. Thomas J. RICHARDSON
88 Corporate Gift Officer .... Mr. Gregory FREEDLAND
18 Asst VP Facilities .... Mr. Thomas A. WALTZ, JR.
53 Dean Education & Human Services .... Dr. George DRAKE
79 Dean Arts/Human & Social Sci .... Dr. Diane UMBLE
81 Dean Science & Technology .... Dr. Michael JACKSON
58 Dean Grad Studies & Adult Lrng .... Dr. Victor DESANTIS
06 Registrar .... Ms. Alison HUTCHINSON
07 Director of Admissions .... Ms. Katy FERRIER
36 Assoc Director Career Management .... Ms. Margo J. SASSAMAN
38 Director Counseling/Human Devel .... Dr. Kelsey K. BACKELS
19 Chief of University Police .... Mr. Peter J. ANDERS
23 Medical Director .... Vacant
41 Director of Intercollegiate Ath .... Mr. Miles GALLAGHER
40 Manager University Bookstore .... Ms. Audrey HERR
42 Campus Minister .... Mr. Duane METZLER

30 AVP Advancement & Dir External Rels ..... Mr. Steven A. DIGUISEPPE
44 Assoc VP for Advancement ..... Ms. Alice MCMURRY
09 Director Institutional Research ..... Dr. Joseph E. REVELT
88 Senior Major Gift Officer ..... Ms. Martha P. MACADAM
102 Dir Sponsored Pgms & Research Admin ..... Dr. Rene MUNOZ
96 Director of Purchasing/Campus Svcs ... Mr. David C. ERRICKSON
12 Director of Visual & Perform Arts ..... Ms. Laura KENDALL
26 Director of Communications ..... Ms. Janet KACSKOS
106 Director of Online Programs ..... Ms. Lauren EDGELL
29 Director Alumni Engagement ..... Ms. Denise BERG
43 Dir Legal Services/General Counsel ..... Mr. Jeffrey HAWKINS

*Shippensburg University of Pennsylvania (A)

1871 Old Main Drive, Shippensburg PA 17257-2200

County: Cumberland FICE Identification: 003326
Unit ID: 216010
Telephone: (717) 477-7447 Carnegie Class: Masters/L
FAX Number: (717) 477-1273 Calendar System: Semester
URL: www.ship.edu
Established: 1871 Annual Undergrad Tuition & Fees (In-State): $10,052
Enrollment: 7,355 Coed
Affiliation or Control: State IRS Status: 501(c)3
Highest Offering: Doctorate
Accreditation: M, BUS, CACREP, CS, ENG, JOUR, SW, TED

02 President ..... Dr. George F. HARPSTER
05 Provost & Executive Vice President ..... Dr. Barbara G. LYMAN
84 VP for Enroll Mgmt/Tech/Library ..... Dr. Rick RUTH
10 Vice Pres Administration/Finance ..... Vacant
32 VP for Student Affairs ..... Dr. Roger L. SERR
26 Interim VP Ext & Univ Relations ..... Dr. Leslie FOLMER CLINTON
15 Assoc VP for Human Resources ..... Dr. David TOPPER
102 Pres Shippensburg Univ Foundation ..... Mr. John CLINTON
21 Assoc VP & Chief Financial Officer ..... Ms. Melinda D. FAWKS
20 Assoc Provost/Dean of Graduate ..... Dr. Tracy A. SCHOOLCRAFT
51 Interim Dean of Prof/Cont/Dist Ed ..... Dr. Carolyn CALLAGHAN
35 Dean of Students ..... Dr. David L. LOVETT
06 Registrar ..... Ms. Cathy J. SPRENGER
36 Director Career Development ..... Ms. Victoria KERR BUCHBAUER
37 Director Financial Aid ..... Ms. Trina SNYDER
29 Exec Dir University/Alumni Rels ..... Vacant
26 Director Publications & Advertising ..... Ms. Laura LUDLAM
08 Dean Library & Multi-Media Services ..... Dr. Dennis MATHES
22 Director Social Equity ..... Mr. Cecil E. HOWARD
88 Director Womens Center ..... Ms. Stephanie ERDICE
09 Director Inst Research & Planning ..... Mr. Mark PILGRIM
25 Dir Sponsored Pgms/Inst Public Svc . Mr. Christopher WONDERS
38 Director Counseling Services ..... Dr. Philip W. HENRY
88 Director of Conferences ..... Mr. Randy HAMMOND
53 Dean College Education & Human Svcs .. Dr. James R. JOHNSON
49 Dean College Arts & Science ..... Dr. James MIKE
50 Dean College of Business ..... Dr. John KOOTI
88 Dean Academic Engagement & Student ..... Dr. Sarah STOKELY
18 Chief Facilities/Physical Plant ..... Mr. Lance BRYSON
96 Director of Purchasing/Contracting ..... Ms. Deborah MARTIN
19 Director Public Safety ..... Ms. Cytha D. GRISSOM
41 Athletic Director ..... Mr. Jeff A. MICHAELS
04 Exec Asst to the President ..... Ms. Robin MAUN
101 Secretary of the Institution/Board ..... Ms. Robin MAUN
104 Director Study Abroad ..... Ms. Mary BURNETT
39 Director Student Housing ..... Mr. Barry MCCLANAHAN

*Slippery Rock University of Pennsylvania (B)

1 Morrow Way, Slippery Rock PA 16057-1326

County: Butler FICE Identification: 003327
Unit ID: 216038
Telephone: (724) 738-9000 Carnegie Class: Masters/L
FAX Number: (724) 738-2169 Calendar System: Semester
URL: www.sru.edu
Established: 1889 Annual Undergrad Tuition & Fees (In-State): $9,645
Enrollment: 8,495 Coed
Affiliation or Control: State IRS Status: 501(c)3
Highest Offering: Doctorate
Accreditation: M, ART, ACBSP, #ARCPA, CAATE, CACREP, CARTE, CS, DANCE, EXSC, MUS, NRPA, NUR, PTA, SW, TED, THEA

02 President ..... Dr. Cheryl NORTON
05 Provost/Vice Pres Acad & Stdnt Affs ..... Dr. Philip WAY
10 Vice Pres Finance/Administration ..... Dr. Amir MOHAMMADI
30 Vice President for Univ Advancement ..... Vacant
21 Asst Vice Pres for Finance ..... Ms. Molly MERCER
18 Asst Vice Pres for Facilities/Plng ..... Mr. Scott ALBERT
23 Exec Dir Student Health & Wellness ..... Vacant
32 Exec Dir for Student Services ..... Ms. Debra PINCEK
35 Exec Dir for Student Development ..... Vacant
15 Asst Vice Pres Human Resources ..... Ms. Lynne M. MOTYL
28 Asst VP Diversity & Equal Oppty ..... Ms. Holly M. MCCOY
100 Chief of Staff ..... Ms. Tina L. MOSER
84 Assoc Provost Enrollment Services ..... Dr. Amanda A. YALE
13 Assoc Provost Info Technology ..... Dr. John ZIEGLER
102 Exec Director Univ Foundation ..... Dr. Edward R. BUCHA
26 Exec Director Public Relations ..... Ms. Rita E. ABENT
37 Director Student Financial Aid ..... Ms. Alyssa DOBSON
19 Director Public Safety ..... Mr. Paul NOVAK
19 Director University Police ..... Mr. Michael SIMMONS
09 Assoc Prov Inst Rsrch/Acad Fin Mgmt ..... Ms. Carrie J. BIRCKBICHLER
08 Manager of Library Operations ..... Ms. Jennifer J. BARTEK
14 Director of Info & Adm Tech Svcs ..... Mr. Henry MAGUSIAK
06 Director Acad Records/Summer School ..... Mr. Eliott G. BAKER
07 Director Undergraduate Admissions ..... Mr. Michael MAY
23 Director Health Services ..... Ms. Kristina BENKESER
36 Associate Director Career Services ..... Mr. John F. SNYDER
29 Director Alumni Affairs ..... Ms. Kelly BAILEY
76 Interim Dean Col Health Environ/Sci ..... Dr. Jerry CHMIELEWSKI
07 Director Graduate Admissions ... Ms. Brandi WEBER-MORTIMER
41 Athletic Director ..... Mr. Paul A. LUEKEN
39 Director of Residence Life ..... Mr. Patrick T. BESWICK
85 Director International Services ..... Vacant
25 Director Grants & Sponsored Rsrch . Ms. Nancy L. CRUIKSHANK
38 Director of Student Counseling ..... Dr. Chris CUBERO
93 Director of Minority Students ..... Ms. Corinne J. GIBSON
96 Director of Purchasing ..... Mr. Mark S. COMBINE
88 Interim Assoc Provost Trans Exper ..... Dr. Bradley WILSON
49 Interim Dean Col Liberal Arts ..... Ms. Jennifer KELLER
50 Dean College of Business ..... Dr. Lawrence SHAO
53 Dean College of Education ..... Dr. Keith DILS
88 Assoc Provost Student Success ..... Mr. David WILMES

*West Chester University of Pennsylvania (C)

University & High Street, West Chester PA 19383-0001

County: Chester FICE Identification: 003328
Unit ID: 216764
Telephone: (610) 436-1000 Carnegie Class: Masters/L
FAX Number: (610) 436-3115 Calendar System: Semester
URL: www.wcupa.edu
Established: 1871 Annual Undergrad Tuition & Fees (In-State): $9,462
Enrollment: 16,086 Coed
Affiliation or Control: State IRS Status: 501(c)3
Highest Offering: Doctorate
Accreditation: M, ART, BUS, CAATE, CACREP, COARC, CS, DIETD, EXSC, FEPAC, MUS, NURSE, PH, SP, SPAA, SW, TED, THEA

02 Interim President ..... Dr. Chris FIORENTINO
100 COS and Exec Deputy to President ..... Dr. John VILLELLA
04 Sr Assoc to the President ..... Ms. Rebecca HOOK
22 Director Social Equity ..... Ms. Lynn KLINGENSMITH
05 Provost & VP for Academic Affairs .. Dr. R. Lorraine BERNOTSKY
11 Vice President Admin/Finance ..... Mr. Mark P. MIXNER
13 Vice President Info Services ..... Dr. Dikran KASSABIAN
30 Vice President Advancement ..... Dr. Mark G. PAVLOVICH
12 Interim Dir for External Operations ..... Ms. Lisa MONTGOMERY
32 VP Student Affs/Dean of Students ..... Vacant
46 Assoc VP Planning and Acad Admin ..... Vacant
58 Assoc Prov & Dean Grad Studies ..... Dr. Jeffery OSGOOD
07 Director Admissions ..... Ms. Marsha L. HAUG
53 Dean College Education/Social Work ..... Dr. Kenneth D. WITMER
50 Dean College of BPM ..... Dr. Michelle PATRICK
81 Interim Dean College Science & Math ..... Dr. Jack WABER
76 Dean College Health Science ..... Dr. Linda ADAMS
57 Dean College Arts & Humanities ..... Dr. Timothy V. BLAIR
25 Assoc VP Sponsored Research ..... Dr. Gautam PILLAY
23 Director Health Center ..... Ms. Robyn SPRAGINS
15 Assoc Vice Pres Human Resources ..... Mr. Michael T. MALOY
35 Asst Vice Pres Student Affairs ..... Ms. Sara HINKLE
35 Asst Vice Pres Student Affairs ..... Vacant
10 Asst VP Finance/Business Svcs ..... Vacant
84 Asst Prov & Asst VP Enrollment Mgmt . Mr. Joseph SANTIVASCI
85 Interim Dir International Programs ..... Dr. Peter LOEDEL
102 Exec Director WCU Foundation ..... Mr. Richard T. PRZYWARA
18 Assoc VP for Facilities ..... Mr. Jim LEWIS
88 Dir Facilities Finance/Support Svcs ..... Ms. Susan MILLER
21 Dir Accounting/Financial Reporting ..... Mr. Kevin MCCADDEN
09 AVP Institutional Research ..... Ms. Lisa YANNICK
21 Bursar/Director Student Finan Svcs ..... Mr. Daniel PAULETTI
88 Director Budget ..... Ms. Ilene MATES
26 Executive Director Communications ..... Ms. Nancy GAINER
88 Director Publications/Printing Svcs ..... Mr. Matthew BORN
31 Director Cultural/Community Affairs ..... Mr. John RHEIN
88 Director Conference Services ..... Ms. Mary Beth KURIMAY
08 Director Library Services ..... Vacant
88 Director Teacher Education Center ..... Dr. James B. PRICE
36 Director Career Devel Center ..... Ms. Rebecca ROSS
88 Dir Acad Development Pgm ..... Dr. John CRAIG
88 Dir Learning Asst/Resource ..... Ms. Gerardina MARTIN
37 Director Financial Aid ..... Mr. Dana C. PARKER
38 Director Counseling Center ..... Dr. Julie PERONE
29 Director Alumni Relations ..... Ms. Debbie NAUGHTON
41 Director Athletics ..... Dr. Edward M. MATEJKOVIC
88 Director Sports Information ..... Mr. James ZUHLKE
28 Director Multicultural Affairs ..... Mr. Jerome HUTSON
88 Director Women's Center ..... Ms. Alicia HAHN-MURPHY
19 Director Public Safety ..... Mr. Michael D. BICKING
96 Director Business Services ..... Ms. Marianne PEFFALL
88 Dir Environmental Health/Safety ..... Ms. Gail FELLOWS
88 Director Network & Telecom ..... Mr. Joseph SINCAVAGE
91 Dir Administrative Computing Systms ..... Mr. Patrick LENZI
88 Dir IT Strategic Sourcing/Planning ..... Ms. Chaw-ye CHANG
105 Director Content and Web Svcs ..... Ms. Kimberly SLATTERY
90 Spec Asst to VP Information Svcs ..... Dr. James FABREY
89 Director New Student Programs ..... Mr. Jared BROWN
88 Asst Dean Student Dev & Involvmnt ..... Mr. Peter GALLOWAY
39 Director Residence Life ..... Ms. Marion MCKINNEY
88 Director Student Conduct ..... Ms. Christina BRENNER
88 Director Campus Recreation ..... Dr. Stephen GAMBINO
88 Dir Student Leadership/Involve ..... Mr. Charles WARNER
109 Director Sykes Student Union ..... Mr. David TIMMANN
88 Dir Fraternity & Sorority Life ..... Ms. Cara JENKINS
88 Dir Service Lrng & Volunteer Pgm ..... Ms. Jodi ROTH-SAKS
88 Int Dir Acad Dev Pgm/Act 101 Pgm ..... Dr. Francis ATUAHENE
88 Dir Pre-major Academic Advising ..... Dr. Ann COLGAN
92 Director Honors College ..... Dr. Kevin DEAN
104 Asst VP for International Programs ..... Vacant
106 Exec Director Distance Education ..... Dr. Rui LI
88 Exec Dir Student Service Inc ..... Ms. Donna SNYDER
40 Student Svcs Inc Bookstore Manager ..... Mr. Stephen MANNELLA

* *Clarion University Venango College* (D)

1801 W First Street, Oil City PA 16301-3297

Telephone: (814) 676-6591 FICE Identification: 003319
Accreditation: &M, ADNUR, COARC, NAIT, NUR

† Regional accreditation is carried under the parent institution in Clarion, PA

* *Lock Haven University Clearfield Branch Campus* (E)

201 University Drive, Clearfield PA 16830

Telephone: (814) 768-3405 Identification: 770186
Accreditation: &M

† Regional accreditation is carried under the parent institution in Lock Haven, PA

Philadelphia College of Osteopathic Medicine (F)

4170 City Avenue, Philadelphia PA 19131-1694

County: Philadelphia FICE Identification: 003352
Unit ID: 215123
Telephone: (215) 871-6100 Carnegie Class: Spec-4-yr-Med
FAX Number: (215) 871-6719 Calendar System: Trimester
URL: www.pcom.edu
Established: 1899 Annual Graduate Tuition & Fees: N/A
Enrollment: 2,806 Coed
Affiliation or Control: Independent Non-Profit IRS Status: 501(c)3
Highest Offering: Doctorate; No Undergraduates
Accreditation: M, ARCPA, CLPSY, IPSY, OSTEO

01 President & CEO ..... Dr. Jay S. FELDSTEIN
05 Provost/Senior VP Acad Affairs/Dean ..... Dr. Kenneth J. VEIT
10 Vice Pres Finance/Treasurer/CFO ..... Mr. Peter DOULIS
58 Vice Pres Grad Pgms/Academic Plng ... Dr. Robert G. CUZZOLINO
17 Chief Acad Ofcr-PCOM Mednet-Opti ..... Dr. Richard A. PASCUCCI
43 Chief Legal Affairs Officer ..... Mr. David F. SIMON
63 Dean Osteopathic Med Pgm-GA Campus ..... Dr. William CRAVER, III
67 Dean School of Pharmacy ..... Dr. Mark P. OKAMOTO
20 Assoc Dean Graduate Medical Educ ..... Dr. David KUO
20 Assoc Dean Clinical Education ..... Dr. Joseph KACZMARCZYK
35 Asst Dean Pharmacy Student Affairs ..... Dr. Michael LEE
20 Assoc Dean Curriculum ..... Dr. Kerin FRESA
20 Assoc Dean Curriculum ..... Dr. Bonnie BUXTON
12 Chief Campus Officer-Georgia Campus ..... Mr. Bryan GINN
46 Chief Science Officer ..... Dr. Mindy GEORGE-WEINSTEIN
32 Chief Student Affair Officer ..... Dr. Tina WOODRUFF
26 Chief Marketing/Communications Ofcr ... Ms. Wendy W. ROMANO
37 Chief Student Financial Aid Officer ..... Mr. Michael WISNIEWSKI
15 Chief Human Resources Officer ..... Mr. Edward J. POTTS
07 Chief Admissions Officer ..... Ms. Deborah A. BENVENGER
28 Chief Diversity Officer ..... Dr. Lisa M. MCBRIDE
13 Chief Technology Officer ..... Mr. James A. WILLIAMS
88 Chief Compliance Officer ..... Dr. Allan MCLEOD
88 Chief Risk Management Officer ..... Ms. Laura G. BELL
18 Chief Facilities/Plant Operations ..... Mr. Frank H. WINDLE
30 Chief Advancement Officer ..... Ms. Carrie COLLINS
08 Chair of Library/Exec Director ..... Ms. Stephanie FERRETTI
06 Registrar ..... Ms. Deborah A. CASTELLANO
96 Director of Purchasing ..... Vacant

Philadelphia University (G)

4201 Henry Avenue, Philadelphia PA 19144

County: Philadelphia FICE Identification: 003354
Unit ID: 215099
Telephone: (215) 951-2700 Carnegie Class: Masters/L
FAX Number: (215) 951-2569 Calendar System: Semester
URL: www.philau.edu
Established: 1884 Annual Undergrad Tuition & Fees: $36,670
Enrollment: 3,762 Coed
Affiliation or Control: Independent Non-Profit IRS Status: 501(c)3
Highest Offering: Doctorate
Accreditation: M, ACBSP, ARCPA, ART, CIDA, ENG, LSAR, MIDWF, OT, OTA

01 President ..... Dr. Stephen SPINELLI, JR.
11 VP for Administration/COO ..... Dr. Geoffrey CROMARTY
10 Chief Financial Officer/Treasurer ..... Vacant
05 Provost ..... Mr. Matt BAKER
30 VP Development & Alumni Relations ..... Mr. Jesse SHAFER
26 Vice Pres Marketing/Public Rels ..... Ms. Patricia M. BALDRIDGE
13 Vice President/CIO ..... Mr. Jeff CEPULL
18 Asst Vice Pres for Operations ..... Mr. J. Thomas BECKER
15 Director Human Resources ..... Ms. Michele GILBERT
84 Dean of Enrollment Management ..... Ms. Christine GREB
32 Dean of Students ..... Dr. Henry HUMPHREYS
48 Exec Dean College of Architecture ..... Dr. Barbara KLINKHAMMER
81 Exec Dean Col Science & Health ..... Dr. Mike DRYER
54 Exec Dean Col Design Engr/Comm ..... Dr. Ron KANDER

50 Dean School of Business Admin .... Dr. Monica LAM
58 Director Acad Pgm Continuing Stds .... Ms. Susan CALDER
08 Director of Library Services .... Ms. Karen ALBERT
38 Director Advising/Counseling .... Vacant
41 Athletic Director .... Mr. Thomas R. SHIRLEY, JR.
29 Director Alumni Relations .... Ms. Melissa GARONZIK
36 Director of Career Services .... Ms. Tracy DEPEDRO
40 Director Bookstore .... Ms. Shirley A. LANDIS
37 Director Financial Aid .... Ms. Lisa J. COOPER
23 Director Health Services .... Ms. Megan O. GRUGAN
06 Interim Registrar .... Ms. Juanita WOMACK
39 Director of Residence Life Educ .... Mr. Dillon EPPENSTEIN
19 Director Safety & Security .... Mr. Jeffrey BAIRD
35 Assoc Dean Student Engagement .... Mr. Timothy J. BUTLER
09 Director of Institutional Research .... Mr. Mark PALLADINO
07 Director of Admissions .... Ms. Kidesti TEKLEGIORGIS

Pittsburgh Career Institute (A)

421 Seventh Avenue, Pittsburgh PA 15219-1907
County: Allegheny FICE Identification: 022023
Unit ID: 216782
Telephone: (412) 281-2600 Carnegie Class: Spec 2-yr-Health
FAX Number: (412) 227-0807 Calendar System: Other
URL: www.pci.edu
Established: 2014 Annual Undergrad Tuition & Fees: $17,850
Enrollment: 114 Coed
Affiliation or Control: Proprietary IRS Status: Proprietary
Highest Offering: Associate Degree
Accreditation: ACICS, COARC, DMS

01 Campus President .... Patti L. YAKSHE

Pittsburgh Institute of Aeronautics (B)

5 Allegheny County Airport, West Mifflin PA 15122-2674
County: Allegheny FICE Identification: 005310
Unit ID: 215381
Telephone: (412) 346-2100 Carnegie Class: Spec 2-yr-Tech
FAX Number: (412) 466-0513 Calendar System: Quarter
URL: www.pia.edu
Established: 1929 Annual Undergrad Tuition & Fees: $20,345
Enrollment: 382 Coed
Affiliation or Control: Independent Non-Profit IRS Status: 501(c)3
Highest Offering: Associate Degree
Accreditation: ACCSC

01 President/CFO .... Mr. John GRAHAM, III
03 Executive Vice President/Director .... Ms. Suzanne MARKLE
05 Director of Compliance .... Mr. Jason MONGAN
07 Director of Admissions .... Mr. Steven SABOLD

Pittsburgh Institute of Mortuary Science (C)

5808 Baum Boulevard, Pittsburgh PA 15206-3706
County: Allegheny FICE Identification: 010814
Unit ID: 215390
Telephone: (412) 362-8500 Carnegie Class: Spec 2-yr-A&S
FAX Number: (412) 362-1684 Calendar System: Trimester
URL: www.pims.edu
Established: 1939 Annual Undergrad Tuition & Fees: N/A
Enrollment: 217 Coed
Affiliation or Control: Independent Non-Profit IRS Status: 501(c)3
Highest Offering: Associate Degree
Accreditation: FUSER

01 President & CEO .... Eugene C. OGRODNIK
06 Registrar .... Karen S. ROCCO

Pittsburgh Technical Institute (D)

1111 McKee Road, Oakdale PA 15071-3205
County: Allegheny FICE Identification: 007437
Unit ID: 215415
Telephone: (412) 809-5100 Carnegie Class: Assoc/MT-VT-High Trad
FAX Number: (412) 809-5320 Calendar System: Quarter
URL: www.pti.edu
Established: 1946 Annual Undergrad Tuition & Fees: $16,192
Enrollment: 2,045 Coed
Affiliation or Control: Proprietary IRS Status: Proprietary
Highest Offering: Associate Degree
Accreditation: M, MAC, PNUR, SURGT

01 President .... Mr. Gregory DEFEO
03 Executive Vice President .... Mr. George PRY
05 Sr Vice Pres Academic Affairs .... Mr. Mark SCOTT
10 Sr Vice Pres Financial Affairs .... Mr. Terry FARRELL
26 Vice President of Marketing .... Mr. Bart LEVITT
10 Vice President of Business Affairs .... Mr. Chuck CUBELIC
21 Vice President Financial Services .... Mrs. Connie FRIEDBERG
32 Vice President Student Services .... Mr. Keith MERLINO
20 Vice President Education .... Ms. Eileen STEFFAN
30 Vice President of Inst Advancement .... Mrs. Ruth DELACH
09 Vice Pres of Strategic Initiatives .... Mr. Jeff BELSKY
43 General Counsel .... Mr. William KIEFER
06 Registrar .... Mrs. Patricia TARVIN
36 Director of Career Services .... Mrs. Josephine SMITH
27 Director of Public Relations .... Mrs. Linda ALLAN
15 Director of Human Resources .... Ms. Nancy SHEPPARD
13 IT Department Director .... Mr. Bill SHOWERS
19 Director of Public Safety .... Dr. James LAURIA
39 Director of Resident Life .... Ms. Gloria RITCHIE
88 Director of Compliance .... Ms. Melissa BROWN
40 Campus Store Manager .... Mrs. Cynthia KLEIN
29 Alumni Coordinator .... Mrs. Christine IOLI
105 Web Marketing Coordinator .... Mr. Tom ESTLACK
18 Director of Facilities Services .... Mr. Tom VUCELICH
37 Director Student Financial Aid .... Ms. Denise FISHER

Pittsburgh Theological Seminary (E)

616 N. Highland Avenue, Pittsburgh PA 15206-2596
County: Allegheny FICE Identification: 003356
Unit ID: 215424
Telephone: (412) 362-5610 Carnegie Class: Spec-4-yr-Faith
FAX Number: (412) 363-3260 Calendar System: Quarter
URL: www.pts.edu
Established: 1794 Annual Graduate Tuition & Fees: N/A
Enrollment: 219 Coed
Affiliation or Control: Presbyterian Church (U.S.A.) IRS Status: 501(c)3
Highest Offering: Doctorate; No Undergraduates
Accreditation: M, THEOL

01 President .... Dr. David V. ESTERLINE
05 VP Academic Affs/Dean of Faculty .... Dr. Heather H. VACEK
30 VP Strategic Advance/Mktg .... Vacant
32 VP Student Svcs/Dean of Students .... Mr. John WELCH
45 VP Planning/Inst Effectiveness .... Dr. James DOWNEY
10 Vice Pres Finance & Administration .... Ms. Ann GETKIN
06 Registrar .... Ms. Anne E. MALONE
08 Director of the Library .... Ms. Michelle SPOMER
88 Director of Field Education .... Dr. Catherine M. BRALL
29 Director of Alumni/ae Services .... Ms. Carolyn CRANSTON
88 Director Doctor of Ministry Program .... Dr. Susan KENDALL
51 Director Continuing Education .... Dr. Helen BLIER
37 Director of Financial Aid .... Ms. Cheryl DEPAOLIS
84 Director of Enrollment Mgmt .... Rev. Derek DAVENPORT
07 Director of Admissions .... Rev. Anthony RIVERA

Point Park University (F)

201 Wood Street, Pittsburgh PA 15222-1984
County: Allegheny FICE Identification: 003357
Unit ID: 215442
Telephone: (412) 391-4100 Carnegie Class: Masters/L
FAX Number: (412) 392-3998 Calendar System: Semester
URL: www.pointpark.edu
Established: 1960 Annual Undergrad Tuition & Fees: $28,250
Enrollment: 3,737 Coed
Affiliation or Control: Independent Non-Profit IRS Status: 501(c)3
Highest Offering: Doctorate
Accreditation: M, DANCE, ENGT, IACBE

01 President .... Dr. Paul HENNIGAN
05 Provost .... Dr. John PEARSON
10 Sr VP Finance and Operations .... Ms. Bridget MANCOSH
43 Sr VP and General Counsel .... Ms. Amy Elizabeth MCCALL
26 VP of External Affairs .... Ms. Mariann K. GEYER
84 Vice Pres Enrollment Management .... Mr. Gary BRACKEN
30 Vice Pres Development/Alumni Rels ...... Ms. Sharon M. NAVONEY
32 VP of Student Affairs .... Mr. Keith PAYLO
15 VP of Human Resources .... Ms. Lisa STEFANKO
07 Asst Vice Pres for Admissions .... Ms. Trudy WILLIAMS
96 Asst VP Procurement/Business Svcs .... Ms. Ruth RAULUK
18 Vice President of Operations .... Mr. Christopher J. HILL
19 AVP Public Safety/Chief Police .... Mr. Jeffrey D. BESONG
09 AVP Institutional Research .... Mr. Christopher E. CHONCEK
21 AVP of Finance .... Mr. Jim HARDT
53 Chair Education .... Dr. Darlene MARNICH
79 Chair Humanities/Human Science .... Dr. Brent ROBBINS
54 Chair Natural Science/Engr Tech .... Dr. Gregg JOHNSON
88 Chair Criminal Justice/Intell Stds .... Mr. Michael BOTTA
88 Chair Management .... Mr. Steve TANZILLI
50 Chair Business .... Mr. Ed SCOTT
88 Chair Theatre .... Ms. Sheila MCKENNA
88 Chair Dance .... Mr. Ruben GRACIANI
88 Chair Cinema .... Vacant
88 Chair Literary Arts .... Dr. Sarah PERRIER
60 Chair School of Communication .... Dr. Thom BAGGERMAN
04 Exec Assistant to the President .... Ms. Margaret SMITH
06 University Registrar .... Ms. Jennifer FEDELE
08 Director/Librarian/Academic Svcs .... Ms. Liz EVANS
27 Mng Dir Marketing/Public Relations .... Mr. Louis CORSARO
39 Director of Campus Life .... Ms. Janet D. EVANS
07 Director of Admissions .... Ms. Joell MINFORD
41 Director of Athletics .... Mr. Dan SWALGA
88 Dir Conference & Event Services .... Ms. Christina MORTON
38 Student Counseling .... Ms. Taffie BUCCI
106 Dir Online Education/E-learning .... Mr. Nelson CHIPMAN
29 Director Alumni Relations .... Ms. Sarah MYKSIN
37 Director Student Financial Aid .... Mr. George SANTUCCI
44 Director Annual or Planned Giving .... Ms. Greta DANIELS

Reading Area Community College (G)

PO Box 1706, Reading PA 19603-1706
County: Berks FICE Identification: 010388
Unit ID: 215585
Telephone: (610) 372-4721 Carnegie Class: Assoc/HT-Mix Trad/Non
FAX Number: (610) 372-4264 Calendar System: Semester
URL: www.racc.edu
Established: 1971 Annual Undergrad Tuition & Fees (In-District): $5,130
Enrollment: 4,198 Coed
Affiliation or Control: State/Local IRS Status: 501(c)3
Highest Offering: Associate Degree
Accreditation: M, ADNUR, COARC, MLTAD, PNUR

84 Dean of Enrollment Management .... Ms. Kay LITMAN
01 President .... Dr. Anna D. WEITZ
05 Sr VP of Academic Affairs/Provost .... Dr. Susan D. LOONEY
10 Sr VP Fin & Admin Svcs/Treasurer .... Mr. Kenneth DEARSTYNE
103 VP Workforce Dev/Community Educ .... Vacant
30 VP External Aff/Exec Dir Foundation .... Mr. Michael NAGEL
32 Dean of Student Affairs .... Ms. Maria MITCHELL
21 Assoc VP for Bus Svcs/Controller .... Ms. Dolores PETERSON
62 Asst Dean Library Svcs/Learning Res ... Ms. Mary Ellen HECKMAN
15 Director Human Resources .... Vacant
26 Director Marketing/Communications .... Vacant
13 Director Information Technology .... Mr. Chet WINTERS
09 Dir of Asessment/Research/Planning .... Ms. Mary FLAGG
37 Director Financial Aid/Registrar ..... Mr. Benjamin ROSENBERGER
57 Dir of Miller Center for the Arts .... Ms. Cathleen STEPHEN
25 Dir Grant Dev/Mgmt/Title IX Coord .... Ms. Patricia HELFENSTEIN
96 Purchasing Manager .... Mr. Michael HODOWANEC
19 Director of Safety & Security .... Vacant
35 Coordinator of Student Activities .... Ms. Kimberly UPHOLD
04 Exec Admin Asst to the President .... Ms. Sandra STRAUSE
50 Asst Dean of Business Division .... Ms. Linda BELL
76 Asst Dean of Health Professions .... Dr. Amelia CAPOTOSTA
79 Asst Dean of Comm/Arts/Humanities .... Mr. Kevin COOTS
81 Asst Dean of Science/Math .... Dr. Gloria OIKELOME
83 Int Asst Dean of Soc Sci/Hum Svc .... Dr. Robin ECKERT
07 Dir Admiss & Enrollment Svcs .... Dr. Agibail WERNICKI
20 Dean of Instruction .... Ms. Cynthia SEAMAN

Reconstructionist Rabbinical College (H)

1299 Church Road, Wyncote PA 19095-1898
County: Montgomery FICE Identification: 022734
Unit ID: 215619
Telephone: (215) 576-0800 Carnegie Class: Spec-4-yr-Faith
FAX Number: (215) 576-6143 Calendar System: Semester
URL: www.rrc.edu
Established: 1968 Annual Graduate Tuition & Fees: N/A
Enrollment: 45 Coed
Affiliation or Control: Jewish IRS Status: 501(c)3
Highest Offering: Doctorate; No Undergraduates
Accreditation: M

01 President .... Rabbi Deborah WAXMAN
05 Vice Pres Academic Affairs .... Dr. Elsie STERN
10 Int VP/CFO/Chief Admin Officer .... Mr. Ken HUTTON
31 Int VP Community Engagement .... Rabbi David TEUTSCH
45 VP Strategic Advancement .... Dr. Josh PESKIN
32 VP Student Development .... Rabbi Amber POWERS
30 Asst Vice Pres Development .... Ms. Barbara G. LISSY
08 Acting Library Director .... Mr. Alan LAPAYOVER

Reformed Episcopal Seminary (I)

826 Second Avenue, Blue Bell PA 19422-1257
County: Montgomery Identification: 667050
Unit ID: 216348
Telephone: (610) 292-9852 Carnegie Class: Not Classified
FAX Number: (610) 292-9853 Calendar System: Quarter
URL: www.reseminary.edu
Established: 1887 Annual Graduate Tuition & Fees: N/A
Enrollment: N/A Coed
Affiliation or Control: Reformed Episcopal Church IRS Status: 501(c)3
Highest Offering: Master's; No Undergraduates
Accreditation: THEOL

01 Chancellor and President .... Rt Rev. David L. HICKS
05 Dean and Vice President .... Rev Dr. Jonathan S. RICHES
08 Librarian .... Rev. Russell BUCHANAN
07 Director of Admissions & Recruiting .... Mr. David A. FRANCE
18 Maintenance/Grounds Supervisor .... Mr. Shawn RILEY
13 Director Information & Technology .... Mr. Gregory R. WRIGHT

Reformed Presbyterian Theological Seminary (J)

7418 Penn Avenue, Pittsburgh PA 15208-2594
County: Allegheny FICE Identification: 003358
Unit ID: 215628
Telephone: (412) 731-6000 Carnegie Class: Spec-4-yr-Faith
FAX Number: (412) 731-4834 Calendar System: Quarter
URL: www.rpts.edu
Established: 1810 Annual Graduate Tuition & Fees: $11,520
Enrollment: 76 Coed
Affiliation or Control: Reformed Presbyterian Church IRS Status: 501(c)3
Highest Offering: Doctorate; No Undergraduates
Accreditation: THEOL

01 President .... Dr. Jerry F. O'NEILL
05 Dean of the Faculty .... Mr. Barry YORK
06 Registrar/Head Librarian .... Mr. Thomas G. REID, JR.
40 Bookstore Manager .... Mrs. Vicki SMITH
10 Treasurer .... Mr. James MCFARLAND
07 Director of Admissions .... Mr. Edwin BLACKWOOD
37 Director of Financial Aid .... Mrs. Sharon SAMPSON
30 Dir of Institutional Advancement .... Mr. Mark SAMPSON
04 Administrative Asst to President .... Mrs. Vicki SMITH
18 Chief Facilities/Physical Plant .... Rev. Andrew JACKSON
32 Chief Student Affairs/Student Life .... Rev. Edwin BLACKWOOD

The Restaurant School at Walnut Hill College (A)

4207 Walnut Street, Philadelphia PA 19104-3518
County: Philadelphia FICE Identification: 021928
Unit ID: 215637
Telephone: (215) 222-4200 Carnegie Class: Spec-4-yr-Other
FAX Number: (215) 222-4219 Calendar System: Other
URL: www.walnuthillcollege.edu
Established: 1974 Annual Undergrad Tuition & Fees: $23,550
Enrollment: 396 Coed
Affiliation or Control: Proprietary IRS Status: Proprietary
Highest Offering: Baccalaureate
Accreditation: ACCSC

01 President ... Mr. Daniel LIBERATOSCIOLI
03 Executive Vice President ... Mr. Karl D. BECKER
11 Vice President Administrative Svcs ... Ms. Peggy LIBERATOSCIOLI
10 Vice President of Operations ... Mr. Dennis LIBERATI
88 Vice President of Culinary Arts ... Chef Gary TREVISANI
05 Chief Academic Officer ... Mr. David MORROW
07 Director of Admissions ... Mr. John ENGLISH
21 Chief Business Officer ... Mr. Chris MOLZ
32 Dir Student/Community Engagement ... Ms. Meghan BLOOME
37 Director Financial Aid ... Ms. Caitlin SNEDEKER
50 Director School of Management ... Mr. David MORROW

Robert Morris University (B)

6001 University Boulevard,
Moon Township PA 15108-1189
County: Allegheny FICE Identification: 003359
Unit ID: 215655
Telephone: (412) 397-6400 Carnegie Class: DU-Mod
FAX Number: (412) 397-5958 Calendar System: Semester
URL: www.rmu.edu
Established: 1921 Annual Undergrad Tuition & Fees: $27,194
Enrollment: 5,555 Coed
Affiliation or Control: Independent Non-Profit IRS Status: 501(c)3
Highest Offering: Doctorate
Accreditation: M, BUS, CS, ENG, NMT, NURSE, TEAC

01 President ... Dr. Christopher HOWARD
10 Sr Vice Pres for Business Affairs ... Mr. Dan W. KIENER
05 Provost/Sr VP Academic Affairs ... Mr. David L. JAMISON
30 Sr VP Institutional Advancement ... Mr. Jay T. CARSON
43 Vice President & General Counsel ... Ms. Renee T. CAVALOVITCH
21 Vice President Financial Operations ... Mr. Jeffrey A. LISTWAK
15 Vice President of Human Resources ... Ms. Ellen G. WIECKOWSKI
106 Vice President & Sr Vice Provost ... Dr. Derya A. JACOBS
84 VP Enrollment Management ... Ms. Wendy C. BECKEMEYER
32 Vice President for Student Life ... Mr. John MICHALENKO
30 Vice President for Development ... Ms. Kimberley A. HAMMER
13 Vice Pres Information Technology ... Ms. Ellen G. WIECKOWSKI
18 Vice Pres for Facilities ... Mr. Perry F. ROOFNER
26 Vice Pres Public Rels/Marketing ... Mr. Jonathan POTTS
20 Vice Provost for Academic Affairs ... Dr. Lawrence A. TOMEI
46 Vice Pres & Senior Vice Provost ... Dr. Derya JACOBS
09 Vice Provost ... Dr. David R. MAJKA
60 Dean School Comm/Info Systems ... Dr. AnnMarie M. LEBLANC
50 Acting Dean School of Business ... Dr. Lois D. BRYAN
54 Dean School of Engr/Math/Science ... Dr. Maria V. KALEVITCH
53 Dean Sch Education/Social Sciences ... Dr. Mary Ann RAFOTH
66 Dean School Nursing/Health ... Dr. Valerie M. HOWARD
88 Dir Univ Sponsorships/Athletic Fund ... Mr. Matthew B. MILLET
07 Dean of Admissions ... Ms. Kellie L. LAURENZI
88 Exec Dir Bayer Ctr Nonprofit Mgmt ... Ms. Peggy M. OUTON
35 Assistant Dean of Students ... Mrs. Maureen H. KEEFER
41 Director of Athletics ... Dr. Craig S. COLEMAN
08 Director University Library ... Dr. Timothy M. SCHLAK
21 Chief Accounting Officer/Controller ... Ms. Melissa A. MICCO
06 Registrar/Exec Dir of Academic Svcs ... Mr. Frank E. PERRY
19 Director Public Safety ... Mr. Randy L. MINK
36 Director Career Center ... Ms. Kishma DECASTRO-SALLIS
39 Director Residence Life ... Mrs. Anne L. LAHODA
38 Director Center for Student Success ... Ms. Cassandra L. ODEN
28 Chief Diversity/Inclusion Officer ... Dr. Yasmin S. PUROHIT
27 Senior Director Public Relations ... Mr. Jonathan POTTS
109 Sr Director Financial Operations ... Anita NILKANT
37 Director Student Financial Aid ... Ms. Stephanie N. HENDERSHOT
29 Asst Dir Alumni Relations ... Mary C. GERAD

Rosedale Technical Institute (C)

215 Beecham Drive, Suite 2, Pittsburgh PA 15205-9791
County: Allegheny FICE Identification: 012050
Unit ID: 215682
Telephone: (412) 521-6200 Carnegie Class: Spec 2-yr-Tech
FAX Number: (412) 521-2520 Calendar System: Semester
URL: www.rosedaletech.org
Established: 1949 Annual Undergrad Tuition & Fees: $12,770
Enrollment: 440 Coed
Affiliation or Control: Independent Non-Profit IRS Status: 501(c)3
Highest Offering: Associate Degree
Accreditation: ACCSC

01 President ... Dennis F. WILKE
05 Director of Education ... Kara CHAN
07 Director of Admissions ... Debbie BIER

Rosemont College (D)

1400 Montgomery Avenue, Rosemont PA 19010-1699
County: Montgomery FICE Identification: 003360
Unit ID: 215691
Telephone: (610) 527-0200 Carnegie Class: Masters/M
FAX Number: (610) 527-0341 Calendar System: Semester
URL: www.rosemont.edu
Established: 1921 Annual Undergrad Tuition & Fees: $32,500
Enrollment: 890 Coed
Affiliation or Control: Roman Catholic IRS Status: 501(c)3
Highest Offering: Master's
Accreditation: M

37 Dir Enrollment Svcs/Fin Compliance ... Ms. Deborah CAWLEY
05 Provost/VP Academic/Student Affairs ... Dr. B. Christopher DOUGHERTY
10 VP for Finance & Administration ... Dr. Randy ELDRIDGE
30 Vice Pres College Relations ... Ms. Christyn MORAN
32 Dean of Students ... Mr. Troy CHIDDICK
84 Vice President for Enrollment Mgmt ... Mr. Dennis J. MURPHY
88 Vice President for Mission ... Sr. Jeanne Marie HATCH, SHCJ
08 Exec Director of Library Services ... Mrs. Catherine FENNELL
58 Dean Schools Graduate/Prof Studies ... Dr. Dennis R. DOUGHERTY
20 Academic Dean Undergrad College ... Mrs. Paulette HUTCHINSON
06 Registrar/Dir of Inst Research ... Ms. Jennifer HAWKES
29 Director of Alumni Relations ... Mr. Kevin GARY
26 Managing Director of Communications ... Ms. Roberta PERRY
41 Director of Athletics ... Ms. Lynn S. ROTHENHOEFER
38 Director Student Counseling ... Ms. Bonnie MARSHALL
15 Asst VP Human Resources ... Ms. Jane FEDEROWICZ
42 Director of Campus Ministry ... Mr. Jay VERZOSA
18 Director of Operations ... Mr. Raymond A. BROWN
39 Asst Director of Residence Life ... Ms. Devan EVERETT
19 Director of Public Safety ... Mr. Osmond MBAERI
07 Associate Director of Admissions ... Ms. Bettsy THOMMEN
01 President ... Dr. Sharon LATCHAW HIRSH
21 Controller ... Ms. Faith BYRNE

Saint Charles Borromeo Seminary (E)

100 E Wynnewood Road, Wynnewood PA 19096-3099
County: Montgomery FICE Identification: 003364
Unit ID: 216047
Telephone: (610) 667-3394 Carnegie Class: Spec-4-yr-Faith
FAX Number: (610) 667-7635 Calendar System: Semester
URL: www.scs.edu
Established: 1832 Annual Undergrad Tuition & Fees: $20,050
Enrollment: 204 Male
Affiliation or Control: Roman Catholic IRS Status: 501(c)3
Highest Offering: Master's
Accreditation: M, THEOL

01 Rector & President ... M.Rev. Timothy C. SENIOR
05 Vice President for Academic Affairs ... Rev. Robert A. PESARCHICK
03 Vice Rector Theology/Dir of Liturgy ... Rev. Patrick J. WELSH
03 Vice Rector of the College ... Rev. Joseph SHENOSKY
10 Chief Financial Officer ... Mr. Stephen DOLAN
108 VP Info Services & Assessment ... Mrs. Cait KOKOLUS
33 Dean of Men Theology ... Rev. Brian KANE
33 Dean of Men College ... Rev. George SZPARAGOWSKI
08 Director of Library Services ... Mr. James HUMBLE
06 Registrar ... Mrs. Shura SULLIVAN
42 Dir Spiritual Formation College ... Fr. Herb SPERGER
42 Dir Spiritual Formation Theology ... Fr. Ned SHLESINGER
88 Director Pastoral/Apostolic Form ... Rev. Augustine ESPOSITO
73 Dean School of Theological Studies ... Rev. John AMES
64 Director of Music ... Mr. Rudolph LUCENTE
21 Director of Financial Services ... Ms. Barbara COADY
37 Director Student Financial Aid ... Ms. Nora DOWNEY
19 Director of Safety and Security ... Mr. Nicholas MANCINI

Saint Francis University (F)

PO Box 600, Loretto PA 15940-0600
County: Cambria FICE Identification: 003366
Unit ID: 215743
Telephone: (814) 472-3000 Carnegie Class: Masters/L
FAX Number: (814) 472-3003 Calendar System: Semester
URL: www.francis.edu
Established: 1847 Annual Undergrad Tuition & Fees: $32,178
Enrollment: 2,667 Coed
Affiliation or Control: Roman Catholic IRS Status: 501(c)3
Highest Offering: Doctorate
Accreditation: M, ARCPA, ENG, EXSC, IACBE, NURSE, OT, PTA, SW

01 President ... Rev. Malachi VAN TASSELL, TOR
05 Provost ... Dr. Wayne POWEL
10 Vice President for Finance ... Mr. Jeffrey SAVINO
32 Vice Pres for Student Development ... Dr. Frank MONTECALVO
42 Director of Mission Integration ... Rev. Joseph LEHMAN
30 Vice President for Advancement ... Mr. Robert CRUSCIEL
84 Vice Pres for Enrollment Management ... Ms. Erin E. MCCLOSKEY
08 Dean of Library Services ... Ms. Sandra A. BALOUGH
97 Assoc Dean of General Education ... Ms. Martha O'BRIEN
06 Registrar ... Dr. Stephen R. ROMBOUTS
09 Director of Institutional Research ... Ms. Kate DEATER
37 Financial Aid Director ... Mr. Jamie KOSH
26 Director Marketing & Public Affairs ... Ms. Marie YOUNG
44 Director of Development ... Ms. Marie B. MELUSKY
38 Director of Counseling Center ... Mr. David P. WILSON
13 Director Computer Services ... Mr. George F. PYO
29 Director of Alumni Relations ... Ms. Jaimie STEEL
51 Director Continuing Education ... Ms. Julie BARRIS
18 Director of Physical Plant ... Mr. Doug EPPLEY
21 Controller ... Mr. Thomas R. FRITZ
41 Director of Athletics ... Mr. Bob S. KRIMMEL
88 Dir Small Business Devel Center ... Mr. Barry SURMA
19 University Police ... Capt. Robert FATULA
39 Director of Residence Life ... Mr. Donald MILES
42 Director of Campus Ministry ... Rev. Christopher DOBSON
88 Dir Center for Academic Success ... Ms. Renee BERNARD
35 Dir of Student Engagement ... Mr. Bobby ANDERSON
15 Director of Human Resources ... Ms. Marian BENDER
28 Director of Multicultural Affairs ... Ms. Lynne BANKS
96 Director of Purchasing ... Mr. Caleb DRENNING
20 Associate Provost ... Dr. Peter R. SKONER
40 Manager of Bookstore ... Ms. Barbara SHINGLE

Saint Joseph's University (G)

5600 City Avenue, Philadelphia PA 19131-1376
County: Philadelphia FICE Identification: 003367
Unit ID: 215770
Telephone: (610) 660-1000 Carnegie Class: Masters/L
FAX Number: (610) 660-3300 Calendar System: Semester
URL: www.sju.edu
Established: 1851 Annual Undergrad Tuition & Fees: $42,180
Enrollment: 8,974 Coed
Affiliation or Control: Roman Catholic IRS Status: 501(c)3
Highest Offering: Doctorate
Accreditation: M, BUS, BUSA, CS

01 President ... Dr. Mark C. REED
05 Provost ... Dr. Jeanne F. BRADY
88 Associate Provost for Mission ... Dr. E. Springs STEELE
32 VP Student Life/Assoc Provost ... Dr. Cary M. ANDERSON
11 Vice Pres Administrative Services ... Mr. Kevin W. ROBINSON
30 VP University Advancement ... Mr. Martin F. FARRELL
26 Vice President External Affairs ... Ms. Joan F. CHRESTAY
10 Vice President Financial Affairs ... Mr. David R. BEAUPRE
15 VP Human Resources ... Ms. Sharon O'GRADY EISENMANN
27 VP Marketing & Communications ... Mr. Joseph M. LUNARDI
39 VP Campus Life ... Dr. John A. JEFFERY
43 General Counsel ... Ms. Marianne SCHIMELFINIG
100 Assistant Vice President ... Ms. Sarah F. QUINN
20 Associate Provost Faculty Support ... Dr. Paul ASPAN
49 Interim Dean Col Arts & Sciences ... Dr. Richard A. WARREN
50 Dean Haub School of Business ... Dr. Joseph A. DIANGELO, JR.
41 Vice Pres/Director Athletics ... Mr. Dominick J. DIJULIA
58 Exec Dir Graduate A&S ... Dr. Elisabeth M. WOODWARD
84 Int Assoc Provost Enrollment Mgt ... Mr. Robert J. MCBRIDE
06 University Registrar ... Mr. Scott J. SPENCER
08 Director Drexel Library ... Ms. Anne Z. KRAKOW
21 Assoc VP Fin Planning & Analysis ... Ms. Stephanie PRICKEN
21 Assoc VP & Controller ... Mr. Joseph CASSIDY
86 Asst VP Govt & Community Rels ... Mr. Wadell RIDLEY, JR.
35 Asst VP Student Educ Support Svcs ... Dr. Kimberly M. ALLEN-STUCK
29 Asst Vice Pres Alumni Relations ... Mr. Thomas MONAGHAN
13 Chief Information Officer ... Mr. Francis J. DISANTI
88 Asst Provost for Operations ... Ms. Dawn M. BURDSALL
88 Asst VP Student Development ... Dr. Mary Elaine PERRY
24 Exec Dir Acad Tech/Dist Learning ... Dr. David LEES
07 Asst Prov Undergrad Admiss/Enroll ... Ms. Maureen MATHIS
42 Director Campus Ministry ... Mr. Thomas J. SHEIBLEY
36 Exec Director Career Dev Center ... Ms. Trish SHAFER
38 Director Counseling/Pers Dev Ctr ... Dr. Gregory NICHOLLS
18 Director Facilities Management ... Mr. Kevin M. KANE
37 Dir Student Records/Financial Svcs ... Ms. Eileen TUCKER
28 Director of Inclusion and Diversity ... Ms. Monica M. SMITH
19 Director Public Safety & Security ... Mr. John GALLAGHER
96 Director Purchasing ... Mr. William O. ANDERSON
23 Director Student Health Service ... Ms. Laura HURST
35 Dir Student Leadership/Activities ... Dr. Beth HAGOVSKY
09 Asst Prov Inst Effectiveness/Rsrch ... Ms. Wenjun CHI
04 Executive Asst to President ... Ms. Helene TAYLOR
102 Dir Foundation/Corporate Relations ... Ms. Georgette HAMATY
104 Director International Programs ... Mr. Thomas L. KESARIS
25 Director Academic Research Svcs ... Mr. Thomas J. KAEO
44 Director Planned Giving ... Ms. Anat BECKER

St. Tikhon's Orthodox Theological Seminary (H)

PO Box 130, South Canaan PA 18459-0130
County: Wayne FICE Identification: 039193
Unit ID: 216180
Telephone: (570) 561-1818 Carnegie Class: Not Classified
FAX Number: N/A Calendar System: Semester
URL: www.stots.edu
Established: 1938 Annual Undergrad Tuition & Fees: N/A
Enrollment: N/A Coed
Affiliation or Control: Other IRS Status: 501(c)3
Highest Offering: First Professional Degree
Accreditation: THEOL

01 President ... Metr. Tikhon MOLLARD
03 Rector/CEO ... Abp. Michael DAHULICH
05 Dean/COO ... V.Rev. Steven A. VOYTOVICH
10 Chief Financial Officer ... V.Rev. Dennis SWENCKI
04 Administrative Asst to Dean/COO ... Ms. Teresa VAUX-MICHEL
06 Registrar ... Prof. Sergei D. ARHIPOV
20 Asst to Dean Academic Affairs ... Dr. Paul J. WITEK
30 Chief Development/Advancement ... Mr. Seraphim DANCKAERT

Saint Vincent College (A)

300 Fraser Purchase Road, Latrobe PA 15650-2690

County: Westmoreland | FICE Identification: 003368
Unit ID: 215798
Telephone: (724) 805-2500 | Carnegie Class: Bac-A&S
FAX Number: (724) 805-2019 | Calendar System: Semester
URL: www.stvincent.edu
Established: 1846 | Annual Undergrad Tuition & Fees: $32,392
Enrollment: 1,829 | Coed
Affiliation or Control: Roman Catholic | IRS Status: 501(c)3
Highest Offering: Doctorate
Accreditation: M, ACBSP

01 President .... Br. Norman W. HIPPS, OSB
03 Executive Vice President .... Rev. Paul TAYLOR, OSB
05 VP Academic Affairs .... Dr. John SMETANKA
10 VP/Chief Finance/Admin Officer .... Mr. Richard WILLIAMS
32 VP Student Affairs .... Ms. Mary COLLINS
26 VP Marketing and Communication .... Ms. Suzanne ENGLISH
07 Dean of Admissions .... Mr. Stephen NEITZ
13 Chief Information Officer .... Mr. Peter E. MAHONEY
20 Dean of Studies .... Ms. Alice J. KAYLOR
50 Dean McKenna Sch Bus/Econ/Govt .... Dr. Gary QUINLIVAN
60 Dean Sch Soc Sci/Communication/Educ .... Dr. MaryBeth SPORE
79 Dean Humanities & Fine Arts .... Rev. Rene KOLLAR, OSB
81 Dean Science/Math & Computing .... Dr. Stephen M. JODIS
06 Registrar .... Ms. Celine R. BRUDNOK
08 Librarian .... Bro. David KELLY, OSB
29 Director of Alumni Affairs .... Mr. Shawn GOUCH
27 Director of Public Relations .... Mr. Donald A. ORLANDO
36 Director Career Services .... Ms. Courtney BAUM
15 Director of Human Resources .... Ms. Judith MAHER
42 Director of Campus Ministry .... Rev. Killian LOCH, OSB
23 Director Wellness Center .... Ms. Gretchen FLOCK
19 Director Public Safety .... Mr. Steve BROWN
41 Athletic Director .... Rev. Myron KIRSCH, OSB
39 Director Resident Life .... Mr. Robert BAUM
96 Dir of Purchasing/Chief Fire Dept .... Mr. Terry NOEL
09 Director of Institutional Research .... Ms. Julia CAVALLO
18 Director of Facility Management .... Mr. Larry HENDRICK
40 Manager Book Center .... Rev. Anthony GROSSI, OSB
88 Exec Dir Fred Rogers Center .... Mr. Rick FERNANDES
58 Coord of Graduate Studies .... Ms. Amanda GUNTHER
04 Administrative Asst to President .... Ms. Patricia OWENS
104 Director Study Abroad .... Ms. Sara HART
37 Director Student Financial Aid .... Ms. Mary GAZAL
102 Dir Foundation/Govt/Corporate Rels .... Ms. Christine FOSCHIA
43 Dir Legal Services/General Counsel .... Mr. Bruce ANTKOWIAK

Saint Vincent Seminary (B)

300 Fraser Purchase Road, Latrobe PA 15650-2690

County: Westmoreland | Identification: 666018
Unit ID: 215813
Telephone: (724) 805-2592 | Carnegie Class: Spec-4-yr-Faith
FAX Number: (724) 532-5052 | Calendar System: Semester
URL: www.saintvincentseminary.edu
Established: 1846 | Annual Undergrad Tuition & Fees: N/A
Enrollment: 45 | Coed
Affiliation or Control: Roman Catholic | IRS Status: 501(c)3
Highest Offering: Master's
Accreditation: THEOL

01 Rector .... V.Rev. Edward M. MAZICH, OSB
88 Director of Spiritual Formation .... Rev. Boniface N. HICKS, OSB
05 Academic Dean .... Rev. Patrick T. CRONAUER, OSB
20 Director of Human Formation .... Rev. John-Mary TOMPKINS, OSB
03 Vice-Rector .... Rev. John-Mary TOMPKINS, OSB
42 Director of Liturgy .... Rev. Cyprian G. CONSTANTINE, OSB
88 Director of Pastoral Formation .... Rev. Nathan MUNSCH, OSB
32 Dean of Students .... Rev. Emmanuel O. AFUNUGO
38 Dir of Pre-Theologian Formation .... Dr. Lawrence SUTTON

Salus University (C)

8360 Old York Road, Elkins Park PA 19027-1516

County: Philadelphia | FICE Identification: 003311
Unit ID: 214564
Telephone: (215) 780-1400 | Carnegie Class: Spec-4-yr-Other Health
FAX Number: (215) 780-1325 | Calendar System: Quarter
URL: www.salus.edu
Established: 1919 | Annual Undergrad Tuition & Fees: N/A
Enrollment: 1,124 | Coed
Affiliation or Control: Independent Non-Profit | IRS Status: 501(c)3
Highest Offering: Doctorate
Accreditation: M, #ARCPA, AUD, OPT, OPTR, OT, @SP

01 President .... Dr. Michael H. MITTLEMAN
05 Vice President Faculty Affairs .... Dr. Janice SCHARRE
10 Vice Pres Finance/Business Affairs .... Mr. Donald KATES
17 Vice Pres Clinical Services .... Dr. John GAAL
45 Vice President for Inst Planning .... Dr. Lawrence MCCLURE
32 Dean Student Affairs .... Dr. James CALDWELL
20 Exec Assistant to the Provost .... Ms. Karen BOYKIN
09 Asst Dir Research Admin .... Ms. Lydia PARKE
06 Registrar .... Ms. Shannon BOSS
13 Chief Information Officer .... Mr. William BRICHTA
38 Director Personal/Prof Development .... Dr. James CALDWELL
37 Assoc Dean Student Financial Affs .... Dr. H. Lawrence MCCLURE
18 Director Physical Plant .... Mr. Richard ECHEVARRI
30 Director of Development .... Ms. Lynne CORBOY
26 Director Publications/Communication .... Ms. Alexis ABATE
29 Director Alumni Relations/Giving .... Ms. Jamie LEMISCH
51 Coord Continuing/Post-Graduate Educ .... Mrs. Melissa VITEK
58 Chairperson Graduate Studies .... Vacant
40 Bookstore Manager .... Mr. Joe NOCE
24 Director Instructional Media .... Mr. Glenn ROEDEL
36 Dir Student Placement/Student Affs .... Vacant
84 Director Enrollment Management .... Dr. Jim CALDWELL
88 Exec Dir Inst Visually Impaired .... Dr. Audrey SMITH
08 Head Librarian .... Ms. Marietta DOOLEY
19 Director of Security .... Mr. Wayne PANCZA
15 Dir Human Res/Affirm Action/Facil .... Ms. Maura KEENAN
96 Director of Purchasing .... Ms. Lydia FRIEL

Seton Hill University (D)

1 Seton Hill Drive, Greensburg PA 15601-1599

County: Westmoreland | FICE Identification: 003362
Unit ID: 215947
Telephone: (724) 834-2200 | Carnegie Class: Masters/M
FAX Number: (724) 830-4611 | Calendar System: Semester
URL: www.setonhill.edu
Established: 1883 | Annual Undergrad Tuition & Fees: $32,420
Enrollment: 2,247 | Coed
Affiliation or Control: Roman Catholic | IRS Status: 501(c)3
Highest Offering: Master's
Accreditation: M, ARCPA, DENT, DIETC, IACBE, MFCD, MUS, SW

01 President .... Dr. Mary FINGER
32 VP Mission .... Sr. Vivien LINKHAUER, SC
05 Acting Provost .... Sr. Susan YOCHUM
10 Vice Pres Finance & Business .... Vacant
11 Vice Pres Administration/Registrar .... Mrs. Barbara C. HINKLE
44 Vice Pres Institutional Advancement .... Ms. Christine MUESELER
13 Chief Information Officer .... Ms. Melissa ALSING
84 Vice Pres Enrollment Management .... Mr. Brett FRESHOUR
21 Controller .... Mr. Paul EDSALL
35 Dean of Student Services .... Dr. Charmaine F. STRONG
07 Director Admissions .... Ms. Ashley JOSAY ZULLO
08 Director of Library .... Mr. David STANLEY
30 Director Development .... Ms. Molly ROBB SHIMKO
29 Director of Alumni Relations .... Ms. Mary COX
37 Director of Financial Aid .... Ms. Tracey DE BAEZ SNYDER
36 Director of Career Development .... Ms. Renee STAREK
15 Director Personnel Services .... Mrs. Darlene SAUERS
18 Director Facilities .... Mr. Bill VOKES
41 Executive Athletic Director .... Mr. Chris SNYDER
42 Director Campus Ministry .... Sr Maureen O'BRIEN
04 Assistant to the President .... Mrs. Carol BILLMAN
06 Registrar .... Ms. Barbara HINKLE
38 Director Student Counseling .... Ms. Teresa BASSI-COOK
09 Director of Institutional Research .... Mrs. Edith COOK
26 Chief Public Relations Officer .... Ms. Jennifer REEGER
96 Director of Purchasing .... Mr. Charles O'NEILL
19 Director Security/Safety .... Vacant
22 Dir Affirmative Action/EEO .... Ms. Darlene SAUERS
25 Chief Contracts/Grants Admin .... Ms. Cynthia FERRARI
39 Director Student Housing .... Mr. Cory CAMPBELL
86 Director Government Relations .... Mrs. Carol BILLMAN

South Hills School of Business and Technology (E)

541 58th Street, Altoona PA 16602

Telephone: (814) 944-6134 | Identification: 770772
Accreditation: ACICS, CAHIIM, MAAB

South Hills School of Business and Technology (F)

480 Waupelani Drive, State College PA 16801-4516

County: Centre | FICE Identification: 013263
Unit ID: 216083
Telephone: (814) 234-7755 | Carnegie Class: Assoc/MT-VT-High Trad
FAX Number: (814) 234-0926 | Calendar System: Quarter
URL: www.southhills.edu
Established: 1970 | Annual Undergrad Tuition & Fees: $16,521
Enrollment: 630 | Coed
Affiliation or Control: Proprietary | IRS Status: Proprietary
Highest Offering: Associate Degree
Accreditation: ACICS, CAHIIM, DMS, MAAB

00 Owner .... Mrs. Maralyn MAZZA
01 President .... Mr. S. Paul MAZZA, III
05 Director .... Mr. Mark MAGGS

Summit University of Pennsylvania (G)

538 Venard Road, Clarks Summit PA 18411-1297

County: Lackawanna | FICE Identification: 002670
Unit ID: 211024
Telephone: (570) 586-2400 | Carnegie Class: Spec-4-yr-Faith
FAX Number: (570) 586-1753 | Calendar System: Semester
URL: www.summit.edu
Established: 1932 | Annual Undergrad Tuition & Fees: $21,850
Enrollment: 836 | Coed
Affiliation or Control: Baptist | IRS Status: 501(c)3
Highest Offering: Doctorate
Accreditation: M, BI

01 President .... Dr. James R. LYTLE
05 VP of Academics .... Dr. William J. HIGLEY
10 CFO & COO .... Mr. Michael NOLAN
30 VP of Institutional Advancement .... Mrs. Lisa KONZELMAN
27 VP Communications/External Rels .... Mr. Mel WALKER
20 Interim Seminary Dean .... Dr. Wayne SLUSSER
32 VP of Student Development .... Mr. Roddy HANNAH
33 Associate Dean of Men .... Mr. Ted BOYKIN
34 Associate Dean of Women .... Mrs. Faye MOORE
04 Exec Dir of President's Office .... Dr. Lee KLIEWER
11 Exec Dir of Administrative Svcs .... Mr. Allen R. DREYER
08 Librarian .... Mr. Jeremy MCGINNISS
37 Interim Director of Financial Aid .... Mrs. Deb CRAGLE
26 Director Communications/Marketing .... Ms. Dena CAMBRA
19 Director Safety/Security .... Mr. Ken MORRIS
84 Exec Dir for Enrollment Management .... Mr. Drew WHIPPLE
18 Chief Facilities/Physical Plant .... Mr. Wayne STEVENS
13 Director of Information Technology .... Mr. Douglas HEITNER
73 Dean School of Theology .... Dr. David A. LACKEY
53 Dean of School of Education .... Dr. Ritch KELLEY
49 Dean of School of Arts & Sciences .... Dr. Janet K. HICKS
15 Director of Human Resources .... Mrs. Renelle THEODORE
106 Director of Distance Education .... Dr. Jim KING
41 Athletic Director .... Mr. Mike MCCARTY

Susquehanna University (H)

514 University Avenue, Selinsgrove PA 17870-1025

County: Snyder | FICE Identification: 003369
Unit ID: 216278
Telephone: (570) 374-0101 | Carnegie Class: Bac-A&S
FAX Number: (570) 372-4040 | Calendar System: Semester
URL: www.susqu.edu
Established: 1858 | Annual Undergrad Tuition & Fees: $42,040
Enrollment: 2,093 | Coed
Affiliation or Control: Evangelical Lutheran Church In America
IRS Status: 501(c)3
Highest Offering: Baccalaureate
Accreditation: M, BUS, MUS

01 President .... Dr. L. Jay LEMONS
100 VP & Chief of Staff .... Dr. Philip E. WINGER
05 Co-COO/Provost/Dean of Faculty .... Dr. Linda A. MCMILLIN
10 Co-COO & VP for Finance & Admin .... Mr. Michael COYNE
26 Vice President for Univ Relations .... Mr. Ronald A. COHEN
84 VP for Enrollment & Marketing .... Ms. Madeleine E. RHYNEER
32 VP Student Engagement & Success .... Ms. Lisa M. SCOTT
20 Assoc Provost/Dean A&S .... Dr. Valerie G. MARTIN
50 Dean Weis School of Business .... Dr. Marsha KELLIHER
27 Chief Communications Officer .... Ms. Angie BURROWS
30 Asst Vice President Gift Planning .... Mr. Doug SEABERG
04 Assistant to the President .... Ms. Joann B. MIERES
04 Senior Admin Asst to the President .... Ms. Sharon POPE
38 Asst Dean & Director of Counseling .... Dr. Stacey PEARSON-WHARTON
89 Director of First Year Experience .... Ms. Katherine BURR
28 Asst Dean Intercultural/Cmty Engage .... Ms. Dena SALERNO
07 Director of Admissions .... Mr. Philip BETZ
08 Director of the Library .... Ms. Katherine FURLONG
37 Director of Student Financial Svcs .... Ms. Erin M. WOLFE
06 Registrar .... Ms. Alison A. RICHARD
42 University Chaplain .... Rev. Scott M. KERSHNER
13 Chief Information Officer .... Mr. Mark D. HUBER
41 Director of Athletics .... Dr. Pamela SAMUELSON
18 Director of Facilities Management .... Mr. Chris C. BAILEY
36 Asst Provost Post-Graduate Outcomes .... Ms. Michaeline SHUMAN
88 Director of Event Management .... Ms. Brenda MULL
29 Asst VP Alumni/Parent & Donor .... Ms. Becky DEITRICK
09 Dir Institute Research/Asst Provost .... Dr. Colleen FLEWELLING
25 Grants Coordinator .... Mr. Malcolm DERK
104 Dean of Global Programs .... Dr. Scott MANNING
15 Director Human Resources .... Ms. Jennifer BUCHER
19 Director Public Safety .... Mr. David GARDNER
44 Director of the Annual Fund .... Vacant
92 Director of Honors Program .... Dr. Dave RAMSARAN

Swarthmore College (I)

500 College Avenue, Swarthmore PA 19081-1390

County: Delaware | FICE Identification: 003370
Unit ID: 216287
Telephone: (610) 328-8000 | Carnegie Class: Bac-A&S
FAX Number: (610) 328-8673 | Calendar System: Semester
URL: www.swarthmore.edu
Established: 1864 | Annual Undergrad Tuition & Fees: $47,442
Enrollment: 1,542 | Coed
Affiliation or Control: Independent Non-Profit | IRS Status: 501(c)3
Highest Offering: Baccalaureate
Accreditation: M, ENG

01 President .... Valerie A. SMITH
05 Provost .... Thomas STEPHENSON
10 Vice President Finance & Admin .... Gregory N. BROWN
30 Vice President Alumni/Development .... Karl CLAUSS
18 Vice Pres Facilities & Services .... C. Stuart HAIN
15 Vice Pres for Human Resources .... Pamela PRESCOD-CAESAR
26 VP/Communications & Secretary/Col .... Nancy NICELY
07 Vice Pres & Dean of Admissions .... Jim BOCK
21 Asst Vice Pres Finance & Controller .... Eileen E. PETULA
32 Dean of Students .... H. Elizabeth BRAUN
28 Assoc Dean of Diversity/Inclusion .... Sha Duncan SMITH
06 Registrar .... Martin O. WARNER

08	College Librarian	Peggy SEIDEN
09	Director Institutional Research	Robin H. SHORES
29	Director of Alumni Relations	Lisa LEE
37	Director of Financial Aid	Varo L. DUFFINS
36	Director Career Services	Nancy BURKETT
19	Director of Public Safety	Michael HILL
43	General Counsel/Asst Sec of College	Sharmaine LAMAR
23	Director Worth Health Center	Alice HOLLAND
38	Director Psychological Services	David RAMIREZ
41	Director Physical Educ/Athletics	Adam HERTZ
44	Director Annual and Parent Giving	Lisa SHAFER
13	Chief Info Technology Officer	Joel COOPER
35	Director Student Engagement	Rachel HEAD
104	Director Off-Campus Study	Pat MARTIN
39	Asst Dir Residential Communities	Isaiah THOMAS
04	Special Assistant to the President	Susan EAGAR

Talmudical Yeshiva of Philadelphia (A)

6063 Drexel Road, Philadelphia PA 19131-1296

County: Philadelphia FICE Identification: 012523
Unit ID: 216311
Telephone: (215) 473-1212 Carnegie Class: Spec-4-yr-Faith
FAX Number: (215) 477-5065 Calendar System: Semester
Established: 1953 Annual Undergrad Tuition & Fees: $8,750
Enrollment: 120 Male
Affiliation or Control: Independent Non-Profit IRS Status: 501(c)3
Highest Offering: Second Talmudic Degree
Accreditation: RABN

05	Dean	Rabbi Shmuel KAMENETSKY
05	Dean	Rabbi Yehuda SVEI
05	Dean	Rabbi Sholom KAMENETSKY

Temple University (B)

1801 N. Broad Street, Philadelphia PA 19122-6072

County: Philadelphia FICE Identification: 003371
Unit ID: 216339
Telephone: (215) 204-7000 Carnegie Class: DU-Highest
FAX Number: (215) 204-5694 Calendar System: Semester
URL: www.temple.edu
Established: 1884 Annual Undergrad Tuition & Fees (In-State): $15,188
Enrollment: 37,485 Coed
Affiliation or Control: State Related IRS Status: 501(c)3
Highest Offering: Doctorate
Accreditation: M, #ARCPA, ART, BUS, CAATE, CAHIIM, CARTE, CLPSY, DANCE, DENT, ENG, ENGT, HSA, IPSY, JOUR, LAW, LSAR, MED, MUS, NRPA, NURSE, OT, PCSAS, PH, PHAR, PLNG, POD, PTA, SCPSY, SP, SW, THEA

01	Acting President	Dr. Richard M. ENGLERT
03	VP for Public Affairs	Mr. William T. BERGMAN, JR.
05	Exec VP and Provost	JoAnne A. EPPS
43	VP & University Counsel	Mr. Michael B. GEBHARDT
32	VP for Student Affairs	Dr. Theresa A. POWELL
13	VP Computer/CIO	Cindy LEAVITT
17	Sr EVP for Health Affairs	Dr. Larry R. KAISER
03	Sr Vice Provost Strategic Comm	Dr. Elizabeth LEEBRON TUTELMAN
10	VP/CFO & Treasurer	Mr. Kenneth H. KAISER
29	VP Alumni Relations	Mr. Kenneth LAWRENCE, JR.
26	VP Strategic Marketing	Ms. Karen B. CLARKE
35	Assoc VP/Dean of Students	Dr. Stephanie IVES
30	VP Institutional Advancement	Mr. James DICKER
46	VP for Research Administration	Dr. Michele M. MASUCCI
18	VP Construction/Facilities & Ops	Mr. Gennaro J. LEVA
21	Sr Assoc VP Finance	Mr. William J. WILKINSON
88	Assoc VP Business Services	Mr. Michael D. SCALES
15	Assoc VP Human Resources	Ms. Sharon I. BOYLE
21	Assoc VP/Controller	Mr. David MARINO
22	Asst VP Inst Diversity	Dr. Tiffenia D. ARCHIE
11	Asst VP Fin/Admin & VP-CFO & Treas	Ms. Kathryn P. D'ANGELO
88	Vice Provost for Faculty Affairs	Dr. Kevin J. DELANEY
84	Senior Vice Provost Enrollment Mgmt	Mr. William N. BLACK
20	Sr Vice Provost Undergrad Studies	Dr. Peter JONES
20	Vice Prov Acad Affs/Assessment/ IR	Dr. Jodi LEVINE LAUFGRABEN
08	Dean for University Libraries	Mr. Joseph P. LUCIA
06	Registrar	Mr. Bhavesh BAMBHROLIA
41	Exec VP and COO	Mr. Kevin G. CLARK
38	Director Tuttleman Counseling Svcs	Dr. John L. DIMINO
36	Sr Director Career Services	Ms. Rosalie SHEMMER
09	Director IR/Assessment	Ms. Sally M. FRAZEE
88	Interim VP International Affairs	Martyn MILLER
88	Asst VP Student Affairs	Ms. Brooke WALKER
88	Asst VP Study Abroad	Ms. Denise A. CONNERTY
23	Sr Admin Student & Employee Health	Dr. Mark DENYS
37	Director Student Financial Services	Mr. Craig FENNELL
88	Vice Provost University College	Dr. Vicki Lewis MCGARVEY
96	Director Procurement/Purchasing	Ms. Donna SCHWEIBENZ
88	Assistant VP/Bursar	Mr. David R. GLEZERMAN
97	Director General Education	Dr. Istvan L. VARKONYI
12	Director TU Center City	Mr. William PARSHALL
88	Assoc Director Admissions	Ms. Laura S. REDDICK
40	Bookstore Manager	Ms. Amanda HOWE
49	Interim Dean Liberal Arts	Dr. William STULL
53	Dean of Education	Dr. Greg ANDERSON
61	Interim Dean Law School	Gregory M. MANDEL
64	Dean Boyer College of Music	Dr. Robert T. STROKER
57	Interim Dean Tyler School of Art	Ms. Hester STINNETT
50	Dean Tourism/Hospitality Mgmt	Dr. Moshe PORAT
52	Dean of Dentistry	Dr. Amid ISMAIL
63	Sr Exec VP Health Dean of Medicine	Dr. Larry KAISER
67	Dean of Pharmacy	Dr. Peter H. DOUKAS
54	Dean Engineering	Dr. Keya SADEGHIPOUR
88	Dean Podiatric Medicine	Dr. John A. MATTIACCI
72	Dean Science & Technology	Dr. Michael KLEIN
60	Dean Media & Communication	Mr. David BOARDMAN
76	Dean Health Prof & Social Work	Dr. Laura SIMINOFF
88	Dean of Tourism/Hospitality Mgmt	Dr. Moshe PORAT
88	Dean Temple Japan	Dr. Bruce STRONACH
88	Dean Temple Rome	Dr. Hilary L. LINK
07	Director of Admissions	Ms. Karin W. MORMANDO
101	VP & Secretary of Board of Trustees	Ms. Anne K. NADOL
19	Executive Director Public Safety	Mr. Charles LEONE

Thaddeus Stevens College of Technology (C)

750 E King Street, Lancaster PA 17602-3198

County: Lancaster FICE Identification: 007912
Unit ID: 216296
Telephone: (717) 299-7730 Carnegie Class: Assoc/HVT-High Trad
FAX Number: (717) 299-7748 Calendar System: Semester
URL: www.stevenscollege.edu
Established: 1905 Annual Undergrad Tuition & Fees (In-State): $7,430
Enrollment: 913 Coed
Affiliation or Control: State IRS Status: 501(c)3
Highest Offering: Associate Degree
Accreditation: M

01	President	Dr. William E. GRISCOM
05	Int Vice President Academic Affs	Dr. William THOMPSON
10	Vice President Finance and Admin	Mrs. Betty TOMPOS
32	Director for Student Services	Mr. Christopher METZLER
84	Dir Enrollment Services/Admissions	Dr. Erin NELSEN
08	Learning Resources Center Director	Ms. Sharon MCILHENNEY
108	Director Assessment/Accountability	Ms. Cheryl LUTZ
15	Director of Personnel Services	Ms. Sue EMSWILER
26	Dir of Marketing/Public Information	Mr. Adam AURAND
38	Director of Student Counseling	Ms. Debra SCHUCH
28	Director Multicultural Affairs	Mr. Paul CULBRETH
29	Alumni Foundation Exec Director	Mr. Alex MUNRO
37	Director Financial Aid/Registrar	Mr. Michael DEGROFT
41	Athletic Director	Mr. Christopher METZLER
30	Director of Development	Mr. Allen TATE
36	Director of Career Services	Ms. Laurie GROVE
39	Residence Life Advisor	Mr. Ernie BROWN
18	Facilities Maintenance Manager	Mr. Eugene DUNCAN, JR.

† Qualified individuals are eligible for full scholarships based on family/financial status.

Thiel College (D)

75 College Avenue, Greenville PA 16125-2181

County: Mercer FICE Identification: 003376
Unit ID: 216357
Telephone: (724) 589-2000 Carnegie Class: Bac-A&S
FAX Number: (724) 589-2850 Calendar System: Semester
URL: www.thiel.edu
Established: 1866 Annual Undergrad Tuition & Fees: $28,868
Enrollment: 1,074 Coed
Affiliation or Control: Evangelical Lutheran Church In America
IRS Status: 501(c)3
Highest Offering: Baccalaureate
Accreditation: M

01	President	Dr. Susan TRAVERSO
05	VP Academic Affairs/Dean of College	Dr. Lynn FRANKEN
30	Int Vice Pres College Advancement	Ms. Roberta LEONARD
10	Vice President Finance/Management	Mr. Robert SCHMOLL
13	Chief Information Officer	Vacant
04	Administrative Asst to President	Mrs. Linda NOCHTA
32	VP of Student Life	Mr. Michael MCKINNEY
84	VP Enrollment Management	Mr. Stephen LAZOWSKI
20	Assoc Academic Dean	Vacant
26	Dir Communications/Marketing	Mr. Jonathan L. SHEARER
41	Director of Athletics	Ms. Amy SCHAFER
44	Dir of Special & Planned Giving	Mr. Mario MARINI
29	Director of Alumni Development	Mr. Kraig SMITH
44	Director of Alumni Relations	Ms. Kelly SANZARI
18	Director of Facilities	Mr. Michael SHULTZ
08	Director Library	Mr. Allen MORRILL
15	Director Human Resources	Mrs. Jennifer CLARK
36	Assoc Dean of Career Development	Mr. Martin BLACK
19	Chief of Police/Dir Public Safety	Mr. Eric ALLEN
06	Registrar	Ms. Denise UREY
35	Assoc Dean of Students	Ms. Bobbi MUTINELLI
42	Campus Pastor	Rev. Jayne M. THOMPSON
07	Sr Assoc Director of Admissions	Mrs. Sonya L. LAPIKAS
37	Exec Director Financial Aid	Ms. Cynthia H. FARRELL
23	Director Student Health Services	Ms. Christine CIANCI

Thomas Jefferson University (E)

11th and Walnut Streets, Philadelphia PA 19107-5083

County: Philadelphia FICE Identification: 012393
Unit ID: 216366
Telephone: (215) 955-6000 Carnegie Class: Spec-4-yr-Med
FAX Number: (215) 955-3739 Calendar System: Quarter
URL: www.jefferson.edu
Established: 1824 Annual Undergrad Tuition & Fees: N/A
Enrollment: 3,606 Coed
Affiliation or Control: Independent Non-Profit IRS Status: 501(c)3
Highest Offering: Doctorate
Accreditation: M, ANEST, #ARCPA, CYTO, DENT, DMS, MED, MFCD, MT, NMT, NURSE, OT, PAST, PH, PHAR, PTA, RAD, RADDOS, RADMAG, RTT

01	President & CEO	Dr. Stephen K. KLASKO
03	EVP & Chief Operating Officer	Ms. Kathleen GALLAGHER
05	Provost	Dr. Mark L. TYKOCINSKI
26	Senior VP Univ Marketing/Relations	Vacant
10	Exec VP and CFO	Mr. Peter DEANGELIS
30	Sr VP Institutional Advancement	Dr. Elizabeth DALE
43	Sr VP & University Counsel	Ms. Cristina G. CAVALIERI
46	Assoc Provost Clinical Research	Dr. David WHELLAN
18	Sr Vice Pres for Facilities Mgmt	Mr. Ronald E. BOWLAN
15	SVP Human Resources	Mr. Jeffrey STEVENS
11	Vice President University Affairs	Ms. Janice MARINI
58	Dean Jeff College of Biomed Science	Dr. Gerald GRUNWALD
63	Dean Sidney Kimmel Medical College	Dr. Mark L. TYKOCINSKI
66	Dean Jefferson College of Nursing	Dr. Beth Ann SWAN
67	Dean Jefferson College of Pharmacy	Dr. Rebecca FINLEY
76	Interim Dean Jeff Coll Health Prof	Dr. Debra ZELNICK
69	Dean Jefferson Sch of Pop Health	Dr. David NASH
32	Dean of Student & Admissions SKMC	Dr. Clara A. CALLAHAN
07	Director of Admissions	Dr. Elizabeth BROOKS
06	University Registrar	Dr. Raelynn COOTER
29	Exec Director of Alumni Assoc SKMC	Ms. Cristina GESO
08	University Librarian	Mr. Anthony FRISBY
23	Medical Director Univ Health Svcs	Dr. Ellen M. O'CONNOR
24	Director Medical Media Services	Mr. Pejman MAKARECHI
35	Assoc VP Student Affairs	Ms. Jennifer FOGERTY
39	Manager Housing/Residence Life	Ms. Laurie YUNKE
37	Univ Director Student Financial Aid	Ms. Susan MCFADDEN
40	Director Bookstore	Ms. Charity MARSHALL
91	Chief Information Officer	Mr. Praveen CHOPRA
19	Director of Security	Mr. Joseph BYHAM
85	Dir International Exchange Services	Ms. Janice M. BOGEN
07	Dir Admission/Recruitment/Grad Stds	Mr. Marc STEARNS
28	Assoc Dean Diversity/Minority Affs	Dr. Bernard LOPEZ
96	Director of Purchasing	Mr. Robert C. BURKHOLDER
35	Associate Provost Student Affairs	Dr. Charles A. POHL
04	Executive Associate to President	Ms. Grace L. HARDESKI
09	Director of Institutional Research	Dr. Carolyn GIORDANO
101	Secretary of the Institution/Board	Ms. Michele R. DOUGHERTY
102	Dir Foundation/Corporate Relations	Ms. Molly GERBER
103	Dir Workforce/Career Development	Ms. Jennifer M. GRONSKY
105	Director Web Services	Ms. Chris MCNAMEE-SMITH
25	Chief Contracts/Grants Admin	Mr. Brian N. SQUILLA
36	Director Student Placement	Ms. Jennifer GRONSKY
38	Director Student Counseling	Dr. Deanna NOBLEZA
44	Director Annual or Planned Giving	Ms. Lisa REPKO
45	Chief Institutional Planning	Mr. John EKARIUS
84	Director Enrollment Management	Ms. Erin M. FINN
86	Director Government Relations	Mr. Hugh J. LAVERY
90	Director Academic Computing	Mr. Kenneth M. OEFFLER
22	Dir Affirmative Action/EEO	Mr. Joseph HILL
100	Chief of Staff	Mr. John EKARIUS
104	Director Study Abroad	Ms. Janice BOGEN
108	Director Institutional Assessment	Dr. Carolyn GIORDANO
13	Chief Info Technology Officer (CIO)	Mr. Praveen CHOPRA

Triangle Tech (F)

191 Performance Road, Sunbury PA 17801

Telephone: (570) 988-0700 Identification: 770586
Accreditation: ACCSC

Triangle Tech, Bethlehem (G)

3184 Airport Road, Bethlehem PA 18017

Telephone: (610) 691-1300 Identification: 770587
Accreditation: ACCSC

Triangle Tech, Dubois (H)

225 Tannery Row Rd, Falls Creek PA 15840

County: Clearfield FICE Identification: 021744
Unit ID: 216454
Telephone: (814) 371-2090 Carnegie Class: Assoc/HVT-Mix Trad/Non
FAX Number: (814) 371-9227 Calendar System: Semester
URL: www.triangle-tech.edu
Established: 1982 Annual Undergrad Tuition & Fees: $16,629
Enrollment: 147 Coed
Affiliation or Control: Proprietary IRS Status: Proprietary
Highest Offering: Associate Degree
Accreditation: ACCSC

01	Director	Mrs. Stephanie A. CRAIG
03	Assistant Director	Mr. Steve CURLL
05	Academic Affairs Advisor	Mrs. Joan HOCKMAN
07	Admiss/Recruiting/Training Coord	Mr. Drew GORDON
07	Admiss/Recruiting/Training Coord	Mrs. Joy BURKE
36	Career Advisor	Mr. Jarred HETRICK
37	Financial Aid Administrator	Ms. Michelle L. JASHINSKI

Triangle Tech, Erie (I)

2000 Liberty Street, Erie PA 16502-2594

County: Erie FICE Identification: 020902
Unit ID: 216427
Telephone: (814) 453-6016 Carnegie Class: Spec 2-yr-Tech
FAX Number: (814) 454-2818 Calendar System: Semester
URL: www.triangle-tech.edu
Established: 1976 Annual Undergrad Tuition & Fees: $16,383
Enrollment: 46 Coed

Affiliation or Control: Proprietary　IRS Status: Proprietary
Highest Offering: Associate Degree
Accreditation: ACCSC

00	CEO	Mr. James R. AGRAS
01	Campus Director	Mr. Ken ADAMS
03	Executive Vice President	Mr. Rudy K. AGRAS
07	Vice President of Admissions	Vacant

Triangle Tech, Greensburg (A)

222 E Pittsburgh Street, Suite A,
Greensburg PA 15601-3304
County: Westmoreland　FICE Identification: 021290
Unit ID: 216445
Telephone: (724) 832-1050　Carnegie Class: Spec 2-yr-Tech
FAX Number: (724) 834-0325　Calendar System: Semester
URL: www.triangle-tech.edu
Established: 1944　Annual Undergrad Tuition & Fees: $16,589
Enrollment: 186　Coed
Affiliation or Control: Proprietary　IRS Status: Proprietary
Highest Offering: Associate Degree
Accreditation: ACCSC

00	Chairman/CEO	James R. AGRAS
01	President	Timothy J. MCMAHON
11	Dir School Compliance/Operations	Deborah G. HEPBURN
12	Director of Branch Campus/CEO	George THIELER

Triangle Tech, Pittsburgh (B)

1940 Perrysville Avenue, Pittsburgh PA 15214-3897
County: Allegheny　FICE Identification: 007839
Unit ID: 216436
Telephone: (412) 359-1000　Carnegie Class: Assoc/HVT-High Non
FAX Number: (412) 359-1012　Calendar System: Semester
URL: www.triangle-tech.edu
Established: 1944　Annual Undergrad Tuition & Fees: $16,589
Enrollment: 226　Coed
Affiliation or Control: Proprietary　IRS Status: Proprietary
Highest Offering: Associate Degree
Accreditation: ACCSC

00	Chairman/CEO	James R. AGRAS
01	President	Timothy J. MCMAHON
07	Director of Admissions	Terry KUCIC
05	Senior Director	Deborah G. HEPBURN
12	School Director	Kendall THOMAS

Trinity Episcopal School for Ministry (C)

311 11th Street, Ambridge PA 15003-2397
County: Beaver　FICE Identification: 022993
Unit ID: 216463
Telephone: (724) 266-3838　Carnegie Class: Spec-4-yr-Faith
FAX Number: (724) 266-4617　Calendar System: Semester
URL: www.tsm.edu
Established: 1976　Annual Graduate Tuition & Fees: N/A
Enrollment: 173　Coed
Affiliation or Control: Protestant Episcopal　IRS Status: 501(c)3
Highest Offering: Doctorate; No Undergraduates
Accreditation: THEOL

01	Dean/President	V.Rev. Justyn TERRY
05	Academic Dean	Rev Dr. Mark STEVENSON
30	Dean Advancement/Dir DMin Degree	Rev Dr. H. Lawrence THOMPSON, III
32	Director of Student Life	Mr. Geoffrey MACKEY
06	Registrar/Financial Aid Director	Ms. Stacey WILLIARD
07	Director of Recruitment	Rev. Aidan SMITH
08	Library Director	Ms. Susanah HANSON
11	Dean of Administration	Mrs. Karen GETZ
44	Director of Development	Mr. Jerry MOTE
04	Administrative Asst to President	Ms. Megan CAREY
26	Director of Communications	Rev. Christopher M. KLUKAS

The University of the Arts (D)

320 S Broad Street, Philadelphia PA 19102-4944
County: Philadelphia　FICE Identification: 003350
Unit ID: 215105
Telephone: (215) 717-6000　Carnegie Class: Spec-4-yr-Arts
FAX Number: (215) 717-6045　Calendar System: Semester
URL: www.uarts.edu
Established: 1876　Annual Undergrad Tuition & Fees: $39,908
Enrollment: 1,894　Coed
Affiliation or Control: Independent Non-Profit　IRS Status: 501(c)3
Highest Offering: Master's
Accreditation: M, ART, MUS

01	President	Dr. David YAGER
05	Provost	Dr. Patricia KUCKER
30	Vice Pres Advancement	Ms. Josephine BURRI
100	Chief of Staff	Ms. Anna NAGY
10	Vice Pres Finance/Administration	Mr. Stephen LIGHTCAP
13	Vice Pres Technology & Info Svcs	Mr. Thomas CARNWATH
84	VP Enroll Mgmt/Retention/Stdnt Affs	Mr. Rick LONGO
06	Registrar	Mr. Shawn GREEN
04	Sr Administrative Assistant	Ms. Francina GIRARD

University of Pennsylvania (E)

1 College Hall, Room 100, Philadelphia PA 19104-6830
County: Philadelphia　FICE Identification: 003378
Unit ID: 215062
Telephone: (215) 898-5000　Carnegie Class: DU-Highest
FAX Number: (215) 898-5756　Calendar System: Semester
URL: www.upenn.edu
Established: 1740　Annual Undergrad Tuition & Fees: $49,536
Enrollment: 24,806　Coed
Affiliation or Control: Independent Non-Profit　IRS Status: 501(c)3
Highest Offering: Doctorate
Accreditation: M, ANEST, BUS, CEA, CLPSY, CS, DENT, ENG, IPSY, LAW, LSAR, MED, MIDWF, NURSE, PAST, PCSAS, PH, PLNG, SW, VET

01	President	Dr. Amy GUTMANN
03	Executive Vice President	Mr. Craig CARNAROLI
05	Provost	Dr. Vincent PRICE
06	Registrar	Mr. Adam B. SHERR
07	Dean of Admissions	Mr. Eric J. FURDA
32	Vice Provost University Life	Dr. Valarie S. MCCOULLUM
10	Vice Pres Finance & Treasurer	Ms. MaryFrances MCCOURT
18	Vice Pres Facil/Real Est Svcs	Ms. Anne PAPAGEORGE
17	CEO Univ of PA Health System	Dr. Ralph W. MULLER
08	Vice Provost/Dir of Libraries	Mr. Harry C. ROGERS
13	Vice Pres Info Technology/CIO	Mr. Thomas H. MURPHY
100	Vice Pres & Chief of Staff	Mr. Gregory S. ROST
88	Vice Pres Institutional Affairs	Ms. Joann MITCHELL
30	Vice Pres Dev/Alumni Relations	Mr. John H. ZELLER
15	Vice Pres Human Resources	Dr. John J. HEUER
86	Vice Pres Govt & Comm Relations	Mr. Jeffrey COOPER
19	Vice President Public Safety	Ms. Maureen RUSH
26	Vice Pres for Univ Communications	Mr. Stephen J. MACCARTHY
88	Vice Pres Business Services	Ms. Marie D. WITT
45	Vice Pres Budget Mgmt Analysis	Ms. Bonnie C. GIBSON
43	Senior Vice Pres/General Counsel	Ms. Wendy S. WHITE
101	VP & Secretary of the University	Ms. Leslie L. KRUHLY
20	Vice Provost for Education	Dr. Beth A. WINKELSTEIN
20	Vice Provost Faculty Affairs	Dr. Anita L. ALLEN
29	Asst Vice Pres Alumni Relations	Mr. Fredrick H. WAMPLER
88	Vice Provost for Research	Dr. Dawn A. BONNELL
88	Assoc Vice Pres Rsrch Svcs	Ms. Elizabeth D. PELOSO
14	Assoc Vice Pres Networking/Telecom	Vacant
88	Assoc VP Audit Compl & Privacy	Mr. Gregory J. FELLICANO
31	Assoc VP/Dir Ctr Cmty Partnerships	Dr. Ira HARKAVY
28	Assoc Vice Prov Equity & Access	Rev. William GIPSON
21	Comptroller	Mr. John F. HORN
63	Exec Vice Pres/Dean Sch of Medicine	Dr. J. L. JAMESON
49	Dean School Arts & Sciences	Dr. Steven J. FLUHARTY
54	Dean School of Engr/Applied Science	Dr. Vijay KUMAR
66	Dean School of Nursing	Dr. Antonia VILLARRUEL
50	Dean Wharton School	Dr. Geoffrey GARRETT
60	Dean Annenberg Sch Communications	Dr. Michael X. DELLI CARPINI
52	Dean School of Dental Medicine	Dr. Denis F. KINANE
48	Dean School of Design	Dr. Frederick STEINER
53	Dean Graduate School Education	Dr. Pam GROSSMAN
61	Dean School of Law	Dr. Theodore W. RUGER
70	Dean School Social Policy/Practice	Dr. John L. JACKSON
74	Dean School of Veterinary Medicine	Dr. Joan C. HENDRICKS
107	Vice Dean Liberal & Prof Studies	Ms. Nora E. LEWIS
35	Assoc VP Student Reg/Fin Svcs	Dr. Michelle H. BROWN-NEVERS
09	Assoc VP Inst Rsrch/Sr Adv to Pres	Ms. Stacey J. LOPEZ
85	Dir Intl Student & Scholar Svcs	Dr. Rodolfo R. ALTAMIRANO
36	Dir of Career Services	Ms. Patricia L. ROSE
37	Dir Student Financial Aid	Ms. Elaine P. VARAS
35	Assoc Vice Prov for Student Affairs	Mr. Hikaru KOZUMA
38	Dir Counseling/Psych Services	Dr. William B. ALEXANDER
102	Exec Dir Corp & Found Rels	Dr. Diana B. ALTEGOER
22	Exec Dir Affirm Action & Equal Op	Mr. Sam B. STARKS
23	Exec Dir Student Health Services	Dr. Giang T. NGUYEN
88	Mgng Dir Annenberg Cr/Penn Presents	Dr. Michael J. ROSE
88	Exec Dir Morris Arboretum	Mr. Paul W. MEYER
88	Dir Institute of Contempory Art	Ms. Amy SADAO
88	Dir Museum of Archlgy/Anthrplgy	Mr. Julian F. SIGGERS
41	Dir Intercollegiate Athletics	Ms. M. Grace CALHOUN
24	IT Director	Mr. James F. JOHNSON
91	IT Exec Dir Admin Info Tech	Ms. Jeanne F. CURTIS
39	Exec Dir Col Houses & Acad Svcs	Mr. Martin REDMAN
42	University Chaplain	Rev. Charles L. HOWARD
104	Director Study Abroad	Mr. Nigel COSSAR
106	Exec Director Online Learning Init	Ms. Amy BENNET
04	Administrative Asst to President	Ms. Jodi SARKISIAN
105	Dir Web Strategy & Visual Comm	Mr. Steven MINICOLA
44	Exec Dir Gift Plng/Assoc Gen Couns	Ms. Marcie L. MERZ
96	Director of Purchasing	Mr. Mark MILLS

University of Phoenix Philadelphia Campus (F)

30 South 17th Street, 2nd Floor, Philadelphia PA 19103
Telephone: (267) 234-2000　Identification: 770933
Accreditation: &NH, ACBSP

† Branch campus of University of Phoenix, Tempe, AZ.

University of Pittsburgh (G)

4200 Fifth Avenue, Pittsburgh PA 15260-3583
County: Allegheny　FICE Identification: 003379
Unit ID: 215293
Telephone: (412) 624-4141　Carnegie Class: DU-Highest
FAX Number: N/A　Calendar System: Semester
URL: www.pitt.edu
Established: 1787　Annual Undergrad Tuition & Fees (In-State): $18,192
Enrollment: 28,617　Coed
Affiliation or Control: State Related　IRS Status: 501(c)3
Highest Offering: Doctorate
Accreditation: M, ANEST, ARCPA, AUD, BUS, CAATE, CACREP, CAHIIM, CEA, CLPSY, CORE, DENT, DH, DIETC, DIETD, ENG, HSA, HT, IPSY, LAW, LIB, MED, @MIDWF, NURSE, OPE, CT, PCSAS, PERF, PH, PHAR, PTA, SP, SPAA, SW, THEA

01	Chancellor and Chief Exec Officer	Dr. Patrick GALLAGHER
05	Sr Vice Chancellor & Provost	Dr. Patricia E. BEESON
63	Sr VC Health Sci/Dean Sch of Med	Dr. Arthur S. LEVINE
101	Secy of Board of Trustees	Dr. Kathy HUMPHREY
10	Senior Vice Chancellor and CFO	Mr. Arthur G. RAMICONE
30	Vice Chancellor Inst Advancement	Mr. Albert J. NOVAK, JR.
43	Sr Vice Chanc & Chief Legal Officer	Ms. Geovette WASHINGTON
26	Vice Chanc for Communications	Ms. Susan ROGERS
100	Sr VC for Engmnt and Chief of Staff	Dr. Kathy HUMPHREY
11	Sr VC Business and Operations	Mr. Gregory A. SCOTT
86	Vice Chanc Community & Govt Rels	Mr. Paul A. SUPOWITZ
15	Assoc Vice Chanc Human Resources	Vacant
27	Interim Director University News	Mr. Joseph T. MIKSCH
20	Vice Provost Undergraduate Studies	Dr. Juan J. MAFREDI
58	Vice Provost Graduate Studies	Dr. Alberta M. SBRAGIA
45	Vice Prov Acad Plng/Resource Mgmt	Dr. David N. DEJONG
29	Assoc Vice Chanc Alumni Relations	Mr. Jeffery T. GLEIM
39	Associate Vice Chancellor Business	Mr. Eli SHORAK
102	Assoc VC Corp & Found Rel	Mr. Thomas P. CRAWFORD
19	Assoc VC Public Safety & Emer Mngmt	Mr. Ted P. FRITZ
18	Assoc VC Facilities Mgmt	Mr. Scott C. BERNOTAS
16	Asst VC Human Resources	Mr. Stephen M. FERBER
06	University Registrar	Ms. Patti J. MATHAY
41	Athletic Director	Mr. Scott BARNES
07	Chief Enrollment Officer	Mr. Marc L. HARDING
32	Int Vice Prov & Dean of Students	Mr. Kenyon R. BONNER
46	Vice Provost Research	Dr. Mark S. REDFERN
49	Dean Deitrich Sch Arts & Sci/CGS	Dr. N. John COOPER
92	Dean University Honors College	Dr. Edward M. STRICKER
50	Dean Jos M Katz Gr Sch Bus	Dr. Arjang A. ASSAD
53	Dean of School of Education	Dr. Alan M. LESGOLD
54	Dean Swanson School of Engineering	Dr. Gerald D. HOLDER
61	Dean of School of Law	Mr. William M. CARTER
80	Dean Grad Sch Public/Intl Affs	Dr. John T. KEELER
70	Dean School of Social Work	Dr. Larry E. DAVIS
62	Dean School Information Sciences	Dr. Ronald L. LARSEN
52	Dean School of Dental Medicine	Dr. Thomas W. BRAUN
66	Dean of School of Nursing	Dr. Jacqueline DUNBAR-JACOB
67	Dean School of Pharmacy	Dr. Patricia D. KROBOTH
69	Dean Grad School Public Health	Dr. Donald S. BURKE
76	Dean Sch of Health & Rehabilitation	Dr. Anthony DELITTO
12	President Johnstown Campus	Dr. Jem M. SPECTAR
12	President Greensburg Campus	Dr. Sharon P. SMITH
12	President Bradford and Titusville	Dr. Livingston ALEXANDER
104	Sr Dir Intl Pgms & Dir UCIS	Dr. Ariel ARMONY
40	Director Book Centers	Ms. Debra R. FYOCK
24	Dir Ctr Instruct Dev/Distance Educ	Ms. Cynthia GOLDEN
13	Dir Computer Svcs/Systems Devel	Ms. Jinx P. WALTON
09	Director Institutional Research	Mr. Robert D. GOGA
21	Director Internal Audit	Mr. John P. ELLIOTT
36	Int Assoc Dean & Dir Career Dev	Ms. Cheryl S. FINLAY
08	Interim Dir Univ Library System	Ms. Fern E. BRODY
19	Chief University Police	Mr. James K. LOFTUS
23	Director Student Health Svcs	Ms. Marian S. VANEK
96	Manager Purchasing Services	Mr. Thomas E. YOUNGS, JR.
44	Sr Exec Director Planned Giving	Mr. Walter E. BROWN, JR.
04	Exec Asst to the Chancellor	Ms. Mary Jo RACE
106	Dir Online Programs	Ms. Lorna R. KEARNS
37	Director Financial Aid	Dr. Randall MCCREADY
38	Director Counseling Center	Dr. Ed MICHAELS
28	Assoc VChanc Diversity & Inclusion	Ms. Pamela W. CONNELLY
88	Vice Chanc Economic Partnerships	Ms. Rebecca BAGLEY

University of Pittsburgh at Bradford (H)

300 Campus Drive, Bradford PA 16701-2812
Telephone: (814) 362-7500　FICE Identification: 003380
Accreditation: &M, ADNUR, CAATE, NUR

† Regional accreditation is carried under the parent institution in Pittsburgh, PA.

University of Pittsburgh at Greensburg (I)

150 Finoli Drive, Greensburg PA 15601-5898
Telephone: (724) 837-7040　FICE Identification: 003381
Accreditation: &M

† Regional accreditation is carried under the parent institution in Pittsburgh, PA.

University of Pittsburgh at Johnstown (J)

450 Schoolhouse Road, Johnstown PA 15904-2990
Telephone: (814) 269-7000　FICE Identification: 003382
Accreditation: &M, COARC, ENGT, SURGT

† Regional accreditation is carried under the parent institution in Pittsburgh, PA.

University of Pittsburgh at Titusville (K)

504 E Main, Titusville PA 16354-2097
Telephone: (814) 827-4400　FICE Identification: 003383
Accreditation: &M, ADNUR, PTAA

† Regional accreditation is carried under the parent institution in Pittsburgh, PA.

University of the Sciences in Philadelphia (A)

600 S 43rd Street, Philadelphia PA 19104-4495
County: Philadelphia FICE Identification: 003353
Unit ID: 215132
Telephone: (215) 596-8800 Carnegie Class: Spec-4-yr-Other Health
FAX Number: (215) 895-1100 Calendar System: Semester
URL: www.usciences.edu
Established: 1821 Annual Undergrad Tuition & Fees: $37,466
Enrollment: 2,748 Coed
Affiliation or Control: Independent Non-Profit IRS Status: 501(c)3
Highest Offering: Doctorate
Accreditation: M, ACBSP, #ARCPA, OT, PHAR, PTA

01 President Dr. Kathleen MAYES
05 Provost Dr. Peter J. MILLER
10 VP Finance and Administration Vacant
30 VP for Institutional Advancement Ms. Teresa F. WINSLOW
86 Director Govt and Cmty Affairs Mr. David L. FORDE
26 Director Marketing/ Communications Mr. Michael SCHWARTZMAN
102 Dir of Corporate & Foundation Rels Ms. Rebecca POWERS
13 Exec Dir Information Technology Mr. John MASCIANTONIO
14 Associate Provost/CIO Dr. Mark NESTOR
37 Director of Financial Aid Ms. Pamela RAMANATHAN
06 Registrar Ms. Therese ANDERSON
29 Director of Alumni Relations Mr. Casey RYAN
08 Director of Library Services Mr. Charles MYERS
32 Dean of Students Dr. William J. CUNNINGHAM
67 Dean of Pharmacy Dr. Lisa LAWSON
49 Dean Misher College Arts & Sci Dr. Suzanne K. MURPHY
76 Dean Samson College of Health Sci Dr. Mickey COHEN
88 Dean of Mayes College Dr. Andrew PETERSON
15 Exec Director Human Resources Mr. Michael G. JANES
19 Director Public Safety Ms. Kim C. CARTER
41 Athletic Director Dr. Mark CASERIO
88 Director of Student Engagement Mr. Ross RADISH
35 Director of Student Life Ms. Susanne E. FERRIN
39 Associate Director of Student Life Mr. Anthony FLORENDO
85 Director of Multicultural Affairs Mr. Walter PERRY
09 Director of Institutional Research Dr. Dale TRUSHEIM
21 Controller/Asst VP Finance Ms. Brigid K. ISACKMAN
36 Director Career Services Ms. Kimberly BRYANT
38 Assoc Director Student Counseling Dr. Karen LEVINSON
96 Manager University Purchasing Mr. Vincent HORN
20 Associate Provost Academic Affairs Dr. John CONNORS
88 Director Academic Advising Mr. Joseph CANADAY
18 Director of Facilities Mr. Dan SEVERINO
04 Executive Asst to President Ms. Beth PILIPZECK
104 Director Study Abroad Mr. James YARRISH
106 Director Academic Technology Dr. Rodney B. MURRAY
84 Director Enrollment Management Mr. Peter NACY

The University of Scranton (B)

800 Linden St, Scranton PA 18510-4622
County: Lackawanna FICE Identification: 003384
Unit ID: 215929
Telephone: (570) 941-7400 Carnegie Class: Masters/L
FAX Number: (570) 941-6369 Calendar System: Semester
URL: www.scranton.edu
Established: 1888 Annual Undergrad Tuition & Fees: $41,044
Enrollment: 5,589 Coed
Affiliation or Control: Roman Catholic IRS Status: 501(c)3
Highest Offering: Doctorate
Accreditation: M, ANEST, BUS, CACREP, CORE, CS, CSHSE, ENG, HSA, NURSE, OT, PTA, TEAC

01 President Rev. Kevin P. QUINN, SJ
05 Int Sr VP Acad Affairs & Provost Dr. Joseph H. DREISBACH
10 Sr VP Finance & Administration Mr. Edward J. STEINMETZ, JR.
30 VP for University Advancement Mr. Gary R. OLSEN
26 VP Enroll Mgmt/External Affairs Mr. Gerald C. ZABOSKI
21 Asst VP Budget/Financial Planning Mr. Patrick R. DONOHUE
13 Assoc Vice President Info Tech/CIO Vacant
15 Assoc Vice Pres Human Resources Ms. Patricia L. TETREAULT
42 Interim Dir of Campus Ministry Rev. Richard G. MALLOY, SJ
43 General Counsel Mr. Robert B. FARRELL
100 Chief of Staff Mr. Robert W. DAVIS, JR.
49 Dean Arts & Sciences Dr. Brian P. CONNIFF
50 Dean Kania School Management Dr. Michael O. MENSAH
107 Dean Panuska Col of Prof Studies Dr. Debra A. PELLEGRINO
08 Dean of the Library/Info Fluency Mr. Charles E. KRATZ, JR.
51 Asst Dir for OL/Off Campus-Programs Mrs. Lisa M. LOBASSO
32 Vice Prov Std Formation/Campus Life Dr. Anitra M. MCSHEA
108 Int Assoc Prov Inst Effectiveness Dr. Patricia HARRINGTON
07 Assoc VP Admiss & Undergrad Enroll Mr. Joseph M. ROBACK
07 Asst VP Admissions & Enrollment Ms. Mary Kay ASTON
18 Assoc VP Facilities Operations Mr. James DEVERS
29 Assoc VP Annual Fund/Alumni Rels Ms. Melissa D. STARACE
06 Registrar Ms. Helen H. STAGER
37 Director of Financial Aid Mr. William R. BURKE
36 Director of Career Services Mrs. Constance F. MCDONNELL
28 Director of Equity/Diversity Office Ms. Jennifer LAPORTA
09 Director of Institutional Research Ms. Robyn DICKINSON
38 Director of Counseling Center Mr. Thomas P. SMITH
96 Director of Purchasing Mr. Gary S. ZAMPANO

University of Valley Forge (C)

1401 Charlestown Road, Phoenixville PA 19460-2399
County: Chester FICE Identification: 003306
Unit ID: 216542
Telephone: (610) 935-0450 Carnegie Class: Bac-Diverse
FAX Number: (610) 935-9353 Calendar System: Semester
URL: www.valleyforge.edu
Established: 1939 Annual Undergrad Tuition & Fees: $20,394
Enrollment: 885 Coed
Affiliation or Control: Assemblies Of God Church IRS Status: 501(c)3
Highest Offering: Master's
Accreditation: M, SW

01 Interim President Dr. Byron D. KLAUS
03 Executive VP & VP of Development Dr. Daniel W. MORTENSEN
05 VP of Academic Affairs Dr. Kevin E. BEERY
10 VP of Finance Mr. Jonathan CAPECI
32 VP of Student Life Rev. Jennifer D. GALE
20 Associate Dean Rev. Stuart P. ROSS
21 Controller Mrs. Myra D. OCASIO
49 Arts & Sciences Dept Chair Mrs. Laura BROOKINS
83 Behavioral Sciences Dept Chair Dr. Debra BROWN
50 Business Dept Chair Dr. William CLARKSON
73 Church Ministry Dept Chair Dr. Jerome DOUGLAS
73 Deaf Pastoral Ministries Dept Chair Dr. JoAnn SMITH
72 Digital Media/Commun Dept Chair Mr. Leone BILOTTA
53 Education Dept Chair Dr. A. Glenn MCCLURE
88 Intercultural Studies Dept Chair Rev. David KIM
64 Music Dept Chair Dr. William DESANTO
88 Director of Accounting Mrs. Betty SMITH
07 Director of Admissions Rev. Joseph OCASIO
30 Coordinator of Development Mrs. Darlene GRUBER
41 Director of Athletics Mr. Jon MACK
36 Director Career Services Rev. Amy THURSTON
37 Director of Financial Aid Mrs. Linda STEIN
15 Director Human Resources Mrs. Veronica BIRD
13 Director of Information Technology Mrs. Varinia ROBINSON
105 Web Master Mr. Steve THURSTON
08 Librarian/Dir Storms Research Ctr Mrs. Deborah HIRNEISEN
26 Director of Marketing Mrs. Michelle MALONEY
06 Registrar Dr. Troy GEARHART
23 Nurse Mrs. Lauren BORN
35 Campus Director Rev. Wendy BEERY
35 Campus Director Vacant
39 Residence Director Mrs. Katharyn MCLELLAN
39 Residence Director Mr. Yung Won PARK
04 Administrative Asst to President Ms. Chrysta M. ARCHER

Ursinus College (D)

PO Box 1000, 601 East Main Street, Collegeville PA 19426-1000
County: Montgomery FICE Identification: 003385
Unit ID: 216524
Telephone: (610) 409-3000 Carnegie Class: Bac-A&S
FAX Number: (610) 489-0627 Calendar System: Semester
URL: www.ursinus.edu
Established: 1869 Annual Undergrad Tuition & Fees: $47,700
Enrollment: 1,681 Coed
Affiliation or Control: Independent Non-Profit IRS Status: 501(c)3
Highest Offering: Baccalaureate
Accreditation: M

01 President Dr. Brock BLOMBERG
05 Interim Dean & Exec VP Acad Affairs Dr. April KONTOSTATHIS
10 Vice Pres Finance & Administration Ms. Annette PARKER
30 Senior Vice Pres for Advancement Ms. Jill A. MARSTELLER
84 Vice President for Enrollment Mr. David TOBIAS
32 Vice Pres of Student Affairs/Dean Ms. Deborah O. NOLAN
21 Associate Vice Pres/Controller Ms. Andrea BOHN
07 Director of Admissions Ms. Dana MATASSINO
44 Exec Director of Planned Giving Mr. Mark P. GADSON
08 Special Library Collections Mr. Charles JAMISON
36 Director of Career Services Mrs. Carla M. RINDE
18 Director of Physical Facilities Mr. Jason VAN BUREN
41 Director of Athletics Mrs. Laura MOLIKEN
26 Chief Communications Officer Mr. Thomas YENCHO
37 Director Student Financial Services Mrs. Suzanne SPARROW
06 Registrar Ms. Barbara A. BORIS
29 Director of Alumni Relations Ms. Pamela PANARELLA
20 Associate Dean of the College Dr. Jay MILLER
15 Director Human Resources Ms. Kelley WILLIAMS
09 Director of Institutional Research Ms. Annemarie BARTLETT
102 Dir Foundation/Corporate Relations Mr. Edmond CLARKE
13 Chief Info Technology Officer (CIO) Mr. Eugene SPENCER
28 Coord of Diversity/Inclusion Mr. Terrence WILLIAMS
04 Executive Asst to President Ms. Teri A. LOBO

Valley Forge Military College (E)

1001 Eagle Road, Wayne PA 19087-3695
County: Delaware FICE Identification: 003386
Unit ID: 216551
Telephone: (610) 989-1451 Carnegie Class: Not Classified
FAX Number: (610) 975-9642 Calendar System: Semester
URL: www.vfmac.edu
Established: 1935 Annual Undergrad Tuition & Fees: $29,975
Enrollment: 322 Coed
Affiliation or Control: Independent Non-Profit IRS Status: 501(c)3
Highest Offering: Associate Degree
Accreditation: M

01 President Military Academy/College Col. John C. CHURCH
05 Head of School Academy Ms. Sandra YOUNG
10 Chief Financial Officer/COO Mr. Vincent VUONO
32 Commandant of Cadets Col. Gerard A. TERTYCHNY
30 Vice Pres Institutional Advance/Dev Mr. Douglas HASBROUCK
84 VP Enrollment Mgmt/Marketing Mr. Jamieson BILELLA
18 Director of Facilities Mr. Bryan K. GEILING
07 Director College Admissions Ms. Kristen ROSE
08 Director of Library Services Ms. Dana KERRIGAN
15 Director of Human Resources Ms. Marianne MEADE
13 Director Information Technology Mr. Michael G. BROCK
41 Director of Athletics Mr. Richard CASEY
35 Dean Student Activities Ms. Lauren WOCHOK
06 Assistant Dean/Registrar Mrs. Maureen MALONE
88 Transfer Advisor Ms. Joann MCCRACKEN

Vet Tech Institute (F)

125 Seventh Street, Pittsburgh PA 15222-3400
County: Allegheny FICE Identification: 008568
Unit ID: 213914
Telephone: (412) 391-7021 Carnegie Class: Spec 2-yr-Health
FAX Number: (412) 232-4348 Calendar System: Semester
URL: www.vettechinstitute.edu
Established: 1958 Annual Undergrad Tuition & Fees: $14,860
Enrollment: 372 Coed
Affiliation or Control: Proprietary IRS Status: Proprietary
Highest Offering: Associate Degree
Accreditation: ACCSC

01 Director Mrs. Jackie FLYNN

Villanova University (G)

800 Lancaster Avenue, Villanova PA 19085-1699
County: Delaware FICE Identification: 003388
Unit ID: 216597
Telephone: (610) 519-4500 Carnegie Class: DU-Mod
FAX Number: (610) 519-5000 Calendar System: Semester
URL: www.villanova.edu
Established: 1842 Annual Undergrad Tuition & Fees: $47,616
Enrollment: 10,735 Coed
Affiliation or Control: Roman Catholic IRS Status: 501(c)3
Highest Offering: Doctorate
Accreditation: M, ANEST, BUS, BUSA, CACREP, CS, ENG, LAW, NURSE, SPAA

01 President Rev. Peter M. DONOHUE, OSA
43 Vice President & General Counsel Ms. Debra FICKLER
05 Provost Dr. Patrick G. MAGGITTI
30 Sr Vice Pres University Advancement Mr. Michael O'NEILL
10 Exec VP Administration/Finance Mr. Kenneth G. VALOSKY
13 Vice Pres/Chief Information Officer Mr. Stephen FUGALE
32 Vice President for Student Life Rev. John P. STACK, OSA
26 Vice Pres University Communication Ms. Ann DIEBOLD
42 Vice Pres for Mission & Ministry Dr. Barbara E. WALL
20 Vice Provost for Academics Dr. Craig WHEELAND
35 Assoc Vice Pres for Student Life Ms. Kathleen J. BYRNES
15 AVP Human Res/Affirm Action Ofcr Ms. Ellen KRUTZ
109 Assoc Vice Pres for Auxiliary Svcs Mr. Anthony ALFANO
29 Assoc Vice Pres Alumni Relations Mr. George R. KOLB
46 Assoc Vice Provost for Research Dr. Amanda GRANNAS
28 Assoc Vice Prov Diversity/Inclusion Dr. Teresa A. NANCE
84 Dean Enrollment Management Mr. Stephen R. MERRITT
09 Exec Dir Planning/Inst Research Dr. James F. TRAINER
18 Vice Pres Facilities Management Mr. Robert MORRO
07 Director University Admission Mr. Michael M. GAYNOR
08 Librarian & Dir of Falvey Library Ms. Millicent GASKELL
35 Dean of Students Mr. Paul F. PUGH
49 Dean Liberal Arts & Sciences Dr. Adele LINDENMEYR
50 Dean Villanova Sch of Business Dr. Joyce RUSSELL
58 Dean Graduate Studies LA&S Dr. Christine PALUS
61 Dean Widger School of Law Mr. Mark ALEXANDER
66 Dean of Nursing Dr. M. Louise FITZPATRICK
54 Dean of Engineering Dr. Gary A. GABRIELE
88 Dir Ctr Worship/Spirituality Ms. Linda JACZYNSKI
88 Dir Ctr Service/Social Justice Ms. Irene KING
88 Director Center for Worship Rev. Joseph MOSTARDI, OSA
88 Dir Ctr Grad Pastoral Ministry Educ Ms. Joyce ZAVARICH
107 Dean Col of Professional Studies Dr. Deborah J. TYKSINSKI
85 Dir Intl Students & Human Services Mr. Stephen T. MCWILLIAMS
37 Director Financial Assistance Ms. Bonnie Lee BEHM
19 Director of Public Safety Mr. David TEDJESKE
36 Director Career Services Vacant
92 Director of the Honors Program Dr. Thomas W. SMITH
38 Director of Univ Counseling Center Dr. Joan G. WHITNEY
94 Dir Gender & Women's Studies Dr. Lisa SEWELL
39 Director Office of Residence Life Mr. Thomas DE MARCO
96 Director of Procurement Mr. John R. DURHAM
27 Director of Media Relations Mr. Jonathan GUST
41 Director of Athletics Mr. Mark JACKSON
23 Director Student Health Center Dr. Mary MCGONIGLE
23 Medical Director Student Health Ctr Dr. Brian BULLOCK
06 Registrar Ms. Pamela BRAXTON
22 Asc Dir Center Multicultural Affs Ms. Linda COLEMAN
88 University Compliance Officer Ms. Leyda L. BENITEZ
100 Executive Assistant to President Ms. Teisa BROWN
106 Exec Dir Online Programs Ms. Kristy IRWIN
53 Assoc Vice Prov Teach/Learning Dr. Randy WEINSTEIN

Washington & Jefferson College (H)

60 S Lincoln Street, Washington PA 15301-4801
County: Washington FICE Identification: 003389
Unit ID: 216667
Telephone: (724) 503-1001 Carnegie Class: Bac-A&S
FAX Number: (724) 223-6534 Calendar System: 4/1/4
URL: www.washjeff.edu

Established: 1781 Annual Undergrad Tuition & Fees: $43,226
Enrollment: 1,362 Coed
Affiliation or Control: Independent Non-Profit IRS Status: 501(c)3
Highest Offering: Master's
Accreditation: M

01 President ...Dr. Tori HARING-SMITH
05 VP Academic Affairs/Dean of Faculty ...Dr. Judy KIRKPATRICK
10 CFO/VP Business/Finance ...Mr. Dennis MCMASTER
30 VP Development/Alumni Relations ...Mr. Michael P. GRZESIAK
84 Vice President for Enrollment ...Mr. Robert J. GOULD
21 Assoc VP for Business & Finance ...Mr. Thomas SZEJKO
32 VP and Dean of Student Life ...Ms. Eva CHATTERJEE-SUTTON
44 Dir of Campaigns & Advancement Oper ...Ms. Lori DOUGHERTY
20 Associate Dean of the Faculty ...Dr. Sharon TAYLOR
58 Assoc Dean Grad/Continuing Studies ...Dr. Michael SHAUGHNESSY
28 Asst Dean Stdnt Life/Dir Diver Pgm ...Ms. Ketwana SCHOOS
20 Asst Dean for Academic Affairs ...Dr. Steven MALINAK
18 Dir of Campus Operations & Planning ...Mr. Jim MILLER
26 Dir Marketing/Communications ...Mr. Erik RUETER
06 Registrar ...Ms. Leslie MAXIN
29 Assoc VP Alumni Relations & Dev ...Ms. Michele HUFNAGEL
07 Director of Admission ...Mr. Robert ADKINS
84 Associate VP of Enrollment ...Ms. Michelle ANDERSON
13 Dir of Information/Technology Svcs ...Mr. Daniel FAULK
15 Director Human Resources ...Mr. Robert ALLISON
19 Director Protection Services ...Mr. Robert COCCO
36 Director Career Services ...Ms. Roberta CROSS
40 Bookstore Manager ...Ms. Cynthia BRICELAND
41 Director of Athletics ...Mr. Scott MCGUINNESS
08 Director of Library Services ...Vacant
102 Foundation & Corp Relations Officer ...Ms. Julie THROCKMORTON
91 Assoc Director for Admin Computing ...Mr. Michael A. TIMKO
104 Director of Study Abroad ...Ms. Sara KOCHUBA
108 Dir of Assessment & Inst Research ...Ms. Lindsey GUINN
88 Director of Academic Advising ...Ms. Elizabeth MCCLINTOCK
88 Director Conferences and Events ...Ms. Maureen VALENTINE
38 Director of Counseling Services ...Ms. Lisa HAMILTON
39 Director of Residence Life ...Mr. Tyler KOWCHECK

Waynesburg University (A)

51 W College Street, Waynesburg PA 15370-1222
County: Greene FICE Identification: 003391
Unit ID: 216694
Telephone: (724) 627-8191 Carnegie Class: Masters/L
FAX Number: N/A Calendar System: Semester
URL: www.waynesburg.edu
Established: 1849 Annual Undergrad Tuition & Fees: $22,030
Enrollment: 2,039 Coed
Affiliation or Control: Presbyterian Church (U.S.A.) IRS Status: 501(c)3
Highest Offering: Doctorate
Accreditation: M, CAATE, CACREP, IACBE, NURSE

00 Chancellor ...Dr. Timothy R. THYREEN
01 President ...Mr. Doug LEE
05 Provost ...Dr. Dana BAER
10 Chief Financial Officer ...Mr. John OLON
32 VP of Student Services ...Rev. James TINNEMEYER
06 Registrar ...Mrs. Vicki WILSON
41 Athletic Director ...Mr. Larry MARSHALL
13 VP Information Technology Services ...Mr. William DUMIRE
08 Director Eberly Library ...Mr. Rea REDD
26 Communication Specialist ...Ms. Ashley WISE
36 Director of Placement ...Mrs. Marie E. COFFMAN
38 Student Counselor ...Mrs. Jane S. OWEN
21 Business Ofc Supervisor/Controller ...Mr. Dave MARTIN
23 Director of Health Services ...Ms. Jennifer SHIRING
15 Director Human Resources ...Mr. Tom HELMICK
37 Director Student Financial Aid ...Mr. Matthew STOKAN

Westminster College (B)

319 South Market Street, New Wilmington PA 16172-0001
County: Lawrence FICE Identification: 003392
Unit ID: 216807
Telephone: (724) 946-8761 Carnegie Class: Bac-A&S
FAX Number: (724) 946-7132 Calendar System: Semester
URL: www.westminster.edu
Established: 1852 Annual Undergrad Tuition & Fees: $34,105
Enrollment: 1,307 Coed
Affiliation or Control: Presbyterian Church (U.S.A.) IRS Status: 501(c)3
Highest Offering: Master's
Accreditation: M, MUS

01 President ...Dr. Kathy B. RICHARDSON
05 Vice Pres Academic Affs/Dean of Col ...Vacant
30 VP Inst Advancement/Chief Dev Ofcr ...Mr. Matthew P. STINSON
10 Vice Pres Finance/Mgmt Services ...Mr. Kenneth J. ROMIG
06 Registrar ...Mr. Scott D. WIGNALL
07 Vice President for Enrollment ...Dr. Thomas H. STEIN
42 Dean of the Chapel ...Rev. James R. MOHR
32 VP Student Affairs/Dean of Students ...Dr. Neal A. EDMAN
35 Assoc Dean of Student Affairs ...Ms. Gina M. VANCE
37 Director Student Financial Aid ...Ms. Cheryl GERBER
08 Assoc Dean Library/Info Service ...Ms. Erin T. SMITH
36 Director of Career Center ...Ms. Kathryn K. DEMEDAL
29 Director of Alumni Relations ...Ms. Kara H. MONTGOMERY
26 Sr Dir Marketing/Communications ...Mr. Richard A. SHERLOCK
20 Assoc Dean Academic Affairs ...Dr. Jamie G. MCMINN
58 Dir Graduate School/Adult Studies ...Dr. Robert L. ZORN
41 Athletic Director ...Mr. James E. DAFLER
18 Director of Physical Plant ...Mr. Ronald J. PENNINGTON
21 Business Manager ...Ms. Jane M. SMITH
19 Director of Public Safety ...Mr. James D. WALKER
09 Director of Institutional Research ...Dr. Jamie G. MCMINN
23 Director Health Services ...Ms. Melissa M. BARON
40 Bookstore Manager ...Ms. Kay A. GALANSKI
21 Controller ...Ms. Christine A. MILLER
15 Director of Human Resources ...Ms. Kimberlee K. CHRISTOFFERSON
38 Counselor ...Ms. Barbara I. QUINCY
28 Director of Diversity Services ...Ms. Jeannette HUBBARD

Westminster Theological Seminary (C)

2960 Church Road, Glenside PA 19038
County: Montgomery FICE Identification: 003393
Unit ID: 216816
Telephone: (215) 887-5511 Carnegie Class: Spec-4-yr-Faith
FAX Number: (215) 887-5404 Calendar System: Semester
URL: www.wts.edu
Established: 1929 Annual Graduate Tuition & Fees: N/A
Enrollment: 560 Coed
Affiliation or Control: Independent Non-Profit IRS Status: 501(c)3
Highest Offering: Doctorate; No Undergraduates
Accreditation: M, THEOL

01 President ...Dr. Peter A. LILLBACK
05 Provost/Executive Vice President ...Dr. Jeffrey K. JUE
30 Vice Pres Development/Gen Counsel ...Mr. James M. SWEET
32 VP for Campus Life/Dean of Students ...Mr. Steven J. CARTER
44 Vice Pres Advancement Operations ...Mr. Chun LAI
20 Associate Dean for Academic Affairs ...Mr. John KIM
06 Registrar ...Ms. Melinda E. DUGAN
07 Director of Admissions ...Mr. Jonathan M. BRACK
08 Director of Library Services ...Mr. Alexander (Sandy) FINLAYSON
73 Director DMin/Supervised Ministry ...Mr. Timothy Z. WITMER
40 Director Bookstore ...Mr. Chun LAI
37 Financial Aid Officer ...Ms. Fiona E. DAVENPORT
13 Information Systems Director ...Mr. Mike HALPIN
18 Physical Plant Manager ...Mr. Richard W. MAIENSHEIN
04 Administrative Asst to President ...Ms. Abigail DAISE

Westmoreland County Community College (D)

145 Pavilion Lane, Youngwood PA 15697-1895
County: Westmoreland FICE Identification: 010176
Unit ID: 216825
Telephone: (724) 925-4000 Carnegie Class: Assoc/MT-VT-Mix Trad/Non
FAX Number: (724) 925-1150 Calendar System: Semester
URL: www.wccc.edu
Established: 1970 Annual Undergrad Tuition & Fees (In-District): $4,830
Enrollment: 5,638 Coed
Affiliation or Control: Local IRS Status: 501(c)3
Highest Offering: Associate Degree
Accreditation: M, ACFEI, ADNUR, DA, DH, DMS, MAC

01 President ...Dr. Tuesday STANLEY
05 Vice Pres Acad Affs/Stdnt Svcs ...Dr. Kristy BISHOP
11 Vice Pres Administrative Services ...Mr. Steve CIPPIELLO
51 VP Cont Educ/Workforce & Cmty Devel ...Dr. Patrick E. GERITY
10 Chief Business Officer ...Vacant
25 Director of Grants ...Ms. Debra J. WILLIAMS
15 Director Human Resources ...Ms. Lauren M. FARRELL
106 Dir Distance Edu/Learning Resources ...Ms. Annette BOYER
50 Dean Business/Math/Science/Engineer ...Ms. Cynthia PROCTOR
76 Dean Health Profess/Culinary Arts ...Dr. Cindy KOMARINSKI
72 Dean Technology ...Mr. Frank J. KORDALSKI
79 Dean Public Svc/Human/Soc Science ...Dr. Andrew BARNETTE
106 Dean Dist Educ & Educ Centers ...Ms. Tara ZIKEL
84 Vice Pres Enrollment Mgmt ...Ms. Sydney BEELER
102 Exec Director Education Foundation ...Ms. Debra D. WOODS
37 Director Financial Aid ...Vacant
18 Director Facilities ...Vacant
21 Controller ...Mr. Timothy W. STAHL
13 Director Information Technology ...Mr. Steve BUDNY
109 Director College Services ...Mr. Ronald A. KRIVDA
26 Director Public Relations ...Ms. Anna Marie PALATELLA
07 Director Admissions ...Ms. Janice T. GRABOWSKI
41 Director Student Life/Athletics ...Mr. Richard G. HOLLER
09 Dir Institutional Research/Data Svc ...Vacant
96 Director of Purchasing ...Mr. James LUTZ

Widener University (E)

One University Place, Chester PA 19013-5792
County: Delaware FICE Identification: 003313
Unit ID: 216852
Telephone: (610) 499-4000 Carnegie Class: DU-Mod
FAX Number: N/A Calendar System: Semester
URL: www.widener.edu
Established: 1821 Annual Undergrad Tuition & Fees: $41,224
Enrollment: 4,912 Coed
Affiliation or Control: Independent Non-Profit IRS Status: 501(c)3
Highest Offering: Doctorate
Accreditation: M, BUS, CLPSY, ENG, HSA, IPSY, LAW, NURSE, PTA, SW, TED

01 President ...Dr. Julie E. WOLLMAN
05 Sr Vice President/Provost ...Dr. Stephen C. WILHITE
10 Sr Vice Pres Administration/Finance ...Mr. Joseph J. BAKER
30 Vice Pres University Advancement ...Ms. Linda S. DURANT
13 Interim Chief Information Officer ...Mr. Chris SMITH
21 Associate VP & Controller ...Ms. Catherine MCGEEHAN
11 Associate VP of Administration ...Mr. George E. HASSEL
26 Asst Vice Pres University Relations ...Ms. Lou Anne BULIK
18 Director of Operations ...Mr. Carl G. PIERCE
58 Assoc Provost Grad Studies ...Vacant
20 Associate Provost Undergraduate ...Dr. Geraldine A. BLOEMKER
32 Assoc Provost/Dean of Students ...Dr. Denise D. GIFFORD
54 Dean School of Engineering ...Dr. Fred A. AKL
49 Dean College Arts & Sciences ...Dr. Sharon M. MEAGHER
50 Dean School of Business Admin ...Dr. Jayati GHOSH
66 Dean School of Nursing ...Dr. Laura C. DZUREC
51 Dean Sch of Educ/Innov/Cont Studies ...Dr. Shawn M. FITZGERALD
88 Dean Sch Human Svc Professions ...Dr. Paula SILVER
21 Bursar ...Ms. Diana BARRACLOUGH
08 Librarian ...Mr. Oscar LANZA-GALINDO
84 Assoc VP for Enrollment Services ...Mr. Thomas K. MALLOY
06 Director of Records/Registration ...Ms. Kristen CHANDO
29 Director of Alumni Engagement ...Ms. Tina A. PHILLIPS
09 Dir of Inst Res & Effectiveness ...Dr. Stephen W. THORPE
36 Placement Director ...Ms. Jan MOPPERT
41 Director of Athletics ...Mr. Jack L. SHAFER
85 Director International Student Svcs ...Ms. Kandy TURNER
19 Director of Campus Safety ...Mr. Patrick SULLIVAN
23 Director of Health Services ...Ms. Lynn A. NELSON-RUSSOM
24 Head of Multimedia/Classroom Spprt ...Mr. Eric WOEBKENBERG
40 Manager Campus Bookstore ...Vacant
91 Director Information Systems ...Mrs. Linda TAYLOR
88 Director Technical Resources ...Mr. Perry M. DRAYFAHL
15 Director of Human Resources ...Ms. Beth GLASSMAN
96 Director of Purchasing ...Ms. Michelle SHELTON
89 Dir Student Success/Retention ...Mr. Timothy J. CAIRY
97 Dir Honors Program in General Educ ...Dr. Ilene LIEBERMAN
94 Director of Women's Studies ...Dr. Annalisa CASTALDO
86 Director Government Relations ...Ms. Julie DIETRICH

† See Delaware listing of Widener University School of Law.

Widener University Commonwealth Law School (F)

3800 Vartan Way, PO Box 69380,
Harrisburg PA 17106-9380
Telephone: (717) 541-3900 Identification: 667244
Accreditation: &M, LAW

† Branch campus of Widener University, Chester, PA.

Wilkes University (G)

84 W South Street, Wilkes-Barre PA 18766-0001
County: Luzerne FICE Identification: 003394
Unit ID: 216931
Telephone: (570) 408-5000 Carnegie Class: Masters/L
FAX Number: (570) 408-2934 Calendar System: Semester
URL: www.wilkes.edu
Established: 1933 Annual Undergrad Tuition & Fees: $32,356
Enrollment: 4,562 Coed
Affiliation or Control: Independent Non-Profit IRS Status: 501(c)3
Highest Offering: Doctorate
Accreditation: M, ACBSP, CEA, ENG, NURSE, PHAR

01 President ...Dr. Patrick F. LEAHY
05 Provost & Sr Vice President ...Dr. Anne SKLEDER
30 Vice Pres University Advancement ...Mr. Michael WOOD
10 Vice President & General Counsel ...Mr. Loren D. PRESCOTT
21 Controller ...Ms. Janet KOBYLSKI
84 Vice President Enrollment Services ...Vacant
32 Vice President Student Affairs ...Dr. Paul S. ADAMS
15 Chief Human Resource Officer ...Mr. Joseph HOUSENICK
35 Dean of Students ...Mr. Mark R. ALLEN
88 Associate Dean Student Affairs ...Vacant
54 Dean of Science & Engineering ...Dr. William HUDSON
49 Dean College Arts & Humanities ...Dr. Paul RIGGS
67 Dean Nesbitt Col Pharmacy ...Dr. Bernard GRAHAM
88 VP of Strategic Initiatives ...Dr. Michael SPEZIALE
50 Dean Sidhu School of Business ...Dr. Jeffrey ALVES
62 Dean Library ...Mr. John STACHACZ
09 Exec Director Info/Analysis/Plng ...Mr. Brian BOGERT
29 Director Alumni Relations ...Ms. Bridget GIUANTA
41 Director of Athletics ...Ms. Addy MALATESTA
23 Director Health Services ...Ms. Diane E. O'BRIEN
36 Director Career Services ...Mrs. Carol A. BOSACK-KOSEK
39 Director Residence Life ...Ms. Elizabeth ROVEDA
58 Director Graduate Teach Education ...Ms. Grace SURDOVEL
06 Registrar ...Mrs. Susan A. HRITZAK
37 Interim Director of Financial Aid ...Ms. Delaina JAYNE
26 Assoc VP Marketing Communications ...Mr. Jack A. CHIELLI
18 Director Facilities Services ...Mr. Charles CARY
07 Director of Admissions ...Mr. Alex SPERRAZZA
28 Exec Director of Diversity ...Ms. Georgia COSTALAS
96 Dir Procurement & Financial Svcs ...Ms. Alicia BOND
25 Director of Sponsored Programs ...Ms. Amanda MODROVSKY
27 Director of Marketing ...Mrs. Kim D. BOWER SPENCE
04 Assistant to the President ...Ms. Dawn LEAS

Williamson College of the Trades (H)

106 S New Middletown Road, Media PA 19063-5299
County: Delaware FICE Identification: 041238
Unit ID: 216940
Telephone: (610) 566-1776 Carnegie Class: Not Classified
FAX Number: (610) 566-6502 Calendar System: Semester

URL: www.williamson.edu
Established: 1888 Annual Undergrad Tuition & Fees: N/A
Enrollment: N/A Male
Affiliation or Control: Independent Non-Profit IRS Status: 501(c)3
Highest Offering: Associate Degree
Accreditation: ACCSC

01 President .... Mr. Michael J. ROUNDS
10 Exec Vice President and COO .... Mr. Gregory L. LINDEMUTH
05 Vice President of Education & CAO .... Mr. Samuel H. WRIGHTSON
30 Vice President of Inst Advancement .... Mrs. Arlene A. SNYDER
32 Dean of Students .... Mr. Thomas J. MOFFITT
07 Dean of Admissions .... Mr. Jason C. MERILLAT
41 Director of Athletics .... Mr. Dale H. PLUMMER
42 Chaplain/Counselor .... Rev. Mark A. SPECHT
06 Registrar .... Ms. Anne M. HAYES
36 Director of Placement .... Ms. Margaret T. KINGHAM
26 Director of Public Relations .... Mr. Carl A. VAIRO

Wilson College (A)

1015 Philadelphia Avenue, Chambersburg PA 17201-1285
County: Franklin FICE Identification: 003396
Unit ID: 217013
Telephone: (717) 262-4141 Carnegie Class: Bac-Diverse
FAX Number: (717) 264-1578 Calendar System: 4/1/4
URL: www.wilson.edu
Established: 1869 Annual Undergrad Tuition & Fees: $24,392
Enrollment: 771 Coed
Affiliation or Control: Presbyterian Church (U.S.A.) IRS Status: 501(c)3
Highest Offering: Master's
Accreditation: M

01 President .... Dr. Barbara K. MISTICK
05 VP for Academic Affairs/Dean of Fac .... Dr. Elissa HEIL
30 VP for Institutional Advancement .... Ms. Camilla B. RAWLEIGH
10 Vice Pres Finance & Administration .... Mr. Brian ECKER
84 Vice President for Enrollment .... Ms. Mary Ann NASO
32 Vice President for Student Dev/Dean .... Dr. Mary Beth WILLIAMS
26 VP for Marketing and Communications .... Mr. Brian SPEER
100 Chief of Staff .... Ms. Melissa J. IMES
06 Registrar .... Ms. Jean B. HOOVER
37 Dean of Financial Aid .... Ms. Linda D. BRITTAIN
09 Director of Institutional Effective .... Mr. Andrew S. ABEL
08 AVP for Technology and Library Svcs .... Mr. Jose DIEUDONNE
18 Director of Physical Plant .... Mr. Jack KELLY
27 Manager of Media Relations .... Ms. Cathy MENTZER
40 College Store Coordinator .... Ms. Robin HERRING
41 Athletic Director .... Ms. Lori FREY
51 Director of Conferences .... Mr. Joel PAGLIARO
29 Director of Alumnae Programs .... Ms. Marybeth FAMULARE
44 Director of Annual Fund .... Ms. Carolyn WOODS
15 Director Human Resources .... Ms. Bonnie COURTNEY
20 Assoc Dean of Academic Advising .... Dr. Deborah AUSTIN
21 Assoc VP for Finance/Admin .... Ms. Lori TOSTEN
36 Director of Career Development .... Ms. Linda A. BOECKMAN
38 Director of Student Counseling .... Ms. Cindy SHOEMAKER
88 Director of Women With Children Pgm .... Ms. Katherine KOUGH
37 Coordinator of Financial Aid .... Ms. Christine KNOUSE
28 Coordinator of Diversity .... Vacant
42 Chaplain .... Rev. Emily MORGAN
39 Director of Residence Life .... Ms. Sherri SADOWSKI
102 Dir Foundation/Corporate Relations .... Ms. Margaret LIGHT
07 Director of Admissions .... Mr. Michael MONTANA

Won Institute of Graduate Studies (B)

137 S Easton Road, Glenside PA 19038
County: Montgomery FICE Identification: 039493
Unit ID: 442064
Telephone: (215) 884-8942 Carnegie Class: Spec-4-yr-Other Health
FAX Number: (215) 884-9002 Calendar System: Trimester
URL: www.woninstitute.edu
Established: 2002 Annual Graduate Tuition & Fees: N/A
Enrollment: 94 Coed
Affiliation or Control: Independent Non-Profit IRS Status: 501(c)3
Highest Offering: Master's; No Undergraduates
Accreditation: M, ACUP

01 President .... Dr. Bokin KIM
11 Chief Administrative Officer .... Ms. Colleen O'CONNELL
10 Chief Financial Officer .... Ms. Maria PERRY
05 Chief Academic Officer .... Ms. Gloria NOUEL
06 Registrar .... Vacant
08 Librarian .... Mrs. Sandy HOSTETTER
85 International Student Advisor .... Rev. Hojin PARK
13 Chief Info Technology Officer (CIO) .... Ms. Elizabeth REED
26 Chief Public Relations/Marketing .... Mr. Zach BREMMER

The Workforce Institute's City College (C)

1231 North Broad Street, Philadelphia PA 19122
County: Philadelphia FICE Identification: 031091
Unit ID: 214023
Telephone: (215) 568-9215 Carnegie Class: Spec 2-yr-Tech
FAX Number: (215) 568-3511 Calendar System: Semester
URL: www.citycollege-careers.org
Established: 1974 Annual Undergrad Tuition & Fees: $12,097
Enrollment: 31 Coed
Affiliation or Control: Independent Non-Profit IRS Status: 501(c)3
Highest Offering: Associate Degree
Accreditation: ACCSC

01 President .... Dr. Richard COHEN
11 Executive Director .... Ms. Wendy-Anne ROBERTS-JOHNSON
10 Controller .... Ms. Mary DURSO
05 Interim Director of Education .... Ms. Wendy-Anne ROBERTS-JOHNSON
37 Financial Aid Director .... Ms. Madeline SARGENT
07 Admissions Representative .... Mr. Eric MAISTER
36 Career Manager .... Mr. Eric MAISTER

WyoTech-Blairsville (D)

500 Innovation Drive, Blairsville PA 15717-8060
Telephone: (724) 459-9500 Identification: 666305
Accreditation: ACCSC

† Branch campus of Wyoming Technical Institute, Laramie, WY.

Yeshiva Beth Moshe (E)

930 Hickory Street, Scranton PA 18505-2196
County: Lackawanna FICE Identification: 013134
Unit ID: 217040
Telephone: (570) 346-1747 Carnegie Class: Spec-4-yr-Faith
FAX Number: (570) 346-2251 Calendar System: Semester
Established: 1965 Annual Undergrad Tuition & Fees: $8,600
Enrollment: 55 Male
Affiliation or Control: Independent Non-Profit IRS Status: 501(c)3
Highest Offering: Second Talmudic Degree
Accreditation: RABN

01 Chief Executive Officer .... Rabbi Yaakov SCHNAIDMAN
03 Executive Director .... Rabbi Avraham PRESSMAN

York College of Pennsylvania (F)

Country Club Road, York PA 17403-3651
County: York FICE Identification: 003399
Unit ID: 217059
Telephone: (717) 846-7788 Carnegie Class: Masters/S
FAX Number: (717) 849-1607 Calendar System: Semester
URL: www.ycp.edu
Established: 1787 Annual Undergrad Tuition & Fees: $18,240
Enrollment: 5,067 Coed
Affiliation or Control: Independent Non-Profit IRS Status: 501(c)3
Highest Offering: Doctorate
Accreditation: M, ACBSP, ANEST, COARC, CS, ENG, MUS, NRPA, NURSE

01 President .... Dr. Pamela J. GUNTER-SMITH
05 Provost & Dean Academic Affairs .... Dr. Laura NIESEN DE ABRUNA
10 Chief Financial Officer .... Mr. Matthew SMITH
20 Assoc Dean Academic Affairs .... Dr. Carl SEAQUIST
20 Interim Dean of Academic Services .... Dr. Joshua LANDAU
32 Dean of Student Affairs .... Mr. Joseph F. MERKLE
18 Dean of Campus Operations .... Dr. Kenneth M. MARTIN
30 Dean of College Advancement .... Dr. Jane HOGGE
50 Associate Dean Business .... Dr. James NORRIE
41 Asst Dean Athletics & Recreation .... Mr. Paul SAIKIA
84 Interim Dean Enrollment Management .... Dr. Darrien DAVENPORT
26 Asst Dean Institutional Advancement .... Ms. Mary E. DOLHEIMER
44 Asst Dean Development .... Mr. Zane GIZZI
07 Director of Admissions .... Vacant
06 Registrar .... Mr. William BENTON
08 Librarian .... Vacant
37 Director of Financial Aid .... Mr. Calvin H. WILLIAMS
13 CIO .... Vacant
29 Director Alumni Relations .... Mrs. Kristin SCHAB
36 Asst Dean Career Development .... Ms. Beverly A. EVANS
06 Assistant Registrar .... Mr. Matthew ROSS
19 Director of Public Safety .... Mr. Edward C. BRUDER
39 Director of Residence Life .... Mr. Robbie BACON
15 Director Human Resources .... Mrs. Vicki L. STEWART
38 Director Counseling Services .... Mr. Darrell WILT
91 Dir Administrative Computer Center .... Mr. Brian K. SMELTZER
23 Director Health Services .... Mrs. Amy DOWNS
40 Director Bookstore .... Mrs. Lynn P. FERRO
88 Director Campus & Special Events .... Ms. Sherry HEFLIN
102 Dir Corporate/Foundation/Govt Rels .... Mr. Jeffrey VERMEULEN
27 College Editor .... Mrs. Gail HUGANIR
42 Coordinator Religious Activities .... Mrs. Louise WORLEY
31 Dean Ctr for Community Engagement .... Dr. Dominic F. DELLICARPINI
09 Director of Institutional Research .... Ms. Sarah GALLIMORE
35 Asst Dean Student Affairs .... Dr. Darrien DAVENPORT
24 Dir Center for Teaching & Learning .... Mrs. Cindy CRIMMINS
44 Sr Dir Principal & Planned Gifts .... Mr. Mark RANK
04 Executive Asst to President .... Mrs. Cynthia E. REISINGER

YTI Career Institute (G)

2900 Fairway Drive, Altoona PA 16602
County: Blair FICE Identification: 030819
Unit ID: 375939
Telephone: (814) 944-5643 Carnegie Class: Assoc/HVT-High Trad
FAX Number: (814) 944-5309 Calendar System: Quarter
URL: www.yti.edu
Established: 2006 Annual Undergrad Tuition & Fees: N/A
Enrollment: 334 Coed
Affiliation or Control: Proprietary IRS Status: Proprietary
Highest Offering: Associate Degree
Accreditation: ACCSC, #COARC, MAC

01 Campus President .... Ms. Natalie LOMBARDO
05 Director of Education .... Mr. Jack MARQUIS

YTI Career Institute (H)

3050 Hempland Road, Lancaster PA 17601
Telephone: (717) 295-1100 Identification: 770588
Accreditation: ACCSC, CAHIIM, MAC

YTI Career Institute (I)

1405 Williams Road, York PA 17402-9017
County: York FICE Identification: 021274
Unit ID: 217077
Telephone: (717) 757-1100 Carnegie Class: Assoc/HVT-High Trad
FAX Number: (717) 757-4964 Calendar System: Quarter
URL: www.yti.edu
Established: 1967 Annual Undergrad Tuition & Fees: N/A
Enrollment: 1,677 Coed
Affiliation or Control: Proprietary IRS Status: Proprietary
Highest Offering: Associate Degree
Accreditation: ACCSC, ACFEI, MAC

01 Chairman and CEO .... Mr. Timothy FOSTER
12 President - York .... Ms. Adrienne SCOTT
12 President - Lancaster .... Ms. Sherry ERNEY
12 President - Altoona .... Mrs. Natalie LOMBARDO
12 President - MTC .... Ms. Adrienne SCOTT
05 Sr VP Education & Regulatory .... Vacant

RHODE ISLAND

Brown University (J)

Providence RI 02912
County: Providence FICE Identification: 003401
Unit ID: 217156
Telephone: (401) 863-1000 Carnegie Class: DU-Highest
FAX Number: (401) 863-3700 Calendar System: Semester
URL: www.brown.edu
Established: 1764 Annual Undergrad Tuition & Fees: $49,346
Enrollment: 9,181 Coed
Affiliation or Control: Independent Non-Profit IRS Status: 501(c)3
Highest Offering: Doctorate
Accreditation: EH, ENG, IPSY, MED, PDPSY, PH

01 President .... Christina H. PAXSON
05 Provost .... Richard M. LOCKE
30 Sr Vice Pres for Univ Advancement .... Patricia WATSON
102 Exec Vice Pres Planning & Policy .... Russell C. CAREY
10 Exec VP Finance/Administration .... Barbara D. CHERNOW
26 VP for Communications .... Cass CLIATT
43 Vice President/General Counsel .... Beverly E. LEDBETTER
13 Vice Pres Computing/Info Services .... Ravindra PENDSE
29 Vice President Alumni Relations .... Todd G. ANDREWS
18 Vice Pres for Facilities Management .... Stephen M. MAIORISI
46 Vice President for Research .... David SAVITZ
15 Vice Pres for Human Resources .... Karen DAVIS
32 Vice Pres Campus Life/Student Svcs .... Vacant
20 Deputy Provost .... Joseph S. MEISEL
28 Assoc Provost Acad Devel/Diversity .... Liza CARIAGA-LO
63 Dean Medicine & Biological Sciences .... Jack ELIAS
58 Dean of Graduate School .... Andrew G. CAMPBELL
20 Dean of the Faculty .... Kevin MCLAUGHLIN
20 Dean of the College .... Maud MANDEL
07 Dean of Admission .... Logan POWELL
31 Director State/Community Relations .... Albert A. DAHLBERG
08 University Librarian .... Harriette HEMMASI
21 University Controller/Assistant VP .... Donald S. SCHANCK
41 Director of Athletics .... Jack HAYES
06 Registrar .... Robert F. FITZGERALD
37 Director of Financial Aid .... James TILTON
19 Dir Public Safety/Chief of Police .... Mark J. PORTER
38 Director Psychological Services .... Sherri NELSON
09 Director of Institutional Research .... Katharine T. BARNES
96 Director of Procurement .... Jeanne HEBERT

Bryant University (K)

1150 Douglas Pike, Smithfield RI 02917-1291
County: Providence FICE Identification: 003402
Unit ID: 217165
Telephone: (401) 232-6000 Carnegie Class: Masters/M
FAX Number: (401) 232-6319 Calendar System: Semester
URL: www.bryant.edu
Established: 1863 Annual Undergrad Tuition & Fees: $39,808
Enrollment: 3,462 Coed
Affiliation or Control: Independent Non-Profit IRS Status: 501(c)3
Highest Offering: Beyond Master's But Less Than Doctorate
Accreditation: EH, #ARCPA, BUS

00 Chairman Board of Trustees .... Mr. William CONATY
01 President .... Mr. Ronald K. MACHTLEY
04 Exec Asst to the President .... Dr. Roger ANDERSON
05 Provost .... Mr. Glenn SULMASY
32 VP & Dean Student Affairs .... Dr. John SADDLEMIRE
82 VP International Affairs .... Dr. Hong YANG
10 VP Business Affairs .... Mr. Barry F. MORRISON
30 VP University Advancement .... Mr. David WEGRZYN
13 VP Information Services/CIO .... Mr. Chuck LOCURTO
15 Assoc VP Human Resources .... Ms. Linda S. LULLI

18 Asst VP Campus Management .... Mr. Brian J. BRITTON
21 Asst VP Business & Controller .... Mr. Farokh BHADA
49 Dean College of Arts & Sciences .... Dr. Wendy SAMTER
50 Int Dean College of Business .... Dr. Madan ANNAVARJULA
58 Asst Dean Graduate School .... Mr. Tony WHEELER
84 VP Enrollment Management .... Ms. Michelle CLOUTIER
51 Dir Exec Development Center .... Ms. Annette CERILLI
88 Exec Dir Inst for Family Enterprise .... Dr. William T. O'HARA
88 Dir RI Export Assistance Center .... Mr. Raymond FOGARTY
89 Dir Academic Center for Excellence .... Dr. Laurie L. HAZARD
20 Asst VP Teaching and Learning .... Vacant
06 Registrar .... Ms. Susan MCLACKEN
20 Asst to VP Academic Affairs .... Ms. Elizabeth A. POWERS
35 Assoc Dean of Students .... Mr. Robert E. SLOSS
39 Assoc Dean Residence Life .... Mr. John DENIO
35 Assoc Dean Student Life .... Ms. Judy KAWAMOTO
88 Dir Bryant Center Operations .... Mr. Richard DANKEL
36 Dir Career Services .... Ms. Barbara FINEMAN
42 Chaplain Campus Ministry .... Rev. Philip DEVENS
38 Dir Counseling Services .... Mr. William PHILLIPS
23 Dir Health Services .... Ms. Susan CURRAN
28 Dir Intercultural Center .... Dr. Mailee KUE
19 Dir Public Safety .... Mr. Stephen BANNON
31 Dir Student Involvement Center .... Mr. John LINDSAY
88 Asst Dir Women's Center .... Ms. Kelly BOUTIN
07 Dir Transfer Admission .... Ms. Brenda DORAN
07 Sr Assoc Dir Mulitcult Admission .... Ms. Priscilla ALICEA
07 Assoc Dir International Admission .... Mr. John ERIKSEN
37 Dir Financial Aid .... Mr. John B. CANNING
88 Dir Conferences & Special Events .... Ms. Sheila GUAY
96 Dir Purchasing & Support Services .... Ms. Paulette RATTIGAN
44 Exec Dir Development .... Mr. Edward MAGRO
29 Dir Alumni Relations .... Ms. Robin T. WARDE
90 Dir Acad Computing & Media Svcs .... Mr. Phillip LOMBARDI
91 Dir Admin Systems .... Ms. Christine BIGWOOD
14 Dir Computer & Telecomm Svcs .... Mr. Richard SIEDZIK
08 Dir Library Services .... Ms. Mary F. MORONEY
16 Assoc Dir Human Resources .... Ms. Catherine CURRIE
41 Dir Athletics .... Mr. Bill SMITH
09 Dir Planning & Inst Research .... Mr. Robert JONES
88 Exec Dir US-China Institute .... Dr. Hong YANG
40 Manager Bookstore .... Mr. Stanley STOWIK
26 Chief Public Relations/Marketing .... Ms. Ellizabeth O'NEILL
104 Director Study Abroad .... Ms. Cyndi LEWIS
102 Dir Foundation/Corporate Relations .... Ms. Robin RICHARDSON

Community College of Rhode Island (A)

400 East Avenue, Warwick RI 02886-1807
County: Kent FICE Identification: 003408
Unit ID: 217475
Telephone: (401) 825-1000 Carnegie Class: Assoc/HT-High Trad
FAX Number: (401) 825-2166 Calendar System: Semester
URL: www.ccri.edu
Established: 1964 Annual Undergrad Tuition & Fees (In-State): $4,266
Enrollment: 17,553 Coed
Affiliation or Control: State IRS Status: 501(c)3
Highest Offering: Associate Degree
Accreditation: EH, ACBSP, ADNUR, ART, COARC, COMTA, DA, DH, DMS, HT, MLTAD, MUS, OTA, PNUR, PTAA, RAD

01 President .... Dr. Meghan HUGHES
05 Interim VP for Academic Affairs .... Dr. Rosemary COSTIGAN
10 Vice President for Business Affairs .... Mr. David B. PATTEN
32 VP Stdnt Affs & Chf Outcomes Ofcr .... Ms. Sara ENRIGHT
30 Assoc VP Institutional Advancement .... Ms. Izabel D. DEARAUJO-RIVERA
32 Assoc VP for Student Services .... Dr. Ronald L. SCHERTZ
84 Int Dean of Enrollment Services .... Mr. Joel A. FRIEDMAN
18 Director of Physical Plant .... Mr. Kenneth F. MCCABE
49 Int Dean Arts/Humanities/Soc Sci .... Mr. John W. COLE
66 Interim Assistant Nurse Education .... Dr. Hilary JANSSON
50 Dean Business/Science/Technology .... Dr. Peter N. WOODBERRY
51 Assoc Vice President of CWCE .... Ms. Robin Ann SMITH
08 Dean of Learning Resources .... Ms. Ruth D. SULLIVAN
35 Dean of Students .... Mr. Michael J. CUNNINGHAM, II
21 Controller .... Ms. Sharon A. PICARD
35 Assoc Dean Student Life/Svc Lrng .... Dr. Rebecca H. YOUNT
15 Director of Human Resources .... Ms. Sheri L. NORTON
13 Chief Information Officer .... Mr. Anthony J. PARZIALE
19 Director of Safety & Security .... Mr. Dale R. WETHERELL
26 Director Marketing & Communications .... Vacant
41 Director of Athletics .... Mr. Joseph PAVONE
09 Director Inst Research/Planning .... Dr. William LEBLANC
21 Bursar .... Mr. Dennis J. GRASSINI
88 Director Access to Opportunity .... Ms. Tracy KARASINSKI
40 Director Bookstore Operations .... Ms. Colleen D. TURCOTTE
29 Director of Alumni Affairs .... Ms. Marisa ALBINI
22 Dir AA/EEO/Div/Incl/Title IX Coord .... Mr. Alphonso ATKINS, JR.
96 Director of Purchasing .... Ms. Lisa M. CONSIVINE-FONTES
21 Business Manager .... Ms. Ruth A. BARRINGTON
36 Coordinator Career Services .... Ms. Camille NUMRICH
37 Director of Financial Aid .... Mr. Joel A. FRIEDMAN

Johnson & Wales University (B)

8 Abbott Park Place, Providence RI 02903-3703
County: Providence FICE Identification: 003404
Unit ID: 217235
Telephone: (401) 598-1000 Carnegie Class: Masters/L
FAX Number: (401) 598-2880 Calendar System: Quarter
URL: www.jwu.edu
Established: 1914 Annual Undergrad Tuition & Fees: $29,566
Enrollment: 9,955 Coed
Affiliation or Control: Independent Non-Profit IRS Status: 501(c)3
Highest Offering: Doctorate
Accreditation: EH, #ARCPA, DIETD

00 Chairman of the Board .... Mr. James H. HANCE, JR.
01 Chancellor .... Mr. John J. BOWEN
12 COO/Providence Campus President .... Ms. Mim L. RUNEY
32 Vice President of Student Affairs .... Mr. Ronald MARTEL
05 Executive Vice Chancellor/Provost .... Mr. Thomas L. DWYER
30 Vice President of Resource Developm .... Ms. Page C. SCIOTTO
88 Vice Pres of Student Acad Fin Svcs .... Ms. Lynn ROBINSON
10 Treasurer and CFO .... Mr. Joseph J. GREENE
43 General Counsel .... Mr. Bud REMILLARD
36 VP of Experiential Educ/Career Svcs .... Ms. Maureen DUMAS
84 Sr VP of Enrollment Management .... Mr. Kenneth F. DISAIA
15 Vice President of Human Resources .... Ms. Diane D'AMBRA
50 Dean of College of Mgmt .... Mr. Lou DIABROSCO
49 Dean of Arts & Sciences .... Ms. Angela RENAUD
54 Dean of the School of Engr & Design .... Mr. Frank TWEEDIE
88 Dean of Culinary Education .... Mr. Peter LEHMULLER
109 Vice President of Auxiliary Service .... Mr. Michael DOWNING
18 VP of Facilities and Const Mgmt .... Mr. Robert TAYLOR
13 Chief Information Officer .... Mr. Akhi GUPTA
11 Senior Vice Pres of Administration .... Ms. Marie BERNARDO-SOUSA
100 Chief of Staff & Corp Secretary .... Ms. Emily GILCREAST
96 Director of Procurement .... Mr. Michael GILLARDI
36 Director of Ext Educ & Career Svcs .... Ms. Sheri ISPIR
09 Director of Institutional Research .... Mr. George REZENDES
19 Chief Security Officer .... Major Michael P. QUINN
21 University Budget Director .... Ms. Eileen T. HASKINS
88 Director of Student Communications .... Ms. Kristine E. MCNAMARA
88 Dean of Academic Program Develop .... Mr. Paul J. MCVETY
106 Dean School Online & Cont Educ .... Ms. Cynthia L. PARKER
88 Director Center for Acad Support .... Ms. Mary Ann CANNING MCCOMISKEY
06 University Registrar .... Ms. Tammy HARRIGAN
08 Dean of Libraries .... Ms. Rosita HOPPER
39 Director Residential Life .... Mr. Jev KRAGULJEVIC
41 Director of Athletics .... Ms. Jamie MARCOUX
86 VP Comm/Government Relations .... Ms. Lisa PELOSI

New England Institute of Technology (C)

One New England Tech Blvd., East Greenwich RI 02818
County: Kent FICE Identification: 007845
Unit ID: 217305
Telephone: (800) 736-7744 Carnegie Class: Bac/Assoc-Mixed
FAX Number: (401) 886-0859 Calendar System: Quarter
URL: www.neit.edu
Established: 1940 Annual Undergrad Tuition & Fees: $23,031
Enrollment: 2,922 Coed
Affiliation or Control: Independent Non-Profit IRS Status: 501(c)3
Highest Offering: Master's
Accreditation: EH, ADNUR, #COARC, ENGT, NUR, OT, OTA, PTAA, SURGT

01 President .... Mr. Richard I. GOUSE
03 Executive Vice President .... Mr. Seth KURN
05 Senior Vice President and Provost .... Dr. Douglas H. SHERMAN
10 Sr VP Financial Affs & Endowment .... Ms. Cheryl C. CONNORS
32 Vice Pres Student Support Services .... Ms. Catherine E. KENNEDY
21 VP of Finance & Business Admin .... Mr. Robert R. THEROUX
20 Associate Provost .... Dr. Henry YOUNG
07 Director of Admissions .... Mr. Michael CARUSO
37 Director Financial Aid .... Ms. Anna KELLY
08 Director Library .... Ms. Susan WARTHMAN
36 Director of Career Services .... Ms. Patricia BLAKEMORE
109 Director Auxiliary Services .... Mr. Patrick TRACEY
06 Registrar .... Ms. Doreen LASIEWSKI
35 Director Student Affairs .... Ms. Lee PEEBLES
30 Dir of Development & Alumni Rels .... Ms. Joan SEGERSON
09 Director of Institutional Research .... Dr. Henry YOUNG
106 Dir Online Education/E-learning .... Mr. Larry BOUTHILLIER
13 Chief Info Technology Officer (CIO) .... Mr. Jacques LAFLAMME
18 Chief Facilities/Physical Plant .... Mr. Patrick TRACEY
26 Chief Public Relations/Marketing .... Mr. Steven H. KITCHIN
84 Director Enrollment Management .... Ms. Kathleen EHLERS
103 Dir Workforce/Career Development .... Mr. Steven H. KITCHIN
19 Director Security/Safety .... Mr. Robert WARREN
29 Director Alumni Relations .... Ms. Joan SEGERSON
43 Dir Legal Services/General Counsel .... Mr. Philip PARSONS
96 Director of Purchasing .... Mr. William MENARD

Providence College (D)

1 Cunningham Square, Providence RI 02918-0001
County: Providence FICE Identification: 003406
Unit ID: 217402
Telephone: (401) 865-1000 Carnegie Class: Masters/L
FAX Number: (401) 865-2057 Calendar System: Semester
URL: www.providence.edu
Established: 1917 Annual Undergrad Tuition & Fees: $45,400
Enrollment: 4,533 Coed
Affiliation or Control: Roman Catholic IRS Status: 501(c)3
Highest Offering: Master's
Accreditation: EH, BUS, MUS, SW

01 President .... Rev. Brian J. SHANLEY, OP
03 Executive Vice President/Treasurer .... Rev. Kenneth R. SICARD, OP
04 Asst to Pres & Exec Vice President .... Ms. Ann MANCHESTER-MOLAK
05 Sr VP Academic Affairs/Provost .... Dr. Hugh F. LENA, III
10 Sr VP for Finance & Business/CFO .... Mr. John M. SWEENEY
30 Sr VP for Institutional Advancement .... Mr. Gregory T. WALDRON
32 Vice Pres Student Affairs .... Ms. Kristine C. GOODWIN
43 Vice President/General Counsel .... Ms. Marifrances MCGINN
42 Vice Pres for Mission & Ministry .... Rev. R. Gabriel PIVARNIK, OP
21 Assoc VP for Finance/Asst Treasurer .... Ms. Jacqueline M. WHITE
35 Assoc VP for Student Affairs .... Dr. Steven A. SEARS
20 Assoc VP for Academic Affairs .... Dr. Brian J. BARTOLINI
41 Assoc VP for Athletics/Athletic Dir .... Mr. Robert G. DRISCOLL
15 Assoc Vice Pres for Human Resources .... Ms. Kathleen M. ALVINO
28 Assoc VP/Chief Diversity Officer .... Mr. Rafael A. ZAPATA
26 Assoc VP Public Affairs/Cmty Rels .... Mr. Steven J. MAURANO
20 Asst Vice Pres for Academic Affairs .... Mr. Charles J. HABERLE
21 Asst Vice Pres for Business Svcs .... Mr. Warren S. GRAY
29 Asst Vice Pres for Alumni Relations .... Mr. Robert FERREIRA
44 Asst Vice Pres for Development .... Ms. Lynne FRASER
45 Asst VP Capital Projects & Fac Plng .... Mr. Mark F. RAPOZA
58 Dean of Undergrad & Grad Studies .... Rev. Mark D. NOWEL, OP
49 Dean School of Arts & Sciences .... Dr. Sheila A. LIOTTA
107 Dean School of Professional Studies .... Dr. Brian M. MCCADDEN
07 Assoc VP Admissions/Financial Aid .... Mr. Raul A. FONTS
50 Dean School of Business .... Dr. Sylvia MAXFIELD
51 Dean School of Continuing Education .... Dr. Janet L. CASTLEMAN
35 AVP Stdnt Affs/Asst Dean of Stdnts .... Ms. Tiffany D. GAFFNEY
84 Dean of Enrollment Services .... Ms. Yvonne D. ARRUDA
104 Dean of International Studies .... Mr. Adrian G. BEAULIEU
35 Director of Student Activities .... Ms. Sharon L. HAY
84 Associate Dean of Enrollment Svcs .... Ms. Ann E. BARONE
37 Exec Director of Financial Aid .... Ms. Sandra J. OLIVEIRA
19 Exec Director Safety & Security .... Mr. John J. LEYDEN
88 Asst VP Integrated Learning & Admin .... Ms. Patricia A. GOFF
18 Exec Director of Physical Plant .... Mr. William J. HARTIGAN
08 Director of Library .... Dr. Donald R. BAILEY
09 Director of Institutional Research .... Ms. Melanie R. SULLIVAN
90 Dir Enterprise Infrastructure & Ops .... Mr. Carmine R. PISCOPO
92 Director Liberal Arts Honors .... Dr. Stephen J. LYNCH
96 Director Central Purch/Receiving .... Mr. Mark S. MCGOVERN
88 Director of Academic Svcs/Wrt Ctr .... Mr. Bryan D. MARINELLI
38 VP Student Development & Compliance .... Dr. James F. CAMPBELL
13 Chief Info Technology Officer (CIO) .... Mr. Paul V. FONTAINE

Rhode Island College (E)

600 Mount Pleasant Avenue, Providence RI 02908-1991
County: Providence FICE Identification: 003407
Unit ID: 217420
Telephone: (401) 456-8000 Carnegie Class: Masters/L
FAX Number: (401) 456-8379 Calendar System: Semester
URL: www.ric.edu
Established: 1854 Annual Undergrad Tuition & Fees (In-State): $8,197
Enrollment: 8,641 Coed
Affiliation or Control: State IRS Status: 501(c)3
Highest Offering: Doctorate
Accreditation: EH, ART, CACREP, MUS, NURSE, SW, TED

01 President .... Dr. Frank A. SANCHEZ
05 Vice President Academic Affairs .... Dr. Ronald E. PITT
10 Vice Pres Administration & Finance .... Mr. David A. GINGERELLA
32 Int Vice President Student Affairs .... Dr. Scott KANE
30 Int VP College Advance & Col Rels .... Mr. Clark M. GREENE
107 Assoc VP Prof Studies & Cont Educ .... Ms. Jenifer GIROUX
20 Asst VP Acad Affairs/Enroll Mgmt .... Dr. Holly L. SHADOIAN
21 Controller .... Mr. Stephen J. NEDDER
13 Asst VP Information Services .... Ms. Pamela CHRISTMAN
44 Assc VP for Develop & External Rels .... Mr. Edwin R. PACHECO
15 Director of Human Resources .... Ms. Maggie SULLIVAN
49 Dean Faculty Arts & Sciences .... Dr. Earl L. SIMSON
53 Dean Sch Education & Human Dev .... Dr. Donald C. HALQUIST
66 Dean School of Nursing .... Dr. Jane WILLIAMS
50 Dean School of Management .... Dr. Jeffrey MELLO
70 Dean School of Social Work .... Dr. Roberta S. PEARLMUTTER
58 Int Dean of Graduate Studies .... Dr. Leslie SCHUSTER
08 Director of the Library .... Ms. Carissa DELIZIO
100 Coordinator of President's Staff .... Vacant
26 Dir of Communications & Marketing .... Vacant
105 Director Web Services .... Ms. Karen M. RUBINO
07 Director of Admissions .... Mr. John MCLAUGHLIN
06 Director of Records .... Ms. Tamecka C. HARDMON
37 Director Student Financial Aid .... Mr. Kenneth S. FERUS
25 Director of Research & Creative Act .... Ms. Lisa SMOLSKI
18 Director Facilities & Operations .... Mr. James M. JERUE
90 Director User Support Services .... Mr. Paul MORRIS
91 Director MIS .... Dr. Bin YU
14 Director Network/Telecommunications .... Mr. Henk E. SONDER
19 Director of Security & Safety .... Mr. Frederick W. GHIO
09 Dir Inst Research & Planning .... Dr. Christopher P. HOURIGAN
96 Director of Purchasing .... Ms. Jessica L. SILVA
41 Dir of Athletics & AVP for Admin .... Mr. Donald E. TENCHER
39 Director Residential Life/Housing .... Ms. Teresa L. BROWN
36 Int Director Career Dev Center .... Ms. Demetria MORAN
23 Director College Health Services .... Ms. Lynn A. WACHTEL
38 Director Counseling Center .... Dr. Thomas J. LAVIN
29 Director Alumni Affairs .... Ms. Suzanna ALBA
40 Manager Campus Store .... Mr. Steven PLATT
104 Director of Study Abroad .... Dr. Olga JUZYN
88 Director of Budget .... Mr. Robert EATON
102 Int Director RIC Foundation .... Mr. Clark GREENE
28 Director of Diversity .... Ms. Antoinette GOMES
22 Dir Affirmative Action/EEO .... Ms. Robinette KELLEY

Rhode Island School of Design (A)

2 College Street, Providence RI 02903-2784

County: Providence | FICE Identification: 003409 | Unit ID: 217493
Telephone: (401) 454-6100 | Carnegie Class: Spec-4-yr-Arts
FAX Number: (401) 454-6320 | Calendar System: 4/1/4
URL: www.risd.edu
Established: 1877 | Annual Undergrad Tuition & Fees: $45,840
Enrollment: 2,449 | Coed
Affiliation or Control: Independent Non-Profit | IRS Status: 501(c)3
Highest Offering: Master's
Accreditation: EH, ART, LSAR

Code	Title	Name
01	President	Ms. Rosanne SOMERSON
04	Executive Assistant to President	Ms. Jessica HODGDEN
05	Provost	Mr. Pradeep SHARMA
30	Vice Pres Institutional Engagement	Mr. William KRAMER
15	Vice Pres Human Resources	Ms. Candace BAER
26	Exec Dir Marketing & Communications	Ms. Kerci M. STROUD
88	Director RISD Museum of Art	Mr. John W. SMITH
45	VP Integrated Planning	Ms. Mara HERMANO
10	Chief Financial Officer	Mr. Samuel SOLOMON
20	Assoc Provost Acad Affairs	Ms. Tracie COSTANTINO
48	Dean Architecture & Design	Ms. Nancy SKOLOS
57	Dean of Fine Arts	Ms. Sheri WILLS
89	Dean of Foundation Studies	Ms. Joanne STRYKER
49	Dean of Liberal Arts	Dr. Daniel CAVICCHI
51	Exec Dir Continuing Education	Ms. Sarah CAGGIANO
08	Director Library Services	Vacant
84	VP Enrollment Management	Vacant
07	Assoc VP Enrollment	Mr. Edward NEWHALL, JR.
37	Asst VP for Enrollment Services	Mr. Anthony GALLONIO
13	CIO	Mr. Richard MICKOOL
18	VP Facilities & EHS	Mr. Jack SILVA
32	Dean of Students	Ms. Margaret BALCH
105	Sr Dir Digital Media Communication	Mr. Brian CLARK
43	General Counsel	Mr. Steven MCDONALD
27	Director of Media Relations	Ms. Jaime MARLAND
19	Director Public Safety	Mr. Normand GAMACHE
09	Director Institutional Research	Mr. Yi NI
108	Director Institutional Assessment	Vacant
21	Director Budget	Mr. Robert HANKE
21	Controller	Mr. Thomas MATTOS
86	Director Government Relations	Ms. Babette ALLINA
29	Director of Alumni Relations	Ms. Christina HARTLEY
88	AVP Strategic Initiatives	Mr. Brian GOLDBERG
44	Director Annual Fund	Ms. Sarah SLIGO
06	Registrar	Vacant
96	Director Procurement Services	Mr. Christopher SWEZEY
14	Director Network Services	Mr. Steven BOUDREAU
27	Director Editorial Services/Media	Ms. Liisa SILANDER
23	Director Health Services	Ms. Mary Jo MACKINNON
39	Director of Residence Life	Mr. Kevin FORTI
38	Dir Student Development/Counseling	Ms. Shauna SUMMERS
102	Dir Corp/Found & Govt Partnerships	Ms. Sara SULLIVAN
101	Director Trustee Relations	Mr. Andrew GAMMON
40	Director RISD Store	Ms. Tila ADAMS
35	Assistant Dean Student Affairs	Mr. Anthony JOHNSON
104	Director RISD Global	Ms. Gwen FARRELLY
109	Dir of Auxiliary Services	Ms. Ginnie DUNLEAVY

Roger Williams University (B)

One Old Ferry Road, Bristol RI 02809-2921

County: Bristol | FICE Identification: 003410 | Unit ID: 217518
Telephone: (401) 253-1040 | Carnegie Class: Masters/M
FAX Number: N/A | Calendar System: Semester
URL: www.rwu.edu
Established: 1956 | Annual Undergrad Tuition & Fees: $31,800
Enrollment: 4,884 | Coed
Affiliation or Control: Independent Non-Profit | IRS Status: 501(c)3
Highest Offering: First Professional Degree
Accreditation: EH, BUS, CONST, ENG, LAW

Code	Title	Name
01	President	Dr. Donald J. FARISH
05	Provost/Sr VP Academic Affairs	Dr. Andrew A. WORKMAN
10	EVP Finance/Administration	Mr. Jerome WILLIAMS
100	Chief of Staff	Mr. Richard HALE
84	VP Enrollment Management	Vacant
21	VP for Accounting/Treasury Mgmt	Mr. Marc LEONETTI
32	Vice President for Student Life	Mr. John J. KING
30	VP Institutional Advancement	Ms. Lisa RAIOLA
45	VP University Outreach/Engagement	Mr. Peter B. WILBUR
08	Dean University Library	Ms. Betsy P. LEARNED
35	Dean of Students	Vacant
88	Asst VP Enrollment Management	Ms. Tracy M. DACOSTA
28	Director Intercultural Center	Mr. Don MAYS
61	Dean RWU School of Law	Mr. Michael J. YELNOSKY
48	Dean Sch Arch/Art & Hist Preserv	Mr. Stephen E. WHITE
50	Dean Gabelli School of Business	Dr. Susan MCTIERNAN
54	Dean Sch Engrng/Comput/Constr Mgmt	Dr. Robert A. POTTER
61	Dean School of Justice Studies	Dr. Stephanie PICOLO MANZI
20	Vice Provost Academic Affairs	Dr. Robert A. COLE
07	Director Graduate Admissions	Mr. Marcus HANSCOM
49	Dean Feinstein Col Arts & Sciences	Dr. Robert EISINGER
07	Dir Admissions Operations/Outreach	Ms. Amanda MARSILI
26	Director of Marketing	Ms. Lori COCHRANE
96	Director of Purchasing	Mr. Thomas KANE
29	Assoc Dean/Dir of Conferences	Ms. Allison CHASE PADULA
06	Registrar	Ms. Joan ROMANO
19	Director of Public Safety	Mr. Steven MELARAGNO

(continued)

Code	Title	Name
41	Director of Athletics	Mr. Dave KEMMY
18	Director of Facilities Management	Mr. John TAMEO
36	Assoc Dean/Dir Ctr Career/Prof Dev	Mr. Stephen CANTINE
38	Director Counseling & Student Devel	Dr. James A. AZAR
23	Director Health Services	Vacant
39	Director of Housing	Mr. Anthony MONTEFUSCO
46	Director of Prospect Research	Ms. Nancy L. RAMOS
39	Director Residence Life/Women's Ctr	Ms. Jennifer STANLEY
09	Director Institutional Research	Ms. Jennifer DUNSEATH
40	Manager Bookstore	Vacant

Salve Regina University (C)

100 Ochre Point Avenue, Newport RI 02840-4192

County: Newport | FICE Identification: 003411 | Unit ID: 217536
Telephone: (401) 847-6650 | Carnegie Class: Masters/M
FAX Number: (401) 341-2925 | Calendar System: Semester
URL: www.salve.edu
Established: 1947 | Annual Undergrad Tuition & Fees: $36,740
Enrollment: 2,739 | Coed
Affiliation or Control: Roman Catholic | IRS Status: 501(c)3
Highest Offering: Doctorate
Accreditation: EH, ART, CORE, IACBE, NURSE, SW

Code	Title	Name
01	President	Dr. Jane GERETY, RSM
05	Vice President Academic Affairs	Dr. Scott ZEMAN
32	Vice President Student Affairs	Dr. Barbara LOMONACO
30	VP University Rels/Advancement	Mr. Michael L. SEMENZA
10	Vice President Administration & CFO	Mr. William B. HALL
84	Vice Pres Enrollment Management	Mr. James R. FOWLER
88	Vice Pres Mission Integration	Dr. Leona MISTO, RSM
26	Assoc Vice Pres Univ Rels/CCO	Ms. Kristine HENDRICKSON
21	Assoc Vice Pres Finance/ Controller	Mr. Michael N. GRANDCHAMP
13	Sr Director Info Technology	Mr. Glenn CLARK
15	Director Human Resources	Ms. Cynthia DONNELLY
20	Associate Provost	Dr. Donna M. COOK
09	Asst VP for Research & Compliance	Dr. Frederick C. PROMADES
07	Dean of Undergraduate Admissions	Ms. Colleen EMERSON
35	Assoc VP and Dean of Students	Mr. J. Malcolm SMITH
107	Dean of Academics	Dr. Alison SHAKARIAN
06	Registrar	Ms. Louise MONAST
37	Director of Financial Aid	Ms. Anne MCDERMOTT
29	Director Alumni & Parent Pgms	Dr. Gerry WILLIS
41	Athletic Director	Ms. Jody MOORADIAN
08	Director of Library Services	Ms. Kathleen BOYD
39	Director of Campus Life	Dr. Jim MOURNIGHAN
90	Director Academic Computing	Mr. Brian A. MCDONNELL
18	Director of Facilities	Mr. Eric MILNER
19	Director of Security/Safety	Mr. Michael CARUOLO
40	Director of Bookstore	Mr. Michael LEDDY
44	Sr Dir Advancement Operations/ Pgms	Ms. Victoria DUCLOS-BARRETT
23	Manager of Health Services	Ms. Sharon Q. CAPUANO
35	Director of Student Activities	Ms. Chiquita BAYLOR
36	Director of Career Development	Mr. Michael WISNEWSKI
96	Director of Purchasing	Ms. Francine LUNN
104	Director of International Programs	Ms. Erin FITZGERALD
38	Dir of Student Counseling Services	Ms. Meghan M. DECARVALHO

University of Rhode Island (D)

Kingston RI 02881-0806

County: Washington | FICE Identification: 003414 | Unit ID: 217484
Telephone: (401) 874-1000 | Carnegie Class: DU-Higher
FAX Number: (401) 874-7149 | Calendar System: Semester
URL: www.uri.edu
Established: 1892 | Annual Undergrad Tuition & Fees (In-State): $12,862
Enrollment: 16,571 | Coed
Affiliation or Control: State | IRS Status: 501(c)3
Highest Offering: Doctorate
Accreditation: EH, BUS, BUSA, CLPSY, CYTO, DIETD, DIETI, ENG, LIB, LSAR, MFCD, MUS, NURSE, PHAR, PTA, SCPSY, SP, TED

Code	Title	Name
01	President	Dr. David M. DOOLEY
100	Chief of Staff	Ms. Michelle CURRERI
05	Provost/Vice Pres Academic Affairs	Dr. Donald H. DEHAYES
46	Vice Pres Research/Economic Devel	Dr. Gerald SONNENFELD
10	Vice Pres for Admin & Finance	Dr. Christina VALENTINO
88	Assoc VP Res/Int Prop Mgmt/Comm	Mr. Michael KATZ
88	Dir Univ Res External Relations	Ms. Melissa MCCARTHY
88	Dir Research Development	Ms. Karen MARKIN
25	Director Sponsored Projects	Ms. Winifred NWANGWU
88	Dir Research Integrity	Mr. Theodore A. MYATT
29	Exec Dir Alumni Relations/Secy Assn	Ms. Michele NOTA
86	Dir Legislative and Govt Rels	Ms. Kelly MAHONEY
26	Exec Dir Cmty & Community Rels	Ms. Linda A. ACCIARDO
88	Dir Publications and Creative Svcs	Vacant
21	Dir Budget & Financial Planning	Ms. Linda BARRETT
21	Controller	Ms. Sharon B. BELL
15	Asst Vice Pres Human Resource Admin	Ms. Anne Marie COLEMAN
16	Director Personnel Services	Ms. Laura KENERSON
18	Asst Vice Pres Business Services	Mr. J. Vernon WYMAN
19	Int Director Public Safety	Mr. Stephen N. BAKER
12	Dir W.A. Jones Campus	Ms. Maria DISANO
88	Assoc Dean Business Administration	Dr. Deborah ROSEN
88	Dir Capital Projects	Mr. Paul DEPACE
88	Dir Campus Planning and Design	Mr. Christopher MCMAHAN
88	Dir Facility Services	Mr. Jerome SIDIO
88	Dir Property & Support Svc	Mr. Bill MATTESON
96	Director Purchasing & Univ Stores	Ms. Betty GIL
28	Assoc VP Comm/Equity/Diversity	Ms. Naomi THOMPSON
43	General Counsel	Mr. Louis J. SACCOCCIO
32	Vice President Student Affairs	Ms. Kathy M. COLLINS
109	Dir Dining Services/Auxiliary	Mr. Steven MELLO
41	Director of Athletics	Mr. Thorr D. BJORN
103	Dir Career and Experiential Edu	Ms. Kim STACK
38	Director Counseling Center	Dr. Robert SAMUELS
88	Dir Recreational Services	Ms. Jodi HAWKINS
35	Asst VP Stdnt Affs & Dean of Stdnts	Dr. Mary J. GONZALES
88	Dir Special Pgms/Talent Devel	Mr. Gerald WILLIAMS
88	Mgr Conf & Spec Pgm Dev	Mr. Joseph PITTLE
35	Asst VP Student Affs & Dir HRL	Mr. John SEARS
39	Interim Dir Housing & Res Life	Dr. Jeffrey PLOUFFE
23	Director Health Services	Ms. Ellen REYNOLDS
40	Administrator Bookstore	Mr. Paul WHITNEY
88	Spec Asst to the Prov for Acad Plng	Ms. Ann M. MORRISSEY
88	Vice Prov Acad Finance/Personnel	Dr. Clifford H. KATZ
09	Director of Institutional Research	Vacant
84	Vice Provost Enrollment Management	Mr. Dean LIBUTTI
07	Dean of Admissions	Ms. Cynthia L. BONN
06	Dir Enrollment Services	Dr. Carnell JONES
101	Vice Provost Faculty Affairs	Dr. Laura BEAUVAIS
13	Chief Information Officer	Vacant
90	Dir Media & Technology Services	Mr. David S. PORTER
91	Dir University Computing Systems	Mr. Charlie SCHIFINO
51	Dean Col Education & Prof Studies	Dr. Lori CICCOMASCOLO
49	Dean of Arts & Sciences	Dr. Winifred E. BROWNELL
50	Dean Business Administration	Dr. Maling EBRAHIMPOUR
54	Dean of Engineering	Dr. Raymond M. WRIGHT
88	Dean Univ Col & Spec Acad Pgms	Dr. Jayne E. RICHMOND
58	Dean of Graduate School	Dr. Nasser H. ZAWIA
66	Interim Dean of Nursing	Dr. Barbara E. WOLFE
67	Interim Dean of Pharmacy	Dr. Paul LARRAT
69	Dean Human Sciences & Services	Dr. Gary LIQUORI
53	Director School of Education	Dr. David BYRD
88	Dean Grad School Oceanography	Dr. Bruce CORLISS
88	Dean of Environment & Life Sciences	Dr. John KIRBY
08	Dean University Libraries	Mr. Karim B. BOUGHIDA
22	Director Affirm Act/Equal Oppty/Div	Ms. Roxanne GOMES
37	Sr Assoc Dir Enrol Svcs/Fin Aid	Mr. Paul LANGHAMMER
92	Director Honors Program	Dr. Lynne DERBYSHIRE
102	President URI Foundation	Ms. Elizabeth O'ROURKE
85	Dir Intl Students and Scholars	Dr. Dania BRANDFORD-CALVO
106	Dir Learning/Assessment & Online	Dr. Diane GOLDSMITH
94	Dir Gender and Women Studies	Dr. Rosaria PISA
105	Manager Web Services	Ms. Lisa CHEN
30	Dir Advancement Services	Mr. John PELTIER
44	Director Annual or Planned Giving	Ms. Bernadine SADWIN

University of Rhode Island Feinstein Providence Campus (E)

80 Washington Street, Providence RI 02903

Telephone: (401) 277-5000 | Identification: 770118
Accreditation: &EH

† Regional accreditation is carried under the parent institution in Kingston, RI

University of Rhode Island Narragansett Bay Campus (F)

215 South Ferry Road, Narragansett RI 02882-1197

Telephone: (401) 874-6222 | Identification: 770129
Accreditation: &EH

† Regional accreditation is carried under the parent institution in Kingston, RI

SOUTH CAROLINA

Aiken Technical College (G)

PO Drawer 696, Aiken SC 29802-0696

County: Aiken | FICE Identification: 010056 | Unit ID: 217615
Telephone: (803) 508-7263 | Carnegie Class: Assoc/MT-VT-High Trad
FAX Number: (803) 593-6641 | Calendar System: Semester
URL: www.atc.edu
Established: 1972 | Annual Undergrad Tuition & Fees (In-District): $4,352
Enrollment: 2,351 | Coed
Affiliation or Control: State/Local | IRS Status: 501(c)3
Highest Offering: Associate Degree
Accreditation: SC, ACBSP, ADNUR, DA, MAC, PNUR, RAD, SURGT

Code	Title	Name
01	President	Dr. Forest E. MAHAN
04	Executive Assistant to President	Ms. Jill UHLER
30	Director Foundation & Alumni	Ms. Mary COMMONS
05	Vice President Education & Training	Dr. Gemma FROCK
76	Dean of Health Sciences	Dr. Hermecender WALTON
72	Dean of Technical Education	Vacant
97	Dean of General Education	Fr. Frederick ROGERS
51	Dean Business/Computer Technolog	Dr. Steven SIMMONS
10	Vice Pres Administrative Services	Mr. Andy JORDAN
37	Director of Financial Aid	Ms. Sue SIMS
13	Director of Info Systems Mgmt	Mr. Walter BUSBEE
15	Director of Human Resources	Ms. Sylvia BYRD
21	Director of Financial Accounting	Mr. Don TRUE

96 Director of Purchasing .... Ms. Toni MARSHALL
18 Director Facilities & Operations .... Ms. Dorenda SPROWL
84 Vice President Enrollment Mgmt .... Dr. Vinson BURDETTE
07 Director of Intake Services .... Mrs. Jessica MOON
06 Registrar .... Mrs. Dawn BUTTS
38 Director Counseling/Disabilities .... Mr. Rich WELDON
26 Int Dir Marketing & Publications .... Ms. Nikasha DICKS

Allen University (A)

1530 Harden Street, Columbia SC 29204-1085
County: Richland FICE Identification: 003417
Unit ID: 217624
Telephone: (803) 376-5700 Carnegie Class: Bac-A&S
FAX Number: N/A Calendar System: Semester
URL: www.allenuniversity.edu
Established: 1870 Annual Undergrad Tuition & Fees: $13,140
Enrollment: 660 Coed
Affiliation or Control: African Methodist Episcopal IRS Status: 501(c)3
Highest Offering: Baccalaureate
Accreditation: **SC**

01 President .... Dr. Lady June COLE
05 VP Academic/Student Life .... Dr. Charlene SPEAREN
84 VP Enrollment Mgmt .... Mrs. Marilyn DEBERRY
10 Chief Finanical Officer .... Ms. Ruby FIELDING
88 Executive Director of Tiltle III .... Mr. William ROBINSON
07 Interim Director of Admissions .... Mr. Adam DILLIHAY
15 Exec Dir Human Resources & Admin .... Mrs. Paige MOORE
26 Executive Director Marketing .... Dr. Flavia ELDEMIRE
18 Facilities/Physical Plant .... Mr. Timothy TAYLOR
09 Coord Inst Effectiveness/Assessment .... Ms. Kimberly LEBBY
29 Director of Alumni Relations .... Mr. Gaurachandra GARRETT
37 Director of Student Financial Aid .... Mrs. Veronica GRIFFITH
38 Director Counseling Services .... Vacant
04 Exec Assistant to President .... Ms. Geraldine LIVINGSTON
08 Head Librarian .... Ms. Carol BOWERS
19 Director Security/Safety .... Chief Kelvin DAVIS
41 Athletic Director .... Mr. Chad WASHINGTON
06 Registrar .... Ms. Marilyn DEBERRY

Anderson University (B)

316 Boulevard, Anderson SC 29621-4035
County: Anderson FICE Identification: 003418
Unit ID: 217633
Telephone: (864) 231-2000 Carnegie Class: Masters/M
FAX Number: (864) 231-2004 Calendar System: Semester
URL: www.andersonuniversity.edu
Established: 1911 Annual Undergrad Tuition & Fees: $24,860
Enrollment: 3,112 Coed
Affiliation or Control: Other IRS Status: 501(c)3
Highest Offering: Doctorate
Accreditation: **SC**, ACBSP, ART, MUS, NURSE, TED

01 President .... Dr. Evans P. WHITAKER
05 Provost .... Vacant
10 VP for Finance and Operations .... Dr. Danny M. PARKER
30 VP for Development .... Mr. James W. LANDRITH
84 VP of Enrollment Management .... Ms. Pam ROSS
42 VP for Christian Life .... Dr. J. Robert CLINE
32 VP for Student Development .... Dr. James A. FEREIRA
13 Chief Information Officer .... Mr. Peter B. HARVIN
28 VP for Presidential Affairs .... Dr. Beverly R. MCADAMS
44 VP for Principal Gifts .... Mr. Dean WOODS
18 Assoc VP for Facil & Procurement .... Mr. Dane S. SLAUGHTER
06 Dean of Enrollment Svcs & Registrar .... Mrs. Carol A. PARKER
20 Vice Provost .... Mrs. Susan B. WOOTEN
07 Dean of Admissions .... Ms. Pam ROSS
41 Director of Athletics .... Mr. Bill J. D'ANDREA
32 Dean of Student Life .... Mr. Jonathan GROPP
08 Director of Library Services .... Mr. Kent A. MILLWOOD
09 Director of External Reporting .... Mr. Daryl A. IVERSON
37 Director of Financial Aid Planning .... Ms. Allison SULLIVAN
26 Director Marketing & Communications .... Mr. Barry D. RAY
38 Director of Counseling Services .... Ms. Erin C. MAURER
29 Director of Alumni Relations .... Vacant
36 Director Career Services .... Ms. Kelly A. BELL
23 Director Health Services .... Mrs. Deb A. TAYLOR
88 Dir of The Ctr for Student Success .... Ms. L. Dianne KING
15 Director of Human Resources .... Mrs. Rose Mariee ALLISON
39 Assoc Dean of Residence Life .... Ms. Melissa JONES
21 Controller .... Ms. Kristie C. COLE
35 Director of Student Activities .... Ms. Sara MUDD
04 Exec Assistant to the President .... Mrs. Diane SUTHERLAND
104 Director of International
Programs .... Dr. Ann-Margaret J. THEMISTOCLEOUS
19 Director of Campus Safety .... Mr. James KINES

The Art Institute of Charleston (C)

24 North Market Street, Charleston SC 29401-2623
Telephone: (843) 727-3500 Identification: 770976
Accreditation: &SC

† Regional accreditation is carried under the parent institution in Atlanta, GA

Benedict College (D)

Harden and Bland Streets, Columbia SC 29204-1086
County: Richland FICE Identification: 003420
Unit ID: 217721
Telephone: (803) 253-5000 Carnegie Class: Bac-Diverse
FAX Number: (803) 253-5059 Calendar System: Semester
URL: www.benedict.edu
Established: 1870 Annual Undergrad Tuition & Fees: $18,288
Enrollment: 2,444 Coed
Affiliation or Control: Independent Non-Profit IRS Status: 501(c)3
Highest Offering: Baccalaureate
Accreditation: **SC**, ACBSP, ART, NRPA, SW, TED

01 President .... Dr. David H. SWINTON
05 Senior Vice Pres Academic Affairs .... Dr. Janeen WITTY
03 Executive Vice President .... Dr. Ruby W. WATTS
10 Vice President Business/Finance .... Ms. Brenda WALKER
32 Vice President Student Affairs .... Mr. Gary E. KNIGHT
30 Vice Pres Institutional Advancement .... Mrs. Barbara C. MOORE
20 Assoc Vice Pres Academic Affairs .... Dr. George A. DEVLIN
21 Asst VP for Business & Finance .... Ms. Jackie BROWN
26 Asst VP for Comm & Marketing .... Ms. Kymm HUNTER
07 Asst VP for Admissions/Student Mktg .... Mrs. Phyllis THOMPSON
29 Assistant VP for Alumni Relations .... Mrs. Ada A. BELTON
13 Dir Information Technology .... Mr. Dave MEDEIROS
27 Chief Information Officer .... Mr. Dan MURPHY
15 Director of Human Resources .... Mrs. Betty A. JENKINS
06 Registrar/Director Student
Records .... Mrs. Wanda A. SCOTT-KINNEY
41 Athletics Director .... Mr. Willie WASHINGTON
38 Director Service Learning & Leaders .... Ms. Tondaleya JACKSON
42 Dir Campus Ministry/Dean of Chapel .... Mr. Thomas DAVIS
19 Director Campus Safety .... Mr. Haywood M. EAZEMORE
36 Director Career Services .... Ms. Karen W. RUTHERFORD
37 Director Financial Aid .... Ms. Sul BLACK
19 Director Physical Plant .... Ms. Chorte' MARTIN
08 Director of Library .... Mrs. Darlene ZINNERMAN-BETHEA
09 Director Institutional Research .... Mr. Jesse EELLINGER
108 Director Institutional Assessment .... Vacant
25 Coordinator Title III .... Mrs. Doris W. JOHNSON
96 Manager Procurement Services .... Ms. Sharling THOMPSON
49 Dean Sch Human/Arts/Soc Sci .... Dr. Charles AUSTIN
50 Dean School of Business/Econ .... Mr. Gerald SMALLS
88 Dean School of Health Human Service .... Dr. Tanya BRICE
53 Dean School of Education .... Dr. Damara HIGHTOWER
72 Dean Sch Science/Tech/Engrng/
Math .... Dr. Samir S. RAYCHOUDHURY
92 Dean School of Honors .... Dr. Warren ROBINSON
57 Chair Fine Arts .... Ms. Gina MOORE
50 Chair Business Admin/Mgmt/Mktg .... Dr. Tracy H. DUNN
88 Chair Education and Family Studies .... Dr. Tracy MIDDLETON
70 Int Chair Social Work .... Mrs. Brenda CLARK
88 Chair English/Foreign Language Dept .... Dr. Herman HOWARD
88 Chair Bio/Chem/Enviroment Hlth Sci .... Dr. Helene TAMBOUE
81 Chair Math/Computer Science .... Ms. Fereshtah ZAHED
54 Chair Physics/Engineering .... Dr. Fouzi H. ARAMMASH
88 Int Chair Economics/Finance/Acctg .... Dr. Syed MAHDI

Bob Jones University (E)

1700 Wade Hampton Boulevard,
Greenville SC 29614-0001
County: Greenville FICE Identification: 003421
Unit ID: 217749
Telephone: (864) 242-5100 Carnegie Class: Spec-4-yr-Faith
FAX Number: (864) 235-6661 Calendar System: Semester
URL: www.bju.edu
Established: 1927 Annual Undergrad Tuition & Fees: $14,900
Enrollment: 3,108 Coed
Affiliation or Control: Proprietary IRS Status: Proprietary
Highest Offering: Doctorate
Accreditation: @SC, TRACS, ENG

00 Chancellor .... Dr. Bob JONES, III
01 President .... Dr. Stephen D. PETTIT
05 Exec Vice Pres for Academic Affairs .... Dr. Gary M. WEIER
11 Executive Vice Pres for Operations .... Mr. Marshall E. FRANKLIN
30 VP Advancement & Alumni Relations .... Mr. John D. MATTHEWS
42 VP for Ministerial Advancement .... Dr. Samuel E. HORN
27 Chief Communication Officer .... Ms. Carol A. KEIRSTEAD
20 Vice Provost/Chief Admin Officer .... Dr. David A. FISHER
10 Chief Financial Officer .... Mr. Kenrie M. STILL
32 Dean of Students/Chief SLO .... Dr. Eric C. NEWTON
26 Chief Publication Officer .... Mr. Bill APELIAN
15 Chief Human Resources Officer .... Mr. Kevin TAYLOR
18 Chief Facilities Management Officer .... Mr. Steve L. HENSLEY
13 Chief Information Officer .... Mr. Marvin P. REEM
84 Chief Enrollment Officer .... Dr. Bobby WOOD
49 Dean College of Arts and Science .... Dr. Renae WENTWORTH
73 Dean School of Religion & Seminary .... Dr. Samuel E. HORN
57 Dean Sch Fine Arts & Communication .... Dr. Darren E. LAWSON
53 Dean School of Education .... Dr. Brian A. CARRUTHERS
50 Dean School of Business .... Mr. Mike BUITER
73 Assoc Dean School of Religion .... Dr. Royce B. SHORT
73 Assoc Dean Seminary/GrdSch Religion .... Dr. Stephen J. HANKINS
06 Registrar .... Dr. Daniel SMITH
33 Dean of Men .... Mr. Jonathan G. DAULTON
34 Dean of Women .... Ms. Deneen LAWSON
07 Director of Admission .... Mr. Gary A. DEEDRICK
88 Director of Ministry Training .... Dr. Nathan CROCKETT
41 Athletic Director .... Mr. Neal RING
37 Director of Financial Aid .... Mrs. Susan YOUNG
08 Libraries Manager .... Mr. Van CARPENTER
09 Sr Dir Planning/Rsrch/Assessment .... Rev. Phil GERARD

Brown Mackie College-Greenville (F)

75 Beattie Place, Ste. 100, Greenville SC 29601-2155
Telephone: (864) 239-5301 Identification: 666781
Accreditation: **ACICS**, OTA

† Branch campus of Brown Mackie College, Tucson, AZ.

Central Carolina Technical College (G)

506 N Guignard Drive, Sumter SC 29150-2499
County: Sumter FICE Identification: 003995
Unit ID: 218858
Telephone: (803) 778-1961 Carnegie Class: Assoc/HVT-Mix Trad/Non
FAX Number: (803) 778-7880 Calendar System: Semester
URL: www.cctech.edu
Established: 1962 Annual Undergrad Tuition & Fees (In-State): $4,481
Enrollment: 3,963 Coed
Affiliation or Control: State IRS Status: 501(c)3
Highest Offering: Associate Degree
Accreditation: **SC**, ADNUR, MAC, PNUR, SURGT

01 President .... Dr. Tim HARDEE
05 Vice Pres Academics .... Vacant
10 Vice President for Business Affairs .... Ms. Terry L. BOOTH
32 Vice President for Student Affairs .... Ms. Lisa BRACKEN
04 Assistant to the President .... Ms. Diana REARDON
51 Director Cont Educ/Workforce Devel .... Ms. Elizabeth WILLIAMS
08 Dean of Learning Resources .... Ms. Nancy BISHOP
102 Director Foundation .... Ms. Meree MCALISTER
26 Director Public Relations .... Ms. Becky RICKENBAKER
15 Director of Personnel .... Mrs. Ronalda S. STOVER
13 Director Information Systems .... Mr. Brian DAVIS
06 Registrar .... Ms. Henrietta SCOTT
37 Director Student Financial Aid .... Ms. Tiffany WILSON
09 Dir Research/Institutional Effect .... Mr. Bryan MAY
07 Director of Admissions & Counseling .... Mrs. Barbara WRIGHT
54 Dean of Industrial and Engineering .... Mr. Brent RUSSELL
76 Dean of Health Sciences .... Dr. Karen COWELL
53 Dean of General Education .... Mr. Myles WILLIAMS

Charleston School of Law (H)

81 Mary Street, PO Box 535, Charleston SC 29402
County: Charleston FICE Identification: 040963
Unit ID: 451510
Telephone: (843) 329-1000 Carnegie Class: Spec-4-yr-Law
FAX Number: (843) 720-7899 Calendar System: Semester
URL: www.charlestonlaw.edu
Established: 2003 Annual Graduate Tuition & Fees: N/A
Enrollment: 449 Coed
Affiliation or Control: Proprietary IRS Status: Proprietary
Highest Offering: First Professional Degree; No Undergraduates
Accreditation: **LAW**

01 President .... Mr. J. Edward BELL, III
05 Dean .... Mr. Andrew L. ABRAMS
20 Associate Dean Academic Affairs .... Ms. Margaret M. LAWTON
07 Associate Dean Admission .... Ms. Jacqueline B. BELL
32 Assoc Dean of Students .... Mr. Brett BARKER
13 Assoc Dean of Info Services .... Ms. Lisa SMITH-BUTLER
10 Chief Financial Officer .... Ms. Wende WOOD
06 Registrar .... Ms. Jennifer SUMMERS

Charleston Southern University (I)

PO Box 118087, Charleston SC 29423-8087
County: Charleston FICE Identification: 003419
Unit ID: 217688
Telephone: (843) 863-7000 Carnegie Class: Masters/M
FAX Number: (843) 863-8074 Calendar System: Semester
URL: www.csuniv.edu
Established: 1964 Annual Undergrad Tuition & Fees: $23,440
Enrollment: 3,367 Coed
Affiliation or Control: Southern Baptist IRS Status: 501(c)3
Highest Offering: Master's
Accreditation: **SC**, CAATE, CS, IACBE, MUS, NUR, TED

01 President .... Dr. Jairy C. HUNTER, JR.
03 Executive Vice President .... Dr. Michael BRYANT
05 Vice President Academic Affairs .... Dr. Jacqueline FISH
10 Vice President for Business Affairs .... Mr. Luke BLACKMON
04 Exec Assistant to the President .... Mrs. Faye WOOD
84 Vice Pres Enrollment Management .... Dr. George METZ
26 Vice Pres Advancement & Marketing .... Mr. David BAGGS
88 Asst to the VP for Retention .... Dr. Scott YARBROUGH
30 Executive Director of Development .... Mr. Bill WARD
32 Dean of Students .... Mr. Clark CARTER
91 Director of Administrative Services .... Mr. Shannon PHILLIPS
08 Director of the Library .... Mrs. Sandra HUGHES
06 Registrar .... Mrs. Amanda SISSION
29 Director of BUC Club .... Mr. Tyler DAVIS
21 Associate Business Officer .... Mrs. Janet MIMS
27 Director of Integrated Marketing .... Mr. John STRUBEL
09 Dir of Institutional Effectiveness .... Mr. Jeffrey BABETZ
58 Director MBA Program .... Dr. Darin GERDES
41 Athletic Director .... Mr. Hank SMALL
42 Director Campus Ministry .... Mr. Jon DAVIS
19 Director Security .... Mr. John WILSON
90 Director Computing & Info Science .... Mr. James ROBERTS
18 Director Physical & Auxiliary Svcs .... Mr. Nick CIMORELLI
29 Director of Alumni Relations .... Mrs. Rebecca POISION
07 Director of Admission .... Mr. James M. RHOTON
15 Director of Personnel Services .... Mrs. Lindsey WALKE
36 Director Career Planning .... Mrs. Hester YOUNG
38 Director Student Counseling .... Mr. Wesley SENN

96 Director of Purchasing .... Mrs. Lisa OROZCO
37 Director Student Financial Aid .... Mrs. Teri KARGES
39 Director Residence Life .... Mr. Tyler DAVIS
50 Dean of Business .... Dr. John B. DUNCAN
83 Dean Humanities/Social Sciences .... Dr. Keith CALLIS
81 Dean Science & Mathematics .... Dr. Todd ASHBY
66 Dean of Nursing .... Dr. Andreea TOADER
53 Dean of Education .... Dr. Melanie MURPHY
76 Dean College of Health Sci .... Vacant
107 College of Adult Professional Stds .... Dr. Marc EMBLER
28 Director of Diversity .... Mr. Marcus BRYANT

The Citadel, The Military College of South Carolina (A)

171 Moultrie Street, Charleston SC 29409-0001
County: Charleston FICE Identification: 003423
Unit ID: 217864
Telephone: (843) 225-3294 Carnegie Class: Masters/L
FAX Number: (843) 953-5287 Calendar System: Semester
URL: www.citadel.edu
Established: 1842 Annual Undergrad Tuition & Fees (In-State): $11,364
Enrollment: 3,592 Coed
Affiliation or Control: State IRS Status: 501(c)3
Highest Offering: Beyond Master's But Less Than Doctorate
Accreditation: SC, BUS, CACREP, CAEP, CS, ENG, TED

01 President .... LtGen. John W. ROSA
05 Provost/Dean of College .... BGen. Connie L. BOOK
11 Vice Pres for Operations .... Col. Thomas G. PHILIPKOSKY
10 Vice President of Finance .... Col. Joseph GARCIA
32 Commandant of Cadets .... Capt. Eugene PALUSO
26 Vice President for Comm & Marketing .... LtCol. W. Brett ASHWORTH
41 Director Intercollegiate Athletics .... Mr. James E. SENTER
30 VP Inst Advanc/Citadel Fndtn Ex Dir .... Mr. Jay DOWD
04 Executive Assistant to President .... Cdr. William LIND
18 Assoc VP/Facilities & Engr .... Col. Ben WHAM
43 General Counsel .... Mr. Mark C. BRANDENBURG
20 Assoc Provost Academic Affairs .... Col. Mark A. BEBENSEE
20 Assoc Prov Plng/Assess/Evaluation .... Col. Tara F. HORNOR
58 Assoc Provost/Citadel Graduate .... Col. Bob H. MCNAMARA
07 Director of Admissions .... LtCol. John W. POWELL, JR.
06 Registrar .... LtCol. Sylvia L. NESMITH
21 Treasurer .... Ms. Julie WELCH
29 Director Alumni Affairs/Placement .... Col. J. Laurence HUTTO
08 Director of Library .... LtCol. David S. GOBLE
13 Dir Info Technology Services .... Mr. Kyle HERRON
37 Director Financial Aid/ Scholarships .... LtCol. Henry M. FULLER, JR.
15 Director of Human Resources .... Maj. Leah S. SCHONFELD
36 Director of Career Services .... Vacant
38 Director of Student Counseling .... Dr. Suzanne BUFANO
09 Institutional Research Director .... Ms. Lisa L. PACE
19 Director Security/Safety .... Col. William A. FLETCHER
23 College Physician .... Dr. Carey M. CAPELL
40 Director of the Cadet Store .... Mr. Kenneth A. WOODRUFF
42 Chaplain/Dir Religious Activities .... Cdr. Joe MOLINA
92 Director Honors Program .... Col. Jack W. RHODES
86 Director Govt & Community Affairs ... Col. Cardon B. CRAWFORD
96 Director of Purchasing .... LtCol. James P. DE LUCA
28 Chief Diversity Officer .... Ms. Shawn EDWARDS
50 Dean of the School of Bus Admin ..... Col. William N. TRUMBULL
53 Dean of the School of Education .... Col. Larry DANIEL
54 Dean of the School of Engineering .... Col. Ronald W. WELCH
81 Int Dean School of Science/Math .... Col. John WEINSTEIN
79 Dean Sch Humanities/Social Sciences .... Col. Winifred B. MOORE
101 Spec Asst to President/Brd Matters .... Vacant
85 Director Multicultural Affairs .... LtCol. Robert P. PICKERING
16 Human Resources Deputy Director .... Mr. Wesley S. SAMS
25 Grants Writer .... Ms. Sylvia R. WILLIAMS

Claflin University (B)

400 Magnolia Street, Orangeburg SC 29115-4477
County: Orangeburg FICE Identification: 003424
Unit ID: 217873
Telephone: (803) 535-5000 Carnegie Class: Bac-A&S
FAX Number: (803) 531-2860 Calendar System: Semester
URL: www.claflin.edu
Established: 1869 Annual Undergrad Tuition & Fees: $15,520
Enrollment: 1,866 Coed
Affiliation or Control: United Methodist IRS Status: 501(c)3
Highest Offering: Master's
Accreditation: SC, ACBSP, MUS, TED

01 President .... Dr. Henry N. TISDALE
11 Vice President for Administration .... Mr. Drexel B. BALL
05 Provost/Chief Academic Officer .... Dr. Karl S. WRIGHT
10 Vice President for Fiscal Affairs .... Mrs. Tijuana R. HUDSON
30 Vice Pres Institutional Advancement .... Rev. Whittaker V. MIDDLETON
32 Vice Pres Student Devel & Services .... Dr. Leroy A. DURANT
45 VP Plng/Assessment/Information Svcs .... Dr. Zia HASAN
20 Vice Provost for Academic Programs .... Dr. Angela W. PETERS
26 Interim Assistant VP Communications .... Mr. Joseph COTTON
35 Asst VP Student Devel & Services .... Mr. Devin L. RANDOLPH
108 AVP Institutional Effectiveness .... Dr. Bridget P. DEWEES
07 Director of Admissions .... Mr. Michael ZEIGLER
79 Dean Sch Humanities & Soc Science .... Dr. Donald G. PACE
50 Dean School of Business .... Dr. Charles RICHARDSON, JR.
53 Dean School of Education .... Dr. Ronald SPEIGHT
81 Dean Sch Natural Sciences & Math .... Dr. Verlie A. TISDALE
13 Asst VP Information Tech Svcs .... Mr. James E. BRENN
51 Exec Dir for Prof & Cont Studies .... Dr. Cindye T. RICHBURG
08 Library Director .... Ms. Marilyn Y. GIBBS
37 Director of Financial Aid .... Ms. Terria C. WILLIAMS
36 Director of Career Development .... Mrs. Carolyn R. SNELL
41 Athletic Director .... Dr. Jerome H. FITCH
15 Director of Human Resources .... Ms. Shirley A. BIGGS
06 Registrar .... Mrs. Roe B. HUNT
29 Director Alumni Affairs/Annual Fund .... Mrs. Zelda LEE
19 Chief of Campus Public Safety .... Mr. Steven A. PEARSON
109 Director of Auxiliary Services .... Mr. Rodeny B. HUDSON
25 Director of Sponsored Programs .... Ms. Veronica GOODMAN
04 Executive Admin Asst to President .... Ms. Melvenia WILLIAMS
09 Director of Institutional Research .... Dr. Corey L. AMAKER
84 Director Enrollment Management .... Mrs. Roe HUNT

Clemson University (C)

201 Sikes Hall, Clemson SC 29634-0001
County: Pickens FICE Identification: 003425
Unit ID: 217882
Telephone: (864) 656-3311 Carnegie Class: DU-Highest
FAX Number: (864) 656-4040 Calendar System: Semester
URL: www.clemson.edu
Established: 1889 Annual Undergrad Tuition & Fees (In-State): $14,272
Enrollment: 21,857 Coed
Affiliation or Control: State IRS Status: 501(c)3
Highest Offering: Doctorate
Accreditation: SC, ART, BUS, BUSA, CACREP, CONST, CS, CVT, DIETD, ENG, ENGR, IPSY, LSAR, NRPA, NURSE, PLNG, TED

01 President .... Dr. James P. CLEMENTS
05 Provost .... Dr. Robert H. JONES
43 General Counsel .... Mr. W.C. (Chip) HOOD
20 Assoc Provost for Faculty Develop .... Dr. Nadim M. AZIZ
10 Chief Financial Officer .... Mr. Brett A. DALTON
32 Interim VP Student Affairs .... Dr. Almeda JACKS
101 Executive Secretary to the Board .... Ms. Angie LEIDINGER
30 Vice President for Advancement .... Mr. A. Neill CAMERON, JR.
103 Vice Pres Public Svc .... Dr. George R. ASKEW
46 Vice President for Research .... Dr. Larry DOOLEY
88 Vice President for Economic Develop .... Dr. John M. BALLATO
13 Vice Prov Computer/Info Technology .... Mr. James R. BOTTUM
88 Vice Provost for International Affs .... Ms. Sharon NAGY
100 Chief of Staff .... Mr. Max ALLEN
29 Chief Alumni Officer .... Mr. Brian J. O'ROURKE
18 Chief Facilities Officer .... Mr. Robert J. WELLS, JR.
35 Associate VP/Dean of Students .... Dr. Joy S. SMITH
88 Associate Provost for Faculty Devel .... Dr. Nadim AZIZ
26 Chief Public Affairs Officer .... Mr. Mark D. LAND
08 Dean of Libraries .... Ms. Mary M. FARRELL
07 Director of Admissions .... Mr. Robert S. BARKLEY
06 Interim Registrar .... Mrs. Debra SPARACINO
37 Director of Financial Aid .... Mr. Richard RITZMAN
36 Director of Career Center .... Mr. Burton O'NEIL
38 Director Counseling/Psych Services .... Dr. Raquel J. CONTRERAS
47 Dean Col Agric/Forestry/Life Sci .... Dr. Thomas R. SCOTT
58 Dean Graduate School/Vice Provost .... Dr. Jason W. OSBORN
48 Dean Col Arch/Arts/Humanities .... Dr. Richard E. GOODSTEIN
54 Dean Col Engr/Sciences .... Dr. Anand GRAMOPADHYE
83 Dean Col of Behavioral/Social Sci .... Dr. Brett WRIGHT
09 Director Institutional Research .... Dr. S. Wickes WESTCOTT, III
39 Executive Director of Housing .... Ms. Verna G. HOWELL
41 Director of Athletics .... Mr. Dan RADAKOVICH
44 Director of Estate & Planned Giving .... Ms. Jovanna J. KING
22 Director Access & Equity .... Mr. Byron A. WILEY
28 Director of Diversity .... Mr. Lee A. GILL
23 Director Student Health Services .... Mr. George W. CLAY
15 Chief Human Resources .... Ms. Michelle PIEKUTOWSKI
91 Executive Director Enterprise Appl .... Mr. Barrett KENDJORIA
25 Director Sponsored Programs .... Ms. Sheila T. LISCHWE
19 Director Law Enforcement & Safety .... Chief Johnson LINK
96 Director of Purchasing .... Mr. Michael NEBESKY
04 Int Asst to the President/Vice Prov .... Dr. Jeremy R. KING
88 Dir Teaching Effectiveness & Innova .... Ms. Linda TILSON
88 Director of Bridge to Clemson Pgm .... Ms. Susan WHORTON
104 Director Study Abroad .... Dr. Uttiyo RAYCHAUDHURI
108 Director Institutional Assessment .... Dr. David K. KNOX

Clinton College (D)

1029 Crawford Road, Rock Hill SC 29730-5152
County: York FICE Identification: 004923
Unit ID: 217891
Telephone: (803) 327-7402 Carnegie Class: Bac/Assoc-Mixed
FAX Number: (803) 327-3261 Calendar System: Semester
URL: www.clintoncollege.edu
Established: 1894 Annual Undergrad Tuition & Fees: $7,251
Enrollment: 194 Coed
Affiliation or Control: African Methodist Episcopal Zion Church
IRS Status: 501(c)3
Highest Offering: Baccalaureate
Accreditation: TRACS

01 President .... Dr. Elaine J. COPELAND
04 Assistant to the President .... Ms. Cheryl A. WEBB
05 VP for Academic Affairs/Dean .... Ms. Janis S. PENDLETON
30 VP for Development .... Mr. Raymond CORLEY
32 VP for Student Affairs .... Dr. Robert M. COPELAND, JR.
10 VP for Business & Finance .... Ms. Archinya INGRAM
06 Registrar .... Mrs. Altavese HUNT-ALLEN
37 Financial Aid .... Ms. Pamela WHITE
08 Librarian .... Ms. Minora HICKS
41 Athletic Director .... Mr. Larry MULLINS
18 Director Facilities/Bldgs/Grounds .... Rev. Lloyd SNIPES
07 Admissions .... Ms. Kim SHEPARD
35 Director Student Support Services .... Ms. Judith COWAN

Coastal Carolina University (E)

PO Box 261954, Conway SC 29528-6054
County: Horry FICE Identification: 003451
Unit ID: 218724
Telephone: (843) 347-3161 Carnegie Class: Masters/L
FAX Number: (843) 349-2990 Calendar System: Semester
URL: www.coastal.edu
Established: 1954 Annual Undergrad Tuition & Fees (In-State): $10,530
Enrollment: 9,976 Coed
Affiliation or Control: State IRS Status: 501(c)3
Highest Offering: Doctorate
Accreditation: SC, ART, BUS, CS, MUS, NUR, TED, THEA

01 President .... Dr. David A. DECENZO
05 Provost/Exec VP Acad/Student Affs .... Dr. J. Ralph BYINGTON
10 Vice Pres Finance/Administration .... Ms. Staci A. BOWIE
30 Vice Pres Philanthropy .... Mr. Mark ROACH
32 VP Student Life & Campus Engagement ...... Dr. Deborah CONNER
88 VP Stdnt Rights & Responsibilities .... Mr. Travis E. OVERTON
26 Vice Pres Univ Communications .... Mr. William PLATE
50 Dean Business Administration .... Dr. Barbara RITTER
53 Dean of Education .... Dr. Edward JADALLAH
79 Dean of Humanities & Fine Arts .... Dr. Daniel ENNIS
81 Dean of Science .... Dr. Michael H. ROBERTS
13 Chief Information & Technology Ofcr .... Mr. Abdallah HADDAD
20 Assoc Provost Admin/Academic .... Ms. Sallie CLARKSON
108 Assoc Prov Assessment/Accreditation .... Dr. John P. BEARD
58 Assoc Provost/Dir Graduate Studies .... Dr. James O. LUKEN
09 Exec Dir of Inst Rsrch/Assessment .... Ms. Christine L. MEE
06 University Registrar .... Mr. Daniel M. LAWLESS
19 Director Public Safety .... Mr. David ROPER
21 Controller .... Ms. Lori CHURCH
28 Dir Multicultural Student Services .... Ms. Patricia SINGLETON-YOUNG
41 Director of Athletics .... Mr. Matthew L. HOGUE
38 Director of Counseling Services .... Dr. Jennie M. CASSIDY
85 Director of International Programs .... Mr. Geoffrey J. PARSONS
39 Director of Housing/Residence Life .... Mr. Steve HARRISON
37 Dir Financial Aid & Scholarship .... Ms. Wendy WATTS
92 Director Honors Program .... Dr. Michael RUSE
36 Director Career Services .... Dr. Tom WOODLE
96 Dir Procurement/Business Services .... Mr. Dean P. HUDSON
18 Interim Director of Facilities .... Mr. T. Rein MUNGO
27 Chief Public Relations Officer .... Ms. Martha S. HUNN
29 Director Alumni Relations .... Ms. Jean Ann BRAKEFIELD
104 Assoc Provost Global Initiatives . Dr. Darla J. DOMKE-DAMONTE
07 Asst Provost Admiss & Merit Award . Ms. Amanda E. CRADDOCK
15 Director Human Resources/EEO Office . Ms. Kimberly SHERFESEE
43 Dir Legal Services/General Counsel .... Mr. Timothy E. MEACHAM
90 Director Academic Computing .... Mr. Fadi N. BAROODY

Coker College (F)

300 E College Avenue, Hartsville SC 29550-3797
County: Darlington FICE Identification: 003427
Unit ID: 217907
Telephone: (843) 383-8000 Carnegie Class: Bac-Diverse
FAX Number: (843) 383-8048 Calendar System: Semester
URL: www.coker.edu
Established: 1908 Annual Undergrad Tuition & Fees: $26,568
Enrollment: 1,219 Coed
Affiliation or Control: Independent Non-Profit IRS Status: 501(c)3
Highest Offering: Master's
Accreditation: SC, ART, MUS, SW, TED

01 President .... Dr. Robert L. WYATT
05 Provost & Dean of the College .... Dr. Tracy PARKINSON
10 EVP Administration & Legal Counsel .... Mr. Tony FLOYD
78 Asst Dean/Dir CTR Engaged Learning .... Ms. Darlene SMALL
26 VP Institutional Identity & IT .... Mr. R. Kyle SAVERANCE
32 Dean of Students .... Ms. Whitney WATTS
41 VP Athletics & Athletic Facilities .... Dr. Lynn GRIFFIN
20 VP Acad Affairs/Dean of Faculty .... Dr. Will CARSWELL
07 Assoc VP for Enrollment Management .... Mr. Adam CONNOLLY
11 VP for Administration .... Ms. Brianna DOUGLAS
06 Dir Academic Records/Inst Research .... Ms. Marcy KERSHNER
18 Director of Facilities .... Vacant
21 Director of Accounting & Reporting .... Mrs. Robin A. PERDUE
37 Director of Financial Aid .... Mrs. Betty B. WILLIAMS
44 Gift Officer .... Ms. Peggy SMITH
29 Director of Alumni Engagement .... Ms. Shelli WILSON
07 Director of Admissions .... Mr. Jeremy NERE
08 Director of Library .... Mr. Todd RIX
19 Director of Campus Safety .... Mr. George MITCHELL

College of Charleston (G)

66 George Street, Charleston SC 29424-0100
County: Charleston FICE Identification: 003428
Unit ID: 217819
Telephone: (843) 953-5507 Carnegie Class: Masters/L
FAX Number: (843) 953-5811 Calendar System: Semester
URL: www.cofc.edu
Established: 1770 Annual Undergrad Tuition & Fees (In-State): $11,322
Enrollment: 11,456 Coed
Affiliation or Control: State IRS Status: 501(c)3

Highest Offering: Master's
Accreditation: SC, BUS, BUSA, CAATE, CS, MUS, SPAA, TED, THEA

01 President ....Mr. Glenn F. MCCONNELL
101 Vice Pres Col Events/Exec Sec BOT ....Ms. Elizabeth W. KASSEBAUM
05 Provost & Exec Vice Pres Admin ....Dr. Brian MCGEE
10 Exec VP Business Affairs ....Mr. Steven C. OSBORNE
11 VP for Admin & Planning ....Mr. Paul D. PATRICK
100 Sr Exec Admin for the Pres ....Ms. Debbie HAMMOND
26 Dir of College Mktg & Comm ....Mr. Mark E. BERRY
30 Exec VP Institutional Advancement ....Mr. George P. WATT, JR.
32 Dean of Students ....Dr. Jeri O. CABOT
43 General Counsel Legal Affairs ....Ms. Angela B. MULHOLLAND
20 Associate Provost ....Dr. Consuela FRANCIS
19 Chief of Police/Dir Public Saf ....Chief Robert S. REESE
20 Associate Provost ....Dr. Deanna M. CAVENY-NOECKER
20 Associate Vice Pres ....Dr. Lynne E. FORD
104 Assoc Provost International Educ ....Dr. Andrew M. SOBIESUO
13 Senior VP/Chief Information Officer ....Dr. Robert E. CAPE
30 Senior VP Economic Development ....Mr. Robert W. MARLOWE
18 VP Facilities Planning ....Ms. Monica R. SCOTT
21 VP Fiscal Services ....Ms. Priscilla D. BURBAGE
21 Dir of Financial Srvcs ....Ms. Debye B. ALDERMAN
109 Dir Business & Auxiliary Services ....Ms. Janet J. BREWTON
96 Procurement Director ....Ms. Wendy E. WILLIAMS
30 Vice President Development ....Mr. Christopher TOBIN
15 VP of Human Resources ....Mr. Edward POPE
22 Dir Equal Opportunity Programs ....Ms. Kimberly A. GERTNER
84 Assoc Vice Pres Enrollment Planning ....Vacant
09 Assoc VP Institutional Research ....Dr. James T. POSEY
28 Associate VP Diversity ....Dr. John BELLO-OGUNU
88 Asst VP New Student Programs ....Ms. Melinda MILEY
06 Registrar ....Ms. Mary C. BERGSTROM
21 Controller ....Ms. Dawn E. WILLAN
21 Treasurer ....Mr. David G. KATZ
58 Dean Graduate School ....Dr. Amy T. MCCANDLESS
57 Dean School of the Arts ....Ms. Valerie B. MORRIS
50 Dean School of Business ....Dr. Alan T. SHAO
53 Dean School of Education ....Dr. Frances C. WELCH
82 Dean School of Languages ....Dr. Antonio D. TILLIS
81 Dean School of Science & Math ....Dr. Michael AUERBACH
79 Dean Sch of Humanitites/Social Sci ....Dr. Jerold L. HALE
107 Dean College of Charleston North ....Dr. Godfrey GIBBISON
51 Director CCEPD ....Dr. Alice M. HAMILTON
92 Dean Honors College ....Dr. Trisha H. FOLDS-BENNETT
41 Director Athletics ....Mr. Joe HULL
25 Director Research and Grants ....Ms. Susan A. RIVALEAU
37 Dir Financial Asst/Veteran Affairs ....Mr. Donald R. GRIGGS
07 Exec Dir of Admissions ....Ms. Suzette STILLE
88 Dir Center for Academic Advising ....Ms. Karen HAUSCHILD
88 Dir Center for Student Learning ....Ms. Melissa M. THOMAS
108 Dir Academic Assessment & Planning ....Dr. Karin ROOF
88 Ombudsperson ....Ms. Denise MITCHELL
22 Dir Ctr for Disabilities Services ....Ms. Deborah F. MIHAL
35 Director Student Life ....Ms. Susan PAYMENT
36 Director Career Services ....Vacant
38 Dir Counseling & Substance Abuse ....Mr. Frank C. BUDD
23 Director Health Services ....Ms. Jane RENO-MUNRO
39 Director Residence Life ....Ms. Melantha ARDREY
19 Dir of Fire and Life Safety ....Mr. Richard N. KRANTZ
88 Dir Enviro Health and Safety ....Mr. Randy L. BEAVER
21 Associate Vice President ....Mr. Samuel B. JONES
88 Director of ECDC ....Ms. Candace L. JARUSZEWICZ
88 AVP Student Affairs Dir HSLC ....Mr. K. Michael DUNCAN
18 Director of Sustainability ....Mr. P. Brian FISHER
88 Director Avery Research Center ....Ms. Patricia WILLIAMS LESSANE
31 Sr Dir of Community Relations ....Ms. Evelyn H. NADEL
88 Dir Undergrad Academic Services ....Ms. Michelle G. FUTRELL

Columbia College (A)

1301 Columbia College Drive, Columbia SC 29203-5998
County: Richland FICE Identification: 003430
Unit ID: 217334
Telephone: (803) 786-3178 Carnegie Class: Masters/M
FAX Number: (803) 786-3752 Calendar System: Semester
URL: www.columbiasc.edu
Established: 1854 Annual Undergrad Tuition & Fees: $28,100
Enrollment: 1,221 Female
Affiliation or Control: United Methodist IRS Status: 501(c)3
Highest Offering: Master's
Accreditation: SC, ART, DANCE, MUS, SW, TED

01 President ....Ms. Elizabeth A. DINNDORF
05 Provost/VP for Academic Affairs ....Dr. Laurie B. HOPKINS
10 Vice President for Finance ....Mr. John C. SIRCY
84 Vice Pres for Enrollment Management ....Mr. Ken HUUS
88 Ex Dir Inst Lship & Prof Excellenc ....Ms. Chris LACOLA
30 VP for Advancement ....Mr. Francis G. SCHODOWSKI
32 Dean Student Affairs ....Ms. LaNae R. BRIGGS
29 Exec Director of Alumnae Relations ....Ms. Carla L. MOORE
06 Registrar/Dir Institutional Rsrch ....Dr. Scott A. SMITH
08 Director of Library ....Ms. Jane TUTTLE
19 Chief of Police ....Chief Howard M. COOK
37 Director of Financial Aid ....Ms. Donna QUICK
36 Director of Ctr for Career Coaching ....Ms. Kenetta PIERCE
13 Dir of Info Technology Services ....Mr. Floyd STAYNER
18 Director of Facilities Management ....Ms. Gaby HICKMAN
26 Exec Director Mktg & Communications ....Ms. Monique MCDANIELS
41 Director of Athletics ....Ms. Kellyanne STUBBLEFIELD
40 Director Bookstore ....Ms. Cory CORP
38 Director Counseling Services ....Ms. Mimi MERIWETHER
04 Executive Assistant to President ....Ms. Joye G. HIPP
07 Director of Admissions ....Ms. Julie A. KING
92 Director Honors Program/Faculty Dev ....Dr. John ZUBIZARRETA

Columbia International University (B)

7435 Monticello Road, Columbia SC 29203
County: Richland FICE Identification: 003429
Unit ID: 217925
Telephone: (803) 754-4100 Carnegie Class: Masters/M
FAX Number: (803) 786-4209 Calendar System: Semester
URL: www.ciu.edu
Established: 1923 Annual Undergrad Tuition & Fees: $20,430
Enrollment: 1,103 Coed
Affiliation or Control: Independent Non-Profit IRS Status: 501(c)3
Highest Offering: Doctorate
Accreditation: SC, BI, CACREP, THEOL

01 President ....Dr. William H. JONES
00 Chancellor ....Dr. George W. MURRAY
05 Senior Vice President/Provost ....Dr. Jim LANPHER
44 Sr Vice Estate & Gift Planning ....Mr. D. Keith MARION
30 Sr VP of Institutional Advancement ....Vacant
73 Dean Seminary & School of Ministry ....Dr. John HARVEY
49 Dean College of Arts and Sciences ....Dr. Bryan BEYER
53 Dean College of Education ....Dr. Connie MITCHELL
104 Dean College Intercultural Studies ....Dr. Edward SMITHER
09 Dir Institutional Research/Assess ....Dr. Ben BRYAN
101 Assoc Provost Online Studies ....Dr. Brian SIMMONS
08 Director of Library ....Mrs. Cynthia SNELL
06 University Registrar ....Mrs. Jennifer BOOTH
15 Director Human Resources ....Mr. Donald E. JONES
29 Int Director of Alumni ....Mrs. Diane MULL
32 Dean of Students ....Mr. Rick SWIFT
07 Director University Admissions ....Mr. Michael SAPIENZA
13 Corporate IT Coordinator ....Mr. Tirrel HOWELL
18 Director Physical Plant ....Mr. Dave MAGNUSON
10 Chief Financial Officer ....Mr. Keith STOKELD
30 Director Development ....Mrs. Diane MULL
37 Director Financial Aid ....Mrs. Patty HIX
36 Director Student Placement ....Mr. Rick SWIFT
04 Administrative Asst to President ....Mrs. Debbie GERMANY
19 Director Security/Safety ....Mr. Bob REGISTER
41 Athletic Director ....Mr. James WHITAKER

Converse College (C)

580 E Main, Spartanburg SC 29302-0006
County: Spartanburg FICE Identification: 003431
Unit ID: 217961
Telephone: (864) 596-9000 Carnegie Class: Masters/M
FAX Number: (864) 596-9158 Calendar System: 4/1/4
URL: www.converse.edu
Established: 1889 Annual Undergrad Tuition & Fees: $16,500
Enrollment: 1,389 Female
Affiliation or Control: Independent Non-Profit IRS Status: 501(c)3
Highest Offering: Beyond Master's But Less Than Doctorate
Accreditation: SC, ART, CIDA, MFCD, MUS, TED

01 President ....Ms. Krista L. NEWKIRK
05 Provost ....Dr. Jeffrey R. BARKER
10 Vice Pres Finance/Administration ....Mr. William JOHNSON
30 VP External Affairs/Univ Relations ....Mrs. Charlotte VERREAULT
79 Dean Humanities/Sciences/Education ....Mrs. Ann PLETCHER
57 Dean School of the Arts ....Dr. Boone HOPKINS
32 Dean of Community Life ....Ms. Rhonda MINGO
08 Librarian ....Mr. Wade WOODWARD
37 Director of Financial Planning ....Mr. James KELLAM
06 Registrar ....Mrs. Mary L. BROWN
15 Human Resources Director ....Ms. Dennis HUGHES
13 Chief Information Officer ....Mr. Zach CORBITT
36 Dean of Professional Development ....Ms. Witney FISHER
26 Director of Media/Communications ....Mrs. Beth LANCASTER
04 Assistant to the President ....Mrs. Stacey BREWER
38 Director of Counseling Services ....Ms. Bethany GARR
09 Director Institutional Research ....Dr. Yongmei LI
07 Assoc Vice Pres of Enrollment Mgmt ....Mr. Trevor PITTMAN
18 Chief Facilities/Physical Plant ....Mr. Robert BROWN
109 Facilities Planner ....Mr. Rick JOLLEY

Denmark Technical College (D)

PO Box 327, Denmark SC 29042-0327
County: Bamberg FICE Identification: 005363
Unit ID: 217989
Telephone: (803) 793-5176 Carnegie Class: Assoc/HVT-High Trad
FAX Number: (803) 793-5942 Calendar System: Semester
URL: www.denmarktech.edu
Established: 1948 Annual Undergrad Tuition & Fees (In-State): $2,926
Enrollment: 1,678 Coed
Affiliation or Control: State IRS Status: 501(c)3
Highest Offering: Associate Degree
Accreditation: SC, ACBSP, ENGT

01 President ....Dr. Leonard MCINTYRE
09 VP for Inst Research/Plng/Dev ....Dr. Lamin DRAMMEH
05 Interim VP for Academic Affairs ....Mrs. Tia WRIGHT-RICHARDS
10 Interim VP for Fiscal Affairs ....Mr. Ramon WIDEMAN
84 VP for Enrollment Management ....Mr. Marcus CORBETT
15 Interim Director of Human Resources ....Ms. Cheryl WASHINGTON
32 Associate VP for Student Services ....Ms. Avis GATHERS
08 Dean of Learning Resources Ctr ....Ms. Carolyn FORTSON
13 Director of Information Technology ....Mr. Fred BOVE
19 Chief of Public Safety ....Mr. Elton SHULER
25 Director of Grants & Contracts ....Mrs. Teresa MACK
36 Director Career Plng/Placement ....Mrs. Leslie HOLMAN-BROOKS
37 Director of Financial Aid ....Mrs. Laura FOGLE
40 Interim Dean of Public Service ....Mrs. Wanda NETTLES
49 Interim Dean of Arts & Sciences ....Mr. Stephan BRITANAK
54 Dean of Industrial/Related Tech ....Dr. Ambrish LAVANIA
50 Dean Business/Computer/Related Tech ....Mrs. Tia WRIGHT-RICHARDS
60 Int Dean of Transitional Studies ....Ms. Carla JACKSON
07 Interim Director of Recruitment ....Ms. Crystal BRAILEY
103 AVP Economic/Workforce Development ....Mr. Stephen MASON
39 Director Student Housing ....Ms. Charlene DICKERSON
06 Registrar ....Ms. Carolyn GRIMES

ECPI University-Charleston (E)

7410 Northside Drive, Ste G101,
North Charleston SC 29420
Telephone: (843) 414-0350 Identification: 770955
Accreditation: &SC, MAAB

† Regional accreditation is carried under the parent institution in Virginia Beach, VA

ECPI University-Columbia (F)

250 Berryhill Road, Ste 300, Columbia SC 29210-6467
Telephone: (803) 773-3333 Identification: 770956
Accreditation: &SC, MAAB

† Regional accreditation is carried under the parent institution in Virginia Beach, VA

ECPI University-Greenville (G)

1001 Keys Drive, Ste 100, Greenville SC 29615
Telephone: (864) 288-2828 Identification: 770954
Accreditation: &SC, MAAB

† Regional accreditation is carried under the parent institution in Virginia Beach, VA

Edward Via College of Osteopathic Medicine-Carolinas Campus (H)

350 Howard Street, Sparntanburg SC 29303
Telephone: (864) 327-9800 Identification: 770941
Accreditation: OSTEO

† Branch campus of Edward Via College of Osteopathic Medicine, Blacksburg, VA.

Erskine College (I)

PO Box 338, 2 Washington Street,
Due West SC 29639-0338
County: Abbeville FICE Identification: 003432
Unit ID: 217998
Telephone: (864) 379-2131 Carnegie Class: Bac-A&S
FAX Number: (864) 379-2167 Calendar System: 4/1/4
URL: www.erskine.edu
Established: 1837 Annual Undergrad Tuition & Fees: $33,315
Enrollment: 753 Coed
Affiliation or Control: Other IRS Status: 501(c)3
Highest Offering: Doctorate
Accreditation: SC, #CAATE, TED, THEOL

01 President ....Dr. Paul D. KOOISTRA
05 Sr VP of Academic Affairs ....Dr. N. Bradley CHRISTIE
10 Sr VP for Finance & Operations ....Mr. Gregory W. HASELDEN
30 Vice President Advancement ....Mr. Buddy FERGUSON
41 Vice Pres for Athletics ....Mr. Mark L. PEELER
26 Vice President for Communications ....Mr. Cliff L. SMITH
73 Vice Pres Theological Seminary ....Dr. Christopher H. WISDOM
32 Dean Student Services ....Ms. Wendi SANTEE
06 Registrar ....Mrs. Tracy M. SPIRES
37 Director of Student Financial Aid ....Mrs. A. Michelle LODATO
13 Director of Information Technology ....Mr. Robert S. CLARKE, III
09 Director of Institutional Research ....Mr. Buck F. BROWN, JR.
42 RUF Campus Minister ....Mr. Paul G. PATRICK
21 Controller ....Mr. Christian M. HABEGER
15 Director Human Resources ....Mrs. Barbara PECK
19 Chief of Erskine Police ....Mr. Charles R. ESTEP
36 Coordinator for Student Transitions ....Mr. Trent D. PAYNE
29 Director of Alumni Affairs ....Mr. William L. FERGUSON
04 Administrative Asst to President ....Mrs. Dena S. HODGE
07 Director of Admissions ....Ms. Tobe R. FRIERSON
105 Director of Comm Technology ....Mr. Brian K. SMITH
108 Assoc Dean of Inst Effectiveness ....Mr. John F. KENNERLY, JR.
39 Asst Dean Residential Lrng/Devel ....Mr. James VAN STENSEL

Florence - Darlington Technical College (J)

PO Box 100548, Florence SC 29502-0548
County: Florence FICE Identification: 003990
Unit ID: 218025
Telephone: (843) 661-8324 Carnegie Class: Assoc/MT-VT-High Trad
FAX Number: (843) 661-8011 Calendar System: Semester
URL: www.fdtc.edu
Established: 1964 Annual Undergrad Tuition & Fees (In-District): $4,078

Enrollment: 6,215 Coed
Affiliation or Control: State/Local IRS Status: 501(c)3
Highest Offering: Associate Degree
Accreditation: SC, ADNUR, CAHIIM, COARC, CSHSE, DA, DH, MLTAD, RAD, SURGT

01 President ..... Dr. Ben P. DILLARD, III
05 Vice President Academic Affairs ..... Dr. Suresh TIWARI
10 Vice Pres Business Affairs ..... Dr. Douglas LANGE
30 Vice Pres Institutional Advancement ..... Ms. Jill LEWIS
26 Vice Pres Marketing/Public Affs ..... Mr. Edward BETHEA
10 Assoc Vice Pres Business Office ..... Ms. Connie MORRIS
76 Assoc VP Allied Health ..... Dr. Maureen DEVER-BUMBA
13 Assoc Vice Pres Info Tech/CIO ..... Mr. Tyron JONES
15 Assoc VP Internal Relations/EEO ..... Ms. Terry DINGLE
09 Director Institutional Research ..... Ms. Melissa MILLER
06 Registrar ..... Vacant
37 Director Financial Aid ..... Mr. Joseph DURANT

Forrest College (A)

601 E River Street, Anderson SC 29624-2405
County: Anderson FICE Identification: 004924
Unit ID: 218043
Telephone: (864) 225-7653 Carnegie Class: Assoc/HVT-Mix Trad/Non
FAX Number: (864) 261-7471 Calendar System: 4/1/4
URL: www.forrestcollege.edu
Established: 1946 Annual Undergrad Tuition & Fees: $9,420
Enrollment: 111 Coed
Affiliation or Control: Proprietary IRS Status: Proprietary
Highest Offering: Associate Degree
Accreditation: ACICS, MAC

00 Chairman Board of Directors ..... Dr. John RE
01 Acting President ..... Dr. Cosmo J. RE
05 Academic Dean ..... June STEWART
11 Administrative Dean/Mgr IT Services ..... Scott PETERSON
101 Secy/Treasurer Board of Directors ..... Charles PALMER
06 Registrar ..... Chris HRENKO
08 Librarian ..... Brandy ROSCOE
76 Actg Medical Assisting Pgm Coord ..... Celina CHASTAIN
07 Coordinator of Admissions ..... Katie WILSON
07 Admissions Rep ..... Joshua CLYNE
07 Admissions Rep ..... Candace BENTLEY
37 Financial Aid Officer ..... Kathryn MONTGOMERY

Francis Marion University (B)

PO Box 100547, Florence SC 29501-0547
County: Florence FICE Identification: 009226
Unit ID: 218061
Telephone: (843) 661-1362 Carnegie Class: Masters/S
FAX Number: (843) 661-1202 Calendar System: Semester
URL: www.fmarion.edu
Established: 1970 Annual Undergrad Tuition & Fees (In-State): $10,100
Enrollment: 3,944 Coed
Affiliation or Control: State IRS Status: Exempt
Highest Offering: Master's
Accreditation: SC, #ARCPA, ART, BUS, NUR, TED, THEA

01 President ..... Dr. Luther F. CARTER
05 Provost/Dean Col of Liberal Arts ..... Dr. Peter D. KING
10 Vice President Business Affairs ..... Mr. John J. KISPERT
11 Vice President Administration ..... Dr. Charlene WAGES
30 Vice President Devel/Exec Dir ..... Mr. Darryl BRIDGES
26 VP Public & Community Affairs ..... Mr. Tucker MITCHELL
32 Vice President for Student Affairs ..... Mrs. Teresa RAMEY
20 Assoc Provost For Academic Affairs ..... Dr. Christopher KENNEDY
21 Asst Vice Pres for Accounting ..... Mr. M. Augustus MCDILL
88 Asst Vice Pres Financial Services ..... Mr. Thomas WELCH
50 Dean School of Business ..... Dr. Hari K. RAJAGOPALAN
53 Dean School of Educaion ..... Dr. Shirley BAUSMITH
76 Dean School of Health Sciences .. Dr. Ruth A. WITTMANN-PRICE
08 Dean of the Library ..... Mrs. Joyce M. DURANT
84 Assoc Provost of Enrollment Mgmt ..... Dr. Alissa WARTERS
37 Financial Assistance Director ..... Ms. Kimberly M. ELLISOR
41 Athletic Director ..... Mr. Murray G. HARTZLER
06 Registrar ..... Ms. Dollie NEWHOUSE
38 Director Counseling and Testing ..... Dr. Rebecca L. LAWSON
18 Director of Facilities Management ..... Mr. Ralph U. DAVIS
36 Director Career Development ..... Dr. Ronald E. MILLER, JR.
07 Director of Admissions ..... Mrs. Perry T. WILSON
35 Asst Dean of Students ..... Ms. R. Daphne CARTER
29 Director of Alumni Affairs ..... Mr. Julian M. YOUNG
96 Director of Purchasing ..... Mr. Eric L. GARRIS
92 Director of Honors Program ..... Dr. Pamela A. ROOKS
13 Chief Information Officer ..... Mr. John DIXON
04 Administrative Asst to President ..... Mrs. Kim DAVIS
105 Media Production/Web Design Coord ..... Mr. Larry B. FALCK
19 Chief of Campus Police ..... Mr. Donald R. TARBELL
39 Director Student Housing ..... Mrs. Cheryl R. TUTTLE
43 Dir Legal Services/General Counsel ... Mr. Jonathan P. EDWARDS

Furman University (C)

3300 Poinsett Highway, Greenville SC 29613-0001
County: Greenville FICE Identification: 003434
Unit ID: 218070
Telephone: (864) 294-2000 Carnegie Class: Bac-A&S
FAX Number: (864) 294-3001 Calendar System: Semester
URL: www.furman.edu
Established: 1826 Annual Undergrad Tuition & Fees: $46,012
Enrollment: 2,973 Coed
Affiliation or Control: Independent Non-Profit IRS Status: 501(c)3
Highest Offering: Master's
Accreditation: SC, MUS, TED

01 President ..... Dr. Elizabeth DAVIS
05 VP Academic Affairs & Provost ..... Dr. George S. SHIELDS
10 VP for Finance & Administration ..... Ms. Mary Lou MERKT
07 Vice President for Enrollment ..... Mr. Michael HENDRICKS
32 Vice President for Student Life ..... Ms. Connie L. CARSON
30 Vice President for Development ..... Mr. Michael D. GATCHELL
26 VP University Communications ..... Mr. Tom EVELYN
20 Int Dean of Faculty ..... Dr. Ken PETERSON
20 Associate Academic Dean ..... Dr. Paula S. GABBERT
06 University Registrar ..... Mr. Brad E. BARRON
58 Director Graduate Studies ..... Dr. Troy M. TERRY
08 Director Libraries ..... Dr. Janis M. BANDELIN
19 Chief of Police ..... Mr. Tom SACCENTI
108 Asst Vice President Assessment ..... Dr. David EUBANKS
09 Director Inst Assessment & Research ..... Mr. Donald E. PIERCE
37 Assoc Vice Pres of Financial Aid ..... Mr. Forrest M. STUART
29 Director of Alumni Association ..... Mr. Mike WILSON
07 Assoc Vice President of Admissions ..... Mr. Brad POCHARD
44 Director of Annual Giving ..... Mr. John KEMP
44 Director of Planned Giving ..... Mr. Steve PERRY
25 Grants Administrator ..... Ms. Judith J. ROMANO
28 Director of Multicultural Affairs ..... Vacant
94 Dir Women's/Gender/Sexuality Study ..... Dr. Karni BHATI
15 Asst VP Human Resources/AAO ..... Mr. Robert BIERLY
13 Chief Information Officer ..... Mr. Fred MILLER
85 Asst Dean Intl Educ/Study Away ..... Vacant
36 Director Career Services ..... Dr. John D. BARKER
109 Auxiliary Services Director ..... Ms. Rebecca VUKSTA
18 Asst VP for Facilities Services ..... Mr. Jeff P. REDDERSON
51 Director Continuing Education ..... Dr. Brad BECHTOLD
41 Director of Athletics ..... Mr. Mike BUDDIE
46 Director UG Research & Internships ..... Dr. Tim G. FEHLER
88 Director CTL ..... Dr. Jane LOVE
17 Director Student Health Services ..... Dr. Jill GOLDEN
38 Director Counseling Center ..... Dr. Stephen DAWES
39 Director University Housing ..... Mr. Ronald C. THOMPSON
88 Director Accessibility Resources ..... Ms. Judy BAGLEY
42 Chaplain ..... Dr. Vaughn CROWETIPTON
40 Director Bookstore ..... Ms. K. C ROBINSON
04 Assistant to President ..... Ms. Cindy ALEXANDER
21 Assoc VP Finance Budget Director ..... Ms. Amy BLACKWELL
96 Director of Purchasing ..... Mr. Clay WOODY
35 Director Student Activities ..... Ms. Jessica BERKEY
104 Director Study Abroad ..... Vacant
43 Dir Legal Services/General Counsel ... Ms. Angela F. LITTLEJOHN

Golf Academy of America (D)

1900 Mr. Joe White Ave., Myrtle Beach SC 29577
Telephone: (800) 342-7342 Identification: 666490
Accreditation: ACICS

† Branch campus of Virginia College, Birmingham, AL.

Greenville Technical College (E)

PO Box 5616, Greenville SC 29606-5616
County: Greenville FICE Identification: 003991
Unit ID: 218113
Telephone: (864) 250-8000 Carnegie Class: Assoc/HVT-High Trad
FAX Number: (864) 250-8507 Calendar System: Semester
URL: www.gvltec.edu
Established: 1962 Annual Undergrad Tuition & Fees (In-State): $4,224
Enrollment: 12,592 Coed
Affiliation or Control: State IRS Status: 501(c)3
Highest Offering: Associate Degree
Accreditation: SC, ACBSP, ACFEI, ADNUR, CAHIIM, COARC, DA, DH, DMS, EMT, ENGT, MAC, MLTAD, OTA, PTAA, RAD, SURGT

01 President ..... Dr. Keith MILLER
05 Vice President for Academic Affairs ..... Dr. Lenna YOUNG
10 Vice President for Finance ..... Mrs. Jacqueline R. DIMAGGIO
32 Vice President Student Services ..... Dr. Matteel JONES
51 Vice Pres Corp & Economic Devel ..... Vacant
45 VP Institutional Effectiveness ..... Mrs. Lauren SIMER

Horry-Georgetown Technical College (F)

2050 Highway 501 E, Conway SC 29526-9521
County: Horry FICE Identification: 004925
Unit ID: 218140
Telephone: (843) 347-3186 Carnegie Class: Assoc/MT-VT-High Trad
FAX Number: (843) 347-4207 Calendar System: Semester
URL: www.hgtc.edu
Established: 1966 Annual Undergrad Tuition & Fees (In-District): $3,960
Enrollment: 7,335 Coed
Affiliation or Control: State/Local IRS Status: 501(c)3
Highest Offering: Associate Degree
Accreditation: SC, ACBSP, ACFEI, ADNUR, DA, DH, DMS, EMT, PNUR, PTAA, RAD, SURGT

01 President ..... Mr. Neyle WILSON
05 Senior VP/VP Academic Affairs ..... Dr. Marilyn FORE
10 Vice President for Business/Finance ..... Mr. Harold HAWLEY
13 Vice Pres of Technology ..... Mr. John DOVE
103 VP Wrkfc Dev/Prov GS/Georgetwn Camp . Mr. Gregory MITCHELL
84 AVP Enrollment Dev/Registration ..... Mr. George SWINDOLL
32 Asc VP Student Affs/Campus Life ..... Dr. Melissa BATTEN
20 AVP Acad Affs/Dean Academic Support ..... Dr. Becky BOONE
20 AVP Acad Affs/Dn Univ Paral/Engr ..... Dr. Shirley BUTLER
20 AVP Acad Affs/Dn Nur/Health Science ..... Dr. Christy CIMINERI
15 AVP Human Res/Employee Relations .... Ms. Jacqueline BARRETT
08 AVP/Dn Library/Learning Resources ..... Ms. Peggy SAYLOR
20 AVP Acad Affs/Dn Bus/Dental ..... Dr. Philip RENDER
21 AVP/Controller ..... Ms. Ellen BLACK
84 AVP Student Enrollment Services ..... Ms. Cynthia JOHNSTON
26 Dir Public Relations/Marketing ..... Ms. Mary EADDY
18 Superintendent Buildings & Grounds ..... Mr. Kevin BROWN
37 Dir of Financial Aid/Veterans Affs ..... Ms. Susan THOMPSON
07 Dir Stdnt Recruitment/Admissions ..... Ms. Thyssene FREDERICK
36 Career Resource Ctr Coordinator ..... Ms. April GARNER
09 Dir Institutional Rsrch/Assessment ..... Ms. Lori HEAFNER
96 Procurement Manager ..... Ms. Dianna CECALA
105 Web Services Coordinator ..... Ms. Melissa MONOLO
19 Director Security/Safety ..... Mr. Barry MARSH

Lander University (G)

320 Stanley Avenue, Greenwood SC 29649-2099
County: Greenwood FICE Identification: 003435
Unit ID: 218229
Telephone: (864) 388-8000 Carnegie Class: Bac-Diverse
FAX Number: (864) 388-8890 Calendar System: Semester
URL: www.lander.edu
Established: 1872 Annual Undergrad Tuition & Fees (In-State): $10,752
Enrollment: 2,787 Coed
Affiliation or Control: State IRS Status: 501(c)3
Highest Offering: Master's
Accreditation: SC, ART, BUS, MACTE, MUS, NURSE, TED

01 President ..... Dr. Richard E. COSENTINO
05 Provost/Vice Pres Academic Affairs ..... Dr. David MASH
10 Vice Pres Business/Administration ..... Mr. Greg LOVINS
32 Vice President for Student Affairs ..... Mr. H. Randall BOUKNIGHT
30 Vice President for Univ Advancement ..... Mr. Ralph PATTERSON
86 VP for Governmental Relations ..... Mr. Adam TAYLOR
84 VP for Enrollment & Access Mgmt ..... Mr. Andy BENOIT
08 Librarian ..... Ms. Lisa WIECKI
38 Director Counseling ..... Ms. Debra J. FRANKS
41 Vice President/Athletic Director ..... Mr. Jefferson J. MAY
15 Director Human Resources ..... Ms. Jeannie MCCALLUM
19 Director University Police ..... Mr. Eddie BRIGGS
26 Director of Public Information ..... Mrs. Megan PRICE
37 Director of Financial Aid ..... Mr. Fred HARDIN
36 Director of Career Services ..... Mrs. Amanda MORGAN
21 Controller ..... Mr. Tom COVAR
40 Dir Bookstore/Procurement/Print Svc ..... Mrs. Mary W. MCDANIEL
13 Dir Office Intern Tech Services ..... Mr. Robin P. LAWRENCE
07 Director of Admissions ..... Mrs. Jennifer M. MATHIS
18 Director Physical Plant/Engr Svcs ..... Mr. Jeff S. BEAVER
06 Registrar ..... Ms. Kelly PROCTOR
29 Director Alumni Relations ..... Ms. Myra GREENE
09 Director of Institutional Research ..... Mr. Mac KIRKPATRICK

Limestone College (H)

1115 College Drive, Gaffney SC 29340-3799
County: Cherokee FICE Identification: 003436
Unit ID: 218238
Telephone: (864) 489-7151 Carnegie Class: Bac-Diverse
FAX Number: (864) 487-8706 Calendar System: Semester
URL: www.limestone.edu
Established: 1845 Annual Undergrad Tuition & Fees: $23,900
Enrollment: 3,214 Coed
Affiliation or Control: Independent Non-Profit IRS Status: 501(c)3
Highest Offering: Master's
Accreditation: SC, #CAATE, MUS, SW, TED

01 President ..... Dr. Walt R. GRIFFIN
05 Exec Vice Pres/VP Academic Affairs ..... Dr. Karen W. GAINEY
10 Vice President Financial Affairs ..... Mr. L. Wayde DAWSON
30 VP Institutional Advancement ..... Ms. Kelly T. CURTIS
84 Vice President Enrollment Services . Mr. Christopher N. PHENICIE
32 Vice President Student Services ..... Mr. Robert A. OVERTON
13 Vice Pres Information Technology ..... Mr. C. R. HORTON
41 Vice Pres Intercollegiate Athletics ..... Mr. Michael H. CERINO
14 Assoc VP Information Technology ..... Vacant
20 Assoc Vice Pres Academic Affairs ..... Dr. Mark A. REGER
45 Assoc Vice Pres Planning/Assessment ..... Dr. Bonnie M. WRIGHT
88 Dean Academic Support ..... Vacant
106 Dean Extended Campus Program ..... Dr. Mark A. REGER
04 Administrative Asst to President ..... Mrs. Nani Lou S. COOPER
56 Dir Extended Campus Classroom Pgm ... Mrs. Donna P. HUDSON
06 Registrar ..... Ms. Pennie D. HUGHES
37 Director Financial Aid ..... Mr. Bobby T. GREER
44 Director Development ..... Vacant
08 Director Library ..... Ms. Lizah ISMAIL
26 Director Communications ..... Mr. Charles W. WYATT
35 Director Student Services ..... Ms. Jessica D. GOINS
36 Director Career Services ..... Ms. Ileka L. LEAKS
90 Director Server Services ..... Dr. Scott D. BERRY
18 Director Physical Plant ..... Mr. Logan RICHARDSON
92 Director Academic Honors Program ..... Ms. Carol R. TAYLOR
83 Assoc Dean/Director Social Work ..... Mr. Jackie A. PUCKETT
19 Chief Campus Security ..... Mr. Richard E. SIMMONS
21 Controller ..... Ms. Iuliana WATSON
23 Campus Nurse ..... Mrs. Sandy B. GREEN
44 Director Advancement Services ..... Mrs. Brandi P. HARTMAN
20 Director Academic Advising ..... Ms. Pennie D. HUGHES
29 Director Development & Alumni ..... Ms. Candace R. WATERS
88 Dir Christian Ed/Leadership Program ..... Rev. J. Ron SINGLETON

109 Director Food Services ....Mr. Joe FIELDS
42 College Chaplain ....Rev. J. Ron SINGLETON
88 Dir Accessibility Services/PALS ....Ms. Andrea ALLISON
15 Dir Human Resources/AAEEO Officer ......Ms. Brenda F. WATKINS
50 Director MBA Program ....Mr. Brandon J. GIBSON
88 Sr Assoc Athletics Dir Compliance ....Mr. Dennis L. BLOOMER
88 Asst Athletics Dir Media Relations ....Mr. Ernest G. MEYERS
88 Asst Athletics Dir Sports Perform ....Mr. Curtis S. LAMB
88 Assoc Dir Athletic Facilities ....Mr. Jimmy D. MARTIN
88 Assoc Athletic Dir External Rels ....Mr. C. Mike SMITH
88 Assc Dir Extend Campus Internet Pgm ....Mrs. Katie P. JONES
105 Dir Extended Campus Internet Pgm ....Mr. Josh HERRON
07 Assoc Director Admissions ....Mr. Travis MCDOWELL
40 Campus Store Manager ....Mrs. Patti H. MCCRAW
38 College Counselor ....Mrs. Mary B. CAMPBELL
107 Chair Div Professional Studies ....Dr. Paul R. LEFRANCOIS
65 Chair Div Natural Sciences ....Mr. Brian F. AMELING
49 Chair Div Arts & Letters ....Dr. Gena E. POOVEY
83 Chair Div Social & Behav Sciences ....Dr. Betsy A. WITT
53 Chair Div Educ/Phys Ed/Teacher Educ ....Dr. Shelly A. MEYERS

Medical University of South Carolina (A)

179 Ashley Avenue, Charleston SC 29425

County: Charleston FICE Identification: 003438
Unit ID: 218335
Telephone: (843) 792-2300 Carnegie Class: Spec-4-yr-Med
FAX Number: N/A Calendar System: Semester
URL: www.musc.edu
Established: 1824 Annual Undergrad Tuition & Fees (In-State): N/A
Enrollment: 2,898 Coed
Affiliation or Control: State IRS Status: Exempt
Highest Offering: Doctorate
Accreditation: SC, ANEST, ARCPA, DENT, DIETI, HSA, HT, IPSY, MED, NURSE, OT, PERF, PHAR, PTA

01 President ....Dr. David J. COLE
100 Chief of Staff ....Dr. Sabra C. SLAUGHTER
05 VP Academic Affairs & Provost ....Dr. Lisa SALADIN
17 Dean Col of Medicine ....Dr. Raymond DUBOIS
10 Exec Vice President Finance & Admin ....Ms. Lisa P. MONTGOMERY
30 Vice President Development ....Mr. Jim J. FISHER
17 VP Clinical Operations ....Dr. Patrick J. CAWLEY
13 VP Information Technology/CIO ....Mr. Michael P. CAPUTO
20 Assoc Prov Education/Student Life ....Dr. Darlene L. SHAW
46 VP Research ....Dr. Kathleen T. BRADY
52 Interim Dean of Dental Medicine ....Dr. Patricia L. BLANTON
76 Interim Dean of Health Professions ....Dr. James ZOLLER
58 Dean of Graduate Studies ....Dr. Paula TRAKTMAN
66 Dean of Nursing ....Dr. Gail W. STUART
67 Int Campus Dean SC Col of Pharmacy ....Dr. Philip D. HALL
08 Director of Libraries ....Ms. Shannon JONES
84 Director Enrollment Management ....Mr. George W. OHLANDT
28 Director Student Programs ....Mr. Kevin SMUNIEWSKI
43 General Counsel ....Ms. Annette R. DRACHMAN
26 Chief Communication & Marketing Ofc ......Ms. Sheila CHAMPLIN
22 Dir Affirm Act/Equal Opportunity .....Mr. Michael VANDERHURST
07 Director of Admissions ....Ms. Lyla HUDSON
18 Chief Facilities/Physical Plant ....Mr. Greg WEIGLE
06 Registrar ....Ms. Sandra L. MORRIS
15 Director Personnel Services ....Ms. Susan H. CARULLO
09 Dir Integrated Planning & Space Mgm .... Dr. Andrew GELASCO
38 Director Student Counseling ....Dr. Alice Q. LIBET
29 Director Alumni Affairs ....Ms. Sallie HUTTON SISTARE
37 Director Student Financial Aid .... Mr. Joseph M. DURANT
96 Director of Purchasing ....Ms. Velma STAMP

† Tuition varies by degree program.

Midlands Technical College (B)

PO Box 2408, Columbia SC 29202-2408

County: Richland FICE Identification: 003993
Unit ID: 218353
Telephone: (803) 738-8324 Carnegie Class: Assoc/MT-VT-High Trad
FAX Number: (803) 738-7784 Calendar System: Semester
URL: www.midlandstech.edu
Established: 1974 Annual Undergrad Tuition & Fees (In-District): $3,988
Enrollment: 11,424 Coed
Affiliation or Control: State/Local IRS Status: 501(c)3
Highest Offering: Associate Degree
Accreditation: SC, ACBSP, ADNUR, CAHIIM, COARC, DA, DH, ENGT, MAC, MLTAD, NMT, PNUR, PTAA, RAD, SURGT

01 President ....Dr. Ronald RHAMES
05 Vice President Academic Affairs ....Dr. Ronald DRAYTON
10 Interim VP for Business Affairs ....Mrs. Debbie WALKER
32 Vice Pres Student Development Svcs ....Ms. Sandi OLIVER
30 VP for Institutional Support ....Ms. Starnell BATES
51 VP Corporate/Continuing Educ/Comm ....Dr. Barrie KIRK
43 General Counsel ....Ms. Crystal ROOKARD
102 Associate VP of Foundation ....Mr. Jack HOEKSTRA
06 Registrar ....Ms. Carla KAISER
13 Director Information Resource Mgmt ....Mr. Tony HOUGH
37 Director of Student Financial Aid ....Mrs. Angela WILLIAMS
84 Director of Enrollment Services ....Ms. Sylvia LITTLEJOHN
26 Director of Public Affairs ....Mr. Todd GAVIN
15 Human Resource Director ....Mrs. Mary Beth LAMPE
07 Director of Admissions ....Mr. Derrah CASSIDY

Miller-Motte Technical College (C)

2451 Highway 501 East, Conway SC 29526
Telephone: (843) 591-1101 Identification: 770778
Accreditation: ACICS

† Branch campus of Miller-Motte Technical College Lynchburg, VA

Miller-Motte Technical College (D)

8085 Rivers Avenue, Suite E, North Charleston SC 29406
Telephone: (843) 574-0101 Identification: 666256
Accreditation: ACICS, MAC, SURGT

† Branch campus of Miller-Motte Technical College Clarksville, TN.

Morris College (E)

100 W College Street, Sumter SC 29150-3599

County: Sumter FICE Identification: 003439
Unit ID: 218399
Telephone: (803) 934-3200 Carnegie Class: Bac-Diverse
FAX Number: (803) 773-3687 Calendar System: Semester
URL: www.morris.edu
Established: 1908 Annual Undergrad Tuition & Fees: $12,649
Enrollment: 780 Coed
Affiliation or Control: Baptist IRS Status: 501(c)3
Highest Offering: Baccalaureate
Accreditation: SC, ACBSP, TED

01 President ....Dr. Luns C. RICHARDSON
05 Academic Dean ....Dr. Leroy STAGGERS
10 Director of Business Affairs ....Mr. Robert EAVES
45 Dir Planning/Govt Relations/IR ....Ms. Dorothy S. CHEAGLE
32 Dean Student Affairs ....Dr. Juana DAVIS-FREEMAN
15 Dir Business Supp Svcs/Personnel ....Mr. Roy GRAHAM
30 Director Inst Advanc/Church Rels ....Rev. Melvin MACK
42 College Minister ....Dr. Charles M. PEE
07 Dir Admissions & Records/Registrar ...Ms. Deborah C. CALHOUN
37 Director of Financial Aid ....Mrs. Sandra S. GIBSON
108 Director of Assessment ....Dr. Lewis P. GRAHAM, JR.
13 Director MIS/Computer Center ....Vacant
21 Chief Accountant ....Mrs. Bernice IRBY
29 Director Alumni Affairs ....Mrs. Altovia A. FELDER-DEAS
26 Director Public Relations ....Vacant
88 Director Learning Resources Ctr ....Ms. Janet S. CLAYTON
36 Director Career Services Center ..Dr. Gloria SEABROOK WRIGHT
20 Dir Academic Administrative Svcs ....Dr. Kay M. RHOADS
38 Director Counseling ....Dr. Quanca D. SIMS
39 Director Residential Life ....Mrs. Venessa F. JEFFERSON
41 Director of Athletics ....Mr. Clarence M. HOUCK
23 Director of Health Services ....Mrs. Johnell ROGERS
89 Director of Freshmen Studies ....Mr. Robert ZALIMAS
92 Director of Honors Program ....Dr. Joseph K. POPOOLA
40 Bookstore Manager ....Ms. Jeanette MOSES-HOLMES
35 Coordinator Student Activities ....Mr. Alston FREEMAN
19 Coordinator Campus Safety Services ....Ms. Lucille W. WILLIAMS

Newberry College (F)

2100 College, Newberry SC 29108-2126

County: Newberry FICE Identification: 003440
Unit ID: 218414
Telephone: (800) 845-4955 Carnegie Class: Bac-Diverse
FAX Number: (803) 321-5627 Calendar System: Semester
URL: www.newberry.edu
Established: 1856 Annual Undergrad Tuition & Fees: $25,000
Enrollment: 1,093 Coed
Affiliation or Control: Evangelical Lutheran Church In America IRS Status: 501(c)3
Highest Offering: Baccalaureate
Accreditation: SC, MUS, NURSE, TED

01 President ....Dr. Maurice W. SCHERRENS
05 VP Academic Affairs & Dean ....Dr. Timothy G. ELSTON
10 VP for Admin Affairs & CFO ....Ms. Kathy WORSTER
30 VP for Institutional Advancement ....Mr. Scott JOYNER
84 Dean of Enrollment Management ....Mr. Joe VANDER HORST
32 Dean of Student Affairs ....Dr. Sandra ROUSE
41 Interim Director of Athletics ....Mr. Ralph PATTERSON
15 Director of Human Resources ....Mrs. Peggy SHULER
09 Dir Institutional Effectiveness ....Dr. Sid PARRISH
06 Registrar ....Mrs. Carol A. BICKLEY
29 Assoc Dir of Alumni Relations ....Mr. Jeff WICKER
08 Librarian ....Ms. Nancy ROSENWALD
18 Director of Facilities ....Mr. Fred ERRIGO
42 Chaplain ....Rev. Ernie WORMAN
21 Director of Accounting ....Mrs. Landee BUZHARDT
38 Dir Health & Counselling Services ....Ms. Martha DORRELL
37 Director of Financial Aid ....Mrs. Danielle BELL
26 Director of Marketing & PR ....Ms. Jill JOHNSON
19 Director Security/Safety ....Mr. Paul WHITMAN

North Greenville University (G)

PO Box 1892, Tigerville SC 29688-1892

County: Greenville FICE Identification: 003441
Unit ID: 218441
Telephone: (864) 977-7000 Carnegie Class: Masters/S
FAX Number: (864) 977-7021 Calendar System: Semester
URL: www.ngu.edu
Established: 1892 Annual Undergrad Tuition & Fees: $16,290
Enrollment: 2,569 Coed
Affiliation or Control: Southern Baptist IRS Status: 501(c)3
Highest Offering: Doctorate
Accreditation: SC, MUS, TED

01 Interim President/CEO ....Dr. Randall J. PANNELL
04 Admin Assistant for President ....Ms. Elise STYLES
05 Vice President Academics ....Dr. Randall PANNELL
32 Vice President Student Services ....Dr. Tony BEAM
20 Asst VP Acads/Dean Communication ....Dr. Linwood HAGIN
58 Vice President Graduate Studies ....Dr. J. Samuel ISGETT
10 Vice President Business Affairs ....Ms. Michelle L. SABOU
07 VP Enrollment Services ....Ms. Keli SEWELL
30 Vice President Advancement ....Vacant
88 Vice President Church Relations ....Rev. Mayson EASTERLING
42 Vice President Campus Ministries ....Dr. Steve CROUSE
102 VP Corp Found Giving/Crusader Club ....Vacant
35 Director Student Services ....Mr. Billy WATSON
09 Director of Institutional Research ...... Dr. George A. HOPSON, JR.
06 Registrar ....Ms. Pam FARMER
18 Director of University Properties ....Mr. Larry MATHIS
41 Athletic Director ....Ms. Jan MCDONALD
34 Director Residential Living Women ....Ms. Lorry GREEN
33 Director Residential Living Men ....Mr. Dillon KEY
08 Director of Hester Library ....Ms. Carla MCMAHAN
19 Director Campus Security ....Mr. Rick MORRIS
88 Dean of Graduate Academic Services .... Mrs. Tawana SCOTT
26 Director Public Rels/Stewardship ....Mr. LaVerne B. HOWELL
29 Dir Alumni Affairs/Planned Giving .... Mrs. Julie STYLES
15 Human Resource Manager ....Mrs. Beth HOUCK
40 Bookstore Manager ....Mrs. Cindy COWAN
38 Personal Counselor Men ....Mr. Steve BIELBY
38 Personal Counselor Women ....Mrs. Sue SUOMI
36 Career Services Coordinator .... Mr. Joshua PUTNAM
23 Director Health Services ....Ms. Kathy BAILEY
30 Executive Director Development ....Rev. Joe F. HAYES
44 Director of Development ....Mr. Jason ROSS
13 Asst VP Information Tech Services ....Mr. Paul GARRETT
37 Director Financial Planning ....Mr. Michael JORDAN
53 Dean Education ....Dr. Constance WRIGHT
79 Dean Humanities ....Dr. H. Paul THOMPSON
57 Dean Fine Arts ....Dr. Jacquelyn H. GRIFFIN
81 Dean Science & Mathematics ....Dr. Tom ALLEN
73 Dean Christian Studies ....Dr. Walter JOHNSON
50 Dean Business & Sport Professions ....Dr. Ralph JOHNSON
88 Asst VP for Online Education ....Dr. Lena MASLENNIKOVA

Northeastern Technical College (H)

1201 Chesterfield Hwy, Cheraw SC 29520

County: Chesterfield FICE Identification: 007602
Unit ID: 217837
Telephone: (843) 921-6900 Carnegie Class: Assoc/HVT-High Trad
FAX Number: (843) 537-6148 Calendar System: Semester
URL: www.netc.edu
Established: 1969 Annual Undergrad Tuition & Fees (In-State): $3,846
Enrollment: 1,090 Coed
Affiliation or Control: State IRS Status: 501(c)3
Highest Offering: Associate Degree
Accreditation: SC

01 President ....Dr. Ron BARTLEY
05 Vice Pres Instruction/Student Svcs ....Dr. Forest MAHAN
10 Vice Pres Administration & Finance ....Mrs. Debbie Q. CHEEK
30 Director for Inst Advancement ....Mrs. Erin FANN
15 Director for Human Resources ....Mrs. Donna CHAVIS
06 Coordinator for Student Records ....Ms. Anne JONES
26 Coordinator for Public Relations ....Mrs. Shannon JUSTICE
84 Director of Enrollment Management ....Mr. Darin COLEMAN
08 Head Librarian ....Mrs. Kulcey STAFFORD
09 Director of Institutional Research .... Mrs. Elizabeth HAMRICK

Orangeburg-Calhoun Technical College (I)

3250 Saint Matthews Road, Orangeburg SC 29118-8299

County: Orangeburg FICE Identification: 006815
Unit ID: 218487
Telephone: (803) 536-0311 Carnegie Class: Assoc/HVT-High Trad
FAX Number: (803) 535-1388 Calendar System: Semester
URL: www.octech.edu
Established: 1966 Annual Undergrad Tuition & Fees (In-State): $4,045
Enrollment: 3,060 Coed
Affiliation or Control: State IRS Status: 501(c)3
Highest Offering: Associate Degree
Accreditation: SC, ACBSF, ADNUR, COARC, ENGT, MAC, PNUR, PTAA, RAD

01 President ....Dr. Walt TOBIN, JR.
05 Vice Pres Academic Affairs ....Mrs. Donna ELMORE
10 Vice President Business Affairs ....Mr. Kim HUFF
32 Vice President of Student Services ....Mrs. Sandra S. DAVIS
11 Assoc VP of Administration ....Mr. Mike HAMMOND
36 AVP Corp Training/Econ Development ....Mrs. Sandra MOORE
06 Registrar ....Ms. Amy OTT
30 Dean Development/Marketing .... Ms. Faith MCCURRY
46 Dean Planning/Research/Development .... Ms. Faith MCCURRY
13 Director Information Technology ....Mr. Gary A. FOLEY
62 Dean Learning Resource Center ....Mrs. Harris MURRAY
18 Chief Facilities/Physical Plant ....Mr. James S. BRYANT, III
37 Director Student Financial Aid ....Ms. Bichevia GREEN
08 Director Library Services ....Ms. Harris MURRAY
07 Director of Admissions ....Vacant
19 Chief of Safety/Security ....Mr. Douglas STOKES
09 Dir Acad Support/Inst Effectiveness ....Mr. Cleveland WILSON

15 Human Resource Director ... Ms. Marie HOWELL
96 Procurement Manager ... Mrs. Scarlet GEDDINGS
84 Enrollment/Records Mgmt Specialist ... Ms. Phyllis STOUDENMIRE

Piedmont Technical College (A)

620 N. Emerald Road, Greenwood SC 29646
County: Greenwood
FICE Identification: 003992
Unit ID: 218520
Telephone: (864) 941-8324
Carnegie Class: Assoc/HVT-High Trad
FAX Number: (864) 941-8555
Calendar System: Semester
URL: www.ptc.edu
Established: 1966
Annual Undergrad Tuition & Fees (In-District): $4,049
Enrollment: 5,694
Coed
Affiliation or Control: State/Local
IRS Status: 501(c)3
Highest Offering: Associate Degree
Accreditation: SC, ADNUR, COARC, CVT, ENGT, FUSER, MAC, OTA, RAD, SURGT

01 President ... Dr. L. Rayburn BROOKS
10 Vice Pres Business & Finance ... Ms. K. Paige CHILDS
05 Vice President Academic Affairs ... Dr. Jack BAGWELL
32 Assoc Vice Pres Student Affairs ... Mr. Andy OMUNDSON
51 Assoc Vice Pres Cont Educ/Econ Dev ... Mr. Rusty DENNING
24 Assoc VP Instructional Technology ... Dr. Joel GRIFFIN
108 Assoc VP Assessment/Compliance ... Ms. Donna FOSTER
84 Assoc VP Enrollment/Communications ... Mr. Joshua BLACK
12 Dean County Centers ... Dr. Jennifer WILBANKS
76 Dean Health Sciences ... Mr. Jerry ALEWINE
54 Dean Engr/Indust Technologies ... Mr. David KIBLER
66 Dean Nursing ... Ms. Tara HARRIS
35 Dean of Students ... Mr. David R. ROSENBAUM
07 Dean of Admissions ... Ms. Renae FRAZIER
09 Director Institutional Reporting ... Ms. Zeolean F. KINARD
26 Director Marketing/Public Relations ... Mr. Russell MARTIN
88 Director Genesis Initiatives ... Mr. Steve B. COLEMAN
18 Director Facilities Management ... Mr. Chad TEAGUE
102 Asst VP Development/PTC Foundation ... Ms. Fran K. WILEY
08 Head Librarian ... Ms. Meredith DANIEL
19 Director Campus Police/Security ... Mr. Terry LEDFORD
37 Director of Financial Aid ... Ms. Missy PERRY
06 Registrar ... Ms. Tamatha SELLS
21 Controller ... Ms. Paige CHILDS
15 Director Human Resources ... Ms. Alesia BROWN
21 Manager Business Office ... Ms. Crystal PITTMAN

Presbyterian College (B)

503 S Broad Street, Clinton SC 29325-2865
County: Laurens
FICE Identification: 003445
Unit ID: 218539
Telephone: (864) 833-2820
Carnegie Class: Bac-A&S
FAX Number: (864) 833-8481
Calendar System: Semester
URL: www.presby.edu
Established: 1880
Annual Undergrad Tuition & Fees: $36,130
Enrollment: 1,460
Coed
Affiliation or Control: Presbyterian Church (U.S.A.)
IRS Status: 501(c)3
Highest Offering: Doctorate
Accreditation: SC, MUS, PHAR, TED

01 President ... Mr. Robert E. STATON
101 Executive Asst to the President ... Ms. Christie L. MUELLER
04 Sr Admin Asst to the President ... Mrs. Jenny G. BOGAN
84 Dean of Enrollment Management ... Mr. Brian J. FORTMAN
07 Associate Dean of Admissions ... Mr. Mark O. FOX, II
05 Provost ... Dr. Donald R. RABER, II
20 Dean of Academic Programs ... Dr. J. Alicia ASKEW
37 VP for Enrollment & Financial Aid ... Mrs. Suzanne M. PETRUSCH
09 Director of Institutional Research ... Dr. Norman B. BRYAN, JR.
08 Director of Thomason Library ... Mr. David W. CHATHAM
24 Director of Media Services ... Mr. Douglas J. WALLACE
104 Director of International Programs ... Mr. Viet X. HA
85 Asst Dir of International Programs ... Ms. Elizabeth M. DILLE
06 Registrar & Director of Records ... Ms. Kendra B. WOODSON
67 Dean School of Pharmacy ... Dr. L. Clifton FUHRMAN, JR.
07 Dir of Admissions Pharmacy School ... Ms. Katherine J. KANE
10 VP Finance/Administration ... Ms. Susan A. MADDUX
21 Controller ... Ms. Dawn W. DURHAM
18 Exec Director of Campus Services ... Mr. Michael D. CRISP
37 Director of Financial Aid ... Ms. Linda J. MCANNALLY
13 Director of Information Technology ... Mr. H. William ROACH
90 Academic Computing Services Coord ... Dr. Robert W. HOWILER
91 Desktop Support/Aux Systems Sr Tech ... Ms. Nellie R. SHELTON
109 Manager of Auxiliary Services ... Mr. Jason T. KOENIG
32 VP for Campus Life/Dean of Students ... Dr. Joy S. SMITH
39 Assoc Dean Students/Residence Life ... Mr. Andrew T. PETERSON
36 Assoc Dean Students/Career Dev ... Vacant
42 Director of Campus Ministries ... Ms. Rachel E. PARSONS-WELLS
19 Director of Safety & Risk Mgmt ... Mr. Lawrence P. MULHALL
38 Director Counseling Services ... Ms. Susan C. GENTRY-WRIGHT
28 Asst Dir of Multicultural Programs ... Ms. Lashawna A. WRIGHT
30 VP for Advancement/Mktg/PR/Comm ... Mr. Grady B. JONES
44 Director of Annual Fund ... Mr. Alex K. SCULL
88 Director of Athletic Major Gifts ... Mr. R. Matthew CAIN
29 Director Alumni Relations ... Ms. Leni N. PATTERSON
41 Director of Athletics ... Mr. Brian P. REESE
15 VP of Human Resources ... Ms. Barbara H. FAYAD

Professional Golfers Career College (C)

4454 Bluffton Pk Crescent, Ste 200, Bluffton SC 29910
Telephone: (843) 759-9611
Identification: 770779
Accreditation: ACICS

† Branch campus of Professional Golfers Career College, Temecula, CA

Sherman College of Chiropractic (D)

PO Box 1452, Spartanburg SC 29304-1452
County: Spartanburg
FICE Identification: 020637
Unit ID: 218751
Telephone: (864) 578-8770
Carnegie Class: Spec-4-yr-Other Health
FAX Number: (864) 599-4860
Calendar System: Quarter
URL: www.sherman.edu
Established: 1973
Annual Graduate Tuition & Fees: N/A
Enrollment: 346
Coed
Affiliation or Control: Independent Non-Profit
IRS Status: 501(c)3
Highest Offering: Doctorate; No Undergraduates
Accreditation: SC, CHIRO

01 President ... Dr. Edwin CORDERO
03 Executive Vice President ... Dr. Neil COHEN
05 Provost ... Dr. Robert IRWIN
20 Vice Pres of Academic Affairs ... Dr. Joseph DONOFRIO
84 Sr Director for Enrollment Services ... Mrs. Kristy SHEPHERD
10 Vice Pres for Business & Finance ... Mrs. Karen CANUP
32 Dean of Student Affairs ... Mrs. LaShanda HUTTO-HARRIS
29 Dir Alumni Rels/Instl Advancement ... Ms. Marggi ROLDAN
06 Registrar ... Ms. Melody SABIN
08 Librarian ... Mrs. Chandra PLACER
37 Director of Financial Aid ... Mrs. Tina CASEY-CORREA
45 Dir Institutional Effectiveness ... Mrs. Crissy LEWIS
04 Admin Asst to President/EVP ... Ms. Roberta THOMAS
26 Director of Public Relations ... Ms. Karen RHODES
09 Director of Institutional Research ... Dr. Pengju George LUO
106 Dir Online Education/E-learning ... Dr. Billie HARRINGTON
15 Director Personnel Services ... Mrs. Mandy SMITH
19 Director Security/Safety ... Mr. Patrick LAUSIER

South Carolina State University (E)

300 College Street, NE, Orangeburg SC 29117-0001
County: Orangeburg
FICE Identification: 003446
Unit ID: 218733
Telephone: (803) 536-7000
Carnegie Class: Masters/M
FAX Number: (803) 533-3622
Calendar System: Semester
URL: www.scsu.edu
Established: 1896
Annual Undergrad Tuition & Fees (In-State): $10,088
Enrollment: 3,331
Coed
Affiliation or Control: State
IRS Status: 501(c)3
Highest Offering: Doctorate
Accreditation: SC, AAFCS, ART, BUS, CACREP, CORE, CS, DIETD, ENG, ENGT, MUS, SP, SW, TED

01 President ... Mr. James E. CLARK
04 Exec Asst to the President ... Ms. Shondra N. ABRAHAM
05 Acting Provost ... Dr. Learie B. LUKE
10 Int Vice Pres for Finance/Mgmt ... Mr. Edward PATRICK
32 Vice Pres for Student Affairs ... Dr. Tamara JEFFERIES-JACKSON
30 AVP Institutional Advancement ... Mr. A. L. FLEMING
46 VP Research/Economic Development ... Mr. Delbert T. FOSTER
11 Interim VP of Administration ... Dr. Rita J. TEAL
43 General Counsel ... Mr. Craig E. BURGESS
20 Associate Provost ... Vacant
26 VP External Affairs/Communications ... Ms. Sonja A. BENNETT-BELLAMY
84 VP Enrollment Management ... Ms. Betty R. BOATWRIGHT
46 Int Assoc Provost/Sponsored Program ... Mr. Elbert R. MALONE
72 Dean Col Sci/Math/Engineering Tech ... Dr. Kenneth LEWIS
53 Int Dn Col Educ/Humanities/Soc Sci ... Dr. Albert G. HAYWARD
58 Int Dean Col of Graduate Studies ... Dr. Frederick M G. EVANS
50 Interim Dean School of Business ... Dr. Barbara L. ADAMS
08 Dean Library & Information Services ... Ms. Adrienne C. WEBBER
88 Interim Dir Stdnt Success Retent ... Ms. Sandra E. SCOTT
06 Registrar/Director Veterans Affairs ... Ms. Ann BELTON
07 Asst Dir Admissions/Recruitment ... Ms. LaSandra ROBINSON
13 Dir Univ Computing/Info Tech Svcs ... Dr. James L. MYERS
37 Director of Financial Aid ... Mrs. C C JACKSON
38 Director Counseling/Student Dev ... Dr. Cherilyn Y. TAYLOR-MINNIEFIELD
21 Controller ... Ms. Teare BREWINGTON
09 Exec Dir Institutional Research ... Dr. Rita TEAL
27 Director of Public Relations ... Mrs. Elizabeth MOSELY-HAWKINS
36 Int Director of Career Placement ... Mr. Joseph THOMAS
15 Director Human Resource Mgmt ... Vacant
41 Director Athletics ... Mr. Paul BRYANT
18 Director of Facilities Mgmt ... Mr. Ken DAVIS
96 Director Procurement Services ... Ms. Jessica FAVOR
39 Director of Residential Life ... Dr. Kelvin RACHELL
19 Interim Chief of Campus Police ... Mr. Mernard CLARKSON
92 Interim Dean Honors College ... Dr. Harriet A. ROLAND
88 Interim Director Sports Information ... Mr. Kendrick D. LEWIS
35 Asst Director of Student Life ... Ms. Cammy D. GRATE
88 Director of Internal Audit ... Vacant
25 Dir Grants & Contract ... Ms. Gwendolyn F. MITCHELL
88 Director of Title III ... Ms. Gloria D. PYLES
88 Director of Staff Development ... Ms. Patricia GIBSON-HAIGLER
28 Director of Multicultural Affairs ... Ms. Carolyn G. FREE
88 Station Manager WSSB-FM ... Mr. Carlito D. A'SEE
88 Athletics Compliance Coordinator ... Mr. Eric M. SEIFARTH
101 Secretary/Board of Trustees ... Ms. Eartha J. MOSLEY
104 Dir International/National Exchange ... Dr. Learie LUKE
105 Web Services ... Mr. Jason BARR
29 Director Alumni Relations ... Ms. Iva GARDNER
54 Dean of Engineering ... Dr. Kenneth LEWIS

South University Columbia Campus (F)

9 Science Court, Columbia SC 29203-6400
Telephone: (803) 799-9082
FICE Identification: 004922
Accreditation: &SC, ACBSP, CACREP, MAC, NURSE, OT, PHAR, @PTAA

† Regional accreditation is carried under the parent institution in Savannah, GA.

Southern Wesleyan University (G)

907 Wesleyan Drive, PO Box 1020, Central SC 29630-1020
County: Pickens
FICE Identification: 003422
Unit ID: 217776
Telephone: (864) 644-5000
Carnegie Class: Masters/L
FAX Number: (864) 644-5900
Calendar System: Semester
URL: www.swu.edu
Established: 1906
Annual Undergrad Tuition & Fees: $23,620
Enrollment: 1,778
Coed
Affiliation or Control: Wesleyan Church
IRS Status: 501(c)3
Highest Offering: Master's
Accreditation: SC, MUS, TED

01 President ... Dr. Todd S. VOSS
05 Provost ... Dr. Tonya STRICKLAND
10 VP for Finance & Auxiliary Services ... Mr. Mark T. REEVES
13 Director Information Technology ... Mr. Mike PREUSZ
37 Director of Financial Aid ... Mrs. Melanie GILLESPIE
18 Director of Physical Plant ... Mr. Jonathan CATRON
09 Assoc VP for Planning & Assessment ... Dr. Corey AMAKER
06 Registrar ... Ms. Janet HARTSOE
08 Int Director of Library Services ... Mrs. Shannon BROOKS
84 VP for Enrollment Management ... Mr. Chad PETERS
07 Dir of Admissions & Enrollment Mgmt ... Mr. David SLABAUGH
32 Vice President for Student Life ... Dr. W. Joseph BROCKINTON
42 AVP Spiritual Life/Univ Chaplain ... Rev. Ken DILL
30 Vice President for Development ... Dr. Lisa MCWHERTER
29 Exec Dir of Alumni/Constituent Rels ... Mrs. Joy L. BRYANT
15 Director of Human Resources ... Mrs. Dana L. FROST
04 Administrative Asst to President ... Ms. Amy JARRETT
106 Dir Online Education/E-learning ... Mr. Tyler WATTS
38 Director Student Counseling ... Ms. Monica PEREZ
41 Athletic Director ... Mr. Chris WILLIAMS
50 Dean of the School of Business ... Dr. Jeannie TRUDEL
53 Dean of the School of Education ... Dr. Sandra MCLENDON

Spartanburg Community College (H)

107 Community College Drive, Spartanburg SC 29303
County: Spartanburg
FICE Identification: 003994
Unit ID: 218830
Telephone: (864) 592-4600
Carnegie Class: Assoc/HVT-High Trad
FAX Number: (864) 592-4642
Calendar System: Semester
URL: www.sccsc.edu
Established: 1963
Annual Undergrad Tuition & Fees (In-State): $4,192
Enrollment: 5,495
Coed
Affiliation or Control: State
IRS Status: 501(c)3
Highest Offering: Associate Degree
Accreditation: SC, ACBSP, ACFEI, ADNUR, COARC, DA, EMT, ENGT, MAC, MLTAD, RAD, SURGT

01 President ... Mr. Henry C. GILES, JR.
05 Sr Vice President Academic Affairs ... Dr. Cheryl COX
10 Vice Pres for Business Affairs ... Mr. Ray SWITZER
102 Exec Dir Advancement/SCC Foundation ... Mr. Samuel S. HOOK
32 Vice President for Student Affairs ... Mr. Ron JACKSON
12 Asc Vice Pres Enroll Mgt/Retention ... Mrs. Lynn F. DALE
20 Assoc Vice Pres of Instruction ... Mrs. Patricia JONES
51 Exec Asst to Pres/Dir Economic Dev ... Mr. Michael P. FORRESTER
12 Executive Director Cherokee Campus ... Mr. Daryl SMITH
12 Exec Director Tyger River Campus ... Dr. Anya SEBASTIEN
12 Exec Director Downtown Campus ... Mrs. Judy SIEG
12 Site Coord Union County Campus ... Mrs. Kathy LANCASTER
108 Director Eval/Accreditation/Plng ... Mr. Jay JACKSON
88 Dean of CCE ... Mr. Robert LESLIE
08 Dean of Learning Resources ... Mr. Mark ROSEVEARE
76 Dean Health & Human Services ... Dr. Berta HOPKINS
49 Dean of Arts & Sciences ... Mrs. Kem HARVEY
07 Director of Admissions ... Ms. Alison CANN
15 Director of Human Resources ... Mr. Rick TEAL
13 Director Information Technologies ... Mr. Peter C. GALLEN
09 Director of Institutional Research ... Mr. Jack R. BOURGEOIS
26 Chief Public Relations Officer ... Mrs. Cheri A. HUCKS
29 Alumni Relations Coordinator ... Ms. Kim FOGEL
38 Director Student Counseling ... Vacant
14 Director Computer Center ... Mrs. Tina S. REID
18 Chief Facilities/Physical Plant ... Mr. Gladden SMOKE
19 Director Security/Safety ... Mr. Andre KERR
06 Registrar ... Ms. Celia N. BAUSS
96 Director Purchasing Office ... Mr. Cecil L. HUTCHERSON
21 Director of Finance ... Mrs. Mary FUHRMAN
37 Director of Financial Aid ... Mr. Jeffery BOYLE
106 Dir Online Education/E-learning ... Mr. Neil GRIFFIN
25 Chief Contracts/Grants Admin ... Mrs. Elena RUSH
54 Dean of Engineering ... Mr. Jeff HUNT
04 Administrative Asst to President ... Ms. Betty HALL
36 Director Student Placement ... Ms. Jennifer LITTLE
90 Director Academic Computing ... Mr. Roy SMITH

Spartanburg Methodist College (A)

1000 Powell Mill Road, Spartanburg SC 29301-5899
County: Spartanburg FICE Identification: 003447
Unit ID: 218821
Telephone: (864) 587-4000 Carnegie Class: Assoc/HT-High Trad
FAX Number: (864) 587-4355 Calendar System: Semester
URL: www.smcsc.edu
Established: 1911 Annual Undergrad Tuition & Fees: $16,700
Enrollment: 793 Coed
Affiliation or Control: United Methodist IRS Status: 501(c)3
Highest Offering: Associate Degree
Accreditation: SC

01 President ....Mr. W. Scott COCHRAN
05 Exec VP for Acad Affairs/Studen Dev ....Dr. Anita K. BOWLES
10 Executive VP for Business Affairs ....Mr. Eric MCDONALD
30 Vice Pres Institutional Advancement ....Mrs. Jennifer DILLENGER
84 Vice President of Enrollment ....Mr. Wells SHEPARD
26 Vice President for Marketing ....Mrs. Lisa WARE
88 Vice President for Prof Development ....Ms. Courtney SHELTON
32 Interim Dean of Students ....Dr. Art HARTZOG
06 Registrar ....Ms. Jill R. JOHNSON
08 Library Director ....Mrs. Erin WASHINGTON
04 Admin Assistant to the President ....Mrs. Cheryl SOMERSET
13 Exec Dir Information Technology ....Mr. Trey ARRINGTON
44 Director of Development ....Mr. Don TATE
37 Director of Financial Aid ....Ms. Kendra STRANGE
38 Director of Student Counseling ....Mr. Pete AYLOR
42 Chaplain/Director of Church Rels ....Rev. Candice Y. SLOAN
41 Director of Athletics ....Mr. Tim WALLACE
18 Director Facilities Management ....Mr. Marty WOODS
29 Director of Alumni Relations ....Mrs. Leah L. PRUITT
15 Exec Director of Human Resources ....Mrs. Jeanette R. DUNN
44 Director of Church Funding ....Rev. Michael E. BOWERS
19 Chief of Campus Safety ....Ms. Teresa D. FERGUSON
09 Director of Assessment Activities ....Mr. Robert W. ISENHOWER
39 Director Student Housing ....Mrs. Stacey MASON

Technical College of the Lowcountry (B)

921 S Ribaut Road, PO Box 1288,
Beaufort SC 29901-1288
County: Beaufort FICE Identification: 009910
Unit ID: 217712
Telephone: (843) 525-8211 Carnegie Class: Assoc/MT-VT-High Trad
FAX Number: (843) 525-8330 Calendar System: Semester
URL: www.tcl.edu
Established: 1969 Annual Undergrad Tuition & Fees (In-State): $4,180
Enrollment: 2,529 Coed
Affiliation or Control: State IRS Status: 501(c)3
Highest Offering: Associate Degree
Accreditation: SC, ACBSP, ADNUR, COMTA, PNUR, PTAA, RAD, SURGT

01 President ....Dr. Richard J. GOUGH
11 Vice Pres Administrative Services ....Mr. Hayes WISER
05 Vice President for Academic Affairs ....Dr. Gina MOUNFIELD
32 Vice President for Student Affairs ....Ms. Nancy WEBER
35 AVP for Student Affairs ....Mr. Rodney ADAMS
09 Director for Research/Planning ....Ms. Camille MYERS
15 Human Resources Director ....Ms. Sonya LYTTLE
20 Director for Learning Resources ....Ms. Sasha BISHOP
50 Div Dean Business Technologies ....Dr. Kenneth FLICK
49 Div Dean Arts & Sciences ....Dr. Gayle TREMBLE
76 Dean Health Sciences ....Dr. Glenn LEVICKI
13 Director of Information Technology ....Mr. Floyd HENDERSON
37 Director Financial Aid ....Ms. Julia DENNIS
30 VP for Inst Advancement ....Ms. Mary Lee CARNS
26 AVP for Public Relations ....Ms. Leigh COPELAND
40 Bookstore Director ....Ms. Louise RENNIX
18 Director of Facility Management ....Mr. Larry BECKLER
96 Director of Purchasing ....Ms. Carol MACK
06 Registrar ....Ms. Allison CANNING
36 Career & Transfer Services Manager ....Ms. Melanie GALLION
04 Administrative Asst to President ....Ms. Ann CULLEN

Tri-County Technical College (C)

PO Box 587, Pendleton SC 29670-0587
County: Anderson FICE Identification: 004926
Unit ID: 218885
Telephone: (864) 646-8361 Carnegie Class: Assoc/HT-High Trad
FAX Number: (864) 646-1895 Calendar System: Semester
URL: www.tctc.edu
Established: 1962 Annual Undergrad Tuition & Fees (In-District): $3,967
Enrollment: 6,386 Coed
Affiliation or Control: State/Local IRS Status: 501(c)3
Highest Offering: Associate Degree
Accreditation: SC, ACBSP, ADNUR, DA, MAC, MLTAD, PNUR, SURGT

01 President ....Dr. Ronnie L. BOOTH
05 Senior Vice President ....Mr. Galen DEHAY
10 Vice Pres Business Affairs ....Ms. Cara HAMILTON
102 Executive Director Foundation ....Mr. Grayson KELLY
20 AVP Instruction & Effectiveness ....Vacant
51 Dean of Continuing Education ....Mr. Rick COTHRAN
84 Dean of Transition to College ....Ms. Jenni CREAMER
32 Dean of Student Development ....Mr. Mark DOUGHERTY
49 Dean Arts & Sciences Division ....Dr. Alfred WHEELER
72 Dean Engineering Technology Div ....Ms. Amanda ORZECHOWSKI
50 Dean Business/Human Services Div ....Mrs. Jackie BLAKLEY
76 Dean Health Education Division ....Dr. Lynn LEWIS
08 Head Librarian ....Ms. Marla ROBERSON
37 Student Financial Aid Director ....Mr. Adam GHILONI
13 CIO/Information Technology Dir ....Mr. Matthew EDWARDS
26 Dir Public Relations/Communication ....Mrs. Rebecca W. EIDSON
30 Director of Development ....Ms. Courtney WHITE
44 Director of Annual Giving ....Mrs. Tammy FISK
15 Asst VP Human Resources ....Mrs. Sharon COLCOLOUGH
07 Director of Admissions ....Ms. Tiffini BLACKWELL
06 Registrar ....Mr. Scott HARVEY
09 Director of Institutional Research ....Mr. Chris MARINO
18 Chief Facilities/Physical Plant ....Mr. Ken KOPERA
21 Director of Fiscal Affairs ....Ms. Tracy WACTOR
96 Director of Purchasing ....Ms. Kristal DOHERTY
38 Director of Student Life/Counseling ....Ms. Croslena JOHNSON
04 Administrative Asst to President ....Mrs. Kathy BRANT
19 Director Security/Safety ....Mr. Jonathan FINCH
25 Chief Contracts/Grants Admin ....Ms. Laneika MUSALINI
86 Dir Econ Dev/Government Relations ....Mr. Dan COOPER
109 Chief Auxiliary Services Officer ....Mr. Kevin STEELE

Trident Technical College (D)

PO Box 118067, Charleston SC 29423-8067
County: Charleston FICE Identification: 004920
Unit ID: 218894
Telephone: (843) 574-6111 Carnegie Class: Assoc/MT-VT-High Trad
FAX Number: (843) 574-6541 Calendar System: Semester
URL: www.tridenttech.edu
Established: 1964 Annual Undergrad Tuition & Fees (In-District): $4,039
Enrollment: 16,136 Coed
Affiliation or Control: State/Local IRS Status: 501(c)3
Highest Offering: Associate Degree
Accreditation: SC, ACBSP, ACFEI, ADNUR, COARC, CSHSE, DA, DH, EMT, MAC, MLTAD, OTA, PNUR, PTAA, RAD

01 President ....Dr. Mary THORNLEY
10 Vice Pres Finance & Administration ....Mr. Scott POELKER
05 Vice President Academic Affairs ....Dr. Patricia ROBERTSON
32 Vice President Student Services ....Dr. Patrice MITCHELL
30 Vice President Advancement ....Ms. Meg HOWLE
51 Vice Pres Continuing Educ/Econ Dev ....Mr. Robert WALKER
13 Vice Pres Information Technology ....Mr. Bernie STRAUB
45 Assoc VP Planning/Accreditation ....Ms. Cathy ALMQUIST
20 Asst Vice Pres Academic Programs ....Ms. Susan NORTON
51 Asst Vice Pres Continuing Education ....Ms. Yvonne BROWN
72 Asst Vice Pres Info Technology ....Vacant
35 Asst Vice Pres for Student Svcs ....Ms. Lynne ANKERSEN
20 Asst Vice President Instruction ....Mr. Eddie SIMMONS
15 Director Human Resources ....Ms. DeVetta HUGHES
96 Dir Procurement/Risk Management ....Ms. Carol BELCHER
40 Dir Auxiliary Enterprises/Bookstore ....Ms. Jloundia PINCKNEY
18 Director Facilities ....Mr. Eric HAMILTON
21 Director Finance ....Ms. Melody TAYLOR
26 Director Marketing ....Ms. Tina AHLEMANN
27 Director Public Info ....Mr. David HANSEN
88 Director High School Programs ....Ms. Melissa STOWASSER
30 Associate VP Development ....Ms. Kimberley HALLIN
14 Dir Information Technology Training ....Mr. Joseph GIBSON
36 Dean of Student Employment ....Mr. Brian ALMQUIST
81 Dean Science & Mathematics ....Mr. Bill LANDRY
79 Dean Humanities & Social Sciences ....Dr. Tim BROWN
88 Dean of The Learning Center ....Mr. David HARRIS
50 AVP Educ Tech/The Online College ....Ms. Connie JOLLY
76 Dean Allied Health Sciences ....Dr. Shelley DIVINEY
57 Dean Film Media and Visual Arts ....Ms. Pat FOX
54 Dean Industrial/Engineering Tech ....Ms. Christine LANG
88 Dean Culinary Inst of Charleston ....Mr. Mike SABOE
61 Dean Law-Related Studies ....Mr. John UNGARO
66 Dean Nursing ....Ms. Marilyn BRADY
38 Dean Student Development ....Ms. Pamela BROWN
88 Dean Comm/Family/Child Studies ....Ms. Stephany HEWITT
84 Dean Enrollment Management ....Mr. John JAMROGOWICZ
75 Dean Aeronautical Studies ....Dr. Barry FRANCO
12 Dean Berkeley Campus ....Ms. Karen WRIGHTEN
12 Dean Mount Pleasant Campus ....Mr. Michael PATTERSON
12 Dean Palmer Campus ....Dr. Louester ROBINSON
19 Director Public Safety ....Mr. Lawrence SAVIDGE
06 Registrar ....Ms. Pamela DROSTE
07 Director of Admissions ....Ms. Clara MARTIN
09 Director of Institutional Research ....Mr. James GREEN
37 Director Student Financial Aid ....Ms. Charlotte SORG

University of Phoenix Columbia SC Campus (E)

1001 Pinnacle Point Drive, Columbia SC 29223-5727
Telephone: (803) 699-5096 Identification: 770223
Accreditation: &NH, ACBSP

† No longer accepting campus-based students.

University of South Carolina Columbia (F)

Columbia SC 29208-0001
County: Richland FICE Identification: 003448
Unit ID: 218663
Telephone: (803) 777-7000 Carnegie Class: DU-Highest
FAX Number: (803) 777-0101 Calendar System: Semester
URL: www.sc.edu
Established: 1801 Annual Undergrad Tuition & Fees (In-State): $11,482
Enrollment: 32,971 Coed
Affiliation or Control: State IRS Status: 501(c)3
Highest Offering: Doctorate
Accreditation: SC, ANEST, ART, BUS, BUSA, CAATE, CACREP, CEA, CLPSY, CORE, CS, DANCE, ENG, HSA, IPSY, JOUR, LAW, LIB, MED, MUS, NURSE, PH, PHAR, PTA SCPSY, SP, SPAA, SW, TED, THEA

01 President ....Dr. Harris PASTIDES
13 Vice President for IT & CIO ....Dr. William F. HOGUE
100 Chief of Staff & Spec Asst to Pres ....Mr. Cantey HEATH
83 University Treasurer ....Mr. Patrick LARDNER
83 Assoc Athletics Dir for Compliance ....Mr. Chance MILLER
83 Exec Dir of Audit & Advisory Svcs ....Ms. Pam DORAN
83 Sr V Prov & Dean for U Grad Studies ....Dr. Helen DOERPINGHAUS
05 Exec VP Acad Affairs and Provost ....Dr. Joan T. GABEL
11 Sr VP for Administration & COO ....Mr. Edward I. WALTON
10 CFO & VP for Finance ....Mrs. Leslie G. BRUNELLI
32 V Prov Acad Supp & Dean of Students ....Dr. Dennis A. PRUITT
15 Vice President Human Resources ....Mr. Christopher D. BYRD
30 VP Development & Alumni Relations ....Ms. Jancy HOUCK
12 VC Palmetto College and V Provost ....Dr. Chris P. PLYLER
46 Vice President for Research ....Dr. Prakash NAGARKATTI
26 Chief Communications Officer ....Mr. Wesley HICKMAN
21 Assoc VP Business Affairs ....Dr. Helen T. ZEIGLER
101 Secretary to Board of Trustees ....Ms. Amy E. STONE
53 Sr Vice Prov & Dean Grad Studies ....Dr. Lacy K. FORD
85 Vice Provost & Dir Global Carolina ....Dr. Allen MILLER
84 Asst V Prov Enrl Mgmt & Dean UG Adm ....Mr. Scott VERZYL
63 Exec Dean School of Medicine ....Dr. Les HALL
03 Dean of University Libraries ....Dr. Tom MCNALLY
43 Gen Counsel & Exec Dir Compliance ....Mr. Walter H. PARHAM
09 Exec Dir Inst Rsch/Assess/Analytics ....Ms. Sabrina ANDREWS
18 VP for Facilities & Transportation ....Mr. Derrick E. HUGGINS
19 Assoc VP Law Enfr & Chief of Police ....Mr. Christopher L. WUCHENICH
37 Dir Student Fin Aid & Scholarship ....Dr. Edgar MILLER
36 Director Career Center ....Mr. Thomas HALASZ
06 University Registrar ....Mr. Aaron C. MARTERER
22 Exec Asst to Pres Equal Oppty Pgm ....Mr. Bobby D. GIST
83 NCAA Compliance Coord ....Mr. Christopher ROGERS
07 Director of Admissions ....Dr. Mary WAGNER
39 Director Housing/Business Opers ....Mr. Parker LEAKE
23 Exec Director Student Health Svcs ....Dr. Deborah C. BECK
41 Athletic Director ....Mr. Ray TANNER
35 Assoc VP for Student Life ....Mr. Jerry T. BREWER
27 Director News & Internal Relations ....Mr. Wesley T. HICKMAN
96 Director of Purchasing ....Mrs. Venis MANIGO
29 Exec Director Alumni Association ....Mr. Jack CLAYPOOLE
83 VP for System Planning ....Dr. Mary Anne FITZPATRICK
83 Chancellor Palmetto College ....Dr. Susan ELKINS
83 Dean Hospitality/Retail/Sport HMgt ....Dr. Haemoon OH
50 Dean Moore School of Business ....Dr. Peter J. BREWS
53 Dean College of Education ....Dr. Lemuel WATSON
54 Dean Col Engineering & Computing ....Dr. Hossein HAJ-HARIRI
69 Dean Arnold School of Public Health ....Dr. G. Thomas CHANDLER
60 Dean Col of Info & Communications ....Mr. Charles BIERBAUER
61 Dean School of Law ....Dr. Robert M. WILCOX
63 Int Dean School of Medicine ....Dr. Caughman TAYLOR
63 Dean Greenville School of Medicine ....Dr. Jerry R. YOUKEY
64 Dean College of Pharmacy ....Dr. Stephen J. CUTLER
49 Interim Dean Col of Arts & Sciences ....Mr. Roger SAWYER
64 Dean School of Music ....Dr. Tayloe HARDING
92 Dean SC Honors College ....Dr. Steve LYNN
66 Dean College of Nursing ....Dr. Jeannette ANDREWS
67 Intr Exec Dean SC Col of Pharmacy ....Dr. Randall C. ROWEN
70 Dean College of Social Work ....Dr. Anna M. SCHEYETTE
92 Dir Fellowships & Scholar Programs ....Ms. Novella BESKID
88 Asst Provost Academic Programs ....Dr. Kristia H. FINNIGAN
88 Executive Director USC Connect ....Dr. Irma J. VANSCOY
28 Chief Diversity Officer ....Mr. John DOZIER
86 Director Govt & Community Relations ....Ms. Shirley D. MILLS
88 Director of Economic Engagement ....Mr. William B. KIRKLAND

University of South Carolina Aiken (G)

471 University Parkway, Aiken SC 29801-6399
County: Aiken FICE Identification: 003449
Unit ID: 218645
Telephone: (803) 648-6851 Carnegie Class: Bac-Diverse
FAX Number: (803) 641-3362 Calendar System: Semester
URL: www.usca.edu
Established: 1961 Annual Undergrad Tuition & Fees (In-State): $9,878
Enrollment: 3,444 Coed
Affiliation or Control: State IRS Status: 501(c)3
Highest Offering: Master's
Accreditation: SC, BUS, MUS, NURSE, TED

01 Chancellor ....Dr. Sandra JORDAN
05 Exec Vice Chanc Academic Affairs ....Dr. Jeff M. PRIEST
30 Vice Chanc Advance & External Rels ....Ms. Mary DRISCOLL
32 Vice Chancellor Student Life & Svcs ....Dr. Deborah KLADIVKO
13 Vice Chancellor Information Tech ....Mr. Ernest PRINGLE
10 VC for Admin and Finance/CFO ....Mr. Joe SOBIERALSKI
20 Asst Vice Chanc Academic Affairs ....Dr. Tim LINTNER
84 Assoc Vice Chanc Enrollment Svcs ....Mr. Daniel J. ROBB
79 Col Coord Humanitie & Soc Science ....Vacant
83 College Coordinator Sciences ....Vacant
50 Dean School of Business Admin ....Dr. Michael FEKULA
53 Dean of the School of Education ....Dr. Judy BECK
66 Dean of the School of Nursing ....Dr. Thayer MCGAHEE
09 Dir Inst Effect/Research/Compliance ....Dr. Lloyd A. DAWE
08 Interim Library Director ....Dr. Natalia BOWDOIN
25 Director Sponsored Research ....Dr. Bill PIRKLE
40 Director of Pacer Shoppe ....Ms. Heidi DIFRANCO

88 Dir Campus Support Services .... Mr. Jeff JENIK
88 Director Children's Center .... Ms. Lynn WILLIAMS
88 Dir USCA Convocation Center .... Mr. Josh SMALL
109 Director of Dining Services .... Mr. Joseph TRAMONTANA
12 Exec Dir of Etherredge Center .... Mr. Jack BENJAMIN
21 Controller .... Mr. Kevin CRAWFORD
15 Dir Human Resources & Affirm Action .... Ms. Maria CHANDLER
88 Dir Campus Recreation & Wellness .... Ms. Mila PADGETT
07 Director of Admissions .... Mr. Andrew HENDRIX
58 Coord Citizenshp Residenc Grad Stds .... Vacant
36 Director of Career Services .... Mr. Corey FERALDI
37 Director Financial Aid .... Linda A. HIGGINS
06 Registrar .... Ms. Vivian D. GRICE
14 Director of Client Services .... Mr. Chris SPIRES
90 Dir Communications & Hardware .... Mr. Bob WIESNER
105 Dir Network Systems/Arch & Infra .... Ms. Joann WILLIAMSON
41 Director of Athletics .... Mr. Douglas R. WARRICK, JR.
38 Director Counseling & Disabilities .... Ms. Cynthia B. GELINAS
23 Director Student Health Center .... Ms. Cynthia B. GELINAS
39 Director of Housing .... Mr. Deri WILLS
28 Dir Global Stds/Multicult Engagemnt .... Mr. Mutombo KABASELE
35 Asst Vice Chanc Student Life .... Mr. Ahmed SAMAHA
19 Chief of Police .... Mr. Kevin LILES
29 Dir Alumni Rels/Cmty Partnerships .... Mr. Randy DUCKETT
51 Dir Conferences & Continuing Educ .... Vacant
44 Director of Major Gifts .... Ms. Robin CALLICOTT
26 Dir Marketing & Community Relations .... Mr. James RABY
105 Coord Web Comm & Social Media .... Ms. Lauren COULS
88 Director Instructional Services .... Mr. Keith PIERCE

University of South Carolina Beaufort (A)

1 University Boulevard, Bluffton SC 29909-6085
County: Beaufort — FICE Identification: 003450
Unit ID: 218654
Telephone: (843) 208-8000 — Carnegie Class: Bac-Diverse
FAX Number: (843) 208-8299 — Calendar System: Semester
URL: www.uscb.edu
Established: 1959 — Annual Undergrad Tuition & Fees (In-State): $9,848
Enrollment: 1,794 — Coed
Affiliation or Control: State — IRS Status: 501(c)3
Highest Offering: Baccalaureate
Accreditation: SC, NURSE, TED

01 Chancellor .... Dr. Al M. PANU
05 Exec VC for Acad Affairs .... Dr. Eric SKIPPER
10 Vice Chanc Finance/Operations .... Mr. Earle HOLLEY
26 Vice Chanc University Advancement .... Dr. Lynn MCGEE
32 Vice Chanc for Student Development .... Dr. Douglas OBLANDER
84 Vice Chanc for Enrollment Mgmt .... Mr. Mack PALMOUR
41 Athletic Director .... Mr. Quin MONAHAN
13 Chief Information Officer .... Mr. Eddie KING
20 Assoc Vice Chanc for Acad Affairs .... Dr. Martha MORIARTY
30 Asst Vice Chanc for Development .... Vacant
08 Interim Director of Libraries .... Ms. Geni FLOWERS
19 Director Public Safety .... Mr. Henry GARBADE
15 Director of Human Resources .... Dr. Sue GOLABEK
37 Director of Financial Aid .... Ms. Patricia GREENE
09 Dir Inst Effectiveness/Research .... Mr. Brian MALLORY
18 Director of Facilities .... Mr. Mike PARROTT
36 Director of Career Services .... Ms. Leta SALAZAR
06 Registrar .... Dr. James TISDALE
35 Director of Student Life .... Ms. Kate VERMILYEA
39 Director Housing and Judicial .... Ms. Deonne WHALEY

University of South Carolina Lancaster (B)

PO Box 889, Lancaster SC 29721-0889
Telephone: (803) 313-7000 — FICE Identification: 003453
Accreditation: &SC, ACBSP, ADNUR, PNUR

† Regional accreditation is carried under University of South Carolina - Columbia.

University of South Carolina Salkehatchie (C)

PO Box 617, Allendale SC 29810-0617
County: Allendale — FICE Identification: 003454
Unit ID: 218681
Telephone: (803) 584-3446 — Carnegie Class: Assoc/HT-High Trad
FAX Number: (803) 584-5038 — Calendar System: Semester
URL: uscsalkehatchie.sc.edu
Established: 1965 — Annual Undergrad Tuition & Fees (In-State): $6,878
Enrollment: 1,076 — Coed
Affiliation or Control: State — IRS Status: 501(c)3
Highest Offering: Associate Degree
Accreditation: &SC

01 Dean .... Dr. Ann C. CARMICHAEL
05 Interim Academic Dean .... Dr. Aaron ARD
32 Asc Dean Student Svcs/Dir Athletics .... Ms. Jane T. BREWER
08 Head Librarian .... Mr. Daniel JOHNSON
11 Director of Finance .... Ms. Jessica ALT
37 Director Financial Aid .... Ms. Julie HADWIN
18 Dir Facilities/Safety/HR Director .... Dr. William A. SANDIFER
40 Bookstore Manager .... Mr. Lamar HEWETT
15 Director of Human Resources .... Dr. William A. SANDIFER
07 Director of Admissions .... Ms. Carmen BROWN
30 Chief Development .... Dr. Ann C. CARMICHAEL
84 Director Enrollment Mgmt Svcs .... Mr. Mike SMITH
88 Asst Director Leadership Institute .... Ms. Terri BOONE
88 Dir Ctr Leadership Development .... Mr. Warren CHAVOUS
88 Sports Information Director .... Mr. Trent KINARD

† Regional accreditation is carried under University of South Carolina - Columbia.

University of South Carolina School of Medicine Greenville (D)

607 Grove Road, Greenville SC 29605
County: Greenville — Identification: 667114
Telephone: (864) 455-7992 — Carnegie Class: Not Classified
FAX Number: (864) 455-8404 — Calendar System: Semester
URL: greenvillemed.sc.edu
Established: 2010 — Annual Graduate Tuition & Fees: N/A
Enrollment: N/A — Coed
Affiliation or Control: State — IRS Status: 501(c)3
Highest Offering: Doctorate; No Undergraduates
Accreditation: MED

01 Dean .... Dr. Jerry R. YOUKEY
05 Associate Dean for Faculty Affairs .... Dr. Robert BEST
32 Associate Dean for Student Affairs .... Dr. Paul CATALANA
10 Chief Business Officer .... David SUDDUTH
06 Registrar & Financial Aid Director .... Casey WILEY
30 Director of Development .... Susan WARD
15 HR Director .... Claire GREGG
13 Director of IT and Facilities .... Ron KNAPPENBERGER

University of South Carolina Sumter (E)

200 Miller Road, Sumter SC 29150-2498
County: Sumter — FICE Identification: 003426
Unit ID: 218690
Telephone: (803) 775-8727 — Carnegie Class: Assoc/HT-High Trad
FAX Number: (803) 775-2180 — Calendar System: Semester
URL: www.uscsumter.edu
Established: 1966 — Annual Undergrad Tuition & Fees (In-State): $6,878
Enrollment: 878 — Coed
Affiliation or Control: State — IRS Status: 501(c)3
Highest Offering: Associate Degree
Accreditation: &SC

01 Regional Campus Dean .... Mr. Michael SONNTAG
05 Exec Assoc Dean Acad/Stdnt Affairs .... Mr. Eric REISENAUER
32 Associate Dean Student Affairs .... Mr. Lynwood WATTS
10 Assoc Dean for Admin/Financial Svcs .... Mr. Bruce K. BLUMBERG
09 Institutional Research Analyst .... Mr. Chuck W. WRIGHT
08 Head Librarian .... Ms. Sharon H. CHAPMAN
07 Director of Admissions Services .... Mr. Keith E. BRITTON
51 Director of Continuing Education .... Ms. Susan S. BRABHAM
26 Dir of Public Relations/Marketing .... Ms. Misty HATFIELD
25 Pgm Director Opp Scholars Program .... Ms. Lisa ROSDAIL
40 Bookstore Manager .... Ms. Julie MCCOY
15 Human Resources Officer .... Ms. Marchetta L. WILLIAMS
88 Program Dir Opportunity Scholars .... Ms. Lisa ROSDAIL
87 Director Shaw AFB Programs .... Mr. Rick BOYD
18 Superintendent Buildings & Grounds .... Mr. Jeff LINGEFELT
20 Academic Affairs Assistant .... Ms. Carol REYNOLDS
41 Athletic Director .... Mr. Lynwood WATTS

† Regional accreditation is carried under University of South Carolina - Columbia.

University of South Carolina Union (F)

PO Drawer 729, Union SC 29379-0729
County: Union — FICE Identification: 004927
Unit ID: 218706
Telephone: (864) 429-8728 — Carnegie Class: Assoc/HT-High Non
FAX Number: (864) 427-3682 — Calendar System: Semester
URL: uscunion.sc.edu
Established: 1965 — Annual Undergrad Tuition & Fees (In-State): $6,878
Enrollment: 679 — Coed
Affiliation or Control: State — IRS Status: 501(c)3
Highest Offering: Associate Degree
Accreditation: &SC

01 Dean/Distinguished Prof Emeritus .... Dr. John CATALANO
05 Associate Dean Acad Affairs .... Dr. Randy LOWELL
84 Director Enrollment Manager .... Mr. M. Bradley GREER
37 Director Financial Aid .... Mr. Robert HOLCOMBE
15 Human Resources .... Ms. Susan P. JETT
40 Administration Bookstore .... Ms. Tanja BLACK
13 Director of Information Technology .... Mr. Keith CAMP
30 Director of Marketing & Development .... Ms. Annie SMITH
08 Library Manager .... Ms. Sharon L. RUPP
51 Coord Cont Ed/Career Svcs/Acad Succ .... Mr. Bill MOORE
10 Director of Budget and Business Ops .... Ms. Michele LEE
12 USC Laurens Location Director .... Mr. Matt DEAN
19 Health and Safety/Security Director .... Mr. Tony GREGORY
18 Maintenance Director .... Mr. Donald LAWSON

† Regional accreditation is carried under University of South Carolina - Columbia.

University of South Carolina Upstate (G)

800 University Way, Spartanburg SC 29303-4996
County: Spartanburg — FICE Identification: 006951
Unit ID: 218742
Telephone: (864) 503-5000 — Carnegie Class: Bac-Diverse
FAX Number: (864) 503-5375 — Calendar System: Semester
URL: www.uscupstate.edu
Established: 1967 — Annual Undergrad Tuition & Fees (In-State): $10,818
Enrollment: 5,585 — Coed
Affiliation or Control: State — IRS Status: 501(c)3
Highest Offering: Master's
Accreditation: SC, ART, BUS, CAHIIM, CS, ENGT, NURSE, TED

01 Interim Chancellor .... Dr. Mary Anne FITZPATRICK
05 Interim Sr Vice Chanc Acad Affair .... Dr. Clif FLYNN
13 Interim Vice Chanc Information Tech .... Mr. Chris HANKE
10 Vice Chanc Admin & Business Affs .... Ms. Sheryl TURNER-WATTS
30 Int VChanc Advance Upstate Found .... Mr. Donald HALE
45 VC Cmty-based Res/Engagement/Plng .... Ms. Kathleen BRADY
13 Vice Chanc Info Tech & Svcs .... Vacant
12 Dir Acad Engagement Greenville Ctr .... Dr. Judith PRINCE
20 Assoc VC Academic Affairs .... Vacant
32 VC Student Affs/Dean of Students .... Ms. Laura PUCKETT-BOLER
06 Registrar .... Ms. Mary David FOX
84 Vice Chanc Enrollment Services .... Ms. Donette STEWART
38 Director Counseling Services .... Ms. Frances L. JARRATT
08 Dean Library .... Ms. Frieda M. DAVISON
37 Director Financial Aid .... Ms. Bonnie C. CARSON
49 Dean Arts & Sciences .... Dr. Dirk SCHLINGMANN
50 Dean Johnson Col Business & Econ .... Dr. Frank RUDISILL
53 Dean Education .... Dr. Lee HURREN
66 Dean Nursing .... Dr. Katharine GIBB
58 Director Graduate Education .... Dr. Tina HERZBERG
29 Director of Alumni Relations .... Ms. Charlianne NESTLEN
102 Director Dev & Found Scholarships .... Mrs. Bea W. SMITH
40 Director Bookstore .... Mr. Jerry CARROLL
41 Athletic Director .... Mr. Lee FOWLER
18 Director Custodial Services .... Mr. Paul SCHMIDT
19 Dir Public Safety & Chief of Police .... Mr. Klay PETERSON
35 Asst Dean/Director Student Life .... Ms. Khrystal SMITH
39 Dir Housing Residential Life .... Ms. Mandy WHITTEN
23 Director Health Services .... Ms. Mary BUCHER
26 Exec Dir Univ Boards & Public Affs .... Mr. John F. PERRY
09 Dir Inst Effectiveness & Compliance .... Dr. Sam COOPER
88 Dir for Fitness and Campus Rec .... Mr. Mark RITTER
22 Dir Disability Services .... Ms. Wendy WOODSBY
51 Dir Continuing Education .... Dr. Faruk TANYEL
21 Budget Manager .... Ms. Vintress BROWN
22 Dir Equal Opp & Employee Relations .... Ms. Sharon WOODS
104 Dir Intl Studies & Language Svcs .... Dr. Deryle HOPE
25 Dir Sponsored Awards .... Ms. Elaine MARSHALL
106 Dir Distance Education .... Dr. David MCCURRY
92 Interim Dir Honors Program .... Dr. Cathy CANINO
88 Dir Ctr Teaching Excellence .... Dr. June CARTER

Virginia College (H)

7201 Two Notch Road, Columbia SC 29223
Telephone: (803) 509-7100 — Identification: 770829
Accreditation: ACICS, MAAB, SURGT

† Branch campus of Virginia College, Birmingham, AL

Virginia College (I)

2400 David H. McLeod Blvd, Suite F, Florence SC 29501
Telephone: (843) 407-2200 — Identification: 770832
Accreditation: ACICS, MAAB

† Branch campus of Virginia College, Birmingham, AL

Virginia College (J)

78 Global Drive, Greenville SC 29607
Telephone: (864) 679-4900 — Identification: 770838
Accreditation: ACICS, ACFEI, MAAB, SURGT

† Branch campus of Virginia College, Birmingham, AL

Virginia College (K)

6185 Rivers Avenue, North Charleston SC 29406-4999
Telephone: (843) 614-4300 — Identification: 770830
Accreditation: ACICS, MAAB, SURGT

† Branch campus of Virginia College, Birmingham, AL

Virginia College (L)

8150 Warren H. Abernathy Highway, Spartanburg SC 29301-2450
Telephone: (864) 504-3200 — Identification: 770831
Accreditation: ACICS, MAAB

† Branch campus of Virginia College, Birmingham, AL

Voorhees College (M)

PO Box 678, Denmark SC 29042-0678
County: Bamberg — FICE Identification: 003455
Unit ID: 218919
Telephone: (803) 780-1234 — Carnegie Class: Bac-Diverse

FAX Number: (803) 780-1015 Calendar System: Semester
URL: www.voorhees.edu
Established: 1897 Annual Undergrad Tuition & Fees: $12,630
Enrollment: 468 Coed
Affiliation or Control: Protestant Episcopal IRS Status: 501(c)3
Highest Offering: Baccalaureate
Accreditation: SC, ACBSP

- 01 President ... Dr. W. Franklin EVANS
- 05 Int Exec VP Academic/Student Affs ... Dr. Lugenia ROCHELLE
- 10 VP Fiscal/Admin Affairs/CFO ... Mrs. V. Diane O'BERRY
- 30 AVP Institutional Advancement ... Mrs. Sonia KING GASS
- 45 VP Planning/Information Mgmt/Tech ... Mr. Samuel BLACKWELL
- 32 AVP Student Affairs/Dean Students ... Mr. Adrian WEST
- 44 AVP Institutional Advancement ... Mrs. Teesa BRUNSON
- 20 AVP Academic Affairs/Registrar ... Mrs. Melika JACKSON
- 21 AVP Fiscal Affairs/Admin Affairs ... Mr. Augusta KITCHEN
- 35 Director Student Support Services ... Ms. Lynda JEFFERSON
- 08 Director of Library Services ... Dr. Marie MARTIN
- 18 Director of Physical Plant ... Mr. Eddie PATTERSON
- 29 Director Alumni Affairs ... Mrs. Dorothy PATTERSON
- 36 Director Career Planning & Outreach ... Vacant
- 42 Chaplain ... Rev. James YARSIAH
- 41 Director of Athletics ... Mr. Willie JEFFERSON
- 19 Director of Safety/Security ... Mr. James WELDON
- 23 Director of Health Services ... Ms. Kimberly SOLOMON
- 07 Director of Admissions/Recruitment ... Mrs. Diondra SMALLS
- 15 Director of Human Resources ... Mrs. Constance COLTER-BRABHAM
- 13 Chief Technology Officer ... Mr. Timothy KENTOPP
- 40 Bookstore Manager ... Mrs. Shanda FOGLE
- 04 Exec Assistant to the President ... Ms. Jade JENKINS
- 50 Div Chair Business/Prof Studies ... Dr. Tywana BRANCH
- 81 Int Chair Natural Sciences/Health ... Dr. Zhabiz GOLKAR

Williamsburg Technical College (A)

601 Martin Luther King, Jr. Avenue,
Kingstree SC 29556-4103
County: Williamsburg FICE Identification: 009322
Unit ID: 218955
Telephone: (843) 355-4110 Carnegie Class: Assoc/HVT-High Trad
FAX Number: (843) 355-4296 Calendar System: Semester
URL: www.wiltech.edu
Established: 1969 Annual Undergrad Tuition & Fees (In-District): $4,008
Enrollment: 717 Coed
Affiliation or Control: State/Local IRS Status: 501(c)3
Highest Offering: Associate Degree
Accreditation: SC, ACBSP

- 01 President ... Dr. Patricia A. LEE
- 05 VP for Academic/Student Affairs ... Dr. Clifton R. ELLIOTT
- 10 VP Administration & Finance ... Ms. Melissa A. COKER
- 30 Assoc VP for Inst Advancement ... Mr. Andrew MULLER
- 32 Assoc VP for Student Affairs ... Dr. Alexis WRIGHT-DUBOSE
- 18 Asst VP for Facilities Management ... Mr. Tyrone THOMAS
- 20 Dean of Instruction ... Mrs. Margaret CHANDLER
- 08 Library Director ... Ms. Caren AGATA
- 07 Director of Admissions/Advisement ... Ms. Cheryl DUBOSE
- 26 Director of Development/Public Rels ... Mrs. Mona B. DUKES
- 37 Director of Financial Aid ... Mrs. Jean BOOS
- 13 Director MIS ... Mr. J. Brent LEE
- 15 Human Resources Manager ... Mrs. Jennifer STRONG
- 103 Dean Cont Education/Workforce Dev ... Mr. James BOSTIC

Winthrop University (B)

Oakland Avenue, Rock Hill SC 29733-0001
County: York FICE Identification: 003456
Unit ID: 218964
Telephone: (803) 323-2211 Carnegie Class: Masters/L
FAX Number: (803) 323-3001 Calendar System: Semester
URL: www.winthrop.edu
Established: 1886 Annual Undergrad Tuition & Fees (In-State): $14,456
Enrollment: 6,024 Coed
Affiliation or Control: State IRS Status: 501(c)3
Highest Offering: Beyond Master's But Less Than Doctorate
Accreditation: SC, ART, BUS, CAATE, CACREP, CIDA, CS, DANCE, DIETD, DIETI, JOUR, MUS, SW, TED, THEA

- 01 President ... Dr. Daniel F. MAHONY
- 05 Provost/Exec VP Academic Affairs ... Dr. Debra C. BOYD
- 10 Vice President Finance & Business ... Mr. J. P. MCKEE
- 30 Vice Pres Institutional Advancement ... Dr. William D. NICHOLSON, II
- 32 Vice President of Student Life ... Dr. Frank P. ARDAIOLO
- 84 VP Access & Enrollment Management ... Mr. Eduardo PRIETO
- 100 Chief of Staff ... Dr. Kimberly A. FAUST
- 26 Sr Counsel to Pres Public Affairs ... Dr. Jeffrey PEREZ
- 19 Asst VP/Chief Campus Police ... Chief Frank J. ZEBEDIS
- 20 Vice Prov Acad Quality/Innovation ... Dr. Meg WEBBER
- 88 Asst VP Curriculum/Program Support ... Mr. Tim DRUEKE
- 21 Associate VP Finance/Business ... Ms. Amanda F. MAGHSOUD
- 18 Assoc VP Facilities Management ... Mr. Walter A. HARDIN
- 15 VP Human Res/Empl Div & Wellness ... Ms. Lisa COWART
- 88 Assoc VP Institutional Advancement ... Mr. Ken SHEETZ
- 11 Vice Provost for Administration ... Ms. Karen JONES
- 27 Assoc VP/Exec Dir University Rels ... Ms. Ellen M. WILDER-BYRD
- 58 Dean of Graduate School ... Dr. Jack DEROCHI
- 49 Dean College Arts & Science ... Dr. Karen M. KEDROWSKI
- 50 Dean Col of Business Administration ... Dr. Roger D. WEIKLE
- 53 Dean College of Education ... Dr. Jennie RAKESTRAW
- 64 Dean College of Visual/Perf ... Dr. David WOHL
- 08 Dean Library Services ... Dr. Mark Y. HERRING
- 88 Dean University College ... Dr. Gloria JONES
- 35 Dean of Students ... Ms. Bethany MARLOWE
- 41 Athletic Director ... Mr. Ken HALPIN
- 90 Asst Vice Pres Comp & Info Tech ... Mr. Patrice BRUNEAU
- 06 Registrar ... Ms. Gina G. JONES
- 07 Director of Admissions ... Ms. Deborah G. BARBER
- 37 Director of Financial Aid ... Ms. Michelle HARE
- 39 Asst VP for Student Life ... Ms. Cynthia A. CASSENS
- 36 Director Career Development/Svcs ... Ms. Ellin MCDONOUGH
- 96 Director Procurement/Risk Mgmt ... Mr. Bob REID
- 53 Director Teaching/Learning Ctr ... Dr. John BIRD
- 23 Dir Health/Counseling Services ... Ms. Jackie CONCODORA
- 85 Director-International Center ... Dr. Leigh POOLE
- 44 Exec Dir Alumni Rels/Annual Giving ... Ms. Lori TUTTLE
- 88 Director Advancement Services ... Mr. Ryan SHEEHAN
- 105 Director Web Development ... Ms. Kimberly BYRD
- 106 Director of Online Learning ... Dr. Kimarie WHETSTONE

Wofford College (C)

429 N Church Street, Spartanburg SC 29303-3663
County: Spartanburg FICE Identification: 003457
Unit ID: 218973
Telephone: (864) 597-4000 Carnegie Class: Bac-A&S
FAX Number: (864) 597-4018 Calendar System: 4/1/4
URL: www.wofford.edu
Established: 1854 Annual Undergrad Tuition & Fees: $38,705
Enrollment: 1,658 Coed
Affiliation or Control: United Methodist IRS Status: 501(c)3
Highest Offering: Baccalaureate
Accreditation: SC

- 01 President ... Dr. Nayef H. SAMHAT
- 10 Chief Financial Officer ... Ms. Bernie F. JEFFERSON
- 05 Provost ... Dr. Michael J. SOSULSKI
- 30 Sr Vice Pres for Advancement ... Dr. David S. WOOD
- 11 Sr Vice Pres for Administration ... Mr. David M. BEACHAM
- 32 Vice President for Student Affairs ... Ms. Roberta H. BIGGER
- 13 VP for Information Technology ... Mr. Jason H. WOMICK
- 84 Vice President for Enrollment ... Mr. Brand R. STILLE
- 26 VP for Marketing and Communications ... Ms. Annie S. MITCHELL
- 18 Assoc VP Facilities/Cap Projects ... Mr. Jason H. BURR
- 21 Assoc VP for Finance and Controller ... Mr. Chris L. GARDNER
- 08 Dean of Library ... Mr. Kevin J. REYNOLDS
- 82 Dean of International Programs ... Ms. Amy E. LANCASTER
- 23 Assoc Dean Students/Dir Health Svcs ... Ms. Beth D. WALLACE
- 04 Exec Admin Asst to President ... Ms. Crystal M. HOLMES
- 41 Director of Athletics ... Mr. Richard A. JOHNSON
- 06 College Registrar ... Ms. Jennifer R. ALLISON
- 42 Chaplain ... Dr. Ronald R. ROBINSON
- 15 Human Resources Director ... Ms. Carole B. LISTER
- 07 Director of Admissions ... Mr. John W. BIRNEY
- 09 Director of Institutional Research ... Mr. Raymond H. RUFF
- 101 Secretary to the Board of Trustees ... Mr. David M. BEACHAM
- 108 Dir Institutional Effectiveness ... Dr. John D. MILES
- 19 Director Campus Safety ... Col. James R. HALL
- 102 Dir Found/Corp & Govt Relations ... Ms. Mary Beth KNIGHT
- 28 Director of Diversity/Inclusion ... Ms. Jennifer M. GUITERREZ-CALDWELL
- 29 Director Alumni & Parents ... Ms. Debbi N. THOMPSON
- 36 Exec Director The Space ... Mr. P. Curtis MCPHAIL
- 37 Director Financial Aid ... Ms. Carolyn B. SPARKS
- 39 Asst Dean of Students for Res Life ... Mr. Brian J. LEMERE
- 44 Director Gift Planning ... Ms. Lisa H. DE FREITAS
- 96 Director Purchasing/Risk Management ... Mr. Daniel P. DEETER

York Technical College (D)

452 S Anderson Road, Rock Hill SC 29730-3395
County: York FICE Identification: 003996
Unit ID: 218991
Telephone: (803) 327-8000 Carnegie Class: Assoc/HVT-High Trad
FAX Number: (803) 327-8059 Calendar System: Semester
URL: www.yorktech.edu
Established: 1964 Annual Undergrad Tuition & Fees (In-State): $4,339
Enrollment: 5,061 Coed
Affiliation or Control: State IRS Status: 501(c)3
Highest Offering: Associate Degree
Accreditation: SC, ACBSP, ADNUR, DA, DH, ENGT, MLTAD, PNUR, RAD, SURGT

- 01 President ... Dr. Greg F. RUTHERFORD
- 05 Exec Vice Pres Acad/Student Affs ... Dr. Stacey MOORE
- 10 VP Business Services ... Dr. Marc TARPLEE
- 32 Assoc VP Academic/Student Affairs ... Vacant
- 30 Vice President for Advancement ... Ms. Melanie E. JONES
- 50 Assoc VP Business/Computer/AA/AS ... Ms. Yolanda WILSON
- 76 Assoc VP Health & Human Services ... Ms. Linda WEAVER-GRIGGS
- 54 Assoc VP Industry/Engineering Tech ... Vacant
- 103 Assoc VP Economic/Workforce Dev ... Vacant
- 08 Librarian ... Ms. Erinrae BAKER
- 84 Dean of Enrollment Services ... Ms. Monique PERRY
- 35 Dean for Student Engagement ... Mr. James B. ROBSON
- 88 Dean Center for Teaching/Learning ... Ms. Kathy L. HOELLEN
- 71 ReadySC Area Director ... Ms. Marianne BORDERS
- 09 Director of Institutional Research ... Ms. Mary Beth SCHWARTZ
- 15 Director of Human Resources ... Ms. Edwina ROSEBORO-BARNES
- 37 Director Student Financial Aid ... Ms. Elizabeth J. ROLLINS
- 13 Information Services Director ... Mr. Richard PARTRIDGE
- 18 Facilities Management Director ... Mr. Robert L. BROWN
- 06 Registrar ... Vacant
- 26 Director of Strategic Communication ... Vacant
- 04 Administrative Asst to President ... Mrs. Jennifer GAMMON

SOUTH DAKOTA

Augustana University (E)

2001 S Summit, Sioux Falls SD 57197-0001
County: Minnehaha FICE Identification: 003458
Unit ID: 219000
Telephone: (605) 274-0770 Carnegie Class: Bac-Diverse
FAX Number: (605) 274-5299 Calendar System: 4/1/4
URL: www.augie.edu
Established: 1860 Annual Undergrad Tuition & Fees: $30,090
Enrollment: 1,825 Coed
Affiliation or Control: Evangelical Lutheran Church In America
IRS Status: 501(c)3
Highest Offering: Master's
Accreditation: NH, CAATE, MUS, NURSE, TED

- 01 President ... Mr. Robert C. OLIVER
- 05 Interim Sr VP Academic Affairs ... Dr. Jerry JORGENSEN
- 32 Vice President Student Services ... Dr. James B. BIES
- 10 Vice Pres Finance/Administration ... Mr. Thomas MEYER
- 30 Vice President for Advancement ... Mr. Robert PRELOGER
- 07 Vice President for Admission ... Ms. Nancy DAVIDSON
- 11 Assoc VP Admin/Chief Info Officer ... Mr. Daniel D. DRENKOW
- 21 Assoc Vice President for Finance ... Ms. Carol SPILLUM
- 20 Assoc VP for Academic Affairs ... Dr. Mitchell G. KINSINGER
- 51 Assoc VP of Grad and Cont Educ ... Dr. Jerry JORGENSEN
- 35 Asst Dean of Students & Dir of Div ... Mr. Mark BLACKBURN
- 15 Director of Human Resources ... Ms. Deanna VERSTEEG
- 37 Director of Financial Aid ... Ms. Tresse EVENSON
- 08 Director of Library ... Ms. Ronelle THOMPSON
- 36 Director Career Center ... Vacant
- 13 Director Mgmt Information Systems ... Ms. Debra FREDERICK
- 18 Chief Facilities/Physical Plant ... Mr. Frank HUGHES
- 29 Director of Alumni Relations ... Ms. Adrienne MCKEOWN
- 41 Athletic Director ... Mr. Slade LARSCHEID
- 06 Registrar/Asst Dean of Instr Data ... Ms. Joni KRUEGER
- 36 Exec Director of Career/Success Ctr ... Ms. Billie STREUFERT
- 88 Dir of Student Acad Support Service ... Ms. Susan BIES
- 104 Director of International Prgrams ... Mr. Donn GRINNAGER
- 108 Director of Assessment ... Dr. David SORENSON
- 19 Director of Campus Safety ... Mr. Rick TUPPER
- 09 Director of Institutional Research ... Vacant

Dakota Wesleyan University (F)

1200 W University, Mitchell SD 57301-4398
County: Davison FICE Identification: 003461
Unit ID: 219091
Telephone: (605) 995-2600 Carnegie Class: Bac-Diverse
FAX Number: (605) 995-2699 Calendar System: Semester
URL: www.dwu.edu
Established: 1885 Annual Undergrad Tuition & Fees: $24,800
Enrollment: 870 Coed
Affiliation or Control: United Methodist IRS Status: 501(c)3
Highest Offering: Master's
Accreditation: NH, ADNUR, CAATE, IACBE, NURSE

- 01 President ... Dr. Amy C. NOVAK
- 10 Executive Vice President ... Ms. Theresa KRIESE
- 05 Provost ... Dr. Joseph ROIDT
- 26 Vice Pres of Marketing and Communic ... Ms. Lori ESSIG
- 30 VP for Institutional Advancement ... Ms. Kitty ALLEN
- 07 Dean of Admissions ... Ms. Fredel THOMAS
- 06 Registrar ... Ms. Karen KNOELL
- 88 Dir Kelley Ctr for Entrepreneurship ... Dr. Ryan VAN ZEE
- 88 Executive Director McGovern Center ... Dr. Alisha VINCENT
- 08 Chief Info Ofcr/Dir Lrng Resources ... Mr. Kevin KENKEL
- 29 Director of Alumni Relations ... Ms. Jackie WENTWORTH
- 37 Director of Financial Aid ... Ms. Mary ALEXANDER
- 15 Director of Human Resources ... Ms. Janet HAYEN
- 42 Campus Pastor ... Rev. Eric VAN METER
- 41 Athletic Director ... Mr. Jon HART
- 18 Director of Physical Plant ... Mr. Louis SCHOENFELDER
- 32 Director of Student Life ... Dr. Diana GOLDAMMER
- 35 Director Student Support Services ... Mr. Tim BOENDER
- 38 Student Support Services Counselor ... Ms. Linda CIMPL
- 40 Director of University Services ... Ms. Lori SOLBERG
- 88 Dean Col Ldrshp & Pub Service ... Dr. W. Jesse WEINS
- 88 Dean Col Adult and Prof Studies ... Dr. Derek DRIEDGER
- 79 Dean College Arts & Humanities ... Dr. Vince REDDER
- 81 Dean Col Health/Fitness & Science ... Dr. Mike CATALANO
- 04 Administrative Asst to President ... Ms. Emily GEORGE
- 39 Director Student Housing ... Mr. Danny SANDBERG
- 40 Chair of Nursing ... Ms. Diane SANDHOFF
- 50 Chair of Business ... Dr. Monty BOHRER
- 53 Chair of Education ... Dr. Ashley DIGMANN

Globe University (G)

5101 South Broadband Lane, Sioux Falls SD 57108
Telephone: (605) 977-0705 Identification: 770780
Accreditation: ACICS, MAAB

† Branch campus of Globe University, Woodbury, MN

John Witherspoon College (A)

4021 Range Road, Rapid City SD 57702
County: Pennington Identification: 667246
Telephone: (605) 342-0317 Carnegie Class: Not Classified
FAX Number: N/A Calendar System: Semester
URL: www.johnwitherspooncollege.org
Established: 2004 Annual Undergrad Tuition & Fees: N/A
Enrollment: N/A Coed
Affiliation or Control: Independent Non-Profit IRS Status: 501(c)3
Highest Offering: Baccalaureate
Accreditation: @TRACS

01 President ....Dr. C. Richard WELLS
03 Provost and Director of Leadership ....Dr. Debra SHATTUCK
05 Vice President of Academic Affairs ....Dr. Ronald LEWIS
08 Director of Learning Resources ....Dr. Bret SAUNDERS
10 Director of Business Affairs ....Carol HARRIS
108 Director Institutional Assessment ....Dr. Jamin HUBNER
26 Marketing Officer ....Sandy BROCKHOUSE
32 Director of Student Services ....Jessica HUBNER

Lake Area Technical Institute (B)

1201 Arrow Avenue, PO Box 730,
Watertown SD 57201-2869
County: Codington FICE Identification: 005309
Unit ID: 219143
Telephone: (605) 882-5284 Carnegie Class: Assoc/HVT-High Trad
FAX Number: (605) 882-6299 Calendar System: Semester
URL: www.lakeareatech.edu
Established: 1965 Annual Undergrad Tuition & Fees (In-District): $5,056
Enrollment: 1,654 Coed
Affiliation or Control: Local IRS Status: 501(c)3
Highest Offering: Associate Degree
Accreditation: NH, DA, EMT, MAC, MLTAD, OTA, PNUR, PTAA

01 President ....Mr. Michael D. CARTNEY
03 Executive Vice President ....Ms. Diane STILES
84 Director of Enrollment ....Mr. Eric SCHULTZ
05 Dean of Academics ....Ms. Kim BELLUM
32 Director of Student Services ....Ms. LuAnn STRAIT
88 Corporate Education Coordinator ....Mr. Steven HAUCK
32 Director of Support Services ....Mr. Shane ORTMEIER
37 Director of Financial Aid ....Ms. Marlene SEEKLANDER
38 Academic Counselor ....Ms. Megan HOWARD
18 Chief Facilities/Physical Plant ....Mr. Doug BUTALA

Mitchell Technical Institute (C)

1800 E Spruce, Mitchell SD 57301-2002
County: Davison FICE Identification: 008284
Unit ID: 219189
Telephone: (605) 995-3025 Carnegie Class: Assoc/HVT-High Trad
FAX Number: (605) 995-3083 Calendar System: Semester
URL: www.mitchelltech.edu
Established: 1968 Annual Undergrad Tuition & Fees (In-District): $5,880
Enrollment: 1,245 Coed
Affiliation or Control: Local IRS Status: 501(c)3
Highest Offering: Associate Degree
Accreditation: NH, ACFEI, MAC, MLTAD, RAD, RTT

01 President ....Mr. Mark WILSON
03 Vice President ....Mr. John HEEMSTRA
103 Director of Advanced Technical Educ ....Mr. Doug GREENWAY
90 Director of Technology ....Mr. David BOOS
05 Dean of Academics ....Dr. Carol GRODE-HANKS
26 Director of Communications ....Ms. Julie BROOKBANK
10 Dean of Fiscal Operations ....Mr. Jared HOFER
84 Director of Enrollment Services ....Mr. Clayton DEUTER
32 Director of Student Services ....Mr. Scott FOSSUM
09 Accred & Inst Effectiveness Dir ....Ms. Marla SMITH
18 Buildings & Grounds Director ....Mr. John SIEVERDING
15 Human Resources Manager ....Ms. Elizabeth KITCHENS
30 Foundation Director ....Ms. Heather LENTZ
36 Career Svcs & Advising Dir ....Ms. Janet GREENWAY
06 Registrar ....Ms. Darla KOTRBA
37 Director Student Financial Aid ....Ms. Morgan HUBER

Mount Marty College (D)

1105 W 8th, Yankton SD 57078-3724
County: Yankton FICE Identification: 003465
Unit ID: 219198
Telephone: (605) 668-1011 Carnegie Class: Masters/S
FAX Number: (605) 668-1607 Calendar System: Semester
URL: www.mtmc.edu
Established: 1936 Annual Undergrad Tuition & Fees: $24,406
Enrollment: 1,236 Coed
Affiliation or Control: Roman Catholic IRS Status: 501(c)3
Highest Offering: Master's
Accreditation: NH, ANEST, CACREP, NURSE

01 President ....Dr. Marcus LONG
101 Asst to the Pres/Asst Sec to Board ....Ms. Carla ENG
05 VP for Academic Affairs ....Dr. Jane WOOD
10 VP for Finance ....Ms. Tabitha LIKNESS
32 VP of Student Affairs ....Ms. Sarah CARDA
30 VP for Advancement ....Ms. Barb REZAC
11 Chief Operations Officer ....Mr. Greg HEINE
09 Director of Inst Effectiveness ....Ms. Kristen WELKER
66 Director of Nurse Anesthesia ....Dr. Mary Anne KROGH
42 Director of Campus Ministry ....Sr. Maribeth WENTZLAFF
12 Director of Watertown Location ....Dr. Calvin KROGMAN
37 Director Student Financial Aid ....Mr. Ken KOCER
06 Registrar ....Ms. Jonna SUPURGECI
13 Chief Information Officer ....Mr. Christian HUNHOFF
08 Director of Library ....Ms. Sandra BROWN
40 Dir Bookstore/Central Scheduling ....Ms. Mary ABBOTT
36 Dir Career Planning/Disability Svcs ....Ms. Tracy TAYLOR
41 Athletic Director ....Mr. Chuck IVERSON
15 Director of Human Resources ....Ms. Julie DATHER
26 Dir of Marketing & Communications ....Ms. Kristen HICKS
44 Director of Annual/Planned Giving ....Ms. Shannon VIERECK
19 Director Security/Safety ....Ms. Sonja OLSON
29 Director Alumni Relations ....Mr. David DICKES

National American University (E)

5301 S Highway 16, Rapid City SD 57701-8932
County: Pennington FICE Identification: 004057
Unit ID: 219204
Telephone: (605) 394-4800 Carnegie Class: Bac-Diverse
FAX Number: (605) 721-5241 Calendar System: Quarter
URL: www.national.edu
Established: 1941 Annual Undergrad Tuition & Fees: $13,647
Enrollment: 1,479 Coed
Affiliation or Control: Proprietary IRS Status: Proprietary
Highest Offering: Doctorate
Accreditation: NH, CAHIIM, IACBE, MAC, NURSE

01 University President ....Dr. Jerry L. GALLENTINE
11 COO ....Dr. Ronald SHAPE

National American University-Sioux Falls (F)

5801 S Corporate Place, Sioux Falls SD 57108
Telephone: (605) 336-4600 Identification: 770388
Accreditation: &NH

† Regional accreditation is carried under the parent institution in Rapid City, SD

Oglala Lakota College (G)

Box 490, Kyle SD 57752-0490
County: Shannon FICE Identification: 014659
Unit ID: 219277
Telephone: (605) 455-6000 Carnegie Class: Tribal
FAX Number: (605) 455-2787 Calendar System: Semester
URL: www.olc.edu
Established: 1971 Annual Undergrad Tuition & Fees: $2,684
Enrollment: 1,427 Coed
Affiliation or Control: Tribal Control IRS Status: 501(c)3
Highest Offering: Master's
Accreditation: NH, SW

01 President ....Mr. Thomas H. SHORTBULL
05 Vice President for Instruction ....Dr. Dawn FRANK
10 Vice President for Business ....Ms. Julie JOHNSON
06 Registrar ....Ms. Leslie MESTETH
08 Director Learning Resources ....Ms. Michelle MAY
15 Personnel Director ....Ms. Faith RICHARDS
37 Financial Aid Director ....Ms. Billi HORNBECK
84 Director Enrollment Management ....Dr. Adetokunbo OREDEIN
07 Director of Admissions ....Ms. Leslie MESTETH
09 Director of Institutional Research ....Dr. Dawn FRANK
96 Assoc Business Ofcr/Dir Purchasing ....Ms. Arlis POURIER
29 Director Alumni Relations ....Ms. Marilyn POURIER
89 Director of Freshman Studies ....Mr. Theodore HAMILTON
13 MIS Director ....Mr. Cliff DELONG
32 Director Student Affairs ....Mr. Lance CHRISTENSEN
30 Inst Development Coordinator ....Ms. Marilyn POURIER
51 Community/Cont Education Coord ....Ms. Kateri MONTILEAUX
88 Applied Science Department Chair ....Mr. David WHITE BULL
81 Math & Science Department Chair ....Ms. Karla WITT
49 Art & History Department Chair ....Ms. Kim BETTELYOUN
53 Education Department Chair ....Ms. Shannon AMIOTTE
66 Nursing Department Chair ....Ms. Jessica ZEPHIER
83 Human Services Department Chair ....Ms. Monique APPLE
88 LAKOTA Studies Department Chair ....Ms. Karen LONE HILL
18 Chief Facilities/Physical Plant ....Mr. Leonard FERGUSON

Presentation College (H)

1500 N Main Street, Aberdeen SD 57401-1280
County: Brown FICE Identification: 003467
Unit ID: 219295
Telephone: (605) 225-1634 Carnegie Class: Spec-4-yr-Other Health
FAX Number: (605) 229-8330 Calendar System: Semester
URL: www.presentation.edu
Established: 1951 Annual Undergrad Tuition & Fees: $18,358
Enrollment: 729 Coed
Affiliation or Control: Roman Catholic IRS Status: 501(c)3
Highest Offering: Baccalaureate
Accreditation: NH, IACBE, MAC, NUR, NURSE, RAD, SURGT, SW

01 President ....Dr. Margaret HUBER
05 Vice Pres for Academics ....Dr. Michelle METZINGER
10 Vice Pres for Finance ....Ms. Cathy HALL
84 Vice Pres for Enrollment ....Mr. Michael MATTISON
32 Vice Pres for Student Services ....Mr. Bob SCHUCHARDT
30 Vice President for Advancement ....Ms. Cynthia WHITNEY
88 Executive Director for Mission ....Sr. Pam DONELAN
06 Registrar ....Ms. Genny SIKES
37 Director Student Financial Aid ....Ms. Maureen SCHUCHARDT
108 Assessment Coordinator ....Dr. Nancy VANDER HOEK
15 Director of Human Resources ....Mr. Jason PETTIGREW
04 Administrative Asst to President ....Ms. Stacy BAUER
26 Dir of Marketing/Public Relations ....Mr. Tim BECKHAM

Sinte Gleska University (I)

PO Box 105, Mission SD 57555-0105
County: Todd FICE Identification: 021437
Unit ID: 219374
Telephone: (605) 856-5880 Carnegie Class: Tribal
FAX Number: (605) 856-5401 Calendar System: Semester
URL: www.sintegleska.edu
Established: 1970 Annual Undergrad Tuition & Fees: $3,154
Enrollment: 641 Coed
Affiliation or Control: Independent Non-Profit IRS Status: 501(c)3
Highest Offering: Master's
Accreditation: NH

01 President ....Mr. Lionel BORDEAUX
05 Vice Pres Academic Affairs ....Ms. Cheryl MEDEARIS
32 Vice Pres Student Services ....Mr. Mike BENGE
10 Vice Pres of Finance ....Ms. Lynette BORDEAUX
31 VP Community Education ....Ms. Sherry RED OWL
06 Registrar ....Mr. Harvey HERMAN
08 Int Library Director ....Ms. Diana DILLION
20 Chief Finance Officer ....Ms. Sarah AROBBA
37 Director Financial Aid ....Mr. William HAY
55 Director Adult Education ....Mr. James SHERMAN, III
15 Personnel Director ....Ms. Michelle ZEPHIER-SWIFT

Sioux Falls Seminary (J)

2100 S Summit Ave, Sioux Falls SD 57105-2729
County: Minnehaha FICE Identification: 004056
Unit ID: 219240
Telephone: (605) 336-6588 Carnegie Class: Spec-4-yr-Faith
FAX Number: (605) 335-9090 Calendar System: 4/1/4
URL: www.sfseminary.edu
Established: 1858 Annual Graduate Tuition & Fees: N/A
Enrollment: 195 Coed
Affiliation or Control: North American Baptist IRS Status: 501(c)3
Highest Offering: Doctorate; No Undergraduates
Accreditation: #NH, THEOL

01 President ....Mr. Gregory J. HENSON
05 Chief Academic Officer & Dean ....Dr. Larry W. CALDWELL
10 Chief Financial Officer ....Mr. Nathan M. HELLING
84 Director of Enrollment Management ....Mr. Dustin J. BROUWER
37 Assoc Dir of Enrollment & Fin Aid ....Ms. Tracy A. JONES
26 Chief Creative Ofcr/VP Proj Design ....Ms. Shanda L. STRICHERZ
29 Dir of Church & Alumni Relations ....Dr. Randall C. TSCHETTER
21 Office Manager ....Ms. Sheryl L. SLETTEN
58 Director of Doctoral Studies ....Dr. Gary E. STRICKLAND
83 Director of Counseling Programs ....Dr. Gretchen L. HARTMANN
88 Dir of Luther House of Study ....Dr. Chris M. CROGHAN
88 Dir of Wesley House of Study ....Dr. Steve A. TREFZ

Sisseton-Wahpeton College (K)

PO Box 689, Sisseton SD 57262-0689
County: Roberts FICE Identification: 022773
Unit ID: 219408
Telephone: (605) 698-3966 Carnegie Class: Tribal
FAX Number: (605) 698-3132 Calendar System: Semester
URL: www.swc.tc
Established: 1979 Annual Undergrad Tuition & Fees (In-District): $4,410
Enrollment: 165 Coed
Affiliation or Control: Local IRS Status: 501(c)3
Highest Offering: Associate Degree
Accreditation: NH

01 President ....Dr. Harvey DUMARCE
05 Vice President of Academic Affairs ....Dr. Jeanette GRAVDAHL
10 Chief Financial Officer ....Ms. Tanya LAFROMEOISE
37 Financial Aid Director ....Ms. Donnette RED BEAR
07 Director of Admissions/Registrar ....Mrs. Darlene REDDAY
66 Director Nursing ....Ms. Nola RAGAN
29 Alumni Director ....Mr. Tyler BIRNEY
18 Director Facilities ....Mr. Russell EBERHARDT
13 Director Information Technology ....Mr. Derrick LAWRENCE

*South Dakota State Board of Regents System Office (L)

306 E Capitol Avenue, Suite 200, Pierre SD 57501-2545
County: Hughes FICE Identification: 033438
Telephone: (605) 773-3455 Carnegie Class: N/A
FAX Number: (605) 773-5320
URL: www.sdbor.edu

01 Executive Director & CEO ....Dr. Mike G. RUSH
10 System VP Finance & Administration ....Dr. Monte KRAMER
05 System VP Academic Affairs ....Dr. Paul TURMAN
46 Asst VP Research & Economic Dev ....Mr. Nathan LUKKES
43 General Counsel ....Mr. Guilherme COSTA
15 Director of Human Resources ....Ms. Kayla BASTIAN
26 Director of Communications ....Dr. Janelle TOMAN

32 System Director of Student Affairs ... Ms. Molly WEISGRAM
09 Director of Institutional Research ... Dr. Daniel PALMER
13 System CIO ... Mr. David HANSEN
20 Associate Academic Officer ... Dr. Jay PERRY

*The University of South Dakota (A)

414 E Clark, Vermillion SD 57069-2390
County: Clay FICE Identification: 003474
Unit ID: 219471
Telephone: (605) 677-5011 Carnegie Class: DU-Higher
FAX Number: (605) 677-5073 Calendar System: Semester
URL: www.usd.edu
Established: 1862 Annual Undergrad Tuition & Fees (In-State): $8,457
Enrollment: 10,061 Coed
Affiliation or Control: State IRS Status: 501(c)3
Highest Offering: Doctorate
Accreditation: NH, ADNUR, ARCPA, ART, AUD, BUS, CACREP, CLPSY, DH, #JOUR, LAW, MED, MUS, NURSE, OT, PTA, SP, SPAA, SW, TED, THEA

02 President ... Mr. James W. ABBOTT
05 Provost/VP Academic Affairs ... Dr. James D. MORAN, III
17 Vice President Health Affairs ... Dr. Mary DEKKER NETTLEMAN
10 Vice Pres Finance - CFO ... Ms. Sheila GESTRING
46 Vice President for Research ... Dr. Mary BERRY
26 VP Marketing/Enroll Svcs/Univ Rels ... Mr. Scott POHLSON
11 Vice Pres Admin/Technology ... Ms. Roberta S. AMBUR
20 Assoc Vice Pres Academic Affairs ... Vacant
28 Associate VP of Diversity ... Vacant
08 Dean of Libraries ... Mr. Daniel R. DAILY
32 VP Student Svcs & Dean of Students ... Dr. Kimberly GRIEVE
96 Director of Purchasing ... Mr. Darby GANSCHOW
15 Vice President Human Resources ... Mr. E. Lee FELDER, JR.
22 Affirmative Action Officer ... Ms. Khara IVERSON
18 Asst VP Facilities Management ... Mr. Bob OEHLER
37 Director of Financial Aid ... Ms. Julie H. PIER
09 Director of Institutional Research ... Vacant
36 Dir Ctr for Academic & Career Plng ... Mr. Steve WARD
06 Registrar ... Ms. Jennifer M. THOMPSON
41 Athletic Director ... Mr. David HERBSTER
38 Director Student Counseling ... Vacant
19 Director Public Safety ... Mr. Peter E. JENSEN
84 Dean of Enrollment ... Mr. Mark PETTY
49 Dean College Arts & Sciences ... Dr. Matthew C. MCEN
50 Dean School of Business ... Dr. A. R VENKATACHALAM
51 Assoc Provost/Cont & Distance Educ ... Dr. Michael CARD
53 Dean School of Education ... Dr. Donald EASTON-BROCKS
57 Dean College Fine Arts ... Dr. Larry SCHOU
63 Dean Sanford School of Medicine ... Dr. Mary DEKKER NETTLEMAN
61 Dean School of Law ... Mr. Thomas GEU

*Black Hills State University (B)

1200 University Street, Spearfish SD 57799-9500
County: Lawrence FICE Identification: 003459
Unit ID: 219046
Telephone: (605) 642-6111 Carnegie Class: Masters/S
FAX Number: (605) 642-6763 Calendar System: Semester
URL: www.bhsu.edu
Established: 1883 Annual Undergrad Tuition & Fees (In-State): $8,004
Enrollment: 4,489 Coed
Affiliation or Control: State IRS Status: 501(c)3
Highest Offering: Master's
Accreditation: NH, BUS, MUS, TED

02 President ... Dr. Tom JACKSON, JR.
05 Provost/Vice Pres Academic Affairs ... Dr. Chris CRAWFORD
10 Vice President Finance/Admin ... Ms. Kathy J. JOHNSON
30 Vice Pres University Advancement ... Mr. Steve L. MEEKER
32 VP for Enrollment & Student Affairs ... Dr. Lois FLAGSTAD
26 Director Univ & Community Relations ... Ms. Corinne HANSEN
13 Chief Info Technology Officer ... Dr. Warren WILSON
37 Director Student Financial Aid ... Ms. Deb HENRIKSEN
38 Director Counseling Center ... Dr. Lois FLAGSTAD
39 Director Residence Life ... Dr. Michael L. ISAACSON
35 Director Student Services ... Dr. Jane KLUG
15 Director of Human Resources ... Mr. Nick OAKS
06 Registrar ... Ms. April M. MEEKER
07 Director of Admissions ... Ms. Beth OAKS
21 Director of Business Services ... Mr. Rob HOUDEK
18 Director Facilities/Physical Plant ... Mr. Randy CULVER
29 Director Alumni Relations ... Mr. Tom WHEATON
09 Director of Institutional Research ... Mr. Rich LOOSE
08 Director Library Operations ... Mr. Scott AHOLA
104 Director International Studies ... Ms. Katie WILDMAN
30 Director of Development ... Ms. Shauna JUNEK
19 Director Security/Safety ... Mr. Philip PESHECK
40 Director University Bookstore ... Mr. Michael JASTORFF
41 Director of Athletics ... Mr. Jhett ALBERS
14 Director Network & Computer Svcs ... Mr. Fred NELSON
49 Dean College of Liberal Arts ... Dr. Amy FUCUA
50 Dean Col of Business & Natural Sci ... Dr. Priscilla ROMKEMA
53 Dean Col of Educ & Behavioral Sci ... Dr. Sharman ADAMS
04 Administrative Asst to President ... Ms. Judy A. BAUER
25 Chief Contracts/Grants Admin ... Mr. William KELLY

*Dakota State University (C)

820 N Washington Avenue, Madison SD 57042-1799
County: Lake FICE Identification: 003463
Unit ID: 219082
Telephone: (605) 256-5111 Carnegie Class: Masters/S
FAX Number: (605) 256-5316 Calendar System: Semester
URL: www.dsu.edu
Established: 1881 Annual Undergrad Tuition & Fees (In-State): $7,974
Enrollment: 3,047 Coed
Affiliation or Control: State IRS Status: 501(c)3
Highest Offering: Doctorate
Accreditation: NH, ACBSP, CAHIIM, COARC, TED

02 President ... Dr. José-Marie GRIFFITHS
04 Executive Assistant to President ... Ms. Kelli WHITEING
05 Provost & VP Academic Affairs ... Dr. Richard HANSON
10 Vice Pres for Business & Admin Svcs ... Mr. Stacy L. KRUSEMARK
32 Vice Pres/Dean Student Affairs ... Mr. Marcus GARSTECKI
13 CIO & VP for Technology ... Mr. David E. OVERBY
102 Vice Pres Institutional Advancement ... Mr. Bob OTTERSON
41 Director of Athletics ... Mr. Jeff L. DITTMAN
49 Dean College of Arts and Sciences ... Dr. Benjamin F. JONES
50 Dean Col Business/Info Systems ... Vacant
53 Dean College of Education ... Dr. Crystal PAULI
58 Dean of Graduate Studies/Research ... Dr. Mark HAWKES
09 Director of Assessment ... Dr. Jay KAHL
08 Director of Library ... Ms. Jan BRUE ENRIGHT
56 Director Extended Programs ... Ms. Sarah RASMUSSEN
25 Director of Sponsored Programs ... Ms. Kacie M. FODNESS
06 Registrar ... Ms. Kathryn CALLIES
21 Controller ... Ms. Amy L. DOCKENDORF
18 Director of Physical Plant ... Mr. Corey BRASKAMP
15 Director Human Resources ... Ms. Angi KAPPENMAN
25 Director of Budget & Grants Admin ... Ms. Sara HARE
25 Dir of Ctr for Adv of HIT ... Mr. Dan FRIEDRICH
36 Asst VP Stdnt Affs/Dir Career Svcs ... Dr. Marie A. LOHSANDT
84 Assoc VP of Enrollment ... Ms. Amy S. CRISSINGER
35 Asst Dean for Student Affairs ... Mr. Steven J. BARTEL
40 Director of Bookstore ... Ms. Heather GILLESPIE
28 Diversity Coordinator ... Vacant
38 Asst Dean for Student Development ... Mr. O. Keith BUNDY
37 Director Financial Aid ... Ms. Denise R. GRAYSON
07 Asst Director of Admissions ... Ms. Amber SCHMIDT
85 International Programs Director ... Ms. Jacy FRY
88 Dir Technical Ops & Development ... Mr. Brent VANAARTSEN
29 Director of Alumni ... Ms. Jona M. SCHMIDT
30 Development Officer ... Ms. Jill RUHD

*Northern State University (D)

1200 S Jay Street, Aberdeen SD 57401-7198
County: Brown FICE Identification: 003466
Unit ID: 219259
Telephone: (605) 626-3011 Carnegie Class: Masters/S
FAX Number: (605) 626-3022 Calendar System: Semester
URL: www.northern.edu
Established: 1901 Annual Undergrad Tuition & Fees (In-State): $7,387
Enrollment: 3,531 Coed
Affiliation or Control: State IRS Status: 501(c)3
Highest Offering: Master's
Accreditation: NH, ACBSP, ART, MUS, TED

02 President ... Dr. Timothy DOWNS
05 Vice Pres Academic Affs/Provost ... Dr. Alan LAFAVE
10 Vice Pres Finance/Administration ... Ms. Veronica PAULSON
32 Vice President for Student Affairs ... Ms. JoEllen LINDNER
20 Associate VP Academic Affairs ... Dr. Joelle LIEN
13 Chief Information Tech Officer ... Dr. Debbi BUMPOUS
44 Director of Annual Funds ... Vacant
102 President/CEO of Foundation ... Mr. Todd JORDRE
06 Registrar ... Ms. Peggy HALLSTROM
07 Director of Admissions ... Vacant
08 Director of Library ... Mr. Robert RUSSELL
38 Director of Counseling Center ... Vacant
09 Institutional Research Officer ... Ms. Heather SCOTT
25 Director Grants Sponsored Research ... Ms. Karen MARCHANT
37 Director of Financial Aid ... Ms. Sharon KIENOW
39 Director of Residence Life ... Mr. Marlin SABOLO
21 Controller ... Ms. Kay FREDRICK
15 Director of Human Resources ... Ms. Susan BOSTIAN
26 Director of University Relations ... Vacant
43 General Counsel ... Mr. John MEYER
18 Director of Facilities Management ... Mr. Monte MEHLHOFF
49 Dean College of Arts & Science ... Dr. Joshua HAGEN
50 Dean School of Business ... Dr. Willard BROUCEK
53 Dean School of Education ... Dr. Kelly DUNCAN
57 Dean School of Fine Arts ... Dr. Kenneth BOULTON
58 Director of Graduate Studies ... Dr. Joelle LIEN
41 Director of Athletics ... Mr. Joshua MOON
40 Director of Bookstore ... Ms. Beth RASMUSSON
96 Director of Purchasing ... Mr. Earl WEISENBURGER
92 Director of Honors Program ... Dr. Erin FOUBERG
71 Director of Special Initiatives ... Vacant
28 Interim Multicultural Advisor ... Ms. Sarah BOTKIN
35 Director of Student Activities ... Ms. Sarah BOTKIN
04 Administrative Asst to President ... Ms. Lisa GROTE
104 Study Abroad Coordinator ... Ms. Jennifer BENGS
106 Dir Online Education/E-learning ... Mr. Ronald BROWNIE
36 Director Student Placement ... Ms. Britt LORENZ

*South Dakota School of Mines and Technology (E)

501 E Saint Joseph, Rapid City SD 57701-3995
County: Pennington FICE Identification: 003470
Unit ID: 219347
Telephone: (605) 394-2511 Carnegie Class: Spec-4-yr-Eng
FAX Number: (605) 394-6131 Calendar System: Semester
URL: www.sdsmt.edu
Established: 1885 Annual Undergrad Tuition & Fees (In-State): $11,170
Enrollment: 2,798 Coed
Affiliation or Control: State IRS Status: 501(c)3
Highest Offering: Doctorate
Accreditation: NH, CS, ENG

02 President ... Dr. Heather WILSON
05 Provost/VP Academic Affairs ... Dr. Demitris KOURIS
10 Vice Pres Finance/Administration ... Mr. Stephen MALOTT
46 Vice President of Research ... Dr. Jan A. PUSZYNSKI
32 VP Student Affs/Dean of Students ... Dr. Patricia G. MAHON
15 Vice President Human Resources ... Ms. Kelli R. SHUMAN
20 Associate Provost Academic Affairs ... Dr. Kathryn E. ALLEY
07 Assoc Provost Acad Administration ... Ms. Molly MOORE
96 Purchasing Manager ... Ms. Barbara MUSTARD
26 Dir of Marketing & Communications ... Ms. Ann M. BRENTLINGER
29 Director of Alumni Association ... Dr. Larry SIMONSON
90 Director Information Tech Svcs ... Mr. Bryan J. SCHUMACHER
08 Director Devereaux Library ... Ms. Patricia M. ANDERSEN
36 Director Career Services ... Dr. Darrell R. SAWYER
37 Director of Financial Aid ... Mr. David W. MARTIN
88 Dir Inst Atmospheric Sciences ... Dr. Andrew G. DETWILER
41 Director of Athletics ... Mr. Joel LEUKEN
102 President SDSM&T Foundation ... Mr. Joel KINCART
18 Director of Facilities Services ... Ms. Jerilyn C. ROBERTS
21 Director of Finance/Controller ... Ms. Heather FORNEY
39 Dir Residence Life/Student Conduct ... Dr. Daniel SEPION
85 Director Ivanhoe International Ctr ... Ms. Susan R. AADLAND
58 Dean of Graduate Education ... Dr. Douglas WELLS
38 Director Counseling/ADA Svcs ... Ms. Megan REDER-SCHOPP
06 Registrar and Dir Academic Services ... Ms. Carla TIU
40 Manager College Bookstore ... Mr. Marlin L. KINZER
35 Student Activities Coordinator ... Mr. Michael KEEGAN
28 Director of Multicultural Affairs ... Mr. Jesse HERRERA

*South Dakota State University (F)

Brookings SD 57007-2298
County: Brookings FICE Identification: 003471
Unit ID: 219356
Telephone: (605) 688-4151 Carnegie Class: DU-Higher
FAX Number: (605) 688-5822 Calendar System: Semester
URL: www.sdstate.edu
Established: 1881 Annual Undergrad Tuition & Fees (In-State): $8,172
Enrollment: 12,543 Coed
Affiliation or Control: State IRS Status: 501(c)3
Highest Offering: Doctorate
Accreditation: NH, AAB, CAATE, CIDA, CONST, CORE, CS, DIETD, @DIETI, ENG, EXSC, JOUR, MT, MUS, NURSE, PHAR, TED

02 President ... Dr. Barry H. DUNN
05 Int Provost/Vice Pres Acad Affairs ... Dr. Dennis HEDGE
32 Vice President Student Affairs ... Dr. Michaela WILLIS
45 VP for Research/Economic Dev ... Dr. Kevin KEPHART
13 VP for Tech/Security ... Dr. Michael ADELAINE
10 Vice Pres Finance & Business/CFO ... Mr. Wesley G. TSCHETTER
20 Assoc Vice Pres for Academic Affs ... Dr. Mary Kay HELLING
18 Asst Vice Pres Facilities Services ... Mr. Dean KATTELMANN
88 Asst VP AA Intl Affairs/Outreach ... Dr. Kathleen FAIRFAX
15 Asst Vice Pres Human Resources ... Mr. Marc SERRETT
04 Asst to the President ... Ms. Karyn WEBER
08 Dean of the Library ... Dr. Kristi TORNQUIST
97 Dean of University College ... Dr. Keith CORBETT
07 Director of Admissions ... Ms. Tracy WELSH
06 Registrar ... Ms. Joyce KEPFORD
38 Director Wellness ... Mr. Jeffrey HUSKEY
37 Financial Aid Officer ... Ms. Carolyn HALGERSON
102 President & CEO of Foundation ... Mr. Steve ERPENBACH
29 President & CEO Alumni Affairs ... Ms. Andi FOUBERG
14 Director Admin Information Svcs ... Mr. William (Joe) MOORE
19 Chief Security/Safety ... Mr. Tim HEATON
39 Director of Residential Life ... Mr. Jeffrey HALE
40 Director of Bookstore ... Mr. Derek PETERSON
41 Director of Athletics ... Mr. Justin SELL
28 Dir of Diversity/Equal Opportunity ... Vacant
56 Interim Director of Extension ... Dr. Karla TRAUTMAN
26 Dir Marketing & Communications ... Mr. Michael LOCKREM
96 Purchasing Director ... Ms. Vicki SOREN
43 University Legal Counsel ... Dr. Tracy GREENE
25 Director of Grants/Contracts ... Ms. Jackie NELSON
24 Mgr Instructional Design Services ... Dr. Shouhong ZHANG
85 Mgr International Students/Scholars ... Mr. Greg WYMER
47 Int Dean Agriculture/Biological Sci ... Dr. Daniel SCHOLL
49 Dean of Arts & Sciences ... Dr. Dennis PAPINI
54 Dean of Engineering ... Dr. Lewis BROWN
53 Dean Education & Human Science ... Dr. Jill THORNGREN
66 Dean of Nursing ... Dr. Nancy FAHRENWALD
67 Acting Dean of Pharmacy ... Dr. Jane MORT
58 Dean of Graduate School ... Dr. Kinchel DOERNER
92 Dean Honors College ... Dr. Timothy NICHOLS
51 Dir Continuing & Distance Educ ... Ms. Lindsey HAMLIN
09 Coordinator Institutional Research ... Ms. Jennifer VANDER WAL

Southeast Technical Institute (G)

2320 N Career Avenue, Sioux Falls SD 57107-1302
County: Minnehaha FICE Identification: 007764
Unit ID: 219426
Telephone: (605) 367-7624 Carnegie Class: Assoc/HVT-High Trad
FAX Number: (605) 367-8305 Calendar System: Semester
URL: www.southeasttech.edu
Established: 1968 Annual Undergrad Tuition & Fees (In-District): $5,280
Enrollment: 2,332 Coed
Affiliation or Control: Local IRS Status: 501(c)3

Highest Offering: Associate Degree
Accreditation: NH, ADNUR, CVT, DMS, NDT, NMT, SURGT

01 President .... Vacant
05 Vice President of Academics .... Mr. James JACOBSEN
10 Vice President Finance & Operations .... Mr. Richard KLUIN
32 Vice Pres Student Affs/Inst Rsrch .... Mr. Tracy NOLDNER
35 Director of Students .... Mr. Jim ROKUSEK
50 Training Solutions Institute .... Mr. Lon HIRD
06 Registrar .... Ms. Kristie VORTHERMS
15 Human Resources Specialist .... Ms. Kathy STRUCK
20 Director of Academic Support .... Dr. Craig PETERS
26 Marketing Coordinator .... Ms. Margaret PENNOCK
37 Financial Aid Director .... Ms. Lynette GRABOWSKA
102 Foundation Associate .... Ms. Chellee NEMEC
21 Business Manager .... Mr. James WESTCOTT
38 Student Personal Counselor .... Ms. Nicole MCMILLIN

University of Sioux Falls (A)

1101 W 22nd Street, Sioux Falls SD 57105-1699
County: Minnehaha FICE Identification: 003469
Unit ID: 219383
Telephone: (605) 331-5000 Carnegie Class: Masters/M
FAX Number: (605) 331-6615 Calendar System: 4/1/4
URL: www.usiouxfalls.edu
Established: 1883 Annual Undergrad Tuition & Fees: $26,240
Enrollment: 1,419 Coed
Affiliation or Control: American Baptist IRS Status: 501(c)3
Highest Offering: Beyond Master's But Less Than Doctorate
Accreditation: NH, IACBE, NURSE, SW, TED

01 President .... Dr. Mark BENEDETTO
04 Exec Assistant to the President .... Ms. Karen BANGASSER
05 Provost/Vice Pres Academic Affairs .... Dr. Brett BRADFIELD
10 VP for Business and Finance .... Ms. Marsha DENNISTON
30 VP for Institutional Advancement .... Dr. Bruce BLUMER
44 VP for Principal Gifts .... Mr. Jon HIATT
15 VP of Human Resources .... Ms. Julie GEDNALSKE
32 Dean of Students .... Mr. Corey ROSS
13 VP Information Technology .... Mr. William BARTELL
42 Dean of the Chapel .... Rev. Dennis L. THUM
06 Registrar .... Ms. Anna HECKENLAIBLE
21 Controller .... Ms. Susan THIE
37 Director of Financial Aid .... Ms. Karrie MORGAN
07 Director of Admissions .... Ms. Aimee VANDER FEEN
08 Director of Library Services .... Ms. Rachel CROWLEY
18 Director of Facilities Services .... Ms. Traci LINDSTEN
41 Director Intercollegiate Athletics .... Mr. Josh SNYDER
88 Director of Degree Comp Program .... Ms. LuAnn GROSSMAN
19 Director of Campus Safety .... Mr. Kevin GREBIN
29 Director Annual Giving & Alumni Rel .... Ms. Kelsey FREIDEL-NELSON
104 Director of International Education .... Mr. Randy NELSON
106 Director of Online Education .... Ms. Veda IVERSON
40 Bookstore Manager .... Ms. Jennifer KNUTSON
50 Dean School of Bus & Entrep Ldrshp .... Dr. Deb HERB-SEPICH
53 Chair Fredrikson School of Educ .... Ms. Julie MCAREAVEY
57 Chair Visual & Performing Arts .... Mr. Jonathan NEIDERHISER
81 Chair of Natural Sciences .... Dr. William SOEFFING
79 Chair of Humanities .... Ms. Nicholle SCHUELKE
66 Director of School of Nursing .... Ms. Jessica CHERENEGAR
83 Chair of Social Sciences .... Ms. Beth O'TOOLE

Western Dakota Technical Institute (B)

800 Mickelson Drive, Rapid City SD 57703-4018
County: Pennington FICE Identification: 010170
Unit ID: 219480
Telephone: (605) 394-4034 Carnegie Class: Assoc/HVT-High Trad
FAX Number: (605) 394-1789 Calendar System: Semester
URL: www.wdt.edu
Established: 1968 Annual Undergrad Tuition & Fees (In-District): $6,200
Enrollment: 840 Coed
Affiliation or Control: Local IRS Status: 501(c)3
Highest Offering: Associate Degree
Accreditation: #NH, EMT, SURGT

01 President .... Dr. Ann BOLMAN
05 Dean of Academics .... Ms. Kelly OEHLERKING
10 Dean of Fiscal Operations .... Mr. Brian WATLAND
30 Dean of Accreditation & Advancement .... Mr. Stephen BUCHHOLZ
20 Associate Dean of Academics .... Ms. Jennifer SEALS
37 Manager of Financial Aid .... Ms. Jill ELDER
15 Human Resources Manager .... Ms. Theresa SCHARN
07 Admissions Director .... Ms. Jill ELDER
08 Registrar .... Ms. Debbie TOMS
18 Chief Facilities/Physical Plant .... Mr. Daryl LEMME
26 Chief Public Relations Officer .... Ms. Megan NICOLAISEN
36 Director of Student Placement .... Ms. Chandra CALVERT
84 Director Enrollment Management .... Ms. Jill ELDER
96 Director of Purchasing .... Mr. Brian WATLAND

TENNESSEE

American Baptist College (C)

1800 Baptist World Center Drive, Nashville TN 37207
County: Davidson FICE Identification: 010460
Unit ID: 219505
Telephone: (615) 256-1463 Carnegie Class: Spec-4-yr-Faith
FAX Number: (615) 226-7855 Calendar System: Semester
URL: www.abcnash.edu
Established: 1924 Annual Undergrad Tuition & Fees: $10,074
Enrollment: 157 Coed
Affiliation or Control: Baptist IRS Status: 501(c)3
Highest Offering: Baccalaureate
Accreditation: BI

01 President .... Dr. Forrest E. HARRIS, SR.
03 Executive Vice President .... Atty. Richard JACKSON
05 Academic Vice President/Dean .... Dr. Renita WEEMS
32 Asst VP Campus Life .... Mr. Martin ESPINOSA
06 Registrar .... Ms. Pamela TABOR
10 Chief Financial Officer .... Ms. Clara A. WILLIAMS
08 Director Library Services .... Ms. Nicole WHITE
04 Executive Assistant to President .... Ms. Mary CARPENTER
35 Assoc Dean Student Success Services .... Ms. LaShante WALKER
09 Director of Institutional Research .... Dr. Regina PRUDE
07 Dir Admissions/Public Relations .... Ms. Dee BOMER

American National University (D)

1328 Highway 11 W, Bristol TN 37620-8530
Telephone: (423) 878-4440 Identification: 666500
Accreditation: ACICS, MAC

† Branch campus of American National University, Salem, VA

American National University (E)

8415 Kingston Pike, Knoxville TN 37919
Telephone: (865) 539-2011 Identification: 770786
Accreditation: ACICS, MAC

† Branch campus of American National University, Salem, VA

Aquinas College (F)

4210 Harding Pike, Nashville TN 37205-2005
County: Davidson FICE Identification: 003477
Unit ID: 219578
Telephone: (615) 297-7545 Carnegie Class: Spec-4-yr-Other Health
FAX Number: (615) 279-3898 Calendar System: Semester
URL: www.aquinascollege.edu
Established: 1961 Annual Undergrad Tuition & Fees: $20,550
Enrollment: 472 Coed
Affiliation or Control: Roman Catholic IRS Status: 501(c)3
Highest Offering: Master's
Accreditation: SC, ADNUR, NUR

01 President .... Sr. Mary Sarah GALBRAITH, OP
10 Vice Pres of Finance & Admin .... Vacant
05 Provost and Vice Pres for Academics .... Sr. Thomas More STEPNOWSKI, OP
32 Vice Pres for Student Life .... Sr. Mary Cecilia GOODRUM, OP
20 Associate Provost .... Dr. William SMART
26 Dir of Communications/Marketing .... Mr. Paul DOWNEY
07 Director of Admissions .... Ms. Connie HANSOM
06 Registrar .... Ms. Michele PRIDDY
08 Librarian .... Mr. Mark HALL
30 Director of Development .... Mr. Kevin T. LEE
40 Bookstore Manager .... Mr. Alan BRADLEY
66 Dean School of Nursing .... Dr. Elizabeth COOPER
66 Director of ASN Nursing Program .... Mrs. Margaret DANIEL
53 Dean School of Education .... Sr. Mary Anne ZUBERBUELER, OP
37 Director of Financial Aid .... Ms. Cynthia PIANA
21 Business Manager .... Ms. Deb WELSH
35 Director of Student Affairs .... Mr. Bryant MORIN
09 Director of Institutional Research .... Dr. William SMART
29 Director of Alumni Relations .... Ms. Rachel HUDSON
18 Chief of Facilities/Physical Plant .... Mr. John WALL
88 Director of Student Learning Svcs .... Mrs. Suzette TELLI
88 Director of Catechetics .... Mr. Jason GALE
49 Dean School of Arts and Sciences .... Dr. Aaron URBANCZYK
50 Dean School of Business .... Vacant
88 Dir Center for Catholic Education .... Sr. Elizabeth Anne ALLEN, OP
19 Director Security/Safety .... Mr. Anthony ATWOOD
39 Director Student Housing .... Ms. Marisa QUINN
84 Vice Pres for Inst Engagement .... Mr. Jesse FORTNEY
91 Director Administrative Computing .... Mr. Ron HAZEN
04 Administrative Asst to President .... Mrs. Brenda L. KINCAID
101 Secretary of the Institution/Board .... Sr. Mary Agnes GREIFFENDORF, OP
104 Director Study Abroad .... Ms. Maria KOSHUTE
36 Career Services Coordinator .... Ms. Cathy HENDON
13 Chief Info Technology Officer (CIO) .... Mrs. Joyce WALL
38 Director Student Counseling .... Sr. Mary Cecilia GOODRUM, OP
45 Chief Institutional Planning .... Mr. Mario MARTINEZ

Argosy University, Nashville (G)

100 Centerview Drive, Suite 225,
Nashville TN 37214-3438
Telephone: (615) 525-2800 Identification: 666668
Accreditation: &WC, ACBSP

† Regional accreditation is carried under the parent institution in Orange, CA.

The Art Institute of Tennessee-Nashville (H)

100 Centerview Dr., Ste 250, Nashville TN 37214-3439
Telephone: (615) 874-1067 Identification: 770975
Accreditation: &SC

† Regional accreditation is carried under the parent institution in Atlanta, GA

Baptist College of Health Sciences (I)

1003 Monroe Avenue, Memphis TN 38104-3199
County: Shelby FICE Identification: 034403
Unit ID: 219639
Telephone: (901) 575-2247 Carnegie Class: Spec-4-yr-Other Health
FAX Number: (901) 572-2461 Calendar System: Trimester
URL: www.bchs.edu
Established: 1994 Annual Undergrad Tuition & Fees: $10,892
Enrollment: 1,170 Coed
Affiliation or Control: Independent Non-Profit IRS Status: 501(c)3
Highest Offering: Baccalaureate
Accreditation: SC, COARC, DMS, MT, NMT, NURSE, RAD, RTT

01 President .... Dr. Betty S. MCGARVEY
04 Administrative Asst to President .... Ms. Joyce J. PERKINS
10 Vice President Financial & Business .... Ms. Leanne SMITH
11 Vice President Admin Svcs/HR .... Dr. Adonna CALDWELL
05 Chief Academic Officer/Provost .... Dr. Loredana C. HAEGER
97 Dean General Educ & Health Studies .... Dr. Barry SCHULTZ
66 Dean Nursing .... Dr. Anne M. PLUMB
76 Dean Allied Health .... Dr. Carol WARREN
32 Dean Student Services .... Ms. Nancy REED
06 Registrar .... Mr. John BERGER
07 Director of Admissions .... Ms. Lissa MORGAN
09 Dir of Institutional Effectiveness .... Dr. Mitzi C. ROBERTS
29 Director Alumni Relations .... Ms. Megan M. BURSI
35 Director Student Services & Housing .... Mr. Jeremy WILKES
37 Director Financial Aid .... Ms. Joanna DARDEN
84 Dean Enrollment Management .... Dr. Arnold ARREDONDO

Belmont University (J)

1900 Belmont Boulevard, Nashville TN 37212-3757
County: Davidson FICE Identification: 003479
Unit ID: 219709
Telephone: (615) 460-6000 Carnegie Class: Masters/L
FAX Number: (615) 460-6446 Calendar System: Semester
URL: www.belmont.edu
Established: 1890 Annual Undergrad Tuition & Fees: $30,000
Enrollment: 7,244 Coed
Affiliation or Control: Christian Churches And Churches of Christ
IRS Status: 501(c)3
Highest Offering: Doctorate
Accreditation: SC, ART, BUS, BUSA, ENGT, LAW, MUS, NURSE, OT, PHAR, PTA, SW, TED, THEA

01 President .... Dr. Robert C. FISHER
05 Provost .... Dr. Thomas D. BURNS
100 Vice President/Chief of Staff .... Dr. Susan H. WEST
11 Vice Pres for Admin & Univ Counsel .... Dr. Jason ROGERS
30 VP for Institutional Effectiveness .... Dr. Paula GILL
30 VP for Develop & External Relations .... Dr. Perry MOULDS
10 Vice President Finance & Operations .... Mr. Steven T. LASLEY
42 VP Spiritual Development .... Dr. Todd LAKE
13 Assoc VP/Chief Information Officer .... Mr. William INGRAM
32 Assoc Provost/Dean of Students .... Dr. Jeffery BURGIN
20 Assoc Provost for Academic Affairs .... Dr. Beverly SCHNELLER
84 Assoc Provost/Dean Enrollment Svcs .... Dr. David MEE
09 Assoc Provost/Assess/Inst Research .... Vacant
88 Assoc Provost ISGE .... Dr. Mimi BARNARD
50 Dean College of Business .... Dr. Patrick RAINES
88 Dean College Visual/Performing Arts .... Dr. Stephen EAVES
88 Dean College of Ent & Music Bus .... Mr. Doug HOWARD
49 Dean Col of Lib Arts & Soc Sci .... Dr. Bryce SULLIVAN
81 Dean Col of Sciences & Mathematics .... Dr. Thomas SPENCE
76 Dean Col Health Sciences/Nursing .... Dr. Cathy TAYLOR
73 Dean of Col Theol & Christian Min .... Dr. Darrell GWALTNEY
61 Dean College of Law .... Dr. Alberto GONZALES
67 Dean College of Pharmacy .... Dr. Phil JOHNSTON
06 University Registrar .... Mr. Steven REED
35 Asst Dean of Students .... Dr. Molly ZLOCK
35 Asst Dean of Students .... Ms. Angie BRYANT
39 Assistant Dean of Students .... Mr. Anthony DONOVAN
07 Director of University Admissions .... Ms. Brooke BRANNIN
15 Director of Human Resources .... Ms. Heather BEMIS
37 Director of Financial Aid .... Mrs. Patricia SMEDLEY
29 Director of Alumni Relations .... Ms. Suzanne THIGPEN
18 Director of Facilities Management .... Mr. Robert CHAVES
19 Chief of Campus Security .... Mr. Pat CUNNINGHAM
90 Director Technology Services .... Mr. Randall REYNOLDS
08 Director of Library Services .... Ms. Sue MASZAROS
41 Athletics Director .... Mr. Scott CORLEY
40 Manager Bookstore .... Mrs. Catherine MURPHY
36 Dir Career & Professional Develop .... Vacant
26 Director of Communications .... Mr. Greg S. PILLON
38 Director Student Counseling .... Ms. Peg LEONARD-MARTIN
104 Director Study Abroad .... Ms. Shelley JEWELL
85 Director of International Education .... Ms. Katherine SKINNER
43 Dir Legal Services/General Counsel .... Dr. Jason ROGERS

Bethel University (K)

325 Cherry Avenue, McKenzie TN 38201-1705
County: Carroll FICE Identification: 003480
Unit ID: 219718
Telephone: (731) 352-4000 Carnegie Class: Masters/L
FAX Number: (731) 352-4069 Calendar System: Semester
URL: www.bethelu.edu
Established: 1842 Annual Undergrad Tuition & Fees: $15,714
Enrollment: 6,229 Coed
Affiliation or Control: Cumberland Presbyterian IRS Status: 501(c)3
Highest Offering: Master's

Accreditation: SC, ARCPA, CAATE, NURSE, TED

01 President ... Mr. Walter BUTLER
05 Chief Academic Officer ... Dr. Phyllis CAMPBELL
49 VP College of Arts and Sciences ... Ms. Nancy BEAN
107 VP College of Prof Studies ... Ms. Kelly SANDERS-KELLEY
06 University Registrar ... Ms. Becky HAMES
10 VP of Finance ... Mr. David HUSS
84 Dean of Enrollment CLA ... Mrs. Tina HODGES
30 Vice President for Development ... Dr. Dale HENRY
32 Dean of Student Development ... Mr. James STEWART
37 Director of Financial Aid ... Ms. Janie BURNS
26 Director of Public Relations ... Ms. Jennifer GLASS
88 Director of College Orientation ... Mrs. Sandy LOUDEN
42 Chaplain ... Rev. Anne HAMES
08 Library Director ... Ms. Jill WHITFILL
15 Human Resource Director ... Ms. Carolyn DOTSON
41 Athletic Director ... Mr. Dale KELLEY
09 Director of Institutional Effective ... Dr. Lisa NORRIS
29 Director Alumni Relations ... Mrs. Myra CARLOCK
76 Director of Col of Health Sciences ... Dr. Joe HAMES
07 Assoc Dean of Enrollment Services ... Ms. Kim HOUSTON
18 Chief Facilities/Physical Plant ... Mr. Randy TANAKA
35 Director Student Affairs ... Mr. James STEWART

Brightwood College (A)

750 Envious Lane, Nashville TN 37217-1342

County: Davidson | FICE Identification: 023262
Unit ID: 246202
Telephone: (615) 279-8300 | Carnegie Class: Spec 2-yr-Other
FAX Number: (615) 297-6678 | Calendar System: Other
URL: www.brightwood.edu
Established: 1981 | Annual Undergrad Tuition & Fees: N/A
Enrollment: 369 | Coed
Affiliation or Control: Proprietary | IRS Status: Proprietary
Highest Offering: Associate Degree
Accreditation: ACICS

01 Executive Director ... Ms. Haley JOHNSON

Bryan College (B)

721 Bryan Drive, Dayton TN 37321-6275

County: Rhea | FICE Identification: 003536
Unit ID: 219790
Telephone: (423) 775-2041 | Carnegie Class: Masters/S
FAX Number: (423) 775-7330 | Calendar System: Semester
URL: www.bryan.edu
Established: 1930 | Annual Undergrad Tuition & Fees: $23,300
Enrollment: 1,599 | Coed
Affiliation or Control: Independent Non-Profit | IRS Status: 501(c)3
Highest Offering: Master's
Accreditation: SC, IACBE

01 President ... Dr. Stephen D. LIVESAY
04 Exec Assistant to the President ... Ms. Margaret A. LEGG
05 Academic Vice President ... Dr. Kevin L. CLAUSON
10 VP of Finance and Enrollment ... Mr. Rick J. TAPHORN
30 Vice Pres of College Advancement ... Mr. Chuck S. BAKER
32 VP Student Services/Ministries ... Mr. Timothy J. HOSTETLER
13 Vice Pres Information Systems ... Vacant
58 Dean Sch of Adult & Graduate Stds ... Dr. Paul R. RICKERT
35 Dean of Students ... Mr. Bruce A. MORGAN
37 Director of Financial Aid ... Mr. David L. HAGGARD
14 Director of Information Systems ... Mr. James SULLIVAN
06 Registrar ... Ms. Janet M. PIATT
08 Director of Library Sciences ... Dr. Gary N. FITSIMMONS
15 Director Personnel Services ... Mrs. Angie C. PRICE
41 Athletic Director ... Mr. Taylor HASTY
18 Director of Physical Plant ... Mr. David A. MORGAN
29 Director of Alumni Affairs ... Mrs. Paulakay HALL
07 Director of Admissions ... Mr. Joshua D. HOOD
88 Accreditation Liaison ... Mr. Samuel J. YOUNGS

Carson-Newman University (C)

1646 Russell Avenue, PO Box 557,
Jefferson City TN 37760-2204

County: Jefferson | FICE Identification: 003481
Unit ID: 219806
Telephone: (865) 471-2000 | Carnegie Class: Masters/M
FAX Number: (865) 471-3502 | Calendar System: Semester
URL: www.cn.edu
Established: 1851 | Annual Undergrad Tuition & Fees: $25,360
Enrollment: 2,362 | Coed
Affiliation or Control: Southern Baptist | IRS Status: 501(c)3
Highest Offering: Doctorate
Accreditation: SC, AAFCS, ART, CACREP, DIETD, MUS, NURSE, TED

01 President ... Dr. J. Randall O'BRIEN
05 Vice Pres Academic Affairs/Provost ... Dr. Paul PERCY
30 Vice President for Advancement ... Ms. Valerie I. DAY
32 Vice President Student Affairs ... Dr. Ross BRUMMETT
35 Dean of Student Affairs ... Mrs. Shelley BALL
08 Dean of Library Services ... Mr. Bruce KOCOUR
26 Exec Dir University Relations ... Mrs. Mary LEIDIG
37 Director Financial Aid ... Mrs. Danette SEALE
38 Director Counseling Services ... Mrs. Jennifer CATLETT
13 Director of IT ... Mr. David TUELL
18 Chief Facilities/Physical Plant ... Mr. Ondes WEBSTER
84 Dean of Enrollment Management ... Mr. Aaron PORTER

92 Director of Honors Program ... Dr. Andrew SMITH
15 Director of Human Resources ... Mr. Jimmy WYATT
41 Athletic Director ... Mr. Allen MORGAN
10 Chief Financial/Business Officer ... Mrs. Martha CHAMBERS
85 Dean of Global Education ... Dr. Regina SULLIVAN
06 Registrar ... Mrs. Sheryl GRAY

Chattanooga College (D)

248 Northgate Mall Drive, Suite 130,
Chattanooga TN 37415

County: Hamilton | FICE Identification: 022042
Unit ID: 220118
Telephone: (423) 624-0077 | Carnegie Class: Assoc/HVT-High Non
FAX Number: (423) 624-1575 | Calendar System: Quarter
URL: www.chattanoogacollege.edu
Established: 1968 | Annual Undergrad Tuition & Fees: $10,690
Enrollment: 347 | Coed
Affiliation or Control: Proprietary | IRS Status: Proprietary
Highest Offering: Associate Degree
Accreditation: ACCSC

01 President ... Mr. William G. FAOUR
03 Vice President ... Mr. Toney C. MCFADDEN
37 Director Financial Aid ... Mrs. Evelyn DAVIS

Christian Brothers University (E)

650 East Parkway S, Memphis TN 38104-5581

County: Shelby | FICE Identification: 003482
Unit ID: 219833
Telephone: (901) 321-3000 | Carnegie Class: Masters/M
FAX Number: (901) 321-3494 | Calendar System: Semester
URL: www.cbu.edu
Established: 1871 | Annual Undergrad Tuition & Fees: $30,166
Enrollment: 1,667 | Coed
Affiliation or Control: Roman Catholic | IRS Status: 501(c)3
Highest Offering: Master's
Accreditation: SC, #ARCPA, ENG, NURSE, TED

01 President ... Dr. John SMARRELLI, JR.
05 Interim VP Academics & Student Life ... Dr. Paul HAUGHT
10 CFO & VP Administration ... Ms. Carolyn HEAD
30 Vice Pres Institutional Advancement ... Mr. Steve CRISMAN
84 VP for Enrollment Management ... Dr. Anne KENWORTHY
32 Dean of Students ... Ms. Karen CONWAY
13 Dir Network Infrastructure/Support ... Mr. Aaron LAMEY
06 Registrar ... Mrs Melody L NABORS
36 Director Career Center ... Mrs. Amy WARE
08 Director of Plough Library ... Ms Kay CUNNINGHAM
07 Director of Admissions ... Ms. Kristi FORMAN
38 Director of Counseling ... Mrs. Sadie LISENBY
37 Director Financial Resources ... Mr. John LEWIS
09 Dir Inst Research/Effectiveness ... Ms. Melissa S. HANSON
39 Director Residence Life ... Mr. Alton WADE
35 Associate VP for Student Life ... Dr. Timothy DOYLE
42 Director of Ministry and Mission ... Br. Dominic EHRMANTRAUT
92 Director Honors Program ... Dr. Tracie L. BURKE
41 Athletic Director ... Mr. Brian SUMMERS
44 Sr Director Development ... Ms Jordan SCARLESKI
29 Director Alumni ... Mr. Terez WILSON
21 Controller ... Mr. Thomas COCHRAN
15 Director of Personnel ... Mr. Greg ELLER
18 Chief Facility/Physical Plant ... Mr. Philip R. YELVINGTON
19 Director of Security ... Mr. John D. LOTRIONTE
40 Director Bookstore ... Ms. Shannon DAVIS
50 Dean School of Business ... Dr. Jack HARGETT
54 Dean School of Engineering ... Dr. Pong MALASRI
49 Interim Dean School of Arts ... Dr Scott GEIS
81 Dean School of Science ... Dr Johnny B. HOLMES
107 Dir Graduate/Professional Stds Pgms ... Ms. Toni ROSS
58 Director Graduate Education Program ... Dr Samantha ALPERIN
58 Director MBA Program ... Dr. Scott LAWYER
66 Director Nursing Program ... Dr. Sue I. LEHMAN-TRZYNKA
88 Director Physician Assistant Stds ... Mr. Gary TOOLEY
04 Senior Executive Asst to President ... Mrs. Donna M. FREEMAN
104 Director Study Abroad ... Dr. Emily FORSDICK
25 Chief Contracts/Grants Admin ... Mr. Robert ARNOLD
101 Secretary of the Institution/Board ... Ms. Melanie BREMER

Concorde Career College (F)

5100 Poplar Avenue, Suite 132, Memphis TN 38137-0132

County: Shelby | FICE Identification: 021571
Unit ID: 219903
Telephone: (901) 761-9494 | Carnegie Class: Spec 2-yr-Health
FAX Number: (901) 761-3293 | Calendar System: Semester
URL: www.concorde.edu
Established: 1967 | Annual Undergrad Tuition & Fees: N/A
Enrollment: 1,310 | Coed
Affiliation or Control: Proprietary | IRS Status: Proprietary
Highest Offering: Associate Degree
Accreditation: COE, COARC, DA, DH, OTA, POLYT, PTAA, RAD, SURGT

01 Campus President ... Mrs. Lori SPENCER
11 Regional Vice President Operations ... Mr. Tommy STEWART

The Crown College of the Bible (G)

2307 W. Beaver Creek Drive, Powell TN 37849

County: Knox | Identification: 667141
Telephone: (865) 938-8186 | Carnegie Class: Not Classified
FAX Number: (865) 938-8188 | Calendar System: Semester
URL: thecrowncollege.com
Established: 1991 | Annual Undergrad Tuition & Fees: N/A
Enrollment: N/A | Coed
Affiliation or Control: Baptist | IRS Status: 501(c)3
Highest Offering: Master's
Accreditation: @TRACS

01 Founder & President ... Clarence SEXTON
05 Vice President of Academics ... Tim TOMLINSON

Cumberland University (H)

1 Cumberland Square, Lebanon TN 37087-3554

County: Wilson | FICE Identification: 003485
Unit ID: 219949
Telephone: (615) 547-1290 | Carnegie Class: Masters/M
FAX Number: (615) 444-2569 | Calendar System: Semester
URL: www.cumberland.edu
Established: 1842 | Annual Undergrad Tuition & Fees: $21,210
Enrollment: 1,481 | Coed
Affiliation or Control: Independent Non-Profit | IRS Status: 501(c)3
Highest Offering: Master's
Accreditation: SC, ACBSP, #CAATE, NUR, NURSE, TED

01 President ... Dr. Paul STUMB
05 Provost/Vice Pres Academic Affairs ... Dr. William MCKEE
10 Vice President of Finance ... Ms. Judy G. JORDAN
30 Vice President of Advancement ... Mr. Rusty RICHARDSON
18 Vice Pres IT/Campus Services ... Mr. Joe GRAY
32 AVP/Dean of Students ... Ms. Stephanie WALKER
66 Dean Nursing and Health Sciences ... Dr. Carol Anne BACH
100 Executive Coordinator to President ... Ms. Leslie STEELE
44 Exec Dir Development/Alumni Rels ... Mr. Jonathan HAWKINS
08 Director Library Services ... Vacant
84 Exec Director Enrollment Services ... Mr. Eddie LOVIN
41 Director of Athletics ... Mr. Ron PAVAN
06 Registrar ... Ms. Tammi PAVAN
15 Human Resources Generalist ... Ms. Renee JONES
13 Director of Information Technology ... Mr. Brian RADFORD
09 Director of Institutional Research ... Mr. Larry F. VAUGHAN
26 Exec Dir Communications/Marketing ... Mr. Phillip CARTER
36 Dir of Career Services/Internships ... Mrs. Ronie MCPEAK

Daymar College (I)

2691 Trenton Road, Clarksville TN 37040-6718

Telephone: (931) 552-7600 | Identification: 666492
Accreditation: ACICS, PTAA

† Branch campus of Daymar College, Nashville, TN.

Daymar College (J)

415 Golden Bear Court, Murfreesboro TN 37128-5508

Telephone: (615) 217-9347 | Identification: 666392
Accreditation: ACICS

† Branch campus of Daymar College, Nashville, TN.

Daymar College (K)

560 Royal Parkway, Nashville TN 37214

County: Davidson | FICE Identification: 004934
Unit ID: 220002
Telephone: (615) 361-7555 | Carnegie Class: Bac/Assoc-Mixed
FAX Number: (615) 367-2736 | Calendar System: Quarter
URL: www.daymarcollege.edu
Established: 1884 | Annual Undergrad Tuition & Fees: $17,000
Enrollment: 89 | Coed
Affiliation or Control: Proprietary | IRS Status: Proprietary
Highest Offering: Baccalaureate
Accreditation: ACICS

01 President ... Mr. Joel MUSGROVE
05 Campus Dean ... Ms. Laurna TAYLOR
10 Director of Financial Services ... Ms. Denise JERNIEAN
36 Director of Career Services ... Ms. Angela PEARROW
06 Registrar ... Mr. Ryan PALOMBO

Fisk University (L)

1000 17th Avenue N, Nashville TN 37208-3051

County: Davidson | FICE Identification: 003490
Unit ID: 220181
Telephone: (615) 329-8500 | Carnegie Class: Bac-A&S
FAX Number: N/A | Calendar System: Semester
URL: www.fisk.edu
Established: 1866 | Annual Undergrad Tuition & Fees: $21,480
Enrollment: 772 | Coed
Affiliation or Control: Independent Non-Profit | IRS Status: 501(c)3
Highest Offering: Master's
Accreditation: SC, ACBSP, MUS

01 Interim President ... Mr. Frank L. SIMS
05 VP of Academic Affairs & Provost ... Dr. Rodney S. HANLEY
10 Vice President for Finance and CFO ... Mrs. Sydney R. LEO
04 Exec Assistant to the President ... Mrs. Sherri B. RUCKER
30 Vice President of Inst Advancement ... Dr. Jens FREDERIKSEN
09 AVP for Inst Effectiveness Accredit ... Dr. Jason R. CURRY
32 VP of Student Engagement & Enroll ... Vacant
20 Vice Provost Academic Initiatives ... Dr. Arnold BURGER
13 Infrastructure Manager ... Mr. Drew JENKINS

29 Exec Director of Alumni Affairs .... Mrs. Adrienne LATHAM
07 Dean of Recruitment & Admission ....Ms. Juliet JOHNSON
37 Director of Financial Aid ....Ms. Bianca MATLOCK
06 Registrar ....Ms. Fantina CARTER
08 University Librarian ....Dr. Jessie C. SMITH
81 Dean Sch Natural Science/Math/Bus ....Dr. Lee LIMBIRD
79 Dean School Humanities/Social Sci .... Dr. Reavis MITCHELL
41 Dir of Athletics & Intramural Pgms .... Dr. Larry GLOVER
42 Dean of the Chapel .... Dr. Jason CURRY
25 Dir Sponsored Research & Programs .... Dr. Amelia HUNTER
44 Director of Planned Giving ....Ms. Sheila SMITH
18 Director of Facilities .... Mr. Norman RAPP
19 Chief/Director of Campus Safety ....Mr. Mickey WEST
96 Director of Purchasing ....Vacant
36 Director Career Development .... Ms. Latreace WELLS
38 Coordinator of Student Counseling .... Dr. Sheila PETERS
15 Director of Human Resources .... Dr. JaCenda DAVIDSON
21 Comptroller ....Mr. Warren IRONS
102 Dir Foundation/Corporate Relations ....Mr. Van PINNOCK
105 Webmaster ....Mr. George DOTSON
39 Director Student Housing ....Dr. Christopher DUKE
43 Dir Legal Services/General Counsel ....Ms. Stacey GARRETT
106 Dir Online Education/E-learning ....Dr. Shirley BROWN
86 Director Government Relations ....Dr. Edwina HAMBY

Fortis Institute (A)

1025 Highway 111, Cookeville TN 38501-4305
County: Putnam FICE Identification: 023263
Unit ID: 418870
Telephone: (931) 526-3660 Carnegie Class: Spec 2-yr-Health
FAX Number: (931) 372-2603 Calendar System: Quarter
URL: www.fortis.edu/cookeville-tennessee.php
Established: 1970 Annual Undergrad Tuition & Fees: $13,715
Enrollment: 226 Coed
Affiliation or Control: Proprietary IRS Status: Proprietary
Highest Offering: Associate Degree
Accreditation: #COE, MLTAD, RAD, SURGT

06 Registrar ....Ms. Wendy BANDY
07 Director of Admissions ....Mr. Brett TADLOCK
10 Chief Business Officer ....Ms. Melissa LEWIS
36 Director Student Placement ....Ms. Cindy GARRISON
37 Director Student Financial Aid ....Ms. Lisa WALLING

Fortis Institute-Nashville (B)

3354 Perimeter Hill Drive, Nashville TN 37211
Telephone: (615) 320-5917 Identification: 770509
Accreditation: ABHES, CVT, MLTAD, RAD, SURGT, SURTEC

† Branch campus of Fortis Institute, Baton Rouge, LA.

Fountainhead College of Technology (C)

3203 Tazewell Pike, Knoxville TN 37918
County: Knox FICE Identification: 007439
Unit ID: 221795
Telephone: (865) 688-9422 Carnegie Class: Spec-4-yr-Other Tech
FAX Number: (865) 688-2419 Calendar System: Semester
URL: www.fountainheadcollege.edu
Established: 1947 Annual Undergrad Tuition & Fees: $14,750
Enrollment: 123 Coed
Affiliation or Control: Proprietary IRS Status: Proprietary
Highest Offering: Baccalaureate
Accreditation: ACCSC

00 CEO ....Mr. Richard W. RACKLEY
01 Campus President ....Ms. Casey C. RACKLEY
32 Director Student Services .... Ms. Fran CLEMMONS

Freed-Hardeman University (D)

158 E Main, Henderson TN 38340-2398
County: Chester FICE Identification: 003492
Unit ID: 220215
Telephone: (731) 989-6000 Carnegie Class: Masters/S
FAX Number: N/A Calendar System: Semester
URL: www.fhu.edu
Established: 1869 Annual Undergrad Tuition & Fees: $21,500
Enrollment: 1,867 Coed
Affiliation or Control: Churches Of Christ IRS Status: 501(c)3
Highest Offering: Doctorate
Accreditation: SC, ACBSP, NURSE, SW, TED, @THEOL

01 President ....Dr. Joe WILEY
04 Executive Assistant to President ....Mrs. Donna STEELE
10 Exec VP and CFO ....Dr. Dwayne WILSON
30 VP for Univ Advancement ....Mr. Dave CLOUSE
05 Provost and VP Academics ....Dr. Charles VIRES
32 VP Student Services ....Dr. Wayne SCOTT
84 VP for Enrollment Management ....Dr. Matt VEGA
20 Associate VP for Academics ....Dr. Vicki JOHNSON
41 Director of Athletics ....Mr. Michael MCCUTCHEN
29 Director of Alumni Relations ....Mrs. Donna STEELE
07 Director of Admissions ....Mr. Joseph ASKEW
35 Dean of Students ....Mr. Stuart VARNER
35 Dean of Student Life ....Mr. Tony ALLEN
06 Registrar ....Mr. Jared GOTT
37 Director Student Financial Services ....Mrs. Summer JUDD

40 University Book Store Manager ....Ms. Katie NIXON
08 Library Director ....Mr. Wade OSBURN
70 Director of Social Work Program ....Mrs. Nadine MCNEAL
24 A-V Supervisor ....Mrs. Gail NASH
21 Controller ....Mrs. Courtney INSELL
45 Dir Institutional Effectiveness ....Mr. A.B WHITE
09 Director of Institutional Research ....Mr. Micah SMITH
15 Human Resources Coordinator ....Mr. Jay SATTERFIELD
18 Director of Facilities ....Dr. Dwayne WILSON
73 Dean College of Biblical Studies ....Dr. Billy R. SMITH
50 Dean College of Business ....Dr. Jason BRASHIER
53 Dean College of Educ & Behav Sci ....Dr. Sharen CYPRESS
49 Dean College of Arts & Sciences ....Dr. LeAnn SELF-DAVIS
92 Dean of Honors College ....Dr. Jenny JOHNSON
104 Dir of International Studies ....Dr. Jenny JOHNSON
38 Director of Counseling ....Mrs. Nicole YOUNG
36 Director of Univ Career Center ....Dr. Wayne SCOTT
96 Purchasing Coordinator ....Mr. Chris CURRY

Harding School of Theology (E)

1000 Cherry Road, Memphis TN 38117-5499
Telephone: (901) 761-1350 FICE Identification: 004081
Accreditation: &NH, THEOL

† Regional accreditation is carried under Harding University, Searcy, AR.

Hiwassee College (F)

225 Hiwassee College Drive, Madisonville TN 37354
County: Monroe FICE Identification: 003494
Unit ID: 220312
Telephone: (423) 442-2001 Carnegie Class: Bac/Assoc-Mixed
FAX Number: (423) 420-1929 Calendar System: Semester
URL: www.hiwassee.edu
Established: 1850 Annual Undergrad Tuition & Fees: $15,543
Enrollment: 424 Coed
Affiliation or Control: United Methodist IRS Status: 501(c)3
Highest Offering: Baccalaureate
Accreditation: TRACS, DH

01 President ....Dr. Robin J. TRICOLI
05 Int Vice Pres for Academic Affairs ....Dr. Jason LEONARD
10 VP Business Affairs & Treasurer ....Mr. David WATTS
84 Assoc Vice Pres for Enrollment ....Mr. John CAGLE
06 Registrar ....Jane DYE

Huntington College of Health Sciences (G)

117 Legacy View Way, Knoxville TN 37918
County: Knox Identification: 666971
Unit ID: 371274
Telephone: (800) 290-4226 Carnegie Class: Not Classified
FAX Number: (865) 524-8339 Calendar System: Semester
URL: www.hchs.edu
Established: 1985 Annual Undergrad Tuition & Fees: N/A
Enrollment: N/A Coed
Affiliation or Control: Proprietary IRS Status: Proprietary
Highest Offering: Doctorate
Accreditation: DEAC

01 Chief Executive Officer/President ....Dr. Art PRESSER
05 Provost ....Mr. Gene BRUNO
10 Chief Financial Officer ....Mr. Robert SCHMAEF
11 Sr VP Admin & Academic Affairs ....Ms. Jennifer GREEN
07 Director of Admissions ....Ms. Kim MARQUIS
10 Director of Finance ....Ms. Jeannette MINIX

John A. Gupton College (H)

1616 Church Street, Nashville TN 37203-2920
County: Davidson FICE Identification: 008859
Unit ID: 220464
Telephone: (615) 327-3927 Carnegie Class: Spec 2-yr-A&S
FAX Number: (615) 321-4518 Calendar System: Semester
URL: www.guptoncollege.edu
Established: 1946 Annual Undergrad Tuition & Fees: $10,590
Enrollment: 129 Coed
Affiliation or Control: Independent Non-Profit IRS Status: 501(c)3
Highest Offering: Associate Degree
Accreditation: SC, FUSER

01 President ....Mr. B. Steven SPANN
08 Library Director ....Mr. William P. BRUCE
06 Registrar ....Ms. Lisa MOFFITT
07 Director of Admissions ....Ms. Terri PURCELL

Johnson University (I)

7900 Johnson Drive, Knoxville TN 37998-0001
County: Knox FICE Identification: 003495
Unit ID: 220473
Telephone: (865) 573-4517 Carnegie Class: Spec-4-yr-Faith
FAX Number: (865) 251-2337 Calendar System: Semester
URL: www.johnsonu.edu
Established: 1893 Annual Undergrad Tuition & Fees: $12,650
Enrollment: 1,124 Coed
Affiliation or Control: Christian Churches And Churches of Christ
IRS Status: 501(c)3
Highest Offering: Doctorate
Accreditation: SC, BI, CACREP

01 President ....Dr. Gary E. WEEDMAN
03 Chancellor/Vice Provost Florida ....Michael CHAMBERS
05 VP for Academic Affairs/Provost ....Dr. Thomas SMITH
84 VP for Enrollment Services ....Vacant
10 VP for Finance ....Cindy BARNARD
30 VP for External Relations ....Richard CLARK
32 VP for Student Services ....David LEGG
11 VP for Administration ....Cliff MCCARTNEY
09 Assoc Provost Inst Effectiveness ....Cindy LEWIS
20 Vice Provost for Academic Services ....Dr. Greg LINTON
106 Assoc Provost for Online Education ....Dr. John KETCHEN
42 Dean of the Chapel ....Bill WOLF
08 Head Librarian ....Carrie Beth LOWE
15 Director Human Resources ....Ruthanne BEAM
18 Director of Plant Services ....Ben LUTZ, JR.
07 Director of Graduate Admissions ....Penny GIBONS
88 Director of Program Administration ....Joy WINGFIELD
37 Assoc Dean/Director Financial Aid ....Vacant
13 IT Manager ....Glenn FEASTER
41 Athletic Director ....Ken UNDERWOOD

King University (J)

1350 King College Road, Bristol TN 37620-2699
County: Sullivan FICE Identification: 003496
Unit ID: 220516
Telephone: (423) 968-4861 Carnegie Class: Masters/L
FAX Number: (423) 968-4456 Calendar System: Other
URL: www.king.edu
Established: 1867 Annual Undergrad Tuition & Fees: $26,480
Enrollment: 2,897 Coed
Affiliation or Control: Presbyterian Church (U.S.A.) IRS Status: 501(c)3
Highest Offering: Doctorate
Accreditation: SC, #CAATE, NURSE, SW

01 President ....Dr. Alexander W. WHITAKER, IV
05 Vice Pres Acad Affairs/Acad Dean ....Dr. Matthew ROBERTS
10 Vice President for Admin & Finance ....Mr. James P. DONAHUE
32 Vice President for Student Affairs ....Dr. Robert A. LITTLETON
84 Assoc VP of Enrollment Mgmt ....Mr. Micah R. CREWS
26 Vice Pres Marketing ....Mrs. A. LeAnn HUGHES
08 Dean of Library Services ....Ms. Erika BRAMMER
35 Assoc VP/Dean of Student Success ....Mr. Matthew S. PELTIER
04 Executive Assistant to President ....Mrs. Gerri S. BROCKWELL
06 Registrar/Dir Regist & Records ....Mrs. Jessica SWINEY
30 Chief Development Officer ....Mr. John W. KING
30 Director of Development ....Mrs. Denise ASBURY
42 Chaplain ....Dr. Brian ALDERMAN
21 Director of Business Operations .... Mr. Thomas R. LARSON
36 Director of Career Development ....Ms. Donna H. FELTY
41 Athletic Director ....Mr. J. David HICKS
38 Director of Counseling .... Mr. Charles S. THOMPSON
88 Sports Information Director ....Mr. Travis L. CHELL
40 Bookstore Manager ....Ms. Susan D. MARSHALL
37 Director Student Financial Aid ....Mr. Richard BRAND
18 Chief Facilities/Physical Plant ....Mr. Todd THOMAS
92 Director of Honors Program ....Dr. Craig STREETMAN
27 Director Marketing & Communications .....Ms. Sarah CLEVINGER
27 Assoc Director of Communication ....Mrs. Laura K. BOGGAN

Lane College (K)

545 Lane Avenue, Jackson TN 38301-4598
County: Madison FICE Identification: 003499
Unit ID: 220598
Telephone: (731) 426-7500 Carnegie Class: Bac-Diverse
FAX Number: (731) 427-3987 Calendar System: Semester
URL: www.lanecollege.edu
Established: 1882 Annual Undergrad Tuition & Fees: $9,930
Enrollment: 1,262 Coed
Affiliation or Control: Christian Methodist Episcopal IRS Status: 501(c)3
Highest Offering: Baccalaureate
Accreditation: SC

01 President ....Dr. Logan C. HAMPTON
03 Executive Vice President/Chaplain ....Dr. Moses GOLDMON
05 Vice President Academic Affairs ....Dr. Michelle STEWART
10 Vice President Business & Finance ....Mr. Melvin R. HAMLETT
32 Vice President Student Affairs ....Vacant
30 Vice Pres Inst Advance/Dir Alum Aff ..... Mr. Richard H. DONNELL
13 Assoc VP Information Technology ...Mr. Earnest L. MITCHELL, III
04 Exec Assistant to the President .... Ms. Darlette C. SAMUELS
18 Chief Facilities/Physical Plant .... Mr. Michael BATES
26 Chief Public Relations Officer .... Ms. Darlette C. SAMUELS
09 Director Institutional Research .... Ms. Charlise ANDERSON
08 Librarian ....Ms. Lan WANG
07 Director of Admissions ....Ms. Monica SCOTT
06 Registrar ....Mr. Terry W. BLACKMON
37 Director of Financial Aid ....Mr. Tony CALHOUN
20 Director Academic Assessment ....Dr. Juanita MORRIS
84 Director Enrollment Management ....Dr. Monica CLAYBORNE-SCOTT
89 Director of Freshman Studies ....Vacant
96 Director of Purchasing ....Ms. Troneka DUNLAP
36 Director Placement Services ....Ms. Virginia S. CRUMP
15 Director of Personnel ....Ms. Juanita MARSHALL
19 Director Security ....Mr. Ernest BOYD
40 Director Bookstore ....Mr. Jeremy MORRIS
19 Director of Safety ....Ms. Aleshia COX-THOMPSON
20 Associate Academic Officer ....Vacant
21 Associate Business Officer ....Mr. Duan ROBINSON

41 Director of Athletics .... Mr. Derrick BURROUGHS
29 Director Alumni Relations .... Ms. Tori HALIBURTON
35 Dean of Students .... Mr. William SMITH, III
27 Chief Information Officer .... Vacant
38 Director Student Counseling .... Dr. April SMITH

L'Ecole Culinaire Memphis (A)

1245 North Germantown Parkway, Cordova TN 38016
Telephone: (901) 754-7115 Identification: 770841
Accreditation: ACCSC

† Branch campus of Vatterott College-Des Moines, Des Moines, IA

Lee University (B)

1120 N Ocoee Street, Cleveland TN 37320-3450
County: Bradley FICE Identification: 003500
Unit ID: 220613
Telephone: (423) 614-8000 Carnegie Class: Masters/M
FAX Number: (423) 614-8083 Calendar System: Semester
URL: www.leeuniversity.edu
Established: 1918 Annual Undergrad Tuition & Fees: $15,000
Enrollment: 4,965 Coed
Affiliation or Control: Church Of God IRS Status: 501(c)3
Highest Offering: Beyond Master's But Less Than Doctorate
Accreditation: SC, ACBSP, CAATE, MFCD, MUS, NURSE, TED

01 President .... Dr. C. Paul CONN
04 Executive Assistant to President .... Mrs. Stephanie TAYLOR
10 Vice President Business & Finance .... Mr. Chris CONINE
05 Vice President for Academic Affairs .... Dr. Deborah MURRAY
84 Vice President for Enrollment .... Mr. Phil COOK
26 VP for University Relations .... Dr. Jerome HAMMOND
32 VP for Student Development .... Dr. Mike HAYES
13 VP for Information Services .... Dr. Jayson VANHOOK
20 Assistant VP for Academic Affairs .... Dr. Eric MOYEN
11 Assistant VP for Operations .... Mr. Cole STRONG
21 Comptroller .... Mr. Duane PACE
37 Director of Financial Aid .... Mrs. Marian DILL
35 Dean of Students .... Mr. Alan MCCLUNG
15 Director of Human Resources .... Mrs. Ann MCELRATH
14 Director of IT Operations .... Mr. Chris GOLDEN
14 Director of IT Systems .... Mr. Nate TUCKER
29 Director of Alumni Relations .... Mrs. Patti CAWOOD
39 Director of Residential Life .... Vacant
06 Registrar .... Ms. Cathy THOMPSOM
21 Bursar .... Ms. Kristy HARNER
08 Librarian .... Dr. Louis MORGAN
42 Director of Campus Ministries .... Rev. Jimmy HARPER
25 Director of Grants .... Mrs. Vanessa HAMMOND
19 Director of Campus Safety .... Mr. Matt BRINKMAN
23 Director of Health Services .... Mr. Mickey MOORE
27 Director of Public Information .... Mr. Brian CONN
73 Dean School of Religion .... Dr. Terry CROSS
49 Dean College of Arts & Sciences .... Dr. Matthew MELTON
53 Dean College of Education .... Dr. William ESTES
64 Dean School of Music .... Dr. William GREEN
66 Dean School of Nursing .... Dr. Sara CAMPBELL
51 Exec Dir of Div of Adult Learning .... Dr. Joshua BLACK
07 Director of Graduate Enrollment .... Vacant
38 Director Counseling & Testing .... Dr. David QUAGLIANA
18 Director of Physical Plant .... Mr. Larry BERRY
41 Athletic Director .... Mr. Larry CARPENTER
104 Director of Global Perspectives .... Mrs. Angeline MCMULLIN
36 Director of Calling and Career .... Dr. Sheila CORNEA
07 Director of Admissions .... Mr. Darren ECHOLS
09 Director of Institutional Research .... Dr. Stacey TUCKER

LeMoyne-Owen College (C)

807 Walker Avenue, Memphis TN 38126-6595
County: Shelby FICE Identification: 003501
Unit ID: 220604
Telephone: (901) 435-1000 Carnegie Class: Bac-Diverse
FAX Number: (901) 435-1699 Calendar System: Semester
URL: www.loc.edu
Established: 1862 Annual Undergrad Tuition & Fees: $10,680
Enrollment: 1,006 Coed
Affiliation or Control: Multiple Protestant Denominations
IRS Status: 501(c)3
Highest Offering: Baccalaureate
Accreditation: SC, TED

01 President .... Dr. Andrea LEWIS MILLER
05 VP Academic and Student Affairs .... Dr. Alfred HALL
10 VP Finance and Administration .... Ms. Loretta STUBBS
88 Director Title III Administration .... Ms. Shirley HILL
32 Dean of Students .... Mr. Kenneth QUINN
30 VP Institutional Advancement .... Vacant
84 Exec Dir Strategic Enrollment Mgmt .... Dr. Delphia HARRIS
15 Director of Human Resources .... Ms. Neva BURKE
08 Librarian .... Ms. Annette BERHE
37 Director Student Financial Services .... Ms. Phyllis TORRY
06 Registrar .... Mr. Addie HARVEY
100 Chief of Staff .... Mr. Mark YATES
29 Director of Alumni Relations .... Ms. Frankie JEFFRIES
21 Controller .... Ms. Colleen GIBSON
09 Director Institutional Research .... Mr. Reoungenria MCFARLAND
92 Director Du Bois Honors Program .... Mr. Dorsey PATTERSON
50 Chair Div Business & Econ Devel .... Dr. Katherine CAUSEY
53 Chair Education Division .... Dr. Ralph CALHOUN
57 Chair Div Fine Arts & Humanities .... Mr. Claybourne FOSTER
65 Chair Div Natural & Math Science .... Dr. Sherry PAINTER
83 Chair Div Social & Behavioral Sci .... Mr. Michael ROBINSON
38 Director Student Counseling .... Mr. Tony WHITSON
26 Dir Public Relations & Marketing .... Ms. Daphne J. THOMAS
41 Director of Athletics .... Mr. Clint JACKSON
11 Director Administrative Services .... Mr. Jesse CHATMAN
88 Exec Director Engaged Student Learn .... Dr. Linda WHITE
07 Director of Admissions .... Mr. Samuel KING
04 Administrative Asst to President .... Ms. Velma GRAY
18 Chief Facilities/Physical Plant .... Mr. Anthony COWAN
39 Director Student Housing .... Ms. Carolyn BISHOP
25 Grant Writer .... Ms. Michelle COWAN

Lincoln College of Technology Nashville (D)

1524 Gallatin Road, Nashville TN 37206-3298
County: Davidson FICE Identification: 007440
Unit ID: 221148
Telephone: (615) 226-3990 Carnegie Class: Spec 2-yr-Tech
FAX Number: (615) 262-8466 Calendar System: Other
URL: www.lincolncollegeoftechnology.com
Established: 1919 Annual Undergrad Tuition & Fees: N/A
Enrollment: 1,782 Coed
Affiliation or Control: Proprietary IRS Status: Proprietary
Highest Offering: Associate Degree
Accreditation: ACCSC

01 President .... Mr. Jim COAKLEY
05 Academic Dean .... Ms. Jackie RODDY
07 Vice President of Admissions .... Mr. Shayne PULVER
37 Director of Financial Aid .... Mr. Chris BIDDLE
06 Registrar .... Mr. Gary WHITE

Lincoln Memorial University (E)

6965 Cumberland Gap Parkway,
Harrogate TN 37752-1901
County: Claiborne FICE Identification: 003502
Unit ID: 220631
Telephone: (423) 869-3611 Carnegie Class: Masters/L
FAX Number: (423) 869-6250 Calendar System: Semester
URL: www.lmunet.edu
Established: 1897 Annual Undergrad Tuition & Fees: $20,546
Enrollment: 3,735 Coed
Affiliation or Control: Independent Non-Profit IRS Status: 501(c)3
Highest Offering: Doctorate
Accreditation: SC, ACBSP, ADNUR, ANEST, ARCPA, #CAATE, CACREP, #LAW, MT, NUR, OSTEO, SW, TED, @VET

01 President .... Dr. B. James DAWSON
11 VP for Administration .... Ms. Lisa B. COX
30 VP University Advancement .... Ms. Cynthia L. WHITT
05 Provost/Vice Pres for Acad Affairs .... Dr. Clayton HESS
10 Vice President of Finance .... Ms. Christy GRAHAM
61 VP/Dean School of Law .... Judge Gary WADE
84 VP Pres Student Enrollment Svcs .... Dr. James (Chip) WEISGERBER
53 Dean of School of Education .... Dr. Sylvia LYNCH
81 Dean of Mathematics & Sciences .... Dr. Amiel JARSTFER
66 Dean Sch of Nursing/VP Ext Sites .... Dr. Mary Anne MODRCIN
50 Dean School of Business .... Dr. James HURLEY
32 VP of Student/Enrollment Services .... Dr. Jonathan LEO
04 Exec Assistant to the President .... Mrs. Janet SMITH
37 Executive Director of Financial Aid .... Ms. Tammy TOMFOHRDE
09 Director of Institutional Research .... Vacant
41 Athletic Director .... Mr. Matthew GREEN
18 Director Properties/Physical Plant .... Mr. Rodney COCHRAN
15 Director of Human Resources .... Ms. Libby KING
96 Director Purchasing .... Ms. Pat TENNYSON
06 Registrar .... Ms. Helen BAILEY
42 University Chaplain .... Vacant
43 Legal Counsel/VP Public Affairs .... Mr. Mark CUSHING
13 Chief Information Officer .... Mr. Jason MCCONNELL
26 Senior Director of Marketing .... Mrs. Kate M. REAGAN
29 Director Alumni Services .... Ms. Sheliah COSBY
40 Bookstore Manager .... Mr. Nathan ADKINS
49 Dean of Arts/Humanities/Social Sci .... Dr. Martin SELLERS
108 Director of Assessment .... Dr. Travis WRIGHT

Lipscomb University (F)

One University Park Dr., Nashville TN 37204-3951
County: Davidson FICE Identification: 003486
Unit ID: 219976
Telephone: (615) 966-1000 Carnegie Class: DU-Mod
FAX Number: (615) 966-1798 Calendar System: Semester
URL: www.lipscomb.edu
Established: 1891 Annual Undergrad Tuition & Fees: $28,624
Enrollment: 4,489 Coed
Affiliation or Control: Churches Of Christ IRS Status: 501(c)3
Highest Offering: Doctorate
Accreditation: SC, ACBSP, CACREP, DIETD, DIETI, ENG, MUS, NUR, PHAR, SW, TED, THEOL

01 President .... Dr. L. Randolph LOWRY, III
05 Provost .... Dr. W. Craig BLEDSOE
32 Senior VP Student Life .... Dr. Scott MCDOWELL
10 Senior VP Finance & Administration .... Mr. Danny F. TAYLOR
53 Int VP & Dean Col of Education .... Dr. Deborah BOYD
88 VP University Relations .... Mr. Walt LEAVER
29 Vice Pres Alumni Relations .... Mr. Phil ELLENBURG
84 VP Enrollment Management .... Mr. Rick HOLAWAY
86 VP External Affairs .... Dr. John LOWRY
26 Sr VP Communications & Marketing .... Ms. Deby K. SAMUELS
42 Vice President for Church Services .... Dr. Scott SAGER
13 Vice President Info Technology/CIO .... Mr. Mike GREEN
20 Vice Prov Acad Admin & Fin Affairs .... Dr. Susan C. GALBREATH
100 Senior Advisor to the President .... Dr. Jim THOMAS
43 General Counsel .... Dr. David WILSON
30 Senior Development Counsel .... Mr. Dale ARMSTRONG
41 Director of Athletics .... Mr. Philip HUTCHESON
20 Associate Provost Academic Support .... Mr. Steve PREWITT
58 Vice Provost for Grad Studies .... Dr. Randy BOULDIN
88 Assoc Prov for Inst Effectiveness .... Dr. Elaine GRIFFIN
88 Assoc Provost Sponsored Programs .... Vacant
79 Dean College of Arts & Sciences .... Dr. Norma BURGESS
73 Dean College of Bible & Ministry .... Dr. C. Leonard ALLEN
50 Int Dean College of Business .... Dr. Ray ELDRIDGE
81 Dean College of Engineering .... Dr. Justin MYRICK
67 Dean College of Pharmacy .... Dr. Roger DAVIS
107 Int Dean College of Prof Studies .... Dr. Nina MOREL
55 Dean School of Computing/Technology .... Dr. Fortune MHLANGA
66 Exec Assoc Dean Sch of Nursing .... Dr. Beth YOUNGBLOOD
35 Dean of Student Life .... Dr. Sam SMITH
21 Associate VP Finance .... Mr. Darrell DUNCAN
102 Assoc VP Donor Rel & Stewardship .... Mr. David ENGLAND
44 Asst VP Annual Giving & Advanc Svcs .... Mrs. Carrie THOMPSON
06 Registrar .... Ms. Teresa WILLIAMS
37 Director of Financial Aid .... Ms. Tiffany SUMMERS
08 Director of Library Services .... Ms. Sandra PARHAM
19 Dir of Campus Security & Safety .... Mr. Darrin BELLOWS
36 Director of Career Development Ctr .... Mrs. Monica WENTWORTH
88 Senior Director of Student Success .... Dr. Brian MAST
88 Director of Student Advocacy .... Ms. Carla BROOKINS
55 Int Dean Adult Degree Program .... Dr. Nina MOREL
73 Assoc Dir Hazelip Sch of Theology .... Dr. Mark BLACK
88 Dir of Grad Exercise & Nutrit Sci .... Dr. Karen ROBICHAUD
83 Chair Grad Studies in Psychology .... Dr. Shanna RAY
88 Managing Dir Inst for ConflictMgmt .... Dr. Steve JOINER
88 Dir Inst for Christian Spirituality .... Dr. Kris MILLER
88 Dir Inst for Law Justice & Society .... Dr. Randy SPIVEY
88 Found Dir Inst for Civic Leadership .... Ms. Linda SCHACHT
88 Found Dir Inst for Sustain Practice .... Mr. Dodd GALBREATH
88 Director of Global Learning .... Mr. Michael WINEGEART
38 Director Counseling Center .... Dr. Frank SCOTT
88 Senior Campus Minister .... Mr. Steve DAVIDSON
28 Asst Dean Intercultural Development .... Ms. Lisa STEELE
09 Director of Institutional Research .... Mr. Matt REHBEIN
15 Director Human Resources .... Mr. Stan LOWERY
18 Director of Campus Plant .... Mr. Jeff WILSON
96 Director of Procurement .... Ms. Deidra PIATT
105 Director of Information Security .... Mr. Dave WAGNER

Martin Methodist College (G)

433 W Madison Street, Pulaski TN 38478-2799
County: Giles FICE Identification: 003504
Unit ID: 220701
Telephone: (931) 363-9800 Carnegie Class: Bac-Diverse
FAX Number: (931) 363-9818 Calendar System: Semester
URL: www.martinmethodist.edu
Established: 1870 Annual Undergrad Tuition & Fees: $23,200
Enrollment: 1,037 Coed
Affiliation or Control: United Methodist IRS Status: 501(c)3
Highest Offering: Master's
Accreditation: SC, NURSE

01 President .... Dr. Ted R. BROWN
05 Vice President of Academic Affairs .... Dr. Judy B. CHEATHAM
10 VP for Finance & Administration .... Mr. David J. STEPHENS
32 VP Campus Life/Enrollment Mgmt .... Mr. Robby C. SHELTON
30 Vice Pres for College Advancement .... Mr. David JONES
06 Registrar .... Mrs. Casey CAPPS
41 Athletic Director .... Mr. Jeff N. BAIN
42 Chaplain .... Rev. Laura KIRKPATRICK
08 Librarian .... Mr. Richard MADDEN
40 Director of Bookstore .... Mrs. Margaret W. JACKSON
29 Alumni Affairs Director .... Mrs. Edna LUNA
04 Assistant to the President .... Mrs. Kim W. HARRISON
84 VP for Campus Life/Enrollment .... Mr. Robby SHELTON
15 Director Personnel Services .... Mr. James R. HLUBB
21 Controller .... Ms. Rhonda CLINARD
37 Director Student Financial Aid .... Mrs. Emma HLUBB
18 Chief Facilities/Physical Plant .... Mr. Fred HYDE
26 Director of Public Relations .... Ms. Sissy GARNER
38 Dir Student Counseling/Career/Svcs .... Ms. Doris F. WOSSUM
85 Director Foreign Students .... Ms. Robin HOOD
13 Director of Technology .... Mr. Edward MARTIN
09 Director of Institutional Research .... Vacant
11 Chief of Administration .... Ms. Mae SANDERS
19 Director Security/Safety .... Mr. Joe MCNAIRY

Maryville College (H)

502 E Lamar Alexander Parkway,
Maryville TN 37804-5907
County: Blount FICE Identification: 003505
Unit ID: 220710
Telephone: (865) 981-8000 Carnegie Class: Bac-A&S
FAX Number: (865) 981-8010 Calendar System: Semester
URL: www.maryvillecollege.edu
Established: 1819 Annual Undergrad Tuition & Fees: $32,866
Enrollment: 1,213 Coed
Affiliation or Control: Presbyterian Church (U.S.A.) IRS Status: 501(c)3

Highest Offering: Baccalaureate
Accreditation: SC, MUS

01 President ... Dr. William T. BOGART
04 Assistant to President ... Ms. Laura M. CASE
05 Vice President & Dean of College ... Dr. Barbara WELLS
10 VP of Finance & Administration ... Mr. Jeffery S. INGLE
32 Vice President & Dean of Students ... Ms. Vandy KEMP
30 VP for Institutional Advancement ... Ms. Suzy BOOKER
07 Exec Dir Admissions/Fin Aid ... Ms. Cyndi SWEET
26 Exec Dir for Mktg & Communications ... Ms. Karen ELDRIDGE
09 Associate Dean & Dir of IR ... Dr. Martha P. CRAIG
06 Registrar ... Ms. Kathi WILSON
21 Controller ... Ms. Julie RAMSEY
35 Assistant Dean of Students ... Ms. Allison NORRIS
39 Director Campus Life ... Ms. Kristin GOURLEY
85 Director of International Education ... Ms. Kirsten SHEPPARD
13 Director of Information Technology ... Mr. John BERRY
90 Dir of Instructional Technology ... Dr. Steven JAMES
88 Director of Learning Services ... Ms. Kim D. OCHSENBEIN
36 Director of the Career Center ... Ms. Christy MCDONALD
37 Director of Financial Aid ... Ms. Alayne BOWMAN
41 Athletic Director ... Ms. Kandis SCHRAM
08 Director of the Library ... Ms. Angela QUICK
18 Director of Physical Plant ... Mr. Andy K. MCCALL
42 Campus Minister ... Rev. Anne MCKEE
15 Director of Human Resources ... Ms. Keni LANAGAN
38 Director of Counseling ... Mr. Bruce HOLT
88 Director of Development ... Mr. Eric BELLAH
88 Asst Director of Maryville Fund ... Ms. Meghan FAGG
29 Dir of Alumni Affairs & Stewardship ... Ms. Angela MILLER
44 Director of Major Gifts ... Ms. Diana CANACARIS
22 Director of Multicultural Affairs ... Mr. Larry ERVIN
40 Bookstore Manager ... Mr. Jeff HUFFMAN
88 Gen Mgr Clayton Center for the Arts ... Mr. Blake SMITH
19 Director of Safety & Security ... Mr. Jack PIEPENBRING

Meharry Medical College (A)

1005 Dr. D. B. Todd Jr. Boulevard,
Nashville TN 37208-3501
County: Davidson | FICE Identification: 003506 | Unit ID: 220792
Telephone: (615) 327-6111 | Carnegie Class: Spec-4-yr-Med
FAX Number: (615) 327-6540 | Calendar System: Semester
URL: www.mmc.edu
Established: 1876 | Annual Graduate Tuition & Fees: N/A
Enrollment: 802 | Coed
Affiliation or Control: Independent Non-Profit | IRS Status: 501(c)3
Highest Offering: Doctorate; No Undergraduates
Accreditation: SC, DENT, MED, PH

01 President/Chief Executive Ofcr ... Dr. James E.K HILDRETH
63 Sr VP Health/Dean Sch of Medicine ... Dr. Marquetta FAULKNER
10 Sr Vice Pres Administration ... Dr. Soletta HOLLOWAY
26 SVP Marketing/Communications ... Ms. Janet CALDWELL
10 Sr Vice President Finance/CFO ... Mrs. LaMel BANDY-NEAL
35 Sr Vice Pres Student Affairs ... Dr. A. Dexter SAMUELS
45 Vice President for Research ... Dr. Russell POLAND
30 VP Development/Faculty Affairs ... Dr. Patricia MATTHEWS-JUAREZ
31 Asst VP External Affairs ... Mr. Lawrence HALL, JR.
13 Assoc VP Information Technology ... Mr. Andrew JACKSON
15 Assoc Vice Pres Human Resources ... Mr. Mark SMITH
21 Assoc Vice Pres Financial Systems ... Mr. Larry HOLDEN
46 Assoc VP for Research-Grants Mgmt ... Vacant
44 Assoc VP Development ... Mrs. Linda WITT
25 Asst Vice Pres Grants & Contracts ... Mr. George WILLIAMS
43 SVP General Counsel/Corp Sec/Sr VP ... Mrs. Ivanetta DAVIS-SAMUELS
58 Dean Graduate Studies and Research ... Dr. Maria DE FATIMA LIMA
32 Int Assoc Dean Student/Academic Aff ... Dr. Mildred D. COLLINS
51 Director Lifelong Learning ... Dr. Allyson FLEMING
76 Dean Allied Health Professions ... Vacant
52 Dean School of Dentistry ... Dr. Cherae FARMER-DIXON
29 Executive Director Alumni Affairs ... Dr. Henry MOSES
07 Int Dir Admissions & Recruitment ... Dr. Allyson F. FLEMING
08 Director of Library ... Dr. Fatima MNCUBE-BARNES
19 Director Campus Safety & Security ... Ms. Theresa MCKINNON
37 Director Student Financial Aid ... Ms. Barbara THARPE
09 Director Institutional Research ... Dr. Chau-Kuang CHEN
100 Chief of Staff ... Mrs. Sandra ANDERSON-WILLIAMS
18 Director Facilities ... Mr. George N. KELLY
38 Director Counseling Center ... Ms. Sharda D. MISHRA
06 Registrar ... Ms. Sonja COGGINS VIENTOS
45 Dir Inst Effectiveness & Planning ... Dr. Juanita BUFORD

Memphis College of Art (B)

1930 Poplar Avenue, Memphis TN 38104
County: Shelby | FICE Identification: 003507 | Unit ID: 220808
Telephone: (901) 272-5100 | Carnegie Class: Spec-4-yr-Arts
FAX Number: (901) 272-5104 | Calendar System: Semester
URL: www.mca.edu
Established: 1936 | Annual Undergrad Tuition & Fees: $30,250
Enrollment: 435 | Coed
Affiliation or Control: Independent Non-Profit | IRS Status: 501(c)3
Highest Offering: Master's
Accreditation: SC, ART

01 President ... Dr. Ronald L. JONES
05 Dean & VP Academic Affairs ... Mr. Remy MILLER
10 VP Operation/Chf Financial Ofcr ... Mr. George NINAN
30 Vice President Advancement ... Ms. Laura HINE
32 Vice President Student Affairs ... Ms. Susan S. MILLER
26 Vice Pres Communications/Mrktng ... Ms. Carrie CORBETT
21 Assoc Vice Pres for Operations ... Mr. Jonathan WELDEN
08 Librarian ... Mr. Derrick CASEY
04 Assistant to President ... Ms. Anne BALLAM
07 Dean of Admissions ... Ms. Annette JAMES-MOORE
35 Director Student Life ... Ms. Nicholous DARMSTAEDTER
37 Director Financial Aid ... Mr. Aaron WHITE
06 Registrar ... Ms. Erica SIMPSON
36 Director Career Development ... Ms. Carrie Allison BROOKS
19 Director Campus Security ... Vacant
109 Business Office Manager ... Ms. Heather RAGLAND
31 Director Community Education ... Ms. Cecelia PALAZOLA

Memphis Theological Seminary (C)

168 East Parkway S at Union, Memphis TN 38104-4395
County: Shelby | FICE Identification: 010529 | Unit ID: 220871
Telephone: (901) 458-8232 | Carnegie Class: Spec-4-yr-Faith
FAX Number: (901) 452-4051 | Calendar System: Semester
URL: www.memphisseminary.edu
Established: 1852 | Annual Graduate Tuition & Fees: N/A
Enrollment: 279 | Coed
Affiliation or Control: Cumberland Presbyterian | IRS Status: 501(c)3
Highest Offering: Doctorate; No Undergraduates
Accreditation: SC, THEOL

01 President ... Dr. Daniel J. EARHEART-BROWN
05 Vice President Academic Affs & Dean ... Dr. Robert S. WOOD
30 Vice President of Advancement ... Dr. Keith GASKIN
08 Librarian ... Ms. Jane K. WILLIAMSON
51 Assoc Dean Continuing Education ... Mr. Pete GATHJE
10 Vice President of Operations/ CFO ... Mrs. Cassandra F. PRICE-PERRY
32 Director of Student Services ... Dr. Barry L. ANDERSON
108 Assoc Dean Inst Effectiveness ... Dr. Gail ROBINSON
06 Dir Acad Rec/Regist & Accreditation ... Dr. Gail D. ROBINSON
26 Communications Coordinator ... Ms. Felecia DONELSON

Meridian Institute of Surgical Assisting (D)

1507 County Hospital Road, Nashville TN 37218
County: Davidson | FICE Identification: 041650 | Unit ID: 461324
Telephone: (877) 954-1500 | Carnegie Class: Not Classified
FAX Number: (615) 746-6765 | Calendar System: Semester
URL: www.meridian-institute.edu
Established: 1999 | Annual Undergrad Tuition & Fees: N/A
Enrollment: 383 | Coed
Affiliation or Control: Proprietary | IRS Status: Proprietary
Highest Offering: Associate Degree
Accreditation: ABHES, SURGA

01 President ... Mr. Dennis STOVER

Mid-America Baptist Theological Seminary (E)

2095 Appling Road, Cordova TN 38016-4911
County: Shelby | FICE Identification: 029172 | Unit ID: 220914
Telephone: (901) 751-8453 | Carnegie Class: Not Classified
FAX Number: (901) 751-8454 | Calendar System: Semester
URL: www.mabts.edu
Established: 1972 | Annual Undergrad Tuition & Fees: N/A
Enrollment: N/A | Coed
Affiliation or Control: Independent Non-Profit | IRS Status: 501(c)3
Highest Offering: Doctorate
Accreditation: SC

01 President ... Dr. Michael R. SPRADLIN
03 Executive Vice President ... Dr. Bradley THOMPSON
05 Academic Vice President ... Dr. Timothy SEAL
10 Vice Pres for Finance & Operations ... Mr. Randy REDD
30 Chief Development Officer ... Mr. Duffy GUYTON
20 Dean of Masters & Associate Pgm ... Dr. Kirk KILPATRICK
12 Director NE Branch ... Dr. Michael HAGGARD
06 Registrar ... Mrs. Rose MINK
08 Director of Library Services ... Mr. Terrence BROWN
42 Director of Practical Missions ... Dr. Kirk KILPATRICK
07 Director of Admissions ... Dr. Tanner HICKMAN
04 Admin Assistant to the President ... Mrs. Maria WOOTEN
18 Supt of Buildings & Grounds ... Mr. Gene APPLEBURY
40 Manager Bookstore ... Mr. David FOUST

Mid-South Christian College (F)

PO Box 181056, Memphis TN 38181
County: Shelby | Identification: 667046 | Unit ID: 481225
Telephone: (901) 375-4400 | Carnegie Class: Spec-4-yr-Faith
FAX Number: (901) 375-4085 | Calendar System: Semester
URL: www.midsouthchristian.edu
Established: 1959 | Annual Undergrad Tuition & Fees: $5,018
Enrollment: 21 | Coed
Affiliation or Control: Independent Non-Profit | IRS Status: 501(c)3
Highest Offering: Baccalaureate
Accreditation: BI

01 President ... Mr. Larry GRIFFIN
05 Academic Dean ... Dr. Robert GRIFFIN
32 Director of Student Services ... Mr. Brent LINN
04 Executive Assistant ... Mrs. Jane GIBSON
06 Registrar ... Mr. Keith GRAHAM
08 Head Librarian ... Mrs. Judi HOMAN
10 Business Manager ... Mrs. Renae MASK
37 Director Student Financial Aid ... Mrs. Mary JACKSON

Middle Tennessee School of Anesthesia (G)

PO Box 417, 315 Hospital Drive, Madison TN 37116-6414
County: Davidson | FICE Identification: 007783 | Unit ID: 220996
Telephone: (615) 868-6503 | Carnegie Class: Spec-4-yr-Other Health
FAX Number: (615) 868-9885 | Calendar System: Quarter
URL: www.mtsa.edu
Established: 1950 | Annual Graduate Tuition & Fees: N/A
Enrollment: 141 | Coed
Affiliation or Control: Independent Non-Profit | IRS Status: 501(c)3
Highest Offering: Doctorate; No Undergraduates
Accreditation: SC, ANEST

01 President ... Dr. Christopher P. HULIN
05 Dean ... Dr. Mana OVERSTREET
10 VP for Finance & Administration ... Sam L. MINTEN
30 VP for Advancement & Alumni ... James B. CLOSSER
20 Program Administrator ... Dr. Rachel M. BROWN
88 Dir of Inst Effectiveness & LR ... Dr. Amy C. GIDEON
07 Coord Admissions/Recruitment ... Pam NIMMO

Miller-Motte Technical College (H)

6397 Lee Highway, Suite 100, Chattanooga TN 37421
Telephone: (423) 510-9675 | Identification: 770781
Accreditation: ACICS, MAC, SURGT

Miller-Motte Technical College (I)

1820 Business Park Drive, Clarksville TN 37040-6023
County: Montgomery | FICE Identification: 026142 | Unit ID: 382771
Telephone: (931) 553-0071 | Carnegie Class: Spec 2-yr-Health
FAX Number: (931) 552-2916 | Calendar System: Quarter
URL: www.miller-motte.edu
Established: 1916 | Annual Undergrad Tuition & Fees: $9,800
Enrollment: 404 | Coed
Affiliation or Control: Proprietary | IRS Status: Proprietary
Highest Offering: Associate Degree
Accreditation: ACICS, #COARC, MAC, POLYT, SURGT

01 Campus Director ... Ms. Kala FIELDER
05 Director of Education ... Ms. Shannon MANZELLA
37 Financial Aid Director ... Ms. Debbie STRATMAN
36 Director of Career Development ... Mr. John MCCASLIN
07 Director of Admissions ... Ms. Gail MASSEY

Miller-Motte Technical College (J)

1515 North Gallatin Pike, Madison TN 37115
Telephone: (615) 859-8090 | Identification: 770782
Accreditation: ACICS

Milligan College (K)

2010 Milligan College PO Box 500,
Milligan College TN 37682-4000
County: Carter | FICE Identification: 003511 | Unit ID: 221014
Telephone: (423) 461-8700 | Carnegie Class: Masters/S
FAX Number: (423) 461-8755 | Calendar System: Semester
URL: www.milligan.edu
Established: 1866 | Annual Undergrad Tuition & Fees: N/A
Enrollment: 1,164 | Coed
Affiliation or Control: Independent Non-Profit | IRS Status: 501(c)3
Highest Offering: Doctorate
Accreditation: SC, NURSE, OT, TED, THEOL

01 President ... Dr. William B. GREER
05 Vice Pres Academic Affairs/Dean ... Dr. Garland YOUNG
32 Vice Pres Athletics & Student Dev ... Mr. Mark FOX
30 Vice Pres Institutional Advancement ... Mr. Jack SIMPSON
84 Vice Pres Enrollment Management ... Dr. Lee HARRISON
10 Vice Pres Business & Finance ... Mrs. Jacqui STEADMAN
06 Registrar/Assoc Dean ... Mrs. Sue SKIDMORE
07 Director of Admissions ... Ms. Kristin WRIGHT
08 Director of Library Services ... Mr. Gary DAUGHT
35 Director of Student Activities ... Mr. Jason ONKS
29 Director of Alumni Relations ... Ms. Theresa GARBE
15 Director Personnel Services ... Ms. Donna GRIFFITH
09 Director of Institutional Research ... Ms. Cindy WYMER
37 Coordinator of Financial Aid ... Ms. Diane KEASLING
26 Director of Church Relations ... Mrs. Phyllis FOX
36 Director Student Placement ... Ms. Beth ANDERSON
18 Service Manager Facilities ... Mr. Ken BROYLES
28 Director of Diversity ... Mr. Jeff SMITH
27 Dir of Public Relations/Marketing ... Ms. Chandrea SHELL

National College (A)
5760 Stage Road, Bartlett TN 38134
Telephone: (901) 213-1681 Identification: 770783
Accreditation: ACICS, MAC

National College (B)
900 Madison Square, Madison TN 37115
Telephone: (615) 612-3015 Identification: 770784
Accreditation: ACICS, CAHIIM, MAC

National College (C)
2526 Thousand Oaks Cove, Memphis TN 38118
Telephone: (901) 363-9046 Identification: 770785
Accreditation: ACICS, CAHIIM, MAC

National College (D)
1638 Bell Road, Nashville TN 37211
County: Davidson FICE Identification: 004617
Unit ID: 388043
Telephone: (615) 333-3344 Carnegie Class: Assoc/HVT-High Non
FAX Number: (615) 333-3429 Calendar System: Quarter
URL: www.national-college.edu
Established: 1991 Annual Undergrad Tuition & Fees: $11,466
Enrollment: 517 Coed
Affiliation or Control: Proprietary IRS Status: Proprietary
Highest Offering: Baccalaureate
Accreditation: ACICS, MAC

01 Director .... Ms. Debra TOLLADAY

North Central Institute (E)
168 Jack Miller Boulevard, Clarksville TN 37042-4810
County: Montgomery FICE Identification: 030791
Unit ID: 418889
Telephone: (931) 431-9700 Carnegie Class: Spec 2-yr-Tech
FAX Number: (931) 431-9771 Calendar System: Semester
URL: www.nci.edu
Established: 1988 Annual Undergrad Tuition & Fees: N/A
Enrollment: 102 Coed
Affiliation or Control: Proprietary IRS Status: Proprietary
Highest Offering: Associate Degree
Accreditation: COE

01 President .... Tamela K. TALIENTO
06 Registrar .... Michelle HARTSON
07 Director of Admissions .... Dale WOOD

Nossi College of Art (F)
590 Cheron Road, Nashville TN 37115
County: Davidson FICE Identification: 025782
Unit ID: 368452
Telephone: (615) 514-2787 Carnegie Class: Spec-4-yr-Arts
FAX Number: (615) 514-2788 Calendar System: Trimester
URL: www.nossi.edu
Established: 1973 Annual Undergrad Tuition & Fees: $17,800
Enrollment: 261 Coed
Affiliation or Control: Proprietary IRS Status: Proprietary
Highest Offering: Baccalaureate
Accreditation: ACCSC

01 President .... Ms. Nossi VATANDOOST
03 Executive Vice President .... Mr. Cyrus VATANDOOST
05 Vice President for Academic Affairs .... Dr. Byron EDWARDS
07 Admissions Director .... Ms. Mary ALEXANDER
37 Financial Aid Director .... Ms. Mary KIDD
06 Registrar .... Mrs. Mindy GILBERT
08 Head Librarian .... Mrs. Kolleen LONGMIRE
26 Chief Public Relations/Marketing .... Mrs. Libby LUFF
10 Business Office Manager .... Mrs. Kristi BINKLEY
32 Chief Student Affairs/Student Life .... Ms. Libby FUNKE-LUFF
36 Director Student Placement .... Mr. Dax GOMEZ

O'More College of Design (G)
423 S Margin Street, Franklin TN 37064
County: Williamson FICE Identification: 021064
Unit ID: 221254
Telephone: (615) 794-4254 Carnegie Class: Spec-4-yr-Arts
FAX Number: (615) 790-1662 Calendar System: Semester
URL: www.omorecollege.edu
Established: 1970 Annual Undergrad Tuition & Fees: $27,360
Enrollment: 172 Coed
Affiliation or Control: Independent Non-Profit IRS Status: 501(c)3
Highest Offering: Baccalaureate
Accreditation: ACCSC, CIDA

01 President .... Dr. David ROSEN
30 Director of Development & Marketing .... Ms. Amy SHELTON
10 Controller .... Ms. Rena MAHAFFEY
19 Director of Security .... Mr. DeWayne PULLIAM
07 Director of Admissions .... Ms. Tori BAGSBY
08 Director of Information Resources .... Ms. Nicole FOX
88 Chair School of Fashion .... Ms. Jamie ATLAS
88 Chair School of Interior Design .... Ms. Kelly GORE
88 Chair School of Interior Design .... Ms. Rebecca ANDREWS
88 Chair School of Visual Design .... Ms. Jess SMITH
32 Director of Student Affairs .... Ms. Jamie SHAFFER
18 Director of Facilities .... Mr. Jimmy FOX
06 Registrar .... Ms. Lauren RICHERT
04 Executive Assistant .... Ms. Emily KYNERD
10 Director of Finance & Admin .... Ms. Lea VOIGT
37 Financial Aid Coordinator .... Ms. Sara MARTIN

Oxford Graduate School (H)
500 Oxford Drive, Dayton TN 37321-6736
County: Rhea FICE Identification: 038403
Unit ID: 461120
Telephone: (423) 775-6596 Carnegie Class: Spec-4-yr-Faith
FAX Number: (423) 775-6599 Calendar System: Semester
URL: www.ogs.edu
Established: 1981 Annual Graduate Tuition & Fees: N/A
Enrollment: 88 Coed
Affiliation or Control: Independent Non-Profit IRS Status: 501(c)3
Highest Offering: Doctorate; No Undergraduates
Accreditation: TRACS

01 President .... Dr. Kimberly GEIGER
00 Chancellor .... Dr. Rollin VAN BROEKHOVEN
05 Dean of Faculty .... Dr. Robert ANDREWS
11 Vice President of Administration .... Dr. Paul LAWHORN
07 Director of Admissions & Phys Opers .... Dr. Gwen BOLLANT
108 Institutional Assessment Officer .... Dr. Joshua REICHARD
10 Business Officer .... Ms. Sharlene DANIEL
29 Director Alumni Relations .... Dr. Bonnie LIBHART
42 Chaplain .... Dr. David WARD
06 Registrar .... Dr. Paul LAWHORN

Pentecostal Theological Seminary (I)
900 Walker Street, NE, Cleveland TN 37311
County: Bradley FICE Identification: 021883
Unit ID: 219842
Telephone: (423) 478-1131 Carnegie Class: Spec-4-yr-Faith
FAX Number: (423) 478-7711 Calendar System: 4/1/4
URL: www.ptseminary.edu
Established: 1975 Annual Graduate Tuition & Fees: N/A
Enrollment: 244 Coed
Affiliation or Control: Church Of God IRS Status: 501(c)3
Highest Offering: Doctorate; No Undergraduates
Accreditation: SC, THEOL

01 President .... Dr. Michael L. BAKER
05 VP for Academics .... Dr. David S. HAN
42 VP for Inst Effect/Accreditation .... Dr. Oliver L. MCMAHAN
10 Director of Finance .... Mr. Caleb PEACOCK
30 VP for Institutional Advancement .... Rev. Ken R. DAVIS
04 Exec Assistant to the President .... Mrs. Teresa GILBERT
84 Senior Director of Enrollment .... Dr. Weltor WRISTON
06 Director of Acad Records/Registrar .... Ms. Anita F. BLEVINS
15 Dir Admin Svcs & Donor/Alumni Rels .... Rev. Joylita W. TERPSTRA
18 Dir of Facilities/Support Services .... Mr. Phillip WOODS
32 Coordinator of Student Services .... Rev. Florentin GHITA
37 Director of Financial Aid .... Mrs. Robin SLUDER
07 Director of Admissions .... Ms. Regina TOWLES WILHELM

Remington College (J)
2710 Nonconnah Boulevard, Memphis TN 38132-2110
Telephone: (901) 345-1000 Identification: 666062
Accreditation: ACCSC

† Branch campus of Remington College, Mobile, AL.

Remington College (K)
441 Donelson Pike, Suite 150, Nashville TN 37214-3558
Telephone: (615) 889-5520 Identification: 666307
Accreditation: ACCSC, DH

† Branch campus of Remington College, Mobile, AL.

Rhodes College (L)
2000 North Parkway, Memphis TN 38112-1690
County: Shelby FICE Identification: 003519
Unit ID: 221351
Telephone: (901) 843-3000 Carnegie Class: Bac-A&S
FAX Number: N/A Calendar System: Semester
URL: www.rhodes.edu
Established: 1848 Annual Undergrad Tuition & Fees: $43,224
Enrollment: 2,054 Coed
Affiliation or Control: Presbyterian Church (U.S.A.) IRS Status: 501(c)3
Highest Offering: Master's
Accreditation: SC, MUS

01 President .... Dr. William E. TROUTT
05 Dean of Academic Affairs .... Dr. Milton MORELAND
10 VP for Finance & Business Affairs .... Mr. Kyle WEBB
13 Vice Pres for Information Services .... Dr. Robert M. JOHNSON, JR.
30 Vice President for Development .... Ms. Jennifer G. WADE
84 Vice Pres Enrollment/Communications .... Mr. Carey THOMPSON
32 Dean of Students .... Ms. Carol E. CASEY
35 Associate Dean of Students .... Ms. Kathleen LAAKSO
20 Assoc Dean of Academic Affairs .... Dr. Brian W. SHAFFER
28 Assoc Dean of Diversity & Inclusion .... Dr. Nicole CHADDOCK
20 Assoc Dean of Academic Affairs .... Dr. Michelle MATTSON
06 Registrar .... Ms. DeAnna ADAMS
37 Director of Financial Aid .... Mr. Michael MORGAN
08 Director of Library .... Ms. Darlene D. BROOKS
29 Director of Alumni Relations .... Ms. Tracy PATTERSON
15 Director of Human Resources .... Ms. Claire R. SHAPIRO
14 Director of Info Tech Services .... Mr. Richard TRENTHEM
19 Director of Campus Safety .... Mr. Ike SLOAS
41 Director of Athletics .... Mr. Jeff CLEANTHES
36 Director of Career Services .... Ms. Sandra G. TRACY
38 Director of Counseling Services .... Mr. Robert B. DOVE
18 Director of Physical Plant .... Mr. Brian E. FOSHEE
44 Director of Planned Giving .... Mr. Jim DUNCAN
26 Director of Communications .... Mr. Ken WOODMANSEE
09 Director of Institutional Research .... Ms. Dawn CLEMENT CORNIES
04 Exec Assistant to the President .... Ms. Melody H. RICHEY
07 Director of Admissions .... Mr. Jeffery NORRIS

Richmont Graduate University (M)
1815 McCallie Avenue, Chattanooga TN 37404
County: Hamilton FICE Identification: 033554
Unit ID: 441104
Telephone: (423) 266-4574 Carnegie Class: Spec-4-yr-Other Health
FAX Number: (423) 265-7375 Calendar System: Semester
URL: www.richmont.edu
Established: 1933 Annual Graduate Tuition & Fees: N/A
Enrollment: 260 Coed
Affiliation or Control: Independent Non-Profit IRS Status: 501(c)3
Highest Offering: Master's; No Undergraduates
Accreditation: SC, CACREP

01 President .... Mr. Bob RODGERS, JR.
05 Academic Dean/Dean Sch Counseling .... Dr. Stephen BRADSHAW
10 VP of Finance .... Mr. Tim MCPHERSON
13 VP of Information Technology .... Mr. Darwin BLANDON
07 Assoc VP of Enrollment Management .... Ms. Roxanne SHELLABARGER
32 Dean of Students .... Dr. Amanda BLACKBURN
73 Dean School of Ministry .... Dr. Michael STEWART
88 Dean of Clinical Affairs .... Dr. Vanessa SNYDER
04 Assistant to the President .... Ms. Sarah GOFF

SAE Institute Nashville (N)
7 Music Circle North, Nashville TN 37203
County: Davidson FICE Identification: 038303
Unit ID: 446525
Telephone: (615) 244-5848 Carnegie Class: Assoc/HVT-High Trad
FAX Number: (615) 244-3192 Calendar System: Semester
URL: nashville.sae.edu
Established: 1976 Annual Undergrad Tuition & Fees: $18,731
Enrollment: 143 Coed
Affiliation or Control: Proprietary IRS Status: Proprietary
Highest Offering: Associate Degree
Accreditation: ACCSC, ACICS

01 Director .... Ms. Lynn DORTON

Sewanee: The University of the South (O)
735 University Avenue, Sewanee TN 37383-1000
County: Franklin FICE Identification: 003534
Unit ID: 221519
Telephone: (931) 598-1000 Carnegie Class: Bac-A&S
FAX Number: (931) 598-1145 Calendar System: Semester
URL: www.sewanee.edu
Established: 1857 Annual Undergrad Tuition & Fees: $38,700
Enrollment: 1,714 Coed
Affiliation or Control: Protestant Episcopal IRS Status: 501(c)3
Highest Offering: Doctorate
Accreditation: SC, THEOL

01 Vice Chancellor & President .... Dr. John M. MCCARDELL, JR.
05 Executive Vice President & Provost .... Dr. John R. SWALLOW
30 Vice President for Advancement .... Mr. Jay FISHER
11 Vice President for Admin Svcs .... Mr. Frank GLADU
45 Vice Provost for Planning and Admin .... Dr. Nancy BERNER
88 Vice President Risk Management .... Mr. Eric HARTMAN
13 Assoc Provost Info Tech/Librarian .... Dr. Vicki G. SELLS
49 Dean College of Arts & Sciences .... Dr. Terry L. PAPILLON
73 Dean School of Theology .... Rt Rev. J. Neil ALEXANDER
32 Dean of Students .... Dr. Marichal GENTRY
09 Asst Dir of Inst Research .... Ms. Sarah STAPLETON
06 Assistant Provost for Academic Svcs .... Mr. Paul G. WILEY
07 Dean of Admission & Financial Aid .... Ms. Lee Ann M. BACKLUND
37 Assoc Dean Student Financial Aid .... Ms. Beth CRAGAR
20 Associate Dean for Academic Affairs .... Dr. Alex M. BRUCE
26 Exec Dir Marketing/Communications .... Mr. Parker OLIVER
15 Director of Human Resources .... Ms. Mary WILSON
41 Director of Athletics .... Mr. Mark F. WEBB
29 Director of Alumni Relations .... Ms. Susan S. ASKEW
36 Director of Career Services .... Ms. Kim D. HEITZENRATER
38 Director of Wellness Center .... Dr. Nicole NOFFSINGER-FRAZIER
93 Director of Minority Affairs .... Mr. Eric V. BENJAMIN
18 Director of Physical Plant Services .... Mr. Michael D. GARDNER
43 University Legal Counsel .... Ms. Donna L. PIERCE
19 Chief of Police .... Ms. Marie ELDRIDGE
10 Treasurer .... Dr. Douglass WILLIAMS

23 Director of Univ Health Services ....Ms. Karen THARP
24 Director of Media Services ....Mr. Larry E. WOOD
42 University Chaplain & Dean ....VRev. Thomas E. MACFIE
28 Assoc Dean Fac Dev & Inclu ....Dr. Elizabeth SKOMP
104 Assoc Dean of Global Education ....Dr. Scott WILSON

South College (A)

3904 Lonas Drive, Knoxville TN 37909-3323
County: Knox FICE Identification: 004938
Unit ID: 220552
Telephone: (865) 251-1800 Carnegie Class: Masters/S
FAX Number: (865) 584-7335 Calendar System: Quarter
URL: www.southcollegetn.edu
Established: 1882 Annual Undergrad Tuition & Fees: $19,425
Enrollment: 1,241 Coed
Affiliation or Control: Proprietary IRS Status: Proprietary
Highest Offering: Doctorate
Accreditation: SC, ARCPA, DMS, MAC, NMT, NUR, OTA, PHAR, @PTA, PTAA, RAD, SURGT

01 President ....Mr. Stephen A. SOUTH
05 Executive VP and Provost ....Dr. Kim B. HALL
32 VP Acad Supp & Student Services ....Dr. Stacy WADDELL
84 VP Enrollment Management ....Mr. Walter HOSEA
13 VP Information Tech/Facilities ....Mr. Ron HALL
86 VP Admin & Regulatory Compliance ....Mr. Steve WOODFORD
108 Director of Inst Effectiveness ....Dr. Lisa SATTERFIELD
08 Head Librarian ....Ms. Anya MCKINNEY
10 Chief Financial Officer ....Mr. Brad ADAMS
06 Registrar ....Ms. Kim WOOD
36 Career Services Coordinator ....Mr. Gary TAYLOR
37 Sr Director of Financial Aid ....Mr. Larry BROADWATER
72 Director Instructional Technology .....Mr. Derrick MACGILLIVRAY
07 Director for Admissions ....Ms. Carrie MAJOR

Southern Adventist University (B)

Box 370, 5010 University Drive,
Collegedale TN 37315-0370
County: Hamilton FICE Identification: 003518
Unit ID: 221661
Telephone: (423) 236-2000 Carnegie Class: Masters/M
FAX Number: (423) 236-1000 Calendar System: Semester
URL: www.southern.edu
Established: 1892 Annual Undergrad Tuition & Fees: $20,650
Enrollment: 3,175 Coed
Affiliation or Control: Seventh-day Adventist IRS Status: 501(c)3
Highest Offering: Doctorate
Accreditation: SC, ADNUR, CACREP, CS, IACBE, MUS, NUR, SW, TED

01 President ....Dr. David C. SMITH
05 Vice Pres Academic Administration ....Dr. Robert YOUNG
10 Vice President Financial Admin ....Mr. Tom VERRILL
32 Vice President Student Services ....Mr. Dennis NEGRON
45 Director Strategic Initiatives ....Mrs. Barb EDENS
30 Vice President Advancement ....Mrs. Carolyn HAMILTON
84 Vice Pres Enrollment Management ....Mr. Marc A. GRUNDY
20 Associate VP Academic Admin ....Dr. Volker HENNING
21 Associate VP Financial Admin ....Mr. Marty HAMILTON
13 Assoc VP Information Systems ....Mr. Gary SEWELL
09 Director Inst Research/Planning ....Dr. Hollis JAMES
08 Director of Libraries ....Mr. Daniel MAXWELL
06 Director Records & Advisement ....Mrs. Joni I. ZIER
15 Director Human Resources ....Mrs. Brenda FLORES-LOPEZ
26 Director Marketing Univ Relation ....Ms. Ingrid SKANTZ
29 Director Alumni Relations ....Ms. Evonne CROOK
38 Director Student Success Center ....Dr. Jim WAMPLER
33 Dean of Men ....Mr. Dwight E. MAGERS
34 Dean of Women ....Ms. Lisa HALL
50 Dean School of Business/Mgmt ....Dr. Mark HYDER
53 Dean School of Education/Psych ....Dr. John MCCOY
57 Dean School of Visual Art/Design ....Mr. Randy CRAVEN
60 Dean School of Journalism/Comm ....Dr. Linda CRUMLEY
64 Dean School of Music ....Dr. Scott BALL
66 Dean School of Nursing ....Dr. Barbara JAMES
68 Dean Sch of Phys Ed/Health/Wellness ....Dr. Robert BENGE
73 Dean School of Religion ....Dr. Greg KING
77 Dean School of Computing ....Dr. Rick HALTERMAN
70 Dean Social Work/Family Studies ....Dr. Kristie WILDER
72 Chair Technology ....Dr. Mark HYDER
81 Chair Mathematics ....Dr. Kevin BROWN
76 Chair Biology/Allied Health ....Dr. Keith SNYDER
88 Chair Chemistry ....Dr. Brent HAMSTRA
88 Chair English ....Dr. Keely TARY
88 Chair History & Political Studies ....Dr. Kris ERSKINE
88 Chair Physics ....Dr. Chris HANSEN
18 Director Plant Services ....Mr. Eric SCHOONARD
35 Director Student Affairs & Life Act ....Ms. Kari SHULTZ
37 Director Student Finance ....Mrs. Paula WALTERS
96 Director of Purchasing Services ....Mr. Russell ORRISON
04 Administrative Asst to President ....Mrs. Joylynn SCOTT

Southern College of Optometry (C)

1245 Madison Avenue, Memphis TN 38104-2222
County: Shelby FICE Identification: 003517
Unit ID: 221670
Telephone: (901) 722-3200 Carnegie Class: Spec-4-yr-Other Health
FAX Number: (901) 722-3279 Calendar System: Trimester
URL: www.sco.edu
Established: 1932 Annual Graduate Tuition & Fees: N/A
Enrollment: 527 Coed
Affiliation or Control: Independent Non-Profit IRS Status: 501(c)3
Highest Offering: Doctorate; No Undergraduates
Accreditation: SC, OPT, OPTR

01 President ....Dr. Lewis REICH
04 Executive Admin Assistant to Pres ....Ms. Sandra S. STEPHENS
05 VP for Academic Affairs ....Dr. John B. CAMPBELL
30 Vice President for Inst Advancement .....Dr. Kristin K. ANDERSON
102 Dir of Corp & Foundation Relations ....Ms. Christine M. WEINREICH
10 Vice President for Finance & Admin ....Mr. David L. WEST
13 Exec Dir of Information Services ....Mr. Dean SWICK
18 Director of Physical Plant ....Mr. Danny ANDERSON
17 Vice Pres for Clinical Programs ....Dr. James E. VENABLE
23 Director of Clinic Operations ....Mr. Gary SNUFFIN
06 Vice President for Student Services ....Mr. Joseph H. HAUSER
07 Dir of Admissions/Enrollment Svcs . Mr. Michael N. ROBERTSON
07 Director of Student Recruitment ....Ms. Sunnie EWING
08 Director of Library ....Ms. Leslie HOLLAND
26 Dir of Communications/Media Svcs ....Mr. Jim HOLLIFIELD
15 Vice President for Human Resources ....Ms. Ann Z. FIELDS
37 Director of Financial Aid ....Ms. Cindy GARNER
09 Director of Institutional Research ....Dr. Michael CHRISTENSEN
108 Director Institutional Assessment ....Ms. Pamela MOSS
19 Manager of Security/Safety ....Mr. Don HENSON
101 Secretary of the Institution/Board ....Ms. Sandra STEPHENS
29 Director of Alumni & Spec Events ....Ms. Beth FISHER
44 Annual Giving Coordinator ....Ms. Cecily FREEMAN

*Tennessee Board of Regents Office (D)

1415 Murfreesboro Road, Nashville TN 37217-2833
County: Davidson FICE Identification: 029031
Unit ID: 409379
Telephone: (615) 366-4400 Carnegie Class: N/A
FAX Number: (615) 366-3922
URL: www.tbr.edu

01 Acting Chancellor ....Mr. David GREGORY
05 Vice Chanc Academic Affairs ....Dr. Tristan DENLEY
10 Vice Chanc Business & Finance ....Mr. Dale SIMS
11 Vice Chanc Admin & Fac Mgmt ....Mr. David B. GREGORY
12 VC TN Colleges of Applied Tech ....Mr. James KING
13 Vice Chanc Information Systems ....Mr. Tom DANFORD
88 Vice Chanc for Community Colleges ....Dr. Warren NICHOLS
43 General Counsel ....Ms. Mary MOODY
09 Asst Vice Chanc Research/Assessment ....Mr. Chris TINGLE
32 Assoc Vice Chanc Student Affairs ....Ms. Heidi LEMING
20 Assoc Vice Chanc Academic Affairs ....Dr. Pamela KNOX
15 Asst Vice Chanc for Human Resources ....Ms. April PRESTON
21 Assistant Vice Chancellor Business ....Ms. Renee STEWART
88 Exec Dir of Operations for ROCC ....Dr. Patrick WILSON
26 Interim Communications Director ....Mr. Rick LOCKER

*Austin Peay State University (E)

601 College Street, Clarksville TN 37044-0002
County: Montgomery FICE Identification: 003478
Unit ID: 219602
Telephone: (931) 221-7011 Carnegie Class: Masters/L
FAX Number: (931) 221-7475 Calendar System: Semester
URL: www.apsu.edu
Established: 1927 Annual Undergrad Tuition & Fees (In-State): $7,501
Enrollment: 10,111 Coed
Affiliation or Control: State IRS Status: 501(c)3
Highest Offering: Beyond Master's But Less Than Doctorate
Accreditation: SC, ART, ENGT, MT, MUS, NUR, RAD, RTT, SW, TED

02 President ....Dr. Alisa WHITE
04 Exec Asst to the President ....Ms. Carol D. CLARK
05 Provost/VP Academic Affairs ....Dr. Rex GANDY
10 Vice President for Finance & Admin ....Mr. Mitch ROBINSON
43 University Attorney ....Ms. Stephanie REEVERS
32 VP for Student Affairs ....Dr. Sherryl BYRD
46 VP Advancement/Comm/Strategic Init ....Mr. Derek VAN DER MERWE
21 Senior Assoc VP for Finance ....Vacant
20 Asst Provost/Asst VP Acad Affairs ....Dr. Lynne CROSBY
84 Assoc Provost for Enrollment Mgmt ....Dr. Beverly BOGGS
30 Exec Director Univ Advancement ....Mr. Kristopher PHILLIPS
31 Dir Community/Business Rels ....Ms. Carol CLARK
26 Exec Dir Marketing/Public Rels ....Mr. Bill PERSINGER
12 Exec Dir APSU Fort Campbell ....Dr. William COX
29 Director of Alumni Relations ....Ms. Nicole PETERSON
21 Director Budgets ....Ms. Sonja STEWART
08 Director Library ....Mr. Joe WEBER
13 Assoc VP & Chief Info Officer ....Ms. Judith MOLNAR
09 Dir Inst Research & Effectiveness ....Ms. Melissa HUNTER
07 Director of Admissions ....Ms. Amy CORLEW
06 Registrar ....Ms. Telaina WRIGLEY
18 Director of Plant Administration ....Mr. Thomas HUTCHINS
45 Dir University Design/Construction ....Mr. Marc BRUNNER
41 Athletic Director ....Mr. Ryan IVEY
27 Director of Sports Information ....Vacant
37 Director of Student Financial Aid ....Ms. Donna PRICE
88 Dir Ctr for Teaching & Learning ....Dr. Loretta GRIFFY
38 Dir of Student Counseling Services ....Dr. Jeff RUTTER
35 Assoc Vice Pres & Dean of Students .....Mr. Gregory SINGLETON
88 Dir African Amer Cultural Ctr ....Vacant
15 Asst VP & Chief HR Officer ....Mr. Michael HAMLET
16 Director of Human Resources ....Ms. Fonda FIELDS
19 Director Public Safety ....Mr. Michael KASITZ
39 Asst Vice President Student Affairs ....Mr. F. Joe MILLS
21 Director Internal Audit ....Mr. Blayne CLEMENTS
25 Exec Dir Research & Sponsored Pgms ....Vacant
96 Director of Purchasing ....Ms. Judy BLAIN
22 Dir Equal Opport & Affirm Action ....Ms. Sheila M. BRYANT
36 Director of Career Services ....Ms. Amanda WALKER
49 Dean College Arts & Letters ....Dr. Dixie WEBB
81 Dean Col Science & Math ....Dr. Jaime TAYLOR
83 Dean Col Behav Health Science ....Dr. David DENTON
58 Assoc Prov/Dean Coll Grad Studies ....Dr. Raja DAKSHINAMURTHY
51 Exec Dir Extended & Distance Educ ....Vacant
104 Director of International Education ....Dr. Marissa CHANDLER
50 Interim Dean Col of Business ....Dr. Charles MOSES
53 Dean College of Education ....Dr. Carlette HARDIN

*East Tennessee State University (F)

1276 Gilbreath Drive, Johnson City TN 37614-1700
County: Washington FICE Identification: 003487
Unit ID: 220075
Telephone: (423) 439-1000 Carnegie Class: DU-Mod
FAX Number: (423) 439-5770 Calendar System: Semester
URL: www.etsu.edu
Established: 1911 Annual Undergrad Tuition & Fees (In-State): $8,153
Enrollment: 14,434 Coed
Affiliation or Control: State IRS Status: 501(c)3
Highest Offering: Doctorate
Accreditation: SC, ART, #AUD, BUS, BUSA, CACREP, CLPSY, COARC, CS, CSHSE, DH, DIETD, DIETI, ENGR, ENGT, MED, MUS, NURSE, PH, PHAR, PTA, RAD, SP, SW, TED, THEA

02 President ....Dr. Brian E. NOLAND
100 Chief of Staff/Assoc VP Health Affs ....Dr. Jane M. JONES
100 Chief of Staff External Operations ....Mr. Jeremy B. ROSS
05 Provost/Vice Pres Academic Affairs ....Dr. Bert C. BACH
10 Vice Pres Finance & Administration ....Dr. David D. COLLINS
17 Vice President Health Affairs ....Dr. Wilsie S. BISHOP
30 VP University Advancement ....Ms. Pamela S. RITTER
41 Athletic Director ....Dr. Richard L. SANDER
28 Spec Asst to Pres Equity/Diversity ....Ms. Mary V. JORDAN
88 Director of Internal Audit ....Ms. Rebecca B. LEWIS
43 University Counsel ....Mr. Edward J. KELLY
26 Exec Director of Univ Relations ....Mr. Joseph E. SMITH
84 Vice Provost Enrollment Services ....Dr. Ramona A. WILLIAMS
51 Dean Cont Studies & Acad Outreach ....Dr. Richard E. OSBORN
46 Vice Prov Research/Sponsored Pgms ....Dr. William R. DUNCAN
32 Vice Pres Student Affairs ....Dr. Joe H. SHERLIN
20 Vice Provost Academic Affairs ....Dr. M. Marshall GRUBE
20 VProv Ugrad Ed/Dir Plan & Analysis ..Dr. William G. KIRKWOOD
18 Assoc VP for Facilities Management ....Mr. William B. RASNICK, JR.
35 Dean of Students ....Dr. Jeffery S. HOWARD
13 CIO/Sr Vice Provost for ITS ....Dr. Karen D. KING
11 Assoc VP Administrative Services ....Dr. Katherine M. KELLEY
21 Sr Assoc VP Finance & Admin ....Dr. B. J. KING
44 Exec Director for Planned Giving ....Ms. Sunny SANDOS
29 Assoc VP Univ Adv/Exec Dir Alumni ....Dr. Robert M. PLUMMER
86 Assoc VP for Comm & Gov Relations ....Ms. Bridget R. BAIRD
49 Dean College Arts & Science ....Dr. Gordon K. ANDERSON
50 Dean College of Business/Technology ....Dr. Dennis R. DEPEW
76 Dean College of Clin/Rehab Sci ....Dr. Donald A. SAMPLES
53 Dean College of Education ....Dr. Terence HICKS
92 Interim Dean Honors College ....Dr. Judith B. SLAGLE
63 Dean College of Medicine ....Dr. Robert T. MEANS, JR.
67 Dean College of Pharmacy ....Dr. Debbie C. BYRD
66 Dean College of Nursing ....Dr. Wendy M. NEHRING
69 Dean College of Public Health ....Dr. Randolph F. WYKOFF
58 Dean School of Graduate Studies ....Dr. Cecilia A. MCINTOSH
08 Dean of Libraries ....Ms. Patricia R. VAN ZANDT
06 University Registrar ....Ms. Sheryl L. BURNETTE
07 Director of Admissions ....Mr. Brian L. HENLEY
36 Director University Career Services ....Dr. David E. MAGEE, JR.
38 Director Counseling Center ....Dr. Steve D. BROWN
37 Interim Director of Financial Aid ....Ms. Cruzita LUCERO
92 Director University Honors Program ....Dr. Joy E. WACHS
39 Director Student Housing ....Dr. Bonnie L. BURCHETT
85 Dir International Programs/Services ....Dr. Maria D. COSTA
93 Multicultural Director ....Ms. Laura C. TERRY
19 Director Public Safety ....Chief Jack R. COTREL
25 Director of Sponsored Programs ....Ms. Wendy ECKERT
87 Director Summer & Winter Sessions ....Dr. Sarah E. HARKNESS
94 Director of Women's Studies ....Dr. Phyllis A. THOMPSON
105 Web Manager ....Ms. Michaele D. LAWS
15 Dir Empl Relations/Compensation/Dev ....Ms. Diana D. MCCLAY
16 Director Benefits/Retirement/HRIS ....Ms. Tammy S. HAMM
108 Dir Institutional Effectiveness ....Dr. Cheri CLAVIER
45 Assoc VP/Chief Planning Officer ....Dr. Michael B. HOFF

*Middle Tennessee State University (G)

1301 E Main Street, Murfreesboro TN 37132-0001
County: Rutherford FICE Identification: 003510
Unit ID: 220978
Telephone: (615) 898-2300 Carnegie Class: DU-Mod
FAX Number: (615) 898-5538 Calendar System: Semester
URL: www.mtsu.edu
Established: 1911 Annual Undergrad Tuition & Fees (In-State): $8,080
Enrollment: 22,729 Coed
Affiliation or Control: State IRS Status: 501(c)3
Highest Offering: Doctorate
Accreditation: SC, AAB, AAFCS, ART, BUS, BUSA, CAATE, CACREP, #CIDA, CS, DIETD, ENGT, JOUR, MUS, NAIT, NRPA, NURSE, SW, TED, THEA

02 President .... Dr. Sidney A. MCPHEE
05 Interim University Provost .... Dr. Mark E. BYRNES
10 Interim VP Business & Finance .... Mr. Alan R. THOMAS
30 Vice President Devel/Univ Relations .... Mr. William J. BALES
32 VP Student Affairs .... Dr. Debra K. SELLS
13 VP Info Tech/Chief Info Officer .... Mr. Bruce PETRYSHAK
58 Vice Provost Rsrch/Dean Grad Stds .... Dr. Jackie ELLER
88 Vice Provost for Student Success .... Dr. Richard SLUDER
43 Univ Counsel & Asst to the Pres .... Ms. Heidi ZIMMERMAN
04 Exec Assistant to the President .... Ms. Kimberly S. EDGAR
22 Exec Dir Institutional Equity/Com .... Ms. Barbara L. PATTON
88 Assistant to the President .... Dr. Gloria L. BONNER
07 Assoc Vice Prov Admis & Enroll Svcs .. Dr. Laurie B. WITHEROW
14 Assoc Vice Pres Info Technology .... Mr. Tom WALLACE
21 Assoc Vice Pres Business Office .... Vacant
35 Assoc Vice Pres/Dean Student Life .... Ms. Sarah SUDAK
26 Vice Pres Mktg/Communications .... Mr. Andrew OPPMANN
15 Asst Vice Pres Human Resource Svcs .... Ms. Kathy I. MUSSELMAN
18 Asst Vice Pres Facilities Services .... Mr. Joe WHITEFIELD
11 Asst Vice Pres Admin/Business Svcs .... Ms. Kathryn CRISP
91 Assoc Vice Pres Enterprise Res Plng .... Mrs. Lisa C. ROGERS
90 Asst Vice Pres Acad & Instruct Tech .... Ms. Barbara J. DRAUDE
81 Dean Col Basic/Applied Science .... Dr. Robert U. FISCHER, JR.
83 Dean College Behavioral & Hlth Sci ... Dr. Harold D. WHITESIDE
60 Dean College Media & Entertain .... Dr. Ken A. PAULSON
50 Dean College of Business .... Dr. David J. URBAN
53 Dean College of Education .... Dr. Lana C. SEIVERS
49 Interim Dean Col of Liberal Arts .... Dr. Karen K. PETERSEN
51 Dean University College .... Dr. David GOTCHER
92 Dean University Honors College .... Dr. John R. VILE
08 Dean University Library .... Ms. Bonnie J. ALLEN
09 Asst Vice Provost for IEPR .... Mr. Chris BREWER
36 Dir Career & Employment Center .... Mr. Bill FLETCHER
88 Asst Vice Prov Student Success .... Mr. Vincent WINDROW
37 Dir of Financial Aid & Scholarship .... Mr. Stephen F. WHITE
25 Dir Research Services .... Mr. Jeffry PORTER
29 Director Alumni Relations .... Ms. Ginger C. FREEMAN
40 Director Bookstore .... Mr. Jeff WHITWELL
24 Manager Center for Educational Med .... Mr. Anthony TATE
38 Director Counseling Services .... Dr. Jane TIPPS
44 Director Development Office .... Vacant
06 Director Enrollment Technical Sys .... Ms. Teresa W. THOMAS
27 Director News & Media Relations .... Mr. Jimmy W. HART
41 Director of Athletics .... Mr. Chris J. MASSARO
23 Director of Health Services .... Mr. Richard L. CHAPMAN
06 Registrar .... Ms. Susan FIELDHOUSE
19 Chief of Police/Dir Public Safety .... Mr. Carl S. PEASTER

*Tennessee State University (A)

3500 John A Merritt Boulevard, Nashville TN 37209-1561
County: Davidson FICE Identification: 003522
Unit ID: 221838
Telephone: (615) 963-5000 Carnegie Class: DU-Mod
FAX Number: (615) 963-7412 Calendar System: Semester
URL: www.tnstate.edu
Established: 1912 Annual Undergrad Tuition & Fees (In-State): $7,112
Enrollment: 9,027 Coed
Affiliation or Control: State IRS Status: 501(c)3
Highest Offering: Doctorate
Accreditation: **SC**, AAFCS, ADNUR, ART, BUS, CAHIIM, COARC, COPSY, CS, DH, DIETD, ENG, MUS, NAIT, NUR, OT, PH, PTA, SP, SPAA, SW, TED

02 President .... Dr. Glenda GLOVER
05 Vice President Academic Affairs .... Dr. Mark G. HARDY
04 Senior Office Assistant .... Ms. Zanetta GOOCH
10 VP Business & Finance .... Mrs. Cynthia BROOKS
11 VP Administrative Affairs .... Ms. Jane JACKSON
32 Assoc VP Student Affairs .... Dr. Michael FREEMAN
30 VP Institutional Advancement .... Ms. Robin WATSON
41 Athletic Director .... Mrs. Teresa LAWRENCE-PHILLIPS
43 University Legal Counsel .... Mr. Laurence PENDLETON
84 Assoc Provost Enrollment Mgmt .... Dr. John CADE
20 Assoc VP Academic Affairs .... Dr. Patricia CROOK
20 AVP Academic Affairs/Extended Educ .... Dr. Evelyn NETTLES
15 Assoc VP/Dir Human Resources .... Ms. Linda C. SPEARS
21 Assoc VP Financial Services .... Mr. Bradley WHITE
18 Assoc VP Facilities/Physical Plant .... Mr. Ronnie BROOKS
88 Asst VP Budget/Travel .... Mr. Bradley WHITE
09 Dir Inst Effectiveness & Research ..... Dr. G. Pamela BURCH-SIMS
28 Dir Equity Diversity & Compliance .... Ms. Tiffa COX
37 Director Financial Aid .... Ms. Amy B. WOOD
06 Registrar .... Mrs. Thelria HARDAWAY
26 Director Media Relations .... Mr. Richard DELAHAYA
19 Chief TSU Police Department .... Mr. Richard BRIGGANCE
08 Dean Libraries & Media Centers .... Dr. Murle KENERSON
49 Dean College of Liberal Arts .... Dr. Gloria C. JOHNSON
50 Dean College of Business .... Dr. Millicent LOWNES-JACKSON
53 Int Dean College of Education .... Dr. Celeste WILLIAMS
54 Dean College of Engr/Tech/Comp Sci ..... Dr. S. Keith HARGROVE
47 Dn Agriculture/Human & Natural Sci .... Dr. Chandra REDDY
76 Int Dean Col Health Sciences .... Dr. Ronald BARREDO

*Tennessee Technological University (B)

1000 N Dixie Avenue, Cookeville TN 38505-0001
County: Putnam FICE Identification: 003523
Unit ID: 221847
Telephone: (931) 372-3101 Carnegie Class: DU-Mod
FAX Number: (931) 372-3898 Calendar System: Semester
URL: www.tntech.edu
Established: 1915 Annual Undergrad Tuition & Fees (In-State): $8,011
Enrollment: 11,339 Coed
Affiliation or Control: State IRS Status: 501(c)3
Highest Offering: Doctorate
Accreditation: **SC**, AAFCS, ART, BUS, BUSA, CACREP, CS, DIETD, ENG, ENGT, MUS, NAIT, NURSE, TED

02 President .... Dr. Philip B. OLDHAM
05 Provost/Vice President Acad Affairs .... Dr. Bahman GHORASHI
10 Vice Pres Planning & Finance .... Dr. Claire STINSON
32 Vice President Student Affairs .... Mr. Marc BURNETT
35 Asst VP Student Affairs .... Mr. Ed BOUCHER
46 VP Research & Economic Development .... Dr. Bharat SONI
86 Director Government Relations .... Dr. Terry SALTSMAN
46 Assoc VP for Research .... Dr. Francis O. OTUONYE
30 Vice President Univ Advancement .... Dr. Kevin BRASWELL
20 Sr Assoc VP Academic Affairs .... Dr. Mark STEPHENS
20 Assoc Provost/Vice Pres Acad Affs .... Dr. Xiaoming (Sharon) HUO
13 Interim CIO Info Tech Svcs .... Dr. Terry SALTSMAN
37 Director Financial Aid .... Mr. Lester MCKENZIE
08 Director Library & Learning Assist .... Dr. Doug BATES
09 Director Institutional Research .... Dr. Glenn W. JAMES
45 Director of Institutional Planning .... Dr. Claire STINSON
15 Assoc VP Human Resources .... Dr. Leslie CRICKENBERGER
19 Director of University Police .... Mr. Tony NELSON
39 Director of Housing .... Mr. Charles MACKE
41 Director of Athletics .... Mr. Mark WILSON
18 Assoc VP Physical Plant .... Mr. Jack BUTLER
38 Director Counseling Center .... Ms. Patricia SMITH
23 Director of Health Svcs .... Ms. Leigh A. FAY
36 Director Career Services .... Ms. Lynn HALEY
26 Assoc VP Communications & Mkting .... Ms. Karen LYKINS
85 Director International Education .... Mr. Charles WILKERSON
06 Registrar .... Ms. Brandi HILL
92 Director Honors Program .... Dr. Rita BARNES
93 Asst VP Multicultural Affairs .... Dr. Robert OWENS
96 Director of Purchasing .... Ms. Judy M. HULL
21 Associate VP Business .... Mr. Jeff YOUNG
43 Director University Counsel .... Ms. Kae CARPENTER
29 Director Alumni Relations .... Mr. Kevin ANDERSON
88 Director of Internal Audit .... Ms. Deanna METTS
28 Dir of AA & Employee Relations .... Ms. Elizabeth GAYS
07 Asst VP Admissions .... Dr. Brandy CARTMELL
19 Dir Envir Health & Safety .... Mr. James COBB
84 Assoc VP Enr Mgmt & Student Success .... Dr. Robert HODUM
49 Dean of Arts & Sciences .... Dr. Paul SEMMES
54 Dean of Engineering .... Dr. Joseph RENCIS
47 Dean Agric & Human Ecology .... Dr. Liz MULLENS
50 Dean of Business Admin .... Dr. Thomas PAYNE
53 Dean College of Education .... Dr. Jennifer SHANK
66 Dean School of Nursing .... Dr. Huey-Ming TZENG
88 Int Dean Interdisciplinary Studies .... Dr. Alice CAMUTI
58 Int Assoc Dean of Graduate Studies .... Dr. Bedelia RUSSELL
04 Administrative Asst to President .... Ms. Terri TAYLOR
105 Director Web Services .... Mr. David WILLIS
108 Director Institutional Assessment .... Dr. Theresa ENNIS
44 Director Annual or Planned Giving .... Mr. Brandon BOYD
90 Director Academic Computing .... Dr. Yvette CLARK
91 Director Administrative Computing .... Mr. Rick CUMBY
106 Assoc VP Digital & Distance Educ .... Dr. Patrick WILSON

*The University of Memphis (C)

Memphis TN 38152
County: Shelby FICE Identification: 003509
Unit ID: 220862
Telephone: (901) 678-2000 Carnegie Class: DU-Higher
FAX Number: N/A Calendar System: Semester
URL: www.memphis.edu
Established: 1912 Annual Undergrad Tuition & Fees (In-State): $8,903
Enrollment: 21,059 Coed
Affiliation or Control: State IRS Status: 501(c)3
Highest Offering: Doctorate
Accreditation: **SC**, ART, AUD, BUS, BUSA, CACREP, CIDA, CLPSY, COPSY, CORE, CS, DIETD, DIETI, ENG, ENGT, HSA, IPSY, JOUR, LAW, MUS, NURSE, PH, PLNG, SCPSY, SP, SPAA, SW, TED, THEA

02 President .... Dr. M. David RUDD
05 Provost .... Dr. Karen WEDDLE-WEST
20 Vice Provost Academic Innvoation .... Dr. Richard IRWIN
10 Vice President Business & Finance .... Mr. David G. ZETTERGREN
88 Asst VP Campus Planning Design .... Mr. Tony POTEET
18 Asst VP Physical Plant .... Mr. Ron BROOKS
21 Asst VP Business Services .... Dr. Edwina WASHINGTON
19 Chief of Police .... Mr. Bruce HARBER
88 Chief Audit Executive .... Mr. Byron MORGAN
30 Chief Development Officer .... Mr. Bobby A. PRINCE
32 Vice President Student Affairs .... Dr. Rosie P. BINGHAM
35 Asst VP Student Aff/Dev .... Dr. Stephanie BLAISDELL
26 VP External Relations .... Ms. Tammy HEDGES
46 Vice President for Research .... Dr. Andrew W. MEYERS
41 Director of Athletics .... Mr. Tom BOWEN
43 University Counsel .... Ms. Melanie MURRY
88 Dir of Institutional Equity .... Mr. Michael S. WASHINGTON
13 Int CIO/Vice Provost for Info Tech .... Dr. Robert JACKSON
84 Vice Provost Enrollment Svcs .... Mr. Steve MCKELLIPS
58 Vice Prov/Dean Graduate School .... Dr. Jasbir DHALIWAL
21 Assistant Vice President Finance .... Ms. Jeannie SMITH
15 Asst Vice Pres Human Resources .... Ms. Maria ALAM
08 Dean U of M Libraries .... Dr. Sylverna V. FORD
09 Director Institutional Research .... Dr. Gary L. DONHARDT
36 Director Career & Employment Svcs .... Ms. Alisha D. ROSE
06 Registrar .... Vacant
37 Director of Student Aid .... Mr. Richard RITZMAN
96 Director of Purchasing .... Ms. Canty ROBBINS
29 Director of Alumni Relations .... Ms. Kristie GOLDSMITH
92 Director University Honors Program .... Dr. Melinda L. JONES
07 Director of Admissions .... Mr. Stephen MCKELLIPS
28 Director of Diversity Initiatives .... Dr. Karen WEDDLE-WEST
88 Int Dn Com Sciences Disorders ...... Dr. Linda D. JARMULOWICZ
49 Dean of Arts & Sciences .... Dr. Thomas J. NENON
50 Dean Business & Economics .... Dr. Rajiv GROVER
53 Int Dean of Educ Health/Human Sci .... Dr. Ernest A. RAKOW
54 Dean of Engineering .... Dr. Richard J. SWEIGARD
88 Dean University College .... Dr. Dan L. LATTIMORE
57 Dean Communication & Fine Arts .... Dr. Richard R. RANTA
61 Dean School of Law .... Mr. Peter V. LETSOU
66 Dean School of Nursing .... Dr. Lin ZHAN
69 Int Dean School of Public Health .... Dr. James G. GURNEY
76 Dir School of Health Studies .... Dr. Richard J. BLOOMER

*Chattanooga State Community College (D)

4501 Amnicola Highway, Chattanooga TN 37406-1097
County: Hamilton FICE Identification: 003998
Unit ID: 219824
Telephone: (423) 697-4400 Carnegie Class: Assoc/MT-VT-High Trad
FAX Number: N/A Calendar System: Semester
URL: www.chattanoogastate.edu
Established: 1965 Annual Undergrad Tuition & Fees (In-State): $3,973
Enrollment: 9,332 Coed
Affiliation or Control: State IRS Status: 501(c)3
Highest Offering: Associate Degree
Accreditation: **SC**, ACBSP, ADNUR, CAHIIM, COARC, DA, DH, DMS, EMT, ENGR, ENGT, MAC, NMT, PTAA, RAD, RTT, SURGT

02 President .... Dr. Flora TYDINGS
04 Special Assistant to the President .... Mr. Joe HELSETH
45 Int VP IE/Rsrch & Planning .... Mr. Robert DENN
05 Vice Pres Academic Affairs .... Dr. Dana NICHOLS
10 Exec Vice Pres Business & Finance .... Ms. Tammy SWENSON
32 Vice President Student Services .... Ms. Debbie ADAMS
13 Vice President Technology .... Dr. James BARROTT
30 Vice Pres Col Advance & Public Rels ..... Ms. Nancy PATTERSON
21 Asst Vice Pres Business & Finance .... Ms. Susan JOSEPH
35 Asst Vice Pres Student Affairs .... Mr. Brad MCCORMICK
18 Asst VP Plant Operations/Facil Plng .... Mr. Steve HUSKINS
56 Asst VP Distributed Education .... Ms. Judy LOWE
25 Asst VP Grants/Contracts/Stdnt Acct .... Ms. Debbie MAILEN
09 Director Institutional Research .... Ms. Bonnie RIGGS
26 Director Marketing .... Ms. Patty BROWN
15 Director Human Resources .... Mr. Brian EVANS
36 Director Career Services/Counseling .... Ms. Sheila ALBRITTON
37 Director Student Financial Aid .... Ms. Julae GROSZ
07 Director of Admissions/Records .... Ms. Gail CAMPBELL
28 Director Diversity .... Ms. Mary KNAFF
41 Athletic Director .... Vacant
08 Dean Library Services .... Ms. Susan JENNINGS
76 Dean Allied Health & Nursing .... Dr. Mark KNUTSEN
79 Dean Humanities & Fine Arts .... Mr. Darrin HASSEVOORT
83 Dean Social/Behavioral Science .... Mr. John HAWORTH
81 Interim Dean Math & Sciences .... Mr. Roy SOFIELD
50 Dean Business/Info Tech .... Mr. Barry JENNISON
32 Dean Student Life/Judicial Affairs .... Ms. Sandy RUTTER
75 Dean Tennessee Technology Center .... Dr. Mike RICKETTS
54 Dean Engineering Technology .... Mr. Tim MCGHEE
84 Dir Welcome Center/Recruiting .... Ms. Kisha CALDWELL
22 Dir Affirmative Action/EEO .... Mr. Jerome GOBER
108 Director Assessment & Planning .... Ms. Sherry MARLOW-ORMSBY

*Cleveland State Community College (E)

PO Box 3570, Cleveland TN 37320-3570
County: Bradley FICE Identification: 003999
Unit ID: 219879
Telephone: (423) 472-7141 Carnegie Class: Assoc/HT-High Trad
FAX Number: (423) 478-6255 Calendar System: Semester
URL: www.clevelandstatecc.edu
Established: 1967 Annual Undergrad Tuition & Fees (In-State): $3,947
Enrollment: 3,522 Coed
Affiliation or Control: State IRS Status: 501(c)3
Highest Offering: Associate Degree
Accreditation: **SC**, ACBSP, ADNUR, MAC, NAIT

02 President .... Dr. William SEYMOUR
05 Vice President for Academic Affairs .... Dr. Denise KING
32 Vice President for Student Services .... Dr. Michael STOKES
10 Vice President Admin & Finance .... Dr. Thomas WRIGHT
09 Director of Institutional Research .... Mr. David KNOPP
37 Director of Financial Aid .... Mrs. Jamie HAMBY
30 Exec Director of Inst Advancement .... Dr. Thomas WRIGHT
26 Director Marketing & Promotions .... Mr. Tony BARTOLO
06 Asst Dir Enrollment Svcs/Registrar .... Mrs. Gail GREENWOOD
15 Director of Human Resources .... Mrs. Joan BATES
08 Director of the Library .... Vacant
13 Director of College Computing .... Mr. Chris MOWERY
19 Coordinator Campus Security .... Mr. Mike HODGES
50 Dean of Business & Technology .... Ms. Susan WEBB-CURTIS
66 Director of Nursing .... Mrs. Nancy LABINE
79 Dean Humanities/Social Sciences .... Dr. Robert BRANDON
81 Dean Math/Science/Health/Wellness .... Dr. Mitchell RHEA
38 Dir Student Development/ACCESS Ctr .... Mr. Mark WILSON
103 Dir Workforce Development .... Mr. Rick CREASY

18 Director of Plant Operations .... Mr. Guy DAVIS
21 Business Manager .... Ms. Alisha FOX
84 Director of Enrollment Services .... Mr. Jason SEWELL
07 Asst Director of Admissions .... Ms. Suzanne BAYNE
41 Athletic Director .... Mr. Mike POLICASTRO

*Columbia State Community College (A)

1665 Hampshire Pike, Columbia TN 38401-5653
County: Maury FICE Identification: 003483
Unit ID: 219888
Telephone: (931) 540-2722 Carnegie Class: Assoc/HT-High Trad
FAX Number: (931) 540-2535 Calendar System: Semester
URL: www.columbiastate.edu
Established: 1966 Annual Undergrad Tuition & Fees (In-State): $3,919
Enrollment: 5,117 Coed
Affiliation or Control: State IRS Status: 501(c)3
Highest Offering: Associate Degree
Accreditation: SC, ACBSP, ADNUR, COARC, EMT, NAIT, RAD

02 President .... Dr. Janet F. SMITH
05 Executive Vice President/Provost .... Dr. Margaret D. SMITH
10 Vice Pres Financial/Admin Services .... Vacant
30 Executive for Advancement .... Ms. Bethany LAY
20 Assoc VP Faculty/Curric & Programs .... Ms. Joni L. LENIG
32 VP Student Services .... Dr. Sean FOX
13 Assoc VP Info Technology .... Dr. Emily SICIENSKY
21 Assoc VP Business Services .... Ms. Elaine CURTIS
26 Director of Communications .... Ms. Amy SPEARS-BOYD
28 Asst to Pres for Access & Diversity .... Dr. Christa S. MARTIN
06 Director Records .... Ms. Sharon G. BOWEN
15 Director Human Resources .... Ms. Christie MILLER
08 Director Library .... Vacant
38 Dir Student Succ Counseling .... Dr. Phillip OWENS
09 Dir Inst Effectiveness & Planning .... Ms. Tammy BORREN
37 Director Financial Aid .... Ms. Cherry JOHNSON
41 Director Athletics .... Mr. Johnny LITTRELL
18 Director Facility Services & Safety .... Mr. Tim HALLMARK
56 Assoc VP Wiliamson Campus .... Dr. Shanna JACKSON
96 Coordinator Purchasing .... Mr. Jon ARNOLD
84 Chief Enrollment Svcs Officer .... Ms. Jill RILEY
103 Dir Workforce/Career Development .... Ms. LK BROWNING
104 Director Study Abroad .... Ms. Ana BASOA-MCMILLAN
106 Dir Online Education/E-learning .... Dr. Marilia GERGES
108 Director Institutional Assessment .... Vacant
19 Director Security/Safety .... Mr. Randy CARROLL

*Dyersburg State Community College (B)

1510 Lake Road, Dyersburg TN 38024-2450
County: Dyer FICE Identification: 006835
Unit ID: 220057
Telephone: (731) 286-3200 Carnegie Class: Assoc/HT-Mix Trad/Non
FAX Number: (731) 286-3333 Calendar System: Semester
URL: www.dscc.edu
Established: 1967 Annual Undergrad Tuition & Fees (In-State): $3,947
Enrollment: 2,847 Coed
Affiliation or Control: State IRS Status: 501(c)3
Highest Offering: Associate Degree
Accreditation: SC, ACBSP, ADNUR, CAHIIM, EMT

02 President .... Dr. Karen A. BOWYER
05 Vice President for the College .... Dr. Teri MADDOX
10 Vice President Finance/Admin Svcs .... Mr. Lowell (Bud) HOFFMANN
30 VP Inst Advancement/Cont Education .... Dr. Kimberly MARTIN
13 Vice President Technology .... Ms. Diane CAMPER
32 Dean of Student Services .... Ms. Larenda FULTZ
08 Dean Learning Resources Center .... Ms. Susan CHARLEY
37 Director of Financial Aid .... Mrs. Kacee HARDY
09 Institutional Research Specialist .... Ms. Mary RICKS
15 Director Human Resources .... Ms. Sheila GILLAHAN
103 Director of Workforce Development .... Ms. Margaret PRATER
29 Director of Alumni Relations .... Ms. Amy FINCH
38 Academic/Career Counselor .... Ms. Sherry BAKER
41 Director of Athletics .... Mr. Alan BARNETT
18 Director of Physical Plant .... Mr. Kent JETTON
07 Director of Admissions & Records .... Ms. Heather PAGE
26 Director of Public Information .... Ms. Amy FINCH
96 Director of Purchasing .... Vacant
21 Business & Student Fin Svcs Manager .... Ms. Donna MEALER
49 Dean Arts & Sciences .... Mr. James BARHAM
72 Dean Business/Tech/Allied Health .... Ms. Julie FRAZIER
66 Dean Nursing/Allied Health Div .... Ms. Amy JOHNSON
04 Administrative Asst to President .... Ms. Edith CARLTON

*Jackson State Community College (C)

2046 North Parkway, Jackson TN 38301-3797
County: Madison FICE Identification: 004937
Unit ID: 220400
Telephone: (731) 424-3520 Carnegie Class: Assoc/HT-Mix Trad/Non
FAX Number: (731) 425-2647 Calendar System: Semester
URL: www.jscc.edu
Established: 1965 Annual Undergrad Tuition & Fees (In-State): $3,933
Enrollment: 4,924 Coed
Affiliation or Control: State IRS Status: 501(c)3
Highest Offering: Associate Degree
Accreditation: SC, ACBSP, ADNUR, EMT, MLTAD, NAIT, PTAA, RAD

02 President .... Dr. Bruce BLANDING
05 VP of Academic Affairs .... Dr. Larry BAILEY
10 Vice Pres of Finance & Admin Affs .... Mr. Horace W. CHASE
30 Dir of Development/Alumni Relations .... Ms. Dee HENDERSON
32 VP of Student Services .... Mr. Brian GANN
30 VP of Institutional Advancement .... Vacant
88 Internal Auditor .... Mrs. Angela P. BROWN
15 Dir Human Resources/Affirm Action .... Ms. Amy WEST
09 Dir Inst Research & Accountability .... Mrs. Sara VONDERHEIDE
13 Director of Information Technology .... Ms. Dana NAILS
21 Director of Business Services .... Mr. Tim DELLINGER
18 Director of Physical Plant .... Mr. Gerald BATCHELOR
96 Director of Purchasing .... Mr. Robert D. HEMRICK
12 Director Lexington Campus .... Ms. Sandy STANFILL
12 Director Savannah Campus .... Mrs. Meda FALLS
12 Director Humboldt Campus .... Ms. Lisa BARKER
26 Coordinator of PR and Marketing .... Vacant
37 Director Student Financial Aid .... Ms. Dewana LATIMER
07 Director of Admissions and Records .... Ms. Robin MAREK
08 Head Librarian .... Mr. Scott COHEN
19 Director Security/Safety .... Mr. Darron BILLINGS

*Motlow State Community College (D)

PO Box 8500, Lynchburg TN 37352-8500
County: Moore FICE Identification: 006836
Unit ID: 221096
Telephone: (931) 393-1500 Carnegie Class: Assoc/HT-High Trad
FAX Number: (931) 393-1681 Calendar System: Semester
URL: www.mscc.edu
Established: 1969 Annual Undergrad Tuition & Fees (In-State): $3,949
Enrollment: 4,758 Coed
Affiliation or Control: State IRS Status: 501(c)3
Highest Offering: Associate Degree
Accreditation: SC, ACBSP, ADNUR, NAIT

02 President .... Dr. Anthony KINKEL
05 Interim VP for Academic Affairs .... Ms. Melody EDMONDS
10 Vice Pres for Finance & Admin .... Ms. Hilda TUNSTILL
30 VP for Advancement & Marketing .... Vacant
88 VP Quality Assur & Performance Fund .... Dr. Scott COOK
13 Chief Information Officer .... Ms. Cynthia LOGAN
32 Vice Pres for Student Affairs .... Ms. Cheryl HYLAND
72 Dean Career & Tech Programs .... Mr. Fred RASCOE
88 Asst Dean CTP & DE .... Ms. Debra SMITH
12 Interim Dean McMinnville Campus .... Mr. David PALMER
76 Dean Allied Health/Dir of Nursing .... Ms. Pat HENDRIX
12 Dean of Moore County Campus .... Vacant
12 Assn Dean Fayetteville Campus .... Ms. Lisa SMITH
12 Dean of Smyrna Campus .... Vacant
35 Dean of Students .... Ms. Kirsten MOSS
18 Director of Facilities .... Mr. Brian GAFFORD
14 Director of Technical Operations .... Mr. Matt HULVEY
88 Director of Special Events .... Ms. Brenda CANNON
36 Director of Career Readiness .... Vacant
08 Director of Libraries .... Mr. Stuart GAETJENS
102 Director of the Foundation .... Ms. Jan ROGERS
37 Executive Director of Financial Aid .... Mr. Joe MYERS
38 Director of Disability & Testing .... Ms. Sonya HOOD
07 Director of Admissions & Records .... Ms. Greer ALSUP
19 Director of Public Safety .... Mr. Ray HIGGINBOTHAM
41 Director of Athletics .... Mr. C. Scott SHASTEEN
09 Dir of Inst Effectiveness/Research .... Ms. Sylvia COLLINS
91 Director Admin Computing .... Ms. Rexann BUMPUS
88 Director Student Success .... Ms. Rhonda COTHAM
84 Director of Recruitment .... Vacant
103 Dir of Workforce Dev & Extended .... Mr. Tom DILLINGHAM
15 Director of Human Resources .... Ms. Laura JENT
96 Director of Fiscal Services .... Ms. Sandy SCHAFFER
04 Admin Assistant to the President .... Ms. Christy GLENN

*Nashville State Community College (E)

120 White Bridge Road, Nashville TN 37209-4515
County: Davidson FICE Identification: 008145
Unit ID: 221184
Telephone: (615) 353-3333 Carnegie Class: Assoc/HT-Mix Trad/Non
FAX Number: (615) 353-3713 Calendar System: Semester
URL: www.nscc.edu
Established: 1969 Annual Undergrad Tuition & Fees (In-State): $3,873
Enrollment: 10,044 Coed
Affiliation or Control: State IRS Status: 501(c)3
Highest Offering: Associate Degree
Accreditation: SC, ACBSP, ACFEI, ADNUR, NAIT, OTA, SURGT

02 President .... Dr. George H. VAN ALLEN
05 Vice President of Academic Affairs .... Vacant
10 Vice Pres Finance & Administration .... Mrs. Mary M. CROSS
09 VP of Institutional Effectiveness .... Dr. Flora R. SETAYESH
45 Assoc VP Planning/Assessment .... Mr. Ted M. WASHINGTON
30 Exec Dir of Devel/Dir Public Affs .... Ms. Karin F. WEAVER
32 Dean of Students .... Dr. Carol J. MARTIN-OSORIO
21 Internal Auditor .... Vacant
06 Registrar .... Mr. Lance L. WOODARD
07 Director of Admissions .... Mrs. Laura P. MORAN
13 Director of Computer Services .... Mr. Paul A. KAMINSKY
19 Director of Safety and Security .... Mr. Derrek G. SHEUCRAFT
37 Director of Financial Aid .... Mr. James J. MORAN
15 Dir Human Res/Affirm Act/Diversity .... Mr. Justin L. HARRIS
18 Director of Operations/Maintenance .... Mr. Jim T. DAWSON
103 Dir Workforce and Community Dev .... Vacant
26 Manager of Publications .... Ms. Ellen L. ZINK
106 Director of Online Learning .... Ms. Shelley J. GROSS-GRAY
83 Dean of Social and Life Sciences .... Dr. Julie E. WILLIAMS
72 Dean of Comp/Eng Technologies .... Dr. Reginald J. GARDNER
81 Dean Math & Natural Sciences .... Dr. Sarah E. ROBERTS
79 Dean English/Humanities & Arts .... Dr. Patricia J. ARMSTRONG
62 Dean Lrng Resources & Distance Educ .... Dr. Faye M. JONES
50 Dean Business & Applied Arts .... Ms. Karen L. STEVENSON
96 Director of Purchasing .... Ms. Jo SMITH
66 Director of Nursing .... Dr. Cynthia G. WALLER
04 Administrative Asst to President .... Mrs. Judy I. COOK
36 Director Student Placement .... Mr. Stephen L. HOOKS

*Northeast State Community College (F)

PO Box 246, 2425 Highway 75, Blountville TN 37617-0246
County: Sullivan FICE Identification: 005378
Unit ID: 221908
Telephone: (423) 323-3191 Carnegie Class: Assoc/HT-High Trad
FAX Number: (423) 279-7636 Calendar System: Semester
URL: www.northeaststate.edu
Established: 1965 Annual Undergrad Tuition & Fees (In-State): $3,936
Enrollment: 5,865 Coed
Affiliation or Control: State IRS Status: 501(c)3
Highest Offering: Associate Degree
Accreditation: SC, ACBSP, ADNUR, CVT, DA, EMT, MLTAD, NAIT, SURGT

02 President .... Dr. Janice H. GILLIAM
04 Exec Assistant to the President .... Ms. Cindy S. CHRISTIAN
05 Vice Pres Academic Affairs .... Dr. Allana R. HAMILTON
10 Chief Financial Officer .... Dr. Steven CAMPBELL
11 Vice Pres Administrative Svcs .... Mr. Fred LEWIS
32 Vice President Student Affairs .... Mr. Matt DELOZIER
12 VP for Northeast State at Kingsport .... Mr. Jeff D. MCCORD
56 Asst VP Evening/Distance Educ .... Dr. Pashia HOGAN
20 Asst Vice Pres Academic Affairs .... Mr. Don COLEMAN
06 Registrar/Admissions & Records .... Ms. Deidra CLOSE
15 Director Human Resources .... Ms. Tyra COPAS
31 Director Community Relations .... Mr. Robert CARPENTER
26 Director of Marketing .... Ms. Amanda ADAMS
09 Institutional Effectiveness Officer .... Dr. Susan E. GRAYBEAL
08 Dean Library .... Mr. Christopher DEMAS
79 Dean Humanities .... Mr. William WILSON
81 Dean Math .... Ms. Malissa TRENT
76 Dean Health Related Profession .... Ms. Connie MARSHALL
72 Dean Advance Technologies .... Mr. Sam S. ROWELL
83 Dean Behavior/Social Sciences .... Dr. Xiaoping WANG
81 Dean Science .... Dr. Carolyn MCCRACKEN
50 Dean Business Technologies .... Mr. Danny L. LAWSON
66 Dean Nursing .... Dr. Melessia D. WEBB
84 Dean of Enrollment Management .... Ms. Jennifer STARLING
07 VA Admissions/Records Tech Clerk .... Mr. John ADCOX

*Pellissippi State Community College (G)

PO Box 22990, Knoxville TN 37933-0990
County: Knox FICE Identification: 012693
Unit ID: 221643
Telephone: (865) 694-6400 Carnegie Class: Assoc/HT-Mix Trad/Non
FAX Number: (865) 539-7240 Calendar System: Semester
URL: www.pstcc.edu
Established: 1974 Annual Undergrad Tuition & Fees (In-State): $3,988
Enrollment: 10,099 Coed
Affiliation or Control: State IRS Status: 501(c)3
Highest Offering: Associate Degree
Accreditation: SC, ACBSP, ACFEI, ADNUR, NAIT

02 President .... Dr. L. Anthony WISE
05 Vice President of Academic Affairs .... Dr. Ted A. LEWIS
13 Vice President Information Services .... Ms. Audrey J. WILLIAMS
10 Vice President Business & Finance .... Mr. Ronald L. KESTERSON
30 VP College Advancement/Exec Dir Fdn .... Ms. Peggy M. WILSON
32 Vice President of Student Affairs .... Dr. Rebecca L. ASHFORD
103 Exec Dir Business/Workforce Dev .... Ms. Teri T. BRAHAMS
12 Campus Dean Blount County Programs .... Ms. Holly L. BURKETT
12 Campus Dean Strawberry Pl Program .... Dr. Mike NORTH
12 Campus Dean Magnolia Ave Programs .... Ms. Rosalyn P. TILLMAN
12 Campus Dean Division Street Program .... Ms. Esther L. DYER
35 Asst Vice President/Dean of Student .... Ms. Mary C. BLEDSOE
21 Asst VP Business Services .... Ms. Renee MOORE
20 Asst VP of Academic Affairs .... Dr. Beth NORTON
84 Asst VP Enrollment Services .... Ms. Leigh A. TOUZEAU
22 Exec Director Equity & Compliance .... Dr. Patrick SHIPWASH
35 Dir of Student Life & Recreation .... Ms. Kim THOMAS-LARUE
36 Director of Placement .... Ms. Cynthia ATCHLEY
22 Director of Disability Services .... Ms. Ann E. SATKOWIAK
38 Director Counseling Department .... Dr. Elizabeth E. FIRESTONE
26 Director Marketing & Communications .... Ms. Julia H. WOOD
06 Registrar .... Ms. Melanie M. PARADISE
08 Director of Library Services .... Mr. J. Peter NERZAK
24 Dir Educ Technology Svcs .... Mr. Brandon BALLENTINE
37 Director of Financial Aid .... Mr. Dick SMELSER
09 Dir Inst Effective/Assess/Planning .... Ms. Nancy A. RAMSEY
18 Director of Facilities .... Ms. Regina MCNEW
19 Director Safety/Security .... Mr. Fred BREINER
21 Director/Budget & Payroll .... Ms. Nancy DONAHUE
96 Director of Purchasing .... Mr. John S. CLARK
15 Director Human Resources .... Ms. Carole GARY
25 Interim Director Grant Development .... Mr. David CAZALET
104 Exec Dir TnCIS/International Educ .... Ms. Tracey BRADLEY

44 Director Major Gift Development ....Ms. Marilyn RODDY
44 Director of Annual & Planned Giving ..Ms. Aneisa L. MCDONALD
29 Dir Cmty Outreach/Donor Engagement ....Ms. Patricia T. MYERS
91 Dir Applications Programming Sup ..... Mr. James (Dean) COPPLE
88 Dir of Network & Technical Services ....Mr. Larry BATES
07 Director of Admissions & Records ..... Ms. Melanie M. PARADISE
28 Director of Access & Diversity ....Ms. Gayle E. WOOD
88 Director of Academic Testing ....Ms. Joan NEWMAN
88 Dir Curriculum & New Programs ....Ms. Judy GOSCH
88 Director of Advising ....Ms. Rachael C. CRAGLE
88 Dir Academic Support Programs .... Ms. Marilyn A. HARPER
88 Bursar ....Ms. Mandy BENTZ
88 Director of Internal Audit .... Ms. Suzanne WALKER
88 Director of QEP .... Ms. Kellie TOON
88 Director of New Student Orientation .... Ms. Rebecca MILAM
88 Director TRIO Student Support Svcs .... Dr. Mark S. COTTER

*Roane State Community College (A)

276 Patton Lane, Harriman TN 37748-5011

County: Roane FICE Identification: 009914
Unit ID: 221397

Telephone: (865) 354-3000 Carnegie Class: Assoc/HT-High Trad
FAX Number: (865) 882-4585 Calendar System: Semester
URL: www.roanestate.edu
Established: 1971 Annual Undergrad Tuition & Fees (In-State): $3,906
Enrollment: 5,832 Coed
Affiliation or Control: State IRS Status: 501(c)3
Highest Offering: Associate Degree
Accreditation: SC, ACBSP, ADNUR, CAHIIM, COARC, COMTA, DH, EMT, OPD, OTA, POLYT, PTAA, RAD

02 President ....Dr. Chris WHALEY
05 Vice Pres for Student Learning/CAO ....Dr. Diane WARD
10 Exec Vice Pres Business & Finance ....Mr. Danny C. GIBBS
103 VP Workforce Develop/Student Affs ....Ms. Teresa S. DUNCAN
30 VP Inst Advancement & Cmty Rels .... Ms. Melinda HILLMAN
21 Asst VP Fiscal/Auxiliary Services ....Ms. Jamie WILMOTH
13 Asst Vice Pres of Info Technology ....Mr. Timothy D. CARROLL
09 Asst VP Institutional Research ....Ms. Karen L. BRUNNER
22 Coordinator Affirmative Action ....Mr. Odell FEARN
08 Director of Library Services ....Mr. Robert M. BENSON
06 Director of Records & Registration .... Ms. Brenda RECTOR
18 Director Physical Plant & Expo Ctr .... Mr. Stan R. STARKEY
29 Director Alumni Relations ....Ms. Tamsin MILLER
96 Director of Purchasing ....Mrs. Dana WEST
36 Workforce Placement & Job Placement ....Ms. Kim HARRIS
04 Executive Assistant to President ....Mrs. Pam WOODY
19 Director Security/Safety ....Mr. Thomas STUFANO
26 Chief Public Relations/Marketing ....Mr. Owen DRISKILL
41 Athletic Director ....Mr. Randy NESBIT
104 Director Study Abroad ....Dr. Adolf KING
106 Dean of Academic Student Services ....Ms. Kathryn RHODES

*Southwest Tennessee Community College (B)

PO Box 780, Memphis TN 38101-0780

County: Shelby FICE Identification: 010439
Unit ID: 221485

Telephone: (901) 333-5000 Carnegie Class: Assoc/MT-VT-Mix Trad/Non
FAX Number: (901) 333-4645 Calendar System: Semester
URL: www.southwest.tn.edu
Established: 2000 Annual Undergrad Tuition & Fees (In-State): $3,963
Enrollment: 10,227 Coed
Affiliation or Control: State IRS Status: 501(c)3
Highest Offering: Associate Degree
Accreditation: SC, ACBSP, ACFEI, ADNUR, #DIETT, EMT, ENGT, MLTAD, PHLEB, PTAA, RAD

02 President ....Dr. Tracy D. HALL
04 Assistant to the President ....Ms. Katrina MULDROW
05 Vice President of Academic Affairs .... Dr. Christopher C. EZELL
86 Exec Asst to Pres/Govt Relations .... Mr. Sherman D. GREER
30 Vice Pres Institutional Advancement ....Mrs. Karen F. NIPPERT
10 Vice Pres Finance & Admin Services ... Mr. Stanley L. ROBINSON
32 Vice Pres Student Affairs ....Mrs. Jacqueline A. FAULKNER
84 Exec Dir of Enrollment Operations ....Ms. Thalia WILSON
26 Exec Director of Comm & Marketing ....Mr. Robert G. MILLER
15 Exec Director Human Resources ....Mr. Steven B. MASSIE
06 Registrar .... Ms. Barbara WELLS
18 Director Physical Plant ....Vacant
96 Director of Purchasing .... Mr. Charles FENNELL
37 Director of Financial Aid .... Mrs. Lechelle D. DAVENPORT
09 Institutional Research Analyst .... Mr. Donald C. MYERS
13 Exec Dir Info Systems (CIO) .... Mr. Michael D. BOYD
19 Director Public Safety ....Mrs. Lezley A. WEBB
88 Exec Dir Equity and Compliance ....Mrs. Monika L. JOHNSON

*Volunteer State Community College (C)

1480 Nashville Pike, Gallatin TN 37066-3188

County: Sumner FICE Identification: 009912
Unit ID: 222053

Telephone: (615) 452-8600 Carnegie Class: Assoc/MT-VT-Mix Trad/Non
FAX Number: (615) 230-3577 Calendar System: Semester
URL: www.volstate.edu
Established: 1970 Annual Undergrad Tuition & Fees (In-State): $3,925
Enrollment: 7,664 Coed
Affiliation or Control: State IRS Status: 501(c)3
Highest Offering: Associate Degree
Accreditation: SC, ACBSP, CAHIIM, COARC, DA, DMS, EMT, MLTAD, POLYT, PTAA, RAD

02 President ....Dr. Jerry FAULKNER
05 Vice President Academic Affairs .... Dr. George PIMENTEL
10 Vice President Business & Finance ....Ms. Beth COOKSEY
32 Vice President Student Services ....Dr. Emily SHORT
30 Vice Pres for Resource Development .... Ms. Karen MITCHELL
45 Vice Pres Inst Planning/Research ....Ms. Jane MCGUIRE
20 Asst VP of Academic Affairs ....Dr. Michael TORRENCE
21 Asst Vice Pres Business & Finance .... Ms. Renee AUSTIN
35 Asst VP Student Svcs/Enrollment Mgt ....Vacant
51 Asst VP/Dean Continuing Education ......Mrs. Hilary B. MARABETI
76 Dean of Health ....Mr. Elvis BRANDON
79 Dean Humanities ....Dr. Jennifer BREZINA
53 Dean Social Science/Education ....Ms. Phyllis FOLEY
81 Dean Math & Science .... Dr. Philip CLIFFORD
50 Dean of Business ....Ms. Patricia ANDERSON
88 Director of Development Studies Pgm .... Ms. Kay DAYTON
15 Dir Personnel/Affirm Act/Human Res .... Ms. Lori CUTRELL
08 Director Library Services .... Ms. Sarah SMITH
07 Dir Admissions & College Registrar ....Mr. Tim AMYX
13 Director Information Technology ....Mr. Kevin BLANKENSHIP
37 Director Student Financial Aid .... Mrs. Sue H. PEDIGO
26 Director Public Relations .... Ms. Tami WALLACE
18 Senior Director Physical Plant .... Mr. William NEWMAN
19 Chief Security & Safety ....Mr. William D. ROGAN
41 Director of Athletics ....Mr. Bobby HUDSON
106 Director Distance Learning ....Ms. Rhonda GREGORY
88 Special Adult Programs/ADA Director .... Ms. Kathy SOWELL
09 Director of Institutional Research ....Mrs. Ann Marie CALDERON
96 Director Purchasing .... Mr. Chris HARRISON
24 Director Media Services .... Mr. Terry HEINEN
88 Director Retention Support Services ....Ms. Heather HARPER
36 Director of Career Placement .... Dr. Rick PARRENT
38 Director Counseling & Testing ....Mr. Terry BUBB
28 Director Student Life & Diversity .... Dr. Kenny YARBROUGH
88 Dir Health Sciences Ctr of Emphasis ....Ms. Terri CRUTCHER
44 Director of Development ....Ms. Debra DAUGHERTY
06 Registrar ....Mr. Tim AMYX

*Walters State Community College (D)

500 S Davy Crockett Parkway, Morristown TN 37813-6899

County: Hamblen FICE Identification: 008863
Unit ID: 222062

Telephone: (423) 585-2600 Carnegie Class: Assoc/HT-High Trad
FAX Number: (423) 585-6853 Calendar System: Semester
URL: www.ws.edu
Established: 1969 Annual Undergrad Tuition & Fees (In-State): $3,936
Enrollment: 6,005 Coed
Affiliation or Control: State IRS Status: 501(c)3
Highest Offering: Associate Degree
Accreditation: SC, ACBSP, ACFEI, ADNUR, CAHIIM, COARC, EMT, MAIT, PTAA, SURGT

02 President ....Dr. Anthony R. MIKSA
04 Int Exec Director to the President ....Ms. Leann LONG
05 Vice President Academic Affairs ....Dr. Lori CAMPBELL
10 Int Vice President Business Affairs ....Dr. Mark HURST
32 Vice President Student Affairs ....Vacant
30 Vice Pres for College Advancement ....Dr. Mark HURST
45 VP for Planning/Research/Assessment . Dr. Debbie L. MCCARTER
20 Asst Vice Pres for Academic Affairs ....Dr. John LAPRISE
35 Asst Vice Pres Student Affairs .... Mr. Michael A. CAMPBELL
18 Ast Vice Pres Facilities Management ....Mr. Max E. WILLIAMS
21 Asst Vice Pres Business Affairs ....Ms. Heather CARRIER
28 Spec Asst to Pres for Diversity ....Ms. W. Ann BOWEN
08 Dean of Library ....Dr. Jamie POSEY
31 Dean/Dir Cmty & Economic Devel .... Dr. Joseph L. COMBS
19 Dean of Public Safety Division ....Mr. Thomas STRANGE
17 Dean Health Programs ....Ms. Marty K. RUCKER
12 Dean Greenville/Greene Co Center .... Ms. Drucilla W. MILLER
12 Dean Sevier County Campus ....Dr. Jama SUTTON
83 Dean of Behavioral/Social Sciences ....Vacant
50 Dean of Business .... Dr. Amy ROSS
79 Dean of Humanities ....Mr. Chippy MCLAIN
81 Dean of Mathematics .... Mr. John C. KNIGHT
49 Dean of Natural Science ....Dr. Jeffrey T. HORNER
75 Dean of Technical Education ....Mr. Thomas R. SEWELL
06 Dean Student Info System/Records ....Ms. Linda MASON
103 Dean Ctr for Workforce Development ....Vacant
37 Dean of Financial Aid ....Ms. Terri STANSBERRY
38 Exec Director Counseling/Testing ....Dr. Andy HALL
15 Exec Dir of Human Resources ....Ms. Tammy GOODE
26 Vice President Public Information ....Mr. James E. PECTOL
13 Exec Director for Information .... Mr. Joe E. SARGENT
41 Director of Athletics ....Mr. Mike CAMPBELL
07 Director of Admissions .... Ms. Avery SWINSON
19 Chief of Campus Police .... Ms. Sarah ROSE
89 Director Freshmen Studies ....Vacant
36 Director Student Placement ....Dr. Andy HALL
92 Director Honors Program .... Ms. Janice M. DONAHUE
96 Director of Purchasing ....Ms. Jerri L. HAMER
105 Director of Network Services ....Mr. Bill R. MOREFIELD
29 Coordinator of Alumni Relations .... Ms. Wanda HARRELL
84 Director Enrollment Development .... Ms. Avery SWINSON
93 Coord Minority Student Recruit ....Ms. Roxanne BOWEN
108 Exec Dir of Planning & Assessment .... Dr. Deanna GARMAN

Tennessee Wesleyan College (E)

204 East College St., Athens TN 37303

County: McMinn FICE Identification: 003525
Unit ID: 221731

Telephone: (423) 745-7504 Carnegie Class: Bac-Diverse
FAX Number: (423) 744-9968 Calendar System: Semester
URL: www.twcnet.edu
Established: 1857 Annual Undergrad Tuition & Fees: $22,900
Enrollment: 1,006 Coed
Affiliation or Control: United Methodist IRS Status: 501(c)3
Highest Offering: Master's
Accreditation: SC, NURSE

01 President ....Dr. Harley KNOWLES
05 Vice President for Academic Affairs ....Dr. Kim E. SPEZIO
10 Vice Pres Financial/Business Affs .... Mrs. Gail HARRIS
32 Vice President for Student Life ....Dr. Scott MASHBURN
30 Vice President of Advancement ....Mr. Randy NELSON
07 Asst Vice President for Admissions .... Ms. Joanne LANDERS
09 VP Institutional Effectiveness .... Mrs. Traci N. WILLIAMS
04 Executive Assistant to President ....Mrs. Gail ROGERS
08 Assoc Dir of Library & Info Svcs .... Ms. Julie ADAMS
06 Registrar ....Mrs. Julie MCCASLIN
37 Director of Financial Aid .... Ms. Lacey WEESE
41 Athletic Director ....Mr. Donny MAYFIELD
15 Human Resources Director ....Mr. Kyle FULBRIGHT
18 Chief of Facilities/Physical Plant ....Mr. Mike INGRAM
26 Director of Communications ....Ms. Bridgette RAPER
35 Assoc Dean of Students ....Ms. Kerrie LYNN
13 Exec Director of Information Tech .... Mr. Brandon LAMBDIN

Trevecca Nazarene University (F)

333 Murfreesboro Road, Nashville TN 37210-2877

County: Davidson FICE Identification: 003526
Unit ID: 221892

Telephone: (615) 248-1200 Carnegie Class: DU-Mod
FAX Number: (615) 248-7728 Calendar System: Semester
URL: www.trevecca.edu
Established: 1901 Annual Undergrad Tuition & Fees: $23,748
Enrollment: 2,606 Coed
Affiliation or Control: Church Of The Nazarene IRS Status: 501(c)3
Highest Offering: Doctorate
Accreditation: SC, ARCPA, CACREP, MUS, NURSE, SW, TED

01 President ....Dr. Dan BOONE
05 University Provost ....Dr. Stephen M. PUSEY
10 Exec Vice Pres Finance & Admin .... Mr. David CALDWELL
26 Vice President External Relations ....Mrs. Peggy J. COONING
51 Assoc Provost Graduate-Cont Stds ....Dr. Tim EADES
20 Assoc Vice Pres Academic Services .... Dr. Tom MIDDENDORF
20 Assoc Vice Pres Academic Programs ....Dr. Jim HIATT
51 Assoc Vice Pres Graduate/Cont Stds .... Dr. Heidi FREDERICK
27 Assoc Vice Pres Marketing & Comm .... Mr. Matthew TOY
32 Assoc Provost/Dean of Student Dev .... Mr. Stephen A. HARRIS
84 Assoc Provost/Dean of Enroll Mgmt .... Ms. Holly WHITBY
42 University Chaplain .... Ms. Shawna GAINES
73 Dean School of Theol/Christian Min ....Dr. Timothy M. GREEN
50 Dean of Business and Technology ....Dr. Jim HIATT
35 Assoc Dean Student Community Life .... Mr. Matt SPRAKER
39 Asc Dean Students Residential Life .... Mrs. Ronda LILIENTHAL
53 Dean of the School of Education ....Dr. Suzann HARRIS
49 Dean of School of Arts & Science ....Dr. Lena WELCH
64 Dean School of Music & Worship Arts ....Dr. David DIEHL
13 Chief Information Officer/ITS ....Mr. John EBERLE
08 Director Library Services .... Mrs. Ruth KINNERSLEY
108 Dir Institutional Effectiveness .... Ms. Donna K. TUDOR
09 Director of Academic Data Mgmt ....Dr. Eugenia HARRIS
06 Registrar ....Ms. Katrina CHAPMAN
19 Director of Security .... Mr. Norm ROBINSON
07 Director of Admissions ....Ms. Melinda MILLER
41 Athletic Director ....Mr. Mark ELLIOTT
88 Director Ctr/Ldrshp Calling Service ....Ms. Michelle GAERTNER
36 Director Counseling Services ....Dr. Sara HOPKINS
28 Coord Student Engagement/Diversity .... Mr. Brodrick THOMAS
88 Coordinator of Sophomore Year Pgm ....Ms. Jennifer NEELY
88 Coordinator of Senior Year Programs .... Ms. Nicole HUBBS
106 Director Online Learning .... Ms. LaMetrius DANIELS
21 Director of Financial Services ....Mr. Chuck SEAMAN
15 Director Human Resources .... Mr. Steve SEXTON
37 Director of Financial Aid ....Mr. Eddie WHITE
76 Director Physician Asst Pgm ....Mr. Bret REEVES
18 Director Plant Operations ....Mr. Glen LINTHICUM
29 Director of Alumni Engagement .... Mr. Michael JOHNSON
27 Mgr of Content & Media Relations ....Ms. Mandy CROW

Tusculum College (G)

60 Shiloh Road, Greeneville TN 37743-9997

County: Greene FICE Identification: 003527
Unit ID: 221953

Telephone: (423) 636-7300 Carnegie Class: Masters/M
FAX Number: (423) 638-7166 Calendar System: Other
URL: www.tusculum.edu
Established: 1794 Annual Undergrad Tuition & Fees: $22,670
Enrollment: 1,921 Coed
Affiliation or Control: Presbyterian Church (U.S.A.) IRS Status: 501(c)3
Highest Offering: Master's
Accreditation: SC, #CAATE

01 President ....Dr. Nancy B. MOODY
05 VP Academic Affairs ....Dr. Ron MAY
30 VP Institutional Advancement .... Ms. Heather PATCHETT
10 Vice Pres/Chief Financial Officer ....Mr. Steve GEHRET
84 VP for Enrollment Management ....Ms. LeAnn HUGHES
20 Asst VP for Academic Affairs ....Dr. Lisa JOHNSON

32 Dean of Students ... Dr. David MCMAHAN
35 Associate Dean of Students ... Ms. Jonita ASHLEY-PAULEY
06 Registrar ... Ms. Bobbie CLARKSTON
21 Controller ... Ms. Tracey JULIAN
07 Director of Operations/Admissions ... Ms. Melissa RIPLEY
45 Asst to Pres Inst Plng/Effectivenes ... Dr. Carl LARSEN
15 Director Human Resources ... Ms. Mary SONNER
36 Director Career Counseling ... Ms. Robin LAY
08 Librarian ... Ms. Kathy HICKS
37 Director of Financial Aid ... Ms. Karen SARTAIN
41 Athletic Director ... Mr. Doug JONES
26 Director of Communications ... Ms. Suzanne RICHEY
13 Director of Information Systems ... Dr. Blair HENLEY
18 Director Facilities Management ... Mr. David MARTIN
92 Director of Honors Program ... Ms. Megan STARK
40 Bookstore Manager ... Mr. Cliff HOY
19 Director of Campus Safety ... Mr. Jonathan GRESHAM
49 Dean School of Arts and Sciences ... Mr. Wayne THOMAS
50 Dean School of Business ... Dr. Michael DILLON
53 Dean School of Education ... Dr. Paul FOX
66 Dean School of Nursing ... Dr. Lois EWEN

Union University (A)

1050 Union University Drive, Jackson TN 38305-3697
County: Madison FICE Identification: 003528
Unit ID: 221971
Telephone: (731) 668-1818 Carnegie Class: DU-Mod
FAX Number: (731) 661-5175 Calendar System: 4/1/4
URL: www.uu.edu
Established: 1823 Annual Undergrad Tuition & Fees: $29,190
Enrollment: 3,846 Coed
Affiliation or Control: Southern Baptist IRS Status: 501(c)3
Highest Offering: Doctorate
Accreditation: SC, ANEST, ART, BUS, CAATE, ENG, MUS, NURSE, PHAR, SW, TED

01 President ... Dr. Samuel (Dub) W. OLIVER
05 Provost/VP Academic Affairs ... Dr. C. Ben MITCHELL
10 Sr Vice Pres Business Services ... Mr. Gary L. CARTER
30 Vice Pres Institutional Advancement . Mrs. Catherine KWASIGROH
84 Vice Pres Enrollment Services ... Mr. Dan GRIFFIN
32 Dean of Students ... Dr. Bryan CARRIER
26 Vice Pres for University Ministries ... Dr. Todd BRADY
108 Vice Pres Institutional Assessment ... Dr. Jimmy H. DAVIS
04 Exec Assistant to the President ... Mrs. Gaye CHRISTY
21 Assoc Vice Pres Business Svcs ... Mr. Robert SIMPSON
08 Acting Director of the Library ... Mrs. Melissa MOORE
27 Assoc VP University Communications ... Mr. Tim ELLSWORTH
90 Assoc VP Information Technology ... Mr. James AVERY
15 Assoc VP Business Svcs/Human Res ... Mr. John CARBONELL
07 Asst VP for Undergraduate Admiss ... Mr. Robbie GRAVES
37 Director Student Financial Planning ... Mr. John WINDHAM
49 Dean College Arts & Sciences ... Dr. John NETLAND
50 Interim Dean School of Business ... Dr. Bill NANCE
66 Dean School of Nursing ... Dr. Kelly HARDEN
53 Exec Dean Col Educ/Human Studies ... Dr. Tom ROSEBROUGH
88 Dean Sch of Theology Missions ... Dr. Nathan FINN
67 Dean School of Pharmacy ... Dr. Sheila MITCHELL
91 Assoc Dir Information Technology ... Miss Karen MCWHERTER
36 Asst Dean Students/Dir Career Svcs ... Mrs. Jackie TAYLOR
13 Director of Data Management ... Mr. David PORTER
06 Registrar ... Mrs. Susan HOPPER
19 Director of Security/Safety ... Mr. Yancey PETTIGREW
41 Director of Athletics ... Mr. Tommy SADLER
18 Chief Facilities/Physical Plant ... Mr. David MCBRIDE

University of Phoenix Memphis Campus (B)

65 Germantown Court, Cordova TN 38018-7290
Telephone: (901) 751-1086 Identification: 770224
Accreditation: &NH, ACBSP

† No longer accepting campus-based students.

University of Phoenix Nashville Campus (C)

616 Marriott Drive, Nashville TN 37214-5048
Telephone: (615) 872-0188 Identification: 770225
Accreditation: &NH, ACBSP

† No longer accepting campus-based students.

*University of Tennessee System Office (D)

800 Andy Holt Tower, Knoxville TN 37996-0180
County: Knox FICE Identification: 008051
Unit ID: 221722
Telephone: (865) 974-1000 Carnegie Class: N/A
FAX Number: (865) 974-3753
URL: www.tennessee.edu

01 President ... Dr. Joe DIPIETRO
03 Executive Vice President ... Dr. David E. MILLHORN
05 VP Academic Affairs/Student Success ... Dr. Katherine N. HIGH
30 CEO Foundation/VP Devel/Alumni ... Mr. Ricky N. MCCURRY
86 VP for Government Rels/Advocacy ... Mr. Anthony HAYNES
45 Vice President for Research ... Dr. David E. MILLHORN
10 Int Treasurer & CFO ... Mr. James (Ron) R. MAPLES
43 VP/General Counsel/Secretary ... Ms. Catherine S. MIZELL
15 Vice President for Human Resources ... Ms. Linda HENDRICKS HARIG
86 Vice Pres Institute for Public Svc ... Dr. Herb BYRD
26 VP Communications & Marketing ... Dr. Tonjanita JOHNSON
13 Chief Information Officer ... Mr. Les MATHEWS
04 Exec Assistant to the President ... Mr. Keith CARVER
21 Exec Dir Auditing/Consulting Svcs ... Ms. Sandy JANSEN
29 Exec Dir UT Natl Alumni Assn ... Mr. Lofton K. STUART

*University of Tennessee, Knoxville (E)

1331 Circle Park, Andy Holt Tower,
Knoxville TN 37996-0184
County: Knox FICE Identification: 003530
Unit ID: 221759
Telephone: (865) 974-1000 Carnegie Class: DU-Highest
FAX Number: (865) 974-1182 Calendar System: Semester
URL: www.utk.edu
Established: 1794 Annual Undergrad Tuition & Fees (In-State): $12,436
Enrollment: 30,386 Coed
Affiliation or Control: State IRS Status: 501(c)3
Highest Offering: Doctorate
Accreditation: SC, ANEST, ART, AUD, BUS, BUSA, CACREP, CIDA, CLPSY, COPSY, CORE, CS, DENT, DIETD, DIETI, ENG, IPSY, JOUR, LAW, LIB, LSAR, MT, MUS, NRPA, NURSE, PAST, PH, RAD, SCPSY, SP, SW, TED, THEA, VET

02 Chancellor ... Dr. Jimmy G. CHEEK
100 Chancellor's Executive Assistant ... Ms. Debra K. THOMAS
05 Provost/Senior VC for Acad Affairs ... Dr. Susan D. MARTIN
32 Vice Chancellor for Student Life ... Dr. Vincent CARILLI
46 Vice Chancellor Research/Engagement ... Dr. Taylor EIGHMY
10 Vice Chanc Finance & Administration ... Mr. Chris CIMINO
26 Vice Chanc for Communications ... Ms. Margie NICHOLS
30 Vice Chanc Development/Alumni Affs ... Mr. Scott RABENOLD
20 Vice Provost for Academic Affairs ... Dr. RJ HINDE
20 Vice Provost Academic Operations ... Vacant
58 Vice Provost/Dean Graduate School ... Dr. Dixie THOMPSON
40 Ast VC Student Life/Dean of Student ... Dr. Melissa SHIVERS
39 Asst VC/Exec Dir Univ Housing ... Dr. Frank CUEVAS
51 Asst Provost Univ Outrch/Cont Educ ... Dr. Norvel BURKETT
07 Asst Provost Enrollment Svcs ... Ms. Kari ALLDREDGE
18 Assoc Vice Chanc Facilities Svcs ... Mr. Dave IRVIN
41 Vice Chancellor/Dir Athletics ... Mr. Dave HART
28 Assoc Vice Chanc Equity & Diversity ... Ms. Jennifer RICHTER
37 Director of Financial Aid ... Mr. Jeffrey G. GERKIN
09 Dir Inst Research/Assessmt ... Ms. Denise GARDNER
38 Director of Student Counseling ... Dr. Victor BARR
06 Registrar ... Ms. Monique W. ANDERSON
27 Director of Marketing ... Ms. Caitlin MCCLEARY
47 Dean Ag Sciences/Natural Resources ... Dr. Caula BEYL
48 Dean of Architecture and Design ... Dr. Scott POOLE
50 Dean Business Administration ... Dr. Steve MANGUM
60 Dean Communication/Information ... Dr. Michael WIRTH
53 Dean Educ/Health/Human Sciences ... Dr. Robert RIDER
54 Dean of Engineering ... Dr. Wayne DAVIS
61 Dean of Law ... Prof. Melanie WILSON
49 Dean of Arts & Sciences ... Dr. Theresa LEE
66 Dean of Nursing ... Dr. Victoria NIEDERHAUSER
70 Dean of Social Work ... Dr. Karen SOWERS
74 Dean of Veterinary Medicine ... Dr. James P. THOMPSON
47 Dean of Agricultural Extension Svc ... Dr. Tim L. CROSS
08 Dean of Libraries ... Dr. Steve SMITH

*University of Tennessee at Chattanooga (F)

615 McCallie Avenue, Chattanooga TN 37403-2504
County: Hamilton FICE Identification: 003529
Unit ID: 221740
Telephone: (423) 425-4111 Carnegie Class: Masters/L
FAX Number: (423) 425-2200 Calendar System: Semester
URL: www.utc.edu
Established: 1886 Annual Undergrad Tuition & Fees (In-State): $8,356
Enrollment: 11,670 Coed
Affiliation or Control: State IRS Status: 501(c)3
Highest Offering: Doctorate
Accreditation: SC, ANEST, ART, BUS, BUSA, CAATE, CACREP, CIDA, CS, DIETD, ENG, ENGT, JOUR, MUS, NURSE, OT, PTA, SPAA, SW, TED, THEA

02 Chancellor ... Dr. Steven R. ANGLE
05 Provost & Sr Vice Chancellor ... Dr. Jerald AINSWORTH
108 Vice Provost for Academic Affairs ... Dr. David RAUSCH
30 Vice Chanc University Advancement ... Dr. Bryan ROWLAND
10 Exec Vice Chanc Fin/Operations & IT ... Dr. Richard BROWN
46 Vice Chancellor for Research ... Dr. Joanne ROMAGNI
32 Vice Chanc Student Development ... Dr. John DELANEY
20 Assoc Provost for Academic Affairs ... Vacant
21 Assoc Vice Chanc Business/Fin Affs ... Ms. Vanasia Conley PARKS
26 Vice Chanc Mktg and Communications ... Mr. Kirk ENGLEHARDT
41 Vice Chanc & Dir of Athletics ... Mr. David BLACKBURN
26 Assoc VC University Relations ... Mr. Chuck CANTRELL
18 Asst VC Operations/Fac Plng & Mgt ... Mr. Tom M. ELLIS
91 Assoc VC & CIO ... Mr. Tom HOOVER
35 Asst VC Student Development ... Dr. Dee Dee ANDERSON
100 Chief of Staff ... Ms. Terry DENNISTON
08 Dean of UTC Library ... Ms. Theresa LIEDTKA
88 Assoc Dean of Student Life ... Mr. Jim HICKS
84 Asst Provost Enrollment Services ... Mr. Yancy FREEMAN
06 Director of Records and Registrar ... Ms. Linda ORTH
13 Director of Enterprise Systems ... Mr. Ron BAKER
09 Dir of Planning/Eval/Inst Research ... Dr. Karen ADSIT
36 Int Dir Placemt/Student Employment ... Mrs. Donna COOPER
15 Interim Director of Human Resources ... Ms. Laure POU
38 Director of Counseling ... Dr. Nancy BADGER
37 Director of Financial Aid ... Ms. Jennifer BUCKLES
58 Dean of the Graduate School ... Dr. Joanne ROMAGNI
49 Dean of Arts & Sciences ... Dr. Jeff ELWELL
50 Dean of Business Administration ... Dr. Robert DOOLEY
53 Dean of Health/Educ/Prof Studies ... Dr. Valerie RUTLEDGE
54 Dean Engineering/Comp Science ... Dr. Daniel PACK
66 Director of Nursing ... Dr. Chris SMITH
22 Director of Equity & Diversity ... Dr. Bryan SAMUEL
78 Director of Cooperative Education ... Vacant
25 Director of Sponsored Programs ... Ms. Meredith PERRY
29 Director of Alumni Affairs ... Ms. Jayne HOLDER
96 Mgr of Business Svcs (Purchasing) ... Mr. Charles SCOTT
19 Chief of Police ... Mr. Robert RATCHFORD
39 Director Student Housing ... Ms. Valara SAMPLE
92 Dean Honors College ... Dr. Linda FROST
88 Director of Community Partnerships ... Ms. Ann YOACHIM
104 Exec Director International Program ... Mr. Takeo SUZUKI
43 Dir Legal Services/General Counsel ... Mr. Yousef A. HAMADEH

*University of Tennessee at Martin (G)

554 University Street, Martin TN 38238-0001
County: Weakley FICE Identification: 003531
Unit ID: 221768
Telephone: (731) 881-7000 Carnegie Class: Masters/M
FAX Number: (731) 881-7019 Calendar System: Semester
URL: www.utm.edu
Established: 1900 Annual Undergrad Tuition & Fees (In-State): $8,326
Enrollment: 7,042 Coed
Affiliation or Control: State IRS Status: 501(c)3
Highest Offering: Master's
Accreditation: #SC, AAFCS, BUS, CEA, DIETD, DIETI, ENG, JOUR, MUS, NUR, SW, TED

02 Interim Chancellor ... Dr. Robert M. SMITH
05 Provost & Vice Chanc for Acad Affs ... Dr. E. Jerald OGG
10 Int Vice Chanc for Finance & Admin ... Ms. Petra R. MCPHEARSON
32 Vice Chancellor for Student Affairs ... Dr. Margaret Y. TOSTON
30 Vice Chancellor for Univ Advancemnt ... Mr. Andrew A. WILSON
20 Assoc Vice Chanc for Academic Affr ... Dr. Victoria S. SENG
13 Interim Chief Information Officer ... Mr. Terry W. LEWIS
21 Int Dir Budget & Mgmt Report ... Ms. Ann PAYNE
35 Asst Vice Chanc for Student Affairs ... Mr. John ABEL
44 Asst VChanc Devel & Planned Giving . Ms. Jeanna C. SWAFFORD
04 Exec Assistant to the Chancellor ... Ms. Edie B. GIBSON
29 Assoc Vice Chanc for Alumni Rels ... Mr. Charley T. DEAL
06 Int Dir of Acad Records & Registrar ... Ms. Martha BARNETT
28 Int Equity & Diversity Ofcr-AA/EEO ... Mr. Joe T. HENDERSON
15 Director of Human Resources ... Mr. James (Phillip) BRIGHT
09 Int Dir Institutional Research ... Dr. Desiree A. MCCULLOUGH
41 Int Dir Intercollegiate Athletics ... Mr. D. Kevin MCMILLAN
08 Int Director of Library ... Mr. Sam S. RICHARDSON
18 Director of Physical Plant Opers ... Mr. Tim J. NIPP
19 Director of Public Safety ... Mr. Scott D. ROBBINS
96 Purchasing Agent ... Ms. Lori A. DONAVANT
38 Dir Student Health & Counseling Svc ... Ms. Shannon DEAL
39 Director of Student Housing ... Vacant
26 Chief Communications Officer ... Mr. Robert (Bud) D. GRIMES
85 Dir Tenn Intensive English Pgm ... Ms. Amy E. FENNING
47 Dean Col Agri & App Sciences ... Dr. Todd A. WINTERS
50 Dean Col Business & Global Affairs ... Dr. Ross N. DICKENS
53 Dean Col Educ/Health/Behav Sci ... Ms. Cynthia L. WEST
79 Dean Col Humanities/Fine Arts ... Dr. Lynn M. ALEXANDER
54 Dean Col Engr & Natural Sci ... Dr. Richard J. HELGESON
105 Director Web Services ... Mr. Brian C. INGRAM
106 Int Dir Exec Online Educ/E-learning ... Dr. Brian DONAVANT
25 Chief Contracts/Grants Admin ... Dr. Joan K. WEST
84 Exec Dir Enroll Svcs/Stdnt Engagmnt ... Dr. James D. MANTOOTH
07 Director of Admissions ... Ms. Destin TUCKER
104 Dir International Education ... Dr. Malcolm KOCH
37 Int Dir Financial Aid & Scholarship ... Ms. Amy MISTRIC

University of Tennessee Health Science Center (H)

920 Madison Ave, Memphis TN 38163-0002
County: Shelby FICE Identification: 006725
Unit ID: 221704
Telephone: (901) 448-5500 Carnegie Class: Not Classified
FAX Number: (901) 448-7750 Calendar System: Semester
URL: www.uthsc.edu
Established: 1911 Annual Undergrad Tuition & Fees (In-State): N/A
Enrollment: N/A Coed
Affiliation or Control: State IRS Status: 501(c)3
Highest Offering: Doctorate
Accreditation: SC, ANEST, #ARCPA, CAHIIM, CYTO, DENT, DH, HT, IPSY, MED, MT, NURSE, OT, PHAR, PTA

01 Chancellor ... Dr. Steve J. SCHWAB
03 Executive Vice Chancellor/COO ... Dr. Kennard D. BROWN
05 VC Academic/Faculty/Student Affs ... Dr. Lori GONZALEZ
10 Vice Chancellor Finance/Operations ... Mr. Anthony A. FERRARA
13 VC Information Technology Services ... Dr. Jan VAN DER AA
46 Vice Chancellor Research ... Dr. Steven R. GOODMAN
30 VC Development and Alumni Affairs ... Dr. Randy L. FARMER
32 Assoc VC Student Affairs ... Dr. Sonya G. SMITH
52 Dean Dentistry ... Dr. Timothy L. HOTTEL
58 Dean Graduate Health Sciences ... Dr. Donald B. THOMASON
76 Dean Health Professions ... Dr. Noma B. ANDERSON
63 Executive Dean Medicine ... Dr. David M. STERN
63 Dean Medicine Chattanooga ... Dr. David C. SEABERG

63 Dean Medicine Knoxville .... Dr. James J. NEUTENS
66 Dean Nursing .... Dr. Wendy M. LIKES
67 Dean Pharmacy .... Dr. Marie A. CHISHOLM-BURNS
06 Interim Registrar .... Dr. Sonya G. SMITH
07 Interim Director of Admissions .... Ms. Melodie PATTERSON
37 Director of Financial Aid .... Mr. Samuel MATHENY
08 Interim Director Library .... Mr. Rick FOUGHT
15 Assc VC Human Resources .... Ms. Chandra ALSTON
18 Assoc VC Facilities Administration .... Mr. Emile DAVID
19 Interim Chief of Police .... Mr. Bruce HOLDEN
22 Asst VC Equity and Diversity .... Dr. Michael ALSTON
26 Interim Asst VC Comm/Marketing .... Ms. Peggy REISSER

Vanderbilt University (A)

2305 West End Avenue, Nashville TN 37203
County: Davidson FICE Identification: 003535
Unit ID: 221999
Telephone: (615) 322-7311 Carnegie Class: DU-Highest
FAX Number: (615) 343-7765 Calendar System: Semester
URL: www.vanderbilt.edu
Established: 1873 Annual Undergrad Tuition & Fees: $44,712
Enrollment: 12,686 Coed
Affiliation or Control: Independent Non-Profit IRS Status: 501(c)3
Highest Offering: Doctorate
Accreditation: SC, AUD, BUS, CACREP, CLPSY, CS, DENT, DIETI, DMS, ENG, IPSY, LAW, MED, MIDWF, MT, MUS, NDT, NMT, PERF, PH, SP, TED, THEOL

01 Chancellor .... Dr. Nicholas ZEPPOS
05 Provost/Vice Chancellor .... Dr. Susan R. WENTE
17 Vice Chanc Hlth Affs/Dean Med Sch .... Dr. Jeffrey R. BALSER
10 Vice Chancellor Finance/CFO .... Mr. Brett SWEET
11 Vice Chanc Administration .... Mr. Eric KOPSTAIN
30 Vice Chanc Dev & Alumni Relations .... Ms. Susie STALCUP
12 Vice Provost for Research .... Dr. Padma RAGHAVAN
13 Vice Chanc for Investments and CIO .... Mr. Anders W. HALL
28 VC Equity/Diversity/Inclusion .... Dr. George C. HILL
15 Chief Human Resources Ofcr .... Ms. Barbara CARROLL
26 VC Univ Affairs and Athletics .... Dr. David WILLIAMS
20 Assoc Vice Chanc Academic Affairs .... Ms. Susan HART
18 Deputy VC Facilities & Environment .... Mr. Judson NEWBERN
27 Vice Chancellor for Public Affairs .... Ms. Beth FORTUNE
09 Exec Dir Institutional Research .... Dr. Roberta BELL
20 Vice Provost Learning & Res Affairs .... Ms. Cynthia J. CYRUS
88 Vice Prov Acad & Strat Affairs .... Dr. John G. GEER
58 Dean of the Graduate School .... Dr. Mark T. WALLACE
08 University Librarian .... Dr. Valerie HOTCHKISS
27 Dean of Student Publicats/Comm .... Mr. F. Clark WILLIAMS
21 Asst V Chanc for Finance/Controller .... Ms. Dalana ROBERTSON
06 Registrar .... Mr. Bart P. QUINET
84 Vice Provost Univ Enrollment Affs .... Dr. Douglas CHRISTIANSEN
07 Dir Undergraduate Admissions .... Mr. John GAINES
37 Director Student Financial Aid .... Mr. Brent B. TENER
38 Director Psych Counseling Center .... Dr. Catherine FUCHS
36 Exec Dir Ctr for Student Prof Devel .... Dr. Katharine S. BROOKS
25 Assoc Director Contract Mgmt .... Mr. Jeff NEWMAN
14 Vice Chancellor Information Tech .... Mr. John M. LUTZ
32 Dean of Students/Assoc Provost .... Mr. Mark BANDAS
106 Assoc Provost for Digital Learning .... Dr. John M. SLOOP
49 Dean College of Arts and Science .... Dr. Lauren BENTON
54 Dean School of Engineering .... Dr. Philippe M. FAUCHET
66 Dean School of Nursing .... Dr. Linda NORMAN
53 Dean Education & Human Development .... Dr. Camilla P. BENBOW
64 Dean Blair School of Music .... Dr. Mark WAIT
73 Dean of the Divinity School .... Dr. Emilie M. TOWNES
61 Dean of the School of Law .... Dr. Chris GUTHRIE
50 Dean Owen Grad School of Mgmt .... Dr. M. Eric JOHNSON
88 Dean of the Ingram Commons .... Dr. Vanessa BEASLEY
42 Associate Chaplain .... Rev. Gretchen PERSON
19 Chief of Police/Asst Vice Chanc .... Mr. August J. WASHINGTON
22 Dir EO/AA & Disability Svcs .... Ms. Anita JENIOUS
41 Dir Sport Operations/Asst Vice Chan .... Mr. Brockton WILLIAMS
104 Director Global Support Services .... Ms. Kathryn HOFELDT
39 Sr Director Housing Operations .... Mr. James S. KRAMKA
43 Vice Chancellor/General Counsel .... Ms. Audrey J. ANDERSON
44 Asst Vice Chancellor Annual Giving .... Mr. Kyle D. MCGOWAN
86 Asst Vice Chanc Federal Relations .... Ms. Christina D. WEST

Vatterott Career College (B)

6991 Appling Farms Parkway, Memphis TN 38133
Telephone: (901) 372-2399 Identification: 770592
Accreditation: ACCSC

† Branch campus of Vatterott College-Des Moines, Des Moines, IA

Vatterott College-Memphis (C)

2655 Dividend Drive, Memphis TN 38132-1713
Telephone: (901) 761-5730 Identification: 666308
Accreditation: ACCSC

† Branch campus of Vatterott College-NorthPark, Berkeley, MO.

Virginia College School of Business and Health (D)

721 Eastgate Loop, Chattanooga TN 37411-5600
Telephone: (423) 893-2000 Identification: 666136
Accreditation: ACICS, ACFEI, MAAB

† Branch campus of Virginia College, Birmingham, AL

Virginia College School of Business and Health (E)

5003 North Broadway Street, Knoxville TN 37918
Telephone: (865) 745-4500 Identification: 770828
Accreditation: ACICS, MAAB

† Branch campus of Virginia College, Birmingham, AL

Visible Music College (F)

200 Madison Avenue, Memphis TN 38103
County: Shelby FICE Identification: 039823
Unit ID: 449764
Telephone: (901) 381-3939 Carnegie Class: Spec-4-yr-Arts
FAX Number: (901) 377-0544 Calendar System: Semester
URL: www.visible.edu
Established: 2000 Annual Undergrad Tuition & Fees: $19,500
Enrollment: 112 Coed
Affiliation or Control: Independent Non-Profit IRS Status: 501(c)3
Highest Offering: Baccalaureate
Accreditation: TRACS

01 President .... Dr. Ken STEORTS
05 Vice President of Academics .... Dr. Cameron HARVEY
32 Director of Students .... JD WILSON
30 Vice President of Advancement .... Geordy WELLS
10 Vice President of Business .... Ben RAWLEY
07 Director of Admissions .... Susan HARRIS
37 Director of Financial Aid .... Cynthia BROWN
06 Registrar .... Scott LENCKE
21 Business Office Manager .... Tom MELTON
18 Operations Manager .... Matt BROWN
84 Director Enrollment Management .... Brian DUFFY

Watkins College of Art, Design & Film (G)

2298 Rosa L. Parks Boulevard, Nashville TN 37228-1306
County: Davidson FICE Identification: 030888
Unit ID: 392840
Telephone: (615) 383-4848 Carnegie Class: Spec-4-yr-Arts
FAX Number: (615) 383-4849 Calendar System: Semester
URL: www.watkins.edu
Established: 1885 Annual Undergrad Tuition & Fees: $20,790
Enrollment: 304 Coed
Affiliation or Control: Independent Non-Profit IRS Status: 501(c)3
Highest Offering: Master's
Accreditation: SC, ART, CIDA

01 President .... Dr. J. KLINE
30 Vice Pres Institutional Advancement .... Ms. Autumn PARROT
05 Vice President for Academic Affairs .... Ms. Joy MCKENZIE
10 Vice Pres Finance and Operations .... Ms. Mary Ellen LOTHAMER
07 Int Director Admissions .... Ms. Jenna MAURICE
26 Director of Communications .... Mr. Brendan TAPLEY
06 Registrar .... Ms. Tracie JOHNSON
37 Director Financial Aid .... Ms. Regina GILBERT
08 Library Director .... Ms. Amy KAMMERMAN
13 Director Information Technology .... Mr. Shawn MAGGARD
18 Director of Facilities .... Mr. Martin DILLINGHAM
88 Chair Film School .... Mr. Richard GERSHMAN
57 Chair Fine Art Department .... Ms. Kristi HARGROVE
88 Chair Graphic Design Department .... Mr. Dan BRAWNER
88 Chair Interior Design Department .... Vacant
88 Chair Photography Department .... Ms. Kristy HARGROVE
97 Director General Education .... Ms. Cary Beth MILLER
51 Director Community Education .... Ms. Anna MCKEOWN
32 Director Student Life .... Ms. Kristina KRAUWAYMIRE

Welch College (H)

3606 West End Avenue, Nashville TN 37205-2498
County: Davidson FICE Identification: 030018
Unit ID: 220206
Telephone: (615) 844-5000 Carnegie Class: Bac-Diverse
FAX Number: (615) 844-5004 Calendar System: Semester
URL: www.welch.edu
Established: 1942 Annual Undergrad Tuition & Fees: $17,398
Enrollment: 329 Coed
Affiliation or Control: Free Will Baptist IRS Status: 501(c)3
Highest Offering: Master's
Accreditation: SC, BI

01 President .... Dr. J. Matthew PINSON
05 Provost .... Dr. Paul G. KETTEMAN
10 Vice President Financial Affairs .... Mr. Craig MAHLER
45 Dir Institutional Planning/Assess .... Dr. Kevin HESTER
30 Vice Pres Institutional Advancement .... Mr. David WILLIFORD
32 VP Student Svcs/Dean of Students .... Dr. Jon FORLINES
34 Dean of Women .... Mrs. Susan FORLINES
21 Staff Accountant .... Mrs. Leigh Ann SMITH
08 Librarian .... Mrs. Carol REID
18 Director of Plant Operations .... Mr. Sandy GOODFELLOW
84 Dir of Enrollment Services .... Mrs. Debbie MOUSER
106 Dir of Online and Adult Studies .... Mr. Allan CROWSON
09 Director of Institutional Research .... Mr. Wayne SPRUILL
41 Athletic Director .... Mr. Garr TURNER
04 Exec Assistant to the President .... Mrs. Martha FLETCHER
06 Registrar .... Mr. Matthew BRACEY
37 Student Financial Aid Coordinator .... Mrs. Angie EDGMON
44 Director of the Annual Fund .... Mr. Mike EDWARDS
26 Chief Public Relations/Marketing .... Mr. Josh OWENS

Williamson College (I)

274 Mallory Station Road, Franklin TN 37067
County: Williamson FICE Identification: 035135
Unit ID: 443340
Telephone: (615) 771-7821 Carnegie Class: Spec-4-yr-Faith
FAX Number: (615) 771-7810 Calendar System: Semester
URL: www.williamsoncc.edu
Established: 1996 Annual Undergrad Tuition & Fees: $11,300
Enrollment: 72 Coed
Affiliation or Control: Non-denominational IRS Status: 501(c)3
Highest Offering: Baccalaureate
Accreditation: BI

01 President .... Dr. Ed SMITH
05 Vice Pres Academic Affairs .... Dr. Todd BRADLEY
88 Dean Emeritus .... Dr. Sharon LANDER
11 Vice President for Operations .... Ms. Susan MAYS
06 Registrar/Dir Instl Effectiveness .... Ms. Karen HUDSON
37 Dir Financial Aid/Veteran Affairs .... Ms. Jennifer SPEER
08 Librarian .... Ms. Elizabeth HUTCHISON
04 Executive Team Coordinator .... Ms. Laura FLOWERS

TEXAS

Abilene Christian University (J)

ACU Box 29100, Abilene TX 79699-9100
County: Taylor FICE Identification: 003537
Unit ID: 222178
Telephone: (325) 674-2000 Carnegie Class: Masters/L
FAX Number: (325) 674-2202 Calendar System: Semester
URL: www.acu.edu
Established: 1906 Annual Undergrad Tuition & Fees: $30,830
Enrollment: 4,427 Coed
Affiliation or Control: Churches Of Christ IRS Status: 501(c)3
Highest Offering: Doctorate
Accreditation: SC, BUS, CIDA, CS, DIETD, @DIETI, JOUR, MFCD, MUS, NURSE, OT, SP, SW, TEAC, THEOL

01 President .... Dr. Phil SCHUBERT
100 Senior Advisor to the President .... Ms. Suzanne ALLMON
03 Vice President of the University .... Dr. Gary D. MCCALEB
05 Provost .... Dr. Robert RHODES
88 Exec VP Academic Affairs-Dallas .... Dr. Jay GOIN
30 VP for Advancement .... Mr. Jim ORR
32 VP for Student Life .... Mr. Chris RILEY
10 VP & Chief Financial Officer .... Mr. Steven HOLLEY
20 VP Academic Affairs-Dallas .... Dr. Stephen JOHNSON
88 Chief Investment Ofcr/Pres ACIMCO .... Mr. Jack W. RICH
43 Vice President & General Counsel .... Mr. Slade SULLIVAN
00 Chancellor .... Dr. Royce MONEY
88 Exec Assistant to the Chancellor .... Mr. Jim HOLMANS
102 Vice Chancellor/Pres ACU Foundation .... Mr. Dan T. GARRETT
20 Vice Provost .... Dr. Susan LEWIS
84 Asst VP Enrollment-Dallas .... Ms. Jessica MANNING
49 Dean College of Arts & Sciences .... Dr. Greg STRAUGHN
73 Dean College of Biblical Studies .... Dr. Ken R. CUKROWSKI
50 Dean College of Business Admin .... Dr. Brad CRISP
53 Dean College of Educ & Human Svcs .... Dr. Donnie SNIDER
92 Dean Honors College .... Dr. Jason MORRIS
58 Int Dean Graduate School .... Dr. Donnie SNIDER
66 Dean School of Nursing .... Dr. Becky HAMMACK
08 Dean Library/Educational Technology .... Dr. John WEAVER
104 Director of the Ctr Intl Educ .... Dr. Stephen SHEWMAKER
106 Managing Director Online Programs .... Mr. Corey PATTERSON
35 Dean of Students .... Mr. Mark LEWIS
36 Director Career Center .... Mrs. Jill FORTSON
06 Registrar/Dir 1st Year Program .... Dr. Eric GUMM
84 Chief Enroll Ofcr/Dir Stdnt Fin Svc .... Mr. Kevin CAMPBELL
26 Chief Marketing Officer .... Mr. Jason GROVES
39 Director Residence Life .... Dr. Bob STRADER
38 Director Univ Counseling Center .... Mr. Steve ROWLANDS
88 Dir Center for Christian Service .... Dr. Jan MEYER
11 VP of Operations .... Mr. Kevin J. ROBERTS
18 Exec Dir Facilities/Campus Develop .... Mr. Corey RUFF
13 Exec Dir of Information Technology .... Mrs. Kay REEVES
24 Exec Dir Adams Ctr Teaching/Lrng .... Dr. Jennifer SHEWMAKER
29 Dir of Alumni Rels & Annual Project .... Mr. Craig FISHER
19 Chief of Police .... Mr. Jimmy ELLISON
44 Director of Major Gifts .... Mr. Don GARRETT
41 Director of Athletics .... Mr. Lee DE LEON
15 Director of HR .... Mrs. Wendy JONES
88 Director of Faculty Enrichment .... Dr. Laura CARROLL
09 Asst Provost for Inst Effectiveness .... Dr. Tom A. MILHOLLAND
96 Director of Procurement .... Ms. Sandy HALL
40 Chief Business Services Officer .... Mr. Anthony T. WILLIAMS
101 Secretary to the Board of Trustees .... Mr. Slade SULLIVAN
04 Exec Assistant Office of President .... Mrs. Stephanie A. WOODLEE
46 Director Research/Sponsored Progams .... Dr. Megan ROTH
58 Dean College Grad/Professional Stds .... Dr. Jamie GOFF
07 Director of Admissions .... Ms. Tamara LONG
88 Title IX Coordinator .... Mrs. Sherita NICKERSON
37 Director of Student Finance .... Ms. Candi HAMMETT

*Alamo Community College District Central Office (A)

201 W. Sheridan, San Antonio TX 78204-1429
County: Bexar FICE Identification: 003607
Unit ID: 222497
Telephone: (210) 485-0020 Carnegie Class: N/A
FAX Number: (210) 486-9166
URL: www.alamo.edu

01 Chancellor .... Dr. Bruce LESLIE
05 Vice Chanc for Academic Success .... Dr. Jo-Carol FABIANKE
11 Vice Chanc for Finance & Admin .... Ms. Diane E. SNYDER
32 Vice Chancellor for Student Success .... Dr. Adelina SILVA
103 Vice Chanc Economic/Workforce Devel ... Dr. Federico ZARAGOZA
44 VC Plng/Performance/Inform/Systems .... Dr. Thomas CLEARY
15 Assoc Vice Chanc Human Resources . Ms. Linda BOYER-OWENS
26 Assoc Vice Chanc Communications .... Mr. Leo ZUNIGA
18 Assoc Vice Chanc Facilities .... Mr. John STRYBOS
10 Assoc VC Finance & Fiscal Services ...... Ms. Pamela ANSBOURY
04 Deputy to the Chancellor .... Ms. Michelle PERALES
30 Exec Director Inst Advancement .... Mr. Jim ESKIN
21 Director of Internal Audit .... Vacant
96 Director Acquisitions & Admin Svcs .... Mr. Gary O'BAR
19 Chief Department of Public Safety .... Mr. Don ADAMS
21 Comptroller .... Ms. Gettie MORENO
12 President Northwest Vista College .... Dr. Ric BASER
12 President San Antonio College .... Dr. Robert VELA
12 President St Philip's College .... Dr. Adena WILLIAMS LOSTON
12 President Palo Alto College .... Dr. Michael FLORES
12 Pres Northeast Lakeview College .... Vacant
37 Director Student Financial Aid .... Mr. Harold WHITIS
43 Dir Legal Services/General Counsel .... Mr. Ross LAUGHEAD
09 Dist Dir Inst Rsch/Effect/Planning .... Mr. Velda VILLARREAL

*Northeast Lakeview College (B)

1201 Kitty Hawk Rd, Universal City TX 78148
County: Bexar Identification: 667278
Telephone: (210) 486-5000 Carnegie Class: Not Classified
FAX Number: N/A Calendar System: Semester
URL: www.alamo.edu/nlc
Established: 2007 Annual Undergrad Tuition & Fees (In-District): N/A
Enrollment: N/A Coed
Affiliation or Control: Local IRS Status: 501(c)3
Highest Offering: Associate Degree
Accreditation: @SC

02 Interim President .... Dr. Thomas CLEARY
11 Vice Pres of College Services .... Dr. Tangila DOVE

*Northwest Vista College (C)

3535 N Ellison Drive, San Antonio TX 78251-4217
County: Bexar FICE Identification: 033723
Unit ID: 420398
Telephone: (210) 486-4000 Carnegie Class: Assoc/HT-High Trad
FAX Number: (210) 486-9105 Calendar System: Semester
URL: www.alamo.edu/nvc
Established: 1995 Annual Undergrad Tuition & Fees (In-District): $2,088
Enrollment: 15,797 Coed
Affiliation or Control: Local IRS Status: 501(c)3
Highest Offering: Associate Degree
Accreditation: SC

02 President .... Dr. Ric N. BASER
03 Vice President for College Services .... Mrs. Erin L. SHERMAN
05 Vice President for Academic Success .... Dr. Amy F. WHITWORTH
32 Vice President for Student Success .... Mrs. Deborah GAITAN
30 Director Institutional Advancement .... Mrs. Lynne DEAN
08 Learning Resources Chair .... Vacant
35 Dean of Student Success .... Mrs. Jennifer COMEDY-HOLMES
26 Dir of Public Relations & Marketing .... Mrs. Renata SERAFIN
13 Director Info/Communications Tech .... Mr. Felix SALINAS
37 Associate Director of Financial Aid .... Mrs. Rosalinda ENCINA
10 Assistant Bursar .... Mrs. Patricia SANCHEZ
15 Sr Human Resources Generalist .... Mrs. Jessica SACAL-TRENT
45 Director of Resources & College Dev .... Ms. Judy V. CAMARGO
18 Superintendent NVC .... Mr. Bernie ZERTUCHE
103 Dean of Workforce Development .... Mr. Patrick FONTENOT
49 Dean of Arts and Sciences .... Vacant
09 Director of Institutional Research .... Dr. Eliza HERNANDEZ
84 Director of Enrollment Management .... Mrs. Robin SANDBERG
07 Associate Director of Admissions .... Mrs. Yvonne GUERRA
04 Executive Assistant to President .... Mrs. Lydia BEAVER

*Palo Alto College (D)

1400 W Villaret Boulevard, San Antonio TX 78224-2499
County: Bexar FICE Identification: 023413
Unit ID: 246354
Telephone: (210) 486-3000 Carnegie Class: Assoc/HT-High Non
FAX Number: (210) 921-5005 Calendar System: Semester
URL: www.alamo.edu
Established: 1985 Annual Undergrad Tuition & Fees (In-District): $2,088
Enrollment: 8,376 Coed
Affiliation or Control: Local IRS Status: 501(c)3
Highest Offering: Associate Degree
Accreditation: SC

02 President .... Dr. Mike FLORES
05 Vice President for Academic Success .... Ms. Elizabeth TANNER
10 Vice President of College Services .... Dr. Beatriz JOSEPH
32 Vice President for Student Success .... Mr. Gilberto BECERRA
49 Dean Arts & Sciences .... Dr. Mary Ellen JACOBS
72 Dean Career/Technical Education .... Vacant
08 Dean of Learning Resources .... Ms. Tina MESA
35 Dean of Student Success .... Ms. Katherine BEAUMONT DOSS
26 Director of Public Relations .... Mr. Jerry ARELLANO
21 Assistant Bursar .... Ms. Sarah MISNER
84 Director of Enrollment Management .... Ms. Elizabeth AGUILAR-VILLARUAL
37 Assc Dir Student Financial Services .... Ms. Shirley LEIJA
41 Athletic Director .... Vacant
18 Facilities Superintendnt/Phys Plant .... Mr. Sergio RIVERA
38 Counselor .... Vacant
29 Coordinator Alumni Relations .... Ms. Leticia INOCENCIO
09 Dir Inst Rsrch/Plng/Effectiveness .... Mr. George GUAJARDO
30 Director of Advancement .... Vacant
06 Chief Records Officer .... Ms. Diane BURRESS
04 Administrative Asst to President .... Mrs. Connie ACOVIO
100 Executive Asst to the President .... Mrs. Leticia DE LA ROSA
13 Chief Info Technology Director .... Mr. Christopher DELGADO

*St. Philip's College (E)

1801 Martin Luther King, San Antonio TX 78203-2098
County: Bexar FICE Identification: 003608
Unit ID: 227854
Telephone: (210) 486-2000 Carnegie Class: Assoc/HVT-High Non
FAX Number: N/A Calendar System: Semester
URL: www.alamo.edu/spc/
Established: 1898 Annual Undergrad Tuition & Fees (In-District): $2,088
Enrollment: 10,514 Coed
Affiliation or Control: Local IRS Status: 501(c)3
Highest Offering: Associate Degree
Accreditation: SC, ACFEI, CAHIIM, COARC, CVT, HT, MLTAD, OTA, PTAA, RAD, SURGT

02 President .... Dr. Adena WILLIAMS LOSTON
05 Vice Pres of Academic Success .... Ms. Maureen CARTLEDGE
32 Vice Pres of Student Success .... Dr. Mordecai BROWNLEE
11 Vice President for College Svcs .... Ms. Lacy HAMPTON
12 Int Dean of Southwest Campus .... Dr. Josha SCOTT
35 Dean Student Success .... Dr. Paul MACHEN
08 Dean Interdisciplinary Programs .... Dr. Natasha SCHMITTOU
75 Dean Applied Science & Tech .... Mr. Christopher BEARDSALL
49 Dean Arts & Science .... Mr. Randall DAWSON
76 Dean of Health Sciences .... Ms. Rose STERLING
37 Asst Director of Financial Aid .... Ms. Grace ZAPATA
45 Director Planning & Research .... Dr. Maria HINOJOSA
10 Assistant Bursar .... Ms. Sophia GONZALEZ
26 Dir Community & Public Relations ....Ms. Tracy ROSS-GARCIA
30 Director Institutional Advancement .... Dr. Sharon CROCKETT-RAY
72 Director Instructional Technology .... Mr. John ORONA
18 Chief Facilities/Physical Plant .... Ms. Bertha NORWOOD
29 Director Alumni Relations .... Dr. Sharon CROCKETT-RAY
84 Director Enrollment Management .... Ms. Beautrice BUTLER
96 Chief Budget Manager .... Mr. Paul BORREGO

*San Antonio College (F)

1300 San Pedro Avenue, San Antonio TX 78212-4299
County: Bexar FICE Identification: 009163
Unit ID: 227924
Telephone: (210) 486-0000 Carnegie Class: Assoc/HT-Mix Trad/Non
FAX Number: N/A Calendar System: Semester
URL: www.alamo.edu/sac
Established: 1925 Annual Undergrad Tuition & Fees (In-District): $2,088
Enrollment: 21,280 Coed
Affiliation or Control: Local IRS Status: 501(c)3
Highest Offering: Associate Degree
Accreditation: SC, ADNUR, CEA, DA, EMT, FUSER, MAC

02 President .... Dr. Robert H. VELA
05 Vice Pres Student/Academic Success .... Dr. Lisa ALCORTA
11 Vice President of College Services .... Vacant
32 Int Dean of Student Success .... Mr. Richard FARIAS
72 Dean Professional & Tech Educ .... Ms. Vernell E. WALKER
49 Dean of Arts & Sciences .... Dr. Conrad KRUEGER
51 Dean Cont Educ/Training Network .... Mr. Tim ROCKEY
08 Dean of Learning Resources .... Dr. Alice JOHNSON
88 Dean of Performance Excellence .... Dr. David WOOD
84 Director of Enrollment Services .... Mr. J. Martin ORTEGA
85 Coordinator International Students .... Ms. Martha BUCHANAN
26 Director Public Relations .... Ms. Vanessa TORRES
45 Director Resource & College Devel .... Ms. Susan B. ESPINOZA
18 Chief Facilities/Physical Plant .... Mr. David ORTEGA
23 Director Health Services .... Ms. Paula DAGGETT
37 Coordinator of Financial Aid .... Mr. Tom CAMPOS
29 Coordinator of Alumni and Friends .... Vacant

Alvin Community College (G)

3110 Mustang Road, Alvin TX 77511-4898
County: Brazoria FICE Identification: 003539
Unit ID: 222567
Telephone: (281) 756-3500 Carnegie Class: Assoc/MT-VT-Mix Trad/Non
FAX Number: (281) 756-3854 Calendar System: Semester
URL: www.alvincollege.edu
Established: 1948 Annual Undergrad Tuition & Fees (In-District): $1,514
Enrollment: 4,837 Coed
Affiliation or Control: Local IRS Status: 501(c)3
Highest Offering: Associate Degree
Accreditation: SC, ADNUR, COARC, DMS, NDT, POLYT

01 President .... Dr. Christal M. ALBRECHT
05 Vice President Instruction .... Dr. Cynthia GRIFFITH
10 VP Administrative Services .... Mr. Karl STAGER
32 VP Student Services .... Ms. Marilyn DEMENT
49 Dean of Arts & Sciences .... Dr. Drew NELSON
76 Dean Legal and Health Sciences .... Dr. John BETHSCHEIDER
51 Dean/Exec Dir Cont Ed/Wkforce Devel .... Mr. Jim SIMPSON
97 Dean General Educ/Academic Support .... Dr. Nadezhda (Nadia) NAZARENKO
88 Dean Prof/Tech/Human Performance .... Dr. Linda AUSTIN
06 Registrar .... Ms. Irene M. ROBINSON
08 Director Library Services .... Ms. Rebecca MCCLAIN
21 Director Fiscal Affairs/Controller .... Ms. Deborah KRAFT
13 Director Information Technology .... Mr. Jeff CERNOCH
37 Dir Student Financial Aid Placement .... Ms. Dora SIMS
15 Exec Director Human Resources .... Ms. Karen EDWARDS
18 Director Physical Plant .... Mr. Mark PUTNAM
29 Director Alumni Relations .... Ms. Wendy DEL BELLO
07 Director Advising Services .... Ms. Stephanie STOCKSTILL
09 Director of Inst Effective/Research .... Mr. Patrick SANGER
30 Chief Development .... Ms. Wendy DEL BELLO
26 Chief Public Relations Officer .... Ms. Wendy DEL BELLO
88 Assistant Director Fiscal Affairs .... Ms. Laurel JOSEPH
35 Coordinator Student Activities .... Ms. Amanda SMITHSON
04 Administrative Asst to President .... Ms. Tammy GIFFROW
19 Director Security/Safety .... Mr. Howard I. HAMRICK

Amarillo College (H)

PO Box 447, Amarillo TX 79178-0001
County: Potter FICE Identification: 003540
Unit ID: 222576
Telephone: (806) 371-5000 Carnegie Class: Assoc/MT-VT-High Trad
FAX Number: (806) 371-5370 Calendar System: Semester
URL: www.actx.edu
Established: 1929 Annual Undergrad Tuition & Fees (In-District): $2,010
Enrollment: 10,336 Coed
Affiliation or Control: State/Local IRS Status: 501(c)3
Highest Offering: Associate Degree
Accreditation: SC, ADNUR, COARC, DH, EMT, FUSER, MLTAD, MUS, NMT, OTA, PTAA, RAD, RTT, SURGT

01 President .... Dr. Russell LOWERY-HART
03 Executive Vice President .... Mr. Mark D. WHITE
05 VP of Academic Affairs .... Dr. Deborah L. VESS
10 VP of Business Affairs .... Mr. Steve G. SMITH
51 Dean of Continuing Education .... Ms. Toni B. GRAY
32 VP of Student Affairs .... Mr. Robert C. AUSTIN
102 Dir AC Foundation/Development .... Mrs. Kathleen B. DOWDY
76 Director Ctr Cont Health Care Educ .. Mrs. Kimberly A. CROWLEY
18 Director Physical Plant .... Mr. Bruce COTGREAVE
37 Director Financial Aid .... Ms. Kelly PRATER
08 Director AC Library Network .... Ms. Emily R. GILBERT
06 Registrar .... Mrs. Diane BRICE
27 General Mgr Communication/Mktg .... Mr. Chris HAYES
15 VP for Employee and Org Dev .... Ms. Lyndy D. FORRESTER
19 Chief of Police .... Mr. Steve L. CHANCE
26 Dir Foundation Mktg/Special Events .. Mrs. Tracy D. DOUGHERTY
09 Exec Dir Decision Analytics & IR .. Mr. Collin C. WITHERSPOON
35 Assoc VP of Student Affairs .... Mrs. April L. SESSLER
38 Director Advising & Counseling .... Mr. Jason A. NORMAN
88 Director Amarillo Museum of Art .... Mrs. Kim B. MAHAN
88 Director Criminal Justice Program .... Mr. Eric C. WALLACE
96 Director of Purchasing/Records Ret .... Ms. Kimberly L. CARLILE
66 Dean of Nursing .... Dr. Richard L. PULLEN
49 Dean of Liberal Arts .... Vacant
81 Dean of STEM .... Vacant
76 Dean of Health Sciences .... Mr. Mark E. ROWH
72 Dean of Technical Education .... Ms. Megan E. EIKNER
88 Dean School of Creative Arts .... Ms. Victoria TAYLOR-GORE
88 Dean of Academic Success .... Dr. Tamara T. CLUNIS
100 Chief of Staff .... Ms. Cara J. CROWLEY
84 Recruitment Spec/Enrollment Mgmt .... Mr. Richie GARZA
13 Asst Chief Information Technology .... Mr. Terry L. KLEFFMAN
04 Administrative Asst to President .... Ms. Joy D. BRENNEMAN
106 Dir Online Education/E-learning .... Ms. Heather L. VORAN
108 Director Institutional Assessment .... Ms. Kristin D. MCDONALD-WILLEY
25 Chief Contracts/Grants Admin .... Ms. Teresa G. CLEMONS

Amberton University (I)

1700 Eastgate Drive, Garland TX 75041
County: Dallas FICE Identification: 022594
Unit ID: 222628
Telephone: (972) 279-6511 Carnegie Class: Masters/L
FAX Number: (972) 279-9773 Calendar System: Quarter
URL: www.amberton.edu
Established: 1971 Annual Undergrad Tuition & Fees: N/A
Enrollment: 1,381 Coed
Affiliation or Control: Independent Non-Profit IRS Status: 501(c)3
Highest Offering: Master's
Accreditation: SC

01 President .... Dr. Melinda REAGAN
05 Academic Dean .... Dr. Jonathan SCHULTZ
30 Dean Univ Advance/VP Strategic Svcs .... Dr. Jo Lynn LOYD
10 Chief Business Officer .... Mr. Brent BRADSHAW
06 Registrar .... Mrs. Marge MASSEY
32 Interim Director Student Services .... Ms. Heather MILLER
84 Director for Recruiting .... Mr. Glenn SORRELLS

08 Head Librarian .... Ms. Bridget BARRY THOMAS
29 Dir Alumni Relations & Inst Rsch .... Dr. Jo Lynn LOYD
07 Director of Admissions .... Dr. Don HEBBARD

American College of Acupuncture and Oriental Medicine (A)

9100 Park West Drive, Houston TX 77063-4104
County: Harris FICE Identification: 031533
Unit ID: 429085
Telephone: (713) 780-9777 Carnegie Class: Spec-4-yr-Other Health
FAX Number: (713) 781-5781 Calendar System: Trimester
URL: www.acaom.edu
Established: 1991 Annual Graduate Tuition & Fees: N/A
Enrollment: 136 Coed
Affiliation or Control: Proprietary IRS Status: Proprietary
Highest Offering: Doctorate; No Undergraduates
Accreditation: SC, ACUP

01 President .... Dr. John Paul LIANG
11 Vice President of Operations .... Ms. Angel GUINARA
05 Dean of Academic Affairs .... Dr. Wen HUANG
20 Dean of Clinical Training .... Dr. Baisong ZHONG
06 Registrar .... Ms. Vicki ROSSMAN
09 Dir Inst Research/Effectiveness .... Mr. Michael Dale STAFFORD
37 Financial Aid Ofcr/Inst Compliance .... Ms. Theresa LIGON

American InterContinental University-Houston Campus (B)

9999 Richmond Avenue, Houston TX 77042-4516
Telephone: (832) 201-3600 Identification: 666335
Accreditation: &NH, ACBSP

† Regional accreditation is carried under the parent institution in Hoffman Estates, IL.

Ana G. Mendez University System-Dallas (C)

3010 N. Stemmons Fwy, Dallas TX 75247
Telephone: (469) 341-7300 Identification: 770947
Accreditation: &M

† Regional accreditation is carried under the parent institution in Rio Piedras, PR

Angelina College (D)

PO Box 1768, Lufkin TX 75902-1768
County: Angelina FICE Identification: 006661
Unit ID: 222822
Telephone: (936) 639-1301 Carnegie Class: Assoc/MT-VT-Mix Trad/Non
FAX Number: (936) 639-4299 Calendar System: Semester
URL: www.angelina.edu
Established: 1966 Annual Undergrad Tuition & Fees (In-District): $2,310
Enrollment: 5,148 Coed
Affiliation or Control: State/Local IRS Status: 501(c)3
Highest Offering: Associate Degree
Accreditation: #SC, COARC, DMS, EMT, RAD, SURGT

01 President .... Dr. Michael SIMON
05 Vice Pres Academic Affairs .... Dr. Cynthia CASPARIS
10 Vice President Business Services .... Mr. Chris SULLIVAN
31 Vice Pres of Community Services .... Mr. Tim DITORO
32 Dean of Student Services .... Mr. Steve HUDMAN
13 Dir Management Information Systems .... Mr. Kenneth STREET
37 Director Student Financial Aid .... Mrs. Sue JONES
18 Chief Facilities/Physical Plant .... Mr. Steve CAPPS
09 Coord Inst Effectiveness & QEP .... Dr. Monica PETERS
26 Coord of Communications .... Mrs. Nancy REYNOLDS
15 Director Human Resources .... Mrs. Tifini WHIDDON
06 Registrar .... Mrs. Sandra COX
88 Assoc Dean Academic Support Svcs .... Ms. Sellestine HUNT
106 Director Distance Education .... Mrs. Judy WRIGHT
21 Controller .... Mrs. Michaelyn GREENE

AOMA Graduate School of Integrative Medicine (E)

4701 West Gate Boulevard, Austin TX 78745
County: Travis FICE Identification: 031564
Unit ID: 429094
Telephone: (512) 454-1188 Carnegie Class: Spec-4-yr-Other Health
FAX Number: (512) 454-7001 Calendar System: Quarter
URL: www.aoma.edu
Established: 1993 Annual Graduate Tuition & Fees: N/A
Enrollment: 196 Coed
Affiliation or Control: Proprietary IRS Status: Proprietary
Highest Offering: Doctorate; No Undergraduates
Accreditation: SC, ACUP

01 President .... Dr. Betty EDMOND
05 Vice President of Faculty .... Dr. Qianzhi (Jamie) WU
10 Interim Chief Financial Officer .... Ms. Linda FONTAINE
32 Dean of Students .... Mr. Robert LAGUNA
45 Program and Research Director .... Dr. John FINNELL
88 Program Director Clinical Education .... Ms. Lesley HAMILTON
08 Head Librarian .... Mr. David YORK
07 Dir Admissions .... Mr. Greg GREEN
06 Registrar .... Ms. Kristen BORTHWICK
58 Dean of Academics .... Dr. Yuxin HE
88 Director of Herbal Studies .... Dr. Dongxin MA
88 Director Acupuncture .... Dr. Zheng ZENG
23 Clinic Business Director .... Ms. Stephanee OWENBY
18 Facilities Manager .... Mr. Pedro CARRION
20 Academic Advisor .... Mr. Robert LAGUNA
26 Dir of Mktg/Community Relations .... Mr. Rob DAVIDSON
81 Director of Biomedical Sciences .... Dr. Raja MANDYAM
37 Director Student Financial Aid .... Ms. Estella SEARS
13 Director of Information Technology .... Mr. Mario CASTILLO
09 Dir Inst Effectiveness/Cont Educ .... Ms. Cara EDMOND

Argosy University, Dallas (F)

5001 Lyndon B. Johnson Freeway, Farmers Branch TX 75244
Telephone: (214) 890-9900 Identification: 666181
Accreditation: &WC, ACBSP, CACREP, HT, MLTAD

† Regional accreditation is carried under the parent institution in Orange, CA.

Arlington Baptist College (G)

3001 W Division, Arlington TX 76012-3497
County: Tarrant FICE Identification: 020814
Unit ID: 222877
Telephone: (817) 461-8741 Carnegie Class: Spec-4-yr-Faith
FAX Number: (817) 274-1138 Calendar System: Semester
URL: www.arlingtonbaptistcollege.edu
Established: 1939 Annual Undergrad Tuition & Fees: $11,000
Enrollment: 250 Coed
Affiliation or Control: Baptist IRS Status: 501(c)3
Highest Offering: Master's
Accreditation: BI

01 President .... Dr. D. L MOODY
05 Academic Dean .... Ms. Janie TAYLOR
32 Dean of Students .... Mr. Richard KOONS
10 Business Manager/Dir Financial Aid .... Mr. David INGRAM
06 Registrar .... Ms. Janie TAYLOR
08 Head Librarian .... Vacant
18 Director Physical Plant .... Mr. Stan SPENCE
40 Director Bookstore .... Mrs. Vickie BRYANT
30 Director Institutional Advancement .... Mrs. Kim MARVIN
41 Athletic Director .... Mr. Cliff MCDANIEL
106 Dir Online Education/E-learning .... Dr. Carl JOHNSON
37 Director Student Financial Aid .... Mrs. Cindy TREAT

The Art Institute of Austin (H)

101 W. Louis Henna Blvd, Ste 100, Austin TX 78728
Telephone: (512) 691-1707 Identification: 770973
Accreditation: &SC CIDA

† Regional accreditation is carried under the parent institution in Houston, TX

Art Institute of Dallas (I)

8080 Park Lane, Suite 100, Dallas TX 75231-5993
Telephone: (214) 692-8080 FICE Identification: 025396
Accreditation: &SC ACFEI, CIDA

† Regional accreditation is carried under the parent institution, South University, Savannah, GA.

The Art Institute of Fort Worth (J)

7000 Calmont Ave, Ste 150, Fort Worth TX 76116
Telephone: (817) 210-0808 Identification: 770918
Accreditation: &SC

† School is in teach-out plan.

The Art Institute of Houston (K)

4140 Southwest Freeway, Houston TX 77027
County: Harris FICE Identification: 021171
Unit ID: 222938
Telephone: (713) 623-2040 Carnegie Class: Spec-4-yr-Arts
FAX Number: (713) 966-2700 Calendar System: Quarter
URL: www.aih.aii.edu
Established: 1978 Annual Undergrad Tuition & Fees: $17,664
Enrollment: 1,887 Coed
Affiliation or Control: Proprietary IRS Status: Proprietary
Highest Offering: Baccalaureate
Accreditation: SC, ACFEI, CIDA

01 President .... Susanne BEHRENS
05 Dean of Academic Affairs .... Dr. Gary EATON
32 Dean of Student Affairs .... Daryl CONTE
10 Director of Accounting .... Trena DEAN
07 Senior Director of Admissions .... Jane CHASTANT
15 Human Resources Generalist .... Elizabeth WHITTINGTON
37 Dir of Student Financial Services .... Kelly GARRETT
06 Registrar .... Grace JACKSON
04 Administrative Asst to President .... Teresa SMITH

The Art Institute of San Antonio (L)

10000 IH-10 W, Ste 200, San Antonio TX 78230
Telephone: (210) 338-7320 Identification: 770974
Accreditation: &SC

† Regional accreditation is carried under the parent institution in Houston, TX

Austin College (M)

900 N Grand Avenue, Sherman TX 75090-4400
County: Grayson FICE Identification: 003543
Unit ID: 222983
Telephone: (903) 813-2000 Carnegie Class: Bac-A&S
FAX Number: (903) 813-3199 Calendar System: 4/1/4
URL: www.austincollege.edu
Established: 1849 Annual Undergrad Tuition & Fees: $36,230
Enrollment: 1,301 Coed
Affiliation or Control: Presbyterian Church (U.S.A.) IRS Status: 501(c)3
Highest Offering: Master's
Accreditation: SC

01 President .... Dr. Marjorie HASS
05 VP Academic Affairs/Dean of Faculty .... Dr. Sheila A. PINERES
32 Vice Pres Student Affairs/Athletics .... Mr. Timothy P. MILLERICK
30 Vice Pres Institutional Advancement .... Mrs. Allison M. DAWSON
10 Vice President for Business Affairs .... Ms. Heidi B. ELLIS
84 Vice President for Inst Enrollment .... Ms. Nan M. DAVIS
21 Assoc VP Business Affairs .... Ms. Rana ASKINS
07 Asst VP Institutional Enrollment .... Mr. Matthew KROV
44 Sr Assoc VP for Inst Advancement .... Ms. Cary E. WACKER
29 Dir Alumni Programming .... Ms. Kate SHELLEY
37 AVP/Exec Director Financial Aid .... Ms. Laurie COULTER
88 Exec Dir Admission .... Ms. Amanda KISSELLE
42 Chaplain/Dir of Church Relations .... Dr. John D. WILLIAMS
35 Dean of Student Life .... Mr. Michael DEEN
06 Registrar .... Dr. Dawn REMMERS
08 College Librarian/Library Director .... Ms. Barbara CORNELIUS
79 Dean of Humanities .... Dr. Max GROBER
81 Dean of Sciences .... Dr. Steve GOLDSMITH
83 Dean of Social Sciences .... Dr. David GRIFFITH
15 Director of Human Resources .... Mr. Keith L. LAREY
36 Director Career Services .... Ms. Margie A. NORMAN
13 Exec Director IT .... Mr. Charles CURTIS
58 Director of Graduate Program .... Dr. Julia SHAHID
104 Study Abroad Coordinator .... Ms. Jade FERNBERG
26 Director of Public Affairs .... Dr. Lynn Z. WOMBLE
19 Chief of Police .... Mr. James PERRY
40 Manager of Campus Store .... Mr. Kenton BEAL
27 Sr Dir Editorial Communications .... Ms. Vickie S. KIRBY
18 Exec Director of Facilities .... Mr. John L. JENNINGS
96 Purchasing Representative .... Ms. Debra REED
102 Dir Corp & Foundation Reltns .... Ms. Britanny DEREBERY
41 Athletic Director .... Mr. David NORMAN
09 Dir Institutional Research & Assess .... Mr. David SNYDER
101 Asst to Pres/Asst Sec of Board .... Ms. Genna BETHEL
38 Coordinator Student Counseling .... Ms. Janie WOOD

Austin Community College District (N)

5930 Middle Fiskville Road, Austin TX 78752-4390
County: Travis FICE Identification: 012015
Unit ID: 222992
Telephone: (512) 223-7000 Carnegie Class: Assoc/MT-VT-High Non
FAX Number: (512) 223-7185 Calendar System: Semester
URL: www.austincc.edu
Established: 1972 Annual Undergrad Tuition & Fees (In-District): $2,550
Enrollment: 40,949 Coed
Affiliation or Control: State/Local IRS Status: 501(c)3
Highest Offering: Associate Degree
Accreditation: SC, ACBSP, ACFEI, ADNUR, CAHIIM, DH, DMS, EMT, MLTAD, OTA, PHLEB, PNUR, PTAA, RAD, SURGT

01 President/CEO .... Dr. Richard M. RHODES
03 Provost/Exec Vice Pres .... Dr. Charles COOK
10 EVP Finance & Administration .... Mr. Neil W. VICKERS
11 EVP Campus Planning & Operation .... Dr. Ben B. FERRELL
05 VP Instruction .... Mr. Michael T. MIDGLEY
32 VP Student Services .... Dr. Virginia FRAIRE
15 VP Human Resources .... Ms. Geraldine TUCKER
09 VP Effectiveness & Accountability .... Ms. Soon O. MERZ
20 AVP College Access Programs .... Dr. Stephanie HAWLEY
13 VP Information Technology .... Mr. Stanley T. GUNN
35 AVP Student Success .... Dr. Richard R. ARMENTA
04 VP External Affairs .... Dr. Molly Beth MALCOLM
45 VP Inst Planning/Develop & Eval .... Dr. Mary E. HARRIS
18 VP Facilities & Construction .... Mr. William S. MULLANE
26 Exec Dir Public Info & College Mktg .... Ms. Brette E. LEA
102 Executive Director ACC Foundation .... Ms. Stephanie C. DEMPSEY
06 Registrar .... Ms. Glynis MILLER
07 Executive Director of Admissions .... Ms. Linda KLUCK
08 Dean Library Services .... Dr. Julie TODARO
19 Chief of Police .... Mr. Lynn DIXON
37 Executive Director Financial Aid .... Ms. Teresita BAZAN
96 Director of Purchasing .... Mr. Anthony OWENS
29 Director Alumni Relations .... Ms. Mary Ann CICALA

Austin Graduate School of Theology (O)

7640 Guadalupe Street, Austin TX 78752
County: Travis FICE Identification: 023628
Unit ID: 247825
Telephone: (512) 476-2772 Carnegie Class: Spec-4-yr-Faith
FAX Number: (512) 476-3919 Calendar System: Semester
URL: www.austingrad.edu
Established: 1976 Annual Undergrad Tuition & Fees: N/A
Enrollment: 40 Coed
Affiliation or Control: Independent Non-Profit IRS Status: 501(c)3
Highest Offering: Master's

Accreditation: SC

01 President .... Dr. Stanley G. REID
37 Vice President/Dir Financial Aid .... Mr. Dave ARTHUR
07 Director Recruiting & Admissions .... Mrs. Dawn BOND
30 Director of Development .... Mr. Neil HANEY

Austin Presbyterian Theological Seminary (A)

100 E 27th Street, Austin TX 78705-5797
County: Travis FICE Identification: 003544
Unit ID: 223001
Telephone: (512) 472-6736 Carnegie Class: Spec-4-yr-Faith
FAX Number: (512) 479-0738 Calendar System: Semester
URL: www.austinseminary.edu
Established: 1902 Annual Graduate Tuition & Fees: N/A
Enrollment: 145 Coed
Affiliation or Control: Presbyterian Church (U.S.A.) IRS Status: 501(c)3
Highest Offering: Doctorate; No Undergraduates
Accreditation: SC, THEOL

01 President .... Rev. Theodore J. WARDLAW
05 Academic Dean .... Dr. David H. JENSEN
10 Vice Pres Finance/Administration .... Ms. Karen MONTGOMERY
30 Vice Pres Institutional Advancement .... Ms. Donna SCOTT
32 Vice Pres Student Affairs/Vocation .... Rev. Jackie SAXON
07 Vice President for Admissions .... Rev. John H. BARDEN
51 VP Education Beyond the Walls .... Ms. Melissa WIGINTON
29 Director Alumni & Church Relations .... Rev. Lemuel GARCIA-ANOYO
08 Director of the Stitt Library .... Dr. Timothy LINCOLN
06 Asst Dean Academic Affs/Registrar .... Ms. Jacqueline D. HEFLEY
37 Director of Financial Aid .... Ms. Glenna BALCH

Bakke Graduate University (B)

8515 Greenville Ave, S206, Dallas TX 75243-7039
County: Dallas FICE Identification: 031108
Unit ID: 420705
Telephone: (214) 329-4447 Carnegie Class: Spec-4-yr-Faith
FAX Number: (214) 347-9367 Calendar System: Semester
URL: www.bgu.edu
Established: 1990 Annual Graduate Tuition & Fees: N/A
Enrollment: 186 Coed
Affiliation or Control: Independent Non-Profit IRS Status: 501(c)3
Highest Offering: Doctorate; No Undergraduates
Accreditation: TRACS

01 President .... Dr. Brad SMITH
05 Academic Dean .... Dr. Judi MELTON
10 Chief Operations/Financial Ofcr .... Ms. Carolyn COCHRAN
06 Registrar .... Dr. Judi MELTON
07 Admissions Coordinator .... Ms. Diana BAKKE
08 Head Librarian .... Ms. Jennifer ROMAN
106 Dir Online Education/E-learning .... Dr. Dale DAN
37 Director Student Financial Aid .... Ms. Carolyn COCHRAN

Baptist Health System School of Health Professions (C)

8400 Datapoint Drive, San Antonio TX 78229
County: Bexar FICE Identification: 006606
Unit ID: 223083
Telephone: (210) 297-9636 Carnegie Class: Spec-4-yr-Other Health
FAX Number: (210) 297-0075 Calendar System: Semester
URL: www.bshp.edu
Established: 1903 Annual Undergrad Tuition & Fees: $1,488
Enrollment: 500 Coed
Affiliation or Control: Proprietary IRS Status: Proprietary
Highest Offering: Baccalaureate
Accreditation: ABHES, ADNUR, NUR, RAD, SURGT, SURTEC

01 President .... Dr. Marion JEWEL
04 Administrative Asst to President .... Diane TYLER
07 Director of Admissions .... Jillian DENMAN
08 Director of Library .... Vacant
05 Director of Gen Educ and Online .... Lucinda FLORES
10 Director of Finance .... Priti LAXMI
37 Director of Student Financial Aid .... Patrick REYNA
13 Director of Information Systems .... Nancy ORTIZ
06 Registrar .... Christopher ESPINOZA
06 Registrar .... Tavianna SIEGEL

† Tuition varies by degree program.

Baptist Hospitals of Southeast Texas School of Radiologic Technology (D)

3030 Fannin Ste A, Beaumont TX 77704
County: Jefferson Identification: 667153
Telephone: (409) 212-5724 Carnegie Class: Not Classified
FAX Number: N/A Calendar System: Semester
URL: www.bhset.net
Established: 1952 Annual Undergrad Tuition & Fees: N/A
Enrollment: N/A Coed
Affiliation or Control: Independent Non-Profit IRS Status: 501(c)3
Highest Offering: Associate Degree
Accreditation: RAD

01 Program Director .... Deborah SMITH
11 Chief of Administration .... David PARMER

Baptist Missionary Association Theological Seminary (E)

P.O. Box 670, 1530 East Pine Street, Jacksonville TX 75766-5407
County: Cherokee FICE Identification: 023312
Unit ID: 223117
Telephone: (903) 586-2501 Carnegie Class: Spec-4-yr-Faith
FAX Number: (903) 586-0378 Calendar System: Semester
URL: www.bmats.edu
Established: 1957 Annual Undergrad Tuition & Fees: $5,700
Enrollment: 137 Coed
Affiliation or Control: Baptist IRS Status: 501(c)3
Highest Offering: Master's
Accreditation: SC, THEOL

01 President .... Dr. Charley HOLMES
05 Dean-Registrar .... Dr. Philip ATTEBERY
04 Assistant to the President .... Keri SOUTHERN
09 Director of Institutional Research .... Dr. James BLAYLOCK

Baptist University of the Americas (F)

7838 Barlite Blvd., San Antonio TX 78224-1336
County: Bexar FICE Identification: 037333
Unit ID: 444398
Telephone: (210) 924-4338 Carnegie Class: Spec-4-yr-Faith
FAX Number: (210) 924-0888 Calendar System: Semester
URL: www.bua.edu
Established: 1947 Annual Undergrad Tuition & Fees: $7,200
Enrollment: 174 Coed
Affiliation or Control: Baptist IRS Status: 501(c)3
Highest Offering: Baccalaureate
Accreditation: BI

01 President .... Mr. Rene MACIEL
10 Vice Pres for Admin and Finance .... Mr. Barry TYLER
30 Vice Pres for Development .... Mr. Teo CISNEROS
05 Vice Pres for Academic Affairs .... Dr. Marconi MONTEIRO
32 Vice Pres for Student Svcs/Enroll .... Ms. Mary RANJEL
88 Vice Pres for Ext Affairs/Dean BBI .... Dr. Moises RODRIGUEZ
37 Financial Aid Administrator .... Mrs. Araceli ACOSTA

Baylor College of Medicine (G)

One Baylor Plaza, Houston TX 77030-3411
County: Harris FICE Identification: 004949
Unit ID: 223223
Telephone: (713) 798-4951 Carnegie Class: Spec-4-yr-Med
FAX Number: (713) 798-3692 Calendar System: Quarter
URL: www.bcm.edu
Established: 1900 Annual Graduate Tuition & Fees: N/A
Enrollment: 1,584 Coed
Affiliation or Control: Independent Non-Profit IRS Status: 501(c)3
Highest Offering: Doctorate; No Undergraduates
Accreditation: SC, ANEST, ARCPA, IPSY, MED, OPE

00 Chancellor .... Dr. Bobby R. ALFORD
01 President and CEO .... Dr. Paul KLOTMAN
05 Provost/SVP Acad & Faculty Affairs .... Dr. Alicia MONROE
17 Vice Pres/Chief Medical Officer .... Dr. Steve SIGWORTH
10 Sr VP/Chief Business Officer .... Mrs. Kimberly C. DAVID
30 Vice Pres Philanthropy .... Ms. Kristi SHERWOOD COOPER
43 Sr Vice Pres/General Counsel .... Mr. Robert F. CORRIGAN, JR.
26 VP Communications/Cmty Outreach .... Ms. Claire M. BASSETT
15 Vice President Human Resources .... Mr. Dane FRIEND
46 Sr Vice President/Dean Research .... Dr. Adam KUSPA
13 VP Information Technology .... Dr. Alexander IZAGUIRRE
86 Vice Pres Government Relations .... Mr. Tom KLEINWORTH
88 Dean Natl Sch Tropical Medicine .... Dr. Peter J. HOTEZ
21 VP Finance/CFO .... Ms. Julie NICKELL
63 Dean of Medical Education .... Dr. Jennifer CHRISTNER
58 Dean Grad School of Biomed Sciences .... Dr. Deborah JOHNSON
76 Dean School Allied Health Sciences .... Dr. Robert MCLAUGHLIN
88 Senior Associate Dean .... Dr. James L. PHILLIPS
07 Associate Dean Admissions .... Dr. Karen E. JOHNSON
63 Sr VP/Dean of Medical Education .... Dr. C. Michael FORDIS, JR.
20 Interim Sr Assoc Dean Med Education .... Dr. Mary L. BRANDT
63 Sr Assoc Dean Grad Medical Educ .... Dr. Linda ANDREWS
88 Associate Dean Res Assurances .... Dr. Stacey L. BERG
88 Sr Assoc Dean Graduate Education .... Dr. Barbara R. SLAUGHTER
88 Asst Dean Graduate Medical Educ .... Dr. Jacqueline LEVESQUE
88 Assistant Dean for Admissions .... Dr. Jesus G. VALLEJO
35 Assistant Dean Student Affairs .... Dr. Toi B. HARRIS
88 Assoc Dean Medical Education .... Dr. Jerry C. GOODMAN
21 Controller .... Mr. Douglas R. SPADE
37 Director Student Financial Planning .... Ms. Hilda DELEON
32 Director of Student Affairs .... Mr. John RAPP
88 Director Environmental Safety .... Mr. Paul MURACA
23 Director Occupational Medicine .... Dr. James E. KELAHER
29 Director Alumni Affairs .... Mr. Alexander M. HOPKINS
19 Exec Director of Security .... Mr. John A. ROBERSON
96 Director Supply Chain Management .... Vacant
28 Sr Assoc Dean Diversity Council .... Dr. Barbara R. SLAUGHTER
06 Registrar .... Ms. Latoya R. WHITAKER

Baylor University (H)

One Bear Place #97096, Waco TX 76798-7096
County: McLennan FICE Identification: 003545
Unit ID: 223232
Telephone: (254) 710-1011 Carnegie Class: DU-Higher
FAX Number: (254) 710-3557 Calendar System: Semester
URL: www.baylor.edu
Established: 1845 Annual Undergrad Tuition & Fees: $40,198
Enrollment: 16,263 Coed
Affiliation or Control: Baptist IRS Status: 501(c)3
Highest Offering: Doctorate
Accreditation: SC, BUS, BUSA, CAATE, CIDA, CLPSY, CS, DIETD, DIETI, ENG, HSA, JOUR, LAW, MIDWF, MUS, NURSE, PAST, PH, PTA, SP, SW, TED, THEA, THEOL

01 Interim President .... Dr. David E. GARLAND
05 Exec Vice Pres & Provost .... Dr. Greg JONES
100 Chief of Staff to the President .... Dr. Robyn L. DRISKELL
10 Senior VP for Operations & CFO .... Dr. Reagan RAMSOWER
30 Sr VP for Univ Development .... Mr. David P. ROSSELLI
32 Vice President Student Life .... Dr. Kevin JACKSON
26 Acting President Marketing & Comm .... Mrs. Karen W. KEMP
13 VP for Info Tech/Dean of Libraries .... Ms. Pattie ORR
31 Vice Pres Constituent Engagement .... Ms. Tommye Lou DAVIS
43 Interim General Counsel .... Mr. Christopher W. HOLMES
41 Director of Athletics .... Mr. Mack RHOADES, IV
88 VP for Governance/Risk & Compliance .... Dr. Juan ALEJANDRO
09 Director Inst Research/Testing .... Dr. Kathleen MORLEY
84 Assoc VP for Summer & Strat Initiat .... Mrs. Diana M. RAMEY
21 Assoc VP Financial Svcs & Treasurer .... Mr. Bob C. SPENCE
21 AVP Ops Plng & Budget Dir .... Mr. Wilson E. MCGREGOR
18 VP for Operations & Facilities Mgmt .... Mr. Brian W. NICHOLSON
15 Assoc Vice Pres Human Resources .... Mrs. Cheryl GOCHIS
91 Assoc VP Info Sys/Svcs & Dpty CIO .... Mrs. Becky L. KING
08 Assoc Dean of the Libraries .... Mr. John WILSON
35 Associate Vice Pres Student Life .... Dr. Martha Lou SCOTT
06 Registrar .... Mr. Jonathan C. HELM
88 Assoc VP Strategic Initiatives .... Mr. Chris KRAUSE
90 Assoc Vice Pres Electronic Library .... Mr. Timothy M. LOGAN
108 Vice Provost Inst Effectiveness .... Dr. Michael MATIER
97 Vice Provost Undergrad Education .... Dr. Wesley NULL
20 Vice Prov/Academic Affs & Policy .... Dr. James BENNIGHOFF
46 Vice Provost for Research .... Dr. Truell HYDE
07 Asst VP of Undergrad Enrollment .... Ms. Jennifer CARRON
88 Asst Vice President & Controller .... Ms. Susan ANZ
88 Asst VP Stdnt Fin Svcs & Strat Plng .... Mrs. Jackie DIAZ
88 Chief Investment Officer .... Mr. R. Brian WEBB
19 Chief of Police .... Mr. Brad WIGTIL
93 Director Multiculture Affairs .... Mrs. Pearlie BEVERLY
20 Director Academic Support Programs .... Ms. Sally E. FIRMIN
23 Medical Director Health Center .... Dr. Sharon STERN
36 Exec Dr Career & Professional Dev .... Dr. Marjorie N. ELLIS
25 Director Sponsored Programs .... Ms. Lisa H. MCKETHAN
38 Director Counseling Svcs .... Dr. James G. MARSH
40 Director Baylor Bookstore .... Mr. Paul BEAULIEU
86 Director Governmental Relations .... Ms. Rochonda FARMER-NEAL
96 Director Procurement Services .... Mr. Tom HOFFMEYER
31 Director Community Relations .... Ms. Gabriela COLMAN
49 Dean College of Arts/Sciences .... Dr. Lee C. NORDT
50 Dean School of Business .... Dr. Terry S. MANESS
53 Dean School of Education .... Dr. Michael MCLENDON
61 Dean School of Law .... Mr. Bradley J B. TOBEN
64 Dean School of Music .... Dr. Gary MORTENSON
66 Dean School of Nursing .... Dr. Shelley F. CONROY
58 Vice Provost & Dean Graduate School .... Dr. Larry LYON
73 Dean Truett Theological Sem .... Dr. Todd STILL
54 Dean Engineering & Computer Science .... Dr. Dennis O'NEAL
92 Dean Honors College .... Dr. Thomas S. HIBBS
85 Vice Provost for Global Engagement .... Dr. Jeffrey HAMILTON
35 Dean Student Development .... Dr. Elizabeth PALACIOS
39 Dean Student Learning & Engagement .... Dr. Jeff DOYLE
42 University Chaplain .... Dr. Burt BURLESON
88 Assoc Dean Student Conduct Admin .... Ms. Bethany J. MCCRAW
37 Asst VP for Stdnt Financial Aid .... Ms. Lyn KINYON
88 Assoc VP Public Safety & Security .... Mr. Mark CHILDERS

B.H. Carroll Theological Institute (I)

6500 N Belt Line Road, Suite 100, Irving TX 75063-6056
County: Tarrant Identification: 667089
Telephone: (972) 580-7600 Carnegie Class: Not Classified
FAX Number: (972) 756-0600 Calendar System: Semester
URL: www.bhcarroll.edu
Established: 2004 Annual Graduate Tuition & Fees: N/A
Enrollment: N/A Coed
Affiliation or Control: Southern Baptist IRS Status: 501(c)3
Highest Offering: Doctorate; No Undergraduates
Accreditation: BI, @THEOL

01 President .... Dr. C. Gene WILKES
10 CFO/Director Business Affairs .... Dr. Bruce MUSKRAT
06 Registrar .... Dr. Stan MOORE
07 Director of Admissions .... Ms. Meredith CHACIN
08 Dir Library & Information Services .... Mr. Don DAY
09 Dir of Institutional Effectiveness .... Ms. Amanda CRANE

Blinn College (J)

902 College Avenue, Brenham TX 77833-4098
County: Washington FICE Identification: 003549
Unit ID: 223427
Telephone: (979) 830-4000 Carnegie Class: Assoc/HT-High Trad
FAX Number: (979) 830-4030 Calendar System: Semester

URL: www.blinn.edu
Established: 1883 Annual Undergrad Tuition & Fees (In-District): $2,256
Enrollment: 18,850 Coed
Affiliation or Control: State/Local IRS Status: 501(c)3
Highest Offering: Associate Degree
Accreditation: SC, ADNUR, DH, EMT, IFSAC, PTAA, RAD

01 District President/CEO .... Dr. Mary HENSLEY
03 Exec Vice Pres/General Counsel .... Mr. Mel WAXLER
88 Special Asst to EVP/Gen Counsel .... Ms. Laurie CLARK
32 Vice Pres Student Services .... Dr. Dennis CROWSON
10 CFO/Sr VP Finance/Admin Svcs .... Ms. Kelli SHOMAKER
05 Asst Vice Pres Instruction .... Ms. Karen BUCK
12 Vice President Bryan Campus .... Vacant
86 Assoc VP Government & Public Affair .... Ms. Cathy BOEKER
20 Dean Academic Affairs .... Dr. John BEAVER
09 Dean Inst Effectiveness/Enroll Mgt .... Mr. Joe BAUMANN
06 Dean Admissions/Records/Registrar .... Ms. Andrea LINER
88 Judicial Officer .... Vacant
35 Dean of Student Success .... Mr. Jeremy THOMAS
43 Legal Counsel .... Mr. Ted HAJOVSKY
102 Executive Director Foundation .... Ms. Susan MYERS
18 Exec Dir Facilities/Planning/Constr .... Mr. Richard O'MALLEY
12 Director Schulenburg Campus .... Ms. Rebecca GARLICK
12 Director Sealy Campus .... Ms. Lisa CATON
72 Dean Technical/Prof Programs .... Ms. Megan COSTANZA
22 Director Disability Services (Bre) .... Ms. Patricia MORAN
22 Dir Disability Services (Bryan) .... Ms. Brenda JONES-WILKINS
04 Admin Asst to District President .... Ms. Becky KREBS
21 Director Accounting .... Mr. Thomas BRAZZEL
08 Dean Library Services .... Vacant
38 Director of Counseling .... Mr. Robert LOVELIDGE
13 Dir Administrative Computing Svcs .... Ms. Christine WIED
37 Dean Financial Aid/Scholarships .... Mr. Brent WILLIFORD
15 Asst VP Human Resources .... Ms. Marie KIRBY
41 Athletic Dir/Mens Head Bsktbl Coach .... Mr. Scott SCHUMACHER
19 Chief College Police Department .... Mr. Craig WIESEPAPE
96 Director Purchasing/Transportation .... Mr. Ross SCHROEDER
07 Director Admissions & Records .... Ms. Kristi URBAN
26 Dir Marketing/Media Relations .... Mr. Jeff TILLEY
35 Dir Student Leadership/Activities .... Mr. David G. MICHENER
39 Housing Director .... Mr. James REED
27 Assoc Dir Marketing/Communications .... Mr. Richard BRAY

Brazosport College (A)

500 College Drive, Lake Jackson TX 77566-3199
County: Brazoria FICE Identification: 007287
Unit ID: 223506
Telephone: (979) 230-3000 Carnegie Class: Bac/Assoc-Assoc Dom
FAX Number: (979) 230-3443 Calendar System: Semester
URL: www.brazosport.edu
Established: 1968 Annual Undergrad Tuition & Fees (In-District): $2,385
Enrollment: 4,155 Coed
Affiliation or Control: Local IRS Status: 501(c)3
Highest Offering: Baccalaureate
Accreditation: SC, EMT

01 President .... Dr. Millicent M. VALEK
05 VP Academic & Student Affairs .... Dr. Lynda VILLANUEVA
31 VP Industry & Community Resources .... Ms. Anne BARTLETT
30 VP College Advancement .... Ms. Serena ANDREWS
11 VP Administrative Services .... Mr. Fred SCOTT
15 VP Human Resources .... Mr. Marshall CAMPBELL
10 VP Financial Services & CFO .... Mr. David MARSHALL
32 Dean of Student Services .... Ms. Jo GREATHOUSE
20 Dean of Instruction .... Mr. Jeffrey DETRICK
09 Dean of Planning/IR .... Dr. Aaron GRACZYK
09 Director Institutional Research .... Mr. Scott FURTWENGLER
07 Director Admissions/Registrar .... Ms. Priscilla SANCHEZ
38 Director Counseling and Testing .... Mr. Arnold RAMIREZ
26 Director Marketing & Communications .... Mr. Kyle SMITH
13 Director Information Technology .... Mr. Ron PARKER
37 Director of Financial Aid .... Ms. Kay WRIGHT
08 Director Library & Learning Service .... Ms. Cassie BRUNER
18 Director Facility Services .... Mr. John DITTO
88 Director Small Business Dev Center .... Dr. Janice GOINES
51 Director Community Education .... Ms. Catherine HANSON
88 Director Children's Center .... Ms. Julie LITTLEFIELD
25 Director Grant Administration .... Ms. Rebecca SHAWVER
109 Director Business Services .... Ms. Ginger WOOSTER
21 Internal Auditor .... Ms. Cynthia STRADER

Brightwood College (B)

2241 South Watson Road, Arlington TX 76010
Telephone: (972) 623-4700 Identification: 770544
Accreditation: ACICS

Brightwood College (C)

6115 Eastex Freeway, Suite A-142, Beaumont TX 77706
Telephone: (409) 833-2722 Identification: 770545
Accreditation: ACICS

Brightwood College (D)

1900 North Expressway, Brownsville TX 78521
Telephone: (956) 547-8200 Identification: 770595
Accreditation: ACICS

Brightwood College (E)

1620 S Padre Island Drive, Ste 600,
Corpus Christi TX 78416
Telephone: (361) 852-2900 Identification: 770597
Accreditation: ACICS

Brightwood College (F)

12005 Ford Road, Suite 100, Dallas TX 75234
County: Dallas FICE Identification: 032723
Unit ID: 382896
Telephone: (972) 385-1446 Carnegie Class: Assoc/HVT-Mix Trad/Non
FAX Number: (972) 385-0641 Calendar System: Other
URL: www.brightwood.edu
Established: Annual Undergrad Tuition & Fees: N/A
Enrollment: 435 Coed
Affiliation or Control: Proprietary IRS Status: Proprietary
Highest Offering: Associate Degree
Accreditation: ACICS, PTAA

01 Executive Director .... Ms. Michelle OWENS

Brightwood College (G)

8360 Burnham Road, Ste 100, El Paso TX 79907
County: El Paso FICE Identification: 025919
Unit ID: 246266
Telephone: (915) 595-1935 Carnegie Class: Assoc/HVT-High Non
FAX Number: (915) 595-6619 Calendar System: Other
URL: www.brightwood.edu
Established: Annual Undergrad Tuition & Fees: N/A
Enrollment: 576 Coed
Affiliation or Control: Proprietary IRS Status: Proprietary
Highest Offering: Associate Degree
Accreditation: ACICS

01 President .... Ms. Dawn MICHELLE
05 Director of Education .... Ms. Ramona GARCIA

Brightwood College (H)

2001 Beach Street, Suite 201, Fort Worth TX 76103
Telephone: (817) 413-2000 Identification: 770598
Accreditation: ACICS

Brightwood College (I)

711 East Airtex Drive, Houston TX 77073
County: Harris FICE Identification: 023122
Unit ID: 229036
Telephone: (281) 443-8900 Carnegie Class: Not Classified
FAX Number: (281) 443-0777 Calendar System: Other
URL: www.brightwood.edu
Established: 1983 Annual Undergrad Tuition & Fees: N/A
Enrollment: 334 Coed
Affiliation or Control: Proprietary IRS Status: Proprietary
Highest Offering: Associate Degree
Accreditation: ACICS, MAC

01 Campus President .... Mr. Richard SAMBRANO

Brightwood College (J)

6410 McPherson, Laredo TX 78041
Telephone: (956) 717-5909 Identification: 770546
Accreditation: ACICS

Brightwood College (K)

1500 S Jackson Road, McAllen TX 78503
Telephone: (956) 630-1499 Identification: 770596
Accreditation: ACICS

Brightwood College (L)

7142 San Pedro Avenue, Suite 100,
San Antonio TX 78216
County: Bexar FICE Identification: 009466
Unit ID: 364955
Telephone: (210) 733-0777 Carnegie Class: Assoc/HVT-Mix Trad/Non
FAX Number: (210) 340-6603 Calendar System: Other
URL: brightwood.edu
Established: Annual Undergrad Tuition & Fees: N/A
Enrollment: 574 Coed
Affiliation or Control: Proprietary IRS Status: Proprietary
Highest Offering: Associate Degree
Accreditation: ACICS, MAC

01 President .... Sandra MUSKOPS

Brightwood College (M)

6441 NW Loop 410, San Antonio TX 78238
County: Bexar FICE Identification: 031158
Unit ID: 431886
Telephone: (210) 308-8584 Carnegie Class: Spec 2-yr-Health
FAX Number: (210) 308-8985 Calendar System: Other
URL: www.brightwood.edu
Established: Annual Undergrad Tuition & Fees: N/A
Enrollment: 556 Coed
Affiliation or Control: Proprietary IRS Status: Proprietary
Highest Offering: Associate Degree
Accreditation: ACICS, CAHIIM

01 President .... Ms. Liza CANCHOLA

Brightwood College-Friendswood (N)

3208 FM 528, Friendswood TX 77546
Telephone: (281) 648-0880 Identification: 667051
Accreditation: ACICS, MAC

† Branch campus of Brightwood College, Houston, TX.

Brite Divinity School (O)

2925 Princeton Street, Fort Worth TX 76129-0001
County: Tarrant Identification: 666228
Unit ID: 450304
Telephone: (817) 257-7575 Carnegie Class: Spec-4-yr-Faith
FAX Number: (817) 257-6932 Calendar System: Semester
URL: www.brite.tcu.edu
Established: 1873 Annual Graduate Tuition & Fees: N/A
Enrollment: 196 Coed
Affiliation or Control: Independent Non-Profit IRS Status: 501(c)3
Highest Offering: Doctorate; No Undergraduates
Accreditation: SC, THEOL

01 President & Chief Executive Officer .... Dr. D. Newell WILLIAMS
05 Exec Vice President/Dean .... Dr. Joretta MARSHALL
10 Vice President Business/Finance .... Ms. Michele G. SMITH
07 Director of Admission .... Dr. Valerie FORSTMAN

Brown Mackie College - Dallas/Ft. Worth (P)

2200 North Hwy 121, Suite 250, Bedford TX 76021
Telephone: (817) 799-0500 Identification: 770798
Accreditation: ACICS, OTA, SURTEC

† Branch campus of The Art Institute of Phoenix, Phoenix, AZ

Brown Mackie College - San Antonio (Q)

4715 Fredericksburg Road, Suite 100,
San Antonio TX 78229
Telephone: (877) 460-1714 Identification: 770799
Accreditation: ACICS, SURTEC

† Branch campus of The Art Institute of Phoenix, Phoenix, AZ

Cardiotech Ultrasound School (R)

12135 Bissonnet, Ste E, Houston TX 77099
FICE Identification: 041385
Unit ID: 458034
Telephone: (281) 495-0078 Carnegie Class: Not Classified
FAX Number: (281) 495-5618 Calendar System: Semester
URL: www.cardiotech.org
Established: 2003 Annual Undergrad Tuition & Fees: $10,233
Enrollment: 43 Coed
Affiliation or Control: Proprietary IRS Status: Proprietary
Highest Offering: Associate Degree
Accreditation: ABHES

Career Point College (S)

4522 Fredericksburg Rd, Suite A-18,
San Antonio TX 78201
County: Bexar FICE Identification: 025911
Unit ID: 224439
Telephone: (210) 732-3000 Carnegie Class: Bac/Assoc-Mixed
FAX Number: (210) 734-9225 Calendar System: Other
URL: www.careerpointcollege.edu
Established: 1921 Annual Undergrad Tuition & Fees: $19,350
Enrollment: 1,208 Coed
Affiliation or Control: Proprietary IRS Status: Proprietary
Highest Offering: Baccalaureate
Accreditation: ACICS

01 Director .... Ms. Debbie ROBBINS

Carrington College - Mesquite (T)

3733 West Emporium Circle, Mesquite TX 75150
Telephone: (972) 682-2800 Identification: 770967
Accreditation: &WJ

† Regional accreditation is carried under the parent institution in Sacramento, CA

Center for Advanced Legal Studies (U)

800 W Sam Houston Pkwy, S Suite 100,
Houston TX 77042
County: Harris FICE Identification: 026047
Unit ID: 379782
Telephone: (713) 529-2778 Carnegie Class: Spec-4-yr-Other
FAX Number: (855) 422-4466 Calendar System: Other
URL: www.paralegal.edu
Established: 1987 Annual Undergrad Tuition & Fees: N/A
Enrollment: 206 Coed

Affiliation or Control: Proprietary IRS Status: Proprietary
Highest Offering: Associate Degree
Accreditation: **ACICS**, COE

01 School Director/Co-Founder .... Mr. Doyle HAPPE
05 Dean .... Mr. Thomas SWANSON
07 Director of Admissions .... Mr. James SCHEFFER

Central Texas College (A)

PO Box 1800, Killeen TX 76540-9990
County: Bell FICE Identification: 004003
Unit ID: 223816
Telephone: (254) 526-7161 Carnegie Class: Assoc/HT-High Non
FAX Number: (254) 526-0817 Calendar System: Semester
URL: www.ctcd.edu
Established: 1965 Annual Undergrad Tuition & Fees (In-District): $2,280
Enrollment: 20,547 Coed
Affiliation or Control: Local IRS Status: 501(c)3
Highest Offering: Associate Degree
Accreditation: **SC**, ADNUR, EMT, MLTAD

01 Chancellor .... Mr. Jim YEONOPOLUS
03 Deputy Chanc US Campus Operations .... Dr. Tina ADY
11 Deputy Chanc Finance & Admin .... Ms. Michele CARTER
05 Deputy Chanc Acad & Student Svcs .... Dr. Dana WATSON
12 Dean Ft Hood/Service Area Campus .... Mr. Raul GARCIA
12 Dean Central Campus .... Ms. Janice ANDERSON
32 Dean Student Services .... Dr. Johnelle WELSH
08 Dean Library Services .... Ms. Deba SWAN
38 Director Guidance/Counseling .... Ms. Jennilee WILLIAMS
06 Associate Dean Admin/Reg/Records ...... Mr. Stephen O'DONOVAN
10 Comptroller .... Mr. Bob LIBERTY
15 Director Human Resource Mgmt .... Ms. Holly JORDAN
106 Director Distance Education/Ed Tech .... Ms. Sharon DAVIS
18 Director Facilities Management .... Mr. Mark HARMSEN
21 Director Business Services .... Ms. Carol GRAY
30 Director College Development .... Ms. Amy BAWCOM
09 Director Institutional Effectivenes .... Dr. Lelia HACKETT
13 Director Information Technology .... Mr. Cliff GAINES
07 Director Admissions/Recruitment .... Ms. Shannon BRALLEY
88 Director Testing .... Ms. JoAnna JOHNSON
85 Director International Student Svcs .... Ms. Rosemary YARGICI
22 Director Disability Support Svcs .... Vacant
88 Director Substance Abuse Resource . Dr. Gerald MAHONE-LEIWS
36 Director Career Planning/Placement .... Ms. Keisha HOLMAN
26 Dir Community Relations/Marketing .... Ms. Barbara MERLO
88 Liaison Military Programs .... Ms. Diana CASTILLO
19 Chief Police/Security Services .... Ms. Mary WHEELER
40 Manager Bookstore .... Ms. Regina MARTINEZ-WOODRUFF
37 Director Student Financial Aid .... Ms. Annabelle SMITH
96 Director of Purchasing .... Ms. Carol GRAY
04 Administrative Asst to President .... Ms. Debra HAVENS
43 Dir Legal Services/General Counsel .... Ms. Deborah SHIBLEY
86 Director Government Relations .... Mr. Brian SUNSHINE

Chamberlain College of Nursing-Houston Campus (B)

11025 Equity Drive, Houston TX 77041
Telephone: (713) 277-9800 Identification: 770500
Accreditation: **&NH**, NURSE

† Regional accreditation is carried under the parent institution in Addison, IL

Chamberlain College of Nursing-Irving (C)

4800 Regent Blvd., Irving TX 75063
Telephone: (469) 706-6705 Identification: 770853
Accreditation: **&NH**, NURSE

† Regional accreditation is carried under the parent institution in Addison, IL

Chamberlain College of Nursing-Pearland (D)

12000 Shadow Creek Pkwy, Pearland TX 77584
Telephone: (832) 664-7000 Identification: 770934
Accreditation: **&NH**, NURSE

† Branch campus of Chamberlain College of Nursing-Addison, Addison, IL.

Cisco College (E)

101 College Heights, Cisco TX 76437-1900
County: Eastland FICE Identification: 003553
Unit ID: 223898
Telephone: (254) 442-5000 Carnegie Class: Assoc/MT-VT-High Trad
FAX Number: (254) 442-5100 Calendar System: Semester
URL: www.cisco.edu
Established: 1940 Annual Undergrad Tuition & Fees (In-State): $3,510
Enrollment: 3,608 Coed
Affiliation or Control: State IRS Status: 501(c)3
Highest Offering: Associate Degree
Accreditation: **SC**, COARC, MAC, SURGT

01 President .... Dr. Thad ANGLIN
05 Chief Instruction Officer .... Dr. Carol DUPREE
32 Vice President for Student Services .... Dr. Jerry DODSON
13 Exec Dir of Information Technology .... Mr. Steve POWELL
09 Vice President of Research/Mkting .... Mr. Joe CARTER
84 Dean of Enrollment Services .... Mr. Olin O. ODOM, III
38 Dean of Counseling .... Mr. Randy LEATH
30 Director of Development .... Ms. Martha MONTGOMERY
37 Director of Financial Aid .... Ms. Linda SELLERS
15 Director of Human Resources .... Ms. Pamela G. PAGE
08 Director of Library Services .... Ms. Donna CLARK
19 Director Campus Safety .... Mr. Roger TIGHE
07 Director of Admissions .... Ms. Shirley DOVE
04 Administrative Asst to President .... Ms. Sydni RABB
103 Dir Workforce/Career Development .... Ms. Charlotte SPEEGLE
106 Dir Online Education/E-learning .... Ms. Sheron CATON
39 Director Student Housing .... Mr. Ryan JOHNSON
10 Dean of Business Svcs/CFO .... Ms. Audra TAYLOR
96 Director of Purchasing .... Ms. Beverly MASSEY

Clarendon College (F)

PO Box 968, Clarendon TX 79226-0968
County: Donley FICE Identification: 003554
Unit ID: 223922
Telephone: (806) 874-3571 Carnegie Class: Assoc/HVT-Mix Trad/Non
FAX Number: (806) 874-3201 Calendar System: Semester
URL: www.clarendoncollege.edu
Established: 1898 Annual Undergrad Tuition & Fees (In-District): $2,424
Enrollment: 1,394 Coed
Affiliation or Control: State/Local IRS Status: 501(c)3
Highest Offering: Associate Degree
Accreditation: **SC**

01 President .... Dr. Robert RIZA
05 Exec VP Academic/Student Affairs .... Mr. Tex BUCKHAULTS
10 Vice Pres Administrative Services .... Mrs. Lana RITCHIE
08 Librarian .... Ms. Pamela REED
37 Associate Dean of Financial Aid .... Mrs. Susan RUSSELL
81 Division Chair Science/Health .... Mrs. Scarlet ESTLACK
49 Division Chair Liberal Arts .... Mrs. Kim JEFFREY
09 Director of Institutional Research .... Dr. Robert TAYLOR
26 Marketing Coordinator .... Mrs. Ashlee ESTLACK
41 Athletic Director .... Mr. Brad VANDEN BOOGAARD
13 Director of Information Technology .... Mr. Will THOMPSON
20 Assoc Dean of General Education .... Mr. Brian FULLER
84 Assoc Dean of Enrollment Services .... Mrs. Becky GREEN

Coastal Bend College (G)

3800 Charco Road, Beeville TX 78102-2197
County: Bee FICE Identification: 003546
Unit ID: 223320
Telephone: (361) 358-2838 Carnegie Class: Assoc/HVT-High Trad
FAX Number: (361) 354-2333 Calendar System: Semester
URL: www.coastalbend.edu
Established: 1965 Annual Undergrad Tuition & Fees (In-District): $3,576
Enrollment: 3,759 Coed
Affiliation or Control: State/Local IRS Status: 501(c)3
Highest Offering: Associate Degree
Accreditation: **SC**, DH, RAD

01 President .... Dr. Beatriz T. ESPINOZA
05 Dean of Academics .... Mr. Mark SECORD
20 Director of Academics .... Dr. Kevin BEHR
32 Dean of Student Services .... Ms. Lupe GANCERES
07 Director of Admissions/Registrar .... Ms. Candy FULLER
26 Dir Institutional Advancement/PR .... Ms. Monica CRUZ
25 Grant Writer .... Ms. Veronica MOLINA
37 Director of Financial Aid .... Ms. Nora MORALES
12 Director of Alice Campus .... Ms. Dee Dee ARISMENDEZ
12 Director of Kingsville Campus .... Ms. Amanda BARRERA
09 Institutional Research Director .... Dr. Paula KENNEY-WALLACE
10 Exec Director of Business Services .... Ms. Dela CASTILLO
08 Director Library Services .... Vacant
15 Human Resources Director .... Ms. Esther MARTINEZ
90 Director of IT Services/Webmaster .... Mr. Amador RAMIREZ
18 Chief Facilities/Physical Plant .... Mr. Jacinto (JC) COLMENERO
04 Executive Asst to President .... Ms. Stacie YANTA
103 Dean of Workforce Training .... Ms. Julia GARCIA

College of Biblical Studies-Houston (H)

7000 Regency Square Boulevard, Houston TX 77036-3298
County: Harris FICE Identification: 034224
Unit ID: 388520
Telephone: (713) 785-5995 Carnegie Class: Spec-4-yr-Faith
FAX Number: (713) 785-5998 Calendar System: Semester
URL: www.cbshouston.edu
Established: 1976 Annual Undergrad Tuition & Fees: $6,946
Enrollment: 496 Coed
Affiliation or Control: Independent Non-Profit IRS Status: 501(c)3
Highest Offering: Baccalaureate
Accreditation: **SC**, BI

01 President .... Dr. Bill BLOCKER
04 Executive Assistant .... Mrs. Vicki PATTERSON
05 VP Academic Affairs/Acad Dean .... Dr. Joseph D. PARLE
03 VP Admin and Student Affairs .... Mr. Paul KEITH
10 Chief Financial Officer .... Vacant
84 Exec Director Enrollment Services .... Dr. Lisa STEWART
26 Exec Director of Marketing and PR .... Ms. Melinda MERILLAT
21 Director Accounting .... Ms. Shaffer GAYLA
18 Dir Real Estate Operations .... Mr. Terry BRYAN
06 Registrar .... Mr. Chad KNIFFEN
08 Director of Library Services .... Mr. Artis LOVELADY, III
09 Dir Inst Effect and Accreditation .... Dr. Bryce F. HANTLA
07 Director of Admissions .... Ms. Maggie RODRIGUEZ
106 Assoc Dean Dist Educ Operations .... Mr. Shane BOOTHE
20 Assoc Dean Faculty and Curr Dev .... Dr. Brittany BURNETTE
37 Senior Financial Aid Officer .... Vacant

The College of Health Care Professions (I)

6505 Airport Blvd, Suite 102, Austin TX 78752
County: Travis FICE Identification: 034263
Unit ID: 437635
Telephone: (512) 892-2835 Carnegie Class: Spec 2-yr-Health
FAX Number: (512) 892-6643 Calendar System: Other
URL: www.chcp.edu
Established: Annual Undergrad Tuition & Fees: N/A
Enrollment: 260 Coed
Affiliation or Control: Proprietary IRS Status: Proprietary
Highest Offering: Associate Degree
Accreditation: **ABHES**

01 President .... Ms. Sara RAMBIKUR

The College of Health Care Professions (J)

240 Northwest Mall, Houston TX 77092
County: Harris FICE Identification: 031281
Unit ID: 392257
Telephone: (713) 425-3100 Carnegie Class: Spec 2-yr-Health
FAX Number: (713) 425-3192 Calendar System: Other
URL: www.chcp.edu
Established: 1988 Annual Undergrad Tuition & Fees: N/A
Enrollment: 1,172 Coed
Affiliation or Control: Proprietary IRS Status: Proprietary
Highest Offering: Associate Degree
Accreditation: **ABHES**, SURGT, SURTEC

01 Campus President .... Terri LOWERY

The College of Health Care Professions-Dallas (K)

8390 Lyndon B. Johnson Fwy, Ste 300, Dallas TX 75243
Telephone: (214) 420-3400 Identification: 770531
Accreditation: **ABHES**

The College of Health Care Professions-Fort Worth (L)

4248 North Freeway, Fort Worth TX 76137
Telephone: (817) 632-5900 Identification: 770532
Accreditation: **ABHES**

The College of Health Care Professions-McAllen (M)

1917 Nolana Avenue, Ste 100, McAllen TX 78504
Telephone: (713) 425-3125 Identification: 770963
Accreditation: **ABHES**

The College of Health Care Professions-San Antonio (N)

4738 Northwest Loop 410, San Antonio TX 78229
Telephone: (210) 298-3600 Identification: 770964
Accreditation: **ABHES**, SURGT

College of the Mainland (O)

1200 Amburn Road, Texas City TX 77591-2499
County: Galveston FICE Identification: 007096
Unit ID: 226408
Telephone: (409) 933-8271 Carnegie Class: Assoc/MT-VT-High Trad
FAX Number: (409) 933-8010 Calendar System: Semester
URL: www.com.edu
Established: 1966 Annual Undergrad Tuition & Fees (In-District): $1,773
Enrollment: 3,858 Coed
Affiliation or Control: Local IRS Status: 501(c)3
Highest Offering: Associate Degree
Accreditation: **SC**, ADNUR, CAHIIM, EMT, MAC

01 President .... Dr. Beth LEWIS
05 Vice President for Instruction .... Dr. Pam MILLSAP
10 Vice President for Fiscal Affairs .... Dr. Clen BURTON
32 Vice President for Student Services .... Dr. Vicki STANFIELD
20 Dean Gen Education Programs .... Dr. Pam MILLSAP
35 Assoc VP Student Success & Conduct .... Ms. Kris KIMBARK
06 Assoc VP for Enrollment/Registrar .... Mrs. Kelly MUSICK
18 Assoc VP Facility Services .... Mr. Charles KING
08 Director Library Services .... Ms. Kathryn PARK
13 Chief Information Officer .... Mr. James TAGLIARENI
37 Director of Student Financial Svcs .... Mr. Carl GORDON
28 Director of Diversity & Equity .... Ms. Lonica BUSH
96 Director of Purchasing .... Ms. Sonja BLINKA
09 Research Specialist .... Ms. Cheryl YOUNG

Collin County Community College District (A)

3452 Spur 399, McKinney TX 75069
County: Collin FICE Identification: 023614
Unit ID: 247834
Telephone: (972) 758-3800 Carnegie Class: Assoc/HT-Mix Trad/Non
FAX Number: (972) 758-3807 Calendar System: Semester
URL: www.collin.edu
Established: 1985 Annual Undergrad Tuition & Fees (In-District): $1,174
Enrollment: 27,991 Coed
Affiliation or Control: State/Local IRS Status: 501(c)3
Highest Offering: Associate Degree
Accreditation: SC, ACFEI, ADNUR, CAHIIM, COARC, DH, EMT, POLYT, SURGT

01 District President ....Dr. H. Neil MATKIN
05 Exec VP/Chief Academic Officer ....Dr. Brenda K. KIHL
88 Sr VP Acad/Workforce/Enroll Svcs ....Dr. Sherry L. SCHUMANN
88 Sr VP Org Effectiveness ....Ms. Kimberly K. DAVISON
10 Acting VP Admin Services & CFO ....Mr. Kenneth LYNN
15 VP Human Resources ....Ms. Norma L. ALLEN
30 VP Advancement ....Ms. Lisa R. VASQUEZ
45 VP Policy & Planning ....Dr. Scott J. PARKE
103 VP Workforce & Economic Dev ....Ms. Jennifer BLALOCK
20 VP Academic Services ....Dr. Dani R. DAY
32 VP Student & Enrollment Services ....Dr. Albert TEZENO
12 VP/Provost Spring Creek Campus ....Dr. Mary S. MCRAE
12 VP/Provost Preston Ridge Campus ....Dr. Abe JOHNSON
12 VP/Provost Central Park Campus ....Dr. Jon H. HARDESTY
106 Assoc VP Academic Outreach ....Mr. Joe R. BUTLER
51 Assoc VP Cont Educ/Workforce Dev ....Vacant
09 Assoc VP Institutional Research ....Dr. Thomas K. MARTIN
21 Assoc VP Financial Svcs & Reporting ....Ms. Barbara A. JINDRA
21 Assoc VP Controller/Stdnt Fin Svcs ....Ms. Julie M. BRADLEY
88 Assoc VP P-12 Partnerships ....Mr. Raul J. MARTINEZ
50 Dean Business & Computer Systems ....Mr. William J. BLITT
88 Dean Developmental Education ....Mr. James N. BARKO
57 Dean Fine Arts ....Ms. Gaye M. COOKSEY
76 Int Dean Health Sci/Emergency Svcs ....Ms. Michelle MILLEN
66 Dean Nursing ....Ms. Donna M. HATCH
49 Dean Academic Affairs Central Park ....Ms. Brenda C. CARTER
79 Dean Comm/Hum/Soc Sci Preston Ridge ....Ms. Wendy A. GUNDERSON
81 Interim Dean STEM Preston Ridge ....Dr. Dawn J. RICHARDSON
79 Dean Comm & Hum Spring Creek ....Dr. Donald L. WEASENFORTH
81 Dean Math & Nat Sci Spring Creek ....Dr. L. Cameron NEAL, JR.
83 Dean Soc & Behav Sci Spring Creek ....Mr. Gary B. HODGE
88 Dean Strategic Initiatives ....Mr. Mark S. GARCIA
84 Dean Student Enroll Svcs Central Pk ....Dr. Alicia L. HUPPE
84 Dean Stdnt Enrol Svcs Spring Creek ....Mr. Douglas G. WILLIS
84 Dean Stdnt Enrol Svcs Preston Ridge ....Ms. Stephanie MEINHARDT
35 Dean of Students ....Mr. Terrence P. BRENNAN
38 Assoc Dean Counseling/Career Svcs ....Dr. Linda R. QUALIA
06 Director of Admissions/Registrar ....Mr. Todd E. FIELDS
13 Assoc VP/Chief Info Sys Officer ....Mr. David R. HOYT
18 Dist Dir Safety/Secur/Facil/Const ....Mr. Ed C. LEATHERS
19 Chief of Police ....Mr. William F. TAYLOR
08 Exec Dir Central Park Library ....Dr. Greg G. REID
08 Exec Dir Preston Ridge Library ....Mr. John C. MULLIN
08 Exec Dir Spring Creek Library ....Ms. Linda A. KYPRIOS
102 Exec Dir Foundation/Development ....Vacant
41 Director Athletics ....Dr. Albert TEZENO
96 Director Purchasing ....Ms. Cynthia L. WHITE
37 Director Financial Aid/Vets Affairs ....Mr. Alan D. PIXLEY
85 Coordinator International Students ....Ms. Rebecca C. CROWELL

Commonwealth Institute of Funeral Service (B)

415 Barren Springs, Houston TX 77090-5913
County: Harris FICE Identification: 003556
Unit ID: 366261
Telephone: (281) 873-0262 Carnegie Class: Spec 2-yr-A&S
FAX Number: (281) 873-5232 Calendar System: Quarter
URL: www.commonwealth.edu
Established: 1936 Annual Undergrad Tuition & Fees: $12,495
Enrollment: 228 Coed
Affiliation or Control: Independent Non-Profit IRS Status: 501(c)3
Highest Offering: Associate Degree
Accreditation: FUSER

01 President/CEO ....Dr. Jason C. ALTIERI
10 Vice President/Treasurer ....Mr. W. Blair WALTRIP
05 Chief Academic Officer ....Mr. Stuart MOEN
20 Associate Academic Officer ....Mr. Christopher LAYTON
37 Director Student Financial Aid ....Ms. Marlene PERRY
06 Registrar ....Ms. Patricia MORENO
08 Head Librarian ....Ms. Melissa DAVIS

Concorde Career College (C)

12606 Greenville Avenue, Suite 130, Dallas TX 75243
Telephone: (469) 221-3411 Identification: 770593
Accreditation: ACCSC, #COARC, DH, PTAA, SURGT

† Branch campus of Concorde Career College, Aurora, CO

Concorde Career College (D)

4803 NW Loop 410, Suite 200, San Antonio TX 78229
Telephone: (210) 428-2000 Identification: 770594
Accreditation: ACCSC, #COARC, DH, PTAA, SURGT

† Branch campus of Concorde Career College, Kansas City MO

Concorde Career Institute (E)

3015 West I-20, Grand Prairie TX 75052
County: Tarrant FICE Identification: 035423
Unit ID: 441742
Telephone: (469) 348-2500 Carnegie Class: Spec 2-yr-Health
FAX Number: (469) 348-2580 Calendar System: Semester
URL: www.concorde.edu
Established: 1991 Annual Undergrad Tuition & Fees: N/A
Enrollment: 987 Coed
Affiliation or Control: Proprietary IRS Status: Proprietary
Highest Offering: Associate Degree
Accreditation: ACCSC, NDT, POLYT, SURGT

01 Campus President ....Mr. Mike LOVEJOY

Concordia University Texas (F)

11400 Concordia University Drive, Austin TX 78726
County: Travis FICE Identification: 003557
Unit ID: 224004
Telephone: (512) 313-3000 Carnegie Class: Masters/L
FAX Number: (512) 313-3339 Calendar System: Semester
URL: www.concordia.edu
Established: 1926 Annual Undergrad Tuition & Fees: $28,160
Enrollment: 2,504 Coed
Affiliation or Control: Lutheran Church - Missouri Synod
IRS Status: 501(c)3
Highest Offering: Doctorate
Accreditation: SC, IACBE, NURSE

01 President/CEO ....Dr. Donald CHRISTIAN
04 Executive Asst to Pres/CEO ....Ms. Kathy ARNOLD
03 Exec VP & Chief Mission Officer ....Dr. Kristi KIRK
05 Provost/CAO ....Dr. Erik ANKERBERG
11 VP Administration & COO ....Ms. Beth ATHERTON
10 Chief Financial Officer ....Ms. Sarah LOGHIN
45 Chief Strategy Officer ....Dr. Shane SOKOLL
42 Campus Pastor ....Rev. Steve FICK
20 AVP Academics Graduate ....Dr. Lynette GILLIS
20 AVP Academics Undergraduate ....Dr. Allen BROWN
20 Assistant Provost ....Dr. Chris WINKLER
07 AVP of Admissions ....Ms. Kristin COULTER
30 AVP External Relations ....Mr. James CANDIDO
26 AVP Marketing/Communications ....Ms. Lisa KESSLER
18 AVP Facilities Services ....Mr. Dan GREGORY
21 Controller ....Ms. Jennifer GONZALES
107 Dean Professional Studies ....Dr. Janet WHITSON
49 Dean Arts & Sciences ....Dr. Carl TROVALL
106 Center Dean Online ....Dr. Alex HERRON
66 Dir School of Nursing Program ....Dr. Kathy LAUCHNER
53 Dir School of Education ....Dr. Michael WALLACE
50 Dir School of Business/Comm ....Dr. Erik GREEN
57 Dir School of Fine Arts ....Dr. Kelly GORDON
81 Dir School of Nat/Applied Sciences ....Dr. Philip SCHIELKE
79 Dir School of Humanities ....Dr. Marchelle SCARNIER
06 Registrar ....Ms. Connie BERAN
37 Director Student Financial Services ....Mr. Russell JEFFREY
41 Athletic Director ....Ms. Ronda SEAGRAVES
38 Director Student Success Center ....Ms. Ruth COOPER
36 Director Career Center ....Ms. Randa SCOTT
32 Dean of Students ....Dr. Elizabeth MEDINA
39 Director of Residential Life ....Mr. Jakob ADAM
08 Director of Library Services ....Ms. Mikail MCINTOSH-DOTY
58 Director MEA Graduate Program ....Dr. Elise BRAZIER
13 Sr Dir of Information Technology ....Mr. Ian VARGA
19 Chief of Police ....Mr. H.E. JENKINS
43 Inside Counsel/Sr Dir Risk & Comp ....Ms. Rachael MARESH
15 Director Human Resources ....Ms. Angela CLEMENTS
29 Dir Donor & Alumni Relations ....Mr. Jeff FROSCH
102 Dir Foundation Relations ....Ms. Meghann BOLTON
44 Dir Donor Relations ....Ms. Tina HAMILTON
90 Director Academic Computing ....Mr. Joel RAHN
40 Bookstore Manager ....Ms. Jessica BRIGHT

Criswell College (G)

4010 Gaston Avenue, Dallas TX 75246-1537
County: Dallas FICE Identification: 041218
Unit ID: 475608
Telephone: (214) 821-5433 Carnegie Class: Not Classified
FAX Number: (214) 370-0497 Calendar System: Semester
URL: www.criswell.edu
Established: 1970 Annual Undergrad Tuition & Fees: $8,230
Enrollment: 343 Coed
Affiliation or Control: Independent Non-Profit IRS Status: 501(c)3
Highest Offering: Master's
Accreditation: SC

01 President ....Barry CREAMER
05 Vice President Academic Affairs ....Joseph WOODDELL
10 Chief Business Officer/VP Finance ....Kevin STILLEY
84 Vice Pres Enrollment Services ....Russell MARRIOTT
100 Chief of Staff ....Daisy REYNOLDS
30 Director of Development ....Mike GOFF

Culinary Institute LeNotre (H)

7070 Allensby Street, Houston TX 77022-4322
County: Harris FICE Identification: 037233
Unit ID: 444565
Telephone: (713) 692-0077 Carnegie Class: Spec 2-yr-A&S
FAX Number: (713) 692-7399 Calendar System: Other
URL: www.culinaryinstitute.edu
Established: 1998 Annual Undergrad Tuition & Fees: $15,938
Enrollment: 430 Coed
Affiliation or Control: Proprietary IRS Status: Proprietary
Highest Offering: Associate Degree
Accreditation: ACCSC, ACFEI

01 School Director ....Isabel OLIVAS

Culinary Institute of America San Antonio (I)

312 Pearl Parkway, Bldg 3, San Antonio TX 78215
Telephone: (210) 554-6400 Identification: 770131
Accreditation: &M

† Regional accreditation is carried under the parent institution in Hyde Park, NY

Dallas Baptist University (J)

3000 Mountain Creek Parkway, Dallas TX 75211-9299
County: Dallas FICE Identification: 003560
Unit ID: 224226
Telephone: (214) 333-7100 Carnegie Class: DU-Mod
FAX Number: (214) 333-5447 Calendar System: 4/1/4
URL: www.dbu.edu
Established: 1898 Annual Undergrad Tuition & Fees: $24,890
Enrollment: 5,445 Coed
Affiliation or Control: Baptist IRS Status: 501(c)3
Highest Offering: Doctorate
Accreditation: SC, ACBSP, CEA, MUS

01 Chancellor ....Dr. Gary COOK
01 President ....Dr. Adam WRIGHT
04 Asst to Chancellor/Dir Gift Acctng ....Mr. Mitch BENNETT
46 Vice Pres for Executive Affairs ....Dr. Norma HEDIN
10 Vice President Financial Affairs ....Dr. Matt MURRAH
30 VP Advancement & Graduate Affairs ....Dr. Cory HINES
11 Vice Pres for Admin Affairs ....Mr. Jonathan TEAT
26 Vice Pres for Communications ....Dr. Blake KILLINGSWORTH
32 Vice President for Student Affairs ....Mr. Jay HARLEY
85 Vice Pres for International Affairs ....Mr. Randy BYERS
05 Provost ....Dr. Denny DOWD
20 Associate Provost ....Mrs. Deemie NAUGLE
20 Asst Provost/Director Hybrid Educ ....Dr. Mark HALE
20 Academic Dean ....Dr. Gail LINAM
35 Dean of Students ....Mr. Dan GIBSON
42 Dean of Spiritual Life ....Mr. John BORUM
58 Acting Dean of Cook School of Ldshp ....Dr. Jack GOODYEAR
50 Dean College of Business ....Dr. Dale SIMS
81 Dean College Natural Science & Math ....Dr. Dionisio FLEITAS
53 Dean College of Education ....Dr. Neil DUGGER
57 Dean College of Fine Arts ....Mr. Ron BOWLES
73 Dean College of Christian Faith ....Dr. Steve MULLEN
79 Dean Col Humanities/Social Sciences ....Dr. Rob SULLIVAN
88 Dean College Professional Studies ....Dr. Donovan FREDRICKSEN
106 Dean of Online Education ....Mrs. Sena BAKER
58 Director of Graduate Programs ....Mrs. Kit MONTGOMERY
55 Director of Weekend College ....Ms. Joyce WALLACE
06 Registrar ....Ms. Linda RONEY
07 Director of Undergrad Admissions ....Mr. Bobby SOTO
29 Asst VP Advanc/Dir Alumni Relations ....Mr. Andrew BRISCOE
84 Asst Vice Pres for Enrollment Svcs ....Mr. Jason WILLIAMS
08 Director of Library ....Ms. Debra COLLINS
15 Director of Human Resources ....Mrs. Tamy ROGERS
37 Asst Vice Pres for Financial Aid ....Mr. Lee FERGUSON
43 General Counsel ....Mr. Dan MALONE
85 Dir Intl Admissions & Immigration ....Mr. Timothy WATTS
88 Director of Intl Student Services ....Mrs. Susie CASSEL
35 Director of Student Life ....Ms. Debora BLAKE
41 Director of Athletics ....Mr. Connor SMITH
36 Director of Career Services ....Mrs. Marion HILL-HUBBARD
38 Dir Counseling & Spiritual Care ....Dr. Jordan DAVIS
27 Director of Marketing ....Mrs. Layna EVANS
39 Director of University Housing ....Mr. Zach BEAN
39 Director of Residence Life ....Mrs. Kelly ANDERSON
24 Director of Media Services ....Mr. Rob LEWIS
42 Dir Intercessory Prayer Ministry ....Ms. Cyndi PETTIT
19 Chief of University Police ....Mr. John SHAW
19 Director of Campus Security ....Mr. Donald KABETZKE
21 Controller ....Mrs. Mendi MCMAHAN
09 Coord Institutional Effectiveness ....Mrs. Carol REID
09 Coord of Institutional Research ....Mrs. Pam NEUMANN
88 Academic Projects Administrator ....Ms. Lou ESPARZA
40 Manager Bookstore ....Mrs. Lauren FENNELL

Dallas Christian College (K)

2700 Christian Parkway, Dallas TX 75234-7299
County: Dallas FICE Identification: 006941
Unit ID: 224244
Telephone: (972) 241-3371 Carnegie Class: Spec-4-yr-Faith
FAX Number: (972) 241-8021 Calendar System: 4/1/4
URL: www.dallas.edu
Established: 1950 Annual Undergrad Tuition & Fees: $16,536
Enrollment: 309 Coed
Affiliation or Control: Christian Churches And Churches of Christ
IRS Status: 501(c)3

Highest Offering: Baccalaureate
Accreditation: BI

01 President — Dr. Brian D. SMITH
05 VP for Academic Affairs — Dr. Perry STEPP
26 VP for Communications — Mr. Matthew MEEKS
30 VP for Institutional Advancement — Mr. Mark WORLEY
10 VP of Finance & Operations — Ms. Andrea SHORT
32 Dean of Students — Mr. Eric HINTON
09 Dir Institutional Effectiveness — Mr. Bruce LONG
06 Registrar — Mrs. Crystal LAIDACKER
37 Dir of Student Financial Svcs — Ms. Breanda GILLASPIE
07 Dean of Admissions — Dr. Mark FISH
18 Director of Facilities — Mr. Gary ADAMS
04 Executive Assistant to the Pres — Ms. Dottie FARLEY
08 Director of Library Services — Ms. Jane REYNOLDS

*Dallas County Community College District Office (A)

1601 South Lamar Street, Dallas TX 75215
County: Dallas — FICE Identification: 009331
Unit ID: 224253
Telephone: (214) 378-1601 — Carnegie Class: N/A
FAX Number: (214) 378-1810
URL: www.dcccd.edu

01 Chancellor — Dr. Joe D. MAY
100 Exec Vice Chanc/Chief of Staff — Dr. Justin LONON
05 Exec Dist Dir WF Educ & Compliance — Mr. Don PERRY
18 Asc Vice Chanc Facil Mgmt/Architect — Mr. Clyde PORTER
43 District Legal Counsel — Mr. Robert WENDLAND
86 Vice Chanc Public & Govt Affairs — Mr. Isaac FAZ
30 Assoc Vice Chanc for Advancement — Mrs. Pyeper WILKINS
15 Chief Talent Officer — Mrs. Susan HALL
45 Assoc VChanc Strategic Initiative — Ms. Mary BRUMBACH
96 Director of Purchasing — Mr. Steve PARK
10 Chief Financial Officer — Mr. John ROBERTSON
13 Chief Info Technology Officer (CIO) — Dr. Tim MARSHALL

*Brookhaven College (B)

3939 Valley View, Dallas TX 75244-4997
County: Dallas — FICE Identification: 021002
Unit ID: 223524
Telephone: (972) 860-4700 — Carnegie Class: Assoc/HT-High Non
FAX Number: (972) 860-4897 — Calendar System: Semester
URL: www.brookhavencollege.edu
Established: 1978 — Annual Undergrad Tuition & Fees (In-District): $1,770
Enrollment: 12,403 — Coed
Affiliation or Control: State/Local — IRS Status: 501(c)3
Highest Offering: Associate Degree
Accreditation: SC, ADNUR, ART, EMT, RAD

02 President — Dr. Thom D. CHESNEY
05 Vice President of Academic Affairs — Mr. Donald SMITH
10 Vice President of Business Services — Mr. George HERRING
32 Vice Pres Student Dev/Enroll Mgmt — Mr. Oscar LOPEZ
04 Exec Assistant to President — Ms. Edna LOVE
50 Exec Dean Business Studies — Mr. Sandy WYCHE
36 Assoc VP Career & Program Resources — Mrs. Marilyn K. KOLESAR-LYNCH
103 Assoc VP Workforce/Continuing Educ — Mr. Vernon L. HAWKINS
30 Assoc Vice Pres Development — Ms. Marilyn K. LYNCH
45 Exec Dean Educational Resources — Ms. Sarah FERGUSON
57 Exec Dean Fine Arts/Physical Educ — Mr. Rick MAXWELL
81 Exec Dean Science/Math — Dr. Kathryn WETZEL
23 Exec Dean of Health/Human Svcs — Dr. Juanita FLINT
09 AVP Plng/Rsrch/Inst Effectiveness — Dr. Michael DENNEHY
13 Director Information Technology — Mr. Michael DEASON
83 Exec Dean Social Sci/Distance Lrng — Mr. Sam GOVEA
26 Executive Dean Communications — Mrs. Kendra VAGLIENTI
88 Exec Dean Stdnt Success/Enroll Svcs — Ms. Brenda DALTON
27 Asst Dir Marketing & Public Info — Mrs. Meridith DANFORTH
07 Director of Admissions/Registrar — Ms. Thoa Hoang VO
41 Director of Athletics — Ms. Lynne LEVESQUE
21 Director of Business Office — Ms. Willadean MARTIN
36 Director Career Services — Ms. Dominica MCCARTHY
88 Dir Brookhaven Geotech Institute — Ms. Melanie GAMBLE
18 Director of Facilities — Mr. Tommy GALLEGOS
15 Exec Dir of Human Resources — Ms. Terri EDRICH
20 Assoc Instructional Dean — Mr. Grant SISK
35 Dir Office of Student Life — Mr. Brian BORSKI
19 Captain of College Police — Mr. John KLINGENSMITH
23 Nurse Health Services — Ms. Mildred KELLEY
04 Assistant to President — Ms. Carrie SCHWEITZER
88 Exec Dean Educational Partnerships — Ms. Doris ROUSEY
88 Exec Dean World Languages — Mr. Grant SISK

*Cedar Valley College (C)

3030 N Dallas Avenue, Lancaster TX 75134-3799
County: Dallas — FICE Identification: 003561
Unit ID: 223773
Telephone: (972) 860-8201 — Carnegie Class: Assoc/MT-VT-High Non
FAX Number: (972) 682-7075 — Calendar System: Semester
URL: www.cedarvalleycollege.edu
Established: 1974 — Annual Undergrad Tuition & Fees (In-District): $1,770
Enrollment: 6,759 — Coed
Affiliation or Control: State/Local — IRS Status: 501(c)3
Highest Offering: Associate Degree
Accreditation: SC

02 President — Dr. Jennifer L. WIMBISH
05 Vice President for Instruction — Ms. Audra BARRETT
32 Int VP Student Svcs/Enroll Mgmt — Dr. Karen LALJIANI
10 Vice President Business Services — Mr. Huan LUONG
81 Director Dean Math/Science/Health — Mr. Eddy RAWLINSON
09 Dir Inst Research/Effectiveness — Ms. Nicole NAAN
49 Division Dean Liberal Arts — Dr. Elsie BURNETT
50 Div Dean Bus/Science/Technology — Dr. Ruben JOHNSON
20 Int Dean Instr Supp Distance Educ — Dr. Maria BOCCALANDRO
51 Executive Dean Cmty & Resource Dev — Mrs. Patricia DAVIS
08 Assoc Dean Educ Resource/Librarian — Ms. Vidya KRISHNASWAMY
07 Director of Admissions — Ms. Linda OSAGIE
18 Director Facilities Management — Mrs. Cindy A. ROGERS
26 Dir Marketing & Public Relations — Mr. Henry MARTINEZ
15 Interim Director Human Resources — Ms. Mary MALLARD
37 Director of Financial Aid — Ms. Cathryn ADAMS
88 Director of Upward Bound — Ms. Olivia GUERRA
88 Int Director of Independent Study — Mr. Joe COLBERT
35 Coordinator Office Student Life — Ms. Myioshi U. HOLMES
36 Senior Placement Coordinator — Ms. Lathera ADDISON
06 Registrar — Ms. Linda OSAGIE
29 Director Alumni Relations — Ms. Patricia DAVIS
38 Director Student Counseling — Ms. Jarlene DECAY
84 Int Director Enrollment Mgmt — Dr. Karen LALJIANI
96 Director of Purchasing — Ms. Susan PIERCE

*Eastfield College (D)

3737 Motley Drive, Mesquite TX 75150-2099
County: Dallas — FICE Identification: 008510
Unit ID: 224572
Telephone: (972) 860-7100 — Carnegie Class: Assoc/MT-VT-High Non
FAX Number: (972) 860-8373 — Calendar System: Semester
URL: www.eastfieldcollege.edu
Established: 1970 — Annual Undergrad Tuition & Fees (In-District): $1,770
Enrollment: 15,112 — Coed
Affiliation or Control: State/Local — IRS Status: 170(c)1
Highest Offering: Associate Degree
Accreditation: SC

02 President — Dr. Jean L. CONWAY
05 Exec VP Academic Affairs — Mr. Michael J. GUTIERREZ
10 VP Business Services — Dr. Adrian H. DOUGLAS
15 Exec Director Human Resources — Mr. Larry L. WILSON
32 Exec Dean Student Development — Mr. Paul M. GOERTEMILLER
12 Exec Dir Pleasant Grove Campus — Mr. Javier E. OLGUIN
09 Director Institutional Research — Mr. Ricardo RODRIGUEZ
20 Assoc VP Academic Affairs — Ms. Rachel B. WOLF
103 Associate Dean of Workforce Dev — Mr. Johnnie O. BELLAMY
81 Executive Dean STEM — Dr. Gretchen K. RIEHL
83 Executive Dean Social Sciences — Dr. Michael D. WALKER
88 Director Workforce Devel — Mrs. Christa K. JONES
08 Executive Dean Library — Ms. Karla J. GREER
20 Assoc VP Academic Affairs — Dr. Kimberly M. LOWRY
57 Exec Dean Arts and Communications — Ms. Courtney CARTER-HARBOUR
21 Exec Dean of Financial Affairs — Ms. Heidi M. BASSETT
18 Director Facilities Management — Mr. Michael BRANTLEY
45 Dean Planning/Research/Inst Effect — Dr. Kimberly K. CHANDLER
46 Dean Resource Development — Dr. Tricia THOMAS-ANDERSON
51 Exec Dean Continuing Education — Ms. Judith C. DUMONT
26 Director of Marketing — Ms. Donielle R. JOHNSON
106 Dean Inst Support & Distance Educ — Mr. Abuzafar M. BASHET
27 Associate Director College Comm — Ms. Sharon L. COOK
07 Exec Dean Student & Enrollment — Mr. Robert C. HARPER

*El Centro College (E)

801 Main Street, Dallas TX 75202-3604
County: Dallas — FICE Identification: 004453
Unit ID: 224615
Telephone: (214) 860-2000 — Carnegie Class: Assoc/MT-VT-High Non
FAX Number: (214) 860-2335 — Calendar System: Semester
URL: www.elcentrocollege.edu
Established: 1966 — Annual Undergrad Tuition & Fees (In-District): $1,770
Enrollment: 10,549 — Coed
Affiliation or Control: State/Local — IRS Status: 501(c)3
Highest Offering: Associate Degree
Accreditation: SC, ACFEI, ADNUR, COARC, CVT, DMS, EMT, MAC, MLTAD, PNUR, RAD, SURGT

02 President — Dr. Jose ADAMES
05 VP Academic Affairs — Dr. Charles MORRIS
45 VP Community/Economic Devel — Ms. Sondra G. FLEMMING
32 VP of Student Svcs & Enrollment — Dr. Chemene L. CRAWFORD
10 VP Business Services — Mr. David A. BROWNING
30 Assoc VP of Development — Ms. Lenora REECE
17 Exec Dean Health Occ/Legal Studies — Dr. Mary L. MCPHERSON
88 Exec Dean Academic Transfer — Dr. Anthony MANSUETO
81 Exec Dean STEM — Ms. Beth STALL
50 Int Exec Dean Bus/Des/Pub Svc — Ms. Elizabeth GUERRA
103 Exec Dean Workforce/Cont Educ — Ms. Jennie POLLARD
106 Dean Instruct Innovation/Acad Sup — Ms. Karla DAMRON
108 Dean Curriculum Assessment — Ms. Karen MONGO
09 Dean Institutional Effectiveness — Ms. Teresa S. ISBELL
35 Dean Student Support Services — Ms. Karen ROYSTER
35 Dean Student Success — Mr. Cornelius JOHNSON
08 Asst Dean Educational Resources — Dr. Norman HOWDEN
07 Assoc Dean Enroll Services — Ms. Rebecca J. GARZA
12 Exec Director West Campus — Ms. Kathy ACOSTA
15 Exec Director Human Resources — Ms. Dawn M. SEGROVES

19 College Director College Police — Mr. Joseph HANNIGAN
26 Dir Marketing/Communications — Ms. Priscilla A. STALEY
18 Col Director Facilities Services — Mr. Jeremy MCCLELLAND
21 Dir Business Operations — Ms. Keisha FARRINGTON
88 Assoc Dean Stdnt Recruit/Outreach — Mr. Monty E. FRANCIS
37 Dir Student Financial Aid — Ms. Pam A. LUCAS
13 Director Information Technology — Mr. Michael C. JOHNSON
85 Director College Programs — Mr. Robert G. REYES
36 Pgm Svcs Coord Career Services — Ms. Christol JOHNSON
40 Manager Bookstore — Mr. Richard SCHLEIFFER

*Mountain View College (F)

4849 W Illinois, Dallas TX 75211-6599
County: Dallas — FICE Identification: 008503
Unit ID: 226930
Telephone: (214) 860-8680 — Carnegie Class: Assoc/HT-High Non
FAX Number: (214) 860-8521 — Calendar System: Semester
URL: www.mountainviewcollege.edu
Established: 1970 — Annual Undergrad Tuition & Fees (In-District): $1,770
Enrollment: 8,950 — Coed
Affiliation or Control: State/Local — IRS Status: 501(c)3
Highest Offering: Associate Degree
Accreditation: SC

02 President — Dr. Robert GARZA
05 Vice President of Instruction — Dr. Lori DODDY
32 VP Student Svcs/Enrollment Mgmt — Dr. Leonard GARRETT
10 Vice President of Business Services — Dr. Sharon DAVIS
84 Exec Dean Student Support Svcs — Mr. Matthew SANCHEZ
90 Exec Dean Curriculum & Instruction — Dr. Karen VALENCIA
45 Dean Education Center/Dir Title V — Vacant
06 Assoc Dean Admission/Enrollment — Ms. Glenda GARRETT
18 Director Facilities Services — Mr. Allan KNOTT
09 Dir of Planning/Research & IE — Ms. Iva BERGERON
37 Director Financial Aid — Ms. Bianca MATLOCK
35 Director of Student Life — Ms. Cathy EDWARDS
103 Exec Dean of Workforce/Cont Educ — Ms. Pat WEBB
26 Director Public Info/Marketing — Ms. Jill LAIN
21 Director of Business Operations — Mr. Jose RODRIGUEZ
07 Asst Director of Admissions — Mr. Kenne EVANS
38 Director of Advising — Vacant
15 Exec Director Human Resources — Mr. Jarred DAVIS
36 Director Career Development — Ms. Regina GARNER
45 Dean Resource Development — Ms. Heather A. MARSH
04 Administrative Asst to President — Ms. Brenda EPPERSON
08 Head Librarian — Ms. Jean BAKER
19 Director Security/Safety — Mr. Marvis MOSLEY
41 Athletic Director — Mr. Keith MCKINNON

*North Lake College (G)

5001 N MacArthur Boulevard, Irving TX 75038-3899
County: Dallas — FICE Identification: 020774
Unit ID: 227191
Telephone: (972) 273-3000 — Carnegie Class: Assoc/HT-High Non
FAX Number: (972) 273-3014 — Calendar System: Semester
URL: www.dcccd.edu
Established: 1977 — Annual Undergrad Tuition & Fees (In-District): $1,770
Enrollment: 10,744 — Coed
Affiliation or Control: State/Local — IRS Status: 501(c)3
Highest Offering: Associate Degree
Accreditation: SC, CONST

02 President — Dr. Christa SLEJKO
05 Vice President Academic Affairs — Dr. Martha HUGHES
103 VP Workforce Education — Dr. Paul KELEMEN
10 Interim Vice Pres Business Services — Dr. Eddie TEALER
45 Vice Pres Planning & Development — Ms. Candace CASTILLO
84 VP Stdnt Svcs/Enrollment Mgmt — Ms. Mary CIMINELLI
88 Director of Learning Resources — Mr. Kent SEAVER
07 Director Admissions & Registration — Ms. Francyenne MAYNARD
26 Director Marketing & Public Info — Ms. Gina FEDERER
12 Ex Director North and South Campus — Mr. Arthur JAMES
08 Head Librarian — Dr. Enrique CHAMBERLAIN
18 Director Facilities Services — Mr. John WATSON
19 Director Campus Police — Mr. Randy REED
88 Int Director of Decision Support — Ms. Peggy SINDELAR
15 Director Human Resources — Mr. Willie NEAL
21 Director Business Operations — Ms. Elsy CARRANZA
32 Dir Student Programs/Resources — Ms. Beth NIKOPOULOS
103 Director Workforce Dev/CE — Mr. Tim SAMUELS
38 Dir Acad Advising Career Edu Pl — Vacant
83 Executive Dean Liberal Arts — Dr. Shawnda FLOYD
81 Exec Dean Math/Science — Dr. Marilyn MAYS
50 Exe Dean Arts/Bus/Sports Sci Tech — Dr. David EVANS
12 Exec Dean West Campus — Mr. Mike COOLEY

*Richland College (H)

12800 Abrams Road, Dallas TX 75243-2199
County: Dallas — FICE Identification: 008504
Unit ID: 227766
Telephone: (972) 238-6194 — Carnegie Class: Assoc/HT-High Non
FAX Number: (972) 238-6978 — Calendar System: Semester
URL: www.rlc.dcccd.edu
Established: 1972 — Annual Undergrad Tuition & Fees (In-District): $1,770
Enrollment: 19,343 — Coed
Affiliation or Control: State/Local — IRS Status: 501(c)3
Highest Offering: Associate Degree
Accreditation: SC, MAC

02 President ....Dr. Kathryn K. EGGLESTON
04 Dean/Exec Assistant to President ....Ms. Janet C. JAMES
05 Exec VP Acad Affs & Stdnt Success .Dr. Zarina BLANKENBAKER
32 VP for Student Development ....Vacant
10 VP for Business Services ....Mr. Ron M. CLARK
84 Assoc VP Enrollment/Supt RCHS ....Ms. Donna WALKER
50 Exec Dean Sch of Engr/Business/Tech ....Ms. Martha A. HOGAN
79 Exec Dean Human/Fine & Perf Arts ....Ms. Diane HILBERT
81 Exec Dean of Math/Science/Hlth Prof ....Dr. Raymond P. CANHAM
09 Assoc VP Plng/Rsrch/Inst Effect ....Ms. Fonda L. VERA
60 Exec Dean World Lang/Cultures/Comm ...Ms. Susan E. BARKLEY
88 Inst Dean Lrng Enrich & Acad Dev ....Mr. Thales GEORGIOU
83 Inst Dean School of Social Science ....Dr. LaQueta WRIGHT
06 Registrar ....Vacant
41 Director Athletic Programs ....Mr. Guy SIMMONS
35 Director of Student Life ....Vacant
08 Dean Educational Services ....Ms. Laura MCKINNON
26 Dir College Comm and Marketing ....Ms. Whitney ROSENBALM
18 Director of Facilities Services ....Mr. Kenneth DUNSON
15 Executive Director Human Resources ....Dr. Bill DIAL
19 Chief of College Police ....Mr. Robert D. BAKER
88 Principal Richland Collegiate HS ....Mr. Craig HINKLE

Dallas Institute of Funeral Service (A)

3909 S Buckner Boulevard, Dallas TX 75227-4314

County: Dallas FICE Identification: 010761
Unit ID: 224271
Telephone: (214) 388-5466 Carnegie Class: Spec 2-yr-A&S
FAX Number: (214) 388-0316 Calendar System: Quarter
URL: www.dallasinstitute.edu
Established: 1945 Annual Undergrad Tuition & Fees: $11,150
Enrollment: 128 Coed
Affiliation or Control: Independent Non-Profit IRS Status: 501(c)3
Highest Offering: Associate Degree
Accreditation: FUSER

01 President ....Mr. James M. SHOEMAKE

Dallas Nursing Institute (B)

12170 North Abrams Road, Suite 125, Dallas TX 75243

County: Dallas FICE Identification: 034165
Unit ID: 437732
Telephone: (469) 941-8300 Carnegie Class: Spec 2-yr-Health
FAX Number: (214) 575-9090 Calendar System: Semester
URL: www.dni.edu
Established: 1991 Annual Undergrad Tuition & Fees: N/A
Enrollment: 160 Coed
Affiliation or Control: Proprietary IRS Status: Proprietary
Highest Offering: Baccalaureate
Accreditation: ABHES

01 Executive Director ....Dr. Ronald HYSON
32 Director of Student Affairs ....Ms. Brigit MATTIX

Dallas Theological Seminary (C)

3909 Swiss Avenue, Dallas TX 75204-6493

County: Dallas FICE Identification: 003562
Unit ID: 224305
Telephone: (214) 887-5000 Carnegie Class: Spec-4-yr-Faith
FAX Number: (214) 887-5532 Calendar System: Semester
URL: www.dts.edu
Established: 1924 Annual Graduate Tuition & Fees: N/A
Enrollment: 2,088 Coed
Affiliation or Control: Independent Non-Profit IRS Status: 501(c)3
Highest Offering: Doctorate; No Undergraduates
Accreditation: SC, THEOL

01 President ....Dr. Mark L. BAILEY
05 Vice Pres Academic Affs/Acad Dean ....Dr. Mark M. YARBROUGH
32 VP Dean Stdnt Svcs/Dean of Students ....Dr. Robert J. GARIPPA
10 Vice President Business & Finance ....Mr. Dale C. LARSON
30 Vice President for Advancement ....Ms. Kimberly B. TILL
11 Vice President Campus Operations ....Mr. Robert F. RIGGS
26 Exec Dir Communications/Ed Tech ....Mr. John C. DYER
102 President Dallas Sem Foundation ....Mr. Stephen M. GOLDING
108 Dean of Assessment ....Dr. Eugene W. POND
20 Dean of Academic Administration ....Dr. James H. THAMES
12 Dean of DTS Houston ....Dr. Bruce W. FONG
58 Director of PhD Studies ....Dr. Richard A. TAYLOR
58 Director of DMin Studies ....Dr. D. Scott BARFOOT
09 Dir of Institutional Effectiveness ....Mr. David HIONIDES
06 Registrar ....Mr. Billy R. TODD, JR.
88 Exec Dir of Leadership Center ....Dr. Bill HENDRICKS
88 Exec Dir of Cultural Engagement ....Dr. Darrell L. BOCK
07 Director of Admissions ....Mr. Nate MCKANNA
08 Library Director ....Mr. Marvin T. HUNN, II
29 Dean of Enrollment/Alumni
Services ....Mr. Gregory A. HATTEBERG
36 Director of Placement ....Dr. Paul E. PETTIT
24 Director of Audio/Visual Support ....Mr. James W. HOOVER
42 Chaplain ....Dr. Joe ALLEN
34 Adviser to Women Students ....Ms. Lynn Etta G. MANNING
93 Adviser to African-American Studnts ...Dr. Terrance S. WOODSON
13 Director of Information Technology ....Mr. Kevin COX
19 Chief of Campus Police ....Mr. John S. BLOOM
39 Director of Housing & Food Services ......Mr. Drew H. WILLIAMS
106 Dir Online and External Studies ....Mr. Robert M. ABEGG
88 Director of Online Chinese Studies ....Dr. Samuel CHIA
38 Director of Counseling Services ....Dr. Kelly CHEATHAM
21 Controller ....Ms. Patricia MAYABB
40 Bookstore Manager ....Mr. Kevin D. STERN
85 International Student Adviser ....Ms. Rachel O'BRIEN
04 Administrative Asst to President ....Ms. Michelle B. SCHIWIETZ
15 Director Personnel Services ....Ms Karen G. HOLDER
44 Director Annual or Planned Giving ....Ms. Kimberley B. TILL
91 Director Administrative Computing ....Mr. Kevin B. COX
105 Director Web Services ....Mr. John C. DYER
37 Director Student Financial Aid ....Ms Karen G. HOLDER

Del Mar College (D)

101 Baldwin Blvd., Corpus Christi TX 78404-3897

County: Nueces FICE Identification: 003563
Unit ID: 224350
Telephone: (361) 698-1200 Carnegie Class: Assoc/MT-VT-High Trad
FAX Number: (361) 698-1559 Calendar System: Semester
URL: www.delmar.edu
Established: 1935 Annual Undergrad Tuition & Fees (In-District): $2,546
Enrollment: 10,439 Coed
Affiliation or Control: Local IRS Status: 501(c)3
Highest Offering: Associate Degree
Accreditation: SC, ACFEI, ADNUR, ART, CAHIIM, COARC, DA, DH, DMS, MLTAD, MUS, NMT, OTA, PTAA, RAD, SURGT, THEA

01 President ....Dr. Mark ESCAMILLA
43 General Counsel ....Mr. Augustin RIVERA, JR.
05 Provost/VP for Academic Affairs ....Dr. Beth LEWIS
35 Vice President for Student Affairs ....Dr. Rito SILVA
10 Int Chief Financial Officer ....Dr. Cathy WEST
103 VP Workforce Dev/Strategic Init ....Ms. Lenora KEAS
26 Exec Dir Strategic Communications ....Ms Claudia JACKSON
30 Exec Director of Development ....Ms. Mary MCQUEEN
07 Dean Student Outreach/Enroll
Svcs ....Ms. Patricia BENAVIDES-DOMINGUEZ
84 Dean Student Engagement & Retention ....Ms. Cheryl SANDERS
49 Dean Division Arts & Sciences ....Dr. Jonda HALCOMB
17 Dean Health Sciences & Prof ....Dr. Shannon YDOYAGA
75 Dean Bus/Ind/Public Safety ....Mr. Charles MCKINNY
15 Exec Director HR & Administration ....Ms. Tammy MCDONALD
21 Comptroller ....Mr. John J. JOHNSON
96 Director of Purchasing/Business Svc ....Mr. David DAVILA
13 Chief Information Officer ....Mr. August ALFONSO
19 Int Chief of Security ....Ms. Lauren WHITE
88 Dir Environ/Health/Safety/Risk Mgmt ....Mr. Kelly L. WHITE
37 Director of Financial Aid ....Ms. Nancy M. BRISENO
06 Registrar ....Ms. Elizabeth ADAMSON
32 Dir Student Leadership/Campus Life ....Ms. Beverly CAGE
88 Dir of Financial Services/Bursar ....Ms. D'Ann POLAND
08 Int Director of Libraries ....Ms. Sally BICKLEY
09 Director of Institutional Research ....Mr. Sushil PALLEMONI
16 Director of Human Resources ....Mr. Jerry W. HENRY
88 Director of Payroll ....Ms. Katrina GARCIA

DeVry University - Houston Campus (E)

11125 Equity Drive, Houston TX 77041-8217

Telephone: (713) 973-3000 Identification: 666219
Accreditation: &NH, ENGT, MT

† Campus is in teach-out. Regional accreditation is carried under the parent institution in Downers Grove, IL.

DeVry University - Irving Campus (F)

4800 Regent Boulevard, Ste 200, Irving TX 75063-2439

Telephone: (972) 929-6777 FICE Identification: 010139
Accreditation: &NH, ENGT

† Regional accreditation is carried under the parent institution in Downers Grove, IL.

East Texas Baptist University (G)

One Tiger Drive, Marshall TX 75670-1498

County: Harrison FICE Identification: 003564
Unit ID: 224527
Telephone: (903) 935-7963 Carnegie Class: Bac-Diverse
FAX Number: (903) 938-1705 Calendar System: Semester
URL: www.etbu.edu
Established: 1912 Annual Undergrad Tuition & Fees: $24,218
Enrollment: 1,299 Coed
Affiliation or Control: Southern Baptist IRS Status: 501(c)3
Highest Offering: Master's
Accreditation: SC, #CAATE, MUS, NURSE

01 President ....Dr. J. Blair BLACKBURN
84 Vice Pres Enrollment/Admin Affairs ....Mr. Kevin CAFFEY
05 Provost/Vice Pres Academic Affairs ....Dr. Thomas SANDERS
30 Vice Pres University Advancement ....Mrs. Susan ROSSMAN
42 Vice Pres Spiritual Development ....Dr. Scott BRYANT
10 Sr Vice Pres Financial Affairs ....Mr. Ned CALVERT
32 Vice President for Student Affairs ....Dr. Heather HADLOCK
51 Vice Pres for Adult Education ....Mr. Vince BLANKENSHIP
35 Asst Dean Student Affs Operations ....Mr. Blair PREVOST
09 Dean Acad Services & Inst Research ....Vacant
07 Admissions Coordinator ....Mr. Madison MCGAUGHEY
13 Director of Inst Technology ....Mr. Barry HALE
06 University Registrar ....Mr. Chris WOOD
29 Director of Alumni Relations ....Mrs. Allison PETEET
107 Dean School of Professional Studies ....Dr. Joseph BROWN
08 Director of Library ....Ms. Cynthia PETERSON
26 Director of Public Relations ....Vacant
37 Director of Financial Aid ....Mr. Tommy YOUNG
41 Director of Athletics ....Mr. Kent REEVES
88 Director Baptist Student Ministry ....Mr. Mark YATES
40 Director of Bookstore ....Ms. Karan SUSTAIRE
18 Director of Physical Facilities ....Mr. Stephen RATCLIFF
88 Director Rec & Athletic Facilities ....Mr. Randy PRINGLE
88 Director Great Commission Center ....Dr. Lisa SEELEY
53 Dean School of Education ....Dr. John SARGENT
88 Dean School of Christian Studies ....Dr. John HARRIS
83 Dean School of Nat/Soc Sciences ....Dr. Lynn NEW
50 Dean School of Business ....Vacant
79 Dean School of Humanities ....Dr. Jerry SUMMERS
85 Dir Global Educ/Grt Commission Ctr ....Dr. Lisa SEELEY
21 Director of Financial Services ....Mr. Richard HUTSELL
88 Director of Student Success ....Mrs. Kelley PAUL
57 Dean School of Comm & Perf Arts ....Dr. Tom WEBSTER
88 Asst Prov of Leadership Development ....Dr. Emily PREVOST
25 Director Design & Media Relations ....Mrs. Becky DAVIS
27 Director of Marketing ....Ms. Emily ROBERSON

El Paso Community College (H)

9050 Viscount Boulevard, El Paso TX 79925

County: El Paso FICE Identification: 010387
Unit ID: 224642
Telephone: (915) 831-3722 Carnegie Class: Assoc/HT-High Trad
FAX Number: (915) 831-6507 Calendar System: Semester
URL: www.epcc.edu
Established: 1969 Annual Undergrad Tuition & Fees (In-District): $2,386
Enrollment: 28,308 Coed
Affiliation or Control: Local IRS Status: 501(c)3
Highest Offering: Associate Degree
Accreditation: SC, ADNUR, CAHIIM, COARC, DA, DH, DMS, EMT, MAC, MLTAD, PTAA, RAD, SURGT

01 President ....Dr. William SERRATA
05 Vice President Instruction ....Mr. Steve SMITH
11 Vice Pres Financial and Admin Ops .Ms. Josette SHAUGHNESSY
13 Vice Pres Information Tech/CIO ....Dr. Jenny GIRON
32 Vice President Student Services ....Ms. Linda GONZALEZ
10 Interim AVP Budget and Fin Svcs ....Mr. Fernando FLORES
20 AVP Instruction and Student Success ....Dr. Julie PENLEY
103 AVP Workforce and CE ....Dr. Jaime FARIAS
15 Assoc VP Employee Relations ....Ms. Nancy N. NELSON
26 Dir Marketing & Community Rels ....Ms. Joyce CORDELL
12 Dean Instruct Programs-MDP Campus ....Vacant
76 Dean Health Career/TechEd/Math/Sci ....Dr. Paula MITCHELL
60 Dean Arts/Comm/Career/TechEd/SoSc ....Dr. Eileen CONKLIN
83 Dean Arts/Comm & Soc Sci ....Ms. Janet EVELER
79 Dean ESL Reading Social Science ....Ms. Susana RODARTE
57 Dean Comm/Performing Arts ....Vacant
53 Dean Education/Career/Tech Pgms ....Vacant
66 Dean Nursing ....Ms. Paula G. MEAGHER
12 Dean Instructional Pgms-NW Campus ....Dr. Lydia TENA
81 Dean Math/Sci/Career Tech Educ ....Mr. Ernest R. WEBB, II
88 Assoc Dean Dual Credit & Early Col ....Mr. Carlos GONZALEZ
37 Exec Director Student Financial Aid ....Mr. Raul H. LERMA
45 Dir Institutional Effectiveness ....Dr. Ron STROUD
08 Director Library Technical Services ....Mr. Luis CHAPARRO
21 Comptroller ....Mr. Fernando FLORES
36 Director Career Services ....Ms. Carla CARDOZA
18 Executive Director Physical Plant ....Mr. Richard L. LOBATO
19 Chief of Police ....Mr. Jose L. RAMIREZ
16 Exec Dir Human Resources ORMS ..Ms. Elizabeth OLGUIN-RYAN
07 Exec Director Admissions/
Registrar ....Dr. Cassandra M. LACHICA-CHAVEZ
96 Dir Purchasing & Contract Mgmt ....Mr. Ruben C. GALLARDO
09 Director Institutional Research ....Dr. Carol KAY
88 Director Human Resources Devel ....Mr. Alex HERNANDEZ
21 Director Budget ....Ms. Laura TELLEZ
88 Director Workplace Literacy Pgm ....Mrs. Sara MARTINEZ
102 Exec Dir Resource Dev/Foundation ....Ms. Dolores GROSS
22 Dir Ctr for Students w/Disabilities ....Ms. Janet M. LOCKHART
88 Director Recruitment/School Rels ....Ms. Nita CORRAL-NAVA
88 Exec Dir Outreach Transition Svcs ....Dr. Marisa E. PIERCE
25 Director Grants Management ....Mr. Alfred C. LAWRENCE
103 Director Workforce Development ....Ms. Luz E. TABOADA
106 Director Distance Education ....Mr. Robert P. JONES
88 Director Student Success ....Ms. Lucia M. RODRIGUEZ
88 Dir Law Enforcement Trng Academy ....Mr. Barry J. BOGLE
28 Director of Diversity Programs ....Mrs. Olga CHAVEZ
41 Athletic Director ....Mr. Felix HINOJOSA

Everest College (I)

300 Six Flags Drive, Suite 100, Arlington TX 76011

Telephone: (817) 652-7790 Identification: 770788
Accreditation: ACICS

† Branch campus of Everest College, Henderson, NV

Everest College (J)

4200 South Freeway, Suite 1940, Fort Worth TX 76115

Telephone: (817) 556-7700 Identification: 770790
Accreditation: ACICS

† Branch campus of Everest College, Colorado Springs, CO

Fortis College (K)

401 East Palace Pkwy Ste 100, Grand Prairie TX 75050

Telephone: (972) 375-0006 Identification: 770937
Accreditation: ABHES, RAD, SURGT, SURTEC

† Branch campus of Fortis Institute, Baton Rouge, LA.

Fortis College (A)

1201 West Oaks Mall, Houston TX 77082
County: Harris FICE Identification: 034244
Unit ID: 392415
Telephone: (713) 266-6594 Carnegie Class: Not Classified
FAX Number: (713) 782-5873 Calendar System: Quarter
URL: fortiscollege.edu
Established: Annual Undergrad Tuition & Fees: N/A
Enrollment: 287 Coed
Affiliation or Control: Proprietary IRS Status: Proprietary
Highest Offering: Associate Degree
Accreditation: COE, SURGT

01 Campus President .... Sidney CAREY

Frank Phillips College (B)

PO Box 5118, Borger TX 79008-5118
County: Hutchinson FICE Identification: 003568
Unit ID: 224891
Telephone: (806) 457-4200 Carnegie Class: Assoc/HVT-High Non
FAX Number: (806) 457-4224 Calendar System: Semester
URL: www.fpctx.edu
Established: 1948 Annual Undergrad Tuition & Fees (In-District): $3,052
Enrollment: 1,348 Coed
Affiliation or Control: Local IRS Status: 501(c)3
Highest Offering: Associate Degree
Accreditation: SC

01 President .... Dr. Jud HICKS
11 Vice Pres Administrative Services .... Dr. Jud HICKS
05 Vice President of Academic Affairs .... Dr. Shannon CARROLL
103 Dean of Career & Technical Educ .... Mr. David CARR
08 Director of the Library .... Mr. Jason PRICE
18 Director Physical Plant .... Ms. Regina HANEY
30 Director Advancement .... Ms. Nicole SIDDENS
37 Dir Student Financial Services .... Ms. Beverly FIELDS
38 Director Student Counseling/Testing .... Ms. Deborah JOHNSON
07 Director Admissions & Records .... Ms. Michele STEVENS
56 Director of Extended Education .... Ms. Tiffany THOMAS
10 Director of Accounting .... Ms. Bridey MCCORMACK

Galen College of Nursing (C)

7411 John Smith Drive, Suite 300, San Antonio TX 78229
Telephone: (210) 733-3056 Identification: 770538
Accreditation: &SC

† Regional accreditation is carried under the parent institution in Louisville, KY

Galveston College (D)

4015 Avenue Q, Galveston TX 77550-7496
County: Galveston FICE Identification: 004972
Unit ID: 224961
Telephone: (409) 944-4242 Carnegie Class: Assoc/MT-VT-High Non
FAX Number: (409) 944-1500 Calendar System: Semester
URL: www.gc.edu
Established: 1966 Annual Undergrad Tuition & Fees (In-District): $1,900
Enrollment: 2,048 Coed
Affiliation or Control: State/Local IRS Status: 501(c)3
Highest Offering: Associate Degree
Accreditation: SC, ADNUR, EMT, NMT, RAD, RTT

01 President .... Dr. Myles SHELTON
05 Vice President of Instruction .... Dr. Cissy MATTHEWS
11 VP for Administration/Finance .... Vacant
30 VP Community Engagement/Spec Proj .... Dr. Gaynelle H. HAYES
32 Actg VP of Student Svcs/Dir Fin Aid .... Mr. Ron C. CRUMEDY
75 Dean of Tech & Prof Education .... Ms. Vera LEWIS-JASPER
30 Dir of Development/GC Foundation .... Ms. Maria TRIPOVICH
10 Director of Business Services .... Mr. M. Jeff ENGBROCK
13 Dir of Information Technology .... Mr. Kelly KLIMPT
26 Director of Public Affairs .... Mr. Joseph E. HUFF, III
15 Dir Human Resources/Risk Management .... Dr. Mary Jan LANTZ
41 Athletic Director/Head Coach .... Mr. Ken DELCAMBRE
07 Director Admissions/Registrar .... Mr. Scott BRANUM
66 Director of Nursing .... Dr. Sandra BRANNAN
09 Director Inst Effectiveness/Rsrch .... Dr. Larry ROOT
18 Director of Facilities/Security .... Mr. Tim W. SETZER
62 Dir of Library/Learning Resources .... Dr. Alan M. UYEHARA
04 Executive Assistant .... Ms. Carla D. BIGGERS

Golf Academy of America (E)

1861 Valley View Lane, Suite 100,
Farmers Branch TX 75234
Telephone: (972) 763-8100 Identification: 770621
Accreditation: ACICS

† Branch campus of Virginia College, Birmingham, AL

Grace School of Theology (F)

3705 College Park Drive, The Woodlands TX 77384
County: Montgomery Identification: 667100
Unit ID: 481401
Telephone: (877) 476-8674 Carnegie Class: Not Classified
FAX Number: (877) 735-2867 Calendar System: Semester
URL: www.gsot.edu
Established: 2002 Annual Undergrad Tuition & Fees: $4,754
Enrollment: 153 Coed
Affiliation or Control: Independent Non-Profit IRS Status: 501(c)3
Highest Offering: Doctorate
Accreditation: TRACS

01 President .... Dr. Dave ANDERSON
43 Exec Vice President/General Counsel .... Mr. Tom KRUPPSTADT
05 Vice Pres Academic Affairs .... Dr. Al LETTING, III
30 Vice Pres Advancement .... Mr. Simon EASTWICK

Graduate Institute of Applied Linguistics (G)

7500 W Camp Wisdom Road, Dallas TX 75236-5629
County: Dallas FICE Identification: 038513
Telephone: (972) 708-7340 Carnegie Class: Not Classified
FAX Number: (972) 708-7292 Calendar System: Other
URL: www.gial.edu
Established: 1999 Annual Undergrad Tuition & Fees: N/A
Enrollment: N/A Coed
Affiliation or Control: Independent Non-Profit IRS Status: 501(c)3
Highest Offering: Master's
Accreditation: SC

01 President .... Dr. David A. ROSS
05 Dean of Academic Affairs .... Dr. Doug TIFFIN
10 Vice President of Finance .... Mr. Rod JENKINS
11 Vice President of Operations .... Mr. David HARRELL
32 Dean of Students .... Ms. Meg TRIHUS
06 Registrar .... Mrs. Lynne M. LAMIMAN
07 Director of Admissions .... Mrs. Maggie A. JOHNSON
08 Library Director .... Ms. Ferne L. WEIMER
30 Director of Development .... Ms. Judy POLLOCK
09 Director of Inst Research/Svcs .... Mr. Richard E. LYNCH
13 Director of Computing Services .... Mr. Chuck WALEK
21 Business Manager .... Mr. Paul W. SETTER
37 Financial Aid Administrator .... Ms. Margaret JOHNSON
88 Veterans' Officer .... Mrs. Mary Sue TIFFIN
42 Chaplain .... Mr. Victor JACKSON
29 Alumni Relations .... Mrs. Allison PYLE
04 Administrative Asst to President .... Ms. Gail DYKSTRA

Grayson College (H)

6101 Grayson Drive, Denison TX 75020-8299
County: Grayson FICE Identification: 003570
Unit ID: 225070
Telephone: (903) 465-6030 Carnegie Class: Assoc/MT-VT-Mix Trad/Non
FAX Number: (903) 463-5284 Calendar System: Semester
URL: www.grayson.edu
Established: 1963 Annual Undergrad Tuition & Fees (In-District): $1,872
Enrollment: 4,636 Coed
Affiliation or Control: State/Local IRS Status: 501(c)3
Highest Offering: Associate Degree
Accreditation: SC, ADNUR, DA, EMT, MLTAD

01 President .... Dr. Jeremy P. MCMILLEN
05 Vice Pres Academic/Student Affs .... Dr. Regina ORGAN
10 Vice President of Business Services .... Mr. Giles BROWN
13 VP Info Technology/Dir of Library .... Mr. Gary PAIKOWSKI
102 Exec Dir Grayson College Foundation .... Mr. Randy TRUXAL
07 Director of Admissions/Registrar .... Mrs. Christy KLEMIUK
37 Director of Financial Aid .... Ms. Donna KING
14 Director of Network Services .... Mr. Mike BROWN
19 Chief of Campus Police .... Mr. Andrew MACPHERSON
26 Dir Marketing/Public Information .... Ms. Amy EVANS
21 Director of Fiscal Services .... Mr. Danny HYATT
41 Athletic Director .... Mr. Mike MCBRAYER
40 Bookstore Manager .... Ms. Venus MCGUIRE

Hallmark University (I)

10401 IH-10 W, San Antonio TX 78230-1737
County: Bexar FICE Identification: 010509
Unit ID: 225201
Telephone: (210) 690-9000 Carnegie Class: Bac/Assoc-Assoc Dom
FAX Number: (210) 697-8225 Calendar System: Other
URL: www.hallmarkuniversity.edu
Established: 1969 Annual Undergrad Tuition & Fees: N/A
Enrollment: 372 Coed
Affiliation or Control: Independent Non-Profit IRS Status: 501(c)3
Highest Offering: Master's
Accreditation: ACCSC

00 CEO .... Mr. Joseph B. FISHER
01 University President .... Mr. Brent FESSLER
11 Sr Vice President of Operations .... Mr. Donald GREGSON
05 Dean of Academics .... Dr. Darla KENWARD
26 VP Public/Media Engagement .... Ms. Sonia ROSS
06 Registrar .... Ms. Racquel SULLEMUN
36 Director of Student Affairs .... Ms. Evonn SHORT
37 Director Student Financial Aid .... Ms. Grace CALIXTO
07 Director of Admissions Aviation .... Mr. Slava ROSS
08 Head Librarian .... Ms. Christina REEDY
10 Chief Business Officer .... Ms. Roxanne DARTY
13 Chief Info Technology Officer (CIO) .... Mr. Taylor MERCIER
18 Director of University Support .... Mr. Christopher SHORT

Hardin-Simmons University (J)

2200 Hickory, Abilene TX 79698-0001
County: Taylor FICE Identification: 003571
Unit ID: 225247
Telephone: (325) 670-1000 Carnegie Class: Masters/M
FAX Number: (325) 670-1267 Calendar System: Semester
URL: www.hsutx.edu
Established: 1891 Annual Undergrad Tuition & Fees: $24,500
Enrollment: 2,084 Coed
Affiliation or Control: Baptist IRS Status: 501(c)3
Highest Offering: Doctorate
Accreditation: SC, ACBSP, CAATE, MUS, NURSE, PTA, SW, THEOL

01 President .... Dr. Eric I. BRUNTMYER
05 Provost & Chief Academic Officer .... Dr. Thomas V. BRISCO
10 Vice President for Finance .... Mrs. Brenda ALEXANDER
30 VP for Institutional Advancement .... Mr. Mike HAMMACK
32 Vice Pres for Student Life .... Dr. Dave ROZEBOOM
84 VP for Enrollment Management .... Mrs. Vicki HOUSE
07 Assoc VP for Enrollment Svcs .... Mr. Jim JONES
53 Dean Irvin School of Education .... Dr. Pamela K. WILLIFORD
49 Dean College of Liberal Arts .... Dr. Alan STAFFORD
50 Dean Kelley College of Business .... Mr. Michael MONHOLLON
64 Dean College of Fine Arts .... Dr. Robert TUCKER
73 Dean Logsdon School of Theology .... Dr. Don WILLIFORD
58 Dean of Graduate Studies .... Dr. Nancy KUCINSKI
66 Dean School of Nursing .... Dr. Nina OUIMETTE
81 Dean School Sciences/Mathematics .... Dr. Christopher L. MCNAIR
13 Assoc Vice Pres Technical Services .... Mr. Travis P. SEEKINS
21 Asst VP For Finance/Controller .... Mrs. Jessica GARCIA
38 Assoc VP Academic Advising/Retent .... Mrs. Gracie CARROLL
08 Dean/Dir of University Libraries .... Mrs. Elizabeth J. WORLEY
09 Director of Institutional Research .... Mrs. Lori BLAKE
06 Registrar .... Mrs. Kacey HIGGINS
35 Dean of Students .... Mr. Brian DAWSON
29 Director of Alumni Relations .... Mrs. Britt E. JONES
19 Chief of Police .... Mr. Frank LOZA
23 University Nurse .... Mrs. Sue A. BIGGS
42 Chaplain .... Dr. Kelly PIGOTT
39 Director of Residence Life .... Mr. Johnathan YORKOWITZ
15 Director of Human Resources .... Mr. John SNAPP
27 Dir of Univ Communications .... Mr. James STONE
37 Dir Student Fin Aid & Scholarships .... Mrs. Bridget MOORE
18 Facilities Services Director .... Mr. Tim MCCARRY
41 Athletic Director .... Mr. John M. NEESE
85 Director of International Studies .... Dr. Allan J. LANDWER
26 Public Relations Director .... Mrs. Cheryl SAWYERS
93 Coordinator of Minority Studies .... Dr. Joe H. ALCORTA
28 Coord of Student Diversity Programs .... Dr. Kelvin J. KELLEY

Hill College (K)

112 Lamar Drive, Hillsboro TX 76645-2711
County: Hill FICE Identification: 003573
Unit ID: 225371
Telephone: (254) 659-7500 Carnegie Class: Assoc/HVT-Mix Trad/Non
FAX Number: (254) 582-7591 Calendar System: Semester
URL: www.hillcollege.edu
Established: 1923 Annual Undergrad Tuition & Fees (In-District): $2,220
Enrollment: 4,020 Coed
Affiliation or Control: Local IRS Status: 501(c)3
Highest Offering: Associate Degree
Accreditation: SC, CVT, EMT

01 President .... Dr. Pamela BOEHM
04 Executive Asst to the President .... Ms. Vonnie MORPHEW
05 Vice President Instruction .... Mr. Rex PARCELLS
25 Vice President External Affairs .... Ms. Jessyca BROWN
10 Vice Pres Administrative Services .... Mr. Billy D. CURBO
32 Vice President Student Services .... Ms. Lizza TRENKLE
13 Vice Pres Information Technology .... Mr. Jessie WHITE
21 Dean Financial Services .... Mrs. Debbie GERIK
08 Librarian - Hill Campus .... Mr. Joseph SHAUGHNESSY
08 Librarian - Cleburne Campus .... Mr. John LAMBERTH
15 Director Human Resources .... Vacant
12 Exec Dir JCC/Dean of Students .... Mr. Bill GILKER
41 Athletic Director .... Mr. Paul BROWN
26 Director of Marketing & Public Rels .... Mr. Derik MOORE
09 Dir of Institutional Effectiveness .... Ms. Sherry DAVIS
37 Director of Financial Aid .... Ms. Kathleen PUSTEJOVSKY
18 Director Physical Plant .... Mr. Frank WILLIAMS
29 Director Alumni Relations .... Mr. Preston MCREYNOLDS

Houston Baptist University (L)

7502 Fondren Road, Houston TX 77074-3298
County: Harris FICE Identification: 003576
Unit ID: 225399
Telephone: (281) 649-3000 Carnegie Class: Masters/M
FAX Number: (281) 649-3012 Calendar System: Semester
URL: www.hbu.edu
Established: 1960 Annual Undergrad Tuition & Fees: $29,800
Enrollment: 3,128 Coed
Affiliation or Control: Southern Baptist IRS Status: 501(c)3
Highest Offering: Doctorate
Accreditation: SC, NUR

01 President .... Dr. Robert B. SLOAN, JR.
05 Provost .... Dr. Cynthia SIMPSON
10 Vice President Financial Operations .... Ms. Sandra N. MOONEY
30 Vice President for Advancement .... Mrs. Sharon SAUNDERS
26 Vice Pres University Relations .... Mrs. Sharon E. SAUNDERS
84 Vice Pres Enrollment Management .... Mr. James STEEN
20 Associate Provost .... Ms. Ritamarie TAUER
20 Associate Provost .... Dr. Michael ROSATO
21 Planning & Budget Director .... Mr. Michael DEI

79 Dean School of Humanities .... Dr. Jodey HINZE
50 Dean School of Business .... Dr. Michael WEEKS
81 Dean College of Science & Math .... Dr. Doris C. WARREN
92 Director Honors College .... Dr. Gary HARTENBURG
53 Interim Dean School of Education .... Dr. Carol MCGAUGHEY
57 Dean School of Fine Arts .... Dr. Jason LESTER
66 Dean Sch Nursing & Allied Hlth .... Dr. Renae SCHUMANN
41 Athletic Director .... Mr. Steve C. MONIACI
06 University Registrar .... Ms. Erinn HUGHES
40 Director of University Store .... Mr. Anthony MARTIN
07 Director of Admissions .... Ms. Amy RICE
08 Interim Director of Libraries .... Mr. Dean RILEY
42 University Minister .... Vacant
21 Assoc VP Financial Operations .... Ms. Loree WATSON
29 Dir of Alumni Relations & Advance .... Ms. Amy YOUNGBLOOD
39 Director Housing Operations .... Vacant
13 Chief Information Officer (IT) .... Mr. Glen JOHNSON
19 Chief of Police .... Mr. Charles RAGAIN
09 Dir Inst Research & Effectiveness .... Mr. Todd COCKRELL
32 Vice President Student Life .... Mr. Whittington GOODWIN
88 SACS Liaison .... Ms. Ritamarie TAUER
04 Admin Asst to the President .... Ms. Karen FRANCIES
15 Director of Human Resources .... Mrs. Jennifer BOHRNSTEDT
18 Dir of Maintenance & Operations .... Mr. Gary DYKE
36 Dir of Career & Calling .... Ms. Colette CROSS
37 Sr Dir Financial Aid & Scholarships .... Ms. Veronica GABBARD
96 Cost Control Analyst .... Ms. Jody WILDING-FARRELL
105 Director Web Services .... Mr. Alan PRESLEY

Houston College of Law (A)

1303 San Jacinto Street, Houston TX 77002-7000

County: Harris | FICE Identification: 004977 | Unit ID: 228194
Telephone: (713) 659-8040 | Carnegie Class: Spec-4-yr-Law
FAX Number: (713) 646-2909 | Calendar System: Semester
URL: www.hcl.edu
Established: 1923 | Annual Graduate Tuition & Fees: N/A
Enrollment: 1,116 | Coed
Affiliation or Control: Independent Non-Profit | IRS Status: 501(c)3
Highest Offering: First Professional Degree; No Undergraduates
Accreditation: LAW

01 President & Dean .... Mr. Donald J. GUTER
03 Executive Vice President .... Vacant
05 Vice President & Associate Dean .... Ms. Maxine GOODMAN
101 Sr Exec Assistant to President/Dean .... Ms. Jennifer M. HUDSON
10 Vice President and CFO .... Mr. Gregory A. BROTHERS
30 Sr VP of Institutional Advancement .... Ms. Maya FREDRICKSON
09 Vice Pres Strategic Plng/Inst Rsrch .... Mr. Jeffrey L. RENSBERGER
08 Director Library Svcs .... Ms. Colleen MANNING
20 Vice President & Associate Dean .... Mr. Bruce MCGOVERN
20 Vice President & Associate Dean .... Mr. T. Gerald TREECE
20 Vice President & Associate Dean .... Ms. Catherine G. BURNETT
20 Vice President & Associate Dean .... Mr. John WORLEY
13 Vice President Technology .... Mr. Randy MARAK
15 VP for HR and General Counsel .... Mr. Steve ALDERMAN
38 Asst Dean for Academic Assistance .... Ms. Gena L. SINGLETON
06 Registrar .... Ms. Mandi GIBSON
36 Director of Career Resources .... Ms. Nazleen JIWANI
07 Assistant Dean for Admissions .... Ms. Alicia CRAMER
21 Controller .... Ms. Nancy N. JOHNSON
37 Director of Financial Aid .... Ms. Pat MILLIGAN
26 Dir Marketing/Communications .... Ms. Diane SUMMERS
32 Assistant Dean .... Ms. Wanda MORROW
19 Director Security .... Mr. Kent BRAZELTON
09 Exec Dir of Institutional Research .... Dr. Ryan BEARD
24 Dir Instructional Technology Svcs .... Mr. Terry SMITH
14 Director Information Services .... Mr. George MILZ
43 General Counsel .... Mr. Steve ALDERMAN
30 Director of Development/Major Gifts .... Ms. Mindy GUTHRIE
44 Director of Annual Giving .... Ms. Susan DIEDERICH
29 Director of Alumni Relations .... Ms. Megan GRAF
102 Dir of Foundation & Govt Relations .... Ms. Ashley ESTES
18 Chief Facilities/Physical Plant .... Mr. William HILL
96 Manager of Purchasing .... Ms. Sandra KASPER

Houston Community College (B)

3100 Main Street, Houston TX 77002

County: Harris | FICE Identification: 010633 | Unit ID: 225423
Telephone: (713) 718-2000 | Carnegie Class: Assoc/HT-High Trad
FAX Number: N/A | Calendar System: Semester
URL: www.hccs.edu
Established: 1971 | Annual Undergrad Tuition & Fees (In-State): $1,632
Enrollment: 58,276 | Coed
Affiliation or Control: State | IRS Status: 501(c)3
Highest Offering: Associate Degree
Accreditation: SC, ACBSP, CAHIIM, COARC, DA, DH, DMS, EMT, ENGT, HT, MAC, MLTAD, NMT, OTA, PTAA, RAD, SURGT

01 Chancellor .... Dr. Cesar MALDONADO
100 Chief of Staff .... Dr. Melissa GONZALEZ
04 Exec Assistant to the Chancellor .... Ms. Keiana BLAKE
10 Senior VC Finance & Administration .... Ms. Teri ZAMORA
43 General Counsel .... Mr. E. Ashley SMITH
05 VC Instructional Services/CAO .... Dr. Kimberly BEATTY
32 Vice Chancellor Student Services .... Dr. Athos BREWER
13 Vice Chancellor Information Tech .... Dr. William E. CARTER
45 VC Planning and Inst Effectiveness .... Vacant
20 Assoc VC of Instructional Services .... Dr. Steve LEVEY
88 Assoc VC of College Readiness .... Dr. Catherine O'BREIN
84 Assoc VC of Enrollment Services .... Ms. Shantay GRAYS
35 Assoc VC of Student Success .... Dr. Cheryl STERLING
85 Assoc VC of Intl Students .... Dr. Parvin BACHERPOUR
18 Chief Facilities Officer .... Mr. Charles SMITH
15 Chief Human Resource Officer .... Ms. Janet MAY
22 Director EEO/Compliance .... Mr. David CROSS
21 Controller .... Dr. Kara BENDER
21 Treasurer .... Mr. Ron E DEFALCO
26 Director Communication Services .... Ms. Frederica GUTHRIE
66 Department Chair Vocational Nursing .... Ms. Deborah SIMMONS-JOHNSON
07 Director of Admissions & Registrar .... Ms. Mary LEMBURG
09 Exec Dir of Inst Research & Innov .... Dr. Martha OBURN
46 Director of Resource Development .... Vacant
102 Executive Director Foundation .... Ms. Carmetha WILLIAMS
12 President-Northeast College .... Dr. Margaret FORD FISHER
12 President-Southwest College .... Dr. Madeline BURILLO
12 President-Central College .... Dr. William HARMON
12 President-Southeast College .... Dr. Irene PORCARELLO
12 President-Northwest College .... Dr. Zachary HODGES
12 President-Coleman College .... Dr. Phillip NICOTERA
29 Alumni Relations Specialist .... Ms. Zandra HENDERSON
96 Ex Dir Purchasing/Procurement Oper .... Mr. Rogelio ANASAGASTI
88 Director Student/Financial Services .... Mr. Hernando MALDONADO
37 Exec Director Student Financial Aid .... Ms. JoEllen SOUCIER
88 Director Internal Auditing .... Mr. Terance CORRINGAN
50 COE Dean Business .... Mr. Jesus RODRIGUEZ
88 COE Dean English .... Ms. Amy TAN
46 COE Director Construction .... Mr. Kris ASPER
88 COE Director Consumer Arts & Sci .... Mr. Anthony HANCOCK
88 COE Director Digital & Info Tech .... Mr. Doug ROWLETT
88 COE Dean Earth Life Natural Sci .... Mr. Jerome DRAIN
54 COE Director Engineering .... Mr. John VASSELLI
88 COE Director Global Energy .... Mr. Morteza SAMEEI
76 COE Director Health Science .... Vacant
49 COE Dean Liberal Arts & Humanities .... Mr. Theodore HANLEY
88 COE Director Logistics .... Ms. Cynthia GARZA
88 COE Director Manufacturing .... Mr. Frederick HEARD
88 COE Director Material Science .... Dr. Tam LE
81 COE Dean Mathematics .... Mr. Timor SERVER
72 COE Director Media Arts & Tech .... Mr. Jimmy ADAMS
88 COE Director Public Safety .... Mr. Johnny SESSUMS
83 COE Dean Social & Behavioral Sci .... Mr. Aaron KNIGHT
86 AVC Government & External Relations .... Mr. Remmele YOUNG

Houston Graduate School of Theology (C)

4300-C West Bellfort, Houston TX 77035

County: Harris | FICE Identification: 023202 | Unit ID: 246345
Telephone: (713) 942-9505 | Carnegie Class: Spec-4-yr-Faith
FAX Number: (713) 942-9506 | Calendar System: Semester
URL: www.hgst.edu
Established: 1983 | Annual Graduate Tuition & Fees: N/A
Enrollment: 167 | Coed
Affiliation or Control: Independent Non-Profit | IRS Status: 501(c)3
Highest Offering: Doctorate; No Undergraduates
Accreditation: THEOL

01 President .... Dr. James H. FURR
05 Academic Dean .... Dr. David B. CAPES
20 Assoc Acad Dean/Dir DMin Program .... Dr. Becky L. TOWNE
10 Chief Financial Officer .... Vacant
07 Dir of Admissions/Recruiting .... Ms. Gloria FIKES
06 Registrar .... Ms. Laura HAMILTON
08 Director of Library Services .... Ms. Janet KENNARD

Howard College (D)

1001 Birdwell Lane, Big Spring TX 79720-3799

County: Howard | FICE Identification: 003574 | Unit ID: 225520
Telephone: (432) 264-5000 | Carnegie Class: Assoc/HT-High Trad
FAX Number: (432) 264-5082 | Calendar System: Semester
URL: www.howardcollege.edu
Established: 1945 | Annual Undergrad Tuition & Fees (In-District): $2,542
Enrollment: 3,756 | Coed
Affiliation or Control: State/Local | IRS Status: 501(c)3
Highest Offering: Associate Degree
Accreditation: SC, ADNUR, COARC, DH, EMT, RAD, SURGT

01 President .... Dr. Cheryl T. SPARKS
05 Vice President Academic Affairs .... Dr. Amy BURCHETT
20 Dean Academic Affairs SWCID .... Mr. Danny CAMPBELL
32 Dean Student Affairs SWCID .... Ms. Nancy BONURA
12 Executive Dean San Angelo .... Ms. Jamie RAINEY
12 Executive Dean Big Spring Area .... Vacant
10 Chief Business Officer .... Mr. Steve SMITH
18 Chief Facilities Operations Officer .... Mr. Terry HANSEN
10 Chief Financial Officer .... Ms. Brenda CLAXTON
08 Dean of Libraries .... Mr. Luis KINCADE
13 Dean Information Technology .... Mr. Eric HANSEN
106 Director eLearning Services .... Ms. Kym CLARK
37 Dean Financial Aid .... Mrs. Candice MALDONADO
26 Director Effectiveness/Information .... Ms. Cindy SMITH
41 Athletic Director .... Vacant
103 Dean Career Technical Education .... Ms. Gayla WILLIAMS
15 Director Human Resources/Payroll .... Ms. Rhonda KERNICK
20 Dean Teaching and Learning .... Ms. Pam CALLAN
06 Dean Student Affairs/Registrar .... Mrs. Taneal RICHARDSON
88 Director Campus Programming .... Ms. Carlea ULRICH
21 Director Student Accounting .... Ms. Margaret CERVANTES
30 Director Institutional Advancement .... Mrs. Jan FORESYTH
76 Dean Health Professions .... Ms. Luci GABEHART
09 Research and Reporting Official .... Ms. Rebecca VILLANUEVA
21 Director Financial Accounting .... Ms. Jeannie CARROLL
04 Executive Asst to the President .... Ms. Julie BAILEY

Howard Payne University (E)

1000 Fisk Street, Brownwood TX 76801-2794

County: Brown | FICE Identification: 003575 | Unit ID: 225548
Telephone: (325) 646-2502 | Carnegie Class: Bac-Diverse
FAX Number: (325) 649-8975 | Calendar System: Semester
URL: www.hputx.edu
Established: 1889 | Annual Undergrad Tuition & Fees: $25,600
Enrollment: 1,137 | Coed
Affiliation or Control: Baptist | IRS Status: 501(c)3
Highest Offering: Master's
Accreditation: SC, CAATE, MUS, SW

01 President .... Dr. William N. ELLIS
05 Provost/Chief Academic Officer .... Dr. Mark TEW
10 Int Chief Financial Officer .... Mr. Mike RODGERS
32 Vice Pres Stdnt Life/Dean Stdnts .... Dr. Magen BUNYARD
44 Vice President Development .... Mr. Randy YEAKLEY
84 Assoc VP for Enrollment Management .... Mr. Kevin KIRK
15 Asst VP for Bus & Hum Resources .... Mr. Bill FISHBACK
18 AVP Facilities/Planning .... Mr. Terry PRITCHETT
06 Registrar .... Mrs. Lana WAGNER
37 Director Financial Aid .... Mrs. Glenda HUFF
07 Director of Admission .... Mrs. P.J GRAMLING
36 Dir Academic Testing/Career Svcs .... Ms. Wendy MCNEELEY
26 Director of Publications .... Mr. Kyle C. MIZE
09 Director Institutional Research .... Vacant
41 Athletic Director .... Mr. Hunter SIMS
91 Database Administrator .... Mr. Tyler CHRISTIANSEN
90 Computer Network Administrator .... Mr. Russell EZZELL
29 Coordinator of Alumni Relations .... Mr. Stephen SULLIVAN
88 Special Events Coordinator .... Ms. Kathy JAMES
04 Executive Assistant to President .... Ms. Tammy LOWREY
38 University Counselor .... Mrs. Toni DAMRON
56 Dean Extended Education .... Dr. Robert BICKNELL
08 Dean of Libraries .... Mrs. Alexia RIGGS
81 Dean School of Science & Math .... Dr. Pam BRYANT
50 Dean School of Business .... Vacant
53 Dean School of Education .... Vacant
64 Dean School of Music & Fine Arts .... Dr. Richard FIESE
73 Dean School of Christian Studies .... Dr. Donnie AUVENSHINE
79 Dean School of Humanities .... Vacant

Huston-Tillotson University (F)

900 Chicon Street, Austin TX 78702-2795

County: Travis | FICE Identification: 003577 | Unit ID: 225575
Telephone: (512) 505-3000 | Carnegie Class: Bac-Diverse
FAX Number: (512) 505-3190 | Calendar System: Semester
URL: www.htu.edu
Established: 1875 | Annual Undergrad Tuition & Fees: $14,346
Enrollment: 1,031 | Coed
Affiliation or Control: Multiple Protestant Denominations | IRS Status: 501(c)3
Highest Offering: Master's
Accreditation: SC, ACBSP

01 President & CEO .... Dr. Colette PIERCE BURNETTE
04 Executive Assistant to President .... Vacant
100 Chief of Staff/Clerk to Board .... Mr. Wayne KNOX
10 VP for Administration & Finance .... Mrs. Valerie D. HILL
05 Int Prov/VP Academic & Stdnt Affs .... Dr. Archibald W. VANDERPUYE
32 Dean of Student Affairs .... Dr. LaTanya LOWERY
08 Director Library & Media Services .... Ms. Patricia A. WILKINS
36 Director Career & Grad Development .... Mr. Paul LEVERINGTON
41 Director of Athletics .... Ms. Ellen J. MCEWEN
84 Dean of the University College .... Dr. Jeffrey G. WILSON
06 University Registrar .... Mrs. Earnestine J. STRICKLAND
25 Dir Sponsored PRGs/Title III Coord .... Ms. Rhonda M. MOSES
09 Int Dir IR/Planning/Assessment .... Ms. Sara SUMMERS
13 Dir Information Technology .... Mr. Mario A. LEAL
26 Director University Relations .... Mrs. Linda Y. JACKSON
18 Director of Facilities .... Mr. William S. GRIMES
30 Director of Development .... Vacant
29 Dir of Alumni Affairs/Advancement .... Mrs. Bridgett C. LEE
35 Director of Campus Life .... Dr. Kyle N. BOONE
88 Dir of Ctr for Academic Excellence .... Ms. Ericka D. JONES
15 Director of Human Resources .... Ms. Joy S. KING
38 Dir Counseling & Consultation Ctr .... Ms. Barbara L. FOUNTAIN
42 University Chaplain .... Rev. Donald E. BREWINGTON
07 Director of Admission .... Mr. Dwayne R. SHORTER
49 Interim Dean of Arts & Sciences .... Dr. Rosalee R. MARTIN
50 Dean of Business & Technology .... Vacant
37 Int Director Student Financial Aid .... Ms. Sheila BROWN
22 Director of Disability Services .... Ms. Barbara L. FOUNTAIN
23 University Nurse .... Ms. Ebony S. BEST

Interactive College of Technology (G)

213 West Southmore, Ste 101, Pasadena TX 77502

County: Harris | FICE Identification: 023313 | Unit ID: 440776
Telephone: (713) 920-1120 | Carnegie Class: Not Classified

FAX Number: (713) 477-0348 Calendar System: Semester
URL: www.ict.edu
Established: Annual Undergrad Tuition & Fees: N/A
Enrollment: 34 Coed
Affiliation or Control: Proprietary IRS Status: Proprietary
Highest Offering: Associate Degree
Accreditation: COE

01 Campus Director .... Michael SANFILIPO

Jacksonville College (A)

105 B. J. Albritton Drive, Jacksonville TX 75766-4759
County: Cherokee FICE Identification: 003579
Unit ID: 225876
Telephone: (903) 586-2518 Carnegie Class: Assoc/HT-High Non
FAX Number: (903) 586-0743 Calendar System: Semester
URL: www.jacksonville-college.edu
Established: 1899 Annual Undergrad Tuition & Fees: $7,275
Enrollment: 543 Coed
Affiliation or Control: Baptist IRS Status: 501(c)3
Highest Offering: Associate Degree
Accreditation: SC

01 President .... Dr. Mike SMITH
05 Academic Dean/Registrar .... Mrs. Marolyn WELCH
32 Dean of Students .... Mr. Donny SADDLER
10 Business Officer .... Ms. Jennifer GUERRA
41 Athletic Director .... Ms. Leasa AILSHIE
06 Registrar .... Ms. Jodye JAY
07 Director of Admissions .... Mrs. Sandra CLAY
18 Chief Facilities/Physical Plant .... Mr. Dan SHOFFNER
26 Chief Public Relations Officer .... Dr. David HEFLIN
29 Director of Alumni Relations .... Mr. Randy DECKER
30 Chief Development Officer .... Mr. Buddy AULTMAN
37 Director Student Financial Aid .... Mr. Paul GALYEAN
39 Director Student Housing .... Mr. David WHITE

Jarvis Christian College (B)

Highway 80 E., PR 7631, Hawkins TX 75765-1470
County: Wood FICE Identification: 003637
Unit ID: 225885
Telephone: (903) 730-4890 Carnegie Class: Bac-Diverse
FAX Number: (903) 769-4842 Calendar System: Semester
URL: www.jarvis.edu
Established: 1912 Annual Undergrad Tuition & Fees: $11,720
Enrollment: 763 Coed
Affiliation or Control: Christian Church (Disciples Of Christ)
IRS Status: 501(c)3
Highest Offering: Baccalaureate
Accreditation: SC, ACBSP

01 President .... Dr. Lester C. NEWMAN
05 Provost/Vice Pres Academic Affairs .... Dr. Glenell PRUITT
10 Vice Pres Administration & Finance .... Mr. Dexter ODOM
30 VP Institutional Advancement/Devel .... Ms. Sunya YOUNG
45 Vice Pres for Inst Effectiveness .... Dr. William SMIALEK
13 Director Information Technology .... Mr. Quinton LATIN
06 Interim Registrar .... Ms. Rubye A. FREEMAN-TAYLOR
39 Director of Housing .... Mr. Cory GIPSON
32 AVP Student/Enrollment Services .... Mr. William HAMPTON
07 Dir Admissions & Enrollment Svcs .... Mr. Brandon BYRD
26 Director Public Relations/Publicity .... Vacant
04 Exec Asst to the President .... Mrs. Cynthia HOLLMAN-STANCIL
08 Head Librarian .... Mr. Rodney ATKINS
38 Director Career Services .... Mr. Chestley TALLEY
37 Director of Financial Aid .... Mr. Eric KING
41 Athletic Director .... Vacant
42 Chaplain/Director of Religious Life .... Mr. Olin FREGIA
15 Dir Human Resources .... Dr. Daphne SINGLETON
09 Dir Institutional Research .... Ms. Celestine KEMAH
108 AVP Inst Effect/Rsch/Assessment .... Dr. Belinda PRIHODA
18 Chief Facilities/Physical Plant .... Mr. Willie SANDIFER

KD Conservatory College of Film and Dramatic Arts (C)

2600 N Stemmons Fwy, Suite 117, Dallas TX 75207-2111
County: Dallas FICE Identification: 023182
Unit ID: 225991
Telephone: (214) 638-0484 Carnegie Class: Spec 2-yr-A&S
FAX Number: (214) 630-5140 Calendar System: Semester
URL: www.kdstudio.com
Established: 1979 Annual Undergrad Tuition & Fees: $16,625
Enrollment: 162 Coed
Affiliation or Control: Proprietary IRS Status: Proprietary
Highest Offering: Associate Degree
Accreditation: THEA

00 Chief Executive Officer .... Ms. Kathy TYNER
01 President .... Mr. Gary TYNER, JR.
05 Director/CAO .... Mr. T. A TAYLOR
88 Program Chair - MT .... Mr. Michael SERRECCHIA
88 Program Chair - Film Program .... Mr. Dennis BISHOP
11 Head of Operations .... Mr. Kaleb WADE
32 Head of Student Services .... Ms. Ashlyn NICHOLS
37 Student Financial Aid .... Ms. Linda CRAFT
08 Chief Library Officer .... Ms. Judith HEAD

Kilgore College (D)

1100 Broadway, Kilgore TX 75662-3299
County: Gregg FICE Identification: 003580
Unit ID: 226019
Telephone: (903) 984-8531 Carnegie Class: Assoc/MT-VT-High Trad
FAX Number: (903) 983-8600 Calendar System: Semester
URL: www.kilgore.edu
Established: 1935 Annual Undergrad Tuition & Fees (In-District): $1,464
Enrollment: 5,768 Coed
Affiliation or Control: Local IRS Status: 501(c)3
Highest Offering: Associate Degree
Accreditation: SC, ADNUR, EMT, PTAA, SURGT

01 President .... Dr. Brenda S. KAYS
05 Vice President of Instruction .... Dr. Michael H. TURPIN
11 Vice Pres Administrative Services .... Mr. Duane MCNANEY
32 Vice President Student Development .... Dr. Mike JENKINS
09 Vice Pres Institutional Planning .... Mrs. Staci MARTIN
57 Div Dean Liberal & Fine Arts .... Mrs. Becky JOHNSON
81 Div Dean Science/Math/Health Sci .... Mrs. Louise WILEY
50 Div Dean Business/Tech/Lang Devel/ .... Mr. Randy LEWELLEN
88 Div Dean of Public Services .... Mr. Randy LEWELLEN
75 Dir of Adult Voc Educ .... Ms. Martha WOODRUFF
12 Div Dean of Longview Center .... Dr. Julie H. FOWLER
06 Registrar .... Mr. Chris GORE
15 Director of Human Resources .... Mr. Tony JOHNSON
13 Director of Information Technology .... Mr. John COLVILLE
08 Director Library .... Ms. Kathy FAIR
40 Manager of Bookstore .... Mr. Corrie THIBODEAUX
19 Chief of Police .... Chief Heath CARIKER
84 Dir of Marketing & Enrollment Mgmt .... Mr. Trey HATTAWAY
04 Assistant to the President .... Mrs. Nancy LAW
30 Director of Development .... Mrs. Leah GORMAN
37 Financial Aid Officer .... Mrs. Annette MORGAN
85 International Student Advisor .... Ms. Estonia GRAVES
26 Coordinator of Public & Sports Info .... Mr. Chris CRADDOCK
09 Coord of Institutional Research .... Ms. Jane LEWIS
29 Coordinator of Alumni Relations .... Mrs. Paula JAMERSON
38 Coordinator of Counseling .... Mrs. Pam GATTON
96 Purchasing Agent .... Ms. Tammie PASCOE
39 Director of Residential Life .... Mr. Edward WILLIAMS
07 Director of Admissions .... Mr. Chris GORE
106 Dir Online Education/E-learning .... Ms. Charleen WORSHAM

The King's University (E)

2121 E. Southlake Boulevard, South Lake TX 76092-6507
County: Tarrant FICE Identification: 035163
Unit ID: 439701
Telephone: (817) 722-1700 Carnegie Class: Spec-4-yr-Faith
FAX Number: N/A Calendar System: Quarter
URL: tku.edu/
Established: 1997 Annual Undergrad Tuition & Fees: $12,990
Enrollment: 692 Coed
Affiliation or Control: Independent Non-Profit IRS Status: 501(c)3
Highest Offering: Doctorate
Accreditation: BI, TRACS

01 President .... Dr. John SPURLING
03 Executive Vice President .... Dr. Pete SANCHEZ
11 Vice Pres Business Admin/Advance .... Mr. Charles SCOTT
84 Vice Pres Enrollment Management .... Dr. David COLE
05 Academic Dean .... Dr. Daniel DAVIS
10 Director of Finance .... Ms. Ashley GREEN
106 Dean/Administrator Online Education .... Prof. Donald C. BRUBAKER
09 Dir Institutional Effectiveness .... Dr. Bobbi STRINGER
32 Dean of Student Life .... Mr. Shawn BRANN
07 Director of Admissions .... Mr. Tyler MAXEY
06 Assoc Dir Student Recruitment .... Ms. Angela TRANEL
37 Director Financial Aid .... Ms. Jackie WADLEIGH
08 Director of Library Services .... Mr. Tracey R. LANE
30 Chief Development .... Mr. Lee S. MIMMS
13 Director Computing & Info Mgmt .... Mr. Edmond M. MUGWANYA
21 Student Accounts Officer .... Ms. June M. HADLEY
90 Dir Acad Computing/Dir Student Affs .... Prof. Donald C. BRUBAKER
29 Director Alumni Relations .... Mrs. Maureen A. BRODERSON
96 Director of Purchasing .... Mr. Bob CARON
28 Director of Diversity .... Dr. Michael J. GREGG
102 Dir Foundation/Corporate Relations .... Mr. Lee S. MIMMS
26 Dir of Marketing/Communications .... Ms. Jovan OVERSHOWN

Laredo Community College (F)

West End Washington Street, Laredo TX 78040-4395
County: Webb FICE Identification: 003582
Unit ID: 226134
Telephone: (956) 722-0521 Carnegie Class: Assoc/MT-VT-High Trad
FAX Number: (956) 721-5381 Calendar System: Semester
URL: www.laredo.edu
Established: 1946 Annual Undergrad Tuition & Fees (In-District): $3,410
Enrollment: 8,307 Coed
Affiliation or Control: Local IRS Status: 501(c)3
Highest Offering: Associate Degree
Accreditation: SC, ADNUR, OTA, PTAA, RAD

01 President .... Dr. Ricardo SOLIS
05 VP Instruction & Student Services .... Dr. Vincent R. SOLIS
25 Vice President for Resource Develop .... Dr. Nora R. GARZA
26 Communications & IE Officer .... Ms. Deirdre REYNA
13 Information Technology Officer .... Mr. Luciano RAMON
10 Chief Financial Officer .... Ms. Nora STEWART
18 Chf Ofcr Facilities/Oil & Gas Inst .... Mr. Orlando J. ZEPEDA
10 Comptroller .... Mr. Cesar E. VELA, JR.
49 Dean of Arts & Sciences .... Dr. Marisela RODRIGUEZ
89 Dean of College Readiness .... Ms. Marissa GUERRERO-LONGORIA
76 Dean Health Sciences & Dual Enroll .... Mr. J. Alfredo INIGUEZ-JIMENEZ
35 Dean of Student Affairs .... Ms. Raquel A. PENA
84 Dean of Enrollment & Reg Services .... Ms. Priscilla G. MEDINA
09 Dir Institutional Research & Plng .... Mrs. Maria Luisa RAMIREZ
08 Director of Library .... Mr. Dale SAENZ
18 Director Physical Plant .... Mr. Jerome ROSALES
27 Dir Marketing/Public Relations .... Mr. Esteban TREVINO, JR.
37 Director of Financial Aid .... Mr. Steven AGUILAR
51 Dir of Adult & Continuing Education .... Ms. Sandra L. CORTEZ
41 Athletic Director .... Mr. Troy G. VAN BRUNT
06 Registrar .... Ms. Olga D. RUBIO
15 Director of Human Resources .... Ms. Veronica CARDENAS
102 Dir Donor Relations & Spec Proj .... Ms. Sara A. POMPA
38 Director of Student Success Ctr .... Ms. Andrea LOPEZ
96 Director of Purchasing .... Ms. Diana AGUILAR
19 Chief of Campus Police .... Mr. Ray CORTEZ
23 Director of Health Services .... Ms. Melissa GARCIA
20 Assoc VP for Instruction .... Dr. Federico SOLIS, JR.
32 Assoc VP for Student Services .... Mr. Robert L. OCHOA

Le Cordon Bleu College of Culinary Arts in Austin (G)

3110 Esperanza Crossing Suite 100, Austin TX 78758
County: Travis FICE Identification: 025693
Unit ID: 364973
Telephone: (512) 837-2665 Carnegie Class: Spec 2-yr-A&S
FAX Number: (512) 977-9753 Calendar System: Other
URL: www.chefs.edu/austin
Established: 1981 Annual Undergrad Tuition & Fees: $13,808
Enrollment: 643 Coed
Affiliation or Control: Proprietary IRS Status: Proprietary
Highest Offering: Associate Degree
Accreditation: ACICS, ACFEI

01 President .... Steve SMITH

† In teach-out mode through September 2017.

Le Cordon Bleu College of Culinary Arts in Dallas (H)

11830 Webb Chapel Road, Suite 1200, Dallas TX 75234
Telephone: (214) 647-8505 Identification: 666728
Accreditation: ACICS, ACFEI

† In teach-out mode through September 2017. Branch campus of Le Cordon Bleu College of Culinary Arts, Austin, TX.

Lee College (I)

511 S Whiting, PO Box 818, Baytown TX 77522-0818
County: Harris FICE Identification: 003583
Unit ID: 226204
Telephone: (281) 427-5611 Carnegie Class: Assoc/HVT-High Trad
FAX Number: (281) 425-6555 Calendar System: Semester
URL: www.lee.edu
Established: 1934 Annual Undergrad Tuition & Fees (In-District): $1,672
Enrollment: 6,481 Coed
Affiliation or Control: State/Local IRS Status: 501(c)3
Highest Offering: Associate Degree
Accreditation: SC, ADNUR, CAHIIM

01 President .... Dr. Dennis BROWN
100 Senior Assistant to the President .... Ms. Leslie D. GALLAGHER
10 VP Finance & Administration .... Mr. Steve EVANS
05 Interim VP Instruction .... Ms. DeDe GRIFFITH
32 VP Student Affairs .... Dr. Donnetta SUCHON
103 VP Student Success/Workforce & RD .... Dr. Christina PONCE
12 Dean of Huntsville Center at TDCJ .... Ms. Donna P. ZUNIGA
09 Exec Dir Institutional Research .... Dr. Michael K. FLEMING
13 Chief Information Officer .... Dr. Carolyn A. LIGHTFOOT
103 Exec Dir of Workforce & Comm Educ .... Ms. Debi JORDAN
06 Registrar .... Mr. Scott BENNETT
15 Director Human Resources .... Ms. Amanda SUMMERS
26 Director Marketing & Public Affairs .... Ms. Susan SMEDLEY
37 Director Financial Aid .... Ms. Sharon STEELE
102 Director of Foundation & Donor Dev .... Ms. Pam WARFORD
96 Director Purchasing .... Mr. Mike SPARKES

LeTourneau University (J)

PO Box 7001, 2100 S Mobberly Ave, Longview TX 75607-7001
County: Gregg FICE Identification: 003584
Unit ID: 226231
Telephone: (903) 233-3000 Carnegie Class: Masters/M
FAX Number: (903) 233-3101 Calendar System: Semester
URL: www.letu.edu
Established: 1946 Annual Undergrad Tuition & Fees: $27,900
Enrollment: 2,667 Coed
Affiliation or Control: Independent Non-Profit IRS Status: 501(c)3
Highest Offering: Master's
Accreditation: SC, ENG, ENGT, IACBE

01 President ... Dr. Dale A. LUNSFORD
05 Provost & Executive Vice President ... Dr. Philip COYLE
30 Int Executive Director Development ... Mr. Steve SHARPE
10 VP Finance/Administration ... Mr. Mike HOOD
32 Dean of Students ... Ms. Kristy MORGAN
84 VP Enrollment Services ... Mr. Carl ARNOLD
20 Assoc Prov & COO Residential Campus ... Dr. Steven D. MASON
20 Assoc Provost & COO Global Campus ... Dr. Stephanie KIRSCHMANN
26 Associate VP-Global Enrollment Svcs ... Mr. Christopher W. FONTAINE
18 Asst VP of Facilities Services ... Mr. Ben HAYWOOD
53 Dean School of Education ... Dr. Larry FRAZIER
50 Dean School of Business ... Dr. Ron DELAP
54 Dean Sch Engineering & Engr Tech ... Dr. Ronald DELAP
49 Dean School of Arts & Sciences ... Dr. Larry FRAZIER
88 Dean School of Aeronautical Science ... Mr. Fred L. RITCHEY
35 Assoc Dean Student Engagement ... Mr. Steve CONN
08 Director Learning Resource Center ... Shelby WAVE
41 Director of Athletics ... Ms. Terri DEIKE
46 Director Office of Sponsored Pgms ... Mr. Paul R. BOGGS
106 Director Distance Learning ... Ms. Colleen HALUPA
13 Chief Information Officer ... Mr. Matthew HENRY
15 Director of Human Resources ... Mrs. Phyllis TURNER
23 Director Health Services ... Mrs. Jerrie REYNOLDS
42 University Chaplain ... Vacant
19 Chief of Police ... Mr. Michael SCHULTZ
36 Director of Career Services ... Mrs. Deena SHELTON
06 University Registrar ... Ms. Kathy MAJZNER
07 Director of Admissions ... Mr. Michael VANBROCKLIN
29 Director of Alumni & Parent Rels ... Ms. Jamie DEYOUNG
27 Director of University Relations ... Ms. Janet RAGLAND
27 Director Marketing & Communication ... Ms. Kate GRONEWALD
44 Dir of Gift Planning and Endowed ... Vacant
88 Dir Curriculum/Academic Resources ... Vacant
21 Controller ... Ms. Vikki KEILERS
09 Asst VP for Quality Assurance ... Dr. Pamela JOHNSON
88 Development Officer ... Mr. Stephen SHARPE
96 Purchasing Agent ... Vacant
88 Executive Dir Ctr for Faith & Work ... Mr. Bill PEEL
04 Administrative Asst to President ... Mrs. Denise BAILEY
28 Director of Diversity ... Mr. Carlton MITCHELL
37 Director Student Financial Aid ... Ms. Tracy WATKINS
38 Dir Ctr Student Counselng/Psych ... Mrs. Judi COYLE
20 Associate Provost-Quality Assurance ... Mrs. Stephanie KIRSCHMANN
104 Chief Global Initatives Officer ... Mr. Alan CLIPPERTON
88 VP Online & Global Enrollment ... Vacant
83 Dean Col Hlth Sciences/Prof Studies ... Dr. Melanie ROUDKOVSKI
26 VP Marketing & Communications ... Mr. Don EGLE
73 Acting Dean School of Theology ... Dr. Viktor ROUDKOVSKI

Lincoln College of Technology (A)

2915 Alouette Drive, Grand Prairie TX 75052

County: Tarrant | FICE Identification: 008353 | Unit ID: 226277
Telephone: (972) 660-5701 | Carnegie Class: Not Classified
FAX Number: (972) 660-6148 | Calendar System: Other
URL: www.lincolntech.com
Established: | Annual Undergrad Tuition & Fees: N/A
Enrollment: 947 | Coed
Affiliation or Control: Proprietary | IRS Status: Proprietary
Highest Offering: Associate Degree
Accreditation: ACCSC

01 Campus President ... Mr. Cory HUGHES

Lone Star College System (B)

5000 Research Forest Drive,
The Woodlands TX 77381-4356

County: Harris | FICE Identification: 011145 | Unit ID: 227182
Telephone: (832) 813-6500 | Carnegie Class: Assoc/HT-Mix Trad/Non
FAX Number: N/A | Calendar System: Semester
URL: www.lonestar.edu
Established: 1972 | Annual Undergrad Tuition & Fees (In-District): $1,504
Enrollment: 69,395 | Coed
Affiliation or Control: State/Local | IRS Status: 501(c)3
Highest Offering: Associate Degree
Accreditation: SC, ADNUR, CAHIIM, CEA, COARC, DH, DMS, EMT, MAC, MUS, OTA, PTAA, RAD, SURGT

01 Chancellor ... Dr. Stephen HEAD
03 Executive Vice Chancellor ... Vacant
10 Vice Chanc for Admin & Finance ... Vacant
13 Vice Chanc/Chief Info Officer ... Mr. Link ALANDER
26 Vice Chanc Govt & Public Relations ... Mr. Amos MCDONALD
32 AVC Student Success ... Vacant
43 General Counsel ... Mr. Mario CASTILLO
100 Vice Chanc/Chief of Staff ... Ms. Helen CLOUGHERTY
12 President of LSC-Kingwood ... Dr. Katherine PERSSON
12 President of LSC-Tomball ... Dr. Lee Ann NUTT
12 President of LSC-North Harris ... Dr. Gerald NAPOLES
12 President of LSC-Montgomery ... Dr. Rebecca RILEY
12 President of LSC-CyFair ... Dr. Seelpa KESHVALA
12 President of LSC-University Park ... Mr. Shah ARDALAN
27 AVC Marketing & Comm ... Vacant
18 Vice Chanc Facilities/Construction ... Mr. Jimmy MARTIN
15 AVC Human Resources ... Mr. Mark YURAN
105 Director Portal Services ... Mr. Harry KHEHRA
88 Director Compliance & Training ... Vacant
05 AVC Academic Affairs ... Mr. Michael KRALL
21 AVC Admin & Finance ... Ms. Tammy CORTES
21 Associate CFO ... Ms. Carin HUTCHINS
21 AVC Accounting ... Ms. Diane NOVAK
106 AVC LSC-Online ... Ms. Wendi PRATER
45 Exec Dir Strategic Plng & Assess ... Dr. Christopher TKACH
14 AVC Office Tech Services ... Mr. Mario BERRY
08 Director Library/LSC-Kingwood ... Mr. Anthony MCMILLIAN
08 Director Library/LSC-Tomball ... Ms. Pamela SHAFER
08 Director Library/LSC-North Harris ... Ms. Pradeep LELE
08 Director Library/LSC-Cy Fair ... Mr. Michael STAFFORD
08 Director Library/LSC-Montgomery ... Dr. Janice PEYTON
08 Director Library/LSC-Univ Park ... Ms. Shannon HAUSINGER
37 Exec Dir Financial Aid ... Ms. Tracie HUNTER
21 Exec Director Internal Audit ... Ms. Leticia CHARBONNEAU
19 Chief of Police/Dir Pub Safety ... Mr. Paul WILLINGHAM
96 Director of Purchasing ... Mr. William DODD
04 Executive Asst to Chancellor ... Ms. Eva BORSCH
30 Chief Advancement Officer ... Vacant
29 Director of Constituent Engagement ... Ms. Susan SUMMERS

Lubbock Christian University (C)

5601 19th Street, Lubbock TX 79407-2099

County: Lubbock | FICE Identification: 003586 | Unit ID: 226383
Telephone: (806) 796-8800 | Carnegie Class: Masters/M
FAX Number: (806) 720-7255 | Calendar System: Semester
URL: www.lcu.edu
Established: 1957 | Annual Undergrad Tuition & Fees: $20,360
Enrollment: 1,902 | Coed
Affiliation or Control: Churches Of Christ | IRS Status: 501(c)3
Highest Offering: Master's
Accreditation: SC, NUR, SW, @THEOL

01 President ... Mr. L. Timothy PERRIN
03 Executive Vice President ... Dr. Brian STARR
05 Provost & Chief Academic Officer ... Dr. Rodney B. BLACKWOOD
43 General Counsel ... Dr. Bart PRUITT
30 Vice Pres University Advancement ... Mr. Raymond RICHARDSON
10 Chief Financial Officer ... Mr. Brandon GOEN
13 Vice President for Technology ... Dr. Karl MAHAN
26 Vice Pres for University Relations ... Mr. Warren MCNEILL
107 Dean Col of Professional Studies ... Dr. Tony ROGERS
49 Dean College Liberal Arts/Education ... Dr. Susan BLASSINGAME
73 Dean Col Biblical Stds/Behavior Sci ... Dr. Jesse LONG
09 Asst VP for Instl Effectiveness ... Mr. Randy SELLERS
41 Athletic Director ... Mr. Paul HISE
06 Registrar ... Mrs. Janice STONE
37 Director of Financial Assistance ... Mrs. Amy HARDESTY
32 Dean of Students ... Mr. Josh STEPHENS
08 Director of Library Services ... Ms. Paula GANNAWAY
18 Director of Campus Facilities ... Mr. Mike SELLECK
38 Director Student Counseling ... Mr. John MAPLES
92 Director of Honors Program ... Dr. Stacy PATTY
23 Director of Medical Clinic ... Dr. Jeff SMITH
14 Director of Technology Services ... Mr. Robert SMITH
88 Director of Disability Services ... Vacant
39 Director of Residential Life ... Mrs. Sunny PARK
07 Director of Admissions ... Mr. Chris HAYES
15 Human Resources Director ... Mrs. Brenda LOWE
29 Director Alumni Relations ... Mrs. Sheila DYE
19 Director of Security ... Mr. Michael SMITH
40 Bookstore Manager ... Mrs. Denise MCNEILL
04 Administrative Asst to President ... Ms. Rhonda SHOOTER
101 Secretary of the Institution/Board ... Ms. Page PRATHER
84 Director Enrollment Management ... Mr. Mondy BREWER
50 Dean School of Business ... Mr. Tracy MACK

Lutheran Seminary Program of the Southwest (D)

PO Box 4790, Austin TX 78765

Telephone: (512) 477-2666 | Identification: 770081
Accreditation: &NH

† Regional accreditation is carried under the parent institution in Chicago, IL

McLennan Community College (E)

1400 College Drive, Waco TX 76708-1498

County: McLennan | FICE Identification: 003590 | Unit ID: 226578
Telephone: (254) 299-8000 | Carnegie Class: Assoc/MT-VT-Mix Trad/Non
FAX Number: (254) 299-8654 | Calendar System: Semester
URL: www.mclennan.edu
Established: 1965 | Annual Undergrad Tuition & Fees (In-District): $2,760
Enrollment: 8,294 | Coed
Affiliation or Control: State/Local | IRS Status: 501(c)3
Highest Offering: Associate Degree
Accreditation: SC, ADNUR, CAHIIM, COARC, EMT, MAC, MLTAD, OTA, PTAA, RAD, SURGT

01 President ... Dr. Johnette MCKOWN
10 Vice Pres Finance & Administration ... Mr. Gene GOOCH
05 Vice President Instruction ... Dr. Donald BALMOS
22 Equal Employment Opportunity Ofcr ... Mr. Al POLLARD
32 Vice President Student Success ... Dr. Drew CANHAM
09 Vice Pres Research/Effectiveness ... Dr. Phil RHODES
102 Exec Director MCC Foundation ... Mr. Harry HARELIK
11 Director Administrative Services ... Ms. Lori SOUTHERN
37 Director Financial Aid ... Mr. James KUBACAK
26 Director Marketing & Communication ... Ms. Lisa WILHELMI
41 Director Athletics ... Mr. Shawn TROCHIM
06 Director Records & Registration ... Mr. Herman V. TUCKER
07 Director Admissions & Recruitment ... Mrs. Karen CLARK
08 Director Library Services ... Mr. Daniel MARTINSEN
15 Director Human Resources ... Ms. Missy KITTNER
18 Director Physical Plant ... Mrs. Dianne E. FEYERHERM
21 Director Financial Services ... Mrs. Terry LECHLER
76 Dean Health Professions ... Ms. Glynnis GAINES
49 Dean Arts & Sciences ... Dr. Fred HILLS
51 Dean Continuing Education ... Mr. Frank GRAVES

McMurry University (F)

1400 Sayles Boulevard, Abilene TX 79697-0002

County: Taylor | FICE Identification: 003591 | Unit ID: 226587
Telephone: (325) 793-3800 | Carnegie Class: Bac-Diverse
FAX Number: (325) 793-4800 | Calendar System: Semester
URL: www.mcm.edu
Established: 1923 | Annual Undergrad Tuition & Fees: $25,763
Enrollment: 1,007 | Coed
Affiliation or Control: United Methodist | IRS Status: 501(c)3
Highest Offering: Master's
Accreditation: SC, NURSE

01 President ... Dr. Sandra HARPER
05 Vice Pres Academic Affairs ... Dr. James HUNT
10 Vice Pres Finance & Administration ... Mrs. Lisa L. WILLIAMS
30 Vice Pres Institutional Advancement ... Ms. Debra HULSE
18 AVP Facilities & Campus Planning ... Mr. Brad POORMAN
84 Vice Pres for Enrollment Management ... Mr. David HERINGER
105 Webmaster ... Mr. Jim QUINNETT
14 Director of Customer Services ... Mr. Freddie FAMBLE, JR.
13 Director of Administrative Systems ... Ms. Kathy DENSLOW
06 Registrar ... Mrs. Carolyn A. CALVERT
08 Director Jay-Rollins Library ... Ms. Terry YOUNG
32 Dean of Student Affairs ... Ms. Vanessa ROBERTS-BRYAN
66 Interim Dean School of Nursing ... Dr. Sheila GARLAND
35 Director of Student Activities ... Ms. Megan BALDREE
37 Director of Financial Aid ... Ms. Lori HERRICK
21 Controller ... Ms. Shelby GIBBS
15 Director of Human Resources ... Ms. Lecia HUGHES
108 Dir of Institutional Effectiveness ... Dr. Thomas BENOIT
09 Director of Institutional Research ... Ms. Terry NIXON
26 AVP of Marketing & Communications ... Mr. Daniel MANSON
29 Director Alumni Relations ... Ms. Suzann COUTS
38 Director Counseling & Career Svcs ... Mr. James GREER
41 Director of Athletics ... Mr. Sam FERGUSON
42 Dir of Religious Life/Univ Chaplain ... Rev. Jeff LUST
19 Director of Campus Security ... Mr. Mark R. ODOM
23 Director of Health Services ... Ms. Ronda HOELSCHER
39 Director of Residence Life ... Vacant
102 Executive Director Donor Relations ... Ms. Nancy SMITH
92 Director Honors Program ... Dr. Philip LE MASTERS
106 Director of Online Education ... Dr. Matt DODD

Messenger College (G)

400 S Industrial Boulevard, Euless TX 76040

County: Tarrant | FICE Identification: 030926 | Unit ID: 417752
Telephone: (817) 554-5950 | Carnegie Class: Spec-4-yr-Faith
FAX Number: (817) 391-4003 | Calendar System: Semester
URL: www.messengercollege.edu
Established: 1987 | Annual Undergrad Tuition & Fees: $8,756
Enrollment: 163 | Coed
Affiliation or Control: Pentecostal Church of God | IRS Status: 501(c)3
Highest Offering: Baccalaureate
Accreditation: TRACS

01 President ... Rev. Randall K. LAWRENCE
04 Administrative Asst to President ... Sharon TOW
05 VP of Academic Affairs ... Dr. Candace RAYBURN
07 Director of Enrollment Services ... Carrie UNDERWOOD
08 Head Librarian ... Mary THOMASON
10 VP of Business Affairs ... Angela HEPPNER
32 VP of Student Development ... Fiona PARKER
37 Director Student Financial Aid ... Diana SPEEGLE

Midland College (H)

3600 N Garfield, Midland TX 79705-6397

County: Midland | FICE Identification: 009797 | Unit ID: 226806
Telephone: (432) 685-4500 | Carnegie Class: Bac/Assoc-Assoc Dom
FAX Number: (432) 685-4714 | Calendar System: Semester
URL: www.midland.edu
Established: 1969 | Annual Undergrad Tuition & Fees (In-District): $1,968
Enrollment: 4,618 | Coed
Affiliation or Control: Local | IRS Status: 501(c)3
Highest Offering: Baccalaureate
Accreditation: SC, CAHIIM, COARC, DMS, EMT

01 President ... Dr. Steve THOMAS
03 Executive Vice President ... Dr. Richard C. JOLLY
88 Special Advisor to President ... Dr. Deana SAVAGE
10 Vice Pres Administrative Services ... Mr. Rick BENDER
32 Vice President Student Services ... Ms. Rita Nell DIFFIE
13 Vice Pres Info Tech/Facilities ... Mr. Dennis SEVER

101 Asst to President/Sec to Board .... Mrs. Bahola EDWARDS
106 Dean of Distance Learning/Cont Educ .... Mr. Dale BEIKIRCH
57 Dean of Fine Arts/Communication .... Mr. William FEELER
72 Dean of Applied Technology .... Mr. Curt PERVIER
76 Dean of Health Sciences .... Ms. Carmen EDWARDS
81 Dean of Math/Natural Sciences .... Dr. Margaret WADE
83 Dean Adult/Developmental Education .... Mrs. Lynda WEBB
30 Exec Dir Inst Advancement/Col Fndn .... Ms. Kathy FLETCHER
06 Registrar .... Mrs. Angela BALCH
08 Head Librarian .... Mr. John DEATS
15 Director of Human Services .... Mrs. Natasha MORGAN
18 Director Physical Plant .... Mr. Ken RILEY
19 Chief of Police .... Mr. Richard MCKEE
26 Dean of Public Information .... Ms. Rebecca BELL
35 Student Life Director .... Mr. Ty SOLIZ
41 Athletic Director .... Mr. Forrest ALLEN
09 Dir Institutional Effect/Planning .... Ms. Karen WAGGONER
37 Director Student Financial Aid .... Ms. Yolanda RAMOS
96 Purchasing Director .... Ms. Barbara FENNELL
84 Dean of Enrollment Management .... Ms. Liz ZENTENO
07 Director of Admissions/Recruitment .... Mr. Jeremy MARTINEZ

Midwestern State University (A)

3410 Taft Boulevard, Wichita Falls TX 76308-2095
County: Wichita FICE Identification: 003592
Unit ID: 226833
Telephone: (940) 397-4000 Carnegie Class: Masters/M
FAX Number: (940) 397-4042 Calendar System: Semester
URL: www.mwsu.edu
Established: 1922 Annual Undergrad Tuition & Fees (In-State): $8,005
Enrollment: 5,874 Coed
Affiliation or Control: State IRS Status: 501(c)3
Highest Offering: Master's
Accreditation: SC, ART, BUS, CAATE, COARC, DH, ENG, MUS, NURSE, RAD, SW, TED, THEA

01 President .... Dr. Suzanne SHIPLEY
05 Provost .... Dr. Betty STEWART
10 VP Business Affairs & Finance .... Dr. Marilyn FOWLE
30 VP Univ Advncmnt & Stdnt Affairs .... Mr. Anthony VIDMAR
32 VP Student Affairs/Enrollment Mgmt .... Dr. Keith LAMB
18 Assoc VP Facilities Services .... Mr. Kyle OWEN
35 Assoc VP Student Affairs/Enrol Mgmt .... Mr. Matthew PARK
13 Chief Information Systems .... Mr. Jim HALL
06 Registrar .... Ms. Darla INGLISH
08 University Librarian .... Dr. Clara LATHAM
37 Director of Student Financial Aid .... Ms. Kathy PENNARTZ-BROWNING
38 Director of Counseling Center .... Dr. Pam MIDGETT
51 Director of Extended Education .... Dr. Pamela MORGAN
07 Director of Admissions .... Ms. Gayonne BEAVERS
19 Chief of Police .... Mr. Patrick COGGINS
26 Director Public Info/Marketing .... Ms. Julie GAYNOR
30 Dir Donor Services and Scholarships .... Ms. Laura PETERSON
36 Director Career Management Center .... Mr. Dirk WELCH
41 Director of Athletics .... Mr. Charles CARR
15 Director of Human Resources .... Ms. Dawn FISHER
09 Director Inst Research & Planning .... Mr. Mark MCCLENDON
21 Controller .... Mr. Chris STOVALL
23 Director Vinson Health Center .... Dr. Keith WILLIAMSON
20 Associate VP Academic Affairs .... Vacant
50 Dean College Business Admin .... Dr. Terry PATTON
53 Dean College of Education .... Dr. Matthew CAPPS
57 Dean College of Fine Arts .... Dr. Martin CAMACHO
76 Dean Col Health Sci/Human Svcs .... Dr. James JOHNSTON
79 Dean College Humanities/Social Sci .. Dr. Samuel E. WATSON, III
81 Dean College of Science & Math .... Dr. Margaret BROWN MARSDEN
86 Director Board & Govt Relations .... Ms. Deborah L. BARROW
29 Director of Alumni Relations .... Ms. Leslee PONDER
88 Director of Academic Success Center .... Ms. Naoma CLARK
105 Webmaster .... Mr. Jonathan SHIREY
96 Director of Purchasing .... Mr. Stephen SHELLEY
22 Dir Disability Support Services .... Ms. Debra HIGGINBOTHAM
39 Director Housing & Residence Life .... Ms. Kristi SCHULTE
30 Director University Development .... Mr. Steve SHIPP
104 Director of Study Abroad .... Vacant
88 Director Testing Center .... Ms. Lynn DUCIOAME
85 Director International Services .... Dr. Randy GLEAN
88 Director Budget & Management .... Ms. Valarie MAXWELL
88 Director Museum .... Dr. Francine CARRARO
88 Director Student Support Services .... Ms. Lisa ESTRADA-HAMBY
88 Campus Postal Supervisor .... Mr. Jon LANE
92 Coordinator Honors Program .... Mrs. Juliana LEHMAN-FELTS
43 Dir Legal Services/General Counsel .... Mr. Barry MACHA

National American University-Austin (B)

13801 Burnet Road, Suite 300, Austin TX 78727
Telephone: (512) 651-4700 Identification: 770411
Accreditation: &NH, MAC

† Regional accreditation is carried under the parent institution in Rapid City, SD

National American University-Georgetown (C)

1015 W University Avenue, Suite 700, Georgetown TX 78628
Telephone: (512) 942-6750 Identification: 770413
Accreditation: &NH, MAC

† Regional accreditation is carried under the parent institution in Rapid City, SD

National American University Harold D. Buckingham Graduate School (D)

6838 Austin Center Blvd, Ste 270, Austin TX 78731
Telephone: (512) 813-2300 Identification: 770931
Accreditation: &NH

† Branch campus of National American University, Rapid City, SD.

National American University-Houston (E)

11511 Katy Freeway Ste 200, Houston TX 77079
Telephone: (832) 619-7300 Identification: 770930
Accreditation: &NH

† Branch campus of National American University, Rapid City, SD.

National American University-Lewisville (F)

475 State Hwy 121 Bypass #150, Lewisville TX 75067
Telephone: (972) 829-2150 Identification: 770415
Accreditation: &NH

† Regional accreditation is carried under the parent institution in Rapid City, SD

National American University-Mesquite (G)

18600 LBJ Freeway, Mesquite TX 75150
Telephone: (972) 773-8800 Identification: 770416
Accreditation: &NH

† Regional accreditation is carried under the parent institution in Rapid City, SD

National American University-Richardson (H)

300 N Coit Road, Suite 225, Richardson TX 75080
Telephone: (972) 773-8650 Identification: 770414
Accreditation: &NH

† Regional accreditation is carried under the parent institution in Rapid City, SD

National American University-South Austin (I)

6800 Westgate Boulevard, #102, Austin TX 78945
Telephone: (512) 651-4750 Identification: 770412
Accreditation: &NH

† Regional accreditation is carried under the parent institution in Rapid City, SD

Navarro College (J)

3200 W Seventh Avenue, Corsicana TX 75110-4899
County: Navarro FICE Identification: 003593
Unit ID: 227146
Telephone: (903) 874-6501 Carnegie Class: Assoc/MT-VT-High Trad
FAX Number: (903) 874-4636 Calendar System: Semester
URL: www.navarrocollege.edu
Established: 1946 Annual Undergrad Tuition & Fees (In-District): $2,218
Enrollment: 9,999 Coed
Affiliation or Control: Local IRS Status: 501(c)3
Highest Offering: Associate Degree
Accreditation: SC, ADNUR, EMT, MLTAD, OTA, @PTAA

01 Interim Chancellor .... Dr. Richard M. SANCHEZ
12 President Ellis Co Campuses .... Dr. Kenneth MARTIN
05 Interim Vice Pres Academic Affs .... Ms. Carol HANES
10 Vice President Finance & Admin .... Ms. Thomas TERESA
30 VP Oper/Institutional Advancement .... Dr. Harold HOUSLEY
32 Vice President Student Services .... Ms. Maryann HAILEY
84 Interim VP Enroll Mgmt/Inst Effect .... Ms. Sina RUIZ
15 VP Human Resources .... Ms. Marcy BALLEW
88 Dean of Midlothian Campus .... Dr. Alex KAJSTURA
26 Director of Mktg/Public Relations .... Vacant
41 Athletic Director .... Mr. Roark MONTGOMERY
20 Interim Exec Dean of Acad Studies .... Mr. Terry PETERMAN
50 Exec Dean Business/Workforce Educ .... Ms. Judy CUTTING
106 Dean of Online Instruction .... Mr. Matthew MILLER
76 Dean of Health Professions .... Mr. Guy FEATHERSTON
12 Dean of Navarro College South .... Dr. Joel MICHAELIS
21 Comptroller .... Ms. Aaron YORK-LANGSTON
103 Dean of Workforce & Cont Ed .... Ms. Darla LITTREL
08 Dean of Libraries .... Mr. Tim KEVIL
07 Dir of Admissions/Registrar .... Ms. Tammy ADAMS
18 Exec Director of Facilities .... Mr. Karl HUMPHRIES
13 Interim CIO .... Mr. Jeff GAMBLIN
37 Director Student Financial Aid .... Ms. Kristal NICHOLSON
39 Director of Residence Life .... Mr. Charles BETTS
104 Director of International Programs .... Ms. Elizabeth PILLANS
88 Academic Dean of Ellis County .... Ms. Terry GIBSON
88 Interim Dean of Sci/Kines/Dev Stds .... Ms. Christina MIMS
71 Dir Navarro College TJJD Program .... Ms. Sheri SHORT
35 Dean of Student Guidance .... Mr. Michael DAVILA
35 Dean of Student Services Ellis Cty .... Ms. Kristin WALKER
09 Director of Institutional Research .... Ms. Elizabeth CHIVERS

North American University (K)

11929 W. Airport Boulevard, Stafford TX 77477
County: Harris FICE Identification: 041795
Unit ID: 461795
Telephone: (832) 230-5555 Carnegie Class: Bac-Diverse
FAX Number: N/A Calendar System: Semester
URL: www.na.edu
Established: 2010 Annual Undergrad Tuition & Fees: $11,900
Enrollment: 473 Coed
Affiliation or Control: Non-denominational IRS Status: 501(c)3
Highest Offering: Master's
Accreditation: ACICS

01 President & Professor .... Dr. Reg R. PECEN
05 Vice Pres Academic Affairs-Provost .... Dr. John C. TOPUZ
04 Administrative Asst to President .... Vacant
06 Registrar .... Antera SHARP
07 Int Director of Admissions .... Shawn WASHINGTON
08 Head Librarian .... Gary CHAUFFEE
106 Dir Online Education/E-learning .... Mustafa MALDAR
13 Chief Info Technology Officer (CIO) .... Khudoyor S. ORTIKOV
32 Chief Student Affairs/Student Life .... Osman KANLIOGLU
37 Assoc Dir Student Financial Aid .... Tya SIMON

North Central Texas College (L)

1525 W. California Street, Gainesville TX 76240-4699
County: Cooke FICE Identification: 003558
Unit ID: 224110
Telephone: (940) 668-7731 Carnegie Class: Assoc/HT-High Trad
FAX Number: (940) 668-6049 Calendar System: Semester
URL: www.nctc.edu
Established: 1924 Annual Undergrad Tuition & Fees (In-District): $1,680
Enrollment: 10,169 Coed
Affiliation or Control: State/Local IRS Status: 501(c)3
Highest Offering: Associate Degree
Accreditation: SC, ADNUR, EMT, SURGT

01 President .... Dr. G. Brent WALLACE
05 Vice Pres Instruction/Student Svcs .... Dr. Andrew FISHER
32 Vice President of Student Services .... Vacant
10 Vice President Financial Services .... Dr. Janie NEIGHBORS
11 Vice Pres Administrative Affairs .... Mr. Robbie BAUGH
30 Vice Pres External Affairs .... Ms. Debbie SHARP
15 Assoc Vice Pres Human Resources .... Mr. Bill WINANS
103 Associate VP Academic Partnerships .... Dr. Emily KLEMENT
13 Chief Information Officer .... Ms. Denise CASON
108 Sr Dir Assessment & Strategic Plng .... Mr. David BROWN
06 Registrar/Director of Admissions .... Ms. Melinda CARROLL
08 Director of Libraries .... Ms. Diane ROETHER
37 Director Financial Aid .... Ms. Ashley TATUM
38 Director Advisement .... Ms. Tracey FLENIKEN
26 Dir Marketing and Public Relations .... Mrs. Dianne WALTERSCHEID
41 Athletic Director .... Mr. Van HEDRICK
35 Director of Student Life .... Ms. Daisy GARCIA
76 Dean of Health Science .... Mrs. Gie ARCHER
72 Dean of Instruction Gainesville .... Mrs. Debbie HUFFMAN
49 Dean of Instruction Corinth .... Dr. Larry GILBERT
49 Dean of Instruction Flower Mound .... Mrs. Sara ALFORD
19 Police Chief .... Mr. James FITCH
35 Dean of Students .... Dr. Rodney LIPSCOMB
12 Dean of Denton County Campuses .... Mr. Roy CULBERSON
12 Director of Flower Mound Campus .... Ms. Jessica DEROCHE
12 Director of Bowie Campus .... Dr. Jose DASILVA
12 Director of Graham Campus .... Ms. Kim BIRDWELL

Northeast Texas Community College (M)

PO Box 1307, Mount Pleasant TX 75456-1307
County: Titus FICE Identification: 023154
Unit ID: 227225
Telephone: (903) 434-8100 Carnegie Class: Assoc/MT-VT-Mix Trad/Non
FAX Number: (903) 572-6712 Calendar System: Semester
URL: www.ntcc.edu
Established: 1984 Annual Undergrad Tuition & Fees (In-District): $2,506
Enrollment: 3,186 Coed
Affiliation or Control: Local IRS Status: 501(c)3
Highest Offering: Associate Degree
Accreditation: SC, EMT, MAC, MLTAD, PTAA

01 President .... Dr. Brad W. JOHNSON
04 Executive Asst to the President .... Ms. Pat L. TALLANT
05 Executive Vice Pres for Instruction .... Dr. Ron CLINTON
11 Interim Vice Pres Administrative Se .... Mr. Mitchell WALKER
30 Vice Pres Institutional Advancement .... Dr. Jonathan W. MCCULLOUGH
32 VP for Student & Outreach Services .... Dr. Josh STEWART
103 Assoc VP for Workforce Development .... Dr. Kevin ROSE
37 Dean Enroll/Dir Student Fin Assist .... Ms. Kim LAWRENCE
76 Dean of Allied Health Professions .... Dr. Shannon COX-KELLEY
84 Associate Dean of Outreach Services .... Ms. Melody HENRY
18 Director of Plant Services .... Mr. Tom RAMLER
08 Director Learning Resource Center .... Mr. Ron BOWDEN
91 Director of Computer Services .... Mr. Kenneth GOODSON
26 Director Marketing/Public Relations .... Ms. Jodi WEBER
06 Registrar .... Ms. Betsy GOODING
15 Director Human Resources .... Ms. Amy ADKINS
10 Controller .... Ms. Jaci M. MERRITT
09 Dir Institutional Effectiveness .... Ms. Toni LABEFF
88 Advisor/Retention Specialist .... Mr. John COLEMAN
36 Career Development/Advisor .... Ms. Lynda WATSON

Northwood University (N)

1114 West FM 1382, Cedar Hill TX 75104
Telephone: (972) 293-5400 Identification: 770280

Accreditation: &NH, ACBSP

† Regional accreditation is carried under the parent institution in Midland, MI

Oblate School of Theology (A)

285 Oblate Drive, San Antonio TX 78216-6693
County: Bexar FICE Identification: 003595
Unit ID: 227289
Telephone: (210) 341-1366 Carnegie Class: Spec-4-yr-Faith
FAX Number: (210) 341-4519 Calendar System: Semester
URL: www.ost.edu
Established: 1903 Annual Graduate Tuition & Fees: N/A
Enrollment: 132 Coed
Affiliation or Control: Roman Catholic IRS Status: 501(c)3
Highest Offering: Doctorate; No Undergraduates
Accreditation: SC, PAST, THEOL

01 President ... Rev. Ronald ROLHEISER
05 Vice Pres Academic Affairs/Dean ... Dr. Scott WOODWARD
10 Vice Pres Finance/Human Resources ... Mr. Rene ESPINOSA
11 Vice Pres Administrative Affairs ... Rev. David KALERT
30 Vice Pres Institutional Advancement ... Mrs. Lea KOCHANEK
20 Associate Dean ... Sr. Linda GIBLER
51 Assoc Dean of Continuing Education ... Mrs. Rose MARDEN
88 Director Oblate Renewal Center ... Mrs. K.T COCKERELL
18 Director of Physical Plant ... Mr. Pedro CANTU
08 Director of the Library ... Ms. Maria GARCIA
06 Registrar & Director of Admissions ... Mr. Mario PORTER
88 Director Lay Ministry Institute ... Mrs. Bonnie ABADIE
88 Director Ministry to Ministers Pgm ... Rev. James MYERS
09 Dir Instl Research/Plng/Assessment ... Rev. David KALERT
88 Director DMin Program ... Rev. Wayne CAVALIER
88 Director PhD Program ... Rev. John MARKEY
26 Director of Communications ... Mr. Michael PARKER

Odessa College (B)

201 W University Boulevard, Odessa TX 79764-7127
County: Ector FICE Identification: 003596
Unit ID: 227304
Telephone: (432) 335-6400 Carnegie Class: Assoc/MT-VT-Mix Trad/Non
FAX Number: (432) 335-6860 Calendar System: Semester
URL: www.odessa.edu
Established: 1946 Annual Undergrad Tuition & Fees (In-District): $2,580
Enrollment: 5,059 Coed
Affiliation or Control: Local IRS Status: 501(c)3
Highest Offering: Associate Degree
Accreditation: SC, ADNUR, EMT, MUS, PTAA, RAD

01 President ... Dr. Gregory D. WILLIAMS
05 Vice President for Instruction ... Ms. Valorie JONES
10 Vice President Business Affairs ... Ms. Virginia E. CHISUM
32 VP Student Svcs/Enrollment Mgmt ... Ms. Kimberly MCKAY
13 Vice President for Information Tech ... Mr. Shawn SHREVES
09 VP for Institutional Effectiveness ... Dr. Donald WOOD
30 Exec Director for Advancement ... Mr. Jeffrey MEYERS
11 Exec Dir of Administration & HR ... Mr. Ken ZARTNER
49 Dean of Arts & Sciences ... Dr. Eric YEAGER
84 Exec Director Enrollment Services ... Mr. Louis GONZALES
06 Registrar ... Ms. Karen DOUGHTY
41 Director Intercollegiate Athletics ... Mr. Wayne BAKER
37 Director Student Financial Svcs ... Ms. Dee NESMITH
18 Director Facilities & Construction ... Mr. Bryan HEIFNER
26 Exec Director of Marketing ... Mr. Frank RICH
38 Exec Director Student Completion ... Ms. Kristi CLEMMER
96 Dir of Purchasing/Business Services ... Ms. Cindy CURNUTT

Our Lady of the Lake University (C)

411 SW 24th Street, San Antonio TX 78207-4689
County: Bexar FICE Identification: 003598
Unit ID: 227331
Telephone: (210) 434-6711 Carnegie Class: Masters/L
FAX Number: (210) 431-3928 Calendar System: Semester
URL: www.ollusa.edu
Established: 1895 Annual Undergrad Tuition & Fees: $26 148
Enrollment: 3,173 Coed
Affiliation or Control: Roman Catholic IRS Status: 501(c)3
Highest Offering: Doctorate
Accreditation: SC, ACBSP, COPSY, MFCD, SP, SW

01 President ... Dr. Diane MELBY
11 Vice President Administration ... Ms. Rosalinda GARCIA
05 Vice President for Academic Affairs ... Dr. Marcheta EVANS
32 Vice President of Student Life ... Mr. Jack L. HANK
10 Vice President Finance & Facilities ... Mr. Allen R. KLAUS
30 Vice Pres Institutional Advancement ... Mr. Daniel YOXALL
84 Vice Pres of Enrollment Management ... Ms. Mary SCOTKA
26 Vice Pres Communications/Marketing ... Mr. Daniel YOXALL
42 Vice President of Mission/Ministry ... Ms. Gloria URRABAZO
13 Chief Technology Officer ... Mr. Joseph G. DECK
108 Asst VP for I/E & Accreditation ... Dr. Kara LARKAN-SKINNER
18 Director Physical Plant ... Mr. Darrell R. GLASSCOCK
15 Director Human Resources ... Mr. Phillip VARGAS
06 Registrar ... Ms. Betty GALVAN
14 Director Network & Telecomm ... Mr. David LYTLE
19 Chief of Police/Dir Campus Safety ... Mr. David JUAREZ
39 Director Residence Life ... Mr. Mark R. CENTER
36 Director Career Counsel/Placement ... Mr. Andres JAIME
38 Director of Counseling Services ... Dr. Rosa ESPINOSA

23 Director of Health Services ... Ms. Julie STUCKEY
40 Director Bookstore ... Ms. Jennifer WOLFF
102 Corporate Relations Officer ... Ms. Roxanne SANCHEZ
46 Director of Advancement Services ... Mr. John SANCHEZ
44 Dir of Stewardship/Constituent Rels ... Ms. Debora GUZMAN
37 Director of Financial Aid ... Ms. Esmarelda FLORES
09 Dir Institutional Research ... Ms. Frances FREY
07 Asst Dir of Undergrad Admissions ... Ms. Shannon TIJERINA

Panola College (D)

1109 West Panola Street, Carthage TX 75633-2397
County: Panola FICE Identification: 003600
Unit ID: 227386
Telephone: (903) 693-2000 Carnegie Class: Assoc/T-High Trad
FAX Number: (903) 693-1167 Calendar System: Semester
URL: www.panola.edu
Established: 1947 Annual Undergrad Tuition & Fees (In-District): $1,752
Enrollment: 2,564 Coed
Affiliation or Control: Local IRS Status: 501(c)3
Highest Offering: Associate Degree
Accreditation: SC, ADNUR, CAHIIM, EMT, MLTAD, OTA

01 President ... Dr. Gregory S. POWELL
05 Vice President of Instruction ... Dr. Joe SHANNON
32 Vice President of Student Services ... Mr. Don CLINTON
10 Vice President of Fiscal Services ... Mr. Troy CASERTA
76 Dean of Health Sciences ... Dr. Barbara CORDELL
08 Director of Library ... Mrs. Cristie FERGUSON
07 Director of Admissions/Registrar ... Mr. Jeremy DORMAN
103 Dir of Workforce & Economic Devel ... Mrs. Whitney MCBEE
30 Dir Institutional Advancement ... Mrs. Jessica PACE
09 Director of Institutional Research ... Mrs. Trythera BLEDSOE
106 Dir Distance Education/Webmaster ... Mrs. Teresa BROOKS
12 Director of Shelby County Operation ... Mrs. Natalie OSWALT
12 Director of Marshall Operations ... Mrs. Laura WOOD
13 Computer Services Director ... Mr. Allen WEST
11 Director of Administrative Services ... Mr. Mike EDENS
19 Campus Police Chief ... Mr. Bryan RICKERT
37 Director Student Financial Aid ... Mrs. Denise WELCH
26 Marketing Coordinator ... Ms. Teresa BEASLEY

Paris Junior College (E)

2400 Clarksville Street, Paris TX 75460-6298
County: Lamar FICE Identification: 003601
Unit ID: 227401
Telephone: (903) 785-7661 Carnegie Class: Assoc/HVT-Mix Trad/Non
FAX Number: (903) 782-0370 Calendar System: Semester
URL: www.parisjc.edu
Established: 1924 Annual Undergrad Tuition & Fees (In-District): $1,548
Enrollment: 5,086 Coed
Affiliation or Control: State/Local IRS Status: 501(c)3
Highest Offering: Associate Degree
Accreditation: SC, ADNUR, EMT, #RAD, SURGT

01 President ... Dr. Pamela D. ANGLIN
05 Vice President of Academic Studies ... Vacant
103 Vice President Workforce Education ... Mr. John SPRADLING
32 Assoc VP Student Access/Success ... Mrs. Sheila REECE
60 Dean Communications/Arts ... Dr. Ken HALEY
07 Director of Admissions ... Mrs. Amie CATO
06 Registrar ... Mrs. Rita TAPP
10 Controller ... Mrs. Keitha CARLTON
37 Director Student Financial Aid ... Mrs. Linda SLAWSON
38 Director Counseling ... Vacant
09 Director Institutional Research ... Mrs. Beverly MATTHEWS
30 Director Institutional Advancement ... Mr. Donald BULLS
35 Director Student Life ... Mr. Kenneth WEBB
13 Director Information Technology ... Mr. David NICHOLS
26 Chief Public Relations Officer ... Ms. Margaret RUFF
18 Manager Plant Operations ... Mr. Randall COX

Parker University (F)

2540 Walnut Hill Lane, Dallas TX 75229-5609
County: Dallas FICE Identification: 023053
Unit ID: 243823
Telephone: (972) 438-6932 Carnegie Class: Spec-4-yr-Other Health
FAX Number: (214) 902-2496 Calendar System: Trimester
URL: www.parker.edu
Established: 1982 Annual Undergrad Tuition & Fees: $15,052
Enrollment: 977 Coed
Affiliation or Control: Independent Non-Profit IRS Status: 501(c)3
Highest Offering: Doctorate
Accreditation: SC, CHIRO, COMTA, OTA

01 President ... Dr. William E. MORGAN
05 Provost ... Dr. Gery HOCHANADEL
63 Dir of Clinics/Col of Chiropractic ... Dr. Patrick BODNAR
29 Director Alumni Relations ... Ms. Donna WALD

Paul Quinn College (G)

3837 Simpson Stuart Road, Dallas TX 75241-4398
County: Dallas FICE Identification: 003602
Unit ID: 227429
Telephone: (214) 376-1000 Carnegie Class: Bac-Diverse
FAX Number: (214) 379-5559 Calendar System: Semester
URL: www.pqc.edu
Established: 1872 Annual Undergrad Tuition & Fees: $8,275
Enrollment: 273 Coed
Affiliation or Control: African Methodist Episcopal IRS Status: 501(c)3
Highest Offering: Baccalaureate
Accreditation: TRACS

01 President ... Dr. Michael J. SORRELL
05 Vice Pres Academic Affairs ... Dr. Kizuwanda GRANT
10 Chief Financial Officer ... Mr. Bruce BRINSON
32 Dean of Student Talent ... Ms. Stacy CHERONES
06 Registrar ... Ms. Twyla GILLS
08 Librarian/Director LRC ... Ms. Clarice MEDLEY-WEEKS
13 Director of Technology ... Ms. Tynia HICKMAN
41 Dir Athletics/Intramural Sports ... Ms. Kelsel THOMPSON
37 Interim Director of Financial Aid ... Ms. Mildred MARTINEZ
35 Director Student Support Svcs ... Ms. Crystal JACKSON
18 Interim Director of Facilities ... Mr. Ed WOODS
09 Instl Research Representative ... Dr. Chris DOWDY
30 Director of Development ... Mr. Dennis COLEMAN
23 Nurse ... Ms. Glenda DAVIS
07 Director of Recruiting ... Mrs. Jessika LARA

Pima Medical Institute-El Paso (H)

8375 Burnham Drive, El Paso TX 79935
Telephone: (520) 323-5987 Identification: 770962
Accreditation: ABHES

† Branch campus of Pima Medical Institute-Tucson, Tucson, AZ

Pima Medical Institute-Houston (I)

10201-C Katy Freeway, Houston TX 77024
Telephone: (713) 778-0778 Identification: 770510
Accreditation: ABHES, #COARC, DH, PTAA, RAD

† Branch campus of Pima Medical Institute-Tucson, Tucson, AZ

Quest College (J)

5430 Fredericksburg Road, Ste 310,
San Antonio TX 78229
County: Bexar FICE Identification: 034003
Unit ID: 439507
Telephone: (210) 366-2701 Carnegie Class: Not Classified
FAX Number: (210) 366-0738 Calendar System: Semester
URL: www.questcollege.edu
Established: 1995 Annual Undergrad Tuition & Fees: N/A
Enrollment: 296 Coed
Affiliation or Control: Proprietary IRS Status: Proprietary
Highest Offering: Associate Degree
Accreditation: COE

00 Owner/Administrator ... Ms. Jeanne MARTIN
01 School Director ... Ms. Sandy CLAUSS

Ranger College (K)

1100 College Circle, Ranger TX 76470-3298
County: Eastland FICE Identification: 003603
Unit ID: 227687
Telephone: (254) 647-3234 Carnegie Class: Assoc/HVT-High Trad
FAX Number: (254) 647-1656 Calendar System: Semester
URL: www.rangercollege.edu
Established: 1926 Annual Undergrad Tuition & Fees (In-District): $2,370
Enrollment: 2,031 Coed
Affiliation or Control: Local IRS Status: 501(c)3
Highest Offering: Associate Degree
Accreditation: SC

01 President ... Dr. William J. CAMPION
12 Vice President Brownwood ... Dr. Orlando MORENO
12 Vice President Erath County ... Dr. Kerry SCHINDLER
84 Dean of Enrollment Management ... Mr. John SLAUGHTER
10 Chief Financial Officer ... Mr. Robert CULVERHOUSE
32 Dean of Students ... Mr. Manuel MCGRIFF
05 Dean of Student Learning ... Dr. Billy ADAMS
11 Dean of Administration ... Mrs. Cherie BELTRAN
06 Registrar ... Mr. John SLAUGHTER
08 Director of Learning Resources ... Vacant
18 Director of Maintenance & Grounds ... Mr. Charles LEMASTER
37 Director of Financial Aid ... Mr. Don HILTON
41 Athletic Director ... Mr. Billy GILLISPIE
15 Director of Personnel ... Ms. DeLinda SPENCER
36 Director Student Placement ... Vacant
38 Dir Academic Counseling & Testing ... Dr. Elizabeth PRICE
21 Bursar ... Ms. Evonne CHERRY
40 Director Bookstore ... Miss Cindy STRINGER
07 Admissions Assistant ... Ms. Mary LUCKY

Redeemer Theological Seminary (L)

6060 N Central Expressway, Ste. 700, Dallas TX 75206
County: Dallas Identification: 667055
Telephone: (214) 528-8600 Carnegie Class: Not Classified
FAX Number: N/A Calendar System: Semester
URL: www.redeemer.edu
Established: 1999 Annual Graduate Tuition & Fees: N/A
Enrollment: N/A Coed
Affiliation or Control: Independent Non-Profit IRS Status: 501(c)3
Highest Offering: Master's; No Undergraduates
Accreditation: THEOL

01 President ... Dr. Martin BAN
05 Academic Dean ... Dr. Douglas M. GROPP

10 Director of Operations/Finance ....Ms. Tami FOWLER
06 Registrar ....Ms. Mary-Chris SAYRE

Remington College-Dallas Campus (A)

1800 Eastgate Drive, Garland TX 75041-5513
County: Dallas FICE Identification: 030265
Unit ID: 223463
Telephone: (972) 686-7878 Carnegie Class: Bac/Assoc-Assoc Dom
FAX Number: (972) 686-5116 Calendar System: Quarter
URL: www.remingtoncollege.edu
Established: 1987 Annual Undergrad Tuition & Fees: $14,566
Enrollment: 822 Coed
Affiliation or Control: Independent Non-Profit IRS Status: 501(c)3
Highest Offering: Baccalaureate
Accreditation: ACCSC

01 Campus President ....Mr. Skip WALLS
05 Academic Dean ....Ms. Michelle FRIEDERICHS

Remington College-Fort Worth Campus (B)

300 E Loop 820, Fort Worth TX 76112-1225
Telephone: (817) 451-0017 Identification: 666063
Accreditation: ACCSC

Remington College-Houston Southeast Campus (C)

20985 Interstate 45 South, Webster TX 77598
Telephone: (281) 554-1700 Identification: 770601
Accreditation: ACCSC

Remington College-North Houston Campus (D)

11310 Greens Crossing, Suite 300, Houston TX 77067
Telephone: (281) 885-4450 Identification: 770600
Accreditation: ACCSC

Rice University (E)

PO Box 1892, Houston TX 77251-1892
County: Harris FICE Identification: 003604
Unit ID: 227757
Telephone: (713) 348-0000 Carnegie Class: DU-Highest
FAX Number: N/A Calendar System: Semester
URL: www.rice.edu
Established: 1891 Annual Undergrad Tuition & Fees: $42,253
Enrollment: 6,621 Coed
Affiliation or Control: Independent Non-Profit IRS Status: 501(c)3
Highest Offering: Doctorate
Accreditation: SC, BUS, ENG

01 President ....Mr. David W. LEEBRON
101 Deputy Sec to Board of Trustees ....Ms. Cynthia L. WILSON
05 Provost ....Dr. Marie L. MIRANDA
11 Vice President Administration ....Dr. Kevin KIRBY
10 Vice President Finance ....Ms. Kathy COLLINS
30 Vice Pres Development/Alumni Rels ....Mr. Darrow ZEIDENSTEIN
88 Vice Pres Investments/Treasurer ....Ms. Allison THACKER
84 Vice President for Enrollment ....Mr. Chris MUNOZ
26 Vice President for Public Affairs ....Ms. Linda THRANE
13 Vice President IT & CIO ....Ms. Klara JELINKOVA
46 Vice Provost Research ....Dr. Yousif SHAMOO
20 Vice Provost for Academic Affairs ....Dr. Paula SANDERS
08 Vice Provost/University Librarian ....Ms. Sara LOWMAN
88 Vice President Strategic Inits ....Dr. Caroline LEVANDER
15 Associate Vice Pres Human Resources ....Ms. Mary A. CRONIN
91 Associate Vice Pres for Admin Systems ....Mr. Randy CASTIGLIONI
43 VP & General Counsel ....Mr. Richard A. ZANSITIS
06 Registrar ....Mr. David TENNEY
29 Asst VP for Alumni Relations ....Ms. Martha GOLDEN
37 Director Student Financial Services ....Ms. Anne E. WALKER
25 AVP Sponsored Proj/Res Compliance ....Ms. Melinda COTTEN
41 Director of Athletics ....Dr. Joseph KARLGAARD
85 Assoc Vice Provost Intl Education ....Dr. Adria BAKER
39 Assoc Vice Pres Housing & Dining ....Mr. Mark DITMAN
23 Director Student Health Services ....Dr. Stacy WARE
09 Assoc VP Institutional Research ....Mr. Sivakumar JAGANATHAN
21 University Controller ....Mr. Bradley FRALIC
21 Director of Internal Audit ....Ms. Janet COVINGTON
19 Chief of Campus Police ....Mr. Johnny WHITEHEAD
22 Director of Affirmative Action ....Mr. Russell BARNES
27 Sr Dir of News & Media Relations ....Mr. B.J ALMOND
21 Director Administrative Services ....Mr. Eugen RADULESCU
07 Director of Admissions ....Mr. Dan WARNER
28 Director of Diversity ....Dr. Roland B. SMITH
38 Director of Student Counseling ...Dr. Timothy K. BAUMGARTNER
36 Dir Center for Career Development ....Ms. Nicole VAN DEN HEUVEL
96 Director of Procurement ....Mr. Brian SOIKA
79 Dean of School of Humanities ....Dr. Nicolas SHUMWAY
58 Dean Graduate/Postdoctoral Stds ....Dr. Seiichi MATSUDA
97 Dean of Undergraduate Education ....Dr. John S. HUTCHINSON
48 Dean of Architecture ....Dr. Sarah M. WHITING
64 Dean of Shepherd School of Music ....Dr. Robert YEKOVICH
54 Dean GR Brown School Engineering ....Dr. Ned THOMAS
50 Dean JH Jones Graduate Sch Business ....Dr. Peter RODRIGUEZ
83 Dean of Social Sciences ....Dr. Antonio MERLO
81 Dean of Wiess Sch Natural Science ....Dr. Peter ROSSKY
51 Dean Glasscock Sch Continuing Stds ....Dr. Mary MCINTIRE
88 Asst Dean Stdnt Counsel/Jud Pgms ....Dr. Donald OSTDIEK
22 Director of Compliance ....Mr. Ken LIDDLE
18 Chief Facilities/Physical Plant ....Ms. Kathy JONES

Rio Grande Bible Institute (F)

4300 South US Highway 281, Edinburg TX 78539-9650
County: Hidalgo Identification: 666395
Unit ID: 475185
Telephone: (956) 380-8100 Carnegie Class: Spec-4-yr-Faith
FAX Number: (956) 380-8256 Calendar System: Semester
URL: www.riogrande.edu
Established: 1946 Annual Undergrad Tuition & Fees: $2,430
Enrollment: 132 Coed
Affiliation or Control: Independent Non-Profit IRS Status: 501(c)3
Highest Offering: Baccalaureate
Accreditation: BI

01 President ....Dr. Lawrence B. WINDLE
04 Administrative Assistant to Pres ....Mrs. Ruth WINDLE
05 Vice President of Education ....Mr. David LOYOLA
10 Vice President of Administration ....Dr. John TARWATER
32 Dean of Students ....Mr. Nelson MATUS
21 Comptroller ....Mr. Jonathan WHITE
08 Librarian ....Mrs. Donna ANTONIUK
06 Registrar ....Mr. Keith SWARTZBAUGH
15 Personnel Director ....Mr. Daniel DELEON
18 Vice President of Campus Services ....Mr. Gary WILLIAMS
26 Vice Pres Ministerial Advancement ....Dr. Robert CRANE

St. Edward's University (G)

3001 S Congress Avenue, Austin TX 78704-6489
County: Travis FICE Identification: 003621
Unit ID: 227845
Telephone: (512) 448-8400 Carnegie Class: Masters/L
FAX Number: (512) 448-8492 Calendar System: Semester
URL: www.stedwards.edu
Established: 1885 Annual Undergrad Tuition & Fees: $38,720
Enrollment: 4,686 Coed
Affiliation or Control: Independent Non-Profit IRS Status: 501(c)3
Highest Offering: Master's
Accreditation: SC, SW

01 President ....Dr. George E. MARTIN
03 Executive Vice President ....Sr. Donna M. JURICK
10 Vice President Financial Affairs ....Ms. Kimberly KVAAL
05 Vice President for Academic Affairs ....Dr. Mary K. BOYD
30 Vice President for Advancement ....Mr. Joe DEMEDEIROS
26 Vice Pres Marketing/Enrollment Mgmt ....Ms. Paige BOOTH
32 Vice President for Student Affairs ....Dr. Lisa L. KIRKPATRICK
13 Vice President Information Tech ....Mr. David E. WALDRON
42 Director of Campus Ministry ....Fr. Peter J. WALSH
09 Assoc VP Inst Effectiveness/Rsrch ....Mr. Bhuban R. PANDEY
88 Assoc VP for Global Initiatives ....Mr. William J. CLABBY
21 Assoc VP for Finance ....Mr. Erin DELFFS
20 Assoc VP for Academic Affairs ....Dr. Molly E. MINUS
88 Assoc VP Faculty Development ....Ms. Lori W. PETERSON
07 Assoc VP/Dean of Admission ....Ms. Tracy L. MANIER
37 Assoc VP Student Financial Services ....Ms. Doris F. CONSTANTINE
35 Dean of Students ....Mr. Steven J. PINKENBURG
88 Assoc VP Stdnt Acad Support Svcs ....Ms. Nicole G. TREVINO
27 Assoc VP for Marketing ....Ms. Christie CAMPBELL
44 Executive Director of Development ....Mr. Michael V. MORELIUS
18 Assoc VP Facilities ....Mr. Michael W. PETERSON
91 Assoc VP Digital Effectiveness ....Ms. Angela M. SVOBODA
88 Assoc VP Digital Innovation ....Mr. Benjamin R. HOCKENHULL
109 Assistant VP for Business Services ....Ms. Cyndy JOHNSON
15 Assistant VP of Human Resources ....Ms. Rosemary RUDNICKI
19 Assistant VP for Campus Safety ....Mr. Scott G. BURNOTES
100 Chief of Staff/Sustainability Coord ....Ms. Cristina L. BORDIN
88 Chief Data Officer/Data Strategy ....Mr. Justin M. SLOAN
83 Dean Behavioral & Social Sciences ....Dr. Brenda J. VALLANCE
50 Dean The Munday School of Business ....Dr. Nancy SCHREIBER
53 Dean School of Education ....Dr. Glenda BALLARD
79 Dean School of Humanities ....Dr. Sharon D. NELL
81 Dean School of Natural Sciences ....Dr. Gary MORRIS
55 Interim Dean of New College ....Dr. Ramsey FOWLER
97 Director of General Education ....Dr. Cory LOCK
89 Director Freshman Studies ....Ms. Alexandra L. BARRON
88 Director Capstone Program ....Dr. Todd D. ONDERDONK
92 Director Honors Program ....Dr. Steven M. RODENBORN
08 Director of Munday Library ....Mr. Pongracz SENNYEY
06 Registrar ....Dr. Lance R. HAYES
36 Dir Career & Prof Development ....Mr. Raymond C. ROGERS
29 Director of Alumni & Parent Pgms ....Ms. Karin DICKS
108 Dir of Institutional Assessment ....Mr. David A. BLAIR
104 Director Ofc of Global Engagement ....Ms. Lesley J. ROBINSON
24 Director Info Technology Resources ....Vacant
90 Dir Instructional & Emerging Tech ....Ms. Rebecca F. DAVIS
105 Midware/User Experience Architect ....Mr. Tim TASHJIAN
27 Director of Communications ....Ms. Mischelle R. DIAZ
38 Director of Health & Counseling Ctr ....Dr. Calvin A. KELLY
102 Director Foundation Relations ....Ms. Allison M. RASP
37 Director Student Financial Services ....Ms. Jennifer M. BECK
41 Director of Athletics ....Ms. Debora W. TAYLOR
35 Director of Student Life ....Mr. Thomas B. SULLIVAN
39 Director Residence Life ....Ms. Alicia L. VELA
04 Admin Assistant to President ....Ms. Lorraine M. PAGAN
40 Campus Stores Director ....Mr. Tim JACKSON

St. Mary's University (H)

One Camino Santa Maria, San Antonio TX 78228-8572
County: Bexar FICE Identification: 003623
Unit ID: 228149
Telephone: (210) 436-3011 Carnegie Class: Masters/L
FAX Number: (210) 436-3500 Calendar System: Semester
URL: www.stmarytx.edu
Established: 1852 Annual Undergrad Tuition & Fees: $27,160
Enrollment: 3,712 Coed
Affiliation or Control: Roman Catholic IRS Status: 501(c)3
Highest Offering: Doctorate
Accreditation: SC, BUS, CACREP, ENG, LAW, MFCD, MUS

01 President ....Mr. Thomas M. MENGLER
05 Provost/VP Academic Affairs ....Dr. Aaron TYLER
10 Vice Pres Administration & Finance ....Ms. Rebeckah J. DAY
84 Vice Prov Enrollment Management ....Dr. Rosalind ALDERMAN
32 Int Assoc Provost Student Dev ....Mr. Timothy BESSLER
30 Vice Pres University Advancement ....Mr. Richard (Rick) KIMBROUGH, II
88 Vice President Mission & Rector ....Rev. Tim EDEN, SM
50 Dean/Bill Greehey Sch Business ....Dr. Tanuja SINGH
79 Dean Humanities & Social Science ....Dr. Janet B. DIZINNO
54 Dean Science/Engrng/Technology ....Dr. Winston EREVELLES
58 Interim Dean Graduate Studies ....Dr. Megan MUSTAIN
61 Dean of Law ....Mr. Steve SHEPPARD
39 Director Residence Life ....Mr. James VILLARREAL
100 Chief of Staff/Office of President ....Ms. Dianne L. PIPES
06 Registrar ....Ms. Christina VILLANUEVA
07 Dean of Admission ....Vacant
08 Exec Director Louis J Blume Library ....Ms. Caroline BYRD
37 Director Financial Assistance ....Mr. David R. KRAUSE
38 Int Director Student Counseling ....Ms. Deidra COLEMAN
90 Exec Dir/Instructor Acad Tech ....Mr. Jeff SCHOMBURG
15 Director Human Resources ....Ms. Elsa YBANEZ
72 Vice Pres Info Tech/Library Svcs ....Mr. Curtis WHITE
91 Exec Dir Resource Mgmt/Planning ....Ms. Louisa A. MARTIN
13 Dir Network Security Administration ...Mr. Robert STOOKSBERRY
14 Director Systems Support Services ....Mr. Frank NIEWIERSKI
42 Director University Ministry ....Mr. Wayne ROMO
29 Executive Director Alumni Relations ....Mr. Peter HANSEN
21 Director of Finance ....Ms. Mei-Lin LEE
21 Director of Accounting Operations ....Ms. Sheila NIX
26 Dir Media Relations/Communications ....Mrs. Gina FARRELL
18 Exec Dir Facilities Administration ....Mr. Aaron HANNA

*San Jacinto College District (I)

4624 Fairmont Parkway, Pasadena TX 77504-3323
County: Harris FICE Identification: 029137
Unit ID: 227988
Telephone: (281) 998-6150 Carnegie Class: N/A
FAX Number: N/A
URL: www.sanjac.edu

01 Chancellor ....Dr. Brenda HELLYER
03 Deputy Chancellor and President ....Dr. Laurel WILLIAMSON
10 Vice Chancellor Fiscal Affairs ....Mr. Chet LEWIS
15 Vice Chanc Human Resources ....Mr. Stephen TRNCAK
13 CIO ....Mr. Rob STANICIC
26 Vice Chanc Marketing/Govt Rels ....Mrs. Teri CRAWFORD
45 Vice Chanc Strategic Initiatives ....Dr. Allatia HARRIS
84 Dean Enroll Mgmt/College Registrar ....Ms. Wanda MUNSON
09 Director of Research ....Mr. George GONZALEZ
37 Dean Financial Aid Services ....Mr. Robert MERINO
96 Director Contracts & Purchasing ....Ms. Ann KOKX-TEMPLET

*San Jacinto College Central (J)

8060 Spencer Highway, Pasadena TX 77505-5903
County: Harris FICE Identification: 003609
Unit ID: 227979
Telephone: (281) 998-6150 Carnegie Class: Assoc/MT-VT-Mix Trad/Non
FAX Number: (281) 476-1892 Calendar System: Semester
URL: www.sanjac.edu
Established: 1960 Annual Undergrad Tuition & Fees (In-District): $1,408
Enrollment: 27,911 Coed
Affiliation or Control: Local IRS Status: 501(c)3
Highest Offering: Associate Degree
Accreditation: &SC, ACFEI, ADNUR, COARC, DMS, EMT, MLTAD, RAD, SURGT

02 Deputy Chancellor and President ....Dr. Laurel WILLIAMSON
05 Provost ....Mr. Van A. WIGGINTON
32 Associate VC Student Services ....Ms. Joanna ZIMMERMAN
06 College Registrar ....Dr. Wanda MUNSON
49 Dean Liberal Arts & Science ....Dr. Kelly SIMONS
75 Dean Business & Technology ....Mr. Jeffrey PARKS
76 Dean Health Sciences ....Mr. Michael KANE
11 Dean Administration ....Dr. James BRASWELL
07 Dean Enrollment Services ....Mr. Kevin MCKISSON
35 Dean Student Development ....Ms. Shelley RINEHART
37 Dean Financial Aid Services ....Mr. Robert MERINO
88 Dean Compliance & Judicial Affairs ....Ms. Clare IANNELLI
92 Director Honors Program ....Dr. Eddie WELLER
88 Director Dual Credit ....Ms. Nicole BARNES
08 Director Library ....Ms. Karen BLANKENSHIP
88 Director Campus Services ....Mr. Christopher CRUMLEY
41 Athletic Director ....Ms. Sharon NELSON
88 Director Student Success ....Ms. Christy KEITH
88 Director Education Planning ....Ms. Christine TORRES

† Regional accreditation is carried under the parent institution (district office) in Pasadena, TX.

*San Jacinto College North (A)
5800 Uvalde Road, Houston TX 77049-4599
County: Harris Identification: 666747
Unit ID: 227997
Telephone: (281) 458-4050 Carnegie Class: Not Classified
FAX Number: (281) 459-7125 Calendar System: Semester
URL: www.sanjac.edu
Established: 1974 Annual Undergrad Tuition & Fees (In-District): N/A
Enrollment: N/A Coed
Affiliation or Control: Local IRS Status: 501(c)3
Highest Offering: Associate Degree
Accreditation: &SC, ACFEI, CAHIIM, EMT, MAC

02 Deputy Chancellor and President .... Dr. Laurel WILLIAMSON
05 Provost .... Dr. William RAFFETTO
32 Associate VC Student Services .... Ms. Joanna ZIMMERMAN
07 Dean Enrollment Services .... Mr. Kevin MCKISSON
11 Dean Administration .... Dr. Jerrel WADE
76 Dean Natural and Health Sciences .... Ms. Rhonda BELL
50 Dean Business and Technology .... Dr. Kerry MIX
88 Dean Comp & Judicial Affairs .... Ms. Clare IANNELLI
62 Director Library .... Ms. Lyn GARNER
49 Dean Liberal Arts .... Mr. Shawn SILMAN
06 College Registrar .... Dr. Wanda MUNSON
41 Athletic Director .... Mr. Tom ARRINGTON
92 Director Honors Program .... Dr. Eddie WELLER
88 Dual Credit Director .... Ms. Jennifer MOWDY
55 Director Evening/Weekend Services .... Mr. Don SPIES
88 Director Student Success Center .... Ms. Erika HERNANDEZ
37 Dean Financial Aid Services .... Mr. Robert MERINO
32 Dean Student Development .... Ms. Tami KELLY
88 Dir Educational Planning & Counsel .... Ms. Sonia TOWNSEND

† Regional accreditation is carried under the parent institution (district office) in Pasadena, TX.

*San Jacinto College South (B)
13735 Beamer Road, Houston TX 77089-6099
County: Harris Identification: 666748
Unit ID: 22797902
Telephone: (281) 484-1900 Carnegie Class: Not Classified
FAX Number: (281) 922-3401 Calendar System: Semester
URL: www.sanjac.edu
Established: 1979 Annual Undergrad Tuition & Fees (In-District): N/A
Enrollment: N/A Coed
Affiliation or Control: Local IRS Status: 501(c)3
Highest Offering: Associate Degree
Accreditation: &SC, ADNUR, PTAA

02 Deputy Chancellor and President .... Dr. Laurel WILLIAMSON
05 Provost .... Dr. Brenda JONES
32 Associate VC Student Services .... Ms. Joanna ZIMMERMANN
49 Dean of Liberal Arts & College Prep .... Ms. Ann TATE
50 Dean Business & Technology .... Mr. Kevin MORRIS
76 Dean Health and Natural Sciences .... Dr. Alexander OKWONNA
11 Dean Administration .... Mr. Joseph HEBERT
07 Dean Enrollment Services .... Mr. Kevin MCKISSON
88 Dean Comp & Judicial Affairs .... Ms. Clare IANNELLI
92 Director Honors Program .... Dr. Eddie WELLER
55 Director Evening Division .... Mr. John BOGGS
62 Director Library .... Mr. Richard MCKAY
41 Director Athletics .... Ms. Kelly SAENZ
88 Dual Credit Director .... Ms. Kristen ROSS
06 College Registrar .... Dr. Wanda MUNSON
32 Dean Student Development .... Ms. Debbie SMITH
88 Director Education Planning .... Ms. Tanesha ANTOINE
88 Director Student Success Center .... Ms. Diana SHOKRALLA
37 Dean Financial Aid Services .... Mr. Robert MERINO

† Regional accreditation is carried under the parent institution (district office) in Pasadena, TX.

Sanford-Brown College (C)
4511 Horizon Hill Boulevard, San Antonio TX 78229
Telephone: (210) 530-9449 Identification: 666733
Accreditation: ACICS

† Branch campus of International Academy of Design and Technology, Tampa, FL. School is in teach out plan.

School of Automotive Machinists & Technology (D)
1911 Antoine Drive, Houston TX 77055
County: Harris FICE Identification: 030323
Unit ID: 377218
Telephone: (713) 683-3817 Carnegie Class: Not Classified
FAX Number: (713) 683-7077 Calendar System: Semester
URL: www.samtech.edu
Established: 1985 Annual Undergrad Tuition & Fees: N/A
Enrollment: 185 Coed
Affiliation or Control: Proprietary IRS Status: Proprietary
Highest Offering: Associate Degree
Accreditation: ACCSC

01 President/Dir of Education .... Judson MASSINGILL
11 CEO/Sch Exec Director/Administrator .... Linda MASSINGILL
07 Director of Admissions .... Scott MORRIS
37 Financial Aid Director .... Susie FAERMAN

Schreiner University (E)
2100 Memorial Boulevard, Kerrville TX 78028-5611
County: Kerr FICE Identification: 003610
Unit ID: 228042
Telephone: (830) 896-5411 Carnegie Class: Bac-A&S
FAX Number: (830) 896-3232 Calendar System: Semester
URL: www.schreiner.edu
Established: 1923 Annual Undergrad Tuition & Fees: $25,086
Enrollment: 1,128 Coed
Affiliation or Control: Presbyterian Church (U.S.A.) IRS Status: 501(c)3
Highest Offering: Master's
Accreditation: SC, NURSE

01 President .... Dr. Timothy SUMMERLIN
05 Provost/Vice Pres Acad Affairs .... Dr. Charlie T. MCCORMICK
10 Vice Pres Administration & Finance .... Mr. Bill MUSE
30 Vice Pres Advancement .... Mr. Mark TUSCHAK
84 Vice Pres Enrollment Services .... Dr. Larry CANTU
06 Assistant Provost & Registrar .... Ms. Darlene BANNISTER
20 Dean of Student Success .... Dr. Candice SCOTT
26 Vice President for Marketing .... Ms. Lane H. TAIT
21 Controller .... Mr. Sam WEBB
42 Campus Minister .... Rev. Virginia NORRIS-LANE
84 Dean of Enrollment Services .... Ms. Toni BRYANT
32 Dean of Students .... Dr. Charlie HUEBER
27 Director of Communications .... Ms. Amy ARMSTRONG
41 Athletic Director .... Mr. Ron MACOSKO
15 Director of Human Resource Services .... Ms. Wendy BLAETTNER
18 Director Facilities Services .... Mr. Dale MYERS
29 Associate Director Alumni Relations .... Mr. Paul CAMFIELD
38 Director Student Counseling .... Ms. Kimberly J. WOODS
36 Director Advising & Career Devel .... Ms. Cristina MARTINEZ
09 Director of Institutional Research .... Dr. Lucien COSTLEY
07 Assoc Dean of Enrollment Services .... Ms. Caroline RANDALL

Seminary of the Southwest (F)
Box 2247, Austin TX 78768-2247
County: Travis FICE Identification: 003566
Unit ID: 224712
Telephone: (512) 472-4133 Carnegie Class: Spec-4-yr-Faith
FAX Number: (512) 472-3098 Calendar System: 4/1/4
URL: www.ssw.edu
Established: 1952 Annual Graduate Tuition & Fees: N/A
Enrollment: 98 Coed
Affiliation or Control: Protestant Episcopal IRS Status: 501(c)3
Highest Offering: Master's; No Undergraduates
Accreditation: SC, THEOL

01 Dean & President .... V.Rev. Cynthia Briggs KITTREDGE
05 Academic Dean .... Dr. Scott BADER-SAYE
03 Executive Vice President .... Mr. Fred CLEMENT
26 VP of Communications .... Ms. Nancy SPRINGER-BALDWIN
10 Accounting Director .... Ms. Kathy LEBRUN
06 Registrar/Director of Assessment .... Ms. Madelyn SNODGRASS
08 Director of the Booher Library .... Ms. Alison POAGE
18 Director of Facilities Management .... Mr. Tigh WALTERS
13 Director Information Technology .... Mr. Erik MORROW
84 Enrollment Manager .... Ms. Beth JORDON

South Plains College (G)
1401 College Avenue, Levelland TX 79336-6595
County: Hockley FICE Identification: 003611
Unit ID: 226158
Telephone: (806) 894-9611 Carnegie Class: Assoc/MT-VT-Mix Trad/Non
FAX Number: (806) 894-5274 Calendar System: Semester
URL: www.southplainscollege.edu
Established: 1957 Annual Undergrad Tuition & Fees (In-State): $2,240
Enrollment: 9,661 Coed
Affiliation or Control: State IRS Status: 501(c)3
Highest Offering: Associate Degree
Accreditation: SC, ADNUR, COARC, EMT, PTAA, SURGT

01 President .... Dr. Robin SATTERWHITE
05 Vice President Academic Affairs .... Dr. Ryan GIBBS
10 Vice Pres Business Affairs .... Ms. Teresa GREEN
32 Vice President of Student Affairs .... Mrs. Cathy MITCHELL
30 Vice Pres Institutional Advancement .... Mr. Stephen S. JOHN
49 Dean of Arts & Sciences .... Mr. Yancy NUNEZ
76 Dean of Health Occupations .... Ms. Sue Ann LOPEZ
75 Dean of Technical Education .... Mr. Robbie M. BLAIR
51 Dean Continuing & Distance Educ .... Mr. Ronald SPEARS
11 Dean Administrative Services .... Mr. Ronnie WATKINS
07 Dean of Admissions & Records .... Mrs. Andrea RANGEL
12 Dean of Reese Center .... Ms. Kara MARTINEZ
35 Dean of Students .... Vacant
09 Assoc Dean of Research & Reports .... Mr. Ryan FITZGERALD
26 Assoc Dean of College Relations .... Mr. Dane DEWBRE
13 Assoc Dean Information Technology .... Mr. James HOWELL
88 Assoc Dean Dual Credit .... Mr. Ron SPEARS
103 Assoc Dean Workforce Development .... Mr. Rafael AGUILERA
20 Assoc Dean of Students .... Ms. Urisonya FLUNDER
38 Director of Counseling & Guidance .... Mrs. Christi ANDERSON
37 Director of Financial Aid .... Ms. Jim Ann BATENHORST
08 Director of Libraries .... Ms. Fran COTTON
30 Director of Development .... Ms. Julie GERSTENBERGER
15 Director of Human Resources .... Mrs. Jeri Ann DEWBRE
41 Director of Athletics .... Mr. Joe TUBB
06 Registrar .... Mr. Andrew RUIZ
18 Director of Physical Plant .... Mr. Cary MARROW

84 Director of Enrollment Management .... Mrs. Kimbra QUINN
21 Controller .... Ms. Teresa GREEN
40 Bookstore Manager .... Mr. Roger SHULL
28 Diversity Coord/Career Counselor .... Ms. Maria LOPEZ-STRONG

South Texas College (H)
3201 W Pecan, McAllen TX 78501
County: Hidalgo FICE Identification: 031034
Unit ID: 409315
Telephone: (956) 872-5051 Carnegie Class: Bac/Assoc-Assoc Dom
FAX Number: (956) 971-3739 Calendar System: Semester
URL: www.southtexascollege.edu
Established: 1993 Annual Undergrad Tuition & Fees (In-District): $3,486
Enrollment: 30,180 Coed
Affiliation or Control: State/Local IRS Status: 501(c)3
Highest Offering: Baccalaureate
Accreditation: SC, ACBSP, CAHIIM, COARC, EMT, OTA, PTAA

01 President .... Dr. Shirley A. REED
05 Int Vice Pres Academic Affs/CAO .... Dr. Anahid PETROSIAN
10 VP Finance/Administrative Svcs .... Ms. Maria G. ELIZONDO
32 Int VP Student Affairs/Enroll Mgmt .... Ms. Wanda GARCIA
13 Int VP Info Services/Planning .... Dr. David PLUMMER
30 Vice Pres Institutional Advancement .... Vacant
88 Exec Officer for NAAMRIE .... Ms. Wanda GARZA
83 Dean Liberal Arts/Soc Sci .... Dr. Margaretha BISCHOFF
50 Dean Business/Technology .... Mr. Mario REYNA
76 Int Dean Nursing/Allied Health .... Ms. Melba TREVINO
81 Dean Math/Science/BA Programs .... Dr. Ali ESMAEILI
88 Dean Bach Deg Prog/Univ Rels .... Dr. Ali ESMAEILI
24 Dir Instructional Technologies .... Mr. Cody GREGG
37 Assoc Dean Student Financial Svcs .... Mr. Mike CARRANZA
21 Comptroller .... Ms. Maria ELIZONDO
15 Director Human Resources .... Ms. Brenda Jo BALDERAZ
51 Dir Cont/Prof & Workforce Education .... Mr. Juan Carlos AGUIRRE
96 Director Purchasing .... Ms. Rebecca CAVAZOS
09 Dir Research/Analytical Svcs .... Mr. Serkan CELTEK
38 Dean Student Support Svcs .... Mr. Paul HERNANDEZ, JR.
18 Director Operations/Maintenance .... Mr. George MCCALEB
18 Director Facilities Plan/Construct .... Mr. Ricardo DE LA GARZA
25 Grants/Contracts Compliance Officer .... Ms. Samantha URIEGAS
12 Campus Administrator Starr Cty .... Dr. Arthuro MONTIEL
12 Campus Administrator Mid-Valley .... Mr. Daniel MONTEZ
88 Employee Relations Officer .... Vacant
106 Dean Distance Learning .... Dr. Erasmus ADDAE
26 Director Public Rels/Marketing .... Mr. Daniel RAMIREZ
88 Dir Outreach/Orient/Wel Centers .... Ms. Kimberly MCKAY
84 Dean Enrollment Services/Registrar .... Mr. Matthew HEBBARD
88 Assoc Dean Prof/Organizational Dev .... Ms. Lee GRIMES ETHERIDGE
20 Asst to VP Instructional Svcs .... Dr. Anahid PETROSIAN
19 Director Security .... Mr. Paul VARVILLE
62 Dean Library Services/Instr Tech .... Mr. Cody GREGG
103 Assc Dean Cmty Engage/Wkfrc Dev .... Vacant
13 Chief Information Officer .... Ms. Alicia GOMEZ
14 Director for IT Services .... Mr. Daniel DE LEON
08 Director Library Technical Services .... Mr. Jesus CAMPOS
08 Director Library Public Services .... Ms. Noemi GARZA
88 Dir Student Lrg Outcomes/Achievemnt .... Mr. Oscar HERNANDEZ
88 Int Dir Centers for Lrg Excellence .... Ms. Jennifer KNECHT
88 Administrator High School Programs .... Mr. Nicolas GONZALEZ
90 Dir Info Commons Open Labs .... Dr. Lelia SALINAS
35 Dean Student Affairs .... Mr. Pablo HERNANDEZ, JR.
88 Chief Information Security Officer .... Mr. Victor GONZALEZ
88 Assoc Dean Curriculum/Student Lrng .... Ms. Kristina WILSON

South University (I)
1220 W. Louis Henna Boulevard, Round Rock TX 78681
Telephone: (512) 516-8800 Identification: 770917
Accreditation: &SC, ACBSP, NURSE, PTAA

† Regional accreditation is carried under the parent institution in Savannah, GA

Southern Methodist University (J)
6425 Boaz Lane, Dallas TX 75205-0100
County: Dallas FICE Identification: 003613
Unit ID: 228246
Telephone: (214) 768-2000 Carnegie Class: DU-Higher
FAX Number: (214) 768-1001 Calendar System: Semester
URL: www.smu.edu
Established: 1911 Annual Undergrad Tuition & Fees: $48,190
Enrollment: 11,272 Coed
Affiliation or Control: United Methodist IRS Status: 501(c)3
Highest Offering: Doctorate
Accreditation: SC, ART, BUS, CLPSY, CS, DANCE, ENG, LAW, MUS, THEA, THEOL

01 President .... Dr. R. Gerald TURNER
05 Provost/VP Academic Affairs .... Dr. Steven C. CURRALL
10 Vice President Business & Finance .... Ms. Chris C. REGIS
32 VP for Student Affairs .... Dr. Pamela D. ANTHONY
30 Vice Pres Devel & External Affairs .... Mr. Brad E. CHEVES
43 Gen Counsel/VP Leg Affs/Govt Rels .... Mr. Paul J. WARD
11 Vice President Executive Affairs .... Dr. Harold W. STANLEY
49 Dean Dedman College .... Dr. Thomas DIPIERO
35 Dean of Student Life .... Dr. Joanne E. VOGEL
88 Assoc VP/Chief Risk Officer .... Ms. Ellen S. HOLLAND
45 Associate Vice President/Budgets .... Mr. Ernie BARRY
26 Assoc Vice President Public Affairs .... Vacant

44 Asst Vice Pres Univ Development ... Ms. Pam CONLIN
15 Assoc VP/Chief Human Res Officer ... Ms. Sheri STARKEY
84 Assoc VP Enroll Management ... Mr. Wes K. WAGGONER
109 Assoc VP of Campus Services ... Ms. Alison TWEEDY
88 Exec Dir of Program Services ... Ms. Dana AYRES
57 Dean Meadows Sch of the Arts ... Dr. Sam HOLLAND
61 Dean Dedman School of Law ... Ms. Jennifer M. COLLINS
54 Dean Lyle School of Engr ... Dr. Marc CHRISTENSEN
73 Dean Perkins School of Theology ... Dr. Craig C. HILL
50 Dean Cox School of Business ... Dr. Albert W. NIEMI, JR.
58 Director of Graduate Studies ... Ms. Reva POLLACK
46 Assoc VP Research/Dean Grad Studies ... Dr. James E. QUICK
53 Interim Dean Sch of Educ/Human Dev ... Dr. Paige D. WARE
08 Dean/Dir Central Univ Libraries ... Ms. Gillian M. MCCOMBS
20 Assoc Provost ... Ms. Julie FORRESTER
20 Assoc Provost ... Mr. Douglas A. REINELT
25 Director of Sponsored Projects ... Ms. Kathleen FURR
41 Director of Athletics ... Mr. Richard L. HART
06 Registrar ... Mr. John A. HALL
37 Exec Director Financial Aid ... Mr. Marc PETERSON
39 AVP Student Affairs/Dean of Housing ... Dr. Troy T. BEHRENS
13 Chief Information Officer ... Mr. Joe GARGIULO
38 Director of Counseling Services ... Dr. Cathey SOUTTER
23 Assoc Dean of Health Services ... Dr. Randy P. JONES
04 Ex Ast to Pres/Ex Dir Inst Acc/Eqt ... Ms. Samantha THOMAS
09 Director of Institutional Research ... Dr. Michael D. TUMEO
88 Treasurer/Chief Investment Officer ... Vacant
96 Director of Procurement ... Ms. Shannon BROWN
42 University Chaplain ... Dr. Stephen RANKIN
24 Asst Dean Central Univ Libraries ... Dr. Bill DWORACZYK
29 Exec Dir Alumni Relations ... Ms. Marianne B. PIEPENBURG
12 Executive Director SMU-in-Taos ... Mr. Michael ADLER
12 Interim Campus Dir SMU-in-Plano ... Mr. Jim KRAMB
104 Director Study Abroad ... Dr. Catherine WINNIE
108 Director Assessment/Accreditation ... Dr. Patricia ALVEY
18 Assoc VP Facilities Plng/Management ... Mr. Philip JABOUR
27 Exec Dir of Integrated Marketing ... Mr. Neil ROBINSON
19 Chief of Police ... Mr. Richard SHAFER
22 Dir Institutional Access and Equity ... Ms. Carolyn HERNANDEZ
07 Interim Dean of Admissions ... Mr. Byron W. LEWIS

Southwest Texas Junior College (A)

2401 Garner Field Road, Uvalde TX 78801-6221
County: Uvalde FICE Identification: 003614
Unit ID: 228316
Telephone: (830) 278-4401 Carnegie Class: Assoc/HT-High Trad
FAX Number: (830) 591-7354 Calendar System: Semester
URL: www.swtjc.edu
Established: 1946 Annual Undergrad Tuition & Fees (In-District): $2,116
Enrollment: 5,572 Coed
Affiliation or Control: Local IRS Status: 501(c)3
Highest Offering: Associate Degree
Accreditation: SC

01 President ... Dr. Hector GONZALES
11 Vice President Administrative Svcs ... Mr. Raul REYES
32 Vice President Student Services ... Mrs. Margo MATA
10 Vice President Finance ... Dr. Anne TARSKI
05 Vice President Academic Services ... Dr. Mark UNDERWOOD
30 AVP Institutional Advancement ... Vacant
12 Vice President Del Rio ... Mr. Derek M. SANDOVAL
12 Vice President Eagle Pass ... Mr. Gilbert S. BERMEA
88 Dean of College of Applied Science ... Mr. Juan Johnny C. GUZMAN
103 Dean of Workforce Education ... Ms. Romelia ARANDA
49 Dean of College of Liberal Arts ... Dr. Cheryl L. SANCHEZ
35 Director of Academic Advising ... Ms. Lorena LOPEZ
37 Director of Financial Aid ... Ms. Yvette HERNANDEZ
13 Director of Information Technology ... Mr. Scott BAKER
18 Physical Plant Director ... Mr. Jesus J. MARTINEZ
35 Director Student Success ... Ms. Randa SCHELL
15 Human Resources Coordinator ... Mr. Oscar S. GARCIA
09 Director of Institutional Research ... Ms. Carol LARUE
06 Registrar ... Mr. Luis FERNANDEZ
08 Head Librarian ... Ms. April COLE
19 Director Security/Safety ... Mr. Robert DOUCET
96 Director of Purchasing ... Ms. Maggie CAMSTRA

Southwest University at El Paso (B)

1414 Geronimo Drive, El Paso TX 79925
County: El Paso FICE Identification: 041317
Unit ID: 451556
Telephone: (915) 778-4001 Carnegie Class: Bac/Assoc-Assoc Dom
FAX Number: (915) 778-1575 Calendar System: Other
URL: www.southwestuniversity.edu
Established: 2001 Annual Undergrad Tuition & Fees: $15,000
Enrollment: 1,337 Coed
Affiliation or Control: Proprietary IRS Status: Proprietary
Highest Offering: Baccalaureate
Accreditation: ABHES, DMS, RAD

01 School Director ... Ms. Yolanda ARRIOLA

Southwestern Adventist University (C)

100 W Hillcrest Street, Keene TX 76059-0567
County: Johnson FICE Identification: 003619
Unit ID: 228468
Telephone: (817) 645-3921 Carnegie Class: Bac-Diverse
FAX Number: (817) 202-6744 Calendar System: Semester
URL: www.swau.edu
Established: 1893 Annual Undergrad Tuition & Fees: $19,916
Enrollment: 810 Coed
Affiliation or Control: Seventh-day Adventist IRS Status: 501(c)3
Highest Offering: Master's
Accreditation: SC, IACBE, NURSE

01 President ... Dr. Ken SHAW
05 VP for Academic Administration ... Dr. Amy ROSENTHAL
10 VP for Financial Administration ... Mr. Joel WALLACE
84 VP for Enrollment ... Ms. Enga ALMEIDA
32 VP for Student Services ... Mr. James THE
42 VP for Spiritual Development ... Mr. Russ LAUGHLIN
30 VP for Univ Advancement ... Mrs. Tami CONDON
09 Director of Institutional Research ... Dr. Thomas G. BUNCH
37 Asst VP for Student Finance ... Mr. Duane VALENCIA
21 Asst VP Financial Administration ... Mr. Greg A. WICKLUND
06 Registrar ... Dr. Robert GARDNER
08 Librarian ... Ms. Cristina M. THOMSEN
34 Dean of Women ... Mrs. Janelle D. WILLIAMS
33 Dean of Men ... Mr. William IVERSON
13 Dir Information Technology Svcs ... Mr. E. Charles LEWIS
18 Plant Engineer ... Mr. Dale E. HAINEY
26 Director of Marketing ... Ms. Darcy FORCE
29 Director of Alumni Relations ... Vacant
38 Director of Counseling & Testing ... Dr. R. Mark ALDRIDGE
22 Director of Disability Services ... Mrs. Dorie CRUZ
88 Dir Ctr for Acad Success/Advising ... Dr. Andrew SMITH
07 Director of Admissions ... Ms. Rahneeka HAZELTON
15 Director of Human Resources ... Mrs. Denise RIVERA
19 Director Security/Safety ... Mr. Sean AMOS

Southwestern Assemblies of God University (D)

1200 Sycamore, Waxahachie TX 75165-2397
County: Ellis FICE Identification: 003616
Unit ID: 228325
Telephone: (972) 937-4010 Carnegie Class: Masters/S
FAX Number: (972) 923-0488 Calendar System: Semester
URL: www.sagu.edu
Established: 1927 Annual Undergrad Tuition & Fees: $19,180
Enrollment: 1,984 Coed
Affiliation or Control: Assemblies Of God Church IRS Status: 501(c)3
Highest Offering: Doctorate
Accreditation: SC, IACBE

01 President ... Dr. Kermit S. BRIDGES
05 Vice President for Academics ... Dr. Paul BROOKS
32 Vice President for Student Develop ... Rev. Terry PHIPPS
10 Vice Pres for Business & Finance ... Rev. David W. WILLEMSEN
30 Vice President for Univ Advancement ... Rev. Irby MCKNIGHT
84 Vice Pres Enrollment & Retention ... Rev. Eddie DAVIS
20 Dean of Academic Services ... Rev. Donny LUTRICK
58 Dean of Graduate Studies ... Dr. Robert HARDEN
73 Dean Col Bible & Church Ministries ... Dr. Michael CLARENSAU
50 Dean Col of Business & Education ... Dr. Larry GOODRICH
64 Dean Col of Music & Comm Arts ... Mr. Del GUYNES
09 Assoc Dean of Inst Effectiveness ... Dr. Kim BERNECKER
106 Asst Dean for Distance Education ... Rev. Joseph HARTMAN
06 Registrar ... Ms. Heather FRANCIS
35 Dean of Students ... Rev. Lance MECHE
88 Director of Learning Centers ... Mr. Nolan JONES
13 Sr Dir Information Technology ... Mr. James GRISSOM
29 Director of Alumni Relations ... Mr. Devin FERGUSON
08 Director of Learning Resources ... Mr. Eugene HOLDER
14 Director of Campus Software ... Mr. Mark WALKER
21 Dir of Business Services ... Mr. Landon ORRILL
88 Senior Director of Accounting ... Ms. Candee LUTRICK
37 Sr Director of Financial Aid ... Mr. Jeff FRANCIS
19 Director of Security ... Mr. Ron CRANE
07 Assistant Dean of Admissions ... Mr. Joshua MARTIN
24 Director of Media Services ... Mr. John COOKMAN
88 Director of Accounts Receivable ... Mr. Chris BACA
36 Director of Career Services ... Ms. Beverly ROBINSON
41 Athletic Director ... Mr. Jesse GODDING
26 Director of University Marketing ... Mr. Ryan MCELHANY
15 Director of Human Resources ... Mrs. Ruth ROBERTS
88 Director of Educator Cert ... Ms. Janice WHITAKER
38 Counselor ... Dr. Tim MYERS
88 Admissions Counselor ... Ms. Pat THOMPSON
88 Director of On Campus Admissions ... Mr. Joshua DUNN
88 Director of Online Admissions ... Mr. Jarrod PACE
04 Executive Asst to President ... Ms. Patricia BROOKS

Southwestern Baptist Theological Seminary (E)

PO Box 22607, Fort Worth TX 76122-0150
County: Tarrant FICE Identification: 003617
Unit ID: 228477
Telephone: (817) 923-1921 Carnegie Class: Not Classified
FAX Number: (817) 921-8766 Calendar System: Semester
URL: www.swbts.edu
Established: 1908 Annual Undergrad Tuition & Fees: N/A
Enrollment: N/A Coed
Affiliation or Control: Southern Baptist IRS Status: 501(c)3
Highest Offering: Doctorate
Accreditation: SC, MUS, THEOL

01 President ... Dr. Paige PATTERSON
05 Executive Vice President/Provost ... Dr. Craig A. BLAISING
10 Vice Pres Business Administration ... Mr. Kevin ENSLEY
30 Vice Pres Institutional Advancement ... Mr. Mike C. HUGHES
32 Vice Pres for Student Services/Comm ... Dr. Steven SMITH
45 Vice Pres of Strategic Initiatives ... Dr. Charles PATRICK
108 Assoc VP Inst Assessment ... Dr. Mark LEEDS
73 Dean of the School of Theology ... Dr. Jeffrey BINGHAM
53 Dean Sch of Church & Fam Ministries ... Dr. Waylan OWENS
64 Dean School of Church Music ... Dr. Leo DAY
12 Dean Havard Sch for Theol Studies ... Dr. Denny AUTREY
73 Dean Sch of Evangelism & Missions ... Dr. Keith EITEL
49 Dean College at Southwestern ... Dr. Mike WILKINSON
94 Dean of Women's Programs ... Dr. Terri STOVALL
56 Dean Center for Extension Education ... Dr. Deron BILES
88 Dean of the School of Preaching ... Mr. David ALLEN
35 Dean of Students ... Mr. Kyle WALKER

Southwestern Christian College (F)

Box 10, Terrell TX 75160-9002
County: Kaufman FICE Identification: 003618
Unit ID: 228486
Telephone: (972) 524-3341 Carnegie Class: Bac/Assoc-Assoc Dom
FAX Number: (972) 563-7133 Calendar System: Semester
URL: www.swcc.edu
Established: 1949 Annual Undergrad Tuition & Fees: $7,764
Enrollment: 164 Coed
Affiliation or Control: Churches Of Christ IRS Status: 501(c)3
Highest Offering: Baccalaureate
Accreditation: SC

01 President ... Dr. Jack EVANS, SR.
30 Vice President for Instl Expansion ... Dr. James MAXWELL
05 Vice President Academic Affairs ... Mrs. Zoa Ann TURNER
10 Vice President Fiscal Affairs ... Mr. Douglas HOWIE
32 Vice President Student Affairs ... Mr. Ben FOSTER
08 Librarian ... Mrs. Doris JOHNSON
07 Director of Admissions ... Mr. Warren ROBERTS
37 Director of Financial Aid ... Ms. Tonya DEAN
44 Director of Development ... Mr. Jack EVANS, JR.

Southwestern University (G)

1001 E University Avenue, Georgetown TX 78626-6144
County: Williamson FICE Identification: 003620
Unit ID: 228343
Telephone: (512) 863-6511 Carnegie Class: Bac-A&S
FAX Number: (512) 863-5788 Calendar System: Semester
URL: www.southwestern.edu
Established: 1840 Annual Undergrad Tuition & Fees: $37,560
Enrollment: 1,538 Coed
Affiliation or Control: United Methodist IRS Status: 501(c)3
Highest Offering: Baccalaureate
Accreditation: SC, MUS

01 President ... Dr. Edward B. BURGER
42 University Chaplain ... Rev. Megan DANNER
04 Dir Admin Svcs for Pres & Trustees ... Ms. Meaghan M. MCCLELLAN
05 Dean of Faculty ... Dr. Alisa GAUNDER
32 Vice President for Student Life ... Ms. Jaime WOODY
13 VP for Information Services and CIO ... Dr. Pam MCQUESTEN
10 VP for Finance and Administration ... Mr. Craig ERWIN
30 Vice Pres for University Relations ... Mr. Paul SECORD
20 Assoc VP Academic Administration ... Ms. Julie A. COWLEY
26 Chief Marketing Officer ... Vacant
15 Assoc VP for Human Resources ... Ms. Elma F. BENAVIDES
39 Dean of Students/Dir Resident Life ... Vacant
29 Assoc VP for Alumni & Parents ... Ms. Megan FRISQUE
41 Assoc VP/Dir Intercollegiate Athl ... Dr. Glada C. MUNT
21 Controller ... Ms. Brenda THOMPSON
19 Chief of Police ... Mr. Brad DUNN
37 Director of Financial Aid ... Mr. James GAETA
36 Director Career Services ... Mr. Daniel OROZCO
20 Assoc Dir Academic Success ... Mr. David SEILER
88 Dir Paideia Program/Assoc Professor ... Dr. Sherry E. ADRIAN
85 Director Intercultural Learning ... Ms. Tisha TEMPLE
09 Director Institutional Research ... Vacant
28 Asst Dean Multicultural Affairs ... Ms. Terri JOHNSON
31 Director Civic Engagement ... Dr. Sarah BRACKMANN
07 Director of Admission ... Mr. Robert BALDWIN
08 Dir of Library Resources ... Ms. Amy ANDERSON
84 Dean of Enrollment Services ... Ms. Christine D. BOWMAN
91 Director Administrative Computing ... Ms. Jennifer O'DANIEL

Stephen F. Austin State University (H)

2008 Alumni Drive, Rusk 206,
Nacogdoches TX 75961-3940
County: Nacogdoches FICE Identification: 003624
Unit ID: 228431
Telephone: (936) 468-2011 Carnegie Class: Masters/L
FAX Number: (936) 468-2202 Calendar System: Semester
URL: www.sfasu.edu
Established: 1921 Annual Undergrad Tuition & Fees (In-State): $7,560
Enrollment: 12,801 Coed
Affiliation or Control: State IRS Status: 501(c)3
Highest Offering: Doctorate
Accreditation: SC, AAFCS, ART, BUS, CAATE, CACREP, CEA, CIDA, CORE, CS, DIETD, DIETI, MUS, NUR, SP, SW, TED, THEA

01 President ... Dr. Baker PATTILLO
05 Provost/VP Academic Affairs ... Dr. Stephen A. BULLARD
10 Vice Pres Finance/Administration ... Dr. Danny R. GALLANT
32 Vice Pres for University Affairs ... Dr. Steve WESTBROOK

30 Vice Pres University Advancement ... Ms. Jill STILL
29 Exec Director Alumni ... Mr. Craig A. TURNAGE
20 Assoc Provost/VP Academic Affairs ... Dr. Mary Nelle BRUNSON
84 Exec Dir of Enrollment Management ... Ms. Monique COSSICH
26 Exec Dir Univ Mktg Comm ... Ms. Shirley A. LUNA
43 General Counsel ... Mr. Damon DERRICK
06 Registrar ... Ms. Lynda LANGHAM
09 Director Institutional Research ... Ms. Karyn HALL
08 Library Director ... Ms. Shirley DICKERSON
39 Director of Residence Life ... Mr. Winston BAKER
18 Director of Physical Plant ... Mr. Lee BRITTAIN
37 Director of Financial Aid ... Ms. Rachele GARRETT
22 Director Affirmative Action ... Vacant
13 Director of ITS ... Mr. Paul DAVIS
15 Director of Human Resources ... Vacant
19 Chief of University Police ... Mr. Marc COSSICH
23 Director Health Services ... Vacant
41 Director of Intercol Athletics ... Mr. Robert W. HILL
35 Dean Student Affairs ... Dr. Adam PECK
36 Director of Counseling ... Ms. Jill MILEM
96 Director of Procurement ... Ms. Kay JOHNSON
46 Dir Research/Sponsored Programs ... Vacant
58 Dean Graduate School ... Dr. Richard BERRY
49 Dean College Liberal/Applied Arts ... Dr. Brian MURPHY
47 Dean College Forestry/Agriculture ... Vacant
53 Dean of College of Education ... Dr. Judy A. ABBOTT
57 Dean College Fine Arts ... Dr. A.C. (Buddy) HIMES
50 Dean College of Business ... Dr. Timothy BISPING
81 Dean College Sciences & Math ... Dr. Kimberly M. CHILDS
04 Special Asst to President ... Ms. Susan H. WILLLIAMS
101 Coordinator of Board Affairs ... Ms. Judith P. BUCKINGHAM
102 Exec Director of Development ... Dr. Joel L. TURNER, III
104 Director International Programs ... Ms. Heather CATTON
105 University Webmaster ... Mr. Jason L. JOHNSTONE
106 Director Instructional Technology ... Dr. Randy MCDONALD
108 Director Institutional Assessment ... Dr. Larry J. KING
38 Asst Dean Stdnt Affairs Support ... Dr. Michael E. WALKER
07 Associate Director of Admissions ... Mr. Kevin L. DAVIS

Tarrant County College District (A)

1500 Houston Street, Fort Worth TX 76102-6599
County: Tarrant FICE Identification: 003626
Unit ID: 228547
Telephone: (817) 515-5100 Carnegie Class: Assoc/HT-Mix Trad/Non
FAX Number: (817) 515-5350 Calendar System: Semester
URL: www.tccd.edu
Established: 1965 Annual Undergrad Tuition & Fees (In-District): $1 320
Enrollment: 50,595 Coed
Affiliation or Control: State/Local IRS Status: 501(c)3
Highest Offering: Associate Degree
Accreditation: **SC**, ACFEI, ADNUR, CAHIIM, COARC, CONST, DH, DIETT, EMT, PTAA, RAD, SURGT

01 Chancellor ... Dr. Eugene V. GIOVANNINI
11 Vice Chanc Admin and Gen Counsel ... Mrs. Angela ROBINSON
10 Vice Chancellor for Finance ... Mr. Mark MCCLENDON
13 Vice Chanc Inst Intel & Technology ... Vacant
05 Vice Chanc Acad Affs/Stdnt Success ... Dr. L. Joy GATES BLACK
18 Vice Chanc Real Estate/Facilities ... Ms. Nina PETTY
26 VC Communications/External Affairs ... Mr. Reginald GATES
20 VP Academic Affairs SO ... Dr. Dana GROVE
20 VP Academic Affairs NE ... Linda s. BRADDY
20 VP Academic Affairs NW ... Dr. Leann ELLIS
20 VP Academic Affairs SE ... Dr. Zena JACKSON
20 VP Academic Affairs TR ... Dr. Bryan STEWART
20 VP Academic Affairs TCC Connect ... Dr. Kelvin BENTLEY
32 VP Student Dev Services NE ... Dr. Magdalena DELA TEJA
32 VP Student Dev Services SE ... Dr. Lyvier LEFFLER
32 VP Student Dev Services SO ... Dr. Larry RIDEAUX
32 VP Student Dev Services TR ... Mr. Adrian RODRIGUEZ
32 VP Student Dev Services NW ... Dr. Joe RODE
32 VP Acad Outreach & SS TCC Connect ... Dr. Aubra J. GANNT
12 President South Campus ... Dr. Peter JORDAN
12 President Northwest Campus ... Dr. Elva C. LEBLANC
12 President Northeast Campus ... Dr. Allen GOBEN
12 President Southeast Campus ... Dr. William COPPOLA
12 President Trinity River Campus ... Dr. Stephen S. MADISON
12 President TCC Connect ... Dr. Carlos MORALES
84 Assoc Vice Chanc Enrollment Svcs ... Mr. David XIMENEZ
88 Assoc Vice Chanc Student Success ... Dr. Jade BORNE
15 Assoc Vice Chanc Human Resources ... Dr. Ricardo CORONADO
25 Assoc Vice Chanc Grants Dev/Compl ... Ms. Jackie MAKI
21 Assoc Vice Chancellor Finance ... Mrs. Nancy H. CHANG
20 Assoc Vice Chanc Academic Affairs ... Dr. Nancy CURE
103 Assoc Vice Chanc Econ/Workforce Dev ... Mr. Benjamin RAND
30 Executive Director of Development ... Dr. Joe MCINTOSH
09 Exec Dir Inst Intell Research ... Dr. Rosemary REYNOLDS
27 Exec Dir Comm PR Mkt ... Ms. Suzanne COTTRAUX
18 Assoc Vice Chan Real Estate/Facs ... Mr. Gary PREATHER
19 Chief of Police ... Mr. Shaun WILLIAMS
20 Dist Reg & Dir Academic Supp Svcs ... Mr. John D. SPENCER
88 Exec Dir International Initiatives ... Dr. Sheryl O. HARRIS
08 Director Library Services NE ... Mr. Mark DOLIVE
08 Director Library Services SO ... Ms. Linda JENSON
08 Director Library Services NW ... Ms. Kristyn S. HELGE
08 Director Library Services SE ... Ms. Jotisa KLEMM
08 Director Library Services TR ... Ms. Suzanne BECKETT
06 Registrar South Campus ... Mr. Samuel (Tex) RUEGG
06 Registrar Northeast Campus ... Mr. Brian D. BARRETT
06 Registrar Northwest Campus ... Ms. Rebecca (Becki) GRIFFITH
06 Registrar Southeast Campus ... Mr. Juan C. TORRES
06 Registrar Trinity Campus ... Mr. Vikas RAJPUROHIT
38 Director of Counseling SO ... Ms. Ticiy MEDLEY
38 Director of Counseling NE ... Dr Condoa PARRENT
38 Director of Counseling NW ... Dr. Charles (Ricks) EDMONDSON
38 Director of Counseling SE ... Dr. Michael DUPONT
38 Director of Counseling TR ... Dr. Louann T SCHULZE
37 District Director Financial Aid ... Ms. Samantha STALNAKER
37 Director of Financial Aid SO ... Ms. JoLynn H. SPROLE
37 Director of Financial Aid NE ... Ms. Mary BLEDSOE
37 Director of Financial Aid NW ... Ms. Trina SMITH-PATTERSON
37 Director of Financial Aid SE ... Ms. Elizabeth LANDWERMEYER
37 Director of Financial Aid TR ... Mr. William MCMULLEN
35 Dir Student Develop Svcs NE ... Mr. Victor BALLESTEROS
35 Dir Student Develop Svcs SO ... Dr. Jared M. COBB
35 Dir Student Develop Svcs NW ... Dr. Vesta M. MARTINEZ
35 Dir Student Develop Svcs SE ... Mr. Douglas C. PEAK
35 Dir Student Develop Svcs TR ... Vacant
96 Director of Business Services ... Mrs. Kathy M. CRUSTO-WAY
96 Exec Dir of Procurement ... Mr. Michael (Mike) HERNDON
18 Exec Dir Inst Strategic Development ... Ms. Margaret K. LUTTON
07 Dist Dir of Admissions & Records ... Ms. Nichole MANCONE
28 Dir of Inst Div & Inclusion ... Mr Andrew DUFFIELD
29 Alumni and Comm Specialist ... Ms. Gloria FISHER

Temple College (B)

2600 S First Street, Temple TX 76504-7435
County: Bell FICE Identification: 003627
Unit ID: 228608
Telephone: (254) 298-8282 Carnegie Class: Assoc/-T-High Trad
FAX Number: (254) 298-8266 Calendar System: Semester
URL: www.templec.edu
Established: 1926 Annual Undergrad Tuition & Fees (In-District): $2.268
Enrollment: 5,200 Coed
Affiliation or Control: Local IRS Status: 501(c)3
Highest Offering: Associate Degree
Accreditation: **SC**, ADNUR, COARC, DH, DMS, EMT, SURGT

01 President ... Dr. Glenda C. BARRON
05 Vice Pres of Educational Services ... Dr. Mark A. SMITH
13 AVP Finance/Information Tech Svcs ... Mr. Gary JACKSON
10 Vice Pres Administrative Svcs/CIO ... Dr. Van MILLER
31 AVP Acad Outreach & Ext Programs ... Dr. Dan SPENCER
15 Assoc VP Resource Management ... Dr. Randy BACA
09 AVP Comm Init & Spec Programs ... Dr. Jimmy ROBERTS
106 Dir Web Applications & System ... Mr. Joe TEAKELL
84 Div Dir Student & Enrollment Svcs ... Mrs. Carey ROSE
08 Div Director of Learning Resources ... Mr. Kevin HENARD
102 Exec Dir Temple College Foundation ... Mrs Jennifer GRAHAM
38 Director Student Advising ... Ms. Amy FLINN
04 Assistant to the President & Board ... Mrs Judith DOHNALIK
37 Director of Financial Aid ... Ms. Peggy WATTS
26 Director Marketing & Media Relation ... Ms. Ellen DAVIS
18 Dir Facilities/Physical Plant ... Mr. Skeet POWELL
96 Director of Purchasing ... Mr. Brian SUPAK
32 Director Student Life ... Mrs. Ruth BRIDGES
06 Registrar ... Mrs. Toni CUELLAR
41 Athletic Director ... Mr. Craig MCMURTRY
19 Chief of Police ... Mr Michael MARKUM

Texarkana College (C)

2500 N Robison Road, Texarkana TX 75501-3099
County: Bowie FICE Identification: 003628
Unit ID: 228699
Telephone: (903) 823-3456 Carnegie Class: Assoc/HVT-Mix Trad/Non
FAX Number: (903) 823-3451 Calendar System: Semester
URL: www.texarkanacollege.edu
Established: 1927 Annual Undergrad Tuition & Fees (In-District): $1,952
Enrollment: 4,061 Coed
Affiliation or Control: Local IRS Status: 501(c)3
Highest Offering: Associate Degree
Accreditation: **SC**, ADNUR

01 President ... Mr James H. RUSSELL
05 Vice President of Instruction ... Mrs. Donna MCDANIEL
10 Chief Finance Officer ... Mrs. Kim JONES
32 Dean of Students ... Mr. Robert JONES
13 Chief Info Technology Officer ... Mr. Mike DUMDEI
30 Director Foundation/Development ... Mrs. Katie ANDRUS
09 Director Inst Rsrch & Effectiveness ... Mrs. Phyllis DEESE
18 Director Facilities Services ... Mr. Rick BOYETTE
26 Director Inst Adv/Public Relations ... Mrs. Suzy IRWIN
88 Director KTXK Radio ... Mr. Steve MITCHELL
15 Director Human Resources ... Mrs. Phyllis DEESE
103 Dean Workforce & Cont Education ... Mrs. Ronda DOZIER
81 Dean STEM ... Dr Catherine HOWARD
76 Dean Health Sciences ... Mrs. Courtney SHOALMIRE
49 Dean Liberal & Performing Arts ... Mrs. Mary E. YOUNG
07 Director of Admissions ... Mr. Lee WILLIAMS
88 Director Advising & Registration ... Dr. Lori ROCHELLE
08 Director Library/Student Support ... Dr. Tonja MACKEY
06 Registrar ... Mr Brandon HIGGINS
37 Director Student Financial Aid ... Mrs. Susan JOHNSTON
04 Presidential Events Coordinator ... Mrs. Mindy PRESTON

*The Texas A & M University System Office (D)

301 Tarrow Street, 7th Floor, College Station TX 77840
County: Brazos FICE Identification: 003629
Unit ID: 228732
Telephone: (979) 458-6000 Carnegie Class: N/A
FAX Number: (979) 458-6044
URL: www.tamus.edu

01 Chancellor ... Mr. John SHARP
05 Vice Chanc for Academic Affairs ... Dr. James HALLMARK
86 Vice Chanc for Federal & State Rels ... Mr. Tommy WILLIAMS
10 Exec VC & Chief Financial Officer ... Mr. Billy HAMILTON
26 Vice Chanc for Marketing & Comm ... Mr. Laylan COPELIN
88 Chief Auditor ... Mr. Charlie HRNCIR
43 General Counsel ... Mr. Ray BONILLA
46 Vice Chancellor for Research ... Dr. Jon MOGFORD
21 Vice Chanc for Business Affairs ... Mr. Phillip RAY
13 Chief Information Officer ... Mr. Mark STONE
21 Treasurer ... Ms. Maria ROBINSON
100 Exec Assistant to the Chancellor ... Ms. Stephanie BJUNE

*Prairie View A & M University (E)

P.O. Box 519, Prairie View TX 77446-0519
County: Waller FICE Identification: 003630
Unit ID: 227526
Telephone: (936) 261-3311 Carnegie Class: DU-Mod
FAX Number: (936) 261-2115 Calendar System: Semester
URL: www.pvamu.edu
Established: 1876 Annual Undergrad Tuition & Fees (In-State): $9,745
Enrollment: 8,429 Coed
Affiliation or Control: State IRS Status: 501(c)3
Highest Offering: Doctorate
Accreditation: **SC**, BUS, CS, DIETD, DIETI, ENG, ENGT, MUS, NUR, NURSE, SW

02 President ... Dr. George C. WRIGHT
05 Provost/Sr VP Academic Affairs ... Dr. Felicia M. NAVE
20 Assoc Prov & Assoc VP Acad Afairs ... Dr. James J. WILSON, JR.
10 Sr Vice President Business Affairs ... Dr. Corey S. BRADFORD, SR.
32 VP for Student Affs/Inst Relations ... Dr. Lauretta F. BYARS
46 Vice Pres Research/Dean Grad School ... Dr. Cajetan M. AKUJUOBI
109 Vice Pres Auxiliary Services ... Mr. Fred E. WASHINGTON
11 Vice President Administration ... Dr. Michael L. MCFRAZIER
100 Chief of Staff ... Dr. Michael L. MCFRAZIER
84 Assoc Provost Enrollment Mgmt ... Mr. Don BYARS
88 Asst VP for Financial Accounting ... Mr. Rod MIRELES
88 Asst VP for Financial Services ... Ms. Patricia BAUGHMAN
92 Director of Honors Program ... Dr. James J. WILSON, JR.
109 Asst VP Auxiliary Enterprises ... Ms. Tressey D. WILSON
30 Director of Development ... Vacant
09 Director Institutional Research ... Mr. Dean WILLIAMSON
07 Int Dir of Undergraduate Admissions ... Ms. Lenice BROWN
18 Int Assistant VP of Physical Plant ... Mr. Charles MUSE
08 Director of Library ... Dr. Rosie L. ALBRITTON
15 Director of Human Resources ... Ms. Radhika AYYAR
37 Director of Financial Aid ... Vacant
36 Program Coord Residence Life ... Mr. Charles E. CROCKETT
63 Director Undergrad Med Acad ... Dr. Dennis E. DANIELS
41 Director of Athletics ... Mr. Ashley N. ROBINSON
13 Chief Information Officer ... Mr. Rodney MOORE
58 Dean of the Graduate School ... Dr. Willie F. TROTTY
50 Dean College of Business ... Dr. Munir QUDDUS
53 Acting Dean College of Education ... Dr. Sarina PHILLIPS
54 Dean College of Engineering ... Dr. Kendall T. HARRIS
47 Dean Col Agriculture/Human Sci ... Dr. Alton B. JOHNSON
66 Dean College of Nursing ... Dr. Betty ADAMS
49 Dean College of Arts & Sciences ... Dr. Danny R. KELLEY
48 Dean School of Architecture ... Dr. Ikhlas SABOUNI
88 Dean Col of Juv Just/Psychology ... Dr. Tamara L. BROWN
21 Director of Treasury Services ... Ms. Equilla JACKSON
23 Director Health Center ... Ms. Thelma J. PIERRE
56 Administrator Coop Extension ... Dr. Carolyn J. WILLIAMS
19 Chief of Police ... Ms. Zena A. STEPHENS
29 Alumni/Special Events Officer ... Ms. Carol CAMPBELL
06 Registrar/Records ... Ms. Deborah J. DUNGEY
12 Exec Dir University College ... Ms. Lettie M. RAAB
28 Director of Diversity ... Ms. Elma D. GONZALEZ
85 Immigration Services Coord ... Mrs. Evelyn J. MCGINTY
96 Procurement Sup/HUB Coordinator ... Mr. Jim A. NELMS
88 Director Budget & Reconciliation ... Mrs. Diane T. EVANS

*Tarleton State University (F)

1333 W Washington, Box T-0001,
Stephenville TX 76402-0001
County: Erath FICE Identification: 003631
Unit ID: 228529
Telephone: (254) 968-9000 Carnegie Class: Masters/L
FAX Number: (254) 968-9920 Calendar System: Semester
URL: www.tarleton.edu
Established: 1899 Annual Undergrad Tuition & Fees (In-State): $6,630
Enrollment 11 681 Coed
Affiliation or Control: State IRS Status: 501(c)3
Highest Offering: Doctorate
Accreditation: **SC**, ACBSP, DMOLS, ENG, HT, MLTAD, MT, MUS, NURSE, SW

02 President ... Dr. F. Dominic DOTTAVIO
100 Chief of Staff ... Dr. David WEISSENBURGER
05 Provost/Exec VPAA ... Dr. Karen MURRAY
30 Vice Pres Inst Advancement ... Dr. Kyle W. MCGREGOR
10 Vice Pres Finance/Administration ... Mr. Tye MINCKLER
32 VP Student Life/Dean Students ... Ms. Laura BOREN
84 Assoc VP Enrollment/Info Mgmt ... Dr. Javier GARZA
20 Assoc VP for Academic Affairs ... Dr. Dwayne SNIDER
36 Director of Career Services ... Ms. Alana HEFNER
46 Exec Dir Office of Faculty Research ... Dr. Roger WITTIE
18 Director of Facilities ... Mr. Aaron WAND
21 Asst VP Finance/Controller ... Ms. Lori BEATY

35 AVP Student Success/Multicul Init ....Dr. Jennifer T. EDWARDS
26 Assoc VP Marketing/Communications .... Ms. Janice HORAK
35 Asst VP Student Life Studies ....Dr. Ashley TULL
49 Dean College Science & Technology .... Dr. James PIERCE
50 Dean Col of Business Administration .... Dr. Steve STEED
47 Dean Col Agricul & Environ Sciences .... Dr. Steve DAMRON
53 Dean College of Education ....Dr. Jordan BARKLEY
57 Dean College Liberal/Fine Arts .... Ms. Kelli STYRON
58 Dean College of Graduate Studies .... Dr. Barry LAMBERT
07 Director Undergraduate Admissions ....Ms. Cynthia HESS
22 Dir Student Disability Services ....Ms. Trina GEYE
08 University Librarian ....Mrs. Donna SAVAGE
31 Asst VP External Relations .... Ms. Janice HORAK
37 Director Student Financial Aid .... Ms. Kathy PURVIS
09 Director Institutional Research ....Dr. Mike HAYNES
13 CIO/Exec Dir Information Tech Svcs .... Ms. Rebecca GRAY
15 Asst VP Employee Services .... Ms. Angela C. BROWN
35 Asst VP for Student Life ....Ms. Darla DOTY
41 Athletic Director ....Mr. Lonn REISMAN
23 Director Student Health Center ....Ms. Bridgette BEDNARZ
19 University Police Chief ....Mr. Matt WELCH
88 Exec Dir of Student Engagement .... Mr. Darrell BROWN
28 Dir Ofc Diversity/Inclusion ....Dr. Lora HELVIE-MASON
24 Dir Center for Instr Innovation .... Dr. Kelli SHAFFER
44 Asst VP of Advancement ....Ms. Sabra GUERRA
104 Dir International Academic Programs ......Dr. Marilyn ROBITAILLE
06 Registrar ....Mr. David SUTTON
96 Director of Purchasing/HUB ....Ms. Elaine CHEW
25 Contract Specialist ....Ms. Kim MEDFORD
40 Manager Campus Store .... Ms. Carrie MCCANN
105 Web Administrator ....Ms. Daphne HUNT
04 Administrative Asst to President .... Ms. Tauna BERTSCH
29 Director Alumni Relations .... Ms. Jessica EVANS

*Texas A & M International University (A)

5201 University Boulevard, Laredo TX 78041-1900

County: Webb FICE Identification: 009651
Unit ID: 226152
Telephone: (956) 326-2001 Carnegie Class: Masters/L
FAX Number: (956) 326-2348 Calendar System: Semester
URL: www.tamiu.edu
Established: 1969 Annual Undergrad Tuition & Fees (In-State): $6,635
Enrollment: 7,554 Coed
Affiliation or Control: State IRS Status: 501(c)3
Highest Offering: Doctorate
Accreditation: SC, BUS, NUR, SPAA

02 Interim President ....Dr. Pablo ARENAZ
05 Interim Provost ....Dr. Thomas R. MITCHELL
10 Vice Pres Finance & Administration ...Mr. Juan J. CASTILLO, JR.
30 Vice Pres Institutional Advancement .... Ms. Rosanne PALACIOS
32 Vice Pres for Student Success .... Dr. Minita RAMIREZ
11 Assoc Vice Pres for Administration ....Mr. Trevor C. LIDDLE
88 Assoc Vice Pres for Compliance ....Mrs. Lisa M. PAUL
13 Assoc VP Information Technology/CIO ... Dr. Leebrian E. GASKINS
88 Associate Provost ....Dr. Kevin D. LINDBERG
49 Dean College Arts & Sciences .... Dr. Claudia E. SAN MIGUEL
50 Dean AR Sanchez Jr Sch of Business ....Dr. Steve R. SEARS
66 Dean Canseco School of Nursing ....Dr. Glenda C. WALKER
08 Dir Sue & Radcliffe Killam Library .... Mr. Douglas M. FERRIER
07 Director Admissions ....Mrs. Rosie A. DICKINSON
06 University Registrar ....Mr. Juan G. GARCIA, JR.
15 Director of Human Resources ....Ms. Martha O. GONZALEZ
26 Director Public Rels Mktg/Info Svcs ....Mr. Steve K. HARMON
37 Director Financial Aid ....Mrs. Laura M. ELIZONDO
41 Director of Athletics .... Mr. Gilbert G. ZIMMERMANN
18 Director Physical Plant .... Mr. Roberto A. GARZA
29 Director Alumni Relations ....Mrs. Yelitza M. HOWARD
36 Executive Director Career Services .. Mrs. Cassandra L. WHEELER
23 Interim Dir of SHS/Cl Asst Prof ....Ms. Angelica M. MICHELANGELI
39 Director of Residence Life/Housing .... Ms. Mirasol TABAREZ
38 Dir Student Couns/Disb Svcs ....Ms. Aracely C. HERNANDEZ
96 Dir Purchasing & Support Services .... Ms. Ann E. GUTIERREZ
92 Assoc Prof Director Honors Pgm ..... Dr. Deborah L. BLACKWELL
21 Comptroller ....Ms. Elena M. MARTINEZ
35 Associate VP of Student Affairs ....Vacant
88 Dir Recruitment/School Relations ....Ms. Scheiby C. FISHER
88 Assoc Dir Student Orien Lead Engage .....Mr. Miguel A. TREVINO
09 Director of Institutional Research ....Ms. Elizabeth MARTINEZ
108 Assoc VP Institutional Assessment ....Dr. Karyn E. MILLER
54 Dean of University College ....Dr. Catheryn J. WEITMAN

*Texas A & M University (B)

1246 TAMU, College Station TX 77843-1246

County: Brazos FICE Identification: 003632
Unit ID: 228723
Telephone: (979) 845-2217 Carnegie Class: DU-Highest
FAX Number: (979) 845-5027 Calendar System: Semester
URL: www.tamu.edu
Established: 1876 Annual Undergrad Tuition & Fees (In-State): $10,176
Enrollment: 61,642 Coed
Affiliation or Control: State IRS Status: 501(c)3
Highest Offering: Doctorate
Accreditation: SC, BUS, BUSA, CAATE, CEA, CLPSY, CONST, COPSY, CS, DENT, DH, DIETD, DIETI, ENG, ENGT, FEPAC, HSA, IPSY, LAW, LSAR, MED, NRPA, NURSE, PH, PLNG, SCPSY, SPAA, VET

02 President .... Mr. Michael K. YOUNG
05 Provost/Exec Vice President ....Dr. Karan L. WATSON
03 Interim Senior Vice President HSC .... Dr. Paul E. OGDEN
10 Sr VP Finance & Admin (CFO) ....Dr. Jerry STRAWSER
26 Sr VP Marketing/Communications ....Ms. Amy B. SMITH
13 Vice President IT & CIO ....Ms. M. Dee CHILDS
15 VP HR & Org Effectiveness .... Dr. Barbara A. ABERCROMBIE
32 Vice President Student Affairs ....Dr. Daniel J. PUGH, SR.
46 Vice President Research ....Dr. Glen A. LAINE
86 Vice Pres Governmental Relations .... Mr. Michael O'QUINN
26 Vice President Brand & Business Dev .... Mr. Shane HINCKLEY
12 Int VP TAMU/Pres TAMU-Galveston ....Dr. Douglas J. PALMER
28 Vice Pres/Assoc Prov Diversity ....Dr. Christine A. STANLEY
20 Vice Provost for Academic Affairs ....Dr. Michael BENEDIK
43 Deputy General Counsel ....Mr. Scott A. KELLY
47 Dean Agriculture & Life Science ....Dr. Mark A. HUSSEY
48 Dean Architecture .... Dr. Jorge VANEGAS
50 Dean Business ....Dr. Eli JONES
52 Dean Dentistry ....Dr. Lawrence E. WOLINSKY
53 Dean Education & Human Development .... Dr. Joyce M. ALEXANDER
54 Dean Engineering ....Dr. M. Katherine BANKS
65 Dean Geosciences ....Dr. Kate C. MILLER
80 Dean Govt & Public Policy ....Gen. Mark A. WELSH, III
61 Dean Law .... Dr. Andrew P. MORRISS
49 Dean Liberal Arts ....Dr. Pamela R. MATTHEWS
63 Interim Dean Medicine ....Dr. Paul E. OGDEN
66 Dean Nursing ....Dr. Sharon A. WILKERSON
67 Dean Pharmacy .... Dr. Indra K. REDDY
69 Dean Public Health .... Dr. Jay MADDOCK
81 Dean Science .... Dr. Meigan C. ARONSON
74 Dean Vet Med & Biomed Sciences ....Dr. Eleanor M. GREEN
08 Dean/Director Libraries .... Mr. David H. CARLSON
88 Dir Inst Biosciences & Tech ....Dr. Cheryl L. WALKER
12 Dean & COO TAMU Qatar ....Dr. Cesar MALAVE
20 Dean of Faculties/Assoc Prov ....Dr. John R. AUGUST
20 Assoc Prov Undergrad Studies ....Dr. Ann KENIMER
107 Assoc Prov Grad & Prof Studies ....Dr. Karen L. BUTLER-PURRY
07 Dir Admissions/Asst VP Acad Svcs .... Mr. Scott MCDONALD
37 Exec Dir Student Financial Aid ....Ms. Delisa F. FALKS
06 Registrar .... Ms. Venesa A. HEIDICK
36 Exec Dir Career Center ....Dr. J. Leigh TURNER
14 Exec Dir Computing & Info Svcs .... Mr. Pete MARCHBANKS
23 Director Student Health Center ....Dr. Martha C. DANNENBAUM
38 Exec Dir Student Counseling Svcs ....Dr. Maggie GARTNER
39 Director Residence Life/Housing ....Ms. Chareny L. RYDL
92 Exec Director Honors Programs ....Dr. Sumana DATTA
104 Director Study Abroad ....Dr. Jane FLAHERTY
96 Exec Director Strategic Sourcing ....Mr. Rex JANNE
09 Exec Dir Data & Research Svcs ....Dr. David J. MARTIN
102 President Texas A&M Foundation ....Mr. Tyson VOELKEL
29 Pres Assoc of Former Students ....Mr. Porter GARNER
100 Liaison to the President .... Ms. Jessica RUBIE
19 Chief University Police ....Mr. J. Michael E. REAGAN
41 Athletic Director ....Mr. Scott WOODWARD

*Texas A & M University - Central Texas (C)

1001 Leadership Place, Killeen TX 76549

County: Bell Identification: 667086
Unit ID: 483036
Telephone: (245) 519-5400 Carnegie Class: Masters/L
FAX Number: (245) 519-5482 Calendar System: Semester
URL: www.tamuct.edu
Established: 1999 Annual Undergrad Tuition & Fees (In-State): N/A
Enrollment: 2,316 Coed
Affiliation or Control: State IRS Status: 501(c)3
Highest Offering: Master's
Accreditation: SC, ACBSP, NURSE, @SW

02 President ....Dr. Marc A. NIGLIAZZO
04 Administrative Asst to President ....Ms. Donna J. DOBSON
05 Chief Academic Officer .... Dr. Peg GRAY-VICKREY
07 Director of Admissions .... Mr. Clifton JONES
08 Head Librarian ....Ms. Bridgit MCCAFFERTY
09 Director of Institutional Research .... Dr. Paul TURCOTTE
10 Chief Business Officer ....Ms. Gaylene NUNN
13 Chief Info Technology Officer (CIO) ....Mr. Todd LUTZ
15 Director Personnel Services ....Mr. Charlie ROSENBLUM
18 Chief Facilities/Physical Plant ....Vacant
28 Dir Affirmative Action/EEO ....Ms. Deserie RIVERA
26 Chief Public Relations/Marketing ....Mrs. Jill CLOUD
30 Exec Dir Advancement & Alumni Svcs ....Dr. Karén CLOS
32 Chief Student Affairs/Student Life ....Mr. Brandon GRIGGS
36 Director Student Placement ....Ms. Cortina MERRITT
37 Director Student Financial Aid .... Mr. Clifton JONES
50 Dean of Business ....Dr. Larry GARNER
53 Dean of Education ....Vacant
86 Director Government Relations ....Vacant
49 Dean of Arts & Science ....Dr. Jerry JONES

*Texas A & M University - Commerce (D)

PO Box 3011, Commerce TX 75429-3011

County: Hunt FICE Identification: 003565
Unit ID: 224554
Telephone: (903) 886-5102 Carnegie Class: DU-Higher
FAX Number: (903) 886-5888 Calendar System: Semester
URL: www.tamuc.edu
Established: 1889 Annual Undergrad Tuition & Fees (In-State): $6,202
Enrollment: 12,111 Coed
Affiliation or Control: State IRS Status: 501(c)3
Highest Offering: Doctorate
Accreditation: SC, ART, BUS, CACREP, ENG, MUS, NURSE, SW

02 Interim President & CEO ....Dr. Ray M. KECK, III
05 Provost/VP Academic Affairs .... Dr. Adolfo BENAVIDES
10 Vice Pres Business & Administration ....Ms. Alicia CURRIN
35 VP for Student Access & Success ....Dr. Mary HENDRIX
30 Vice Pres Institutional Advancement ....Mr. Randy VAN DEVEN
100 Chief of Staff ....Ms. Linda KING
31 Director Community Engagement ....Mr. Noah NELSON
26 Exec Director Mktg Communications .... Ms. Lisa MARTINEZ
41 Athletic Director .... Mr. Tim MCMURRAY
28 Chief Diversity Officer ....Dr. Edward W. ROMERO
20 Associate Provost Academic Affairs ....Dr. Betty A. BLOCK
20 Assistant Provost ....Dr. Madeline JUSTICE
20 Assoc VP Student Access & Success .... Dr. Ricky DOBBS
09 Exec Dir Inst Effectiveness & Rsrch .... Dr. Shonda GIBSON
88 SACSCOC Accreditation Liaison ....Dr. Marila PALMER
84 Dean of Enrollment Mgmt & Retention ....Ms. Dina SOSA-HEGARTY
21 Assoc VP Business Admin/Comptroller ....Ms. Paula HANSON
21 Asst VP and Chief Budget Officer ....Ms. Tina LIVINGSTON
06 Registrar ....Ms. Paige BUSSELL
88 Dir of Acct & Financial Reporting ....Ms. Sarah BAKER
08 Library Director ....Mr. Gregory MITCHELL
12 Exec Dir Extended University ....Dr. Berri O'NEAL
13 Chief Information Officer .... Mr. Tim MURPHY
37 Director of Fin Aid & Scholarships .... Ms. Maria RAMOS
36 Director of Career Development ....Mrs. Tina BOITNOTT
58 Vice Prov of Research/Dean of Grad ....Dr. Arlene HORNE
53 Dean Education & Human Services ....Dr. Tim LETZRING
79 Dean of Humanities/Soc Sci & Art .... Dr. Salvatore ATTARDO
92 Dean of the Honors College ....Dr. Ray GREEN
81 Dean of Science & Engineering ....Dr. Brent DONHAM
50 Dean of Business ....Dr. John HUMPHREYS
47 Interim Dir School of Agriculture ....Dr. Jose LOPEZ
88 Dean of University College ....Dr. Tabetha ADKINS-SHATO
07 Director of Undergrad Admissions ....Mr. Jody TODHUNTER
108 Director of Student Assessment ....Ms. Wendy GRUVER
32 Asst VP/Dean of Students ....Dr. Tomas A. AGUIRRE
29 Director of Alumni Relations ....Mr. Derryle PEACE
19 Chief of Police ....Mrs. Donna SPINATO
12 Director Metroplex Center ....Mr. Russell BLANCHETT
12 Director Navarro Partnership ....Dr. Jeanetta GROCE
12 Rockwall Site Coordinator ....Vacant
38 Director Counseling Center ....Dr. Linda T. CLINTON
39 Dir Residential Living & Learning ....Mr. Michael STARK
88 Dir of Safety & Risk Management .... Mr. Derek PREAS
23 Director Student Health Services ....Ms. Maxine MENDOZA-WELCH
85 Dir International Student Services ....Mr. John Mark JONES
96 Chief Procurement Offcr & HUB Coor ....Mr. Travis BALL
04 Assistant to the President ....Ms. Rhonda FERGUSON
104 Exec Dir Global Prog/Study Abroad ....Mr. Jacques FUQUA
105 Web Application Developer ....Mr. Rick BARR
15 Chief Human Resource Officer ....Mrs. Barbara CORVEY
88 Chief Compliance Officer ....Ms. Heidi R. WRIGHT
18 Exec Dir Facilities Support Svcs ....Mr. David MCKENNA
22 Title IX Administrator ....Mrs. Michele VIEIRA
88 Director of Advancement Services ....Mrs. Brenda MORRIS

*Texas A & M University - Corpus Christi (E)

6300 Ocean Drive, Corpus Christi TX 78412

County: Nueces FICE Identification: 011161
Unit ID: 224147
Telephone: (361) 825-5700 Carnegie Class: DU-Mod
FAX Number: (361) 825-5887 Calendar System: Semester
URL: www.tamucc.edu
Established: 1947 Annual Undergrad Tuition & Fees (In-State): $7,976
Enrollment: 11,256 Coed
Affiliation or Control: State IRS Status: 501(c)3
Highest Offering: Doctorate
Accreditation: SC, BUS, BUSA, #CAATE, CACREP, CS, ENGR, ENGT, MT, MUS, NURSE

02 President/CEO ....Dr. Flavius C. KILLEBREW
05 Prov/VP for Acad Affairs ....Dr. Kelly QUINTANILLA
10 Exec VP for Finance/Admin ....Mr. Terry TATUM
30 Vice Pres Institutional Advancement ....Dr. S. Trent HILL
32 VP Student Engagement & Success .... Dr. Don ALBRECHT
46 VP Rsrch/Commercialization/Outreach .... Dr. Luis CIFUENTES
20 Assoc Vice Pres Academic Affairs ....Dr. Amy ALDRIDGE SANFORD
100 Chief of Staff .... Dr. Mary SHERWOOD
13 Assoc VP for Info Technology/CIO .... Mr. Edward EVANS
20 Assoc VP for Academic Affairs .... Dr. David BILLEAUX
84 Assoc VP Enrollment Management ....Ms. Margaret DECHANT
35 Assoc Vice Pres/Dean of Students ....Ms. Ann DEGAISH
20 Assoc VP Academic Affairs .... Ms. Christine SHUPALA
08 Director Bell Library .... Dr. Catherine RUDOWSKY
09 Assoc VP Planning & Inst Research ....Dr. Leona URBISH
26 Director of Marketing .... Ms. Ashley LARRABEE
29 Exec Director Development ....Ms. Jill JACOBS
06 Univ Registrar/Dir Veterans Affrs ....Mr. Michael RENDON
07 Exec Director of Admissions ....Mr. Oscar REYNA
37 Director of Financial Assistance .... Ms. Jeannie GAGE
31 Director Community Outreach ....Mr. Joseph MILLER
15 Director of Human Resources ....Ms. Debra CORTINAS
36 Director Career Services ....Ms. Terri HOWE
38 Dir Student Counseling/Development ....Dr. Carla BERKICH
28 Dir Employee Develop/Compliance Svc ....Mr. Sam RAMIREZ

11 Exec Dir Administrative Services .... Ms. Judy HARRAL
96 Dir Procurement & Disbursements .... Mr. Will HOBART
21 Bursar .... Ms. Christina HOLZHEUSER
58 Dean College of Graduate Studies .... Dr. Jo Ann CANALES
49 Dean College of Liberal Arts .... Dr. Mark HARTLAUB
50 Dean College of Business .... Dr. John E. GAMBLE
53 Dean College of Education .... Dr. Arthur HERNANDEZ
54 Dean College of Science & Engrng .... Dr. Frank PEZOLD
66 Dean College of Nursing/Health Sci .... Dr. Mary Jane HAMILTON

*Texas A & M University - Kingsville (A)

700 University Boulevard, Kingsville TX 78363-8202
County: Kleberg FICE Identification: 003639
Unit ID: 228705
Telephone: (361) 593-2111 Carnegie Class: DU-Mod
FAX Number: (361) 593-3107 Calendar System: Semester
URL: www.tamuk.edu
Established: 1925 Annual Undergrad Tuition & Fees (In-State): $7,700
Enrollment: 13,246 Coed
Affiliation or Control: State IRS Status: 501(c)3
Highest Offering: Doctorate
Accreditation: **SC**, CS, CIETD, DIETI, ENG, MUS, NAIT, PHAR, SP, SW

02 President .... Dr. Steven H. TALLANT
100 Chief of Staff .... Mr. Randy HUGHES
43 Director of Compliance .... Ms. Karen B. ROYAL
05 Provost & Vice Pres Acad Affs .... Dr. Heidi ANDERSON
32 Sr VP Student Affairs & Admin .... Dr. Terisa RILEY
88 Assistant Director of Budgets .... Ms. Jennifer ALEXANDER
10 Associate VP Finance & Comptroller .... Ms. Joanne MACIAS
88 Risk Management .... Dr. Shane CREEL
36 Exec Director of Career Services .... Mr. Christian FERRIS
109 Director of Auxiliary Services .... Mr. Crispin TREVINO
88 Dir of Campus Rec & Fitness .... Mr. Charles ESPINOSA
84 VP Enrollment Management .... Dr. Terisa RILEY
13 Chief Information Officer .... Mr. Robert PAULSON
14 Assoc CIO .... Mr. Lonnie NAGEL
88 Dir Enterprise Applications .... Mr. Lee MOORE
35 Dean of Students .... Ms. Kristin COMPARY
20 Associate VP Academic Affairs .... Dr. Duane GARDINER
85 Dir International Studies .... Mr. Peter LI
88 Dir Center Teaching Effectiveness .... Dr. Jaya GOSWAMI
58 Assoc VP Research & Grad Studies .... Dr. Allen RASMUSSEN
88 Asst VP Student Access .... Dr. Mary GONZALEZ
47 Interim Dean College Agriculture .... Dr. Shad NELSON
49 Dean Arts & Sciences .... Dr. Dolores GUERRERO
50 Dean Business Administration .... Dr. Natalya DELCOURE
53 Dean Education & Human Performance .... Dr. Alberto RUIZ
54 Dean Engineering .... Dr. Stephan NIX
89 Assoc VP for Student Success .... Dr. Nancy KING SANDERS
26 Exec Dir Markting/Communications .... Ms. Cheryl CAIN
08 Librarian .... Mr. Bruce R. SCHUENAMAN
108 Dir Planning & Assessment .... Vacant
88 Director Citrus Center .... Dr. John DA GRACA
88 Director King Ranch Institute .... Dr. Clay P. MATHIS
88 Exec Director CKWRI .... Dr. Fred BRYANT
88 Exec Co-Director Nat Toxins Res Ctr .... Dr. Elda E. SANCHEZ
88 Director Inst Sust Energy & Env .... Dr. Kim JONES
06 Interim Registrar .... Ms. Mildred SLAUGHTER
07 Director of Admissions .... Ms. Shelly KEY
30 Chief Development/Advancement .... Mr. Bradley WALKER
29 Director Development and Alumni Rel .... Mr. Justin MUNOZ
41 VP Intercollegiate Athletics & Camp .... Mr. Scott GINES
40 Director Bookstore .... Ms. Mary GUTIERREZ
106 Director Distance Learning .... Ms. Michelle DURAN
44 Exec Dir Development & Alumni .... Ms. Lori RUSSEK
23 Director Studet Health & Wellness .... Ms. Jo Elda CASTILLO-ALANIZ
09 Director Institutional Research .... Ms. Miao ZHUANG
88 Director John E Conner Museum .... Mr. Jonathan PLANT
15 Exec Dir Human Resources .... Mr. Leon BAZAR
18 Exec Director Physical Plant .... Mr. John CAMISCIONI
96 Assoc VP Support Services .... Mr. Ralph STEPHENS
25 Contract Administrator .... Ms. Rachel L. BUENTELLO
39 Director Residence Life .... Mr. Tom MARTIN
46 Exec Dir Strategic Programs .... Ms. Maria MARTINEZ
35 Director Student Activities .... Ms. Erin MCCLURE
19 Director of University Police .... Mr. Felipe GARZA
37 Director Student Financial Aid .... Ms. Jessica THOMAS
38 Asst Director Counseling Services .... Ms. Renee WIESS
88 Supervisor Business Services .... Mr. Carlos MARTINEZ
88 Advisor Pre-profession Programs .... Ms. Amanda MUNIZ
88 Bible Chair Baptist .... Mr. Mike CERVANTES
88 Bible Chair Catholic .... Ms. Nina JOINER
04 Sr Exec Asst to President .... Ms. Margarita M. GALVAN
104 Director Study Abroad .... Mr. Peter LI

*Texas A & M University-San Antonio (B)

One University Way, San Antonio TX 78224
County: Bexar Identification: 666689
Unit ID: 22870501
Telephone: (210) 784-1000 Carnegie Class: Not Classified
FAX Number: (210) 784-6219 Calendar System: Semester
URL: www.tamusa.edu
Established: 2009 Annual Undergrad Tuition & Fees (In-District): N/A
Enrollment: N/A Coed
Affiliation or Control: State/Local IRS Status: 501(c)3
Highest Offering: Master's
Accreditation: **SC**

02 President .... Dr. Cynthia TENIENTE-MATSON
05 Provost/VP Academic Affairs .... Dr. Michael O'BRIEN
10 Vice Pres Finance/Administration .... Mr. Darrell MORRISON
32 Vice President for Student Affairs .... Dr. Melissa MAHAN
30 VP for University Advancement .... Dr. Richard ORTEGA
09 Director of Institutional Research .... Ms. Jane MIMS
50 Dean College of Business .... Dr. Tracy HURLEY
49 Dean College of Arts & Sciences .... Dr. Mirley BALASUBRAMANYA
53 Dean College of Education & Devel .... Dr. Eric LOPEZ

*Texas A & M University - Texarkana (C)

7101 University Avenue, Texarkana TX 75503
County: Bowie FICE Identification: 031703
Unit ID: 224545
Telephone: (903) 223-3000 Carnegie Class: Masters/M
FAX Number: (903) 832-8890 Calendar System: Semester
URL: www.tamut.edu
Established: 1971 Annual Undergrad Tuition & Fees (In-State): $6,411
Enrollment: 1,865 Coed
Affiliation or Control: State IRS Status: 501(c)3
Highest Offering: Doctorate
Accreditation: **SC**, CACREP, NURSE

53 Dean College Education/Liberal Art .... Dr. Delbert DOUGHTY
02 President .... Dr. Emily FOURMY CUTRER
05 Provost/Vice Pres Academic Affairs .... Vacant
10 VP Finance & Administration .... Mr. James SCOGIN
32 Asst Vice Pres for Student Success .... Mrs. Elizabeth PATTERSON
30 Assoc VP University Advancement .... Mrs. LeAnne WRIGHT
84 AVP Enrollment Management .... Ms. Kathy WILLIAMS
100 Chief of Staff President's Office .... Mrs. Vicki HUCKABEE
13 Chief Information Technology .... Mr. Jeff HINTON
20 Assoc Provost/SACSCOC Liaison .... Dr. Nancy JORDAN
81 Dean College of STEM .... Dr. Donald PETERSON
50 Dean College of Business .... Dr. Gary STADING
21 Controller .... Mrs. Jackie ELDER
37 Dir Financial Aid & Veteran Svcs .... Mr. Michael FULLER
15 Director Human Resources & EEO .... Mr. Ricky NORTON
08 Director Library .... Mrs. Teri STOVER
18 Director Physical Plant .... Mr. Richard LYNES
18 Police Chief/Director Security .... Mr. Alex SERRANO
96 Director Purchasing .... Mrs. Cynthia HENDERSON
88 Director Payroll .... Mrs. Ramona GREEN
35 Director Student & Career Services .... Mr. Carl GREIG
84 Director Enrollment Management .... Mr. Toney FAVORS
26 Director Communications .... Ms. Carol LANGSTON
58 Dean of Graduate Studies & Research .... Dr. William MCHENRY
41 Director of Athletics .... Mr. Michael GALVAN
04 Administrative Asst to President .... Ms. Loren LOFTIN
06 Registrar .... Mrs. Jana BOATRIGHT
38 Director Student Counseling .... Mrs. Barbara WILSON

*West Texas A & M University (D)

2403 Russell C. Long Blvd., Canyon TX 79015
County: Randall FICE Identification: 003665
Unit ID: 229814
Telephone: (806) 651-0000 Carnegie Class: Masters/L
FAX Number: (806) 651-2126 Calendar System: Semester
URL: www.wtamu.edu
Established: 1910 Annual Undergrad Tuition & Fees (In-State): $7,041
Enrollment: 8,972 Coed
Affiliation or Control: State IRS Status: 501(c)3
Highest Offering: Doctorate
Accreditation: **SC**, BUS, #CAATE, CS, ENG, MUS, NURSE, SP, SW, THEA

02 President/CEO .... Dr. James R. HALLMARK
05 Provost/Vice Pres Acad Affairs .... Dr. Wade SHAFFER
10 Vice Pres for Business and Finance .... Mr. Randy RIKEL
32 Vice President for Student Affairs .... Mr. Michael J. KNOX
30 Vice Pres Institutional Advancement .... Mr. Tim BYNUM
84 Vice Pres of Enrollment Management .... Mr. Dan D. GARCIA
28 Chief Diversity/Inclusion Officer .... Ms. Angela ALLEN
06 Registrar .... Ms. Tana J. MILLER
07 Director of Admissions .... Mr. Kyle MOORE
08 Dir Information/Library Resources .... Ms. Shawna J. KENNEDY-WITTHAR
36 Dir Career Planning/Placement .... Ms. Denese SKINNER
37 Director Student Financial Aid .... Ms. Marian K. GIESECKE
51 Dir Education on Demand .... Ms. Andrea PORTER
23 Director Medical Service .... Dr Jim GIBBS
19 Police Chief .... Chief Shawn G. BURNS
26 Director Communication Services .... Ms. Ann UNDERWOOD
29 Director of Alumni Relations .... Ms. Becky STOGNER
38 Director Counseling Services .... Mr. Orvie NIX
41 Director of Athletics .... Mr. Michael MCBROOM
09 Director Institutional Research .... Mr. Jarvis D. HAMPTON
13 Chief Information Officer .... Mr. James D. WEBB
96 Director of Purchasing .... Mr. Brian GLENN
40 Manager Bookstore .... Mr. Terry S. NEPPER
15 Director Personnel Services .... Mr. David KOHLER
47 Dean Col Agr/Nat Sciences .... Dr. Dean HAWKINS
50 Dean College of Business .... Dr. Neil W. TERRY
53 Dean Col Education & Social Science .... Dr. Eddie W. HENDERSON
57 Dean College Fine Arts/Humanities .... Dr. Jessica MALLARD
54 Dean Col Eng/Comp Sci/Mathematics .... Dr. Emily HUNT
46 VP for Research & Compliance .... Dr. Angela SPAULDING
66 Dean College of Nursing/Health Sci .... Dr. Dirk NELSON
104 Director Study Abroad .... Ms. Carolina GALLOWAY
04 Administrative Asst to President .... Ms. Tracee POST

*Texas A & M University at Galveston (E)

PO Box 1675, Galveston TX 77553-1675
Telephone: (409) 740-4414 FICE Identification: 010298
Accreditation: &SC, ENG, ENGT

† Regional accreditation is carried under the parent institution Texas A & M University, College Station, TX.

Texas Chiropractic College (F)

5912 Spencer Highway, Pasadena TX 77505-1699
County: Harris FICE Identification: 003635
Unit ID: 228866
Telephone: (281) 487-1170 Carnegie Class: Spec-4-yr-Other Health
FAX Number: (281) 487-2009 Calendar System: Trimester
URL: www.txchiro.edu
Established: 1908 Annual Undergrad Tuition & Fees: N/A
Enrollment: 260 Coed
Affiliation or Control: Independent Non-Profit IRS Status: 501(c)3
Highest Offering: Doctorate
Accreditation: **SC**, CHIRO

01 President .... Dr. Steve FOSTER
10 Chief Financial Officer .... Mr. Bill QUINN
05 Dean of Academic Affairs .... Dr. John MROZEK
84 VP of Enrollment Management .... Dr. Fred ZUKER
30 Dean Institutional Advancement .... Dr. Sandra HUGHES
88 Dean of Postgraduate Studies .... Dr. Paul JASKOVIAK
06 Registrar .... Dr. Karlene DENBY
15 Director of Human Resources .... Mrs. Sue ARNOLD
26 Director of Communications .... Mr. Max ARCHER
08 Director of Library Services .... Ms. Carol WEBB
37 Director Financial Aid .... Mr. Arthur GOUDEAU
29 Director of Alumni Relations .... Ms. Gabrielle GREENWADE
32 Director of Student Services .... Ms. Kristina HANSON
07 Director of Admission .... Ms. Monique LEWIS
04 Admin Asst to President .... Ms. Glenda RAMIREZ
18 Physical Plant Supervisor .... Mr. Perry LATIOLAIS

Texas Christian University (G)

2800 S University Drive, Fort Worth TX 76129-2800
County: Tarrant FICE Identification: 003636
Unit ID: 228875
Telephone: (817) 257-7000 Carnegie Class: DU-Higher
FAX Number: (817) 257-7333 Calendar System: Semester
URL: www.tcu.edu
Established: 1873 Annual Undergrad Tuition & Fees: $40,720
Enrollment: 10,033 Coed
Affiliation or Control: Christian Church (Disciples Of Christ)
IRS Status: 501(c)3
Highest Offering: Doctorate
Accreditation: **SC**, ANEST, ART, BUS, BUSA, CAATE, CIDA, CS, DANCE, DIETC, DIETD, ENG, #JOUR, MUS, NURSE, SP, SW

01 Chancellor .... Dr. Victor J. BOSCHINI, JR.
05 Provost/Vice Chanc Academic Affairs .... Dr. R. Nowell DONOVAN
10 Vice Chanc Finance & Administration .... Mr. Brian G. GUTIERREZ
30 Vice Chanc University Advancement .... Mr. Donald J. WHELAN, JR.
32 Vice Chancellor Student Affairs .... Dr. Kathryn CAVINS-TULL
26 Vice Chanc Mktg & Communication .... Ms. Tracy SYLER-JONES
15 Vice Chancellor Human Resources .... Ms. Yohna CHAMBERS
41 Director Athletics .... Mr. Christopher DEL CONTE
88 Chief Investment Officer .... Mr. Jim HILLE
13 Chief Technology Officer .... Mr. Bryan LUCAS
88 Chief University Compliance Officer .... Ms. Andrea NORDMANN
100 Chief of Staff .... Ms. Jean MRASEK
88 Chancellor's Intern .... Mr. Michael MARSHALL
29 Assoc Vice Chanc Alumni Relations .... Ms. Kristi M. HOBAN
88 Assoc Vice Chanc Advancement Ops .... Dr. Roby V. KEY
16 Assoc Vice Chanc Human Resources .... Ms. Faith PERKINS
35 Assoc VC/Dean Student Development .... Dr. Barbara B. HERMAN
35 Assoc Vice Chanc/Dean Campus Life .... Dr. David COZZENS
21 Assoc Vice Chanc & Controller .... Ms. Cheryl L. WILSON
18 Assoc Vice Chanc for Facilities .... Mr. Todd S. WALDVOGEL
88 Associate VC Donor Relations .... Julie WHITT
35 Assoc VC of Student Affairs .... Mr. Darron TURNER
44 Assoc VC University Development .... Mr. David NOLAN
88 Asst VC School & College Dev .... Mr. Adam BAGGS
09 Assoc Provost Research .... Dr. Bonnie MELHART
20 Assoc Provost Academic Support .... Dr. Leo W. MUNSON
20 Asst Provost Academic Plng/Budget .... Ms. Megan M. SOYER
108 Assoc Provost Inst Effectiveness .... Dr. Catherine WEHLBURG
88 Assoc Provost Devel Academic Future .... Dr. David WHILLOCK
49 Dean Addran College of Liberal Arts .... Dr. Andrew SCHOOLMASTER
50 Dean Neeley School of Business .... Dr. Homer EREKSON
60 Dn Bob Scheffer Col Communication .... Dr. Kristie BUNTON
53 Dean College of Education .... Dr. Mary PATTON
57 Dean College of Fine Arts .... Dr. Anne HELMREICH
66 Dean Harris Col Nursing/Hlth Sci .... Dr. Susan WEEKS
54 Dean Col of Science & Engineering .... Dr. Phil HARTMAN
92 Dn John V Roach Honors College .... Dr. Diane SNOW
08 Dean of the Library .... Dr. June KOELKER
07 Dean of Admission .... Mr. Raymond A. BROWN
22 Affirmative Action Officer .... Mr. Darron TURNER

06 Registrar/Dir Enrollment Management .... Ms. Mary KINCANNON
19 Chief TCU Police .... Mr. Steve G. MCGEE
42 Minister to the University .... Rev. Angela KAUFMAN
21 Asst Vice Chanc Finance .... Mr. Kenneth JANAK
106 Asst Provost of Educ Tech/Fac Dev .... Ms. Romana HUGHES
85 Director International Education .... Dr. Jane KUCKO
25 Director Contract Administration .... Mr. Matthew WALLIS
16 Director Employee Relations .... Ms. Kristen TAYLOR
51 Director Extended Education .... Mr. David A. GREBEL
88 Assoc Dean Dir Freshman Admission .... Mr. Heath EINSTEIN
88 Director Transfer Admission .... Ms. Amanda NICKERSON
23 Director Health Services .... Dr. Jane TORGERSON
09 Director Institutional Research .... Dr. Cathan COGHLAN
24 Int Dir Instructional Services .... Ms. Deana RAY
85 Director International Student Svcs .... Mr. John L. SINGLETON
38 Director Mental Health Services .... Dr. Linda WOLSZON
96 Warehouse/Purchasing Agent .... Mr. Roger D. FULLER
39 Director Housing & Residential Life .... Mr. Craig ALLEN
37 Dir Scholarships & Financial Aid .... Mr. Michael H. SCOTT
105 Director Website Management .... Mr. Victor NEIL
25 Director Sponsored Programs .... Ms. Linda FREED
36 Exec Director Career Services .... Dr. John THOMPSON

Texas College (A)

2404 N Grand Avenue, Tyler TX 75702-1962
County: Smith FICE Identification: 003638
Unit ID: 228884
Telephone: (903) 593-8311 Carnegie Class: Bac-Diverse
FAX Number: (903) 593-0588 Calendar System: Semester
URL: www.texascollege.edu
Established: 1894 Annual Undergrad Tuition & Fees: $10,008
Enrollment: 813 Coed
Affiliation or Control: Christian Methodist Episcopal IRS Status: 501(c)3
Highest Offering: Baccalaureate
Accreditation: SC

01 President .... Dr. Dwight FENNELL
05 Vice President Academic Affairs .... Dr. Cynthia MARSHALL-BIGGINS
10 Vice Pres Business & Finance .... Mr. James HARRIS
32 Dean of Students .... Mr. Isaac WILLIAMS
30 Development Officer .... Mrs. Angelia FENNELL
84 Dean of Enrollment Services .... Vacant
07 Coordinator of Admission .... Mr. Ronald MCDOWELL
06 Registrar .... Mr. John ROBERTS
09 Dir Inst Research/ Effectiveness .... Dr. Cynthia MARSHALL-BIGGINS
08 Director of Library Services .... Mrs. Linda SIMMONS-HENRY
13 Asst Dir Information Technology .... Mr. Ocie FISHER
15 Director Human Resources .... Ms. Lois BOWIE
21 Comptroller .... Mr. Walter MOSLEY
41 Athletic Director .... Ms. Elissia BURWELL
37 Director Financial Aid .... Mrs. Angela SPEECH
18 Director Physical Plant .... Mr. Anthony PARKER
26 Coordinator Public Relations .... Ms. Christie HOWARD
29 Coordinator Alumni Affairs .... Ms. Orenthia MASON
19 Director Security/Safety .... Dr. Willie CHAMPION

Texas Health and Science University (B)

4005 Manchaca Road, Austin TX 78704-6737
County: Travis FICE Identification: 031795
Unit ID: 430704
Telephone: (512) 444-8082 Carnegie Class: Spec-4-yr-Other Health
FAX Number: (512) 444-6345 Calendar System: Trimester
URL: www.thsu.edu
Established: 1990 Annual Undergrad Tuition & Fees: N/A
Enrollment: 98 Coed
Affiliation or Control: Proprietary IRS Status: Proprietary
Highest Offering: Master's; No Lower Division
Accreditation: ACICS, ACUP

01 President .... Ms. Lisa (Ping-Hui) LIN
20 VP of Academics/Assessment .... Dr. David G. VEQUIST
10 Director of Development/Operations .... Mr. Paul LIN
05 Academic Dean/Bioen Dir/DAOM Dir .... Dr. Maoyi CAI
88 Director of Acupuncture Department .... Dr. Hai Tao CAO
88 Director of Herbal Department .... Ms. Jiahe JIN
46 Director Research/Clinic Director .... Dr. Lin-Ying TAN
88 ESL Director .... Ms. Maria B. DURAN
03 MBA Director .... Mr. Dan PUHL
32 Dir Student Affairs/Strat Ops .... Ms. Sha-Lene PUNG
35 Dean of Students/Assoc Dir .... Ms. Marty CALLIHAM
06 Registrar/Administrator .... Ms. Brittany D. DEAN
37 Financial Aid/Intl Student Advisor .... Dr. Jiao-sheng JIANG
08 Librarian .... Ms. Leissa KIMBALL
07 Admissions Coordinator .... Mr. Kanok LI
12 Academic Dean San Antonio Campus .... Mr. Roberto GUERRERO

† Offers a doctorate degree but ACICS's scope of recognition by USDE & CHEA does not currently include doctorate degrees.

Texas Lutheran University (C)

1000 W Court Street, Seguin TX 78155-5999
County: Guadalupe FICE Identification: 003641
Unit ID: 228981
Telephone: (830) 372-8000 Carnegie Class: Bac-Diverse
FAX Number: (830) 372-8096 Calendar System: Semester
URL: www.tlu.edu
Established: 1891 Annual Undergrad Tuition & Fees: $27,900
Enrollment: 1,320 Coed
Affiliation or Control: Evangelical Lutheran Church In America
IRS Status: 501(c)3
Highest Offering: Master's
Accreditation: SC, ACBSP, CAATE, MUS, NURSE, TEAC

01 President .... Dr. Stuart B. DORSEY
05 Vice Pres for Academic Affairs .... Dr. Debbie COTTRELL
11 Asst to Pres Admin/Public Affairs .... Mr. Stephen P. ANDERSON
10 Vice President Finance .... Mr. Andrew NELSON
84 Vice President Enrollment Services .... Mr. Thomas OLIVER
30 VP for Development/Alumni Relations .... Mr. Rick ROBERTS
32 VP/Dean of Student Life & Learning .... Ms. Kristi QUIROS
26 Vice President for Marketing Comm .... Ms. Sarah STORY
06 Director of Records & Registration .... Mr. Glenn YOCKEY
08 Library Director .... Ms. Martha RINN
37 Director of Financial Aid .... Ms. Bonnie TREVINO
42 Campus Pastor .... Rev. Kara STEWART
36 Director Career Development .... Ms. LaTonya HENRY
38 Director Counseling Services .... Ms. Terry WEERS
07 Director of Admissions .... Mr. Adam NAVARRO-JUSINO
15 Human Resources Manager .... Ms. Toi TURNER
41 Director of Athletics .... Mr. Bill MILLER
09 Director of Institutional Research .... Ms. Jean CONSTABLE
04 Exec Assistant to the President .... Ms. Susan RINN
101 Secretary of the Institution/Board .... Ms. Susan RINN
102 Dir Foundation/Corporate Relations .... Mr. Sam EHRLICH
104 Director Study Abroad .... Ms. Charla BAILEY
105 Director Web Services .... Ms. Jenni MORIN
108 Director Institutional Assessment .... Dr. Michael CZUCHRY
13 Chief Info Technology Officer (CIO) .... Mr. William SENTER
18 Chief Facilities/Physical Plant .... Mr. Kirk HERBOLD
19 University Police Chief .... Chief Gary HOPPER
29 Director Alumni Relations .... Ms. Taylor CARLETON
39 Director of Residence Life .... Ms. Pesha MABRIE
44 Director Annual Giving .... Ms. Taylor CARLETON
86 Director Government Relations .... Mr. Steve ANDERSON
22 Dir Affirm Action/EEO/Diversity .... Ms. Toi TURNER
43 Dir Legal Services/General Counsel .... Mr. James FROST

Texas Southern University (D)

3100 Cleburne Street, Houston TX 77004-4584
County: Harris FICE Identification: 003642
Unit ID: 229063
Telephone: (713) 313-7011 Carnegie Class: DU-Mod
FAX Number: (713) 313-1092 Calendar System: Semester
URL: www.tsu.edu
Established: 1927 Annual Undergrad Tuition & Fees (In-State): $8,726
Enrollment: 9,233 Coed
Affiliation or Control: State IRS Status: 170(c)1
Highest Offering: Doctorate
Accreditation: SC, BUS, CAHIIM, COARC, DIETD, ENGT, LAW, MT, NAIT, PHAR, PLNG, SPAA, SW, TED

01 President .... Dr. Austin A. LANE
05 Int Provost/VP Academic Affairs .... Dr. Bobby WILSON
10 Vice President for Admin & Finance .... Mr. E. Craig NESS
30 Vice Pres University Advancement .... Ms. Wendy H. ADAIR
100 Chief of Staff .... Ms. Heidi SMITH
43 General Counsel .... Mr. Andrew C. HUGHEY
41 VP Intercollegiate Athletics .... Dr. Charles F. MCCLELLAND
32 VP Student Svcs/Dean of Students .... Dr. William T. SAUNDERS
09 Int Assoc Provost/Assoc VP Research .... Dr. Adebayo O. OYEKAN
88 Dir Title III & Ofc of Sponsored Pr .... Ms. Demetria JOHNSON-WEEKS
15 Assoc VP of Human Resources .... Dr. Brian K. DICKENS
26 Assoc VP of Communications .... Ms. Eva K. PICKENS
84 Assoc VP Enrollment Management .... Mr. Hasan JAMIL
06 University Registrar .... Ms. Marilyn C. SQUARE
08 Exec Director Libraries/Museums .... Dr. Janice L. PAYTON
50 Dean School of Business .... Dr. Ronald A. JOHNSON
51 Int Dir Office of Cont Education .... Dr. Melanie LAWSON
53 Dean College of Education .... Dr. Lillian B. POATS
80 Dean School of Public Affairs .... Dr. Robert D. BULLARD
61 Dean School of Law .... Dr. Dannye HOLLEY
67 Int Dean Col Pharmacy & Health Sci .... Dr. Edward STEMLEY
72 Dean College of Science/Technology .... Dr. Lei YU
60 Dean School of Communications .... Dr. James W. WARD
19 Exec Dir/Chief of Police .... Chief Remon P. GREEN
39 Asst VP of Student Housing .... Dr. William A. THOMAS
92 Dean Freeman Honors College .... Dr. Elizabeth A. BROWN-GUILLORY
96 Exec Dir Procurement Services .... Mr. Gregory G. WILLIAMS
18 Exec Director Facilities & Maint .... Mr. Tim RYCHLEC
13 Chief Information Officer .... Mr. Luis VILLARREAL
20 Assoc Provost/Assoc VP Acad Affairs .... Vacant
58 Dean Graduate School .... Dr. Gregory H. MADDOX
21 Exec Dir Provost of Business Svcs .... Mr. Charles E. HENRY
21 Controller .... Ms. Christina ORDONEZ-CAMPOS
88 Dir Acad Ret Svcs Spec Asst/Provost .... Ms. Lori A. LABRIE
109 Asst VP of Student Auxiliary Svcs .... Dr. Najla F. NAJIEB
88 Exec Director Budget .... Mr. Elias HAILU
88 Assoc VP Treasurer & Budget .... Mr. Louis W. EDWARDS
108 Int Ex Dir Inst Assess/Plng/Effect .... Dr. Rajanel CROCKEM
29 Exec Dir Alumni Rels/Spec Events .... Ms. Connie L. COCHRAN
88 Asst Dean of Student Support Svcs .... Ms. Michara N. DELANEY
88 Director of Scholarships .... Ms. Cynthia LEE
88 Int Dir Teaching & Learning Center .... Dr. Bernnell PELZIER-GLAZE
88 Program Director Urban Academic Vil .... Mr. Darnell JOSEPH
88 Associate Director of QEP Office .... Dr. Arbolina L. JENNINGS
106 Dir Online Education/E-learning .... Mr. Remi ADEMOLA
37 Director Student Financial Aid .... Ms. Linda BALLARD
86 Director Government Relations .... Dr. Leonard H. SPEARMAN

Texas Southmost College (E)

80 Fort Brown, Brownsville TX 78520-4993
County: Cameron FICE Identification: 003643
Unit ID: 229072
Telephone: (956) 295-3600 Carnegie Class: Assoc/HT-Mix Trad/Non
FAX Number: (956) 295-3384 Calendar System: Semester
URL: www.tsc.edu
Established: 1926 Annual Undergrad Tuition & Fees (In-District): N/A
Enrollment: N/A Coed
Affiliation or Control: State/Local IRS Status: 501(c)3
Highest Offering: Associate Degree
Accreditation: SC, ADNUR

01 Interim President .... Mr. Mike SHANNON

Texas State Technical College Waco (F)

3801 Campus Drive, Waco TX 76705-1695
County: McLennan FICE Identification: 003634
Unit ID: 228680
Telephone: (254) 799-3611 Carnegie Class: Assoc/HVT-High Trad
FAX Number: (254) 867-2006 Calendar System: Semester
URL: www.tstc.edu
Established: 1965 Annual Undergrad Tuition & Fees (In-State): N/A
Enrollment: 4,114 Coed
Affiliation or Control: State IRS Status: 501(c)3
Highest Offering: Associate Degree
Accreditation: SC, CAHIIM, DH, EMT, MAC, SURGT

00 Chancellor .... Mr. Mike REESER
11 VC & Chief Operations Officer .... Dr. Elton E. STUCKLY, JR.
86 VC & Chief Govt Affairs Officer .... Mr. Roger MILLER
10 VC & Chief Financial Officer .... Mr. Jonathan HOEKSTRA
88 VC & Chf Business Intelligence Ofcr .... Dr. J. Gary HENRICKS
45 VC & Chief Execution Officer .... Mr. Randall WOOTEN
100 Chief Culture Officer .... Mrs. Gail LAWERENCE
13 VC & Chief Technology Officer .... Mr. Rick HERRERA
26 VC & Chief Marketing Officer .... Mr. Jeff KILGORE
43 VC & Chief Legal Officer .... Mr. Ray RUSHING
88 VC & Chief Policy Officer .... Mr. Michael A. BETTERSWORTH
12 Provost Waco .... Mr. Adam C. HUTCHISON
12 Provost Harlingen .... Dr. Stella E. GARCIA
12 Provost Marshall .... Mr. Barton DAY
12 Provost West Texas .... Ms. Eliska SMITH
12 Provost North Texas .... Mr. Marcus BALCH
12 Provost Williamson County .... Mr. Edgar PADILLA
30 Sr Exec Dir Inst Advancement .... Dr. Terry CONROY

*The Texas State University System (G)

208 E 10th Street, Suite 600, Austin TX 78701-2407
County: Travis FICE Identification: 033442
Telephone: (512) 463-1808 Carnegie Class: N/A
FAX Number: (512) 463-1816
URL: www.tsus.edu

01 Chancellor .... Brian MCCALL
05 Vice Chanc for Academic Affairs .... Perry MOORE
43 Vice Chanc & General Counsel .... Fernando C. GOMEZ
10 Vice Chancellor for Finance .... Roland K. SMITH
86 Vice Chanc Government Relations .... Sean CUNNINGHAM
25 Vice Chanc Contract Administration .... Peter E. GRAVES
88 Associate General Counsel .... Diane CORLEY
18 Assoc Vice Chanc Facilities .... Rob Roy PARNELL
26 Assoc VC Govt Rels/Dir of Commun .... Mike WINTEMUTE
21 Director of Audits & Analysis .... Carole M. FOX
11 Director of Administration .... Carol TREADWAY

*Lamar Institute of Technology (H)

PO Box 10043, Beaumont TX 77710-0043
County: Jefferson FICE Identification: 036273
Unit ID: 441760
Telephone: (409) 880-8321 Carnegie Class: Assoc/HVT-High Trad
FAX Number: (409) 880-1711 Calendar System: Semester
URL: www.lit.edu
Established: 1995 Annual Undergrad Tuition & Fees (In-State): $4,401
Enrollment: 2,799 Coed
Affiliation or Control: State IRS Status: 501(c)3
Highest Offering: Associate Degree
Accreditation: SC, CAHIIM, COARC, DH, DMS, EMT, RAD

02 President .... Dr. Lonnie HOWARD
05 Vice President for Academic Affairs .... Dr. Daniel WRIGHT
10 Vice President Finance & Operations .... Ms. Bonnie ALBRIGHT
32 Vice President for Student Services .... Dr. Jason SMITH
15 Vice President for Human Resources .... Mrs. Catherine BLANCHARD
20 Dean of Instruction .... Ms. Melissa ARMENTOR
103 Vice President for Workforce Dev .... Mr. Patrick CALHOUN
37 Director of Student Financial Aid .... Ms. Lisa SCHROEDER
13 Director of Technology Services .... Ms. Susan COOK
30 Dir of Develop/Dir LIT Foundation .... Ms. Joanne BROWN
26 Director of Public Info/Marketing .... Ms. Juliana SPENCER
18 Facilities Coordinator .... Mr. Jack WIGGINS
36 Job Plcmnt/Student Activities Coord .... Vacant
09 Coord Inst Effectiveness and Grants .... Mr. David MOSLEY
04 Administrative Asst to President .... Mrs. Paula TANNER
06 Registrar .... Mr. David SHORT

*Lamar University (A)

PO Box 10009, Beaumont TX 77710-0009
County: Jefferson
FICE Identification: 003581
Unit ID: 226091
Telephone: (409) 880-7011
Carnegie Class: DU-Mod
FAX Number: (409) 880-8404
Calendar System: Semester
URL: www.lamar.edu
Established: 1923
Annual Undergrad Tuition & Fees (In-State): $8,002
Enrollment: 14,895
Coed
Affiliation or Control: State
IRS Status: 501(c)3
Highest Offering: Doctorate
Accreditation: SC, ACFEI, ADNUR, ART, AUD, BUS, CACREP, CONST, CS, DIETD, DIETI, ENG, MUS, NUR, SP, SW, TED

02 President .... Dr. Kenneth R. EVANS
05 Provost/Vice Pres Academic Affairs .... Dr. James W. MARQUART
10 Vice Pres Finance/Operations .... Dr. Cruse MELVIN
30 Vice Pres University Advancement .... Mr. Juan ZABALA
13 Vice Pres Information Technology .... Ms. Priscilla PARSONS
20 Sr Assoc Provost for Academic Affs .... Dr. Kevin B. SMITH
15 Assoc Vice Pres Human Resources .... Ms. Catherine BLANCHARD
18 Assoc Vice Pres Facilities Mgmt .... Mr. Michael RULAND
21 Assoc Vice Pres Finance/Controller .... Ms. Twila BAKER
32 Assoc VP Undergrad Student Success .... Ms. Sherry BENOIT
58 Dean of Graduate Studies .... Dr. William HARN
49 Dean College Arts & Sciences .... Dr. Brenda NICHOLS
50 Dean College of Business .... Dr. Henry VENTA
53 Dean College of Education .... Dr. Robert SPINA
54 Dean College of Engineering .... Dr. Srinivas PALANKI
57 Dean Col Fine Arts & Communication .... Dr. Derina HOLTZHAUSEN
08 Director Library Services .... Mr. David J. CARROLL
06 Registrar .... Mr. David SHORT, JR.
106 Dir Division of Distance Learning .... Dr. Paula NICHOLS
20 Director of Academic Services .... Mr. James C. RUSH
44 Director of Development .... Dr. La Tanya AFOLAYAN
09 Director Institutional Research .... Dr. Gregory MARSH
36 Dir Career Development/Placement .... Ms. Angela THOMAS
23 Director Health Services .... Ms. Shawn GRAY
19 Chief University Police .... Mr. Hector FLORES
26 Public Relations Director .... Mr. Brian SATTLER
29 Director Alumni Relations .... Ms. Shannon COPELAND
37 Director Student Financial Aid .... Ms. Jill ROWLEY
96 Director of Purchasing .... Mr. William GATES
07 Director of Admissions .... Ms. Melissa C. GALLIEN

*Lamar State College-Orange (B)

410 Front Street, Orange TX 77630-5802
County: Orange
FICE Identification: 023582
Unit ID: 226107
Telephone: (409) 883-7750
Carnegie Class: Assoc/HVT-High Trad
FAX Number: (409) 882-3374
Calendar System: Semester
URL: www.lsco.edu
Established: 1969
Annual Undergrad Tuition & Fees (In-State): $3,950
Enrollment: 2,259
Coed
Affiliation or Control: State
IRS Status: 501(c)3
Highest Offering: Associate Degree
Accreditation: SC

02 President .... Dr. J. Michael SHAHAN
05 Vice President Academic Affairs .... Dr. Gwen WHITEHEAD
10 Vice President Finance & Operations .... Mrs. Dana ROGERS
32 VP Student Svcs & Auxiliary Ent .... Mr. Michael YEATER
08 Director of Library Services .... Ms. Mary MCCOY
06 Registrar .... Mrs. Becky J. MCANELLEY
37 Director Student Financial Aid .... Mr. Kerry J. OLSON
15 Human Resources Director .... Mrs. Alicia GRAY
18 Director of Physical Plant .... Mr. David GOINS
13 Coord Information Resources .... Ms. Linda G. BURNETT
09 Coordinator Institutional Research .... Dr. Hunter KEENEY
25 Contracts/Grants Administrator .... Mrs. Dana N. ROGERS
76 Dean Health Sciences/Workforce Educ .... Ms. Gina A. SIMAR
81 Director Education & Mathematics .... Ms. Suzonne CROCKETT
49 Dir Arts/Humanities/Social Sciences .... Mr. Andy PRESLAR
96 Director of Purchasing .... Vacant

*Lamar State College-Port Arthur (C)

1500 Procter Street, Port Arthur TX 77640-6604
County: Jefferson
FICE Identification: 023485
Unit ID: 226116
Telephone: (409) 983-4921
Carnegie Class: Spec 2-yr-Health
FAX Number: (409) 984-6032
Calendar System: Semester
URL: www.lamarpa.edu
Established: 1909
Annual Undergrad Tuition & Fees (In-State): $5,533
Enrollment: 2,077
Coed
Affiliation or Control: State
IRS Status: 501(c)3
Highest Offering: Associate Degree
Accreditation: SC, SURGT

02 President .... Dr. Betty REYNARD
05 Vice President Academic Affairs .... Dr. Gary D. STRETCHER
10 Vice President for Finance .... Ms. Mary WICKLAND
32 Dean of Student Services .... Dr. Deborrah HEBERT
04 Admin Assistant to the President .... Mrs. Donna SCHION
08 Dean Library Services .... Mr. Peter B. KAATRUDE
06 Registrar .... Ms. Connie NICHOLAS
37 Director Financial Aid .... Ms. Connie RILEY
45 Director Inst Effectiveness .... Mr. James M. KNOWLES
18 Director of Physical Plant .... Mr. Stephen ARNOLD
26 Public Information Officer .... Mr. Gerry DICKERT
56 Dir Inmate Instructional Program .... Dr. Barbara HUVAL
13 Dir Information Technology Services .... Mr. Samir GHORAYEB
15 Director Human Resources .... Ms. Tammy RILEY
07 Director of Admissions .... Ms. Connie NICHOLAS
09 Director of Institutional Research .... Mrs. Petra UZORUO
51 Dean Workforce/Continuing Educ Pgms .... Dr. Ben STAFFORD
72 Dean Technical Programs .... Ms. Sheila TRAHAN
81 Department Head Science & Math .... Dr. Percy JORDAN
50 Dept Head Business/CIS Technology .... Mrs. Sheila GUILLOT
83 Department Head Liberal Arts .... Dr. Barbara HUVAL
39 Director Student Housing .... Dr. Deborrah HEBERT
41 Athletic Director .... Mr. Scott STREET
96 Purchasing Manager .... Mrs. Allison WRIGHT

*Sam Houston State University (D)

1806 Avenue J, Suite 303, Huntsville TX 77341-0001
County: Walker
FICE Identification: 003606
Unit ID: 227881
Telephone: (936) 294-1111
Carnegie Class: DU-Mod
FAX Number: (936) 294-1465
Calendar System: Semester
URL: www.shsu.edu
Established: 1879
Annual Undergrad Tuition & Fees (In-State): $7,618
Enrollment: 19,573
Coed
Affiliation or Control: State
IRS Status: 501(c)3
Highest Offering: Doctorate
Accreditation: SC, ART, BUS, CACREP, CIDA, CLPSY, CS, DIETD, DIETI, FEPAC, MUS, NUR, NURSE, TED

02 President .... Dr. Dana G. HOYT
05 Interim Provost/VPAA .... Dr. Richard EGLSAER
10 VP for Finance & Operations .... Dr. Carlos HERNANDEZ
30 VP for University Advancement .... Mr. Frank HOLMES
84 VP for Enrollment Management .... Dr. Heather THIELEMANN
32 VP for Student Services .... Mr. Frank PARKER
13 VP for Information Technology .... Mr. Mark ADAMS
41 Athletic Director .... Mr. Bobby WILLIAMS
100 Chief of Staff .... Ms. Kathy GILCREASE
20 Interim Vice Provost .... Dr. Mary ROBBINS
58 Dean Graduate Studies .... Dr. Ken HENDRICKSON
25 Assoc VP Research/Sponsored Program .... Dr. Jerry COOK
106 Assoc VP Distance Learning .... Dr. William ANGROVE
21 Asst VP Finance & Operations .... Ms. Sylvia RAPPE
18 Assoc VP Facilities Management .... Mr. Juan NUNEZ
15 Assoc VP for HR & Risk Management .... Mr. David HAMMONDS
26 Assoc VP Marketing & Comm .... Ms. Kris KASKEL-RUIZ
44 Assoc VP for Development .... Ms. Thelma MOONEY
88 Assoc VP Enrollment Management .... Mr. Scot MERTZ
35 Assoc VP Student Svcs/Rec Sports .... Dr. Keith JENKINS
14 Assoc VP Infrustructure/Support Svc .... Mr. Terrance HARRIS
88 Assoc VP Enterprise Services .... Mr. Jacob CHANDLER
09 Asst VP Institutional Effectiveness .... Ms. Donna ARTHO
50 Dean of Business Administration .... Dr. Mitchell MUEHSAM
61 Dean of Criminal Justice .... Dr. Phillip LYONS
53 Dean of Education .... Dr. Stacey EDMONSON
57 Dean of Fine Arts/Mass Comm .... Dr. Ronald SHIELDS
76 Interim Dean of Health Sciences .... Dr. Rhonda CALLAWAY
83 Dean of Humanities/Social Sciences .... Dr. Abbey ZINK
81 Dean of Sciences .... Dr. John PASCARELLA
08 Director Library Services .... Ms. Ann HOLDER
19 Director Public Safety Services .... Mr. Kevin MORRIS
06 Registrar .... Ms. Teresa RINGO
07 Director Undergraduate Admissions .... Vacant
37 Director Financial Aid .... Ms. Lydia HALL
39 Director Residence Life .... Ms. Joellen TIPTON
38 AVP SS/Student Hlth & Couns Center .... Dr. Drew MILLER
29 Director Alumni Relations .... Mr. Charlie VIENNE
35 Dean of Students .... Mr. John YARABECK
108 Asst VP Planning & Assessment .... Dr. Somer FRANKLIN
43 Dir Legal Services/General Counsel .... Ms. Rhonda BEASSIE
88 Interim Controller .... Ms. Amanda WITHERS

*Sul Ross State University (E)

PO Box C-114, Alpine TX 79832-0001
County: Brewster
FICE Identification: 003625
Unit ID: 228501
Telephone: (432) 837-8032
Carnegie Class: Masters/L
FAX Number: (432) 837-8334
Calendar System: Semester
URL: www.sulross.edu
Established: 1917
Annual Undergrad Tuition & Fees (In-State): $5,927
Enrollment: 2,873
Coed
Affiliation or Control: State
IRS Status: 501(c)3
Highest Offering: Master's
Accreditation: SC

02 President .... Dr. Bill KIBLER
05 Exec VP Academic/Stdnt Affs/Provost .... Dr. Jim CASE
10 Vice Pres for Finance & Operations .... Mr. Cesario E. VALENZUELA
84 Vice Pres Enrollment Management .... Vacant
11 Assoc VP Fac/Plng/Construct/Ops .... Mr. Jim W. CLOUSE
30 Assoc Vice Pres University Services .... Mr. Leo G. DOMINGUEZ
12 Associate Provost & Dean RGC .... Dr. Paul SORRELS
11 Exec Asst to President/Dir Admin .... Ms. Yvonne REALIVASQUEZ
06 Director Records & Registration .... Ms. Pamela S. PIPES
08 Dean Library & Info Technology .... Mr. Don DOWDEY
32 Dean of Students .... Mr. Leo DOMINGUEZ
92 Dir Honors Prog/Acad Ctr Excellence .... Dr. Kathy STEIN
26 Director News & Publications .... Mr. Stephen W. LANG
37 Dir Financial Assistance .... Mr. Mickey CORBETT
49 Dean Arts & Science .... Dr. Jay DOWNING
107 Dean Education & Professional Stds .... Vacant
47 Dean Agricult/Natural Resource Sci .... Dr. Robert J. KINUCAN
15 Director of Human Resources .... Mrs. Gail COLLIER
18 Asst Director of Physical Plant .... Mr. Edmundo NATERA
19 Director Dept of Public Safety .... Mr. Johnnie L. HOLBROOKS
21 Director of Accounting Services .... Mr. Santiago CASTILLO
39 Director Residential Living .... Vacant
41 Director of Athletics .... Mr. Bobby S. MESKER
38 Director of Counseling Ctr .... Ms. Mary SCHWARTZE
13 Chief Information Officer .... Mr. David W. GIBSON
96 Director of Purchasing .... Mr. Noe HERNANDEZ
88 Dir Center for Big Bend Studies .... Mr. Andy CLOUD
29 Director Alumni Relations .... Ms. Aida LUEVANOS
88 Director Museum of the Big Bend .... Ms. Elizabeth JACKSON
88 Director of Upward Bound .... Ms. Barbara VEGA
88 Director of University Archives .... Ms. Melleta BELL
88 Director Small Business Devel Ctr .... Ms. Patricia K. LONG
88 Director Law Enforcement Academy .... Dr. Robert HUNTER
07 Director Admissions & Records .... Ms. Claudia WRIGHT
88 Mail Service Supervisor .... Ms. Leticia GONZALES
88 Internal Auditor .... Mr. Scott A. CUPP
36 Coord Career Services & Testing .... Ms. Jan L. RUEB
09 Dir of Institutional Effectiveness .... Dr. Jeanne QVARMSTROM

*Texas State University (F)

601 University Drive, San Marcos TX 78666-4615
County: Hays
FICE Identification: 003615
Unit ID: 228459
Telephone: (512) 245-2111
Carnegie Class: DU-Higher
FAX Number: (512) 245-3040
Calendar System: Semester
URL: www.txstate.edu
Established: 1899
Annual Undergrad Tuition & Fees (In-State): $9,348
Enrollment: 36,739
Coed
Affiliation or Control: State
IRS Status: 170(c)1
Highest Offering: Doctorate
Accreditation: SC, BUS, BUSA, CAATE, CACREP, CAHIIM, CEA, CIDA, COARC, COARCP, CONST, CS, DIETD, DIETI, ENG, HSA, IPSY, JOUR, MT, MUS, NRPA, NURSE, PTA, RTT, SP, SPAA, SW, TEAC

02 President .... Dr. Denise M. TRAUTH
05 Provost/Vice Pres Academic Affairs .... Dr. Gene BOURGEOIS
100 Special Assistant to the President .... Dr. Vicki S. BRITTAIN
32 Vice President Student Affairs .... Dr. Joanne H. SMITH
10 Vice Pres Finance/Support Services .... Mr. Eric ALGOE
30 Vice Pres University Advancement .... Dr. Barbara BREIER
13 Vice Pres Information Technology .... Mr. Kenneth PIERCE
83 Dean College of Applied Arts .... Dr. T. Jaime CHAHIN
50 Dean McCoy Col of Business Admin .... Dr. Denise T. SMART
57 Dean College Fine Arts & Comm .... Dr. John FLEMING
53 Dean College of Education .... Dr. Stan CARPENTER
76 Dean College Health Professions .... Dr. Ruth B. WELBORN
83 Dean College Liberal Arts .... Dr. Michael HENNESSY
81 Dean College of Science & Engr .... Dr. Christine HAILEY
58 Dean The Graduate College .... Dr. Andrea GOLATO
97 Dean Univ Col & Dir PACE Center .... Dr. Daniel BROWN
92 Dean Honors College .... Dr. Heather GALLOWAY
20 Assoc Vice Pres Academic Affairs .... Dr. Debbie M. THORNE
15 Asst VP of Human Resources .... Mr. John E. MCBRIDE
20 Associate Provost .... Dr. Cynthia L. OPHEIM
18 Associate VP of Facilities .... Mr. Thomas F. SHEWAN
86 Assoc VP Research & Dir of Fed Rels .... Vacant
35 Assoc VP Stdnt Affs/Dean of Stdnt .... Dr. Margarita M. ARELLANO
20 Assoc Vice Pres for Inst Effective .... Dr. Beth E. WUEST
21 Assoc VP Financial Services .... Mr. Darryl BORGONAH
84 Assoc VP Enrollment Mgmt/Marketing .... Vacant
08 Associate VP University Library .... Ms. Joan L. HEATH
20 Assistant VP for Academic Services .... Dr. Ronald C. BROWN
38 Director Counseling Center .... Dr. Kathlyn C. DAILEY
07 Asst VP Enroll Mgmt/Dir Ungrad Adm .... Ms. Stephanie ANDERSON
28 AVP/Dir Student Diversity/Inclusion .... Dr. Sherri BENN
44 Asst VP University Advancement .... Mr. Dan PERRY
44 Asst VP University Advancement .... Mr. Matt FLORES
89 Asst Dean of University College .... Ms. Laurie HINDSON
88 Assoc VP Finance/Support Svcs Plng .... Ms. Nancy NUSBAUM
14 Assoc VP for Technology Resources .... Mr. Mark HUGHES
90 Assoc VP Instructional Tech Supp .... Dr. Carlos SOLIS
106 Dir Distance & Extended Learning .... Mr. Dana WILLETT
06 University Registrar .... Mr. Louis E. JIMENEZ
91 Director Enterprise Systems .... Mr. Martin MILLS
37 Director of Fin Aid & Scholarships .... Dr. Christopher MURR
36 Director Career Services .... Ms. Norma GUERRA GAIER
41 Director of Athletics .... Dr. Lawrence B. TEIS
29 Director of Alumni Affairs .... Ms. Kim GANNON
27 Director Univ News Services .... Mr. Jayme L. BLASCHKE
12 Asst VP Round Rock Campus .... Dr. Edna REHBEIN
25 Director of Sponsored Programs .... Mr. W. Scott ERWIN
19 Director University Police .... Mr. Jose BANALES
23 Director Student Health Center .... Dr. Emilio CARRANCO
39 Director Housing & Residential Life .... Dr. Rosanne PROITE
40 Manager University Bookstore .... Vacant
24 Interim Dir Educational Tech Ctr .... Ms. Rori SHEFFIELD
09 Director of Institutional Research .... Mr. Joseph M. MEYER
22 Chief Diversity/Dir Equity & Access .... Dr. Gilda GARCIA
93 Dir Center for Multicul/Gender Stds .... Dr. Audwin ANDERSON
96 Director Purchasing .... Ms. Jacque ALLBRIGHT
26 Director of University Marketing .... Mr. Daniel W. EGGERS
88 Director of Audit & Compliance .... Mr. Steve R. MCGEE
88 Director Campus Recreation .... Dr. Glenn HANLEY
88 Director LBJ Student Center .... Mr. Jack RAHMANN
88 Director Retention Mgmt & Planning .... Dr. Jen BECK

22 Director Disability Services .... Mr. Clint-Michael RENEAU
108 Dir Univ Planning & Assessment .... Dr. Ana Lisa GARZA
104 Asst VP for International Affairs .... Dr. Ryan BUCK

*Texas Tech University System (A)

2500 Broadway Ave., Admin Bldg,
Lubbock TX 79409-2013
County: Lubbock — Identification: 667242
Telephone: (806) 742-0012 — Carnegie Class: N/A
FAX Number: N/A
URL: www.texastech.edu

01 Chancellor .... Mr. Robert L. DUNCAN
05 Vice Chancellor Academic Affairs .... Dr. John OPPERMAN
10 Vice Chancellor & CFO .... Mr. Jim BRUNJES
30 Vice Chancellor Inst Advancement .... Ms. Lisa D. CALVERT
86 Vice Chanc Government Relations .... Ms. Martha BROWN
18 Vice Chanc Facil Plng/Construction .... Mr. Michael MOLINA

*Angelo State University (B)

2601 West Avenue N, San Angelo TX 76909-0001
County: Tom Green — FICE Identification: 003541
Unit ID: 222831
Telephone: (325) 942-2555 — Carnegie Class: Masters/L
FAX Number: N/A — Calendar System: Semester
URL: www.angelo.edu
Established: 1928 — Annual Undergrad Tuition & Fees (In-State): $6,892
Enrollment: 6,494 — Coed
Affiliation or Control: State — IRS Status: 501(c)3
Highest Offering: Doctorate
Accreditation: SC, ACBSP, MUS, NURSE, PTA, SW, TED

02 President .... Dr. Brian J. MAY
05 Provost/Vice Pres Academic Affairs .... Dr. Donald R. TOPLIFF
30 Exec Dir Development & Alumni Rels .... Ms. Jamie AKIN
10 VP for Finance and Administration .... Ms. Angelina WRIGHT
32 VP for Student Affs & Enroll Mgmt .... Dr. Javier FLORES
58 Dean College of Graduate Studies .... Dr. Susan KEITH
54 Dean of College of Sci & Engr .... Dr. Paul SWETS
50 Dean College Business .... Dr. Clifton JONES
53 Dean College of Education .... Dr. John MIAZGA
66 Dean College Health & Human Service .... Dr. Leslie MAYRAND
79 Dean College of Arts & Humanities ...... Ms. Carolyn GASCOIGNE
06 Director of Registrar Services .... Ms. Cindy WEEAKS
89 Dean Freshman College .... Dr. John WEGNER
09 Director of Accountability .... Ms. Brandy HAWKINS
08 Exec Director of Library .... Dr. Maurice G. FORTIN
36 Director Career Development .... Ms. Julie J. RUTHENBECK
15 Director of Human Resources .... Mr. Kurtis R. NEAL
37 Director of Student Financial Aid .... Mr. William BLOOM
26 Director of Communications & Mktg .... Ms. Rebekah BRACKIN
29 Director Development & Alumni Svcs .... Ms. Kimberly ADAMS
35 Exec Director of Student Affairs .... Dr. Bradley PETTY
18 Director of Facilities Management .... Mr. Jay HALBERT
39 Dir of Housing & Residential Pgm .... Ms. Tracy W. BAKER
40 Manager Bookstore .... Ms. Michaela REYNOLDS
41 Athletic Director .... Mr. James REID
19 Chief of University Police .... Mr. James E. ADAMS
13 Assoc VP Information Technology/CIO .... Mr. Douglas FOX
21 Director of Business Services .... Ms. Jessica MANNING
96 Director Purchasing and Travel .... Ms. Michelle MICHAELIS
92 Director of Honors Program .... Dr. Shirley EOFF
04 Executive Asst to the President .... Ms. Adelina C. MORALES
104 Director of International Studies .... Ms. Meghan PACE
07 Director of Admissions .... Ms. Sharla ADAM
38 Director of Counseling Services .... Mr. Cleave POOL
84 Director Enrollment Management .... Mr. Jeffrey SEFCIK
43 Sr Exec Asst to Pres/Gen Counsel .... Mr. Joe MUNOZ

† Affiliated with Texas Tech University in Lubbock, TX

*Texas Tech University (C)

2500 Broadway Avenue, Lubbock TX 79409-2005
County: Lubbock — FICE Identification: 003644
Unit ID: 229115
Telephone: (806) 742-2121 — Carnegie Class: DU-Highest
FAX Number: (806) 742-2138 — Calendar System: Semester
URL: www.ttu.edu
Established: 1923 — Annual Undergrad Tuition & Fees (In-State): $8,028
Enrollment: 35,158 — Coed
Affiliation or Control: State — IRS Status: 170(c)1
Highest Offering: Doctorate
Accreditation: SC, ARCPA, ART, BUS, BUSA, CACREP, #CIDA, CLPSY, COPSY, CS, DANCE, DIETD, DIETI, ENG, IPSY, LAW, LSAR, MFCD, MIDWF, MUS, SPAA, SW, TED, THEA

00 Chancellor .... Mr. Robert L. DUNCAN
02 Interim President .... Dr. John OPPERMAN
101 Sec Board Regents/Ex Asst to Chanc .... Mr. Ben W. LOCK
05 Provost and Senior Vice President ...... Dr. Lawrence SCHOVANEC
10 Chief Operating Ofcr/SVP Admin/Fin .... Ms. Noel SLOAN
30 Vice Chanc Inst Advancement .... Ms. Lisa CALVERT
86 Vice Chancellor Govt Relations .... Ms. Martha BROWN
43 Vice Chanc & General Counsel .... Mr. John HUFFAKER
18 VC Facilities Planning Construction .... Mr. Michael MOLINA
20 Vice Provost Academic Affairs .... Dr. Peggy MILLER
100 President's Chief of Staff .... Ms. Grace HERNANDEZ
29 EVP & CEO Texas Tech Alumni Assoc .... Dr. Bill DEAN
46 Vice President for Research .... Dr. Robert DUNCAN
28 Vice Pres Institutional Diversity .... Dr. Juan S. MUNOZ
84 Sr Assoc Vice Provost Enrollment Management ... Dr. James BURKHALTER
20 Assoc Vice Provost Academic Affairs .... Dr. Gary ELBOW
20 Sr Vice Provost .... Dr. Rob STEWART
26 Director of External Relations .... Ms. Suzanne TAYLOR
21 Asst Vice Pres & Controller .... Ms. Sharon WILLIAMSON
82 Assoc Vice Prov International Affs .... Mr. Tibor P. NAGY
13 Assoc VP Information Technology .... Mr. Sam SEGRAN
08 Dean of Libraries .... Dr. Donald DYAL
60 Dean Media & Communications .... Dr. David PERLMUTTER
32 Asst Dean of Students .... Ms. Denise TIJERINA
37 Managing Dir Financial Aid .... Ms. Becky WILSON
14 Chief Information Officer .... Ms. Kay RHODES
06 Registrar .... Ms. Bobbie BROWN
07 Managing Director of Admissions .... Dr. Ethan LOGAN
27 Managing Dir Commun & Marketing .... Mr. Chris COOK
104 Interim Director Study Abroad .... Ms. Elizabeth A. MCDANIEL
04 Executive Asst to President .... Ms. Jessica CARRILLO
31 Director Community Engagment .... Dr. Heather MARTINEZ
44 Senior Dir Annual Giving Programs ...... Ms. Deborah FINLAYSON
23 Director Student Health Services .... Ms. Evelyn MCPHERSON
39 Managing Dir Student Housing .... Mr. Sean DUGGAN
36 Managing Director Career Center .... Mr. Jay KILLOUGH
15 Managing Director of HR Management .. Ms. Jodie BILLINGSLEY
22 Asst Vice Chanc Admin/Dir EEO .... Ms. Charlotte BINGHAM
38 Managing Dir Student Counseling .... Dr. Eileen NATHAN
41 Director of Athletics .... Mr. Kirby HOCUTT
47 Dean Agriculture Sci/Natural Res .... Dr. Michael GALYEAN
49 Dean of Arts & Sciences .... Dr. Brent LINDQUIST
48 Dean of Architecture .... Mr. Andrew VERNOOY
50 Dean Business Administration .... Dr. Lance NAIL
53 Dean of Education .... Dr. Scott RIDLEY
54 Dean of Engineering .... Dr. Albert SACCO
88 Dean of Human Sciences .... Dr. Linda HOOVER
61 Dean School of Law .... Darby DICKERSON
58 Dean of Graduate School .... Dr. Mark SHERIDAN
92 Interim Dean Honors College .... Dr. Stephen FRITZ
57 Dean Visual & Performing Arts .... Dr. Carol EDWARDS
19 Chief of Police .... Mr. Ronald SEACRIST
09 Managing Dir Institutional Research .... Ms. Vicki WEST
96 Dir Purchasing & Contracting .... Ms. Jennifer ADLING

*Texas Tech University Health Sciences Center (D)

3601 4th Street, Lubbock TX 79430-0001
County: Lubbock — FICE Identification: 010674
Unit ID: 229337
Telephone: (806) 743-1000 — Carnegie Class: Spec-4-yr-Med
FAX Number: N/A — Calendar System: Semester
URL: www.ttuhsc.edu
Established: 1969 — Annual Undergrad Tuition & Fees (In-State): N/A
Enrollment: 4,931 — Coed
Affiliation or Control: State — IRS Status: 501(c)3
Highest Offering: Doctorate
Accreditation: SC, AUD, CAATE, CORE, DMOLS, MED, MT, NURSE, OT, PHAR, PTA, SP

02 President .... Dr. Tedd L. MITCHELL
10 Exec Vice Pres for Finance Admin .... Mr. Elmo M. CAVIN, JR.
05 Exec Vice Pres Academic Affairs .... Dr. Rial D. ROLFE
26 Exec Dir Communications & Mktg .... Ms. Mary CROYLE
17 Exec Vice Pres Rural/Community Hlth .. Dr. Billy U. PHILIPS, JR.
13 Vice Pres Info Tech/Chief Info Ofcr .... Dr. Chip SHAW
86 VP Federal and State Relations .... Mr. Ryan HENRY
100 Chief of Staff .... Ms. Didit MARTINEZ
43 Senior Assoc General Counsel .... Mr. Jon MCGOUGH
21 Assoc Vice Pres Business Affairs .... Mr. Mike CROWDER
46 Senior Vice President for Research .... Dr. Michael CONN
19 Information Security Officer .... Mr. Andrew HOWARD
15 Asst Vice Pres of Human Resources .... Dr. Gena JONES
18 Asst Vice Pres of Physical Plant .... Mr. George MORALES
63 Dean of Medical School .... Dr. Steven L. BERK
58 Dean Grad Sch Biomed Sciences .... Dr. Brandt L. SCHNEIDER
66 Dean of Nursing School .... Dr. Michael L. EVANS
76 Dean of Allied Health Sciences Sch .... Dr. Lori RICE-SPEARMAN
67 Dean of Pharmacy School .... Dr. Quentin R. SMITH
63 Reg Dean Medicine Amarillo Campus .... Dr. Richard JORDAN
63 Reg Dean Medicine Odessa Campus .... Dr. Gary VENTOLINI
66 Reg Dean Nursing Abilene .... Ms. Pearl E. MERRITT
66 Reg Dean Nursing Odessa Campus .... Dr. Sharon CANNON
76 Reg Dean Allied Health Amarillo .... Dr. Michael HOOTEN
76 Reg Dean Allied Health Odessa .... Dr. Neeraj KUMAR
67 Reg Dean Pharmacy Abilene .... Dr. Cindy RAEHL
67 Reg Dean Pharmacy Amarillo .... Dr. Thomas THEKKUMKARA
67 Reg Dean Pharmacy Dallas .... Dr. Roland PATRY
67 Reg Dean Pharmacy Lubbock .... Dr. Charles E. SEIFERT
06 Registrar .... Ms. Tamara N. KRAUSER
08 Exec Director of HSC Libraries .... Vacant
21 Managing Dir Accounting Services .... Ms. Melody OLIPHINT
22 Director of Equal Employment .... Ms. Charlotte BINGHAM
25 Director of Sponsored Programs .... Ms. Erin WOODS
37 Director of Financial Aid .... Mr. Marcus WILSON
25 Sr Director of Contracting .... Mr. Jim LEWIS
96 Managing Director of Purchasing .... Mr. John G. HAYNES
09 Chief Analyst Inst Research .... Mr. Kevin MCINTYRE
32 AVP Student Services .... Ms. Margret DURAN
29 Director of Alumni Relations .... Ms. Julie DOSS
21 Asst Vice Pres of Budget .... Ms. Penny HARKEY
30 Asst VC Development .... Ms. Kendra BURRIS
88 Sr Director Office of Global Health ...... Ms. Michelle ENSMINGER
108 Asst VP Academic Affairs .... Dr. Kari DICKSON
88 Vice President of Health Policy .... Dr. Cynthia JUMPER
28 VP of Diversity & Inclusion .... Dr. Kim PECK
88 Asst Vice Pres Compliance .... Ms. Sonya CASTRO-QUIRINO

*Texas Tech University Health Sciences Center at El Paso (E)

5001 El Paso Drive, El Paso TX 79905
Telephone: (915) 215-4300 — Identification: 667243
Accreditation: &SC, MED, NURSE

† Regional accreditation is carried under the parent institution in Lubbock, TX

Texas Wesleyan University (F)

1201 Wesleyan, Fort Worth TX 76105-1536
County: Tarrant — FICE Identification: 003645
Unit ID: 229160
Telephone: (817) 531-4444 — Carnegie Class: DU-Mod
FAX Number: (817) 531-4425 — Calendar System: Semester
URL: www.txwes.edu
Established: 1890 — Annual Undergrad Tuition & Fees: $24,454
Enrollment: 2,376 — Coed
Affiliation or Control: United Methodist — IRS Status: 501(c)3
Highest Offering: Doctorate
Accreditation: SC, ACBSP, ANEST, BUS, #CAATE, MUS

01 President .... Mr. Frederick G. SLABACH
05 Provost .... Dr. Allen HENDERSON
10 Sr VP Finance & Administration .... Mrs. Donna NANCE
30 VP University Advancement .... Mr. Jim LEWIS
84 VP for Enrollment & Student Svcs .... Ms. Pati ALEXANDER
26 Vice Pres Marketing/Communications .... Mr. John VEILLEUX
20 Assoc Provost Academic Affairs .... Dr. Steven DANIELL
20 Associate Provost .... Dr. Helena BUSSELL
41 Athletic Director .... Mr. Steven TRACHIER
53 Dean School of Education .... Dr. Carlos MARTINEZ
50 Dean of School of Business .... Dr. Hector QUINTANILLA
49 Dean School Arts & Letters .... Vacant
83 Dean School of Natural & Social Sci ..... Dr. Ricardo RODRIGUEZ
32 Dean of Students .... Mr. Dennis HALL
39 Asst Dn of Students/Dir Resid Life .... Mr. Jon BARTLETT
06 Registrar .... Ms. Kay VANTOORN
08 Library Science Assoc Professor .... Ms. Elizabeth HOWARD
21 Controller .... Ms. Caron PATTON
07 Enrollment Services Assistant VP .... Mr. Chadd BRIDWELL
37 Director Financial Aid .... Ms. Laurie ROSENKRANTZ
42 Chaplain .... Vacant
38 Director of Counseling .... Dr. Linda METCALF
29 Director Alumni Relations .... Mrs. DeAwna WOOD
15 AVP of Human Resources .... Vacant
96 Director of Purchasing .... Ms. Deborah CAVITT
36 Director of Career Services .... Ms. Robyn BONE
18 Exec Dir of Facil/Opers/Emr Svcs .... Mr. Brian FRANKS
25 Sr Dir of Sponsored Programs .... Mr. Shawn FARRELL
13 Associate Vice President & CIO .... Mr. Marcus KERR
04 Executive Assistant to the Pres .... Ms. Judi D. PARDUE
04 Executive Assistant to the Pres .... Mrs. Sherry SANDLES
09 Director Institutional Research .... Ms. Sherri CARABALLO
100 Chief of Staff and General Counsel .... Ms. Patti GEARHART TURNER
103 Director Career Services/Counselor .... Ms. Robyn BONE

Texas Woman's University (G)

Box 425587, Denton TX 76204-5587
County: Denton — FICE Identification: 003646
Unit ID: 229179
Telephone: (940) 898-2000 — Carnegie Class: DU-Mod
FAX Number: (940) 898-3198 — Calendar System: Semester
URL: www.twu.edu
Established: 1901 — Annual Undergrad Tuition & Fees (In-State): $6,948
Enrollment: 15,071 — Coed
Affiliation or Control: State — IRS Status: 501(c)3
Highest Offering: Doctorate
Accreditation: SC, ACBSP, CACREP, COPSY, DANCE, DH, DIETD, DIETI, HSA, IPSY, LIB, MFCD, MUS, NURSE, OT, PTA, SCPSY, SP, SW

01 President/Chancellor .... Dr. Carine FEYTEN
05 Provost & VP Academic Affairs .... Dr. Robert NEELY
10 Interim VP Finance/Administration .... Ms. BJ CRAIN
32 Vice President Student Life .... Dr. Monica MENDEZ-GRANT
13 Chief Information Officer .... Dr. Rob PLACIDO
20 Senior Associate Provost .... Dr. Jennifer MARTIN
09 Assoc Prov Inst Improve & Data Mgmt .... Dr. Mark S. HAMNER
26 Assoc Vice Pres Mktg/Communication .... Ms. Cindy POLLARD
84 Vice Pres Enrollment Services .... Mr. Gary RAY
21 Associate Vice President Finance .... Ms. Pam WILSON
18 Assoc Vice Pres Facilities .... Mr. Joe STANDRIDGE, JR.
15 Assoc Vice Pres Human Resources .... Mr. Lewis BENAVIDES
49 Dean College Arts & Sciences .... Dr. Abigail TILTON
69 Dean College Health Sciences .... Dr. Christopher T. RAY
107 Int Dean College Prof Education .... Dr. Jerry WHITWORTH
58 Dean Graduate School .... Dr. Larry LEFLORE
07 Director of Admissions .... Ms. Erma M. NIETO-BRECHT
43 General Counsel .... Ms. Destinee WAITERS
08 Director of Libraries .... Ms. Suzanne SEARS
37 Director Student Financial Aid .... Mr. Governor E. JACKSON
36 Director Career & Employment Svcs .... Ms. Lisa GARZA
38 Director Counseling Center .... Dr. Denise LUCERO-MILLER
27 Director News & Information .... Ms. Amanda SIMPSON

19 Director of Public Safety ... Ms. Liz PAULEY
06 Registrar ... Mr. Bobby LOTHRINGER
41 Athletic Director ... Ms. Chalese CONNORS
23 Director Student Health Services ... Dr. Connie MENARD
39 Director University Housing ... Ms. Jill ECKARDT
29 Director Alumni Relations ... Ms. Anne SCOTT
96 Procurement Services ... Ms. Vanna PARR
04 Executive Asst to Chancellor/Pres ... Ms. Lori HUSLIG
04 Coord Events Outreach & Communic ... Ms. Rachel PRIDE
100 Chief of Staff ... Mr. Christopher JOHNSON
104 Director Study Abroad ... Ms. Annie PHILLIPS
105 Director Univ Web Communications ... Mr. Scott BYNUM
106 Dir Teach & Learn w/Technology ... Dr. Lynda MURPHY
108 Director Academic Assessment ... Dr. Terry SENNE
30 Vice President Advancement ... Ms. Heidi TRACY
50 Director School of Management ... Dr. Margaret A. YOUNG
86 Dir Governmental & Legis Affairs ... Mr. Kevin CRUSER

Trinity University (A)

One Trinity Place, San Antonio TX 78212-7200

County: Bexar
FICE Identification: 003647
Unit ID: 229267
Telephone: (210) 999-7011
Carnegie Class: Masters/S
FAX Number: (210) 999-7696
Calendar System: Semester
URL: www.trinity.edu
Established: 1869
Annual Undergrad Tuition & Fees: $37,856
Enrollment: 2,432
Coed
Affiliation or Control: Independent Non-Profit
IRS Status: 501(c)3
Highest Offering: Master's
Accreditation: SC, BUS, ENG, HSA, TED

01 President ... Dr. Danny ANDERSON
05 VP Faculty and Student Affairs ... Dr. Michael R. FISCHER
10 VP Finance and Administration ... Mr. Gary LOGAN
30 VP Alumni Relations & Develop ... Mr. Michael BACON
26 VP Info Resources/Marketing & Comm ... Dr. Charles B. WHITE
20 Assoc VP Student Academic Issues ... Dr. Sheryl R. TYNES
20 Assoc VP Faculty Recruitment & Dev ... Dr. Duane COLTHARP
20 Assoc VP Budget & Research ... Dr. Mark BRODL
21 Assoc VP Budget/Business Ops ... Ms. Ana M. WINDHAM
07 Assoc VP Enrollment & Student Reten ... Vacant
08 University Librarian ... Ms. Diane J. GRAVES
06 Registrar ... Mr. Alfred RODRIGUEZ
37 Asst VP Student Financial Svcs ... Ms. Glendi GADDIS
38 Director Counseling/Health Svcs ... Dr. Gary W. NEAL
32 Assoc VP Stdnt Affs/Dean of Stdnt ... Mr. David M. TUTTLE
31 Dir Campus/Community Involvement ... Ms. Jamie THOMPSON
36 Director of Career Services ... Ms. Twyla HOUGH
15 Assistant VP Human Resources ... Ms. Pamela JOHNSTON
13 Dir/Chief Info Technology Officer ... Mr. Fred ZAPATA
27 Asst VP External Relations ... Ms. Sharon JONES SCHWEITZER
30 Asst VP Alumni Relations & Dev ... Vacant
44 Director of Planned Giving ... Ms. Kristine HOWLAND
29 Senior Director of Alumni Relations ... Dr. MaryKay COOPER
51 AVP Conferences/Special Pgms ... Ms. Ann G. KNOEBEL
04 Assistant to the President ... Ms. Claire SMITH
19 Asst VP Public Safety/Ent Risk Mgmt ... Mr. Paul CHAPA
18 Director Facility Services ... Mr. Mike SCHWEITZER
40 Director of Bookstore ... Vacant
42 Chaplain ... Rev. Stephen R. NICKLE
09 Assoc VP/Dir Institutional Research ... Dr. Diane G. SAPHIRE
96 Director of Purchasing ... Ms. Cynthia LARA
28 Director Diversity ... Ms. Jamie THOMPSON
41 Athletic Director ... Mr. Bob KING

Trinity Valley Community College (B)

100 Cardinal Drive, Athens TX 75751-2734

County: Henderson
FICE Identification: 003572
Unit ID: 225308
Telephone: (903) 677-8822
Carnegie Class: Assoc/MT-VT-High Non
FAX Number: (903) 675-6316
Calendar System: Semester
URL: www.tvcc.edu
Established: 1946
Annual Undergrad Tuition & Fees (In-District): $2,340
Enrollment: 4,983
Coed
Affiliation or Control: State/Local
IRS Status: 501(c)3
Highest Offering: Associate Degree
Accreditation: SC, ADNUR, EMT, SURGT

01 President Pro Tem ... Dr. Jerry KING
05 Vice President for Instruction ... Dr. Jerry KING
30 VP of Institutional Advancement ... Ms. Kristen BENNETT
32 Vice President Student Services ... Dr. Jay KINZER
13 VP of Information Technology ... Mr. Brett DANIEL
10 Vice Pres Administrative Services ... Mrs. Jean MCSPADDEN
20 Assoc VP Instruction Academic Educ ... Dr. Wendy ELMORE
103 Associate VP of Workforce Education ... Mr. David MCANALLY
91 Assoc VP of Information Technology ... Vacant
21 Associate Business Officer ... Ms. Courtney WALKER
12 Assoc VP of TDCJ Programs ... Dr. Sam HURLEY
18 Asst VP of Facilities Management ... Mr. David GRAEM
76 Provost Health Occupations ... Dr. Helen REID
12 Provost Kaufman County Campus ... Dr. Algia ALLEN
12 Provost Anderson County Campus ... Dr. Jeff WATSON
06 Registrar/Dean Enrollment Mgmt ... Dr. Colette HILLIARD
09 Dir Strategic Planning/SACS ... Ms. Tina RUMMEL
08 Director Learning Resource Center ... Ms. Karla BRYAN
36 Dir of Student Pathways/Success ... Ms. Tammy DENNEY
26 Public Information Officer ... Mr. Mark MEREDITH
07 Director School Relations ... Ms. Audrey HAWKINS
37 Dir Student Finan Aid/Veteran's Svc ... Ms. Jennifer EVILSIZER
41 Athletic Director ... Mr. Brad SMILEY

19 Director of Campus Police ... Mr. Stewart NEWBY
36 Placement Officer ... Vacant
40 Bookstore Manager ... Mrs. Beth Ann KIDD
35 Director Student Activities ... Mr. Harold JONES
31 Director Community Services ... Ms. Gayle ROBERTS
15 Int Director of Human Resources ... Ms. Jarene DOTTS
96 Director of Purchasing ... Ms. Judith MCGILVRAY

Tyler Junior College (C)

PO Box 9020, Tyler TX 75711-9020

County: Smith
FICE Identification: 003648
Unit ID: 229355
Telephone: (903) 510-2200
Carnegie Class: Assoc/MT-VT-High Trad
FAX Number: (903) 510-2632
Calendar System: Semester
URL: www.tjc.edu
Established: 1926
Annual Undergrad Tuition & Fees (In-District): $2,410
Enrollment: 11,163
Coed
Affiliation or Control: State/Local
IRS Status: 170(c)1
Highest Offering: Baccalaureate
Accreditation: SC, CAHIIM, COARC, DH, DMS, EMT, MLTAD, OTA, @PTAA, RAD, SURGT

01 President ... Dr. L. Michael METKE
10 Vice President Business Affairs ... Ms. Sarah E. VAN CLEEF
30 Int Exec Dir Inst Advance/Ext Affrs ... Mr. Dennis M. ANDREWS
32 Provost/Vice Pres Acad & Stdnt Affs ... Dr. Juan E. MEJIA
81 Dean Engineering/Math and Sciences ... Dr. Kenneth E. MURPHY
76 Dean Nursing & Health Professions ... Mr. Paul R. MONAGAN
72 Acting Dean Professional/Tech Progs ... Mr. Jason WALLER
84 Dean Enrollment Management ... Mrs. Janna L. CHANCEY
09 Exec Dir Inst Effect/Plng & Rsrch ... Dr. Cheryl L. ROGERS
62 Director Library Services ... Ms. Marian D. JACKSON
51 Dean Continuing Studies ... Dr. Aubrey D. SHARPE
21 Controller ... Ms. Carol A. HUTSON
06 Dir Academic Svcs/Registrar ... Mr. Thomas ELDER
37 Director Financial Aid ... Mrs. Devon WIGGINS
26 Dir Public Affairs and Grant Dev ... Mr. Fred M. PETERS
35 Director Student Life ... Mrs. Lauren TYLER
29 Director Alumni Affairs ... Mr. Donald L. FRASER
36 Coordinator Career Services ... Mrs. Maggie RUELLE
07 Director Admissions ... Mrs. Nidia HASSAN
15 Exec Dir Human Resources ... Mr. S. Kevin FOWLER
88 Asst VP Student Engagement ... Dr. Timothy S. DRAIN
09 Dir Institutional Research ... Ms. Jacquelyn MESSINGER
18 Exec Dir Facilities & Construction ... Mr. William L. KING
96 Director Campus Services ... Mr. Michael CARUSO
35 Asst VP Student Services ... Dr. Thomas A. JOHNSON
13 Chief Information Officer ... Mr. Larry MENDEZ
109 Director Auxiliary Services ... Ms. Diana KAROL
44 Int Exec Dir Marketing/Media/Comm ... Mrs. Kimberly LESSNER
36 Director Testing ... Mr. Roger GRIMM
88 Director Academic Advising ... Mrs. Jan ADAMS
88 Dean Student Success ... Ms. Lisa M. HARPER
88 Director SBDC ... Mr. Donald W. PROUDFOOT
04 Exec Asst to President ... Ms. Ellen MATTHEWS

University of Dallas (D)

1845 E Northgate Drive, Irving TX 75062-4736

County: Dallas
FICE Identification: 003651
Unit ID: 224323
Telephone: (972) 721-5000
Carnegie Class: Masters/L
FAX Number: (972) 721-5017
Calendar System: Semester
URL: www.udallas.edu
Established: 1956
Annual Undergrad Tuition & Fees: $35,800
Enrollment: 2,548
Coed
Affiliation or Control: Roman Catholic
IRS Status: 501(c)3
Highest Offering: Doctorate
Accreditation: SC, BUS

01 President ... Mr. Thomas W. KEEFE
04 Exec Admin Asst to the President ... Ms. Cathy MCCALEB
84 Sr VP Enroll Mgmt & Student Service ... Dr. John PLOTTS
10 VP and Chief Financial Officer ... Dr. Brian MURRAY
05 Provost and Chief Academic Officer ... Dr. Charles W. EAKER
30 VP for Advancement ... Ms. Joan CANTY
26 Executive VP for External Affairs ... Mr. Robert M. GALECKE
43 General Counsel ... Ms. Karin RILLEY
11 Assoc VP for Administration ... Mr. Patrick DALY
50 Dean College of Business ... Dr. Brett LANDRY
49 Dean of Constantin College ... Dr. Jonathan J. SANFORD
58 Dean Grad School of Liberal Arts ... Dr. Joshua S. PARENS
73 Dean School of Ministry ... Dr. Ted WHAPHAM
08 Dean of Libraries and Research ... Ms. Cherie L. HOHERTZ
88 Assoc Dean for Constantin College ... Dr. Scott CRIDER
06 Registrar ... Mrs. Kathy MCGRAW
19 Campus Safety Supervisor ... Mr. Charles STEADMAN
13 Director Information Technology ... Mr. Richard HAYTER
14 Director of IT User Support Service ... Mr. Sabyasachi SANYAL
44 Director of Annual Giving ... Vacant
41 Director of Athletics ... Mr. Richard STROCKBINE
42 Director of Campus Ministry ... Mrs. Denise PHILLIPS
18 Director of Facilities ... Mr. Jerry HABA
21 Director of Finance ... Mr. Leonard A. ROBERTSON
15 Asst Vice President for HR ... Dr. Richard HUNTLEY
09 Director of Institutional Research ... Mrs. Tanisha BARREN
27 Director of Marketing & Comm ... Mr. William HARTLEY
96 Director of Purchasing ... Mr. Alan STERLING
104 Director for Rome/Summer Programs ... Mrs. Becky DAVIES
23 Director of Student Health ... Dr. Lora RODRIGUEZ
36 Director of Career Services ... Ms. Julie JANIK

*University of Houston System (E)

4302 University Dr., 212 E. Cullen,
Houston TX 77204-2018

County: Harris
FICE Identification: 011721
Unit ID: 229407
Telephone: (713) 743-1000
Carnegie Class: N/A
FAX Number: N/A
URL: www.uhsa.uh.edu

01 Chancellor ... Dr. Renu KHATOR
05 Sr VC for Academic Affairs/Provost ... Dr. Paula M. SHORT
43 Vice Chancellor/General Counsel ... Ms. Dona H. CORNELL
10 VC Administration/Finance ... Mr. Jim MCSHAN
32 Vice Chancellor Student Affairs ... Dr. Richard WALKER
30 VC University Advancement ... Ms. Eloise D. STUHR
26 VP Univ Mktg/Communications/Media ... Vacant
27 Assoc VP Mktg/Comm/Media ... Ms. Lisa K. HOLDEMAN
13 Assoc VC CIO/Information Technology ... Dr. Dennis FOUTY
21 Associate Vice Chancellor Finance ... Mr. Raymond BARTLETT
11 Assoc VC Administration ... Dr. Emily MESSA
86 Vice Chanc Govt Relations ... Mr. Jason S. SMITH
88 Asst VC for Planning & Policy ... Mr. Chris STANICH
15 Exec Director Human Resources ... Ms. Joan M. NELSON
21 Director Internal Auditing ... Mr. Don GUYTON
88 Treasurer ... Ms. Roberta (Robbi) PURYEAR
100 Chief of Staff ... Mr. Michael JOHNSON

*University of Houston (F)

4302 University Dr., 212 E. Cullen,
Houston TX 77204-2018

County: Harris
FICE Identification: 003652
Unit ID: 225511
Telephone: (713) 743-1000
Carnegie Class: DU-Highest
FAX Number: N/A
Calendar System: Semester
URL: www.uh.edu
Established: 1927
Annual Undergrad Tuition & Fees (In-State): $8,759
Enrollment: 40,914
Coed
Affiliation or Control: State
IRS Status: Exempt
Highest Offering: Doctorate
Accreditation: SC, AAFCS, BUS, BUSA, CAATE, CEA, CLPSY, CONST, COPSY, CS, DIETD, DIETI, ENG, ENGT, IPSY, LAW, MUS, NAIT, OPT, OPTR, PHAR, SCPSY, SP, SW

02 President ... Dr. Renu KHATOR
05 Sr VC/VP Academic Affs/Provost ... Dr. Paula M. SHORT
10 VC/VP Administration/Finance ... Mr. Jim MCSHAN
44 VC/VP University Advancement ... Ms. Eloise D. STUHR
32 VC/VP Student Affairs ... Dr. Richard WALKER
26 Int AVP for Mktg/Commun/Media Rels ... Ms. Lisa K. HOLDEMAN
20 Vice Provost Academic Programs ... Dr. Bruce A. JONES
86 VC/VP Govt & Community Relations ... Mr. Jason S. SMITH
43 VC/VP Legal Affairs & Gen Counsel ... Ms. Dona H. CORNELL
46 Int VC/VP Research/Tech Transfer ... Dr. Ramanan KRISHNAMOORTI
31 VP for Community Rels & Inst Access ... Dr. Elwyn C. LEE
88 Vice Provost Global Strategies ... Dr. Jaime ORTIZ
29 Assoc VP Alumni Association ... Mr. Mike PEDE
13 Assoc VP Information Tech/CIO ... Dr. Dennis FOUTY
27 Executive Director Media Relations ... Mr. Mike S. ROSEN
20 Vice Provost & Dean UG Stdnts ... Dr. Teri E. LONGACRE
58 Vice Provost & Dean Grad School ... Mr. Dimitri LITVINOV
88 Int Assoc Provost Fac Dev/Affairs ... Dr. Mark CLARKE
21 Assoc Provost Finance & Admin ... Dr. Sabrina HASSUMANI
30 Assoc VP for Univ Development ... Mr. Cliff REDD
35 Assoc VC/VP Student Affairs ... Mr. Daniel MAXWELL
88 Assoc VP Stdnt Affs/Dean of Stdnts ... Dr. William MUNSON
91 Assoc VP Enterprise Sys Adm ... Dr. Arun JAIN
21 Associate VC/VP Finance ... Mr. Raymond BARTLETT
88 Assoc Prov Educ Innov & Tech ... Dr. Jeff MORGAN
22 Asst VC/VP Equal Opportunity ... Dr. Richard A. BAKER
45 AVC/Assoc Prov Inst Plng/Analy ... Mr. Chris M. STANICH
88 Assoc Prov Strategic Enroll Plng ... Dr. Maureen G. CROFT
41 VP Intercollegiate Athletics ... Mr. Hunter YURACHEK
37 Exec Dir Scholarships & Fin Aid ... Mr. Sal LORIA
15 Exec Director Human Resources ... Ms. Joan NELSON
18 Int Dir Facilities Management ... Mr. Carlos VILLARREAL
51 Director Continuing Education ... Ms. Mercedes SURATY-CLARKE
06 University Registrar ... Ms. Debbie HENRY
07 Executive Director of Admissions ... Ms. Djuana YOUNG
19 Asst VC/VP Public Safety Secu ... Mr. Malcolm DAVIS
96 Director of Purchasing ... Mr. Jack TENNER
49 Int Dean Col Liberal Arts/Soc Sci ... Dr. Steven CRAIG
81 Dean Col Natural Sci & Math ... Dr. Dan WELLS
88 Dean College of Optometry ... Dr. Earl L. SMITH
72 Int Dean College of Technology ... Dr. Neil ELDIN, III
66 Dean School of Nursing ... Dr. Kathryn M. TART
54 Dean Cullen College of Engineering ... Dr. Joseph W. TEDESCO
48 Dean College of Architecture ... Ms. Patricia Belton OLIVER
70 Dean Graduate Col of Social Work ... Dr. Alan DETLAFF
67 Dean College of Pharmacy ... Dr. Lamar PRITCHARD
53 Dean College of Education ... Dr. Robert MCPHERSON
50 Dean Bauer Col Business Admin ... Dr. Latha RAMCHAND
88 Dean Hilton Col Htl/Restaurant Mgt ... Dr. Dennis REYNOLDS
08 Dean University Libraries ... Ms. Lisa A. GERMAN
92 Dean Honors College ... Dr. William MONROE
61 Dean UH Law Center ... Mr. Leonard M. BAYNES
11 Assoc VC/VP Administration ... Dr. Emily MESSA
88 Chief Energy Officer ... Dr. Ramanan KRISHNAMOORTI
17 Interim Chief Health Officer ... Dr. Earl L. SMITH

*University of Houston - Clear Lake (A)

2700 Bay Area Boulevard, Houston TX 77058
County: Harris FICE Identification: 011711
Unit ID: 225414
Telephone: (281) 283-7600 Carnegie Class: Masters/L
FAX Number: (281) 283-2219 Calendar System: Semester
URL: www.uhcl.edu
Established: 1971 Annual Undergrad Tuition & Fees (In-State): $5,802
Enrollment: 8,665 Coed
Affiliation or Control: State IRS Status: 501(c)3
Highest Offering: Doctorate
Accreditation: SC, BUS, BUSA, CS, ENG, ENGR, MFCD, SW, TED

02 President ... Dr. William A. STAPLES
05 Int Sr Vice Pres for Acad Affairs ... Dr. Glen HOUSTON
10 Vice Pres Administration & Finance ... Ms. Michelle DOTTER
04 Executive Assoc to the President .. Ms. Mary Ann H. SHALLBERG
13 Assoc VP Information Resources ... Dr. A. Glen HOUSTON
20 Assoc Vice Pres Academic Affairs ... Dr. Mrinal Mugdh VARMA
30 Assoc VP University Advancement ... Ms. Rhonda THOMPSON
32 Assoc Vice Pres Student Services ... Dr. Darlene BIGGERS
21 Associate Vice President Finance ... Ms. Usha MATHEW
84 Assoc Vice Pres Enrollment Mgmt ... Dr. Yvette BENDECK
18 Assoc VP Facilities Mgmt/Construct ... Mr. Ward MARTAINDALE
50 Dean School Business ... Dr. Wm. Theodore CUMMINGS
81 Dean School Science/Computer Engr ... Dr. Zbigniew CZAJKIEWICZ
79 Dean Sch Human Sci/Humanities ... Dr. Rick SHORT
53 Dean School Education ... Dr. Mark D. SHERMIS
35 Interim Dean of Students ... Mr. David A. RACHITA
28 Asst Dean Student Diversity ... Ms. Linda C. BULLOCK
08 Exec Director Neumann Library ... Ms. Karen WIELHORSKI
85 Exec Dir Intl Admissions/Programs ... Dr. Sameer PANDE
45 Exec Dir Planning and Assessment ... Ms. Pat CUCHENS
15 Executive Director Human Resources ... Ms. Nichole ESLINGER
14 Exec Director University Computing ... Mr. Rodger CARR
21 Exec Dir of Procurement & Payables ... Ms. Debra CARPENTER
25 Exec Dir Sponsored Programs ... Mr. Paul MEYERS
37 Executive Director Financial Aid ... Dr. Billy SATTERFIELD
88 Exec Dir Environment Inst Houston ... Dr. George GUILLEN
06 Registrar/Director Academic Records ... Dr. Billy SATTERFIELD
56 Director Distance/Off-Campus Educ ... Ms. Lisa GABRIEL
26 Exec Dir University Communications ... Ms. Theresa PRESSWOOD
29 Dir Development & Alumni Relations ... Mr. Dwayne BUSBY
19 Interim Chief of Police ... Mr. Allen HILL, JR.
36 Ex Dir Counseling/Hlth/Career Svcs ... Dr. Cindy COOK
91 Assoc Dir Data Management ... Vacant
12 Dir Camp Operat/UHCL Pearland Camp ... Dr. Kathy DUPREE
23 Dir Health & Disability Services ... Ms. Regina PICKETT
07 Exec Director of Admissions ... Ms. Rauchelle JONES
40 Manager Bookstore ... Ms. Laura FORGEY

*University of Houston - Downtown (B)

One Main Street, Houston TX 77002-1014
County: Harris FICE Identification: 003612
Unit ID: 225432
Telephone: (713) 221-8001 Carnegie Class: Masters/S
FAX Number: (713) 221-8075 Calendar System: Semester
URL: www.uhd.edu
Established: 1974 Annual Undergrad Tuition & Fees (In-State): $5,780
Enrollment: 14,439 Coed
Affiliation or Control: State IRS Status: Exempt
Highest Offering: Master's
Accreditation: SC, BUS, ENGT, SW

02 Interim President ... Dr. Michael A. OLIVAS
04 Executive Assoc to President ... Ms. Vanessa PIGEON
88 Special Asst to the President ... Vacant
05 Int Provost/Sr VP Acad & Stdnt Affs ... Mr. Edward HUGETZ
20 Assoc VP for Academic Affairs ... Dr. Faiza KHOJA
32 Assoc VP Student Affairs ... Dr. Tomikia P. LEGRANDE
50 Dean College of Business ... Dr. Michael FIELDS
79 Dean Col Humanities/Social Sci ... Dr. DoVeanna FULTON
88 Int Dean College of Public Service ... Dr. Leigh VAN HORN
81 Dean Col Sciences & Tech ... Dr. Akif UZMAN
97 Dean University College ... Dr. Chris BIRCHAK
88 Int Dir Comm Engage & Svc Learning ... Dr. Poonam GULATI
08 Executive Director WI Dykes Library ... Ms. Pat ENSOR
08 Asst Dir Library Plng & Assessment ... Ms. Lisa BERRY
106 Exec Director Distance Education ... Mr. Louis D. EVANS, III
09 Director of Institutional Research ... Ms. Carol M. TUCKER
46 Asst VP Research/Sponsored Pgms ... Dr. Jerry JOHNSON
25 Dir Grant Writing & Assessment ... Dr. Kwame OPUNI
108 Director of Academic Assessment ... Dr. Lea CAMPBELL
108 Dir Co-Curricular & Oper Assessment ... Dr. Angela KOPONEN
88 Director Creative Services ... Mr. Joe WYNNE
88 Director O'Kane Gallery ... Mr. Mark CERVENKA
92 Exec Director of Scholars Academy ... Dr. Mary Jo PARKER
88 Dir Teaching & Learning Excel ... Dr. Gregory DEMENT
88 Exec Dir Academic Advising Center ... Dr. Wendy WILSON
88 Director FTIC Retention Services ... Ms. Jemma SYLVESTER-CAESAR
88 Director of Advising Services ... Ms. Reyna ROMERO
88 Director of Academic Support Center ... Dr. Isidro GRAU
88 Exec Dir Presidential Affairs & Ops ... Vacant
88 Exec Dir Academic Admin & Ops ... Ms. Elaine PEARSON
88 Dir Strategic Initiatives & Project ... Ms. Lucy BOWEN
92 Director Honors Porgram ... Dr. Mari NICHOLSON-PREUSS
11 Dir College Admin & Operation ... Vacant
72 Dir Applied Business/Technology Ctr ... Mr. G. V. KRISHNAN
88 Director English Language Institute ... Dr. Gail KELLERSBERGER
88 Director Criminal Justice Center ... Mr. Rex WHITE
51 Director Continuing Education ... Ms. Clara ROJAS ALVAREZ LOPEREN
88 Dir Center for Entrepreneurship ... Mr. William DUDLEY
88 Dir Insurance & Risk Management Ctr ... Vacant
88 Dir COB Career Dev Center ... Mr. Brett HOBBY
88 Dir Assurance Learning & Assessment ... Mr. Isiah BROWN
88 Dir of Retail Mgmt Center ... Mr. James DAVIS
10 VP Administration & Finance ... Mr. David M. BRADLEY
13 Assoc VP Information Technology ... Mr. Hossein SHAHROKHI
91 Director Enterprise Systems ... Mr. Kong YIN
88 Dir Technology Learning Services ... Mr. John LANE
88 Director Technical Services ... Ms. Grace DAVILA
88 Dir Comp/Telecom & Video Networks ... Mr. Miguel RUIZ
90 Director User Support Services ... Mr. Said FATTOUH
88 Dir IT Business Services ... Ms. Jacqueline SMITH
88 Dir Info Security & IT Compliance ... Mr. Jon GARZA
109 Dir University Business Services ... Ms. Mary TORRES
88 Director Emergency Management ... Ms. Carol MANOUSOS
88 Director of Budget & Procurement ... Ms. Theresa MENELEY
21 Asst VP Business Affairs ... Mr. George W. ANDERSON
88 Dir Financial Reporting ... Ms. Delethia MURRAY
25 Director Risk Mgmt & Compliance ... Ms. Mary COOK
18 Asst VP Facilities Management ... Mr. Chris MCCALL
88 Dir Maintenance & Renovations ... Mr. Abraham FLORES
88 Dir MEP ... Mr. Kris ZIMMERMAN
19 Interim Chief of Police ... Mr. David DELEON
88 Dir Student Accounts & Collection ... Ms. Lauren BELLENGER
88 Dir Accounts Payable ... Ms. Cynthia CONNER
15 VP Employment Svcs & Operations ... Ms. Ivonne MONTALBANO
16 Exec Dir Employ Services & Opers ... Mr. Shawn MCCANN
88 Dir Benefits & Compensation ... Ms. Erica MORALES
88 Director Employment Operations ... Ms. April FRANK
88 Asst Dean Enrollment Management .. Mr. Christopher CHEATHAM
35 Asst VP Stdnt Success/Dean of Stdnt ... Dr. Patrick JEFFERSON
35 Asst Dn Student Affs/Title IV Coord ... Mr. Tommy THOMASON
88 Int Dir Student Activities & Events ... Ms. Sara T. CRASS
28 Dir Ctr Stdnt Diversity Equ & Incl ... Dr. John HUDSON
07 Interim Director of Admissions ... Ms. Ceshia LOVE
37 Director of Scholarships & Fin Aid ... Ms. LaTasha GOUDEAU
41 Director Sports & Fitness ... Mr. Richard SEBASTIANI
36 Director Career Development Center ... Ms. Laura A. WESELEY
22 Director Disability Services ... Dr. Meritza TAMEZ
88 Director Veterans Services ... Mr. Richard SELVERA
88 Director Testing Services ... Mr. Robert ALONZO
88 Dir Events & Conference Services ... Ms. Mary A. WHITE
88 Interim Director Talent Search ... Ms. Marta ALVARENGA
88 Director Upward Bound ... Ms. Dawanna LEWIS
88 Int Pgm Title V Stdnt Success Grant ... Mr. Branden KUZMICK
30 VP Advancement & External Rels ... Ms. Johanna WOLFE
26 Exec Dir of University Relations ... Ms. Elisa CROSSLAND
102 Director Corporate Relations ... Mr. Jacob LIPP
88 Director Individual Giving ... Ms. Jaha WILLIAMS
88 Dir Advancement Services & Bus Ops ... Mr. Brian DRAKE
29 Director Alumni Relations ... Ms. Liza ALONZO

*University of Houston - Victoria (C)

3007 N Ben Wilson, Victoria TX 77901-4450
County: Victoria FICE Identification: 013231
Unit ID: 225502
Telephone: (361) 570-4848 Carnegie Class: Masters/L
FAX Number: (361) 580-5534 Calendar System: Semester
URL: www.uhv.edu
Established: 1973 Annual Undergrad Tuition & Fees (In-State): $7,086
Enrollment: 4,407 Coed
Affiliation or Control: State IRS Status: 501(c)3
Highest Offering: Master's
Accreditation: SC, BUS, CACREP, NURSE

02 President ... Dr. Raymond V. MORGAN, JR.
11 Vice Pres Administration & Finance ... Mr. Wayne B. BERAN
05 Interim Provost/VP Acad Affairs ... Dr. Don N. SMITH
32 Vice President Student Affairs ... Dr. Jay LAMBERT
49 Dean Arts & Sciences ... Dr. Jeffrey DILEO
50 Dean Business Administration ... Dr. Farhang NIROOMAND
53 Dean Education & Human Development ... Dr. Freddie LITTON
30 VP Advancement & External Relations ... Mr. Jesse D. PISORS
08 Senior Director of Library ... Dr. Joe F. DAHLSTROM
13 Sr Dir Academic & Student Tech Svcs ... Mr. Joseph S. FERGUSON
15 Dir Human Resource/Affirmative Act ... Ms. Laura L. SMITH
84 Asst VP for Enrollment Mgmt ... Dr. Denee THOMAS
88 Dir Small Business Development Ctr ... Mr. Joe HUMPHREYS
06 Registrar ... Ms. Trudy WORTHAM
14 Director Administrative Technology ... Mr. Randy FAULK
37 Director Financial Aid ... Ms. Carolyn R. MALLORY
18 Director Facilities ... Mr. John BURKE
10 Director Business Services ... Mr. Tim MICHALSKI
21 Comptroller ... Ms. Valerie WALDEN
41 Director Athletics ... Mr. Ashley WALYUCHOW
26 Director Marketing & Communications ... Ms. Paula COBLER
38 Director of Counseling Center ... Vacant
35 Director of Student Life & Services ... Mr. Michael WILKINSON
09 Director Institutional Research ... Dr. Tong-Ai ZHANG
88 Director of Budget ... Ms. Karen SANDERS
39 Director Residence Life & Univ Comm ... Mr. Brandon w. LEE
88 Director Capital Projects ... Ms. Brenda SVETLIK
04 Executive Adm Asst to President ... Ms. Kathy WALTON
25 Dir Research Adm & Sponsored Pgms ... Ms. Angela HARTMANN
108 Dir Institutional Effectiveness ... Dr. Sharon M. BAILEY
102 Sr Dir Foundation/Corp Relations ... Ms. Courtney M. SIDES
29 Director Alumni Relations ... Ms. Kira MUDD

University of the Incarnate Word (D)

4301 Broadway, San Antonio TX 78209-6397
County: Bexar FICE Identification: 003578
Unit ID: 225627
Telephone: (210) 829-6000 Carnegie Class: Masters/L
FAX Number: (210) 829-1220 Calendar System: Semester
URL: www.uiw.edu
Established: 1881 Annual Undergrad Tuition & Fees: $27,798
Enrollment: 8,745 Coed
Affiliation or Control: Roman Catholic IRS Status: 501(c)3
Highest Offering: Doctorate
Accreditation: SC, ACBSP, #CAATE, CIDA, DIETD, DIETI, HSA, MUS, NMT, NURSE, OPT, OPTR, @OSTEO, PHAR, PTA, THEA

01 Acting President ... Dr. Denise DOYLE
00 Chancellor ... Dr. Denise DOYLE
88 Vice President Mission and Ministry ... Sr. Walter MAHER
04 Executive Assistant to President ... Ms. Vanessa LOPEZ
26 Asst to the President/Communication ... Mr. Lou FOX
43 Vice President/General Counsel ... Ms. Cindy ESCAMILLA
05 Provost ... Dr. Kathleen LIGHT
84 Vice Pres Enrollment Mgt/Stdnt Svcs . Dr. David M. JURENOVICH
30 Vice Pres Institutional Advancement ... Sr. Kathleen COUGHLIN
10 Vice Pres for Business & Finance ... Mr. Douglas ENDSLEY
104 Vice Pres International Programs ... Mr. Marcos FRAGOSO
56 Vice Pres of Ext Academic Programs ... Dr. Cyndi WILSON-PORTER
13 Vice Pres Information Resources/CIO ... Ms. Lisa BAZLEY
21 Comptroller ... Ms. Edith COGDELL
50 Dean H-E-B Sch Business & Admin ... Dr. Forrest F. AVEN
57 Dean Humanities Arts & Social Sci ... Dr. Kevin VICHCALES
66 Dean Nursing & Health Professions ... Dr. Mary HOKE
53 Dean Dreeben School of Education ... Dr. Denise STAUDT
54 Dean Math Science Engineering ... Dr. Carlos GARCIA
88 Dean Interactive Media & Design ... Dr. Sharon WELKEY
67 Dean Feik School of Pharmacy ... Dr. Arcelia JOHNSON-FANNIN
88 Dean School of Optometry ... Dr. Timothy WINGERT
58 Dean of Grad Studies/Research ... Dr. Osman OZTURGUT
62 Dean of Library Services ... Dr. Cheryl ANDERSON
108 Assoc Provost/Dir of Assessment ... Dr. Glenn JAMES
55 Dean Sch of Extended Studies ... Mr. Vincent PORTER
89 Dean Univ Preparatory Programs ... Mr. Daniel OCHOA
88 Dean School Physical Therapy ... Dr. Caroline GOULET
29 Director of Alumni Relations ... Dr. Lisa MCNARY
27 Director of Public Relations ... Ms. Debra DEL TORO
84 Dean of Enrollment ... Ms. Jennielle STROTHER
32 Dean of Student Success ... Ms. Sandy MCMAKIN
38 Director of Counseling ... Dr. Christie MELONSON
20 Director of Academic Advising ... Ms. Sonia JASSO
88 Director Learning Assistance Center ... Ms. Cristina ARIZA
06 Registrar ... Dr. Bobbye G. FRY
37 Director of Financial Aid ... Ms. Amy CARCANAGUES
32 Dean of Campus Life ... Dr. Renee MOORE
39 Director of Residence Life ... Ms. Diane SANCHEZ
35 Director of Campus Engagement ... Mr. Paul AYALA
23 Director of Health Services ... Vacant
42 Chaplain ... Fr. Tom DYMOWSKI
42 Director of Campus Ministry ... Ms. Elisabeth VILLARREAL
15 Director of Human Resources ... Ms. Annette THOMPSON
96 Director of Purchasing ... Mr. Sam WAGES
18 Director Facilities Mgmt & Services ... Mr. Steve HEYING
41 Director of Athletics ... Mr. John WILLIAMS
88 Director of Infrastructure Support ... Mr. Carl HAYWOOD
88 Director of Enterprise Applications ... Ms. Iris SOLCHER
88 Director Instructional Technology ... Ms. Ana GONZALES
72 Director of Technology Support ... Mr. Anthony RAMOS
09 Director of Institutional Research ... Ms. Robin LOGAN
07 Director of Admissions ... Mr. Javier LARA
36 Coordinator of Career Services ... Ms. Abreeta GOODE
100 Chief of Staff ... Mr. Vincent RODRIGUEZ
102 Dir Foundation/Corporate Relations ... Mr. Robert SOSA
105 Director Web Development ... Mr. Troy KINCKERBOCKER
19 Chief of Police ... Mr. Robert CHAVEZ
44 Dir of Major Gifts/Planned Giving ... Mr. Alex CASTANEDA
63 Dean School of Osteopathic Medicine ... Dr. Robyn PHILLIPS-MADSON

University of Mary Hardin-Baylor (E)

900 College Street, Belton TX 76513-2578
County: Bell FICE Identification: 003588
Unit ID: 226471
Telephone: (254) 295-8642 Carnegie Class: Masters/M
FAX Number: (254) 295-4535 Calendar System: Semester
URL: www.umhb.edu
Established: 1845 Annual Undergrad Tuition & Fees: $26,100
Enrollment: 3,740 Coed
Affiliation or Control: Southern Baptist IRS Status: 501(c)3
Highest Offering: Doctorate
Accreditation: SC, ART, CACREP, MUS, NURSE, @PTA, SW

01 President/CEO ... Dr. Randy G. O'REAR
03 Sr Vice Pres Admin/COO ... Dr. Steve THEODORE
05 Interim Provost/Sr VP Academic Affs ... Dr. Danny MYNATT
45 Vice Pres Campus Planning & Support ... Mr. Rick MARTINEZ
30 Vice Pres for Development ... Dr. Rebecca O'BANION
102 Vice Pres Communication/Spec Proj ... Dr. Paula TANNER
32 Vice Pres for Student Life ... Dr. Byron WEATHERSBEE
41 Vice Pres Athletics ... Mr. Randy MANN
10 Vice Pres Business/Finance/CFO ... Mrs. Jennifer RAMM
15 Vice Pres Human Resources ... Mrs. Susan OWENS
13 Vice Pres Information Tech ... Mr. Brent HARRIS

84 Vice Pres Enrollment Mgmt .... Dr. Gary LAMM
18 Assoc Vice Pres for Campus Planning .... Mr. Bob PATTEE
21 Controller .... Mrs. Charla KAHLIG
50 Dean McLane College of Business .... Dr. Ken SMITH
79 Dean of Humanities & Sciences .... Dr. Danny MYNATT
66 Dean of Nursing .... Dr. Sharon SOUTER
53 Dean of Education .... Dr. Marlene ZIPPERLEN
58 Dean Graduate School .... Dr. Colin WILBORN
88 Dean of Christian Studies .... Dr. Tim CRAWFORD
57 Dean Visual/Performing Arts .... Mr. Ted BARNES
35 Dean of Students .... Mr. Ray MARTIN
39 Assoc Dean Students/Dir Residence .... Ms. Donna PLANK
04 Executive Assistant .... Mrs. Phyllis ROGERS
06 Registrar .... Mrs. Amy MCGILVRAY
88 Dir Grad Student Services/Engagemt .... Ms. Melissa WILLIAMS
07 Director of Admissions & Recruiting .... Dr. Brent BURKS
08 Director Learning Resources .... Ms. Denise KARIMKHANI
26 Director Marketing/Public Relations .... Mr. James STAFFORD
09 Director Institutional Research .... Ms. Jen JONES
37 Director Financial Aid .... Mr. Ron BROWN
92 Director Honors Program .... Dr. David HOLCOMB
19 Director Campus Police .... Mr. Gary SARGENT
96 Purchasing Manager .... Mrs. Jennifer WEBB
29 Director Alumni Relations .... Dr. Brandon SKAGGS
42 University Chaplain .... Dr. George LOUTHERBACK
36 Director Career Services .... Mr. Don OWENS
38 Director Couns Testing & Health .... Mr. Nate WILLIAMS
85 Dir International Student Services .... Mrs. Elizabeth TANAKA
44 Director Planned Giving .... Mrs. Melissa BRAGG
40 Bookstore Manager .... Ms. Debbie COTTRELL

University of North Texas (A)

1155 Union Circle #311277, Denton TX 76203-5013
County: Denton FICE Identification: 003594
Unit ID: 227216
Telephone: (940) 565-2000 Carnegie Class: DU-Highest
FAX Number: (940) 565-7600 Calendar System: Semester
URL: www.unt.edu
Established: 1890 Annual Undergrad Tuition & Fees (In-State): $9,730
Enrollment: 36,486 Coed
Affiliation or Control: State IRS Status: 501(c)3
Highest Offering: Doctorate
Accreditation: SC, ART, AUD, BUS, BUSA, CACREP, CEA, CIDA, CLPSY, COPSY, CORE, CS, ENG, ENGT, FEPAC, JOUR, LIB, MUS, SP, SPAA, SW, TED

01 President .... Dr. Neal SMATRESK
00 Chancellor .... Mr. Lee F. JACKSON
05 Provost/Vice Pres Academic Affairs .... Dr. Finley GRAVES
10 Vice Pres Finance/Administration .... Mr. Bob BROWN
46 VP Research/Economic Development .... Dr. Thomas J. MCCOY
32 Vice President Student Affairs .... Dr. Elizabeth WITH
43 Vice Chancellor/General Counsel .... Ms. Nancy S. FOOTER
26 Vice President University Relations .... Ms. Deborah S. LELIAERT
30 VP for Advancement/Dir of Develop .... Ms. Eileen P. MORAN
84 VP for Enrollment .... Mr. Shannon M. GOODMAN
13 Vice President for Univ Info Svcs .... Dr. Vernon A. CLARK
20 Vice Provost for Academic Affairs .... Dr. Christy CRUTSINGER
20 Vice Provost for Academic Resources .... Mr. Robert A. WATLING
20 Vice Provost for Faculty Success .... Dr. Michael MCPHERSON
41 Athletic Director .... Mr. Henry H. DICKENSON
35 Dean Students .... Dr. Maureen MCGUINNESS
13 Vice President for Information Tech .... Vacant
21 Assoc VP Budget & Analytics .... Ms. Beverly COTTON
28 VP Institutional Equity & Diversity .... Dr. Joanne WOODARD
88 Vice Prov for Transfer Articulation .... Dr. Celia WILLIAMSON
18 Assoc Vice President for Facilities .... Mr. David REYNOLDS
08 Dean of Libraries .... Dr. Martin HALBERT
37 Director Financia Aid .... Ms. Zelma DELEON
49 Dean College of Arts/Sciences .... Dr. David HOLDEMAN
50 Dean College Business .... Dr. Marilyn WILEY
53 Dean College of Education .... Dr. Bertina COMBES
57 Dean Col Visual Arts & Design .... Dr. Eric LIGON
88 Dean Col Public Affs/Community Svc .... Dr. Thomas L. EVENSON
64 Dean College of Music .... Dr. John W. RICHMOND
59 Dean Col of Merch/Hosp & Tourism .... Dr. Judith FORNEY
62 Dean College of Information .... Dr. KINSHUK
58 Vice Provost Toulouse Grad School .... Dr. Victor PRYBUTOK
92 Dean Honors College .... Dr. Glenisson DE OLIVEIRA
60 Dean Mayborn Sch of Journalism .... Dr. Dorothy BLAND
54 Dean College of Engineering .... Dr. Costas TSATSOULIS
90 Director Acad Computing/User Svcs .... Dr. Philip C. BACZEWSKI
09 Director Institutional Research .... Dr. Mary BARTON
108 Assoc Vice Provost DAIR .... Dr. Jason F. SIMON
88 Director of Accreditation .... Ms. Elizabeth VOGT
07 Director of Admissions .... Dr. Rebecca LOTHRINGER
51 Dir Ctr for Achvmnt & Lifelng Lrng .... Ms. Marilyn D. WAGNER
06 Registrar .... Ms. Lynn MCCREARY
15 Assoc Vice Chancellor HR .... Mr. Luis LEWIN
36 Dir Career & Counseling Svcs .... Mr. Dan NAEGELI
38 Director of Counseling & Testing .... Vacant
19 Director/Chief of Police .... Mr. Ed REYNOLDS
39 Director Housing .... Mr. Gina VANACORE
85 Vice Provost International Affairs .... Ms. Amy SHENBERGER
23 Dir Stdnt Health Ctr/Wellness Svcs .... Dr. Herschel VOORHEES
29 Exec Dir Alum Rels/N Texas Exes .... Mr. Robert MCINTURF
04 Administrative Asst to President .... Ms. Ruby RAINES
101 Secretary of the Institution/Board .... Dr. Rosemary R. HAGGETT
25 Asst VP Research/Sponsored Pgm .... Dr. David SCHULTZ
104 Director Study Abroad .... Ms. Amy SHENBERGER

University of North Texas at Dallas (B)

7300 University Hills Blvd, Dallas TX 75241
County: Dallas Identification: 667124
Unit ID: 484905
Telephone: (972) 780-3600 Carnegie Class: Not Classified
FAX Number: (972) 780-3606 Calendar System: Semester
URL: www.untdallas.edu
Established: 2000 Annual Undergrad Tuition & Fees (In-State): $7,650
Enrollment: 2,575 Coed
Affiliation or Control: State IRS Status: 501(c)3
Highest Offering: Doctorate
Accreditation: SC

01 President .... Dr. Ronald MONG
10 Chief Financial Officer .... Dr. Daniel EDELMAN
05 Provost .... Dr. Lois BECKER

University of North Texas Health Science Center at Fort Worth (C)

3500 Camp Bowie Boulevard, Fort Worth TX 76107-2699
County: Tarrant FICE Identification: 009768
Unit ID: 228909
Telephone: (817) 735-2000 Carnegie Class: Spec-4-yr-Med
FAX Number: (817) 735-2486 Calendar System: Semester
URL: www.unthsc.edu
Established: 1966 Annual Graduate Tuition & Fees: N/A
Enrollment: 2,243 Coed
Affiliation or Control: State IRS Status: 501(c)3
Highest Offering: Doctorate; No Undergraduates
Accreditation: SC, ARCPA, HSA, OSTEO, PH, @PHAR, PTA

01 President .... Dr. Michael WILLIAMS
10 Senior VP for Finance and CFO .... Mr. John A. HARMAN
88 Executive VP Clinical Affairs .... Mr. Michael R. HICKS
86 Vice President Governmental Affairs .... Mr. Dan JENSEN
63 Dean Texas Col of Osteopathic Med .... Dr. Don PESKA
32 Vice Pres Student Affairs .... Dr. Thomas MOORMAN
15 Vice Pres Human Resource Svcs .... Vacant
45 VP Research & Innovation .... Vacant
51 Assoc VP for Professional/Cont Edu .... Ms. Pam MCFADDEN
58 Dean Grad Sch Biomedical Sciences .... Dr. Meharvan SINGH
76 Dean School of Health Professions .... Dr. Claire PEEL
69 Dean of School of Public Health .... Vacant
37 Director Student Financial Aid .... Mr. Joseph SANCHEZ
84 Executive Director Enrollment Svcs .... Mr. A.J RANDOLPH
19 Chief of Police .... Mr. Gary GAILLIARD
30 VP Institutional Advancement .... Mr. Doug WHITE
09 VP Strategy & Measurement .... Dr. Thomas FAIRCHILD
21 Vice President Finance & Planning .... Mr. Geoff SCARPELLI
07 Asst Dean of Admissions & Outreach .... Vacant
18 Vice President for Operations .... Mr. Stephen BARRETT
06 Registrar .... Mr. A.J RANDOLPH
100 Chief of Staff .... Mrs. Jennifer TREVINO
03 Executive VP/Chief People Officer .... Mr. Steven R. SOSLAND
05 Provost and Exec VP .... Mr. Thomas YORIO
08 Director of Lewis Library .... Mr. Daniel BURGARD
13 Chief Info Technology Officer (CIO) .... Ms. Lynley DUNGAN

University of Phoenix Austin Campus (D)

10801-2 MoPac Expressway, Suite 300, Austin TX 78759-5459
Telephone: (512) 344-1400 Identification: 770226
Accreditation: &NH, ACBSP

† No longer accepting campus-based students.

University of Phoenix Dallas Campus (E)

12400 Coit Road, Dallas TX 75251-2004
Telephone: (972) 385-1055 Identification: 770227
Accreditation: &NH, ACBSP

† Regional accreditation is carried under the parent institution in Tempe, AZ

University of Phoenix El Paso Campus (F)

1340 Adabel Drive, El Paso TX 79936-5900
Telephone: (915) 599-5900 Identification: 770228
Accreditation: &NH, ACBSP

† Regional accreditation is carried under the parent institution in Tempe, AZ

University of Phoenix Houston Campus (G)

11451 Katy Freeway, Houston TX 77079-2004
Telephone: (713) 465-9966 Identification: 770229
Accreditation: &NH, ACBSP

† Regional accreditation is carried under the parent institution in Tempe, AZ

University of Phoenix San Antonio Campus (H)

8200 IH-10 West, Suite 1000, San Antonio TX 78230-3876
Telephone: (210) 524-2100 Identification: 770231
Accreditation: &NH, ACBSP

† Regional accreditation is carried under the parent institution in Tempe, AZ

University of St. Augustine for Health Sciences (I)

5401 La Crosse Ave, Austin TX 78739
Telephone: (512) 394-9766 Identification: 770940
Accreditation: &WC, OT, PTA

† Branch campus of University of St. Augustine for Health Sciences, San Marcos, CA.

University of St. Thomas (J)

3800 Montrose Boulevard, Houston TX 77006-4696
County: Harris FICE Identification: 003654
Unit ID: 227863
Telephone: (713) 522-7911 Carnegie Class: Masters/L
FAX Number: (713) 525-2125 Calendar System: Semester
URL: www.stthom.edu
Established: 1947 Annual Undergrad Tuition & Fees: $30,310
Enrollment: 3,448 Coed
Affiliation or Control: Roman Catholic IRS Status: 501(c)3
Highest Offering: Doctorate
Accreditation: SC, BUS, NURSE, TEAC, THEOL

01 President .... Dr. Robert IVANY
04 Special Assistant to the President .... Ms. Cindy VIAUD
04 Exec Assistant to the President .... Ms. Anne LAMBERT
10 Vice President for Finance .... Ms. Elizabeth CONDIC
05 Provost and VP Academic Affairs .... Dr. Dominic AQUILA
11 Assoc VP of Human Resources .... Mr. Randy GRAHAM
49 Dean Arts & Sciences .... Dr. Chris EVANS
73 Dean School of Theology .... Dr. Sandra C. MAGIE, CM
50 Dean Cameron School of Business .... Dr. Beena GEORGE
53 Dean School of Educ & Human Svcs .... Dr. Paul PAESE
08 Dean of Libraries .... Mr. James PICCININNI
58 Dir Center for Thomistic Studies .... Dr. Thomas OSBORNE
82 Director Center for Intl Studies .... Dr. Hans STOCKTON
88 Director Center for Irish Studies .... Ms. Lori GALLAGHER
88 Dir Center for Ethical Leadership .... Dr. Joseph CERAMI
13 Vice Pres Information Technology .... Mr. Gary MCCORMACK
30 Vice President for Inst Advancement .... Ms. Cynthia COLBERT RILEY
84 Vice Pres Marketing & Enroll Mgmt .... Ms. Vickie ALLEMAN
88 Director Center for Faith & Culture .... Vacant
06 Registrar .... Ms. Debra LOVELESS
90 Dir of Network & Campus Computing .... Mr. Tony REYNA
90 Director Technology Support Svcs .... Mr. Mark HENDERSON
91 Dir Administrative Computing Svcs .... Ms. Joanna E. PALASOTA
32 Vice Pres Student Affairs .... Ms. Patricia MCKINLEY
35 Dean of Students .... Ms. Lindsey MCPHERSON
38 Exec Dir Counseling & Disability .... Dr. Rose SIGNORELLO
35 Assistant VP of Campus Life .... Mr. Matthew PRASIFKA
42 Dir of Campus Ministry/Chaplain .... Fr. Michael BUENTELLO
39 Director Residence Life .... Vacant
88 Asst Dir of Recreational Sports .... Ms. Mary Ann SHAW
18 Asst VP Facilities Operations .... Mr. Howard A. ROSE
21 Controller .... Ms. Brandy SHAW
88 Treasurer .... Ms. Susan ROSE
84 Asst VP of Enrollment Management .... Mr. Arthur ORTIZ
07 Dir of Transfer Adm & Veteran Svcs .... Mr. Phil BUTCHER
37 Dean of Scholarships/Financial Aid .... Ms. Lynda MCKENDREE
26 Director of Communications .... Ms. Sandra SOLIZ
88 Director of Creative Services .... Ms. Marionette MITCHELL
108 Assoc VP Institutional Assessment .... Dr. Siobhan FLEMING
19 Chief of Police .... Mr. James TATE
41 Athletic Director .... Mr. Todd SMITH
104 Director Study Abroad .... Dr. Ulyses BALDERAS
29 Director Alumni Relations .... Mr. Hank EMERY

*University of Texas System Administration (K)

601 Colorado Street, Austin TX 78701-2982
County: Travis FICE Identification: 003655
Unit ID: 229090
Telephone: (512) 499-4201 Carnegie Class: N/A
FAX Number: (512) 499-4215
URL: www.utsystem.edu

01 Chancellor .... Mr. William H. MCRAVEN
03 Deputy Chancellor .... Mr. David E. DANIEL
05 Exec VC Academic Affairs .... Dr. Steve LESLIE
17 Exec Vice Chanc Health Affairs .... Dr. Raymond S. GREENBERG
10 Exec Vice Chanc Business Affairs .... Dr. Scott C. KELLEY
43 Vice Chanc & General Counsel .... Mr. Dan SHARPHORN
86 Vice Chanc for Govt Relations .... Mr. Barry MCBEE
26 Vice Chanc for External Relations .... Dr. Randa S. SAFADY
86 Vice Chanc Federal Relations .... Mr. William SHUTE
45 Vice Chanc Strategic Initiatives .... Dr. Stephanie A. BOND-HUIE
18 Assoc VC Facil Plng/Construction .... Mr. Michael O'DONNELL
13 Assoc VC & Chief Info Officer .... Mr. Mark MILSTEIN
21 Assc VC/Controller/Chief Budget Ofc .... Mr. Randy WALLACE
15 Assoc Vice Chanc Employee Services .... Mr. Dan STEWART
27 Executive Director Public Affairs .... Ms. Jenny LACOSTE-CAPUTO
88 Executive Director Real Estate .... Mr. Kirk TAMES
30 Dir Development/Gift Planning Svcs .... Ms. Julie LYNCH
19 Director of Police .... Mr. Michael J. HEIDINGSFIELD
04 Administrative Asst to President .... Ms. Katherine IANNESSA

*The University of Texas at Arlington (A)

701 S Nedderman Drive, Arlington TX 76013
County: Tarrant FICE Identification: 003656
Unit ID: 228769
Telephone: (817) 272-2101 Carnegie Class: DU-Highest
FAX Number: (817) 272-5656 Calendar System: Semester
URL: www.uta.edu
Established: 1895 Annual Undergrad Tuition & Fees (In-State): $9,208
Enrollment: 39,740 Coed
Affiliation or Control: State IRS Status: 170(c)1
Highest Offering: Doctorate
Accreditation: SC, ART, BUS, BUSA, CAATE, CEA, CIDA, CS, ENG, LSAR, MUS, NURSE, PLNG, SPAA, SW, TED

02 President .... Dr. Vistasp M. KARBHARI
05 Interim Provost & VP Acad Affairs .... Dr. Linda JOHNSRUD
10 Chief Financial Officer and VP .... Ms. Kelly DAVIS
32 VP Student Affairs .... Dr. Tim QUINNAN
30 VP Development and Alumni Relations .... Mr. Michael KINGAN
46 Vice President Research .... Dr. Duane DIMOS
13 Vice Pres Information Technology .... Vacant
11 Vice Pres Admin & Campus Operations .... Mr. John D. HALL
26 Vice President of Communications .... Ms. Lynne WATERS
15 Vice President for Human Resources .... Ms. Jean HOOD
84 Sr Assoc VP Student Enrollment Svcs .... Dr. Dale WASSON
45 Assoc Vice Provost Inst Eff/Report .... Dr. Loraine PHILLIPS
16 Asst Vice Pres Human Resources .... Ms. Eunice M. CURRIE
27 Asst Vice President Media Services .... Ms. Kristin SULLIVAN
18 Asst VP Campus Operation/Facilities .... Mr. Bill POOLE
88 Interim Director for Univ College .... Ms. Liz HANNABAS
04 Special Assistant to the President .... Ms. Salma ADEM
58 Assoc Dean of Graduate Studies .... Mr. Raymond L. JACKSON
48 Dean of Arch/Urban & Public Affairs .... Dr. Nan ELLIN
50 Dean Business Administration .... Dr. Rachel CROSON
54 Dean of Engineering .... Dr. Khosrow BEHBEHANI
49 Interim Dean of Liberal Arts .... Dr. Elisabeth CAWTHON
66 Dean of Nursing .... Dr. Anne BAVIER
81 Dean of Science .... Dr. Morteza KHALEDI
70 Dean School of Social Work .... Dr. Scott RYAN
53 Interim Dean College of Education .... Dr. John SMITH
92 Dean Honors College .... Dr. Karl PETRUSO
08 Dean of Libraries .... Dr. Rebecca BICHEL
07 Exec Director Admissions & Records .... Dr. Hans GATTERDAM
12 Exec Dir of UTA Ft Worth Center .... Mr. Mike WEST
37 Director of Financial Aid .... Dr. Karen KRAUSE
23 Director Student Health Center .... Mr. Robert BLUM
22 Director Equal Opportunity Services .... Mr. Eddie FREEMAN
24 Director of Art Services .... Mr. Joel QUINTANS
41 Athletic Director .... Mr. Jim BAKER
19 Dir Environmental Health Safety .... Ms. Leah HOY
85 Executive Director Intl Education .... Mr. Jay HORN
88 Director Multicultural Outreach .... Mr. Casey GONZALES
88 Director Multicultural Affairs .... Ms. Leticia MARTINEZ
86 Director Government Relations .... Mr. Jeff JETER
09 Director of Institutional Research .... Ms. Loraine PHILLIPS
43 Dir Legal Services/General Counsel .... Mr. Shelby BOSEMAN
96 Director of Purchasing .... Ms. Julia CORNWELL
29 Exec Dir for Alumni & Donor Rels .... Ms. Julie BARFIELD

*University of Texas at Austin (B)

Austin TX 78712-1111
County: Travis FICE Identification: 003658
Unit ID: 228778
Telephone: (512) 471-3434 Carnegie Class: DU-Highest
FAX Number: (512) 471-2942 Calendar System: Semester
URL: www.utexas.edu
Established: 1883 Annual Undergrad Tuition & Fees (In-State): $9,806
Enrollment: 51,313 Coed
Affiliation or Control: State IRS Status: 170(c)1
Highest Offering: Doctorate
Accreditation: SC, ART, AUD, BUS, BUSA, CAATE, CEA, CIDA, CLPSY, COPSY, CORE, DANCE, DIETC, DIETD, ENG, IPSY, JOUR, LAW, LIB, LSAR, #MED, MUS, NURSE, PHAR, PLNG, SCPSY, SP, SPAA, SW

02 President .... Dr. Gregory L. FENVES
05 Interim Executive VP & Provost .... Dr. Judith H. LANGLOIS
10 VP & Chief Financial Officer .... Mr. Darrell BAZZELL
28 VP Diversity & Community Engagement .... Mr. Gregory J. VINCENT
11 Vice Pres for University Operations .... Dr. Patricia L. CLUBB
46 Vice President Research .... Dr. Juan M. SANCHEZ
13 Chief Information Officer .... Mr. Bradley G. ENGLERT
27 Chief Communications Officer .... Ms. Maria M. ARRELLAGA
43 Vice President Legal Affairs .... Ms. Patricia A. OHLENDORF
26 Director University Media Relations .... Mr. Gary J. SUSSWEIN
88 Deputy to the Pres Strategy/Policy .... Dr. Harrison A. KELLER
100 Deputy to the President .... Ms. Nancy A. BRAZZIL
04 Executive Assistant to President .... Ms. Rebecca L. BAUGHMAN
88 Sr Vice Prov Resource Management .... Dr. Daniel T. SLESNICK
88 Sr Vice Provost Enroll/Grad Mgmt .... Dr. David A. LAUDE
32 Vice President Student Affairs .... Dr. Gage E. PAINE
84 Vice Provost for Enrollment Mgmt .... Vacant
20 Vice Provost for Faculty Affairs .... Dr. Janet M. DUKERICH
88 Vice Provost for Biomed Sciences .... Dr. Robert O. MESSING
46 Assoc VP Rsrch/Dir Spnsrd Projects .... Dr. Jason D. RICHTER
08 Vice Provost/Director UT Libraries .... Dr. Lorraine J. HARICOMBE
06 Vice Provost & Registrar .... Mr. Vincent (Shelby) STANFIELD
104 Vice Provost International Programs .... Dr. Janet L. ELLZEY
58 Interim Dean Graduate Studies .... Dr. Marvin L. HACKERT
88 Vice Provost Inst Accred .... Dr. Linda N. DICKENS
86 Assoc VP for Governmental Relations .... Mr. Carlos E. MARTINEZ
86 Assoc VP for Governmental Relations .... Ms. Gwen W. GRIGSBY
21 Associate VP for Finance .... Ms. Mary E. KNIGHT
21 Budget Director .... Ms. Elvia H. ROSALES
09 Director Institutional Research .... Ms. Tracy H. BROWN
88 Associate Vice Provost .... Ms. Kathryn V. FOSTER
88 Associate Vice Provost .... Ms. Carolyn K. CONNERAT
88 Associate Vice Provost .... Mr. Phil D. LONG
88 Associate Vice President .... Ms. Renee L. WALLACE
30 Executive Director for Development .... Vacant
19 Assoc VP Campus Safety/Security .... Dr. Gerald (Bob) R. HARKINS
18 Sr Assoc VP Facilities Management .... Mr. David L. REA
15 Associate Vice Pres Human Resources .... Dr. Debra G. KRESS
22 Asst VP Institutional Equity .... Dr. Sherri L. SANDERS
23 Director University Health Services .... Ms. Jamie L. SHUTTER
37 Director Student Financial Svcs .... Ms. Diane C. TODD SPRAGUE
35 Sr Assoc Vice Pres/Dean of Students .... Dr. Soncia R. REAGINS-LILLY
39 Director Housing & Food Service .... Mr. Rene RODRIGUEZ
41 Interim Athletics Director .... Mr. Michael PERRIN
41 Women's Athletics Director .... Ms. Christine A. PLONSKY
29 CEO/Exec Director Texas Exes .... Ms. Leslie CEDAR
19 Chief University Police .... Mr. David CARTER
48 Dean of Architecture .... Dr. Frederick R. STEINER
50 Dean McCombs School of Business .... Dr. Jay C. HARTZELL
60 Dean of Communication .... Dr. Jay M. BERNHARDT
53 Dean of Education .... Dr. Manuel J. JUSTIZ
54 Dean of Engineering .... Dr. Sharon L. WOOD
57 Dean of Fine Arts .... Dr. Douglas J. DEMPSTER
62 Dean School of Information .... Dr. Andrew P. DILLON
65 Dean Jackson School of Geosciences .... Dr. Sharon MOSHER
61 Dean School of Law .... Mr. Ward FARNSWORTH
49 Dean of Liberal Arts .... Dr. Randy L. DIEHL
63 Vice President for Medical Affairs .... Dr. S. Claiborne JOHNSTON
81 Dean of Natural Sciences .... Dr. Linda A. HICKE
66 Dean of Nursing .... Dr. Alexa M. STUIFBERGEN
67 Dean of Pharmacy .... Dr. M. Lynn CRISMON
80 Dean LBJ School Public Affs .... Dr. Robert H. WILSON
70 Dean Social Work .... Dr. Luis H. ZAYAS
97 Dean of Undergrad Studies .... Dr. Brent L. IVERSON
51 Associate Director Internal Audits .... Mr. Jeff D. TREICHEL
88 Director Internal Audits .... Mr. Michael W. VANDERVORT
18 Associate VP Utilities/Energy Mgmt .... Mr. Juan M. ONTIVEROS
88 Executive Director Univ Union .... Mr. Mulugeta FEREDE
27 Director Univ of Texas Press .... Mr. David S. HAMRICK
88 Assoc Athl Dir/Dir Spec Events Ctr .... Mr. John M. GRAHAM
96 Assistant VP/Dir of Procurement .... Vacant
07 Director of Admissions .... Ms. Susan L. KEARNS

*The University of Texas at Dallas (C)

800 West Campbell Road, Richardson TX 75080
County: Collin FICE Identification: 009741
Unit ID: 228787
Telephone: (972) 883-2111 Carnegie Class: DU-Highest
FAX Number: (972) 883-2237 Calendar System: Semester
URL: www.utdallas.edu
Established: 1969 Annual Undergrad Tuition & Fees (In-State): $10,864
Enrollment: 23,095 Coed
Affiliation or Control: State IRS Status: 501(c)3
Highest Offering: Doctorate
Accreditation: SC, ACAE, AUD, BUS, BUSA, CS, ENG, IPSY, SP, SPAA

02 President .... Dr. Richard BENSON
05 Provost/Exec VP Academic Affairs .... Dr. B. Hobson WILDENTHAL
10 Vice President for Business Affairs .... Dr. Calvin D. JAMISON
32 Vice President Student Affairs .... Dr. Gene FITCH
46 Vice President Research .... Dr. Bruce GNADE
20 Vice Provost .... Dr. John WIORKOWSKI
30 Vice President for Advancement .... Vacant
26 VP/Chief Information Officer .... Mr. R. David CRAIN
28 Vice President of Diversity .... Dr. George W. FAIR
45 Interim Budget Director .... Mr. David GAARDER
21 VP Finance & Controller .... Mr. Terry PANKRATZ
09 Exec Director Strategic Planning .... Dr. Lawrence J. REDLINGER
35 Interim Dean of Students .... Dr. Amanda SMITH
58 Dean Graduate Studies .... Dr. Marion UNDERWOOD
53 Dean Undergraduate Education .... Dr. Andrew BLANCHARD
79 Dean School Arts & Humanities .... Dr. Dennis KRATZ
50 Dean School of Management .... Dr. Hasan PIRKUL
81 Dean Sch of Natural Science/Math .... Dr. Bruce NOVAK
83 Dean School of Econ/Pol/Policy Sci .... Dr. Denis J. DEAN
76 Dean Sch Behavioral/Brain Science .... Dr. James BARTLETT
37 Dean School General Studies .... Dr. George W. FAIR
54 Dean EJ Sch of Engr/Computer Sci .... Dr. Mark W. SPONG
88 Dean Sch Arts/Tech & Emerg Media .... Dr. Anne BALSAMO
08 Director of Libraries .... Dr. Ellen SAFLEY
06 Registrar .... Ms. Jennifer MCDOWELL
12 Exec Director of Callier Center .... Dr. Thomas F. CAMPBELL
25 Assoc VP Research Administration .... Mr. Rafael MARTIN
18 Assoc VP Facilities Management .... Mr. Richard DEMPSEY
15 Asst VP Human Resource Management .... Ms. Colleen DUTTON
96 Exec Dir Procurement Management .... Ms. Debbie REYNOLDS
19 Chief of Police .... Mr. Larry ZACHARIAS
36 Director Career Services .... Vacant
38 Director Student Counseling .... Mr. James P. CANNICI
88 Director of Audit and Compliance .... Ms. Toni STEPHENS
41 Athletics Director .... Mr. Bill PETITT
78 Assoc Dir Co-operative Education .... Mr. Michael J. CHOATE
90 Director Tech Customer Services .... Mr. Donald L. DAVIS
29 Director of Alumni Relations .... Ms. Melinda MENDOZA
04 Executive Associate to President .... Ms. Kimberly GOODFRIEND
105 Assistant VP Web Services .... Mr. Cary DELMARK
106 Director E-learning .... Mr. Darren CRONE
39 Asst VP Residential Life .... Mr. Ryan WHITE
104 Director Study Abroad .... Ms. Lisabeth LASSITER
37 Director Student Financial Aid .... Ms. Beth TOLAN
43 University Attorney .... Mr. Timothy SHAW
84 Asst Provost Enrollment Management .... Mr. Wray WELDON
86 VP Public Affairs .... Ms. Amanda O. ROCKOW

*University of Texas at El Paso (D)

500 W University Avenue, El Paso TX 79968-8900
County: El Paso FICE Identification: 003661
Unit ID: 228796
Telephone: (915) 747-5000 Carnegie Class: DU-Higher
FAX Number: (915) 747-5111 Calendar System: Semester
URL: www.utep.edu
Established: 1914 Annual Undergrad Tuition & Fees (In-State): $7,259
Enrollment: 23,079 Coed
Affiliation or Control: State IRS Status: 501(c)3
Highest Offering: Doctorate
Accreditation: SC, BUS, BUSA, CORE, CS, ENG, MT, MUS, NURSE, OT, PH, PTA, SP, SPAA, SW

02 President .... Dr. Diana S. NATALICIO
05 Provost .... Dr. Howard DAUDISTEL
03 Executive Vice President .... Mr. Ricardo ADAUTO, III
04 Assistant to the President .... Ms. Estrella ESCOBAR
10 Interim VP Business Affairs .... Mr. Ricardo ADAUTO
46 Vice President for Research .... Dr. Roberto OSEGUEDA
09 Vice Pres Info Resources & Planning .... Dr. Steve RITER
58 Dean of Graduate School .... Dr. Charles AMBLER
32 Vice President Student Affairs .... Dr. Gary EDENS
50 Dean of Business Administration .... Dr. Robert NACHTMANN
53 Dean of Education .... Dr. Cynthia A. GIORGIS
54 Dean of Engineering .... Dr. Carlos M. FERREGUT
49 Dean of Liberal Arts .... Dr. Patricia WITHERSPOON
76 Interim Dean of Health Sciences .... Dr. Osama MIKHAIL
81 Dean of Science .... Dr. Robert KIRKEN
66 Dean of School of Nursing .... Dr. Elias PROVENCIO-VASQUEZ
18 Assoc VP Business Affs/Facilities .... Mr. Greg L. MCNICOL
08 Assoc Vice President Library .... Mr. Robert L. STAKES
26 Asst Vice Pres University Relations .... Mr. Beto LOPEZ
27 Assoc VP University Communications .... Ms. Robin STANTON GERROW
22 Asst Vice Pres EO/AA Dept .... Ms. Sandy VASQUEZ
29 Asst VP Development/Alumni Rels .... Dr. Richard DANIEL
46 Assoc Provost for Resource Mgmt .... Ms. Elizabeth FLORES
84 Asst VP Enrollment Services .... Ms. Amanda VASQUEZ
15 Assoc VP Human Resources Svcs .... Mr. Roger BROWN
19 Chief Campus Police .... Mr. Clifton WALSH
37 Assoc Dir of Student Financial Aid .... Mr. Ron WILLIAMS
23 Director of Student Health Center .... Ms. Louise P. CASTRO
36 Director of Career Services .... Mr. George W. BARTON
35 Associate VP/Dean of Students .... Ms. Catherine M. MCCORRY-ANDALIS
46 Assoc VP Inst Eval/Rsrch & Planning .... Dr. Roy MATHEW
39 Director of Housing Services .... Mr. Charlie E. GIBBENS
40 Director of University Bookstore .... Mr. Fernando PADULA
41 Athletics Director .... Mr. Robert W. STULL
38 Director Counseling Services .... Ms. Sherri I. TERRELL
96 Dir Purchasing/General Services .... Ms. Diane N. DEHOYOS
07 Dir Admissions/Recruitment .... Vacant
21 Assoc Vice Pres Business Affairs .... Mr. Anthony TURRIETTA
30 Assoc VP Institutional Advancement .... Mr. Robert STAKES

*The University of Texas Rio Grande Valley (E)

1201 W University Drive, Edinburg TX 78539-2970
County: Hidalgo FICE Identification: 003599
Unit ID: 227368
Telephone: (888) 882-4026 Carnegie Class: DU-Mod
FAX Number: (956) 665-2150 Calendar System: Semester
URL: www.utrgv.edu
Established: 2015 Annual Undergrad Tuition & Fees (In-State): $7,292
Enrollment: 21,015 Coed
Affiliation or Control: State IRS Status: 501(c)3
Highest Offering: Doctorate
Accreditation: SC, ARCPA, BUS, CORE, DIETC, ENG, #MED, MT, MUS, NURSE, OT, SP, SW, TED, THEA

02 President .... Dr. Guy BAILEY
100 Chief of Staff & VP for Operations .... Dr. Janna ARNEY
05 Provost/EVP Academic Affairs .... Dr. Havidan RODRIGUEZ
10 EVP for Finance and Administration .... Mr. Rick ANDERSON
46 Sr VP for Research/Innov & Economic .... Dr. Theresa A. MALDONADO
30 VP for Advancement .... Dr. Kelly CRONIN
86 VP for Governmental & Community Rel .... Ms. Veronica GONZALES
20 Deputy Provost .... Dr. Cynthia BROWN
88 Vice Provost for Faculty Affairs .... Dr. Ala QUBBAJ
100 Assistant Provost & Chief of Staff .... Ms. Nina YOUNG
32 VP for Student Success .... Dr. Kristin CROYLE
07 VP for Strategic Enrollment .... Dr. Maggie HINOJOSA
21 VP for Finance and Public Policy .... Ms. Mirna GONZALEZ
11 Sr Assoc VP for Operations .... Mr. Doug ARNEY
45 Assoc VP for Planning & Analysis .... Mr. Juan C. GONZALEZ
18 Assoc VP for Facilities .... Ms. Marta SALINAS-HOVAR
19 Assoc VP for Security & Campus Affs .... Mr. Ben REYNA
30 Assoc VP for Development .... Mr. Alicia M. KING
44 Assoc VP for Advancement Services .... Ms. Lydia ALEMAN
88 Assoc VP for Governmental Relations .... Mr. Richard P. SANCHEZ

26 Assoc VP for University Marketing .... Mr. Patrick GONZALES
88 Assoc VP for Shared Research Infras . Dr. Andreas HOLZENBURG
102 Assoc VP for Economic Development .... Mr. Irv DOWNING
21 Asst VP for Finance & Admin ....Ms. Karla LOYA
109 Asst VP for Campus Auxiliary Svcs ....Ms. Leticia BENAVIDES
31 Asst VP for Community Engagement ....Ms. Cris TREJO
09 AVP Strategic Analysis and Inst Res .... Ms. Susan BROWN
53 Dean College of Education & P-16 .....Dr. Patricia A. MCHATTON
50 Dean Col Business Entrepreneurship .... Dr. Mark KROLL
81 Dean College of Sciences ....Dr. Parwinder GREWAL
54 Dean College Engr/Computer Science .... Dr. Alex DOMIJAN
76 Dean College of Health Affairs .... Dr. Michael LEHKER
49 Dean College of Fine Arts ....Dr. Steven BLOCK
83 Dean College of Liberal Arts ....Dr. Walter DIAZ
63 Interim Dean School of Medicine .... Dr. Steven LIEBERMAN
17 Assoc Dean Clinical Affairs ....Dr. William G. MARSHALL
43 Chief Legal Officer ....Ms. Karen ADAMS
15 Chief Human Resources Officer ....Mr. Mike JAMES
22 Chief Compliance Officer .... Ms. Diane SHEPPARD
13 Chief Information Officer ....Dr. Jeffrey GRAHAM
29 Exec Dir of Alumni Relations ....Ms. Isis LOPEZ
41 Athletics Director .... Mr. Christopher KING
46 Director for Strategic Research Dev ....Dr. Pam MEREDITH

*University of Texas at San Antonio (A)

One UTSA Circle, San Antonio TX 78249-0169

County: Bexar FICE Identification: 010115
Unit ID: 229027
Telephone: (210) 458-4011 Carnegie Class: DU-Higher
FAX Number: (210) 458-4187 Calendar System: Semester
URL: www.utsa.edu
Established: 1969 Annual Undergrad Tuition & Fees (In-State): $7,447
Enrollment: 28,628 Coed
Affiliation or Control: State IRS Status: 501(c)3
Highest Offering: Doctorate
Accreditation: SC, ART, BUS, BUSA, CACREP, CEA, CIDA, CONST, ENG, MUS, SPAA, SW

02 President ....Dr. Ricardo ROMO
05 Int Provost/Vice Pres Academic Affs ....Dr. Mauli AGRAWAL
10 Vice Pres for Business Affairs .... Ms. Kathryn FUNK-BAXTER
46 Int Vice President for Research ....Dr. Bernard ARULANANDAM
32 Vice President for Student Affairs .... Mr. Samuel GONZALES
31 Vice President Community Services ....Dr. Jude VALDEZ
30 VP External Rels/Chief Dev Ofcr ....Ms. Marjorie M. FRENCH
11 Assoc Vice Pres for Administration ....Ms. Pamela BACON
20 Exec Vice Provost/Sr Intl Ofcr ....Ms. Rene ZENTENO
09 V Prov Acad Compliance/Inst Effect ....Dr. Sandra T. WELCH
12 Vice Provost for Downtown Campus ....Dr. Jesse T. ZAPATA
13 Vice Provost Information Tech/CIO ....Mr. Bryan WILSON
20 V Prov Acad Supt/Dean UGrad Studies ....Dr. Lawrence R. WILLIAMS
21 Associate VP Financial Affairs ....Ms. Lenora CHAPMAN
15 Associate VP Human Resources .. Ms. Barbara BARAN-CENTENO
08 Dean of Libraries .... Dr. Krisellen MALONEY
92 Dean of Honors College .... Dr. Richard A. DIEM
58 Vice Provost/Dean Graduate School ....Dr. DeBrenna LaFa AGBENYIGA
50 Dean of College of Business .... Dr. Wm Gerard (Gerry) Y. SANDERS
57 Dean College of Liberal & Fine Arts ....Dr. Daniel J. GELO
54 Dean of College of Engineering ....Dr. Joann BROWNING
83 Dean of College of Sciences ....Dr. George PERRY
48 Dean School of Architecture ....Prof. John MURPHY
53 Dean College Educ/Human Development ....Dr. Margo DELLI CARPINI
80 Dean of College of Public Policy ....Dr. Rogelio SAENZ
19 Chief of Police ....Mr. Steve V. BARRERA
41 Assoc VP Director Intcollegiate Ath ....Ms. Lynn HICKEY
29 Director Alumni Program Marketing .... Ms. Anne ENGLERT
43 Chief Legal Officer ....Ms. Gail JENSEN
26 Associate VP for Comm/Marketing ....Mr. Joe IZBRAND
86 Director of External Affairs .... Mr. Albert A. CARRISALEZ
04 Executive Assistant Office of Pres .... Ms. Patricia CARDENAS
06 Registrar .... Dr. Joseph R. DECRISTOFORO
07 Director of Admissions ....Ms. Beverly WOODSON DAY
100 Chief of Staff .... Ms. Sonia V. MARTINEZ
36 Director of Career Services ....Ms. Audrey J. MAGNUSON
104 Interim Dir of Educ Abroad Services ....Ms. Cristina SANCHEZ
105 Associate Director of Web/Portal .... Mr. Shashi B. PINHEIRO
106 Director of Online Learning ....Mr. Michael W. ANDERSON
108 Assistant Vice Provost Assessment .... Dr. Kasey NEECE-FIELDER
18 Associate VP for Facilities ....Mr. David J. RIKER
22 Director Equal Opportunity Services .... Mr. Leonard FLAUM
25 Director of Grants/Contracts .... Ms. Shannyn ADKINS
28 Associate Provost ....Col. Lisa C. FIRMIN
37 Director of Student Financial Aid .... Ms. Diana S. MARTINEZ
38 Director of Counseling Services ....Mr. Thomas BAEZ
39 Director Student Housing/Residence ....Mr. Daniel L. GOCKLEY
44 Director of Fin Ops & Gift Services ...... Ms. Rebecca ANDERSON
84 Director Student Enrollment Svcs ....Ms. Erika M. COX
90 Director of Academic Computing ....Mr. John P. SOUDAH
91 Exec Director of Enterprise System ....Mr. Bryan P. WILSON
96 Director Purchasing/Dist Services ....Mr. Robert I. DICKENS

*University of Texas at Tyler (B)

3900 University Boulevard, Tyler TX 75799-6699

County: Smith FICE Identification: 011163
Unit ID: 228802
Telephone: (903) 566-7000 Carnegie Class: Masters/L
FAX Number: (903) 566-7068 Calendar System: Semester
URL: www.uttyler.edu
Established: 1971 Annual Undergrad Tuition & Fees (In-State): $7,312
Enrollment: 8,036 Coed
Affiliation or Control: State IRS Status: 501(c)3
Highest Offering: Doctorate
Accreditation: SC, BUS, CACREP, ENG, MUS, NAIT, NURSE, @PHAR

02 President ....Dr. Rodney H. MABRY
05 Provost/VP Academic Affairs ....Dr. Amir MIRMIRAN
30 Vice President Univ Advancement .... Mr. Wendell JEFFREYS
32 Vice Pres for Student Affairs .... Dr. Howard PATTERSON
13 Vice President & CIO IT ....Dr. Sherri WHATLEY
20 Vice Provost AA/Grad Studies ....Dr. William GEIGER
46 VP for Research & Technology Transf .... Dr. Michael ODELL
10 VP for Business Affairs .... Mr. William O'DONNELL
15 Director of Human Resources ....Ms. Amy CLEM
21 Assoc VP for Business Affairs ....Ms. Carrie CLAYTON
86 AVP for Legislative Relations ....Ms. Laura JACKSON
84 AVP for Enrollment Management ....Ms. Sarah BOWDIN
108 Asst Vice Pres for Assessment/IE ....Dr. Lou Ann BERMAN
35 Asst VP Student Affs/Dean Students .... Ms. Ona TOLLIVER
49 Dean College of Arts & Sciences ....Dr. Martin SLANN
50 Dean College Business & Technology ....Dr. James LUMPKIN
53 Dean College Educ & Psych ....Dr. Ross SHERMAN
54 Interim Dean College Engineering ....Dr. Michael MCGINNIS
66 Dean College Nursing & Health Sci ....Dr. Yong TAI WANG
08 Exec Director of the Library ....Ms. Jeanne STANDLEY
21 Director of Financial Services ....Ms. Cindy TROYER
18 AVP for Facilities Management ....Mr. Jerry STUFF
29 Director of Alumni Relations ....Ms. Brittany CHILDS
26 Exec Dir Marketing & Communication ....Ms. Beverley GOLDEN
38 Dir Stdnt Svc/Stdnt Couns/Test Ctr .... Ms. Kim HARVEY-LIVINGSTON
39 Director of Residence Life ....Dr. Jennifer WATERS
06 Registrar ....Ms. Sonja MORALE
09 Director of Institutional Analysis ....Ms. Shari KOUKL
19 Chief University Police ....Mr. Mike W. MEDDERS
04 Executive Asst to President ....Ms. Janet ROBERTSON
07 Interim Director of Admissions ....Ms. Angela COPELAND
37 Director of Student Financial Aid ....Mr. Scott LAPINSKI
43 General Counsel ....Mr. Michael DONLEY

*The University of Texas Health Science Center at Houston (UTHealth) (C)

PO Box 20036, Houston TX 77225-0036

County: Harris FICE Identification: 004951
Unit ID: 229300
Telephone: (713) 500-4472 Carnegie Class: Spec-4-yr-Med
FAX Number: (713) 500-3026 Calendar System: Semester
URL: www.uth.edu
Established: 1972 Annual Undergrad Tuition & Fees (In-State): N/A
Enrollment: 4,556 Coed
Affiliation or Control: State IRS Status: 501(c)3
Highest Offering: Doctorate
Accreditation: SC, ANEST, DENT, DH, DIETI, ENGR, MED, NURSE, PERF, PH

02 President ....Dr. Giuseppe N. COLASURDO
11 CFO/COO & Exec VP for Admin ....Mr. T. Kevin DILLON
63 Dean Medical School ....Dr. Barbara J. STOLL
69 Dean School of Public Health ....Dr. Eric BOERWINKLE
52 Dean School of Dentistry ....Dr. John A. VALENZA
58 Dean Grad Sch Biomedical Sciences ..... Dr. Michael BLACKBURN
66 Dean School of Nursing ....Dr. Lorraine FRAZIER
88 Dean Sch of Biomed Informatics ....Dr. Jiajie W. ZHANG
05 Exec VP & Chief Academic Officer ... Dr. Michael R. BLACKBURN
45 Senior VP for Strategic Planning ....Dr. Osama I. MIKHAIL
10 Sr VP Finance & Business Svcs .... Mr. Michael TRAMONTE
46 Vice Dn Rsrch/Dir Molecular Med ....Dr. John HANCOCK
30 Vice Pres Development ....Mr. Kevin J. FOYLE
15 VP/Chief Human Resources Officer ....Mr. Eric FERNETTE
43 Interim VP/Chief Legal Officer ....Mr. Daniel J. REAT
86 VP Govt Relations ....Mr. Scott FORBES
88 VP Research & Technology ....Dr. Bruce C. BUTLER
109 VP Auxiliary Enterprises ....Mr. Charles A. FIGARI
13 VP/Chief Information Officer ....Mr. Richard L. MILLER
18 VP Facilities Planning & Engr ....Mr. Richard L. MCDERMOTT
90 Asst VP Academic Technology ....Dr. William A. WEEMS
21 Asst VP & Chief Audit Officer ....Mr. Daniel SHERMAN
06 Registrar ....Mr. Robert JENKINS
19 Chief of Police ....Mr. William ADCOX
41 Director Recreation/Intramural Pgms ....Ms. Pauline M. HABETZ
85 Director International Affairs ....Ms. Rose Mary VALENCIA
39 Director University Housing ....Mr. Billy C. HINTON
26 Executive Director Media Relations ....Ms. Meredith RAINE
37 Director Student Financial Svcs ....Ms. Aracel ALVAREZ
25 Assoc VP Sponsored Projects Admin ...... Ms. Kathleen KREIDLER
14 Director Data Center Operations .... Mr. Kevin B. GRANHOLD
88 Director Educational Tech Nursing ....Ms. Linda L. CRAYS
88 Director Biomedical Info Tech Med ....Dr. Stephen J. FATH
07 Vice Dean Admissions/Stdt Aff-Med ....Dr. Margaret MCNEESE
29 Assoc Dean Student & Alumni-SOD ....Dr. Hugh P. FIERPONT
32 Dir of Student Affairs-SBMI ....Ms. Jaime HARGRAVE
32 Director Student Affairs-SON ....Ms. Diana PRESSLEY
35 Assoc Dean of Student Affairs-SPH ....Dr. Mary A. SMITH
09 Director of Institutional Research ....Ms. Deanne HERNANDEZ

*University of Texas Health Science Center at San Antonio (D)

7703 Floyd Curl Drive, San Antonio TX 78229-3900

County: Bexar FICE Identification: 003659
Unit ID: 228644
Telephone: (210) 567-7000 Carnegie Class: Spec-4-yr-Med
FAX Number: (210) 567-2025 Calendar System: Other
URL: www.uthscsa.edu
Established: 1959 Annual Undergrad Tuition & Fees (In-State): N/A
Enrollment: 3,147 Coed
Affiliation or Control: State IRS Status: 501(c)3
Highest Offering: Doctorate
Accreditation: SC, ARCPA, COARC, DENT, DH, DIETC, EMT, HT, IPSY, MED, MT, NURSE, OT, PTA, RADDOS

02 President .... Dr. William L. HENRICH
03 Sr Exec Vice President & COO ....Mr. Michael E. BLACK
11 Exec VP for Facility Planning/Admin ....Mr. James D. KAZEN
10 Vice President & CFO ....Ms. Andrea M. MARKS
05 VP Acad/Fac & Student Affairs ....Dr. Jacqueline L. MOK
13 Vice Pres & Chief Information Ofcr ....Mr. Yeman COLLIER
46 Vice President for Research ....Dr. Andrea GIUFFRIDA
86 VP for Governmental Relations ....Mr. Armando DIAZ
30 VP for Institutional Advancement ....Ms. Deborah H. MORRILL
15 Vice Pres of Human Resources ....Mr. J. Michael TESH
100 VP & Chief of Staff ....Ms. Mary G. DELAY
21 Asst Vice Pres for Business Affairs ....Mr. Gerard E. LONG
09 Asst VP Research ....Dr. Mark J. NIJLAND
18 Asst VP for Strategic Initiatives ....Mr. Darrell MAATSCH
63 Dean School of Medicine ....Dr. Francisco GONZALEZ-SCARANO
52 Dean Dental School ....Dr. William W. DODGE
58 Dean Graduate Biomed Science ....Dr. David WEISS
76 Dean School Health Professions ....Dr. David C. SHELLEDY
66 Dean School of Nursing ....Dr. Eileen T. BRESLIN
32 Exec Dir for Student Services ....Vacant
06 Registrar .... Ms. Blanca GUERRA
08 Senior Director of Libraries ....Mr. Owen H. ELLARD
19 Chief of Police ....Mr. Michael PARKS
88 Exec Dir Acad/Fac/Studnt Ombudspers .... Dr. Bonnie L. BLANKMEYER
37 Director of Financial Aid ....Ms. Ellen NYSTROM
38 Director of Student Counseling .... Dr. Mia VIVE
43 Asst VP/Chief Legal Officer ....Mr. Jack C. PARK
96 Sr Dir Supply Chain Mngmt/HUB Coord ....Mr. Eric R. WALLS
07 Director of Admissions ....Vacant
102 Dir Foundation/Corporate Relations ....Vacant
26 Chief Marketing Officer ....Ms. Heather ADKINS
44 Sr Director Planned Giving ....Mr. W. Kent HAMILTON

*The University of Texas Health Science Center at Tyler (E)

11937 US Hwy 271, Tyler TX 75708-3154

County: Smith Identification: 667206
Telephone: (903) 877-7777 Carnegie Class: Not Classified
FAX Number: N/A Calendar System: Semester
URL: www.uthct.edu
Established: 1977 Annual Graduate Tuition & Fees: N/A
Enrollment: N/A Coed
Affiliation or Control: State IRS Status: 501(c)3
Highest Offering: Master's; No Undergraduates
Accreditation: SC

02 President and CEO ....Dr. Kirk A. CALHOUN
03 Exec VP/Chief of Staff ....Joseph F. WOELKERS
05 Sr VP Clinical & Academic Affairs ....Dr. Jeffrey L. LEVIN
46 Sr VP Research & Graduate Studies ....Dr. Steven IDELL
23 Sr VP/CMO & Physician in Chief ....Dr. Steven W. COX
88 Sr VP Population Health ....Dr. David L. LAKEY
88 Sr VP/CAO/Hospital & Clinics ....Timothy G. OCHRAN
10 VP Finance and CFO ....Kris KAVASCH
15 VP Human Resources/CHRO ....Cynthia SCOTT-LUNAU
43 VP/Chief Legal Officer ....Terry WITTER
45 VP Planning & Public Policy ....Daniel DESLATTE
13 VP Information Technology (CIO) ....John YODER
30 VP Institutional Advancement ....Derrith BONDURANT
18 Assoc VP Physical Plant ....Thomas BRUNETTE
20 Assoc VP Academic Affairs .....Dr. Pierre F. NEUENSCHWANDER
32 Director of Student Affairs ....Dr. Mickey SLIMP
08 Director of Library Services ....Thomas CRAIG
09 Director of Institutional Research ....Sara SHEPHERD
86 Dir University & Community Affairs ....Kimberly ASHLEY
96 Director of Purchasing ....Crystal SMITH
37 Director Student Financial Aid ....Araceli ALVAREZ
06 Registrar ....Robert JENKINS
04 Administrative Asst to President ....Carol DAVIS
19 Chief of Police .... Chief Robert CROMLEY
26 Chief Public Affair/Market Exec ....Rhonda SCOBY

*The University of Texas MD Anderson Cancer Center (F)

1515 Holcombe Boulevard, Houston TX 77030-4000

County: Harris FICE Identification: 025554
Unit ID: 416801
Telephone: (713) 792-6161 Carnegie Class: Spec-4-yr-Other Health
FAX Number: N/A Calendar System: Semester
URL: www.mdanderson.org
Established: 1941 Annual Undergrad Tuition & Fees (In-District): N/A
Enrollment: 303 Coed
Affiliation or Control: State/Local IRS Status: 501(c)3
Highest Offering: Doctorate
Accreditation: SC, CETECH, CYTO, DENT, DMOLS, HT, MT, PAST, RAD, RADDOS, RADMAG, RTT

02 President ....Dr. Ronald DEPINHO
11 Exec Vice Pres/Administration .... Mr. Dan FONTAINE
88 Exec Vice Pres/Physician-in-Chief ....Dr. Thomas BUCHHOLZ

05 Provost/Executive Vice President ....Dr. Ethan DMITROVSKY
100 Chief of Staff ....Mr. Steven C. HENDERSON

*The University of Texas Medical Branch (A)

301 University Boulevard, Galveston TX 77555-0100
County: Galveston FICE Identification: 004952
Unit ID: 228653
Telephone: (409) 772-1011 Carnegie Class: Spec-4-yr-Med
FAX Number: N/A Calendar System: Semester
URL: www.utmb.edu
Established: 1891 Annual Undergrad Tuition & Fees (In-State): N/A
Enrollment: 3,211 Coed
Affiliation or Control: State IRS Status: 170(c)1
Highest Offering: Doctorate
Accreditation: SC, ARCPA, BBT, COARC, DENT, @DIETI, MED, MT, NURSE, OT, PH, PTA

02 President ....Dr. David L. CALLENDER
04 Exec Asst to the President ....Ms. Jandee ALARID
05 Exec VP/Provost/Dean Sch of Med ....Dr. Danny O. JACOBS
23 Exec VP & CEO Health System .. Ms. Donna K. SOLLENBERGER
10 Exec VP & Chief Business/Fin Ofcr ....Ms. Cheryl SADRO
86 Sr VP Health Policy & Legis Affairs ....Dr. Ben G. RAIMER
88 VP & Chief Physician Executive .... Dr. Rex M. MCCALLUM
17 Chief Medical Officer ....Dr. Selwyn O. ROGERS
20 VP Education & Dean Sch of Nursing .....Dr. Pamela G. WATSON
76 VP & Dean Sch of Health Professions .....Dr. Elizabeth J. PROTAS
58 VP & Dean Grad Sch of Biomed Sci ....Dr. David W. NIESEL
15 VP HR & Employee Services ....Dr. Ronald B. MCKINLEY
13 VP Information Services & CIO ....Mr. Todd A. LEACH
21 VP Finance Academic Enterprise ....Ms. Frances HUTCHISON
18 VP Business Oper & Facilities ....Mr. Michael B. SHRINER
11 Interim VP/Chief Oper Officer AE ....Mr. Steven SLOATE
21 VP Finance Clinical Enterprise ......Mr. David M. CONNAUGHTON
45 VP for Strategic Mgmt ....Dr. Rebecca SAAVEDRA
43 Sr VP General Counsel ....Ms. Carolee KING
26 VP Marketing & Communications ....Mr. Stephen CAMPBELL
81 Assoc Dean Grad Sch Biomed Sci ....Dr. Jose M. BARRAL
07 Assoc Dean Admissions Sch of Med ....Dr. Jeffrey RABEK
32 Assoc Dean Student Affairs/Adm SON .....Ms. Dorothy PEARROW
46 Assoc VP Research Admin ....Ms. Toni J. D'AGOSTINO
08 Assoc VP Academic Res/Library ....Ms. Patricia A. CIEJKA
09 Assoc VP Inst Effectiveness ....Dr. John C. MCKEE
27 Assoc VP Public Affairs ....Ms. Mary G. HAVARD
21 Assoc VP Fin Plng & Perf Mgmt ....Mr. Matthew FURLONG
21 Assoc VP Budget & Analysis .... Ms. Celia BAILEY-OCHOA
88 Assoc VP Audit Services ....Ms. Kimberly K. HAGARA
30 Assoc VP Chief Develop Officer ....Ms. Betsy B. CLARDY
29 Asst VP Alumni Relations ....Vacant
28 VP & Chief Compliance Officer ....Mr. Tobin R. BOENIG
06 AVP Univ Student Svcs & Registrar ....Mr. William S. BOEH
19 Chief of University Police ....Mr. Thomas ENGELLS
22 Dir of Diversity and Inclusion ....Vacant
96 AVP Supply Chain Management ....Mr. Frank REIGHARD
38 Director Student Counseling ....Ms. Cynthia DESANTOS
100 Chief of Staff ....Ms. Sheila LIDSTONE
16 Assoc VP HR Talent Manager ....Mr. Ian BARRETT
105 Director Digital Communications ....Mr. Eduardo VALDES
106 Dir Online Education/E-learning ....Dr. Trish RICHARD
108 Asst Dir Institutional Effectivenes ....Mr. Jay HOWELL
37 Director Student Financial Aid ....Ms. Carol CROMIE
39 AVP BOF Student Housing ....Mr. Carlos ESCOBAR
41 Athletic Director ....Mr. Gerald CLEVELAND
44 Director Annual or Planned Giving ....Ms. Marie MACZAK
90 Asst Director Academic Computing ....Mr. David DEL PINO KLOQUES

*University of Texas of the Permian Basin (B)

4901 E University Boulevard, Odessa TX 79762-0001
County: Ector FICE Identification: 009930
Unit ID: 229018
Telephone: (432) 552-2020 Carnegie Class: Masters/M
FAX Number: (432) 552-2374 Calendar System: Semester
URL: www.utpb.edu
Established: 1969 Annual Undergrad Tuition & Fees (In-State): $5,250
Enrollment: 5,560 Coed
Affiliation or Control: State IRS Status: 501(c)3
Highest Offering: Master's
Accreditation: SC, ART, BUS, CAATE, ENG, MUS, NURSE, SW, TED

53 Int Dean School of Education ....Dr. Roy HURST
02 President ....Dr. W. David WATTS
04 Assistant to the President ....Ms. Danielle JESENSKY
05 Provost/Vice Pres Academic Affairs ....Dr. Dan HEIMMERMANN
10 Vice President Business Affairs ....Mr. Mark MCGURK
32 Sr AVP Academic & Student Services ....Ms. Teresa SEWELL
58 AVP Research/Dean Graduate Studies ....Dr. Juli RATHEAL
13 Chief Information Officer ....Mr. Lowell BALLARD
49 Dean College of Arts & Science ....Dr. Michael ZAVADA
50 Dean School of Business ....Dr. William PRICE
30 Director Institutional Advancement ....Ms. Lee Anna GOOD
07 Director Admissions ....Mr. Scott SMILEY
06 Registrar ....Mr. Joe SANDERS
37 Director Financial Aid ....Mr. C. Edward KERESTLY
08 Director of Library Services ....Mr. Howard MARKS
15 Director Human Resources ....Ms. Sharon BURKE
51 Director Continuing Education ....Mr. Rey LASCANO
26 Interim Public Information Officer ....Ms. Travis WOODWARD

41 Director Athletics ....Dr. Steve AICINENA
19 Chief of Police ....Chief Tom HAIN
18 Chief Facilities/Physical Plant ....Mr. Jay HANEY
36 Dir Student Placement/Counseling ....Mr. Tony LOVE
96 Interim Director of Purchasing ....Ms. Ynez ALDERSON
09 Director of Institutional Research ....Dr. Denise WATTS
29 Alumni Relations ....Mrs. Maribea MERRITT
39 Director Student Housing ....Ms. Chermae PEEL

*University of Texas Southwestern Medical Center (C)

5323 Harry Hines Boulevard, Dallas TX 75390-9002
County: Dallas FICE Identification: 010019
Unit ID: 228635
Telephone: (214) 648-3111 Carnegie Class: Spec-4-yr-Med
FAX Number: N/A Calendar System: Other
URL: www.utsouthwestern.edu
Established: 1943 Annual Undergrad Tuition & Fees (In-State): N/A
Enrollment: 2,341 Coed
Affiliation or Control: State IRS Status: 501(c)3
Highest Offering: Doctorate
Accreditation: SC, ARCPA, CLPSY, CORE, DIETC, IPSY, MED, OPE, PAST, PTA, RTT

02 President ....Dr. Daniel K. PODOLSKY
100 Vice President & Chief of Staff ....Dr. Robin M. JACOBY
05 Exec VP Acad Affs/Provost/Dean SMS ....Dr. Gregory FITZ
03 Exec VP Health System Affairs ....Dr. Bruce A. MEYER
10 Exec Vice Pres Business Affairs ....Mr. Arnim DONTES
46 Vice Provost/Dean of Basic Research ....Dr. David W. RUSSELL
32 Vice President Clinical Operations ...... Dr. John D. RUTHERFORD
88 Vice President/CEO University Hosp ....Dr. John WARNER
88 Chief Quality Officer ....Dr. Gary REED
21 Vice President Financial Affairs ....Mr. Michael SERBER
86 Vice Pres Govt Affairs & Policy ....Ms. Angelica MARIN-HILL
26 Vice Pres Comm Mktg & Publ Affs ....Mr. Steve MOORE
15 Vice President Chief HR Officer ....Mr. Ivan THOMPSON
43 Vice President Legal Affairs ....Ms. Leah A. HURLEY
72 Vice Pres Technology Development ....Mr. Frank P. GRASSLER
30 Vice President Development ....Ms. Amanda BILLINGS
102 Vice Pres Community and Corp Rels ......Mr. Ruben E. ESQUIVEL
13 Vice Pres Information Resources ....Mr. Kirk A. KIRKSEY
18 Vice President Facilities Mgmt ....Mr. Juan M. GUERRA, JR.
29 Vice Pres Stdnt/Alumni Affs/Admiss ....Mr. J. W. NORRED
09 Vice Pres Research Administration ....Ms. Angela WISHON
20 Vice President COO Academic Affairs .... Mr. Cameron SLOCUM
88 Assoc Vice Pres Ambulatory Care ....Dr. Stan TAYLOR
88 Chief Med Officer University Hosp ....Dr. Steven LEACH
88 Assoc Vice Pres Chief Nursing Ofcr ....Ms. Susan HERNANDEZ
96 Asst Vice Pres Materials Mgmt ....Mr. Charles COBB
88 Assoc Vice Pres Parkland HHS Aff ....Dr. Christopher MADDEN
27 Asst Vice Pres Marketing ....Ms. Dorothea BONDS
88 Asst Vice President Communication ....Vacant
21 Asst Vice Pres Acctg Fiscal Svcs ....Ms. Sharon LEARY
08 Asst Vice Pres Library Services ....Ms. Kelly GONZALEZ
20 Sr Assoc Dean Academic Admin ....Dr. Charles M. GINSBURG
45 Sr Assoc Dean Strategic Development ....Dr. Dwain L. THIELE
28 Assoc Dean Faculty Diversity & Dev .... Dr. Byron L. CRYER
88 Assoc Dean Global Health ....Dr. Fiemu E. NWARIAKU
51 Assoc Dean Graduate Medical Education ....Dr. Bradley MARPLE
63 Assoc Dean Undergrad Medical Educ ....Dr. Robert REGE
32 Assoc Dean Student Affairs ....Dr. Angela MIHALIC
32 Assoc Dean Student Affairs ....Dr. James M. WAGNER
93 Assoc Dean Student Diversity & Incl ....Dr. Shawna NESBITT
88 Associate Dean ....Dr. Perrie M. ADAMS
58 Dean Grad School Biomedical Science ....Dr. Andrew ZINN
76 Dean School of Health Professions ....Dr. Jon WILLIAMSON
06 Associate Registrar ....Mr. Timothy WILLIAMSON
07 Assoc Director of Admissions ....Ms. Anne P. MCLANE
11 Assoc VP/Chief Operating Officer ....Ms. Becky MCCULLEY
17 Assoc Vice Pres UTSW Health System ....Mr. Suresh GUNASEKARAN
88 Assoc VP Academic & Admin Sys ....Ms. Dipti RANGANATHAN
108 Asst Vice Pres Academic Plng/Assess ....Mr. James DRAKE

Vernon College (D)

4400 College Drive, Vernon TX 76384-4092
County: Wilbarger FICE Identification: 010060
Unit ID: 229504
Telephone: (940) 552-6291 Carnegie Class: Assoc/MT-VT-High Non
FAX Number: (940) 553-3902 Calendar System: Semester
URL: www.vernoncollege.edu
Established: 1970 Annual Undergrad Tuition & Fees (In-District): $2,940
Enrollment: 2,989 Coed
Affiliation or Control: State/Local IRS Status: 501(c)3
Highest Offering: Associate Degree
Accreditation: SC, CAHIIM, SURGT

01 President ....Dr. Dusty R. JOHNSTON
04 Admin Secretary to the President ....Ms. Mary KING
05 Dean of Instructional Services ....Dr. Gary Don HARKEY
10 Dean of Administrative Services ....Mr. Garry DAVID
32 Dean of Student Services ....Mr. James NORDONE
07 Dean Admiss/Registr/Financial Aid ....Mr. Joe HITE
103 Assoc Dean of Instructional Service ....Ms. Shana DRURY
30 Director of Inst Advancement ....Ms. Michelle ALEXANDER
88 Director of Quality Enhancement ....Ms. Criquett LEHMAN
09 Dir of Institutional Effectiveness ....Mrs. Betsy HARKEY
37 Director Financial Aid ....Mrs. Melissa J. ELLIOTT
08 Director of Library Services ....Ms. Marion GRONA

18 Director Physical Plant ....Mr. Lyle BONNER
15 Director of Human Resources ....Mrs. Haven DAVID
39 Director of Housing ....Ms. Kelly EASON
35 Assoc Dean of Student Services ....Mrs. Kristin HARRIS
06 Director of Admissions & Records ....Mrs. Amanda RAINES
66 Dir Associate Degree in Nursing ....Mrs. Mary RIVARD
66 Dir Licensed Vocational Nursing ....Ms. Sherri DENHEM
35 Director of Student Activities ....Ms. Shealeigh JONES
19 Director of Campus Police ....Mr. Kevin HOLLAND
41 Athletic Director ....Mrs. Julie MYERS-KUHN

Vet Tech Institute of Houston (E)

4669 Southwest Freeway, Suite 100, Houston TX 77027
County: Harris FICE Identification: 021448
Unit ID: 223472
Telephone: (713) 629-8940 Carnegie Class: Spec 2-yr-Health
FAX Number: (713) 629-0059 Calendar System: Semester
URL: www.vettechinstitute.edu/houston
Established: 2007 Annual Undergrad Tuition & Fees: $14,200
Enrollment: 216 Coed
Affiliation or Control: Proprietary IRS Status: Proprietary
Highest Offering: Associate Degree
Accreditation: ACICS

01 Director/Chief Academic Officer ....Mr. Elbert HAMILTON, JR.

Victoria College (F)

2200 E Red River, Victoria TX 77901-4494
County: Victoria FICE Identification: 003662
Unit ID: 229540
Telephone: (361) 573-3291 Carnegie Class: Assoc/MT-VT-High Trad
FAX Number: (361) 572-3850 Calendar System: Semester
URL: www.victoriacollege.edu
Established: 1925 Annual Undergrad Tuition & Fees (In-District): $2,640
Enrollment: 4,146 Coed
Affiliation or Control: Local IRS Status: 501(c)3
Highest Offering: Associate Degree
Accreditation: SC, ADNUR, #COARC, EMT, PTAA

01 President ....Dr. David HINDS
05 Vice President of Instruction ....Ms. Marjorie PRICE-SEEGER
10 Vice Pres Administrative Svcs ....Mr. Keith BLUNDELL
32 Vice President of Student Services ....Dr. Florinda CORREA
30 VP College Advance/External Affairs ....Ms. Jennifer L. YANCEY
09 Dir Inst Effect/Research/Assess ....Ms. Patricia REHAK
08 Director of Libraries ....Dr. Joe F. DAHLSTROM
07 Director of Enrollment Services ....Ms. Missy KLIMITCHEK
18 Director Physical Plant ....Mr. Robert DUFFIE
37 Director Financial Aid ....Ms. Kim OBSTA
15 Director Human Resources ....Ms. Terri KURTZ
26 Dir Marketing & Communications ....Mr. Darin KAZMIR
38 Director Advising/Counseling ....Mr. Robert CUBRIEL, III
96 Director of Purchasing ....Ms. Lydia HUBER
21 Director of Finance ....Ms. Tracey BERGSTROM
35 Student Center/Activities Director ....Ms. Elaine EVERETT-HENSLEY
13 Director Technology Services ....Mr. Andy FARRIOR
04 Exec Admin Asst to President ....Ms. Mary Ann RODRIGUEZ
102 Exec Dir of College Advance & Found ....Ms. Amy MUNDY

Virginia College (G)

5005 50th Street, Lubbock TX 79414
Telephone: (806) 784-1900 Identification: 770547
Accreditation: ACICS

† Branch campus of Virginia College, Birmingham, AL

Virginia College Austin (H)

14200 North Interstate 35, Austin TX 78728
Telephone: (512) 371-3500 Identification: 666074
Accreditation: ACICS, #COARC, DMS, MAAB, SURGT

† Branch campus of Virginia College, Birmingham, AL.

Vista College (I)

3440 Bell Street, Suite 100, Amarillo TX 79109
Telephone: (806) 372-3700 Identification: 770548
Accreditation: COE

Vista College (J)

6101 Montana Avenue, El Paso TX 79925-2021
County: El Paso FICE Identification: 025720
Unit ID: 365204
Telephone: (915) 779-8031 Carnegie Class: Assoc/HVT-High Non
FAX Number: (915) 779-8097 Calendar System: Semester
URL: www.vistacollege.edu
Established: 1987 Annual Undergrad Tuition & Fees: $15,760
Enrollment: 2,951 Coed
Affiliation or Control: Proprietary IRS Status: Proprietary
Highest Offering: Associate Degree
Accreditation: #COE

01 Campus Director ....Mr. Antonio RICO
06 Registrar ....Ms. Valerie PARKS
07 Assoc Director of Admissions ....Mr. Andre ROYOS
36 Director Career Services ....Vacant

37 Director Student Financial Aid .... Ms. Adrianna DURAN
63 Director Medical .... Ms. Juana CERVANTES

Vista College (A)

4620 50th Street, Lubbock TX 79414
Telephone: (806) 785-2100 Identification: 770549
Accreditation: COE

Vista College-Online (B)

300 N. Coit Road, Suite 300, Richardson TX 75080
County: Davis FICE Identification: 025728
Unit ID: 377342
Telephone: (972) 707-8600 Carnegie Class: Bac/Assoc-Assoc Dom
FAX Number: (972) 707-8575 Calendar System: Other
URL: www.vistacollege.edu/online/
Established: Annual Undergrad Tuition & Fees: N/A
Enrollment: 266 Coed
Affiliation or Control: Proprietary IRS Status: Proprietary
Highest Offering: Baccalaureate
Accreditation: ACCSC

01 Director .... Mr. Art WALLER

Wade College (C)

1950 Stemmons Fwy, Ste 4080, LB 562, Dallas TX 75207
County: Dallas FICE Identification: 010130
Unit ID: 226879
Telephone: (214) 637-3530 Carnegie Class: Bac/Assoc-Mixed
FAX Number: (214) 637-0827 Calendar System: Trimester
URL: www.wadecollege.edu
Established: 1962 Annual Undergrad Tuition & Fees: $13,310
Enrollment: 207 Coed
Affiliation or Control: Proprietary IRS Status: Proprietary
Highest Offering: Baccalaureate
Accreditation: SC

01 President .... Dr. Harry DAVROS
03 Vice President .... Mr. John CONTE
05 Director of Academic Affairs .... Ms. Elizabeth JOHNSTON
11 Director of Institutional Support .... Ms. Kim PARKER
08 Head Librarian .... Mrs. Bobbie BAUMGARTEN
36 Director of Career Services .... Mrs. Jennifer MAGEE
07 Director of Admissions .... Mr. John FLORES
37 Director Student Financial Aid .... Ms. Lisa HOOVER

Wayland Baptist University (D)

1900 West Seventh, Plainview TX 79072-6998
County: Hale FICE Identification: 003663
Unit ID: 229780
Telephone: (806) 291-1000 Carnegie Class: Masters/L
FAX Number: (806) 291-1960 Calendar System: Semester
URL: www.wbu.edu
Established: 1908 Annual Undergrad Tuition & Fees: $13,680
Enrollment: 5,536 Coed
Affiliation or Control: Southern Baptist IRS Status: 501(c)3
Highest Offering: Doctorate
Accreditation: SC, MUS, NUR

01 President .... Dr. Bobby L. HALL
05 Vice Pres Academics .... Vacant
84 Vice Pres Enrollment Management .... Dr. D. Claude LUSK
20 Vice Pres of External Campuses .... Dr. Elane SEEBO
10 Chief Financial Officer .... Ms. Lezlie HUKILL
20 Associate Academic Vice President .... Dr. Stan DEMERRITT
12 Exec Dir/Campus Dean Albuquerque .... Dr. Tom FISHER
12 Exec Dir/Campus Dean Altus .... Dr. Jerry FAUGHT
12 Exec Dir/Campus Dean Amarillo .... Dr. J. B BOREN
12 Exec Dir/Campus Dean Anchorage .... Dr. Eric ASH
12 Exec Dir/Campus Dean Clovis .... Dr. Gary MITCHELL
12 Exec Dir/Campus Dean Fairbanks .... Vacant
12 Exec Dir/Campus Dean Hawaii .... Dr. Dan JACOBSON
12 Exec Dir/Campus Dean Lubbock .... Dr. David BISHOP
12 Exec Dir/Campus Dean Phoenix .... Dr. D. Glenn SIMMONS
12 Exec Dir/Campus Dean San Antonio .... Dr. James ANTENEN
12 Exec Dir/Campus Dean Sierra Vista .... Vacant
12 Exec Dir/Campus Dean Wichita Falls .... Dr. Dean DANIEL
83 Acad Dean School Behav & Soc Sci .... Dr. Peter BOWEN
50 Academic Dean School of Business .... Dr. Barry W. EVANS
53 Academic Dean School of Education .... Dr. Gene WHITFILL
57 Academic Dean School of Fine Arts .... Dr. Marti R. RUNNELS
79 Academic Dean School of Lang & Lit .... Dr. Cindy M. MCCLENAGAN
81 Academic Dean School Math/Sciences .... Dr. Scott FRANKILIN
64 Academic Dean School of Music .... Dr. Ann B. STUTES
66 Academic Dean School of Nursing .... Dr. Diane FRAZOR
73 Academic Dean Religion & Philosophy .... Dr. Clinton LOWEN
06 Registrar .... Mrs. Julie BOWEN
32 Exec Dir Student Development .... Vacant
30 Executive Dir Univ Advancement .... Mr. Mike MELCHER
21 Controller .... Vacant
41 Athletic Director .... Mr. Rick COOPER
07 Exec Dir Admissions Recruitmt .... Mr. Chad CAIN
07 Director Admissions .... Mrs. Debbie STENNETT
29 Director Alumni Development .... Mr. Danny ANDREWS
88 Director Church Services .... Vacant
44 Director Annual Fund .... Mrs. Teresa YOUNG
44 Director Donor Relations .... Ms. Amber MCCLOUD
37 Director Financial Aid .... Mrs. Karen LAQUEY
58 Director of Graduate Studies .... Ms. Amanda STANTON
15 Director Human Resources .... Mr. Ron APPLING
13 Director Information Technology .... Mrs. Katrina SMITH
09 Dir Inst Research/Effectiveness .... Dr. Andy PAGEL
12 Director Kenya Campus .... Dr. Richard SHAW
08 Director Library .... Dr. Polly R. LACKEY
88 Director Property Management .... Mr. Danny W. MURPHREE
26 Director Public Relations .... Mr. Jonathan PETTY
88 Director Special Projects .... Mrs. Penny POOLE
23 Director of Health Services .... Vacant
39 Director Student Housing .... Mrs. Nancy KEITH
38 Dir Counseling/Career/Disability .... Ms. Teresa MOORE
42 Director Student Ministries .... Mr. Donnie BROWN
40 Director University Services .... Vacant
106 Director Virtual Campus .... Dr. Trish TRIFILO
105 Director Web Services .... Mrs. Charlotte SCHUMACHER
88 Director External Records .... Mr. Daniel BROWN
19 Chief of Police/WBU .... Mr. Lonnie BURTON
18 Chief Facilities/Physical Plant .... Mr. David MURPHREE
04 Exec Admin Asst to President .... Mrs. Cynthia TREVINO

Weatherford College (E)

225 College Park Drive, Weatherford TX 76086-5699
County: Parker FICE Identification: 003664
Unit ID: 229799
Telephone: (817) 594-5471 Carnegie Class: Assoc/HT-High Trad
FAX Number: (817) 598-6210 Calendar System: Semester
URL: www.wc.edu
Established: 1869 Annual Undergrad Tuition & Fees (In-District): $2,400
Enrollment: 5,613 Coed
Affiliation or Control: Local IRS Status: 501(c)3
Highest Offering: Associate Degree
Accreditation: SC, ADNUR, COARC, DMS, EMT, OTA, PHLEB, PTAA, RAD

01 President .... Dr. Kevin EATON
04 Exec Asst to the President .... Mrs. Theresa R. HUTCHISON
32 VP of Inst & Student Services .... Mr. Michael ENDY
10 Exec VP Financial/Admin Affairs .... Mrs. Andra R. CANTRELL
30 Vice Pres Institutional Advancement .... Mr. Brent BAKER
76 Dean of Health & Human Sciences .... Ms. Katherine BOSWELL
05 Executive Dean of Academics .... Mr. Michael ENDY
53 Dean Educational/Instructional Sppt .... Ms. Rhonda TORRES
35 Executive Dean of Student Services .... Mr. Adam FINLEY
103 Dean Workforce & Economic Devel .... Ms. Kay YOUNG
26 Dir Communications/Public Relations .... Mrs. Crystal BROWN
31 Dean of Community Programs .... Mr. Duane DURRETT
88 Director Truck Driving .... Vacant
09 Dir Inst Research and Assessment .... Mr. Lee BUTLER
35 Exec Director Student Development .... Mr. Doug JEFFERSON
36 Dir of Career and Transfer Center .... Mr. John TURNTINE
109 Director Food Services .... Ms. Erin DAVIDSON
37 Director Student Financial Aid .... Mr. Donnie PURVIS
21 Controller .... Mrs. Rebecca DEPUY
15 Director Human Resources .... Mrs. Ralinda STONE
07 Director of Admissions/Veterans .... Mr. Ralph WILLINGHAM
13 Director Technology Services .... Mr. Greg SHRADER
08 Director of Library Services .... Mrs. Valerie STARR
18 Director of Facilities .... Ms. Rhonda SWAN
96 Director of Purchasing .... Mrs. Jeanie HOBBS
45 Director of Resource Development .... Vacant
19 Chief of Campus Police .... Mr. Paul STONE
38 Student Counseling .... Ms. Phyllis TIFFIN
88 Director Upward Bound .... Mr. Jeff KHALDEN
29 Director Alumni Relations .... Mr. Brent BAKER
103 Director of Workforce Education .... Ms. Jaretta KRUSE
53 Director of Teacher Education .... Dr. Joyce MELTON PAGES
06 Registrar .... Mrs. Vicki TRAWEEK
88 Director of Testing .... Ms. Leta MORRIS
88 Dir of Outreach/Student Success .... Ms. Kay LANDRUM
88 Director Special Populations .... Mrs. Dawn KAHLDEN
39 Director Student Housing .... Miss Faith STIFFLER
41 Athletic Director .... Mr. Bob MCKINLEY

West Coast University (F)

8435 N Stemmons Freeway, Dallas TX 75247-3900
Telephone: (214) 453-4533 Identification: 770485
Accreditation: &WC

† Regional accreditation is carried under the parent institution in North Hollywood, CA

Western Technical College (G)

9451 Diana Drive, El Paso TX 79924-6936
Telephone: (915) 566-9621 Identification: 666103
Accreditation: ACCSC

Western Technical College (H)

9624 Plaza Circle, El Paso TX 79927-2105
County: El Paso FICE Identification: 020983
Unit ID: 224679
Telephone: (915) 532-3737 Carnegie Class: Assoc/HVT-High Trad
FAX Number: (915) 532-6946 Calendar System: Other
URL: www.westerntech.edu
Established: 1969 Annual Undergrad Tuition & Fees: N/A
Enrollment: 990 Coed
Affiliation or Control: Proprietary IRS Status: Proprietary
Highest Offering: Associate Degree
Accreditation: ACCSC, PTAA

01 President/Director .... Mr. Allan SHARPE
88 Assistant Director .... Mr. Randy KUYKENDALL
11 Chief Administrative Officer .... Mr. Bill TERRELL
12 Executive VP/Campus School Director .... Ms. Mary CANO
05 Academic Dean (Plaza) .... Ms. Lynda CERVANTES
05 Academic Dean (Diana) .... Ms. Marsha LAWLER
10 Accounting Controller .... Ms. Laura PLUMMER
37 Student Financial Services Director .... Ms. Danielle PICCHI
36 Director Career Services .... Ms. Helen GARCIA
07 Director Admission .... Mr. Marco MARTINEZ
13 Director Information Technology .... Mr. Jose PEREZ

Western Texas College (I)

6200 College Avenue, Snyder TX 79549-6189
County: Scurry FICE Identification: 009549
Unit ID: 229832
Telephone: (325) 573-8511 Carnegie Class: Assoc/MT-VT-High Non
FAX Number: (325) 573-9321 Calendar System: Semester
URL: www.wtc.edu
Established: 1969 Annual Undergrad Tuition & Fees (In-District): $1,898
Enrollment: 2,067 Coed
Affiliation or Control: State/Local IRS Status: 501(c)3
Highest Offering: Associate Degree
Accreditation: SC

01 President .... Dr. Barbara R. BEEBE
04 Assistant to the President .... Ms. Melanie SCHWERTNER
10 Chief Financial Officer .... Ms. Patricia CLAXTON
11 Chief Operation Officer .... Mr. Mike THORTON
09 Dean Inst Research & Effectiveness .... Mr. Britt CANADA
05 Dean of Instructional Affairs .... Ms. Stephanie DUCHENEAUX
32 Dean of Student Services .... Mr. Ralph RAMON
72 Dean of Technology .... Mr. Roy BARTELS
103 Dean Workforce Development .... Vacant
41 Athletic Director .... Ms. Tammy DAVIS
06 Registrar .... Ms. Ann GALYEAN
37 Director Financial Aid .... Mr. Greg TORRES
21 Controller .... Ms. Marjann MORROW
15 Director of Human Resources .... Ms. Sheila WILLIAMSON
85 Dir International Student Services .... Ms. Melissa DOUCETTE
96 Director of Purchasing & Compliance .... Mr. Mitch CALHOUN

Wharton County Junior College (J)

911 Boling Highway, Wharton TX 77488-3298
County: Wharton FICE Identification: 003668
Unit ID: 229841
Telephone: (979) 532-4560 Carnegie Class: Assoc/MT-VT-Mix Trad/Non
FAX Number: (979) 532-6545 Calendar System: Semester
URL: www.wcjc.edu
Established: 1946 Annual Undergrad Tuition & Fees (In-District): $2,222
Enrollment: 7,152 Coed
Affiliation or Control: Local IRS Status: 501(c)3
Highest Offering: Associate Degree
Accreditation: SC, CAHIIM, CSHSE, DH, EMT, PTAA, RAD, SURGT

01 President .... Ms. Betty A. MCCROHAN
05 Vice President of Instruction .... Mrs. Leigh Ann COLLINS
10 Vice President Administrative Svcs .... Mr. Bryce KOCIAN
13 Vice President of Technology & IR ... Ms. Pamela YOUNGBLOOD
32 Vice President of Student Services .... Mr. David LEENHOUTS
21 Dean of Financial & Business Svcs .... Mr. Gus WESSELS
26 Director of Marketing & Comm .... Ms. Zina CARTER
06 Registrar .... Ms. Karen PREISLER
37 Director of Financial Aid .... Mr. Richard D. HYDE
08 Director Library Info/Tech Services .... Ms. Kwei HSU
18 Director of Facilities Management .... Mr. Mike FEYEN
15 Director of Human Resources .... Ms. Judy JONES
09 Director of Inst Effectiveness .... Dr. Danson JONES
96 Director of Purchasing .... Mr. Philip WUTHRICH

Wiley College (K)

711 Wiley Avenue, Marshall TX 75670-5199
County: Harrison FICE Identification: 003669
Unit ID: 229887
Telephone: (903) 927-3300 Carnegie Class: Bac-Diverse
FAX Number: (903) 938-8100 Calendar System: Semester
URL: www.wileyc.edu
Established: 1873 Annual Undergrad Tuition & Fees: $11,828
Enrollment: 1,351 Coed
Affiliation or Control: United Methodist IRS Status: 501(c)3
Highest Offering: Baccalaureate
Accreditation: SC, ACBSP

01 President and CEO .... Dr. Haywood L. STRICKLAND
03 Executive Vice President .... Dr. Glenda F. CARTER
10 Vice Pres for Business & Finance .... Dr. James BATTEN
05 Provost/VP Academic Affairs .... Dr. Gloria P. JAMES
32 Vice President Student Affairs .... Dr. Joseph L. MORALE
30 Vice Pres Institutional Advancement ...... Mr. Anthony HOLLOMAN
84 Vice Pres for Enrollment Services .... Mr. Antonio M. BOYLE
13 Acting Director Info Technology .... Mr. Chris WATSON
21 Director of Finance .... Mrs. Dawn JONES
53 Dean of Education .... Dr. Calandra LOCKHART
42 College Chaplain .... Vacant
04 Special Assistant to the President .... Mrs. Karen HELTON
50 Dean of Business & Technology .... Dr. Abdalla F. HAGAN
49 Dean of Sciences .... Dr. John G. STUART
79 Dean Social Sciences & Humanities .... Dr. Sherlynn H. BYRD
26 Director of Public Relations .... Ms. Tammy TAYLOR

08 Director of Library Services .... Mr. Christopher ALTNAU
06 Registrar .... Ms. Laura LANDER
07 Director of Admissions .... Ms. Jamecia MURRAY
15 Director of Human Resources .... Mrs. Krystal MOODY
18 Superintendent of Facilities .... Vacant
37 Director of Financial Aid .... Ms. Cecelia K. JONES
29 Director of Alumni Relations .... Ms. Alvena JONES
09 Director of Institutional Research .... Mr. Daniel NYACHUBA
11 Director Administrative Svcs .... Mr. O. Ivan WHITE
23 College Nurse .... Ms. Shonte EPPERSON
36 Dir Student Placement/Counseling .... Ms. LaDonna GAUT
41 Acting Director of Athletics .... Dr. Joseph L. MORALE
96 Director of Purchasing .... Mr. Darius Z. KIMBLE
35 Director of Student Development .... Ms. LaDonna GAUT
101 Secretary of the Institution/Board .... Mrs. Cassandra M. JOHNSON
106 Dir Online Education/E-learning .... Dr. Kim C. LONG
19 Director Security/Safety .... Mr. Winston ROBINSON
39 Director of Residence Life .... Mr. Howard FISHER
43 Dir Legal Services/General Counsel .... Dr. Kim BEATON
44 Director Major Gifts/Planned Giving .... Mr. Charles CORNISH
90 Director Academic Computing .... Vacant
100 Chief of Staff .... Dr. Charles N. SMITH

UTAH

Argosy University, Salt Lake City (A)

121 Election Road Suite 300, Draper UT 84020-7724
Telephone: (801) 601-5000 Identification: 666655
Accreditation: &WC, ACBSP, MFCD

† Regional accreditation is carried under the parent institution in Orange, CA.

The Art Institute of Salt Lake City (B)

121 West Election Road, Draper UT 84020
Telephone: (801) 601-4700 Identification: 666694
Accreditation: #ACICS

† Branch campus of The Art Institute of Phoenix, AZ. School is in teach-out plan.

Brigham Young University (C)

Provo UT 84602-0002
County: Utah FICE Identification: 003670
Unit ID: 230038
Telephone: (801) 422-4000 Carnegie Class: DU-Higher
FAX Number: (801) 422-0684 Calendar System: Semester
URL: www.byu.edu
Established: 1875 Annual Undergrad Tuition & Fees: $5,150
Enrollment: 30,484 Coed
Affiliation or Control: Latter-day Saints IRS Status: 501(c)3
Highest Offering: Doctorate
Accreditation: NW, ART, BUS, BUSA, CAATE, CLPSY, CONST, COPSY, CS, DANCE, DIETD, DIETI, ENG, ENGR, ENGT, IPSY, JOUR, LAW, MFCD, MT, MUS, NRPA, NURSE, PH, SP, SPAA, SW, TEAC, THEA

01 President .... Dr. Kevin J. WORTHEN
05 Academic Vice President .... Dr. Brent W. WEBB
11 Administrative Vice President .... Mr. Brian K. EVANS
44 Advancement Vice President .... Dr. Matthew O. RICHARDSON
13 Vice Pres Info Tech/Chief Info Ofcr .... Dr. J. Kelly FLANAGAN
88 International Vice President .... Dr. Sandra ROGERS
32 Student Life Vice President .... Dr. Janet S. SCHARMAN
43 Asst to President/General Counsel .... Mr. Michael R. ORME
45 Asst to Pres Planning/Assessment ..... Mr. James D. GORDON, III
27 Asst to Pres Univ Communications .... Mrs. Carri P. JENKINS
20 Assoc Acad Vice President Faculty .... Dr. Craig H. HART
20 Assoc Acad VP Undergraduate Stds .... Dr. Brad L. NEIGER
46 Assoc Acad VP Research/Grad Stds .... Dr. Alan R. HARKER
35 Assoc Student Life Vice Pres .... Dr. Ronald K. CHAPMAN
10 Chief Financial Officer .... Mr. Brian K. EVANS
18 Asst Admin VP Physical Facilities .... Mr. Ole M. SMITH
15 Asst Admin VP Human Resource Svcs .... Mr. Forrest FLAKE
35 Asst Admin VP/Stdnt Auxiliary Svc .... Mr. Mark CLEGG
26 Managing Dir Alumni/Ext Rels .... Mr. McKay CHRISTENSEN
30 Managing Dir LDS Philanthropies .... Dr. Tanise CHUNG-HOON
36 Exec Dir Stdnt Acad/Advisement Svcs .... Vacant
35 Dean Student Life .... Mr. Vernon L. HEPERI
37 Director Financial Aid/Scholarships .... Mr. Stephen E. HILL
88 Dean Undergraduate Education .... Dr. Joseph D. PARRY
08 University Librarian .... Ms. Jennifer PAUSTENBAUGH
58 Dean Graduate Studies .... Dr. Wynn C. STIRLING
51 Dean Continuing Education .... Dr. Lee GLINES
47 Dean Life Sciences .... Dr. James P. PORTER
54 Dean Engineering & Technology .... Dr. Michael E. JENSEN
83 Dean Family Home & Social Science .... Dr. Benjamin M. OGLES
57 Dean Fine Arts & Communications .... Dr. Edward E. ADAMS
79 Dean Humanities .... Dr. J. Scott MILLER
61 Dean Law School .... Dr. D. Gordon SMITH
50 Dean Marriott School Management .... Dr. Lee T. PERRY
53 Dean McKay School of Education .... Dr. Mary Ann PRATER
81 Dean Physical & Math Science .... Dr. Scott D. SOMMERFELDT
66 Dean Nursing .... Dr. Patricia RAVERT
73 Dean Religious Education .... Dr. Brent TOP
38 Director Counseling & Career Ctr .... Dr. Steve A. SMITH
09 Dir Institutional Assess/Analysis .... Dr. Danny R. OLSEN
06 Registrar .... Mr. Barry ALLRED
07 Director of Admissions .... Vacant
96 Director of Purchasing .... Mr. W. Timothy HILL
88 Dir University Accessibility Center .... Dr. Gerilynn VORKINK
19 Director Security/Safety .... Mr. Larry STOTT
39 Director Student Housing .... Ms. Julie FRANKLIN
41 Athletic Director .... Mr. Tom HOLMOE

Broadview Entertainment Arts University (D)

240 East Morris Avenue, Salt Lake City UT 84115
Telephone: (801) 300-4300 Identification: 770809
Accreditation: ACICS

Broadview University (E)

1902 W 7800 S, West Jordan UT 84088-4021
County: Salt Lake FICE Identification: 011166
Unit ID: 230056
Telephone: (801) 304-4224 Carnegie Class: Spec-4-yr-Other Health
FAX Number: (801) 304-4229 Calendar System: Quarter
URL: www.broadviewuniversity.edu
Established: 1971 Annual Undergrad Tuition & Fees: $13,500
Enrollment: 219 Coed
Affiliation or Control: Proprietary IRS Status: Proprietary
Highest Offering: Master's
Accreditation: ACICS, MAAB

01 President .... Mr. Terry MYHRE
05 Director .... Ms. Deeann KERR

Eagle Gate College (F)

915 North 400 West, Layton UT 84041
Telephone: (801) 546-7500 Identification: 770812
Accreditation: ACICS

Eagle Gate College (G)

5588 S Green Street, Suite 150, Murray UT 84123-6965
County: Salt Lake FICE Identification: 021785
Unit ID: 230366
Telephone: (801) 333-8100 Carnegie Class: Bac/Assoc-Mixed
FAX Number: (801) 263-6520 Calendar System: Other
URL: www.eaglegatecollege.edu
Established: 1979 Annual Undergrad Tuition & Fees: $15,262
Enrollment: 238 Coed
Affiliation or Control: Proprietary IRS Status: Proprietary
Highest Offering: Baccalaureate
Accreditation: ACICS

01 President .... Mr. Chris NICKELL
03 Campus VP .... Mr. Bill HALE

Fortis College (H)

3949 South 700 East, Suite 150, Salt Lake City UT 84107
Telephone: (801) 713-0915 Identification: 666762
Accreditation: ACCSC, ADNUR, DH

† Tuition varies by degree program.

Independence University (I)

4021 South 700 East, Suite 400,
Salt Lake City UT 84107-2453
County: Salt Lake FICE Identification: 022061
Unit ID: 465812
Telephone: (800) 972-5149 Carnegie Class: Spec-4-yr-Other Health
FAX Number: (801) 263-0345 Calendar System: Other
URL: www.independence.edu
Established: 1978 Annual Undergrad Tuition & Fees: $16,968
Enrollment: 4,478 Coed
Affiliation or Control: Proprietary IRS Status: Proprietary
Highest Offering: Master's
Accreditation: ACCSC, COARC

01 President .... Mr. Eric JUHLIN

LDS Business College (J)

95 North 300 West, Salt Lake City UT 84101-3500
County: Salt Lake FICE Identification: 003672
Unit ID: 230418
Telephone: (801) 524-8100 Carnegie Class: Assoc/MT-VT-High Trad
FAX Number: (801) 524-1900 Calendar System: Semester
URL: www.ldsbc.edu
Established: 1886 Annual Undergrad Tuition & Fees: $3,160
Enrollment: 2,006 Coed
Affiliation or Control: Latter-day Saints IRS Status: 501(c)3
Highest Offering: Associate Degree
Accreditation: NW, #MAC

01 President .... Mr. Larry J. RICHARDS
04 Executive Admin Asst .... Ms. Jolynn T. WOLFGRAMM
05 Chief Academic Officer .... Mr. Bruce C. KUSCH
13 Chief Information Officer .... Mr. Mark R. AUGHENBAUGH
10 Vice President Finance/Controller .... Mr. Bob H. WISER
30 Vice President Advancement .... Mr. Craig V. NELSON
50 Director of Strategic Initiatives .... Mr. Robert O. SALMON
88 Director of Academic Programs .... Ms. Cathy T. CAREY
20 Dean of Instructional Support .... Mr. Tyler S. MORGAN
32 Chief Student Services Officer .... Mr. Adrian T. JUCHAU
15 Director of Human Resources .... Mr. Brady J. KIMBER
26 Director of Public Affairs .... Mr. Howard M. COLLETT
36 Director of Career Services .... Mr. Justin K. JONES
06 Registrar .... Ms. Tamra TAYLOR
07 Asst Director of Admissions .... Ms. Dawn FELLOWS
88 Director of Instructional Design .... Mr. Jared WRIGHT
88 Director of Business Solutions .... Mr. Glenn MCGETTIGAN
08 Dir of Library/Inform Resources .... Ms. Sarah SORENSEN
88 Accounting Program Director .... Mr. Bruce SCHREINER
50 Business Skills Program Director .... Mr. Scott NEWMAN
88 Entrepreneurship Program Director .... Mr. Doug MCDOUGAL
88 Professional Sales Program Director .... Ms. Jennifer WARNAS
72 Applied Technology Program Director ...... Mr. Mitch PENDLETON
76 Health Professions Program Director .... Ms. Olivia WEST
88 Paralegal Program Director .... Ms. Kimberly GARNER
97 General Studies Program Director .... Ms. Christine GRAHAM
88 Interior Design Program Director .... Mr. Miles HUNSAKER
50 Business Info Tech Program Dir .... Mr. Spencer DEGRAW
88 Social Media Marketing Program Dir ... Mr. Barett CHRISTENSEN
88 GSO/Proj Mgmt Program Director .... Mr. Brent ANDRUS
73 Institute of Religion Director .... Mr. Keith BURKHART
21 Controller .... Mr. Chris REITZ
37 Student Financial Services Manager .... Ms. Melanie CONOVER
40 Bookstore Manager .... Ms. Rachel BINGHAM
88 Director of Student Support .... Ms. Gail SINGLEY
108 Director Institutional Assessment .... Mr. Michael R. DAVISON

Midwives College of Utah (K)

1174 E Graystone Way Suite 2,
Salt Lake City UT 84106-2671
County: Utah Identification: 666281
Unit ID: 480985
Telephone: (866) 680-2756 Carnegie Class: Spec-4-yr-Other Health
FAX Number: (866) 207-2024 Calendar System: Semester
URL: www.midwifery.edu
Established: 1980 Annual Undergrad Tuition & Fees: $6,340
Enrollment: 217 Coed
Affiliation or Control: Independent Non-Profit IRS Status: 501(c)3
Highest Offering: Master's
Accreditation: MEAC

01 President .... Ms. Kristi RIDD-YOUNG
05 Academic Dean .... Ms. Nicole CROFT
17 Clinical Dean .... Ms. Sarah CARTER
06 Registrar .... Ms. Laura PARK
08 Head Librarian .... Ms. Kaylee RIDD
07 Admissions .... Ms. Mel SMITH-TOURVILLE
13 Chief Info Technology Officer (CIO) .... Mr. Alan BELLOWS
37 Financial Aid Director .... Ms. Whitney MESYEF
58 Graduate Dean .... Ms. Courtney EVERSON
10 Chief Business Officer .... Ms. Julie DELONG

Neumont University (L)

143 South Main, Salt Lake City UT 84111
County: Salt Lake FICE Identification: 010098
Unit ID: 445692
Telephone: (801) 302-2800 Carnegie Class: Spec-4-yr-Other Tech
FAX Number: (801) 302-2811 Calendar System: Quarter
URL: www.neumont.edu
Established: 2003 Annual Undergrad Tuition & Fees: $24,000
Enrollment: 431 Coed
Affiliation or Control: Proprietary IRS Status: Proprietary
Highest Offering: Master's
Accreditation: ACICS

01 President/Campus Dir Utah .... Shaun MCALMONT
05 Provost .... Aaron REED
32 Dean of Students .... Erin MCCORMACK
06 Registrar/Dir Academic Programs .... Larry CRANDALL
07 Director of Admissions .... Karick HEATON

New Charter University (M)

50 W. Broadway, Suite 300, Salt Lake City UT 84101
County: Salt Lake FICE Identification: 041292
Unit ID: 420361
Telephone: (801) 883-8336 Carnegie Class: Not Classified
FAX Number: (801) 855-5922 Calendar System: Trimester
URL: www.new.edu
Established: 1994 Annual Undergrad Tuition & Fees: N/A
Enrollment: N/A Coed
Affiliation or Control: Proprietary IRS Status: Proprietary
Highest Offering: Master's
Accreditation: DEAC

01 President .... Mr. David ROSS
05 Academic Dean .... Ms. Diane JOHNSON
10 Exec Director Business Operations .... Ms. Debbie AUSTIN
32 Manager Operations/Student Affairs .... Ms. Char BOSEN

Nightingale College (N)

4155 Harrison Blvd, Ste 100, Ogden UT 84403
County: Weber FICE Identification: 038383
Unit ID: 444787
Telephone: (801) 689-2160 Carnegie Class: Not Classified
FAX Number: (801) 689-3114 Calendar System: Semester
URL: www.nightingale.edu
Established: 2010 Annual Undergrad Tuition & Fees: N/A
Enrollment: 156 Coed
Affiliation or Control: Proprietary IRS Status: Proprietary

Highest Offering: Baccalaureate
Accreditation: **ABHES**, ADNUR

01 President/CEO .... Mr. Mikhail SHNEYDER
10 Vice Pres Operations/Controller .... Ms. Kara HARMON
26 Vice Pres Marketing & Admission .... Mr. Jonathan TANNER

Ogden-Weber Applied Technology College (A)

200 North Washington Boulevard, Ogden UT 84404-4089
County: Weber FICE Identification: 023465
Unit ID: 230490
Telephone: (801) 627-8300 Carnegie Class: Not Classified
FAX Number: (801) 395-3727 Calendar System: Other
URL: www.owatc.edu
Established: 1971 Annual Undergrad Tuition & Fees (In-District): N/A
Enrollment: 2,615 Coed
Affiliation or Control: State/Local IRS Status: 501(c)3
Highest Offering: Associate Degree
Accreditation: **COE**, MAC, PNUR

01 President & Chief Executive Officer .... Collette MERCIER
05 VP for Instructional Services .... James R. TAGGART
32 VP for Student Services .... Rhonda LAURITZEN
10 VP for College Services/CFO .... Tyler CALL
04 Administrative Asst to President .... Tina SMITH
06 Registrar .... Kari MARLER
102 Dir Foundation/Corporate Relations .... Monica SCHWENK
15 Director Personnel Services .... Theresa WALKER
19 Director Security/Safety .... Fred FRAZIER
26 Dir Marketing & Diversity .... Juliane KETTERING
37 Director Student Financial Aid .... Jan BURTON

† Campus of Utah College of Applied Technology, Salt Lake City, UT.

Provo College (B)

1450 W 820 N, Provo UT 84601-1305
County: Utah FICE Identification: 023608
Unit ID: 380438
Telephone: (801) 818-8900 Carnegie Class: Assoc/HVT-High Non
FAX Number: (801) 375-9728 Calendar System: Other
URL: www.provocollege.edu
Established: 1984 Annual Undergrad Tuition & Fees: $14,377
Enrollment: 372 Coed
Affiliation or Control: Proprietary IRS Status: Proprietary
Highest Offering: Associate Degree
Accreditation: **ACICS**, ADNUR, PTAA

01 Campus President .... Mr. Todd SMITH
05 Academic Dean .... Mrs. Jana COLYAR
10 Business Manager .... Ms. Julie BRADFORD
07 Director of Admissions .... Ms. Tania ROWLAND
37 Financial Services Assoc Director .... Ms. Julie TRUJILLO
06 Registrar .... Mrs. April ACUNA
32 Director of Student Services .... Ms. Liz TIDWELL
36 Director of Career Services .... Ms. Karna OWENS

Rocky Mountain University of Health Professions (C)

122 East 1700 South, Building C, Provo UT 84606-7379
County: Utah FICE Identification: 041932
Unit ID: 475495
Telephone: (801) 375-5125 Carnegie Class: Spec-4-yr-Other Health
FAX Number: (801) 375-2125 Calendar System: Trimester
URL: www.rmuohp.edu
Established: 1998 Annual Graduate Tuition & Fees: N/A
Enrollment: 501 Coed
Affiliation or Control: Proprietary IRS Status: Proprietary
Highest Offering: Doctorate; No Undergraduates
Accreditation: **NW**, #ARCPA, NURSE, PTA

01 President .... Dr. Richard P. NIELSEN
05 Exec VP Academic Affairs/Provost .... Dr. Hani GHAZI-BIRRY
11 Chief Operation Officer .... Dr. Michael SKURJA
10 Vice President Finance .... Mr. Jeff B. BATE
31 VP Inst Effect/Cmty Engagement .... Dr. Jessica D. EGBERT
84 VP Enrollment Management .... Dr. Erin NOSEL
09 Exec VP Inst Effect/Strategic Int .... Dr. Sandra PENNINGTON
46 Director of Research .... Dr. Brent ALVAR
51 Director Continuing Education .... Dr. Michael SKURJA
32 Director Student Services .... Dr. Erin NOSEL

Stevens-Henager College (D)

755 South Main Street, Logan UT 84321
Telephone: (435) 792-6970 Identification: 770603
Accreditation: **ACCSC**, MAC

Stevens-Henager College (E)

1890 South 1350 West, Ogden UT 84401
County: Weber FICE Identification: 003674
Unit ID: 230621
Telephone: (801) 622-1567 Carnegie Class: Spec-4-yr-Other Health
FAX Number: (801) 621-0853 Calendar System: Quarter
URL: www.stevenshenager.edu
Established: 1891 Annual Undergrad Tuition & Fees: $16,968
Enrollment: 321 Coed
Affiliation or Control: Independent Non-Profit IRS Status: 501(c)3
Highest Offering: Baccalaureate
Accreditation: **ACCSC**, MAC, SURGT

01 Pres of Ogden Campus/Regional Dir .... Ms. Vicky DEWSNUP
07 Director of Admissions .... Ms. Wynn HURTADO
32 Director of Student Services .... Mr. Doug BURCH
05 Chief Academic Officer .... Dr. Wayne HUNSAKER
10 Chief Business Officer .... Mr. Leland NEIL
36 Director Career Services .... Mr. Doug BURCH

Stevens-Henager College (F)

1476 S Sandhill Road, Orem UT 84058-7310
Telephone: (801) 418-1450 FICE Identification: 030030
Accreditation: **ACCSC**, #MAC

Stevens-Henager College (G)

720 South River Road, Suite C-130, St. George UT 84790
Telephone: (435) 628-9902 Identification: 770604
Accreditation: **ACCSC**

Stevens-Henager College (H)

383 W Vine Street, Salt Lake City UT 84123
Telephone: (801) 281-7620 Identification: 666038
Accreditation: **ACCSC**, COARC

† Branch campus of Stevens-Henager College, Ogden, UT.

Uintah Basin Applied Technology College (I)

1100 East Lagoon Street, Roosevelt UT 84066
County: Duchesne FICE Identification: 011165
Unit ID: 230676
Telephone: (435) 722-6900 Carnegie Class: Not Classified
FAX Number: (435) 722-6999 Calendar System: Semester
URL: www.ubatc.edu
Established: 1968 Annual Undergrad Tuition & Fees (In-State): N/A
Enrollment: 1,389 Coed
Affiliation or Control: State IRS Status: 501(c)3
Highest Offering: Associate Degree
Accreditation: **COE**, PNUR

01 Campus President .... Aaron E. WEIGHT
32 Vice Pres of Student Services .... Robert PETERSON
10 Vice President Fiscal Services .... Keith SPROUSE
05 Vice President Instruction .... Bob NAYLOR
04 Exec Assistant to the President .... Trenna BALLOU
06 Registrar .... Julene OLSEN
37 Financial Aid Coordinator .... Karen SECREST
07 Admissions .... Jim LAMUTH
15 Human Resources Dir/Controller .... Shawn METCALF

† Campus of Utah College of Applied Technology, Salt Lake City, UT.

University of Phoenix Utah Campus (J)

5373 South Green Street, Salt Lake City UT 84123-4642
Telephone: (801) 263-1444 Identification: 770232
Accreditation: **&NH** ACBSP, CACREP

† Regional accreditation is carried under the parent institution in Tempe, AZ

The Utah College of Dental Hygiene at Careers Unlimited (K)

1176 S 1480 W, Orem UT 84058-4905
County: Utah FICE Identification: 034633
Unit ID: 448239
Telephone: (801) 426-8234 Carnegie Class: Spec-4-yr-Other Health
FAX Number: (801) 224-5437 Calendar System: Other
URL: www.ucdh.edu
Established: 2006 Annual Undergrad Tuition & Fees: N/A
Enrollment: 177 Coed
Affiliation or Control: Proprietary IRS Status: Proprietary
Highest Offering: Baccalaureate
Accreditation: **ACCSC**, DH

01 College President .... Mr. Brent MOLEN
10 College Vice President/CFO .... Ms. Krista MCCLURE
00 Director Emeritus/CEO .... Mr. Kenneth MOLEN

*Utah System of Higher Education (L)

The Gateway, 60 S 400 W, Salt Lake City UT 84101-1284
County: Salt Lake FICE Identification: 009339
Telephone: (801) 321-7101 Carnegie Class: N/A
FAX Number: (801) 321-7199
URL: www.higheredutah.org

01 Exec Ofcr/Comm of Higher Education .... Mr. David L. BUHLER
05 Assoc Commissioner Academic Affairs .... Dr. Elizabeth J. HITCH
10 Assoc Commissioner Fin/Facilities .... Dr. Gregory STAUFFER
37 Exec Director Student Financial Aid .... Mr. David A. FEITZ
88 UESP Executive Director .... Ms. Lynne WARD

*The University of Utah (M)

201 South 1460 East, Salt Lake City UT 84112-1107
County: Salt Lake FICE Identification: 003675
Unit ID: 230764
Telephone: (801) 581-7200 Carnegie Class: DU-Highest
FAX Number: (801) 581-3007 Calendar System: Semester
URL: www.utah.edu
Established: 1850 Annual Undergrad Tuition & Fees (In-State): $8,197
Enrollment: 31,515 Coed
Affiliation or Control: State IRS Status: 501(c)3
Highest Offering: Doctorate
Accreditation: **NW**, ARCPA, #AUD, BUS, BUSA, CAATE, CEA, CLPSY, COPSY, CYTO, DANCE, DENT, DIETC, EMT, ENG, ENGR, HSA, IPSY, LAW, MED, MIDWF, MT, MUS, NMT, NRPA, NURSE, OT, PH, PHAR, PLNG, PTA, SCPSY, SP, SPAA, SW, TEAC

02 President .... Dr. David W. PERSHING
05 Sr Vice Pres Academic Affairs .... Dr. Ruth WATKINS
17 Sr VP Hlth Sci/CEO Univ Ut Hlth Ctr .... Dr. Vivian S. LEE
43 Interim Chief General Counsel .... Ms. Elizabeth DOLAN WINTER
11 Vice Pres Administrative Services .... Mr. Arnold B. COMBE
10 Chief Business Officer .... Mr. John E. NIXON
32 Vice President Student Affairs .... Dr. Barbara H. SNYDER
30 Vice Pres Institutional Advancement .... Mr. Fred C. ESPLIN
86 Vice President Government Relations .... Mr. Jason PERRY
15 Assoc Vice Pres for Human Resources .... Ms. Joan GINES
46 Vice President Research .... Dr. Thomas N. PARKS
04 Exec Asst to the President .... Ms. Julia JONES
13 Chief Information Officer .... Mr. Stephen HESS
21 Chief Strategy Officer .... Ms. Patricia A. ROSS
88 Chief Global Officer .... Dr. Michael L. HARDMAN
16 Chief Human Resources Officer .... Mr. Jeff HERRING
26 Chief Mktg & Communications Officer .... Mr. William J. WARREN
20 Sr AVP AA & Dean Undergrad Studies .... Dr. Martha S. BRADLEY
84 Sr Assoc VP for Enrollment Mgmt .... Ms. Mary G. PARKER
45 Assoc VP Acad Affs/Budget/Planning .... Ms. Cathy ANDERSON
18 Int VP Admin Services/Facilities .... Mr. Ken NYE
10 Assoc VP Admin/Finance & Bus Svcs .... Mr. Jeffrey J. WEST
20 Int Assoc VP Equity/Diversity .... Dr. Kathryn B. STOCKTON
88 Associate Vice President Research .... Dr. Cynthia M. FURSE
88 Assoc VP Acad Affairs/Faculty .... Dr. Amy WILDERMUTH
35 AVP Student Affs/Bus/Auxil Svcs .... Dr. Jerry L. BASFORD
109 Assoc VP Admin Svc/Auxiliary Svc .... Mr. Gordon N. WILSON
58 Dean Graduate School .... Dr. David B. KIEDA
48 Dean Architecture & Planning .... Dr. Keith D. MOORE
50 Dean David Eccles Sch of Business .... Dr. Taylor RANDALL
52 Interim Dean School of Dentistry .... Dr. Glen HANSON
53 Dean College of Education .... Dr. Maria FRANQUIZ
54 Dean College of Engineering .... Dr. Richard B. BROWN
57 Dean Col of Fine Arts/AVP the Arts .... Dr. Raymond TYMAS-JONES
68 Dean College of Health .... Dr. David H. PERRIN
92 Dean Honors College .... Dr. Sylvia TORTI
79 Dean College of Humanities .... Dr. Dianne HARRIS
61 Dean S J Quinney College of Law .... Dr. Robert ADLER
65 Dean Coll of Mines & Earth Science .... Dr. Francis H. BROWN
63 Dean School of Medicine .... Dr. Vivian S. LEE
66 Dean College of Nursing .... Dr. Patricia MORTON
67 Interim Dean College of Pharmacy .... Dr. Kristen A. KEEFE
81 Dean College of Science .... Dr. Henry WHITE
83 Int Dean Col Social/Behav Science .... Dr. Cynthia BERG
70 Dean College of Social Work .... Mr. Hank LIESE
88 Dean of Students .... Ms. Lori MCDONALD
06 University Registrar .... Mr. Timothy J. EBNER
23 CEO University Hospitals & Clinics .... Mr. David E. ENTWISTLE
91 Exec Dir Proj/Apps/Univ Info Tech .... Ms. Deborah B. RAKHSHA
88 Director Institutional Review Board .... Mr. John P. STILLMAN
86 Director Purchasing .... Mr. James T. PARKER
94 Director Gender Studies .... Dr. Susie PORTER
77 Department Chair Sch of Computing .... Mr. Ross T. WHITAKER
52 Dir Dental Clinic/Gen Prac Residency .... Dr. James BEKKER
07 Director Admissions .... Mr. Matthew LOPEZ
29 Exec Director Alumni Association .... Mr. M. John ASHTON
44 Director Planned Giving .... Ms. Karin S. HARDY
37 Dir Financial Aid & Scholarships .... Mr. John CURL
08 Dean MLIB/University Librarian .... Ms. Alberta COMER
62 Dir Eccles Health Sciences Library .... Ms. Jean P. SHIPMAN
62 Dir S J Quinney Col of Law/Lib .... Ms. Melissa BERNSTEIN
36 Director of Career Services .... Mr. Stan D. INMAN
38 Director Counseling Center .... Dr. Lauren WEITZMAN
39 Director Housing & Res Education .... Ms. Barbara REMSBURG
39 Director Univ Student Apartments .... Mr. Richard L. JAMES
88 Dir Natural History Museum of Utah .... Dr. Sarah B. GEORGE
19 Chief of Police .... Mr. Dale G. BROPHY
40 Director Campus Bookstore .... Mr. Daniel L. ARCHER
85 Director International Center .... Ms. Chalimar L. SWAIN
41 Director Athletics .... Dr. Chris HILL
25 Dir Office of Sponsored Projects .... Mr. Brent K. BROWN
31 Dir Univ Neighborhood Partners .... Dr. Sarah MUNRO
09 Director Institutional Analysis .... Dr. Paul A. GORE

*Southern Utah University (N)

351 W University Blvd, Cedar City UT 84720-2470
County: Iron FICE Identification: 003678
Unit ID: 230603
Telephone: (435) 586-7700 Carnegie Class: Masters/L
FAX Number: (435) 586-5475 Calendar System: Semester
URL: www.suu.edu
Established: 1897 Annual Undergrad Tuition & Fees (In-State): $6,300
Enrollment: 7,656 Coed
Affiliation or Control: State IRS Status: 501(c)3
Highest Offering: Master's

Accreditation: NW, ART, BUS, CAATE, CAEP, CS, DANCE, ENG, ENGT, MUS, NURSE, SPAA

02 President .... Mr. Scott L. WYATT
05 Provost .... Dr. Bradley COOK
10 Vice Pres of Finance & Admin .... Mr. Marvin DODGE
32 Asst VP/Dean Student Services .... Mr. Jason RAMIREZ
30 Vice Pres Advance/Enrollment Mgmt .... Mr. Stuart JONES
58 Assoc Provost/Dean of Graduate Stds .... Dr. James SAGE
07 Director of Admissions .... Mr. Brandon WRIGHT
18 Executive Director of FM .... Mr. Tiger FUNK
26 Exec Director Brand Strategy .... Ms. Ellen TREANOR
28 Exec Director of Access/Inclusion .... Mr. Jonathan PUENTE
08 Dean/Director Library/Univ Studies .... Dr. Richard SAUNDERS
51 Dean of Continuing/Profess Studies .... Mr. Mark ATKINSON
21 Asst VP of Budget and Planning .... Mr. Mitchell BEALER
75 Director CTE .... Mr. David A. WARD
06 Registrar .... Mr. John ALLRED
15 Director Human Resources .... Mr. David T. MCGUIRE
88 Dean Integrative/Engaged Learning .... Dr. Patrick CLARKE
37 Director of Financial Aid .... Ms. Jan CAREY-MCDONALD
29 Vice Pres Alumni/Community Rels .... Ms. Mindy BENSON
41 Athletic Director .... Mr. Jason BUTIKOFER
43 Legal Counsel .... Ms. Ann Marie ALLEN
79 Dean Col Humanities/Soc Sci .... Dr. James MCDONALD
50 Dean School of Business .... Dr. Carl R. TEMPLIN
53 Dean College of Education .... Dr. Shawn L. CHRISTIANSEN
81 Dean College of Sci and Engineering .... Dr. Robert EVES
57 Dean College Performing/Visual Arts .... Mrs. Shauna MENDINI
96 Director of Purchasing .... Mr. Bradley BROWN
09 Exec Dir Inst Research/Assessment .... Mr. Christian REINER
38 Director Student Counseling .... Dr. Curtis HILL

*Dixie State University (A)

225 S University Avenue, Saint George UT 84770-3876

County: Washington FICE Identification: 003671
Unit ID: 230171
Telephone: (435) 652-7500 Carnegie Class: Bac/Assoc-Mixed
FAX Number: (435) 656-4001 Calendar System: Semester
URL: www.dixie.edu
Established: 1911 Annual Undergrad Tuition & Fees (In-State): $4,620
Enrollment: 8,570 Coed
Affiliation or Control: State IRS Status: 501(c)3
Highest Offering: Baccalaureate
Accreditation: NW, ACBSP, ADNUR, COARC, DH, EMT, MT, MUS, NUR, PTAA, RAD, SURGT, TEAC

02 President .... Dr. Richard B. WILLIAMS
11 Vice Pres Administrative Services .... Mr. Paul MORRIS
05 Exec Vice Pres Academic Services .... Dr. Michael LACOURSE
32 VP Student Services/Govt Relations .... Mr. Frank LOJKO
30 Vice Pres Advancement .... Mr. Brad LAST
49 Dean School of Humanities .... Dr. Richard FEATHERSTONE
66 Dean School Health Sciences .... Dr. Carole GRADY
50 Dean School Business .... Dr. Kyle WELLS
81 Dean Science & Technology .... Dr. Eric PEDERSEN
53 Dean Sch Education/Family Studies .... Dr. Brenda SABEY
51 Dean Academic & Community Outreach .... Ms. Becky SMITH
35 Dean of Students .... Mr. Del BEATTY
13 Chief Information Officer .... Mr. Gary J. KOEVEN
10 Asst VP of Business Services .... Mr. A. Scott TALBOT
15 Exec Director of Human Resources .... Mr. Travis ROSENBERG
18 Executive Director Campus Services .... Ms. Sherry RUESCH
08 Director Library .... Mr. Richard PAUSTENBAUGH
109 Executive Director Auxiliaries .... Mr. Don STECK
37 Exec Director Student Financial Aid .... Mr. J. D ROBERTSON
84 Exec Dir Enrollment Services .... Mr. David ROOS
06 Registrar .... Ms. Julie STENDER
07 Director of Admissions .... Mr. Brett SCHWARTS
38 Director Student Counseling .... Mr. Mike OLSEN
26 Director Public Relations .... Ms. Jyl HALL
18 Director Facilities Operation .... Mr. Doug WHITEHEAD
19 Director Security/Safety .... Mr. Don C. REID
41 Athletic Director .... Mr. Jason BOOTHE
39 Director Resident Life .... Mr. Seth GUBLER
09 Director of Institutional Research .... Ms. Andrea BROWN
04 Exec Assistant to the President .... Mrs. Marilyn LAMOREAUX
35 Director of Student Involvement .... Mr. Luke KEROUAC
96 Director of Purchasing .... Ms. Jackie FREEMAN
29 Director of Alumni Relations .... Ms. Kalynn LARSON
103 Dir Workforce/Career Development .... Mr. Steve BRINGHURST
105 Director of Network Services .... Mr. Jerry MATSON
25 Chief Contracts/Grants Admin .... Mr. Bill O'NEILL
28 Director of Diversity .... Ms. Christina DUNCAN
43 Dir Legal Services/General Counsel .... Mr. Doajo HICKS
91 Director Administrative Computing .... Mr. James MILLER

*Utah State University (B)

Logan UT 84322-0001

County: Cache FICE Identification: 003677
Unit ID: 230728
Telephone: (435) 797-1000 Carnegie Class: DU-Higher
FAX Number: (435) 797-3880 Calendar System: Semester
URL: www.usu.edu
Established: 1888 Annual Undergrad Tuition & Fees (In-State): $7,260
Enrollment: 27,662 Coed
Affiliation or Control: State IRS Status: 501(c)3
Highest Offering: Doctorate
Accreditation: NW, ART, AUD, BUS, BUSA, CEA, CIDA, CORE, CS, DIETC, DIETD, DIETI, ENG, ENGR, IPSY, LSAR, MFCD, MUS, PSPSY, SP, SW, TEAC

02 President .... Dr. Stan L. ALBRECHT
05 Provost .... Dr. Noelle E. COCKETT
43 General Counsel .... Ms. Mica MCKINNEY
10 Vice President Business & Finance .... Mr. Dave COWLEY
32 Vice President Student Services .... Mr. James MORALES
56 Vice Pres Extension & Agriculture .... Dr. Kenneth L. WHITE
46 VP Research/Dn Sch Graduate Stds .... Dr. Mark R. MCLELLAN
30 VP Univ Advance/Commercialization .... Mr. Robert BEHUNIN
13 CIO/Assoc VP Information Technology .... Dr. Eric HAWLEY
18 Associate VP for Facilities .... Mr. Charles DARNELL
07 Asst VP Recruitment/Enrollment Svcs .... Mr. John MORTENSEN
20 Vice Provost .... Dr. Laurens H. SMITH
51 Vice Prov Regional Camp/Dist Educ .... Mr. Travis PETERSON
08 Interim Dean Libraries .... Mr. Brad COLE
26 Exec Dir Public Relations/Marketing .... Mr. Tim VITALE
09 Dir Analysis Assess/Accreditation .... Mr. Michael TORRENS
22 Director Affirmative Action/EEO .... Ms. Stacy STURGEON
41 Athletic Director .... Mr. John HARTWELL
25 Exec Director Sponsored Programs .... Mr. Kevin PETERSON
86 Director Government Relations .... Mr. Neil N. ABERCROMBIE
15 Interim Exec Dir of Human Resources .... Mr. Chris NELSON
19 Director University Police Dept .... Mr. Steven J. MECHAM
06 Registrar .... Mr. Roland SQUIRE
36 Exec Dir Career Services/Coop Educ .... Ms. Donna E. CROW
37 Director of Financial Aid .... Ms. Patti KOHLER
38 Director Counseling Center .... Dr. David BUSH
40 Director of Campus Store .... Mr. David HANSEN
92 Director of Honors .... Ms. Kristine MILLER
96 Director of Purchasing .... Mr. Jeff CROSBIE
47 Dean of Agriculture .... Dr. Kenneth L. WHITE
57 Dean of Arts .... Dr. Craig JESSOP
50 Dean of Business .... Mr. Douglas D. ANDERSON
53 Dean of Education .... Dr. Beth FOLEY
54 Dean of Engineering .... Dr. Christine HAILEY
79 Dean Humanities/Social Science .... Dr. John C. ALLEN
65 Dean of Natural Resources .... Dr. Chris LUECKE
81 Interim Dean of Science .... Ms. Lisa BERREAU

*Utah Valley University (C)

800 W University Parkway, Orem UT 84058-5999

County: Utah FICE Identification: 004027
Unit ID: 230737
Telephone: (801) 863-8000 Carnegie Class: Masters/S
FAX Number: (801) 226-5207 Calendar System: Semester
URL: www.uvu.edu
Established: 1941 Annual Undergrad Tuition & Fees (In-State): $5,386
Enrollment: 31,332 Coed
Affiliation or Control: State IRS Status: 501(c)3
Highest Offering: Master's
Accreditation: NW, ADNUR, BUS, CAEP, CEA, CS, DH, EMT, ENG, IFSAC, MUS, NUR, SW, TEAC

02 President .... Dr. Matthew S. HOLLAND
05 Senior Vice Pres Academic Affairs .... Dr. Jeffery E. OLSON
11 Vice Pres Finance & Administration .... Dr. Val L. PETERSON
32 Vice President Student Affairs .... Dr. Michelle O. TAYLOR
30 Vice Pres Development/Alumni .... Mr. Scott COOKSEY
26 Vice Pres University Relations .... Dr. Cameron K. MARTIN
45 VP Planning/Budgets & HR .... Ms. Linda MAKIN
10 Assoc Vice Pres Finance .... Vacant
20 Assoc Vice Pres Engaged Learning .... Dr. Frederick H. WHITE
18 Assoc Vice Pres Facilities Planning .... Mr. Frank YOUNG
20 Assoc VP Programs .... Dr. Maureen ANDRADE
27 Assoc VP College Mktg/Communication .... Mr. Chris TAYLOR
20 Assoc VP Academic Affairs/Admin .... Dr. Kathren BROWN
35 Assoc VP Student Success/Retention .... Ms. Michelle KEARNS
88 Sr Dir Community College Programs .... Dr. Darrel L. HAMMON
21 Asst VP/Controller Business Svcs .... Mr. Kedric BLACK
07 Sr Director Admissions/One Stop .... Vacant
72 Dean Computing/Technology .... Dr. Michael SAVOIE
57 Dean School of the Arts .... Dr. Newell DAYLEY
81 Dean Science & Health .... Dr. Daniel FAIRBANKS
50 Dean School of Business .... Dr. Norman WRIGHT
97 Dean University College .... Dr. Forrest G. WILLIAMS
75 Dean Aviation and Public Services .... Dr. David MCENTIRE
53 Dean School of Education .... Dr. Parker C. FAWSON
15 Assoc VP Human Res/Equity Officer .... Mr. Mark WIESENBERG
37 Director Financial Aid/Scholarship .... Ms. Trish HOWARD
19 Dir Public Safety/Chief of Police .... Mr. John BREWER
44 Director of Planned Giving .... Ms. Cristina PIANEZZOLA
09 Director Institutional Research .... Mr. Robert LOVERIDGE
41 Assoc VP Athletics .... Mr. Vince OTOUPAL
24 Director Studios & Engineering .... Mr. Will MCKINNON
40 Director Bookstore .... Ms. Louise BRIDGE
06 Registrar .... Ms. LuAnn SMITH
28 Dir Multicultural Student Services .... Mr. Barney NYE
29 Director Alumni Relations .... Ms. Jeri L. ALLPHIN
38 Dir Career & Academic Counseling .... Mr. Adam BLACK
96 Director of Purchasing .... Mr. Ryan LINDSTROM
04 Executive Asst to President .... Ms. Candice L. GARDNER
08 Director Library .... Ms. Lesli BAKER
100 Chief of Staff .... Vacant
102 Dir Foundation/Corporate Relations .... Vacant
103 Dir Workforce/Career Development .... Ms. Sherry HARWARD
104 Director Study Abroad .... Mr. Baldomero LAGO
105 Director Web Services .... Mr. Nathan GERBER
108 Institutional Review Board Chair .... Mr. Andrew CREER
13 Assoc Vice Pres CIO/IT .... Mr. Ray WALKER
90 Director Academic IT & Analytics .... Ms. Laura BUSBY

*Weber State University (D)

3850 Dixon Parkway, Ogden UT 84408

County: Weber FICE Identification: 003680
Unit ID: 230782
Telephone: (801) 626-6000 Carnegie Class: Masters/L
FAX Number: (801) 626-7922 Calendar System: Semester
URL: www.weber.edu
Established: 1889 Annual Undergrad Tuition & Fees (In-State): $5,321
Enrollment: 25,954 Coed
Affiliation or Control: State IRS Status: 501(c)3
Highest Offering: Master's
Accreditation: NW, ADNUR, ART, BUS, BUSA, CAATE, CAHIIM, CEA, CIDA, COARC, CONST, CS, DH, EMT, ENG, ENGT, HSA, MLTAD, MT, MUS, NUR, SW, TEAC

02 President .... Dr. Charles A. WIGHT
05 Provost .... Dr. Madonne MINER
10 Vice Pres Administrative Services .... Dr. Norm TARBOX
30 Vice Pres for Univ Advancement .... Dr. Brad MORTENSEN
32 Vice President Student Affairs .... Dr. Janet WINNIFORD
13 VP for Information Technology .... Dr. Bret R. ELLIS
88 Vice Provost Innovation & Econo Dev .... Mr. Alexander LAWRENCE
51 Vice Prov & Dean Continuing Educ .... Dr. Bruce DAVIS
35 Assoc VP for Student Affairs .... Dr. Brett PEROZZI
21 Asst VP for Financial Services .... Mr. Steven E. NABOR
15 Asst Vice Pres for Human Resources .... Ms. Cherrie NELSON
11 Asst VP for Administrative Services .... Mr. Jerry G. GRAYBEAL
18 Assoc VP for Facilities Management .... Mr. Kevin HANSEN
84 Asst Prov for Enrollment Services .... Dr. Bruce BOWEN
20 Asst Prov & Dean of Undergraduates .... Dr. Ryan THOMAS
76 Dean Health Professions .... Dr. Yasmen SIMONIAN
50 Dean Business/Economics .... Dr. Jeffrey STEAGALL
53 Dean of Education .... Dr. Jack L. RASMUSSEN
83 Dean Social Behavioral Science .... Dr. Frank HARROLD
79 Interim Dean of Arts & Humanities .... Dr. Catherine ZUBLIN
81 Dean of Science .... Dr. David MATTY
72 Dean of Applied Science & Tech .... Dr. David FERRO
35 Dean of Students .... Dr. Jeffrey J. HURST
06 Registrar .... Mr. Casey D. BULLOCK
19 Director Public Safety .... Vacant
29 Exec Director Alumni Association .... Ms. Nancy COLLINWOOD
38 Dir Counseling & Psycholog Services .... Dr. Dianna K. ABEL
36 Director of Career Services .... Dr. Winn STANGER
37 Director of Financial Aid .... Mr. Jed SPENCER
27 Director of Media Relations .... Mr. John L. KOWALEWSKI
07 Director of Admissions .... Mr. Scott TEICHERT
08 University Librarian .... Ms. Joan HUBBARD
22 Dir Equal Opportunity/Affirm Action .... Dr. Barry G. GOMBERG
41 Dir of Intercollegiate Athletics .... Mr. Jerry BOVEE
40 Bookstore Director .... Mr. Tim ECK
25 Director Sponsored Projects .... Mr. James TAYLOR
85 Director Services Intl Students .... Mr. Morteza EMAMI
23 Director Student Health Center .... Ms. Juliana P. LARSEN
26 Director Public Relations .... Ms. Allison B. HESS
91 Director Administrative Computing .... Vacant
43 University Counsel .... Dr. G. Richard HILL
39 Director Housing & Residence Life .... Mr. Daniel KILCREASE
96 Director of Purchasing .... Ms. Nancy E. EMENGER
28 Chief Diversity Officer .... Dr. Adrienne G. GILLESPIE
92 Director of Honors Program .... Dr. Judy ELSLEY
88 Director Budget & Investments .... Mr. Brian L. SHUPPY
94 Coordinator of Women's Studies .... Dr. Parrilla DE KOKAL

*Snow College (E)

150 College Avenue, Ephraim UT 84627-1299

County: Sanpete FICE Identification: 003679
Unit ID: 230597
Telephone: (435) 283-7000 Carnegie Class: Bac/Assoc-Assoc Dom
FAX Number: (435) 283-6879 Calendar System: Semester
URL: www.snow.edu
Established: 1888 Annual Undergrad Tuition & Fees (In-State): $3,484
Enrollment: 4,779 Coed
Affiliation or Control: State IRS Status: 501(c)3
Highest Offering: Baccalaureate
Accreditation: NW, ACBSP, ADNUR, MUS, PNUR, THEA

02 President .... Dr. Gary L. CARLSTON
05 Vice President for Academic Affairs .... Dr. Steven HOOD
10 VP Finance/Administrative Services .... Mr. Jacob DETTINGER
32 Vice President Student Success .... Mr. Craig MATHIE
35 Director of Student Life .... Ms. Michelle BROWN
75 Dean Business & Applied Tech .... Mr. Mike MEDLEY
36 Director of Student Success .... Vacant
08 Director Library/Information Svcs .... Mr. Jon OSTLER
09 Director Institutional Research .... Ms. Beckie HERMANSEN
15 Director Human Resource Development .... Mr. Wayne SQUIRE
18 Director Campus Services Ephraim .... Ms. Leslee COOK
24 Director TTC .... Mr. Chase MITCHELL
39 Director Student Housing .... Ms. Jessica SIEGFRIED
41 Athletic Director .... Mr. Robert NIELSON
06 Registrar .... Mr. Micah STRAIT
07 Director Admissions .... Mr. Jeffrey SAVAGE
21 Budget Director .... Ms. Sherri HANSEN
26 Director Public Relations .... Mr. John STEVENS
35 Director Student Affairs .... Mr. Mike ANDERSON
37 Director Student Financial Aid .... Mr. Jack DALENE
38 Director Student Counseling .... Mr. Allen RIGGS
96 Director of Purchasing .... Mr. Michael JORGENSEN
30 Chief Development Officer .... Ms. Rosie CONNOR

27 Director of Campus Relations .... Ms. Heidi STRINGHAM
04 Administrative Asst to President .... Ms. Marci LARSEN
13 Chief Info Technology Officer (CIO) .... Mr. Phil ALLRED

*Salt Lake Community College (A)

4600 S Redwood Road, Salt Lake City UT 84123-3197
County: Salt Lake FICE Identification: 005220
Unit ID: 230746
Telephone: (801) 957-4111 Carnegie Class: Assoc/HT-Mix Trad/Non
FAX Number: (801) 957-4444 Calendar System: Semester
URL: www.slcc.edu
Established: 1948 Annual Undergrad Tuition & Fees (In-State): $3,569
Enrollment: 30,248 Coed
Affiliation or Control: State IRS Status: 501(c)3
Highest Offering: Associate Degree
Accreditation: NW, ACBSP, ACFEI, ADNUR, DH, FUSER, MAC, OTA, PTAA, RAD, SURGT

02 President .... Dr. Deneece HUFTALIN
05 Provost .... Dr. Clifton SANDERS
10 Business Services Vice Pres .... Mr. Dennis KLAUS
32 Student Services Vice President .... Dr. Charles LEPPER
30 Vice Pres Institutional Advancement .... Ms. Alison MCFARLANE
86 Govt & Community Relations VP .... Mr. Tim SHEEHAN
108 Vice Pres Inst Effectiveness .... Ms. Barbara GROVER
28 Spec Asst to President .... Dr. Roderic LAND
103 Assoc Provost/Workforce & Econ Dev .... Mr. Rick BOUILLON
20 Assoc Provost Academic Support .... Dr. Nate SOUTHERLAND
88 Assoc VP Student Success/Completion .... Dr. Nancy SINGER
88 Int Asst Provost Lrng Advancement .... Dr. David HUBERT
21 Asst Vice Pres of Budget Services .... Mr. Darren MARSHALL
35 Dean of Students/Asst Vice Pres .... Dr. Marlin CLARK
15 Asst Vice Pres of Human Resources .... Mr. Craig GARDNER
18 Assistant VP of Facilities .... Mr. Robert ASKERLUND
45 Asst VP Student Plng/Support .... Dr. Nancy SINGER
84 Asst VP Student Enrollment Services .... Mr. Eric WEBER
26 Asst VP Inst Mktg/Communications .... Mr. Michael NAVARRE
09 Asst VP Strategy & Analysis .... Mr. Jeff AIRD
88 Dean Arts/Communication/Media .... Mr. Richard SCOTT
50 Dean School of Business .... Dr. Dennis BROMLEY
79 Dean Humanities & Social Sciences .... Dr. John MCCORMICK
76 Dean School of Health Sciences .... Dr. JoAnne WRIGHT
81 Dean Science/Math & Engineering .... Dr. Craig CALDWELL
75 Dean Technical Specialties .... Mr. Rick BOUILLON
41 Athletic Director .... Mr. Kevin M. DUSTIN
88 Dean SAT/Prof Development .... Mr. Kevin BROCKBANK
109 Sr Dir Student Ctr/Auxiliary Svc .... Mr. Jason BEAL
88 Director Technical Productions .... Mr. Seth MILLER
38 Director Academic Advising .... Ms. Sonia PARKER
36 Director Career/Student Employment .... Mr. Jack HESLEPH
88 Director Testing & Placement .... Ms. Diana HARVEY
06 Registrar .... Ms. MaryEtta CHASE
37 Director Financial Aid .... Ms. Cristi MILLARD
19 Director Public Safety .... Mr. Shane CRABTREE
13 Chief Information/Security Officer .... Mr. Bill ZOUMADAKIS
21 Controller/Business Manager .... Mr. Douglas HANSEN
22 EEO Director .... Ms. Mozelle ORTON
96 Director of Purchasing .... Ms. Lois WIESEMANN
25 Director Sponsored Projects .... Ms. Nicole OMER
70 Exec Director of Development .... Ms. Nancy MICHALKO
88 Risk Manager .... Ms. Mikel BIRCH
29 Alumni Coordinator .... Vacant
04 Admin Asst to President & Board Sec .... Ms. Janice SCHMIDT

*Utah State University Eastern (B)

451 E 400 N, Price UT 84501-2699
Telephone: (435) 613-5000 FICE Identification: 003676
Accreditation: &NW, ADNUR, PNUR

† Regional accreditation is carried under the parent institution in Logan, UT.

Western Governors University (C)

4001 S 700 E, Suite 700, Salt Lake City UT 84107-2533
County: Salt Lake FICE Identification: 033394
Unit ID: 433387
Telephone: (801) 274-3280 Carnegie Class: Masters/L
FAX Number: (801) 274-3305 Calendar System: Other
URL: www.wgu.edu
Established: 1996 Annual Undergrad Tuition & Fees: $6,070
Enrollment: 57,821 Coed
Affiliation or Control: Independent Non-Profit IRS Status: 501(c)3
Highest Offering: Master's
Accreditation: NW, CAHIIM, NURSE, TED

01 President .... Dr. Scott D. PULSIPHER
05 Provost/Chief Academic Officer .... David LEASURE
10 Vice Pres Finance/Administration .... David GROW
09 Vice Pres Quality/Inst Research .... Jason LEVIN
88 Vice Pres of Strategic Relations .... Vacant
26 Vice President of Marketing .... Carey HILDERBRAND
15 Vice President of Human Resources .... Bonnie PATTEE
37 Vice Pres of Financial Aid .... Bob COLLINS
27 Vice President of Public Relations .... Joan MITCHELL
20 Associate Provost Student Mentoring .... Mitsu PHILLIPS
20 Associate Provost Academic Services .... Dr. Stacey LUDWIG-JOHNSON
76 Dean College of Health Professions .... Jan JONES-SCHENK
88 Chief Marketing Officer .... Patrick PARTRIDGE
86 Director Government Relations .... Chris BONNELL

Westminster College (D)

1840 S 1300 E, Salt Lake City UT 84105-3697
County: Salt Lake FICE Identification: 003681
Unit ID: 230807
Telephone: (801) 484-7651 Carnegie Class: Masters/L
FAX Number: (801) 466-6916 Calendar System: Semester
URL: www.westminstercollege.edu
Established: 1875 Annual Undergrad Tuition & Fees: $31,528
Enrollment: 2,991 Coed
Affiliation or Control: Independent Non-Profit IRS Status: 501(c)3
Highest Offering: Master's
Accreditation: NW, AAB, ACBSP, ANEST, MACTE, NURSE, PH, TEAC

01 President .... Mr. Stephen F. MORGAN
05 Provost .... Dr. Lisa GENTILE
30 Vice Pres Institutional Advancement .... Mrs. Staci CARSON
10 Vice Pres Finance & Administration .... Mr. Curtis W. RYAN
84 Vice President Enrollment Mgmt .... Vacant
26 Exec Dir Intgrated Marketing Comm .... Ms. Sheila YORKIN
49 Dean School of Arts & Sciences .... Dr. Lance NEWMAN
66 Dean School of Nursing/Hlth Science .... Dr. Sheryl STEADMAN
50 Dean School of Business .... Mrs. Melissa KOERNER
53 Dean School of Education .... Dr. Melanie AGNEW
32 Dean of Students .... Mr. Mark FERNE
29 Director Alumni Relations .... Ms. Michelle BARBER-LYHNAKIS
09 Director of Inst Research/Assess .... Ms. Nichole GREENWOOD
88 Assoc VP of College Relations .... Ms. Annalisa HOLCOMBE
13 Chief Information Officer .... Mr. Robert ALLRED
43 General Counsel/Risk Management .... Ms. Kathryn HOLMES
21 Director of Accounting Services .... Ms. Jennifer MEDRANO
15 Director of Human Resources .... Ms. Julie FREESTONE
06 Registrar .... Ms. Mindy WENNERGREN
37 Director of Financial Aid .... Ms. Jenny RYAN
07 Director of Admissions .... Ms. Darlene DILLEY
18 Director Plant/Facilities .... Mr. Richard A. BROCKMYER
36 Director of Career Resource Center .... Vacant
08 Director Giovale Library .... Mr. Robert ALLRED
35 Assistant Dean of Students .... Mr. Karnell BLACK
39 Director of Student Involvement .... Mr. Ryan COOK
88 Director Start Center .... Ms. Deborah VICKERY
88 Director of Conferences .... Mr. Jeff BROWN
19 Director of Campus Safety .... Mr. Saeed REZAI
41 Director of Athletics .... Mr. Shay WYATT
42 Director of Spiritual Life .... Ms. Jan SAAED
38 Director of Campus Counseling .... Ms. Lisa JONES
92 Director of Honors Program .... Dr. Richard BADENHAUSEN
91 Database Administrator .... Mr. Kyle RIMA
04 Administrative Asst to President .... Ms. Emmalee SZWEDKO
22 Title IX Coordinator/EEO Complaince .... Mr. Jason SCHWARTZ
101 Secretary of the Institution/Board .... Ms. Annalisa HOLCOMBE

VERMONT

Bennington College (E)

One College Drive, Bennington VT 05201-6003
County: Bennington FICE Identification: 003682
Unit ID: 230816
Telephone: (802) 442-5401 Carnegie Class: Bac-A&S
FAX Number: (802) 447-4269 Calendar System: Semester
URL: www.bennington.edu
Established: 1932 Annual Undergrad Tuition & Fees: $48,220
Enrollment: 755 Coed
Affiliation or Control: Independent Non-Profit IRS Status: 501(c)3
Highest Offering: Master's
Accreditation: EH

01 President .... Dr. Mariko SILVER
05 Provost/Dean of the College .... Ms. Isabel ROCHE
10 VP for Finance & Administration .... Mr. Brian MURPHY
45 Sr VP for Institutional Initiatives .... Mr. David G. REES
88 Sr VP for Strategic Partnerships .... Ms. Paige BARTELS
30 VP for Institutional Advancement .... Mr. Matt RIZZO
26 VP for Communications .... Ms. Janet L. MARSDEN
07 VP/Dean of Admissions & Fin Aid .... Mr. Hung BUI
18 AVP for Facilities Mgmt & Planning .... Mr. Andy SCHLATTER
20 Assoc Provost/Dean of Studies .... Mr. Duncan DOBBELMANN
32 Dean of Students .... Ms. Xenia MARKOWITT
09 Dean of Research/Plng/Assessment .... Mr. Zeke BERNSTEIN
15 Director of Human Resources .... Ms. Heather FALEY
29 Director of Alumni Relations .... Ms. Marie LEAHY
37 Director of Financial Aid .... Ms. Heather CLIFFORD

Champlain College (F)

163 S Willard Street, Burlington VT 05402-0670
County: Chittenden FICE Identification: 003684
Unit ID: 230852
Telephone: (802) 860-2700 Carnegie Class: Masters/M
FAX Number: (802) 860-2750 Calendar System: Semester
URL: www.champlain.edu
Established: 1956 Annual Undergrad Tuition & Fees: $37,536
Enrollment: 3,585 Coed
Affiliation or Control: Independent Non-Profit IRS Status: 501(c)3
Highest Offering: Master's
Accreditation: EH, ART, RAD, SW

01 President .... Mr. Donald J. LAACKMAN
05 Provost .... Dr. Laurie QUINN
10 Vice President Finances .... David J. PROVOST
84 Vice President Enrollment .... Lisa BLUNDERS
30 Vice President Advancement .... David J. PROVOST
32 Vice President Student Life .... Dr. Leslie AVERILL
15 Vice President People & Technology .... Mary Margaret LEE
101 VP Strategic Communications & Exten .... Katie HAWLEY
21 Vice President Finance .... Shelley NAVARI
13 Asst Vice Pres Information Systems .... Theodore LASKARIS
36 Director Career Collaborative .... Dr. Tanja Hinterstoisser BOERA
20 Senior Associate Provost .... Dr. Michelle MILLER
104 Associate Provost-Education Abroad .... Dr. James CROSS
53 Dean Education/Human Stds Div .... Dr. Laurel BONGIORNO
88 Dean Comm/Creative Media Div .... Dr. Paula WILLOQUET-MARICONDI
50 Dean Business Division .... Dr. Wes BALDA
77 Int Dean Information Tech/Science .... Dr. Scott STEVENS
51 Dean Continuing Professional Stds .... Dr. Mika NASH
07 Director of Undergrad Admissions .... Chris PERLONGO
06 Registrar .... Rebecca PETERSON
37 Director of Financial Aid .... Kristi JOVELL
38 Dir of Counseling & Accomodations .... Skip HARRIS
18 Director of Physical Plant .... Thomas BONNETTE
19 Director of Security & Safety .... Vacant
23 Director Health Services .... Skip HARRIS
22 Director of Affirmative Action .... Dana HUTCHINSON
39 Director of Residential Life .... Danelle BERUBE
85 Foreign Students Advisor .... Kathy LYNN
26 Public Information & News Director .... Stephen MEASE
29 Director of Alumni Relations .... Hannah CAMPBELL
08 Director Library .... Janet COTTRELL
28 Dir Student Diversity/Inclusion .... Ame LAMBERT
103 Director Workforce Development .... Melissa HERSH
88 Director Philanthropy .... Sarah ANDRIANO
04 Executive Assistant .... Linda MURPHY
40 Bookstore Manager .... Kevin MCCANN
106 Director E-learning .... Ursula JONES
108 Director Learning Assessment .... Ellen ZEMAN
105 Director Web Services .... Brian ANDREWS
25 Chief Contracts/Grants Admin .... Ted WINOKUR

College of St. Joseph (G)

71 Clement Road, Rutland VT 05701-3899
County: Rutland FICE Identification: 003685
Unit ID: 231077
Telephone: (802) 773-5900 Carnegie Class: Bac-Diverse
FAX Number: (802) 776-5258 Calendar System: Semester
URL: www.csj.edu
Established: 1956 Annual Undergrad Tuition & Fees: $21,900
Enrollment: 332 Coed
Affiliation or Control: Roman Catholic IRS Status: 501(c)3
Highest Offering: Master's
Accreditation: EH

01 Interim President .... Mr. Larry JENSEN
05 Int VP Academic Affs/Dean of Fac .... Dr. Jonas PRIDA
10 Vice President Business Affairs .... Mrs. Kristie JOHNSON
32 VP Student Affs/Dean of Students .... Ms. Melissa PARADEE
15 Vice Pres Human Resources .... Ms. Judy FRAZIER
11 Associate VP of Administration .... Ms. Judy MORGAN
37 Director of Financial Aid .... Mrs. Julie ROSMUS
07 Director of Admissions .... Mr. Ken LABATE
30 Dir Development/Alumni Relations .... Mr. Bates CHILDRESS
41 Athletics Director .... Mr. Jeffrey BROWN
06 Registrar .... Mr. Greg CHAMBERLAND
13 CIS Administrator .... Mr. Raymond GIBBS
35 Director of Learning Center .... Ms. Susan BOYCE
26 Assoc VP Marketing/External Affairs .... Mr. James LAMBERT
21 Controller .... Mrs. Karen REYNOLDS
18 Director of Maintenance .... Mr. Thomas BELAND
08 Librarian .... Ms. Doreen MCCULLOUGH
49 Chair Arts & Sciences Division .... Dr. David BALFOUR
50 Chair Business Division .... Dr. Robert GODDARD
53 Chair Education Division .... Dr. David ST. GERMAIN
83 Chair Psychology/Human Services Div .... Dr. Michael W. KESLER

Goddard College (H)

123 Pitkin Road, Plainfield VT 05667-9432
County: Washington FICE Identification: 003686
Unit ID: 230889
Telephone: (800) 468-4888 Carnegie Class: Masters/M
FAX Number: (802) 454-1029 Calendar System: Semester
URL: www.goddard.edu
Established: 1863 Annual Undergrad Tuition & Fees: $15,476
Enrollment: 538 Coed
Affiliation or Control: Independent Non-Profit IRS Status: 501(c)3
Highest Offering: Master's
Accreditation: EH

01 Interim President .... Mr. Robert KENNY
05 Academic Dean .... Dr. Lewis JONES
10 Chief Financial Officer .... Vacant
100 Spec Asst to Pres/Chief of Staff .... Vacant
30 Chief Advancement Officer .... Vacant
32 Associate Dean of Community Life .... Ms. Susan A. WILSON
06 Registrar .... Mr. Josh CASTLE
15 Director of Human Resources .... Ms. Gloria ABBIATI
37 Director of Financial Aid .... Ms. Beverly JENE
88 Director of Campus Services .... Mr. Paul SHPER
08 Director of Information Access .... Ms. Clara BRUNS
18 Director of Facilities Operations .... Mr. Scott BLANCHARD
21 Director of Business Office .... Ms. Sherri MOLLEUR
07 Director of Admissions .... Mr. Gariot LOUIMA
88 Manager of WGDR/WGDH Radio .... Mr. Kris GRUEN

Green Mountain College (A)

1 Brennan Circle, Poultney VT 05764-1199
County: Rutland FICE Identification: 003687
Unit ID: 230898
Telephone: (802) 287-8000 Carnegie Class: Masters/S
FAX Number: (802) 287-8099 Calendar System: Semester
URL: www.greenmtn.edu
Established: 1834 Annual Undergrad Tuition & Fees: $35,340
Enrollment: 833 Coed
Affiliation or Control: Independent Non-Profit IRS Status: 501(c)3
Highest Offering: Master's
Accreditation: EH

01 President .... Mr. Robert W. ALLEN
03 Executive Vice President .... Mr. Chris HALNON
05 Vice President Academic Affairs .... Dr. Thomas MAUHS-PUGH
32 Vice President Student Affairs .... Dr. Joseph E. PETRICK
84 Dean of Enrollment Mgmt/Marketing .... Mr. Jeffrey MON
04 Executive Assistant to President .... Ms. Jeanne V. ROOT
20 Dean of Faculty .... Dr. James HARDING
07 Director of Admissions .... Mr. Ryan LONGE
30 Director of Development .... Ms. Mary Lou WILLITS
06 Registrar .... Ms. Sharon L. HOFFMAN
18 Director of Facilities .... Mr. William BALLARD
19 Director of Public Safety .... Mr. Steven BROWN
26 Director of Public Relations .... Mr. Kevin COBURN
41 Athletic Director .... Mr. Kip SHIPLEY
08 Director Library & Information Svcs .... Mr. Paul MILLETTE
85 Director of International Pgms .... Vacant
13 Director Computing & Info Mgmt .... Mr. Jeffrey WRIGHT
42 Chaplain .... Ms. Shirley OSKAMP
29 Dir Alumni Relations/Annual Giving .... Ms. Michele ALMEIDA
36 Director of Career Counseling .... Ms. Serena GUILES
92 Director of College Honors Program .... Dr. Jennifer SELLERS
37 Director Student Financial Aid .... Ms. Wendy ELLIS
15 Director Human Resources .... Ms. Janie EVANS
38 Director Student Counseling .... Vacant
09 Director of Institutional Research .... Ms. Sharon L. HOFFMAN

Landmark College (B)

19 River Road South, Putney VT 05346
County: Windham FICE Identification: 025326
Unit ID: 247649
Telephone: (802) 387-4767 Carnegie Class: Bac/Assoc-Assoc Dom
FAX Number: (802) 387-6868 Calendar System: Semester
URL: www.landmark.edu
Established: 1985 Annual Undergrad Tuition & Fees: $51,330
Enrollment: 518 Coed
Affiliation or Control: Independent Non-Profit IRS Status: 501(c)3
Highest Offering: Baccalaureate
Accreditation: EH

01 President .... Dr. Peter A. EDEN
05 VP Academic Affairs .... Dr. Gail GIBSON SHEFFIELD
30 VP Institutional Advancement .... Ms. Ellen SMITH
10 VP Administration/Finance .... Mr. Jon A. MACCLAREN
32 VP Student Affairs .... Mr. Michael LUCIANI
84 VP Enrollment Management .... Mr. James VANDER HOOVEN
88 VP Educational Research/Innovation .... Ms. Manju BANERJEE
04 Assistant to the President .... Ms. Tiffany KERYLOW
20 Academic Dean .... Dr. Adrienne MAJOR
88 Dir Transfer/Career/Internship Svc .... Ms. Jan COPLAN
26 Director Marketing & Communications .... Mr. Mark DIPIETRO
18 Dir Facilities/Planning/Operations .. Mr. Corrado PARAMITHIOTTI
08 Head Librarian .... Ms. Jennifer LANN
13 Chief Technology Officer .... Ms. Corinne BELL
06 Registrar .... Ms. Karen DAMIAN
41 Director Athletics .... Mr. Steve STANLEY
37 Director Student Financial Aid .... Mr. Michael MERTES
38 Director of Counseling/Wellness .... Ms. Jacala MILLS
23 Director of Health Services .... Mr. Michael DALEY
40 Bookstore Manager .... Ms. Kimberly JUDD
15 Dir of Human Resources .... Ms. Carolyn LEBAIL
21 Controller .... Mr. Mark HIGGINS
35 Dean of Students .... Mr. Patrick CONNELLY
07 Senior Director Enrollment Services .... Ms. Carroll PARE
19 Director Campus Safety .... Mr. Stephen MURRELL
29 Associate Director Alumni Affairs .... Ms. Tricia STANLEY

Marlboro College (C)

PO Box A, Marlboro VT 05344-9999
County: Windham FICE Identification: 003690
Unit ID: 230940
Telephone: (802) 257-4333 Carnegie Class: Bac-A&S
FAX Number: (802) 257-4154 Calendar System: Semester
URL: www.marlboro.edu
Established: 1946 Annual Undergrad Tuition & Fees: $39,250
Enrollment: 230 Coed
Affiliation or Control: Independent Non-Profit IRS Status: 501(c)3
Highest Offering: Master's
Accreditation: EH

01 President .... Mr. Kevin F. QUIGLEY
10 Chief Financial Officer .... Ms. Anne PRATT
05 Dean of Faculty/Chief Academic Ofcr .... Mr. Richard GLEJZER
07 Dean of Admissions .... Ms. Brigid LAWLER
32 Dean of Students .... Mr. Luis ROSA
58 Assoc Dean Graduate/Professional St .... Ms. Kate JELLEMA
08 Library Director .... Ms. Beth RUANE
06 Asst Registrar .... Ms. Diane HEILEMAN
102 Dir Corp & Foundation Relations .... Ms. Hillary TWINING
26 Dir of Marketing/Communications .... Mr. Matthew BARONE
44 Annual Giving Director .... Mr. Pete SMITH
18 Director of Plant Operations .... Mr. Dan J. COTTER
82 World Studies Director .... Mr. Seth HARTER
40 Bookstore Manager .... Ms. Rebecca BARTLETT
04 Asst to President .... Ms. Vanessa REDFIELD
29 Director Alumni Relations .... Ms. Kathy WATERS

Marlboro College Graduate School (D)

28 Vernon Street, Brattleboro VT 05301
Telephone: (802) 258-9200 Identification: 770120
Accreditation: &EH

† Regional accreditation is carried under the parent institution in Marlboro, VT

Middlebury Bread Loaf School of English (E)

75 Franklin Street, Middlebury VT 05753
Telephone: (802) 443-5418 Identification: 770119
Accreditation: &EH

† Bread Loaf School of English is a summer graduate program and the enrollment figure is for the summer term.

Middlebury College (F)

Old Chapel, Middlebury VT 05753-6200
County: Addison FICE Identification: 003691
Unit ID: 230959
Telephone: (802) 443-5000 Carnegie Class: Bac-A&S
FAX Number: (802) 443-2071 Calendar System: 4/1/4
URL: www.middlebury.edu
Established: 1800 Annual Undergrad Tuition & Fees: $47,828
Enrollment: 2,533 Coed
Affiliation or Control: Independent Non-Profit IRS Status: 501(c)3
Highest Offering: Doctorate
Accreditation: EH

01 President .... Dr. Laurie L. PATTON
05 Provost .... Dr. Susan BALDRIDGE
88 VP for Academic Development .... Dr. Tim SPEARS
10 VP for Finance/Treasurer .... Mr. Patrick J. NORTON
03 Sr Vice Pres/Philanthropic Advisor .... Mr. Michael SCHOENFELD
88 VP Lang Sch/Sch Abroad/Risk Officer .... Dr. Michael GEISLER
30 VP for Advancement .... Mr. James R. KEYES
88 VP Academic Affairs/Dean of Faculty .... Dr. Andrea LLOYD
26 VP for Communications & Marketing .... Mr. Bill BURGER
32 VP Student Affairs/Dean of College .... Dr. Katy SMITH ABBOTT
58 VP Acad Affs/Dean of the Institute .... Dr. Jeffrey DAYTON-JOHNSON
07 Dean of Admissions .... Mr. Gregory B. BUCKLES
104 Dean of International Programs .... Dr. Jeffrey CASON
101 Special Asst to Pres/Sec of Corp .... Mr. David A. DONAHUE
45 Assoc Provost for Planning .... Mr. LeRoy GRAHAM
08 Dean of the Library .... Mr. Michael D. ROY
37 Assoc VP Student Financial Services ... Ms. Kim DOWNS-BURNS
79 Dean of the Language Schools .... Dr. Stephen SNYDER
20 Dean of Curriculum .... Dr. Suzanne GURLAND
09 Dean for Faculty Dev & Research .... Dr. James RALPH
21 Asst Treasurer/Dir of Business Svcs .... Mr. Thomas CORBIN
29 Assoc VP Alumni Rels/Annual Giving .... Ms. Margaret STOREY GROVES
38 Exec Dir Health & Counseling Svcs .... Dr. Augustus JORDAN
42 Chaplain .... Ms. Laurie JORDAN
41 Director of Athletics .... Mr. Erin QUINN
35 Assoc Dn of the Col/Dir Pub Safety .Ms. Elizabeth B. BURCHARD
06 Registrar .... Ms. Jennifer THOMPSON
15 Acting Assoc VP for Human Resources .... Ms. Cheryl MULLINS
40 Bookstore Manager .... Ms. Erin JONES-POPPE

† Tuition figure is a comprehensive fees figure.

New England Culinary Institute (G)

7 School Street, Montpelier VT 05602-9720
County: Washington FICE Identification: 022540
Unit ID: 230977
Telephone: (802) 223-6324 Carnegie Class: Spec-4-yr-Other
FAX Number: (802) 225-3280 Calendar System: Quarter
URL: www.neci.edu
Established: 1980 Annual Undergrad Tuition & Fees: N/A
Enrollment: 422 Coed
Affiliation or Control: Proprietary IRS Status: Proprietary
Highest Offering: Baccalaureate
Accreditation: ACCSC

01 CEO/President .... Mr. Francis VOIGT
10 Chief Financial Officer .... Mr. Phillip HARKER
05 Dean of Education/Dept Chr Cul Arts .... Mr. Lyndon VIRKLER
88 Exec Chef & VP Culinary Operations .... Chef Jean-Louis GERIN
88 Chair Baking & Pastry Programs .... Chef Kathleen KESSLER
88 Chair Food/Beverage Business Mgmt .... Ms. Michelle FORD
20 Director of Compliance/Academics .... Ms. Laureen GAUTHIER
106 Chair Online Programs .... Chef Peg CHECCI
06 Registrar .... Ms. Gail MACDONALD
07 Director of Admissions .... Mr. Dwight CROSS
08 Head Librarian .... Ms. Rachel BORNSTEIN
15 Director Human Resources .... Ms. Jennifer ZETARSKI
18 Director of Facilities .... Mr. William COLGAN
36 Career Services Manager .... Ms. Eunice JORDAN
20 Sr Dir Operations & Education .... Chef David MILES
37 Director Financial Aid .... Ms. Jessica CHAPPEL

Norwich University (H)

158 Harmon Drive, Northfield VT 05663-1000
County: Washington FICE Identification: 003692
Unit ID: 230995
Telephone: (802) 485-2000 Carnegie Class: Masters/L
FAX Number: (802) 485-2032 Calendar System: Semester
URL: www.norwich.edu
Established: 1819 Annual Undergrad Tuition & Fees: $36,092
Enrollment: 3,672 Coed
Affiliation or Control: Independent Non-Profit IRS Status: 501(c)3
Highest Offering: Master's
Accreditation: EH, ACBSP, #CAATE, ENG, NURSE

01 President .... Dr. Richard W. SCHNEIDER
05 Senior VPAA & Dean of Faculty .... Dr. Guiyou HUANG
107 VP & Dean CGCS .... Dr. William CLEMENTS
84 VP Technology and Student Affairs .... Dr. Frank VANECEK
30 VP Alumni & Development Relations .... Mr. David J. WHALEY
13 VP Strategic Partnership .... Mr. Phillip SUSMANN
84 VP of Enrollment Management .... Mr. Greg MATTHEWS
107 Dean Col of Professional Schools .... Mr. Aron TEMKIN
83 Dean College of Liberal Arts .... Dr. Andrea TALENTINO
81 Dean College of Science/Mathematics .... Dr. Michael MCGINNIS
88 Dean School of National Services .... Col. Robert KUCKUK
29 Assoc VP Alumni Relations .... Ms. Diane SCOLARO
20 Associate VP Academic Affairs .... Dr. Joseph BYRNE
04 Exec Assistant to President .... Ms. Laura AMELL
10 Chief Financial Officer .... Ms. Lauren WOBBY
11 Chief Administrative Officer .... Mr. David MAGIDA
88 Director Center for Student Success .... Ms. Shelby GILE
32 Dean of Students .... Ms. Martha MATHIS
08 Interim Head Librarian .... Mr. Greg SAUER
41 Athletic Director .... Mr. Anthony A. MARIANO
18 Director Facilities/Operations .... Mr. Bizhan YAHYAZADEH
37 Director Student Financial Aid .... Mr. Martin DANIELS
38 Director Student Counseling .... Dr. Melvin MILLER
07 Director of Admissions .... Mr. Tim REARDON
06 Registrar & Inst Research Dir .... Dr. Diane DOUGLAS
88 Asst VP Office of Communications .... Ms. Kathy MURPHY-MORIARITY
102 Dir Foundation/Corporate Relations .... Vacant
103 Dir Career Development .... Ms. Kathryn PROVOST
19 Director Security/Safety .... Vacant
15 Director of Human Resources .... Ms. Lisa YAEGER

Saint Michael's College (I)

One Winooski Park, Colchester VT 05439-0001
County: Chittenden FICE Identification: 003694
Unit ID: 231059
Telephone: (802) 654-2000 Carnegie Class: Bac-A&S
FAX Number: (802) 654-2297 Calendar System: Semester
URL: www.smcvt.edu
Established: 1904 Annual Undergrad Tuition & Fees: $40,750
Enrollment: 2,618 Coed
Affiliation or Control: Roman Catholic IRS Status: 501(c)3
Highest Offering: Master's
Accreditation: EH, CEA

01 President .... Dr. John J. NEUHAUSER
04 Assistant to the President .... Ms. Tara L. ARCURY
05 Vice Pres Academic Affairs .... Dr. Karen A. TALENTINO
10 Vice President for Finance .... Mr. Neal ROBINSON
32 Vice President for Student Affairs .... Dr. Dawn M. ELLINWOOD
84 Vice Pres Enrollment/Marketing .... Dr. Sarah M. KELLY
15 Vice President for HR & Admin Svcs .... Mr. Michael J. NEW
30 VP for Institutional Advancement .... Mr. Patrick J. GALLIVAN
20 Dean of the College .... Dr. Jeffrey M. AYRES
42 Director Edmundite Campus Ministry .... Rev. Brian J. CUMMINGS, SSE
07 Director of Admission .... Mr. Michael STEFANOWICZ
37 Director Student Financial Services .... Mr. Daniel R. COUTURE
06 Registrar .... Mr. John D. SHEEHEY
29 Director of Alumni/Parent Relations .... Ms. Angela ARMOUR
35 Director Student Activities .... Ms. Grace A. KELLY
93 Dir Multicultural Student Affairs .... Mr. Moise ST. LOUIS
39 Director of Residence Life .... Mr. Louis DIMASI
88 Associate Dean of the College .... Dr. Jonathan L. D'AMORE
104 Director of Study Abroad .... Ms. Peggy H. IMAI
92 Honors Program Faculty Coordinator .... Dr. Jim BYRNE
94 Coord of Gender/Women's Studies .... Dr. Patricia DELANEY
08 Dir Library & Information Services .... Mr. John K. PAYNE
13 Chief Information Officer .... Mr. William O. ANDERSON
19 Director of Public Safety .... Mr. Peter D. SOONS
18 Dir of Facilities/College Architect .... Mr. James P. FARRINGTON
38 Director of Personal Counseling .... Ms. Linda HOLLINGDALE
36 Director of Career Development .... Ms. Christine CLARY
23 Director of Health Services .... Ms. Mary MASSON
41 Director of Athletics .... Dr. Christopher KENNEY
44 Director of Advancement Services .... Ms. Linda V. DONAHUE
102 Director of Foundation Relations .... Ms. Angela IRVINE
96 Director of Business Services .... Mr. Robert ROBINSON
105 Dir of Web Site Development .... Mr. Brian MACDONALD
44 Director of Individual Giving .... Ms. Terri P. SELBY
88 Financial Accounting Manager .... Ms. Shirley J. GOODELL-LACKEY
40 Bookstore Manager .... Mr. Stephen MCMAHON
26 Marketing/Communications Manager .... Ms. Lindsay DAMICI

School for International Training (SIT) (A)

1 Kipling Road, Brattleboro VT 05302-0676
County: Windham FICE Identification: 008860
Unit ID: 231068
Telephone: (802) 257-7751 Carnegie Class: Spec-4-yr-Other
FAX Number: (802) 258-3248 Calendar System: Other
URL: www.sit.edu
Established: 1964 Annual Undergrad Tuition & Fees: N/A
Enrollment: 414 Coed
Affiliation or Control: Independent Non-Profit IRS Status: 501(c)3
Highest Offering: Master's
Accreditation: EH

01 President ... Mr. Don STEINBERG
10 CFO ... Mr. Kote LOMIDZE
100 Chief Of Staff ... Ms. Bethaney LACLAIR
11 Vice President Operations ... Ms. Rachel HENRY
43 General Counsel ... Ms. Lisa RAE
58 Interim Dean SIT Graduate Institute ... Mr. Kenneth WILLIAMS
84 Dean External Rels/Strtgc Enrol Mgt ... Ms. Laurie BLACK
30 Vice President Philanthropy ... Mr. Tom NAVIN
88 Program Coord Language & Culture ... Ms. Sharon BROOKS
15 Executive Director Human Resources ... Ms. Anne BRNGER
07 Interim Director of Admissions ... Ms. Joan PERREAULT
06 Registrar ... Ms. Ginny NELLIS
37 Director Financial Aid ... Ms. Cathy MULLINS
32 Director of Campus Life ... Mr. Stephen SWEET
26 Director of Marketing ... Ms. Mary Kate O'BRIEN
04 Executive Asst to CEO & President ... Ms. Adelee AUSTIN
104 Vice Provost for Study Abroad ... Ms. Priscilla STONE
108 Dean Institutional Assessment ... Ms. Ellen HOLMES
13 Exec Director of IT ... Mr. Tom TOLBERT
28 Director of Diversity ... Vacant
29 Director of Alumni Engagement ... Ms. Carla LINEBACK
38 Director Student Counseling ... Ms. Jane BUCKINGHAM
39 Director Student Housing ... Mr. David FINCK
36 Director Career & Practicum Service ... Ms. Squeak STONE

Southern Vermont College (B)

982 Mansion Drive, Bennington VT 05201-6002
County: Bennington FICE Identification: 003693
Unit ID: 231086
Telephone: (802) 442-5427 Carnegie Class: Bac-Diverse
FAX Number: (802) 447-4695 Calendar System: Semester
URL: www.svc.edu
Established: 1926 Annual Undergrad Tuition & Fees: $23,260
Enrollment: 457 Coed
Affiliation or Control: Independent Non-Profit IRS Status: 501(c)3
Highest Offering: Baccalaureate
Accreditation: EH, NURSE, RAD

01 President ... Dr. David R. EVANS
10 VP Admin and Finance ... Ms. Jennifer MACKSEY
05 Provost and Dean of College ... Dr. James C. WHITE
04 Executive Assistant ... Vacant
20 Asst Provost Faculty Affairs ... Dr. Stacey HILLS
66 Chair Nursing ... Dr. Mary BOTTER
79 Chair of Humanities ... Dr. Jennifer BURG
81 Chair of Science and Technology ... Dr. Jennifer NELSON
83 Chair of Social Sciences ... Mr. Scott STEIN
32 Assoc Prov Stdnt Aff/Dn of Students ... Ms. Heather QUIRE
07 VP of Admissions ... Mr. Daniel SUMMERS, II
08 Director Library ... Ms. Sarah SANFILIPPO
06 Registrar/Dir Inst Research ... Mr. Jason SAMPLER
36 Coord Career Dev/Internships ... Ms. Elizabeth DUNHAM
18 Director of Facilities ... Mr. Mark J. KLAUDER
41 Director of Athletics ... Mr. Michael MCDONOUGH
38 Director of Counseling ... Ms. Louise BINETTE
39 Director of Residence Life ... Vacant
19 Director of Campus Safety ... Mr. James G. WALDON
37 Director of Student Fin Svcs ... Ms. Susan ROCHETTE
15 Director of Human Resources ... Ms. Carole SHERINGHAM
88 Coord Learning Disabilities ... Mr. David A. LINDENBERG
13 Director Information Technology ... Mr. Michael KEEN
26 Sr Adv Public Relations/Marketing ... Ms. Susan BIGGS
27 Asst Director of Communication ... Ms. Marion WHITEFORD
28 Director of Diversity Initiatives ... Dr. Ivan FIGUEROA
30 VP Advancement ... Ms. Nina MOSER

Sterling College (C)

PO Box 72, Craftsbury Common VT 05827-0072
County: Orleans FICE Identification: 021435
Unit ID: 231095
Telephone: (802) 586-7711 Carnegie Class: Bac-A&S
FAX Number: (802) 586-2596 Calendar System: Semester
URL: www.sterlingcollege.edu
Established: 1958 Annual Undergrad Tuition & Fees: $34,890
Enrollment: 116 Coed
Affiliation or Control: Independent Non-Profit IRS Status: 501(c)3
Highest Offering: Baccalaureate
Accreditation: EH

01 President ... Mr. Matthew DERR
05 Dean of Academics ... Dr. Carol DICKSON
07 Director of Admission ... Mr. Tim PATTERSON
30 Director of Advancement Services ... Mr. Topher BORDEAU
10 Director of Finance/Operations ... Ms. Deborah CLARK
08 Librarian ... Ms. Petra VOGEL
18 Director of Facilities ... Mr. Kelly JONES
32 Dean of Community ... Ms. Favor ELLIS
06 Registrar ... Ms. Laura Lea BERRY
26 Director of Communications ... Ms. Christian FEUERSTEIN
29 Director of Alumni Relations ... Mr. Topher BORDEAU
37 Director of Financial Aid ... Ms. Barbara STUART

University of Vermont (D)

South Prospect Street, Burlington VT 05405-0160
County: Chittenden FICE Identification: 003696
Unit ID: 231174
Telephone: (802) 656-3131 Carnegie Class: DU-Higher
FAX Number: N/A Calendar System: Semester
URL: www.uvm.edu
Established: 1791 Annual Undergrad Tuition & Fees (In-State): $16,768
Enrollment: 12,856 Coed
Affiliation or Control: State IRS Status: 501(c)3
Highest Offering: Doctorate
Accreditation: EH, BUS, CAATE, CACREP, CLPSY, DENT, DIETC, DIETD, ENG, IPSY, MED, MT, NMT, NURSE, PTA, RTT, SP, SPAA, SW, TED

01 President ... Dr. E. Thomas SULLIVAN
05 Senior Vice President & Provost ... Dr. David V. ROSOWSKY
10 VP for Finance & Treasurer ... Mr. Richard H. CATE
86 VP University Relations & Admin ... Dr. Thomas J. GUSTAFSON
46 VP Research ... Dr. Richard A. GALBRAITH
30 CEO & President The UVM Foundation ... Mr. O. Richard BUNDY, III
43 VP Legal Affairs & General Counsel ... Ms. Francine T. BAZLUKE
84 VP Enrollment Management ... Ms. Stacey R. KOSTELL
20 Assoc Prov Faculty Affairs ... Dr. Jim VIGOREAUX
20 Assoc Provost Teaching & Learning ... Dr. Brian V. REED
32 Vice Provost for Student Affairs ... Dr. Annie STEVENS
28 VP for Human Resources & Diversity ... Dr. Wanda R. HEADING-GRANT
100 VP for Executive Operations ... Dr. Gary L. DERR
18 Assoc VP Admin & Facility Services ... Mr. William P. BALLARD
15 Director Benefits & Employee Svcs ... Mr. Harold J. PIERCE
35 Dean of Students ... Dr. David A. NESTOR
29 Assoc VP for Alumni Relations ... Mr. Alan E. RYEA
63 Dean College of Medicine ... Dr. Frederick C. MORIN, III
66 Dean Nursing & Health Sciences ... Dr. Patricia A. PRELOCK
49 Dean Arts & Sciences ... Dr. William A. FALLS
47 Dean Agriculture & Life Sciences ... Dr. Thomas C. VOGELMANN
54 Dean Engineering & Math Sciences ... Dr. Luis A. GARCIA
53 Dean Education & Social Svcs ... Dr. Scott THOMAS
50 Dean Business Administration ... Dr. Sanjay SHARMA
92 Interim Dean Honors College ... Dr. Lisa J. SCHNELL
65 Dean Environment & Natural Resource ... Dr. Nancy E. MATHEWS
56 Dean Extension ... Dr. Douglas O. LANTAGNE
58 Dean Graduate College ... Dr. Cynthia J. FOREHAND
51 Dean Continuing & Distance Educ ... Ms. Cynthia L. BELLIVEAU
08 Dean Libraries & Learning Res & CIO ... Ms. Mara R. SAULE
06 Registrar ... Mr. Keith P. WILLIAMS
09 Director Institutional Research ... Vacant
26 Director University Communications ... Mr. Enrique CORREDERA
13 Assoc Chief Information Officer ... Ms. Julia H. RUSSELL
25 Assoc VP Research Admin ... Ms. Jennifer GAGNON
21 University Budget Director ... Mr. Alberto CITARELLA
19 Chief of Police Services ... Ms. Lianne M. TUOMEY
41 Director of Athletics ... Mr. Jeffrey L. SCHULMAN
36 Director Career Services ... Ms. Pamela K. GARDNER
23 Director Ctr for Health & Wellbeing ... Dr. Jon K. PORTER
38 Counsel/Psych Services Program Dir ... Dr. Todd N. WEINMAN
39 Acting Director Residential Life ... Ms. Kim PARKER
40 Director University Bookstore ... Mr. Jay E. MENNINGER
85 Director Intl Education Services ... Ms. Kimberly A. HOWARD
102 COO & VP The UVM Foundation ... Mr. Mark W. DORGAN
44 Senior Development Coordinator ... Ms. Donna BURKE
22 Director AA & EO ... Mr. Jes S. KRAUS
07 Director Graduate Admissions ... Ms. Sydnee VIRAY
07 Director Undergraduate Admissions ... Dr. Elizabeth A. WISER
37 Director Student Financial Services ... Ms. Marie D. JOHNSON
96 Director Purchasing Services ... Ms. Natalie L. GUILLETTE
94 Director Women's Center ... Ms. Sarah G. WARRINGTON
24 Access/Media Services Librarian ... Mr. Aaron F. NICHOLS
101 Board of Trustees Coordinator ... Ms. Corinne B. THOMPSON

Vermont College of Fine Arts (E)

36 College Street, Montpelier VT 05602-3145
County: Washington FICE Identification: 003697
Unit ID: 455992
Telephone: (802) 828-8600 Carnegie Class: Masters/M
FAX Number: (802) 828-8649 Calendar System: Semester
URL: www.vcfa.edu
Established: 2008 Annual Graduate Tuition & Fees: N/A
Enrollment: 369 Coed
Affiliation or Control: Independent Non-Profit IRS Status: 501(c)3
Highest Offering: Master's; No Undergraduates
Accreditation: EH

01 President ... Mr. Thomas Christopher GREENE
05 Academic Dean ... Mr. Matthew MONK
10 Chief Financial Ofcr/VP for Admin ... Ms. Erica HARE
04 Administrative Asst to President ... Ms. Angela PALADINO
26 Dir of Marketing & Communications ... Mr. Jay ERICSON
06 Registrar ... Ms. Jody MAUNSELL
08 Head Librarian ... Mr. Jim NOLTE
13 Chief Info Technology Officer (CIO) ... Mr. Peter TIMPONE
18 Chief Facilities/Physical Plant ... Mr. Bill CAMERON
29 Director Alumni Relations ... Ms. Sabrina FADIAL
84 Director Enrollment Management ... Mr. David MARKOW

† Carnegie Graduate Instructional Program classification is Postbac-A&S

Vermont Law School (F)

164 Chelsea Street, PO Box 96, South Royalton VT 05068-0096
County: Windsor FICE Identification: 011934
Unit ID: 231147
Telephone: (802) 831-1000 Carnegie Class: Spec-4-yr-Law
FAX Number: (802) 831-1163 Calendar System: Semester
URL: www.vermontlaw.edu
Established: 1972 Annual Graduate Tuition & Fees: N/A
Enrollment: 642 Coed
Affiliation or Control: Independent Non-Profit IRS Status: 501(c)3
Highest Offering: First Professional Degree; No Undergraduates
Accreditation: EH, LAW

01 President and Dean ... Mr. Marc MIHALY
05 Vice Dean for Faculty ... Mr. David MEARS
11 Vice Dean for Administration ... Ms. Stephanie WILLBANKS
10 Vice President for Finance ... Ms. Lorraine ATWOOD
100 Chief of Staff ... Ms. Kimberly EVANS
88 Assoc Dean/Director Env Law Ctr ... Ms. Melissa SCANLAN
32 Assoc Dean Student Affs & Diversity ... Ms. Shirley JEFFERSON
20 Dep Vice Dean for Academic Affairs ... Ms. Beth MCCORMACK
106 Assoc Director of Distance Learning ... Ms. Adrienne SOLER
07 Assoc Dean of Admissions ... Mr. John MILLER
30 Vice President of Advancement ... Ms. Mary WELZ
15 Human Resources Manager ... Ms. Chantelle BRACKETT
08 Library Director ... Mr. Cynthia LEWIS
21 Comptroller ... Mr. Robert WEBBER
06 Registrar ... Ms. Maureen MORIARTY
37 Director of Financial Aid ... Ms. Melody DEFLORIO
18 Facilities Manager ... Mr. Andrew BRACKETT
26 Director of Communications ... Ms. Maryellen APELQUIST
13 Technology Operations Manager ... Mr. Sean LEE
04 Exec Asst to the President/Dean ... Ms. Stephanie CHIARELLA
40 Bookstore Manager ... Ms. Amy MCDOWELL
29 Asst Director of Alumni Affairs ... Ms. Melissa SCHLOBOHM

*Vermont State Colleges Office of the Chancellor (G)

PO Box 7, Montpelier VT 05601
County: Washington FICE Identification: 029162
Unit ID: 231156
Telephone: (802) 224-3000 Carnegie Class: N/A
FAX Number: (802) 224-3035
URL: www.vsc.edu

01 Chancellor ... Mr. Jeb SPAULDING
04 Exec Assistant to the Chancellor ... Ms. Elaine SOPCHAK
43 Vice President/General Counsel ... Mr. William REEDY
10 Vice Pres/Chief Financial Officer ... Mr. Stephen WISLOSKI
05 Chief Academic/Tech Officer ... Dr. Yasmine ZIESLER
86 Dir External/Governmental Affairs ... Ms. Tricia COATES
26 Chief Information Officer ... Ms. Dianne POLLAK
18 Director of Facilities ... Mr. Richard ETHIER
91 Director Admin Information Systems ... Mr. Kevin CONROY
13 Director of System Info Tech ... Vacant
15 Director of Human Resources ... Ms. Nancy SHAW
09 Director of Institutional Research ... Ms. Hope BAKER-CARR
88 Director of Payroll/Benefits ... Ms. Tracy SWEET
25 Grants Coordinator ... Mr. David RUBIN

*Castleton University (H)

62 Alumni Drive, Castleton VT 05735-4454
County: Rutland FICE Identification: 003683
Unit ID: 230834
Telephone: (802) 468-5611 Carnegie Class: Bac-Diverse
FAX Number: (802) 468-6470 Calendar System: Semester
URL: www.castleton.edu
Established: 1787 Annual Undergrad Tuition & Fees (In-State): $11,282
Enrollment: 2,133 Coed
Affiliation or Control: State IRS Status: 501(c)3
Highest Offering: Master's
Accreditation: EH, CAATE, NURSE, SW

02 President ... Mr. David S. WOLK
04 Exec Assistant to the President ... Ms. Rita B. GENO
05 Academic Dean ... Dr. Jonathan SPIRO
11 Dean of Administration ... Mr. Scott DIKEMAN
10 Director of Finance ... Ms. Laura JAKUBOWSKI
32 Dean of Students ... Mr. Dennis PROULX
84 Dean of Enrollment ... Mr. Maurice OUIMET
15 Director of Human Resources ... Ms. Janet HAZELTON
35 Associate Dean of Students ... Ms. Victoria ANGIS
06 Registrar ... Ms. Lori ARNER
08 Director Calvin Coolidge Library ... Ms. Jami YAZDANI
37 Director Student Financial Aid ... Ms. Kathy O'MEARA
53 Director of Student Teaching ... Dr. Richard REARDON
18 Director of Physical Plant ... Mr. Chuck LAVOIE
30 Dean of Advancement ... Mr. Jeff WELD
36 Dir of Career Development ... Ms. Renee BEAUPREWHITE
23 Wellness Center Director ... Ms. Martha COULTER
38 Director Student Counseling ... Vacant

*Community College of Vermont (A)

PO Box 489, Montpelier VT 05601
County: Washington FICE Identification: 011167
Unit ID: 230861
Telephone: (802) 828-2800 Carnegie Class: Assoc/HT-High Non
FAX Number: (802) 828-2805 Calendar System: Semester
URL: www.ccv.edu
Established: 1970 Annual Undergrad Tuition & Fees (In-State): $6,054
Enrollment: 6,019 Coed
Affiliation or Control: State IRS Status: 501(c)3
Highest Offering: Associate Degree
Accreditation: EH, MAAB

02 President Ms. Joyce M. JUDY
11 Dean of Administration Dr. Barbara MARTIN
05 Dean of Academic Services Ms. Deborah STEWART
32 Dean of Student Services Ms. Heather WEINSTEIN
84 Dean Enrollment Services Ms. Pam CHISHOLM
20 Associate Academic Dean Ms. Darlene MURPHY
20 Associate Academic Dean Ms. Diane HERMANN-ARTIM
12 Exec Director of Academic Center Ms. Penne LYNCH
12 Exec Director of Academic Center Mr. Eric SAKAI
12 Exec Director of Academic Center Ms. Katie MOBLEY
12 Exec Director of Academic Center Ms. Tapp BARNHILL
24 Dean of Learning Technologies Mr. Eric SAKAI
15 Director Human Resources Mr. Robert FINNEGAN
06 Registrar Mr. Thomas ARNER
07 Director of Admissions Mr. Adam WARRINGTON
09 Dir Institutional Research/Planning Ms. Laura MASSELL
26 Chief Public Relations Officer Mr. Josh LARKIN
88 Director of Secondary Initiatives Ms. Natalie SEARLE
36 Director of Career Training Program Vacant
27 Dir of Marketing/Communications Ms. Janette SHAFFER
10 Chief Financial/Business Officer Mr. Nathan HOCK

*Johnson State College (B)

337 College Hill, Johnson VT 05656
County: Lamoille FICE Identification: 003688
Unit ID: 230913
Telephone: (802) 635-1240 Carnegie Class: Masters/S
FAX Number: N/A Calendar System: Semester
URL: www.jsc.edu
Established: 1828 Annual Undergrad Tuition & Fees (In-State): $11,018
Enrollment: 1,613 Coed
Affiliation or Control: State IRS Status: 501(c)3
Highest Offering: Master's
Accreditation: EH

02 President Dr. Elaine C. COLLINS
05 Academic Dean Dr. Dan REGAN
11 Dean of Administration and CIO Ms. Sharron R. SCOTT
32 Dean of Student Life & College Rels Dr. David BERGH
84 Associate Dean of Enrollment Ms. Penny HOWRIGAN
35 Associate Dean of Students Ms. Michele WHITMORE
06 Registrar Mr. Douglas EASTMAN
51 Co-Director of External Degree Prgm Ms. Valerie EDWARDS
18 Director of Physical Plant Mr. Woody DIONNE
41 Director of Athletics & Recreation Mr. Jamey VENTURA
38 Director of Counseling Services Ms. Kate MCCARTHY
30 Director Development/Alumni Rels Ms. Lauren PHILIE
36 Director of Advising Ms. Sara KINERSON
89 Director of First-Year Experience Ms. Margo WARDEN
19 Director Safety & Security Mr. Michael PALAGONIA
26 Dir College Communications Ms. Deborah BOUTON
37 Director Student Financial Aid Ms. Lisa CUMMINGS
15 Director Human Resources Ms. Sharron SCOTT
07 Director of Admissions Mr. Patrick ROGERS
08 Librarian Mr. Joseph FARARA
79 Chair Humanities Dr. Paul SILVER
53 Chair Education Dept Dr. Kathleen BRINEGAR
65 Chair Environ/Health Sciences Dr. Elizabeth DOLCI
88 Chair Performing Arts Mr. Stephen BLAIR
57 Chair Fine Arts Mr. Ken LESLIE
50 Chair Business/Economics Mr. James BLACK
60 Chair Writing/Literature Dr. Sharon TWIGG
81 Chair Mathematics Dr. Julie THEORET
83 Chair Behavioral Sciences Dr. Susan GREEN
04 Executive Asst to President Ms. Cecilia NORTH

*Lyndon State College (C)

1001 College Road, PO Box 919,
Lyndonville VT 05851-0919
County: Caledonia FICE Identification: 003689
Unit ID: 230931
Telephone: (802) 626-6200 Carnegie Class: Bac-Diverse
FAX Number: (802) 626-9770 Calendar System: Semester
URL: www.lyndonstate.edu
Established: 1911 Annual Undergrad Tuition & Fees (In-State): $11,018
Enrollment: 1,430 Coed
Affiliation or Control: State IRS Status: 501(c)3
Highest Offering: Master's
Accreditation: EH, EXSC

02 President Dr. Joseph A. BERTOLINO
05 Interim Dean of Academic Affairs Dr. Nolan T. ATKINS
10 Dean of Administration Ms. Loren W. LOOMIS HUBBELL
20 Associate Dean of Faculty Mr. Thomas K. ANDERSON
32 Dean of Student Affairs Mr. Jonathan M. DAVIS
07 Director of Admissions Mr. Vincent U. MALONEY
18 Director of Physical Plant Mr. Thomas R. ARCHER
91 Chief Technology Officer Mr. Michael A. DENTE
44 Director of Development Ms. Jennifer K. HARRIS
08 Library Director Mr. Samuel C. BOSS
06 Registrar Ms. Miranda D. FOX
35 Director of Student Life Ms. Erin S. ROSSETTI
41 Director of Athletics Mr. Christopher T. UMMER
37 Director of Financial Aid Ms. Tanya W. BRADLEY
36 Director of Career Services Ms. Amy L. WRIGHT
88 Dir of Student Academic Development Ms. Debra M. BAILIN
26 Executive Director of Communication Ms. Sylvia PLUMB
88 Director of Advising Resources Ms. Kathleen E. GOLD
15 Director of Human Resources Ms. Sandra L. FRANZ

*Vermont Technical College (D)

PO Box 500, Randolph Center VT 05061-0500
County: Orange FICE Identification: 003698
Unit ID: 231165
Telephone: (802) 728-1000 Carnegie Class: Bac/Assoc-Mixed
FAX Number: (802) 728-1508 Calendar System: Semester
URL: www.vtc.edu
Established: 1866 Annual Undergrad Tuition & Fees (In-State): $13,490
Enrollment: 1,542 Coed
Affiliation or Control: State IRS Status: 501(c)3
Highest Offering: Master's
Accreditation: EH, ADNUR, COARC, DH, ENGT, NUR, PNUR

02 President Mr. Daniel P. SMITH
05 Dean Academic Affairs Mr. Philip PETTY
32 Dean of Student Affairs Mr. John PATERSON
20 Dean Academic Pgm Development Mr. Brent SARGENT
11 Dean of Administration Mr. Littleton TYLER
13 Chief Technology Officer Mr. James SMITH
30 Assoc Dean Inst Advancement Vacant
66 Assoc Dean of Nursing Ms. Cindy MARTINDILL
06 Registrar Ms. Sarah LEVIN
10 Controller Ms. Eileen DONOVAN
37 Director Financial Aid Ms. Catherine MCCULLOUGH
29 Assoc Dean Enrollment/Alumni Affs Mr. Dwight CROSS
19 Director Public Safety Mr. Emile FREDETTE
18 Director Physical Plant Mr. Daniel KOLOSKI
36 Director Career Developmenet Ms. Karry BOOSKA
15 Director of Human Resources Ms. Pamela ANKUDA
26 Dir Marketing/Communications Ms. Amanda CHAULK
40 Manager Bookstore Mr. Joe HIRAK
07 Director of Admissions Ms. Jessica VAN DEREN
08 Library Director Ms. Jane KEARNS

VIRGINIA

Advanced Technology Institute (E)

5700 Southern Boulevard, Virginia Beach VA 23462-2409
County: City of Virginia Beach FICE Identification: 031275
Unit ID: 231411
Telephone: (757) 490-1241 Carnegie Class: Spec 2-yr-Tech
FAX Number: (757) 499-5929 Calendar System: Semester
URL: www.auto.edu
Established: 1993 Annual Undergrad Tuition & Fees: $13,250
Enrollment: 717 Coed
Affiliation or Control: Proprietary IRS Status: Proprietary
Highest Offering: Associate Degree
Accreditation: ACCSC

01 Campus President Mr. Dick DAIGLE
05 Chief Academic Officer Mr. Chenek PICKA
07 Director of Admissions Mr. Mike CORCORAN
32 Director of Student Services Mr. Kirk CLAYTON
37 Director Student Financial Aid Mr. Chad MARTS
06 Registrar Mrs. Shannon VOIGT
15 Director Personnel Services Mr. Rey LIZAN
36 Director Student Placement Mr. Kirk CLAYTON
39 Director Student Housing Mr. Kirk MANGHAM

American College of Commerce and Technology (F)

803 W. Broad Street #100, Falls Church VA 22046
Identification: 667273
Telephone: (703) 942-6200 Carnegie Class: Not Classified
FAX Number: (703) 942-8791 Calendar System: Quarter
URL: www.acct.edu
Established: 2010 Annual Undergrad Tuition & Fees: N/A
Enrollment: N/A Coed
Affiliation or Control: Proprietary IRS Status: Proprietary
Highest Offering: Master's
Accreditation: ACICS

01 President & CEO Dr. William SCHIPPER

American National University (G)

1813 E Main Street, Salem VA 24153-4598
County: Independent City FICE Identification: 003726
Unit ID: 232797
Telephone: (540) 986-1800 Carnegie Class: Bac/Assoc-Mixed
FAX Number: (540) 986-1344 Calendar System: Quarter
URL: www.an.edu
Established: 1886 Annual Undergrad Tuition & Fees: $11,466
Enrollment: 1,337 Coed
Affiliation or Control: Proprietary IRS Status: Proprietary
Highest Offering: Master's
Accreditation: ACICS, CEA, EMT, MAC

01 President Mr. Frank E. LONGAKER
10 Exec VP of Campus Operations Mr. Jason TOWERS
21 Exec VP of Campus Support Operation Ms. Cathy PLUNKETT
88 Regional Vice Pres Operations Mr. Greg GOSSETT
88 Regional Vice Pres Operations Mr. Paul WOLF
88 Regional Vice Pres Operations Mr. Sean KUHN

American National University (H)

3926 Seminole Trail, Charlottesville VA 22911-8397
Telephone: (434) 295-0136 Identification: 666501
Accreditation: ACICS, MAC

American National University (I)

336 Old Riverside Drive, Danville VA 24541-1819
Telephone: (434) 793-6822 Identification: 666502
Accreditation: ACICS, MAC, SURGT

American National University (J)

1515 Country Club Road, Harrisonburg VA 22801-9709
Telephone: (540) 432-0943 Identification: 666503
Accreditation: ACICS, MAC, SURGT

American National University (K)

104 Candlewood Court, Lynchburg VA 24502-2653
Telephone: (434) 239-3500 Identification: 666504
Accreditation: ACICS, MAC

American National University (L)

905 N. Memorial Boulevard, Martinsville VA 24112-2420
Telephone: (276) 632-5621 Identification: 666505
Accreditation: ACICS, MAC

Appalachian College of Pharmacy (M)

1060 Dragon Road, Oakwood VA 24631
County: Buchanan FICE Identification: 041806
Unit ID: 449922
Telephone: (276) 498-4190 Carnegie Class: Spec-4-yr-Other Health
FAX Number: (276) 498-4193 Calendar System: Semester
URL: www.acpharm.org
Established: 2003 Annual Graduate Tuition & Fees: N/A
Enrollment: 214 Coed
Affiliation or Control: Independent Non-Profit IRS Status: 501(c)3
Highest Offering: Doctorate; No Undergraduates
Accreditation: SC, PHAR

01 President Mr. Michael G. MCGLOTHLIN
05 Dean Dr. Susan L. MAYHEW
10 Chief Financial Officer Ms. Holli HARMAN
07 Dir of Admissions/Fin Aid/Registrar Ms. Vickie KEENE
103 Dir of Institutional Development Mr. Terry KILGORE
32 Dir Student Services/Alumni Affairs Mr. Jason MCGLOTHLIN
13 Dir Information Technology/Safety Mr. Michael DEEL

Appalachian School of Law (N)

1169 Riverside Drive, Grundy VA 24614-2825
County: Buchanan FICE Identification: 035593
Unit ID: 432348
Telephone: (800) 895-7411 Carnegie Class: Spec-4-yr-Law
FAX Number: (276) 935-8261 Calendar System: Semester
URL: www.asl.edu
Established: 1995 Annual Undergrad Tuition & Fees: N/A
Enrollment: 160 Coed
Affiliation or Control: Independent Non-Profit IRS Status: 501(c)3
Highest Offering: First Professional Degree
Accreditation: LAW

01 Interim Dean and COO Ms. Sandra K. MCGLOTHLIN
05 Associate Dean of Academic Affairs Mr. Mason HEIDT
08 Acting Director of Library Ms. Glenna OWENS
36 Director of Career Services Mr. Jeremy WILLIAMS
13 Director of Information Services Mr. Brian PRESLEY
15 Director Cmty Service & Personnel Ms. Jina M. SAULS
32 Director of Admissions Ms. Corie RIFE
06 Registrar Ms. Beth STANLEY
37 Financial Aid Officer Mr. David BROOKSHIRE

Argosy University, Washington DC (O)

1550 Wilson Boulevard, Suite 600,
Arlington VA 22209-2435
Telephone: (703) 526-5800 Identification: 666788
Accreditation: &WC, ACBSP, CACREP, CLPSY

† Regional accreditation is carried under the parent institution in Orange, CA.

The Art Institute of Virginia Beach (P)

4500 Main Street, Ste 100, Virginia Beach VA 23462
Telephone: (757) 493-6700 Identification: 770977
Accreditation: &SC

† Regional accreditation is carried under the parent institution in Atlanta, GA

The Art Institute of Washington (A)

1820 North Fort Myer Drive, Arlington VA 22209-1802
Telephone: (703) 358-9550 Identification: 770945
Accreditation: &SC, ACFEI, CIDA

† Branch campus of The Art Institute of Atlanta, Atlanta, GA.

Atlantic University (B)

215 67th Street, Virginia Beach VA 23451-8101
County: Virginia Beach Identification: 666653
Unit ID: 231402
Telephone: (757) 631-8101 Carnegie Class: Not Classified
FAX Number: (757) 631-8096 Calendar System: Trimester
URL: www.atlanticuniv.edu
Established: 1930 Annual Graduate Tuition & Fees: N/A
Enrollment: N/A Coed
Affiliation or Control: Independent Non-Profit IRS Status: 501(c)3
Highest Offering: Master's; No Undergraduates
Accreditation: DEAC

01 CEO .... Kevin TODESCHI
05 Dir Academic & Administrative Affs .... James VAN AUKEN
88 Education Services Manager .... Rachel ALVIDREZ
84 Enrollment Clerk .... Megan STORY

Averett University (C)

420 W Main Street, Danville VA 24541-3692
County: Independent City FICE Identification: 003702
Unit ID: 231420
Telephone: (434) 791-5600 Carnegie Class: Bac-Diverse
FAX Number: (434) 791-7181 Calendar System: Semester
URL: www.averett.edu
Established: 1859 Annual Undergrad Tuition & Fees: $30,900
Enrollment: 872 Coed
Affiliation or Control: Independent Non-Profit IRS Status: 501(c)3
Highest Offering: Master's
Accreditation: SC, #CAATE, NURSE

01 President .... Dr. Tiffany M. FRANKS
32 Executive Vice President .... Mr. Charles S. HARRIS
05 Vice Pres for Academic Affairs .... Dr. Timothy FULOP
10 Vice President Business & Finance .... Mr. Aaron HOWELL
30 Vice Pres Institutional Advancement .... Mr. Albert RAWLEY
15 Director of Human Resources .... Mrs. Kathie TUNE
84 Vice Pres Enrollment Management .... Ms. Stacy GATO
37 Director Student Financial Services .... Mr. Carl BRADSHER
21 Controller .... Ms. Lisa STEWART
08 Director of Library .... Ms. Elaine DAY
36 Director of Career Development .... Ms. Angie MCADAMS
06 Registrar .... Mrs. Janet ROBERSON
26 Dir of Marketing/Communications .... Ms. Cassie JONES
29 Director Alumni Relations .... Mr. Dan HAYES
09 Dir Institutional Research/Effect .... Dr. Pam MCKIRDY
07 Director of Admissions .... Mr. Joel NESTER
18 Chief Facilities/Physical Plant .... Mr. Alonzo JONES
35 Director of Student Affairs .... Ms. Lesley VILLARCSE
38 Director of Student Counseling .... Mrs. Joan KAHWAJY-ANDERSON

Baptist Theological Seminary at Richmond (D)

8040 Villa Park Drive, Richmond VA 23228
County: Independent City FICE Identification: 031169
Unit ID: 366793
Telephone: (804) 355-8135 Carnegie Class: Spec-4-yr-Faith
FAX Number: (804) 355-8182 Calendar System: Semester
URL: www.btsr.edu
Established: 1991 Annual Graduate Tuition & Fees: N/A
Enrollment: 78 Coed
Affiliation or Control: Independent Non-Profit IRS Status: 501(c)3
Highest Offering: Doctorate; No Undergraduates
Accreditation: THEOL

01 President .... Dr. Ronald W. CRAWFORD
05 Dean .... Dr. Timothy GILBERT
30 VP Institutional Advancement .... Mr. Rob FOX
10 Dir Business Affairs & Facilities .... Dr. James F. PEAK, JR.
07 Director Admissions & Recruitment .... Dr. Melissa FALLEN
06 Registrar .... Rev. Susan BLANCHARD
13 Chief Info Technology Officer (CIO) .... Ms. Eryn VAN LEAR
26 Communications Manager .... Ms. Lacy KENDRICK

Bethel College (E)

1705 Todds Lane, Hampton VA 23666
County: Hampton City FICE Identification: 041538
Unit ID: 458113
Telephone: (757) 826-1883 Carnegie Class: Spec-4-yr-Faith
FAX Number: (757) 826-5436 Calendar System: Semester
URL: www.bethel-college.com
Established: 2004 Annual Undergrad Tuition & Fees: $8,100
Enrollment: 57 Coed
Affiliation or Control: Assemblies Of God Church IRS Status: 501(c)3
Highest Offering: Baccalaureate
Accreditation: BI

01 Acting President .... Dr. Ron DE BERRY
05 Academic Dean/Exec Vice President .... Dr. Ron DEBERRY
32 Student Affairs .... Ms. Nanette BARTHOLOMEW
06 Registrar .... Ms. Shawn LABADIE
08 Librarian .... Ms. Janell SANFORD
30 Director Institutional Advancement .... Ms. Audrey SOMERO

Bluefield College (F)

3000 College Avenue, Bluefield VA 24605-1799
County: Tazewell FICE Identification: 003703
Unit ID: 231554
Telephone: (276) 326-3682 Carnegie Class: Bac-Diverse
FAX Number: (276) 326-4288 Calendar System: Semester
URL: www.bluefield.edu
Established: 1922 Annual Undergrad Tuition & Fees: $23,296
Enrollment: 944 Coed
Affiliation or Control: Baptist IRS Status: 501(c)3
Highest Offering: Master's
Accreditation: SC, NURSE, TEAC

01 President .... Dr. David W. OLIVE
04 Assistant to the President .... Mrs. Diane T. SHOTT
05 VP for Academic Affairs .... Dr. Marshal FLOWERS
30 VP for Advancement .... Mrs. Ruth BLANKENSHIP
10 VP for Finance & Admin .... Mrs. Ruth BLANKENSHIP
32 VP for Student Development .... Mr. Trent ARGO
84 VP for Enrollment Management .... Mr. Trent ARGO
06 Registrar .... Ms. Jennifer LAMB
08 Director of Library Services .... Ms. Barbara GILLESPIE
26 Director of Public Relations .... Mr. Chris SHOEMAKER
29 Director of Alumni Relations .... Mr. Josh GRUBB
09 Director of Institutional Research .... Mr. Bryan FRAZIER
37 Director of Financial Aid .... Ms. Carly KESTNER
42 Campus Minister .... Rev. Henry CLARY
41 Athletic Director .... Mr. Mike WHITE
40 Campus Store Manager .... Mrs. Judy AKERS
18 Director of Maintenance .... Mr. Blair TAYLOR
19 Coordinator of Campus Safety .... Mr. Will ROBINSON
15 Human Resources Director .... Ms. Judy PEDNEAU
106 Dir of Online Programs .... Mr. Andrew LAWRENCE
13 Chief Info Technology Officer .... Mr. Steve KESSINGER
53 Dean School of Education .... Dr. Donna WATSON

Bon Secours Memorial College of Nursing (G)

8550 Magellan Parkway, Ste 1100, Richmond VA 23227
County: Henrico FICE Identification: 010043
Unit ID: 233356
Telephone: (804) 627-5300 Carnegie Class: Spec-4-yr-Other Health
FAX Number: (804) 627-5330 Calendar System: Semester
URL: www.bsmcon.edu
Established: 1961 Annual Undergrad Tuition & Fees: N/A
Enrollment: 489 Coed
Affiliation or Control: Independent Non-Profit IRS Status: 501(c)3
Highest Offering: Baccalaureate
Accreditation: ACICS, NURSE

05 Vice Pres Academic Affairs/Provost .... Dr. Melanie H. GREEN
66 Dean of Nursing .... Dr. Barbara C. SORBELLO
10 Dean of Administration and Finance .... Dr. Regina E. WELCH
32 Dean of Student Services .... Ms. Leslie WINSTON

Bridgewater College (H)

402 E College Street, Bridgewater VA 22812-1599
County: Rockingham FICE Identification: 003704
Unit ID: 231581
Telephone: (540) 828-8000 Carnegie Class: Bac-A&S
FAX Number: (540) 828-5479 Calendar System: 4/1/4
URL: www.bridgewater.edu
Established: 1880 Annual Undergrad Tuition & Fees: $31,480
Enrollment: 1,785 Coed
Affiliation or Control: Church Of The Brethren IRS Status: 501(c)3
Highest Offering: Baccalaureate
Accreditation: SC, CAATE

01 President .... Dr. David W. BUSHMAN
03 Executive Vice President .... Mr. Roy W. FERGUSON, JR.
05 Provost/VP for Academic Affairs .... Dr. Leona SEVICK
10 Vice Pres for Finance & Treasurer .... Ms. Anne B. KEELER
30 Vice Pres for Institutional Advance .... Dr. Maureen SILVA
26 Exec Dir Marketing & Communications .. Ms. Abbie PARKHURST
84 Vice President for Enrollment Mgmt .... Mr. Reggie WEBB
18 Director of Sustainability .... Mr. Teshome H. MOLALENGE
40 Bookstore Manager .... Ms. Sarah LANDIS
20 Associate Dean of Academic Affairs .... Dr. Robert B. ANDERSEN
32 VP for Student Life/Dean of Student .... Dr. Leslie FRERE
36 Director of Career Services .... Ms. Sherry TALBOTT
88 Director of Academic Support Svcs .... Dr. Raymond W. STUDWELL, II
42 Chaplain .... Rev. Robert R. MILLER
07 Director of Admissions .... Mr. Jarret L. SMITH
37 Director of Financial Aid .... Mr. Scott D. MORRISON
21 Director of Budget & Analysis .... Mr. Jeffrey FIKE
13 Director of Info Tech Center .... Ms. Kristy K. RHEA
41 Director of Athletics .... Mr Curtis L. KENDALL
38 Director of Counseling Services .... Mr. Randall HOOK
29 Director of Alumni Relations .... Ms. Ellen B. MILLER
09 Director of Institutional Research .... Ms. Dawn S. DALBOW
15 Director of Human Resources .... Mrs. Kimberly P. HARPER
08 Library Director .... Mr. Andrew L. PEARSON
06 Registrar .... Ms. Cynthia K. HOWDYSHELL
21 Controller .... Ms. Mary S. SCHWAB
27 Editor/Dir of Media Relations .... Mr. Charles R. CULBERTSON
18 Director of Facilities .... Mr. David R. VANDEVANDER
19 Campus Police Chief .... Mr. Nicholas P. PICERNO
28 Minority Mentor .... Mr. James E. RAEFORD
23 Director of Student Health Services .... Ms. Paige FRENCH
28 Director of Multicultural Services .... Ms. Joanne HARRIS-DUFF
109 Director of Dining Services .... Ms. Mary SPEIR
04 Administrative Asst to President .... Mrs. Elaine C. DELLINGER
39 Director Student Housing .... Ms. Dawn OHANESSIAN
104 Director International Education .... Mrs. Anne MARSH

Bryant & Stratton College (I)

8141 Hull Street Road, North Chesterfield VA 23235-6411
Telephone: (804) 745-2444 Identification: 666496
Accreditation: &M, ADNUR, MAC

† Regional accreditation is carried under the parent institution (corporate office) in Buffalo, NY.

Bryant & Stratton College (J)

301 Centre Pointe Drive, Virginia Beach VA 23462-4417
Telephone: (757) 499-7900 FICE Identification: 010061
Accreditation: &M, MAC

† Regional accreditation is carried under the parent institution (corporate office) in Buffalo, NY.

California University of Management and Sciences Virginia (K)

4300 Wilson Blvd, Suite 140, Arlington VA 22203
Telephone: (703) 663-8088 Identification: 666734
Accreditation: ACICS

† Branch campus of California University of Management and Sciences, Anaheim, CA.

Centra College of Nursing (L)

905 Lakeside Drive, Suite A, Lynchburg VA 24501
County: Independent City FICE Identification: 021758
Unit ID: 232618
Telephone: (434) 200-3070 Carnegie Class: Spec 2-yr-Health
FAX Number: (434) 200-5505 Calendar System: Semester
URL: www.centracon.edu
Established: 2011 Annual Undergrad Tuition & Fees: N/A
Enrollment: 151 Coed
Affiliation or Control: Independent Non-Profit IRS Status: 501(c)3
Highest Offering: Associate Degree
Accreditation: ABHES, ADNUR, PNUR

01 Dean .... Dr. Melody SHARP
66 Assoc Director ADN Program .... Dr. Jim EMERSON
66 Assoc Director PN Program .... Ms. Dana GRANT
05 Director of Academic Progression .... Dr. Diane ELMORE
37 Financial Aid/Enrollment Manager .... Mr. Aaron ELLENBURG

Centura College (M)

932 Ventura Way, Chesapeake VA 23320
Telephone: (757) 549-2121 Identification: 770608
Accreditation: ACCSC

Centura College (N)

616 Denbigh Boulevard, Newport News VA 23608
Telephone: (757) 874-2121 Identification: 770606
Accreditation: ACCSC

Centura College (O)

7020 N Military Highway, Norfolk VA 23518-4202
Telephone: (757) 853-2121 Identification: 770605
Accreditation: ACCSC

Centura College (P)

7914 Midlothian Turnpike, North Chesterfield VA 23235
County: Chesterfield FICE Identification: 031264
Unit ID: 427982
Telephone: (804) 330-0111 Carnegie Class: Spec 2-yr-Health
FAX Number: (804) 330-3809 Calendar System: Semester
URL: www.centuracollege.edu
Established: 1992 Annual Undergrad Tuition & Fees: $16,337
Enrollment: 167 Coed
Affiliation or Control: Proprietary IRS Status: Proprietary
Highest Offering: Associate Degree
Accreditation: ACCSC

01 Campus Executive Director .... Zoe THOMPSON
11 Director of Compliance and Admin .... Grace BLEVINS
05 Director of Education .... Ann TRIBBEY
07 Director of Admissions .... Paul WILLIAMS
06 Registrar .... Virginia GOODWIN
37 Financial Aid .... Korey HUGHES
10 Bursar .... Leslie CROCKER
32 Student Services .... Helena COOPER

36 Career Services .... Steven TERRY
08 Head Librarian .... Towana HATCHER

Centura College (A)

2697 Dean Drive, Suite 100,
Virginia Beach VA 23452-7431
County: City of Virginia Beach FICE Identification: 023344
Unit ID: 232016
Telephone: (757) 340-2121 Carnegie Class: Bac/Assoc-Mixed
FAX Number: (757) 340-9704 Calendar System: Semester
URL: www.centuracollege.edu
Established: 1969 Annual Undergrad Tuition & Fees: $16,887
Enrollment: 181 Coed
Affiliation or Control: Proprietary IRS Status: Proprietary
Highest Offering: Baccalaureate
Accreditation: ACCSC

01 Campus Executive Director .... Ben CLARK
11 Assistant Campus Executive Director .... Dennis RYAN
05 Director of Education .... Marcus WESSON
07 Director of Admissions .... Dustin SAUNDERS
06 Registrar .... Dennis RYAN
37 Financial Aid Officer .... Jennifer BROADWELL
10 Bursar .... Bernadene ALFRED
32 Student Services Coordinator .... Mary MORGAN
36 Career Services Coordinator .... Brenda HOUCK
36 Career Services Coordinator .... Shawn HUTCHINGS
08 Librarian .... Jeffery BARBOUR

Chamberlain College of Nursing-Arlington Campus (B)

2450 Crystal Drive, Arlington VA 22202
Telephone: (703) 416-7300 Identification: 770497
Accreditation: &NH, NURSE

† Regional accreditation is carried under the parent institution in Addison, IL

Chester Career College (C)

751 West Hundred Road, Chester VA 23836-2516
County: Chesterfield FICE Identification: 034095
Telephone: (804) 751-9191 Carnegie Class: Not Classified
FAX Number: (804) 751-2599 Calendar System: Semester
URL: www.chestercareercollege.edu
Established: 1997 Annual Undergrad Tuition & Fees: N/A
Enrollment: N/A Coed
Affiliation or Control: Proprietary IRS Status: Proprietary
Highest Offering: Associate Degree
Accreditation: COE

01 Campus Director .... Ms. Debbie HARRIS
05 Academic Dean .... Ms. Sandra KERRICK
06 Registrar .... Ms. Annette WHITE
08 Head Librarian .... Ms. Kathy PHILO
36 Director Job Placement .... Mrs. Tamara KNIGHT
37 Director Student Financial Aid .... Ms. Jennifer GLOVER

Christendom College (D)

134 Christendom Drive, Front Royal VA 22630-6534
County: Warren FICE Identification: 036653
Unit ID: 231703
Telephone: (540) 636-2900 Carnegie Class: Not Classified
FAX Number: (540) 636-1655 Calendar System: Semester
URL: www.christendom.edu
Established: 1977 Annual Undergrad Tuition & Fees: N/A
Enrollment: N/A Coed
Affiliation or Control: Roman Catholic IRS Status: 501(c)3
Highest Offering: Master's
Accreditation: SC

01 President .... Dr. Timothy T. O'DONNELL
10 Executive Vice President/CFO/COO .... Mr. Kenneth H. FERGUSON
05 Vice President Academic Affairs .... Dr. Gregory TOWNSEND
30 Vice President for Advancement .... Mr. John F. CISKANIK
18 Vice Pres Operations/Facility Plng .... Mr. Michael S. FOECKLER
84 Vice Pres Enrollment & Marketing .... Mr. Thomas MCFADDEN
21 Controller .... Mr. Luke FIER
32 Dean of Student Life .... Mr. Chris VANDER WOUDE
20 Academic Dean .... Mr. Mark WUNSCH
06 Registrar .... Mr. Walter A. JANARO
07 Director of Admissions .... Mr. Sam PHILLIPS
08 Director of Christendom Library ...... Mr. Andrew V. ARMSTRONG
37 Financial Aid Officer .... Mrs. Alisa L. POLK
29 Asst Dir Alumni/Donor Relations .... Mr. Vince CRISTE
13 Director of Computer Services .... Mr. Douglas S. BRIGGS
88 Registrar/Business Officer NDGS .... Miss Heidi KALIAN
41 Athletic Director .... Mr. Patrick QUEST
30 Dir Advancement Operations/Svcs .... Mr. Paul JALSEVAC
04 Exec Assistant to the President .... Ms. Brenda SEELBACH
58 Dean of the Graduate School .... Dr. Kristen BURNS

Christopher Newport University (E)

1 Avenue of the Arts, Newport News VA 23606-3072
County: Independent City FICE Identification: 003706
Unit ID: 231712
Telephone: (757) 594-7000 Carnegie Class: Masters/S
FAX Number: N/A Calendar System: Semester
URL: www.cnu.edu
Established: 1960 Annual Undergrad Tuition & Fees (In-State): $12,526
Enrollment: 5,221 Coed
Affiliation or Control: State IRS Status: 501(c)3
Highest Offering: Master's
Accreditation: SC, BUS, ENG, MUS, SW, THEA

01 President .... Hon. Paul S. TRIBLE, JR.
100 Chief of Staff .... Mrs. Cynthia R. PERRY
05 Provost .... Dr. David C. DOUGHTY
10 Executive Vice President/CFO .... Mr. William L. BRAUER
43 University Counsel .... Ms. Maureen MATSEN
30 Vice Pres for Univ Advancement .... Mrs. Adelia P. THOMPSON
15 Director of Human Resources .... Mrs. Lorraine M. WESTPHAL
04 Exec Assistant to President/Board ...... Mrs. Beverley D. MUELLER
07 Dean of Admission .... Mr. Robert J. LANGE
32 Dean of Students .... Dr. Kevin M. HUGHES
49 Dean College Arts & Humanities .... Dr. Lori J. UNDERWOOD
83 Dean College of Social Sciences .... Dr. Robert E. COLVIN
83 Dean College Nat/Behav Science .... Dr. Nicole R. GUAJARDO
50 Dean Luter School of Business .... Dr. George H. EBBS
41 Director of Athletics .... Mr. Kyle S. MCMULLIN
21 University Comptroller .... Mrs. A. Diane REED
06 University Registrar .... Mrs. Julianna M. WAIT
37 Director of Financial Aid .... Ms. Christina L. RUSSELL
39 Assistant Director of Housing .... Mr. Andrew H. KOERNERT
09 Director of Institutional Research .... Ms. Donna A. VARNER
13 Chief Information Officer .... Mr. Andrew B. CRAWFORD
45 Director of Planning & Budget .... Ms. Patricia L. MCDERMOTT
88 Director of University Audit .... Ms. Faith D. BELOTE
108 Director of Assessment & Evaluation .... Mr. Jason C. LYONS
96 Director of Materiel Management .... Mr. Ryan A. FEREBEE
08 University Librarian .... Ms. Mary K. SELLEN
19 Chief of University Police .... Mr. Andrew H. ENGEMANN, JR.
18 Director of Facilities Mgmt .... Mr. G. Scott GESELE
44 Sr Dir Advancement/Gift Planning .... Ms. Lucy L. LATCHUM
102 Dir Foundation & Corporate Giving .... Mr. Keith D. ROOTS
26 Exec Dir of University Relations .... Mrs. Amie G. DALE
27 Director of External Relations .... Mr. Thomas E. KRAMER
29 Director of Alumni Relations .... Mr. M. Baxter VENDRICK
22 Director of Title IX and EO .... Ms. Michelle L. MOODY
38 Exec Dir Counseling/Health Services .... Dr. William V. RITCHEY
36 Director Center of Career Planning ...... Ms. Elizabeth K. WESTLEY
104 Director of Study Abroad .... Ms. Amanda K. PIERCE

College of William & Mary (F)

PO Box 8795, Williamsburg VA 23187-8795
County: Independent City FICE Identification: 003705
Unit ID: 231624
Telephone: (757) 221-4000 Carnegie Class: DU-Higher
FAX Number: (757) 221-1259 Calendar System: Semester
URL: www.wm.edu
Established: 1693 Annual Undergrad Tuition & Fees (In-State): $19,372
Enrollment: 8,437 Coed
Affiliation or Control: State IRS Status: 501(c)3
Highest Offering: Doctorate
Accreditation: SC, BUS, BUSA, CACREP, IPSY, LAW, TED

01 President .... Mr. W. Taylor REVELEY, III
05 Provost .... Dr. Michael HALLERAN
10 Sr VP for Finance & Administration .... Mr. Samuel E. JONES
30 VP for University Advancement .... Mr. Matthew T. LAMBERT
45 Vice Pres for Strategic Initiatives .... Mr. Henry R. BROADDUS
32 Vice President for Student Affairs .... Dr. Virginia M. AMBLER
41 Director of Athletics .... Mr. Edward (Terry) C. DRISCOLL
29 Assoc VP/Ex Dir Alumni Engagement . Ms. Marilyn W. MIDYETTE
49 Dean Faculty of Arts & Sciences .... Dr. Katharine CONLEY
50 Dean Mason School of Business .... Mr. Lawrence B. PULLEY
53 Dean School of Education .... Dr. Spencer NILES
61 Dean William & Mary Law School ...... Mr. Davison M. DOUGLAS
88 Dean and Director of VIMS .... Dr. John T. WELLS
08 Dean University Libraries .... Ms. Carrie COOPER
43 University Counsel .... Ms. Deborah A. LOVE
20 Vice Prov Academic & Faculty Affs .... Ms. Susan S. GROVER
82 Vice Prov Intl Affairs/Reves Ctr .... Dr. Stephen E. HANSON
46 Vice Provost Rsch & Grad Prof Stds .... Dr. Dennis M. MANOS
13 Chief Information Officer .... Mr. Courtney CARPENTER
14 Deputy CIO .... Ms. Bernadette KENNEY
108 Assoc Provost Inst Accred .... Dr. Susan L. BOSWORTH
07 Dean of Admission/Assoc Prov Enroll .... Mr. Tim A. WOLFE
06 Assoc Provost & Univ Registrar .... Ms. Sara L. MARCHELLO
09 Director of Institutional Research .... Mr. Evan DAVIES
106 Assoc Provost ELearning Initiatives .... Dr. Michele H. JACKSON
88 Dean for Educational Policy .... Dr. Lu Ann HOMZA
58 Dean Graduate Studies & Research .... Dr. Virginia TORCZON
92 Dean Honors/Interdisciplinary Stds .... Dr. Joel D. SCHWARTZ
88 Dean of Undergraduate Studies .... Dr. Janice L. ZEMAN
104 Director of Global Education .... Ms. Sylvia MITTERNDORFER
86 Assoc VP Government Relations .... Ms. Frances C. BRADFORD
26 Chief Com Officer Univ Web/Design .... Mr. Brian WHITSON
88 Assoc VP Development/Campaign Dir .... Mr. Mark L. BEGLY
44 Assoc VP University Development .... Mr. Earl T. GRANGER
18 Assoc Vice Pres Facilities Mgmt .... Mr. Van DOBSON
35 Dean of Students .... Ms. Marjorie THOMAS
25 Director of Sponsored Programs .... Ms. Jane LOPEZ
22 Asst Director of Equal Opportunity .... Ms. Sharron GATLING
37 Director Student Financial Aid .... Mr. Edward P. IRISH
15 Chief Human Resources Officer .... Mr. John POMA
38 Director Counseling Center .... Dr. Warrenetta C. MANN
36 Director Career Development .... Ms. Kathleen L. POWELL
19 Chief W&M Police Department .... Ms. Deborah CHEESEBRO
21 Asst VP Financial Operations .... Vacant
23 Director Student Health Services .... Dr. Virginia D. WELLS
28 Dir of Ctr for Student Diversity .... Dr. Vernon HURTE
39 Assoc VP Stdnt Affs/Dir of Res Life .... Ms. Deborah BOYKIN
96 Dir of Procurement & Fixed Assets ...... Mr. Gregory W. JOHNSON
40 Manager W&M Bookstore .... Ms. Cathy PACHECO
100 Asst to President/Chief of Staff .... Mr. Michael J. FOX
101 Secretary to the Board of Visitors .... Mr. Michael J. FOX
04 Executive Asst to President .... Ms. Cynthia A. BRAUER
105 Director of University Web & Design .... Ms. Tina L. COLEMAN
88 Assoc VP for Health & Wellness .... Dr. Robert K. CRACE

Columbia College (G)

8300 Merrifield Avenue, Fairfax VA 22031
County: Fairfax FICE Identification: 041273
Unit ID: 455983
Telephone: (703) 206-0508 Carnegie Class: Assoc/HT-High Trad
FAX Number: (703) 206-0488 Calendar System: Other
URL: www.ccdc.edu
Established: 1999 Annual Undergrad Tuition & Fees: N/A
Enrollment: 428 Coed
Affiliation or Control: Proprietary IRS Status: Proprietary
Highest Offering: Associate Degree
Accreditation: ACICS, COE

01 President .... Dr. Richard K. KIM

Culinary Institute of Virginia (H)

2428 Almeda Avenue, Ste 106, Norfolk VA 23513
Telephone: (757) 858-2433 Identification: 770960
Accreditation: &SC

† Regional accreditation is carried under the parent institution in Virginia Beach, VA

Danville Regional Medical Center School of Health Professions (I)

142 South Main Street, Danville VA 24541
County: Independent City FICE Identification: 021116
Telephone: (434) 799-4510 Carnegie Class: Not Classified
FAX Number: (434) 799-3718 Calendar System: Semester
URL: www.danvilleregional.com
Established: 1898 Annual Undergrad Tuition & Fees: N/A
Enrollment: N/A Coed
Affiliation or Control: Proprietary IRS Status: Proprietary
Highest Offering: Associate Degree
Accreditation: ABHES, RAD

01 Director Radiology Pgms/Tech .... Mr. Kevin MURRAY

DeVry University - Arlington Campus (J)

2450 Crystal Drive, Arlington VA 22202-3887
Telephone: (703) 414-4000 Identification: 666220
Accreditation: &NH, ENGT

† Regional accreditation is carried under the parent institution in Downers Grove, IL.

Eastern Mennonite University (K)

1200 Park Road, Harrisonburg VA 22802-2462
County: Independent City FICE Identification: 003708
Unit ID: 232043
Telephone: (540) 432-4000 Carnegie Class: Masters/S
FAX Number: (540) 432-4444 Calendar System: Semester
URL: www.emu.edu
Established: 1917 Annual Undergrad Tuition & Fees: $32,300
Enrollment: 1,695 Coed
Affiliation or Control: Mennonite Church IRS Status: 501(c)3
Highest Offering: Master's
Accreditation: SC, CACREP, NURSE, PAST, SW, TED, THEOL

01 Interim President .... Dr. Lee F. SNYDER
05 Provost .... Dr. Fred L. KNISS
30 Vice President for Advancement .... Mr. Kirk L. SHISLER
10 Vice President for Finance .... Mr. Daryl W. BERT
84 Vice Pres Enrollment & Marketing .... Vacant
32 Vice President for Student Life .... Dr. Kenneth L. NAFZIGER
20 Vice Pres & Undergrad Academic Dean .... Dr. Deirdre SMELTZER
73 Seminary Dean .... Dr. Michael A. KING
06 University Registrar .... Mr. David A. DETROW
26 Director of Marketing Services .... Ms. Andrea S. WENGER
07 Director Undergraduate Admissions .... Mr. Matthew RUTH
08 Director of Libraries .... Dr. G. Marcille H. FREDERICK
37 Director of Financial Assistance .... Ms. Michele R. HENSLEY
36 Director Career Services/Testing .... Ms. Kimberly PHILLIPS
29 Director of Alumni/Parent Relations .... Mr. Jeffrey A. SHANK
09 Director Institutional Research .... Dr. Scott BARGE
04 Assistant to the President .... Ms. Twila K. YODER
41 Athletic Director .... Mr. David A. KING
42 Campus Pastor .... Mr. Brian M. BURKHOLDER
13 Director of Information Systems .... Mr. Benjamin S. BEACHY
18 Director of Physical Plant .... Mr. Ed LEHMAN
15 Director Human Resources .... Ms. Marcia J. ENGLE
21 Controller .... Mr. Timothy STUTZMAN
27 Chief Public Information Officer .... Mr. Michael J. ZUCCONI
35 Director Student Affairs .... Ms. Rachel R. SAWATZKY
38 Director Student Counseling .... Ms. Pamela D. COMER

Eastern Virginia Career College (A)

10304 Spotsylvania Avenue, Ste. 400,
Fredericksburg VA 22408-8605
County: Spotsylvania FICE Identification: 036543
Unit ID: 441858
Telephone: (540) 373-2200 Carnegie Class: Spec 2-yr-Health
FAX Number: (540) 373-4465 Calendar System: Other
URL: www.evcc.edu
Established: 2000 Annual Undergrad Tuition & Fees: N/A
Enrollment: 203 Coed
Affiliation or Control: Proprietary IRS Status: Proprietary
Highest Offering: Associate Degree
Accreditation: COE, OTA

01 Chief Executive Officer/President ....Ms. A. Christine CARROLL

Eastern Virginia Medical School (B)

Box 1980, Norfolk VA 23501-1980
County: Independent City FICE Identification: 010338
Unit ID: 231970
Telephone: (757) 446-5600 Carnegie Class: Spec-4-yr-Med
FAX Number: (757) 446-5135 Calendar System: Other
URL: www.evms.edu
Established: 1973 Annual Graduate Tuition & Fees: N/A
Enrollment: 1,049 Coed
Affiliation or Control: Independent Non-Profit IRS Status: 501(c)3
Highest Offering: Doctorate; No Undergraduates
Accreditation: SC, ARCPA, CLPSY, IPSY, MED, PH, SURGA

01 President/Provost/Dean ....Dr. Richard V. HOMAN
04 Sr Exec Assistant to the President .... Ms. Barbara C. ALBRIGHT
88 Director Internal Audit ....Mr. Robert B. WOOD
100 VP of Operations/Chief of Staff ....Mr. Brant M. COX
17 Vice Pres/Dean Sch of Health Prof ....Dr. Charles D. COMBS
88 Assoc Dean for Health Professions ....Dr. Jeffrey A. JOHNSON
10 Vice Pres Administration/Finance ..... Mr. Mark R. BABASHANIAN
19 Chief of Police ....Mr. Andrew J. MITCHELL
18 Director Facilities/Physical Plant ....Mr. Doug MARTIN
28 Vice President for Diversity ....Mr. Mekbib L. GEMEDA
45 Vice Dean for Faculty Affairs ....Dr. Elza MYLONA
88 Vice Dean Clinical Affairs .... Dr. Alfred Z. ABUHAMAD
23 CEO EVMS Medical Group ....Mr. James F. LIND
05 Vice Dean Academic Affairs ....Dr. Ronald W. FLENNER
43 Vice President and General Counsel ....Ms. Stacy R. PURCELL
58 Vice Dean Grad Medical Education ....Dr. Linda R. ARCHER
46 Vice Dean for Research ....Dr. Jerry L. NADLER
09 Sr Assoc Dean for Research ....Dr. William J. WASILENKO
88 Assoc Dean Hum Sub Protection/IRB ....Dr. Harry J. TILLMAN
50 Assoc Dean Business/Admin Affairs ....Mr. David E. HUBAND
84 Assoc Dean Admissions and Enroll ....Dr. Donald C. MEYER
32 Assoc Dean for Student Affairs ....Dr. Ann E. CAMPBELL
20 Asst Dean for Academic Affairs ..... Dr. Senthil K. RAJASEKARAN
08 Assoc Dean Library/Lrng Resource ....Ms. Judith R. MERCER
35 Asst Dean Student Affairs ....Dr. Tereasa W. BABINEAU
07 Asst Dean of Admissions ....Dr. Thomas D. KIMBLE
93 Asst Dean for Diversity ....Ms. Gail C. WILLIAMS
06 Registrar ....Mr. Michael J. DONLAN
15 Director Human Resources ....Mr. Matthew R. SCHENK
21 Asst VP for Financial Services .... Ms. Helen S. HESELIUS
72 Director for Technology Transfer .... Mr. Paul B. DIMARCO
37 Director Student Financial Aid .... Ms. Margaret L. MURPHY
21 Director for Business Management ......Ms. Tammy A. CHRISMAN
96 Director of Materials Management ....Mr. Steven LEE
13 Chief Information Officer ....Ms. Deborah A. TAYLOR
26 Chief Comm and Marketing Officer ....Dr. Vincent A. RHODES
29 Exec Director for Alumni Affairs .... Ms. Melissa W. LANG
30 Asst VP Development ....Ms. Connie L. MCKENZIE
88 Director of the Brock Institute ....Dr. Cynthia ROMERO
51 Director for Continuing Med Educ ....Ms. Drucie A. PAPAFIL
88 Director Occupational Health ....Ms. Heather SINGLETON
25 Director Sponsored Programs ....Ms. Yolanda F. DEMORY
88 Director Rad Safety Env Health ....Mr. Courtney A. KERR
88 Director Risk Management ....Ms. Donita M. LAMARAND

† Member of Virginia Consortium for Professional Psychology.

ECPI University (C)

5555 Greenwich Road, Virginia Beach VA 23462-6554
County: Independent City FICE Identification: 010198
Unit ID: 248934
Telephone: (757) 671-7171 Carnegie Class: Bac/Assoc-Mixed
FAX Number: (757) 671-8661 Calendar System: Semester
URL: www.ecpi.edu
Established: 1966 Annual Undergrad Tuition & Fees: $14,755
Enrollment: 10,932 Coed
Affiliation or Control: Proprietary IRS Status: Proprietary
Highest Offering: Master's
Accreditation: SC, ACFEI, MAAB, NUR

01 President ....Mr. Mark B. DREYFUS
12 Campus President .... Mr. Kevin PAVEGLIO
13 VP Info Systems/Financial Aid ....Mr. Jeff ARTHUR

ECPI University-Northern Virginia (D)

10021 Balls Ford Road, Ste 100, Manassas VA 20109
Telephone: (703) 563-8000 Identification: 770957
Accreditation: &SC, MAAB, RAD, SURTEC

† Regional accreditation is carried under the parent institution in Virginia Beach, VA

ECPI University-Richmond/Innsbrock (E)

4305 Cox Road, Glen Allen VA 23060
Telephone: (804) 934-0100 Identification: 770961
Accreditation: &SC

† Regional accreditation is carried under the parent institution in Virginia Beach, VA

ECPI University-Richmond/Moorefield (F)

800 Moorefield Park Drive, Richmond VA 23236
Telephone: (804) 330-5533 Identification: 770958
Accreditation: &SC, MAAB, SURTEC

† Regional accreditation is carried under the parent institution in Virginia Beach, VA

ECPI University-Roanoke (G)

5234 Airport Road, Roanoke VA 24012
Telephone: (540) 563-8000 Identification: 770959
Accreditation: &SC, MAAB

† Regional accreditation is carried under the parent institution in Virginia Beach, VA

Edward Via College of Osteopathic Medicine (H)

2265 Kraft Drive, Blacksburg VA 24060
County: Montgomery FICE Identification: 037093
Unit ID: 442806
Telephone: (540) 231-4000 Carnegie Class: Spec-4-yr-Med
FAX Number: (540) 231-5252 Calendar System: Semester
URL: www.vcom.vt.edu
Established: 2002 Annual Graduate Tuition & Fees: N/A
Enrollment: 1,444 Coed
Affiliation or Control: Independent Non-Profit IRS Status: 501(c)3
Highest Offering: Doctorate; No Undergraduates
Accreditation: OSTEO

01 President ....Dr. Dixie TOOKE-RAWLINS
05 Provost/EVP & Founding Dean ....Dr. Dixie TOOKE-RAWLINS
10 Associate Vice Pres Finance/CFO ....Mr. Marc HAMRIC
32 Vice Pres Student Services ....Mr. William KING
46 Assoc Vice Pres Research/Grad Stds .... Dr. Hara P. MISRA
11 Vice President Operations ....Mr. Bill PRICE
12 Vice Dean Carolinas Campus ....Dr. Timothy J. KOWALSKI
12 Dean Virginia Campus ....Dr. Jan M. WILLCOX
58 Vice Dean Post-Bac/Pre-med Program ... Dr. Francine ANDERSON
63 Vice Dean Post-Bacc/Medical Pgm .... Dr. Brian W. HILL
21 Sr Exec Dir Administrative Svcs ....Ms. Patty SMITH

Emory & Henry College (I)

PO Box 947, 30461 Garnand Drive,
Emory VA 24327-0947
County: Washington FICE Identification: 003709
Unit ID: 232025
Telephone: (276) 944-4121 Carnegie Class: Bac-A&S
FAX Number: (276) 944-6934 Calendar System: Semester
URL: www.ehc.edu
Established: 1836 Annual Undergrad Tuition & Fees: $30,900
Enrollment: 1,038 Coed
Affiliation or Control: United Methodist IRS Status: 501(c)3
Highest Offering: Doctorate
Accreditation: SC, #CAATE, @PTA, TEAC

01 President ....Mr. Jake B. SCHRUM
43 Exec Asst to Pres/General Counsel ....Mr. Mark R. GRAHAM
05 VP Academic Affairs/Dean ....Dr. David P. HANEY
10 VP for Business and Finance ....Mr. Richard K. GAUMER
32 VP Student Life/Dean of Students ....Ms. Pamela L. GOURLEY
30 VP for Institutional Advancement ....Mr. Joseph P. TAYLOR
84 Vice Pres for Enrollment Management ....Mr. Dave VOSKUIL
09 Dir Institutional Research/Effect ....Mr. Gregory G. STEINER
29 Director of Alumni Affairs ....Ms. Monica S. HOEL
37 Director of Financial Aid ....Ms. Scarlett BLEVINS
06 Registrar/Dir of CSA ....Ms. Lynn ELLIOTT
36 Director of Career Planning .... Ms. Amanda GARDNER
38 Director Student Counseling .... Ms. Jill M. SMELTZER
26 Director Public Relations ....Mr. Dirk S. MOORE
13 Chief Information Officer/Librarian ...... Ms. Lorraine N. ABRAHAM
18 Dir of Facilities Management .... Mr. Scott E. WILLIAMS
40 Bookstore Manager ....Mr. Terry RICHARDSON
42 Chaplain ....Rev Mary K. BRIGGS
15 Human Resources Manager .... Ms. Kim STEINER
20 Associate VP Academic Affairs ....Dr. Michael J. PUGLISI
35 Assistant Dean of Students .... Mr. Kyle CUTSHAW
21 Associate VP Business/Finance ....Ms. Benita BARE
07 Director of Admissions .... Mr. Matthew CRISMAN
39 Director of Housing .... Ms. Lacey SOUTHWICK
41 Director of Athletics ....Ms. Myra SIMS
19 Chief of Campus Police .... Mr. Scott POORE
102 Dir Foundation/Corporate Relations ....Ms. Kathi BOATWRIGHT
104 Director Study Abroad .... Dr. Celeste GAIA
105 Director Web Services ....Mr. Kevin CALL
44 Director Annual or Planned Giving .... Ms. Ronan KING
53 Director of Education Center ....Dr. Janet CRICKMER

Everest College (J)

825 Greenbrier Circle, Chesapeake VA 23320
County: Chesapeake City Identification: 667298
Unit ID: 438647
Telephone: (757) 361-3900 Carnegie Class: Spec 2-yr-Other
FAX Number: (757) 361-3917 Calendar System: Other
URL: www.everest.edu
Established: Annual Undergrad Tuition & Fees: N/A
Enrollment: 671 Coed
Affiliation or Control: Proprietary IRS Status: Proprietary
Highest Offering: Associate Degree
Accreditation: ACICS

Everest College (K)

803 Diligence Drive, Newport News VA 23606
County: Independent City FICE Identification: 009267
Unit ID: 232502
Telephone: (757) 873-1111 Carnegie Class: Assoc/HVT-High Non
FAX Number: (757) 873-0728 Calendar System: Other
URL: www.everest.edu
Established: 1941 Annual Undergrad Tuition & Fees: $9,960
Enrollment: 433 Coed
Affiliation or Control: Proprietary IRS Status: Proprietary
Highest Offering: Associate Degree
Accreditation: ACICS

01 President ....Mr. Aaron MORRIS
05 Director of Education ....Ms. Wanda FLEMING

† In teach-out mode. Tuition varies by degree program.

Faith Bible College (L)

6330 Newtown Rd, Ste 211, Norfolk VA 23502
Identification: 667285
Telephone: (757) 423-2095 Carnegie Class: Not Classified
FAX Number: (757) 222-1341 Calendar System: Semester
URL: www.faithbiblecollege.com
Established: 1995 Annual Undergrad Tuition & Fees: N/A
Enrollment: N/A Coed
Affiliation or Control: Independent Non-Profit IRS Status: 501(c)3
Highest Offering: Associate Degree
Accreditation: @BI

01 President ....Dr. Hap STRUTHERS
05 Provost .... Dr. Cherral MASON

Ferrum College (M)

PO Box 1000, 215 Ferrum Mtn Road,
Ferrum VA 24088-9001
County: Franklin FICE Identification: 003711
Unit ID: 232089
Telephone: (540) 365-2121 Carnegie Class: Bac-Diverse
FAX Number: (540) 365-4269 Calendar System: Semester
URL: www.ferrum.edu
Established: 1913 Annual Undergrad Tuition & Fees: $30,835
Enrollment: 1,451 Coed
Affiliation or Control: United Methodist IRS Status: 501(c)3
Highest Offering: Baccalaureate
Accreditation: SC, SW

01 President ....Dr. Joseph C. SPOONER
05 VP for Academic Affairs ....Dr. Gail SUMMER
10 VP for Business and Finance ....Mr. Chris BURNLEY
30 Vice Pres Institutional Advancement ....Mr. George SEALS
84 Vice Pres Enrollment Services ....Vacant
32 Vice President of Student Affairs .... Dr. Andrea P. ZUSCHIN
42 Dean of Chapel ....Dr. Jan C. NICHOLSON ANGLE
04 Presidential Assistant .... Ms. Courtney L. BROWN
06 Registrar ....Mrs. Yvonne S. WALKER
07 Dean of Admissions .... Mr. Jason D. BYRD
09 Director of Inst Research ....Mrs. Ursa JOHNSON
08 Director Stanley Library ....Ms. Brandi PORTER
37 Director of Financial Aid ....Ms. Heather HOLLANDSWORTH
29 Director Alumni & Family Programs .... Mrs. Tracy S. HOLLEY
26 Director of Public Relations ....Vacant
41 Director of Athletics ....Mr. J. Abraham NAFF
44 Regional Gift Officer .... Mr. Gene BOURNE
18 Director of Physical Plant .... Mr. Brad BISHOP
35 Dir Student Leadership & Engagement ....Mr. Justin MUSE
13 Dir of Network & Computer Svcs ....Mr. Daniel K. HODGES
15 Dir of Human Resources ....Mr. Chris CHANDLER
40 Bookstore Manager ....Mr. Josh JUSTUS
19 Chief of Ferrum College Police Dept ....Chief J. F. OWENS
36 Dir Career Svcs/Student Employment ....Vacant
88 Director of Academic Accessibility ....Ms. Nancy S. BEACH
91 Dir Administrative Computing ....Mr. Tim BELCHER
79 Dean School Arts & Humanities ....Dr. David B. HOWELL
81 Dean School Natural Science & Math ....Dr. Jinnie GARRETT
83 Dean School Social Sciences ....Dr. Kevin REILLY

Fortis College (N)

6300 Center Drive, Building 22, Norfolk VA 23502
County: Independent City FICE Identification: 023427
Unit ID: 233329
Telephone: (757) 499-5447 Carnegie Class: Spec 2-yr-Health
FAX Number: N/A Calendar System: Quarter
URL: www.fortis.edu/campuses

Established: Annual Undergrad Tuition & Fees: $17,804
Enrollment: 315 Coed
Affiliation or Control: Proprietary IRS Status: Proprietary
Highest Offering: Associate Degree
Accreditation: **ACICS**

01 President .... Ms. Darleen CERNOCH

Fortis College (A)

2000 Westmoreland Street, Suite A, Richmond VA 23230
Telephone: (804) 323-1020 Identification: 770815
Accreditation: **ACICS**, DA, SURGT

George Mason University (B)

4400 University Drive - MSN 3A1, Fairfax VA 22030-4444
County: Fairfax FICE Identification: 003749
Unit ID: 232186
Telephone: (703) 993-1000 Carnegie Class: DU-Highest
FAX Number: N/A Calendar System: Semester
URL: www.gmu.edu
Established: 1957 Annual Undergrad Tuition & Fees (In-State): $10,952
Enrollment: 33,729 Coed
Affiliation or Control: State IRS Status: 501(c)3
Highest Offering: Doctorate
Accreditation: **SC**, ART, BUS, BUSA, CAATE, CEA, CLPSY, CS, ENG, EXSC, HSA, IPSY, LAW, MUS, NRPA, NURSE, PH, SPAA, SW, TED

01 President .... Dr. Ángel CABRERA
05 Provost & Executive Vice President .... Dr. S. David WU
10 Senior VP of Administration/Finance .... Ms. Jennifer (J.J.) DAVIS
100 Chief of Staff .... Mr. Frank NEVILLE
07 Vice Pres Enrollment Management .... Mr. David BURGE
18 Vice President for Facilities .... Mr. Thomas G. CALHOUN
86 VP Government & Community Relations .... Mr. Paul LIBERTY
30 VP Univ Advancement & Alumni Rels .... Dr. Janet BINGHAM
13 VP Information Technology/CIO .... Ms. Marilyn SMITH
32 Vice President for University Life .... Ms. Rose PASCARELL
46 Vice President for Research .... Dr. Deborah CRAWFORD
22 VP Compliance/Diversity & Ethics .... Mr. Julian WILLIAMS
15 VP for HR/Payroll & Fac/Staff Life .... Ms. Linda HARBER
43 University Counsel .... Mr. Thomas M. MONCURE
45 Asst VP & Chief Budget Officer .... Mr. David MOORE
21 Assoc VP/Controller Fiscal Services .... Ms. Lisa KEMP
20 Vice Provost Academic Affairs .... Dr. Michelle MARKS
20 Assoc Prov for Undergrad Education .... Dr. Janette MUIR
88 Assoc Prov for Academic Admin .... Ms. Renate H. GUILFORD
58 Assoc Prov for Graduate Education .... Dr. Cody EDWARDS
35 Exec Dir Ofc of Student Involvement .... Ms. Lauren LONG
35 Assistant Vice Pres University Life .... Dr. Kahan SABLO
06 University Registrar .... Ms. Eve DAUER
37 Director Student Financial Aid .... Dr. Sandra TARBOX
36 Interim Director Univ Career Svcs .... Ms. Saskia CLAY-ROOKS
08 University Librarian .... Mr. John G. ZENELIS
23 Exec Director Student Health Svcs .... Dr. Wagida A. ABDALLA
29 Assoc VP Alumni Affairs .... Ms. Christine CLARK-TALLEY
41 Dir of Intercollegiate Athletics .... Mr. Brad EDWARDS
19 Interim Chief of Police .... Mr. Thomas LONGO
49 Dean Col of Humanities/Social Sci .... Dr. Deborah BOEHM-DAVIS
61 Dean School of Law .... Dr. Henry BUTLER
80 Dean School of Policy/Govt .... Dr. Mark ROZELL
50 Dean School of Business .... Dr. Sarah NUTTER
53 Dean College of Educ & Human Devel .... Dr. Mark R. GINSBERG
54 Dean Volgenau School of Engineering .... Dr. Kenneth BALL
66 Dean College of Health/Human Svcs .... Dr. Thomas R. PROHASKA
81 Dean College of Science .... Dr. Peggy AGOURIS
88 Dean Sch Conflict Analysis & Resol .... Dr. Kevin AVRUCH
88 Dean CVPA/Exec Dir HPAC .... Dr. Rick DAVIS
38 Exec Dir Counseling Center .... Dr. Barbara MEEHAN
09 Assoc Prov Institutional Research .... Dr. Thulasi KUMAR
96 Director of Purchasing and AP .... Mr. Cliff SHORE
04 Director of Presidential Admin .... Ms. Sharon CULLEN
101 Secretary pro tem to the Board .... Ms. Kathy CAGLE
39 Ast Dean Univ Life/Housing/Res Life .... Dr. Thomas HARDY
104 Exec Director Global Strategy .... Dr. Solon SIMMONS
108 Acting Dir Institutional Assessment .... Dr. Stephanie HAZEL
25 Asc VP Rsrch Ops Ofc Sponsored Pgms .... Mr. Mike LASKOFSKI
26 VP Communications & Marketing .... Vacant
44 Director Annual Giving .... Mr. Nick HERMAN

Global Health College (C)

6101 Stevenson Avenue, Alexandria VA 22304
County: Independent City FICE Identification: 041400
Unit ID: 455390
Telephone: (703) 212-7410 Carnegie Class: Spec 2-yr-Health
FAX Number: (703) 212-7414 Calendar System: Other
URL: www.global.edu
Established: 2004 Annual Undergrad Tuition & Fees: $19,037
Enrollment: 361 Coed
Affiliation or Control: Proprietary IRS Status: Proprietary
Highest Offering: Baccalaureate
Accreditation: **ACICS**, PNUR

01 President .... Mariatu KARGBO
10 Vice Pres Administration/Fiscal Svc .... Bernard FRISBY

Hampden-Sydney College (D)

College Road, PO Box 128,
Hampden-Sydney VA 23943-0667
County: Prince Edward FICE Identification: 003713
Unit ID: 232256
Telephone: (434) 223-6000 Carnegie Class: Bac-A&S
FAX Number: (434) 223-6350 Calendar System: Semester
URL: www.hsc.edu
Established: 1775 Annual Undergrad Tuition & Fees: $41,730
Enrollment: 1,105 Male
Affiliation or Control: Presbyterian Church (U.S.A.) IRS Status: 501(c)3
Highest Offering: Baccalaureate
Accreditation: **SC**

01 President .... Dr. John L. STIMPERT
05 Provost and Dean of Faculty .... Dr. Dennis G. STEVENS
20 Associate Dean of the Faculty .... Dr. Walter M. MCDERMOTT
10 VP Business Affairs & Finance .... Mr. W. Glenn CULLEY, JR.
30 VP Institutional Advancement .... Dr. H. Lee KING, JR.
11 VP Strategy/Admin & Board Affairs .... Dr. V. Dale JONES
07 Dean of Admissions .... Ms. Anita H. GARLAND
32 Dean of Students .... Dr. David A. KLEIN
20 Associate Dean Academic Success .... Ms. Lisa A. BURNS
41 Director of Athletics .... Mr. Richard P. EPPERSON, II
08 Director of the Library & Computing .... Ms. Shaunna E. HUNTER-MCKINNEY
06 Registrar .... Ms. Dawn L. CONGLETON
37 Director of Financial Aid .... Ms. Zita M. BARREE
29 Director of Alumni Relations .... Mr. James E. BARTON
18 Director of Physical Plant .... Mr. John C. PRENGAMAN
36 Dir Career Ed/Vocational Reflection .... Ms. Ellen Lea MASTERS
23 Director of Student Health Center .... Ms. Andrea R. JONES
15 Director of Human Resources .... Ms. Barbara S. ARMENTROUT
19 Int Dir Public Safety/Chf of Police .... Mr. Scott E. WILLIAMS
40 Bookstore Manager .... Ms. Kimberly S. MICHAUX
09 Assoc Dean Inst Effectiveness .... Dr. Christine C. ROSS
26 Director Communications & Marketing .... Mr. Thomas H. SHOMO
21 Controller .... Mr. Michael A. SMITH
35 Dir of Student Affairs Operations .... Ms. Sandy P. COOKE
39 Director of Residence Life .... Mr. John R C. RAMSAY
25 Director Grants & Special Projects .... Ms. P. J. TOWNSEND
104 Dir Global Education & Study Abroad .... Dr. Daniella WIDDOWS

Hampton University (E)

100 E. Queen Street, Hampton VA 23668
County: Independent City FICE Identification: 003714
Unit ID: 232265
Telephone: (757) 727-5000 Carnegie Class: Masters/M
FAX Number: (757) 727-5085 Calendar System: Semester
URL: www.hamptonu.edu
Established: 1868 Annual Undergrad Tuition & Fees: $23,112
Enrollment: 4,393 Coed
Affiliation or Control: Independent Non-Profit IRS Status: 501(c)3
Highest Offering: Doctorate
Accreditation: **SC**, AAB, CACREP, CS, ENG, IACBE, JOUR, MUS, NURSE, PHAR, PTA, SP, TED

01 President .... Dr. William R. HARVEY
05 Executive Vice President & Provost .... Dr. JoAnn W. HAYSBERT
10 Vice Pres Business Affs/Treasurer .... Mrs. Doretha J. SPELLS
11 Vice Pres for Administrative Svcs .... Dr. Barbara L. INMAN
43 Vice President/General Counsel .... Atty. Faye HARDY-LUCAS
30 Vice President for Development .... Mrs. Iris RAMEY
04 Executive Assistant to President .... Dr. Charrita D. DANLEY
32 Assoc Vice Pres for Student Affairs .... Vacant
21 Asst VP Business Affs/Comptroller .... Mrs. Denise NICHOLS
25 Asst Vice Pres Grants Management .... Mrs. Lillie F. GREEN
20 Asst Provost Academic Affairs .... Dr. Pollie MURPHY
13 Assistant Provost Technology .... Vacant
26 Asst VP for Marketing .... Ms. B. DaVida PLUMMER
45 Asst Prov Research & Grantsmanship .... Dr. Michelle PENN-MARSHALL
88 Dean of Judicial Affairs .... Mr. Woodson H. HOPEWELL, JR.
39 Dean of Residential Life .... Miss Jewel B. LONG
07 Dean of Admissions .... Mrs. Angela BOYD
06 Registrar .... Mrs. Jorsene COOPER
36 Dir Career Counsel/Planning Ctr .... Mrs. Vivian DAVID
38 Int Director Counseling Center .... Dr. Linda KIRKLAND-HARRIS
08 Administrator University Libraries .... Vacant
29 Director of Alumni Affairs .... Ms. Brint MARTIN
15 Director of Human Resources .... Ms. Rikki THOMAS
14 Director Computer Center .... Mr. Darien HAWKINS
37 Financial Aid Officer .... Mr. Martin MILES
27 Director of University Relations .... Mrs. Yuri Rodgers MILLIGAN
09 Director Institutional Research .... Mrs. Michelle CLAWSON
23 Director Student Health Services .... Dr. Karen WILLIAMS
42 University Chaplain .... Rev. Debra L. HAGGINS
18 Director Buildings & Grounds .... Mr. Randall HARDY
87 Director of Summer Sessions .... Dr. Pollie MURPHY
19 Chief of Campus Police .... Mr. David GLOVER
86 Director Government Relations .... Mr. Wilbert L. THOMAS
96 Director of Purchasing .... Vacant
40 University Bookstore Manager .... Ms. Michelle R. MILLER
53 Dean School of Liberal Arts .... Dr. Linda MALONE-COLON
66 Interim Dean School of Nursing .... Dr. Hilda WILLIAMSON
81 Assistant Dean School of Science .... Dr. Michelle CLAVILLE
51 Dean Sch Educ/Human Development .... Dr. Cassandra HERRING
50 Dean School of Business .... Dr. Sid H. CREDLE
54 Dean Sch of Engineering/Technology .... Dr. Eric J. SHEPPARD
67 Dean School of Pharmacy .... Dr. Wayne HARRIS
58 Dean the Graduate College .... Dr. Michelle PENN-MARSHALL
60 Dean Scripps Howard Sch Journ/Comm .... Mr. Brett PULLEY
88 Dean University College .... Dr. Almarie MUNLEY

Hollins University (F)

PO Box 9688, Roanoke VA 24020-1688
County: Roanoke FICE Identification: 003715
Unit ID: 232308
Telephone: (540) 362-6000 Carnegie Class: Bac-A&S
FAX Number: (540) 362-6642 Calendar System: 4/1/4
URL: www.hollins.edu
Established: 1842 Annual Undergrad Tuition & Fees: $35,635
Enrollment: 770 Female
Affiliation or Control: Independent Non-Profit IRS Status: 501(c)3
Highest Offering: Master's
Accreditation: **SC**, TEAC

01 President .... Ms. Nancy O. GRAY
10 Vice Pres Finance/Administration .... Ms. Kerry EDMONDS
30 Vice Pres for External Relations .... Ms. Audrey STONE
84 Vice President of Enrollment .... Mr. Jason HAMILTON
05 Chair of the Faculty .... Mr. Michael GETTINGS
32 Dean of Students .... Ms. Patty O'TOOLE
20 Dean Academic Services .... Ms. Rebecca BEACH
28 Associate Dean Intercultural Pgms .... Ms. Jeri L. SUAREZ
04 Executive Assistant to President .... Ms. Brook E. DICKSON
88 Director Alumnae & Donor Relations .... Vacant
06 Registrar .... Ms. Patricia BROKKEN
08 Director of the Library .... Mr. Luke VILELLE
15 Director of Human Resources .... Ms. Alicia GODZWA
26 Director of Public Relations .... Mr. Jeff HODGES
29 Director of Alumnae Relations .... Ms. Nikki WILLIAMS
36 Director Career Development Center .... Ms. Ashley GLENN
37 Director Financial Aid .... Ms. Mary Jean CORRISS
41 Director of Athletics .... Mr. William MANNINO
09 Asst Dir Institutional Research .... Ms. Katie READ
18 Director Plant Operations/Services .... Ms. Mae RAMSEY
104 Director International Programs .... Vacant
13 Chief Info Technology Officer .... Ms. Carol REED
19 Director Security/Safety .... Mr. David CARLSON
39 Dir Housing & Residential Life .... Ms. Melissa HINE
07 Director of Admissions .... Ms. Ashley BROWNING

iGlobal University (G)

7700 Little River Turnpike, Ste 600, Annandale VA 22003
County: Fairfax Identification: 667105
Unit ID: 483780
Telephone: (703) 941-2020 Carnegie Class: Not Classified
FAX Number: (703) 941-2025 Calendar System: Quarter
URL: www.iglobaluniversity.org
Established: 2008 Annual Undergrad Tuition & Fees: $13,820
Enrollment: 173 Coed
Affiliation or Control: Proprietary IRS Status: Proprietary
Highest Offering: Master's
Accreditation: **ACICS**

01 President & CEO .... Dr. David Y. SOHN
05 Director .... Mr. Dustin CASSELL

Institute for the Psychological Sciences (H)

2001 Jefferson Davis Hwy, Ste 511,
Arlington VA 22202-3609
County: Arlington FICE Identification: 038724
Unit ID: 445869
Telephone: (703) 416-1441 Carnegie Class: Spec-4-yr-Other Health
FAX Number: (703) 416-8588 Calendar System: Semester
URL: www.ipsciences.edu
Established: 1998 Annual Graduate Tuition & Fees: N/A
Enrollment: 101 Coed
Affiliation or Control: Independent Non-Profit IRS Status: 501(c)3
Highest Offering: Doctorate; No Undergraduates
Accreditation: **SC**, CLPSY

Ivy Christian College (I)

9401 Mathy Drive, Ste 200, Fairfax VA 22031
County: Fairfax Identification: 667213
Telephone: (703) 425-4143 Carnegie Class: Not Classified
FAX Number: (703) 425-4148 Calendar System: Quarter
URL: www.iccvau.org
Established: 2006 Annual Undergrad Tuition & Fees: N/A
Enrollment: N/A Coed
Affiliation or Control: Independent Non-Profit IRS Status: 501(c)3
Highest Offering: Baccalaureate
Accreditation: **TRACS**

01 President .... Dr. David Y. PAK
05 Academic Dean .... Pastor Youn LEE

James Madison University (J)

800 S Main Street, Harrisonburg VA 22807-0001
County: Independent City FICE Identification: 003721
Unit ID: 232423
Telephone: (540) 568-6211 Carnegie Class: Masters/L
FAX Number: N/A Calendar System: Semester
URL: www.jmu.edu
Established: 1908 Annual Undergrad Tuition & Fees (In-State): $10,018
Enrollment: 20,855 Coed
Affiliation or Control: State IRS Status: 501(c)3
Highest Offering: Doctorate
Accreditation: **SC**, ARCPA, ART, AUD, BUS, BUSA, CAATE, CACREP, CS, DANCE, DIETD, ENG, ENGR, IPSY, MUS, NURSE, OT, PSPSY, SP, SPAA, SW, TED, THEA

01 President ....Mr. Jonathan R. ALGER
05 Provost/Senior VP Academic Affairs ....Dr. Jerry BENSON
10 Sr Vice Pres Administration/Finance ....Mr. Charles W. KING
32 Sr VP Student Affairs/Univ Planning ....Dr. Mark J. WARNER
30 Vice Pres University Advancement ....Dr. Nick LANGRIDGE
84 VP Access and Enrollment Mgmt ....Ms. Donna L. HARPER
04 Exec Assistant to the President .Mrs. Maggie BURKHART-EVANS
81 Dean College Science/Math ....Dr. Cynthia BAUERLE
49 Dean College Arts/Letters ....Dr. David K. JEFFREY
76 Dean Col of Health & Behav Studies ....Dr. Sharon LOVELL
50 Dean College of Business ....Dr. Mary GOWAN
57 Dean College Visual Performing Arts ....Dr. George E. SPARKS
53 Dean College of Education ....Dr. Phillip M. WISHON
72 Dean College of Int Science & Engr ....Dr. Robert KOLVOORD
58 Dean Graduate School ....Dr. Jie CHEN
97 Dean University Studies ....Dr. Linda C. HALPERN
08 Dean of Libraries/Educ Technologies ....Dr. Adam A. MURRAY
43 University Counsel ....Ms. Susan L. WHEELER
45 Asst Vice Pres Budget Management ....Ms. Diane L. STAMP
07 Dean of Admissions ....Mr. Michael D. WALSH
37 Dir Financial Aid & Scholarships ....Ms. Lisa L. TUMER
15 Director Human Resources ....Ms. Diane YERIAN
09 Director Institutional Research ....Dr. Frank J. DOHERTY
41 Director of Athletics ....Mr. Jeffrey T. BOURNE
26 Dir Comm & Univ Spokesperson ....Mr. Bill J. WYATT
06 University Registrar ....Ms. Michele M. WHITE
19 Chief of Police ....Mr. Lee A. SHIFFLETT
22 Dir of EEO ....Mr. James R. ROBINSON
29 Director Alumni Relations ....Ms. Ashley E. PRIVOTT
27 Senior Advancement Marketing Dir ....Mr. David R. TAYLOR

Jefferson College of Health Sciences (A)

101 Elm Avenue S.E., Roanoke VA 24013

County: Independent City FICE Identification: 006622
Unit ID: 231837
Telephone: (540) 985-8483 Carnegie Class: Spec-4-yr-Other Health
FAX Number: (540) 224-6703 Calendar System: Semester
URL: www.jchs.edu
Established: 1982 Annual Undergrad Tuition & Fees: $24,400
Enrollment: 1,131 Coed
Affiliation or Control: Independent Non-Profit IRS Status: 501(c)3
Highest Offering: Doctorate
Accreditation: SC, ARCPA, COARC, EMT, MT, NURSE, OT, OTA, PTAA, SURGT

01 President ....Dr. Nathaniel L. BISHOP
05 Dean Academic Affairs ....Dr. Lisa ALLISON-JONES
11 Dean Administrative Services ....Ms. Anna S. MILLIRONS
32 Dean Student Affairs ....Mr. B. Scott HILL
18 Safety/Physical Plant Officer ....Ms. Susan L. BOOTH
108 Dean for Inst Effectiveness ....Dr. Glen R. MAYHEW
84 Sr Director Enrollment Management ....Ms. Connie S. COOK
30 Director of Development ....Mr. Erik W. WILLIAMS
49 Chair Arts & Sciences ....Dr. Francis C. DANE
66 Chair Nursing ....Dr. Ava G. PORTER
88 Chair Rehab/Wellness ....Dr. Glen R. MAYHEW
88 Pgm Director Physician Assistant ....Dr. Sarah L. NICELY
88 Pgm Director Health & Exercise Sci . Dr. Allison H. BOWERSOCK
88 Pgm Director Emergency Services ....Mr. John C. COOK
88 Director Biomed/Science/Math ....Dr. Robin L. DAVIES
88 Pgm Director Physical Therapy Asst ....Ms. Rebecca DUFF
88 Pgm Director Doctor Occ Therapy ....Dr. David A. HAYNES
79 Director Humanities & Soc Sciences .....Dr. Courtney D. WATSON
88 Pgm Director Medical Lab Science ....Ms. Laura R. LINK
88 Pgm Director Occ Therapy Assistant ....Ms. Ave M. MITTA
88 Pgm Dir Family Nurse Practitioner ....Dr. Rhoda R. MURRAY
88 Pgm Director Healthcare Mgmt BS ....Ms. Carey H. PEERMAN
88 Pgm Director Respiratory Therapy ....Dr. Chase POULSEN
88 Pgm Director Surgical Technology ....Mr. John D. RATLIFF
88 Pgm Director Health Psychology ....Dr. Robert C. REESE
88 Program Dir Doctor Health Sciences ....Dr. Robert C. RIMKIS
88 Program Director RN-to-BSN ....Dr. Milena STAYKOVA
88 Program Director Doctor Nursing ....Dr. Patty M. VARI
88 Director InterProfessional Educ ....Ms. Kimberly WHITER
88 Pgm Director Health
Sciences ....Dr. Diana L. WILLEMAN-BUCKELEW
88 Pgm Director Accelerated/Trad BSN ....Dr. Kimberly M. WILSON
21 Bursar ....Ms. Tonia Y. ANDREWS
40 Manager Bookstore ....Ms. Suzanne M. ANDERSON
35 Student Life Administrator ....Ms. Elizabeth A. COSTA
25 Sponsored Projects Coordinator ....Ms. Amanda M. ELLINGER
04 Admin Assistant to President ....Ms. Andrea G. WELLMAN
37 Director of Financial Aid ....Ms. Debra J. JOHNSON
26 Senior Consultant Communications ....Mr. Mark A. LAMBERT
07 Director of Admissions ....Ms. Judith O. MCKEON
09 Director Institutional Research ....Dr. Timothy R. MILLARD
88 Director of Academic Support Svcs ....Mr. Al W. OVERSTREET
39 Residence Life Coordinator ....Ms. Stephanie SIMPSON
38 Director Counseling and Wellness ....Dr. Jennifer J. SLUSHER
08 Director Library ....Ms. Ramona H. THISS
106 Dir Online & Continuing Education ....Ms. Margie B. VEST
06 Registrar ....Ms. Linda C. WILLIAMS
88 Disability Services Coordinator ....Ms. Katie BOUCHARD

The John Leland Center for Theological Studies (B)

1306 N Highland Street, Arlington VA 22201

County: Arlington Identification: 666340
Telephone: (703) 812-4757 Carnegie Class: Not Classified
FAX Number: (703) 812-4764 Calendar System: Other
URL: www.leland.edu
Established: 1998 Annual Graduate Tuition & Fees: N/A
Enrollment: N/A Coed
Affiliation or Control: Baptist IRS Status: 501(c)3
Highest Offering: Master's; No Undergraduates
Accreditation: THEOL

01 President ....Dr. Mark J. OLSON
05 Academic Dean ....Dr. John LEE
04 Assistant to the President ....Ms. Shana WRIGHT
08 Librarian ....Ms. Monica LEAK
06 Registrar ....Ms. Andrea BAKKE
07 Director Recruiting/Admissions ....Mr. Daniel BRIDGEFORTH
10 Chief Business Officer ....Mr. Mel HARRIS
21 Associate Business Officer ....Mr. Jonathan RIDER
26 Chief Public Relations Officer ....Ms. Vicki BOHANNON

Kings Park University (C)

4613-D Pinecrest Office Park Drive, Alexandria VA 22312

County: Fairfax Identification: 667158
Telephone: (703) 354-3533 Carnegie Class: Not Classified
FAX Number: (703) 354-3577 Calendar System: Trimester
URL: www.kpu.us
Established: 2000 Annual Graduate Tuition & Fees: N/A
Enrollment: N/A Coed
Affiliation or Control: Independent Non-Profit IRS Status: 501(c)3
Highest Offering: Master's; No Undergraduates
Accreditation: ACUP

01 President ....Rev. Tae JONG PARK

Liberty University (D)

1971 University Boulevard, Lynchburg VA 24515

County: Independent City FICE Identification: 020530
Unit ID: 232557
Telephone: (434) 582-2000 Carnegie Class: DU-Mod
FAX Number: (434) 582-2304 Calendar System: Semester
URL: www.liberty.edu
Established: 1971 Annual Undergrad Tuition & Fees: $20,109
Enrollment: 81,459 Coed
Affiliation or Control: Other IRS Status: 501(c)3
Highest Offering: Doctorate
Accreditation: SC, ACBSP, CAATE, CACREP, CS, ENG, EXSC, LAW, MUS, NURSE, @OSTEO, @SW, TED

01 President ....Mr. Jerry FALWELL, JR.
03 Executive Vice President & COO ....Mr. Randy SMITH
05 Provost ....Dr. Ronald E. HAWKINS
10 Chief Financial Officer ....Mr. Don MOON
32 Sr Vice President Student Affairs ....Dr. Mark L. HINE
84 Sr VP Enrollment Management ....Mr. Chris JOHNSON
109 Senior VP for Auxiliary Services ....Mr. Lee BEAUMONT
26 Executive VP for Marketing ....Mr. Ron KENNEDY
15 Vice President Human Resources ....Mrs. Laura J. WALLACE
88 Vice Pres for Spiritual Development ....Mr. David NASSER
45 AVP for Institutional Effectiveness ....Dr. F. William WHEELER
13 Chief Information Officer ....Mr. Matthew J. ZEALAND
06 Registrar ....Mr. Luke GENTALA
43 General Counsel ....Mr. David M. CORRY
29 Director of Alumni Affairs ....Mr. Tyler FALWELL
08 Dean Jerry Falwell Library ....Ms. Angela RICE
86 Dean Helms School of Government ....Mr. Shawn D. AKERS
37 Sr VP University Financial Services ....Dr. Robert L. RITZ
45 Sr VP for Planning & Construction ....Mr. Charles SPENCE
07 VP of Admissions ....Dr. Steve PETERSON
31 VP Community Relations ....Dr. Barry MOORE
88 VP Special Proj & Bus Development ....Mr. Chris CARROLL
88 Vice Provost for LUO Academy ....Dr. Jay SPENCER
41 Director of Athletics ....Mr. Jeff BARBER
49 Dean College of Arts & Sciences ....Dr. Roger D. SCHULTZ
50 Dean School of Business ....Dr. Scott M. HICKS
60 Dean School of Communication ....Dr. Norm MINTLE
97 Dean CASAS ....Dr. Brian YATES
73 Dean School of Divinity ....Dr. Ed HINDSON
53 Dean School of Education ....Dr. Heather SCHOFFSTALL
35 Director of Campus Recreation ....Mr. Chris MISIANO
18 Vice Pres of Field Operations ....Mr. Scott STARNES
19 Chief of Police LUPD ....Col. Richard HINKLEY
72 Dean School of Engineering and CSCI ....Mr. David DONAHOO
28 Dir Ctr for Multicltrl Enrichment ....Ms. Melany PEARL
106 Exec Director LUO Enrollment ......Mrs. Tamela CRICKENBERGER
88 Vice Provost for Academic Op ....Dr. Kevin D. CORSINI
61 Dean School of Law ....Mr. Keith FAULKNER
88 Dean School of Aeronautics ....Mr. Jim MOLLOY
88 Dir Center for Teaching Excellence ....Mrs. Sharon WHEELER
97 Vice Provost for UG Education ....Dr. Emily HEADY
88 Dean English Language Institute ....Dr. Bill WEGERT
58 Vice Provost for Grad Education ....Dr. Doug MANN
76 Dean School of Health Sciences ....Dr. Ralph LINSTRA
63 Dean College of Osteopathic Med ....Dr. Ronnie MARTIN
64 Dean School of Music ....Dr. Vernon WHALEY
88 Vice Provost for Academic Admin ....Dr. Ben GUTIERREZ
35 Dean of Students ....Mr. Robert MULLEN
88 Director of Risk Management ....Mr. Robert WELLS
66 Dean School of Nursing ....Dr. Deanna BRITT
88 Dean of Resident Admissions ....Mr. Terry ELAM

Longwood University (E)

201 High Street, Farmville VA 23909-1801

County: Prince Edward FICE Identification: 003719
Unit ID: 232566
Telephone: (434) 395-2000 Carnegie Class: Masters/M
FAX Number: (434) 395-2635 Calendar System: Semester
URL: www.longwood.edu
Established: 1839 Annual Undergrad Tuition & Fees (In-State): $11,910
Enrollment: 5,096 Coed
Affiliation or Control: State IRS Status: 501(c)3
Highest Offering: Master's
Accreditation: SC, BUS, CAATE, EXSC, MUS, NRPA, NURSE, SP, SW, TED, THEA

01 President ....Mr. W. Taylor REVELEY, IV
05 Provost/Vice Pres Academic Affairs ....Dr. Joan NEFF
10 Vice Pres Administration & Finance ....Mr. Kenneth COPELAND
32 Vice President for Student Affairs ....Dr. Tim J. PIERSON
86 VP for Commonwealth Relations ....Ms. Courtney HODGES
45 VP for Strategic Operations ....Ms. Victoria KINDON
13 Chief Information Officer ....Ms. Victoria KINDON
84 Assoc VP Enrollment Management ....Dr. Jennifer K. GREEN
26 Assoc VP Publ/Mktg/Communications ....Ms. Sabrina BROWN
09 Interim Dir Assess/Inst Research ....Dr. David LEHR
06 Registrar ....Mrs. Susan HINES
08 Interim Dean of Library ....Ms. Tammy HINES
29 Assistant VP for Alumni Relations ....Mr. Ryan CATHERWOOD
28 Dir Citizen Ldrshp/Soc Justice Educ ....Mr. Jonathan E. PAGE
38 Director Student Counseling ....Dr. Maureen J. WALLS-MCKAY
36 Director University Career Center ....Ms. Ashley CRUTE
37 Director Student Financial Aid ....Ms. Melissa D. SHEPHERD
15 Chief Human Resources Officer ....Ms. Lisa MOONEY
18 Dir Facilities Operations Services ....Mr. Alvin B. MYERS
96 Director of Materiel Management ....Ms. Cathryn B. MOBLEY
100 Chief of Staff ....Mr. Justin POPE
41 Athletic Director ....Mr. Troy AUSTIN

Lynchburg College (F)

1501 Lakeside Drive, Lynchburg VA 24501-3199

County: Independent City FICE Identification: 003720
Unit ID: 232609
Telephone: (434) 544-8100 Carnegie Class: Masters/M
FAX Number: (434) 544-8499 Calendar System: Semester
URL: www.lynchburg.edu
Established: 1903 Annual Undergrad Tuition & Fees: $35,555
Enrollment: 2,736 Coed
Affiliation or Control: Christian Church (Disciples Of Christ)
IRS Status: 501(c)3
Highest Offering: Doctorate
Accreditation: SC, ACBSP, #ARCPA, CAATE, EXSC, MUS, NURSE, PTA

01 President ....Dr. Kenneth R. GARREN
05 Vice Pres & Dean for Academic Affs ....Dr. Sally SELDEN
10 Vice President Business & Finance ....Mr. Steve BRIGHT
30 Sr Vice President Advancement ....Dr. J. Michael BONNETTE
84 Vice Pres Enrollment Management ....Mrs. Rita DETWILER
32 Vice Pres & Dean of Student Develop .....Mr. Hayward GUENARD
09 Vice Pres Institutional Research ....Mrs. Debbie DRISCOLL
26 Assistant VP Communications & Mktg ....Mr. Mike JONES
50 Dean School Business & Economics ....Dr. Joseph TUREK
53 Dean School Education/Human Devel ....Dr. Roger JONES
60 Dean Sch Communications & The Arts ....Dr. Oeida HATCHER
79 Dean Sch Humanities/Social Science ....Dr. Charles WATSON
81 Dean School of Sciences ....Dr. Barry LOBB
76 Dean Sch Health Science/Human Perf ....Dr. Jean ST. CLAIR
06 Registrar/Asst Dean Acad/Stdnt Info ....Mr. Jay K. WEBB
08 Director of the Library .. Mr. Christopher A. MILLSON-MARTULA
37 Assoc Director of Financial Aid ....Ms. Michelle DAVIS
07 Director of Admissions ....Ms. Sharon WALTERS-BOWER

Mary Baldwin University (G)

318 Prospect Street, Staunton VA 24401

County: Augusta FICE Identification: 003723
Unit ID: 232672
Telephone: (540) 887-7000 Carnegie Class: Bac-A&S
FAX Number: (540) 886-5561 Calendar System: Other
URL: www.mbc.edu
Established: 1842 Annual Undergrad Tuition & Fees: $30,331
Enrollment: 1,754 Female
Affiliation or Control: Presbyterian Church (U.S.A.) IRS Status: 501(c)3
Highest Offering: Doctorate
Accreditation: SC, #ARCPA, OT, @PTA, SW, TEAC

01 President ....Dr. Pamela FOX
05 Interim Provost ....Dr. Oliver EVANS
10 Exec Vice President Finance/Admin ....Mr. David MOWEN
84 VP Enrollment Mgmt ....Ms. Lois H. WILLIAMS
30 Vice Pres University Advancement ....Ms. Sherri MYLOTT
26 SVP of University Relations ....Ms. Crista CABE
76 VP of MDCHS ....Dr. Linda SEESTEDT-STANFORD
88 Assoc VP for Inclusive
Excellence ....Rev. Andrea CORNELL-SCOTT
88 Commandant VWIL/Spec Asst to Pres .....BGen. Teresa A. DJURIC
88 Dir of Accred/Spec Asst to Pres ....Dr. Lewis D. ASKEGAARD
11 Dir of Admin & Student Success ....Ms. Lallon POND
09 Institutional Repts/Research Coord ....Ms. Carrie BOYD
13 Chief Information Officer ....Mr. Angus MCQUEEN
06 Registrar ....Ms. Kimberlely D. ROBINSON
08 Director of Library ....Ms. Carol CREAGER
49 Dean of College of Arts & Sciences ....Dr. Martha J. WALKER
50 Dean of Col Business & Prof
Stds ....Dr. Joseph R. SPRANGEL, JR.
53 Dean of College of Education ....Dr. Rachel POTTER
57 Director MLitt/MFA ....Dr. Paul MENZER
88 Dir Program for Exception Gifted ....Vacant

15 Director of Human Resources .... Ms. Shelly IRVINE
32 Assoc VP of Student Life .... Ms. Lisa WELLS
18 Director Facilities Management .... Mr. Brent DOUGLASS
21 Dir of Budgets/Business Operation .... Mr. Rick CZERWINSKI
29 Director of Alumni Relations .... Ms. Kim M. HUTTO
36 Director Career to Career Center .... Ms. Nell DESMOND
37 Director of Financial Aid .... Ms. Robin DIETRICH
04 Executive Presidential Assistant .... Ms. Sharon S. BOSSERMAN
41 Athletic Director .... Ms. Lynda J. ALANKO
07 Dir of Admiss for Adult & Grad Stds .... Mr. Daryl L. KINGREY
19 Director Security/Safety .... Mr. Thomas L. BYERLY

Marymount University (A)

2807 N Glebe Road, Arlington VA 22207-4299
County: Arlington FICE Identification: 003724
Unit ID: 232706
Telephone: (703) 522-5600 Carnegie Class: Masters/L
FAX Number: (703) 284-1637 Calendar System: Semester
URL: www.marymount.edu
Established: 1950 Annual Undergrad Tuition & Fees: $28,310
Enrollment: 3,441 Coed
Affiliation or Control: Roman Catholic IRS Status: 501(c)3
Highest Offering: Doctorate
Accreditation: SC, ACBSP, CACREP, CAEP, CIDA, HSA, NURSE, PTA, TED

01 President .... Dr. Matthew D. SHANK
05 Interim Provost & VP Acad Affairs .... Dr. Rita WONG
10 Vice Pres for Financial Affairs .... Mr. Alphonso V. DIAZ
30 Vice Pres University Advancement .... Mr. Joseph FOSTER
32 Vice Pres for Student Affairs .... Dr. Linda MCMURDOCK
09 Assoc VP Planning & Inst Effect .... Mr. Michael SCHUCHERT
20 Assoc VP Academic Affairs .... Mrs. Bridget MURPHY
84 Assoc VP Enrollment Mgmt & Dir Grad ...... Mrs. Francesca REED
21 Asst Vice Pres and Controller .... Mr. Ronald SOMERVELL
109 Asst Vice Pres Campus Plng & Mgmt .... Mr. Upendra MALANI
08 Dean Library & Learning Services .... Dr. Zary MOSTASHARI
35 Dean Student Life .... Mrs. Christina RAJMAIRA
36 Dean Student Success .... Dr. David WILMES
49 Dean Arts & Sciences .... Dr. Christina CLARK
50 Dean Business Administration .... Dr. James RYERSON
53 Dean Education & Human Services .... Dr. Lois STOVER
66 Dean Health Professions .... Dr. Jeanne MATTHEWS
58 Assoc Dean for Grad & Prof Studies .... Dr. Jason CRAIG
89 Assoc Dean First Year Experience .... Ms. Yolanda GIBSON
88 Asst Dean Student Engagement .... Mr. Vernon WILLIAMS
06 University Registrar .... Mrs. Simone WOUNG
12 Executive Director Reston Center .... Mr. Lawrence HOFFMAN
13 Exec Director IT Services .... Mr. Steve MUNSON
15 Exec Dir Human Resource Svcs .... Vacant
104 Exec Dir Center for Global Studies .... Mr. Victor BETANCOURT SANTIAGO
88 Int Exec Dir Ctr Teaching/Learning .... Mrs. Marcia DURSI
07 Director of Undergrad Admissions .... Vacant
18 Director of Physical Plant .... Vacant
19 Dir of Campus Safety/Transportation .... Mr. Eric HOLS
23 Director Student Health Center .... Mrs. Catherine BROCKER
25 Dir Office of Sponsored Research .... Mrs. Cheryl GREEN
29 Director Alumni Relations .... Vacant
37 Director Financial Aid .... Ms. Deborah RAINES
38 Director Student Counseling .... Ms. Natalie MITCHELL
39 Dir Campus & Residential Svcs .... Ms. Tina SHEPPARD
41 Director Athletics .... Ms. Jamie REYNOLDS
42 Director Campus Ministry .... Fr. Thomas YEHL
44 Director Annual Fund .... Vacant
71 Dir Campus Pgms & Leadership Dev .... Mr. Vincent STOVALL
85 Director International Student Svcs .... Mrs. Aline ORFALI
91 Dir of Admin Information Services .... Ms. Gale KNOEDLER
92 Director Honors Program .... Dr. Stacy LOPRESTI-GOODMAN
105 Director Integrated Tech Solutions .... Mr. Joseph LUCKETT
106 Dir Distance Educ & Instr Design .... Dr. Susan CONRAD
108 Dir Assessment & Inst Effectiveness .... Ms. Ann BOUDINOT
88 Director Acad Affairs Info Systems .... Mr. Louis FRISENDA
88 Director Budget & Risk Mgmt .... Mrs. Margaret AXELROD
88 Director Enrollment Mgmt Systems .... Mrs. Sara MEEHAN
88 Director Experiential Learning .... Mr. David POMEROY
88 Director Infrastructure & Security .... Mr. David LUTES
88 Director IT Support Services .... Mr. John TAMBERT
88 Director Planning & Service Quality .... Mrs. Anne STANCIL
88 Dir Special Events & Conferences .... Ms. Soo PETERSON
88 Director Student Access Services .... Mrs. Hope FISHER
88 Dir Stdnt Conduct & Acad Integrity ..... Mr. Christopher FIORELLO
88 Director Training/Org Development .... Mrs. Bernadette COSTELLO
16 Asst Director Employment .... Ms. Lisa IGIEHON
88 Bursar .... Mr. Anantha GORTI
24 Manager Student Tech Resources .... Mr. Oscar VENTURA-MENDOZA
40 Manager B&N Bookstore .... Ms. Kandice LARGE
96 Coordinator of Purchasing .... Mrs. Amy PAPPAS
04 Administrative Asst to President .... Mrs. Hilary PHILLIPS

Medical Careers Institute (B)

1001 Omni Boulevard Suite 200,
Newport News VA 23606-4388
Telephone: (757) 873-2423 FICE Identification: 022472
Accreditation: &SC, CAHIIM, MAAB, PTAA, RAD

† Regional accreditation is carried under the parent institution, ECPI College of Technology, in Virginia Beach, VA.

Medical Careers Institute (C)

2809 Emerywood Parkway, Suite 400,
Richmond VA 23294
Telephone: (804) 521-5999 Identification: 667038
Accreditation: &SC, MAAB

† Regional accreditation is carried under the parent institution ECPI College of Technology, Virginia Beach, VA.

Miller-Motte Technical College (D)

1011 Creekside Lane, Lynchburg VA 24502-4353
County: Lynchburg FICE Identification: 004992
Unit ID: 233091
Telephone: (434) 239-5222 Carnegie Class: Assoc/HVT-High Non
FAX Number: (434) 239-1069 Calendar System: Quarter
URL: www.miller-motte.edu
Established: 1997 Annual Undergrad Tuition & Fees: $10,288
Enrollment: 409 Coed
Affiliation or Control: Proprietary IRS Status: Proprietary
Highest Offering: Associate Degree
Accreditation: ACICS, MAC, SURGT

01 Director .... Ms. Susie ROWLAND

Miller-Motte Technical College (E)

4444-A Electric Road, Roanoke VA 24018
Telephone: (540) 597-1010 Identification: 770816
Accreditation: ACICS

Norfolk State University (F)

700 Park Avenue, Norfolk VA 23504-8000
County: Independent City FICE Identification: 003765
Unit ID: 232937
Telephone: (757) 823-8600 Carnegie Class: Masters/M
FAX Number: (757) 823-2067 Calendar System: Semester
URL: www.nsu.edu
Established: 1935 Annual Undergrad Tuition & Fees (In-State): $8,366
Enrollment: 6,027 Coed
Affiliation or Control: State IRS Status: 501(c)3
Highest Offering: Doctorate
Accreditation: SC, BUS, CLPSY, CS, DIETD, ENG, JOUR, KIN, MT, MUS, NAIT, NUR, SW, TED

01 President .... Mr. Eddie N. MOORE, JR.
05 Provost/Vice Pres Academic Affs .... Dr. Sandra J. DELOATCH
10 Vice Pres Finance and Admin .... Mr. Gerald E. HUNTER
30 Interim Vice Pres Univ Advancement .... Dr. Deborah C. FONTAINE
32 Vice President for Student Affairs .... Mr. Edward M. WILLIS
20 Vice Provost .... Dr. Mildred K. FULLER
20 Vice Provost .... Dr. Clarence D. COLEMAN
84 Asst Vice Pres Enrollment Mgmt .... Vacant
108 AVP Inst Research/Assessment/Plng .... Vacant
43 University Counsel .... Ms. Pamela F. BOSTON
07 Dir of Recruitment & Admissions .... Mrs. Lakeisha E. MAYES
19 Chief of Campus Police .... Mr. Troy COVINGTON
38 Director of Counseling .... Ms. Vanessa C. JENKINS
06 Registrar .... Mr. Michael CARPENTER
08 Dean of Library Services .... Vacant
37 Director of Financial Aid .... Mr. Kevin J. BURNS
36 Director of Career Services .... Vacant
15 Assoc VP Human Resources .... Ms. Mona ADKINS-EASLEY
29 Dir Alumni Relations/Annual Giving .... Ms. Michelle D. HILL
49 Dean of Liberal Arts .... Dr. Belinda C. ANDERSON
50 Interim Dean of Business .... Dr. Bidhu D. MOHANTY
53 Interim Dean of Education .... Dr. Denise LITTLETON
76 Act Dean of Science/Eng/Technology .... Dr. Larry MATTIX
70 Interim Dean of Social Work .... Dr. Rowena G. WILSON
92 Dean of Honors College .... Dr. Page LAWS
58 Dean of Graduate Studies & Research . Dr. George E. MILLER, III
86 Legislative Liaison .... Mr. Robert L. TURNER
13 Information Technology Manager .... Ms. Regina ENGLISH
26 Int Dir Communications & Marketing ..... Ms. Stevalynn R. ADAMS
09 Dir Institutional Research .... Dr. Alona SMOLOVA
39 Exec Dir Housing & Residence Life ... Mrs. Faith M. FITZGERALD
40 Bookstore Manager .... Ms. Angela HARRISON
41 Athletics Director .... Mr. Marty L. MILLER
18 Assoc Vice Pres Facilities Mgmt .... Mr. Anton KASHIRI
85 Dir International Student Services .... Mrs. Beverly HARRIS
96 Director of Procurement .... Mr. Eugene ANDERSON
21 University Controller .... Mrs. Karla J. AMAYA GORDON
35 Dean of Students .... Ms. Tracci JOHNSON
88 Assoc Vice Pres for Student Affairs .... Mrs. Julia WINGARD
108 Director of Assessment .... Ms. Katrice HAWTHORNE

† Member of Virginia Consortium for Professional Psychology.

Old Dominion University (G)

5115 Hampton Boulevard, Norfolk VA 23529-0001
County: Independent City FICE Identification: 003728
Unit ID: 232982
Telephone: (757) 683-3000 Carnegie Class: DU-Higher
FAX Number: (757) 683-4505 Calendar System: Semester
URL: www.odu.edu
Established: 1930 Annual Undergrad Tuition & Fees (In-State): $9,480
Enrollment: 24,932 Coed
Affiliation or Control: State IRS Status: 501(c)3
Highest Offering: Doctorate
Accreditation: SC, ANEST, ART, BUS, BUSA, CAATE, CACREP, CLPSY, CYTO, DH, ENG, ENGT, EXSC, MT, MUS, NMT, NRPA, NURSE, PH, PTA, SP, SPAA, TED, THEA

01 President .... Mr. John R. BRODERICK
05 Provost/VP Academic Affairs .... Dr. Austin AGHO
10 Vice President Admin & Finance .... Vacant
46 Vice President for Research .... Dr. Morris W. FOSTER
15 Vice Pres for Human Resources ... Ms. September C. SANDERLIN
30 Vice Pres University Advancement .... Mr. Alonzo C. BRANDON
32 VP Student Engagement & Enroll Svcs ...... Dr. Ellen J. NEUFELDT
88 Vice Provost for Faculty/Pgm Devel .... Vacant
88 Vice Prov Academic Programs .... Dr. Brian K. PAYNE
20 Assoc Vice Pres Academic Affairs .... Mr. James P. DUFFY
21 Assoc VP for Financial Services ...... Ms. Deborah L. SWIECINSKI
88 Asst VP Regional/Higher Educ Ctrs .... Ms. Renee E. OLANDER
56 Assoc VP Distance Learning .... Mr. Andrew R. CASIELLO
84 Assoc Vice Pres Enrollment Mgmt .... Ms. Jane H. DANE
44 Assoc Vice Pres for Advancement .... Mr. Daniel J. GENARD
88 Assoc VP Student Engagement .... Dr. Johnny W. YOUNG
109 Asst Vice Pres Auxiliary Services .... Mr. Todd K. JOHNSON
21 Asst VP Finance/Univ Controller .... Ms. Mary C. DENEEN
13 CIO/Assoc VP for University Svcs .... Mr. James R. WATERFIELD
31 Asst Vice Pres Community Engagement .... Ms. Karen F. MEIER
35 Dean Students/AVP Stdnt Engagement .... Dr. Donald M. STANSBERRY
20 Asst VP Undergraduate Studies .... Ms. Judith M. BOWMAN
29 Asst Vice Pres of Alumni Relations .... Ms. Joy L. JEFFERSON
26 AVP Marketing & Communications ..... Ms. Giovanna M. GENARD
22 Asst VP Inst Equity & Diversity .... Ms. ReNee S. DUNMAN
58 Associate VP for Graduate Studies .... Dr. Robert WOJTOWICZ
49 Dean College Arts & Letters .... Dr. Dana HELLER
81 Dean College of Sciences .... Dr. Chris PLATSOUCAS
76 Dean College of Health Sciences .... Dr. Shelley C. MISHOE
50 Dean Strome College of Business .... Dr. Jeff F. TANNER
53 Dean Darden College of Education .... Dr. Jane S. BRAY
54 Dean Batten Col Engineering & Tech ...... Dr. Stephanie G. ADAMS
92 Dean Honors College .... Dr. David D. METZGER
20 Exec Dir Ctr High Impact Practices .... Ms. Lisa MAYES
36 Int Exec Dir Career Management Ctr .... Ms. Beverly FORBES
93 Exec Dir of Intercultural Relations .... Ms. Lesa C. CLARK
43 Asst Atty Gen/Assoc Univ Counsel .... Mr. Richard E. NANCE
85 Exec Dir International Programs .... Dr. Marcelo E. SILES
08 University Librarian .... Mr. George J. FOWLER
11 Chief Operating Officer .... Mr. David F. HARNAGE
06 Interim University Registrar .... Mr. Humberto PORTELLEZ
07 Exec Director of Admissions .... Dr. J. Christopher FLEMING
41 Director of Athletics .... Dr. C. Wood SELIG
37 Director Student Financial Aid .... Ms. Vera E. RIDDICK
31 Director of Community Relations .... Ms. Cecelia T. TUCKER
88 Director Military Affairs .... Mr. Robert E. CLARK
38 Sr Exec Director Counseling Svcs .... Vacant
23 Director Student Health Center .... Ms. Jennifer J. FOSS
85 Director Intl Students/Scholar Svcs .... Ms. Robbin S. FULMORE
39 Exec Director of Student Housing .... Ms. April H. KONVALINKA
18 Director Facilities Management .... Mr. R. Dillard GEORGE
19 VP for Public Safety & Chief Police .... Ms. Rhonda L. HARRIS
28 Dir Inst Equity/Diversity/EO/AA .... Ms. Lanay NEWSOM
109 Actg Dir of Procurement Services .... Ms. Etta A. HENRY
94 Director Women's Studies .... Dr. Jennifer N. FISH
16 Dir of HR Employee Rels/Strat Init .... Ms. Kathleen C. WILLIAMSON
35 Dir Leadership/Student Involvement .... Ms. Nicole C. KIGER
40 University Bookstore Manager .... Mr. Darryl ATKINSON
04 Asst to the President/Asst to COO .... Ms. Velvet L. GRANT
86 Asst to Pres for Govt Relations .... Ms. Elizabeth A. KERSEY

† Member of Virginia Consortium for Professional Psychology.

Patrick Henry College (H)

Ten Patrick Henry Circle, Purcellville VA 20132
County: Loudoun FICE Identification: 039513
Telephone: (540) 338-1776 Carnegie Class: Not Classified
FAX Number: (540) 441-8709 Calendar System: Semester
URL: www.phc.edu
Established: 2000 Annual Undergrad Tuition & Fees: N/A
Enrollment: N/A Coed
Affiliation or Control: Independent Non-Profit IRS Status: 501(c)3
Highest Offering: Baccalaureate
Accreditation: TRACS

00 Chancellor .... Dr. Michael P. FARRIS
01 President .... Mr. Jack HAYE
10 VP for Administration & Finance .... Mr. Daryl WOLKING
09 VP for Institutional Effectiveness .... Mr. Rodney J. SHOWALTER
30 Vice President for Advancement .... Mr. Tom ZIEMNICK
05 Dean of Academic Affairs .... Dr. Frank GULIUZZA
32 Dean of Student Affairs .... Ms. Sandra K. CORBITT
08 Director of the Library .... Ms. Sara E. PENSGARD
07 Director of Admissions .... Mr. Stephen C. ALLEN

Protestant Episcopal Theological Seminary in Virginia (I)

3737 Seminary Road, Alexandria VA 22304-5201
County: Independent City FICE Identification: 003731
Unit ID: 233259
Telephone: (703) 370-6600 Carnegie Class: Not Classified
FAX Number: (703) 370-6234 Calendar System: Semester
URL: www.vts.edu
Established: 1823 Annual Graduate Tuition & Fees: N/A
Enrollment: N/A Coed
Affiliation or Control: Protestant Episcopal IRS Status: 501(c)3

Highest Offering: Doctorate; No Undergraduates
Accreditation: THEOL

01 Dean and President .... Rev. Ian S. MARKHAM
05 VP of Academic Affairs .... Rev. Melody D. KNOWLES
10 VP for Administration and Finance .... Mrs. Heather ZDANCEWICZ
30 VP of Institutional Advancement ....Rev. J. Barney HAWKINS
15 VP for HR and Inst Effectiveness ....Ms. Katie GLOVER
32 Assoc Dean of Students .... Vacant
06 Registrar .... Mrs. Tamara A. SHEPHERD
08 Head Librarian ....Dr. Mitzi J. BUDDE
26 Director of Communications ....Mr. Curtis PRATHER
07 Director of Admissions .... Ms. Janice SIENKIEWICZ

Radford University (A)

801 East Main Street, Radford VA 24142
County: Radford City FICE Identification: 003732
Unit ID: 233277
Telephone: (540) 831-5000 Carnegie Class: Masters/L
FAX Number: N/A Calendar System: Semester
URL: www.radford.edu
Established: 1910 Annual Undergrad Tuition & Fees (In-State): $9,809
Enrollment: 9,798 Coed
Affiliation or Control: State IRS Status: 170(c)1
Highest Offering: Doctorate
Accreditation: SC, ART, BUS, #CAATE, CACREP, CIDA, COPSY, CS, DIETD, MUS, NRPA, NURSE, OT, PTA, SP, SW, TED, THEA

01 President ....Ms. Penelope W. KYLE
05 Provost/VP Academic Affairs ....Dr. Joseph SCARTELLI
10 VP Finance and Administration/CFO ....Mr. Richard ALVAREZ
13 VP Information Technology/CIO ....Mr. Danny KEMP
32 VP Student Affairs .... Dr. Mark SHANLEY
26 VP University Relations/CCO ....Mr. Larry CARPENTER
30 VP University Advancement ....Ms. Melissa WOHLSTEIN
50 Dean Business and Economics ....Dr. George LOW
53 Dean Education and Human Devel .... Dr. Kenna COLLEY
76 Dean Health and Human Services .... Dr. Kenneth COX
83 Dean Humanities and Behavioral Sci ....Dr. Katherine HAWKINS
81 Dean Science and Technology ....Dr. J. Orion ROGERS
57 Dean Visual and Performing Arts ....Ms. Margaret DEVANEY
58 Dean Graduate Studies and Research .... Dr. Dennis GRADY
07 Dean of Admissions/Enrollment Mgmt ....Mr. James PENNIX
08 Dean of the Library ....Mr. Steven HELM
06 Registrar ....Mr. Matthew BRUNNER
37 Director of Financial Aid ....Ms. Barbara PORTER
29 Executive Dir of Alumni Relations ....Ms. Laura TURK
41 Director Intercollegiate Athletics ....Mr. Robert LINEBURG
15 Exec Dir & Chief HR Officer .... Ms. Theresa SLAUGHTER
19 Asst VP for Public Safety ....Ms. Colleen ROBERTS
09 Director of Institutional Research ....Dr. Eric LOVIK
101 Secretary of the Board of Visitors ..... Ms. Michele SCHUMACHER

Randolph College (B)

2500 Rivermont Avenue, Lynchburg VA 24503-1555
County: Independent City FICE Identification: 003734
Unit ID: 233301
Telephone: (434) 947-8000 Carnegie Class: Bac-A&S
FAX Number: (434) 947-8139 Calendar System: Semester
URL: www.randolphcollege.edu
Established: 1891 Annual Undergrad Tuition & Fees: $35,410
Enrollment: 693 Coed
Affiliation or Control: United Methodist IRS Status: 501(c)3
Highest Offering: Master's
Accreditation: SC, TEAC

01 President ....Dr. Bradley W. BATEMAN
05 VP Academic Affs & Dean of College ....Dr. Carl A. GIRELLI
10 Vice Pres Institutional Advancement ... Mr. Kenneth ST. CHARLES
10 Vice Pres Finance & Administration .... Mr. James MANARO
32 VP Student Affs & Dean of Students .... Dr. Matha THORNTON
84 VP Enrollment Management .... Mr. Michael J. QUINN
100 VP & Chief of Staff .... Mr. Wesley FUGATE
20 Associate Dean of the College ....Ms. Paula J. WALLACE
29 Director Alumnae & Alumni Pgm .... Vacant
09 Dir IR/Planning & Assessment ....Dr. John F. KEENER
15 Director Human Resources .... Ms. Sharon SAUNDERS
18 Chief Facilities/Physical Plant ....Mr. J.W WOOD
21 Director of Finance ....Mr. Jonathan TYREE
38 Director Student Counseling .... Dr. Anne HERSHBELL
08 Librarian ....Mr. Theodore J. HOSTETLER
06 Registrar .... Ms. Barbara S. THRASHER
37 Dir Student Financial Services .....Ms. Debi WOODALL-STEVENS
36 Director of Career Development .... Ms. Krista LEIGHTON
13 Director of Information Technology .... Mr. Victor GOSNELL
04 Administrative Asst to President ....Ms. Cindy LYONS
07 Director of Admissions ....Ms. Nelson DAVIS
19 Director Security/Safety ....Mr. Kris IRWIN
41 Athletic Director .... Ms. Tina HILL

Randolph-Macon College (C)

204 Henry Street, PO Box 5005, Ashland VA 23005-5505
County: Hanover FICE Identification: 003733
Unit ID: 233295
Telephone: (804) 752-7200 Carnegie Class: Bac-A&S
FAX Number: (804) 752-7231 Calendar System: Other
URL: www.rmc.edu
Established: 1830 Annual Undergrad Tuition & Fees: $37,600
Enrollment: 1,394 Coed
Affiliation or Control: United Methodist IRS Status: 501(c)3
Highest Offering: Baccalaureate
Accreditation: SC, TEAC

01 President ....Mr. Robert R. LINDGREN
05 Provost/VP for Academic Affairs ....Dr. William T. FRANZ
10 Vice Pres of Admin & Finance ....Mr. Paul DAVIES
30 Vice Pres for College Advancement .... Ms. Diane M. LOWDER
84 Vice Pres for Enroll/Admiss/Fin Aid ....Dr. David L. LESESNE
32 Vice President for Student Affairs ....Dr. Grant L. AZDELL
04 Executive Assistant to the Pres ....Ms. Jennifer L. THOMPSON
88 Exec Dir Ctr Personal/Career Dev .... Ms. Cindy SZADOKIERSKI
07 Director of Admissions ....Mr. Anthony F. AMBROGI
29 Exec Director Alumni Relations ....Mrs. Susan H. DONAVANT
26 Dir of Marketing & Communications ....Mrs. Anne Marie LAURANZON
37 Director of Financial Aid ....Mrs. Mary Y. NEAL
13 CIO and ITS Director ....Mr. Kirk BAUMBACH
06 Registrar ....Mrs. Alana DAVIS
36 Director of Counseling Services .... Dr. D. Craig ANDERSON
09 Director of Institutional Research .... Vacant
18 Dir of Operations & Physical Plant ....Mr. Thomas P. DWYER
42 Chaplain ....Rev. Kendra SWAGER
19 Director of Campus Safety ....Mr. Maurice J. KIELY
41 Athletic Director ....Mr. Jeffrey S. BURNS
15 Director Human Resources ....Mrs. Sharon E. JACKSON
21 Controller .... Ms. Barbara A. DAUBERMAN
20 Associate Dean of the College ....Dr. Lauren C. BELL
36 Director of Professional Develop ....Ms. Catherine A. ROLLMAN
35 Asst Dean of Students ....Mr. James D. MCGHEE, JR.
40 Bookstore Manager .... Mrs. Barclay F. DUPRIEST
21 Director of Budget/Financial Analys .... Mrs. Caroline C. BUSCH

Reformed Theological Seminary (D)

1651 Old Meadow Road, Suite 300, McLean VA 22102
Telephone: (703) 448-3393 Identification: 666079
Accreditation: &SC, THEOL

† Regional accreditation is carried under the parent institution in Jackson, MS.

Regent University (E)

1000 Regent University Drive, Virginia Beach VA 23464-9800
County: Independent City FICE Identification: 030913
Unit ID: 231651
Telephone: (757) 352-4127 Carnegie Class: DU-Mod
FAX Number: (757) 352-4381 Calendar System: Semester
URL: www.regent.edu
Established: 1977 Annual Undergrad Tuition & Fees: $16,478
Enrollment: 5,914 Coed
Affiliation or Control: Independent Non-Profit IRS Status: 501(c)3
Highest Offering: Doctorate
Accreditation: SC, ACBSP, CACREP, CLPSY, LAW, TEAC, THEOL

01 Chancellor & CEO ....Dr. M.G. (Pat) ROBERTSON
05 Executive VP for Academic Affairs ... Dr. Gerson MORENO-RIANO
10 Chief Financial Officer ....Mr. Robert OWEN
32 Executive VP for Student Life .... Dr. Joseph UMIDI
43 Senior VP & General Counsel ....Mr. Louis A. ISAKOFF
30 Vice President for Advancement .... Mrs. Ann LEBLANC
26 VP for Marketing & Public Relations .... Mrs. Sherri MILLER
10 Vice President for Finance ....Mr. Dean A. WOOTEN
15 VP for Human Resources & Admin ....Mrs. Martha J. SMITH
20 Associate VP for Academic Affairs ....Mr. Douglas COOK
88 Associate VP for Teaching/Learning ....Dr. Jason BAKER
61 Dean School of Law ....Mr. Michael HERNANDEZ
49 Dean College of Arts & Sciences .... Dr. Gerson MORENO-RIANO
08 Interim Dean of University Library ....Dr. Leanne STRUM
50 Dean School of Business/Leadership .... Dr. Doris GOMEZ
80 Dean School of Government .... Dr. Eric PATTERSON
53 Dean School of Education ....Dr. Donald FINN
38 Dean Psychology & Counseling .... Dr. William HATHAWAY
60 Dean Communication & the Arts ....Dr. Mitch LAND
73 Dean School of Divinity ....Dr. Corne BEKKER
06 Registrar ....Ms. Erica LEMELLE
84 Assistant VP of Enrollment Mgmt ....Mrs. Heidi CECE
35 Director of Student Activities ....Mr. Roger CHEEKS
106 Director of CTL ....Dr. Tonya AMANKWATIA
37 Director of Financial Aid ....Mrs. Dotti DAVIDSON
09 Director of Institutional Research ....Dr. Amanda WYNN
18 Dir of Facilities & Engineering ....Mr. Richard JEMIOLA
29 Director of Alumni Relations ....Ms. Melissa FUQUAY
42 Director of Campus Ministries ....Mr. Jason PEAKS
108 Director of Assessment ....Mr. Ryan MURNANE
88 Dir of Graduate & Military Admiss ....Mr. Bob HABIB
39 Director of Residence Life ....Mr. Adam WILLIAMS
96 Manager of Purchasing ....Mrs. Pauline CARRAWAY
04 Admin Assistant to the President .... Mrs. Carol DIXON

Richard Bland College (F)

8311 Halifax Road, Petersburg VA 23805-7100
County: Independent City FICE Identification: 003707
Unit ID: 233338
Telephone: (804) 862-6100 Carnegie Class: Spec 2-yr-Other
FAX Number: (804) 862-6207 Calendar System: Semester
URL: www.rbc.edu
Established: 1960 Annual Undergrad Tuition & Fees (In-State): $5,493
Enrollment: 1,525 Coed
Affiliation or Control: State IRS Status: 501(c)3
Highest Offering: Associate Degree
Accreditation: SC

01 President ....Dr. Debbie L. SYDOW
05 Dean of Faculty/CAO ....Dr. Vern L. LINDQUIST
10 Dean Finance/Admin/COO ....Ms. Penny HOWARD
26 Chief Information/Strategy/Innovat .... Mr. Kenneth LATESSA
19 Chief Campus Safety/Security ....Mr. Jeffrey BROWN
30 Director Advancement/Alumni ....Ms. Mary Beth POMA
07 Dean of Enrollment Services ....Dr. James T. HART
06 Registrar ....Ms. Lois WRAY
08 Director of Library ....Ms. Aimee JOYAUX
13 Director of Info Tech Services .... Ms. Deborah JAMES
37 Director of Financial Aid .... Ms. Michelle BYERS
15 Director of Human Resources .... Ms. Bethany HARRIS
88 Manager of Proj & Telecomm ....Mr. George JELLERSON
38 Dir of Counseling/Student Support ....Ms. Evanda WATTS-MARTINEZ
41 Director of Athletics ....Mr. Chuck MOORE
27 Director of Communications ....Ms. Joanne WILLIAMS
39 Assoc Director of Residence Life ....Ms. Corey SCOTT

Riverside College of Health Careers (G)

316 Main Street, Newport News VA 23601
County: Independent City FICE Identification: 021400
Unit ID: 233408
Telephone: (757) 240-2200 Carnegie Class: Spec 2-yr-Health
FAX Number: (757) 240-2225 Calendar System: Semester
URL: www.riverside.edu
Established: 1916 Annual Undergrad Tuition & Fees: N/A
Enrollment: 270 Coed
Affiliation or Control: Independent Non-Profit IRS Status: 501(c)3
Highest Offering: Associate Degree
Accreditation: ABHES, DNUR, PNUR, PTAA, RAD, SURGT, SURTEC

01 System Director of Education ....Robin M. NELHUEBEL
06 Registrar ....Lori WHITTAKER
08 Head Librarian ....Cassandra MOORE

Roanoke College (H)

221 College Lane, Salem VA 24153-3747
County: Independent City FICE Identification: 003736
Unit ID: 233426
Telephone: (540) 375-2500 Carnegie Class: Bac-A&S
FAX Number: (540) 375-2205 Calendar System: Semester
URL: www.roanoke.edu
Established: 1842 Annual Undergrad Tuition & Fees: $39,791
Enrollment: 2,050 Coed
Affiliation or Control: Evangelical Lutheran Church In America
IRS Status: 501(c)3
Highest Offering: Baccalaureate
Accreditation: SC, ACBSP, CAATE, TEAC

01 President ....Mr. Michael C. MAXEY
05 Vice President/Dean of the College ....Dr. Richard A. SMITH
84 VP of Enroll Svcs/Dean Adm/Fin Aid ....Dr. Brenda P. POGGENDORF
32 Vice President Student Affairs ....Mr. Aaron L. FETROW
10 Vice President Business Affairs .... Mr. Mark P. NOFTSINGER
30 Vice President Resource Development ... Ms. Connie K. CARMACK
37 VP Enrollment/Dir Admiss/Fin Aid ..Dr. Brenda P. POGGENDORF
43 General Counsel ....Mr. G. Michael PACE, JR.
13 Chief Information Officer ....Ms. Rebecca F. SANDLIN
09 Dir Institutional Research ....Dr. Jack K. STEEHLER
20 Assoc Dean Academic Affairs/Admin ... Dr. Jennifer K. BERENSON
06 Assoc Dean Acad Affairs/Registrar .... Ms. Leah L. RUSSELL
07 Director of Admissions ....Ms. Patricia N. LEDONNE
35 AVP/Dean of Students/Student Affs ....Dr. Brian T. CHISOM
39 Director of Residence Life/Housing ....Mr. Jimmy R. WHITED
92 Director of Honors Programs .... Dr. Michael A. HAKKENBERG
08 Director of the Library .... Ms. Elizabeth MCCLENNEY
36 Director of Career Services ....Ms. Toni D. MCLAWHORN
24 Media Technology Director .... Mr. David H. MULFORD
31 Dir of Community Programs ....Ms. Tanya RIDPATH
26 Director of Public Relations ....Ms. Teresa T. GEREAUX
44 Director of Gift Planning ....Mr. Richard J. POGGENDORF
29 Dir of Alumni/Family Relations ....Mr. Jonathan E. LEE
21 Director of Finance & Budget ....Ms. Kathryn A. VANNESS
91 Database Director ....Ms. Mitzi B. STEELE
15 Director Human Resources ....Ms. Cathy S. DICKERSON
40 Bookstore Coordinator/Buyer ....Ms. Melissa B. RUTLEDGE
19 Director Campus Safety ....Mr. Thomas A. RAMBO
23 Dir Student Health/Counseling Svcs ....Ms. Sandra W. MCGHEE
41 Athletic Director ....Mr. M. Scott ALLISON
42 Chaplain/Dean of the Chapel ....Rev. Christopher M. BOWEN
104 Director International Education ...... Dr. Pamela A. SEROTA COTE
28 Director of Multicultural Affairs ....Ms. Juliet J. LOWERY
04 Executive Assistant to President ....Ms. Joyce A. SINK

Saint Michael College of Allied Health (I)

8305 Richmond Hwy, Ste 10A, Alexandria VA 22309
County: Independent City Identification: 667226
Telephone: (703) 746-8708 Carnegie Class: Not Classified
FAX Number: (703) 746-8709 Calendar System: Other
URL: www.stmichaelcollegeva.us
Established: 2007 Annual Undergrad Tuition & Fees: N/A
Enrollment: N/A Coed
Affiliation or Control: Proprietary IRS Status: Proprietary
Highest Offering: Associate Degree

Accreditation: COE

01 Director .... Dr. Michael ADEDOKUN

Sentara College of Health Sciences (A)

1441 Crossways Boulevard, Ste 105,
Chesapeake VA 23320
County: Chesapeake City FICE Identification: 031065
Unit ID: 232885
Telephone: (757) 388-2900 Carnegie Class: Spec-4-yr-Other Health
FAX Number: (757) 222-7694 Calendar System: Semester
URL: www.sentara.edu
Established: 1892 Annual Undergrad Tuition & Fees: N/A
Enrollment: 367 Coed
Affiliation or Control: Independent Non-Profit IRS Status: 501(c)3
Highest Offering: Baccalaureate
Accreditation: ACICS, CVT, NURSE, SURGT

01 Dean Sentara Col of Health Sciences .... Ms. Shelly COHEN
05 Dean Academic Affairs .... Dr. Angela TAYLOR
45 Asst Dean Institutional Effective .... Ms. Metta ALSOBROOK
11 Asst Dean Administration & Finance .... Mr. Christopher NELSON
84 Director of Enrollment Management .... Mr. Joseph HOWE
08 Librarian .... Ms. Suzanne DUNCAN
37 Financial Aid Advisor .... Ms. Mary Ann RIVERA
07 Admissions Recruiter .... Mr. Jeremy BROFFT
07 Admissions Recruiter .... Mr. Kevin LAWRENCE

Shenandoah University (B)

1460 University Drive, Winchester VA 22601-5195
County: Independent City FICE Identification: 003737
Unit ID: 233541
Telephone: (540) 665-4500 Carnegie Class: DU-Mod
FAX Number: N/A Calendar System: Semester
URL: www.su.edu
Established: 1875 Annual Undergrad Tuition & Fees: $30,760
Enrollment: 3,693 Coed
Affiliation or Control: United Methodist IRS Status: 501(c)3
Highest Offering: Doctorate
Accreditation: SC, ARCPA, BUS, CAATE, COARC, MIDWF, MUS, NURSE, OT, PHAR, PTA, TEAC

01 President .... Dr. Tracy FITZSIMMONS
05 VP for Academic Affairs .... Dr. Adrienne G. BLOSS
10 Vice Pres Administration/Finance .... Mr. Robert L. KEASLER
32 Vice President for Student Life .... Rev Dr. Rhonda VANDYKE COLBY
30 Senior VP & VP for Advance & Plng .... Mr. Mitchell L. MOORE
84 VP for Enrol Mgmt & Student Success .... Dr. Clarresa MORTON
35 Dean of Students .... Ms. Sue O'DRISCOLL
29 Assoc Vice Pres for Alumni Affairs .... Ms. Jane D. PITTMAN
26 Director of Media Relations .... Ms. Emily BURNER
49 Dean of College of Arts & Sciences .... Dr. Jeff COKER
50 Dean of Byrd School of Business .... Dr. Miles DAVIS
64 Dean of Shenandoah Conservatory .... Dr. Michael J. STEPNIAK
67 Dean of Dunn School of Pharmacy .... Dr. Robert DICENZO
07 Exec of Recruitment & Admissions .... Mr. Andy WOODALL
35 Dir of Student Engagement .... Mr. Doug STUMP
08 Director of Library Services .... Mr. Christopher A. BEAN
06 Registrar .... Ms. Emily HOLLINS
21 Asst VP for Admin & Finance .... Ms. Courtney JARRETT
37 Director of Financial Aid .... Ms. Karen H. BUCHER
36 Director of Career Services .... Ms. Jennifer A. SPATARO-WILSON
18 Director of Physical Plant .... Mr. Barry SCHNOOR
23 Director of Wellness Center .... Mr. Ronald G. STICKLEY
15 Director of Human Resources .... Ms. Marie C. LANDES
41 Athletic Director .... Mr. Doug ZIPP
91 Database & System Administrator .... Mr. Seth BURKE
13 Director of Institutional Computing .... Mr. Quaiser ABSAR
66 Dean Custer School of Nursing .... Dr. Kathleen LASALA
88 Director Div of Athletic Training .... Dr. Rose A. SCHMIEG
88 Dir Div of Occupational Therapy .... Dr. Cathy SHANHOLTZ
88 Interim Dir Div of Physical Therapy .... Dr. Sheri HALE
88 Sr Dir Advancement - Conservatory .... Mr. Bradley C. SNOWDEN
19 Chief of Public Safety .... Mr. Robin EBERSOLE
102 Dir of Grant Supp & Foundation Rels .... Ms. Jennifer BOUSQUET
109 Director Auxiliary Services .... Ms. Pamela B. SMULOVITZ
88 Dir Div of Physician Asst Studies .... Dr. Rachel CARLSON
20 Director Learning Services .... Ms. Holli PHILLIPS
42 Dean of Spiritual Life .... Rev Dr. Justin ALLEN
88 Dir Division of Respiratory Care .... Ms. Stephanie CROSS
09 Director Institutional Research .... Dr. Howard BALLENTINE
40 Bookstore Manager .... Ms. Kimberly OTYENOH
96 Purchasing/Accounts Payable Manager .... Ms. Amy DILL
24 Coordinator Media Services .... Ms. Val GANGWER
38 Director Student Counseling .... Ms. Nancy SCHULTE
04 Executive Asst to President .... Ms. Kim KECKLEY
101 Secretary of the Board of Trustees .... Vacant
53 Director School of Education .... Dr. Dennis KELLISON
104 Director International Programs .... Ms. Bethany GALIPEAU-KONATE
44 Director Annual or Planned Giving .... Ms. Kara JENKINS
90 Director Insitutional Computing .... Mr. Quaiser ABSAR

South Baylo University (C)

7535 Little River Tnpk Unit 325-A, Annandale VA 22003
Telephone: (703) 642-7518 Identification: 770912
Accreditation: @ACUP

† Branch campus of South Baylo University, Anaheim, CA

South University (D)

2151 Old Brick Road, Richmond VA 23060
Telephone: (804) 727-6800 Identification: 770919
Accreditation: &SC, ACBSP, CACREP, NURSE, PTAA

† Regional accreditation is carried under the parent institution in Savannah, GA

South University (E)

301 Bendix Road, Suite 100, Virginia Beach VA 23452
Telephone: (757) 493-6900 Identification: 770920
Accreditation: &SC, ACBSP, CACREP, NURSE, PTAA

† Regional accreditation is carried under the parent institution in Savannah, GA

Southern Virginia University (F)

1 University Hill Drive, Buena Vista VA 24416-3097
County: Rockbridge FICE Identification: 003738
Unit ID: 233611
Telephone: (540) 261-8400 Carnegie Class: Bac-A&S
FAX Number: (540) 266-3859 Calendar System: Semester
URL: www.svu.edu
Established: 1867 Annual Undergrad Tuition & Fees: $14,900
Enrollment: 705 Coed
Affiliation or Control: Independent Non-Profit IRS Status: 501(c)3
Highest Offering: Baccalaureate
Accreditation: SC

01 President .... Dr. Reed N. WILCOX
05 Int Provost .... Dr. Scott DRANSFIELD
10 VP Finance .... Mr. Robert E. HUCH
30 VP Institutional Advancement .... Mr. Ron SEAMONS
88 University Ambassador .... Dr. Richard G. WHITEHEAD
07 VP Enrollment and Marketing .... Mr. Brett GARCIA
32 VP Student Life .... Mr. Charley BOWEN
46 VP Educational Research & Dev .... Dr. Karen M. WALKER
11 Exec Dir of Campus Operations .... Mr. Arthur FURLER
04 Administrative Asst to President .... Mrs. Kristie GIBBONS
06 Registrar .... Ms. Whitney M. LARSEN
08 Director of Library Services .... Mrs. Stephanie K. HARDY
104 Director of Travel Study .... Mrs. Carrie P. BROTHERSON
20 Associate Provost .... Dr. Jeremy JOHN
57 Division Chair Fine & Perf Arts .... Dr. LaRae CARTER
79 Division Chair Humanities .... Dr. Thomas R. PORTER
81 Div Chair Science & Mathematics .... Dr. Richard GARDNER
83 Div Chair Social & Behavioral Sci .... Dr. Frances MACDONNELL
53 Director of Teacher Education .... Mrs. Kimberly KEARNEY
09 Director of Institutional Research .... Dr. Alan WHITEHURST
21 Controller & Dir of Business Ops .... Mr. Jesse SEEGMILLER
37 Director of Financial Aid .... Mr. John BRANDT
15 Assoc Director Human Resources .... Mr. Tyson COOPER
88 Title IX Coordinator .... Mr. Jacob SMITH
96 Senior Accountant .... Mr. Trenton DESPAIN
44 Director of Institutional Advance .... Mr. William BRADDY
07 Director of Admissions .... Vacant
41 Athletic Director .... Mr. Jason LAMB
26 Director of Communications .... Mr. Chris PENDLETON
88 Senior Women's Athletic Admin .... Mrs. Deidra DRYDEN
29 Alumni Relations Coordinator .... Mr. Cameron CROWTHER
35 Dean of Students .... Mr. Joseph BOUCHELLE, III
38 Director of Student Support .... Mr. Michael GIBBONS
36 Director Career Development Center .... Mr. Cameron T. CROWTHER
23 Director of Student Health Services .... Mrs. Ginger LANIER
85 Foreign Students PDSO .... Ms. Whitney M. LARSEN
19 Director Security/Safety .... Mr. Jacob SMITH
11 Director of Campus Operations .... Mr. Joseph WHETSTONE
109 Director of Food Services .... Mrs. Effie WALLACE
18 Asst Dir Facilities/Physical Plant .... Mr. Byron PORTER
13 IT Support Manager .... Ms. Stephanie GILMER

Southside Regional Medical Center Professional Schools (G)

430 Clairmont Court, Suite 200,
Colonial Heights VA 23834
County: Independent City FICE Identification: 012744
Unit ID: 233082
Telephone: (804) 765-5800 Carnegie Class: Spec 2-yr-Health
FAX Number: (804) 765-5944 Calendar System: Semester
URL: www.srmconline.com
Established: 1895 Annual Undergrad Tuition & Fees: N/A
Enrollment: 123 Coed
Affiliation or Control: Proprietary IRS Status: Proprietary
Highest Offering: Associate Degree
Accreditation: ABHES, ADNUR, DMS, RAD

01 Vice Pres for Professional Schools .... Ms. Cynthia PARSONS

Standard Healthcare Services College of Nursing (H)

7704 Leesburg Pike, Suite 1000, Falls Church VA 22043
County: Fairfax Identification: 667129
Unit ID: 483814
Telephone: (703) 891-1787 Carnegie Class: Not Classified
FAX Number: (703) 891-1789 Calendar System: Other
URL: www.standardcollege.edu
Established: 2004 Annual Undergrad Tuition & Fees: N/A
Enrollment: 246 Coed
Affiliation or Control: Proprietary IRS Status: Proprietary
Highest Offering: Associate Degree
Accreditation: ABHES

01 Executive Director .... Ms. Isibor J. NOSEGBE
06 Registrar .... Ms. Lisley M. ANCO
05 Director of Education .... Mr. Sakpa S. AMARA
66 Program Director .... Mrs. Sage WILLIAMS
32 Dean of Student Services .... Mrs. Sondra BROWN
37 Financial Aid .... Mrs. Brenda GARCES
07 Admissions .... Mrs. Candice SAVICE

Stratford University (I)

7777 Leesburg Pike, Suite 1LN, Falls Church VA 22043
County: Fairfax FICE Identification: 025412
Unit ID: 438498
Telephone: (703) 821-8570 Carnegie Class: Masters/L
FAX Number: N/A Calendar System: Quarter
URL: www.stratford.edu
Established: 1976 Annual Undergrad Tuition & Fees: $15,135
Enrollment: 2,971 Coed
Affiliation or Control: Proprietary IRS Status: Proprietary
Highest Offering: Master's
Accreditation: ACICS, ACFEI, CEA, MAAB, NURSE

01 President .... Dr. Richard SHURTZ
05 Chief Academic Officer .... Vacant
12 Campus Director DC Metro .... Voytek PANAS
20 Campus Dean .... Dr. Richelle RESTO
13 Chief Info Technology Officer (CIO) .... Kevin COUGHENOUR
26 Chief Public Relations/Marketing .... Mary Ann SHURTZ

Stratford University (J)

11104 West Broad Street, Glen Allen VA 23060
Telephone: (804) 290-4231 Identification: 770819
Accreditation: ACICS, ACFEI, MAAB

Stratford University (K)

836 J. Clyde Morris Boulevard,
Newport News VA 23601-1303
Telephone: (757) 873-4235 Identification: 770818
Accreditation: ACICS, ACFEI, MAAB

Stratford University (L)

14340 Gideon Drive, Woodbridge VA 22192
Telephone: (703) 897-1982 Identification: 770817
Accreditation: ACICS, ACFEI, MAAB

Sweet Briar College (M)

134 Chapel Road, Sweet Briar VA 24595-9998
County: Amherst FICE Identification: 003742
Unit ID: 233718
Telephone: (434) 381-6100 Carnegie Class: Bac-A&S
FAX Number: (434) 381-6173 Calendar System: Semester
URL: www.sbc.edu
Established: 1901 Annual Undergrad Tuition & Fees: $34,935
Enrollment: 700 Female
Affiliation or Control: Independent Non-Profit IRS Status: 501(c)3
Highest Offering: Master's
Accreditation: SC, ENG

01 President .... Mr. Phillip C. STONE
11 Vice Pres of Admin/General Counsel .... Ms. Nancyellen KEANE
04 Exec Asst Office of the President .... Mrs. Dawn GATEWOOD
09 Director Institutional Research .... Ms. Christy C. COLE
05 Dean of Academic Affairs .... Ms. Pamela DEWEESE
84 Dean of Enrollment Management .... Mr. Bill ALLEN
08 Dir Integrated Information Systems .... Mr. Joe MALLOY
41 Director of Athletics .... Ms. Teresa BOYLAN
104 Director Junior Year in Spain .... Ms. Giulia V. WITCOMBE
32 Dean of Student Life/Academic Supp .... Mrs. Kelly KRAFT-MEYER
10 Vice Pres Finance and Treasurer .... Mr. Timothy KLOCKO
21 Assoc VP Finance/Administration .... Ms. Debbie FARIS
15 Director of Human Resources .... Ms. Nicole WHITEHEAD
18 Director Physical Plant .... Mr. Steve BAILEY
19 Director of Campus Safety .... Mr. Brian MARKER
37 Director Financial Aid .... Ms. Wanda SPRADLEY
40 Book Shop Manager .... Ms. Lynn LEWIS
96 Director Purchasing .... Ms. Cynthia L. PONTON
88 Coordinator Benefits .... Mrs. Judy SPROUSE
88 Director of Hospitality .... Ms. Cathy MAYS
44 Vice Pres Alumnae Relations/Develop .... Ms. Mary Pope HUTSON
38 Mental Health Counselor/Health Svcs .... Ms. Elizabeth S. BLEVINS
36 Director Career Services .... Ms. Barbara WATTS
39 Director Residence Life & Housing .... Ms. Kerri BOND
26 Director of Media/Marketing & Comm .... Ms. Joelle ZIEMIAN
06 Registrar .... Ms. Deborah POWELL
07 Director of Admissions .... Mrs. Marcia THOM-KALEY
13 Chief Info Technology Officer (CIO) .... Mr. Aaron MAHLER
25 Chief Contracts/Grants Admin .... Ms. Kathleen PLACIDI
29 Director Alumni Relations .... Ms. K.P PAPADIMITRIOU

Union Presbyterian Seminary (N)

3401 Brook Road, Richmond VA 23227-4597
County: Independent City FICE Identification: 003743
Unit ID: 233842

Telephone: (804) 355-0671 Carnegie Class: Spec-4-yr-Faith
FAX Number: (804) 355-3919 Calendar System: Semester
URL: www.upsem.edu
Established: 1812 Annual Graduate Tuition & Fees: N/A
Enrollment: 180 Coed
Affiliation or Control: Presbyterian Church (U.S.A.) IRS Status: 501(c)3
Highest Offering: Doctorate; No Undergraduates
Accreditation: **SC**, THEOL

01 President ....Dr. Brian K. BLOUNT
10 Vice Pres Finance & Administration ...Mr. Michael B. CASHWELL
30 Vice President Advancement ....Mr. Richard WONG
84 VP Student Life/Enrollment Mgmt ....Ms. Michelle WALKER
05 Dean Union Presby Sem (Richmond) ..Dr. Kenneth J. MCFAYDEN
12 Dean Union Presby Sem (Charlotte) ....Dr. Richard N. BOYCE
20 Associate Dean Academic Programs ....Dr. E. Carson BRISSON
07 Director of Admissions ....Ms. Mairi RENWICK
06 Registrar ....Mr. J. Stanley HARGRAVES
08 Seminary Librarian ....Dr. Christopher RICHARDSON
13 Director Technology Services ....Mr. John R. WILSON
36 Director Student Placement ....Dr. Susan E. FOX
37 Director of Financial Aid ....Ms. Michelle WALKER

University of Fairfax (A)

3361 Melrose Ave, NW, Roanoke VA 24017
County: Independent City Identification: 667094
Telephone: (888) 980-9151 Carnegie Class: Not Classified
FAX Number: N/A Calendar System: Other
URL: www.ufairfax.edu
Established: 2002 Annual Undergrad Tuition & Fees: N/A
Enrollment: N/A Coed
Affiliation or Control: Other IRS Status: Proprietary
Highest Offering: Doctorate
Accreditation: **DEAC**

05 Academic Dean ....Dr. Scott MENSCH
11 Administrative Dean ....Keith NORDMANN
26 VP Marketing & Communications ....Chuck STEENBURGH

† Tuition is $895 per semester credit.

University of Management & Technology (B)

1901 Fort Myer Drive, Suite 700, Arlington VA 22209-1609
County: Arlington FICE Identification: 041103
Unit ID: 437097
Telephone: (703) 516-0035 Carnegie Class: DU-Mod
FAX Number: (703) 516-0985 Calendar System: Semester
URL: www.umtweb.edu
Established: 1998 Annual Undergrad Tuition & Fees: $9,450
Enrollment: 1,020 Coed
Affiliation or Control: Proprietary IRS Status: Proprietary
Highest Offering: Doctorate
Accreditation: **DEAC**

01 President ....Dr. Yanping CHEN
05 Academic Dean ....Dr. J. Davidson FRAME

University of Mary Washington (C)

1301 College Avenue, Fredericksburg VA 22401-5300
County: Independent City FICE Identification: 003746
Unit ID: 232681
Telephone: (540) 654-1000 Carnegie Class: Masters/L
FAX Number: (540) 654-1073 Calendar System: Semester
URL: www.umw.edu
Established: 1908 Annual Undergrad Tuition & Fees (In-State): $11,130
Enrollment: 4,535 Coed
Affiliation or Control: State IRS Status: 501(c)3
Highest Offering: Master's
Accreditation: **SC**, MUS

01 President ....Dr. Troy PAINO
05 Provost ....Dr. Jonathan LEVIN
100 Chief of Staff ....Dr. Martin A. WILDER
10 VP for Admin & Finance ....Mr. Richard R. PEARCE
32 Vice President Student Affairs ....Dr. Juliette LANDPHAIR
30 Vice Pres for Advance & Univ Rels ....Mr. Salvatore M. MERINGOLO
102 CEO of UMW Foundation ....Mr. Jeffrey W. ROUNTREE
13 Actg CIO ....Mr. Hall CHESHIRE
88 Exec Dir Economic Development ....Mr. Brian J. BAKER
15 Asst Vice Pres/Human Res/AAEEO ....Ms. Sabrina C. JOHNSON
105 Director of Digital Communication ....Ms. Shelley KEITH
21 Asst Vice Pres Business Svcs/CPO ....Ms. Erma A. BAKER
20 Associate Provost ....Dr. John T. MORELLO
18 Assoc Vice Pres Facilities Services ....Mr. John P. WILTENMUTH, III
09 Asst Prov Inst Analy & Effect ....Mr. Taiwo A. ANDE
84 Assoc Prov for Enrollment Mgmt ....Ms. Kimberley BUSTER-WILLIAMS
53 Int Dean of College of Education ....Dr. Nina MIKHALEVSKY
50 Dean College of Business ....Dr. Lynne D. RICHARDSON
20 Dean College of Arts & Sciences ....Dr. Richard FINKELSTEIN
35 Dean of Student Life ....Mr. Cedric B. RUCKER
37 Director of Financial Aid ... Ms. Heidi HUNTER-GOLDSWORTHY
09 Director of Institutional Research ....Mr. Mathew C. WILKERSON
21 Internal Audit Director ....Ms. Tera D. KOVANES
39 Director of Residence Life ....Ms. Christine M. PORTER
06 Registrar ....Ms. Rita DUNSTON
41 Director of Athletics ....Mr. Ken D. TYLER
08 University Librarian ....Ms. Rosemary ARNESON
88 Director of Publications ....Ms. Neva S. TRENIS
24 Director of Dodd Auditorium ....Mr. Doug NOBLE
88 Assoc Dean of Advising Services ....Ms. Sallie W. BRAXTON
19 Chief of University Police ....Mr. Michael W. HALL
29 Exec Director Alumni Relations ....Mr. Mark THADEN
38 Director of Counseling/Psych Svcs ....Mr. Tevya ZUKOR
88 Director of Disability Resources ....Ms. Sandra FRITTON
23 University Physician ....Dr. P. Thomas RILEY
88 Director of University Galleries ..Ms. Rosemary K. JESIONOWSKI
28 Spec Asst Diversity & Inclusion ....Dr. Leah COX
26 Associate VP University Rels ....Ms. Anna B. BILLINGSLEY
27 Director Media & Public Relations ....Ms. Marty G. MORRISON
27 Director of Marketing ....Mr. Malcolm HOLMES
88 Director of Design Services ....Ms. AJ NEWELL
29 Director National Alumni Engagement ....Vacant
44 Assoc VP Univ Advancemnt/Alumni Rel ....Mr. Kenneth L. STEEN

University of North America (D)

8618 Westwood Center Dr., Ste 100, Vienna VA 22182
County: Fairfax Identification: 667241
Telephone: (571) 633-9651 Carnegie Class: Not Classified
FAX Number: (703) 890-3372 Calendar System: Semester
URL: www.uona.edu
Established: Annual Undergrad Tuition & Fees: N/A
Enrollment: N/A Coed
Affiliation or Control: Independent Non-Profit IRS Status: 501(c)3
Highest Offering: Master's
Accreditation: **ACICS**

00 Chancellor ....Marty MARTIN
01 President ....Jill MARTIN
05 VP of Academics/Outreach ....John HOUGH
20 VP of Education ....Jason KOO
37 Director Student Financial Affairs ....Padmanjali POKHAREL

University of Phoenix Richmond-Virginia Beach Campus (E)

9750 West Broad Street, Glen Allen VA 23060-4169
Telephone: (804) 281-3900 Identification: 770233
Accreditation: &NH, ACBSP

† No longer accepting campus-based students.

University of the Potomac (F)

2070 Chain Bridge Road Suite G100, Vienna VA 22182
Telephone: (888) 380-1192 Identification: 666178
Accreditation: &M

† Regional accreditation is carried under the parent institution in Washington, DC.

University of Richmond (G)

28 Westhampton Way, Richmond VA 23173-1903
County: Independent City FICE Identification: 003744
Unit ID: 233374
Telephone: (804) 289-8000 Carnegie Class: Bac-A&S
FAX Number: (804) 287-6540 Calendar System: Semester
URL: www.richmond.edu
Established: 1830 Annual Undergrad Tuition & Fees: $48,090
Enrollment: 4,182 Coordinate
Affiliation or Control: Independent Non-Profit IRS Status: 501(c)3
Highest Offering: Doctorate
Accreditation: **SC**, BUS, BUSA, LAW, TEAC

01 President ....Dr. Ronald A. CRUTCHER
05 Provost & VP Academic Affairs ....Dr. Jacquelyn FETROW
10 Vice President Business & Finance ....Mr. David B. HALE
32 Vice President Student Affairs ....Dr. Stephen D. BISESE
30 Vice President Advancement ....Mr. Thomas C. GUTENBERGER
13 Vice Pres for Information Services ....Mr. Keith J. MCINTOSH
84 Vice Pres Enrollment Management ....Dr. Stephanie DUPAUL
100 Chief of Staff ....Dr. Lori G. SCHUYLER
101 Secretary Board of Trustees ....Ms. Ann Lloyd BREEDEN
04 Special Assistant to President ....Mrs. Carolyn R. MARTIN
88 CEO Spider Mgmt Company ....Mr. Steve KNEELEY
15 Assoc Vice Pres Human Resources ....Mr. Carl K. SORENSEN
18 Assoc Vice Pres Facilities ....Mr. Andrew S. MCBRIDE
29 Asst VP Alumni & Career Services ....Ms. Kristin J. WOODS
102 Asst VP Foundation/Corp/Govt Rels ... Ms. Michelle E. WAMSLEY
42 University Chaplain ....Rev. Craig T. KOCHER
07 Asst VP and Dean of Admissions ....Mr. Gil VILLANUEVA
08 University Librarian ....Mr. Kevin BUTTERFIELD
09 Dir Institutional Effectiveness ....Dr. Patricia B. MURPHY
06 University Registrar ....Ms. Susan D. BREEDEN
37 Director of Financial Aid ....Ms. Cynthia B. DEFFENBAUGH
36 Director Career Services ....Ms. Leslie W. STEVENSON
38 Director of CAPS ....Dr. Peter O. LEVINESS
96 Director Strategic Sourcing ....Ms. Jean C. HINES
35 Assoc VP Student Development ....Dr. Tinina Q. CADE
41 Director of Athletics ....Mr. Keith GILL
104 Director Study Abroad ....Ms. Michele D. COX
105 Director Web Services ....Mr. Eric F. PALMER
33 Dean of Richmond College ....Dr. Joseph R. BOEHMAN
34 Dean Westhampton College ....Dr. Juliette L. LANDPHAIR
49 Dean School of Arts & Sciences ....Dr. Kathleen R. SKERRETT
50 Dean School of Business ....Dr. Nancy A. BAGRANOFF
61 Dean School of Law ....Dr. Wendy C. PERDUE
51 Dean School Continuing Studies ....Dr. Jamelle WILSON
88 Dean Jepson School Leader Stds ....Dr. Sandra J. PEART
19 Assoc VP Public Sfty/Chief of Police ....Mr. David M. MCCOY
23 Director Health Center ....Dr. Lynne P. DEANE
25 Asst VP for Communications ....Mr. John M. BARRY
40 Manager University Bookstore ....Mr. Roger L. BROOKS
23 Director Common Ground ....Dr. Glyn HUGHES
39 Director Student Housing ....Ms. Joan D. LACHOWSKI
43 VP & General Counsel ....Ms. Shannon E. SINCLAIR
91 Manager Admin Systems ....Mr. Lee PARKER, III

University of Virginia (H)

Charlottesville VA 22903
County: Independent City FICE Identification: 003745
Unit ID: 234076
Telephone: (434) 924-0311 Carnegie Class: DU-Highest
FAX Number: (434) 924-0938 Calendar System: Semester
URL: www.virginia.edu
Established: 1819 Annual Undergrad Tuition & Fees (In-State): $15,192
Enrollment: 23,732 Coed
Affiliation or Control: State IRS Status: 501(c)3
Highest Offering: Doctorate
Accreditation: **SC**, BUS, BUSA, CAATE, CACREP, CLPSY, CS, DENT, DIETI, ENG, IPSY, LAW, LSAR, MED, NURSE, PAST, PCSAS, PH, PLNG, PSPSY, SP, TEAC

01 President ....Dr. Teresa A. SULLIVAN
101 Secretary Board of Visitors ....Ms. Susan G. HARRIS
05 Exec Vice President & Provost ....Dr. Thomas C. KATSOULEAS
17 Exec Vice Pres for Health Affairs ....Dr. Richard P. SHANNON
30 Vice Pres for Advancement ....Mr. Mark M. LUELLEN
03 Exec Vice Pres/Chief Operating Ofcr ....Mr. Patrick D. HOGAN
32 Vice Pres/Chief Student Affs Ofcr ....Ms. Patricia M. LAMPKIN
46 Interim Sr Vice Pres for Research ....Mr. Phillip A. PARRISH
28 VP/Chief Officer Diversity/Equity ....Mr. Marcus L. MARTIN
41 Dir Intercollegiate Athletic Pgms ....Mr. Craig K. LITTLEPAGE
23 CEO Medical Center ....Ms. Pamela M. SUTTON-WALLACE
15 Interim VP/Chief HR Officer ....Mr. Bryan E. GAREY
11 Sr Vice President for Operations ....Ms. Colette SHEEHY
10 Vice President for Finance ....Ms. Melody BIANCHETTO
13 Chief Info Officer ....Ms. Virginia EVANS
88 Health Sys CFO/Bus Dev Officer ....Mr. Larry L. FITZGERALD
100 Chief of Staff/Assoc VP for Admin ....Ms. Nancy A. RIVERS
20 Vice Prov for Academic Affairs ....Mr. Archie L. HOLMES, JR.
88 Vice Prov Faculty Affairs ....Ms. Kerry ABRAMS
88 Vice Provost for Global Affairs ....Mr. Jeffrey w. LEGRO
11 Vice Prov for Admin/Chief of Staff ....Ms. Anda L. WEBB
88 Vice Provost for the Arts ....Mr. Jody K. KIELBASA
88 Assoc VP Business Operations ....Mr. Richard A. KOVATCH
37 Asst Vice Pres Student Finan Svcs ....Mr. Stephen A. KIMATA
25 Asst VP Research Admin ....Ms. Elizabeth H. ADAMS
26 VP for Communication/Chief Mktg Of ....Mr. David W. MARTEL
18 Assoc VP & Chief Facilities Officer ....Mr. Donald E. SUNDGREN
88 Chief Investment Officer ....Mr. Lawrence E. KOCHARD
06 Registrar ....Ms. Carol A J. STANLEY
07 Dean of Admission ....Mr. Gregory W. ROBERTS
61 Dean School of Law ....Mr. Paul G. MAHONEY
49 Dean School of Arts & Sciences ....Mr. Ian BAUCOM
63 Dean School of Medicine ....Dr. David S. WILKES
66 Dean School of Nursing ....Ms. Dorrie K. FONTAINE
54 Dean Schl Engr/Applied Science ....Mr. Craig BENSON
48 Dean School of Architecture ....Ms. Elizabeth K. MEYER
50 Dean School of Commerce ....Mr. Carl P. ZEITHAML
80 Dean Sch Leadership/Public Policy ....Mr. Allan C. STAM
53 Dean School of Education ....Mr. Robert C. PIANTA
50 Dean Grad School Business Admin ....Mr. Scott C. BEARDSLEY
51 Interim Dean Cont & Prof Studies ....Mr. Steven E. LAYMON
35 Associate VP/Dean of Students ....Mr. Allen W. GROVES
23 Exec Director Student Health ....Dr. Christopher HOLSTEGE
43 Gen Counsel & Corporate Secretary ....Mr. Roscoe C. ROBERTS
22 Asst VP for Equal Opportunity Pgms ....Ms. Catherine SPEAR
08 Univ Librarian/Dean of Libraries ....Mr. John M. UNSWORTH
09 Assoc Prov Inst Assess & Studies ....Ms. Christina MORELL
88 Exec Director The Jefferson Trust ....Mr. Wayne COZART
36 Assoc VP Career & Prof Development ....Mr. Everette FORTNER
88 Dir Summer & Special Academic Pgms ....Mr. Dudley J. DOANE
104 Dir International Studies Office ....Mr. Dudley J. DOANE
19 Chief of Police ....Mr. Michael A. GIBSON
39 Exec Dir Housing & Residence Life ....Ms. Gay PEREZ
40 Executive Director of UVa Bookstore ....Mr. Jonathan A. KATES
93 Dean African-American Affairs ....Dr. Maurice APPREY
94 Dir Study in Women Gender Sexuality ....Ms. Charlotte PATTERSON
96 Director of Procurement Services ....Mr. Eric N. DENBY

The University of Virginia's College at Wise (I)

One College Avenue, Wise VA 24293-4412
County: Wise FICE Identification: 003747
Unit ID: 233897
Telephone: (276) 328-0100 Carnegie Class: Bac-A&S
FAX Number: (276) 376-1012 Calendar System: Semester
URL: www.uvawise.edu
Established: 1954 Annual Undergrad Tuition & Fees (In-State): $9,220
Enrollment: 2,183 Coed
Affiliation or Control: State IRS Status: 501(c)3
Highest Offering: Baccalaureate
Accreditation: **SC**, CS, ENG, NURSE, TEAC

01 Chancellor Dr. Donna P. HENRY
05 Provost/Vice Chan for Acad Affairs Dr. Sanders HUGUENIN
30 Vice Chanc Devel/College Relations Mr. Robert S. BRAGG
10 Vice Chanc Finance/Administration Mr. Sim E. EWING
84 Vice Chancellor Enrollment Mgmt Mr. Russell D. NECESSARY
20 Academic Dean Dr. Amelia J. HARRIS
32 Dean of Students Vacant
21 Comptroller Mrs. Kristy KISER
06 Registrar Ms. Narda PORTER
08 Director of the Library Mr. Robin P. BENKE
15 Director of Human Resources Ms. Stephanie D. PERRY
88 Director of College Services Mr. Joseph B. KISER
26 Director of News & Media Relations Ms. Kathy STILL
44 Director of Development Ms. Valerie LAWSON
29 Director of Alumni Relations Ms. Pamela J. COLLIE
37 Director of Financial Aid Ms. Rebecca HUFFMAN
35 Asst Dir of Student Activities Ms. Sarah SMITH
36 Director of Career Development Ms. Neva BRYAN
38 Personal Counselor/Health Services Ms. Rachel ROSE
19 Campus Police Chief Mr. Ronnie SHORTT
12 Site Director UVA-Wise Programs Ms. Courtney L. CONNER
18 Interim Dir Facility Planning/Mgmt Mr. David SHORT
27 Associate Vice Chancellor of Info Dr. P. Scott BEVINS
24 Director of Media Services Ms. Rosa BOTT
40 Bookstore Manager Mr. Scott LAWSON
39 Director of Residence Life Mr. Josh JUSTICE
108 Director Institutional Assessment Mr. David KLOCEK
100 Chief of Staff Ms. Huda ADEN

Virginia Baptist College (A)

4105 Plank Road, Fredericksburg VA 22407-4803
County: Spotsylvania FICE Identification: 038626
Unit ID: 482228
Telephone: (540) 785-5440 Carnegie Class: Spec-4-yr-Faith
FAX Number: (540) 785-5441 Calendar System: Semester
URL: www.vbc.edu
Established: 1984 Annual Undergrad Tuition & Fees: $5,540
Enrollment: 94 Coed
Affiliation or Control: Baptist IRS Status: 501(c)3
Highest Offering: Master's
Accreditation: TRACS

00 Chancellor Dr. Don FORRESTER
01 President Daniel STEVENS
05 Chief Academic Officer John EDMONDS
32 Chief Student Affairs/Student Life Adam DAVIS
10 Chief Financial Officer Sherry DAVIS
37 Director Student Financial Aid Meg POLIVKA
39 Director Student Housing Adam DAVIS
108 Director Institutional Assessment Ann RILL

Virginia Beach Theological Seminary (B)

2221 Centerville Turnpike, Virginia Beach VA 23464-6847
County: Virginia Beach FICE Identification: 039663
Telephone: (757) 479-3706 Carnegie Class: Not Classified
FAX Number: (757) 479-4232 Calendar System: Semester
URL: www.vbts.edu
Established: 1995 Annual Graduate Tuition & Fees: N/A
Enrollment: N/A Coed
Affiliation or Control: Baptist IRS Status: 501(c)3
Highest Offering: Master's; No Undergraduates
Accreditation: TRACS

01 President Dr. Daniel K. DAVEY
05 Chief Academic Officer Dr. Eric J. LEHNER
07 Director of Admissions Mr. Edward R. ESTES
10 Financial Officer Dr. Thomas A. KEISER
06 Registrar Dr. Mark HASSLER
09 Dir Institutional Effectiveness Dr. Robert J. TOMENENDAL

Virginia College (C)

7200 Midlothian Turnpike, Richmond VA 23225
Telephone: (804) 977-5100 Identification: 770837
Accreditation: ACICS, ACFEI, MAAB, OTA

† Branch campus of Virginia College, Birmingham, AL

Virginia Commonwealth University (D)

901 W Franklin Street, Box 842527,
Richmond VA 23284-2527
County: Independent City FICE Identification: 003735
Unit ID: 234030
Telephone: (804) 828-0100 Carnegie Class: DU-Highest
FAX Number: N/A Calendar System: Semester
URL: www.vcu.edu
Established: 1838 Annual Undergrad Tuition & Fees (In-State): $12,772
Enrollment: 30,848 Coed
Affiliation or Control: State IRS Status: 501(c)3
Highest Offering: Doctorate
Accreditation: SC, ANEST, ART, BUS, BUSA, CACREP, CEA, CIDA, CLPSY, COPSY, CORE, CS, DANCE, DENT, DH, DIETI, EMT, ENG, FEPAC, HSA, IPSY, JOUR, MED, MT, MUS, NMT, NUR, OT, PAST, PDPSY, PH, PHAR, PLNG, PTA, RAD, RTT, SPAA, SW, TED, THEA

01 Pres VCU/Pres & Chair VCU Hlth Sys Dr. Michael RAO
05 Provost & VP for Academic Affair Dr. Gail HACKETT
17 VP Health Sci/CEO VCU Health Sys Dr. Marsha RAPPLEY
17 VPres Clincial Svcs/CEO of VCU Hosp Mr. John DUVAL
10 VP for Finance and Budget Ms. Karol GRAY
46 Vice President for Research Dr. Francis L. MACRINA
30 Vice Pres Development & Alumni Rel Ms. Marsha HEIL
86 Exec Dir Govt Rels & Health Pol Ms. Karah L. GUNTHER
32 Interim Vice Prov Student Affairs Dr. Charles J. KLINK
88 Int Vice Prov for Life Sciences Dr. Leonard A. SMOCK
09 Vice Prov Planning & Decision Supp Ms. Kathleen SHAW
84 Vice Prov for Strategic Enrollment Mr. Luke D. SCHULTHEIS
13 Chief Information Officer Tech Svcs Mr. Alexander L. HENSON
18 Interim Assoc VPres Facilities Mgmt Mr. Richard F. SILWOSKI
84 Asst Vice Provost Enroll Svcs Ms. Anjour HARRIS
15 Asst Vice Pres for Human Resource Ms. Cathleen C. BURKE
08 University Librarian Mr. John E. ULMSCHNEIDER
43 University Counsel Ms. Madelyn F. WESSEL
41 Assoc VP and Director of Athletics Mr. Edward K. MCLAUGHLIN
88 Asst Vice Pres of Business Services Ms. Diane L. REYNOLDS
39 Exec Dir Residential Life & Housing Mr. Curtis ERWIN
06 Univ Registrar & Dir Records/Regis Mr. Bernard C. HAMM
07 Assoc VProv Strat Enrollment Mgmt Ms. Sybil C. HALLORAN
37 Executive Director of Financial Aid Mr. Marc VERNON
38 Dir of Counseling Services Dr. Jihad N. AZIZ
36 Dir of University Career Center Ms. Heidi A. MCCORMICK
35 Assoc Vice Prov/Dean Student Affs Dr. Reuban B. RODRIGUEZ
29 Assoc VP University Alum Relations Mr. Gordon A. MCDOUGALL
88 Exec Dir Global Education Office Dr. R. McKenna BROWN
88 Dir Ctr for Environmental Studies Dr. Gregory C. GARMAN
25 Sr Assoc VP Rsrch Admin/Compliance Ms. Susan E. ROBB
19 Chief of Police Mr. John A. VENUTI
31 VProv/Div Community Engagement Dr. Catherine W. HOWARD
94 Chair Women's Studies Dr. Kimberly M. BROWN
92 Dean Honors College Dr. Barry L. FALK
67 Dean of Pharmacy Dr. Joseph T. DIPIRO
66 Dean of School of Nursing Dr. Jean GIDDENS
63 Dean of School of Medicine Dr. Jerome F. STRAUSS
53 Dean School of Education Dr. Andrew P. DAIRE
52 Dean of Dentistry Dr. David C. SARRETT
50 Dean School of Business Mr. Ed A. GRIER
49 Dean Humanities & Sciences Dr. Monsterrat FUENTES
57 Interim Dean School of Arts Mr. James FRAZIER
70 Dean School of Social Work Dr. James E. HINTERLONG
76 Dean Allied Health Professions Dr. Cecil B. DRAIN
58 Dean Graduate School Dr. F. Douglas BOUDINOT
54 Dean of School of Engineering Dr. Barbara D. BOYAN
96 Director Procurement Payment Svcs Ms. Brenda MOWEN
26 Vice President University Relations Ms. Pamela D. LEPLEY
104 Director Study Abroad Ms. Stephanie DAVENPORT TIGNOR
28 Sr Asst to Pres & Int VP Inclusiv Dr. Kevin ALLISON
100 Sr Exec Dir Ofc Pres/Int VP Admin Mr. Brian D. SHAW
106 Director of Online Academic Program Mr. Jonathan D. BECKER
90 Dir Academic Technologies Ms. Colleen BISHOP

*Virginia Community College System Office (E)

300 Arboretum Place, Suite 200, Richmond VA 23236
County: Independent City FICE Identification: 008904
Unit ID: 234146
Telephone: (804) 819-4901 Carnegie Class: N/A
FAX Number: (804) 819-4760
URL: www.vccs.edu

01 Chancellor Dr. Glenn DUBOIS
10 Vice Chanc Administrative Services Ms. Donna VANCLEAVE
05 Vice Chancellor Academic Services Dr. Sharon MORRISSEY
103 Vice Chanc Workforce Development Dr. Craig HERNDON
13 Vice Chanc Information Tech Svcs Dr. James DAVIS
30 Vice Chanc Institutional Advance Dr. Jennifer SAGER GENTRY
15 Assoc Vice Chanc Human Resource Svc Dr. Christopher LEE
18 Assoc Vice Chanc/Facility Mgmt Mr. Bert JONES
43 General Counsel Ms. Greer SAUNDERS
88 Director of Internal Audit Mr. Whit MADERE
21 Controller Mr. Dave MAIR
04 Exec Assistant to the Chancellor Ms. Rose Marie OWEN

*Blue Ridge Community College (F)

PO Box 80, Weyers Cave VA 24486-0080
County: Augusta FICE Identification: 006819
Unit ID: 231536
Telephone: (540) 234-9261 Carnegie Class: Assoc/HT-Mix Trad/Non
FAX Number: (540) 234-8189 Calendar System: Semester
URL: www.brcc.edu
Established: 1967 Annual Undergrad Tuition & Fees (In-State): $5,019
Enrollment: 4,388 Coed
Affiliation or Control: State IRS Status: 501(c)3
Highest Offering: Associate Degree
Accreditation: SC, ADNUR

02 President Dr. John A. DOWNEY
32 Vice Pres Instruction/Student Svcs Dr. Robert YOUNG
10 VP Finance/Administrative Svcs Ms. Cynthia PAGE
15 Director of Human Resources Mr. Tim NICELY
30 Executive Director Development Ms. Amy LASER KIGER
05 Dean of Academic Affairs Ms. Marlena JARBOE
05 Dean of Academic Affairs Dr. David URSO
103 Dean of Workforce & Continuing Ed Dr. Kevin B. RATLIFF
88 Dean Student Support Services Ms. Annette WILLIAMS
08 Head Librarian Mr. Kyle MCCARRELL
26 Chief Public Relations Officer Ms. Bridget BAYLOR
06 Registrar/Admissions Ms. Erika MABREY
21 Financial Services Manager Ms. Franki HAMPTON
19 Security & Compliance Coordinator Mr. Wayne MARTIN
09 Coordinator Institutional Research Dr. Susan E. CROSBY
37 Financial Aid Coordinator Ms. Megan HARTLESS
36 Coord Career Services/ Recruitment Ms. Carmel MURPHY-NORRIS
84 Enrollment Services Specialist Ms. Amanda BLAND

*Central Virginia Community College (G)

3506 Wards Road, Lynchburg VA 24502-2498
County: Independent City FICE Identification: 004988
Unit ID: 231697
Telephone: (434) 832-7600 Carnegie Class: Assoc/HT-High Non
FAX Number: (434) 386-4700 Calendar System: Semester
URL: www.cvcc.vccs.edu
Established: 1966 Annual Undergrad Tuition & Fees (In-State): $4,470
Enrollment: 4,519 Coed
Affiliation or Control: State IRS Status: 501(c)3
Highest Offering: Associate Degree
Accreditation: SC, COARC, EMT, RAD

02 President Dr. John CAPPS
05 VP Student & Academic Services Dr. Muriel MICKLES
10 Vice President Finance & Admin Svcs Mr. Lewis BRYANT, III
103 VP Workforce Solutions & Cmty Educ Dr. Ruth HENDRICK
30 Vice Pres Institutional Advancement Mr. Michael BRADFORD
13 Vice Pres of Information Technology Mr. James D. LIGHTFOOT
45 Dean Inst Effectiveness/Planning Ms. Kristen OGDEN
32 Dean of Student Services Ms. Patricia SAFFIOTI
88 Director of Strategic Initiatives Mr. William SANDIDGE
29 Director Alumni/Public Relations Mr. Kenneth BUNCH
84 Dean of Enrollment Management Mr. Michael FARRIS
15 Human Resource Manager Mr. Randall FRANKLIN
18 Capital Outlay Project Engineer Mr. Tom BUSHLEY
56 Distance Education Supervisor Mr. Ed MCGEE
08 Coordinator of Library Services Mr. Michael T. FEIN
78 Coord Apprenticeship/Coop Education Vacant
79 Dean Humanities/Social Science Dr. Peter DORMAN
50 Dean of Business & Allied Health Dr. James LEMONS
81 Dean of Science/Math/Engineering Dr. Jeffrey W. LAUB
04 General Administration Coordinator Ms. Dianne SYKES
38 Director Student Counseling Ms. Lisa CHILTON

*Dabney S. Lancaster Community College (H)

1000 Dabney Drive, Clifton Forge VA 24422-1000
County: Alleghany FICE Identification: 004996
Unit ID: 231873
Telephone: (540) 863-2800 Carnegie Class: Assoc/HT-High Non
FAX Number: (540) 863-2915 Calendar System: Semester
URL: www.dslcc.edu
Established: 1962 Annual Undergrad Tuition & Fees (In-State): $4,350
Enrollment: 1,257 Coed
Affiliation or Control: State IRS Status: 501(c)3
Highest Offering: Associate Degree
Accreditation: SC, ACFEI, ADNUR

02 President Dr. John J. RAINONE
49 Vice President of Academic Affairs Dr. Benjamin WORTH
10 Vice President Finance/Admin Svcs Mrs. Angela GRAHAM
51 VP Continuing Educ/Workforce Svcs Mr. Gary S. KEENER
32 Director of Student Services Mr. Matthew MCGRAW
30 Director of Inst Advancement Ms. Rachael G. THOMPSON
08 Director of Learning Resources Ms. Nova WRIGHT
13 Director of Technology Services Ms. Tamra LIPSCOMB
15 Director of Human Resources Ms. April TOLLEY
108 Director Inst Effectiveness Dr. Chris OREM
18 Buildings & Grounds Supervisor Mr. Steven N. RICHARDS
21 Business Manager Ms. Deidre WOLFE
88 Special Assistant to President Ms. Gail JOHNSON
37 Coord of Student Financial Aid Mrs. Joy BROYLES
06 Registrar Ms. Lorrie FERGUSON
04 Executive Asst to President Vacant
07 Admissions Officer Ms. Rachel RIDDER
29 Alumni Relations Coordinator Ms. Jodi BURGESS
84 Retention Coordinator Mr. Joseph HAGY

*Danville Community College (I)

1008 S Main Street, Danville VA 24541-4088
County: Independent City FICE Identification: 003758
Unit ID: 231882
Telephone: (434) 797-2222 Carnegie Class: Assoc/MT-VT-High Non
FAX Number: (434) 797-8514 Calendar System: Semester
URL: www.dcc.vccs.edu
Established: 1967 Annual Undergrad Tuition & Fees (In-State): $4,365
Enrollment: 3,982 Coed
Affiliation or Control: State IRS Status: 501(c)3
Highest Offering: Associate Degree
Accreditation: SC

02 President Dr. Bruce R. SCISM
05 Vice Pres Academic/Student Services Dr. Debra HOLLEY
10 Vice Pres Financial/Admin Services Mr. Scott BARNES
30 Vice President of Development Mr. Shannon HAIR
09 Dir of Plng/Effectiveness/Research Mr. George STILL
26 Public Relations/Marketing Manager Ms. Kimberly BUCK

*Eastern Shore Community College (A)

29300 Lankford Highway, Melfa VA 23410-9755

County: Accomack FICE Identification: 003748
Unit ID: 232052
Telephone: (757) 789-1789 Carnegie Class: Assoc/MT-VT-Mix Trad/Non
FAX Number: (757) 789-1737 Calendar System: Semester
URL: www.es.vccs.edu
Established: 1971 Annual Undergrad Tuition & Fees (In-State): $4,395
Enrollment: 839 Coed
Affiliation or Control: State IRS Status: 501(c)3
Highest Offering: Associate Degree
Accreditation: SC

02 President .... Dr. Linda THOMAS-GLOVER
05 VP of Academic & Student Svcs .... Dr. Kimberly BRITT
10 Vice Pres Finance & Administration .... Mrs. Annette EDWARDS
32 Coordinator of Student Services .... Mrs. Cheryll MILLS
08 Director Learning Resources .... Mrs. Janet JUSTIS
06 Registrar .... Vacant
09 Director of Institutional Research .... Ms. Judith GRIER
26 Marketing and Development Officer .... Mr. William LECATO
37 Financial Aid Coordinator .... Ms. Carole READ
15 Human Resource Officer .... Mr. Michael DRISCOLL
18 Chief Facilities/Physical Plant .... Mr. Bobby MEARS
29 Director Alumni Relations/Devel .... Ms. Eve BELOTE
20 Assistant to the VP of Academics .... Mrs. Robin RICH-COATES

*Germanna Community College (B)

2130 Germanna Highway, Locust Grove VA 22508-2102

County: Orange FICE Identification: 008660
Unit ID: 232195
Telephone: (540) 423-9030 Carnegie Class: Assoc/HT-Mix Trad/Non
FAX Number: (540) 727-3207 Calendar System: Semester
URL: www.germanna.edu
Established: 1970 Annual Undergrad Tuition & Fees (In-State): $4,560
Enrollment: 7,282 Coed
Affiliation or Control: State IRS Status: 501(c)3
Highest Offering: Associate Degree
Accreditation: SC, ADNUR, DA, @PTAA

02 President .... Dr. David A. SAM
04 Exec Assistant to the President .... Ms. Pamela S. DUFF
05 VP Academic & Student Services .... Mr. Thomas PERIN
10 VP Finance & Administrative Svcs .... Mr. Richard BREHM
103 VP Workforce & Community Educ .... Dr. Jeanne WESLEY
30 VP Institutional Advancement .... Mr. Doug ELLIOTT
32 Dean of Student Services .... Ms. Pam FREDERICK
09 Exec Dir of Planning & Assessement .... Dr. John M. DAVIS
08 Head Librarian .... Ms. Tamara REMHOF
06 Registrar .... Ms. Cheri MAEA
72 Dean Professional & Technical Study .... Ms. Denise GUEST
55 Dean Distance Educ & Lrng Resources .... Dr. Yanyan YONG
66 Dean of Nursing & Health Technology .... Dr. Patti LISK
15 Associate VP of Human Resources .... Mrs. Laurie BOURNE
18 Building & Ground Supervisor .... Mr. Garland FENWICK
13 Manager Technology Services .... Ms. Jacque LARSEN
26 Director of Marketing .... Vacant
49 Dean of Arts & Sciences .... Dr. Shashuna GRAY
103 Dean of Workforce Prof Development .... Ms. Martha O'KEEFE
19 Chief of Police .... Mr. Craig BRANCH
37 Director Student Financial Aid .... Mr. Aaron WHITACRE

*J. Sargeant Reynolds Community College (C)

PO Box 85622, Richmond VA 23285-5622

County: Henrico FICE Identification: 003759
Unit ID: 232414
Telephone: (804) 371-3000 Carnegie Class: Assoc/MT-VT-Mix Trad/Non
FAX Number: (804) 371-3650 Calendar System: Semester
URL: www.reynolds.edu
Established: 1972 Annual Undergrad Tuition & Fees (In-State): $4,653
Enrollment: 11,861 Coed
Affiliation or Control: State IRS Status: 501(c)3
Highest Offering: Associate Degree
Accreditation: SC, ACFEI, ADNUR, COARC, DA, DT, EMT, MLTAD, OPD

02 President .... Dr. Gary L. RHODES
03 Executive Vice President .... Dr. Genene D. LEROSEN
05 Vice President Academic Affairs .... Dr. David R. LOOPE
30 Vice President Advancement .... Mrs. Elizabeth S. LITTLEFIELD
103 VP Comm Col Workforce Alliance .... Mr. Louis L. MCGINTY
10 VP Finance and Administration .... Ms. Amelia M. BRADSHAW
32 VP Student Affairs/Title IX Coord .... Dr. Thomas N. HOLLINS, JR.
45 Assoc VP Policy/Inst Effectiveness .... Dr. Timothy MERRILL
13 Vice President Technology .... Dr. Mark D. WEBSTER
79 Dean School of Humanities/Soc Sci .... Dr. Barbara M. GLENN
50 Dean School of Business .... Mr. David J. BARRISH
76 Dean School of Nursing/Allied Hlth .... Dr. Susan S. HUNTER
81 Dean School of Math Sci Engineering .... Mr. Raymond A. BURTON
20 Dean Educational Support Services .... Mr. Ty CORBIN
09 Director Office Inst Effectiveness .... Dr. Jackie R. BOURQUE
15 Assoc VP HR/Equal Emp Oppty Ofcr .... Ms. Corliss B. WOODSON
37 Director of Financial Aid .... Mrs. Kiesha L. POPE
07 Director of Admissions & Records .... Mrs. Karen M. PETTIS-WALDEN
88 Director Outreach and Recruitment .... Ms. Tracy S. GREEN
27 Director Communications .... Mr. Joseph SHILLING
26 Director of Marketing .... Ms. Kelly A. SMITH
08 Director of Info/Library Services .... Ms. Hong WU
88 Director of Learning Communities .... Mr. Charles PETERSON, JR.
18 Director Facilities Mgmt/Planning .... Mr. Michael VERDU
21 Director of Financial Operations .... Ms. Shirley L. HOPKINS
30 Director of Development .... Ms. Marianne S. MCGHEE
88 Director of Middle College .... Ms. Mary Jo WASHKO
84 Director of Enrollment Services .... Mr. Brian A. RICHARDSON
06 Registrar .... Ms. Denise S. TUNSTALL
96 Purchasing Manager .... Mr. Christopher L. COLE
19 Chief of Police .... Mr. Paul L. RONCA

*John Tyler Community College (D)

13101 Jefferson Davis Highway, Chester VA 23831-5316

County: Chesterfield FICE Identification: 004004
Unit ID: 232450
Telephone: (804) 796-4000 Carnegie Class: Assoc/HT-Mix Trad/Non
FAX Number: (804) 796-4163 Calendar System: Semester
URL: www.jtcc.edu
Established: 1965 Annual Undergrad Tuition & Fees (In-State): $4,345
Enrollment: 9,875 Coed
Affiliation or Control: State IRS Status: 501(c)3
Highest Offering: Associate Degree
Accreditation: SC, ADNUR, FUSER

02 President .... Dr. Edward E. RASPILLER
04 Executive Assistant to President .... Ms. Mara M. HILLIAR
05 VP Learning & Student Success .... Dr. William FIEGE
10 VP Finance & Administration .... Mr. William F. TAYLOR
103 Vice Pres for CC Workforce Alliance .... Mr. Mac L. MCGINTY
32 Dean of Students .... Ms. Sandra KIRKLAND
54 Interim Dean Engr/Bus/Public Svcs .... Dr. Julie RANSON
49 Dean Arts/Humanities/Soc Sciences .... Dr. Mikell BROWN
81 Dean Math/Natural & Health Sci .... Dr. Johanna WEISS
09 Dir Institutional Effectiveness .... Dr. Donna JOVANOVICH
08 Librarian Chester Campus .... Ms. Linda LUEBKE
15 AVP of Human Resources .... Ms. Susan GRINNAN
37 Director Financial Aid .... Mr. Tony JONES
19 Security Manager .... Mr. Frank MEDAGLIA
35 Coordinator Student Activities .... Vacant
36 Director Counseling Chester Campus .... Vacant
36 Dir Counseling Midlothian Campus .... Dr. Ruth VARNEY
18 Director Facilities Operations .... Mr. Greg A. DUNAWAY
08 Librarian Midlothian Campus .... Ms. Helen MCKANN
06 Registrar .... Ms. Joy L. JAMES
96 Director of Purchasing .... Ms. Nancy M. JIMISON
30 VP Institutional Advancement .... Ms. Rachel BIUNDO

*Lord Fairfax Community College (E)

173 Skirmisher Lane, Middletown VA 22645-1745

County: Frederick FICE Identification: 008659
Unit ID: 232575
Telephone: (540) 868-7000 Carnegie Class: Assoc/HT-Mix Trad/Non
FAX Number: (540) 868-7100 Calendar System: Semester
URL: www.lfcc.edu
Established: 1970 Annual Undergrad Tuition & Fees (In-State): $4,424
Enrollment: 6,996 Coed
Affiliation or Control: State IRS Status: 501(c)3
Highest Offering: Associate Degree
Accreditation: SC, EMT, SURGT

02 President .... Dr. Cheryl THOMPSON-STACY
05 VP of Academic & Student .... Dr. Kim BLOSSER
10 VP of Financial & Admin Services .... Mr. Chris BOIES
103 VP Workforce Solutions/Cont Educ .... Ms. Jeanian CLARK
15 Assoc VP of Human Resource Manager .... Ms. Karen N. FOREMAN
30 Director of Development .... Ms. Liv HEGGOY
25 Director TAACCCT Project/K2W .... Dr. John MILAM
76 Dean Health Professions .... Ms. Patricia F. LAWSON
50 Dean Business/Educ/HLM & Technology .... Dr. Karen KELLISON
81 Dean Science/Eng/Math & Health .... Dr. J. Brandon SHAW
83 Dean Hum/Social Sciences/Stdnt Dev .... Dr. James GILLISPIE
12 Dean Fauquier Campus .... Ms. Caroline WOOD
32 Dean Academic/Stdnt Aff & Outreach .... Ms. Brenda K. BYARD
08 Director Learning Resources Center .... Mr. David R. GRAY
72 Coordinator Network Sec/IT Sp Proj .... Mr. Douglas M. SHRIER
38 Director Advising & Stdnt Support .... Ms. Amber FOLTZ
37 Director of Financial Aid .... Vacant
88 Librarian .... Mr. Gregory MACDONALD
88 Librarian .... Ms. Kerry KILPATRICK
88 Dir Transition Programs/Title IX .... Ms. Linda KISER
35 Coord Student Life & Recruitment .... Ms. Brandy BOIES
71 Associate Dean of Academic Support .... Dr. Mia S. DEZURA
88 Director TRIO Student Support Svcs .... Ms. Sarah WILLIAMS
88 Coord Business/Industry Trng WSCE .... Mr. Bill PENCE
88 Coord Business/Industry Trng WSCE .... Mr. Larry BAKER
88 Coord Marketing/Business/Ind Trng .... Mr. Guy E. CURTIS, III
84 Associate Dean of Instruction .... Ms. Heather BURTON
88 Counselor - Fauquier Campus .... Ms. Andrea M. LO
88 Counselor .... Ms. Kelly REDMON

*Mountain Empire Community College (F)

3441 Mountain Empire Road,
Big Stone Gap VA 24219-4634

County: Wise FICE Identification: 009629
Unit ID: 232788
Telephone: (276) 523-2400 Carnegie Class: Assoc/MT-VT-Mix Trad/Non
FAX Number: (276) 523-8297 Calendar System: Semester
URL: www.mecc.edu
Established: 1972 Annual Undergrad Tuition & Fees (In-State): $4,365
Enrollment: 2,718 Coed
Affiliation or Control: State IRS Status: 501(c)3
Highest Offering: Associate Degree
Accreditation: SC, ADNUR, COARC, NAIT

02 President .... Dr. Scott HAMILTON
05 VP Academic & Student Services .... Ms. Vickie RATLIFF
10 Vice Pres Finance & Admin Services .... Mr. Ron VICARS
30 Vice Pres Institutional Advancement .... Ms. Donna G. STANLEY
32 Dean of Student Services .... Mr. Brandon DOTSON
07 Director of Enrollment Services .... Ms. Kristy HALL
08 Director of Library Services .... Mr. Michael GILLEY
51 Dir Continuing & Distance Education .... Ms. Sue Ella BOATRIGHT-WELLS
37 Dir Financial Aid/Enrollment Svcs .... Ms. Kristy HALL
13 Dir Ctr Computing & Info Technology .... Mr. Tony ROBINSON
15 Director Personnel Services .... Ms. Pam GILES
18 Chief Facilities/Physical Plant .... Mr. Preston LAYNE
49 Dean Arts & Sciences .... Ms. Harriett ARRINGTON
72 Dean of Industrial Tech/Health Sci .... Mr. Tommy CLEMENTS
50 Dean of Business & Info Tech .... Mr. Tommy CLEMENTS
26 Chief Public Relations Officer .... Ms. Amy GREEAR
19 Chief of Police .... Mr. Russell CYPHERS

*New River Community College (G)

5251 College Drive, Dublin VA 24084-1127

County: Pulaski FICE Identification: 005223
Unit ID: 232867
Telephone: (540) 674-3600 Carnegie Class: Assoc/HT-High Non
FAX Number: (540) 674-3642 Calendar System: Semester
URL: www.nr.edu
Established: 1969 Annual Undergrad Tuition & Fees (In-State): $4,352
Enrollment: 4,585 Coed
Affiliation or Control: State IRS Status: 501(c)3
Highest Offering: Associate Degree
Accreditation: SC

02 President .... Dr. Jack M. LEWIS
05 VP for Instruction/Student Svcs .... Dr. Patricia B. HUBER
10 Vice Pres for Finance & Technology .... Mr. John L. VAN HEMERT
30 VP for W/D and External Relations .... Dr. Mark C. ROWH
88 Assoc Dir ASLP/Emer Prep Coord .... Mrs. Amy J. HALL
88 Director of ASLP .... Mrs. Jill WILLIAMS
49 Dean of Arts & Sciences .... Dr. Janice SHELTON
50 Dean of Business & Technologies .... Dr. Peter ANDERSON
06 Registrar .... Mrs. Tammy SMITH
09 Dir Inst Effectiveness/Research .... Dr. Frederick M. STREFF
15 Dir of Human Resources & Bus Oper .... Ms. Melissa P. ANDERSON
32 Director of Student Affairs .... Mrs. Deborah KENNEDY
37 Director of Student Financial Aid .... Ms. Lori A. NUNN
102 Executive Director of Foundation .... Ms. Angie E. COVEY
96 Inventory and Purchasing Technician .... Ms. Monica W. CARDEN
56 Dir Dist Educ/Offsite Campus Svcs .... Mrs. Linda C. CLAUSSEN
08 Coordinator of Library Services .... Mrs. Sandra B. SMITH
07 Coord Admissions/Records/Stdnt Svcs .... Mrs. Tammy SMITH
18 Chief Facilities/Physical Plant .... Mr. Anthony J. NICOLO
88 Coordinator of WorkKeys Center .... Mrs. Patricia RYAN
84 Enrollment Manager Coordinator .... Mrs. Deborah D. KENNEDY
26 Public Relations Specialist .... Ms. Joyce K. TAYLOR
22 Coord Ctr for Disability Services .... Ms. Lucy J. HOWLETT

*Northern Virginia Community College (H)

4001 Wakefield Chapel Road, Annandale VA 22003-3796

County: Fairfax FICE Identification: 003727
Unit ID: 232946
Telephone: (703) 323-3000 Carnegie Class: Assoc/HT-Mix Trad/Non
FAX Number: (703) 323-3767 Calendar System: Semester
URL: www.nvcc.edu
Established: 1965 Annual Undergrad Tuition & Fees (In-State): $5,138
Enrollment: 51,487 Coed
Affiliation or Control: State IRS Status: 501(c)3
Highest Offering: Associate Degree
Accreditation: SC, ADNUR, CAHIIM, COARC, DA, DH, DMS, EMT, MLTAD, OTA, PTAA

02 President .... Dr. Scott RALLS
05 Exec VP/Chief Academic Officer .... Dr. Mel D. SCHIAVELLI
10 Vice President Finance .... Ms. Dimitrina DIMKOVA
11 Acting Vice Pres/Chief Admin Ofcr .... Ms. Dimitrina DIMKOVA
13 Vice Pres of Information Technology .... Dr. Steven G. SACHS
103 VP of Workforce Development .... Mr. Steve PARTRIDGE
09 VP Inst Effectiveness & Student Suc .... Dr. George E. GABRIEL
20 Assoc VP Academic Services .... Dr. Sharon N. ROBERTSON
84 Assoc VP Stdnt Svcs & Enroll Mgmt .... Dr. Elizabeth HARPER
12 Provost Alexandria Campus .... Dr. Annette HAGGRAY
12 Provost Annandale Campus .... Dr. Pamela HILBERT
12 Provost Loudoun Campus .... Dr. Julie LEIDIG
12 Acting Provost Manassas Campus .... Dr. Molly LYNCH
12 Provost Medical Education Campus .... Dr. Anne LOOCHTAN
12 Provost Woodbridge Campus .... Dr. Sam HILL
102 Exec Dir NVCC Education Foundation .... Mr. John J. RUFFINO
06 College Registrar .... Ms. Alethea HAMILTON
22 Director of Diversity .... Mr. Everett V. EBERHARDT
102 Assistant Dir NVCC Educ Foundation .... Ms. Mary BRAMLEY
25 Director of Grants .... Dr. Syedur RAHMAN
15 Director of Human Resources .... Ms. Charlotte M. CALOBRISI
96 Director of Purchasing .... Mr. Edward J. MELLON
37 Dir Stdnt Financial Aid/Support Svc .... Ms. Joan A. ZANDERS

21 Acting Associate VP .... Mr. Frederick TITTMANN
18 Director of Facilities .... Mr. Steven PATTERSON
26 Director of Media Relations .... Ms. Kathy THOMPSON
19 Director Security/Safety .... Chief Daniel DUSSEAU
86 Director Government Affs/Cmty Rels .... Mr. Dana KAUFFMAN

*Patrick Henry Community College (A)

645 Patriot Avenue, Martinsville VA 24112

County: Henry
FICE Identification: 003751
Unit ID: 233019
Telephone: (276) 638-8777
Carnegie Class: Assoc/HT-High Non
FAX Number: (276) 656-0320
Calendar System: Semester
URL: www.ph.vccs.edu
Established: 1962
Annual Undergrad Tuition & Fees (In-State): $4,360
Enrollment: 2,853
Coed
Affiliation or Control: State
IRS Status: 501(c)3
Highest Offering: Associate Degree
Accreditation: SC, ADNUR, EMT

02 President .... Dr. Angeline D. GODWIN
05 VP Academic/Student Develop Svcs .... Dr. Kristin WESTOVER
10 VP Finance & Admin Services .... Mr. John HANBURY
103 VP Workforce/Economic/Community Dev .... Mrs. Rhonda HODGES
30 VP Institutional Advancement .... Dr. Greg HODGES
20 Dean Academic Success/Col Transfer .... Vacant
81 Dean Science/Tech/Engineering/Math .... Mr. Steve BRANCH
76 Dean Prof Tech/Health Sciences .... Mr. Jeff FIELDS
72 Dean of Technology .... Mr. David DEAL
15 Director of Human Resources .... Ms. Lori MCCARTY
84 Dir of Enrollment Mgmt .... Dr. Colin FERGUSON
07 Coord Admiss & Accel Lrng .... Ms. Meghan EGGLESTON
26 Public Relations & Mktg Mgr .... Mr. James BOVE
06 Registrar .... Ms. Jessica CARTER
37 Financial Aid/Veterans Admin .... Mrs. Cindy KELLER
08 Head Librarian .... Mr. Barry REYNOLDS
25 Chief Contracts/Grants Admin .... Ms. Sarah B. MORRISON
41 Athletic Director .... Mr. Brian HENDERSON
09 Research Analyst .... Ms. Lisa FINLEY
18 Chief Facilities/Physical Plant .... Ms. Roberta WRIGHT
19 Director Security/Safety .... Mr. Gary DOVE
96 Director of Purchasing .... Ms. Lori CONNER
04 Administrative Asst to President .... Ms. Jencie GIBSON

*Paul D. Camp Community College (B)

100 N College Drive, Franklin VA 23851-0737

County: Independent City
FICE Identification: 009159
Unit ID: 233037
Telephone: (757) 569-6700
Carnegie Class: Assoc/HT-High Non
FAX Number: (757) 569-6795
Calendar System: Semester
URL: www.pdc.edu
Established: 1970
Annual Undergrad Tuition & Fees (In-State): $4,340
Enrollment: 1,259
Coed
Affiliation or Control: State
IRS Status: 501(c)3
Highest Offering: Associate Degree
Accreditation: SC

02 President .... Dr. Daniel W. LUFKIN
05 VP Academic/Student Development .... Dr. Tara ATKINS-BRADY
10 VP Finance/Admin Svcs .... Dr. Joe EDENFIELD
30 VP Institutional Advancement .... Dr. Renee FELTS
32 Dean Student Services .... Ms. Trina JONES
20 Dean of Suffolk Academic Programs .... Dr. Justin OLIVER
20 Dean of Franklin Campus .... Ms. Antoinette JOHNSON
08 Librarian .... Mr. Troy HAND
12 Academic Director-Smithfield .... Dr. Justin OLIVER
103 VP of Workforce Development .... Mr. Randy BETZ
09 Coord Inst Research/Assessment .... Ms. Damay J. BULLOCK
18 Chief Facilities/Physical Plant .... Vacant
15 Human Resources Analyst .... Mr. Shawn BURKS
26 Public Relations Specialist .... Ms. Wendy HARRISON
37 Financial Aid Coordinator .... Ms. Teresa HARRISON
04 Assistant to the President .... Ms. Cathy CUTCHINS

*Piedmont Virginia Community College (C)

501 College Drive, Charlottesville VA 22902-7589

County: Independent City
FICE Identification: 009928
Unit ID: 233116
Telephone: (434) 977-3900
Carnegie Class: Assoc/HT-High Non
FAX Number: (434) 971-8232
Calendar System: Semester
URL: www.pvcc.edu
Established: 1972
Annual Undergrad Tuition & Fees (In-State): $4,445
Enrollment: 5,554
Coed
Affiliation or Control: State
IRS Status: 501(c)3
Highest Offering: Associate Degree
Accreditation: SC, ADNUR, DMS, EMT, RAD, SURGT

02 President .... Dr. Frank FRIEDMAN
05 VP Instruction/Student Svcs .... Dr. John DONNELLY
10 Vice President Finance/Admin Svcs .... Mr. Kim MCMANUS
30 Vice Pres Advancement/Development .... Vacant
79 Dean Humanities/Fine Arts/Soc Sci .... Dr. Clifford W. HAURY
50 Dean Business/Math/Technologies .... Dr. Adam HASTINGS
17 Dean Health & Life Sciences .... Dr. Jean CHAPPELL
103 Dean Workforce Services .... Ms. Valerie PALAMOUNTAIN
32 Director of Student Services .... Ms. Mary Lee WALSH
13 Dir Information Technology/CIO .... Ms. Sue HAAS
09 Dir Instl Research/Planning/Effect .... Dr. Jolene HAMM

06 Registrar .... Ms. Allyson REA
96 Business Manager .... Ms. Tracy CERSLEY
18 Facilities Manager .... Mr. Dennis WEIR
15 Human Resources Manager .... Mrs. Teresa WILLIS
26 Marketing/Media Relations Director .... Ms. Leigh-Anne LAWRENCE
84 Outreach Manager .... Ms. Denise MCCLANAHAN
08 Coordinator Library Services .... Ms. Crystal NEWELL
37 Coordinator Financial Aid .... Vacant
36 Coordinator Advising & Transfer .... Mr. Kemper STEELE

*Rappahannock Community College (D)

12745 College Drive, Glenns VA 23149-0287

County: Gloucester
FICE Identification: 009160
Unit ID: 233310
Telephone: (804) 758-6700
Carnegie Class: Assoc/HT-High Non
FAX Number: (804) 758-3852
Calendar System: Semester
URL: www.rappahannock.edu
Established: 1970
Annual Undergrad Tuition & Fees (In-State): $4,460
Enrollment: 3,569
Coed
Affiliation or Control: State
IRS Status: 501(c)3
Highest Offering: Associate Degree
Accreditation: SC, ADNUR

02 President .... Dr. Elizabeth H. CROWTHER
32 VP Instruction/Student Development .... Dr. A. Donna ALEXANDER
10 Vice Pres Finance/Admin Services .... Mr. William DOYLE
103 Vice Pres Workforce/Cmty Devel .... Mr. Jason PERRY
05 Academic Dean .... Ms. Martha BROOKS
35 Dean Student Development .... Dr. Dave KEEL
106 Dean of Distance Learning/Tech .... Ms. Virginia JONES
30 Dean of College Advancement .... Ms. Sarah POPE
108 Dean Research/Effectiveness/Plng .... Dr. Glenda D. HAYNIE
06 College Registrar .... Ms. Felicia B. PACKETT
37 Financial Aid/Veteran Affairs Ofcr .... Ms. Sherika CHARITY
15 Director Human Resources .... Mrs. Caroline W. STELTER
18 Facilities/Physical Plant Manager .... Mr. Mark P. BEAVER
10 Business Manager .... Ms. Susan S. BROADDUS
08 Library Coordinator .... Mr. Dan REAM

*Southside Virginia Community College (E)

109 Campus Drive, Alberta VA 23821-2930

County: Brunswick
FICE Identification: 008661
Unit ID: 233639
Telephone: (434) 949-1000
Carnegie Class: Assoc/MT-VT-High Non
FAX Number: (434) 949-7863
Calendar System: Semester
URL: www.southside.edu
Established: 1970
Annual Undergrad Tuition & Fees (In-State): $4,350
Enrollment: 5,352
Coed
Affiliation or Control: State
IRS Status: 501(c)3
Highest Offering: Associate Degree
Accreditation: SC, ADNUR, EMT

02 President .... Dr. Al ROBERTS
05 Vice Pres Academics/Student Affs .... Ms. Tara CARTER
10 Vice Pres Finance & Administration .... Mr. Peter G. HUNT
25 VP Adult Education & Grants .... Dr. Linda SHEFFIELD
13 Chief Information Officer .... Mr. Chad WOLLENBERG
84 Dean Enrollment Management .... Mrs. Shannon FEINMAN
20 Dean of Instruction .... Ms. Dixie DALTON
20 Dean of Instruction .... Mr. Chad PATTON
20 Dean of Instruction .... Ms. Michelle EDMONDS
09 Dean Institutional Effectiveness .... Vacant
66 Dean of Nursing/Health Technology .... Ms. Michelle K. EDMONDS
102 Exec Director SVCC Foundation .... Mrs. Mary Jane ELKINS
08 College Librarian .... Ms. Marika PETERSON
26 Public Relations & Mktg Specialist .... Ms. Christie C. HALES
37 Director of Financial Aid .... Ms. Sally THARRINGTON
15 Human Resources Manager .... Ms. Bethany W. HARRIS
18 Buildings/Grounds Supt Christanna .... Mr. Roger WRAY
38 Dir Student Counseling Christanna .... Ms. Bernadette BATTLE
38 Director Student Counseling Daniel .... Mrs. Dorethea SIZEMORE
21 Business Manager .... Mrs. Juanita GRIZZARD
29 Alumni Relations SVCC .... Mrs. Mary Jane ELKINS
06 Ofcr for Admiss/Registration Team .... Ms. Robin NELSON

*Southwest Virginia Community College (F)

Box SVCC, Richlands VA 24641-1101

County: Tazewell
FICE Identification: 007260
Unit ID: 233648
Telephone: (276) 964-2555
Carnegie Class: Assoc/HT-Mix Trad/Non
FAX Number: (276) 964-9307
Calendar System: Semester
URL: www.sw.edu
Established: 1967
Annual Undergrad Tuition & Fees (In-State): $4,335
Enrollment: 2,546
Coed
Affiliation or Control: State
IRS Status: 501(c)3
Highest Offering: Associate Degree
Accreditation: SC, ADNUR, EMT, OTA, RAD

02 President .... Dr. J. Mark ESTEPP
05 VP Academics & Student Services .... Dr. Barbara J. FULLER
10 Vice Pres Finance & Admin Svcs .... Mr. Windell TURNER
04 General Admin Coordinator .... Ms. Rhonda L. VANDYKE
79 Dean Humanit/Sci/Math/Health Tech .... Ms. Cathy SMITH-COX
50 Dean Business/Engr & Indust Tech .... Mr. James DYE

103 Dean Cmty/Workforce & Econ Sol .... Vacant
32 Dean Student Success .... Ms. Dyan E. LESTER
09 Institutional Research Officer .... Dr. Edmond C. SMITH
102 Exec Dir SWCC Educ Foundation & Dev .... Ms. Susan L. HAGY LOWE
15 Human Resources Director .... Ms. Martha L. RASNAKE
19 Campus Police Chief .... Mr. Ronnie KISER
21 Business Manager .... Mr. Michael BALES
18 Physical Plant Superintendent .... Mr. Tony MCGHEE
26 Public Relations Coordinator .... Ms. Patsy G. BUSSARD
08 Coordinator of Library Services .... Ms. Teresa A. YEAROUT
106 Director Distance Learning .... Vacant
25 Grants Coordinator .... Ms. Phyllis ROBERTS

*Thomas Nelson Community College (G)

99 Thomas Nelson Drive, Hampton VA 23666

County: Independent City
FICE Identification: 006871
Unit ID: 233754
Telephone: (757) 825-2700
Carnegie Class: Assoc/HT-Mix Trad/Non
FAX Number: (757) 825-2763
Calendar System: Semester
URL: www.tncc.edu
Established: 1967
Annual Undergrad Tuition & Fees (In-State): $4,416
Enrollment: 10,436
Coed
Affiliation or Control: State
IRS Status: 501(c)3
Highest Offering: Associate Degree
Accreditation: SC, ADNUR, DH

02 President .... Dr. John T. DEVER
05 Int Vice Pres for Academic Affairs .... Mr. Charles SWAIM
32 Vice President for Student Affairs .... Dr. Daniel LUFKIN
11 Vice President for Admin/Finance .... Mr. Charles A. NURNBERGER
103 Vice Pres for Workforce Development .... Dr. Deborah G. WRIGHT
44 Vice Pres Institutional Advancement .... Ms. Cynthia CALLAWAY
35 Assoc VP for Student Affairs .... Dr. Vicki RICHMOND
13 Director of Information Tech .... Mr. Wayne DAVIS
106 Dir Distance/Distributive Learning .... Ms. Ruth SMITH
84 Int Dean of Enrollment Management .... Ms. Kris RARIG
10 Assoc VP for Financial Services .... Ms. Teresa BAILEY
103 Assoc VP for Workforce Training/CE .... Dr. Carmen BURROWS
60 Dean Communications/Social Sciences .... Mr. Patrick TOMKINS
81 Int Dean Science/Engr/Technology .... Ms. Riham MAHFOUZ
50 Int Dean Bus/Public Svcs/IT/Math .... Mr. Bryan JONES
76 Dean Health Professions .... Dr. Christy HAWKINS
37 Dir Financial Aid/Veteran Affairs .... Ms. Kathryn ANDERSON
18 Mgr Facilities/Plan/Capital Outlay .... Mr. Mark KRAMER
26 Director Public Relations/Marketing .... Ms. Cecilia RAMIREZ
30 Director of Development .... Vacant
08 Director of Learning Resources .... Mr. Richard HODGES
09 Dir Inst Research and Effectiveness .... Mr. Steven FELKER
21 Business Office Manager .... Mr. Phillip BRADSHAW
15 Director of Human Resources .... Ms. Joy COOKE

*Tidewater Community College (H)

121 College Place, Norfolk VA 23510

County: Independent City
FICE Identification: 003712
Unit ID: 233772
Telephone: (757) 822-1122
Carnegie Class: Assoc/HT-Mix Trad/Non
FAX Number: (757) 822-1060
Calendar System: Semester
URL: www.tcc.edu
Established: 1968
Annual Undergrad Tuition & Fees (In-State): $5,171
Enrollment: 27,646
Coed
Affiliation or Control: State
IRS Status: 501(c)3
Highest Offering: Associate Degree
Accreditation: SC, ACFEI, ADNUR, CAHIIM, COARC, DMS, EMT, FUSER, MLTAD, OTA, PTAA, RAD

02 President .... Dr. Edna V. BAEHRE-KOLOVANI
05 VP Academic Affairs/Chief Acad Ofcr .... Dr. Daniel T. DEMARTE
32 Int VP for Student Affairs .... Dr. Michael D. SUMMERS
10 Vice President Finance .... Ms. Phyllis F. MILLOY
26 VP Public Affairs & Communications .... Dr. James P. TOSCANO
30 VP Inst Advancement/Exec Dir Devel .... Ms. Felecia W. BLOW
18 Exec Dir Real Estate Dev/COO Facil .... Mr. Matthew J. BAUMGARTEN
13 Acting VP Information Systems .... Mr. Curtis K. AASEN
103 VP for Workforce Solutions .... Dr. Corey L. MCCRAY
12 Provost Chesapeake Campus .... Dr. Lisa B. RHINE
12 Provost Portsmouth Campus .... Dr. Michelle W. WOODHOUSE
12 Provost Norfolk Campus .... Dr. Jeffrey S. BOYD
12 Provost Virginia Beach Campus .... Dr. Michael D. SUMMERS
09 Dir Institutional Effectiveness .... Mr. Curtis K. AASEN
15 Associate VP for Human Resources .... Ms. Beth LUNDE
100 Chief of Staff .... Ms. Susan M. JAMES
20 AVP Academics .... Dr. Kellie C. SOREY
20 AVP Faculty Professional Dev .... Mr. Frederick E. STEMPLE, JR.
20 AVP Learning Tech Applications .... Mr. John MOREA
08 AVP for Libraries .... Mr. Steve E. LITHERLAND
84 AVP Recruitment/Admission/Enroll .... Dr. Karen D. CAMPBELL
106 Dean for the Center of eLearning .... Ms. Virginia K. ZILLGES
27 AVP Interactive Com/Pub Info Office .... Ms. Marian L. ANDERFUREN
35 AVP for Student Success .... Ms. Christine DAMROSE-MAHLMANN
50 Dean Bus/Pub Svc/Tech Chesapeake .... Mr. James E. PERKINSON, JR.
79 Dean of Humanities & Soc Sciences .... Ms. Diane N. RYAN
81 Dean Sci/Tech/Eng/Math Chesapeake .... Mr. Thomas B. STOUT
35 Dean of Student Svcs Chesapeake .... Dr. James E. EDWARDS
50 Dean Bus/SC/P Svcs/Tech Norfolk .... Ms. Johnna C. HARRELL

81 Dean Lang/Math/Science Norfolk ... Dr. Kerry S. RAGNO
35 Dean of Student Svcs Norfolk ... Mr. Emmanuel CHESTNUT
50 Dean Bus/Pub Svcs/Tech Portsmouth ... Ms. Ann P. AMBROSE
81 Dean Lang/Math/Science Portsmouth ... Ms. Jenefer D. SNYDER
35 Dean of Student Svcs Portsmouth ... Ms. Dana M. SINGLETON
66 Dean Beazley School Nurs Portsmouth ... Dr. Phyllis M. EATON
54 Dean Math Eng & Ind Tech Va Beach ... Mr. David A. EKKER
76 Dean Health Professions ... Mr. Thomas G. CALOGRIDES, JR.
50 Dean IT & Business Va Beach ... Mr. William CLEMENT
81 Dean Natural Sciences Va Beach ... Mr. Gregory P. FRANK
83 Dean Social Sci/Pub Svcs Va Beach ... Mr. Joseph J. FAIRCHILD
79 Dean Humanities Va Beach ... Ms. Marcanne ANDERSEN
35 Dean of Student Svcs Va Beach ... Dr. Marilyn R. HODGE
88 Dir Reg Automotive Ctr Chesapeake ... Mr. Beno RUBIN
14 Dir Programming Systems & Develop ... Mr. Ken BALLARD
14 Dir Network & Telecom Services ... Vacant
06 College Registrar ... Mrs. Laura BURNHAM
57 Interim Director Visual Arts Center ... Ms. Corrine LILYARD-MITCHELL
18 Director Facilities Management ... Mr. David R. GUGLIELMO
19 Director Safety & Security ... Mr. George J. OKATY
88 Director of Emergency Preparedness ... Mr. Pete F. SOMMER
88 Exec Dir Ctr Military Veterans Educ ... Dr. Bruce H. BRUNSON
88 Exec Dir Roper Performing Arts Ctr ... Mr. Paul H. LASAKOW
21 Director Fiscal Services ... Ms. Reyne D. BUCHHOLZ
96 Director Material Mgmt Procurement ... Ms. Robin S. MOORE
37 Director Central Financial Aid ... Ms. Jennifer E. HARPHAM
109 Director Auxiliary Services ... Ms. Bridgett M. PASSAUER
21 Dir Fin Info Systems & Operations ... Ms. Heather H. TAYLOR
88 Dir Gen Educ Assess Trans Partnrshp ... Ms. Jennifer FERGUSON
88 Dir Std Mental Health & Behavior ... Dr. Jessica SMITH
45 Dir of Planning & Accountability ... Dr. Kimberly M. BOVEE
45 Director Grants/Sponsored Programs ... Ms. Laverne ELLERBE
88 Director of Intercultural Learning ... Dr. Jeanne B. NATALI
88 Director Marketing ... Mr. Curt J. WYNN
105 Chief Web Communications Officer ... Ms. Allison H. TRELOAR
04 Administrative Asst to President ... Ms. Latesha JOHNSON

*Virginia Highlands Community College (A)

PO Box 828, Abingdon VA 24212-0828

County: Washington FICE Identification: 007099
Unit ID: 233903
Telephone: (276) 739-2400 Carnegie Class: Assoc/HT-Mix Trad/Non
FAX Number: (276) 739-2590 Calendar System: Semester
URL: www.vhcc.edu
Established: 1967 Annual Undergrad Tuition & Fees (In-State): $4,365
Enrollment: 2,505 Coed
Affiliation or Control: State IRS Status: 501(c)3
Highest Offering: Associate Degree
Accreditation: SC, ADNUR

02 President ... Dr. Gene C. COUCH, JR.
05 VP Instruction & Student Services ... Dr. Stacy THOMAS
10 VP Financial/Administrative Svcs ... Ms. Christine FIELDS
30 Vice Pres Institutional Advancement ... Dr. Joey GILBERT
49 Business Humanities & Science Div ... Ms. Barbara MANUEL
72 Director of Institutional Advance ... Mr. Robert E. MAY
66 Dean of Nursing and Allied Health ... Ms. Kathy J. MITCHELL
103 VP Workforce Training & Cont Educ ... Ms. Melinda T. LELAND
08 Coordinator of Library Services ... Mr. Joel RUDY
37 Director of Financial Aid ... Ms. Karen T. CHEERS
07 Director Admission/Records ... Ms. Karen T. CHEERS
06 Registrar ... Ms. Charlene EASTRIDGE
15 Human Resource Manager ... Ms. Laura MCCLELLAN
32 Coord PR/Marketing & Alumni ... Ms. Anne DUNHAM
88 Coordinator Talent Search ... Mr. Justin NECESSARY
88 Director Project EXCEL ... Ms. Beth PAGE
38 Coordinator of Student Success ... Mr. Stacy THOMAS
21 Business Manager ... Ms. Mary SNEAD
96 Director of Purchasing ... Ms. Chelsa TAYLOR
88 Institutional Effectiveness ... Ms. Jennifer D. ADDISON
90 Coord Academic Computing/Technology ... Mr. Glen JOHNSON
26 Public Relations Officer ... Ms. Anne M. DUNHAM
09 Institutional Research Officer ... Mr. Jeff D. RUSSELL
18 Chief Facilities/Physical Plant ... Mr. Ernest L. NUNLEY
19 Campus Police Chief ... Mr. Blake ANDIS
36 Career Plng/Placement Specialist ... Mr. Michael MCBRIDE

*Virginia Western Community College (B)

PO Box 14007, Roanoke VA 24038-4007

County: Independent City FICE Identification: 003760
Unit ID: 233949
Telephone: (540) 857-8922 Carnegie Class: Assoc/HT-High Non
FAX Number: (540) 857-6526 Calendar System: Semester
URL: www.virginiawestern.edu
Established: 1966 Annual Undergrad Tuition & Fees (In-State): $4,713
Enrollment: 8,632 Coed
Affiliation or Control: State IRS Status: 501(c)3
Highest Offering: Associate Degree
Accreditation: SC, ACBSP, ACFEI, DH, RAD, RTT

02 President ... Dr. Robert H. SANDEL
10 Vice Pres of Finance/Admin Services ... Ms. Lisa RIDPATH
05 Vice Pres Academic/Student Affs ... Dr. Elizabeth WILMER
30 Vice Pres Institutional Advancement ... Dr. Angela M. FALCONETTI
103 Vice Pres Workforce Development Svc ... Dr. Milian HAYWARD
45 Dean Institutional Effectiveness ... Ms. Rachelle KOUDELIK-JONES
49 Dean Liberal Arts/Social Sciences ... Ms. Amy ANGUIANO
76 Dean Health Professions ... Ms. Carole GRAHAM
81 Dean Science/Tech/Engineering/Math ... Dr. John ANDERSON
50 Dean Business/Trades/Technology ... Ms. Deborah YANCEY
24 Dean Learning Resources ... Mr. Christopher PORTER
32 Dean of Student Services ... Ms. Lori BAKER
09 Director Institutional Research ... Ms. Carol ROWLETT
18 Director of Facilities Planning ... Mr. Kevin G. WITTER
26 Coord for Marketing/Strategic Comm ... Mr. Josh MEYER
06 Registrar ... Ms. Karin COLE
19 Campus Police Chief ... Mr. Craig HARRIS
37 Coord Financial Aid/Veterans Affs ... Mr. Chad SARTINI
103 Workforce Operations Supervisor ... Ms. Cassandra DOVE
13 Dir Information Educ Technology ... Mr. Shivaj SAMANTA
15 Assoc VP of Human Resources ... Ms. Jennifer PITTMAN
21 Business Manager ... Mrs. Fredina AARON
84 Coordinator for Enrolment Services ... Ms. Brooke FERGUSON
08 Coordinator of the Library ... Vacant
36 Coordinator Career Services ... Ms. Rhonda PERDUE
25 Coord Grants Dev & Special Projects ... Ms. Marilyn J. HERBERT-ASHTON
29 Coordinator of Development ... Ms. Carole TARRANT

*Wytheville Community College (C)

1000 E Main Street, Wytheville VA 24382-3308

County: Wythe FICE Identification: 003761
Unit ID: 234377
Telephone: (276) 223-4700 Carnegie Class: Assoc/HT-Mix Trad/Non
FAX Number: (276) 223-4778 Calendar System: Semester
URL: www.wcc.vccs.edu
Established: 1963 Annual Undergrad Tuition & Fees (In-State): $4,380
Enrollment: 3,302 Coed
Affiliation or Control: State IRS Status: 501(c)3
Highest Offering: Associate Degree
Accreditation: SC, ADNUR, DH, MLTAD, PTAA

02 President ... Dr. Dean SPRINKLE
05 Vice Pres Instruction/Student Devel ... Dr. Lorri HUFFARD
10 Vice Pres Finance & Admin Services ... Ms. Crystal Y. CREGGER
09 Director of Institutional Research ... Dr. Kent E. GLINDEMANN
30 Vice Pres of College Development ... Dr. Rhonda E. CATRON-WOOD
103 Director of Workforce ... Mr. Perry HUGHES
83 Dean of Transfer & Social Sciences ... Mr. Jacob SURRATT
76 Dean of Health & Occupational Pgms ... Mr. Jamie EDWARDS
32 Dean of Student Services ... Ms. Renee THOMAS
13 Director Acad/Admin Computing ... Mr. Shawn MCREYNOLDS
06 Registrar ... Ms. Karen ALEXANDER
15 Human Resources Manager ... Ms. Malinda EVERSOLE
26 Public Relations Coordinator ... Vacant
08 Coordinator of Library Services ... Mr. George E. MATTIS, JR.
96 Procurement Officer ... Ms. Vivian FANNING
106 Dir of Distance & Distrib Learning ... Mr. Kenneth E. FAIRBANKS
37 Coordinator Financial Aid ... Ms. Mary Beth GALLAGHER
04 Administrative Asst to President ... Ms. Denita BURNETT
88 Development Services Coordinator ... Ms. Jill W. ROSS

Virginia International University (D)

11200 Waples Mill Road, Suite 360, Fairfax VA 22030

County: Fairfax FICE Identification: 041440
Telephone: (703) 591-7042 Carnegie Class: Not Classified
FAX Number: (703) 591-7046 Calendar System: Semester
URL: www.viu.edu
Established: 1998 Annual Undergrad Tuition & Fees: N/A
Enrollment: N/A Coed
Affiliation or Control: Independent Non-Profit IRS Status: 501(c)3
Highest Offering: Master's
Accreditation: ACICS

01 President ... Dr. Isa SARAC
03 Vice President University Affairs ... Ms. Christine KOONTS

Virginia Military Institute (E)

319 Letcher Avenue, Lexington VA 24450-0304

County: Independent City FICE Identification: 003753
Unit ID: 234085
Telephone: (540) 464-7230 Carnegie Class: Bac-A&S
FAX Number: (540) 464-7583 Calendar System: Semester
URL: www.vmi.edu
Established: 1839 Annual Undergrad Tuition & Fees (In-State): $16,536
Enrollment: 1,700 Coed
Affiliation or Control: State IRS Status: 501(c)3
Highest Offering: Baccalaureate
Accreditation: SC, BUS, ENG

01 Superintendent ... Gen. J. H. Binford PEAY
05 Dean of the Faculty ... BGen. Jeffrey G. SMITH
10 Deputy Superintendent Finance/Admin ... BGen. Robert L. GREEN
32 Commandant of Cadets ... Col. William J. WANOVICH
100 Chief of Staff ... Col. James P. INMAN
04 Exec Asst to the Superintendent ... LtCol. Sean P. HARRINGTON
21 Assoc Business Exec/Treasurer ... Col. Jeffrey L. LAWHORNE
07 Director of Admissions ... Col. Vernon L. BEITZEL
88 Exec Director Museum Programs ... Col. Keith E. GIBSON
37 Director of Financial Aid ... Maj. Thomas A. BRASHEARS
35 Deputy Commandant ... Col. L. E. HURLBUT
36 Director of Career Services ... Col. R. Samuel RATCLIFFE
41 Director Intercollegiate Athletics ... Mr. David L. DILES
26 Director Communications & Marketing ... Col. Stewart D. MACINNIS
29 Executive VP Alumni Association ... Col. Adam C. VOLANT
102 Exec VP VMI Foundation/Fund Raising ... Mr. Brian S. CROCKETT
88 Exec VP Keydet Club/Athletic Fund ... Mr. Gregory M. CAVALLARO
06 Registrar ... Col. Janet M. BATTAGLIA
15 Director Human Resources ... Col. Robert B. SPORE
18 Director Physical Plant ... Col. James L. WILLIAMS, JR.
09 Director Institutional Research ... LtCol. Lee L. RAKES
109 Director Auxiliary Services ... Col. David P. WILLIAMS
40 Manager Bookstore ... Mr. Bradley N. MCDOUGAL
42 Institute Chaplain ... Col. James S. PARK
17 Institute Physician ... Dr. David L. COPELAND
88 Director of Athletic Communications ... Mr. Wade H. BRANNER
08 Head Librarian ... Col. Donald H. SAMDAHL, JR.
38 Director of Cadet Counseling ... LtCol. Sarah L. JONES
13 Director Information Technology ... Col. Thomas F. HOPKINS
96 Director of Purchasing ... Maj. Kathy H. TOMLIN

† Tuition includes required room and board and quartermaster charges.

Virginia Polytechnic Institute and State University (F)

Blacksburg VA 24061-0202

County: Montgomery FICE Identification: 003754
Unit ID: 233921
Telephone: (540) 231-6000 Carnegie Class: DU-Highest
FAX Number: (540) 231-9263 Calendar System: Semester
URL: www.vt.edu
Established: 1872 Annual Undergrad Tuition & Fees (In-State): $12,485
Enrollment: 31,224 Coed
Affiliation or Control: State IRS Status: 501(c)3
Highest Offering: Doctorate
Accreditation: SC, ART, BUS, BUSA, CACREP, CEA, CIDA, CLPSY, CONST, CS, DIETD, DIETI, ENG, IPSY, LSAR, MFCD, MUS, PCSAS, PH, PLNG, SPAA, TED, THEA, VET

01 President ... Timothy D. SANDS
05 Executive Vice President & Provost ... Thanassis RIKAKIS
11 Vice President for Administration ... Sherwood G. WILSON
13 Vice Pres for Information Tech ... Scott F. MIDKIFF
32 Vice President Student Affairs ... Patricia A. PERILLO
30 Vice Pres for Advancement ... Charles D. PHLEGAR
29 Sr Assoc Vice Pres Alumni Relations ... Matthew M. WINSTON, JR.
28 Vice Provost Inclusion & Diversity ... Menah PRATT-CLARKE, JR.
46 Vice Provost Research & Innovation ... Theresa MEYER
20 Vice Prov for Undergrad Acad Affs ... Rachel L. HOLLOWAY
58 Vice President and Dean Grad Educ ... Karen P. DEPAUW
56 VP Outreach/International Affs ... Guru GHOSH
10 Vice President for Finance and CFO ... M. Dwight SHELTON, JR.
07 Assoc VP/Dir Undergrad Admissions ... Mildred JOHNSON
35 Dean of Students ... Thomas BROWN
15 Assoc Vice Pres for Administration ... Lisa WILKES
09 Assoc Provost Inst Effectivness ... Steven CULVER
43 University Counsel ... Kay K. HEIDBREDER
84 Vice Prov for Enroll & Degree Mgmt ... Wanda H. DEAN
37 Dir of Scholarships/Financial Aid ... Elizabeth ARMSTRONG
20 Vice Provost Faculty Affairs ... Jack FINNEY
45 Vice Provost Resource Management ... Kenneth SMITH
23 Director Schiffert Health Center ... Kanitta CHAROENSIRI
18 Assoc Vice Pres/Chief Facilities ... Christopher KIWUS
109 Director of Dining Services ... Ted FAULKNER
39 Dir Housing and Residential Life ... Eleanor FINGER
41 Athletic Director ... Whit BABCOCK
26 Assoc Vice Pres Univ Relations ... Tracy VOSBURGH
38 Director Student Counseling ... Chris FLYNN
40 Executive Director Bookstore ... Donald J. WILLIAMS
62 Dean of Libraries ... Tyler WALTERS
47 Dean of Agriculture/Life Sciences ... Alan GRANT
48 Dean of Architecture/Urban Studies ... Jack DAVIS
49 Dean College of Science ... Sally C. MORTEN
50 Dean of Business ... Robert T. SUMICHRAST
54 Int Dean of Engineering ... G. Don TAYLOR
79 Dean Liberal Arts & Human Sciences ... Elizabeth SPILLER
74 Dean of Veterinary Medicine ... Cyril R. CLARKE
65 Dean of Natural Resources & Environ ... Paul M. WINISTORFER
96 Director of Procurement ... Mary HELMICK
91 Assoc Vice Pres for Enterprise Sys ... Deborah M. FULTON
12 VP for the National Capital Region ... Steven H. MCKNIGHT
102 CEO Virginia Tech Foundation ... John E. DOOLEY
04 Sr Executive Asst to President ... Sandy SMITH
06 University Registrar ... Rick SPARKS
100 Chief of Staff ... Kim O'ROURKE
104 Director Global Education Office ... Theresa C. JOHANSSON
105 Director Web Communications ... John JACKSON
106 Exec Dir Tech-enhanced Learning ... Dale PIKE
88 Asst Provost Regional Accreditation ... Kristen BUSH
19 Chief of Police/Dir of Security ... Kevin FOUST
22 Dir Affirmative Action/EEO ... Karisa MOORE
25 Chief Contracts/Grants Admin ... Frank FITZGERALD
44 Director Annual or Planned Giving ... Randy HOLDEN
86 Exec Director Government Relations ... Chris YIANILOS

Virginia State University (G)

One Hayden Drive,
Virginia State University VA 23806-0001

County: Chesterfield FICE Identification: 003764
Unit ID: 234155
Telephone: (804) 524-5000 Carnegie Class: Masters/M
FAX Number: (804) 524-6506 Calendar System: Semester
URL: www.vsu.edu
Established: 1882 Annual Undergrad Tuition & Fees (In-State): $8,226
Enrollment: 5,025 Coed
Affiliation or Control: State IRS Status: 501(c)3

Highest Offering: Doctorate
Accreditation: SC, ART, BUS, CS, DIETD, DIETI, ENG, ENGR, ENGT, MUS, NAIT, SW, TED

01 President .... Dr. Makola M. ABDULLAH
10 Vice President for Finance .... Mr. Kevin DAVENPORT
05 Provost/VP for Academic Affairs .... Dr. Donald PALM
32 VP for Student Success & Engagement .... Dr. Letizia GAMBRELL-BOONE
30 VP for Institutional Advancement .... Ms. Reshunda MAHONE
11 Vice President for Administration .... Mr. Hubert D. HARRIS
20 Vice Provost .... Dr. James E. HUNTER
15 Assoc VP for Human Resource .... Vacant
84 Asst VP/Student Enrollment Services .... Mr. Henry DEBOSE
21 Assoc Vice President for Finance .... Ms. Sheila MCNAIR
50 Dean Reginald F Lewis Col Business . Dr. Emmanuel OMOJOKUN
54 Dean College of Engineering & Tech . Dr. Keith M. WILLIAMSON
79 Dean Col of Humanities & Soc Sci .... Dr. Andrew KANU
47 Dean College of Agriculture .... Vacant
58 Dean Graduate Studies .... Dr. James E. HUNTER
62 Dean Library & Library Services .. Dr. Elsie S. WEATHERINGTON
76 Dean College of Natural Health Sci .... Dr. Larry BROWN
44 Director of Development .... Vacant
06 Registrar .... Mrs. Debera BONNER
09 Director Inst Planning/Assessment .... Dr. Emmett L. RIDLEY
37 Director of Financial Aid .... Mrs. Myra PHILLIPS
19 Chief of Police and Public Safety .... Mr. David BRAGG
27 Media Specialist .... Mr. Jesse VAUGHAN
18 Director of Facilities .... Mr. Gilbert HANZLIK
07 Director for Enrollment Services .... Mr. Rodney HALL
26 Interim Director for Communication .... Mrs. Gwen WILLIAMS DANDRIDGE
22 Human Resources Manager .... Ms. Gayle O'NEAL
39 Director Residence Facilities .... Dr. Kelvin RACHELL
36 Director Career Services .... Mr. Joseph LYONS
40 Bookstore Manager .... Mr. Kevin POWELL
92 Director Honors Program .... Mr. Daniel M. ROBERTS
41 Athletic Director .... Mrs. Peggy DAVIS
42 Minister .... Rev. Delano DOUGLAS
29 Director of Alumni Relations .... Vacant
13 Deputy Chief Information Officer .... Mr. Justin D. GRIFFIN
23 Director of Student Health Services .... Dr. Darylnet LYTTLE
25 Contract Manager .... Ms. Linda SCOTT
87 Director Summer School Session .... Dr. Vykuntapathi THOTA
96 Director of Purchasing .... Mrs. Yolanda BUCK
38 Director University Counseling .... Dr. Kendra L. PUGH
88 Special Assistant to the President .... Mr. Osubi CRAIG
04 Executive Assistant to President .... Dr. Chris WALLACE
101 Special Asst to President & Board .... Dr. Annie REDD
43 General Counsel .... Ms. Ramona L. TAYLOR

Virginia Tech Carilion School of Medicine (A)

2 Riverside Circle, Suite M140, Roanoke VA 24016
County: Independent City — Identification: 667148
Unit ID: 459082
Telephone: (540) 526-2559 — Carnegie Class: Not Classified
FAX Number: (540) 581-0741 — Calendar System: Other
URL: www.vtc.vt.edu
Established: 2007 — Annual Graduate Tuition & Fees: N/A
Enrollment: 167 — Coed
Affiliation or Control: Independent Non-Profit — IRS Status: 501(c)3
Highest Offering: Doctorate; No Undergraduates
Accreditation: SC, MED

01 President & Dean .... Dr. Cynda Ann JOHNSON

Virginia Union University (B)

1500 N Lombardy Street, Richmond VA 23220-1784
County: Independent City — FICE Identification: 003766
Unit ID: 234164
Telephone: (804) 257-5600 — Carnegie Class: Bac-A&S
FAX Number: (804) 257-5818 — Calendar System: Semester
URL: www.vuu.edu
Established: 1865 — Annual Undergrad Tuition & Fees: $15,746
Enrollment: 1,715 — Coed
Affiliation or Control: Baptist — IRS Status: 501(c)3
Highest Offering: Doctorate
Accreditation: SC, ACBSP, SW, TED, THEOL

01 Acting President .... Dr. Joseph F. JOHNSON
05 VP Academic Affairs .... Dr. Zakir HOSSAIN
32 VP Enroll Mgmt & Student Affs .... Dr. A. Zachary FAISON
10 VP Financial Affairs .... Mr. Gregory LEWIS
30 Vice Pres Institutional Advancement .... Mr. Dennis C. WASHINGTON
09 VP Research/Planning & Spec Pgms .... Dr. Joy P. GOODRICH
26 Chief of Staff/Dir Public Relations .... Ms. Vanessa COOMBS
53 Dean Evelyn R Syphax Sch Ed/Psy .... Dr. David A. ADEWUYI
81 Dean Math/Science & Technology .... Dr. Latrelle A. GREEN
50 Dean Sydney Lewis Sch of Business ....Dr. Brenda J. PONSFORD
79 Dean Sch of Humanities/Soc Sci .... Dr. Michael OROK
73 Sr VP/Dean School of Theology .... Dr. John W. KINNEY
25 Asst to President Title III Pgms .... Mr. Samuel T. RHOADES
15 Director Human Resources .... Ms. Hollace J. ENOCH
06 Registrar .... Ms. Marilyn A. BROOKS
38 Director Counseling .... Dr. Remy J. THOMPSON
29 Director of Alumni Relations .... Ms. Charmica D. EPPS
08 Library Director .... Ms. Pamela B. FOREMAN
37 Director Financial Aid .... Mrs. Antionette T. HOUSE
13 Director Information Technology .... Mr. Robert R. GRAY
36 Director Career Services .... Ms. Takeish N. BROWN
84 Director of Enrollment Management .... Ms. Kristie L. WHITE
42 University Pastor .... Rev. Angelo V. CHATMON
41 Athletic Director .... Mr. Joseph TAYLOR
19 Chief University Police .... Col. Carlton G. EDWARDS
24 Audio Visual Coordinator .... Mr. JaPrince L. CARTER
21 Asst VP Finan Affairs/Comptroller .... Ms. Stephanie M. WHITE
40 Bookstore Manager .... Ms. Terri WYATT
39 Director of Residence Life .... Mr. Mandrake T. MILLER
31 Int Dir of Community & Student Rels .... Ms. Tyciee L. FAISON
18 Director Facilities .... Mr. David E. GORDON
96 Director of Purchasing .... Mr. Michael T. ADKINS
04 Administrative Asst to President .... Ms. Renee W. JOLLEY
104 Dir Ctr for International Studies .... Dr. David A. ADEWUYI
106 Dir Online Education/E-learning .... Dr. Laurene E. COLLINS
108 Director Institutional Assessment .... Dr. Patty R. YOUNG
22 Dir Affirmative Action/EEO .... Ms. Hollace J. ENOCH
44 Director Annual or Planned Giving .... Ms. Lisa D. WINN

Virginia University of Lynchburg (C)

2058 Garfield Avenue, Lynchburg VA 24501-6417
County: Independent City — FICE Identification: 003762
Unit ID: 234137
Telephone: (434) 528-5276 — Carnegie Class: Spec-4-yr-Faith
FAX Number: (434) 528-4257 — Calendar System: Semester
URL: www.vul.edu
Established: 1886 — Annual Undergrad Tuition & Fees: $7,880
Enrollment: 324 — Coed
Affiliation or Control: Independent Non-Profit — IRS Status: 501(c)3
Highest Offering: Doctorate
Accreditation: TRACS

01 President .... Dr. Kathy C. FRANKLIN
05 Provost/Executive Vice President .... Dr. John BOREK
10 Vice President of Finance .... Dr. Donald LESLIE
32 Vice Pres Div Student Affairs .... Dr. Phillip E. CAMPBELL
30 VP for Institutional Advancement .... Vacant
06 Registrar .... Ms. Sarah CUNNINGHAM
84 Dir Enrollment Management/Fin Aid .... Ms. Rita B. WALKER
07 Dir of Admissions/Univ Recruiter .... Mr. Houston D. WALTHALL
106 Dir Online Education/E-learning .... Ms. Katrina V. FRANKLIN
19 Director Security/Safety .... Mr. Robert CABLER, JR.
25 Chief Contracts/Grants Admin .... Mr. Jason J. RANDOO
37 Director Student Financial Aid .... Mrs. Daphne BOOKER
41 Athletic Director .... Mr. Don LEE

Virginia University of Oriental Medicine (D)

9401 Mathy Drive, Fairfax VA 22031
County: Fairfax — Identification: 667208
Telephone: (703) 323-5690 — Carnegie Class: Not Classified
FAX Number: (703) 323-5692 — Calendar System: Quarter
URL: www.vuom.org
Established: — Annual Undergrad Tuition & Fees: N/A
Enrollment: N/A — Coed
Affiliation or Control: Independent Non-Profit — IRS Status: 501(c)3
Highest Offering: Master's
Accreditation: ACICS, ACUP

01 President .... John SHIN
05 Vice Pres Academic Affairs .... Tae CHEONG-CHOO

Virginia Wesleyan College (E)

1584 Wesleyan Drive, Norfolk VA 23502-5599
County: Independent City — FICE Identification: 003767
Unit ID: 234173
Telephone: (757) 455-3200 — Carnegie Class: Bac-A&S
FAX Number: (757) 461-4944 — Calendar System: 4/1/4
URL: www.vwc.edu
Established: 1961 — Annual Undergrad Tuition & Fees: $34,428
Enrollment: 1,501 — Coed
Affiliation or Control: United Methodist — IRS Status: 501(c)3
Highest Offering: Baccalaureate
Accreditation: SC, NRPA, SW

01 President .... Dr. Scott D. MILLER
05 VP Academic Affs/Dean of College .... Dr. Timothy G. O'ROURKE
10 Vice President of Finance .... Mr. Cary A. SAWYER
32 VP for Student Affairs .... Dr. Keith MOORE
30 VP for Advancement .... Dr. Mort GAMBLE
11 VP for Facilities and Operations .... Mr. Bruce F. VAUGHAN
07 Vice President of Enrollment .... Mr. David WAGGONER
100 Exec Asst to Pres/Chief of Staff .... Ms. Laynee H. TIMLIN
45 Senior Researcher/Policy Analyst .... Mr. Donald STAUFFER
88 Exec Dir Quality Enhancement Plan .... Dr. Sara SEWELL
26 Director of Communications .... Ms. Leona BAKER
88 Assoc VP for Advancement .... Ms. Suzanne SAVAGE
20 Associate Dean for Academic Support .... Ms. Debbie L. HICKS
20 Assoc Dean of the College .... Dr. Sally SHEDD
39 Director of Residence Life .... Ms. McCarren CAPUTA
13 Chief Information Officer .... Mr. Robert LEITGEB
41 Director of Athletics .... Ms. Joanne M. RENN
55 Asst Dir of Adult Studies Program .... Ms. Pamela PARAMORE
08 Library Director .... Mrs. Susan ERICKSON
15 Director of Human Resources .... Ms. Karla R. RASMUSSEN
06 Registrar .... Ms. Regina BYNUM
37 Director of Financial Aid .... Ms. Teresa L. RHYNE
96 Director of Purchasing .... Ms. Midge ZIMMERMAN
31 Director of Community Service .... Ms. Diane E. HOTALING
36 Director of Career Development .... Ms. LaShay MCQUEEN
19 Director of Campus Security .... Mr. Jerry MANCE, JR.
29 Director of Alumni Relations .... Ms. Lina GREEN
18 Director of Physical Plant .... Mr. Robert LEVINSKY
42 Chaplain .... Rev. Greg WEST
38 Director of Counseling Services .... Mr. Bill BROWN
88 Director of Special Constituencies .... Ms. Tiffany WILLIAMS
44 Dir of Corporate and Annual Giving .... Ms. Lori MCCAREL
92 Director Honors and Scholars .... Dr. Joyce B. EASTER
88 Director of Student Activities .... Ms. Kate GRIFFIN
23 Director of Health Services .... Ms. Valerie L. COVINGTON
40 Bookstore Manager .... Ms. Kim S. BROWN
04 Administrative Asst to President .... Ms. Jodi BRYANT

Washington and Lee University (F)

204 W Washington Street, Lexington VA 24450-2116
County: Independent City — FICE Identification: 003768
Unit ID: 234207
Telephone: (540) 458-8400 — Carnegie Class: Bac-A&S
FAX Number: (540) 458-8945 — Calendar System: Other
URL: www.wlu.edu
Established: 1749 — Annual Undergrad Tuition & Fees: $46,417
Enrollment: 2,264 — Coed
Affiliation or Control: Independent Non-Profit — IRS Status: 501(c)3
Highest Offering: Doctorate
Accreditation: SC, BUS, JOUR, LAW, TEAC

01 President .... Dr. Kenneth P. RUSCIO
05 Interim Provost .... Dr. Marc CONNER
20 Associate Provost .... Dr. Elizabeth KNAPP
10 Vice Pres for Finance and Admin .... Mr. Steven G. MCALLISTER
30 Vice Pres University Advancement .... Mr. Dennis W. CROSS
32 VP Student Affs & Dean of Students .... Ms. Sidney S. EVANS
101 Sr Asst to Pres/Sec of University .... Mr. James D. FARRAR
43 General Counsel .... Ms. Leanne M. SHANK
22 Assoc Gen Counsel Compliance Spprt .... Ms. Jennifer E. KIRKLAND
49 Dean of the College .... Dr. Suzanne P. KEEN
50 Dean of Commerce/Economics/Politics .... Mr. Robert D. STRAUGHAN
61 Dean of Law School .... Mr. Brant J. HELLWIG
26 Exec Dir of Comm/Public Affairs .... Mr. Brian ECKERT
35 Dean of Student Life .... Mr. David M. LEONARD
35 Assoc Dean of Students .... Ms. Tamara Y. FUTRELL
35 Assoc Dean of Students .... Ms. Tammi R. SIMPSON
30 Exec Dir of University Development .... Mr. Tres MULLIS
41 Director of Athletics .... Ms. Janine M. HATHORN
89 Asst Dean for 1st Yr Experience .... Mr. Jason L. RODOCKER
07 Dean of Admissions/Financial Aid .... M. Sally S. RICHMOND
09 Asst Provost for Inst Effectiveness .... Mr. Bryan PRICE
06 University Registrar .... Mr. Scott DITTMAN
08 University Librarian .... Mr. John TOMBARGE
85 Director International Education .... Dr. Mark E. RUSH
29 Exec Director of Alumni Affairs .... Mr. Waller T. DUDLEY
15 Exec Director of Human Resources .... Ms. Mary E. MAIN
37 Director of Financial Aid .... Mr. James D. KASTER
18 Exec Dir Facilities/Capital Plng .... Mr. John HOOGAKKER
21 Associate Treasurer & Controller .... Mrs. Deborah Z. CAYLOR
13 Chief Technology Officer .... Mr. David SAACKE
24 Senior Academic Technologist .... Mr. Brandon R. BUCY
36 Director Career Development .... Mr. John A. JENSEN
23 Director Student Health/Counseling .... Dr. Jane T. HORTON
109 Director of Dining Services .... Mr. Michael R. ZANIE
40 Director of Administrative Services .... Mr. K. C SCHAEFER

Washington University of Virginia (G)

4300 Evergreen Lane, Annandale VA 22003
County: Fairfax — Identification: 666234
Telephone: (703) 333-5904 — Carnegie Class: Not Classified
FAX Number: (703) 333-5906 — Calendar System: Semester
URL: www.wuv.edu
Established: — Annual Undergrad Tuition & Fees: N/A
Enrollment: N/A — Coed
Affiliation or Control: Baptist — IRS Status: 501(c)3
Highest Offering: Doctorate
Accreditation: BI, @THEOL

01 President .... Dr. Peter M. CHANG
03 Executive Vice President .... Mrs. Joyce G. PARK
07 Admissions Advisor .... Mr. David Y. LEE

Wave Leadership College (H)

1000 North Great Neck Road, Virginia Beach VA 23454
County: Independent City — Identification: 667210
Telephone: (757) 481-5005 — Carnegie Class: Not Classified
FAX Number: (757) 496-6697 — Calendar System: Semester
URL: www.wavecollege.com
Established: 2000 — Annual Undergrad Tuition & Fees: N/A
Enrollment: N/A — Coed
Affiliation or Control: Independent Non-Profit — IRS Status: 501(c)3
Highest Offering: Associate Degree
Accreditation: @BI

01 President .... Steve KELLY
03 Executive Vice President .... Derek P. HOLSER
05 Academic Dean .... Sarah HUMMEL
32 Dean of Students .... Dave M. HALL

06 Registrar .... Jacquie EVANS
08 Librarian .... Sasha MATTHEWS
37 Financial Aid Director .... James KNARR

WASHINGTON

Antioch University Seattle (A)

2326 Sixth Avenue, Seattle WA 98121-1814
Telephone: (206) 441-5352 Identification: 666812
Accreditation: &NH, CACREP, MFCD

† Regional accreditation is carried under the parent institution in Yellow Springs, Ohio.

Argosy University, Seattle (B)

2601 A Elliott Avenue, Seattle WA 98121-1318
Telephone: (206) 283-4500 Identification: 666080
Accreditation: &WC, ACBSP

† Regional accreditation is carried under the parent institution in Orange, CA.

The Art Institute of Seattle (C)

2323 Elliott Avenue, Seattle WA 98121-1622
County: King FICE Identification: 022913
Unit ID: 234492
Telephone: (206) 448-0900 Carnegie Class: Spec-4-yr-Arts
FAX Number: (206) 448-2501 Calendar System: Quarter
URL: www.ais.edu
Established: 1946 Annual Undergrad Tuition & Fees: $17,556
Enrollment: 1,378 Coed
Affiliation or Control: Proprietary IRS Status: Proprietary
Highest Offering: Baccalaureate
Accreditation: NW, ACFEI, CIDA

01 President .... Carol MENCK
05 Dean of Academic Affairs .... Dr. Scott CARNZ
15 Director of Human Resources .... Vacant
32 Dean of Student Affairs .... Angela HEDWALL
07 Senior Director of Admissions .... Vacant
10 Regional Finance Director .... Greg WOODARD
36 Director Career Services .... Vacant

Bastyr University (D)

14500 Juanita Drive NE, Kenmore WA 98028-4966
County: King FICE Identification: 022425
Unit ID: 235547
Telephone: (425) 602-3000 Carnegie Class: Spec-4-yr-Other Health
FAX Number: (425) 823-6222 Calendar System: Quarter
URL: www.bastyr.edu
Established: 1978 Annual Undergrad Tuition & Fees: N/A
Enrollment: 1,202 Coed
Affiliation or Control: Independent Non-Profit IRS Status: 501(c)3
Highest Offering: Doctorate
Accreditation: NW, ACUP, DIETD, DIETI, MEAC, NATUR

01 President .... Dr. Mac POWELL
05 Senior Vice President/Provost .... Dr. Timothy C. CALLAHAN
10 Vice President for Finance & Admin .... Mr. Glenn R. FORD
100 Chief of Staff .... Ms. Coquina L. DEGER
30 Chief Development Officer .... Vacant
32 Vice President of Student Affairs .... Ms. Susan WEIDER
07 Asst Vice Pres Recruitment & Retent .... Ms. Christine MASTERSON
08 Director of Library Services .... Ms. Jane SAXTON
29 Dir Career and Alumni Svcs .... Ms. Susan FARLEY
23 Chf Medical Ofcr Ctr Natural Health .... Dr. Jamey WALLACE
15 Vice Presiden of Human Resources .... Mr. Keith W. WOODY
13 Director of Information Technology .... Mr. John GAYTHORPE
09 Director of Research Development .... Dr. Mark MARTZEN
26 Assoc Vice President of Marketing .... Ms. Cathy SANTINI
46 Senior Research Scientist .... Dr. Leanna STANDISH
40 Bookstore Manager .... Mr. Marty PETERSEN
07 Associate Director of Admissions .... Ms. Lauren SCHOEN
37 Director Financial Aid .... Ms. Danette CARTER
18 Director Facilities and Safety .... Mr. Daniel CLARK
21 Assistant Controller .... Ms. Jeanette FRAZIER
38 Director Counseling .... Ms. Cheryln STOVER
06 Registrar .... Ms. Aracelly SALAZAR
101 Secretary of the Institution/Board .... Ms. Margaret BREVOORT
108 Director Institutional Assessment .... Mr. Kai CHANG
19 Director Security/Safety .... Mr. Daniel CLARK
22 VP Affirmative Action/EEO .... Mr. Keith W. WOODY
25 Chief Contracts/Grants Admin .... Mr. Dave HAMMOND
28 Director of Diversity .... Ms. Safiya MCCARTER
04 Exec Admin Asst to President .... Ms. Nicola FRANCIS
44 Senior Major Gifts Officer .... Ms. Nina MCGUINNESS

Bates Technical College (E)

1101 S Yakima Avenue, Tacoma WA 98405-4895
County: Pierce FICE Identification: 005306
Unit ID: 235671
Telephone: (253) 680-7000 Carnegie Class: Assoc/HVT-High Non
FAX Number: (253) 680-7101 Calendar System: Quarter
URL: www.bates.ctc.edu
Established: 1940 Annual Undergrad Tuition & Fees (In-State): $3,681
Enrollment: 2,907 Coed
Affiliation or Control: State IRS Status: 501(c)3
Highest Offering: Associate Degree
Accreditation: NW, ACFEI, DA, DT, OTA

01 President .... Dr. Ron LANGRELL
05 Exec VP of Instruction/Student Svcs .... Mr. Al GRISWOLD
04 Exec Asst to the President .... Ms. Becky WELCH
32 Vice President of Student Services .... Ms. Lin ZHOU
15 Director of Human Resources .... Mr. Gary NILSSON
11 Vice Pres Administrative Services .... Ms. Holly WOODMANSEE
30 Director of College Relations .... Ms. Kimberly PLEGER
18 Director Facilities & Operations .... Mr. Marty MATTES
96 General Services Manager .... Mr. Alexander KENESSON
37 Financial Aid Officer .... Ms. Susan NEESE
13 Int Director Information Technology .... Mr. Pat TAYLOR
84 Dir of Enrollment Mgt/Admission .... Ms. Jaime SERENO
28 College Diversity Coordinator .... Ms. Kathy FLORES
09 Director of Institutional Research .... Mr. Jon BOLAS
19 Director Security/Safety .... Mr. Derick NELONS

Bellevue College (F)

3000 Landerholm Circle, SE, Bellevue WA 98007-6484
County: King FICE Identification: 003769
Unit ID: 234669
Telephone: (425) 564-1000 Carnegie Class: Bac/Assoc-Assoc Dom
FAX Number: (425) 564-4065 Calendar System: Quarter
URL: www.bellevuecollege.edu
Established: 1965 Annual Undergrad Tuition & Fees (In-State): $3,619
Enrollment: 13,469 Coed
Affiliation or Control: State IRS Status: 501(c)3
Highest Offering: Baccalaureate
Accreditation: NW ADNUR, CIDA, DMS, NDT, NMT, NURSE, RADDOS, RTT

01 President .... Dr. David RULE
04 Exec Asst to the President .... Ms. Lisa CORCORAN
11 Vice Pres Administrative Services .... Mr. Ray WHITE
05 Vice President of Instruction .... Mr. Tom NIELSEN
15 Vice President of Human Resources .... Mr. Aaron HILLIARD
30 Vice Pres Institutional Advancement .... Ms. Gayle BARGE
32 Vice President of Student Affairs .... Dr. Ata KARIM
103 Vice Pres of Econ & Wkfrc Dev .... Mr. Albert LEWIS
28 Int Vice President of Diversity .... Dr. Sayumi IREY
13 Vice Pres of Information Resources .... Mr. Russell BEARD
09 Assoc VP Effect & Strat Planning .... Ms. Patricia JAMES
51 Dean Continuing Education .... Vacant
79 Dean of Arts and Humanities .... Ms. Margaret HARADA
76 Dean of HSEWI .... Ms. Leslie HEIZER NEWQUIST
83 Dean of Social Science .... Ms. Virginia BRIDWELL
88 Associate Dean of Student Programs .... Mr. Faisal JASWAL
35 Dean of Student Affairs .... Vacant
85 Dean of Intl Educ & Global Init .... Mr. Jean D'ARC CAMPBELL
10 Exec Dir of Finance & Auxiliary Svc .... Ms. Jennifer STROTHER
08 Dean of Library Media Center .... Ms. Vivienne MCCLENDON
26 Director of Marketing .... Ms. Alonda WILLIAMS
37 Director Financial Aid .... Ms. Melanie RUIZ
19 Director of Public Safety .... Mr. Tommy VU
13 Director Computing Services .... Mr. Jason AQUI
91 Manager Networking Svcs & Security .... Mr. Gary FARRIS
41 Director of Athletics .... Mr. Bill O'CONNOR
38 Student Counseling .... Mr. Harlan LEE
40 Director Bellevue College Bookstore .... Ms. Kristen CONNELY
96 Exec Director Physical Plant Ops .... Mr. Dexter JOHNSON

Bellingham Technical College (G)

3028 Lindebergh Avenue, Bellingham WA 98225-1599
County: Whatcom FICE Identification: 004999
Unit ID: 234696
Telephone: (360) 752-7000 Carnegie Class: Assoc/HVT-High Non
FAX Number: (360) 676-2798 Calendar System: Quarter
URL: www.btc.edu
Established: 1957 Annual Undergrad Tuition & Fees (In-District): $3,389
Enrollment: 2,301 Coed
Affiliation or Control: State/Local IRS Status: 501(c)3
Highest Offering: Associate Degree
Accreditation: NW, ACFEI, DA, DH, SURGT

01 President .... Dr. Kimberly PERRY
04 Exec Assistant to the President .... Ms. Ronda LAUGHLIN
05 Vice President of Instruction .... Dr. Frank POWERS
32 Vice President of Student Services .... Dr. Linda FOSSEN
11 VP of Administrative Services .... Ms. Chad STITELER
72 Dean of Professional Technical Educ .... Mr. Walter HUDSICK
30 Exec Director College Advancement .... Mr. Dean FULTON
15 Director Human Resources .... Ms. Camille GATZA
37 Director Financial Aid .... Ms. Crystal BAGBY
06 Director Registration/Enrollment .... Ms. Joan KAMMERZELL
13 Dir Computer/Inform Support Svcs .... Mr. Curtis PERERA
08 Director Library .... Ms. Jane BLUME
18 Chief Facilities/Physical Plant .... Mr. David JUNGKUNTZ
26 Director of Communications .... Ms. Marni SALING MAYER
07 Director of Admissions .... Ms. Karen BADE
09 Dir of Inst Research & Planning .... Ms. RaeLyn AXLUND MCBRIDE

† Granted candidacy at the Baccalaureate level.

Big Bend Community College (H)

7662 Chanute Street NE, Moses Lake WA 98837-3299
County: Grant FICE Identification: 003770
Unit ID: 234711
Telephone: (509) 793-2222 Carnegie Class: Assoc/MT-VT-Mix Trad/Non
FAX Number: (509) 762-6329 Calendar System: Quarter
URL: www.bigbend.edu
Established: 1962 Annual Undergrad Tuition & Fees (In-State): $3,846
Enrollment: 2,016 Coed
Affiliation or Control: State IRS Status: 501(c)3
Highest Offering: Associate Degree
Accreditation: NW, ADNUR

01 President .... Dr. Terry LEAS
10 Vice Pres Administrative Services .... Ms. Linda SCHOONMAKER
05 Vice Pres Instruction/Student Svcs .... Mr. Bob MOHRBACHER
15 VP of Human Resources & Labor .... Mrs. Kim GARZA
75 Dean Prof Technical Education .... Ms. Daneen BERRY-GUERIN
49 Dean of Arts & Sciences .... Ms. Kara GARRETT
53 Dean Educ/Health/Language Skills .... Vacant
32 Director of Student Programs .... Ms. Kim JACKSON
37 Director of Financial Aid .... Mr. Jeremy IVERSON
06 Registrar .... Ms. Ruth COFFIN
08 Dean of Library Resources .... Mr. Tim FUHRMAN
41 Director of Athletics .... Mr. Preston WILKS
102 Dir Inst Advancement/Exec Dir Found .... Mrs. LeAnne PARTON
26 Publication & Information Director .... Vacant
21 Director of Business Services .... Ms. Charlene RIOS
40 Director of Bookstore .... Mrs. Caren COURTRIGHT
96 Director of Purchasing .... Mr. Joe AUVIL
39 Residence Hall Coordinator .... Mr. Hugh SCHOLTE
09 Dean of Institutional Research .... Ms. Valerie PARTON
13 Chief Info Technology Officer (CIO) .... Mr. Rick SPARKS
19 Director Security/Safety .... Mr. Kyle FOREMAN
04 Administrative Asst to President .... Ms. Melinda DOURTE
18 Chief Facilities/Physical Plant .... Mr. James SAUCEDA

Carrington College - Spokane (I)

10102 E Knox Ave., Suite 200, Spokane WA 99206-4187
Telephone: (509) 532-8888 Identification: 666385
Accreditation: &WJ, MAAB, RAD

† Regional accreditation is carried under the parent institution in Sacramento, CA.

Cascadia College (J)

18345 Campus Way, NE, Bothell WA 98011-8205
County: King FICE Identification: 034835
Unit ID: 439190
Telephone: (425) 352-8000 Carnegie Class: Assoc/HT-Mix Trad/Non
FAX Number: (425) 352-8313 Calendar System: Quarter
URL: www.cascadia.edu
Established: 2000 Annual Undergrad Tuition & Fees (In-District): $3,748
Enrollment: 2,759 Coed
Affiliation or Control: State/Local IRS Status: Exempt
Highest Offering: Associate Degree
Accreditation: NW

01 President .... Dr. Eric MURRAY
05 Vice Pres Student Learning/Success .... Dr. Rosemary SUTTON
20 Dean for Student Learning .... Dr. Erik TINGELSTAD
20 Dean for Student Learning .... Dr. Todd LUNDBERG
32 Dean for Student Services .... Ms. Erin BLAKENEY
06 Registrar .... Ms. Arlene HRUBY
09 Dir Institutional Research .... Mr. Glenn COLBY
10 Chief Business Officer .... Mr. Terrence HSIAO
15 Director Personnel Services .... Ms. Gina LORENZ
18 Chief Facilities/Physical Plant .... Vacant
26 Exec Director College Relations .... Ms. Meagan WALKER
35 Director of Student Life .... Ms. Becky RIOPEL
37 Director Student Financial Aid .... Ms. Deann HOLIDAY
30 Chief Development .... Vacant
38 Director Student Counseling .... Mr. Gordon DUTRISAC
84 Director Enrollment Management .... Mr. Shawn MILLER

† Granted candidacy at the Baccalaureate level.

Central Washington University (K)

400 E University Way, Ellensburg WA 98926-7501
County: Kittitas FICE Identification: 003771
Unit ID: 234827
Telephone: (509) 963-2111 Carnegie Class: Masters/L
FAX Number: (509) 963-3206 Calendar System: Quarter
URL: www.cwu.edu
Established: 1890 Annual Undergrad Tuition & Fees (In-State): $8,688
Enrollment: 11,799 Coed
Affiliation or Control: State IRS Status: 501(c)3
Highest Offering: Master's
Accreditation: NW, BUS, CACREP, CONST, DIETD, DIETI, EMT, ENGT, IPSY, MUS

01 President .... Dr. James L. GAUDINO
05 Provost/VP Academic & Student Life .... Dr. Katherine FRANK
10 Int VP Business & Financial Affairs .... Mr. Joel KLUCKING
100 Chief of Staff .... Ms. Linda SCHACTLER
20 Assoc Provost Faculty Affairs .... Ms. Anne CUBILIE
88 Assoc Provost Accreditation .... Dr. Bernadette JUNGBLUT
21 Int Dir Student Financial Services .... Ms. Kelley CHRISTIANSON
84 Vice Pres Enrollment Management .... Ms. Sharon O'HARE
32 Dean of Student Success .... Dr. Sarah SWAGER
35 Assoc Dean Student Development .... Mr. Keith CHAMPAGNE
88 Int Assoc Dean Student Achievement .... Ms. Mindie DIEU
15 Executive Director of HR .... Ms. Staci SLEIGH-LAYMAN
18 Dir Plant Operations and Maintenenc .... Mr. Michael MOON
16 Dir Faculty and Labor Relations .... Mr. Don ANDERSON
11 Int VP of Operations .... Mr. Gene SHODA
58 Dean Graduate Studies/Research .... Dr. Kevin ARCHER
49 Dean College of Arts/Humanities .... Dr. Stacey ROBERTSON

50 Dean College of Business .... Dr. Kathryn MARTELL
53 Dean College of Educ/Prof Studies .... Dr. Paul BALLARD
83 Dean College of the Sciences .... Dr. Tim ENGLUND
08 Dean of Library Services .... Dr. Patricia CUTRIGHT
30 Vice Pres University Advancement .... Mr. Scott WADE
85 Exec Dir Intl Studies & Programs .... Dr. Ann RADWAN
06 Registrar .... Ms. Lindsey BROWN
41 Director Athletics .... Mr. Dennis FRANCOIS
12 Exec Director Extended Learning .... Ms. Melanie PALM
07 Director of Admissions .... Ms. Kathy GAER-CARLTON
37 Int AVP Financial Planning/Analysis .... Mr. Adrian NARANJO
39 Assoc Dean Student Living .... Mr. Richard DESHIELDS
19 Dir Police and Parking Services .... Chief Michael LUVERA
26 Exec Director Public Affairs .... Ms. Linda SCHACTLER
108 Exec Dir Inst Effectiveness .... Ms. Nina OMAN
28 Director of Diversity .... Dr. Delores CLEARY
29 Sr Dir Alumni/Constituent Rels .... Mr. Bob FORD
36 Director Career Services .... Ms. Vicki SANNUTO
38 Director of Counseling .... Ms. Rhonda MCKINNEY
96 Director of Contracts/Procurement .... Mr. Stuart THOMPSON
21 Assoc VP Fin & Bus Auxiliaries .... Mr. Joel KLUCKING
13 Assoc VP Info Svcs & Security .... Mr. Andreas BOHMAN

Centralia College (A)

600 Centralia College Boulevard,
Centralia WA 98531-4035
County: Lewis FICE Identification: 003772
Unit ID: 234845
Telephone: (360) 736-9391 Carnegie Class: Bac/Assoc-Assoc Dom
FAX Number: (360) 330-7108 Calendar System: Quarter
URL: www.centralia.edu
Established: 1925 Annual Undergrad Tuition & Fees (In-State): $4,188
Enrollment: 3,317 Coed
Affiliation or Control: State IRS Status: 501(c)3
Highest Offering: Baccalaureate
Accreditation: NW

01 President .... Dr. Robert MOHRBACHER
05 Vice President Instruction .... Mr. John MARTENS
32 Vice President of Students .... Mr. Robert COX
10 Vice Pres Finance/Administration .... Mr. Steve WARD
15 VP Human Resources/Legal Affairs .... Ms. Julie LEDFORD
103 Dean Workforce Education .... Ms. Durelle SULLIVAN
08 Dean of Library Services/E-Learning .... Ms. Sue KENNEDY
88 Dean of Academic Transfer Programs .... Mr. Christian BRUHN
09 Director of Institutional Research .... Vacant
103 Dir WorkFirst & Worker Retraining .... Ms. Margret FRIEDLEY
84 Director of Enrollment Services .... Ms. Kimberly INGRAM
37 Director of Financial Aid .... Ms. Tracy DAHL
13 Director Information Technology .... Mr. Patrick ALLISON
41 Director of Sports Programs .... Mr. Bob PETERS
29 Director Alumni Relations .... Ms. Julie JOHNSON
96 Director of Purchasing .... Ms. Bonnie MYER
26 Dir College Relations & Events .... Ms. Amanda HAINES
06 Registration Specialist .... Ms. Rosanna SCHLAGEL
40 Bookstore Manager .... Ms. Tammy STRODEMIER
97 Program Coordinator .... Ms. Joanie ROGERSON

Charter College (B)

17200 SE Mill Plain Blvd, Suite 100, Vancouver WA 98683
Telephone: (360) 448-2000 Identification: 770822
Accreditation: ACICS

† Branch campus of Charter College, Anchorage, AK

Charter College-Fife (C)

3700 Pacific Highway E, Suite 150, Fife WA 98424
Telephone: (775) 525-2117 Identification: 770623
Accreditation: ACICS

† Branch campus of Charter College, Anchorage, AK

City University of Seattle (D)

521 Wall Street, Suite 100, Seattle WA 98121
County: King FICE Identification: 013022
Unit ID: 234915
Telephone: (206) 239-4500 Carnegie Class: Masters/L
FAX Number: (206) 239-4802 Calendar System: Quarter
URL: www.cityu.edu
Established: 1973 Annual Undergrad Tuition & Fees: N/A
Enrollment: 2,545 Coed
Affiliation or Control: Independent Non-Profit IRS Status: 501(c)3
Highest Offering: Master's
Accreditation: NW, ACBSP, CACREP, CS

01 President .... Vacant
101 Exec Asst Office of the President .... Ms. Novelette COTTER
32 Vice President Student Services .... Dr. Melissa E. MECHAM
05 Provost/Vice Pres Academic Affairs .... Dr. Kurt KIRSTEIN
10 SVP Business & Administration .... Mr. Bruce K. BRYANT
88 Vice President European Operations .... Dr. Jan REBRO
84 Vice Pres Enrollment Management .... Mr. Matt HANUSA
50 Dean School of Management .... Mr. Tom CAREY
53 Dean School of Education .... Dr. Craig SCHIEBER
108 Director of Inst Effectiveness .... Vacant
21 Director of Finance .... Ms. Stephany KEELEY
15 Director of Human Resources .... Ms. Janet O'LEARY
08 Director Library Services .... Ms. Mary MARA
37 Assoc Dir Student Financial Svcs .... Ms. Linda COOKE
29 Alumni Relations Manager .... Mr. Alex WEBSTER
90 Director of Information Technology .... Mr. Kevin H. BROWN
07 Director Admissions .... Ms. Amy PORTWOOD
85 Director Intl Student Office .... Ms. Sabine SAWAY
18 Facilities Manager .... Mr. Troy CRABREE

† Accredited at the Doctorate level.

Clark College (E)

1933 Fort Vancouver Way, Vancouver WA 98663-3598
County: Clark FICE Identification: 003773
Unit ID: 234933
Telephone: (360) 992-2000 Carnegie Class: Assoc/MT-VT-Mix Trad/Non
FAX Number: (360) 992-2871 Calendar System: Quarter
URL: www.clark.edu
Established: 1933 Annual Undergrad Tuition & Fees (In-State): $3,456
Enrollment: 10,911 Coed
Affiliation or Control: State IRS Status: 501(c)3
Highest Offering: Associate Degree
Accreditation: NW, ADNUR, DH, MAC, RAD

01 President .... Mr. Robert KNIGHT
05 Vice President of Instruction .... Dr. Tim COOK
32 Vice President of Student Affairs .... Mr. William BELDEN
11 Vice President of Admin Services .... Mr. Bob WILLIAMSON
15 Assoc Vice Pres of Human Resources .... Vacant
45 Assoc VP Planning/Instl Effective .... Ms. Shanda DIEHL
51 Assoc VP Corp & Continuing Educ .... Mr. Kevin WITTE
84 Interim Dir of Enrollment/Registrar .... Ms. Mirranda SAARI
50 Dean Business/Technology .... Ms. Genevieve HOWARD
79 Int Dean Engl/Comm/Hum/Basic Educ .... Ms. Deena GODWIN
76 Dean Life Sci/Health & Phys Ed .... Vacant
83 Dean Social Sciences/Fine Arts .... Mr. Miles JACKSON
66 Assoc Dean of Nursing .... Ms. Cynthia MYERS
52 Director of Dental Hygiene .... Ms. Brenda WALSTEAD
04 Exec Assistant to the President .... Ms. Leigh KENT
41 Director of Athletics .... Ms. Ann WALKER
16 Associate Director Human Resources .... Ms. Sue WILLIAMS
08 Dir of Library Services .... Ms. Michelle BAGLEY
18 Director of Plant Services .... Mr. Tim PETTA
26 Chief Comm & Information Officer .... Mr. Chato HAZELBAKER
36 Director Career/Employment Services .... Ms. Edie BLAKELY
37 Director of Financial Aid .... Ms. Chippi BELLO
07 Assoc Dir of Entry Services .... Vacant
10 Director of Business Services .... Ms. Sabra SAND
35 Dir Stdnt Life/Multicult Stdnt Affs .... Ms. Sarah GRUHLER
38 Director Advising & Counseling .... Ms. Kelsey DUPRIE
25 Director of Grant Development .... Ms. Lori SILVERMAN
28 Director of Equity & Diversity .... Vacant
19 Director of Security & Safety .... Mr. Ken PACHECO
85 International Recruitment Manager .... Ms. Jane WALSTER
40 Bookstore Manager .... Ms. Monica KNOWLES
88 Mature Learning & Travel Stds Mgr .... Ms. Tracy REILLY-KELLY
96 Purchasing Manager .... Ms. Lisa NELSON
102 Foundation CEO .... Ms. Lisa GIBERT
105 Information Technology Specialist .... Mr. Chris CONCANNON
29 Director Alumni Relations .... Ms. Vivian MANNING

† Granted candidacy at the Baccalaureate level.

Clover Park Technical College (F)

4500 Steilacoom Boulevard, SW,
Lakewood WA 98499-4004
County: Pierce FICE Identification: 005752
Unit ID: 234951
Telephone: (253) 589-5800 Carnegie Class: Bac/Assoc-Assoc Dom
FAX Number: (253) 589-5601 Calendar System: Quarter
URL: www.cptc.edu
Established: 1942 Annual Undergrad Tuition & Fees (In-State): $5,382
Enrollment: 3,682 Coed
Affiliation or Control: State IRS Status: 501(c)3
Highest Offering: Associate Degree
Accreditation: NW, DA, HT, MAC, MLTAD, SURGT

01 Interim President .... Dr. Joyce LOVEDAY
04 Executive Assistant .... Cherie STEELE
05 Int Vice President Instruction .... Mabel EDMONDS
10 Vice President Finance & Admin Svcs .... Larry CLARK
32 Interim VP Student Success .... Juanita RICKS
06 VP Strategic Development .... Tawny DOTSON
15 Human Resources Director .... Shelby FRITZ
103 Dir of Workforce Development .... Cristeen CROUCHET
13 Dir Information Technology .... Michael TAYLOR
37 Director Financial Aid .... Wendy JOSEPH
18 Director Facilities Services .... John KANISS
12 Dir Northwest Career/Technical HS .... Loren DAVIS
84 Director of Enrollment Services .... Cynthia MOWRY
96 Purchasing Coord/Capital Projects .... Kate PURATICH
26 Marketing/Outreach Coordinator .... Janet HOLM
36 WorkFirst Special Projects Coord .... Vacant
09 Institutional Researcher .... Dr. Margie TOMSIC
40 Bookstore Coordinator .... Donna KOEHLER
18 Custodial Maintenance Coordinator .... Morris MILLER
06 Registrar .... Cynthia MOWRY
88 Int Dean Division I .... Claire KORSCHINOWSKI
88 Dean Division II .... Michelle HILLESLAND
88 Int Dean Division III .... Tanya SORENSON
30 Executive Director Foundation .... Lyman GIFFORD

† Granted candidacy at the Baccalaureate level.

Columbia Basin College (G)

2600 N 20th Avenue, Pasco WA 99301-3397
County: Franklin FICE Identification: 003774
Unit ID: 234979
Telephone: (509) 547-0511 Carnegie Class: Bac/Assoc-Assoc Dom
FAX Number: (509) 546-0404 Calendar System: Quarter
URL: www.columbiabasin.edu
Established: 1955 Annual Undergrad Tuition & Fees (In-State): $4,194
Enrollment: 6,385 Coed
Affiliation or Control: State IRS Status: 170(c)1
Highest Offering: Baccalaureate
Accreditation: NW, ADNUR, DH, EMT, MAC, SURGT

01 President .... Dr. Richard CUMMINS
05 Vice President Instruction .... Dr. Virginia TOMLINSON
10 Vice President of Administration .... Mr. Tyrone BROOKS
32 Vice President of Student Services .... Ms. Patricia CAMPBELL
15 VP Human Resources/Legal Affairs .... Ms. Camilla GLATT
09 Dean for Organizational Learning .... Dr. Jason ENGLE
49 Dean Arts & Humanities .... Mr. Bill MCKAY
62 Assoc Dean Library Services .... Ms. Melissa MCBURNEY
102 Executive Director Foundation .... Mr. Eric CLEMENTS
13 Director of Technology Services .... Mr. Brian DEXTER
40 Bookstore Director .... Ms. Debra BRUCE
18 Director of Plant Operations .... Mr. Chuck SCHMIDT
41 Athletic Director .... Mr. Scott ROGERS
26 Director of Communications .... Mr. Frank MURRAY
35 Director of Student Programs .... Ms. Alice SCHLEGEL
37 Director Student Financial Aid .... Mr. Ben BEUS
96 Director of Purchasing .... Ms. Sarah BROOKS
06 Associate Registrar .... Ms. Donna KORSTAD
04 Executive Asst to President .... Ms. Lupe PEREZ

*Community Colleges of Spokane District 17 (H)

501 N Riverpoint Boulevard, Ste 126,
Spokane WA 99217-6000
County: Spokane FICE Identification: 010784
Telephone: (509) 434-5107 Carnegie Class: N/A
FAX Number: (509) 434-5120
URL: www.ccs.spokane.edu

01 Chancellor .... Dr. Christine JOHNSON
12 Pres Spokane Community College .... Dr. Ryan CARSTENS
12 Pres Spokane Falls Comm College .... Dr. Janet GULLICKSON
05 Provost/Chief Learning Officer .... Dr. Nancy FAIR-SZOFRAN
20 Vice President of Learning SCC .... Ms. Rebecca RHODES
20 Vice President of Learning SFCC .... Vacant
32 VP of Student Services SCC .... Dr. Glen COSBY
32 VP of Student Services SFCC .... Mr. Darren PITCHER
10 Chief Financial Officer .... Ms. Lisa HJALTALIN
11 Chief Administration Officer .... Mr. Greg L. STEVENS
13 Chief Information Officer .... Mr. David O'NEILL
26 Public Information Officer .... Ms. Carolyn CASEY
41 Dist Director of Athletics PE/Rec .... Mr. Ken BURRUS
102 Executive Director CCS Foundation .... Mr. Tony D. HIGLEY
40 Director College Bookstores .... Ms. Shami R. RUGGLES
18 District Director of Facilities .... Vacant
103 Dist Dir Wkforce/Cont Ed/Corp Trng .... Ms. Sara SEXTON-JOHNSON
07 District Outreach Coordinator .... Mr. Tim CHURCHILL
96 Purchasing Manager .... Mr. Rod RAMER

*Spokane Community College (I)

North 1810 Greene Street, Spokane WA 99217-5499
County: Spokane FICE Identification: 003793
Unit ID: 236692
Telephone: (509) 533-7000 Carnegie Class: Assoc/HVT-Mix Trad/Non
FAX Number: (509) 533-8839 Calendar System: Quarter
URL: www.scc.spokane.edu
Established: 1963 Annual Undergrad Tuition & Fees (In-State): $3,388
Enrollment: 9,974 Coed
Affiliation or Control: State IRS Status: 501(c)3
Highest Offering: Associate Degree
Accreditation: NW, ACFEI, ADNUR, CAHIIM, COARC, CVT, DA, DMS, MAC, RAD, SURGT

00 District Chancellor .... Dr. Christine JOHNSON
02 President .... Dr. Ryan CARSTENS
05 Acting VP of Instruction .... Ms. Jenni MARTIN
32 Vice President of Student Services .... Dr. Glen COSBY
32 Director Student Success & Outreach .... Ms. Lori HUNT
07 Director Admissions & Registration .... Ms. Roxanne BELOIT
35 Associate Dean Student Development .... Mr. Connan CAMPBELL
51 Dean Adult Basic Education .... Mr. Ragu HEGDE
49 Dean Arts & Sciences .... Ms. Vicki TRIER
50 Dean Business/Hospitality/Info Tech .... Mr. Jeff BROWN
88 Assoc Dean Corrections Education .... Mr. Kevin HOUSE
56 Dean Extended Learning .... Vacant
76 Dean Health & Environmental Science .... Dr. J.L HENRIKSEN
66 Associate Dean of Nursing .... Dr. Cheri OSLER
75 Dean for Technical Education .... Mr. Dave COX
41 Director Athletics/PE/Recreation .... Mr. Ken BURRUS
09 Director of Planning & Research .... Vacant
51 Acting Asst Dean Adult Basic Ed .... Ms. Sarah STIFFLER
88 Assistant Dean PACE Services .... Ms. Linda AMES
06 Registrar .... Ms. Roxanne BELOIT
37 Director Financial Aid .... Ms. Tammy ZIBELL
10 Chief Financial Officer .... Ms. Lisa HJALTALIN

40 Director of College Bookstores ... Ms. Shami RUGGLES
11 Chief Administration Officer ... Mr. Greg STEVENS
26 Chief Public Information Officer ... Ms. Carolyn CASEY
30 District Development Officer ... Mr. Tony HIGLEY
20 District Provost ... Dr. Nancy FAIR-SZOFRAN
38 Student Counseling Department Chair ... Mr. Bill RAMBO
96 Director of Purchasing ... Mr. Rodney RAMER
04 Executive Asst to President ... Ms. Kathleen ROBERSON
13 Chief Info Technology Officer (CIO) ... Dr. David O'NEILL
88 Asst Dean of Arts & Sciences ... Ms. Gwendolyn JAMES

*Spokane Falls Community College (A)

3410 W Fort George Wright Drive,
Spokane WA 99224-5288
County: Spokane FICE Identification: 009544
Unit ID: 236708
Telephone: (509) 533-3500 Carnegie Class: Assoc/HT-High Non
FAX Number: (509) 533-3237 Calendar System: Quarter
URL: www.spokanefalls.edu
Established: 1967 Annual Undergrad Tuition & Fees (In-State): $3,388
Enrollment: 5,970 Coed
Affiliation or Control: State IRS Status: Exempt
Highest Offering: Associate Degree
Accreditation: NW, OTA, PTAA

02 President ... Dr. Janet GULLICKSON
04 Exec Asst to the President ... Ms. Jan CARPENTER
05 Vice President of Learning ... Vacant
32 Vice President of Student Services ... Dr. Darren PITCHER
81 Dean Computing/Math & Science ... Mr. James BRADY
83 Dean Soc Sci/Acct/Econ/Hum Svcs ... Dr. Joseph JOZWIAK
79 Dean Humanities ... Dr. Linda BEANE-BOOSE
57 Dean Visual & Performing Arts ... Dr. Bonnie BRUNT
50 Dean Bus/Prof Stds/Workforce ... Ms. Lora SENF
36 Dean Student Support Services ... Ms. Chrissy DAVIS JONES
06 Assoc Dean Enrollment Services ... Mr. Steven BAYS
07 Dir Recruit/New Stdnt Entry Center ... Ms. Chrissy DAVIS JONES
38 Co-Chair of Student Counseling ... Mr. Loren PEMBERTON
38 Co-Chair of Student Counseling ... Ms. Cynthia VIGIL
37 Director of Financial Aid ... Ms. Marjorie DAVIS
41 Athletic Director ... Mr. Ken BURRUS
19 Security & Safety Supervisor ... Mr. Kenneth DEMELLO
09 Dir Inst Effectiveness/Research ... Ms. Sally JACKSON
15 Chief Human Resources Officer ... Mr. Greg STEVENS
10 Chief Business Officer ... Ms. Lisa HJALTALIN
13 Chief Info Technology Officer (CIO) ... Dr. David O'NEILL
102 Exec Director CCS Foundation ... Mr. Tony HIGLEY
85 Vice Prov Strategic Partnerships ... Dr. Kevin BROCKBANK
08 District Director of Libraries ... Dr. Mary Ann GOODWIN
106 Interim District Dir e-Learning ... Dr. Kevin BROCKBANK
103 Chief Workforce Development Officer ... Mr. Mark MATTKE
26 Public Information Officer ... Ms. Carolyn CASEY
18 Director of Facilities ... Vacant
96 Director of Purchasing ... Mr. Rod RAMER

† Granted candidacy at the Baccalaureate level.

Cornish College of the Arts (B)

1000 Lenora Street, Seattle WA 98121-2707
County: King FICE Identification: 012315
Unit ID: 235024
Telephone: (206) 726-5151 Carnegie Class: Spec-4-yr-Arts
FAX Number: (206) 720-1011 Calendar System: Semester
URL: www.cornish.edu
Established: 1914 Annual Undergrad Tuition & Fees: $37,240
Enrollment: 767 Coed
Affiliation or Control: Independent Non-Profit IRS Status: 501(c)3
Highest Offering: Baccalaureate
Accreditation: NW, ART

01 President ... Mr. Chris KEVORKIAN
05 Provost ... Ms. Moira SCOTT PAYNE
30 VP Institutional Advancement ... Ms. Sarah PERRY
10 VP of Finance and Administration ... Mr. Jeffrey R. RIDDELL
84 VP of Enrollment Management ... Vacant
06 Dean of Academic Services/Registrar . Ms. Adrienne M. BOLYARD
32 Dean of Student Life ... Mr. Jerry HEKKEL
26 Director of Communications ... Ms. Rosemary JONES
15 Director of Human Resources ... Vacant
13 Director of Information Technology ... Mr. Mark LEDESMA
21 Controller ... Ms. Tina CHAMBERLAIN
08 Director of Library Services ... Ms. Hollis NEAR
07 Director of Admissions ... Ms. Sharron STARLING
18 Facilities Director ... Ms. Jenny FRAZIER
19 Dir of Campus Safety & Security ... Mr. Brandon BIRD
37 Director of Financial Aid ... Ms. Monique THERIAULT
38 Director Student Counseling ... Ms. Lori KORSHORK

DigiPen Institute of Technology (C)

9931 Willows Road, NE, Redmond WA 98052
County: King FICE Identification: 037243
Unit ID: 443410
Telephone: (425) 558-0299 Carnegie Class: Bac-Diverse
FAX Number: (425) 558-0378 Calendar System: Semester
URL: www.digipen.edu
Established: 1988 Annual Undergrad Tuition & Fees: $27,800
Enrollment: 1,018 Coed
Affiliation or Control: Proprietary IRS Status: Proprietary
Highest Offering: Master's
Accreditation: ACCSC, ENG

01 President ... Mr. Claude COMAIR
32 Sr VP Student & External Affairs ... Ms. Angela KUGLER
35 Dean of Students ... Mr. Marshal TRAVERSE
07 Director of Admissions ... Ms. Danial POWERS
37 Director Student Financial Aid ... Ms. Trinity HUTTNER

Eastern Washington University (D)

526 5th Street, Cheney WA 99004-1619
County: Spokane FICE Identification: 003775
Unit ID: 235097
Telephone: (509) 359-6200 Carnegie Class: Masters/L
FAX Number: (509) 359-6927 Calendar System: Quarter
URL: www.ewu.edu
Established: 1882 Annual Undergrad Tuition & Fees (In-State): $7,866
Enrollment: 13,453 Coed
Affiliation or Control: State IRS Status: 501(c)3
Highest Offering: Doctorate
Accreditation: NW, BUS, CAATE, CACREP, CS, DH, ENG, ENGT, MUS, NRPA, OT, PLNG, PTA, SP, SPAA, SW

01 President ... Dr. Mary CULLINAN
05 Interim Prov/VP of Academic Affs ... Dr. Mary Ann KEOGH HOSS
10 Vice President for Business/Finance ... Ms. Mary VOVES
32 Vice President for Student Affairs . Ms. Stacey MORGAN FOSTER
30 Vice President of Advancement ... Mr. Michael WESTFALL
13 VP Info Technology/CIO ... Dr. Gary PRATT
20 Vice Prov Academic Admin ... Dr. Linda KIEFFER
88 Vice Prov Acad Plng/Grants & Res ... Dr. Colin ORMSBY
88 Vice Prov Undergrad & Stdnt Success ... Dr. Chuck LOPEZ
08 Dean of Libraries ... Dr. Suzanne MILTON
06 Registrar/Enrollment Svcs ... Ms. Angela ANDERSON
41 Director Intercollegiate Athletics ... Mr. William CHAVES
21 Assoc VP Finance/Chief Fin Officer ... Ms. Toni HABEGGER
18 Assoc Vice Pres for Facilities ... Mr. Shawn KING
84 Assoc Vice Pres Enrollment Mgmt ... Dr. Neil WOOLF
04 Exec Assistant to the President/BOT ... Ms. Catherine MOSS
100 Assoc to the President ... Ms Laurie CONNELLY
86 Director of Government Relations ... Mr. David BURI
36 Dir Career Services Center ... Ms. Virginia HINCH
92 Director of University Honors ... Dr. Dana ELDER
07 Director of Admissions ... Ms. Cathy SLEETH
37 Director of Fin Aid & Scholarships ... Mr. Bruce DEFRATES
40 Dir of Bookstore/Pence Union Bldg ... Mr. Robert ANDERSON
51 Dir of Continuing Education & RS ... Vacant
06 Director of Registration & Records ... Ms. Debra FOCKLER
58 Vice Provost/Graduate Research ... Dr. Colin ORMSBY
15 Director of Human Resources ... Ms. Jolynn ROGERS
29 Director of Alumni Advancement ... Ms. Lisa POPLAWSKI
109 Assoc VP/Business Auxiliary Svcs ... Ms. LeeAnn CASE
39 Sr Director Housing/Resid Life ... Mr. Josh ASHCROFT
38 Director Counseling & Psych Svcs ... Dr. Robert QUACKENBUSH
19 Director Public Safety/Chief Police ... Chief Timothy L. WALTERS
44 Assoc Director of Annual Giving ... Ms. Pa SPANJER
27 Director of Media Relations ... Mr. David MEANY
22 Dir Equal Opp/Affirm Action Coord ... Ms. Gayla THOMAS
50 Dean Business & Public Admin ... Dr. Martine DUCHATELET
49 Dean College Arts/Letters/Education ... Dr. Roy SONNEMA
83 Dean Col Social/Behav Sci/Soc Work ... Dr. Vickie SHIELDS
81 Dean Col Science Math & Technology ... Dr. Judd CASE
66 Dean Health Science & Public Health ... Dr. Lauren O'HANLON
35 Assoc VP/Dean of Student Life ... Dr. Amy JOHNSON
09 Assoc Director/Institutional Rsrch ... Ms. Bamby FIELDS
26 Chief Public Relations Officer ... Ms. Teresa CONWAY
104 Dir Office of Global Initiatives ... Ms. Catherine DIXON
106 Exec Director E-Learning ... Mr. Ben MEREDITH
25 Exec Dir Grants & Research Dev ... Ms. Ruth GALM

Edmonds Community College (E)

20000 68th Avenue W, Lynnwood WA 98036-5999
County: Snohomish FICE Identification: 005001
Unit ID: 235103
Telephone: (425) 640-1459 Carnegie Class: Assoc/MT-VT-High Non
FAX Number: (425) 771-3366 Calendar System: Quarter
URL: www.edcc.edu
Established: 1967 Annual Undergrad Tuition & Fees (In-State): $3,758
Enrollment: 8,993 Coed
Affiliation or Control: State IRS Status: 501(c)3
Highest Offering: Associate Degree
Accreditation: NW, CA, CONST

01 President ... Dr. Jean HERNANDEZ
05 Exec Vice President Instruction ... Dr. Charlie CRAWFORD
10 Vice Pres/Chief Financial Officer ... Mr. Kevin MCKAY
30 Vice Pres Col Relations/Advancement ... Dr. Tonya DRAKE
15 Int Exec Director Human Resources ... Ms. Suzanne MOREAU
32 Vice President Student Services ... Ms. Christina CASTORENA
103 VP Workforce Development/Training ... Dr. Terry COX
85 Vice Pres International Education ... Mr. David CORDELL
84 Dean Student Enroll/Financial Svcs ... Mr. Saovra EAR
35 Dean Student Life/Development ... Mr. Daniel JOHNSON
36 Dean Student Success/Retention ... Vacant
88 Interim Director Advising ... Ms. Heidi FARANI
04 Executive Asst to the President ... Ms. Patty MICHAJLA
102 Director College Foundation ... Mr. Brad THOMAS
25 Director Grants & Research ... Vacant
26 Director Communications/Marketing ... Ms. Marisa PIERCE
13 Director Information Technology ... Ms. Eva SMITH
18 Dir Facilites Planning & Operations ... Ms. Stephanie TEACHMAN
28 Int Director Equity & Inclusion ... Ms. Michele DOMINGO
96 Director of Purchasing ... Ms. Marian PAANANEN

27 Public Information Officer ... Mr. Nathan MACDONALD
19 Director Safety & Security ... Mr. Daniel GUERRERO
41 Athletic Director ... Mr. Jorge DE LA TORRE
85 Dir International Student Services ... Ms. Lisa THOMPSON
09 Institutional Researcher ... Ms. Pat HUFFMAN
108 Director Institutional Assessment ... Mr. James MULIK

Everett Community College (F)

2000 Tower Street, Everett WA 98201-1390
County: Snohomish FICE Identification: 003776
Unit ID: 235149
Telephone: (425) 388-9100 Carnegie Class: Assoc/MT-VT-High Non
FAX Number: (425) 388-9129 Calendar System: Quarter
URL: www.everettcc.edu
Established: 1941 Annual Undergrad Tuition & Fees (In-State): $3,643
Enrollment: 7,516 Coed
Affiliation or Control: State IRS Status: 501(c)3
Highest Offering: Associate Degree
Accreditation: NW, ADNUR, MAC

01 President ... Dr. David BEYER
04 Sr Exec Asst to President ... Ms. Melissa GERAGHTY
05 Int EVP Instruction/Student Svcs ... Ms. Gail MIULLI
30 Vice Pres of College Advancement ... Dr. John OLSON
10 Vice Pres of Administrative Svcs ... Ms. Jennifer L. HOWARD
26 Vice Pres of College Services ... Mr. Patrick SISNEROS
12 Exec Dir Univ Ctr North Puget Sound ... Vacant
60 Dean Communication/Social Sciences ... Mr. Eugene MCAVOY
32 Dean of Student Development ... Mr. Anthony WILLIAMS
81 Dean of Math & Science ... Mr. Al FRIEDMAN
62 Dean of Arts & Learning Resources ... Ms. Jeanne LEADER
76 Dean Health Sciences/Public Safety ... Mr. Jason SMITH
53 Dean of Basic & Adult Education ... Ms. Katie JENSEN
28 Chief Diversity & Equity Officer ... Ms. Maria PENA
51 Director Continuing Education ... Ms. Karen LANDRY
84 Dean Enrollment/Student Finan Svcs ... Ms. Laurie FRANKLIN
50 Dean of Business & Applied Tech ... Mr. Ryan DAVIS
19 Dir of Campus Safety & Security ... Vacant
88 Vice Pres of Corporate Training ... Mr. John B. BONNER
09 Director Institutional Research ... Vacant
41 Director of Athletics ... Mr. Larry WALKER
40 Director of Bookstore ... Mr. Wes MORROW
22 Dir Center for Disability Services ... Ms. Karen EHNAT

The Evergreen State College (G)

2700 Evergreen Parkway, NW, Olympia WA 98505-0005
County: Thurston FICE Identification: 008155
Unit ID: 235167
Telephone: (360) 867-6000 Carnegie Class: Masters/M
FAX Number: N/A Calendar System: Quarter
URL: www.evergreen.edu
Established: 1967 Annual Undergrad Tuition & Fees (In-State): $8,380
Enrollment: 4,219 Coed
Affiliation or Control: State IRS Status: 501(c)3
Highest Offering: Master's
Accreditation: NW

01 President ... Dr. George S. BRIDGES
05 Interim Provost ... Dr. Ken TABBUTT
20 Vice President for Academic Affairs ... Dr. Michael ZIMMERMAN
32 Vice President Student Affairs ... Dr. Wendy ENDRESS
10 Vice President Finance/Admin ... Dr. John HURLEY
30 Vice President College Advancement ... Ms. Amanda WALKER
84 Assoc Vice Pres for Enrollmt Mgmt ... Mr. Steve HUNTER
15 Assoc Vice Pres for Human Resources ... Ms. Laurel UZNANSKI
08 Dean of Library Services ... Mr. Greg MULLINS
35 Dir of Academic and Career Advising ... Ms. Kitty JONES
100 Chief of Staff/Secretary to BOT ... Mr. John CARMICHAEL
45 Director of Planning and Budget ... Ms. Lisa DAWN-FISHER
22 Affirm Act/Equal Opp Officer ... Ms. Lorie MASTIN
13 Director Computing/Communications ... Mr. Antonio ALFONSO
26 Chief Communications Officer ... Ms. Michelle MA
37 Director of Financial Aid ... Ms. Tracy HALL
06 Registrar ... Ms. Elaine HAYASHI-PETERSEN
09 Director of Institutional Research ... Ms. Laura COGHLAN
18 Director of Facilities ... Ms. Jeanne RYNNE
21 Director of Business Services ... Mr. Dave KOHLER
36 Director Career Development Center ... Mr. Steve LAING
38 Dir Counseling & Health Services ... Ms. Elizabeth MCHUGH
96 Purchasing and Contracts Manager ... Mr. Jay FIELD
07 Director of Admissions ... Mr. Eric PEDERSEN
88 Director of Sustainability ... Mr. Scott MORGAN

Faith Evangelical College & Seminary (H)

3504 N Pearl Street, Tacoma WA 98407-2607
County: Pierce FICE Identification: 036894
Unit ID: 443049
Telephone: (253) 752-2020 Carnegie Class: Spec-4-yr-Faith
FAX Number: (253) 759-1790 Calendar System: Quarter
URL: www.faithseminary.edu
Established: 1969 Annual Undergrad Tuition & Fees: $7,840
Enrollment: 320 Coed
Affiliation or Control: Interdenominational IRS Status: 501(c)3
Highest Offering: Doctorate
Accreditation: TRACS

01 President ... Dr. Michael J. ADAMS

05 Vice Pres Academic Affs/Provost .... Dr. H. Wayne HOUSE
104 VP Intl Affs/Dean Korean Division .... Dr. Kyu H. LEE
11 VP Administrative Affs/Registrar .... Mr. John WHEELER
32 Dir Student Svcs/Korean Division .... Dr. Wookuk SUH
10 Chief Financial Officer .... Dr. Douglas COLLIER
07 Director of Admissions .... Mrs. Lorrie WHATELY
08 Library Director .... Dr. Timothy HYUN
35 Director Student Services .... Ms. Nor BOICE
04 Exec Administrative Assistant .... Ms. Kimberly ADAMS

Gonzaga University (A)

502 E Boone Avenue, Spokane WA 99258-0001
County: Spokane FICE Identification: 003778
Unit ID: 235316
Telephone: (509) 313-4220 Carnegie Class: Masters/L
FAX Number: (509) 313-5718 Calendar System: Semester
URL: www.gonzaga.edu
Established: 1887 Annual Undergrad Tuition & Fees: $37,990
Enrollment: 7,352 Coed
Affiliation or Control: Roman Catholic IRS Status: 501(c)3
Highest Offering: Doctorate
Accreditation: NW, ANEST, BUS, BUSA, CACREP, CEA, CS, ENG, LAW, MUS, NURSE, TED

01 President .... Dr. Thayne M. MCCULLOH
100 Chief of Staff .... Mr. John SKLUT
05 Academic Vice President .... Dr. Patricia OCONNELL KILLEN
10 Vice President for Finance .... Mr. Charles J. MURPHY
88 VP for Mission & Ministry .... Vacant
32 VP for Student Development .... Dr. Judith BIGGS GARBUIO
30 VP for University Advancement .... Mr. Joe POSS
45 VP for Policy/Planning & Admin .... Dr. Robert MYERS
20 Assoc Academic Vice President .... Dr. Ron LARGE
28 Assoc AVP/Chief Diversity Officer .... Dr. Raymond REYES
06 Asst Academic Vice Pres/Registrar .... Ms. Jolanta A. WEBER
15 Asst Vice President Human Resources ... Mr. Kirk WOOD-GAINES
88 Assistant VP for Marketing/Comm .... Mr. Dave SONNTAG
88 Assistant VP for Mission .... Fr. Jim VOISS, SJ
36 Asst VP for Student Devel/Career .... Mr. O. Ray ANGLE
88 Vice President of the University .... Fr. Frank E. CASE, SJ
07 Dean of Admission .... Ms. Julie A. MCCULLOH
88 Dean of Student Well Being/Healthy .... Mr. Eric BALDWIN
08 Dean of Library Services .... Mr. Paul J. BRACKE
37 Dean of Student Finance Services .... Mr. James WHITE
13 Interim Chief Information Officer .... Mr. Jim JONES
26 Director Cmty/Public Relations .... Ms. Mary Joan HAHN
29 Director Alumni .... Mr. Bob D. FINN
36 Director Career Center .... Dr. Mary HEITKEMPER
38 Director of Counseling Services .... Dr. Fernando ORTIZ
49 Dean Arts & Sciences .... Dr. Elisabeth MERMANN-JOZWIAK
50 Dean School of Business .... Dr. Kenneth ANDERSON
107 Acting Dean School of Prof Studies .... Dr. Joe ALBERT
53 Dean of Education .... Dr. Vincent C. ALFONSO
54 Dean of Engineering & Applied Scien .... Dr. Steve SILLIMAN
61 Dean of Law .... Ms. Jane KORN
09 Director of Institutional Research .... Ms. Jolanta A. WEBER
41 Director of Athletics .... Mr. Michael L. ROTH
42 Director of University Ministry .... Mrs. Michelle M. WHEATLEY
43 General Counsel .... Ms. Maureen MCGUIRE
18 Director Plant Services .... Mr. Kenneth R. SAMMONS
92 Director Honors Program .... Rev. Tim R. CLANCY, SJ
96 Manager of Purchasing .... Mr. Steve M. LUNDEN
104 Director Study Abroad .... Mr. Richard O. MENARD
25 Director Sponsored Research & Pgm .... Dr. Joann WAITE
108 Faculty Director of Assessment .... Dr. Patrick T. MCCORMICK
66 Dean of Nursing & Human Physiology .... Dr. Brenda STEVENSON MARSHALL
20 Asst AVP for Global Engagement .... Dr. Joseph J. KINSELLA
35 Dean of Student Engagement .... Mr. Matt LAMSMA
106 Dean of Virtual Campus .... Dr. Michael CAREY
71 Director of Gonzaga-In-Florence .... Dr. Jason HOUSTON
100 Faculty Advisor to the President .... Dr. Ellen M. MACCARONE
21 Assoc Vice President of Finance .... Mr. Joe SMITH
88 Controller .... Ms. Deena PRESNELL
88 Sr Publications Ed & Content Strat .... Ms. Kathryn VANSKIKE
11 Chancellor .... Fr. Bernard J. COUGHLIN, SJ
19 Director Security/Safety .... Mr. Scott SNIDER
22 Dir Affirmative Action/EEO .... Ms. Chris PURVIANCE
39 Director Student Housing .... Mr. Dennis COLESTOCK
04 Executive Asst to President .... Ms. Julia BJORDAHL
101 Secretary of the Institution/Board .... Ms. Maureen MCGUIRE
44 Director of Annual Giving .... Ms. Stephanie ROCKWELL

Grays Harbor College (B)

1620 Edward P. Smith Drive, Aberdeen WA 98520-7500
County: Grays Harbor FICE Identification: 003779
Unit ID: 235334
Telephone: (360) 532-9020 Carnegie Class: Assoc/HVT-High Non
FAX Number: (360) 538-4299 Calendar System: Quarter
URL: www.ghc.edu
Established: 1930 Annual Undergrad Tuition & Fees (In-District): $3,688
Enrollment: 2,006 Coed
Affiliation or Control: State/Local IRS Status: 501(c)3
Highest Offering: Associate Degree
Accreditation: #NW, ADNUR

01 President .... Dr. James MINKLER
04 Senior Admin Assistant to President .... Ms. Sandra ZELASKO
05 Vice President for Instruction .... Ms. Laurie CLARY
10 Chief Financial Officer .... Vacant
32 Vice President for Student Services .... Mr. Jason HOSENEY
13 Chief Info Technology Officer/CIO .... Vacant
75 Assoc Dean Vocational Instruction .... Mr. Mike KELLY
35 Assoc Dean for Student Services .... Vacant
08 Assoc Dean Library/Media Services .... Mr. Ahniwa FERRARI
07 Assoc Dean of Admissions .... Vacant
15 Chief Human Resources Officer .... Mr. Darrin JONES
37 Director Student Financial Aid .... Ms. Stacey SAVINO
18 Dir Campus Operations/Sfty/Security .... Mr. Lance JAMES
38 Director of Counseling .... Vacant
30 Chief Development Officer .... Ms. Jan JORGENSON
26 Director Public Relations .... Ms. Jane F. GOLDBERG
09 Chief Instl Effect/Research/Plng .... Ms. Kristy ANDERSON
06 Registrar .... Ms. Nancy DEVERSE
41 Athletic Director .... Mr. Tom SUTERA
106 Dir Online Education/E-Learning .... Mr. James UMPHRES

† Granted candidacy at the Baccalaureate level.

Green River College (C)

12401 SE 320th Street, Auburn WA 98092-3699
County: King FICE Identification: 003780
Unit ID: 235343
Telephone: (253) 833-9111 Carnegie Class: Bac/Assoc-Assoc Dom
FAX Number: (253) 288-3470 Calendar System: Quarter
URL: www.greenriver.edu
Established: 1965 Annual Undergrad Tuition & Fees (In-State): $4,344
Enrollment: 7,915 Coed
Affiliation or Control: State IRS Status: 501(c)3
Highest Offering: Baccalaureate
Accreditation: NW, OTA, PTAA

01 Interim President .... Mr. Scott MORGAN
05 Int Vice Pres of Instruction .... Dr. Deborah CASEY POWELL
13 Exec Dir of Information Technology .... Ms. Camella MORGAN
10 Vice President Business Affairs .... Ms. Shirley BEAN
15 Vice President for Human Resources ...... Mr. Marshall SAMPSON
32 Vice President of Student Services . Dr. Deborah CASEY POWELL
56 VP Intl Programs/Extended Learning .... Mr. Wendy STEWART
75 Int Dn Prof/Tech Ed/Trades & Tech .... Mr. Jeff MCCAULEY
49 Dean Fine Arts/Math/Soc Sci/Library ...... Ms. Christie GILLILAND
88 Director of Capital Projects .... Vacant
84 Dean of Enrollment & Completion .... Mr. David LARSEN
06 Director of Enrollment Services .... Ms. Denise BENNATTS
37 Director of Financial Aid .... Ms. Mary EDINGTON
30 Exec Director of Development/Found .... Mr. George FRASIER
21 Director of Budget .... Ms. Janee SOMMERFELD
21 Controller .... Ms. Leda VOIGT
18 Director of Facilities .... Mr. Robert OLSON
26 Exec Director of College Relations .... Ms. Allison FRIEDLY
51 Dean for Branch Campuses & CE .... Ms. Leslie MOORE
09 Exec Dir Institutional Effectivenes .... Mr. Christopher JOHNSON
28 Dir Diversity/Equity & Incluion .... Vacant
96 Director of Procurement .... Ms. Laura LOWE
19 Director of Campus Safety .... Mr. Derek RONNFELTD
41 Director Athletics .... Mr. Robert KICKNER
04 Executive Assistant to President .... Ms. Suzanne MCCUDDEN

Heritage University (D)

3240 Fort Road, Toppenish WA 98948-9599
County: Yakima FICE Identification: 003777
Unit ID: 235422
Telephone: (509) 865-8500 Carnegie Class: Masters/S
FAX Number: (509) 865-7976 Calendar System: Semester
URL: www.heritage.edu
Established: 1982 Annual Undergrad Tuition & Fees: $19,122
Enrollment: 1,241 Coed
Affiliation or Control: Independent Non-Profit IRS Status: 501(c)3
Highest Offering: Master's
Accreditation: NW, #ARCPA, MT, SW

01 President .... Dr. John E. BASSETT
05 Provost/VP Academic Affairs .... Dr. Laurie FATHE
32 VP Student Affairs & Enrollment .... Dr. Celestino LIMAS
100 Chief of Staff .... Ms. Veronica NARANJO
30 VP Advancement & Marketing .... Mr. David WISE
84 Assoc VP Enrollment Management .... Vacant
10 VP Business Services & CFO .... Mr. John VORNBROCK
06 Registrar .... Mr. Luis GUTIERREZ
53 Dean of Education & Psychology .... Ms. Merrilou HARRISON
18 Director Physical Plant/Maintenance .... Mr. Jeff BEEHLER
37 Director of Financial Aid .... Mr. Oscar VERDUZCO
08 Reference Librarian .... Mr. Ron HODGE
13 VP Information Technology/CIO .... Mr. Jim BUSH
07 Director of Recruitment .... Ms. Erica TAIT
26 Communications Officer .... Ms. Bonnie HUGHES
04 Manager President's Office .... Ms. Betty J. SAMPSON
09 Director of Institutional Research .... Vacant
15 Director Human Resources .... Ms. Veronica NARANJO
49 Dean Arts & Sciences .... Dr. Kazuhiro SONODA
35 Asst VP Student Affairs .... Ms. Melissa HILL
88 Director Academic Advising .... Ms. Irma DEPRIETO
88 Director Business Services .... Ms. Donnita MARSH
20 Associate Provost .... Vacant
21 Controller .... Mr. Mark MCNABB
29 Director of Alumni Relations .... Vacant

Highline College (E)

PO Box 98000, 2400 S 240th Street, Des Moines WA 98198-9800
County: King FICE Identification: 003781
Unit ID: 235431
Telephone: (206) 878-3710 Carnegie Class: Bac/Assoc-Assoc Dom
FAX Number: (206) 870-3779 Calendar System: Quarter
URL: www.highline.edu
Established: 1961 Annual Undergrad Tuition & Fees (In-State): $3,846
Enrollment: 6,443 Coed
Affiliation or Control: State IRS Status: 501(c)3
Highest Offering: Associate Degree
Accreditation: NW, ADNUR, COARC, MAC

01 President .... Dr. Jack BERMINGHAM
11 Vice Pres Administrative Services .... Mr. Michael PHAM
05 Vice Pres for Academic Affairs .... Mr. Jeff WAGNITZ
30 VP Inst Advancement/Cmty Rels .... Dr. Lisa SKARI
32 Vice Pres for Student Services .... Ms. Toni CASTRO
20 Dean of Instruction-Vocational .... Ms. Alice MADSEN
20 Dean of Instruction-Academics .... Dr. Rolita EZEONU
24 Dean Instructional Resources .... Ms. Monica LUCE
35 Assoc Dean Student Programs .... Mr. Jonathan BROWN
31 Exec Dir Community Education .... Ms. Judy PERRY
84 Assoc Dean Enrollment Services .... Ms. Lorraine ODOM
26 Director Communications & Marketing .... Mr. Tony JOHNSON
15 Exec Director of Human Resources .... Ms. Sue WILLIAMSON
10 Director Financial Services .... Ms. Shirley BEAN
13 Director Information Technology Services .... Mr. Tim WRYE
18 Director Plant Operations .... Mr. Barry HOLLDORF
19 Dir Safety/Sec & Emergency Manager .... Mr. Jim BAYLOR
41 Director Athletics .... Mr. John DUNN
44 Director Resources & Development .... Mr. Rod STEPHENSON
09 Manager Institutional Research .... Ms. Emily COATES
38 Assoc Dean Counseling/Judicial .... Dr. Allison LAU
40 Bookstore Manager .... Ms. Kristi DOPP
96 Manager of Purchasing .... Ms. Dianna THIELE
06 Registrar .... Ms. Debbie FAISON
07 Director of Admissions .... Ms. L. Michelle KUWASAKI
22 Program Asst Multicultural Affairs .... Ms. Barbara TALKINGTON
29 Coordinator Alumni Relations .... Ms. Madison GRIDLEY

† Granted candidacy at the Baccalaureate level.

Lake Washington Institute of Technology (F)

11605 132nd Avenue NE, Kirkland WA 98034-8506
County: King FICE Identification: 005373
Unit ID: 235699
Telephone: (425) 739-8100 Carnegie Class: Bac/Assoc-Assoc Dom
FAX Number: (425) 739-8299 Calendar System: Quarter
URL: www.lwtech.edu
Established: 1949 Annual Undergrad Tuition & Fees (In-State): $3,880
Enrollment: 3,660 Coed
Affiliation or Control: State IRS Status: 170(c)1
Highest Offering: Baccalaureate
Accreditation: NW, ACFEI, ADNUR, DA, DH, FUSER, MAC, OTA, PTAA

01 President .... Dr. Amy M. MORRISON GOINGS
04 Exec Assistant to the President .... Ms. Heather DEGRAW
32 VP Student Services .... Dr. Ruby HAYDEN
05 VP of Instruction .... Dr. Elliot STERN
10 VP Administrative Services .... Mr. Bill THOMAS
86 Exec Dir Legislative & Ext Rels .... Ms. Terry BYINGTON
13 Exec Dir Information Technology .... Mr. Mike POTTER
102 Exec Director Foundation .... Ms. Elisabeth SORENSEN
15 Exec Director Human Resources .... Ms. Melissa LAMY
88 Spec Asst to Pres College Advance .... Ms. Andrea I. OLSON
53 Dean Gen Educ/Hospitality & Svcs .... Mr. Douglas J. EMORY
76 Dean Instruction Allied Health .... Ms. Jamilyn PENN
72 Dean Applied Design Programs .... Dr. Suzanne AMES
89 Principal/Dean High School Programs .... Dr. Kim INFINGER
08 Library Program Coordinator .... Ms. Cheyenne M. RODUIN
26 Director Communications/Marketing .... Ms. Leslie COHAN
76 Dir Phys Therapist Assistant Pgm .... Ms. Molly VERSCHUYL
88 Director Funeral Services .... Ms. Jamye CAMERON
66 Director of Nursing .... Ms. Antwinett LEE
104 Director International Programs .... Ms. Sarah ROSS
106 Director of eLearning .... Ms. Rhonda DEWITT
18 Director Facilities & Operations .... Mr. Tim WHEELER
37 Director Financial Aid .... Mr. Bill CHANEY
103 Director Workforce Development .... Ms. Demetra BIROS
25 Dir of Research & Grant Development .... Ms. Cathy COPELAND
07 Director Admissions & Outreach .... Ms. Christina HARTER
88 Director TRiO Student Support Svcs .... Dr. Patricia HUNTER
21 Controller .... Mr. Xieng LIM
109 Manager Food Service Operations .... Mr. Joe TREVINO
96 Purchasing Manager .... Mr. Gordy FUNAI
105 Website/Digital Content Specialist .... Ms. Alisa SHTROMBERG
88 Manager Student Programs .... Ms. Sheila WALTON
40 Manager Bookstore .... Mr. Russ MERKOW
19 Director Security/Safety .... Mr. Anthony BOWERS
54 Dean of Industrial Technology .... Dr. Sharon BUCK
84 Director Enrollment Services .... Ms. Larisa AKSELRUD
35 Director Student Development .... Ms. Andrea FECHNER
09 Director Research & Grants .... Ms. Cathy COPELAND
28 Interim Diversity Program Coord .... Ms. Neera MEHTA

Lower Columbia College (G)

PO Box 3010, Longview WA 98632-0310
County: Cowlitz FICE Identification: 003782
Unit ID: 235750
Telephone: (360) 442-2311 Carnegie Class: Assoc/HVT-High Non
FAX Number: (360) 442-2109 Calendar System: Quarter
URL: www.lowercolumbia.edu
Established: 1934 Annual Undergrad Tuition & Fees (In-State): $4,131
Enrollment: 3,208 Coed

Affiliation or Control: State IRS Status: 170(c)1
Highest Offering: Associate Degree
Accreditation: NW, ADNUR, MAC

01 President .... Mr. Christopher C. BAILEY
05 Vice President of Instruction .... Mr. Brendan GLASER
11 Vice President Administrative Svcs .... Mr. Nolan WHEELER
32 Vice President of Student Services .... Ms. Sue ORCHARD
103 Int Dean Workforce/Continuing Educ .... Ms. Tamra BELL
20 Dean Instructional Programs .... Mr. Kyle HAMMON
76 Executive Dean Allied Health/Nurse .... Ms. Karen JOINER
09 Director Effectiveness & Marketing .... Ms. Wendy HALL
18 Director of Campus Services .... Mr. Richard HAMILTON
102 Director of Foundation .... Ms. Kendra SPRAGUE
41 Athletic Director .... Mr. Kirc J. ROLAND
21 Controller .... Ms. Kelley WEST
15 Director of Personnel Services .... Ms. Kendra SPRAGUE
37 Financial Aid Officer .... Ms. Marisa GEIER
08 Associate Dean Resource Svcs .... Ms. Melinda HARBAUGH
13 Director of Information Technology .... Mr. Brandon RAY
40 Director of Bookstore .... Mr. Cliff HICKS
07 Director Admissions/Registrar .... Ms. Nichole SEROSHEK
10 Chief Business Officer .... Mr. Nolan WHEELER
96 Director of Purchasing .... Ms. Sherry GOHN
04 Executive Assistant .... Ms. Linda J. CLARK
06 Registrar .... Ms. Nichole SEROSHEK
106 Dir Online Education/E-learning .... Ms. Sarah GRIFFITH
19 Director Security/Safety .... Mr. Jason ARROWSMITH
29 Director Alumni Relations .... Ms. Sheila BURGIN

Moody Bible Institute-Spokane (A)

611 E Indiana Avenue, Spokane WA 99207
Telephone: (509) 570-5900 Identification: 770082
Accreditation: &NH

† Regional accreditation is carried under the parent institution in Chicago, IL

Northwest College of Art & Design (NCAD) (B)

16301 Creative Drive NE, Poulsbo WA 98370-8651
County: Kitsap FICE Identification: 026021
Unit ID: 377546
Telephone: (360) 779-9993 Carnegie Class: Spec-4-yr-Arts
FAX Number: (360) 779-9933 Calendar System: Semester
URL: www.ncad.edu
Established: 1982 Annual Undergrad Tuition & Fees: $19,050
Enrollment: 94 Coed
Affiliation or Control: Proprietary IRS Status: Proprietary
Highest Offering: Baccalaureate
Accreditation: ACCSC

01 President .... Craig FREEMAN
05 Director of Education .... Julius FINLEY
11 Director of Operations .... Kim PERIGARD
06 Registrar .... Danielle MACKELWICH
13 IT Admin .... Skye CARLSON
07 Admissions Representative .... Brigette WATSON
37 Financial Aid .... Mac FOX
08 Head Librarian .... Tiffany SUDELA

Northwest Indian College (C)

2522 Kwina Road, Bellingham WA 98226-9278
County: Whatcom FICE Identification: 021800
Unit ID: 380377
Telephone: (360) 676-2772 Carnegie Class: Tribal
FAX Number: (360) 738-0136 Calendar System: Quarter
URL: www.nwic.edu
Established: 1978 Annual Undergrad Tuition & Fees: $4,407
Enrollment: 637 Coed
Affiliation or Control: Tribal Control IRS Status: 501(c)3
Highest Offering: Baccalaureate
Accreditation: NW

01 President .... Dr. Justin GUILLORY
10 Chief Financial Officer .... Mr. Steve ZAWOYSKY
05 Vice Pres Instruction/Student Svcs .... Ms. Carole RAVE
11 Vice Pres Campus Development .... Mr. David OREIRO
46 VP for Research/Sponsored Programs .... Ms. Barbara ROBERTS
04 Exec Assistant to the President .... Ms. Frances SELLARS
106 Dean of Academic/Distant Learning .... Ms. Bernice PORTERVINT
32 Dean of Student Life .... Ms. Victoria RETASKET
37 Asc Dn Students/Fin Aid Dir/Admiss .... Vacant
13 IS Director .... Mr. Michael JAMES
08 Library Director .... Ms. Valerie MCBETH
06 Registrar .... Ms. Patricia CUEVA
09 Director of Institutional Research .... Ms. Carmen BLAND
15 Director Human Resources .... Ms. Linda SCHNELL
18 Director of Facilities Maintenace .... Mr. Jon DAVIS
19 Security Manager .... Mr. Jerry EMORY
30 Director of NWIC Foundation .... Mr. Greg MASTEN
41 Athletic Director .... Ms. Krista MAHLE
96 Purchasing Manager .... Mr. Charlie ROBERTS

Northwest School of Wooden Boatbuilding (D)

42 N Water Street, Port Hadlock WA 98339-8706
County: Jefferson FICE Identification: 041550
Unit ID: 458140
Telephone: (360) 385-4948 Carnegie Class: Spec 2-yr-Tech
FAX Number: (360) 385-5089 Calendar System: Other
URL: www.nwswb.edu
Established: 1981 Annual Undergrad Tuition & Fees: $14,550
Enrollment: 61 Coed
Affiliation or Control: Independent Non-Profit IRS Status: 501(c)3
Highest Offering: Associate Degree
Accreditation: ACCSC

01 Executive Director .... Ms. Betsy DAVIS

Northwest University (E)

PO Box 579, Kirkland WA 98083-0579
County: King FICE Identification: 003783
Unit ID: 236133
Telephone: (425) 822-8266 Carnegie Class: Masters/M
FAX Number: (425) 889-5224 Calendar System: Semester
URL: www.northwestu.edu
Established: 1934 Annual Undergrad Tuition & Fees: $28,087
Enrollment: 1,862 Coed
Affiliation or Control: Assemblies Of God Church IRS Status: 501(c)3
Highest Offering: Doctorate
Accreditation: NW, ACBSP, NURSE

01 President .... Dr. Joseph CASTLEBERRY
05 Provost .... Dr. Jim HEUGEL
10 Chief Financial Officer .... Mr. John JORDAN
30 Senior VP of Advancement .... Mr. Ken CORNELL
42 Campus Pastor .... Rev. Phil RASMUSSEN
06 Registrar .... Mrs. Sandy HENDRICKSON
07 Director of Admissions .... Mr. Andy HALL
37 Director of Financial Aid .... Mr. Roger WILSON
41 Athletic Director .... Mr. Gary MCINTOSH
08 College Librarian .... Mr. Adam EPP
38 Director of Counseling Services .... Ms. Teresa REGAN
29 Dir of Alumni Svcs/Parent Rels .... Ms. Leanne KONZELMAN
15 Director Human Resources .... Ms. Victoria CLARK
36 Director Student Success .... Mrs. Amy JONES
32 Dean of Students .... Mr. Rick ENGSTROM
26 Director of Marketing .... Mr. Steve BOSTROM
04 Administrative Asst to President .... Mrs. Patti THOMAS
50 Dean Sch of Business & Management .... Dr. Teresa GILLESPIE
53 Dean College of Education .... Dr. Ron JACOBSON

Olympic College (F)

1600 Chester Avenue, Bremerton WA 98337-1699
County: Kitsap FICE Identification: 003784
Unit ID: 236188
Telephone: (360) 792-6050 Carnegie Class: Bac/Assoc-Assoc Dom
FAX Number: (360) 475-7151 Calendar System: Quarter
URL: www.olympic.edu
Established: 1946 Annual Undergrad Tuition & Fees (In-State): $3,837
Enrollment: 7,349 Coed
Affiliation or Control: State IRS Status: 501(c)3
Highest Offering: Baccalaureate
Accreditation: NW, ACFEI, ADNUR, MAC, NURSE, PTAA

01 President .... Dr. David C. MITCHELL
05 Vice President for Instruction .... Dr. Mary GARGUILE
10 Vice President for Administration .... Dr. Kay ASH
32 Vice President for Student Services .... Dr. Damon BELL
26 Vice President Equity & Inclusion .... Ms. Cheryl NUÑEZ
15 Exec Director Human Resource Svcs .... Vacant
51 Director of Continuing Education .... Vacant
04 Exec Assistant to the President .... Ms. Shawna BLISS
37 Director Student Financial Services .... Ms. Heidi TOWNSEND
27 Director of Communications .... Mr. Shawn DEVINE
84 Dean of Enrollment Services .... Ms. Jennifer GLASIER
18 Dir Facilities Svcs/Capital Project .... Mr. Robert PASQUARIELLO
21 Director of Business Services .... Ms. Janell WHITELEY
96 Procurement Officer .... Ms. Diana LAKE
36 Director Career Center .... Ms. Teresa MCDERMOTT
09 Exec Dir Inst Plng/Assessment/Rsrch .... Ms. Summer KENESSON
28 Supervisor Multicltrl/Student Pgms .... Ms. Jodie COLLINS
103 Dean Workforce Development .... Ms. Amy HATFIELD
08 Dean Library/Lrng Resources/eLrng .... Ms. Erica COE
35 Dean of Student Development .... Vacant
50 Dean Business & Technology .... Dr. Norma WHITACRE
81 Dean Math/Engineer/Sci/Health .... Dr. Mark HARRISON
79 Dean Humanities/Social Science .... Vacant
13 Exec Dir of Technical Services .... Ms. Evelyn HERNANDEZ
19 Director of Campus Safety .... Mr. Daniel WALKUP
25 Director of Grants .... Vacant
29 Exec Dir of Foundation/Alumni Assn .... Mr. David EMMONS
41 Director of Athletics .... Mr. Barry JANUSCH

Pacific Lutheran University (G)

12180 Park Avenue S., Tacoma WA 98447-0003
County: Pierce FICE Identification: 003785
Unit ID: 236230
Telephone: (253) 531-6900 Carnegie Class: Masters/M
FAX Number: (253) 535-8320 Calendar System: 4/1/4
URL: www.plu.edu
Established: 1890 Annual Undergrad Tuition & Fees: $37,950
Enrollment: 3,242 Coed
Affiliation or Control: Evangelical Lutheran Church In America
IRS Status: 501(c)3
Highest Offering: Master's
Accreditation: NW, BUS, CS, ENG, MFCD, MUS, NURSE, SW, TED

01 President .... Dr. Thomas W. KRISE
100 Senior Advisor to the President .... Ms. Kris H. PLAEHN
04 Exec Assoc to the President .... Ms. Deidre N. HILL
101 Director of Admin & Sec to Board .... Ms. Vicky L. WINTERS
05 Provost/Senior VP Academic Affairs .... Dr. Rae Linda BROWN
10 Vice President Finance & Operations .... Mr. Allan BELTON
30 Vice Pres for Advancement .... Mr. Daniel J. LEE
32 Vice Pres for Student Life .... Dr. Joanna C. ROYCE-DAVIS
07 Dean for Enrollment Svcs .... Mr. David E. GUNOVICH
26 Vice Pres Marketing & Communication .... Ms. Donna L. GIBBS
20 Assoc Provost for Undergrad Program .... Dr. Jan P. LEWIS
21 Controller .... Mr. Steve M. WHITEHOUSE
08 Assoc Provost for Information Tech .... Dr. Frank X. MOORE
42 University Pastor .... Rev. Jen RUDE
57 Dean School of Arts & Communication .... Dr. Cameron D. BENNETT
50 Dean of School of Business .... Dr. Chung-Shing LEE
53 Dean School of Educ & Kinesiology .... Dr. Terry BERGESON
66 Dean School of Nursing .... Dr. Sheila K. SMITH
79 Dean of Humanities .... Dr. Kevin J. O'BRIEN
88 Dean of Natural Sciences .... Dr. Matthew J. SMITH
83 Dean of Social Sciences .... Dr. David R. HUELSBECK
35 Dean of Students .... Dr. Eva R. FREY
51 Assoc Provost for Grad & Cont Educ .... Dr. Geoffrey E. FOY
88 Exec Dir Wang Ctr for Global Educ .... Dr. Tamara R. WILLIAMS
88 Director Academic Advising .... Mr. Hal R. DELAROSBY
41 Director Athletics & Recreation .... Ms. Laurie L. TURNER
06 Registrar .... Mr. Kevin A. BERG
39 Assoc VP for Campus Life .... Mr. Tom A. HUELSBECK
18 Assoc VP for Facilities Management .... Mr. Ray ORR
19 Director of Campus Safety & Info .... Mr. Greg V. PREMO
36 Director of Career Connections .... Ms. Donna L. MILLER
23 Director Health & Counseling Srv .... Ms. Kimberly E. RIANO
15 Assoc Vice Pres Human Resources .... Ms. Teri P. PHILLIPS
90 Dir of Enterprise Systems & Comm .... Mr. David P. ALLEN
37 Director of Student Financial Aid .... Mr. Michael T. FRECHETTE
40 Manager of Bookstore .... Ms. Amanda B. HAWKINS
09 Dir Assessment/Accreditation/Rsrch .... Dr. David A. VEAZEY
102 Corporate & Foundation Mgr .... Ms. Danielle N. CRYER
44 Director Annual Giving .... Ms. Alicia A. HINCKLEY

† Granted candidacy at the Doctorate level.

Pacific Northwest University of Health Sciences (H)

111 University Parkway, Suite 202, Yakima WA 98901
County: Yakima FICE Identification: 041305
Unit ID: 455406
Telephone: (509) 452-5100 Carnegie Class: Spec-4-yr-Med
FAX Number: (509) 452-5101 Calendar System: Semester
URL: www.pnwu.edu
Established: 2005 Annual Graduate Tuition & Fees: N/A
Enrollment: 431 Coed
Affiliation or Control: Independent Non-Profit IRS Status: 501(c)3
Highest Offering: Doctorate; No Undergraduates
Accreditation: @NW, OSTEO

01 President .... Dr. Keith WATSON
05 Senior Advisor to the President .... Dr. Robert E. SUTTON
10 Chief Financial Officer .... Ms. Ann HITTLE
11 Chief Operations Officer .... Mr. Frank D. ALVAREZ
30 Chief Advancement Officer .... Vacant
63 Dean Col of Osteopathic Medicine .... Dr. Thomas SCANDALIS
09 Chief Research Officer .... Vacant
08 Head Librarian .... Ms. Anita CLEARY
13 Chief Info Technology Officer (CIO) .... Mr. John DEVORE
15 Director Personnel Services .... Ms. Stefanie DURAND
18 Chief Facilities/Physical Plant .... Mr. Dave WARNER
19 Director Security/Safety .... Mr. Ben HITTLE
26 Chief Public Relations/Marketing .... Mr. Dean O'DRISCOLL
29 Director Alumni Relations .... Mr. Adam STORY
37 Director Student Financial Aid .... Ms. Laura PENDLETON
45 Chief Institutional Planning .... Ms. Angie GIRARD
04 Administrative Asst to President .... Ms. Vikki GORE
07 Director of Enrollment Services .... Ms. LeAnn HUNTER
108 Dir Institutional Effectiveness .... Ms. Lori FULTON
32 Assoc Dean Student Affairs .... Dr. Stephen LAIRD
96 Asst Dir Procurement/Asset Mgmt .... Ms. Cindy BLONDE

Peninsula College (I)

1502 East Lauridsen Boulevard,
Port Angeles WA 98362-6698
County: Clallam FICE Identification: 003786
Unit ID: 236258
Telephone: (360) 452-9277 Carnegie Class: Bac/Assoc-Assoc Dom
FAX Number: (360) 457-8100 Calendar System: Quarter
URL: www.pencol.edu
Established: 1961 Annual Undergrad Tuition & Fees (In-District): $4,191
Enrollment: 2,342 Coed
Affiliation or Control: State/Local IRS Status: 501(c)3
Highest Offering: Baccalaureate
Accreditation: NW, ADNUR

01 President .... Dr. Luke ROBINS
05 Vice President Instruction .... Vacant
11 Vice President Administrative Svcs .... Ms. Deborah FRAZIER
32 Vice President Student Services .... Mr. Jack HULS
45 VP Institutional Effectiveness .... Dr. Paula DOHERTY
50 Dir Cmty/Business Education .... Ms. Linty HOPIE
55 Dean Adult Basic Education .... Dr. Evelyn SHORT

35 Dean of Student Services ....Ms. Maria PENA
37 Assoc Dean Fin Aid/Enrollment Svcs .... Ms. Krista FRANCIS
41 Assoc Dean Athletics/Student Prgms ....Mr. Rick ROSS
13 Director Information Technology ....Mr. Steven BAXTER
04 Executive Asst to the President ....Ms. Pattie FISCHER
26 Director Public Information ....Ms. Phyllis L. VAN HOLLAND
15 Director Human Resources ....Mr. Kraig MICHELS
85 Dir Intl Stdnt Pgm/Stdnt Recruit .. Ms. Sophia ILIAKIS-DOHERTY
102 Exec Director College Foundation ....Ms. Mary HUNCHBERGER
09 Int Dir of Institutional Research ....Ms. Katie BRENKMAN
18 Director Physical Plant ....Mr. Rick CROOT
40 Bookstore Manager ....Mrs. Camilla RICO
88 Manager High School Program ....Ms. Cindy LAUDERBACK

Perry Technical Institute (A)

2011 W. Washington Avenue, Yakima WA 98903
County: Yakima FICE Identification: 009387
Unit ID: 236212
Telephone: (509) 453-0374 Carnegie Class: Not Classified
FAX Number: (509) 453-0375 Calendar System: Quarter
URL: www.perrytech.edu
Established: 1939 Annual Undergrad Tuition & Fees: N/A
Enrollment: 791 Coed
Affiliation or Control: Independent Non-Profit IRS Status: 501(c)3
Highest Offering: Associate Degree
Accreditation: ACCSC

01 President ....Christine COTE

Pierce College District (B)

1601 39th Avenue SE, Puyallup WA 98374
County: Pierce FICE Identification: 005000
Unit ID: 235237
Telephone: (253) 964-6500 Carnegie Class: Assoc/HT-High Non
FAX Number: N/A Calendar System: Quarter
URL: www.pierce.ctc.edu
Established: 1967 Annual Undergrad Tuition & Fees (In-State): $3,643
Enrollment: 5,927 Coed
Affiliation or Control: State IRS Status: 501(c)3
Highest Offering: Associate Degree
Accreditation: NW, ADNUR, DH

01 District Chancellor ....Dr. Michele JOHNSON
12 President Pierce College Puyallup ....Dr. Marty CAVALLUZZI
12 President Fort Steilacoom ....Ms. Denise YOCHUM
05 VP Learning/Student Success-PY .... Dr. Matthew CAMPBELL
05 Vice Pres Learning/Stdnt Success-FS ....Dr. Debra GILCHRIST
10 Vice Pres Administrative Services .... Mr. Choi HALLADAY
30 Vice President of Advancement ....Ms. Deidre SOILEAU
15 Vice President for Human Resources ....Ms. Holly GORSKI
13 Dean of Institutional Technology .... Mr. Mike STOCKE
06 Registrar/Dean of Enroll Svcs-Dist ....Ms. Anne WHITE
08 Dean Libraries & Learning Resources ....Ms. Christie FLYNN
26 Dir Marketing and Communications .... Mr. Brian BENEDETTI
32 Dean of Student Services ....Ms. Agnes STEWARD
35 Dir Student Programs-Ft Steilacoom ....Mr. Cameron COX
41 Director of Athletics .... Mr. Duncan STEVENSON
18 Director of Facilities & Const Mgt ....Mr. Jim TAYLOR
35 Dir of Student Life-Puyallup ....Mr. Sean COOKE
85 Exec Dir of International Education ....Ms. Myung PARK
19 District Manager Campus Safety .... Mr. Chris MACKERSIE
21 Director of Budget and Finance ....Ms. Sylvia JAMES
37 Director Financial Aid ....Ms. Isabelle MORA
84 Director Enrollment Services-Puy ....Ms. Els DEMING
09 Institutional Researcher .... Mr. Erik GIMNESS
49 District Dean Arts & Humanities ....Dr. Holly SMITH
88 District Dean Transitional Educ ....Ms. Lori GRIFFIN
76 District Dean Tech/Allied Health ....Mr. Ronald MAY
81 District Dean Natural Sciences ....Mr. Thomas BROXSON
83 District Dean Social Sciences ....Dr. Sachi HORBACK
29 Alumni Relations Manager ....Ms. Marion SHARP
96 Procurement Officer ....Mr. Curtis LEE

† Granted candidacy at the Baccalaureate level.

Pima Medical Institute-Renton (C)

555 South Renton Village Place, Renton WA 98057
Telephone: (425) 228-9600 Identification: 770517
Accreditation: ABHES, COARC, OTA

† Branch campus of Pima Medical Institute-Tucson, Tucson, AZ

Pima Medical Institute-Seattle (D)

9709 3rd Avenue NE, Suite 400, Seattle WA 98115-2052
Telephone: (206) 322-6100 Identification: 666172
Accreditation: ABHES, DH, OTA, PTAA, RAD

† Branch campus of Pima Medical Institute-Tucson, Tucson, AZ

Pinchot University (E)

220 2nd Avenue South, Suite 400,
Seattle WA 98104-2617
County: King FICE Identification: 041612
Unit ID: 458159
Telephone: (206) 855-9559 Carnegie Class: Spec-4-yr-Bus
FAX Number: (206) 682-0504 Calendar System: Quarter
URL: www.pinchot.edu
Established: 2002 Annual Undergrad Tuition & Fees: N/A
Enrollment: 108 Coed
Affiliation or Control: Independent Non-Profit IRS Status: 501(c)3
Highest Offering: Master's
Accreditation: ACICS

01 President .... Ms. Jill BAMBURG
05 Dean of Academic Affairs/Faculty ....Dr. Mary Kay CHESS
10 CFO/Vice President of Operations .... Ms. Sandra POSSIN
06 Registrar ....Ms. Lynn BRAUN
07 Director of Admissions .... Ms. Becca BALYEAT
32 Director of Student/Academic Affs ....Ms. Bethany LINDSEY

Renton Technical College (F)

3000 NE Fourth Street, Renton WA 98056-4123
County: King FICE Identification: 010434
Unit ID: 236382
Telephone: (425) 235-2352 Carnegie Class: Assoc/HVT-High Non
FAX Number: (425) 235-7832 Calendar System: Quarter
URL: www.rtc.edu
Established: 1942 Annual Undergrad Tuition & Fees (In-State): $4,836
Enrollment: 3,359 Coed
Affiliation or Control: State IRS Status: 501(c)3
Highest Offering: Associate Degree
Accreditation: NW, ACFEI, DA, MAC, SURGT

01 President ....Dr. Kevin D. MCCARTHY
10 VP Finance/Administration ....Ms. Melinda M. MERRELL
05 Vice President Instruction ....Mr. Angel REYNA
32 VP Student Services ....Ms. Jessica GILMORE ENGLISH
97 Dean Basic Studies ....Ms. Jodi NOVOTNY
76 Dean Allied Health .... Mr. Christopher CARTER
103 Executive Dean Workforce/Econ Dev ....Mr. Jacob JACKSON
50 Dean Bus/Educ/Hum Svcs/Gen Educ ....Ms. Sarah WAKEFIELD
72 Dean Automotive/Tech/Distance Educ ....Vacant
102 Foundation Executive Director ....Ms. Carrie SHAW
13 Chief Information Officer ....Mr. Paul CORRIGLIANO
07 Director Enrollment Services ....Mr. Patrick BROWN
46 Exec Dir Institutional Advancement ....Ms. Michelle CAMPBELL
08 Director Library ....Ms. Cheyenne RODUIN
21 Director Financial Services ....Mr. Mark JOHNSON
15 Executive Director Human Resources ....Ms. Lesley HOGAN
37 Director Financial Aid ....Ms. Debbie SOLOMON
18 Director Plant Operations ....Mr. Barry A. BAKER
40 Bookstore Manager ....Mr. Jose A. PERDOMO
19 Safety & Security Manager ....Mr. Matthew VIELBIG
88 Dean Culinary Arts ....Mr. Doug MEDBURY
26 Dir College Relations/Marketing .... Mr. Roberto BONACCORSO
38 Dean Counseling & Advising .... Mr. Scott LATIOLAIS
35 Director Student Programs ....Ms. Jessica SUPINSKI
06 Registration Coordinator ....Ms. Ly CHANG
88 Custodial Manager ....Mr. Mark DANIELS
88 Director Outreach/Entry Services .... Ms. Andrea LANCASTER
04 Executive Asst to President ....Ms. Di BEERS

† Granted candidacy at the Baccalaureate level.

Saint Martin's University (G)

5000 Abbey Way, SE, Lacey WA 98503-7500
County: Thurston FICE Identification: 003794
Unit ID: 236452
Telephone: (360) 491-4700 Carnegie Class: Masters/M
FAX Number: (360) 459-4124 Calendar System: Semester
URL: www.stmartin.edu
Established: 1895 Annual Undergrad Tuition & Fees: $33,194
Enrollment: 1,801 Coed
Affiliation or Control: Roman Catholic IRS Status: 501(c)3
Highest Offering: Master's
Accreditation: NW, ACBSP, ENG, NURSE, SW, TEAC

00 Chancellor .... Abbot Neal G. ROTH, OSB
01 President .... Dr. Roy F. HEYNDERICKX
05 Provost & Vice President ....Dr. Molly E. SMITH
10 Vice President of Finance ....Mr. Ed BARTON
30 Vice Pres Inst Advancement ....Ms. Cecelia LOVELESS
85 Vice Pres Intl Programs/Development ....Ms. Josephine YUNG
26 VP of Marketing/
Communications ....Ms. Genevieve CANCEKO CHAN
13 Associate Vice President/CIO ....Mr. Greg DAVIS
15 Associate VP of Human Resources .... Ms. Cynthia JOHNSON
49 Dean Col of Arts & Sciences ....Dr. Jeff CRANE
53 Dean of Education ....Dr. Kate BOYLE
50 Dean of Business ....Dr. Richard BEER
54 Dean of Engineering ....Dr. David OLWELL
32 Dean Student Services ....Ms. Melanie RICHARDSON
84 Dean Enrollment Management .. Ms. Pamela HOLSINGER-FUCHS
07 Dean Admission/Stdnt Financial Svcs ....Vacant
21 Controller .... Ms. Linda NEWMAN
37 Director Financial Aid .... Mr. Michael GROSSO
29 Director Alumni Relations ....Vacant
06 Assistant Registrar ....Ms. Ronda VANDERGIFF
18 Director Facilities Management ....Mr. Philip CHEEK
44 Dir of Development/Planned Giving ....Ms. Katie WOJKE
36 Director of Career Placement ....Ms. Ann ADAMS
41 Athletic Director ....Mr. Bob GRISHAM
56 Director Extension Programs ....Mr. Cruz ARROYO
08 Library Director ....Mr. Scot HARRISON
42 Director Campus Ministry ....Ms. Angela CARLIN
39 Director of Housing/Residence Life ....Mr. Tim MCCLAIN
38 Director Counseling Center ....Ms. Jan BERNEY
09 Director Institutional Grants/Rsrch ....Ms. Erin HOILAND

Sanford-Brown College (H)

645 Andover Park West, Seattle WA 98188-3319
Telephone: (206) 575-1865 Identification: 666265
Accreditation: ACICS

† Branch campus of International Academy of Design and Technology, Tampa, FL. School is in teach out plan.

*Seattle Colleges (I)

1500 Harvard Avenue, Seattle WA 98122-3803
County: King FICE Identification: 010106
Unit ID: 236498
Telephone: (206) 934-4100 Carnegie Class: N/A
FAX Number: (206) 934-3883
URL: www.seattlecolleges.edu

01 Chancellor .... Dr. Shouan PAN
03 Interim Vice Chancellor .... Dr. Mary Ellen O'KEEFFE
10 Vice Chanc for Finance & Technology .... Dr. Kurt BUTTLEMAN
15 Chief Human Resources Officer ....Dr. David BLAKE
26 Communications Director ....Dr. Earnest PHILLIPS
30 Assoc Vice Chanc for Advancement .... Ms. Julie COLEMAN
12 President South Seattle College ....Mr. Gary OERTLI
12 President North Seattle College ....Dr. Warren BROWN
12 Int Pres Seattle Central College ......Dr. Sheila EDWARDS LANGE

*North Seattle College (J)

9600 College Way N, Seattle WA 98103-3599
County: King FICE Identification: 009704
Unit ID: 236072
Telephone: (206) 934-3600 Carnegie Class: Bac/Assoc-Assoc Dom
FAX Number: (206) 934-3606 Calendar System: Quarter
URL: www.northseattle.edu
Established: 1970 Annual Undergrad Tuition & Fees (In-State): $4,458
Enrollment: 6,493 Coed
Affiliation or Control: State IRS Status: 170(c)1
Highest Offering: Baccalaureate
Accreditation: NW, ADNUR, MAC

02 President ....Dr. Warren J. BROWN
05 Vice President for Instruction ....Dr. Kristen JONES
32 Vice Pres Student Development ....Ms. Marci MYER
11 Vice President of Administration ....Ms. Andrea JOHNSON
36 Exec Dean Career/Workforce Educ ....Mr. John LEDERER
79 Dean Art/Humanities/Social Sciences .... Dr. Julianne KIRGIS
81 Dean Math & Science ....Ms. Alissa AGNELLO
17 Dean Health & Human Services ....Dr. Steven THOMAS
50 Dean Business/Eng Info Tech ....Dr. Laura HOPKINS
08 Dean Library & Media Services ....Ms. Sharon SIMES
35 Assoc Dean Student Develop Svcs ....Ms. Alice MELLING
88 Dean Basic/Transitional Stds ....Mr. Curtis BONNEY
30 Executive Director of Advancement ....Ms. Traci RUSSELL
26 Dir Marketing & Public Relations ....Ms. Melissa MIXON
84 Dean Enrollment Svcs/Registrar ....Ms. Kathy RHODES
51 Director Continuing Education ....Ms. Christy ISAACSON
37 Director Financial Aid Services ....Ms. Brianne SANCHEZ
35 Dir Student Ldrshp/Multi Cult Pgms ....Mr. Jeffrey VASQUEZ
103 Director Workforce Education ....Ms. Lindsay CAEL
09 Dir Institutional Effectiveness ....Dr. Stephanie DYKES
104 Director International Programs ....Mr. Ryan PACKARD
15 Director of Human Resources ....Mr. Martin LOGAN
18 Dir Facilities & Plant Operations ....Mr. Jeffrey CAULK
38 Lead Counselor ....Dr. Lydia MINATOYA
13 Chief Info Technology Officer ....Ms. Cindy RICHE
19 Director Security/Safety ....Mr. Darryl JOHNSON
28 Director of Diversity & Inclusion ....Ms. Pam RACANSKY
07 Coordinator Admissions/Residency .... Mr. Fleetwood L. WILSON
04 Executive Asst to President ....Ms. Toni STANKOVIC
10 Director Business Operations ....Mr. Dennis YASUKOCHI
25 Director of Grants ....Ms. Ann RICHARDSON
41 Athletic Director ....Ms. Carianya NAPOLI

*Seattle Central College (K)

1701 Broadway, Seattle WA 98122-2400
County: King FICE Identification: 003787
Unit ID: 236513
Telephone: (206) 587-3800 Carnegie Class: Bac/Assoc-Assoc Dom
FAX Number: (206) 344-4390 Calendar System: Quarter
URL: seattlecentral.edu
Established: 1966 Annual Undergrad Tuition & Fees (In-State): $3,891
Enrollment: 6,773 Coed
Affiliation or Control: State IRS Status: 170(c)1
Highest Offering: Baccalaureate
Accreditation: NW, ACFEI, ADNUR, COARC, DH, OPD, SURGT

02 President ....Dr. Sheila EDWARDS LANGE
05 Vice Pres of Instruction ....Mr. Bradley LANE
11 Vice Pres Administrative Services ....Mr. Bruce RIVELAND
32 Vice Pres Student Services ....Ms. Yoshiko HARDEN
103 Assoc Vice President Workforce Educ ....Mr. Al GRISWOLD
09 Exec Dir Inst Effectiveness ....Dr. Wai-Fong LEE
35 Dean of Student Resources & Support ....Ms. Brigid MCDEVITT
37 Director of Financial Aid ....Ms. Noel MCBRIDE
102 Executive Director Foundation ....Ms. Lauren GUZAUSKAS
26 Director of Communications ....Mr. David SANDLER
08 Exec Dean Instructional Resources ....Dr. Wai-Fong LEE
49 Dean Basic Studies ....Ms. Laura DIZAZZO
50 Dean Business IT & Creative Arts ....Vacant

76 Dean of Allied Health ... Mr. David GOURD
81 Dean Science & Mathematics ... Dr. Wendy ROCKHILL
83 Dean Humanities/Social Sciences ... Dr. Bradley LANE
88 Exec Dean International Education ... Dr. Andrea INSLEY
35 Dean Student Life & Engagement ... Ms. Lexie EVANS
13 Assoc Dean Information Technology ... Ms. Harriet WASSERMAN
12 Asst Dean Seattle Maritime Academy ... Dr. Matthew VON RUDEN
12 Director Seattle Culinary Academy ... Ms. Joy GULMON-HURI
51 Director Cmty Educ/Evening Pgm ... Mr. Jeff WEST
84 Dean Enrollment Services/Registrar ... Ms. Diane COLEMAN
19 Director Public Safety ... Mr. Elman MCCLAIN
18 Dir Facilities/Plant Operations ... Mr. Chuck DAVIS

*South Seattle Community College (A)

6000 16th Avenue, SW, Seattle WA 98106-1499
County: King FICE Identification: 009706
Unit ID: 236504
Telephone: (206) 934-5300 Carnegie Class: Bac/Assoc-Assoc Dom
FAX Number: (206) 934-5393 Calendar System: Quarter
URL: www.southseattle.edu
Established: 1969 Annual Undergrad Tuition & Fees (In-State): $4,130
Enrollment: 5,535 Coed
Affiliation or Control: State IRS Status: 501(c)3
Highest Offering: Baccalaureate
Accreditation: NW

02 President ... Mr. Gary L. OERTLI
05 Vice Pres Instruction ... Mr. Pete LORTZ
11 Int Vice Pres Administrative Svcs ... Ms. Irina MINASOVA
32 Vice President Student Services ... Dr. Rosie RIMANDO
30 Assoc Vice Pres College Advancement ... Dr. Elizabeth A. PLUHTA
45 Dean Instructional Resources ... Ms. Mary Jo WHITE
12 Exec Dean of Georgetown Campus ... Ms. Holly MOORE
97 Dean Basic & Transitional Studies ... Mr. John BOWERS
20 Dean of Academic Programs ... Ms. Stephanie DELANEY
35 Dean Student Life ... Vacant
103 Dn Professional/Tech/Workforce Educ ... Ms. Veronica WADE
17 Dean Hosp & Service Occupations ... Mr. Robert GLATT
88 Dean Multi-Trades/Info Technology ... Mr. Duncan BURGESS
84 Dean Enrollment Services ... Ms. Joyce ALLEN
88 Dean of Aviation ... Ms. Kim ALEXANDER
20 Assoc Dean Academic Programs ... Ms. Laura KINGSTON
06 Assistant Registrar ... Ms. Marilyn ANDERSON-BURT
51 Director Continuing Education ... Ms. Luisa MOTTEN
103 Dir Worksource Dev/Employment Svcs ... Ms. Deborah WHITE
37 Dir Student Financial Assistance ... Ms. Corinne SOLTIS
26 Interim Director Communications ... Mr. Ty SWENSON
15 Director Human Resources ... Ms. Linda MANNING
108 Dir of Planning/Research/Assessment ... Mr. Greg DEMPSEY
13 Dir Business Operation/IT ... Ms. Irina MINASOVA
18 Dir Facilities & Plant Operations ... Mr. Eric STEEN
28 Director of Diversity & Retention ... Vacant
19 Manager Safety/Security ... Mr. James E. LEWIS
40 Manager Bookstore ... Ms. Kayleigh WOLD

Seattle Institute of Oriental Medicine (B)

444 Ravenna Boulevard, Suite 101, Seattle WA 98115
County: King FICE Identification: 032803
Unit ID: 439914
Telephone: (206) 517-4541 Carnegie Class: Spec-4-yr-Other Health
FAX Number: N/A Calendar System: Trimester
URL: www.siom.edu
Established: 1994 Annual Undergrad Tuition & Fees: N/A
Enrollment: 42 Coed
Affiliation or Control: Proprietary IRS Status: Proprietary
Highest Offering: Master's; No Lower Division
Accreditation: ACUP

01 President ... Craig MITCHELL
05 Academic Dean ... Lisa TAYLOR-SWANSON
06 Registrar ... Vacant

Seattle Pacific University (C)

3307 Third Avenue W, Seattle WA 98119-1997
County: King FICE Identification: 003788
Unit ID: 236577
Telephone: (206) 281-2111 Carnegie Class: DU-Mod
FAX Number: (206) 281-2115 Calendar System: Quarter
URL: www.spu.edu
Established: 1891 Annual Undergrad Tuition & Fees: $37,086
Enrollment: 4,217 Coed
Affiliation or Control: Free Methodist IRS Status: 501(c)3
Highest Offering: Doctorate
Accreditation: NW, BUS, CACREP, CLPSY, DIETD, ENG, MFCD, MUS, NURSE, TED, @THEOL

01 President ... Dr. Daniel J. MARTIN
05 Provost ... Dr. Jeffrey B. VAN DUZER
11 Sr VP for Planning & Administration ... Mr. Donald W. MORTENSON
32 VP for Student Life ... Dr. Jeffrey C. JORDAN
30 VP for Advancement ... Mrs. Louise S. FURROW
10 VP for Business & Finance ... Mr. Craig G. KISPERT
84 VP for Enrollment Mgmt & Mktg ... Mr. Nate MOUTTET
20 Vice Provost Academic Affairs ... Dr. Cynthia J. PRICE
13 Assoc VP Information/Data Mgmt ... Vacant
18 Asst VP Facility Management ... Mr. David B. CHURCH
43 Asst VP Risk Mgmt & Univ Counsel ... Mr. Nick GLANCY
14 Asst VP Technology Services ... Mr. David W. TINDALL
102 President of Seattle Pacific Fdn ... Vacant
50 Dean School of Business/Govt/Econ ... Dr. Ross STEWART
53 Dean School of Education ... Dr. Rick EIGENBROOD
66 Dean School of Health Sciences ... Dr. Lorie WILD
81 Dean CAS - Sciences Division ... Dr. Bruce D. CONGDON
49 Dean CAS - Arts & Humanities Div ... Dr. Debra-L SEQUEIRA
88 Dean School of Psych/Fam & Cmty ... Dr. Katy TANGENBERG
73 Dean School of Theology ... Dr. Douglas M. STRONG
42 Dean of Students for Cmty Life ... Mr. Chuck STRAWN
36 Dean Stdnt Lrng/Dir Ctr Career Coun ... Dr. Jacqui S. SMITH-BATES
08 University Librarian ... Mr. Michael PAULUS
38 Director Student Counseling Center ... Dr. Steven A. MAYBELL
07 Sr Dir Recruitment and Admissions ... Mr. Jobe S. KORB-NICE
07 Director Undergraduate Admissions ... Ms. Ineliz SOTO FULLER
06 University Registrar ... Mrs. Kenda GATLIN
26 Co-Director Univ Communications ... Mrs. Alison ESTEP
26 Co-Director Univ Communications ... Mr. Dale KEGLEY
88 Asst VP UG Enrollment Mgmt ... Mr. Jordan L. GRANT
27 News & Media Relations Manager ... Ms. Tracy C. NORLEN
45 Assoc Director Projects & Planning ... Mr. Wayne H. ELLING
31 Director of University Services ... Ms. Alexis CRUIKSHANK
19 Director of Safety & Security ... Mr. Mark REID
44 Director of Advancement ... Ms. Maribeth MARTIN LOPIT
29 Director of Alumni Relations ... Mr. Bryan H. JONES
41 Director of Athletics ... Vacant
15 Director of Human Resources ... Mr. Gary E. WOMELSDUFF
28 Director of the John Perkins Center ... Mr. Tali HAIRSTON
39 Director of Residence Life ... Mr. Gabe JACOBSEN
35 Director Student Programs ... Ms. Whitney BROETJE
88 Dean of Multi-Ethnic/Wellness Pgms ... Mrs. Susan OKAMOTO LANE
104 Director of Study Abroad ... Ms. Gail DEBELL
04 Executive Asst to President ... Mrs. Ruth JACOBSEN

The Seattle School of Theology and Psychology (D)

2501 Elliot Avenue, Seattle WA 98121-1177
County: King FICE Identification: 034664
Unit ID: 441131
Telephone: (206) 876-6100 Carnegie Class: Spec-4-yr-Other Health
FAX Number: (206) 876-6195 Calendar System: Trimester
URL: www.theseattleschool.edu
Established: 2001 Annual Graduate Tuition & Fees: N/A
Enrollment: 297 Coed
Affiliation or Control: Independent Non-Profit IRS Status: 501(c)3
Highest Offering: Master's; No Undergraduates
Accreditation: THEOL

01 President ... Dr. Keith R. ANDERSON
05 Sr Vice Pres Academic Affs/CAO ... Dr. J. Derek MCNEIL
10 Chief Financial Officer ... Mr. Phil BISHOP
30 Vice Pres Advancement ... Ms. Cathy LOERZEL
32 Dean of Students ... Mr. Paul STEINKE
08 Dir Library Svcs/Inst Assessment ... Ms. Cheryl GOODWIN
06 Dir Academic Services/Registrar ... Ms. Kristen HOUSTON
84 Director of Enrollment Management ... Ms. Nicole GREENWALD
13 Director Computer & Info Services ... Ms. Grace LA TORRA
15 Human Resources ... Ms. Kartha HEINZ

Seattle University (E)

901 12th Avenue, Seattle WA 98122-1090
County: King FICE Identification: 003790
Unit ID: 236595
Telephone: (206) 296-6000 Carnegie Class: Masters/L
FAX Number: N/A Calendar System: Quarter
URL: www.seattleu.edu
Established: 1891 Annual Undergrad Tuition & Fees: $39,690
Enrollment: 7,273 Coed
Affiliation or Control: Roman Catholic IRS Status: 501(c)3
Highest Offering: Doctorate
Accreditation: NW, BUS, CACREP, DMS, ENG, LAW, MFCD, MIDWF, NURSE, SPAA, SW, THEOL

01 President ... Rev. Stephen V. SUNDBORG, SJ
05 Interim Provost ... Dr. Robert DULLEA
11 Executive Vice President Admin ... Dr. Timothy LEARY
10 Chief Financial Officer ... Ms. Connie KANTER
43 Vice Pres and University Counsel ... Ms. Mary S. PETERSEN
30 VP University Advancement ... Mr. Michael PODLIN
32 VP Student Development ... Dr. Michele MURRAY
88 Vice President Mission & Ministry ... Rev. Peter ELY, SJ
45 Vice Pres University Planning ... Dr. Robert DUNIWAY
84 Vice President for Enrollment Svcs ... Ms. Marilyn CRONE
26 Vice President for Communications ... Mr. Scott MCCLELLAN
15 Vice President Human Resources ... Mr. Gerald HUFFMAN
49 Dean of Arts & Sciences ... Dr. David POWERS
50 Dean of Business & Economics ... Dr. Joseph M. PHILLIPS
53 Dean of Education ... Dr. Deanna SANDS
66 Dean of Nursing ... Dr. Kristen SWANSON
54 Dean of Science & Engineering ... Dr. Michael QUINN
79 Interim Dean of Humanities ... Dr. Paulette KIDDER
61 Dean of Law ... Ms. Annette C. CLARK
73 Dean of Theology & Ministry ... Dr. Mark MARKULY
08 University Librarian ... Mr. John P. POPKO
20 Assoc Provost Academic Achievement ... Dr. Charles LAWRENCE
20 Assoc Provost Global Engagement ... Dr. Russell POWELL
46 Assoc Provost Research & Grad Educ ... Dr. William EHMANN
13 Chief Information Officer ... Mr. Charles PORTER
21 Assoc VP of Finance ... Mr. Andrew O'BOYLE
18 Assoc VP Facilities Administration ... Mr. Robert SCHWARTZ
29 Asst VP Alumni Relations ... Ms. Susan VOSPER
14 Executive Director ... Mr. Dennis GENDRON
44 Sr Director of Planned Giving ... Ms. Sarah FINNEY
44 Director of Annual Giving ... Ms. Cathy REILLY
102 Dir of Foundation & Corporate Rels ... Ms. Jane SPALDING
35 Assoc Vice Pres Student Development ... Dr. Alvin STURDIVANT
06 Associate Registrar ... Mr. Andrew ANDERSON
07 Dean of Admissions ... Ms. Melore NIELSEN
09 Director of Institutional Research ... Dr. Irina VOLOSHIN
42 Director Campus Ministry ... Ms. Tammy LIDDELL
37 Director Student Financial Services ... Mr. Jeff SCOFIELD
41 Director of Athletics ... Mr. Bill HOGAN
19 Executive Director of Public Safety ... Mr. Timothy MARRON
35 Dean of Students ... Mr. Darrell GOODWIN
85 Director International Student Ctr ... Mr. Ryan GREENE
104 Director Education Abroad ... Ms. Gina LOPARDO
36 Executive Director Career Services ... Ms. Sarah THOMSON
38 Director Counseling Center ... Dr. Kimberly CALUZA
28 Director of Multicultural Affairs ... Ms. Tiffany GRAY
39 Dir Housing & Resid Life ... Ms. Kathleen BAKER
25 Director Research & Sponsored Proj ... Dr. Nalini IYER
96 Director of Purchasing ... Ms. Marie PETERSON
23 Director Student Health Center ... Ms. Maura O'CONNOR
04 Executive Secretary to President ... Ms. Liz PILATI
100 Assistant to the President ... Ms. Kathy YBARRA
105 Web Communications Manager ... Mr. Jason BEARD
51 Dean New and Continuing Studies ... Dr. Richard FEHRENBACHER
22 Dir Professional Dev/EEO ... Ms. Helaina SOREY
86 Director of External Affairs ... Mr. Solynn MCCURDY
88 Associate Chief Information Officer ... Mr. Travis NATION

Shoreline Community College (F)

16101 Greenwood Avenue N, Shoreline WA 98133-5696
County: King FICE Identification: 003791
Unit ID: 236610
Telephone: (206) 546-4101 Carnegie Class: Assoc/MT-VT-High Non
FAX Number: (206) 546-4630 Calendar System: Quarter
URL: www.shoreline.edu
Established: 1964 Annual Undergrad Tuition & Fees (In-State): $3,730
Enrollment: 6,015 Coed
Affiliation or Control: State IRS Status: 170(c)1
Highest Offering: Associate Degree
Accreditation: NW, ADNUR, CAHIIM, DH, MLTAD

01 President ... Dr. Cheryl ROBERTS
05 VP Academic & Student Affairs ... Ms. Alison STEVENS
11 Vice Pres Administrative Svcs ... Vacant
15 VP Human Resources/Legal Affairs ... Mr. Stephen SMITH
26 Exec Dir Communication/Marketing ... Ms. Martha G. LYNN
96 Exec Dir Budget/Capitol Finance ... Ms. Dawn VINBERG
04 Exec Asst to the President ... Ms. Lori YONEMITSU
85 Exec Dir International Programs ... Ms. Diana SAMPSON
72 Director Technology Support Service ... Mr. Gary KALBFLEISCH
06 Registrar ... Ms. Chris MELTON
18 Director Facilities ... Mr. Jason FRANCOIS
19 Director Safety & Security ... Ms. Robin BLACKSMITH
66 Program Director Nursing ... Ms. Lynn VON SCHLIEDER
37 Director Financial Aid ... Ms. Chris MELTON
38 Assoc Dean Equity/Engage Counseling ... Dr. Yvonne L. TERRELL-POWELL
109 Exec Dir Auxiliary/Logistical Svcs ... Vacant
09 Dir Institutional Effectiveness ... Ms. Bayta MARING
08 Dean Library Services ... Mr. Chris MATZ
32 Dean of Students ... Ms. Kim THOMPSON
103 Dean Workforce/Cont Educ/Automotive ... Vacant
31 Dean Capital Projects/Cmty Rels ... Vacant
79 Dean Humanities Division ... Ms. Kathy HUNT
70 Dean Social Science ... Ms. Amy KINSEL
81 Dean Math/Science ... Mr. Guy HAMILTON
27 Asst Dir Communication/Marketing ... Mr. Sean DUKE
30 Chief Development/Advancement ... Ms. Mary BRUEGGEMAN
41 Athletic Director ... Mr. Steve ESKRIDGE

Skagit Valley College (G)

2405 College Way, Mount Vernon WA 98273-5899
County: Skagit FICE Identification: 003792
Unit ID: 236638
Telephone: (360) 416-7600 Carnegie Class: Bac/Assoc-Assoc Dom
FAX Number: (360) 416-7890 Calendar System: Quarter
URL: www.skagit.edu
Established: 1926 Annual Undergrad Tuition & Fees (In-State): $4,200
Enrollment: 4,993 Coed
Affiliation or Control: State IRS Status: 501(c)3
Highest Offering: Associate Degree
Accreditation: NW, ACFEI, ADNUR, MAC

01 President ... Dr. Thomas KEEGAN
05 Vice President for Instruction ... Dr. Kenneth LAWSON
10 Vice Pres Administrative Services ... Mr. Ed JARAMILLO
12 Vice President of Whidbey Campus ... Dr. Laura CAILLOUX
32 Vice Pres Student Services ... Dr. David PAUL
13 Dean of Information Technology ... Mr. Andy HEISER
103 Dean Workforce Education ... Mr. Darren GREENO
20 Dean Academic Education ... Dr. Gabriel MAST
84 Assoc Dean Enrollment Services ... Ms. Sinead PLAGGE
37 Director of Financial Aid ... Ms. Crystal ALLISON
15 Exec Director of Human Resources ... Ms. Carolyn TUCKER
18 Director of Facilities & Operations ... Mr. Dave SCOTT

26 Director of Public Information ....Ms. Arden AINLEY
104 Director of International Programs ....Ms. Christa SCHULZ
40 Bookstore Manager ....Ms. Kim HALL
41 Athletic Director ....Mr. Steve EPPERSON
09 Director of Institutional Research ....Dr. Maureen PETTITT

† Granted candidacy at the Baccalaureate level.

South Puget Sound Community College (A)

2011 Mottman Road, SW, Olympia WA 98512-6292
County: Thurston FICE Identification: 005372
Unit ID: 236656
Telephone: (360) 754-7711 Carnegie Class: Assoc/MT-VT-High Non
FAX Number: (360) 664-0780 Calendar System: Quarter
URL: www.spscc.edu
Established: 1962 Annual Undergrad Tuition & Fees (In-State): $3,957
Enrollment: 4,881 Coed
Affiliation or Control: State IRS Status: 501(c)3
Highest Offering: Associate Degree
Accreditation: NW, ACFEI, DA, IFSAC, MAC

01 President ....Dr. Timothy STOKES
04 Special Assistant to the President ....Ms. Diana TOLEDO
05 Vice President for Instruction ....Dr. Michelle ANDREAS
32 Vice President for Student Services ....Dr. David PELKEY
11 Vice Pres Administrative Services ....Mr. Albert BROWN
07 Dean of Enrollment Services ....Mr. Steven ASHPOLE
18 Director of Facilities ....Ms. Laura PRICE
26 Dir of Public Relations & Events ....Ms. Kelly GREEN
35 Dean Student Engagement/Retention ....Ms. Jennifer MANLEY
37 Dean of Student Financial Services ....Ms. Johanna DWYER
15 Chief Human Resources Officer ....Mr. Kennith HARDEN
102 Exec Director of College Foundation ....Ms. Tanya MOTE
28 Director of Diversity & Equity ....Ms. Eileen YOSHINA
09 Director of Institutional Research ....Ms. Jennifer TUIA
06 Director of Enrollment/Registrar ....Ms. Heidi DEARBORN
08 Dean of Academic Support Services ....Dr. Kevin ASMAN
19 Director of Safety & Security ....Mr. Robert SHAILOR
13 Chief Information Officer ....Ms. Lori CASILE
72 Dean of Applied Technology ....Ms. Kathy HOOVER
76 Dean of Natural & Applied Sciences ....Vacant
79 Dean of Humanities/Communications ....Ms. Mary SOLTMAN
83 Dean of Social Sciences & Business ....Ms. Valerie SUNDBY-THORP
96 Procurement & Supply Specialist 4 ....Ms. Vida SHERRARD-HANNON

Tacoma Community College (B)

6501 S 19th Street, Tacoma WA 98466-6100
County: Pierce FICE Identification: 003796
Unit ID: 236753
Telephone: (253) 566-5000 Carnegie Class: Assoc/MT-VT-High Non
FAX Number: (253) 566-5169 Calendar System: Quarter
URL: www.tacomacc.edu
Established: 1965 Annual Undergrad Tuition & Fees (In-State): $4,194
Enrollment: 7,189 Coed
Affiliation or Control: State IRS Status: 501(c)3
Highest Offering: Associate Degree
Accreditation: NW, ADNUR, CAHIIM, COARC, DMS, EMT, RAD

01 President ....Dr. Sheila RUHLAND
05 Exec VP Academic/Student Affairs ....Dr. Tod TREAT
11 Vice Pres Administrative Services ....Mr. Tim GOULD
32 Vice Pres Student Services ....Ms. Mary CHIKWINYA
88 Dir Conduct/Compliance & Partners ....Ms. Dolores HAUGEN
07 Dean for Entry & Enrollment Svcs ....Ms. Betsy ABTS
38 Dean for Advising and Counseling ....Ms. Shema HANEBUTTE
108 Dean Org Learning & Effectiveness ....Dr. Mecca SALAHUDDIN
18 Director Facilities/CapitalProjects ....Mr. Greg RANDALL
35 Director of Student Engagement ....Ms. Sonja MORGAN
37 Director Student Financial Aid ....Ms. Kim MATISON
04 Executive Asst to President ....Ms. Judy COLARUSSO
09 Director of Institutional Research ....Ms. Kelley SADLER
15 Director of Human Resources ....Ms. Beth BROOKS
30 Vice Pres for College Advancement ....Mr. Bill RYBERG
41 Athletic Director ....Mr. Jason PRENEVOST
10 Director Financial Services ....Ms. Janice STROH
13 Director of IT ....Mr. Clay KRAUSS

† Granted candidacy at the Baccalaureate level.

University of Phoenix Western Washington Campus (C)

7100 Fort Dent Way, Suite 100, Tukwila WA 98188-8553
Telephone: (425) 572-1600 Identification: 770234
Accreditation: &NH, ACBSP

† Regional accreditation is carried under the parent institution in Tempe, AZ

University of Puget Sound (D)

1500 N Warner St., Tacoma WA 98416-0002
County: Pierce FICE Identification: 003797
Unit ID: 236328
Telephone: (253) 879-3100 Carnegie Class: Bac-A&S
FAX Number: (253) 879-3500 Calendar System: Semester
URL: www.pugetsound.edu
Established: 1888 Annual Undergrad Tuition & Fees: $44,976
Enrollment: 2,826 Coed
Affiliation or Control: Independent Non-Profit IRS Status: 501(c)3
Highest Offering: Doctorate
Accreditation: NW, IPSY, MUS, OT, PTA

01 President ....Dr. Isiaah CRAWFORD
101 Board Secy/Dir Ofc of President ....Ms. Mary Elizabeth COLLINS
05 Academic VP/Dean of University ....Dr. Kristine M. BARTANEN
10 Vice Pres Finance & Admin ....Ms. Sherry B. MONDOU
26 Vice President University Relations ....Mr. David BEERS
84 Interim Vice President Enrollment ....Ms. Christine MICA
32 VP Student Affairs/Dean of Students ....Mr. Mike SEGAWA
21 Assoc VP Accounting/Budget Svcs ....Ms. Janet S. HALLMAN
15 Assoc Vice Pres Human Resources ....Ms. Cindy MATERN
21 Assoc Vice Pres Business Services ....Mr. John M. HICKEY
18 Assoc Vice Pres Facilities Services ....Mr. Bob KIEF
37 Assoc VP for Student Financial Svcs ....Ms. Maggie A. MITTUCH
27 Executive Dir of Communications ....Ms. Gayle MCINTOSH
13 Chief Information Officer ....Mr. Jeremy L. CUCCO
28 Dean Diversity and Inclusion ....Mr. Michael BENITEZ
20 Associate Academic Dean ....Dr. Martin JACKSON
20 Associate Academic Dean ....Dr. Sunil KUKREJA
20 Associate Academic Dean ....Dr. Renee HOUSTON
09 Dir Inst Research & Retention ....Ms. C. Ellen PETERS
06 Registrar ....Mr. Brad TOMHAVE
08 Library Director ....Ms. Jane CARLIN
41 Director of Athletics ....Ms. Amy E. HACKETT
29 Director Alumni & Parent Relations ....Ms. Allison CANNADY-SMITH
85 Director International Programs ....Mr. Roy ROBINSON
53 Dean School of Education ....Dr. John WOODWARD
50 Dir School of Business/Leadership ....Dr. Alva BUTCHER
64 Director of School of Music ....Dr. Keith C. WARD
88 Director of Occupational Therapy ....Dr. George TOMLIN
88 Director of Physical Therapy ....Dr. Jennifer D. HASTINGS

University of Washington (E)

Seattle WA 98195-0001
County: King FICE Identification: 003798
Unit ID: 236948
Telephone: (206) 543-2100 Carnegie Class: DU-Highest
FAX Number: (206) 543-9285 Calendar System: Quarter
URL: www.washington.edu
Established: 1861 Annual Undergrad Tuition & Fees (In-State): $11,839
Enrollment: 44,784 Coed
Affiliation or Control: State IRS Status: 501(c)3
Highest Offering: Doctorate
Accreditation: NW, ARCPA, AUD, BUS, BUSA, CAHIIM, CEA, CLPSY, CONST, DENT, DIETC, EMT, ENG, HSA, IPSY, JOUR, LAW, LIB, LSAR, MED, MIDWF, MT, NURSE, OPE, OT, PAST, PDPSY, PH, PHAR, PLNG, PTA, SCPSY, SP, SPAA, SW

01 President ....Dr. Ana Mari CAUCE
05 Provost/Exec Vice Pres ....Dr. Gerald J. BALDASTY
12 Chancellor Bothell Campus ....Dr. Bjong W. YEIGH
12 Chancellor Tacoma Campus ....Dr. Mark PAGANO
10 Int Vice Pres Finance/Facilities ....Ms. Elizabeth CHERRY
28 Int VP Minority Affs/Vice Prov Div ....Dr. Rickey HALL
17 Exec VP Med Affs/CEO UW Med/Dean ....Dr. Paul G. RAMSEY
30 Vice Pres for Univ Advancement ....Dr. Connie KRAVAS
15 Vice President Human Resources ....Ms. Mindy KORNBERG
13 VP & Vice Prov UW Info Tech ....Ms. Kelli TROSVIG
26 Chief Marketing & Communications ....Ms. Mary GRESCH
46 Vice Provost Research ....Dr. Mary E. LIDSTROM
51 V Provost UW Educational Outreach ....Dr. Rovy BRANON
45 Assoc Vice Prov Plng & Budgeting ....Ms. Sarah NORRIS HALL
20 Vice Prov/Dean Undergrad Acad Affs ....Dr. Ed TAYLOR
32 Vice Pres Student Life ....Mr. Denzil SUITE
88 V Provost for Academic Personnel ....Dr. Cheryl A. CAMERON
88 V Prov for Innovation/CoMotion ....Dr. Vikram JANDHYALA
86 Director Federal Relations ....Ms. Sarah CASTRO
43 Division Chief Attorney General ....Ms. Karin NYROP
06 University Registrar ....Ms. Helen GARRETT
29 Assoc VP Alum Relations ....Mr. Paul RUCKER
17 Interim Dir UW Medical Ctr Admin ....Mr. Geoff P. AUSTIN
37 AVP Student Life/Dir Fin Aid ....Ms. Kay LEWIS
86 Chief Strategy Officer ....Ms. Margaret A. SHEPHERD
84 Asst VP Enrollment/Admissions ....Dr. Philip BALLINGER
09 Director Institutional Analysis ....Ms. Carol DIEM
36 Director Career Center ....Ms. Susan TERRY
14 CFO/UW Information Technology ....Mr. Bill FERRIS
18 Assoc VP Capital Planning Devel ....Mr. Michael MCCORMICK
92 Director Honors Program ....Dr. Victoria LAWSON
41 Director Athletics ....Ms. Jennifer COHEN
08 VP for Digital Init/Dean Libraries ....Ms. Lizabeth A. WILSON
96 Director Procurement Services ....Mr. Mark CONLEY
58 Vice Prov/Dean Graduate School ....Dr. David L. EATON
49 Dean Arts & Sciences ....Dr. Robert STACEY
47 Dean Col of Built Environments ....Dr. John SCHAUFELBERGER
22 Dir EOAA ....Ms. Alexia WHITAKER
50 Dean Business School ....Dr. Jim JIAMBALVO
54 Dean Engineering ....Dr. Michael B. BRAGG
61 Dean Law School ....Dr. Kellye Y. TESTY
70 Dean Social Work ....Dr. Edwina UEHARA
52 Dean Dentistry ....Dr. Joel H. BERG
63 Dean Medicine ....Dr. Paul G. RAMSEY
66 Dean Nursing ....Dr. Azita EMAMI
67 Dean Pharmacy ....Dr. Sean SULLIVAN
69 Dean School of Public Health ....Dr. Howard FRUMKIN
53 Dean Education ....Dr. Mia TUAN
80 Dean of Public Affairs ....Dr. Sandra O. ARCHIBALD
88 Dean Information School ....Dr. Harry BRUCE
88 Dean Col of the Environment ....Dr. Lisa GRAUMLICH
04 Administrative Asst to President ....Ms. Lenina ARENAS-FUENTES

07 Director of Admissions ....Mr. Paul SEEGERT
104 Director Study Abroad ....Mr. Peter MORAN
108 Director Institutional Assessment ....Dr. Nana LOWELL
19 Director Security/Safety ....Mr. John N. VINSON
38 Director Student Counseling ....Dr. Natacha F. KUNE
39 Director Student Housing ....Ms. Pam SCHREIBER

Walla Walla Community College (F)

500 Tausick Way, Walla Walla WA 99362-9267
County: Walla Walla FICE Identification: 005006
Unit ID: 236887
Telephone: (509) 522-2500 Carnegie Class: Assoc/HVT-High Non
FAX Number: (509) 527-4480 Calendar System: Quarter
URL: www.wwcc.edu
Established: 1967 Annual Undergrad Tuition & Fees (In-State): $4,203
Enrollment: 4,851 Coed
Affiliation or Control: State IRS Status: 170(c)1
Highest Offering: Associate Degree
Accreditation: NW, ADNUR, MAC

01 President ....Dr. Derek R. BRANDES
05 Vice President of Instruction ....Dr. Marleen RAMSEY
32 Vice Pres of Student Affairs ....Mr. Jose DA SILVA
10 VP Financial & Admin Services ....Mrs. Davina K. FOGG
76 Dean of Health Sciences Education ....Ms. Kathleen ADAMSKI
30 Director of Resource Development ....Mr. Doug BAYNE
07 Director of Admissions/Registrar ....Mr. Carlos E. DELGADILLO
38 Dean Student Success ....Ms. Kristi WELLINGTON-BAKER
37 Financial Aid Director ....Ms. Danielle HODGEN
08 Director of Library Services ....Mrs. Stacy PREST
12 Interim Director Clarkston Campus ....Dr. Chad MILTENBERGER
41 Athletic Director ....Mr. Jeffrey E. REINLAND
15 Vice President of Human Resources ....Mrs. Sharon M. HARTFORD
18 Director of Plant Facilities ....Mr. Shane LOPER
106 Director of eLearning ....Ms. Lisa CHAMBERLIN
88 Dean of Transitional Studies ....Ms. Darlene SNIDER
40 Bookstore Manager ....Ms. Alecia ANGELL
31 Coordinator of Community Education ....Ms. Jodi WORDEN
26 Dir Marketing & Communications ....Ms. Melissa THIESSEN
06 Registrar ....Mr. Carlos DELGADILLO
09 Director of Institutional Research ....Dr. Nicholas VELLUZZI
103 Dean Ag Science/Energy/Water Mgmt ....Mr. Jerry ANHORN, JR.
13 Director Technology Svcs ....Mr. Kevin COMBS
56 Dean Entrep Pgm Extend Learning ....Ms. Jessica GILMORE

Walla Walla University (G)

204 S College Avenue, College Place WA 99324-1198
County: Walla Walla FICE Identification: 003799
Unit ID: 236896
Telephone: (509) 527-2615 Carnegie Class: Masters/M
FAX Number: (509) 527-2397 Calendar System: Quarter
URL: www.wallawalla.edu
Established: 1892 Annual Undergrad Tuition & Fees: $26,382
Enrollment: 1,887 Coed
Affiliation or Control: Seventh-day Adventist IRS Status: 501(c)3
Highest Offering: Master's
Accreditation: NW, ACBSP, ACFEI, ENG, MUS, NUR, NURSE, SW

01 President ....Dr. John MCVAY
05 Vice Pres Academic Administration ....Dr. Bob CUSHMAN
10 Vice Pres Financial Administration ....Mr. Steve ROSE
32 Vice Pres Student Life and Mission ....Dr. David RICHARDSON, JR.
84 VP University Relations and Advance ....Ms. Jodi WAGNER
28 Asst to President for Diversity ....Dr. Pedrito MAYNARD-REID
04 Executive Asst Office of President ....Ms. Deirdre BENWELL
20 Associate Vice Pres Academic Admin ....Dr. Scott LIGMAN
21 Associate Vice Pres Financial Admin ....Mr. Ken VYHMEISTER
35 Asst VP/Dean of Students ....Ms. Hilary CATLETT
08 Director of Libraries ....Ms. Carolyn GASKELL
06 Registrar ....Ms. Carolyn DENNEY
42 Chaplain ....Mr. Paddy MCCOY
29 Director of Alumni Relations ....Mrs. Terri DICKINSON NEIL
13 Director Information Services ....Mr. Scott MCFADDEN
37 Assoc Director Financial Aid ....Ms. Nancy CALDERA
15 Director Human Resources ....Ms. Jennifer CARPENTER
18 Director of Plant Services ....Mr. George BENNETT
26 Dir Marketing/University Relations ....Ms. Holley BRYANT
07 Director of Admissions ....Mr. Dallas WEIS
36 Director Career Development Center ....Mr. David LINDSTROM
38 Director Counseling/Testing ....Mr. Don WALLACE
09 Director of Institutional Research ....Mr. Brian HARTMAN
41 Athletic Director ....Mr. Gerry LARSON
19 Campus Security Director ....Ms. Courtney BRYANT
44 Director Gift Planning ....Ms. Dorita TESSIER
58 Dean of Graduate Programs ....Dr. Pam CRESS
66 Dean of School of Nursing ....Dr. Lucille KRULL
73 Dean of School of Theology ....Dr. David THOMAS
54 Dean of School of Engineering ....Dr. Doug LOGAN
50 Dean of Business ....Mr. Josefer MONTES
53 Dean of Education ....Dr. Denise DUNZWEILER
70 Dean of Social Work/Sociology ....Dr. Susan SMITH

Washington State University (H)

PO Box 645910, Pullman WA 99164-5910
County: Whitman FICE Identification: 003800
Unit ID: 236939
Telephone: (509) 335-3564 Carnegie Class: DU-Highest
FAX Number: N/A Calendar System: Semester
URL: www.wsu.edu
Established: 1890 Annual Undergrad Tuition & Fees (In-District): $11,967

Enrollment: 28,686 Coed
Affiliation or Control: State/Local IRS Status: 501(c)3
Highest Offering: Doctorate
Accreditation: NW, BUS, BUSA, CAATE, CEA, CIDA, CLPSY, CONST, COPSY, CS, DIETC, ENG, HSA, IPSY, LSAR, MUS, NURSE, PHAR, SP, SPAA, VET

01 President .... Dr. Kirk SCHULZ
05 Provost/Exec Vice President .... Dr. Daniel BERNADO
10 Interim VP Finance/Administration .... Ms. Olivia YANG
30 VP Advancement/CEO WSU Foundation .... Mr. John GARDNER
106 VP Academic Outreach/Innovation .... Dr. David CILLAY
32 Int VP Student Affairs/Dn Students .... Dr. Melynda HUSKEY
13 VP Information Tech & CIO .... Mr. Sasi PILLAY
46 Vice President Research .... Dr. Christopher KEANE
86 VP External AffairsGovernment Rels .... Ms. Colleen KERR
20 Vice Provost for Faculty Affairs .... Dr. Frances MCSWEENEY
12 Chancellor WSU Spokane .... Dr. Lisa BROWN
12 Chancellor WSU Tri-Cities .... Dr. Keith MOO-YOUNG
12 Chancellor WSU Vancouver .... Dr. Mel NETZHAMMER
43 Div Chief State Attorney Gen Office .... Ms. Danielle HESS
47 Dean Agric/Human Natl Res Sci .... Dr. Ron MITTELHAMMER
50 Dean Carson College of Business .... Dr. Chip HUNTER
53 Dean College of Education .... Dr. Michael TREVISAN
54 Int Dean Engineering & Architecture .... Dr. Don BENDER
66 Dean College of Nursing .... Dr. Joyce GRIFFIN-SOBEL
67 Dean College of Pharmacy .... Dr. Gary POLLACK
60 Int Dean College of Communication .... Dr. Bruce PINKLETON
49 Dean College of Arts & Sciences .... Dr. Daryll DEWALD
74 Dean College of Veterinary Medicine .... Dr. Bryan K. SLINKER
92 Dean Honors College .... Dr. M. Grant NORTON
21 Assoc VP & Chief Budget Officer .... Ms. Joan KING
18 Assoc VP Facilities Services .... Ms. Olivia YANG
71 Dean University College .... Dr. Mary F. WACK
08 Dean Libraries .... Mr. Joseph STARRATT
06 Registrar .... Ms. Julia POMERENK
07 Director Admissions .... Ms. Wendy PETERSON
09 Assoc Dir Institutional Research .... Ms. Fran HERMANSTON
37 Director Financial Aid .... Mr. Brian DIXON
41 Director Intercollegiate Athletics .... Mr. William H. MOOS
88 Director Internal Audit .... Ms. Heather LOPEZ
26 Dir Marketing Communications .... Ms. Kathy BARNARD

Washington State University-Spokane (A)

412 East Spokane Falls Blvd, Spokane WA 99207-9600
Telephone: (509) 358-7500 Identification: 770948
Accreditation: &NW

† Regional accreditation is carried under the parent institution in Pullman, WA

Washington State University-Tri Cities (B)

2710 Crimson Way, Richland WA 99354-1671
Telephone: (509) 372-7000 Identification: 770949
Accreditation: &NW

† Regional accreditation is carried under the parent institution in Pullman, WA

Washington State University-Vancouver (C)

14204 NE Salmon Creek Ave, Vancouver WA 98686-9600
Telephone: (360) 546-9788 Identification: 770950
Accreditation: &NW

† Regional accreditation is carried under the parent institution in Pullman, WA

Wenatchee Valley College (D)

1300 Fifth Street, Wenatchee WA 98801-1799
County: Chelan FICE Identification: 003801
Unit ID: 236975
Telephone: (509) 682-6800 Carnegie Class: Assoc/MT-VT-Mix Trad/Non
FAX Number: (509) 682-6541 Calendar System: Quarter
URL: www.wvc.edu
Established: 1939 Annual Undergrad Tuition & Fees (In-State): $3,800
Enrollment: 3,510 Coed
Affiliation or Control: State IRS Status: 501(c)3
Highest Offering: Associate Degree
Accreditation: NW, ADNUR, MAC, MLTAD

01 President .... Mr. James RICHARDSON
04 Exec Assistant to President .... Ms. Janet FRANZ
05 Vice President of Instruction .... Dr. Carli SCHIFFNER
11 VP of Administrative Services .... Ms. Suzie BENSON
38 Vice President Student Development .... Dr. Chio FLORES
49 Dean Lib Arts/Sciences/Basic Skills .... Mr. Tony THOMAS
12 Dean Omak Campus .... Vacant
103 Dean Workforce Education .... Vacant
76 Dean Allied Health/Nursing .... Ms. Jenny CAPELO
15 Director Human Resources .... Ms. Reagan BELLAMY
45 Dir Institutional Effectiveness .... Vacant
32 Director Student Programs/Outreach .... Mr. Donte QUININE
37 Director Financial Aid .... Mr. Kevin BERG
18 Facilities & Operations Manager .... Mr. Rich PETERS
06 Registrar .... Mr. Bruce MAXWELL
08 Dn Libraries/Learning Technologies .... Mr. Andrew HERSH-TUDOR
10 Director of Fiscal Services .... Ms. Janice FREDSON
26 Communications Manager .... Ms. Libby SIEBENS
20 Coordinator of Adult Basic Skills .... Mr. Aaron PARROTT
27 Marketing/Graphic Design Specialist .... Mr. Nick WINTERS

† Granted candidacy at the Baccalaureate level.

Western Washington University (E)

516 High Street, Bellingham WA 98225-5950
County: Whatcom FICE Identification: 003802
Unit ID: 237011
Telephone: (360) 650-3000 Carnegie Class: Masters/L
FAX Number: (360) 650-3022 Calendar System: Quarter
URL: www.wwu.edu
Established: 1893 Annual Undergrad Tuition & Fees (In-State): $8,611
Enrollment: 15,060 Coed
Affiliation or Control: State IRS Status: 501(c)3
Highest Offering: Beyond Master's But Less Than Doctorate
Accreditation: NW, ART, BUS, CACREP, CORE, CS, ENGT, MUS, NRPA, NURSE, SP, TED

01 President .... Dr. Sabah RANDHAWA
05 Vice Pres Academic Affairs/Provost .... Dr. Brent CARBAJAL
10 Vice Pres Business/Financial Affs .... Mr. Richard D. VAN DEN HUL
84 VP Enrollment/Student Services .... Dr. Eileen V. COUGHLIN
26 Vice Pres for University Relations .... Mr. Steve SWAN
30 Vice Pres University Advancement .... Ms. Stephanie BOWERS
32 Asst VP Enrollment/Student Services .... Dr. Kunle OJIKUTU
13 Vice Prov Info/Chief Info Officer .... Dr. Greg SMITH
58 Vice Prov Rsch/Dean Grad Sch .... Dr. Kathleen KITTO
53 Vice Prov Undergraduate Education .... Dr. Steven L. VANDERSTAAY
22 Vice Prov Equal Oppty/Employmt Div .... Dr. Sue GUENTER-SCHLESINGER
51 Vice Provost Extended Education .... Dr. Earl F. GIBBONS
35 Dean of Students .... Mr. Theodore W. PRATT, JR.
15 Asst VP for Human Resources .... Ms. Chyerl WOLFE-LEE
06 Registrar .... Mr. David BRUNNEMER
07 Exec Dir Admissions/Financial Aid .... Ms. Clara CAPRON
36 Director Career Services Center .... Ms. Tina LOUDON
37 Director Financial Aid .... Ms. Clara CAPRON
29 Executive Director Alumni Relations .... Ms. Deborah DEWEES
27 Director University Communications .... Mr. Paul COCKE
44 Dir Plan Giving/Sr Advisor to Pres .... Vacant
08 Dean of Libraries .... Dr. Mark GREENBERG
39 Director University Residences .... Mr. Leonard JONES
04 Sr Executive Assistant to President .... Dr. Paul DUNN
09 Director of Institutional Research .... Dr. Ming ZHANG
18 Director of Facilities Management .... Mr. John F. FURMAN
19 Director of Public Safety .... Mr. Darin RASMUSSEN
41 Athletic Director .... Mr. Steven CARD
92 Director of Honors Program .... Dr. Scott LINNEMAN
96 Director of Business Services .... Mr. Pete HEILGEIST
79 Dean College of Humanities/Soc Sci .... Dr. Brent MALLINCKRODT
72 Dean College of Science/Technology .... Dr. Catherine CLARK
50 Dean College Business & Econ .... Dr. Scott YOUNG
65 Dean Huxley Col of the Environment .... Dr. Steven HOLLENHORST
57 Dean College of Fine & Perf .... Dr. Christopher SPICER
53 Dean Woodring College of Education .... Dr. Francisco RIOS
12 Dean Fairhaven College .... Dr. Jack HERRING
101 Secretary to the Board of Trustees .... Ms. Barbara A. SANDOVAL
104 Director Int Programs & Exchanges .... Ms. Liz PARTOLAN-FRAY
25 Contracts Assistant .... Ms. Monica MORROW
38 Director Counseling Center .... Dr. Nancy CORBIN
43 AAG/Chief Legal Advisor .... Ms. Kerena HIGGINS
86 Director Government Relations .... Ms. Becca KENNA-SCHENK

Whatcom Community College (F)

237 W Kellogg Road, Bellingham WA 98226-8003
County: Whatcom FICE Identification: 010364
Unit ID: 237039
Telephone: (360) 383-3000 Carnegie Class: Assoc/HT-Mix Trad/Non
FAX Number: (360) 383-4000 Calendar System: Quarter
URL: www.whatcom.ctc.edu
Established: 1970 Annual Undergrad Tuition & Fees (In-State): $4,311
Enrollment: 4,176 Coed
Affiliation or Control: State IRS Status: 501(c)3
Highest Offering: Associate Degree
Accreditation: NW, ADNUR, MAC, PTAA

01 President .... Dr. Kathi HIYANE-BROWN
05 Vice President for Instruction .... Mr. Curt FREED
11 Int VP for Administrative Services .... Mr. Nate LANGSTRAAT
32 Vice Pres for Student Services .... Dr. Luca LEWIS
20 Dean for Instruction .... Mr. Ed HARRI
08 Library Director .... Mr. Howard FULLER
10 Director for Business & Finance .... Mr. Ken BRONSTEIN
06 Registrar .... Mr. Michael SINGLETARY
37 Director of Financial Aid .... Mr. David KLAFFKE
41 Assoc Dir Student/Athletic Pgms .... Mr. Greg SPURGETIS
85 Director of International Programs .... Mr. Kelly KESTER
26 Director for Comm/Marketing .... Ms. Mary VERMILLION
40 Bookstore Manager .... Mr. Jon SPORES
18 Senior Facilities Director .... Mr. Brian KEELEY
04 Special Assistant to the President .... Ms. Rafeeka KLOKE
15 Executive Director Human Resources .... Ms. Becky RAWLINGS
09 Director for Institutional Research .... Dr. Anne Marie KARLBERG
30 Exec Dir Institutional Advancement .... Ms. Anne BOWEN
27 Public Information Officer .... Ms. Mary VERMILLION

† Granted candidacy at the Baccalaureate level.

Whitman College (G)

345 Boyer Avenue, Walla Walla WA 99362-2083
County: Walla Walla FICE Identification: 003803
Unit ID: 237057
Telephone: (509) 527-5411 Carnegie Class: Bac-A&S
FAX Number: (509) 527-5859 Calendar System: Semester
URL: www.whitman.edu
Established: 1882 Annual Undergrad Tuition & Fees: $46,138
Enrollment: 1,498 Coed
Affiliation or Control: Independent Non-Profit IRS Status: 501(c)3
Highest Offering: Baccalaureate
Accreditation: NW

01 President .... Dr. Kathleen MURRAY
05 Provost/Dean of Faculty .... Dr. Alzada TIPTON
30 Vice President for Development .... Mr. John W. BOGLEY
10 Treasurer/Chief Financial Officer .... Mr. Peter W. HARVEY
32 Dean of Students .... Mr. Charles E. CLEVELAND
20 Associate Dean of Faculty .... Dr. Lisa R. PERFETTI
84 Dean of Admission/Financial Aid .... Mr. Tony A. CABASCO
13 Chief Technology Officer .... Mr. Dan M. TERRIO
18 Chief Facilities/Physical Plant .... Mr. Daniel L. PARK
08 Librarian .... Mrs. Dalia L. CORKRUM
91 Director of Enterprise Technology .... Mr. Michael OSTERMAN
07 Director of Admissions .... Mr. Adam MILLER
09 Director of Institutional Research .... Dr. Neal J. CHRISTOPHERSON
20 Assistant Dean of Faculty .... Ms. Kendra J. GOLDEN
35 Associate Dean of Students .... Ms. Barbara A. MAXWELL
26 Chief Communications Officer .... Mr. Joshua JENSEN
38 Director Student Counseling .... Mr. F. 'Thatcher' CARTER
39 Director Residence Life & Housing .... Ms. Nancy J. TAVELLI
29 Director Alumni Relations .... Ms. Nancy L. MITCHELL
104 Director of Off-Campus Studies .... Ms. Susan H. HOLME
15 Director Human Resources .... Mr. Dennis T. HOPWOOD
06 Registrar .... Ms. Stacey J. GIUSTI
19 Director of Security .... Mr. Mattew STROE
23 Director Health Services .... Ms. Claudia L. NESS
36 Director of Career Center .... Ms. Gayle TOWNSEND
37 Director of Financial Aid Services .... Ms. Marilyn K. PONTI
41 Athletic Director .... Mr. Dean C. SNIDER
42 Coordinator of Spiritual Life .... Mr. Adam M. KIRTLEY
04 Executive Assistant to President .... Ms. Jennifer A. CASPER
44 Director of Annual Giving .... Mr. Brian DOHE

Whitworth University (H)

300 W Hawthorne Road, Spokane WA 99251-0001
County: Spokane FICE Identification: 003804
Unit ID: 237066
Telephone: (509) 777-1000 Carnegie Class: Masters/S
FAX Number: (509) 777-4763 Calendar System: 4/1/4
URL: www.whitworth.edu
Established: 1890 Annual Undergrad Tuition & Fees: $39,096
Enrollment: 2,654 Coed
Affiliation or Control: Presbyterian IRS Status: 501(c)3
Highest Offering: Master's
Accreditation: NW, CAATE, MUS, NURSE

01 President .... Dr. Beck A. TAYLOR
05 Provost & Executive Vice President .... Dr. Caroline J. SIMON
100 Chief of Staff .... Vacant
04 Exec Asst to President/Board Secy .... Ms. Ruth R. PELLS
10 VP Finance & Administration .... Mr. Lawrence K. PROBUS
32 VP for Student Life/Title IX .... Ms. Rhosetta R. RHODES
84 VP Admissions & Financial Aid .... Mr. Greg ORWIG
30 VP Institutional Advancement .... Dr. Scott A. MCQUILKIN
15 Assoc VP Human Resources .... Ms. Dolores J. HUMISTON
21 Assoc VP Finance & Administration .... Ms. Luz I. MERKEL
27 Chief Information Officer .... Mr. Kenneth BROWN
42 Dean Spiritual Life .... Dr. Forrest BUCKNER
41 Director of Athletics .... Mr. Timothy DEMANT
88 Director of Athletic Training .... Ms. Cynthia WRIGHT
20 Associate Provost of Instruction .... Dr. Randall B. MICHAELIS
88 Assoc Provost Fac Devel/Schlrshp .... Dr. Kathleen H. STORM
25 Dir Sponsored Program/Grants .... Ms. Lynn NOLAND
42 Dir Office of Church Engagement .... Dr. Terry P. MCGONIGAL
28 Asst Dean Student Diversity .... Mr. David GARCIA
53 Dean of School of Education .... Dr. Barbara SANDERS
88 Director MIT .... Dr. David CHERRY
50 Dean School of Business .... Dr. Timothy J. WILKINSON
49 Dean College of Arts & Sciences .... Dr. Noelle WIERSMA
51 AVP Grad Admissions & Cont Studies .... Ms. Cheryl D. VAWTER
88 Dir Graduate Studies in Education .... Ms. Roberta WILBURN
06 Registrar .... Ms. Beverly S. KLEEMAN
88 Dir Instructional Resources .... Mr. Kenneth D. PECKA
88 Assoc Dean Com Standards/Compliance .... Dr. Craig CHATRIAND
29 Dir Alumni/Parent Relations .... Mr. Dale W. HAMMOND
07 Director of Admissions .... Ms. Marianne W. HANSEN
18 Director of Facilities Services .... Mr. Christopher EICHORST
23 Director of Health Center .... Ms. Edelweiss WHITSON
37 Director of Financial Aid .... Ms. Traci L. STENSLAND
35 Assoc Dean of Students/Dir HUB .... Ms. Dayna L. COLEMAN
39 Assoc Director of Student Housing .... Mr. Alan B. JACOB
32 Director of Residence Life .... Mr. Timothy CALDWELL
40 Manager of Bookstore .... Vacant
26 Director of Communications .... Ms. Nancy G. HINES
38 Director of Counseling Services .... Ms. Monica WHITLOCK
09 Director of Institutional Research .... Ms. Wendy L. OLSON
08 Director Library .... Ms. Amanda C. CLARK
19 Supr II Security Services .... Ms. Jacquelyn CHRISTENSEN
88 Director MA Theology .... Dr. Jeremy WYNNE
104 Dir of International Education Ctr .... Ms. Sue JACKSON
88 Dir US Cultural Studies .... Dr. Stacy GEORGE
88 Director MBA .... Mr. John HENGESH
88 Dir Evening Teacher Certification .... Dr. Corey MCKENNA
88 Assoc Dean Organiz Management .... Ms. Christie ANDERSON

Yakima Valley College (A)

PO Box 22520, S 16th Ave & Nob Hill, Yakima WA 98907-2520

County: Yakima FICE Identification: 003805
Unit ID: 237109
Telephone: (509) 574-4600 Carnegie Class: Bac/Assoc-Assoc Dom
FAX Number: (509) 574-6860 Calendar System: Quarter
URL: www.yvcc.edu
Established: 1928 Annual Undergrad Tuition & Fees (In-State): $4,225
Enrollment: 3,950 Coed
Affiliation or Control: State IRS Status: 170(c)1
Highest Offering: Baccalaureate
Accreditation: NW, ADNUR, DH, MAC, SURGT

01 President ....Dr. Linda KAMINSKI
05 Vice Pres Instruction/Student Svcs ....Mr. Tomas YBARRA
10 Vice Pres Administrative Services ....Ms. Teresa HOLLAND
12 Dean Basic Skills/Grandview Campus ....Dr. Bryce HUMPHREYS
13 Director Tech Services ....Mr. Scott TOWSLEY
32 Dean Student Services ....Ms. Leslie BLACKABY
49 Dean Arts & Sciences ....Ms. Kerrie CAVANESS
75 Dean Workforce Education ....Ms. Paulette LOPEZ
08 Library Director ....Vacant
37 Director Student Financial Aid ....Ms. Janet CANTELON
06 Registrar/Director of Admissions ....Mr. Quinn HALE
09 Dir Institutional Effectiveness ....Ms. Sheila DELQUADRI
29 Director Alumni Relations ....Ms. Deborah WILSON
26 Community Relations Coordinator ....Ms. Nicole HOPKINS
15 Director Human Resources ....Mr. Mark ROGSTAD
18 Director Facilities/Physical Plant ....Mr. Jeff WOOD
21 Director Accounting Services ....Ms. Clarissa WOLFE
35 Student Life Coordinator ....Ms. Caitlin GOODWILL

WEST VIRGINIA

Alderson Broaddus University (B)

101 College Hill Drive, Philippi WV 26416-4600

County: Barbour FICE Identification: 003806
Unit ID: 237118
Telephone: (304) 457-1700 Carnegie Class: Bac-Diverse
FAX Number: (304) 457-6239 Calendar System: Semester
URL: www.ab.edu
Established: 1871 Annual Undergrad Tuition & Fees: $24,140
Enrollment: 1,108 Coed
Affiliation or Control: American Baptist IRS Status: 501(c)3
Highest Offering: Master's
Accreditation: NH, ARCPA, CAATE, NUR, TEAC

01 President ....Dr. James (Tim) BARRY
05 Provost/Executive Vice President ....Dr. Joan L. PROPST
11 Vice Pres for Administration ....Mr. Bruce A. BLANKENSHIP
84 Vice Pres Enrollment Management ....Dr. Eric M. SHOR
10 Vice Pres for Finance/CFO ....Mr. Dennis E. STARK
32 Dean of Student Affairs ....Mr. Bruce A. BLANKENSHIP
20 Associate Provost ....Dr. Andrea J. BUCKLEW
63 Dean Col of Physician Asst Studies ....Mr. Thomas F. MOORE
76 Dean College of Health Sciences ....Ms. Kimberly L. WHITE
53 Dean College of Education and Music ....Dr. Joseph F. SUPER
50 Dean Col of Business & Management ....Mr. Richard T. FOLEY
79 Dean Col of Humanities & Soc Sci ....Dr. James M. OWSTON
81 Dean College of Science/Tech/Math ....Dr. Ross A. BRITTAIN
06 Registrar ....Dr. Saundra E. HOXIE
08 Director of Library Services ....Mr. David E. HOXIE
41 Athletic Director ....Mr. Dennis W. CREEHAN
42 Chaplain ....Dr. Carl W. GITTINGS
08 Dir Academic Ctr for Educ Success ....Dr. Amy MASON
21 Controller ....Mr. Jeff ROGERS
29 Director of Alumni Relations ....Mr. Joshua D. ALLEN
44 Director of Annual Giving ....Ms. Christy L. MULLENS-SHAW
40 Director of Campus Services ....Mr. Ed BURDA
36 Director of Career Services ....Ms. Teresa D. VAN ALSBURG
38 Director of Counseling Services ....Mr. Chad HOSTETLER
37 Director of Financial Aid ....Ms. Amy L. KING
18 Director of Facilities ....Mr. Lawrence J. TALLMAN
27 Dir of Information and Research ....Ms. Julia M. MORRIS
13 Director of Information Technology ....Ms. Carol WEAVER
26 Director of Mktg/Communications ....Mr. Craig J. BUTLER
39 Director Student Housing ....Mr. David A. FALLETA
19 Director Security/Safety ....Mr. Matthew SISK
04 Exec Asst to Pres/Sec to the Board ....Ms. Juliet A. SPRUILL
105 Web Content Editor ....Ms. Eva M. TREFETHEN
07 Director of Admissions ....Ms. Erika L. THON
09 Director of Institutional Research ....Dr. Bob S. BUCKINGHAM
102 Dir Foundation/Corporate Relations ....Ms. Vicki W. GLASOW

American National University (C)

110 Park Center Drive, Parkersburg WV 26101

Telephone: (304) 699-3005 Identification: 770787
Accreditation: ACICS, MAC

† Branch campus of American National University, Salem, VA

American National University (D)

421 Hilltop Drive, Princeton WV 24740

Telephone: (304) 487-3845 Identification: 666499
Accreditation: ACICS, MAC

† Branch campus of American National University, Salem, VA

American Public University System (E)

111 W Congress Street, Charles Town WV 25414-1621

County: Jefferson FICE Identification: 035393
Unit ID: 449339
Telephone: (304) 724-3700 Carnegie Class: Masters/L
FAX Number: (304) 724-3780 Calendar System: Other
URL: www.apus.edu
Established: 1991 Annual Undergrad Tuition & Fees: $6,880
Enrollment: 57,539 Coed
Affiliation or Control: Proprietary IRS Status: Proprietary
Highest Offering: Master's
Accreditation: NH, ACBSP, NURSE

01 President/CEO ....Dr. Karan H. POWELL
05 Exec VP & Provost ....Vacant
26 Exec VP Programs & Marketing ....Ms. Carol S. GILBERT
10 Exec VP & CFO ....Mr. Richard SUNDERLAND, JR.
11 SVP/Chief Admin Officer ....Mr. Pete W. GIBBONS
13 SVP/Chief Information Officer ....Ms. Tracy WOODS
20 SVP/Academic Opers Officer ....Dr. Gwen HALL
20 SVP/Acad Prgm Dev & Outreach ....Mr. Michael NETZER
06 VP/Registrar ....Ms. Michelle NEWMAN
84 VP Enrollment Mgt & Student Support ....Ms. Terry GRANT
31 VP Community Relations ....Dr. John HOUGH
32 VP Student Services ....Ms. Caroline SIMPSON
09 VP Institutional Research ....Dr. Dave BECHER
08 VP Library and Educ Materials ....Dr. Hedi BENAICHA
88 VP Military/Veteran & CC Outreach ....Mr. John ALDRICH
15 VP Human Resources ....Ms. Amy PANZARELLA
37 VP Financial Aid & Compliance ....Mr. Keith WELLINGS
88 VP Ombudsman ....Ms. Lynn C. WALLACE

Appalachian Bible College (F)

161 College Drive, Mount Hope WV 25880

County: Raleigh FICE Identification: 007544
Unit ID: 237136
Telephone: (304) 877-6428 Carnegie Class: Spec-4-yr-Faith
FAX Number: (304) 877-5082 Calendar System: Semester
URL: abc.edu
Established: 1950 Annual Undergrad Tuition & Fees: $13,590
Enrollment: 302 Coed
Affiliation or Control: Independent Non-Profit IRS Status: 501(c)3
Highest Offering: Master's
Accreditation: NH, BI

01 President ....Dr. Daniel L. ANDERSON
05 Vice President for Academics ....Mr. Daniel S. HANSHEW
10 Vice President for Business ....Mr. Kenneth E. LILLY
30 Vice President for Development ....Rev. Jonathan A. RINKER
32 Vice President for Student Services ....Rev. David E. CHILDS
42 Vice Pres for Extension Ministries ....Mr. David J. HOLLOWAY
33 Dean of Men ....Mr. Kevin GULLION
34 Dean of Women ....Mrs. Linda J. CHILDS
06 Registrar ....Dr. John RINEHART
07 Director of Admissions ....Mr. Benjamin CALE
08 Librarian ....Mr. David W. DUNKERTON
37 Director of Financial Aid ....Mrs. Deana B. STEINKE
04 Admin Assistant to the President ....Mrs. Elisabeth I. GOLDEN
26 Director of Public Relations ....Miss Karisa A. CLARK

Bethany College (G)

31 E. Campus Drive, Bethany WV 26032-3002

County: Brooke FICE Identification: 003808
Unit ID: 237181
Telephone: (304) 829-7000 Carnegie Class: Bac-A&S
FAX Number: (304) 829-7700 Calendar System: 4/1/4
URL: www.bethanywv.edu
Established: 1840 Annual Undergrad Tuition & Fees: $26,500
Enrollment: 757 Coed
Affiliation or Control: Christian Church (Disciples Of Christ)
IRS Status: 501(c)3
Highest Offering: Master's
Accreditation: NH, SW, TED

01 President ....Dr. Tamara N. RODENBERG
05 Int Vice Pres for Academic Affairs ....Dr. Gary KAPPEL
10 Vice President for Finance ....Mrs. Eileen GREAF
03 Senior Vice President ....Mr. Sven DE JONG
04 Asst to the President ....Ms. Stephanie GORDON
20 Asst Vice President Academic Affs ....Ms. Katherine SHELEK-FURBEE
32 Dean of Students ....Mr. Gerald STEBBINS
37 Director of Financial Aid ....Mr. Jason MCCLAIN
41 Director of Athletics & Recreation ....Mr. Brian ROSE
09 Dir Institutional Research/Records ....Mr. Richard MILLER
88 Director of McCann Learning Center ....Ms. Heather TAYLOR
88 Dir Student Engag/Responsibility ....Ms. Alyssa FEDEROFF
89 Director of First Year Experience ....Ms. Heather TAYLOR
104 Director of International Programs ....Dr. Harald MENZ
36 Director of Career Services ....Mr. John OSBORNE
23 Director of the Byrd Health Center ....Mrs. Carol TYLER
26 Director of Communications ....Ms. Rebecca ROSE
29 Director of Alumni/Parent Relations ....Ms. Ashley KANOTZ
30 Director of Advancement Services ....Ms. Shirley KEMP
88 Director of Sports Information ....Mr. Jerrod PLATE
88 Director of Church Relations ....Dr. Larry GRIMES
18 Director of Physical Plant ....Mr. Jay EISENHAUER
21 Asst Vice President for Finance ....Ms. Deidra R. PARR
21 Director of Business Affairs ....Ms. Saralyn DAGUE
19 Director of Safety & Security ....Mr. Larry PALMER
15 Director of Human Resources ....Mrs. Stephanie LAFLAM
39 Director of Residence Life ....Mr. Andrew LEWIS
35 Director of Student Activities ....Mr. Samuel GOODGE
42 Chaplain ....Rev. Scott THAYER
08 Director of the Libraries ....Mrs. Heather MAY-RICCIUTI
24 Dir Media Services/Classroom Tech ....Mr. Thomas V. FURBEE
88 Public Services Librarian ....Vacant
06 Registrar ....Ms. Lisa CUCARESE
84 Vice Pres of Enrollment Management ....Ms. Mollie CECERE
88 General Manager Conference Center ....Ms. Donna WHITE
109 Director of Dining Services ....Mrs. Necol M. DUNSON
40 Manager of the Bookstore ....Ms. Rosemary BERNTH
38 College Counselor ....Ms. Renee STOCK

Catholic Distance University (H)

115 West Congress Street, Charles Town WV 25414

County: Jefferson FICE Identification: 041242
Unit ID: 475398
Telephone: (304) 724-5000 Carnegie Class: Not Classified
FAX Number: (304) 724-5017 Calendar System: Other
URL: www.cdu.edu
Established: 1983 Annual Undergrad Tuition & Fees: N/A
Enrollment: 186 Coed
Affiliation or Control: Independent Non-Profit IRS Status: 501(c)3
Highest Offering: Master's
Accreditation: DEAC

01 President ....Dr. Marianne E. MOUNT
05 Academic Dean ....Dr. Peter BROWN
20 Faculty Chair ....Dr. Matthew BUNSON
88 Dean of Catechetical Programs ....Sr. Mary Margaret SCHLATHER
06 Registrar ....Ms. Theresa SNIDER
06 Continuing Education Registrar ....Mrs. Kathleen WOODDELL
26 Director of Communications ....Vacant
07 Director of Admissions ....Ms. Carol CIULLO
10 Bursar ....Mrs. Amy SHOUSE
13 Director of Technology ....Mrs. Carol DALEY

Davis & Elkins College (I)

100 Campus Drive, Elkins WV 26241-3996

County: Randolph FICE Identification: 003811
Unit ID: 237358
Telephone: (304) 637-1900 Carnegie Class: Bac-A&S
FAX Number: (304) 637-1413 Calendar System: 4/1/4
URL: www.dewv.edu
Established: 1904 Annual Undergrad Tuition & Fees: $27,492
Enrollment: 846 Coed
Affiliation or Control: Presbyterian Church (U.S.A.) IRS Status: 501(c)3
Highest Offering: Baccalaureate
Accreditation: NH, ADNUR, #IACBE, THEA

01 President ....Mr. Chris A. WOOD
10 VP for Business & Finance ....Ms. Greta J. TROASTLE
05 Vice President for Academic Affairs ....Vacant
32 Vice President for Student Affairs ....Mr. Scott D. GODDARD
30 Vice President for Development ....Vacant
15 Director Human Resources ....Ms. M. J. COREY
06 Registrar ....Dr. Stephanie C. HAYNES
18 Director of Physical Plant ....Mr. Ron SELDERS
37 Director Financial Planning ....Mr. Matthew A. SUMMERS
08 Assistant Director Booth Library ....Ms. Mary Jo DEJOICE
42 Chaplain ....Rev. Kevin M. STARCHER
41 Director of Athletics ....Mr. Jamie JOSS
19 Director of Security ....Mr. Martin WHITE
04 Executive Asst to the President ....Ms. Robin PRICE
13 Chief Information Officer ....Mr. Tim GIBSON
29 Director of Alumni Engagement ....Ms. Wendy MORGAN
84 Vice Pres for Enrollment Mgmt ....Ms. Sandy NEEL
09 Director of Institutional Research ....Vacant
26 Dir Communications & Marketing ....Ms. Nanci BROSS-FREGONARA

Future Generations Graduate School (J)

390 Road Less Traveled, Franklin WV 26807-9201

County: Pendleton Identification: 666714
Unit ID: 481030
Telephone: (304) 358-2000 Carnegie Class: Spec-4-yr-Other
FAX Number: (304) 358-3008 Calendar System: Other
URL: www.future.edu
Established: 2003 Annual Graduate Tuition & Fees: N/A
Enrollment: 38 Coed
Affiliation or Control: Independent Non-Profit IRS Status: 501(c)3
Highest Offering: Master's; No Undergraduates
Accreditation: NH

01 Executive Director ....Dr. Daniel TAYLOR
11 Chief Operating Officer ....Stephanie HARTMAN
32 Chief Student Affairs/Student Life ....Christie HAND
108 Director Institutional Assessment ....Dr. Jesse PAPPAS
06 Registrar ....Jodie WIMER

Huntington Junior College (K)

900 Fifth Avenue, Huntington WV 25701-2004

County: Cabell FICE Identification: 009047
Unit ID: 237437

Telephone: (304) 697-7550 Carnegie Class: Assoc/HVT-High Non
FAX Number: (304) 697-7554 Calendar System: Quarter
URL: www.huntingtonjuniorcollege.edu
Established: 1936 Annual Undergrad Tuition & Fees: $7,800
Enrollment: 648 Coed
Affiliation or Control: Proprietary IRS Status: Proprietary
Highest Offering: Associate Degree
Accreditation: NH, MAC

01 President ..... Carolyn A. SMITH
03 Director ..... Dr. Catherine E. SNODDY
05 Academic Affairs Director ..... Linda J. WEST
10 Chief Fiscal Officer ..... Sharon SNODDY

Martinsburg College (A)

341 Aikens Center, Martinsburg WV 25404
County: Berkeley Identification: 667035
Telephone: (304) 263-6262 Carnegie Class: Not Classified
FAX Number: (866) 703-6611 Calendar System: Other
URL: www.martinsburgcollege.edu
Established: 1980 Annual Undergrad Tuition & Fees: N/A
Enrollment: N/A Coed
Affiliation or Control: Proprietary IRS Status: Proprietary
Highest Offering: Associate Degree
Accreditation: DEAC

01 President ..... Paul VIBOCH
05 Chief Academic Officer ..... Stella GARLICK
07 Director of Admissions ..... Laurie MAURO
06 Registrar ..... Debra HAYTAS

Mountain State College (B)

1508 Spring Street, Parkersburg WV 26101
County: Wood FICE Identification: 005008
Unit ID: 237598
Telephone: (304) 485-5487 Carnegie Class: Spec 2-yr-Health
FAX Number: (304) 485-3524 Calendar System: Quarter
URL: www.msc.edu
Established: 1888 Annual Undergrad Tuition & Fees: $6,215
Enrollment: 158 Coed
Affiliation or Control: Proprietary IRS Status: Proprietary
Highest Offering: Associate Degree
Accreditation: ACICS

01 President ..... Mrs. Judith SUTTON

Ohio Valley University (C)

1 Campus View Drive, Vienna WV 26105-8000
County: Wood FICE Identification: 003819
Unit ID: 237640
Telephone: (304) 865-6000 Carnegie Class: Bac-Diverse
FAX Number: (304) 865-6001 Calendar System: Semester
URL: www.ovu.edu
Established: 1958 Annual Undergrad Tuition & Fees: $19,840
Enrollment: 431 Coed
Affiliation or Control: Churches Of Christ IRS Status: 501(c)3
Highest Offering: Master's
Accreditation: NH, IACBE

01 President ..... Dr. Harold SHANK
10 CFO ..... Mr. Jeffrey A. DIMICK
00 Chancellor ..... Dr. Keith STOTTS
05 VP for Academic Affairs ..... Dr. Joy JONES
41 Athletic Director ..... Mr. Chad PORTER
30 VP Advancement ..... Vacant
04 President's Office Manager ..... Mrs. Missy WAYT
18 Director of Campus Operations ..... Mr. David STEWART
36 Director of Career Services ..... Mrs. Kathy MULLER
32 Dean of Student Life ..... Mr. Jason DOUGHERTY
08 Library Director ..... Mrs. Janice HEDDEN
06 Registrar ..... Mrs. Amy GHERKE
07 Director of Admissions Management ..... Mrs. Kay GROSE
09 Director of OIE ..... Mrs. Rebecca CLARK
13 Chief Info Technology Officer ..... Mr. Christopher LANG
26 Director of Marketing ..... Mr. Marty DAVIS
19 Director Security/Safety ..... Ms. Hope ASH
37 Director Student Financial Aid ..... Mrs. Lindsay COLE
50 Dean College of Business ..... Dr. Dan BLAIR
53 Dean College of Education ..... Mrs. Glenda J. PENNINGTON

Salem International University (D)

223 W Main Street, Box 500, Salem WV 26426-0500
County: Harrison FICE Identification: 003820
Unit ID: 237783
Telephone: (304) 326-1109 Carnegie Class: Masters/M
FAX Number: (304) 326-1246 Calendar System: Semester
URL: www.salemu.edu
Established: 1888 Annual Undergrad Tuition & Fees: $17,700
Enrollment: 536 Coed
Affiliation or Control: Proprietary IRS Status: Proprietary
Highest Offering: Master's
Accreditation: NH, TED

01 President ..... Mr. Dan NELANT
04 Executive Asst to President ..... Mrs. Barbara L. MCCLAIN
03 Executive Vice President ..... Dr. Cecil E. KIRKLAND
05 Provost ..... Dr. Craig S. MCCLELLAN
37 Dir Financial Aid & Compliance ..... Mr. Donald RONAN
13 Director of Information Technology ..... Mr. Anthony GRANT
11 VP Operations ..... Vacant
07 Director of Admissions ..... Ms. Iris ROBERTSON
10 Chief Financial Officer ..... Mr. William WINKOWSKI
21 Controller ..... Ms. Ginger RICHARDS
85 Intl Student Dir & Business Mgr ..... Mrs. Stephanie ROBERTS
06 Registrar ..... Mr. Joseph E. FERLIC
50 Dean of Business ..... Dr. Marc D. GETTY
53 Dean of Education ..... Dr. Craig S. MCCLELLAN
66 Director of Nursing Education ..... Mrs. Cheryl MICHAELS
08 Dean of Library Services ..... Dr. Phyllis D. FREEDMAN
32 Dean of Student Affairs ..... Dr. Dennis MCNABOE
19 Director of Campus Security ..... Mr. Joseph E. SHAVER
41 Director of Athletics ..... Mr. Jamie SHOEMAKER

University of Charleston (E)

2300 Maccorkle Avenue, SE, Charleston WV 25304-1099
County: Kanawha FICE Identification: 003818
Unit ID: 237312
Telephone: (304) 357-4800 Carnegie Class: Masters/S
FAX Number: (304) 357-4715 Calendar System: Semester
URL: www.ucwv.edu
Established: 1888 Annual Undergrad Tuition & Fees: $26,100
Enrollment: 2,111 Coed
Affiliation or Control: Independent Non-Profit IRS Status: 501(c)3
Highest Offering: Doctorate
Accreditation: NH, #ARCPA, CAATE, CIDA, DMS, NUR, CTA, PHAR, RAD, TEAC

01 President ..... Dr. Edwin H. WELCH
05 Exec VP/Provost/Dean of Faculty ..... Dr. Letha ZOOK
10 Exec VP Administration & Finance ..... Mrs. Cleta M. HARLESS
30 Vice Pres for Development ..... Ms. Deborah MORRIS
07 Exec VP/Chief Admissions/Mktg Ofcr ..... Ms. Joan CLARK
32 Dean of Students ..... Dr. Mordecai BROWNLEE
26 Director of Marketing ..... Mr. David TRAUBE
100 Chief of Staff ..... Dr. Jerry FORSTER
06 Registrar ..... Ms. Carol SPRADLING
29 Director of Alumni Relations ..... Ms. Catherine ECKLEY
21 Controller ..... Ms. Terri UNDERHILL
13 Chief Information Officer ..... Mr. Scott TERRY
08 Director of Library Services ..... Mr. John ADKINS
85 Director International Student Pgms ..... Ms. Elizabeth SLACK
37 Associate Director Financial Aid ..... Ms. Nina MORTON
35 Assistant Dean of Students ..... Ms. Virginia MOORE
35 Dir of Student Involvement ..... Ms. Sarah CAMPFIELD
40 Bookstore Manager ..... Mr. Glenn JOHNSON
18 Director of Facilities Services ..... Mr. Gary BOYD
41 Athletic Director ..... Dr. Bren STEVENS
88 VP/Chief Innovation Executive ..... Ms. Ronda HOLEHOUSE
09 Director of Institutional Research ..... Ms. Lisa DAWKINS
50 Dean Graduate School of Business ..... Dr. Scott BELLAMY
67 Dean School of Pharmacy ..... Dr. Michelle EASTON
49 Dean School of Arts & Sciences ..... Dr. Barbara WRIGHT
76 Dean School of Health Sciences ..... Dr. Pamela ALDERMAN

Valley College - Beckley Campus (F)

120 New River Town Center, Suite C, Beckley WV 25801
County: Raleigh FICE Identification: 030844
Unit ID: 377652
Telephone: (304) 252-9547 Carnegie Class: Spec 2-yr-Other
FAX Number: (304) 252-1694 Calendar System: Other
URL: www.valley.edu
Established: 1983 Annual Undergrad Tuition & Fees: $15,700
Enrollment: 331 Coed
Affiliation or Control: Proprietary IRS Status: Proprietary
Highest Offering: Associate Degree
Accreditation: ACICS

01 President ..... Mr. Tony PALMIERI
05 Vice President Campus Operations ..... Ms. Beth GARDNER
10 Vice President Administration ..... Mr. Matt JENKINS

Valley College - Martinsburg Campus (G)

287 Aikens Center, Martinsburg WV 25404-6203
County: Berkeley FICE Identification: 026094
Unit ID: 377661
Telephone: (304) 263-0979 Carnegie Class: Spec 2-yr-Health
FAX Number: (304) 263-2413 Calendar System: Other
URL: www.valley.edu
Established: 1983 Annual Undergrad Tuition & Fees: N/A
Enrollment: 140 Coed
Affiliation or Control: Proprietary IRS Status: Proprietary
Highest Offering: Associate Degree
Accreditation: ACICS

01 Campus Director ..... Mr. Brandon BOWERS

Valley College - Princeton Campus (H)

616 Harrison Street, Princeton WV 24740
County: Mercer FICE Identification: 030842
Unit ID: 377670
Telephone: (304) 425-2323 Carnegie Class: Not Classified
FAX Number: (304) 425-5890 Calendar System: Other
URL: www.valley.edu
Established: 1986 Annual Undergrad Tuition & Fees: N/A
Enrollment: 89 Coed
Affiliation or Control: Proprietary IRS Status: Proprietary
Highest Offering: Associate Degree
Accreditation: ACICS

01 Campus Director ..... Ms. Misty TESTERMAN

West Virginia Business College (I)

116 Pennsylvania Avenue, Nutter Fort WV 26301-4516
Telephone: (304) 624-7695 Identification: 666507
Accreditation: ACICS

† Branch campus of West Virginia Business College, Wheeling, WV.

West Virginia Business College (J)

1052 Main Street, Wheeling WV 26003-2702
County: Ohio FICE Identification: 010861
Unit ID: 237978
Telephone: (304) 232-0361 Carnegie Class: Assoc/HVT-High Trad
FAX Number: (304) 232-0363 Calendar System: Quarter
URL: www.wvbc.edu
Established: 1881 Annual Undergrad Tuition & Fees: $9,700
Enrollment: 125 Coed
Affiliation or Control: Proprietary IRS Status: Proprietary
Highest Offering: Associate Degree
Accreditation: ACICS

01 General Manager ..... Mr. James WEIR

*West Virginia Council for Community & Technical College Education (K)

1018 Kanawha Boulevard E, Suite 700,
Charleston WV 25301-2800
County: Kanawha Identification: 666993
Telephone: (304) 558-0265 Carnegie Class: N/A
FAX Number: (304) 558-1646
URL: www.wvctcs.org

01 Chancellor ..... Sarah A. TUCKER

*Blue Ridge Community and Technical College (L)

13650 Apple Harvest Drive, Martinsburg WV 25403
County: Berkeley FICE Identification: 039573
Unit ID: 446774
Telephone: (304) 260-4380 Carnegie Class: Assoc/HT-High Non
FAX Number: (304) 260-1788 Calendar System: Semester
URL: www.blueridgectc.edu
Established: 1974 Annual Undergrad Tuition & Fees (In-State): $3,696
Enrollment: 5,528 Coed
Affiliation or Control: State IRS Status: 501(c)3
Highest Offering: Associate Degree
Accreditation: NH, ADNUR, EMT, PTAA

02 President ..... Dr. Peter G. CHECKOVICH
05 Vice President of Instruction ..... Dr. George PERRY
103 VP Economic and Workforce Devel ..... Dr. Ann M. SHIPWAY
84 VP of Enrollment Management ..... Ms. Leslie C. SEE
10 Chief Financial Officer ..... Dr. Craig MILLER
06 Registrar ..... Dr. Angie M. KINDER
32 Associate Dean of Students ..... Ms. Brenda NEAL
15 Vice President Human Resources ..... Mr. Justin RUBLE
13 Vice President of IT ..... Mr. Michael BYERS
37 Director of Financial Aid ..... Ms. Anna CRAWFORD

*BridgeValley Community & Technical College (M)

2001 Union Carbide Drive, South Charleston WV 25303
County: Kanawha FICE Identification: 040386
Unit ID: 445018
Telephone: (304) 205-6600 Carnegie Class: Not Classified
FAX Number: N/A Calendar System: Semester
URL: www.bridgevalley.edu
Established: 2014 Annual Undergrad Tuition & Fees (In-District): N/A
Enrollment: N/A Coed
Affiliation or Control: State/Local IRS Status: Exempt
Highest Offering: Associate Degree
Accreditation: NH, ADNUR, COARC, DH, ENGT, MLTAD, NMT

02 President ..... Dr. Eunice BELLINGER
05 Sr Vice Pres Academic/Student Affs ..... Dr. Kristin MALLORY
103 Sr Vice Pres WF/Economic Develop ..... Mr. Jeff WYCO
88 VP Workforce Education ..... Ms. Laura MCCULLOUGH
32 Dean of Students ..... Mr. James MCDOUGLE
97 Dean of General Education ..... Ms. Kim LOVINSKI
76 Dean of Health ..... Ms. Suzette BREEDEN
06 Chief Records Officer/Registrar ..... Mr. Roy SIMMONS
15 Chief Human Resources Officer ..... Ms. Michelle BISSELL
10 Chief Financial Officer ..... Ms. Cathy AQUINO
04 Executive Asst to President ..... Ms. Alicia SYNER
08 Director of Library Services ..... Ms. Heather LAUER
09 Chief Banner Officer ..... Mr. James FAUVER
18 Chief IT/Operations Officer ..... Mr. Jason STARK
19 Chief of Police ..... Mr. Bazra FAKHIR
26 Chief Marketing Officer ..... Mr. Brian BOLYARD

50 Dean Business/Legal/Human Svcs ....Ms. Megan LORENZ
72 Dean of Technology ....Mr. Norm MORTENSEN
84 Dean of Enrollment Services ....Ms. Joyce SURBAUGH
37 Director of Financial Aid ....Ms. Mary BLIZZARD
36 Director of Student Placement ....Ms. Judy WHIPKEY
38 Director of Counseling Svcs ....Ms. Carla BLANKENBUEHLER
96 Chief Procurement Officer ....Mr. John POWELL

*Eastern West Virginia Community and Technical College (A)

316 Eastern Drive, Moorefield WV 26836-1155
County: Hardy FICE Identification: 041190
Unit ID: 438708
Telephone: (304) 434-8000 Carnegie Class: Assoc/MT-VT-High Non
FAX Number: (304) 434-7000 Calendar System: Semester
URL: www.easternwv.edu
Established: 1999 Annual Undergrad Tuition & Fees (In-State): $3,060
Enrollment: 914 Coed
Affiliation or Control: State IRS Status: Exempt
Highest Offering: Associate Degree
Accreditation: NH, ADNUR

02 President ....Dr. Charles TERRELL
11 Exec Dean for Administrative Svcs ....Ms. Penny REARDON
05 Dean for Teaching & Learning ....Ms. Debra BACKUS
32 Dean of Student Access & Success ....Ms. Monica WILSON
20 Assoc Dean Academic & Student Svcs ....Ms. Sherry BECKER-GORBY
103 Assoc Dean Workforce Education ....Ms. Sherry WATTS
31 Dean of Community Engagement ....Ms. Briana LAVORGNA
04 Administrative Asst to President ....Ms. Michael O'LEARY

*Mountwest Community and Technical College (B)

1 Mountwest Way, Huntington WV 25701
County: Cabell FICE Identification: 040414
Unit ID: 444954
Telephone: (304) 710-3141 Carnegie Class: Assoc/HT-High Non
FAX Number: (304) 710-3187 Calendar System: Semester
URL: www.mctc.edu
Established: 1975 Annual Undergrad Tuition & Fees (In-District): $3,816
Enrollment: 2,026 Coed
Affiliation or Control: State/Local IRS Status: 501(c)3
Highest Offering: Associate Degree
Accreditation: NH, ACBSP, CAHIIM, COARC, EMT, MAC, PTAA

02 President ....Dr. Keith J. COTRONEO
05 Exec Vice Pres/Chief Academic Ofcr ....Dr. Harry R. FAULK
10 Vice Pres Finance/Business/CFO ....Mr. Daniel J. FIGLER
32 Vice President of Student Services ....Ms. Billie K. BROOKS
13 VP Operations/Info Technology ......Mrs. Terri L. TOMBLIN-BYRD
06 Registrar ....Ms. Angela ROSS

*New River Community and Technical College (C)

280 University Drive, Beaver WV 25813
County: Raleigh FICE Identification: 039603
Unit ID: 447582
Telephone: (304) 929-6703 Carnegie Class: Assoc/MT-VT-Mix Trad/Non
FAX Number: (304) 929-6719 Calendar System: Semester
URL: www.newriver.edu
Established: 2003 Annual Undergrad Tuition & Fees (In-State): $3,706
Enrollment: 1,957 Coed
Affiliation or Control: State IRS Status: 501(c)3
Highest Offering: Associate Degree
Accreditation: NH, EMT, #PTAA

02 President ....Dr. L. Marshall WASHINGTON
04 Exec Secretary to the President ....Ms. Lori A. MIDKIFF
05 Vice Pres Academic Affairs ....Vacant
11 Vice Pres Administrative Services ....Ms. Leah A. TAYLOR
13 Vice Pres Technology/Library Svcs ....Dr. David J. AYERSMAN
15 Director Human Resources ....Ms. Amanda L. BAKER
27 Chief Communications Officer ....Ms. Elizabeth M. BELCHER
12 Regional Director of Operations ....Ms. Jill HOLLIDAY
12 Regional Director of Operations ....Mr. Roger D. GRIFFITH
12 Regional Director of Operations ....Ms. Mary IGO
09 Int Dir of Institutional Research ....Mr. James M. FEDDERS
06 Registrar ....Ms. Janelle SCHOFIELD
08 Staff Librarian ....Mr. Robert H. COSTON
37 Director of Financial Aid ....Ms. Patricia HARMON
96 Director of Purchasing ....Ms. Twana JACKSON
10 Chief Financial Officer ....Ms. Heike I. SOEFFKER-CULICERTO
18 Director of Physical Plant ....Mr. Robert RUNION
26 Director of Public Relations ....Ms. Jenni CANTERBURY
84 Director of Enrollment Services ....Ms. Tracy L. EVANS
88 Dean of Transfer and Preprof ....Ms. Marianne LAYER

*Pierpont Community & Technical College (D)

1201 Locust Avenue, Fairmont WV 26554-2470
County: Marion FICE Identification: 040385
Unit ID: 443492
Telephone: (304) 367-4692 Carnegie Class: Assoc/HVT-Mix Trad/Non
FAX Number: (304) 367-4881 Calendar System: Semester
URL: www.pierpont.edu
Established: 1974 Annual Undergrad Tuition & Fees (In-State): $4,460
Enrollment: 2,311 Coed
Affiliation or Control: State IRS Status: 501(c)3
Highest Offering: Associate Degree
Accreditation: NH, ACFEI, CAHIIM, #COARC, EMT, MLTAD, NAIT, PTAA

02 President ....Vacant
10 VP for Finance and Administration ....Mr. Dale R. BRADLEY
05 Provost/VP for Academic Affairs ....Ms. Leslie LOVETT
86 VP for Organization and Development ....Mr. Stephen E. LEACH
13 VP Information Technology/CIO ....Mr. Rob LINGER
103 VP Workforce & Economic Development ..Mr. Paul SCHREFFLER
04 Exec Assistant to the President ....Ms. Cyndee SENSIBAUGH
50 Dean Sch of Business/Aviation/Tech ....Dr. Gerald BACZA
76 Dean School of Health Careers ....Dr. Rosemarie ROMESBURG
79 Dean School of Human Services ....Dr. Brian FLOYD

*Southern West Virginia Community and Technical College (E)

P. O. Box 2900, Mount Gay WV 25637-2900
County: Logan FICE Identification: 003816
Unit ID: 237817
Telephone: (304) 792-7098 Carnegie Class: Assoc/MT-VT-High Trad
FAX Number: (304) 792-7046 Calendar System: Semester
URL: www.southernwv.edu
Established: 1971 Annual Undergrad Tuition & Fees (In-State): $3,412
Enrollment: 1,859 Coed
Affiliation or Control: State IRS Status: 501(c)3
Highest Offering: Associate Degree
Accreditation: NH, ADNUR, COARC, EMT, MLTAD, RAD, SURGT

02 President ....Dr. Robert E. GUNTER
10 VP for Finance & Administration ....Mr. Samuel M. LITTERAL
05 VP Academic Affairs ....Dr. Jack D. DILBECK, SR.
103 VP Economic & Workforce Development .....Mr. Allyn S. BARKER
13 Chief Information Officer ....Mr. Gary HOLEMAN
30 Vice President for Development ....Mr. Ronald E. LEMON
15 Interim Human Resources Director ....Ms. Debbie C. DINGESS
04 Exec Asst to President & BOG ....Ms. Emma L. BAISDEN
09 Dir Institutional Effectiveness ....Vacant
12 Director Wyoming Campus Operations ....Mr. David LORD
12 Dir Williamson Campus Operations ....Ms. Rita G. ROBERSON
12 Director Logan Campus Operations ....Mr. Randy SKEENS
12 Director Boone Campus Operations ....Mr. William COOK
50 Division Head HealthCare & Business ....Mr. Steven HALL
88 Div Head Applied & Industrial Tech ....Mr. Guy LOWES, JR.
88 Div Head Soc Sci/Educ & Non-Trad ....Mr. Steven LACEK
88 Div Head University Transfer ....Ms. Melinda D. SAUNDERS
06 Interim Registrar ....Ms. Teri WELLS
37 Dir Student Financial Assistance ....Mr. August KAFER
08 Director of Libraries ....Ms. Kimberly L. MAYNARD
96 Director of Purchasing ....Vacant
84 Dir Enroll Mgmt/Stdnt Engagement ....Mr. Darrell TAYLOR
88 Public Relations Specialist ....Ms. Carol A. COLE
22 Dir Affirmative Action/EEO ....Ms. Debbie C. DINGESS
44 Director Annual or Planned Giving ....Mr. Ronald E. LEMON
26 Public Relations Specialist ....Ms. Carol COLE

*West Virginia Northern Community College (F)

1704 Market Street, Wheeling WV 26003-3643
County: Ohio FICE Identification: 009054
Unit ID: 238014
Telephone: (304) 233-5900 Carnegie Class: Assoc/MT-VT-Mix Trad/Non
FAX Number: (304) 232-4651 Calendar System: Semester
URL: www.wvncc.edu
Established: 1972 Annual Undergrad Tuition & Fees (In-State): $3,530
Enrollment: 1,923 Coed
Affiliation or Control: State IRS Status: 501(c)3
Highest Offering: Associate Degree
Accreditation: NH, ACFEI, ADNUR, CAHIIM, MAC, RAD, SURGT

02 President ....Dr. Vicki RILEY
05 Vice President Academic Affairs ....Dr. Carry DEATLEY
10 CFO & VP Administrative Services ....Mr. Jeff SAYRE
32 Vice President Student Services ....Mrs. Janet FIKE
31 Dean Community Relations ....Mr. Robert DEFRANCIS
18 Director of Facilities ....Mr. Jim BALLER
15 Chief Human Resource Officer ....Mrs. Peggy CARMICHAEL
12 Dean New Martinsville & Weirton ....Mr. Larry TACKETT
35 Director Student Union Activities ....Mrs. Shannon PAYTON
04 Administrative Asst to President ....Ms. Stephanie KAPPEL
06 Registrar ....Ms. Ashley MORAN

*New River Technical College Greenbrier Valley Campus (G)

101 Church Street, Lewisburg WV 24901-1303
Telephone: (304) 647-6560 Identification: 770468
Accreditation: &NH

† Regional accreditation is carried under the parent institution in Beaver, WV

*New River Technical College Mercer County Campus (H)

1397 Stafford Drive, Princeton WV 24740-8230
Telephone: (304) 818-2009 Identification: 770469
Accreditation: &NH

† Regional accreditation is carried under the parent institution in Beaver, WV

*New River Technical College Nicholas County Campus (I)

6101 Webster Road, Summersville WV 26651
Telephone: (304) 872-1236 Identification: 770470
Accreditation: &NH

† Regional accreditation is carried under the parent institution in Beaver, WV

*Southern West Virginia Community and Technical College-Boone/Lincoln Campus (J)

3505 Daniel Boone Parkway, Suite A, Foster WV 25608-8126
Telephone: (304) 369-2952 Identification: 770471
Accreditation: &NH

† Regional accreditation is carried under the parent institution in Mount Gay, WV

*Southern West Virginia Community and Technical College-Williamson Campus (K)

1601 Armory Drive, Williamson WV 25661
Telephone: (304) 235-6046 Identification: 770473
Accreditation: &NH

† Regional accreditation is carried under the parent institution in Mount Gay, WV

*Southern West Virginia Community and Technical College-Wyoming/McDowell Campus (L)

128 College Drive, Saulsville WV 25876
Telephone: (304) 294-8346 Identification: 770472
Accreditation: &NH

† Regional accreditation is carried under the parent institution in Mount Gay, WV

*West Virginia Northern Community College (M)

141 Main Street, New Martinsville WV 26155
Telephone: (304) 455-4684 Identification: 770474
Accreditation: &NH

† Regional accreditation is carried under the parent institution in Wheeling, WV

*West Virginia Northern Community College (N)

150 Park Avenue, Weirton WV 26062
Telephone: (304) 723-2210 Identification: 770475
Accreditation: &NH

---

*West Virginia Higher Education Policy Commission (O)

1018 Kanawha Boulevard E, Ste 700, Charleston WV 25301-2887
County: Kanawha FICE Identification: 033440
Unit ID: 237941
Telephone: (304) 558-2101 Carnegie Class: N/A
FAX Number: (304) 558-5719
URL: www.wvhepc.edu

01 Chancellor ....Dr. Paul L. HILL
88 Chancellor Community College ....Dr. Sarah TUCKER
88 Director of Science and Research ....Dr. Jan TAYLOR
26 Associate Vice Chancellor for Comm ....Ms. Jessica TICE
05 Vice Chancellor for Academic Affs ....Dr. Corley DENNISON
10 Vice Chancellor for Finance ....Dr. Edward MAGEE
32 Vice Chancellor for Student Affairs ....Dr. Adam GREEN
45 Vice Chancellor Policy and Planning ....Dr. Neal HOLLY
15 Vice Chancellor for Human Resources ....Ms. Trish CLAY
43 General Counsel ....Mr. Bruce R. WALKER
11 Exec Vice Chancellor Administration ....Mr. Matt TURNER
35 Dir Student/Educational Services ....Mr. Daniel E. CROCKETT
37 Senior Director of Financial Aid ....Mr. Brian WEINGART
88 Director Administrative Services ....Ms. Cindy L. ANDERSON

*Bluefield State College (P)

219 Rock Street, Bluefield WV 24701-2198
County: Mercer FICE Identification: 003809
Unit ID: 237215
Telephone: (304) 327-4000 Carnegie Class: Bac-Diverse
FAX Number: (304) 325-7747 Calendar System: Semester
URL: www.bluefieldstate.edu
Established: 1895 Annual Undergrad Tuition & Fees (In-State): $6,120
Enrollment: 1,563 Coed
Affiliation or Control: State IRS Status: 501(c)3
Highest Offering: Baccalaureate
Accreditation: NH, ACBSP, ADNUR, ENGT, NURSE, RAD, TED

02 President ....Dr. Marsha V. KROTSENG
05 Interim VP Academic Affs/Provost ....Dr. Angela LAMBERT
10 Vice Pres Financial/Admin Affairs ....Ms. Shelia JOHNSON

32 Vice President Student Affairs ....Dr. JoAnn ROBINSON
04 Dir Inst/Media Rels/Asst to Pres ....Mr. James A. NELSON
88 Executive Dir Title III ....Dr. Guy SIMS
06 Registrar ....Ms. Terry THOMPSON
08 Director Library Services ....Ms. Joanna THOMPSON
24 Interim Chief Technology Officer ....Mr. Tom G. COOK
13 Director of Computer Services ....Mr. Tom G. COOK
36 Director of Placement ....Vacant
07 Director of Admissions ....Vacant
37 Director of Financial Aid ....Mr. Thomas ILSE
15 Director of Human Resources ....Ms. Jonette AUGHENBAUGH
18 Admin Asst Senior of Physical Plant ....Ms. Diana GIBSON
19 Director Public Safety ....Mr. Jason BROOKS
09 Director of Institutional Research ....Dr. Tracey ANDERSON
38 Director of Counseling ....Dr. Cravor JONES
29 Director Alumni Affairs ....Ms. Deirdre GUYTON
40 Manager Bookstore ....Vacant
41 Athletic Director ....Mr. John LEWIS
50 Dean School of Business ....Vacant
49 Dean School of Arts and Sciences ....Dr. Martha EBORALL
54 Dean School of Eng Tech/Comp Sci ....Dr. Shannon BOWLING
53 Interim Dean School of Education .Dr. Shelia SARGENT-MARTIN
66 Dean School Nursing/Allied Health ....Ms. Angela LAMBERT
66 ADN Program Director ....Ms. Sandra WYNN
66 BSN Program Director ....Ms. Beth PRITCHETT
88 Program Dir of Radiologic Tech ....Ms. Melissa HAYE
61 Program Dir Criminal Justice ....Vacant
28 Asst to Pres Equity/Divers/Inclusn ....Dr. Guy SIMS
96 Director of Purchasing ....Mr. Paul RUTHERFORD
30 Director of Advancement/Planning ....Ms. Betty CARROLL

*Concord University (A)

PO Box 1000, Athens WV 24712-1000

County: Mercer FICE Identification: 003810
Unit ID: 237330
Telephone: (304) 384-3115 Carnegie Class: Masters/S
FAX Number: (304) 384-9044 Calendar System: Semester
URL: www.concord.edu
Established: 1872 Annual Undergrad Tuition & Fees (In-State): $6,902
Enrollment: 2,545 Coed
Affiliation or Control: State IRS Status: 501(c)3
Highest Offering: Master's
Accreditation: NH, CAATE, SW, TED

02 President ....Dr. Kendra BOGGESS
05 VP & Academic Dean ....Dr. Peter VISCUSI
30 VP for Advancement ....Mrs. Alicia BESENYEI
20 Associate Dean ....Dr. Cheryl BARNES
32 VP Student Affairs ....Dr. Marjie FLANIGAN
10 VP for Business & Finance ....Dr. Charles P. BECKER
11 VP of Administration ....Mr. Rick DILLON
13 VP of Information Technology ....Mr. Charles ELLIOTT
84 VP for Enrollment Management ....Mr. Greg KING
06 Registrar ....Mrs. Carolyn COX
08 Director of Libraries ....Mrs. Connie SHUMATE
37 Director of Student Financial Aid ....Mrs. Debra TURNER
29 Director of Alumni Relations ....Ms. Sarah TURNER
88 Director Bonner Scholars Program ....Mrs. Kathy BALL
15 Human Resources Director ....Mr. Daniel FITZPATRICK
18 Director Physical Plant ....Mr. Gerry VONVILLE
19 Director of Public Safety ....Chief Mark STELLA
36 Director of Career Services ....Vacant
38 Director of Counseling ....Mr. David BAILEY
40 Bookstore Manager ....Mr. Randy JONES
41 Athletic Director ....Mr. Kevin GARRETT
21 Financial Reporting Officer ....Ms. Elizabeth J. CAHILL
24 Ctr for Academic Technologies ....Mr. Steve MEADOWS
26 Public Relations/Mktg Specialist ....Mr. Lance MCDANIEL
25 Director of Grants and Contracts ....Mrs. Melanie FARMER
12 Director of the Beckley Center ....Dr. Susan WILLIAMS
96 Contract Specialist ....Mr. Gary HYLTON
88 Director of Retention ....Ms. Sarah BEASLEY
88 Administrative Secretary to Pres ....Mrs. Trena STOVALL
04 Executive Secretary to President ....Mrs. Lora WOOLWINE
102 Interim Director of the Foundation ....Mrs. Bren YEAGER
39 Director Student Housing ....Mr. Bill FRALEY

*Fairmont State University (B)

1201 Locust Avenue, Fairmont WV 26554-2470

County: Marion FICE Identification: 003812
Unit ID: 237367
Telephone: (304) 367-4000 Carnegie Class: Masters/S
FAX Number: (304) 367-4789 Calendar System: Semester
URL: www.fairmontstate.edu
Established: 1865 Annual Undergrad Tuition & Fees (In-State): $6,620
Enrollment: 4,035 Coed
Affiliation or Control: State IRS Status: 501(c)3
Highest Offering: Master's
Accreditation: NH, ACBSP, ADNUR, ENGR, ENGT, NURSE, TED

53 Dean School Educ/Hlth/Hum Perf ....Dr. Carolyn CRISLIP-TACY
02 President FSU ....Dr. Maria C. ROSE
05 Provost/VP Academic Affairs ....Dr. Christina M. LAVORATA
10 Vice Pres Admin & Fiscal Affairs ....Ms. Deborah STILES
13 VP/Chief Information Officer ....Mr. John LYMPANY
32 Vice Pres Student Services ....Dr. Timothy OXLEY
108 VP Inst Assessment & Effectiveness ....Dr. Timothy OXLEY
04 Executive Asst to the President ....Ms. Judith E. BIAFORE
20 Assoc Provost for Academic Affs ....Dr. Jack R. KIRBY
26 AVP University Communications ....Ms. Ann B. BOOTH
18 Asst Vice Pres for Facilities ....Mr. Tom T. TUCKER
15 AVP for Human Resources ....Mrs. Cynthia S. CURRY
06 Registrar ....Dr. Shayne GERVAIS
49 Dean College of Liberal Arts ....Dr Deanna J. SHIELDS
72 Dean College of Science/Tech ....Dr Donald E. TRISEL
50 Dean School of Business ....Dr Richard C. HARVEY
57 Int Dean School of Fine Arts ....Dr. Robert E. MILD
66 Dean School of Nursing ....Dr. Sharon BONI
07 Director of Admissions/Recruitment ....Ms. Amie M. FAZALARE
29 Director Alumni Relations ....Ms. Emily L. SWAIN
91 Dir of Applications Develop Svcs ....Mr Andy FAISOVICH
41 Director of Athletics ....Mr. Timothy A. MCNEELY
19 Dir of Emerg Mgmt/Chief of Police ....Mr Jack A. CLAYTON
38 Dir of Counseling and Disab Srvs ....Ms. Andrea M. PAMMER
37 Dir Financial Aid/Scholarships ....Ms. Tresa WEIMER
39 Director of Housing ....Ms. Alicia KALKA
08 Director of Library Services ....Ms. Thelma J. HUTCHINS
96 Director of Procurement ....Ms. Monica J. COCHRAN
27 Director of Public Relations ....Ms. Amy E. PELLEGRIN
36 Dir of Career Development Center ....Ms. Amy V. DRVAR
90 Director of Solutions Center ....Ms. Joanie FAISOVICH
23 Director of Student Health Services ....Ms. Trish WATSON

*Glenville State College (C)

200 High Street, Glenville WV 26351-1292

County: Gilmer FICE Identification: 003813
Unit ID: 237385
Telephone: (304) 462-7361 Carnegie Class: Bac-Diverse
FAX Number: (304) 462-7610 Calendar System: Semester
URL: www.glenville.edu
Established: 1872 Annual Undergrad Tuition & Fees (In-State): $7,032
Enrollment: 1,802 Coed
Affiliation or Control: State IRS Status: 501(c)3
Highest Offering: Baccalaureate
Accreditation: NH, TED

02 President ....Dr. Peter B. BARR
05 VP Academic Affairs ....Dr Milan C. VAVREK
10 Exec Vice Pres Business & Finance .Mr. Robert O. HARDMAN, II
26 SVP for Student/External Relations ....Mr. James W. SPEARS
30 VP Advancement/Exec Dir GSC Found ......Mr. Dennis J. POUNDS
04 Executive Assistant to President ....Ms. Teresa G. STERNS
53 Dean of Teacher Education ....Dr. Kevin G. CAIN
15 Chief Human Resources Officer ....Ms. Krystal D. SMITH
37 Director of Financial Aid ....Ms. Karen D. LAY
18 Exec Director of Physical Plant ....Mr Thomas R. RATLIFF
39 Director of Residence Life ....Mr. Jerry L. BURKHAMMER
41 Director of Athletics ....Mr. Marcal LAZENBY
23 Director Campus Health Services ....Ms. Ronda L. WILLIAMS
08 Director of Library ....Ms. Gail L. WESTBROOK
21 Controller ....Mr. Richard E. ACCORD
96 Director of Purchasing ....Ms. Joyce E. RIDDLE
29 Director of Alumni Affairs ....Ms. Debra A. NAGY
32 Director of Student Activities ....Ms. Jodi WALTERS
06 Registrar ....Ms. Ann M. REED
13 Manager of Database Admin ....Mr. Neal L. BENSON
36 Academic Support Counselor ....Mr. Bill LILLY
38 Professional Counselor ....Mr. Timothy J. UNDERWOOD
07 Int Director of Admissions ....Ms. Teresa G. STERNS
19 Associate Director of Public Safety ....Mr. Ronald K. TAYLOR

*Marshall University (D)

1 John Marshall Drive, Huntington WV 25755-0001

County: Cabell FICE Identification: 003815
Unit ID: 237525
Telephone: (304) 696-3170 Carnegie Class: Masters/L
FAX Number: (304) 696-6565 Calendar System: Semester
URL: www.marshall.edu
Established: 1837 Annual Undergrad Tuition & Fees (In-State): $6,814
Enrollment: 13,381 Coed
Affiliation or Control: State IRS Status: 501(c)3
Highest Offering: Doctorate
Accreditation: NH, ADNUR, ANEST, BUS, BUSA, CAATE, CAHIIM, CLPSY, COARC, CYTO, DIETD, DIETI, ENG, ENGR, FEPAC, JOUR, MED, MLTAD, MT, MUS, NUR, PHAR, PTA, SP, SW, TED

02 President ....Dr. Jerome A. GILBERT
05 Provost/Sr VP Academic Affairs ....Dr. Gayle L. ORMISTON
03 Sr VP Exec Affairs & Gen Counsel ....Mr. F. Layton COTTRILL
10 Sr VP Finance/CFO ....Ms. Mary Ellen HEUTON
26 Senior VP Communication/Marketing .....Ms. Virginia R. PAINTER
63 Dean of Medicine ....Dr. Joseph I. SHAPIRO
102 CEO MU Foundation Inc ....Dr. Ron AREA
11 Sr VP for Administration ....Ms. Brandi D. JACOBS
46 VP Research ....Mr. John MAHER
53 Dean College of Education ....Dr. Teresa EAGLE
29 Executive Director Alumni Relations ....Mr. Matthew D. HAYES
44 Vice President Development ....Mr. Lance WEST
28 Assoc VP Intercultural Affairs ....Mr Maurice R. COOLEY
13 Chief Technology Officer ....Mr. Allen TAYLOR
07 Dir Admission Undergrad/Grad Pgms ....Ms. Tammy JOHNSON
32 Dean Student Affairs ....Mr. Cedric GATHINGS
106 Asst VP for OnLine learning Lib/IT ....Ms. Monica BROOKS
58 Interim Dean Graduate College ....Dr. David FITTENGER
49 Dean College Liberal Arts ....Dr. Robert BOCKWALTER
50 Dean College of Business ....Dr. Haiyang CHEN
57 Dean College of Arts & Media ....Mr. Donald L. VAN HORN
67 Dean School of Pharmacy ....Dr Kevin W. YINGLING
66 Dean College of Health Prof ....Dr Michael PREWITT
54 Dean Col of Info Tech/Engr ....Dr. Wael ZATAR
81 Dean College of Science ....Dr. Charles SOMERVILLE
41 Director of Athletics ....Mr. Mike HAMRICK
06 Registrar ....Ms. Roberta FERGUSON
37 Director Student Financial Aid ....Ms. Kathy BIALK
36 Director Career Services ....Ms. Denise HOGSETT
15 Director Human Resource Services ....Mr. Bruce B. FELDER
19 Director of Public Safety ....Mr. James E. TERRY
96 Director of Purchasing ....Ms. Stephanie SMITH
18 Interim Director of Physical Plant ....Mr. Richard OSBURN
39 Director Residence Services ....Vacant
09 Asst to Pres/Sr VP Inst Rsch/Plng ......Mr. Michael J. MCGUFFEY
85 Dir Ctr for Intl Programs ....Vacant
22 Director Equity Programs ....Ms. Debra HART
88 Director Recruitment ....Ms. Elizabeth WOLFE
43 Assoc General Counsel ....Ms. Jendonnae HOUDYSCHELL
86 Asst to Pres for External Liaison ....Mr. William BURDETTE
88 Budget Director ....Mr. Mark ROBINSON

*Shepherd University (E)

PO Box 5000, Shepherdstown WV 25443-5000

County: Jefferson FICE Identification: 003822
Unit ID: 237792
Telephone: (304) 876-5000 Carnegie Class: Bac-A&S
FAX Number: (304) 876-3101 Calendar System: Semester
URL: www.shepherd.edu
Established: 1871 Annual Undergrad Tuition & Fees (In-State): $6,830
Enrollment: 4,041 Coed
Affiliation or Control: State IRS Status: 501(c)3
Highest Offering: Doctorate
Accreditation: NH, ART, IACBE, MUS, NRPA, NURSE, SW, TED

02 President ....Dr. Mary HENDRIX
05 Provost ....Dr. Christopher AMES
10 Vice President Finance ....Mr. Tony MAJOR
32 Vice President Student Affairs ....Dr. Thomas SEGAR
30 Vice Pres of University Advancement ....Mr. Chris SEDLOCK
84 Vice President Enrollment Mgmt ....Mr. Bill SOMMERS
43 General Counsel ....Mr. K. Alan PERDUE
100 Chief of Staff ....Vacant
11 Vice President Administration ....Mr. James VIGIL
35 Asst VP Stdnt Aff/Student Success ....Vacant
81 Dean Sch of Natural Sciences/Math ....Dr. Colleen NOLAN
79 Dean School of Arts & Humanities ....Mr. Dow BENEDICT
50 Dean Sch of Bus/Social Sciences ....Dr. Ann M. LEGREID
53 Dean Sch Educ/Profess Studies ....Dr. Virginia HICKS
58 AVPAA/Dean Grad Studies/Cont Educ ....Dr. Scott BEARD
88 Dean Teaching & Learning ....Dr. Laura RENNINGER
26 Exec Director Univ Communications ....Ms. Valerie OWENS
09 Director Institutional Research ....Ms. Sara MAENE
39 Director Residence Life ....Ms. Elizabeth SECHLER
21 Director of Finance ....Ms. Rebecca STOTTLEMEYER
35 Asst VP Student Aff/Student Engage ....Ms. Holly FRYE
15 Director Human Resources ....Dr. Marie DEWALT
13 Director Info Technology Services ....Mr. Joey DAGG
06 Registrar ....Ms. Tracy SEFFERS
07 Director of Admissions ....Ms. Kristen DESANTIS
37 Director of Financial Aid ....Ms. Joyce CABRAL
19 Univ Police Chief ....Mr. John MCAVOY
53 Director Teacher Education ....Dr. Douglas KENNARD
18 Director of Facilities ....Mr. Eric SHULER
41 Athletics Director ....Vacant
96 Director of Procurement Services ....Ms. Debra LANGFORD
38 Director Student Counseling ....Ms. Shanan SPENCER
29 Director Alumni Relations ....Ms. Alexis REED
92 Director Honors Program ....Dr. Mark CANTRELL
44 Director Annual Giving ....Vacant
104 Director Study Abroad ....Vacant
25 Dr of Grant Support/Corp/Found Rela ....Ms. Jessica KUMP
08 Dean Library ....Dr. David GANSZ
04 Admin Coord for the Pres ....Mrs. Sonya SHOLLEY

*West Liberty University (F)

208 University Drive, West Liberty WV 26074

County: Ohio FICE Identification: 003823
Unit ID: 237932
Telephone: (304) 336-5000 Carnegie Class: Bac-Diverse
FAX Number: (304) 336-8403 Calendar System: Semester
URL: www.westliberty.edu
Established: 1837 Annual Undergrad Tuition & Fees (In-State): $6,702
Enrollment: 2,694 Coed
Affiliation or Control: State IRS Status: 501(c)3
Highest Offering: Master's
Accreditation: NH, ARCPA, CAATE, DH, IACBE, MT, MUS, NURSE, SW, TED

02 President ....Dr. Stephen G. GREINER
05 Provost ....Dr. Brian L. CRAWFORD
43 Vice President & General Counsel ....Vacant
32 VP of Student Services/Registrar ....Mr. Scott A. COOK
10 Executive Vice President & CFO ....Ms. Stephanie HOOPER
81 Dean College of Sciences ....Dr. Robert KREISBERG
49 Interim Dean College Liberal Arts ....Dr. Tammy L. MCCLAIN
57 Interim Dean College Arts & Comm ....Dr. Matthew HARDER
53 Dean College of Education ....Dr. Keely O. CAMDEN
66 Dir of Nursing Programs ....Dr. Rose M. KUTLENIOS
50 Dean College of Business ....Dr. Michael TURRENTINE
35 Executive Director Student Services ....Ms. Marcella T. SNYDER
15 Chief Human Resources Officer ....Ms. Diana L. HARTO
13 Chief Technology Officer ....Mr. James T. CLARK
09 Dir of Inst Research & Assessment ....Ms. Paula J. TOMASIK
41 Director of Athletics ....Dr. Aaron C. HUFFMAN
07 Dir of Admissions & Recruitment ....Ms. Brenda M. KING
51 Director of Cont Educ/Special Pgm ....Vacant

08 Director of Library .... Ms. Cheryl R. HARSHMAN
29 Exec Dir of Alumni/Cmty Relations .... Mr. Ron A. WITT
37 Director Financial Aid .... Mrs. Katie R. COOPER
30 VP of Institutional Advancement .... Mr. Jason W. KOEGLER
109 Director of Auxiliary Services .... Vacant
18 Chief of Operations .... Mr. Patrick J. HENRY
38 Director of Counseling .... Ms. Bridgette DAWSON
92 Director of the Honors Program .... Dr. Shannon D. HALICKI
88 Director Dental Hygiene Programs .... Ms. Stephanie MEREDITH
88 Dir Clinical Lab Science Program .... Dr. William C. WAGENER
21 Associate Business Officer .... Vacant
23 Director of Health Services .... Ms. Cheryl C. BENNINGTON
88 Director Physican Assistant Program .... Dr. William A. CHILDERS, JR.
85 Coord International Student Rec .... Ms. Mihaela A. SZABO
26 Executive Director of Marketing .... Ms. Tammi SECRIST
101 Secretary of the Institution/Board .... Ms. Mary A. EDWARDS
104 Director Study Abroad .... Dr. Sannon HALICKI
105 Director Web Services .... Ms. Whitney M. INKSTER
106 Dir Online Education/E-learning .... Ms. Lucy KEFAUVER
19 Director Security/Safety .... Vacant
39 Director Housing & Residence Life .... Ms. Marcella T. SNYDER
96 Director of Purchasing .... Ms. Katrina A. HYDE
06 Registrar .... Mr. Scott A. COOK

*West Virginia School of Osteopathic Medicine (A)

400 N Lee Street, Lewisburg WV 24901-1196

County: Greenbrier FICE Identification: 011245
Unit ID: 237880

Telephone: (304) 645-6270 Carnegie Class: Spec-4-yr-Med
FAX Number: (304) 645-4859 Calendar System: Semester
URL: www.wvsom.edu
Established: 1972 Annual Graduate Tuition & Fees: N/A
Enrollment: 815 Coed
Affiliation or Control: State IRS Status: 501(c)3
Highest Offering: First Professional Degree; No Undergraduates
Accreditation: NH, OSTEO

02 President .... Dr. Michael D. ADELMAN
05 Vice Pres Academic Affairs & Dean .... Dr. Craig BOISVERT
10 Vice Pres Finance & Facilities .... Mr. Larry WARE
11 Vice Pres for Administration .... Dr. James W. NEMITZ
15 Associate VP of Human Resources .... Ms. Leslie BICKSLER
100 Associate VP Administrative Affairs .... Ms. Marilea BUTCHER
43 Vice Pres/General Counsel .... Mr. Jeffrey SHAWVER
04 Administrative Assistant Senior .... Ms. Marietta CHANEY
20 Assoc Dean Osteopathic Medical Educ ...... Dr. Robert W. FOSTER
20 Assoc Dean Graduate Med Education .... Dr. Victoria SHUMAN
20 Assoc Dean Preclinical Education .... Dr. Edward BRIDGES
20 Assoc Dean Predoctoral Clin Educ .... Dr. George BOXWELL
108 Assoc Dean Assessment/Educ Devel .... Dr. Machelle LINSENMEYER
20 Assoc Dean Affiliated/Spons Pgms .... Dr. Malcolm MODRZAKOWSKI
32 Assistant Dean Student Affairs .... Dr. Rebecca MORROW
88 Director of Clinical Evaluation Ctr .... Dr. Gail SWARM
88 Director National Boards Office .... Dr. Robert FISK
13 Director Information Technology .... Ms. Kimberly RANSOM
16 Human Resources Manager .... Ms. Tiffany BURNS
06 Registrar .... Ms. Jennifer SEAMS
37 Director Financial Aid .... Ms. Sharon L. HOWARD
30 Director Institutional Development .... Ms. Heather ANTOLINI
29 Director of Alumni Relations .... Ms. Shannon WARREN
07 Director of Admissions .... Ms. Patricia PERKINS
96 Director of Contracts .... Ms. Betty BAKER
08 Director of Library .... Ms. Mary ESSIG
26 Director of Marketing and PR .... Ms. Amy GOETZ
24 Director of Media Services .... Mr. Richard MCMAHAN
18 Director of Physical Plant II .... Mr. William ALDER
35 Program Administrator Senior .... Ms. Belinda EVANS
09 Coordinator Institutional Research .... Mr. Lance RIDPATH
40 Business Manager/Bookstore .... Ms. Cindi KNIGHT

*West Virginia State University (B)

PO Box 1000, Institute WV 25112-1000

County: Kanawha FICE Identification: 003826
Unit ID: 237899

Telephone: (304) 766-3000 Carnegie Class: Bac-A&S
FAX Number: (304) 720-2075 Calendar System: Semester
URL: www.wvstateu.edu
Established: 1891 Annual Undergrad Tuition & Fees (In-State): $6,662
Enrollment: 2,884 Coed
Affiliation or Control: State IRS Status: 501(c)3
Highest Offering: Master's
Accreditation: NH, ACBSP, SW, TED

02 President .... Dr. Anthony L. JENKINS
10 VP for Business and Finance .... Mr. Melvin JONES
05 Provost and VP for Academic Affairs .... Dr. Kumara JAYASURIYA
09 Coord Institutional Research .... Dr. Danny R. CANTRELL
32 Vice President for Student Affairs .... Ms. Katherine MCCARTHY
30 VP for University Advancement .... Ms. Patricia J. SCHUMANN
20 Assoc Provost & Assoc VP Acad Affs .... Dr. Scott WOODARD
35 Asst Vice Pres Student Affairs .... Mr. Joseph ODEN, JR.
26 Chief of Staff and VP for Leg Affs .... Mr. Thomas BENNETT, II
86 VP for Research & Public Service .... Dr. Orlando F. MCMEANS
79 Int Dean Col of Arts & Humanities .... Dr. Robert WALLACE
81 Int Dean Col of Natural Sci/Math .... Dr. Naveed ZAMAN
107 Dean Col of Prof Studies .... Dr. Paige CARNEY
50 Dean Col of Bus Admin/Soc Sci .... Dr. David BEJOU
27 Director of Public Relations .... Mr. Jack BAILEY
13 Director of Information Technology .... Mr. Alan SKIDMORE
09 Dir of Inst Research/Effective .... Ms. Vicky MORRIS-DUEER
18 Director Physical Facilities .... Mr. Marvin SMITH
06 Director Records & Registration .... Ms. Donna L. HUNTER
19 Director of Public Safety .... Chief Joseph SAUNDERS
21 Asst VP for Business & Finance .... Ms. Kristi WILLIAMS
08 Director of Drain-Jordan Library .... Dr. Willette STINSON
37 Director of Student Financial Asst .... Ms. JoAnn L. ROSS
29 Director of Alumni Relations .... Ms. Belinda FULLER
15 Director of Human Resources .... Ms. Joyce CHANEY
36 Dir of Career Services & Coop Educ .... Ms. Sandhya (Sandy) G. MAHARAJ
07 Director of Admissions .... Ms. Ashley WEIR
88 Director of New Student Programs .... Mrs. Sharon S. BANKS
96 Director of Purchasing .... Mrs. Janis A. BENNETT
106 Dir of Center for Online Learning .... Dr. Thomas KIDDIE
41 Athletic Director .... Mr. Nathan BURTON
04 Executive Asst to the President .... Ms. Crystal WALKER

*West Virginia University (C)

1500 University Avenue, Morgantown WV 26506-0002

County: Monongalia FICE Identification: 003827
Unit ID: 238032

Telephone: (304) 293-0111 Carnegie Class: DU-Highest
FAX Number: (304) 293-5883 Calendar System: Semester
URL: www.wvu.edu
Established: 1867 Annual Undergrad Tuition & Fees (In-State): $7,632
Enrollment: 29,175 Coed
Affiliation or Control: State IRS Status: 501(c)3
Highest Offering: Doctorate
Accreditation: NH, ART, AUD, BUS, BUSA, CAATE, CACREP, CLPSY, COPSY, CORE, CS, DENT, DH, DIETD, DIETI, DMS, ENG, ENGR, FEPAC, HT, IPSY, JOUR, LAW, LSAR, MED, MT, MUS, NMT, NURSE, OT, PA, PAST, PH, PHAR, PTA, RAD, RADMAG, RTT, SP, SPAA, SW, TED, THEA

02 President/Chief Exec Officer .... Mr. E. Gordon GEE
05 Provost & VP Acad Affairs .... Ms. Joyce MCCONNELL
10 Vice President for Admin & Finance ..... Mr. Narvel G. WEESE, JR.
26 Vice Pres for University Relations .... Ms. Sharon L. MARTIN
17 Vice Pres & Ex Dean of Hlth Sci .... Dr. Clay B. MARSH
32 Vice President Student Affairs .... Dr. William SCHAFER
46 Vice President for Research .... Mr. Fred L. KING
102 President & CEO WVU Found .... Ms. Cindi ROTH
15 VP for Human Resources .... Mr. Cris DEBORD
58 Vice Pres Health Sci Res/Grad Educ .... Dr. Glen DILLON
20 Sr Assoc Provost Academic Affairs .... Dr. Russell K. DEAN
20 Assoc Provost Academic Personnel .... Dr. Cecil B. WILSON
88 Director Research & Rural Health .... Ms. Jodie JACKSON
100 VP Fed Relations & Sr Advis to Pres .... Mr. John J. COLE
88 Exec Officer for Policy Development .... Dr. Jennifer L. FISHER
43 VP Legal Affairs/General Counsel .... Mr. Rob ALSOP
21 Assoc VP & Chief Financial Officer .... Ms. Paula R. CANGELIO
21 Sr Assoc Vice Pres for Finance .... Mr. Daniel A. DURBIN
56 Dean & Director of Extension Svcs .... Dr. Steve C. BONANNO
13 Assoc Provost IT/CIO .... Dr. John P. CAMPBELL
18 Sr Assoc VP Facilities & Svcs .... Mr. Randy HUDAK
35 Assoc Vice Pres Student Affairs .... Mr. Michael A. ELLINGTON
88 Asst VP Hlth Sci & Tech Academy .... Ms. Ann L. CHESTER
84 Assoc VP Enroll Mgmt Svcs .... Mr. Stephen LEE
45 Assoc Vice Pres Planning & Treasury .... Ms. Elizabeth P. REYNOLDS
86 Assoc VP State/Corporate Relations .... Ms. Sarah A. SMITH
25 Asst VP Office of Research Admin .... Mr. Alan B. MARTIN
09 Director of Institutional Research .... Dr. Nicolas VALCIK
39 Director Res Life/Dean of Students .... Ms. Trish CENDANA
41 Director Intercollegiate Athletics .... Mr. Shane LYONS
23 Director of Health Services .... Dr. Jan E. PALMER
27 Spec Asst VP Univ Relations .... Ms. Rebecca B. LOFSTEAD
29 Exec Director Alumni Association .... Mr. Sean FRISBEE
37 Director Financial Aid .... Ms. Sandra K. OERLY-BENNETT
07 Exec Director Admissions .... Dr. Stephen E. LEE
06 University Registrar .... Ms. Aimee PFEIFER
08 Dean of Library Services .... Jon E. CAWTHORNE
38 Asst VP Student Wellness .... Dr. Catherine A. YURA
21 Director Financial Services .... Ms. Lisa A. LIVELY
19 Chief of Police/Univ Police Dept .... Capt. Bob E. ROBERTS
96 Asst VP Procurement/Cont & Pay .... Mr. David BEAVER
88 Assoc VP Intl & Global Outreach .... Dr. David C. STEWART
50 Dean Business and Economics .... Dr. Javier REYES
49 Dean of Arts & Sciences .... Dr. Gregory DUNAWAY
57 Dean College Creative Arts .... Dr. Paul K. KREIDER
53 Dean Educ & Human Resources .... Dr. Gypsy DENZINE
61 Dean of Law .... Mr. Gregory W. BOWMAN
63 Executive Dean of Medicine .... Dr. Clay MARSH
52 Dean of Dentistry .... Dr. Tom BORGIA
54 Dean of Engr/Mineral Resources .... Dr. Eugene V. CILENTO
47 Dean of Agriculture & Forestry .... Dr. Daniel J. ROBISON
67 Dean of Pharmacy .... Dr. Patricia A. CHASE
60 Dean of College of Media .... Dr. Maryanne REED
68 Dean Physical Education .... Dr. Dana D. BROOKS
66 Dean of Nursing .... Dr. Tara HULSEY
92 Dean of Honors College .... Mr. Kenneth P. BLEMINGS
88 Assoc Provost UG Acad Affairs .... Dr. Susan D. DAY-PERROOTS
36 Director Career Services .... Mr. David L. DURHAM
88 Assoc Provost Intl Acad Affairs .... Dr. Michael LASTINGER
88 Campus Provost-WVUIT .... Dr. Nigel N. CLARK
88 Assoc Provost Grad Acad Affairs .... Dr. Katherine A. KARRAKER
35 Assoc VP & Dean of Students .... Mr. G. Corey FARRIS
28 VP Diversity Equity & Inclusion .... Mr. David M. FRYSON
105 Director Web Services .... Ms. Cathy ORNDORFF
106 Dir Online Education/E-learning .... Ms. Lucinda HART
88 Asst VP Strategic & Acad Com .... Dr. Ann CLAYCOMB
88 Asst VP Entrepreneurship & Innovat .... Ms. Melinda WALLS

*West Virginia University at Parkersburg (D)

300 Campus Drive, Parkersburg WV 26104-8647

County: Wood FICE Identification: 003828
Unit ID: 237686

Telephone: (304) 424-8000 Carnegie Class: Bac/Assoc-Mixed
FAX Number: (304) 424-8315 Calendar System: Semester
URL: www.wvup.edu
Established: 1961 Annual Undergrad Tuition & Fees (In-State): $3,216
Enrollment: 2,985 Coed
Affiliation or Control: State IRS Status: 501(c)3
Highest Offering: Baccalaureate
Accreditation: NH, ACBSP, ADNUR, NUR, SURGT, TED

02 President .... Dr. Fletcher LAMKIN
04 Executive Asst to the President .... Mr. Brady WHIPKEY
05 Sr Vice Pres of Academic Affairs .... Dr. Jane MILLEY
32 Vice President for Student Services .... Mr. Anthony UNDERWOOD
20 Dean for Academic Success .... Dr. Cinthia GISSY
103 Exec Dir Workforce/Community Educ .... Ms. Michele WILSON
10 Vice Pres Finance/Administration .... Ms. Alice HARRIS
26 Director Marketing/Communications .... Mrs. Katie WOOTTON
13 Chief Information Officer .... Mr. Doug ANTHONY
22 Special Asst to President .... Mrs. Debbie RICHARDS
12 Director Jackson County Center .... Mr. John GORRELL
102 Director of Development .... Ms. Senta GOUDY
18 Director Facilities & Services .... Mr. David WHITE
15 Director Human Resources .... Mr. Scott POE
09 Dir Inst Rsrch/Outcomes Assessment .... Mr. Jeremy STARKEY
06 Registrar .... Mrs. Leslie SIMS
07 Dean of Enrollment .... Mrs. Christine POST
37 Director of Financial Aid .... Mrs. Heather SKIDMORE
21 Director of Business Services .... Ms. Jeannine RATLIFFE
35 Director Student Activities .... Mr. Tom YENCHA
08 Director of Library .... Mr. Stephen HUPP
50 Chair Business/Economics/Math Div .... Dr. Larry MULLER
53 Chair Education/Humanities Division .... Dr. David LANCASTER
76 Chair Health Sciences Division .... Dr. Rose BEEBE
83 Chair Social Science/Languages Div .... Mrs. Kim KORCMAROS
72 Chair Science/Technology Division .... Mr. Jared GUMP

*Marshall University-South Charleston Campus (E)

100 Angus E Peyton Drive, South Charleston WV 25303

Telephone: (304) 746-2500 Identification: 770467
Accreditation: &NH

† Regional accreditation is carried under the parent institution in Huntington, WV

*Potomac State College of West Virginia University (F)

101 Fort Avenue, Keyser WV 26726

Telephone: (304) 788-6800 FICE Identification: 003829
Accreditation: &NH

† Regional accreditation is carried under the parent institution in Morgantown, WV

*West Virginia University Institute of Technology (G)

405 Fayette Pike, Montgomery WV 25136-2436

Telephone: (304) 442-1000 FICE Identification: 003825
Accreditation: &NH, CS, ENG, ENGT

† Regional accreditation is carried under the parent institution in Morgantown, WV

West Virginia Junior College (H)

1000 Virginia Street East, Charleston WV 25301-2817

County: Kanawha FICE Identification: 010573
Unit ID: 237987

Telephone: (304) 345-2820 Carnegie Class: Assoc/HVT-High Non
FAX Number: (304) 345-1425 Calendar System: Quarter
URL: www.wvjc.edu
Established: 1892 Annual Undergrad Tuition & Fees: $12,625
Enrollment: 162 Coed
Affiliation or Control: Proprietary IRS Status: Proprietary
Highest Offering: Associate Degree
Accreditation: ACICS

01 Campus President .... Mr. Chad T. CALLEN

West Virginia Junior College (I)

148 Willey Street, Morgantown WV 26505-5596

County: Monongalia FICE Identification: 005007
Unit ID: 237996

Telephone: (304) 296-8282 Carnegie Class: Assoc/HVT-Mix Trad/Non
FAX Number: (304) 581-6990 Calendar System: Quarter
URL: www.wvjc.edu
Established: 1922 Annual Undergrad Tuition & Fees: $13,090
Enrollment: 373 Coed
Affiliation or Control: Proprietary IRS Status: Proprietary

Highest Offering: Associate Degree
Accreditation: ACICS

01 President & CEO .... Mr. Chad CALLEN
05 Academic Director .... Ms. Brittany NUZZO
36 Career Services .... Ms. Samantha ESPOSITO
37 Financial Aid Director .... Ms. Patricia CALLEN

West Virginia Junior College-Bridgeport (A)

176 Thompson Drive, Bridgeport WV 26330
Telephone: (304) 842-4007 Identification: 770823
Accreditation: ACICS

West Virginia Wesleyan College (B)

59 College Avenue, Buckhannon WV 26201-2699
County: Upshur FICE Identification: 003830
Unit ID: 237969
Telephone: (304) 473-8000 Carnegie Class: Masters/S
FAX Number: N/A Calendar System: Semester
URL: www.wvwc.edu
Established: 1890 Annual Undergrad Tuition & Fees: $28,792
Enrollment: 1,511 Coed
Affiliation or Control: United Methodist IRS Status: 501(c)3
Highest Offering: Master's
Accreditation: NH, #CAATE, MUS, NUR, TED

01 President .... Dr. Pamela BALCH
05 VP Academic Affairs & Dean of Col .... Dr. Boyd CREASMAN
10 VP Administration & Finance .... Dr. Barry PRITTS
32 VP Student Affairs .... Vacant
84 VP Enrollment Management .... Mr. John WALTZ
30 VP Advancement .... Mr. Robert SKINNER
42 Dean of the Chapel .... Rev. Christopher SCOTT
102 Director Foundation/Govt Relations .... Ms. Nicki BENTLEY-COLTHART
11 Director of Administrative Services .... Mr. Robert KIMBLE
37 Director Financial Aid .... Ms. Susan GEORGE
29 Assoc VP Adv & Alumni Relations .... Mr. William ARMISTEAD
08 Director of Library Services .... Ms. Paula MCGREW
06 Dir Acad & Career Svcs/Registrar .... Ms. Alice CREASMAN
39 Director Campus Life & Housing .... Ms. Alisa LIVELY
09 Director of Institutional Research .... Ms. Tammy CRITES
15 Director of Human Resources .... Ms. Vickie CROWDER
18 Director of the Physical Plant .... Mr. Kenneth ANDREW
30 Director Advancement Operations .... Ms. Rose Ellen LOUDIN
88 Director of Learning Center .... Dr. Shawn KUBA
41 Director of Athletics .... Mr. Randall TENNEY
21 Controller .... Mr. Randall CRITES
40 Retail Store Manager .... Ms. Bethaney MCKISIC
92 Director Honors Program .... Mr. Douglas VAN GUNDY
93 Director Multicultural Programs .... Mr. Robert QUARLES
44 Planned Giving Coordinator .... Rev. David PETERS
38 Director of Counseling Services .... Ms. Lori THOMPSON
31 Dir of Leadership Development .... Ms. LeeAnn BROWN
13 Director of Computing Services .... Mr. Neil ROTH
23 Director of Health Services .... Ms. Angela MAHAFFEY
04 Administrative Asst to President .... Ms. Deborah K. MULLENS
19 Director of Security .... Mr. David PARKS
43 Dir Legal Services/General Counsel .... Mr. David W. MCCAULEY
101 Secretary of the Institution/Board .... Mrs. Deborah K. MULLENS
36 Director of Career Services .... Mrs. Barbara MORRISSETTE

Wheeling Jesuit University (C)

316 Washington Avenue, Wheeling WV 26003-6295
County: Ohio FICE Identification: 003831
Unit ID: 238078
Telephone: (304) 243-2000 Carnegie Class: Masters/M
FAX Number: (304) 243-2243 Calendar System: Semester
URL: www.wju.edu
Established: 1954 Annual Undergrad Tuition & Fees: $28,030
Enrollment: 1,575 Coed
Affiliation or Control: Roman Catholic IRS Status: 501(c)3
Highest Offering: Doctorate
Accreditation: NH, ACBSP, CAATE, COARC, NURSE, PTA, TEAC

01 President .... Rev. James FLEMING, SJ
03 Executive Vice President & Counsel .... Mr. George JOSEPH
05 Chief Academic Officer .... Dr. Robert PHILLIPS
10 Chief Financial Officer/VP Admin .... Mr. Gene P. GRILLI
88 VP for Mission & Ministry .... Fr. William RICKLE, SJ
15 Dir of HR/Assoc VP Administration .... Mr. Don KAMINSKI
32 Interim Dean of Student Development .... Fr. William RICKLE, SJ
58 Dean Graduate & Professional Stds .... Mr. Chris PETROSINO
13 Assoc VP for Info Tech Services .... Mr. Daniel T. FEELEY
37 Director Financial Aid .... Ms. Christie L. TOMCZYK
06 Registrar .... Mr. Wilson TURNER
08 Librarian .... Ms. Kelly MUMMERT
91 Systems Administrator .... Mr. Richard M. KLEMPA
42 Director of Campus Ministry .... Mr. Jamey BROGAN
41 Athletic Director .... Mr. Kevin FORDE
18 Director of Physical Plant .... Mr. Frank P. CONNELLY
85 Intl Admissions Representative .... Ms. Jasmin ILOVAR
04 Administrative Asst to President .... Ms. Mary Jo HABURSKY
100 Chief of Staff .... Mr. Mark PHILLIPS
102 Dir Foundation/Corporate Relations .... Ms. Jasmine LO
105 Director Web Services .... Mr. Christopher KREGER
106 Dir Online Education/E-learning .... Mr. D. Jason FRITZMAN
19 Director Security/Safety .... Mr. Stephen HABURSKY
29 Director Alumni Relations .... Ms. Kelly KLUBERT
38 Director Student Counseling .... Mr. Paul BELLOTTE
07 Dean of Undergraduate Admissions .... Mr. Dustin JARRETT
44 Director Annual Giving .... Mr. Noah MULL

WISCONSIN

Alverno College (D)

3400 S 43rd Street, Box 343922,
Milwaukee WI 53234-3922
County: Milwaukee FICE Identification: 003832
Unit ID: 238193
Telephone: (414) 382-6000 Carnegie Class: Masters/M
FAX Number: (414) 382-6066 Calendar System: Semester
URL: www.alverno.edu
Established: 1887 Annual Undergrad Tuition & Fees: $25,660
Enrollment: 2,389 Female
Affiliation or Control: Independent Non-Profit IRS Status: 501(c)3
Highest Offering: Master's
Accreditation: NH, MUS, NURSE

01 President .... Dr. Andrea J. LEE, IHM
10 Sr Vice Pres Finance & Mgmt Svcs .... Mr. James OPPERMANN
05 Sr Vice Pres Academic Affairs .... Vacant
30 Vice President College Advancement .... Ms. Julie QUINLAN BRAME
20 Exec Director Academic Services .... Sr. Marlene NEISES
84 VP for Enrollment Services .... Ms. Kate LUNDEEN
32 Assoc VP/Dean of Students .... Dr. Wendy POWERS
07 Director of Admissions .... Vacant
20 Vice President for Student Success .... Dr. Kathy LAKE
20 Associate Vice President Academic .... Dr. Jeanna ABROMEIT
06 Registrar .... Ms. Patricia HARTMANN
08 Director Library .... Mr. Larry DUERR
36 Director Career Development .... Ms. Joanna PATTERSON
13 Exec Dir Information Technology .... Ms. Anita EIKENS
37 Dir Student Financial Plng .... Ms. Amy CHRISTEN
29 Director Alumnae Relations .... Ms. Kim MUENCH
38 Director Advising .... Ms. Kate TISCH
51 Dir Institute Educational Outreach .... Ms. Judith REISETTER-HART
15 Director Human Resources .... Ms. Mary CASEY
41 Director of Athletics .... Mr. Brad DUCKWORTH
42 Campus Minister .... Ms. Connie POPP
96 Purchasing Agent .... Ms. Anne MCCARRON
09 Director of Institutional Research .... Dr. Glen ROGERS
14 Chief Information Officer .... Mr. Jim HILBY
50 Dean School of Business .... Dr. Eileen SHERMAN
66 Interim Dean School of Nursing .... Ms. Margaret RAUSCHENBERGER
53 Interim Dean of School of Education .... Dr. Patricia LUEBKE
49 Dean School of Arts & Sciences .... Dr. Kevin CASEY
50 Director Master of Business Admin .... Dr. Patricia JENSEN
79 Assoc Dean Humanities Division .... Dr. John SAVAGIAN
81 Asc Dean Natl Science/Math/Tech Div .... Dr. Angela FREY
83 Assoc Dean Behavioral Sciences Div .... Dr. Julie ULLMAN
72 Assoc Dean Comm & Tech Div .... Dr. Jennifer MIKULAY
57 Assoc Dean Arts Div .... Dr. Kat GILBERT
28 Sp Asst to VP Acad Affs/Multclt Iss .... Vacant
04 Director of Presidential Operations .... Ms. Jill DESMOND
101 Executive Assistant .... Ms. Melissa KALLENBERGER
18 Chief Facilities/Physical Plant .... Mr. John MARKS
19 Director Security/Safety .... Lt. Michelle ENGEL

The Art Institute of Wisconsin (E)

320 East Buffalo Street, Suite 100, Milwaukee WI 53202
Telephone: (877) 285-4234 Identification: 770824
Accreditation: #ACICS

† School is in teach-out plan.

Bellin College, Inc. (F)

3201 Eaton Road, Green Bay WI 54311
County: Brown FICE Identification: 006639
Unit ID: 238324
Telephone: (920) 433-6699 Carnegie Class: Spec-4-yr-Other Health
FAX Number: (920) 433-1923 Calendar System: Semester
URL: www.bellincollege.edu
Established: 1909 Annual Undergrad Tuition & Fees: $20,500
Enrollment: 351 Coed
Affiliation or Control: Independent Non-Profit IRS Status: 501(c)3
Highest Offering: Master's
Accreditation: NH, NURSE, RAD

01 President & CEO of the College .... Dr. Connie J. BOERST
10 Vice President Business & Finance .... Mrs. Ginger B. KRUMMEN SCHRAVEN
66 Dean of Nursing .... Dr. Stephanie M. STEWART
76 Dean of Allied Health Sciences .... Mr. Mark A. BAKE
32 Dean of Student Services .... Dr. Nancy M. BURRUSS
30 Vice President Development & PR .... Mr. Matt G. RENTMEESTER
13 Director of Technology .... Mr. Travis A. SMITH
06 Registrar .... Mr. Russell J. LEARY
37 Director Financial Aid .... Ms. Lena C. GOODMAN
84 Director of Enrollment Mgmt .... Mrs. Kathryn WALL
04 Administrative Asst to President .... Ms. Jamie L. CAMPBELL
08 Head Librarian .... Ms. Cindy M. REINL

Beloit College (G)

700 College Street, Beloit WI 53511-5595
County: Rock FICE Identification: 003835
Unit ID: 238333
Telephone: (608) 363-2000 Carnegie Class: Bac-A&S
FAX Number: (608) 363-2717 Calendar System: Semester
URL: www.beloit.edu
Established: 1846 Annual Undergrad Tuition & Fees: $45,050
Enrollment: 1,303 Coed
Affiliation or Control: Independent Non-Profit IRS Status: 501(c)3
Highest Offering: Baccalaureate
Accreditation: NH

01 President .... Dr. Scott BIERMAN
05 Provost .... Dr. Ann DAVIES
100 Chief of Staff .... Mr. Daniel J. SCHOOFF
45 VP Budget & Planning .... Vacant
30 VP Development & Alumni Relations .... Ms. Beth MONTEIRO
15 VP Human Resources and Operations .... Ms. Lori RHEAD
84 VP Enrollment .... Dr. Robert MIRABILE
32 Dean of Students .... Dr. Christina KLAWITTER
13 Chief Information Officer .... Vacant
26 Chief Comm & Integ Mktg Officer .... Vacant
108 Dir Strategic Research & Assessment .... Ms. Ellie O'BYRNE
09 Dir Strategic Research & Planning .... Ms. Ruth VATER
06 Registrar .... Ms. Mary BOROS-KAZAI
07 Director of Admissions .... Mr. Patrick WALSH
07 Director of Intl Admissions .... Ms. Erin GUTH
18 Director of Facilities .... Mr. Karl WILLIAMS
29 Exec Dir of Dev & Alumni Engage .... Mr. Mark C. WOLD
39 Director Resident Life/Conferences .... Mr. John F. WINKELMANN
36 Director of Career Development .... Ms. Jessica FOX-WILSON
38 College Counselor .... Vacant
37 Director of Financial Aid .... Ms. Michelle CURTIS
28 Sr Dir Acad Diversity & Inclusion .... Ms. Nicole TRUESDELL
41 Athletic Director .... Mr. Tim SCHMIECHEN
40 Bookstore Director .... Mr. Peter FRONK

Bryant & Stratton College (H)

310 W Wisconsin Avenue, Suite 500 E,
Milwaukee WI 53203
Telephone: (414) 276-5200 FICE Identification: 005009
Accreditation: &M, ADNUR, MAC

† Regional accreditation is carried under the parent institution (corporate office) in Buffalo, NY.

Cardinal Stritch University (I)

6801 N Yates Road, Milwaukee WI 53217-3985
County: Milwaukee FICE Identification: 003837
Unit ID: 238430
Telephone: (414) 410-4000 Carnegie Class: DU-Mod
FAX Number: (414) 410-4239 Calendar System: Semester
URL: www.stritch.edu
Established: 1937 Annual Undergrad Tuition & Fees: $27,540
Enrollment: 3,811 Coed
Affiliation or Control: Roman Catholic IRS Status: 501(c)3
Highest Offering: Doctorate
Accreditation: NH, ACBSP, NUR, NURSE, TED

01 President .... Dr. James P. LOFTUS
00 Chancellor .... Vacant
04 Exec Assistant to the President .... Ms. Kathryn HOWELL
05 Provost & VP Academic Affairs .... Dr. Jeffrey D. SENESE
30 Vice President for Univ Advancement .... Dr. Robert J. BUCKLA
10 Vice President Business & Finance .... Vacant
84 Vice President Enrollment Services .... Mr. Allan M. MITCHLER
13 Chief Information Officer .... Mr. David W. WEINBERG-KINSEY
66 Dean College Nursing/Health Science .... Dr. Kelly J. DRIES
50 Dean College of Business & Mgmt .... Dr. Phillip T. ANDERSON
53 Dean College of Education & Ldrship .... Dr. Freda R. RUSSELL
49 Dean College of Arts & Sciences .... Dr. Daniel J. SCHOLZ
41 Director of Athletics .... Dr. Tim M. VAN ALSTINE
15 Director of Human Resources/Payroll .... Mr. Michael D. HOFFMAN
06 Registrar .... Ms. Kristin A. HILDEBRANDT
21 Bursar .... Ms. Lisa M. LEWIN
37 Dir of Financial Aid .... Mr. Mark W. QUISTORF
21 Dir Treasury & Risk Management .... Mr. Scott A. HELLRUNG
20 Director of Academic Affairs .... Ms. Kristin A. HILDEBRANDT
32 Sr Director Student Success .... Ms. Tracy A. FISCHER
88 Dir of Mission Engagement .... Mr. Sean T. LANSING
32 Dean of Students .... Ms. Donney MORONEY
36 Career Education .... Mr. Tom E. KIPP
38 Dir for Counseling/Mental Wellness .... Vacant
104 Coord International Education .... Ms. Sarah R. SWEENEY
09 Dir of Institutional Effectiveness .... Mr. William L. MARCOU
91 Director of Enterprise Systems .... Ms. Susan L. INGLES
08 Director of University Library .... Ms. Laurie G. SWARTWOUT
102 Exec Dir Corporate & Foundation Rel .... Ms. Tonya M. MANTILLA
44 Director Major Gifts/Planned Giving .... Ms. Lisa M. HANDLER
26 Sr Dir Media Relations Adv Comm .... Ms. Mary M. REINKE
29 Dir Alumni Relations/Annual Giving .... Ms. Corrine M. ANSHUS
18 Director of Facilities .... Mr. John B. GLYNN
19 Director of Security .... Mr. Andrew DE RUBERTIS

Carroll University (J)

100 N East Avenue, Waukesha WI 53186-5593
County: Waukesha FICE Identification: 003838
Unit ID: 238458
Telephone: (262) 547-1211 Carnegie Class: Masters/S
FAX Number: (262) 524-7646 Calendar System: Semester
URL: www.carrollu.edu
Established: 1846 Annual Undergrad Tuition & Fees: $29,535
Enrollment: 3,446 Coed
Affiliation or Control: Presbyterian Church (U.S.A.) IRS Status: 501(c)3

Highest Offering: Doctorate
Accreditation: NH, ARCPA, CAATE, NURSE, PTA

01 President .... Dr. Doug N. HASTAD
05 Provost .... Dr. Joanne PASSARO
10 Vice President for Finance .... Mr. Ron LOSTETTER
84 Vice President for Enrollment .... Mr. James V. WISEMAN
30 Vice President for Advancement .... Mr. Stephen KUHN
32 Vice President Student Affairs .... Dr. Theresa BARRY
06 Registrar .... Ms. Ann HANDFORD
21 Controller .... Ms. Deidre ERWIN
26 Dir of Communications/Marketing .... Ms. Jeannine SHERMAN
15 Director of Human Resources .... Ms. Lorraine FORCINITO
08 Interim Library Director .... Ms. Brittany LARSON
37 Director of Student Financial Svcs .... Ms. Dawn M. SCOTT
41 Athletic Director .... Mr. Joe BAKER
88 Assoc Director of Part-Time Studies .... Ms. Linda SKLANDER
28 Director of Cultural Diversity .... Ms. Nicole DAVIS
29 Director Alumni Relations .... Ms. Dolores M. BROWN
96 Director of Purchasing .... Ms. Char RICHARDS
07 Director of Admissions .... Ms. Kelly J. HEIMAN
18 Chief Facilities/Physical Plant .... Mr. Alan PESCHL
38 Director Student Counseling .... Ms. Angie R. BRANNAN
04 Exec Assistant to the President .... Ms. Gina M. EHLER

Carthage College (A)

2001 Alford Park Drive, Kenosha WI 53140-1994
County: Kenosha | FICE Identification: 003839
Unit ID: 238476
Telephone: (262) 551-8500 | Carnegie Class: Bac-A&S
FAX Number: (262) 551-6208 | Calendar System: 4/1/4
URL: www.carthage.edu
Established: 1847 | Annual Undergrad Tuition & Fees: $38,375
Enrollment: 2,948 | Coed
Affiliation or Control: Evangelical Lutheran Church In America
IRS Status: 501(c)3
Highest Offering: Master's
Accreditation: NH, CAATE, MUS, SW

01 President .... Dr. Gregory S. WOODWARD
100 Executive Director .... Ms. Karen HOWELL
05 Provost/VP Academic Affairs .... Dr. David GARCIA
88 Chief Investment Officer .... Mr. William R. ABT
10 Chief Financial Officer .... Mr. Randy BARFIELD
30 VP for Institutional Advancement .... Ms. Evelyn BUCHANAN
26 VP for Communications .... Ms. Molly POLK
84 VP for Enrollment .... Mr. Nick MULVEY
32 Dean of Students/VP Student Life .... Dr. Kimberlie GOLDSBERRY
101 Secretary to the Board .... Mr. Paul HEGLAND
100 Chief of Staff/VP Strategic Init .... Mr. Thomas KLINE

College of Menominee Nation (B)

PO Box 1179, Keshena WI 54135-1179
County: Menominee | FICE Identification: 031251
Unit ID: 413617
Telephone: (800) 567-2344 | Carnegie Class: Tribal
FAX Number: (715) 799-1336 | Calendar System: Semester
URL: www.menominee.edu
Established: 1992 | Annual Undergrad Tuition & Fees: $6,200
Enrollment: 560 | Coed
Affiliation or Control: Tribal Control | IRS Status: 501(c)3
Highest Offering: Baccalaureate
Accreditation: NH, ADNUR

01 Interim President .... Dr. Diana MORRIS
05 Chief Academic Officer .... Dr. Diana MORRIS
10 Comptroller .... Mr. Mwata CHISHA
12 Int Vice Pres CMN Green Bay Campus .... Ms. Kathy DENOR
26 Dean External Relations .... Vacant
32 Dean of Student Services .... Ms. Nicole FISH
49 Dean of Letters & Science .... Dr. Chad WAUKECHON
66 Dean of Nursing .... Ms. Karen BIALCIK
75 Dean of Technical Education .... Vacant
51 Dean of Continuing Education .... Mr. Brian BOWALKOWSKI
04 Assistant to the President .... Ms. Melinda COOK
09 Director Institutional Research .... Vacant
30 Director Advancement .... Ms. Irene KIEFER
25 Director of Sponsored Programs .... Mrs. Jill MARTIN
13 IT Director .... Vacant
18 Director of Operations .... Vacant
21 Business Manager .... Vacant
15 Human Resources Director .... Ms. Rachel RICE-TUMA
06 Registrar/Bursar .... Ms. Geraldine SANAPAW
07 Int Admissions/Financial Aid Mgr .... Ms. Crystal LEPSCIER
29 Dir Alumni Relations/Development .... Ms. Susan WAUKAU
88 Vocational Rehab Director .... Ms. Myrna WARRINGTON
08 Library Director .... Ms. Maria ESCALANTE
40 Director of Bookstore .... Vacant

College of Menominee Nation Oneida Campus (C)

2733 S Ridge Road, Green Bay WI 54304
Telephone: (920) 965-0070 | Identification: 770424
Accreditation: &NH

† Regional accreditation is carried under the parent institution in Keshena, WI

Columbia College of Nursing (D)

4425 N Port Washington Rd, Milwaukee WI 53212-1099
County: Milwaukee | FICE Identification: 006640
Unit ID: 238573
Telephone: (414) 326-2330 | Carnegie Class: Spec-4-yr-Other Health
FAX Number: (414) 236-2331 | Calendar System: Semester
URL: www.ccon.edu
Established: 1901 | Annual Undergrad Tuition & Fees: N/A
Enrollment: 151 | Coed
Affiliation or Control: Independent Non-Profit | IRS Status: 501(c)3
Highest Offering: Master's
Accreditation: NH, NURSE

01 President & Dean .... Dr. Jill M. BERG
10 Chief Financial/Business Officer .... Ms. Christina ITALIANO
05 Associate Dean of Academic Affairs .... Ms. Heather VARTANIAN
04 Exec Assistant to the President .... Ms. Gail PETERSON
37 Director Student Financial Aid .... Ms. Wendy HILVO
24 Director Educational Media .... Mr. Keith JACKSON
07 Admissions Specialist .... Mr. Tyler LORENZ

Concordia University Wisconsin (E)

12800 N Lake Shore Drive, Mequon WI 53097-2402
County: Ozaukee | FICE Identification: 003842
Unit ID: 238616
Telephone: (262) 243-5700 | Carnegie Class: Masters/L
FAX Number: (262) 243-4351 | Calendar System: 4/1/4
URL: www.cuw.edu
Established: 1881 | Annual Undergrad Tuition & Fees: $27,100
Enrollment: 8,161 | Coed
Affiliation or Control: Lutheran Church - Missouri Synod
IRS Status: 501(c)3
Highest Offering: Doctorate
Accreditation: NH, #ARCPA, CAATE, DMS, IACBE, MAC, NURSE, OT, PHAR, PTA, SW

01 President .... Rev Dr. Patrick T. FERRY
11 Executive VP & Chief Oper Ofcr .... Mr. Allen J. PROCHNOW
05 Senior VP of Academics .... Dr. William R. CARIO
07 Senior VP of Enrollment Services .... Mr. Kenneth K. GASCHK
88 Senior VP Unviersity Affairs .... Ms. Gretchen M. JAMESON
30 VP of Advancement .... Rev Dr. Roy PETERSON
10 VP Finance & CFO .... Ms. Joan M. SCHOLZ
13 VP of Information Technology .... Mr. Thomas G. PHILLIP
26 VP of Integrated Marketing .... Ms. Anita R. CLARK
32 VP of Student Life .... Mr. Steven P. TAYLOR
20 Asst VP Academics/Cont & Dist Ed .... Dr. Bernard D. BULL
20 Asst VP Academics Faculty Dev .... Dr. Leah M. DVORAK
20 Asst VP Academics/Student Success .... Dr. Elizabeth A. POLZIN
88 Asst VP Advancement .... Mr. Andrew G. LOCKE
27 Asst VP Strategic Communications .... Ms. Lisa LILJEGREN
42 Campus Pastor .... Rev. Steven N. SMITH
88 Chair Faculty Senate .... Dr. Robert S. BURLAGE
49 Dean School Arts/Sciences .... Dr. Steven R. MONTREAL
50 Dean School of Business .... Dr. Daniel S. SEM
53 Dean School of Education .... Dr. Michael D. UDEN
76 Dean School of Health Professions .... Dr. Linda M. SAMUEL
66 Dean School of Nursing .... Dr. Sharon L. CHAPPY
67 Dean School of Pharmacy .... Dr. Dean L. ARNESON
32 Dean of Students .... Dr. Steven W. GERNER
06 Registrar .... Dr. Carl R. BUTZ
29 Director of Alumni Relations .... Ms. Michelle L. WAGNER
41 Director of Athletics .... Dr. Rob M. BARNHILL
42 Director Campus Ministry .... Dcn. Kim C. BUELTMANN
19 Director Campus Safety .... Mr. Mario VALDES
38 Director of Counseling .... Mr. David T. ENTERS
36 Director of Career Services .... Mr. Ben B. ROHDE
37 Director of Financial Aid .... Mr. Robert J. NOWAK
15 Director Human Resources .... Ms. Hilary F. VATTER
09 Director of Institutional Research .... Dr. Tamara R. FERRY
24 Director Instructional Technology .... Mr. Sean B. YOUNG
08 Director of Library Services .... Mr. Christian R. HIMSEL
39 Director of Residence Life .... Ms. Beckie KRUSE
88 Exec Director - Centers & Acceler .... Ms. Rochelle R. REGENAUER
51 Exec Director Cont & Dist Ed .... Ms. Sarah A. PECOR
85 Exec Director International Educ .... Rev Dr. David C. BIRNER
18 Superintendent Buildings & Grounds .... Mr. Steven V. HIBBARD
40 Bookstore Manager .... Ms. Kia LOR

Edgewood College (F)

1000 Edgewood College Drive, Madison WI 53711-1997
County: Dane | FICE Identification: 003848
Unit ID: 238661
Telephone: (608) 663-4861 | Carnegie Class: DU-Mod
FAX Number: (608) 663-3291 | Calendar System: Semester
URL: www.edgewood.edu
Established: 1927 | Annual Undergrad Tuition & Fees: $26,550
Enrollment: 2,980 | Coed
Affiliation or Control: Roman Catholic | IRS Status: 501(c)3
Highest Offering: Doctorate
Accreditation: NH, ACBSP, #MFCD, NURSE

01 President .... Dr. Scott FLANAGAN
05 VP Academic Affs/Academic Dean .... Dr. Dean PRIBBENOW
32 VP Student Devel/Dean of Students .... Dr. Tony CHAMBERS
10 VP Business & Finance .... Mr. Michael GUNS
84 VP Enrollment Mgmt .... Ms. Christine BENEDICT
88 VP Dominican Life & Mission .... Sr. Maggie HOPKINS, OP
30 VP Inst Advancement .... Mr. Gary KLEIN
20 Associate Academic Dean .... Dr. Kelley GRORUD
49 Dean School of Arts & Sciences .... Dr. John FIELDS
50 Dean School of Business .... Dr. Stevie WATSON
53 Dean School of Education .... Dr. Timothy SLEKAR
71 Dean School of Integrative Studies .... Dr. Kristine MICKELSON
66 Dean School of Nursing .... Dr. Margaret NOREUIL
07 Director Freshman Admissions .... Mr. Derek JOHNSON
13 Director Information Technology .... Mr. Deron KLING
09 Director Inst Assessment & Research .... Dr. Edward J. KEELEY
06 Registrar .... Ms. Michelle KELLEY
106 Director Online Learning .... Dr. Karen FRANKER
08 Library Director .... Dr. Sylvia CONTRERAS
36 Director Career Education .... Ms. Shawn JOHNSON
29 Alumni Director .... Ms. Cassie WICKERSHAM
26 Director Marketing & Communication .... Mr. Edward TAYLOR
15 Director Human Resources .... Ms. Pamela LAVALLIERE
18 Director Facilities & Operations .... Ms. Susan VANDERSANDEN
38 Director Personal Counseling Svcs .... Dr. Megan COBB
21 Controller .... Ms. Jane WILHELM
28 Director Diversity & Inclusion .... Mr. Tony GARCIA
37 Director Student Financial Aid .... Ms. Kari GRIBBLE
23 Director Student Health Services .... Ms. Kimberly MORELAND
41 Director Athletics .... Mr. Al BRISACK

George Williams College of Aurora University (G)

350 Constance Boulevard, Williams Bay WI 53191
Telephone: (262) 245-5531 | Identification: 770066
Accreditation: &NH

† Regional accreditation is carried under the parent institution in Aurora, IL

Globe University-Appleton (H)

5045 West Grande Market Drive, Grande Chute WI 54914
Telephone: (920) 364-1100 | Identification: 770800
Accreditation: ACICS, MAAB

† Branch campus of Globe University, Woodbury, MN

Globe University-Eau Claire (I)

4955 Bullis Farm Road, Eau Claire WI 54702
Telephone: (715) 855-6600 | Identification: 770801
Accreditation: ACICS, MAAB

† Branch campus of Globe University, Woodbury, MN

Globe University-La Crosse (J)

2651 Midwest Drive, Third FL, Onalaska WI 54650
Telephone: (608) 779-2600 | Identification: 770803
Accreditation: ACICS, MAAB

† Branch campus of Globe University, Woodbury, MN

Globe University-Madison East (K)

4901 Eastpark Boulevard, Madison WI 53718
Telephone: (608) 216-9400 | Identification: 770804
Accreditation: ACICS, MAAB

† Branch campus of Globe University, Woodbury, MN

Globe University-Wausau (L)

1480 County Road XX, Rothschild WI 54474
Telephone: (715) 301-1300 | Identification: 770806
Accreditation: ACICS, MAAB

† Branch campus of Globe University, Woodbury, MN

Herzing University (M)

5218 E Terrace Drive, Madison WI 53718-8340
County: Dane | FICE Identification: 009621
Unit ID: 240392
Telephone: (608) 249-6611 | Carnegie Class: Masters/M
FAX Number: (608) 249-8593 | Calendar System: Semester
URL: www.herzing.edu
Established: 1965 | Annual Undergrad Tuition & Fees: $13,090
Enrollment: 2,649 | Coed
Affiliation or Control: Independent Non-Profit | IRS Status: 501(c)3
Highest Offering: Master's
Accreditation: NH, ADNUR, IACBE, NURSE

01 President .... Ms. Renee HERZING
12 Campus President .... Mr. William VINSON
10 CFO & Vice President of Finance .... Mr. Robert HERZOG
05 Academic Dean .... Ms. Christine HOOVER
37 Educational Funding Manager .... Mr. Clayton GROTH
32 Director of Student Services/Regist .... Ms. Amy HERFEL
07 Director of Admissions .... Mr. Nile MCKIBBEN
36 Director of Career Development .... Mr. Jeff WESTRA

Herzing University Brookfield Campus (N)

555 South Executive Drive, Brookfield WI 53005
Telephone: (262) 649-1710 | Identification: 770429
Accreditation: &NH, NURSE, @PTAA

† Regional accreditation is carried under the parent institution in Madison, WI

Herzing University Kenosha Campus (A)

4006 Washington Road, Kenosha WI 53144
Telephone: (262) 671-0675 Identification: 770430
Accreditation: &NH, MAAB, NURSE

† Regional accreditation is carried under the parent institution in Madison, WI

Herzing University Online (B)

W140N8917 Lilly Road, Menomonee Falls WI 53051
Telephone: (866) 508-0748 Identification: 770431
Accreditation: &NH, CAHIIM, MAAB

† Regional accreditation is carried under the parent institution in Madison, WI

Lac Courte Oreilles Ojibwa Community College (C)

13466 W Trepania Road, Hayward WI 54843-2181
County: Sawyer FICE Identification: 025322
Unit ID: 260372
Telephone: (715) 634-4790 Carnegie Class: Tribal
FAX Number: (715) 634-5049 Calendar System: Semester
URL: www.lco.edu
Established: 1982 Annual Undergrad Tuition & Fees: $4,590
Enrollment: 352 Coed
Affiliation or Control: Tribal Control IRS Status: 501(c)3
Highest Offering: Associate Degree
Accreditation: #NH

01 President .... Dr. Diane VERTIN
05 VP of Academic & Student Affairs .... Ms. Barb LUNDBERG
11 Vice President of Admin Services .... Ms. Rita MUELLER
10 Chief Financial Officer .... Ms. Jill MATCHETT
51 Dean of Continuing Education .... Ms. Amber MARLOW
09 Director of Institutional Research .... Mr. Tyler TURPIN
32 Dean of Student Svcs & Enrollment .... Ms. Karen BREIT
20 Interim Academic Dean .... Ms. Gerralynne BERG
108 Director of Assessment/Accred .... Mr. Tom ANTELL
25 Office of Sponsored Programs Dir .... Mr. Dan GRETZ
37 Financial Aid Director .... Ms. Kelly QUARDERER

Lakeland College (D)

PO Box 359, Sheboygan WI 53082-0359
County: Sheboygan FICE Identification: 003854
Unit ID: 238980
Telephone: (920) 565-1000 Carnegie Class: Masters/L
FAX Number: (920) 565-1060 Calendar System: Semester
URL: www.lakeland.edu
Established: 1862 Annual Undergrad Tuition & Fees: $25,050
Enrollment: 3,973 Coed
Affiliation or Control: United Church Of Christ IRS Status: 501(c)3
Highest Offering: Master's
Accreditation: NH, TEAC

01 President .... Mr. Dan W. ECK
04 Assistant to the President .... Ms. Ann M. FLAD-JESION
05 Provost/Dean of College .... Dr. Margaret L. ALBRINCK
30 Vice President for Advancement .... Ms. Beth BORGEN
84 Vice Pres Enrollment Management .... Mr. Zach R. VOELZ
10 VP/Chief Financial Officer .... Mrs. Carole ROBERTSON
06 Registrar .... Ms. Jacquelyn MORGAN
07 Senior Dir Recruitment/Admissions .... Ms. Kristen ENGELS
103 Director of Career Development .... Mrs. Jessica LAMBRECHT
09 Director of Institutional Research .... Mr. Paul WHITE
32 Chief of Student Affairs .... Mr. Eric BLACKNALL
08 Director of Library Services .... Ms. Ann K. PENKE
37 Director of Financial Aid .... Ms. Patty L. TAYLOR
26 Director of Communications .... Mr. David D. GALLIANETTI
21 Controller .... Ms. Sharon L. ROOB
29 Dir Alumni & Church Relations .... Ms. Linda BOSMAN
15 Director of Human Resources .... Mr. Peter G. PLATTEN
41 Director of Athletics .... Ms. April ARVAN
18 Dir Facilities/Mgmt & Planning .... Mr. Rich N. HAEN
38 Director of Student Counselling .... Dr. Carey A. KNIER
19 Director Security/Safety .... Mr. David SIMON
39 Director of Residence Life .... Mr. Jim BAJCZYK
105 Director of Web Services .... Mr. Eric LAROSE

Lawrence University (E)

711 E. Boldt Way, Appleton WI 54911
County: Outagamie FICE Identification: 003856
Unit ID: 239017
Telephone: (920) 832-7000 Carnegie Class: Bac-A&S
FAX Number: (920) 832-6978 Calendar System: Other
URL: www.lawrence.edu
Established: 1847 Annual Undergrad Tuition & Fees: $43,740
Enrollment: 1,511 Coed
Affiliation or Control: Independent Non-Profit IRS Status: 501(c)3
Highest Offering: Baccalaureate
Accreditation: NH, MUS

01 President .... Mr. Mark BURSTEIN
04 Executive Asst to the President .... Ms. Alice BOECKERS
05 Provost and Dean of the Faculty .... Dr. David BURROWS
10 VP Finance & Administration .... Mr. Christopher LEE
30 VP Development/Alumni Rels .... Mr. Calvin D. HUSMANN
32 VP Student Affairs & Dean .... Ms. Nancy D. TRUESDELL
29 VP Alumni/Constituency Engagement .... Mr. Mark D. BRESEMAN
26 Assoc Vice Pres Communications .... Mr. Craig L. GAGNON
44 Campaign Dir/Principal Gifts Ofcr .... Ms. Kristen M. PIEKEMSON
30 Assoc Vice Pres Development .... Ms. Stacy J. MARA
21 Controller .... Ms. Amy PRICE
64 Dean Conservatory of Music .... Mr. Brian G. PERTL
36 Dean of Career Services .... Ms. Mary T. MEANY
35 Dean Student Academic Services .... Vacant
20 Associate Dean of the Faculty .... Dr. Robert F. WILLIAMS
28 Asst Dean Students Multicul Affs .... Ms. Pa Lee MOUA
09 Director of Research Administration .... Ms. Kristin L. MCKINLEY
07 Dean of Admissions & Financial Aid .... Mr. Kenneth L. ANSELMENT
37 Director of Financial Aid .... Ms. Sara C. HOLMAN
06 Registrar .... Ms. Anne S. NORMAN
08 Librarian .... Mr. Peter J. GILBERT
41 Athletic Director .... Ms. Christyn ABARAY
13 Director Information Tech Svcs .... Mr. Steven M. ARMSTRONG
15 Director of Human Resources .... Ms. Rochelle L. BLINDAUER
18 Director of Facility Services .... Mr. Daniel R. MEYER
38 Assoc Dean Stdnts Health/Wellness .... Mr. Scott W. RADTKE

Madison Media Institute-College of Media Arts (F)

2702 Agriculture Drive, Madison WI 53718-6787
County: Dane FICE Identification: 010913
Unit ID: 364168
Telephone: (800) 236-4997 Carnegie Class: Spec-4-yr-Other Tech
FAX Number: (608) 442-0141 Calendar System: Semester
URL: www.mediainstitute.edu
Established: 1969 Annual Undergrad Tuition & Fees: $18,690
Enrollment: 372 Coed
Affiliation or Control: Proprietary IRS Status: Proprietary
Highest Offering: Baccalaureate
Accreditation: ACICS

01 President .... Mr. Mike BAILEY
10 Controller .... Mr. Kert SHEPLER
07 Admissions Director .... Ms. Susan ARRAY
05 Acting Academic Dean .... Mr. Mike BAILEY
36 Director Student Placement .... Ms. Susan ARRAY

Maranatha Baptist University (G)

745 West Main Street, Watertown WI 53094-7600
County: Jefferson FICE Identification: 023172
Unit ID: 239071
Telephone: (920) 261-9300 Carnegie Class: Bac-Diverse
FAX Number: (920) 261-9109 Calendar System: Semester
URL: www.mbu.edu
Established: 1968 Annual Undergrad Tuition & Fees: $13,940
Enrollment: 1,064 Coed
Affiliation or Control: Independent Non-Profit IRS Status: 501(c)3
Highest Offering: Doctorate
Accreditation: NH, NURSE

01 President .... Dr. Martin MARRIOTT
03 Executive Vice President .... Dr. Matthew DAVIS
05 Vice President for Academic Affairs .... Dr. William LICHT
30 Vice President for Inst Advancement .... Dr. Jim H. HARRISON
10 Vice President for Business Affairs .... Dr. Mark W. STEVENS
32 Dean of Students .... Dr. John DAVIS
06 Registrar .... Mr. Steve CARLSON
07 Director of Admissions .... Dr. Jim H. HARRISON
30 Director of Development .... Mr. Steve BOARD
09 Director of Institutional Research .... Mr. Jonathan COLEMAN
15 Director Personnel Services .... Mr. Curt OBERHOLTZER
26 Chief Public Relations Officer .... Mr. Peter WRIGHT
41 Athletic Director .... Mr. Robert THOMPSON
08 Librarian .... Mr. Mark HANSON
35 Director Student Affairs .... Mr. David ANDERSON
29 Director Alumni Relations .... Dr. John DAVIS
37 Director Student Financial Aid .... Mr. Randy HIBBS
13 Chief Info Technology Officer (CIO) .... Dr. Werner LUMM
19 Director Security/Safety .... Mr. Timothy JOHNS
106 Dir Online Education/E-learning .... Dr. Werner LUMM
108 Director Institutional Assessment .... Mr. Jonathan COLEMAN
105 Director Web Services .... Mr. Peter WRIGHT
18 Chief Facilities/Physical Plant .... Dr. Werner LUMM
50 Director School of Business .... Mr. Tracy FOSTER
53 Director School of Education .... Mr. David HANDYSIDE

Marian University (H)

45 S National Avenue, Fond Du Lac WI 54935-4699
County: Fond Du Lac FICE Identification: 003861
Unit ID: 239080
Telephone: (920) 923-7600 Carnegie Class: Masters/M
FAX Number: (920) 923-7154 Calendar System: Semester
URL: www.marianuniversity.edu
Established: 1936 Annual Undergrad Tuition & Fees: $27,210
Enrollment: 2,130 Coed
Affiliation or Control: Roman Catholic IRS Status: 501(c)3
Highest Offering: Doctorate
Accreditation: NH, IACBE, NURSE, RAD, SW, TED

01 President .... Dr. Andrew P. MANION
05 VP Academic Affairs .... Dr. Russell K. MAYER
10 VP Business & Finance .... Ms. Janeen M. MEIFERT
84 VP Enrollment Management .... Ms. Stacey L. AKEY
32 VP for Student Engagement .... Ms. Kate CANDEE
30 Senior VP for University Relations .... Dr. George E. KOONCE, JR.
44 Vice Pres Advancement .... Ms. Tracy L. MILKOWSKI
04 Executive Assistant to President .... Ms. Carey C. GARDIN
45 Interim VP Inst Effectiveness .... Dr. Julie A. LUETSCHWAGER
53 Dean School of Education .... Dr. Kelly A. CHANEY
66 Dean Nursing/Health Prof .... Dr. Linda K. MATHESON
49 Dean Arts/Sciences .... Dr. Michelle MAJEWSKIE
50 Dean Business/Public Safety .... Dr. Jeffrey G. REED
35 Dean of Student Engagement .... Dr. Paul KRIKAU
08 Director of Libraries .... Ms. Kathryn A. JOHNSTON
18 General Manager/Facilities .... Mr. Artie L. GOLD
06 Registrar .... Ms. Cheryl A. TEICHMILLER
09 Director of Institutional Research .... Mr. Thomas P. RICHTER
37 Director of Financial Aid .... Ms. Pamela WARREN
42 Director of Campus Ministry .... Sr. Marie SCOTT, CSA
26 Director University Relations .... Ms. Tracy QUALMANN
29 Director Alumni Relations .... Ms. Mary ENDRIES
07 Dean of Admission .... Ms. Shannon S. LALUZERNE
15 Director of Human Resources .... Ms. Amanda L. DUVAL
41 Director of Athletics .... Mr. Jason BARTELT
88 Dean Advising/Academic Services .... Ms. Cathy M. MATHWEG
23 Director of Health Services .... Ms. Jodi S. SCHRAUTH
36 Director of Career Services .... Ms. Mary J. HATLEN
109 Director of Campus Dining Services .... Ms. Nikki A. KRAMER
13 Director of Information Technology .... Dr. Daniel C. PARIZO
40 Director of Bookstore .... Ms. Mary MANGAN-FLOOD
38 Director of Counseling .... Vacant
92 Director Honors Program .... Dr. Mathew P. SZROMBA
108 Director of Inst Assessment .... Dr. Moreen K. CARVAN
39 Director of Student Services .... Ms. Dee HARMSEN
104 Coordinator of Study Abroad .... Ms. Andelys BOLANOS
19 Director Security/Safety .... Mr. Matt D. ROSE

Marquette University (I)

PO Box 1881, Milwaukee WI 53201-1881
County: Milwaukee FICE Identification: 003863
Unit ID: 239105
Telephone: (414) 288-7700 Carnegie Class: DU-Higher
FAX Number: (414) 288-3300 Calendar System: Semester
URL: www.marquette.edu
Established: 1881 Annual Undergrad Tuition & Fees: $37,170
Enrollment: 11,745 Coed
Affiliation or Control: Roman Catholic IRS Status: 501(c)3
Highest Offering: Doctorate
Accreditation: NH, ARCPA, BUS, BUSA, CAATE, CACREP, CLPSY, COPSY, DENT, ENG, LAW, MIDWF, MT, NURSE, PTA, SP, THEA

01 President .... Dr. Michael R. LOVELL
05 Provost .... Dr. Daniel J. MYERS
31 Vice President Public Affairs .... Ms. Rana H. ALTENBURG
43 Vice President and General Counsel .... Ms. Cynthia M. BAUER
15 Vice President Human Resources .... Mr. Octavio CASTRO
32 Vice President Student Affairs .... Dr. Xavier A. COLE
09 Vice Pres Research and Innovation .... Dr. Jeanne M. HOSSENLOPP
10 Vice President Finance .... Mr. John C. LAMB
42 Interim Vice Pres Mission Ministry .... Rev. Edward MATHIE, SJ
20 Senior Vice Prov Faculty Affairs .... Dr. Gary MEYER
26 Vice Pres Marketing & Communication .... Mr. David MURPHY
41 Vice Pres and Director of Athletics .... Mr. Bill SCHOLL
30 Vice Pres University Advancement .... Mr. Michael VANDERHOEF
84 Vice Provost Enrollment Management .... Dr. John BAWOROWSKY
88 Vice Prov Strategic & Academic Plan .... Vacant
88 Vice Provost Academic Affairs .... Dr. John J. SU
06 Registrar .... Ms. Georgia D. MCRAE
07 Interim Dean of Admissions .... Ms. Jean BURKE
76 Dean of Health Sciences .... Dr. William CULLINAN
60 Dean of Communication .... Dr. Kimo AH YUN
53 Dean of Education .... Dr. William A. HENK
49 Dean of Arts & Sciences .... Dr. Richard C. HOLZ
61 Dean of the Law School .... Mr. Joseph D. KEARNEY
52 Dean of Dentistry .... Dr. William K. LOBB
66 Interim Dean of Nursing .... Dr. Donna MCCARTHY
54 Dean of Engineering .... Dr. Kristina ROPELLA
50 Dean of Business Administration .... Dr. Brian D. TILL
08 Dean of Libraries .... Ms. Janice WELBURN
58 Dean of Graduate School .... Dr. Douglas WOODS
101 Assistant to Pres/Corp Secretary .... Mr. Steven W. FRIEDER
13 Chief Information Officer .... Ms. Kathy J. LANG
35 Dean of Students .... Dr. Stephanie QUADE
28 Exec Director Diversity & Inclusion .... Dr. William WELBURN
88 Assoc Vice Prov Acad Support Pgm .... Ms. Anne D. DEAHL
90 Assoc Vice Provost Educational Tech .... Mr. G. Jon PRAY
88 Senior Director of Development .... Mr. Timothy RIPPINGER
21 Senior Assoc Vice President Finance .... Ms. Mary Lou AUSTIN
45 Assoc VP Finance/Univ Architect .... Ms. Lora STRIGENS
35 Assistant Vice Pres Student Affairs .... Dr. Jeff JANZ
39 Exec Dir Housing and Residence Life .... Ms. Mary JANZ
25 Exec Dir Research & Sponsored Prog .... Ms. Katherine DURBEN
23 Exec Dir University Medical Clinic .... Dr. Carolyn S. SMITH
36 Director Career Services Center .... Ms. Laura F. KESTNER-RICKETTS
38 Director of Counseling Center .... Dr. Michael J. ZEBROWSKI
18 Dir Facilities & Campus Services .... Mr. Gregory ADAMS
37 Director of Financial Aid .... Ms. Susan M. TEERINK
104 Dir International Education Office .... Mr. Terence MILLER
40 Director Marquette Spirit Shop .... Mr. James K. GRAEBERT
29 Engagement Director .... Mr. Daniel DEWEERDT
19 Chief of Police .... Mr. Paul MASCARI
96 Director of Purchasing .... Ms. Jenny ALEXANDER

Medical College of Wisconsin (A)

PO Box 26509, Milwaukee WI 53226-0509
County: Milwaukee FICE Identification: 024535
Unit ID: 239169
Telephone: (414) 955-8296 Carnegie Class: Spec-4-yr-Med
FAX Number: (414) 955-6560 Calendar System: Other
URL: www.mcw.edu
Established: 1893 Annual Graduate Tuition & Fees: N/A
Enrollment: 1,209 Coed
Affiliation or Control: Independent Non-Profit IRS Status: 501(c)3
Highest Offering: Doctorate; No Undergraduates
Accreditation: NH, AA, DENT, MED, PDPSY, PH

01 President & CEO ... Dr. John R. RAYMOND, SR.
03 Dean/Executive Vice President ... Dr. Joseph E. KERSCHNER
04 Administrative Asst to President ... MS. Cheryl A. DYER
05 VP Academic Outreach ... Dr. Cheryl A. MAURANA
10 Sr Vice Pres Finance/Administration ... Mr. Christopher KOPS
88 Dean Grad Sch Biomedical Science ... Dr. Ravi P. MISRA
30 Vice Pres of Development ... Ms. Alice ARCHABAL
15 Vice President Human Resources ... Ms. Sherri DUCHARME-WHITE
86 Vice Pres Government/Community Affs ... Ms. Kathryn A. KUHN
28 VP Corporate Compliance Risk Mgmt ... Mr. Daniel WICKEHAM
27 VP Comm/Experience & Brand Mgmt ... Ms. Mara LORD
26 Sr Assoc Vice Pres Communications .. Mr. Richard N. KATSCHKE
20 Sr Assoc Dean for Academic Affs ... Dr. William J. HUESTON
22 Sr Asc Dean Faculty Affs/Diversity ... Dr. Alonzo P. WALKER
32 Assoc Dean Student Affs & Diversity ... Dr. Dawn S. BRAGG
63 Sr Assoc Dean Graduate Med Educ ... Dr. Kenneth B. SIMONS
46 Director Neuroscience Research Ctr ... Dr. Cecilia J. HILLARD
20 Associate Dean Curriculum ... Dr. Travis WEBB
21 Director Budget ... Vacant
13 Director Application Development ... Ms. Rebecca L. MORRISON
08 Director Medical Libraries ... Vacant
07 Interim Director Admissions ... Ms. Alexis MEYER
06 Registrar ... Ms. Kerry GROSSE
18 Sr Dir Campus Operations ... Mr. Jeffrey BORNEMANN
37 Director Student Financial Services ... Ms. Linda L. PASCHAL
25 Director Grants & Contracts ... Ms. April HAVERTY
29 Exec Director Alumni Relations ... Mr. Seth M. FLYNN
21 Director Business Services ... Vacant
40 Manager of Bookstore ... Ms. Cathy GRANFIELD
19 Director Public Safety ... Mr. David C. FELLER
43 General Counsel ... Mr. John NEWSOME
10 Chief Financial Officer ... Vacant
67 Dean School of Pharmacy ... Dr. George MACKINNON
25 Contract Administrator ... Mr. Jeffrey WOJNOWSKI
45 Sr Assoc Dean for Research ... Dr. Ann NATTINGER

Midwest College of Oriental Medicine (B)

6232 Bankers Road, Racine WI 53403-9747
County: Racine FICE Identification: 030612
Unit ID: 383020
Telephone: (800) 593-2320 Carnegie Class: Spec-4-yr-Other Health
FAX Number: (262) 554-7475 Calendar System: Quarter
URL: www.acupuncture.edu
Established: 1979 Annual Undergrad Tuition & Fees: N/A
Enrollment: 93 Coed
Affiliation or Control: Proprietary IRS Status: Proprietary
Highest Offering: Master's; No Lower Division
Accreditation: ACUP

01 President ... Dr. William J. DUNBAR
05 Director of Academics ... Dr. Robert CHELNICK
12 Evanston Campus Director ... Dr. Kristine L. LA POINT
37 Director of Financial Aid ... Ms. Elizabeth M. HOJAN
07 Admissions Coord/Transfer Credit ... Mr. Lawrence PILOCZEWSKI
06 Records Officer/Registrar ... Ms. Amy L. BENISH
08 Dean of Students/Librarian ... Mr. John BALLARINI
32 Dean of Students ... Ms. Olga GAJDOSIK
09 Research Director ... Mr. Jin Hua XIE
85 Dean of Foreign Students ... Dr. Duckin SUH
108 Clinic Tracking/Inst Evaluation ... Ms. Deirdre M. DUNBAR
91 Information Systems ... Mr. William H. LEHMAN
26 Marketing/Student Affairs ... Mr. Chris A. KRAJNIAK
88 Office Manager ... Ms. Stephanie M. PITTMAN

Milwaukee Career College (C)

3077 North Maryfair Road, Suite 300,
Milwaukee WI 53222
County: Milwaukee FICE Identification: 041174
Unit ID: 449861
Telephone: (800) 754-1009 Carnegie Class: Not Classified
FAX Number: (414) 727-9557 Calendar System: Other
URL: www.mkecc.edu
Established: 2002 Annual Undergrad Tuition & Fees: N/A
Enrollment: 92 Coed
Affiliation or Control: Proprietary IRS Status: Proprietary
Highest Offering: Associate Degree
Accreditation: ABHES

01 President ... Jack TAKAHASHI

Milwaukee Institute of Art & Design (D)

273 E Erie Street, Milwaukee WI 53202-6003
County: Milwaukee FICE Identification: 020771
Unit ID: 239309
Telephone: (414) 847-3200 Carnegie Class: Spec-4-yr-Arts
FAX Number: (414) 291-8077 Calendar System: Semester
URL: www.miad.edu
Established: 1974 Annual Undergrad Tuition & Fees: $33,560
Enrollment: 622 Coed
Affiliation or Control: Independent Non-Profit IRS Status: 501(c)3
Highest Offering: Baccalaureate
Accreditation: NH, ART

01 President ... Mr. Jeff MORIN
05 VP of Academic Affairs ... Mr. David MARTIN
84 VP for Enrollment Management ... Ms. Mary C. SCHOPP
04 Executive Assistant to President ... Ms. Mary EGGERT
09 Assoc VP Academic Plng/Assessment ... Ms. Cynthia LYNCH
10 VP for Financial Affairs ... Ms. Brenda JONES
26 VP of Development & Communications ... Ms. Vivian M. ROTHSCHILD
30 Vice President of Development ... Ms. Vivian ROTHSCHILD
39 Director of Residential Living ... Ms. Marianne HONRATH
32 Dean of Students ... Mr. Tony J. NOWAK
37 Executive Director of Financial Aid ... Ms. Carol MASSE
07 Director of Admissions ... Mr. David SIGMAN
88 Enroll Communications Specialist ... Ms. Stacey STEINBERG
08 Director of Library Services ... Ms. Cynthia D. LYNCH
36 Director of Career Services ... Mr. Duane P. SEIDENSTICKER
51 Dir Pre-College & Adult Learning ... Mr. Corbett TOOMSEN
19 Director Security/Safety ... Mr. Keith A. KOTOWICZ
06 Director of Registration Services ... Ms. Jean WEIMER
38 Director of College Advising ... Ms. Michelle GROSS
29 Mgr of Alumni Engagment/ Development ... Mr. Benno ROTHSCHILD
15 Director of Human Resources ... Ms. April FORRAY
20 Director of Academic Operations ... Ms. Marie KAMINSKI
18 Building Maintenance Manager ... Mr. Michael A. GOETZ
13 Director of Technology ... Mr. Matt OGDEN
25 Exe Dir AIM HIGH Wisconsin ... Ms. Sharon CROWE

Milwaukee School of Engineering (E)

1025 N Broadway, Milwaukee WI 53202-3109
County: Milwaukee FICE Identification: 003868
Unit ID: 239318
Telephone: (414) 277-7300 Carnegie Class: Masters/S
FAX Number: (414) 277-7454 Calendar System: Quarter
URL: www.msoe.edu
Established: 1903 Annual Undergrad Tuition & Fees: $36,540
Enrollment: 2,810 Coed
Affiliation or Control: Independent Non-Profit IRS Status: 501(c)3
Highest Offering: Master's
Accreditation: NH, CONST, ENG, ENGT, NURSE, PERF

01 President ... Dr. John WALZ
05 Int Vice President Academics ... Dr. Steven BIALEK
10 Vice President of Finance and CFO ... Ms. Dawn THIBEDEAU
30 Interim VP of Development ... Mr. Jonathan KOWALSKI
18 VP of Operations ... Mr. Kevin MORIN
84 VP of Enroll Mgmt & Dean of Student ... Dr. Timothy VALLEY
09 Dean of Institutional Research ... Dr. Deborah JACKMAN
25 Dean Grants & Projects ... Mr. Sheku KAMARA
48 Chair Architectural Engr Dept ... Dr. Blake WENTZ
50 Chair School of Business ... Mr. Steve BIALEK
54 Chair Electrical Engr/CPU Sci Dept ... Dr. Stephen WILLIAMS
97 Chair General Studies Department ... Dr. Alicia DOMACK
81 Chair Mathematics Department ... Vacant
54 Chair Mechanical Engineering Dept ... Dr. Cynthia BARNICKI
81 Chair Physics/Chemistry Dept ... Dr. Matey KALTCHEV
66 Chair Nursing Department ... Dr. Debra JENKS
21 Controller ... Ms. Janda VAVRICKA
06 Registrar ... Ms. Mary F. NIELSEN
13 Director of IT Services ... Mr. Paul FABIAN
26 Director Marketing Public Affairs ... Ms. Sandra L. EVERTS
27 Director Public & Media Relations ... Ms. JoEllen BURDUE
15 Director of Human Resources ... Mr. Kevin A. MORIN
37 Director of Financial Aid ... Mr. Steve MIDTHUN
44 Director of Development ... Mr. Jonathan V. KOWALSKI, JR.
38 Director of Counseling ... Mr. Joseph P. MELOY
32 Director Student Activities ... Mr. Nick SEIDLER
39 Director Residence Halls ... Dr. William E. BREESE
41 Director Athletics ... Mr. Dan I. HARRIS
08 Director of Library & Info Services ... Mr. Gary S. SHIMEK
105 Director of Services/Webmaster ... Mr. Kent A. PETERSON
19 Director of Public Safety ... Mr. William P. FADROWSKI
88 Director Fluid Power Institute ... Mr. Tom S. WANKE
29 Director Alumni Affairs ... Ms. Cathy VAREBROOK
07 Director of Admissions ... Ms. Seandra MITCHELL
36 Director Student Placement ... Ms. Mary SPENCER
40 Bookstore Manager ... Mr. David P. ABRAHAMSON

Mount Mary University (F)

2900 N Menomonee River Parkway,
Milwaukee WI 53222-4597
County: Milwaukee FICE Identification: 003869
Unit ID: 239390
Telephone: (414) 930-3000 Carnegie Class: Masters/M
FAX Number: (414) 930-3712 Calendar System: Semester
URL: www.mtmary.edu
Established: 1913 Annual Undergrad Tuition & Fees: $26,760
Enrollment: 1,385 Female
Affiliation or Control: Roman Catholic IRS Status: 501(c)3
Highest Offering: Doctorate
Accreditation: NH, CACREP, #CIDA, DIETC, DIETI, OT, SW

01 President ... Dr. Eileen SCHWALBACH
03 Exec VP Administrative Services ... Ms. Beth WNUK
05 VP Academic/Student Affairs ... Dr. Karen FRIEDLEN
10 Senior Vice Pres Finance ... Vacant
84 Vice Pres Enrollment Services ... Mr. David WEGENER
30 Vice Pres Development ... Ms. Pamela OWENS
88 Vice President Mission/ Identity ... Sr. Joan PENZENSTADLER, SSND
20 Dean Academic Affairs ... Dr. Wendy WEAVER
32 Dean Student Affairs ... Ms. Sarah OLEJNICZAK
58 Dean of Graduate Education ... Vacant
21 Controller ... Ms. Sharon ROOB
06 Registrar ... Dr. Mary KARR
44 Senior Director of Development ... Ms. Lisa BREITSPRECKER
26 Senior Dir of Mktg/Public Relations ... Mr. Scott RUDIE
29 Director of Alumnae Relations ... Ms. Andrea MILLER
07 Director of Graduate Admission ... Mr. Kirk MESSER
07 Director of Undergraduate Admission ... Ms. Rebecca SURGES
09 Director of Inst Research ... Dr. Jill MEYER
08 Director of Library ... Mr. Eric ROBINSON
13 Director of Information Technology ... Mr. Marc BELANGER
37 Director Financial Aid ... Ms. Debra DUFF
35 Director of Student Engagement ... Ms. Kayla SELL
39 Director of Residence Life ... Mr. Erich ZEIMANTZ
36 Dir of Advising/Career Development ... Ms. Michelle PLIML
104 Director of International Studies ... Ms. Nan METZGER
15 Director of Human Resources ... Vacant
41 Athletic Director ... Mr. Marc HEIDORF
42 Director of Campus Ministry ... Ms. Lea ROSENBERG
18 Director of Buildings & Grounds ... Ms. Rebecca JOHNSON
19 Director of Public Safety ... Mr. Paul LESHOK
40 Mgr Barnes & Noble Bookstore ... Mr. Timothy STERNKE
04 Executive Assistant to President ... Ms. Pamela SALOUN

Nashotah House (G)

2777 Mission Road, Nashotah WI 53058-9793
County: Waukesha FICE Identification: 003874
Unit ID: 239424
Telephone: (262) 646-6500 Carnegie Class: Spec-4-yr-Faith
FAX Number: (262) 646-6504 Calendar System: Semester
URL: www.nashotah.edu
Established: 1842 Annual Graduate Tuition & Fees: N/A
Enrollment: 100 Coed
Affiliation or Control: Protestant Episcopal IRS Status: 501(c)3
Highest Offering: Doctorate; No Undergraduates
Accreditation: THEOL

01 Dean-President ... Rev. Steven A. PEAY
10 Associate Dean of Administration ... Rev. Philip J. CUNNINGHAM
13 IT/Database Administrator ... Mr. Matt BILLS
05 Associate Dean for Academic Affairs ... Rev. Andrew GROSSO
06 Registrar ... Rev. Rick HARTLEY
32 Associate Dean of Students ... Rev. Rick HARTLEY
35 Student Affairs Associate ... Mrs. Kelly MEDINA
07 Director of Student Recruitment ... Vacant
08 Library Director ... Dr. David G. SHERWOOD
30 Associate Dean of Inst Advancement ... Ms. Diane PLANTENBERG
26 Marketing/Communications ... Mr. Alex CIANO
18 Chief Facilities/Physical Plant ... Mr. Ricco MEDINA
101 Secretary of the Board of Trustees ... Rev. R. Brien KOEHLER
09 Dir of Institutional Research ... Rev. Esther KRAMER
29 Dir of Alumni Relations ... Mrs. Jan WATTER

Northland College (H)

1411 Ellis Avenue, Ashland WI 54806-3999
County: Ashland FICE Identification: 003875
Unit ID: 239512
Telephone: (715) 682-1699 Carnegie Class: Bac-A&S
FAX Number: (715) 682-1308 Calendar System: Other
URL: www.northland.edu
Established: 1892 Annual Undergrad Tuition & Fees: $32,754
Enrollment: 584 Coed
Affiliation or Control: United Church Of Christ IRS Status: 501(c)3
Highest Offering: Baccalaureate
Accreditation: NH

01 President ... Dr. Michael MILLER
05 Academic Dean ... Dr. Leslie ALLDRITT
30 VP of Institutional Advancement ... Ms. Margot ZELENZ
10 VP Finance & Administration ... Mr. Robert JACKSON
32 Interim Dean of Students ... Ms. Patti FENNER-LEINO
88 Exec Director Environmental Inst ... Mr. Mark PETERSON
88 Exec Director of Development ... Ms. Kristy LIPHART
20 Associate Academic Dean ... Dr. Alan BREW
07 Director of Admissions ... Mr. Teege METTILLE
06 Interim Registrar ... Ms. Michelle BITZER
08 Library Director ... Ms. Julia WAGGONER
29 Director of Alumni Relations ... Ms. Jackie MOORE
13 Information Service Manager ... Mr. Todd PYDO
41 Athletic Director ... Ms. Kim FALKENHAGEN
15 Director Human Resources ... Mr. Paul SKORACZEWSKI
37 Director of Student Financial Aid ... Ms. Heather SHELLY
21 Controller ... Mr. Matt HULMER
44 Director of Annual Giving ... Ms. Carrie SLATER-DUFFY
09 Institutional Research Specialist ... Ms. Petra HOFSTEDT

04 Exec Assistant to the President .... Ms. Dawn RIVARD
39 Director of Residential Life .... Ms. Melissa HARVEY
42 College Chaplain .... Mr. Mark RICKER
25 Director of Grant Dev and Admin .... Ms. Lisa WILLIAMSON
26 Exec Director of Inst Marketing .... Ms. Demeri MULLIKIN

Ottawa University Wisconsin (A)

245 South Executive Drive, Brookfield WI 53005-4204
Telephone: (262) 879-0200 Identification: 666084
Accreditation: &NH

† Regional accreditation is carried under the parent institution in Ottawa, KS.

Rasmussen College - Appleton (B)

3500 E. Destination Drive, Appleton WI 54915
Telephone: (920) 750-5900 Identification: 667059
Accreditation: &NH, MAAB

† Regional accreditation is carried under the parent institution in Saint Cloud, MN. The tuition figure is an average, actual tuition may vary.

Rasmussen College - Green Bay (C)

904 South Taylor Street, Building 1, Green Bay WI 54303
Telephone: (920) 593-8400 Identification: 667063
Accreditation: &NH, CAHIIM, MAAB, MLTAD

† Regional accreditation is carried under the parent institution in Saint Cloud, MN. The tuition figure is an average, actual tuition may vary.

Rasmussen College - Wausau (D)

1101 Westwood Drive, Wausau WI 54401
Telephone: (715) 841-8000 Identification: 667068
Accreditation: &NH, MAAB

† Regional accreditation carried under the parent institution in Saint Cloud, MN. The tuition figure is an average, actual tuition may vary.

Ripon College (E)

300 West Seward Street, PO Box 248,
Ripon WI 54971-0248
County: Fond du Lac FICE Identification: 003884
Unit ID: 239628
Telephone: (920) 748-8115 Carnegie Class: Bac-A&S
FAX Number: (920) 748-7243 Calendar System: Semester
URL: www.ripon.edu
Established: 1851 Annual Undergrad Tuition & Fees: $36,514
Enrollment: 840 Coed
Affiliation or Control: Independent Non-Profit IRS Status: 501(c)3
Highest Offering: Baccalaureate
Accreditation: NH

01 President .... Zachariah P. MESSITTE
04 Admin Asst to President .... Vacant
101 Special Assistant to the President .... Margaret A. CARNE
05 VP & Dean of Faculty .... Ed WINGENBACH
30 VP for Advancement .... Vacant
10 Vice President for Finance .... Thomas M. PONTO
32 Vice President Dean of Students .... Christophor M. OGLE
84 Vice President for Enrollment .... Jennifer MACHACEK
06 Assoc Dean of Faculty/Registrar .... Michele A. WITTLER
88 Exec Dir Ctr for Social Responsib .... Lindsay A. BLUMER
07 Dean of Admissions .... Leigh D. MLODZIK
21 Controller .... Lori A. SCHULZE
08 User Services Librarian .... Andrew R. PRELLWITZ
35 Dir Student Activities/Orientation .... Melissa L. BEMUS
88 Director Student Support Svcs .... Daniel J. KRHIN
39 Director of Residence Life .... Jessica L. JOANIS
26 Exec Dir Marketing & Communications .... Melissa K. ANDERSON
27 Dir of Creative & Social Media .... Richard T. DAMM
44 Exec Director of Development .... Larry P. MALCHOW
13 Exec Dir of Information Technology .... Tara A. LACHAPELL
109 General Manager Food Service .... Allison OTTO
18 Director Physical Plant .... Brian SKAMRA
41 Director of Athletics .... Julie H. JOHNSON
102 Dir Foundation & Govt Relations .... Terri L. HOLZMAN
44 Director Annual Fund .... Nancy L. HINTZ
36 Dir Constit Engagemnt & Career Svcs .... Amy L. GERRETSEN
15 Human Resource Administrator .... Jennifer FRANZ
38 Director of Counseling Services .... Cynthia S. VIERTEL
40 Bookstore Manager .... Rose OLKIEWICZ
37 Director Financial Aid .... David B. WOODWARD

Sacred Heart Seminary and School of Theology (F)

7335 S Highway 100, P.O. Box 429,
Hales Corners WI 53130-0429
County: Milwaukee FICE Identification: 020780
Unit ID: 239637
Telephone: (414) 425-8300 Carnegie Class: Spec-4-yr-Faith
FAX Number: (414) 529-6999 Calendar System: Semester
URL: www.shsst.edu
Established: 1933 Annual Graduate Tuition & Fees: N/A
Enrollment: 98 Coed
Affiliation or Control: Roman Catholic IRS Status: 501(c)3
Highest Offering: Master's; No Undergraduates
Accreditation: NH, THEOL

01 President-Rector .... Msgr. Ross A. SHECTERLE
10 VP Finance .... Ms. Sally A. SMITS
05 VP Intellectual Formation .... Dr. Patrick J. RUSSELL
20 VP Pastoral Formation .... Dr. John OLESNAVAGE
42 VP Spiritual Formation .... Rev. Paul KELLY, SCJ
08 Director Library & Acad Tech Svcs .... Ms. Susanna PATHAK
07 VP External Affairs .... Dr. Jeremy BLACKWOOD
06 Registrar .... Ms. Julie O'CONNOR
26 Director Communications .... Mr. Jonathan DRAYNA
18 Director Plant Operations .... Mr. Michael J. ERATO
04 Executive Asst to President-Rector .... Ms. Theresa M. ILLINGWORTH
13 Information Systems Coordinator .... Ms. Mary GRIEGER

Saint Norbert College (G)

100 Grant Street, De Pere WI 54115-2099
County: Brown FICE Identification: 003892
Unit ID: 239716
Telephone: (920) 403-3181 Carnegie Class: Bac-A&S
FAX Number: (920) 403-4008 Calendar System: Semester
URL: www.snc.edu
Established: 1898 Annual Undergrad Tuition & Fees: $34,237
Enrollment: 2,169 Coed
Affiliation or Control: Roman Catholic IRS Status: 501(c)3
Highest Offering: Master's
Accreditation: NH

01 President .... Mr. Thomas KUNKEL
05 Vice Pres Acad Affs/Dean of Col .... Dr. Jeffrey FRICK
10 Vice President Business & Finance .... Ms. Eileen JAHNKE
30 Vice Pres Institutional Advancement .... Mr. Phil OSWALD
32 Vice Pres Mission & Student Affairs .... Rev. Jay J. FOSTNER
84 Vice Pres Enrollment Mgmt/Comm .... Mr. Edward LAMM
44 Assoc Vice Pres Inst Advancement .... Ms. Lynette GREEN
09 AVP Institutional Effectiveness .... Dr. Ray ZURAWSKI
20 Associate Academic Dean .... Dr. Michael ROSEWALL
36 Director Career Services .... Ms. Mary Ellen OLSON
35 Associate Dean Student Life .... Vacant
38 Dir Counseling/Career Programs .... Mr. Bruce ROBERTSON
07 Actg Exec Director of Admissions .... Mr. Mark SELIN
29 Director Alumni & Parent Relations .... Mr. Todd DANEN
21 Director of Finance .... Mr. Curt KOWALESKI
37 Director of Financial Aid .... Ms. Jessica RAFELD
26 Director Communications/Marketing .... Mr. Drew VAN FOSSEN
08 Director of Library .... Dr. Kristin D. VOGEL
15 Director Human Resources .... Ms. Sue BRINKMAN
41 Director Physical Educ/Athletics .... Mr. Tim BALD
06 Registrar .... Ms. Lauren GAECKE
13 Vice Pres & Chief Info Officer .... Mr. Lee REID
104 Assoc Academic Dir Global Affairs .... Ms. Gratzia VILLARROEL
28 Dir Multicultural Student Services .... Ms. Bridgit MARTIN
18 Director Facilities/Physical Plant .... Mr. Patrick WRENN
40 Manager Bookstore Operations .... Ms. Monica WITTROCK
04 Administrative Asst to President .... Ms. Jamie MCGUIRE
102 Dir Foundation/Corporate Relations .... Ms. Amy KUNDINGER
100 Chief of Staff .... Ms. Amy SORENSON
19 Director Security/Safety .... Mr. Steve JAKUPS
39 Director Student Housing .... Mr. Michael PECKHAM

Silver Lake College of the Holy Family (H)

2406 S Alverno Road, Manitowoc WI 54220-9319
County: Manitowoc FICE Identification: 003850
Unit ID: 239743
Telephone: (920) 684-6691 Carnegie Class: Masters/S
FAX Number: (920) 684-7082 Calendar System: Semester
URL: www.sl.edu
Established: 1935 Annual Undergrad Tuition & Fees: $25,320
Enrollment: 629 Coed
Affiliation or Control: Roman Catholic IRS Status: 501(c)3
Highest Offering: Master's
Accreditation: NH, MUS, NURSE

01 President .... Dr. Chris E. DOMES
05 VP for Academic Affairs .... Mr. Matthew SOUCY
10 VP of Finance & Business .... Mr. Brian RISTE
30 VP Advancement/External Relations .... Mr. Marc BARBEAU
42 Exec Dir of Mission Integration .... Sr. Lorita GAFFNEY
06 Registrar/Dir Institutional Rsrch .... Ms. Amy ECKLEY
08 Head Librarian .... Ms. Natalie LONG
37 Director Student Financial Aid .... Ms. Erica PLOECKELMAN
29 Director Alumni/Special Events .... Ms. Tammy REIGEL
13 Director Technology Services .... Mr. Jeff RAHMLOW
15 VP of Human Resources .... Ms. Sandy ISSELMANN
36 Dir Career Res/Experiential Lrng .... Ms. Jan L. ALGOZINE
26 Dir PR/Grant Writing .... Ms. Suzanne WEISS
19 Director of Campus Safety .... Mr. Aaron DUSZYNSKI
44 Assoc Dir Annual Giving/Advanc Svcs .... Ms. Katie RUNNOE
07 Director of Admissions .... Ms. Jamie GRANT
41 Athletic Director .... Mr. Ben WIDEMAN
32 Dir Residence/Student Life .... Ms. Rachel FISCHER
39 Director Student Housing .... Ms. Juanita SOTO
84 Dir Retention/Enrollment Services .... Mr. Dan CONNOLLY
04 Executive Asst to President .... Ms. RK GREENING

University of Phoenix Milwaukee Main Campus (I)

10850 West Park Place, Suite 150,
Milwaukee WI 53224-3606
Telephone: (414) 410-7900 Identification: 770235
Accreditation: &NH, ACBSP

† No longer accepting campus-based students.

*University of Wisconsin System (J)

1220 Linden Dr, 1720 Van Hise Hall,
Madison WI 53706-1559
County: Dane FICE Identification: 003894
Unit ID: 240435
Telephone: (608) 262-2321 Carnegie Class: N/A
FAX Number: (608) 262-3985
URL: www.wisconsin.edu

01 President .... Ray W. CROSS
05 Vice Pres Academic/Student Affairs .... James P. HENDERSON
11 Sr VP Administration/Fiscal Affairs .... David MILLER
10 Int Vice President Finance .... Julie GORDON
30 Assoc VP Economic Development .... David BRUKARDT
15 Sr AVP Human Res/Workforce Div .... Shenita BROKENBURR
20 AVP Academic Pgms/Educ Innovation .... Stephen KOLISON
13 Assoc VP Learning/Info Tech .... Sasi PILLAY
45 Assoc VP Budget & Planning .... Freda J. HARRIS
26 Exec Dir Integr Mktg/Communications .... Alex HUMMEL
43 General Counsel .... Tomas L. STAFFORD
100 Chief of Staff .... Jessica TORMEY

*University of Wisconsin-Madison (K)

500 Lincoln Drive, Madison WI 53706-1380
County: Dane FICE Identification: 003895
Unit ID: 240444
Telephone: (608) 262-1234 Carnegie Class: DU-Highest
FAX Number: (608) 262-8123 Calendar System: Semester
URL: www.wisc.edu
Established: 1848 Annual Undergrad Tuition & Fees (In-State): $10,415
Enrollment: 42,598 Coed
Affiliation or Control: State IRS Status: 501(c)3
Highest Offering: Doctorate
Accreditation: NH, ARCPA, ART, AUD, BUS, BUSA, CAATE, CIDA, CLPSY, COPSY, CORE, CYTO, DANCE, DIETD, DMS, ENG, IPSY, LAW, LIB, LSAR, MED, MUS, NURSE, OT, PCSAS, PH, PHAR, PLNG, PTA, RAD, SCPSY, SP, SW, THEA, VET

02 Chancellor .... Dr. Rebecca BLANK
05 Provost Academic Affairs .... Dr. Sarah MANGELSDORF
11 Vice Chancellor Administration .... Mr. Laurent HELLER
13 CIO/Vice Provost Info Technology .... Mr. Bruce MAAS
100 Chancellor's Chief of Staff .... Mr. Matt MAYRL
30 Vice Chanc University Relations .... Mr. Charles HOSLET
84 Vice Provost Enrollment Management .... Mr. Steven HAHN
18 Assoc Vice Chanc Facil Plng/Mgmt .... Mr. William ELVEY
28 Vice Provost Diversity/Climate .... Dr. Patrick SIMS
20 Assoc Vice Chanc Faculty/Staff Pgms .... Dr. Michael BERNARD-DONALS
20 Assoc Vice Chanc Teaching/Learning .... Dr. Steven M. CRAMER
10 Asst Vice Chanc Business Services .... Ms. Martha KERNER
32 Dean of Students .... Ms. Lori BERQUAM
58 Dean Graduate School .... Dr. Marsha R. MAILICK
58 Assoc Dean Graduate School .... Ms. Petra SCHROEDER
49 Dean College Letters & Science .... Dr. John K. SCHOLZ
63 Dean Medicine and Public Health .... Dr. Robert N. GOLDEN
53 Dean School of Education .... Dr. Diana HESS
50 Dean School of Business .... Dr. Francois ORTALO-MAGNE'
67 Dean School of Pharmacy .... Dr. Steven M. SWANSON
54 Dean of College of Engineering .... Dr. Ian ROBERTSON
47 Dean of Agricultural/Life Sciences .... Dr. Kathryn VANDENBOSCH
66 Dean of School of Nursing .... Dr. Linda SCOTT
59 Dean of Human Ecology .... Dr. Soyeon SHIM
74 Dean of Veterinary Medicine .... Dr. Mark D. MARKEL
61 Dean of the Law School .... Dr. Margaret RAYMOND
82 Dean International Studies .... Dr. Guido PODESTÁ
43 Director of Admin Legal Services .... Mr. Raymond P. TAFFORA
88 Director Environmental Studies .... Dr. Paul ROBBINS
41 Director Intercollegiate Athletics .... Mr. Barry L. ALVAREZ
88 Director of Physical Plant .... Mr. Robert D. LAMPPA
88 Int Director of Arboretum .... Dr. Donna M. PAULNOCK
88 Director State Lab of Hygiene .... Dr. Charles BROKOPP
88 Director of Wisconsin Union .... Mr. Mark C. GUTHIER
07 Director of Admissions .... Mr. Derek KINDLE
08 Director of Libraries .... Mr. Edward VANGEMERT
26 Director University Communications .... Mr. John LUCAS
102 President UW Foundation .... Dr. Michael M. KNETTER
29 Director of Alumni Association .... Ms. Paula E. BONNER
37 Director Student Financial Services .... Ms. Susan FISCHER
38 Director of Counseling Services .... Dr. Danielle OAKLEY
15 Director Human Resources .... Mr. Robert LAVIGNA
39 Director of University Housing .... Dr. Jeffrey NOVAK
51 Dean Continuing Studies .... Dr. Jeffrey RUSSELL
19 Director of University Police .... Ms. Susan RISELING
88 Director of Archives .... Mr. David NULL
23 Director University Health Service .... Dr. Sarah A. VAN ORMAN
88 Director of Space Management .... Mr. Douglas N. ROSE
17 President Hospital & Clinics .... Ms. Donna KATEN-BAHENSKY
109 Dir Auxiliary Operations Analysis .... Ms. Donna HALLERAN
06 Registrar .... Mr. Scott OWCZAREK
88 Secretary of the Faculty .... Mr. Steven K. SMITH
88 Secretary of Academic Staff .... Ms. Heather M. DANIELS
88 Director of Recreational Sports .... Mr. John HORN
16 Director of Academic Personnel .... Mr. Stephen R. LUND
16 Director Classified Personnel .... Mr. Mark WALTERS
85 Dir International Student Services .... Ms. Laurie COX
22 Dir Office of Equity & Diversity .... Mr. Luis A. PINERO

96 Director of Purchasing .... Ms. Martha KERNER
09 Dir Instl Rsrch/Acad Plng/Analysis .... Dr. Jocelyn L. MILNER
88 Special Asst to Provost .... Dr. Eden INOWAY-RONNIE
86 Sr Special Asst to Chanc Fed Rels .... Mr. Ben J. MILLER

*University of Wisconsin-Eau Claire (A)

105 Garfield Avenue, PO Box 4004,
Eau Claire WI 54702-4004

County: Eau Claire | FICE Identification: 003917
Unit ID: 240268
Telephone: (715) 836-2637 | Carnegie Class: Masters/M
FAX Number: (715) 836-2902 | Calendar System: Semester
URL: www.uwec.edu
Established: 1916 | Annual Undergrad Tuition & Fees (In-State): $8,822
Enrollment: 10,721 | Coed
Affiliation or Control: State | IRS Status: 501(c)3
Highest Offering: Doctorate
Accreditation: NH, BUS, CAATE, #JOUR, MUS, NURSE, SP, SW

02 Chancellor .... Dr. James C. SCHMIDT
05 Prov/Vice Chanc Academic Affairs .... Dr. Patricia A. KLEINE
100 Special Assistant to the Chancellor .... Ms. Mary Jane BRUKARDT
32 Vice Chanc Student Affairs .... Dr. Beth A. HELLWIG
46 Asst VC Research/Sponsored Pgm .... Dr. Karen G. HAVHOLM
18 Asst Chanc Facilities/Univ Rels .... Mr. Michael J. RINDO
20 Int Assoc Vice Chanc Academic Affs .... Dr. Mary F. HOFFMAN
20 Assoc Vice Chanc Academic Affairs .... Dr. Michael J. CARNEY
28 Exec Director Diversity & Inclusion .... Ms. Jodi M. THESING-RITTER
45 Executive Director Mktg & Planning ... Ms. Mary Jane BRUKARDT
22 Director of Affirmative Action .... Ms. Teresa E. O'HALLORAN
102 Pres UWEC Found/Dir Univ Advance .... Ms. Kimera K. WAY
10 Director of Budget & Resource Plan .... Ms. Kristen M. HENDRICKSON
32 Dean of Students .... Dr. Joseph J. ABHOLD
07 Director of Admissions .... Ms. Heather M. KRETZ
28 Asst Director of Multicultural Affs .... Mr. Charles C. VUE
08 Director of Libraries .... Mr. John H. POLLITZ
13 Chief Information Officer .... Mr. Chip P. ECKARDT
14 Dir Learning & Technology Services .... Mr. Craig A. MEY
15 Director of Human Resources .... Mr. David J. MILLER
37 Director of Financial Aid .... Ms. Kathleen A. SAHLHOFF
38 Director of Counseling .... Ms. Lynn Y. WILSON
06 Registrar .... Ms. Tessa A. PERCHINSKY
36 Assoc Director Career Services .... Ms. Staci L. HEIDTKE
19 Director of University Police .... Mr. David W. SPRICK
23 Director of Student Health Services .... Ms. Laura G. CHELLMAN
39 Director of Housing & Res Life .... Mr. J. Quincy CHAPMAN
41 Director of Athletics .... Mr. Daniel J. SCHUMACHER
51 Director Continuing Education .... Mr. Durwin LONG
85 Interim Director Intl Education .... Ms. Colleen C. MARCHWICK
102 Director Corporate Relations .... Mr. John G. BACHMEIER
92 Director of Honors Program .... Dr. Jefford B. VAHLBUSCH
26 Chief Public Relations Officer .... Mr. Michael J. RINDO
27 Director of Integrated Marketing .... Ms. Rebecca J. DIENGER
30 Chief Development/Alumni Relations .... Ms. Kimera K. WAY
96 Purchasing Agent .... Ms. Karen E. MCINTYRE
09 Institutional Planner .... Mr. Andrew J. NELSON
108 Director of Assessment .... Dr. Jennifer J. FAGER
49 Dean College of Arts & Sciences .... Dr. David E. LEAMAN
66 Dean Col of Nursing/Health Sciences .... Dr. Linda K. YOUNG
53 Dean Col Education/Human Sciences .... Dr. Carmen K. MANNING
50 Interim Dean College of Business .... Dr. Timothy S. VAUGHAN
04 Executive Asst to Chancellor .... Ms. Suzanne C. OLSON

*University of Wisconsin-Green Bay (B)

2420 Nicolet Drive, Green Bay WI 54311-7001

County: Brown | FICE Identification: 003899
Unit ID: 240277
Telephone: (920) 465-2000 | Carnegie Class: Masters/S
FAX Number: (920) 465-2032 | Calendar System: Semester
URL: www.uwgb.edu
Established: 1965 | Annual Undergrad Tuition & Fees (In-State): $7,824
Enrollment: 6,927 | Coed
Affiliation or Control: State | IRS Status: 501(c)3
Highest Offering: Master's
Accreditation: NH, ART, CAHIIM, DIETD, DIETI, MUS, NURSE, SW

02 Chancellor .... Dr. Gary L. MILLER
05 Provost/Vice Chancellor .... Dr. Gregory DAVIS
10 Vice Chanc Business & Finance .... Ms. Sheryl VAN GRUENSVEN
30 Vice Chanc University Advancement .... Mr. Lance CAVANAUGH
32 Dean of Students .... Dr. Brenda AMENSON-HILL
20 Assoc Provost for Academic Affairs .... Dr. Clifton GANYARD
107 Dean Professional Studies .... Dr. Sue JOSEPH MATTISON
49 Dean Liberal Arts & Sciences .... Dr. Scott FURLONG
07 Director of Admissions .... Ms. Jennifer JONES
15 Director of Human Resources .... Ms. Christine OLSON
18 Dir Facilities Management/Planning .... Mr. Paul PINKSTON
19 Director Public Safety .... Mr. Thomas KUJAWA
41 Director Athletics .... Ms. Mary Ellen GILLESPIE
21 Controller .... Ms. SuAnn DETAMPEL
09 Director Institutional Research .... Dr. Deborah FURLONG
84 Dean Enrollment .... Ms. Christina TROMBLEY
46 Director of Institute for Research .... Ms. Lidia NONN
37 Director Financial Aid .... Mr. James P. ROHAN
39 Director of Residence Life .... Ms. Gail SIMS-AUBERT
40 Director Bookstore .... Mr. Gregory KANNENBERG
24 Director Media Svcs/Telecomm .... Mr. William HUBBARD

23 Director Health Services .... Ms. Amy HENNIGES
38 Director Counseling Services .... Mr. Gregory L. SMITH
100 Chief of Staff .... Mr. Ron PFEIFER
26 Director University Communications .. Mr. Christopher SAMPSON
36 Director Career Services ...... Ms. Linda G. PEACOCK-LANDRUM
29 Director Alumni Relations .... Ms. Kari MOODY
35 Director Student Life .... Ms. Lisa TETZLOFF
06 Registrar .... Vacant
04 Administrative Asst to President .... Ms. Paula MARCEC
08 Library Director .... Ms. Paula GANYARD
104 Director Study Abroad .... Mr. Brent BLAHNIK
28 Director of Diversity .... Dr. Justin MALLETT
44 Director of Development .... Vacant

*University of Wisconsin-La Crosse (C)

1725 State Street, La Crosse WI 54601-3788

County: La Crosse | FICE Identification: 003919
Unit ID: 240329
Telephone: (608) 785-8000 | Carnegie Class: Masters/L
FAX Number: (608) 785-8492 | Calendar System: Semester
URL: www.uwlax.edu
Established: 1909 | Annual Undergrad Tuition & Fees (In-State): $8,832
Enrollment: 10,669 | Coed
Affiliation or Control: State | IRS Status: 501(c)3
Highest Offering: Doctorate
Accreditation: NH, ARCPA, BUS, CAATE, MUS, NMT, NRPA, OT, PH, PTA, RADDOS, RTT

02 Chancellor .... Dr. Joe GOW
05 Provost/Vice Chanc Acad Affairs .... Dr. Betsy MORGAN
30 Vice Chancellor Advancement .... Mr. Greg REICHERT
10 Vice Chancellor Admin & Finance .... Dr. Bob HETZEL
84 Assoc Vice Chanc Enrollment Mgmt .... Dr. Fred PIERCE
50 Dean of Business Administration .... Dr. Laura MILNER
53 Director School of Education .... Dr. Marcie WYCOFF-HORN
79 Dean of Liberal Studies .... Dr. Julia JOHNSON
76 Dean Science Health .... Dr. Bruce RILEY
58 Assoc V Chan Acad/Dir Univ Grad Std .... Dr. Robert HOAR
32 Asst Chancellor & Dean of Students .... Dr. Paula M. KNUDSON
13 Chief Information Officer .... Dr. Mohamed ELHINDI
15 Director of Human Resources .... Ms. Madeline HOLZEM
51 Director Continuing Educ/Exten .... Ms. Penny TIEDT
08 Director of Library .... Ms. Catherine LAVALLÉE-WELCH
85 Director International Education .... Mr. Fred M. PIERCE
07 Director ES/Admissions .... Mr. Corey SJOQUIST
06 Registrar .... Dr. Christine S. BAKKUM
37 Director ES/Financial Aid .... Ms. Louise L. JANKE
38 Director Counseling/Testing .... Ms. Gretchen REINDERS
36 Director of Career Services .... Ms. Gail BEAUSOLEIL
41 Athletic Director .... Ms. Kim BLUM
26 Director News and Marketing .... Mr. Brad R. QUARBERG
29 Director Alumni Relations .... Ms. Janie M. MORGAN
23 Director Student Health Center .... Dr. Brian K. ALLEN
09 Director Institutional Research .... Ms. Natalie SOLVERSON
19 Interim Chief of University Police .... Mr. Scott MC COLLOUGH
18 Director Physical Plant .... Mr. Hank M. KLOS
28 Assoc Dean Campus Climate/Diversity . Ms. Barbara E. STEWART
22 Director Affirmative Action .... Mr. Nizam ARAIN
106 Dir Online Education/E-learning .... Dr. Brian UDERMANN
39 Director Student Housing .... Mr. Nick NICKLAUS

*University of Wisconsin-Milwaukee (D)

PO Box 413, Milwaukee WI 53201-0413

County: Milwaukee | FICE Identification: 003896
Unit ID: 240453
Telephone: (414) 229-1122 | Carnegie Class: DU-Highest
FAX Number: (414) 229-6329 | Calendar System: Semester
URL: www.uwm.edu
Established: 1885 | Annual Undergrad Tuition & Fees (In-State): $9,429
Enrollment: 27,596 | Coed
Affiliation or Control: State | IRS Status: 501(c)3
Highest Offering: Doctorate
Accreditation: NH, BUS, BUSA, CAATE, CEA, CLPSY, COPSY, CS, DANCE, DMS, ENG, LIB, MT, MUS, NURSE, OT, PLNG, PTA, RAD, SCPSY, SP, SW

02 Chancellor .... Dr. Mark MONE
05 Provost/Vice Chanc Academic Affairs .... Dr. Johannes BRITZ
10 Vice Chanc Finance & Admin Affs .... Ms. Robin L. VAN HARPEN
26 Vice Chanc Univ Rels/Communications .... Mr. Thomas L. LULJAK
46 Interim Vice Provost of Research .... Dr. Mark T. HARRIS
32 Int Vice Chancellor Student Affairs .... Mr. James HILL
30 Vice Chancellor Development .... Dr. Patricia A. BORGER
88 Vice Chanc Global Inclusion & Engag .... Dr. Joan M. PRINCE
20 Assoc Vice Chanc Academic Affairs .... Dr. Devarajan VENUGOPALAN
20 Assoc Vice Chanc Academic Affs .... Dr. Phyllis KING
28 Associate Vice Chancellor Diversity .... Vacant
84 Assoc Vice Chanc Enrollment Mgmt .... Vacant
13 Chief Information Officer .... Dr. Robert J. BECK
18 Assoc VC Facilities Planning/Mgmt .... Mr. Geoffrey HURTADO
04 Senior Advisor to the Chancellor .... Mr. David H. GILBERT
76 Dean College Health Sciences .... Dr. Ronald A. CISLER
48 Dean Architecture & Urban Planning .... Dr. Robert C. GREENSTREET
50 Int Dean School of Business .... Dr. Kanti PRASAD
53 Dean of the School of Education .... Dr. Alan R. SHOHO
54 Dean Col Engr & Applied Science .... Dr. Brett PETERS
57 Dean Peck School of the Arts .... Dr. Scott EMMONS
46 Senior Dir/Assoc Dean of Research .... Dr. J. Val KLUMP

69 Int Dean School of Public Health .... Dr. Ronald PEREZ
58 Dean Graduate School .... Dr. Marija GAJDARDZISKA-JOSIFOVSKA
49 Dean College Letters & Science .... Dr. Rodney SWAIN
62 Dean School Information Studies .... Dr. Tomas LIPINSKI
66 Interim Dean of College of Nursing .... Dr. Kim LITWACK
70 Dean Helen Bader Sch Social Welfare .... Dr. Stan STOJKOVIC
51 Int Dean School of Continuing Educ .... Dr. Paula M. RHYNER
35 Dean of Students .... Dr. Timothy GORDON
22 Dir Equity/Diversity Services .... Ms. Jazmin TAYLOR
08 Int AVP/Director of the Library .... Mr. Michael DOYLEN
43 Director Legal Affairs .... Ms. Joely B. URDAN
06 Registrar .... Mr. Seth J. ZLOTOCHA
15 Assoc VC Human Resources .... Mr. Timothy DANIELSON
19 Chief of University Police .... Mr. Joseph LEMIRE
25 Director Office Sponsored Research .... Mr. Thomas MARCUSSEN
23 Director Health Center .... Dr. Julia BONNER
09 Dir Assessment/Institutional Rsrch .... Dr. Gesele DURHAM
85 Exec Dir Center for Intl Education .... Ms. Sarah TULLY
37 Int Exec Dir Financial Aid .... Mr. Mark LEVINE
39 Director of Residence Life .... Mr. Scott S. PEAK
41 Athletic Director .... Ms. Amanda BRAUN
40 Director Bookstore .... Mr. Erik G. HEMMING
36 Int Dir Career Development Center .... Ms. Cindy PETRITES
27 Director of Media Services .... Ms. Michelle JOHNSON
21 Dir Business & Financial Svcs .... Mr. Jerry TARRER
29 Director Alumni Relations .... Ms. Adrienne BASS
96 Purchasing Manager .... Ms. Joan C. AGUADO-WARE
45 Dir Budget & Planning .... Ms. Cindy KLUGE
07 Director of Admissions & Recruiting .... Vacant

*University of Wisconsin-Oshkosh (E)

800 Algoma Boulevard, Oshkosh WI 54901-3551

County: Winnebago | FICE Identification: 003920
Unit ID: 240365
Telephone: (920) 424-1234 | Carnegie Class: Masters/L
FAX Number: (920) 424-7317 | Calendar System: Semester
URL: www.uwosh.edu
Established: 1871 | Annual Undergrad Tuition & Fees (In-State): $7,487
Enrollment: 14,541 | Coed
Affiliation or Control: State | IRS Status: 501(c)3
Highest Offering: Doctorate
Accreditation: NH, BUS, CAATE, CACREP, CS, CSHSE, EXSC, IFSAC, JOUR, MUS, NURSE, SW

02 Chancellor .... Dr. Andrew J. LEAVITT
05 Provost & Vice Chancellor .... Dr. Lane R. EARNS
20 Asst Vice Chanc Curricular Affairs ..... Dr. Carleen VANDE ZANDE
20 Asst Vice Chanc Acad Support .... Dr. Sylvia CAREY-BUTLER
51 Asst Vice Chanc Lifelong Learning .... Dr. Charles HILL
32 Vice Chancellor Student Affairs .... Dr. Brandon MILLER
10 Vice Chancellor Administrative Svcs .... Ms. Lori WORM
21 Associate Vice Chanc Admin Svcs .... Ms. Lori M. WORM
06 Registrar .... Ms. Lisa M. DANIELSON
22 Affirmative Action Officer .... Ms. Ameerah MCBRIDE
09 Director of Institutional Research .... Mr. Michael W. WATSON
38 Director of Counseling Center .... Dr. Sandy COX
13 CIO Director Info Technology .... Ms. Anne MILKOVICH
50 Dean Business .... Dr. Scott BEYER
66 Dean Nursing .... Dr. Leslie NEAL BOYLAN
53 Dean Education & Human Services .... Dr. Frederick L. YEO
49 Dean Letters & Sciences .... Dr. John J. KOKER
102 Pres Univ of Wisc Oshkosh Foundatn ...... Mr. Arthur H. RATHJEN
29 Director of Alumni Association .... Ms. Christine M. GANTNER
37 Director of Financial Aid .... Mr. Kim DONAT
26 Exec Director Integrated Marketing .... Ms. Jamie CEMAN
25 Director Grants/Faculty Development ...... Mr. Robert W. ROBERTS
35 Dean of Students .... Dr. Sharon KIPETZ
58 Director Graduate Studies .... Mr. Gregory WYPISZYNSKI
07 Director of Admissions .... Ms. Jill M. ENDRIES
15 Director of Human Resources .... Ms. Laurie TEXTOR
18 Facilities/Physical Plant Director .... Vacant
36 Director of Career Services .... Ms. Jaime PAGE-STADLER
96 Purchasing/Printing Manager .... Mr. Barry GAUTHIER
92 Director University Honors Program .... Dr. Laurence CARLIN
08 Director Library .... Mr. Patrick J. WILKINSON
04 Administrative Asst to President .... Ms. Suzette THIBADEAU
104 Director Study Abroad .... Ms. Jenna GRAFF
28 Director of Diversity .... Vacant
39 Director Student Housing .... Mr. Tom FOJTIK
41 Athletic Director .... Mr. Darryl SIMS
90 Director Academic Computing .... Ms. Laura KNAAPEN

*University of Wisconsin-Parkside (F)

900 Wood Road, Box 2000, Kenosha WI 53141-2000

County: Kenosha | FICE Identification: 005015
Unit ID: 240374
Telephone: (262) 595-2345 | Carnegie Class: Bac-A&S
FAX Number: (262) 595-2202 | Calendar System: Semester
URL: www.uwp.edu
Established: 1968 | Annual Undergrad Tuition & Fees (In-State): $7,341
Enrollment: 4,543 | Coed
Affiliation or Control: State | IRS Status: 501(c)3
Highest Offering: Master's
Accreditation: NH, BUS

02 Chancellor .... Deborah L. FORD
05 Provost/Vice Chancellor .... Robert DUCOFFE
10 Vice Chanc Admin/Fiscal Affairs .... Melvin KLINKNER
32 Dean of Students .... Tammy MCGUCKIN

30 Asst Chanc Univ Rels/Advancement .... John JARACZEWSKI
20 Associate Provost ....Gary WOOD
20 Assoc VC Ofc of Academic Affairs .... Kimberly KELLEY
28 University Diversity & Inclusion .... Heather KIND-KEPPEL
50 Dean Col of Bus Econ & Comput .... Dirk BALDWIN
49 Dean College of Arts/Humanities .... Lesley WALKER
81 Dean College of Nat & Hlth Sciences .... Emmanual OTU
83 Int Dean Social Sci & Prof Studies .... Peggy JAMES
31 Int Exec Dir Ctr for Cmty Partners .... Debra KARP
08 Director of the Library .... Anna STADICK
13 Chief Information Officer .... Vacant
93 Director Minority Student Services .... Damian EVANS
21 Dir Business Services/Controller .... Scott MENKE
15 Int Director Human Resources .... Linda BUSHA
19 Dir Campus Police/Public Safety .... James HELLER
37 Director Financial Aid .... Kristina KLEMENS
29 Coord Donor Relations & Stewardship .... Melissa GREINER
06 Registrar .... Rhonda KIMMEL
36 Dir of Advising/Career Center .... Gwen JONES
18 Director Facilities Management .... Donald A. KOLBE
94 Director of Women's Studies .... Linda CRAFTON
96 Director of Purchasing .... Vacant
35 Assoc Dean of Students .... Steve WALLNER
38 Dir Health/Counseling/Disability .... Renee KIRBY
40 Manager Bookstore .... Kim FLANNERY
07 Director Recruit & Admissions .... Troy MOLDENHAUER
04 Administrative Asst to Chancellor .... Diane DONNELLY
88 Admin Program Manager Intl Educ .... Elaine PHILIPPA
39 Director Residence Life .... Joseph BERTHIAUME
41 Athletic Director .... Tamie FALK-DAY
105 Director Web Services .... Elizabeth MCGEE
26 Chief Public Relations/Marketing .... John MIELKE

*University of Wisconsin-Platteville (A)

1 University Plaza, Platteville WI 53818-3099

County: Grant — FICE Identification: 003921
Unit ID: 240462
Telephone: (608) 342-1491 — Carnegie Class: Masters/L
FAX Number: (608) 342-1232 — Calendar System: Semester
URL: www.uwplatt.edu
Established: 1866 — Annual Undergrad Tuition & Fees (In-State): $7,488
Enrollment: 8,901 — Coed
Affiliation or Control: State — IRS Status: 501(c)3
Highest Offering: Master's
Accreditation: NH, ENG, MUS, NAIT

02 Chancellor .... Mr. Dennis J. SHIELDS
05 Act Provost/Vice Chanc Acad Affairs .... Dr. Liz THROOP
26 Vice Chanc University Relations .... Ms. Rose M. SMYRSKI
10 Vice Chanc Administrative Services .... Mr. Robert G. CRAMER
32 Assoc Vice Chanc Student Affairs .... Dr. Laura BAYLESS
30 Exec Dir Development/Alumni Rels ..... Mr. Steven M. RAMIG, JR.
58 Director Graduate School .... Dr. Dominic BARRACLOUGH
06 Registrar .... Mr. David S. KIECKHAFER
84 Vice Chanc Enroll/Student Support ... Ms. Angela M. UDELHOFEN
37 Director of Financial Aid .... Vacant
38 Director Student Counseling .... Ms. Deirdre L. DALSING
26 Dir Univ Info/Comm/Public Rels .... Mr. Paul J. ERICKSON
41 Int Dir Intercollegiate Athletics .... Mr. Mike EMENDORFER
39 Director of Residence Life .... Mrs. Linda MULROY-BOWDEN
15 Director Human Resources/AA/EED .... Ms. Janelle CROWLEY
19 Director Security/Safety .... Chief Joseph HALLMAN
93 Dir Multicultural Educ Resource Ctr .... Ms. Angela M. MILLER
96 Director of Purchasing .... Mr. Lewis BETTINGER
08 Interim Director of Library .... Mr. Jon MUSSELMAN
18 Director of Facilities Management .... Mr. Pete D. DAVIS
36 Director of Career Center .... Dr. Jennifer L. WILLIAMSON-MENDEZ
51 Director Continuing Education .... Ms. Kerie WEDIGE
49 Int Dean Col Liberal Arts/Education .... Dr. Melissa E. GORMLEY
54 Dean Col of Engr/Math/Science .... Dr. Molly GRIBB
47 Dean Business Life Sci/Agric .... Dr. Wayne C. WEBER
28 Chief Diversity Officer .... Ms. Angela M. MILLER
20 Acting Asst Provost Academic Affs .... Dr. Patrick HAGEN
20 Actg Asst Provost Academic Plng .... Dr. Chanaka MENDIS
108 Exec Dir Inst Effectiveness .... Ms. Nettie DANIELS
13 Asst Vice Chanc/Chief Info Ofcr .... Ms. Suzanne A. TRAXLER
106 Exe Dir Alternative Delivery System .... Ms. Dawn M. DRAKE
106 Director Distance Learning Center .... Mr. Daniel R. AVENARIUS
106 Asst Exec Director Alt Delivery Sys .... Mr. Michael GAU
21 Comptroller .... Ms. Cathy J. RIEDL-FARREY
35 Dean of Students .... Ms. Sherry C. NEVINS
07 Director Admissions .... Ms. Heidi TUESCHER-GILLE
23 Director Student Health Services .... Vacant
88 Director PACCE .... Dr. Kevin J. BERNHARDT
88 Director Student Support Services .... Ms. Laura A. FRANKLIN
104 Director International Programs .... Ms. Donna L. ANDERSON
88 Director Retention Initiatives .... Ms. Karen MCLEER

*University of Wisconsin-River Falls (B)

410 S Third Street, River Falls WI 54022-5013

County: Pierce — FICE Identification: 003923
Unit ID: 240471
Telephone: (715) 425-3911 — Carnegie Class: Masters/M
FAX Number: (715) 425-4487 — Calendar System: Semester
URL: www.uwrf.edu
Established: 1874 — Annual Undergrad Tuition & Fees (In-State): $7,937
Enrollment: 6,198 — Coed
Affiliation or Control: State — IRS Status: 501(c)3
Highest Offering: Beyond Master's But Less Than Doctorate
Accreditation: NH, BUS, CACREP, MACTE, MUS, SP, SW

02 Chancellor .... Dr. Dean A. VAN GALEN
05 Int Vice Chancellor & Provost .... Dr. Faye PERKINS
10 Assistant Chancellor Bus/Finance .... Ms. Elizabeth FRUEH
13 Assistant Chancellor of Advancement .... Mr. Chris MUELLER
85 Int Asst VC for International Pgms .... Ms. Katrina LARSEN
20 Associate VC Academic Affairs .... Dr. Wesley CHAPIN
32 Assoc Vice Chanc Student Affs .... Mr. Gregg HEINSELMAN
21 Controller .... Mr. Joel HEUSCHELE
47 Dean Agricult/Food/Environ Sci .... Dr. Dale GALLENBERG
53 Int Dean Education/Profess Studies .... Dr. Michael HARRIS
49 Dean of Arts & Sciences .... Dr. Bradley J. CASKEY
50 Dean Business & Economics .... Dr. Michael FROEMMUELLER
13 Co-Int Chief Information Officer .... Mrs. Sara SOLLAND
13 Co-Int Chief Information Officer .... Mr. Jason WINGET
15 Interim Human Resources Director .... Ms. Deb SCHWAB
18 Exec Dir Facilities/Planning/Mgmt .... Mr. Michael J. STIFTER
22 Interim Director Affirmative Action .... Mrs. Brenda CREIGHTON
88 Director Enrollment/Student Success .... Mr. Mark R. MEYDAM
06 Registrar .... Mr. Daniel VANDE YACHT
07 Director of Admissions .... Mrs. Sarah EGERSTROM
46 Director Grants & Research .... Ms. Diane BENNETT
08 Director of Library .... Ms. Valerie I. MALZACHER
35 Director of Student Life .... Mr. Paul SHEPHERD
41 Interim Athletic Director .... Mrs. Crystal LANNING
37 Director Financial Assistance .... Mr. Robert BODE
45 Director Campus Planning .... Mr. Dale K. BRAUN
19 Director of Protective Services .... Mr. Karl FLEURY
96 Director Purchasing Services .... Ms. Gail ANDERSON
88 Dir Academic Success Center .... Ms. Chuayi YANG
35 Dir Student Services & Programs ..... Mr. Gregg M. HEINSELMAN
29 Director Alumni Relations .... Mr. Daniel E. MCGINTY
09 Director of Institutional Research .... Mrs. Jennifer DREWS
92 Director Honors Program .... Ms. Kathleen HUNZER
38 Director Student Counseling .... Ms. Alice REILLY-MYKLEBUST
56 Outreach Program Manager .... Ms. Pamela BOWEN
88 McNair Scholars Director .... Dr. Natalie STROBACH
26 Director of Communications and ER .... Ms. Susan WALKER
39 Director of Student Housing .... Ms. Karla THOENNES
40 Manager Bookstore .... Ms. Sherry REHNELT
04 Administrative Asst to Chancellor .... Ms. Sherri SKOGEN
100 Chief of Staff .... Ms. Beth SCHOMMER

*University of Wisconsin-Stevens Point (C)

2100 Main Street, Stevens Point WI 54481-3871

County: Portage — FICE Identification: 003924
Unit ID: 240480
Telephone: (715) 346-0123 — Carnegie Class: Masters/S
FAX Number: (715) 346-4841 — Calendar System: Semester
URL: www.uwsp.edu
Established: 1894 — Annual Undergrad Tuition & Fees (In-State): $7,672
Enrollment: 9,330 — Coed
Affiliation or Control: State — IRS Status: 501(c)3
Highest Offering: Doctorate
Accreditation: NH, ART, AUD, CAATE, CIDA, DANCE, DIETD, ENG, MT, MUS, NURSE, SP, SW, THEA

02 Chancellor .... Dr. Bernie PATTERSON
05 Provost & Vice Chancellor .... Dr. Greg SUMMERS
10 Vice Chancellor Business Affairs .... Mr. Gregory M. DIEMER
32 Vice Chancellor Student Affairs .... Dr. Al THOMPSON
20 AVC for Tech/Learning/Acad Pgms .... Dr. Todd HUSPENI
100 Chief of Staff .... Dr. Robert MANZKE
15 AVC Person/Bdgt/Grants/Summer Pgms .... Dr. Katie JORE
51 Exec Dir UWSP Continuing Education .... Mr. Tom GOSPODARCZYK
07 Director Admissions .... Mr. Bill JORDAN
37 Director of Financial Aid .... Ms. Mandy ELOWINSKI
19 Director Safety & Loss Control .... Mr. Jeff KARCHER
30 Vice Chanc Univ Advancement .... Mr. Chris RICHARDS
29 Director of Alumni Affairs .... Ms. Laura GEHRMAN-ROTTIER
26 Interim Dir Univ Relations/Comm .... Mr. Gary WESCOTT
16 Director of Personnel .... Ms. Pam DOLLARD
38 Director Counseling Center .... Dr. Stacey GERKEN
13 Dir of Information Technology .... Mr. Jim BARRETT
22 Director Equity/Affirmative Action .... Ms. Pam DOLLARD
08 Director University Library .... Dr. Kathy DAVIS
06 Registrar .... Mr. Ed LEE
18 Chief Facilities/Physical Plant .... Mr. Paul HASLER
36 Interim Director Career Services .... Ms. Sue KISSINGER
96 Purchasing Manager .... Ms. Heidi WALLNER
57 Int Dean Col Fine Arts/Commun .... Dr. Rhonda SPRAGUE
49 Dean College of Letters & Science .... Dr. Christopher CIRMO
65 Dean Coll of Natural Resources .... Dr. Christine L. THOMAS
107 Dean Col of Professional Studies .... Dr. Marty LOY
09 Director of Institutional Research .... Vacant
28 Director of Multicultural Affairs .... Mr. Ron STREGE
35 Director Student Affairs .... Dr. Al THOMPSON
04 Administrative Asst to President .... Ms. Jean SCHERER
104 Director Study Abroad .... Dr. Eric YONKE
41 Athletic Director .... Dr. Daron MONTGOMERY
50 Dean of Business .... Dr. Gary MULLINS
84 Director Enrollment Management .... Mr. Jim BARRETT
86 Director Government Relations .... Dr. Robert MANZKE
39 Director Student Housing .... Mr. Brian FAUST

*University of Wisconsin-Stout (D)

712 South Broadway, Menomonie WI 54751-2458

County: Dunn — FICE Identification: 003915
Unit ID: 240417
Telephone: (715) 232-1122 — Carnegie Class: Masters/L
FAX Number: (715) 232-1416 — Calendar System: 4/1/4
URL: www.uwstout.edu
Established: 1891 — Annual Undergrad Tuition & Fees (In-State): $9,203
Enrollment: 9,394 — Coed
Affiliation or Control: State — IRS Status: 501(c)3
Highest Offering: Beyond Master's But Less Than Doctorate
Accreditation: NH, ACBSP, ART, CACREP, CIDA, CONST, CORE, CS, DIETD, DIETI, ENG, ENGT, MFCD, TED

53 Dean Col of Ed/Hosp/Hlth/Hum Sci .... Dr. Robert SALT
02 Chancellor .... Dr. Robert MEYER
05 Provost & Vice Chancellor .... Dr. Patrick GUILFOILE
10 Vice Chanc for Admin/Student Life .... Mr. Phil LYONS
20 Associate Vice Chancellor .... Dr. Glendali RODRIQUEZ
30 Vice Chanc Univ Advance/Mktg .... Mr. Mark PARSON
32 Asst VC Student Life Svcs .... Mr. Scott GRIESBACH
28 Asst Vice Chanc for Diversity .... Vacant
45 Asst Chanc Plng/Assess/Rsrch/Qual .. Dr. Meridith DRZAKOWSKI
49 Dean Col Arts/Humanities/Social Sci .... Dr. Maria ALM
81 Dean Col of Science/Tech/Engr/Math .... Dr. Charles BOMAR
35 Interm Dean of Students .... Ms. Sandi SCOTT DUEX
06 Registrar .... Mr. Scott CORRELL
84 Director Enrollment Management .... Vacant
36 Interim Director Career Services .... Mr. Bryan BARTS
08 Interm Director University Library .... Ms. Susan LINDAHL
04 Special Assistant to the Chancellor .... Ms. Kristi KRIMPELBEIN
37 Director Student Financial Aid .... Ms. Beth BOISEN
26 Director University Communications .... Mr. Doug MELL
21 Director Business/Financial Svcs .. Ms. Kim SCHULTE-SHOBERG
13 Chief Information Officer .... Mr. Doug J. WAHL
76 Exec Director Health & Safety .... Mr. James UHLIR
15 Interim Director Human Resources .... Ms. Kristi KRIMPELBEIN
38 Director Counseling Center .... Dr. John ACHTER
23 Director Student Health Services .... Ms. Janice LAWRENCE-RAMAEKER
40 Director Bookstore .... Ms. Cathy CLOSE
44 Director of the Annual Fund .... Ms. Jennifer RUDIGER
85 Director International Education .... Vacant
18 Director Physical Plant .... Ms. Shirley KLEBESADEL
96 Director Procurement/Materials Mgmt .... Mr. Brent TILTON
39 Dir University Housing .... Ms. Sandra SCOTT DUEX
41 Director Athletics .... Mr. Duey NAATZ
29 Director Alumni Relations .... Ms. Juliet FOX
19 Dir of Safety & Risk Management .... Mr. Dean A. SANKEY
19 Coordinator University Police .... Ms. Lisa A. WALTER
106 Assoc Dir Online Educ/E-learning .... Dr. Amy GULLIXSON

*University of Wisconsin-Superior (E)

Belknap and Catlin, PO Box 2000, Superior WI 54880-4500

County: Douglas — FICE Identification: 003925
Unit ID: 240426
Telephone: (715) 394-8101 — Carnegie Class: Bac-Diverse
FAX Number: (715) 394-8454 — Calendar System: Semester
URL: www.uwsuper.edu
Established: 1893 — Annual Undergrad Tuition & Fees (In-State): $8,036
Enrollment: 2,600 — Coed
Affiliation or Control: State — IRS Status: 501(c)3
Highest Offering: Beyond Master's But Less Than Doctorate
Accreditation: NH, MUS, SW

02 Chancellor .... Dr. Renee WACHTER
05 Int Provost/Vice Chanc Acad Affairs .... Dr. Jackie WEISSENBURGER
30 Vice Chanc University Advancement ... Ms. Jeanne E. THOMPSON
32 Dean of Students .... Mr. Harry ANDERSON
21 Controller .... Mr. Robert B. WAKSDAHL
10 Vice Chanc Administration/Finance .... Ms. Gigi KOENIG
15 Int Assoc Director Human Resources .... Mr. Steve MARSHALL
18 Director Facilities Management .... Mr. Dustin JOHNSON
26 Dir Communications/Government Rels .... Mr. Daniel FANNING
06 Registrar .... Mr. Jeff KIRSHLING
08 Interim Librarian .... Ms. Laura JACOBS
07 Director of Admissions .... Mr. Robert STRAND
41 Interim Athletic Director .... Mr. Nick BURSIK
37 Director Student Financial Aid .... Ms. Donna R. DAHLVANG
13 Director Administrative Info Svcs .... Vacant
51 Dir Center Cont Educ/Online Svcs .... Mr. Ryan MATARA
56 Int Dir Distance Learning/Cont Educ .... Ms. Karen HEIKEL
40 Director Bookstore .... Mr. Vaughn N. RUSSOM
29 Director Alumni Relations .... Mr. Thomas K. BERGH
38 Director Advisement .... Ms. Courtney ALEXANDER
28 Interim Director of Diversity .... Ms. Gabriela THEIS
84 Director Enrollment Management .... Dr. Christopher TREMBLAY

*University of Wisconsin-Whitewater (F)

800 W Main, Whitewater WI 53190-1790

County: Walworth — FICE Identification: 003926
Unit ID: 240189
Telephone: (262) 472-1918 — Carnegie Class: Masters/L
FAX Number: (262) 472-1518 — Calendar System: Semester
URL: www.uww.edu
Established: 1868 — Annual Undergrad Tuition & Fees (In-State): $7,637
Enrollment: 12,176 — Coed
Affiliation or Control: State — IRS Status: 501(c)3
Highest Offering: Doctorate
Accreditation: NH, ART, BUS, CACREP, ENGR, MUS, SP, SW, THEA

02 Chancellor .... Dr. Beverly A. KOPPER

05 Prov/Exec Vice Chanc Academic Affs ... Dr. Susan ELROD
32 Vice Chancellor Student Affairs ... Dr. Thomas R. RIOS
30 VC Univ Advance/Foundation Pres ... Mr. Jonathan ENSLIN
11 Vice Chanc Administrative Affs ... Mr. Jeff (Dean) ARNOLD
20 Assoc Vice Chanc Academic Affairs ... Dr. Greg COOK
13 Asst Vice Chanc Tech/Info Resource ... Dr. Elena POKOT
84 Asst Vice Chanc Enroll/Retention ... Mr. Matt ASCHENBRENER
09 Director of Institutional Research ... Ms. Lynsey SCHWABROW
20 AVC Multicult Affs/Stdnt Success ... Dr. Richard MCGREGORY
37 Director of Financial Aid ... Ms. Carol A. MILLER
10 Chief Business Officer ... Mr. Jeff (Dean) ARNOLD
26 Chief Public Relations Officer ... Ms. Sara KUHL
21 Director of Budget ... Ms. Aimee C. ARNOLD
07 Director of Admissions ... Dr. Jeremy REED
06 Registrar ... Ms. Jodi M. HARE-PAYNTER
36 Director of Career Services ... Mr. Ron BUCHHOLZ
15 Director Human Resources/Diversity ... Ms. Judith M. TRAMPF
85 Dir Center for Global Education ... Ms. Candace A. CHENOWETH
44 Exec Dir University Development ... Ms. Kate LOFTUS
18 Director Facility Planning/Mgmt ... Mr. Greg SWANSON
38 Exec Dir Univ Health/Counseling Svc ... Dr. Richard L. JAZDZEWSKI
96 Director of Purchasing ... Mr. Michael T. HIRSCHFIELD
28 Director of Diversity ... Dr. Elizabeth OGUNSOLA
92 Director of Honors Program ... Dr. Elizabeth KIM
88 Int Dir Acad Advising/Explor Ctr ... Ms. Pamela TANNER
35 Dean of Students ... Ms. Artanya WESLEY
57 Dean Arts/Communication ... Dr. Robert MERTENS
50 Dean of Business & Economics ... Dr. John CHENOWETH
53 Dean Education/Professional Studies ... Dr. Katharina E. HEYNING
49 Dean Letters & Sciences ... Dr. David TRAVIS
58 Dean Grad Stds/Continuing Educ ... Dr. Seth MEISEL
04 Executive Asst to the Chancellor ... Mrs. Kari HEIDENREICH
41 Athletic Director ... Ms. Amy EDMONDS

*University of Wisconsin Colleges (A)

432 N. Lake Street, Room 401, Madison WI 53706
County: Dane — FICE Identification: 003897
Unit ID: 240055
Telephone: (608) 262-3786 — Carnegie Class: Assoc/HT-High Trad
FAX Number: (608) 262-7872 — Calendar System: Semester
URL: www.uwc.edu
Established: 1964 — Annual Undergrad Tuition & Fees (In-State): $5,148
Enrollment: 14,045 — Coed
Affiliation or Control: State — IRS Status: 501(c)3
Highest Offering: Baccalaureate
Accreditation: NH

02 Chancellor ... Dr. Cathy SANDEEN
05 Provost/Vice Chancellor ... Dr. Gregory P. LAMPE
10 Vice Chancellor Admin & Fin Svcs ... Mr. Steve C. WILDECK
32 Assoc VC Stdt Svcs & Enroll Mgmt ... Dr. Richard BARNHOUSE
20 Assoc Vice Chancellor Acad Affairs ... Dr. Joseph FOY
21 Assoc VC Admin & Finance ... Ms. Colleen GODFRIAUX
84 Exec Dir Marketing & Enrollment ... Ms. Vicki KEEGAN
13 Chief Information Officer ... Mr. Werner GADE
15 Asst Vice Chanc Human Resources ... Mr. Jason BEIER
06 Registrar ... Mr. Larry GRAVES
37 Director Student Financial Aid ... Mr. William TRIPPETT
26 Exec Director University Relations ... Vacant
28 Dir Equity/Diversity & Inclusion ... Ms. Christine CURLEY
104 Director International Programs ... Mr. Tim URBONYA
100 Chief of Staff to the Chancellor ... Ms. Molly VIDAL
12 Northeast Regional Dean ... Dr. Martin RUDD
12 Southwest Regional Dean ... Dr. Charles E. CLARK
12 North Regional Dean ... Dr. Keith MONTGOMERY
12 Southeast Regional Dean ... Dr. Jackie JOSEPH-SILVERSTEIN

*University of Wisconsin Baraboo/Sauk County (B)

1006 Connie Road, Baraboo WI 53913
Telephone: (608) 355-5200 — Identification: 770450
Accreditation: &NH

† Regional accreditation is carried under the parent institution in Madison, WI

*University of Wisconsin Barron County (C)

1800 College Drive, Rice Lake WI 54868
Telephone: (715) 234-8176 — Identification: 770457
Accreditation: &NH

† Regional accreditation is carried under the parent institution in Madison, WI

*University of Wisconsin Fond du Lac (D)

400 University Drive, Fond du Lac WI 54935
Telephone: (920) 929-1100 — Identification: 770451
Accreditation: &NH

† Regional accreditation is carried under the parent institution in Madison, WI

*University of Wisconsin Fox Valley (E)

1478 Midway Road, Menasha WI 54952
Telephone: (920) 832-2600 — Identification: 770456
Accreditation: &NH

† Regional accreditation is carried under the parent institution in Madison, WI

*University of Wisconsin Manitowoc (F)

705 Viebahn Street, Manitowoc WI 54220-6699
Telephone: (920) 683-4700 — Identification: 770453
Accreditation: &NH

† Regional accreditation is carried under the parent institution in Madison, WI

*University of Wisconsin-Marathon County (G)

518 South 7th Avenue, Wausau WI 54401
Telephone: (715) 261-6100 — Identification: 770461
Accreditation: &NH

† Regional accreditation is carried under the parent institution in Madison, WI

*University of Wisconsin Marinette (H)

750 W Bay Shore Street, Marinette WI 54143-4253
Telephone: (715) 735-4300 — Identification: 770454
Accreditation: &NH

† Regional accreditation is carried under the parent institution in Madison, WI

*University of Wisconsin Marshfield/Wood County (I)

2200 West 5th Street, Marshfield WI 54449
Telephone: (715) 389-6530 — Identification: 770455
Accreditation: &NH

† Regional accreditation is carried under the parent institution in Madison, WI

*University of Wisconsin Richland (J)

1200 Highway 14 West, Richland Center WI 53581-1316
Telephone: (608) 647-6186 — Identification: 770458
Accreditation: &NH

† Regional accreditation is carried under the parent institution in Madison, WI

*University of Wisconsin Rock County (K)

2909 Kellogg Avenue, Janesville WI 53546
Telephone: (608) 758-6565 — Identification: 770452
Accreditation: &NH

† Regional accreditation is carried under the parent institution in Madison, WI

*University of Wisconsin Sheboygan (L)

One University Drive, Sheboygan WI 53081-4760
Telephone: (920) 459-6600 — Identification: 770459
Accreditation: &NH

† Regional accreditation is carried under the parent institution in Madison, WI

*University of Wisconsin Washington County (M)

400 University Drive, West Bend WI 53095
Telephone: (262) 335-5200 — Identification: 770462
Accreditation: &NH

† Regional accreditation is carried under the parent institution in Madison, WI

*University of Wisconsin Waukesha (N)

1500 N University Drive, Waukesha WI 53188-2799
Telephone: (262) 521-5200 — Identification: 770460
Accreditation: &NH

† Regional accreditation is carried under the parent institution in Madison, WI

Viterbo University (O)

900 Viterbo Court, La Crosse WI 54601-8802
County: La Crosse — FICE Identification: 003911
Unit ID: 240107
Telephone: (608) 796-3000 — Carnegie Class: Masters/L
FAX Number: (608) 796-3050 — Calendar System: Semester
URL: www.viterbo.edu
Established: 1890 — Annual Undergrad Tuition & Fees: $25,050
Enrollment: 2,804 — Coed
Affiliation or Control: Roman Catholic — IRS Status: 501(c)3
Highest Offering: Doctorate
Accreditation: NH, ACBSP, CACREP, DIETC, DIETI, MUS, NURSE, SW, TED

01 President ... Dr. Richard B. ARTMAN
05 Vice President for Academic Affairs ... Dr. Glena TEMPLE
32 Vice President Student Development ... Dr. Diane L. BRIMMER
10 Vice Pres Administration/Finance ... Mr. Todd M. ERICSON
30 Vice Pres Institutional Advancement ... Mr. Wendell SNODGRASS
26 Vice Pres Communications/Marketing ... Mr. Paul WILHELMSON
21 Assistant Vice President Finance ... Mr. Eugene R. ALBERTS
07 Dean of Admission ... Mr. Robert L. FORGET
42 Chaplain ... Fr. Conrad A. TARGONSKI
66 Int Dean College of Nursing/Health ... Dr. Mary Lu GERKE
53 Int Dean Col of Education/Sci/Math ... Dr. Jerry KEMBER
49 Dean School Letters & Sciences ... Dr. Glena G. TEMPLE
57 Dean School of Fine Arts/Humanities ... Dr. Timothy B. SCHORR
50 Dean Dahl School of Business ... Dr. Thomas E. KNOTHE
58 Dean Graduate/Prof/Adult Education ... Vacant
88 Director of Ethics in Leadership ... Dr. Richard L. KYTE
06 Registrar ... Ms. Kori SALASKI
08 Director of Library ... Ms. Gretel L. STOCK-KUPPERMAN
13 Director Instruct/Info Technology ... Ms. Sarah BEARBOWER
41 Athletic Director ... Mr. Barry J. FRIED
37 Director of Financial Aid ... Ms. Terry W. NORMAN
29 Director Alumni Relations ... Ms. Kathleen A. DUERWACHTER
36 Director Career Planning/Placement ... Ms. Beth D. DOLDER-ZIEKE
15 Director of Human Resources ... Ms. Heather BUTTERFIELD
09 Director Institutional Research ... Ms. Naomi R. STENNES-SPIDAHL
18 Director Physical Plant ... Mr. Eugene M. MCCURDY
38 Dir Counseling/Student Development ... Ms. Lesley A. STUGELMAYER
39 Director of Residence Life ... Ms. Crystal LILLGE
53 Director Grad Studies in Education ... Ms. Jeanette ARMSTRONG
88 Dir Faculty Dev/Internship Coord ... Dr. Theresa MOORE
88 Director of Global Education ... Mr. Shaojie JIANG
19 Director Campus Safety ... Ms. Lisa JOSVAI
07 Associate Director of Admissions ... Mr. Eric R. SCHMIDT
04 Executive Admin Asst to President ... Ms. Sheila SEVERSON

Wisconsin Lutheran College (P)

8800 W Bluemound Road, Milwaukee WI 53226-4699
County: Milwaukee — FICE Identification: 021366
Unit ID: 240338
Telephone: (414) 443-8800 — Carnegie Class: Bac-Diverse
FAX Number: (414) 443-8514 — Calendar System: Semester
URL: www.wlc.edu
Established: 1973 — Annual Undergrad Tuition & Fees: $27,040
Enrollment: 1,179 — Coed
Affiliation or Control: Independent Non-Profit — IRS Status: 501(c)3
Highest Offering: Master's
Accreditation: NH, NURSE

01 President ... Dr. Daniel W. JOHNSON
05 Provost & VP of Academic Affairs ... Dr. John D. KOLANDER
32 Vice President Student Life ... Rev. Nathan STROBEL
10 Vice Pres Finance & Administration ... Mr. Gary SCHMID
26 Exec Dir Marketing & Communication ... Mr. James BRANDT
30 Vice Pres Development ... Mr. Richard MANNISTO
15 Vice Pres of Human Resources ... Mr. Steven SCHROEDER
21 Asst Vice Pres Finance ... Mrs. Diane HOEHNKE
07 Exec Director of Admissions ... Mr. Lucas FAUST
06 Registrar ... Mr. Brett VALERIO
08 Director of Library Services ... Mrs. Starla C. SIEGMANN
37 Director Student Financial Aid ... Mrs. Linda L. LOEFFEL
42 Campus Pastor ... Rev. Wayne SHEVEY
53 Director Teacher Education ... Prof. James HOLMAN
39 Director Residential Life/Housing ... Mr. Adam VOLBRECHT
41 Athletic Director ... Mr. Edward NOON
88 Director of Arts Programming ... Mr. Daniel SCHMAL
13 Director of Information Technology ... Mr. John MEYER
29 Director of Alumni Relations ... Mrs. Lisa LEFFEL
44 Sr Director of Planned Giving ... Vacant
09 Information Systems Analyst ... Mrs. Olya FINNEGAN
102 Director Corp/Foundation Relations ... Ms. Sharon PATTERSON
18 Chief Facilities/Physical Plant ... Mr. Gary SCHMID
24 Media Services Coordinator ... Mr. Tim SNYDER

Wisconsin School of Professional Psychology (Q)

9120 W Hampton Avenue, Milwaukee WI 53225-4960
County: Milwaukee — FICE Identification: 022713
Unit ID: 240213
Telephone: (414) 464-9777 — Carnegie Class: Spec-4-yr-Other Health
FAX Number: (414) 358-5590 — Calendar System: Semester
URL: www.wspp.edu
Established: 1979 — Annual Graduate Tuition & Fees: N/A
Enrollment: 91 — Coed
Affiliation or Control: Independent Non-Profit — IRS Status: 501(c)3
Highest Offering: Doctorate; No Undergraduates
Accreditation: NH, CLPSY

01 President ... Dr. Kathleen M. RUSCH
05 Dean ... Dr. Dale A. BESPALEC
04 Office Manager ... Ms. Veronica V. EGERSON
17 Director Clinical Training ... Dr. Susan DVORAK
08 Head Librarian ... Ms. Rebecca DOUGHERTY
37 Director Student Financial Aid ... Mr. Erik MOZOLIK

*Wisconsin Technical College System (R)

PO Box 7874, Madison WI 53707-7874
County: Dane — Identification: 666185
Telephone: (608) 266-1207 — Carnegie Class: N/A
FAX Number: (608) 266-1285
URL: www.wtcsystem.edu

01 President ... Ms. Morna K. FOY
03 Executive Vice President ... Mr. James ZYLSTRA

05 Provost/Vice President .... Ms. Kathleen CULLEN
45 Dir Strategic Advancement .... Mr. Conor SMYTH

*Blackhawk Technical College (A)

PO Box 5009, Janesville WI 53547-5009
County: Rock FICE Identification: 005390
Unit ID: 238397
Telephone: (608) 758-6900 Carnegie Class: Assoc/HVT-High Trad
FAX Number: (608) 757-7740 Calendar System: Semester
URL: www.blackhawk.edu
Established: 1912 Annual Undergrad Tuition & Fees (In-District): $4,045
Enrollment: 2,471 Coed
Affiliation or Control: State/Local IRS Status: 501(c)3
Highest Offering: Associate Degree
Accreditation: NH, ACFEI, ADNUR, DA, DMS, #MAC, MLTAD, PTAA, RAD

02 President .... Dr. Tracy P. PIERNER
05 Vice President Learning .... Dr. Diane NYHAMMER
10 Vice President Finance/College Oper .... Ms. Renea L. RANGUETTE
15 Vice President Human Resources .... Mr. Brian B. GOHLKE
32 Vice President Student Services .... Mr. Edward G. ROBINSON
09 Dir Institutional Effectiveness .... Mr. G. Scott DAVIS
04 Asst to President/Board Liaison .... Ms. Jacqueline J. PINS
13 Chief Information Officer .... Vacant
26 Marketing & Communications Mgr .... Mr. Gary KOHN
97 Dean Gen Ed/Academic Support .... Dr. Sally VOGL-BAUER
88 Assoc Dean Gen Ed/Academic Supp .... Mr. Darian SNOW
76 Dean Health Sciences .... Ms. Nancy R. LIGHTFIELD
88 Dean Public Safety .... Mr. Gary TRULSON
19 Manager of Campus Safety & Security .... Mr. Brad K. SMITH
88 EMS Fire Service & Paramedic Coord .... Mr. Robert BALSAMO
66 Assoc Dean Nursing .... Dr. Doris G. ELLISON
72 Dean Advanced Mfg & Transportation .... Dr. Garry D. KRAUSE
50 Dean Business and Econ Dev .... Dr. Gina MCCONOUGHEY
12 Director of Monroe Campus .... Mr. Matthew URBAN
21 Controller .... Mr. Gerri DOWNING
25 Manager Grants Administration .... Mr. Andrew S. MCGRATH
37 Director of Financial Aid .... Ms. Deena WETTSTEIN
06 Director Student Development .... Ms. Kerry K. FROEHLICH-MUELLER
18 Facilities Director .... Mr. Steve KORMANAK
96 Manager Purchasing/Fac Design .... Mr. Thomas PELLIZZI
51 Continuing Education Manager .... Ms. Kerry OSMOND
08 Director of Learning Resources .... Dr. Elizabeth REZEL
30 Director of Advancement & Comm Rel .... Vacant

*Chippewa Valley Technical College (B)

620 W Clairemont Avenue, Eau Claire WI 54701-6162
County: Eau Claire FICE Identification: 005304
Unit ID: 240116
Telephone: (715) 833-6200 Carnegie Class: Assoc/HVT-Mix Trad/Non
FAX Number: (715) 833-6470 Calendar System: Semester
URL: www.cvtc.edu
Established: 1912 Annual Undergrad Tuition & Fees (In-District): $4,159
Enrollment: 6,074 Coed
Affiliation or Control: Local IRS Status: 501(c)3
Highest Offering: Associate Degree
Accreditation: NH, ADNUR, CAHIIM, COARC, DH, DMS, EMT, MAC, MLTAD, PTAA, RAD, SURGT

02 President .... Bruce A. BARKER
05 Vice President Education .... Julie FURST-BOWE
11 Vice President Operations .... Tom G. HUFFCUTT
32 Vice President Student Services .... Margo A. KEYS
12 Exec Dean Health/Emer Svcs & RF .... Shelly OLSON
12 Chippewa Falls Campus Manager .... Angela ECKMAN
12 Menomonie Campus Manager .... Daniel LYTLE
12 Director of B&I Services .... Roxann VANDERWYST
46 Director Plng/Research & Grants .... Margaret A. DICKENS
75 Dean Skilled Trades & Engineering .... Jeff SULLIVAN
06 Registrar .... Jessica SCHWARTZ
84 Director of Enrollment Services .... Paige WEGNER
37 Financial Aid Officer .... Barbara CLOUTIER
31 Dir of Mktg & Community Relations .... Pam HALLER
10 Director of Budget & Finance .... Kirk L. MOIST
88 Director of Prof Development .... Debra WALSH
13 Director of Info Technology .... Tom J. LANGE
35 Student Central Manager .... Laura ERICSON
35 Student Life Specialist .... Alisa S. SCHLEY
96 Purchasing Representative .... Doug D. DEKAN
21 Budget & Purchasing Manager .... Tracy M. DRIER
19 Public Safety Manager .... William HENNING
28 Diversity Manager .... Dang YANG
88 Director Advisement & Services .... Natalyn M. MARLAIRE
35 Dean Academic and Develop Services .... Jennifer ANDEREGG
102 Exec Dir CVTC Found/Alumni Assoc .... Aliesha R. CROWE
25 Grants & Accreditation Manager .... Shana SCHMIDT
108 Intake Assesment Data Analyst .... Philip V. PALSER
50 Dean Business & Academic Initiative .... Lynette LIVINGSTON
18 Director of Facilities .... Rod BAGLEY
15 Human Resources Director .... Tam BURGAU
21 Business Office Manager .... Sara J. NICK
97 Dean Gen Educ & Liberal Arts .... Cherrie BERGANDI
88 Dean Ag/Energy/Transportation .... Adam WEHLING
88 Criminal Justice Director .... Eric ANDERSON
88 Curr Spec/Instr Designer .... Jodi RUST
76 Assoc Dean of Health .... Jennifer MCSORLEY
04 Executive Asst to President .... Lauren SULLIVAN

*Fox Valley Technical College (C)

1825 N Bluemound Drive, Appleton WI 54914-1543
County: Outagamie FICE Identification: 009744
Unit ID: 238722
Telephone: (920) 735-5600 Carnegie Class: Assoc/HVT-High Non
FAX Number: (920) 735-2582 Calendar System: Semester
URL: www.fvtc.edu
Established: 1967 Annual Undergrad Tuition & Fees (In-District): $4,373
Enrollment: 10,519 Coed
Affiliation or Control: State/Local IRS Status: 501(c)3
Highest Offering: Associate Degree
Accreditation: NH, ACFEI, ADNUR, CAHIIM, DA, DH, EMT, MAC, OTA

02 President .... Dr. Susan A. MAY
05 CAO/VP Instructional Services .... Dr. Christopher MATHENY
11 VP Facilities & Operations .... Ms. Jill MCEWEN
32 VP Student/Community Development .... Dr. Patti JORGENSEN
15 VP Human Resources .... Ms. Deb GORMAN
72 Dean Manufacturing & Agriculture .... Mr. Steve STRAUB
10 VP Financial Services/CFO .... Ms. Amy VAN STRATEN
13 VP Information Tech/CIO .... Mr. Troy KOHL
97 Dean General Studies .... Ms. Carol MAY
102 Exec Dir FVTC Foundation/Cmty Rels .... Ms. Mary DOWNS
12 Oshkosh Campus Director .... Ms. Melissa KOHN
37 Director Student Financial Svcs .... Ms. Stacy DORAN
06 Registrar .... Mr. Brian BUSS
26 Director College Marketing .... Ms. Barb DREGER
88 Director Compensation & Benefits .... Ms. Barb KIEFFER
88 Director Venture Center .... Ms. Amy PIETSCH
46 Director College Effectiveness .... Dr. Patti FROHRIB

*Gateway Technical College (D)

3520 30th Avenue, Kenosha WI 53144-1690
County: Kenosha FICE Identification: 005389
Unit ID: 238759
Telephone: (262) 564-2200 Carnegie Class: Assoc/HVT-High Non
FAX Number: (262) 564-2201 Calendar System: Semester
URL: www.gtc.edu
Established: 1912 Annual Undergrad Tuition & Fees (In-District): $4,090
Enrollment: 7,410 Coed
Affiliation or Control: State/Local IRS Status: 501(c)3
Highest Offering: Associate Degree
Accreditation: NH, ACBSP, ADNUR, DA, PTAA, SURGT

02 President .... Dr. Bryan D. ALBRECHT
05 Exec VP/Prov/Chief Academic Officer .... Ms. Zina HAYWOOD
12 Dean Racine Campus .... Mr. Ray KOUKARI
12 Dean Elkhorn Campus .... Mr. Michael O'DONNELL
12 Dean Kenosha Campus .... Mr. Gary FLYNN
10 Vice President Finance .... Ms. Bane THOMEY
86 VP Government/Community Relations .... Ms. Stephanie SKLBA
103 VP Workforce/Economic Develop Div .... Ms. Debbie DAVIDSON
32 Asst Provost/VP IE/Student Success .... Dr. John THIBODEAU
35 Associate VP Student Success .... Ms. Stacy RILEY
88 Dean Learning Success .... Dr. Tammi SUMMERS
06 Registrar .... Ms. Chrystal MOEZ
09 Associate VP Institutional Research .... Ms. Anne WHYNOTT
15 VP Human Resources and Facilities .... Mr. William WHYTE
26 Marketing Director .... Ms. Jayne HERRING
07 Director of College Access .... Ms. Amanda VIRZI
18 Chief Facilities/Physical Plant .... Mr. William WHYTE
21 Controller .... Ms. Sharon JOHNSON
37 Director Student Financial Aid .... Mr. Justin KEHRING
28 Director of Diversity .... Ms. Debbie MILLER
102 Foundation Executive Director .... Dr. Jennifer CHARPENTIER
13 Chief Info Technology Officer (CIO) .... Mr. Jeff ROBSHAW

*Lakeshore Technical College (E)

1290 North Avenue, Cleveland WI 53015-1414
County: Manitowoc FICE Identification: 009194
Unit ID: 239008
Telephone: (920) 693-1000 Carnegie Class: Assoc/HVT-High Non
FAX Number: (920) 693-8078 Calendar System: Semester
URL: www.gotoltc.edu
Established: 1913 Annual Undergrad Tuition & Fees (In-District): $4,064
Enrollment: 3,008 Coed
Affiliation or Control: State/Local IRS Status: 501(c)3
Highest Offering: Associate Degree
Accreditation: NH, ADNUR, EMT, RAD

02 President .... Dr. Michael LANSER
04 Executive Assistant .... Ms. Heidi SOODSMA
05 Vice President of Instruction .... Dr. Barbara DODGE
32 Vice President of Student Services .... Dr. Douglas GOSSEN
103 Vice President Workforce & Econ Dev .... Mr. Peter THILLMAN
15 Chief Human Resources Officer .... Ms. Kathleen KOTAJARVI
10 Chief Financial Officer .... Ms. Cindy DROSS
09 Quality/Continuous Improvement Mgr .... Ms. Cheryl TERP
26 Director of Marketing .... Ms. Julie MIRECKI
28 Diversity Coordinator .... Ms. Nicole YANG
88 Associate Dean Mgf & Appr .... Ms. Sheila SCHETTER
50 Dean Business & Technology .... Mr. Ed JANAIRO
97 Dean General & Pre-College Educ .... Ms. Rachelle PHAKITTHONG
47 Exec Dean Mfg Trades/Agriculture .... Mr. Richard HOERTH
07 Enrollment Services Manager .... Mr. George HENZE
37 Financial Aid Manager .... Ms. Jessica HEMENWAY
36 Career Placement Ctr Manager .... Ms. Foua HANG
18 Physical Plant Supervisor .... Mr. Bryan KOESER
08 Library Manager .... Ms. Kelly CARPENTER
22 Affirmative Action Officer .... Ms. Kathleen KOTAJARVI
40 Bookstore Manager .... Ms. Kelly WOLFERT
13 Director of Information Technology .... Ms. Wendy NASGOVITZ
30 Director of Advancement .... Ms. Karla ZAHN
44 Development Director .... Ms. Katie WILLINGER
47 Dean of Energy & Agriculture .... Mr. Patrick STASZAK
88 Dean of Health & Human Services .... Mr. James LEMEROND
88 Dean of Public Safety .... Mr. Ryan SKABROUD
88 Assoc Dean of Culinary/Hospitality .... Dr. Rufina GARAY

*Madison Area Technical College (F)

1701 Wright Street, Madison WI 53704-2599
County: Dane FICE Identification: 004007
Unit ID: 238263
Telephone: (608) 246-6100 Carnegie Class: Bac/Assoc-Assoc Dom
FAX Number: (608) 246-6880 Calendar System: Semester
URL: www.madisoncollege.edu
Established: 1912 Annual Undergrad Tuition & Fees (In-District): $4,217
Enrollment: 16,759 Coed
Affiliation or Control: State/Local IRS Status: 501(c)3
Highest Offering: Associate Degree
Accreditation: NH, ACFEI, ADNUR, COARC, CSHSE, DH, EMT, MAC, MLTAD, OPTT, OTA, PTAA, RAD, SURGT

02 President .... Dr. Jack E. DANIELS, III
04 Admin Asst to the President .... Ms. Judith CASTRO-ROMAKER
05 Provost .... Dr. Turina BAKKEN
32 Sr VP Student Dev & Success .... Dr. Keith T. CORNILLE
26 Int Dir Commun/Strategic Marketing .... Mr. Cary R. HEYER
15 Asst VP Human Resources .... Ms. Kristin GEBHARDT
45 VP Institutional Learning/Effect .... Mr. Timothy L. CASPER
11 VP Administrative Services .... Mr. Mark THOMAS
13 Chief Information Officer .... Mr. Mirwais QADER
103 Dean Workforce Education .... Ms. Schauna RASMUSSEN
88 Dean Academic Advancement .... Mr. Christopher P. VANDALL
54 Dean Applied Science Engr & Tech .... Ms. Denise REIMER
49 Dean Arts & Sciences .... Dr. Todd H. STEBBINS
50 Dean Business & Applied Arts .... Mr. Bryan M. WOODHOUSE
76 Dean Health Education .... Dr. Mark C. LAUSCH
88 Assoc Dean Academic Advancement .... Ms. Janice L. METTAUER
51 Dean Community & Corporate Learning .... Ms. Kathleen A. RADIONOFF
38 Assoc Dean Guidance & Counseling .... Dr. Geraldo G. VILACRUZ
88 Dean Human & Protective Services .... Dr. Shawna M. CARTER
35 Director Student Life .... Ms. Renee M. ALFANO
12 Dean Northern Region .... Mr. James FALCO
12 Dean Eastern Region .... Ms. Jennifer BAKKE
88 Dean Ctr Excellence Teaching/Learn .... Ms. Sarah FRITZ
19 Director Public Safety .... Mr. James A. BOTTONI
104 Dir International Education .... Dr. Geoffrey W. BRADSHAW
88 Dir Retention & Student Svcs .... Ms. Carlotta V. CALMESE
36 Dir College & Career Transitions .... Ms. Juanita COMEAU
06 Manager Records/Admissions .... Vacant
08 Director Library Services .... Ms. Julie C. GORES
41 Athletic Director .... Mr. Stephen C. HAUSER
21 Budget Director .... Ms. Sylvia RAMIREZ
108 Director Testing and Assessment .... Mr. James A. MERRITT
10 Controller .... Ms. Lauralynn M. GRIGG
12 IBPS Administrator .... Vacant
25 Director Grants & Special Projects .... Ms. Emily J. SANDERS
84 Dean Enrollment Services .... Ms. Lori A. SEBRANEK
18 Director Facilities Services .... Mr. Michael M. STARK
102 Chief Exec Officer Foundation .... Ms. Tammy THAYER
09 Dir Inst Research & Effectiveness .... Mr. Ali R. ZARRINNAM
12 Regional Campus Manager South .... Ms. Valentina AHEDO
21 Assistant Controller .... Ms. Dorothy CONDUAH
40 Bookstore Manager .... Mr. Scott R. HEIMAN
37 Dean Financial Aid .... Ms. Melissa HABERMAN
28 VP Equity/Diversity/Cmty Relations .... Ms. Lucia NUNEZ

*Mid-State Technical College (G)

500 32nd Street N, Wisconsin Rapids WI 54494-5599
County: Wood FICE Identification: 005380
Unit ID: 239220
Telephone: (715) 422-5300 Carnegie Class: Assoc/HVT-High Non
FAX Number: (715) 422-5345 Calendar System: Semester
URL: www.mstc.edu
Established: 1967 Annual Undergrad Tuition & Fees (In-District): $4,211
Enrollment: 2,779 Coed
Affiliation or Control: State/Local IRS Status: 501(c)3
Highest Offering: Associate Degree
Accreditation: NH, ADNUR, CAHIIM, COARC, EMT, MAC, PHLEB, SURGT

02 President .... Dr. Susan BUDJAC
05 Vice President Academic Affairs .... Ms. Sandy KIDDOO
32 Vice Pres Student Affairs .... Dr. Mandy LANG
10 Vice Pres Finance & IT .... Mr. Nelson D. DAHL
15 Vice President Human Resources .... Mr. Richard O'SULLIVAN
50 Dean General Education & Business .... Vacant
75 Dean Technical/Industrial Division .... Mr. Alan JAVOROSKI
76 Dean Service & Health Div .... Ms. Barb JASCOR
12 Dean Stevens Point Campus .... Mr. Volker GAUL
12 Dean Marshfield Campus .... Ms. Brenda DILLENBURG
84 Dean of Enrollment Management .... Mr. Aamer CHAUHDRI
26 Director of Communications .... Mr. Karl EASTTORP
30 Dir Inst Effectiveness/Academics .... Dr. Debra HAGEN-FOLEY
102 Director Foundation and Alumni .... Ms. Jill STECKBAUER
18 Director of Facilities/Procurement .... Vacant
35 Director Student Support .... Ms. Christina LORGE-GROVER
96 Director of Purchasing .... Vacant

06 Registrar .... Ms. Denise BORLAND
08 Librarian .... Ms. Maria HERNANDEZ
37 Financial Aid Manager .... Mrs. Mary Jo GREEN

*Milwaukee Area Technical College (A)

700 W State Street, Milwaukee WI 53233-1443
County: Milwaukee FICE Identification: 003866
Unit ID: 239248
Telephone: (414) 297-6600 Carnegie Class: Assoc/HVT-High Trad
FAX Number: (414) 297-7990 Calendar System: Semester
URL: www.matc.edu
Established: 1912 Annual Undergrad Tuition & Fees (In-District): $4,360
Enrollment: 16,712 Coed
Affiliation or Control: Local IRS Status: 501(c)3
Highest Offering: Associate Degree
Accreditation: NH, ACFEI, ADNUR, COARC, CVT, DH, #FUSER, MAC, MLTAD, OTA, PHLEB, PNUR, PTAA, RAD, SURGT

02 President .... Dr. Vicki J. MARTIN
05 Provost .... Dr. Mohammad DAKWAR
32 Vice Pres Student Services .... Dr. Trevor KUBATZKE
10 Int Vice President of Finance .... Mr. Jeffrey HOLLOW
43 Vice President & Legal Counsel .... Ms. Janice FALKENBERG
13 Assoc VP Information Technology .... Mr. Michael WALSH
23 Dean Health Occupation .... Dr. Dessie LEVY
50 Int Dean Business & Graphic Arts .... Dr. Richard BUSALACCHI
24 General Manager Public Television .... Mr. Bohdan ZACHARY
35 Director Student Life .... Mr. Archie GRAHAM
08 Director of Library .... Vacant
37 Director Admissions/Financial Aid .... Ms. Camille NICOLAI
90 Director Technical Services .... Mr. Michael GAVIN
21 Controller .... Ms. Eva KUETHER
19 Director Public Safety .... Ms. Aisha BARKOW
06 Registrar .... Ms. Sarah ADAMS
09 Director Institutional Research .... Dr. Yan WANG
84 Manager Recruitment .... Ms. Sophia WILLIAMS
29 Director Alumni Relations .... Ms. Christine MCGEE
38 Director Counseling & Advising Svcs .... Mr. Walter LANIER
26 Chief Public Relations Officer .... Ms. Kathleen HOHL
96 Procurement Manager .... Ms. Laura MOORE
41 Coordinator Athletics .... Mr. Randy CASEY

*Moraine Park Technical College (B)

235 N National Avenue, Fond Du Lac WI 54936-1940
County: Fond Du Lac FICE Identification: 009256
Unit ID: 239372
Telephone: (920) 922-8611 Carnegie Class: Assoc/HVT-High Non
FAX Number: (920) 929-2471 Calendar System: Semester
URL: www.morainepark.edu
Established: 1967 Annual Undergrad Tuition & Fees (In-District): $4,322
Enrollment: 6,280 Coed
Affiliation or Control: State/Local IRS Status: 501(c)3
Highest Offering: Associate Degree
Accreditation: NH, ADNUR, CAHIIM, COARC, EMT, MAC, MLTAD, RAD, SURGT

02 President .... Bonnie BAERWALD
05 Vice Pres Academic Affairs .... James R. EDEN
10 VP Finance/Administrative Services .... Carrie KASUBASKI
32 Vice President Student Affairs .... Stanley CRAM
15 Vice President Human Resources .... Kathleen M. BROSKE
30 VP Marketing/College Advancement .... Sharon N. HOLMES
13 Chief Information Officer .... Jerry RICHARDS
84 Vice Pres of Enrollment Management .... Bethany M. RAFFAELLI
30 Director of College Advancement .... Dana KNEBEL
12 WB & Online Campus/Cmty Partner .... Peter J. RETTLER
12 Beaver Dam Campus/Cmty Prtnr .... Karen COLEY
20 Executive Dean of Instruction .... James V. EDEN
24 Exec Dean Instructional Support .... Gerald R. EDGREN, III
76 Exec Dean Hlth Sciences/Public Svcs .... Kathy S. VANEERDEN
88 Dean of Health Sciences/Public Svcs .... Kristin M. FINNEL
06 Registrar .... Amanda HRUSKA
26 Dir Marketing/Communications .... Melissa WORTHINGTON
07 Recruitment & Retention Associate .... Sally A. RUBACK
08 Library Services Coordinator .... Hans BAIERL
109 Auxiliary Services Associate .... Jon A. SHAPIRO
18 Facilities Associate .... Timothy J. FLOOD
22 Employment/Affirmative Action Assoc .... Beth A. MENDOZA
96 Purchasing Associate .... Charles E. BIRRINGER
37 Student Financials Partner .... Karen A. ZUEHLKE

*Nicolet Area Technical College (C)

5364 College Drive, PO Box 518,
Rhinelander WI 54501-0518
County: Oneida FICE Identification: 005384
Unit ID: 239442
Telephone: (715) 365-4493 Carnegie Class: Assoc/HVT-Mix Trad/Non
FAX Number: (715) 365-4445 Calendar System: Semester
URL: www.nicoletcollege.edu
Established: 1967 Annual Undergrad Tuition & Fees (In-State): $4,532
Enrollment: 1,139 Coed
Affiliation or Control: State IRS Status: 501(c)3
Highest Offering: Associate Degree
Accreditation: NH, ADNUR, DH, MAC

02 President .... Dr. Richard R. NELSON
05 VP of Academic Services .... Mr. Ron SKALLERUD
32 VP of Student Services .... Ms. Kathleen FERREL
10 Chief Financial Officer .... Mr. John VAN DE LOO
26 Executive Director .... Ms. Sandy KINNEY
15 Director of Human Resources .... Dr. Dan GROLEAU
13 CIO/Interim Dir Library Services .... Mr. Greg MILJEVICH
66 Dean of Health Occupations .... Dr. Lenore BLEMKE
103 Dean of Workforce/Economic Dev .... Ms. Sandy BISHOP
49 Dean of Liberal Arts/Business .... Dr. Emily STUCKENBRUCK
88 Dean of Trade/Industry/Apprentice .... Mr. Jeff LABS
19 Assoc Dean/Dir Pub Safety/Security .... Mr. Jason GOELDNER
18 Director of Facilities .... Mr. Pete VANNEY
37 Director of Financial Aid .... Ms. Jill PRICE
102 Foundation Executive Director .... Ms. Heather SCHALLOCK
09 Planning/Development/Evaluation Mgr .... Ms. Kelly HAVERKAMPF
45 Managing Dir Strategic Initiative .... Mr. Chuck KOMP
06 Registrar .... Ms. Kyle GRUENING
04 Exec Asst to President/Board .... Ms. Anne E. BONACK

*Northcentral Technical College (D)

1000 W Campus Drive, Wausau WI 54401-1880
County: Marathon FICE Identification: 005387
Unit ID: 239460
Telephone: (715) 675-3331 Carnegie Class: Assoc/HVT-High Non
FAX Number: (715) 675-9776 Calendar System: Semester
URL: www.ntc.edu
Established: 1912 Annual Undergrad Tuition & Fees (In-District): $4,230
Enrollment: 4,377 Coed
Affiliation or Control: Local IRS Status: 501(c)3
Highest Offering: Associate Degree
Accreditation: NH, ADNUR, DH, EMT, MAC, MLTAD, PHLEB, RAD, SURGT

02 President .... Dr. Lori A. WEYERS
05 Vice President for Learning .... Dr. Shelly MONDEIK
32 Vice President of Student Services .... Dr. Jeannie M. WORDEN
10 Vice President of Finance & CFO .... Ms. Roxanne LUTGEN
13 Chief Information Officer .... Mr. Chet A. STREBE
18 Director of Facilities .... Mr. Rob ELLIOTT
26 Director of Marketing & PR .... Mrs. Katrina FELCH
19 Dean Public Safety .... Ms. Sara GOSSFELD-BENZING
47 Dean Agricultural Sciences .... Dr. Vicky PIETZ
50 Dean Business/Cmty Svc/Intl Educ .... Mr. Christopher SEVERSON
12 Dean Regional Campuses .... Ms. Bobbi DAMROW
76 Dean of Health Sciences .... Ms. Lorraine ZOROMSKI
22 Employment Coord/Affirm Action Ofcr .... Ms. Cindy THELEN
88 Director Quality/Continuous Improv .... Mrs. Beth ELLIE
35 Director of Student Relations .... Mr. Shawn P. SULLIVAN
19 Director of Security .... Mr. Dan JACOBSON
06 Registrar .... Mr. Nick BLANCHETTE
84 Dean of College Enrollment .... Ms. Sarah DILLON
15 Director of Human Resources .... Ms. Karen BRZEZINSKI
97 Dean ESS/Interim Dean Gen Studies .... Ms. Debra STENCIL
36 Director of Transfer & Placement .... Ms. Suzi MATHIAS
38 Dean of Student Success .... Mrs. Shannon LIVINGSTON
75 Dean of Technical & Trades .... Mr. Darren ACKLEY
51 Dean Continuing Ed/Virtual College .... Mr. Brad GAST
04 Executive Asst to President .... Mrs. PaHnia THAO
09 Director of Institutional Research .... Mrs. Angela M. SERVI
37 Director Student Financial Aid .... Mr. Jeff CICHON

*Northeast Wisconsin Technical College (E)

PO Box 19042, 2740 W Mason Street,
Green Bay WI 54307-9042
County: Brown FICE Identification: 005301
Unit ID: 239488
Telephone: (920) 498-5444 Carnegie Class: Assoc/HVT-Mix Trad/Non
FAX Number: (920) 498-6260 Calendar System: Semester
URL: www.nwtc.edu
Established: 1913 Annual Undergrad Tuition & Fees (In-District): $4,280
Enrollment: 10,406 Coed
Affiliation or Control: State/Local IRS Status: 501(c)3
Highest Offering: Associate Degree
Accreditation: NH, ADNUR, CAHIIM, COARC, DA, DH, DMS, EMT, ENGT, MAC, MLTAD, PTAA, RAD, SURGT

02 President .... Dr. H. Jeffrey RAFN
05 Vice President of Learning .... Ms. Lori SUDDICK
32 Vice President of Student Services .... Vacant
30 Vice Pres of College Advancement .... Ms. Karen SMITS
15 Vice President of Human Resources .... Ms. Sandy RYCZKOWSKI
13 Chief Information Officer .... Ms. Linda HARTFORD
10 VP Business & Finance .... Mr. Robert MATHEWS
12 Dean Regional Learning .... Ms. Jan SCOVILLE
50 Dn Business/Information Technology .... Mr. Randy SMITH
76 Dean Health Science .... Ms. Kay TUPALA
72 Dean Trades & Engr Technologies .... Dr. Mark WEBER
97 Dean General Education .... Ms. Michaeline SCHMIT
20 Dean Learning Solutions .... Ms. Anne KAMPS
103 Dean Corp Training & Economic Devel .... Mr. Dean STEWART
38 Dean of Student Success .... Ms. Vickie LOCK
07 Dean Enrollment Services/Registrar .... Mr. Mark FRANKS
84 Mgr Assessment/Academic Coaching .... Mr. George SKENANDORE
37 Financial Aid Director .... Ms. Emily YSEBAERT
96 Director of Purchasing .... Mr. Mark CICHON
102 Foundation Director .... Ms. Crystal HARRISON
40 Director Bookstore .... Mr. Patrick SORELLE
26 Public Relations/Comm Specialist .... Ms. Kathleen FRYDA
18 Director of Facilities .... Mr. Chet LAMERS
08 Manager Library Services .... Ms. Kim LAPLANTE
104 Mgr Student Involvement/Intl Pgm .... Ms. Megan POPKEY
21 Director of Financial Operations .... Vacant
04 Administrative Asst to President .... Ms. Mary Jo TILOT
09 Institutional Researcher .... Mr. Jeff GREBINOSKI

105 Director Web Services .... Ms. Erica PLAZA
28 Director of Diversity .... Mr. Mohammed BEY

*Southwest Wisconsin Technical College (F)

1800 Bronson Boulevard, Fennimore WI 53809-9778
County: Grant FICE Identification: 007669
Unit ID: 239910
Telephone: (608) 822-3262 Carnegie Class: Assoc/HVT-Mix Trad/Non
FAX Number: (608) 822-6019 Calendar System: Semester
URL: www.swtc.edu
Established: 1967 Annual Undergrad Tuition & Fees (In-District): $4,164
Enrollment: 2,334 Coed
Affiliation or Control: State/Local IRS Status: 501(c)3
Highest Offering: Associate Degree
Accreditation: NH, ADNUR, MAC, MEAC, MLTAD, PTAA

02 President .... Dr. Jason S. WOOD
10 VP for Administrative Services .... Mr. Caleb WHITE
05 Chief Academic Officer/Exec Dean .... Ms. Kathleen E. GARRITY
50 Dean Business/Mgmt/General Studies .... Dr. Richard AMMON
47 Dean of Industry/Trades/Agriculture .... Dr. Derek DACHELET
32 Dean of Students .... Ms. Holly MILLER
15 Director of Human Resources .... Ms. Krista WEBER
30 Director Institutional Advancement .... Ms. Barbara TUCKER
102 Exec Dir of Foundation/Real Estate .... Ms. Holly CLENDENEN
13 Continuous Improvement/IT Supervsr .... Ms. Lisa RILEY
101 Executive Asst to Board/President .... Ms. Karen M. CAMPBELL
18 Director of Facilities .... Mr. Dan IMHOFF
37 Financial Aid Manager .... Ms. Joy A. KITE
19 Public Safety Supervisor .... Ms. Kris WUBBEN
88 Business & Industry Services Mgr .... Ms. Amy CHARLES
20 Innovative/Alternative Learning Mgr .... Ms. Kim MAIER
21 Controller .... Ms. Kelly KELLY
88 Supervisor of Pre-College Programs .... Ms. Julie PLUEMER
06 Registrar .... Ms. Danielle SEIPPEL
36 Career Services Manager .... Ms. Heather FIFRICK

*Waukesha County Technical College (G)

800 Main Street, Pewaukee WI 53072-4696
County: Waukesha FICE Identification: 005294
Unit ID: 240125
Telephone: (262) 691-5566 Carnegie Class: Assoc/HVT-High Non
FAX Number: (262) 691-5593 Calendar System: Semester
URL: www.wctc.edu
Established: 1923 Annual Undergrad Tuition & Fees (In-District): $4,250
Enrollment: 8,692 Coed
Affiliation or Control: State/Local IRS Status: 501(c)3
Highest Offering: Associate Degree
Accreditation: NH, ACFEI, ADNUR, CAHIIM, DH, EMT, ENGT, MAC, SURGT

02 President .... Ms. Kaylen A. BETZIG
05 VP Learning .... Ms. Denine ROOD
32 VP Student Services .... Ms. Nicole GAHAGAN
10 VP Finance .... Ms. Cary A. TESSMANN
15 VP Human Resource Svcs .... Mr. David BROWN
11 VP Strat Mktg Innov & Effectiveness .... Dr. Ann KRAUSE-HANSON
13 Chief Information Officer .... Mr. Rodney NOBLES
102 Dir Foundation/Corporate Relations .... Ms. Ellen PHILLIPS
50 Dean Business Occupations .... Dr. Bradley PIAZZA
75 Dean Industrial Occupations .... Mr. Michael SHIELS
76 Dean Service Occupations .... Dr. Greg WEST
97 Dean Academic Support .... Ms. Bethany LEONARD
76 Dean Health Occupations .... Ms. Sandra STEARNS
103 Dean Center/Business Performance .... Dr. Joseph WEITZER
35 Director Student Development .... Dr. Rinardo REDDICK
18 Director Facilities Services .... Mr. Jeffrey LEVERENZ
06 Registrar .... Ms. Penny STEFFEN
38 Director Counsel/Acad Sup/Spec Svcs .... Dr. Christopher DAOOD
36 Mgr Career Development Services .... Ms. Debra WEBER
26 Marketing & Communications Mgr .... Ms. Susan STERN
07 Mgr Admissions/Testing Svcs .... Ms. Kathleen KAZDA
106 Director Academic Technology .... Mr. Randall COOROUGH
25 Director of Grants & Contracts .... Ms. Linda J. MILLER
09 Director Inst Rsrch & Effectiveness .... Vacant
88 Associate Registrar .... Ms. Rachel BURLING
37 Manager Financial Aid .... Mr. Timothy K. JACOBSON
35 Student Life Coordinator .... Mr. Jonathan N. PEDRAZA
08 Director of Library Services .... Ms. Terry KEMPER
19 Enviro Health & Safety Supervisor .... Mr. Bruce NEUMANN
27 Specialist Public Relations .... Ms. Shelly KUHN
96 Purchasing Specialist .... Ms. Victoria NASH
28 Diversity Coordinator .... Mr. Rolando DELEON
40 Bookstore Manager .... Mr. James DRAEGER
85 International Educ Coordinator .... Mr. K. Austin BAADE
04 Administrative Asst to President .... Ms. Carolyn TINDALL

*Western Technical College (H)

400 N Seventh Street, La Crosse WI 54601-3368
County: La Crosse FICE Identification: 003840
Unit ID: 240170
Telephone: (608) 785-9200 Carnegie Class: Assoc/HVT-High Trad
FAX Number: (608) 785-9205 Calendar System: Trimester
URL: www.westerntc.edu
Established: 1912 Annual Undergrad Tuition & Fees (In-District): $3,779
Enrollment: 4,130 Coed
Affiliation or Control: State/Local IRS Status: 501(c)3
Highest Offering: Associate Degree

Accreditation: NH, ADNUR, CAHIIM, COARC, DA, EMT, MAC, MLTAD, OTA, PTAA, RAD, SURGT

02 President .... Dr. J. Lee RASCH
10 Vice President Finance/Operations .... Mr. Wade HACKBARTH
05 Vice President of Academic Affairs .... Dr. Roger STANFORD
32 VP Student Development & Success .... Dr. Denise T. VUJNOVICH
45 VP Strategic Effectiveness & Engag .... Ms. Amy THORNTON
12 Director of Ops-Regional Locations .... Ms. Jennifer BRAVE
102 Executive Director Foundation .... Mr. Michael SWENSON
13 Director Computer/Telecomm Svcs .... Mr. Bruce E. MATHEW
37 Financial Aid Manager .... Ms. Jerolyn R. GRANDALL
21 Controller .... Ms. Amy SCHMIDT
56 Director Business & Industry Svcs .... Ms. Patti BALACEK
38 Director Counseling Enroll Svcs .... Ms. Ann BRANDAU-HYNEK
29 Manager Alumni Relations .... Ms. Sally EMERSON
07 Manager Admissions/Registration .... Ms. Sandy PETERSON
35 Dean of Students .... Ms. Shelley MCNEELY
08 Manager Library Services .... Vacant
26 Assoc Director Information Services .... Ms. Joan PIERCE
40 Bookstore Manager .... Mr. David R. WIGNES
72 Dean Integrated Technology .... Mr. Josh GAMER
76 Dean Health & Public Safety .... Ms. Diane NEEFE
97 Dean General Education .... Dr. Douglas STRAUSS
50 Dean Business Education .... Mr. Gary BROWN

*Wisconsin Indianhead Technical College (A)

505 Pine Ridge Drive, Shell Lake WI 54871-9300
County: Washburn FICE Identification: 011824
Unit ID: 240198
Telephone: (715) 468-2815 Carnegie Class: Assoc/HVT-High Non
FAX Number: (715) 468-2819 Calendar System: Semester
URL: www.witc.edu
Established: 1968 Annual Undergrad Tuition & Fees (In-State): $4,545
Enrollment: 3,045 Coed
Affiliation or Control: State IRS Status: Exempt
Highest Offering: Associate Degree
Accreditation: NH, ADNUR, CAHIIM, MAC, OTA

02 President .... Mr. John WILL
10 Vice Pres Business & Tech Svcs/CFO .... Mr. Steven DECKER
05 Vice President Academic Affairs .... Dr. Bonny COPENHAVER
32 Vice President Student Affairs .... Mr. Steve BITZER
51 Vice President Cont Educ/Foundation .... Mr. Craig FOWLER
09 VP Institutional Effectiveness ..... Ms. Susan YOHNK LOCKWOOD
15 VP Human Resources/Risk Mgmt .... Ms. Cher VINK
13 Sr Director Technology Services .... Mr. James DAHLBERG
37 Director Financial Aid .... Mr. Terry KLEIN
06 Registrar .... Mr. Shane EVENSON
08 Director Learning Resources .... Mr. Scott VRIEZE
84 Director of Enrollment .... Ms. Laura SULLIVAN
26 Director Marketing & Recruitment .... Ms. Jena VOGTMAN

*Chippewa Valley Technical College-Chippewa Falls Campus (B)

770 Scheidler Road, Chippewa Falls WI 54729
Telephone: (715) 738-3841 Identification: 770419
Accreditation: &NH

† Regional accreditation is carried under the parent institution in Eau Claire, WI

*Chippewa Valley Technical College-Gateway (C)

2320 Alpine Road, Eau Claire WI 54703
Telephone: (715) 874-4600 Identification: 770420
Accreditation: &NH

† Regional accreditation is carried under the parent institution in Eau Claire, WI

*Chippewa Valley Technical College Menomonie Campus (D)

403 Technology Drive East, Menomonie WI 54751
Telephone: (715) 232-2685 Identification: 770422
Accreditation: &NH

† Regional accreditation is carried under the parent institution in Eau Claire, WI

*Chippewa Valley Technical College River Falls Campus (E)

500 South Wasson Lane, River Falls WI 54022
Telephone: (715) 425-3301 Identification: 770423
Accreditation: &NH

† Regional accreditation is carried under the parent institution in Eau Claire, WI

*Chippewa Valley Technical College-West (F)

4000 Campus Road, Eau Claire WI 54703
Telephone: (715) 852-1394 Identification: 770421
Accreditation: &NH

† Regional accreditation is carried under the parent institution in Eau Claire, WI

*Fox Valley Technical College (G)

150 N Campbell Road, Oshkosh WI 54902
Telephone: (920) 233-9191 Identification: 770425
Accreditation: &NH

† Regional accreditation is carried under the parent institution in Appleton, WI

*Gateway Technical College Burlington Center (H)

496 McCanna Parkway, Burlington WI 53105
Telephone: (262) 767-5200 Identification: 770426
Accreditation: &NH, EMT

† Regional accreditation is carried under the parent institution in Kenosha, WI

*Gateway Technical College Elkhorn Campus (I)

400 County Road H, Elkhorn WI 53121
Telephone: (262) 741-8200 Identification: 770427
Accreditation: &NH, MAC

† Regional accreditation is carried under the parent institution in Kenosha, WI

*Gateway Technical College Racine Campus (J)

1001 S Main Street, Racine WI 53403
Telephone: (262) 619-6200 Identification: 770428
Accreditation: &NH, CAHIIM

† Regional accreditation is carried under the parent institution in Kenosha, WI

*Madison Area Technical College Commercial Avenue Education Center (K)

2125 Commercial Avenue, Madison WI 53704
Telephone: (608) 246-6100 Identification: 770436
Accreditation: &NH

† Regional accreditation is carried under the parent institution in Madison, WI

*Madison Area Technical College Downtown Education Center (L)

211 North Carroll Street, Madison WI 53703
Telephone: (608) 246-6100 Identification: 770437
Accreditation: &NH

† Regional accreditation is carried under the parent institution in Madison, WI

*Madison Area Technical College Portage (M)

330 West Collins Street, Portage WI 53901
Telephone: (608) 745-3100 Identification: 770438
Accreditation: &NH

† Regional accreditation is carried under the parent institution in Madison, WI

*Madison Area Technical College Fort Atkinson (N)

827 Banker Road, Fort Atkinson WI 53538
Telephone: (920) 563-7200 Identification: 770435
Accreditation: &NH

† Regional accreditation is carried under the parent institution in Madison, WI

*Madison Area Technical College Reedsburg (O)

300 Alexander Avenue, Reedsburg WI 53959
Telephone: (608) 524-7800 Identification: 770439
Accreditation: &NH

† Regional accreditation is carried under the parent institution in Madison, WI

*Madison Area Technical College Watertown (P)

1300 West Main Street, Watertown WI 53098
Telephone: (920) 206-8000 Identification: 770440
Accreditation: &NH

† Regional accreditation is carried under the parent institution in Madison, WI

*Mid-State Technical College Marshfield Campus (Q)

2600 West 5th Street, Marshfield WI 54449
Telephone: (715) 387-2538 Identification: 770441
Accreditation: &NH

† Regional accreditation is carried under the parent institution in Wisconsin Rapids, WI

*Mid-State Technical College Stevens Point Campus (R)

1001 Centerpoint Drive, Stevens Point WI 54481
Telephone: (715) 344-3063 Identification: 770442
Accreditation: &NH

† Regional accreditation is carried under the parent institution in Wisconsin Rapids, WI

*Milwaukee Area Technical College (S)

5555 West Highlands Road, Mequon WI 53092
Telephone: (262) 238-2200 Identification: 770443
Accreditation: &NH

† Regional accreditation is carried under the parent institution in Milwaukee, WI

*Milwaukee Area Technical College (T)

6665 South Howell Avenue, Oak Creek WI 53154-1107
Telephone: (414) 571-4500 Identification: 770444
Accreditation: &NH

† Regional accreditation is carried under the parent institution in Milwaukee, WI

*Milwaukee Area Technical College (U)

1200 South 71st Street, West Allis WI 53214-3110
Telephone: (414) 456-5500 Identification: 770445
Accreditation: &NH, DIETT

† Regional accreditation is carried under the parent institution in Milwaukee, WI

*Moraine Park Technical College (V)

700 Gould Street, Beaver Dam WI 53916
Telephone: (920) 887-1428 Identification: 770446
Accreditation: &NH

† Regional accreditation is carried under the parent institution in Fond Du Lac, WI

*Moraine Park Technical College (W)

2151 North Main Street, West Bend WI 53090
Telephone: (262) 335-5713 Identification: 770447
Accreditation: &NH

† Regional accreditation is carried under the parent institution in Fond Du Lac, WI

*Northeast Wisconsin Technical College-Marinette Campus (X)

1601 University Drive, Marinette WI 54143
Telephone: (715) 735-9361 Identification: 770448
Accreditation: &NH

† Regional accreditation is carried under the parent institution in Green Bay, WI

*Northeast Wisconsin Technical College-Sturgeon Bay Campus (Y)

229 N 14th Avenue, Sturgeon Bay WI 54235
Telephone: (920) 746-4900 Identification: 770449
Accreditation: &NH

† Regional accreditation is carried under the parent institution in Green Bay, WI

*Wisconsin Indianhead Technical College-Ashland Campus (Z)

2100 Beaser Avenue, Ashland WI 54806
Telephone: (715) 682-8040 Identification: 770463
Accreditation: &NH, MAC

† Regional accreditation is carried under the parent institution in Shell Lake, WI

*Wisconsin Indianhead Technical College-New Richmond Campus (a)

1019 S Knowles Avenue, New Richmond WI 54017
Telephone: (715) 246-6561 Identification: 770464
Accreditation: &NH, MAC

† Regional accreditation is carried under the parent institution in Shell Lake, WI

*Wisconsin Indianhead Technical College-Rice Lake Campus (b)

1900 College Drive, Rice Lake WI 54868
Telephone: (715) 234-7082 Identification: 770465
Accreditation: &NH, DA, EMT, MAC

† Regional accreditation is carried under the parent institution in Shell Lake, WI

* *Wisconsin Indianhead Technical College-Superior Campus* (A)

600 North 21st Street, Superior WI 54880

Telephone: (715) 394-6677 Identification: 770466
Accreditation: &NH

† Regional accreditation is carried under the parent institution in Shell Lake, WI

Wright Graduate University for the Realization of Human Potential (B)

N7698 County Highway H, Elkhorn WI 53121

County: Walworth Identification: 667224
Telephone: (262) 742-4444 Carnegie Class: Not Classified
FAX Number: (262) 721-0752 Calendar System: Quarter
URL: www.wrightgrad.edu
Established: 2006 Annual Graduate Tuition & Fees: N/A
Enrollment: N/A Coed
Affiliation or Control: Independent Non-Profit IRS Status: 501(c)3
Highest Offering: Master's; No Undergraduates
Accreditation: ACICS

01 CEO .... Dr. Bob WRIGHT
05 Dean of Faculty & Curriculum .... Dr. Judith WRIGHT

WYOMING

Carbon County Higher Education Center/Rawlins (C)

812 E. Murray Street, Rawlins WY 82301-4466

Telephone: (307) 328-9204 Identification: 770481
Accreditation: &NH

† Regional accreditation is carried under the parent institution in Rock Springs, WY

Casper College (D)

125 College Drive, Casper WY 82601-2458

County: Natrona FICE Identification: 003928
Unit ID: 240505
Telephone: (307) 268-2110 Carnegie Class: Assoc/MT-VT-High Non
FAX Number: (307) 268-2682 Calendar System: Semester
URL: www.caspercollege.edu
Established: 1945 Annual Undergrad Tuition & Fees (In-District): $2,640
Enrollment: 3,824 Coed
Affiliation or Control: Local IRS Status: 501(c)3
Highest Offering: Associate Degree
Accreditation: NH, ACBSP, ADNUR, ART, COARC, DANCE, EMT, MLTAD, MUS, OTA, RAD, THEA

01 President .... Dr. Darren D. DIVINE
05 Vice President Academic Affairs .... Dr. Shawn POWELL
32 Vice President Student Services .... Ms. Kim BYRD
10 Vice Pres Administrative Services .... Ms. Lynnde COLLING
51 Exec Dean of Continuing Education .... Dr. Laura DRISCOLL
15 Int Director Human Resources .... Mr. Scott MILLER
07 Director Admissions/Student Records .... Ms. Kyla FOLTZ
26 Director of Public Relations .... Mr. Chris LORENZEN
18 Director Physical Plant .... Mr. Michael SAWYER
38 Director Student Counseling .... Ms. Teresa WALLACE
08 Director of the Library .... Mr. Brad MATTHIES
13 Director Information Technology .... Mr. Kent BROOKS
36 Director of Student Success Service .... Ms. Leanne LOYA
39 Director of Housing .... Ms. Barb MERYHEW
41 Athletic Director .... Ms. Angel SHARMAN
19 Director Campus Security .... Mr. Lance JONES
102 Exec Director Foundation .... Ms. Paulann DOANE
09 Institutional Researcher .... Ms. Lynn FLETCHER
37 Director of Student Financial Aid .... Mrs. Shannon ESKAM
21 Dir Financial Services/Controller .... Ms. Robyn LANDEN
96 Purchasing Coordinator .... Mr. Paul CHRISTMAN
06 Registrar .... Ms. Linda NICHOLS
29 Director Alumni Relations .... Ms. Linda NIX
04 Executive Asst to President .... Ms. Janice DALGARNO
108 Director Institutional Assessment .... Dr. Melissa STAHLEY-CUMMINGS
25 Grant Coordinator .... Ms. Katie MCMILLAN

Central Wyoming College (E)

2660 Peck Avenue, Riverton WY 82501-1520

County: Fremont FICE Identification: 007289
Unit ID: 240514
Telephone: (307) 855-2000 Carnegie Class: Assoc/HT-High Non
FAX Number: (307) 855-2095 Calendar System: Semester
URL: www.cwc.edu
Established: 1966 Annual Undergrad Tuition & Fees (In-District): $2,712
Enrollment: 2,082 Coed
Affiliation or Control: Local IRS Status: 501(c)3
Highest Offering: Associate Degree
Accreditation: NH, ADNUR

01 President .... Dr. Cristobal O. VALDEZ
04 Exec Asst to the President/Board .... Ms. Linda BENDER
03 Vice Pres Academic Affairs .... Dr. Brad TYNDALL
10 Vice Pres Admin Svcs/CFO .... Mr. Ron GRANGER
32 Vice Pres Student Affairs .... Ms. Cory DALY
13 Chief Information Officer .... Mr. John WOOD
18 Chief Facilities/Physical Plant .... Mr. Wayne ROBINSON
08 Director of Library Services .... Ms. Nicole POUGET
26 Director of Marketing .... Ms. Lori RIDGWAY
15 Exec Dir for Human Resources .... Mr. Ray QUAN
21 Finance Officer .... Ms. Lindy PASKETT
19 Director of Campus Safety/Security .... Mr. Chuck CARR
103 Dean Business/Technical & Workforce .... Ms. Lynne MCAULIFFE
41 Director of Athletics .... Mr. Steve BARLOW
06 Registrar .... Ms. Connie NYBERG
49 Dean for Arts & Sciences .... Dr. Mark NORDEEN
76 Dean for Health & Sciences .... Ms. Kathy WELLS
44 Director Annual or Planned Giving .... Ms. Becky RUTHENBECK

CollegeAmerica Cheyenne (F)

6101 Yellowstone Road, Cheyenne WY 82009

Telephone: (307) 637-2044 Identification: 770609
Accreditation: ACCSC

† Branch campus of CollegeAmerica Denver, Denver, CO

Eastern Wyoming College (G)

3200 W C Street, Torrington WY 82240-1699

County: Goshen FICE Identification: 003929
Unit ID: 240596
Telephone: (307) 532-8200 Carnegie Class: Assoc/HVT-High Non
FAX Number: (307) 532-8229 Calendar System: Semester
URL: ewc.wy.edu/
Established: 1948 Annual Undergrad Tuition & Fees (In-District): $2,568
Enrollment: 1,704 Coed
Affiliation or Control: State/Local IRS Status: 501(c)3
Highest Offering: Associate Degree
Accreditation: NH

01 President .... Dr. Richard PATTERSON
04 Exec Asst to President/Board .... Ms. Holly L. BRANHAM
05 VP for Academic Services .... Dr. Michelle LANDA
10 VP for Admin Services .... Mr. Ron LAHER
32 VP for Student Services .... Dr. Rex COGDILL
20 Associate VP for Outreach .... Mr. Roger HUMPHREY
20 Associate VP for Converse County .... Mrs. Margaret FARLEY
30 Dir of Institutional Development .... Mr. John HANSEN
08 Director of Library Services .... Mrs. Casey DEBUS
41 Director of College Athletics .... Mr. Tom ANDERSEN
26 Director of College Relations .... Ms. Tami AFDAHL
18 Director of Physical Plant .... Mr. Keith JARVIS
39 Director of Residence Life .... Mr. Kyle RICE
37 Director of Financial Aid .... Ms. Susan STEPHENSON
15 Director Human Resources .... Mr. Edward MEYER
21 Business Office Director .... Ms. Karen PARRIOTT

Eastern Wyoming College-Douglas Campus (H)

800 South Wind River Drive, Douglas WY 82633

Telephone: (307) 624-7000 Identification: 770476
Accreditation: &NH

† Regional accreditation is carried under the parent institution in Torrington, WY

Gillette College (I)

300 West Sinclair, Gillette WY 82718

Telephone: (888) 544-5538 Identification: 770478
Accreditation: &NH

† Regional accreditation is carried under the parent institution in Sheridan, WY

Institute of Business and Medical Careers (J)

1854 Dell Range Boulevard, Cheyenne WY 82009

Telephone: (307) 433-8363 Identification: 666738
Accreditation: ACICS

† Branch campus of Institute of Business and Medical Careers, Fort Collins, CO.

Laramie County Community College (K)

1400 E College Drive, Cheyenne WY 82007-3299

County: Laramie FICE Identification: 009259
Unit ID: 240620
Telephone: (307) 778-5222 Carnegie Class: Assoc/HT-High Non
FAX Number: (307) 778-1399 Calendar System: Semester
URL: www.lccc.wy.edu
Established: 1968 Annual Undergrad Tuition & Fees (In-District): $3,144
Enrollment: 4,388 Coed
Affiliation or Control: State/Local IRS Status: 501(c)3
Highest Offering: Associate Degree
Accreditation: NH, ADNUR, DH, DMS, EMT, PTAA, RAD, SURGT

01 President .... Dr. Joe SCHAFFER
05 Interim VP of Academic Affairs .... Ms. Therese HARPER
10 Vice Pres of Administration/Finance .... Mr. Rick JOHNSON
32 Vice President of Student Services .... Ms. Judy HAY
13 Chief Technology Officer .... Mr. Chad MARLEY
15 Executive Director Human Resources .... Ms. Tammy MAAS
30 Assoc VP Inst Advancement .... Ms. Lisa MURPHY
12 Assoc VP of Albany County Campus .... Dr. James MALM
45 Assc VP Institutional Effectiveness .... Dr. Kim BENDER
08 Librarian .... Ms. Karen LANGE
37 Director of Financial Aid .... Ms. Julie WILSON
26 Director of Public Relations .... Mr. Ty STOCKTON
18 Director of Physical Plant .... Mr. Timothy MACNAMARA
21 Director of Accounting Services .... Mr. Herry ANDREWS
29 Dir Alumni Affairs/Event Planning .... Ms. Lisa TRIMBLE
44 Dir Scholarships & Annual Giving .... Vacant
09 Manager of Institutional Research .... Ms. Ann MURRAY
07 Dir of Admissions and Welcome Ctr .... Ms. Sarah HANNES
06 Registrar .... Ms. Stacy MAESTAS
49 Dean School of Arts & Humanities .... Dr. Daniel POWELL
50 Dean Sch of Bus/Ag & Tech Studies .... Mr. Melvin O. HAWKINS, JR.
76 Int Dean Sch of Health Sci & Well .... Ms. Cindy HENNING
81 Interim Dean School Math & Science .... Ms. Ami WANGELINE
103 Dean Sch of Outreach/Workforce Dev .... Ms. Maryellen TAST
20 Dir Instructional Technologies .... Mr. Les BALSIGER
19 Director Campus Safety & Security .... Mr. James CROSBY
41 Director of Athletics .... Mr. Scott NOBLE

Laramie County Community College Albany County Campus (L)

1125 Boulder Drive, Laramie WY 82070

Telephone: (307) 721-5138 Identification: 770477
Accreditation: &NH

† Regional accreditation is carried under the parent institution in Cheyenne, WY

Northern Wyoming Community College District (M)

PO Box 1500, 3059 Coffeen Avenue, Sheridan WY 82801-1500

County: Sheridan FICE Identification: 003930
Unit ID: 240666
Telephone: (307) 674-6446 Carnegie Class: Assoc/MT-VT-High Non
FAX Number: (307) 674-4293 Calendar System: Semester
URL: www.sheridan.edu
Established: 1948 Annual Undergrad Tuition & Fees (In-District): $2,952
Enrollment: 4,374 Coed
Affiliation or Control: Local IRS Status: 501(c)3
Highest Offering: Associate Degree
Accreditation: NH, ADNUR, DH

01 President .... Dr. Paul R. YOUNG
05 VP Academic Affairs .... Dr. Richard HALL
10 VP Admin & Finance/CFO .... Ms. Cheryl A. HEATH
12 VP Gillette College/CEO .... Dr. Mark G. ENGLERT
86 VP External Affairs .... Dr. Susan BIGELOW
06 Dean Enrollment Services .... Ms. Sharon ELWOOD
32 Dean of Students .... Ms. Carol GARCIA
49 Dean Arts/Humanies & Social Science .... Dr. Mercedes AGUIRRE BATTY
75 Dean Career/Technical Education .... Mr. Jed JENSEN
15 Director Human Resources .... Ms. Jennifer MCARTHUR
26 Dir Marketing/College Information .... Ms. Wendy M. SMITH
37 Director Financial Aid Services .... Ms. Kristen GAST
13 Dir Information Technology Services .... Mr. Brady R. FACKRELL
09 Director of Institutional Research .... Mr. Jason BROWNING
21 Controller .... Ms. Karen B. BURTIS
07 Executive Director of Admissions .... Mr. Joe B. MUELLER
39 Director Housing/Residential Educ .... Ms. Larissa B. BONNET
88 Director Veteran Services .... Mr. Tyler JENSEN
18 Director Facilities/Physical Plant .... Mr. Kent A. ANDERSEN
18 Director Gillette Facilities .... Mr. Mark N. ANDERSEN
103 Dir Workforce Development & CE .... Ms. Karen ST. CLAIR
08 Librarian .... Ms. Katrina M. BROWN
19 Director Security/Safety .... Mr. Jason VELA
41 Athletic Director .... Ms. Jenni WINTER
04 Administrative Asst to President .... Ms. Mary Jo JOHNSON

Northwest College (N)

231 W 6th St, Powell WY 82435

County: Park FICE Identification: 003931
Unit ID: 240657
Telephone: (307) 754-6000 Carnegie Class: Assoc/HT-Mix Trad/Non
FAX Number: (307) 754-6245 Calendar System: Semester
URL: www.nwc.edu
Established: 1946 Annual Undergrad Tuition & Fees (In-District): $2,789
Enrollment: 1,652 Coed
Affiliation or Control: State/Local IRS Status: 501(c)3
Highest Offering: Associate Degree
Accreditation: NH, ADNUR, ART, MUS

01 President .... Dr. Stefani HICSWA
05 Vice Pres Academic Affairs .... Dr. Gerald GIRAUD
32 Interim Vice Pres Student Affairs .... Dr. Gerald GIRAUD
11 Vice Pres Admin Services .... Ms. Lisa WATSON
26 Vice Pres College Relations .... Mr. Mark KITCHEN
102 Executive Director NWC Foundation .... Ms. Shelby WETZEL
20 Dean Student Learning/Acad Support .... Dr. Matthew EWERS
103 Dean Extended Campus/Workforce .... Ms. Ronda PEER
08 Library Director .... Dr. Susan RICHARDS
10 Finance Director .... Mr. Brad BOWEN
15 Human Resources Director .... Ms. Jill ANDERSON
13 Computing Services Director .... Mr. Casey DEARCORN

18	Facilities Director	Mr. David PLUTE
06	Registrar/Admissions Director	Mr. Brad HAMMOND
37	Financial Aid/Scholarships Director	Mr. Shaman QUINN
39	Residence/Campus Life Director	Mr. Dee HAVIG
04	Exec Secretary to President & Board	Ms. Cindy CICCI
07	Admissions Manager	Mr. West HERNANDEZ
09	Institutional Researcher	Ms. Lisa SMITH
105	Web Developer	Ms. Carey MILLER
108	Assessment Coordinator	Ms. Aura NEWLIN
19	Campus Security Coordinator	Mr. Lee BLACKMORE
25	Grant Writer	Ms. Megan WILSON
44	Development Manager	Ms. Carol BELL

Oyster Ridge Higher Education/Kemmerer (A)

PO Box 423, Kemmerer WY 83101
Telephone: (307) 877-6958 Identification: 770479
Accreditation: &NH

† Regional accreditation is carried under the parent institution in Rock Springs, WY

University of Wyoming (B)

1000 E University Avenue, Dept 3434,
Laramie WY 82071-3434
County: Albany FICE Identification: 003932
Unit ID: 240727
Telephone: (307) 766-1121 Carnegie Class: DU-Higher
FAX Number: (307) 766-2271 Calendar System: Semester
URL: www.uwyo.edu
Established: 1886 Annual Undergrad Tuition & Fees (In-State): $4,892
Enrollment: 12,820 Coed
Affiliation or Control: State IRS Status: 501(c)3
Highest Offering: Doctorate
Accreditation: NH, BUS, CACREP, CLPSY, CS, DIETD, ENG, LAW, MUS, NURSE, PHAR, SP, SW, TED

01	President	Dr. Laurie NICHOLS
05	Vice President Academic Affairs	Dr. David JONES
10	Vice President Administration	Mr. Bill MAI
86	Vice Pres Govt & Community Affairs	Mr. Chris BOSWELL
46	Vice Pres Research & Economic Dev	Dr. William A. GERN
32	Vice President Student Affairs	Dr. Sara L. AXELSON
13	Vice President Information Tech	Mr. Robert R. AYLWARD
30	Vice Pres Institutional Advancement	Mr. W. Ben BLALOCK, III
43	Vice President & General Counsel	Mr. Richard H. MILLER
41	Director Intercollegiate Athletics	Mr. Tom BURMAN
20	Associate VP Academic Affairs	Dr. Anne ALEXANDER
20	Interim Assoc VP Academic Affairs	Dr. Tami BENHAM-DEAL
20	Interim Assoc VP Academic Affairs	Dr. Ann HILD
11	Assoc Vice Pres Operations	Mr. Mark A. COLLINS
21	Assoc VP Fiscal Administration	Ms. Janet S. LOWE
21	Asst Vice Pres Budget/Inst Analysis	Ms. Arley WILLIAMS
88	Assoc Vice President Research	Ms. Dorothy C. YATES
35	AVP Student Affairs/Dn of Students	Mr. Sean BLACKBURN
88	Assoc VP Institutional Advancement	Mr. John D. STARK
26	Assoc VP Communication/Marketing	Mr. Chad BALDWIN
47	Dean of Agriculture	Dr. Frank D. GALEY
49	Dean of Arts & Sciences	Dr. Paula LUTZ
50	Dean of Business	Dr. Sanjay PUTREVU
53	Dean of Education	Dr. Ray REUTZEL
54	Dean of Engineering	Dr. Michael PISHKO
76	Dean of Health Sciences	Dr. Joseph F. STEINER
61	Dean of Law	Dr. Klint ALEXANDER
56	Dean Outreach	Dr. Susan FRYE
12	Assoc Dean UW at Casper	Dr. Scott SEVILLE
08	Interim Dean of Libraries	Ms. Lori PHILLIPS
65	Director Haub Sch Env/Nat Resources	Dr. Ingrid BURKE
07	Director of Admissions	Ms. Shelley DODD
36	Director Advising/Career Services	Ms. Evelyn J. CHYTKA
28	Director Affirmative Action/EEO	Ms. Oneida BLAGG
29	Exec Director Alumni Affairs	Mr. Keener FRYE
88	Acting Dir American Heritage Center	Mr. Rick EWIG
88	Director School of Energy Resources	Dr. Mark NORTHAM
88	Director Art Museum	Ms. Susan MOLDENHAUER
88	Director Campus Recreation	Mr. Patrick MORAN
45	Director Facilities Planning	Mr. Larry BLAKE
109	Director Auxiliary Services	Ms. Carolyn SMITH
15	Interim Director Human Resources	Mr. Mark BERCHENI
18	Interim Director Physical Plant	Mr. John DAVIS
92	Interim Director Honors Program	Dr. Susan ARONSTEIN
86	Spec Advis to the Pres for Ext Rels	Ms. Meredith ASAY
39	Exec Dir Res Life/Dining/Stdnt Un	Mr. Eric WEBB
37	Director Student Financial Aid	Ms. Kathy BOBBITT
06	Interim Registrar	Mr. Lane BUCHANAN
23	Director Student Health Service	Dr. Joanne E. STEANE
19	Chief University Police Dept	Mr. Mike SAMP
38	Dir University Counseling Center	Dr. Keith EVASHEVSKI

Western Wyoming Community College (C)

2500 College Drive, Rock Springs WY 82902-0428
County: Sweetwater FICE Identification: 003933
Unit ID: 240693
Telephone: (307) 382-1600 Carnegie Class: Assoc/MT-VT-High Non
FAX Number: (307) 382-1636 Calendar System: Semester
URL: www.westernwyoming.edu
Established: 1959 Annual Undergrad Tuition & Fees (In-District): $2,424
Enrollment: 3,472 Coed
Affiliation or Control: State/Local IRS Status: 501(c)3
Highest Offering: Associate Degree
Accreditation: NH, ADNUR

01	President	Dr. Karla N. LEACH
05	VP for Student Learning	Dr. Kim FARLEY
32	VP for Student Success Services	Dr. Philip PARNELL
11	VP for Administrative Services	Mr. Sheldon FLOM
07	Director of Admissions	Ms. Erin GREY
06	Registrar	Ms. Kay LEUM
37	Director of Financial Aid	Ms. Nicole CASTILLON
08	Director of Library Services	Ms. Janice GROVER-ROOSA
18	Director of Physical Resources	Vacant
39	Dir Residence Halls/Student Life	Mr. Dustin CONOVER
40	Bookstore Manager	Ms. Natalie LANE
41	Athletic Director	Dr. Lu SWEET
92	Director of Honors Program	Mr. Richard KEMPA
09	Director of Planning & Improvement	Ms. Dianna RENZ
15	Director Human Resources	Ms. Shaundria WILLIAMS
26	Coord of Marketing/Public Info	Mr. Christopher SHEID
30	Director Community College Relation	Mr. David TATE
36	Dir Student Engagement & Completion	Mr. Mark REMBACZ
10	Director of Finance and Controller	Ms. Debbie BAKER
38	Dir Student Counseling/Disability	Ms. Amy GALLEY
96	Director of Purchasing	Ms. Tammy REGISTER
04	Executive Asst to President	Ms. Randy FRINK
19	Protective Services Supervisor	Mr. Mark PADILLA
106	Director of Distance Learning	Ms. Nancy JOHNSON
13	Director of Information Technology	Mr. Derek ROBINSON
20	Dean of Academics	Dr. Clifford WITTSTRUCK

Western Wyoming Community College Outreach Afton/Star Valley (D)

247 N Washington, Box 1237, Afton WY 83110
Telephone: (307) 886-3834 Identification: 770483
Accreditation: &NH

† Regional accreditation is carried under the parent institution in Rock Springs, WY

Western Wyoming Community College Outreach Evanston (E)

1013 Cheyenne Drive, Evanston WY 82930
Telephone: (307) 789-3988 Identification: 770482
Accreditation: &NH

† Regional accreditation is carried under the parent institution in Rock Springs, WY

Wyoming Catholic College (F)

1400 City Park Dr, PO Box 750, Lander WY 82520
County: Fremont Identification: 667227
Telephone: (307) 332-2930 Carnegie Class: Not Classified
FAX Number: (307) 332-2918 Calendar System: Semester
URL: www.wyomingcatholiccollege.com
Established: 2005 Annual Undergrad Tuition & Fees: N/A
Enrollment: N/A Coed
Affiliation or Control: Roman Catholic IRS Status: 501(c)3
Highest Offering: Baccalaureate
Accreditation: @NH

01	President	Dr. Glenn ARBERY
05	Academic Dean	Dr. Thaddeus KOZINSKI
10	VP for Operations & Finance	Mr. Richard ROLLINO
30	Vice Pres for Advancement	Mr. Jonathan TONKOWICH
30	Asst Vice Pres of Advancement	Ms. Mary MURRAY
32	Director of Student Services	Ms. Hillary ROWNEY

WyoTech (G)

4373 N 3rd Street, Laramie WY 82072-9519
County: Albany FICE Identification: 009157
Unit ID: 240718
Telephone: (307) 742-3776 Carnegie Class: Spec 2-yr-Tech
FAX Number: (307) 721-4854 Calendar System: Other
URL: www.wyotech.edu
Established: 1966 Annual Undergrad Tuition & Fees: N/A
Enrollment: 1,085 Coed
Affiliation or Control: Proprietary IRS Status: Proprietary
Highest Offering: Associate Degree
Accreditation: ACCSC

01	President	Mr. Caleb PERRITON
84	Director of Student Success	Mr. Kyle MORRIS
36	Director of Career Services	Mr. Martin AXLUND
88	Manager of Student Finance	Ms. Brenda COSSITT
88	Enrollment Manager	Mr. Glenn HALSEY
06	Registrar	Ms. Revalee WEERHEIM
39	Housing Manager	Mr. Gabe LUCERO

US SERVICE SCHOOLS

Air Force Institute of Technology (H)

2950 Hobson Way, Wright Patterson AFB OH 45433-7765
County: Greene FICE Identification: 003009
Unit ID: 200697
Telephone: (937) 255-2321 Carnegie Class: DU-Mod
FAX Number: (937) 656-7600 Calendar System: Quarter
URL: www.afit.edu
Established: 1919 Annual Graduate Tuition & Fees: N/A
Enrollment: 860 Coed
Affiliation or Control: Federal IRS Status: Exempt
Highest Offering: Doctorate; No Undergraduates
Accreditation: NH, ENG, ENGR

01	Chancellor	Dr. Todd I. STEWART
05	Provost/Vice Chancellor	Dr. Sivaguru S. SRITHARAN
54	Dean Graduate School of Engr & Mgt	Dr. Adedeji B. BADIRU
46	Dean for Research	Dr. Heidi R. RIES
10	Chief Financial Officer	Ms. Amber L. RICHEY
09	Director Institutional Research	Dr. Nancy J. ROSZELL
06	Director Admissions/Registrar	Ms. Kathleen K. HALL
32	Dean of Students	Vacant
20	Associate Dean for Academic Affairs	Dr. Paul J. WOLF
13	Dir Communications & Information	Major Jeremy MILLAR
08	Director D'Azzo Research Library	Dr. Ellis BETECK
15	Director Personnel Services	Ms. Leanne HEAGLE
18	Chief Facilities/Physical Plant	Mr. Anthony KING
29	Manager Alumni Affairs	Ms. Kathleen E. SCOTT
35	Director Student Services	Ms. Kathleen HALL
85	Director of Intl Student Affairs	Ms. Annette D. ROBB
40	Bookstore Supervisor	Mr. Joseph SCOTT
106	Dir Online Education/E-learning	Mr. John A. REISNER

Air University (I)

55 LeMay Plaza South, Maxwell AFB AL 36112-6335
County: Montgomery FICE Identification: 001001
Telephone: (334) 953-5613 Carnegie Class: Not Classified
FAX Number: (334) 953-2749 Calendar System: Other
URL: www.au.af.mil
Established: 1946 Annual Undergrad Tuition & Fees: N/A
Enrollment: N/A Coed
Affiliation or Control: Federal IRS Status: Exempt
Highest Offering: Doctorate
Accreditation: SC

01	Commander and President	MajGen. Steven L. KWAST
03	Vice Commander	MajGen. Timothy J. LEAHY
05	Vice President for Academic Affairs	Dr. Matthew C. STAFFORD
06	Registrar	Dr. Michael J. MASTERSON
20	Deputy Director Academic Affairs	Mr. Jay WARWICK
20	Director Academic Affairs	Dr. Chris CAIN

† Parent institution of Community College of the Air Force, School of Advanced Air and Space Studies, and the Air Force Institute of Technology

Community College of the Air Force (J)

100 South Turner Blvd,
Maxwell AFB, Gunter Annex AL 36114-3011
Telephone: (334) 649-5000 FICE Identification: 012308
Accreditation: &SC, PTAA

† Regional accreditation is carried under the parent institution, Air University, Maxwell AFB, AL.

Defense Language Institute (K)

1759 Lewis Road, Monterey CA 93944
County: Monterey FICE Identification: 001195
Unit ID: 428222
Telephone: (831) 242-5291 Carnegie Class: Not Classified
FAX Number: (831) 242-6495 Calendar System: Other
URL: www.dliflc.edu
Established: 1941 Annual Undergrad Tuition & Fees: N/A
Enrollment: N/A Coed
Affiliation or Control: Federal IRS Status: Exempt
Highest Offering: Associate Degree
Accreditation: WJ

01	Commandant	Col. Phillip DEPPERT
05	Provost	Dr. Betty Lou LEAVER
20	Associate Provost	Dr. Hiam KANBAR
06	Registrar	Dr. Peter SILZER

† Associate Arts in Foreign Language authorized by US Congress in December 2001 and approved by ACCJC/WASC in June 2002.

59th Dental Training Squadron (L)

Bldg 3352, Lackland AFB TX 78236
Telephone: (210) 292-7251 Identification: 770122
Accreditation: &M

† Regional accreditation is carried under the parent institution in Bethesda, MD

Joint Forces Staff College (M)

7800 Hampton Boulevard, Norfolk VA 23511-1702
Telephone: (757) 443-6124 Identification: 770121
Accreditation: &M

† Regional accreditation is carried under the parent institution in Washington, DC

The Judge Advocate General's Legal Center & School (N)

600 Massie Road, Charlottesville VA 22903-1781
County: Albemarle Identification: 666974
Telephone: (434) 971-3300 Carnegie Class: Not Classified
FAX Number: (434) 971-3338 Calendar System: Quarter
URL: www.jagcnet.army.mil/tjaglcs

Established: 1951 Annual Graduate Tuition & Fees: N/A
Enrollment: N/A Coed
Affiliation or Control: Federal IRS Status: Exempt
Highest Offering: Master's; No Undergraduates
Accreditation: LAW

01 Commander/Commandant BGen. Paul S. WILSON
05 Dean Col. Randall J. BAGWELL
20 Associate Dean of Academics Mr. Maurice A. LESCAULT, JR.
32 Associate Dean of Students LtCol. Andrew D. FLOR

Marine Corps University (A)

2076 South Street, Quantico VA 22134-5068
County: Prince William Identification: 666745
Unit ID: 438513
Telephone: (703) 784-2105 Carnegie Class: Not Classified
FAX Number: (703) 784-1271 Calendar System: Semester
URL: www.mcu.usmc.mil
Established: 1989 Annual Graduate Tuition & Fees: N/A
Enrollment: N/A Coed
Affiliation or Control: Federal IRS Status: Exempt
Highest Offering: Master's; No Undergraduates
Accreditation: SC

01 President BGen. Thomas GORRY
05 Vice President for Academic Affairs Dr. James ANDERSON
11 VP for Operations & Planning Mr. Jay HATTON
10 VP Business Affairs Mr. Keil GENTRY
20 Director Academic Support Division Mr. Richard JAQUES
09 Director Institutional Research Dr. Susan JOHNSTON

National Defense University (B)

Fort Lesley J. McNair, Washington DC 20319-5066
FICE Identification: 031893
Unit ID: 423494
Telephone: (202) 685-3924 Carnegie Class: Not Classified
FAX Number: (202) 685-3920 Calendar System: Semester
URL: www.ndu.edu
Established: 1976 Annual Graduate Tuition & Fees: N/A
Enrollment: N/A Coed
Affiliation or Control: Federal IRS Status: Exempt
Highest Offering: Master's; No Undergraduates
Accreditation: M

01 President MajGen. Frederick M. PADILLA
03 Senior Vice President Amb. Donald YAMAMOTO
05 Provost/Vice Pres Academic Affairs Dr. John W. YAEGER
11 Chief Operating Officer Mr. Robert C. KANE
43 General Counsel Ms. Mollie MURPHY
46 Sr Dir Research/Strategic Support Dr. Richard D. HOOKER, JR.
88 Chancellor CISA Dr. Michael S. BELL
88 Commandant ES COL. Paul H. FREDENBURGH, III
88 Commandant NWC BGen. Darren E. HARTFORD
88 Chancellor iCollege Ms. Janice M. HAMBY
88 Commandant JFSC RADM. Brad WILLIAMSON
107 Deputy Director CAPSTONE Ms. Bonnie SWANSON
20 Deputy Vice Pres Academic Affairs Dr. Tim RUSSO
32 Associate Provost Student/Acad Svcs Vacant
06 University Registrar Mr. Larry JOHNSON
42 Chaplain COL. Jeffery ZUST
26 Director of Strategic Communication Mr. Mark PHILLIPS
13 Chief Information Officer Ms. Diane WEBBER
105 Web/Social Media Manager Ms. Jennifer RUSSELL
10 Director Resource Management Mr. Jay HELMING
25 Director Contracting Ms. Jenifer CUOZZO
23 Director Health Fitness Mr. Tony SPINOSA
15 Director Human Resources Mr. Tim ROBERTSON
08 Director Libraries Ms. Helen (Meg) TULLOCH
85 Dir International Student Mgmt Ofc Dr. John GODWIN
18 Chief Facilities/Physical Plant Mr. Charles FANSHAW
19 Director Security Mr. Joe PALLANEZ
88 Events Director Vacant
102 Int President/CEO NDU Foundation Amb. Walter STADTLER

National Intelligence University (C)

200 MacDill Boulevard, Washington DC 20340-5100
Identification: 666393
Unit ID: 131380
Telephone: (202) 231-3344 Carnegie Class: Not Classified
FAX Number: (202) 231-3294 Calendar System: Quarter
URL: www.ni-u.edu
Established: 1962 Annual Undergrad Tuition & Fees: N/A
Enrollment: N/A Coed
Affiliation or Control: Federal IRS Status: Exempt
Highest Offering: Master's
Accreditation: M

01 President Dr. David R. ELLISON
04 Executive Assistant to President Ms. Mary BERGMANN
100 Chief of Staff Col. Michael E. SENN
05 Exec VP & Provost Dr. Susan M. STUDDS
09 VP Research Dr. Terrence C. MARKIN
46 Dir Ctr for Strategic Intel Rsrch Dr. Cathryn Q. THURSTON
108 Dir Institutional Effectiveness Ms. Ellen ROSENTHAL
10 VP Finance & Administration Mr. Paul LEGERE
11 Director of Univ Operations Mr. Stephen J. KERDA
18 Facilities Dr. Richard MESTAS
19 Security Officer Ms. Thelma FLAMER
06 Registrar Mr. Eric H. STUPAR
08 Director Library Services Ms. Denise CAMPBELL
58 Dean College Strategic Intel Dr. Donald HANLE
12 Director NSA Campus Mr. Dax NORMAN
12 Director NGA Campus Mr. Timothy J. CHRISTENSON
12 Director Reserve Monthly Pgm LCDR. Rachael L. LEWIS
12 Director European Academic Ctr Dr. Samiah E. BARONI
12 Director Southern Academic Ctr Mr. Kevin TALIAFERRO
12 Director Quantico Academic Ctr Mr. Kevin LOGAN
58 Dean School of Science & Tech Intel Dr. Brian R. SHAW
26 VP Outreach Mr. Frederick HAMMERSEN
29 Dir Outreach & Alumni Affairs Mr. Thomas VAN WAGNER

Naval Postgraduate School (D)

1 University Circle, Room M10, Monterey CA 93943-5100
County: Monterey FICE Identification: 001310
Unit ID: 119678
Telephone: (831) 656-2441 Carnegie Class: DU-Higher
FAX Number: (831) 656-2921 Calendar System: Quarter
URL: www.nps.edu
Established: 1909 Annual Undergrad Tuition & Fees: N/A
Enrollment: 2,869 Coed
Affiliation or Control: Federal IRS Status: Exempt
Highest Offering: Doctorate
Accreditation: WC, BUS, ENG, SPAA

01 President VAdm. Ronald A. ROUTE, RET.
100 Chief of Staff Capt. Deidre MCLAY
05 Provost/Academic Dean Dr. Steven R. LERMAN
100 Chief of Staff Capt. Anthony J. PARISI
20 Vice Provost for Academic Affairs Dr. Orrin Douglas MOSES
46 Dean of Research Dr. Jeffrey D. PADUAN
54 Dean Grad Sch Engr/Applied Sci Dr. Clyde SCANDRETT
58 Dean Sch of Intl Graduate Studies Dr. James J. WIRTZ
50 Dean Grad Sch Bus/Public Policy Dr. William R. GATES
72 Dean Grad Sch Oper & Info Sciences Dr. Gordon MCCORMICK
32 Dean of Students Capt. Matthew R. VANDERSLUIS
10 Comptroller Mr. Kevin K. LITTLE
13 Director Information Technology Mr. Joseph LOPICCOLO
18 Director Facilities Management Mr. Andrew (Pete) BOERLAGE
08 University Librarian Ms. Eleanor S. UHLINGER
06 Registrar Mr. Mike ANDERSEN
15 Director Human Resources Ms. Ermelinda RODRIGUEZ-HEFFNER
29 Director of Alumni Relations Mr. Kari L. MIGLAW
19 Sr Lecturer NPS/Chief Security Ofcr Capt. Robert SIMERAL, RET.
28 EEO Director Ms. Deborah A. BAITY
56 Director of CED3 Mr. Tom M. MASTRE
07 Director of Admissions Ms. Sue DOOLEY
88 Director of Programs Cmdr. James V. WALSH

Naval War College (E)

686 Cushing Road, Newport RI 02841-1207
County: Newport FICE Identification: 003413
Unit ID: 432320
Telephone: (401) 841-3089 Carnegie Class: Not Classified
FAX Number: (401) 841-1297 Calendar System: Trimester
URL: www.usnwc.edu
Established: 1884 Annual Graduate Tuition & Fees: N/A
Enrollment: N/A Coed
Affiliation or Control: Federal IRS Status: Exempt
Highest Offering: Master's; No Undergraduates
Accreditation: EH

01 President RADM. Jeffrey A. HARLEY
04 Exec Assistant to the President LCDR. Jay BREWER
05 Provost Dr. Lewis M. DUNCAN
88 Chief of Staff to the Provost Mr. Richard R. MENARD
20 Associate Provost Prof. William R. SPAIN
100 Chief of Staff CAPT. Francis MOLINARI
20 Dean of Academic Affairs Dr. John GAROFANO
09 Dean Center for Warfare Studies Prof. Thomas CULORA
32 Dean of Students CAPT. Pat KEYES
08 Director Library Services Dr. Allen C. BENSON
56 Dir College of Distance Education Dr. Jay HICKEY
06 Registrar Ms. Michele BLACKBURN
46 Chairman Strategy & Policy Dr. Michael PAVKOVIC
88 Chairman National Security Affairs Dr. David COOPER
88 Chairman Joint Military Operations CAPT. Alan ABRAMSON
10 Chief Business Officer Mr. Robert SAMPSON
15 Director Military Personnel Svcs CDR. Melanie HA'O
15 Civilian Human Resources Officer Ms. Charlene HANSON
18 Chief Facilities/Physical Plant Ms. Beth LEINBERRY
26 Chief Public Relations Officer CDR. Kelly BRANNON
13 Chief Information Officer Mr. Joseph PANGBORN
19 Director of Security Mr. Paul GATELY
29 Director Alumni Affairs Ms. Julia GAGE
88 Director Writing Center Vacant
104 Director International Programs Prof. Thomas MANGOLD
88 Dean Col Operatnl/Strategic Ldrshp Prof. James KELLY
88 Director of Events Ms. Karen SELLERS

School of Advanced Air and Space Studies (F)

125 Chennault Circle, Maxwell AFB AL 36112-6424
Telephone: (334) 953-5155 Identification: 666746
Accreditation: &SC

† Regional accreditation is carried under the parent institution, Air University, Maxwell AFB, AL.

Uniformed Services University of the Health Sciences (G)

4301 Jones Bridge Road, Bethesda MD 20814-4799
County: Montgomery FICE Identification: 021610
Unit ID: 164137
Telephone: (301) 295-3013 Carnegie Class: Not Classified
FAX Number: (301) 295-3431 Calendar System: Quarter
URL: www.usuhs.edu
Established: 1972 Annual Graduate Tuition & Fees: N/A
Enrollment: N/A Coed
Affiliation or Control: Federal IRS Status: Exempt
Highest Offering: Doctorate; No Undergraduates
Accreditation: M, ANEST, CLPSY, DENT, ENGR, MED, NURSE, PH

01 President Dr. Richard W. THOMAS
05 Sr Vice Pres University Programs Dr. Thomas TRAVIS
10 Vice Pres Finance & Admin Mr. Walter TINLING
26 Vice Pres External Affairs Dr. Jeffrey LONGACRE
46 Vice President for Research Dr. Yvonne MADDOX
04 Exec Assistant to the President Ms. Mary L. SCHWARTZ
100 Chief of Staff Mr. Robert J. THOMPSON
63 Dean School of Medicine Dr. Arthur KELLERMANN
58 Assoc Dean Graduate Education Dr. Gregory MUELLER
07 Assoc Dean Admiss & Recruiting SOM COL. Aaron SAGUIL
88 Assoc Dean Graduate Medical Educ CAPT. Jerri CURTIS
32 Assoc Dean Student Affairs COL. Lisa MOORES
88 Assistant Dean Academic Support Dr. William WITTMAN
88 Assistant Dean Clinical Sciences CAPT. Patricia MCKAY
66 Dean Graduate School of Nursing Dr. Carol ROMANO
20 Assoc Dean Academic Affairs GSN Dr. Diane SEIBERT
46 Director AFRRI COL. Lester HUFF
13 Chief Information Officer Mr. Timothy RAPP
43 General Counsel Mr. Jason KAAR
06 AVP & University Registrar Ms. Gail-Selina HEWITT-CLARKE
15 Director Civilian Human Res Mr. Darryl BROWN
08 Acting University Librarian Ms. Linda SPITZER
18 Director of Facilities Ms. Cheryl KING
96 Director of Contracting Mr. Anthony REVENIS
21 AVP Resource Management Ms. Antoinette WHITMEYER
29 Director Alumni Relations Ms. Sharon HOLLAND
20 Assoc Dean for Curriculum Dr. Arnyce POCK
88 Assoc Dean for Faculty Dr. Brian REAMY
88 Assoc Dean for Medical Education Dr. William GILLILAND
52 Dean Naval Postgrad Dental School CAPT. Glenn MUNRO
52 Dean Air Force Postgrad Dental Sch COL. Drew FALLIS
52 Executive Dean Postgrad Dental Dr. Thomas R. SCHNEID

United States Air Force Academy (H)

2304 Cadet Drive, Suite 2400,
USAF Academy CO 80840-5002
County: El Paso FICE Identification: 001369
Unit ID: 128328
Telephone: (719) 333-3070 Carnegie Class: Bac-Diverse
FAX Number: (719) 333-3647 Calendar System: Semester
URL: www.usafa.af.mil/
Established: 1954 Annual Undergrad Tuition & Fees: N/A
Enrollment: 3,952 Coed
Affiliation or Control: Federal IRS Status: Exempt
Highest Offering: Baccalaureate
Accreditation: NH, BUS, CS, DENT, ENG

01 Superintendent LtGen. Michelle D. JOHNSON

United States Army Command and General Staff College (I)

100 Stimson Avenue, Fort Leavenworth KS 66027
County: Leavenworth FICE Identification: 001947
Unit ID: 156055
Telephone: (913) 684-3097 Carnegie Class: Not Classified
FAX Number: (913) 684-2906 Calendar System: Trimester
URL: usacac.army.mil/cac2/cgsc/
Established: 1881 Annual Graduate Tuition & Fees: N/A
Enrollment: N/A Coed
Affiliation or Control: Federal IRS Status: Exempt
Highest Offering: Master's; No Undergraduates
Accreditation: NH

01 Commandant LtGen. Robert B. BROWN
03 Deputy Commandant BGen. John S. KERN
04 Assistant Deputy Commandant Col. Leona C. KNIGHT
05 Dean of Academics Dr. Wendell C. KING
100 Chief of Staff Mr. Jeffrey P. LA MOE
58 Director Graduate Degree Programs Dr. Robert BAUMANN
08 Director of Library Mr. Ed BURGESS
32 Director CGSS School Col. Douglas C. CARDINALE
06 Registrar Mr. Thomas E. CREVISTON
26 Chief Public Relations Officer Mr. Harry SARLES

United States Army War College (J)

122 Forbes Avenue, Carlisle PA 17013-5050
County: Cumberland Identification: 666235
Telephone: (717) 245-4711 Carnegie Class: Not Classified
FAX Number: (717) 245-4721 Calendar System: Other
URL: www.carlisle.army.mil
Established: 1901 Annual Graduate Tuition & Fees: N/A
Enrollment: N/A Coed
Affiliation or Control: Federal IRS Status: Exempt
Highest Offering: Master's; No Undergraduates

Accreditation: M

01 Commandant .... MajGen. William E. RAPP
05 Provost .... Dr. Lance BETROS

United States Coast Guard Academy (A)

15 Mohegan Avenue, New London CT 06320-8100
County: New London FICE Identification: 001415
Unit ID: 130624
Telephone: (860) 444-8444 Carnegie Class: Bac-Diverse
FAX Number: (860) 444-8288 Calendar System: Semester
URL: www.cga.edu
Established: 1876 Annual Undergrad Tuition & Fees: $942
Enrollment: 896 Coed
Affiliation or Control: Federal IRS Status: Exempt
Highest Offering: Baccalaureate
Accreditation: EH, BUS, ENG

01 Superintendent .... RADM. James E. RENDON
03 Assistant Superintendent .... CAPT. Ronald A. LABREC
45 Planning Officer .... CDR. Gregory K. SABRA
05 Dean of Academics .... Dr. Kurt J. COLELLA
20 Associate Dean .... CDR. Gregory HALL
45 Director of Academic Resources .... Dr. Eric PAGE
07 Director of Admissions .... CAPT. Robert E. MCKENNA
32 Commandant of Cadets .... CAPT. Melissa L. RIVERA
06 Registrar .... Mr. Donald E. DYKES
08 Librarian .... Ms. Lucia MAZIAR
10 Comptroller .... LCDR. Francisco A. ESTEVEZ
26 Communication Director .... Mr. David M. SANTOS
09 Institutional Research .... Dr. Leonard M. GIAMBRA
13 Head of Information Services .... CDR. Robert F. TAYLOR
16 Personnel Management Specialist .... Mrs. Sunnie ROBINSON
15 Chief Personnel/Administration .... CDR. David BURNS
18 Chief Facilities Engineer .... CDR. Joshua W. FANT
19 Security Chief .... CDR. Robert F. TAYLOR
22 Civil Rights Officer .... Mr. Roy P. ZIEGENGEIST
23 Chief Health Services .... CAPT. Ernest E. SULLIVENT
38 Chief Cadet Counselor .... Dr. Robert MURRAY
40 Bookstore Manager .... Ms. Lauri KERP
41 Director of Athletics .... Mr. Timothy M. FITZPATRICK
42 Command Chaplain .... CAPT. Michael J. PARISI
43 Staff Legal Officer .... CDR. Ben G. KARPINSKI
85 International Cadet Advisor .... Dr. Kassim M. TARHINI
28 Instructor Inclusion and Diversity .... Dr. Aram DEKOVEN

† There is a one-time entrance fee of $3,000 to cover uniform, laptop, and supplies.

United States Merchant Marine Academy (B)

300 Steamboat Road, Kings Point NY 11024-1634
County: Nassau FICE Identification: 002892
Unit ID: 197027
Telephone: (516) 773-5000 Carnegie Class: Bac-Diverse
FAX Number: (516) 773-5582 Calendar System: Trimester
URL: www.usmma.edu
Established: 1943 Annual Undergrad Tuition & Fees: $1,107
Enrollment: 961 Coed
Affiliation or Control: Federal IRS Status: Exempt
Highest Offering: Master's
Accreditation: M, ENG

01 Superintendent .... RADM. James A. HELIS
03 Deputy Superintendent .... RDML. Susan L. DUNLAP
32 Commandant of Midshipmen .... CAPT. David SOSA
05 Assistant Academic Dean .... Ms. Dianne TAHA
18 Asst Supt for Facilities .... Capt. Theodore DOGONNIUCK
30 Director Office of External Affairs .... Mr. Ben BENSON
07 Director of Admissions .... Vacant
06 Registrar .... Ms. Lisa JERRY
13 Director Computer/Information Mgmt .... Mr. Kevin CLARKE
15 Director Human Resources .... Mr. Andrew GREEN
10 Chief Financial Officer .... Vacant
29 Director Alumni Relations .... Mr. Jim TOBIN
35 Director Student Affairs .... Mr. Nicholas RACHOWICZ
36 Dir of Prof Develop/Career Services .... Capt. Gene ALBERT
37 Director Student Financial Aid .... Mr. Joseph BECKER
96 Director of Purchasing .... Mr. Max DIAH
09 Director of Institutional Research .... Vacant
41 Athletic Director .... Ms. Maureen WHITE
108 Director Institutional Assessment .... Ms. Lori TOWNSEND
43 Dir Legal Services/General Counsel .... Ms. Ilene KREITZER

United States Military Academy (C)

West Point NY 10996-5000
County: Orange FICE Identification: 002893
Unit ID: 197036
Telephone: (845) 938-4041 Carnegie Class: Bac-A&S
FAX Number: (845) 938-3021 Calendar System: Semester
URL: www.westpoint.edu
Established: 1802 Annual Undergrad Tuition & Fees: N/A
Enrollment: 4,414 Coed
Affiliation or Control: Federal IRS Status: Exempt
Highest Offering: Baccalaureate
Accreditation: M, CS, ENG

01 Superintendent/President .... LTG. Robert CASLEN, JR.
05 Dean of Academic Board .... BG. Cindy JEBB
20 Vice Dean .... Dr. Jean BLAIR
32 Commandant of Cadets .... BG. Diana M. HOLLAND
100 Chief of Staff .... COL. Wayne A. GREEN
88 Garrison Commander .... COL. Andrew HANSON
07 Director of Admissions .... COL. Deborah MCDONALD
06 Assoc Dean Operations/Registrar .... Dr. James DALTON
45 Associate Dean for Research .... LTC. John GRAHAM
09 Institutional Research .... LTC. Holly WEST
13 Chief Information Officer .... LTC. Edward TEAGUE
10 Director of Resource Management .... Mr. Leslie BREHM
26 Public Affairs Officer .... LTC. Kasker CHRISTOPHER
08 USMA Library .... Mr. Christopher BARTH
29 President Association of Graduates .... Mr. Robert MCCLURE
38 Dir Center for Personal Development .... LTC. Darcy SCHNACK
41 Director Intercollegiate Athletics .... Mr. Boo CORRIGAN
18 Chief Facilities/Physical Plant .... Mr. Matthew TALABER
15 Dir Center for Faculty Excellence .... Dr. Mark EVANS
35 Dir Ctr for Enchanced Performance .... LTC. Pete JENSEN
88 Director of Cadet Activities .... COL. Tom HANSBARGER
43 Chief Legal Assistance .... Mr. Micheal BARRETT
28 Director of Diversity .... Dr. Donald OUTING

United States Naval Academy (D)

121 Blake Road, Annapolis MD 21402-5000
County: Anne Arundel FICE Identification: 030430
Unit ID: 164155
Telephone: (410) 293-1000 Carnegie Class: Bac-A&S
FAX Number: (410) 293-3734 Calendar System: Semester
URL: www.usna.edu
Established: 1845 Annual Undergrad Tuition & Fees: N/A
Enrollment: 4,511 Coed
Affiliation or Control: Federal IRS Status: Exempt
Highest Offering: Baccalaureate
Accreditation: M, CS, ENG

01 Superintendent .... VADM. Walter E. CARTER, JR.
32 Commandant of Midshipmen .... COL. Stephen LISZEWSKI
05 Academic Dean & Provost .... Dr. Andrew T. PHILLIPS
20 Vice Academic Dean .... Dr. Boyd A. WAITE
07 Dean of Admissions .... Capt. Bruce J. LATTA
10 Associate Dean for Finances .... Capt. Peter A. NARDI
20 Assoc Dean for Academic Affairs .... Dr. Jennifer WATERS
08 Assoc Dean Information Svcs/Library .... Mr. James RETTIG
21 CFO/Deputy for Finance .... Mr. Joseph RUBINO
100 Chief of Staff .... Capt. George E. LANG, JR.
11 CO Naval Support Activity Annapolis .... Capt. Thomas L. REESE
06 Registrar .... Dr. Christopher A. DAVIS
26 Public Affairs Officer .... CDR. John SCHOFIELD
29 Exec Director Alumni Association .... Mr. William OCONNER
21 Comptroller .... CDR. Todd W. HAUGE
13 Chief Information Officer .... CDR. Louis J. GIANNOTTI
88 Director Academic Center .... Dr. Bruce J. BUKOWSKI
09 Director Institutional Research .... Capt. Glenn F. GOTTSCHALK
18 Public Works Officer .... Capt. Nicholas MERRY
41 Athletic Director .... Mr. Chet GLADCHUK
42 Command Chaplain .... Capt. Michael PARISI
30 Director Officer Development .... Capt. Mike MICHEL
15 Director Human Resources .... Mr. William COFFIN
28 Director of Diversity .... Capt. Pat WILLIAMS

AMERICAN SAMOA

American Samoa Community College (E)

PO Box 2609, Pago Pago AS 96799-2609
County: American Samoa FICE Identification: 010010
Unit ID: 240736
Telephone: (684) 699-9155 Carnegie Class: Bac/Assoc-Assoc Dom
FAX Number: (684) 699-6259 Calendar System: Semester
URL: www.amsamoa.edu
Established: 1970 Annual Undergrad Tuition & Fees (In-State): $3,550
Enrollment: 1,276 Coed
Affiliation or Control: State IRS Status: 501(c)3
Highest Offering: Baccalaureate
Accreditation: WJ

01 President .... Dr. Seth P. GALEA'I
09 Director of Inst Effectiveness .... Mr. Sonny J. LEOMITI
05 VP of Academic and Student Affairs .... Dr. Rosevonne PATO
88 Director of Samoan Studies Inst .... Mrs. Okenaisa FAUOLO-MANILA
88 Director of Land Grant/ACNR .... Mr. Ropeti ARETA
88 Director of UCEDD .... Ms. Taaimamao TUPUOLA
51 Director of Adult Education-LEL .... Mr. Tauvela FALE
88 Director of Small Business Devel .... Dr. Herbert THWEATT
11 VP of Administration and Finance .... Dr. Mikaele ETUALE
20 Dean of Academic Affairs .... Mrs. Letupu MOANANU
53 Director of Teacher Education .... Dr. Lina GALEA'I-SCANLAN
72 Director of Trades & Technology .... Mr. Michael LEAU
108 Director of Curriculum & Assessment ...... Mrs. Evelyn V. FRUEAN
32 Dean of Student Services .... Dr. Emilia LE'I
10 Chief Financial Officer .... Mrs. Emey S LAFAU-TOA
13 Chief Information Officer .... Ms. Grace TULAFONO
18 Physical Facilities Maint Officer .... Mr. Loligi SEUMANUTAFA
15 Human Resources Officer .... Mrs. Serema ASIFOA
96 Procurement Officer .... Mrs. Jessie SU'ESU'E
38 Program Director of Counseling .... Ms. Annie PANAMA
08 Program Director of Library Svcs .... Mr. Elvis ZODIACAL

06 Records Officer .... Mrs. Sifagatogo TUITASI
07 Admission Officer .... Mrs. Elizabeth LEUMA
37 Financial Aid Officer .... Mr. Peteru K. LAM YUEN
40 Bookstore Manager .... Mrs. Alofia AFALAVA

FEDERATED STATES OF MICRONESIA

College of Micronesia-FSM (F)

PO Box 159 Kolonia, Pohnpei FM 96941-0159
FICE Identification: 010343
Unit ID: 243638
Telephone: (691) 320-2480 Carnegie Class: Assoc/HT-High Non
FAX Number: (691) 320-2479 Calendar System: Semester
URL: www.comfsm.fm
Established: 1963 Annual Undergrad Tuition & Fees (In-State): $5,541
Enrollment: 2,344 Coed
Affiliation or Control: State IRS Status: 501(c)3
Highest Offering: Associate Degree
Accreditation: WJ

01 President/CEO .... Dr. Joseph M. DAISY
09 Vice President IEQA .... Ms. Frankie HARRISS
05 Vice Pres Instructional Affairs .... Mrs. Karen SIMION
84 Vice Pres Enroll Mgmt/Student Svcs .... Mr. Joey ODUCADO
56 VP Coop Research/Ext (Land Grant) ..... Mr. Walter James CURRIE
11 Vice President Admin Services .... Mr. Joseph HABUCHMAI
12 Dean Chuuk Campus .... Mr. Kind KANTO
12 Dean Kosrae Campus .... Mr. Nena MIKE
12 Dean Yap Campus .... Ms. Lourdes ROBOMAN
10 Comptroller .... Mrs. Roselle TOGONON
12 Director FSM-FMI Campus .... Mr. Matthias EWARMAI
45 Director Research & Planning .... Mr. Jimmy HICKS
15 Director Human Resources .... Ms. Rencelly NELSON
20 Dean of Academic Programs .... Mrs. Maria DISION
08 Director Learning Resource Center .... Mrs. Jennifer HELIEISAR
75 Dir Career & Technical Education .... Mr. Grilly JACK
18 Director Physical Plant/Maintenance ..... Mr. Francisco MENDIOLA
06 Registrar .... Vacant
21 Business Officer Manager .... Mr. Doman DAOAS
37 Director of Financial Aid .... Mr. Faustino YAROFAISUG
38 Counselor .... Ms. Penselyn SAM
13 Director Information Technology .... Mr. Gordon SEGAL
39 Director Residential/Campus Life .... Ms. Krystilyn M. ATKINSON
100 Chief of Staff .... Ms. Universe YAMASE
19 Supervisor Security/Safety .... Mr. Warren CHING
96 Director of Procurement .... Mr. Roberto (Bobby) J. SANTOS

GUAM

Guam Community College (G)

PO Box 23069, Barrigada GU 96921-3069
County: Guam FICE Identification: 015361
Unit ID: 240745
Telephone: (671) 735-5531 Carnegie Class: Assoc/MT-VT-Mix Trad/Non
FAX Number: (671) 734-5238 Calendar System: Semester
URL: www.guamcc.edu
Established: 1977 Annual Undergrad Tuition & Fees (In-District): $3,414
Enrollment: 2,458 Coed
Affiliation or Control: State/Local IRS Status: 501(c)3
Highest Offering: Associate Degree
Accreditation: WJ, ACFEI, MAC

01 President .... Dr. Mary Y. OKADA
05 Vice President Academic Affairs .... Dr. R. Ray D. SOMERA
10 Vice Pres Finance & Administration .... Ms. Carmen K. SANTOS
21 Controller .... Mr. Edwin E. LIMTUATCO
75 Dean Trades & Professional Services .... Dr. Virginia C. TUDELA
32 Dean Technology & Student Services .... Dr. Michael L. CHAN
26 Asst Dir Communications & Promo .... Ms. Jayne T. FLORES
04 Private Secretary .... Ms. Esther A. MUNA
101 Admin Secretary II BOT-Pres Ofc .... Ms. Bertha M. GUERRERO
07 Coordinator Admissions/Registration .... Mr. Patrick L. CLYMER
45 Asst Dir Planning & Development .... Ms. Doris U. PEREZ
103 Asst Dir Cont Educ & Workforce Dev .... Ms. Rowena Ellen PEREZ
88 Assoc Dean Trade & Prof Svcs .... Ms. Pilar WILLIAMS
88 Assoc Dean Trade & Prof Svcs .... Dr. Elizabeth A. DIEGO
35 Assoc Dean Tech & Student Svcs .... Mr. Ronald G. HARTZ
15 Administrator Human Resources .... Ms. Joann W. MUNA
18 Facilities Engineer Administrator .... Vacant
08 Librarian .... Ms. Christine B. MATSON
20 Admin Ofcr VP's Ofc-Academic Affs .... Ms. Ana Mari C. ATOIGUE
09 Asst Director AIER .... Ms. Marlena O. MONTAGUE
88 Pgm Spc Adult Basic Educ .... Ms. Ava M. GARCIA
88 Pgm Spc CACGP .... Ms. Fermina A. SABLAN
35 Pgm Spc Ctr Student Involvement .... Ms. Barbara B. LEON GUERRERO
23 School Health Counselor .... Ms. Eva Marie L. MUI
88 Program Specialist .... Mr. Wesley T. GIMA
37 Coordinator Student Financial Aid .... Ms. Esther A. RIOS
88 Pgm Spc TRIO Programs .... Dr. Julie ULLOA-HEATH
29 Pgm Specialist Alum & Fundraising .... Ms. Bonnie Mae M. DATUIN
29 Pgm Spc Alum & Fundraising .... Mr. Danilo Philbert BILONG
96 Supply Management Administrator . Ms. Joleen M. EVANGELISTA
13 Data Processing Administrator .... Mr. Francisco C. CAMACHO
51 Pgm Spc Continuing Educ .... Ms. Terry L. BARNHART
51 Pgm Spc Continuing Educ .... Mr. Philip C. GUERRERO

40 Bookstore Manager Mr. Daniel T. OKADA
55 Prgm Spc Night Administrator Mr. Huan HOSEI
19 Safety Admin Envir Safety Ofcr Mr. Gregorio T. MANGLONA
88 Pgm Spc Accomodative Svcs Mr. John F. PAYNE
88 Sustainability Coordinator Mr. Francisco E. PALACIOS
88 Pgm Spc P&D Ms. Priscilla C. JOHNS

Pacific Islands University (A)

172 Kinney's Road, Mangilao GU 96913
County: Guam FICE Identification: 034383
Unit ID: 439862
Telephone: (671) 734-1812 Carnegie Class: Spec-4-yr-Faith
FAX Number: (671) 734-1813 Calendar System: Semester
URL: www.piu.edu
Established: 1976 Annual Undergrad Tuition & Fees: $5,128
Enrollment: 72 Coed
Affiliation or Control: Independent Non-Profit IRS Status: 501(c)3
Highest Offering: Master's
Accreditation: TRACS

01 President/CEO Dr. David L. OWEN
10 VP Finance/Administration Mr. Nino T. PATE
05 Provost/Academic Vice President Mr. Juan FLORES
20 Seminary Dean Mr. Malcolm James SAWYER
88 Liberal Studies Chair Mr. James MASON
88 Biblical Studies Chair Ms. Iotaka CHORAM
32 Dean of Students Ms. Celeste HEIMBACH
21 Operations Director/Bookkeeper Ms. Celia ATOIGE
04 Exec Assistant to the President Vacant
08 Library Director Mr. Paul DRAKE
15 Human Resource Director Mr. Nino T. PATE

University of Guam (B)

UOG Station, Mangilao GU 96923-1800
County: Guam FICE Identification: 003935
Unit ID: 240754
Telephone: (671) 735-2990 Carnegie Class: Masters/M
FAX Number: (671) 734-2296 Calendar System: Semester
URL: www.uog.edu
Established: 1952 Annual Undergrad Tuition & Fees (In-State): $5,338
Enrollment: 3,958 Coed
Affiliation or Control: State IRS Status: 501(c)3
Highest Offering: Master's
Accreditation: WC, IACBE, NUR, SW, TED

01 President Dr. Robert A. UNDERWOOD
05 Sr VP Academic & Student Affairs Dr. Anita B. ENRIQUEZ
10 Vice Pres Administration & Finance Mr. Randall V. WIEGAND
58 AVP Graduate Studies/Research & SP Dr. John A. PETERSON
43 University Legal Counsel Ms. Victorina M Y. RENACIA
13 Chief Information Officer Mr. Rommel HILDAGO
88 Institutional Compliance Officer Vacant
04 Executive Assistant to President Ms. Louise M. TOVES
26 Director Integrated Mktg & Comm Mr. Jonas D. MACAPINLAC
45 Chief Planning Officer Mr. David S. OKADA
29 Director Dev & Alumni Affairs Mr. Norman ANALISTA
102 Exec Director Endowment Foundation Ms. Janiece A. SABLAN
108 Dir Academic Assess/Inst Research Ms. Deborah D. LEON GUERRERO
49 Dean Col of Lib Arts & Social Sci Dr. James D. SELLMANN
47 Dean Col of Natural & Applied Sci Dr. Lee S. YUDIN
50 Dean Sch Business & Pub Admin Dr. Annette T. SANTOS
53 Dean School of Education Dr. John SANCHEZ
66 Dean of Nursing & Hlth Sci Dr. Margaret HATTORI-UCHIMA
84 Dean Enroll Mgmt & Stdnt Svcs Mr. Michael GUNN
06 Registrar Ms. Remy B. CRISTOBAL
37 Financial Aid Director Mr. Mark A. DUARTE
32 Student Life Officer Ms. Sallie MCDONALD
88 Director Guam CEDDERS Dr. Heidi E. SAN NICOLAS
08 Interim Director Learning Resources Dr. Monique STORIE
13 Dir Info Tech Resource/Computer Ctr Dr. Luan P. NGUYEN
88 Dir Micronesia Area Res Center Dr. Monique C. STORIE
88 Director Marine Laboratory Dr. Terry DONALDSON
88 Dir Watr Env Rsrch Inst Wstrn Pac Dr. Shahram KHOSROWPANAH
88 Dir Ctr for Island Sustainability Dr. John A. PETERSON
88 Actg Director Prof/Intl Program Mr. Carlos TAITANO
88 Director TRIO Programs Mr. Yoichi K. RENGIIL
15 Chief Human Resources Officer Mr. Larry GAMBOA
18 Chief Plant Fac Ofcr Fac & Util Mr. Sonny P. PEREZ
41 Field House/Athletics Director Mr. Doug PALMER
19 Safety Administrator Mr. Felix MANSAPIT
40 Director Bookstore & Auxiliary Svcs Ms. Ann S A. LEON GUERRERO
21 Comptroller Ms. Zeny ASUNCION-NACE
39 Director of Residence Halls Mr. Jonathan TRIPLET

MARSHALL ISLANDS

College of the Marshall Islands (C)

PO Box 1258, Majuro MH 96960-1258
County: Marshalls FICE Identification: 030224
Unit ID: 376695
Telephone: (692) 625-3394 Carnegie Class: Assoc/HT-High Trad
FAX Number: (692) 625-7203 Calendar System: Semester
URL: www.cmi.edu
Established: 1989 Annual Undergrad Tuition & Fees (In-State): $4,885
Enrollment: 1,087 Coed
Affiliation or Control: State IRS Status: 501(c)3
Highest Offering: Associate Degree
Accreditation: WJ

01 President Dr. Theresa B. KOROIVULAONO
05 VP Academic & Student Affairs Vacant
11 Vice Pres Administration Mr. William REIHER
10 Chief Financial Officer Mr. Stevenson KOTTON
20 Dean of Academic Affairs Ms. Vasemaca SAVU
32 Dean of Student Services Ms. Rachel SALOMON
06 Registrar Ms. Monica GORDON
07 Director of Admissions & Records Ms. Jomi CAPELLE
08 Director of Library Services Mr. Chris SEBASTIAN
15 Human Resources Director Ms. Agnes KOTOISUVA
51 Director Continuing/Adult Education Ms. Rosana JERICHO
18 Director Physical Plant Mr. Emil DEBRUM
13 Director Information & Technology Mr. Bonifacio SANCHEZ
88 Director Nuclear Institute Ms. Mary L. SILK
37 Financial Aid Director Ms. Jacinta SAMUEL
49 Chair Liberal Arts Ms. Elizabeth SWITAJ
50 Chair Business & IT Ms. Meitaka KENDALL-DOMNICK
66 Chair Nursing Ms. Florence L. PETER
19 Director Security/Safety Mr. David DEBRUM
38 Dir Counseling/Career & Transfer Mr. Terry HAZARD
09 Dir Inst Research & Planning Ms. Cherly T. VILA
108 Dir Inst Integrity & Effectiveness Ms. Ruth ABBOTT

NORTHERN MARIANAS

Northern Marianas College (D)

PO Box 501250, Saipan MP 96950-1250
FICE Identification: 030330
Unit ID: 240790
Telephone: (670) 234-5498 Carnegie Class: Bac/Assoc-Mixed
FAX Number: (670) 234-1270 Calendar System: Semester
URL: www.marianas.edu
Established: 1976 Annual Undergrad Tuition & Fees (In-District): $2,820
Enrollment: 1,186 Coed
Affiliation or Control: State/Local IRS Status: 501(c)3
Highest Offering: Baccalaureate
Accreditation: WC

01 Interim President Mr. David J. ATTAO
05 Dean of Academic Programs & Svcs Ms. Barbara K. MERFALEN
32 Dean of Student Services Mr. Leo PANGELINAN
10 Chief Financial Officer Ms. Tracy GUERRERO
11 Dean of Admin/Resource Development Mr. David ATTAO
31 Dean of CREES Dr. Timothy KOCK
04 Executive Secretary to President Ms. Becky SABLAN
13 Director of Information Technology Mr. Jonathan LIWAG
09 Dir Institutional Effectiveness Ms. Jacqueline CHE
08 Director Library Services Mr. Christopher TODD
53 Director School of Education Ms. Charlotte R. CEPEDA
51 Director of Adult Basic Education Ms. Lorraine T. CABRERA
38 Acting Director of Counseling Svcs Ms. Joan TORRES
37 Director of Financial Aid Ms. Daisy MANGLONA-PROPST
96 Procurement Manager Ms. Anita C. CAMACHO
15 Human Resources Ms. Novelyn TENORIO
21 Chief Accountant Ms. Solita K. BARNES
36 Career Planning/Placement Coord Ms. Neda C. DELEON GUERRERA
18 Facilities Manager Mr. John GUERRERO
29 President NMC Alumni Association Mr. Jack O. KIYOSHI
106 Director of Distance Learning & ALO Ms. Amanda ALLEN
06 Registrar Mr. Leo PANGELINAN
101 Secretary of the Institution/Board Ms. Helen B. CAMACHO
26 Director of External Relations Mr. Frankie M. ELIPTICO

PALAU

Palau Community College (E)

PO Box 9, Koror PW 96940-0009
County: Koror FICE Identification: 011009
Unit ID: 243647
Telephone: (680) 488-2470 Carnegie Class: Assoc/HVT-High Trad
FAX Number: (680) 488-2447 Calendar System: Semester
URL: www.palau.edu
Established: 1969 Annual Undergrad Tuition & Fees: $3,250
Enrollment: 604 Coed
Affiliation or Control: Federal IRS Status: Exempt
Highest Offering: Associate Degree
Accreditation: WJ

01 President Dr. Patrick U. TELLEI
05 Vice President Education & Training Vacant
11 Vice Pres Administration & Finance Mr. Jay OLEGERIIL
46 Vice Pres Cooperative Rsrch/Exten Mr. Thomas TARO
04 Exec Assistant to the President Mr. Todd NGIRAMENGIOR
32 Dean of Students Mr. Sherman DANIEL
20 Dean of Academic Affairs Mr. Robert RAMARUI
51 Dean of Continuing Education Mr. William WALLY
30 Director of Development Mr. Tzuchie TADAO
07 Director Admissions & Financial Aid Mrs. Dahlia M. KATOSANG
06 Registrar Ms. Lesley B. ADACHI
15 Director of Human Resources Mr. Omdasu T. UEKI
18 Director of Physical Plant Mr. Clement KAZUMA
13 Director of Computer Systems Mr. Bruce RIMIRCH
35 Director of Student Life Ms. Hilda REKLAI
10 Director of Finance Ms. Uroi N. SALII
38 Counselor Ms. Maurine ALEXANDER
38 Counselor Ms. Glendalynn NGIRMERIIL
91 System Analyst Ms. Grace ALEXANDER
88 Accreditation Liaison Officer Ms. Deikola OLIKONG
08 Director of Library Services Vacant
09 Director of Institutional Research Ms. Deikola OLIKONG

PUERTO RICO

American University of Puerto Rico (F)

Box 2037, Bayamon PR 00960-2037
County: Bayamon FICE Identification: 011941
Unit ID: 241100
Telephone: (787) 620-2040 Carnegie Class: Masters/S
FAX Number: (787) 785-7377 Calendar System: Other
URL: www.aupr.edu
Established: 1963 Annual Undergrad Tuition & Fees: $5,811
Enrollment: 832 Coed
Affiliation or Control: Independent Non-Profit IRS Status: 501(c)3
Highest Offering: Master's
Accreditation: M

01 President Vacant
03 Executive Vice President Mr. Jaime GONZALEZ
05 Vice President Acad/Student Affairs Dr. Jose RAMIREZ-FIGUEROA
10 Vice Pres Finance & Admin Affairs Mrs. Magda A. CANCEL-PEREZ
32 Dean Student Affairs Prof. Claribel RODRIGUEZ-VARGAS
06 Registrar Prof. Maria RODRIGUEZ-PAZ
07 Admissions Officer Ms. Keren LLANOS
08 Learning Resources Center Director Ms. Dirza ALMESTICA
37 Director Financial Aid Mrs. Yahaira MELENDEZ
21 Director Accounting Mrs. Jeanette AVILES-FERRAN
38 Director Guidance Counseling Mrs. Luz S. HERNANDEZ
24 Director Educational Media Ms. Carol SANTIAGO
41 Athletic Director Mr. Manfredo VEGA
15 Director Personnel Services Mrs. Ginette OPPENHEIMER
12 Director Manati Campus Prof. Milagros RIVERA-OTERO
09 Dir Research/Institutional Planning Vacant
18 Chief Facilities/Physical Plant Mr. Efrain LUGO
36 Director of Student Placement Vacant
96 Director of Purchasing Mrs. Celeste TRAVERSO
92 Director of Honors Program Prof. Claribel RODRIGUEZ
30 Chief Development Mr. Jaime GONZALEZ
20 Associate Academic Officer Prof. Zahira GARCIA
13 Director Computer Center Vacant
53 Dept Chair School of Education Dr. Jose RAMIREZ
50 Dept Chair Business Admin/Sec Sci Vacant
49 Department Chair Arts & Sciences Vacant
100 Chief of Staff Ms. Rosabel VAZQUEZ
102 Dir Foundation/Corporate Relations Dr. Adela VAZQUEZ
105 Director Web Services Vacant
19 Director Security/Safety Ms. Rosabel VAZQUEZ
45 Chief Institutional Planning Prof. Bolivar RAMIREZ-CARLO, III
04 Administrative Asst to President Mrs. Carmen ARROYO

Atenas College (G)

Paseo de las Atenas #101, Manati PR 00674
FICE Identification: 035443
Unit ID: 440651
Telephone: (787) 884-3838 Carnegie Class: Spec-4-yr-Other Health
FAX Number: (787) 854-4530 Calendar System: Semester
URL: www.atenascollege.edu
Established: 1996 Annual Undergrad Tuition & Fees: $6,945
Enrollment: 1,363 Coed
Affiliation or Control: Independent Non-Profit IRS Status: 501(c)3
Highest Offering: Baccalaureate
Accreditation: ACCSC, @PTAA

01 President Dra. Maria L. HERNÁNDEZ NÚÑEZ
05 Vice President Academic Affairs Prof. Widalys GONZÁLEZ
20 Associate Dean of Academic Affairs Dra. Cenia K. ROMANO
20 Associate Dean Academic Affairs Prof. Rosa M. MORALES
20 Associate Dean of Academic Affairs Mrs. Brenda HERNÁNDEZ-AVEVEDO
88 Associate Dean Acad & Adm Affairs Mrs. Luz C. REYES
07 Recruitment and Admissions Director Mr. Joel FIGUEROA
88 Dir Learning Res Ctr Tech & DE Mrs. Annette DAVILA
36 Director Student Placement Mrs. Sally SANTA
11 Vice Pres of Administrative Affairs Mrs. Ingrid Y. COLÓN
10 VP Finance & Acad Adm Affairs Mrs. Astrid Y. MELÉNDEZ HERNÁNDEZ
45 VP Inst Planning and Innovation Dra. Nereida NALES PÉREZ
09 VP Inst Planning and Effectiveness Mrs. María C. MEDINA
26 Marketing Coordinator Mrs. Angianette RESTO
15 Human Resources and Security Dir Mrs. Aurea FIGUEROA
18 Operation Manager Mr. Carlos R. VÁZQUEZ
10 Accounting Director Mrs. Zulay SOTO
37 Financial Aid Administrator Mr. Manuel RAMÍREZ
06 Registrar Mrs. Walitza HERNÁNDEZ
38 Guidance and Counseling Mrs. Keila OJEDA FERNÁNDEZ
08 Librarian Mrs. Sonia N. FERRER MEDINA
88 Coordinator Simulation Center Prof. Diana N. RAMOS MARTÍNEZ
04 Admn Svcs Coordinator for President Mrs. Diana RODRÍGUEZ ALVARADO

Atlantic University College (A)

PO Box 3918, Guaynabo PR 00970
County: Guaynabo FICE Identification: 025054
Unit ID: 241216
Telephone: (787) 720-1022 Carnegie Class: Spec-4-yr-Other Tech
FAX Number: (787) 720-1092 Calendar System: Quarter
URL: www.atlanticu.edu
Established: 1983 Annual Undergrad Tuition & Fees: $7,425
Enrollment: 1,496 Coed
Affiliation or Control: Independent Non-Profit IRS Status: 501(c)3
Highest Offering: Baccalaureate
Accreditation: ACICS

01 President ....Dr. Teresa DE DIOS UNANUE
13 Exec Vice Pres/Dean Technology/ Mktg ....Prof. Heri MARTINEZ DE DIOS
05 Academic Dean ....Prof. Ivette CARBONELL
10 Dean of Administration ....Prof. Heriberto MARTINEZ-ABREU
88 Dean of Digital Arts/Sciences ....Prof. Frances GRAU
06 Registrar ....Ms. Edna I. GUTIERREZ
38 Dir Student Counseling/ Placement ....Prof. Maria C. LOPEZ-CEPERO RAMOS
37 Director Financial Aid ....Mrs. Janice RIVERA
08 Head Librarian ....Mrs. Tania DIAZ
07 Director of Admissions ....Mr. Joel MONTERO
21 Director Business Office ....Mrs. María del C MONTESINO
15 Officer of Human Resources ....Ms. Viviana SANTIAGO

Caribbean University (B)

Box 493, Bayamon PR 00960-0493
County: Bayamon FICE Identification: 012525
Unit ID: 241377
Telephone: (787) 780-0070 Carnegie Class: Masters/S
FAX Number: (787) 785-0101 Calendar System: Semester
URL: www.caribbean.edu
Established: 1969 Annual Undergrad Tuition & Fees: $5,080
Enrollment: 1,959 Coed
Affiliation or Control: Independent Non-Profit IRS Status: 501(c)3
Highest Offering: Doctorate
Accreditation: M, ENG, @TEAC

01 President/CEO ....Dr. Ana E. CUCURELLA-ADORNO
03 Executive Director ....Mr. Victor T. ADORNO
05 Vice President of Academic Affairs ....Dr. Luis J. DELGADO
45 Vice President of Planning and Info ....Mr. Jorge RIEFKOHL
11 Dean Administration Affairs ....Mr. Israel RODRIGUEZ
32 Dean of Student Affairs ....Mr. Luis J. DELGADO
13 IT Interim Director ....Mr. Luis N. PRATTS
15 Human Resources Director ....Mrs. Teresita RIVERA
37 Director Student Financial Aid ....Mr. Javier VAZQUEZ
06 Registrar ....Ms. Maranjani BORRERO
08 Librarian/Director Audio-Visual ....Mrs. Carmen L. APONTE
07 Director of Admissions ....Mrs. Rosalie MORALES
12 Director of Carolina Campus ....Prof. Jose CUETO
12 Director of Ponce Campus ....Prof. Sonia PACHECO
12 Director Vega Baja Campus ....Vacant
20 Provost ....Ms. Lillian MATOS
71 Director Special Service Program ....Mrs. Maryliz AUBRET
26 Public Relations Director ....Dr. Enrique ROSARIO
58 Assoc Dean of Graduate Programs ....Dr. Luis MEJIAS
49 Director Department Arts/Science ....Prof. William PEREZ
50 Director Dept Business Admin/Sec Sc ....Mr. Jose M. CUETO
76 Health Services ....Ms. Mara MEDINA
54 Director Department of Engineering ....Dr. Hermes CALDERON
66 Director Department of Nursing ....Dr. Mildred FLORES
53 Director Department Education ....Dr. Edgardo REYES
77 Director of Computer Science ....Dr. Augusto CARVAJAL
18 Chief Facilities/Physical Plant ....Mr. Henry SEVILLA
43 Legal Advisor ....Mr. Rafael SANTIAGO
38 Director Counseling Center (CIOSE) .... Dr. David BAEZ MOJICA
41 Athletic Director ....Mr. Rafael MARRERO PEREZ
22 Director of Compliance ....Mrs. Elena GARCIA
84 Director Enrollment Management ....Vacant
09 Director of Institutional Research ....Dr. Luz D. SERRANO
96 Director of Purchasing ....Mrs. Carmen J. ROSA

Carlos Albizu University (C)

Box 9023711, San Juan PR 00902-3711
County: San Juan FICE Identification: 010724
Unit ID: 241331
Telephone: (787) 725-6500 Carnegie Class: Spec-4-yr-Other Health
FAX Number: (787) 721-7187 Calendar System: Semester
URL: www.albizu.edu
Established: 1966 Annual Undergrad Tuition & Fees: $7,006
Enrollment: 1,063 Coed
Affiliation or Control: Independent Non-Profit IRS Status: 501(c)3
Highest Offering: Doctorate
Accreditation: M, CLPSY, SP

00 Chair Board of Trustees ....Mr. Jaime L. ALBORS BIGAS
01 Interim President ....Dr. Sylvia LOPEZ-JORGE
12 Chancellor of San Juan Campus . Dr. Jose J. CABIYA-MORALES
12 Int Chancellor of Miami Campus ....Dr. Irene BRAVO
07 Director Admissions/Student Affs .... Mr. Carlos RODRIGUEZ
11 Spec Asst to Chanc for Admin Affs .... Mr. Luis ECHEGARAY
05 Interim Provost ....Dr. Daniel MARTINEZ ORTIZ
88 Special Assistant to Vice President ....Ms. Sylvia LOPEZ
32 Dean of Student Services ....Ms. Carmen RIVERA
10 Director of Finance ....Mr. Hector PENA
46 Director Research Training .... Dr. Lymaries PADILLA-COTTO
88 Director General Psychology Program ....Dr. Jaime VERAY
51 Director Continuing Education ....Ms. Isabel HERNANDEZ
88 Director Internship ....Dr. Aica GARCIA
37 Director Financial Aid ....Mrs. Doris QUERO-MENDEZ
08 Director Library ....Ms. Yolanda ROSARIO-ROSARIO
06 Registrar ....Mr. Nieves RIVERA
88 Dir Industrial/Org Psych Program ... Dr. Miguel MARTINEZ-LUGO
13 Dir Information Technology Svcs ....Mr. Luis CAMACHO
88 Administrator Community Svcs Clinic ....Mr. Rafael ORTIZ
31 Director Community Services Clinic ....Dr. Jose RODRIGUEZ-QUINONES
88 Dir PhD Clinical Psychology Program ....Dr. Jose CABIYA
88 Dir PsyD Clinical Psychology Pgm ....Dr. Julio SANTANA MARINO
15 Exec Director of Human Resources ....Ms. Angela RAMOS
30 Director Development ....Vacant
88 Director Clinical Training ....Dr. Noel QUINTERO-JIMENEZ
88 Director Bachelor's Program ....Dr. Jaime VERAY
38 President Student Counseling ....Mr. Ricardo DEL RIO-MORALES
11 Director Administration ....Mr. John FERNANDEZ
26 Director Communication ....Ms. Norma BORGES
29 Director Alumni Relations ....Ms. Angeles PEREZ
09 Dir Inst Research/Assessment ....Mr. Rafael MELENDEZ

Center for Advanced Studies On Puerto Rico and the Caribbean (D)

PO Box 902-3970, Old San Juan PR 00902-3970
County: San Juan FICE Identification: 021660
Unit ID: 241793
Telephone: (787) 723-4481 Carnegie Class: Spec-4-yr-Other
FAX Number: (787) 723-1023 Calendar System: Semester
URL: www.ceaprc.edu
Established: 1976 Annual Graduate Tuition & Fees: N/A
Enrollment: 489 Coed
Affiliation or Control: Independent Non-Profit IRS Status: 501(c)3
Highest Offering: Doctorate; No Undergraduates
Accreditation: M

01 Chancellor ....Mr. Miguel A. RODRIGUEZ-LOPEZ
05 Academic Dean ....Dr. Jaime L. RODRIGUEZ-CANCEL
06 Registrar ....Mrs. Mayra I. RAMIREZ
08 Head Librarian ....Mr. Francis J. MOJICA
10 Administration Dean ....Mrs. Lizzette CARRILLO
04 Chancellor's Assistant .... Ms. Clarissa SANTIAGO-TORO
07 Marketing and Enrollment Director .....Mrs. Monica D. GONZALEZ
37 Financial Aid Officer ....Mrs. Lillian M. OLIVER
101 Secretary of the Institution/Board . Ms. Clarissa SANTIAGO-TORO
32 Student Affairs Officer .... Mr. Jose F. PEREZ-RODRIGUEZ

Centro de Estudios Multidisciplinarios (E)

Calle Degetau #25, Bayamon PR 00961
Telephone: (787) 780-8900 Identification: 770590
Accreditation: ACCSC

Centro de Estudios Multidisciplinarios (F)

Calle Dr. Vidal #8 y #53, Humacao PR 00791
Telephone: (787) 850-8333 Identification: 770589
Accreditation: ACCSC

Centro de Estudios Multidisciplinarios (G)

Calle Cristy #56, Mayaguez PR 00681
Telephone: (787) 986-7440 Identification: 770591
Accreditation: ACCSC

Centro de Estudios Multidisciplinarios (H)

Calle 13 #1206, Ext San Agustin, Rio Piedras PR 00926
County: San Juan FICE Identification: 021891
Unit ID: 241517
Telephone: (787) 765-4210 Carnegie Class: Spec-4-yr-Other Health
FAX Number: (787) 765-4277 Calendar System: Semester
URL: www.cempr.edu
Established: 1980 Annual Undergrad Tuition & Fees: $6,640
Enrollment: 892 Coed
Affiliation or Control: Independent Non-Profit IRS Status: 501(c)3
Highest Offering: Baccalaureate
Accreditation: ACCSC

01 President ....Mr. Juan C. PAGANI-SOTO
05 Academic Dean ....Dr. Nereida MORA
07 Director of Admissions ....Mr. Juan RESTO TORRES
06 Registrar ....Mrs. Margarita RIVERA
10 Finance Director ....Mr. Carlos RODRIGUEZ
12 Branch Director ....Mrs. Brenda COLON
15 Human Resources Director ...... Mrs. Lilliana M. LOPEZ-MEDERO

Colegio de Cinematografia, Artes y Television (I)

51 Dr. Veve St, Degetau St Corner, Bayamon PR 00961
County: Bayamon FICE Identification: 031576
Unit ID: 430935
Telephone: (787) 779-2500 Carnegie Class: Assoc/MT-VT-High Trad
FAX Number: (787) 995-2525 Calendar System: Semester
URL: www.ccatpr.com/nosotros/
Established: 1993 Annual Undergrad Tuition & Fees: $6,560
Enrollment: 900 Coed
Affiliation or Control: Proprietary IRS Status: Proprietary
Highest Offering: Associate Degree
Accreditation: ACCSC

01 President ....Ms. Carola GARCIA

Colegio Universitario de San Juan (J)

180 Jose R. Oliver Street, San Juan PR 00918
County: San Juan FICE Identification: 010567
Unit ID: 241720
Telephone: (787) 480-2400 Carnegie Class: Bac-Diverse
FAX Number: (787) 250-7395 Calendar System: Semester
URL: www.cunisanjuan.edu
Established: 1972 Annual Undergrad Tuition & Fees (In-District): $2,370
Enrollment: 1,405 Coed
Affiliation or Control: Local IRS Status: 501(c)3
Highest Offering: Baccalaureate
Accreditation: M, ADNUR

01 Chancellor ....Dr. Haydee M. ZAYAS-HERNÁNDEZ
45 Dir Planning/Inst Research/Ext Rels ....Prof. Ana I. LANDRON-ARANA
05 Dean Academic Affairs ....Dr. Phaedra GELPI-RODRÍGUEZ
32 Dean Student Affairs ....Dr. Melvin VEGA-GONZALEZ
11 Dean Administrative Affairs ....Prof. Gilberto OLIVO-CRUZ
51 Dir Continuing Educ/Extension Pgm ....Mrs. Annelis RIVERA-MARQUEZ
37 Manager Student Financial Aid .... Mrs. Kennia I. SANTOS-PEREZ
08 Head Librarian ....Mrs. Sheila VERA-MORALES
06 Registrar ....Mrs. Evelyn GUZMAN-LOPEZ
38 Counselor ....Mrs. Mara MALAVE-LASSO
36 Placement Officer .... Prof. Waleska Y. ROSA-NUÑEZ
13 Administrator Info Systems/ Telecomm ....Mr. Zacarias POURIET-DE LA CRUZ
72 Director Science & Technology ....Prof. Marcus DROZ
76 Director Health Related Science ....Prof. Elizabeth ROSARIO-RODRIGUEZ
50 Director Business Administration .... Prof. Nilda E. RODRIGUEZ-MOLINA
97 Manager General Education .... Prof. Carmen J. RODRIGUEZ
88 Dir Behavior Related Profession ....Prof. María T. PEREZ-CASANOVA

Columbia Central University (K)

PO Box 8517, Caguas PR 00726-8517
County: Caguas FICE Identification: 008902
Unit ID: 241304
Telephone: (787) 743-4041 Carnegie Class: Spec-4-yr-Other Health
FAX Number: (787) 746-5616 Calendar System: Semester
URL: www.columbiaco.edu
Established: 1966 Annual Undergrad Tuition & Fees: $6,520
Enrollment: 1,864 Coed
Affiliation or Control: Proprietary IRS Status: Proprietary
Highest Offering: Master's
Accreditation: M

01 President ....Mrs. Daritza R. MULERO
05 VP Academic Affairs ....Mrs. Carmen J. LOPEZ
03 Senior VP of Operations ....Mrs. Carmen M. RIVERA
10 VP Finance and Administration ....Mrs. Yesenia CARRION
32 VP Student Affairs ....Mrs. Brendaliz ZAYAS
26 VP Marketing and Communication .... Mr. Angel QUIÑONES
12 Chancellor of Caguas Campus ....Dra. Gladys SERRANO
12 Chancellor of Yauco Branch ....Ms. Jannette MENDEZ
35 Executive Director Student Affairs ....Mrs. Belmarie HUERTAS
20 Dean Academic Affairs ....Mr. Luis LOPEZ
08 Institutional Librarian ....Ms. Luz NEGRON
11 Administrative Support Director .... Ms. Carmen I. ROJAS
37 Financial Aid Director .... Mrs. Gloria MIRABAL
07 Coordinator of Admissions ....Mrs. Linnette MILETTI
06 Registrar ....Ms. Wilmarie TORRES
38 Student Counselor .... Ms. Ingrid CARRION
15 Director Human Resources ....Ms. Elsie M. TORRES
36 Director Student Placement ....Ms. Iris TIZOL
18 Facilities & Development Director ....Mr. Jesus M. RIVERA

Columbia Centro Universitario (L)

Box 3062, Yauco PR 00698-3062
Telephone: (787) 856-0945 Identification: 666036
Accreditation: &M

† Regional accreditation is carried under the parent institution in Caguas, PR.

Conservatory of Music of Puerto Rico (M)

951 Ponce de Leon Ave. Miramar, Santurce PR 00907
County: San Juan FICE Identification: 010819
Unit ID: 241766
Telephone: (787) 751-0160 Carnegie Class: Spec-4-yr-Arts
FAX Number: (787) 766-1216 Calendar System: Semester
URL: www.cmpr.edu
Established: 1959 Annual Undergrad Tuition & Fees (In-State): $3,370
Enrollment: 481 Coed
Affiliation or Control: State IRS Status: 501(c)3
Highest Offering: Master's
Accreditation: M

01 Chancellor ... Mr. Luis HERNANDEZ
05 Interim Dean of Academic Affairs ... Mrs. Ilsama HERNANDEZ
10 Dean of Finance/Administration ... Dr. Ivan SARIEGO
32 Dean Student Affairs/Financial Aid ... Mr. Luis R. DIAZ
88 Director of Preparatory School ... Mr. Orlando MALDONADO
07 Admission Coordinator ... Mrs. Ana M. ARRAIZA
08 Librarian ... Mrs. Damaris CORDERO
30 Development & Public Relations Dir ... Vacant
15 Human Resources Director ... Ms. Alba DAVILA
38 Counselor ... Mrs. Pilar RUIBAL
06 Registrar ... Mr. Jose A. MATOS
09 Director of Institutional Research ... Mrs. Eutimia SANTIAGO
18 Chief Facilities/Physical Plant ... Mr. Armando TOLEDO

Dewey University (A)

PO Box 19538, San Juan PR 00910-1538
County: San Juan FICE Identification: 031121
Unit ID: 431309
Telephone: (787) 753-0039 Carnegie Class: Not Classified
FAX Number: (787) 764-6303 Calendar System: Trimester
URL: www.dewey.edu
Established: 1992 Annual Undergrad Tuition & Fees: $7,495
Enrollment: 41 Coed
Affiliation or Control: Independent Non-Profit IRS Status: 501(c)3
Highest Offering: Baccalaureate
Accreditation: ACICS

01 President/CEO ... Mr. Carlos A. QUINONES
03 Executive Vice Presidenet ... Ms. Yelitza FELICIANO
10 Director of Finance ... Mr. Jaime MARTIR

Dewey University-Bayamon (B)

Road 2 Corujo Industrial Park, Bayamon PR 00959
Telephone: (787) 778-1200 Identification: 770777
Accreditation: ACICS

Dewey University-Carolina (C)

Road 3 Compound 11, Lot 7, Carolina PR 00986
Telephone: (787) 769-1515 Identification: 770776
Accreditation: ACICS

Dewey University-Fajardo (D)

267 General Valero Street, Fajardo PR 00738
Telephone: (787) 860-1212 Identification: 770775
Accreditation: ACICS

Dewey University-Juana Diaz (E)

Rd 149, KM 55.9 Lomas Industrial PK,
Juana Diaz PR 00795
Telephone: (787) 260-1023 Identification: 770774
Accreditation: ACICS

Dewey University-Manati (F)

Rd 604,KM 49.1,Tierra Nueva Salient, Manati PR 00674
Telephone: (789) 854-3800 Identification: 770807
Accreditation: ACICS

Dominican Study Center of the Caribbean (G)

PO Box 1968, Bayamon PR 00960-1968
County: Bayamon Identification: 666337
Telephone: (787) 786-4508 Carnegie Class: Not Classified
FAX Number: (787) 798-2712 Calendar System: Semester
URL: www.cedoc.edu
Established: 1980 Annual Undergrad Tuition & Fees: N/A
Enrollment: N/A Coed
Affiliation or Control: Independent Non-Profit IRS Status: 501(c)3
Highest Offering: Master's
Accreditation: THEOL

01 Dean ... Rev Dr. Yamil A. SAMALOT-RIVERA, OP

EDIC College (H)

PO Box 9120, Caguas PR 00726-9120
County: Caguas FICE Identification: 030219
Unit ID: 376321
Telephone: (787) 704-1020 Carnegie Class: Assoc/HVT-High Non
FAX Number: (787) 746-0048 Calendar System: Semester
URL: ediccollege.edu
Established: 1987 Annual Undergrad Tuition & Fees: $6,700
Enrollment: 1,148 Coed
Affiliation or Control: Proprietary IRS Status: Proprietary
Highest Offering: Associate Degree
Accreditation: ACICS

01 President/CEO ... Mr. Jose A. CORDOVA
11 Administrator ... Mrs. Milagros CARTAGENA
88 Licensing & Accreditation Director ... Mrs. Loida R. RAMIREZ
12 Director of Branch Campus ... Mr. Reinaldo GONZALEZ
12 Director of Branch Campus ... Mr. Ricardo FLORES
05 Chief Academic Officer ... Mrs. Betsy VIDAL
10 Comptroller ... Mr. Francis HILARIO

EDP University of Puerto Rico (I)

PO Box 192303, San Juan PR 00919-2303
County: San Juan FICE Identification: 021651
Unit ID: 243832
Telephone: (787) 765-3560 Carnegie Class: Bac-Diverse
FAX Number: (787) 777-0025 Calendar System: Semester
URL: www.edpuniversity.edu
Established: 1968 Annual Undergrad Tuition & Fees: $5,940
Enrollment: 1,568 Coed
Affiliation or Control: Independent Non-Profit IRS Status: 501(c)3
Highest Offering: Master's
Accreditation: M, ADNUR

01 President ... Mrs. Gladys T. NIEVES
03 Executive Vice President ... Dr. Marilyn PASTRANA
05 Academic Dean ... Mrs. Yadirah SOTO
10 Vice President Finance ... Mr. Luis RIVERA
26 VP Institutional/International Rels ... Ms. Sandra ARROYO
108 VP Acreditation & Inst Assessment ... Dr. Alberto LOPEZ
13 AVP Administration and Technology ... Eng. Luis FUSTER
85 AVP International Affairs ... Ms. Sandra ARROYO
21 AVP Finance ... Mrs. Marie Luz PASTRANA
108 AVP Assessment ... Mrs. Nydia RIVERA
14 Inst Information Systems Dean ... Dr. Ramon MALLOL
06 Registrar ... Mrs. Marian DEJESUS
08 Librarian ... Mrs. Igrí ENRIQUEZ
32 Student Services Dean ... Mr. Oscar MORALES
37 Director of Financial Aid ... Mrs. Maria COLON
07 Director of Admissions ... Mrs. Dendy VILA
15 Director Human Resources ... Mr. Hector VAZQUEZ

EDP University of Puerto Rico (J)

PO Box 1674, 49 Betances Street,
San Sebastian PR 00685-1674
Telephone: (787) 896-2137 Identification: 666488
Accreditation: &M, ADNUR

† Regional accreditation is carried under the parent institution in San Juan, PR.

Escuela de Artes Plasticas de Puerto Rico (K)

PO Box 9021112, San Juan PR 00902-1112
County: San Juan FICE Identification: 025694
Unit ID: 241951
Telephone: (787) 725-8120 Carnegie Class: Spec-4-yr-Arts
FAX Number: (787) 725-8111 Calendar System: Semester
URL: www.eap.edu
Established: 1966 Annual Undergrad Tuition & Fees (In-State): $3,248
Enrollment: 555 Coed
Affiliation or Control: State IRS Status: 501(c)3
Highest Offering: Baccalaureate
Accreditation: M, ART

01 Interim Chancellor ... Mr. Carlos E. RIVERA PÉREZ
11 Int Dean of Administration ... Ms. Limaris SOLO AQUINO
05 Int Dean Academic Affairs ... Prof. Teresa LOPEZ
06 Registrar ... Ms. Ileana MALDONADO
07 Officer of Admissions ... Ms. Nitza MELENDEZ
13 Chief Information Technology ... Ms. Limaris SOTO AQUINO
37 Director Student Financial Aid ... Mr. Alfred DIAZ
20 Acting Asst Dean Academic Affairs ... Ms. Ivette MUNOZ
45 Director of Planning & Budget ... Mr. Carlos E. RIVERA
09 Assistant Institutional Research ... Dr. Shirley A. TAVARES
10 Chief Financial Officer ... Ms. Mayra E. DIAZ
18 Coord Facilities/Physical Plant ... Mr. Edwin ALICEA
56 Coordinator Extension Program ... Ms. Liliam NIEVES
38 Counselor Stdnt Life/Counseling ... Ms. Susanne GOTAY
88 Coordinator Cultural Activities ... Mr. Adrian O. RIVERA NEGRON
105 Director Web Services ... Mr. Celso E. PORTELA IRIGOYEN
08 Library Director ... Ms. Estrella VÁZQUEZ
20 Int Asst Dean Acad/Student Affairs ... Ms. Ivette MUÑOZ
15 Director Human Resources ... Ms. Ivette RODRÍGUEZ
28 Director of Projects ... Dr. Shirley A. TAVARES
53 Director Education ... Prof. Noemi RIVERA
97 Director General Studies ... Dr. Maria VAZQUEZ
88 Director Fashion/Apparel Design ... Prof. Ana COLORADO
88 Director Industrial/Product Design ... Prof. Vladimir GARCIA
88 Dir Design/Visual Communications ... Prof. Guillermo VÁZQUEZ
88 Director Painting ... Prof. Carlos MARCIAL
88 Director Sculpture ... Prof. Linda SÁNCHEZ PINTOR
88 Director Graphics ... Prof. Haydee LANDING

Evangelical Seminary of Puerto Rico (L)

Ponce De Leon Avenue 776, San Juan PR 00925-2207
County: San Juan FICE Identification: 006823
Unit ID: 243498
Telephone: (787) 763-6700 Carnegie Class: Spec-4-yr-Faith
FAX Number: (787) 751-0847 Calendar System: Semester
URL: www.se-pr.edu
Established: 1919 Annual Undergrad Tuition & Fees: N/A
Enrollment: 231 Coed
Affiliation or Control: Interdenominational IRS Status: 501(c)3
Highest Offering: Doctorate
Accreditation: M, THEOL

01 President ... Dra. Doris GARCIA RIVERA
05 Academic Dean/Chaplain ... Dr. Francisco J. GOITIA PADILLA
10 Director Administration & Finances ... Ms. Myrna E. PEREZ-LOPEZ
06 Registrar ... Mrs. Keina TRONCOSO FERNANDEZ
08 Head Librarian ... Mrs. Milka VIGO VERESTÍN
30 Official of Development/Planning ... Ms. Ruth M. DIAZ SEMPRIT
37 Student Financial Aid ... Ms. Lourdes JESUS CESAREO

Huertas College (M)

PO Box 8429, Caguas PR 00726-8429
County: Caguas FICE Identification: 022608
Unit ID: 242112
Telephone: (787) 746-1400 Carnegie Class: Assoc/HVT-High Non
FAX Number: (787) 747-0170 Calendar System: Semester
URL: www.huertas.edu
Established: 1945 Annual Undergrad Tuition & Fees: $6,635
Enrollment: 1,184 Coed
Affiliation or Control: Proprietary IRS Status: Proprietary
Highest Offering: Baccalaureate
Accreditation: M, CAHIIM, PTAA

01 President ... Maria del Mar LOPEZ-AVILES
03 Exec Vice President and Compliance ... Raul HERNANDEZ-RODRIGUEZ
05 Vice Pres Academic/Student Affairs ... Amarillys GARCIA-ACOSTA
30 VP Planning and Development ... Ruth BONILLA
15 VP of Human Resources ... Leslie Ann GUZMAN
32 Associate VP of Student Success ... Maribel CONTRERAS
06 Registrar ... Krishna MARQUEZ
08 Head Librarian ... Maribel CONTRERAS
38 Director Student Counseling ... Evelyn COTTO
10 Director of Revenue ... Eva VEGA
22 Compliance Officer ... Vacant
04 Administrative Asst to President ... Iris COLON
07 Director of Admissions ... Hector MORALES
18 Chief Facilities/Physical Plant ... Ruben LOPEZ
26 Chief Public Relations/Marketing ... Amarilis LOPEZ
36 Director Student Placement ... Veronica RUIZ

Humacao Community College (N)

PO Box 9139, Humacao PR 00792-9139
County: Humacao FICE Identification: 023406
Unit ID: 242121
Telephone: (787) 852-1430 Carnegie Class: Bac/Assoc-Mixed
FAX Number: (787) 850-1577 Calendar System: Trimester
URL: www.hccpr.edu
Established: 1978 Annual Undergrad Tuition & Fees: $5,382
Enrollment: 639 Coed
Affiliation or Control: Independent Non-Profit IRS Status: 501(c)3
Highest Offering: Baccalaureate
Accreditation: ACICS

01 President ... Lic. Jorge E. MOJICA
03 Executive Vice President ... Prof. Aida E. RODRIGUEZ
05 Exec Director/Chief Academic Ofcr ... Dr. Gladys E. FLECHA
55 Director of Evening Session ... Prof. Ada BAEZ
88 Title V Project Director ... Dr. Brenda L. MORALES
81 STEM Projec Director ... Mr. Jaime RIVERA
37 Director Student Financial Aid ... Mrs. Cheryle PEREZ
36 Student Placement Officer ... Mrs. Ada BAEZ
36 Student Placement Officer ... Mrs. Damaris APONTE
07 Director Admissions ... Mrs. Adela APONTE
51 Continuing Education Officer ... Mrs. Maria M. GONZALEZ
06 Registar Assistant ... Mr. Jorge CARRERO
06 Registrar ... Mrs. Nildalee MELENDEZ
08 Head Librarian ... Mrs. Lourdes ELIZA
10 Treasury Officer (Finance) ... Mrs. Diana RODRIGUEZ
38 Student Counselor ... Mrs. Maria RODRIGUEZ
11 Chief College Administrator ... Mrs. Marianne BERRIOS
04 Admin Asst to Pres/Dir Personnel ... Mrs. Nilda E. RODRIGUEZ

ICPR Junior College (O)

558 Munoz Rivera Avenue, Hato Rey PR 00919-0304
County: San Juan FICE Identification: 011940
Unit ID: 243841
Telephone: (787) 753-6000 Carnegie Class: Assoc/HVT-Mix Trad/Non
FAX Number: (787) 622-3416 Calendar System: Semester
URL: www.icprjc.edu
Established: 1946 Annual Undergrad Tuition & Fees: $6,450
Enrollment: 688 Coed
Affiliation or Control: Proprietary IRS Status: Proprietary
Highest Offering: Associate Degree
Accreditation: M

01 President/Chief Executive Officer ... Dr. Olga RIVERA
12 Hato Rey Campus Director ... Mrs. Maria de los M. RIVERA
05 Academic Affairs Dean ... Mrs. Elsa RODRIGUEZ
07 Dir Admissions/Marketing Hato Rey ... Mrs. Beatriz FLORES
07 Director Admissions Mayaguez ... Mrs. Aracelis GASTON
07 Director Admissions Arecibo ... Ms. Meysaliz GARCIA
07 Director Admissions Manati ... Mrs. Viviana TORRES
10 Finance and Accounting Director ... Mrs. Arelis DIAZ
37 Financial Aid Director ... Ms. Jennifer HERNANDEZ
12 Mayaguez Campus Director ... Dr. Luz M. ORTIZ
12 Arecibo Campus Director ... Mrs. Ivette CHARRIEZ
12 Manati Campus Director ... Mr. Fernando GONZALEZ
06 Registrar Hato Rey ... Ms. Naphtali CAULDRON
06 Registrar Mayaguez ... Mrs. Olga NEGRON
06 Registrar Arecibo ... Mrs. Glenda PADIN

06 Registrar Manati ....Mrs. Vanessa TRINIDAD
06 Registrar Bayamon Extension ....Mrs. Diana FREYTES
26 Director of Admissions/Marketing ....Ms. Beatriz FLORES
13 Information Systems Director ....Mr. Nelson MEJIAS
08 Learning Res Librarian Hato Rey ....Mrs. Sulynet TORRES
08 Lrng Resources Librarian Mayaguez ....Mrs. Jessica CARO
08 Lrng Resources Librarian Arecibo ....Mrs. Irma JIMENEZ
08 Learning Resources Librarian ....Mr. Martin ROSADO
38 Professional Counselor Mayaguez ....Mrs. Barbarita CUMPIANO
38 Professional Counselor Arecibo ....Mrs. Milagros AGUILAR
38 Professional Counselor Manati ....Mrs. Lourdes RIOS
38 Professional Counselor Hato Rey ....Mrs. Yarelis COLON
15 Human Resources Director ....Mrs. Daisy CASTRO
43 Institutional Compliance Director ....Mrs. Lizzette VARGAS
56 Bayamon Extension Director ....Mr. Manuel MELO
20 Academic Coordinator Mayaguez ....Mrs. Ravel BONILLA
20 Academic Coordinator Arecibo ....Mrs. Edith RAMOS
20 Academic Coordinator Manati ....Mrs. Maribel TORRES
20 Academic Coordinator Hato Rey ....Mr. Josue CINTRON

ICPR Junior College-Arecibo Campus (A)

PO Box 146007, Arecibo PR 00614-0067
Telephone: (787) 878-6000 Identification: 770166
Accreditation: &M

† Regional accreditation is carried under the parent institution in Hato Rey, PR

ICPR Junior College-Manati Branch Campus (B)

PO Box 49, Manati PR 00674-0049
Telephone: (787) 884-6000 Identification: 770168
Accreditation: &M

† Regional accreditation is carried under the parent institution in Hato Rey, PR

ICPR Junior College-Mayaguez Campus (C)

PO Box 1108, Mayaguez PR 00681-9913
Telephone: (787) 832-6000 Identification: 770167
Accreditation: &M

† Regional accreditation is carried under the parent institution in Hato Rey, PR

Instituto de Banca y Comercio (D)

709 Ferrocarril Street, Ponce PR 00717
Telephone: (787) 840-6119 Identification: 770773
Accreditation: ACICS

Instituto de Banca y Comercio (E)

61 Ponce de Leon Ave, San Juan PR 00917
Identification: 667107
Telephone: (787) 754-7120 Carnegie Class: Not Classified
FAX Number: (787) 754-7143 Calendar System: Other
URL: www.ibanca.net
Established: 1975 Annual Undergrad Tuition & Fees: N/A
Enrollment: N/A Coed
Affiliation or Control: Proprietary IRS Status: Proprietary
Highest Offering: Associate Degree
Accreditation: ACICS

01 President ....Sr. Guillermo NIGAGLIONI
05 Director ....Mrs. Ana Jacqueline RIVERA

*Inter American University of Puerto Rico Central Office (F)

GPO Box 363255, San Juan PR 00936-3255
County: San Juan FICE Identification: 008242
Unit ID: 242671
Telephone: (787) 766-1912 Carnegie Class: N/A
FAX Number: (787) 751-3375
URL: www.inter.edu

01 President ....Mr. Manuel L. FERNOS
05 Vice Pres Academic & Student Affrs ....Mr. Agustin ECHEVARRIA
10 VP Financial Affairs/Services ....Mr. Luis ESQUILIN
42 Vice President Religious Affairs ....Rev. Norberto DOMINGUEZ
20 Associate VP Academic Affairs ....Dr. Rafael CABRERA
21 Assoc VP Financial Affairs/Services ....Ms. Olga LUNA
32 Associate Vice Pres Student Affairs ....Vacant
100 Exec Dir to Pres/Chief of Staff ....Mr. Dominique GILORMINI-DE GRACIA
26 Exec Dir Public Rels/Communications ....Mrs. Zaima NEGRON
84 Int Dir Inst Prom/Stdnt Recruitment ....Mr. Porfirio RIVERA
09 Exec Director Inst Research ....Dr. Isaac SANTIAGO
13 Exec Dir Information/Telecom ....Mrs. Jossie SALGUERO
43 Exec Director Legal Services ....Mrs. Lorraine JUARBE
43 Exec Director Federal Legal Svcs ....Mr. Vladimir ROMAN
15 Exec Director Human Resources ....Ms. Maggie COLON
30 Exec Director Devel/Alumni Affairs .. Dr. Nelda RIVERA-CLAUDIO

*Inter American University of Puerto Rico Aguadilla Campus (G)

Box 20000, Aguadilla PR 00605-9001
County: Aguadilla FICE Identification: 003939
Unit ID: 242626
Telephone: (787) 891-0925 Carnegie Class: Masters/S
FAX Number: (787) 882-3020 Calendar System: Other
URL: www.aguadilla.inter.edu
Established: 1957 Annual Undergrad Tuition & Fees: $5,534
Enrollment: 4,668 Coed
Affiliation or Control: Independent Non-Profit IRS Status: 501(c)3
Highest Offering: Master's
Accreditation: M, ADNUR, NUR, TEAC

02 Chancellor ....Dr. Elie AGESILAS
05 Dean of Studies ....Mrs. Nilsa M. ROMAN
32 Dean of Student Affairs ....Mrs. Ana C. LAUSELL
13 Director Information and Technology ....Mr. Asdrubal JIMENEZ
90 Information Systems Administrator ....Mr. Jossue MORALES
10 Dean of Administrative Affairs ....Mr. Israel AYALA
20 Associate Dean of Studies ....Dr. Luis A. ACEVEDO
30 Development Director ....Miss Sacha M. RUIZ
08 Library Director ....Mrs. Monserrate YULFO
07 Admissions Director ....Mrs. Doris PEREZ
06 Registrar ....Mrs. Maria PEREZ
37 Financial Aid Director ....Mrs. Gloria CORTES
21 Bursar ....Mr. Harry MUNIZ
15 Human Resources Director ....Mr. Jose R. AREIZAGA
96 Purchasing Officer ....Mrs. Wanda VARGAS
35 Student Support Services Director ....Mrs. Ivonne ACEVEDO
81 Director of Science and Technology ....Prof. Jose SOLORZANO
79 Director of Education & Hum Studies ....Mrs. Ramonita ROSA
50 Director Economic Science & Admin ....Dra. Maria G. ROSA
53 Dir of Social & Behavioral Sciences ....Prof. Gerardo LOPEZ
42 Chaplain ....Dr. Pablo E. ROJAS
88 Director of Upward Bound Program ....Ms. Mayra ROZADA
88 Dir Campus Learning Center ....Ms. Yamilette PROSPER
18 Dir Building Maintenance/Univ Guard ....Mr. Jose CABAN
38 Director of Counseling Office ....Ms. Dary ACEVEDO
41 Sports Director ....Ms. Yolanda PAGAN
84 Enrollment Manager ....Prof. Myriam MARCIAL

*Inter American University of Puerto Rico Arecibo Campus (H)

PO Box 4050, Arecibo PR 00614-4050
County: Arecibo FICE Identification: 005026
Unit ID: 242635
Telephone: (787) 878-5475 Carnegie Class: Masters/M
FAX Number: (787) 880-1624 Calendar System: Semester
URL: www.arecibo.inter.edu
Established: 1957 Annual Undergrad Tuition & Fees: $4,962
Enrollment: 4,713 Coed
Affiliation or Control: Independent Non-Profit IRS Status: 501(c)3
Highest Offering: Master's
Accreditation: M, ANEST, NUR, SW, TEAC

02 Chancellor ....Dr. Rafael RAMIREZ-RIVERA
05 Dean of Academic Affairs ....Dr. Annette VEGA
11 Dean of Administrative Affairs ....Lic. Antonio PEREZ-LÓPEZ
32 Dean of Student Affairs ....Mrs. Ilvis AGUIRRE
20 Assoc Dean of Academic Affairs ....Dr. Wanda I. BALSEIRO
08 Educational Resources Center Dir ....Mrs. Sara ABREU
10 Bursar ....Mr. Victor MALDONADO
37 Student Financial Aid Director ....Mr. Ramon DE JESUS
06 Registrar ....Mrs. Carmen RODRIGUEZ
07 Director of Admissions ....Mrs. Provi MONTALVO
04 Executive Assistant to Chancellor ....Mrs. Enid ARBELO
56 Distance Learning Director ....Prof. Ebigaly OLIVER
45 Planning Director ....Mrs. Enid ARBELO
42 Religious Life Director ....Mr. Amilcar SOTO
15 Personnel Director ....Vacant
41 Athletic Department ....Ms. Ileana MORALES
50 Director Econ & Adms Sciences Dept ....Prof. Elba TORO
51 Continuing Education Director ....Mrs. Mariel LLERANDI
53 Director of Education Department ....Dr. Auris MARTINEZ
66 Director of Nursing Department ....Dr. Frances CORTES
79 Dir of Humanities Department ....Vacant
81 Director of Sciences & Tech Dept ....Dr. Lizbeth ROMERO
83 Director of Social Sciences Dept ....Dr. Lourdes CARRION
30 Development Director ....Vacant
38 Director Student Counseling ....Ms. Abigail TORRES
13 Director of Computing Center ....Mr. Jose SEGARRA
58 Director Graduate Program in Educ ....Dra. Ramonita DIAZ
18 Chief Facilities/Physical Plant ....Vacant
84 Director Enrollment Management ....Mrs. Carmen MONTALVO
88 Dir Graduate Program Anesthesia ....Prof. Josue RAMOS
96 Purchasing Officer ....Mrs. Sonia VILLAIZAN
92 Coordinator Honor Program ....Ms. Vilmaris VAZQUEZ
108 Director Institutional Assessment ....Dr. Pedro RIVERA
26 Director of Marketing ....Mr. Juan RODRIGUEZ

*Inter American University of Puerto Rico Barranquitas Campus (I)

PO Box 517, Barranquitas PR 00794-0517
County: Barranquitas FICE Identification: 005027
Unit ID: 242644
Telephone: (787) 857-3600 Carnegie Class: Bac-Diverse
FAX Number: (787) 857-2244 Calendar System: Semester
URL: www.br.inter.edu
Established: 1957 Annual Undergrad Tuition & Fees: $5,014
Enrollment: 2,146 Coed
Affiliation or Control: Independent Non-Profit IRS Status: 501(c)3
Highest Offering: Master's
Accreditation: M, TEAC

02 Chancellor ....Dr. Irene FERNANDEZ
05 Dean Academic Affairs ....Dr. Patricia ALVAREZ
11 Dean Administrative Affairs ....Mr. Jose E. ORTIZ-ZAYAS
32 Dean Student Affairs ....Mrs. Aramilda CARTAGENA
84 Enrollment Manager ....Mrs. Lydia ARCE
81 Dir Natural Sciences/Technology ....Prof. Jose PEREZ
37 Financial Aid Director ....Mr. Eduardo FONTANEZ
15 Director Human Resources ....Mr. Victor SANTIAGO
10 Bursar Director ....Mr. Antonio J. ROSARIO
06 Registrar ....Mrs. Sandra M. MORALES
07 Director of Admissions ....Mr. Edgardo CINTRON
53 Dir Education/Social Sci/Humanities ....Dr. Filomena CINTRON
76 Dir Health Department ....Dr. Omar GUERRERO
09 Director of Institutional Research ....Dr. Maribel LÓPEZ
38 Director Upward Bound Program ....Mrs. Saraliz GONZALEZ
51 Director Continuing Education ....Mrs. Aixa SERRANO
84 Director Recruitment/Promotion ....Mrs. Ana Isabel COLON
29 Director Alumni Relations ....Mr. Elvin J. ORTIZ
08 Librarian ....Mrs. Maria del C RIVERA
41 Athletic Director ....Mr. Israel RIVERA

*Inter American University of Puerto Rico Bayamon Campus (J)

500 Dr. John Will Harris Road, Bayamon PR 00957
County: Bayamon FICE Identification: 005028
Unit ID: 242705
Telephone: (787) 279-1912 Carnegie Class: Bac-Diverse
FAX Number: (787) 279-2205 Calendar System: Semester
URL: bayamon.inter.edu
Established: 1912 Annual Undergrad Tuition & Fees: $4,962
Enrollment: 4,826 Coed
Affiliation or Control: Independent Non-Profit IRS Status: 501(c)3
Highest Offering: Master's
Accreditation: M, AAB, ENG, OPTR

02 Chancellor ....Prof. Juan F. MARTINEZ
04 Assistant to Chancellor ....Mr. Antonio L. PANTOJA
04 Assistant to Chancellor ....Vacant
30 Chief Development ....Mr. Jaime COLON
05 Chief Academic Officer ....Dr. Carlos J. OLIVARES
20 Associate Academic Officer ....Vacant
08 Head Librarian ....Mrs. Sandra ROSA
88 Internships and Exchanges Officer ....Mrs. Maritza ZAMBRANA
88 Dean School of Aeronautics ....Prof. Jorge CALAF
54 Interim Dean School of Engineering ....Dr. Amilcar RINCON
54 Director Electrical Engr Dept ....Prof. Miguel MUÑIZ
54 Director Industrial Engr Dept ....Vacant
54 Director Mechanical Engr Dept ....Dr. Eduardo PEREZ
81 Director Mathematics/Sciences ....Dr. Rafael CANALES
50 Dir Business Administration Dept ....Dra. Grace D. LEO
60 Director Communications Dept ....Prof. Ruth E. HERNANDEZ
77 Director Computer Sciences Dept ....Prof. Jose RODRIGUEZ
76 Director of Health Science ....Prof. Jose M. CRUZ
79 Director Humanities/Language Dept ....Dra. Isabel GARAYTA
75 Director Tech Institute ....Mrs. Liza FREYTES
32 Chief Students Life Officer ....Mrs. Gema C. TORRES
35 Student Affairs Assistant ....Mrs. Grace GOMEZ
38 Director Student Counseling ....Mrs. Magali PALMER
35 Student Activities Director ....Mrs. Cybel BETANCOURT
41 Athletic Director ....Mr. Reynaldo ROLON
23 Infirmary ....Mrs. Maria ROSADO
10 Chief Financial/Business Officer ....Mr. Juan C. HERNANDEZ
96 Purchasing Officer ....Mrs. Gladys ARROYO
21 Associate Business Officer ....Mr. Serafin RIVERA
18 Chief Facilities/Physical Plant ....Eng. Jose A. FUENTES
15 Human Resources Director ....Mrs. Migdalia ORTIZ
20 Associate Academic Officer ....Dr. Bert RIVERA
84 Director Enrollment Services ....Miss Ivette NIEVES
35 Director of Students Services ....Mrs. Aurelis BAEZ
06 Registrar ....Mr. Eddie AYALA
13 Director Information Technology ....Mr. Edwin RIVERA
42 Director of Chaplaincy Office ....Rvda. Carmen I. PEREZ
106 Dir Online Education/E-learning ....Dr. Jose G. SANTIAGO
09 Director of Institutional Research ....Vacant
39 Housing Administrator ....Mr. Gerardo BURGOS
88 International Relations Director ....Mr. Luis ALCARAZ

*Inter American University of Puerto Rico Fajardo Campus (K)

Call Box 70003, Fajardo PR 00738-7003
County: Fajardo FICE Identification: 022828
Unit ID: 242680
Telephone: (787) 863-2390 Carnegie Class: Bac-Diverse
FAX Number: (787) 860-3470 Calendar System: Semester
URL: fajardo.inter.edu
Established: 1960 Annual Undergrad Tuition & Fees: $4,905
Enrollment: 2,272 Coed
Affiliation or Control: Independent Non-Profit IRS Status: 501(c)3
Highest Offering: Master's
Accreditation: M, SW, TEAC

02 Chancellor ....Dr. Ismael SUAREZ-HERRERO
05 Dean Academic Affairs ....Dr. Paula SAGARDIA OLIVERAS
11 Dean Administrative Affairs .....Ms. Lydia E. SANTIAGO ROSADO
32 Dean for Student Affairs ....Dr. Javier MARTINEZ
06 Registrar ....Mrs. Arlene PARRILLA
07 Director of Admissions ....Mrs. Ada CARABALLO
37 Director Student Financial Aid ....Mrs. Marilyn MARTINEZ
08 Librarian ....Ms. Angie COLON
15 Director of Personnel Office ....Mrs. Maria A. RAMOS

09 Planning Director ....Ms. Hilda L. ORTIZ
41 Athletic Director ....Mr. Jose RUIZ
18 Physical Plant Supervisor ....Mr. Angel J. RUIZ
42 Chaplain/Director Campus Ministry ....Rev. Rafael HIRALDO
50 Chairperson Business Department ....Prof. Wilfredo DEL VALLE
53 Chairperson Educ & Social Sci Dept ....Dr. Porfirio MONTES
79 Chairperson Humanities Dept ..Prof. Lourdes PEREZ DEL VALLE
81 Chairperson Math/Science Dept ....Prof. Irma MORALES
84 Director Enrollment Management ....Mrs. Glenda DIAZ

*Inter American University of Puerto Rico Guayama Campus (A)

Call Box 10004, Guayama PR 00785
County: Guayama FICE Identification: 022827
Unit ID: 242699
Telephone: (787) 864-2222 Carnegie Class: Bac-Diverse
FAX Number: (787) 866-5006 Calendar System: Semester
URL: www.guayama.inter.edu
Established: 1958 Annual Undergrad Tuition & Fees: $5,589
Enrollment: 2,151 Coed
Affiliation or Control: Independent Non-Profit IRS Status: 501(c)3
Highest Offering: Master's
Accreditation: M, TEAC

02 President ....Mr. Manuel J. FERNOS
00 Chancellor ....Prof. Carlos E. COLON-RAMOS
06 Registrar ....Mr. Luis A. SOTO
08 Librarian ....Mrs. Edny SANTIAGO
10 Bursar ....Ms. Teresa MANAUTOU
05 Dean of Studies ....Dr. Angela DE JESUS
11 Dean of Administration ....Mr. Nestor A. LEBRON
32 Dean of Students ....Dr. Rosa J. MARTINEZ
07 Director Admissions ....Mrs. Laura FERRER
37 Director Financial Aid ....Mr. Jose A. VECHINI
29 Director Alumni Relations ....Dr. Rosa J. MARTINEZ
51 Director Continuing Education ....Mrs. Diannie RIVERA
15 Human Resources Officer ....Mrs. Maria MARES
18 Chief Facilities/Physical Plant ....Mr. Benjamin AYALA
45 Dir Evaluation & Strategic Planning ....Mrs. Claribel RODRIGUEZ
30 Chief Devel/Dir Annual Plan Giv ....Vacant
42 Chaplain Director ....Rvdo. Arnaldo CINTRON
84 Director Enrollment Management ....Mrs. Eileen RIVERA
96 Director of Purchasing ....Mrs. Maria VAZQUEZ
31 Dir of Community & New Student Rels ....Mrs. Luz ORTIZ
23 Director Health Services ....Mrs. Arcilia RIVERA
66 Director Nursing Program ....Dr. Minerva MULERO
88 Dir Adult Higher Education Program ....Mrs. Carmen G. RIVERA
50 Dir Dept Business Admin/Econ Sci ....Dr. Rosalia MORALES
53 Dir Dept Education/Soc Sci/Hum Std ....Dr. Ray ROBLES
81 Dir Dept Natural & Applied Science ....Prof. Carmen TORRES
09 Director of Institutional Research ....Mr. Tomas JIMENEZ

*Inter American University of Puerto Rico / Metropolitan Campus (B)

PO Box 191293, San Juan PR 00919-1293
County: San Juan FICE Identification: 003940
Unit ID: 242653
Telephone: (787) 250-1912 Carnegie Class: DU-Mod
FAX Number: (787) 250-0742 Calendar System: Trimester
URL: www.metro.inter.edu
Established: 1962 Annual Undergrad Tuition & Fees: $7,122
Enrollment: 9,649 Coed
Affiliation or Control: Independent Non-Profit IRS Status: 501(c)3
Highest Offering: Doctorate
Accreditation: M, ADNUR, MT, NUR, SW, TEAC

02 Chancellor ....Prof. Marilina L. WAYLAND
05 Dean of Studies ....Prof. Migdalia TEXIDOR
32 Dean of Students ....Dr. Carmen OQUENDO
10 Dean of Administration ....Mr. Jimmy CANCEL
11 Dean of Faculty Cs Economics & Adm ....Prof. Fredrick VEGA
53 Dean of Education & Behavioral Sci ....Dr. Carmen COLLAZO
83 Director School of Psychology ....Dr. Jaime SANTIAGO
79 Dean Faculty of Humanities ....Dr. Oscar CRUZ
66 Director of Nursing ....Dr. Ivette CORA
72 Director of Medical Technology ....Dr. Ida A. MEJIAS
81 Dean Faculty of Science & Technolog ....Dr. Yogani GOVENDER
06 Registrar ....Ms. Lisette RIVERA
84 Enrollment Management ....Mr. Luis E. RUIZ
20 Associate Dean of Studies ....Ms. Blanca M. GONZALEZ
08 Dir of Ctr for Access Info ....Ms. Maria de Lourdes RESTO
15 Human Resources Officer ....Mrs. Darlin TORRES
37 Director of Financial Aid ....Ms. Lillian CONCEPCION
18 Dir Conservation & General Services ....Ing. Marina O. RIVERA
38 Dir Student Placement/Guidanc/Couns ....Ms. Beatriz RIVERA
83 Director School of Social Work ....Dr. Elizabeth MIRANDA
58 Director School of Education ....Dr. Maria D. RUBERO
85 Coord International Rels Office ....Prof. Ramon AYALA
73 Dir School of Theology ....Dr. Angel VELEZ
88 Dir School of Criminal Justice ....Prof. Luis SOTO
13 Director Informatic/Telecomm Center ....Mr. Eduardo ORTIZ
36 Director Student Placement ....Mrs. Adabel-Vanessa COLON
07 Director of Admissions ....Ms. Janies OLIVIERI
09 Dean Inst Research/External Rsrch ....Vacant
30 Development & Fund Raising ....Mrs. Evelyn VEGA
96 Purchasing Officer ....Mrs. Patricia GONZALEZ
92 Coordinator of Honors Program ....Prof. Mariusz JACKO
88 Bursar ....Ms. Carmen RIVERA
106 Dir Online Education/E-learning ....Mr. Jairo PULIDO
19 Director Security/Safety ....Mr. George RIVERA
41 Athletic Director ....Mr. Jesus CORA

*Inter American University of Puerto Rico Ponce Campus (C)

104 Turpo Industrial Park Road, #1, Mercedita PR 00715-1602
County: Ponce FICE Identification: 005029
Unit ID: 242662
Telephone: (787) 284-1912 Carnegie Class: Masters/S
FAX Number: (787) 841-0103 Calendar System: Semester
URL: ponce.inter.edu
Established: 1962 Annual Undergrad Tuition & Fees: $4,962
Enrollment: 5,788 Coed
Affiliation or Control: Independent Non-Profit IRS Status: 501(c)3
Highest Offering: Doctorate
Accreditation: M, OTA, PTAA, RAD, TEAC

02 Chancellor ....Dr. Vilma E. COLON
05 Dean of Academic Affairs ....Dr. Jacqueline ALVAREZ
32 Dean of Students ....Mrs. Edda COSTAS
11 Dean of Administrative Affairs ....Eng. Victor A. FELIBERTY
10 Financial Officer ....Mrs. Maria DE P. MENDEZ
08 Director Education Resource Center ....Mrs. Maria SILVESTRINI
35 Director Student Services ....Mrs. Miriam MARTINEZ
10 Bursar ....Mr. Brian HERNANDEZ
06 Registrar ....Mrs. Maria del C PEREZ
30 Director of Development ....Mrs. Hilda V. STELLA
07 Director of Admissions ....Mr. Franco L. DIAZ
15 Human Resource Director ....Mrs. Waleska FLORES
19 Supervisor of University Guard ....Mr. Reinaldo ROSADO
37 Director Student Financial Aid ....Ms. Karen CAQUIAS
41 Athletic Director ....Mr. Raul HERNANDEZ
58 Director of Graduate Programs ....Dr. Delma SANTIAGO
50 Director Business & Administration ....Mrs. Vivien MATTEI
51 Director Continuing Education ....Mrs. Evelyn CASTILLO
79 Act Dir Humanistics/Pedagogical Std ....Mrs. Santy CORREA
81 Director Mathematics/Sciences ....Dr. Hector W. COLON
83 Dir Social/Behavioral Science ....Ms. Lidis L. JUSINO
76 Associate Dean of Health Science ....Dr. Omayra CARABALLO
38 Dir Univ Integration Services Ofc ....Mr. Hector MARTINEZ
13 Director Computer Center ....Mr. Antonio RAMOS
26 Public Relations Officer ....Vacant
04 Chief Executive Assistant ....Mrs. Yinaira SANTIAGO
27 Dir Marketing & Student Promotion ....Mrs. Vanessa PAGAN
106 Director Distance Education Program ....Mr. Rolando MENDEZ
88 Accreditation/Certification Officer ....Vacant
45 Director of Evaluation & Planning ....Vacant
18 Chief Facilities/Physical Plant ....Vacant
36 Director Student Placement ....Mr. Hector MARTINEZ
84 Enrollment Manager ....Mrs. Miriam MARTINEZ
42 Chaplain ....Rev. Lucy ROSARIO
51 Adult Education Director ....Mrs. Marilyn OLIVERAS
20 Assoc Dean Acad Affs/Distance Educ ....Dr. Omayra CARABALLO
21 Assoc Dean Administrative Affairs ....Mr. Julio MUNOZ
96 Purchasing Officer ....Mrs. Vivian ARMSTRONG

*Inter American University of Puerto Rico San German Campus (D)

PO Box 5100, San German PR 00683-9801
County: San German FICE Identification: 003938
Unit ID: 242617
Telephone: (787) 264-1912 Carnegie Class: Masters/M
FAX Number: (787) 892-6350 Calendar System: Semester
URL: www.intersg.edu
Established: 1912 Annual Undergrad Tuition & Fees: $4,962
Enrollment: 5,223 Coed
Affiliation or Control: Independent Non-Profit IRS Status: 501(c)3
Highest Offering: Doctorate
Accreditation: M, IACBE, MT, RAD, TEAC

02 Chancellor ....Prof. Agnes MOJICA
05 Dean of Academic Affairs ....Dr. Nyvia ALVARADO
11 Dean of Administration ....Mrs. Frances CARABALLO
32 Dean of Students ....Mr. Raúl MEDINA
20 Associate Dean of Academic Affairs ....Prof. Vilma MARTÍNEZ
21 Auxiliary Dean of Administration ....Mrs. Marisol GONZÁLEZ
15 Director of Human Resources ....Mrs. Evelyn TORRES
18 Chief Facilities/Physical Plant ....Mr. José A. RIVERA
37 Director Financial Aid ....Mrs. María Inés LUGO
06 Registrar ....Mrs. Arleen SANTANA
07 Director of Admissions ....Mrs. Mildred CAMACHO
08 Director of Library ....Mrs. Mayra RODRÍGUEZ
38 Director Student Counseling ....Mrs. Daisy PÉREZ
09 Dir Plng Evaluation/Inst Studies ....Miss María MORALES MARTÍNEZ
19 Director of Security ....Vacant
13 Director of Computer Center ....Mr. Rogelio TORO-ZAPATA
41 Athletic Director ....Prof. Francisco ACEVEDO
39 Director of Men Student Housing ....Mrs. Erlinda VEGA
39 Director of Women Student Housing ....Mrs. Hilda CRUZ
42 Dir Chaplaincy/Spiritual Well-being ....Rev. Pablo CARABALLO
04 Special Assistant of the Chancellor ....Mrs. Tary GARCÍA
35 Manager of Student Services ....Mrs. María Gil MARTÍNEZ
51 Director of Continuing Education ....Vacant
58 Director Graduate Programs ....Dr. Ailín T. PADILLA
109 Manager of Food Services ....Mrs. Judy ROSADO
17 Director of Medical Services ....Vacant
109 Auxiliary Dean of Students ....Mrs. Janet RIVERA
30 Chief Development Officer ....Miss Leticia MARTÍNEZ
96 Director of Purchasing ....Mr. Israel CRUZ
10 Director Bursar's Office ....Mr. Carlos SEGARRA
53 Director of Education ....Dr. Miriam PADILLA
83 Director of Social Scieces & Libera ....Dr. Felipe MARTÍNEZ
50 Director of Entreprenurial & Mgmt ....Dr. Milsa MORALES
88 Director of Biology & Environmental ....Prof. Iris SEDA
72 Director of Technical Studies ....Prof. Mildred ORTIZ
57 Director of Fine Arts ....Prof. Samuel ROSADO
76 Director of Health Sciences ....Prof. Maritza ORTIZ
88 Director of Language & Literature ....Dr. María BODEGA
81 Director of Math & Applied Sciences ....Prof. Yvonne AVILÉS
92 Director of Honor Program ....Miss Sulmarie MORALES
26 Director of External Resources ....Prof. Mildred DE SANTIAGO
106 Dir Online Education/E-learning ....Prof. Luis ZORNOSA

*Inter American University of Puerto Rico School of Law (E)

PO Box 70351, San Juan PR 00936-8351
County: San Juan Identification: 666813
Unit ID: 242723
Telephone: (787) 751-1912 Carnegie Class: Spec-4-yr-Law
FAX Number: (787) 751-2975 Calendar System: Semester
URL: www.derecho.inter.edu
Established: 1961 Annual Graduate Tuition & Fees: N/A
Enrollment: 849 Coed
Affiliation or Control: Independent Non-Profit IRS Status: 501(c)3
Highest Offering: First Professional Degree; No Undergraduates
Accreditation: M, LAW

02 President ....Mr. Manuel J. FERNÓS
61 Dean ....Dr. Julio E. FONTANET-MALDONADO
05 Dean for Academic Affairs ....Dr. Yanira REYES-GIL
32 Dean of Students ....Dr. Iris M. CAMACHO-MELÉNDEZ
11 Dean of Administration ....Mr. Heriberto SOTO-LÓPEZ
06 Registrar ....Mrs. Sonia I. MONTALVO-COLÓN
08 Head Librarian ....Mr. Hector R. SANCHEZ-FERNANDEZ
61 Director of Legal Aid Clinic ..Mr. Rafael E. RODRÍGUEZ-RIVERA
37 Director of Financial Aid ....Mr. Ricardo CRESPO
07 Director of Admissions ....Mrs. Angela TORRES
18 Chief Facilities/Physical Plant ....Mr. Jose A. RIVERA
96 Director of Purchasing ....Vacant
88 Director of Bursar Office ....Mrs. Ileana PIÑERO
45 Planning/Eval & Development Ofc ....Mrs. Ecith C. PABON-RODRIGUEZ
88 Academic Support Program ....Mrs. Patricia OTÓN-OLIVIERI
88 Master Program Coordinator ....Dr. Luis E. ROMERO-NIEVES
04 Executive Asst to President ....Mr. Dominique GILORMINI
13 Chief Info Technology Officer ....Ms. Olga I. CRUZ-PABÓN
15 Director Personnel Services ....Mrs. Milagros AMALBERT
19 Acting Director Security/Safety ....Mr. Rafael ORTIZ-ORTIZ
30 Dir Development/Alumni Rels ....Mrs. Sheila GÓMEZ
36 Director Student Placement/Counsel ....Vacant
51 Dir of Continuing Legal Education ....Mr. Cesar ALVARADO-TORRES

*Inter American University of Puerto Rico School of Optometry (F)

500 John Will Harris Road, Bayamon PR 00957-6257
County: San Juan Identification: 666601
Unit ID: 404222
Telephone: (787) 765-1915 Carnegie Class: Spec-4-yr-Other Health
FAX Number: (787) 767-3920 Calendar System: Semester
URL: www.optonet.inter.edu
Established: 1981 Annual Graduate Tuition & Fees: N/A
Enrollment: 231 Coed
Affiliation or Control: Independent Non-Profit IRS Status: 501(c)3
Highest Offering: First Professional Degree; No Undergraduates
Accreditation: M, OPT

02 Dean ....Dr. Andres PAGAN
05 Dean for Academic Affairs ....Dr. Angel ROMERO
10 Dean of Administration ....Mr. Francisco RIVERA
32 Dean of Student Affairs ....Dra. Iris CABELLO
42 Director Religious Life ....Dra. Ileana VARGAS
30 Director Development ....Mrs. Maria J. AULET
17 Dean of Clinical Affairs ....Dra. Damaris PAGAN
08 Library Director ....Mrs. Wilma MARRERO
15 Director Human Resources ....Mrs. Jackeline MEJIAS
37 Financial Aid Officer ....Mrs. Sirimarie MARTÍNEZ
04 Executive Assistant of the Dean ....Mrs. Arleen E. CORREA
06 Registrar ....Mrs. Luz OCASIO
26 Director Marketing/Promotion ....Mrs. Jaqueline PABON

Mech-Tech College (G)

PO Box 6118, Caguas PR 00726
County: Caguas FICE Identification: 030255
Unit ID: 414461
Telephone: (787) 744-1060 Carnegie Class: Assoc/HVT-High Trad
FAX Number: (787) 744-1035 Calendar System: Quarter
URL: www.mechtech.edu
Established: 1984 Annual Undergrad Tuition & Fees: $9,042
Enrollment: 3,101 Coed
Affiliation or Control: Proprietary IRS Status: Proprietary
Highest Offering: Associate Degree
Accreditation: CNCE

01 President ....Mr. Edwin J. COLON COSME

Monteclaro: Escuela de Hoteleria y Artes Culinarias (A)

PO Box 447 Palmer, Rio Grande PR 00721
FICE Identification: 034143
Unit ID: 437705
Telephone: (787) 888-1135 Carnegie Class: Not Classified
FAX Number: (787) 888-1252 Calendar System: Semester
URL: www.monteclaro.edu
Established: Annual Undergrad Tuition & Fees: N/A
Enrollment: 4 Coed
Affiliation or Control: Independent Non-Profit IRS Status: 501(c)3
Highest Offering: Associate Degree
Accreditation: ACCSC

National University College (B)

MSC 452, PO Box 144035, Arecibo PR 00614
Telephone: (787) 879-5044 Identification: 666489
Accreditation: &M

† Regional accreditation is carried under the parent institution in Bayamon, PR

National University College (C)

P.O. Box 2036, Bayamon PR 00960
County: Puerto Rico FICE Identification: 022606
Unit ID: 242972
Telephone: (787) 780-5134 Carnegie Class: Spec-4-yr-Other Health
FAX Number: (787) 786-9093 Calendar System: Trimester
URL: www.nuc.edu
Established: 1982 Annual Undergrad Tuition & Fees: $6,495
Enrollment: 5,320 Coed
Affiliation or Control: Proprietary IRS Status: Proprietary
Highest Offering: Master's
Accreditation: M, @PTAA, TEAC

01 President .... Dr. Gloria E. BAQUERO
88 VP of Compliance .... Mr. Desi LOPEZ
05 VP Academic Affairs .... Dr. Maria ESTRADA
32 VP of Student Affairs .... Ms. Ana M. LUCUMI
108 Institutional Dir of Assessment .... Ms. Lydia COLLAZO
46 Director Research & Development .... Mr. Angel AVILES
37 Institutional Dir Financial Aid .... Ms. Elizabeth CRUZ
06 Registrar .... Ms. Glorimar RODRIGUEZ

National University College (D)

190 Ave Gautier Benýtez esquina Ave, Caguas PR 00725
Telephone: (787) 653-4733 Identification: 770928
Accreditation: &M

† Branch campus of National University College, Bayamon, PR.

National University College Ponce Campus (E)

SR #506 KM 1.00, Bo Coto Laurel, Ponce PR 00716
Telephone: (787) 840-4474 Identification: 770169
Accreditation: &M

† Regional accreditation is carried under the parent institution in Bayamon, PR

National University College Rio Grande Campus (F)

Carr.#3 Km 22.01, Bo. Cienaga Baja,
Rio Grande PR 00745
Telephone: (787) 809-5100 Identification: 770170
Accreditation: &M

† Regional accreditation is carried under the parent institution in Bayamon, PR

Ponce Paramedical College (G)

1213 Acacia Street Villa Flores Urb,
Ponce PR 00716-2901
County: Ponce FICE Identification: 025349
Unit ID: 243072
Telephone: (787) 848-1589 Carnegie Class: Spec 2-yr-Health
FAX Number: (787) 259-0169 Calendar System: Other
URL: www.popac.edu
Established: 1983 Annual Undergrad Tuition & Fees: N/A
Enrollment: 2,607 Coed
Affiliation or Control: Proprietary IRS Status: Proprietary
Highest Offering: Associate Degree
Accreditation: ACCSC

01 President .... Mrs. Wilda VELEZ
05 Academic Dean .... Mrs. Rosa E. CRUZ
06 Registrar .... Mrs. Ivette OLIVERAS
37 Director Student Financial Aid .... Mr. Lunill LOPEZ

Ponce School of Medicine & Health Sciences (H)

PO Box 7004, Ponce PR 00732-7004
County: Ponce FICE Identification: 024824
Unit ID: 243081
Telephone: (787) 840-2575 Carnegie Class: Masters/S
FAX Number: (787) 840-9756 Calendar System: Semester
URL: www.psm.edu
Established: 1977 Annual Graduate Tuition & Fees: N/A
Enrollment: 701 Coed
Affiliation or Control: Independent Non-Profit IRS Status: 501(c)3
Highest Offering: Doctorate; No Undergraduates
Accreditation: M, CLPSY, IPSY, MED, PH

01 President/CEO .... Dr. David LENIHAN
05 Vice Pres Academic Affairs .... Dr. Jose TORRES-RUIZ
32 Vice Pres Student Affairs .... Dr. Emil RUIZ
11 Chief Operations Officer .... Ms. Ann COSS
10 Chief Financial Officer .... Mr. Carlos ROJAS

The Pontifical Catholic University of Puerto Rico (I)

2250 Las Americas Avenue, Suite 564,
Ponce PR 00717-9997
County: Ponce FICE Identification: 003936
Unit ID: 241410
Telephone: (787) 841-2000 Carnegie Class: DU-Mod
FAX Number: (787) 651-2034 Calendar System: Semester
URL: www.pucpr.edu
Established: 1948 Annual Undergrad Tuition & Fees: $5,130
Enrollment: 8,079 Coed
Affiliation or Control: Roman Catholic IRS Status: 501(c)3
Highest Offering: Doctorate
Accreditation: M, CORE, LAW, MT, NUR, SW, TEAC

00 Chancellor .... M.Rev. Ruben A. GONZALEZ MEDINA, CMF
01 President .... Dr. Jorge I. VELEZ AROCHO
04 Executive Assistant to President .... Lic. Liza RIESTRA
05 Vice President Academic Affairs .... Dr. Leandro COLON
10 Vice President of Finance .... Prof. Irma I. RODRIGUEZ
32 Vice President for Student Affairs .... Prof. Freddie MARTINEZ
20 Assoc Vice Pres Academic Affairs .... Prof. Maria MUNIZ
35 Asst to Vice Pres Student Affairs .... Prof. Myriam D. LOPEZ
09 Vice President Inst Rsrch/Dev Plng .... Dr. Felix CORTES
12 Rector Arecibo Branch .... Dr. Edwin HERNANDEZ
12 Rector Mayaguez Branch .... Dr. Olga HERNÁNDEZ
06 Registrar .... Prof. Ivan DAVILA
07 Director of Admissions .... Dr. Ana C. BONILLA
08 Director of the Library .... Prof. Macca VARGAS
37 Director of Student Aid .... Mrs. Maria NOLASCO
36 Director of Placement Services .... Vacant
13 Director Computer Center .... Mr. Moises CABRERA
55 Director of Evening Studies .... Prof. Caridad ALVAREZ
24 Director Educational Technology .... Dr. Edgar RODRIGUEZ
79 Dean of Arts & Humanities .... Rev. Juan Luis NEGRON DELGADO
81 Dean of Sciences .... Dra. Alma L. SANTIAGO
61 Dean of the School of Law .... Lic. Jose A. FRONTERA
50 Dean Business Administration .... Dr. David ZAYAS
53 Dean of Education .... Dr. Myriam ZAYAS
58 Dean Institute of Graduate Studies .... Dr. Hernan VERA
48 Dean School of Architecture .... Mr. Luis V. BADILLO-LOZANO
51 Coord Continuing Education Inst .... Mrs. Karen G. MORALES
27 Communications .... Mrs. Julibeth RODRIGUEZ
29 Alumni Relations Officer .... Mrs. Maria S. MASCARO
15 Director Human Resources .... Mr. Wilfredo CORNIER
40 Director Bookstore .... Mrs. Ashley VELEZ
41 Athletic Director .... Mr. Ramon HERNANDEZ
42 Chaplain .... Rev. Juan C. RIVERA
109 Director Auxiliary Enterprises .... Mr. Julio FELIU
26 Director Public Relations .... Mrs. Irem POVENTUD
38 Director Student Counseling .... Dr. Arvin BAEZ
18 Physical Plant/Safety & Security .... Mr. Julio PALMER
21 Treasurer Bursar's Office .... Mr. Juan E. ROMAN
96 Interim Director of Purchasing .... Mrs. Nelly VELAZQUEZ
88 Exec Dir International Relations .... Dra. Enid MIRANDA
88 Director of Biotechnology .... Dra. Carilu SANTIAGO
88 Accreditation Liaison Officer .... Dr. Carmen J. ACOSTA-FUMERO
30 Infrastructure Director .... Ing. Armando RODRIGUEZ
84 Coord Institutional Recruitment .... Sr. Rene MARRERO
89 Director of Freshmen .... Prof. Carmen Z. TORRES
106 Dir Online Education/E-learning .... Dr. Carmen BETANCOURT
19 Director Security/Safety .... Mr. Julio PALMER
43 Dir Legal Services/General Counsel .... Lic. Carolyn COSTAS
86 Director Government Relations .... Mr. Ruben COLON
100 Chief of Staff .... Lic. Liza RIESTRA
108 Director Institutional Assessment .... Dr. Jose N. CARABALLO
39 Director Student Housing .... Mr. Francisco LUGO
39 Director Student Housing .... Ms. Magda PEREZ

Pontifical Catholic University of Puerto Rico-Arecibo Campus (J)

Box 144045, Arecibo PR 00614-4045
Telephone: (787) 881-1212 Identification: 666603
Accreditation: &M

† Regional accreditation is carried under the parent institution in Ponce, PR.

Pontifical Catholic University of Puerto Rico-Mayaguez Campus (K)

Box 1326, Mayaguez PR 00681-1326
Telephone: (787) 834-5151 Identification: 666605
Accreditation: &M

† Branch campus of The Pontifical Catholic University of Puerto Rico, Ponce, PR.

San Juan Bautista School of Medicine (L)

PO Box 4968, Carretera 172, Caguas PR 00726-4968
County: San Juan FICE Identification: 031773
Unit ID: 430670
Telephone: (787) 743-3038 Carnegie Class: Spec-4-yr-Med
FAX Number: (787) 743-3042 Calendar System: Semester
URL: www.sanjuanbautista.edu
Established: 1978 Annual Graduate Tuition & Fees: $9,360
Enrollment: 330 Coed
Affiliation or Control: Proprietary IRS Status: Proprietary
Highest Offering: First Professional Degree; No Undergraduates
Accreditation: M, MED

01 President/Dean .... Dr. Yocasta BRUGAL-MENA
11 Dean of Administration .... Mr. Carlos F. ABREU
05 Chief Academic Officer .... Dr. Irving MALDONADO
06 Registrar .... Mr. Israel LÓPEZ
08 Head Librarian .... Mr. Carlos ALTAMIRANO
10 Chief Business Officer .... Mr. Juan C. CASTRO
32 Chief Student Affairs/Student Life .... Dr. Yolanda MIRANDA
37 Director Student Financial Aid .... Miss Beatriz DE LEÓN

Seminario Teologico de Puerto Rico (M)

Calle Jose Canals #458, Oficina 301, San Juan PR 00918
Telephone: (787) 274-1142 Identification: 770142
Accreditation: &M

† Regional accreditation is carried under the parent institution in Nyack, NY

*Sistema Universitario Ana G. Mendez (N)

Apartado 21345, Rio Piedras PR 00928-1341
County: San Juan FICE Identification: 029078
Unit ID: 242060
Telephone: (787) 751-0178 Carnegie Class: N/A
FAX Number: (787) 766-1706
URL: www.suagm.edu

01 President .... Mr. Jose F. MENDEZ
03 Executive Vice President .... Mr. Jose F. MENDEZ, JR.
05 Vice President for Academic Affairs .... Mr. Jorge L. CRESPO
10 Vice Pres Financial Affairs .... Mr. Alfonso L. DAVILA
32 VP Student/Marketing Affairs .... Dr. Mayra CRUZ
45 Vice President Planning & Research .... Mr. Jorge CRESPO
11 Vice Pres Administrative Affairs .... Mr. Ricardo RODRIGUEZ
15 Vice President Human Resources .... Dr. Victoria DE JESUS
104 Vice President International Affs .... Dr. David MENDEZ
13 Chief Information Officer .... Sr. Kenneth MALDONADO
26 Director Public Relations .... Ms. Maria MARTINEZ
04 Exec Assistant to President .... Ms. Lydia I. MASSARI
06 Registrar .... Ms. Elisa QUILES
07 Director of Admissions .... Ms. Ramonita FUENTES

*Universidad Ana G. Mendez (O)

PO Box 21345, Bayamon PR 00928-1345
County: Bayamon Identification: 667292
Telephone: (787) 288-1118 Carnegie Class: Not Classified
FAX Number: (787) 288-1141 Calendar System: Semester
URL: agmvirtual.suagm.edu
Established: Annual Graduate Tuition & Fees: N/A
Enrollment: N/A Coed
Affiliation or Control: Independent Non-Profit IRS Status: 501(c)3
Highest Offering: Master's; No Undergraduates
Accreditation: M

02 Chancellor .... Dr. Migdalia TORRES
03 Vice Chancellor .... Dr. Wilfredo COLON-GUASO

*Universidad del Este (P)

PO Box 2010, Carolina PR 00984-2010
County: San Juan FICE Identification: 003941
Unit ID: 243346
Telephone: (787) 257-7373 Carnegie Class: Masters/L
FAX Number: (787) 776-1220 Calendar System: Semester
URL: www.suagm.edu/une
Established: 1949 Annual Undergrad Tuition & Fees: $5,820
Enrollment: 13,331 Coed
Affiliation or Control: Independent Non-Profit IRS Status: 501(c)3
Highest Offering: Master's
Accreditation: M, ACBSP, ACFEI, SW, TEAC

02 Chancellor .... Dr. Mildred HUERTAS SOLÁ
05 Acting Vice Chanc Academic Affairs .... Ms. Nilda ROSADO
11 Vice Chanc Admin Affs/Ofce of Chanc .... Mrs. Maria S. DIAZ
32 Vice Chancellor Student Affairs .... Dr. María G. VEAZ
24 Vice Chanc Information Resources .... Mrs. Carmen ORTEGA
46 Vice Chanc External Resources .... Mrs. Mayra M. FERRAN
20 Assoc VC Licensing/Accreditation .... Ms. Nilda I. ROSADO
88 Assoc Vice Chanc Admin Affairs .... Mrs. Magalie ALVARADO
35 Assoc Vice Chanc Student Affairs .... Mrs. Gisela NEGRON
84 Assoc VC Enrollment Management .... Mrs. Magda E. OSTOLAZA
23 AVC Stdnt Quality of Life/Wellness .... Mrs. Carmen G. VELAZQUEZ
07 Asst Vice Chan Admiss/Financial Aid .... Vacant
09 Asst Vice Chanc Academic Effective .... Dr. Claribette RODRIGUEZ

36 Exec Director Employment Placement ... Mrs. Diana M. COLON
30 Asst VC for University Advancement ... Mrs. Maria I. DE GUZMAN
15 Asst Vice Pres Human Resources ... Mrs. Marisol MUÑOZ
10 Assistant Vice President of Budget ... Mr. Jorge A. TORRES
45 Asst Vice President of Planning ... Mr. Alberto J. CAMACHO
88 Dean Intl Sch Hosp/Culinary Arts ... Mrs. Terestella GONZÁLEZ
107 Dean Professional Studies ... Mrs. Mildred Y. RIVERA
18 Physical Plant/Operations VC ... Mr. Edgar D. RODRIGUEZ
06 Registrar ... Mrs. Elisa QUILES
37 Director of Financial Aid ... Mrs. Eigna DE JESUS
08 Director of Library ... Mrs. Elsa MARIANI
26 Director Public Relations ... Mrs. Ivonne D. ARROYO
29 Director Alumni ... Ms. Lorna M. MORLA
13 Information/Telecommunications Dir ... Mr. Rigoberto TERRERO
41 Athletic Director ... Mr. Julio FIGUEROA
19 Director Safety & Security ... Mr. Carlos E. BERROA
53 Dean of Education ... Dr. Maria del Carmen ARRIBAS
50 Dean of Business Administration ... Dr. Maritza I. ESPINA
72 Dean of Science and Technology ... Dr. Marielis E. RIVERA
76 Dean of Health Science ... Dr. Silvio VÉLEZ
83 Dean of Social Science ... Dr. Luis MAYO
51 Exec Director Continuing Education ... Mrs. Litza A. RIVERA
104 Director of International Affairs ... Mrs. Laurie A. MELIN

*Universidad Del Turabo (A)

Estacion Universidad, Box 3030, Gurabo PR 00778-3030
County: Gurabo | FICE Identification: 011719
Unit ID: 243601
Telephone: (787) 743-7979 | Carnegie Class: DU-Mod
FAX Number: (787) 744-5394 | Calendar System: Semester
URL: www.suagm.edu
Established: 1972 | Annual Undergrad Tuition & Fees: $5,820
Enrollment: 17,325 | Coed
Affiliation or Control: Independent Non-Profit | IRS Status: 501(c)3
Highest Offering: Doctorate
Accreditation: M, BUS, #DIETC, ENG, @NATUR, NURSE, SP, SW, TEAC

02 Chancellor ... Dr. Dennis ALICEA
11 Vice Chancellor of Admin Affairs ... Dr. Gladys BETANCOURT
05 Vice Chancellor Academic Affairs ... Dr. Roberto LORAN
32 Vice Chancellor of Student Affairs ... Dra. Brunilda APONTE
08 Vice Chancellor Information Res ... Dr. Sarai LASTRA
92 Vice Chancellor Honors Program ... Ms. Maricarmen SANTOS
88 Asst Vice Chanc Eval & Development ... Ms. Keila J. ROCHE
21 Asst Vice Chanc Admin Affairs ... Mrs. Edna ORTA
53 Dean Education ... Mr. Israel RODRÍGUEZ
50 Dean Business and Entrepreneurship ... Dr. Juan Carlos SOSA
54 Dean Engineering ... Dr. Hector RODRÍGUEZ
72 Dean Natural Science & Technology ... Dr. Teresa LIPSETT
83 Dean Social Sciences & Commun ... Dra. María del C. SANTOS
48 Dean Architecture/Design ... Arq. Aurorisa MATEO
76 Dean Health Sciences ... Dra. Nydia BOU
88 Dean Technical Studies ... Ms. Maria E. FLORES
107 Dean Professional Studies ... Ms. Mildred Y. RIVERA
51 Dean Continuing Education ... Mrs. Lizbeth RIVERA
58 Associate Dean of Graduate Studies ... Dr. Sharon CANTRELL
06 Registrar ... Mrs. Zoraida ORTIZ
97 Dean of General Studies ... Mr. Felix R. HUERTAS
27 Director of Marketing ... Ms. Melba G. SÁNCHEZ
37 Director Office of Financial Aid ... Mrs. Carmen J. RIVERA
26 Director Public Relations ... Ms. Iris SERRANO
18 Chief Facilities/Physical Plant ... Eng. Mayra RODRIGUEZ
29 Coordinator Alumni Relations ... Ms. René S. RONDA
30 Chief Development Officer ... Ms. Alba RIVERA
96 Director of Purchasing ... Mr. Jose BERRIOS
07 Director of Admissions ... Mrs. Diriee Y. RODRIGUEZ
45 Aux Vice President of Planning ... Ms. Mari G. GONZALEZ
15 Director Personnel Services ... Mrs. Iris BERRIOS
36 Assoc Vice Chanc Student Placement ... Ms. Carmen PULLIZA
84 Director Enrollment Management ... Ms. Maria V. FIGUEROA
10 Chief Business Officer ... Vacant
38 Assoc Vice Chanc Student Counseling ... Ms. Samaris COLLAZO
106 Dir Online Education/E-learning ... Dra. Pilar DAVILA
108 Director Institutional Assessment ... Mr. Ernesto ESPINOZA
41 Assoc Dean/Athletic Director ... Mr. Jorge H. GAROFALO

*Universidad Metropolitana (B)

PO Box 21150, Rio Piedras PR 00928-1150
County: San Juan | FICE Identification: 025875
Unit ID: 241739
Telephone: (787) 766-1717 | Carnegie Class: Masters/L
FAX Number: (787) 759-7663 | Calendar System: Quarter
URL: www.suagm.edu/umet
Established: 1980 | Annual Undergrad Tuition & Fees: $5,820
Enrollment: 13,773 | Coed
Affiliation or Control: Independent Non-Profit | IRS Status: 501(c)3
Highest Offering: Doctorate
Accreditation: M, ACBSP, ADNUR, NUR

02 SUAGM President ... Dr. José F. MENDEZ
00 Chancellor ... Dr. Carlos M. PADIN
05 Vice Chancellor Academic Affairs ... Dr. Juan OTERO
108 Asst Vice Chanc Inst Assessment ... Dr. Carmen M. LUNA
29 Asst Vice Chanc Inst Development ... Ms. Belissa AQUINO
32 Vice Chanc for Student Affairs ... Mrs. Carmen ROSADO
88 Executive Director Intl Affairs ... Dr. Zaida VEGA
88 Int Vice Chanc External Resources ... Mrs. Molly HARDIGREE
88 Int Assoc Vice Chanc Accred/Lic ... Mrs. Alma RESTO
11 Assoc Vice Chanc for Admin Affairs ... Dr. Gregorio VILLEGAS
15 Asst Vice Pres for Human Resources ... Mr. Jorge RODRIGUEZ
13 Vice Pres Information Resources ... Mr. Carlos M. DELGADO
30 Assoc Vice Chanc Dev/Retention ... Mrs. Awilda PEREZ
10 Asst Vice Pres Analysis & Budget ... Mrs. Aixa ALDARONDO
45 Asst Vice President of Planning ... Dr. Mariela COLLAZO
44 Director Retention/Develop ... Mr. Ariel MENDEZ
83 Int Dean Soc Scienc/Human & Commun ... Dr. Mariveliz CABAN
50 Int Dean of Business ... Dr. Teresita IBARRA
53 Dean of Education ... Dr. Luis A. MOJICA
76 Dean of Health Science ... Dr. Lourdes MALDONADO
81 Dean of Science & Technology ... Dr. Karen GONZALEZ
65 Dean of Environmental Affairs ... Dr. María C. ORTIZ
83 Assoc Dean of Social Sciences ... Vacant
107 Assoc Dean of Professional Studies ... Ms. Melissa GUILLIANI
60 Int Assoc Dean of Communications ... Mrs. Sugelenia COTTO
79 Assoc Dean of Humanities ... Dr. Roxanna D. DOMENECH
75 Dean of Technical Studies ... Mrs. Laura E. APONTE
51 Exec Director Continuing Education ... Ms. Lorna MARTINEZ
53 Assoc Dean of Education ... Ms. Barbara PONCE
53 Assoc Dean of Education ... Dr. Mariwilda PADILLA
08 Head Librarian ... Mr. Gabriel LOPEZ
18 Vice Chanc Operations & Facilities ... Eng. Francisco CABALLERO
76 Director of Respiratory Therapy ... Mrs. Katherine GARCÍA
66 Int Director of Nursing ... Dr. Yanilda RODRIGUEZ
26 Director Public Relations ... Ms. Yvonne GUADALUPE
06 Registrar ... Mrs. Beatriz NIEVES
12 Additional Location Dir Bayamón ... Dr. Guillermo VAZQUEZ
12 Additional Location Dir Aguadilla ... Mr. Luis A. RUIZ
12 Additional Location Dir Jayuya ... Mrs. Irma del Pilar CRUZ
12 Additional Location Dir Comerío ... Mr. Jessie HERNANDEZ
07 Admissions Director ... Ms. Yadira RIVERA LUGO
41 Athletic Director ... Mr. Ariel ORTIZ

Trinity College of Puerto Rico (C)

PO Box 7313, Ponce PR 00732
FICE Identification: 031159
Unit ID: 431929
Telephone: (787) 848-5739 | Carnegie Class: Not Classified
FAX Number: (787) 284-2537 | Calendar System: Semester
URL: www.trinitypr.edu
Established: 1969 | Annual Undergrad Tuition & Fees: $6,795
Enrollment: 246 | Coed
Affiliation or Control: Independent Non-Profit | IRS Status: 501(c)3
Highest Offering: Associate Degree
Accreditation: ACICS

01 Executive Director ... Maria DEL PILAR BONNIN OROZCO
05 Academic Director ... Elizabeth PEREZ TOLEDO
10 Director of Finance Office ... Margarita PEREZ DE JESUS
06 Registrar ... Ana SOTO I COLON

Universal Technology College of Puerto Rico (D)

111 Comercio Street, Aguadilla PR 00603
County: Aguadilla | FICE Identification: 030297
Unit ID: 376385
Telephone: (787) 882-2065 | Carnegie Class: Spec-4-yr-Other Health
FAX Number: (787) 891-2370 | Calendar System: Semester
URL: www.unitecpr.edu
Established: 1987 | Annual Undergrad Tuition & Fees: N/A
Enrollment: 412 | Coed
Affiliation or Control: Independent Non-Profit | IRS Status: 501(c)3
Highest Offering: Baccalaureate
Accreditation: ACICS

01 Chief Executive Officer ... Mrs. Keila LOPEZ
11 Administrative Manager ... Vacant
04 Executive Secretary ... Mrs. Marilyn GONZALEZ
05 Chief Academic Officer ... Vacant
06 Registrar ... Ms. Maria ALVAREZ
08 Director of Library ... Ms. Airlyn VAZQUEZ
10 Accountant ... Ms. Nancy MORALES
12 Director of Branch Campus ... Ms. Nelida CARDONA
13 Director Computer Center ... Mr. Zain CORDERO
15 Director Human Resources ... Ms. Luz ESTRELLA
18 Chief Facilities/Physical Plant ... Mr. Danily NIEVES
32 Director Student Affairs ... Vacant
36 Student Placement Officer ... Ms. Luz ESTRELLA
45 Director Planning & Development ... Mrs. Evelyn TORRES
37 Director Student Financial Aid ... Mr. Samuel HERNANDEZ
38 Director Student Counsel ... Mrs. Dalia SANTIAGO
96 Purchasing Officer ... Mrs. Dolores MITJANS
23 Healthcare Services ... Mr. Silverio JIMENEZ
07 Coordinator of Admissions ... Mrs. Teresita RIVERA
50 Dir General Studies/Business Admin ... Mrs. Sandra GONZALEZ
72 Director of Industrial Technology ... Mr. Eduardo FIGUEROA

Universidad Adventista de las Antillas (E)

Box 118, Mayaguez PR 00681-0118
County: Mayaguez | FICE Identification: 005019
Unit ID: 241191
Telephone: (787) 834-9595 | Carnegie Class: Bac-Diverse
FAX Number: (787) 834-9597 | Calendar System: Semester
URL: www.uaa.edu
Established: 1961 | Annual Undergrad Tuition & Fees: $6,850
Enrollment: 1,360 | Coed
Affiliation or Control: Seventh-day Adventist | IRS Status: 501(c)3
Highest Offering: Master's
Accreditation: M, ANEST, NUR

01 President ... Dr. Obed JIMENEZ
05 Vice President for Academic Affairs ... Dr. Myrna COLON
10 Vice President Financial Affairs ... Mr. Misael JIMENEZ
32 Vice President for Students Affairs ... Mr. Jaime LOPEZ
30 VP Planning and Development ... Dr. Jose D. GOMEZ
42 Religious Affairs Director ... Mr. Abiezer RODRIGUEZ
20 Associate VP Academic Affairs ... Mrs. Yolanda PEREZ
21 Associate Financial Vice President ... Mrs. Madeline CRUZ
88 Director Student Finance Office ... Mrs. Naobelin CASIANO
66 Dean of the School of Nursing ... Dr. Maria ROSA
66 Director School of Nursing ... Mrs. Maria CRUZ
53 Dean of the School of Education ... Dr. Maritza LAMBOY
50 Director of Business Administration ... Dr. David L. RAMOS
81 Director Mathematics/Sciences/Comp ... Mrs. Alicia MORADILLOS
73 Director Theology Department ... Dr. Efren PAGAN
06 Registrar ... Mrs. Ana D. TORRES
07 Director of Admissions ... Mrs. Yolanda FERRER
37 Director of Student Financial Aid ... Mrs. Awilda MATOS
26 Dir Public Relations & Promotion ... Miss Lorell VARELA
108 Dir of Institutional Effectiveness ... Dr. Aúrea ARAÚJO
13 Director Computing and Information ... Mr. Heber VAZQUEZ
08 Librarian ... Mrs. Aixa VEGA
38 Counselor ... Mrs. Ivelisse PEREZ
88 Environmental Services Director ... Mr. Legna VARELA
18 Chief Facilities/Physical Plant ... Mr. Abel RODRIGUEZ
34 Dean of Women ... Mrs. Felicita CRUZ
33 Dean of Men ... Mr. Rigoberto SANTIAGO
09 Institutional Researcher ... Dr. Digna M. WILLIAMS

Universidad Central de Bayamon (F)

PO Box 1725, Bayamon PR 00960-1725
County: Bayamon | FICE Identification: 005022
Unit ID: 241225
Telephone: (787) 786-3030 | Carnegie Class: Masters/M
FAX Number: (787) 740-2200 | Calendar System: Semester
URL: www.ucb.edu.pr
Established: 1961 | Annual Undergrad Tuition & Fees: $6,220
Enrollment: 2,360 | Coed
Affiliation or Control: Roman Catholic | IRS Status: 501(c)3
Highest Offering: Master's
Accreditation: M, CORE, SW

01 President ... Dr. Lillian NEGRON
05 Academic Dean ... Dr. Luz C. VALENTIN
11 Interim Administrative Dean ... Mrs. Enid RIVERA
32 Dean of Students ... Mrs. Niza ZAYAS
49 Dir College Liberal Arts/Humanities ... Fr. Yamil SAMALOT
53 Dir Col of Education and Behavior ... Dr. Caroline GONZALEZ
50 Dir Business Development & Tech ... Dr. Nidia COLON
08 Director Learning Resources ... Mrs. Annette VALENTIN
15 Director of Human Resources ... Mrs. Elaine NUNEZ
30 Int Dir Institutional Development ... Mr. Pedro BERMUDEZ
07 Director of Admissions ... Mrs. Wanda APONTE
37 Director Student Financial Aid ... Mrs. Edna ORTIZ
38 Dir Guidance/Counseling Center ... Mrs. Milagros M. RIVERA
06 Registrar ... Mr. Victor COLON
35 Dir Center Learning Stre (CFAEE) ... Mrs. Myrna PEREZ
13 Director of Information System ... Mr. Jose R. AVILES
18 Director Physical Facilities ... Mr. Eliezer GARCIA
26 Int Marketing Director ... Ms. Magdalis LOPEZ
96 Purchase Officer ... Mrs. Jessica OJEDA
09 Institutional Research Officer ... Mrs. Luz M. PALACIOS
66 Nursing Program Coordinator ... Prof. Zaida RUIZ
20 Associate Academic Dean ... Mr. Pedro BERMUDEZ
29 Alumni Relations ... Mrs. Niza ZAYAS
81 Dir College Sciences/Health Profes ... Dr. Pedro ROBLES
03 Executive Vice President ... Mr. Angel VALENTIN
04 Administrative Asst to President ... Mrs. Luz N. VALLELLANES
101 Secretary of the Institution/Board ... Prof. Marcelina VELEZ
105 Director Web Services ... Mr. Manuel ECHEANDIA
106 Dir Online Education/E-learning ... Mr. Jorge L. DIAZ
108 Director Institutional Assessment ... Dr. Judith TORRES
41 Athletic Director ... Mr. Edwin MORALES

Universidad Central Del Caribe (G)

PO Box 60-327, Bayamon PR 00960-6032
County: Bayamon | FICE Identification: 021633
Unit ID: 243568
Telephone: (787) 798-3001 | Carnegie Class: Spec-4-yr-Med
FAX Number: (787) 798-6836 | Calendar System: Semester
URL: www.uccaribe.edu
Established: 1976 | Annual Undergrad Tuition & Fees: $10,470
Enrollment: 467 | Coed
Affiliation or Control: Independent Non-Profit | IRS Status: 501(c)3
Highest Offering: Doctorate
Accreditation: M, MED

01 President ... Dr. Jose Ginel RODRIGUEZ
05 Dean for Academic Affairs ... Dr. Nereida DIAZ-RODRIGUEZ
20 Asst Dean of Curriculum Development ... Dr. Alvaro PÉREZ
11 Dean Administrative Affairs ... Ms. Emilia SOTO
32 Dean Student Affairs ... Dr. Omar PEREZ
17 Dean of Medicine ... Dr. Jose Ginel RODRIGUEZ
63 Associate Dean of Medicine ... Mrs. Zilka RIOS
53 Asst Dean Professional Services ... Ms. Emilia SOTO
06 Registrar ... Ms. Nilda MONTANEZ-LOPEZ
07 Director of Admissions ... Ms. Irma L. CORDERO
37 Director Student Financial Aid ... Ms. Mayra SERRANO
10 Director of Finances ... Mrs. Iris J. FONT
08 Librarian ... Ms. Mildred RIVERA
51 Director of Continuing Education ... Dr. Frances GARCIA

38 Counselor .... Ms. Mariana T. HERNÁNDEZ
46 Dean of Research and Graduate Pgms .... Dr. Luis A. CUBANO
20 Dean for Clinical & Faculty Affairs .... Dr. Harry MERCADO
30 Director Inst Development Office .... Ms. Yvonne CORSINO

Universidad Pentecostal Mizpa (A)

RR16 Box 4800, San Juan PR 00926
County: San Juan | FICE Identification: 031983
Unit ID: 441690
Telephone: (787) 720-4476 | Carnegie Class: Spec-4-yr-Faith
FAX Number: (787) 720-2012 | Calendar System: Semester
URL: www.mizpa.edu
Established: 1937 | Annual Undergrad Tuition & Fees: $4,120
Enrollment: 407 | Coed
Affiliation or Control: Pentecostal Church of God | IRS Status: 501(c)3
Highest Offering: Master's
Accreditation: BI

01 President .... Mr. Luis A. HERNANDEZ RAMIREZ
05 Dean of Academic Affairs .Mr. Jose G. TORRACA MONDRIGUEZ
10 Dean Administration/Finance .... Mr. Ismael SOTO MALDONADO
32 Dean of Student Affairs .... Mr. Jorge A. BURGOS
42 Coordinator Ministerial Formation .... Mr. Harry MUNOZ
06 Registrar .... Mr. Leonardo MELENDEZ LEON
08 Librarian .... Mrs. Melanie RODRIGUEZ
37 Student Financial Aid Officer .... Mrs. Myriam JUARBE
26 Chief Public Relations Officer .... Mr. Rafael LABOY
04 Administrative Asst to President .... Mrs. Maria E. VARGAS

Universidad Politecnica De Puerto Rico (B)

Ponce de Leon 377, Box 192017, San Juan PR 00919
County: San Juan | FICE Identification: 021000
Unit ID: 243577
Telephone: (787) 622-8000 | Carnegie Class: Spec-4-yr-Eng
FAX Number: (787) 754-8268 | Calendar System: Trimester
URL: www.pupr.edu
Established: 1966 | Annual Undergrad Tuition & Fees: $8,040
Enrollment: 4,507 | Coed
Affiliation or Control: Independent Non-Profit | IRS Status: 501(c)3
Highest Offering: Master's
Accreditation: M, ENG, ENGR, IACBE, LSAR

01 President .... Prof. Ernesto VAZQUEZ-BARQUET
03 Executive Vice President .... Mr. Ernesto VAZQUEZ-MARTINEZ
84 Vice Pres Enrollment Management .... Mr. Carlos PEREZ
05 Chief Academic Officer .... Dr. Miguel A. RIESTRA
06 Registrar .... Mrs. Mayra I. LOPEZ
07 Director Admissions .... Mrs. Teresa CARDONA
08 Head Librarian .... Mrs. Mirta COLON
37 Director Financial Aid .... Mr. Sergio VILLOLDO
09 Director of Institutional Research .... Dr. Miguel A. RIESTRA
15 Director Personnel Services .... Ms. Ana CASTELLANO
18 Chief Facilities/Physical Plant .... Mr. Herminio ROMERO
29 Alumni Relations .... Ms. Lourdes ALCRUDO
32 Director Student Affairs .... Mr. Carlos PEREZ
36 Director Student Placement .... Mrs. Angie ESCALANTE
38 Director Student Counseling .... Ms. Claribel DIAZ-DIAZ
10 Associate Business Officer .... Mrs. Olga CANCEL
96 Director of Purchasing .... Mr. Ramon RIVERA
19 Director Security/Safety .... Mr. Miguel ALBARRAN
41 Athletic Director .... Mr. Roberto MEDINA-ORTIZ
50 Dean of Business .... Dr. Eugenio A. LONGO
49 Dean of Arts and Science/Education .... Dr. Catalina VICENS
54 Dean of Engineering .... Dr. Carlos J. GONZALEZ
106 Dir Online Education/E-learning .... Mrs. Heyda DELGADO

Universidad Teologica Del Caribe (C)

PO Box 901, Saint Just PR 00978-0901
County: Trujillo Alto | FICE Identification: 023355
Unit ID: 241614
Telephone: (787) 761-0640 | Carnegie Class: Spec-4-yr-Faith
FAX Number: (787) 748-9220 | Calendar System: Semester
URL: www.utcpr.edu
Established: 1956 | Annual Undergrad Tuition & Fees: $3,784
Enrollment: 250 | Coed
Affiliation or Control: Church Of God | IRS Status: 501(c)3
Highest Offering: Master's
Accreditation: BI

01 President .... Francisco ORTIZ
05 Academic Dean .... Carmen AYALA
06 Registrar .... Maria Judith CARABALLO
10 Administration Dean .... Frankie NEGRON
32 Students Dean .... Wilfredo ADORNO
37 Financial Aid Director .... Claudia RODRIGUEZ
08 Librarian .... Velma Leticia SOSA
45 Planning & Development Officer .... Ana CEPERO
106 Online Program Coordinator .... Luis COLON
58 Graduate School Coordinator .... Glenda VELAZQUEZ
12 North-Central (Dorado) Campus Coord .... Richard D'COSTA
07 Admissions Officer .... Raul MCCLIN

*University of Puerto Rico-Central Administration (D)

1187 Flamboyan Street, San Juan PR 00926-1117
County: San Juan | FICE Identification: 003942
Unit ID: 243160
Telephone: (787) 250-0000 | Carnegie Class: N/A
FAX Number: (787) 759-6917
URL: www.upr.edu

01 President .... Dr. Uroyoan F. WALKER-RAMOS
03 Executive Director .... Lic. Manuel E. CAMARA-MONTULL
05 Vice President for Academic Affairs .... Dra. Celia M. CAMACHO
09 Vice Pres Research/Investigation .... Dr. Jose A. LASALDE-DOMINICCI
32 Vice Pres for Student Affairs .... Dra. Margarita E. VILLAMIL-TORRES
12 Chancellor UPR-Rio Piedras Campus .... Dr. Carlos E. SEVERINO-VALDEZ
12 Chancellor UPR-Mayaguez Campus .... Dr. John FERNANDEZ
12 Chanc UPR-Medical Sciences Campus .... Dr. Noel J. AYMAT-SANTANA
12 Chancellor UPR-Cayey Campus .... Dr. Mario MEDINA-CABAN
12 Chancellor UPR-Humacao Campus .... Dr. Efrain VAZQUEZ-VERA
12 Chancellor UPR-Bayamon Campus .... Prof. Margarita FERNANDEZ-ZAVALA
12 Chancellor UPR-Ponce Campus .... Dr. Leonardo MORALES-TOMASSINI
12 Chancellor UPR-Carolina Campus .. Dr. Moises ORENGO-AVILES
12 Chancellor UPR-Utuado Campus .... Dra. Raquel G. VARGAS-GOMEZ
12 Chancellor UPR-Aguadilla Campus .... Dr. Nelson A. VERA-HERNANDEZ
12 Chancellor UPR-Arecibo Campus .Dr. Otilio GONZALEZ-CORTES
30 Dir Devel & Alumni Affairs Office .... Sra. Gretchen KRANS
88 Dir Ctrl Designer Construction .... Arq. Alejandro ARGUELLES
10 Director Finance Office .... CPA. Norberto GONZALEZ
15 Director Human Resources Office .... Sra. Erika DIAZ-RIOS
11 Director Administrative Service .... Mr. Juan M. ORTIZ-VAZQUEZ
13 Director Information Systems Office .... Mr. Victor DIAZ-RODRIGUEZ
37 Director Student Financial Aid .... Vacant
43 Director Legal Affairs Office .... Lic. Cristina ALCARAZ-EMMANUELLI
88 Administrator Botanical Garden .... Sr. Juan M. ORTIZ-VAZQUEZ
26 University Press & Communications . Sra. Olga L. VELEZ-ROLON
101 Exec Secretary University Board .... Sra. Mayra M. FLORES-SANTOS
21 Director Budget Office .... Mr. Basilio RIVERA-ARROYO
18 Dir Physical Dev/Infrastrcture Ofc .... Arq. Fernando PLA-GOMEZ

*University of Puerto Rico-Aguadilla (E)

PO Box 6150, Aguadilla PR 00604-6150
County: Aguadilla | FICE Identification: 012123
Unit ID: 243106
Telephone: (787) 890-2681 | Carnegie Class: Bac-Diverse
FAX Number: (787) 891-3455 | Calendar System: Semester
URL: www.uprag.edu
Established: 1972 | Annual Undergrad Tuition & Fees (In-State): $2,019
Enrollment: 2,927 | Coed
Affiliation or Control: State | IRS Status: 501(c)3
Highest Offering: Baccalaureate
Accreditation: M, ACBSP, ENGT, TED

02 Chancellor .... Dr. Nelson A. VERA HERNANDEZ
05 Dean Academic Affairs .... Dr. Herminia ALEMANY-VALDEZ
11 Dean Administration .... Mr. Luis ALVAREZ-RUIZ
32 Dean Student Affairs .... Dr. Migdalia GONZALEZ-GUERRA
06 Registrar .... Mrs. Zaida SERRANO
07 Admissions Officer .... Mrs. Melba SERRANO
08 Head Librarian .... Prof. Elsa MATOS
13 Director of Computer Center .... Mr. Ismael VILLANUEVA
15 Director of Personnel .... Mrs. Nilsa MORALES TORRES
19 Director of Security/Safety .... Mr. Edwin VAZQUEZ MEDINA
37 Director Student Financial Aid .... Mrs. Yanira MATOS
51 Director Continuing Education .... Prof. Luis R. RIVERA
38 Director Student Counseling .... Dr. Gilberto HERRERA
45 Dir Planning/Inst Research Office .... Mr. Gerardo JAVARIZ
18 Chief Facilities/Physical Plant .... Mr. Luis GARCIA
29 Director Alumni Relations .... Mrs. Jeannette AQUINO
96 Purchasing Supervisor .... Mrs. Widylia MEDINA

*University of Puerto Rico at Arecibo (F)

Call Box 4010, Arecibo PR 00614-4010
County: Arecibo | FICE Identification: 007228
Unit ID: 243115
Telephone: (787) 815-0000 | Carnegie Class: Bac-Diverse
FAX Number: (787) 880-2245 | Calendar System: Semester
URL: www.upra.edu
Established: 1967 | Annual Undergrad Tuition & Fees (In-State): $2,049
Enrollment: 3,790 | Coed
Affiliation or Control: State | IRS Status: 501(c)3
Highest Offering: Baccalaureate
Accreditation: M, ACBSP, ADNUR, CS, ENGT, JOUR, NUR TED

02 Chancellor .... Dr. Otilio GONZALEZ CORTES
05 Dean of Academic Affairs .... Dra. Ana GARCIA ADARNE
11 Dean of Administrative Affairs .... Prof. Rafael GARCIA TOULET
32 Dean of Student Affairs .... Dra. Nayla BAEZ
09 Dir Planning/Institutional Research .... Prof. Sylka TORRES
06 Registrar .... Mrs. Adilia RODRIGUEZ
07 Director of Admissions .... Mrs. Magaly MENDEZ
08 Head Librarian .... Prof. Robert ROSADO
15 Director Human Resources .... Dr. Luis LARACUENTE
38 Director Student Counseling .... Dra. Pilar CORDERO

04 Assistant to the Chancellor .... Prof. Juan PUIG
51 Dir Continuing Education/Prof Stds .... Mrs. Carmen TORRES
37 Director Student Financial Aid .... Ms. Daliana FRESSE
41 Athletic Director .... Mrs. Ruth NIEVES
13 Computing & Information Management .... Prof. Luis COLON
20 Assoc Dean of Academic Affairs .... Dra. Wanda DELGADO RODRIGUEZ
29 Director Alumni Relations .... Mrs. Mariely ORTIZ
92 Director Honors Program .... Dra. Jane ALBERDESTON
96 Director of Purchasing .... Mrs. Rosaura QUINTANA
18 Chief Facilities/Physical Plant .... Mr. Edwin RAMOS

*University of Puerto Rico at Bayamon (G)

Carr. 174 #170 Industrial Minillas, Bayamon PR 00959-1911
County: Bayamon | FICE Identification: 010975
Unit ID: 243133
Telephone: (787) 993-0000 | Carnegie Class: Bac-Diverse
FAX Number: (787) 993-8900 | Calendar System: Semester
URL: www.uprb.edu
Established: 1971 | Annual Undergrad Tuition & Fees (In-State): $2,014
Enrollment: 4,974 | Coed
Affiliation or Control: State | IRS Status: 501(c)3
Highest Offering: Baccalaureate
Accreditation: M, ACBSP, CS, ENGT, TED

02 Chancellor .... Prof. Margarita FERNÁNDEZ-ZAVALA
05 Dean Academic Affairs .... Prof. Carmen SKERRETT-LLANOS
32 Dean Student Affairs .... Ms. Ivonne MARCIAL-VEGA
06 Registrar .... Ms. Carmen CINTRON-OTERO
07 Director Admissions .... Mrs. Carmen MONTES-BURGOS
08 Director Learning Resources .... Prof. Maria de los Angeles ZAVALA-COLÓN
11 Interim Dean Administrative Affairs .... Mr. Melysa RODRÍGUEZ-BONANO
15 Director Human Resources .... Mrs. Mayra DIAZ
35 Director Student Activities .... Mrs. Maribelle PERGOLA-RIVERA
36 Director Student Placement .... Prof. Nelson VÁZQUEZ-ESPEJO
37 Director Student Financial Aid .... Mr. Marcos DE JESÚS
38 Director Student Counseling ... Ms. Guadalupe VEGA-GUTIERREZ
81 Director Biology .... Dr. Nilda APONTE-AVELLANET
50 Director Business Administration .... Prof. Norma PÉREZ
09 Director Planning & Inst Research .... Mr. Javier ZAVALA-QUIÑONES
53 Director Education .... Prof. María A. GONZÁLEZ DE RESENDE
54 Director Engineering .... Prof. Jorge VELAR-PRIETO
68 Director Physical Education .... Prof. Carlos MARICHAL-LUGO
79 Director Humanities .... Dr. Nora RODRÍGUEZ-VALLÉS
83 Director Social Sciences .... Dr. Elizabeth CRESPO-KEBLER
77 Director Computer Science .... Dr. Nelliud TORRES-BATISTA
75 Director Secretarial Sciences .... Prof. Nancy JIMÉNEZ-PÉREZ
72 Director Electronics .... Prof. Jesús ORTIZ-CINTRÓN
23 Director Health Services .... Dr. Adelaida L. ORTIZ-GÓMEZ
96 Director Purchasing .... Ms. María I. CRESPO-MARTÍNEZ
88 Director Special Services .... Ms. Shelciy COLLAZO-CASTRO
81 Director Physics .... Dr. Solange BENITEZ-RAMÍREZ
88 Director English .... Prof. Catherine TORO-CAMACHO
88 Director Spanish .... Dr. Raúl GUADALUPE
81 Director Mathematics .... Prof. Angel MORERA-GONZÁLEZ
88 Director Chemistry .... Dr. Solange BENÍTEZ-RAMÍREZ
18 Coord Facilities/Physical Plant .... Mr. Melysa RODRÍGUEZ-BONANO
10 Director Finance .... Ms. Evelyn AVILES-CABAN
21 Director Budget .... Mr. Wilfredo ORTIZ-RUÍZ
13 Director Information Systems .... Ms. Marcia RODRÍGUEZ-ORTIZ
105 Director Web Services .... Mr. Orlando ORENGO-ORTEGA
19 Director Security/Safety .... Ms. Yermarie COSME-FERNANDEZ
41 Athletic Director .... Mr. Gerardo BATISTA-SANTIAGO
43 Dir Legal Services/General Counsel ... Ms. Maribel GORBEA-DÍAZ

*University of Puerto Rico-Carolina (H)

PO Box 4800, Carolina PR 00984-4800
County: San Juan | FICE Identification: 030160
Unit ID: 243142
Telephone: (787) 257-0000 | Carnegie Class: Bac-Diverse
FAX Number: (787) 750-7940 | Calendar System: Quarter
URL: www.uprc.edu
Established: 1974 | Annual Undergrad Tuition & Fees (In-State): $3,056
Enrollment: 3,843 | Coed
Affiliation or Control: State | IRS Status: 501(c)3
Highest Offering: Baccalaureate
Accreditation: M, ACBSP

02 Chancellor .... Dr. Moises ORENGO
05 Dean of Academic Affairs .... Dr. Awilda NUNEZ
11 Dean Administrative Affairs .... Prof. Víctor PÉREZ
32 Dean Student Affairs .... Prof. Nitza AVILA
06 Registrar .... Mr. Abelardo MARTINEZ
15 Human Resources Director .... Mr. Gregory BERMUDEZ
09 Director of Planning/Inst Research .... Prof. Cristina MARTINEZ
08 Director Learning Resources Center .... Prof. Stanley PORTELA
51 Director Continuing Education .... Mrs. Luaida OYOLA
07 Admissions Officer .... Mrs. Celia MENDEZ
13 Coord/Dir Computer Sys Center .... Mr. Liberty ROLON
37 Financial Aid Director .... Mr. Rafael RUIZ
22 Affirmative Action Officer .... Mrs. Rosa QUINONES
88 Director Graphic Arts/Advertising .... Dr. Carmen ORTIZ
50 Director Banking/Finance/Insurance .... Prof. George OTERO
81 Director Natural Sciences .... Dr. Luis TORRES

88 Director Secretarial Sciences ... Dr. Ana FALCON
83 Director Social Sciences ... Dr. Gerardo PERFECTO
68 Director Physical Education ... Prof. Walbert MARCANO
88 Director Auto Tech/Mech Engineering ... Dr. Angel MALDONADO
79 Director Humanities ... Dr. Gerardo PERFECTO
88 Director Spanish ... Dr. Mayra ENCARNACION
88 Director English ... Prof. Wanda RODRIGUEZ
88 Dean Hotel Administration School ... Dr. Paul RIVERA
23 Director Health Care ... Dr. Zaida DIAZ
18 Supt Operations & Maintenance ... Mr. Herman MUNIZ
41 Athletic Director ... Mr. Arcadio OCASIO
10 Chief Business Officer ... Mrs. Sarahi GUADALUPE

*University of Puerto Rico at Cayey (A)

PO BOX 372230, Cayey PR 00737-2230
County: Cayey FICE Identification: 007206
Unit ID: 243151
Telephone: (787) 738-2161 Carnegie Class: Bac-A&S
FAX Number: (787) 738-8039 Calendar System: Semester
URL: www.cayey.upr.edu
Established: 1967 Annual Undergrad Tuition & Fees (In-State): $2,049
Enrollment: 3,687 Coed
Affiliation or Control: State IRS Status: 501(c)3
Highest Offering: Baccalaureate
Accreditation: M, ACBSP, TED

02 Chancellor ... Dr. Mario MEDINA
05 Dean of Academic Affairs ... Dr. Raul CASTRO
11 Dean of Administration Affairs ... Prof. Belma BORRAS
32 Dean of Student Affairs ... Dr. Rochellie MARTINEZ
08 Director Library ... Prof. Angel RIOS
06 Registrar ... Mrs. Daisy RAMOS
15 Director Human Resources ... Mrs. Gema FIGUEROA
56 Head Extension Division ... Mr. Jesus MARTINEZ
37 Director Student Financial Aid ... Mrs. Sonia PLACERES
38 Director Student Counseling ... Dr. Lino HERNANDEZ
36 Interim Director Student Placement ... Mrs. Rosa ORTIZ
13 Director Computer Center ... Mrs. Minerva DIAZ
45 Director Planning & Development ... Prof. Fernando VAZQUEZ-CALLE
07 Director Admissions ... Mr. Wilfredo LOPEZ
18 Director Facilities/Physical Plant ... Mr. Hector FELIX
23 Director Health Services ... Vacant
19 Director Security/Safety ... Mr. Carlos VAZQUEZ
92 Director Honor Program ... Prof. Irmannette TORRES-LUGO
20 Associate Academic Officer ... Vacant
41 Director Athletic Program ... Mr. Isamel RAMOS
29 Director Alumni Relations ... Mrs. Leilany C. RIVERA
96 Director Purchasing ... Mrs. Maria CORTES
43 Director Legal Services ... Mr. Francisco MORENO
88 Student Ombudsman ... Prof. Rolando CID
53 Education ... Dr. Ricardo MOLINA
79 Humanities ... Prof. Harry HERNANDEZ
83 Social Sciences ... Dr. Angel RODRIGUEZ
88 Hispanic Studies ... Prof. Miguel FORNERIN
88 English ... Prof. David LIZARDI
81 Chemistry ... Dr. Mayra PAGAN
65 Natural Science ... Dr. Glorivee ROSARIO
88 Biology ... Dr. Rosa del C TORRES
94 Women's Studies ... Vacant
09 Director Assess & Inst Research ... Prof. Fernando VAZQUEZCALLE
10 Chief Business Officer ... Mr. Jose COLON
88 Director Budgeting ... Mrs. Maria SANTIAGO
81 Mathematics-Physics ... Dr. Jose ALONSO
50 Business Administration ... Vacant
68 Physical Education ... Vacant
88 RISE Program ... Dr. Robert ROSS
88 Commission on Prevention of Viol ... Dr. Jose VARGAS
88 Interdisciplinary Research Inst ... Ms. Vionex MARTI
88 Museum ... Mr. Jonathan BERRIOS
100 Chief of Staff ... Prof. Gladys RAMOS
101 Secretary of the Institution/Board ... Mrs. Sylvia TUBENS
104 Director Study Abroad ... Vacant
105 Director Web Services ... Mr. William SANDOVAL
26 Chief Public Relations/Marketing ... Ms. Yari RIVAS

*University of Puerto Rico-Humacao (B)

Call Box 860, Humacao PR 00792
County: Humacao FICE Identification: 003943
Unit ID: 243179
Telephone: (787) 850-0000 Carnegie Class: Bac-Diverse
FAX Number: (787) 852-4638 Calendar System: Semester
URL: www.uprh.edu
Established: 1962 Annual Undergrad Tuition & Fees (In-State): $2,049
Enrollment: 3,628 Coed
Affiliation or Control: State IRS Status: 501(c)3
Highest Offering: Baccalaureate
Accreditation: M, ACBSP, ENGT, NUR, PTAA, SW, TED

02 Chancellor ... Dr. Jose M. ENCARNACION
05 Dean of Academic Affairs ... Dr. Carlos GALIANO
11 Dean Administrative Affairs ... Prof. Luis R. RODRIGUEZ
04 Assistant to the Chancellor ... Lic. Ricardo DIAZ
32 Dean of Student Affairs ... Prof. Ricardo ROHENA
20 Assistant Dean of Academic Affairs ... Dr. Anibal MUÑOZ
09 Dir Planning/Accreditation/IR ... Dr. Ivelisse BLASINI
06 Registrar ... Mr. Jorge ACEVEDO
07 Director of Admissions ... Mrs. Milagros ALVAREZ
08 Director of the Library ... Mr. Luis RODRIGUEZ
13 Dir Computer/Commun & Info Mgmt ... Mr. Jorge DAVILA
15 Director Human Resources ... Mrs. Janice A. MARTINEZ
10 Director of Finance ... Mrs. Ines SANCHEZ
37 Asst Financial Aid Officer ... Mrs. Brunilda LÓPEZ
88 Director Interdis/Intreg Dev Std ... Dr. Castula SANTIAGO
51 Dir Continuing Education/Extension ... Mr. Rody RIVERA
23 Director Health Services ... Vacant
18 Chief Facilities/Physical Plant ... Eng. Daniel ROSARIO
19 Director Security/Transit ... Mr. Ricky HERNANDEZ
96 Purchase Supervisor ... Mr. Javier A. MUYET
88 Student Ombuds Person ... Prof. Elizabeth R. HODGES
41 Athletic Activities Director ... Mr. Elmer WILLIAMS
21 Director of Budget Office ... Mrs. Iris N. CARRASQUILLO
108 Office of Institutional Assessment ... Prof. Viviana CRUZ
88 Director Svcs Population Disabil ... Prof. Magaly RODRIGUEZ
101 Sec of Academic Senate/Adm Board ... Prof. Amelia MALDONADO
29 Alumni Relations ... Mrs. Jose N. GONZALEZ
88 Envir Health & Occupational Safety ... Mrs. Angelica TORRES
26 Press Relations ... Mrs. Iraida CINTRON
50 Director of Business Administration ... Prof. Enrique SUAREZ
88 Director of Biology Dept ... Dr. Hector AYALA
88 Director of Chemistry Dept ... Dr. Rolando TREMONT
60 Director of Communication Dept ... Prof. Hector PIÑERO
53 Director of Education Dept ... Dr. Luz I. RIVERA
88 Director of English Dept ... Dr. Giovanna BALAGUER
79 Director of Humanities Dept ... Dr. Zoe JIMENEZ
81 Director of Mathematics Dept ... Prof. Barbara SANTIAGO
66 Director of Nursing Dept ... Prof. Alba PEREZ
88 Dir of Occupational Therapy Dept ... Prof. Mayra LEBRON
88 Director of Office System Adm Dept ... Prof. Ivelisse REYES
88 Director of Physical Therapy Dept ... Dr. Moises CARTAGENA
88 Dir of Physics & Electronics Dept ... Dr. Rogerio FURLAN
83 Director of Social Science Dept ... Dr. Alice OUSLAN
70 Director of Social Work Dept ... Dr. Evelyn CRUZ
88 Director of Spanish Dept ... Dr. Carmen ORAMA
92 Dir of Academic Honor Program Dept ... Dr. Maria MULERO
88 Dir of Communication Competences ... Prof. Margarita PARRILLA
88 Graphics Art Supervisor ... Mr. Carlos LAZU
22 Dir Affirmative Action/EEO ... Mrs. Mariolga ROTGER
46 Dir Subsidized Research & Programs ... Dr. Lilliam CASILLAS
88 Director Day Care Center ... Mrs. Carmen LUNA
88 Museum Director ... Dr. Cruz ORTIZ
88 Student Support Service Director ... Prof. Olga BERRÍOS
88 Upward Bound Director ... Mrs. Myriam CINTRON

*University of Puerto Rico-Mayaguez Campus (C)

PO Box 9000, Mayaguez PR 00681-9000
County: Mayaguez FICE Identification: 003944
Unit ID: 243197
Telephone: (787) 832-4040 Carnegie Class: Masters/M
FAX Number: (787) 834-3031 Calendar System: Semester
URL: www.uprm.edu
Established: 1911 Annual Undergrad Tuition & Fees (In-State): $2,049
Enrollment: 12,130 Coed
Affiliation or Control: State IRS Status: 501(c)3
Highest Offering: Doctorate
Accreditation: M, ENG, NUR, TED

02 Chancellor ... Dr. John FERNANDEZ VAN CLEVE
05 Dean of Academic Affairs ... Dr. Jaime SEGUEL
10 Dean of Administration ... Prof. Lucas N. AVILES
32 Dean of Students ... Dr. Francisco MALDONADO FORTUNET
49 Dean of Arts & Sciences ... Dr. Manuel VALDÉS PIZZINI
54 Dean of Engineering ... Dr. Agustín RULLÁN
47 Acting Dean Agricultural Sciences ... Dr. Raul MACCHIAVELLI
50 Dean Business Administration ... Prof. Ana MARTIN
58 Acting Director of Graduate Studies ... Dr. Didier VALDES
13 Director of Computer Center ... Mr. Martin MELENDEZ
06 Registrar ... Mrs. Xenia RAMÍREZ
08 Director of the Library ... Prof. Luis CASIANO TORRES
07 Director of Admissions ... Sra. Maria ALEMAÑY
37 Dir Student Financial Aid ... Mrs. Nannette HERNÁNDEZ
36 Director Student Placement ... Mrs. Nancy NIEVES
26 Press Office Director ... Mrs. Mariam L. ROSA VELEZ
45 Director Inst Research/Planning ... Prof. Mercedes FERRER
29 Director Alumni Association ... Mr. Luciano FIGUEROA-YOMARACHALIFF
15 Director Personnel Services ... Mrs. Lissette V. GONZÁLEZ
18 Acting Director Physical Resources ... Eng. Wilson ORTIZ
38 Int Director Student Counseling ... Dra. Zaida CALDERON
21 Director Financial Services ... Mr. Angél F. PÉREZ PACHECO
51 Director Continuing Education ... Prof. Silvestre COLÓN
19 Acting Director Security/Safety ... Ms. Marisabel FERNANDEZ
23 Director Health Services ... Mrs. Rosie TORRES
41 Director Athletic Activities ... Mr. Ray QUINONES
43 Director Legal Services ... Lcda. Gretchen HUYKE
108 Director Institutional Assessment ... Prof. Betsy MORALES

*University of Puerto Rico-Medical Sciences Campus (D)

PO Box 365067, San Juan PR 00936-5067
County: San Juan FICE Identification: 024600
Unit ID: 243203
Telephone: (787) 758-2525 Carnegie Class: Spec-4-yr-Med
FAX Number: (787) 758-2556 Calendar System: Other
URL: www.rcm.upr.edu
Established: 1950 Annual Undergrad Tuition & Fees (In-State): N/A
Enrollment: 2,221 Coed
Affiliation or Control: State IRS Status: 501(c)3
Highest Offering: Doctorate
Accreditation: M, ANEST, AUD, CAHIIM, CYTO, DA, DENT, DIETI, HSA, MED, MT, NMT, NURSE, OT, PH, PHAR, PTA, RAD, SP

02 Chancellor ... Dr. Noel J. AYMAT SANTANA
05 Dean Academic Affairs ... Dr. Ramon GONZALEZ
32 Dean Students Affairs ... Dr. Nitza RIVERA
11 Dean of Administration ... Prof. Carlos ORTIZ
63 Dean School of Medicine ... Dr. Edgar COLON NEGRON
52 Dean School Dental Medicine ... Dr. Ana LOPEZ
69 Dean Grad School Public Health ... Dr. Ralph RIVERA
67 Dean School of Pharmacy ... Dr. Wanda MALDONADO
76 Dean School Health Prof ... Dr. Barbara SEGARRA
66 Dean School of Nursing ... Dr. Suane SANCHEZ
100 Chief of Staff ... Mrs. Lilia FIGUERA
20 Associate Academic Officer ... Dr. Jose CAPRILES
13 Ctr Informatics/Technology Director ... Mr. Jose Luis QUINONES
43 Director Legal Services ... Mr. Raul BANDS DEL PILAR
26 Chief Information Officer ... Mr. Angel HOYOS
06 Registrar ... Mr. Reinaldo POMALES
08 Library Director ... Dr. Irma QUINONES
09 Director Inst & Academic Research ... Dr. Wanda BARRETO
24 Director Educational Media ... Prof. Luis ESTREMERA
35 Assoc Dean Student Affairs ... Mrs. Rosa VELEZ
07 Director of Admissions ... Mrs. Maribel ORTIZ
38 Director of Student Counseling ... Prof. Blanca AMOROS
37 Director of Student Financial Aid ... Mrs. Yolanda RIVERA
10 Chief Financial Officer ... Mrs. Yolanda QUIÑONES
15 Director Personnel Services ... Mrs. Maria Teresa GONZALEZ
18 Chief Facilities/Physical Plant ... Mr. Julio A. COLLAZO
96 Director of Purchasing ... Mr. Jose CARDONA
19 Director Security Office ... Mr. William FIGUEROA
108 Director Institutional Assessment ... Prof. Lillian RIOS
25 Chief Contracts/Grants Admin ... Dr. Marcia CRUZ

*University of Puerto Rico at Ponce (E)

PO Box 7186, Ponce PR 00732-7186
County: Ponce FICE Identification: 009652
Unit ID: 243212
Telephone: (787) 844-8181 Carnegie Class: Bac-Diverse
FAX Number: (787) 844-8679 Calendar System: Semester
URL: www.uprp.edu
Established: 1970 Annual Undergrad Tuition & Fees (In-State): $2,014
Enrollment: 3,230 Coed
Affiliation or Control: State IRS Status: 501(c)3
Highest Offering: Baccalaureate
Accreditation: M, ACBSP, ENGT, PTAA, TED

02 Chancellor ... Dr. Doris S. TORRES
04 Executive Officer III ... Vacant
04 Assistant to the Chancellor ... Prof. Lizzette ROIG
05 Dean Academic Affairs ... Prof. Carmen A. BRACERO
11 Dean Administrative Affairs ... Mr. Isaac COLON
32 Dean Student Affairs ... Mrs. Acmin VELAZQUEZ
20 Associate Academic Dean ... Dr. Joycette SANTOS
45 Dir Inst Research/Planning Officer ... Dr. Jennifer ALICEA
08 Director Library ... Prof. Brett DIAZ
06 Registrar ... Mrs. Marya Z. SANTIAGO
38 Director of Student Counseling ... Dr. Efrain RIOS
07 Director of Admissions ... Mrs. Emily MATOS
37 Director of Financial Aid ... Mr. Arturo ALMODOVAR
15 Director of Personnel Services ... Mr. Juan C. LEON
88 Director of Cultural Activities ... Dr. Jose L. PONS
13 Director of Computer Center ... Mr. Juan VEGA
18 Chief Facilities/Physical Plant ... Mr. Alberto GARCIA
40 Director Bookstore ... Vacant
41 Athletic Director ... Mrs. Lesbia COLON
23 Director Health Services ... Dr. Pedro COLLAZO
29 Director Alumni Relations ... Mrs. Valerie DÍAZ
30 Chief Development ... Vacant
19 Director of Security/Traffic ... Mr. German PIMENTEL
88 Coordinator Security/Safety ... Mrs. Celia GONZÁLEZ
22 Coordinator Affirmative Action ... Mrs. Marlene RODRIGUEZ

*University of Puerto Rico-Rio Piedras Campus (F)

PO Box 23300, Rio Piedras PR 00931-3300
County: San Juan FICE Identification: 007108
Unit ID: 243221
Telephone: (787) 763-7099 Carnegie Class: DU-Higher
FAX Number: (787) 764-8799 Calendar System: Semester
URL: www.uprrp.edu
Established: 1903 Annual Undergrad Tuition & Fees (In-State): $2,019
Enrollment: 15,659 Coed
Affiliation or Control: State IRS Status: 501(c)3
Highest Offering: Doctorate
Accreditation: M, ACBSP, BUS, CORE, CS, DIETD, JOUR, LAW, LIB, PLNG, SPAA, SW, TED

00 Chancellor ... Dr. María de los A. CASTRO ARROYO
02 Interim President ... Dr. Celeste FREYTES
05 Dean Academic Affairs ... Dr. Carmen H. RIVERA VEGA
11 Dean of Administration ... Dr. Grisel E. MELÉNDEZ RAMOS
32 Dean of Students ... Dr. Gloria DÍAZ URBINA
20 Associate Dean Academic Affairs ... Dr. Sunny CABRERA
50 Dean Business Administration ... Dr. José A. GONZÁLEZ TABOADA
48 Dean of Architecture ... Arq. Mayra JIMÉNEZ
81 Dean of Natural Sciences ... Dr. Carlos GONZÁLEZ
83 Dean of Social Sciences ... Dr. Isabel MONTAÑEZ

61 Dean of Law ... Ms. Vivian NEPTUNE
97 Dean of General Studies ... Dr. Vicky MUÑIZ
79 Dean of Humanities ... Dr. Agnes BOSCH
58 Dean Graduate Studies/ Research ... Dr. Pedro J. RODRIGUEZ ESQUERDO
53 Dean of Education ... Dr. Roamé TORRES
35 Asst Dean Student Affairs ... Ms. Estela PEREZ RIESTRA
38 Director of Student Counseling ... Mrs. Maria JIMENEZ CHAFEY
30 Int Dir Devel & Alumni Relations ... Mrs. Elsa MARIN
06 Registrar ... Mr. Juan M. APONTE
08 Director of Library System ... Dr. Miguel SANTIAGO
15 Director of Human Resources ... Vacant
07 Director of Admissions ... Mr. Ángel ECHEVARRÍA
13 Director of Computer Center ... Mr. Reinaldo RIVERA
62 Director Grad Sch Library/Info Sci ... Dr. José SÁNCHEZ
60 Director School of Communication ... Dr. Jorge SANTIAGO
58 Dir Graduate Sch of Planning ... Dr. Carmen CONCEPCIÓN
51 Dir Continuing Educ/Extension ... Dr. Carlos ROSADO
09 Director of Institutional Research ... Prof. Zulyn RODRIGUEZ
18 Chief Planning/Physical Devel Ofc ... Arq. Miguel PAGÁN
26 Chief Public Relations Officer ... Mrs. Lorna CASTRO
37 Director of Student Financial Aid ... Mr. Anibal ALVALLE
96 Director of Purchasing ... Mr. Ángel DÍAZ

*University of Puerto Rico at Utuado (A)

PO Box 2500, Utuado PR 00641-2500

County: Utuado | FICE Identification: 029384 | Unit ID: 243188

Telephone: (787) 894-2828 | Carnegie Class: Bac/Assoc-Mixed

FAX Number: (787) 894-1081 | Calendar System: Semester

URL: www.uprutuado.edu

Established: 1979 | Annual Undergrad Tuition & Fees (In-State): $2,049

Enrollment: 1,385 | Coed

Affiliation or Control: State | IRS Status: 501(c)3

Highest Offering: Baccalaureate

Accreditation: M, ACBSP, TED

02 Chancellor ... Dr. Raquel G. VARGAS GOMEZ
05 Academic Dean ... Prof. Melquiades ADAMES
10 Chief Business Officer ... Dr. Lisette MARRERO
32 Chief Student Life Officer ... Prof. Ana ARCE
08 Library Director ... Prof. Regina OQUENDO
09 Director Institutional Research ... Dr. Javier LUGO
06 Registrar ... Mrs. Ivelisse RIVERA
07 Director of Admission ... Mrs. María V. ROBLES
15 Int Director Human Resources ... Ms. Luz E. MARTÍNEZ
38 Director Student Counseling ... Mr. Amilcar GONZALEZ
37 Director Student Financial Aid ... Mrs. Edymariel CORTES
13 Director Information Systems ... Mr. Hector L. LOPEZ
19 Director Security/Safety ... Mr. Miguel TORRES
41 Director of Athletics ... Mr. Miguel RODRIGUEZ
47 Director of Agriculture ... Prof. Eladio GONZALEZ
50 Dir Office Systems/Business Admin ... Dr. Luis A. TAPIA
96 Director of Purchasing ... Ms. Dalimary MATOS
51 Director Continuing Education ... Mr. Miguel SALVA
53 Director Education ... Mrs. Vilmaris CESTEROS
65 Director Natural Sciences ... Dr. Vilmari LÓPEZ
79 Director Humanities/Spanish/English ... Prof. Hector M. REYES

University of the Sacred Heart (B)

PO Box 12383, San Juan PR 00914-8505

County: San Juan | FICE Identification: 003937 | Unit ID: 243443

Telephone: (787) 728-1515 | Carnegie Class: Masters/M

FAX Number: (787) 728-1692 | Calendar System: Semester

URL: www.sagrado.edu

Established: 1935 | Annual Undergrad Tuition & Fees: $5,780

Enrollment: 5,261 | Coed

Affiliation or Control: Roman Catholic | IRS Status: 501(c)3

Highest Offering: Master's

Accreditation: M, NURSE, SW, TED

01 President ... Dr. Gilberto MARXUACH-TORROS
84 Chief of Staff/Dir Enrollment Mgmt ... Mrs. Lourdes BERTRAN-PASARELL
05 Chief Academic Officer ... Dr. Eloísa GORDON
11 Dean of Administration ... Mr. Jose L. RICCI
30 VP University Relations and Develop ... Mr. Eduardo AROSEMENA
10 Int Chief Financial Officer ... Mrs. Rebecca QUINTERO
20 Associate Academic Dean ... Prof. Yezmin HERNANDEZ-SOTO
32 Associate Students Dean ... Prof. Pedro FRAILE
09 Director of Inst Research Office ... Dr. Maria DEL C. RODRIGUEZ
07 Director of Admissions ... Mr. Edwin RIOS
06 Registrar ... Ms. Mildred PINEIRO
26 Communications & Digital Media Dir ... Mrs. Sandra POMALES
21 Director of Budgeting ... Mrs. Maribel VALENTIN
91 Chief Information Technology Office ... Mr. Severo ALICEA
18 Chief Facilities/Physical Plant ... Mr. Jose L. RICCI
15 Director Human Resources ... Mrs. Marilyn FIGUEROA
29 Director Alumni Relations ... Mrs. Arelis MARRERO
08 Head Librarian ... Mrs. Sonia DIAZ
37 Director of Financial Aid ... Ms. June C. ANDRADE
39 Director Student Housing ... Mr. Carlos MOLL
41 Athletic Director ... Mrs. Mari BATISTA
50 Director Business Administration ... Prof. Arturo FIGUEROA
53 Director Education Department ... Dr. Migdalia OQUENDO
81 Director Natural Sciences ... Prof. Agda CARDERO
79 Dir Fac Intdspln Human/Social Stds ... Dr. Sylvia ALVAREZ
21 Internal Auditor ... Mr. Ricardo AGUIRRE
51 Assoc Director Continuing Education ... Mrs. Elvia AGOSTO
19 Director Security/Safety ... Capt. Jose LOZADA

VIRGIN ISLANDS

University of the Virgin Islands (C)

#2 John Brewers Bay, Saint Thomas VI 00802-9990

FICE Identification: 003946 | Unit ID: 243665

Telephone: (340) 776-9200 | Carnegie Class: Masters/S

FAX Number: (340) 693-1005 | Calendar System: Semester

URL: www.uvi.edu

Established: 1962 | Annual Undergrad Tuition & Fees (In-State): $5,014

Enrollment: 2,280 | Coed

Affiliation or Control: State | IRS Status: 501(c)3

Highest Offering: Doctorate

Accreditation: M, ADNUR, NUR

01 President ... Dr. David HALL
88 VP/Business Development/Innovation ... Dr. Haldane DAVIES
04 Director of Presidential Operations ... Ms. Una DYER
101 Liaison to the Board ... Ms. Gail T. STEELE
05 Provost/VP for Academic Affairs ... Dr. Camille A. MCKAYLE
46 Interim Vice Provost/ECC/RPS ... Dr. Frank MILLS
53 Dean School of Education ... Dr. Linda V. THOMAS
81 Interim Dean College of Sci & Math ... Dr. Sandra ROMANO
50 Dean School of Business ... Dr. Stephen A. REAMES
79 Dean College Liberal Arts/Soc Sci ... Dr. Emily ALLEN-WILLIAMS
66 Dean School of Nursing ... Ms. Beverley A. LANSIQUOT
104 Director of Study Abroad ... Dr. James S. MADDIRALA
84 Interim VP Access/Enroll Services ... Stephan T. MOORE
07 Dir Undergrad Recruit/Admissions ... Dr. Xuri M. ALLEN
06 Registrar ... Ms. Monifa J. POTTER
37 Director of Financial Aid ... Ms. Cheryl A. ROBERTS
41 Interim Athletic Director ... Dr. David SANTESTEBAN
31 Dir Community/Personal Develop ... Ms. ILene HEYWARD
32 Dean of Students-STT Campus ... Ms. Verna J. RIVERS
36 Dir Counseling & Career Services ... Ms. Patricia TOWAL
38 Director of Counseling Services ... Ms. Dahlia STRIDIRON
39 Asst Dir Student Affairs/Admissions ... Ms. Nicole F. JACKSON
32 Dean of Students-AAS Campus ... Mr. Stephan T. MOORE
106 Exec Director of Student Success ... Dr. Stephen W. MOORE
30 VP Institutional Advancement ... Mr. Mitchell NEAVES
29 Dir Annual Giving/Alumni Affairs ... Ms. Linda SMITH
44 Capital Campaign Manager ... Mr. Jose Raul CARRILLO
26 Director Public Relations ... Vacant
88 Special Events Coordinator ... Ms. Liza MARGOLIS
102 Dir Corp/Foundation/Govt Relations ... Mr. Richard G. CLEAVER
96 Purchasing Supervisor ... Mr. Eric CHRISTIAN
105 Webmaster ... Ms. Moneca K. PINKETT-WILKINS
10 VP Administration & Finance ... Ms. Shirley L. LAKE-KING
21 Controller ... Ms. Peggy SMITH
15 Director of HR/Org Development ... Mr. Charles Ronald MEEK
16 Assoc Dir HR/Org Development ... Vacant
40 Bookstore Manager-STT Campus ... Mr. Mervin Y. TAYLOR
40 Bookstore Manager-AAS Campus ... Ms. Shanta ROBERTS
19 Acting Chief/Campus Police/ Security ... Mr. Theodore E. GLASFORD
18 Director of Physical Plant ... Mr. Charles MARTIN
13 VP of ITS and Assessment ... Mrs. Tina M. KOOPMANS
14 Assistant Chief Information Officer ... Ms. Sharlene J. HARRIS
08 Director of Libraries ... Ms. Judith V. ROGERS
27 Marketing Manager/CELL ... Ms. Caroline FOLYDORE-SIMON

University of the Virgin Islands-St. Croix (D)

RR1 10.000, Kingshill VI 00850-9781

Telephone: (340) 778-1620 | Identification: 770173

Accreditation: †M

† Regional accreditation is carried under the parent institution in Saint Thomas, VI

Index of Key Administrators

A

ABU-GHAZALEH, Nabil 619-644-7100 45 J
nabil.abu-ghazaleh@gcccd.edu
ABU-SHAHEEN, Dania 914-813-9212 329 K
dshaheen@sarahlawrence.edu
ABUHAMAD, Alfred, Z 757-446-7979 489 B
abuhamaz@evms.edu
ABUKHALAF, Ronnie 561-912-2166 99 J
rabukhalaf@evergladesuniversity.edu
ABUSHABAN, Sahar 619-660-4654 45 I
sahar.abushaban@gcccd.edu
ABUTIN, Albert 714-992-7076 54 H
aabutin@fullcoll.edu
ABUZNEID, Abdelshakour, A 203-576-4113 89 C
abuzneid@bridgeport.edu
ACARDO, John 630-637-5754 149 H
jjacardo@noctrl.edu
ACCAPADI, Mamta, M 407-646-2185 107 O
maccapadi@rollins.edu
ACCARDI, Michael 978-837-5062 225 E
accardim@merrimack.edu
ACCIARDO, Linda, A 401-874-2116 426 D
lindaa@uri.edu
ACCORD, Richard, D 304-462-6182 513 C
richard.accord@glenville.edu
ACEBO, Kayla 918-631-2565 389 E
kayla-acebo@utulsa.edu
ACEVEDO, Beatriz 212-924-5900 336 I
bursar@swedishinstitute.edu
ACEVEDO, Dary 787-891-0925 533 G
dacevedo@aguadilla.inter.edu
ACEVEDO, Francisco 787-264-1912 534 D
facevedo@intersg.edu
ACEVEDO, Gerald, C 847-592-6600 151 D
gacevedo@princeinstitute.edu
ACEVEDO, Helmi 407-447-7305 102 D
hacevedo@ftcollege.edu
ACEVEDO, Ivonne 787-891-0925 533 G
iaecheva@ns.inter.edu
ACEVEDO, Jorge 787-850-9380 538 B
jorge.acevedo4@upr.edu
ACEVEDO, Luis, A 787-891-0925 533 G
luacevedo@aguadilla.inter.edu
ACEVES, Salvador, D 303-458-4144 82 L
saceves@regis.edu
ACEY, Denise 573-334-9181 267 C
denise@metrobusinesscollege.edu
ACHAN, Jennifer 661-395-4482 47 J
ACHARYA, Suresh 269-749-7666 240 A
sacharya@olivetcollege.edu
ACHEMIRE, Roy 918-293-3800 386 B
roy.achemire@okstate.edu
ACHENBACH, David 508-793-3320 217 C
dachenba@holycross.edu
ACHENBACH, USMS, Gerard 231-995-1203 239 C
gachenbach@nmc.edu
ACHENBACH, Laurie 618-453-7984 154 I
laurie@science.siu.edu
ACHESON, Carol 503-253-3443 393 D
cacheson@ocom.edu
ACHING, Gerard, L 607-255-4625 312 A
gla23@cornell.edu
ACHS, Carol 480-461-7742 14 D
carol.achs@mesacc.edu
ACHTER, John 715-232-2468 521 D
achterj@uwstout.edu
ACHTERBERG, Cheryl, L 614-292-2461 375 A
achterberg.1@osu.edu
ACHTERMAN, Douglas 408-848-4809 44 I
dachterman@gavilan.edu
ACIERNO, Lou 212-752-1530 318 F
lou.acierno@limcollege.edu
ACKERLEY, Roseanne 513-487-3234 315 F
rackerley@huc.edu
ACKERMAN, Aidan 617-262-5000 216 A
aidan.ackerman@the-bac.edu
ACKERMAN, Dean 812-888-4447 169 A
dackerman@vinu.edu
ACKERMAN, Debbie 217-732-3155 146 B
dackerman@lincolncollege.edu
ACKERMAN, Denise 845-758-7625 304 F
ackerman@bard.edu
ACKERMAN, Kathy 828-395-1522 350 E
kackerman@isothermal.edu
ACKERMAN, Tom 352-271-2905 109 C
thomas.ackerman@sfcollege.edu
ACKERMANN, Arthur, J 314-935-5582 274 N
ackermann@wustl.edu
ACKERMANN, Stephanie 309-341-5327 136 C
sackermann@sandburg.edu
ACKLAND, Terri 520-494-5227 12 J
terri.ackland@centralaz.edu
ACKLEH, Azmy 337-482-6986 201 D
asa5773@louisiana.edu
ACKLEY, Brian 607-844-8222 337 G
ackleyb@tc3.edu
ACKLEY, Darren 715-675-3331 524 D
ackley@ntc.edu
ACKLEY, Lavon 229-430-0415 116 A
lackley@albanytech.edu
ACOLASTE, Ras 703-878-2800 93 F
ACOSTA, Araceli 210-924-4338 452 F
araceli.acosta@bua.edu
ACOSTA, Esmeralda, M 623-845-3012 14 C
esmeralda.acosta@gccaz.edu
ACOSTA, Kathy 214-860-1416 456 E
kacosta@dcccd.edu
ACOSTA, Lydia, M 954-262-4640 105 J
lacosta@nsu.nova.edu
ACOSTA, Maria 773-838-7984 137 H
macosta68@ccc.edu
ACOSTA, Pilar 407-708-2432 109 E
acostap@seminolestate.edu
ACOSTA, R. Alexander 305-348-1118 111 A
ACOSTA, Vanessa 714-966-8500 73 G
vacosta@ves.edu
ACOSTA-FUMERO, Carmen, J 787-841-2000 535 I
cacosta@pucpr.edu
ACOVIO, Connie 210-486-3000 450 D
cacovio@alamo.edu
ACQUAAH, George 301-860-3610 212 D
gacquaah@bowiestae.edu
ACREE, Cheryl 229-333-2126 130 A
cheryl.acree@wiregrass.edu
ACREE, Elizabeth, A 520-621-5200 17 I
acree@email.arizona.edu
ACREE, Jenny 785-243-1435 179 N
jacree@cloud.edu
ACTON, Anne 617-422-7282 226 H
aacton@nesl.edu
ACTON, James 312-567-5000 142 I
jacton@iit.edu
ACTOR-ENGEL, Rose 215-635-7300 404 D
raengel@gratz.edu
ACUNA, Angela 602-787-7029 14 E
angela.l.acuna@paradisevalley.edu
ACUNA, April 801-818-8900 481 B
ADA, Raymond 719-632-7626 80 P
rada@intellitec.edu
ADACHI, Lesley, B 680-488-2471 530 E
lbadachi@gmail.com
ADACHI, Themy 510-430-3285 52 J
themy@mills.edu
ADADE, Anthony 508-929-8714 222 F
aadade@worcester.edu
ADAIR, Adam 870-512-7801 19 C
adam_adair@asun.edu
ADAIR, Brian 510-466-7269 57 E
badair@peralta.edu
ADAIR, Brian 541-885-1600 393 G
brian.adair@oit.edu
ADAIR, Charles 631-420-2198 335 E
charles.adair@farmingdale.edu
ADAIR, Kathy 906-248-3354 231 N
kadair@bmcc.edu
ADAIR, Matt 952-829-2459 244 J
matt.adair@bethfel.org
ADAIR, Russell, K 203-432-4469 90 D
russell.adair@yale.edu
ADAIR, Shandra 303-837-0825 76 L
sadair@aii.edu
ADAIR, Wendy, H 713-313-7455 470 D
adairw@tsu.edu
ADAM, Baba 530-895-2987 29 F
adamba@butte.edu
ADAM, Charles, A 563-333-6151 176 D
adamcharlesa@sau.edu
ADAM, Iddi 651-779-3447 249 A
iddi.adam@century.edu
ADAM, Jakob 512-313-3000 455 F
jakob.adam@concordia.edu
ADAM, Michelle 305-809-3279 100 N
ADAM, Nabil 973-353-5541 296 C
adam@adam.rutgers.edu
ADAM, Sharla 325-942-2041 472 B
sharla.adam@angelo.edu
ADAMES, Jose 214-860-2010 456 E
jose.adames@dcccd.edu
ADAMES, Melquiades 787-894-2828 539 A
melquiades.adames@upr.edu
ADAMO, Clare 860-632-3009 88 B
library@holyapostles.edu
ADAMO, Paul, J 607-436-2535 331 F
paul.adamo@oneonta.edu
ADAMS, Adam 712-722-6006 171 J
adam.adams@dordt.edu
ADAMS, Adam 870-759-4142 24 J
aadams@wbcoll.edu
ADAMS, Alexandra 443-412-2345 208 A
avictor@harford.edu
ADAMS, Allison 904-743-1122 103 G
aladams@jones.edu
ADAMS, Amanda 423-354-5143 446 F
acadams@northeaststate.edu
ADAMS, Amy 614-236-6242 364 N
aadams@capital.edu
ADAMS, Ann 312-491-2869 150 F
a-adams@northwestern.edu
ADAMS, Ann 360-438-4382 506 G
aadams@stmartin.edu
ADAMS, Ann Clay 404-687-4524 119 D
adamsa@ctsnet.edu
ADAMS, Anthony, T 334-229-5176 1 D
anthony-adams@alasu.edu
ADAMS, Barbara, B 847-866-3939 140 G
barbara.adams@garrett.edu
ADAMS, Barbara, L 803-536-8980 432 E
badams@scsu.edu
ADAMS, Barresa 478-445-7305 121 A
barresa.adams@gcsu.edu
ADAMS, Betty 713-797-7000 467 E
bnadams@pvamu.edu
ADAMS, Billy 254-267-7039 463 K
badams@rangercollege.edu
ADAMS, Blake 678-839-5053 129 E
badams@westga.edu
ADAMS, Brad 865-251-1800 444 A
badams@southcollegetn.edu
ADAMS, Brenda 501-450-1226 20 F
adams@hendrix.edu
ADAMS, Brett, C 443-352-4250 211 A
bcadams@stevenson.edu
ADAMS, Bruce 504-286-5432 199 I
badams@suno.edu
ADAMS, Carey 314-719-3609 265 C
cadams@fontbonne.edu
ADAMS, Carol 678-717-2233 128 F
carol.adams@ung.edu
ADAMS, Carole 515-643-6601 175 B
cadams1@mercydesmoines.org
ADAMS, Caroline 805-893-3285 70 E
caroline.adams@ucsb.edu
ADAMS, Catherine 706-396-8105 125 H
cladams@paine.edu
ADAMS, Cathryn 972-860-8269 456 C
cadams@dcccd.edu
ADAMS, Chadd 205-665-6155 9 B
cadams3@montevallo.edu
ADAMS, Charles, H 813-974-3087 112 C
chadams@honors.usf.edu
ADAMS, Chris 573-840-9666 273 A
cadams@trcc.edu
ADAMS, Christopher, J 631-451-4118 336 D
adamsc@sunysuffolk.edu
ADAMS, Clint 303-373-2008 83 B
president@rvu.edu
ADAMS, Corey 607-729-1581 312 E
cadams@davisny.edu
ADAMS, Dana 773-508-8077 146 G
dadams2@luc.edu
ADAMS, Dania 305-348-3875 111 A
dania.pearson_adams@fiu.edu
ADAMS, Dean 270-384-8036 191 E
adamsd@lindsey.edu
ADAMS, DeAnna 901-843-3885 443 L
registrar@rhodes.edu
ADAMS, Debbie 423-697-2493 445 D
debbie.adams@chattanoogastate.edu
ADAMS, Denise 530-895-2329 29 F
adamsde@butte.edu
ADAMS, Don 210-485-0088 450 A
dadams@alamo.edu
ADAMS, Edward 646-312-1190 307 A
edward.adams@baruch.cuny.edu
ADAMS, Edward, E 801-422-8271 480 C
ed_adams@byu.edu
ADAMS, Elizabeth 912-583-3242 118 B
eadams@bpc.edu
ADAMS, Elizabeth, H 434-924-4274 495 H
eha3w@virginia.edu
ADAMS, Elizabeth, T 818-677-2969 34 A
elizabeth.t.adams@csun.edu
ADAMS, Ellen 718-631-6269 309 E
eadams@qcc.cuny.edu
ADAMS, Gary 972-241-3371 455 K
gadams@dallas.edu
ADAMS, Grantley 860-738-6333 87 A
gadams@nwcc.edu
ADAMS, Gregory 414-288-1492 517 I
gregory.adams@marquette.edu
ADAMS, Jacob 909-607-3318 38 I
jacob.adams@cgu.edu
ADAMS, James, E 325-942-2071 472 B
james.adams@angelo.edu
ADAMS, Jan 903-510-3287 473 C
jada@tjc.edu
ADAMS, Jane, A 352-392-4574 112 A
jane-adams@ufl.edu
ADAMS, Janieth 601-979-0928 258 D
janieth.f.wilson_adams@jsums.edu
ADAMS, Jason 303-762-6936 79 I
jason.adams@denverseminary.edu
ADAMS, Jeff 479-788-7221 23 A
jeff.adams@uafs.edu
ADAMS, Jeffrey, M 336-841-4581 345 A
jeadams@highpoint.edu
ADAMS, Jeffrey, R 717-871-7462 415 F
jeffrey.adams@millersville.edu
ADAMS, Jennifer 925-473-7302 41 J
jadams@losmedanos.edu
ADAMS, Jennifer 334-347-2623 3 H
jadams@escc.edu
ADAMS, Jennifer 315-792-7810 336 C
jennifer.adams@sunyit.edu
ADAMS, Jennifer 614-236-6170 364 N
jadams@capital.edu
ADAMS, Jim, J 909-599-5433 48 K
jjadams@lifepacific.edu
ADAMS, Jimmy 713-718-2093 459 B
jimmy.adams@hccs.edu
ADAMS, John 415-485-9467 40 C
jadams@marin.edu
ADAMS, Jordan 918-540-6211 384 F
jordan.m.adams@neo.edu
ADAMS, Joshua 707-524-1731 63 G
jadams2@santarosa.edu
ADAMS, Julie 423-746-5251 447 E
jadams@twcnet.edu
ADAMS, Julie 973-655-7067 293 A
adamsju@mail.montclair.edu
ADAMS, Karen 785-242-5200 183 M
karen.adams@ottawa.edu
ADAMS, Karen 812-856-5596 162 F
kadams@iu.edu
ADAMS, Karen 918-495-7163 386 H
kaadams@oru.edu
ADAMS, Karen 956-296-1416 476 E
karen.adams@utrgv.edu
ADAMS, Karen, H 812-856-5596 162 E
kadams@indiana.edu
ADAMS, Kelly, L 315-792-3047 339 B
kadams@utica.edu
ADAMS, Ken 814-453-6016 420 I
ADAMS, Kent 620-672-5641 184 D
kenta@prattcc.edu
ADAMS, Kimberly 325-942-2122 472 B
kadams15@angelo.edu
ADAMS, Kimberly 253-752-2020 503 H
kimadams@faithseminary.edu
ADAMS, Kris 620-252-7137 180 B
adams.kris@coffeyville.edu
ADAMS, Lauretta 404-225-4604 117 A
lhannon@atlantatech.edu
ADAMS, Linda 706-379-3111 130 B
leadams@yhc.edu
ADAMS, Linda 610-738-3892 416 C
ladams@wcupa.edu
ADAMS, Lita 413-748-3695 228 E
ladams@springfieldcollege.edu
ADAMS, Mack 575-527-7552 301 C
madams@nmsu.edu
ADAMS, Mark 208-885-4977 134 G
marka@uidaho.edu
ADAMS, Mark 936-294-1158 471 D
ucs_mca@shsu.edu
ADAMS, Marsha 256-824-6345 8 F
marsha.adams@uah.edu
ADAMS, Mary, A 303-991-1575 76 I
mary.adams@americansentinel.edu
ADAMS, Matthew 570-454-6172 410 F
matthew.adams@mccann.edu
ADAMS, Melvin 207-255-1305 205 C
melvin.adams@maine.edu
ADAMS, Michael 310-506-4443 56 J
michael.adams@pepperdine.edu
ADAMS, Michael 910-893-1686 342 F
adams@campbell.edu
ADAMS, Michael, J 888-777-7675 503 H
mjadams@faithseminary.edu
ADAMS, Michelle 773-291-6100 137 G
madams@ccc.edu
ADAMS, Molly-Dodd 352-588-8291 108 C
molly-dodd.adams@saintleo.edu
ADAMS, Neale, J 515-574-1284 173 F
adams_n@iowacentral.edu
ADAMS, Patrick 516-876-3194 333 C
adamsp@oldwestbury.edu
ADAMS, Paul 785-628-5866 180 I
padams@fhsu.edu
ADAMS, Paul, S 570-408-4114 423 G
paul.adams@wilkes.edu
ADAMS, Perrie, M 214-648-2258 478 C
perrie.adams@utsouthwestern.edu
ADAMS, Phillip, D 912-358-3059 126 F
adamsp@savannahstate.edu
ADAMS, Randall 202-885-8664 94 E
radams@wesleyseminary.edu
ADAMS, Rebecca 252-940-6321 347 E
rebecca.adams@beaufortccc.edu
ADAMS, Rita, S 618-393-2982 142 B
adamsr@iecc.edu
ADAMS, Robert 575-492-2597 300 H
radams@nmjc.edu
ADAMS, Robert, J 386-226-6119 99 A
adamsr@erau.edu
ADAMS, Rodney 843-525-8219 433 B
radams@tcl.edu
ADAMS, Ron 541-737-2111 393 H
osu.provost@oregonstate.edu
ADAMS, Sally Ann 479-575-2000 22 I

ADAMS, Sarah .... 414-297-6595.. 524 A
adamss4@matc.edu

ADAMS, Sharman .... 605-642-6551.. 437 B
sharman.adams@bhsu.edu

ADAMS, Shawn .... 404-225-4005.. 117 A
sadams@atlantatech.edu

ADAMS, Sheila, V .... 662-329-7299.. 259 E
svadams@muw.edu

ADAMS, Sherman .... 859-846-5417.. 191 G
sadams@midway.edu

ADAMS, Shirley, M .... 860-515-3836.... 85 D
sadams@charteroak.edu

ADAMS, Stephanie, G ..... 757-683-4244.. 492 G
sgadams@odu.edu

ADAMS, Stephen .... 413-572-5394.. 222 E
sadams@westfield.ma.edu

ADAMS, Stevalynn, R ...... 757-823-8373.. 492 F

ADAMS, Susanne, H ...... 910-755-7302.. 347 H
adamss@brunswickcc.edu

ADAMS, Tammy .... 903-875-7348.. 462 J
tammy.adams@navarrocollege.edu

ADAMS, Terri .... 202-806-7040.... 93 A
tadams-fuller@howard.edu

ADAMS, Tiffany .... 563-425-5959.. 177 D
adamst26@uiu.edu

ADAMS, Tila .... 401-277-4909.. 426 A
madams@risd.edu

ADAMS, Vic .... 859-442-1175.. 189 D
vic.adams@kctcs.edu

ADAMS, Wesley .... 252-940-6423.. 347 E
wesley.adams@beaufortccc.edu

ADAMS COWES, Sheila ... 810-762-9532.. 236 C
sadams@kettering.edu

ADAMS-DUNFORD, Jane . 828-227-7234.. 359 A
jdunford@wcu.edu

ADAMS-GASTON,
Javaune .... 614-292-9334.. 375 A
adams-gaston.1@osu.edu

ADAMS-KEANE, Helen ..... 518-861-2596.. 320 A
hadamskeane@mariacollege.edu

ADAMS O'REGAN,
Michelle .... 603-641-7243.. 287 G
mkadams@anselm.edu

ADAMS SOMERLOT, Lisa 678-839-6428.. 129 E
ladams@westga.edu

ADAMSKI, Kathleen .... 509-527-4240.. 508 F
kathleen.adamski@wwcc.edu

ADAMSKI, M. Patricia ..... 516-463-6800.. 316 D
patricia.adamski@hofstra.edu

ADAMSON, Bonnie, J ..... 910-630-7307.. 346 E
adamson@methodist.edu

ADAMSON, Craig .... 215-416-3723.. 406 C
craigadamson@iirp.edu

ADAMSON, Elizabeth ...... 361-698-1297.. 457 D
eadamson@delmar.edu

ADAMSON, Richard .... 320-363-3164.. 254 N
radamson@csbsju.edu

ADAMSON, Wendy .... 218-855-8062.. 248 N
wadamson@clcmn.edu

ADAMUS, Anne M, G ...... 248-204-2208.. 237 B
aadamus@ltu.edu

ADANK, Nicki .... 507-453-2676.. 250 C
nadank@southeastmn.edu

ADANU, Sesime .... 607-778-5024.. 332 D
adanusk@sunybroome.edu

ADAUTO, Ricardo .... 915-747-5555.. 476 D
radauto@utep.edu

ADAUTO, III, Ricardo ..... 915-747-5555.. 476 D
radauto@utep.edu

ADCOX, John .... 423-354-5198.. 446 F
jmadcox@northeaststate.edu

ADCOX, Kathy, S .... 252-451-8274.. 351 F
kadcox@nashcc.edu

ADCOX, William .... 713-792-2275.. 477 C
william.adcox@uth.tmc.edu

ADDAE, Erasmus .... 956-872-2129.. 465 H
eaddae@southtexascollege.edu

ADDERLY-HENRY,
Denelta .... 727-873-4838.. 112 D
denelta@usf.edu

ADDINGTON, Eric, J ...... 218-299-3010.. 246 A
eaddingt@cord.edu

ADDINGTON, Gary .... 719-384-6859.... 82 A
gary.addington@ojc.edu

ADDISON, Jennifer, D ..... 276-739-2458.. 499 A
jaddison@vhcc.edu

ADDISON, Lathera .... 972-860-8146.. 456 C
laddison@dcccd.edu

ADDISON, Lynn .... 912-583-3285.. 118 B
laddison@bpc.edu

ADDISON, Marcia .... 330-494-6170.. 377 J
maddison@starkstate.edu

ADDISON, Steve .... 501-450-3199.... 24 G
saddison@uca.edu

ADDISON, Tricia .... 478-825-6301.. 120 F
addisont@fvsu.edu

ADDISON, Trip .... 912-478-1583.. 122 B
taddison@georgiasouthern.edu

ADDISON REID, Barbara . 617-349-8500.. 220 B
baddison@lesley.edu

ADDLEMAN, Eleanor, M . 717-766-2511.. 410 J
eaddlema@messiah.edu

ADDY, Cathryn, L .... 860-733-1700.... 87 E
caddy@txcc.commnet.edu

ADEBAYO, Bob .... 308-432-7078.. 281 H
badebayo@csc.edu

ADEBIYI, Songie .... 708-596-2000.. 154 E
sadebiyi@ssc.edu

ADEDOKUN, Michael ..... 703-746-8708.. 493 I

ADEGBOYE, David, S ..... 504-286-5327.. 199 I
dadegboye@suno.edu

ADELABU, Detris Honora 617-879-2184.. 229 G
dadelabu@wheelock.edu

ADELAINE, Michael .... 605-688-4988.. 437 F
michael.adelaine@sdstate.edu

ADELANI, Lateef .... 314-340-3319.. 265 H
adelanil@hssu.edu

ADELMAN, Michael, D ..... 304-647-6200.. 514 A
madelman@osteo.wvsom.edu

ADELSBERG, Lester .... 504-762-3224.. 196 D
ladels@dcc.edu

ADELSPERGER, Donna .... 219-989-2436.. 166 F
adelsper@pnw.edu

ADEM, Salma .... 817-272-2101.. 476 A
adem@uta.edu

ADEMOLA, Remi .... 713-313-4835.. 470 D
ademolara@tsu.edu

ADEN, Huca .... 276-376-3452.. 495 I
ha3d@uvawise.edu

ADEN-FOX Nancy .... 402-472-4344.. 282 M
naden1@unl.edu

ADER, Elaine .... 916-558-2062.... 51 D
adere@scc.losrios.edu

ADERHOLD, Mary .... 770-537-5719.. 129 M
mary.aderhold@westgatech.edu

ADERO, Chad .... 301-846-2531.. 207 F
cadero@frederick.edu

ADEWUMI, Michael, A .... 814-863-4030.. 412 F
m2a@psu.edu

ADEWUYI, David, A .... 804-257-5742.. 500 B
daadewuyi@vuu.edu

ADEWUYI, David, A .... 804-342-3937.. 500 B
daadewuyi@vuu.edu

ADEY, Penelope, S .... 518-388-6109.. 338 H
adeyp@union.edu

ADEYANJU, Matthew .... 231-591-2324.. 233 L
matthewadeyanju@ferris.edu

ADIA, Trish .... 305-507-5800.... 93 F

ADIA, Trish .... 305-507-5700.... 93 F

ADIA, Trish .... 954-378-2400.... 93 F

ADIA, Trish .... 561-904-3000.... 93 F

ADISHIAN-ASTONE,
Deborah .... 559-278-2083.... 32 F
debbiea@csufresno.edu

ADKINS, Adele .... 937-328-3857.. 366 E
adkinsa@clarkstate.edu

ADKINS, Amy .... 903-434-8121.. 462 M
aadkins@ntcc.edu

ADKINS, Andi .... 937-319-6074.. 363 D
aadkins@antiochcollege.org

ADKINS, Barbara .... 918-631-5003.. 389 E
barbara-adkins@utulsa.edu

ADKINS, Cathy, L .... 828-689-1395.. 346 C
cadkins@mhu.edu

ADKINS, Ernest .... 480-517-8202.... 14 G
ernest.adkins@riosalado.edu

ADKINS, Heather .... 210-567-2041.. 477 D
adkinsh3@uthscsa.edu

ADKINS, John .... 304-357-4779.. 511 E
johnadkins@ucwv.edu

ADKINS, Justin .... 814-332-3353.. 397 A
jadkins@allegheny.edu

ADKINS, Kay .... 606-326-2043.. 188 N
kay.adkins@kctcs.edu

ADKINS, Kenneth, R .... 734-487-8460.. 233 J
kadkins5@emich.edu

ADKINS, Marc .... 440-826-2768.. 363 M
madkins@bw.edu

ADKINS, Michael, T .... 804-257-5752.. 500 B
mtadkins@vuu.edu

ADKINS, Nathan .... 423-869-6306.. 441 E
nathan.adkins@lmunet.edu

ADKINS, Robert .... 724-503-1001.. 422 H
radkins@washjeff.edu

ADKINS, Shannyn .... 210-458-4229.. 477 A
shannyn.adkins@utsa.edu

ADKINS, Sheldon .... 405-425-5250.. 385 C
sheldon.adkins@oc.edu

ADKINS-EASLEY, Mona .... 757-823-8160.. 492 F
madkins-easley@nsu.edu

ADKINS-SHATO, Tabetha . 903-886-5876.. 468 D
tabetha.adkins@tamuc.edu

ADKISON, Steve .... 870-230-5134.... 20 E
sadkison@hsu.edu

ADLEBURG, Frances .... 850-973-1603.. 105 H
adleburgf@nfcc.edu

ADLEMAN, Chris .... 517-321-0242.. 235 C
cadleman@glcc.edu

ADLER, Ayden .... 765-658-4437.. 160 F
aydenadler@depauw.edu

ADLER, Brian .... 610-758-3375.. 408 H
bla212@lehigh.edu

ADLER, Brian D .... 580-774-3063.. 338 C
brian.adler@swosu.edu

ADLER, Brian U .... 229-928-1361.. 122 C
brian.adler@gsw.edu

ADLER, Kate .... 212-343-1234.. 321 B
kadler@mcny.edu

ADLER, Laurie .... 626-472-5121.... 42 I
ladler@esgvrop.org

ADLER, Michael .... 214-768-1864.. 465 J
madler@smu.edu

ADLER, Niall .... 408-855-5127.... 74 G
niall.adler@missioncollege.edu

ADLER, Robert .... 801-581-3791.. 481 M
robert.adler@law.utah.edu

ADLER, Shmuel .... 773-463-7738.. 155 J
sadler@telshe.edu

ADLER, Wendy .... 508-541-1542.. 217 G
wadler@dean.edu

ADLING, Jennifer .... 806-742-3844.. 472 C
jennifer.adling@ttu.edu

ADLISH, John .... 702-651-5664.. 284 H
john.adlish@csn.edu

ADMON, Hadass .... 626-264-8880.... 71 D

ADNEY, Chris .... 918-444-2500.. 384 G
adneyc@nsuok.edu

ADOLPH, Laurie .... 563-336-3351.. 172 A
ladolph@eicc.edu

ADORNETTO, Anthony ..... 740-588-1205.. 382 C
aadornetto@zanestate.edu

ADORNO, Margaret .... 909-621-8147.... 58 A
margaret.adorno@pomona.edu

ADORNO, Victor, T .... 787-780-0070.. 531 B
vadorno@caribbean.edu

ADORNO, Wilfredo .... 787-761-0640.. 537 C
decanoestudiantes@utcpr.edu

ADRIAN, Jane .... 913-360-7117.. 178 I
jadrian@benedictine.edu

ADRIAN, Loretta, P .... 714-241-6152.... 39 E
ladrian@coastline.edu

ADRIAN, Sherry, E .... 512-863-1905.. 466 G
adrians@southwestern.edu

ADRIANCE, Anne .... 212-229-5600.. 322 E
adrianca@newschool.edu

ADRIANO, Jonalee .... 707-638-5259.... 68 C
jonalee.adriano@tu.edu

ADSIT, Jason .... 716-829-7731.. 313 A
adsitj@dyc.edu

ADSIT, Karen .... 423-425-4007.. 448 F
karen-adsit@utc.edu

ADU-MIREKU, Samuel .... 910-672-1042.. 356 E
sadu-mireku@uncfsu.edu

ADUKAITIS, Megan .... 610-796-8225.. 397 D
megan.adukaitis@alvernia.edu

ADWELL, Jack .... 217-875-7211.. 152 C
jadwell@richland.edu

ADY, Tina .... 254-526-1402.. 454 A
tady@ctcd.edu

AEFSKY, Fern .... 352-588-7276.. 108 C
fern.aefsky@saintleo.edu

AEILTS, Larry .... 734-973-3480.. 242 G
laeilts@wccnet.edu

AELION, C. Marjorie .... 413-545-2526.. 220 F
maelion@schoolph.umass.edu

AESCHLIMANN,
Rodney, L .... 775-784-1113.. 285 A
rod@admin.edu

AFALAVA, Aotoia .... 684-699-9155.. 529 E
a.afalava@amsamoa.edu

AFDAHL, Tami .... 307-532-8206.. 526 G
tami.afdahl@ewc.wy.edu

AFFLECK-GRAVES,
John, F .... 574-631-4700.. 168 B
affleck-graves.1@nd.edu

AFFLERBACH, Kathie .... 215-248-6324.. 409 D
kafflerbach@ltsp.edu

AFFUSO, Paul .... 626-264-8880.... 71 D

AFOLABI, Rachael, O .... 412-578-6244.. 400 C
roafolabi@carlow.edu

AFOLAYAN, La Tanya .... 409-880-8422.. 471 A
latanya.afolayan@lamar.edu

AFROOKHTEH, Afshin ..... 714-816-0366.... 68 E
afshin.afrookhteh@trident.edu

AFSAHI, Armin .... 303-871-2647.... 84 B
armin.afsahi@du.edu

AFUNUGO, Emmanuel O 724-805-2473.. 419 B
emmanuel.afunugo@stvincent.edu

AFZAL, Cameron .... 914-395-2303.. 329 K
cafzal@sarahlawrence.edu

AGAN, Jeffrey .... 706-295-6974.. 121 F
jagan@gntc.edu

AGARWAL, Vaibhav .... 574-631-0946.. 168 B
vagarwal@nd.edu

AGATA, Caren .... 843-355-4131.. 435 A
agatac@wiltech.edu

AGATHA, Rachelle .... 619-388-2990.... 60 G
ragatha@sdccd.edu

AGBARAJI, Casmir .... 505-786-4113.. 300 E
cagbaraji@navajotech.edu

AGBAYANI, Amefil .... 808-956-4567.. 131 F
agbayani@hawaii.edu

AGBENYIGA,
DeBrenna LaFa .... 210-458-6878.. 477 A
debrenna.agbenyiga@utsa.edu

AGBOLI-ESEDEBE,
Angela .... 703-329-9100.... 93 F

AGBOOLA, Isaac .... 202-651-5224.... 92 C
isaac.agboola@gallaudet.edu

AGEE, Deborah, G .... 530-752-2396.... 69 A
dgagee@ucdavis.edu

AGEE, Doug, A .... 636-584-6714.. 264 M
doug.agee@eastcentral.edu

AGEE, Patty, A .... 660-263-3900.. 263 A
pattyagee@cccb.edu

AGEE, Steve .... 405-208-5276.. 385 E
sagee@okcu.edu

AGESILAS, Elie .... 787-891-0925.. 533 G
eagesila@aguadilla.inter.edu

AGHAYAN, Ali .... 805-893-8533.... 70 E
ali.aghayan@ehs.ucsb.edu

AGHO, Austin .... 757-683-3079.. 492 G
aagho@odu.edu

AGIDIUS, Erin .... 208-885-4285.. 134 G
erina@uidaho.edu

AGJMURATI, Nick .... 212-592-2000.. 330 C
nagjmurati@sva.edu

AGLAN, Heshmat .... 334-727-8355...... 8 A
aglan@mytu.tuskegee.edu

AGNE, Anissa .... 904-620-2698.. 112 B
anissa.agne@unf.edu

AGNELLO, Alissa .... 206-934-3746.. 506 J
alissa.agnello@seattlecolleges.edu

AGNELLO-VAZQUEZ,
Jacqueline .... 914-633-2548.. 317 B
jagnellovazquwz@iona.edu

AGNELLO-VELEY,
Josephine .... 860-906-5007.... 86 B

AGNER, Susan .... 704-637-4411.. 343 B
sagner@catawba.edu

AGNESI, Peter .... 954-201-5321.... 96 I
pagnesi@broward.edu

AGNETTA, Daniel, E .... 269-471-3302.. 230 H
agnetta@andrews.edu

AGNEW, Donna .... 847-578-8316.. 153 A
donna.agnew@rosalindfranklin.edu

AGNEW, F. Raymond ...... 518-327-6317.. 326 B
ragnew@paulsmiths.edu

AGNEW, Ina .... 918-293-4761.. 386 B
ina.agnew@okstate.edu

AGNEW, Melanie .... 801-832-2474.. 483 D
magnew@westminstercollege.edu

AGNOSTAK, Harry, M ...... 848-932-3929.. 295 F
harry.agnostak@rutgers.edu

AGO, Emmanuel .... 718-862-7996.. 319 L
emmanuel.ago@manhattan.edu

AGOONS, Akwai .... 478-827-3229.. 120 F
akwaia@fvsu.edu

AGOSTA, Frank .... 212-592-2000.. 330 C
fagosta@sva.edu

AGOSTO, Elilzabeth, L ..... 603-646-3124.. 286 J
elizabeth.lee.agosto@dartmouth.edu

AGOSTO, Elvia .... 787-728-1515.. 539 B
eagosto@sagrado.edu

AGOURIS, Peggy .... 703-993-1362.. 490 B
pagouris@gmu.edu

AGRAS, James, R .... 412-359-1000.. 420 I

AGRAS, James, R .... 412-359-1000.. 421 B
jagras@triangle-tech.edu

AGRAS, James, R .... 412-359-1000.. 421 A
jagras@triangle-tech.edu

AGRAS, Rudy, K .... 412-359-1000.. 420 I

AGRAWAL, Gail, B .... 319-335-9034.. 169 H
gail-agrawal@uiowa.edu

AGRAWAL, Jagdish .... 510-885-3291.... 32 E
jagdish.agrawal@csueastbay.edu

AGRAWAL, Mauli .... 210-458-4110.. 477 A
mauli.agrawal@utsa.edu

AGRE-KIPPENHAN,
Susan .... 503-883-2409.. 392 B
sagreki@linfield.edu

AGRELA, Ramona .... 949-824-5962.... 69 C
ragrela@uci.edu

AGREY, Loren .... 937-395-8837.. 371 D
loren.agrey@kc.edu

AGUADO-WARE, Joan, C 414-229-4304.. 520 D
aguadowa@uwm.edu

AGUE, Paul, E .... 619-201-8701.... 60 D
paul.ague@sdcc.edu

AGUIAR, Aracely .... 310-287-4374.... 50 E
aguiara@wlac.edu

AGUIAR, Jenny .... 617-730-7102.. 226 J
jenny.aguiar@newbury.edu

AGUILA, Nayda, G .... 617-964-1100.. 214 D
naguila@ants.edu

AGUILAR, Carmen .... 508-678-2811.. 223 A
carmen.aguilar@bristolcc.edu

AGUILAR, Charmaine .... 570-674-6247.. 410 K
caguilar@misericordia.edu

AGUILAR, Cheryl, M .... 909-607-1232.... 38 J
cheryl.aguilar@cmc.edu

AGUILAR, Diana .... 956-721-5126.. 460 F
diana.aguilar@laredo.edu
AGUILAR, Jose, A .... 951-827-3878.... 70 B
jose.aguilar@ucr.edu
AGUILAR, Milagros .... 787-878-6000.. 532 O
maguilar@icprjc.edu
AGUILAR, Steven .... 956-721-5361.. 460 F
steven.aguilar@laredo.edu
AGUILAR-VILLARUAL,
Elizabeth .... 210-486-3713.. 450 D
eaguilar-villar@alamo.edu
AGUILERA, Mary .... 503-581-8600.. 391 B
maguilera@corban.edu
AGUILERA, Rafael .... 806-894-9611.. 465 G
raguilera@southplainscollege.edu
AGUINALDO, Teresa .... 847-543-2288.. 138 C
com401@clcillinois.edu
AGUIRRE, Arturo .... 213-487-0110.... 42 H
info@dula.edu
AGUIRRE, Ilvis .... 787-878-5475.. 533 H
iaguirre@arecibo.inter.edu
AGUIRRE, Isaiah .... 951-343-5067.... 29 H
iaguirre@calbaptist.edu
AGUIRRE, Juan Carlos ..... 956-872-6782.. 465 H
jcaguirre@southtexascollege.edu
AGUIRRE, Katherine .... 631-451-4022.. 336 E
aguirrk@sunysuffolk.edu
AGUIRRE, Maria .... 928-317-6180.... 11 J
maria.aguirre@azwestern.edu
AGUIRRE, Maria, E .... 928-317-6180.... 11 J
maria.aguirre@azwestern.edu
AGUIRRE, Raymund .... 619-388-6411.... 60 E
raguirre@sdccd.edu
AGUIRRE, Ricardo .... 787-728-1515.. 539 B
raguirre@sagrado.edu
AGUIRRE, Tina .... 760-355-6467.... 46 J
tina.aguirre@imperial.edu
AGUIRRE, Tomas, A .... 903-886-5153.. 468 D
tomas.aguirre@tamuc.edu
AGUIRRE BATTY,
Mercedes .... 307-674-6446.. 526 M
mbatty@sheridan.edu
AGUNDEZ, Adrian .... 661-763-7737.... 67 F
aagundez@taftcollege.edu
AGWUNOBI, Andrew .... 860-679-2594.... 89 D
agwunobi@uchc.edu
AH YUN, Kimo .... 414-288-7133.. 517 I
james.ahyun@marquette.edu
AHA, Christian .... 856-225-6042.. 296 A
christian.aha@camden.rutgers.edu
AHEARN, Michael, J .... 978-867-4004.. 219 A
michael.ahearn@gordon.edu
AHEDO, Valentina .... 608-246-6461.. 523 F
vahedo@madisoncollege.edu
AHEE, Renee .... 313-927-1438.. 237 E
rahee@marygrove.edu
AHERN, Catherine .... 585-785-1273.. 314 D
catherine.ahern@flcc.edu
AHERN, Jack .... 413-545-2710.. 220 F
jfa@ipo.umass.edu
AHERN, Joseph, F .... 845-758-7178.. 304 F
ahern@bard.edu
AHERN, Karen .... 508-362-2131.. 223 C
kahern@capecod.edu
AHERN, Martin .... 617-984-1635.. 227 F
mahern@quincycollege.edu
AHERON, Michelle .... 919-497-3306.. 346 B
maheron@louisburg.edu
AHLBAUM, Mitch .... 212-772-4946.. 308 D
mahlbaum@hunter.cuny.edu
AHLEMANN, Tina .... 843-574-6142.. 433 D
tina.ahlemann@tridenttech.edu
AHLQUIST, Michelle .... 320-762-4918.. 248 J
michellea@alextech.edu
AHLUWALIA, Anoop .... 732-224-1987.. 289 I
aahluwalia@brookdalecc.edu
AHMAD, Maria .... 765-455-9203.. 163 A
activities@iuk.edu
AHMAD, Shahzad .... 320-308-4287.. 252 A
shah@stcloudstate.edu
AHMED, Andrea .... 520-383-8401.... 17 E
aahmed@tocc.edu
AHMED, Haroon .... 909-962-6762.... 39 A
hahmed@cst.edu
AHMED, Haseeb .... 419-448-2284.. 369 G
hahmed@heidelberg.edu
AHMED, Jameel .... 812-877-8956.. 166 H
ahmed@rose-hulman.edu
AHMED, Juzar .... 812-465-7160.. 168 E
juzar@usi.edu
AHMED, M. Monir .... 909-537-3132.... 34 C
mahmed@csusb.edu
AHMED, Mirza, F .... 313-496-2674.. 242 H
fahmed1@wcccd.edu
AHMED, Mustaq .... 419-358-3237.. 364 D
ahmedm@bluffton.edu
AHMED, Shahzad .... 320-308-5151.. 252 A
shah@stcloudstate.edu
AHMED, Shariq .... 909-748-8352.... 71 K
shariq_ahmed@redlands.edu
AHN, David .... 805-267-1690.... 48 F
AHN, Hee Young .... 323-731-2383.... 55 J
president@psuca.edu
AHN, Hongjun .... 714-533-3946.... 35 E
hjahn@calums.edu
AHN, Kelly .... 212-229-5600.. 322 E
ahnk@newschool.edu
AHN, Young Jin .... 714-533-1495.... 65 B
admission@southbaylo.edu
AHO, Lynn .... 906-524-8313.. 236 D
laho@kbocc.edu
AHO, Marie .... 906-227-2981.. 239 B
mariaho@nmu.edu
AHOLA, Scott .... 605-642-6359.. 437 B
scott.ahola@bhsu.edu
AHORRIO, Beatriz .... 212-694-1000.. 305 I
bahorrio@boricuacollege.edu
AHRENS, Emily .... 218-285-2203.. 251 F
emily.ahrens@rainyriver.edu
AHRENS, Rebecca .... 417-873-7523.. 264 H
bahrens@drury.edu
AHUMADA, Martin .... 928-724-6669.... 12 T
mahumada@dinecollege.edu
AHUMADA, Martin .... 928-724-6671.... 12 T
mahumada@dinecollege.edu
AICINENA, Steve .... 432-552-2675.. 478 B
aicinena_s@utpb.edu
AIELLO, Sara .... 808-689-2710.. 131 G
saiello@hawaii.edu
AIER, Justin .... 617-868-3450.. 218 E
AIKEN, Adel, G .... 724-847-5002.. 404 B
aaiken@geneva.edu
AIKEN, Donn .... 518-464-8765.. 314 A
daiken@excelsior.edu
AIKEN, Irene .... 910-521-6271.. 358 C
irene.aiken@uncp.edu
AIKEN, Ryan .... 413-775-1309.. 223 D
aikenr@gcc.mass.edu
AIKEN, William .... 910-272-3230.. 352 E
waiken@robeson.edu
AIKENS, Jane .... 641-472-7000.. 175 A
jaikens@mum.edu
AILSHIE, Leasa .... 903-586-2518.. 460 A
lailshie@jacksonville-college.edu
AILSTOCK, M. Stephen .... 410-777-2230.. 206 B
smailstock@aacc.edu
AIMONE, Chris .... 812-877-8498.. 166 H
aimone@rose-hulman.edu
AINLAY, Stephen, C .... 518-388-6101.. 338 H
ainlays@union.edu
AINLEY, Arden .... 360-416-7716.. 507 G
arden.ainley@skagit.edu
AINSLEIGH, Susan .... 413-565-1000.. 215 A
sainsleigh@baypath.edu
AINSLEY, Sharon .... 610-647-4400.. 406 B
sainsley@immaculata.edu
AINSLIE, Andrew .... 585-275-3316.. 338 K
andrew.ainslie@simon.rochester.edu
AINSLIE, Carolyn, N .... 609-258-1447.. 294 D
ainslie@princeton.edu
AINSWORTH, Emma, L ... 662-685-4771.. 257 A
eainsworth@bmc.edu
AINSWORTH, Jerald .... 423-425-4633.. 448 F
jerald-ainsworth@utc.edu
AINSWORTH, Patricia ...... 978-542-6446.. 222 D
painsworth@salemstate.edu
AIRD, Jeff .... 801-957-4090.. 483 A
jeffrey.aird@slcc.edu
AIREY, Linda .... 317-738-8225.. 160 J
lairey@franklincollege.edu
AIRHIHENBUWA, Collins 314-977-3240.. 271 K
airhihenbuwaco@slu.edu
AIROZO, Paul .... 508-830-5051.. 222 C
pairozo@maritime.edu
AISTRUP, Joseph .... 334-844-4026...... 1 G
jaa0025@auburn.edu
AITKEN, Derek .... 510-885-3877.... 32 E
derek.aitken@csueastbay.edu
AITSON-ROESSLER,
Mechelle .... 405-733-7308.. 387 I
maitson-roessler@rose.edu
AIZAWA, Hatsue .... 620-241-0723.. 179 L
hatsue.aizawa@centralchristian.edu
AIZENSTAT, Stephen .... 805-969-3626.... 56 B
saizenstat@pacifica.edu
AJE, John .... 609-984-1130.. 297 F
jaje@tesu.edu
AJIBADE, Victoria .... 718-368-6896.. 308 F
victoria.ajibade@kbcc.cuny.edu
AKAKPO, Koffi .... 419-755-4702.. 373 G
kakakpo@ncstatecollege.edu
AKANDE, Benjamin .... 573-592-5315.. 275 E
akande@westminster-mo.edu
AKBAR, Maksood .... 847-290-6425.. 150 C
provost@nwsc.edu
AKBARI, Hamid .... 507-457-5014.. 252 G
hakbari@winona.edu
AKCHIN, Lisa, G .... 410-455-2889.. 211 G
akchin@umbc.edu
AKE, Barbara .... 505-566-3218.. 301 J
akeb@sanjuancollege.edu
AKENS, Cathy .... 305-919-5943.. 111 A
akens@fiu.edu
AKERMAN, Patricia .... 320-308-5966.. 252 B
pakerman@sctcc.edu
AKERS, Judy .... 276-326-4260.. 487 F
jvannoy@bluefield.edu
AKERS, Lex, A .... 309-677-2721.. 136 B
lakers@bradley.edu
AKERS, Mary Anne .... 443-885-3225.. 209 F
maryanne.akers@morgan.edu
AKERS, Matthew, P .... 330-972-7954.. 378 G
akers1@uakron.edu
AKERS, Shawn, D .... 434-592-5451.. 491 D
sdakers@liberty.edu
AKEY, Lynn .... 507-389-2419.. 250 E
lynn.akey@mnsu.edu
AKEY, Stacey, L .... 920-923-7652.. 517 H
sakey@marianuniversity.edu
AKHATAR, Sumaira .... 510-356-4760.... 76 E
AKHAVI, Seyed .... 212-594-4000.. 337 F
sakhavi@tricollege.edu
AKHTAR, Shama .... 301-860-3402.. 212 D
sakhtar@bowiestate.edu
AKIE, Ronald, E .... 617-928-4790.. 226 B
reakie@mountida.edu
AKIN, Christopher, L .... 813-974-0898.. 112 C
cakin@usf.edu
AKIN, Daniel, L .... 919-761-2222.. 355 I
dakin@sebts.edu
AKIN, Hudson .... 765-641-4232.. 158 J
hakin@anderson.edu
AKIN, Jamie .... 325-942-2116.. 472 B
jamie.akin@angelo.edu
AKIN, JJ .... 507-933-7510.. 246 J
jakin@gustavus.edu
AKIN, Joeleen .... 404-471-6133.. 115 J
jakin@agnesscott.edu
AKIN, Renea .... 270-534-3461.. 190 H
renea.akin@kctcs.edu
AKINKUOYE, Nicholas .... 760-355-6215.... 46 J
nicholas.akinkuoye@imperial.edu
AKINLEYE, Johnson .... 919-530-6230.. 357 A
johnson.akinleye@nccu.edu
AKINS, Ceciley .... 847-866-3971.. 140 G
ceciley.akins@garrett.edu
AKINS, Mike .... 904-596-2464.. 113 J
makins@tbc.edu
AKKAWI, Kayed .... 312-935-6025.. 152 D
kakkawi@robertmorris.edu
AKL, Fred, A .... 610-499-4036.. 423 E
faakl@widener.edu
AKL, Hatem .... 732-255-0400.. 293 E
hakl@ocean.edu
AKMAN, Jeffrey, S .... 202-741-2880.... 92 D
akman@gwu.edu
AKOB, Joe .... 570-422-3291.. 414 H
jakob@esu.edu
AKOJIE, Patricia, A .... 270-686-4200.. 187 C
patricia.akojie@brescia.edu
AKRIDGE, Travis .... 478-299-3530.. 127 E
takridge@southeasterntech.edu
AKRIGHT, Jan .... 217-228-5520.. 136 A
akrightj@brcn.edu
AKS, Richard, M .... 848-932-3787.. 295 F
richard.aks@rutgers.edu
AKSELRUD, Larisa .... 425-739-8515.. 504 F
larisa.akselrud@lwtech.edu
AKSU, Mert .... 313-994-6620.. 241 G
aksumn@udmercy.edu
AKUJUOBI, Cajetan, M ... 936-261-1550.. 467 E
cmakujuobi@pvamu.edu
AL-AMIN, John .... 323-953-4000.... 49 H
alminja@lacitycollege.edu
AL-ASSAF, Yousef .... 585-475-2411.. 327 E
ymacad@rit.edu
AL-HAZZAM DAWASARI,
Elizabeth .... 480-860-2700.... 13 G
edawsari@taliesin.edu
ALADE, Ayodele, J .... 410-651-6327.. 212 B
ajalade@umes.edu
ALAI, Meghan .... 732-906-2622.. 292 E
malai@middlesexcc.edu
ALAIMO, Joseph .... 215-951-1974.. 407 A
alaimo@lasalle.edu
ALAIMO, Kathleen .... 773-298-3191.. 153 H
alaimo@sxu.edu
ALAIMO, Kathleen .... 773-298-3090.. 153 H
alaimo@sxu.edu
ALAM, Maria .... 901-678-2867.. 445 C
malam@memphis.edu
ALAM, Mohammad .... 212-220-1299.. 307 B
malam@bmcc.cuny.edu
ALAMAT, Natalie .... 303-477-7240.... 80 H
nataliea@heritage-education.com
ALAMEIDA, Marshall .... 415-485-9326.... 40 C
malameida@marin.edu
ALANDER, Link .... 832-813-6842.. 461 B
link.s.alander@lonestar.edu
ALANGAR, Sadhana .... 734-864-4202.. 232 F
sadhana@cleary.edu
ALANKO, Lynda, J .... 540-887-7161.. 491 G
lalanko@mbc.edu
ALARID, Jandee .... 409-772-9868.. 478 A
jalarid@utmb.edu
ALASIO, Claire .... 732-571-3463.. 292 F
calasio@monmouth.edu
ALATORRE, Helen, M ...... 405-466-3445.. 383 M
halatorre@langston.edu
ALAVALAPATI, Janaki, R . 334-844-1007...... 1 G
jra0024@auburn.edu
ALAVI, Maryam .... 404-894-2600.. 121 D
maryam.alavi@scheller.gatech.edu
ALBA, Suzanna .... 401-456-8086.. 425 E
salba@ric.edu
ALBANESE, Karli .... 909-599-5433.... 48 K
kalbanese@lifepacific.edu
ALBANESE, Linda .... 516-323-4025.. 321 H
lalbanese@molloy.edu
ALBANESE, Marc .... 610-282-1100.. 402 B
marc.albanese@desales.edu
ALBANO, John .... 209-386-6777.... 52 E
albano.j@mccd.edu
ALBANO, Ralph .... 202-319-5218.... 92 A
albano@cua.edu
ALBANO, Stephen, D .... 609-984-1100.. 297 F
salbano@tesu.edu
ALBARRAN, Agustin .... 619-644-7161.... 45 J
agustin.albarran@gcccd.edu
ALBARRAN, Charo .... 707-256-7105.... 53 H
calbarran@napavalley.edu
ALBARRAN, Miguel .... 787-622-8000.. 537 B
malbarran@pupr.edu
ALBAWANEH, Mahmoud . 949-783-4807.... 74 A
malbawaneh@westcoastuniversity.edu
ALBAWANEH, Mahmoud . 562-985-5462.... 33 B
mahmoud.albawaneh@csulb.edu
ALBAYYARI, Jay .... 419-586-0341.. 381 H
jay.albayyari@wright.edu
ALBERDESTON, Jane .... 787-815-0000.. 537 F
jane.alberdeston@upr.edu
ALBERS, Jhett .... 605-642-6885.. 437 B
jhett.albers@bhsu.edu
ALBERT, Angelique .... 406-275-4820.. 278 E
angelique_albert@skc.edu
ALBERT, Barbara, J .... 570-326-3761.. 413 O
balbert@pct.edu
ALBERT, David .... 773-702-9800.. 156 D
dalbert@medicine.bsd.uchicago.edu
ALBERT, Gene .... 516-773-5000.. 529 B
albertg@usmma.edu
ALBERT, Jennifer .... 631-656-2128.. 314 F
jennifer.albert@ftc.edu
ALBERT, Joe .... 509-313-3564.. 504 A
albert@gonzaga.edu
ALBERT, Juline .... 712-274-6400.. 177 I
juline.albert@witcc.edu
ALBERT, Karen .... 215-951-2843.. 416 G
albertk@philau.edu
ALBERT, Katrice .... 612-624-0594.. 255 H
ka225@umn.edu
ALBERT, Marianne .... 724-222-5330.. 412 E
malbert@penncommercial.edu
ALBERT, Neil .... 315-228-7397.. 310 G
nalbert@colgate.edu
ALBERT, Patricia .... 336-272-7102.. 344 G
patricia.albert@greensboro.edu
ALBERT, OP, Peg .... 517-264-7000.. 241 A
palbert@sienaheights.edu
ALBERT, Rita .... 561-237-7231.. 104 O
ralbert@lynn.edu
ALBERT, Robert .... 606-783-5158.. 191 H
r.albert@moreheadstate.edu
ALBERT, Scott .... 724-738-9000.. 416 B
ALBERT, Wendy .... 717-867-6302.. 408 F
walbert@lvc.edu
ALBERT-KNOPP, Heather . 207-801-5640.. 202 H
halbert-knopp@coa.edu
ALBERT LINK, Cindy .... 617-266-1400.. 215 G
ALBERTA, Vince .... 702-895-5165.. 284 L
vince.alberta@unlv.edu
ALBERTO, Paul, A .... 404-413-8100.. 122 D
palberto@gsu.edu
ALBERTS, Eugene, R .... 608-796-3849.. 522 O
eralberts@viterbo.edu
ALBERTS, Kristin, R .... 904-256-7180.. 103 D
kalbert@ju.edu
ALBERTS, Trev .... 402-554-2305.. 283 B
talberts@unomaha.edu
ALBERTSON, Hattie .... 701-228-5454.. 361 D
hattie.c.albertson@dakotacollege.edu
ALBERTSON, Kay, H .... 919-735-5151.. 354 A
kha@waynecc.edu
ALBIERI, Guilherme .... 212-938-5500.. 334 F
galbieri@sunyopt.edu
ALBIN-HILL, Jill .... 708-524-6980.. 139 F
jalbin@dom.edu
ALBINA, Adam, R .... 603-641-7266.. 287 G
aalbina@anselm.edu
ALBINI, Marisa .... 401-333-7150.. 425 A
malbini@ccri.edu

ALI, Abe .... 661-336-5141.... 47 I
abeali@kccd.edu
ALI, Cheryl .... 609-497-7756.. 294 C
cheryl.ali@ptsem.edu
ALI, Craig .... 419-755-4705.. 373 G
cali@ncstatecollege.edu
ALI, Hesham .... 402-554-2380.. 283 B
hali@unomaha.edu
ALI, Ibrahim .... 909-274-4225.... 53 C
iali@mtsac.edu
ALI, Mahmood .... 641-472-1126.. 175 A
housing@mum.edu
ALI, Masoom .... 516-572-7113.. 322 C
masoom.ali@ncc.edu
ALI, Mohammad .... 937-376-6235.. 365 H
mali@centralstate.edu
ALI, Nicholas, D .... 412-531-4433.. 401 K
info@deantech.edu
ALI, Noorjhan .... 847-679-3135.. 144 G
nali@ksi.edu
ALI, Richard, D .... 412-531-4433.. 401 K
info@deantech.edu
ALI, Rita .... 309-694-5561.. 141 F
rali@icc.edu
ALIBERTI, Fred .... 518-629-7210.. 316 G
f.aliberti@hvcc.edu
ALIBRANDI, Cynthia, A .... 315-445-4462.. 318 E
alibraca@lemoyne.edu
ALIC, Mersiha .... 260-203-2914.. 167 E
alicm@trine.edu
ALICANDRO, Jean .... 860-832-1664.... 85 F
alicandro@ccsu.edu
ALICEA, Dennis .... 787-743-7979.. 536 A
ut_dalicea@suagm.edu
ALICEA, Edwin .... 787-725-8120.. 532 K
ealicea@eap.edu
ALICEA, Jennifer .... 787-844-8181.. 538 E
jennifer.alicea@upr.edu
ALICEA, Joseph .... 718-518-4377.. 308 C
jalicea@hostos.cuny.edu
ALICEA, Marisa .... 312-362-8772.. 139 C
malicea@depaul.edu
ALICEA, Priscilla .... 401-232-6715.. 424 K
palicea@bryant.edu
ALICEA, Severo .... 787-728-1515.. 539 B
salicea@sagrado.edu
ALICEA, Victor, G .... 212-694-1000.. 305 I
valicea@boricuacollege.edu
ALICEA-MALDONADO,
Rafael .... 585-345-6820.. 315 C
ralicea-maldonado@genesee.edu
ALIFFI, Kelley .... 651-730-5100.. 246 I
kaliffi@globeuniversity.edu
ALIG, Julie .... 978-934-2506.. 221 A
julie_alig@uml.edu
ALINIAZEE, M, T .... 847-290-6425.. 150 C
president@nwsc.edu
ALIPOE, Dovi .... 601-877-6543.. 256 F
alipoe@alcorn.edu
ALISHIO, Kip, C .... 513-529-4634.. 372 K
alishikc@miamioh.edu
ALIX, Jeff .... 419-289-5093.. 363 J
jalix@ashland.edu
ALKALY, Benjamin .... 310-338-7854.... 51 E
benjamin.alkaly@lmu.edu
ALKANAT, Gokhan .... 334-244-4023...... 2 A
galkanat@aum.edu
ALKIRE, Amy .... 612-330-1188.. 244 I
alkire@augsburg.edu
ALKIRE, Laurie .... 308-635-6036.. 283 D
alkirel@wncc.edu
ALLADA, Venkata .... 573-341-4573.. 274 B
allada@mst.edu
ALLAN, Bill .... 316-295-5567.. 181 B
ballan@friends.edu
ALLAN, Linda .... 412-809-5100.. 417 D
allan.linda@pti.edu
ALLAN, Mark .... 215-951-1395.. 407 A
allanm@lasalle.edu
ALLAN, Sarah .... 740-374-8716.. 381 A
sallan@wscc.edu
ALLARD, Don .... 919-761-2310.. 355 I
dallard@sebts.edu
ALLARD, Elaine .... 603-535-2458.. 288 F
eallard@plymouth.edu
ALLARD, Ingrid, M .... 518-262-5919.. 303 E
allardi@mail.amc.edu
ALLARD, Lee .... 518-782-6737.. 330 E
lallard@siena.edu
ALLARD, Michael .... 518-828-4181.. 311 D
allard@sunycgcc.edu
ALLARD, Nicholas, W .... 718-780-7901.. 305 L
nicholas.allard@brooklaw.edu
ALLBAUGH, Jonathan .... 714-556-3610.... 73 B
jonathan.allbaugh@vanguard.edu
ALLBRIGHT, Jacque .... 512-245-2521.. 471 F
ja14@txstate.edu
ALLBRITTEN, Jeffery .... 239-489-9211.. 101 F
president@fsw.edu
ALLCORN, Terry, A .... 417-268-6003.. 262 H
tallcorn@gobbc.edu
ALLDREDGE, Annita .... 415-749-4560.... 61 B
aalldredge@sfai.edu
ALLDREDGE, Brian .... 415-514-0421.... 70 D
brian.alldredge@ucsf.edu
ALLDREDGE, Kari .... 865-974-1350.. 448 E
kalldre1@utk.edu
ALLDRITT, Leslie .... 715-682-1358.. 518 H
lalldritt@northland.edu
ALLEE, Kelly .... 217-234-5215.. 145 D
kallee@lakeland.cc.il.us
ALLEGRETTA, Kerri .... 516-403-5392.. 339 G
kallegretta@webb.edu
ALLEM, Deb .... 970-247-7212.... 80 D
allen_d@fortlewis.edu
ALLEMAN, Vickie .... 713-942-3466.. 475 J
alleman@stthom.edu
ALLEMAN-BEYERS,
Natalie .... 913-468-8500.. 182 A
nalleman@jccc.edu
ALLEN, Al .... 386-822-8808.. 113 B
aallen@stetson.edu
ALLEN, Algia .... 972-563-9573.. 473 B
aallen@tvcc.edu
ALLEN, Amanda .... 670-237-6722.. 530 D
amanda.allen@marianas.edu
ALLEN, Amy .... 320-762-4591.. 248 J
amya@alextech.edu
ALLEN, Andrew .... 651-227-9171.. 253 S
andrew.allen@mitchellhamline.edu
ALLEN, Andrew, T .... 619-260-4553.... 72 B
provost@sandiego.edu
ALLEN, Angela .... 806-651-8482.. 469 D
aallen@mail.wtamu.edu
ALLEN, Anita, L .... 215-898-4032.. 421 E
aallen@law.upenn.edu
ALLEN, Ann Marie .... 435-586-7700.. 481 N
mciffallen@suu.edu
ALLEN, Anna, M .... 215-951-1374.. 407 A
aallen@lasalle.edu
ALLEN, Anthony .... 718-933-6700.. 321 I
aallen@monroecollege.edu
ALLEN, Anthony, W .... 573-629-3252.. 265 G
anthony.allen@hlg.edu
ALLEN, Augusta .... 610-341-5870.. 403 B
aallen6@eastern.edu
ALLEN, Betsy .... 270-824-1727.. 190 B
betsy.allen@kctcs.edu
ALLEN, Bill .... 434-381-6142.. 494 M
ballen@sbc.edu
ALLEN, Bonita .... 251-405-7040...... 2 D
ballen@bishop.edu
ALLEN, Bonnie, J .... 615-898-2772.. 444 G
bonnie.allen@mtsu.edu
ALLEN, Brenda .... 303-315-2104.... 84 A
brenda.j.allen@ucdenver.edu
ALLEN, Brenda .... 336-750-2200.. 359 B
allenba@wssu.edu
ALLEN, Brian .... 815-939-5258.. 150 I
ballen@olivet.edu
ALLEN, Brian, K .... 608-785-8558.. 520 C
ballen@uwlax.edu
ALLEN, C. Leonard .... 615-966-6064.. 441 F
leonard.allen@lipscomb.edu
ALLEN, Calhoun .... 318-869-5120.. 194 I
callen@centenary.edu
ALLEN, Carol, M .... 443-412-2144.. 208 A
caallen@harford.edu
ALLEN, Carolyn, H .... 479-575-6702.... 22 I
challen@uark.edu
ALLEN, SJ, Charles, H .... 203-254-4000.... 87 G
executive@fairfield.edu
ALLEN, Charley, B .... 270-809-3919.. 192 A
callen@murraystate.edu
ALLEN, Chris .... 503-223-8188.. 394 H
ALLEN, Cindy .... 517-787-0800.. 235 G
allencynthiaa@jccmi.edu
ALLEN, Clifford .... 503-725-5053.. 394 G
cliffa@pdx.edu
ALLEN, Craig .... 817-257-7865.. 469 G
c.allen2@tcu.edu
ALLEN, Dana .... 505-277-5808.. 302 F
ALLEN, Daniel .... 602-331-7500.... 11 K
dallen@aii.edu
ALLEN, Daniel, T .... 267-502-2636.. 398 J
daniel.allen@brynathyn.edu
ALLEN, Darren .... 205-929-6361...... 5 D
dallen@lawsonstate.edu
ALLEN, David .... 508-678-2811.. 223 A
david.allen@bristolcc.edu
ALLEN, David .... 817-923-1921.. 466 E
dallen@swbts.edu
ALLEN, JR., David .... 386-481-2497.... 96 H
allend@cookman.edu
ALLEN, David, D .... 662-915-7265.. 261 B
allen@olemiss.edu
ALLEN, David, N .... 520-621-7262.... 17 I
allendn@email.arizona.edu
ALLEN, David, P .... 253-535-7524.. 505 G
david.allen@plu.edu
ALLEN, David, W .... 916-339-4336.... 53 F
dallen@mticollege.edu
ALLEN, Dee Dee .... 501-450-1228.... 20 F
allendd@hendrix.edu
ALLEN, Dennis .... 541-776-9942.. 394 A
ALLEN, Diane .... 312-935-6023.. 152 D
dallen@robertmorris.edu
ALLEN, Diane, D .... 410-548-3374.. 213 A
ddallen@salisbury.edu
ALLEN, Donna, Y .... 870-235-4012.... 22 F
dyallen@saumag.edu
ALLEN, Douglas, W .... 320-222-5201.. 251 G
douglas.allen@ridgewater.edu
ALLEN, OP,
Elizabeth Anne .... 615-297-7545.. 438 F
sreanne@aquinascollege.edu
ALLEN, Emily .... 302-343-4500.... 33 C
eallen3@calstatela.edu
ALLEN, Emily .... 405-208-5000.. 385 E
ALLEN, Eric .... 724-589-2186.. 420 D
eallen@thiel.edu
ALLEN, Erika .... 208-792-2458.. 134 A
elallen@lcsc.edu
ALLEN, Erin .... 319-335-3305.. 169 H
allene@uifoundation.org
ALLEN, Erin .... 704-991-0261.. 353 E
eallen4640@stanly.edu
ALLEN, Forrest .... 432-685-4580.. 461 H
fallen@midland.edu
ALLEN, Gary, K .... 573-882-9200.. 273 D
allengk@umsystem.edu
ALLEN, Gary, K .... 573-882-9200.. 273 E
allengk@missouri.edu
ALLEN, George .... 517-607-2556.. 235 E
gallen@hillsdale.edu
ALLEN, Greg .... 402-557-7581.. 278 I
greg.allen@bellevue.edu
ALLEN, Helen .... 205-348-7949...... 8 D
helen.allen@ua.edu
ALLEN, Hilary .... 919-760-8548.. 346 D
allenh@meredith.edu
ALLEN, Ivan .... 478-757-3501.. 118 G
iallen@centralgatech.edu
ALLEN, Ivan, H .... 478-988-6833.. 118 H
iallen@centralgatech.edu
ALLEN, James .... 618-536-3465.. 154 H
jsallen@siu.edu
ALLEN, JR., James .... 301-387-3006.. 207 G
james.allen@garrettcollege.edu
ALLEN, James, S .... 618-453-7653.. 154 I
jsallen@siu.edu
ALLEN, Janine .... 503-581-8166.. 391 B
jallen@corban.edu
ALLEN, Jason, K .... 816-414-3700.. 268 D
president@mbts.edu
ALLEN, Jay, S .... 270-707-3705.. 189 G
jay.allen@kctcs.edu
ALLEN, Jeff .... 252-492-2061.. 353 H
allenjl@vgcc.edu
ALLEN, Jen .... 706-419-1119.. 119 G
jen.allen@covenant.edu
ALLEN, Jennie .... 909-447-2502.... 39 A
jallen@cst.edu
ALLEN, Jerry .... 510-594-3641.... 29 K
jallen@cca.edu
ALLEN, Jim .... 419-434-4207.. 381 E
jallen@winebrenner.edu
ALLEN, Jo .... 919-760-8511.. 346 D
jallen@meredith.edu
ALLEN, Jody .... 405-692-3130.. 384 C
jallen@macu.edu
ALLEN, Joe .... 214-887-5362.. 457 C
jallen@dts.edu
ALLEN, John, A .... 614-885-5585.. 376 G
jallen@pcj.edu
ALLEN, John, C .... 435-797-1195.. 482 B
john.allen@usu.edu
ALLEN, John, W .... 580-327-8594.. 384 M
jwallen@nwosu.edu
ALLEN, Joseph .... 218-935-0417.. 256 E
joseph.allen@wetcc.edu
ALLEN, Joshua, D .... 304-457-6392.. 510 B
allenjd@ab.edu
ALLEN, Joyce .... 206-934-5378.. 507 A
joyce.allen@seattlecolleges.edu
ALLEN, Judy .... 207-801-5680.. 202 H
jallen@coa.edu
ALLEN, Julia .... 704-922-6511.. 350 A
allen.julia@gaston.edu
ALLEN, Justin .... 540-535-3561.. 494 B
jallen3@su.edu
ALLEN, Kanya .... 270-707-3827.. 189 G
kanya.allen@kctcs.edu
ALLEN, Karen .... 812-855-6090.. 162 F
karealle@indiana.edu
ALLEN, Katherine .... 313-593-5300.. 242 A
kmaallen@umich.edu
ALLEN, Kathy .... 501-279-4263.... 20 D
kallen@harding.edu
ALLEN, Kathy .... 828-694-1773.. 347 G
allenkc@blueridge.edu
ALLEN, Kellie .... 606-326-2044.. 188 N
kellie.allen@kctcs.edu
ALLEN, Kent .... 405-425-5194.. 385 C
kent.allen@oc.edu
ALLEN, Kirsten .... 316-322-3192.. 179 E
kallen2@butlercc.edu
ALLEN, Kitty .... 605-995-2612.. 435 F
kiallen1@dwu.edu
ALLEN, Larry, K .... 518-564-3282.. 334 A
lalle001@plattsburgh.edu
ALLEN, Linda .... 417-865-2815.. 265 B
allenl@evangel.edu
ALLEN, Linda, A .... 319-296-4201.. 173 B
linda.allen@hawkeyecollege.edu
ALLEN, Linda, D .... 617-373-2307.. 227 B
ALLEN, Lindsay .... 508-793-7666.. 217 B
liallen@clarku.edu
ALLEN, Lonny .... 419-448-3359.. 378 A
lallen@tiffin.edu
ALLEN, Lori .... 575-527-7727.. 301 C
allen@nmsu.edu
ALLEN, Lynne .... 617-353-3350.. 216 E
cfadean@bu.edu
ALLEN, Marjorie .... 847-925-6967.. 141 A
mallen@harpercollege.edu
ALLEN, Mark .... 719-384-6830.... 82 A
mark.allen@ojc.edu
ALLEN, Mark .... 313-577-4311.. 243 F
fp0431@wayne.edu
ALLEN, Mark .... 918-293-4830.. 386 B
mark.allen@okstate.edu
ALLEN, Mark, R .... 570-408-4103.. 423 G
mark.allen@wilkes.edu
ALLEN, Martha .... 218-935-0417.. 256 E
martha.allen@wetcc.edu
ALLEN, Mary .... 410-225-4255.. 209 B
mallen01@mica.edu
ALLEN, Matt .... 406-683-7450.. 277 A
matt.allen@umwestern.edu
ALLEN, Max .... 864-656-3413.. 428 C
maallen@clemson.edu
ALLEN, Melissa .... 607-431-4130.. 315 E
allenm2@hartwick.edu
ALLEN, Michael .... 406-496-4399.. 277 G
mallen@mtech.edu
ALLEN, Michael .... 818-364-7635.... 49 J
ALLEN, Michael .... 559-453-2038.... 44 F
michael.allen@fresno.edu
ALLEN, Michael, K .... 818-364-7635.... 49 J
allenm@lamission.edu
ALLEN, Michael, S .... 202-319-5619.... 92 A
allen@cua.edu
ALLEN, Michele .... 816-604-4023.. 267 K
michele.allen@mcckc.edu
ALLEN, Myrna, L .... 386-312-4249.. 108 B
myrnaallen@sjrstate.edu
ALLEN, Nancy .... 303-871-2094.... 84 B
nallen@du.edu
ALLEN, Norma, L .... 972-599-3159.. 455 A
nsmith@collin.edu
ALLEN, Patricia .... 503-534-7022.. 392 D
pallen@marylhurst.edu
ALLEN, Philip, D .... 229-333-5952.. 129 G
pdallen@valdosta.edu
ALLEN, Rachael .... 503-821-8920.. 394 B
rallen@pnca.edu
ALLEN, Remy, E .... 504-568-4802.. 198 A
rall1@lsuhsc.edu
ALLEN, Renee .... 505-346-2346.. 302 E
renee.allen@bie.edu
ALLEN, Robert .... 334-420-4266...... 7 G
rallen@trenholmstate.edu
ALLEN, Robert .... 910-755-7321.. 347 H
allenr@brunswickcc.edu
ALLEN, Robert, W .... 802-287-8201.. 484 A
allenr@greenmtn.edu
ALLEN, Robin .... 610-796-8392.. 397 D
robin.allen@alvernia.edu
ALLEN, Rondall, E .... 410-651-8350.. 212 B
reallen@umes.edu
ALLEN, Rosemary .... 502-863-8146.. 188 I
rosemary_allen@georgetowncollege.edu
ALLEN, Rusty .... 620-947-3121.. 185 B
rustya@tabor.edu
ALLEN, Ryan .... 757-881-5100.... 93 F
ALLEN, Scott, T .... 203-596-4590.... 88 F
scallen@post.edu
ALLEN, Seth .... 909-621-8134.... 58 A
seth.allen@pomona.edu
ALLEN, Seth .... 866-931-4300.. 270 I
library@rockbridge.edu
ALLEN, Shannon .... 270-824-1785.. 190 B
shannon.allen@kctcs.edu
ALLEN, Sharlene .... 218-299-6894.. 250 D
sharlene.allen@minnesota.edu
ALLEN, Sharon .... 928-428-8342.... 13 B
sharon.allen@eac.edu
ALLEN, Sheila, W .... 706-542-3461.. 128 E
sallen01@uga.edu
ALLEN, Shelli, R .... 636-584-6565.. 264 M
shelli.allen@eastcentral.edu
ALLEN, Sheryl .... 601-635-2111.. 257 F
sallen@eccc.edu

ALVAREZ, Jackie .... 541-737-2131.. 393 H
jackie.alvarez@oregonstate.edu

ALVAREZ, Jacqueline ...... 413-542-2354.. 214 C
jalvarez@amherst.edu

ALVAREZ, Jacqueline .... 787-284-1912.. 534 C
jalvarez@ponce.inter.edu

ALVAREZ, Lourdes .... 203-932-7257.... 90 A
lavarez@newhaven.edu

ALVAREZ, Maria .... 787-882-2065.. 536 D
registraduria@unitecpr.net

ALVAREZ, Maria, L .... 305-899-3085.... 96 D
malvarez@barry.edu

ALVAREZ, Milagros .... 787-850-9301.. 538 B
milagros.alvarez@upr.edu

ALVAREZ, Patricia .... 787-857-3600.. 533 I
palvarez@br.inter.edu

ALVAREZ, Patricia .... 559-730-3988.... 40 E
patriciaa@cos.edu

ALVAREZ, Raul .... 714-484-7128..... 54 G
ralvarez@cypresscollege.edu

ALVAREZ, Richard .... 540-831-5411.. 493 A
ralvarez@radford.edu

ALVAREZ, Richard .... 718-997-5929.. 309 D
richard.alvarez@qc.cuny.edu

ALVAREZ, Silvia .... 212-431-2872.. 323 H
silvia.alvarez@nyls.edu

ALVAREZ, Sylvia .... 787-728-1515.. 539 B
salvarez@sagrado.edu

ALVAREZ, Timothy .... 701-231-7701.. 361 A
timothy.alvarez@ndsu.edu

ALVAREZ-ROBINSON,
Sonia .... 404-385-3306.. 121 D
sonia@consulting.gatech.edu

ALVAREZ-RUIZ, Luis .... 787-890-2681.. 537 E
luis.alvarez8@upr.edu

ALVARO, Tammy .... 989-386-6622.. 238 B
talvaro@midmich.edu

ALVERSON, Amelia, J .... 212-851-7929.. 311 E
amelia.alverson@columbia.edu

ALVES, Eddie .... 541-881-5590.. 395 E
ealves@tvcc.cc

ALVES, Jeffrey .... 570-408-4725.. 423 G
jeffrey.alves@wilkes.edu

ALVES, Stephanie .... 925-969-2082..... 41 I
salves@dvc.edu

ALVEY, Patricia .... 214-768-4519.. 465 J
palvey@smu.edu

ALVIDREZ, Rachel .... 757-631-8101.. 487 B
rachel.alvidrez@atlanticuniv.edu

ALVINO, Kathleen, M .... 401-865-2430.. 425 D
kalvino@providence.edu

ALVIS, Robert .... 812-357-6543.. 167 B
ralvis@saintmeinrad.edu

ALVITI, Eileen .... 617-266-1400.. 215 G

ALY, Mai .... 773-481-8061.. 137 I
maly@ccc.edu

ALZAHABI, Basem .... 810-762-7893.. 236 C
balzahab@kettering.edu

AMACK, April .... 970-542-3187..... 81 H
april.amack@morgancc.edu

AMADI, Emmanual .... 662-254-3363.. 260 A
amadi@mvsu.edu

AMADO, Manuel .... 303-458-4122..... 82 L
mamado@regis.edu

AMADOR, Lui .... 657-278-8660..... 33 A
lamador@fullerton.edu

AMAKER, Corey .... 864-644-5001.. 432 G
camaker@swu.edu

AMAKER, Corey, L .... 803-535-5075.. 428 B
camaker@claflin.edu

AMALBERT, Milagros .... 787-751-1912.. 534 E
mamalber@juris.inter.edu

AMAN, Rick, K .... 208-535-5366.. 133 G
strick.aman@my.eitc.edu

AMANKWATIA, Tonya ...... 757-352-4886.. 493 E
tamankwatia@regent.edu

AMAR, Vikram .... 217-333-0931.. 157 A
amar@illinois.edu

AMARA, Sakpa, S .... 703-891-1787.. 494 H

AMARI, Neil, D .... 918-836-6886.. 388 E
neil.amari@spartan.edu

AMARO, Jovana .... 336-322-2122.. 351 H
jovana.amaro@piedmontcc.edu

AMASON, Allen .... 912-478-2622.. 122 B
aamason@georgiasouthern.edu

AMASON, Amy .... 706-776-0104.. 125 J
aamason@piedmont.edu

AMATO, John .... 515-271-2849.. 171 K
john.amato@drake.edu

AMATO, Paula, A .... 603-428-2461.. 287 C
pamato@nec.edu

AMATO, Roseann .... 407-708-2713.. 109 E
amator@seminolestate.edu

AMATOR, Shelley .... 505-566-3466.. 301 J
amators@sanjuancollege.edu

AMAVIZCA, Gabriela .... 520-417-4708..... 12 L
amavizcag@cochise.edu

AMAYA, Mercedes .... 305-237-2325.. 105 D
mamaya@mdc.edu

AMAYA GORDON,
Karla, J .... 757-823-8275.. 492 F
kjagordon@nsu.edu

AMBACH, Robert .... 513-556-2413.. 379 A
robert.ambach@uc.edu

AMBAR, Carmen, T .... 610-606-4612.. 400 E
president@cedarcrest.edu

AMBELANG, Charlie .... 408-551-1940..... 63 E
cambelang@scu.edu

AMBLER, Charles .... 915-747-5950.. 476 D
cambler@utep.edu

AMBLER, Virginia, M .... 757-221-1236.. 488 F
vmambl@wm.edu

AMBRA, Stephen .... 603-271-6484.. 286 F
sambra@ccsnh.edu

AMBROGI, Anthony, F ...... 804-752-7362.. 493 C
aambrogi@rmc.edu

AMBRON, Sueann .... 303-315-8001..... 84 A
sueann.ambron@ucdenver.edu

AMBROSE, Ann, P .... 757-822-2301.. 498 H
aambrose@tcc.edu

AMBROSE, AnneMarie ...... 315-866-0300.. 316 A
ambroseac@herkimer.edu

AMBROSE, Charles, M ...... 660-543-4112.. 273 C
ambrose@ucmo.edu

AMBROSE, Daniel .... 847-233-7700.. 150 D
dambrose@nc.edu

AMBROSE, Danielle .... 503-493-6508.. 391 A
dambrose@cu-portland.edu

AMBROSE, James .... 315-786-2490.. 317 H
jambrose@sunyjefferson.edu

AMBROSE, Molly, B .... 617-228-2457.. 223 B
mambrose@bhcc.mass.edu

AMBROSE, Pam .... 312-915-7602.. 146 G
pambros@luc.edu

AMBROSE, Susan .... 617-373-2170.. 227 B

AMBROSIA, Todd .... 212-614-6110.. 326 C
tambrosia@chpnet.org

AMBUR, Roberta, S .... 605-677-5661.. 437 A
roberta.ambur@usd.edu

AMBURGEY, Jeff, S .... 859-985-3082.. 187 B
jeff_amburgey@berea.edu

AMBUSKE, Joseph .... 614-236-6116.. 364 N
jambuske@capital.edu

AMDUR, Nick .... 617-619-1900.. 219 G
nick.amdur@faculty.hult.edu

AMEER, Inge-Lise .... 603-643-3113.. 286 J
inge-lise.ameer@dartmouth.edu

AMEIGH, Michael .... 315-312-3500.. 333 D
michael.ameigh@oswego.edu

AMELING, Brian, F .... 864-488-8200.. 430 H
bameling@limestone.edu

AMELL, Laura .... 802-485-2065.. 484 H
lamell@norwich.edu

AMELSBERG, James .... 641-585-8164.. 177 F
amelsbergj@waldorf.edu

AMEN, Barbara, A .... 503-777-7259.. 394 I
barbara.amen@reed.edu

AMEND, John .... 402-554-2242.. 283 B
jamend@unomaha.edu

AMENDOLA, Luigi .... 815-836-5875.. 145 H
amendolu@lewisu.edu

AMENSON-HILL, Brenda .. 218-477-2171.. 250 F
brenda.amensonhill@mnstate.edu

AMENSON-HILL, Brenda . 920-465-2159.. 520 B
hillb@uwgb.edu

AMENTA, Paula .... 847-214-7273.. 140 A
pamenta@elgin.edu

AMERIN, Kylea, C .... 580-327-8601.. 384 M
kcamerin@nwosu.edu

AMERIO, Barbara .... 661-763-7881..... 67 F
bamerio@taftcollege.edu

AMERO, Carolina .... 678-466-4217.. 119 A
carolinaamero@clayton.edu

AMERSHEK, Tom .... 620-235-4775.. 184 C
tamershek@pittstate.edu

AMES, Christopher .... 304-876-5176.. 513 E
cames@shepherd.edu

AMES, David .... 617-964-1100.. 214 D
dames@ants.edu

AMES, John .... 610-785-6287.. 418 E
james@scs.edu

AMES, Linda .... 509-279-6258.. 502 I
linda.ames@scc.spokane.edu

AMES, Lynda, J .... 518-564-3310.. 334 A
amesl j@plattsburgh.edu

AMES, Marilyn .... 914-337-9300.. 311 F
marilyn.ames@concordia-ny.edu

AMES, Scott .... 203-837-9014..... 85 I
amess@wcsu.edu

AMES, Suzanne .... 425-739-8410.. 504 F
suzanne.ames@lwtech.edu

AMES, Trevor, R .... 612-624-6244.. 255 H
amesx001@umn.edu

AMEY, Carol, J .... 859-858-3511.. 186 J
camey@asbury.edu

AMEY, Tracey .... 570-327-4503.. 413 O
tamey@pct.edu

AMEZCUA, Jason .... 217-228-5432.. 151 F
amezcja@quincy.edu

AMEZCUA, Victoria .... 626-396-2278..... 27 L
victoria.amezcua@artcenter.edu

AMI, Dawn .... 505-346-2339.. 302 E
dawn.ami@bie.edu

AMICK, Patricia, A .... 816-604-1130.. 267 F
patricia.amick@mcckc.edu

AMICO, David .... 315-792-5318.. 321 G
damico@mvcc.edu

AMIDON, Howard .... 978-921-4242.. 225 G
howard.amidon@montserrat.edu

AMIDON, Jacob, E .... 585-785-1418.. 314 D
jacob.amidon@flcc.edu

AMIDON, James, L .... 765-361-6364.. 169 C
amidonj@wabash.edu

AMIDON, JR., James, L . 765-361-6364.. 169 C
amidonj@wabash.edu

AMIE, Torrion .... 952-358-8505.. 251 A
torrion.amie@normandale.edu

AMINY, Marina .... 949-582-4365..... 65 G
maminy@saddleback.edu

AMIOTTE, Shannon .... 605-455-6012.. 436 G
samiotte@olc.edu

AMIRIDIS, Michael .... 312-413-3350.. 156 F
chancellor@uic.edu

AMIRIDIS, Michael .... 312-413-3350.. 156 E
amiridis@uic.edu

AMIRTHARAJ, Merlin .... 704-991-0207.. 353 E
mamirtharaj5283@stanly.edu

AMIS, Eric, J .... 330-972-7500.. 378 G
amis@uakron.edu

AMITH, Charles .... 888-488-4968..... 47 D

AMLANER, Charles, J .... 470-578-6738.. 123 J
camlaner@kennesaw.edu

AMLER, Robert, W .... 914-594-4531.. 323 I
robert_amler@nymc.edu

AMMAR, Salwa .... 718-862-7440.. 319 L
salwa.ammar@manhattan.edu

AMMETER, Tony .... 662-915-6748.. 261 B
tammeter@olemiss.edu

AMMIDOWN, Darla .... 603-577-6533.. 286 I
dammidown@dwc.edu

AMMIGAN, Ravi .... 302-831-2115..... 91 F
rammigan@udel.edu

AMMON, Darryl, C .... 660-263-3900.. 263 A
darrylammon@cccb.edu

AMMON, Janice, S .... 609-497-7890.. 294 C
chapel@ptsem.edu

AMMON, Richard .... 608-822-2421.. 524 F
rammon@swtc.edu

AMMONS, Brian .... 828-298-3325.. 359 F
bammons@warren-wilson.edu

AMMONS, Don .... 704-922-6240.. 350 A
ammons.don@gaston.edu

AMMONS, Kevin .... 334-347-2623...... 3 H
kammons@escc.edu

AMMONS, Lee .... 205-391-5830...... 6 G
wammons@sheltonstate.edu

AMMONS, Lee .... 334-420-4479...... 7 G
lammons@trenholmstate.edu

AMMONS, Sandy .... 910-630-7114.. 346 E
sammons@methodist.edu

AMOA, Kwesi .... 914-606-6789.. 340 C
kwesi.amoa@sunywcc.edu

AMODIO, Francis .... 845-569-3154.. 322 B
francis.amodio@msmc.edu

AMODIO, Greg .... 203-582-3621..... 88 G
greg.amodio@quinnipiac.edu

AMOKE, William .... 619-298-1829..... 66 D
wamoke@ssu.edu

AMON, Julie .... 856-225-6108.. 296 A
julie.amon@camden.rutgers.edu

AMOO, Judith, L .... 308-635-6702.. 283 D
amooj@wncc.edu

AMORIM, Daniel .... 617-730-7018.. 226 J
daniel.amorim@newbury.edu

AMOROS, Blanca .... 787-758-2525.. 538 D
blanca.amoros@upr.edu

AMOS, Anthea .... 850-484-4436.. 106 H
aamos@pensacolastate.edu

AMOS, Maureen, T .... 773-442-5000.. 149 J
m-amos@neiu.edu

AMOS, Ralph .... 765-494-0764.. 166 D
ralphamos@purdue.edu

AMOS, Sean .... 817-202-6740.. 466 C
samos@swau.edu

AMOTT, Teresa, L .... 309-341-7210.. 145 A
tamott@knox.edu

AMPARO, Frank .... 623-935-8872..... 14 A
frank.amparo@estrellamountain.edu

AMRHEIN, Rick .... 219-464-5777.. 168 F
rick.amrhein@valpo.edu

AMRHEIN, Rick .... 219-464-6777.. 168 F
rick.amrhein@valpo.edu

AMRIKHAS, Violet .... 818-947-2533..... 50 D
amrikhv@lavc.edu

AMSBERRYAUGIER, Lora 504-280-5563.. 198 D
slamsberr@uno.edu

AMSEL, Shimshon .... 732-370-1560.. 289 C

AMSPAUGH, Melissa, A .. 440-525-7357.. 371 F
mamspaugh@lakelandcc.edu

AMSTER, Yosef .... 347-619-9074.. 341 H

AMSTUTZ, Margaret .... 706-542-0383.. 128 E
mastutz@uga.edu

AMUNDSEN,
Minakshi, M .... 207-859-5002.. 202 G
mina.amundsen@colby.edu

AMUNDSEN, Scott .... 714-816-0366..... 68 E
scott.amundsen@trident.edu

AMUNDSON, Bret .... 218-625-4983.. 245 J
bamundson@css.edu

AMUNDSON,
Elizabeth, A .... 202-994-4900..... 92 D
amundson@gwu.edu

AMUNDSON, Jhennifer ..... 847-628-1019.. 144 B
jamundson@judson.edu

AMUNDSON, Shannon ...... 319-895-4174.. 171 A
samundson@cornellcollege.edu

AMYOT, Maribeth .... 513-745-3445.. 381 I
amyotm@xavier.edu

AMYX, Tim .... 615-230-3614.. 447 C
tim.amyx@volstate.edu

AN, Nana .... 202-885-2729..... 91 J
nanaan@american.edu

ANACKER, Gayne .... 951-343-4682..... 29 H
ganaker@calbaptist.edu

ANAGNOS, Thalia .... 408-924-5360..... 35 C
thalia.anagnos@sjsu.edu

ANAHITA, Sine .... 907-474-6515..... 10 G
sine.anahita@alaska.edu

ANALISTA, Norman .... 671-735-2586.. 530 B
nanalista@uguam.uog.edu

ANANIA, Cheryle .... 515-271-2191.. 171 K
cheryle.anania@drake.edu

ANANOU, Simeon .... 518-956-8080.. 331 A
ssananou@albany.edu

ANASAGASTI, Rogelio ...... 713-718-5001.. 459 B
rogelio.anasagasti@hccs.edu

ANASTASIO, Michael .... 718-933-6700.. 321 I
manastasio@monroecollege.edu

ANASTASSIOU,
Pamela, L .... 928-523-2109..... 15 H
pamela.anastassiou@nau.edu

ANAWALT, Deborah .... 410-626-2504.. 210 D
debbie.anawalt@sjc.edu

ANAYA, Angela .... 505-888-8898.. 302 B
financialaid@acupuncturecollege.edu

ANAYA, James .... 303-492-8047..... 83 K
james.anaya@colorado.edu

ANAYA, Jose .... 310-660-6464..... 42 J
janaya@elcamino.edu

ANAYA, Nena .... 505-424-2331.. 299 L
nanaya@iaia.edu

ANCHETA, Rachel .... 707-864-7122..... 65 A
rachel.ancheta@solano.edu

ANCHOR, Mike .... 706-771-4021.. 117 C
manchor@augustatech.edu

ANCHOR, Rebecca, E .... 585-245-5100.. 333 B
anchor@geneseo.edu

ANCI, Diane .... 740-427-5778.. 371 C
ancid@kenyon.edu

ANCO, Lisley, M .... 703-891-1787.. 494 H
registrar@standardcollege.edu

ANCTIL, Robin .... 641-844-5571.. 173 J
robin.anctil@iavalley.edu

ANDE, Taiwo, A .... 540-654-1282.. 495 C
tande@umw.edu

ANDELIBI, Jila .... 714-867-5009..... 65 D
jandelibi@southcoastcollege.com

ANDELMAN, Julia .... 212-678-8893.. 317 I
juandelman@jtsa.edu

ANDELORA, Jeffrey .... 480-461-7343..... 14 D
jeffrey.andelora@mesacc.edu

ANDERECK, Barbara, S .... 740-368-3773.. 376 B
bsandere@owu.edu

ANDEREGG, Jennifer .... 715-833-6361.. 523 B
janderegg2@cvtc.edu

ANDERFUREN, Marian, L 757-822-1940.. 498 H
manderfuren@tcc.edu

ANDERLEY, Gerald, M ...... 651-962-6061.. 256 C

ANDERMAN, Lynea .... 610-892-1524.. 414 B
landerman@pit.edu

ANDERS, Lee .... 620-862-5252.. 178 F
andle@barclaycollege.edu

ANDERS, Peter, J .... 717-871-5972.. 415 F
peter.anders@millersville.edu

ANDERSEN, Brooke .... 914-633-2625.. 317 B
bandersen@iona.edu

ANDERSEN, Catherine ...... 410-837-6205.. 213 C
candersen@ubalt.edu

ANDERSEN, Jim .... 209-384-6396..... 52 E
andersen.j@mccd.edu

ANDERSEN, Kathy .... 717-728-2503.. 400 F
kathyandersen@centralpenn.edu

ANDERSEN, Kent .... 205-226-4679...... 2 C
kanderse@bsc.edu

ANDERSEN, Kent, A .... 307-674-6446.. 526 M
kandersen@sheridan.edu

ANDERSEN, Leslie .... 714-816-0366..... 68 E
leslie.andersen@trident.edu

ANDERSEN, Marcanne .... 757-822-7184.. 498 H
mandersen@tcc.edu

ANDERSEN, Mark, N .... 307-686-0254.. 526 M
mandersen@sheridan.edu
ANDERSEN, Mary .... 719-775-8873.... 81 H
mary.andersen@morgancc.edu
ANDERSEN, Mike .... 831-656-1062.. 528 D
manderse@nps.edu
ANDERSEN, Patricia, M ... 605-394-1261.. 437 E
patricia.andersen@sdsmt.edu
ANDERSEN, Robert, B ..... 540-828-5350.. 487 H
randerse@bridgewater.edu
ANDERSEN, Sherry .... 508-362-2131.. 223 C
sanderse@capecod.edu
ANDERSEN, Stephen .... 706-764-6936.. 121 F
sandersen@gntc.edu
ANDERSEN, Thomas Ove 828-884-8320.. 342 C
ove.andersen@brevard.edu
ANDERSEN, Tom .... 307-532-8321.. 526 G
tom.andersen@ewc.wy.edu
ANDERSON, Aime .... 662-562-3305.. 260 C
aanderson@northwestms.edu
ANDERSON, Al .... 406-275-4833.. 278 E
al_anderson@skc.edu
ANDERSON, Amanda .... 620-241-0723.. 179 L
amanda.anderson@centralchristian.edu
ANDERSON, Amber .... 661-763-7870.... 67 F
aanderson@taftcollege.edu
ANDERSON, Amy .... 512-863-1639.. 466 G
andersoa@southwestern.edu
ANDERSON, Amy .... 269-782-1367.. 241 C
aanderson@swmich.edu
ANDERSON, Amy .... 352-340-4801.. 106 F
andersa@phsc.edu
ANDERSON, Amy .... 828-898-8845.. 345 G
andersona@lmc.edu
ANDERSON, Amy, A .... 917-493-4501.. 319 M
aanderson@msmnyc.edu
ANDERSON, Andrea .... 419-995-8020.. 370 G
anderson.a@rhodesstate.edu
ANDERSON, Andrew .... 206-296-5858.. 507 E
registrar@seattleu.edu
ANDERSON, Angela .... 509-359-6200.. 503 D
ANDERSON, Angela, B .... 740-376-4711.. 372 A
angela.anderson@marietta.edu
ANDERSON, Angela, D .... 301-546-0699.. 210 C
andersad@pgcc.edu
ANDERSON, Angela, R .... 252-328-6747.. 356 C
andersona@ecu.edu
ANDERSON, Antje .... 402-461-7351.. 280 D
aanderson@hastings.edu
ANDERSON, Ashley .... 410-888-9048.. 209 C
aanderson1@muih.edu
ANDERSON, Ashley .... 785-784-6606.. 178 G
andersona@bartonccc.edu
ANDERSON, Audrey, J ..... 615-322-8965.. 449 A
audrey.j.anderson@vanderbilt.edu
ANDERSON, Audwin .... 512-245-2361.. 471 F
aa04@txstate.edu
ANDERSON, Barry, L .... 901-334-5806.. 442 C
banderson@memphisseminary.edu
ANDERSON, Belinda, C .... 757-823-8118.. 492 F
bcanderson@nsu.edu
ANDERSON, Ben .... 859-572-5282.. 192 B
andersonb5@nku.edu
ANDERSON, Benjamin, J 828-298-3325.. 359 F
benjand@warren-wilson.edu
ANDERSON, Beth .... 423-461-8316.. 442 K
banderson@milligan.edu
ANDERSON, Betty, H ...... 337-475-5615.. 200 H
anderson@mcneese.edu
ANDERSON, Betty, L .... 573-629-3055.. 265 G
banderson@hlg.edu
ANDERSON, Betty-Jo ...... 918-335-6238.. 386 F
banderson@okwu.edu
ANDERSON, Bobby .... 209-386-6730.... 52 E
robert.anderson@mccd.edu
ANDERSON, Bobby .... 814-472-3386.. 418 F
banderson@francis.edu
ANDERSON, Bradford ...... 805-756-5210.... 31 I
bpanders@calpoly.edu
ANDERSON, Brett, B .... 970-491-7530.... 78 Q
brett.anderson@colostate.edu
ANDERSON, Brian .... 662-329-7386.. 259 E
banderson@muw.edu
ANDERSON, Bridges .... 334-222-6591...... 5 F
banderson@lbwcc.edu
ANDERSON, Bridgette ..... 845-431-8655.. 312 G
banderso@sunydutchess.edu
ANDERSON, Brooke .... 617-627-4975.. 228 H
brooke.anderson@tufts.edu
ANDERSON, Bryan .... 352-365-3677.. 104 J
andersob@lssc.edu
ANDERSON, C. Colt .... 718-817-4802.. 314 G
coltanderson@fordham.edu
ANDERSON, Carl, A .... 202-526-3799.... 93 E
canderson@johnpaulii.edu
ANDERSON, Carrie .... 319-398-5500.. 174 I
carrie.anderson@kirkwood.edu
ANDERSON, Cary, M ...... 610-660-1045.. 418 G
cander01@sju.edu
ANDERSON, Cathleen ...... 716-286-8717.. 324 E
cra@niagara.edu
ANDERSON, Cathy .... 801-581-6940.. 481 M
cathy.anderson@hsc.utah.edu
ANDERSON, JR.,
Charles .... 606-487-3058.. 189 E
chuck.anderson@kctcs.edu
ANDERSON, Charlise .... 731-426-7500.. 440 K
ANDERSON, Charlotte ..... 785-227-3380.. 178 J
andersonc@bethanylb.edu
ANDERSON, Cheryl .... 912-344-2586.. 116 E
cheryl.anderson@armstrong.edu
ANDERSON, Cheryl .... 210-829-3837.. 474 D
cheryla@uiwtx.edu
ANDERSON, Chris .... 507-537-6272.. 252 E
chris.anderson@smsu.edu
ANDERSON, Chris .... 973-408-3910.. 291 B
cjanders@drew.edu
ANDERSON, Christi .... 806-894-9611.. 465 G
canderson@southplainscollege.edu
ANDERSON, Christie .... 509-777-4218.. 509 H
canderson@whitworth.edu
ANDERSON, Christina ..... 218-855-8027.. 248 N
canderson@clcmn.edu
ANDERSON, Christina ..... 815-394-4388.. 152 G
canderson@rockford.edu
ANDERSON, Christopher . 716-375-2310.. 328 B
canderso@sbu.edu
ANDERSON, Cincy .... 918-463-2931.. 383 F
cindy.anderson@connorsstate.edu
ANDERSON, Cincy, L ...... 304-558-4016.. 512 O
cindy.anderson@wvhepc.edu
ANDERSON, Cliff .... 763-433-1100.. 248 K
clifford.anderson@anokaramsey.edu
ANDERSON, Clifford .... 763-433-1100.. 248 L
clifford.anderson@anokaramsey.edu
ANDERSON, Cody .... 828-835-4287.. 353 G
canderson@tricountycc.edu
ANDERSON, Colin, T .... 734-764-7254.. 241 J
colina@umich.edu
ANDERSON, Corey .... 541-684-7354.. 393 B
canderson@nwcu.edu
ANDERSON, Cynthia .... 828-398-7161.. 347 D
cynthiaianderson@abtech.edu
ANDERSON, Cynthia .... 708-974-5347.. 148 G
anderson@morainevalley.edu
ANDERSON, Cynthia .... 928-523-7618.... 15 H
cynthia.anderson@nau.edu
ANDERSON, Cynthia .... 419-372-6389.. 364 E
cynthia@bgsu.edu
ANDERSON, D. Craig ...... 804-752-7270.. 493 C
canderson@rmc.edu
ANDERSON, Daisy .... 717-766-2511.. 410 J
anderson@messiah.edu
ANDERSON, Dan, J .... 515-574-2813.. 173 F
anderson_dan@iowacentral.edu
ANDERSON, Daniel, J ..... 336-278-7410.. 344 D
andersd@elon.edu
ANDERSON, Daniel, L ..... 304-877-6428.. 510 F
president@abc.edu
ANDERSON, Danny .... 210-999-8401.. 473 A
tupresident@trinity.edu
ANDERSON, Danny .... 901-722-3204.. 444 C
danderson@sco.edu
ANDERSON, Daryl .... 718-779-1430.. 326 D
danderson1@mail.plazacollege.edu
ANDERSON, Dave .... 877-476-8674.. 458 F
ANDERSON, David .... 920-206-2347.. 517 G
david.anderson@mbu.edu
ANDERSON, David .... 616-234-3638.. 234 E
danderso@grcc.edu
ANDERSON, David .... 405-682-7400.. 385 D
danderson@occc.edu
ANDERSON, David, B ...... 202-994-9120.... 92 D
dbanderson@gwu.edu
ANDERSON, David, R ...... 507-786-3000.. 254 P
anderson@stolaf.edu
ANDERSON, Dawn, L .... 619-260-7733.... 72 B
dawn@sandiego.edu
ANDERSON, Deborah, L .. 815-224-0406.. 143 C
deborah_anderson@ivcc.edu
ANDERSON, Dee Dee ...... 423-425-4761.. 448 F
deedee-anderson@utc.edu
ANDERSON, Delia, C ...... 617-732-2910.. 225 C
delia.anderson@mcphs.edu
ANDERSON, Denise .... 973-596-3434.. 293 D
denise.anderson.2@njit.edu
ANDERSON, Diane, K ..... 269-387-2152.. 243 H
diane.anderson@wmich.edu
ANDERSON, Diann .... 256-372-8094...... 1 A
diane.anderson@aamu.edu
ANDERSON, Dianne .... 505-277-1807.. 302 F
danderson@unm.edu
ANDERSON, Don .... 509-963-2290.. 501 K
andersond1@cwu.edu
ANDERSON, Don, K .... 515-964-0601.. 172 F
andersond@faith.edu
ANDERSON, Donna, L ..... 608-342-1739.. 521 A
anderdon@uwplatt.edu
ANDERSON, Dorothy .... 505-277-5824.. 302 F
unmvphr@unm.edu
ANDERSON, Douglas .... 314-246-7406.. 275 B
danderson11@webster.edu
ANDERSON, Douglas D . 435-797-2376.. 482 B
douglas.anderson@usu.edu
ANDERSON, Elliott .... 847-628-5052.. 144 B
elliott.anderson@judsonu.edu
ANDERSON, Eric .... 208-885-6739.. 134 G
esanderson@uidaho.edu
ANDERSON, Eric .... 712-707-7132.. 176 B
eric.anderson@nwciowa.edu
ANDERSON, Eric .... 715-855-7512.. 523 B
eanderson72@cvtc.edu
ANDERSON, Eric, R .... 614-236-6606.. 364 N
eanderson@capital.edu
ANDERSON, Eugene .... 305-284-4643.. 114 H
genea@miami.edu
ANDERSON, Eugene .... 757-823-8045.. 492 F
eanderson@nsu.edu
ANDERSON, Faith .... 912-443-5776.. 126 G
fanderson@savannahtech.edu
ANDERSON, Francine ...... 540-231-4000.. 489 H
ANDERSON, G. Scott ...... 212-220-8051.. 307 B
sanderson@bmcc.cuny.edu
ANDERSON, Gail .... 715-425-3232.. 521 B
gail.anderson@uwrf.edu
ANDERSON, George W .. 713-221-8449.. 474 B
andersong@uhd.edu
ANDERSON, Geri .... 970-339-6617.... 76 H
geri.anderson@aims.edu
ANDERSON, Gordon, K ... 423-439-5671.. 444 F
andersgk@etsu.edu
ANDERSON, Gordon, L ... 612-343-4741.. 253 Y
glanders@northcentral.edu
ANDERSON, Grace .... 406-771-4399.. 277 F
grace.anderson3@gfcmsu.edu
ANDERSON, Greg .... 215-204-8017.. 420 B
gregoryanderson@temple.edu
ANDERSON, Gregory .... 912-344-3185.. 116 E
greg.anderson@armstrong.edu
ANDERSON, Gregory .... 650-306-3353.... 62 G
andersong@smccd.edu
ANDERSON, Harry .... 715-394-8241.. 521 E
handerso@uwsuper.edu
ANDERSON, Heidi .... 361-593-3106.. 469 A
heidi.anderson@tamuk.edu
ANDERSON, Ian .... 207-699-5033.. 203 F
ianderson@meca.edu
ANDERSON, Jacqui .... 620-343-4600.. 180 H
jaanderson@fhtc.edu
ANDERSON, Jade .... 208-467-8061.. 134 D
jadeanderson@nnu.edu
ANDERSON, James .... 208-426-2384.. 132 I
jamesanderson@boisestate.edu
ANDERSON, James .... 703-784-6917.. 528 A
james.anderson@usmc.mil
ANDERSON, James .... 570-208-5858.. 406 J
jamesanderson@kings.edu
ANDERSON, James, A ..... 910-672-1141.. 356 E
janderson@uncfsu.edu
ANDERSON, James, T ..... 973-655-7022.. 293 A
andersonja@mail.montclair.edu
ANDERSON, Janice .... 254-526-1116.. 454 A
janice.anderson@ctcd.edu
ANDERSON, Jean .... 479-619-4208.... 21 D
janderso@nwacc.edu
ANDERSON, Jeanette .... 626-571-8811.... 72 E
jeanettea@uwest.edu
ANDERSON, Jeff .... 808-245-8384.. 132 B
jeffa@hawaii.edu
ANDERSON, Jeffrey .... 352-588-8657.. 108 C
jeffrey.anderson@saintleo.edu
ANDERSON, Jeffrey .... 518-255-5413.. 334 D
andersjm@cobleskill.edu
ANDERSON, Jeffrey, J ..... 847-574-5210.. 145 C
janderson@lfgsm.edu
ANDERSON, Jennifer .... 203-254-4000.... 87 G
janderson@fairfield.edu
ANDERSON, Jennifer .... 614-287-5581.. 367 C
jander02@cscc.edu
ANDERSON, Jeremy .... 606-337-1533.. 187 I
janderson@ccbbc.edu
ANDERSON, Jerry .... 515-271-3985.. 171 K
jerry.anderson@drake.edu
ANDERSON, Jessica .... 815-825-9786.. 144 F
jessica.anderson@kishwaukeecollege.edu
ANDERSON, Jill .... 307-754-6401.. 526 N
jill.anderson@nwc.edu
ANDERSON, Jillian .... 508-929-8072.. 222 F
jillian.anderson@worcester.edu
ANDERSON, Joan, E .... 508-793-3644.. 217 C
janderso@holycross.edu
ANDERSON, Joanna .... 660-596-7223.. 272 G
janderson@sfccmo.edu
ANDERSON, Joel, E .... 501-569-3200.... 23 B
jeanderson@ualr.edu
ANDERSON, Joelle .... 651-255-6107.. 255 C
janderson@unitedseminary.edu
ANDERSON, John .... 540-857-7273.. 499 B
janderson@virginiawestern.edu
ANDERSON, John, A .... 470-578-3132.. 123 J
janders2@kennesaw.edu
ANDERSON, John, M .... 717-871-7001.. 415 F
mupresident@millersville.edu
ANDERSON, Joyce .... 208-376-7731.. 132 H
janderson@boisebible.edu
ANDERSON, JP .... 585-594-6400.. 327 D
anderson_jp@roberts.edu
ANDERSON, Judith .... 507-538-0162.. 245 E
anderson.judith@mayo.edu
ANDERSON, Judy .... 620-341-5379.. 180 G
jander21@emporia.edu
ANDERSON, Julie .... 507-222-6824.. 245 C
janderso@carleton.edu
ANDERSON, Julie .... 218-723-6021.. 245 J
ANDERSON, Justin .... 603-646-3661.. 286 J
justin.anderson@dartmouth.edu
ANDERSON, Karen .... 515-643-6791.. 175 B
kanderson8@mercydesmoines.org
ANDERSON, Kathleen ...... 410-837-5249.. 213 C
kanderson@ubalt.edu
ANDERSON, Kathleen, M 563-333-6344.. 176 D
officeofthepresident@sau.edu
ANDERSON, Kathryn .... 757-825-2851.. 498 G
andersonk@tncc.edu
ANDERSON, Kay .... 478-445-6286.. 121 A
kay.anderson@gcsu.edu
ANDERSON, Keith .... 704-216-6248.. 346 A
kanderson@livingstone.edu
ANDERSON, Keith, R .... 206-876-6101.. 507 D
kanderson@theseattleschool.edu
ANDERSON, Kelly .... 214-333-5433.. 455 J
kellya@dbu.edu
ANDERSON, Kelly .... 505-566-3775.. 301 J
andersonk@sanjuancollege.edu
ANDERSON, Kelly .... 419-772-2073.. 374 J
k-anderson@onu.edu
ANDERSON, Kelsi .... 734-995-7350.. 232 I
kelsi.anderson@cuw.edu
ANDERSON, Kenneth .... 509-313-3404.. 504 A
anderson@jepson.gonzaga.edu
ANDERSON, Kevin .... 617-266-1400.. 215 G
ANDERSON, Kevin .... 301-314-0013.. 211 E
kevina@umd.edu
ANDERSON, Kevin .... 931-372-6554.. 445 B
kanderson@tntech.edu
ANDERSON, Kevin, L ...... 563-589-0211.. 177 H
kanderson@wartburgseminary.edu
ANDERSON, Kim .... 484-365-7565.. 409 B
kanderson@lincoln.edu
ANDERSON, Kirk, D .... 309-794-7203.. 135 D
kirkanderson@augustana.edu
ANDERSON, Kristin, K ..... 901-722-3216.. 444 C
kanderson@sco.edu
ANDERSON, Kristine .... 231-777-0447.. 238 G
kristine.anderson@muskegoncc.edu
ANDERSON, Kristy .... 360-538-4151.. 504 B
kanderso@ghc.edu
ANDERSON, Larry .... 218-879-0842.. 249 C
larrya@fdltcc.edu
ANDERSON, Larry .... 218-879-0822.. 249 C
larrya@fdltcc.edu
ANDERSON, Larry .... 318-797-5371.. 198 C
larry.anderson@lsus.edu
ANDERSON, Latrice .... 305-626-3713.. 101 A
latrice.anderson@fmuniv.edu
ANDERSON, OFM,
Lawrence .... 518-783-2332.. 330 E
landerson@siena.edu
ANDERSON, Layne .... 218-477-2447.. 250 F
layne.anderson@mnstate.edu
ANDERSON, Leesa, P ...... 706-778-3000.. 125 J
landerson@piedmont.edu
ANDERSON, Leif, B .... 612-330-1497.. 244 I
andersol@augsburg.edu
ANDERSON, Leslie .... 870-733-6732.... 19 A
landerson@asumidsouth.edu
ANDERSON, Linda .... 256-726-7095...... 6 B
landerson@oakwood.edu
ANDERSON, Linda .... 503-297-5544.. 393 C
landerson@ocac.edu
ANDERSON, Linda, S ...... 816-604-2380.. 267 I
linda.anderson@mcckc.edu
ANDERSON, Lisa .... 218-723-6738.. 245 J
landerso@css.edu
ANDERSON, Lisa .... 718-270-5000.. 309 B
lisa@mec.cuny.edu
ANDERSON, Lisa .... 479-619-2227.... 21 D
landerson7@nwacc.edu
ANDERSON, Lois .... 301-387-3042.. 207 G
lois.anderson@garrettcollege.edu
ANDERSON, Louise .... 269-488-4777.. 235 I
landerson@kvcc.edu
ANDERSON, Lydia .... 559-442-8222.... 67 C
lydia.anderson@fresnocitycollege.edu
ANDERSON, Marie .... 909-469-5485.... 74 K
manderson@westernu.edu
ANDERSON, Mark .... 860-628-4751.... 88 C
manderson@lincolncollegene.edu
ANDERSON, Mark, R .... 470-578-6160.. 123 J
mande126@kennesaw.edu
ANDERSON, Marlene .... 701-224-5578.. 361 C
marlene.anderson@bismarckstate.edu
ANDERSON, Martha .... 602-285-7553.... 14 F
martha.anderson@phoenixcollege.edu

ANDERSON, Mary .... 218-723-6436.. 245 J manders1@css.edu
ANDERSON, Maureen ...... 352-854-2322.... 97 R andersom@cf.edu
ANDERSON, Melinda, F .. 318-619-2916.. 197 J manderson@lsua.edu
ANDERSON, Melissa, K .. 920-748-8365.. 519 E andersonmk@ripon.edu
ANDERSON, Melissa, L ... 336-841-9220.. 345 A manderson@highpoint.edu
ANDERSON, Melissa, P .. 540-674-3635.. 497 G manderson@nr.edu
ANDERSON, Michael .... 218-755-2015.. 248 M manderson@bemidjistate.edu
ANDERSON, Michael, J ... 718-951-5000.. 307 D
ANDERSON, Michael, W . 210-458-5949.. 477 A michael.anderson1@utsa.edu
ANDERSON, Michelle ...... 312-788-1125.. 157 H manderson@vandercook.edu
ANDERSON, Michelle ...... 724-503-1001.. 422 H manderson@washjeff.edu
ANDERSON, Mike .... 435-283-7393.. 482 E mike.anderson@snow.edu
ANDERSON, Monique, W 865-974-2101.. 448 E manders3@utk.edu
ANDERSON, Myron .... 303-556-3022.... 81 G mande118@msudenver.edu
ANDERSON, N. Douglas . 740-376-4536.. 372 A doug.anderson@marietta.edu
ANDERSON, Nancy .... 978-867-4828.. 219 A nancy.anderson@gordon.edu
ANDERSON, Nickoel .... 218-733-5990.. 249 H n.anderson@lsc.edu
ANDERSON, Nina .... 732-571-7551.. 292 F nanderso@monmouth.edu
ANDERSON, Noma, B ..... 901-448-5581.. 448 H nander13@uthsc.edu
ANDERSON, Patricia .... 775-753-2115.. 284 I pat.anderson@gbcnv.edu
ANDERSON, Patricia .... 615-230-3300.. 447 C patricia.anderson@volstate.edu
ANDERSON, Patty .... 386-752-1822.. 100 L patty.anderson@fgc.edu
ANDERSON, Pauline .... 954-201-7877.... 96 I panderso@broward.edu
ANDERSON, Per .... 218-299-3932.. 246 A anderson@cord.edu
ANDERSON, Peter .... 540-674-3607.. 497 G ptanderson@nr.edu
ANDERSON, Phillip, T ..... 414-410-4004.. 515 I ptanderson@stritch.edu
ANDERSON, Randy .... 323-953-4000.... 49 H andersr@lacitycollege.edu
ANDERSON, Ray .... 480-965-0983.... 11 H ray.anderson@asu.edu
ANDERSON, Rayelle .... 208-769-5978.. 134 C rayelle_anderson@nic.edu
ANDERSON, Rebecca .... 210-458-4132.. 477 A rebecca.anderson@utsa.edu
ANDERSON, Rebecca .... 704-337-2485.. 355 A andersonr@queens.edu
ANDERSON, Rebekah ...... 503-251-5718.. 396 C reanderson@uws.edu
ANDERSON, Rhonda, C ... 989-837-4455.. 239 D rca@northwood.edu
ANDERSON, Rick .... 252-940-6417.. 347 E rick.anderson@beaufortccc.edu
ANDERSON, Rick .... 956-665-2121.. 476 E rick.anderson@utrgv.edu
ANDERSON, Rick, L .... 785-670-1634.. 185 H rick.anderson@washburn.edu
ANDERSON, Robert .... 517-629-0446.. 230 E banderson@albion.edu
ANDERSON, Robert .... 509-359-2531.. 503 D randerson@ewu.edu
ANDERSON, Robin, D ...... 503-943-7224.. 396 B anderson@up.edu
ANDERSON, Roger .... 908-852-1400.. 290 D andersonr@centenarycollege.edu
ANDERSON, Roger .... 401-232-6088.. 424 K randerso@bryant.edu
ANDERSON, Ron .... 651-201-1498.. 248 I ron.anderson@so.mnscu.edu
ANDERSON, Ronald, M ... 859-858-3511.. 186 J ron.anderson@asbury.edu
ANDERSON, Russell .... 601-266-4153.. 261 E rusty.anderson@usm.edu
ANDERSON, Ryan .... 718-405-3403.. 310 H ryan.anderson@mountsaintvincent.edu
ANDERSON, Sandy .... 907-745-3201........ 9 H sanderson@akbible.edu
ANDERSON, Scott, R .... 815-599-3604.. 141 E scott.anderson@highland.edu
ANDERSON, Sharee .... 208-535-5333.. 133 G sharee.anderson@my.eitc.edu
ANDERSON, Sharon .... 805-756-7745.... 31 I sander17@calpoly.edu
ANDERSON, Sharon, D .... 336-734-7735.. 349 G sanderson@forsythtech.edu
ANDERSON, Shawn .... 218-299-6535.. 250 D shawn.anderson@minnesota.edu
ANDERSON, Shayna .... 661-362-2203.... 52 A sanderson@masters.edu
ANDERSON, Stephanie .... 512-245-2803.. 471 F sa35@txstate.edu
ANDERSON, Stephen, P .. 830-372-8020.. 470 C sanderson@tlu.edu
ANDERSON, Steve .... 803-372-8022.. 470 C sanderson@tlu.edu
ANDERSON, Susan .... 978-656-3483.. 224 A andersons@middlesex.mass.edu
ANDERSON, Susan .... 216-373-6396.. 374 B andersons@ndc.edu
ANDERSON, Susan, M ..... 530-898-6472.... 32 C sanderson@csuchico.edu
ANDERSON, Suzanne, M 540-853-0691.. 491 A srmcquire@carilionclinic.org
ANDERSON, Sylvia .... 919-530-6681.. 357 A sander55@nccu.edu
ANDERSON, Sylvia, C ..... 919-530-6681.. 357 A sander55@nccu.edu
ANDERSON, Tamara .... 508-565-1661.. 228 F tanderson@stonehill.edu
ANDERSON, Therese .... 215-596-8813.. 422 A registrar@usciences.edu
ANDERSON, Thomas, K .. 802-626-6497.. 486 C thomas.anderson@lyndonstate.edu
ANDERSON, Timothy, J .. 413-545-6388.. 220 F tjanderson@ecs.umass.edu
ANDERSON, Tina, K .... 229-333-2119.. 130 A tina.anderson@wiregrass.edu
ANDERSON, Todd .... 910-521-6371.. 358 C todd.anderson@uncp.edu
ANDERSON, Todd, J .... 213-624-1200.... 43 J tjanderson@fidm.edu
ANDERSON, Tracey .... 304-327-4331.. 512 P tanderson@bluefieldstate.edu
ANDERSON, Ty .... 580-559-5225.. 383 H tydand@ecok.edu
ANDERSON, Vanessa ...... 303-797-5930.... 76 J vanessa.anderson@arapahoe.edu
ANDERSON, Wanda .... 302-736-2443.... 91 G wanda.anderson@wesley.edu
ANDERSON, William .... 845-431-8961.. 312 G william.anderson@sunydutchess.edu
ANDERSON, William .... 336-316-2907.. 344 H andersonwj@guilford.edu
ANDERSON, William, L .... 301-546-0622.. 210 C anderswl@pgcc.edu
ANDERSON, William, O .. 802-654-2252.. 484 I wanderson@smcvt.edu
ANDERSON, William, O .. 610-660-1276.. 418 G banderso@sju.edu
ANDERSON, Yolanda, B .. 919-530-6738.. 357 A yandersn@nccu.edu
ANDERSON-BINA, Cindy . 218-235-2121.. 252 F c.bina@vcc.edu
ANDERSON-BURT, Marilyn .... 206-934-5144.. 507 A marilyn.anderson-burt@seattlecolleges.edu
ANDERSON MARTINEZ, Richard .... 207-602-2826.. 205 F randerson@une.edu
ANDERSON-SAPATA, Barbara .... 847-233-7700.. 150 D banderson-sapata@nc.edu
ANDERSON WIECK, Patricia .... 503-594-6000.. 390 F patricia.anderson@clackamas.edu
ANDERSON-WILLIAMS, Sandra .... 615-327-6683.. 442 A williamss@mmc.edu
ANDIS, Blake .... 276-739-2582.. 499 A bandis@vhcc.edu
ANDORS, Allison .... 516-686-7737.. 323 G aandors@nyit.edu
ANDRACKI, Jason .... 814-332-4351.. 397 A jandrack@allegheny.edu
ANDRADE, Alicia .... 559-453-2220.... 44 F alicia.andrade@fresno.edu
ANDRADE, June, C .... 787-728-1515.. 539 B jandrade@sagrado.edu
ANDRADE, Kim .... 405-422-1267.. 387 E andradek@redlandscc.edu
ANDRADE, Maureen .... 801-863-6158.. 482 C maureen.andrade@uvu.edu
ANDRADE, Raul .... 312-939-0111.. 139 G raul@eastwest.edu
ANDRAOS, Amale .... 212-854-3473.. 311 E aa3217@columbia.edu
ANDRE, Nicholas .... 570-662-4834.. 415 E nandre@mansfield.edu
ANDREA, Francine .... 201-559-6181.. 291 K andreaf@felician.edu
ANDREA, JR., Robert, K . 518-956-8206.. 331 A randrea@albany.edu
ANDREANI, Scott .... 330-494-6170.. 377 J sandreani@starkstate.edu
ANDREAS, Marc .... 616-222-3000.. 236 F mandreas@kuyper.edu
ANDREAS, Michelle .... 360-596-5209.. 508 A mandreas@spscc.edu
ANDREASEN, Michael, C 541-346-0869.. 395 G miandrea@uoregon.edu
ANDRECHAK, Michael ..... 404-727-9252.. 120 E michael.j.andrechak@emory.edu
ANDREINI, Janelle, S ...... 402-465-2414.. 281 K jsa@nebrwesleyan.edu
ANDREJCZYK, Rose, L .... 413-205-3248.. 214 B rose.andrejczyk@aic.edu
ANDREO, Eddie .... 620-441-7101.. 180 D andreoe@cowley.edu
ANDREOLA, Michael .... 412-536-1096.. 406 K michael.andreola@laroche.edu
ANDREOTTI, Carole .... 617-588-1369.. 215 E candreotti@bfit.edu
ANDRESEN, Julie, A .... 573-629-4001.. 265 G jandresen@hlg.edu
ANDRESEN, Sharla .... 541-383-7208.. 390 D sandresen@cocc.edu
ANDRESEN REID, Marcia 507-284-3627.. 245 F andresen.marcia@mayo.edu
ANDRESS-MARTIN, Holly 583-288-6421.. 264 F handress@culver.edu
ANDREU, Angel, E .... 585-292-3031.. 321 J aandreu@monroecc.edu
ANDREU, Frank .... 305-821-3333.. 101 B fandreu@fnu.edu
ANDREW, Barbara .... 973-720-3657.. 298 G andrewb@wpunj.edu
ANDREW, Damon, P .... 225-578-1258.. 197 I damonandrew@lsu.edu
ANDREW, Kenneth .... 304-473-8367.. 515 B andrew_k@wvwc.edu
ANDREW, Martha .... 575-758-8914.. 300 D marcya@midwiferycollege.edu
ANDREW, Matthew .... 320-308-4072.. 252 A mjandrew@stcloudstate.edu
ANDREW, Melissa .... 870-762-3118.... 18 G mandrew@smail.anc.edu
ANDREW, Paul .... 617-495-1000.. 219 D paul_andrew@harvard.edu
ANDREW, Ruth Aletha ..... 919-735-5151.. 354 A raandrew@waynecc.edu
ANDREWS, Aaron .... 870-759-4105.... 24 J aandrews@wbcoll.edu
ANDREWS, Adrienne .... 530-344-5716.... 51 C andrewa@flc.losrios.edu
ANDREWS, AnneMarie ...... 845-431-8980.. 312 G amandrews@sunydutchess.edu
ANDREWS, Beverly .... 269-467-9945.. 234 B bandrews@glenoaks.edu
ANDREWS, Bradley, J ..... 620-229-6223.. 184 J brad.andrews@sckans.edu
ANDREWS, Brett .... 316-942-4291.. 183 I andrewsb@newmnau.edu
ANDREWS, Brian .... 802-865-6431.. 483 F andrews@champlain.edu
ANDREWS, Chip, L .... 770-534-6759.. 118 A candrews@brenau.edu
ANDREWS, Danny .... 806-291-3600.. 479 D andrewsd@wbu.edu
ANDREWS, David .... 858-642-8801.... 54 A dandrews@nu.edu
ANDREWS, David, W .... 410-516-7820.. 208 D davidandrews@jhu.edu
ANDREWS, Dennis, M ...... 903-510-2034.. 473 C mand@tjc.edu
ANDREWS, Diane, L .... 814-865-5423.. 412 F dla6@psu.edu
ANDREWS, Donald, R ..... 225-771-5640.. 199 H jazandrews@yahoo.com
ANDREWS, George .... 305-237-3316.. 105 D gandrews@mdc.edu
ANDREWS, Herry .... 307-778-1231.. 526 K handrews@lccc.wy.edu
ANDREWS, Jeannette .... 803-777-3862.. 433 F jandrews@mailbox.sc.edu
ANDREWS, Jeff .... 601-318-6741.. 261 I jeff.andrews@wmcarey.edu
ANDREWS, Kattia .... 620-365-5116.. 178 A andrews@allencc.edu
ANDREWS, Kim .... 318-335-3944.. 196 A kimandrews@cltcc.edu
ANDREWS, Kim .... 660-543-8059.. 273 C andrews@ucmo.edu
ANDREWS, Linda .... 713-798-4620.. 452 G landrews@bcm.edu
ANDREWS, Loretta .... 406-447-4508.. 276 B landrews@carroll.edu
ANDREWS, Lynn .... 503-554-2112.. 391 D landrews@georgefox.edu
ANDREWS, Margaret .... 810-762-3420.. 242 B mmandrew@umflint.edu
ANDREWS, Mark .... 770-228-7367.. 127 F mandrews@sctech.edu
ANDREWS, Mark, A .... 718-990-5897.. 328 F andrewsm@stjohns.edu
ANDREWS, Michael .... 585-273-4734.. 338 K michael.andrews@rochester.edu
ANDREWS, Michael, F .... 503-943-8628.. 396 B andrews@up.edu
ANDREWS, Nancy .... 919-684-2455.. 343 J nancy.andrews@mc.duke.edu
ANDREWS, Nikki .... 508-373-9701.. 215 D nikki.andrews@becker.edu
ANDREWS, Rebecca .... 615-794-4254.. 443 G randrews@omorecollege.edu
ANDREWS, Richard .... 916-691-7423.... 51 B andrewr@crc.losrios.edu
ANDREWS, Richard .... 405-733-7516.. 387 I randrews@rose.edu
ANDREWS, Robert .... 423-775-6596.. 443 H
ANDREWS, Robert .... 704-847-5600.. 355 J randrews@ses.edu
ANDREWS, Robert .... 573-592-5251.. 275 E robert.andrews@westminster-mo.edu
ANDREWS, Roy .... 503-255-0332.. 392 G randrews@multnomah.edu
ANDREWS, Sabrina .... 803-777-0395.. 433 F andrews1@mailbox.sc.edu
ANDREWS, Serena .... 979-230-3245.. 453 A serena.andrews@brazosport.edu
ANDREWS, Sheila .... 317-632-5553.. 165 L sandrews@lincolntech.edu
ANDREWS, Sona .... 503-725-5257.. 394 G sona.andrews@pdx.edu
ANDREWS, Spring .... 831-477-5220.... 29 G spandrew@cabrillo.edu
ANDREWS, Stacie .... 814-254-0557.. 401 A standrews@pa.gov
ANDREWS, Tangela .... 561-912-2166.... 99 J taandrews@evergladesuniversity.edu
ANDREWS, Tim .... 913-360-7363.. 178 I tandrews@benedictine.edu
ANDREWS, Todd, G .... 401-863-6331.. 424 J todd_andrews@brown.edu
ANDREWS, Todd, J .... 860-727-6937.... 87 H tandrews@goodwin.edu
ANDREWS, Tonia, Y .... 540-985-9784.. 491 A tyandrews@jchs.edu
ANDREWS, Traci .... 954-923-4440.. 104 G financialaid@keycollege.edu
ANDREWS, Warren .... 914-654-5926.. 311 A wandrews@cnr.edu
ANDREWS, Wayne, D .... 606-783-2022.. 191 H w.andrews@moreheadstate.edu
ANDREWS-O'HARA, Carla .... 928-523-7221.... 15 H caohara@nau.edu
ANDRIANO, Sarah .... 802-860-2778.. 483 F sandriano@champlain.edu
ANDRIASSIAN, Alen .... 323-953-4000.... 49 H andriaar@lacitycollege.edu
ANDRIATCH, Michael .... 585-395-5809.. 332 E mandriat@brockport.edu
ANDRICK, Jason .... 301-687-4162.. 212 F jpandrick@frostburg.edu
ANDRICK, John .... 701-845-7302.. 361 B john.andrick@vcsu.edu
ANDRIOLA, Tom .... 510-987-0405.... 68 L tom.andriola@ucop.edu
ANDRITO, Neil .... 978-542-6000.. 222 D neil.andrito@salemstate.edu
ANDROUIN, George .... 904-620-4222.. 112 B gandroui@unf.edu
ANDRUK, Robert .... 203-591-7348.... 88 F randruk@post.edu
ANDRUS, Brent .... 801-524-1955.. 480 J brenta51@ldsbc.edu
ANDRUS, Dionne .... 225-216-8221.. 195 H andrusd@mybrcc.edu
ANDRUS, Katie .... 903-823-3125.. 467 C katie.andrus@texarkanacollege.edu
ANDRZJEWSKI, Linda, M 302-356-6754.... 91 I linda.m.andrzjewski@wilmu.edu
ANDUJAR-WENDLAND, Sandra .... 212-686-9040.. 340 D s.andujar@woodtobecoburn.edu
ANEMA, Elizabeth, A .... 413-542-2313.. 214 C alumni@amherst.edu
ANG, Catharina .... 808-373-2849.. 132 G cathyang2008@gmail.com
ANGE, Crystal .... 252-940-6216.. 347 E crystal.ange@beaufortccc.edu
ANGEL, Andrea .... 501-683-7208.... 23 B alangel@ualr.edu
ANGEL, David, P .... 508-793-7320.. 217 B dangel@clarku.edu
ANGEL, Julian .... 305-899-2908.... 96 D jangel@barry.edu
ANGELI, Valerie, G .... 717-867-6232.. 408 F angeli@lvc.edu
ANGELIS, Peter .... 310-825-4941.... 69 D pangelis@ha.ucla.edu
ANGELL, Alecia .... 509-527-3683.. 508 F alecia.angell@wwcc.edu
ANGELL, Lance .... 617-879-1209.. 229 G langell@wheelock.edu
ANGELL, Mary .... 505-473-6322.. 302 A mary.angell@santafeuniversity.edu

ANGELL, Townsend .... 503-777-7763.. 394 I
townsend.angell@reed.edu
ANGELO, Caroline .... 706-227-5375.. 116 H
cangelo@athenstech.edu
ANGELO, Lisa .... 215-968-8306.. 399 A
lisa.angelo@bucks.edu
ANGELONE, Ida .... 973-353-5459.. 296 C
angelone@andromeda.rutgers.edu
ANGELONI, Lisa .... 609-771-3080.. 290 F
angeloni@tcnj.edu
ANGEMI, Karen .... 909-621-8384.... 46 A
karen_angemi@hmc.edu
ANGEMI, Karen .... 909-621-8384.... 46 A
kangemi@hmc.edu
ANGER, Donna .... 907-474-6131.... 10 G
dmanger@alaska.edu
ANGER, Paul .... 928-428-6260.... 13 B
paul.anger@eac.edu
ANGERMEIER, Jaclyn ...... 856-222-9311.. 295 C
jangermeier@rcbc.edu
ANGEVINE, Roger, L .... 606-878-4801.. 190 E
roger.angevine@kctcs.edu
ANGIS, Victoria .... 802-468-1231.. 485 H
victoria.angis@castleton.edu
ANGLE, Nick .... 810-766-4056.. 231 D
nangle02@baker.edu
ANGLE, O. Ray .... 509-313-4100.. 504 A
angle@gonzaga.edu
ANGLE, Perry .... 559-442-4600.... 67 C
perry.angle@fresnocitycollege.edu
ANGLE, Ray .... 919-962-4481.. 357 D
rayangle@email.unc.edu
ANGLE, Steven, R .... 423-425-4141.. 448 F
steven-angle@utc.edu
ANGLIM, Sean .... 315-568-3092.. 323 A
sanglim@nycc.edu
ANGLIN, Jennifer .... 866-251-3244.. 106 A
ANGLIN, Pamela, D .... 903-785-7661.. 463 E
panglin@parisjc.edu
ANGLIN, Roland .... 216-687-5269.. 366 I
r.anglin@csuohio.edu
ANGLIN, Thad .... 254-442-5111.. 454 E
thad.anglin@cisco.edu
ANGRISANI, Vincent .... 718-997-5600.. 309 D
vincent.angrisani@qc.cuny.edu
ANGROVE, William .... 936-294-2774.. 471 D
wla002@shsu.edu
ANGST, JR., Arthur, H ..... 516-876-3094.. 333 C
angsta@oldwestbury.edu
ANGUIANO, Amy .... 540-857-7254.. 499 B
aanguiano@virginiawestern.edu
ANGUIANO, Maria .... 951-827-7310.... 70 B
maria.anguiano@ucr.edu
ANGULO, Michael .... 609-652-4295.. 297 C
michael.angulo@stockton.edu
ANGULO, Susan .... 305-628-6566.. 108 E
cangulo@stu.edu
ANHORN, JR., Jerry .... 509-527-4299.. 508 F
jerry.anhorn@wwcc.edu
ANICH, Kenneth .... 563-876-3353.. 171 I
kanich@dwci.edu
ANID, Nada .... 516-686-7931.. 323 G
nanid@nyit.edu
ANILOWSKI, Jennifer ...... 860-253-3090.... 86 A
janilowski@asnuntuck.edu
ANKE, Sharla, M .... 724-287-8711.. 399 B
sharla.anke@bc3.edu
ANKENY, Mark .... 503-352-2924.. 394 C
mankeny@pacificu.edu
ANKER, Laura, M .... 516-876-3460.. 333 C
ankerl@oldwestbury.edu
ANKER, Perryne .... 310-824-1586.... 24 L
panker@ajrca.org
ANKERBERG, Erik .... 512-313-3000.. 455 F
erik.ankerberg@concordia.edu
ANKERSEN, Lynne .... 843-574-6137.. 433 D
lynne.ankersen@tridenttech.edu
ANKERSON, Katherine ..... 402-472-0243.. 282 M
ANKSORUS, Remington ... 815-928-5554.. 150 I
rjanksorus@olivet.edu
ANKUDA, Pamela .... 802-728-1530.. 486 D
pankuda@vtc.edu
ANNA, Gary, M .... 309-677-3150.. 136 B
gma@bradley.edu
ANNAN, Jack .... 970-521-6690.... 81 O
jack.annan@njc.edu
ANNARELLI, James, J ...... 727-864-8243.... 98 L
annarejj@eckerd.edu
ANNAVARJULA, Madan ... 401-232-6227.. 424 K
mannavar@bryant.edu
ANNE, Kirk .... 585-245-5577.. 333 B
kma@geneseo.edu
ANNEAR, Patricia, T .... 724-287-8711.. 399 B
patricia.annear@bc3.edu
ANNETT, JR., Bruce, J .... 248-204-2200.. 237 B
bannett@ltu.edu
ANNETTE, Harold .... 218-322-2353.. 249 G
harold.annette@itascacc.edu
ANNINO, Louis .... 203-932-7153.... 90 A
lannino@newhaven.edu

ANNIS, David, L .... 405-325-2300.. 389 B
dannis@ou.edu
ANNUNZIATA, Marisa ..... 914-323-1345.. 319 N
marissa.annunziata@mville.edu
ANSARI, Shahid .... 781-239-4277.. 214 G
sansari@babson.edu
ANSBOURY, Pamela .... 210-485-0307.. 450 A
pansboury@alamo.edu
ANSEL, Stuart .... 718-252-7800.. 337 I
sansel@touro.edu
ANSELMENT, Kenneth, L . 920-832-6992.. 517 E
ken.anselment@lawrence.edu
ANSHUS, Corrine, M .... 414-410-4203.. 515 I
cmanshus@stritch.edu
ANSON, Catherine, T .... 216-397-4520.. 370 H
canson@jcu.edu
ANSTEY, Barbara .... 603-271-6484.. 286 F
banstey@ccsnh.edu
ANSTOETTER, Donald ..... 314-792-6120.. 266 F
anstoetter@kenrick.edu
ANSTROM, Deborah .... 828-298-3325.. 359 F
danstrom@warren-wilson.edu
ANSTROM, Deborah .... 828-298-3325.. 359 F
purchasing@warren-wilson.edu
ANT, Susan .... 952-358-8906.. 251 A
susan.ant@normandale.edu
ANTCZAK, Frederick .... 616-331-2495.. 234 F
antczakf@gvsu.edu
ANTCZAK, Laura .... 239-985-3475.. 101 F
lantczak@fsw.edu
ANTEL, Lisa .... 203-596-4585.... 88 F
lantel@post.edu
ANTELL, Tom .... 715-634-4790.. 517 C
tantell@lco.edu
ANTELMAN, Kristin .... 626-395-6416.... 30 H
kristin.antelman@caltech.edu
ANTENEN, James .... 210-826-7595.. 479 D
antenenj@wbu.edu
ANTER, David .... 805-378-1415.... 73 D
danter@vcccd.edu
ANTHONY, Cynthia .... 205-391-5880...... 6 G
canthony@sheltonstate.edu
ANTHONY, David .... 315-464-8047.. 332 C
anthonyd@upstate.edu
ANTHONY, Doug .... 304-424-8280.. 514 D
doug.anthony@wvup.edu
ANTHONY, Elayne .... 601-979-2151.. 258 D
elayne.j.hayes-anthony@jsums.edu
ANTHONY, Hannah .... 773-244-4585.. 149 I
hkanthony@northpark.edu
ANTHONY, Kathy .... 610-526-6045.. 405 B
kanthony@harcum.edu
ANTHONY, Linda .... 612-338-7224.. 256 D
linda.anthony@laureate.net
ANTHONY, Mark .... 808-983-4149.. 130 I
manthony@tokai.edu
ANTHONY, Michael .... 507-285-7217.. 251 I
michael.anthony@rctc.edu
ANTHONY, Miriam .... 708-596-2000.. 154 E
manthony@ssc.edu
ANTHONY, Pamela, D .... 214-768-2821.. 465 J
pdanthony@smu.edu
ANTHONY, Philadelphia .. 336-750-3301.. 359 B
philadelphiawa@wssu.edu
ANTHONY, Sharon .... 215-572-2850.. 397 G
anthony@arcadia.edu
ANTHONY, Yvonne, E .... 617-933-7445.. 224 F
yanthony@rcc.mass.edu
ANTHWAL, Sunny .... 845-398-4061.. 329 G
sunny@stac.edu
ANTILLA, Margaret .... 503-338-2428.. 390 G
mantilla@clatsopcc.edu
ANTKOWIAK, Alex .... 410-337-6061.. 207 H
alex.antkowiak@goucher.edu
ANTKOWIAK, Bruce .... 724-805-2940.. 419 A
bruce.antkowiak@stvincent.edu
ANTMAN, Karen, H .... 617-638-5300.. 216 E
kha4@bu.edu
ANTOINE, Kevin .... 718-270-1361.. 332 B
kevin.antoine@downstate.edu
ANTOINE, Linda, B .... 225-771-4580.. 199 H
linda_antoine@subr.edu
ANTOINE, Tanesha .... 281-922-3453.. 465 B
tanesha.antoine@sjcd.edu
ANTOLINI, Heather .... 304-647-6374.. 514 A
hantolini@osteo.wvsom.edu
ANTOLOVIC, Laurie, G ..... 812-856-5844.. 162 F
lantolov@iu.edu
ANTONAKAKIS, Helen ...... 856-227-7200.. 290 B
hantonakakis@camdencc.edu
ANTONELLO, Michael .... 561-237-7960.. 104 O
mantonello@lynn.edu
ANTONETTI, Nina .... 413-369-4044.. 217 E
antonetti@csld.edu
ANTONICH, Cheryl .... 708-456-0300.. 156 C
cherylantonich@triton.edu
ANTONIO, Anjanette .... 718-289-5800.. 307 C
anjanette.antonio@bcc.cuny.edu
ANTONIO, Edward .... 303-765-3163.... 80 M
eantonio@iliff.edu

ANTONIUK, Donna .... 956-380-8128.. 464 F
dantoniuk@riogrande.edu
ANTONOWICZ, Joseph ..... 908-737-3150.. 292 C
jantonow@kean.edu
ANTONS, Christopher ...... 415-482-1932.... 42 G
christopher.antons@dominican.edu
ANTONUCCI, Carl .... 860-832-2099.... 85 F
antonucci@ccsu.edu
ANTONUCCI, Robert, V .... 800-838-2580.. 226 C
rantonucci@ngs.edu
ANTONUCCI, Toni, C .... 734-763-5846.. 241 J
tca@umich.edu
ANTROBUS, Barbara .... 859-858-2285.. 186 I
ANTROP-GONZALEZ,
Rene .... 651-999-5959.. 250 A
rene.antropgonzalez@metrostate.edu
ANTUNES, Nancy .... 781-891-2686.. 215 F
nantunes@bentley.edu
ANTURKAR, Anjali, N .... 734-764-5132.. 241 J
anturkar@umich.edu
ANUMBA, Chimay .... 352-392-4836.. 112 A
anumba@ufl.edu
ANWAY, Amy .... 419-559-2371.. 377 M
aanway01@terra.edu
ANYANWU, FitzPatrick ..... 337-421-6905.. 197 B
fitzpatrick.anyanwu@sowela.edu
ANYANWU,
Fitzpatrick, U .... 337-421-6905.. 197 B
fitzpatrick.anyanwu@sowela.edu
ANZ, Susan .... 254-710-8641.. 452 H
susan_anz@baylor.edu
ANZALDUA, Ricardo .... 212-237-8316.. 308 E
ranzaldua@jjay.cuny.edu
ANZALONE, Alessandro .. 813-253-7960.. 102 R
aanzalone2@hccfl.edu
ANZALONE, Roseann ...... 518-743-2242.. 335 A
anzalonr@sunyacc.edu
ANZINGER, John .... 240-629-7858.. 207 F
janzinger@frederick.edu
AOUN, Joseph, E .... 617-373-2101.. 227 B
APANEL, Stephen, J .... 570-577-1195.. 398 L
stephen.apanel@bucknell.edu
APANOVICH, Val .... 570-674-6749.. 410 K
vapanovi@misericordia.edu
APAW, David .... 410-225-2464.. 209 B
dapaw@mica.edu
APEKEY, Stella, G .... 571-553-3537.... 92 D
sapekey@gwu.edu
APEL, Scott .... 562-985-4031.... 33 B
scott.apel@csulb.edu
APELIAN, Eil .... 864-242-5100.. 427 E
APELQUIST, Maryellen .... 802-831-1228.. 485 F
mapelquist@vermontlaw.edu
APER, Jeffery, P .... 217-424-6220.. 148 D
japer@millikin.edu
APFELTHALER, Gerhard ... 805-493-3352.... 31 C
apfeltha@callutheran.edu
APICERNO, Amy .... 727-864-8217.... 98 L
apiceral@eckerd.edu
APIGIAN, Caitlin .... 719-389-6705.... 77 J
caitlin.apigian@coloradocollege.edu
APLIN, Greg .... 334-222-6591...... 5 F
jgaplin@lbwcc.edu
APODACA, Phillip, C .... 719-389-6613.... 77 J
papodaca@coloradocollege.edu
APOLLO, Richard, M .... 516-463-5405.. 316 D
richard.apollo@hofstra.edu
APONTE, Adela .... 787-285-2525.. 532 N
adela.aponte@hccpr.edu
APONTE, Arcelio .... 973-353-5541.. 296 C
arcelio.aponte@rutgers.edu
APONTE, Brunilda .... 787-743-7979.. 536 A
baponte@suagm.edu
APONTE, Carmen, L .... 787-780-0070.. 531 B
caponte@caribbean.edu
APONTE, Damaris .... 787-852-1430.. 532 N
d.aponte.r@hccpr.edu
APONTE, Juan, M .... 787-764-0000.. 538 F
juan.aponte6@upr.edu
APONTE, Julio .... 787-274-1142.. 325 C
japonte@stdpr.org
APONTE, Laura, E .... 787-766-1717.. 536 B
um_laporte@suagm.edu
APONTE, Wanda .... 787-786-3030.. 536 F
waponte@ucb.edu.pr
APONTE-AVELLANET,
Nilda .... 787-993-8861.. 537 G
nilda.aponte2@upr.edu
APPAVOO, Suresh .... 415-485-3598.... 42 G
sappavoo@dominican.edu
APPEL, Elizabeth, H .... 410-777-7383.. 206 B
ehappel@aacc.edu
APPEL, Heidi .... 419-530-6031.. 380 D
heidi.appel@utoledo.edu
APPEL, Marie-Noel .... 212-229-5662.. 322 E
appelm@newschool.edu
APPELBAUM, Marla .... 212-229-5192.. 322 E
marla@newschool.edu
APPELGET, Kristin .... 609-258-3018.. 294 D
appelget@princeton.edu

APPELL, Breck, H .... 515-964-0601.. 172 F
appellb@faith.edu
APPELSMITH, Jacob, A ..... 530-754-6295.... 69 A
jappelsmith@ucdavis.edu
APPELT, Uschi .... 812-866-7221.. 161 C
appelt@hanover.edu
APPIAH-PADI,
Stephen, K .... 570-577-3796.. 398 L
s.appiahpadi@bucknell.edu
APPIARIUS, Donald, B .... 260-399-7700.. 168 D
dappiarius@sf.edu
APPLE, Carl .... 616-632-2843.. 231 A
cpa001@aquinas.edu
APPLE, Mark .... 317-955-6775.. 165 N
mapple@marian.edu
APPLE, Monique .... 605-455-6055.. 436 G
mapple@olc.edu
APPLE, Ryan .... 517-321-0242.. 235 C
rapple@glcc.edu
APPLE VANALSTINE,
Judy .... 317-788-3271.. 168 A
japplevanal@uindy.edu
APPLEBURY, Gene .... 901-751-8453.. 442 E
gapplebury@mabts.edu
APPLEBY, Charley .... 870-680-8717.... 19 C
charley_appleby@asun.edu
APPLEBY, Karen .... 208-282-2783.. 133 H
applekare@isu.edu
APPLEGATE, J. Phillip ..... 918-631-2070.. 389 E
phil-applegate@utulsa.edu
APPLEGATE, John .... 812-855-9198.. 162 E
jsapple@iu.edu
APPLEGATE, John, S .... 812-855-9198.. 162 F
jsapple@iu.edu
APPLEGRAD, Yaakov .... 732-367-1060.. 289 G
APPLEMAN, Boomer .... 508-559-5208.. 383 H
bappleman@ecok.edu
APPLETON, Judith, A ...... 607-255-9970.. 312 A
jaa2@cornell.edu
APPLETON, Kevin .... 410-651-6230.. 212 B
kappleton@umes.edu
APPLETON, Lea .... 909-445-2590.... 39 A
lappleton@cst.edu
APPLIN, Mary Beth .... 601-857-3253.. 258 A
mary.applin@hindscc.edu
APPLING, Ron .... 806-291-3451.. 479 D
applingr@wbu.edu
APPOLONIA, Terry .... 814-938-6711.. 415 B
terry.appolonia@iup.edu
APPREY, Augustine .... 717-290-8747.. 408 B
aapprey@lancasterseminary.edu
APPREY, Maurice .... 434-924-7923.. 495 H
ma9h@virginia.edu
APSEY, Curt .... 406-447-5479.. 276 B
capsey@carroll.edu
APSEY, Curt .... 208-426-1781.. 132 I
capsey@boisestate.edu
AQUI, Jason .... 425-564-4128.. 501 F
jason.aqui@bellevuecollege.edu
AQUILA, Dominic .... 713-525-2164.. 475 J
aquilad@stthom.edu
AQUILA, Jennifer, K .... 610-799-1120.. 408 G
jaquila@lccc.edu
AQUILA, Scott, W .... 610-799-1550.. 408 G
saquila@lccc.edu
AQUINO, Belissa .... 787-766-1717.. 536 B
beaquino@suagm.edu
AQUINO, Carlos .... 815-740-3398.. 157 F
caquino@stfrancis.edu
AQUINO, Cathy .... 304-734-6611.. 511 M
cathy.aquino@bridgevalley.edu
AQUINO, Jeannette .... 787-890-2681.. 537 E
jeanette.aquino@upr.edu
ARABIA, Caprice .... 716-926-8942.. 316 B
carabia@hilbert.edu
ARADHYA, Jennifer, M .... 781-280-3511.. 224 A
aradhyaj@middlesex.mass.edu
ARAGON, Paul .... 575-769-4165.. 299 G
paul.aragon@clovis.edu
ARAGON, Ruben .... 505-454-3330.. 300 F
rubenaragon@nmhu.edu
ARAIMO, Angelo, G .... 718-390-3412.. 339 F
aaraimo@wagner.edu
ARAIN, Nizam .... 608-785-8541.. 520 C
narain@uwlax.edu
ARAIZA, Claudia .... 619-298-1829.... 66 D
caraiza@ssu.edu
ARAIZA, William .... 718-780-7520.. 305 L
bill.araiza@brooklaw.edu
ARALDI, Mary-Jane, S ..... 518-471-3260.. 320 F
maryjane.araldi@sphp.com
ARAMMASH, Fouzi, H ...... 803-705-4311.. 427 D
arammashf@benedict.edu
ARANA, Sloane .... 918-540-6393.. 384 F
scbrown@neo.edu
ARANAS, Theodore .... 415-239-3546.... 38 E
taranas@ccsf.edu
ARANDA, Eileen .... 909-667-4411.... 38 G
president@claremontlincoln.edu
ARANDA, Romelia .... 830-758-4125.. 466 A
rdaranda@swtjc.edu

ARANEO, Mary Lou .... 631-451-4611.. 336 D
araneom@sunysuffolk.edu
ARANT, Mark .... 918-444-2060.. 384 G
arant@nsuok.edu
ARANT, T.J .... 678-407-5200.. 121 B
tjarant@ggc.edu
ARAQUE, Maria .... 312-915-8777.. 146 G
maraque@luc.edu
ARAS, Kate .... 949-794-9090.... 66 H
karas@stanbridge.edu
ARAUJO, Lisa .... 516-877-3230.. 303 B
araujo@adelphi.edu
ARAÚJO, Aúrea .... 787-834-9595.. 536 E
aaraujo@uaa.edu
ARBALLO, Madelyn .... 909-594-5611.... 53 C
marballo@mtsac.edu
ARBELO, Enid .... 787-878-5475.. 533 H
earbelo@arecibo.inter.edu
ARBERY, Glen .... 307-332-2930.. 527 F
garbery@wyomingcatholiccollege.com
ARBIDE, Donna, A .... 305-284-2873.. 114 H
darbide@miami.edu
ARBONEAUX, Annette ..... 985-448-4041.. 201 A
annette.arboneaux@nicholls.edu
ARBUCKLE, Joanne .... 212-217-4680.. 314 B
joanne_arbuckle@fitnyc.edu
ARBUSTO, Joan .... 203-575-8091.... 86 G
jarbusto@nv.edu
ARBUTHNOT, Beth .... 706-864-1440.. 128 F
beth.arbuthnot@ung.edu
ARCARESE, Chris .... 303-352-3032.... 79 F
chris.arcarese@ccd.edu
ARCARIO, Paul .... 718-482-5400.. 309 A
arcariop@lagcc.cuny.edu
ARCE, Ana .... 787-894-2828.. 539 A
ana.arce1@upr.edu
ARCE, Elsa, M .... 412-365-1282.. 400 G
arce@chatham.edu
ARCE, Frank .... 312-752-2478.. 144 E
frank.arce@kendall.edu
ARCE, Joshua .... 785-749-8482.. 181 E
jarce@haskell.edu
ARCE, Katherine .... 310-338-2881.... 51 E
katherine.arce@lmu.edu
ARCE, Lydia .... 787-857-3600.. 533 I
larce@br.inter.edu
ARCELUS, Victor, J .... 860-439-2834.... 87 F
victor.arcelus@conncoll.edu
ARCENEAUX, Alex .... 985-448-4004.. 201 A
alex.arceneaux@nicholls.edu
ARCH, Xan .... 503-943-7310.. 396 B
arch@up.edu
ARCHABAL, Alice .... 414-955-4718.. 518 A
aarchabal@mcw.edu
ARCHAMBAULT, Karen, L 856-222-9311.. 295 C
karchambault@rcbc.edu
ARCHAMBAULT, Marc ..... 270-745-6208.. 194 D
marc.archambault@wku.edu
ARCHBALD, Patrick, T ..... 413-545-2125.. 220 F
archbald@umass.edu
ARCHBOLD, David, J .... 248-370-3358.. 239 K
archbold@oakland.edu
ARCHER, Chris .... 603-623-0313.. 287 D
chrisarcher@nhia.edu
ARCHER, Chrysta, M .... 610-914-1402.. 422 C
cmarcher@valleyforge.edu
ARCHER, Daniel, L .... 801-581-6326.. 481 M
darcher@campusstore.utah.edu
ARCHER, Elizabeth .... 619-876-4250.... 68 I
earcher@usuniversity.edu
ARCHER, III, Frank .... 229-430-3686.. 115 K
frank.archer@asurams.edu
ARCHER, Gie .... 940-668-7731.. 462 L
marcher@nctc.edu
ARCHER, Keith, A .... 309-341-7212.. 145 A
kaarcher@knox.edu
ARCHER, Kevin .... 509-963-3101.. 501 K
kevin.archer@cwu.edu
ARCHER, Len .... 407-303-5619.... 95 C
len.archer@adu.edu
ARCHER, Linda, R .... 757-446-6190.. 489 B
archerlr@evms.edu
ARCHER, Lynn .... 412-536-1182.. 406 K
lynn.archer@laroche.edu
ARCHER, Max .... 281-998-6024.. 469 F
marcher@txchiro.edu
ARCHER, Nicole .... 415-351-3553.... 61 B
narcher@sfai.edu
ARCHER, Patrick, C .... 563-333-6263.. 176 D
archerpatrickc@sau.edu
ARCHER, Rebecca .... 321-674-7571.. 100 M
rarcher@fit.edu
ARCHER, Ron .... 714-879-3901.... 46 F
rarcher@hiu.edu
ARCHER, Ryan .... 316-295-5410.. 181 B
archerr@friends.edu
ARCHER, Thomas, R .... 802-626-6454.. 486 C
thomas.archer@lyndonstate.edu
ARCHER-RIERSON, Abby . 620-242-0439.. 183 C
archera@mcpherson.edu
ARCHEY, Larry .... 413-559-5767.. 219 C

ARCHIBALD, Michael ...... 909-621-8152.... 64 A
marchiba@scrippscollege.edu
ARCHIBALD, Sandra, O ... 206-616-1648.. 508 E
sarch@uw.edu
ARCHIE, Tiffenia, D .... 215-204-9213.. 420 B
tiffenia.archie@temple.edu
ARCHINAL, Ginette .... 336-278-7230.. 344 D
garchinal@elon.edu
ARCHULETA, Irma .... 408-223-6749.... 62 D
irma.archuleta@evc.edu
ARCHULETA, Leticia .... 505-454-2502.. 299 M
larchuleta@luna.edu
ARCHULETA, Renee .... 303-914-6345.... 82 I
renee.archuleta@rrcc.edu
ARCILA, Luz .... 727-864-7748.... 98 L
arcilal@eckerd.edu
ARCUINO, Cathy, L .... 620-235-4680.. 184 C
carcuino@pittstate.edu
ARCURY, Tara, L .... 802-654-2212.. 484 I
tarcury@smcvt.edu
ARD, Aaron .... 803-584-3446.. 434 C
ajard@mailbox.sc.edu
ARDAGNA, Wendy .... 856-776-2370.. 290 I
wardagna@cccnj.edu
ARDAIOLO, Frank, P .... 803-323-2251.. 435 B
ardaiolof@winthrop.edu
ARDALAN, Shah .... 281-290-2777.. 461 B
shah.ardalan@lonestar.edu
ARDEN, Warwick, A .... 919-515-2195.. 357 B
warwick_arden@ncsu.edu
ARDIS, Ann .... 302-831-2054.... 91 F
aardis@udel.edu
ARDREY, Melantha .... 843-953-3257.. 428 G
ardreym@cofc.edu
AREA, Ron .... 304-696-2826.. 513 D
area@marshall.edu
AREIZAGA, Jose, R .... 787-891-0925.. 533 G
jareizag@aguadilla.inter.edu
ARELLANO, Jerry .... 210-486-3884.. 450 D
jarellano59@alamo.edu
ARELLANO, Margarita, M 512-245-2124.. 471 F
ma33@txstate.edu
AREMU, Kola .... 256-761-6175...... 7 F
karemu@talladega.edu
ARENA, Maryanne .... 585-345-6802.. 315 C
mcarena@genesee.edu
ARENA, Meaghan .... 585-245-5619.. 333 B
arena@geneseo.edu
ARENA, Michael .... 646-664-9319.. 306 M
michael.arena@cuny.edu
ARENAS-FUENTES,
Lenina .... 206-543-5010.. 508 E
mlenina@uw.edu
ARENAS-RIVERA,
Edith, N .... 212-346-1257.. 325 J
earenas@pace.edu
ARENAZ, Pablo .... 956-326-2320.. 468 A
president@tamiu.edu
AREND, Lori .... 412-536-2506.. 406 K
lori.arend@laroche.edu
AREND, Matthew .... 517-629-0521.. 230 E
marend@albion.edu
ARENDT, Ben .... 616-526-6000.. 232 A
ARENDT, Thomas, K .... 562-902-3355.... 66 A
tomarendt@scuhs.edu
ARENIVAS, Marisol .... 520-417-4115..... 12 L
arenivasm@cochise.edu
ARENS, Dave .... 712-279-1715.. 170 B
dave.arens@briarcliff.edu
ARENS, Timothy, E .... 312-329-4191.. 148 F
timothy.arens@moody.edu
ARENS, Trente .... 630-829-6077.. 135 F
tarens@ben.edu
ARESON, Ann, H .... 814-332-6556.. 397 A
aareson@allegheny.edu
ARETA, Ropeti .... 684-699-1575.. 529 E
a.areta@amsamoa.edu
ARETS, Wiel .... 312-567-3263.. 142 I
wiel.arets@iit.edu
ARETZ, Anthony .... 406-791-5300.. 278 G
anthony.aretz@ugf.edu
AREVALO-HILLEN,
Jessica .... 510-594-3788.... 29 K
jarevalo@cca.edu
AREY, Emily .... 704-669-4139.. 348 F
areye@clevelandcc.edu
AREY, George, A .... 617-552-4725.. 216 C
george.arey@bc.edu
AREY, Jason .... 207-216-4399.. 204 B
jarey@yccc.edu
AREY, Sherrie .... 406-791-5309.. 278 G
sherrie.arey@ugf.edu
ARGENTIERI, Colleen ...... 607-587-3932.. 334 G
argentch@alfredstate.edu
ARGIRI, Elizabeth .... 586-445-7306.. 237 C
argiril@macomb.edu
ARGO, Linda .... 202-885-2753.... 91 J
largo@american.edu
ARGO, Mike, A .... 870-235-4083.... 22 F
maargo@saumag.edu

ARGO, Scott .... 706-667-4095.. 117 D
sargo@augusta.edu
ARGO, Trent .... 276-326-4217.. 487 F
targo@bluefield.edu
ARGUELLES, Adrianna ..... 718-939-5100.. 319 A
aarguelles@libi.edu
ARGUELLES, Alejandro .... 787-250-0000.. 537 D
alejandro.arguelles@upr.edu
ARGYRIS, Steven, G .... 510-649-2430.... 45 G
sargyris@gtu.edu
ARHIN, Afua .... 910-672-1924.. 356 E
aarhin@uncfsu.edu
ARHIPOV, Sergei, D .... 570-581-1818.. 418 H
sergei.arhipov@stots.edu
ARIAS, Hamlet .... 305-273-4499.... 97 M
hamelet.arias@cbt.edu
ARIAS, Michael, R .... 949-824-3868.... 69 C
mrarias@uci.edu
ARICK, Bruce, E .... 317-940-9481.. 159 K
barick@butler.edu
ARICK, Elaine, C .... 330-471-8138.. 371 J
earick@malone.edu
ARIDA, Lisa, A .... 716-839-8218.. 312 D
larida@daemen.edu
ARILSON, Barbara .... 440-375-7000.. 371 E
barilson@lec.edu
ARIOLA-SUKISAKI,
Kainoa .... 808-932-7777.. 131 E
kariola@hawaii.edu
ARISMENDEZ, Dee Dee ... 361-664-2981.. 454 G
deedeea@coastalbend.edu
ARISTIZABAL,
Humberto, X .... 410-543-6426.. 213 A
hxarisitzabal@salisbury.edu
ARIZA, Cristina .... 210-829-3870.. 474 D
mariza@uiwtx.edu
ARIZA, Diane, M .... 203-582-8939.... 88 G
diane.ariza@quinnipiac.edu
ARIZA, Ricardo, M .... 402-280-2469.. 279 H
ariza@creighton.edu
ARJUNE, Ricky, B .... 904-620-2502.. 112 B
rarjune@unf.edu
ARLINGTON, David, L ...... 716-851-1987.. 313 H
arlington@ecc.edu
ARLITSCH, Kenning .... 406-994-6978.. 277 C
kenning.arlitsch@montana.edu
ARMAGOST, Mark, S .... 814-863-4308.. 412 F
msa17@psu.edu
ARMBRUSTER, Shirley ..... 559-278-2795.... 32 F
shirleya@csufresno.edu
ARMENDARIZ, John .... 617-373-2133.. 227 B
ARMENT, Susan .... 660-263-4100.. 269 D
susana@macc.edu
ARMENTA, Richard, R ...... 512-223-7795.. 451 N
rarmenta@austincc.edu
ARMENTOR, Melissa .... 409-880-8853.. 470 H
mfarmentor@lit.edu
ARMENTROUT,
Barbara, S .... 434-223-6220.. 490 D
barmentrout@hsc.edu
ARMENTROUT, Renae ...... 319-208-5015.. 176 J
rarmentrout@scciowa.edu
ARMES, Traci .... 812-941-2260.. 163 F
trarmes@ius.edu
ARMIJO, Danny .... 575-624-8250.. 300 I
darmijo@nmmi.edu
ARMIJO, Lillian .... 575-835-5780.. 300 G
larmijo@admin.nmt.edu
ARMINANA, Ruben .... 707-664-2156.... 35 D
ruben.arminana@sonoma.edu
ARMINGTON, Thomas ..... 610-526-1391.. 397 E
tom.armington@theamericancollege.edu
ARMINI, Michael, A .... 617-373-5718.. 227 B
ARMINIAK, Anthony .... 734-374-3227.. 242 H
aarmini1@wcccd.edu
ARMISTEAD, Katya .... 805-893-8912.... 70 E
katya.armistead@sa.ucsb.edu
ARMISTEAD, Lisa, P .... 404-413-2091.. 122 D
larmistead@gsu.edu
ARMISTEAD, William .... 304-473-8509.. 515 B
armistead_w@wvwc.edu
ARMOND, Pashuan .... 919-466-4400.... 93 F
ARMONY, Ariel .... 412-648-7374.. 421 G
armony@pitt.edu
ARMOR, Thomas, W .... 317-738-8045.. 160 J
tarmor@franklincollege.edu
ARMOUR, Angela .... 802-654-2527.. 484 I
aarmour@smcvt.edu
ARMOUR, Janet .... 662-862-8383.. 258 C
jyarmour@iccms.edu
ARMOUR, Lisa .... 352-381-3642.. 109 C
lisa.armour@sfcollege.edu
ARMOUR, Robert .... 606-546-1799.. 193 E
rarmour@unionky.edu
ARMOUR, Robin .... 925-473-7501.... 41 J
rarmour@losmedanos.edu
ARMOZA, Marcela .... 718-260-4999.. 309 C
marmoza@citytech.cuny.edu
ARMS, Gina .... 516-686-7902.. 323 G
garms@nyit.edu

ARMSTRONG, Albert .... 305-899-3250.... 96 D
aarmstrong@barry.edu
ARMSTRONG, Amy .... 830-792-7405.. 465 E
anarmstrong@schreiner.edu
ARMSTRONG, Andrew ...... 310-655-6970.... 55 E
aarmstrong@otis.edu
ARMSTRONG, Andrew, V 540-636-2900.. 488 D
armstrong@christendom.edu
ARMSTRONG, Booker .... 816-604-4125.. 267 K
booker.armstrong@mcckc.edu
ARMSTRONG, Connie .... 334-291-4981...... 2 H
connie.armstrong@cv.edu
ARMSTRONG, Dale .... 615-966-5148.. 441 F
dale.armstrong@lipscomb.edu
ARMSTRONG, David .... 706-865-2134.. 128 D
darmstrong@truett.edu
ARMSTRONG, David .... 507-389-7206.. 252 D
david.armstrong@southcentral.edu
ARMSTRONG, David, A ..... 859-344-3348.. 193 C
darmstrong@thomasmore.edu
ARMSTRONG, David, M .. 816-501-2423.. 262 G
david.armstrong@avila.edu
ARMSTRONG, Elizabeth ... 540-231-7197.. 499 F
beth1@vt.edu
ARMSTRONG, Franca .... 315-334-7701.. 321 G
farmstrong@mvcc.edu
ARMSTRONG, Gary .... 816-415-7651.. 275 F
armstrongg@william.jewell.edu
ARMSTRONG, JR.,
J. David .... 954-201-7401.... 96 I
darmstro@broward.edu
ARMSTRONG, Jeanette .... 608-796-3395.. 522 O
jearmstrong@viterbo.edu
ARMSTRONG, Jeffrey, D .. 805-756-1111.... 31 I
presidentsoffice@calpoly.edu
ARMSTRONG, Katelynn .. 618-634-3270.. 154 B
katelynna@shawneecc.edu
ARMSTRONG, Keith .... 719-590-6758.... 79 D
karmstrong@coloradotech.edu
ARMSTRONG, Kelli, J .... 617-552-0585.. 216 C
kelli.armstrong@bc.edu
ARMSTRONG, Kevin .... 402-375-7510.. 281 J
kearmst1@wsc.edu
ARMSTRONG, Kim .... 501-337-5000.... 19 K
karmstrong@coto.edu
ARMSTRONG, Kimberly ... 717-358-3985.. 403 J
kim.armstrong@fandm.edu
ARMSTRONG, Lee, F .... 334-844-5176...... 1 G
armstlf@auburn.edu
ARMSTRONG, Lori, B .... 410-704-3570.. 213 B
larmstrong@towson.edu
ARMSTRONG, Mary Beth 205-665-6720...... 9 B
armstrom@montevallo.edu
ARMSTRONG, Molly .... 252-246-1396.. 354 D
marmstrong@wilsoncc.edu
ARMSTRONG, Myeshia ..... 562-908-3404.... 58 I
marmstrong@riohondo.edu
ARMSTRONG, Nancy, A .. 419-772-2251.. 374 J
n-armstrong@onu.edu
ARMSTRONG, Neal, R ...... 520-621-3513.... 17 I
nra@email.arizona.edu
ARMSTRONG, Patricia, J .. 615-353-3758.. 446 E
patricia.armstrong@nscc.edu
ARMSTRONG, Peter .... 402-465-2153.. 281 K
parmstro@nebrwesleyan.edu
ARMSTRONG, Shirley .... 334-291-4964...... 2 H
shirley.armstrong@cv.edu
ARMSTRONG, Steven, M . 920-832-6769.. 517 E
steven.m.armstrong@lawrence.edu
ARMSTRONG, Susan .... 318-675-5406.. 198 B
sarmst@lsuhsc.edu
ARMSTRONG, Terri, A ..... 530-251-8839.... 48 E
tarmstrong@lassencollege.edu
ARMSTRONG, Tonya .... 919-572-1625.. 341 M
tarmstrong@apexsot.edu
ARMSTRONG, Virginia ..... 760-921-5444.... 56 E
virginia.armstrong@paloverde.edu
ARMSTRONG, Vivian .... 787-284-1912.. 534 C
varmstro@ponce.inter.edu
ARMSTRONG, William, L 303-963-3350.... 77 I
warmstrong@ccu.edu
ARMUSEWICZ, Allison ..... 716-614-6238.. 324 D
aarmusewicz@niagaracc.suny.edu
ARN, Diana .... 501-977-2001.... 24 B
arn@uaccm.edu
ARNADE, Peter .... 808-956-6460.. 131 F
parnade@hawaii.edu
ARNAK, Sonja .... 949-582-4602.... 65 G
slopezarnak@saddleback.edu
ARNDT, Steve, A .... 919-515-8851.. 357 B
saarndt@ncsu.edu
ARNDT, Steven, E .... 910-521-6209.. 358 C
steven.arndt@uncp.edu
ARNDT, Wayne .... 732-987-2237.. 292 A
warndt@georgian.edu
ARNER, Joseph .... 352-588-7548.. 108 C
joseph.arner@saintleo.edu
ARNER, Lori .... 802-468-1211.. 485 H
lori.arner@castleton.edu
ARNER, Lynette .... 330-263-2139.. 367 A
larner@wooster.edu

ARNER, Thomas .... 802-828-2800.. 486 A
arnert@ccv.edu
ARNESON, Dean, L .... 262-243-5700.. 516 E
dean.arneson@cuw.edu
ARNESON, Rosemary ...... 540-654-1000.. 495 C
rarneso3@umw.edu
ARNETT, David, J .... 978-478-3400.. 227 C
darnett@northpoint.edu
ARNETT, Donna .... 859-218-2247.. 193 G
donna.arnett@uky.edu
ARNETT, Harold .... 620-441-6584.. 180 D
harold.arnett@cowley.edu
ARNEY, Doug .... 956-296-1535.. 476 E
doug.arney@utrgv.edu
ARNEY, Janna .... 956-665-2100.. 476 E
janna.arney@utrgv.edu
ARNN, Larry .... 517-607-2301.. 235 E
larnn@hillsdale.edu
ARNO, Marlene .... 716-851-1431.. 313 H
arno@ecc.edu
ARNOLD, Aimee, C .... 262-472-5955.. 521 F
mccanna@uww.edu
ARNOLD, Angela .... 952-358-9045.. 251 A
angela.arnold@normandale.edu
ARNOLD, Carl .... 903-233-4310.. 460 J
carlarnold@letu.edu
ARNOLD, Carolyn .... 510-723-6965.... 37 B
carnold@chabotcollege.edu
ARNOLD, Christina .... 616-234-3532.. 234 E
carnold@grcc.edu
ARNOLD, Clinton, E .... 562-903-4816.... 28 E
clinton.arnold@biola.edu
ARNOLD, David .... 575-492-2124.. 302 M
darnold@usw.edu
ARNOLD, Gertrude, L ...... 208-426-3236.. 132 I
gertiarnold@boisestate.edu
ARNOLD, Harvey .... 772-462-6210.. 103 B
harnold@irsc.edu
ARNOLD, Jane .... 412-536-1786.. 406 K
jane.arnold@laroche.edu
ARNOLD, Jeanne .... 717-337-6375.. 404 C
jarnold@gettysburg.edu
ARNOLD, Jeff (Dean) .... 262-472-1922.. 521 F
arnoldd@uww.edu
ARNOLD, Jill .... 573-629-3103.. 265 G
jarnold@hlg.edu
ARNOLD, Joan .... 575-624-7261.. 299 J
joan.arnold@roswell.enmu.edu
ARNOLD, Jon .... 714-895-8183.... 39 F
jarnold@gwc.cccd.edu
ARNOLD, Jon .... 931-540-2538.. 446 A
jarnold15@columbiastate.edu
ARNOLD, Joshua .... 909-599-5433.... 48 K
jarnold@lifepacific.edu
ARNOLD, Julie .... 419-448-2953.. 369 G
jarnold3@heidelberg.edu
ARNOLD, Kathy .... 512-313-3000.. 455 F
kathy.arnold@concordia.edu
ARNOLD, Kenneth, L .... 707-256-3331.... 53 H
karnold@napavalley.edu
ARNOLD, Lester .... 336-750-2000.. 359 B
arnoldle@wssu.edu
ARNOLD, Lorene, R .... 260-399-7700.. 168 D
larnold@sf.edu
ARNOLD, Mary, M .... 651-641-8268.. 246 B
marnold@csp.edu
ARNOLD, Michael, A .... 302-831-1916.... 91 F
marnold@udel.edu
ARNOLD, Randall .... 303-245-4797.... 81 I
rarnold@naropa.edu
ARNOLD, Robert .... 901-321-4299.. 439 E
rarnold@cbu.edu
ARNOLD, Rodney .... 870-743-3000.... 21 C
rarnold@northark.edu
ARNOLD, Sally .... 978-232-2029.. 218 D
sarnold@endicott.edu
ARNOLD, Shirley, E .... 828-884-8329.. 342 C
arnoldse@brevard.edu
ARNOLD, Stephen .... 409-984-6249.. 471 C
stephen.arnold@lamarpa.edu
ARNOLD, Sue .... 281-487-1170.. 469 F
sarnold@txchiro.edu
ARNOLD, Susan .... 610-606-4609.. 400 E
swarnold@cedarcrest.edu
ARNOLD, Tai .... 518-587-2100.. 335 D
tai.arnold@esc.edu
ARNOLD, Timothy .... 716-338-1125.. 317 F
timothyarnold@mail.sunyjcc.edu
ARNOLD, Ulises .... 303-352-3038.... 79 F
ARNOLD, Virginia .... 404-872-3593.. 117 B
varnold@johnmarshall.edu
ARNOLD, III, W. Ellis ...... 501-450-1223.... 20 F
arnold@hendrix.edu
ARNONE, Harriet .... 516-686-7517.. 323 G
harnone@nyit.edu
ARNOULD, Karen, A .... 810-762-3344.. 242 B
karnould@umflint.edu
ARNOVE, Theresa .... 410-532-5155.. 210 B
tarnove@ndm.edu
ARNST, Scott .... 810-762-3123.. 242 B
sarnst@umflint.edu

ARNZEN, Diane .... 636-481-3282.. 266 C
darnzen@jeffco.edu
AROBBA, Sarah .... 605-856-5880.. 436 I
sarah.arobba@sintegleska.edu
AROMANDO, Drew, C .... 609-896-5178.. 295 B
aromando@rider.edu
ARON, Deborah .... 215-635-7300.. 404 D
daron@gratz.edu
ARONSON, Ann .... 612-624-6868.. 255 H
aronson@umn.edu
ARONSON, Ed .... 541-881-5875.. 395 E
earonson@tvcc.cc
ARONSON, Linda .... 508-849-3458.. 214 E
laronson@annamaria.edu
ARONSON, Meigan, C ...... 979-845-7361.. 468 B
maronson@tamu.edu
ARONSON, Roberta, C ..... 412-396-1818.. 403 A
aronson@duq.edu
ARONSON, Susan .... 213-624-1200.... 43 J
saronson@fidm.edu
ARONSTAM, Robert, S ..... 570-389-5333.. 414 D
aronstam@bloomu.edu
ARONSTEIN, Susan .... 307-766-4110.. 527 B
aronstei@uwyo.edu
ARORA, Deepa .... 478-934-6588.. 124 E
deepa.arora@mga.edu
ARORA SINGH, Alka .... 623-845-3968.... 14 C
alka.arora.singh@gccaz.edu
AROSEMENA, Eduardo ..... 787-728-1545.. 539 B
earosemena@sagrado.edu
AROZ, Susan, D .... 480-732-7075.... 13 O
sue.aroz@cgc.edu
ARP, Dan .... 541-737-2331.. 393 H
dan.arp@oregonstate.edu
ARP, Robert .... 707-654-1037.... 33 D
rarp@csum.edu
ARPINO, Donald .... 617-879-7899.. 222 A
darpino@massart.edu
ARQUETTE, Mary .... 419-824-3969.. 371 I
marquette@lourdes.edu
ARQUETTE, Robert .... 419-517-7446.. 371 I
rarquette@lourdes.edu
ARQUETTE, Toby .... 630-844-5614.. 135 E
tarquett@aurora.edu
ARRAIZA, Ana, M .... 787-751-0160.. 531 M
aarraiza@cmpr.pr.gov
ARRAY, Susan .... 608-663-2000.. 517 F
sarray@mediainstitute.edu
ARREDONDO, Arnold .... 901-572-2455.. 438 I
arnold.arredondo@bchs.edu
ARREDONDO, Marisol ...... 714-628-7339.... 37 F
arredond@chapman.edu
ARRELLAGA, Maria, M ...... 512-471-6080.. 476 B
arrellaga@utexas.edu
ARRIAZA, Cecilia .... 714-992-7087.... 54 H
carriaza@fullcoll.edu
ARRIBAS,
Maria del Carmen .... 787-257-7373.. 535 P
ue_marribas@suagm.edu
ARRINGTON, Cedric .... 256-551-1711...... 4 F
cedric.arrington@drakestate.edu
ARRINGTON, Doris, B .... 860-906-5085.... 86 B
darrington@ccc.commnet.edu
ARRINGTON, Harriett .... 276-523-2400.. 497 F
harrington@mecc.edu
ARRINGTON, Michelle .... 601-266-6698.. 261 E
michelle.arrington@usm.edu
ARRINGTON, Pam .... 330-966-5460.. 377 J
parrington@starkstate.edu
ARRINGTON, Pamela .... 334-241-9592...... 7 H
parrington@troy.edu
ARRINGTON,
Stephanie, K .... 765-285-8304.. 159 B
skarrington@bsu.edu
ARRINGTON, Tom .... 281-459-7613.. 465 A
tom.arrington@sjcd.edu
ARRINGTON, Trey .... 864-587-4396.. 433 A
arringtont@smcsc.edu
ARRINGTON-JONES,
Angela .... 773-291-6297.. 137 G
aarrington@ccc.edu
ARRIOLA, Yolanda .... 915-778-4001.. 466 B
ARROWOOD, Roarke .... 828-835-4305.. 353 G
rarrowood@tricountycc.edu
ARROWSMITH, Jason .... 360-442-2270.. 504 G
jarrowsmith@lowercolumbia.edu
ARROYO, Carmen .... 787-620-2040.. 530 F
carroyo@aupr.edu
ARROYO, Cheryl .... 219-989-2977.. 166 F
cheryla@pnw.edu
ARROYO, Cruz .... 253-964-4688.. 506 G
carroyo@stmartin.edu
ARROYO, Gladys .... 787-279-1912.. 533 J
garroyo@bayamon.inter.edu
ARROYO, Ivonne, D .... 787-257-7323.. 535 P
iarroyo@suagm.edu
ARROYO, Patti .... 303-404-5111.... 80 E
patti.arroyo@frontrange.edu
ARROYO, Sandra .... 787-765-3560.. 532 I
sarroyo@edpuniversity.edu

ARRUDA, Yvonne, D .... 401-865-2480.. 425 D
yarruda@providence.edu
ARRUTTI, Duane .... 505-277-8125.. 302 F
darrutti@unm.edu
ARSHACK, Susan .... 912-344-2596.. 116 E
susan.arshack@armstrong.edu
ARTALE, Maureen, P .... 607-436-3216.. 331 F
maureen.artale@oneonta.edu
ARTEAGA, Joseph .... 805-546-3205.... 41 L
joseph_arteaga@cuesta.edu
ARTEAGA-JOHNSON
Craig .... 909-607-6643.... 58 A
craig.arteagajohnson@pomona.edu
ARTECONA, Sarah, N .... 305-284-5490.. 114 H
sartecona@miami.edu
ARTENTSEN, Marc .... 508-541-1608.. 217 G
marentsen@dean.edu
ARTER, Neil .... 405-425-5906.. 385 C
neil.arter@oc.edu
ARTERBURN, Dave .... 256-824-6846...... 8 F
david.r.arterburn@uah.edu
ARTHO, Donna .... 936-294-3101.. 471 D
artho@shsu.edu
ARTHUR, Christon .... 269-471-3404.. 230 H
christon@andrews.edu
ARTHUR, Dave .... 512-476-2772.. 451 O
finaid@austingrad.edu
ARTHUR, Gwendolynne ..... 508-793-7384.. 217 B
garthur@clarku.edu
ARTHUR, Jeff .... 757-671-7171.. 489 C
jarthur@ecpi.edu
ARTHUR, Mark .... 405-789-7661.. 388 B
mark.arthur@swcu.edu
ARTHUR, Salinda .... 912-478-5253.. 122 B
sarthur@georgiasouthern.edu
ARTHUR, Scott .... 303-724-8469.... 84 A
scott.arthur@ucdenver.edu
ARTHUR, Virginia .... 651-793-1900.. 250 A
ginny.arthur@metrostate.edu
ARTHURS, Margaret .... 607-431-4061.. 315 E
arthursm@hartwick.edu
ARTIBEE, Jessica .... 952-446-4130.. 246 D
artibeej@crown.edu
ARTIGUES, Jay .... 985-549-2253.. 201 C
ARTIM, Chris .... 219-844-0100.. 159 E
christopher.artim@brightwood.edu
ARTIS, Christine .... 718-933-6700.. 321 I
cartis@monroecollege.edu
ARTIS, Lori .... 618-468-3000.. 145 G
lartis@lc.edu
ARTLEY, James .... 904-256-1162.. 100 E
jartley@fcsl.edu
ARTMAN, Richard, B .... 608-796-3001.. 522 O
rbartman@viterbo.edu
ARTMAN, Vickie .... 618-634-3219.. 154 B
vickiea@shawneecc.edu
ARULANANDAM,
Bernard .... 210-458-6859.. 477 A
bernard.arulanandam@utsa.edu
ARUM, Richard .... 949-824-8026.... 69 C
richard.arum@uci.edu
ARUNACHALAM, Vairam . 573-882-3225.. 273 E
arunachalam@missouri.edu
ARUSH, Ilan .... 661-824-2977.... 53 K
iarush@mps.edu
ARVAN, April .... 920-565-2327.. 517 D
arvanaa@lakeland.edu
ARVELO, Wildolfo .... 603-427-7602.. 286 B
warvelo@ccsnh.edu
ARVIDSON, Susie .... 620-223-2700.. 181 A
susiea@fortscott.edu
ARVIN, Ann .... 650-498-6227.... 66 I
aarvin@stanford.edu
ARVIN, Loraine .... 503-517-7625.. 394 I
arvinl@reed.edu
ARVISO, Jason .... 505-786-4193.. 300 E
jarviso@navajotech.edu
ARVIZU, Mimi .... 408-848-4840.... 44 I
marvizu@gavilan.edu
ARVIZU, Primavera .... 661-763-7815.... 67 F
parvizu@taftcollege.edu
ARZOLA, Fernando .... 646-378-6150.. 325 C
fernando.arzola@nyack.edu
ARZROUNI-CHAHINIAN,
Chaghig .... 510-925-4282.... 26 M
carzrouni@aua.am
ASAD, Ray .... 408-453-9900.... 46 B
rasad@henley-putnam.edu
ASADOORIAN, III,
Malcolm, O .... 781-768-7077.. 227 G
malcolm.asadoorian@regiscollege.edu
ASAMOAH, Yaw, A .... 724-357-2280.. 415 B
yaw.asamoah@iup.edu
ASANTE, Javonda .... 973-313-6211.. 297 A
javonda.asante@shu.edu
ASARO, Diane, C .... 773-508-2543.. 146 G
dasaro@luc.edu
ASARO, Linda .... 212-229-5592.. 322 E
asarol@newschool.edu
ASATO, Susan .... 760-757-2121.... 52 K
sasato@miracosta.edu

ASAWA, Archibald, E .... 949-480-4006.... 64 J
asawa@soka.edu
ASAY, Meredith .... 307-766-2903.. 527 B
masay@uwyo.edu
ASBILL, Jonathan .... 918-456-5511.. 384 G
asbill01@nsuok.edu
ASBURY, Denise .... 423-652-4895.. 440 J
dasbury@king.edu
ASBURY, Jo-Ellen .... 410-334-2181.. 211 A
jasbury@stevenson.edu
ASBURY, Sean .... 614-287-2525.. 367 C
sasbury@cscc.edu
ASCENCIO, Mario .... 626-396-2231.... 27 L
mario.ascencio@artcenter.edu
ASCH, Emily .... 651-690-6650.. 254 M
ejasch@stkate.edu
ASCHENBRENER, Matt ...... 262-472-1570.. 521 F
aschenbm@uww.edu
ASCHENDRENER,
Saundra .... 480-990-3773.... 13 M
ASCHER, Marie .... 914-594-4208.. 323 I
marie_ascher@nymc.edu
ASCHIM, Joan .... 541-463-5591.. 391 G
aschimj@lanecc.edu
ASCHLIMAN, David, A ...... 260-422-5561.. 162 B
daaschliman@indianatech.edu
ASCIONE, Lou .... 619-388-7873.... 60 H
lascione@sdccd.edu
ASDURIAN, Emil .... 718-261-5800.. 305 J
easdurianmd@bramsonort.edu
ASELTYNE, Dennis .... 707-468-3131.... 52 C
daseltyne@mendocino.edu
ASENCIO-PINTO, Aida ...... 708-209-3492.. 138 G
aida.asencio-pinto@cuchicago.edu
ASGARIAN, Spiridoula, K 212-346-1343.. 325 J
sasgarian@pace.edu
ASH, Beth .... 740-477-7788.. 374 G
bash@ohiochristian.edu
ASH, Christine, A .... 216-368-4350.. 365 B
caa2@case.edu
ASH, David, E .... 989-774-3094.. 232 D
ash1de@cmich.edu
ASH, Eric .... 907-375-4515.. 479 D
ash@wbu.edu
ASH, Hope .... 304-865-6015.. 511 C
hope.ash@ovu.edu
ASH, Kay .... 360-475-7500.. 505 F
kash@olympic.edu
ASH, Kenya, D .... 513-529-7157.. 372 K
ashkd@miamioh.edu
ASH, Michael .... 319-208-5050.. 176 J
mash@scciowa.edu
ASH, Steven .... 352-854-2322.... 97 R
ashs@cf.edu
ASHAOLU, John .... 724-480-3470.. 401 F
john.ashaolu@ccbc.edu
ASHBAUGH, Jackie, E ...... 330-972-8973.. 378 H
jackie1@uakron.edu
ASHBURN, Beth, D .... 336-725-8344.. 354 G
ashburnb@piedmontu.edu
ASHBURN, Elyse .... 410-455-2065.. 211 G
eashburn@umbc.edu
ASHBY, Brendan .... 651-846-1314.. 252 C
brendan.ashby@saintpaul.edu
ASHBY, Pamela .... 207-834-7550.. 205 B
pam.ashby@maine.edu
ASHBY, Patti .... 405-912-9017.. 387 D
pashby@hc.edu
ASHBY, Todd .... 843-863-7984.. 427 I
tashby@csuniv.edu
ASHBY, Valerie .... 919-684-4510.. 343 J
asdean@duke.edu
ASHCRAFT, Chester .... 870-460-1018.... 23 D
ashcraftc@uamont.edu
ASHCRAFT, Eric .... 859-846-5781.. 191 G
ewashcraft@midway.edu
ASHCRAFT, Matthew .... 480-461-7215.... 14 D
matthew.ashcraft@mesacc.edu
ASHCROFT, Josh .... 509-359-6916.. 503 D
jashcroft@ewu.edu
ASHDOWN, Jane .... 516-877-4065.. 303 B
jashdown@adelphi.edu
ASHENMACHER,
Robert, J .... 218-723-6075.. 245 J
rashenma@css.edu
ASHER, Adam .... 312-235-3549.. 154 C
a.asher@shimer.edu
ASHER, Bernadette .... 404-627-2681.. 117 G
bernadette.asher@beulah.edu
ASHER, Curt .... 661-654-3042.... 32 A
casher@csub.edu
ASHER, Joy .... 859-238-5284.. 187 H
joy.asher@centre.edu
ASHER, Pamela .... 816-268-5442.. 269 H
pjasher@nts.edu
ASHFORD, Bruce, R .... 919-761-2435.. 355 I
bashford@sebts.edu
ASHFORD, Rebecca, L ...... 865-694-6552.. 446 G
rlashford@pstcc.edu
ASHFORD, Scott .... 541-737-1211.. 393 H
scott.ashford@oregonstate.edu

ASHLEY, Bill .... 601-276-3717.. 260 H
bashley@smcc.edu
ASHLEY, Donna .... 646-717-9706.. 315 B
ashley@gts.edu
ASHLEY, Garrett, P .... 562-951-4625.... 31 H
gashley@calstate.edu
ASHLEY, Kimberly .... 903-877-5739.. 477 E
kimberly.ashley@uthct.edu
ASHLEY, Kurt .... 630-617-6472.. 140 C
kurt.ashley@elmhurst.edu
ASHLEY, Mark .... 909-621-8090.... 46 A
mark_ashley@hmc.edu
ASHLEY, Mary Ellen .... 937-775-4271.. 381 H
maryellen.ashley@wright.edu
ASHLEY, Richard .... 704-272-5463.. 353 B
rashley@spcc.edu
ASHLEY, Sheryl .... 619-660-4030.... 45 I
sheryl.ashley@gcccd.edu
ASHLEY, Tim, M .... 315-267-2222.. 334 B
ashleytm@potsdam.edu
ASHLEY, Traci, D .... 919-209-2563.. 350 G
tdashley@johnstoncc.edu
ASHLEY, SR.,
Willard W.C .... 732-247-5241.. 293 B
washley@nbts.edu
ASHLEY-PAULEY, Jonita .. 423-798-7830.. 447 G
jpauley@tusculum.edu
ASHLOCK, Benjamin .... 415-749-4566.... 61 B
bashlock@sfai.edu
ASHMEN, Jeff .... 912-443-4155.. 126 G
jashmen@savannahtech.edu
ASHMON, Rosa .... 334-872-2533...... 6 F
ASHMYAN, Ilya .... 201-360-4693.. 292 B
iashmyan@hccc.edu
ASHOUR, Cheryl .... 780-744-1150.... 56 F
cashour@palomar.edu
ASHPOLE, Steven .... 360-596-5240.. 508 A
sashpole@spscc.edu
ASHRAF, Tasneem .... 520-335-1883.... 12 L
ashraft@cochise.edu
ASHTON, Andrew .... 845-437-5785.. 339 C
anashton@vassar.edu
ASHTON, Catherine .... 319-385-6227.. 174 A
catherine.ashton@iw.edu
ASHTON, M. John .... 801-581-3055.. 481 M
john.ashton@alumni.utah.edu
ASHTON, Nadine .... 313-664-7673.. 232 G
nashton@collegeforcreativestudies.edu
ASHTON, Sharon .... 904-620-2115.. 112 B
sashton@unf.edu
ASHTON-MILLER,
James, A .... 734-764-7516.. 241 J
jaam@umich.edu
ASHTON-PRITTING,
Randi, L .... 860-768-4268.... 89 G
pritting@hartford.edu
ASHWELL, Dru .... 417-626-1234.. 269 K
dashwell@occ.edu
ASHWORTH, Dennis .... 706-355-5167.. 116 H
dashworth@athenstech.edu
ASHWORTH, Edward, N .. 207-581-3202.. 204 H
edward.ashworth@maine.edu
ASHWORTH, W. Brett ...... 843-953-6779.. 428 A
washwort@citadel.edu
ASIAMAH-ANDRADE,
Akua .... 856-225-6322.. 296 A
andradea@camlink.rutgers.edu
ASIFOA, Sereima .... 684-699-9155.. 529 E
s.asifoa@amsamoa.edu
ASKA, Aaron .... 201-200-3035.. 293 C
aaska@njcu.edu
ASKEGAARD, Lewis, D ..... 540-887-7071.. 491 G
laskegaa@mbc.edu
ASKELSON, Denise .... 218-935-0417.. 256 E
denise.askelson@wetcc.edu
ASKELSON, Mary, M .... 503-788-6644.. 394 I
askelsom@reed.edu
ASKERLUND, Robert .... 801-957-4101.. 483 A
robert.askerlund@slcc.edu
ASKEW, George, R .... 864-656-3140.. 428 C
gaskew@clemson.edu
ASKEW, J. Alicia .... 864-833-8215.. 432 B
jaaskew@presby.edu
ASKEW, Joseph .... 731-989-6651.. 440 D
jaskew@fhu.edu
ASKEW, Rachel .... 561-912-1211.... 99 J
raskew@evergladesuniversity.edu
ASKEW, Susan, S .... 931-598-1710.. 443 O
saskew@sewanee.edu
ASKEW, Tara .... 706-649-1901.. 119 F
taskew@columbustech.edu
ASKEW-ROBINSON,
Jipaum .... 618-634-3364.. 154 B
jipaumr@shawneecc.edu
ASKEY, Angela .... 520-494-5485.... 12 J
angela.askey@centralaz.edu
ASKINS, Rana .... 903-813-2444.. 451 M
raskins@austincollege.edu
ASKREN, Mark .... 402-472-2311.. 282 M
maskren1@unl.edu

ASMAN, Kevin .... 360-596-5448.. 508 A
kasman@spscc.edu
ASMUS, Colleen, M .... 850-474-2642.. 113 A
casmus@uwf.edu
ASONEVICH, Walter, J ..... 814-262-3820.. 413 P
wasonevich@pennhighlands.edu
ASOODEH, Mike, M .... 985-549-2314.. 201 C
asoodeh@selu.edu
ASPAN, Paul .... 610-660-1000.. 418 G
paspan@sju.edu
ASPER, Kris .... 713-718-6858.. 459 B
kris.asper@hccs.edu
ASPERGER, Joseph .... 810-762-9749.. 236 C
jasperge@kettering.edu
ASPINALL, David .... 910-221-2224.. 344 F
daspinall@gcd.edu
ASPINALL, Robin, J .... 909-621-8116.... 38 J
robin.aspinall@cmc.edu
ASPINWALL, Neil .... 337-421-6965.. 197 B
neil.aspinwall@sowela.edu
ASQUINO, Daniel, M .... 978-632-0001.. 224 B
d_asquino@mwcc.mass.edu
ASSAD, Arjang, A .... 412-648-1556.. 421 G
aassad@pitt.edu
ASSAEL, Leon .... 612-624-2424.. 255 H
assael@umn.edu
ASSAF, Michael .... 413-775-1318.. 223 D
assafm@gcc.mass.edu
ASSANIS, Dennis .... 302-831-2111.... 91 F
president@udel.edu
ASSELIN, Edward, E .... 518-255-5215.. 334 D
asselie@cobleskill.edu
ASSELIN, Martha, J .... 581-381-1336.. 330 B
asselimj@sunysccc.edu
ASSERSON, Elizabeth ...... 406-994-4531.. 277 C
basserson@montana.edu
ASTARITA, Susan .... 718-862-7313.. 319 L
susan.astarita@manhattan.edu
ASTEMBORSKI-DECKER,
Cynthia .... 518-381-1353.. 330 B
astembc@sunysccc.edu
ASTI, Martha, S .... 704-233-8008.. 359 H
asti@wingate.edu
ASTI, Tony .... 602-286-8000.... 14 B
anthony.asti@gatewaycc.edu
ASTOLFI, Amy .... 978-232-2001.. 218 D
aastolfi@endicott.edu
ASTON, Lauri .... 724-653-2216.. 402 F
laston@dec.edu
ASTON, Mary Kay .... 570-941-5984.. 422 B
marykay.aston@scranton.edu
ASTON, Rollah .... 575-624-7281.. 299 J
rollah.aston@roswell.enmu.edu
ASTON, Sheree .... 909-706-3502.... 74 K
saston@westernu.edu
ASTORGA, Juan Carlos ... 818-710-2248.... 50 A
astorgjc@piercecollege.edu
ASUKILE, Imani, D .... 727-816-3192.. 106 F
asukili@phsc.edu
ASUNCION-NACE, Zeny .... 671-735-2942.. 530 B
znace@uguam.uog.edu
ATALLAH, Zahi .... 831-755-6960.... 45 L
zatallah@hartnell.edu
ATCHISON, Kathryn Ann . 310-794-0212.... 69 D
katchison@resadmin.ucla.edu
ATCHLEY, Cynthia .... 865-694-6554.. 446 G
catchley@pstcc.edu
ATCHLEY, Stephen .... 562-868-6488.... 47 M
ATENCIO, Elaine .... 619-260-4520.... 72 B
atencio@sandiego.edu
ATENCIO, Wilma .... 719-846-5555.... 83 G
wilma.atencio@trinidadstate.edu
ATES, Clarence .... 508-854-7515.. 224 E
cates@qcc.mass.edu
ATES, Kerry, A .... 410-516-8068.. 208 D
kates1@jhu.edu
ATEWOLOGUN, Adenuga . 507-433-0607.. 251 H
adenuga.atewologun@riverland.edu
ATHANS, Stephan .... 919-718-7287.. 348 D
sathans@cccc.edu
ATHERTON, Beth .... 512-313-3000.. 455 F
beth.atherton@concordia.edu
ATHERTON, Dennis .... 575-492-2763.. 300 H
datherton@nmjc.edu
ATHERTON, Joe .... 707-467-3067.... 52 C
jatherton@mendocino.edu
ATHEY, Rochelle .... 702-895-5541.. 284 L
rochelle.athey@unlv.edu
ATIEH, Lute .... 816-279-7000.. 262 B
lute@abtu.edu
ATIEH, Ramsey .... 816-279-7000.. 262 B
ramsey@abtu.edu
ATIEH, Sam .... 816-279-7000.. 262 B
president@abtu.edu
ATKIN, Michael, B .... 818-947-2600.... 50 D
atkinmb@lavc.edu
ATKINS, JR., Alphonso ..... 401-825-1220.. 425 A
aratkins@ccri.edu
ATKINS, Angie, S .... 662-329-7126.. 259 E
aatkins@muw.edu

ATKINS, Christine .... 203-401-4071.... 85 C
catkins@albertus.edu
ATKINS, Colette .... 319-398-5431.. 174 I
colette.atkins@kirkwood.edu
ATKINS, Darlenna, M .... 318-797-5237.. 198 C
darlenna.atkins@lsus.edu
ATKINS, Deb .... 763-424-0993.. 251 B
datkins@nhcc.edu
ATKINS, Douglas, G .... 603-526-3738.. 285 L
datkins@colby-sawyer.edu
ATKINS, Elizabeth, A .... 856-225-2521.. 296 A
atkins1@camden.rutgers.edu
ATKINS, Garry, L .... 205-726-2763...... 6 E
glatkins@samford.edu
ATKINS, Kemal .... 603-358-2108.. 288 E
kemal.atkins@keene.edu
ATKINS, Marsha .... 312-850-7159.. 138 A
matkins15@ccc.edu
ATKINS, Nolan, T .... 802-626-6406.. 486 C
nolan.atkins@lyndonstate.edu
ATKINS, Norman .... 212-228-1888.. 327 A
ATKINS, Paula, B .... 318-795-2407.. 198 C
paula.atkins@lsus.edu
ATKINS, Priscilla, D .... 616-395-7986.. 235 F
atkinsp@hope.edu
ATKINS, Rodney .... 903-730-4890.. 460 B
ratkins@jarvis.edu
ATKINS-BRADY, Tara ...... 757-569-6713.. 498 B
tatkins-brady@pdc.edu
ATKINSON, Barbara .... 702-895-3524.. 284 L
barbara.atkinson@unlv.edu
ATKINSON, Darryl .... 757-683-3407.. 492 G
datkinso@odu.edu
ATKINSON, Debra .... 620-276-9533.. 181 C
debbie.atkinson@gcccks.edu
ATKINSON, Eva, G .... 270-686-4282.. 187 C
eva.atkinson@brescia.edu
ATKINSON, J. Scott .... 585-395-2501.. 332 E
satkinso@brockport.edu
ATKINSON, James .... 559-325-5200.... 67 B
james.atkinson@scccd.edu
ATKINSON, Jane, M .... 503-768-7200.. 392 A
ATKINSON, Janet .... 208-426-1689.. 132 I
jatkinso@boisestate.edu
ATKINSON, Jeffrey .... 704-233-8117.. 359 H
atkinson@wingate.edu
ATKINSON, Jill .... 775-673-7123.. 284 K
jatkinson@tmcc.edu
ATKINSON, Judith .... 856-415-2115.. 295 D
jatkinson@rcgc.edu
ATKINSON, Justin .... 559-323-2100.... 61 E
jatkinson@sjcl.edu
ATKINSON, Kacey .... 561-276-6520.. 127 D
katkinson@southuniversity.edu
ATKINSON, Krystilyn, M . 691-320-2482.. 529 F
ATKINSON, Linda .... 301-784-5000.. 205 G
latkinson@allegany.edu
ATKINSON, Mark .... 435-586-1966.. 481 N
markatkinson@suu.edu
ATKINSON, Rose .... 406-768-6317.. 276 F
ratkinson@fpcc.edu
ATKINSON, Sander .... 601-484-8707.. 258 F
satkinso@meridiancc.edu
ATKINSON, Simon .... 317-274-1020.. 163 D
ATKINSON, Stacy .... 704-463-3062.. 354 F
stacy.atkinson@pfeiffer.edu
ATKINSON, Susan .... 870-245-5581.... 21 E
atkinsons@obu.edu
ATKINSON, Susan, J .... 714-449-7442.... 51 F
satkinson@ketchum.edu
ATKINSON, Thomas .... 269-782-1276.. 241 C
tatkinson@swmich.edu
ATKINSON, Tyler .... 785-227-3380.. 178 J
atkinsonts@bethanylb.edu
ATKINSON, Vicki .... 847-925-6208.. 141 A
vatkinso@harpercollege.edu
ATKINSON-ALSTON,
Stephanie .... 310-233-4025.... 49 I
atkinssa@lahc.edu
ATKINSON-WILLOUGHBY,
Brenda .... 202-687-5677.... 92 E
ba3@georgetown.edu
ATLAS, Gordan .... 607-871-2924.. 303 F
atlas@alfred.edu
ATLAS, Jamie .... 615-794-4254.. 443 G
jatlas@omorecollege.edu
ATOIGE, Celia .... 671-734-1812.. 530 A
catoige@piu.edu
ATOIGUE, Ana Mari, C ..... 671-735-5527.. 529 G
anamari.atoigue@guamcc.edu
ATTAO, David .... 670-237-6801.. 530 D
david.attao@marianas.edu
ATTAO, David, J .... 670-237-6700.. 530 D
president@marianas.edu
ATTARDO, Salvatore .... 903-886-5166.. 468 D
salvatore.attardo@tamuc.edu
ATTEBERY, Philip .... 903-586-2501.. 452 E
philip.attebery@bmats.edu
ATTERBURY,
G. Burnham 'Burnie' ...... 209-932-2967.... 71 C
batterbury@pacific.edu

ATTIG, Ann, M .... 719-884-5000.... 81 N
amattig@nbc.edu
ATTRIDGE, Daniel, F .... 202-319-5139.... 92 A
attridge@cua.edu
ATUAHENE, Francis .... 610-436-3505.. 416 C
fatuahene@wcupa.edu
ATWATER, Caryn .... 336-272-7102.. 344 G
caryn.atwater@greensboro.edu
ATWATER, Ken .... 813-253-7050.. 102 R
katwater@hccfl.edu
ATWATER, Steve .... 907-474-6440.... 10 G
satwater@alaska.edu
ATWELL, Patrick .... 573-288-6424.. 264 F
patwell@culver.edu
ATWELL, Scott .... 850-644-2761.. 111 C
satwell@fsu.edu
ATWOOD, Anthony .... 615-297-7545.. 438 F
atwooda@aquinascollege.edu
ATWOOD, Kim .... 502-456-6504.. 193 B
katwood@sullivan.edu
ATWOOD, Lorraine .... 802-831-1204.. 485 F
latwood@vermontlaw.edu
ATWOOD, Steve .... 573-840-9708.. 273 A
satwood@trcc.edu
ATWOOD, Tom .... 202-462-2101.... 93 B
atwood@iwp.edu
AU, Gerard .... 909-537-5100.... 34 C
gau@csusb.edu
AU, Peggy .... 510-628-8038.... 49 A
peggyau@lincolnuca.edu
AU, Simon .... 408-435-8989.... 64 G
sau@svuca.edu
AUBIN, Mary Ann .... 314-792-6302.. 266 F
aubin@kenrick.edu
AUBRECHT, Don .... 412-365-1231.. 400 G
daubrecht@chatham.edu
AUBRET, Maryliz .... 787-780-0070.. 531 B
maubret@caribbean.edu
AUBREY, Leonard .... 516-686-1100.. 323 G
laubrey@nyit.edu
AUBRY, Ann .... 309-556-3181.. 143 D
aaubry@iwu.edu
AUBRY, Dawn, M .... 248-370-3228.. 239 K
dmaubry@oakland.edu
AUBRY, Nadine .... 617-373-2154.. 227 B
AUCOIN, Brent .... 765-448-1986.. 160 H
AUCOIN, Judi, F .... 205-726-2728...... 6 E
jfaucoin@samford.edu
AUCOIN, Martin .... 828-339-4217.. 353 D
m_aucoin@southwesterncc.edu
AUDAS, Jean Paul .... 405-325-1710.. 389 B
jaudas@ou.edu
AUDET, Suzanne .... 508-999-8076.. 220 H
saudet@umassd.edu
AUDETTE, Bert .... 207-509-7277.. 204 F
baudette@unity.edu
AUDUS, Kenneth, L .... 785-864-3591.. 185 D
audus@ku.edu
AUDUSSEAU, Loïc .... 718-289-5168.. 307 C
loic.audusseau@bcc.cuny.edu
AUDYATIS, Todd .... 508-531-2608.. 221 C
taudyatis@bridgew.edu
AUER, Matthew, R .... 207-786-6066.. 202 D
mauer@bates.edu
AUERBACH, Michael .... 843-953-5991.. 428 G
auerbachmh@cofc.edu
AUERBACH, Steven .... 808-845-9143.. 132 A
sauerbac@hawaii.edu
AUFDERHEIDE, Keith .... 404-364-8405.. 125 F
kaufderheide@oglethorpe.edu
AUGENSTEIN, Amee .... 260-459-4545.. 164 C
aaugenstein@ibcfortwayne.edu
AUGENSTEIN, Heather ..... 520-515-3649.... 12 L
augensteinh@cochise.edu
AUGHENBAUGH, Barbara 410-837-5719.. 213 C
baughenbaugh@ubalt.edu
AUGHENBAUGH, Jonette 304-327-4049.. 512 P
jaughenbaugh@bluefieldstate.edu
AUGHENBAUGH,
Mark, R .... 801-524-8195.. 480 J
mark@ldsbc.edu
AUGOSTINI,
Christopher, L .... 202-687-7330.... 92 E
cla4@georgetown.edu
AUGSBURGER, Arol, R ..... 312-949-7700.. 142 A
aaugsburger@ico.edu
AUGSBURGER, Carrie, A . 515-964-0601.. 172 F
augsburgerc@faith.edu
AUGSBURGER, Lance, A . 515-964-0601.. 172 F
augsburgerl@faith.edu
AUGSPURGER, Bobbie ..... 417-455-5750.. 264 E
bobbieaugspurger@crowder.edu
AUGUST, Bonne .... 718-260-5560.. 309 C
baugust@citytech.cuny.edu
AUGUST, John, R .... 979-845-4274.. 468 B
j-august@tamu.edu
AUGUST, Michele .... 620-241-0723.. 179 L
michele.august@centralchristian.edu
AUGUST-SCHWARTZ,
Suzanne .... 510-869-6511.... 59 L
saugustschwartz@samuelmerritt.edu

AZAR, Eve 908-835-2335 298 E azar@warren.edu
AZAR, James, A 401-254-3124 426 B jazar@rwu.edu
AZAREKNO, Anita 541-737-0123 393 H
AZARI, Cynthia 805-678-5808 73 E cazari@vcccd.edu
AZDELL, Grant, L 804-752-7266 493 C gazdell@rmc.edu
AZEBEOKHAI, Ignatius, C 501-569-3180 23 B icazebeokhai@ualr.edu
AZEVEDO, Hannah 773-244-4892 149 I hjazevedo@northpark.edu
AZEVEDO, Mario 601-979-7036 258 D mario.j.azevedo@jsums.edu
AZEVEDO, Steve 480-461-7974 14 D steve.azevedo@mesacc.edu
AZHAND, Hamid, U 909-537-5136 34 C hazhand@csusb.edu
AZINGER, Albert 309-438-2453 143 B atazing@ilstu.edu
AZIZ, Jihad, N 804-828-6200 496 D jnaziz@vcu.edu
AZIZ, Nadim 864-656-0542 428 C aziz@clemson.edu
AZIZ, Nadim, M 864-656-3243 428 C aziz@clemson.edu
AZIZAN-GARDNER, Noor 573-882-6282 273 E azizan-gardnern@missouri.edu
AZKOUL, Emilie 616-222-1447 233 A emilie.azkoul@cornerstone.edu
AZURE, Jackie 406-768-3213 276 F jazure@fpcc.edu
AZURE, Lisa 701-255-3285 362 E lazure@uttc.edu
AZURE, Melody 701-854-8020 362 B melodya@sbci.edu
AZURE, Tracy 701-477-7862 362 D tazure@tm.edu
AZZARA, Tom 631-420-2599 335 E azzaratf@farmingdale.edu
AZZARELLO, Tony 419-227-3141 380 A
A'SEE, Carlito, D 803-536-7485 432 E cdasee@scsu.edu

B

BAADE, K. Austin 262-691-5550 524 G kbaade@wctc.edu
BAAKKO, Lori 906-487-7360 234 A lori.baakko@finlandia.edu
BAAR, Rachael 270-831-9803 189 F rachael.baar@kctcs.edu
BAAR, Tricia 501-337-5000 19 K tbaar@coto.edu
BAART, Aaron 712-722-6079 171 J aaron.baart@dordt.edu
BAAS, Jane 269-387-3234 243 H jane.baas@wmich.edu
BAAS, John 712-722-6020 171 J john.baas@dordt.edu
BAAS, Mark 507-332-5876 252 D mark.baas@southcentral.edu
BABALIS, Eva 718-779-1430 326 D ebabalis@mail.plazacollege.edu
BABANI, Henry 305-442-9223 105 F hbabani@mrc.edu
BABASHANIAN, Mark, R 757-446-6003 489 B babashmr@evms.edu
BABB, Brian 386-506-4457 98 E babbb@daytonastate.edu
BABB, Brian, T 386-506-4457 98 E babbb@daytonastate.edu
BABB, Mike 847-925-6825 141 A mbabb@harpercollege.edu
BABB, Stephanie 559-325-5242 67 B stephanie.babb@scccd.edu
BABBITT, Jeff 585-567-9211 316 F jeff.babbitt@houghton.edu
BABBITT, Steven 516-463-5019 316 D steven.babbitt@hofstra.edu
BABBITT, Terry 505-277-8392 302 F tbabbitt@unm.edu
BABBITTS, Judith 914-395-2371 329 K jbabbitts@sarahlawrence.edu
BABCOCK, Bernie 541-881-5706 395 E bbabcock@tvcc.cc
BABCOCK, Deanna 812-535-5299 166 K deanna.babcock@smwc.edu
BABCOCK, Ed 309-694-5337 141 F ebabcock@icc.edu
BABCOCK, Lisa 716-614-6407 324 D lbabcock@niagaracc.suny.edu
BABCOCK, Michael 906-487-7348 234 A michael.babcock@finlandia.edu
BABCOCK, Whit 540-231-3977 499 F hokiead@vt.edu
BABEL, Rebecca 815-753-1395 150 A rbabel@niu.edu
BABEL, Thomas 630-515-3029 139 D tbabel@devrygroup.com
BABENCHUK, Iavoslava 631-451-4409 336 D babenci@sunysuffolk.edu
BABER, James 740-266-0902 368 D jbaber@egcc.edu
BABER, Karen 309-796-5036 135 I baberk@bhc.edu
BABESHOFF, Ruth 714-628-4886 58 H babeshoff_ruth@sccollege.edu
BABETZ, Jeffrey 843-863-7921 427 I jbabetz@csuniv.edu
BABINEAU, Tereasa, W 757-446-5116 489 B babinetw@evms.edu
BABINGTON, Cindy 765-658-4088 160 F cbabington@depauw.edu
BABINGTON, Lynn 203-254-4000 87 G lbabington@fairfield.edu
BABLER, Cheryl 530-895-4050 29 F bablerch@butte.edu
BABLER, Cheryl 530-879-4050 29 F bablerch@butte.edu
BABOOLAL, Alina 212-229-5620 322 E baboolaa@newschool.edu
BABOWICZ, Debra, P 315-684-6078 336 B babowidp@morrisville.edu
BABYAK, Joyce 440-775-8540 374 C joyce.babyak@oberlin.edu
BACA, Amy 575-538-6145 303 A bacaamym@wnmu.edu
BACA, Brad 970-943-2186 84 H bbaca@western.edu
BACA, Chris 972-825-4650 466 D cbaca@sagu.edu
BACA, Jeannie 575-234-9220 301 B jbaca101@nmsu.edu
BACA, Lori 505-747-2186 301 F lbaca@nnmc.edu
BACA, Max 505-454-3117 300 F mbaca@nmhu.edu
BACA, Philip 575-624-8497 300 I baca@nmmi.edu
BACA, Randy 254-298-8582 467 B randy.baca@templejc.edu
BACA, Sylvia 505-426-2048 300 F sbaca@nmhu.edu
BACA-DOSTER, Carmen, E 303-765-3127 80 M cbaca@iliff.edu
BACCAR, Cindy 503-725-5533 394 G baccarc@pdx.edu
BACCHETTA, Aldo 816-802-3334 266 D abacchetta@kcai.edu
BACCUS-HAIRSTON, Nilaya 301-546-7422 210 C baccusnd@pgcc.edu
BACH, Alex 913-234-0610 179 M alex.bach@cleveland.edu
BACH, Bert, C 423-439-4219 444 F bachb@etsu.edu
BACH, Bruce 215-641-6519 410 L bbach@mc3.edu
BACH, Carol Anne 615-547-1200 439 H cbach@cumberland.edu
BACH, Larry, C 612-343-4703 253 Y lcbach@northcentral.edu
BACHAND, Donald, J 989-964-4041 240 F dbachand@svsu.edu
BACHAS, Leonidas, G 305-284-4117 114 H bachas@miami.edu
BACHHER, Jagdeep, S 510-987-0260 68 L jagdeep.baccher@ucop.edu
BACHLE, Lori 402-552-3100 279 D
BACHMAN, Gary 517-338-3333 232 F gbachman@cleary.edu
BACHMAN, Rob 303-762-6970 79 I rob.bachman@denverseminary.edu
BACHMANN, Robin 714-895-8382 39 F rbachmann@gwc.cccd.edu
BACHMEIER, James 616-331-2188 234 F bachmeij@gvsu.edu
BACHMEIER, John, G 715-836-5189 520 A bachmejg@uwec.edu
BACHMEIER, Mark 828-262-6483 356 B bachmeiermd@appstate.edu
BACHOO, Richard, R 860-832-1776 85 F bachoor@ccsu.edu
BACHRACH, Gavriel 847-982-2500 141 D bachrach@htc.edu
BACHRACH, Steven 732-263-5600 292 F sbachrac@monmouth.edu
BACHUS, Dan 602-639-7500 13 I
BACIK, Johanna 216-987-2283 367 E johanna.bacik@tri-c.edu
BACK, Corey 317-921-4538 164 F cback7@ivytech.edu
BACKELS, Kelsey, K 717-871-7821 415 F kelsey.backels@millersville.edu
BACKER, Carol 800-782-2422 31 E cbacker@mail.cnuas.edu
BACKER, Joni 402-375-7200 281 J jobacke1@wsc.edu
BACKHAUS, Kristin 845-257-2930 331 E backhauk@newpaltz.edu
BACKLIN, Bill 785-833-4332 182 F bill.backlin@kwu.edu
BACKLUND, Lee Ann, M 931-598-1238 443 O lafton@sewanee.edu
BACKLUND, Mary, I 845-758-7472 304 F backlund@bard.edu
BACKMAN, Andrea 202-408-2400 93 F
BACKMAN, Carey 585-389-2320 322 D cbackma2@naz.edu
BACKMAN, Danielle 800-371-6105 15 F danielle@nationalparalegal.edu
BACKMAN, Kelli 402-481-8698 278 J kelli.backman@bryanhealthcollege.edu
BACKMAN, Scott 561-912-2166 99 J sbackman@evergladesuniversity.edu
BACKOFEN, Susan 316-684-3356 184 J susan.backofen@sckans.edu
BACKOS, Dean 734-487-4428 233 J dbackos@emich.edu
BACKUS, Amy 216-368-2866 365 B amy.backus@case.edu
BACKUS, Bruce, D 314-935-9882 274 N backusb@wustl.edu
BACKUS, Debra 304-434-8000 512 A debra.backus@easternwv.edu
BACKUS, Robert, H 607-746-4677 335 C backusrh@delhi.edu
BACON, Amy 417-447-2660 270 A bacona@otc.edu
BACON, Curt 541-552-6487 395 A bacon@sou.edu
BACON, Gus 406-395-4875 278 F gbacon@stonechild.edu
BACON, Jack 610-892-1007 414 B jbacon@pit.edu
BACON, Karen 212-340-7700 341 G kbacon@yu.edu
BACON, Lisa 781-239-3175 223 F lbacon@massbay.edu
BACON, Michael 210-999-7328 473 A
BACON, Pamela 210-458-6551 477 A pamela.bacon@utsa.edu
BACON, Robbie 717-815-6818 424 F rbacon2@ycp.edu
BACON, Steve 661-654-2210 32 A sbacon@csub.edu
BACQUE, Heather 504-864-7225 198 E heather.bacque@sodexo.com
BACZA, Gerald 304-367-4632 512 D gerald.bacza@pierpont.edu
BACZEWSKI, Philip, C 940-565-3886 475 A baczewski@unt.edu
BADAL, Amy, A 570-577-1601 398 L amy.badal@bucknell.edu
BADAL, Ashour 209-664-6747 34 E abadal@csustan.edu
BADAL, Joel 317-789-8284 160 E jbadal@crossroads.edu
BADAL, Robert, S 701-252-3467 362 F badal@uj.edu
BADALYAN, Anna 323-953-4000 49 H badalya@lacitycollege.edu
BADE, Karen 360-752-8324 501 G kbade@btc.edu
BADE, Michael 415-502-6460 70 D michael.bade@ucsf.edu
BADE, Robert, E 727-816-3413 106 F badeb@phsc.edu
BADE, William, D 217-786-2326 146 E bill.bade@llcc.edu
BADEAUX, Aimee 225-491-1624 199 B aimee.badeaux@ololcollege.edu
BADENHAUSEN, Richard 801-832-2460 483 D rbadenhausen@westminstercollege.edu
BADER, Greg, R 740-587-5734 368 B baderg@denison.edu
BADER, Irv 718-820-4880 337 I irv.bader@touro.edu
BADER, Jeff 406-994-2205 277 C jeff.bader@montana.edu
BADER-SAYE, Scott 512-472-4133 465 F scott.bader-saye@ssw.edu
BADESSA, Diane 609-586-4800 292 D badessad@mccc.edu
BADGER, Nancy 423-425-4438 448 F nancy-badger@utc.edu
BADIEY, Mohsen 302-831-3687 91 F badiey@udel.edu
BADILLO-LOZANO, Luis, V 787-841-2000 535 I luis_badillo@pucpr.edu
BADIRU, Adedeji, B 937-255-3025 527 H adedeji.badiru@afit.edu
BADOLATO, Michael 978-762-4000 224 C mbadolat@northshore.edu
BADOVINAC, Amanda 406-496-4828 277 G abadovinac@mtech.edu
BADOVINAC, John, C 406-496-4249 277 G jbadovinac@mtech.edu
BADOVINAC, Michele 209-468-9141 67 H mbadovinac@sjcoe.net
BADOWSKA, Eva 718-817-4400 314 G badowska@fordham.edu
BADRY, Jay 909-687-1759 44 H jaybadry@gs.edu
BADWAL, Avi 619-260-2943 72 B abadwal@sandiego.edu
BADZEK, Laurie 910-962-7410 358 D badzekl@uncw.edu
BAE, Chawook 770-220-7914 120 G bae@gcuniv.edu
BAEHRE-KOLOVANI, Edna, V 757-822-1050 498 H ekolovani@tcc.edu
BAENEN, Michael 617-627-3300 228 H michael.baenen@tufts.edu
BAENNINGER, MaryAnn 973-408-3100 291 B president@drew.edu
BAER, Candace 401-454-6426 426 A cbaer@risd.edu
BAER, Catherine, E 845-437-5401 339 C cabaer@vassar.edu
BAER, Dana 724-852-3295 423 A dbaer@waynesburg.edu
BAER, Eugen 315-781-3300 316 C baer@hws.edu
BAER, Marc 616-395-7748 235 F baer@hope.edu
BAER, Natasha 763-433-1707 248 K natasha.baer@anokaramsey.edu
BAER, Ulrich, C 212-998-8695 324 C ulrich.baer@nyu.edu
BAERWALD, Bonnie 920-929-2127 524 B bbaerwald@morainepark.edu
BAESLACK, III, William, A 216-368-4346 365 B william.baeslack@case.edu
BAESSLER, Laura 937-481-2223 381 C laura_baessler@wilmington.edu
BAEZ, Ada 787-852-1430 532 N abaez4@hccpr.edu
BAEZ, Ada 787-285-5457 532 N abaez4@hccpr.edu
BAEZ, Arvin 787-841-2000 535 I arvin_baez@pucpr.edu
BAEZ, Aurelis 787-279-1912 533 J abaez@bayamon.inter.edu
BAEZ, Juan 310-233-4427 49 I baezrj@lahc.edu
BAEZ, Nayla 787-815-0000 537 F nayla.baez@upr.edu
BAEZ, Thomas 210-458-4140 477 A thomas.baez@utsa.edu
BAEZ MILAN, Tony 724-653-2183 402 F tbaez@dec.edu
BAEZ MOJICA, David 787-780-0070 531 B dbaez@caribbean.edu
BAEZA-ORTEGO, Gilda 575-538-6350 303 A ortegog@wnmu.edu
BAFFA, Joe 714-556-3610 73 B joe.baffa@vanguard.edu
BAGAYOKO, Diola 225-771-4845 199 H diola_bagayoko@subr.edu
BAGBY, Crystal 360-752-8320 501 G cbagby@btc.edu
BAGBY, Sara 606-693-5000 191 A srichardson@kmbc.edu
BAGDAZIAN, Robert, A 805-525-4417 67 J rbagdazian@thomasaquinas.edu
BAGEL, George 770-534-6265 118 A gbagel@brenau.edu
BAGEL, Jeffrey 716-851-1991 313 H bagel@ecc.edu
BAGENTS, Bill 256-766-6610 4 B bbagents@hcu.edu
BAGG, Eva 562-938-4736 49 D ebagg@lbcc.edu
BAGG, Mary Beth 317-788-3220 168 A bagg@uindy.edu
BAGGERMAN, Thom 412-392-4761 417 F tbaggerman@pointpark.edu
BAGGETT, Cody 217-641-4360 143 H cbaggett@jwcc.edu
BAGGISH, Mindy 909-593-3511 71 B mbaggish@laverne.edu
BAGGOT, Joseph 507-222-4075 245 C jbaggot@carleton.edu
BAGGOTT, Jacob 205-975-4041 8 E jbaggott@uab.edu
BAGGS, Adam 817-257-6814 469 G a.baggs@tcu.edu
BAGGS, David 843-863-7513 427 I dbaggs@csuniv.edu
BAGGSON, Gulizar 479-619-2203 21 D gbaggson@nwacc.edu
BAGHERPOUR, Parvin 713-718-7733 459 B pr.bagherpour@hccs.edu

BAGILEO, Nick, J ... 202-526-3799 ... 93 E
nbagileo@johnpaulii.edu
BAGLEY, Bob ... 706-233-7240 ... 127 A
bbagley@shorter.edu
BAGLEY, Elizabeth ... 404-471-6339 ... 115 J
ebagley@agnesscott.edu
BAGLEY, Judy ... 864-294-2320 ... 430 C
judy.bagley@furman.edu
BAGLEY, Michelle ... 360-992-2472 ... 502 E
mbagley@clark.edu
BAGLEY, Rebecca ... 412-624-5530 ... 421 G
bagley@pitt.edu
BAGLEY, Rod ... 715-833-6480 ... 523 B
rbagley1@cvtc.edu
BAGLEY, Shawn ... 330-823-2280 ... 379 F
bagleysp@mountunion.edu
BAGNALL, James ... 928-428-8414 ... 13 B
jim.bagnall@eac.edu
BAGNELL, William ... 252-328-6858 ... 356 C
bagnellw@ecu.edu
BAGNELL FINNEGAN,
Kathleen ... 215-951-1234 ... 407 A
finnegan@lasalle.edu
BAGNOLI, Joseph, P ... 641-269-3600 ... 172 I
bagnolij@grinnell.edu
BAGRANOFF, Nancy, A ... 804-289-8550 ... 495 G
nbagrano@richmond.edu
BAGSBY, Tori ... 615-794-4254 ... 443 G
tbagsby@omorecollege.edu
BAGSTAD, Kristi ... 563-588-6314 ... 170 F
kristi.bagstad@clarke.edu
BAGTAZ, Cheryl ... 603-897-8211 ... 287 F
cbagtaz@rivier.edu
BAGWELL, Christopher ... 228-896-2500 ... 259 C
christopher.bagwell@mgccc.edu
BAGWELL, Elizabeth ... 828-251-6511 ... 357 C
bbagwell@unca.edu
BAGWELL, Heidi ... 617-537-6843 ... 147 F
hjbagwell@mckendree.edu
BAGWELL, Jack ... 864-941-8307 ... 432 A
bagwell.j@ptc.edu
BAGWELL, Lydia ... 575-527-7766 ... 301 C
lbagwell@nmsu.edu
BAGWELL, Randall, J ... 434-971-3303 ... 527 N
randall.j.bagwell.mil@mail.mil
BAHAM, Anthony, L ... 985-380-2957 ... 196 K
anthonybaham@scl.edu
BAHAR, Sonya ... 314-516-7150 ... 274 A
bahars@umsl.edu
BAHARANYI, Ntam ... 334-727-8659 ... 8 A
nbaharanyi@tuskegee.edu
BAHLS, Steven, C ... 309-794-7208 ... 135 D
stevenbahls@augustana.edu
BAHNEY, Steve ... 217-245-1488 ... 145 D
steve.bahney@doc.illinois.gov
BAHNSEN, JoEllen ... 309-438-5667 ... 143 B
jbahnse@ilstu.edu
BAHR, Brett ... 218-755-2599 ... 248 M
bbahr@bemidjistate.edu
BAHR, Christine, M ... 618-537-6810 ... 147 F
cmbahr@mckendree.edu
BAHR, Jonathon ... 734-995-7311 ... 232 I
jon.bahr@cuaa.edu
BAI, Kang ... 573-651-2249 ... 272 B
kbai@semo.edu
BAI, Kang ... 815-836-5640 ... 145 H
kbai@lewisu.edu
BAI, Monica ... 928-523-6514 ... 15 H
monica.bai@nau.edu
BAI, Vinglin ... 516-739-1545 ... 323 D
admissions@nyctcm.edu
BAI, Yifeng ... 973-748-9000 ... 289 H
yifeng_bai@bloomfield.edu
BAIA, Larissa ... 603-524-3207 ... 286 C
lbaia@ccsnh.edu
BAIDA, Ana ... 470-578-6555 ... 123 J
abaida@kennesaw.edu
BAIDOO, Christopher, E ... 619-239-0391 ... 36 A
cbaidoo@cwsl.edu
BAIER, Henry, D ... 734-764-3402 ... 241 J
hbaier@umich.edu
BAIER, Valerie, A ... 570-326-3761 ... 413 O
vbaier@pct.edu
BAIERL, Hans ... 920-924-3112 ... 524 B
hbaierl@morainepark.edu
BAIERL, Kenneth, W ... 574-520-4560 ... 163 E
kbaierl@iusb.edu
BAIGENT, Peter, M ... 631-632-6700 ... 332 A
peter.baigent@stonybrook.edu
BAIK, Sang ... 213-763-7007 ... 50 C
baiks@lattc.edu
BAILARD, Rhiannon ... 310-506-4702 ... 56 J
rhiannon.bailard@pepperdine.edu
BAILEY, Alison ... 309-438-2947 ... 143 B
baileya@ilstu.edu
BAILEY, Amanda ... 404-215-2656 ... 124 I
amanda.bailey@morehouse.edu
BAILEY, Ann ... 662-325-3555 ... 259 D
housing@saffairs.msstate.edu
BAILEY, Anthony ... 213-740-2852 ... 72 D
arbailey@usc.edu
BAILEY, Barrye ... 225-768-1701 ... 199 B
barrye.bailey@ololcollege.edu
BAILEY, Beth ... 706-419-1104 ... 119 G
beth.bailey@covenant.edu
BAILEY, Bliss ... 334-844-4511 ... 1 G
bailebn@auburn.edu
BAILEY, Bob ... 620-241-0723 ... 179 L
bob.bailey@centralchristian.edu
BAILEY, Brian ... 312-567-6937 ... 142 I
bbailey4@iit.edu
BAILEY, Brian ... 585-389-2764 ... 322 D
bbailey2@naz.edu
BAILEY, Cassy ... 785-594-8484 ... 178 D
cassy.bailey@bakeru.edu
BAILEY, Charla ... 830-372-8098 ... 470 C
cbailey@tlu.edu
BAILEY, Chris, C ... 570-372-4149 ... 419 H
baileyc@susqu.edu
BAILEY, Christopher, C ... 360-442-2101 ... 504 G
cbailey@lowercolumbia.edu
BAILEY, Clint ... 252-328-2606 ... 356 C
baileyrc@ecu.edu
BAILEY, Dan ... 845-675-4402 ... 325 C
dan.bailey@nyack.edu
BAILEY, Darlene ... 816-415-5943 ... 275 F
baileyd@william.jewell.edu
BAILEY, David ... 304-384-5290 ... 513 A
counseling@concord.edu
BAILEY, David, C ... 574-631-1097 ... 168 B
bailey.77@nd.edu
BAILEY, Denice ... 503-594-3002 ... 390 F
denice.bailey@clackamas.edu
BAILEY, Denise ... 903-233-3100 ... 460 J
denisebailey@letu.edu
BAILEY, Dennis, A ... 850-644-8136 ... 111 C
dbailey@fsu.edu
BAILEY, Dexter ... 631-632-4490 ... 332 A
dexter.bailey@stonybrook.edu
BAILEY, Dexter, A ... 631-632-4811 ... 332 A
dexter.bailey@stonybrook.edu
BAILEY, Donald, R ... 401-865-1188 ... 425 D
drbailey@providence.edu
BAILEY, Donna ... 603-577-6211 ... 286 I
dbailey2@dwc.edu
BAILEY, Duane ... 516-686-1133 ... 323 G
duane.bailey@nyit.edu
BAILEY, Dudley (Skip), L ... 585-292-2833 ... 321 J
dbailey@monroecc.edu
BAILEY, Ed ... 231-995-1215 ... 239 C
ebailey@nmc.edu
BAILEY, Gary ... 616-538-2330 ... 234 D
gbailey@gbcol.edu
BAILEY, Guy ... 956-665-2100 ... 476 E
president@utrgv.edu
BAILEY, Helen ... 423-869-6387 ... 441 E
helen.bailey@lmunet.edu
BAILEY, Jack ... 304-766-4109 ... 514 B
jbaile19@wvstateu.edu
BAILEY, Janie ... 870-633-4480 ... 20 B
jbailey@eacc.edu
BAILEY, Jaye ... 203-392-5552 ... 85 H
baileyj10@southernct.edu
BAILEY, Jeannie ... 775-753-2317 ... 284 I
jeannie.bailey@gbcnv.edu
BAILEY, Jeff ... 870-972-3077 ... 18 J
jbailey@astate.edu
BAILEY, Jessica, H ... 601-984-6300 ... 261 C
jhbailey@umc.edu
BAILEY, Jessika ... 580-559-5252 ... 383 H
jbailey@ecok.edu
BAILEY, Jodi ... 201-200-2116 ... 293 C
jbailey2@njcu.edu
BAILEY, Joseph, A ... 585-345-6900 ... 315 C
jabailey@genesee.edu
BAILEY, Julie ... 432-264-5030 ... 459 D
jbailey@howardcollege.edu
BAILEY, Julie, A ... 774-353-0661 ... 215 D
julie.bailey@becker.edu
BAILEY, Kathy ... 864-977-7170 ... 431 G
kathy.bailey@ngu.edu
BAILEY, Keith ... 706-357-0049 ... 128 E
kdb163@uga.edu
BAILEY, Kelly ... 724-738-4223 ... 416 B
kelly.bailey@sru.edu
BAILEY, Kevin ... 850-474-2214 ... 113 A
baileyk@uwf.edu
BAILEY, Kim ... 952-885-5439 ... 253 Z
kbailey@nwhealth.edu
BAILEY, Larry ... 731-424-3520 ... 446 C
lbailey@jscc.edu
BAILEY, Lee ... 573-592-4381 ... 275 G
lee.bailey@williamwoods.edu
BAILEY, Lisa ... 909-652-6532 ... 37 D
lisa.bailey@chaffey.edu
BAILEY, Lora ... 505-454-3146 ... 300 F
baileyl@nmhu.edu
BAILEY, Mara ... 515-961-1684 ... 176 H
mara.bailey@simpson.edu
BAILEY, Marcia ... 636-584-6551 ... 264 M
marcia.bailey@eastcentral.edu
BAILEY, Margaret ... 760-471-1316 ... 59 H
BAILEY, Mark ... 909-621-8219 ... 57 H
mark_bailey@pitzer.edu
BAILEY, Mark ... 205-853-1200 ... 5 B
mbailey@jeffstateonline.com
BAILEY, Mark, L ... 214-887-5001 ... 457 C
mbailey@dts.edu
BAILEY, Mary Kaye ... 702-651-4362 ... 284 H
marykaye.bailey@csn.edu
BAILEY, Michelle ... 563-441-4152 ... 172 D
mmbailey@eicc.edu
BAILEY, Mike ... 309-341-5336 ... 136 C
mbailey@sandburg.edu
BAILEY, Mike ... 608-663-2000 ... 517 F
mbailey@media institute.edu
BAILEY, Mitchell ... 937-512-3050 ... 377 D
mitchell.bailey@sinclair.edu
BAILEY, Orret ... 205-970-9203 ... 7 B
obailey@sebc.edu
BAILEY, Patrick ... 818-677-2393 ... 34 A
patrick.bailey@csun.edu
BAILEY, Patrick, X ... 504-865-3434 ... 198 E
pbailey@loyno.edu
BAILEY, Paul ... 678-466-4377 ... 119 A
paulbailey@clayton.edu
BAILEY, Peter, A ... 302-295-1191 ... 91 I
peter.a.bailey@wilmu.edu
BAILEY, JR., Philip, S ... 805-756-2226 ... 31 I
pbailey@calpoly.edu
BAILEY, Rita ... 470-578-2364 ... 123 J
rbaile62@kennesaw.edu
BAILEY, Robin ... 847-635-1428 ... 150 G
rbailey@oakton.edu
BAILEY, Sharon, M ... 361-570-4236 ... 474 C
baileysm@uhv.edu
BAILEY, Shaun ... 559-934-2254 ... 74 D
shaunbailey@whccd.edu
BAILEY, Steve ... 434-381-6110 ... 494 M
sbailey@sbc.edu
BAILEY, Teresa ... 757-825-2770 ... 498 G
baileyt@tncc.edu
BAILEY, Terry ... 706-272-2611 ... 119 H
tbailey@daltonstate.edu
BAILEY, William ... 814-393-2323 ... 414 G
wbailey@clarion.edu
BAILEY, William ... 252-493-7434 ... 352 A
wbailey@email.pittcc.edu
BAILEY, William, C ... 309-298-2442 ... 158 A
wc-bailey@wiu.edu
BAILEY-AYE, Regena ... 785-654-2416 ... 178 A
rbailey@allencc.edu
BAILEY-CHEN, Robin ... 661-255-1050 ... 30 E
rbaileychen@calarts.edu
BAILEY-FOURNIER,
Dennis ... 831-479-6317 ... 29 G
debailey@cabrillo.edu
BAILEY-OCHOA, Celia ... 409-772-8909 ... 478 A
cebailey@utmb.edu
BAILEY PENROD, Juliett ... 256-726-7457 ... 6 B
jbpenrod@oakwood.edu
BAILIE, John ... 267-246-5891 ... 406 C
johnbailie@iirp.edu
BAILIN, Debra, M ... 802-626-6210 ... 486 C
debra.bailin@lyndonstate.edu
BAILLARGEON, Betty ... 860-215-9207 ... 87 D
bbaillargeon@trcc.commnet.edu
BAILLIE, Christopher ... 701-255-3285 ... 362 E
cbaillie@uttc.edu
BAILO, Carole Anne ... 480-212-1704 ... 16 R
BAILON, Kathy ... 213-624-1200 ... 43 J
kbailon@fidm.edu
BAILY, Jessica ... 914-674-7611 ... 320 G
jbaily@mercy.edu
BAILY, Scott ... 970-491-7655 ... 78 Q
scott.baily@colostate.edu
BAIMA, Thomas, A ... 847-566-6401 ... 157 G
tbaima@usml.edu
BAIN, Andrew, C ... 410-951-4231 ... 212 E
acbain@coppin.edu
BAIN, Jeff, M ... 931-363-9872 ... 441 G
jbain@martinmethodist.edu
BAIN, Margaret, M ... 315-267-2344 ... 334 B
bainm@potsdam.edu
BAIN, Michael, L ... 404-669-2097 ... 126 A
michael.bain@point.edu
BAIN-DOWELL, Astra ... 718-270-1234 ... 332 B
astra.dowell@downstate.edu
BAINE, Brad ... 870-759-4128 ... 24 J
bbaine@wbcoll.edu
BAINES, Joel, D ... 225-578-9905 ... 197 I
jbaines@lsu.edu
BAINTER, Bradley ... 309-298-1808 ... 158 A
bl-bainter@wiu.edu
BAIR, Ava ... 719-336-1574 ... 81 D
ava.bair@lamarcc.edu
BAIR, Ryan ... 309-677-2697 ... 136 B
rbair@fsmail.bradley.edu
BAIR, Sheila, C ... 410-778-7201 ... 213 E
sbair2@washcoll.edu
BAIR, Susanne, P ... 716-878-4324 ... 332 F
bairsp@buffalostate.edu
BAIRD, Bridget, R ... 423-439-8222 ... 444 F
bairdb@etsu.edu
BAIRD, David ... 860-685-2000 ... 90 C
dbaird@wesleyan.edu
BAIRD, Davis ... 508-793-7673 ... 217 B
dbaird@clarku.edu
BAIRD, Denise ... 317-738-8270 ... 160 J
dbaird@franklincollege.edu
BAIRD, Denise, M ... 317-738-8270 ... 160 J
dbaird@franklincollege.edu
BAIRD, Dion ... 503-594-0760 ... 390 F
dion.baird@clackamas.edu
BAIRD, Geoffrey ... 205-329-7900 ... 3 B
geoffrey.baird@ecacolleges.com
BAIRD, Jeffrey ... 215-951-2620 ... 416 G
bairdj@philau.edu
BAIRD, Karen ... 312-322-1720 ... 155 F
kbaird@spertus.edu
BAIRD, Lynn, N ... 208-885-6534 ... 134 G
lbaird@uidaho.edu
BAIRD, Stephanie ... 405-425-5200 ... 385 C
stephanie.baird@oc.edu
BAIRD, Timothy, R ... 724-847-6490 ... 404 B
trbaird@geneva.edu
BAIRD-JAMES, Allison ... 310-794-8686 ... 69 D
abaird-james@finance.ucla.edu
BAISDEN, Emma, L ... 304-896-7402 ... 512 E
emma.baisden@southernwv.edu
BAISDEN, Vernon, L ... 614-247-6300 ... 375 A
baisden.14@osu.edu
BAISEY, Michael ... 301-624-2892 ... 207 F
mbaisey@frederick.edu
BAITMAN, Clay, L ... 618-235-2700 ... 155 C
clay.baitman@swic.edu
BAITY, Deborah, A ... 831-656-2480 ... 528 D
dbaity@nps.edu
BAJAR, Jane ... 303-753-6046 ... 83 A
jbajar@rmcad.edu
BAJCZYK, Jim ... 920-565-1521 ... 517 D
bajczykja@lakeland.edu
BAK, Doug ... 719-846-5513 ... 83 G
doug.bak@trinidadstate.edu
BAKANE, Samir ... 973-655-7773 ... 293 A
bakanes@mail.montclair.edu
BAKAR, Senem ... 202-885-3352 ... 91 J
bakar@american.edu
BAKARI, Sentwali ... 515-271-2835 ... 171 K
sentwali.bakari@drake.edu
BAKE, Mark, A ... 920-433-6626 ... 515 F
mark.bake@bellincollege.edu
BAKEMEIER, Emily, P ... 203-432-4440 ... 90 D
emily.bakemeier@yale.edu
BAKER, Adria ... 713-348-6095 ... 464 E
abaker@rice.edu
BAKER, Alvin ... 606-326-2422 ... 188 N
alvin.baker@kctcs.edu
BAKER, Amanda, L ... 304-929-6717 ... 512 C
abaker@newriver.edu
BAKER, Amy ... 573-288-6493 ... 264 F
abaker@culver.edu
BAKER, Andrew, R ... 301-447-5295 ... 209 G
baker@msmary.edu
BAKER, Barry ... 407-823-2564 ... 111 E
barry.baker@ucf.edu
BAKER, Barry, A ... 425-235-5839 ... 506 F
bbaker@rtc.edu
BAKER, Betty ... 304-793-6873 ... 514 A
bbaker@osteo.wvsom.edu
BAKER, Brent ... 817-598-6275 ... 479 E
bbaker@wc.edu
BAKER, Brian ... 812-749-1212 ... 166 B
bbaker@oak.edu
BAKER, Brian, J ... 540-286-1302 ... 495 C
bbaker@umw.edu
BAKER, Carey ... 870-235-4042 ... 22 F
clbaker@saumag.edu
BAKER, Caroline ... 410-455-8171 ... 211 G
cbaker@umbc.edu
BAKER, Chuck, S ... 423-775-7136 ... 439 B
cbaker0930@bryan.edu
BAKER, Connie ... 805-289-6400 ... 73 F
cbaker@vcccd.edu
BAKER, Crystal ... 812-237-2215 ... 162 A
crystal.baker@indstate.edu
BAKER, Dave ... 717-728-2272 ... 400 F
davebaker@centralpenn.edu
BAKER, David, A ... 541-737-3871 ... 393 H
david.baker@oregonstate.edu
BAKER, David, E ... 312-567-3561 ... 142 I
bakerd@iit.edu
BAKER, Debbie ... 307-382-1611 ... 527 C
dbaker@westernwyoming.edu
BAKER, Debra ... 662-246-6301 ... 259 B
dbaker@msdelta.edu
BAKER, Denice ... 978-837-5231 ... 225 E
bakerde@merrimack.edu
BAKER, Diane ... 269-927-6287 ... 236 G
baker@lakemichigancollege.edu
BAKER, Douglas, D ... 815-753-9500 ... 150 A
ddbaker@niu.edu

BAKER, Dyann, J .... 860-701-5016.... 88 D
baker_dy@mitchell.edu
BAKER, Eliott, G .... 724-738-2010.. 416 B
eliott.baker@sru.edu
BAKER, Elizabeth .... 252-222-6216.. 348 B
bakere@carteret.edu
BAKER, Erinnae .... 803-981-7075.. 435 D
ebaker@yorktech.edu
BAKER, Erma, A .... 540-654-2043.. 495 C
ebaker@umw.edu
BAKER, Fred .... 501-450-1362.... 20 F
baker@hendrix.edu
BAKER, Gail .... 402-554-2232.. 283 B
gbaker@unomaha.edu
BAKER, Gary .... 941-752-5431.. 110 H
bakerg@scf.edu
BAKER, George, R .... 502-597-5365.. 191 B
george.baker@kysu.edu
BAKER, Gisella .... 319-296-4465.. 173 B
gisella.baker@hawkeyecollege.edu
BAKER, Gordon .... 678-466-4334.. 119 A
gordonbaker@clayton.edu
BAKER, Hilary .... 818-677-7750.... 34 A
hilary.baker@csun.edu
BAKER, James .... 973-300-2100.. 297 D
jbaker@sussex.edu
BAKER, James, P .... 417-836-8501.. 268 I
jbaker@missouristate.edu
BAKER, Janet .... 610-740-3765.. 400 E
jlbaker@cedarcrest.edu
BAKER, Jason .... 757-352-4447.. 493 E
jasobak@regent.edu
BAKER, Jean .... 214-860-8885.. 456 F
jeanbaker@dcccd.edu
BAKER, Jeff .... 859-371-9393.. 186 M
BAKER, Jeffrey, A .... 704-687-8457.. 358 A
jbaker88@uncc.edu
BAKER, Jillian .... 215-951-1430.. 407 A
bakerj@lasalle.edu
BAKER, Jim .... 817-272-2261.. 476 A
jimbaker@uta.edu
BAKER, Jimmy .... 513-562-8762.. 363 H
jbaker@artacademy.edu
BAKER, Jo Nell .... 909-593-3511.... 71 B
jbaker@laverne.edu
BAKER, Joe .... 262-524-7319.. 515 J
jrbaker@carrollu.edu
BAKER, John, C .... 517-355-6509.. 237 I
bakerjj@cvm.msu.edu
BAKER, John, S .... 614-885-5585.. 376 G
BAKER, Joseph, J .... 610-499-4151.. 423 E
jjbaker@widener.edu
BAKER, Josh .... 719-502-3019.... 82 B
josh.baker@ppcc.edu
BAKER, Judith, G .... 585-389-2824.. 322 D
jbaker51@naz.edu
BAKER, Judy .... 650-949-7388.... 44 B
bakerjudy@foothill.edu
BAKER, Karen .... 870-575-8406.... 23 E
BAKER, Kathleen .... 206-296-6305.. 507 E
bakerkat@seattleu.edu
BAKER, Ken .... 716-839-7688.. 312 D
kbaker@daemen.edu
BAKER, Ken .... 419-995-8065.. 370 G
baker.k@rhodesstate.edu
BAKER, Larry .... 540-868-7283.. 497 E
lbaker@lfcc.edu
BAKER, Leona .... 757-455-3366.. 500 E
lbaker@vwc.edu
BAKER, Lesli .... 801-863-8286.. 482 C
bakerle@uvu.edu
BAKER, Linda .... 610-799-1584.. 408 G
lbaker4@lccc.edu
BAKER, Lori .... 540-857-6348.. 499 B
sdeanofstudentservices@virginiawestern.edu
BAKER, LuAnn .... 870-307-7425.... 21 A
luann.baker@lyon.edu
BAKER, Margaret, W .... 415-422-2959.... 72 C
mwbaker@usfca.edu
BAKER, Marilyn .... 816-271-4361.. 269 C
mbaker3@missouriwestern.edu
BAKER, Matt .... 660-562-1219.. 269 J
mcbaker@nwmissouri.edu
BAKER, Matt .... 215-951-2917.. 416 G
mbaker@philau.edu
BAKER, Maureen .... 402-844-7258.. 282 B
maureen@northeast.edu
BAKER, Michael, F .... 508-856-3040.. 221 B
michael.baker@umassmed.edu
BAKER, Michael, L .... 423-478-7702.. 443 I
mbaker@ptseminary.edu
BAKER, Monica .... 928-226-4262.... 12 N
monica.baker@coconino.edu
BAKER, Nancy .... 704-636-6882.. 345 B
nbaker@hoodseminary.edu
BAKER, Natalie .... 404-880-6879.. 118 K
nbaker@cau.edu
BAKER, Neal .... 765-983-1355.. 160 G
bakerne@earlham.edu
BAKER, Neil .... 252-823-5166.. 349 E
bakern@edgecombe.edu
BAKER, Nelson .... 404-894-8920.. 121 D
nelson.baker@pe.gatech.edu
BAKER, Nick .... 989-275-5000.. 236 E
nick.baker@kirtland.edu
BAKER, Nolan .... 850-718-2310.... 97 G
bakern@chipola.edu
BAKER, Pearl .... 606-539-4211.. 193 F
pearl.baker@ucumberlands.edu
BAKER, Richard .... 601-643-8404.. 257 D
richard.baker@colin.edu
BAKER, Richard, A .... 713-743-8834.. 473 F
rabaker4@central.uh.edu
BAKER, Robert .... 617-984-5959.. 227 F
rbaker@quincycollege.edu
BAKER, Robert, D .... 972-238-6174.. 456 H
rbaker1@dcccd.edu
BAKER, Robert, T .... 336-758-5224.. 359 E
bakerrt@wfu.edu
BAKER, Robin, E .... 503-554-2101.. 391 D
rbaker@georgefox.edu
BAKER, Ron .... 423-425-2208.. 448 F
ron-baker@utc.edu
BAKER, Russell, D .... 317-921-4313.. 164 E
rbaker80@ivytech.edu
BAKER, Ruth, E .... 410-334-2815.. 213 G
rbaker@worwic.edu
BAKER, Sallie .... 828-835-4202.. 353 G
sbaker@tricountycc.edu
BAKER, Sandy .... 951-222-8408.... 59 C
sandy.baker@rcc.edu
BAKER, Sarah .... 910-672-1185.. 356 E
sdbaker@uncfsu.edu
BAKER, Sarah .... 903-886-5045.. 468 D
sarah.baker@tamuc.edu
BAKER, Scott .... 830-591-7215.. 466 A
sgbaker@swtjc.edu
BAKER, Scott .... 828-339-4249.. 353 D
scottb@southwesterncc.edu
BAKER, Scott, R .... 740-427-5148.. 371 C
bakersr@kenyon.edu
BAKER, Sena .... 214-333-6923.. 455 J
sena@dbu.edu
BAKER, Sherry .... 731-286-3242.. 446 B
baker@dscc.edu
BAKER, Stephen, N .... 401-874-2109.. 426 D
snbaker@uri.edu
BAKER, Steven .... 561-803-2223.. 106 C
steven_baker@pba.edu
BAKER, Susan .... 727-341-3640.. 108 D
baker.susan@spcollege.edu
BAKER, Susan, D .... 585-292-2124.. 321 J
sbaker@monroecc.edu
BAKER, Tamara .... 504-865-3860.. 198 E
tbaker@loyno.edu
BAKER, Teresa .... 417-626-1234.. 269 K
baker.teresa@occ.edu
BAKER, Thomas, N .... 315-267-2900.. 334 B
bakertn@potsdam.edu
BAKER, Tracy, W .... 325-942-2035.. 472 B
tracy.baker@angelo.edu
BAKER, Twila .... 409-880-8932.. 471 A
twila.baker@lamar.edu
BAKER, Valparisa .... 863-292-3602.. 106 I
vbaker@polk.edu
BAKER, Waylon .... 701-627-4738.. 361 H
wbaker@nhsc.edu
BAKER, Wayne .... 432-335-6574.. 463 B
wbaker@odessa.edu
BAKER, Winston .... 936-468-2601.. 466 H
bakerwa@sfasu.edu
BAKER-BARNES, Kiki .... 504-816-4752.. 195 B
kbarnes@dillard.edu
BAKER-CARR, Hope .... 802-224-3000.. 485 G
hope.baker-carr@vsc.edu
BAKER-DEMARAY, Twyla 701-627-4738.. 361 H
tbaker@nhsc.edu
BAKER-FLOWERS, Kim .... 971-722-5841.. 394 F
kim.bakerflowers@pcc.edu
BAKER-ROUSSAT,
Marilee .... 203-285-2310.... 86 C
mroussat@gwcc.commnet.edu
BAKER-WATSON, Stevie .. 765-658-6075.. 160 F
steviebaker-watson@depauw.edu
BAKEWELL-SACHS,
Susan .... 503-494-7445.. 393 F
sondeansoffice@ohsu.edu
BAKHIT, Norm .... 574-535-7507.. 161 A
nbakhit@goshen.edu
BAKK, Kelly .... 218-749-7765.. 249 I
k.bakk@mesabirange.edu
BAKKE, Andrea .... 703-812-4757.. 491 B
abakke@leland.edu
BAKKE, Diana .... 214-329-4447.. 452 B
diana.bakke@bgu.edu
BAKKE, Jennifer .... 920-568-7224.. 523 F
jbakke@madisoncollege.edu
BAKKE, Lisa .... 702-651-4211.. 284 H
lisa.bakke@csn.edu
BAKKE, Sherrie .... 559-325-3600.... 30 C
sbakke@chsu.org
BAKKEN, Jeffrey .... 309-677-3997.. 136 B
jbakken@bradley.edu
BAKKEN, Turina .... 608-246-6516.. 523 F
bakken@madisoncollege.edu
BAKKUM, Christine, S .... 608-785-8951.. 520 C
cbakkum@uwlax.edu
BAKSH-JARRETT, Gail ..... 718-482-5116.. 309 A
gailbj@lagcc.cuny.edu
BAKSI, Christine .... 717-245-1916.. 402 D
baksic@dickinson.edu
BAKST, M, S .... 248-968-3360.. 244 B
BAKST, Y .... 248-968-3360.. 244 B
BAKY, John, S .... 215-951-1286.. 407 A
baky@lasalle.edu
BAL, Balbir .... 352-588-8599.. 108 C
balbir.bal@saintleo.edu
BALABAN, Mark .... 845-431-8044.. 312 G
BALABUER, Camille .... 407-277-0311.... 99 J
cbalabuer@evergladesuniversity.edu
BALACEK, Patti .... 608-785-9201.. 524 H
balacekp@westerntc.edu
BALACHANDRAN, Betsy .. 847-851-5309.. 135 A
ebalachandran@aiuonline.edu
BALAGUER, Giovanna ..... 787-850-9337.. 538 B
giovanna.balaguer@upr.edu
BALAKRISHNAN, Raju ..... 313-593-5248.. 242 A
rajub@umich.edu
BALANOFF, Janet .... 407-708-2963.. 109 E
balanoffj@seminolestate.edu
BALAS, E. Andrew .... 706-721-2621.. 117 D
andrew.balas@augusta.edu
BALAS, Heather, M .... 330-569-5132.. 369 J
balashm@hiram.edu
BALASH, Amber, L .... 330-471-8241.. 371 J
abalash@malone.edu
BALASKI, Keith .... 320-222-5211.. 251 G
keith.balaski@ridgewater.edu
BALASON, Severo .... 708-974-5346.. 148 G
balasonjrs@morainevalley.edu
BALASUBRAMANYA,
Mirley .... 210-784-2225.. 469 B
mbalasub@tamusa.edu
BALATBAT, Joseph .... 212-924-5900.. 336 I
jbalatbat@swedishinstitute.edu
BALBACH, Donna .... 812-357-6525.. 167 B
dbalbach@saintmeinrad.edu
BALCAZAR, Genaro .... 773-244-5705.. 149 I
gabalcazar@northpark.edu
BALCAZAR, Hector .... 323-563-4815.... 37 G
hectorbalcazar@cdrewu.edu
BALCH, Angela .... 432-685-4508.. 461 H
abalch@midland.edu
BALCH, Glenna .... 512-404-4828.. 452 A
gbalch@austinseminary.edu
BALCH, Marcus .... 254-799-3611.. 470 F
BALCH, Margaret .... 401-454-6655.. 426 A
mbalch@risd.edu
BALCH, Pamela .... 304-473-8181.. 515 B
balch@wvwc.edu
BALCH, Sue Ann .... 229-317-6924.. 120 A
BALCHAK, Sharon .... 216-373-5322.. 374 B
sbalchak@ndc.edu
BALD, Tim .... 920-403-3030.. 519 G
tim.bald@snc.edu
BALDA, Wes .... 802-865-5725.. 483 F
strubler@champlain.edu
BALDASARE, Angela, Y ... 520-626-2885.... 17 I
baldasar@email.arizona.edu
BALDASTY, Gerald, J .... 206-685-3218.. 508 E
baldasty@uw.edu
BALDEMOR, Vince .... 808-544-0209.. 130 H
vbaldemor@hpu.edu
BALDERAS, Ulyses .... 713-525-3533.. 475 J
balderj@stthom.edu
BALDERAZ, Brenda Jo ..... 956-872-5057.. 465 H
brendajb@southtexascollege.edu
BALDIN, Antoinette .... 419-995-8222.. 370 G
baldin.a@rhodesstate.edu
BALDINI, Fred .... 916-278-3551.... 34 B
baldinif@csus.edu
BALDONADO, Hernando . 713-718-5069.. 459 B
nandy.baldonado@hccs.edu
BALDONEDO, Claudia ..... 718-482-5236.. 309 A
claudiab@lagcc.cuny.edu
BALDREE, Megan .... 325-793-4801.. 461 F
baldree.megan@mcm.edu
BALDRIDGE, Amanda ...... 580-387-7200.. 384 D
abaldridge@mscok.edu
BALDRIDGE, Patricia, M . 215-951-0843.. 416 G
baldridgep@philau.edu
BALDRIDGE, Susan .... 802-443-5518.. 484 F
scbaldridge@middlebury.edu
BALDUCCI, Laureen .... 650-949-7823.... 44 B
balduccilaureen@foothill.edu
BALDWIN, Alphonso ...... 847-543-2113.. 138 C
abaldwin@clcillinois.edu
BALDWIN, Anne, E .... 585-245-5547.. 333 B
baldwina@geneseo.edu
BALDWIN, Candice .... 717-871-5360.. 415 F
candice.baldwin@millersville.edu
BALDWIN, Chad .... 307-766-2929.. 527 B
cbaldwin@uwyo.edu
BALDWIN, Charlene .... 714-532-7747.... 37 F
baldwin@chapman.edu
BALDWIN, Cheryl .... 305-237-7239.. 105 D
cbaldwin@mdc.edu
BALDWIN, Christine, A ... 714-850-4800.... 85 A
baldwin@taftu.edu
BALDWIN, Darin .... 334-745-6437...... 7 C
dbaldwin@suscc.edu
BALDWIN, David, N .... 508-626-4645.. 221 E
dbaldwin@framingham.edu
BALDWIN, Deborah, J ..... 501-569-3123.... 23 B
djbaldwin@ualr.edu
BALDWIN, Diane .... 617-353-4377.. 216 E
dbaldwin@bu.edu
BALDWIN, Dirk .... 262-595-2379.. 520 F
baldwin@uwp.edu
BALDWIN, Dorsey .... 912-478-5409.. 122 B
dbaldwin@georgiasouthern.edu
BALDWIN, Eric .... 509-313-4100.. 504 A
baldwine@gonzaga.edu
BALDWIN, Erin .... 515-294-5802.. 169 G
baldwine@iastate.edu
BALDWIN, James .... 518-464-8500.. 314 A
jbaldwin@excelsior.edu
BALDWIN, John .... 413-369-4044.. 217 E
baldwin@csld.edu
BALDWIN, John .... 386-481-2454.... 96 H
baldwinj@cookman.edu
BALDWIN, Michael .... 510-780-4500.... 48 J
mbaldwin@lifewest.edu
BALDWIN, R. Chad .... 636-584-6609.. 264 M
robert.baldwin@eastcentral.edu
BALDWIN, Robert .... 512-863-1200.. 466 G
baldwinb@southwestern.edu
BALDWIN, Ronda .... 740-477-7713.. 374 G
rbaldwin@ohiochristian.edu
BALDWIN, Sarah, T .... 859-858-3511.. 186 J
sarah.baldwin@asbury.edu
BALDWIN, Stan .... 601-925-3321.. 259 A
sbaldwin@mc.edu
BALDWIN, Terri, M .... 740-588-1210.. 382 C
tbaldwin@zanestate.edu
BALDWIN, Tony .... 704-216-6272.. 346 A
tbaldwin@livingstone.edu
BALDWIN, Veria .... 606-589-3018.. 190 G
cookie.baldwin@kctcs.edu
BALDWIN-DIMEO, Caren 603-526-3714.. 285 L
cbaldwin-dimeo@colby-sawyer.edu
BALENTINE, Jerry .... 516-686-3999.. 323 G
jerry.balentine@nyit.edu
BALENTINE, Kim .... 417-626-1234.. 269 K
kbalentine@occ.edu
BALES, Jennifer .... 913-621-8733.. 180 F
jennifer@donnelly.edu
BALES, John .... 208-885-5953.. 134 G
jbales@uidaho.edu
BALES, Kay .... 765-285-5344.. 159 B
kbales@bsu.edu
BALES, Michael .... 276-964-7323.. 498 F
michael.bales@sw.edu
BALES, Richard, C .... 419-772-2205.. 374 J
r-bales@onu.edu
BALES, Stefany .... 208-885-6567.. 134 G
sbales@uidaho.edu
BALES, William, J .... 615-898-5818.. 444 G
joe.bales@mtsu.edu
BALESTRA, Elisa .... 914-813-9242.. 329 K
ebalestra@sarahlawrence.edu
BALESTRERI, Teresa, A ... 314-516-5002.. 274 A
tkb@umsl.edu
BALEY, Heather .... 503-244-0726.. 389 J
heatherbaley@achs.edu
BALFOUR, Charmaine ...... 256-761-6277...... 7 F
ccbalfour@talladega.edu
BALFOUR, David .... 802-776-5213.. 483 G
david.balfour@csj.edu
BALGE, Daniel, N .... 507-354-8221.. 247 J
balgedn@mlc-wels.edu
BALI, Vinita .... 650-949-7077.... 44 B
balivinita@foothill.edu
BALINSKI, Joseph .... 231-439-6347.. 239 A
jbalinski@ncmich.edu
BALINT, Bill .... 724-357-7854.. 415 B
wsbalint@iup.edu
BALIUS, Cheryl .... 601-947-4201.. 259 C
cheryl.balius@mgccc.edu
BALK, Nicholas .... 518-694-7328.. 303 C
nicholas.balk@acphs.edu
BALL, Al .... 239-513-1122.. 102 T
aball@hodges.edu
BALL, Christine .... 706-771-4150.. 117 C
cball@augustatech.edu
BALL, Dave .... 319-296-4204.. 173 B
david.ball@hawkeyecollege.edu
BALL, Deborah .... 816-604-1148.. 267 F
deborah.ball@mcckc.edu

BALL, Deborah, L ... 734-615-4415.. 241 J dball@umich.edu
BALL, Diane ... 239-513-1122.. 102 T dball@hodges.edu
BALL, Don ... 330-494-6170.. 377 J dball@starkstate.edu
BALL, Drexel, B ... 803-535-5263.. 428 B dball@claflin.edu
BALL, Gerald, D ... 828-689-1242.. 346 C gball@mhu.edu
BALL, Gregory, F ... 301-405-1691.. 211 E gball@umd.edu
BALL, James, D ... 410-386-8188.. 206 I jball@carrollcc.edu
BALL, Jason ... 561-297-3440.. 110 K jball@fau.edu
BALL, Jennette ... 315-568-3296.. 323 A jball@nycc.edu
BALL, John ... 504-568-4500.. 198 A jball@lsuhsc.edu
BALL, Joshua ... 606-886-3863.. 189 A jball0079@kctcs.edu
BALL, Justin ... 309-677-3850.. 136 B jball@bradley.edu
BALL, Karen ... 559-791-2420.... 47 L kball@portervillecollege.edu
BALL, Kathy ... 304-384-6009.. 513 A bonner@concord.edu
BALL, Kenneth ... 703-993-1497.. 490 B vsdean@gmu.edu
BALL, Kevin ... 330-941-1560.. 382 A keball@ysu.edu
BALL, Kim ... 704-894-2521.. 343 I kiball@davidson.edu
BALL, Kimberly ... 657-278-4968.... 33 A kball@fullerton.edu
BALL, Linda ... 785-227-3380.. 178 J lsball@bethanylb.edu
BALL, Margaret, T ... 718-817-3010.. 314 G mball@fordham.edu
BALL, Michael ... 859-246-6512.. 189 B michael.ball@kctcs.edu
BALL, Scott ... 423-236-2881.. 444 B sball@southern.edu
BALL, Shelley ... 865-471-3235.. 439 C sball@cn.edu
BALL, Thomas, G ... 724-458-2163.. 404 F tgball@gcc.edu
BALL, Travis ... 903-886-5060.. 468 D travis.ball@tamuc.edu
BALL, Williams, S ... 513-558-7333.. 379 A william.s.ball@uc.edu
BALL-WILLIAMSON, Carrie ... 662-862-8123.. 258 C cbball@iccms.edu
BALLABAN, David, C ... 610-921-7256.. 396 H dballaban@albright.edu
BALLAGH DE TOVAR, Jane ... 913-621-8791.. 180 F jane@donnelly.edu
BALLAM, Anne ... 901-272-5145.. 442 B aballam@mca.edu
BALLANTINE, Clay ... 413-559-5590.. 219 C cballantine@hampshire.edu
BALLANTYNE, Trina ... 201-216-5128.. 297 B trina.ballantyne@stevens.edu
BALLARD, Bethany ... 269-782-1385.. 241 C bballard@swmich.edu
BALLARD, Carol ... 334-670-3182.... 7 H csupri@troy.edu
BALLARD, Carol ... 863-680-6236.. 101 E cballard@flsouthern.edu
BALLARD, Chris ... 217-362-6414.. 148 D cballard@millikin.edu
BALLARD, Debra ... 310-665-6921.... 55 E dballard@otis.edu
BALLARD, Donna ... 662-476-5054.. 257 G dballard@eastms.edu
BALLARD, Glenda ... 512-448-8655.. 464 G gballard@stedwards.edu
BALLARD, Jennifer ... 870-512-7861.... 19 C jennifer_ballard@asun.edu
BALLARD, Jennifer ... 503-883-2509.. 392 B jballard@linfield.edu
BALLARD, Katie ... 270-686-4529.. 190 D katie.ballard@kctcs.edu
BALLARD, Ken ... 757-822-1972.. 498 H kballard@tcc.edu
BALLARD, Linda ... 713-313-7480.. 470 D ballard_lc@tsu.edu
BALLARD, Lowell ... 432-552-2415.. 478 B
BALLARD, Margaret ... 617-745-3876.. 218 A margaret.ballard@enc.edu
BALLARD, Paul ... 509-963-1410.. 501 K pballard@cwu.edu
BALLARD, Steve ... 870-543-5910.... 22 E sballard@seark.edu
BALLARD, Terri ... 412-536-1251.. 406 K terri.ballard@laroche.edu
BALLARD, William ... 802-287-8236.. 484 A ballardb@greenmtn.edu
BALLARD, William, H ... 419-772-2020.. 374 J b-ballard@onu.edu
BALLARD, William, P ... 802-656-2240.. 485 D william.ballard@uvm.edu
BALLARD GORMAN, Shannon ... 518-244-3142.. 327 H ballas@sage.edu
BALLARD-THROWER, Rhea ... 202-806-8047.... 93 A rballard@law.howard.edu
BALLARINI, John ... 262-554-6110.. 518 B jaballarini@yahoo.com
BALLARO, Mollie, A ... 716-827-2418.. 338 E ballarom@trocaire.edu
BALLATO, John, M ... 864-656-3642.. 428 C jballat@clemson.edu
BALLEISEN, Edward ... 919-684-1964.. 343 J eballeis@duke.edu
BALLENGEE, Greg ... 740-351-3574.. 377 C gballengee@shawnee.edu
BALLENTINE, Angela ... 252-492-2061.. 353 H ballentine@vgcc.edu
BALLENTINE, Brandon ... 865-694-6545.. 446 G bcballintine@pstcc.edu
BALLENTINE, Howard ... 540-665-4767.. 494 B hballent@su.edu
BALLENTINE, Leslie ... 970-207-4550.... 81 F leslieb@mckinleycollege.edu
BALLENTINE, Leslie ... 970-207-4500.... 84 F leslieb@uscareerinstitute.edu
BALLER, Jim ... 304-214-8960.. 512 F jballer@wvncc.edu
BALLESTEROS, Victor ... 817-515-6456.. 467 A victor.ballesteros@tccd.edu
BALLEW, Marcy ... 903-875-7330.. 462 J marcy.ballew@navarrocollege.edu
BALLEW, Stacy ... 580-745-2869.. 387 M sballew@se.edu
BALLEW, Steve ... 601-266-4131.. 261 E steve.ballew@usm.edu
BALLINGER, Kevin, M ... 714-432-5015.... 39 G kballinger@occ.cccd.edu
BALLINGER, Marcia, J ... 440-365-5222.. 371 H
BALLINGER, Philip ... 206-221-2305.. 508 E philipba@uw.edu
BALLMAN, Terry ... 909-537-5800.... 34 C tballman@csusb.edu
BALLO, Erlynne ... 949-582-4213.... 65 G eballo@saddleback.edu
BALLOM, Kenneth ... 217-333-2121.. 157 A ballom@illinois.edu
BALLOU, Bradley ... 910-962-7803.. 358 D balloub@uncw.edu
BALLOU, Dawn ... 617-732-2077.. 225 C dawn.ballou@mcphs.edu
BALLOU, Trenna ... 435-722-6900.. 481 I trenna@ubatc.edu
BALMOS, Donald ... 254-299-8602.. 461 E dbalmos@mclennan.edu
BALMUTH RAFFELD, Beth ... 413-585-2020.. 228 D braffelc@smith.edu
BALOG, John ... 914-323-5135.. 319 N john.balog@mville.edu
BALOG, Scott ... 850-201-8632.. 113 E balogs@tcc.fl.edu
BALOGA, Monica ... 321-674-8889.. 100 M mbaloga@fit.edu
BALOGH, Deborah Ware ... 317-788-3212.. 168 A dbalogh@uindy.edu
BALOK, Janet ... 270-809-2546.. 192 A jbalok@murraystate.edu
BALOUGH, Sandra, A ... 814-472-3151.. 418 F sbalough@francis.edu
BALSAM, Carl, E ... 773-244-5610.. 149 I cbalsam@northpark.edu
BALSAMO, Anne ... 972-883-4376.. 476 C axb161831@utdallas.edu
BALSAMO, Michael ... 586-445-7141.. 237 C balsamom@macomb.edu
BALSAMO, Robert ... 608-743-4525.. 523 A rbalsamo@blackhawk.edu
BALSANO, Gregory, R ... 562-903-4704.... 28 E greg.balsano@biola.edu
BALSDON, Edmund ... 619-594-2309.... 35 A ebalsdon@mail.sdsu.edu
BALSEIRO, Wanda, I ... 787-878-5475.. 533 H wbalseiro@arecibo.inter.edu
BALSER, Deborah, B ... 314-516-5146.. 274 A balserd@umsl.edu
BALSER, Jeffrey, R ... 615-936-3030.. 449 A jeff.balser@vanderbilt.edu
BALSIGER, Les ... 307-778-4359.. 526 K lbalsiger@lccc.wy.edu
BALTER-REITZ, Susan ... 406-657-2214.. 277 D sbalter-reitz@msubillings.edu
BALTES, Erin ... 207-859-1327.. 204 E baltese@thomas.edu
BALTES, Tim ... 417-447-2631.. 270 A baltest@otc.edu
BALTHAZAR, Judith ... 610-526-5374.. 398 K jbalthaz@brynmawr.edu
BALTHAZAR, Pierre ... 916-278-6578.... 34 B balthazar@csus.edu
BALTIMORE, Lester, B ... 516-877-3142.. 303 B baltimore@adelphi.edu
BALTODANO, Josefina ... 510-981-2820.... 57 B jbaltodano@peralta.edu
BALTZER, Don ... 602-850-8000.... 16 E dbaltzer@ps.edu
BALTZIS, Basil ... 973-596-3619.. 293 D basil.c.baltzis@njit.edu
BALYEAT, Becca ... 206-855-9559.. 506 E becca.balyeat@pinchot.edu
BALZA, Stephen, J ... 507-354-8221.. 247 J balzasj@mlc-wels.edu
BALZANO, Amanda ... 336-758-4455.. 359 E balzanow@wfu.edu
BAMBARA, Cynthia, S ... 301-784-5000.. 205 G cbambara@allegany.edu
BAMBERGER, Gregory ... 610-683-4095.. 415 C gbamberg@kutztown.edu
BAMBHROLIA, Bhavesh ... 215-204-1224.. 420 B bhavesh@temple.edu
BAMBHROLIA, Savita ... 609-586-4800.. 292 D bambhros@mccc.edu
BAMBINA, Antonia, E ... 812-461-5357.. 168 E adbambina@usi.edu
BAMBURG, Jill ... 206-780-6203.. 506 E jill.bamburg@pinchot.edu
BAME, Kevin ... 618-453-2474.. 154 I kbame@siu.edu
BAMFO, Alex ... 202-238-2666.... 93 A alexander.bamfo@howard.edu
BAMFORD, Ryan ... 413-545-9652.. 220 F rbamford@umass.edu
BAMMAN, Chris ... 660-543-4331.. 273 C bamman@ucmo.edu
BAMONTE, Paul ... 718-409-7254.. 336 A pbamonte@sunymaritime.edu
BAN, Martin ... 214-528-8600.. 463 L
BANA, Mark ... 303-914-6220.... 82 I mark.bana@rrcc.edu
BANACH, Michael ... 718-940-5584.. 328 G mbanach@sjcny.edu
BANACH, Patricia, S ... 860-465-5000.... 85 G banachp@easternct.edu
BANAIAN, King ... 320-308-4791.. 252 A kbanaian@stcloudstate.edu
BANALES, Jose ... 512-245-8336.. 471 F jb1478@txstate.edu
BANASZAK, Larry ... 614-823-1693.. 376 C lbanaszak@otterbein.edu
BANAVAR, Jayanth, F ... 301-405-2316.. 211 E banavar@umd.edu
BANBURY, Doug ... 517-607-2327.. 235 E dbanbury@hillsdale.edu
BANCHOFF, Thomas ... 202-687-5117.... 92 E banchoft@georgetown.edu
BANCROFT, Rose ... 631-451-4064.. 336 D bancror@sunysuffolk.edu
BANDA, Magda ... 708-656-8000.. 149 A magna.banda@morton.edu
BANDAS, Mark ... 615-322-6400.. 449 A mark.bandas@vanderbilt.edu
BANDELIN, Janis, M ... 864-294-2191.. 430 C janis.bandelin@furman.edu
BANDO, Patricia, A ... 617-552-3307.. 216 C patricia.bando@bc.edu
BANDRE, Mark, A ... 785-833-4306.. 182 F mark.bandre@kwu.edu
BANDS DEL PILAR, Raul ... 787-758-2525.. 538 D raul.bandsdelpilar@upr.edu
BANDURSKI, Steven ... 810-762-9517.. 236 C sbandurski@kettering.edu
BANDY, JR., John, W ... 404-413-4600.. 122 D jbandy@gsu.edu
BANDY, Kanoe ... 661-763-7779.... 67 F kbandy@taftcollege.edu
BANDY, Sam ... 815-394-4138.. 152 G sbandy@rockford.edu
BANDY, Wendy ... 931-526-3660.. 440 A wendy.bandy@fortisinstitute.edu
BANDY-NEAL, LaMel ... 615-327-6767.. 442 A lbneal@mmc.edu
BANDYOPADHYAY, Santanu ... 714-484-7330.... 54 G sbandyopadhyay@cypresscollege.edu
BANE, Jason ... 217-206-6600.. 156 G
BANERJEE, Manju ... 802-387-6807.. 484 B manjubanerjee@landmark.edu
BANERJEE-STEVENS, Juni ... 530-898-6345.... 32 C dbanerjee-stevens@csuchico.edu
BANERJI, Debashish ... 323-663-2167.... 71 E debashish.banerji@uprs.edu
BANESS KING, Deborah ... 708-456-0300.. 156 C debbiebaresskirg@triton.edu
BANEY, Todd ... 704-922-6485.. 350 A baney.todd@gaston.edu
BANG, Barbara ... 701-671-2277.. 361 F barbara.bang@ndscs.edu
BANG, Sam ... 626-584-5398.... 44 G sbang@fuller.edu
BANGASSER, Karen ... 605-331-6684.. 438 A karen.bangasser@usiouxfalls.edu
BANGASSER, Kathy ... 815-599-3448.. 141 E kathy.bangasser@highland.edu
BANGASSER, Susan ... 909-384-8650.... 60 C sbangasser@sbccd.cc.ca.us
BANGERT, Stephanie ... 510-869-1528.... 59 L sbangert@samuelmerritt.edu
BANGERT-DROWNS, Robert ... 518-442-4988.. 331 A rbangert@albany.edu
BANGS, Joann ... 651-690-6500.. 254 M jmbangs@stkate.edu
BANIAK, Rick ... 314-516-2366.. 274 A baniakr@umsl.edu
BANICK, Gabrielle, A ... 402-472-5208.. 282 K gbanick@nebraska.edu
BANISTER, Stephen ... 701-858-3855.. 360 F stephen.banister@minotstateu.edu
BANKHEAD, Brad ... 225-216-8256.. 195 H bankheadb@mybrcc.edu
BANKO, Matthew ... 336-506-4243.. 347 C matthew.banko@alamancecc.edu
BANKOLE-MEDINA, Katherine ... 410-951-3431.. 212 E kbankole@coppin.edu
BANKS, Alexis ... 251-981-3771..... 2 I alexis.banks@columbiasouthern.edu
BANKS, Cara ... 309-779-7704.. 156 A cara.banks@trinitycollegeqc.edu
BANKS, Cerri, A ... 518-580-5352.. 330 F cbanks@skidmore.edu
BANKS, Christopher ... 213-613-2200.... 65 H christopher_banks@sciarc.edu
BANKS, Christy ... 631-687-4596.. 328 G cbanks@sjcny.edu
BANKS, Dacia, L ... 315-684-6289.. 336 B banksdl@morrisville.edu
BANKS, James, W ... 631-548-2605.. 336 D banksj@sunysuffolk.edu
BANKS, Jeff ... 402-449-2858.. 280 C jbanks2725@graceu.edu
BANKS, Julie, M ... 937-229-3233.. 379 D jbanks1@udayton.edu
BANKS, Kathryn, M ... 252-638-7367.. 349 B banksk@cravencc.edu
BANKS, Kenneth ... 408-498-5104.... 39 H kbanks@cogswell.edu
BANKS, Kevin ... 443-885-3527.. 209 F kevin.banks@morgan.edu
BANKS, Lucretia ... 252-335-3228.. 356 D lrbanks@ecsu.edu
BANKS, Lynne ... 814-472-3002.. 418 F lbanks@francis.edu
BANKS, M. Katherine ... 979-845-7203.. 468 B k-banks@tamu.edu
BANKS, Mary ... 239-590-1172.. 110 L mbanks@fgcu.edu
BANKS, McRae ... 336-334-5338.. 358 B mcbanks@uncg.edu
BANKS, Melissa ... 912-443-3388.. 126 G mbanks@savannahtech.edu
BANKS, Michael ... 816-604-6544.. 267 G michael.banks@mcckc.edu
BANKS, Nannette ... 773-947-6322.. 147 D nbanks@mccormick.edu
BANKS, Roman ... 225-771-5930.. 199 H roman_banks@subr.edu
BANKS, Ronald ... 502-597-5998.. 191 B ron.banks@kysu.edu
BANKS, Sharon, S ... 304-766-3078.. 514 B banksss@wvstateu.edu
BANKS, Traci ... 201-692-7304.. 291 J traci161_banks@fdu.edu
BANKS, Wayne ... 870-574-4493.... 22 G wbanks@sautech.edu
BANKS, William ... 856-227-7200.. 290 B wbanks@camdencc.edu
BANKS, Willie ... 812-237-8111.. 162 A willie.banks@indstate.edu
BANKS, Yvonne, R ... 651-631-5221.. 256 A yrbanks@unwsp.edu
BANKS-DEAVER, Yolanda, E ... 919-530-6204.. 357 A ybanks@nccu.edu
BANKS-SANTILLI, Linda ... 617-879-2371.. 229 G lsantilli@wheelock.edu
BANKSTON, Patrick ... 219-980-6562.. 163 B pbanks@iun.edu
BANNAN, Denise, A ... 810-766-4272.. 231 C denise.bannan@baker.edu
BANNER, Josephina, E ... 610-558-5548.. 411 E bannerj@neumann.edu
BANNER, Lilliam ... 908-737-0367.. 292 C lbanner@kean.edu
BANNISTER, Darlene ... 830-792-7357.. 465 E bannistr@schreiner.edu

BANNISTER, Mark .... 785-628-5339.. 180 I
markbannister@fhsu.edu
BANN, Brandon .... 318-487-7439.. 195 F
brandon.bannon@lacollege.edu
BANNON, Douglas, F .... 319-398-5517.. 174 I
doug.bannon@kirkwood.cc.ia.us
BANNON, Jan-Marie .... 415-749-4523.... 61 B
jbannon@sfai.edu
BANNON, Stephen .... 401-232-6001.. 424 K
sbannon@bryant.edu
BANSAVICH, John .... 415-422-5529.... 72 C
bansavich@usfca.edu
BANTA, Trudy, W .... 317-274-4111.. 163 D
tbanta@iupui.edu
BANTON, Cris .... 503-554-2167.. 391 D
cbanton@georgefox.edu
BANTZ, Craig .... 740-593-1014.. 375 H
cbantz@ohio.edu
BANTZ, Don .... 907-564-8201.... 10 B
dbantz@alaskapacific.edu
BANUELOS, Javier .... 562-860-2451.... 36 P
jbanuelos@cerritos.edu
BANUSH, David .... 504-865-5000.. 200 C
BANZ, Clint .... 717-560-8233.. 407 E
cbanz@lbc.edu
BAPASOLA, Elizabeth .... 609-771-2455.. 290 F
bapasola@tcnj.edu
BAPTISTE, JoRae .... 808-245-8323.. 132 B
jorae@hawaii.edu
BAPTISTE, Michele .... 212-650-6310.. 307 E
mbaptiste@ccny.cuny.edu
BAQUERA, Jesus .... 505-426-2057.. 300 F
baqueraj@nmhu.edu
BAQUERO, Gloria, E .... 787-780-5134.. 535 C
gbaquero@nuc.edu
BAR, Rosann .... 732-255-0400.. 293 E
rbar@ocean.edu
BARABINO, Gilda .... 212-650-5435.. 307 E
gbarabino@ccny.cuny.edu
BARAJAS, Leticia .... 213-763-7071.... 50 C
barajal@lattc.edu
BARAJAS, Silvia .... 805-378-1412.... 73 D
sbarajas@vcccd.edu
BARAKAT, Nabeel .... 310-233-4351.... 49 I
barakanm@lahc.edu
BARAKAT, Nabeel, M .... 310-233-4351.... 49 I
barakanm@lahc.edu
BARAKEH, Zeina .... 415-351-3571.... 61 B
zbarakeh@sfai.edu
BARAN, Kelley .... 508-531-2492.. 221 C
kelley.baran@bridgew.edu
BARAN-CENTENO,
Barbara .... 210-458-4037.. 477 A
barbara.centeno@utsa.edu
BARANOWSKI, Donna .... 941-907-2262.... 99 J
dbaranowski@evergladesuniversity.edu
BARATO, Ruben .... 914-606-6777.. 340 C
ruben.barato@sunywcc.edu
BARBA, Jesse, D .... 413-542-5485.. 214 C
jbarba@amherst.edu
BARBARAK, Thomas .... 314-256-8886.. 262 D
barbarak@ai.edu
BARBAREE, Joel .... 870-850-4821.... 22 E
jbarbaree@seark.edu
BARBARI, Timothy .... 617-353-2230.. 216 E
barbari@bu.edu
BARBATIS, Peter .... 561-868-3142.. 106 D
barbatip@palmbeachstate.edu
BARBEAU, Marc .... 920-686-6176.. 519 H
marc.barbeau@sl.edu
BARBEE, Brent .... 910-410-1809.. 352 C
btbarbee@richmondcc.edu
BARBEE, Chris .... 616-331-3590.. 234 F
barbeec@gvsu.edu
BARBEE, Dan .... 419-530-1448.. 380 D
BARBEE, Kenneth, A .... 215-895-1335.. 402 G
kenneth.andrew.barbee@drexel.edu
BARBER, Andrea .... 585-785-1216.. 314 D
andrea.barber@flcc.edu
BARBER, Bernadette (BJ) 626-584-5238.... 44 G
bjbarber@fuller.edu
BARBER, Billy .... 252-789-0303.. 351 A
bbarber@martincc.edu
BARBER, Catherine .... 985-448-5916.. 196 E
catherine.barber@fletcher.edu
BARBER, Deborah, G .... 803-323-2191.. 435 B
barberdg@winthrop.edu
BARBER, Elizabeth .... 812-749-1243.. 166 B
bbarber@oak.edu
BARBER, Glynis .... 410-951-3078.. 212 E
gbarber@coppin.edu
BARBER, Jacques .... 516-877-4800.. 303 B
jbarber@adelphi.edu
BARBER, James .... 816-654-7109.. 266 E
jbarber@kcumb.edu
BARBER, Jeff .... 434-582-2100.. 491 D
jbarber2@liberty.edu
BARBER, Jennifer .... 916-278-6295.... 34 B
jbarbar@csus.edu
BARBER, Jeremiah .... 816-501-4587.. 270 J
jeremiah.barber@rockhurst.edu

BARBER, Kimberly .... 850-644-6127.. 111 C
kabarber@admin.fsu.edu
BARBER, Luanne .... 870-612-2119.... 23 H
luanne.barber@uaccb.edu
BARBER, Marcia, A .... 315-470-6611.. 334 E
mabarber@esf.edu
BARBER, Mary .... 904-743-1122.. 103 G
mbarber@jones.edu
BARBER, Michael .... 858-653-6740.... 47 G
mbarber@jpcatholic.com
BARBER, Michael, J .... 406-247-5750.. 277 D
mbarber@msubillings.edu
BARBER, Michelle .... 563-884-5106.. 176 C
michelle.barber@palmer.edu
BARBER, Ray, G .... 812-749-1213.. 166 B
ocuexec@oak.edu
BARBER, Sharon .... 563-355-3500.. 174 E
sbarber@kaplan.edu
BARBER, Tamara .... 701-224-5476.. 361 C
tamara.barber@bismarckstate.edu
BARBER, Tanyka .... 443-885-3559.. 209 F
tanyka.barber@morgan.edu
BARBER, Tracy .... 719-255-7507.... 83 L
tbarber@uccs.edu
BARBER, Trent, J .... 860-512-3353.... 86 E
tbarber@manchestercc.edu
BARBER-LYHNAKIS,
Michelle .... 801-832-2755.. 483 D
mbarber@westminstercollege.edu
BARBERA, Anthony .... 516-876-3135.. 333 C
barberaa@oldwestbury.edu
BARBERI, Heather .... 732-255-0400.. 293 E
hbarberi@ocean.edu
BARBICH, Michelle .... 814-732-1457.. 415 A
mbarbich@edinboro.edu
BARBIERI, Lina .... 610-282-1100.. 402 B
lina.barbieri@desales.edu
BARBOSA, Miguel .... 570-422-3545.. 414 H
mbarbosa@esu.edu
BARBOUR, A. Sandy .... 814-865-1086.. 412 F
asb25@psu.edu
BARBOUR, Cheryl .... 303-546-3565.... 81 I
cheryl@naropa.edu
BARBOUR, Darrell .... 641-585-8138.. 177 F
darrell.barbour@waldorf.edu
BARBOUR, Jeffery .... 757-340-2121.. 488 A
librariancvab@centura.edu
BARBOUR, Monica .... 313-993-1951.. 241 G
barboumm@udmercy.edu
BARBOUR, Suzanne .... 706-542-6392.. 128 E
sbarbour@uga.edu
BARBOUR, Wayne .... 301-846-2565.. 207 F
wbarbour@frederick.edu
BARCHI, Robert, L .... 848-932-7454.. 295 F
president@rutgers.edu
BARCLAY, Kent .... 978-232-2282.. 218 D
kbarclay@endicott.edu
BARCUS, Susan .... 937-395-8607.. 371 D
susan.barcus@ketteringhealth.org
BARD, Elizabeth .... 501-296-1275.... 23 C
ebard@uams.edu
BARD, Jennifer, S .... 513-556-0121.. 379 A
jennifer.bard@uc.edu
BARD, Melissa .... 252-328-9881.. 356 C
bardme@ecu.edu
BARD, Sharon, K .... 704-463-3428.. 354 F
sharon.bard@pfeiffer.edu
BARDEGUEZ, Lemuel .... 405-682-7814.. 385 D
lbardeguez@occc.edu
BARDELL, Kathleen .... 617-449-7430.. 229 B
kathleen.bardell@urbancollege.edu
BARDEN, John, H .... 512-404-4829.. 452 A
jbarden@austinseminary.edu
BARDET, Jean Pierre .... 305-284-6035.. 114 H
bardet@miami.edu
BARDILL MOSCARITOLO,
Lisa .... 914-773-3860.. 325 J
lbardillmoscaritolo@pace.edu
BARDO, John, W .... 316-978-3001.. 185 J
john.bardo@wichita.edu
BARE, Benita .... 276-944-6800.. 489 I
bbare@ehc.edu
BARE, James, S .... 516-739-1545.. 323 D
admin_dean@nyctcm.edu
BAREFIELD, Kevin .... 662-685-4771.. 257 A
kbarefield@bmc.edu
BAREFOOT, Chad .... 919-497-3325.. 346 B
cbarefoot@louisburg.edu
BAREFOOT, Russell .... 908-526-1200.. 295 A
russell.barefoot@raritanval.edu
BARELMAN, Jason .... 402-375-7327.. 281 J
jabarel1@wsc.edu
BARENDS, Frans .... 404-894-5000.. 121 D
frans.barends@business.gatech.edu
BARENTINE, Julie .... 504-816-8595.. 198 H
housing@nobts.edu
BARES, Donna .... 440-375-7075.. 371 E
dbares@lec.edu
BARFIELD, Craig .... 919-760-8516.. 346 D
craigb@meredith.edu

BARFIELD, Julie .... 817-272-2584.. 476 A
barfield@uta.edu
BARFIELD, Kem .... 860-215-9210.... 87 D
kbarfield@trcc.commnet.edu
BARFIELD, Kim .... 336-838-6419.. 354 C
kim.barfield@wilkescc.edu
BARFIELD, Randy .... 262-551-5791.. 516 A
rbarfield@carthage.edu
BARFOOT, D. Scott .... 214-887-5151.. 457 C
sbarfoot@dts.edu
BARG, Sarah .... 402-826-8501.. 280 B
sarah.barg@doane.edu
BARGAS, DeLynn .... 575-562-2175.. 299 I
delynn.bargas@enmu.edu
BARGE, Gayle .... 425-564-2282.. 501 F
gayle.barge@bellevuecollege.edu
BARGE, Scott .... 540-432-4304.. 488 K
scott.barge@emu.edu
BARGE-MILES, Linda .... 850-599-8210.. 110 J
linda.bargemiles@famu.edu
BARGER, Brett .... 618-239-6007.. 266 J
bbarger@lindenwood.edu
BARGER, Debbie, M .... 515-263-6012.. 172 H
dbarger@grandview.edu
BARGER, Debra, E .... 530-898-6105.... 32 C
dbarger@csuchico.edu
BARGER, Eric, C .... 503-943-7337.. 396 B
barger@up.edu
BARGER, Kyle .... 215-248-6325.. 409 D
kbarger@ltsp.edu
BARGER, Peter, S .... 630-637-5362.. 149 H
psbarger@noctrl.edu
BARGER, Robert, C .... 614-235-4136.. 378 C
rbarger@tlsohio.edu
BARHAM, James .... 731-286-3371.. 446 B
jbarham@dscc.edu
BARIL, Kathleen .... 419-772-2180.. 374 J
k-baril@onu.edu
BARILAR, Stephen, J .... 570-577-3333.. 398 L
steve.barilar@bucknell.edu
BARILE, Brandon .... 315-781-3880.. 316 C
barile@hws.edu
BARILLO, Madeline, K .... 203-857-7039.... 87 B
mbarillo@norwalk.edu
BARIOLA, Kristi .... 662-246-6376.. 259 B
kbariola@msdelta.edu
BARISH, Robert .... 312-413-0340.. 156 F
rbarish@uic.edu
BARKALOW, Susan .... 252-823-5166.. 349 E
BARKAN, Chester .... 516-572-7370.. 322 C
chester.barkan@ncc.edu
BARKE, Brady, L .... 573-651-2227.. 272 B
bbarke@semo.edu
BARKELOO, Mary, E .... 308-635-6033.. 283 D
barkeloo@wncc.edu
BARKER, Allyn, S .... 304-896-7404.. 512 E
allyn.barker@southernwv.edu
BARKER, Anita, S .... 530-898-6470.... 32 C
abarker@csuchico.edu
BARKER, Brett .... 843-377-2149.. 427 H
bbarker@charlestonlaw.edu
BARKER, Bruce, A .... 715-833-6221.. 523 B
bbarker@cvtc.edu
BARKER, David, F .... 502-852-4676.. 194 A
david.barker@louisville.edu
BARKER, Ellie .... 301-891-4151.. 213 D
ebarker@wau.edu
BARKER, Helen, G .... 301-369-2800.. 206 H
hgbarker@captechu.edu
BARKER, Jeanette .... 919-530-6367.. 357 A
jbarker@nccu.edu
BARKER, Jeffrey, H .... 864-596-9091.. 429 C
jeff.barker@converse.edu
BARKER, John .... 617-627-4239.. 228 H
john.barker@tufts.edu
BARKER, John, D .... 864-294-2106.. 430 C
john.barker@furman.edu
BARKER, John, F .... 716-286-8220.. 324 E
jfb@niagara.edu
BARKER, Lee .... 773-256-3000.. 147 G
lbarker@meadville.edu
BARKER, Lisa .... 731-425-8835.. 446 C
lbarker@jscc.edu
BARKER, Lorie .... 559-791-2370.... 47 L
lbarker@portervillecollege.edu
BARKER, Michael .... 919-843-5684.. 357 D
michael_barker@unc.edu
BARKER, Neva .... 909-621-8306.... 64 A
neva.barker@scrippscollege.edu
BARKER, Randy .... 910-892-3178.. 344 I
rbarker@heritagebiblecollege.edu
BARKER, Rhonda .... 850-872-3857.. 102 M
rbarker@gulfcoast.edu
BARKER, Rod .... 503-491-7666.. 392 F
rod.barker@mhcc.edu
BARKER, Stephen .... 949-824-8792.... 69 C
barker@uci.edu
BARKER, Tess .... 810-762-3322.. 242 B
tessba@umflint.edu
BARKER-GARCIA, Deb .... 909-667-4484.... 38 G
dbarkergarcia@claremontlincoln.edu

BARKETT, Pamela .... 443-334-2176.. 211 A
pbarkett@stevenson.edu
BARKLEY, Beatrice, L .... 215-368-5000.. 398 C
bbarkley@biblical.edu
BARKLEY, Brian .... 770-836-6830.. 129 M
brian.barkley@westgatech.edu
BARKLEY, Jordan .... 254-968-9089.. 467 F
jbarkley@tarleton.edu
BARKLEY, Leanne .... 508-999-8878.. 220 H
lbarkley@umassd.edu
BARKLEY, Robert, S .... 864-656-5463.. 428 C
rbrtbkl@clemson.edu
BARKLEY, Susan, E .... 972-238-6943.. 456 H
sbarkley@dcccd.edu
BARKLEY, Susanna .... 334-683-5112...... 5 C
sbarkley@judson.edu
BARKLEY-GIFFIN,
Adrienne .... 618-985-3741.. 143 F
adriennebarkley@jalc.edu
BARKO, James, N .... 972-881-5721.. 455 A
jbarko@collin.edu
BARKO, Valerie .... 618-985-3741.. 143 F
valeriebarko@jalc.edu
BARKOFF, Larry .... 734-677-5413.. 242 G
lbarkoff@wccnet.edu
BARKOW, Aisha .... 414-297-7035.. 524 A
barkowa@matc.edu
BARKOWITZ, Daniel .... 386-312-4041.. 108 B
danielbarkowitz@sjrstate.edu
BARKSCHAT, Kate .... 828-395-1163.. 350 E
kbarkschat@isothermal.edu
BARKSDALE, Jeffrey .... 251-981-3771...... 2 I
jeffrey.barksdale@columbiasouthern.edu
BARKSDALE, Tina, M .... 302-356-6940.... 91 I
tina.m.barksdale@wilmu.edu
BARKWELL, LaRue .... 202-806-2500.... 93 A
lbarkwell@howard.edu
BARKWILL, Joseph .... 516-463-6623.. 316 D
joseph.barkwill@hofstra.edu
BARLAND, Karen .... 410-951-3704.. 212 E
kbarland@coppin.edu
BARLETT, Paul .... 913-234-0632.. 179 M
paul.barlett@cleveland.edu
BARLOK, Tracy .... 508-793-3776.. 217 C
tbarlok@holycross.edu
BARLOW, Cathy, C .... 910-962-3867.. 358 D
barlowc@uncw.edu
BARLOW, Charlene .... 859-344-3348.. 193 C
barlowc@thomasmore.edu
BARLOW, Christopher .... 405-744-7665.. 385 G
christopher.barlow@okstate.edu
BARLOW, Douglas .... 479-968-0353.... 19 F
dbarlow@atu.edu
BARLOW, Jean Ann .... 918-647-1200.. 382 I
jbarlow@carlalbert.edu
BARLOW, Justin .... 678-839-5000.. 129 E
jbarlow@westga.edu
BARLOW, Marlene, T .... 215-968-8000.. 399 A
barlowm@bucks.edu
BARLOW, Michael .... 270-706-8614.. 189 C
mbarlow0002@kctcs.edu
BARLOW, Steve .... 307-855-2029.. 526 E
sbarlow@cwc.edu
BARLOW, William .... 440-775-8273.. 374 C
bill.barlow@oberlin.edu
BARLOW-KELLEY, Jill .... 207-801-5633.. 202 H
jbk@coa.edu
BARLOWE, Jamie .... 419-530-2413.. 380 D
jamie.barlowe@utoledo.edu
BARNABY, Mike .... 218-855-8039.. 248 N
mbarnaby@clcmn.edu
BARNARD, Cheryl, A .... 860-231-5267.... 90 B
cbarnard@usj.edu
BARNARD, Cindy .... 865-573-4517.. 440 I
cbarnard@johnsonu.edu
BARNARD, David .... 318-487-7386.. 195 F
david.barnard@lacollege.edu
BARNARD, DeeDee .... 828-286-3636.. 350 E
ddbarnard@isothermal.edu
BARNARD, Kathy .... 208-885-7372.. 134 G
kathybarnard@uidaho.edu
BARNARD, Kathy .... 509-335-3564.. 508 H
BARNARD, Laura .... 440-525-7096.. 371 F
lbarnard@lakelandcc.edu
BARNARD, Mimi .... 615-460-8397.. 438 J
mimi.barnard@belmont.edu
BARNARD, Susan .... 201-447-7938.. 289 E
sbarnard@bergen.edu
BARNARD, Tom .... 217-351-2582.. 151 B
tbarnard@parkland.edu
BARNCART, Victor .... 805-756-7416.... 31 I
vbrancar@calpoly.edu
BARNDS, W. Kent .... 309-794-7314.. 135 D
wkentbarnds@augustana.edu
BARNES, Andre .... 415-239-3151.... 38 E
abarnes@ccsf.edu
BARNES, Andrew .... 850-973-1604.. 105 H
barnesa@nfcc.edu
BARNES, Andrew .... 718-636-3570.. 326 E
awbarnes@pratt.edu
BARNES, Bradley .... 205-934-4073...... 8 E

BARRETT, Scott .... 765-998-4917.. 167 C
scott_barrett@taylor.edu
BARRETT, Stephen .... 817-735-2261.. 475 C
stephen.barrett@unthsc.edu
BARRETT, Susan .... 610-526-6005.. 405 B
sbarrett@harcum.edu
BARRETT, Tim .... 315-445-4155.. 318 E
barrettm@lemoyne.edu
BARRETT, William .... 570-740-0305.. 409 E
wbarrett@luzerne.edu
BARRETT, Zunilka .... 617-287-7005.. 220 E
zbarrett@umassp.edu
BARRETTA, Jacqueline ..... 503-370-6004.. 396 G
mbarretta@willamette.edu
BARRETTE, Catherine .... 313-577-1615.. 243 F
c.barrette@wayne.edu
BARRIER, Jeremy .... 256-766-6610...... 4 B
jbarrier@hcu.edu
BARRINGER, Judy .... 212-659-7215.. 318 D
jbarringer@tkc.edu
BARRINGER, Susan, J ..... 336-217-7221.. 344 G
susan.barringer@greensboro.edu
BARRINGTON, Ruth, A .... 401-825-2184.. 425 A
rbarrington@ccri.edu
BARRIOS, Eugenio .... 212-220-1266.. 307 B
ebarrios@bmcc.cuny.edu
BARRIOS, Francisco .... 573-651-2154.. 272 B
fbarrios@semo.edu
BARRIOS, Sharon, A .... 530-898-4473.... 32 C
sbarrios@csuchico.edu
BARRIS, Brad .... 706-236-2272.. 117 F
bbarris@berry.edu
BARRIS, Julie .... 814-472-3012.. 418 F
jbarris@francis.edu
BARRISH, David, J .... 804-523-5934.. 497 C
dbarrish@reynolds.edu
BARRON, Alexandra, L .... 512-464-8878.. 464 G
alexb@stedwards.edu
BARRON, Brad, E .... 864-294-2033.. 430 C
brad.barron@furman.edu
BARRON, Caulyne .... 602-648-5750.... 13 A
cbarron@dunlap-stone.edu
BARRON, Dori .... 828-448-3170.. 354 B
dbarron@wpcc.edu
BARRON, Eric, J .... 814-865-7611.. 412 F
president@psu.edu
BARRON, Glenda, O .... 254-298-8600.. 467 B
glenda.barron@templejc.edu
BARRON, Jose .... 575-624-8263.. 300 I
barron@nmmi.edu
BARRON, Katie .... 970-542-3108.... 81 H
katie.barron@morgancc.edu
BARRON, Kelly .... 530-895-4047.... 29 F
barronke@butte.edu
BARRON, Maria, V .... 954-308-2180.... 95 K
mbarron@aii.edu
BARRON, Matthew .... 906-786-5802.. 231 O
barronm@baycollege.edu
BARRON, Robert .... 515-263-6195.. 172 H
rbarron@grandview.edu
BARRON CHUNG, Amy ... 415-442-6622.... 45 B
slind@ggu.edu
BARROS, Ligia .... 305-629-2929.. 108 G
lbarros@sanignaciocollege.edu
BARROSO-BURRELL,
Kristina .... 574-472-8585.. 161 N
kbarroso-burrell@hcc-nd.edu
BARROSS, Ben .... 419-530-7877.. 380 D
ben.barros@utoledo.edu
BARROTT, James .... 423-697-3211.. 445 D
jim.barrott@chattanoogastate.edu
BARROW, Carla .... 229-225-5077.. 127 G
cbarrow@southernregional.edu
BARROW, Christine, E .... 301-546-0419.. 210 C
barowce@pgcc.edu
BARROW, Deborah, L ..... 940-397-4212.. 462 A
debbie.barrow@mwsu.edu
BARROW, Ramona .... 270-706-8486.. 189 C
rbarrows0001@kctcs.edu
BARROWS, David .... 217-206-6730.. 156 G
barrows.david@uis.edu
BARROWS, Karen, A .... 585-475-2396.. 327 E
karen.barrows@rit.edu
BARROWS, Karen, A .... 585-475-2396.. 327 E
kab7050@rit.edu
BARROWS, Keith .... 518-738-8847.. 314 A
kbarrows@excelsior.edu
BARROWS, Robert .... 617-228-2241.. 223 B
rbarrows@bhcc.mass.edu
BARROWS, Stephen .... 616-632-2151.. 231 A
spb001@aquinas.edu
BARRY, Ann Marie .... 847-635-1699.. 150 G
annmarie@oakton.edu
BARRY, Barney .... 913-253-5060.. 184 G
bernard.barry@spst.edu
BARRY, Carol .... 225-578-1480.. 197 I
carolbarry@lsu.edu
BARRY, Catherine .... 603-882-6923.. 286 E
cbarry@ccsnh.edu
BARRY, Donna, M .... 973-655-4361.. 293 A
barryd@mail.montclair.edu
BARRY, Ernie .... 214-768-2004.. 465 J
ebarry@smu.edu
BARRY, James (Tim) .... 304-457-6317.. 510 B
barryjt@ab.edu
BARRY, Jeannette .... 402-375-7466.. 281 J
jebarry1@wsc.edu
BARRY, Jessica .... 937-294-0592.. 377 B
jessica@saa.edu
BARRY, John, M .... 804-289-8241.. 495 G
jbarry2@richmond.edu
BARRY, Kevin, G .... 302-295-1170.... 91 I
kevin.g.barry@wilmu.edu
BARRY, Liz .... 858-566-1200.... 42 D
lbarry@disd.edu
BARRY, Matthew .... 207-985-7976.. 203 E
matthewbarry@landingschool.edu
BARRY, Richard .... 610-526-6532.. 398 K
rbarry@brynmawr.edu
BARRY, Sandra .... 617-254-2610.. 227 H
sandy.barry@sjs.edu
BARRY, Seana .... 541-318-3772.. 390 D
sbarry@cocc.edu
BARRY, Terry .... 570-422-3377.. 414 H
tbarry1@esu.edu
BARRY, Theresa .... 262-524-7334.. 515 J
tbarry@carrollu.edu
BARRY-ARQUIT,
Rachel, E .... 503-943-8000.. 396 B
BARRY MCCORMICK,
Joan .... 718-636-3537.. 326 E
jmccormick@pratt.edu
BARRY THIAS, Bridget .... 972-279-6511.. 450 I
bbarrythias@amberton.edu
BARSOM, Michelle .... 229-243-6970.. 117 E
michelle.barsom@bainbridge.edu
BARSTAD, Joel .... 303-715-3184.... 83 C
joel.barstad@archden.org
BARTA, Carol .... 612-436-7576.. 248 F
cbarta@msbcollege.edu
BARTA, Gary .... 319-335-9435.. 169 H
gary-barta@uiowa.edu
BARTA, James, J .... 478-301-5397.. 124 D
barta_jj@mercer.edu
BARTA, Lou .... 217-641-4215.. 143 H
lbarta@jwcc.edu
BARTA, Sharon .... 510-485-7813.... 56 I
sbarta@patten.edu
BARTANEN, Kristine, M .. 253-879-3205.. 508 D
acadvp@pugetsound.edu
BARTEE, Robert .... 402-559-4203.. 283 A
bbartee@unmc.edu
BARTEK, Jennifer, J .... 724-738-2339.. 416 B
jennifer.bartek@sru.edu
BARTEL, Charles, R .... 412-396-6200.. 403 A
bartelc@duq.edu
BARTEL, Kyle, J .... 580-774-3705.. 388 C
kyle.bartel@swosu.edu
BARTEL, Steven, J .... 605-256-5146.. 437 C
steve.bartel@dsu.edu
BARTEL, Tonia .... 660-831-4105.. 269 B
bartelt@moval.edu
BARTELL, William .... 605-331-6703.. 438 A
bill.bartell@usiouxfalls.edu
BARTELMAY, Ryan .... 312-752-2454.. 144 E
ryan.bartelmay@kendall.edu
BARTELS, Dennis .... 614-416-6200.. 364 G
dbartels@bradfordschoolcolumbus.edu
BARTELS, Jean, E .... 912-478-5258.. 122 B
jbartels@georgiasouthern.edu
BARTELS, Kirsten .... 318-357-4577.. 201 B
bartelsk@nsula.edu
BARTELS, Michael .... 563-387-1352.. 174 L
bartmi03@luther.edu
BARTELS, Paige .... 802-440-4300.. 483 E
pbartels@bennington.edu
BARTELS, Richard .... 606-337-1164.. 187 I
rbartels@ccbbc.edu
BARTELS, Roy .... 325-574-7629.. 479 I
rbartels@wtc.edu
BARTELS, Suzanne, M ..... 336-316-2046.. 344 H
bartelssm@guilford.edu
BARTELSON, Gretchen, G 712-324-5061.. 175 G
gbartelson@nwicc.edu
BARTELSON, Jon, C .... 508-831-5725.. 230 C
jonb@wpi.edu
BARTELT, Jason .... 920-923-8090.. 517 H
jbartelt@marianuniversity.edu
BARTFIELD, Joel .... 518-262-7302.. 303 E
bartfi@mail.amc.edu
BARTGES, Ellyn .... 320-308-0125.. 252 A
elbartges@stcloudstate.edu
BARTH, Christopher .... 845-938-3833.. 529 C
christopher.barth@usma.edu
BARTH, Cynthia .... 410-225-4223.. 209 B
cbarth@mica.edu
BARTH, Doug .... 785-594-4526.. 178 D
doug.barth@bakeru.edu
BARTH, Michael .... 406-496-4233.. 277 G
mbarth@mtech.edu
BARTH, Richard, P .... 410-706-7794.. 211 F
rbarth@ssw.umaryland.edu
BARTH, Rick .... 205-665-6239...... 9 B
rbarth@montevallo.edu
BARTHA, Jaimee .... 847-628-2514.. 144 B
jbartha@judsonu.edu
BARTHEL, Jamie .... 763-422-6082.. 248 K
jbarthel@anokatech.edu
BARTHELEMY, Diana .... 773-577-8100.. 139 A
BARTHELL, John .... 405-974-3371.. 388 L
jbarthell@uco.edu
BARTHELMAS, Frederick . 518-587-2100.. 335 D
rick.barthlemas@esc.edu
BARTHOLOMEW, Craig ... 480-990-3773.... 13 M
BARTHOLOMEW, Diane ... 660-831-4146.. 269 B
bartholomewd@moval.edu
BARTHOLOMEW, Lynda .. 256-726-7543...... 6 B
lbartholomew@oakwood.edu
BARTHOLOMEW, Nanette 757-826-1883.. 487 E
studentaffairs@bcva.edu
BARTHOLOMEW-FEIS,
Dixee .... 712-749-2131.. 170 D
bartholomew@bvu.edu
BARTINI, Michael, D .... 207-725-3146.. 202 F
mbartini@bowdoin.edu
BARTKO, Jim .... 559-244-5641.... 32 F
jbartko@csufresno.edu
BARTKOWSKI, Debra .... 954-308-2434.... 95 K
dbartkowski@aii.edu
BARTL, Noelle .... 575-562-2412.. 299 I
noelle.bartl@enmu.edu
BARTLE, Gamin .... 973-408-3106.. 291 B
gbartle@drew.edu
BARTLE, John, R .... 402-554-3989.. 283 B
jbartle@unomaha.edu
BARTLEBAUGH,
Brenda, P .... 318-797-5009.. 198 C
brenda.bartlebaugh@lsus.edu
BARTLETT, Anne .... 979-230-3202.. 453 A
anne.bartlett@brazosport.edu
BARTLETT, Annemarie ..... 610-409-3359.. 422 D
abartlett@ursinus.edu
BARTLETT, James .... 972-883-2355.. 476 C
jbartlet@utdallas.edu
BARTLETT, Jason, T .... 718-390-4080.. 328 F
bartletj@stjohns.edu
BARTLETT, Jon .... 817-531-4870.. 472 F
jdbartlett@txwes.edu
BARTLETT, Julia .... 913-234-0758.. 179 M
julia.bartlett@cleveland.edu
BARTLETT, Noah .... 415-703-9560.... 29 K
nbartlett@cca.edu
BARTLETT, Raymond .... 713-743-5544.. 473 E
rbartlett@uh.edu
BARTLETT, Raymond .... 832-842-5544.. 473 F
rbartlett@uh.edu
BARTLETT, Rebecca .... 802-258-9226.. 484 C
rbartlet@marlboro.edu
BARTLETT, Stacy .... 706-385-1100.. 126 A
stacy.bartlett@point.edu
BARTLETT, Walter, C .... 336-322-2100.. 351 H
walter.bartlett@piedmontcc.edu
BARTLEY, Jacqueline .... 973-748-9000.. 289 H
jackie_bartley@bloomfield.edu
BARTLEY, Kurt .... 303-964-5152.... 82 L
kbartley@regis.edu
BARTLEY, Mary, E .... 515-961-1511.. 176 H
mimi.bartley@simpson.edu
BARTLEY, Patricia, A .... 773-256-0717.. 147 A
pbartley@lstc.edu
BARTLEY, Ron .... 843-921-6901.. 431 H
rbartley@netc.edu
BARTLING, Jonathan .... 815-928-5405.. 150 I
jbartlin@olivet.edu
BARTLING, Kaitlyn .... 641-648-4611.. 173 K
kaitlyn.bartling@iavalley.edu
BARTLING, Kelly, H .... 308-865-8455.. 282 L
bartlingkh@unk.edu
BARTLOW, Jon, A .... 620-235-4761.. 184 C
jbartlow@pittstate.edu
BARTO, Christopher, E .... 212-752-1530.. 318 F
christopher.barto@limcollege.edu
BARTO, Daniel .... 727-341-3051.. 108 D
barto.daniel@spcollege.edu
BARTO, Robert .... 630-466-7900.. 157 K
rbarto@waubonsee.edu
BARTOL, Michelle, M .... 814-641-3432.. 406 F
bartolm@juniata.edu
BARTOLD, Melissa .... 312-225-1700.. 142 A
mbartold@ico.edu
BARTOLI, Andrea .... 973-313-6174.. 297 A
andrea.bartoli@shu.edu
BARTOLINI, Brian, J .... 401-865-1554.. 425 D
bbartoli@providence.edu
BARTOLO, Tony .... 423-478-6208.. 445 E
tbartolo@clevelandstatecc.edu
BARTOLOTTA, Charles ..... 631-451-4790.. 336 D
bartolc@sunysuffolk.edu
BARTOLOTTA, Charles ..... 631-451-4790.. 336 E
bartolc@sunysuffolk.edu
BARTOLOTTA, Theresa ..... 609-652-4501.. 297 C
theresa.bartolotta@stockton.edu
BARTON, Carolina .... 949-214-3093.... 41 F
carolina.barton@cui.edu
BARTON,
Charles (Lennie) .... 919-760-8375.. 346 D
bartonl@meredith.edu
BARTON, Chris .... 386-255-0295.. 115 G
BARTON, Craig .... 312-899-5133.. 154 A
cbarton@saic.edu
BARTON, David .... 660-284-4800.. 265 I
BARTON, Delores .... 404-270-5376.. 128 A
dbarton@spelman.edu
BARTON, Ed .... 360-438-4534.. 506 G
ebarton@stmartin.edu
BARTON, George, W .... 915-747-5640.. 476 D
gwbarton@utep.edu
BARTON, J. Mark .... 479-394-7622.... 22 B
mbarton@rmcc.edu
BARTON, Jacqueline, K ... 626-395-3646.... 30 H
jkbarton@caltech.edu
BARTON, James, E .... 434-223-6148.. 490 D
jbarton@hsc.edu
BARTON, Jennifer, K .... 520-621-3512.... 17 I
barton@email.arizona.edu
BARTON, Judi .... 660-284-4800.. 265 I
registrar@heartlandcollege.edu
BARTON, Mary .... 940-565-2085.. 475 A
mary.barton@unt.edu
BARTON, Michelle .... 760-744-1150.... 56 F
mbarton@palomar.edu
BARTON, Pat .... 678-466-4185.. 119 A
patbarton@clayton.edu
BARTON, Patricia .... 510-136-1220.... 46 E
barton@hnu.edu
BARTON, Sara .... 310-506-4275.... 56 J
sara.barton@pepperdine.edu
BARTOW, Patricia .... 619-216-6694.... 66 E
pbartow@swccd.edu
BARTREM, Richard .... 330-569-5128.. 369 J
bartremrl@hiram.edu
BARTRUG, Reba .... 740-374-8716.. 381 A
rbartrug@wscc.edu
BARTS, Bryan .... 715-232-1469.. 521 D
bartsb@uwstout.edu
BARTSCH, Jonathan .... 617-236-8873.. 218 G
jbartsch@fisher.edu
BARTUNEK, Tami, A .... 913-288-7201.. 182 C
tbartunek@kckcc.edu
BARTUSIK, Lisa Marie ..... 850-484-2014.. 106 H
lbartusik@pensacolastate.edu
BARWICK, Daniel, W .... 620-331-4100.. 181 J
dbarwick@indycc.edu
BARZACCHINI, Mike .... 847-925-6510.. 141 A
mbarzacc@harpercollege.edu
BASALA, Nissim .... 732-370-1560.. 289 C
BASCH, Hersch .... 718-438-1002.. 320 H
BASCO, Chris .... 405-224-3140.. 389 D
cbasco@usao.edu
BASCOM, Shawn .... 208-282-5304.. 133 H
bascshaw@isu.edu
BASER, Ric .... 210-486-4908.. 450 A
rbaser@alamo.edu
BASER, Ric, N .... 210-486-4900.. 450 C
rbaser@alamo.edu
BASFORD, Jerry, L .... 801-581-7793.. 481 M
jbasford@sa.utah.edu
BASGEN, Brian .... 413-565-1000.. 215 A
bbasgen@baypath.edu
BASH, Cassaundra .... 574-936-8898.. 158 I
cassaundra.bash@ancilla.edu
BASH, Lee .... 641-784-5072.. 172 G
bash@graceland.edu
BASHANT, Wendy .... 619-239-0391.... 36 A
wbashant@cwsl.edu
BASHARA, Teri .... 318-678-6000.. 195 I
tbashara@bpcc.edu
BASHAW, Ed .... 620-341-5274.. 180 G
ebashaw@emporia.edu
BASHAW, Edward .... 479-968-0490.... 19 F
ebashaw@atu.edu
BASHET, Abuzafar, M ...... 972-860-7158.. 456 D
azbashet@dcccd.edu
BASHFORD, Joanne .... 305-237-6034.. 105 D
jbashfor@mdc.edu
BASHWINER, Bruce .... 585-273-5798.. 338 K
bruce.bashwiner@rochester.edu
BASIL, Meredith .... 657-278-3057.... 33 A
mbasil@fullerton.edu
BASILE, Elizabeth .... 718-368-4539.. 308 F
ebasile@kbcc.cuny.edu
BASILEO, Paul .... 631-451-4854.. 336 E
basilep@sunysuffolk.edu
BASINGER, David .... 585-594-6550.. 327 D
basingerd@roberts.edu
BASINGER, Randall, G .... 717-796-5375.. 410 J
rbasinge@messiah.edu
BASINSKI, Judith, B .... 716-878-4611.. 332 F
basinsjb@buffalostate.edu
BASIRATMAND, Mehran .. 561-297-0230.. 110 K
mehran@fau.edu
BASKARAN, Christiana .... 523-953-4000.... 49 H
baskarc@lacitycollege.edu

BAUGHMAN, Patricia ...... 936-261-1944.. 467 E
pabaughman@pvamu.edu
BAUGHMAN, Rebecca, L . 512-471-2303.. 476 B
rbaughman@austin.utexas.edu
BAUGUS, John .... 626-815-4622.... 28 A
jbaugus@apu.edu
BAUHARD, Bill .... 402-449-2817.. 280 C
bbauhard6793@graceu.edu
BAUM, Benjamin .... 410-626-2522.. 210 D
BAUM, Christina .... 203-392-5760.... 85 H
baumc1@southernct.edu
BAUM, Courtney .... 724-805-2253.. 419 A
courtney.baum@email.stvincent.edu
BAUM, Cynthia .... 714-620-3700.... 27 I
cbaum@argosy.edu
BAUM, Daniel, B .... 410-777-2011.. 206 B
dbbaum@aacc.edu
BAUM, Keith .... 717-569-7071.. 407 E
kbaum@lbc.edu
BAUM, Richard .... 212-998-4365.. 324 C
rich.baum@nyu.edu
BAUM, Robert .... 724-805-2590.. 419 A
bob.baum@email.stvincent.edu
BAUM, Robin .... 914-594-4882.. 323 I
robin_baum@nymc.edu
BAUMAL, Robert .... 978-656-3244.. 224 A
baumalr@middlesex.mass.edu
BAUMAN, Curtis .... 570-945-8506.. 406 H
curtis.bauman@keystone.edu
BAUMAN, Dallas .... 631-632-6974.. 332 A
dallas.bauman@stonybrook.edu
BAUMAN, David .... 218-723-6179.. 245 J
dbauman@css.edu
BAUMAN, Jerry .... 312-996-7240.. 156 F
jbauman@uic.edu
BAUMAN, Joel .... 386-822-7100.. 113 B
jbauman@stetson.edu
BAUMANN, Benjamin ...... 508-678-2811.. 223 A
ben.baumann@bristolcc.edu
BAUMANN, Erick .... 708-524-5054.. 139 F
ebauman@dom.edu
BAUMANN, Joe .... 979-830-4075.. 452 J
joe.baumann@blinn.edu
BAUMANN, Melissa, J ..... 334-844-5860...... 1 G
mjb0041@auburn.edu
BAUMANN, Robert .... 913-684-2741.. 528 I
robert.baumann@leavenworth.army.mil
BAUMBACH, Kirk .... 804-752-7263.. 493 C
kirkbaumbach@rmc.edu
BAUMEISTER, Bo .... 503-493-6587.. 391 A
bbaumeister@cu-portland.edu
BAUMER, Brian .... 718-990-3292.. 328 F
baumerb@stjohns.edu
BAUMET, Robert, L .... 716-878-5304.. 332 F
baumetrl@buffalostate.edu
BAUMGAERTNER, Jill, P . 630-752-5060.. 158 C
jill.baumgaertner@wheaton.edu
BAUMGARDNER,
Brice, D .... 573-629-3279.. 265 G
bbaumgardner@hlg.edu
BAUMGARDNER, Deidra . 317-738-8189.. 160 J
dbaumgardner@franklincollege.edu
BAUMGARDNER, Marian . 918-495-7442.. 386 H
mbaumgardner@oru.edu
BAUMGARDNER,
Michael .... 518-244-2207.. 327 H
baumgm@sage.edu
BAUMGARDNER, Waylon 951-343-4876.... 29 H
wbaumgardner@calbaptist.edu
BAUMGARDNER,
William, B .... 606-474-3151.. 188 L
wbbaumgardner@kcu.edu
BAUMGART, Reilly .... 618-262-8641.. 142 F
baumgartr@iecc.edu
BAUMGARTEN, Bobbie ... 214-637-3530.. 479 C
bbaumgarten@wadecollege.edu
BAUMGARTEN,
Matthew, J .... 757-822-1780.. 498 H
mbaumgarten@tcc.edu
BAUMGARTNER,
Annmarie .... 419-772-2729.. 374 J
a-baumgartner@onu.edu
BAUMGARTNER, Bruce ... 814-732-2776.. 415 A
bbaumgartner@edinboro.edu
BAUMGARTNER,
David, A .... 319-335-1023.. 169 H
david-baumgartner@uiowa.edu
BAUMGARTNER, Eric, T .. 419-772-2372.. 374 J
e-baumgartner@onu.edu
BAUMGARTNER, Holly, L 419-824-3756.. 371 I
hbaumgartner@lourdes.edu
BAUMGARTNER, Renee .... 408-554-5344.... 63 E
rbaumgartner@scu.edu
BAUMGARTNER,
Timothy, K .... 713-348-4867.. 464 E
timothy.k.baumgartner@rice.edu
BAUMHOVER, Lynne ...... 563-589-0300.. 177 H
lbaumhover@wartburgseminary.edu
BAUMLER, Angela .... 410-532-3150.. 210 B
abaumler@ndm.edu
BAUMLER, Kim .... 563-589-3000.. 177 C
BAUMLER, Scott, J .... 563-588-4990.. 174 K
scott.baumler@loras.edu
BAUN, Dan .... 507-537-6978.. 252 E
dan.baun@smsu.edu
BAUN, Jeffrey, S .... 610-359-5315.. 401 L
jbaun@dccc.edu
BAUR, John .... 309-438-2583.. 143 B
jebaur@ilstu.edu
BAURA, Gail .... 773-508-8070.. 146 G
gbaura@luc.edu
BAUS, Amy .... 563-589-3132.. 177 C
abaus@dbq.edu
BAUSHKE, Ken .... 270-745-3056.. 194 D
ken.baushke@wku.edu
BAUSINGER, Patricia, E .. 570-321-4049.. 409 F
baus@lycoming.edu
BAUSMAN, Marvin .... 319-398-5516.. 174 I
marvin.bausman@kirkwood.edu
BAUSMITH, Shirley .... 843-661-1487.. 430 B
sbausmith@fmarion.edu
BAUSS, Celia, N .... 864-592-4754.. 432 H
baussc@sccsc.edu
BAUTISTA MOLLER,
Lydia, B .... 954-607-4344.. 114 F
BAVER, Chad .... 406-683-7382.. 277 A
chad.baver@umwestern.edu
BAVIER, Anne .... 817-272-2776.. 476 A
bavier@uta.edu
BAVISI, Sanjay .... 505-922-2886.. 299 K
BAWA, Navraj .... 888-775-1514.... 68 J
BAWA, Opinder .... 415-422-2787.... 72 C
osbawa@usfca.edu
BAWCOM, Amy .... 254-526-1472.. 454 A
amy.bawcom@ctcd.edu
BAWOROWSKY, John ..... 414-288-4976.. 517 I
john.baworowsky@marquette.edu
BAXTER, Agnes .... 919-546-8212.. 355 F
abaxter@shawu.edu
BAXTER, Aimee, F .... 318-257-2641.. 200 G
abaxter@latech.edu
BAXTER, Charlene .... 706-880-8311.. 123 K
cbaxter@lagrange.edu
BAXTER, Keith .... 580-745-2250.. 387 M
kbaxter@se.edu
BAXTER, Melissa .... 315-568-3271.. 323 A
mbaxter@nycc.edu
BAXTER, Pat .... 212-229-8947.. 322 E
baxterp@newschool.edu
BAXTER, Randy, A .... 662-720-7576.. 260 B
rabaxter@nemcc.edu
BAXTER, Steven .... 360-417-6300.. 505 I
sbaxter@pencol.edu
BAYARDELLE, Eddy .... 718-289-5185.. 307 C
eddy.bayardelle@bcc.cuny.edu
BAYER, Deborah, A .... 248-232-4311.. 239 E
dabayer@oaklandcc.edu
BAYER, Deborah, A .... 248-232-4211.. 239 E
dabayer@oaklandcc.edu
BAYERL, Sue .... 320-308-2111.. 252 A
sjbayerl@stcloudstate.edu
BAYLES, Kenneth .... 402-559-4945.. 283 A
kbayles@unmc.edu
BAYLESS, Debi .... 573-518-1330.. 268 E
dbayless@mineralarea.edu
BAYLESS, Laura .... 608-342-1854.. 521 A
baylessl@uwplatt.edu
BAYLOR, Bridget .... 540-453-2358.. 496 F
baylorb@brcc.edu
BAYLOR, Chiquita .... 401-341-2225.. 426 C
chiquita.baylor@salve.edu
BAYLOR, Gail .... 828-298-3325.. 359 F
gbaylor@warren-wilson.edu
BAYLOR, Jim .... 206-592-3443.. 504 E
jbaylor@highline.edu
BAYNARD, Donald .... 617-287-7799.. 220 G
donald.baynard@umb.edu
BAYNE, Deann .... 402-872-2226.. 281 I
dbayne@peru.edu
BAYNE, Doug .... 509-527-4253.. 508 F
doug.bayne@wwcc.edu
BAYNE, Sheila .... 617-627-2000.. 228 H
sheila.bayne@tufts.edu
BAYNE, Suzanne .... 423-472-7141.. 445 E
sbayne@clevelandstatecc.edu
BAYNES, Leonard, M ..... 713-743-2478.. 473 F
lbaynes@central.uh.edu
BAYOUMI, Magdy, A ...... 337-482-6147.. 201 D
mab@louisiana.edu
BAYS, Steven .... 509-533-3570.. 503 A
steve.bays@sfcc.spokane.edu
BAYTO, Tammy .... 478-274-7852.. 125 D
tbayto@oftc.edu
BAZAN, Teresita .... 512-223-7950.. 451 N
tbazan@austincc.edu
BAZAN, Yamilet .... 951-785-2100.... 48 A
ybazan@lasierra.edu
BAZANT, Robert, S .... 724-222-5330.. 412 E
rbazant@penncommercial.edu
BAZAR, Leon .... 361-593-2258.. 469 A
kulgb000@tamuk.edu
BAZARNIC, Steve .... 301-784-5000.. 205 G
sbazarnic@allegany.edu
BAZEMORE, Dennis .... 910-893-1540.. 342 F
bazemored@campbell.edu
BAZEMORE,
Haywood, M .... 803-705-4321.. 427 D
bazemoreh@benedict.edu
BAZIL, Ted .... 914-961-8313.. 329 H
ted@svots.edu
BAZILE, Samantha .... 845-398-4102.. 329 G
sbazile@stac.edu
BAZLEY, Lisa .... 210-829-3959.. 474 D
lisa@uiwtx.edu
BAZLUKE, Francine, T ..... 802-656-8585.. 485 D
francine.bazluke@uvm.edu
BAZYLEWICZ, Terry, T ..... 908-852-1400.. 290 D
BAZZELL, Darrell .... 512-471-3434.. 476 B
bazzell@austin.utexas.edu
BEA, David .... 520-206-4519.... 16 F
dbea@pima.edu
BEACH, Bradley .... 330-244-4732.. 380 J
bbeach@walsh.edu
BEACH, Cora .... 541-962-3368.. 391 C
cbeach@eou.edu
BEACH, Nancy, S .... 540-365-4529.. 489 M
nbeach@ferrum.edu
BEACH, Natalie .... 503-399-5105.. 390 E
natalie.beach@chemeketa.edu
BEACH, Rebecca .... 540-362-6414.. 490 F
rbeach@hollins.edu
BEACH, Vince .... 641-585-8133.. 177 F
vince.beach@waldorf.edu
BEACHAM, David, M .... 864-597-4206.. 435 C
beachamdm@wofford.edu
BEACHAM, Ralph .... 620-724-0390.. 181 A
ralphb@fortscott.edu
BEACHNAU, Andrew .... 616-331-2120.. 234 F
beachnaa@gvsu.edu
BEACHY, Benjamin, S ..... 540-432-4478.. 488 K
ben.beachy@emu.edu
BEACON, John .... 812-237-3560.. 162 A
john.beacon@indstate.edu
BEADENKOPF, Scott .... 610-361-5327.. 411 E
beadenks@neumann.edu
BEADLES, Mary .... 706-245-7226.. 120 D
mbeadles@ec.edu
BEAGHAN, John, W .... 248-370-2445.. 239 K
beaghan@oakland.edu
BEAGLE, Donald .... 704-461-6740.. 342 A
donaldbeagle@bac.edu
BEAGLE, Mike .... 541-552-6127.. 395 A
beaglem@sou.edu
BEAHON, Mary Ann .... 573-592-1127.. 275 G
maryann.beahon@williamwoods.edu
BEAIL, Linda .... 619-849-2408.... 57 M
lindabeail@pointloma.edu
BEAKMAN, Andrew, W ..... 315-792-3111.. 339 B
awbeakma@utica.edu
BEAL, Jason .... 801-957-4205.. 483 A
jason.beal@slcc.edu
BEAL, Judy .... 617-521-2139.. 228 C
judy.beal@simmons.edu
BEAL, Kenton .... 903-813-2468.. 451 M
bookstore@austincollege.edu
BEAL, Lee .... 828-835-4233.. 353 G
lbeal@tricountycc.edu
BEAL, Stephen .... 510-594-3630.... 29 K
sbeal@cca.edu
BEALE, Charles, L .... 302-831-8107.... 91 F
cbeale@udel.edu
BEALE, Connie, L .... 973-761-9401.. 297 A
concetta.beale@shu.edu
BEALE, Marjorie, A .... 626-395-6369.... 30 H
mbeale@caltech.edu
BEALER, Mitchell .... 435-586-7723.. 481 N
bealer@suu.edu
BEALES, Sharon .... 610-861-5451.. 411 G
sbeales@northampton.edu
BEALL, David .... 773-508-2391.. 146 G
dbeall@luc.edu
BEALS, Linda, M .... 937-327-6374.. 381 F
lbeals@wittenberg.edu
BEALS, Michael, J .... 714-556-3610.... 73 B
officeofthepresident@vanguard.edu
BEAM, Brian .... 309-438-8404.. 143 B
babeam@ilstu.edu
BEAM, Carla .... 907-786-7711.... 10 E
cjbeam@alaska.edu
BEAM, Gina .... 716-614-6220.. 324 D
gbeam@niagaracc.suny.edu
BEAM, Jay .... 704-971-8500.. 343 E
jbeam@charlottelaw.edu
BEAM, John .... 510-464-3474.... 57 D
jbeam@peralta.edu
BEAM, Julie .... 574-807-7020.. 159 D
julie.beam@bethelcollege.edu
BEAM, Linda .... 310-660-3401.... 42 J
lbeam@elcamino.edu
BEAM, Ruthanne .... 865-573-4517.. 440 I
rubeam@johnsonu.edu
BEAM, Tony .... 864-977-2008.. 431 G
tony.beam@ngu.edu
BEAMAN, Cynthia, A .... 812-888-4125.. 169 A
cbeaman@vinu.edu
BEAMAN, Patricia, L ...... 716-839-8538.. 312 D
pbeaman@daemen.edu
BEAMAN, Riley .... 910-576-6222.. 351 E
beamanr@montgomery.edu
BEAMER, Janet .... 704-499-9200.... 93 F
BEAMON, Jeff .... 912-650-6206.. 127 D
jbeamon@southuniversity.edu
BEAMON, Stanley .... 312-850-7038.. 138 A
sbeamon3@ccc.edu
BEAN, Al .... 207-780-5588.. 205 E
albean@maine.edu
BEAN, Caronda .... 225-771-2191.. 199 H
caronda_bean@subr.edu
BEAN, Christopher, A ...... 540-665-4553.. 494 B
cbean@su.edu
BEAN, Debra .... 925-969-3302.... 47 F
dbean@jfku.edu
BEAN, James, C .... 617-373-2170.. 227 B
BEAN, Joanne .... 207-893-7895.. 204 D
jbean@sjcme.edu
BEAN, Kellie .... 607-431-4400.. 315 E
bwank@hartwick.edu
BEAN, Miho .... 603-206-8101.. 286 D
msbean@ccsnh.edu
BEAN, Nancy .... 731-352-4000.. 438 K
beann@bethelu.edu
BEAN, Paul .... 785-242-5200.. 183 M
paul.bean@ottawa.edu
BEAN, Shirley .... 206-878-3710.. 504 E
sbean@highline.edu
BEAN, Shirley .... 253-833-9111.. 504 C
sbean@greenriver.edu
BEAN, Stacey .... 937-778-7844.. 368 E
sbean@edisonohio.edu
BEAN, Steve .... 218-322-2351.. 249 G
steve.bean@itascacc.edu
BEAN, Zach .... 214-333-2212.. 455 J
zach@dbu.edu
BEANE-BOOSE, Linda ...... 509-533-3567.. 503 A
linda.beane-boose@sfcc.spokane.edu
BEANS, Jessica .... 937-298-3399.. 371 D
jessica.beans@kc.edu
BEAR, Catherine .... 314-529-9466.. 267 B
cbear@maryville.edu
BEAR, Marca .... 813-257-3280.. 114 M
mbear@ut.edu
BEARBOWER, Sarah .... 608-796-3000.. 522 O
sbearbower@viterbo.edu
BEARCE, John .... 702-651-7454.. 284 H
john.bearce@csn.edu
BEARD, Aileen .... 218-625-4834.. 245 J
abeard@css.edu
BEARD, Alison .... 828-726-2311.. 347 I
abeard@cccti.edu
BEARD, Ashley .... 601-477-5454.. 258 E
ashley.beard@jcjc.edu
BEARD, Audrey, W .... 919-530-5327.. 357 A
awbeard@nccu.edu
BEARD, Christopher .... 808-675-3368.. 130 E
christopher.beard@byuh.edu
BEARD, David .... 706-880-8175.. 123 K
dbeard@lagrange.edu
BEARD, Eric .... 719-638-6580.... 80 B
ebeard@cci.edu
BEARD, Gerald .... 662-562-3319.. 260 C
BEARD, Jason .... 206-296-2499.. 507 E
beardj@seattleu.edu
BEARD, John, P .... 843-349-6441.. 428 E
johnb@coastal.edu
BEARD, Katie .... 205-652-3528...... 9 F
kbeard@uwa.edu
BEARD, Mary, A .... 716-851-1675.. 313 H
beard@ecc.edu
BEARD, Richard, L .... 717-867-6363.. 408 F
rbeard@lvc.edu
BEARD, Robert .... 918-495-6588.. 386 H
rbeard@oru.edu
BEARD, Russell .... 425-564-4200.. 501 F
russ.beard@bellevuecollege.edu
BEARD, Ryan .... 713-646-1811.. 459 A
rbeard@hcl.edu
BEARD, Scott .... 304-876-5370.. 513 E
sbeard@shepherd.edu
BEARD, Tanika .... 706-821-8103.. 125 H
recordsofficestaff@paine.edu
BEARD, Timothy, L .... 727-816-3400.. 106 F
beardt@phsc.edu
BEARDMORE, Kevin .... 270-686-4504.. 190 D
kevin.beardmore@kctcs.edu
BEARDMORE, Melissa, A 410-777-2532.. 206 B
mabeardmore@aacc.edu
BEARDON, Sheiron .... 870-780-1206.... 18 G
sbeardon@smail.anc.edu
BEARDSALL, Christopher 210-486-2312.. 450 E
cbeardsall@alamo.edu
BEARDSLEE, Gene .... 402-872-2270.. 281 I
gbeardslee@peru.edu

BEDFORD, Allen .... 267-502-2567.. 398 J
allen.bedford@brynathyn.edu
BEDFORD, April .... 718-951-5214.. 307 D
abedford@brooklyn.cuny.edu
BEDFORD, Brian .... 916-691-7226.... 51 B
BEDFORD, John .... 405-208-5322.. 385 E
jbedford@okcu.edu
BEDFORD, Judy .... 952-446-4177.. 246 D
bedfordj@crown.edu
BEDFORD, Laura .... 315-792-3179.. 339 B
lbedford@utica.edu
BEDFORD, Laurie .... 612-338-7224.. 256 D
laurie.bedford@waldenu.edu
BEDFORD, Norm .... 702-774-8000.. 284 L
norm.bedford@unlv.edu
BEDFORD, Wayne .... 205-652-3687...... 9 F
dbedford@uwa.edu
BEDI, Param, S .... 570-577-1557.. 398 L
param.bedi@bucknell.edu
BEDINGFIELD, Sarah .... 603-427-7631.. 286 B
sbedingfield@ccsnh.edu
BEDINI, Ken .... 860-465-5247.... 85 G
bedini@easternct.edu
BEDNARZ, Bridgette .... 254-968-9271.. 467 F
bednarz@tarleton.edu
BEDNEY, Elynda, A .... 269-471-6040.. 230 H
bedney@andrews.edu
BEDOYA, Eduardo .... 231-777-0332.. 238 G
eduardo.bedoya@muskegoncc.edu
BEDOYA, Theresa .... 410-225-2434.. 209 B
tbedoya@mica.edu
BEDSOLE, Blake .... 205-652-3581...... 9 F
bbedsole@uwa.edu
BEDTKE, James .... 507-457-1458.. 254 O
jbedtke@smumn.edu
BEDWELL, Pamela .... 478-471-2730.. 124 E
pamela.bedwell@mga.edu
BEDWELL, Teresa, M .... 937-775-2313.. 381 H
teresa.bedwell@wright.edu
BEE, Richard .... 562-903-4728.... 28 E
richard.e.bee@biola.edu
BEE, Timothy, S .... 520-621-1737.... 17 I
timbee@email.arizona.edu
BEEBE, Anthony, E .... 805-730-4011.... 63 D
beebe@sbcc.edu
BEEBE, Barbara, R .... 325-574-6501.. 479 I
bbeebe@wtc.edu
BEEBE, Gayle, D .... 805-565-6024.... 75 A
president@westmont.edu
BEEBE, Norman .... 413-775-1333.. 223 D
beebe@gcc.mass.edu
BEEBE, Robert, D .... 909-593-3511.... 71 B
rbeebe@laverne.edu
BEEBE, Rose .... 304-424-8286.. 514 D
rose.beebe@wvup.edu
BEEBY, James, M .... 812-464-1855.. 168 E
jmbeeby@usi.edu
BEECH, Amanda .... 661-255-1050.... 30 E
abeech@calarts.edu
BEECH, Bettina .... 601-984-1020.. 261 C
bbeech@umc.edu
BEECH, JR., Derrick .... 404-756-5294.. 125 A
dbeech@msm.edu
BEECH, Rachel, A .... 520-621-6123.... 17 I
rabeech@email.arizona.edu
BEECHER, Brian .... 847-543-2464.. 138 C
bbeecher@clcillinois.edu
BEECHER, Shan, L .... 515-574-1985.. 173 F
beecher@iowacentral.edu
BEECHING, Angela .... 212-749-2802.. 319 M
abeeching@msmnyc.edu
BEEHLER, Jeff .... 509-865-0446.. 504 D
beehler_j@heritage.edu
BEEHLER, John, M .... 256-782-5881...... 4 H
president@jsu.edu
BEEKE, Joel, R .... 616-977-0599.. 240 B
joel.beeke@prts.edu
BEEKE, Jonathon .... 616-977-0599.. 240 B
jonathon.beeke@prts.edu
BEEKE, Jonathon, D .... 616-432-3408.. 240 B
jonathon.beeke@prts.edu
BEEKMAN, William, R .... 517-353-9818.. 237 I
beekman@msu.edu
BEELEN, Joan .... 616-957-6027.. 232 B
jrb44@calvinseminary.edu
BEELER, Jeremy .... 908-835-2301.. 298 E
jbeeler@warren.edu
BEELER, Monique .... 415-338-1111.... 35 B
mbeeler@sfsu.edu
BEELER, Sydney .... 724-925-4050.. 423 D
beelers@wccc.edu
BEEMAN, Greg .... 845-675-4417.. 325 C
greg.beeman@nyack.edu
BEEMER, Matthew .... 904-596-2473.. 113 J
mbeemer@tbc.edu
BEEMER, Pamela .... 847-491-7505.. 150 F
p-beemer@northwestern.edu
BEEN, Sharon, A .... 501-882-8836.... 18 I
sabeen@asub.edu
BEER, Laura .... 503-699-3361.. 392 D
lbeer@maryhurst.edu
BEER, Patrick .... 478-387-4783.. 121 E
pbeer@gmc.edu
BEER, Richard .... 360-486-8784.. 506 G
jrbeer@stmartin.edu
BEERS, David .... 253-879-3902.. 508 D
dbeers@pugetsound.edu
BEERS, Di .... 425-235-2426.. 506 F
dbeers@rtc.edu
BEERS, Josh .... 717-560-8240.. 407 E
jbeers@lbc.edu
BEERS, Maggie .... 415-338-3613.... 35 B
mbeers@sfsu.edu
BEERS, Peter .... 717-560-8267.. 407 E
pbeers@lbc.edu
BEERS, Stephen, T .... 479-524-7252.... 20 H
sbeers@jbu.edu
BEERT, Brian .... 563-386-3570.. 173 A
bbeert@hamiltontechcollege.com
BEERY, Kevin, E .... 610-917-1401.. 422 C
kebeery@valleyforge.edu
BEERY, Wendy .... 610-917-1429.. 422 C
wmbeery@valleyforge.edu
BEESLEY, Brad .... 918-781-7450.. 382 D
beesleyb@bacone.edu
BEESON, Duane, L .... 712-707-7116.. 176 B
beeson@nwciowa.edu
BEESON, Patricia, E .... 412-624-4223.. 421 G
beeson@pitt.edu
BEETS, Shannon .... 775-831-1314.. 285 G
sbeets@sierranevada.edu
BEEZHOLD, Philip, D .... 616-526-6481.. 232 A
pdb2@calvin.edu
BEG, Christina .... 216-397-1998.. 370 H
cbeg@jcu.edu
BEGANY, James .... 724-357-7544.. 415 B
jbegany@iup.edu
BEGAY, Janice .... 785-749-8419.. 181 E
janice.begay@bie.edu
BEGAY, Karen, F .... 520-626-9809.... 17 I
kfbegay@email.arizona.edu
BEGG, Melissa, D .... 212-854-2691.. 311 E
mdb3@columbia.edu
BEGGS, Crystal .... 701-788-4647.. 360 E
crystal.beggs@mayvillestate.edu
BEGIAN, Jamie .... 203-837-8851.... 85 I
begianj@wcsu.edu
BEGIN, Gene, P .... 508-286-3223.. 229 F
begin_gene@wheatoncollege.edu
BEGLEY, John, B .... 270-384-8505.. 191 E
begleyj@lindsey.edu
BEGLEY, Mary Ann .... 415-338-3885.... 35 B
begley@sfsu.edu
BEGLEY, Thomas .... 518-276-2525.. 327 B
begley@rpi.edu
BEGLY, Mark, L .... 757-221-1009.. 488 F
mlbegly@wm.edu
BEHAN, Joseph .... 718-405-3212.. 310 H
joseph.behan@mountsaintvincent.edu
BEHAN, Lawrence, M .... 413-662-5245.. 222 B
l.behans@mcla.edu
BEHAN KRAUS,
Carolyn, A .... 203-773-8521.... 85 C
cbehan@albertus.edu
BEHAUNEK, Luke .... 515-961-1562.. 176 H
luke.behaunek@simpson.edu
BEHBEHANI, Khosrow .... 817-272-2571.. 476 A
kb@uta.edu
BEHEN, Joseph .... 312-499-4272.. 154 A
jbehen@saic.edu
BEHLING, Laura, L .... 309-341-7216.. 145 A
llbehling@knox.edu
BEHM, Bonnie Lee .... 610-519-6456.. 422 G
bonnie.behm@villanova.edu
BEHMAND, Mojgan .... 415-485-3276.... 42 G
mojgan.behmand@dominican.edu
BEHMER, Scott .... 440-610-2240.. 127 D
sbehmer@southuniversity.edu
BEHN, Julie .... 408-944-6121.. 176 C
julie.behn@palmer.edu
BEHNEN, Erin .... 618-650-3639.. 155 A
etimpe@siue.edu
BEHNKE, Laura .... 215-702-4521.. 399 E
lbehnke@cairn.edu
BEHR, Eileen, W .... 215-571-3548.. 402 G
eileen.w.behr@drexel.edu
BEHR, Fred, C .... 507-786-3636.. 254 P
behr@stolaf.edu
BEHR, John .... 914-961-8313.. 329 H
jbehr@svots.edu
BEHR, Julie .... 706-778-8500.. 125 J
jbehr@piedmont.edu
BEHR, Kate, E .... 914-337-9300.. 311 F
kate.behr@concordia-ny.edu
BEHR, Kevin .... 361-354-2527.. 454 G
kevind@coastalbend.edu
BEHR, Michelle .... 205-226-4650...... 2 C
mbehr@bsc.edu
BEHR, Richard, A .... 239-590-7399.. 110 L
rbehr@fgcu.edu
BEHRE, William .... 732-987-2314.. 292 A
wbehre@georgian.edu
BEHRENDT, Todd .... 315-792-5679.. 321 G
tbehrendt@mvcc.edu
BEHRENS, Ann .... 217-228-5432.. 151 F
behrean@quincy.edu
BEHRENS, Kim .... 559-791-2322.... 47 L
kbehrens@portervillecollege.edu
BEHRENS, Susanne .... 713-623-2040.. 451 K
sbehrens@aii.edu
BEHRENS, Troy, T .... 214-768-2420.. 465 J
tbehrens@smu.edu
BEHRINGER, Marilyn .... 559-324-6476.... 67 A
marilyn.behringer@scccd.edu
BEHRS, David .... 415-451-2802.... 61 D
dbehrs@sfts.edu
BEHUNEK, Sarah .... 303-458-3535.... 82 L
sbehunek@regis.edu
BEHUNIN, Robert .... 435-797-9693.. 482 B
robert.behunin@usu.edu
BEIDLEMAN, David, C .... 717-361-1493.. 403 C
beidlemand@etown.edu
BEIDLER, James .... 614-287-2646.. 367 C
jbeidler@cscc.edu
BEIER, Jason .... 608-890-1066.. 522 A
jason.beier@uwex.uwc.edu
BEIER, Nancy, A .... 410-777-2834.. 206 B
nabeier@aacc.edu
BEIKIRCH, Dale .... 432-685-5539.. 461 H
dbeikirch@midland.edu
BEIL, Cheryl .... 202-994-6712.... 92 D
cbeil@gwu.edu
BEILOCK, Sian .... 773-834-3713.. 156 D
beilock@uchicago.edu
BEIMER, Connie .... 505-277-2498.. 302 F
cbeimer@unm.edu
BEINHOFF, Lisa .... 575-835-5615.. 300 G
lbeinhoff@admin.nmt.edu
BEINKE, Dayna .... 816-415-5902.. 275 F
beinked@william.jewell.edu
BEIRNE, Jay .... 800-838-2580.. 226 C
jbeirne@ngs.edu
BEISE, Elizabeth, J .... 301-405-6836.. 211 E
beise@umd.edu
BEISECKER, Mark .... 805-893-4071.... 70 E
mark.beisecker@bookstore.ucsb.edu
BEISSWENGER, Drew .... 620-331-4100.. 181 J
dbeisswenger@indycc.edu
BEITEL, Leland .... 443-334-2064.. 211 A
lbeitel@stevenson.edu
BEITEY, George .... 619-388-7860.... 60 H
gbeitey@sdccd.edu
BEITLER, Sidney .... 561-868-3484.. 106 D
beitlers@palmbeachstate.edu
BEITZEL, Vernon, L .... 540-464-7211.. 499 E
beitzelvl@vmi.edu
BEJAR, Elizabeth .... 305-348-2151.. 111 A
elizabeth.bejar@fiu.edu
BEJNAROWICZ, Ewa .... 312-553-3193.. 137 D
ebejnarowicz@ccc.edu
BEJOU, David .... 304-766-3025.. 514 B
dbejou@wvstateu.edu
BEJUNE, Matthew .... 508-929-8511.. 222 F
mbejune@worcester.edu
BEKCHIAN, Arina .... 510-925-4282.... 26 M
abekchya@aua.am
BEKE-HARRIGAN, Heidi .... 330-490-7186.. 380 J
hbekeharrigan@walsh.edu
BEKISZ, Pete .... 315-279-5484.. 318 C
pbekisz@keuka.edu
BEKKER, Corne .... 757-352-4401.. 493 E
clbekker@regent.edu
BEKKER, James .... 801-213-3505.. 481 M
james.bekker@hsc.utah.edu
BEKRITSKY, Brett .... 845-848-7405.. 312 F
brett.bekritsky@dc.edu
BELAND, Thomas .... 802-776-5279.. 483 G
tom.beland@csj.edu
BELANGER, OFM,
Brian, C .... 518-783-5047.. 330 E
bbelanger@siena.edu
BELANGER, David, J .... 413-585-2530.. 228 D
dbelange@smith.edu
BELANGER, Jaqueline .... 330-287-1306.. 375 B
belanger.24@osu.edu
BELANGER, Kenneth .... 315-228-7220.. 310 G
kbelanger@colgate.edu
BELANGER, Lisa .... 860-768-4666.... 89 G
belanger@hartford.edu
BELANGER, Marc .... 414-930-3119.. 518 F
belangem@mtmary.edu
BELANGER-HAAS, Aimee .... 937-328-6038.. 366 E
haasa@clarkstate.edu
BELCH, Joe .... 619-594-2473.... 35 A
gbelch@mail.sdsu.edu
BELCHER, Carol .... 843-574-6230.. 433 D
carol.belcher@tridenttech.edu
BELCHER, Chris .... 417-865-2815.. 265 B
belcherc@evangel.edu
BELCHER, Chris, P .... 701-483-2984.. 360 D
chris.belcher@dickinsonstate.edu
BELCHER, Christopher .... 701-483-2984.. 360 D
christopher.belcher@dickinsonstate.edu
BELCHER, Dana .... 580-559-5564.. 383 H
dbelcher@ecok.edu
BELCHER, David, O .... 828-227-7100.. 359 A
dbelcher@wcu.edu
BELCHER, Elizabeth, M .... 304-929-5464.. 512 C
ebelcher@newriver.edu
BELCHER, Jim .... 866-323-0233.... 58 E
president@providencecc.edu
BELCHER, Keith, E .... 912-279-5922.. 119 C
kbelcher@ccga.edu
BELCHER, Lawrence .... 317-788-2397.. 168 A
belcherl@uindy.edu
BELCHER, Michael .... 978-934-3929.. 221 A
michael_belcher@uml.edu
BELCHER, Michael .... 209-946-2537.... 71 C
mbelcher@pacific.edu
BELCHER, Nicholas .... 617-850-1297.. 219 F
nbelcher@hchc.edu
BELCHER, Tim .... 540-365-4366.. 489 M
tbelcher@ferrum.edu
BELD, Jo, M .... 507-786-3632.. 254 P
beld@stolaf.edu
BELDEN, Eric .... 330-490-7337.. 380 J
ebelden@walsh.edu
BELDEN, William .... 360-992-2103.. 502 E
wbelden@clark.edu
BELDONA, Sam .... 415-458-3786.... 42 G
sriram.beldona@dominican.edu
BELECKY, Steven .... 303-963-3000.... 77 I
sbelecky@ccu.edu
BELERIQUE, Rosa .... 424-207-3753.... 55 E
rbelerique@otis.edu
BELETE, Yared .... 303-797-5092.... 76 J
yared.belete@arapahoe.edu
BELFIELD, Kevin, D .... 973-596-3676.. 293 D
kevin.d.belfield@njit.edu
BELFIELD, Sherri .... 704-378-1032.. 345 E
sbelfield@jcsu.edu
BELGARDE, Judy, A .... 701-477-7978.. 362 D
jbelgarde@tm.edu
BELIN, Jackie .... 908-526-1200.. 295 A
jacki.belin@raritanval.edu
BELIN, Joanne .... 205-970-9215...... 7 B
jbelin@sebc.edu
BELINSKI, Victor .... 909-274-4365.... 53 C
vbelinski@mtsac.edu
BELISLE, William, R .... 504-284-5539.. 199 I
wbelisle@suno.edu
BELK, Peter .... 913-469-8500.. 182 A
pbelk@jccc.edu
BELKIN, Betsey .... 440-646-8184.. 380 F
bbelkin@ursuline.edu
BELKNAP, Cindy .... 570-577-3654.. 398 L
cindy.belknap@bucknell.edu
BELKNAP, Monica .... 928-776-2217.... 18 D
monica.belknap@yc.edu
BELKNAP, Peggy .... 928-536-6231.... 15 J
peggy.belknap@npc.edu
BELKO, Dawn .... 763-424-0715.. 251 B
dbelko@nhcc.edu
BELL, Aimee .... 330-569-5279.. 369 J
bella1@hiram.edu
BELL, Amy .... 870-743-3000.... 21 C
abell@northark.edu
BELL, Barbara .... 216-987-4851.. 367 E
barbara.bell@tri-c.edu
BELL, Bonita .... 910-272-3331.. 352 E
bbell@robeson.edu
BELL, Brett .... 619-388-7815.... 60 H
bbell@sdccd.edu
BELL, Carmen .... 575-624-8080.. 300 I
carmen@nmmi.edu
BELL, Carol .... 307-754-6190.. 526 N
carol.bell@nwc.edu
BELL, Christopher .... 207-768-9511.. 205 D
chris@maine.edu
BELL, Corinne .... 802-387-6863.. 484 B
corinnebell@landmark.edu
BELL, Cynthia, M .... 330-941-3101.. 382 A
cmbell02@ysu.edu
BELL, Damon .... 360-475-7474.. 505 F
dbell@olympic.edu
BELL, Danielle .... 803-321-5128.. 431 F
danielle.bell@newberry.edu
BELL, Darrell .... 585-594-6202.. 325 B
bell_darrell@roberts.edu
BELL, Darrell .... 585-594-6200.. 327 D
bell_darrell@roberts.edu
BELL, David .... 646-565-6000.. 337 I
adam.hammerman@touro.edu
BELL, David, D .... 614-823-1300.. 376 C
dbell@otterbein.edu
BELL, Dean .... 312-322-1791.. 155 F
dbell@spertus.edu
BELL, Deborah, H .... 662-915-6867.. 261 B
dbell@olemiss.edu
BELL, Denise .... 508-793-2397.. 217 C
dbell@holycross.edu
BELL, Denise .... 850-973-9481.. 105 H
belld@nfcc.edu

BELL, Dolores ... 678-359-5015 .. 122 E
doloresb@gordonstate.edu
BELL, Geraldine ... 205-929-1715 .. 5 H
gbell@mail.miles.edu
BELL, Gregory, J ... 570-321-4395 .. 409 F
bell@lycoming.edu
BELL, Harold ... 404-270-5269 .. 128 A
hbell@spelman.edu
BELL, Hershey ... 814-866-6641 .. 407 D
hbell@lecom.edu
BELL, III, J. Edward ... 843-377-2426 .. 427 H
ebell@charlestonlaw.edu
BELL, Jacqueline, B ... 843-377-1327 .. 427 H
jbell@charlestonlaw.edu
BELL, James, L ... 580-327-8590 .. 384 M
jlbell@nwosu.edu
BELL, Jennifer ... 856-256-4410 .. 295 E
bellj@rowan.edu
BELL, Jenny ... 205-665-6565 .. 9 B
jbell8@montevallo.edu
BELL, John, D ... 808-675-3455 .. 130 E
john.bell@byuh.edu
BELL, Jorge ... 415-920-6001 .. 38 E
jbell@ccsf.edu
BELL, Julie ... 217-228-5432 .. 151 F
bellju@quincy.edu
BELL, Juliette, B ... 410-651-6101 .. 212 B
jbbell@umes.edu
BELL, Kati ... 415-482-2483 .. 42 G
kathrina.bell@dominican.edu
BELL, Kelly, A ... 864-662-6064 .. 427 B
kbell@andersonuniversity.edu
BELL, Kim ... 912-583-3245 .. 118 B
kbell@bpc.edu
BELL, Laura, G ... 215-871-6609 .. 416 F
laurab@pcom.edu
BELL, Lauren, C ... 804-752-7268 .. 493 C
lbell@rmc.edu
BELL, Leia ... 860-727-6967 .. 87 H
lbell@goodwin.edu
BELL, Leslie, T ... 910-521-6760 .. 358 C
leslie.bell@uncp.edu
BELL, Lillie, F ... 318-357-6171 .. 201 B
belle@nsula.edu
BELL, Linda ... 610-372-4721 .. 417 G
lbell@racc.edu
BELL, Linda ... 212-854-2708 .. 304 I
labell@barnard.edu
BELL, Lisa, G ... 859-246-6564 .. 189 B
lisag.bell@kctcs.edu
BELL, Lynn ... 334-556-2223 .. 3 N
lbell@wallace.edu
BELL, Marty ... 217-228-5432 .. 151 F
bellma@quincy.edu
BELL, Melleta ... 432-837-8388 .. 471 E
mbell@sulross.edu
BELL, Michael, S ... 202-685-8685 .. 528 B
bellm@ndu.edu
BELL, Nathan ... 678-359-5021 .. 122 E
nathanb@gordonstate.edu
BELL, Nikki ... 912-583-3287 .. 118 B
nbell@bpc.edu
BELL, Norma, G ... 205-853-1200 .. 5 B
ngbell@jeffstateonline.com
BELL, Rebecca ... 432-685-4556 .. 461 H
rbell@midland.edu
BELL, Rhonda ... 281-998-6150 .. 465 A
rhonda.bell@sjcd.edu
BELL, Robert, H ... 626-585-7205 .. 56 H
rhbell@pasadena.edu
BELL, Roberta ... 615-322-4359 .. 449 A
roberta.bell@vanderbilt.edu
BELL, Robin ... 229-931-2352 .. 127 C
rbell@southgatech.edu
BELL, Scott ... 907-474-6265 .. 10 G
svbell2@alaska.edu
BELL, Sharon, B ... 401-874-2378 .. 426 D
sbbell@mail.uri.edu
BELL, Sheree ... 636-481-3119 .. 266 C
sbell6@jeffco.edu
BELL, Stephen ... 847-543-2238 .. 138 C
sbell@clcillinois.edu
BELL, Stephen ... 610-558-5549 .. 411 E
bells@neumann.edu
BELL, Steven, K ... 724-847-6530 .. 404 B
skbell@geneva.edu
BELL, Stuart, R ... 205-348-5100 .. 8 D
stuart.bell@ua.edu
BELL, Tamra ... 360-442-2621 .. 504 G
tbell@lowercolumbia.edu
BELL, Tom, J ... 828-884-8142 .. 342 C
bellt@brevard.edu
BELL, Tommy ... 618-453-7250 .. 154 I
tbell@siu.edu
BELL, Trudy ... 805-546-3206 .. 41 L
tbell@cuesta.edu
BELL, Wendy ... 607-735-1750 .. 313 F
wbell@elmira.edu
BELL, William ... 847-233-7700 .. 150 D
wbell@nc.edu
BELL, Wylie ... 910-410-1826 .. 352 C
wdbell@richmondcc.edu
BELL, Yulonda ... 863-669-2305 .. 106 I
ybell@polk.edu
BELL ADAMS, Sandra ... 718-262-2363 .. 310 A
sadams@york.cuny.edu
BELLACERO, Cynthia, M ... 252-638-7328 .. 349 B
bellaceroc@cravencc.edu
BELLAFIORE, April ... 508-678-2811 .. 223 A
april.bellafiore@bristolcc.edu
BELLAH, Eric ... 865-981-8225 .. 441 H
eric.bellah@maryvillecollege.edu
BELLALTA, Maria ... 617-262-5000 .. 216 A
maria.bellalta@the-bac.edu
BELLAMEY, Tim ... 618-634-3221 .. 154 B
timb@shawneecc.edu
BELLAMY, Antoinette, P ... 910-630-7257 .. 346 E
abellamy@methodist.edu
BELLAMY, Johnnie, O ... 972-860-7619 .. 456 D
johnniebellamy@dcccd.edu
BELLAMY, Reagan ... 509-682-6445 .. 509 D
rbellamy@wvc.edu
BELLAMY, Sandra ... 212-694-1000 .. 305 I
sbellamy@boricuacollege.edu
BELLAMY, Scott ... 304-357-6696 .. 511 E
scottbellamy@ucwv.edu
BELLANCA, Rose ... 734-973-3491 .. 242 G
rbellanca@wccnet.edu
BELLATTI, Tom ... 918-495-6913 .. 386 H
tbellatti@oru.edu
BELLAVANCE, Leslie ... 616-451-2787 .. 233 L
lesliebelavance@ferris.edu
BELLAVIA, Rand ... 716-829-7616 .. 313 A
bellavia@dyc.edu
BELLE ISLE, Denell ... 651-213-4678 .. 247 B
BELLEFEUILLLE,
Barbara, K ... 574-807-7250 .. 159 D
barb.bellefeuille@bethelcollege.edu
BELLEMAN, Ben ... 740-420-5933 .. 374 G
bbelleman@ohiochristian.edu
BELLEMORE, Eileen, H ... 508-565-1033 .. 228 F
BELLENGER, Lauren ... 713-221-8197 .. 474 B
bellengerl@uhd.edu
BELLENGHI, Tami ... 503-228-6528 .. 390 A
tbellenghi@aii.edu
BELLER, Wendy ... 217-228-5432 .. 151 F
bellewe@quincy.edu
BELLEW, Kevin ... 859-858-3511 .. 186 J
kevin.bellew@asbury.edu
BELLICINI, Pierre, A ... 814-866-8121 .. 407 D
pbellicini@lecom.edu
BELLINA, Amy ... 732-571-3586 .. 292 F
abellina@monmouth.edu
BELLING, Karen ... 630-752-5021 .. 158 C
karen.belling@wheaton.edu
BELLINGER, Andrew ... 315-792-7141 .. 336 C
abellinger@sunypoly.edu
BELLINGER, Eunice ... 304-205-6613 .. 511 M
eunice.bellinger@bridgevalley.edu
BELLINGER, Jesse ... 803-705-4326 .. 427 D
bellingerj@benedict.edu
BELLINGS, Andy ... 563-588-6420 .. 170 F
andy.bellings@clarke.edu
BELLINI, Michel ... 217-265-5297 .. 157 A
bellini@illinois.edu
BELLINO, Maria ... 480-517-8175 .. 14 G
maria.bellino@riosalado.edu
BELLIPANNI, Domino ... 662-246-6471 .. 259 B
dbellipanni@msdelta.edu
BELLIVEAU, Cynthia, L ... 802-656-3890 .. 485 D
cynthia.belliveau@uvm.edu
BELLO, Chippi ... 360-992-2260 .. 502 E
cbello@clark.edu
BELLO, Debbie ... 215-728-4733 .. 412 B
debbie.bello@jevs.org
BELLO, Diane ... 631-632-6179 .. 332 A
diane.bello@stonybrook.edu
BELLO-DECASTRO, Leigh ... 973-877-3483 .. 291 H
bellodecastro@essex.edu
BELLO-OGUNU, John ... 843-953-5079 .. 428 G
belloogunuj@cofc.edu
BELLOMY, Chasley ... 256-228-6001 .. 5 I
bellomyc@nacc.edu
BELLONA, Steven, J ... 315-859-4502 .. 315 D
sbellona@hamilton.edu
BELLONI, Francis, L ... 914-594-4110 .. 323 I
francis_belloni@nymc.edu
BELLOTTE, Paul ... 304-243-2081 .. 515 C
pbellotte@wju.edu
BELLOWS, Alan ... 801-649-5230 .. 480 K
BELLOWS, Charlene, M ... 508-831-5577 .. 230 C
cbellows@wpi.edu
BELLOWS, Darrin ... 615-966-7600 .. 441 F
darrin.bellows@lipscomb.edu
BELLUCCI, Debbie ... 413-755-4334 .. 224 G
dbellucci@stcc.edu
BELLUCCI, Keith ... 617-732-2145 .. 225 C
keith.bellucci@mcphs.edu
BELLUM, Kim ... 605-882-5284 .. 436 B
bellumk@lakeareatech.edu
BELMAN, David ... 925-473-7423 .. 41 J
dbelman@losmedanos.edu
BELMAR, Ricardo ... 305-607-6123 .. 105 J
belmar@nova.edu
BELMODIS, Cassie ... 503-399-5159 .. 390 E
cassie.belmodis@chemeketa.edu
BELNAP, Jeffrey ... 516-299-2900 .. 319 C
jeffrey.belnap@liu.edu
BELNAP, Ryan ... 907-834-1613 .. 11 A
rkbelnap@pwscc.edu
BELOBRAJDIC, Scott ... 618-650-2298 .. 155 A
sbelobr@siue.edu
BELOIT, Roxanne ... 509-533-7067 .. 502 I
roxanne.beloit@scc.spokane.edu
BELONNI-ROSARIO,
Ruth-Aimée ... 712-290-8709 .. 408 B
rabelonni-rosario@lancasterseminary.edu
BELOTE, Eve ... 757-789-1767 .. 497 A
ebelote@es.vccs.edu
BELOTE, Faith, D ... 757-594-7618 .. 488 E
faith.belote@cnu.edu
BELOTE, Michael, R ... 478-301-2850 .. 124 D
michael r belote@mercer.edu
BELOW, Debbie ... 573-986-6888 .. 272 B
dbelow@semo.edu
BELROSE, Jacqueline ... 978-632-6600 .. 224 B
j_belrose@mwcc.mass.edu
BELSHER, Judy ... 602-243-8200 .. 14 I
judy.belsher@southmountaincc.edu
BELSKY, Jeff ... 412-809-5100 .. 417 D
belsky.jeff@pti.edu
BELSKY, Yisroel ... 718-941-8000 .. 321 A
BELSTRA, James, E ... 708-239-4720 .. 155 M
jim.belstra@trnty.edu
BELTON, Ada, A ... 803-705-4327 .. 427 D
beltona@benedict.edu
BELTON, Allan ... 253-535-7121 .. 505 G
allan.belton@plu.edu
BELTON, Ann ... 803-536-8406 .. 432 E
abelton3@scsu.edu
BELTON, Kenny, B ... 410-651-3087 .. 212 B
kbbelton@umes.edu
BELTON, Ray ... 225-771-4680 .. 199 H
ray_belton@sus.edu
BELTON, Ray, L ... 225-771-4680 .. 199 G
ray_belton@sus.edu
BELTRAME, Grace, J ... 617-928-4041 .. 226 B
gbeltrame@mountida.edu
BELTRAN, Cherie ... 254-267-7038 .. 463 K
cbeltran@rangercollege.edu
BELTRAN, JD ... 415-351-3530 .. 61 B
jdbeltran@sfai.edu
BELTRAN, Philip ... 408-554-4161 .. 63 E
pjbeltran@scu.edu
BELTRONE, Gail ... 212-854-6031 .. 304 I
gbeltron@barnard.edu
BELTZ, Maran ... 386-481-2928 .. 96 H
beltzm@cookman.edu
BEMBRY, Walter ... 785-784-5225 .. 177 D
bembryw@uiu.edu
BEMELEN, Jeff ... 303-871-3256 .. 84 B
jbemelen@du.edu
BEMIS, Heather ... 615-460-6456 .. 438 J
heather.bemis@belmont.edu
BEMIS, Scot, R ... 603-646-3768 .. 286 J
scot.r.bemis@dartmouth.edu
BEMSKI, Peter ... 928-541-7777 .. 15 G
pbemski@ncu.edu
BEMUS, Melissa, L ... 920-748-8112 .. 519 E
bemusm@ripon.edu
BEN AROLS, Gerard, A ... 212-998-1212 .. 324 C
gba1@nyu.edu
BENABESS, Najiba ... 217-424-6285 .. 148 D
nbenabess@millikin.edu
BENAICHA, Hedi ... 617-349-8836 .. 220 B
hbenaicha@lesley.edu
BENAICHA, Hedi ... 304-724-3700 .. 510 E
hbenaicha@apus.edu
BENARD, Mary ... 760-757-2121 .. 52 K
mbenard@miracosta.edu
BENAVIDES, Adolfo ... 903-886-5018 .. 468 D
adolfo.benavides@tamuc.edu
BENAVIDES, Elma, F ... 512-863-1441 .. 466 G
benavide@southwestern.edu
BENAVIDES, Julie ... 323-265-8779 .. 49 G
benavij@elac.edu
BENAVIDES, Leticia ... 956-665-2255 .. 476 E
letty.benavides@utrgv.edu
BENAVIDES, Lewis ... 940-898-3555 .. 472 G
lbenavides@twu.edu
BENAVIDES-DOMINGUEZ,
Patricia ... 361-698-2474 .. 457 D
pbdominguez@delmar.edu
BENAVIDEZ, Antonio ... 520-383-8401 .. 17 E
abenavidez@tocc.edu
BENAVIDEZ, Max ... 909-621-8099 .. 38 J
max.benavidez@cmc.edu
BENBOW, Camilla, P ... 615-322-8407 .. 449 A
camilla.benbow@vanderbilt.edu
BENCHIMOL, Daniel ... 212-875-4497 .. 304 E
dbenchimol@bankstreet.edu
BENCHIMOL, Daniel ... 212-875-4633 .. 304 E
dbenchimol@bankstreet.edu
BENCHOFF, Bryan ... 740-593-0061 .. 375 H
benchoff@ohio.edu
BENDAPUDI, Neeli ... 785-864-4904 .. 185 D
neeli@ku.edu
BENDECK, Yvette ... 281-283-3022 .. 474 A
bendeck@uhcl.edu
BENDEL, Colleen ... 740-593-1642 .. 375 H
bendl@ohio.edu
BENDELE, Jennifer ... 419-227-3141 .. 380 A
jennifer@unoh.edu
BENDER, Dave ... 614-823-1876 .. 376 C
dbender@otterbein.edu
BENDER, David, L ... 989-837-4374 .. 239 D
bender@northwood.edu
BENDER, Don ... 509-335-5593 .. 508 H
bender@wsu.edu
BENDER, Donna ... 504-314-2148 .. 200 C
dbender@tulane.edu
BENDER, Jennie, M ... 606-474-3226 .. 188 L
jbender@kcu.edu
BENDER, Jim ... 651-638-6400 .. 244 L
j-bender@bethel.edu
BENDER, Judy ... 585-475-4315 .. 327 E
jebpsn@rit.edu
BENDER, Karla ... 713-718-8247 .. 459 B
karla.bender@hccs.edu
BENDER, Kim ... 307-778-4337 .. 526 K
kbender@lccc.wy.edu
BENDER, Laurie ... 732-224-2059 .. 289 I
lbender@brookdalecc.edu
BENDER, Linda ... 307-855-2102 .. 526 E
lbender@cwc.edu
BENDER, Loren, J ... 407-582-3408 .. 114 N
lbender2@valenciacollege.edu
BENDER, Marian ... 814-472-3931 .. 418 F
mbender@francis.edu
BENDER, Michael ... 845-207-0330 .. 305 D
BENDER, Rick ... 432-685-4529 .. 461 H
rbender@midland.edu
BENDER, Starr, S ... 407-303-5765 .. 95 C
starr.bender@adu.edu
BENDER, Stephanie ... 410-337-6431 .. 207 H
stephanie.bender@goucher.edu
BENDER, Susan ... 208-885-2539 .. 134 G
benders@uidaho.edu
BENDER, IV, Thomas, B ... 504-866-7426 .. 199 A
librarian@nds.edu
BENDER, Virginia ... 201-761-6024 .. 296 K
vbender@saintpeters.edu
BENDER, Virginia, A ... 201-761-6024 .. 296 K
vbender@saintpeters.edu
BENDER, Yaakov ... 718-868-2300 .. 304 K
BENDICKSON, Kimberly ... 941-487-4668 .. 111 D
kbendickson@ncf.edu
BENDICKSON, Mary ... 813-253-7210 .. 102 R
mbendickson@hccfl.edu
BENEDETTI, Brian ... 253-864-3235 .. 506 B
bbenedetti@pierce.ctc.edu
BENEDETTI, Debbie ... 707-546-4000 .. 42 M
dbenedetti@empirecollege.com
BENEDETTI, Marco, F ... 716-888-2480 .. 306 F
benedet2@canisius.edu
BENEDETTO, Geri ... 908-737-7000 .. 292 C
gbenedet@kean.edu
BENEDETTO, Mark ... 605-331-6684 .. 438 A
mark.benedetto@usiouxfalls.edu
BENEDETTO, William ... 845-431-8096 .. 312 G
benedett@sunydutchess.edu
BENEDICK, Ronald, W ... 614-235-4136 .. 378 C
rbenedick@tlsohio.edu
BENEDICT, Amy ... 607-436-2534 .. 331 F
amy.benedict@oneonta.edu
BENEDICT, Barbara ... 719-549-3039 .. 82 G
barbara.benedict@pueblocc.edu
BENEDICT, Christine ... 608-663-2294 .. 516 F
cbenedict@edgewood.edu
BENEDICT, David ... 860-486-2725 .. 89 D
david.benedict@uconn.edu
BENEDICT, Dow ... 304-876-5393 .. 513 E
dbenedic@shepherd.edu
BENEDICT, Dwight ... 202-651-5064 .. 92 C
dwight.benedict@gallaudet.edu
BENEDICT, Jody, C ... 585-385-8322 .. 328 E
jbenedict@sjfc.edu
BENEDICT, Reeta ... 207-509-7273 .. 204 F
rbenedict@unity.edu
BENEDICT, Stacie ... 559-453-7195 .. 44 F
stacie.benedict@fresno.edu
BENEDICT-BARBIAN,
Amanda ... 701-483-2370 .. 360 D
amanda.benedict@dickinsonstate.edu
BENEDIK, Michael ... 979-845-4016 .. 468 B
benedik@tamu.edu
BENEDUCE, James ... 631-656-2139 .. 314 F
james.beneduce@ftc.edu
BENEFIEL, Lori ... 541-383-7572 .. 390 D
lbenefiel@cocc.edu
BENEFIEL, Ron ... 619-849-2613 .. 57 M
ronbenefiel@pointloma.edu

BENEFIEL, Shannon .... 606-337-1103.. 187 I
sbenefiel@ccbbc.edu
BENEFIELD, John .... 760-757-2121.... 52 K
jbenefield@miracosta.edu
BENEKE, Thomas, J .... 515-574-1050.. 173 F
beneke@iowacentral.edu
BENESH, Gina .... 314-539-5355.. 271 F
gbenesh@stlcc.edu
BENET, Suzeanne .... 616-331-2400.. 234 F
benets@gvsu.edu
BENEVEDES, Julie, K .... 209-667-3440.... 34 E
jbenevedes@csustan.edu
BENFANTI, William, J ..... 716-878-5557.. 332 F
benfanwj@buffalostate.edu
BENFATTI, Angela .... 719-384-6834.... 82 A
angela.benfatti@ojc.edu
BENFER, Pamela, A .... 570-577-1561.. 398 L
pam.benfer@bucknell.edu
BENFORD, Gladys .... 870-575-8405.... 23 E
benfordg@uapb.edu
BENFORD, Jeffrey .... 925-473-7425.... 41 J
jbenford@losmedanos.edu
BENFORD, Kacee .... 575-461-4413.. 300 A
kaceeb@mesalands.edu
BENGE, Mike .... 605-856-5880.. 436 I
mike.benge@sintegleska.edu
BENGE, Robert .... 423-236-2855.. 444 B
rcbenge@southern.edu
BENGEL, Jo Ann .... 626-815-5003.... 28 A
jbengel@apu.edu
BENGFORT, Joseph .... 415-353-4273.... 70 D
joe.bengfort@ucsf.edu
BENGINIA, Francis, A ..... 610-330-5090.. 407 C
benginif@lafayette.edu
BENGS, Jennifer .... 605-626-7802.. 437 D
jennifer.bengs@northern.edu
BENGTSON, Kathy .... 612-767-7051.. 244 D
kathy.bengtson@alfredadler.edu
BENHAM, Maenette .... 808-956-0980.. 131 F
mbenham@hawaii.edu
BENHAM-DEAL, Tami ...... 307-766-4286.. 527 B
benham@uwyo.edu
BENINGHOVE, Linda ...... 201-216-5412.. 297 B
linda.beninghove@stevens.edu
BENISH, Amy, L .... 262-554-2010.. 518 B
albenish@aol.com
BENITEZ, Hubert .... 816-936-8711.. 271 L
hbenitez@saintlukescollege.edu
BENITEZ, Leyda, L .... 610-519-3976.. 422 G
leyda.benitez@villanova.edu
BENITEZ, Michael .... 253-879-3929.. 508 D
mbenitez@pugetsound.edu
BENITEZ-RAMÍREZ,
Solange .... 787-993-8863.. 537 G
solange.benitez@upr.edu
BENITO, Agueda .... 312-752-2094.. 144 E
agueda.benito@kendall.edu
BENJAMIN, Ashu .... 504-286-5279.. 199 I
abenjamin@suno.edu
BENJAMIN, Bill .... 727-873-4199.. 112 D
benjamin@mail.usf.edu
BENJAMIN, Eric, V .... 931-598-1241.. 443 O
ebenjami@sewanee.edu
BENJAMIN, Finbar .... 256-726-7105...... 6 B
fbenjamin@oakwood.edu
BENJAMIN, Gregory .... 610-399-2419.. 414 F
gbenjamin@cheyney.edu
BENJAMIN, Guy .... 808-237-5144.. 130 G
BENJAMIN, Helen .... 925-229-6820.... 41 G
hbenjamin@4cd.edu
BENJAMIN, Jack .... 803-641-3327.. 433 G
BENJAMIN, Jodi .... 402-941-6102.. 280 N
benjamin@midlandu.edu
BENJAMIN, Mary, E .... 870-575-8216.... 23 E
benjaminm@uapb.edu
BENJAMIN, Pamela .... 419-755-4029.. 373 G
benjamin.155@osu.edu
BENJAMIN, Robert .... 617-745-3595.. 218 A
robert.j.benjamin@enc.edu
BENJAMIN, Robert .... 269-471-3310.. 230 H
robertb@andrews.edu
BENKE, Jack .... 573-592-5231.. 275 E
jack.benke@westminster-mo.edu
BENKE, Robin, P .... 276-328-0151.. 495 I
rpb@wise.edu
BENKESER, Kristina .... 724-738-2052.. 416 B
kristina.benkeser@sru.edu
BENLOLO, Henri .... 352-854-2322.... 97 R
benloloh@cf.edu
BENMAMOUN, Elabbas ... 217-333-6677.. 157 A
benmamou@illinois.edu
BENMERGUI, Diana .... 212-960-5277.. 341 G
benmergui@yu.edu
BENN, Sherri .... 512-245-2278.. 471 F
sb17@txstate.edu
BENN, Valerie .... 919-718-7423.. 348 D
vbenn159@cccc.edu
BENN-MARSHALL, Karen 256-726-7005...... 6 B
kmarshall@oakwood.edu

BENNASAR,
Mari Carmen .... 617-327-6777.. 229 H
mari_bennasar@williamjames.edu
BENNATTS, Denise .... 253-833-9111.. 504 C
dbennatts@greenriver.edu
BENNECKE, Margie .... 847-233-7700.. 150 D
mbennecke@nc.edu
BENNEIAN, Teresa .... 717-290-8748.. 408 B
tbenneian@lancasterseminary.edu
BENNER, Brent, W .... 813-253-6211.. 114 M
bbenner@ut.edu
BENNER, Mary .... 405-208-5270.. 385 E
mbenner@okcu.edu
BENNER, Tracy .... 614-823-1580.. 376 C
tbenner@otterbein.edu
BENNET, Amy .... 215-898-0561.. 421 E
amy84@upenn.edu
BENNETT, Amy .... 317-955-6768.. 165 N
abennett@marian.edu
BENNETT, Anthony, T ...... 910-672-1314.. 356 E
abennett@uncfsu.edu
BENNETT, Bo .... 828-448-6197.. 345 G
bennettb@lmc.edu
BENNETT, Bradley .... 785-460-5403.. 180 C
brad.bennett@colbycc.edu
BENNETT, Calvin .... 601-484-8894.. 258 F
cbennett@meridiancc.edu
BENNETT, Cameron, D .... 253-535-7150.. 505 G
bennetcd@plu.edu
BENNETT, Carolyn .... 516-876-3203.. 333 C
bennettc@oldwestbury.edu
BENNETT, Cathryn .... 336-272-7201.. 344 G
cathryn.bennett@greensboro.edu
BENNETT, Christopher ..... 440-375-7000.. 371 E
cbennett@lec.edu
BENNETT, Daniel .... 828-669-8012.. 346 M
dbennett@montreat.edu
BENNETT, David, A .... 606-474-3256.. 188 L
dbennett@kcu.edu
BENNETT, Derwin .... 518-255-5836.. 334 D
bennetdd@cobleskill.edu
BENNETT, Diane .... 715-425-3195.. 521 B
diane.bennett@uwrf.edu
BENNETT, Doug, L .... 740-368-3148.. 376 B
dlbennet@owu.edu
BENNETT, Douglas .... 714-432-5126.... 39 G
dbennett@occ.cccd.edu
BENNETT, Drew, A .... 417-255-7900.. 269 A
wpchancellor@missouristate.edu
BENNETT, Drew, A .... 417-255-7900.. 268 I
drewbennett@missouristate.edu
BENNETT, Elbert .... 870-575-8504.... 23 E
bennette@uapb.edu
BENNETT, Elizabeth, C ..... 949-824-7982.... 69 C
bennette@uci.edu
BENNETT, Elizabeth, P ..... 717-290-8713.. 408 B
ebennett@lancasterseminary.edu
BENNETT, Eric .... 212-659-7290.. 318 D
ebennett@tkc.edu
BENNETT, Gene .... 870-780-1201.... 18 G
gbennett@smail.anc.edu
BENNETT, George .... 509-527-2930.. 508 G
george.bennett@wallawalla.edu
BENNETT, Heather .... 309-796-5301.. 135 I
bennetth@bhc.edu
BENNETT, Herman .... 212-817-7540.. 308 A
hbennett@gc.cuny.edu
BENNETT, Holly, L .... 561-207-5400.. 106 D
bennetth@palmbeachstate.edu
BENNETT, James .... 913-288-7259.. 182 C
jbennett@kckcc.edu
BENNETT, James .... 216-687-5308.. 366 I
j.e.bennett90@csuohio.edu
BENNETT, Jamie .... 213-613-2200.... 65 H
jamie_bennett@sciarc.edu
BENNETT, Janice, G .... 563-588-8000.. 172 E
jbennett@emmaus.edu
BENNETT, Janis, A .... 304-766-3010.. 514 B
bennetja@wvstateu.edu
BENNETT, Jeffrey, L .... 570-321-4031.. 409 F
bennett@lycoming.edu
BENNETT, Jeremy .... 580-559-5256.. 383 H
jbennett@ecok.edu
BENNETT, Jim .... 406-265-3594.. 277 E
james.bennett10@msun.edu
BENNETT, Jim .... 408-551-1910.... 63 E
jbbennett@scu.edu
BENNETT, Jim .... 541-383-7733.. 390 D
jmbennett@cocc.edu
BENNETT, Joan, W .... 848-932-6223.. 295 F
profmycogirl@yahoo.com
BENNETT, JoAnn .... 937-327-6185.. 381 F
jbennett@wittenberg.edu
BENNETT, Josh .... 406-447-6932.. 277 B
josh.bennett@umhelelna.edu
BENNETT, Kari .... 518-438-3111.. 320 A
bennettk@mariacollege.edu
BENNETT, Kevin .... 904-256-7585.. 103 D
kbennet1@ju.edu
BENNETT, Kim .... 260-665-4438.. 167 E
bennettk@trine.edu

BENNETT, Kristen .... 903-670-2664.. 473 B
kristen.bennett@tvcc.edu
BENNETT, Laura .... 541-956-7136.. 394 J
lbennett@roguecc.edu
BENNETT, Linda L, M ..... 812-464-1756.. 168 E
bennettl@usi.edu
BENNETT, Lisa .... 585-594-6804.. 325 B
bennett_lisa@roberts.edu
BENNETT, Lori .... 559-325-5205.... 67 B
lori.bennett@scccd.edu
BENNETT, Marla .... 217-732-3168.. 146 A
hr@lincolnchristian.edu
BENNETT, Martin .... 419-434-4558.. 379 E
bennett@findlay.edu
BENNETT, Marvin .... 405-878-5169.. 387 J
mdbennett@stgrgorys.edu
BENNETT, Matt .... 517-338-3014.. 232 F
mbennett@cleary.edu
BENNETT, Maybelle, T ..... 202-806-4771.... 93 A
maybelle.bennett@howard.edu
BENNETT, Michael, J ...... 727-341-3012.. 108 D
bennett.michael@spcollege.edu
BENNETT, Mitch .... 214-333-5139.. 455 J
mitch@dbu.edu
BENNETT, Patricia .... 850-729-4901.. 105 I
bennettp@nwfsc.edu
BENNETT, Patrick .... 623-245-4600.... 17 G
pbennett@uti.edu
BENNETT, Patrick .... 614-947-6836.. 369 A
patrick.bennett@franklin.edu
BENNETT, II, Richard, E . 518-629-7205.. 316 G
r.bennett@hvcc.edu
BENNETT, Rick .... 408-855-5232.... 74 G
rick.bennett@wvm.edu
BENNETT, Robert .... 518-327-6049.. 326 B
bbennett@paulsmiths.edu
BENNETT, Rodney .... 301-846-2501.. 207 F
rbennett@frederick.edu
BENNETT, Rodney, D .... 601-266-5001.. 261 E
president@usm.edu
BENNETT, Samantha .... 312-235-3511.. 154 C
s.bennett@shimer.edu
BENNETT, Sari, M .... 603-862-4285.. 288 C
sari.bennett@unh.edu
BENNETT, Scott .... 904-620-2002.. 112 B
sbennett@unf.edu
BENNETT, Scott .... 281-425-6396.. 460 I
sbennett@lee.edu
BENNETT, Sherri .... 870-838-2945.... 18 G
sbennett@smail.anc.edu
BENNETT, Stephen, R ...... 507-933-7526.. 246 J
sbennett@gustavus.edu
BENNETT, Tanya .... 678-717-2292.. 128 F
tanya.bennett@ung.edu
BENNETT, II, Thomas ..... 304-766-3112.. 514 B
tbennett3@wvstateu.edu
BENNETT, Todd .... 404-364-8329.. 125 F
tbennett1@oglethorpe.edu
BENNETT, Valerie .... 309-677-3961.. 136 B
vbennett@bradley.edu
BENNETT, Vernell .... 662-846-4150.. 257 E
vbennett@deltastate.edu
BENNETT, Vernell, A .... 502-597-6827.. 191 B
vernell.bennett@kysu.edu
BENNETT-BELLAMY,
Sonja, A .... 803-813-1340.. 432 E
sbennet5@scsu.edu
BENNETT-BELLAMY,
Sonya .... 919-546-8301.. 355 F
sonja.bennett@shawu.edu
BENNETT-CAMPBELL,
Bonnie, L .... 815-224-0481.. 143 C
bonnie_campbell@ivcc.edu
BENNIE, Kevin, M .... 530-226-4978.... 64 H
kbennie@simpsonu.edu
BENNIE, Roanna .... 925-424-1104.... 37 C
rbennie@laspositascollege.edu
BENNIEFIELD, Marcus ...... 619-702-9400.... 31 A
marcus.benniefield@cibu.edu
BENNIGHOFF, James ...... 254-710-6500.. 452 H
james_bennighoff@baylor.edu
BENNING, Tom .... 314-529-9304.. 267 B
tbenning@maryville.edu
BENNINGER, Paul .... 336-917-5460.. 355 E
paul.benninger@salem.edu
BENNINGTON, Cheryl, C 304-336-8049.. 513 F
cbennington@westliberty.edu
BENNION, Paul .... 208-459-5841.. 133 D
pbennion@collegeofidaho.edu
BENOIT, Andy .... 337-482-6474.. 201 D
ajbenoit@louisiana.edu
BENOIT, Andy .... 864-388-8183.. 430 G
abenoit@lander.edu
BENOIT, Anthony .... 617-588-1324.. 215 E
abenoit@bfit.edu
BENOIT, Debra .... 985-493-2563.. 201 A
debi.benoit@nicholls.edu
BENOIT, Doug .... 714-992-7033.... 54 H
dbenoit@fullcoll.edu
BENOIT, Jennifer, D .... 814-865-8753.. 412 F
jdd41@psu.edu

BENOIT, Kathy .... 714-992-7048.... 54 H
kbenoit@fullcoll.edu
BENOIT, Michele .... 541-888-7421.. 395 B
mbenoit@socc.edu
BENOIT, Pam .... 740-593-2600.. 375 H
benoit@ohio.edu
BENOIT, Sherry .... 409-880-1718.. 471 A
sherry.benoit@lamar.edu
BENOIT, Thomas .... 325-793-3869.. 461 F
tbenoit@mcm.edu
BENOL, Christine .... 732-571-7516.. 292 F
cbenol@monmouth.edu
BENOLIEL, Abraham .... 718-339-1090.. 340 O
rabenoliel@mikdashmelech.org
BENOLIEL, Haim .... 718-339-1090.. 340 O
roshyeshiva@mikdashmelech.org
BENOLKEN, Julie .... 651-450-3622.. 249 F
jbenolk@inverhills.edu
BENRUD, Ann .... 612-874-3793.. 247 M
abenrud@mcad.edu
BENSE, Judith, A .... 850-474-2200.. 113 A
jbense@uwf.edu
BENSE, Kim .... 970-675-3335.... 78 J
kim.bense@cncc.edu
BENSEL, Terry .... 814-332-3391.. 397 A
tbensel@allegheny.edu
BENSEN, Steven, P .... 701-788-4761.. 360 E
steven.bensen@mayvillestate.edu
BENSINK, Michael .... 508-678-2811.. 223 A
michael.bensink@bristolcc.edu
BENSON, Allen, C .... 401-841-3397.. 528 E
BENSON, Becca .... 601-925-3830.. 259 A
rbenson@mc.edu
BENSON, Ben .... 516-773-5000.. 529 B
bensonb@usmma.edu
BENSON, Bill .... 541-962-3241.. 391 C
wbenson@eou.edu
BENSON, Brenda .... 310-434-4433.... 63 F
benson_brenda@smc.edu
BENSON, Bruce, D .... 303-860-5600.... 83 J
officeofthepresident@cu.edu
BENSON, Craig .... 434-924-3593.. 495 H
chb4x@virginia.edu
BENSON, Daniel .... 507-389-6838.. 250 E
daniel.benson@mnsu.edu
BENSON, Dawn .... 406-275-4985.. 278 E
dawn_benson@skc.edu
BENSON, Duane .... 712-274-5133.. 175 C
bensond@morningside.edu
BENSON, Ella .... 252-398-6304.. 343 G
bensone@chowan.edu
BENSON, Erin, V .... 207-768-9453.. 205 D
erin.benson@maine.edu
BENSON, Gus .... 859-622-3636.. 188 F
gus.benson@eku.edu
BENSON, Haley .... 847-259-1840.. 137 B
BENSON, Holly .... 334-244-3125...... 2 A
hbenson@aum.edu
BENSON, Jason .... 701-483-2014.. 360 D
jason.bensen@sodexo.com
BENSON, Jennifer .... 706-355-5124.. 116 H
jbenson@athenstech.edu
BENSON, Jerry .... 540-568-3429.. 490 J
bensonaj@jmu.edu
BENSON, Jill, M .... 978-468-7111.. 219 B
jbenson@gcts.edu
BENSON, Jocelyn .... 313-577-3933.. 243 F
jbenson@wayne.edu
BENSON, Mark .... 518-442-2562.. 331 A
mabenson@albany.edu
BENSON, Marla .... 870-864-7146.... 22 D
mbenson@southark.edu
BENSON, Megan .... 602-383-8228.... 17 H
mbenson@uat.edu
BENSON, Michael .... 859-622-2977.. 188 F
michael.benson@eku.edu
BENSON, Mindy .... 435-586-7763.. 481 N
benson@suu.edu
BENSON, Mitchel .... 916-568-3041.... 50 J
bensonm@losrios.edu
BENSON, Neal, L .... 304-462-6119.. 513 C
neal.benson@glenville.edu
BENSON, Patricia .... 610-526-6142.. 405 B
pbenson@harcum.edu
BENSON, Patrick .... 312-788-1133.. 157 H
meca@vandercook.edu
BENSON, Paul, H .... 937-229-2245.. 379 D
pbenson1@udayton.edu
BENSON, Peter .... 203-287-3017.... 88 E
paier.admin@snet.net
BENSON, Richard .... 972-883-2201.. 476 C
benson@utdallas.edu
BENSON, Robert, M .... 865-882-4553.. 447 A
bensonrm@roanestate.edu
BENSON, Robin .... 918-647-1344.. 382 I
rbenson@carlalbert.edu
BENSON, Samantha .... 910-879-5567.. 347 F
sbenson@bladencc.edu
BENSON, Scott, A .... 308-865-8431.. 282 L
bensonsa1@unk.edu

BERMAN, Mark, R 413-205-3008 214 B mark.berman@aic.edu
BERMAN, Mary Jane 513-529-1943 372 K bermanmj@miamioh.edu
BERMAN, Michael 805-437-2099 32 B michael.berman@csuci.edu
BERMAN, Paula 617-277-3915 216 D bermanp@bgsp.edu
BERMAN, Richard 813-974-9694 112 C rberman@usf.edu
BERMAN, Richard, T 740-587-6521 368 B bermanr@denison.edu
BERMAN, Sheryl 562-902-3360 66 A sherylberman@scuhs.edu
BERMAN, Stanley 617-327-6777 229 H stanley_berman@williamjames.edu
BERMANN, Todd 706-864-1451 128 F todd.berrman@ung.edu
BERMEA, Gilbert, S 830-758-4111 466 A gbermea@swtjc.edu
BERMEL, Patricia 619-680-4430 30 A patricia.bermel@cc-sd.edu
BERMINGHAM, Jack 206-878-3710 504 E jbermingham@highline.edu
BERMINGHAM, Jordan 503-226-4391 394 B jbermingham@pnca.edu
BERMUDEZ, Eliezer 812-237-3683 162 A eliezer.bermudez@indstate.edu
BERMUDEZ, Emilia (Lilly) 405-878-5152 387 J elbermudez@stgregorys.edu
BERMUDEZ, Gregory 787-757-1520 537 H gregory.bermudez@upr.edu
BERMUDEZ, Pedro 787-786-3030 536 F pbermudez@ucb.edu.pr
BERNA, Francis, J 215-951-1346 407 A berna@lasalle.edu
BERNABE, Arnaldo 718-518-6888 308 C abernabe@hostos.cuny.edu
BERNAD, Manuel, A 858-499-0202 39 J manuelb@coleman.edu
BERNADELLE, Guary 815-967-7300 152 F bernadelle@rockfordcareercollege.edu
BERNADO, Daniel 509-335-5581 508 H bernado@wsu.edu
BERNAHL, Joni 217-786-9627 146 E joni.bernahl@llcc.edu
BERNAIX, Laura 618-650-3969 155 A lbernai@siue.edu
BERNAL, Deanna 818-785-2726 36 M deanna.bernal@casalomacollege.edu
BERNAL, Erika 714-992-7832 51 F ebernal@ketchum.edu
BERNAL, Jesse, M 616-331-3296 234 F bernalje@gvsu.edu
BERNAL-OLSON, Patricia 937-229-4211 379 D pbernalolson1@udayton.edu
BERNARD, Bill 212-924-5900 336 I wbernard@swedishinstitute.edu
BERNARD, Christopher 570-577-3011 398 L chris.bernard@bucknell.edu
BERNARD, David, K 314-921-9290 274 F dbernard@ugst.edu
BERNARD, Dee 651-450-3522 249 F dbernar@inverhills.edu
BERNARD, Frances 518-438-3111 320 A franb@mariacollege.edu
BERNARD, Kacey 610-341-1459 403 B kbernard@eastern.edu
BERNARD, Kacey 610-341-1389 412 C kbernard@eastern.edu
BERNARD, Marjorie, P 412-578-8880 400 C mpbernard@carlow.edu
BERNARD, Nancy, M 334-844-4744 1 G bernanm@auburn.edu
BERNARD, Pamela 919-684-3955 343 J pam.bernard@duke.edu
BERNARD, Philip 617-989-4162 229 D bernardp@wit.edu
BERNARD, Renee 814-472-2766 418 F rbernard@francis.edu
BERNARD, Richard 405-974-3493 388 L rbernard1@uco.edu
BERNARD, Sue 207-768-2808 203 L sbernard@nmcc.edu
BERNARD, Vicki 314-340-5112 265 H bernardv@hssu.edu
BERNARD-DONALS, Michael 608-262-5246 519 K mfbernarddon@wisc.edu
BERNARDI, Robert 985-448-4794 201 A rob.bernardi@nicholls.edu
BERNARDINO, Maria 209-954-5065 61 F mbernardino@deltacollege.edu
BERNARDIS, Tim 406-638-3113 276 G tim@lbhc.edu
BERNARDO, Lisa, M 209-667-3094 34 E lbernardo@csustan.edu
BERNARDO, Peter, R 216-397-4217 370 H pbernardo@jcu.edu
BERNARDO-SOUSA, Marie 401-598-1754 425 B marie.bernardo-sousa@jwu.edu
BERNAS, Judith, A 602-827-2017 17 I jbernas@email.arizona.edu
BERNAUER, Edmund 808-521-2288 131 A dean@orientalmedicine.edu
BERNDT, Michael 651-779-3493 249 A michael.berndt@century.edu
BERNE, Jennifer 847-925-6975 141 A jbernel@harpercollege.edu
BERNE, Robert 212-998-2283 324 C robert.berne@nyu.edu
BERNECKER, Kim 972-825-4634 466 D kbernecker@sagu.edu
BERNER, JR., Howard, E 314-275-3514 151 E howard.berner@principia.edu
BERNER, Nancy 931-598-1172 443 O nberner@sewanee.edu
BERNEY, Jan 360-438-4513 506 G jberney@stmartin.edu
BERNHARD, Edward, E 574-807-7121 159 D bernhae@bethelcollege.edu
BERNHARD, Mark, C 812-464-1829 168 E mbernhard@usi.edu
BERNHARD, Robert, J 574-631-3902 168 B bernhard.9@nd.edu
BERNHARDSON, Bonnie 218-879-0828 249 C bonnie@fdltcc.edu
BERNHARDSON, Mark 218-879-0703 249 C mbernhar@fdltcc.edu
BERNHARDT, Jay, M 512-471-8100 476 B jay.bernhardt@austin.utexas.edu
BERNHARDT, Kevin, J 608-342-1365 521 A bernhark@uwplatt.edu
BERNHARDT, Regina 215-248-7000 400 H bernhardtr@chc.edu
BERNIER, Jessica 845-437-5320 339 C jebernier@vassar.edu
BERNIER, Jose 386-822-7045 113 B jbernier@stetson.edu
BERNOTAS, Scott, C 412-624-9510 421 G bernotas@pitt.edu
BERNOTSKY, R. Lorraine 610-436-6977 416 C lbernotsky@wcupa.edu
BERNSTEIN, Aimee 718-409-5979 336 A abernstein@sunymaritime.edu
BERNSTEIN, Alan 229-333-5860 129 G abernste@valdosta.edu
BERNSTEIN, David 845-406-4308 340 I
BERNSTEIN, Melissa 801-581-3386 481 M melissa.bernstein@law.utah.edu
BERNSTEIN, Pamela 603-880-8308 288 A pbernstein@thomasmorecollege.edu
BERNSTEIN, Pamela 603-880-8308 288 A tmc@thomasmorecollege.edu
BERNSTEIN, Robin 402-557-7300 278 I robin.bernstein@bellevue.edu
BERNSTEIN, Zeke 802-440-4594 483 E zbernstein@bennington.edu
BERNTH, Rosemary 304-829-7255 510 G rbernth@bethanywv.edu
BERNTSON, Joan, L 218-751-8670 254 A joanberntson@oakhills.edu
BEROKOFF, Mark 405-912-9030 387 D mberokoff@hc.edu
BEROL, Polly 610-341-1386 403 B pberol@eastern.edu
BEROWSKI, Alfred 315-866-0300 316 A berowskfj@herkimer.edu
BERQUAM, Lori 608-263-5700 519 K lberquam@studentlife.wisc.edu
BERQUE, David, A 765-658-4735 160 F dberque@depauw.edu
BERQUIST, Gina 503-255-0332 392 G ginab@multnomah.edu
BERRAHOU, Catherine 248-689-8282 242 F cberraho@walshcollege.edu
BERREAU, Lisa 435-797-3509 482 B lisa.berreau@usu.edu
BERRIDGE, Bob 773-256-0783 147 A bberridg@lstc.edu
BERRIOS, Amy 610-353-7630 398 I
BERRIOS, Iris 787-743-7979 536 A ac_irberrios@suagm.edu
BERRIOS, Jonathan 787-738-2161 538 A jonathan.berrios@upr.edu
BERRIOS, Jose 787-751-0178 536 A ac_jberrios@suagm.edu
BERRIOS, Marianne 787-852-1430 532 N mberrios@hccpr.edu
BERRIOS, William 212-592-2000 330 C wberrios@sva.edu
BERRMAN, Terri 815-455-8783 147 E tberryman@mchenry.edu
BERROA, Carlos, E 787-257-7373 535 P ceberroa@suagm.edu
BERRY, Anthony, T 860-297-2000 89 B
BERRY, Brian 870-777-5722 24 A brian.berry@uacch.edu
BERRY, Carolynn 336-750-2110 359 B berryc@wssu.edu
BERRY, Chad 859-985-3490 187 B chad_berry@berea.edu
BERRY, Clay 870-508-6124 19 B cberry@asumh.edu
BERRY, Donna 559-638-0300 67 D donna.berry@reedleycollege.edu
BERRY, Emily 513-529-9625 372 K emily.berry@miamioh.edu
BERRY, Evan 772-462-7945 103 B eberry@irsc.edu
BERRY, Gwennette, C 319-273-2820 170 A gwenne.berry@uni.edu
BERRY, Jessica 207-778-7295 205 A jess.berry@maine.edu
BERRY, Joanne 603-427-7609 286 B jberry@ccsnh.edu
BERRY, Joe 501-882-4407 18 I jlberry@asub.edu
BERRY, John 419-995-8439 370 G berry.j@rhodesstate.edu
BERRY, John 865-981-8145 441 H john.berry@maryvillecollege.edu
BERRY, Josh 785-442-6031 181 H jberry@highlandcc.edu
BERRY, Joshua 203-582-8695 88 G joshua.berry@quinnipiac.edu
BERRY, Keith 813-253-7714 102 R kberry@hccfl.edu
BERRY, Kimberly, G 518-629-8007 316 G k.berry@hvcc.edu
BERRY, Koop 330-490-7058 380 J kberry@walsh.edu
BERRY, Larry 423-614-8086 441 B lberry@leeuniversity.edu
BERRY, Laura 870-743-3000 21 C lberry@northark.edu
BERRY, Laura Lea 802-586-7711 485 C lberry@sterlingcollege.edu
BERRY, Linda, C 708-209-3209 138 G linda.berry@cuchicago.edu
BERRY, Lisa 713-221-8468 474 B berryl@uhd.edu
BERRY, Mario 281-290-3960 461 B mario.berry@lonestar.edu
BERRY, Mark, A 213-621-2200 39 I
BERRY, Mark, E 843-953-7645 428 G berrym@cofc.edu
BERRY, Mary 605-677-5370 437 A mary.berry@usd.edu
BERRY, Molly 217-424-6335 148 D mberry@millikin.edu
BERRY, Richard 936-468-2807 466 H rberry@sfasu.edu
BERRY, Ronald 318-342-1103 201 E rberry@ulm.edu
BERRY, Scott, D 864-488-4525 430 H sberry@limestone.edu
BERRY, Trey 870-235-4001 22 F tcberry@saumag.edu
BERRY, Virginia 530-541-4660 48 D berry@ltcc.edu
BERRY-GUERIN, Daneen 509-793-2053 501 H daneenb@bigbend.edu
BERRY-JOHNSON, Pamela 478-825-6211 120 F
BERRYMAN, Daniel 520-206-4740 16 F dberryman@pima.edu
BERRYMAN, Davis 405-491-6680 388 A dberryma@snu.edu
BERRYMAN, Jennifer 508-856-2900 221 B jennifer.berryman@umassmed.edu
BERRYMAN, Joanne 502-585-9911 192 E jberryman@spalding.edu
BERRYMAN, Terri 815-455-8783 147 E tberryman@mchenry.edu
BERRYMAN, Theresa 847-543-2890 138 C tberryman@clcillinois.edu
BERRIOS, Olga 787-850-9340 538 B olga.berrios@upr.edu
BERSCHEIDT, Jim 402-280-1272 279 H jimberscheidt@creighton.edu
BERSHAD, Carolyn 607-753-4728 333 A carolyn.bershad@cortland.edu
BERSON, Gail 413-538-2515 226 A gberson@mtholyoke.edu
BERT, Daryl, W 540-432-4101 488 K daryl.bert@emu.edu
BERT, Melissa 320-589-6017 255 F mbert@morris.umn.edu
BERTCH, Dennis 269-488-4205 235 I dbertch@kvcc.edu
BERTEAUX, Susan 508-830-5035 222 C sberteaux@maritime.edu
BERTHEL, Michael 516-299-2606 319 C michael.berthel@liu.edu
BERTHELOT, Yves 404-385-3383 121 D yves.berthelot@provost.gatech.edu
BERTHELSEN, Mike 612-624-6837 255 H berth004@umn.edu
BERTHELSEN, Rita 507-453-1466 250 C rberthelsen@southeastmn.edu
BERTHIAUME, Joseph 262-595-2058 520 F berthiau@uwp.edu
BERTHIAUME, Peter, L 603-526-3675 285 L pberthia@colby-sawyer.edu
BERTHOUMIEUX, Rachel 516-686-1140 323 G rberthou@nyit.edu
BERTI, David, M 617-422-7215 226 H dberti@nesl.edu
BERTINI, Kristine 207-780-5180 205 E kristine.bertini@maine.edu
BERTINI, Vickie 847-619-8840 152 H vbertini@roosevelt.edu
BERTOLINI, Leonard, A 630-829-6003 135 F lbertolini@ben.edu
BERTOLINO, Joseph, A 802-626-6404 486 C joseph.bertolino@lyndonstate.edu
BERTOLUCCI, Linda 619-644-7799 45 J linda.bertolucci@gcccd.edu
BERTOT, John 301-405-4252 211 E jbertot@umd.edu
BERTOZZI, Stefano 510-642-2082 68 M sbertozzi@berkeley.edu
BERTRAM, Alissa 617-236-8827 218 G abertram@fisher.edu
BERTRAM, Brian 517-264-7676 241 A bbertram@sienaheights.edu
BERTRAN-PASARELL, Lourdes 787-728-1515 539 B lbertran@sagrado.edu
BERTRAND, Andre, E 404-215-2717 124 I andre.bertrand@morehouse.edu
BERTSCH, Lynda 701-858-3360 360 F lynda.bertsch@minotstateu.edu
BERTSCH, Tauna 254-968-9921 467 F bertsch@tarleton.edu
BERTSCHE, Allen, P 309-794-8283 135 D allenbertsche@augustana.edu
BERTSCHINGER, Edmund 617-253-1000 225 A
BERTSOS, Daniel 937-775-4172 381 H dan.bertsos@wright.edu
BERUBE, Alaina 952-888-4777 253 Z aberube@nwhealth.edu
BERUBE, Danelle 802-860-2702 483 F dberube@champlain.edu
BERUBE, Eric 661-763-7944 67 F eberube@taftcollege.edu
BERUBE, Patricia 413-572-5415 222 E pberube@westfield.ma.edu
BERUMEN, Yvonne 909-621-8129 57 H yvonne_berumen@pitzer.edu
BERWICK, Robert 386-822-7141 113 B rberwick@stetson.edu
BESADE, Elizabeth 305-899-4758 96 D ebesade@barry.edu
BESANA, GianMario 312-362-5554 139 C gbesana@depaul.edu
BESEDA, Michael 503-370-6021 396 G mbeseda@willamette.edu
BESEL, Karl 219-980-6554 163 B kbesel@iun.edu
BESENYEI, Alicia 304-384-6313 513 A abesenyei@concord.edu
BESHARA, Alexa 732-255-0400 293 E abeshara@ocean.edu
BESHEARS, Brenda 217-228-5520 136 A bbeshears@brcn.edu
BESIKOF, Rudolph 951-487-3404 53 D rbesikof@msjc.edu
BESKID, Novella 803-777-0958 433 F novella@sc.edu
BESNARD, Pamela 909-621-8192 58 A pamela.besnard@pomona.edu
BESNETTE HAUSER, Carrie 970-945-8691 78 B
BESONG, Jeffrey, D 412-392-3819 417 F jbesong@pointpark.edu
BESPALEC, Dale, A 414-464-9777 522 Q bespalec.dale@wspp.edu
BESPALOV, Oleg 818-710-4292 50 A bespalo@piercecollege.edu
BESS, Vivian 301-736-3631 209 A vivian.bess@msbbcs.edu
BESSESEN, Marit 619-594-6578 35 A bessesen@mail.sdsu.edu
BESSETTE, Bill 270-707-3795 189 G bill.bessette@kctcs.edu
BESSETTE, James 740-245-7225 380 C jbessette@rio.edu
BESSETTE, Jeanine 313-577-2116 243 F jeanine.bessette@wayne.edu
BESSETTE, Ray 207-941-7785 202 I bessetter@husson.edu
BESSETTE, Roger 413-755-4390 224 G rbessette@stcc.edu
BESSEY, Dean 207-509-7232 204 F dbessey@unity.edu
BESSIE, Joseph 218-477-2415 250 F joseph.bessie@mnstate.edu

BIERMAN, Matthew, J ..... 309-298-2005.. 158 A
mj-bierman@wiu.edu
BIERMAN, Matthew, J ..... 309-298-1811.. 158 A
mj-bierman@wiu.edu
BIERMAN, Matthew, J ..... 309-298-1800.. 158 A
mj-bierman@wiu.edu
BIERMAN, Scott .... 608-363-2201.. 515 G
biermans@beloit.edu
BIERMANN, Mark .... 219-464-5779.. 168 F
mark.biermann@valpo.edu
BIERNBAUM, John .... 309-298-3320.. 158 A
j-biernbaum@wiu.edu
BIERS, Lisa, M .... 260-422-5561.. 162 B
lmbiers@indianatech.edu
BIERSTER, Susan .... 561-868-3891.. 106 D
bierstes@palmbeachstate.edu
BIES, James, B .... 605-274-4124.. 435 E
jim.bies@augie.edu
BIES, Susan .... 605-274-5503.. 435 E
susan.bies@augie.edu
BIESECKER, James .... 717-337-6700.. 404 C
jbieseck@gettysburg.edu
BIETELCHIES, Wade .... 517-265-5161.. 230 D
BIGARD, Heather .... 859-846-6290.. 191 G
hbigard@midway.edu
BIGBY, Angela, D .... 702-968-2046.. 285 E
abigby@roseman.edu
BIGBY, Cindy .... 918-540-6201.. 384 F
cbigby@neo.edu
BIGCRANE, Michael .... 406-275-4789.. 278 E
michael_bigcrane@skc.edu
BIGDA, Steven, J .... 508-373-1979.. 215 D
steven.bigda@becker.edu
BIGDELI-JAHED, Fariba ... 502-597-6604.. 191 B
fariba.bigdelijahed@kysu.edu
BIGELOW, Gary .... 617-228-3474.. 223 B
gbigelow@bhcc.mass.edu
BIGELOW, Susan .... 307-674-6446.. 526 M
sbigelow@sheridan.edu
BIGG, Dort .... 954-763-9840.... 95 N
executivedirector@atom.edu
BIGGANE, Michael, J ...... 716-851-1416.. 313 H
biggane@ecc.edu
BIGGER, Kimberly .... 870-248-4000.... 19 H
kim.bigger@blackrivertech.edu
BIGGER, Roberta, H .... 864-597-4040.. 435 C
biggerrh@wofford.edu
BIGGERS, Carla, D .... 409-944-1200.. 458 D
cbiggers@gc.edu
BIGGERS, Darlene .... 281-283-3000.. 474 A
biggers@uhcl.edu
BIGGIN, Margot .... 617-627-3287.. 228 H
margot.biggin@tufts.edu
BIGGIO, Nancy .... 205-726-4267...... 6 E
ncbiggio@samford.edu
BIGGS, Curtis .... 973-300-2201.. 297 D
cbiggs@sussex.edu
BIGGS, Jocelyn .... 336-517-1818.. 342 B
jbiggs@bennet.edu
BIGGS, Kristen .... 231-843-5875.. 243 G
kmbiggs@westshore.edu
BIGGS, Patsy .... 501-420-1201.... 18 F
patsy.biggs@arkansasbaptist.edu
BIGGS, Shirley, A .... 803-535-5268.. 428 B
sbiggs@claflin.edu
BIGGS, Sue, A .... 325-670-1314.. 458 J
sbiggs@hsutx.edu
BIGGS, Susan .... 802-447-4041.. 485 B
sbiggs@svc.edu
BIGGS, Vicki .... 314-505-7266.. 263 I
BIGGS GARBUIO, Judith 509-313-4100.. 504 A
biggsgarbuio@gonzaga.edu
BIGNEY, Tracy .... 207-973-3234.. 204 G
bigney@maine.edu
BIGWOOD, Christine .... 401-232-6348.. 424 K
cbigwood@bryant.edu
BILACH, Bernadett .... 480-994-9244.... 17 C
bernadettb@swiha.edu
BILBRUCK, Tom .... 661-362-3235.... 40 A
tom.bilbruck@canyons.edu
BILCHAK, Karen .... 814-254-0471.. 401 A
kbilchak@pa.gov
BILDER, Kevin .... 480-517-8464.... 14 G
kevin.bilder@riosalado.edu
BILDERBACK, Rebecca ..... 620-365-5116.. 178 A
bilderback@allencc.edu
BILDERBACK, Ryan .... 620-365-5116.. 178 A
rbilderback@allencc.edu
BILEK, Mary Lu .... 508-985-1149.. 220 H
mbilek@umassd.edu
BILELLA, Jamieson .... 610-989-1451.. 422 E
jbilella@vfmac.edu
BILES, Brad .... 816-584-6888.. 270 D
brad.biles@park.edu
BILES, Deron .... 817-923-1921.. 466 E
dbiles@swbts.edu
BILGER, Audrey .... 909-621-8137.... 58 A
audrey.bilger@pomona.edu
BILGER, Cindy, L .... 570-577-1631.. 398 L
cbilger@bucknell.edu
BILGER, Jackie .... 570-321-4309.. 409 F
bilger@lycoming.edu
BILICH, Dan .... 330-867-1996.. 373 F
BILLARD, Trisha .... 516-876-3053.. 333 C
billardt@oldwestbury.edu
BILLEAUDEAU, Kim, A .... 337-262-5300.. 201 D
kimberlyb@louisiana.edu
BILLEAUX, David .... 361-825-2393.. 468 E
david.billeaux@tamucc.edu
BILLECI, Celesta .... 805-893-3437.... 70 E
celesta.billeci@sa.ucsb.edu
BILLECI, Jennifer .... 925-631-4600.... 59 I
jbilleci@stmarys-ca.edu
BILLEN, Isabelle .... 405-733-7580.. 387 I
ibillen@rose.edu
BILLEY, Terry, L .... 580-928-5533.. 388 C
terry.billey@swosu.edu
BILLHARTZ, Scott, L .... 618-537-6869.. 147 F
slbillhartz@mckendree.edu
BILLI, John, E .... 734-936-5214.. 241 J
jbilli@umich.edu
BILLICK, Tammy, N .... 971-722-7800.. 394 F
tbillick@pcc.edu
BILLIE, Marie, H .... 410-651-7502.. 212 B
mhbillie@umes.edu
BILLINGER, Kristi, M .... 785-864-7231.. 185 D
kristib@ku.edu
BILLINGHAM, Diana .... 352-365-3545.. 104 J
billingd@lssc.edu
BILLINGS, Amanda .... 214-648-2344.. 478 C
amanda.billings@utsouthwestern.edu
BILLINGS, Charles .... 415-485-3263.... 42 G
charles.billings@dominican.edu
BILLINGS, Christine .... 402-280-2444.. 279 H
christinebillings@creighton.edu
BILLINGS, Darron .... 731-424-3520.. 446 C
dbillings@jscc.edu
BILLINGS, James .... 928-541-7777.... 15 G
jbillings@ncu.edu
BILLINGSLEA, Aldo .... 408-554-4533.... 63 E
abillingslea@scu.edu
BILLINGSLEY, Anna, B .... 540-654-1055.. 495 C
abilling@umw.edu
BILLINGSLEY, Dale, B ..... 502-852-5209.. 194 A
dbbill01@louisville.edu
BILLINGSLEY, Jodie .... 806-742-2020.. 472 C
jodie.billingsley@ttu.edu
BILLINGSLEY, Linda .... 318-487-7630.. 195 F
linda.billingsley@lacollege.edu
BILLINGSLEY, Miron, P ... 919-530-6342.. 357 A
mpbillingsley@nccu.edu
BILLINGSLEY, Tiffany ...... 870-633-4480.... 20 B
tbillingsley@eacc.edu
BILLITIER, Rick .... 585-594-7777.. 327 D
billitier_rick@roberts.edu
BILLMAN, Carol .... 724-838-4204.. 419 D
billman@setonhill.edu
BILLMAN, Kathleen .... 773-256-0770.. 147 A
kbillman@lstc.edu
BILLS, Andy .... 336-841-4538.. 345 A
abills@highpoint.edu
BILLS, Joyce .... 918-465-1777.. 383 I
jbills@eosc.edu
BILLS, Linda, G .... 814-332-3362.. 397 A
lbills@allegheny.edu
BILLS, Matt .... 262-646-6513.. 518 G
mbills@nashotah.edu
BILLS-WINDT, Caryn, A .. 312-413-8145.. 156 F
cabw@uic.edu
BILLUPS, Terry .... 440-646-8109.. 380 F
terry.billups@ursuline.edu
BILLUPS, Vory .... 404-225-4474.. 117 A
vbillups@atlantatech.edu
BILODEAU, Leta .... 207-859-1201.. 204 E
bilodeaul@thomas.edu
BILONG, Danilo Philbert . 671-735-5554.. 529 G
danilophilbert.bilong@guamcc.edu
BILOTTA, Barbara, J .... 716-880-2265.. 320 D
barbara.bilotta@medaille.edu
BILOTTA, Leone .... 610-917-1483.. 422 C
l_bilotta@valleyforge.edu
BILSKY, Edward .... 207-602-2707.. 205 F
ebilsky@une.edu
BIMER, Tammy, C .... 734-763-9954.. 241 J
tammyc@umich.edu
BINA, Shawn .... 218-235-2170.. 252 F
s.bina@vcc.edu
BINARD, Kris .... 303-404-5103.... 80 E
kris.binard@frontrange.edu
BINAU, Brad, A .... 614-235-4136.. 378 C
bbinau@tlsohio.edu
BINDER, Arthur .... 575-528-7070.. 301 C
beagle@nmsu.edu
BINDER, Holly .... 417-873-7654.. 264 H
hbinder@drury.edu
BINDER, Jan .... 602-285-7869.... 14 F
jan.binder@phoenixcollege.edu
BINDEWALD, Kurt .... 504-865-3226.. 198 E
kjbindew@loyno.edu
BINESH, Behzad .... 714-744-7099.... 37 F
binesh@chapman.edu
BINETTE, Louise .... 802-447-6343.. 485 B
lbinette@svc.edu
BING, Andrea .... 415-565-4733.... 69 B
wellesan@uchastings.edu
BING, Richard, N .... 212-998-2391.. 324 C
richard.bing@nyu.edu
BINGAMON, Cindy .... 314-837-6777.. 271 B
cbingamon@stlchristian.edu
BINGEL, Amanda .... 518-388-6117.. 338 H
bingela@union.edu
BINGEL, Laurie, A .... 618-235-2700.. 155 C
laurie.bingel@swic.edu
BINGER, Nancy .... 847-628-2510.. 144 B
nbinger@judsonu.edu
BINGHAM, Charlotte .... 806-742-3627.. 472 C
charlotte.bingham@ttu.edu
BINGHAM, Charlotte .... 806-742-3627.. 472 D
charlotte.bingham@ttu.edu
BINGHAM, Daniel, J .... 406-444-6800.. 277 B
daniel.bingham@umhelena.edu
BINGHAM, Douglas, A ..... 858-784-8469.... 64 B
BINGHAM, Janet .... 703-993-8756.. 490 B
bingham@gmu.edu
BINGHAM, Jeffrey .... 817-923-1921.. 466 E
jbingham@swbts.edu
BINGHAM, Jeri .... 773-252-5131.. 152 B
jeri.bingham@resu.edu
BINGHAM, Michael .... 828-448-6020.. 354 B
mbingham@wpcc.edu
BINGHAM, Rachel .... 801-524-8129.. 480 J
rbingham@ldsbc.edu
BINGHAM, Rosie, P .... 901-678-2114.. 445 C
rbingham@memphis.edu
BINGHAM, Tom .... 808-956-7166.. 131 F
bingham@hawaii.edu
BINGHAM, Vicki, L .... 662-846-4268.. 257 E
vbingham@deltastate.edu
BINK, Cynthia .... 718-260-5030.. 309 C
cbink@citytech.cuny.edu
BINKERD, James .... 707-638-5883.... 68 C
jim.binkerd@tu.edu
BINKLEY, Kristi .... 615-514-2787.. 443 F
kbinkley@nossi.edu
BINKOWSKI, Marcella ...... 215-637-7700.. 405 J
smbinkowski@holyfamily.edu
BINNEY, Craig .... 508-565-1107.. 228 F
cbinney@stonehill.edu
BINNEY, Diane, M .... 626-395-6651.... 30 H
dbinney@caltech.edu
BINNICKER, Paul .... 816-833-0524.. 172 G
binnicke@graceland.edu
BINNING, William, C .... 330-941-3436.. 382 A
wcbinning@ysu.edu
BINNINGTON, Ian .... 814-332-2357.. 397 A
ibinning@allegheny.edu
BINSTOCK, Jonathan .... 585-276-8902.. 338 K
jbinstock@mag.rochester.edu
BIONDO, Drew .... 631-451-4776.. 336 D
biondodr@sunysuffolk.edu
BIOTEAU, Cynthia, A .... 904-632-3222.. 101 G
cynthia.bioteau@fscj.edu
BIR, Chad .... 317-955-6040.. 165 N
cbir@marian.edu
BIRBERICK, Anne .... 815-753-0494.. 150 A
annie@niu.edu
BIRCH, Andrea, C .... 770-718-5325.. 118 A
abirch@brenau.edu
BIRCH, Barbara .... 212-960-5373.. 341 G
birch@yu.edu
BIRCH, Esther .... 301-736-3631.. 209 A
esther.birch@msbbcs.edu
BIRCH, Laura, A .... 217-420-6661.. 148 D
lbirch@millikin.edu
BIRCH, Mikel .... 801-957-4041.. 483 A
mikel.birch@slcc.edu
BIRCHAK, Chris .... 713-221-8007.. 474 B
birchakc@uhd.edu
BIRCHARD, Michael .... 763-424-0850.. 251 B
mbirchard@nhcc.edu
BIRCKBICHLER, Carrie, J 724-738-2150.. 416 B
carrie.birckbichler@sru.edu
BIRD, Brandon .... 206-726-5024.. 503 B
bbird@cornish.edu
BIRD, John .... 803-323-3374.. 435 B
birdj@winthrop.edu
BIRD, Lee, E .... 405-744-5328.. 385 G
lee.bird@okstate.edu
BIRD, Lori .... 419-267-1266.. 374 A
lbird@northweststate.edu
BIRD, Sheila .... 620-278-4247.. 185 A
sbird@sterling.edu
BIRD, Su Ann .... 229-931-2110.. 127 C
sbird@southgatech.edu
BIRD, SuAnn .... 229-931-2110.. 127 C
sbird@southgatech.edu
BIRD, Veronica .... 610-917-1422.. 422 C
rabird@valleyforge.edu
BIRDINE, Phil .... 580-477-7700.. 389 I
phil.birdine@wosc.edu
BIRDSELL, David .... 646-660-6700.. 307 A
david.birdsell@baruch.cuny.edu
BIRDSELL, Jo .... 858-642-8365.... 54 A
jbirdsell@nu.edu
BIRDSONG, Jeff .... 918-540-6348.. 384 F
jbirdsong@neo.edu
BIRDSONG, Ronnie .... 575-562-4614.. 299 I
ronnie.birdsong@enmu.edu
BIRDWELL, Cindy, A .... 517-264-7194.. 241 A
cbirdwell@sienaheights.edu
BIRDWELL, Kim .... 940-521-7101.. 462 L
kbirdwell@nctc.edu
BIRDWHISTELL, Terry, L . 859-218-1871.. 193 G
terry.bird@uky.edu
BIRGE, James, F .... 413-662-5201.. 222 B
j.birge@mcla.edu
BIRGE, Susan, N .... 203-254-4000.... 87 G
sbirge@fairfield.edu
BIRINGER, Bobbi .... 312-261-3550.. 149 B
bobbi.biringer@nl.edu
BIRK, Michelle, L .... 618-235-2700.. 155 C
michelle.birk@swic.edu
BIRKE, Richard .... 503-370-6046.. 396 G
rbirke@willamette.edu
BIRKEDAHL, Patrice .... 510-659-6208.... 55 B
pbirkedahl@ohlone.edu
BIRKEDAHL, Walter .... 510-659-6216.... 55 B
wbirkedahl@ohlone.edu
BIRKENHOLTZ,
Kenneth, I .... 515-961-1512.. 176 H
ken.birkenholtz@simpson.edu
BIRKES, R. Dennis .... 724-287-8711.. 399 B
dennis.birkes@bc3.edu
BIRKHEAD, Mary .... 610-282-1100.. 402 B
mary.birkhead@desales.edu
BIRKHEAD, Susan .... 518-268-5130.. 329 J
susan.birkhead@sphp.com
BIRKHOLZ, Jane .... 218-855-8016.. 248 N
jbirkholz@clcmn.edu
BIRKNER, Linda, M .... 501-977-2006.... 24 B
birkner@uaccm.edu
BIRKS, Robert .... 310-544-6461.... 59 K
robert.birks@usw.salvationarmy.org
BIRKS, Stacy .... 310-544-6405.... 59 K
stacy.birks@usw.salvationarmy.org
BIRKY, Ian, T .... 610-758-3880.. 408 H
itb0@lehigh.edu
BIRKY, Joshua .... 217-351-2376.. 151 B
jbirky@parkland.edu
BIRMINGHAM, Lynne ...... 603-542-7744.. 286 G
lbirmingham@ccsnh.edu
BIRMINGHAM, Stacy, G .. 724-458-3841.. 404 F
sgbirmingham@gcc.edu
BIRNBACH, David, J .... 305-284-2002.. 114 H
dbirnbach@miami.edu
BIRNBAUM, Ben .... 617-552-3353.. 216 C
ben.birnbaum@bu.edu
BIRNER, David, C .... 262-243-5700.. 516 E
david.birner@cuw.edu
BIRNEY, John, W .... 864-597-4135.. 435 C
birneyjw@wofford.edu
BIRNEY, Tyler .... 605-698-3966.. 436 K
tbirney@swc.tc
BIRNIE, Christine, R .... 585-385-8430.. 328 E
cbirnie@sjfc.edu
BIRON, Jackie .... 510-780-4500.... 48 J
jbiron@lifewest.edu
BIRON, Louise .... 518-255-5623.. 334 D
bironl@cobleskill.edu
BIRON, Rebecca, E .... 603-646-3113.. 286 J
rebecca.e.biron@dartmouth.edu
BIROS, Demetra .... 425-739-8315.. 504 F
demetra.biros@lwtech.edu
BIRREN, Susan, J .... 781-736-3451.. 216 F
birren@brandeis.edu
BIRRINGER, Charles, E .... 920-924-3420.. 524 B
cbirringer@morainepark.edu
BIRTWISTLE, Heidi .... 610-341-1738.. 403 B
hbirtwis@eastern.edu
BIRX, Donald, L .... 603-535-2210.. 288 F
dlbirx@plymouth.edu
BISBEE, Chester, A .... 404-413-2000.. 122 D
cbisbee@gsu.edu
BISBEE, Nina .... 610-526-7935.. 398 K
nbisbee@brynmawr.edu
BISBEE, Yolanda .... 208-885-6448.. 134 G
yobiz@uidaho.edu
BISBEY, CDP, Michele .... 412-536-1255.. 406 K
michele.bisbey@laroche.edu
BISCH, Debbie .... 620-227-9209.. 180 E
debbieb@dc3.edu
BISCHOFF, Jeannette .... 916-660-7000.... 64 F
jbischoff@sierracollege.edu
BISCHOFF, Margaretha ..... 956-872-8310.. 465 H
etybuh@southtexascollege.edu
BISCHOFF, Richard, W .... 216-368-5445.. 365 B
richard.bischoff@case.edu
BISER, Bruce .... 651-793-1910.. 250 A
bruce.biser@metrostate.edu
BISESE, Stephen, D .... 804-289-8615.. 495 G
sbisese@richmond.edu
BISH, Courtney, D .... 315-386-7120.. 335 B
bish@canton.edu

BISH, Kevin 859-858-2272 186 I
BISHOP, Brad 540-365-4250 489 M
bradbishop@ferrum.edu
BISHOP, Brandan 616-222-1954 233 A
brandan.bishop@cornerstone.edu
BISHOP, Carl 704-290-5235 353 B
cbishop@spcc.edu
BISHOP, Carla 785-532-1858 182 D
cbishop@ksu.edu
BISHOP, Carol, M 607-746-4582 335 C
bishopcm@delhi.edu
BISHOP, Carolyn 901-435-1755 441 C
carolyn_bishop@loc.edu
BISHOP, Catherine, F 405-325-1543 389 B
cbishop@ou.edu
BISHOP, Christopher 888-384-0849 25 P
cjbishop@allied.edu
BISHOP, Colleen 804-828-9914 496 D
cbishop4@vcu.edu
BISHOP, David 806-785-9285 479 D
bishop@wbu.edu
BISHOP, Dennis 214-638-0484 460 C
dbishop@kdstudio.com
BISHOP, Donald, C 574-631-7505 168 B
dbishop1@nd.edu
BISHOP, Emily, A 601-979-3975 258 D
emily.a.bishop@jsums.edu
BISHOP, Jason 603-271-6484 286 F
jbishop@ccsnh.edu
BISHOP, Jeffrey 314-977-6663 271 K
jbisho12@slu.edu
BISHOP, Kelley 301-314-7236 211 E
kbishop1@umd.edu
BISHOP, Kristy 724-925-4212 423 D
bishopkr@wccc.edu
BISHOP, Kyle, K 240-895-4289 210 E
kkbishop@smcm.edu
BISHOP, Laura 918-495-6151 386 H
lbishop@oru.edu
BISHOP, Lisa, J 812-888-4274 169 A
bishop@vinu.edu
BISHOP, Mary Kay 585-389-2012 322 D
mbishop2@naz.edu
BISHOP, Mike 951-552-8759 29 H
mbishop@calbaptist.edu
BISHOP, Nancy 803-778-6638 427 G
bishopnw@cctech.edu
BISHOP, Nathaniel, L 540-985-8484 491 A
nlbishop@jchs.edu
BISHOP, Norman 606-368-6091 186 B
normbishop@alc.edu
BISHOP, Pamela 614-287-2437 367 C
pbishop2@cscc.edu
BISHOP, Paul 805-965-0581 63 D
pwbishop@sbcc.edu
BISHOP, Phil 206-876-6100 507 D
pbishop@theseattleschool.edu
BISHOP, Rex 770-975-4522 118 J
BISHOP, Richard 860-832-2201 85 F
bishopr@ccsu.edu
BISHOP, Robert, H 813-974-3780 112 C
robertbishop@usf.edu
BISHOP, Sandy 715-365-4564 524 C
sbishop@nicoletcollege.edu
BISHOP, Sasha 843-470-8396 433 B
sbishop@tcl.edu
BISHOP, Selah 904-470-8952 98 N
selah.bisho0911@ewc.edu
BISHOP, Steve 417-447-8152 270 A
bishops@otc.edu
BISHOP, Steve 601-276-3701 260 H
bishop@smcc.edu
BISHOP, Stuart 928-536-6265 15 J
stuart.bishop@npc.edu
BISHOP, Wesley, T 504-286-5325 199 I
wbishop@suno.edu
BISHOP, William 504-861-5431 198 E
wgbishop@loyno.edu
BISHOP, William 916-278-7469 34 B
william.bishop@csus.edu
BISHOP, Wilsie, S 423-439-4811 444 F
bishopws@etsu.edu
BISHOP-MONROE,
Robbie 404-572-3695 124 I
robbie.bishopmonroe@morehouse.edu
BISIGNANO, Chris 914-251-6530 334 C
chris.bisignanoi@purchase.edu
BISKUPIAK, Walter, H 406-447-5420 276 B
bbiskupi@carroll.edu
BISMARK, Jeanie 870-235-4078 22 F
mjbismark@saumag.edu
BISPING, Timothy 936-468-3101 466 H
bispingto@sfasu.edu
BISSELL, Michelle 304-205-6640 511 M
michelle.bissell@bridgevalley.edu
BISSELL, Monika 207-795-2846 203 G
bisselmo@cmhc.org
BISSELL, Sally 419-783-2366 368 A
sbissell@defiance.edu
BISSELL PAULSON, Lisa 707-965-7362 56 A
lpaulson@puc.edu
BISSET, Matthew, S 727-864-8482 98 L
bissetms@eckerd.edu
BISSET, William, J 718-862-7200 319 L
william.bisset@manhattan.edu
BISSINGER, Mary 805-482-2755 59 G
mbissinger@stjohnsem.edu
BISSONETTE, David 218-855-8178 248 N
dbissonette@clcmn.edu
BISSONETTE, Matt 507-379-3335 251 H
matt.bissonette@riverland.edu
BISWAS, Harun 678-466-4240 119 A
harunbiswas@clayton.edu
BITIKOFER, Scott 407-646-2121 107 O
sbitikofer@rollins.edu
BITNER, Hannah 816-322-0110 262 N
hannah.bitner@calvary.edu
BITNER, Justin 314-246-7464 275 B
justinbitner77@webster.edu
BITNER, Scott 410-706-3822 211 F
sbitner@umaryland.edu
BITNER, Teddy 816-322-0110 262 N
teddy.bitner@calvary.edu
BITOK, Abe 928-724-6736 12 T
BITSOI, LeManuel 312-942-0725 153 B
lee_bitsoi@rush.edu
BITTERBAUM, Erik, J 607-753-2201 333 A
erik.bitterbaum@cortland.edu
BITTERSFELD, Y 718-692-0208 340 M
yeshivaht@gmail.com
BITTINGER, Dale 410-455-2278 211 G
bittinger@umbc.edu
BITTINGER, SaraBeth 301-687-3130 212 F
sbittinger@frostburg.edu
BITTLE, Carolyn 910-410-1751 352 C
ctbittle@richmondcc.edu
BITTORF, David, C 240-500-2000 207 I
dcbittorf@hagerstowncc.edu
BITZER, Michael 704-637-4466 343 B
jmbitzer@catawba.edu
BITZER, Michael 704-637-4410 343 B
jmbitzer@catawba.edu
BITZER, Michelle 715-682-1484 518 H
mbitzer@northland.edu
BITZER, Steve 715-682-4591 525 A
steve.bitzer@witc.edu
BIUNDO, Rachel 804-594-1479 497 D
rbiundo@jtcc.edu
BIVINS, Dallas 480-941-1993 44 H
dallasbivins@gs.edu
BIXBY, David, E 626-815-5334 28 A
dbixby@apu.edu
BIXBY, John, L 305-284-2211 114 H
jbixby@miami.edu
BIXEL, Patricia 207-941-7144 202 I
bixelp@husson.edu
BIXLER, Kirk, J 317-738-8801 160 J
kbixler@franklincollege.edu
BIZON, Walter, G 248-204-3020 237 B
wbizon@ltu.edu
BIZOT, Caroline 985-867-2238 199 F
cbizot@sjasc.edu
BJARNSON, Corey 513-241-4338 363 G
corey.bjarnson@antonellicollege.edu
BJELLAND, David 320-762-4407 248 J
davidb@alextech.edu
BJERKE, Keith 701-231-6825 361 A
keith@ndsualumni.com
BJERKLIE, Joseph, R 207-834-8621 205 B
joseph.bjerklie@maine.edu
BJERUM, Joanna 316-284-5326 179 A
jbjerum@bethelks.edu
BJOKNE, Daniel, H 515-964-0601 172 F
bjokned@faith.edu
BJORDAHL, Julia 509-313-6102 504 A
bjordahl@gonzaga.edu
BJORGAN, Heather 309-796-5340 135 I
bjorganh@bhc.edu
BJORK, Ross 662-915-7546 261 B
rbjork@olemiss.edu
BJORKLUND, Robert, B 651-638-6396 244 L
robert-bjorklund@bethel.edu
BJORKMAN, David, J 561-297-0113 110 K
dbjorkm1@fau.edu
BJORKMAN, Karen 419-530-7842 380 D
karen.bjorkman@utoledo.edu
BJORN, Thorr, D 401-874-5245 426 D
tbjorn@uri.edu
BJUNE, Stephanie 979-458-6000 467 D
sbjune@tamus.edu
BLACHFORD, Charles 215-753-3664 400 H
blachfordc@chc.edu
BLACK, Adam 801-863-6378 482 C
blackad@uvu.edu
BLACK, Andrew 727-864-8258 98 L
blackad@eckerd.edu
BLACK, Ann 505-428-1811 301 K
ann.black@sfcc.edu
BLACK, Bettye, R 405-466-3294 383 M
brblack@langston.edu
BLACK, Britt 630-752-5072 158 C
britt.black@wheaton.edu
BLACK, JR., Christopher 815-921-4445 152 E
c.black@rockvalleycollege.edu
BLACK, Christopher, B 260-422-5561 162 B
cbblack@indianatech.edu
BLACK, Connie 208-562-3252 133 F
connieblack@cwidaho.cc
BLACK, Diane 251-442-2209 9 A
dblack@umobile.edu
BLACK, Ellen 843-349-5211 430 F
ellen.black@hgtc.edu
BLACK, Gary 440-826-2900 363 M
gblack@bw.edu
BLACK, Heather 412-365-1281 400 G
hblack@chatham.edu
BLACK, James 802-635-1298 486 B
james.black@jsc.edu
BLACK, Jane 740-695-9500 364 B
jblack@belmontcollege.edu
BLACK, Jason 205-726-3673 6 E
jjblack@samford.edu
BLACK, Jeff 410-972-3303 210 D
jeffrey.black@sjc.edu
BLACK, John 248-689-8282 242 F
jblack@walshcollege.edu
BLACK, John Paul 252-527-6223 350 H
jpblack73@lenoircc.edu
BLACK, John Paul 252-527-6223 350 H
jblack@lenoircc.edu
BLACK, Joshua 864-941-8542 432 A
black.j@ptc.edu
BLACK, Joshua 423-614-8370 441 B
jblack@leeuniversity.edu
BLACK, Josiah 630-620-2130 150 B
jblack@seminary.edu
BLACK, Karnell 801-832-2231 483 D
kblack@westminstercollege.edu
BLACK, Katherine 860-768-4103 89 G
kablack@hartford.edu
BLACK, Kedric 801-863-8536 482 C
kedric.black@uvu.edu
BLACK, Kim 970-351-1102 84 C
kim.black@unco.edu
BLACK, Laura, L 662-329-7135 259 E
llblack@muw.edu
BLACK, Laurie 802-258-3273 485 A
laurie.black@worldlearning.org
BLACK, Lendley, C 218-726-7106 255 D
chan@d.umn.edu
BLACK, Linda 970-351-1638 84 C
linda.black@unco.edu
BLACK, Lisa 619-239-0391 36 A
lblack@cwsl.edu
BLACK, Lynda, K 336-838-6148 354 C
lynda.black@wilkescc.edu
BLACK, Mark 615-966-5709 441 F
mark.black@lipscomb.edu
BLACK, Martin 724-589-2372 420 D
mblack@thiel.edu
BLACK, Michael 404-894-2486 121 D
mike.black@housing.gatech.edu
BLACK, Michael 419-267-1390 374 A
mblack@northweststate.edu
BLACK, Michael, E 210-567-7103 477 D
blackm@uthscsa.edu
BLACK, Michael, M 229-245-6517 129 G
mmblack@valdosta.edu
BLACK, Michael, R 805-922-6966 25
mblack@hancockcollege.edu
BLACK, Nancy Jo 888-488-4968 47 D
BLACK, Norman, S 808-675-3936 130 E
norman.black@byuh.edu
BLACK, Rochelle, A 248-370-3682 239 K
black@oakland.edu
BLACK, Shaun, C 315-445-4569 318 E
blacksc@lemoyne.edu
BLACK, Sul 803-705-4334 427 D
blacks@benedict.edu
BLACK, Tanja 864-429-8728 434 F
trblack@mailbox.sc.edu
BLACK, Thomas 650-723-1550 66 I
thomas.black@stanford.edu
BLACK, William, N 215-204-4760 420 B
william.black@temple.edu
BLACK, Willie 678-839-5344 129 E
wblack@westga.edu
BLACK-ARIAS, Maxine 212-924-5900 336 I
mblakarias@swedishinstitute.edu
BLACK-GOLD, Tonia 704-637-4393 343 B
tblackgo@catawba.edu
BLACKABY, Leslie 509-574-6806 510 A
lblackaby@yvcc.edu
BLACKARD, Gary 417-865-2815 255 B
blackardg@evangel.edu
BLACKARD, Glynis, D 770-720-5600 126 C
gdb@reinhardt.edu
BLACKBOURN,
Richard, L 662-325-3717 259 D
rlb277@msstate.edu
BLACKBURN, Amanda 404-233-3949 443 M
ablackburn@richmont.edu
BLACKBURN, David 423-425-4495 448 F
david-blackburn@utc.edu
BLACKBURN, J. Blair 903-923-2222 457 G
bblackburn@etbu.edu
BLACKBURN, Kristi 562-860-2451 36 P
kblackburn@cerritos.edu
BLACKBURN, Lisa 606-218-5296 194 C
lisablackburn@upike.edu
BLACKBURN, Mark 605-274-4313 435 E
mark.blackburn@augie.edu
BLACKBURN, Michael 713-500-6087 477 C
michael.r.blackburn@uth.tmc.edu
BLACKBURN, Michael, R 713-500-3019 477 C
michael.r.blackburn@uth.tmc.edu
BLACKBURN, Michele 401-841-6597 528 E
BLACKBURN, Sean 307-766-3296 527 B
sean.blackburn@uwyo.edu
BLACKBURN, Steven 860-509-9560 88 A
sblackburn@hartsem.edu
BLACKBURN, Terri 208-467-8673 134 D
tblackburn@nnu.edu
BLACKBURN-SMITH,
Jefferson 614-823-1031 376 C
jblackburnsmith@otterbein.edu
BLACKFORD, Nancy 330-490-7106 380 J
nblackford@walsh.edu
BLACKHURST, Anne 218-477-2243 250 F
anne.blackhurst@mnstate.edu
BLACKIE, Crisanne 207-581-1359 204 H
BLACKKETTER,
Donald, M 406-496-4129 277 G
dblackketter@mtech.edu
BLACKLAW, Stuart 412-237-8182 401 B
sblacklaw@ccac.edu
BLACKLEY, Scott 662-407-1501 258 C
jsblackley@iccms.edu
BLACKMAN, Bret 402-554-2227 283 B
bblackman@unomaha.edu
BLACKMAN, Orville 812-280-7271 183 M
orville.blackman@ottawa.edu
BLACKMAN, Peter 510-666-8248 25 D
pblackman@aimc.edu
BLACKMAN, Terrance 718-270-6417 309 B
tblackman@mec.cuny.edu
BLACKMER, Jennifer 765-285-2783 159 B
jsblackmer@bsu.edu
BLACKMON, Bruce 704-687-7010 358 A
ablackm8@uncc.edu
BLACKMON, Chianti 301-447-6932 209 G
blackmon@msmary.edu
BLACKMON, Luke 843-863-8004 427 I
lblackmon@csuniv.edu
BLACKMON, Paul 334-420-4461 7 G
pblackmon@trenholmstate.edu
BLACKMON, Terry, W 731-426-7601 440 K
tblackmon@lanecollege.edu
BLACKMON, Timothy 630-752-5087 158 C
chaplains.office@wheaton.edu
BLACKMORE, Lee 307-754-6067 526 N
lee.blackmore@nwc.edu
BLACKNALL, Eric 920-565-1043 517 D
blacknallev@lakeland.edu
BLACKSHEAR, Regina, G 314-539-5123 271 F
rblackshear@stlcc.edu
BLACKSMITH, Lourdes 630-466-7900 157 K
lblacksmith@waubonsee.edu
BLACKSMITH, Robin 206-546-4503 507 F
rblacksmith@shoreline.edu
BLACKSTONE, Tondelaya 410-951-4265 212 E
tblackstone@coppin.edu
BLACKWELL, Amy 864-294-3496 430 C
amy.blackwell@furman.edu
BLACKWELL, Ann 601-266-4568 261 E
ann.blackwell@usm.edu
BLACKWELL, Bill 218-755-2590 248 M
wblackwell@bemidjistate.edu
BLACKWELL, David, W 859-257-8939 193 G
dblackwell@uky.edu
BLACKWELL, Deborah 704-355-5970 343 A
debbie.blackwell@carolinascollege.edu
BLACKWELL, Deborah, L 956-326-2628 468 A
dblackwell@tamiu.edu
BLACKWELL, Jody 405-912-9463 387 D
jblackwell@hc.edu
BLACKWELL, Joe 405-789-7661 388 B
joe.blackwell@swcu.edu
BLACKWELL, Mary, D 623-845-3305 14 C
m.blackwell@gccaz.edu
BLACKWELL, Samuel 803-780-1239 434 M
blackwell@voorhees.edu
BLACKWELL, Scott 601-266-4783 261 E
edward.blackwell@usm.edu
BLACKWELL, Simon 301-447-5600 209 G
syblackwell@msmary.edu
BLACKWELL, Tiffini 864-646-1492 433 C
tblackw7@tctc.edu
BLACKWELL, Tina 503-768-7680 392 A
clb@lclark.edu
BLACKWELL, Toni 617-266-1400 215 G

BLACKWELL-CLARK, Edwina ... 937-376-6216.. 365 H
eblackwell-clark@centralstate.edu

BLACKWOOD, Edwin ... 412-731-6000.. 417 J
eblackwood@rpts.edu

BLACKWOOD, James ... 706-880-8050.. 123 K
jblackwood@lagrange.edu

BLACKWOOD, Jeremy ... 414-425-8300.. 519 F
jblackwood@shsst.edu

BLACKWOOD, Kathy ... 650-358-6869.... 62 F
blackwoodk@smccd.edu

BLACKWOOD, Rodney, B 806-720-7402.. 461 C
rod.blackwood@lcu.edu

BLADDICK, Jerry ... 941-955-8862.. 107 M
jbladdick@ringling.edu

BLADES, Dawn ... 845-257-3171.. 331 E
bladesd@newpaltz.edu

BLADWIN, Jenifer ... 215-619-7391.. 410 L
jbaldwin@mc3.edu

BLAETTNER, Wendy ... 830-792-7375.. 465 E
wlblaettner@schreiner.edu

BLAGG, Oneida ... 307-766-3459.. 527 B
oblagg@uwyo.edu

BLAGG, Rosalyn ... 870-508-6128.... 19 B
rblagg@asumh.edu

BLAHNIK, Brent ... 920-465-2190.. 520 B
blahnikb@uwgb.edu

BLAHNIK, Jeffrey, J ... 405-325-2151.. 389 B
jblahnik@ou.edu

BLAICH, Charles, F ... 765-361-6311.. 169 C
blaichc@wabash.edu

BLAIFEDER, Mark ... 212-217-4020.. 314 B
mark_blaifeder@fitnyc.edu

BLAIN, Daniel, S ... 330-325-6261.. 373 H
dblain@neomed.edu

BLAIN, Judy ... 931-221-7691.. 444 E
blainj@apsu.edu

BLAIR, Alan ... 413-572-5582.. 222 E
alan@westfield.ma.edu

BLAIR, Anthony, L ... 717-866-5775.. 403 F
ablair@evangelical.edu

BLAIR, Audrey, D ... 563-333-6364.. 176 D
blairaudreyd@sau.edu

BLAIR, Brian ... 202-885-2842.... 91 J
bblair@american.edu

BLAIR, Brian ... 267-502-2407.. 398 J
brian.blair@brynathyn.edu

BLAIR, Cinnamon ... 505-277-1806.. 302 F
cblair@salud.unm.edu

BLAIR, Dan ... 304-865-6135.. 511 C
dan.blair@ovu.edu

BLAIR, David, A ... 512-428-1286.. 464 G
davidab@stedwards.edu

BLAIR, Doug ... 574-239-8380.. 161 N
dblair@hcc-nd.edu

BLAIR, Eric ... 816-584-6858.. 270 D
eric.blair@park.edu

BLAIR, Jan ... 231-591-2150.. 233 L
janblair@ferris.edu

BLAIR, Jean ... 845-938-3615.. 529 C
jean.blair@usma.edu

BLAIR, Jeff ... 614-251-4735.. 374 I
blairj@ohiodominican.edu

BLAIR, John, P ... 270-745-6520.. 194 D
jp.blair@wku.edu

BLAIR, Kim, M ... 336-841-9044.. 345 A
kblair@highpoint.edu

BLAIR, Kristine ... 330-941-3409.. 382 A
klblair@ysu.edu

BLAIR, Linda ... 502-447-1000.. 192 G
lblair@spencerian.edu

BLAIR, Marilou, C ... 716-851-1832.. 313 H
blair@ecc.edu

BLAIR, Matthew ... 305-899-4013.... 96 D
mblair@barry.edu

BLAIR, Michael, R ... 563-387-1040.. 174 L
blairmic@luther.edu

BLAIR, Neil, B ... 913-253-5090.. 184 G
neil.blair@spst.edu

BLAIR, Patricia ... 707-476-4100.... 40 D
patricia-blair@redwoods.edu

BLAIR, Paul, G ... 574-372-5100.. 161 B
blairp@grace.edu

BLAIR, Robbie, M ... 806-716-2336.. 465 G
rblair@southplainscollege.edu

BLAIR, Sara, B ... 734-764-9290.. 241 J
sbblair@umich.edu

BLAIR, Stanley ... 732-571-3619.. 292 F
sblair@monmouth.edu

BLAIR, Stephen ... 802-635-1314.. 486 B
stephen.blair@jsc.edu

BLAIR, Sylvia ... 410-386-8411.. 206 I
sblair@carrollcc.edu

BLAIR, Thomas, A ... 770-216-2960.. 123 F
tab@ict.edu

BLAIR, Timothy, V ... 610-436-2739.. 416 C
tblair@wcupa.edu

BLAIR, Trent ... 270-745-3253.. 194 D
trent.blair@wku.edu

BLAIR, Wendell ... 312-553-5662.. 137 D
wblair@ccc.edu

BLAIR, Wray ... 301-687-4201.. 212 F
wnblair@plattsburgh.edu

BLAIR, Zulema ... 718-270-6127.. 309 B
zblair@mec.cuny.edu

BLAIS, Jessica ... 727-873-4456.. 112 D
blais@usfsp.edu

BLAIS, Natalie ... 413-545-2211.. 220 F
natalie@chancellor.umass.edu

BLAIS, Roger, N ... 918-631-2554.. 389 E
roger-blais@utulsa.edu

BLAISDELL, Stephanie ... 901-678-5792.. 445 C
sblsdell@memphis.edu

BLAISE, Butterfly, L ... 518-564-3002.. 334 A
bblai001@plattsburgh.edu

BLAISING, Craig, A ... 817-923-1921.. 466 E
cblaising@swbts.edu

BLAKE, Alan ... 603-271-6484.. 286 F
ablake@ccsnh.edu

BLAKE, Brian ... 215-895-2200.. 402 G
mb3545@drexel.edu

BLAKE, Christopher ... 478-471-2712.. 124 E
christopher.blake@mga.edu

BLAKE, Christopher, T ... 631-451-4283.. 336 E
blakec@sunysuffolk.edu

BLAKE, Darcy ... 650-543-3901.... 52 D
dblake@menlo.edu

BLAKE, David ... 206-934-4136.. 506 I
dave.blake@seattlecolleges.edu

BLAKE, Debora ... 214-333-5448.. 455 J
debora@dbu.edu

BLAKE, Diane, T ... 518-388-6104.. 338 H
blaked@union.edu

BLAKE, Erin ... 225-216-8711.. 195 H
blakee@mybrcc.edu

BLAKE, F. Phyllis ... 914-633-2462.. 317 B
pblake@iona.edu

BLAKE, Ira ... 570-389-4308.. 414 D
iblake@bloomu.edu

BLAKE, Joi Lin ... 760-744-1150.... 56 F

BLAKE, Karen ... 203-575-8269.... 86 G
kblake@nv.edu

BLAKE, Keiana ... 713-718-5059.. 459 B
keiana.blake@hccs.edu

BLAKE, Kevin, M ... 716-888-2778.. 306 F
blakek@canisius.edu

BLAKE, Larry ... 307-766-9028.. 527 B
lblake3@uwyo.edu

BLAKE, Lisa ... 309-341-5282.. 136 C
lblake@sandburg.edu

BLAKE, Lori ... 325-670-5896.. 458 J
lblake@hsutx.edu

BLAKE, Paul, A ... 231-591-3797.. 233 L
paulblake@ferris.edu

BLAKE, Peg ... 707-826-3361.... 34 F
plb91@humboldt.edu

BLAKE, Robert, C ... 202-994-6870.... 92 D
rblake@gwu.edu

BLAKE, Scott ... 906-487-7242.. 234 A
scott.blake@finlandia.edu

BLAKE, Susan, N ... 470-578-3576.. 123 J
sblake@kennesaw.edu

BLAKE, William, J ... 330-941-2086.. 382 A
wjblake@ysu.edu

BLAKE-JUDD, Jemma ... 909-274-4750.... 53 C
jbjudd@mtsac.edu

BLAKEFIELD, Mary ... 765-973-8522.. 162 G
mblakefi@iue.edu

BLAKELY, Craig, H ... 502-852-3297.. 194 A
crag.blakely@louisville.edu

BLAKELY, Dee ... 618-634-3247.. 154 B
deeb@shawneecc.edu

BLAKELY, Edie ... 360-992-2239.. 502 E
eblakely@clark.edu

BLAKELY, Robert ... 334-727-8540...... 8 A
rblakely@mytu.tuskegee.edu

BLAKELY, Robert ... 602-212-0501.... 11 N

BLAKELY, Zeledith ... 252-638-1587.. 349 B
blakelyz@cravencc.edu

BLAKEMAN, Donald, L ... 502-863-8091.. 188 I
don_blakeman@georgetowncollege.edu

BLAKEMORE, Jerry, D ... 815-753-1000.. 150 A
jblakemore@niu.edu

BLAKEMORE, Patricia ... 401-739-5000.. 425 C
pblakemore@neit.edu

BLAKENEY, Erin ... 425-352-8307.. 501 J
eblakeney@cascadia.edu

BLAKESLEE, Amber ... 707-826-5702.... 34 F
amber.blakeslee@humboldt.edu

BLAKESLEE, James ... 828-328-7244.. 345 H
james.blakeslee@ellucian.com

BLAKESLEE, Sarah ... 530-898-5029.... 32 C
sblakeslee@csuchico.edu

BLAKEY, Linda ... 734-973-3536.. 242 G
blakey@wccnet.edu

BLAKLEY, Jackie ... 864-646-1305.. 433 C
jblakle1@tctc.edu

BLAKLEY, Linda ... 312-362-7734.. 139 C
lblakley@depaul.edu

BLAKLEY, Ramon ... 478-445-1283.. 121 A
ramon.blakley@gcsu.edu

BLALARK, Frank ... 919-684-2813.. 343 J
registrar@duke.edu

BLALOCK, Jennifer ... 972-985-9717.. 455 A
jblalock@collin.edu

BLALOCK, III, W. Ben ... 307-766-6300.. 527 B
bblalock@uwyo.edu

BLANCHARD, Andrew ... 972-883-6706.. 476 C
ablanch@utdallas.edu

BLANCHARD, Catherine .. 409-880-8375.. 471 A
catherine.blanchard@lamar.edu

BLANCHARD, Catherine .. 409-880-8355.. 470 H
catherine.blanchard@lamar.edu

BLANCHARD, Gina, A ... 740-392-6868.. 373 D
gina.blanchard@mvnu.edu

BLANCHARD, Gordon ... 847-578-3232.. 153 A
gordon.blanchard@rosalindfranklin.edu

BLANCHARD, Jon, A ... 207-768-2795.. 203 L
jblanch@nmcc.edu

BLANCHARD, Joyce ... 207-621-3403.. 204 I
joyceb@maine.edu

BLANCHARD, Loren, J ... 562-951-4710.... 31 H
lblanchard@calstate.edu

BLANCHARD, Marsha, L . 573-888-0513.. 272 B
mblanchard@semo.edu

BLANCHARD, Myrtho ... 202-274-5946.... 94 B
mblanchard@udc.edu

BLANCHARD, Sarah ... 860-231-5355.... 90 B
sblanchard@usj.edu

BLANCHARD, Scott ... 802-322-1640.. 483 H
scott.blanchard@goddard.edu

BLANCHARD, Susan ... 804-204-1218.. 487 D
registrar@btsr.edu

BLANCHET, Robert, C ... 315-684-6046.. 336 B
blanchrc@morrisville.edu

BLANCHETT, Russell ... 972-882-7520.. 468 D
russell.blanchett@tamuc.edu

BLANCHETT, Wanda, J ... 848-932-0747.. 296 B
wanda.blanchett@gse.rutgers.edu

BLANCHETTE, Nick ... 715-675-3331.. 524 D
blanchet@ntc.edu

BLANCHIER, Andree ... 530-242-7510.... 64 D
ablanchier@shastacollege.edu

BLANCO, Mark, E ... 914-337-9300.. 311 F
mark.blanco@concordia-ny.edu

BLANCO, Michael ... 503-883-2616.. 392 B
mblanco@linfield.edu

BLANCO MASIAS, Eva ... 408-554-4700.... 63 E
eblanco@scu.edu

BLAND, Amanda ... 540-234-9261.. 496 F

BLAND, Bartholomew, F .. 718-960-8731.. 308 B
bartholomew.bland@lehman.cuny.edu

BLAND, Byron ... 650-433-3814.... 56 D
bbland@paloaltou.edu

BLAND, Carmen ... 360-676-2772.. 505 C
cbland@nwic.edu

BLAND, Constance ... 662-254-3800.. 260 A
cgbland@mvsu.edu

BLAND, Dorothy ... 940-367-4927.. 475 A
dorothy.bland@unt.edu

BLAND, Glenda ... 256-378-2004...... 2 G
gbland@cacc.edu

BLAND, James ... 937-393-3431.. 377 F
jbland@sscc.edu

BLAND, Janet, L ... 740-376-4741.. 372 A
janet.bland@marietta.edu

BLAND, Jeanie ... 314-921-9290.. 274 F
jbland@ugst.edu

BLAND, John, D ... 704-687-5822.. 358 A
jdbland@uncc.edu

BLAND, Marissa ... 816-415-5938.. 275 F
blandm@william.jewell.edu

BLAND, Terry ... 662-862-8282.. 258 C
tgbland@iccms.edu

BLAND, Wilson, T ... 202-806-6131.... 93 A
wtbland@howard.edu

BLANDFORD, David, K ... 989-463-7147.. 230 F
blandford@alma.edu

BLANDFORD, Holly, R ... 217-544-6464.. 153 G
holly.blandford@stjohnscollegespringfield.edu

BLANDFORD, Jonathan, W ... 502-272-7404.. 187 A
jblandford@bellarmine.edu

BLANDING, Bruce ... 731-424-3520.. 446 C
bblanding@jscc.edu

BLANDON, Darwin ... 423-266-4574.. 443 M
dblandon@richmont.edu

BLANEY, Diana ... 219-464-7867.. 168 F
diana.blaney@valpo.edu

BLANK, Dave, L ... 336-278-6705.. 344 D
dblank@elon.edu

BLANK, James ... 330-672-3614.. 370 I
jblank@kent.edu

BLANK, Michelle ... 419-783-2490.. 368 A
mblank@defiance.edu

BLANK, Rebecca ... 608-262-9946.. 519 K
chancellor@news.wisc.edu

BLANKE, Raymond ... 405-733-7306.. 387 I
rblanke@rose.edu

BLANKENBAKER, Zarina .. 972-238-6025.. 456 H
zblankenbaker@dcccd.edu

BLANKENBUEHLER, Carla ... 304-205-6706.. 511 M
carla.blankenbuehler@bridgevalley.edu

BLANKENHEIM, Kim ... 319-368-6464.. 175 D
kblankenheim@mtmercy.edu

BLANKENHORN, Stacie ... 503-359-1082.. 394 C
bookstore@pacificu.edu

BLANKENSHIP, Bruce, A . 304-457-6340.. 510 B
blankenshipba@ab.edu

BLANKENSHIP, Bruce, A . 304-457-6213.. 510 B
blankenshipba@ab.edu

BLANKENSHIP, Bryan, P . 859-858-2228.. 186 I

BLANKENSHIP, Daniel ... 309-467-6301.. 140 E
dblankenship@eureka.edu

BLANKENSHIP, Karen ... 281-476-1850.. 464 J
karen.blankenship@sjcd.edu

BLANKENSHIP, Kevin ... 615-230-3428.. 447 C
kevin.blankenship@volstate.edu

BLANKENSHIP, Mark, V .. 859-280-1250.. 191 D
mblankenship@lextheo.edu

BLANKENSHIP, Mike ... 601-605-3315.. 258 B
mblankenship@holmescc.edu

BLANKENSHIP, Paul ... 859-256-3100.. 188 M
paul.blankenship@kctcs.edu

BLANKENSHIP, Ruth ... 276-326-4556.. 487 F
rblankenship@bluefield.edu

BLANKENSHIP, Ruth ... 276-326-4556.. 487 F
lrblankenship@bluefield.edu

BLANKENSHIP, Tim ... 404-471-5465.. 115 J
tblankenship@agnesscott.edu

BLANKENSHIP, Vince ... 903-923-2002.. 457 G
vblankenship@etbu.edu

BLANKINSHIP, Blair ... 410-837-5714.. 213 C
bblankinship@ubalt.edu

BLANKMEYER, Bonnie, L 210-567-2691.. 477 D
blankmeyer@uthscsa.edu

BLANKS, Janet ... 561-297-3288.. 110 K
blanks@fau.edu

BLANKSON, Joana ... 404-297-9522.. 122 A
blanksonj@gptc.edu

BLANSETT, Dewey ... 662-329-7396.. 259 E
dblansett@oe.muw.edu

BLANTON, Angela ... 412-268-4925.. 400 D
ablanton@andrew.cmu.edu

BLANTON, Carmen ... 910-755-7332.. 347 H
blantonc@brunswickcc.edu

BLANTON, James ... 205-929-6317...... 5 D
jblanton@lawsonstate.edu

BLANTON, Jason ... 606-783-9361.. 191 H
j.blanton@moreheadstate.edu

BLANTON, Jay, D ... 859-257-3303.. 193 G
jay.blanton@uky.edu

BLANTON, Julie ... 620-665-3510.. 181 I

BLANTON, Patricia, L ... 843-792-3811.. 431 A
blanton@musc.edu

BLANTON, Ryan ... 918-463-2931.. 383 F
ryan.blanton@connorsstate.edu

BLANTON, Sharon ... 808-543-8000.. 130 H
sblanton@hpu.edu

BLANTON, Sharon ... 609-771-3353.. 290 F
blantons@tcnj.edu

BLAPPERT, Gerald ... 985-732-6640.. 196 G

BLASCHKE, Jayme, L ... 512-245-2925.. 471 F
jb71@txstate.edu

BLASE, Frances ... 610-896-1014.. 405 I
fblase@haverford.edu

BLASE, Kristen ... 603-428-2226.. 287 C
kblase@nec.edu

BLASIC, Michael ... 607-735-1830.. 313 F
mblasic@elmira.edu

BLASIG, Jerry, A ... 402-557-7075.. 278 I
jerry.blasig@bellevue.edu

BLASINGAME, David, T ... 314-935-5850.. 274 N
david_blasingame@wustl.edu

BLASINI, Ivelisse ... 787-850-9341.. 538 B
ivelisse.blasini@upr.edu

BLASS, Tammy ... 323-226-6511.... 50 F
tblass@dhs.lacounty.gov

BLASSINGAME, Susan ... 806-720-7602.. 461 C
susan.blassingame@lcu.edu

BLASTING, Ralph ... 716-673-3174.. 331 D
ralph.blasting@fredonia.edu

BLASZAK, Julie ... 616-632-2945.. 231 A
jab008@aquinas.edu

BLASZKOWSKI, Remek ... 561-732-4424.. 108 F
rblaszkowski@svdp.edu

BLATCHFORD, Alicia ... 305-284-5155.. 114 H
awb49@miami.edu

BLATCHLEY, Richard, L ... 651-631-5321.. 256 A
rlblatchley@unwsp.edu

BLATTNER, Alan ... 919-962-2211.. 357 D
allan_blattner@unc.edu

BLATTNER, Nancy ... 973-618-3217.. 290 A
nblattner@caldwell.edu

BLAU, Diane ... 248-476-1122.. 237 H
dblau@mispp.edu

BLAU, Phil ... 740-351-3137.. 377 C
pblau@shawnee.edu

BLAUSTEIN, Marilyn, H ... 413-545-0941.. 220 F
blaustein@oirp.umass.edu

BOATWRIGHT, Betty, R ... 803-536-8556.. 432 E
bboatwright@scsu.edu
BOATWRIGHT, Cassie ..... 850-484-1778.. 106 H
cboatwright@pensacolastate.edu
BOATWRIGHT, Kathi .... 276-944-6541.. 489 I
kboatwright@ehc.edu
BOATWRIGHT, Tamara .... 678-359-5259.. 122 E
tamarab@gordonstate.edu
BOAZ, Matt .... 937-775-3207.. 381 H
matthew.boaz@wright.edu
BOB-PENNYPACKER,
Beaulah .... 928-524-7326.... 15 J
beaulah.bob-pennypacker@npc.edu
BOBAK, Karen, A .... 315-568-3864.. 323 A
kbobak@nycc.edu
BOBART, David .... 410-837-4331.. 213 C
dbobart@ubalt.edu
BOBB, June .... 718-997-5780.. 309 D
june.bobb@qc.cuny.edu
BOBBETT, Tricia .... 417-667-8181.. 264 A
tbobbett@cottey.edu
BOBBIN, Michael, J .... 904-256-7055.. 103 D
mbobbin@ju.edu
BOBBIN, Steffi .... 617-559-8640.. 219 E
sbobbin@hebrewcollege.edu
BOBBITT, Donald, R .... 501-686-2505.... 22 H
dbobbitt@uasys.edu
BOBBITT, Kathy .... 307-766-2116.. 527 B
bobbitt1@uwyo.edu
BOBER, Delia .... 216-987-5137.. 367 E
delia.bober@tri-c.edu
BOBICH, Marni .... 909-607-8533.... 57 H
marni_bobich@pitzer.edu
BOBICK, Aaron, F .... 314-935-6350.. 274 N
afb@wustl.edu
BOBINSKI, Michael .... 404-894-5411.. 121 D
mbobinski@athletics.gatech.edu
BOBO, David .... 205-853-1200...... 5 B
dbobo@jeffstateonline.com
BOBO, Jill .... 870-777-5722.... 24 A
jill.bobo@uacch.edu
BOBO, Lori .... 601-925-3252.. 259 A
lbobo@mc.edu
BOBST, Karen .... 541-485-1780.. 393 A
karenbobst@newhope.edu
BOCANEGRA, Melanie ..... 310-434-3992.... 63 F
bocanegra_melanie@smc.edu
BOCCALANDRO, Maria .... 972-860-8051.. 456 C
mboccalandro@dcccd.edu
BOCCHICCHIO, Rebecca .. 916-660-8000.... 64 F
rbocchicchio@sierracollege.edu
BOCCHINFUSO-COHEN,
Rita .... 559-278-2381.... 32 F
ritab@csufresno.edu
BOCIAN, Terry, M .... 616-632-2475.. 231 A
bociater@aquinas.edu
BOCK, Darrell, L .... 214-887-5251.. 457 C
dbock@dts.edu
BOCK, Jim .... 610-328-8529.. 419 I
jbock1@swarthmore.edu
BOCK, Mike .... 260-665-4878.. 167 E
bockm@trine.edu
BOCK, Wendy .... 309-796-5180.. 135 I
bockw@bhc.edu
BOCKSTEIN, Mindy .... 212-393-6340.. 308 E
mbockstein@jjay.cuny.edu
BOCZER, Amy .... 203-254-4000.... 87 G
aboczer@fairfield.edu
BODDIE-FORBES,
Rasheda .... 662-325-2033.. 259 D
rboddie-forbes@saffairs.msstate.edu
BODDIE-LAVAN, Jeanine . 334-244-3610...... 2 A
jblavan@aum.edu
BODE, Brian .... 816-584-6432.. 270 D
brian.bode@park.edu
BODE, Gerhard .... 314-505-7103.. 263 I
bodeg@csl.edu
BODE, Lori .... 636-949-4925.. 266 J
lbode@lindenwood.edu
BODE, Robert .... 715-425-3141.. 521 B
robert.bode@uwrf.edu
BODEGA, María .... 787-164-1912.. 534 D
maria_dolores_bodega_@intersg.edu
BODEN, Alison .... 609-258-6244.. 294 D
aboden@princeton.edu
BODEN, Janet .... 773-256-0744.. 147 A
jboden@lstc.edu
BODEN, Michael .... 845-431-8952.. 312 G
michael.boden@sunydutchess.edu
BODIN, Susan .... 312-915-7454.. 146 G
sbodin@luc.edu
BODINE, Kari .... 701-845-7534.. 361 B
kari.bodine@vcsu.edu
BODINE, Kasey .... 706-385-1000.. 126 A
kasey.bodine@point.edu
BODINE AL-SHARIF,
Mary .... 405-682-1611.. 385 D
mary.bodineal-sharif@occc.edu
BODMER, Brad, R .... 518-783-2315.. 330 E
BODNAR, Molly .... 719-389-6351.... 77 J
molly.bodnar@coloradocollege.edu
BODNAR, Patrick .... 972-438-6932.. 463 F
pbodnar@parker.edu
BODNAR, Richard .... 718-997-5191.. 309 D
richard.bodnar@qc.edu
BODONI, June .... 978-867-4217.. 219 A
june.bodoni@gordon.edu
BODRATO, Kelli .... 718-405-3234.. 310 H
kelli.bodrato@mountsaintvincent.edu
BODRATTI, Robert .... 518-828-4181.. 311 D
bodratti@sunycgcc.edu
BODRI, Michael .... 706-864-1958.. 128 F
michael.bodri@ung.edu
BODUR, Niyazi .... 516-686-7724.. 323 G
nbodur@nyit.edu
BODVARSSON, Orn .... 916-278-6504.... 34 B
obbodvarsson@csus.edu
BODWIN, Jeffrey .... 218-477-5892.. 250 F
jeffrey.bodwin@mnstate.edu
BOE, Eugene .... 218-739-3375.. 247 H
eboe@lbs.edu
BOE, Susan .... 503-255-0332.. 392 G
sboe@multnomah.edu
BOECK, Mark .... 515-294-8959.. 169 G
mboeck@foundation.iastate.edu
BOECKENSTEDT, Jon .... 312-362-7143.. 139 C
jboecken@depaul.edu
BOECKERMANN,
Gabriele .... 513-569-1550.. 366 D
gabriele.boeckermann@cincinnatistate.edu
BOECKERS, Alice .... 920-832-6525.. 517 E
alice.o.boeckers@lawrence.edu
BOECKMAN, Linda, A ...... 717-262-2006.. 424 A
linda.boeckman@wilson.edu
BOEDEKER, Katrina, P ..... 260-399-7700.. 168 D
kboedeker@sf.edu
BOEDER, John, C .... 507-354-8221.. 247 J
boederjc@mlc-wels.edu
BOEGEL, Tom .... 415-239-3360.... 38 E
tboegel@ccsf.edu
BOEH, William, S .... 409-772-9803.. 478 A
wsboeh@utmb.edu
BOEHLER, Susan .... 217-732-3155.. 146 B
sboehler@lincolncollege.edu
BOEHM, Beth, A .... 502-852-3975.. 194 A
baboeh01@louisville.edu
BOEHM, Christopher .... 205-552-1222...... 3 B
chris.boehm@ecacolleges.com
BOEHM, J. J .... 989-964-4055.. 240 F
jjboehm@svsu.edu
BOEHM, Leslie .... 513-618-1925.. 366 C
lboehm@ccms.edu
BOEHM, Michael .... 574-284-4610.. 167 A
mboehm@saintmarys.edu
BOEHM, Michael, J .... 614-292-5881.. 375 A
boehm.1@osu.edu
BOEHM, Pamela .... 254-659-7501.. 458 K
pboehm@hillcollege.edu
BOEHM-DAVIS, Deborah . 703-993-8715.. 490 B
dbdavis@gmu.edu
BOEHMAN, Joseph, R ..... 804-289-8000.. 495 G
jboehman@richmond.edu
BOEHME, Michael, J .... 320-234-8509.. 251 G
mike.boehme@ridgewater.edu
BOEHMER, Ann .... 636-584-6679.. 264 M
ann.boehmer@eastcentral.edu
BOEHMER, Brian .... 740-364-9535.. 365 D
bboehmer@newark.ohio-state.edu
BOEHMER, Robert, G ...... 478-289-2027.. 120 C
bboehmer@ega.edu
BOEHMLER, Brook, S ...... 641-422-4212.. 175 E
boehmbro@niacc.edu
BOEHNE, Cheryl .... 618-545-3184.. 144 D
cboehne@kaskaskia.edu
BOEHNE, Rhonda .... 618-545-3022.. 144 D
rboehne@kaskaskia.edu
BOEKER, Cathy .... 979-830-4455.. 452 J
cboeker@blinn.edu
BOELCKE, Renee, E .... 269-337-7248.. 235 H
renee.boelcke@kzoo.edu
BOELE, Erin .... 599-278-2345.... 32 F
eboele@csufresno.edu
BOENDER, Tim .... 605-995-2901.. 435 F
tiboende@dwu.edu
BOENIG, Catrina .... 337-475-5145.. 200 H
cboenig@mcneese.edu
BOENIG, Tobin, R .... 409-747-8702.. 478 A
trboenig@utmb.edu
BOENINGER, Candace ..... 740-593-4100.. 375 H
boeningc@ohio.edu
BOER, Keri .... 828-669-8012.. 346 M
kboer@montreat.edu
BOERA,
Tanja Hinterstoisser ...... 802-651-5896.. 483 F
thinterstoisser@champlain.edu
BOERBOOM, Chris .... 701-231-7867.. 361 A
chris.boerboom@ndsu.edu
BOERGERMANN, Gary ..... 918-343-7625.. 387 F
gboergermann@rsu.edu
BOERLAGE,
Andrew (Pete) .... 831-656-3037.. 528 D
aboerlage@nps.edu
BOERNER, Anne .... 503-297-5544.. 393 C
aboerner@ocac.edu
BOERNER, Barbara, B ...... 828-884-8319.. 342 C
boernerb@brevard.edu
BOERNER, William .... 716-673-3358.. 331 D
william.boerner@fredonia.edu
BOERS, Barbara .... 616-526-6127.. 232 A
brb29@calvin.edu
BOERSMA, Paul, H .... 616-395-7145.. 235 F
boersma@hope.edu
BOERST, Connie, J .... 920-433-6622.. 515 F
connie.boerst@bellincollege.edu
BOERWINKLE, Eric .... 713-500-9050.. 477 C
eric.boerwinkle@uth.tmc.edu
BOESCH, Donald .... 410-228-9250.. 212 A
BOESCH, Ron .... 563-884-5567.. 176 C
ron.boesch@palmer.edu
BOESEL, Terry .... 714-997-6818.... 37 F
boesel@chapman.edu
BOEVE, Jim .... 402-461-7468.. 280 D
jboeve@hastings.edu
BOEVE, Traci .... 402-461-7789.. 280 D
tboeve@hastings.edu
BOEVINGLOH, Linda .... 636-481-3488.. 266 C
lboeving@jeffco.edu
BOFFI, William .... 508-213-2428.. 227 A
william.boffi@nichols.edu
BOGAGE, Alan .... 410-386-8339.. 206 I
abogage@carrollcc.edu
BOGAN, Jenny, G .... 864-833-8700.. 432 B
jgbogan@presby.edu
BOGAN, Jeremy .... 518-454-5155.. 311 B
boganj@strose.edu
BOGAN, Kim .... 619-849-2481.... 57 M
kimbogan@pointloma.edu
BOGARD, Karen .... 870-543-5907.... 22 E
kbogard@seark.edu
BOGARD, Michele, K .... 402-280-2775.. 279 H
bogard@creighton.edu
BOGART, Denise .... 229-333-5709.. 129 G
dbogart@valdosta.edu
BOGART, Marti, S .... 630-637-5355.. 149 H
msbogart@noctrl.edu
BOGART, William, T .... 865-981-8101.. 441 H
tom.bogart@maryvillecollege.edu
BOGATSKI, Anatole .... 510-780-4500.... 48 J
abogatski@lifewest.edu
BOGDALEK, Steven, J ...... 248-204-3925.. 237 B
sbogdalek@ltu.edu
BOGDAN, Sharon .... 410-532-5332.. 210 B
sbogdan@ndm.edu
BOGDANOV, Anna .... 215-728-4177.. 412 B
anna.bogdanov@jevs.org
BOGEN, David .... 410-669-9200.. 209 B
dbogen@mica.edu
BOGEN, Janice .... 215-503-4335.. 420 E
janice.bogen@jefferson.edu
BOGEN, Janice, M .... 215-503-4335.. 420 E
janice.bogen@jefferson.edu
BOGER-HAWKINS,
Caitlin .... 860-738-6441.... 87 A
cboger-hawkins@nwcc.edu
BOGERT, Brian .... 570-408-4015.. 423 G
brian.bogert@wilkes.edu
BOGERTMAN, Krista .... 617-745-3895.. 218 A
krista.bogertman@enc.edu
BOGGAN, Jeff .... 678-717-3570.. 128 F
jeff.boggan@ung.edu
BOGGAN, Laura, K .... 423-652-4707.. 440 J
lkboggan@king.edu
BOGGESS, Kendra .... 304-384-5224.. 513 A
president@concord.edu
BOGGIE, Mark .... 520-515-5451.... 12 L
boggiem@cochise.edu
BOGGIO, Pamela, J .... 508-213-2483.. 227 A
pamela.boggio@nichols.edu
BOGGS, Beverly .... 931-221-6540.. 444 E
boggsb@apsu.edu
BOGGS, Brad .... 662-620-5302.. 258 C
bdboggs@iccms.edu
BOGGS, Gretchen, M .... 410-250-1088.. 212 B
contedoc@ezy.net
BOGGS, John .... 281-998-6150.. 465 B
john.boggs@sjcd.edu
BOGGS, Paul, R .... 903-233-3981.. 460 J
paulboggs@letu.edu
BOGGS, Rainie .... 859-253-3637.. 188 G
rainie.boggs@frontier.edu
BOGGS, Sherri .... 419-251-1865.. 372 C
sherri.boggs@mercycollege.edu
BOGH, Wayne .... 909-389-3309.... 60 B
wbogh@craftonhills.edu
BOGHOSSIAN, Fikru .... 443-885-3160.. 209 F
fikru.boghossian@morgan.edu
BOGLE, Barry, J .... 915-831-7116.. 457 H
bbogle@epcc.edu
BOGLE, Brittany .... 408-498-5137.... 39 H
bbogle@cogswell.edu
BOGLE, Christy .... 704-991-0370.. 353 E
cbogle9678@stanly.edu
BOGLE, Yvonne .... 413-782-1594.. 229 E
yvonne.bogle@wne.edu
BOGLEY, John, W .... 509-527-5979.. 509 G
bogleyj@whitman.edu
BOGLIN, Amber .... 404-527-4540.. 118 F
ahamilton@carver.edu
BOGNA, Gina .... 661-362-3376.... 40 A
gina.bogna@canyons.edu
BOGNER, Drew .... 516-323-3200.. 321 H
dbogner@molloy.edu
BOGOMILSKY, Moshe ...... 718-434-0784.. 306 J
BOGOSIAN, Deborah .... 212-229-5600.. 322 E
deborah.bogosian@newschool.edu
BOGUE, Michelle .... 269-782-1486.. 241 C
mbogue@swmich.edu
BOHACH, Gregory .... 662-325-3006.. 259 D
gbohach@dafvm.msstate.edu
BOHACZ, Candy .... 269-467-9945.. 234 B
cbohacz@glenoaks.edu
BOHAM, Kenneth, A .... 828-726-2211.. 347 I
kboham@cccti.edu
BOHAM, Sandra .... 406-275-4974.. 278 E
sandra_boham@skc.edu
BOHAN, David .... 973-378-9801.. 297 A
david.bohan@shu.edu
BOHANNON, Betsy .... 859-622-1500.. 188 F
betsy.bohannon@eku.edu
BOHANNON, Vicki .... 703-812-4757.. 491 B
vbohannon@leland.edu
BOHASKA, Chris .... 410-225-2490.. 209 B
cbohaska@mica.edu
BOHL, Kyle .... 616-538-2330.. 234 D
kbohl@gbcol.edu
BOHLANDER, Brad .... 919-515-2191.. 357 B
BOHLEKE, Briant .... 717-334-6286.. 409 C
bbohleke@ltsg.edu
BOHLEKE,
Henry "Chuck" .... 708-456-0300.. 156 C
henrybohleke@triton.edu
BOHLEN, Greg .... 303-273-3333.... 78 M
gbohlen@imines.edu
BOHLENDER, Kristi .... 970-491-6533.... 78 Q
kristi.bohlender@colostate.edu
BOHM, Tiffany .... 913-288-7274.. 182 C
tbohm@kckcc.edu
BOHMAN, Andreas .... 509-963-2499.. 501 K
bohmana@cwu.edu
BOHMAN, Bob .... 813-393-3675.. 127 D
bbohman@southuniversity.edu
BOHN, Andrea .... 610-409-3562.. 422 D
abohn@ursinus.edu
BOHN, Bill .... 541-506-6090.. 390 I
bbohn@cgcc.edu
BOHN, Crystal, D .... 309-341-7200.. 145 A
cdbohn@knox.edu
BOHN, Michael .... 513-556-0626.. 379 A
bearcad@ucmail.uc.edu
BOHN, Nicole .... 415-405-3583.... 35 B
nbohn@sfsu.edu
BOHNENBLUST, Delyna .. 620-421-6700.. 182 G
delynab@labette.edu
BOHNET, Sandra .... 269-488-4409.. 235 I
sbohnet@kvcc.edu
BOHNETT, Sally .... 419-251-1866.. 372 C
sally.bohnett@mercycollege.edu
BOHNSACK, Jennifer .... 602-331-7500.... 11 K
jbohnsack@aii.edu
BOHNY, David .... 973-618-3440.. 290 A
dbohny@caldwell.edu
BOHREN, Karen .... 231-591-2607.. 233 L
karenbohren@ferris.edu
BOHRER, Joseph, S .... 610-330-3161.. 407 C
bohrerj@lafayette.edu
BOHRER, Monty .... 605-995-2997.. 435 F
mobohrer@dwu.edu
BOHRER, Robert, E .... 717-337-6823.. 404 C
rbohrer@gettysburg.edu
BOHRNSTEDT, Jennifer ..... 281-649-3321.. 458 L
jbohrnstedt@hbu.edu
BOICE, Daniel .... 870-460-1080.... 23 D
boice@uamont.edu
BOICE, Nor .... 253-752-2020.. 503 H
nboice@faithseminary.edu
BOICE-PARDEE, Heath ...... 585-475-2268.. 327 E
hbpvsa@rit.edu
BOIES, Brandy .... 540-868-7161.. 497 E
bboies@lfcc.edu
BOIES, Chris .... 540-868-7129.. 497 E
cboies@lfcc.edu
BOIKE, Allan .... 216-916-7468.. 370 I
aboike1@kent.edu
BOILINI, Laura, L .... 386-312-4199.. 108 B
lauraboilini@sjrstate.edu
BOISE, Craig, M .... 315-443-3678.. 337 A
cmboise@law.syr.edu
BOISEN, Beth .... 715-232-1695.. 521 D
boisenb@uwstout.edu
BOISJOLY, Russell, P ...... 716-673-4813.. 331 D
russell.boisjoly@fredonia.edu
BOISSELLE, Juliet .... 315-781-3952.. 316 C
jhboiselle@hws.edu

BOISSELLE, Vincent 315-781-3549 316 C
boisselle@hws.edu
BOISSONEAULT, Susan 508-678-2811 223 A
susan.boissoneault@bristolcc.edu
BOISVERT, Craig 304-647-6363 514 A
cboisvert@osteo.wvsom.edu
BOITNOTT, Tina 903-886-5110 468 D
tina.boitnott@tamuc.edu
BOJONCA, Victoria 317-299-0333 167 D
victoria.bojonca@tcmi.org
BOKOSKI, Leslie 610-647-4400 406 B
lbokoski@immaculata.edu
BOKSAN, George 610-861-1421 411 B
boksang@moravian.edu
BOKTOR, Monir 949-794-9090 66 H
mboktor@stanbridge.edu
BOLA, William 207-206-2365 205 F
wbola@une.edu
BOLA, William 207-602-2365 205 F
wbola@une.edu
BOLAND, Carolyn 513-244-4717 373 C
carolyn.boland@msj.edu
BOLAND, Kristine 419-783-2469 368 A
kboland@defiance.edu
BOLAND, Mary, G 808-956-8522 131 F
mgboland@hawaii.edu
BOLAND, Mary Kate 610-647-4400 406 B
mboland@immaculata.edu
BOLAND-CHASE, Ann 570-961-4728 409 H
chase@marywood.edu
BOLANOS, Andelys 920-923-7148 517 H
abolanos@marianuniversity.edu
BOLAS, Jon 253-680-7000 501 E
jbolas@bates.ctc.edu
BOLDEN, Errol 410-951-3542 212 E
ebolden@coppin.edu
BOLDMAN, Denise 937-484-1243 380 E
dboldman@urbana.edu
BOLDMAN, Rachel 386-822-8900 113 B
rboldman@stetson.edu
BOLDREY, Penny 989-358-7297 230 G
boldreyp@alpenacc.edu
BOLDT, Bill 503-725-5037 394 G
BOLDT, Deborah 505-428-1704 301 K
deborah.boldt@sfcc.edu
BOLDUC, Michael, C 561-237-7180 104 O
mbolduc@lynn.edu
BOLE, John 406-377-9416 276 D
jbole@dawson.edu
BOLEK, Catherine 410-651-6714 212 B
csbolek@umes.edu
BOLENBAUGH, Peter 406-657-1106 278 D
peter.bolenbaugh@rocky.edu
BOLERATZ, David 606-693-5000 191 A
dboleratz@kmbc.edu
BOLERATZ, Jonathan 814-332-5206 397 A
jboleratz@allegheny.edu
BOLES, Jessica 580-559-5539 383 H
jboles@ecok.edu
BOLES, Susan 970-824-1151 78 J
susan.boles@cncc.edu
BOLEY, Paula 419-995-8218 370 G
boley.p@rhodesstate.edu
BOLGER, Eric 417-690-2278 263 E
bolger@cofo.edu
BOLIN, Alexis 408-848-4742 44 I
0282mgr@fheg.follett.com
BOLIN, Mark 256-352-8102 9 G
mark.bolin@wallacestate.edu
BOLIN, Mary, C 859-257-8701 193 G
marychandler.bolin@uky.edu
BOLING, Cindy 405-974-2547 388 L
cboling@uco.edu
BOLISH, Jennifer 651-905-3428 255 B
jbolish@browncollege.edu
BOLL, Julie 217-228-5432 151 F
bollju@quincy.edu
BOLLANT, Gwen 423-775-6596 443 H
gbollant@ogs.edu
BOLLENBACHER, Brian 773-252-6464 152 B
brian.bollenbacher@resu.edu
BOLLHEIMER, Meredith 814-824-3363 410 H
mbollheimer@mercyhurst.edu
BOLLIER, John, H 203-432-6754 90 D
john.bollier@yale.edu
BOLLING, Phyllis 973-596-3420 293 D
phyllis.bolling@njit.edu
BOLLINGER, Bruce 701-231-6177 361 A
bruce.bollinger@ndsu.edu
BOLLINGER, Larry 617-745-3000 218 A
larry.bollinger@enc.edu
BOLLINGER, Lee, C 212-854-9970 311 E
bollinger@columbia.edu
BOLLINGER, Mary 603-888-1311 287 F
mbollinger@rivier.edu
BOLLMAN, Dan 517-355-3366 237 I
dbollman@ipf.msu.edu
BOLLMAN-DALANSKY,
Terri, L 814-641-3424 406 F
bollmat@juniata.edu
BOLLMANN, Janice, A 314-286-4805 270 G
jabollmann@ranken.edu
BOLMAN, Ann 605-718-2401 438 B
ann.bolman@wdt.edu
BOLMAN, Dave 602-383-8228 17 H
dbolman@uat.edu
BOLOGNA, Brynn 816-584-6714 270 D
brynn.bologna@park.edu
BOLOGNONE,
John (Buddy) 213-624-1200 43 J
bbolognone@fidm.edu
BOLSAKOV, Vlad 858-653-6740 47 G
vbolsakov@jpcatholic.com
BOLSINGER, Tod 626-304-3711 44 G
bolsinger@fuller.edu
BOLSTER, Jeff 619-849-2480 57 M
jeffbolster@pointloma.edu
BOLT, Barb 814-868-9900 403 D
barbb@erieit.edu
BOLT, Barbara 814-864-6666 404 E
barbarab@glit.edu
BOLT, Corrine 606-218-5327 194 C
corrinebolt@upike.edu
BOLT, Dave 559-925-3222 74 E
davebolt@whccd.edu
BOLT, Gary 630-844-6878 135 E
gbolt@aurora.edu
BOLT, Susan 574-284-4556 167 A
sbolt@saintmarys.edu
BOLT, Tracy, L 443-334-2270 211 A
tbolt@stevenson.edu
BOLTON, David 417-328-1538 272 C
dbolton@sbuniv.edu
BOLTON, Denny, G 336-841-9202 345 A
ebolton@highpoint.edu
BOLTON, G. Allen 205-934-5493 8 E
BOLTON, Harry 707-654-1192 33 D
hbolton@csum.edu
BOLTON, Janice 770-962-7580 123 D
jbolton@gwinnetttech.edu
BOLTON, Lance 719-502-2200 82 B
lance.bolton@ppcc.edu
BOLTON, Leigha 251-626-3303 8 B
lbolton@ussa.edu
BOLTON, Meghann 512-313-3000 455 F
meghann.bolton@concordia.edu
BOLTON, Melanie 256-378-4900 2 G
mbolton@cacc.edu
BOLTON, Robert, D 517-750-1200 241 E
rbolton@arbor.edu
BOLTON, Sarah 330-263-2311 367 A
sbolton@wooster.edu
BOLTON, Shantay 334-727-8011 8 A
BOLTON, Tonya, D 870-759-4130 24 J
tbolton@wbcoll.edu
BOLTZ, Fran 716-286-8751 324 E
fboltz@niagara.edu
BOLYAI, Stephen 973-720-2233 298 G
bolyais@wpunj.edu
BOLYARD, Adrienne, M 206-726-5021 503 B
abolyard@cornish.edu
BOLYARD, Brian 304-205-6767 511 M
brian.bolyard@bridgevalley.edu
BOLYARD, Melissa 404-727-0692 120 E
mbolyar@emory.edu
BOMAR, Charles 715-232-4055 521 D
bomarc@uwstout.edu
BOMBA, Jody, L 909-593-3511 71 B
jodybomba@laverne.edu
BOMER, Dee 615-687-6907 438 C
dbomer@abcnash.edu
BOMGAARS, Deb 712-722-6689 171 J
deb.bomgaars@dordt.edu
BOMOTTI, Gerry 702-895-3571 284 L
gerry.bomotti@unlv.edu
BONA, Dennis 218-793-2465 251 C
dennis.bona@northlandcollege.edu
BONACCORSO, Roberto 425-235-2356 506 F
rbonaccorso@rtc.edu
BONACK, Anne, E 715-365-4415 524 C
abonack@nicoletcollege.edu
BONADIE, Heidi 909-599-5433 48 K
hbonadie@lifepacific.edu
BONAHUE, Edward 352-381-3822 109 C
ed.bonahue@sfcollege.edu
BONANNO, Joseph 812-855-4440 162 F
jbonanno@indiana.edu
BONANNO, Steve, C 304-293-6967 514 C
steve.bonanno@mail.wvu.edu
BONAPARTE, Donna 781-239-6434 214 G
dbonaparte@babson.edu
BONAPARTE, Greta 410-644-6400 206 E
BONATO, Frederick 973-655-4280 293 A
bonatof@mail.montclair.edu
BONAVIST, Kathleen 603-526-3729 285 L
kathleen.bonavist@colby-sawyer.edu
BONCUORE, Cheryl 847-574-5159 145 C
cboncuore@lfgsm.edu
BOND, Alicia 570-408-6024 423 G
alicia.bond@wilkes.edu
BOND, Bill, E 406-756-3818 276 E
bbond@fvcc.edu
BOND, Bradley 815-753-9403 150 A
bbond@niu.edu
BOND, Cindy, R 208-732-6454 133 E
cbond@csi.edu
BOND, Dawn 512-476-2772 451 O
admissions@austingrad.edu
BOND, Emma 601-426-6346 260 G
ebond@southeasternbaptist.edu
BOND, Erin 212-431-2199 323 H
erin.bond@nyls.edu
BOND, Helen 202-806-0870 93 A
hbond@howard.edu
BOND, Inge 408-988-2200 74 G
inge.bond@missioncollege.edu
BOND, Jan 912-478-6397 122 B
jbond@georgiasouthern.edu
BOND, Kerri 434-381-6346 494 M
kbond@sbc.edu
BOND, Martha 315-781-3780 316 C
mbond@hws.edu
BOND, Melissa 910-576-6222 351 E
bonds@montgomery.edu
BOND, Meredith, R 216-687-9321 366 I
m.bond40@csuohio.edu
BOND, Michelle 334-386-7275 3 I
mbond@faulkner.edu
BOND, Mollie 312-329-4177 148 F
mollie.bond@moody.edu
BOND, Nola 660-562-1128 269 J
nbond@nwmissouri.edu
BOND, Susan, E 610-359-1222 401 L
sbond@dccc.edu
BOND-HUIE,
Stephanie A 512-499-4798 475 K
shuie@utsystem.edu
BONDAVALLI, Bonnie 815-836-5242 145 H
bondavbo@lewisu.edu
BONDAVALLI, Bruno 773-878-3439 153 E
bbondavalli@staugustine.edu
BONDS, Dorothea 214-648-7500 478 C
dorothea.bonds@utsouthwestern.edu
BONDS, Jess 209-478-0800 46 H
jbonds@humphreys.edu
BONDS, Nechell, T 417-836-5517 268 I
nbonds@missouristate.edu
BONDS, Neil 870-743-3000 21 C
nbonds@northark.edu
BONDS, Thomas 662-862-8130 258 C
tabonds@iccms.edu
BONDURANT, Derrith 903-877-5728 477 E
derrith.bondurant@uthct.edu
BONDURANT, Glenda P 252-246-1333 354 D
gbondurant@wilsoncc.edu
BONDY, Jeff 406-994-2661 277 C
jbondy@montana.edu
BONDY, Kaylyn 701-774-4585 361 G
kaylyn.bondy@willistonstate.edu
BONE, Andrew 503-399-6593 390 E
andrew.bone@chemeketa.edu
BONE, Robyn 817-531-6552 472 F
rbone@txwes.edu
BONE, Robyn 817-531-6595 472 F
rbone@txwes.edu
BONEBREAK, Dawn 918-663-9000 387 B
dawnb@oklattcollege.org
BONEBRIGHT, Terri 501-450-1273 20 F
bonebright@hendrix.edu
BONELLI, Vicky 618-544-8657 142 D
bonelliv@iecc.edu
BONEMERY, Anne 413-755-4297 224 G
bonemery@stcc.edu
BONES, Rafael 252-335-3785 356 D
rabones@ecsu.edu
BONESIO-PETERSON
Jacquelynn 860-832-2553 85 F
bonesio@ccsu.edu
BONEWALD, Karen, I 603-526-3748 285 L
kbonewald@colby-sawyer.edu
BONEY, Leslie 919-843-7338 356 A
lboney@northcarolina.edu
BONEY, Lindsey 251-442-2390 9 A
lboney@umobile.edu
BONEZ, Allison 317-955-6080 165 N
abonez@marian.edu
BONFANTI, Phil 228-896-2507 259 C
phil.bonfanti@mgccc.edu
BONFIGLIO, Robert, A 585-245-5618 333 B
bonfig@geneseo.edu
BONGARTZ, Michael 816-235-1515 273 F
bongartzm@umkc.edu
BONGIORNO, Laurel 802-651-5978 483 F
bongiorno@champlain.edu
BONGO, Catherine, N 973-655-7137 293 A
bongoc@mail.montclair.edu
BONI, Bethyn 315-568-3252 323 A
bboni@nycc.edu
BONI, Sharon 304-367-0205 513 B
sharon.boni@fairmontstate.edu
BONIECKI, Kurt 501-450-3126 24 G
kurtb@uca.edu
BONIFAS, Angela 309-298-2010 158 A
aj-bonifas@wiu.edu
BONIFER, Duane 309-457-2321 148 E
dbonifer@monmouthcollege.edu
BONIFORTI, Alfredo, H 561-237-7173 104 O
aboniforti@lynn.edu
BONIFORTI, Chris, G 561-237-7163 104 O
cboniforti@lynn.edu
BONILLA, Ana, O 787-841-2000 535 I
admisiones@pucpr.edu
BONILLA, Angelita 973-353-1494 296 C
bonillan@andromeda.rutgers.edu
BONILLA, Anie 954-492-5353 97 I
abonilla@citycollege.edu
BONILLA, Carlos 626-529-8403 55 H
cbonilla@pacificoaks.edu
BONILLA, David 406-771-4425 277 F
dbonilla@gfcmsu.edu
BONILLA, Dennis 602-557-3213 17 L
dennis.bonilla@phoenix.edu
BONILLA, Kathleen 559-489-2221 67 C
kathy.bonilla@fresnocitycollege.edu
BONILLA, Mary Kay 406-771-5123 277 F
mbonilla@gfcmsu.edu
BONILLA, Matthew 212-463-0400 337 I
matthew.bonilla3@touro.edu
BONILLA, Ravel 787-832-6000 532 O
rbonilla@icprjc.edu
BONILLA, Ray 979-458-6128 467 D
rbonilla@tamus.edu
BONILLA, Ruth 787-746-1400 532 M
rbonilla@huertas.edu
BONK, Sharon, B 617-588-1356 215 E
sbonk@bfit.edu
BONN, Brenda 719-255-3317 83 L
bbonn@uccs.edu
BONN, Cynthia, L 401-874-7100 426 D
cynthia_bonn@uri.edu
BONNELL, Chris 801-274-3280 483 C
chris.bonnell@wgu.edu
BONNELL, Dawn, A 215-898-7236 421 E
vpr@pobox.upenn.edu
BONNER, A. Frank 704-406-4236 344 E
president@gardner-webb.edu
BONNER, Connie, C 260-359-4006 161 O
cbonner@huntington.edu
BONNER, Davita 386-481-2143 96 H
bonnerd@cookman.edu
BONNER, Debera 804-524-5276 499 G
dbonner@vsu.edu
BONNER, Gloria, L 615-494-7969 444 G
gloria.bonner@mtsu.edu
BONNER, Hugh, W 315-464-6560 332 C
bonnerh@upstate.edu
BONNER, Jo 205-348-6149 8 C
jo.bonner@uasystem.edu
BONNER, John, B 425-276-9520 503 F
jbonner@everettcc.edu
BONNER, Judy 662-325-3742 259 D
judy.bonner@provost.msstate.edu
BONNER, Julia 414-229-4716 520 D
jbonner@uwm.edu
BONNER, Kenyon, R 412-648-1006 421 G
krb114@pitt.edu
BONNER, Lisa 212-229-5600 322 E
lisa.murray@newschool.edu
BONNER, Lyle 940-552-6291 478 D
lbonner@vernoncollege.edu
BONNER, Paula, E 608-262-9630 519 K
pbonner@waastaff.com
BONNER, Tommy 507-222-4199 245 C
tbonner@carleton.edu
BONNER, William 518-736-3622 315 A
bbonner@fmcc.edu
BONNET, Larissa, B 307-674-6446 526 M
lbonnet@sheridan.edu
BONNETTE, J. Michael 434-544-8907 491 F
bonnette@lynchburg.edu
BONNETTE, Thomas 802-860-2705 483 F
bonnette@champlain.edu
BONNEY, Curtis 206-934-4521 506 J
curtis.bonney@seattlecolleges.edu
BONNIN, Linda 205-348-4592 8 D
linda.bonnin@ua.edu
BONNSTETTER, Bret 847-925-6224 141 A
bbonnste@harpercollege.edu
BONOFIGLIO, Carrie 517-338-3314 232 F
cbono@cleary.edu
BONOMO, Nawal 570-389-4199 414 D
nbonomo@bloomu.edu
BONONES, Patrick 404-471-6396 115 J
pbonones@agnesscott.edu
BONSTEEL, Susan 443-334-2320 211 A
shbonsteel@stevenson.edu
BONTINELLI, Stasi 303-751-8700 77 C
bontinelli@bel-rea.com
BONTRAGER, Cindy, A 785-532-6226 182 D
cab@ksu.edu

BONTRAGER, Katie .... 937-481-2280.. 381 C
katie_bontrager@wilmington.edu
BONUCHI, Molly, A .... 308-635-6112.. 283 D
bonuchim@wncc.edu
BONURA, Nancy .... 432-264-3752.. 459 D
nbonura@howardcollege.edu
BONURA, Rocky .... 310-660-3670.... 42 J
rbonura@elcamino.edu
BONURA, Stephen .... 914-337-9300.. 311 F
steve.bonura@concordia-ny.edu
BONVILLIAN, William, B . 202-789-1828.. 225 A
BOOB, Cristene, N .... 814-865-0512.. 412 F
cnb1@psu.edu
BOOCKER, David, J .... 402-554-2338.. 283 B
dboocker@unomaha.edu
BOOG, Melissa, M .... 410-543-6330.. 213 A
mmboog@salisbury.edu
BOOHER, Doug .... 812-855-9529.. 162 F
dbooher@indiana.edu
BOOHER, Mark .... 805-922-6966..... 25 I
mbooher@pcpa.org
BOOK, Connie, L .... 843-953-5007.. 428 A
cbook1@citadel.edu
BOOK, Leon .... 573-334-6825.. 272 A
lbook@sehcollege.edu
BOOKE, Bradly .... 410-778-2800.. 213 E
bbooke2@washcoll.edu
BOOKER, Alicia .... 216-987-3048.. 367 E
alicia.booker@tri-c.edu
BOOKER, Daphne .... 434-528-5276.. 500 C
dbooker@vul.edu
BOOKER, Kevin .... 404-653-7893.. 124 I
kevin.booker@morehouse.edu
BOOKER, Latoya .... 616-632-2455.. 231 A
latoya.booker@aquinas.edu
BOOKER, Lonnie .... 785-833-4360.. 182 F
lonnie.booker@kwu.edu
BOOKER, Marc .... 205-934-9847....... 8 E
mbooker@uab.edu
BOOKER, Michael .... 636-481-3312.. 266 C
mbooker@jeffco.edu
BOOKER, Ndala .... 407-303-6413.... 95 C
ndala.booker@adu.edu
BOOKER, RhaeAnn .... 616-698-7111.. 233 C
rbooker@davenport.edu
BOOKER, Sid .... 814-732-2810.. 415 A
sbooker@edinboro.edu
BOOKER, Steve .... 407-646-2395.. 107 O
sbooker@rollins.edu
BOOKER, Suzy .... 865-981-8203.. 441 H
suzy.booker@maryvillecollege.edu
BOOKMAN, Douglas .... 919-573-5350.. 355 G
BOOKOUT, James .... 334-670-3617....... 7 H
jbookout@troy.edu
BOOKOUT, Jeff .... 870-358-8614..... 19 C
jeff_bookout@asun.edu
BOOKSTAVER, John .... 636-922-8356.. 271 A
jbookstaver@stchas.edu
BOOKSTAVER, John .... 636-922-8722.. 271 A
jbookstaver@stchas.edu
BOOKWALTER, Robert ..... 304-696-2350.. 513 D
bookwalt@marshall.edu
BOOM, Philip .... 563-588-8000.. 172 E
pboom@emmaus.edu
BOOMER, Holly .... 970-675-3258..... 78 J
holly.boomer@cncc.edu
BOOMS, Carole .... 734-432-5811.. 237 D
cbooms@madonna.edu
BOONE, Becky .... 843-349-5274.. 430 F
becky.boone@hgtc.edu
BOONE, Beth .... 352-392-1311.. 112 A
bboone@ufl.edu
BOONE, Cheryl, A .... 513-585-0032.. 366 A
cheryl.boone@thechristcollege.edu
BOONE, Christopher, G ... 480-965-2236..... 11 H
christopher.g.boone@asu.edu
BOONE, Dan .... 615-248-1251.. 447 F
dboone@trevecca.edu
BOONE, Debbie .... 334-291-4927....... 2 H
debbie.boone@cv.edu
BOONE, John, B .... 919-866-5923.. 353 I
jbboone@waketech.edu
BOONE, Kathleen, C .... 716-839-8301.. 312 D
kboone@daemen.edu
BOONE, Kyle, N .... 512-505-3037.. 459 F
knboone@htu.edu
BOONE, Loren .... 320-308-3151.. 252 A
ljboone@stcloudstate.edu
BOONE, M. Scott .... 404-872-3593.. 117 B
sboone@johnmarshall.edu
BOONE, Nick .... 402-941-6016.. 280 N
boone@midlandu.edu
BOONE, Rebecca .... 318-357-5621.. 201 B
booner@nsula.edu
BOONE, Richard .... 707-826-3256..... 34 F
richard.boone@humboldt.edu
BOONE, Steve, E .... 501-686-7348..... 23 C
seboone@uams.edu
BOONE, Terri .... 803-584-3446.. 434 C
booneter@mailbox.sc.edu

BOONE, Zak .... 541-383-7212.. 390 D
zboone@cocc.edu
BOONSTRA, Brenda .... 706-776-0103.. 125 J
bboonstra@piedmont.edu
BOOR, Kathryn, J .... 607-255-2241.. 312 A
kjb4@cornell.edu
BOOREN, Diane .... 303-457-2757..... 80 C
diane.booren@zenith.org
BOOROS, Deborah .... 610-282-1100.. 402 B
deborah.booros@desales.edu
BOOS, David .... 605-995-3065.. 436 C
david.boos@mitchelltech.edu
BOOS, Jean .... 843-355-4167.. 435 A
boosj@wiltech.edu
BOOSE, Barbara .... 515-271-1661.. 171 H
barbara.boose@dmu.edu
BOOSINGER, Timothy, R . 334-844-5771...... 1 G
provost@auburn.edu
BOOSKA, Karry .... 802-728-1320.. 486 D
kbooska@vtc.edu
BOOSTER, Richard .... 541-683-5141.. 391 E
dbooster@gutenberg.edu
BOOTE, Marlys .... 319-335-2043.. 169 H
marlys-boote@uiowa.edu
BOOTH, Ann, B .... 304-367-4047.. 513 B
ann.booth@fairmontstate.edu
BOOTH, Derrick .... 916-484-8403..... 51 A
boothd@arc.losrios.edu
BOOTH, Eric, W .... 770-720-9198.. 126 C
ewb@reinhardt.edu
BOOTH, H. Austin .... 716-645-0983.. 331 C
abooth@buffalo.edu
BOOTH, Jane, E .... 212-854-0286.. 311 E
jeb@gc.columbia.edu
BOOTH, Jennifer .... 803-754-4100.. 429 B
BOOTH, Jocelyn .... 630-844-4647.. 135 E
jbooth@aurora.edu
BOOTH, LaQuita .... 334-229-4124....... 1 D
lbooth@alasu.edu
BOOTH, Molly .... 205-391-3978....... 6 G
mbooth@sheltonstate.edu
BOOTH, Paige .... 512-448-8429.. 464 G
paigeb@stedwards.edu
BOOTH, Ronnie, L .... 864-646-1773.. 433 C
rlbooth@tctc.edu
BOOTH, Scott .... 336-734-7317.. 349 G
sbooth@forsythtech.edu
BOOTH, Susan, A .... 573-629-3002.. 265 G
sbooth@hlg.edu
BOOTH, Susan, L .... 540-224-4640.. 491 A
slbooth1@jchs.edu
BOOTH, Terry, L .... 803-778-6624.. 427 G
boothtl@cctech.edu
BOOTHE, Jason .... 435-652-7526.. 482 A
boothe@dixie.edu
BOOTHE, Shane .... 832-252-4646.. 454 H
shane.boothe@cbshouston.edu
BOOTHMAN, Christopher 870-972-2031..... 18 J
cboothman@astate.edu
BOOTMAN, J, L .... 520-626-1657..... 17 I
bootman@email.arizona.edu
BOOTS, Joshua, D .... 563-588-7329.. 174 K
joshua.boots@loras.edu
BOOZANG, Kathleen .... 973-642-8750.. 297 A
kathleen.boozang@shu.edu
BOOZE, David .... 714-484-7432..... 54 G
dbooze@cypresscollege.edu
BOPKO, Patricia .... 909-652-6152..... 37 D
patricia.bopko@chaffey.edu
BOPP, Jodi, L .... 740-368-3324.. 376 B
jlbopp@owu.edu
BOPP, Ruthane, I .... 847-735-5025.. 145 B
bopp@lakeforest.edu
BOQUET, OSB,
Gregory, M .... 985-867-2232.. 199 F
rector@sjasc.edu
BOQUETTE, Troy .... 810-762-0243.. 238 F
troy.boquette@mcc.edu
BORAH, Jeffrey .... 631-420-2661.. 335 E
borahj@farmingdale.edu
BORASI, Raffaella .... 585-275-0880.. 338 K
raffaella.borasi@rochester.edu
BORCHERDING, Alan .... 314-505-7763.. 263 I
borcherdinga@csl.edu
BORCHERS, Brian .... 208-885-2076.. 134 G
bborcher@uidaho.edu
BORCHERS, Mary Ellen ... 614-236-6814.. 364 N
mborchers@capital.edu
BORCHERS, Mitch .... 913-469-8500.. 182 A
mborchers@jccc.edu
BORCHERS, Tim .... 402-872-2222.. 281 I
tborchers@peru.edu
BORCHERT, Anne, M .... 216-368-0242.. 365 B
amb14@case.edu
BORCK, Pat .... 478-471-2865.. 124 E
pat.borck@mga.edu
BORDEAU, Topher .... 802-586-7711.. 485 C
tbordeau@sterlingcollege.edu
BORDEAUX, Lionel .... 605-856-5880.. 436 I
lionel.bordeaux@sintegleska.edu

BORDEAUX, Lynette .... 605-856-2355.. 436 I
lynette.bordeaux@sintegleska.edu
BORDELON, Deborah .... 708-534-8045.. 140 H
dbordelon@govst.edu
BORDEN, Donald .... 856-227-7200.. 290 B
dborden@camdencc.edu
BORDEN, Jeff .... 352-588-8310.. 108 C
jeff.borden@saintleo.edu
BORDEN, M. Paige .... 407-823-4765.. 111 E
paige.borden@ucf.edu
BORDEN, Sue .... 207-947-4591.. 202 E
sborden@bealcollege.edu
BORDEN, Susan .... 410-626-2506.. 210 D
susan.borden@sjc.edu
BORDER, Debra .... 402-481-3804.. 278 J
deb.border@bryanhealthcollege.edu
BORDERS, Julianna, G ..... 419-334-8400.. 377 M
jborders01@terra.edu
BORDERS, Marianne .... 803-981-7320.. 435 D
borders@sctechsystem.edu
BORDIN, Cristina, L .... 512-464-8893.. 464 G
cristinb@stedwards.edu
BORDNICK, Patrick .... 504-865-5314.. 200 C
bordnick@tulane.edu
BORDONARO, Vilma .... 914-594-4900.. 323 I
vilma_bordonaro@nymc.edu
BOREEN, Jean .... 928-523-6765..... 15 H
jean.boreen@nau.edu
BOREK, Jarrod .... 860-932-4079..... 87 C
jborek@qvcc.edu
BOREK, John .... 434-528-5276.. 500 C
BORELLI, Alysa .... 530-541-4660..... 48 D
borelli@ltcc.edu
BORELLI, Gina .... 714-542-8086..... 29 C
gborelli@bristoluniversity.edu
BORELLI, Tricia, S .... 563-588-7085.. 174 K
tricia.borelli@loras.edu
BOREN, David, L .... 405-325-3916.. 389 B
dboren@ou.edu
BOREN, J. B .... 806-352-5207.. 479 D
borenjb@wbu.edu
BOREN, Laura .... 254-968-9085.. 467 F
lboren@tarleton.edu
BORER, Ralph (Sam), J ... 402-557-7355.. 278 I
sam.borer@bellevue.edu
BORES, Gerald .... 503-552-2007.. 392 H
gbores@nunm.edu
BORFITZ, Joanne .... 315-228-7120.. 310 G
jborfitz@colgate.edu
BORGEN, Beth .... 920-565-1023.. 517 D
borgembm@lakeland.edu
BORGER, Jennika .... 610-861-1583.. 411 B
borgerj@moravian.edu
BORGER, Patricia, A .... 414-229-3013.. 520 D
pborger@uwm.edu
BORGES, Daniel .... 619-482-6336..... 66 E
dborges@swccd.edu
BORGES, Donald .... 209-575-6198..... 76 A
borgesd@mjc.edu
BORGES, Nikki .... 313-993-1538.. 241 G
borgesnl@udmercy.edu
BORGES, Norma .... 787-725-6500.. 531 C
nborges@albizu.edu
BORGIA, Daniel, J .... 716-888-2160.. 306 F
BORGIA, Tom .... 304-293-2521.. 514 C
aborgia@hsc.wvu.edu
BORGLUM, Karen, M .... 407-582-3455.. 114 N
kborglum@valenciacollege.edu
BORGMAN, Cathleen, M . 203-254-4081..... 87 G
cborgman@fairfield.edu
BORGMAN, Kenneth, L ... 989-463-7314.. 230 F
borgman@alma.edu
BORGMANN-INGWERSEN,
Marian .... 402-465-2415.. 281 K
mborgman@nebrwesleyan.edu
BORGOGNONI, Mary, E .. 716-286-8352.. 324 E
meb@niagara.edu
BORGONAH, Darryl .... 512-245-2550.. 471 F
djb129@txstate.edu
BORGSMILLER, Stephen .. 573-472-3210.. 272 B
sjborgsmiller@semo.edu
BORGUS, Donna .... 585-389-2471.. 322 D
dborgus8@naz.edu
BORIA, Selina, M .... 508-854-4368.. 224 E
sboria@qcc.mass.edu
BORICH, Joe .... 419-448-3438.. 378 A
borichj@tiffin.edu
BORING, David .... 231-348-6838.. 239 A
dboring@ncmich.edu
BORIS, Barbara, A .... 610-409-3605.. 422 D
bboris@ursinus.edu
BORISKIN, Ronnie .... 917-493-4583.. 319 M
rboriskin@msmnyc.edu
BORJORQUEZ, Lina .... 213-738-6719..... 66 F
finaid@swlaw.edu
BORK, Eric .... 870-307-7242..... 21 A
eric.bork@lyon.edu
BORKOVICH, Bruce .... 231-591-5000.. 233 L
bruceborkovich@ferris.edu
BORKOWSKI, Donald, V . 207-725-3947.. 202 F
dborkows@bowdoin.edu

BORKOWSKI, Ellen, Y ..... 518-388-6293.. 338 H
borkowse@union.edu
BORLAND, Denise .... 715-422-5502.. 523 G
denise.borland@mstc.edu
BORMANN YOUNG,
Carol .... 651-793-1920.. 250 A
carolbormann.young@metrostate.edu
BORN, Lauren .... 610-917-1465.. 422 C
leborn@valleyforge.edu
BORN, Matthew .... 610-436-2231.. 416 C
mborn@wcupa.edu
BORNE, Jade .... 817-515-5636.. 467 A
jade.borne@tccd.edu
BORNEMANN, Jeffrey .... 414-955-8793.. 518 A
jbornema@mcw.edu
BORNHORST, Mary .... 937-778-7837.. 368 E
mbornhorst@edisonohio.edu
BORNSTEIN, Eva .... 718-960-8232.. 308 B
eva.bornstein@lehman.cuny.edu
BORNSTEIN, Leah, L .... 970-339-6210..... 76 H
leah.bornstein@aims.edu
BORNSTEIN, Rachel .... 802-225-3318.. 484 G
rachel.bornstein@neci.edu
BORNUS, Susan .... 651-523-2929.. 247 A
sbornus@hamline.edu
BORONICO, Jess .... 516-686-7838.. 323 G
jboronic@nyit.edu
BORONKAS, Michele .... 908-526-1200.. 295 A
michele.boronkas@raritanval.edu
BOROS-KAZAI, Mary .... 608-363-2640.. 515 G
boroskaz@beloit.edu
BOROUGHS, SJ,
Philip, L .... 508-793-2525.. 217 C
pborough@holycross.edu
BOROWICK, Matthew .... 973-378-9847.. 297 A
matthew.borowick@shu.edu
BOROWICK, Matthew .... 973-378-9822.. 297 A
matthew.borowick@shu.edu
BOROWICZ, Laurie .... 815-825-9333.. 144 F
laurie.borowicz@kishwaukeecollege.edu
BORR, Mike .... 701-231-9535.. 361 A
mike.borr@ndsu.edu
BORRAS, Belma .... 787-738-2161.. 538 A
belma.borras@upr.edu
BORREGO, Paul .... 210-486-2194.. 450 E
pborrego4@alamo.edu
BORREGO, Susan, E .... 810-762-3322.. 242 B
sborrego@umflint.edu
BORRELL, Anthony .... 813-757-2111.. 102 R
aborrell2@hccfl.edu
BORREN, Tammy .... 931-540-2553.. 446 A
tborren@columbiastate.edu
BORRERO, Jennifer, S ...... 718-982-2335.. 307 F
jennifer.borrero@csi.cuny.edu
BORRERO, Maranjani .... 787-780-0070.. 531 B
mborrero@caribbean.edu
BORSCH, Elva .... 832-813-6571.. 461 B
elva.borsch@lonestar.edu
BORSIG, Jim .... 662-329-7100.. 259 E
jbborsig@muw.edu
BORSKI, Brian .... 972-860-4116.. 456 B
bborski@dcccd.edu
BORST, Charlotte, G .... 208-459-5502.. 133 D
cborst@collegeofidaho.edu
BORSZ, Michael .... 315-498-2097.. 325 G
m.a.borsz@sunyocc.edu
BORTHWICK, Kristen .... 512-492-3011.. 451 E
registrar@aoma.edu
BORTMAN, Lisa .... 310-506-4393..... 56 J
lisa.bortman@pepperdine.edu
BORTMAN, Walter, J .... 818-364-7800..... 49 J
bortmawj@lamission.edu
BORTON, Jeffrey .... 734-462-4400.. 240 H
jborton@schoolcraft.edu
BORTUNK, Ayelet .... 305-653-8770.. 115 H
abortunk@lecfl.com
BORTZ, Carolyn .... 610-861-5434.. 411 G
cbortz@northampton.edu
BORUCKI, Jennifer, C .... 818-947-2433..... 50 D
fongjc@lavc.edu
BORUFF-JONES, Polly ..... 765-455-9343.. 163 A
pboruffj@iuk.edu
BORUM, John .... 214-333-5973.. 455 J
johnb@dbu.edu
BORUNDA, Nicole .... 619-594-2078..... 35 A
nborunda@mail.sdsu.edu
BORUSZEWSKI, Richard .. 517-371-5140.. 243 I
boruszer@cooley.edu
BOS, James .... 712-722-6030.. 171 J
jim.bos@dordt.edu
BOSACK-KOSEK,
Carol, A .... 570-408-5963.. 423 G
carol.bosack@wilkes.edu
BOSCH, Agnes .... 787-767-4300.. 538 F
agnes.bosch@upr.edu
BOSCHINI, JR., Victor, J 817-257-7783.. 469 G
v.boschini@tcu.edu
BOSCHUNG, Milla .... 205-348-6250....... 8 D
mboschun@ches.ua.edu
BOSCO, Carol .... 518-629-7117.. 316 G
c.bosco@hvcc.edu

BOWEN, Pamela .... 715-425-0633.. 521 B
pamela.bowen@uwrf.edu
BOWEN, Patricia, A .... 606-693-5000.. 191 A
pbowen@kmbc.edu
BOWEN, Peter .... 806-291-1171.. 479 D
pbowen@wbu.edu
BOWEN, Rachel .... 610-526-6157.. 405 B
rbowen@harcum.edu
BOWEN, Robin, E .... 479-968-0228.... 19 F
rbowen@atu.edu
BOWEN, Roxanne .... 423-585-6806.. 447 D
roxanne.bowen@ws.edu
BOWEN, Sam .... 320-222-5206.. 251 G
sam.bowen@ridgewater.edu
BOWEN, Sharon, G .... 931-540-2548.. 446 A
sbowen@columbiastate.edu
BOWEN, Sherri, W .... 336-734-7200.. 349 G
sbowen@forsythtech.edu
BOWEN, Terry .... 410-386-8494.. 206 I
tbowen@carrollcc.edu
BOWEN, Tom .... 901-678-5395.. 445 C
tmbowen1@memphis.edu
BOWEN, W. Ann .... 423-585-6892.. 447 D
ann.bowen@ws.edu
BOWENS, Laura Lee .... 201-328-5196.. 290 H
lbowens@ccm.edu
BOWENS, Ollie .... 662-252-8000.. 260 F
obowens@rustcollege.edu
BOWENS, Pacey .... 870-762-3134.... 18 G
pbowens@smail.anc.edu
BOWER, Beth, A .... 978-542-6134.. 222 D
bbower@salemstate.edu
BOWER, David, A .... 812-464-1918.. 168 E
bower@usi.edu
BOWER, Eric .... 216-791-5000.. 366 H
eric.bower@cim.edu
BOWER, Jami .... 678-839-6464.. 129 E
jbower@westga.edu
BOWER, Mike .... 567-661-7200.. 376 D
mike_bower@owens.edu
BOWER SPENCE, Kim, D 570-408-4764.. 423 G
kimberly.bowerspence@wilkes.edu
BOWERS, Angela .... 563-355-3500.. 174 E
abowers@kaplan.edu
BOWERS, Anthony .... 425-739-8135.. 504 F
anthony.bowers@lwtech.edu
BOWERS, Brandon .... 304-263-0979.. 511 G
BOWERS, Brian .... 504-486-7411.. 202 C
bbowers1@xula.edu
BOWERS, Carol .... 803-376-5700.. 427 A
cbowers@allenuniversity.edu
BOWERS, David, A .... 212-938-5666.. 334 F
dbowers@sunyopt.edu
BOWERS, David, G .... 517-338-3021.. 232 F
dbowers@cleary.edu
BOWERS, J, D .... 573-882-4333.. 273 E
bowersjd@missouri.edu
BOWERS, J. Betsy .... 850-474-2637.. 113 A
bbowers@uwf.edu
BOWERS, James, R .... 585-385-8318.. 328 E
jbowers@sjfc.edu
BOWERS, Jan .... 607-436-3488.. 331 F
jan.bowers@oneonta.edu
BOWERS, Jane .... 212-237-8801.. 308 E
jbowers@jjay.cuny.edu
BOWERS, John .... 270-745-4278.. 194 D
john.bowers@wku.edu
BOWERS, John .... 206-934-6869.. 507 A
john.bowers@seattlecolleges.edu
BOWERS, Kathy .... 417-626-1234.. 269 K
kbowers@occ.edu
BOWERS, Kevin .... 618-544-8657.. 142 D
bowersk@iecc.edu
BOWERS, Lynn .... 773-380-6786.. 135 H
lbowers@bexleyseabury.edu
BOWERS, Michael, E .... 864-587-4220.. 433 A
bowersme@smcsc.edu
BOWERS, Rodney .... 321-674-8080.. 100 M
rbowers@fit.edu
BOWERS, Stephanie .... 360-650-2055.. 509 E
stephanie.bowers@wwu.edu
BOWERS, Susan .... 712-279-7969.. 176 E
susan.bowers@stlukescollege.edu
BOWERS, William .... 315-312-2888.. 333 D
william.bowers@oswego.edu
BOWERS-CAMPBELL, Joy 502-863-8172.. 188 I
joy_bowers-campbell@georgetowncollege.edu
BOWERS-GENTRY,
Rebecca .... 619-388-7241.... 60 H
rbowersg@sdccd.edu
BOWERSOCK, Allison, H . 540-985-9943.. 491 A
ahbowersock@jchs.edu
BOWERSOCK, Gary .... 303-273-3330.... 78 M
gbowerso@mines.edu
BOWERSOX, Laurie, A .... 717-270-6310.. 405 C
labowers@hacc.edu
BOWERSOX, Lou Ann ..... 270-852-3118.. 191 C
lbowersox@kwc.edu
BOWES, Bill .... 501-686-6840.... 23 C
wrbowes@uams.edu
BOWES, Kristen .... 914-674-7544.. 320 G
kbowes@mercy.edu
BOWIE, DeWayne .... 337-482-6287.. 201 D
dkbowie@louisiana.edu
BOWIE, Jalonna .... 913-234-0681.. 179 M
jalonna.bowie@cleveland.edu
BOWIE, John .... 207-755-5432.. 203 I
jbowie@cmcc.edu
BOWIE, Linda .... 410-951-3915.. 212 E
lbowie@coppin.edu
BOWIE, Lois .... 903-593-8311.. 470 A
lbowie@texascollege.edu
BOWIE, Michelle .... 202-884-9611.... 94 A
bowiem@trinitydc.edu
BOWIE, Staci, A .... 843-349-2227.. 428 E
sbowie@coastal.edu
BOWIE, Thomas .... 303-458-4040.... 82 L
tbowie@regis.edu
BOWKER, Janet, L .... 814-836-1955.. 415 A
bowker@edinboro.edu
BOWLAN, Ronald, E .... 215-503-7268.. 420 E
ron.bowlan@jefferson.edu
BOWLDS, Joy .... 270-852-8965.. 190 D
joy.bowlds@kctcs.edu
BOWLES, Anita, K .... 864-587-4221.. 433 A
bowlesa@smcsc.edu
BOWLES, Crystal .... 918-293-5274.. 386 B
crystal.bowles@okstate.edu
BOWLES, Diane .... 704-378-1202.. 345 E
dbowles@jcsu.edu
BOWLES, Donna, J .... 812-941-2204.. 163 F
dbowles@ius.edu
BOWLES, James, H .... 270-824-8588.. 190 B
james.bowles@kctcs.edu
BOWLES, Ron .... 214-333-5520.. 455 J
ronb@dbu.edu
BOWLES, Ryan, A .... 507-786-3965.. 254 P
bowles@stolaf.edu
BOWLES, Ulisa .... 910-672-1411.. 356 E
ubowles@uncfsu.edu
BOWLIN, Stephanie .... 909-469-5383.... 74 K
sbowlin@westernu.edu
BOWLING, Damon .... 918-836-6886.. 388 E
damon.bowling@spartan.edu
BOWLING, Dee .... 252-737-1133.. 356 C
bowlingde@ecu.edu
BOWLING, Doug .... 513-569-1752.. 366 D
doug.bowling@cincinnatistate.edu
BOWLING, John, C .... 815-939-5221.. 150 I
jbowling@olivet.edu
BOWLING, Shannon .... 304-327-4131.. 512 P
sbowling@bluefieldstate.edu
BOWLING, Thomas .... 301-687-4311.. 212 F
tbowling@frostburg.edu
BOWLUS, Robin .... 419-358-3453.. 364 D
bowlusr@bluffton.edu
BOWMAN, Alayne .... 865-981-8011.. 441 H
alayne.bowman@maryvillecollege.edu
BOWMAN, Benjamin .... 574-284-4552.. 167 A
bbowman@saintmarys.edu
BOWMAN, Bruce, A .... 410-777-2873.. 206 B
babowman2@aacc.edu
BOWMAN, Christine, D ...... 512-863-1200.. 466 G
bowmanc@southwestern.edu
BOWMAN, Corey, L .... 660-543-4114.. 273 C
bowman@ucmo.edu
BOWMAN, David .... 202-806-7540.... 93 A
david.bowman@howard.edu
BOWMAN, David .... 657-278-2638.... 33 A
dbowman@fullerton.edu
BOWMAN, Elizabeth .... 805-965-0581.... 63 D
bowmane@sbcc.edu
BOWMAN, Gail .... 859-985-3774.. 187 B
bowmang@berea.edu
BOWMAN, Gina .... 870-972-2250.... 18 J
gbowman@astate.edu
BOWMAN, Glen .... 252-335-3424.. 356 D
gcbowman@ecsu.edu
BOWMAN, Gregory, W .... 304-293-3199.. 514 C
gwbowman@mail.wvu.edu
BOWMAN, Heath .... 252-328-6072.. 356 C
bowmanhe15@ecu.edu
BOWMAN, Helen, Y .... 215-895-2803.. 402 G
helen.y.bowman@drexel.edu
BOWMAN, John .... 301-687-4111.. 212 F
jbowman@frostburg.edu
BOWMAN, Judith, M .... 757-683-3260.. 492 G
jbowman@odu.edu
BOWMAN, Katie, M .... 727-816-3236.. 106 F
bowmank@phsc.edu
BOWMAN, Keith .... 415-338-1571.... 35 B
kjbowman@sfsu.edu
BOWMAN, Kevin .... 808-687-7032.. 130 H
kbowman@hpu.edu
BOWMAN, Kimberly .... 717-901-5173.. 405 H
kbowman@harrisburgu.edu
BOWMAN, Lisa .... 918-495-6888.. 386 H
lbowman@oru.edu
BOWMAN, Michael .... 510-659-6064.... 55 B
mbowman@ohlone.edu
BOWMAN, Pam .... 662-685-4771.. 257 A
pbowman@bmc.edu
BOWMAN, Pamela, L .... 309-298-1971.. 158 A
pl-bowman@wiu.edu
BOWMAN, JR.,
Ronald, L .... 330-972-2157.. 378 G
rbowman@uakron.edu
BOWMAN, Scott .... 612-874-3677.. 247 M
scott_bowman@mcad.edu
BOWMAN, Scott, R .... 323-343-3810.... 33 C
sbowman@calstatela.edu
BOWMAN, Stacie .... 978-837-3448.. 225 E
bowmans@merrimack.edu
BOWMAN, Teri, A .... 660-543-4900.. 273 C
tbowman@ucmo.edu
BOWMAN, Ty .... 562-860-2451.... 36 P
tbowman@cerritos.edu
BOWMAN, William .... 202-319-5290.... 92 A
bowmanw@cua.edu
BOWMANN, John .... 636-949-4678.. 266 J
jbowmann@lindenwood.edu
BOWNE, Kristine .... 626-396-2474.... 27 L
kristine.bowne@artcenter.edu
BOWNES, Kim, M .... 603-535-2771.. 288 F
kbownes@plymouth.edu
BOWNES JOHNSON,
Beth .... 256-352-8190...... 9 G
BOWRON, Steve .... 507-433-0695.. 251 H
steve.bowron@riverland.edu
BOWSER, Adam .... 814-443-2522.. 413 P
abowser@pennhighlands.edu
BOWSER, Chris .... 641-683-5155.. 173 C
chris.bowser@indianhills.edu
BOWSER, Steve .... 404-270-5326.. 128 A
sbowser@spelman.edu
BOWYER, Donald .... 870-972-3053.... 18 J
dbowyer@astate.edu
BOWYER, Karen, A .... 731-286-3301.. 446 B
bowyer@dscc.edu
BOX, Catherine, P .... 601-974-1060.. 258 H
BOX, Jay .... 859-256-3132.. 188 M
president@kctcs.edu
BOX, Jean, A .... 205-726-2565...... 6 E
jabox@samford.edu
BOXDORFER, Bill .... 573-288-6571.. 264 F
bboxdorfer@culver.edu
BOXLER, Susan .... 641-673-1284.. 177 J
boxlers@wmpenn.edu
BOXWELL, George .... 304-647-6290.. 514 A
gboxwell@osteo.wvsom.edu
BOYAN, Barbara, D .... 804-828-0190.. 496 D
bboyan@vcu.edu
BOYCE, Brian .... 617-964-1100.. 214 D
brian.boyce@ants.edu
BOYCE, Eric .... 828-251-6951.. 357 C
eboyce@unca.edu
BOYCE, Greg .... 719-846-5530.... 83 G
greg.boyce@trinidadstate.edu
BOYCE, Kelsey .... 563-387-1008.. 174 L
boycke01@luther.edu
BOYCE, Lynn .... 405-224-3140.. 389 D
lboyce@usao.edu
BOYCE, Mary, C .... 212-854-1123.. 311 E
boyce@columbia.edu
BOYCE, Richard, N .... 704-337-2450.. 494 N
rboyce@upsem.edu
BOYCE, Robert .... 301-687-4043.. 212 F
rjboyce@frostburg.edu
BOYCE, Susan .... 802-776-5239.. 483 G
susan.boyce@csj.edu
BOYD, Alan .... 440-775-5666.. 374 C
aboyd@oberlin.edu
BOYD, Amanda .... 701-777-2219.. 360 C
amanda.boyd@und.edu
BOYD, Amanda, L .... 419-866-0261.. 377 L
alboyd@stautzenberger.com
BOYD, Amy .... 402-354-7073.. 281 F
amy.boyd@methodistcollege.edu
BOYD, Angela .... 757-727-5328.. 490 E
angela.boyd@hamptonu.edu
BOYD, Betsy, A .... 541-346-0946.. 395 G
eaboyd@uoregon.edu
BOYD, Bill .... 910-323-5614.. 342 H
billboyd@ccbs.edu
BOYD, Brandon .... 931-372-3997.. 445 B
bboyd@tntech.edu
BOYD, Brian .... 407-823-3016.. 111 E
brian.boyd@ucf.edu
BOYD, Carla .... 520-515-5337.... 12 L
boydc@cochise.edu
BOYD, Carla, L .... 218-726-8795.. 255 D
clboyd@d.umn.edu
BOYD, Carla, M .... 217-443-8753.. 139 B
cboyd@dacc.edu
BOYD, Carrie .... 540-887-7288.. 491 G
cboyd@mbc.edu
BOYD, Chrispher .... 336-770-3322.. 358 E
boydc@uncsa.edu
BOYD, Clarence .... 918-495-7767.. 386 H
cboyd@oru.edu
BOYD, Cristine, D .... 330-569-5288.. 369 J
boydcd@hiram.edu
BOYD, Cynthia .... 770-426-2756.. 124 B
cboyd@life.edu
BOYD, Cynthia, E .... 312-942-6915.. 153 B
cynthia_e_boyd@rush.edu
BOYD, Danielle .... 618-634-3298.. 154 B
danielleb@shawneecc.edu
BOYD, David .... 734-432-5380.. 237 D
daveboyd@madonna.edu
BOYD, David, L .... 714-850-4800.... 67 G
boyd@taftu.edu
BOYD, Deborah .... 615-966-5708.. 441 F
deborah.boyd@lipscomb.edu
BOYD, Debra, C .... 803-323-2220.. 435 B
boydd@winthrop.edu
BOYD, Diane, E .... 334-844-1266...... 1 G
deb0020@auburn.edu
BOYD, Ernest .... 731-426-7531.. 440 K
eboyd@lanecollege.edu
BOYD, JR., Eulas .... 718-780-0395.. 305 L
eulas.boyd@brooklaw.edu
BOYD, Frank, A .... 309-556-3255.. 143 D
fboyd@iwu.edu
BOYD, Gary .... 304-357-4704.. 511 E
garyboyd@ucwv.edu
BOYD, Gerald, L .... 240-629-7840.. 207 F
gboyd@frederick.edu
BOYD, Gwendolyn, E .... 334-229-4202...... 1 D
presgboyd@alasu.edu
BOYD, Heather .... 303-273-3221.... 78 M
hboyd@mines.edu
BOYD, JR., James, I .... 707-965-7203.... 56 A
jboyd@puc.edu
BOYD, Jeffrey, S .... 757-822-1180.. 498 H
jsboyd@tcc.edu
BOYD, John .... 405-682-7501.. 385 D
jboyd@occc.edu
BOYD, John .... 405-682-1611.. 385 D
jboyd@occc.edu
BOYD, John, C .... 828-766-1270.. 351 B
jboyd@mayland.edu
BOYD, Karen, O .... 314-576-5923.. 274 A
boyd@umsl.edu
BOYD, Kathleen .... 401-341-2374.. 426 C
boydk@salve.edu
BOYD, Keisha .... 386-214-3653.... 96 H
boydk@cookman.edu
BOYD, Keith .... 312-942-2694.. 153 B
keith_boyd@rush.edu
BOYD, Ken .... 913-443-5858.. 126 G
kboyd@savannahtech.edu
BOYD, Ken .... 765-998-4965.. 167 C
knboyd@taylor.edu
BOYD, Kim .... 918-495-7108.. 386 H
kboyd@oru.edu
BOYD, Linda, D .... 617-732-2800.. 225 C
linda.boyd@mcphs.edu
BOYD, Lonnie .... 620-229-6136.. 184 J
lonnie.boyd@sckans.edu
BOYD, Mary, K .... 512-448-8741.. 464 G
mboyd@stedwards.edu
BOYD, Michael .... 706-754-7807.. 125 B
mboyd@northgatech.edu
BOYD, Michael .... 815-802-8360.. 144 C
mboyd@kcc.edu
BOYD, Michael, D .... 901-333-4318.. 447 B
mdboyd@southwest.tn.edu
BOYD, Monica .... 336-917-5579.. 355 E
monica.boyd@salem.edu
BOYD, Monique .... 301-314-8280.. 211 E
mboyd1@umd.edu
BOYD, Nick .... 530-283-0202.... 43 G
nboyd@frc.edu
BOYD, Rick .... 803-775-8727.. 434 E
boydrl@uscsumter.edu
BOYD, Robert .... 559-278-4480.... 32 F
robert_boyd@csufresno.edu
BOYD, Ruth .... 580-774-3177.. 388 C
ruth.boyd@swosu.edu
BOYD, Sharon, H .... 910-962-7769.. 358 D
boyds@uncw.edu
BOYD, Steve .... 970-945-8691.... 78 B
BOYD, Steven .... 916-484-8633.... 51 A
boyds@arc.losrios.edu
BOYD, Susan .... 586-445-7408.. 237 C
boyds@macomb.edu
BOYD, Thomas .... 303-273-3020.... 78 M
tboyd@mines.edu
BOYD, Thomas .... 303-273-3247.... 78 M
tboyd@mines.edu
BOYD, Todd, T .... 580-774-3782.. 388 C
todd.boyd@swosu.edu
BOYD MCELROY, Diana .. 816-604-2326.. 267 I
diana.mcelroy@mcckc.edu
BOYD-PUGH, Jennifer, N 305-899-4057.... 96 D
jboydpugh@barry.edu
BOYDSTUN, Morris .... 479-394-7622.... 22 B
mboydstun@rmcc.edu
BOYE-BEAMAN, Joni, M . 989-964-4062.. 240 F
jbb@svsu.edu

- **BOYER**, Annette .. 724-925-4101 .. 423 D boyera@wccc.edu
- **BOYER**, Bruce .. 508-565-1380 .. 228 F bboyer@stonehill.edu
- **BOYER**, Bruce, E .. 573-875-7251 .. 263 F beboyer@ccis.edu
- **BOYER**, Charles .. 406-994-3681 .. 277 C cboyer@montana.edu
- **BOYER**, Debra, A .. 617-228-2403 .. 223 B dboyer@bhcc.mass.edu
- **BOYER**, John, W .. 773-702-8576 .. 156 D jwboyer@uchicago.edu
- **BOYER**, Kim, L .. 518-956-8241 .. 331 A kboyer3@albany.edu
- **BOYER**, Mary .. 215-702-4541 .. 399 E mboyer@cairn.edu
- **BOYER**, Mary Jo .. 610-450-6524 .. 401 L mboyer@dccc.edu
- **BOYER**, Naomi .. 863-298-6854 .. 106 I nboyer@polk.edu
- **BOYER**, Paul, J .. 413-597-4181 .. 230 A paul.j.boyer@williams.edu
- **BOYER**, Scott .. 717-560-8214 .. 407 E sboyer@lbc.edu
- **BOYER**, Suzanne, L .. 410-777-2045 .. 206 B slboyer1@aacc.edu
- **BOYER FERHAT**, Caroline .. 800-995-3159 .. 275 G caroline.boyerferhat@williamwoods.edu
- **BOYER-OWENS**, Linda .. 210-485-0230 .. 450 A lboyer-owens@alamo.edu
- **BOYERS**, Jayson .. 517-586-3012 .. 232 F jboyers@cleary.edu
- **BOYES**, Jerry, S .. 716-878-6533 .. 332 F boyesjs@buffalostate.edu
- **BOYES**, Monica .. 530-895-2936 .. 29 F boyesmo@butte.edu
- **BOYETT**, Chad .. 912-287-5808 .. 119 B cboyett@coastalpines.edu
- **BOYETT**, Chris .. 419-995-8357 .. 370 G boyett.c@rhodestate.edu
- **BOYETT**, James, C .. 501-362-1125 .. 18 I jcboyett@hebersprings.asub.edu
- **BOYETT**, Jennifer .. 870-230-5401 .. 20 E boyett@hsu.edu
- **BOYETT**, Patricia .. 504-865-7880 .. 198 E
- **BOYETTE**, Alan, J .. 336-334-5494 .. 358 B alan_boyette@uncg.edu
- **BOYETTE**, Barbara, G .. 336-316-2825 .. 344 H boyettebg@guilford.edu
- **BOYETTE**, Rick .. 903-823-3274 .. 467 C ricky.boyette@texarkanacollege.edu
- **BOYETTE**, Susan .. 404-413-3456 .. 122 D staylor83@gsu.edu
- **BOYKIN**, Coretta .. 251-578-1313 .. 6 C cboykin@rstc.edu
- **BOYKIN**, Deborah .. 757-221-3178 .. 488 F boykin@wm.edu
- **BOYKIN, III**, George, H .. 919-516-4888 .. 355 D ghboykin@st-aug.edu
- **BOYKIN**, Gregory .. 252-985-5117 .. 354 E gboykin@ncwc.edu
- **BOYKIN**, Karen .. 215-780-1420 .. 419 C kboykin@salus.edu
- **BOYKIN**, Lashanna .. 619-680-4430 .. 30 A lashanna.boykin@cc-sd.edu
- **BOYKIN**, Regena .. 601-635-2111 .. 257 F rboykin@eccc.edu
- **BOYKIN**, Ted .. 570-586-2400 .. 419 G tboykin@summitu.edu
- **BOYLAN**, Ellen .. 570-348-6203 .. 409 H eboylan@marywood.edu
- **BOYLAN**, Stanley, L .. 646-565-6000 .. 337 I stanley.boylan@touro.edu
- **BOYLAN**, Teresa .. 434-381-6337 .. 494 M tboylan@sbc.edu
- **BOYLE**, Allison, J .. 410-576-6316 .. 210 E aboyle@oag.state.md.us
- **BOYLE**, Amy .. 504-865-2445 .. 198 E aboyle@loyno.edu
- **BOYLE**, Ann .. 480-219-6107 .. 262 A aboyle@atsu.edu
- **BOYLE**, Antonio, M .. 903-927-3329 .. 479 K amboyle@wileyc.edu
- **BOYLE**, Carol Ann .. 516-877-3775 .. 303 B boyle@adelphi.edu
- **BOYLE**, Christine .. 201-761-7390 .. 296 K cboyle@saintpeters.edu
- **BOYLE**, Deborah .. 727-341-3153 .. 108 D boyle.deborah@spcollege.edu
- **BOYLE**, Jeanne, E .. 848-932-7505 .. 296 B jeboyle@rulmail.rutgers.edu
- **BOYLE**, Jeffery .. 864-592-4823 .. 432 H boylej@sccsc.edu
- **BOYLE**, Jerry .. 970-410-0456 .. 85 B
- **BOYLE**, Kate .. 360-438-4333 .. 506 G kboyle@stmartin.edu
- **BOYLE**, Kevin .. 973-618-3372 .. 290 A kboyle@caldwell.edu
- **BOYLE**, Lori .. 619-239-0391 .. 36 A lboyle@cwsl.edu
- **BOYLE**, Nuala .. 585-389-2670 .. 322 D nboyle5@naz.edu
- **BOYLE**, Patrick, M .. 773-508-7070 .. 146 G pboyle@luc.edu
- **BOYLE**, Robert, J .. 904-620-4663 .. 112 B rboyle@unf.edu
- **BOYLE**, Sharon, I .. 215-926-2200 .. 420 B sharon.boyle@temple.edu
- **BOYLE**, Taggart .. 617-984-1771 .. 227 F tboyle@quincycollege.edu
- **BOYLE**, Thomas, A .. 630-515-6166 .. 148 C tboyle@midwestern.edu
- **BOYLES**, Elinda .. 740-351-3005 .. 377 C eboyles@shawnee.edu
- **BOYLES**, Joel .. 662-562-3240 .. 260 C jboyles@northwestms.edu
- **BOYLES**, Robin .. 662-846-4804 .. 257 E rboyles@deltastate.edu
- **BOYLES**, Shery .. 919-760-8581 .. 346 D boyless@meredith.edu
- **BOYLL**, Dave .. 303-937-4222 .. 77 K dboyll@chu.edu
- **BOYMELGREEN**, Shaya .. 718-434-0784 .. 306 J
- **BOYNE**, Andrew .. 985-448-7928 .. 196 E andrew.boyne@fletcher.edu
- **BOYNTON**, Andrew, C .. 617-552-4107 .. 216 C andy.boynton@bc.edu
- **BOYNTON**, Antoine .. 706-583-2552 .. 116 H aboynton@athenstech.edu
- **BOYS**, Kevin, S .. 937-393-3431 .. 377 F kboys@sscc.edu
- **BOYS**, Mary, C .. 212-280-1550 .. 338 I mboys@uts.columbia.edu
- **BOYSUN**, Virginia .. 406-377-9404 .. 276 D vboysun@dawson.edu
- **BOYUM**, Ginny .. 507-280-5081 .. 251 I ginny.boyum@rctc.edu
- **BOYUM-BREEN**, Trenda .. 952-806-3910 .. 254 C
- **BOZARTH**, Diane .. 573-288-6473 .. 264 F dbozarth@culver.edu
- **BOZARTH**, Peggy, I .. 270-707-3844 .. 189 G peggy.bozarth@kctcs.edu
- **BOZEMAN-EVANS**, Pamela .. 773-244-5662 .. 149 I pbozeman@northpark.edu
- **BOZINSKI**, Glenn .. 570-674-6434 .. 410 K gbozinsk@misericordia.edu
- **BOZZUTO**, Victoria .. 203-285-2408 .. 86 C vbozzuto@gwcc.commnet.edu
- **BRAATEN**, Pamela, K .. 701-788-4773 .. 360 E pamela.braaten@mayvillestate.edu
- **BRAATZ**, Brady, J .. 913-971-3452 .. 183 D bbraatz@mnu.edu
- **BRAATZ**, Jay .. 312-362-7561 .. 139 C jbraatz@depaul.edu
- **BRABAZON**, Jodi .. 215-574-9600 .. 406 A jbrabazon@hussianart.edu
- **BRABHAM**, Sherry, F .. 212-217-4020 .. 314 B sherry_brabham@fitnyc.edu
- **BRABHAM**, Susan, S .. 803-938-3795 .. 434 E brabhams@uscsumter.edu
- **BRACCIANO**, Susan .. 816-271-4214 .. 269 C braccian@missouriwestern.edu
- **BRACE**, Karen, K .. 260-982-5050 .. 165 M kkbrace@manchester.edu
- **BRACELY**, Kenesha .. 904-470-8445 .. 98 N k.bracely@ewc.edu
- **BRACERO**, Carmen, A .. 787-844-9231 .. 538 E carmen.bracero@upr.edu
- **BRACEY**, Carol .. 951-343-4456 .. 29 H cbracey@calbaptist.edu
- **BRACEY**, Gerald .. 228-897-7101 .. 261 I jerry.bracey@wmcarey.edu
- **BRACEY**, Matthew .. 615-844-5233 .. 449 H mbracey@welch.edu
- **BRACH**, Michael .. 574-239-8368 .. 161 N mbrach@hcc-nd.edu
- **BRACK**, Jonathan, M .. 215-572-3878 .. 423 C jbrack@wts.edu
- **BRACKE**, Paul, J .. 509-313-6533 .. 504 A
- **BRACKEN**, Damien, S .. 617-266-1400 .. 215 G
- **BRACKEN**, Gary .. 412-391-4100 .. 417 F gbracken@pointpark.edu
- **BRACKEN**, James .. 330-672-2962 .. 370 I jbracke1@kent.edu
- **BRACKEN**, Lisa .. 803-778-6652 .. 427 G brackenlm@cctech.edu
- **BRACKETT**, Andrew .. 802-831-1260 .. 485 F abrackett@vermontlaw.edu
- **BRACKETT**, Chantelle .. 802-831-1308 .. 485 F cbrackett@vermontlaw.edu
- **BRACKETT**, Geoffrey, L .. 845-575-3000 .. 320 B geoffrey.brackett@marist.edu
- **BRACKETT**, Robert .. 708-563-1577 .. 142 I rbrackett@iit.edu
- **BRACKETT**, Stacey .. 828-328-7309 .. 345 H stacey.brackett@lr.edu
- **BRACKETT**, Suzanne .. 252-985-5101 .. 354 E sbrackett@ncwc.edu
- **BRACKIN**, Chad .. 225-578-4736 .. 197 H cmb@lsu.edu
- **BRACKIN**, James .. 229-317-6315 .. 120 A james.brackin@darton.edu
- **BRACKIN**, Rebekah .. 325-942-2248 .. 472 B rebekah.brackin@angelo.edu
- **BRACKLEY**, Autumn .. 208-562-3225 .. 133 F autumnbrackley@cwidaho.cc
- **BRACKLEY**, Paul .. 312-329-4225 .. 148 F paul.brackley@moody.edu
- **BRACKMANN**, Sarah .. 512-863-1987 .. 466 G brackmas@southwestern.edu
- **BRACKNELL**, Ann .. 205-391-2958 .. 6 G abracknell@sheltonstate.edu
- **BRACY**, Jucy .. 504-486-7411 .. 202 C jbracy@xula.edu
- **BRACY**, Marion .. 504-520-7507 .. 202 C mbracy@xula.edu
- **BRACY KNIGHT**, Becca .. 310-954-5080 .. 29 D
- **BRADAC**, John .. 607-844-8222 .. 337 G
- **BRADACH**, Carmen .. 218-749-7743 .. 252 F c.bradach@mr.mnscu.edu
- **BRADACH**, Carmen .. 218-749-7743 .. 249 c.bradach@mesabirange.edu
- **BRADBERRY**, J. Chris .. 402-280-2950 .. 279 H jcbradberry@creighton.edu
- **BRADBERRY**, Randall .. 662-476-5064 .. 257 G tbradberry@eastms.edu
- **BRADBERRY**, Richard .. 443-885-3488 .. 209 F richard.bradberry@morgan.edu
- **BRADBURY**, Boyd .. 218-477-2095 .. 250 F bradbury@mnstate.edu
- **BRADBURY**, Jane .. 309-692-4092 .. 147 I jbradbury@midstate.edu
- **BRADDER**, Kelley, L .. 515-961-1621 .. 176 H kelley.bradder@simpson.edu
- **BRADDIX**, D'Andre .. 314-516-5205 .. 274 A braddixd@umsl.edu
- **BRADDY**, Linda, s .. 817-515-6686 .. 467 A linda.braddy@tccd.edu
- **BRADDY**, William .. 540-261-8450 .. 494 F bill.braddy@svu.edu
- **BRADEEN**, N. .. 212-217-4370 .. 314 B
- **BRADEN**, Jeffery, P .. 919-515-2468 .. 357 B jeff_braden@ncsu.edu
- **BRADEN**, Kale .. 916-484-8050 .. 51 A bradenc@arc.losrios.edu
- **BRADEN**, Tracey .. 573-592-5301 .. 275 E bradent@westminster-mo.edu
- **BRADFIELD**, Brett .. 605-331-6712 .. 438 A brett.bradfield@usiouxfalls.edu
- **BRADFIELD**, Carol .. 407-303-9585 .. 95 C carol.bradfield@adu.edu
- **BRADFIELD**, Jennifer, S .. 440-775-8400 .. 374 C jennifer.bradfield@oberlin.edu
- **BRADFIELD**, Tanisha .. 714-432-5509 .. 39 G tbradfield@occ.cccd.edu
- **BRADFIELD**, Terry .. 202-885-8631 .. 94 E tbradfield@wesleyseminary.edu
- **BRADFORD, SR.**, Corey, S .. 936-261-2150 .. 467 E csbradford@pvamu.edu
- **BRADFORD**, Frances C .. 757-221-7802 .. 488 F fcbrad@wm.edu
- **BRADFORD**, Grethel .. 301-891-4139 .. 213 D gbradford@wau.edu
- **BRADFORD**, Jerry .. 256-233-8278 .. 1 F jerry.bradford@athens.edu
- **BRADFORD**, Joy .. 404-880-8049 .. 118 K jbradford@cau.edu
- **BRADFORD**, Julie .. 801-818-8900 .. 481 B julie.bradford@provocollege.edu
- **BRADFORD**, Lawrence .. 323-241-5280 .. 50 B bradfoll@lasc.edu
- **BRADFORD**, Linda .. 205-247-8001 .. 7 E lbradford@stillman.edu
- **BRADFORD**, Michael .. 434-832-7293 .. 496 G bradfordm@cvcc.vccs.edu
- **BRADFORD**, Michele .. 256-439-6822 .. 3 M mbradford@gadsdenstate.edu
- **BRADFORD**, Paul .. 805-565-6237 .. 75 A pbradford@westmont.edu
- **BRADFORD**, Peggy .. 914-606-6712 .. 340 C peggy.bradford@wcc.edu
- **BRADFORD-PERRY**, Emma .. 225-771-4990 .. 199 H emma_perry@subr.edu
- **BRADFORD ROUSE**, Teri .. 805-565-7255 .. 75 A tbradfordrouse@westmont.edu
- **BRADIN**, Bernice .. 617-349-8685 .. 220 B bbradin@lesley.edu
- **BRADLEY**, Akirah .. 303-492-8476 .. 33 K akirah.bradley@colorado.edu
- **BRADLEY**, Alan .. 615-297-7545 .. 438 F alanb@aquinascollege.edu
- **BRADLEY**, Alice .. 704-290-5832 .. 353 B abradley@spcc.edu
- **BRADLEY**, Alvin .. 318-274-3278 .. 200 F bradleya@gram.edu
- **BRADLEY**, Angela .. 228-897-3886 .. 259 C angela.bradley@mgccc.edu
- **BRADLEY**, Brenda .. 712-274-6400 .. 177 I brenda.bradley@witcc.edu
- **BRADLEY**, Cedric .. 228-497-7627 .. 259 C cedric.bradley@mgccc.edu
- **BRADLEY**, Dale, R .. 304-367-4692 .. 512 D dale.bradley@pierpont.edu
- **BRADLEY**, Daniel, J .. 812-237-4000 .. 162 A president@indstate.edu
- **BRADLEY**, David, M .. 713-221-8610 .. 474 B bradleyd@uhd.edu
- **BRADLEY**, DeMethra .. 651-696-6220 .. 247 I dbradley@macalester.edu
- **BRADLEY**, Dennis, J .. 814-732-1030 .. 415 A bradley@edinboro.edu
- **BRADLEY**, Devon .. 517-483-1426 .. 237 A bradled@lcc.edu
- **BRADLEY**, Jane .. 319-296-4230 .. 173 B jane.bradley@hawkeyecollege.edu
- **BRADLEY**, Jennifer .. 319-398-4913 .. 174 I jbradley@kirkwood.edu
- **BRADLEY**, Jennifer .. 334-244-3554 .. 2 A jbradle8@aum.edu
- **BRADLEY**, Jennifer .. 808-734-9890 .. 131 I jbradley@hawaii.edu
- **BRADLEY**, JoAnn .. 718-270-4418 .. 332 B jbradley@downstate.edu
- **BRADLEY**, Joseph .. 410-617-5780 .. 208 G jbradley@loyola.edu
- **BRADLEY**, Julie, M .. 972-758-3821 .. 455 A jbradley@collin.edu
- **BRADLEY**, Kathy .. 717-337-6960 .. 404 C kbradley@gettysburg.edu
- **BRADLEY**, Liz .. 402-557-7266 .. 278 I crumly@bellevue.edu
- **BRADLEY**, Marcy, K .. 607-871-2350 .. 303 F bradlemk@alfred.edu
- **BRADLEY**, Mark .. 360-882-2200 .. 44 H markbradley@gs.edu
- **BRADLEY**, Martha, S .. 801-585-3582 .. 481 M martha.bradley@utah.edu
- **BRADLEY**, Miho .. 808-983-4163 .. 130 I mbradley@tokai.edu
- **BRADLEY**, Monica .. 318-274-6118 .. 200 F bradleym@gram.edu
- **BRADLEY**, Nedra .. 601-484-8674 .. 258 F nbradley@meridiancc.edu
- **BRADLEY**, Patrick, J .. 660-543-4515 .. 273 C pbradley@ucmo.edu
- **BRADLEY**, Paul .. 937-769-1683 .. 363 E pbradley@antioch.edu
- **BRADLEY**, Paul .. 937-769-1683 .. 363 F pbradley@antioch.edu
- **BRADLEY**, Paul, A .. 651-631-5592 .. 256 A pabradley@unwsp.edu
- **BRADLEY**, Roger .. 386-267-0565 .. 98 D director@daytonacollege.edu
- **BRADLEY**, Tanya, W .. 802-626-6218 .. 486 C tanya.bradley@lyndonstate.edu
- **BRADLEY**, Tina .. 870-508-6130 .. 19 B tbradley@asumh.edu
- **BRADLEY**, Todd .. 615-550-3173 .. 449 I todd.bradley@williamsoncc.edu
- **BRADLEY**, Tracey .. 865-539-7158 .. 446 G tcbradley@pstcc.edu
- **BRADLEY**, Vinson .. 251-580-4908 .. 4 D vinson.bradley@hawks.huntingdon.edu
- **BRADLEY BRENNAN**, Dolores .. 404-270-5734 .. 128 A dbradley@spelman.edu
- **BRADLEY-DOPPES**, Peg .. 303-871-3399 .. 84 B pbd@du.edu
- **BRADLEY-HASTY**, Barbara .. 252-536-3386 .. 350 C bhasty399@halifaxcc.edu
- **BRADSHAW**, Amelia, M .. 804-523-5867 .. 497 C abradshaw@reynolds.edu
- **BRADSHAW**, Bob .. 510-659-6191 .. 55 B bbradshaw@ohlone.edu
- **BRADSHAW**, Boyd .. 636-227-2100 .. 267 A
- **BRADSHAW**, Brent .. 972-279-6511 .. 450 I bbradshaw@amberton.edu
- **BRADSHAW**, Debra .. 816-268-5472 .. 269 H dlbradshaw@nts.edu
- **BRADSHAW**, Erin .. 505-224-4000 .. 299 F ebradshaw3@cnm.edu
- **BRADSHAW**, Geoffrey, W .. 608-246-6165 .. 523 F gbradshaw@madisoncollege.edu
- **BRADSHAW**, George .. 909-274-4419 .. 53 C gbradshaw@mtsac.edu
- **BRADSHAW**, Kim .. 704-355-5584 .. 342 E kim.bradshaw@carolinashealthcare.org
- **BRADSHAW**, Kim .. 704-355-5584 .. 343 A kim.bradshaw@carolinascollege.edu
- **BRADSHAW**, Marjorie .. 913-234-0607 .. 179 M marjorie.bradshaw@cleveland.edu
- **BRADSHAW**, Michael .. 601-477-4161 .. 258 E michael.bradshaw@jcjc.edu
- **BRADSHAW**, Phillip .. 757-825-2895 .. 498 G bradshawp@tncc.edu
- **BRADSHAW**, Stephen .. 404-233-3949 .. 443 M sbradshaw@richmont.edu
- **BRADSHAW**, William .. 215-951-1425 .. 407 A bradshaww69@lasalle.edu

BRADSHAW, Wilson, G .... 239-590-1055.. 110 L
president@fgcu.edu
BRADSHER, Carl .... 434-791-5646.. 487 C
cbradshe@averett.edu
BRADT, Jeremy .... 815-599-3500.. 141 E
jeremy.bradt@highland.edu
BRADY, Bridget .... 805-898-4003.... 43 K
blbrady@fielding.edu
BRADY, Christian, M .... 814-865-2631.. 412 F
cmb44@psu.edu
BRADY, Claire .... 352-365-3608.. 104 J
bradyc@lssc.edu
BRADY, David, M .... 203-576-4589.... 89 C
dbrady@bridgeport.edu
BRADY, Diane .... 925-424-1630.... 37 C
dbrady@laspositascollege.edu
BRADY, Douglas .... 716-375-2455.. 328 B
dbrady@sbu.edu
BRADY, Henry, E .... 510-642-5116.... 68 M
hbrady@econ.berkeley.edu
BRADY, James .... 509-533-3680.. 503 A
jim.brady@sfcc.spokane.edu
BRADY, Jeanne, F .... 610-660-1000.. 418 G
BRADY, Kathleen .... 732-987-2415.. 292 A
kbrady@georgian.edu
BRADY, Kathleen .... 864-503-5941.. 434 G
kbrady@uscupstate.edu
BRADY, Kathleen, T .... 843-792-5205.. 431 A
bradyk@musc.edu
BRADY, Lauren .... 480-245-7980.... 13 L
lauren.brady@ibcs.edu
BRADY, Marilyn .... 843-574-6566.. 433 D
marilyn.brady@tridenttech.edu
BRADY, Patricia .... 808-373-2849.. 132 G
BRADY, Scott .... 630-942-2219.. 138 B
bradys310@cod.edu
BRADY, Steven .... 812-877-8878.. 166 H
brady1@rose-hulman.edu
BRADY, Todd .... 731-661-6566.. 448 A
tbrady@uu.edu
BRAESE, Paul .... 828-898-8776.. 345 G
braesep@lmc.edu
BRAEUTIGAM, Ronald, R 847-491-7040.. 150 F
braeutigam@northwestern.edu
BRAGA, Sophia .... 518-464-8580.. 314 A
sbraga@excelsior.edu
BRAGG, Chris .... 208-732-6775.. 133 E
cbragg@csi.edu
BRAGG, Dallas .... 704-808-8044.. 343 E
dbragg@charlottelaw.edu
BRAGG, Darcy .... 229-928-2378.. 122 C
darcy.bragg@gsw.edu
BRAGG, David .... 804-524-5598.. 499 G
dbragg@vsu.edu
BRAGG, Dawn, S .... 414-456-8734.. 518 A
dbragg@mcw.edu
BRAGG, Elizabeth .... 503-760-3131.. 390 B
elizabeth@birthingway.edu
BRAGG, Melissa .... 254-295-4608.. 474 E
mbragg@umhb.edu
BRAGG, Michael, B .... 206-543-1829.. 508 E
mbragg@uw.edu
BRAGG, Robert, S .... 276-328-0129.. 495 I
rsb2e@uvawise.edu
BRAGIN, Marc .... 740-427-5228.. 371 C
braginm@kenyon.edu
BRAHA, Habtu .... 410-951-3014.. 212 E
hbraha@coppin.edu
BRAHA, Habtu .... 410-951-3447.. 212 E
hbraha@coppin.edu
BRAHAMS, Teri, T .... 865-694-6476.. 446 G
tbrahams@pstcc.edu
BRAHM, Gary .... 949-753-4774.... 28 F
chancellor@brandman.edu
BRAIDES, Cheryl .... 215-612-6600.. 398 G
cbraides@chicareers.com
BRAILER, James .... 410-516-8070.. 208 D
jbraile1@jhu.edu
BRAILEY, Crystal .... 803-793-5512.. 429 D
braileyc@denmarktech.edu
BRAIM, Barry .... 413-775-1311.. 223 D
braim@gcc.mass.edu
BRAINARD, Lisa, C .... 518-292-1959.. 327 H
brainl@sage.edu
BRAINARD, Nancy .... 918-495-7119.. 386 H
nbrainard@oru.edu
BRAINER, Charles .... 765-998-5271.. 167 C
chbrainer@taylor.edu
BRAINERD, Thomas .... 208-882-1566.. 134 B
tbrainerd@nsa.edu
BRAIS, Nathan .... 714-546-7600.... 39 E
nbrais@coastline.edu
BRAISHER, Lyndsey .... 405-912-9007.. 387 D
lbraisher@hc.edu
BRAISHER, Mark, H .... 405-912-9013.. 387 D
mbraisher@hc.edu
BRAKEFIELD, Jean Ann ... 843-349-2846.. 428 E
jeanann@coastal.edu
BRAKER, Regina .... 541-962-3509.. 391 C
rbraker@eou.edu

BRAKSICK, Ben .... 317-955-6319.. 165 N
bbraksick@marian.edu
BRALL, Catherine, M .... 412-924-1404.. 417 E
cbrall@pts.edu
BRALLEY, Shannon .... 254-526-1934.. 454 A
shannon.bralley@ctcd.edu
BRALY, JR., Cliff .... 336-272-7102.. 344 G
bralyc@greensboro.edu
BRAMANTE, Paula .... 617-603-6900.. 226 D
paula.bramante@necb.edu
BRAMBLETT, Sandra, J ... 404-894-8874.. 121 D
sandi@gatech.edu
BRAME, David .... 407-438-6000.. 110 A
BRAME, Tracey .... 616-301-6800.. 243 I
bramet@cooley.edu
BRAMLAGE, Jenell .... 215-968-8058.. 399 A
jenell.bramlage@bucks.edu
BRAMLAGE, SC, Nancy .... 513-244-4844.. 373 C
nancy.bramlage@msj.edu
BRAMLETT, Nancy .... 913-758-4372.. 185 F
nancy.bramlett@stmary.edu
BRAMLETTE, Jeff .... 706-291-2121.. 127 A
jbramlette@shorter.edu
BRAMLEY, Mary .... 703-323-3749.. 497 H
mbramley@nvcc.edu
BRAMMELL, Keith .... 606-326-2426.. 188 N
keith.brammell@kctcs.edu
BRAMMER, Erika .... 423-652-6301.. 440 J
ebrammer@king.edu
BRAMMER, Robyn .... 714-895-8125.... 39 F
rbrammer@gwc.cccd.edu
BRAMON, Margie .... 800-995-3159.. 275 G
margie.bramon@williamwoods.edu
BRAMUCCI, Robert, S .... 949-582-4960.... 65 E
rbramucci@socccd.edu
BRANCA, Matthew, P .... 570-326-3761.. 413 O
mbranca@pct.edu
BRANCA, Mickey .... 415-241-2255.... 38 E
mbranca@ccsf.edu
BRANCH, Anna .... 413-545-6237.. 220 F
abranch@soc.umass.edu
BRANCH, Carol .... 310-846-2554.... 55 E
ananse@otis.edu
BRANCH, Craig .... 540-891-3007.. 497 B
cbranch@germanna.edu
BRANCH, Gary .... 256-395-2211.... 7 C
gbranch@suscc.edu
BRANCH, Gary, L .... 251-580-2100.... 4 I
gary.branch@faulknerstate.edu
BRANCH, Rachel, U .... 904-819-6294.... 99 M
rbranch@flagler.edu
BRANCH, Steve .... 276-656-0211.. 498 A
sbranch@patrickhenry.edu
BRANCH, Tywana .... 803-780-1089.. 434 M
tbranch@voorhees.edu
BRANCHEAU, Carrie .... 303-753-6046.... 83 A
cbrancheau@rmcad.edu
BRANCHEAU, Ed .... 858-225-4301.... 30 F
BRANCHINI, Ann, Z .... 516-323-3008.. 321 H
office-of-academic-affairs@molloy.edu
BRANCIFORTE,
Rosemarie .... 407-277-0311.... 99 J
rbranciforte@evergladesuniversity.edu
BRANCOLINI, Kristine .... 310-338-4593.... 51 E
kbrancol@lmu.edu
BRAND, Amy .... 617-253-4078.. 225 A
BRAND, Amy .... 601-553-3455.. 258 F
abrand@meridiancc.edu
BRAND, David .... 910-678-8307.. 349 F
brandd@faytechcc.edu
BRAND, Frederick .... 609-984-1588.. 297 F
fbrand@tesu.edu
BRAND, Jonathan .... 319-895-4324.. 171 A
jbrand@cornellcollege.edu
BRAND, Richard .... 423-968-4861.. 440 J
rjbrand@king.edu
BRANDAU, Janet .... 303-360-4735.... 79 E
janet.brandau@ccaurora.edu
BRANDAU-HYNEK, Ann .... 608-785-9585.. 524 H
brandauhyneka@westerntc.edu
BRANDAUER,
Samantha, C .... 717-245-8068.. 402 D
brandaus@dickinson.edu
BRANDEBURG, Rosanne . 352-365-3515.. 104 J
brandebr@lssc.edu
BRANDEL, Scott .... 312-752-2104.. 144 E
scott.brandel@kendall.edu
BRANDENBURG, Aurelia . 859-985-3173.. 187 B
aurelia_brandenburg@berea.edu
BRANDENBURG,
Mark, C .... 843-953-5252.. 428 A
mark.brandenburg@citadel.edu
BRANDER, Kenneth .... 212-960-5263.. 341 G
brander@yu.edu
BRANDES, Derek, R .... 509-527-4274.. 508 F
derek.brandes@wwcc.edu
BRANDES, Rand .... 828-328-7077.. 345 H
rand.brandes@lr.edu
BRANDFORD-CALVO,
Dania .... 401-874-2018.. 426 D
brandford@uri.edu

BRANDI, Anne, E .... 516-572-7205.. 322 C
anne.brandi@ncc.edu
BRANDI, Erica .... 610-398-5300.. 408 I
ebrandi@lincolntech.edu
BRANDKAMP, Katelyn .... 660-263-4100.. 269 D
katelynb@macc.edu
BRANDON, Alonzo, C .... 757-683-5383.. 492 G
abrandon@odu.edu
BRANDON, Dave, E .... 217-424-6330.. 148 D
dbrandon@millikin.edu
BRANDON, Deborah, L .... 909-869-3427.... 31 J
dlbrandon@cpp.edu
BRANDON, Elvis .... 615-230-3375.. 447 C
elvis.brandon@volstate.edu
BRANDON, Eric .... 828-328-7301.. 345 H
eric.brandon@lr.edu
BRANDON, Felicia .... 914-674-7718.. 320 G
fbrandon@mercy.edu
BRANDON, Kevin .... 708-209-3127.. 138 G
kevin.brandon@cuchicago.edu
BRANDON, Lisa, K .... 618-537-6865.. 147 F
lkbrandon@mckendree.edu
BRANDON, Mark, E .... 205-348-5117.... 8 D
mbrandon@law.ua.edu
BRANDON, Maureen .... 970-247-7264.... 80 D
brandon_m@fortlewis.edu
BRANDON, Michaele .... 505-566-3693.. 301 J
brandonm@sancollege.edu
BRANDON, Robert .... 423-478-6229.. 445 E
rbrandon01@clevelandstatecc.edu
BRANDON, Sonia .... 970-248-1884.... 77 L
sbrandon@coloradomesa.edu
BRANDON, Tracey, P .... 336-599-0032.. 351 H
tracey.brandon@piedmontcc.edu
BRANDSEN, Cheryl .... 616-526-6102.. 232 A
brac@calvin.edu
BRANDSTATER, Nate .... 937-395-8618.. 371 D
nate.brandstater@kc.edu
BRANDT, Amy .... 607-778-5014.. 332 D
brandtac@sunybroome.edu
BRANDT, Elaine .... 573-897-5000.. 272 H
BRANDT, Eric .... 218-733-7600.. 249 H
eric.brandt@lsc.edu
BRANDT, James .... 414-443-8866.. 522 P
jim.brandt@wlc.edu
BRANDT, Jay, J .... 561-237-7947.. 104 O
jbrandt@lynn.edu
BRANDT, John .... 540-261-8467.. 494 F
john.brandt@svu.edu
BRANDT, Lisa .... 402-461-5177.. 280 H
BRANDT, Martin .... 631-420-2333.. 335 E
martin.brandt@farmingdale.edu
BRANDT, Mary, L .... 713-798-3380.. 452 G
brandt@bcm.edu
BRANDT, Scott .... 831-459-2425.... 70 F
sbrandt@ucsc.edu
BRANDT, William .... 973-278-5400.. 305 B
wab@berkeleycollege.edu
BRANDT, William .... 973-278-5400.. 289 F
wab@berkeleycollege.edu
BRANDT-RAUF, Paul .... 312-996-5939.. 156 F
pwb1@uic.edu
BRANDVOLD, Kelli .... 808-734-9575.. 131 I
kellib@hawaii.edu
BRANGMAN, Alan .... 302-831-1110.... 91 F
brangman@udel.edu
BRANHAM, Celeste .... 207-778-7087.. 205 A
cbranham@maine.edu
BRANHAM, Holly, L .... 307-532-8303.. 526 G
holly.branham@ewc.wy.edu
BRANHAM, Keith .... 309-672-5916.. 147 H
kbranham@methodistcol.edu
BRANHAM, LaTonya .... 937-376-6611.. 365 H
lbranham@centralstate.edu
BRANHAM, Lorraine .... 315-443-3627.. 337 A
lbranham@syr.edu
BRANICKY, Michael .... 785-864-3881.. 185 D
mbranicky@ku.edu
BRANIGAN, David, E .... 814-863-9150.. 412 F
deb7@psu.edu
BRANKLE, Steve .... 479-524-7209.... 20 H
sbrankle@jbu.edu
BRANN, Shawn .... 817-722-1700.. 460 E
shawn.brann@tku.edu
BRANNAN, Angie, R .... 262-524-7335.. 515 J
abrannan@carrollu.edu
BRANNAN, Colleen, E .... 607-436-2748.. 331 F
colleen.brannan@oneonta.edu
BRANNAN, Sandra .... 409-944-1387.. 458 D
sbrannan@gc.edu
BRANNAN, Thomas, I .... 205-934-0177.... 8 E
tbrannan@uab.edu
BRANNER, Wade, H .... 540-464-7253.. 499 E
brannerwh@vmi.edu
BRANNIN, Brooke .... 615-460-6364.. 438 J
brooke.brannin@belmont.edu
BRANNON, Jennifer .... 478-934-3352.. 124 E
jennifer.brannon@mga.edu
BRANNON, Kelly .... 401-841-2220.. 528 E
BRANNON, Mark .... 256-306-2500.... 2 F
mark.brannon@calhoun.edu

BRANNON, Tony, L .... 270-809-3328.. 192 A
tbrannon@murraystate.edu
BRANON, Rovy .... 206-685-6313.. 508 E
rbranon@uw.edu
BRANSCOME, Tara .... 256-331-5299.... 6 A
tbranscome@nwscc.edu
BRANSCUM, Cindy .... 417-455-5506.. 264 E
cindybranscum@crowder.edu
BRANSON, Angela .... 312-942-9523.. 153 B
angela_branson@rush.edu
BRANSON, Cathy .... 606-487-3550.. 189 E
cathy.branson@kctcs.edu
BRANSON, Mark .... 312-662-4121.. 134 I
mbranson@adler.edu
BRANSON, Salinda Jo .... 309-649-6217.. 155 G
jo.branson@src.edu
BRANSON, Walter, J .... 573-341-4122.. 274 B
bransonwj@mst.edu
BRANSTETTER, Jeffrey, C 402-280-5530.. 279 H
jbranstetter@creighton.edu
BRANSTETTER, Marie .... 913-288-7211.. 182 C
marie@kckcc.edu
BRANT, Christine .... 734-432-5620.. 237 D
cbrant@madonna.edu
BRANT, David .... 310-506-4349.... 56 J
david.brant@pepperdine.edu
BRANT, Felicia .... 202-274-5000.... 94 B
fbrant@udc.edu
BRANT, Kathy .... 864-646-1774.. 433 C
kbrand@tctc.edu
BRANT, Keith .... 831-459-2654.... 70 F
keithb@ucsc.edu
BRANT, Todd .... 405-789-6400.. 388 A
tbrant@snu.edu
BRANTLEY, Allison .... 205-652-3665.... 9 F
abrantley@uwa.edu
BRANTLEY, Brenda .... 318-678-6000.. 195 I
bbrantley@bpcc.edu
BRANTLEY, Kyle .... 601-925-7634.. 259 A
brantley@mc.edu
BRANTLEY, Linda .... 978-762-4000.. 224 C
lbrantley@northshore.edu
BRANTLEY, Michael .... 972-860-7640.. 456 D
mbrantley@dcccd.edu
BRANTLEY, Will .... 405-585-5000.. 385 B
will.brantley@okbu.edu
BRANTON-HOUSLEY,
Mary .... 970-204-8121.... 80 E
mary.branton-housley@frontrange.edu
BRANUM, Scott .... 409-944-1216.. 458 D
tbranum@gc.edu
BRAS, Duane .... 616-222-3000.. 236 F
dbras@kuyper.edu
BRAS, Rafael .... 404-385-5700.. 121 D
provost@gatech.edu
BRASCA, Meredith .... 904-743-1122.. 103 G
mbrasca@jones.edu
BRASE, Don .... 503-399-5184.. 390 E
don.brase@chemeketa.edu
BRASE, Heather .... 314-744-5342.. 268 F
matlock@mobap.edu
BRASE, Wendell, C .... 949-824-5107.... 69 C
wcbrase@uci.edu
BRASEL, Steve .... 312-329-4194.. 148 F
steve.brasel@moody.edu
BRASFIELD, Julie, A .... 919-515-8008.. 357 B
julie_brasfield@ncsu.edu
BRASHEAR, Kurth .... 402-643-7408.. 279 F
kurth.brashear@cune.edu
BRASHEARS, Randolph .... 978-934-2384.. 221 A
randolph_brashears@uml.edu
BRASHEARS, Thomas, A . 540-464-7184.. 499 E
brashearsta@vmi.edu
BRASHER, Christine .... 337-482-1394.. 201 D
cbrasher@louisiana.edu
BRASHIER, Jason .... 731-989-6571.. 440 D
jbrashier@fhu.edu
BRASIER, Terry .... 828-398-7146.. 347 D
terrygbrasier@abtech.edu
BRASKAMP, Corey .... 605-256-5227.. 437 C
corey.braskamp@dsu.edu
BRASKICH, Brian .... 651-255-6170.. 255 C
bbraskich@unitedseminary.edu
BRASSARD, Kevin, F .... 508-213-2213.. 227 A
kevin.brassard@nichols.edu
BRASSIL, Kristoffer, W .... 617-358-7000.. 216 E
kbrassil@bu.edu
BRASSORD, James, D .... 413-542-2202.. 214 C
jdbrassord@amherst.edu
BRASTETER, Christina .... 856-256-5173.. 295 E
brasteter@rowan.edu
BRASURE, III, Ralph .... 860-515-3873.... 85 D
BRASWELL, Cara Mia .... 334-244-3498.... 2 A
cbraswe2@aum.edu
BRASWELL, Frank .... 651-846-1490.. 252 C
frank.braswell@saintpaul.edu
BRASWELL, James .... 281-476-2771.. 464 J
james.braswell@sjcd.edu
BRASWELL, Jody .... 417-690-3372.. 263 E
braswell@cofo.edu

BRASWELL, Kevin .... 931-372-6092.. 445 B
kbraswell@tntech.edu
BRATHWAITE,
Cicely Horsham .... 212-220-8141.. 307 B
chorshambrathwaite@bmcc.cuny.edu
BRATHWAITE, Edward ..... 909-607-8509.... 38 I
edward.brathwaite@sodexo.com
BRATHWAITE, Joy, E .... 612-343-4165.. 253 Y
jebrathw@northcentral.edu
BRATSCH, John .... 559-730-3830.... 40 E
johnbr@cos.edu
BRATSCH-PRINCE, Dawn . 515-294-6410.. 169 G
deprince@iastate.edu
BRATT, Jonathan .... 585-594-6830.. 327 D
bratt_jonathan@roberts.edu
BRATTOLI, Tamara .... 815-280-2470.. 144 A
tbrattol@jjc.edu
BRATTON, Marissa .... 808-544-0249.. 130 H
mbratton@hpu.edu
BRATTON, Phyllis, K .... 701-252-3467.. 362 F
pbratton@uj.edu
BRATULIN, Paul .... 909-384-8978.... 60 C
pbratulin@sbccd.cc.ca.us
BRAUCHLE, Ken .... 812-237-2334.. 162 A
ken.brauchle@indstate.edu
BRAUCKMULLER, Lois .... 352-854-2322.... 97 R
brauckml@cf.edu
BRAUER, Cynthia, A .... 757-221-1693.. 488 F
cabra1@wm.edu
BRAUER, Douglas .... 217-875-7200.. 152 C
dbrauer@richland.edu
BRAUER, Erinn .... 308-345-8112.. 280 M
brauere@mpcc.edu
BRAUER, Jeanna .... 417-667-8181.. 264 A
jbrauer@cottey.edu
BRAUER, William, L .... 757-594-7040.. 488 E
wbrauer@cnu.edu
BRAULT, Kelly, N .... 248-370-4921.. 239 K
brault@oakland.edu
BRAUN, Abraham .... 845-425-1370.. 325 F
BRAUN, Amanda .... 414-229-6599.. 520 D
abraun25@uwm.edu
BRAUN, Bernie .... 225-578-1295.. 197 I
bbraun@lsu.edu
BRAUN, Dale, K .... 715-425-3840.. 521 B
dale.k.braun@uwrf.edu
BRAUN, Dennis .... 508-767-7541.. 214 F
dbraun@assumption.edu
BRAUN, Eric .... 740-351-3257.. 377 C
ebraun@shawnee.edu
BRAUN, Eric .... 740-351-3542.. 377 C
ebraun@shawnee.edu
BRAUN, H. Elizabeth .... 610-328-8365.. 419 I
lbraun1@swarthmore.edu
BRAUN, Keith .... 518-327-6072.. 326 B
kbraun@paulsmiths.edu
BRAUN, Keith, V .... 727-816-3336.. 106 F
braunk@phsc.edu
BRAUN, Lynn .... 206-780-6221.. 506 E
lynn.braun@pinchot.edu
BRAUN, Mark .... 515-281-6527.. 169 F
mbraun@iastate.edu
BRAUN, Mary, C .... 319-273-6144.. 170 A
mary.braun@uni.edu
BRAUN, Neil, S .... 212-346-1962.. 325 J
nbraun@pace.edu
BRAUN, Raymond .... 419-372-3411.. 364 E
rwbraun@bgsu.edu
BRAUN, Ronald .... 620-947-3121.. 185 B
ronb@tabor.edu
BRAUN, Thomas, W .... 412-648-1938.. 421 G
twb3@pitt.edu
BRAUNGARD,
Elizabeth (Liz), A .... 717-361-1525.. 403 C
braungarde@etown.edu
BRAUNGARD, John .... 518-629-4507.. 316 G
j.braungard@hvcc.edu
BRAUNINGER, Mike .... 504-280-6590.. 198 D
rbraunin@uno.edu
BRAUNSCHWEIG, Jim ..... 712-274-6400.. 177 I
jim.braunschweig@witcc.edu
BRAVAIS-SLYMAN,
Karine .... 312-777-8674.. 142 G
kbravais-slyman@aii.edu
BRAVE, Jennifer .... 608-789-6248.. 524 H
bravej@westerntc.edu
BRAVEMAN, Daan .... 585-389-2004.. 322 D
dbravem7@naz.edu
BRAVER, Joel .... 845-782-1380.. 341 I
BRAVERMAN, David .... 310-243-3784.... 32 D
dgbraverman@csudh.edu
BRAVERMAN, Lisa .... 201-692-2671.. 291 J
BRAVMAN, John, C .... 570-577-1511.. 398 L
john.bravman@bucknell.edu
BRAVO, Irene .... 305-592-1223.. 531 C
BRAWNER, Dan .... 615-383-4848.. 449 G
dbrawner@watkins.edu
BRAXTON, Joanne, E ...... 631-451-4160.. 336 D
braxtoj@sunysuffolk.edu
BRAXTON, Pamela .... 610-519-4032.. 422 G
pamela.braxton@villanova.edu
BRAXTON, Sallie, W .... 540-286-8016.. 495 C
sbraxton@umw.edu
BRAXTON, Weldon .... 218-322-2380.. 249 G
weldon.braxton@itascacc.edu
BRAY, D. John .... 716-829-7818.. 313 A
brayjd@dyc.edu
BRAY, Heather .... 614-222-6191.. 367 B
hbray@ccad.edu
BRAY, Holly .... 860-486-4241.... 89 D
holly.bray@uconn.edu
BRAY, Jane, S .... 757-683-3938.. 492 G
jsbray@odu.edu
BRAY, John .... 765-677-1771.. 164 B
john.bray@indwes.edu
BRAY, Richard .... 979-209-7285.. 452 J
richard.bray@blinn.edu
BRAY, Sean .... 410-617-2838.. 208 G
sbray@loyola.edu
BRAY, Tim .... 612-624-2095.. 255 H
brayx010@umn.edu
BRAYSHAW, Laurie .... 505-424-2305.. 299 L
llogan@iaia.edu
BRAYTON, Kelley .... 310-434-3465.... 63 F
brayton_kelley@smc.edu
BRAYTON, Spencer .... 217-854-3231.. 135 K
spencer.brayton@blackburn.edu
BRAZ, Meredith .... 603-646-2246.. 286 J
meredith.braz@dartmouth.edu
BRAZA, Peter .... 719-255-4550.... 83 L
pbraza@uccs.edu
BRAZDA, Sara .... 978-837-5257.. 225 E
brazdas@merrimack.edu
BRAZEAU, Gayle .... 207-221-4366.. 205 F
gbrazeau@une.edu
BRAZELTON, Kent .... 713-646-1889.. 459 A
kbrazelton@hcl.edu
BRAZES, Spencer .... 503-552-2016.. 392 H
sbrazes@nunm.edu
BRAZIER, Elise .... 512-313-3000.. 455 F
elise.brazier@concordia.edu
BRAZZEL, Thomas .... 979-830-4041.. 452 J
thomas.brazzel@blinn.edu
BRAZZIL, Nancy, A .... 512-471-1232.. 476 B
nancy@po.utexas.edu
BREANDAU, L.A .... 256-924-0511...... 5 E
labreandau@legacyu.net
BREAU, Walter, C .... 413-265-2222.. 217 D
breauw@elms.edu
BREAULT, Donna .... 419-289-5369.. 363 J
dbreault@ashland.edu
BREAULT, Susan .... 860-932-4062.... 87 C
sbreault@qvcc.edu
BREAUX, David .... 662-846-4100.. 257 E
dbreaux@deltastate.edu
BREAUX, Jules .... 337-482-6471.. 201 D
breaux@louisiana.edu
BREAZILE, Chad .... 816-279-7000.. 262 B
chad@abtu.edu
BRECCIAROLI, TJ .... 256-824-6700...... 8 F
thomas.brecciaroli@uah.edu
BRECHBILL, Ryan .... 614-823-1520.. 376 C
rbrechbill@otterbein.edu
BRECHER, Sharon .... 305-534-7050.. 113 F
sbrecher@talmudicu.edu
BRECKENRIDGE, James .. 650-433-3826.... 56 D
jbreckenridge@paloaltou.edu
BRECKENRIDGE, Joyce .. 412-237-3110.. 401 B
jbreckenridge@ccac.edu
BREEDEN, Amy .... 804-527-1000.... 93 F
BREEDEN, Amy .... 804-763-6300.... 93 F
BREEDEN, Ann Lloyd .... 804-289-8732.. 495 G
abreeden@richmond.edu
BREEDEN, Joe .... 580-349-1446.. 385 F
joeb@opsu.edu
BREEDEN, Steven .... 574-372-5100.. 161 B
projectrequests@grace.edu
BREEDEN, Susan, D .... 804-289-8400.. 495 G
sbreeden@richmond.edu
BREEDEN, Suzette .... 304-734-6640.. 511 M
suzette.breeden@bridgevalley.edu
BREEDLOVE, Liz .... 309-854-1715.. 135 I
breedlovel@bhc.edu
BREEDLOVE, Paul .... 541-880-2239.. 391 F
breedlove@klamathcc.edu
BREEMS, Jennifer .... 712-722-6043.. 171 J
jenni.breems@dordt.edu
BREEN, Bill .... 904-680-7674.. 100 E
wbreen@fcsl.edu
BREEN, David, K .... 508-849-3416.. 214 E
dbreen@annamaria.edu
BREEN, Patricia, A .... 626-529-8008.... 55 H
pbreen@pacificoaks.edu
BREEN, Thomas .... 518-292-1926.. 327 H
breent@sage.edu
BREER, Mary .... 217-234-5401.. 145 D
mbreer@lakeland.cc.il.us
BREERWOOD, Adam ..... 601-403-1132.. 260 D
abreerwood@prcc.edu
BREES, Chris .... 641-844-5679.. 173 L
chris.brees@iavalley.edu
BREESE, Jeffrey .... 708-524-6813.. 139 F
jbreese@com.edu
BREESE, Steven .... 203-392-5468.... 85 H
breeses1@southernct.edu
BREESE, William, E .... 414-277-7401.. 518 E
breese@msoe.edu
BREFFLE, Barbara .... 714-449-7448.... 51 F
bbreffle@ketchum.edu
BREGE, Nicholas .... 989-358-7202.. 230 G
bregen@alpenacc.edu
BREHENY, Marie .... 413-775-1397.. 223 D
brehenym@gcc.mass.edu
BREHLER, Elizabeth .... 336-506-4138.. 347 C
elizabeth.brehler@alamancecc.edu
BREHM, Leslie .... 845-938-6947.. 529 C
8drm@usma.edu
BREHM, Richard .... 540-423-9042.. 497 E
rbrehm@germanna.edu
BREIER, Barbara .... 512-245-2396.. 471 F
blb137@txstate.edu
BREILAND, Chris .... 918-333-6151.. 386 F
cbreiland@okwu.edu
BREILAND, Whitney .... 918-333-6151.. 386 F
wbreiland@okwu.edu
BREINER, Fred .... 865-539-7144.. 446 G
fjbreiner@pstcc.edu
BREINER, Ozzie .... 610-758-3500.. 408 H
lb05@lehigh.edu
BREIT, Karen .... 715-634-4790.. 517 C
kbreit@lco.edu
BREITBACH, William .... 530-242-7555.... 64 D
wbreitbach@shastacollege.edu
BREITBARTH,
Jonathan, S .... 651-641-8796.. 246 B
breitbarth@csp.edu
BREITENBACH, Edward .... 231-777-0526.. 238 G
edward.breitenbach@muskegoncc.edu
BREITER, Randy .... 305-442-9223.. 105 F
rbreiter@mrc.edu
BREITHAUPT, Jeff .... 917-493-4702.. 319 M
jbreithaupt@msmnyc.edu
BREITHOLZ, Brian .... 216-523-7221.. 366 I
b.breitholz@csuohio.edu
BREITMEYER, Chris .... 503-338-2425.. 390 G
cbreitmeyer@clatsopcc.edu
BREITSPRECKER, Lisa ..... 414-930-3131.. 518 F
breitspl@mtmary.edu
BREJA, Lisa .... 641-844-5576.. 173 J
lisa.breja@iavalley.edu
BREKKE, Alice .... 701-777-3511.. 360 C
alice.brekke@und.edu
BREKKE, Tom .... 218-723-6717.. 245 J
tbrekke@css.edu
BREKKEN, Kathryn, C ...... 702-651-7535.. 284 H
kc.brekken@csn.edu
BRELAND, Arthur .... 404-627-2681.. 117 G
arthur.breland@beulah.edu
BRELAND, Byron .... 408-288-3725.... 62 E
byron.breland@sjcc.edu
BRELAND, Garry, M .... 601-318-6101.. 261 I
garry.breland@wmcarey.edu
BRELAND, Jason .... 601-528-8424.. 259 C
jason.breland@mgccc.edu
BRELAND, Jennifer, R ..... 205-934-3555...... 8 E
jbreland@uab.edu
BRELAND, Phyllis .... 315-389-4399.. 315 D
pbreland@hamilton.edu
BRELAND, Roger .... 251-442-2216...... 9 A
rbreland@umobile.edu
BRELLIS, Matthew .... 631-687-4561.. 328 G
mbrellis@sjcny.edu
BREMER, Cris, M .... 559-489-2220.... 67 C
crism.bremer@fresnocitycollege.edu
BREMER, Melanie .... 901-321-4482.. 439 E
mbremer@cbu.edu
BREMER-LOPEZ, Jafet ..... 718-357-0500.. 329 E
jbremer-lopez@stpaulsschoolofnursing.edu
BREMMER, Zach .... 215-884-8942.. 424 B
zach.bremmer@vroninstitute.edu
BREMS, Christiane .... 503-352-7330.. 394 C
cbrems@pacificu.edu
BRENCHER, Anastasia ..... 315-684-6020.. 336 B
brencha@morrisville.edu
BRENEMAN, Curt .... 518-276-6305.. 327 B
brenec@rpi.edu
BRENER, Laura .... 503-883-2449.. 392 B
lbrener@linfield.edu
BRENKMAN, Katie .... 360-417-6276.. 505 I
kbrenkman@pencol.edu
BRENN, James, E .... 803-535-5326.. 428 B
jbrenn@claflin.edu
BRENNAN, Blair .... 308-432-6044.. 231 H
bbrennan@csc.edu
BRENNAN,
Christopher, P .... 727-864-8122.... 98 L
brennacp@eckerd.edu
BRENNAN, Deb .... 308-398-7305.. 278 K
dbrennan@cccneb.edu
BRENNAN, Joanne .... 562-977-6053.... 44 D
BRENNAN, John .... 302-831-2072.... 91 F
jbrennan@udel.edu
BRENNAN, Jonathan .... 518-629-7311.. 316 G
j.brennan@hvcc.edu
BRENNAN, Joseph, A ...... 518-956-8150.. 331 A
jabrennan@albany.edu
BRENNAN, Joyce .... 508-678-2811.. 223 A
BRENNAN, Kara .... 914-633-2410.. 317 B
kbrennan@iona.edu
BRENNAN, Kate .... 856-225-6577.. 296 A
katecb@camden.rutgers.edu
BRENNAN, Kelly .... 212-217-3800.. 314 B
kelly_brennan@fitnyc.edu
BRENNAN, Kelly .... 734-487-8898.. 233 J
kelly.brennan@emich.edu
BRENNAN, Kevin .... 860-486-5022.... 89 D
kevin.brennan@uconn.edu
BRENNAN, Leah .... 860-701-5061.... 88 D
brennan_l@mitchell.edu
BRENNAN, Lipa .... 718-438-2727.. 341 J
rlb@novominsk.com
BRENNAN, Rick .... 708-974-5388.. 148 G
brennan@morainevalley.edu
BRENNAN, Robert, J .... 301-447-7432.. 209 G
brennan@msmary.edu
BRENNAN, Susan .... 781-891-2061.. 215 F
sbrennan@bentley.edu
BRENNAN, Terence .... 303-373-2008.... 83 B
tbrennan@rvu.edu
BRENNAN, Terrence, P ... 972-881-5734.. 455 A
tbrennan@collin.edu
BRENNAN, Terry .... 630-953-3707.. 136 H
tbrennan@chamberlain.edu
BRENNAN, William .... 671-405-5921.. 227 F
wbrennan@quincycollege.edu
BRENNAN, William, J ..... 207-326-2220.. 204 C
bill.brennan@mma.edu
BRENNEMAN, Darnell ...... 740-857-1311.. 376 L
dbrenneman@rosedale.edu
BRENNEMAN, David .... 812-855-0608.. 162 F
davabren@indiana.edu
BRENNEMAN, James, E .. 574-535-7180.. 161 A
president@goshen.edu
BRENNEMAN, Joy, D ...... 806-371-5124.. 450 H
jdbrenneman@actx.edu
BRENNEMANN, Kyle .... 573-629-3007.. 265 G
kbrennemann@hlg.edu
BRENNEN, Bernadette ..... 716-286-8360.. 324 E
bmb@niagara.edu
BRENNEN, David, A .... 859-257-1678.. 193 G
david.brennen@uky.edu
BRENNER, Christina .... 610-436-3511.. 416 C
cbrenner@wcupa.edu
BRENNER, David, A .... 858-534-1501.... 70 C
dbrenner@ucsd.edu
BRENNER, Mary, B .... 805-893-7118.... 70 E
betsy@education.ucsb.edu
BRENNER, Rebecca .... 617-243-2152.. 219 I
rbrenner@lasell.edu
BRENNER-SCOTTI, Laura . 609-984-1141.. 297 F
lbrennerscotti@tesu.edu
BRENNIE, Matthew .... 845-688-6068.. 338 F
brenniem@sunyulster.edu
BRENSINGER, Terry .... 559-453-2325.... 44 F
terry.brensinger@fresno.edu
BRENT, Daniel .... 617-327-6777.. 229 H
dan_brent@williamjames.edu
BRENTLINGER, Ann, M ... 605-394-1604.. 437 E
ann.brentlinger@sdsmt.edu
BRENTLINGER, Dustin ..... 419-448-2062.. 369 G
dbrentli@heidelberg.edu
BRENZING, Pam .... 616-331-3490.. 234 F
brenzinp@gvsu.edu
BRESCIANI, Dean .... 701-231-7211.. 361 A
dean.bresciani@ndsu.edu
BRESE, James .... 808-356-5273.. 130 H
jbrese@hpu.edu
BRESEE, Mikel .... 313-664-1546.. 232 G
mbresee@collegeforcreativestudies.edu
BRESEMAN, Mark, D .... 920-832-6519.. 517 E
mark.d.breseman@lawrence.edu
BRESINGHAM, Ann .... 312-935-6710.. 152 D
abresingham@robertmorris.edu
BRESLAUER, Kenneth, J .. 732-445-3956.. 295 F
kjbdna@rci.rutgers.edu
BRESLAWSKI, Terry .... 724-357-3077.. 415 B
terry.breslawski@iup.edu
BRESLIN, Beau .... 518-580-5705.. 330 F
bbreslin@skidmore.edu
BRESLIN, Eileen, T .... 210-567-5800.. 477 D
breslin@uthscsa.edu
BRESLIN, Kathleen, A ..... 610-359-5131.. 401 L
kbreslin@dccc.edu
BRESLIN, Lisa .... 410-857-2225.. 209 D
lbreslin@mcdaniel.edu
BRESNAHAN, Nicole .... 202-885-2822.... 91 J
nlbres@american.edu
BRESSETTE, Andrew .... 706-236-2216.. 117 F
abressette@berry.edu
BRESSLER, Coleen .... 402-844-7006.. 282 B
coleen@northeast.edu

BRESSLER, Rebecca, B .... 662-915-7735.. 261 B rbbressl@olemiss.edu
BRESSO, Michele .... 661-336-5041.... 47 I mbresso@kccd.edu
BRETON, Gary .... 706-236-1756.. 117 F gbreton@berry.edu
BRETSCHER, David .... 217-786-2238.. 146 E david.bretscher@llcc.edu
BRETT, Jennifer .... 203-576-4122.... 89 C acup@bridgeport.edu
BRETT, Jessie .... 541-962-3740.. 391 C jbrett@eou.edu
BRETTSCHNEIDER, Marla, B .... 603-862-1750.. 288 C marla.brettschneider@unh.edu
BRETZ, Brenda, K .... 717-245-1587.. 402 D bretz@dickinson.edu
BREUER, Catherine .... 952-358-8243.. 251 A catherine.breuer@normandale.edu
BREVOORT, Margaret ...... 425-602-3003.. 501 D
BREW, Alan .... 715-682-1329.. 518 H abrew@northland.edu
BREWER, Andrew .... 315-268-4022.. 310 B abrewer@clarkson.edu
BREWER, Athos .... 713-718-5115.. 459 B athos.brewer@hccs.edu
BREWER, Brent .... 269-687-5642.. 241 C bbrewer01@swmich.edu
BREWER, Carol, A .... 507-933-8809.. 246 J cbrewer@gustavus.edu
BREWER, Chris .... 615-494-8803.. 444 G chris.brewer@mtsu.edu
BREWER, Clay .... 618-985-3741.. 143 F claybrewer@jalc.edu
BREWER, Craig .... 650-508-3684.... 54 J cbrewer@ndnu.edu
BREWER, Dawn, M .... 812-888-4225.. 169 A dbrewer@vinu.edu
BREWER, Deborah .... 716-614-5911.. 324 D dbrewer@niagaracc.suny.edu
BREWER, Deborah .... 716-614-6200.. 324 D
BREWER, Dennis .... 479-575-3301.... 22 I dbrewer@uark.edu
BREWER, Dominic .... 212-998-5001.. 324 C dominic.brewer@nyu.edu
BREWER, George .... 706-272-4456.. 119 H gbrewer@daltonstate.edu
BREWER, Helen .... 908-709-7142.. 298 A helen.brewer@ucc.edu
BREWER, Jane, T .... 843-549-6314.. 434 C jtbrewer@mailbox.sc.edu
BREWER, Janet .... 501-760-4313.... 21 B jbrewer@np.edu
BREWER, Janet .... 765-641-4272.. 158 J jlbrewer@anderson.edu
BREWER, Jay .... 401-841-7008.. 528 E
BREWER, Jerry, T .... 803-777-5783.. 433 F jerry-brewer@sc.edu
BREWER, Jim, L .... 870-460-1274.... 23 D brewer@uamont.edu
BREWER, John .... 801-863-8320.. 482 C brewerjc@uvu.edu
BREWER, JR., John, B .... 301-447-5043.. 209 G brewer@msmary.edu
BREWER, Judy .... 319-656-2447.. 176 F
BREWER, Kristina .... 260-665-4161.. 167 E brewerk@trine.edu
BREWER, Michael, H ...... 484-664-3400.. 411 D brewer@muhlenberg.edu
BREWER, Mondy .... 806-720-7803.. 461 C mondy.brewer@lcu.edu
BREWER, Nancy .... 631-451-4469.. 336 E brewern@sunysuffolk.edu
BREWER, Regina, L .... 336-628-4554.. 352 B rlbrewer@randolph.edu
BREWER, Rick .... 916-558-2442.... 51 D brewerr@scc.losrios.edu
BREWER, Rick .... 318-487-7400.. 195 F rick.brewer@lacollege.edu
BREWER, Robert, W .... 336-272-7102.. 344 G rbrewer@greensboro.edu
BREWER, Ryan .... 205-329-7865........ 3 B ryan.brewer@ecacolleges.com
BREWER, Stacey .... 864-596-9050.. 429 C stacey.brewer@converse.edu
BREWER, Susan .... 870-460-1050.... 23 D brewers@uamont.edu
BREWER, Tim .... 704-878-3205.. 351 D tbrewer@mitchellcc.edu
BREWINGTON, Delsey ..... 910-592-8084.. 352 H dbrewington@sampsoncc.edu
BREWINGTON, Donald, E .... 512-505-3054.. 459 F debrewington@htu.edu
BREWINGTON, Holly .... 910-592-8084.. 352 H hbrewington@sampsoncc.edu
BREWINGTON, Mark .... 910-630-7149.. 346 E sbrewington@methodist.edu
BREWINGTON, Mazie, L . 951-222-8307.... 59 C mazie.brewington@rcc.edu
BREWINGTON, Teare .... 803-536-7011.. 432 E tbrewing@scsu.edu
BREWS, Peter, J .... 803-777-3176.. 433 F peter.brews@moore.sc.edu
BREWSTER, Carrie .... 925-631-4643.... 59 I cbrewste@stmarys-ca.edu
BREWSTER, Geoffrey .... 918-610-8303.. 386 I geoff.brewster@ptstulsa.edu
BREWSTER, LaRita .... 256-761-6119...... 7 F lmbrewster@talladega.edu
BREWTON, Janet, J .... 843-953-4820.. 428 G brewtonj@cofc.edu
BREY, Richard .... 208-282-2902.. 133 H breyrich@isu.edu
BREZEL, Allan .... 404-872-3593.. 117 B abrezel@johnmarshall.edu
BREZIL, Chris .... 212-229-5300.. 322 E brezilc@newschool.edu
BREZINA, Jennifer .... 615-230-3214.. 447 C jennifer.brezina@volstate.edu
BREZINA, Katherine .... 508-678-2811.. 223 A katherine.brezina@bristolcc.edu
BREZINSKI, Donald .... 603-645-3109.. 287 I d.brezinski@snhu.edu
BRHEL, Jan, M .... 518-354-5282.. 325 A president@nccc.edu
BRIAN, Robert, M .... 912-583-3107.. 118 B rbrian@bpc.edu
BRIAN, Thomas, J .... 918-631-2200.. 389 E thomas-brian@utulsa.edu
BRIAND, Simone .... 913-234-0810.. 179 M simone.briand@cleveland.edu
BRIAR, Jennifer .... 760-591-3012.... 72 A jbriar@usa.edu
BRIAR, John .... 559-325-3600.... 30 C jbriar@chsu.org
BRIAR-LAWSON, Katharine, H .... 518-442-5324.. 331 A kbriarlawson@albany.edu
BRICE, Diane .... 806-371-5028.. 450 H kdbrice@actx.edu
BRICE, Tanya .... 803-705-4945.. 427 D bricet@benedict.edu
BRICELAND, Cynthia .... 724-503-1001.. 422 H cbriceland@washjeff.edu
BRICENO, Jaime .... 773-380-7045.. 135 H jbriceno@bexleyseabury.edu
BRICHER, Gary .... 860-297-2331.... 89 B gary.bricher@trincoll.edu
BRICHTA, William .... 215-780-1307.. 419 C wbrichta@salus.edu
BRICK, George .... 575-624-8023.. 300 I brick@nmmi.edu
BRICKER, J. Douglas .... 412-396-6361.. 403 A bricker@duq.edu
BRICKER, Susan .... 626-585-7614.... 56 H sbricker@pasadena.edu
BRICKHOUSE, Nancy .... 314-977-2193.. 271 K brickhouse@slu.edu
BRICKHOUSE, Wendy, W 252-335-0821.. 349 A wbrickhouse@albemarle.edu
BRICKLE, Colleen .... 952-358-8158.. 251 A colleen.brickle@normandale.edu
BRICKNER-WOOD, Larry . 603-862-1165.. 288 C larry.brickner-wood@unh.edu
BRIDDES, Bill .... 610-902-8526.. 399 D
BRIDEL, David .... 213-821-4035.... 72 D bridel@usc.edu
BRIDGE, Holly .... 417-328-1806.. 272 C hbridge@sbuniv.edu
BRIDGE, Louise .... 801-863-8689.. 482 C bridgelo@uvu.edu
BRIDGEFORTH, Daniel .... 703-812-4757.. 491 B dbridgeforth@leland.edu
BRIDGEFORTH, Valerie .... 601-318-6188.. 261 I vbridgeforth@wmcarey.edu
BRIDGEMAN, Curtis .... 503-370-6402.. 396 G cbridgem@willamette.edu
BRIDGEMAN, Doris .... 601-977-7836.. 261 A dbridgeman@tougaloo.edu
BRIDGEMAN, Gregory ..... 270-707-3904.. 189 G gbridgeman0001@kctcs.edu
BRIDGENS, Marc, E .... 570-326-3761.. 413 O mbridgen@pct.edu
BRIDGER, Donald .... 303-458-4206.... 82 L dbridger@regis.edu
BRIDGER, Seth .... 614-235-4136.. 378 C sbridger@tlsohio.edu
BRIDGERS, Amy .... 252-399-6397.. 341 P abbridgers@barton.edu
BRIDGES, Ceil, L .... 870-235-4079.... 22 F clbridges@saumag.edu
BRIDGES, Clarence, F ..... 312-413-5946.. 156 F cbridges@uic.edu
BRIDGES, Craig .... 218-723-4822.. 245 J cbridges@css.edu
BRIDGES, Darryl .... 843-661-1295.. 430 B dbridges@fmarion.edu
BRIDGES, David .... 229-391-5050.. 115 I dbridges@abac.edu
BRIDGES, Edward .... 304-647-6439.. 514 A ebridges@osteo.wvsom.edu
BRIDGES, George, S .... 360-867-6100.. 503 G bridges@evergreen.edu
BRIDGES, Harold, A .... 310-338-2700.... 51 E
BRIDGES, J. Thomas .... 704-847-5600.. 355 J jbridges@ses.edu
BRIDGES, Karl .... 208-282-3045.. 133 H bridkarl@isu.edu
BRIDGES, Katie .... 202-462-2101.... 93 B kbridges@iwp.edu
BRIDGES, Kermit, S .... 972-825-4652.. 466 D president@sagu.edu
BRIDGES, Kristina .... 319-399-8100.. 170 G kbridges@coe.edu
BRIDGES, LaDonna .... 508-626-4906.. 221 E lbridges@framingham.edu
BRIDGES, Martin .... 910-410-1818.. 352 C mwbridges@richmondcc.edu
BRIDGES, Michael, W ...... 412-396-1813.. 403 A bridgesm@duq.edu
BRIDGES, Robert .... 417-334-6411.. 263 E rbridges@cofo.edu
BRIDGES, Ruth .... 254-298-8309.. 467 B ruth.bridges@templejc.edu
BRIDGES, Scott, D .... 618-453-6214.. 154 I bridges@siu.edu
BRIDGES, Shelton .... 502-451-0815.. 193 A sbridges@sullivan.edu
BRIDGES, Shelton .... 502-451-0815.. 193 B sbridges@sullivan.edu
BRIDGES, Steven, J .... 812-464-1849.. 168 E sjbridge@usi.edu
BRIDGES, Tharsteen .... 334-874-5700...... 3 A tbridges@ccal.edu
BRIDGES, Vernon, D .... 818-947-2541.... 50 D bridgevd@lavc.edu
BRIDGESMITH, Lance ...... 310-506-4700.... 56 J lance.bridgesmith@pepperdine.edu
BRIDGMAN, Christa, L ...... 828-298-3325.. 359 F cbridgma@warren-wilson.edu
BRIDGMON, Phillip .... 918-456-5511.. 384 G bridgmon@nsuok.edu
BRIDWELL, Chadd .... 817-531-4422.. 472 F cbridwell@txwes.edu
BRIDWELL, Joy .... 406-395-4875.. 278 F jbridwell@stonechild.edu
BRIDWELL, Virginia .... 425-564-2198.. 501 F virginia.bridwell@bellevuecollege.edu
BRIELER, Robert .... 636-481-3337.. 266 C rbrieler@jeffco.edu
BRIELL, Scott .... 641-784-5110.. 172 G sbriell1@graceland.edu
BRIELMAIER, Michele .... 507-389-7385.. 252 D michele.brielmaier@southcentral.edu
BRIEM, Kit .... 651-255-6111.. 255 C kbriem@unitedseminary.edu
BRIEN, Jane .... 845-758-4294.. 304 F brien@bard.edu
BRIERE, Donna .... 603-752-1113.. 286 H dbriere@ccsnh.edu
BRIGDON, Beth, P .... 706-721-9667.. 117 D bbrigdon@augusta.edu
BRIGETY, Reuben, E .... 202-994-6240.... 92 D rbrigety@gwu.edu
BRIGGANCE, Richard .... 615-963-5171.. 445 A rbriggance@tnstate.edu
BRIGGER, Clark, V .... 814-863-4774.. 412 F cvb12@psu.edu
BRIGGLE, Jennifer .... 970-207-4550.... 81 F jenniferbr@mckinleycollege.edu
BRIGGS, Catherine, R ...... 856-222-9311.. 295 C cbriggs@rcbc.edu
BRIGGS, Chad .... 847-628-2018.. 144 B chad.briggs@judsonu.edu
BRIGGS, Charlotte .... 413-565-1000.. 215 A cbriggs@baypath.edu
BRIGGS, Darcy .... 303-797-5623.... 76 J darcy.briggs@arapahoe.edu
BRIGGS, Douglas, S .... 540-636-2900.. 488 D dougb@christendom.edu
BRIGGS, Eddie .... 864-388-8222.. 430 G ebriggs@lander.edu
BRIGGS, Jeff .... 859-344-3352.. 193 C briggsj@thomasmore.edu
BRIGGS, Jeff .... 785-628-4200.. 180 I jbriggs@fhsu.edu
BRIGGS, Jennifer .... 812-488-2602.. 167 I jb610@evansville.edu
BRIGGS, SR., Jerryl .... 662-254-3425.. 260 A jerryl.briggs@mvsu.edu
BRIGGS, Jodi .... 508-541-1656.. 217 G jbriggs@dean.edu
BRIGGS, Julie, A .... 585-245-5616.. 333 B briggsja@geneseo.edu
BRIGGS, Karen .... 619-260-2762.... 72 B karenbriggs@sandiego.edu
BRIGGS, Kenneth .... 860-215-9259.... 87 D kbriggs@trcc.commnet.edu
BRIGGS, Kristin .... 336-249-8186.. 349 C kristin_briggs@davidsonccc.edu
BRIGGS, LaNae, R .... 803-786-3856.. 429 A lrbriggs@columbiasc.edu
BRIGGS, Larry .... 208-769-3474.. 134 C ljbriggs@nic.edu
BRIGGS, Mary, K .... 276-944-6836.. 489 I mkbriggs@ehc.edu
BRIGGS, Paige .... 505-277-0727.. 302 F pdbriggs@unm.edu
BRIGGS, Peter, F .... 517-353-1720.. 237 I pbriggs@msu.edu
BRIGGS, Phillip .... 805-289-6000.... 73 F pbriggs@vcccd.edu
BRIGGS, Stephen, R .... 706-236-2281.. 117 F sbriggs@berry.edu
BRIGGS, Susan .... 406-683-7031.. 277 A susan.briggs@umwestern.edu
BRIGGS, Thyra .... 909-607-4408.... 46 A thyra_briggs@hmc.edu
BRIGGS, Tonya, M .... 610-359-7349.. 401 L tbriggs@dccc.edu
BRIGHAM, Bettie Ann ..... 610-341-5823.. 403 B bbrigham@eastern.edu
BRIGHAM, David, R .... 215-972-2056.. 413 L dbrigham@pafa.org
BRIGHAM, R. Scott .... 773-907-4700.. 137 E sbrigham@ccc.edu
BRIGHT, Brett .... 620-665-3579.. 181 I brightb@hutchcc.edu
BRIGHT, Erin, L .... 503-943-7125.. 396 B bright@up.edu
BRIGHT, George, L .... 610-861-1534.. 411 B brightg@moravian.edu
BRIGHT, Harry .... 641-472-1178.. 175 A hbright@mum.edu
BRIGHT, James (Phillip) . 731-881-7845.. 448 G pbright@utm.edu
BRIGHT, Jessica .... 512-313-3000.. 455 F jessica.bright@concordia.edu
BRIGHT, Marvin .... 727-712-5742.. 108 D bright.marvin@spcollege.edu
BRIGHT, Richard .... 641-269-4850.. 172 I bright@grinnell.edu
BRIGHT, Sarah .... 636-481-3218.. 266 C sbright@jeffco.edu
BRIGHT, Steve .... 434-544-8208.. 491 F bright@lynchburg.edu
BRIGHTON, Robyn .... 407-582-3895.. 114 N rbrighton1@valenciacollege.edu
BRIJBASI, Monique .... 305-628-6648.. 108 E mbrijbasi@stu.edu
BRILEY, Brantley .... 252-527-6223.. 350 H bbriley@lenoircc.edu
BRILEY, Jana .... 912-478-1301.. 122 B janawms@georgiasouthern.edu
BRILL, Ann .... 309-341-7130.. 145 A abrill@knox.edu
BRILL, Ann, M .... 785-864-4755.. 185 D abrill@ku.edu
BRILLER, Vladimir .... 718-636-4245.. 326 E vbriller@pratt.edu
BRILLEY, Amy .... 217-362-6488.. 148 D abrilley@millikin.edu
BRILLHART, David .... 740-366-9319.. 365 D brillhart.5@osu.edu
BRIMHALL, Carrie .... 218-736-1524.. 250 D carrie.brimhall@minnesota.edu
BRIMHALL, Joseph .... 503-251-5712.. 396 C jebrimhall@uws.edu
BRIMHALL-VARGAS, Mark .... 617-627-3323.. 228 H mark.brimhallvargas@tufts.edu
BRIMMER, Diane, L .... 608-796-3801.. 522 O dlbrimmer@viterbo.edu
BRINDLE, Denise .... 978-665-3454.. 221 D dbrindl1@fitchburgstate.edu
BRINDLEY, Roger .... 813-974-1218.. 112 C brindley@usf.edu
BRINDLEY, Roger .... 813-974-0349.. 112 C brindley@usf.edu
BRINEGAR, Kathleen ...... 802-635-1472.. 486 B kathleen.brinegar@jsc.edu
BRINER, Clare .... 708-974-5376.. 148 G brinerc@morainevalley.edu
BRINEY, Colleen, M .... 479-575-5165.... 22 I cbriney@uark.edu
BRINGAZE, Tammy .... 413-572-5491.. 222 E tbringaze@westfield.ma.edu
BRINGER, Michael .... 573-288-6300.. 264 F mbringer@culver.edu
BRINGHURST, Steve .... 435-652-7901.. 482 A brings@dixie.edu
BRINGSJORD, Elizabeth .. 518-320-1251.. 330 H elizabeth.bringsjord@suny.edu
BRINING, Patricia .... 215-968-8091.. 399 A patricia.brining@bucks.edu
BRINK, Benita .... 719-587-7426.... 76 G babrink@adams.edu
BRINK, Laura .... 617-521-2127.. 228 C laura.brink@simmons.edu

BRINK-DRESCHER, Judith ... 516-323-3925 .. 321 H
jdrescher@molloy.edu

BRINKER, Cynthia, S ... 812-464-1774 .. 168 E
cbrinker@usi.edu

BRINKLEY, David ... 270-745-6140 .. 194 D
david.brinkley@wku.edu

BRINKLEY, Martin ... 919-962-4417 .. 357 D
martin92@unc.edu

BRINKMAN, Matt ... 423-614-8395 .. 441 B
mmbrinkman@leeuniversity.edu

BRINKMAN, Sue ... 920-403-3210 .. 519 G
sue.brinkman@snc.edu

BRINKOETTER, Darbe ... 217-875-7200 .. 152 C
dbrinkoetter@richland.edu

BRINNER, Jonda ... 502-410-6200 .. 188 H
jbrinner@galencollege.edu

BRINSON, Anne ... 317-921-4831 .. 164 E
aebrinson@ivytech.edu

BRINSON, Bruce ... 214-379-5573 .. 463 G
bbrinson@pqc.edu

BRINSON, Donna ... 678-341-6607 .. 123 L
dbrinson@laniertech.edu

BRINSON, Leigh ... 312-935-4408 .. 152 D
lbrinson@robertmorris.edu

BRINSON, Marla ... 732-906-2513 .. 292 E
mbrinson@middlesexcc.edu

BRINSON, Reggie ... 904-620-2820 .. 112 B
reggie.brinson@unf.edu

BRINSON, Willie, L ... 919-735-5151 .. 354 A
wlbrinson@waynecc.edu

BRIONES, Eloisa, M ... 650-738-4227 .... 62 I
briones@smccd.edu

BRIOTTA, Richard ... 413-565-1000 .. 215 A
rbriotta@baypath.edu

BRISACK, Al ... 608-663-3289 .. 516 F
abrisack@edgewood.edu

BRISBANE, Frances, L ... 631-444-2139 .. 332 A
frances.brisbane@stonybrook.edu

BRISBON, T. Muriel ... 610-896-1250 .. 405 I
tbrisbon@haverford.edu

BRISCO, Thomas, V ... 325-670-1211 .. 458 J
tbrisco@hsutx.edu

BRISCOE, Andrew ... 214-333-5735 .. 455 J
andrewb@dbu.edu

BRISCOE, Chad ... 574-372-5100 .. 161 B
chad.briscoe@grace.edu

BRISCOE, Connie ... 407-646-2194 .. 107 O
cbriscoe@rollins.edu

BRISEBOIS, Robin ... 619-684-8793 .... 54 C
rbrisebois@newschoolarch.edu

BRISENO, Nancy, M ... 361-698-1293 .. 457 D
nbriseno3@delmar.edu

BRISKEY, Marvin ... 614-947-6002 .. 369 A
marv.briskey@franklin.edu

BRISLIN, Shawn, P ... 607-746-4670 .. 335 C
brislisp@delhi.edu

BRISOLARA, Sharon ... 530-242-7625 .... 64 D
sbrisolara@shastacollege.edu

BRISSON, Caitrin ... 617-603-6900 .. 226 D
caitrin.brisson@necb.edu

BRISSON, E. Carson ... 804-355-0671 .. 494 N
cbrisson@upsem.edu

BRISSON, Michelle ... 973-408-3454 .. 291 B
mbrisson@drew.edu

BRISSON-FARLEY, Andree ... 785-628-4000 .. 180 I
a_brisson@fhsu.edu

BRISTLE, Shawn ... 928-758-3926 .... 15 E
sbristle@mohave.edu

BRISTOL, Cecelia, M ... 815-226-4083 .. 152 G
cbristol@rockford.edu

BRISTOL, Louis ... 860-738-6328 .... 87 A
lbristol@nwcc.edu

BRISTOR, Valerie ... 561-297-3357 .. 110 K
bristor@fau.edu

BRISTOW, Aimee ... 573-592-5364 .. 275 E
aimee.bristow@westminster-mo.edu

BRISTOW, Jessica ... 248-218-2038 .. 240 C
jbristow@rc.edu

BRISTOW, Troy ... 630-637-5559 .. 149 H
tbbristow@noctrl.edu

BRITANAK, Stephan ... 803-793-5109 .. 429 D
britanaks@denmarktech.edu

BRITIGAN, Bradley, E ... 402-599-8878 .. 283 A
bradley.britigan@unmc.edu

BRITSCH, James ... 575-492-2873 .. 300 H
jbritsch@nmjc.edu

BRITT, Ann ... 252-792-1521 .. 351 A
abritt@martincc.edu

BRITT, Anthony ... 252-328-9317 .. 356 C
britta@ecu.edu

BRITT, Deanna ... 434-582-2521 .. 491 D
dbritt@liberty.edu

BRITT, Denise ... 404-752-1500 .. 125 A
dbritt@msm.edu

BRITT, Eddie ... 601-643-8628 .. 257 D
eddie.britt@colin.edu

BRITT, Frank ... 480-947-6644 .... 16 C
frank.britt@pennfoster.edu

BRITT, Jeanette ... 814-824-2247 .. 410 H
jbritt@mercyhurst.edu

BRITT, Julianne ... 781-891-3456 .. 215 F
jbritt@bentley.edu

BRITT, Kenith ... 317-955-6209 .. 165 N
kbritt@marian.edu

BRITT, Kimberly ... 757-789-1748 .. 497 A
kbritt@es.vccs.edu

BRITT, Tammy, T ... 704-233-8111 .. 359 H
tbritt@wingate.edu

BRITTAIN, Lee ... 936-468-3206 .. 466 H
lbrittain@sfasu.edu

BRITTAIN, Linda, D ... 717-264-4141 .. 424 A
lbrittain@wilson.edu

BRITTAIN, Ross, A ... 304-457-6428 .. 510 B
brittainra@ab.edu

BRITTAIN, Vicki, S ... 512-245-2121 .. 471 F
vb01@txstate.edu

BRITTON, Bill ... 805-756-2190 .... 31 I
bibritto@calpoly.edu

BRITTON, Brian, J ... 401-232-6051 .. 424 K
bbritton@bryant.edu

BRITTON, Cathy ... 785-227-3380 .. 178 J
brittoncd@bethanylb.edu

BRITTON, Dana, J ... 717-766-2511 .. 410 J
dbritton@messiah.edu

BRITTON, Ida ... 240-567-5264 .. 209 E
ida.britton@montgomerycollege.edu

BRITTON, Karen ... 781-239-3101 .. 223 F
kbritton@massbay.edu

BRITTON, Keith, E ... 803-938-3882 .. 434 E
kbritton@uscsumter.edu

BRITTON, Lawrence ... 610-399-2302 .. 414 F
fas-lbritton@cheyney.edu

BRITTON, Mark ... 316-295-5787 .. 181 B
mark_britton@friends.edu

BRITTON, Sharon ... 617-573-8536 .. 228 G
sbritton@suffolk.edu

BRITTON-SPEARS, Ona ... 918-463-2931 .. 383 F
ona.britton-spears@connorsstate.edu

BRITZ, Johannes ... 412-229-4501 .. 520 D
britz@uwm.edu

BRIZENDINE, Lyle, W ... 314-516-6788 .. 274 A
brizendinel@umsl.edu

BRIZIARELLI, Susan ... 516-877-4118 .. 303 B
sbriziarelli@adelphi.edu

BRNGER, Anne ... 802-258-3117 .. 485 A
anne.brnger@worldlearning.org

BROADDUS, Henry, R ... 757-221-3987 .. 488 F
hrbroa@wm.edu

BROADDUS, Susan, S ... 804-758-6724 .. 498 D
sbroaddus@rappahannock.edu

BROADHURST, Gary ... 315-792-5573 .. 321 G
gbroadhurst@mvcc.edu

BROADHURST, Robin ... 216-221-8584 .. 380 I
rbroadhust@vmcad.edu

BROADIE, II, Paul ... 203-332-5224 .... 86 D
pbroadie@hcc.commnet.edu

BROADUS, Alicia ... 330-972-8901 .. 378 H
broadus@uakron.edu

BROADWATER, Bonnie ... 301-387-3050 .. 207 G
bonnie.broadwater@garrettcollege.edu

BROADWATER, Larry ... 865-251-1800 .. 444 A
lbroadw@southcollegetn.edu

BROADWAY, Michael, J ... 906-227-2700 .. 239 B
mbroadwa@nmu.edu

BROADWAY, Shane ... 501-660-1001 .... 18 H
sbroadway@asusystem.edu

BROADWELL, Jennifer ... 757-340-2121 .. 488 A
finaid2cvab@centura.edu

BROADWELL, Phyllis ... 912-279-5816 .. 119 C
pbroadwell@ccga.edu

BROCATO, MaryAnne ... 662-332-8750 .. 259 B
mbrocato@msdelta.edu

BROCK, Carly ... 316-323-6939 .. 179 E
cbrock2@butlercc.edu

BROCK, Connie ... 816-271-4237 .. 269 C
cbrock2@missouriwestern.edu

BROCK, Donna ... 404-880-8337 .. 118 K
dbrock@cau.edu

BROCK, Doug ... 319-363-1323 .. 175 D
dbrock@mtmercy.edu

BROCK, Greg ... 541-684-7252 .. 393 B
gbrock@nwcu.edu

BROCK, III, Harry, B ... 205-726-4071 ...... 6 E
bbrock@samford.edu

BROCK, Lynn, A ... 937-766-7846 .. 365 C
brockl@cedarville.edu

BROCK, Marcius ... 507-389-1180 .. 250 E
marcius.brock@mnsu.edu

BROCK, Michael, G ... 610-989-1246 .. 422 E
mbrock@vfmac.edu

BROCK, Michelle ... 704-290-5357 .. 353 B
mbrock@spcc.edu

BROCK, Nikki ... 336-917-5473 .. 355 E
nikki.brock@salem.edu

BROCK, Sabra ... 212-742-8770 .. 337 I
sabra.brock@touro.edu

BROCK, Sharia ... 601-925-7714 .. 259 A
sbrock@mc.edu

BROCK, Summer ... 252-399-6383 .. 341 P
sebrock@barton.edu

BROCK-MURPHY, Angel ... 330-385-1070 .. 376 A

BROCK-SMITH, Cynthia ... 202-806-2530 .... 93 A
cynthia.brocksmith@howard.edu

BROCKBANK, Kevin ... 801-957-5009 .. 483 A
kevin.brockbank@slcc.edu

BROCKBANK, Kevin ... 509-533-3844 .. 503 A
kevin.brockbank@ccs.spokane.edu

BROCKEL, Sarah ... 406-247-5780 .. 277 D
sbrockel@msubillings.edu

BROCKENBROUGH, Karl, B ... 301-860-3470 .. 212 D
kbrockenbrough@bowiestate.edu

BROCKER, Catherine ... 703-284-1610 .. 492 A
catherine.brocker@marymount.edu

BROCKETT, Lori ... 760-750-4405 .... 34 D
brockett@csusm.edu

BROCKGREITENS, Kathy ... 636-922-8229 .. 271 A
kbrockgreitens@stchas.edu

BROCKHOFF, Jennifer ... 502-585-9911 .. 192 E
jbrockhoff@spalding.edu

BROCKHOFF FITZSIMMONS, Lisa, L ... 402-280-3006 .. 279 H
lisabrockhoff@creighton.edu

BROCKHOUSE, Sandy ... 605-342-0317 .. 436 A
sbrockhouse@johnwitherspooncollege.org

BROCKIE, Clarena ... 406-353-2607 .. 275 H
cbrockie@ancollege.edu

BROCKIE, Dixie ... 406-353-2607 .. 275 H
dbrockie@ancollege.edu

BROCKIE, Kimberly ... 406-353-2607 .. 275 H
kbrockie@ancollege.edu

BROCKIE, Michele ... 406-353-2607 .. 275 H
mbrockie@ancollege.edu

BROCKINTON, W. Joseph ... 864-644-5142 .. 432 G
jbrockinton@swu.edu

BROCKLEHURST, Stephanie ... 215-836-2222 .. 397 F
finaid@antonelli.edu

BROCKMAN, Diane ... 660-596-7205 .. 272 G
dbrockman@sfccmo.edu

BROCKMAN, Mark ... 513-745-4842 .. 381 I
brockmanml@xavier.edu

BROCKMUELLER, Angie ... 620-327-8231 .. 181 G
angieb@hesston.edu

BROCKMYER, Richard A ... 801-832-2516 .. 483 D
rbrockmyer@westminstercollege.edu

BROCKWAY, David, J ... 601-318-6199 .. 261 I
david.brockway@wmcarey.edu

BROCKWELL, Gerri, S ... 423-652-4784 .. 440 J
gbrockwell@king.edu

BROD, Catherine ... 914-251-6014 .. 334 C
catherine.brod@purchase.edu

BRODA, Joanna ... 212-346-1652 .. 325 J
jbroda@pace.edu

BRODA, Mary ... 517-750-1200 .. 241 E
mary.broda@arbor.edu

BRODE, Andrea ... 352-638-9724 .... 96 F
abrode@beaconcollege.edu

BRODERICK, Christopher ... 503-725-3773 .. 394 G
christopher.broderick@pdx.edu

BRODERICK, Deborah ... 212-998-6825 .. 324 C
deborah.broderick@nyu.edu

BRODERICK, Jo ... 978-921-4242 .. 225 G
jo.broderick@montserrat.edu

BRODERICK, John, F ... 757-683-3159 .. 492 G
jbroderi@odu.edu

BRODERICK, Mac ... 603-513-1327 .. 288 D
mac.broderick@granite.edu

BRODERICK, Mark, C ... 410-617-2713 .. 208 G
mbroder@loyola.edu

BRODERICK, Marybeth ... 845-848-7824 .. 312 F
marybeth.broderick@dc.edu

BRODERICK, Michael ... 860-515-3885 .... 85 D
mbroderick@charteroak.edu

BRODERICK, Shelley ... 202-274-7332 .... 94 B
sbroderick@udc.edu

BRODERICK, Victor, K ... 217-786-2414 .. 146 E
victor.broderick@llcc.edu

BRODERSON, Maureen, A ... 817-552-3700 .. 460 E
mbroderson@tku.edu

BRODEUR, Thomas ... 860-832-2531 .... 85 F
brodeur@ccsu.edu

BRODHEAD, Richard H ... 919-684-2424 .. 343 J
president@duke.edu

BRODIE, Marilyn ... 408-288-3729 .... 62 E
marilyn.brodie@sjcc.edu

BRODIGAN, Rebecca H ... 207-859-4692 .. 202 G
becky.brodigan@colby.edu

BRODL, Mark ... 210-999-8201 .. 473 A
mbrodl@trinity.edu

BRODLEY, Carla, E ... 617-373-2462 .. 227 B

BRODMERKEL, Darcy ... 570-674-6466 .. 410 K
dbrodmer@misericordia.edu

BRODMERKEL, Douglas ... 516-876-2787 .. 333 C
brodmerkeld@oldwestbury.edu

BRODRICK, Jeff ... 616-538-2330 .. 234 D
jbrodrick@gbcol.edu

BRODSKY, Mikhail ... 510-208-2803 .... 49 A
rector@lincolnuca.edu

BRODSKY, Stephen ... 212-346-1274 .. 325 J
sbrodksy@pace.edu

BRODT, Bonita ... 312-893-7161 .. 140 D
bbrodt@erikson.edu

BRODY, Adam ... 407-277-0311 .... 99 J
abrody@evergladesuniversity.edu

BRODY, Charles, J ... 570-674-6218 .. 410 K
cbrody@misericordia.edu

BRODY, Charmain ... 610-398-5300 .. 408 I
cbrody@lincolntech.edu

BRODY, Fern, E ... 412-648-7747 .. 421 G
feb@pitt.edu

BRODY, Matthew ... 919-962-4651 .. 356 A
msbrody@northcarolina.edu

BRODY, Michael ... 503-777-7521 .. 394 I
brodym@reed.edu

BRODZINSKI, James ... 219-464-6758 .. 168 F
jim.brodzinski@valpo.edu

BROEDER, Jennifer ... 314-246-7988 .. 275 B
jbroeder@webster.edu

BROEKER, Camy ... 317-274-4511 .. 163 D

BROEKER, Christine ... 407-708-2396 .. 109 E
broekerc@seminolstate.edu

BROERING, Naomi ... 619-574-6909 .... 55 G
nbroering@pacificcollege.edu

BROETJE, Whitney ... 206-281-2831 .. 507 C
broetw@spu.edu

BROFFT, Jeremy ... 757-388-2862 .. 494 A
jbroft@sentara.edu

BROGAN, Frank, T ... 717-720-4010 .. 414 C
fbrogan@passhe.edu

BROGAN, Jamey ... 304-243-2385 .. 515 C
jbrogan@wju.edu

BROGAN, Michael, S ... 716-839-8227 .. 312 D
mbrogan@daemen.edu

BROGDEN, Jeff, D ... 919-658-7171 .. 355 K
jbrogden@umo.edu

BROGDON, Jarrod ... 229-333-2100 .. 130 A
jarrod.brogdon@wiregrass.edu

BROGE, Jason ... 989-275-5000 .. 236 E
jason.broge@kirtland.edu

BROGE, Jason ... 314-505-7092 .. 263 I
brogej@csl.edu

BROGHAMMER, Sean, M ... 970-351-2806 .... 84 C
sean.broghammer@unco.edu

BROGLIE, Mary, C ... 914-968-6200 .. 329 C
mary.broglie@archny.org

BROGLIE, Nancy ... 609-292-2108 .. 297 F
nbroglie@tesu.edu

BROIL, D.C ... 913-288-7117 .. 182 C
dcbroil@kckcc.edu

BROILES, Janet ... 870-575-8471 .... 23 E
broilesj@uapb.edu

BROKAW, Tim ... 207-621-3300 .. 204 I
timothy.brokaw@maine.edu

BROKENBURR, Shenita ... 608-262-8299 .. 519 J
sbrokenburr@uwsa.edu

BROKENSHIRE, Catherine ... 312-777-8619 .. 142 G
cbrokenshire@aii.edu

BROKKE, Dan ... 952-829-2470 .. 244 J
dan.brokke@bethfel.org

BROKKE, Derek ... 952-829-1320 .. 244 J
derek.brokke@bethfel.org

BROKKEN, Patricia ... 540-362-6016 .. 490 F
brokkenpe@hollins.edu

BROKOPP, Charles ... 608-890-1569 .. 519 K
cdb@mail.slh.wisc.edu

BROKVIST, Randi ... 904-632-3301 .. 101 G
rbrokvis@fscj.edu

BROLLEY, Francis, R ... 815-224-0466 .. 143 C
fran_brolley@ivcc.edu

BROM, Don ... 215-637-7700 .. 405 J
dbrom@holyfamily.edu

BROMAN, Erica ... 413-552-2747 .. 223 E
ebroman@hcc.edu

BROMAN, Erica ... 413-572-5244 .. 222 E
ebroman@westfield.ma.edu

BROMANDER, Lowell ... 651-523-2225 .. 247 A
lbromander@hamline.edu

BROMFIELD, Christopher ... 305-626-0207 .. 101 A
christopher.bromfield@fmuniv.edu

BROMFIELD, Robert, L ... 415-422-2786 .... 72 C
rlbromfield@usfca.edu

BROMLEY, Dennis ... 801-957-4322 .. 483 A
dennis.bromley@slcc.edu

BROMM, Drew ... 252-334-2043 .. 346 F
drew.bromm@macuniversity.edu

BROMSTRUP, Bryan, T ... 812-877-8205 .. 166 H
bromstru@rose-hulman.edu

BRONDER, James, S ... 419-998-3138 .. 380 A
jsbronde@unoh.edu

BRONET, Frances ... 312-567-3163 .. 142 I
fbronet@iit.edu

BRONFMAN, Jane ... 860-906-5103 .... 86 B
jbronfman@ccc.commnet.edu

BRONISZ, John ... 505-224-3730 .. 299 F
jbronisz@cnm.edu

BRONK, Leslie .... 952-885-5413.. 253 Z
lbronk@nwhealth.edu
BRONKEMA, F. David ... 484-384-2935.. 412 C
semdean@eastern.edu
BRONKEMA, F. David ..... 610-225-5068.. 403 B
dbronkem@eastern.edu
BRONNER, Gwethalyn ..... 847-543-2685.. 138 C
gbronner@clcillinois.edu
BRONNER, Jennifer, L ..... 740-826-8463.. 373 E
jbronner@muskingum.edu
BRONSDON, Chris .... 619-594-7985.... 35 A
cbronsdo@mail.sdsu.edu
BRONSON, Matthew .... 415-257-1345.... 42 G
matthew.bronson@dominican.edu
BRONSTEIN, Fred .... 410-234-4700.. 208 D
fred.bronstein@jhu.edu
BRONSTEIN, Ken .... 360-383-3359.. 509 F
kbronstein@whatcom.ctc.edu
BRONSTEIN, Laura .... 607-777-5572.. 331 B
lbronst@binghamton.edu
BRONSTEIN, Susan .... 716-338-1035.. 317 F
susanbronstein@mail.sunyjcc.edu
BRONSTEIN, Susan .... 239-489-9357.. 101 F
sbronstein@fsw.edu
BROOK, Turner .... 314-423-1900.. 262 C
BROOKBANK, Julie .... 605-995-3026.. 436 C
julie.brookbank@mitchelltech.edu
BROOKBANK, Maureen ... 202-319-5598.... 92 A
brookbank@cua.edu
BROOKE, Georgia .... 518-464-8559.. 314 A
gbrooke@excelsior.edu
BROOKE, Judith .... 321-674-8053.. 100 M
jbrooke@fit.edu
BROOKE, Patrick .... 651-638-6879.. 244 L
pbrooke@bethel.edu
BROOKER, Paulita .... 704-463-7302.. 354 F
paulita.brooker@pfeiffer.edu
BROOKER, Sarah .... 717-564-4112.. 398 F
sbrooker@kaplan.edu
BROOKET, Jenn .... 517-264-7159.. 241 A
jbrooket@sienaheights.edu
BROOKEY, Lauren .... 918-595-7977.. 388 F
lauren.brookey@tulsacc.edu
BROOKEY, Lauren, F .... 918-595-7977.. 388 F
lauren.brookey@tulsacc.edu
BROOKING, David .... 662-329-7138.. 259 E
dmbrooking@muw.edu
BROOKINS, Carla .... 615-966-7076.. 441 F
carla.brookins@lipscomb.edu
BROOKINS, Laura .... 610-917-1451.. 422 C
ljbrookins@valleyforge.edu
BROOKMAN, Kim .... 413-236-1003.. 222 G
kbrookman@berkshirecc.edu
BROOKNER, Laurie .... 415-565-8813.... 69 B
brookner@uchastings.edu
BROOKOVER, Joe .... 515-643-6611.. 175 B
jbrookover@mercydesmoines.org
BROOKS, Aaron .... 662-243-2655.. 257 G
abrooks@eastms.edu
BROOKS, Ann .... 918-302-3617.. 383 I
abrooks@eosc.edu
BROOKS, Anthony .... 919-719-1983.. 355 F
anthony.brooks@shawu.edu
BROOKS, Audrey .... 410-532-5735.. 210 B
abrooks@ndm.edu
BROOKS, Barbara .... 303-871-3631.... 84 B
barbara.l.brooks@du.edu
BROOKS, Beth .... 253-566-5054.. 508 B
bbrooks@tacomacc.edu
BROOKS, Billie, K .... 304-710-3363.. 512 B
billie.brooks@mctc.edu
BROOKS, Blake .... 317-632-5553.. 165 L
bbrooks@lincolntech.edu
BROOKS, Browning .... 850-644-8343.. 111 C
bbrooks@fsu.edu
BROOKS, Carlton .... 719-502-2003.... 82 B
carlton.brooks@ppcc.edu
BROOKS, Carrie Allison .. 901-272-5160.. 442 B
cbrooks@mca.edu
BROOKS, Charles, R .... 973-596-2875.. 293 D
brooks@njit.edu
BROOKS, Christopher ...... 734-207-9581.. 148 F
chris.brooks@moody.edu
BROOKS, Cindy, L .... 610-799-1121.. 408 G
cbrooks@lccc.edu
BROOKS, Constance .... 702-889-8426.. 284 G
constance_brooks@nshe.nevada.edu
BROOKS, Cynthia .... 615-963-7410.. 445 A
cbrooks@tnstate.edu
BROOKS, Dana, D .... 304-293-8026.. 514 C
dbrooks@mail.wvu.edu
BROOKS, Danny, K .... 336-841-9131.. 345 A
dbrooks@highpoint.edu
BROOKS, Darlene, D .... 901-843-3901.. 443 L
brooksd@rhodes.edu
BROOKS, Donnie .... 601-974-1190.. 258 H
brookda@millsaps.edu
BROOKS, II, Earl, D .... 260-665-4101.. 167 E
brookse@trine.edu
BROOKS, Elizabeth .... 215-955-0916.. 420 E
elizabeth.brooks@jefferson.edu
BROOKS, Fred .... 252-451-8233.. 351 F
fbrooks@nashcc.edu
BROOKS, Gail .... 657-278-8213.... 33 A
BROOKS, Gene .... 402-643-7411.. 279 F
gene.brooks@cune.edu
BROOKS, II, H. Gordon .. 337-482-6224.. 201 D
gbrooks@louisiana.edu
BROOKS, Ian .... 510-883-2056.... 42 F
ibrooks@dspt.edu
BROOKS, James, L .... 323-856-7600.... 26 I
jbrooks@afi.com
BROOKS, Jason .... 620-341-5481.. 180 G
jbrooks5@emporia.edu
BROOKS, Jason .... 304-327-4181.. 512 P
jbrooks@bluefieldstate.edu
BROOKS, Jim .... 352-335-2332.... 94 F
BROOKS, Jim, J .... 541-346-6121.. 395 G
brooksja@uoregon.edu
BROOKS, Joanna .... 619-594-6111.... 35 A
jbrooks@mail.sdsu.edu
BROOKS, John .... 912-344-2587.. 116 E
john.brooks@armstrong.edu
BROOKS, John, I .... 910-672-1060.. 356 E
jibrooks@uncfsu.edu
BROOKS, Joseph .... 303-963-3463.... 77 I
jbrooks@ccu.edu
BROOKS, Juliette .... 201-692-7050.. 291 J
juliette_brooks@fdu.edu
BROOKS, Justin, P .... 619-239-0391.... 36 A
jbrooks@cwsl.edu
BROOKS, Karl .... 847-635-1739.. 150 G
kbrooks@oakton.edu
BROOKS, Katharine, S ..... 615-322-2750.. 449 A
katharine.s.brooks@vanderbilt.edu
BROOKS, Keith .... 612-659-6104.. 250 B
keith.brooks@minneapolis.edu
BROOKS, Kelly .... 575-527-7551.. 301 C
kbrooks@nmsu.edu
BROOKS, Kent .... 307-268-2703.. 526 D
kbrooks@caspercollege.edu
BROOKS, Krista .... 559-453-2289.... 44 F
krista.brooks@fresno.edu
BROOKS, L. Rayburn .... 864-941-8301.. 432 A
brooks.r@ptc.edu
BROOKS, Larry .... 701-228-5457.. 361 D
larry.brooks@dakotacollege.edu
BROOKS, LaShon, F .... 662-254-3425.. 260 A
lfbrooks@mvsu.edu
BROOKS, Lisa .... 818-240-1000.... 45 A
lbrooks@glendale.edu
BROOKS, Lois .... 541-737-0739.. 393 H
lois.brooks@oregonstate.edu
BROOKS, Lyvette .... 215-751-8046.. 401 G
lbrooks@ccp.edu
BROOKS, Marilyn, A .... 804-257-5846.. 500 B
mabrooks2@vuu.edu
BROOKS, Mark .... 229-931-2246.. 127 C
mbrooks@southgatech.edu
BROOKS, Mark, D .... 270-901-1117.. 190 F
mark.brooks@kctcs.edu
BROOKS, Martha .... 804-758-6771.. 498 D
mbrooks@rappahannock.edu
BROOKS, Michelle .... 252-328-2872.. 356 C
brooksm@ecu.edu
BROOKS, Monica .... 304-696-6474.. 513 D
brooks@marshall.edu
BROOKS, Nancy, S .... 515-294-8757.. 169 G
nsbrook@iastate.edu
BROOKS, Patricia .... 972-825-4652.. 466 D
pabrooks@sagu.edu
BROOKS, Paul .... 972-825-4616.. 466 D
pbrooks@sagu.edu
BROOKS, Randy, M .... 217-424-6205.. 148 D
rbrooks@millikin.edu
BROOKS, Rena .... 918-647-1217.. 382 I
trbrooks@carlalbert.edu
BROOKS, Robert .... 617-928-4602.. 226 B
rbrooks@mountida.edu
BROOKS, Roger, L .... 804-289-8491.. 495 G
rbrooks@richmond.edu
BROOKS, Ron .... 901-678-2077.. 445 C
rbrooks@memphis.edu
BROOKS, Ronnie .... 615-963-5671.. 445 A
rbrooks6@tnstate.edu
BROOKS, Sarah .... 509-542-4837.. 502 G
sbrooks@columbiabasin.edu
BROOKS, Sean .... 410-951-3455.. 212 E
sbrooks@coppin.edu
BROOKS, Shannon .... 864-644-5072.. 432 G
sbrooks@swu.edu
BROOKS, Sharon .... 802-258-3344.. 485 A
sharon.brooks@sit.edu
BROOKS, Telaekah .... 202-601-1215.. 314 A
tbrooks@excelsior.edu
BROOKS, Teresa .... 903-693-2060.. 463 D
trbrooks@panola.edu
BROOKS, Thom, R .... 828-339-4202.. 353 D
tbrooks@southwesterncc.edu
BROOKS, Thomas .... 641-472-7000.. 175 A
tbrooks@mum.edu
BROOKS, Tim .... 402-280-2564.. 279 H
timbrooks@creighton.edu
BROOKS, Todd .... 706-236-2260.. 117 F
tbrooks@berry.edu
BROOKS, Tyrone .... 509-542-4408.. 502 G
tbrooks@columbiabasin.edu
BROOKS, Vanessa .... 734-973-3621.. 242 G
vbrooks@wccnet.edu
BROOKS, Vera .... 410-462-8500.. 206 D
vbrooks@bccc.edu
BROOKS, Walter, T .... 508-362-2131.. 223 C
wbrooks@capecod.edu
BROOKS, Wendy .... 989-358-7299.. 230 G
brooksw@alpenacc.edu
BROOKS, Wes .... 319-385-6284.. 174 A
wesley.brooks@iw.edu
BROOKS, Will .... 678-033-1434.. 124 B
william.brooks2@life.edu
BROOKS BLAIR,
Sarah, D .... 937-529-2201.. 378 F
sblair@united.edu
BROOKSHIRE, David .... 276-244-1211.. 486 N
dbrookshire@asl.edu
BROOKSHIRE, Kathy .... 601-484-8612.. 258 F
kbrooksh@meridiancc.edu
BROOM, Cheryl .... 760-795-2121.... 52 K
cbroom@miracosta.edu
BROOMALL, James, K ..... 302-831-2795.... 91 F
jbroom@udel.edu
BROOME, Barbara .... 330-672-8799.. 370 I
bbroome1@kent.edu
BROOME, Marion .... 919-684-3786.. 343 J
marion.broome@duke.edu
BROOME, Melba .... 202-274-6118.... 94 B
mbroome@udc.edu
BROOMHEAD, Keiko .... 617-989-4034.. 229 D
broomheadk@wit.edu
BROPHY, Ann .... 314-246-7422.. 275 B
annbrophy26@webster.edu
BROPHY, Dale, G .... 801-585-2677.. 481 M
dale.brophy@dps.utah.edu
BROPHY, Katharine .... 973-655-7761.. 293 A
brophyka@mail.montclair.edu
BROPHY, Michael, S .... 630-829-6004.. 135 F
mbrophy@ben.edu
BROPHY, Timothy, S .... 352-273-4476.. 112 A
tbrophy@aa.ufl.edu
BROPHY, JR., William, E 256-824-6144....... 8 F
william.brophy@uah.edu
BRORBY, Gregory .... 775-753-2260.. 284 I
gregory.brorby@gbcnv.edu
BROSHOUS, Robert, D .... 563-589-3199.. 177 C
bbroshou@dbq.edu
BROSKE, Kathleen, M ..... 920-924-2139.. 524 B
kbroske@morainepark.edu
BROSKY, Lisa .... 520-206-4850.... 16 F
lbrosky@pima.edu
BROSKY, Lisa .... 502-213-2400.. 190 A
lisa.brosky@kctcs.edu
BROSNAN, JoAnna, M .... 607-746-4727.. 335 C
brosnajm@delhi.edu
BROSNAN, Mary .... 516-323-3468.. 321 H
mbrosnan@molloy.edu
BROSS, Scott .... 309-268-8385.. 141 C
scott.bross@heartland.edu
BROSS-FREGONARA,
Nanci .... 304-704-1162.. 510 I
brossfregonaran@dewv.edu
BROSTROM, Nathan, E .... 510-987-9029.... 68 L
nathan.brostrom@ucop.edu
BROTHERS, Gregory, A ... 713-646-1888.. 459 A
gbrothers@hcl.edu
BROTHERS, James, F ...... 937-229-2829.. 379 D
jbrothers1@udayton.edu
BROTHERS, Wes .... 740-477-7757.. 374 G
wbrothers@ohiochristian.edu
BROTHERSON, Carrie, P . 540-261-8534.. 494 F
carrie.brotherson@svu.edu
BROTHERTON, Jeffrey ..... 614-222-4014.. 367 B
jbrotherton@ccad.edu
BROTHERTON,
Thomas, S .... 712-852-5224.. 173 G
tbrotherton@iowalakes.edu
BROUCEK, Willard .... 605-626-2401.. 437 D
willard.broucek@northern.edu
BROUDE, Nancy .... 617-587-5585.. 226 E
brouden@neco.edu
BROUGH, Aimee, B .... 717-736-4122.. 405 C
abbrough@hacc.edu
BROUGHTON, Nancy .... 218-879-0837.. 249 C
sam@fdltcc.edu
BROUHARD,
Nathanael, T .... 215-972-2015.. 413 L
nbrouhard@pafa.edu
BROUILLARD-BRUCE,
Torry .... 209-946-2331.... 71 C
tbrouillard@pacific.edu
BROUILLET, Susan .... 603-230-3576.. 286 A
sbrouillet@ccsnh.edu
BROUILLETTE,
Domenick, R .... 816-604-1370.. 267 F
domenick.brouillette@mcckc.edu
BROUNK, Thomas, M ..... 314-935-5955.. 274 N
tom_brounk@wustl.edu
BROUSSARD, Camille ..... 212-431-2354.. 323 H
camille.broussard@nyls.edu
BROUSSARD, Michael ..... 337-550-1292.. 197 K
mpbrouss@lsue.edu
BROUWER, Dustin, J ...... 605-336-6588.. 436 J
dbrouwer@sfseminary.edu
BROWDER, Steven, K ..... 317-738-8301.. 160 J
sbrowder@franklincollege.edu
BROWER, Bill .... 315-445-5441.. 318 E
browewih@lemoyne.edu
BROWER, Bob .... 619-849-2216.... 57 M
bobbrower@pointloma.edu
BROWER, David, C .... 607-746-4540.. 335 C
browerdc@delhi.edu
BROWER, Jennifer .... 505-224-4669.. 299 F
jbrower@cnm.edu
BROWER, Keith .... 718-862-7345.. 319 L
keith.brower@manhattan.edu
BROWER, Laura .... 805-289-6460.... 73 F
lbrower@vcccd.edu
BROWER, Lynn .... 818-778-5749.... 50 D
browerl@lavc.edu
BROWER, Paul, O .... 508-213-2271.. 227 A
paul.brower@nichols.edu
BROWER, Pearl, K .... 907-852-3333.... 10 D
pearl.brower@ilisagvik.edu
BROWER, Roderick .... 910-695-3994.. 353 A
browerr@sandhills.edu
BROWN, Aaron .... 951-222-8789.... 58 J
aaron.brown@rccd.edu
BROWN, Alanka .... 301-624-2724.. 207 F
albrown@frederick.edu
BROWN, Albert .... 360-596-5268.. 508 A
abrown@spscc.edu
BROWN, Alesia .... 864-941-8611.. 432 A
brown.a@ptc.edu
BROWN, Alfreda .... 330-672-2442.. 370 I
abbrown@kent.edu
BROWN, Allen .... 512-313-3000.. 455 F
allen.brown@concordia.edu
BROWN, Amon .... 202-651-5007.... 92 C
amon.brown@gallaudet.edu
BROWN, Amy, L .... 607-746-4584.. 335 C
brownal@delhi.edu
BROWN, Andrea .... 435-652-7595.. 482 A
abrown@dixie.edu
BROWN, Andrew .... 651-696-6069.. 247 I
dabrown@macalester.edu
BROWN, Angela .... 315-312-4100.. 333 D
angela.brown@oswego.edu
BROWN, Angela, C .... 254-968-9128.. 467 F
abrown@tarleton.edu
BROWN, Angela, P .... 731-425-2347.. 446 C
abrown@jscc.edu
BROWN, Ann .... 919-516-5083.. 355 D
abrown@st-aug.edu
BROWN, Anne .... 617-228-3267.. 223 B
abrown@bhcc.mass.edu
BROWN, Annette .... 410-334-2900.. 213 G
abrown@worwic.edu
BROWN, Ansel, E .... 919-530-7477.. 357 A
browna@nccu.edu
BROWN, Art .... 515-964-6394.. 171 B
acbrown9@dmacc.edu
BROWN, B, T .... 252-536-7245.. 350 C
btbrown920@halifaxcc.edu
BROWN, Barry .... 617-928-4502.. 226 B
barrybrown@mountida.edu
BROWN, Beverly .... 718-262-2238.. 310 A
bbrown@york.cuny.edu
BROWN, Bill .... 863-638-7228.. 115 C
bill.brown@warner.edu
BROWN, Bill .... 919-760-2367.. 346 D
brownw@meredith.edu
BROWN, Bill .... 757-455-5730.. 500 E
bbrown@vwc.edu
BROWN, Bob .... 859-233-8889.. 193 D
robrown@transy.edu
BROWN, Bob .... 940-565-2055.. 475 A
bob.brown@unt.edu
BROWN, Bobbie .... 806-742-3661.. 472 C
bobbie.brown@ttu.edu
BROWN, Bradd .... 405-208-5001.. 385 E
bradd.brown@okcu.edu
BROWN, Braden .... 405-382-9277.. 387 L
b.brown@sscok.edu
BROWN, Bradley .... 435-586-7871.. 481 N
brown@suu.edu
BROWN, Brenda .... 321-674-7420.. 100 M
brendabrown@fit.edu
BROWN, Brenda, L .... 478-218-3288.. 118 H
bbrown@centralgatech.edu
BROWN, Brent, K .... 801-581-3003.. 481 M
brent.brown@osp.utah.edu
BROWN, Brian .... 315-364-3207.. 340 B
bbrown@wells.edu

BROWN, JR., Buck, F 864-379-8805 429 I brown@erskine.edu
BROWN, C. Keith 706-821-8286 125 H ckbrown@paine.edu
BROWN, Calvin 205-348-5966 8 D cbrown@alumni.ua.edu
BROWN, Carl 614-947-6080 369 A carl.brown@franklin.edu
BROWN, Carmen 803-584-3446 434 C cdbrown@mailbox.sc.edu
BROWN, Carol 559-791-2316 47 L cbrown@portervillecollege.edu
BROWN, Carol, J 309-341-7980 145 A cbrown@knox.edu
BROWN, Carolanne 561-803-2050 106 C carolanne_brown@pba.edu
BROWN, Carrie 607-274-3846 317 D brownc@ithaca.edu
BROWN, Catherine 716-614-5950 324 D cbrown@niagaracc.suny.edu
BROWN, Chad 918-647-1200 382 I
BROWN, Chad, M 740-588-1201 382 C cbrown@zanestate.edu
BROWN, Charles 502-456-6773 193 B cbrown@sullivan.edu
BROWN, Charlotte 405-466-3217 383 M cjbrown@langston.edu
BROWN, Chelsea 301-934-2251 207 B cbrown1@csmd.edu
BROWN, Cheryl-Ann 321-674-7581 100 M cbrown@fit.edu
BROWN, Christopher 949-376-6000 48 C cbrown@lcad.edu
BROWN, Christopher, L 212-854-2254 311 E clb2140@columbia.edu
BROWN, Christopher, M 336-334-7551 356 F cmbrown7@ncat.edu
BROWN, Cindy 417-455-5540 264 E cindybrown@crowder.edu
BROWN, Constance 212-854-2011 304 I cbrown@barnard.edu
BROWN, Courtney, L 540-365-4201 489 M cbrown@ferrum.edu
BROWN, Craig 208-562-3412 133 F craigbrown@cwidaho.cc
BROWN, Craig 740-477-7443 374 G jcbrown@ohiochristian.edu
BROWN, Crystal 817-598-6274 479 E cbrown@wc.edu
BROWN, Curressia 662-254-3600 260 A cbrown@mvsu.edu
BROWN, Cynthia 956-665-4025 476 E cynthia.brown@utrgv.edu
BROWN, Cynthia 706-754-7714 125 B cbrown@northgatech.edu
BROWN, Cynthia 901-381-3939 449 F cynthia@visible.edu
BROWN, Cynthia, F 413-662-5242 222 B c.brown@mcla.edu
BROWN, Cynthia, G 508-213-2065 227 A cindy.brown@nichols.edu
BROWN, Dale 402-552-3470 279 D browndale@clarksoncollege.edu
BROWN, Dan 502-863-7035 188 I dan_brown@georgetowncollege.edu
BROWN, Dana 601-979-3060 258 D dana.a.brown@jsums.edu
BROWN, Dana 601-979-5848 258 D dana.a.brown@jsums.edu
BROWN, Danene 619-388-2803 60 G dmbrown@sdccd.edu
BROWN, Daniel 512-245-3579 471 F db70@txstate.edu
BROWN, Daniel 806-291-3575 479 D brownd@wbu.edu
BROWN, Daniel, W 203-582-8927 88 G daniel.brown@quinnipiac.edu
BROWN, Danita 203-857-7004 87 B dbrown@norwalk.edu
BROWN, Darlene 215-248-7158 400 H brown@chc.edu
BROWN, Darrell 254-968-9083 467 F dwbrown@tarleton.edu
BROWN, Darryl 301-295-3412 528 G darryl.brown@usuhs.edu
BROWN, David 314-434-4044 264 C david.brown@covenantseminary.edu
BROWN, David 352-638-9721 96 F dbrown@beaconcollege.edu
BROWN, David 262-691-5346 524 G dbrown@wctc.edu
BROWN, David 910-668-3331 462 L dbrown@nctc.edu
BROWN, Deanie 217-206-6222 156 G brown.deanie@uis.edu
BROWN, Deborah 417-659-9307 268 H brown-deborah@mssu.edu
BROWN, Debra 610-917-3955 422 C dlbrown@valleyforge.edu
BROWN, Dennis 281-425-6300 460 I dbrown@lee.edu
BROWN, Derek 303-404-5492 80 E derek.brown@frontrange.edu
BROWN, Diane 205-929-1461 5 H dbrown@miles.edu
BROWN, Diane, M 484-365-8055 409 B dbrown@lincoln.edu
BROWN, Dina 978-556-3701 224 D dbrown@necc.mass.edu
BROWN, Dolores, M 262-524-7133 515 J docampo@carrollu.edu
BROWN, Donna 660-626-2790 262 A dbrown@atsu.edu
BROWN, Donna 479-248-7236 20 C registrar@ecollege.edu
BROWN, Donna, L 218-477-2721 250 F donna.brown@mnstate.edu
BROWN, Donnie 806-291-3596 479 D brownd@wbu.edu
BROWN, Douglas 508-588-9100 223 G
BROWN, Douglas E 515-964-0601 172 F brownd@faith.edu
BROWN, Edward 334-727-8011 8 A ebrown@tuskegee.edu
BROWN, Eric 530-221-4275 64 C
BROWN, Eric 207-778-7457 205 A brown.eric@maine.edu
BROWN, Erica 205-226-4733 2 C ebrown@bsc.edu
BROWN, Erik 218-726-8891 255 D etbrown@d.umn.edu
BROWN, Erika 404-752-1723 125 A ebrown@msm.edu
BROWN, Erin 405-789-7661 388 B erin.brown@swcu.edu
BROWN, JR., Ermen 701-766-1342 360 A ermen.brown@littlehoop.edu
BROWN, Ernie 717-299-7730 420 C brown@stevenscollege.edu
BROWN, Ethel, M 404-413-1300 122 D ebrown@gsu.edu
BROWN, Evan 708-456-0300 156 C ebrown@triton.edu
BROWN, Felicia 252-335-3642 356 D fdbrown@ecsu.edu
BROWN, Fran 248-476-1122 237 H fbrown@mispp.edu
BROWN, Francis, H 801-581-8767 481 M fbrown@mines.utah.edu
BROWN, Fred 850-872-3843 102 M fbrown@gulfcoast.edu
BROWN, Gary 814-725-7080 410 H gbrown@mercyhurst.edu
BROWN, Gary 608-785-9167 524 H browng@westerntc.edu
BROWN, Gary, L 919-530-7466 357 A gbrown@nccu.edu
BROWN, Geeta, A 714-712-7900 46 N
BROWN, George, H 828-227-7028 359 A ghbrown@wcu.edu
BROWN, Giles 903-463-8620 458 H browng@grayson.edu
BROWN, Gina, S 202-806-7456 93 A gina.brown@howard.edu
BROWN, Gladys 951-827-5604 70 B gladys.brown@ucr.edu
BROWN, Glenn 973-684-5402 294 A gbrown@pccc.edu
BROWN, Glory 850-599-3531 110 J glory.brown@famu.edu
BROWN, Gregory 707-864-7000 65 A gregory.brown@solano.edu
BROWN, Gregory, N 610-328-8316 419 I gbrown3@swarthmore.edu
BROWN, Guilbert 814-732-2585 415 A gbrown@edinboro.edu
BROWN, H. David 816-271-4327 269 C browndav@missouriwestern.edu
BROWN, Harold 415-452-5163 38 E hbrown@ccsf.edu
BROWN, Heather 213-477-2966 53 B hbrown@msmu.edu
BROWN, Isiah 713-221-8001 474 B browni@uhd.edu
BROWN, Ivey 336-750-2105 359 B browniv@wssu.edu
BROWN, J. Steven 202-319-4738 92 A brownj@cua.edu
BROWN, J. T 650-508-3521 54 J jtbrown@ndnu.edu
BROWN, J.J 828-262-2060 356 B brownjj1@appstate.edu
BROWN, Jackie 323-563-5985 37 G jackiebrown@cdrewu.edu
BROWN, Jackie 803-705-4971 427 D brrownjw@benedict.edu
BROWN, James 661-824-2977 53 K jbrown@ntps.edu
BROWN, James 570-389-4410 414 D jbrown@bloomu.edu
BROWN, Janet, M 219-464-5289 168 F janet.brown@valpo.edu
BROWN, Janice 301-846-2484 207 F jbrown@frederick.edu
BROWN, Jared 610-436-3305 416 C jbrown@wcupa.edu
BROWN, Jasmin, K 910-630-7034 346 E jabrown@methodist.edu
BROWN, Jeff 828-250-2350 357 C jbrown@unca.edu
BROWN, Jeff 801-832-2900 483 D jbrown@westminstercollege.edu
BROWN, Jeff 509-533-7373 502 I jeff.brown@scc.spokane.edu
BROWN, Jeffery 573-629-3260 265 G jbrown@hlg.edu
BROWN, Jeffrey 802-776-5216 483 G jeffrey.brown@csj.edu
BROWN, Jeffrey 804-862-6186 493 F jbrown@rbc.edu
BROWN, Jeffrey 217-333-2747 157 A brownjr@illinois.edu
BROWN, Jennifer 203-582-3246 88 G jennifer.brown@quinnipiac.edu
BROWN, Jennifer 785-738-9085 183 J jbrown@ncktc.edu
BROWN, Jeremy 530-541-4660 48 D jjbrown@ltcc.edu
BROWN, Jeremy 951-639-5420 53 D jbrown@msjc.edu
BROWN, Jeremy 970-248-1962 77 L jbrown@coloradomesa.edu
BROWN, Jerry 928-350-2113 16 P jbrown@prescott.edu
BROWN, Jess 309-467-6865 140 E jbrown@eureka.edu
BROWN, Jesse, M 260-359-4028 161 O jbrown@huntington.edu
BROWN, Jessyca 254-659-7504 458 K jbrown@hillcollege.edu
BROWN, Jim 770-229-3455 127 F jbrown@sctech.edu
BROWN, Jim 828-689-1185 346 C jbrown@mhu.edu
BROWN, JoAnn 318-670-9651 199 J jwarren@susla.edu
BROWN, Joanne 409-832-2956 470 H jcbrown@lit.edu
BROWN, John 404-270-5227 128 A jbrow109@spelman.edu
BROWN, John, P 404-215-2659 124 I john.brown@morehouse.edu
BROWN, Jonathan 206-592-3257 504 E jbrown@highline.edu
BROWN, Joseph 910-246-4957 353 A brownj@sandhills.edu
BROWN, Joseph 903-923-2270 457 G jbrown@etbu.edu
BROWN, Joyce 443-885-3015 209 F joyce.brown@morgan.edu
BROWN, Joyce, F 212-217-4000 314 B joyce_brown@fitnyc.edu
BROWN, Julia 662-472-9011 258 B jubrown@holmescc.edu
BROWN, June, E 918-631-2584 339 E june-brown@utulsa.edu
BROWN, Kari 252-492-2061 353 H brownk@vgcc.edu
BROWN, Karen, A 607-436-2524 331 F karen.brown@oneonta.edu
BROWN, Karen, J 603-899-4280 237 A brownkj@franklinpierce.edu
BROWN, Kathleen 641-844-5670 173 L kathleen.brown@iavalley.edu
BROWN, Kathleen, M 574-284-4557 167 A kbrown@saintmarys.edu
BROWN, Kathren 801-863-8517 482 C kbrown@uvu.edu
BROWN, Kathryn, F 612-624-3533 255 H brown059@umn.edu
BROWN, Katie 704-971-8162 343 E kbrown@charlottelaw.edu
BROWN, Karma, M 307-674-6446 526 M kbrown@sheridan.edu
BROWN, Keith 440-365-5222 371 H
BROWN, Keith, A 205-853-1200 5 B kbrown@jeffstateonline.com
BROWN, Kelli 229-333-5952 129 G kellibrown@valdosta.edu
BROWN, Kelly 405-224-3140 389 D kbrown@usao.edu
BROWN, Kevin 252-335-2477 356 D klbrown@ecsu.edu
BROWN, Ken 563-588-8193 170 F ken.brown@clarke.edu
BROWN, Ken 620-278-4217 185 A kbrown@sterling.edu
BROWN, Kendrick 909-748-8359 71 K kendrick_brown@redlands.edu
BROWN, Kennard, D 901-448-4797 448 H kbrown@uthsc.edu
BROWN, Kenneth 509-777-4486 509 H kbrown@whitworth.edu
BROWN, Kent 573-635-4971 266 I kentbrown@molawcenter.com
BROWN, Kevin 843-349-5398 430 F kevin.brown@hgtc.edu
BROWN, Kevin 641-784-5149 172 G brown@graceland.edu
BROWN, Kevin 812-866-7040 161 C brownk@hanover.edu
BROWN, Kevin 212-659-3604 318 D kbrown@tkc.edu
BROWN, Kevin 517-750-1200 241 E kevin.brown@arbor.edu
BROWN, Kevin 218-477-2795 250 F kevin.brown@mnstate.edu
BROWN, Kevin 423-236-2874 444 B kbrown@southern.edu
BROWN, Kevin, A 919-866-5475 353 I kabrown@waketech.edu
BROWN, Kevin, H 206-239-4500 502 D khbrown@cityu.edu
BROWN, Kim, S 757-455-3275 500 E kbrown@vwc.edu
BROWN, Kimberly 515-271-1462 171 H kimberly.brown@dmu.edu
BROWN, Kimberly, M 804-828-3893 496 D knbrown@vcu.edu
BROWN, Kristen, C 336-272-7102 344 G kristen.brown@greensboro.edu
BROWN, Kyle 315-386-7164 335 B brownk@canton.edu
BROWN, Kyle, A 315-267-7164 334 B browkya@potsdam.edu
BROWN, Larry 804-524-1162 499 G lbrown@vsu.edu
BROWN, Laura 413-662-5223 222 B l.brown@mcla.edu
BROWN, Laura 508-270-4116 223 F lbrown@massbay.edu
BROWN, Laura 847-925-6133 141 A lbrown@harpercollege.edu
BROWN, Laura 860-632-3010 88 B admissions@holyapostles.edu
BROWN, LeAnn 651-213-4175 247 B ltbrown@hazeldenbettyford.edu
BROWN, Lee 559-325-5264 67 B lee.brown@scccd.edu
BROWN, LeeAnn 304-473-8160 515 B brown_l@wvwc.edu
BROWN, Lenice 936-261-1068 467 E ldbrown@pvamu.edu
BROWN, JR., Leonard, E 240-895-4208 210 E lebrown1@smcm.edu
BROWN, Levy 252-527-6223 350 H ldbrown53@lenoircc.edu
BROWN, Lewis 605-688-4161 437 F lewis.brown@sdstate.edu
BROWN, Linda 660-359-3948 269 I lbrown@mail.ncmissouri.edu
BROWN, Linda, J 218-299-4206 246 A linbrown@cord.edu
BROWN, Lindsey 509-963-3001 501 K lindsey.brown@cwu.edu
BROWN, Lisa 509-358-7521 508 H lisaj.brown@wsu.edu
BROWN, Lisa 405-682-7896 385 D lbrown@occc.edu
BROWN, Lisa, M 202-687-6457 92 E lbrown@georgetown.edu
BROWN, Lisa, M 216-397-4184 370 H lmbrown@jcu.edu
BROWN, Lori, A 973-313-6132 297 A lori.brown@shu.edu
BROWN, Lucille 203-285-2114 86 C lbrown@gwcc.commnet.edu
BROWN, Lynne 212-998-2350 324 C lynne.brown@nyu.edu
BROWN, M. Christopher 225-771-2360 199 H mc_brown@sus.edu
BROWN, Mandy 641-844-5715 173 L mandy.brown@iavalley.edu
BROWN, Marcia, W 973-353-3709 296 C mwbrown@andromeda.rutgers.edu
BROWN, Marcus 217-875-7200 152 C mbrown@richland.edu
BROWN, Margo 904-819-6474 99 M mbrown@flagler.edu
BROWN, Mark 712-324-5061 175 G mbrown@nwicc.edu
BROWN, Martha 806-742-0012 472 A
BROWN, Martha 806-742-2120 472 C martha.brown@ttu.edu
BROWN, Mary 573-875-8700 263 F mbrown10@ccis.edu
BROWN, Mary, L 864-596-9094 429 C mary.brown@converse.edu
BROWN, Mary Jo 217-544-6464 153 G
BROWN, Mary Lou 573-840-9689 273 A mlbrown@trcc.edu
BROWN, Matt 901-381-3939 449 F matt@visible.edu
BROWN, Max 603-524-3207 286 C

BROWN, Melanie, A .... 904-808-7410.. 108 B
melaniebrown@sjrstate.edu
BROWN, Melissa .... 314-652-0300.. 271 D
mbrown@slchcmail.com
BROWN, Melissa .... 314-625-0300.. 271 D
mbrown@slchcmail.com
BROWN, Melissa .... 412-809-5100.. 417 D
brown.melissa@pti.edu
BROWN, Melissa, S .... 909-607-7855.... 39 B
melissa_brown@kgi.edu
BROWN, Merri .... 215-248-6323.. 409 D
mbrown@ltsp.edu
BROWN, Merv, R .... 208-496-2010.. 132 J
brownme@byui.edu
BROWN, Michael .... 406-447-6947.. 277 B
michael.brown@umhelena.edu
BROWN, Michael .... 937-376-2946.. 376 F
mbrown@payne.edu
BROWN, II, Michael, A .. 336-334-7940.. 356 F
mabrown8@ncat.edu
BROWN, Michael, T .... 805-893-2944.... 70 E
michael.brown@extension.ucsb.edu
BROWN, Michele .... 847-635-1981.. 150 G
mbrown@oakton.edu
BROWN, Michelle .... 678-717-6201.. 128 F
michelle.brown@ung.edu
BROWN, Michelle .... 435-283-7127.. 482 E
michelle.brown@snow.edu
BROWN, Mike .... 574-936-8898.. 158 I
mike.brown@ancilla.edu
BROWN, Mike .... 903-463-8772.. 458 H
mbrown@grayson.edu
BROWN, Mikell .... 804-594-1509.. 497 D
mbrown@jtcc.edu
BROWN, Monica, R .... 240-567-4341.. 209 E
monica.brown@montgomerycollege.edu
BROWN, Morgan .... 310-846-2648.... 55 E
mbrown@otis.edu
BROWN, Naima .... 352-395-5648.. 109 C
naima.brown@sfcollege.edu
BROWN, Nancy .... 516-876-3275.. 333 C
brownn@oldwestbury.edu
BROWN, Natasha .... 404-270-5617.. 128 A
nbrown29@spelman.edu
BROWN, Nedra .... 803-750-2500.... 93 F
BROWN, Nicholas .... 303-410-2407.... 82 K
nbrown@redstone.edu
BROWN, Nick .... 785-539-3571.. 183 B
nick.brown@mccks.edu
BROWN, Nicole .... 708-802-7750.. 140 F
nbrown@foxcolleg.edu
BROWN, Nicole .... 417-208-0636.. 266 E
nbrown@kcumb.edu
BROWN, Nicole, R .... 417-625-3137.. 268 H
brown-n@mssu.edu
BROWN, Owen .... 718-270-5045.. 309 B
obrown@mec.cuny.edu
BROWN, Pamela .... 718-260-5008.. 309 C
pbrown@citytech.cuny.edu
BROWN, Pamela .... 510-987-9251.... 68 L
pamela.brown@ucop.edu
BROWN, Pamela .... 843-574-6246.. 433 D
pamela.brown@tridenttech.edu
BROWN, Patricia, R .... 716-839-8484.. 312 D
pbrown@daemen.edu
BROWN, Patrick .... 217-245-3176.. 141 G
patrick.brown@mail.ic.edu
BROWN, Patrick .... 425-235-2352.. 506 F
pbrown@rtc.edu
BROWN, Patty .... 423-697-2437.. 445 D
patty.brown@chattanoogastate.edu
BROWN, Paul .... 254-659-7860.. 458 K
pbrown@hillcollege.edu
BROWN, Paul, R .... 732-571-3402.. 292 F
president@monmouth.edu
BROWN, Peter .... 540-338-2700.. 510 H
pbrown@cdu.edu
BROWN, Philip .... 219-989-2240.. 166 F
pbrown4@pnw.edu
BROWN, Philip, R .... 207-768-2708.. 203 L
pbrown@nmcc.edu
BROWN, Phillip, J .... 410-864-3613.. 210 F
pbrown@stmarys.edu
BROWN, Phillip, M .... 618-650-3415.. 155 A
phbrown@siue.edu
BROWN, R. McKenna .... 804-828-8471.. 496 D
mbrown@vcu.edu
BROWN, R. Michael .... 724-357-5924.. 415 B
rmbrown@iup.edu
BROWN, Rachel, A .... 202-994-6495.... 92 D
rabrown@gwu.edu
BROWN, Rachel, M .... 615-868-6503.. 442 G
rachel.brown@mtsa.edu
BROWN, Rae Linda .... 253-535-7126.. 505 G
raelinda.brown@plu.edu
BROWN, Randy .... 732-987-2254.. 292 A
rbrown@georgian.edu
BROWN, JR., Randy, D .. 404-413-1800.. 122 D
rdbrown@gsu.edu
BROWN, Rashayla .... 312-629-6869.. 154 A
maffai@saic.edu
BROWN, Ray .... 573-592-5238.. 275 E
ray.brown@westminster-mo.edu
BROWN, Raymond, A .... 610-527-0200.. 418 D
bbrown@rosemont.edu
BROWN, Raymond, A .... 817-257-7490.. 469 G
r.brown@tcu.edu
BROWN, Rebecca .... 850-599-3090.. 110 J
rebecca.brown@famu.edu
BROWN, Rebekkah, L .... 484-664-3247.. 411 D
rbrown@muhlenberg.edu
BROWN, Renee, D .... 419-559-2367.. 377 M
rbrown@terra.edu
BROWN, Reynolda .... 305-626-3711.. 101 A
rbrown@fmuniv.edu
BROWN, Rhonda .... 773-896-2400.. 137 A
rhonda.brown@ctschicago.edu
BROWN, Ricardo .... 601-979-8836.. 258 D
ricardo.a.brown@jsums.edu
BROWN, Richard .... 423-425-4393.. 448 F
richard-brown@utc.edu
BROWN, Richard, B .... 801-581-6912.. 481 M
brown@coe.utah.edu
BROWN, Rick .... 814-641-3311.. 406 F
brownri@juniata.edu
BROWN, Ricky .... 252-493-7259.. 352 A
rbrown@email.pittcc.edu
BROWN, Robert .... 410-386-8224.. 206 I
rbrown@carrollcc.edu
BROWN, Robert .... 502-272-8249.. 187 A
rbrown@bellarmine.edu
BROWN, Robert .... 570-321-4250.. 409 F
brownr@lycoming.edu
BROWN, Robert .... 864-596-9744.. 429 C
robert.brown@converse.edu
BROWN, Robert, A .... 617-353-2200.. 216 E
rabrown@bu.edu
BROWN, Robert, B .... 913-684-5621.. 528 I
BROWN, Robert, C .... 216-368-4306.. 365 B
robert.c.brown@case.edu
BROWN, Robert, K .... 918-781-7218.. 382 D
brownr@bacone.edu
BROWN, Robert, L .... 803-981-7375.. 435 D
rbrown@yorktech.edu
BROWN, Robert, M .... 251-460-6151...... 9 E
rbrown@southalabama.edu
BROWN, Robin, C .... 970-491-2682.... 78 Q
robin.brown@colostate.edu
BROWN, Roger .... 915-747-5202.. 476 D
rbrown6@utep.edu
BROWN, Roger, H .... 617-266-1400.. 215 G
BROWN, Rolanda .... 662-621-4244.. 257 B
rbrown@coahomacc.edu
BROWN, Ron .... 254-295-4517.. 474 E
rbrown@umhb.edu
BROWN, Ronald .... 334-229-7680...... 1 D
rbrown@alasu.edu
BROWN, Ronald, C .... 512-245-2205.. 471 F
rb04@txstate.edu
BROWN, Ronald, T .... 702-895-3693.. 284 L
BROWN, Rosann .... 814-641-3133.. 406 F
brownr@juniata.edu
BROWN, Roxanne .... 773-602-5016.. 137 F
rbrown262@ccc.edu
BROWN, Russ .... 772-462-6004.. 103 B
rbrown@irsc.edu
BROWN, Sabrina .... 434-395-2021.. 491 E
browncs2@longwood.edu
BROWN, Sandra .... 858-534-3526.... 70 C
sandrabrown@ucsd.edu
BROWN, Sandra .... 605-668-1555.. 436 D
sbrown@mtmc.edu
BROWN, Sara .... 501-760-4129.... 21 B
sbrown@np.edu
BROWN, Sarah .... 918-647-1474.. 382 I
sbrown@carlalbert.edu
BROWN, Scott, C .... 330-263-2011.. 367 A
scbrown@wooster.edu
BROWN, Shannon .... 305-899-4834.... 96 D
sbrown@barry.edu
BROWN, Shannon .... 603-668-2211.. 287 I
s.brown8@snhu.edu
BROWN, Shannon .... 267-341-3314.. 405 J
sbrown10@holyfamily.edu
BROWN, Shannon .... 214-768-4909.. 465 J
shannonbrown@smu.edu
BROWN, Shannon .... 828-726-2288.. 347 I
sbrown@cccti.edu
BROWN, Sharon .... 252-335-0821.. 349 A
sharon_brown@albemarle.edu
BROWN, Sheila .... 937-376-6349.. 365 H
sbrown@centralstate.edu
BROWN, Sheila .... 512-505-3031.. 459 F
stbrown@htu.edu
BROWN, Shelley .... 330-490-7134.. 380 J
sbrown@walsh.edu
BROWN, Shirley .... 615-329-8756.. 439 L
sbrown@fisk.edu
BROWN, Simon .... 215-751-8039.. 401 G
sbrown@ccp.edu
BROWN, Sondra .... 703-891-1787.. 494 H
dean@standardcollege.edu
BROWN, Stan .... 229-317-6721.. 120 A
stan.brown@darton.edu
BROWN, Stephanie .... 561-237-7784.. 104 O
scbrown@lynn.edu
BROWN, Stephanie .... 954-262-7456.. 105 J
browstep@nova.edu
BROWN, Stephanie .... 252-451-8257.. 351 F
sbrown@nashcc.edu
BROWN, Stephen, G .... 530-221-4275.... 64 C
sbrown@shasta.edu
BROWN, Steve .... 724-805-2534.. 419 A
steve.brown@email.stvincent.edu
BROWN, Steve, D .... 423-439-4841.. 444 F
browsd02@etsu.edu
BROWN, Steven .... 850-474-2222.. 113 A
sbrown4@uwf.edu
BROWN, Steven .... 802-287-8912.. 484 A
browns@greenmtn.edu
BROWN, Steven, D .... 906-227-1188.. 239 B
stebrown@nmu.edu
BROWN, Sue, C .... 309-655-2206.. 153 F
sue.c.brown@osfhealthcare.org
BROWN, Susan .... 808-932-7095.. 131 E
susanb@hawaii.edu
BROWN, Susan .... 956-665-2383.. 476 E
susan.brown@utrgv.edu
BROWN, Susan, M .... 859-233-8225.. 193 D
subrown@transy.edu
BROWN, Sylvia .... 252-744-6422.. 356 C
brownsy@ecu.edu
BROWN, T. Rhett .... 704-233-8111.. 359 H
r.brown@wingate.edu
BROWN, Takeish, N .... 804-257-5888.. 500 B
tnbrown@vuu.edu
BROWN, Tamara, L .... 936-261-5205.. 467 E
tlbrown@pvamu.edu
BROWN, Tavonda .... 870-743-3000.... 21 C
tbrown@northark.edu
BROWN, Ted, R .... 931-363-9802.. 441 G
tbrown@martinmethodist.edu
BROWN, Teisa .... 610-519-8881.. 422 G
teisa.brown@villanova.edu
BROWN, Teresa .... 404-225-4700.. 117 A
tbrown@atlantatech.edu
BROWN, Teresa, L .... 401-456-8240.. 425 E
tlbrown@ric.edu
BROWN, Terrence .... 901-751-8453.. 442 E
tbrown@mabts.edu
BROWN, Terry .... 716-673-3335.. 331 D
terry.brown@fredonia.edu
BROWN, Terry .... 610-683-4120.. 415 C
tbrown@kutztown.edu
BROWN, Theresa .... 334-874-5700...... 3 A
tbrown@ccal.edu
BROWN, Therese .... 303-404-5535.... 80 E
therese.brown@frontrange.edu
BROWN, Thomas .... 205-929-1061...... 5 H
tbrown@miles.edu
BROWN, Thomas .... 540-231-3787.. 499 F
tbrown@vt.edu
BROWN, Thomas, W .... 507-933-7005.. 246 J
brownie@gustavus.edu
BROWN, Tim .... 843-574-6424.. 433 D
tim.brown@tridenttech.edu
BROWN, Timothy .... 616-392-8555.. 244 A
tim.brown@westernsem.edu
BROWN, Tom .... 352-638-9762.... 96 F
tbrown@beaconcollege.edu
BROWN, Tom .... 310-660-3015.... 42 J
tbrown@elcamino.edu
BROWN, Tomeka, K .... 318-670-9319.. 199 J
tbrown@susla.edu
BROWN, Trachanda .... 215-242-7989.. 400 H
brownt@chc.edu
BROWN, Tracy, H .... 512-471-5974.. 476 B
tracy.brown@austin.utexas.edu
BROWN, Trevor, L .... 614-292-4533.. 375 A
brown.2296@osu.edu
BROWN, Trish .... 256-924-0511...... 5 E
tbrown@legacyu.net
BROWN, Venessa .... 618-650-5867.. 155 A
vbrown@siue.edu
BROWN, Victor .... 937-395-5604.. 371 D
victor.brown@kc.edu
BROWN, Vintress .... 864-503-5553.. 434 G
vbrown@uscupstate.edu
BROWN, JR., Walter, E ... 412-648-3185.. 421 G
walter.brown@ia.pitt.edu
BROWN, Wanda .... 336-750-2000.. 359 B
brownwa@wssu.edu
BROWN, Warren .... 206-934-3601.. 506 I
warren.brown@seattlecolleges.edu
BROWN, Warren, J .... 206-934-3601.. 506 J
warren.brown@seattlecolleges.edu
BROWN, Wayne .... 518-464-8675.. 314 A
wbrown@excelsior.edu
BROWN, Wheeler .... 601-979-2360.. 258 D
wheeler.brown@jsums.edu
BROWN, Wilfred, E .... 805-893-4155.... 70 E
willie.brown@auxiliary.ucsb.edu
BROWN, William .... 970-330-8008.... 76 H
bill.brown@aims.edu
BROWN, William .... 301-696-3402.. 208 B
brownw@hood.edu
BROWN, William .... 812-855-1822.. 162 F
brownwm@indiana.edu
BROWN, William .... 973-408-3976.. 291 B
wbrown1@drew.edu
BROWN, William, H .... 704-894-2143.. 343 I
wibrown@davidson.edu
BROWN, William (Bill) .... 859-846-5358.. 191 G
bbrown@midway.edu
BROWN, William Terry .... 203-332-5060.... 86 D
wbrown@housatonic.edu
BROWN, Winston, D .... 504-520-7577.. 202 C
wbrown@xula.edu
BROWN, Yvette .... 305-899-3600.... 96 D
ybrown@barry.edu
BROWN, Yvonne .... 843-574-6083.. 433 D
yvonne.brown@tridenttech.edu
BROWN, Zachary .... 607-431-4547.. 315 E
brownz@hartwick.edu
BROWN-CORNELIUS,
Denise .... 502-272-8270.. 187 A
dbrowncornelius@bellarmine.edu
BROWN GORDAN, Loria . 601-979-2107.. 258 D
loria.c.brown@jsums.edu
BROWN-GUILLORY,
Elizabeth, A .... 713-313-1983.. 470 D
brown-guillorye@tsu.edu
BROWN MARSDEN,
Margaret .... 940-397-4253.. 462 A
margaret.brownmarsden@mwsu.edu
BROWN MCCLURE,
Fran'Cee .... 404-270-5133.. 128 A
fbrownmc@spelman.edu
BROWN-NEVERS,
Michelle, H .... 215-898-7233.. 421 E
mbnevers@upenn.edu
BROWN-SOW, Lynette ..... 215-751-8859.. 401 G
lbrown@ccp.edu
BROWN-WELTY, Sharon .. 909-537-8101.... 34 C
sharonb@csusb.edu
BROWN YOUNG, Danita . 612-624-3560.. 255 H
dbyoung@umn.edu
BROWNE, Brian .... 718-990-2762.. 328 F
browneb@stjohns.edu
BROWNE, Doug .... 620-417-1201.. 184 I
doug.browne@sccc.edu
BROWNE, Jacob .... 727-864-8846.... 98 L
brownejh@eckerd.edu
BROWNE, Joan, M .... 202-806-7513.... 93 A
jmbrowne@howard.edu
BROWNE, Kevin .... 312-413-3471.. 156 F
kbrowne@uic.edu
BROWNE, Marcus .... 718-522-9073.. 304 D
mbrowne@asa.edu
BROWNE, Patrick .... 503-256-3180.. 396 C
pbrowne@uws.edu
BROWNE, Paul .... 574-631-8696.. 168 B
pbrowne@nd.edu
BROWNE-BOATSWAIN,
Venoreen .... 763-422-6094.. 248 L
venoreen.browne-boatswain@
anokaramsey.edu
BROWNE-BOATSWAIN,
Venoreen .... 763-422-6094.. 248 K
venoreen.browne-boatswain@
anokaramsey.edu
BROWNELL, Beverley ...... 714-895-1190.... 39 F
bbrownell@gwc.cccd.edu
BROWNELL, Claire .... 303-871-4876.... 84 B
claire.brownell@du.edu
BROWNELL, Jayne, E ...... 513-529-4631.. 372 K
browneje@miamioh.edu
BROWNELL, Jennifer ...... 336-506-4140.. 347 C
jennifer.brownell@alamancecc.edu
BROWNELL, Scott .... 612-330-1644.. 244 I
brownell@augsburg.edu
BROWNELL, Winifred, E .. 401-874-4101.. 426 D
winnie@uri.edu
BROWNER, Stephanie ..... 212-229-5100.. 322 E
browners@newschool.edu
BROWNIE, Ronald .... 605-626-2568.. 437 D
ronald.brownie@northern.edu
BROWNING, Ashley .... 540-362-6210.. 490 F
abrowning@hollins.edu
BROWNING, David, A ...... 252-399-6329.. 341 P
dabrowning@barton.edu
BROWNING, David, A ...... 214-860-2015.. 456 E
dbrowning@dcccd.edu
BROWNING, E.R. (Jay) .... 513-556-6153.. 379 A
jay.browning@uc.edu
BROWNING, Eric .... 740-392-6868.. 373 D
eric.browning@mvnu.edu
BROWNING, Gari .... 510-659-6200.... 55 B
gbrowning@ohlone.edu
BROWNING, Jason .... 307-674-6446.. 526 M
jbrowning@sheridan.edu
BROWNING, Joann .... 210-458-7379.. 477 A
joann.browning@utsa.edu

BROWNING, Katherine .... 301-387-3097.. 207 G
katherine.browning@garrettcollege.edu
BROWNING, Kimbrea ...... 513-487-1173.. 378 E
kimbrea.browning@myunion.edu
BROWNING, LK .... 931-540-2841.. 446 A
lkbrowning1@columbiastate.edu
BROWNING, Marian .... 626-529-8500.... 55 H
mbrowning@pacificoaks.edu
BROWNING, Mark .... 208-769-3316.. 134 C
mark_browning@nic.edu
BROWNING, Midge .... 618-374-5776.. 151 E
midge.browning@principia.edu
BROWNING, Peter .... 417-873-7231.. 264 H
pbrowning@drury.edu
BROWNING, Robert .... 303-352-3356.... 79 F
BROWNING, Roger .... 618-393-2982.. 142 B
browningr@iecc.edu
BROWNING, Steve .... 870-235-4102.... 22 F
dsbrowning@saumag.edu
BROWNLEE, Candace .... 309-268-8041.. 141 C
candace.brownlee@heartland.edu
BROWNLEE, David, W ..... 610-558-5628.. 411 E
dbrownle@neumann.edu
BROWNLEE, James, H ..... 330-471-8382.. 371 J
jbrownlee@malone.edu
BROWNLEE, Mordecai ..... 210-486-2252.. 450 E
mbrownlee3@alamo.edu
BROWNLEE, Mordecai ..... 304-357-4957.. 511 E
mordecaibrownlee@ucwv.edu
BROWNLEE, Reb .... 814-262-3842.. 413 P
rbrownlee@pennhighlands.edu
BROWNLEE, Tamarah, D . 260-481-6840.. 163 C
brownlet@ipfw.edu
BROWNLOW, Antonio ...... 662-254-3411.. 260 A
abrownlow@mvsu.edu
BROWNSBERGER,
William .... 660-944-2914.. 263 G
wbrownsberger@conception.edu
BROWNSON, James .... 208-885-5369.. 134 G
jbrownson@uidaho.edu
BROWNSTEIN, Aaron ...... 323-822-9700.... 68 B
aaron.brownstein@touro.edu
BROXSON, Thomas .... 253-840-8338.. 506 B
tbroxson@pierce.ctc.edu
BROYLES, Jennifer .... 848-445-5573.. 296 B
jbroyles@echo.rutgers.edu
BROYLES, Jennifer .... 848-445-5573.. 295 F
jbroyles@echo.rutgers.edu
BROYLES, Joy .... 540-863-2861.. 496 H
jbroyles@dslcc.edu
BROYLES, Ken .... 423-461-8734.. 442 K
kbroyles@milligan.edu
BROYLES, Wendy .... 334-983-6556...... 7 H
whuckabee@troy.edu
BROZ, Roger .... 612-659-6805.. 250 B
roger.broz@minneapolis.edu
BROZA, Dave .... 651-638-6459.. 244 L
d-broza@bethel.edu
BROZOVICH, Mary .... 303-458-4376.... 82 L
mbrozovi@regis.edu
BROZZO, Shirley, A .... 906-227-1000.. 239 B
sbrozzo@nmu.edu
BRUBACHER, Don .... 517-607-3130.. 235 E
dbrubacher@hillsdale.edu
BRUBAKER, Andy .... 229-732-5935.. 116 C
andybrubaker@andrewcollege.edu
BRUBAKER, David .... 585-567-9484.. 316 F
david.brubaker@houghton.edu
BRUBAKER, Donald, C .... 817-552-3700.. 460 E
dbrubaker@ktu.edu
BRUBAKER, Donald, C .... 817-552-3700.. 460 E
dbrubaker@tku.edu
BRUBAKER, Glenn, R ...... 607-587-4750.. 334 G
brubakgr@alfredstate.edu
BRUBAKER, Joel, A .... 724-847-6503.. 404 B
jabrubak@geneva.edu
BRUBAKER, Karl .... 620-327-8216.. 181 G
karlb@hesston.edu
BRUBAKER, Kevin .... 503-375-7030.. 391 B
kbrubaker@corban.edu
BRUBAKER, Linda .... 708-216-3960.. 146 G
lbrubaker@lumc.edu
BRUBAKER, Sara .... 620-242-0413.. 183 C
brubakes@mcpherson.edu
BRUBAKER-COLE, Susie .. 541-737-3626.. 393 H
susie.brubaker-cole@oregonstate.edu
BRUCE, Aaron, I .... 619-594-3319.... 35 A
abruce@mail.sdsu.edu
BRUCE, Alex, M .... 931-598-1919.. 443 O
ambruce@sewanee.edu
BRUCE, Beth .... 870-612-2057.... 23 H
beth.bruce@uaccb.edu
BRUCE, Debra .... 509-542-4604.. 502 G
dbruce@columbiabasin.edu
BRUCE, Douglas .... 770-467-6039.. 127 F
dbruce@sctech.edu
BRUCE, Gonzalo .... 620-341-5374.. 180 G
gbruce@emporia.edu
BRUCE, Harry .... 206-616-0985.. 508 E
harryb@uw.edu
BRUCE, J. Michael .... 812-866-7039.. 161 C
bruce@hanover.edu
BRUCE, Jimmie, D .... 740-264-5591.. 368 D
jbruce@egcc.edu
BRUCE, Karen .... 205-879-5588...... 3 I
kbruce@faulkner.edu
BRUCE, Kathy .... 847-925-6732.. 141 A
kbruce@harpercollege.edu
BRUCE, Linda .... 410-337-6223.. 207 H
linda.bruce@goucher.edu
BRUCE, Lori .... 662-325-7400.. 259 D
lmb102@msstate.edu
BRUCE, Motice .... 601-977-4470.. 261 A
mbruce@tougaloo.edu
BRUCE, Nisa .... 505-566-3490.. 301 J
brucen@sanjuancollege.edu
BRUCE, Philip .... 912-478-5197.. 122 B
pbruce@georgiasouthern.edu
BRUCE, Rob .... 919-962-2646.. 357 D
rob_bruce@unc.edu
BRUCE, Robert (Todd) ..... 216-397-1600.. 370 H
rbruce@jcu.edu
BRUCE, Stanyell .... 410-455-2632.. 211 G
bruce@umbc.edu
BRUCE, Steve .... 574-520-4457.. 163 E
stbruce@iusb.edu
BRUCE, Terry .... 619-393-2982.. 142 B
brucet@iecc.edu
BRUCE, Will .... 805-922-6966.... 25 I
wbruce@hancockcollege.edu
BRUCE, William, P .... 615-327-3927.. 440 H
pbruce@guptoncollege.edu
BRUCH, Courtney .... 303-404-5133.... 80 E
courtney.bruch@frontrange.edu
BRUCIATI, Antoinette .... 203-396-8004.... 88 I
bruciatia@sacredheart.edu
BRUCKI, Mark, J .... 248-204-2310.. 237 B
mbrucki@ltu.edu
BRUCKLER, Michael, L .... 240-895-2045.. 210 E
mlbruckler@smcm.edu
BRUCKMAN, Steve .... 415-452-5321.... 38 E
sbruckman@ccsf.edu
BRUCKNER, Michael, S ... 484-664-3230.. 411 D
bruckner@muhlenberg.edu
BRUDE, Jon .... 719-549-3340.... 82 G
jon.brude@pueblocc.edu
BRUDER, Edward, C .... 717-815-1314.. 424 F
ebruder@ycp.edu
BRUDNICKI, James .... 856-222-9311.. 295 C
jbrudnic@rcbc.edu
BRUDNOK, Celine, R .... 724-805-2720.. 419 A
celine.brudnok@email.stvincent.edu
BRUDVIG, James .... 845-758-7429.. 304 F
brudvig@bard.edu
BRUE ENRIGHT, Jan .... 605-256-5205.. 437 C
jan.brueenright@dsu.edu
BRUECK, Joshua .... 217-641-4320.. 143 H
jbrueck@jwcc.edu
BRUECKEN, John .... 515-271-1471.. 171 H
john.bruecken@dmu.edu
BRUEGGEMAN, Mary ..... 206-533-6724.. 507 F
mbrueggeman@shoreline.edu
BRUEGGEMANN, Chuck .. 618-537-6873.. 147 F
cebrueggemann@mckendree.edu
BRUEHL, Allen, A .... 508-767-7311.. 214 F
abruehl@assumption.edu
BRUEN, Christina, M ..... 508-910-6633.. 220 H
cbruen@umassd.edu
BRUESS, Brian .... 651-690-6778.. 254 M
bjbruess@stkate.edu
BRUESS, Brian .... 651-690-6043.. 254 M
bjbruess@stkate.edu
BRUGAL-MENA, Yocasta . 787-743-3038.. 535 L
ybrugal@sanjuanbautista.edu
BRUGGEMAN, Jared .... 417-625-9574.. 268 H
bruggeman-j@mssu.edu
BRUGGEMAN, John, H .. 513-487-3269.. 315 F
jbruggeman@huc.edu
BRUGH, Larry .... 814-262-3849.. 413 P
lbrugh@pennhighlands.edu
BRUGH, Suzanne .... 814-262-6463.. 413 P
sbrugh@pennhighlands.edu
BRUGMAN, Donna, M ...... 617-984-1776.. 227 F
dbrugman@quincycollege.edu
BRUHN, Christian .... 360-736-9391.. 502 A
cbruhn@centralia.edu
BRUHN, Mark, S .... 812-855-0326.. 162 E
mbruhn@iu.edu
BRUHN, Sheila .... 218-793-2465.. 251 C
sheila.bruhn@northlandcollege.edu
BRUHN, Tobias .... 215-968-8223.. 399 A
tobi.bruhn@bucks.edu
BRUINSMA, Paul .... 618-842-3711.. 142 C
bruinsmap@iecc.edu
BRUKARDT, David .... 608-262-3905.. 519 J
BRUKARDT, Mary Jane .... 715-836-2320.. 520 A
brukarmj@uwec.edu
BRULE, Lise, M .... 203-392-5722.... 85 H
brulel1@southernct.edu
BRUMAGIN, Ruth .... 570-288-8400.. 403 H
ruthb@marcogrp.com
BRUMBACH, Mary .... 214-378-1549.. 456 A
mbrumbach@dcccd.edu
BRUMBERG, Joshua .... 212-817-7215.. 308 A
jbrumberg@gc.cuny.edu
BRUMFIELD, Adele, C ..... 858-534-3156.... 70 C
acbrumfield@ucsd.edu
BRUMFIELD, Robb, T ...... 225-578-2887.. 197 I
robb@lsu.edu
BRUMITT, Jane .... 312-629-6184.. 154 A
jbrumitt@saic.edu
BRUMLEY, Jessica .... 954-262-8835.. 105 J
jw1263@nova.edu
BRUMLEY, Larry, D .... 478-301-5700.. 124 D
brumley_ld@mercer.edu
BRUMMEL, Joe .... 641-628-7648.. 170 E
brummelj@central.edu
BRUMMELS, Lin .... 402-375-7321.. 281 J
librummel@wsc.edu
BRUMMER, James, M ..... 651-962-6595.. 256 C
jbrummer@stthomas.edu
BRUMMER, Joni, M .... 480-732-7226.... 13 C
joni.brummer@cgc.edu
BRUMMETT, Ross .... 865-471-3235.. 439 C
rbrummett@cn.edu
BRUMMUND, Barry, T .... 520-621-0588.... 17 I
brummund@email.arizona.edu
BRUN, James .... 859-371-9393.. 186 M
jbrun@beckfield.edu
BRUNDAGE, Isaac .... 575-538-6339.. 303 A
brundagei@wnmu.edu
BRUNDAGE, Kelly .... 850-474-3063.. 113 A
kbrundage@uwf.edu
BRUNDAGE, Ken .... 814-871-7551.. 404 A
brundage001@gannon.edu
BRUNDAGE, Tracy, L ...... 570-326-3761.. 413 O
tbrundag@pct.edu
BRUNDIDGE, Linda .... 847-317-7023.. 156 B
lbrundid@tiu.edu
BRUNDIECK, Stephanie ... 402-844-7277.. 282 B
stephanie@northeast.edu
BRUNDO-SHARRAR,
Tricia, A .... 402-280-4076.. 279 H
sharrar@creighton.edu
BRUNDY, Curtis .... 319-352-8500.. 177 G
curtis.brundy@wartburg.edu
BRUNE, Carolyn .... 847-574-5154.. 145 C
cbrune@lfgsm.edu
BRUNEAU, Patrice .... 803-323-2266.. 435 B
bruneaup@winthrop.edu
BRUNELLE, Christopher .. 909-652-6591.... 37 D
christopher.brunelle@chaffey.edu
BRUNELLI, Leslie, G .... 803-777-1967.. 433 F
lgbrunel@mailbox.sc.edu
BRUNEN, Meredith .... 479-619-4176.... 21 D
mbrunen@nwacc.edu
BRUNER, Cassie .... 979-230-3308.. 453 A
cassie.bruner@brazosport.edu
BRUNER, Dan, L .... 208-467-8843.. 134 D
dlbruner@nnu.edu
BRUNER, Greg .... 815-939-5249.. 150 I
gbruner@olivet.edu
BRUNER, Jeremy .... 501-450-3183.... 24 G
jbruner@uca.edu
BRUNER, Joe W .... 859-858-3511.. 186 J
joe.bruner@asbury.edu
BRUNER, Judith .... 858-246-1800.... 70 C
jbruner@ucsd.edu
BRUNET EAGAN,
Kathleen .... 973-328-5052.. 290 H
keagan@ccm.edu
BRUNET-KOCH, Cameron 231-348-6601.. 239 A
ckoch@ncmich.edu
BRUNETT, Emerald .... 541-888-7229.. 395 B
emerald.brunett@socc.edu
BRUNETTA, Stephanie ..... 607-431-4000.. 315 E
brunetta@hartwick.edu
BRUNETTE, Thomas .... 903-877-7212.. 477 E
tom.brunette@uthct.edu
BRUNETTO, Jeffrey .... 201-200-2040.. 293 C
jbrunetto@njcu.edu
BRUNGARDT, Cherie ...... 970-521-6787.... 81 O
cherie.brungardt@njc.edu
BRUNGARDT, Heather ..... 970-521-6623.... 81 O
heather.brungardt@njc.edu
BRUNING, Merribeth ...... 765-641-4406.. 158 J
mdbruning@anderson.edu
BRUNING, Steve .... 614-236-6528.. 364 N
sbruning@capital.edu
BRUNJES, Jim .... 806-742-0012.. 472 A
BRUNKOW, Alan .... 402-761-8259.. 232 F
abrunkow@southeast.edu
BRUNNEMER, David .... 360-650-7732.. 509 E
david.brunnemer@wwu.edu
BRUNNER, Diane .... 419-473-2700.. 367 J
dbrunner@daviscollege.edu
BRUNNER, Emily .... 215-702-4300.. 399 E
ebrunner@cairn.edu
BRUNNER, Jon, L .... 239-590-7950.. 110 L
jbrunner@fgcu.edu
BRUNNER, Karen, L .... 865-882-4606.. 447 A
brunnerkl@roanestate.edu
BRUNNER, Ludwig .... 716-375-7666.. 328 B
lbrunner@sbu.edu
BRUNNER, Marc .... 931-221-7887.. 444 E
brunnerm@apsu.edu
BRUNNER, Mark .... 573-876-2381.. 272 I
mbrunner@stephens.edu
BRUNNER, Marta .... 518-580-5506.. 330 F
BRUNNER, Mary, K .... 810-989-5512.. 240 G
mbrunner@sc4.edu
BRUNNER, Matthew .... 540-851-5271.. 493 A
msbrunner@radford.edu
BRUNNER, Thomas .... 908-852-1400.. 290 D
brunnert@centenarycollege.edu
BRUNNER, Tim .... 419-473-2700.. 367 J
tbrunner@daviscollege.edu
BRUNNER, Timothy .... 419-473-2700.. 367 J
tbrunner@daviscolleg.edu
BRUNO, Bonnie .... 336-278-6603.. 344 D
bbruno2@elon.edu
BRUNO, Christopher .... 470-578-5483.. 123 J
cbruno3@kennesaw.edu
BRUNO, Craig .... 412-536-1152.. 406 K
craig.bruno@laroche.edu
BRUNO, Gene .... 800-290-4226.. 440 G
gbruno@hchs.edu
BRUNO, Joanne, Z .... 570-422-3539.. 414 H
provost@esu.edu
BRUNO, Joseph, M .... 617-333-2158.. 217 F
BRUNO, Kimberly .... 504-568-4820.. 198 A
kbruno@lsuhsc.edu
BRUNO, Laura .... 718-281-5212.. 309 E
lbruno@qcc.cuny.edu
BRUNO, Nick, J .... 318-342-1010.. 201 E
bruno@ulm.edu
BRUNO, SC, Teresa .... 973-957-0188.. 288 G
academicdean@acs350.org
BRUNOLD, Timothy .... 213-740-6753.... 72 D
admdean@usc.edu
BRUNS, Clara .... 802-322-1603.. 483 H
clara.bruns@goddard.edu
BRUNS, Jack .... 319-385-6375.. 174 A
jack.bruns@iw.edu
BRUNS, Lisa .... 631-420-2245.. 335 E
lisa.bruns@farmingdale.edu
BRUNS, Sandy .... 712-324-5061.. 175 G
sandy@nwicc.edu
BRUNSON, Bruce, H .... 757-822-7101.. 498 H
bbrunson@tcc.edu
BRUNSON, Claude .... 601-984-1012.. 261 C
cbrunson@umc.edu
BRUNSON, Isaac .... 256-761-6315...... 7 F
isaacbrunson@talladega.edu
BRUNSON, Laura, R .... 405-325-3352.. 389 B
lbrunson@ou.edu
BRUNSON, Mary Nelle ..... 936-468-2707.. 466 H
mbrunson@sfasu.edu
BRUNSON, Rod .... 973-353-5870.. 296 C
rodbruns@andromeda.rutgers.edu
BRUNSON, Teesa .... 803-780-1194.. 434 M
tbrunson@voorhees.edu
BRUNSWICK, Katie .... 703-330-8400.... 93 F
BRUNSWICK, Katie .... 703-729-8800.... 93 F
BRUNT, Bonnie .... 509-533-3339.. 503 A
bonnie.brunt@sfcc.spokane.edu
BRUNTMYER, Eric, I .... 325-670-1227.. 458 J
ebruntmyer@hsutx.edu
BRUNTON, Mark .... 702-579-3528.. 283 I
mbrunton@kaplan.edu
BRUNTZ, Crystal .... 816-501-3600.. 262 G
crystal.bruntz@avila.edu
BRUSATI, Gerianne .... 845-341-4020.. 325 H
gerianne.brusati@sunyorange.edu
BRUSCATO, Brandon .... 318-342-5314.. 201 E
bruscato@ulm.edu
BRUSH, Thomas .... 410-617-2280.. 208 G
tdbrush@loyola.edu
BRUSH, Thomas .... 410-617-1466.. 208 G
tdbrush@loyola.edu
BRUSKI, Kathleen .... 989-358-7335.. 230 G
bruskik@alpenacc.edu
BRUSOE, Suzanne .... 651-423-8205.. 249 B
suzie.brusoe@dctc.edu
BRUSOE, Suzanne .... 651-423-8205.. 249 B
suzanne.brusoe@dctc.edu
BRUSOE, Suzie .... 651-450-3642.. 249 F
BRUSTEIN, William, I .... 614-292-5881.. 375 A
brustein.1@osu.edu
BRUSTKERN, Kari .... 406-447-5422.. 276 B
kbrustkern@carroll.edu
BRUSZEWSKI, Roger .... 717-871-4087.. 415 F
roger.bruszewski@millersville.edu
BRUTON, Muniece .... 323-241-5338.... 50 B
BRUXVOORT, Debra .... 641-628-7671.. 170 E
bruxvoortb@central.edu
BRY, Jay .... 978-665-3131.. 221 D
jbry@fitchburgstate.edu
BRYAN, Ben .... 803-754-4100.. 429 B
BRYAN, Brett .... 541-278-5900.. 390 C
bbryan@bluecc.edu
BRYAN, Charles "Hank" .. 989-386-6622.. 238 B
cbryan@midmich.edu

BRYAN, Doug .... 704-406-4398.. 344 E
dbryan@gardner-webb.edu
BRYAN, James .... 316-322-3232.. 179 E
jbryan8@butlercc.edu
BRYAN, Jaxie .... 919-464-2254.. 350 G
jlbryan1@johnstoncc.edu
BRYAN, John .... 413-545-2554.. 220 F
johnbryan@provost.umass.edu
BRYAN, Karla .... 903-675-6229.. 473 B
kbryan@tvcc.edu
BRYAN, Laura .... 859-233-8121.. 193 D
lbryan@transy.edu
BRYAN, Lois, D .... 412-397-6339.. 418 B
bryan@rmu.edu
BRYAN, Mitzi .... 718-636-3430.. 326 E
mbryan@pratt.edu
BRYAN, Neva .... 276-328-0126.. 495 I
njd8r@uvawise.edu
BRYAN, JR., Norman, B . 864-833-8757.. 432 B
nbbryan@presby.edu
BRYAN, Paul .... 215-893-5252.. 401 J
paul.bryan@curtis.edu
BRYAN, Robert .... 216-987-4684.. 367 E
robert.bryan@tri-c.edu
BRYAN, Royce .... 620-862-5252.. 178 F
royce.bryan@barclaycollege.edu
BRYAN, Sandy .... 520-515-5313.... 12 L
bryans@cochise.edu
BRYAN, Sibley .... 706-453-0378.. 116 H
sbryan@athenstech.edu
BRYAN, Susan .... 417-865-2815.. 265 B
bryans@evangel.edu
BRYAN, Terry .... 832-252-4676.. 454 H
terry.bryan@cbshouston.edu
BRYAN, Timothy, A .... 330-471-8539.. 371 J
tbryan@malone.edu
BRYAN, Wes .... 714-895-8101.... 39 F
wbryan@gwc.cccd.edu
BRYAN WILLIAMS,
Pamela .... 314-529-9614.. 267 B
pbryanwilliams@maryville.edu
BRYANT, JR., Alfred .... 910-775-4009.. 358 C
alfred.bryant@uncp.edu
BRYANT, Angela .... 336-734-7618.. 349 G
abryant@forsythtech.edu
BRYANT, Angela, V .... 229-928-1378.. 122 C
angela.bryant@gsw.edu
BRYANT, Angie .... 615-460-6407.. 438 J
angie.bryant@belmont.edu
BRYANT, Bruce, K .... 206-239-4500.. 502 D
brucebryant@cityu.edu
BRYANT, Bryan .... 719-846-5691.... 83 G
bryant.bryant@trinidadstate.edu
BRYANT, Carlton, G .... 800-782-2422.... 31 E
cbryant@mail.cnuas.edu
BRYANT, Charles .... 909-447-6339.... 39 A
cbryant@cst.edu
BRYANT, Cherie .... 207-741-5726.. 203 M
cbryant@smccme.edu
BRYANT, Clint .... 706-737-1626.. 117 D
cbryant1@augusta.edu
BRYANT, Courtney .... 509-527-2222.. 508 G
courtney.bryant@wallawalla.edu
BRYANT, Daniel, C .... 740-376-4718.. 372 A
dan.bryant@marietta.edu
BRYANT, David, A .... 407-303-9305.... 95 C
david.bryant@adu.edu
BRYANT, David, A .... 580-349-1302.. 385 F
dbryant@opsu.edu
BRYANT, Elisa .... 417-625-3039.. 268 H
bryant-e@mssu.edu
BRYANT, Felicia .... 856-227-7200.. 290 B
fbryant@camdencc.edu
BRYANT, Fred .... 361-593-3922.. 469 A
kffcb00@tamuk.edu
BRYANT, Gerard .... 646-781-5625.. 308 E
gwbryant@jjay.cuny.edu
BRYANT, Holley .... 509-527-2772.. 508 G
holley.bryant@wallawalla.edu
BRYANT, Jack .... 405-422-1260.. 387 E
jack.bryant@redlandscc.edu
BRYANT, III, James, S ... 803-535-1330.. 431 I
bryantj@octech.edu
BRYANT, Jocelyn .... 410-951-3922.. 212 E
jbryant@coppin.edu
BRYANT, Jodi .... 757-455-3200.. 500 E
jbryant@vwc.edu
BRYANT, John .... 309-556-3449.. 143 D
jbryant@iwu.edu
BRYANT, Jordan .... 847-317-7074.. 156 B
jbryant@tiu.edu
BRYANT, Joy, L .... 864-644-5385.. 432 G
jbryant@swu.edu
BRYANT, Kimberly .... 215-895-1121.. 422 A
k.bryant@usciences.edu
BRYANT, Kimberly .... 336-734-7236.. 349 G
kbryant@forsythtech.edu
BRYANT, Kinney .... 405-425-5155.. 385 C
kinney.bryant@oc.edu
BRYANT, III, Lewis .... 434-832-7615.. 496 G
bryantl@cvcc.vccs.edu

BRYANT, Marcus .... 843-863-7352.. 427 I
mdbryant@csuniv.edu
BRYANT, Mark .... 661-722-6300.... 27 B
mbryant6@avc.edu
BRYANT, Michael .... 843-863-7973.. 427 I
mbryant@csuniv.edu
BRYANT, Micki .... 714-564-6079.... 58 G
bryant_micki@sac.edu
BRYANT, Morgan .... 601-925-3354.. 259 A
mbryant@mc.edu
BRYANT, Nicole .... 305-237-5223.. 105 D
nbryant@mdc.edu
BRYANT, Pam .... 325-649-8401.. 459 E
pbryant@hputx.edu
BRYANT, Paul .... 803-536-7000.. 432 E
BRYANT, Ronnie .... 910-755-7483.. 347 H
bryantr@brunswickcc.edu
BRYANT, Rosalynn .... 314-362-9253.. 265 E
rjr9245@bjc.org
BRYANT, Scott .... 903-923-2173.. 457 G
sbryant@etbu.edu
BRYANT, Sheila, M .... 931-221-7178.. 444 E
bryantsm@apsu.edu
BRYANT, Stephanie .... 417-836-4408.. 268 I
stephaniebryant@missouristate.edu
BRYANT, Theresa .... 412-788-7360.. 401 B
tbryant@ccac.edu
BRYANT, Tim .... 513-244-4504.. 373 C
tim.bryant@msj.edu
BRYANT, Toni .... 830-792-7229.. 465 E
tlbryant@schreiner.edu
BRYANT, Vickie .... 817-461-8741.. 451 G
vbryant@arlingtonbaptistcollege.edu
BRYANT, Wayne, H .... 318-670-9230.. 199 J
wbryant@ssla.edu
BRYANT-FRIEDRICH,
Amanda .... 419-530-4968.. 380 D
amanda.bryant-friedrich@utoledo.edu
BRYARS, Beth .... 251-580-2227...... 4 I
beth.bryars@faulknerstate.edu
BRYCE, Jeanne .... 928-428-8261.... 13 B
jeanne.bryce@eac.edu
BRYCE, Mark .... 928-428-8231.... 13 B
mark.bryce@eac.edu
BRYDE, Beverly .... 610-902-8331.. 399 D
beverly.reilly.bryde@cabrini.edu
BRYDEN, David, L .... 336-841-9101.. 345 A
dbryden@highpoint.edu
BRYDON, Lucinda, C .... 607-746-4603.. 335 C
brydonlm@delhi.edu
BRYENTON, John .... 270-686-4615.. 190 D
john.bryenton@kctcs.edu
BRYLINSKY, Jody .... 269-387-2314.. 243 H
jody.brylinsky@wmich.edu
BRYMER, Krystin .... 334-244-3758...... 2 A
kbrymer@aum.edu
BRYNE, Dara .... 212-484-1347.. 308 E
dbyrne@jjay.cuny.edu
BRYS-WILSON, Jessica ... 252-985-5186.. 354 E
jbrys-wilson@ncwc.edu
BRYSON, Allison .... 541-880-2234.. 391 F
bryson@klamathcc.edu
BRYSON, Barbara .... 520-621-5511.... 17 I
bwbryson@email.arizona.edu
BRYSON, Cynthia .... 713-771-5336.. 123 F
cbryson@ict.edu
BRYSON, Lance .... 717-477-1451.. 416 A
jlbrys@ship.edu
BRYSON, Suzanne .... 828-251-6128.. 357 C
sbryson@unca.edu
BRZENIK, Andrea .... 727-736-5082.. 109 D
abrzenik@schiller.edu
BRZEZINSKI, Karen .... 715-675-3331.. 524 D
brzezinski@ntc.edu
BRZORAD, John .... 828-328-7606.. 345 H
john.brzorad@lr.edu
BRZOZOWSKI, Eileen .... 321-433-5687.... 98 K
brzozowskie@easternflorida.edu
BRZYCKI, Shelly .... 847-578-8355.. 153 A
shelly.brzycki@rosalindfranklin.edu
BRZYTWA, MaryClare .... 415-503-6263.... 61 C
mcbrzytwa@sfcm.edu
BUBB, Kevin .... 517-483-9764.. 237 A
bubbk@lcc.edu
BUBB, Terry .... 615-230-3398.. 447 C
terry.bubb@volstate.edu
BUBNOVA, Elena .... 775-673-8239.. 284 K
ebubnova@tmcc.edu
BUCALOS, Anne .... 502-272-8405.. 187 A
abucalos@bellarmine.edu
BUCARO, S. Ted .... 937-229-4122.. 379 D
sbucaro1@udayton.edu
BUCCALO, Nicole .... 410-334-2892.. 213 G
nbuccalo@worwic.edu
BUCCI, Taffie .... 412-392-3959.. 417 F
tbucci@pointpark.edu
BUCCIARELLI, Roseann ... 732-906-4681.. 292 E
rbucciarelli@middlesexcc.edu
BUCCILLI, Michael .... 203-285-2626..... 86 C
mbuccilli@gwcc.commnet.edu

BUCELL, Michael .... 814-732-2252.. 415 A
bucell@edinboro.edu
BUCHA, Edward, R .... 724-738-2183.. 416 B
ebucha@srufoundation.org
BUCHAN, Kristina .... 208-535-5477.. 133 G
kristina.buchan@my.eitc.edu
BUCHANAN, Barbara .... 775-673-7090.. 284 K
bbuchanan@tmcc.edu
BUCHANAN, Cindy .... 413-205-3918.. 214 B
cindy.buchanan@aic.edu
BUCHANAN, Eddie .... 828-766-1227.. 351 B
ebuchanan@mayland.edu
BUCHANAN, Evelyn .... 262-551-6122.. 516 A
ebuchanan@carthage.edu
BUCHANAN, Harvey .... 850-644-2825.. 111 C
buchanan@fsu.edu
BUCHANAN, James .... 707-864-7176.... 65 A
james.buchanan@solano.edu
BUCHANAN, Kelly .... 619-201-8702.... 60 D
kelly.buchanan@sdcc.edu
BUCHANAN, Kent, L .... 405-208-5287.. 385 E
kbuchanan@okcu.edu
BUCHANAN, Lane .... 307-766-5272.. 527 B
lane@uwyo.edu
BUCHANAN, Linda, R ...... 229-732-5926.. 116 C
lindabuchanan@andrewcollege.edu
BUCHANAN, Martha .... 210-486-0116.. 450 F
mbuchanan@alamo.edu
BUCHANAN, Merilyn .... 805-437-8579.... 32 B
merilyn.buchanan@csuci.edu
BUCHANAN, Pamela .... 828-227-7640.. 359 A
pbuchanan@wcu.edu
BUCHANAN, Russell .... 610-292-9852.. 417 I
rbuchanan@reseminary.edu
BUCHANAN, Stephanie ..... 770-426-2884.. 124 B
stephanie.buchanan@life.edu
BUCHANAN, Tony .... 330-337-6403.. 362 I
college@awc.edu
BUCHANAN BERNARD,
Daphne .... 202-806-6530.... 93 A
dbernard@howard.edu
BUCHE, Nathan .... 620-665-3569.. 181 I
buchen@hutchcc.edu
BUCHELE, Ann .... 541-917-4211.. 392 C
buchela@linnbenton.edu
BUCHELI, Hernan .... 925-631-4277.... 59 I
hmb5@stmarys-ca.edu
BUCHER, Jake .... 785-594-8475.. 178 D
jbucher@bakeru.edu
BUCHER, Jasmine, A .... 717-867-6036.. 408 F
bucher@lvc.edu
BUCHER, Jennifer .... 570-372-4157.. 419 H
bucherjennifer@susqu.edu
BUCHER, John, E .... 440-775-6727.. 374 C
john.bucher@oberlin.edu
BUCHER, Karen, H .... 540-665-4621.. 494 B
kbucher@su.edu
BUCHER, Mary .... 864-503-5000.. 434 G
BUCHER, Oskar .... 541-684-7273.. 393 B
obucher@nwcu.edu
BUCHHOLZ, Reyne, D ...... 757-822-1754.. 498 H
rbuchholz@tcc.edu
BUCHHOLZ, Richard .... 405-422-6204.. 387 E
richard.buchholz@redlandscc.edu
BUCHHOLZ, Robert .... 336-278-5500.. 344 D
rbuchholz@elon.edu
BUCHHOLZ, Ron .... 262-472-1498.. 521 F
buchholr@uww.edu
BUCHHOLZ, Stephen .... 605-718-2436.. 438 B
stephen.buchholz@wdt.edu
BUCHHOLZ, Thomas .... 713-792-2121.. 477 F
BUCHKO, Lindsay .... 202-448-7037.... 92 C
lindsay.buchko@gallaudet.edu
BUCHMAN, Ashley .... 870-512-7812.... 19 C
ashley_buchman@asun.edu
BUCHMAN, Irene .... 212-217-4590.. 314 B
irene_buchman@fitnyc.edu
BUCHMAN, Lorne, M .... 626-396-2301.... 27 L
president@artcenter.edu
BUCHOLC, Stanley .... 978-665-3215.. 221 D
sbucholc@fitchburgstate.edu
BUCHWALD, Adam .... 503-768-7227.. 392 A
buchwald@lclark.edu
BUCHWALD, Carrie .... 847-574-5164.. 145 C
cbuchwald@lfgsm.edu
BUCHWALD, Maurissa ...... 580-581-2612.. 382 G
mbuchwald@cameron.edu
BUCHWALD, Rosalinda ..... 626-914-8897.... 38 D
rbuchwald@citruscollege.edu
BUCHWALDER, Mary, P ... 937-229-3131.. 379 D
mbuchwalder1@udayton.edu
BUCK, A. Scott .... 252-328-6910.. 356 C
bucka@ecu.edu
BUCK, Charles .... 208-292-1737.. 134 G
buck@uidaho.edu
BUCK, David .... 208-282-3111.. 133 H
buckdavi@isu.edu
BUCK, James, E .... 937-393-3431.. 377 F
jbuck@sscc.edu
BUCK, John .... 407-447-7300.. 102 D
jbuck@ftccollege.edu

BUCK, John .... 314-246-4463.. 275 B
buckjh@webster.edu
BUCK, Karen .... 979-209-7280.. 452 J
karenbuck@blinn.edu
BUCK, Katherine .... 973-290-4203.. 290 G
kbuck@cse.edu
BUCK, Kavin .... 503-821-8942.. 394 B
kbuck@pnca.edu
BUCK, Kevan, C .... 918-631-3245.. 389 E
kevan-buck@utulsa.edu
BUCK, Kimberly .... 434-797-8458.. 496 I
kimberly.buck@dcc.vccs.edu
BUCK, Leah .... 207-768-2768.. 203 L
lbuck@nmcc.edu
BUCK, Marilyn .... 765-285-5816.. 159 B
mbuck@bsu.edu
BUCK, Marilyn .... 765-285-5818.. 159 B
mbuck@bsu.edu
BUCK, Marilyn, M .... 765-285-3716.. 159 B
mbuck@bsu.edu
BUCK, Mark .... 630-799-0899.. 139 D
mbuck@devry.edu
BUCK, Nick .... 317-931-2378.. 160 B
nbuck@cts.edu
BUCK, Ryan .... 512-245-7966.. 471 F
r_b259@txstate.edu
BUCK, Sharon .... 425-739-8146.. 504 F
sharon.buck@lwtech.edu
BUCK, Sylvia, T .... 812-488-2724.. 167 I
sb79@evansville.edu
BUCK, Yolanda .... 804-524-5297.. 499 G
ybuck@vsu.edu
BUCKALEW, Danielle .... 205-652-3852...... 9 F
bdbuckalew@uwa.edu
BUCKELS, Carol .... 386-738-6686.. 113 B
cbuckels@stetson.edu
BUCKENMEYER, Janet ...... 912-344-3277.. 116 E
janet.buckenmeyer@armstrong.edu
BUCKER, Robert .... 503-725-3340.. 394 G
william.robert.bucker@pdx.edu
BUCKHAULTS, Tex .... 806-874-3571.. 454 F
tex.buckhaults@clarendoncollege.edu
BUCKHAULTS, Tresea, L . 318-342-5240.. 201 E
buckhaults@ulm.edu
BUCKI, SJ, John, P .... 315-445-4110.. 318 E
buckijp@lemoyne.edu
BUCKINGHAM, Bob, S ...... 304-457-6588.. 510 B
buckinghamrs@ab.edu
BUCKINGHAM, Jane .... 802-258-3367.. 485 A
jane.buckingham@worldlearning.org
BUCKINGHAM, John .... 319-656-2447.. 176 F
BUCKINGHAM, Judith, P 936-468-4048.. 466 H
jpbuckingham@sfasu.edu
BUCKINGHAM, Stacy .... 618-985-3741.. 143 F
stacybuckingham@jalc.edu
BUCKLA, Robert, J .... 414-410-4201.. 515 I
rbuckla@stritch.edu
BUCKLE, Eileen .... 732-255-0400.. 293 E
ebuckle@ocean.edu
BUCKLER, C. Adam .... 317-896-9324.. 167 H
abuckler@ubca.org
BUCKLES, Beverly, J .... 909-558-4528.... 49 C
bbuckles@llu.edu
BUCKLES, Dale .... 270-706-8431.. 189 C
dale.buckles@kctcs.edu
BUCKLES, Gregory, B ...... 802-443-5161.. 484 F
deanofadmissions@middlebury.edu
BUCKLES, Jennifer .... 423-425-4677.. 448 F
jennifer-buckles@utc.edu
BUCKLEW, Andrea, J .... 304-457-6438.. 510 B
bucklewaj@ab.edu
BUCKLEW, Kathy .... 863-297-1016.. 106 I
kbucklew@polk.edu
BUCKLEY, Alison .... 443-518-4133.. 208 C
abuckley@howardcc.edu
BUCKLEY, Anne .... 205-934-9518...... 8 E
abuckley@uab.edu
BUCKLEY, Chris .... 910-893-1208.. 342 F
buckley@campbell.edu
BUCKLEY, Cynthia .... 405-466-2231.. 383 M
BUCKLEY, Cynthia, S .... 405-466-3204.. 383 M
csbuckley@langston.edu
BUCKLEY, David .... 530-898-6411.... 32 C
dbuckley@csuchico.edu
BUCKLEY, Debi .... 479-619-4217.... 21 D
dbuckley@nwacc.edu
BUCKLEY, Emily .... 913-621-8731.. 180 F
ebuckley@donnelly.edu
BUCKLEY, Gerard, J .... 585-475-6317.. 327 E
gbuckley@ntid.rit.edu
BUCKLEY, Irene .... 914-674-7308.. 320 G
ibuckley@mercy.edu
BUCKLEY, Jeanne .... 215-572-4019.. 397 G
buckleyj@arcadia.edu
BUCKLEY, Jennifer .... 630-844-6155.. 135 E
jbuckley@aurora.edu
BUCKLEY, Jerry .... 661-362-3410.... 40 A
jerry.buckley@canyons.edu
BUCKLEY, John, M .... 302-857-1200.... 91 C
john.buckley@dtcc.edu

BUOSCIO, Amy .... 708-237-5050.. 150 D
abuoscio@nc.edu
BURAK, Deborah .... 610-861-4137.. 411 G
dburak@northampton.edu
BURAK, Marshall, J .... 510-628-8016.... 49 A
mburak@lincolnuca.edu
BURBA, Dave .... 530-541-4660.... 48 D
burba@ltcc.edu
BURBA, Randy .... 714-997-6763.... 37 F
burba@chapman.edu
BURBACK, Michael .... 202-884-9000.... 94 A
burbackm@trinitydc.edu
BURBAGE, Priscilla, D .... 843-953-5578.. 428 G
burbagep@cofc.edu
BURBANTE, Gilberto .... 985-448-4208.. 201 A
gilberto.burbante@nicholls.edu
BURBEY, Denise .... 716-338-1250.. 317 F
deniseburbey@mail.sunyjcc.edu
BURCH, Beth .... 503-253-3443.. 393 D
bburch@ocom.edu
BURCH, Christopher, L ... 240-895-3115.. 210 E
clburch@smcm.edu
BURCH, Chuck, S .... 704-406-4342.. 344 E
cburch@gardner-webb.edu
BURCH, Doug .... 801-622-1573.. 481 E
doug.burch@stevenhenager.edu
BURCH, Doug .... 801-622-1573.. 481 E
doug.burch@stevenshenager.edu
BURCH, Franki .... 704-406-3522.. 344 E
fburch@gardner-webb.edu
BURCH, Jeremy .... 808-983-4154.. 130 I
jburch@tokai.edu
BURCH, Jim .... 912-443-5874.. 126 G
jburch@savannahtech.edu
BURCH, John .... 270-789-5015.. 187 G
jrburch@campbellsville.edu
BURCH, Rhonda .... 812-866-7014.. 161 C
burch@hanover.edu
BURCH, Sam .... 404-962-3263.. 129 F
sam.burch@usg.edu
BURCH, Susan .... 406-756-3839.. 276 E
sburch@fvcc.edu
BURCH, Wanda .... 949-214-3080.... 41 F
wanda.burch@cui.edu
BURCH-SIMS, G. Pamela 615-963-7043.. 445 A
psims@tnstate.edu
BURCHAM, Timothy .... 870-972-2085.... 18 J
tburcham@astate.edu
BURCHAM, CFRE,
Timothy, R .... 859-256-3100.. 188 M
tim.burcham@kctcs.edu
BURCHARD, Bob, P .... 573-875-7410.. 263 F
rpburchard@ccis.edu
BURCHARD, Elizabeth, B . 802-443-5201.. 484 F
eboudah@middlebury.edu
BURCHARD, Eric .... 740-593-1804.. 375 H
burchard@ohio.edu
BURCHARD, Faye, C .... 573-875-7400.. 263 F
fcburchard@ccis.edu
BURCHETT, Amy .... 432-264-5063.. 459 D
aburchett@howardcollege.edu
BURCHETT, Bonnie, L ..... 423-439-4446.. 444 F
bonnie@etsu.edu
BURCHETT, Dick .... 501-812-2238.... 21 H
dburchett@pulaskitech.edu
BURCHETT, Jody .... 740-588-1277.. 382 C
jburchett@zanestate.edu
BURCHETT, Kevin .... 734-423-2139.. 237 F
BURCHETT, Lance, E .... 501-686-5987.... 23 C
leburchett@uams.edu
BURCHFIELD, Doug .... 828-627-4632.. 350 D
ddburchfield@haywood.edu
BURCHFIELD, Nettie, L .... 985-549-2068.. 201 C
nburchfield@selu.edu
BURCK, Renee .... 517-264-3999.. 230 D
rburck@adrian.edu
BURCKHARDT, Judy .... 303-991-1575.... 76 I
judy.burckhardt@americansentinel.edu
BURD, Gail, D .... 520-626-4099.... 17 I
gburd@email.arizona.edu
BURD, Randy, M .... 520-626-1863.... 17 I
rburd@u.arizona.edu
BURDA, Ed .... 304-457-6238.. 510 B
burdaep@ab.edu
BURDEN, Kathlyn .... 770-229-3328.. 127 F
kburden@sctech.edu
BURDEN, Matthew .... 630-637-5433.. 149 H
mburden@noctrl.edu
BURDEN, Regina .... 334-724-4746...... 8 A
rburden@mytu.tuskegee.edu
BURDEN, Velma .... 912-478-5421.. 122 B
vburden@georgiasouthern.edu
BURDETTE, David .... 270-809-6979.. 192 A
dburdette@murraystate.edu
BURDETTE, Vinson .... 803-508-7244.. 426 G
burdettv@atc.edu
BURDETTE, William .... 304-696-6523.. 513 D
burdette@marshall.edu
BURDI, Glenn .... 718-631-6344.. 309 E
gburdi@qcc.cuny.edu
BURDICK, Evelyn, P .... 708-209-3259.. 138 G
evelyn.burdick@cuchicago.edu
BURDICK, Jonathan .... 585-275-6805.. 338 K
jonathan.burdick@rochester.edu
BURDICK, Mary Ellen .... 315-684-6461.. 336 B
burdicme@morrisville.edu
BURDICK, Phil .... 847-925-6183.. 141 A
pburdick@harpercollege.edu
BURDINE, Mike .... 208-459-5663.. 133 D
mburdine@collegeofidaho.edu
BURDOWSKI, Allen .... 718-489-5324.. 328 D
aburdowski@sfc.edu
BURDSALL, Dawn, M ...... 610-660-1333.. 418 G
dburdsal@sju.edu
BURDUE, JoEllen .... 414-277-7117.. 518 E
burdue@msoe.edu
BURDZINSKI, Donna, R .. 352-797-5001.. 106 F
burdzid@phsc.edu
BURDZINSKI, Kenneth, R 727-816-3412.. 106 F
burdzink@phsc.edu
BURFORD, Kristina .... 501-450-1362.... 20 F
burford@hendrix.edu
BURFORD, Kyla .... 618-252-5400.. 154 G
kyla.burford@sic.edu
BURG, James .... 260-481-4146.. 163 C
burgj@ipfw.edu
BURG, Jennifer .... 802-447-6359.. 485 B
jburg@svc.edu
BURG, Mary, G .... 785-864-3131.. 185 D
mburg@ku.edu
BURGARD, Bambi .... 816-802-3455.. 266 D
bburgard@kcai.edu
BURGARD, Daniel .... 817-735-2589.. 475 C
daniel.burgard@unthsc.edu
BURGAU, Tam .... 715-858-1377.. 523 B
tburgau@cvtc.edu
BURGAY, Stephen, P .... 617-353-1168.. 216 E
burgay@bu.edu
BURGE, Charles .... 954-771-0376.. 104 H
cburge@knoxseminary.edu
BURGE, David .... 703-993-5487.. 490 B
dburge@gmu.edu
BURGE, David .... 717-569-7071.. 407 E
dburge@lbc.edu
BURGE, Jennifer, G .... 309-677-4939.. 136 B
jgruening@bradley.edu
BURGE, Legand .... 334-229-4200...... 1 D
llburge@alasu.edu
BURGE, Monique .... 717-569-7071.. 407 E
mburge@lbc.edu
BURGEE, Lawrence, E ..... 610-558-5596.. 411 E
burgeel@neumann.edu
BURGENER, Kelly, T .... 208-496-1135.. 132 J
burgenerk@byui.edu
BURGER, Arnold .... 615-329-8516.. 439 L
aburger@fisk.edu
BURGER, Bill .... 802-443-5834.. 484 F
bburger@middlebury.edu
BURGER, Cindy, L .... 717-766-2511.. 410 J
cburger@messiah.edu
BURGER, Edward, B .... 512-863-1454.. 466 G
burger@southwestern.edu
BURGER, Lisa .... 701-777-4706.. 360 C
lisa.burger@und.edu
BURGER, Michael .... 334-244-3380...... 2 A
mburger1@aum.edu
BURGER, Rosemary .... 570-340-6054.. 409 H
burger@marywood.edu
BURGES, Jena .... 707-826-4192.... 34 F
jb139@humboldt.edu
BURGESS, Amanda .... 612-330-1791.. 244 I
burgessa@augsburg.edu
BURGESS, Brenda, K .... 580-774-3015.. 388 C
brenda.burgess@swosu.edu
BURGESS, Charlotte, G ... 909-748-8281.... 71 K
char_burgess@redlands.edu
BURGESS, Colleen .... 704-403-3502.. 342 E
colleen.burgess@carolinashealthcare.org
BURGESS, Craig, E .... 803-533-3928.. 432 E
BURGESS, Darren .... 918-444-2186.. 384 G
burgessd@nsuok.edu
BURGESS, Douglas .... 513-556-9900.. 379 A
douglas.burgess@uc.edu
BURGESS, Duncan .... 206-934-6882.. 507 A
duncan.burgess@seattlecolleges.edu
BURGESS, Ed .... 913-758-3033.. 528 I
burgesse@leavenworth.army.mil
BURGESS, James .... 818-401-1030.... 40 G
jburgess@columbiacollege.edu
BURGESS, Jodi .... 540-863-2835.. 496 H
jburgess@dslcc.edu
BURGESS, Kimberly .... 386-481-2668.... 96 H
burgessk@cookman.edu
BURGESS, Marcus .... 305-626-1443.. 101 A
marcus.burgess@fmuniv.edu
BURGESS, Norma .... 615-966-6146.. 441 F
norma.burgess@lipscomb.edu
BURGESS, Shane, C .... 520-621-7621.... 17 I
shaneburgess@email.arizona.edu
BURGESS, Sylvia .... 580-581-2284.. 382 G
sylviab@cameron.edu
BURGESS, Valerie .... 603-880-8308.. 288 A
vburgess@thomasmorecollege.edu
BURGETT, Paul, J .... 585-275-2758.. 338 K
pburgett@admin.rochester.edu
BURGGRAFF, Lucy .... 919-573-5350.. 355 G
BURGHART, Michael .... 707-826-3512.... 34 F
msb39@humboldt.edu
BURGHER, Louis, W .... 402-552-2586.. 279 D
burgherlouis@clarksoncollege.edu
BURGIN, David .... 419-251-7331.. 372 C
david.burgin@mercycollege.edu
BURGIN, Jeffery .... 615-460-6407.. 438 J
jeffery.burgin@belmont.edu
BURGIN, Sheila .... 360-442-2132.. 504 G
sburgin@lowercolumbia.edu
BURGIN, Vicki .... 251-442-2269...... 9 A
vburgin@umobile.edu
BURGIS, Laura .... 909-667-4421.... 38 G
lburgis@claremontlincoln.edu
BURGMAYER, Sharon .... 610-526-5106.. 398 K
sburmay@brynmawr.edu
BURGMEIER, Julie .... 563-588-6374.. 170 F
julie.bergmeier@clarke.edu
BURGNER, Ryan, C .... 308-635-6798.. 283 D
burgnerr@wncc.edu
BURGOS, Gerardo .... 787-279-1912.. 533 J
gburgos@bayamon.inter.edu
BURGOS, Jorge, A .... 787-720-4476.. 537 A
decanatoestudiantes@mizpa.edu
BURGOS, Kathy .... 562-860-2451.... 36 P
kburgos@cerritos.edu
BURGOS, Maida .... 305-821-3333.. 101 B
mburgos@fnu.edu
BURGOS-LOPEZ, Luz .... 410-337-6532.. 207 H
luz.burgoslopez@goucher.edu
BURGOYNE, Bonnie .... 870-512-7740.... 19 C
bonnie_burgoyne@asun.edu
BURI, David .... 360-359-4958.. 503 D
dburi@ewu.edu
BURIK, Larry .... 909-607-2226.... 57 H
larry_burik@pitzer.edu
BURILLO, Madeline .... 713-718-7748.. 459 B
madeline.burillo@hccs.edu
BURISH, Thomas, G .... 574-631-6631.. 168 B
burish.2@nd.edu
BURK, Ann, M .... 308-432-6311.. 281 H
aburk@csc.edu
BURK, Thomas .... 973-328-5037.. 290 H
tburk@ccm.edu
BURKE, Barbara .... 718-260-5173.. 309 C
bburke@citytech.cuny.edu
BURKE, Brian, W .... 413-545-2204.. 220 F
bwburke@external.umass.edu
BURKE, Bridget .... 701-231-6128.. 361 A
bridget.burke@ndsu.edu
BURKE, Carson .... 330-923-9959.. 368 I
cburke@fortiscollege.edu
BURKE, Cathleen, C .... 804-828-0179.. 496 D
ccburke@vcu.edu
BURKE, Chelsey .... 828-251-6501.. 357 C
cburke@unca.edu
BURKE, Christy .... 740-376-4708.. 372 A
christy.burke@marietta.edu
BURKE, Clarence .... 919-572-1625.. 341 M
cburke@apexsot.edu
BURKE, Colleen .... 215-572-2785.. 397 G
burkec@arcadia.edu
BURKE, Courtney .... 518-262-9590.. 303 E
burkec4@mail.amc.edu
BURKE, Dale .... 808-544-9394.. 130 H
dburke@hpu.edu
BURKE, Derek, A .... 252-398-6369.. 343 G
burked@chowan.edu
BURKE, Donald, S .... 412-624-3001.. 421 G
donburke@pitt.edu
BURKE, Donna .... 802-656-3402.. 485 D
donna.burke@uvm.edu
BURKE, Emily .... 617-746-1990.. 219 G
emily.burke@hult.edu
BURKE, Genevieve .... 312-752-2174.. 144 E
genevieve.burke@kendall.edu
BURKE, Greg .... 812-749-1288.. 166 B
gburke@oak.edu
BURKE, Greg .... 318-357-5251.. 201 B
burkeg@nsula.edu
BURKE, Ingrid .... 307-766-5080.. 527 B
indy.burke@uwyo.edu
BURKE, James, A .... 216-397-4484.. 370 H
burke@jcu.edu
BURKE, Jean .... 414-288-7013.. 517 I
jean.burke@marquette.edu
BURKE, Jeanmarie, R .... 315-568-3869.. 323 A
jburke@nycc.edu
BURKE, Joe .... 620-421-6700.. 182 G
joeburke@labette.edu
BURKE, John .... 845-848-4079.. 312 F
john.burke@dc.edu
BURKE, John .... 361-570-4840.. 474 C
burkej@uhv.edu
BURKE, John, D .... 617-552-3387.. 216 C
john.burke.7@bc.edu
BURKE, Jonathan .... 949-376-6000.... 48 C
jburke@lcad.edu
BURKE, Jonathan, L .... 816-604-6620.. 267 G
jon.burke@mcckc.edu
BURKE, Joseph, D .... 256-228-6001...... 5 I
burkej@nacc.edu
BURKE, Joy .... 814-371-2090.. 420 H
jburke@triangle-tech.edu
BURKE, Kathleen, F .... 818-719-6408.... 50 A
kburke@piercecollege.edu
BURKE, Kelly, J .... 336-334-5375.. 358 B
kjburke@uncg.edu
BURKE, Keri .... 503-883-2269.. 392 B
kburke@linfield.edu
BURKE, Kevin .... 717-358-3981.. 403 J
kevin.burke@fandm.edu
BURKE, Kimberly, G .... 601-974-1250.. 258 H
burkekg@millsaps.edu
BURKE, Lillian .... 410-225-4219.. 209 B
lburke@mica.edu
BURKE, Mary .... 617-984-1708.. 227 F
mburke@quincycollege.edu
BURKE, Matthew .... 617-928-4500.. 226 B
mburke@mountida.edu
BURKE, Melinda, W .... 520-621-3557.... 17 I
mwburke@email.arizona.edu
BURKE, Michael, L .... 951-222-8800.... 58 J
michael.burke@rccd.edu
BURKE, Neva .... 901-435-1601.. 441 C
neva_burke@loc.edu
BURKE, Peggy .... 773-325-4605.. 139 C
pburke@depaul.edu
BURKE, Scott .... 617-928-7337.. 226 B
sburke@mountida.edu
BURKE, Scott, M .... 404-413-2088.. 122 D
sburke@gsu.edu
BURKE, Seth .... 540-665-6257.. 494 B
sburke@su.edu
BURKE, Sharon .... 432-552-2747.. 478 B
burke_s@utpb.edu
BURKE, Tanya .... 978-478-3400.. 227 C
tburke@northpoint.edu
BURKE, Ted .... 508-541-1774.. 217 G
tburke@dean.edu
BURKE, Thomas .... 410-864-3602.. 210 F
tburke@stmarys.edu
BURKE, Thomas .... 601-266-5020.. 261 E
thomas.burke@usm.edu
BURKE, Thomas .... 212-343-1234.. 321 B
tburke@mcny.edu
BURKE, Tom, J .... 661-336-5117.... 47 I
tburke@kccd.edu
BURKE, Tracie, L .... 901-321-3357.. 439 E
tburke@cbu.edu
BURKE, Vic .... 912-443-5799.. 126 G
vburke@savannahtech.edu
BURKE, William .... 570-454-6172.. 410 F
william.burke@mccann.edu
BURKE, William, R .... 570-941-7887.. 422 B
william.burke@scranton.edu
BURKE-SULLIVAN,
Eileen, C .... 402-280-3285.. 279 H
e_burkesullivan@creighton.edu
BURKEE, James .... 914-337-9300.. 311 F
james.burkee@concordia-ny.edu
BURKERT, Amy, L .... 412-268-5865.. 400 D
ak11@andrew.cmu.edu
BURKES, Kate .... 479-619-4299.... 21 D
kburkes@nwacc.edu
BURKET, Lisa .... 317-896-9324.. 167 H
lburket@ubca.org
BURKETT, Amy .... 704-330-5940.. 348 E
amy.burkett@cpcc.edu
BURKETT, Holly, L .... 865-981-5302.. 446 G
hlburkett@pstcc.edu
BURKETT, Kaia .... 510-587-7890.... 57 B
kburkett@peralta.edu
BURKETT, Kaia .... 510-587-7890.... 57 E
kburkett@peralta.edu
BURKETT, Kina .... 251-809-1555...... 5 A
kina.burkett@jdcc.edu
BURKETT, Nancy .... 610-328-8651.. 419 I
nburket1@swarthmore.edu
BURKETT, Norvel .... 865-974-3181.. 448 E
nburkett@utk.edu
BURKETT, Timothy .... 704-847-5600.. 355 J
itadmin@ses.edu
BURKEY, Daniel, E .... 402-280-2131.. 279 H
dburkey@creighton.edu
BURKHALTER,
Carmen, L .... 256-765-4288...... 9 C
cburkhalter@una.edu
BURKHALTER, James ...... 806-742-1452.. 472 C
j.burkhalter@ttu.edu
BURKHALTER, Shelia ...... 410-837-4271.. 213 C
sburkhalter@ubalt.edu
BURKHAMMER, Jerry, L . 304-462-6413.. 513 C
jerry.burkhammer@glenville.edu
BURKHARDT, Janet .... 303-871-4757.... 84 B
janet.burkhardt@du.edu

BURKHARDT, Lou Ann .... 312-461-0600.. 134 K
lburkhardt@aaart.edu

BURKHARDT, Paul .... 928-350-4100.... 16 P
pburkhardt@prescott.edu

BURKHARDT, Ronald ...... 856-351-2608.. 296 L
rburkhardt@salemcc.edu

BURKHART, Jenny .... 859-858-2318.. 186 I

BURKHART, Keith .... 801-524-1923.. 480 J
kburkhart@ldsbc.edu

BURKHART, Patricia .... 954-492-5353.... 97 I
pburkhart@citycollege.edu

BURKHART-EVANS,
Maggie .... 540-568-5646.. 490 J
evansmb@jmu.edu

BURKHOLDER, Audrey .... 419-448-2171.. 369 G
aburkhol@heidelberg.edu

BURKHOLDER, Brian, M . 540-432-4132.. 488 K
brian.burkholder@emu.edu

BURKHOLDER, Mary, E ... 419-783-2360.. 368 A
mburkholder@defiance.edu

BURKHOLDER, Robert, C 215-503-6249.. 420 E
robert.burkholder@jefferson.edu

BURKINK, Timothy, J ...... 308-865-8342.. 282 L
burkinktj@unk.edu

BURKMAN, Roger .... 502-585-9911.. 192 E
rburkman@spalding.edu

BURKS, Barry, L .... 336-334-7995.. 356 F
blburks@ncat.edu

BURKS, Brent .... 254-295-4514.. 474 E
bburks@umhb.edu

BURKS, Bryan .... 501-279-4312.... 20 D
bburks@harding.edu

BURKS, Eric .... 785-738-9057.. 183 J
eburks@ncktc.edu

BURKS, Gwenevera, E ..... 559-453-2010.... 44 F
gwen.burks@fresno.edu

BURKS, Laura .... 334-580-2144...... 4 I
laura.burks@faulknerstate.edu

BURKS, Scott, A .... 502-852-4661.. 194 A
scott.burks@louisville.edu

BURKS, Shawn .... 757-569-6791.. 498 B
sburks@pdc.edu

BURKS, Suzanne, M .... 405-744-5458.. 385 G
suzanne.burks@okstate.edu

BURKUM, Karen, J .... 315-268-6576.. 310 B
kburkum@clarkson.edu

BURKWHAT, Louis, E ...... 530-226-4979.... 64 H
lburkwhat@simpsonu.edu

BURLAGE, Robert, S .... 262-243-5700.. 516 E
robert.burlage@cuw.edu

BURLAUD, Patricia .... 516-686-7443.. 323 G
pburlaud@nyit.edu

BURLEIGH-JONES,
Bronté .... 717-245-1943.. 402 D
jonesbro@dickinson.edu

BURLESON, Brooke .... 828-766-1269.. 351 B
bburleson@mayland.edu

BURLESON, Burt .... 254-710-3517.. 452 H
burt_burleson@baylor.edu

BURLESON, Susan .... 336-249-8186.. 349 C
sdburl@davidsonccc.edu

BURLEW, Elizabeth .... 315-655-7375.. 306 H
eburlew@cazenovia.edu

BURLEW, Jon .... 606-679-8501.. 190 E
jon.burlew@kctcs.edu

BURLEW, Lynette .... 318-473-6401.. 197 J
lburlew@lsua.edu

BURLING, Rachel .... 262-691-5266.. 524 G
rburling@wctc.edu

BURLINGAME, Kathy .... 502-410-6200.. 188 H
kburlingame@galencollege.edu

BURMA, William, H .... 515-263-2975.. 172 H
bburma@grandview.edu

BURMAN, Tom .... 307-766-2292.. 527 B
tburman@uwyo.edu

BURMASTER, Elizabeth ... 301-846-2440.. 207 F
eburmaster@frederick.edu

BURNAM, Paul .... 740-362-3435.. 372 D
pburnam@mtso.edu

BURNAM, Scott, M .... 937-778-7849.. 368 E
sburnam@edisonohio.edu

BURNE, Tom .... 828-898-3522.. 345 G
burnet@lmc.edu

BURNER, Emily .... 540-545-7334.. 494 B
eburner@su.edu

BURNES, Michael .... 706-236-2245.. 117 F
mburnes@berry.edu

BURNESS, Maria .... 410-386-8526.. 206 I
mburness@carrollcc.edu

BURNETT, Benjamin .... 601-318-6144.. 261 I
bburnett@wmcarey.edu

BURNETT, Bradley, T .... 405-325-5505.. 389 B
bburnett@ou.edu

BURNETT, Brian, D .... 573-882-3611.. 273 D
burnettbd@umsystem.edu

BURNETT, Catherine, G ... 713-646-1831.. 459 A
cburnett@hcl.edu

BURNETT, Daniel, C .... 606-451-6749.. 190 E
danielc.burnett@kctcs.edu

BURNETT, Denita .... 276-223-4769.. 499 C
dburnett@wcc.vccs.edu

BURNETT, Edward, T ...... 508-286-8381.. 229 F
burnett_edward@wheatoncollege.edu

BURNETT, Elsie .... 972-860-8201.. 456 C
eburnett@dcccd.edu

BURNETT, George, A ...... 928-541-7777.... 15 G
president@ncu.edu

BURNETT, John .... 724-938-4014.. 414 E
burnett@calu.edu

BURNETT, Linda, G .... 409-882-3998.. 471 B
linda.burnett@lsco.edu

BURNETT, Lonnie .... 251-442-2319...... 9 A
lburnett@umobile.edu

BURNETT, Lori, W .... 229-430-6443.. 115 K
lori.burnett@asurams.edu

BURNETT, Marc .... 931-372-3411.. 445 B
mburnett@tntech.edu

BURNETT, Mary .... 717-477-1279.. 416 A
meburnett@ship.edu

BURNETT, Myra .... 404-270-5027.. 128 A
mburnett@spelman.edu

BURNETT, Sharron, T ...... 405-466-3259.. 383 M
stburnett@langston.edu

BURNETT, Tod, A .... 949-582-4722.... 65 G
tburnett@saddleback.edu

BURNETTE, Brittany .... 832-252-0737.. 454 H
brittany.burnette@cbshouston.edu

BURNETTE, Cindy .... 270-745-2755.. 194 D
cindy.burnette@wku.edu

BURNETTE, George .... 336-770-1480.. 358 E
burnetteg@uncsa.edu

BURNETTE, JR., Glen ...... 910-521-6275.. 358 C
glen.burnette@uncp.edu

BURNETTE, Randy .... 252-940-6426.. 347 E
randy.burnette@beaufortccc.edu

BURNETTE, Richard .... 850-644-1532.. 111 C
rburnette@admin.fsu.edu

BURNETTE, Shery, L .... 423-439-4230.. 444 F
burnetts@etsu.edu

BURNETTE, Stephanie ...... 321-433-7271.... 98 K
burnettes@easternflorida.edu

BURNETTE, Teri .... 706-396-8132.. 125 H
tburnette@paine.edu

BURNEY, Christina, M ..... 508-565-1325.. 228 F
cburney@stonehill.edu

BURNEY, David .... 479-524-9500.... 20 H

BURNEY, John .... 402-826-8221.. 280 B
john.burney@doane.edu

BURNEY, Linda .... 910-879-5519.. 347 F
lburney@bladencc.edu

BURNEY, Michelle .... 662-227-2304.. 258 B
mburney@holmescc.edu

BURNEY, Rolanda .... 336-517-2225.. 342 B
rburney@bennett.edu

BURNHAM, Don .... 601-605-3301.. 258 B
dburnham@holmescc.edu

BURNHAM, Laura .... 757-822-1919.. 498 H
lburnham@tcc.edu

BURNHAM, Mark, A .... 517-353-9000.. 237 I
mburnham@msu.edu

BURNIM, Mickey, L .... 301-860-3555.. 212 D
president@bowiestate.edu

BURNIP, David, W .... 330-471-8251.. 371 J
dburnip@malone.edu

BURNISTON, Kay .... 386-506-3658.... 98 E
burnisk@daytonastate.edu

BURNLEY, Chris .... 540-365-4231.. 489 M
cburnley@ferrum.edu

BURNLEY, Lawrence, A ... 937-229-4073.. 379 D
lburnley1@udayton.edu

BURNLEY, Linda .... 646-888-6639.. 319 I
burnleyl@sloankettering.edu

BURNOTES, Scott, G .... 512-448-8445.. 464 G
sburnote@stedwards.edu

BURNS, Andrew .... 970-247-7180.... 80 D
burns_a@fortlewis.edu

BURNS, Anita .... 518-464-8545.. 314 A
aburns@excelsior.edu

BURNS, Ann, K .... 716-673-3333.. 331 D
ann.burns@fredonia.edu

BURNS, Barb .... 314-392-2362.. 268 F
burnsba@mobap.edu

BURNS, Barbara .... 478-471-2502.. 124 E
barbara.burns@mga.edu

BURNS, Candace .... 973-720-2138.. 298 G
burnsc@wpunj.edu

BURNS, Carl, F .... 573-341-4292.. 274 B
carlb@mst.edu

BURNS, Cathy .... 918-343-7791.. 387 F
cburns@rsu.edu

BURNS, Cindy .... 910-678-8564.. 349 F
griffinw@faytechcc.edu

BURNS, Daniel, P .... 985-867-2225.. 199 F
acdean@sjasc.edu

BURNS, Dave .... 309-341-5463.. 136 C
dburns@sandburg.edu

BURNS, David .... 860-444-8201.. 529 A
david.burns@uscg.mil

BURNS, Dianne .... 641-673-1084.. 177 J
burnsd@wmpenn.edu

BURNS, Elizabeth, A ...... 313-927-1208.. 237 E
eburns@marygrove.edu

BURNS, Eric .... 530-741-6838.... 76 D
eburns@yccd.edu

BURNS, Erin .... 510-849-8222.... 55 I
eburns@psr.edu

BURNS, Gary .... 816-501-4854.. 270 J
gary.burns@rockhurst.edu

BURNS, J. Joseph .... 617-552-3273.. 216 C
john.burns@bc.edu

BURNS, Jack .... 734-384-4249.. 238 C
jburns@monroeccc.edu

BURNS, Jacqueline .... 352-392-1784.. 112 A
jkbu@ufl.edu

BURNS, James, R .... 617-552-3900.. 216 C
james.burns.3@bc.edu

BURNS, James, T .... 215-670-9235.. 412 D
jtburns@peirce.edu

BURNS, Jamie .... 252-862-1261.. 352 D
jburns6896@roanokechowan.edu

BURNS, Janie .... 731-352-4253.. 438 K
burnsj@bethelu.edu

BURNS, Jeffrey, S .... 804-752-7367.. 493 C
jburns@rmc.edu

BURNS, Jennifer, A .... 412-365-1849.. 400 G
jburns@chatham.edu

BURNS, Joseph, A .... 607-255-4843.. 312 A
deanoffaculty-mailbox@cornell.edu

BURNS, Kathleen .... 508-678-2811.. 223 A
kathleen.burns@bristolcc.edu

BURNS, Kelli .... 314-539-5371.. 271 F
kburns@stlcc.edu

BURNS, Keri .... 678-839-6431.. 129 E
kburns@westga.edu

BURNS, Kevin, J .... 757-823-8879.. 492 F
kburns@nsu.edu

BURNS, Kimberly .... 215-567-7080.. 397 H
kburns@aii.edu

BURNS, Kristen .... 703-658-4304.. 488 D
krisburns@christendom.edu

BURNS, Laura .... 315-364-3289.. 340 B
lburns@wells.edu

BURNS, Lisa, A .... 434-223-6118.. 490 D
lburns@hsc.edu

BURNS, Lita .... 208-769-3302.. 134 C
lita_burns@nic.edu

BURNS, Lucy .... 502-272-8234.. 187 A
lburns@bellarmine.edu

BURNS, Marie-Elaine ...... 510-436-2501.... 57 E
meburns@peralta.edu

BURNS, Marvin .... 405-466-6150.. 383 M
mburns@langston.edu

BURNS, Matthew .... 585-275-4085.. 338 K
matthew.burns@rochester.edu

BURNS, Max .... 678-359-5015.. 122 E
mburns@gordonstate.edu

BURNS, Michael .... 913-281-7670.. 132 C
mburns@kckcc.edu

BURNS, Michael .... 913-288-7670.. 132 C
mburns@kckcc.edu

BURNS, Michael .... 405-208-6365.. 335 E
mpburns@okcu.edu

BURNS, Patrick .... 970-491-1833.... 78 Q
patrick.burns@colostate.edu

BURNS, Patrick .... 928-776-2055.... 18 D
patrick.burns@yc.edu

BURNS, Peter .... 518-327-6017.. 325 B
pburns@paulsmiths.edu

BURNS, Randy .... 270-384-8170.. 191 E
burnsr@lindsey.edu

BURNS, Sarah, H .... 704-233-8128.. 359 H
shburns@wingate.edu

BURNS, Shawn, G .... 806-651-2300.. 469 D
sburns@mail.wtamu.edu

BURNS, Skipper .... 678-359-5739.. 122 E
skipperb@gordonstate.edu

BURNS, Steven .... 845-398-4176.. 329 G
sburns@stac.edu

BURNS, Susan, E .... 313-577-0157.. 243 F
sburns@wayne.edu

BURNS, Susan, R .... 563-588-6540.. 170 F
susan.burns@clarke.edu

BURNS, Terry .... 937-395-8520.. 371 D
terry.burns@ketteringhealth.org

BURNS, Thomas .... 716-286-8580.. 324 E
tburns@niagara.edu

BURNS, Thomas, D .... 615-460-6400.. 438 J
thomas.burns@belmont.edu

BURNS, Tiffany .... 304-647-6349.. 514 A
tburns@osteo.wvsom.edu

BURNS, Todd .... 309-268-8020.. 141 C
todd.burns@heartland.edu

BURNS, Wendy .... 651-523-2235.. 247 A
wburns@hamline.edu

BURNS, William .... 732-224-2426.. 289 I
wburns@brookdalecc.edu

BURNS, William .... 701-231-7671.. 361 A
william.burns@ndsu.edu

BURNSIDE, Michael .... 404-225-4448.. 117 A
mburnside@atlantatech.edu

BURNSIDE, Virgil .... 859-985-3150.. 187 B
virgil_burnside@berea.edu

BURON, Otha .... 601-979-2339.. 258 D
otha.burton@jsums.edu

BURPO, Jesse .... 405-789-7661.. 388 B
jessie.burpo@swcu.edu

BURR, Alan .... 941-487-4245.. 111 D
aburr@ncf.edu

BURR, Jason, H .... 864-597-4381.. 435 C
burrjh@wofford.edu

BURR, Katherine .... 570-372-4753.. 419 H
burr@susqu.edu

BURR, Kim .... 828-766-1350.. 351 B
kburr@mayland.edu

BURR, Mei Mei .... 937-481-2242.. 381 C
meimei_burr@wilmington.edu

BURR, Stephen .... 313-883-8623.. 240 D
burr.stephen@shms.edu

BURRAGE, Sean .... 580-745-2500.. 387 M
sburrage@se.edu

BURRELL, Becky .... 419-995-8331.. 370 G
burrell.b@rhodesstate.edu

BURRELL, James .... 704-378-1081.. 345 E
jburrell@jcsu.edu

BURRELL, Kari .... 907-474-7907.... 10 G
kari.burrell@alaska.edu

BURRELL, Steven .... 928-523-9998.... 15 H
steven.burrell@nau.edu

BURRELL, Todd, C .... 618-650-3705.. 155 A
tburrel@siue.edu

BURRELL-MCRAE,
Karlene, A .... 207-859-4780.. 202 G
karlene.burrellmcrae@colby.edu

BURRESS, Diane .... 210-486-3000.. 450 D

BURRI, Josephine .... 215-717-6144.. 421 D
jburri@uarts.edu

BURRICHTER, William ..... 585-567-9622.. 316 F
william.burrichter@houghton.edu

BURRILL, Jennifer, R .... 269-471-6601.. 230 H
burrillj@andrews.edu

BURRIS, David .... 530-283-0202.... 43 G
dburris@frc.edu

BURRIS, Deborah, J .... 314-516-5695.. 274 A
dburris@umsl.edu

BURRIS, Janssen .... 225-214-1947.. 199 B
janssen.burris@ololcollege.edu

BURRIS, Kendra .... 806-743-2786.. 472 D
kendra.burris@ttuhsc.edu

BURROUGHS, Carolyn .... 318-678-6000.. 195 I
cburroughs@bpcc.edu

BURROUGHS, Cynthia ..... 501-370-5337.... 21 G
cburroughs@philander.edu

BURROUGHS, Derrick ..... 731-426-7500.. 440 K

BURROUGHS DAVIS,
Robin .... 603-526-3752.. 285 L
rdavis@colby-sawyer.edu

BURROW, Susan .... 256-215-4300...... 2 G
sburrow@cacc.edu

BURROWS, Angie .... 570-372-4120.. 419 H
burrowsa@susqu.edu

BURROWS, Carmen .... 757-825-2939.. 498 G
burrowsc@tncc.edu

BURROWS, David .... 920-832-6528.. 517 E
david.burrows@lawrence.edu

BURROWS, SC,
Joanne, M .... 563-588-6385.. 170 F
joanne.burrows@clarke.edu

BURROWS-SCHUMACHER,
Molly, A .... 563-588-4981.. 174 K
molly.burrowsschumacher@loras.edu

BURRUS, Ken .... 509-533-7220.. 502 I
ken.burrus@ccs.spokane.edu

BURRUS, Ken .... 509-533-3630.. 503 A
ken.burrus@ccs.spokane.edu

BURRUS, Ken .... 509-533-7220.. 502 H
kburrus@ccs.spokane.edu

BURRUS, MiVida .... 248-689-8282.. 242 F
mburrus@walshcollege.edu

BURRUS, Robert .... 910-962-3226.. 358 D
burrusr@uncw.edu

BURRUSS, Jennifer .... 252-789-0247.. 351 A
jburruss@martincc.edu

BURRUSS, Nancy, M .... 920-433-6632.. 515 F
nancy.burruss@bellincollege.edu

BURRUTO, James .... 315-781-3319.. 316 C
burruto@hws.edu

BURRY, Leslie .... 816-995-2820.. 270 H
leslie.burry@researchcollege.edu

BURSE, Raymond, M .... 502-597-6260.. 191 B
raymond.burse@kysu.edu

BURSI, Megan, M .... 901-572-2853.. 438 I
megan.bursi@bchs.edu

BURSIK, Nick .... 715-395-4619.. 521 E
nbursik@uwsuper.edu

BURSON, Todd, E .... 740-427-5181.. 371 C
bursont@kenyon.edu

BURSTEIN, Mark .... 920-832-6525.. 517 E
mark.burstein@lawrence.edu

BURSTEN, Bruce .... 508-831-5222.. 230 C
bbursten@wpi.edu

BURSTON, Gwendolyn ..... 336-334-4822.. 350 B
ggburston@gtcc.edu

BURSTYN, Yaakov .... 305-534-7050.. 113 F
rabbibursty@talmudicu.edu
BURSZTYN, Jacob .... 732-367-1060.. 289 G
jbursztyn@bmg.edu
BURT, Andrea .... 517-264-3100.. 230 D
aburt@adrian.edu
BURT, Bobby .... 256-924-0511.... 5 E
bburt@legacyu.net
BURT, Charles .... 617-745-3725.. 218 A
charles.burt@enc.edu
BURT, Mickey, G .... 563-884-5451.. 176 C
mickey.burt@palmer.edu
BURTI, Ellen .... 718-940-5852.. 328 G
eburti@sjcny.edu
BURTIS, Karen, B .... 307-674-6446.. 526 M
kburtis@sheridan.edu
BURTIS, Ken .... 530-752-4964.... 69 A
provost@ucdavis.edu
BURTLE, Melissa .... 229-217-4210.. 127 G
mburtle@southernregional.edu
BURTLEY, Harold .... 219-980-6539.. 163 B
hburtley@iun.edu
BURTNESS, John .... 303-352-4435.... 81 G
ua@msudenver.edu
BURTNETT, Jody .... 217-875-7211.. 152 C
jburtnett@richland.edu
BURTON, Adam .... 951-343-4286.... 29 H
aburton@calbaptist.edu
BURTON, Adrienne .... 714-895-5103.... 39 F
aburton@gwc.cccd.edu
BURTON, Alan .... 580-745-2731.. 387 M
aburton@se.edu
BURTON, Barbara .... 309-694-8817.. 141 F
barbara.burton@icc.edu
BURTON, Becky .... 706-583-2818.. 116 H
bburton@athenstech.edu
BURTON, Ben .... 317-921-4712.. 164 E
bburton@ivytech.edu
BURTON, Carol .... 828-227-7495.. 359 A
burton@wcu.edu
BURTON, Chet .... 775-445-4236.. 285 B
chester.burton@wnc.edu
BURTON, Clen .... 409-933-8261.. 454 O
clenburton@com.edu
BURTON, Derrick .... 641-585-8671.. 177 F
derrick.burton@waldorf.edu
BURTON, Donald, N .... 602-648-5750.... 13 A
dburton@dunlap-stone.edu
BURTON, Elizabeth .... 610-399-2427.. 414 F
eburton@cheyney.edu
BURTON, Gera, C .... 573-882-4250.. 273 E
burtong@missouri.edu
BURTON, Gregory, A .... 973-761-9362.. 297 A
gregory.burton@shu.edu
BURTON, Heather .... 540-868-7201.. 497 E
hburton@lfcc.edu
BURTON, Jan .... 801-627-8309.. 481 A
burtonj@owatc.edu
BURTON, Jennus, L .... 928-523-2708.... 15 H
jennus.burton@nau.edu
BURTON, Khalilah .... 251-981-3771...... 2 I
khalilah.burton@columbiasouthern.edu
BURTON, Larry .... 336-272-7102.. 344 G
lwburton@greensboro.edu
BURTON, Lonnie .... 806-291-3635.. 479 D
burtonl@wbu.edu
BURTON, Marjorie .... 440-775-5782.. 374 C
marjorie.burton@oberlin.edu
BURTON, Mel .... 770-426-2986.. 124 B
mel.burton@life.edu
BURTON, Melody .... 503-517-1369.. 396 D
mburton@warnerpacific.edu
BURTON, Nathan .... 304-766-4354.. 514 B
nburton2@wvstateu.edu
BURTON, Patrice .... 708-596-2000.. 154 E
pburton@ssc.edu
BURTON, Raymond, A .... 804-523-5374.. 497 C
rburton@reynolds.edu
BURTON, Robert .... 808-984-3245.. 132 D
reburton@hawaii.edu
BURTON, Sharon .... 270-831-9646.. 189 F
sharon.burton@kctcs.edu
BURTON, Stacy .... 775-784-1740.. 285 A
sburton@unr.edu
BURTON, Terrance .... 508-999-8664.. 220 H
tburton@umassd.edu
BURTON, Timothy, P .... 516-877-3385.. 303 B
burton@adelphi.edu
BURTON, JR., Velmer, S 662-915-1081.. 261 B
vsburton@olemiss.edu
BURTON-GOSS, Sadie .... 781-239-6334.. 214 G
sburtongoss@babson.edu
BURTON JONES, Kathy ... 917-493-4717.. 319 M
kjones@msmnyc.edu
BURWELL, Elissia .... 903-593-8311.. 470 A
eburwell@texascollege.edu
BURWELL, Timothy, H .... 828-262-2030.. 356 B
burwellth@appstate.edu
BURY, John .... 918-631-2602.. 389 E
john-bury@utulsa.edu
BURY, Sandra .... 309-677-2808.. 136 B
sandy@bradley.edu
BURY, Sandra .... 309-677-3100.. 136 B
sandy@fsmail.bradley.edu
BURZACHECHI, Nancilee . 412-237-4684.. 401 B
nancilee@ccac.edu
BURZICHELLI, Dominick . 856-415-2292.. 295 D
dburzichelli@rcgc.edu
BURZINSKI, Jody .... 620-421-6700.. 182 G
jodyb@labette.edu
BUSALACCHI, Richard ..... 414-297-6969.. 524 A
busalacr@matc.edu
BUSAM, Leah .... 513-745-4879.. 381 I
busaml@xavier.edu
BUSBEE, Walter .... 803-508-7254.. 426 G
busbeew@atc.edu
BUSBY, Dwayne .... 281-283-2019.. 474 A
busby@uhcl.edu
BUSBY, Laura .... 801-863-8456.. 482 C
lbusby@uvu.edu
BUSBY, Teresa .... 601-446-1211.. 257 D
teresa.busby@colin.edu
BUSCEMI, Vince .... 410-857-2290.. 209 D
vbuscemi@mcdaniel.edu
BUSCH, Brian .... 252-789-0247.. 351 A
bbusch@martincc.edu
BUSCH, Caroline, C .... 804-752-3267.. 493 C
cbusch@rmc.edu
BUSCH, Gregory .... 419-755-4570.. 373 G
gbusch@ncstatecollege.edu
BUSCH, Nancy .... 402-472-2526.. 282 M
nbusch2@unl.edu
BUSCHART, W. David ...... 303-762-6907.... 79 I
david.buschart@denverseminary.edu
BUSCHER, Frank, M .... 630-844-5252.. 135 E
fbuscher@aurora.edu
BUSCHER, Kristin .... 402-872-2298.. 281 I
kbuscher@peru.edu
BUSCHMAN, John, E .... 973-761-9005.. 297 A
john.buschman@shu.edu
BUSE, Jon .... 319-398-4977.. 174 I
jon.buse@kirkwood.edu
BUSE, Kathleen .... 973-618-3411.. 290 A
kbuse@caldwell.edu
BUSE, William .... 212-799-5000.. 318 A
BUSEL, Yaakov .... 732-985-6533.. 294 E
BUSER, Boyd, R .... 606-218-5411.. 194 C
boydbuser@upike.edu
BUSH, Catherine .... 440-525-7119.. 371 F
cbush@lakelandcc.edu
BUSH, Cathy .... 440-525-7112.. 371 F
cbush@lakelandcc.edu
BUSH, Darren .... 657-278-7271.... 33 A
dlbush@fullerton.edu
BUSH, David .... 435-797-1012.. 482 B
david.bush@usu.edu
BUSH, Edward, C .... 916-691-7321.... 51 B
bushe@crc.losrios.edu
BUSH, Jason .... 740-446-4367.. 369 C
jbush@gallipoliscareercollege.edu
BUSH, Jim .... 509-865-8570.. 504 D
bush_j@heritage.edu
BUSH, Katherine .... 845-437-5900.. 339 C
kabush@vassar.edu
BUSH, Keith .... 218-751-8670.. 254 A
it@oakhills.edu
BUSH, Kristen .... 540-231-1796.. 499 F
khbush@vt.edu
BUSH, Lisa, F .... 828-398-7202.. 347 D
lbush@abtech.edu
BUSH, Lonica .... 409-933-8413.. 454 O
lbush@com.edu
BUSH, Michael .... 805-678-5813.... 73 E
mbush@vcccd.edu
BUSH, Mickie .... 503-494-7800.. 393 F
regohsu@ohsu.edu
BUSH, Polly .... 585-340-9500.. 310 F
pbush@crcds.edu
BUSH, TaJuan .... 215-335-0800.. 409 A
tbush@lincolntech.edu
BUSH, Tyre .... 607-962-9540.. 312 B
BUSHA, Cathy .... 503-768-7186.. 392 A
cbusha@lclark.edu
BUSHA, Linda .... 262-595-2230.. 520 F
BUSHER, Edward, J .... 937-328-6095.. 366 E
bushere@clarkstate.edu
BUSHEY, Jane, L .... 480-245-7930.... 13 L
jane.bushey@ibcs.edu
BUSHEY, Stephanie .... 516-463-6853.. 316 D
stephanie.bushey@hofstra.edu
BUSHLEY, Tom .... 434-832-7725.. 496 G
bushleyt@cvcc.vccs.edu
BUSHMAN, David, W .... 540-828-5605.. 487 H
dbushman@bridgewater.edu
BUSHNELL, Lynn, M .... 203-582-8651.... 88 G
lynn.bushnell@quinnipiac.edu
BUSHNELL, Ryan .... 517-321-0242.. 235 C
rbushnell@glcc.edu
BUSHONG, Sara .... 419-372-2856.. 364 E
sbushon@bgsu.edu
BUSHWAY, Deborah .... 952-887-1392.. 253 Z
dbushway@nwhealth.edu
BUSHY, Thomas .... 508-830-5020.. 222 C
tbushy@maritime.edu
BUSKIRK, Susan .... 410-706-4937.. 211 F
sbuskirk@umaryland.edu
BUSROE, Andrew .... 606-368-6113.. 186 B
andrewbusroe@alc.edu
BUSS, Brian .... 920-735-5792.. 523 C
buss@fvtc.edu
BUSS, James, J .... 410-677-6556.. 213 A
jjbuss@salisbury.edu
BUSS, Marney .... 508-213-2101.. 227 A
marney.buss@nichols.edu
BUSSARD, Patsy, G .... 276-964-7332.. 498 F
pat.bussard@sw.edu
BUSSE, Dan .... 850-484-1158.. 106 H
dbusse@pensacolastate.edu
BUSSELL, Helena .... 817-531-4405.. 472 F
hbussell@txwes.edu
BUSSELL, Paige .... 903-468-3209.. 468 D
paige.bussell@tamuc.edu
BUSSELL, Rachelle .... 909-558-4544.... 49 C
rbussell@llu.edu
BUSSELL, Shawn .... 419-824-3785.. 371 I
sbussell@lourdes.edu
BUSSEY, Brenda .... 508-929-8455.. 222 F
bbussey@worcester.edu
BUSSEY, Kevin .... 217-228-5432.. 151 F
busske@quincy.edu
BUSSEY, Tosha .... 404-225-4596.. 117 A
tbussey@atlantatech.edu
BUSTA, Joseph, F .... 251-460-7616...... 9 E
jbusta@southalabama.edu
BUSTAMANTE, Camilla .... 505-428-1388.. 301 K
camilla.bustamante@sfcc.edu
BUSTAMANTE, Chris .... 480-517-8118.... 14 G
chris.bustamante@riosalado.edu
BUSTARD, James .... 217-351-2211.. 151 B
jbustard@parkland.edu
BUSTER-WILLIAMS,
Kimberley .... 540-654-1618.. 495 C
kwilli23@umw.edu
BUSTOS, Adriana .... 303-477-7240.... 80 H
adrianab@heritage-education.com
BUSTOS, Phillip .... 505-224-4741.. 299 F
pbustos@cnm.edu
BUTALA, Doug .... 605-882-5284.. 436 B
doug.butala@lakeareatech.edu
BUTCHER, Alva .... 253-879-3394.. 508 D
abutcher@pugetsound.edu
BUTCHER, Claudette .... 918-293-5256.. 386 B
claudette.butcher@okstate.edu
BUTCHER, Marilea .... 304-647-6367.. 514 A
mbutcher@osteo.wvsom.edu
BUTCHER, Michael .... 912-279-5815.. 119 C
mbutcher@ccga.edu
BUTCHER, Phil .... 713-942-3409.. 475 J
butchep@stthom.edu
BUTCHER, Teri .... 248-218-2042.. 240 C
tbutcher@rc.edu
BUTCHER, Thomas, A .... 616-331-2067.. 234 F
butchert@gvsu.edu
BUTCHER, Tina .... 706-507-8951.. 119 E
butcher_tina@columbusstate.edu
BUTCHKO, Thomas .... 570-208-5928.. 406 J
thomasbutchko@kings.edu
BUTDORFF, Carla .... 419-747-5401.. 373 G
196mgr@fheg.follett.com
BUTERA, Peter .... 716-286-8060.. 324 E
pbutera@niagara.edu
BUTERA, Rae-Anne .... 781-292-2321.. 218 H
rae-anne.butera@olin.edu
BUTERA, Vince .... 847-578-8374.. 153 A
vince.butera@rosalindfranklin.edu
BUTIKOFER, Jason .... 435-865-8330.. 481 N
jasonbutikofer@suu.edu
BUTIN, Dan .... 978-837-5338.. 225 E
dan.butin@merrimack.edu
BUTKOVICH, Michelle ..... 248-204-2111.. 237 B
mbutkovic@ltu.edu
BUTKUS, Bonnie .... 585-475-5498.. 327 E
bjbdar@rit.edu
BUTLER, Alison .... 805-893-2622.... 70 E
alison.butler@ucsb.edu
BUTLER, Allen, P .... 815-455-8999.. 147 E
abutler@mchenry.edu
BUTLER, Andra .... 606-546-1224.. 193 E
abutler@unionky.edu
BUTLER, Andrew .... 508-831-6634.. 230 C
abutler@wpi.edu
BUTLER, Ann .... 910-592-8081.. 352 H
abutler@sampsoncc.edu
BUTLER, Beautrice .... 210-486-2300.. 450 E
bbutler@alamo.edu
BUTLER, Blake .... 501-760-4176.... 21 B
bbutler@np.edu
BUTLER, Brady .... 412-536-1300.. 406 K
brady.butler@laroche.edu
BUTLER, Bruce, D .... 713-500-3369.. 477 C
bruce.d.butler@uth.tmc.edu
BUTLER, Bryant .... 601-968-5930.. 256 I
bbutler@belhaven.edu
BUTLER, Connie .... 402-643-7332.. 279 F
connie.butler@cune.edu
BUTLER, Craig, J .... 304-457-6445.. 510 B
butlercj@ab.edu
BUTLER, Duan .... 540-374-4300.... 93 F
BUTLER, Greg .... 601-477-4113.. 258 E
greg.butler@jcjc.edu
BUTLER, Heidi .... 610-861-5453.. 411 G
hbutler@northampton.edu
BUTLER, Henry .... 703-993-1607.. 490 B
hnbutler@gmu.edu
BUTLER, Jack .... 931-372-3227.. 445 B
jbutler@tntech.edu
BUTLER, Janice, R .... 570-577-3973.. 398 L
janice.butler@bucknell.edu
BUTLER, Jennifer .... 708-656-8000.. 149 A
jennifer.butler@morton.edu
BUTLER, Jody .... 918-463-2931.. 383 F
jody.butler@connorsstate.edu
BUTLER, Joe, R .... 972-599-3121.. 455 A
jrbutler@collin.edu
BUTLER, S.J., John, T .... 617-552-6855.. 216 C
john.butler@bc.edu
BUTLER, Ken .... 484-664-3126.. 411 D
butler@muhlenberg.edu
BUTLER, Kevin .... 702-992-2000.. 284 J
kevin.butler@nsc.edu
BUTLER, Kim, I .... 515-263-2841.. 172 H
maintenance@grandview.edu
BUTLER, Lee .... 817-598-6345.. 479 E
cbutler@wc.edu
BUTLER, LeRoy .... 815-836-5923.. 145 H
butlerle@lewisu.edu
BUTLER, Lisa .... 660-543-4001.. 273 C
ljbutler@ucmo.edu
BUTLER, Lisa .... 573-897-5000.. 272 H
BUTLER, Lynn .... 847-543-2974.. 138 C
lbutler@clcillinois.edu
BUTLER, Marley .... 417-626-1234.. 269 K
recruitment@occ.edu
BUTLER, Mary Edith .... 630-466-7900.. 157 K
mbutler@waubonsee.edu
BUTLER, Michael .... 909-469-5534.... 74 K
mbutler@westernu.edu
BUTLER, Odo .... 518-836-2808.. 330 B
butlero@sunysccc.edu
BUTLER, Patrick, B .... 319-335-3565.. 169 H
patrick-butler@uiowa.edu
BUTLER, Paul, C .... 856-225-6637.. 296 A
pbutler@camden.rutgers.edu
BUTLER, Rainier .... 406-683-7201.. 277 A
rainier.butler@umwestern.edu
BUTLER, Rebecca, A .... 419-434-5797.. 379 E
butlerr@findlay.edu
BUTLER, Robert .... 707-256-7625.... 53 H
rbutler@napavalley.edu
BUTLER, Sandy .... 404-364-8870.. 125 F
sbutler@oglethorpe.edu
BUTLER, Shai .... 518-337-2306.. 311 B
butlers@strose.edu
BUTLER, Sharon .... 517-884-0101.. 237 I
sbutler@msu.edu
BUTLER, Shirley .... 843-349-5218.. 430 F
shirley.butler@hgtc.edu
BUTLER, Stephen, L .... 251-626-3303...... 8 B
sbutler@ussa.edu
BUTLER, Timothy, J .... 215-951-2599.. 416 G
butlert@philau.edu
BUTLER, Vicki .... 870-235-4026.... 22 F
vjbutler@saumag.edu
BUTLER, Walter .... 731-352-4000.. 438 K
butlerw@bethelu.edu
BUTLER-LUDWIG,
John, L .... 773-442-4200.. 149 J
j-butler-ludwig1@neiu.edu
BUTLER-PURRY,
Karen, L .... 979-845-3628.. 468 B
klbutler@tamu.edu
BUTT, Debi, S .... 336-841-4524.. 345 A
debib@highpoint.edu
BUTT, Ryan .... 419-517-8929.. 371 I
rbutt@lourdes.edu
BUTTAFARRO, JR.,
Thomas .... 716-375-2155.. 328 B
tbuttafa@sbu.edu
BUTTENSCHON,
Marianne .... 315-792-5631.. 321 G
mbuttenschon@mvcc.edu
BUTTERFIELD, Heather .. 608-796-3930.. 522 O
hmbutterfield@viterbo.edu
BUTTERFIELD, Kevin .... 804-289-8942.. 495 G
kbutterf@richmond.edu
BUTTERMORE, Jim .... 724-964-8811.. 411 F
jbuttermore@ncstrades.edu
BUTTLEMAN, Kurt .... 206-934-4111.. 506 I
kurt.buttleman@seattlecolleges.edu
BUTTRY, Tonya .... 573-334-6825.. 272 A
tbuttry@sehcollege.edu

C

CAFONCELLI, Kathy, L ..... 610-921-7600.. 396 H
kcafoncelli@albright.edu

CAGE, Beverly .... 361-698-1279.. 457 D
bacage@delmar.edu

CAGE, Patrick .... 773-995-3524.. 136 M
pcage@csu.edu

CAGE, Stephanie .... 318-473-6424.. 197 J
scage@lsua.edu

CAGE, Stephanie .... 636-481-3298.. 266 C
scage@jeffco.edu

CAGGIANO, Marion .... 973-655-3417.. 293 A
caggianom@mail.montclair.edu

CAGGIANO, Sarah .... 401-454-6200.. 426 A
scaggian@risd.edu

CAGIGAS, Marcia .... 323-415-5383.... 49 G
cagigamp@elac.edu

CAGLE, David .... 815-802-8128.. 144 C
dcagle@kcc.edu

CAGLE, David .... 251-442-2226...... 9 A
dcagle@umobile.edu

CAGLE, John .... 423-442-2001.. 440 F
caglejo@hiwassee.edu

CAGLE, Kathy .... 703-993-8627.. 490 B
kcagle@gmu.edu

CAGLE, Randy, L .... 218-477-2477.. 250 F
caglera@mnstate.edu

CAGLE, Sheri .... 815-802-8822.. 144 C
scagle@kcc.edu

CAGNET, Danny .... 248-218-2190.. 240 C
dcagnet@rc.edu

CAHALAN, Jodi .... 515-271-1369.. 171 H
jodi.cahalan@dmu.edu

CAHALAN, SJ, Patrick, J . 310-338-5921.... 51 E
pcahalan@lmu.edu

CAHALL, Perry, J .... 614-885-5585.. 376 G
pcahall@pcj.edu

CAHEN, Robert .... 440-525-7097.. 371 F
bcahen@lakelandcc.edu

CAHILL, Bridget .... 847-925-6889.. 141 A
bcahilli@harpercollege.edu

CAHILL, Elizabeth, J .... 304-384-6003.. 513 A
lcahill@concord.edu

CAHILL, Heather .... 413-205-3972.. 214 B
heather.cahill@aic.edu

CAHILL, Holly .... 701-477-7862.. 362 D
hcahill@tm.edu

CAHILL, Margaret, D .... 651-962-6131.. 256 C
mdcahill@stthomas.edu

CAHILL, Michael, T .... 856-225-6191.. 296 A
michael.cahill@law.rutgers.edu

CAHILL, Regina .... 212-594-4000.. 337 F
rcahill@tcicollege.edu

CAHILL, Richard .... 859-985-3451.. 187 B
richard_cahill@berea.edu

CAHILL, Ryan .... 313-883-8696.. 240 D
cahill.ryan@shms.edu

CAHILL, Tina .... 617-405-5942.. 227 F
tcahill@quincycollege.edu

CAHOON, Faye .... 252-451-8221.. 351 F
fcahoon@nashcc.edu

CAHOON, Kirsten .... 507-786-3268.. 254 P
cahoon@stolaf.edu

CAI, Maoyi .... 512-444-8082.. 470 B
cai@thsu.edu

CAILLET, Barb .... 330-684-8935.. 378 H

CAILLET, Barb .... 330-684-8935.. 378 H
naumoff@uakron.edu

CAILLOUX, Laura .... 360-679-5333.. 507 G
laura.cailloux@skagit.edu

CAIMI, Steve .... 215-785-0111.. 413 K

CAIN, Candace .... 248-218-2040.. 240 C
ccain@rc.edu

CAIN, Chad .... 806-291-3500.. 479 D
chad.cain@wbu.edu

CAIN, Cheryl .... 361-593-2138.. 469 A
cheryl.cain@tamuk.edu

CAIN, Chris .... 334-953-5159.. 527 I
anthony.cain@us.af.mil

CAIN, Christele, N .... 443-518-4148.. 208 C
ccain2@howardcc.edu

CAIN, Darrell .... 317-917-5702.. 164 F
dcain@ivytech.edu

CAIN, John .... 352-397-5829.. 108 C
john.cain@saintleo.edu

CAIN, Katherine .... 314-977-4180.. 271 K
caink@slu.edu

CAIN, Kevin, G .... 304-462-6201.. 513 C
kevin.cain@glenville.edu

CAIN, Marcus .... 816-802-3468.. 266 D
mcain@kcai.edu

CAIN, Michael .... 716-829-2100.. 331 C
vphs@buffalo.edu

CAIN, Michael, E .... 716-829-3955.. 331 C
mcain@buffalo.edu

CAIN, R. Matthew .... 864-833-8296.. 432 B
mcain@presby.edu

CAIN, Ruth .... 816-235-6084.. 273 F
cainre@umkc.edu

CAIN, Sandra .... 508-541-1658.. 217 G
scain@dean.edu

CAIN, Sara Beth .... 619-388-2721.... 60 G
scain@sdccd.edu

CAIN, Stephen, D .... 240-567-1796.. 209 E
stephen.cain@montgomerycollege.edu

CAIN, Thomas, B .... 404-527-4522.. 118 F
tcain@carver.edu

CAIN, Wingate .... 820-652-0632.. 351 C
wingatecain@mcdowelltech.edu

CAIRES, Matthew .... 406-994-2826.. 277 C
mcaires@montana.edu

CAIRNS, Charles, B .... 520-626-0998.... 17 I
cairnsc@email.arizona.edu

CAIRNS, Heather .... 229-226-1621.. 128 B
hcairns@thomasu.edu

CAIRNS, Janet .... 918-631-3101.. 389 E
janet-cairns@utulsa.edu

CAIRNS, Jill .... 207-834-7602.. 205 B
jillb@maine.edu

CAIRNS, Linda .... 303-373-2008.... 83 B
lcairns@rvu.edu

CAIRNS, Mike .... 415-451-2817.... 61 D
mcairns@sfts.edu

CAIRO, Jim, R .... 504-568-4246.. 198 A
jcairo@lsuhsu.edu

CAIROL, Miguel .... 718-260-5600.. 309 C
mcairol@citytech.cuny.edu

CAIRY, Timothy, J .... 610-499-1193.. 423 E
tjcairy@widener.edu

CAISON, Anthony .... 919-866-6101.. 353 I
amcaison@waketech.edu

CAKMAK, Burak .... 212-229-8966.. 322 E
cakmakb@newschool.edu

CAL, John .... 305-348-4001.. 111 A
john.cal@fiu.edu

CAL, Mark .... 575-439-3622.. 301 A
mcal@nmsu.edu

CALA, Catherine .... 330-941-3119.. 382 A
cacala@ysu.edu

CALABRESE, John .... 586-498-4066.. 237 C
calabresej93@macomb.edu

CALABRESE, Nancy .... 410-626-2553.. 210 D
nancy.calabrese@sjc.edu

CALABRESE, Walter .... 252-444-0739.. 349 B
calabresew@cravencc.edu

CALABRIA, Patrick .... 631-420-2400.. 335 E
patrick.calabria@farmingdale.edu

CALAF, Jorge .... 787-279-1912.. 533 J
jcalaf@bayamon.inter.edu

CALAIS, Debra .... 337-482-6199.. 201 D
dcalais@louisiana.edu

CALAMAI, Anthony, G .... 828-262-3078.. 356 B
calamaiag@appstate.edu

CALAMAIO, Caprice .... 913-234-0733.. 179 M
caprice.calamaio@cleveland.edu

CALAMARE, Susan, S .... 617-422-7387.. 226 H
scalamare@nesl.edu

CALAMETTI, Jeffrey, D ..... 251-442-2242...... 9 A
jcalametti@umobile.edu

CALAMIA, James .... 732-255-0400.. 293 E
jcalamia@ocean.edu

CALAMIA, John, J .... 504-865-3946.. 198 E
calamia@loyno.edu

CALANDRELLA, Drew .... 530-898-6131.... 32 C
dcalandrella@csuchico.edu

CALARESO, Jack, P .... 718-940-5902.. 328 G
jcalareso@sjcny.edu

CALARESO, Joe .... 305-595-9500.... 95 A
admissions@amcollege.edu

CALATRELLO, Stephen ...... 256-306-2716...... 2 F
stephen.calatrello@calhoun.edu

CALCADO, Antonio .... 848-445-2474.. 295 F
acalcado@facilities.rutgers.edu

CALDARELLO, Beth .... 660-359-3948.. 269 I
bcaldarello@mail.ncmissouri.edu

CALDER, Susan .... 215-951-0981.. 416 G
calders@philau.edu

CALDER, Tom .... 410-516-7490.. 208 D
tcalder@jhu.edu

CALDERA, Nancy .... 509-527-2315.. 508 G
nancy.caldera@wallawalla.edu

CALDERARA, Kevin .... 907-474-6600.... 10 G
kmcalderara@alaska.edu

CALDERON, Ann Marie ... 615-230-3401.. 447 C
annmarie.calderon@volstate.edu

CALDERON, Gerardo .... 209-954-5052.... 61 F
gcalderon@deltacollege.edu

CALDERON, Hermes .... 787-780-0070.. 531 B
hcalderon@caribbean.edu

CALDERON, Janet .... 407-303-6108.... 95 C
janet.calderon@adu.edu

CALDERON, Nancy, T .... 408-554-4400.... 63 E
ntcalderon@scu.edu

CALDERON, Rosa .... 310-338-8839.... 51 E
rosa.calderon@lmu.edu

CALDERON, Sonny .... 818-333-3558.... 54 B

CALDERON, Zaida .... 787-265-3864.. 538 C
zaida.calderon@upr.edu

CALDERONE, Jackie .... 508-541-1530.. 217 G
0558mgr@fheg.follett.com

CALDERSON, Carl .... 619-201-8780.... 60 D
carl.calderson@sdcc.edu

CALDWELL, Adonna .... 901-572-2592.. 438 I
adonna.caldwell@bchs.edu

CALDWELL, Agnes .... 517-265-5161.. 230 D
acaldwell@adrian.edu

CALDWELL, Angela .... 870-248-4000.... 19 H
angelac@blackrivertech.edu

CALDWELL, Brinda, W ..... 828-398-7134.. 347 D
bcaldwell@abtech.edu

CALDWELL, Cary .... 704-406-3939.. 344 E
ccaldwell@gardner-webb.edu

CALDWELL, Catherine ...... 313-993-1544.. 241 G
caldwecr@udmercy.edu

CALDWELL, Cheryl .... 417-255-7960.. 269 A
cherylcaldwell@missouristate.edu

CALDWELL, Craig .... 801-957-5180.. 483 A
craig.caldwell@slcc.edu

CALDWELL, Dallas .... 405-974-2631.. 388 L
dcaldwell@uco.edu

CALDWELL, Daniel .... 601-318-6115.. 261 I
daniel.caldwell@wmcarey.edu

CALDWELL, David .... 615-248-1311.. 447 F
dcaldwell@trevecca.edu

CALDWELL, Diana .... 574-936-8898.. 158 I
diana.caldwell@ancilla.edu

CALDWELL, Donna .... 706-864-1410.. 128 F
donna.caldwell@ung.edu

CALDWELL, Gail .... 256-726-7024...... 6 B
gcaldwell@oakwood.edu

CALDWELL, Getchel .... 910-672-1661.. 356 E
gcaldwel@uncfsu.edu

CALDWELL, Helen .... 704-378-1014.. 345 E
hcaldwell@jcsu.edu

CALDWELL, Hollie .... 303-369-5151.... 82 F
hollie.caldwell@plattcolorado.edu

CALDWELL,
Jacqueline, H .... 918-631-2691.. 389 E
jacqueline-caldwell@utulsa.edu

CALDWELL, James .... 215-780-1306.. 419 C
jcaldwell@salus.edu

CALDWELL, James .... 215-780-1311.. 419 C
jcaldwell@salus.edu

CALDWELL, James, O .... 303-837-0825.... 76 L
caldwellj@aii.edu

CALDWELL, Janet .... 615-327-6851.. 442 A
jcaldwell@mmc.edu

CALDWELL, Jeff .... 405-733-7395.. 387 I
jcaldwell@rose.edu

CALDWELL, Jim .... 215-780-1313.. 419 C
jcaldwell@salus.edu

CALDWELL, Jodi, K .... 912-478-5541.. 122 B
jodic@georgiasouthern.edu

CALDWELL, Katrina .... 815-753-1554.. 150 A
kcaldwell1@niu.edu

CALDWELL, Kisha .... 423-697-3250.. 445 D
kisha.caldwell@chattanoogastate.edu

CALDWELL, Larry, W .... 605-336-6588.. 436 J
lcaldwell@sfseminary.edu

CALDWELL, Linda .... 251-580-2247...... 4 I
linda.caldwell@faulknerstate.edu

CALDWELL, Michael .... 559-278-3027.... 32 F
mcaldwell@csufresno.edu

CALDWELL, Nina .... 314-529-9485.. 267 B
ncaldwell@maryville.edu

CALDWELL, Patrice .... 575-562-2315.. 299 I
patrice.caldwell@enmu.edu

CALDWELL, Rachel .... 928-344-7501.... 11 J
rachel.caldwell@azwestern.edu

CALDWELL, Richard .... 402-898-1000.. 279 G
rich_c@creativecenter.edu

CALDWELL, Sandra .... 559-638-0300.... 67 D
sandra.caldwell@reedleycollege.edu

CALDWELL, Sheila .... 678-717-3592.. 128 F
sheila.caldwell@ung.edu

CALDWELL, Timothy .... 509-777-1000.. 509 H
tcaldwell@whitworth.edu

CALDWELL, Trish .... 916-484-8354.... 51 A
caldwet@arc.losrios.edu

CALDWELL, Troy .... 740-695-9500.. 364 B
tcaldwell@belmontcollege.edu

CALDWELL, Ward .... 336-770-3283.. 358 E
caldwellw@uncsa.edu

CALDWELL, IV,
William, B .... 478-387-4775.. 121 E
wcaldwell@gmc.edu

CALE, Benjamin .... 304-877-6428.. 510 F
admissions@abc.edu

CALE, Lynn .... 252-823-5166.. 349 E
calel@edgecombe.edu

CALEB, Peter .... 917-493-4507.. 319 M
library@msmnyc.edu

CALEF, Susan, A .... 402-280-5807.. 279 H
scalef@creighton.edu

CALENDA, Marianne .... 717-361-1196.. 403 C
calendam@etown.edu

CALERO, Teofilo .... 773-878-2998.. 153 E
tcalero@staugustine.edu

CALFAS, Karen, J .... 858-822-7552.... 70 C
kcalfas@ucsd.edu

CALHOUN, Annette .... 502-447-1000.. 192 G
macalhoun@spencerian.edu

CALHOUN, Barbara, S ...... 470-578-6258.. 123 J
bcalhoun@kennesaw.edu

CALHOUN, Chantae .... 910-362-7722.. 348 A
ccalhoun@cfcc.edu

CALHOUN, Cheryl .... 352-395-5719.. 109 C
cheryl.calhoun@sfcollege.edu

CALHOUN, Deborah, C ... 803-934-3216.. 431 E
dcalhoun@morris.edu

CALHOUN, Elizabeth .... 520-626-9921.... 17 I
ecalhoun@email.arizona.edu

CALHOUN, John .... 619-849-2784.... 57 M
johncalhoun@pointloma.edu

CALHOUN, Kirk, A .... 903-877-7750.. 477 E
kirk.calhoun@uthct.edu

CALHOUN, Larry .... 912-538-3101.. 127 E
lcalhoun@southeasterntech.edu

CALHOUN, Linda .... 270-686-4473.. 190 D
linda.calhoun@kctcs.edu

CALHOUN, Lozanne .... 870-543-5952..... 22 E
lcalhoun@seark.edu

CALHOUN, M. Grace .... 215-898-7215.. 421 E
athdir@pobox.upenn.edu

CALHOUN, Matthew .... 601-276-3718.. 260 H
mattc@smcc.edu

CALHOUN, Mitch .... 325-574-7612.. 479 I
mcalhoun@wtc.edu

CALHOUN, Patrick .... 409-839-2014.. 470 H
pcalhoun@lit.edu

CALHOUN, Paul .... 518-580-5590.. 330 F
pcalhoun@skidmore.edu

CALHOUN, Paula, M .... 330-471-8236.. 371 J
pcalhoun@malone.edu

CALHOUN, Ralph .... 901-435-1276.. 441 C
ralph_calhoun@loc.edu

CALHOUN, Rica .... 309-298-3070.. 158 A
rh-calhoun@wiu.edu

CALHOUN, Rochelle .... 609-258-3056.. 294 D
rochelle.calhoun@princeton.edu

CALHOUN, Thomas, G .... 703-993-2661.. 490 B
tcalhou2@gmu.edu

CALHOUN, JR.,
Thomas, J .... 773-995-2400.. 136 M
tcalhoun@csu.edu

CALHOUN, Tony .... 731-426-7658.. 440 K
tcalhoun@lanecollege.edu

CALHOUN, Vaughn, A .... 508-373-9736.. 215 D
vaughn.calhoun@becker.edu

CALHOUN-BROWN,
Allison .... 404-413-2067.. 122 D
acalhounbrown@gsu.edu

CALHOUN-FRENCH,
Diane .... 502-213-2621.. 190 A
diane.calhoun-french@kctcs.edu

CALICA, Corinna .... 925-424-1575.... 37 C
ccalica@laspositascollege.edu

CALILAN, James (Kimo) .. 707-864-7264.... 65 A

CALISSI, Barbara .... 516-323-3035.. 321 H
bcalissi@molloy.edu

CALISTO, George, W .... 312-553-3149.. 137 D
gcalisto@ccc.edu

CALIXTO, Grace .... 210-690-9000.. 458 I
gcalixto@hallmarkuniversity.edu

CALKINS, Gregory .... 513-529-3020.. 372 K
calkingp@miamioh.edu

CALL, Alyson .... 620-417-1103.. 184 I
aly.call@sccc.edu

CALL, Christopher, D .... 805-565-6023.... 75 A
ccall@westmont.edu

CALL, Diane .... 718-631-6222.. 309 E
dcall@qcc.cuny.edu

CALL, Kevin .... 276-944-6155.. 489 I
kcall@ehc.edu

CALL, Patrick .... 303-871-5090.... 84 B
patrick.call@du.edu

CALL, Susan .... 989-386-6604.. 238 B
scall@midmich.edu

CALL, Tyler .... 801-627-8451.. 481 A
callt@owatc.edu

CALL, Vickie, G .... 336-838-6146.. 354 C
vickie.call@wilkescc.edu

CALLAGHAN, Aloysius, R 651-962-5777.. 256 C
arcallaghan@stthomas.edu

CALLAGHAN, Carolyn .... 717-477-1348.. 416 A
cmcallaghan@ship.edu

CALLAGHAN, James, E ..... 740-826-8121.. 373 E
jamesc@muskingum.edu

CALLAGHAN, Karen, A ..... 305-899-3401.... 96 D
kcallaghan@barry.edu

CALLAGHAN, MaryEllen .. 914-633-2512.. 317 B
mcallaghan@iona.edu

CALLAHAN, Audra .... 508-999-8620.. 220 H
acallahan@umassd.edu

CALLAHAN, Candice .... 718-779-1499.. 326 D
info@plazacollege.edu

CALLAHAN, Caroline .... 718-779-1499.. 326 D
cmc@plazacollege.edu

CALLAHAN, III,
Charles, E .... 718-779-1499.. 326 D
cec3@plazacollege.edu

CAMPBELL, Joeseph .... 870-680-8725.... 19 C
joe_campbell@asun.edu
CAMPBELL, John .... 530-752-1730.... 69 A
jgcampbell@ucdavis.edu
CAMPBELL, John, B .... 901-722-3372.. 444 C
jbcampbell@sco.edu
CAMPBELL, John, P .... 304-293-4874.. 514 C
jpcampbe@mail.wvu.edu
CAMPBELL, Jonathan .... 870-230-5098.... 20 E
campbej@hsu.edu
CAMPBELL, Karen, D .... 757-822-1447.. 498 H
kcampbell@tcc.edu
CAMPBELL, Karen, M .... 608-822-2300.. 524 F
kcampbell@swtc.edu
CAMPBELL, Kathy .... 503-399-5018.. 390 E
kathy.campbell@chemeketa.edu
CAMPBELL, Keith, E .... 404-413-4465.. 122 D
kcampbell@gsu.edu
CAMPBELL, Kelly, D .... 404-687-4547.. 119 D
campbellk@ctsnet.edu
CAMPBELL, Keni .... 907-796-6509.... 10 H
klcampbell4@alaska.edu
CAMPBELL, Kevin .... 325-674-2765.. 449 J
kac96b@acu.edu
CAMPBELL, Kim .... 614-234-5144.. 373 B
kcampbell@mccn.edu
CAMPBELL, Kimberly .... 405-491-6335.. 388 A
kcampbel@snu.edu
CAMPBELL, Kimberly .... 913-971-3584.. 183 D
kjcampbell@mnu.edu
CAMPBELL, Kirby, D .... 318-342-5147.. 201 E
kcampbell@ulm.edu
CAMPBELL, Kristi .... 870-543-5959.... 22 E
kcampbell@seark.edu
CAMPBELL, Lauren .... 215-637-7700.. 405 J
lcampbell@holyfamily.edu
CAMPBELL, Lea .... 713-221-5548.. 474 B
campbellc@uhd.edu
CAMPBELL, Lisa .... 714-992-7085.... 54 H
lcampbell@fullcoll.edu
CAMPBELL, Lisa .... 775-623-4824.. 284 I
lisa.campbell@gbcnv.edu
CAMPBELL, Lisa, M .... 724-287-8711.. 399 B
lisa.campbell@bc3.edu
CAMPBELL, Lori .... 423-585-6933.. 447 D
lori.campbell@ws.edu
CAMPBELL, Lucy .... 619-684-8783.... 54 C
lcampbell@newschoolarch.edu
CAMPBELL, Mark .... 415-749-4581.... 61 B
mcampbell@sfai.edu
CAMPBELL, Marshall .... 979-230-3474.. 453 A
marshall.campbell@brazosport.edu
CAMPBELL, Mary, B .... 314-935-3617.. 274 N
marycampbell@wustl.edu
CAMPBELL, Mary, B .... 864-488-8280.. 430 H
mcampbell@limestone.edu
CAMPBELL, Mason .... 870-508-6168.... 19 B
mcampbell@asumh.edu
CAMPBELL, Matthew .... 253-840-8419.. 506 B
mcampbell@pierce.ctc.edu
CAMPBELL, Michael .... 760-384-6159.... 47 K
michael.campbell@cerrocoso.edu
CAMPBELL, Michael .... 816-279-7000.. 262 B
michael.campbell@abtu.edu
CAMPBELL, Michael, A .... 423-585-2682.. 447 D
mike.campbell@ws.edu
CAMPBELL, Michelle .... 425-235-2352.. 506 F
mcampbell@rtc.edu
CAMPBELL, Mike .... 423-585-2682.. 447 D
michael.campbell@ws.edu
CAMPBELL, Milt .... 641-673-1074.. 177 J
campbellm@wmpenn.edu
CAMPBELL, Mitchell, L .... 916-558-2426.... 51 D
campbem@scc.losrios.edu
CAMPBELL, Nicole, J .... 405-325-1978.. 389 B
njudice@ou.edu
CAMPBELL, Pam .... 760-384-6178.... 47 K
pagodfre@cerrocoso.edu
CAMPBELL, Patricia .... 509-542-4761.. 502 G
pcampbell@columbiabasin.edu
CAMPBELL, Patricia .... 617-627-3331.. 228 H
patricia.campbell@tufts.edu
CAMPBELL, Phillip, E .... 434-528-5276.. 500 C
pcampbell@vul.edu
CAMPBELL, Phyllis .... 731-352-4046.. 438 K
campbellp@bethelu.edu
CAMPBELL, Randy .... 607-778-5196.. 332 D
campbellrj@sunybroome.edu
CAMPBELL, Rina .... 949-214-3561.... 41 F
rina.campbell@cui.edu
CAMPBELL, Robert .... 410-704-4862.. 213 B
rcampbell@towson.edu
CAMPBELL, Robert, D .... 212-817-7300.. 308 A
rcampbell@gc.cuny.edu
CAMPBELL, Robin .... 336-517-2229.. 342 B
rcampbell@bennett.edu
CAMPBELL, Rosana .... 570-484-2723.. 415 D
rcampbel@lhup.edu
CAMPBELL, Samerah .... 559-244-5989.... 67 A
samerah.campbell@scccd.edu
CAMPBELL, Sara .... 423-614-8525.. 441 B
scampbell@leeuniversity.edu
CAMPBELL, Scott .... 773-834-3390.. 156 D
scottcampbell@uchicago.edu
CAMPBELL, Sharon .... 919-760-8011.. 346 D
sharonca@meredith.edu
CAMPBELL,
Shoshanna, M .... 718-780-7501.. 305 L
shoshanna.campbell@brooklaw.edu
CAMPBELL, Sierra .... 708-802-6181.. 140 F
scampbell@foxcollege.edu
CAMPBELL, Stanley, R ..... 859-238-5271.. 187 H
stan.campbell@centre.edu
CAMPBELL, Stephanie ..... 318-357-5351.. 201 B
campbells@nsula.edu
CAMPBELL, Stephanie ..... 904-470-8114.... 98 N
s.campbell@ewc.edu
CAMPBELL, Stephen .... 216-368-5555.. 365 B
stephen.campbell@case.edu
CAMPBELL, Stephen .... 409-772-9751.. 478 A
stepcamp@utmb.edu
CAMPBELL, Steven .... 423-323-0205.. 446 F
srcampbell@northeaststate.edu
CAMPBELL, Thomas, F .... 214-905-3001.. 476 C
thomas.f.campbell@utdallas.edu
CAMPBELL, Thomas, L .... 610-282-1100.. 402 B
thomas.campbell@desales.edu
CAMPBELL, Timothy, G .... 859-858-3511.. 186 J
tim.campbell@asbury.edu
CAMPBFIELD, Timothy, M .. 443-334-2838.. 211 A
tmcampbell@stevenson.edu
CAMPBELL, Tish .... 912-525-5000.. 126 E
lcampbel@scad.edu
CAMPBELL, Tom .... 714-628-2516.... 37 F
tcampbell@chapman.edu
CAMPBELL, SJ,
William, R .... 508-793-2446.. 217 C
wcampbel@holycross.edu
CAMPBELL-HOOPS,
Toma .... 406-353-2607.. 275 H
thoops@ancollege.edu
CAMPE, Robert, J .... 607-735-1802.. 313 F
rcampe@elmira.edu
CAMPEAU, Tony .... 406-994-2603.. 277 C
tcampeau@montana.edu
CAMPER, Diane .... 731-286-3338.. 446 B
camper@dscc.edu
CAMPER, Shannon .... 845-451-1352.. 312 C
s_camper@culinary.edu
CAMPERI, Marcelo, F ...... 415-422-5939.... 72 C
camperi@usfca.edu
CAMPFIELD, Sarah .... 304-357-4741.. 511 E
sarahcampfield@ucwv.edu
CAMPION, Anne .... 312-777-8559.. 142 G
acampion@aii.edu
CAMPION, James, R .... 518-828-4181.. 311 D
campion@sunycgcc.edu
CAMPION, William, J .... 254-647-3234.. 463 K
bcampion@rangercollege.edu
CAMPLESE, Cole, W .... 773-702-8034.. 156 D
kathiek@uchicago.edu
CAMPO, Carlos .... 419-289-5050.. 363 J
ccampo@ashland.edu
CAMPO, Juan, E .... 805-893-3945.... 70 E
jcampo@religion.ucsb.edu
CAMPO, Regina, Z .... 717-337-6207.. 404 C
rcampo@gettysburg.edu
CAMPOS, Becky .... 714-997-6943.... 37 F
bcampos@chapman.edu
CAMPOS, Cesar .... 312-939-0111.. 139 G
cesar@eastwest.edu
CAMPOS, Connie .... 408-848-4802.... 44 I
ccampos@gavilan.edu
CAMPOS, Darcie, R .... 708-534-5000.. 140 H
dcampos@govst.edu
CAMPOS, Diana .... 575-234-9227.. 301 B
dcampos@nmsu.edu
CAMPOS, Javier .... 559-453-4600.... 44 F
javier.campos@fresno.edu
CAMPOS, Jesus .... 956-872-8330.. 465 H
jhcampos@southtexascollege.edu
CAMPOS, Lisa .... 928-523-5353.... 15 H
lisa.campos@nau.edu
CAMPOS, Nicolette .... 910-521-6695.. 358 C
nicolette.campos@uncp.edu
CAMPOS, Tom .... 210-486-0606.. 450 F
tcampos1@alamo.edu
CAMPS, Manel .... 831-459-2411.... 70 F
mcamps@ucsc.edu
CAMSTRA, Maggie .... 830-591-7342.. 466 A
maggie.camstra@swtjc.edu
CAMUTI, Alice .... 931-372-3366.. 445 B
acamuti@tntech.edu
CANACARIS, Diana .... 865-273-8882.. 441 H
diana.canacaris@maryvillecollege.edu
CANADA, Allison, M .... 410-334-2918.. 213 G
acanada@worwic.edu
CANADA, Britt .... 325-574-7671.. 479 I
bcanada@wtc.edu
CANADA, Clarence .... 706-821-8292.. 125 H
ccanada@paine.edu
CANADA, Mark .... 765-455-9227.. 163 A
canadam@iuk.edu
CANADA, Ruth .... 573-681-5975.. 266 I
canadar@lincolnu.edu
CANADAY, Bruce .... 314-446-8184.. 271 E
bruce.canaday@stlcop.edu
CANADAY, JR., John ...... 719-384-6818.... 82 A
john.canaday@ojc.edu
CANADAY, Joseph .... 215-596-7524.. 422 A
j.canaday@usciences.edu
CANAL, Marcie .... 213-738-6800.... 66 F
administrativeservices@swlaw.edu
CANALES, Carmen, I .... 336-758-3256.. 359 E
ccanales@wfu.edu
CANALES, Jason, G .... 413-662-5413.. 222 B
jason.canales@mcla.edu
CANALES, Jo Ann .... 361-825-3884.. 468 E
joann.canales@tamucc.edu
CANALES, Leticia .... 559-675-4800.... 67 D
leticia.canales@scccd.edu
CANALES, Luis .... 309-438-0287.. 143 B
lacanal@ilstu.edu
CANALES, Rafael .... 787-279-1912.. 533 J
rrcanales@bayamon.inter.edu
CANALS, Alex .... 718-933-6700.. 321 I
acanals@monroecollege.edu
CANAN, Michelle .... 918-293-5494.. 386 B
michelle.canan@okstate.edu
CANAS, Carlos .... 305-626-3698.. 101 A
carlos.canas@fmuniv.edu
CANAVAN, Jessie .... 330-823-2579.. 379 F
canavajl@mountunion.edu
CANAVAN, Linda, T .... 781-292-2341.. 218 H
linda.canavan@olin.edu
CANAVAN, Terry .... 631-499-7100.. 319 A
tcanavan@libi.edu
CANCEKO CHAN,
Genevieve .... 360-491-4700.. 506 G
gchan@stmartin.edu
CANCEL, Jimmy .... 787-250-1912.. 534 B
jcancel@metro.inter.edu
CANCEL, Olga .... 787-754-8000.. 537 B
ocancel@pupr.edu
CANCEL-PEREZ,
Magda, A .... 787-620-2040.. 530 F
mcancel@aupr.edu
CANCELLIERE, Jaclyn ...... 410-287-1034.. 206 J
jcancelliere@cecil.edu
CANCHOLA, Liza .... 210-308-8584.. 453 M
CANCILLA, Devon .... 816-235-1107.. 273 F
cancillad@umkc.edu
CANCILLA, Mike .... 256-549-8311...... 3 M
mcancilla@gadsdenstate.edu
CANDEE, Kate .... 920-923-8727.. 517 H
kcandee@marianuniversity.edu
CANDELA, Natalie .... 810-762-9832.. 236 C
ncandela@kettering.edu
CANDELARIA, J. Randel .. 336-734-7216.. 349 G
jcandelaria@forsythtech.edu
CANDIA-BAILEY,
Antoinette .... 410-704-2516.. 213 B
acandiabailey@towson.edu
CANDIDO, James .... 512-313-3000.. 455 F
james.candido@concordia.edu
CANDLER, George, B .... 212-327-7801.. 327 F
candler@rockefeller.edu
CANDLER, Marietta .... 870-612-2070.... 23 H
marietta.candler@uaccb.edu
CANDREVA, Anne, M .... 412-578-6043.. 400 C
candrevaam@carlow.edu
CANEIRO-LIVINGSTON,
Graciela .... 563-588-6406.. 170 F
graciela.caneiro-livingston@clarke.edu
CANEPA, Janet, A .... 203-254-4280.... 87 G
jcanepa@fairfield.edu
CANEPA, Thomas .... 513-556-2495.. 379 A
tom.canepa@uc.edu
CANEPI, Karen .... 702-968-2033.. 285 E
kcanepi@roseman.edu
CANER, Emir .... 706-865-2134.. 128 D
ecaner@truett.edu
CANFIELD, Clarke .... 207-741-5575.. 203 M
ccanfield@smccme.edu
CANFIELD, Kathleen .... 847-925-6437.. 141 A
kcanfiel@harpercollege.edu
CANFIELD, Kipton .... 309-341-5325.. 136 C
kcanfield@sandburg.edu
CANGELIO, Paula, R .... 304-293-5841.. 514 C
pacongelio@hsc.wvu.edu
CANGELLARIS,
Andreas, C .... 217-333-2150.. 157 A
cangella@illinois.edu
CANGEMI, Livia .... 212-650-3868.. 308 D
livia.cangemi@hunter.cuny.edu
CANHAM, Drew .... 254-299-8645.. 461 E
dcanham@mclennan.edu
CANHAM, Raymond, P .... 972-238-6248.. 456 H
canham@dcccd.edu
CANIA, Lisa, M .... 315-229-5585.. 329 D
lcania@stlawu.edu
CANIDA, II, Robert, L ..... 910-522-5790.. 358 C
canida@uncp.edu
CANIGLIA, Alan, S .... 717-358-3934.. 403 J
alan.caniglia@fandm.edu
CANIGLIA, Jason, J .... 303-458-4160.... 82 L
jcaniglia@regis.edu
CANINO, Cathy .... 864-503-5657.. 434 G
ccanino@uscupstate.edu
CANN, Alison .... 864-592-4991.. 432 H
canna@sccsc.edu
CANNADA, JR.,
Robert, C .... 601-923-1600.. 260 E
rcannada@rts.edu
CANNADAY SAULNY,
Helen .... 202-994-6710.... 92 D
saulnyh@gwu.edu
CANNADY, Sharell .... 704-461-6722.. 342 A
sharellcannady@bac.edu
CANNADY-SMITH,
Allison .... 253-879-3450.. 508 D
acannadysmith@pugetsound.edu
CANNAN, Erin .... 845-758-7454.. 304 F
cannan@bard.edu
CANNELL, Stephen .... 269-488-4241.. 235 I
scannell@kvcc.edu
CANNER-WARD, Laisha ... 352-371-2833.... 98 I
clinicdirector@dragonrises.edu
CANNEY, Catherine .... 978-665-3653.. 221 D
ccanney@fitchburgstate.edu
CANNICI, James, P .... 972-883-2575.. 476 C
cannici@utdallas.edu
CANNIFF, James, F .... 617-228-2435.. 223 B
jfcanniff@bhcc.mass.edu
CANNING, Allison .... 843-525-8210.. 433 B
acanning@tcl.edu
CANNING, Elizabeth .... 508-793-2365.. 217 C
ecanning@holycross.edu
CANNING, John, B .... 401-232-6020.. 424 K
jcanning@bryant.edu
CANNING MCCOMISKEY,
Mary Ann .... 401-598-4689.. 425 B
maryann.canningmccomiskey@jwu.edu
CANNON, Amy .... 270-901-1012.. 190 F
amy.cannon@kctcs.edu
CANNON, Brenda .... 931-393-1546.. 446 D
bcannon@mscc.edu
CANNON, Bruce .... 406-656-9950.. 278 H
CANNON, Bunnie .... 225-578-0302.. 197 I
bcannon@lsu.edu
CANNON, Candy .... 559-325-5282.... 67 B
candy.cannon@scccd.edu
CANNON, Chris .... 251-460-6161...... 9 E
ccannon@southalabama.edu
CANNON, David .... 567-661-7112.. 376 D
david_cannon@owens.edu
CANNON, Glen, D .... 770-962-7580.. 123 D
gcannon@gwinnetttech.edu
CANNON, Gordon .... 601-266-5116.. 261 E
gordon.cannon@usm.edu
CANNON, Gregory .... 845-575-3000.. 320 B
greg.cannon@marist.edu
CANNON, Jason .... 256-840-4150...... 6 H
jcannon@snead.edu
CANNON, Katherine .... 508-793-7499.. 217 B
kcannon@clarku.edu
CANNON, Kathleen .... 503-847-2557.. 396 C
kcannon@uws.edu
CANNON, Mark, B .... 808-675-3803.. 130 E
mark.cannon@byuh.edu
CANNON, Mary .... 614-234-5177.. 373 B
mcannon@mccn.edu
CANNON, Michael, R .... 314-935-5152.. 274 N
michael_cannon@wustl.edu
CANNON, Rebecca .... 225-768-0810.. 199 B
rebecca.cannon@ololcollege.edu
CANNON, Sharon .... 432-703-5270.. 472 D
sharon.cannon@ttuhsc.edu
CANNON, Sharon .... 610-399-2057.. 414 F
scannon@cheyney.edu
CANNON, Sondra .... 732-224-2695.. 289 I
scannon@brookdalecc.edu
CANNON, Tonya .... 404-527-4520.. 118 F
tcannon@carver.edu
CANNON, Tyrone, H .... 415-422-6167.... 72 C
cannont@usfca.edu
CANNY, Eric .... 612-330-1383.. 244 I
canny@augsburg.edu
CANO, Mary .... 915-566-9621.. 479 H
mcano@westerntech.edu
CANON, Susan .... 507-786-3647.. 254 P
canon@stolaf.edu
CANON, Sybil .... 662-560-1103.. 260 C
srcanon@northwestms.edu
CANONICA, James .... 856-227-7200.. 290 B
jcanonica@camdencc.edu
CANOUGH, Corrine, M ...... 585-785-1469.. 314 D
corinne.canough@flcc.edu
CANOY, Eugenio .... 408-274-7900.... 62 D
eugenio.canoy@evc.edu
CANOY, Robert, W .... 704-406-4395.. 344 E
rcanoy@gardner-webb.edu

CAREY, Seamus .... 859-233-8111.. 193 D
president@transy.edu
CAREY, Sidney .... 713-266-6594.. 458 A
CAREY, Thomas, P .... 207-786-6254.. 202 D
tcarey@bates.edu
CAREY, Tim .... 607-274-3225.. 317 D
tcarey@ithaca.edu
CAREY, Tom .... 206-239-4500.. 502 D
CAREY, William .... 845-451-1300.. 312 C
w_carey@culinary.edu
CAREY-BUTLER, Sylvia .... 920-424-0348.. 520 E
careybus@uwosh.edu
CAREY-MCDONALD, Jan . 435-586-7735.. 481 N
careymcdonald@suu.edu
CARFAGNA, Angelo .... 201-692-7025.. 291 J
angelo@fdu.edu
CARFORA, John .... 310-338-6004.... 51 E
jcarfora@lmu.edu
CARGUELLO, Brett, M ..... 315-655-7150.. 306 H
CARHART, Tori .... 315-228-7676.. 310 G
tcarhart@colgate.edu
CARIAGA-LO, Liza .... 401-863-2216.. 424 J
liza_cariaga-lo@brown.edu
CARIDI, James, A .... 614-251-4595.. 374 I
caridij@ohiodominican.edu
CARIGLIO-DORRIS,
Jenna .... 330-569-5134.. 369 J
carigliojd@hiram.edu
CARIKER, Heath .... 903-983-8657.. 460 D
hcariker@kilgore.edu
CARILLI, Vincent .... 865-974-7449.. 448 E
vincent.carilli@tennessee.edu
CARIN, Lawrence .... 919-681-6438.. 343 J
lcarin@duke.edu
CARINGELLA, Santino ..... 312-362-6986.. 139 C
scaringe@depaul.edu
CARIO, William .... 262-243-4263.. 232 I
william.cario@cuw.edu
CARIO, William, R .... 262-243-5700.. 516 E
william.cario@cuw.edu
CARISSIMI, Laura, K .... 440-365-5222.. 371 H
CARITO, Phyllis .... 518-828-4181.. 311 D
carito@sunycgcc.edu
CARKUM, Duane .... 504-520-7490.. 202 C
dcarkum@xula.edu
CARL, Ashley .... 813-253-7158.. 102 R
acarl@hccfl.edu
CARL, Cathy .... 845-431-8635.. 312 G
cathy.carl@sunydutchess.edu
CARL, Diane .... 570-321-4101.. 409 F
carl@lycoming.edu
CARL, Heidi, A .... 765-361-6375.. 169 C
carlh@wabash.edu
CARL, James, C .... 203-396-8454.... 88 I
carlj@sacredheart.edu
CARL, Peggy .... 978-542-6517.. 222 D
pcarl@salemstate.edu
CARL, Steven, B .... 508-767-7267.. 214 F
sb.carl@assumption.edu
CARLAND, Tammy Rae .... 510-594-3649.... 29 K
tcarland@cca.edu
CARLBLOM, Shelia .... 765-677-2191.. 164 B
sheila.carlblom@indwes.edu
CARLETON, Lauren .... 218-869-5748.. 194 I
lcarleton@centenary.edu
CARLETON, Mary Ruth .... 619-594-4562.... 35 A
mcarleto@mail.sdsu.edu
CARLETON, Taylor .... 830-372-8026.. 470 C
tcarleton@tlu.edu
CARLETTA, Charles, F ...... 518-276-6212.. 327 B
carlec@rpi.edu
CARLEY, Michael .... 559-791-2275.... 47 L
mcarley@portervillecollege.edu
CARLI, Gale .... 510-742-3102.... 55 B
gcarli@ohlone.edu
CARLILE, Debra .... 405-878-5422.. 387 J
dlcarlile@stgregorys.edu
CARLILE, Kimberly, L ...... 806-371-5017.. 450 H
k0153833@actx.edu
CARLIN, Angela .... 360-412-6152.. 506 G
acarlin@stmartin.edu
CARLIN, Jane .... 253-879-3118.. 508 D
jcarlin@pugetsound.edu
CARLIN, Laurence .... 920-424-7364.. 520 E
carlin@uwosh.edu
CARLIN, Melanie .... 217-357-9117.. 152 D
mcarlin@robertmorris.edu
CARLIN, Michael .... 704-687-5500.. 358 A
mike.carlin@uncc.edu
CARLIN, Virginia, A .... 630-873-3485.. 140 B
vcarlin@ellis.edu
CARLING SMITH,
Malcolm .... 916-339-4371.... 53 F
mcarlingsmith@mticollege.edu
CARLISLE, Beth .... 602-943-2311.... 18 C
beth.carlisle@west.edu
CARLISLE, Brian .... 909-621-8241.... 57 H
brian_carlisle@pitzer.edu
CARLISLE, David, M .... 323-563-4987.... 37 G
davidcarlisle@cdrewu.edu
CARLISLE, Elizabeth .... 812-749-1241.. 166 B
lcarlisle@oak.edu
CARLISLE, Jerry, H .... 501-882-8835.... 18 I
jhcarlisle@asub.edu
CARLISLE, Sandra .... 320-629-5100.. 251 E
carlisles@pine.edu
CARLISLE, Susan .... 502-213-5200.. 190 A
susan.carlisle@kctcs.edu
CARLO, Jennifer, A .... 412-578-6087.. 400 C
jacarlo@carlow.edu
CARLO, Luis .... 646-378-6171.. 325 C
luis.carlo@nyack.edu
CARLOCK, Danielle .... 480-423-6653.... 14 H
d.carlock@scottsdalecc.edu
CARLOCK, Jennifer .... 309-655-7100.. 153 F
jennifer.carlock@osfhealthcare.org
CARLOCK, Myra .... 731-352-4090.. 438 K
carlockm@bethelu.edu
CARLOCK, Ruth .... 402-363-5704.. 283 G
rmcarlock@york.edu
CARLOS, Raymond .... 909-384-8253.... 60 C
rcarlos@sbccd.cc.ca.us
CARLOS, Terri .... 909-537-7576.... 34 C
tcarlos@csusb.edu
CARLSEN, Paul .... 225-308-4422.. 195 G
paulcarlsen@lctcs.edu
CARLSON, Annie .... 828-669-8012.. 346 M
acarlson@montreat.edu
CARLSON, Bob .... 630-682-6002.. 142 I
carlson@iit.edu
CARLSON, Britt .... 978-867-4221.. 219 A
britt.carlson@gordon.edu
CARLSON, Cameron, B ...... 620-229-6115.. 184 J
cameron.carlson@sckans.edu
CARLSON, Caroline .... 949-376-6000.... 48 C
ccarlson@lcad.edu
CARLSON, Catherina .... 781-891-2989.. 215 F
ccarlson@bentley.edu
CARLSON, Cathy .... 507-222-4075.. 245 C
ccarlson@carleton.edu
CARLSON, Chris .... 951-222-8000.... 58 J
chris.carlson@rcc.edu
CARLSON, Craig .... 203-857-3344.... 87 B
ccarlson@norwalk.edu
CARLSON, David .... 540-362-6675.. 490 F
dcarlson@hollins.edu
CARLSON, David, H .... 979-845-8160.. 468 B
davidcarlson@tamu.edu
CARLSON, Deborah .... 402-354-7023.. 281 F
deb.carlson@methodistcollege.edu
CARLSON, Debra .... 320-308-3296.. 252 A
dlcarlson@stcloudstate.edu
CARLSON, Don .... 218-879-0878.. 249 C
dcarlson@fdltcc.edu
CARLSON, Don .... 925-424-1322.... 37 C
CARLSON, Douglas .... 415-476-4527.... 70 D
doug.carlson@ucsf.edu
CARLSON, Dusten .... 815-965-8616.. 152 F
CARLSON, Gerald, P .... 337-482-6678.. 201 D
gcarlson@louisiana.edu
CARLSON, Gregory .... 701-845-7480.. 361 B
gregory.carlson@vcsu.edu
CARLSON, James .... 847-578-8805.. 153 A
james.carlson@rosalindfrannklin.edu
CARLSON, Jeffrey .... 708-524-6814.. 139 F
jcarlson@dom.edu
CARLSON, Jessica .... 406-586-3585.. 276 I
jessica.carlson@montanabiblecollege.edu
CARLSON, Jim .... 406-586-3585.. 276 I
jim.carlson@montanabiblecollege.edu
CARLSON, Jodi .... 503-375-7000.. 391 B
jcarlson@corban.edu
CARLSON, Julie .... 402-844-7142.. 282 B
juliec@northeast.edu
CARLSON, Kathleen .... 773-298-3305.. 153 H
carlson@sxu.edu
CARLSON, Kathleen .... 574-284-4543.. 167 A
kcarlson@saintmarys.edu
CARLSON, Kenna Lee .... 402-486-2503.. 282 I
kecarlso@ucollege.edu
CARLSON, Kenneth .... 701-777-2127.. 360 C
kenneth.carlson@und.edu
CARLSON, Kevin .... 906-217-4023.. 231 O
kevin.carlson@baycollege.edu
CARLSON, Laina .... 651-450-3654.. 249 F
lcarlso@inverhills.edu
CARLSON, Laura .... 574-631-8052.. 168 B
lcarlson@nd.edu
CARLSON, Malinda, L .... 217-245-3011.. 141 G
mcarlson@mail.ic.edu
CARLSON, Mark .... 651-201-1827.. 248 I
mark.carlson@so.mnscu.edu
CARLSON, Mary .... 616-222-3000.. 236 F
mcarlson@kuyper.edu
CARLSON, Melinda .... 314-977-2824.. 271 K
mcarlson2@slu.edu
CARLSON, Nancy .... 303-914-6389.... 82 I
nancy.carlson@rrcc.edu
CARLSON, Neil .... 616-526-6420.. 232 A
nec4@calvin.edu
CARLSON, Nicki .... 218-683-8546.. 251 C
nicki.carlson@northlandcollege.edu
CARLSON, Nicole .... 763-493-0597.. 251 B
ncarlson@nhcc.edu
CARLSON, Paul .... 815-802-8652.. 144 C
pcarlson@kcc.edu
CARLSON, Paula, J .... 563-387-1001.. 174 L
president@luther.edu
CARLSON, Rachel .... 540-545-7382.. 494 B
rcarlso2@su.edu
CARLSON, Ria, M .... 949-824-7911.... 69 C
ria.carlson@uci.edu
CARLSON, Rich .... 402-486-2508.. 282 I
ricarlso@ucollege.edu
CARLSON, Robert .... 785-227-3380.. 178 J
carlsonr@bethanylb.edu
CARLSON, Rosa, F .... 559-791-2315.... 47 L
rcarlson@portervillecollege.edu
CARLSON, Skye .... 360-779-9993.. 505 B
scarlson@ncad.edu
CARLSON, Steve .... 937-298-3399.. 371 D
steve.carlson@ketteringhealth.org
CARLSON, Steve .... 920-206-2342.. 517 G
steve.carlson@mbu.edu
CARLSON, Steven, T .... 574-372-5100.. 161 B
carlsost@grace.edu
CARLSON, Susan .... 510-987-0728.... 68 L
susan.carlson@ucop.edu
CARLSON, Tammy .... 309-438-8846.. 143 B
tscarls@ilstu.edu
CARLSON, Wayne, E .... 614-292-2872.. 375 A
carlson.8@osu.edu
CARLSON ZINK, Deanna . 701-777-2611.. 360 C
deannac@undfoundation.org
CARLSTON, Gary, L .... 435-283-7010.. 482 E
gary.carlston@snow.edu
CARLSTROM, Lester, H ..... 773-244-5597.. 149 I
lcarlstrom@northpark.edu
CARLTON, Edith .... 731-286-3300.. 446 B
carlton@dscc.edu
CARLTON, Keitha .... 903-785-7661.. 463 E
kcarlton@parisjc.edu
CARLTON, LeAnn, K .... 816-654-7213.. 266 E
lcarlton@kcumb.edu
CARLTON, William .... 912-279-5892.. 119 C
wcarlton@ccga.edu
CARLTON-CAREW,
Miranda .... 704-499-9200.... 93 F
CARMACK, Amy .... 781-272-0222.. 215 A
acarmack@baypath.edu
CARMACK, Connie, K .... 540-375-2230.. 493 H
carmack@roanoke.edu
CARMAN, Beth Anne .... 614-236-6211.. 364 N
bcarman@capital.edu
CARMAN, Kevin .... 775-784-1740.. 285 A
kcarman@unr.edu
CARMEAN, John .... 352-381-3625.. 109 C
john.carmean@sfcollege.edu
CARMEL, Julie .... 508-929-8754.. 222 F
jcarmel@worcester.edu
CARMEN, Kim .... 318-675-5207.. 198 B
shvreg@lsuhsc.edu
CARMICAL, Beth .... 910-272-3343.. 352 E
bcarmical@robeson.edu
CARMICHAEL, Ann, C .... 803-584-3446.. 434 C
anncar@mailbox.sc.edu
CARMICHAEL, Beverly, C 904-819-6290.... 99 M
bcarmichael@flagler.edu
CARMICHAEL, Brenda .... 620-343-4600.. 180 H
bcarmichael@fhtc.edu
CARMICHAEL, Jason .... 970-943-2079.... 84 H
jcarmichael@western.edu
CARMICHAEL, John .... 360-867-6100.. 503 G
carmichj@evergreen.edu
CARMICHAEL, Paul .... 860-343-5787.... 86 F
pcarmichael@mxcc.commnet.edu
CARMICHAEL, Peggy .... 304-214-8901.. 512 F
pcarmichael@wvncc.edu
CARMICHAEL, Stacey .... 770-394-8300.. 116 F
stacey.carmichael@cbre.com
CARMICHAEL, Stacy .... 228-896-2503.. 259 C
stacy.carmichael@mgccc.edu
CARMICHAEL, William ...... 901-369-0835.... 93 F
CARMINE, Kevin .... 718-319-7965.. 308 C
kcarmine@hostos.cuny.edu
CARMODY, Patricia .... 507-537-6206.. 252 E
patricia.carmody@smsu.edu
CARMONA, Gloria .... 760-355-6244.... 46 J
gloria.carmona@imperial.edu
CARNAGHI, Jan .... 317-955-6154.. 165 N
jcarnaghi@marian.edu
CARNAHAN, Diane .... 209-468-9155.... 67 H
dcarnahan@sjcoe.net
CARNAHAN, Scott .... 503-883-2229.. 392 B
scarnah@linfield.edu
CARNAROLI, Craig .... 215-898-6693.. 421 E
carnarol@upenn.edu
CARNE, Kim .... 906-786-5802.. 231 O
carnek@baycollege.edu
CARNE, Margaret, A .... 920-748-8180.. 519 E
carnem@ripon.edu
CARNES, Allen .... 336-770-3320.. 358 E
carnesa@uncsa.edu
CARNES, Gregory, A .... 256-765-4245...... 9 C
gacarnes@una.edu
CARNES, Kathy, M .... 252-493-7220.. 352 A
kcarnes@email.pittcc.edu
CARNES, Peter .... 508-565-1206.. 228 F
pcarnes@stonehill.edu
CARNEVALE, David .... 562-907-4284.... 75 B
dcarneva@whittier.edu
CARNEY, Diane, E .... 412-291-6250.. 397 I
dcarney@aii.edu
CARNEY, Gary .... 610-861-7909.. 411 B
carneyg@moravian.edu
CARNEY, Ginny .... 218-335-4267.. 247 F
ginny.carney@lltc.edu
CARNEY, Joshua .... 630-620-2188.. 150 B
jcarney@seminary.edu
CARNEY, Margaret .... 202-319-5515.... 92 A
CARNEY, Martin .... 216-421-7424.. 366 G
mcarney@cia.edu
CARNEY, Michael, J .... 715-836-4353.. 520 A
carneymj@uwec.edu
CARNEY, Paige .... 304-766-3313.. 514 B
carney3@wvstateu.edu
CARNEY, Randy .... 618-937-2127.. 148 I
rcarney@morthland.edu
CARNEY, Sheila, A .... 412-578-6424.. 400 C
carneysa@carlow.edu
CARNEY, Timothy .... 202-319-5619.... 92 A
carneyt@cua.edu
CARNEY, Timothy, D .... 412-578-8712.. 400 C
tdcarney@carlow.edu
CARNEY-DEBORD, Nan ..... 740-587-6428.. 368 B
carneydebord@denison.edu
CARNEY-HALL, Karla .... 309-556-3111.. 143 D
dstudent@iwu.edu
CARNICOM, Scott .... 570-484-2204.. 415 D
carnicom@lhup.edu
CARNIE, Andrew, H .... 520-621-3471.... 17 I
carnie@email.arizona.edu
CARNLEY, Raymond .... 478-471-2732.. 124 E
raymond.carnley@mga.edu
CARNO, John .... 908-852-1400.. 290 D
carnoj@centenarycollege.edu
CARNS, Mary Lee .... 843-525-5692.. 433 B
mcarns@tcl.edu
CARNWATH, Thomas .... 215-717-6640.. 421 D
tcarnwath@uarts.edu
CARNZ, Scott .... 206-239-2320.. 501 C
scarnz@aii.edu
CARO, Jessica .... 787-832-6000.. 532 O
jcaro@icprjc.edu
CARO, Mary Ellen .... 609-984-1130.. 297 F
mcaro@tesu.edu
CARO, SJ, Robert, V .... 310-338-2987.... 51 E
rcaro@lmu.edu
CAROL, Steve .... 732-987-2414.. 292 A
scarol@georgian.edu
CAROLINA, Kimberly .... 203-575-8056.... 86 G
kcarolina@nv.edu
CARON, Bob .... 817-552-3700.. 460 E
bcaron@tku.edu
CARON, Rick .... 406-447-6937.. 277 B
rick.caron@umhelena.edu
CAROTHERS, Amy .... 775-784-6620.. 285 A
acarothers@unr.edu
CAROTHERS, John .... 775-784-1394.. 285 A
jcarothers@adv.unr.edu
CARP, Richard, M .... 925-631-4443.... 59 I
rmcarp@gmail.com
CARPENTER, Andre .... 504-398-2110.. 200 D
acarpenter@olhcc.edu
CARPENTER, Barbara .... 225-771-2613.. 199 H
carp.subr@aol.com
CARPENTER, Brenda .... 405-682-1611.. 385 D
bcarpenter@occc.edu
CARPENTER, Carol .... 616-977-5520.. 233 A
carol.carpenter@cornerstone.edu
CARPENTER, Carolyn, A .. 573-629-3116.. 265 G
carolyn.carpenter@hlg.edu
CARPENTER, Christina ..... 847-543-2359.. 138 C
ccarpenter1@clcillinois.edu
CARPENTER, Courtney ..... 757-221-2001.. 488 F
cmcarp@wm.edu
CARPENTER, Dale .... 828-227-7311.. 359 A
carpenter@wcu.edu
CARPENTER, Dana .... 225-771-2394.. 199 H
dana_carpenter@subr.edu
CARPENTER, David .... 618-544-8657.. 142 D
carpenterd@iecc.edu
CARPENTER, Debra .... 281-283-2150.. 474 A
carpenter@uhcl.edu
CARPENTER, Dianna, M .. 816-604-2230.. 267 I
dianna.carpenter@mcckc.edu
CARPENTER, Jan .... 509-533-3535.. 503 A
jan.carpenter@sfcc.spokane.edu
CARPENTER, Jennifer ...... 509-527-2683.. 508 G
jennifer.carpenter@wallawalla.edu
CARPENTER, Jessica .... 607-735-1812.. 313 F
jcarpenter@elmira.edu

CARSON, Scott 601-426-6346 260 G scarson@southeasternbaptist.edu

CARSON, Staci 801-832-2750 483 D scarson@westminstercollege.edu

CARSON, Tamika 312-850-7070 138 A tdavenport13@ccc.edu

CARSTARPHEN, Minnie 334-876-9345 4 A mcarstarphen@wccs.edu

CARSTENS, Jeffrey 402-375-7213 281 J jecarst1@wsc.edu

CARSTENS, Lisa 503-352-2141 394 C carstens@pacificu.edu

CARSTENS, Ryan 509-533-7042 502 H ryan.carstens@scc.spokane.edu

CARSTENS, Ryan 509-533-7042 502 I ryan.carstens@scc.spokane.edu

CARSTENSEN, Lundie 619-201-8705 60 D lundie.carstensen@sdcc.edu

CARSWELL, Justin 417-690-3446 263 E carswell@cofo.edu

CARSWELL, Linda 828-448-3110 354 B lcarswell@wpcc.edu

CARSWELL, Pamela 386-752-1822 100 L pamela.carswell@fgc.edu

CARSWELL, Will 843-383-8063 428 F wcarswell@coker.edu

CART, J. Robert 973-655-7028 293 A cartr@mail.montclair.edu

CARTABUKE, Jacqueline 516-877-6004 303 B jcartabuke@adelphi.edu

CARTAGENA, Aramilda 787-857-3600 533 I acartagena@br.inter.edu

CARTAGENA, Carlos 520-515-5485 12 L cartagec@cochise.edu

CARTAGENA, Milagros 787-704-1020 532 H mcartagena@edicollege.edu

CARTAGENA, Moises 787-850-9390 538 B moises.cartagena@upr.edu

CARTE, Mandy 216-368-2595 365 B mmc111@case.edu

CARTER, Abby 229-227-3177 127 G acarter@southernregional.edu

CARTER, Alfonza 919-546-8527 355 F alcarter@shawu.edu

CARTER, Allison, A 906-487-2335 238 A allison@mtu.edu

CARTER, Amber 859-442-1712 189 D amber.carter@kctcs.edu

CARTER, Andy 701-858-3042 360 F andy.carter@minotstateu.edu

CARTER, Angela, M 336-334-4822 350 B amcarter@gtcc.edu

CARTER, Ashley 770-534-6164 118 A acarter@brenau.edu

CARTER, Bates 302-622-8000 90 E bcarter@dcad.edu

CARTER, Bessie 405-945-3211 386 C cartebm@osuokc.edu

CARTER, Beth 910-630-7425 346 E bcarter@methodist.edu

CARTER, Brenda, C 214-491-6271 455 A bcarter@collin.edu

CARTER, Brett 607-778-5003 332 D carterbd@sunybroome.edu

CARTER, Cameron, S 530-754-7764 69 A cscarter@ucdavis.edu

CARTER, Charlotte 205-366-8948 7 E ccarter@stillman.edu

CARTER, Christopher 425-235-2352 506 F ccarter@rtc.edu

CARTER, Cindy 641-585-8130 177 F carterc@waldorf.edu

CARTER, Cindy 559-453-3447 44 F cindy.carter@fresno.edu

CARTER, Clark 843-863-8008 427 I ccarter@csuniv.edu

CARTER, Clay 252-940-6357 347 E clay.carter@beaufortccc.edu

CARTER, Clinton, P 256-765-4233 9 C cpcarter@una.edu

CARTER, Cynthia 229-931-2057 127 C ccarter@southgatech.edu

CARTER, Danette 425-602-3083 501 D dcarter@bastyr.edu

CARTER, Danita 314-918-2625 265 A dcarter@eden.edu

CARTER, Darryl 716-878-6522 332 F carterdc@buffalostate.edu

CARTER, David 512-232-6400 476 B david.carter@austin.utexas.edu

CARTER, Derek, A 240-567-7587 209 E derek.carter@montgomerycollege.edu

CARTER, Dione 310-434-4858 63 F carter_dione@smc.edu

CARTER, Don 928-523-1605 15 H don.carter@nau.edu

CARTER, Ed 256-331-5277 6 A cartere@nwscc.edu

CARTER, Eloise 334-727-8953 8 A ecarter@mytu.tuskegee.edu

CARTER, Emily, J 240-895-3002 210 E ejcarter@smcm.edu

CARTER, Evonne 252-335-0821 349 A evonne_carter@albemarle.edu

CARTER, F. 'Thatcher' 509-527-5195 509 G carterft@whitman.edu

CARTER, Fantina 615-329-8586 439 L fcarter@fisk.edu

CARTER, Gary, L 731-661-5204 448 A gcarter@uu.edu

CARTER, Glenda, F 903-927-3336 479 K gcarter@wileyc.edu

CARTER, Glenn 603-577-6414 286 I gcarter@dwc.edu

CARTER, Helene 706-821-8323 125 H hcarter@paine.edu

CARTER, Holly 812-488-1040 167 I hc110@evansville.edu

CARTER, Hugh 334-222-6591 5 F hcarter@lbwcc.edu

CARTER, Jacque 402-826-8253 280 B jacque.carter@doane.edu

CARTER, JaPrince, L 804-342-3895 500 B jlcarter@vuu.edu

CARTER, Jeffrey, W 800-287-8822 159 C president@bethanyseminary.edu

CARTER, Jennifer, L 724-847-6603 404 B jlcarter@geneva.edu

CARTER, Jennings 618-545-3169 144 D jcarter@kaskaskia.edu

CARTER, Jessica 276-656-0312 498 A jcarter@patrickhenry.edu

CARTER, Joe 254-442-5106 454 E joe.carter@cisco.edu

CARTER, John, B 413-542-2771 214 C jbcarter@amherst.edu

CARTER, Joseph 610-647-4400 406 B jcarter@immaculata.edu

CARTER, Julien, C 617-627-3271 228 H julien.carter@tufts.edu

CARTER, June 864-503-5881 434 G jcarter@uscupstate.edu

CARTER, Kathleen 706-778-8500 125 J kcarter@piedmont.edu

CARTER, Kathryn 978-934-2741 221 A kathryn_cater@uml.edu

CARTER, Kim 712-325-3320 174 B kcarter@iwcc.edu

CARTER, Kim, C 859-257-9420 193 G kccarter.1@uky.edu

CARTER, Kim, C 215-895-1190 422 A k.carter@usciences.edu

CARTER, Kimberly 229-317-6247 120 A kimberly.carter@darton.edu

CARTER, Kimberly 229-317-6248 120 A

CARTER, Kimberly 229-430-4600 115 K kimberly.carter@asurams.edu

CARTER, Lana 719-296-6108 82 G lana.carter@pueblocc.edu

CARTER, LaRae 540-261-8575 494 F larae.carter@svu.edu

CARTER, Laurie 859-622-1842 188 F laurie.carter@eku.edu

CARTER, Lawrence, E 404-215-2608 124 I lawrence.carter@morehouse.edu

CARTER, Lawrence, L 517-321-0242 235 C lcarter@glcc.edu

CARTER, Linda 816-604-3081 267 J linda.carter@mcckc.edu

CARTER, Linda 606-539-4230 193 F linda.carter@ucumberlands.edu

CARTER, Linnie, S 717-780-2321 405 C lscarter@hacc.edu

CARTER, Luther, F 843-661-1210 430 B lcarter@fmarion.edu

CARTER, Martin 404-527-4520 118 F mcarter@carver.edu

CARTER, Matt 505-277-3003 302 F mdcarter@unm.edu

CARTER, Melanie 202-806-2550 93 A melcarter@howard.edu

CARTER, Michael 270-789-5001 187 G mvcarter@campbellsville.edu

CARTER, Michael 661-255-1050 30 E mcarter@calarts.edu

CARTER, Michele 254-526-1331 454 A michele.carter@ctcd.edu

CARTER, Mike 714-879-3901 46 F mcarter@hiu.edu

CARTER, Mike 918-495-7150 386 H mcarter@oru.edu

CARTER, Nick 510-841-1905 26 C ncarter@absw.edu

CARTER, Ninette 580-581-2226 382 G ncarter@cameron.edu

CARTER, Pam 215-751-8737 401 G pcarter@ccp.edu

CARTER, Phillip 615-547-1307 439 H pcarter@cumberland.edu

CARTER, Phyllis 510-464-3232 57 D pcarter@peralta.edu

CARTER, Prudence 510-643-6644 68 M pcarter@berkeley.edu

CARTER, R. Daphne 843-661-1188 430 B rcarter@fmarion.edu

CARTER, Regina, W 501-569-3408 23 B rswade@ualr.edu

CARTER, Richard 309-298-2501 158 A r-carter@wiu.edu

CARTER, Richard 309-298-1929 158 A r-carter@wiu.edu

CARTER, JR., Rodney 717-560-8206 407 E rcarter@lbc.edu

CARTER, Ronald, L 909-558-7616 49 C rcarter@llu.edu

CARTER, Ronald, L 704-378-1006 345 E rcarter@jcsu.edu

CARTER, Sarah 801-649-5230 480 K clinicaldean@midwifery.edu

CARTER, Saundra 202-274-6430 94 B scarter@udc.edu

CARTER, Scott 620-278-4290 185 A scarter@sterling.edu

CARTER, Seth, M 785-460-5400 180 C seth.carter@colbycc.edu

CARTER, Sharon, L 714-879-3901 46 F slcarter@hiu.edu

CARTER, Shawna, M 608-246-6249 523 F smcarter@madisoncollege.edu

CARTER, Sheila 312-369-7994 138 F scarter@colum.edu

CARTER, Shree 714-556-3610 73 B vutrustees@vanguard.edu

CARTER, Shree 714-556-3610 73 B scarter@vanguard.edu

CARTER, Sonja 212-875-4603 304 E scarter@bankstreet.edu

CARTER, Spencer, D 269-471-3395 230 H scarter@andrews.edu

CARTER, Steven, J 215-887-5511 423 C scarter@wts.edu

CARTER, Tara 434-736-2005 498 E tara.carter@southside.edu

CARTER, Tay Sha 479-619-4396 21 D tcarter@nwacc.edu

CARTER, Thomas, E 315-470-6691 334 E tecarter@esf.edu

CARTER, Tiffany 773-291-6315 137 G tcarter63@ccc.edu

CARTER, Todd 620-417-1012 184 I todd.carter@sccc.edu

CARTER, Todd 316-322-3201 179 E tcarter@butlercc.edu

CARTER, Tom 256-331-5263 6 A tom.carter@nwscc.edu

CARTER, JR., Walter, E 410-293-1000 529 D

CARTER, William 320-762-4464 248 J billc@alextech.edu

CARTER, William, E 713-718-8708 459 B william.carter@hccs.edu

CARTER, William, M 412-648-1401 421 G wmc4@pitt.edu

CARTER, Zina 979-532-6417 479 J zinac@wcjc.edu

CARTER-CHAPMAN, Renee, M 907-786-6486 10 F rmcarterchapman@uaa.alaska.edu

CARTER-COLEY, Stacey 252-492-2061 353 H cartercoley@vgcc.edu

CARTER-DOVE, Bernadette 919-209-2025 350 G bjcarterdove@johnstoncc.edu

CARTER-HARBOUR, Courtney 972-860-7335 456 D courtneycarter@dcccd.edu

CARTER-PRIEST, Carol 870-733-6740 19 A clcarter-priest@asumidsouth.edu

CARTER-STEVENS, Marilyn 718-862-7958 319 L marilyn.carter@manhattan.edu

CARTER-TELLISON, Katrina 561-237-7210 104 O kcarter-tellison@lynn.edu

CARTHELL, Sidney, G 270-809-6836 192 A scarthell@murraystate.edu

CARTIER, Jennifer 207-509-7282 204 F jcartier@unity.edu

CARTIER, Jolie, L 619-239-0391 36 A jcartier@cwsl.edu

CARTIER, Missy, M 559-323-2100 61 E mcartier@sjcl.edu

CARTLEDGE, Ernest 240-567-7991 209 E ernest.cartledge@montgomerycollege.edu

CARTLEDGE, Maureen 210-486-2174 450 E mcartledge@alamo.edu

CARTMELL, Brandy 931-372-3888 445 B bcartmell@tntech.edu

CARTMILL, Mark 859-985-3922 187 B cartmillm@berea.edu

CARTNAL, Ryan 805-546-3946 41 L rcartnal@cuesta.edu

CARTNEY, Michael, D 605-882-5284 436 B cartneym@lakeareatech.edu

CARTOLANO, Joseph 718-631-6231 309 E jcartolano@qcc.cuny.edu

CARTWRIGHT, Alexander 518-320-1314 330 H alexander.cartwright@suny.edu

CARTWRIGHT, Bill 415-422-5417 72 C jcartwri@usfca.edu

CARTWRIGHT, Cynthia 716-664-5100 317 E

CARTWRIGHT, Kevin 949-376-6000 48 C kcartwright@lcad.edu

CARTWRIGHT, Michael, G 317-788-3233 168 A mcartwright@uindy.edu

CARTWRIGHT, Rick, E 260-399-7700 168 D rcartwright@sf.edu

CARTY, Cheryl 478-471-5235 124 E cheryl.carty@mga.edu

CARTY, Karenann 718-933-6700 321 I kcarty@monroecollege.edu

CARTY, Raymond, W 573-629-3094 265 G rcarty@hlg.edu

CARULLO, Susan, H 843-792-2071 431 A carullos@musc.edu

CARUOLO, Michael 401-341-2334 426 C michael.caruolo@salve.edu

CARUSO, Anne-Marie 617-989-4174 229 D carusoa@wit.edu

CARUSO, Britni 217-544-6464 153 G britni.caruso@stjohnscollegespringfield.edu

CARUSO, Elizabeth, S 585-395-2414 332 E lcaruso@brockport.edu

CARUSO, Janet 516-572-7599 322 C janet.caruso@ncc.edu

CARUSO, Michael 401-739-5000 425 C mcaruso@neit.edu

CARUSO, Michael 903-510-2420 473 C mcar@tjc.edu

CARUSO, Michele, E 985-448-4081 201 A michele.caruso@nicholls.edu

CARUTHERS, Janet 573-875-7372 263 F jaocaruthers@ccis.edu

CARVAJAL, Augusto 787-780-0070 531 B acarvajal@caribbean.edu

CARVAJAL, Richard 229-317-6705 120 A

CARVALLOZA, Anthony 212-327-7161 327 F anthony.carvalloza@rockefeller.edu

CARVAN, Moreen, K 920-923-8583 517 H mkcarvan31@marianuniversity.edu

CARVER, Andrew 618-453-7661 154 I acarver@siu.edu

CARVER, Billy 828-898-3542 345 G carverb@lmc.edu

CARVER, JR., Curtis, A 205-975-0250 8 E carverc@uab.edu

CARVER, David, S 402-559-7276 283 A dcarver@unmc.edu

CARVER, Doris, W 336-322-2111 351 H doris.carver@piedmontcc.edu

CARVER, Eric 727-341-3664 108 D carver.eric@spcollege.edu

CARVER, Jerelene 919-546-8525 355 F jcarver@shawu.edu

CARVER, Keith 865-974-0782 448 D carverk@tennessee.edu

CARVER, Leslie 858-534-4004 70 C tmcprovost@ucsd.edu

CARVER, Matthew 785-227-3380 178 J carverm@bethanylb.edu

CARVER, Matthew, J 716-880-2288 320 D matthew.j.carver@medaille.edu

CARVER, Nicole 620-241-0723 179 L nichole.carver@centralchristian.edu

CARVER, Petra 207-326-2241 204 C petra.carver@mma.edu

CARVER, Philip, J 617-287-5310 220 G philip.carver@umb.edu

CARVER, II, William, S 252-451-8328 351 F bcarver@nashcc.edu

CARWEIN, Vicky, L 260-481-6103 163 C chancellor@ipfw.edu

CARY, Ann 816-235-1700 273 F caryah@umkc.edu

CARY, Charles 570-408-4553 423 G charles.cary@wilkes.edu

CARY, Kim 407-447-6933 270 A caryk@otc.edu

CARY, Kurt 719-587-7727 76 G kurt_cary@adams.edu

CARY, Stacey 309-796-5225 135 I carys@bhc.edu

CARY, Wendy, M 315-697-8200 338 L wcary@uscny.edu

CASADA, Tracy, L 606-679-8501 190 E tracy.casada@kctcs.edu

CASAINE, Wil 609-771-2602 290 F casainew@tcnj.edu

CASALE, Amanda 301-447-5271 209 G casale@msmary.edu

CASTILLO, Evelyn .... 787-284-1912.. 534 C
ecastillo@ponce.inter.edu
CASTILLO, Henry .... 718-862-7249.. 319 L
bookstore@manhattan.edu
CASTILLO, Jay .... 510-436-1648.... 46 E
jcastillo@hnu.edu
CASTILLO, JR., Juan, J ... 956-326-2380.. 468 A
jjcastillo@tamiu.edu
CASTILLO, Keith .... 951-552-8720.... 29 H
kcastillo@calbaptist.edu
CASTILLO, Lida .... 626-873-2139.... 53 E
lcastillo@mtsierra.edu
CASTILLO, Maggie .... 623-935-8839.... 14 A
maggie.castillo@estrellamountain.edu
CASTILLO, Mario .... 512-492-3005.. 451 E
mcastillo@aoma.edu
CASTILLO, Mario .... 832-813-6508.. 461 B
mario.k.castillo@lonestar.edu
CASTILLO, Marvin .... 619-482-6330.... 66 E
mcastillo@swccd.edu
CASTILLO, Nicole .... 209-946-2496.... 71 C
ncastillo@pacific.edu
CASTILLO, Pio .... 818-364-7866.... 49 J
castilpg@lamission.edu
CASTILLO, Raul, V .... 818-947-2618.... 50 D
castilrv@lavc.edu
CASTILLO, Rosalinda .... 773-442-5300.. 149 J
r-castillo2@neiu.edu
CASTILLO, Salvador .... 541-737-8083.. 393 H
salvador.castillo@oregonstate.edu
CASTILLO, Santiago .... 432-837-8885.. 471 E
santiago.castillo@sulross.edu
CASTILLO, Saundra .... 575-527-7076.. 301 C
scastillo@nmsu.edu
CASTILLO, Sharrese .... 808-983-4146.. 130 I
scastillo@tokai.edu
CASTILLO, Victor .... 773-838-7795.. 137 H
vcastillo@ccc.edu
CASTILLO-ALANIZ,
Jo Elda .... 361-593-3991.. 469 A
jo.alaniz@tamuk.edu
CASTILLO CLARK, Evette . 925-631-4238.... 59 I
ecc4@stmarys-ca.edu
CASTILLO-FRICK, Iliana .... 305-237-0294.. 105 D
ifrick@mdc.edu
CASTILLO-GARRISON,
Estella .... 949-582-4646.... 65 G
egarrison@saddleback.edu
CASTILLON, Nicole .... 307-382-1642.. 527 C
ncastillon@westernwyoming.edu
CASTLE, Ashley .... 757-493-6000.... 93 F
CASTLE, Ashley .... 757-382-9900.... 93 F
CASTLE, Carey .... 218-793-8612.. 251 C
carey.castle@northlandcollege.edu
CASTLE, Carey .... 218-683-8612.. 251 C
carey.castle@northlandcollege.edu
CASTLE, Clinton .... 218-683-8600.. 251 C
clinton.castle@northlandcollege.edu
CASTLE, Josh .... 802-322-1672.. 483 H
josh.castle@goddard.edu
CASTLE, Lyle .... 208-282-3218.. 133 H
castlyle@isu.edu
CASTLE, Lyle, W .... 208-282-7852.. 133 H
castlyle@isu.edu
CASTLE, Ruthie .... 662-562-3213.. 260 C
rcastle@northwestms.edu
CASTLE, Tom .... 319-363-1323.. 175 D
tcastle@mtmercy.edu
CASTLEBERRY, Annettee .. 870-307-7227.... 21 A
annette.castleberry@lyon.edu
CASTLEBERRY, Joseph .... 425-889-4202.. 505 E
joseph.castleberry@northwestu.edu
CASTLEBERRY, Rita, J ..... 580-327-8540.. 384 M
rjcastleberry@nwosu.edu
CASTLEBURY, Lisa .... 812-357-6515.. 167 B
lcastlebury@saintmeinrad.edu
CASTLEMAN, Janet, L ...... 401-865-2816.. 425 D
jcastlem@providence.edu
CASTLEMAN, Louanna ...... 910-678-0141.. 349 F
castleml@faytechcc.edu
CASTO, Benjamin, P .... 240-895-2055.. 210 E
bjcasto@smcm.edu
CASTON, Gay Lynn .... 601-857-3396.. 258 A
glcaston@hindscc.edu
CASTONGUAY, Sharon ...... 860-685-3377.... 90 C
scastonguay@wesleyan.edu
CASTONGUAY, Suzette .... 937-769-1375.. 363 E
scastonguay@antioch.edu
CASTONGUAY, Suzette .... 937-769-1375.. 363 F
scastonguay@antioch.edu
CASTOR, Tammy .... 661-362-3516.... 40 A
tammy.castor@canyons.edu
CASTORENA, Christina .... 425-640-1668.. 503 E
christina.castorena@edcc.edu
CASTRIOTA, Nadia .... 518-445-2361.. 303 D
ncast@albanylaw.edu
CASTRO, Adam .... 973-748-9000.. 289 H
adam_castro@bloomfield.edu
CASTRO, Bernie .... 856-691-8600.. 290 I
bcastro@cccnj.edu
CASTRO, Cynthia .... 208-885-6307.. 134 G
cynthiacastro@uidaho.edu
CASTRO, Daisy .... 787-753-6335.. 532 O
dcastro@icprjc.edu
CASTRO, Evelyn .... 718-270-6046.. 309 B
ecastro@mec.cuny.edu
CASTRO, Francia, L .... 212-694-1000.. 305 I
fcastro@boricuacollege.edu
CASTRO, Ida, L .... 570-504-9647.. 400 I
icastro@tcmc.edu
CASTRO, Jill .... 248-476-1122.. 237 H
jcastro@mispp.edu
CASTRO, Joseph, I .... 559-278-2324.... 32 F
josephcastro@csufresno.edu
CASTRO, Juan, C .... 787-743-3038.. 535 L
jcastro@sanjuanbautista.edu
CASTRO, Kaye .... 239-687-5343.... 95 P
kcastro@avemarialaw.edu
CASTRO, Lorna .... 787-764-0000.. 538 F
lorna.castro@upr.edu
CASTRO, Louise, P .... 915-747-8820.. 476 D
lpcastro@utep.edu
CASTRO, Madelyn .... 813-253-6201.. 114 M
macastro@ut.edu
CASTRO, Melba .... 657-278-5579.... 33 A
melbacastro@fullerton.edu
CASTRO, Octavio .... 414-288-5629.. 517 I
octavio.castro@marquette.edu
CASTRO, Raul .... 787-738-2161.. 538 A
raul.castro@upr.edu
CASTRO, Rodrigo .... 305-899-4062.... 96 D
rcastro@barry.edu
CASTRO, Roz .... 630-953-3681.. 136 H
rcastro@chamberlain.edu
CASTRO, Sarah .... 202-624-1426.. 508 E
smcastro@uw.edu
CASTRO, Toni .... 206-592-3351.. 504 E
tcastro@highline.edu
CASTRO ARROYO,
María de los, A .... 787-763-7099.. 538 F
ma.castro@upr.edu
CASTRO-QUIRINO,
Sonya .... 806-743-3949.. 472 D
sonya.castro@ttuhsc.edu
CASTRO-ROMAKER,
Judith .... 608-246-6678.. 523 F
jcastro-romaker@madisoncollege.edu
CASTROVERDE MOSKOLENKO,
Tania .... 312-431-2391.. 152 H
CASTRUITA, Javier .... 408-741-2042.... 74 F
javier_castruita@wvm.edu
CASWELL, Roger .... 620-341-5372.. 180 G
rcaswekk@emporia.edu
CATALANA, Paul .... 864-455-3510.. 434 D
pcatalana@ghs.org
CATALANO, John .... 864-424-8019.. 434 F
jcat@mailbox.sc.edu
CATALANO, Megan .... 573-288-6570.. 264 F
mcatalano@culver.edu
CATALANO, Mike .... 605-995-2669.. 435 F
micatala@dwu.edu
CATALANO, Steven .... 718-489-5309.. 328 D
scatalano@sfc.edu
CATALDI, Amy, E .... 405-208-5446.. 385 E
acataldi@okcu.edu
CATALDI, Jennifer .... 317-738-8256.. 160 J
jcataldi@franklincollege.edu
CATALFAMO, Kevin .... 856-351-2701.. 296 L
kcatalfamo@salemcc.edu
CATALLOZZI, Lori, A .... 617-228-2048.. 223 B
lacatallozzi@bhcc.mass.edu
CATALON, Linda, H .... 225-771-2520.. 199 G
linda_catalon@sus.edu
CATANZARO, Sam .... 309-438-7018.. 143 B
catanzar@ilstu.edu
CATAUDELLA, Vincent, B 203-576-5616.... 89 A
vincent.cataudella@stvincentscollege.edu
CATCHINGS, Robert .... 202-806-6700.... 93 A
rcatchings@howard.edu
CATE, Fred .... 812-855-1161.. 162 E
fcate@iu.edu
CATE, Fred, H .... 812-856-2096.. 162 F
vpr@iu.edu
CATE, Richard, H .... 802-656-0219.. 485 D
richard.cate@uvm.edu
CATELLA, Rosanne .... 440-934-3101.. 374 F
rcatella@ohiobusinesscollege.edu
CATER, Lisa .... 870-460-1420.... 23 D
caterl@uamont.edu
CATES, Brenda, B .... 919-658-7853.. 355 K
bcates@umo.edu
CATES, Damon .... 773-702-2151.. 156 D
dcates@uchicago.edu
CATES, Jared .... 417-255-7233.. 269 A
jaredcated@missouristate.edu
CATES, John .... 256-824-6633...... 8 F
john.cates@uah.edu
CATH, Tom .... 219-464-5005.. 168 F
tom.cath@valpo.edu
CATHCART, Scott .... 760-744-1150.... 56 F
scathcart@palomar.edu
CATHELINE, Jim .... 724-964-8811.. 411 F
jcatheline@ncstrades.edu
CATHER, Michael .... 410-704-4679.. 213 B
mcather@towson.edu
CATHERMAN, David .... 504-398-2279.. 200 D
dcatherman@olhcc.edu
CATHERWOOD, Ryan .... 434-395-4804.. 491 E
catherwoodrp@longwood.edu
CATHEY, Patrice, A .... 716-878-4055.. 332 F
catheypc@mail.buffalostate.edu
CATHEY, Ron .... 318-257-4336.. 200 G
rcathey@latech.edu
CATHIE, Julie .... 530-541-4660.... 48 D
cathie@ltcc.edu
CATLETT, Deborrah, L ...... 859-246-6810.. 189 B
deborrah.catlett@kctcs.edu
CATLETT, Hilary .... 509-257-2542.. 508 G
hilary.catlett@wallawalla.edu
CATLETT, Jennifer .... 865-471-3530.. 439 C
jcatlett@cn.edu
CATO, Amie .... 903-785-7661.. 463 E
acato@parisjc.edu
CATO, Michael .... 845-437-7605.. 339 C
micato@vassar.edu
CATON, Bonnie .... 410-857-2259.. 209 D
bcaton@mcdaniel.edu
CATON, Brock, E .... 207-778-7033.. 205 A
brock.caton@maine.edu
CATON, Lisa .... 979-627-0286.. 452 J
lisa.caton@blinn.edu
CATON, Rebecca, A .... 630-515-6190.. 148 C
rcaton@midwestern.edu
CATON, Rhonda .... 479-788-7073.... 23 A
rhonda.caton@uafs.edu
CATON, Sheron .... 325-794-4530.. 454 E
sheron.caton@cisco.edu
CATOTA, Claudia .... 661-654-2137.... 32 A
ccatota@csub.edu
CATRON, Greg .... 904-620-2903.. 112 B
greg.catron@unf.edu
CATRON, Jonathan .... 864-644-5662.. 432 G
jcatron@swu.edu
CATRON-WOOD,
Rhonda, K .... 276-223-4772.. 499 C
rcatronwood@wcc.vccs.edu
CATT, Helen .... 229-430-3506.. 116 A
hcatt@albanytech.edu
CATT, Stephen, R .... 724-287-8711.. 399 B
stephen.catt@bc3.edu
CATTANACH, John, R .... 315-516-4100.. 274 A
cattanachj@umsl.edu
CATTANI, Jessica .... 213-624-1200.... 43 J
jcattani@fidm.edu
CATTON, Heather .... 936-468-5597.. 466 H
hcatton@sfasu.edu
CATTOOR, Chad, A .... 314-505-7304.. 263 I
cattoorc@csl.edu
CAUCE, Ana Mari .... 206-543-5010.. 508 E
provost@uw.edu
CAUDA, Lisa .... 585-475-7721.. 327 E
lisa.cauda@rit.edu
CAUDILL, Helene .... 209-667-3407.... 34 E
hcaudill@csustan.edu
CAUDILL, Reggie, J .... 973-596-3019.. 293 D
reggie.j.caudill@njit.edu
CAUDILL, Whitney .... 260-982-2658.. 165 M
wjcaudill@manchester.edu
CAUDLE, Mary Anne .... 252-789-0280.. 351 A
mcaudle@martincc.edu
CAUDLE, Patricia, M .... 909-748-8171.... 71 K
pat_caudle@redlands.edu
CAUGHEY, Martha .... 850-484-1604.. 106 H
mcaughey@pensacolastate.edu
CAUGHMAN, Gretchen .... 706-721-4014.. 117 D
gcaughma@augusta.edu
CAULDRON, Naphtali .... 787-753-6000.. 532 O
mcauldron@icprjc.edu
CAULEY, Phil .... 828-227-2923.. 359 A
cauley@wcu.edu
CAULEY, Thomas .... 215-368-5000.. 398 C
tcauley@biblical.edu
CAULFIELD, Jack .... 508-213-2398.. 227 A
jack.caulfield@nichols.edu
CAULFIELD, Richard .... 907-796-6565.... 10 H
racaulfield@alaska.edu
CAULFIELD, Thomas, M .. 217-351-2477.. 151 B
tcaulfield@parkland.edu
CAULK, Jeffrey .... 206-934-6020.. 506 J
jeffrey.caulk@seattlecolleges.edu
CAULKINS, Amy .... 309-341-5290.. 136 C
acaulkins@sandburg.edu
CAUPP, Jeffrey, G .... 480-245-7979.... 13 L
jeff.caupp@ibcs.edu
CAUSBY, Cory .... 828-227-7218.. 359 A
causby@wcu.edu
CAUSEY, Bruce .... 256-306-2569...... 2 F
bruce.causey@calhoun.edu
CAUSEY, Jana .... 601-554-5506.. 260 D
jcausey@prcc.edu
CAUSEY, Jeffrey .... 336-517-2116.. 342 B
jcausey@bennett.edu
CAUSEY, Joy .... 229-317-6886.. 120 A
joy.causey@darton.edu
CAUSEY, Katherine .... 901-435-1259.. 441 C
katherine_causey@loc.edu
CAUSEY, Mary Frances .... 928-350-1112.... 16 P
mcausey@prescott.edu
CAUSLAND, Luann .... 678-407-5000.. 121 B
lcausland@ggc.edu
CAUTIN, Robin .... 203-396-8020.... 88 I
cautinr@sacredheart.edu
CAUWELS, Beth .... 805-565-6101.... 75 A
bcauwels@westmont.edu
CAVACO, Frank .... 617-964-1100.. 214 D
fcavaco@ants.edu
CAVALIER, Amy .... 617-873-0106.. 217 A
amy.cavalier30@go.cambridgecollege.edu
CAVALIER, Donald, R ...... 218-281-8585.. 255 E
cavalier@umn.edu
CAVALIER, Philip .... 870-307-7202.... 21 A
philip.cavalier@lyon.edu
CAVALIER, Wayne .... 210-341-1366.. 463 A
wcavalier@ost.edu
CAVALIERI, Correne .... 718-779-1499.. 326 D
ccavalieri@plazacollege.edu
CAVALIERI, Cristina, G .... 215-503-9496.. 420 E
cristina.cavalieri@jefferson.edu
CAVALIERI, Thomas .... 856-566-6995.. 295 E
cavalita@rowan.edu
CAVALLARO, Claire .... 657-278-4021.... 33 A
ccavallaro@fullerton.edu
CAVALLARO, Gregory, M 540-464-7328.. 499 E
gcav@vmiaa.org
CAVALLARO, Vito .... 212-938-5500.. 334 F
vito@sunyopt.edu
CAVALLO, Julia .... 724-805-2372.. 419 A
julia.cavallo@email.stvincent.edu
CAVALLUZZI, Marty .... 253-840-8421.. 506 B
mcavalluzzi@pierce.ctc.edu
CAVALOVITCH, Renee, T . 412-397-5262.. 418 B
cavalovitch@rmu.edu
CAVANAGH, Debbie .... 310-338-4493.... 51 E
debbie.cavanagh@lmu.edu
CAVANAGH, Jon .... 765-998-4161.. 167 C
jon.cavanagh@taylor.edu
CAVANAGH, Kevin .... 914-654-5085.. 311 A
kcavanagh@cnr.edu
CAVANAGH, Stephen .... 413-545-5093.. 220 F
dean@nursing.umass.edu
CAVANAUGH, Amy .... 503-943-7201.. 396 B
cavanaug@up.edu
CAVANAUGH, Brian .... 716-829-7878.. 313 A
cavanaub@dyc.edu
CAVANAUGH, SSJ,
Cecelia .... 215-753-3623.. 400 H
ccavanau@chc.edu
CAVANAUGH, Kyle .... 919-684-2826.. 343 J
kyle.cavanaugh@duke.edu
CAVANAUGH, Lance .... 920-465-2018.. 520 B
cavanaul@uwgb.edu
CAVANAUGH, Mary .... 212-396-7549.. 308 D
mary.cavanaugh@hunter.cuny.edu
CAVANAUGH, Mike .... 585-582-8201.. 313 B
michaelcavanaugh@elim.edu
CAVANESS, Kerrie .... 509-574-4870.. 510 A
kcavaness@yvcc.edu
CAVANUAGH, Rachel .... 910-362-7317.. 348 A
rcavenaugh@cfcc.edu
CAVAZOS, Gregoria, A .... 505-922-2886.. 299 K
gregoria.cavazos@eccu.edu
CAVAZOS, Rebecca .... 956-664-4680.. 465 H
beckyc@southtexascollege.edu
CAVENAUGH, Andy .... 910-296-2480.. 350 F
acavenaugh@jamessprunt.edu
CAVENAUGH, Jennifer ...... 407-691-1268.. 107 O
jcavenaugh@rollins.edu
CAVENER, Douglas, R ...... 814-865-9591.. 412 F
drc9@psu.edu
CAVENY-NOECKER,
Deanna, M .... 843-953-5731.. 428 G
cavenyd@cofc.edu
CAVERLEY, Darla .... 320-629-5118.. 251 E
calverleyd@pine.edu
CAVI, Sandra .... 309-438-8489.. 143 B
skcavi@ilstu.edu
CAVICCHI, Daniel .... 401-454-6580.. 426 A
dcavicch@risd.edu
CAVIN, JR., Elmo, M .... 806-743-3080.. 472 D
elmo.cavin@ttuhsc.edu
CAVIN, Glynn .... 334-670-3617...... 7 H
gcavin@troy.edu
CAVIN, Wesley .... 318-255-7950.. 200 G
wes@latechalumni.org
CAVINESS, Debbie, J .... 315-470-6632.. 334 E
dcavines@esf.edu
CAVINESS, Howard .... 318-274-6437.. 200 F
cavinessh@gram.edu
CAVINS-TULL, Kathryn ..... 817-257-7820.. 469 G
k.cavins@tcu.edu
CAVIS, Mark .... 906-487-7315.. 234 A
mark.cavis@finlandia.edu

CHAMPION, Jason .... 918-293-5342.. 386 B
jason.champion@okstate.edu
CHAMPION, John, E .... 336-841-9196.. 345 A
jchampion@highpoint.edu
CHAMPION, Laura .... 616-526-6678.. 232 A
ldc4@calvin.edu
CHAMPION, Thomas .... 510-593-2923.... 63 H
tchampion@saybrook.edu
CHAMPION, Willie .... 903-593-8311.. 470 A
wchampion@texascollege.edu
CHAMPLIN, Sheila .... 843-792-2691.. 431 A
champlin@musc.edu
CHAMPOLI, John .... 207-941-7175.. 202 I
campolij@husson.edu
CHAMRA, Louay, M .... 248-370-2217.. 239 K
chamra@oakland.edu
CHAMSAZ, Amir .... 410-706-3802.. 211 F
achamsaz@umaryland.edu
CHAN, Andy .... 336-758-4662.. 359 E
achan@wfu.edu
CHAN, Bill .... 614-947-6054.. 369 A
bill.chan@franklin.edu
CHAN, Caleb, K .... 517-750-1200.. 241 E
cchan@arbor.edu
CHAN, Chuen .... 510-464-3221.... 57 D
cchan@peralta.edu
CHAN, Claudia .... 718-482-5005.. 309 A
clchan@lagcc.cuny.edu
CHAN, Emily .... 719-389-6679.... 77 J
echan@coloradocollege.edu
CHAN, Eva .... 718-270-6487.. 309 B
echan@mec.cuny.edu
CHAN, Gilen .... 718-260-4981.. 309 C
gchan@citytech.cuny.edu
CHAN, Joe .... 312-281-3279.. 152 H
jchan@roosevelt.edu
CHAN, Kara .... 412-521-6200.. 418 C
kara.chan@rosedaletech.org
CHAN, Larry .... 937-775-2475.. 381 H
larry.chan@wright.edu
CHAN, Michael, L .... 671-735-5573.. 529 G
michael.chan@guamcc.edu
CHAN, Paul, H .... 303-871-4646.... 84 B
phchan@du.edu
CHAN, Regina .... 212-517-0501.. 320 C
rchan@mmm.edu
CHANCE, Bill .... 207-221-4373.. 205 F
wchance@une.edu
CHANCE, Carla .... 513-569-4755.. 366 D
carla.chance@cincinnatistate.edu
CHANCE, Chelsea .... 318-797-5364.. 198 C
chelsea.chance@lsus.edu
CHANCE, Dayne .... 908-709-7089.. 298 A
chance@ucc.edu
CHANCE, Katie .... 256-551-5214...... 4 F
katie.chance@drakestate.edu
CHANCE, Kenneth, B .... 216-368-3266.. 365 B
kenneth.b.chance@case.edu
CHANCE, Steve, L .... 806-371-5161.. 450 H
slchance@actx.edu
CHANCEY, Danny .... 251-442-2491...... 9 A
dbchancey@umobile.edu
CHANCEY, Debra, H .... 251-689-8951...... 9 A
dchancey@umobile.edu
CHANCEY, Janna, L .... 903-510-2298.. 473 C
jcha@tjc.edu
CHANDI, Balbir .... 661-362-5416.... 40 A
balbir.chandi@canyons.edu
CHANDLER, Andrew .... 408-741-2074.... 74 H
andrew.chandler@westvalley.edu
CHANDLER, Brandon .... 856-225-6473.. 296 A
brandonc@rutgers.edu
CHANDLER, Chris .... 540-365-4287.. 489 M
cchandler@ferrum.edu
CHANDLER, Cullen, J .... 570-321-4173.. 409 F
chandler@lycoming.edu
CHANDLER, Derrall .... 619-388-3537.... 60 F
dchandle@sdccd.edu
CHANDLER, G. Thomas ... 803-777-5032.. 433 F
tchandler@sc.edu
CHANDLER, Jacob .... 936-294-3160.. 471 D
ucs_jrc@shsu.edu
CHANDLER, John, M .... 319-399-8622.. 170 G
jchandle@coe.edu
CHANDLER, Kim .... 651-696-6366.. 247 I
kchandle@macalester.edu
CHANDLER, Kimberly, K . 972-860-8388.. 456 D
kimchandler@dcccd.edu
CHANDLER, Kirk .... 336-334-4822.. 350 B
kdchandler@gtcc.edu
CHANDLER, Legail, P ...... 314-362-4930.. 274 N
legail_chandler@wustl.edu
CHANDLER, Linda .... 910-695-3961.. 353 A
chandlerl@sandhills.edu
CHANDLER, Margaret ...... 843-355-4133.. 435 A
chandlerm@wiltech.edu
CHANDLER, Maria .... 803-641-3317.. 433 G
mariac@usca.edu
CHANDLER, Marissa .... 931-221-6424.. 444 E
chandlerm@apsu.edu
CHANDLER, Mary .... 315-445-4300.. 318 E
richermm@lemoyne.edu
CHANDLER, Norma .... 602-787-7073.... 14 E
norma.chandler@paradisevalley.edu
CHANDLER, Rebecca .... 310-338-2723.... 51 E
rchandler@lmu.edu
CHANDLER, Roger .... 251-575-8223...... 1 C
rchandler@ascc.edu
CHANDLER, Roger .... 303-963-3341.... 77 I
rchandler@ccu.edu
CHANDLER, Sabrina, J .... 914-606-6880.. 340 C
sabrina.johnson.chandler@sunywcc.edu
CHANDLER, Shelly .... 352-638-9710.... 96 F
schandler@beaconcollege.edu
CHANDLER, Tess .... 650-949-6149.... 44 A
chandlertess@fhda.edu
CHANDLER, Timothy .... 410-704-2131.. 213 B
tchandler@towson.edu
CHANDO, Kristen .... 610-499-4142.. 423 E
kmchando@widener.edu
CHANDO, Michael .... 856-415-2282.. 295 D
mchando@rcgc.edu
CHANEY, Bill .... 425-739-8119.. 504 F
bill.chaney@lwtech.edu
CHANEY, C. Steven .... 916-348-4689.... 43 A
stevec@chaneyassociates.com
CHANEY, Carmela .... 323-856-7698.... 26 I
cchaney@afi.com
CHANEY, Jayn .... 641-269-3200.. 172 I
chaneyj@grinnell.edu
CHANEY, Joyce .... 304-766-5224.. 514 B
jchaney@wvstateu.edu
CHANEY, Kelly, A .... 920-923-7177.. 517 H
kachaney01@marianuniversity.edu
CHANEY, Kevin .... 740-392-6868.. 373 D
kevin.chaney@mvnu.edu
CHANEY, Laura .... 415-422-2710.... 72 C
lchaney@usfca.edu
CHANEY, Marietta .... 304-647-6400.. 514 A
mchaney@osteo.wvsom.edu
CHANEY, Matthew .... 231-591-2617.. 233 L
matthewchaney@ferris.edu
CHANEY, Rob .... 850-201-6085.. 113 E
chaneyr@tcc.fl.edu
CHANEY, Steve .... 916-367-4786.... 60 D
steve.chaney@sdcc.edu
CHANEY, Susan .... 505-438-8884.. 302 B
susan@acupuncturecollege.edu
CHANG, Caroline .... 408-554-5360.... 63 E
cschang@scu.edu
CHANG, Chaw-ye .... 610-436-3043.. 416 C
cchang@wcupa.edu
CHANG, Christopher .... 845-687-5096.. 338 F
changc@sunyulster.edu
CHANG, Cindy .... 818-719-6425.... 50 A
changck@piercecollege.edu
CHANG, Diane, E .... 808-956-0391.. 131 D
dianec@hawaii.edu
CHANG, Eun-Woo .... 419-289-5051.. 363 J
echang@ashland.edu
CHANG, Frank .... 213-740-4623.... 72 D
fjc@usc.edu
CHANG, George .... 908-737-3600.. 292 C
gchang@kean.edu
CHANG, Gilbert .... 239-513-1135.. 115 F
gchang@wolford.edu
CHANG, Jerry .... 808-932-7339.. 131 E
jerry7@hawaii.edu
CHANG, Jimmy .... 727-341-4305.. 108 D
chang.jimmy@spcollege.edu
CHANG, Judy .... 847-679-3135.. 144 G
judy@ksi.edu
CHANG, Julian .... 520-795-0787.... 11 G
academicdean@asaom.edu
CHANG, Kai .... 425-602-3181.. 501 D
kchang@bastyr.edu
CHANG, Lillian .... 808-373-2849.. 132 G
dr.chang@wmi.edu
CHANG, Ling Ling .... 516-739-1545.. 323 D
library@nyctcm.edu
CHANG, Lvshao .... 408-433-2280.... 38 B
CHANG, Ly .... 425-235-2352.. 506 F
lchang@rtc.edu
CHANG, Mari .... 808-934-2526.. 131 J
changm@hawaii.edu
CHANG, Nancy, H .... 817-515-5222.. 467 A
nancy.chang@tccd.edu
CHANG, Peter, M .... 703-333-5904.. 500 G
mchang@wuv.edu
CHANG, Sheng-Chung ...... 626-571-5110.... 49 B
shengchung@les.edu
CHANG, Tim .... 323-259-2531.... 55 A
tchang@oxy.edu
CHANG, Wendy .... 305-237-0244.. 105 D
wchang1@mdc.edu
CHANLER, Annette .... 318-371-3035.. 196 H
annettechanler@nwltc.edu
CHANNICK, Susan, A .... 619-239-0391.... 36 A
sac@cwsl.edu
CHANTHORN, Amarin .... 218-335-4262.. 247 F
amarin.chanthorn@lltc.edu
CHAO, Gloria .... 212-220-8304.. 307 B
gchao@bmcc.cuny.edu
CHAO-BUSHOVEN, Karin . 559-453-2058.... 44 F
karin.chao-bushoven@fresno.edu
CHAPA, Paul .... 210-999-8328.. 473 A
paul.chapa@trinity.edu
CHAPARRO, Luis .... 915-831-2132.. 457 H
lchapa13@epcc.edu
CHAPDELAINE,
Andrea, E .... 301-696-3855.. 208 B
chapdelaine@hood.edu
CHAPIN, John .... 727-394-6995.. 108 D
chapin.john@spcollege.edu
CHAPIN, Wesley .... 715-425-0629.. 521 B
wes.chapin@uwrf.edu
CHAPMAN, Alisa .... 919-843-8929.. 356 A
chapman@northcarolina.edu
CHAPMAN, Ana .... 201-360-4244.. 292 B
achapman@hccc.edu
CHAPMAN, Ana .... 201-360-4242.. 292 B
achapman@hccc.edu
CHAPMAN, Angela .... 860-515-3889.... 85 D
achapman@charteroak.edu
CHAPMAN, Angela .... 860-515-3880.... 85 D
achapman@charteroak.edu
CHAPMAN, Angela .... 860-515-3889.... 85 D
achapman@charteroak.edu
CHAPMAN, April .... 707-836-2904.... 63 G
achapman@santarosa.edu
CHAPMAN, Brenda, J ...... 404-413-3505.. 122 D
bchapman@gsu.edu
CHAPMAN, Bryce .... 314-744-7631.. 268 F
chapmanb@mobap.edu
CHAPMAN, Dale, T .... 618-468-2001.. 145 G
dchapman@lc.edu
CHAPMAN, Daniel, W .... 774-354-0679.. 215 D
daniel.chapman@becker.edu
CHAPMAN, David, W .... 205-726-2771...... 6 E
dwchapma@samford.edu
CHAPMAN, Dominique ...... 413-572-5295.. 222 E
dchapman@westfield.ma.edu
CHAPMAN, Elaine .... 626-585-7608.... 56 H
efchapman@pasadena.edu
CHAPMAN, J. Quincy ...... 715-836-3630.. 520 A
chapmajq@uwec.edu
CHAPMAN, Katrina .... 651-638-6043.. 244 L
k-chapman@bethel.edu
CHAPMAN, Katrina .... 615-248-1268.. 447 F
klchapman@trevecca.edu
CHAPMAN, Kendall, P ...... 601-643-8364.. 257 D
ken.chapman@colin.edu
CHAPMAN, Lenora .... 210-458-4071.. 477 A
lenora.chapman@utsa.edu
CHAPMAN, Linda .... 618-468-4000.. 145 G
lchapman@lc.edu
CHAPMAN, Lisa .... 919-807-7096.. 347 B
chapmanl@nccommunitycolleges.edu
CHAPMAN, Lorna .... 706-754-7789.. 125 B
lchapman@northgatech.edu
CHAPMAN, Matt .... 707-668-5663.... 42 C
CHAPMAN, Merv .... 816-414-3700.. 268 D
mchapman@mbts.edu
CHAPMAN, Michelle .... 404-756-4054.. 116 I
mchapman@atlm.edu
CHAPMAN, Richard, L ...... 615-898-2988.. 444 G
richard.chapman@mtsu.edu
CHAPMAN, Robbin .... 781-283-3511.. 229 C
rchapman@wellesley.edu
CHAPMAN, Ronald, K ...... 801-422-8157.. 480 C
ron_chapman@byu.edu
CHAPMAN, Sharon, H ...... 803-938-3810.. 434 E
hamptons@uscsumter.edu
CHAPMAN, Steve, J .... 330-569-6107.. 369 J
chapmansj@hiran.edu
CHAPMAN, Tasha .... 314-434-4044.. 264 C
tasha.chapman@covenantseminary.edu
CHAPMAN, Tracy, A .... 402-280-3616.. 279 H
tracychapman@creighton.edu
CHAPP, Belena .... 215-568-4010.. 411 A
bchapp@moore.edu
CHAPPEL, Jessica .... 802-225-3220.. 484 G
jessica.chappel@neci.edu
CHAPPELL, Cindy .... 619-849-2531.... 57 M
cindychappell@pointloma.edu
CHAPPELL, Dorothy, F ..... 630-752-5627.. 158 C
dorothy.chappell@wheaton.edu
CHAPPELL, Jean .... 513-569-1525.. 366 D
jean.chappell@cincinnatistate.edu
CHAPPELL, Jean .... 434-961-5446.. 498 C
jchappell@pvcc.edu
CHAPPELL, Joy, G .... 336-342-4261.. 352 F
chappellj@rockinghamcc.edu
CHAPPELL, Paul .... 661-946-2274.... 73 I
CHAPPELL, Susan .... 318-342-3636.. 201 E
chappell@ulm.edu
CHAPPELL-LONG, Cheryl 808-956-4561.. 131 H
cchappel@hawaii.edu
CHAPPELL-WILLIAMS,
Lynette .... 607-255-3976.. 312 A
lc75@cornell.edu
CHAPPLE, Tarana .... 816-604-4900.. 267 K
tarana.chapple@mcckc.edu
CHAPPY, Sharon, L .... 262-243-5700.. 516 E
sharon.chappy@cuw.edu
CHAPUT, Barbara .... 413-662-5596.. 222 B
barbara.chaput@mcla.edu
CHAPUT, JR., Maury, L .. 410-777-2324.. 206 B
mlchaput@aacc.edu
CHARBONNEAU, Bryan ... 619-684-8803.... 54 C
bcharbonneau@newschoolarch.edu
CHARBONNEAU, Leticia .. 832-813-6246.. 461 B
leticia.t.charbonneau@lonestar.edu
CHARD, David .... 617-879-2211.. 229 G
dchard@wheelock.edu
CHARETTE, Martin .... 860-932-4157.... 87 C
mcharette@qvcc.edu
CHARETTE, Melodie .... 406-657-1022.. 278 D
melodie.charette@rocky.edu
CHARETTE, Reno .... 406-657-2144.. 277 D
rcharette@msubillings.edu
CHARGIN, Jan .... 408-848-4724.... 44 I
jbchargin@gavilan.edu
CHARITY, Sherika .... 804-758-6737.. 498 D
scharity@rappahannock.edu
CHARLES, Amy .... 608-822-2324.. 524 F
acharles@swtc.edu
CHARLES, Claudia .... 314-889-1434.. 265 C
ccharles@fontbonne.edu
CHARLES, Cynthia .... 504-816-4263.. 195 B
ccharles@dillard.edu
CHARLES, D. Maurice ...... 315-781-3671.. 316 C
CHARLES, Jeffrey, R .... 408-554-4607.... 63 E
jcharles@scu.edu
CHARLES, John .... 217-545-8080.. 154 H
jcharles@siu.edu
CHARLES, John .... 617-253-3292.. 225 A
CHARLES, Kevin, E .... 603-862-1098.. 288 C
kevin.charles@unh.edu
CHARLES, Kristin .... 415-239-3303.... 38 E
CHARLES, Mitch .... 916-388-2800.... 36 D
mpcharles@carrington.edu
CHARLES, Olivier .... 334-347-2623...... 3 H
ocharles@escc.edu
CHARLES, Renee .... 309-677-3260.. 136 B
rcharles@fsmail.bradley.edu
CHARLES, Robiaun, R ...... 404-471-6000.. 115 J
rcharles@agnesscott.edu
CHARLES, Roosevelt .... 413-755-4088.. 224 G
rccharles@stcc.edu
CHARLES, Shawn, M .... 504-286-5348.. 199 I
sgulley@suno.edu
CHARLEY, Susan .... 731-286-3226.. 446 B
charley@dscc.edu
CHARLIER, Hara, D .... 218-855-8053.. 248 N
hcharlier@clcmn.edu
CHARLTON, Patricia, A .... 702-651-5667.. 284 H
patty.charlton@csn.edu
CHARNAY, Richard .... 405-682-1611.. 385 D
richard.j.charnay@occc.edu
CHARNAY, Ruth .... 405-682-1611.. 385 D
rcharnay@occc.edu
CHARNEY, Dennis, S .... 212-241-5674.. 317 A
CHARNEY, Len .... 617-262-5000.. 216 A
len.charney@the-bac.edu
CHARNOW, Rebecca .... 917-493-4404.. 319 M
rcharnow@msmnyc.edu
CHAROENSIRI, Kanitta ..... 540-231-5313.. 499 F
charkx@vt.edu
CHARPENTIER, Jennifer ... 262-564-2866.. 523 D
charpentierj@gtc.edu
CHARPENTIER, Paul .... 207-741-5503.. 203 M
pcharpentier@smccme.edu
CHARRIEZ, Ivette .... 787-878-6000.. 532 O
icharriez@icprjc.edu
CHARRON, Michael .... 507-457-1606.. 254 O
mcharron@smumn.edu
CHARTON, Jacques .... 415-485-3227.... 42 G
charton@dominican.edu
CHASE, Anne .... 859-985-3266.. 187 B
anne_chase@berea.edu
CHASE, Christy .... 203-582-8738.... 88 G
christy.chase@quinnipiac.edu
CHASE, David .... 323-856-7609.... 26 I
dchase@afi.com
CHASE, Del .... 719-336-1514.... 81 D
del.chase@frontrange.edu
CHASE, Diane .... 702-895-3301.. 284 L
diane.chase@unlv.edu
CHASE, Gregory, M .... 336-734-7246.. 349 G
gchase@forsythtech.edu
CHASE, Horace, W .... 731-425-2610.. 446 C
hchase@jscc.edu
CHASE, John .... 323-663-2167.... 71 E
registrar@uprs.edu
CHASE, Julie .... 207-741-5874.. 203 M
jchase@smccme.edu
CHASE, Marilyn, O .... 317-788-2192.. 168 A
chase@uindy.edu
CHASE, Mary, E .... 402-280-2703.. 279 H
marychase@creighton.edu

CHESTER, Brandi ... 870-248-4000 ... 19 H brandic@blackrivertech.edu
CHESTER, Cathie ... 914-251-5976 .. 334 C cathie.chester@purchase.edu
CHESTER, Rosalind ... 504-394-7744 .. 200 D rchester@olhcc.edu
CHESTER, Steven ... 860-343-5864 ... 86 F schester@mxcc.commnet.edu
CHESTER, Thomas, P ... 609-652-4384 .. 297 C thomas.chester@stockton.edu
CHESTER, Timothy, M ... 706-542-3145 .. 128 E tchester@uga.edu
CHESTNUT, SR., Coley, C ... 334-874-5700 ... 3 A cchestnut@ccal.edu
CHESTNUT, Emmanuel ... 757-822-1421 .. 498 H echestnut@tcc.edu
CHEU, Susan ... 408-864-8976 ... 44 A cheususan@deanza.edu
CHEUNG, Alvin ... 916-686-8883 ... 31 F
CHEVALIER, David ... 478-289-2370 .. 120 C dchevalier@ega.edu
CHEVALIER, Jason ... 909-652-6904 ... 37 D jason.chevalier@chaffey.edu
CHEVALIER, JR., Joseph . 404-756-5773 .. 125 A jchevalier@msm.edu
CHEVES, Brad, E ... 214-768-2667 .. 465 J bcheves@smu.edu
CHEVRETTE, II, Joseph, M ... 315-733-2300 .. 338 L jchevrette@uscny.edu
CHEW, Elaine ... 254-968-9611 .. 467 F chew@tarleton.edu
CHEW, Kenneth ... 812-237-3939 .. 162 A kenneth.chew@indstate.edu
CHEW, Thomas ... 585-389-2884 .. 322 D tchew3@naz.edu
CHEYNE, Larry ... 503-399-5210 .. 390 E larry.cheyne@chemeketa.edu
CHEZUM, Kelly, O ... 315-268-4483 .. 310 B kchezum@clarkson.edu
CHI, Wenjun ... 610-660-1000 .. 418 G
CHIA, Samuel ... 214-887-5121 .. 457 C schia@dts.edu
CHIANG, Amber ... 661-395-4251 ... 47 J amchiang@bakersfieldcollege.edu
CHIANG, Stacy ... 510-485-7836 ... 56 I schiang@patten.edu
CHIAPPETTA, Anthony ... 202-319-5623 ... 92 A chiappetta@cua.edu
CHIAPPINI, Thomas, A ... 330-494-6170 .. 377 J tchiappini@starkstate.edu
CHIARA, Mary Jo, B ... 718-940-5574 .. 328 G mchiara@sjcny.edu
CHIARELLA, Stephanie ... 802-831-1237 .. 485 F schiarella@vermontlaw.edu
CHIAVELLI, James ... 978-837-5509 .. 225 E chiavellij@merrimack.edu
CHICHESTER, Susan, E ... 585-245-5577 .. 333 B sue@geneseo.edu
CHICK, Brian ... 603-206-8158 .. 286 D bchick@ccsnh.edu
CHICKERING, F. William . 609-896-5111 .. 295 B wchickering@rider.edu
CHICKERING, Fran ... 603-427-7629 .. 286 B fchickering@ccsnh.edu
CHICO HURST, Karen ... 518-442-5540 .. 331 A kchicohurst@albany.edu
CHIDDICK, Troy ... 610-527-0200 .. 418 D tchiddick@rosemont.edu
CHIDIAC, George ... 626-585-7424 ... 56 H gchidiac@pasadena.edu
CHIDUME, Kene ... 312-752-2007 .. 144 E kene.chidume@kendall.edu
CHIELLI, Jack, A ... 570-408-4770 .. 423 G jack.chielli@wilkes.edu
CHIEVES, Kevin ... 912-443-5491 .. 126 G kchieves@savannahtech.edu
CHIGAWA, Steven ... 808-235-7457 .. 132 E chigawa@hawaii.edu
CHIGAZOLA, Deborah ... 707-527-4525 ... 63 G dchigazola@santarosa.edu
CHIGOS, Lisa ... 619-961-4326 ... 68 A lchigos@tjsl.edu
CHIH, Lo-Li ... 808-974-7595 .. 131 E loli@hawaii.edu
CHIKWINYA, Mary ... 253-566-5127 .. 508 B mchikwinya@tacomacc.edu
CHILCOAT, Cynthia, A ... 928-523-6120 ... 15 H cindy.chilcoat@nau.edu
CHILDERS, Amber ... 501-337-5000 ... 19 K amber@coto.edu
CHILDERS, Camille ... 316-978-3620 .. 185 J camille.childers@wichita.edu
CHILDERS, Christopher ... 773-244-5750 .. 149 I cchilders@northpark.edu
CHILDERS, Henry, A ... 520-626-6779 ... 17 I hankc@email.arizona.edu
CHILDERS, Jana ... 415-451-2859 ... 61 D jchilders@sfts.edu
CHILDERS, Joseph ... 951-827-4302 ... 70 B joseph.childers@ucr.edu
CHILDERS, Karen ... 909-384-8987 ... 60 C kchilder@sbccd.cc.ca.us
CHILDERS, Mark ... 254-710-4619 .. 452 H mark_childers@baylor.edu
CHILDERS, Sharon ... 828-565-4094 .. 350 D shchilders@haywood.edu
CHILDERS, JR., William, A ... 304-336-5100 .. 513 F bill.childers@westliberty.edu
CHILDRES, Donna ... 706-236-1714 .. 117 F dchildres@berry.edu
CHILDRESS, Amanda ... 256-840-4210 ... 6 H achildress@snead.edu
CHILDRESS, Bates ... 802-773-5900 .. 483 G bates.childress@csj.edu
CHILDRESS, Jamie ... 919-718-7239 .. 348 D jchildress@cccc.edu
CHILDRESS, Marc ... 913-344-1236 .. 178 D marc.childress@bakeru.edu
CHILDREY, Cynthia, A ... 928-523-6802 ... 15 H cynthia.childrey@nau.edu
CHILDREY, Lauren, T ... 336-272-7102 .. 344 G lauren.childrey@greensboro.edu
CHILDS, Brittany ... 903-566-7444 .. 477 B bchilds@uttyler.edu
CHILDS, Cindy, D ... 301-546-0014 .. 210 C childscd@pgcc.edu
CHILDS, David, E ... 304-877-6428 .. 510 F david.childs@abc.edu
CHILDS, K. Paige ... 864-941-8688 .. 432 A childs.p@ptc.edu
CHILDS, Kimberly, M ... 936-468-2805 .. 466 H kchilds@sfasu.edu
CHILDS, Linda, J ... 304-877-6428 .. 510 F linda.childs@abc.edu
CHILDS, M. Dee ... 979-845-2217 .. 468 B
CHILDS, Paige ... 864-941-8688 .. 432 A childs.p@ptc.edu
CHILDS, Richard, G ... 410-864-4274 .. 210 F rchilds@stmarys.edu
CHILDS, Shannon ... 541-882-3521 .. 391 F childs@klamathcc.edu
CHILDS, Shannon ... 541-880-2210 .. 391 F childs@klamathcc.edu
CHILDS, Sidney ... 419-372-2156 .. 364 E sidneyc@bgsu.edu
CHILDS, Sidney, R ... 989-964-2932 .. 240 F schilds@svsu.edu
CHILES, Kristie ... 702-579-3530 .. 283 I kchiles@kaplan.edu
CHILES, Rebecca ... 503-838-8481 .. 396 E chilesr@wou.edu
CHILES, Thomas ... 617-552-0840 .. 216 C thomas.chiles@bc.edu
CHILICKI, Stacy ... 207-216-4312 .. 204 B schilicki@yccc.edu
CHILLO, Joseph, L ... 617-730-7035 .. 226 J joseph.chillo@newbury.edu
CHILSTRON, Brian ... 714-662-4402 ... 55 F bchilstron@pacific-college.edu
CHILTON, Bette ... 815-825-9308 .. 144 F bette.chilton@kishwaukeecollege.edu
CHILTON, Lisa ... 434-832-6689 .. 496 G chiltonl@cvcc.vccs.edu
CHIMENTI, Vito, R ... 215-670-9297 .. 412 D vrchimenti@peirce.edu
CHIMIENTI, Sonia ... 508-856-2300 .. 221 B sonia.chimienti@umassmemorial.org
CHIN, Deborah ... 203-932-7020 ... 90 A dchin@newhaven.edu
CHIN, Elaine ... 408-924-3601 ... 35 C elaine.chin@sjsu.edu
CHIN, Jean, E ... 706-542-8715 .. 128 E jchin@uga.edu
CHIN, Julie ... 818-299-5500 ... 74 A jchin@westcoastuniversity.edu
CHIN, Penny, J ... 516-876-3137 .. 333 C chinp@oldwestbury.edu
CHIN, Qi ... 219-473-4375 .. 159 L
CHINCHILLA, Gladys ... 312-939-4975 .. 141 B gchinchilla@harrington.edu
CHINERY, Mary ... 732-987-2341 .. 292 A mchinery@georgian.edu
CHING, Doris ... 808-689-2770 .. 131 G dching@hawaii.edu
CHING, Warren ... 691-320-2480 .. 529 F chiefsecurity@comfsm.fm
CHINN, Jeffrey ... 619-961-4235 ... 68 A jchinn@tjsl.edu
CHINNIAH, Nim, S ... 847-491-5534 .. 150 F nim.chinniah@northwestern.edu
CHINNOCK PETROSKI, Mary, J ... 308-865-8655 .. 282 L petroskimj@unk.edu
CHINWAH, Lovette ... 937-376-6210 .. 365 H lchinwah@centralstate.edu
CHINWAH, Lovette ... 937-376-6631 .. 365 H lchinwah@centralstate.edu
CHIOCHIOS, Tim ... 650-543-3722 ... 52 D tim.chiochios@menlo.edu
CHIPMAN, Nelson ... 412-392-4306 .. 417 F nchipman@pointpark.edu
CHIPMAN, Stephanie ... 217-245-3030 .. 141 G stephanie.chipman@mail.ic.edu
CHIPMAN, Wayne ... 417-873-7258 .. 264 H wchipman@drury.edu
CHIPPS, Michael, R ... 402-844-7054 .. 282 B michaelc@northeast.edu
CHIQUITO, Yug Fon ... 626-529-8246 ... 55 H ychiquito@pacificoaks.edu
CHIRICO, Donna ... 718-262-2804 .. 310 A dchirico@york.cuny.edu
CHISEM, Lori ... 205-929-3409 ... 5 D lchisem@lawsonstate.edu
CHISHA, Mwata ... 800-567-2344 .. 516 B mchisha@menominee.edu
CHISHOLM, Arnett ... 734-973-3540 .. 242 G achisholm@wccnet.edu
CHISHOLM, Barbara ... 334-727-8535 ... 8 A chisholm@mytu.tuskegee.edu
CHISHOLM, Brendan, H .. 508-856-4031 .. 221 B brendan.chisholm@umassmed.edu
CHISHOLM, Bruce, T ... 336-322-2146 .. 351 H bruce.chisholm@piedmontcc.edu
CHISHOLM, Douglas, W .. 937-766-7992 .. 365 C chisd@cedarville.edu
CHISHOLM, Kelly ... 603-206-8004 .. 286 D kchisholm@ccsnh.edu
CHISHOLM, Laura ... 610-647-4400 .. 406 B lchisholm@immaculata.edu
CHISHOLM, Pam ... 802-828-2800 .. 486 A chisholp@ccv.edu
CHISHOLM, Rex ... 312-503-3209 .. 150 F r-chisholm@northwestern.edu
CHISHOLM-BURNS, Marie, A ... 901-448-6036 .. 448 H mchisho3@uthsc.edu
CHISLER, Christi, R ... 909-869-3805 ... 31 J crchisler@cpp.edu
CHISMAR, William, G ... 808-956-8866 .. 131 F chismar@hawaii.edu
CHISOLM, Theresa, H ... 813-974-5567 .. 112 C chisolm@usf.edu
CHISOM, Brian, T ... 540-375-2592 .. 493 H chisom@roanoke.edu
CHISUM, Virginia, E ... 432-335-6415 .. 463 B vchisum@odessa.edu
CHITLIK, Judy ... 714-480-7489 ... 58 F chitlik_judy@rsccd.edu
CHITRE, Manoj ... 909-607-9828 ... 38 I manoj.chitre@cgu.edu
CHITWOOD, Ashley ... 504-671-6603 .. 196 D achitw@dcc.edu
CHITWOOD, Charles ... 405-491-6455 .. 388 A cchitwood@snu.edu
CHIU, Edward ... 781-239-5199 .. 214 G echiu4@babson.edu
CHIVERS, Elizabeth ... 903-875-7735 .. 462 J elizabeth.chivers@navarrocollege.edu
CHLIWNIAK, Luba ... 716-614-6450 .. 324 D lchliwniak@niagaracc.suny.edu
CHMIELESKI, Guy ... 316-295-5488 .. 181 B guy_chmieleski@friends.edu
CHMIELEWSKI, Jerry ... 724-738-2489 .. 416 B jerry.chmielewski@sru.edu
CHMURA, Michael ... 781-239-4549 .. 214 G mchmura@babson.edu
CHMURA, Wivinia, A ... 412-578-8762 .. 400 C wachmura@carlow.edu
CHO, Esther ... 714-683-1210 ... 28 D music@buc.edu
CHO, Hyun Sung ... 770-220-7910 .. 120 G revdrcho@gmail.com
CHO, Karen ... 808-235-7404 .. 132 E kcho@hawaii.edu
CHO, Katherine H, S ... 213-413-9500 ... 66 B dean@scusoma.edu
CHO, Nam Hong ... 240-447-1664 .. 120 G akap1997@hotmail.com
CHO, Peter ... 504-762-3188 .. 196 D plcho@dcc.edu
CHOATE, Jim ... 319-398-7612 .. 174 I jchoate@kirkwood.edu
CHOATE, Michael, J ... 972-883-2943 .. 476 C mchoate@utdallas.edu
CHOATE, Regina ... 575-492-2774 .. 300 H rchoate@nmjc.edu
CHOCK, Hansford ... 808-373-2849 .. 132 G hansford.at.wmi@gmail.com
CHOCK, Keala ... 808-845-9229 .. 132 A kaseyc@hawaii.edu
CHODOSH, Hiram, E ... 909-621-8111 ... 38 J hiram.chodosh@cmc.edu
CHODZKO-ZAJKO, Wojciech ... 217-333-6715 .. 157 A wojtek@illinois.edu
CHOE, Tina ... 310-338-2833 ... 51 E tina.choe@lmu.edu
CHOI, Henry ... 714-533-1495 ... 65 B advising@southbaylo.edu
CHOI, Jayoung ... 718-262-2297 .. 310 A jchoi@york.cuny.edu
CHOI, Karen ... 562-926-1023 ... 58 B karenchoi@ptsa.edu
CHOI, Kyunam ... 714-525-0088 ... 45 F qchoi3@yahoo.com
CHOI, Mun ... 860-486-4037 ... 89 D mun.choi@uconn.edu
CHOI, Paul ... 510-592-9688 ... 54 I paul.choi@npu.edu
CHOI, Sooshin ... 313-664-1486 .. 232 G sooshin@collegeforcreativestudies.edu
CHOI, Sun Hee ... 718-639-3975 .. 120 G eastersun@hanmail.net
CHOI, Youngsook ... 562-926-1023 ... 58 B youngsook79@gmail.com
CHOJNACKI, David ... 561-868-3465 .. 106 D chojnacd@palmbeachstate.edu
CHOJNICKI, Linda, M ... 413-782-1315 .. 229 E linda.chojnicki@wne.edu
CHOLETTE, Beth, K ... 585-245-5716 .. 333 B cholette@geneseo.edu
CHONCEK, Christopher, E ... 412-392-3421 .. 417 F cchoncek@pointpark.edu
CHONG, Angela ... 608-771-2201 .. 290 F chonga@tcnj.edu
CHONG, Bruce ... 386-822-7452 .. 113 B bchong@stetson.edu
CHONG, Dawn ... 419-372-2723 .. 364 E dchong@bgsu.edu
CHONG, Frank ... 707-527-4431 ... 63 G fchong@santarosa.edu
CHONG, Philip ... 800-782-2422 ... 31 E pnpchong@gmail.com
CHONKO, Arthur, J ... 740-587-6456 .. 368 B chonko@denison.edu
CHOO, Jeff ... 617-327-6777 .. 229 H jeff_choo@williamjames.edu
CHOONOO, John ... 646-312-2196 .. 307 A john.choonoo@baruch.cuny.edu
CHOPIN, Marc ... 208-885-7146 .. 134 G
CHOPKA, John, A ... 717-796-4780 .. 410 J jchopka@messiah.edu
CHOPP, Rebecca ... 303-871-2111 ... 84 B chancellor@du.edu
CHOPRA, Praveen ... 215-503-5110 .. 420 E praveen.chopra@jefferson.edu
CHORAM, Iotaka ... 671-734-1812 .. 530 A ichoram@piu.edu
CHORBAJIAN, Gil ... 518-694-7394 .. 303 C gil.chorbajian@acphs.edu
CHOROSZY, Melisa, N ... 775-784-6181 .. 285 A choroszy@admin.unr.edu
CHOTTINER, Gregg ... 212-217-3400 .. 314 B gregg_chottiner@fitnyc.edu
CHOU, Lexer ... 808-455-0248 .. 132 C achou@hawaii.edu
CHOU, Victoria ... 708-524-6962 .. 139 F vchou@dom.edu
CHOUDHRY, Rizwan ... 703-330-8400 ... 93 F
CHOW, Raymond ... 650-358-6742 ... 62 F chow@smccd.edu
CHOW, Timothy ... 812-877-8910 .. 166 H timothy.chow@rose-hulman.edu
CHOWDHURY, Faruque ... 908-737-3300 .. 292 C fchowdhu@kean.edu
CHOWN, Deborah ... 413-775-1832 .. 223 D chown@gcc.mass.edu
CHREIST, Ryan ... 303-402-1660 ... 83 K ryan.chreist@colorado.edu
CHRENKO, Sarah, A ... 517-264-7179 .. 241 A schrenko@sienaheights.edu
CHRESTAY, Joan, F ... 610-660-1226 .. 418 G joan.chrestay@sju.edu
CHRISLER, Jennifer, S ... 413-585-2040 .. 228 D jchrisler@smith.edu
CHRISMAN, Dana ... 319-208-5017 .. 176 J dchrisman@scciowa.edu
CHRISMAN, Tammy, A ... 757-446-8447 .. 489 B chrismta@evms.edu
CHRISPENS, Pamela ... 951-785-2002 ... 48 A pchrispe@lasierra.edu
CHRIST, Andrew, P ... 973-596-5774 .. 293 D andrew.p.christ@njit.edu
CHRIST, Brad ... 541-552-6451 .. 395 A christb@sou.edu
CHRIST, Carol ... 510-642-1961 ... 68 M cchrist@berkeley.edu
CHRIST, Suzanne ... 618-545-3069 .. 144 D schrist@kaskaskia.edu
CHRISTAKIS, Michael, N . 518-956-8140 .. 331 A mchristakis@albany.edu
CHRISTALDI, Antoinette ... 610-526-1382 .. 397 E antoinette.christaldi@theamericancollege.edu
CHRISTEL, Mark, A ... 330-263-2483 .. 367 A mchristel@wooster.edu

CIENSKI, John, P ... 631-451-4080 .. 336 E cienskj@sunysuffolk.edu

CIEPLY, Kevin ... 239-687-5305 .... 95 P kcieply@avemarialaw.edu

CIEZ-VOLZ, Kathleen ... 904-361-6257 .. 101 G kathleen.ciez.volz@fscj.edu

CIFRA, Jason, S ... 808-934-2510 .. 131 J cifra@hawaii.edu

CIFUENTES, Geraldo ... 503-517-1017 .. 396 D gcifuentes@warnerpacific.edu

CIFUENTES, Luis ... 361-825-2577 .. 468 E luis.cifuentes@tamucc.edu

CIHA, Lisa ... 319-399-8669 .. 170 G lciha@coe.edu

CIHAK, Michael ... 320-589-6154 .. 255 F cihakmw@morris.umn.edu

CILENTO, Eugene, V ... 304-293-4157 .. 514 C gene.cilento@mail.wvu.edu

CILLAY, David ... 509-335-5454 .. 508 H dcillay@wsu.edu

CIMA, Cara ... 863-680-4390 .. 101 E ccima@flsouthern.edu

CIMALORE, Ann ... 205-853-1200 ...... 5 B acimalore@jeffstateonline.com

CIMAROSSA, Valerie ... 602-383-8228 .... 17 H vcimarossa@uat.edu

CIMBOLIC, Peter ... 614-251-4690 .. 374 I peter.cimbolic@ohiodominican.edu

CIMINELLI, Mary ... 972-273-3130 .. 456 G marygciminelli@dcccd.edu

CIMINELLI, Thomas, E ... 716-888-2250 .. 306 F ciminel1@canisius.edu

CIMINERI, Christy ... 843-477-2166 .. 430 F christy.cimineri@hgtc.edu

CIMINO, Chris ... 865-974-9880 .. 448 E cimino@utk.edu

CIMITILE, Maria ... 616-331-2400 .. 234 F cimitilm@gvsu.edu

CIMOCHOWSKI, Lindsey . 617-585-5000 .. 216 A lindsey.cimochowski@the-bac.edu

CIMORELLI, Abigail ... 973-290-4282 .. 290 G acimorelli@cse.edu

CIMORELLI, Nick ... 843-863-7581 .. 427 I ncimorel@csuniv.edu

CIMPL, Linda ... 605-995-2896 .. 435 F licimpl@dwu.edu

CINAR, Ali ... 312-567-3637 .. 142 I cinar@iit.edu

CINI, Marie ... 301-985-7174 .. 212 C marie.cini@umuc.edu

CINK, Janey ... 412-291-6340 .. 397 I jcink@aii.edu

CINTORINO, Salvatore ... 860-832-1889 .... 85 F cintorino@ccsu.edu

CINTRON, Arnaldo ... 787-864-2222 .. 534 A arnaldo.cintron@guayama.inter.edu

CINTRON, Doris ... 212-650-8166 .. 307 E dcintron@ccny.cuny.edu

CINTRON, Edgardo ... 787-857-3600 .. 533 I ecintron@br.inter.edu

CINTRON, Filomena ... 787-857-3600 .. 533 I scintron@br.inter.edu

CINTRON, Iraida ... 787-850-9374 .. 538 B iraida.cintron@upr.edu

CINTRON, Josue ... 787-753-6000 .. 532 O jcintron@icprjc.edu

CINTRON, Myriam ... 787-850-9302 .. 538 B myriam.cintron1@upr.edu

CINTRON, Nancy, A ... 718-960-8366 .. 308 B nancy.cintron@lehman.cuny.edu

CINTRON-OTERO, Carmen ... 787-993-8922 .. 537 G carmen.cintron2@upr.edu

CIOCE, Michael ... 856-222-9311 .. 295 C mcioce@rcbc.edu

CIOFFI, Laura ... 212-752-1530 .. 318 F laura.cioffi@limcollege.edu

CIOLFI, Michael, A ... 203-576-4278 .... 89 C mciolfi@bridgeport.edu

CIOSEK, Edward ... 413-748-3108 .. 228 E eciosek@springfieldcollege.edu

CIOTOLI, Carlo ... 212-443-1297 .. 324 C carlo.ciotoli@nyu.edu

CIPFL, Joseph, J ... 618-537-6462 .. 147 F jjcipfl@mckendree.edu

CIPOLLA, Anthony ... 845-848-7814 .. 312 F anthony.cipolla@dc.edu

CIPRES, Elizabeth ... 949-451-5410 .... 65 F ecipres@ivc.edu

CIPRIANI, Colleen ... 614-234-5828 .. 373 B ccipriani@mccn.edu

CIPRIANO, Matt, J ... 215-968-8255 .. 399 A cipriano@bucks.edu

CIPRIANO, Michael ... 978-934-2654 .. 221 A michael_cipriano@uml.edu

CIRAULO, Paul ... 212-517-0531 .. 320 C pciraulo@mmm.edu

CIRCE, Scott ... 305-223-4561 .. 108 A scirce@sjvcs.edu

CIRCLE, Kelly ... 303-914-6213 .... 82 I kelly.circle@rrcc.edu

CIRELLI, Rachel ... 718-862-7308 .. 319 L rcirelli01@manhattan.edu

CIRI, Michael ... 907-796-6534 .... 10 H maciri@alaska.edu

CIRI, Michael ... 907-796-6452 .... 10 H maciri@alaska.edu

CIRIACO, Sandy, V ... 402-280-5560 .. 279 H ciriaco@creighton.edu

CIRILLO, Laureen ... 413-565-1006 .. 215 A lcirillo@baypath.edu

CIRILLO, Robert ... 914-606-6981 .. 340 C robert.cirillo@sunywcc.edu

CIRMO, Christopher ... 715-346-4224 .. 521 C ccirmo@uwsp.edu

CIRRINCIONE, AnnaMaria ... 607-753-2336 .. 333 A annamaria.cirrincione@cortland.edu

CISKANIK, John, F ... 800-877-5456 .. 488 D ciskanik@christendom.edu

CISLER, Ronald, A ... 414-229-5663 .. 520 D rac@uwm.edu

CISNA, Shawn ... 309-796-5000 .. 135 I cisnas@bhc.edu

CISNEROS, Maria ... 504-671-5603 .. 196 D mcisne@dcc.edu

CISNEROS, Teo ... 210-924-4338 .. 452 F teo.cisneros@bua.edu

CISSELL, Jason, A ... 502-272-8329 .. 187 A jcissell@bellarmine.edu

CITARELLA, Alberto ... 802-656-3244 .. 485 D alberto.citarella@uvm.edu

CITRON, Chaim ... 323-937-3763 .... 75 G ccitron@yoec.edu

CITTI, Lori, A ... 410-516-6760 .. 208 D lcitti1@jhu.edu

CIUFFO, Patricia ... 646-565-6000 .. 337 I patricia.ciuffo@touro.edu

CIULLO, Carol ... 888-254-4238 .. 510 H cciullo@cdu.edu

CLABBY, William, J ... 512-448-8704 .. 464 G bclabby@stedwards.edu

CLACK, Olivia ... 870-574-4481 .... 22 G oclack@sautech.edu

CLAERBOUT, Libby ... 701-858-4155 .. 360 F libby.claerbout@minotstateu.edu

CLAERHOUT, Cathryn ... 231-995-1034 .. 239 C cclaerhout@nmc.edu

CLAEYS, Aimee, K ... 515-281-6456 .. 169 F akclaeys@iastate.edu

CLAFFEY, George ... 203-837-9800 .... 85 I claffeyg@wcsu.edu

CLAFFEY, JR., George, F ... 860-515-3777 .... 85 D gclaffey@charteroak.edu

CLAFFEY, Joan ... 312-893-7113 .. 140 D jclaffey@erikson.edu

CLAFFEY, Marian, A ... 773-508-7473 .. 146 G mclaffe@luc.edu

CLAGETT, Craig, A ... 410-386-8163 .. 206 I cclagett@carrollcc.edu

CLAGHORN, Patricia ... 856-415-5504 .. 295 D pclaghorn@rcgc.edu

CLAGUE, Roger ... 530-749-3804 .... 76 B rclague@yccd.edu

CLAIRE, Michael ... 650-574-6222 .... 62 H clairem@smccd.edu

CLANCEY, Robert ... 863-669-2321 .. 106 I rclancey@polk.edu

CLANCY, Amanda ... 303-678-3736 .... 80 E amanda.clancy@frontrange.edu

CLANCY, Patricia ... 718-390-3422 .. 339 F patricia.clancy@wagner.edu

CLANCY, SJ, Tim, R ... 509-313-6701 .. 504 A clancy@gonzaga.edu

CLANTON, Ann ... 251-405-7055 ...... 2 D aclanton@bishop.edu

CLANTON, Janet ... 573-897-5000 .. 272 H

CLANTON, Karen ... 256-824-6013 ...... 8 F karen.clanton@uah.edu

CLAPP, Cheryl ... 812-877-8686 .. 166 H clapp@rose-hulman.edu

CLAPP, Jason ... 319-399-8526 .. 170 G jclapp@coe.edu

CLAPP, Kenneth, W ... 704-637-4446 .. 343 B kclapp@catawba.edu

CLAPP, Marlene ... 508-830-5069 .. 222 C mclapp@maritime.edu

CLAPP, Stacey ... 609-343-5632 .. 288 H sclapp@atlantic.edu

CLAPPER, Mark, A ... 717-361-1499 .. 403 C clapperm@etown.edu

CLAPPER-DEWELL, Theophylact ... 315-858-3914 .. 316 E frtheophylact@jordanville.org

CLARDY, Betsy, B ... 409-772-8789 .. 478 A bbclardy@utmb.edu

CLARDY, JR., Mike ... 334-844-9996 ...... 1 G clardch@auburn.edu

CLARENSAU, Michael ... 972-825-4827 .. 466 D mclarensau@sagu.edu

CLARK, Adon ... 478-374-6407 .. 124 E adon.clark@mga.edu

CLARK, Adrian, R ... 816-654-7095 .. 266 E arclark@kcumb.edu

CLARK, Alfred ... 909-593-3511 .... 71 B aclark@laverne.edu

CLARK, Alice ... 662-915-7583 .. 261 B amclark@olemiss.edu

CLARK, Amanda, C ... 509-777-4482 .. 509 H amandaclark@whitworth.edu

CLARK, Amy ... 503-838-8187 .. 396 E clarkaj@wou.edu

CLARK, Andy ... 478-471-5365 .. 124 E andy.clark@mga.edu

CLARK, Anita, R ... 262-243-5700 .. 516 E anita.clark@cuw.edu

CLARK, Ann, B ... 860-727-6761 .... 87 H aclark@goodwin.edu

CLARK, Annette, C ... 206-398-4000 .. 507 E annclark@seattleu.edu

CLARK, Ben ... 757-340-2121 .. 488 A directorcvab@centura.edu

CLARK, Benita, I ... 919-866-7894 .. 353 I biclark@waketech.edu

CLARK, Beverly ... 228-896-2512 .. 259 C beverly.clark@mgccc.edu

CLARK, Bill ... 626-584-5588 .... 44 G billclark@fuller.edu

CLARK, Bob ... 310-506-4798 .... 56 J bob.clark@pepperdine.edu

CLARK, Brandi ... 520-494-5577 .... 12 J brandi.clark@centralaz.edu

CLARK, Brenda ... 803-705-4385 .. 427 D clarkb@benedict.edu

CLARK, Brian ... 401-427-6920 .. 426 A bclark@risd.edu

CLARK, Brian, J ... 207-859-4604 .. 202 G bjclark@colby.edu

CLARK, Brock ... 228-497-7634 .. 259 C brock.clark@mgccc.edu

CLARK, Bryon ... 580-745-2064 .. 387 M bclark@se.edu

CLARK, Carol ... 931-221-7570 .. 444 E clarkc@apsu.edu

CLARK, Carol, D ... 931-221-7570 .. 444 E clarkc@apsu.edu

CLARK, Catherine ... 360-650-6400 .. 509 E catherine.clark@wwu.edu

CLARK, Charles ... 706-737-1738 .. 117 D cwclark@augusta.edu

CLARK, Charles, E ... 920-683-4710 .. 522 A charles.clark@uwc.edu

CLARK, Charles, L ... 309-341-7399 .. 145 A clclark@knox.edu

CLARK, Cheryl ... 318-487-7602 .. 195 F cheryl.clark@lacollege.edu

CLARK, Chris ... 618-634-3233 .. 154 B chrisc@shawneecc.edu

CLARK, Christina ... 703-284-1560 .. 492 A christina.clark@marymount.edu

CLARK, Cynthia, A ... 860-628-4751 .... 88 C cclark@lincolncollegene.edu

CLARK, Dan ... 503-838-8483 .. 396 E clarkd@wou.edu

CLARK, Dana ... 810-766-4028 .. 231 C dana.clark@baker.edu

CLARK, Dana ... 810-766-4028 .. 231 D dlclark07@baker.edu

CLARK, Dana ... 570-740-0422 .. 409 E dclark@luzerne.edu

CLARK, Daniel ... 630-752-5593 .. 158 C daniel.clark@wheaton.edu

CLARK, Daniel ... 616-234-4354 .. 234 E dbclark@grcc.edu

CLARK, Daniel ... 425-602-3064 .. 501 D dclark@bastyr.edu

CLARK, Dave ... 701-224-5434 .. 361 C david.clark@bismarckstate.edu

CLARK, David ... 212-346-1590 .. 325 J dclark@pace.edu

CLARK, David ... 651-638-6553 .. 244 L d-clark@bethel.edu

CLARK, David ... 559-638-0300 .... 67 D david.clark@reedleycollege.edu

CLARK, David ... 301-736-3631 .. 209 A david.clark@msbbcs.edu

CLARK, Dean, T ... 620-229-6364 .. 184 J dean.clark@sckans.edu

CLARK, Debbie ... 309-457-2125 .. 148 E dclark@monmouthcollege.edu

CLARK, Deborah ... 802-586-7711 .. 485 C dclark@sterlingcollege.edu

CLARK, Deborah, E ... 607-871-2170 .. 303 F clarkd@alfred.edu

CLARK, Denise ... 301-405-4282 .. 211 E djclark@umd.edu

CLARK, Dennis ... 510-535-9394 .... 56 I dclark@patten.edu

CLARK, Dennis ... 815-802-8606 .. 144 C dclark@kcc.edu

CLARK, Dewey ... 252-985-5140 .. 354 E dclark@ncwc.edu

CLARK, Dianne ... 318-371-3035 .. 196 H dianneclark@nwltc.edu

CLARK, Donald ... 207-602-2274 .. 205 F dclark@une.edu

CLARK, Donna ... 254-442-5001 .. 454 E donna.clark@cisco.edu

CLARK, Douglas ... 610-341-5810 .. 403 B dclark1@eastern.edu

CLARK, Douglas, L ... 407-646-1520 .. 107 O dclark@rollins.edu

CLARK, Douglas, R ... 951-785-2244 .... 48 A dclark@lasierra.edu

CLARK, Douglas, S ... 510-642-4192 .... 68 M cocdean@berkeley.edu

CLARK, Duwon ... 573-681-5477 .. 266 I clarkd@lincolnu.edu

CLARK, Elizabeth ... 617-541-5332 .. 224 F eclark@rcc.mass.edu

CLARK, Elizabeth ... 660-785-7200 .. 273 B eclark@truman.edu

CLARK, Eric ... 617-984-1741 .. 227 F eclark@quincycollege.edu

CLARK, Eric ... 937-258-8251 .. 370 F eric.clark@icb.edu

CLARK, Frederick ... 508-531-1201 .. 221 C fred.clark@bridgew.edu

CLARK, Gail ... 765-987-1439 .. 160 G clarkga@earlham.edu

CLARK, Gary, A ... 310-825-5108 .... 69 D gclark@admission.ucla.edu

CLARK, Gary, C ... 405-744-6384 .. 385 G gary.clark@okstate.edu

CLARK, Gaye ... 910-410-1804 .. 352 C agclark@richmondcc.edu

CLARK, Ginger ... 813-253-7144 .. 102 R gclark@hccfl.edu

CLARK, Glenn ... 401-341-2400 .. 426 C glenn.clark@salve.edu

CLARK, III, Irvin ... 717-780-2300 .. 405 C

CLARK, Jacqueline ... 256-549-8695 ...... 3 M jclark@gadsdenstate.edu

CLARK, Jacqueline ... 718-270-6994 .. 309 B jaclark@mec.cuny.edu

CLARK, James ... 252-399-6450 .. 341 P jclark@barton.edu

CLARK, James ... 513-556-4615 .. 379 A clark2j9@ucmail.uc.edu

CLARK, James, A ... 334-844-4765 ...... 1 G clarkj3@auburn.edu

CLARK, James, E ... 803-536-7013 .. 432 E jclark25@scsu.edu

CLARK, James, T ... 304-336-8043 .. 513 F clarkj@westliberty.edu

CLARK, Jamie, K ... 740-588-1222 .. 382 C jclark@zanestate.edu

CLARK, Jane, E ... 301-405-2437 .. 211 E jeclark@umd.edu

CLARK, Janet ... 812-535-5182 .. 166 K jclark@smwc.edu

CLARK, Jeanian ... 540-868-7122 .. 497 E jclark@lfcc.edu

CLARK, Jeffrey, A ... 518-580-5929 .. 330 F jclark@skidmore.edu

CLARK, Jennifer ... 724-589-2858 .. 420 D jclark@thiel.edu

CLARK, Jennifer, R ... 312-915-7819 .. 146 G jclark7@luc.edu

CLARK, Jill ... 712-325-3285 .. 174 B jclark@iwcc.edu

CLARK, Jimmy ... 479-979-1484 .... 24 I jclark@ozarks.edu

CLARK, Joan ... 304-357-4750 .. 511 E joanclark@ucwv.edu

CLARK, John, B ... 203-837-8300 .... 85 I clarkj@wcsu.edu

CLARK, John, S ... 865-694-6601 .. 446 G jclark@pstcc.edu

CLARK, Joy ... 334-244-3600 ...... 2 A jclark@aum.edu

CLARK, Karen ... 765-973-8242 .. 162 G krclark@iue.edu

CLARK, Karen ... 254-299-8689 .. 461 E kclark@mclennan.edu

CLARK, Karen, M ... 708-344-4700 .. 146 D kclark@lincolntech.edu

CLARK, Karisa, A ... 304-877-6428 .. 510 F publicrelations@abc.edu

CLARK, Kathleen ... 717-560-8214 .. 407 E kclark@lbc.edu

CLARK, Kathy ... 630-844-5443 .. 135 E kclark@aurora.edu

CLARK, Kevin, G ... 215-204-2452 .. 420 B keviclar@temple.edu

CLARK, Kimberly, M ... 336-342-4261 .. 352 F clarkk@rockinghamcc.edu

CLARK, Kristin ... 559-925-3217 .... 74 E kristinclark@whccd.edu

CLARK, Kyle ... 850-644-4242 .. 111 C kyle@fsu.edu

CLARK, Kym ... 432-264-5144 .. 459 D kclark@howardcollege.edu

CLARK, L. Nathan, N .... 775-856-2266.. 284 A nclark@ccnn4u.com
CLARK, Lanette .... 406-758-6328.. 276 F lclark@fpcc.edu
CLARK, Larry .... 253-589-5602.. 502 F larry.clark@cptc.edu
CLARK, Laura .... 870-777-5722.... 24 A laura.clark@uacch.edu
CLARK, Laurie .... 979-830-4336.. 452 J laurie.clark@blinn.edu
CLARK, Lawrence, S .... 318-797-5234.. 198 C larry.clark@lsus.edu
CLARK, Leanna .... 303-315-7734.... 84 A leanna.clark@ucdenver.edu
CLARK, Lela .... 910-521-6262.. 358 C lela.clark@uncp.edu
CLARK, Leonard .... 318-342-1041.. 201 E leclark@ulm.edu
CLARK, Lesa, C .... 757-683-4406.. 492 G lclark@odu.edu
CLARK, Letitia .... 714-438-4606.... 39 D lclark35@cccd.edu
CLARK, Linda, J .... 360-442-2100.. 504 G lclark@lowercolumbia.edu
CLARK, Lisa .... 910-642-7141.. 353 C lisa.clark@sccnc.edu
CLARK, Lloyd .... 502-597-6000.. 191 B
CLARK, Lynne .... 718-262-2698.. 310 A lclark@york.cuny.edu
CLARK, Margie .... 517-483-1461.. 237 A clarkm@lcc.edu
CLARK, Mark .... 515-964-6213.. 171 B maclark@dmacc.edu
CLARK, Marla .... 269-927-8762.. 236 G mclark@lakemichigancollege.edu
CLARK, Marlin .... 801-957-4004.. 483 A marlin.clark@slcc.edu
CLARK, Mary .... 501-977-2011.... 24 B clark@uaccm.edu
CLARK, Mary .... 202-885-2155.... 91 J mlclark@american.edu
CLARK, Mary .... 252-222-6190.. 348 B clarkm@carteret.edu
CLARK, Matthew .... 612-626-4734.. 255 H mclark@umn.edu
CLARK, OSB, Matthew .... 985-867-2245.. 199 F mrclark@sjasc.edu
CLARK, Melinda .... 813-226-4858.. 108 C melinda.clark@saintleo.edu
CLARK, MelodyAnn .... 219-844-0100.. 159 E melodyann.clark@brightwood.edu
CLARK, Michael .... 719-336-6660.... 81 D michael.clark@lamarcc.edu
CLARK, Michael .... 910-521-6815.. 358 C michael.clark@uncp.edu
CLARK, Michael .... 570-321-4249.. 409 F clark@lycoming.edu
CLARK, Michelle .... 859-858-3511.. 186 J michelle.clark@asbury.edu
CLARK, Murray, B .... 859-323-5220.. 193 G mbclar2@email.uky.edu
CLARK, Naoma .... 940-397-4544.. 462 A naoma.clark@mwsu.edu
CLARK, Nick .... 662-476-5075.. 257 G nclark@eastms.edu
CLARK, Nigel, N .... 304-293-4813.. 514 C nigel.clark@mail.wvu.edu
CLARK, Nuriyah .... 716-851-1205.. 313 H clarkn@ecc.edu
CLARK, Pam .... 989-686-9225.. 233 I pamelaclark@delta.edu
CLARK, Paul, E .... 610-921-7708.. 396 H pclark@albright.edu
CLARK, Reatha .... 601-984-1010.. 261 C rhclark@umc.edu
CLARK, Rebecca .... 304-865-6085.. 511 C becky.clark@ovu.edu
CLARK, Richard .... 404-894-4154.. 121 D rick.clark@admission.gatech.edu
CLARK, Richard .... 702-895-1469.. 284 L richard.clark@unlv.edu
CLARK, Richard .... 865-573-4517.. 440 I rclark@johnsonu.edu
CLARK, Rob .... 585-275-5931.. 338 K rclark@rochester.edu
CLARK, Robert .... 404-880-6623.. 118 K rclark@cau.edu
CLARK, Robert, A .... 207-941-7138.. 202 I clarkr@husson.edu
CLARK, Robert, E .... 757-683-3018.. 492 G reclark@odu.edu
CLARK, II, Robert, E .... 302-736-2508.... 91 G robert.clark@wesley.edu
CLARK, Rodney .... 508-678-2811.. 223 A rodney.clark@bristolcc.edu
CLARK, Ron, M .... 972-238-6277.. 456 H rclark@dcccd.edu
CLARK, Ryan .... 503-699-6268.. 392 D rclark@marylhurst.edu
CLARK, Sandra .... 410-857-2217.. 209 D sgclark@mcdaniel.edu
CLARK, Sara, M .... 417-836-6105.. 268 I saraclark@missouristate.edu
CLARK, Sarah, E .... 863-667-5463.. 109 L seclark@seu.edu
CLARK, Scott .... 415-451-2833.... 61 D sclark@sfts.edu
CLARK, Scott, D .... 716-888-8357.. 306 F clarks@canisius.edu
CLARK, Shani .... 229-317-6926.. 120 A shani.clark@darton.edu
CLARK, Sharon, L .... 813-988-5131.. 100 F clarks@floridacollege.edu
CLARK, Shaun .... 870-777-5722.... 24 A shaun.clark@uacch.edu
CLARK, Steve .... 541-737-4875.. 393 H steve.clark@oregonstate.edu
CLARK, Susan .... 517-629-0798.. 230 E sclark@albion.edu
CLARK, Susan, G .... 330-972-7780.. 378 G sclark1@uakron.edu
CLARK, Tammy, L .... 313-258-7522.. 114 M tclark@ut.edu
CLARK, Tarryl .... 320-308-5377.. 252 B tclark@sctcc.edu
CLARK, Terry .... 618-453-7960.. 154 I tclark@business.siu.edu
CLARK, Thomas .... 919-582-3750.. 355 F tomclark@shawu.edu
CLARK, Todd .... 909-469-5473.... 74 K tclark@westernu.edu
CLARK, Todd, A .... 336-316-2133.. 344 H clarkta@guilford.edu
CLARK, Tracie .... 704-330-6022.. 348 E tracie.clark@cpcc.edu
CLARK, Tracy .... 218-935-0417.. 256 E tracy.clark@wetcc.edu
CLARK, Vernon, A .... 940-565-2453.. 475 A allen.clark@unt.edu
CLARK, Victoria .... 425-822-8266.. 505 E victoria.clark@northwestu.edu
CLARK, Vincent, W .... 718-960-8539.. 308 B vincent.clark@lehman.cuny.edu
CLARK, Wayne, N .... 208-496-2510.. 132 J clarkw@byui.edu
CLARK, William .... 856-351-2602.. 296 L clark@salemcc.edu
CLARK, William .... 330-972-8772.. 378 H bclark3@uakron.edu
CLARK, Yvette .... 603-645-9623.. 287 I y.clark@snhu.edu
CLARK, Yvette .... 931-372-3004.. 445 B yclark@tntech.edu
CLARK ARTIS, Roslyn ..... 305-626-3600.. 101 A roslyn.artis@fmuniv.edu
CLARK-BETANCOURT, Tammy, L .... 217-443-8778.. 139 B tbetancourt@dacc.edu
CLARK-EVANS, Barbara .... 913-288-7504.. 182 C bclark@kckcc.edu
CLARK JOHNSON, Virginia, L .... 701-231-8211.. 361 A virginia.clark@ndsu.edu
CLARK-TALLEY, Christine 703-993-8757.. 490 B cclarkta@gmu.edu
CLARK-WHITE, Patricia .... 949-585-2987.... 28 F pwhite@brandman.edu
CLARKBERG, Marin, E ..... 607-255-9101.. 312 A mec30@cornell.edu
CLARKE, Ann .... 315-443-5889.. 337 A anclarke@syr.edu
CLARKE, Anthony .... 910-642-7141.. 353 C anthony.clarke@sccnc.edu
CLARKE, Calauncra .... 225-771-2552.. 200 A cclarke@sulc.edu
CLARKE, Cara .... 606-759-7141.. 190 C cara.clarke@kctcs.edu
CLARKE, Chris .... 760-252-2411.... 28 B cclarke@barstow.edu
CLARKE, Claudia .... 607-778-5220.. 332 D clarkeck@sunybroome.edu
CLARKE, Cyril, R .... 540-231-7910.. 499 F clarkecr@vt.edu
CLARKE, David .... 518-694-7252.. 303 C david.clarke@acphs.edu
CLARKE, Edmond .... 610-409-3206.. 422 D eclarke@ursinus.edu
CLARKE, Germel .... 202-884-9000.... 94 A clarkeg@trinitydc.edu
CLARKE, Ivan .... 310-233-4436.... 49 I clarkein@lahc.edu
CLARKE, Jaime .... 503-594-3220.. 390 F jaimec@clackamas.edu
CLARKE, Karen, B .... 215-204-8367.. 420 B karen.clarke@temple.edu
CLARKE, Kathy .... 916-348-4689.... 43 A kclarke@epic.edu
CLARKE, Kenneth, I .... 607-255-6002.. 312 A kic2@cornell.edu
CLARKE, Kevin .... 516-773-5000.. 529 B clarkek@usmma.edu
CLARKE, Melanie .... 212-621-4101.. 308 E maclarke@jjay.cuny.edu
CLARKE, Mark .... 713-743-9854.. 473 F mclarke@uh.edu
CLARKE, Megan .... 906-248-8435.. 231 N
CLARKE, Patrick .... 435-586-5479.. 481 N clarke@suu.edu
CLARKE, Rachelle .... 480-517-8544.... 14 G rachelle.clark@riosalado.edu
CLARKE, Robert .... 503-493-6555.. 391 A rclarke@cu-portland.edu
CLARKE, III, Robert, S .... 864-379-8775.. 429 I clarke@erskine.edu
CLARKE, Ryan .... 601-635-2111.. 257 F rclarke@eccc.edu
CLARKE, Shari .... 740-593-2614.. 375 H clarkes@ohio.edu
CLARKE, Sonia .... 985-858-5861.. 196 E sonia.clarke@fletcher.edu
CLARKE-ANDERSON, Shannon .... 718-270-5143.. 309 B shannon@mec.cuny.edu
CLARKE-GLOVER, Jazzmine .... 718-390-3280.. 339 F j.clarke-glover@wagner.edu
CLARKE-TURNER, Kay ...... 973-596-3082.. 293 D kay.turner@njit.edu
CLARKSON, Mernard .... 803-533-3803.. 432 E mclarks1@scsu.edu
CLARKSON, Nancy, E .... 585-785-1344.. 314 D nancy.clarkson@flcc.edu
CLARKSON, Sallie .... 843-349-2448.. 428 E sallie@coastal.edu
CLARKSON, William .... 610-917-1477.. 422 C wmclarkson@valleyforge.edu
CLARKSTON, Bobbie .... 423-636-7300.. 447 G bclarkston@tusculum.edu
CLARY, Bruce .... 620-242-0506.. 183 C claryb@mcpherson.edu
CLARY, Christine .... 802-654-2548.. 484 I cclary@smcvt.edu
CLARY, Dean .... 309-649-6316.. 155 G dean.clary@src.edu
CLARY, Donnie, O .... 252-398-6250.. 343 G claryd@chowan.edu
CLARY, Ernest .... 484-646-5933.. 415 C clary@kutztown.edu
CLARY, Gail .... 229-931-2318.. 127 C gclary@southgatech.edu
CLARY, Henry .... 276-326-4257.. 437 F hclary@bluefield.edu
CLARY, Jason .... 503-228-6528.. 390 A jclary@aii.edu
CLARY, Joshua, R .... 270-686-4332.. 137 C josh.clary@brescia.edu
CLARY, Laurie .... 360-538-4009.. 504 B lclary@ghc.edu
CLARY, Stephanie .... 270-686-9550.. 137 C stephanie.clary@brescia.edu
CLASS, Richard, D .... 212-472-1500.. 324 A rclass@nysid.edu
CLAUSEN, Dave .... 530-251-8826.... 48 E dclausen@lassencollege.edu
CLAUSEN, Doris .... 201-216-5016.. 297 B doris.clausen@stevens.edu
CLAUSEN, Janice .... 661-654-3360.... 32 A jclausen@csub.edu
CLAUSEN, Louise .... 270-852-3284.. 191 C lclausen@kwc.edu
CLAUSEN, Terry .... 870-850-8606.... 22 E tclausen@seark.edu
CLAUSON, Kevin, L .... 423-775-7324.. 439 B kclauson4864@bryan.edu
CLAUSON BASH, Kathleen, M .... 641-784-5064.. 172 G clauson@graceland.edu
CLAUSS, Kari .... 610-690-5707.. 419 I kclauss1@swarthmore.edu
CLAUSS, Sandy .... 210-366-2701.. 463 J
CLAUSSEN, Ann, E .... 610-861-1492.. 411 B claussena@moravian.edu
CLAUSSEN, Linda, C .... 540-674-3614.. 497 G lclaussen@nr.edu
CLAVELLE, Martha .... 619-644-7000.... 45 J martha.clavelle@gcccd.edu
CLAVERIE, Mark .... 518-587-2100.. 335 D mark.claverie@esc.edu
CLAVIER, Cheri .... 423-439-7483.. 444 F clavier@etsu.edu
CLAVIJO, Manuel .... 508-849-3280.. 214 E mclavijo@annamaria.edu
CLAVILLE, Michelle .... 757-727-5239.. 490 E michelle.claville@hamptonu.edu
CLAWSON, Dana .... 318-677-3100.. 201 B roed@nsula.edu
CLAWSON, Michelle .... 757-727-5474.. 490 E michelle.clawson@hamptonu.edu
CLAXTON, Brenda .... 432-264-5160.. 459 D bclaxton@howardcollege.edu
CLAXTON, Patricia .... 325-574-7607.. 479 I pclaxton@wtc.edu
CLAXTON, Stephanie, L .... 315-267-2154.. 334 B claxtosc@potsdam.edu
CLAY, Aileen .... 603-206-8175.. 286 D aclay@ccsnh.edu
CLAY, Antoinette, M .... 732-255-0400.. 293 E aclay@ocean.edu
CLAY, Brian .... 501-370-5336.... 21 G bclay@philander.edu
CLAY, Daniel .... 319-335-5380.. 169 H daniel-clay@uiowa.edu
CLAY, Doreen .... 818-710-2510.... 50 A claydj@piercecollege.edu
CLAY, George, W .... 864-656-0723.. 428 C gclay@clemson.edu
CLAY, Gladys .... 904-470-8087.... 98 N gladys.clay@ewc.edu
CLAY, John, L .... 256-469-7333...... 4 E president@hbc1.edu
CLAY, Karen .... 662-329-7104.. 259 E kgclay@muw.edu
CLAY, Karen .... 541-962-3792.. 391 C karen.clay@eou.edu
CLAY, Lauren .... 662-476-5060.. 257 G lclay@eastms.edu
CLAY, Maggie .... 310-393-0411.... 56 G mclay@rand.org
CLAY, Martyn .... 813-757-2110.. 102 R mclay6@hccfl.edu
CLAY, Melanie, N .... 678-839-0627.. 129 E melaniec@westga.edu
CLAY, Mercedes .... 419-783-2362.. 368 A mclay@defiance.edu
CLAY, Patricia .... 610-282-1100.. 402 B patricia.clay@desales.edu
CLAY, Philip, N .... 508-831-5201.. 230 C pclay@wpi.edu
CLAY, Rex .... 704-922-6243.. 350 A clay.rex@gaston.edu
CLAY, Sandra .... 903-586-2518.. 460 A sclay@jacksonville-college.edu
CLAY, Sharon .... 770-394-8300.. 116 F dbclay@aii.edu
CLAY, Sharon .... 913-758-6108.. 185 F sharon.clay@stmary.edu
CLAY, Trish .... 304-558-2104.. 512 O patricia.clay@wvhepc.edu
CLAY, Victor .... 323-259-2598.... 55 A vclay@oxy.edu
CLAY-ROOKS, Saskia .... 703-993-3738.. 490 B sclayroo@gmu.edu
CLAYBON, John .... 405-682-7855.. 385 D jclaybon@occc.edu
CLAYBORNE, Hannah .... 419-289-5324.. 363 J hclaybor@ashland.edu
CLAYBORNE, Staci, G ...... 618-235-2700.. 155 C staci.clayborne@swic.edu
CLAYBORNE-SCOTT, Monica .... 731-426-7533.. 440 K mclayborne@lanecollege.edu
CLAYBROOK, Jennifer, D 706-880-8032.. 123 K jclaybrook@lagrange.edu
CLAYCOMB, Ann .... 304-293-9919.. 514 C ann.claycomb@mail.wvu.edu
CLAYPOOL, Joe .... 859-333-8888.. 193 G joseph.claypool@uky.edu
CLAYPOOLE, Jack .... 803-777-4111.. 433 F jclaypoole@mycarolina.org
CLAYTER, Seth .... 207-699-5032.. 203 F sclayter@meca.edu
CLAYTON, Carrie .... 903-566-7184.. 477 B cclayton@uttyler.edu
CLAYTON, Dana .... 812-488-2500.. 167 I dc26@evansville.edu
CLAYTON, Ellen .... 443-334-2558.. 211 A eclayton@stevenson.edu
CLAYTON, Jack, A .... 304-842-8269.. 513 B jclayton@fairmontstate.edu
CLAYTON, Jan, L .... 918-595-7901.. 388 F jan.clayton@tulsacc.edu
CLAYTON, Janet, S .... 803-934-3246.. 431 E jclayton@morris.edu
CLAYTON, Jay, B .... 724-653-2202.. 402 F jclayton@dec.edu
CLAYTON, Jeffrey .... 954-492-5353.... 97 I jclayton@citycollege.edu
CLAYTON, Kirk .... 757-490-1241.. 486 E kclayton@auto.edu
CLAYTON, Kori .... 501-337-5000.... 19 K kclayon@coto.edu
CLAYTON, Lisa .... 413-528-7239.. 214 H lclayton@simons-rock.edu
CLAYTON, Loretta .... 478-471-5762.. 124 E loretta.clayton@mga.edu
CLAYTON, Patricia, I .... 336-322-2105.. 351 H patti.clayton@piedmontcc.edu
CLAYTON, Tiffany .... 610-921-7795.. 396 H tclayton@albright.edu
CLAYTON, Tonya, M .... 989-386-6601.. 238 B tmclayton@midmich.edu
CLAYTON, Yvette .... 256-372-5690...... 1 A yvette.clayton@aamu.edu

CLEANTHES, Jeff .... 901-843-3456.. 443 L
cleanthesj@rhodes.edu
CLEARFIELD, Michael ...... 707-638-5982.... 68 C
michael.clearfield@tu.edu
CLEARWATER, Bonnie ..... 954-262-0225.. 105 J
bclearwater@moafl.org
CLEARY, Anita .... 509-452-5100.. 505 H
acleary@pnwu.edu
CLEARY, Brian .... 860-512-2613.... 86 E
bcleary@manchestercc.edu
CLEARY, Charles .... 860-773-3403.... 87 E
ccleary@txcc.commnet.edu
CLEARY, Delores .... 509-963-2152.. 501 K
delores.cleary@cwu.edu
CLEARY, Kathleen .... 937-512-3159.. 377 D
kathleen.cleary@sinclair.edu
CLEARY, Keelan .... 503-534-4051.. 392 D
kcleary@marylhurst.edu
CLEARY, Kelly .... 610-896-1181.. 405 I
kcleary@haverford.edu
CLEARY, Lynn .... 315-464-5387.. 332 C
clearyl@upstate.edu
CLEARY, Paul, C .... 203-785-2867.... 90 D
paul.cleary@yale.edu
CLEARY, Sally .... 973-290-4449.. 290 G
scleary@cse.edu
CLEARY, Thomas .... 210-485-0500.. 450 A
tcleary1@alamo.edu
CLEARY, Thomas .... 210-486-5000.. 450 B
CLEARY, Thomas, R .... 619-260-4297.... 72 B
tcleary@sandiego.edu
CLEARY, Valerie, A .... 503-370-6262.. 396 G
vcleary@willamette.edu
CLEAVER, Richard, G .... 340-693-1042.. 539 C
richard.cleaver@uvi.edu
CLEAVES, Laura .... 603-577-6515.. 286 I
lcleaves@dwc.edu
CLEAVES, Wandamae .... 207-947-4591.. 202 E
bookstore@bealcollege.edu
CLEBSCH, Bill .... 650-725-0056.... 66 I
clebsch@stanford.edu
CLECKLER, Steven .... 205-970-9239...... 7 B
scleckler@sebc.edu
CLECKNER, Lisa .... 315-781-4381.. 316 C
cleckner@hws.edu
CLEEK, Stu .... 805-565-6029.... 75 A
scleek@westmont.edu
CLEGG, Cynthia, B .... 405-325-2190.. 389 B
cclegg@hsc.net.ou.edu
CLEGG, Cynthia, B .... 405-325-2910.. 389 B
cclegg@hsc.net.ou.edu
CLEGG, Mark .... 801-422-3868.. 480 C
mark_clegg@byu.edu
CLEGG, Neill .... 336-272-7102.. 344 G
cleggn@greensboro.edu
CLEM, Amy .... 903-566-7480.. 477 B
aclem@uttyler.edu
CLEM, Cynthia .... 404-880-8048.. 118 K
cclem@cau.edu
CLEM, Randy .... 916-558-2424.... 51 D
clemrj@scc.losrios.edu
CLEMENCE, Patrick .... 319-398-1274.. 174 I
patrick.clemence@kirkwood.edu
CLEMENS, Bonnie .... 909-607-3679.... 38 H
bonnie_clemens@cuc.claremont.edu
CLEMENS, John .... 229-317-6700.. 120 A
john.clemens@darton.edu
CLEMENT, Christopher, D 603-862-3081.. 288 C
christopher.clement@unh.edu
CLEMENT, Fred .... 512-472-4133.. 465 F
fred.clement@ssw.edu
CLEMENT, Gregory .... 978-632-6600.. 224 B
g_clement@mwcc.mass.edu
CLEMENT, James, A .... 205-726-2395...... 6 E
jaclemen@samford.edu
CLEMENT, Linda, M .... 301-314-8430.. 211 E
lclement@umd.edu
CLEMENT, Mercedes .... 386-506-3440.... 98 E
clemenm@daytonastate.edu
CLEMENT, Nancy .... 985-448-7915.. 196 E
nancy.clement@fletcher.edu
CLEMENT, Richard .... 505-277-4241.. 302 F
riclement@unm.edu
CLEMENT, William .... 757-822-7373.. 498 H
wclement@tcc.edu
CLEMENT CORNIES,
Dawn .... 901-843-3745.. 443 L
corniesd@rhodes.edu
CLEMENTE, Amy .... 404-364-8533.. 125 F
aclemente@oglethorpe.edu
CLEMENTS, Angela .... 512-313-3000.. 455 F
angela.clements@concordia.edu
CLEMENTS, Blayne .... 931-221-7466.. 444 E
clementsb@apsu.edu
CLEMENTS, Carole .... 303-546-3584.... 81 I
carole@naropa.edu
CLEMENTS, Eric .... 509-542-4688.. 502 G
eclements@columbiabasin.edu
CLEMENTS, Gary .... 252-527-6223.. 350 H
gclements@lenoircc.edu
CLEMENTS, Geri .... 478-553-2066.. 125 C
gclements@oftc.edu
CLEMENTS, James, P .... 864-656-3413.. 428 C
president@clemson.edu
CLEMENTS, Kieran .... 706-886-6831.. 128 C
clements@tfc.edu
CLEMENTS, Lee Ann .... 904-256-7030.. 103 D
lclemen@ju.edu
CLEMENTS, Mari .... 626-584-5501.... 44 G
clements@fuller.edu
CLEMENTS, Stephen, K ..... 859-858-3511.. 186 J
steve.clements@asbury.edu
CLEMENTS, Tommy .... 276-523-7462.. 497 F
tclements@me.vccs.edu
CLEMENTS, Tommy .... 276-523-7431.. 497 F
tclements@me.vccs.edu
CLEMENTS, Vickie .... 814-864-6666.. 404 E
vickiec@glit.edu
CLEMENTS, William .... 802-485-2370.. 484 H
bclements@norwich.edu
CLEMETSEN, Bruce .... 541-917-4806.. 392 C
clemetb@linnbenton.edu
CLEMMER, Kristi .... 432-335-6865.. 463 B
kclemmer@odessa.edu
CLEMMER, Margaret .... 202-885-2141.... 91 J
megc@american.edu
CLEMMONS, Brian .... 732-906-2509.. 292 E
bclemmons@middlesexcc.edu
CLEMMONS, Fran .... 865-688-9422.. 440 C
CLEMMONS, Raechelle ..... 704-894-3246.. 343 I
raclemmons@davidson.edu
CLEMMONS, Sarah .... 850-718-2213.... 97 G
clemmonss@chipola.edu
CLEMMONS, Val .... 910-362-7373.. 348 A
vclemmons@cfcc.edu
CLEMONS, Brian .... 816-415-7802.. 275 F
clemonsb@william.jewell.edu
CLEMONS, Cassie .... 912-287-5834.. 119 B
cclemons@coastalpines.edu
CLEMONS, Cheryl .... 270-686-4250.. 187 C
cheryl.clemons@brescia.edu
CLEMONS, Chuck .... 352-395-5202.. 109 C
chuck.clemons@sfcollege.edu
CLEMONS, Neil .... 386-506-3813.... 98 E
clemonn@daytonastate.edu
CLEMONS, Rita .... 909-635-0250.. 217 A
rita.clemons@cambridgecollege.edu
CLEMONS, Teresa, G .... 806-345-5548.. 450 H
t0155151@actx.edu
CLENDENEN, Holly .... 608-822-2362.. 524 F
hclendenen@swtc.edu
CLENDENEN, Mike .... 252-493-7645.. 352 A
mclendenen@email.pittcc.edu
CLERE, Ray, R .... 859-257-2746.. 193 G
ray.clere@uky.edu
CLERKIN, Elizabeth .... 440-775-8450.. 374 C
liz.clerkin@oberlin.edu
CLERKIN, Kris .... 603-201-0420.. 287 I
k.clerkin@snhu.edu
CLESCERI, Michael .... 815-479-7833.. 147 E
mclesceri@mchenry.edu
CLEVELAND, SR.,
Alvin, A .... 334-872-2533...... 6 F
aclevesr@aol.com
CLEVELAND, Angela .... 269-965-3931.. 236 A
clevelanda@kellogg.edu
CLEVELAND, III, Carl, S . 913-234-0600.. 179 M
carl.clevelandiii@cleveland.edu
CLEVELAND, Charles, E .... 509-527-5158.. 509 G
clevelan@whitman.edu
CLEVELAND, Conne .... 559-934-2383.... 74 C
conneclevelend@whccd.edu
CLEVELAND, Gerald .... 409-772-3689.. 478 A
gtclevel@utmb.edu
CLEVELAND, Melanie .... 229-243-3007.. 117 E
melanie.cleveland@bainbridge.edu
CLEVELAND, Tracey .... 716-851-1844.. 313 H
clevelandt@ecc.edu
CLEVELAND, Vicki .... 951-552-8650.... 29 H
vdcleveland@calbaptist.edu
CLEVENGER, Brian .... 217-206-6174.. 156 G
clevenger.brian@uis.edu
CLEVENGER, Julie .... 217-786-2365.. 146 E
julie.clevenger@llcc.edu
CLEVENGER, Leah .... 704-406-4255.. 344 E
lclevenger@gardner-webb.edu
CLEVINGER, Sarah .... 423-652-4715.. 440 J
sclevinger@king.edu
CLIATT, Bill .... 213-624-1200.... 43 J
bcliatt@fidm.edu
CLIATT, Cass .... 401-863-2453.. 424 J
cass_cliatt@brown.edu
CLICK, Sally, E .... 317-940-9854.. 159 K
sclick@butler.edu
CLICK, Stanley .... 606-759-7141.. 190 C
stanley.click@kctcs.edu
CLICKNER, David, C .... 518-629-8068.. 316 G
d.clickner@hvcc.edu
CLIFFORD, Alexander .... 207-454-1003.. 204 A
aclifford@wccc.me.edu
CLIFFORD, Bob .... 505-454-3351.. 300 F
bclifford@nmhu.edu
CLIFFORD, Christopher ... 205-934-8229...... 8 E
cbcliff@uab.edu
CLIFFORD, Dale .... 912-525-5000.. 126 E
dcliffor@scad.edu
CLIFFORD, Heather .... 802-440-4325.. 483 E
hclifford@bennington.edu
CLIFFORD, Joan .... 518-244-2410.. 327 H
cliffj3@sage.edu
CLIFFORD, John, P .... 216-397-4963.. 370 H
jclifford@jcu.edu
CLIFFORD, Patrick .... 203-773-6989.... 85 C
pclifford@albertus.edu
CLIFFORD, Paul, J .... 814-865-6516.. 412 F
pjc37@psu.edu
CLIFFORD, Philip .... 615-230-3250.. 447 C
phil.clifford@volstate.edu
CLIFT, Carla .... 256-551-3120...... 4 F
carla.clift@drakestate.edu
CLIFTON, Gaye, B .... 336-342-4261.. 352 F
cliftong@rockinghamcc.edu
CLIFTON, SJ, James, F ..... 402-280-2519.. 279 H
jclifton@creighton.edu
CLIFTON, Jamie .... 951-571-6293.... 59 A
jamie.clifton@mvc.edu
CLIFTON, Jerry .... 501-205-8789.... 19 J
jclifton@cbc.edu
CLIFTON, Lonzy .... 334-876-9251...... 4 A
lonzy.clifton@wccs.edu
CLINARD, Lesley, J .... 269-337-5767.. 235 H
lesley.clinard@kzoo.edu
CLINARD, Rhonda .... 931-363-9820.. 441 G
rclinard@martinmethodist.edu
CLINE, Angela .... 252-493-7679.. 352 A
acline@email.pittcc.edu
CLINE, Cathie .... 870-633-4480.... 20 B
ccline@eacc.edu
CLINE, Elizabeth, W .... 330-325-6498.. 373 H
ecline@neomed.edu
CLINE, Gina .... 321-433-7000.... 98 K
clineg@easternflorida.edu
CLINE, Glen, E .... 607-587-3917.. 334 G
clinege@alfredstate.edu
CLINE, J. Robert .... 864-231-2077.. 427 B
bcline@andersonuniversity.edu
CLINE, Jack .... 240-477-9505.. 185 D
jackcline@ku.edu
CLINE, Joseph .... 775-784-1740.. 285 A
cline@unr.edu
CLINE, Kimberly, R .... 516-299-2501.. 319 B
president@liu.edu
CLINE, Kimberly, R .... 516-299-2501.. 319 C
president@liu.edu
CLINE, Laurel .... 610-796-8317.. 397 D
laurel.cline@alvernia.edu
CLINE, Mariah .... 620-417-1106.. 184 I
mariah.cline@sccc.edu
CLINE, Nicky .... 319-398-5629.. 174 I
nicky.cline@kirkwood.edu
CLINE, Penny .... 785-462-3984.. 180 C
CLINE, Robert, J .... 814-871-5615.. 404 A
cline001@gannon.edu
CLINE, Serena .... 503-517-1026.. 396 D
scline@warnerpacific.edu
CLINE, Stacy .... 585-582-8241.. 313 B
stacycline@elim.edu
CLINE, Tamara .... 530-283-0202.... 43 G
tcline@frc.edu
CLINE, Tricia .... 785-628-4091.. 180 I
tcline@fhsu.edu
CLINGINGSMITH, Aaron .. 406-657-2243.. 277 D
aaron.clingingsmith@msubillings.edu
CLINGMAN, Michele .... 575-492-2545.. 300 H
mclingman@nmjc.edu
CLINKSCALES, Sherard ..... 812-237-4091.. 162 A
sherard.clinkscales@indstate.edu
CLINTON, Antwan, D .... 202-806-1361.... 93 A
aclinton@howard.edu
CLINTON, Christine, M .... 814-886-6380.. 411 C
cclinton@mtaloy.edu
CLINTON, Don .... 903-693-2055.. 463 D
dclinton@panola.edu
CLINTON, Ericka .... 212-924-5900.. 336 I
eclinton@swedishinstitute.edu
CLINTON, John .... 717-477-1377.. 416 A
jeclin@sufoundation.org
CLINTON, Joseph .... 845-848-7700.. 312 F
joseph.clinton@dc.edu
CLINTON, Linda, T .... 903-886-5139.. 468 D
linda.clinton@tamuc.edu
CLINTON, Ron .... 903-434-8186.. 462 M
rclinton@ntcc.edu
CLINTON, Veronica .... 732-906-4661.. 292 E
vclinton@middlesexcc.edu
CLINTON JONES,
Karen, A .... 716-878-6210.. 332 F
joneska@buffalostate.edu
CLIPPERTON, Alan .... 903-233-3160.. 460 J
alanclipperton@letu.edu
CLISH, Colleen .... 651-290-6328.. 253 S
colleen.clish@mitchellhamline.edu
CLITES, Mona .... 301-784-5000.. 205 G
mclites@allegany.edu
CLOAN, Deborah .... 951-222-8000.... 59 C
deborah.cloan@rcc.edu
CLODFELTER, Elaine .... 704-272-5302.. 353 B
eclodfelter@spcc.edu
CLODFELTER, JR.,
Roger, D .... 336-841-9156.. 345 A
rclodfel@highpoint.edu
CLOETE, Marion, E .... 619-239-0391.... 36 A
mcloete@cwsl.edu
CLOHAN, William, C .... 949-783-4800.... 74 A
william.clohan@westcoastuniversity.edu
CLOKEY, Diane .... 860-253-3015.... 86 A
dclokey@asnuntuck.edu
CLONINGER, Jason .... 217-854-5654.. 135 K
jason.cloninger@blackburn.edu
CLONINGER, Mindy, E ..... 620-235-4241.. 184 C
mcloninger@pittstate.edu
CLOONAN, Patricia .... 202-687-7318.... 92 E
cloonanp@georgetown.edu
CLOOS, Kevin, P .... 716-673-3452.. 331 D
kevin.cloos@fredonia.edu
CLOPTON, John, D .... 319-296-4004.. 173 B
john.clopton@hawkeyecollege.edu
CLOS, Karén .... 254-519-5744.. 468 C
karen.bleeker@tamuct.edu
CLOSE, Cathy .... 715-232-1235.. 521 D
closec@uwstout.edu
CLOSE, Deidra .... 423-354-2405.. 446 F
dlclose@northeaststate.edu
CLOSE, Stacey .... 860-465-5000.... 85 G
closes@easternct.edu
CLOSE, Steve .... 443-334-2690.. 211 A
sclose@stevenson.edu
CLOSSER, James, B .... 615-868-6503.. 442 G
jclosser@mtsa.edu
CLOUD, Andy .... 432-837-8179.. 471 E
wacloud@sulross.edu
CLOUD, Chris .... 212-353-4136.. 311 G
cloud@cooper.edu
CLOUD, Gary .... 480-219-6013.. 262 A
gcloud@atsu.edu
CLOUD, Jessica .... 510-549-4711.... 66 J
jcloud@sksm.edu
CLOUD, Jill .... 254-519-5491.. 468 C
jill.cloud@tamuct.edu
CLOUD, Rodney .... 334-387-3877...... 1 E
rodneycloud@amridgeuniversity.edu
CLOUD, Sharon .... 770-412-4000.. 127 F
scloud@sctech.edu
CLOUGH, Susan .... 970-542-3127.... 81 H
susan.clough@morgancc.edu
CLOUGHERTY, Helen .... 832-813-6514.. 461 B
helen.clougherty@lonestar.edu
CLOUNCH, Teresa .... 785-594-8473.. 178 D
teresa.clounch@bakeru.edu
CLOUSE, Andrew, D .... 814-886-6480.. 411 C
aclouse@mtaloy.edu
CLOUSE, Cindy, D .... 606-679-8501.. 190 E
cindy.clouse@kctcs.edu
CLOUSE, Dave .... 731-989-6019.. 440 D
dclouse@fhu.edu
CLOUSE, Jim, W .... 432-837-8777.. 471 E
jclouse@sulross.edu
CLOUSE, Mark .... 405-208-5225.. 385 E
mclouse@okcu.edu
CLOUSE, Monica .... 606-546-1215.. 193 E
mclouse@unionky.edu
CLOUSTON, Heather, O .... 336-633-0286.. 352 B
hoclouston@randolph.edu
CLOUTIER, Barbara .... 715-858-1806.. 523 B
bcloutier@cvtc.edu
CLOUTIER, Michael .... 978-665-3590.. 221 D
mclouti4@fitchburgstate.edu
CLOUTIER, Michelle .... 401-232-6722.. 424 K
mcloutier@bryant.edu
CLOVIS, Stephen .... 503-845-3570.. 392 E
stephen.clovis@mtangel.edu
CLOW, Todd .... 517-607-2456.. 235 E
tclow@hillsdale.edu
CLOW, William, T .... 309-298-1552.. 158 A
wt-clow@wiu.edu
CLOWER, Matthew .... 334-808-6313...... 7 H
mclower@troy.edu
CLOWERS, Laurie, C .... 919-866-5929.. 353 I
lcclowers@waketech.edu
CLOYD, Angela .... 859-858-3581.. 186 I
president@asburyseminary.edu
CLOYD, Benjamin, G .... 601-857-3894.. 258 A
bgcloyd@hindscc.edu
CLOYD, Timothy .... 417-873-7201.. 264 H
jtcloyd16@drury.edu
CLUBB, Patricia, L .... 512-232-7742.. 476 B
pat.clubb@austin.utexas.edu
CLUBB, Sandy Hatfield ..... 515-271-2889.. 171 K
sandra.clubb@drake.edu
CLUCHEY, Cheryl .... 231-591-3811.. 233 L
cherylcluchey@ferris.edu

COHEN, David .... 800-371-6105.... 15 F
david@nationalparalegal.edu
COHEN, Ilene .... 732-255-0400.. 293 E
icohen@ocean.edu
COHEN, Jason .... 413-755-4438.. 224 G
jlcohen@stcc.edu
COHEN, Jennifer .... 206-543-2212.. 508 E
huskyad@uw.edu
COHEN, Joan .... 207-741-5559.. 203 M
jcohen@smccme.edu
COHEN, Joel, J .... 646-660-6060.. 307 A
COHEN, Jonah .... 203-285-2289.... 86 C
jcohen@gwcc.commnet.edu
COHEN, Jonathan .... 207-778-7430.. 205 A
COHEN, Kathleen, L .... 607-735-1728.. 313 F
kcohen@elmira.edu
COHEN, Kristin, E .... 919-508-2206.. 359 G
kris.cohen@peace.edu
COHEN, Laurie .... 480-423-6511.... 14 H
laurie.cohen@scottsdalecc.edu
COHEN, Lee .... 662-915-7178.. 261 B
leecohen@olemiss.edu
COHEN, Lizabeth .... 617-495-8602.. 219 D
lizabeth_cohen@radcliffe.harvard.edu
COHEN, Mark, J .... 202-687-7610.... 92 E
cohenm@georgetown.edu
COHEN, Marvin .... 312-369-7226.. 138 F
mcohen@colum.edu
COHEN, Melissa .... 717-796-5220.. 410 J
mcohen@messiah.edu
COHEN, Michael, E .... 772-466-4822.... 95 R
m.cohen@aviator.edu
COHEN, Mickey .... 215-596-8540.. 422 A
m.cohen@usciences.edu
COHEN, Morris .... 513-862-2743.. 369 E
morris_cohen@email.gscollege.edu
COHEN, Neil .... 864-578-8770.. 432 D
ncohen@sherman.edu
COHEN, Paula .... 215-895-1266.. 402 G
paula.marantz.cohen@drexel.edu
COHEN, Peter .... 718-368-5563.. 308 F
pcohen@kbcc.cuny.edu
COHEN, Pinchas .... 213-740-1354.... 72 D
hassy@usc.edu
COHEN, Richard .... 215-985-2500.. 424 C
rjc@phmc.org
COHEN, Richard, L .... 847-735-5555.. 145 B
cohen@lakeforest.edu
COHEN, Ronald, A .... 570-372-4103.. 419 H
cohen@susqu.edu
COHEN, Scott .... 731-425-2615.. 446 C
scohen@jscc.edu
COHEN, Shaya .... 347-619-9074.. 341 H
COHEN, Shelly .... 757-388-2900.. 494 A
scohen@sentara.edu
COHEN, Susan, J .... 215-574-9600.. 406 A
scohen@hussianart.edu
COHEN, Tamara .... 352-392-1261.. 112 A
tamararc@dso.ufl.edu
COHEN, Vicki .... 201-692-2525.. 291 J
cohen@fdu.edu
COHEN, William, A .... 301-405-9354.. 211 E
wcohen@umd.edu
COHEN, William, A .... 626-350-1500.... 30 D
COHEN, Yehuda .... 347-619-9074.. 341 H
COHEN, Zoe .... 978-837-5121.. 225 E
cohenz@merrimack.edu
COHEN-PERRY,
Carrmela, D .... 919-516-4128.. 355 D
cdcohen-perry@st-aug.edu
COHEN-ROSE, Amy .... 617-277-3915.. 216 D
cohenrose@bgsp.edu
COHN, Stephen, A .... 919-687-3606.. 343 J
stevec@acpub.duke.edu
COHRS, Daniel, L .... 303-963-3352.... 77 I
dcohrs@ccu.edu
COHUNE, Ellen .... 805-756-2527.... 31 I
ecohune@calpoly.edu
COICAUD, Jean-Marc ...... 973-353-3285.. 296 C
jeanmarc.coicaud@rutgers.edu
COKE, Kim .... 573-875-7420.. 263 F
kjcoke@ccis.edu
COKER, Alan .... 208-885-5541.. 134 G
alanc@uidaho.edu
COKER, Amber .... 850-913-3293.. 102 M
acoker@gulfcoast.edu
COKER, Bryan, F .... 410-337-6150.. 207 H
bryan.coker@goucher.edu
COKER, Dawn .... 706-880-8267.. 123 K
dcoker@lagrange.edu
COKER, Jeff .... 540-665-4587.. 494 B
jcoker2@su.edu
COKER, Kim .... 870-574-4533.... 22 G
kcoker@sautech.edu
COKER, Melissa, A .... 843-355-4117.. 435 A
cokerm@wiltech.edu
COKER, Scott, A .... 309-298-1834.. 158 A
sa-coker@wiu.edu
COKER, Sherry .... 417-447-8884.. 270 A
cokers@otc.edu
COKER-KOLO, Doyin .... 812-941-2385.. 163 F
ecokerko@ius.edu
COKKINOS, Michael .... 212-217-4476.. 314 B
michael_cokkinos@fitnyc.edu
COLÓN, Ingrid, Y .... 787-884-3838.. 530 G
administradora@atenascollege.edu
COLÓN, Silvestre .... 787-832-4040.. 538 C
decep@uprm.edu
COLÓN, Victor .... 515-289-9200.. 173 E
vcolon@inste.edu
COLADARCI, Richard .... 603-230-3512.. 286 A
rcoladarci@ccsnh.edu
COLADARCI, Ted, T .... 207-581-1415.. 204 H
theo@maine.edu
COLAGROSS, Glenda .... 256-395-2211...... 7 C
gcolagross@suscc.edu
COLAGROSS, Glenda .... 256-331-5275...... 6 A
colg@nwscc.edu
COLAHAN, Michael .... 610-896-1350.. 405 I
mcolahan@haverford.edu
COLANANNI, Terri .... 501-337-5000.... 19 K
terric@coto.edu
COLANER, Kevin, T .... 909-869-3365.... 31 J
ktcolaner@cpp.edu
COLANGELO, Carmon ..... 314-935-9300.. 274 N
colangelo@wustl.edu
COLAPIETRO, Cathy, L ... 913-971-3298.. 183 D
ccolapietro@mnu.edu
COLARERI, Michael, L ..... 978-468-7111.. 219 B
mcolareri@gcts.edu
COLARIC, Susan .... 727-497-5051.. 108 D
colaric.susan@spcollege.edu
COLARULLI, Guy, C .... 860-768-4749.... 89 G
colarulli@hartford.edu
COLARUSSO, Judy .... 253-566-5136.. 508 B
jcolarusso@tacomacc.edu
COLASURDO,
Giuseppe, N .... 713-500-3000.. 477 C
giuseppe.n.colasurdo@uth.tmc.edu
COLATCH, John, P .... 570-577-1592.. 398 L
john.colatch@bucknell.edu
COLBAN, Tom .... 201-360-4393.. 292 B
tcolban@follett.com
COLBECK, Ellen .... 217-875-7200.. 152 C
ecolbeck@richland.edu
COLBERT, Carly, J .... 315-445-4312.. 318 E
colbercj@lemoyne.edu
COLBERT, Claudia .... 718-997-3009.. 309 D
claudia.colbert@qc.cuny.edu
COLBERT, Joe .... 972-860-2973.. 456 C
jcolbert@dcccd.edu
COLBERT, Mary, J .... 410-857-2214.. 209 D
mcolbert@mcdaniel.edu
COLBERT RILEY, Cynthia 713-525-3119.. 475 J
colbert@stthom.edu
COLBROOK, William .... 217-351-2884.. 151 B
wcolbrook@parkland.edu
COLBS, Sandy .... 309-438-3655.. 143 B
slcolbs@ilstu.edu
COLBY, Adam .... 727-864-7732.... 98 L
colbyac@eckerd.edu
COLBY, Andrew .... 603-862-1568.. 288 C
andy.colby@unh.edu
COLBY, Chuck .... 570-662-4952.. 415 E
ccolby@mansfield.edu
COLBY, Glenn .... 425-352-8420.. 501 J
gcolby@cascadia.edu
COLBY-BOND, Courtney .. 208-562-3084.. 133 F
courtneybond@cwidaho.cc
COLBY CLEMENTS, Paula 978-681-0800.. 225 B
pcolby@mslaw.edu
COLCOLOUGH, Sharon .... 864-646-1790.. 433 C
scolcolo@tctc.edu
COLDREN, Brian .... 404-261-1441.. 125 F
bcoldren@oglethorpe.edu
COLDREN, Mark .... 716-645-8155.. 331 C
mcoldren@buffalo.edu
COLDREN, Stephanie .... 410-337-6118.. 207 H
stephanie.coldren@goucher.edu
COLE, Amber .... 405-945-3310.. 386 C
ambcole@osuokc.edu
COLE, Andrew .... 859-344-3683.. 193 C
colea@thomasmore.edu
COLE, April .... 830-591-7252.. 466 A
acole@swtjc.edu
COLE, Brad .... 435-797-2631.. 482 B
brad.cole@usu.edu
COLE, Brian .... 336-631-1226.. 358 E
coleb@uncsa.edu
COLE, Bruce .... 704-922-6309.. 350 A
cole.bruce@gaston.edu
COLE, Carol .... 304-896-7429.. 512 E
carol.cole@southernwv.edu
COLE, Carol, A .... 304-896-7429.. 512 E
carol.cole@southernwv.edu
COLE, Christopher, L .... 804-523-5843.. 497 C
ccole@reynolds.edu
COLE, Christy, C .... 434-381-6530.. 494 M
ccole@sbc.edu
COLE, Dan .... 402-363-5609.. 283 G
dcole@york.edu
COLE, David .... 817-722-1618.. 460 E
david.cole@tku.edu
COLE, David, J .... 843-792-2211.. 431 A
coledj@musc.edu
COLE, Dayton, T .... 828-262-2751.. 356 B
coledt@appstate.edu
COLE, Donald, R .... 662-915-7111.. 261 B
dcole@olemiss.edu
COLE, Elyne .... 217-333-6677.. 157 A
egcole@illinois.edu
COLE, Frank .... 505-566-3511.. 301 J
colef@sancollege.edu
COLE, Graham .... 847-317-8086.. 156 B
gacole@tiu.edu
COLE, Jack, T .... 717-766-2511.. 410 J
jcole@messiah.edu
COLE, Jeffrey .... 860-439-2030.... 87 F
jcole1@conncoll.edu
COLE, Jeffrey, S .... 724-847-4696.. 404 B
jscole@geneva.edu
COLE, Jill .... 716-926-8933.. 316 B
jillcole@hilbert.edu
COLE, Jim .... 478-301-2994.. 124 D
cole_jm@mercer.edu
COLE, Joey .... 501-812-2243.... 21 H
jcole@pulaskitech.edu
COLE, John, J .... 304-293-8470.. 514 C
jay.cole@mail.wvu.edu
COLE, John, W .... 401-825-2034.. 425 A
jcole@ccri.edu
COLE, Judith, M .... 617-253-8231.. 225 A
COLE, Karin .... 540-857-7236.. 499 B
kcole@virginiawestern.edu
COLE, Katharine, H .... 813-253-6130.. 114 M
kcole@ut.edu
COLE, Kathryn, B .... 601-857-3502.. 258 A
kathryn.cole@hindscc.edu
COLE, Keri .... 601-857-3624.. 258 A
kbcole@hindscc.edu
COLE, Kimberly, M .... 330-972-2603.. 378 G
kmorgan@uakron.edu
COLE, Kristie, C .... 864-231-2067.. 427 B
kcole@andersonuniversity.edu
COLE, Lady June .... 803-376-5701.. 427 A
lcole@allenuniversity.edu
COLE, Lauren .... 334-670-3216...... 7 H
lscole@troy.edu
COLE, Lauren, G .... 910-642-7141.. 353 C
lauren.cole@sccnc.edu
COLE, Lindsay .... 304-865-6077.. 511 C
lindsay.cole@ovu.edu
COLE, Lisa, L .... 318-257-5222.. 200 G
lcole@latech.edu
COLE, Mark .... 305-237-3242.. 105 D
mcole@mdc.edu
COLE, Mark .... 315-312-3672.. 333 D
rmark.cole@oswego.edu
COLE, Nadara, L .... 662-720-7277.. 260 B
ncole@nemcc.edu
COLE, Nathan .... 937-778-1555.. 368 E
ncole@edisonohio.edu
COLE, Nathan .... 937-381-1555.. 368 E
ncole@edisonohio.edu
COLE, Rebecca, S .... 937-775-2350.. 381 H
rebecca.cole@wright.edu
COLE, Richard .... 732-906-4153.. 292 E
rcole@middlesexcc.edu
COLE, Richard .... 678-915-5519.. 123 J
rcole@kennesaw.edu
COLE, JR., Richard .... 914-633-2311.. 317 B
rcole@iona.edu
COLE, Robert .... 413-205-3336.. 214 B
robert.cole@aic.edu
COLE, Robert, A .... 401-254-3149.. 426 B
rcole@rwu.edu
COLE, Ronald, B .... 814-332-3393.. 397 A
rcole@allegheny.edu
COLE, Sercia .... 501-370-5378.... 21 G
scolel@philander.edu
COLE, Stephanie, A .... 716-286-8319.. 324 E
scole@niagara.edu
COLE, Steve .... 870-584-1143.... 23 F
scole@cccua.edu
COLE, Susan, A .... 973-655-4212.. 293 A
coles@mail.montclair.edu
COLE, III, W. Allen .... 859-572-5225.. 192 B
colew1@nku.edu
COLE, W. Scott .... 407-823-2482.. 111 E
scott.cole@ucf.edu
COLE, Wayne .... 563-441-4011.. 172 D
wcole@eicc.edu
COLE, Xavier, A .... 410-778-7752.. 213 E
xcole2@washcoll.edu
COLE, Xavier, A .... 414-288-7206.. 517 I
xavier.a.cole@marquette.edu
COLE-VELASQUEZ,
Colleen .... 575-624-8011.. 300 I
cvelasquez@nmmi.edu
COLEAL, Sharlene .... 661-362-3405.... 40 A
sharlene.coleal@canyons.edu
COLECCHIA, Carlo .... 201-355-1124.. 291 K
colecchiac@felician.edu
COLELLA, Carlo .... 301-405-1105.. 211 E
ccolella@umd.edu
COLELLA, Christine .... 215-885-2360.. 409 G
ccolella@manor.edu
COLELLA, Kurt, J .... 860-444-8275.. 529 A
kurt.j.colella@uscg.mil
COLELLA, Laurie .... 508-831-4922.. 230 C
lcolella@wpi.edu
COLELLI, Marc .... 650-325-5621.... 59 J
marc.colelli@stpatricksseminary.org
COLELLO, Elizabeth .... 315-268-3826.. 310 B
ecolello@clarkson.edu
COLEMAN, Anastasia .... 718-817-3112.. 314 G
acoleman11@fordham.edu
COLEMAN, Andre .... 916-558-2376.... 51 D
colemaa@scc.losrios.edu
COLEMAN, Angela .... 850-599-3183.. 110 J
angela.coleman@famu.edu
COLEMAN, Anne Marie ... 401-874-5270.. 426 D
acoleman@uri.edu
COLEMAN, Annetta .... 317-789-8271.. 160 E
acoleman@crossroads.edu
COLEMAN, Barbara .... 212-875-4472.. 304 E
bcoleman@bankstreet.edu
COLEMAN, Bob, J .... 904-620-2700.. 112 B
jcoleman@unf.edu
COLEMAN, Carmita .... 773-821-2500.. 136 M
ccolem30@csu.edu
COLEMAN, Carole, T .... 928-344-7521.... 11 J
carole.coleman@azwestern.edu
COLEMAN, Catherine, T .. 870-633-4480.... 20 B
ccoleman@eacc.edu
COLEMAN, Chad .... 574-535-7292.. 161 A
chadc@goshen.edu
COLEMAN, Clarence, D .... 757-823-8408.. 492 F
cdcoleman@nsu.edu
COLEMAN, Clinton, R .... 443-885-3022.. 209 F
clinton.coleman@morgan.edu
COLEMAN, Craig, S .... 412-397-4912.. 418 B
colemanc@rmu.edu
COLEMAN, Daniel .... 410-462-8432.. 206 D
dacoleman@bccc.edu
COLEMAN, Danielle .... 252-398-6200.. 343 G
colemd@chowan.edu
COLEMAN, Darin .... 843-921-6936.. 431 H
dcoleman@netc.edu
COLEMAN, David .... 859-622-1403.. 188 F
david.coleman@eku.edu
COLEMAN, Dayna, L .... 509-777-4565.. 509 H
dcoleman@whitworth.edu
COLEMAN, Deanna .... 574-239-8405.. 161 N
dcoleman@hcc-nd.edu
COLEMAN, Deidra .... 210-436-3135.. 464 H
dcoleman@stmarytx.edu
COLEMAN, Dennis .... 214-379-5514.. 463 G
dcoleman@pqc.edu
COLEMAN, Diane .... 206-934-3842.. 506 K
diane.coleman@seattlecolleges.edu
COLEMAN, Don .... 423-354-2533.. 446 F
dscoleman@northeaststate.edu
COLEMAN, Ellen .... 302-736-2508.... 91 G
ellen.coleman@wesley.edu
COLEMAN, Emily .... 606-539-4230.. 193 F
emily.coleman@ucumberlands.edu
COLEMAN, F. Paul .... 607-431-4449.. 315 E
colemanf@hartwick.edu
COLEMAN, Frances, N ..... 662-325-7661.. 259 D
fcoleman@library.msstate.edu
COLEMAN, Hardin, L .... 617-353-3213.. 216 E
hardin@bu.edu
COLEMAN, Helen .... 217-244-8817.. 157 A
hjcolema@illinois.edu
COLEMAN, James .... 928-523-8062.... 15 H
james.coleman@nau.edu
COLEMAN, James, C .... 601-977-7809.. 261 A
jcoleman@tougaloo.edu
COLEMAN, Jay, T .... 319-352-8264.. 177 G
todd.coleman@wartburg.edu
COLEMAN, John .... 612-624-2535.. 255 H
coleman@umn.edu
COLEMAN, John .... 903-434-8104.. 462 M
jcoleman@ntcc.edu
COLEMAN, Jonathan .... 920-206-2346.. 517 G
jonathan.coleman@mbu.edu
COLEMAN, Joyce .... 708-534-4124.. 140 H
jcoleman@govst.edu
COLEMAN, Julie .... 206-934-3227.. 506 I
julie.coleman@seattlecolleges.edu
COLEMAN, June .... 620-341-5407.. 180 G
jcoleman@emporia.edu
COLEMAN, Kristie .... 918-595-8180.. 388 F
kristie.coleman@tulsacc.edu
COLEMAN, Lamar .... 860-465-0147.... 85 G
colemanl@easternct.edu
COLEMAN, Laura .... 906-786-5802.. 231 O
colemanl@baycollege.edu
COLEMAN, Linda .... 610-519-4074.. 422 G
linda.coleman@villanova.edu

COLLINS-HALL, Lori .... 937-319-0069.. 363 D
lcollinshall@antiochcollege.org
COLLINWOOD, Nancy ...... 801-626-6569.. 482 D
ncollinwood@weber.edu
COLLIS, Jennifer .... 440-375-7175.. 371 E
jcollis@lec.edu
COLLMIER, Robert .... 973-748-9000.. 289 H
robert_collmier@bloomfield.edu
COLLOGAN, Jessica .... 904-256-7269.. 103 D
jcollog@ju.edu
COLLOPY, David .... 413-528-7773.. 214 H
dcollopy@simons-rock.edu
COLLUM, Tammy .... 770-975-4000.. 118 J
COLLURA, Dorothy .... 419-289-5031.. 363 J
dcollura@ashland.edu
COLMAN, Avrohom .... 732-367-1060.. 289 G
COLMAN, Gabriela .... 254-710-1421.. 452 H
gabriela_colman@baylor.edu
COLMAN, Glenn .... 870-743-3000.... 21 C
gcoleman@northark.edu
COLMENERO,
Jacinto (JC) .... 361-354-2559.. 454 G
jcolmenero@coastalbend.edu
COLMERAUER, Joanne .... 716-270-2826.. 313 H
colmerauer@ecc.edu
COLOM, Albert, N .... 904-620-2881.. 112 B
colom@unf.edu
COLOMBAT, Andre .... 410-617-2910.. 208 G
acp@loyola.edu
COLOMBO, Samuel .... 607-753-2305.. 333 A
samuel.colombo@cortland.edu
COLON, Adabel-Vanessa . 787-250-1912.. 534 B
avcolon@metro.inter.edu
COLON, Ana Isabel .... 787-857-3600.. 533 I
acolon@br.inter.edu
COLON, Angie .... 787-863-2390.. 533 K
angie.colon@fajardo.inter.edu
COLON, Brenda .... 787-765-4210.. 531 H
bcolon@cempr.edu
COLON, Diana, M .... 787-257-7373.. 535 P
dmcolon@suagm.edu
COLON, Eddie .... 816-279-7000.. 262 B
eddie.colon@abtu.edu
COLON, Hector, W .... 787-284-1912.. 534 C
hwcolon@ponce.inter.edu
COLON, Iris .... 787-746-1400.. 532 M
icolon@huertas.edu
COLON, Isaac .... 787-844-8991.. 538 E
isaaccolondegro@upr.edu
COLON, Jaime .... 787-279-1912.. 533 J
jcolon@bayamon.inter.edu
COLON, Jose .... 787-738-2161.. 538 A
jose.colon29@upr.edu
COLON, Leandro .... 787-841-2000.. 535 I
leandro_colon@pucpr.edu
COLON, Lesbia .... 787-844-8181.. 538 E
lesbia.colon@upr.edu
COLON, Luis .... 787-815-0000.. 537 F
luis.colon19@upr.edu
COLON, Luis .... 787-761-0640.. 537 C
lcolon@utcpr.edu
COLON, Maggie .... 787-763-1912.. 533 F
mcolon@inter.edu
COLON, Maria .... 787-765-3560.. 532 I
mscolon@edpuniversity.edu
COLON, Michelle .... 407-888-8689.. 100 H
mcolon@fcim.edu
COLON, Mirta .... 787-754-8000.. 537 B
mcolon@pupr.edu
COLON, Myrna .... 787-834-9595.. 536 E
mcolon@uaa.edu
COLON, Nidia .... 787-786-3030.. 536 F
ncolon@ucb.edu.pr
COLON, Ruben .... 787-841-2000.. 535 I
ruben_colon@pucpr.edu
COLON, Victor .... 787-786-3030.. 536 F
vcolon@ucb.edu.pr
COLON, Vilma, E .... 787-284-1912.. 534 C
vcolon@ponce.inter.edu
COLON, Yarelis .... 787-753-6000.. 532 O
ycolon@icprjc.edu
COLON-CANALES, Wanda 301-891-4093.. 213 D
wcanales@wau.edu
COLON COSME,
Edwin, J .... 787-744-1060.. 534 G
edwincolon@mechtech.edu
COLON-GUASO, Wilfredo 787-288-1118.. 535 O
COLON NEGRON, Edgar . 787-758-2525.. 538 D
edgar.colon2@upr.edu
COLON-RAMOS,
Carlos, E .... 787-864-2222.. 534 A
carlos.colon@guayama.inter.edu
COLONNO, Daniel, J .... 413-662-5281.. 222 B
d.colonno@mcla.edu
COLORADO, Ana .... 787-725-8120.. 532 K
acolorado0013@eap.edu
COLORETTI, Angela .... 808-735-4787.. 130 F
angela.coloretti@chaminade.edu
COLSON, Darrel, D .... 319-352-8450.. 177 G
president@wartburg.edu
COLSON, Jessica .... 413-265-2454.. 217 D
colsonj@elms.edu
COLSON, Matthew .... 631-632-4932.. 332 A
matthew.colson@stonybrook.edu
COLTER-BRABHAM,
Constance .... 803-780-1189.. 434 M
cbrabham@voorhees.edu
COLTHARP, Duane .... 210-999-8201.. 473 A
dcolthar@trinity.edu
COLTHARP, Glenn .... 417-455-5740.. 264 E
glenncoltharp@crowder.edu
COLTMAN, Heather .... 561-297-3803.. 110 K
coltman@fau.edu
COLTRANE, Scott, L .... 541-346-3186.. 395 G
provost@uoregon.edu
COLTRANE BATTLE,
Donna .... 919-760-8346.. 346 D
battledo@meredith.edu
COLUCCI, David .... 718-779-1499.. 326 D
dcolluci@plazacollege.edu
COLUCCI, Rita .... 508-626-4993.. 221 E
rcolucci@framingham.edu
COLUMBUS, Kristi .... 319-895-4153.. 171 A
kcolumbus@cornellcollege.edu
COLUSSY-ESTES, Kate ...... 404-471-6437.. 115 J
kcolussyestes@agnesscott.edu
COLVEY, Kirsten, S .... 909-389-3327.... 60 B
kcolvey@craftonhills.edu
COLVILLE, John .... 903-988-3747.. 460 D
jcolville@kilgore.edu
COLVIN, Brandon .... 701-228-5452.. 361 D
brandon.colvin@dakotacollege.edu
COLVIN, Christopher .... 508-213-2368.. 227 A
christopher.colvin@nichols.edu
COLVIN, Jenna .... 706-867-4518.. 128 F
jenna.colvin@ung.edu
COLVIN, Robert, E .... 757-594-0723.. 488 E
rcolvin@cnu.edu
COLVSON, W. Mark .... 845-257-3719.. 331 E
colvsonm@newpaltz.edu
COLWELL, Joy .... 219-989-2665.. 166 F
colwell@pnw.edu
COLWELL, Ken .... 860-832-3217.... 85 F
colwell@ccsu.edu
COLWELL, Kim, H .... 217-443-8769.. 139 B
kcolwell@dacc.edu
COLWELL, William, B ...... 618-453-2121.. 154 I
COLYAR, Jana .... 801-818-8900.. 481 B
jana.colyar@provocollege.edu
COMAGE, Rebecca .... 978-542-2404.. 222 D
rebecca.comage@salemstate.edu
COMAIR, Claude .... 425-558-0299.. 503 C
ccomair@digipen.edu
COMALANDER, Tammy .... 251-981-3771...... 2 I
tammy.comalander@columbiasouthern.edu
COMANDA, Peter .... 815-280-6606.. 144 A
pcomanda@jjc.edu
COMAS, Waldemar, A ...... 914-594-4567.. 323 I
waldemar_comas@nymc.edu
COMBE, Arnold, B .... 801-581-6404.. 481 M
arnie.combe@admin.utah.edu
COMBES, Bertina .... 940-565-2231.. 475 A
bertina.combes@unt.edu
COMBINE, Mark, S .... 724-738-2251.. 416 B
mark.combine@sru.edu
COMBS, Brandon .... 859-858-3511.. 186 J
brandon.combs@asbury.edu
COMBS, Charles, D .... 757-446-6090.. 489 B
combscd@evms.edu
COMBS, Delcie .... 606-487-3100.. 189 E
delcie.combs@kctcs.edu
COMBS, Joseph, L .... 423-585-2675.. 447 D
joseph.combs@ws.edu
COMBS, Kevin .... 509-524-5162.. 508 F
kevin.combs@wwcc.edu
COMBS, Kristina, A .... 415-485-9504..... 40 C
kcombs@marin.edu
COMBS, Lisa, H .... 704-894-2000.. 343 I
COMBS, Patricia .... 256-228-6001...... 5 I
combsp@nacc.edu
COMBS, Steven .... 417-873-7204.. 264 H
scombs@drury.edu
COMBS, Vickie .... 606-487-3110.. 189 E
vickie.combs@kctcs.edu
COMEAU, Jeff .... 850-474-2610.. 113 A
jcomeau@uwf.edu
COMEAU, Juanita .... 608-246-6596.. 523 F
jcomeau@madisoncollege.edu
COMEAUX, David, P .... 337-482-0922.. 201 D
dcomeaux@louisiana.edu
COMEAUX, Linda .... 303-914-6403.... 82 I
linda.comeaux@rrcc.edu
COMEAUX, Mark .... 714-879-3901..... 46 F
mcomeaux@hiu.edu
COMEDY-HOLMES,
Jennifer .... 210-486-4857.. 450 C
jcomedy-holmes@alamo.edu
COMEGYS, Marianne .... 318-675-6065.. 198 B
mcomeg@lsuhsc.edu
COMER, Alberta .... 801-585-9521.. 481 M
alberta.comer@utah.edu
COMER, Charlotte .... 501-420-1213.... 18 F
charlotte.comer@arkansasbaptist.edu
COMER, Christopher .... 406-243-2632.. 276 K
chris.comer@umontana.edu
COMER, Crystal .... 612-330-1034.. 244 I
comerc@augsburg.edu
COMER, Kimberly .... 229-928-1373.. 122 C
kim.comer@gsw.edu
COMER, Linda, S .... 863-680-3951.. 101 E
lcomer@flsouthern.edu
COMER, Pamela, D .... 540-432-4314.. 488 K
pam.comer@emu.edu
COMER, Sean .... 513-745-4868.. 381 I
comers@xavier.edu
COMERFORD, Ann .... 309-298-1931.. 158 A
at-comerford@wiu.edu
COMERFORD, John .... 217-854-3231.. 135 K
john.comerford@blackburn.edu
COMERFORD,
Sandra Stefani .... 650-574-6404.... 62 H
comerford@smccd.edu
COMEY, William .... 301-934-7509.. 207 B
billc@csmd.edu
COMMETTE, Jeanne .... 978-232-2344.. 218 D
jcommett@endicott.edu
COMMISSO, Louis .... 631-730-2023.. 305 K
lcommisso@bcl.edu
COMMON, Brandon .... 309-556-3990.. 143 D
bcommon@iwu.edu
COMMONS, Mary .... 803-508-7413.. 426 G
commonsm@atc.edu
COMPAAN, Korey .... 952-446-4233.. 246 D
compaank@crown.edu
COMPARY, Kristin .... 361-593-3606.. 469 A
kristin.compary@tamuk.edu
COMPHER, Jeff .... 252-737-4501.. 356 C
compherj@ecu.edu
COMPLIMENT, Brad .... 562-985-4001.... 33 B
brad.compliment@csulb.edu
COMPTON, Allyssa .... 845-368-7203.. 329 I
allyssa.compton@use.salvationarmy.org
COMPTON, Betsy .... 205-652-3892...... 9 F
bcompton@uwa.edu
COMPTON, Duane, A .... 603-650-1200.. 286 J
duane.a.compton@dartmouth.edu
COMRIE, Andrew, C .... 520-621-1856.... 17 I
comrie@email.arizona.edu
COMRIE, Phyllis .... 828-713-2520.. 346 M
pcomrie@montreat.edu
COMSTOCK, Alysha .... 708-524-6296.. 139 F
acomstock@dom.edu
COMVALIUS-GODDARD,
Sharon .... 617-552-8259.. 216 C
sharon.comvalius-goddard@bc.edu
CONARD, T. Hunt .... 518-580-5940.. 330 F
hconard@skidmore.edu
CONATSER, Sherri .... 405-878-5116.. 387 J
seconatser@stgregorys.edu
CONATY, William .... 401-232-6000.. 424 K
CONAWAY, Kathleen, M .. 814-332-4799.. 397 A
kconaway@allegheny.edu
CONBOY, Sheila (Katie) .. 617-521-2077.. 228 C
katie.conboy@simmons.edu
CONCANNON, Chris .... 360-992-2411.. 502 E
cconcannon@clark.edu
CONCEPCIÓN, Carmen .... 787-764-0000.. 538 F
concepcioncm@yahoo.com
CONCEPCION, Angelica .... 718-390-3420.. 339 F
angelica.concepcion@wagner.edu
CONCEPCION, Beth .... 912-525-5000.. 126 E
bconcepc@scad.edu
CONCEPCION, Lillian .... 787-250-1912.. 534 B
lconcepcion@metro.inter.edu
CONCHA, Lee .... 847-578-8848.. 153 A
lee.concha@rosalindfranklin.edu
CONCILIO, Michael .... 215-335-0800.. 409 A
mconcilio@lincolntech.edu
CONCODORA, Jackie .... 803-323-2206.. 435 B
concodoraj@winthrop.edu
CONDE-FRAZIER,
Elizabeth .... 215-324-0746.. 403 B
econdefr@eastern.edu
CONDELL, Greg .... 617-373-5144.. 227 B
CONDIC, Elizabeth .... 713-525-6960.. 475 J
condice@stthom.edu
CONDON, Jacquelyn, S ... 309-457-2113.. 148 E
jackiec@monmouthcollege.edu
CONDON, Jennifer .... 813-974-6061.. 112 C
jcondon@admin.usf.edu
CONDON, Jennifer, M ..... 515-574-1190.. 173 F
condon@iowacentral.edu
CONDON, Katherine .... 850-474-2230.. 113 A
kcondon@uwf.edu
CONDON, Lisa .... 860-768-4007.... 89 G
lcondon@hartford.edu
CONDON, Patricia .... 508-678-2811.. 223 A
patricia.condon@bristolcc.edu
CONDON, Stephen, M ...... 336-821-2471.. 345 C
scondon@johnwesley.edu
CONDON, Tami .... 817-645-3921.. 466 C
tcondon@swau.edu
CONDON, Terry .... 617-287-7800.. 220 G
terry.condon@umb.edu
CONDRA, Shawn, M .... 785-539-3571.. 183 B
scondra@mccks.edu
CONDRON, Dan .... 707-664-2158.... 35 D
condrond@sonoma.edu
CONDRON, Leanne .... 724-480-3401.. 401 F
leanne.condron@ccbc.edu
CONDUAH, Dorothy .... 608-243-4746.. 523 F
dconduah@madisoncollege.edu
CONE, Allen, J .... 323-265-8913.... 49 G
coneaj@elac.edu
CONE, Angela, W .... 334-420-4216...... 7 G
acone@trenholmstate.edu
CONE, Christopher .... 816-322-0110.. 262 N
CONE, Diana .... 912-478-5258.. 122 B
dcone@georgiasouthern.edu
CONE, Janet, R .... 828-251-6922.. 357 C
jcone@unca.edu
CONELLI, Maria, A .... 718-951-3180.. 307 D
mconelli@brooklyn.cuny.edu
CONEWAY, Raydor .... 478-275-6589.. 125 D
CONEWAY, Raydor .... 478-553-2065.. 125 C
rconeway@oftc.edu
CONFER, Christopher ...... 765-641-4219.. 158 J
clconfer@anderson.edu
CONGDON, Bruce, D .... 206-281-2899.. 507 C
bcongdon@spu.edu
CONGER, Heather .... 609-894-9311.. 295 C
hconger@rcbc.edu
CONGLETON, Dawn, L ..... 434-223-6203.. 490 D
dcongleton@hsc.edu
CONGLETON, Peter .... 212-353-4172.. 311 G
peterc@cooper.edu
CONGLETON, Yasemin .... 859-246-6487.. 189 B
yasemin.congleton@kctcs.edu
CONGRESSI, Karyn .... 386-752-1822.. 100 L
karyn.congressi@fgc.edu
CONIGLIO, Michael .... 706-880-8184.. 123 K
mconiglio@lagrange.edu
CONINE, Chris .... 423-614-8102.. 441 B
cconine@leeuniversity.edu
CONINE, Darren .... 978-837-5154.. 225 E
conined@merrimack.edu
CONINE, Frances .... 318-357-5286.. 201 B
coninef@nsula.edu
CONINE, Richard .... 518-832-7791.. 335 A
coniner@sunyacc.edu
CONISON, Jay .... 704-971-8504.. 343 E
jconison@charlottelaw.edu
CONJAR, Catarin .... 610-647-4400.. 406 B
cconjar@immaculata.edu
CONKLIN, Barbara .... 252-399-6570.. 341 P
baconklin@barton.edu
CONKLIN, David .... 716-488-3026.. 317 E
davidconklin@jbc.edu
CONKLIN, Denise .... 405-912-9005.. 387 D
dconklin@hc.edu
CONKLIN, Eileen .... 915-831-4432.. 457 H
econklin@epcc.edu
CONKLIN, Elizabeth .... 860-486-2943.... 89 D
elizabeth.conklin@uconn.edu
CONKLIN, Kathleen .... 517-371-5140.. 243 I
conklink@cooley.edu
CONKLIN, Lara, L .... 217-443-8798.. 139 B
lconklin@dacc.edu
CONKLIN, Margaret .... 212-355-1501.. 306 L
mconklin@christies.edu
CONKLIN, Peter .... 603-513-1382.. 288 D
peter.conklin@granite.edu
CONKLIN, Robin .... 845-574-4484.. 327 G
rconklin@sunyrockland.edu
CONLEY, Bill .... 402-554-2358.. 283 B
bconley@unomaha.edu
CONLEY, Cary .... 270-831-9610.. 189 F
cary.conley@kctcs.edu
CONLEY, Dennis .... 618-395-7777.. 142 E
conleyd@iecc.edu
CONLEY, Heather .... 319-398-5504.. 174 I
heather.conley@kirkwood.edu
CONLEY, Jeremy, D .... 515-574-1086.. 173 F
conley@iowacentral.edu
CONLEY, Jerome .... 513-529-2800.. 372 K
conleyj@miamioh.edu
CONLEY, John .... 518-562-4219.. 310 C
john.conley@clinton.edu
CONLEY, Johnny .... 909-384-8988.... 60 C
jconley@sbccd.cc.ca.us
CONLEY, Katharine .... 757-221-2470.. 488 F
kconley@wm.edu
CONLEY, Kelli .... 256-840-4101...... 6 H
kconley@snead.edu
CONLEY, Kimberley, S ..... 270-831-9752.. 189 F
kim.conley@kctcs.edu
CONLEY, Laura, H .... 330-972-5793.. 378 G
lhc1@uakron.edu
CONLEY, Maria .... 978-934-2383.. 221 A
maria_conley@uml.edu

CONYERS, Rhyan, M ... 859-233-8500.. 193 D rconyers@transy.edu
CONZATTI, Maria, P ... 516-572-7600.. 322 C maria.conzatti@ncc.edu
CONZEN, Christopher ... 212-752-1530.. 318 F christopher.conzen@limcollege.edu
COOGAN, Jay ... 612-874-3737.. 247 M president@mcad.edu
COOK, Aaron ... 303-546-5284.... 81 I acook@naropa.edu
COOK, Alicia ... 973-748-9000.. 289 H alicia_cook@bloomfield.edu
COOK, Allen, P ... 203-576-4206.... 89 C acook@bridgeport.edu
COOK, Amber ... 814-871-7421.. 404 A cook0692@gannon.edu
COOK, Andrea, P ... 503-517-1212.. 396 D acook@warnerpacific.edu
COOK, Angela ... 207-780-5737.. 205 E
COOK, Anita ... 914-606-6745.. 340 C anita.cook@sunywcc.edu
COOK, Barbara Jo ... 770-467-6038.. 127 F bcook@sctech.edu
COOK, Bradley ... 435-586-7704.. 481 N bradcook@suu.edu
COOK, Brenda, A ... 334-683-2353...... 5 G bcook@marionmilitary.edu
COOK, Brett ... 208-496-3405.. 132 J cookb@byui.edu
COOK, Brian ... 440-525-7720.. 371 F bcook@lakelandcc.edu
COOK, Bruce ... 386-506-4417.... 98 E cookb@daytonastate.edu
COOK, Carey, W ... 208-467-8643.. 134 D cwcook@nnu.edu
COOK, Charles ... 512-223-7612.. 451 N charles.cook@austincc.edu
COOK, Chris ... 806-742-2136.. 472 C chris.cook@ttu.edu
COOK, Cindy ... 281-283-2595.. 474 A cookc@uhcl.edu
COOK, Connie, S ... 540-985-8344.. 491 A cscook@jchs.edu
COOK, Corey ... 208-426-1368.. 132 I coreydcook@boisestate.edu
COOK, Courtney ... 207-699-5060.. 203 F ccook@meca.edu
COOK, Craig ... 530-226-4188.... 64 H ccook@simpsonu.edu
COOK, Darrell ... 202-885-3546.... 91 J dcook@american.edu
COOK, David ... 847-628-1520.. 144 B dcook@judsonu.edu
COOK, David ... 309-694-8551.. 141 F dcook@icc.edu
COOK, David ... 913-897-8400.. 185 D davidcook@ku.edu
COOK, David, E ... 218-722-4000.. 246 E davidc@dbumn.edu
COOK, Debra ... 918-335-6264.. 386 F dcook@okwu.edu
COOK, Don ... 954-201-7538.... 96 I dcook@broward.edu
COOK, Donelda ... 410-617-5171.. 208 G dcook@loyola.edu
COOK, Donna, L ... 575-439-3699.. 301 A donnac@nmsu.edu
COOK, Donna, M ... 401-341-2435.. 426 C donna.cook@salve.edu
COOK, Douglas ... 757-352-4331.. 493 E dougcoo@regent.edu
COOK, Edith ... 724-830-1014.. 419 D ecook@setonhill.edu
COOK, Ellen, D ... 337-482-6306.. 201 D edcook@louisiana.edu
COOK, Elsie ... 510-567-6174.... 67 E drcook@sum.edu
COOK, Gary ... 770-484-1204.. 124 C gary.cook@lutherrice.edu
COOK, Gary ... 214-333-5130.. 455 J chancellor@dbu.edu
COOK, Greg ... 262-472-1077.. 521 F cookg@uww.edu
COOK, Holly ... 970-207-4500.... 84 F hollyc@uscareerinstitute.edu
COOK, Holly ... 970-207-4550.... 81 F hollyc@mckinleycollege.edu
COOK, Howard, M ... 803-786-3343.. 429 A hcook@columbiasc.edu
COOK, James ... 336-734-7311.. 349 G jcook@forsythtech.edu
COOK, Jeffrey ... 657-278-4475.... 33 A jcook@fullerton.edu
COOK, Jeffrey ... 513-569-1579.. 366 D jeffrey.cook@cincinnatistate.edu
COOK, Jerry ... 918-456-5511.. 384 G cookjc@nsuok.edu
COOK, Jerry ... 936-294-3620.. 471 D bio_jlc@shsu.edu
COOK, Jessica ... 302-736-2435.... 91 G jessica.cook@wesley.edu
COOK, Jim ... 573-651-2206.. 272 B jcook@semo.edu
COOK, John, B ... 603-206-8009.. 286 D jcook@ccsnh.edu
COOK, John, B ... 413-755-4906.. 224 G jbcook@stcc.edu
COOK, John, C ... 540-985-8317.. 491 A jccook@jchs.edu
COOK, Jolane ... 870-777-5722.... 24 A jolane.cook@uacch.edu
COOK, Judy, I ... 615-353-3236.. 446 E judy.cook@nscc.edu
COOK, Karen ... 650-723-2300.... 66 I kcook@stanford.edu
COOK, Karen ... 410-777-7370.. 206 B kcook@aacc.edu
COOK, Kevin ... 601-984-4100.. 261 C kcook@umc.edu
COOK, Larry ... 909-389-3384.... 60 B lcook@craftonhills.edu
COOK, Les, P ... 906-487-2465.. 238 A lpcook@mtu.edu
COOK, Leslee ... 435-283-7221.. 482 E leslee.cook@snow.edu
COOK, Lisa, R ... 510-981-2939.... 57 B lrcook@peralta.edu
COOK, Lori ... 918-495-7708.. 386 H lcook@oru.edu
COOK, Mary ... 713-222-5340.. 474 B cookm@uhd.edu
COOK, Melinda ... 617-670-4462.. 218 G mcook1@fisher.edu
COOK, Melinda ... 800-567-2344.. 516 B melcook@menominee.edu
COOK, Melissa ... 207-801-5610.. 202 H mcook@coa.edu
COOK, Michelle ... 405-208-5000.. 385 E michelle.cook@okcu.edu
COOK, Michelle ... 336-750-2184.. 359 B cookm@wssu.edu
COOK, Michelle, G ... 706-583-8195.. 128 E mgcook@uga.edu
COOK, Patrick ... 978-656-3134.. 224 A
COOK, Phil ... 423-614-8500.. 441 B pcook@leeuniversity.edu
COOK, Richard, D ... 585-785-1410.. 314 D richard.cook@flcc.edu
COOK, Robert, G ... 617-627-2546.. 228 H robert.cook@tufts.edu
COOK, Rosalie ... 650-493-4430.... 64 I rosalie.cook@sofia.edu
COOK, Royrickers ... 334-844-5700...... 1 G cookroy@auburn.edu
COOK, Ryan ... 801-832-5303.. 483 D rcook@westminstercollege.edu
COOK, Sandra ... 619-594-4766.... 35 A scook@mail.sdsu.edu
COOK, Sarah ... 404-727-6123.. 120 E sccook@emory.edu
COOK, Scott ... 931-393-1844.. 446 D scook@mscc.edu
COOK, Scott, A ... 304-336-8137.. 513 F cookscot@westliberty.edu
COOK, Sharon, L ... 972-860-7629.. 456 D scook@dcccd.edu
COOK, Stacey, A ... 408-864-8330.... 44 A cookstacey@deanza.edu
COOK, Steve ... 502-895-3411.. 191 F scook@lpts.edu
COOK, Susan ... 409-880-8195.. 470 H slcook@lit.edu
COOK, Terry ... 410-455-2939.. 211 G tcook@umbc.edu
COOK, Thomas ... 239-513-1135.. 115 F tcook@wolford.edu
COOK, Tim ... 909-599-5433.... 48 K tcook@lifepacific.edu
COOK, Tim ... 360-992-2217.. 502 E tcook@clark.edu
COOK, Tom, G ... 304-327-4111.. 512 P tcook@bluefieldstate.edu
COOK, Toni ... 510-748-2135.... 57 C tcook@peralta.edu
COOK, Tracy ... 601-877-6111.. 256 F tmcook@alcorn.edu
COOK, Vicki ... 231-995-1144.. 239 C vcook@nmc.edu
COOK, William ... 304-307-0716.. 512 E william.cook@southernwv.edu
COOK-FRANCIS, Lynette .. 212-237-8100.. 308 E lcook-francis@jjay.cuny.edu
COOK-NOBLES, Robin ... 784-283-2839.. 229 C rcooknob@wellesley.edu
COOKE, Caretta ... 504-816-4222.. 195 B ccooke@dillard.edu
COOKE, Connie, F ... 716-878-4902.. 332 F cookecf@buffalostate.edu
COOKE, Harry ... 704-922-6355.. 350 A cooke.harry@gaston.edu
COOKE, Ilene ... 845-437-7200.. 339 C ilcooke@vassar.edu
COOKE, Joy ... 757-825-2728.. 498 G cookej@tncc.edu
COOKE, Linda ... 206-239-4500.. 502 D lcooke@cityu.edu
COOKE, Peggy, S ... 248-370-2190.. 239 K cooke@oakland.edu
COOKE, Sandy, P ... 434-223-6340.. 490 D scooke@hsc.edu
COOKE, Sean ... 253-840-8472.. 506 B scooke@pierce.ctc.edu
COOKE, Sunita ... 760-757-2121.... 52 K scooke@miracosta.edu
COOKMAN, John ... 972-825-4659.. 466 D jcookman@sagu.edu
COOKSEY, Beth ... 615-230-3560.. 447 C beth.cooksey@volstate.edu
COOKSEY, Gaye, M ... 972-881-5807.. 455 A gcooksey@collin.edu
COOKSEY, Lynita ... 870-972-2030.... 18 J lcooksey@astate.edu
COOKSEY, Scott ... 801-863-8568.. 482 C scott.cooksey@uvu.edu
COOLE, Gloria, G ... 218-722-4000.. 246 E finaid@dbumn.edu
COOLEY, Chantell ... 251-981-3771...... 2 I chantell.cooley@columbiasouthern.edu
COOLEY, Francis ... 203-287-3029.... 88 E paier.dean@snet.net
COOLEY, John ... 614-287-2501.. 367 C jcooley3@cscc.edu
COOLEY, Lisa, K ... 336-322-2200.. 351 H lisa.cooley@piedmontcc.edu
COOLEY, Lynn ... 203-432-2733.... 90 D lynn.cooley@yale.edu
COOLEY, Marianne, B ... 784-283-3344.. 229 C mcooley@wellesley.edu
COOLEY, Maurice, R ... 304-696-5430.. 513 D cooley@marshall.edu
COOLEY, Meghan, M ... 309-794-7314.. 135 D meghancooley@augustana.edu
COOLEY, Mike ... 972-860-7871.. 456 G mcooley@dcccd.edu
COOLEY, Nanette ... 610-330-5114.. 407 C cooleyn@lafayette.edu
COOLEY, Stacey ... 505-224-4000.. 299 F scooley3@cnm.edu
COOLEY, Thomas ... 412-268-4731.. 400 D tkcooley@andrew.cmu.edu
COOLEY, Tom ... 816-604-6538.. 267 G thomas.cooley@mcckc.edu
COOMAR, Parmeshwar ... 734-384-4209.. 238 C pcoomar@monroeccc.edu
COOMBS, Gary, F ... 619-201-8989.... 65 J gcoombs@shadowmountain.org
COOMBS, Robert ... 207-741-5569.. 203 M rcoombs@smccme.edu
COOMBS, Vanessa ... 804-257-5856.. 500 B vcoombs@vuu.edu
COOMER, Sue, B ... 270-384-8024.. 191 E coomers@lindsey.edu
COOMES, Kerrie ... 620-431-2820.. 183 H kcoomes@neosho.edu
COON, David, W ... 415-485-9502.... 40 C dcoon@marin.edu
COON, Lynda ... 479-575-2000.... 22 I
COON, Omayra ... 910-221-2224.. 344 F
COON, Thomas ... 405-744-2474.. 385 G thomas.coon@okstate.edu
COONAN, Patrick, R ... 516-877-4511.. 303 B coonan@adelphi.edu
COONEN, Ned ... 847-214-7557.. 140 A ncoonen@elgin.edu
COONER, Elizabeth ... 908-527-7213.. 298 A elizabeth.cooner@ucc.edu
COONEY, Anita ... 718-636-3630.. 326 E acooney@pratt.edu
COONEY, J.P ... 330-494-6170.. 377 J jcooney@starkstate.edu
COONEY, Marcia, J ... 570-577-1631.. 398 L marcia.cooney@bucknell.edu
COONEY, Terry ... 410-704-2128.. 213 B tcooney@towson.edu
COONEY-CONNOR, Erica . 315-781-3103.. 316 C econnor@hws.edu
COONEY MINER, Dianne, C ... 585-385-8472.. 328 E dcooney-miner@sjfc.edu
COONING, Peggy, J ... 615-248-1355.. 447 F pcooning@trevecca.edu
COONROD, Curtis, C ... 314-516-5211.. 274 A curt_coonrod@umsl.edu
COONROD, Julie ... 505-277-2711.. 302 F jcoonrod@unm.edu
COONROD, Kevin ... 334-844-7170...... 1 G kcc0024@auburn.edu
COONS, Christopher, R ... 607-735-1806.. 313 F ccoons@elmira.edu
COONS, Maria ... 847-925-6143.. 141 A mcoons@harpercollege.edu
COONS, Patrick ... 502-272-8056.. 187 A pcoons@bellarmine.edu
COONS, Robert, A ... 812-877-8007.. 166 H robert.a.coons@rose-hulman.edu
COONTZ, Heather ... 216-373-5316.. 374 B hcoontz@ndc.edu
COOPEE, Scott, J ... 413-782-1246.. 229 E scott.coopee@wne.edu
COOPER, Adrienne ... 386-481-2076.... 96 H coopera@cookman.edu
COOPER, Alan ... 212-678-8065.. 317 I alcooper@jtsa.edu
COOPER, Almeta ... 404-752-1895.. 125 A acooper@msm.edu
COOPER, Amy, M ... 270-384-8053.. 191 E coopera@lindsey.edu
COOPER, Aneita ... 870-759-4184.... 24 J acooper@wbcoll.edu
COOPER, Anne, M ... 727-341-3323.. 108 D cooper.anne@spcollege.edu
COOPER, Barbara, I ... 252-222-6225.. 348 B cooperb@carteret.edu
COOPER, Brett ... 870-759-4107.... 24 J bcooper@wbcoll.edu
COOPER, Candace ... 704-878-3256.. 351 D ccooper@mitchellcc.edu
COOPER, Carrie ... 757-221-3055.. 488 F clcooper@wm.edu
COOPER, Christopher ... 617-274-3398.. 225 C christopher.cooper@mcphs.edu
COOPER, Christopher ... 419-383-5320.. 380 D christopher.cooper@utoledo.edu
COOPER, Chrystal ... 910-672-1073.. 356 E ccooper3@uncfsu.edu
COOPER, Constance ... 502-410-6200.. 188 H ccooper@galencollege.edu
COOPER, Corey ... 765-998-4694.. 167 C crcooper@taylor.edu
COOPER, Cynthia, L ... 585-292-3015.. 321 J ccooper@monroecc.edu
COOPER, Dan ... 864-646-1762.. 433 C dcooper2@tctc.edu
COOPER, David ... 773-777-4220.. 150 D dcooper@nc.edu
COOPER, David ... 401-841-3540.. 528 E
COOPER, Donna ... 423-425-4184.. 448 F donna-cooper@utc.edu
COOPER, Doug ... 404-653-7882.. 124 I douglas.cooper@morehouse.edu
COOPER, Ed ... 229-430-3577.. 116 A ecooper@albanytech.edu
COOPER, Elizabeth ... 615-297-7545.. 438 F coopere@aquinascollege.edu
COOPER, Emmett ... 212-875-4679.. 304 E ecooper@bankstreet.edu
COOPER, Eric ... 707-654-1299.... 33 D ecropper@csum.edu
COOPER, Erik ... 916-660-7512.... 64 F ecooper@sierracollege.edu
COOPER, Frank ... 609-771-2357.. 290 F fcooper@tcnj.edu
COOPER, Franklin ... 406-638-3161.. 276 G cooperf@lbhc.edu
COOPER, Gail, S ... 626-585-7282.... 56 H gscooper@pasadena.edu
COOPER, Gayle ... 870-612-2121.... 23 H gayle.cooper@uaccb.edu
COOPER, Greg ... 765-455-9463.. 163 A gregcoop@iuk.edu
COOPER, Hans ... 443-885-3300.. 209 F hans.cooper@morgan.edu
COOPER, Helena ... 804-330-0111.. 487 P stuadvcrim@centura.edu
COOPER, Ingrid ... 484-654-2373.. 403 B icooper@eastern.edu
COOPER, James ... 773-291-6536.. 137 G jcooper53@ccc.edu
COOPER, James, E ... 334-727-8011...... 8 A cooper@tuskegee.edu
COOPER, James, M ... 619-239-0391.... 36 A jcooper@cwsl.edu
COOPER, Jason ... 269-927-8165.. 236 G cooperj@lakemichigancollege.edu
COOPER, Jeffrey ... 215-898-1388.. 421 E jeffcoop@upenn.edu
COOPER, Joe, J ... 906-487-2622.. 238 A jjcooper@mtu.edu
COOPER, Joel ... 610-328-7679.. 419 I jcooper2@swarthmore.edu
COOPER, John, D ... 563-333-6480.. 176 D cooperjohnd@sau.edu
COOPER, Jorsene ... 757-727-5323.. 490 E jorsene.cooper@hamptonu.edu
COOPER, Josh ... 617-327-6777.. 229 H josh_cooper@williamjames.edu
COOPER, Judi ... 407-708-2138.. 109 E cooperj@seminolestate.edu
COOPER, Karen ... 603-897-8508.. 287 F kcooper@rivier.edu
COOPER, Karen, S ... 650-723-0198.... 66 I karen.cooper@stanford.edu
COOPER, Karla ... 402-826-8111.. 280 B karla.cooper@doane.edu

COOPER, Karyn .... 850-729-6922.. 105 I
cooperk@nwfsc.edu
COOPER, Katie, R .... 304-336-8131.. 513 F
katie.cooper@westliberty.edu
COOPER, Kelly .... 815-921-4092.. 152 E
k.cooper@rockvalleycollege.edu
COOPER, Kelly .... 559-934-2231.... 74 C
kellycooper@whccd.edu
COOPER, Kenneth .... 925-424-1013.... 37 C
kcooper@laspositascollege.edu
COOPER, Kenneth .... 845-758-7461.. 304 F
cooper@bard.edu
COOPER, Kerrie, L .... 315-386-7616.. 335 B
cooper@canton.edu
COOPER, Kevin .... 772-462-7546.. 103 B
kcooper@irsc.edu
COOPER, Linda .... 260-665-4124.. 167 E
cooperl@trine.edu
COOPER, Lisa .... 209-954-5632.... 61 F
lcooper@deltacollege.edu
COOPER, Lisa, A .... 229-931-2921.. 122 C
lcooper@gsw.edu
COOPER, Lisa, J .... 215-951-2940.. 416 G
cooperl@philau.edu
COOPER, Marina .... 410-704-2356.. 213 B
mcooper@towson.edu
COOPER, Mark .... 614-251-4576.. 374 I
cooperm2@ohiodominican.edu
COOPER, Mary-Beth, A ... 413-748-3241.. 228 E
mbcooper@springfieldcollege.edu
COOPER, MaryKay .... 210-999-7011.. 473 A
marykay.cooper@trinity.edu
COOPER, Matthew .... 609-984-1140.. 297 F
mcooper@tesu.edu
COOPER, Michael .... 908-737-4700.. 292 C
mrcooper@kean.edu
COOPER, Monty .... 606-474-3000.. 188 L
COOPER, N. John .... 412-624-1164.. 421 G
cooper@pitt.edu
COOPER, Nani Lou, S ...... 864-488-4617.. 430 H
ncooper@limestone.edu
COOPER, Natalie, F .... 270-824-8599.. 190 B
natalie.cooper@kctcs.edu
COOPER, Patrick .... 812-357-6378.. 167 B
pcooper@saintmeinrad.edu
COOPER, Paul .... 631-451-4445.. 336 D
cooperp@sunysuffolk.edu
COOPER, R. Scott .... 267-502-2681.. 398 J
rscott.cooper@brynathyn.edu
COOPER, Rick .... 251-981-3771...... 2 I
rick.cooper@columbiasouthern.edu
COOPER, Rick .... 806-291-3801.. 479 D
rick.cooper@wbu.edu
COOPER, Ruth .... 512-313-3000.. 455 F
ruth.cooper@concordia.edu
COOPER, Sam .... 864-503-5854.. 434 G
scooper7@uscupstate.edu
COOPER, Sandy .... 918-595-7856.. 388 F
sandy.cooper@tulsacc.edu
COOPER, Shaina .... 202-274-5410.... 94 B
shaina.cooper@udc.edu
COOPER, Stephanie .... 973-300-2161.. 297 D
scooper@sussex.edu
COOPER, Stewart, E .... 219-464-5002.. 168 F
stewart.cooper@valpo.edu
COOPER, Susan .... 657-278-1605.... 33 A
scooper@fullerton.edu
COOPER, Tana .... 620-792-9241.. 178 G
coopert@bartonccc.edu
COOPER, Tara, L .... 606-546-1241.. 193 E
tcooper@unionky.edu
COOPER, Toya .... 805-565-6832.... 75 A
tcooper@westmont.edu
COOPER, Tracey, L .... 440-525-7230.. 371 F
tcooper@lakelandcc.edu
COOPER, Tyson .... 540-261-8463.. 494 F
tyson.cooper@svu.edu
COOPER-WHITE,
Michael, L .... 717-334-6286.. 409 C
mcooper@ltsg.edu
COOPERSMITH, Lynn ...... 609-586-4800.. 292 D
coopersl@mccc.edu
COOROUGH, Randall .... 262-691-5168.. 524 G
rcoorough@wctc.edu
COOTE, Samra .... 404-752-1733.. 125 A
scoote@msm.edu
COOTER, Raelynn .... 215-503-6595.. 420 E
raelynn.cooter@jefferson.edu
COOTER, Robert, B .... 502-272-7992.. 187 A
rcooter@bellarmine.edu
COOTS, Kevin .... 610-372-4721.. 417 G
kcoots@racc.edu
COP, Kenneth, B .... 732-932-7211.. 295 F
kcop@aps.rutgers.edu
COP, Kenneth, B .... 732-932-7211.. 296 B
kcop@aps.rutgers.edu
COPAS, Tyra .... 423-354-5259.. 446 F
tlcopas@northeaststate.edu
COPASS, Ron .... 239-489-9129.. 101 F
rlcopass@fsw.edu

COPE, Marla .... 913-234-0687.. 179 M
marla.cope@cleveland.edu
COPE, Michael .... 310-506-4270.... 56 J
mike.cope@pepperdine.edu
COPE, Tyler .... 714-533-3946.... 35 E
tyler@calums.edu
COPELAND, Angela .... 903-566-7080.. 477 B
jcopeland@uttyler.edu
COPELAND, Boyd .... 636-922-8238.. 271 A
bcopeland@stchas.edu
COPELAND, Brian .... 616-331-2831.. 234 F
copelabr@gvsu.edu
COPELAND, Cathy .... 425-739-8156.. 504 F
cathy.copeland@lwtech.edu
COPELAND, David, L .... 540-464-7218.. 499 E
copelanddl@vmi.edu
COPELAND, Elaine, J .... 803-327-7402.. 428 D
ecopeland@clintoncollege.edu
COPELAND, Gayle .... 530-226-4133.... 64 H
gcopeland@simpsonu.edu
COPELAND, Jeff .... 813-253-7016.. 102 R
hcopeland4@hccfl.edu
COPELAND, Jessica .... 256-469-7333...... 4 E
reg@hbc1.edu
COPELAND, Judson .... 405-425-5129.. 385 C
judson.copeland@oc.edu
COPELAND, Kenneth ...... 434-395-2016.. 491 E
copelandpk@longwood.edu
COPELAND, Leigh .... 843-525-8231.. 433 B
lcopeland@tcl.edu
COPELAND, Louise .... 651-290-6439.. 253 S
louise.copeland@mitchellhamline.edu
COPELAND, Maura .... 912-478-7481.. 122 B
mconley@georgiasouthern.edu
COPELAND, Michele .... 612-659-6248.. 250 B
michele.copeland@minneapolis.edu
COPELAND, Paul .... 302-736-2538.... 91 G
paul.copeland@wesley.edu
COPELAND, JR.,
Robert, M .... 803-327-7402.. 428 D
rcopeland@clintoncollege.edu
COPELAND, Shannon .... 409-880-8922.. 471 A
shannon.copeland@lamar.edu
COPELAND, Wanda .... 610-796-8437.. 397 D
wanda.copeland@alvernia.edu
COPELAND-MORGAN,
Youlonda .... 310-825-2665.... 69 D
ycopeland-morgan@saonet.ucla.edu
COPELIN, Laylan .... 979-458-6425.. 467 D
lcopelin@tamus.edu
COPELY, Pat .... 937-376-2946.. 376 F
pcopely@payne.edu
COPENHAVER, Bonny ...... 715-394-6677.. 525 A
bonny.copenhaver@witc.edu
COPENHAVER, Martin ...... 617-964-1100.. 214 D
mcopenhaver@ants.edu
COPENHAVER, Michael ... 619-644-7000.... 45 J
michael.coppenhaver@gcccd.edu
COPLAN, Jan .... 802-387-7175.. 484 B
jancoplan@landmark.edu
COPLAND, Katherine .... 917-493-4030.. 319 M
kcopland@msmnyc.edu
COPLIN, Kimberly, A .... 740-587-6243.. 368 B
coplin@denison.edu
COPLIN, Louis .... 518-629-7348.. 316 G
l.coplin@hvcc.edu
COPONITI, Laura, I .... 405-224-3140.. 389 D
lcoponiti@usao.edu
COPONITI, Mike .... 405-224-3140.. 389 D
mcoponiti@usao.edu
COPONITI, Mike, D .... 405-224-3140.. 389 D
mcoponiti@usao.edu
COPP, Crista .... 310-338-1745.... 51 E
crista.copp@lmu.edu
COPP, Destini .... 404-432-3475.. 127 D
acopp@southuniversity.edu
COPPEDGE, Robin .... 580-371-2371.. 384 D
rcoppedge@mscok.edu
COPPERSMITH, Clifford ... 406-247-3009.. 277 D
ccoppersmith@msubillings.edu
COPPLE, Chad .... 618-437-5321.. 152 A
copplec@rlc.edu
COPPLE, James (Dean) .. 865-694-6536.. 446 G
jdcopple@pstcc.edu
COPPOLA, David, L .... 570-945-8500.. 406 H
david.coppola@keystone.edu
COPPOLA, Stephen, A ..... 704-687-5965.. 358 A
scoppola@uncc.edu
COPPOLA, William .... 817-515-3001.. 467 A
william.coppola@tccd.edu
COPPRUE, Lisa .... 313-845-9610.. 235 D
lcopprue@hfcc.edu
COQUEREL, Phoebe .... 404-225-4529.. 117 A
pcoquerel@atlantatech.edu
CORA, Ivette .... 787-250-1912.. 534 B
icora@intermetro.com
CORA, Jesus .... 787-250-1912.. 534 B
jacora@metro.inter.edu
CORAZZA, Anthony .... 718-368-5124.. 308 F
acorazza@kbcc.cuny.edu

CORBA, David .... 586-286-2058.. 237 C
corbad@macomb.edu
CORBAT, Carol .... 318-473-6431.. 197 J
ccorbat@[illegible]sua.edu
CORBETT, Ann .... 207-621-3145.. 204 I
annie@maine.edu
CORBETT, Carrie .... 901-272-5111.. 442 B
ccorbett@mca.edu
CORBETT, Christopher ..... 912-525-5000.. 126 E
ccorbett@scad.edu
CORBETT, Diane .... 614-292-8595.. 375 A
corbett.[illegible]68@osu.edu
CORBETT, Faith .... 718-260-5564.. 309 C
fcorbett@citytech.cuny.edu
CORBETT, Heather .... 860-768-2409.... 89 G
hcorbett@hartford.edu
CORBETT, Idra .... 859-572-5379.. 192 B
corbetti[illegible]@nku.edu
CORBETT, Keith .... 605-688-4153.. 437 F
keith.corbett@sdstate.edu
CORBETT, Marcus .... 803-793-5289.. 429 D
corbettm@denmarktech.edu
CORBETT, Martin .... 315-781-3656.. 316 C
corbett@hws.edu
CORBETT, Michele .... 619-849-2510.... 57 M
michelecorbett@pointloma.edu
CORBETT, Mickey .... 432-837-8059.. 471 E
mcorbett@sulross.edu
CORBETT, Tova .... 919-530-5547.. 357 A
tcorbet7@nccu.edu
CORBIN, Amanda .... 912-583-3249.. 118 B
acorbin@bpc.edu
CORBIN, Chuck .... 317-931-3324.. 160 B
ccorbin@cts.edu
CORBIN, Edith .... 856-222-9311.. 295 C
ecorbin@rcbc.edu
CORBIN, Nancy .... 360-650-3000.. 509 E
nancy.corbin@wwu.edu
CORBIN, Russ .... 315-498-2831.. 325 G
corbinr@sunyocc.edu
CORBIN, Thomas .... 802-443-5504.. 484 F
corbin@middlebury.edu
CORBIN, Ty .... 804-523-5726.. 497 C
tcorbin@reynolds.edu
CORBITT, Sandra, K .... 540-338-1776.. 492 H
slife@phc.edu
CORBITT, Timothy .... 315-229-5392.. 329 D
tcorbitt@stlawu.edu
CORBITT, Zach .... 864-596-9215.. 429 C
zach.corbitt@converse.edu
CORBOY, Lynne .... 215-780-1392.. 419 C
lcorboy@salus.edu
CORBY, Linda .... 718-270-2611.. 332 B
linda.corby@downstate.edu
CORCORAN, Carol .... 603-358-2035.. 288 E
carol.corcoran@keene.edu
CORCORAN, Heather, A ... 314-935-9292.. 274 N
hcorcoran@wustl.edu
CORCORAN, Janenne ...... 410-386-8444.. 206 I
jcorcoran@carrollcc.edu
CORCORAN, Jerry, M ...... 815-224-0404.. 143 C
jerry_corcoran@ivcc.edu
CORCORAN, Kevin, J ...... 248-370-2140.. 239 K
corcoran@oakland.edu
CORCORAN, Lisa .... 425-564-2302.. 501 F
lisa.corcoran@bellevuecollege.edu
CORCORAN, Mike .... 757-490-1241.. 486 E
mcorcoran@auto.edu
CORCORAN, Tim .... 619-644-7572.... 45 H
tim.corcoran@gcccd.edu
CORCORAN, William .... 201-612-5234.. 289 E
wcorcoran@bergen.edu
CORCORAN, William, M .. 570-208-5846.. 406 J
wmcorcor@kings.edu
CORDANO, Debbie .... 626-529-8500.... 55 H
dcordano@pacificoaks.edu
CORDANO, Mark .... 978-837-5401.. 225 E
cordanom@merrimack.edu
CORDANO,
Roberta (Bobbi) .... 202-651-5000.... 92 C
CORDEIRO, Wayne .... 808-853-1040.. 131 B
CORDEIRO, Wayne .... 541-485-1780.. 393 A
waynecordeiro@newhope.edu
CORDEIRO, William .... 805-437-8860.... 32 B
william.cordeiro@csuci.edu
CORDELL, Barbara .... 903-694-4003.. 463 D
bcordell@panola.edu
CORDELL, David .... 425-640-1412.. 503 E
dcordell@edcc.edu
CORDELL, Janice, K .... 563-387-1018.. 174 L
cordellj@luther.edu
CORDELL, Joyce .... 915-831-6530.. 457 H
jyamasak@epcc.edu
CORDELL, Michelle .... 479-619-4361.... 21 D
mcordell@nwacc.edu
CORDELL, Peggy .... 706-295-6959.. 121 F
pcordell@gntc.edu
CORDELL, Penny .... 706-272-4498.. 119 H
pcordell@daltonstate.edu
CORDER, Colleen .... 503-552-1702.. 392 H
ccorder@[illegible]unm.edu

CORDERO, Damaris .... 787-751-0160.. 531 M
dcordero@cmpr.gov.pr
CORDERO, Dona .... 847-491-3355.. 150 F
d-cordero@northwestern.edu
CORDERO, Edwin .... 864-578-8770.. 432 D
ecordero@sherman.edu
CORDERO, Heather .... 847-317-7071.. 156 B
hcordero@tiu.edu
CORDERO, Irma, L .... 787-740-1611.. 536 G
irma.cordero@uccaribe.edu
CORDERO, Pilar .... 787-815-0000.. 537 F
pilar.cordero@upr.edu
CORDERO, Zain .... 787-882-2065.. 536 D
mis@unitecpr.net
CORDERY, Simon .... 706-864-1819.. 128 F
simon.cordery@ung.edu
CORDES, Mark .... 815-753-0380.. 150 A
mcordes@niu.edu
CORDES, Molly .... 319-226-2091.. 169 D
molly.cordes@allencollege.edu
CORDIA, Judith .... 775-445-3295.. 285 B
judith.cordia@wnc.edu
CORDISCO, Shelli .... 607-778-5222.. 332 D
cordiscosl@sunybroome.edu
CORDLE, David .... 620-341-5171.. 180 G
dcordle@emporia.edu
CORDLE, Robbie, L .... 301-687-4403.. 212 F
rcordle@frostburg.edu
CORDOVA, David .... 773-878-8756.. 153 E
dcordova@staugustine.edu
CORDOVA, Denise .... 775-682-6708.. 285 A
dcordova@unr.edu
CORDOVA, Francie .... 505-277-5251.. 302 F
fcordova3@unm.edu
CORDOVA, John .... 661-362-5586.... 40 A
john.cordova@canyons.edu
CORDOVA, Jose, A .... 787-704-1020.. 532 H
jcordova@ediccollege.edu
CORDOVA, Matthew .... 505-454-2559.. 299 M
mcordova@luna.edu
CORDOVA, Mitchell .... 239-590-7074.. 110 L
mcordova@fgcu.edu
CORDOVA, Ryan .... 505-747-2288.. 301 F
rcordova@nnmc.edu
CORDOVA QUERO,
Hugo .... 510-549-4705.... 66 J
hquero@sksm.edu
CORDULACK, John .... 217-875-7200.. 152 C
jcordulack@richland.edu
CORDULACK, Tricia .... 217-875-7211.. 152 C
tcordulack@richland.edu
CORENO, Kendra .... 440-449-5368.. 380 F
kcoreno@follett.com
CORESSEL, James .... 419-783-2503.. 368 A
jcoressel@defiance.edu
COREY, Barry, H .... 562-903-4701.... 28 E
president@biola.edu
COREY, Frederick, C .... 602-496-0624.... 11 H
frederick.corey@asu.edu
COREY, George, A .... 413-577-5211.. 220 F
gcorey@uhs.umass.edu
COREY, M, J .... 304-637-1344.. 510 I
coreym@dewv.edu
COREY, Steven .... 312-369-7844.. 138 F
scorey@colum.edu
COREY, Steven, M .... 269-749-7642.. 240 A
scorey@olivetcollege.edu
CORIA, Elizabeth .... 415-239-3382.... 38 E
ecoria@ccsf.edu
CORINO, Mark, A .... 973-618-3412.. 290 A
mcorino@caldwell.edu
CORKERY, John, E .... 312-987-1426.. 143 G
7corkery@jmls.edu
CORKHILL, Kristin .... 239-489-9306.. 101 F
kcorkhill@fsw.edu
CORKILL, Jim, R .... 805-893-5882.... 70 E
jim.corkill@bfs.ucsb.edu
CORKRAN, Ken .... 508-541-1700.. 217 G
kcorkran@dean.edu
CORKRUM, Dalia, L .... 509-527-5193.. 509 G
corkrum@whitman.edu
CORKUM, David .... 617-552-4500.. 216 C
david.corkum@bc.edu
CORLE, Trish .... 814-262-3841.. 413 P
tcorle@pennhighlands.edu
CORLEW, Amy .... 931-221-6131.. 444 E
corlewa@apsu.edu
CORLEY, David .... 530-257-6181.... 48 E
dcorley@lassencollege.edu
CORLEY, Diane .... 512-463-9976.. 470 G
diane.corley@tsus.edu
CORLEY, Raymond .... 803-327-7402.. 428 D
rcorley@clintoncollege.edu
CORLEY, Scott .... 615-460-5547.. 438 J
scott.corley@belmont.edu
CORLEY, Stacey .... 941-359-7674.. 107 M
scorley@ringling.edu
CORLEY, Thomas .... 785-242-5200.. 183 M
thomas.corley@ottawa.edu
CORLISS, Bruce .... 401-874-6222.. 426 D
bruce.corliss@gso.uri.edu

CORLISS, Jon .... 205-975-6092..... 8 E
joncorliss@uab.edu
CORMAN, RJ .... 828-398-7286.. 347 D
richardjcorman@abtech.edu
CORMIER, Cathy .... 318-473-6459.. 197 J
ccormier@lsua.edu
CORMIER, Garth .... 207-941-7626.. 202 I
cormierg@husson.edu
CORMIER, Matthew .... 508-362-2131.. 223 C
mcormier@capecod.edu
CORN, Melanie .... 614-222-3220.. 367 B
CORNACCHIA, Eugene, J . 201-761-6010.. 296 K
ecornacchia@saintpeters.edu
CORNEA, Sheila .... 423-614-8630.. 441 B
scornea@leeuniversity.edu
CORNEJO, Silvia .... 619-216-6755.... 66 E
scornejo@swccd.edu
CORNELIUS, Adrian, R .... 301-314-8249.. 211 E
adrianc@umd.edu
CORNELIUS, Barbara .... 903-813-2536.. 451 M
bcornelius@austincollege.edu
CORNELIUS, Jerod, L .... 651-631-5320.. 256 A
jlcornelius@unwsp.edu
CORNELIUS, Ken .... 334-244-3232...... 2 A
kcornelius@aum.edu
CORNELIUS, Michael .... 480-423-6573.... 14 H
michael.cornelius@scottsdalecc.edu
CORNELIUS, Tim .... 479-619-3117.... 21 D
tcornelius@nwacc.edu
CORNELIUS TAYLOR,
Carmen .... 406-353-2607.. 275 H
ctaylor@ancollege.edu
CORNELL, Brian .... 607-735-1720.. 313 F
bcornell@elmira.edu
CORNELL, Craig .... 740-597-3280.. 375 H
cornellc@ohio.edu
CORNELL, Dennis .... 213-740-2111.... 72 D
dcornell@president.usc.edu
CORNELL, Dona, H .... 832-842-0949.. 473 E
dhcornell@uh.edu
CORNELL, Dona, H .... 713-743-0949.. 473 F
dhcornell@uh.edu
CORNELL, John .... 912-279-5703.. 119 C
jcornell@ccga.edu
CORNELL, Ken .... 425-889-7800.. 505 E
ken.cornell@northwestu.edu
CORNELL-SCOTT, Andrea . 540-887-7270.. 491 G
ascott@mbc.edu
CORNELY, Joe .... 513-244-4955.. 373 C
joseph.cornely@msjl.edu
CORNER, Kimberly .... 402-465-7783.. 281 K
kcorner@nebrwesleyan.edu
CORNER, William, T .... 616-526-6451.. 232 A
wtc2@calvin.edu
CORNERO, Robert .... 732-571-3424.. 292 F
rcornero@monmouth.edu
CORNETT, Doug .... 859-622-2301.. 188 F
doug.cornett@eku.edu
CORNETT, Jeff .... 317-921-4282.. 164 F
jcornett29@ivytech.edu
CORNETT, Megan .... 443-412-2379.. 208 A
mcornett@harford.edu
CORNETT, Scott .... 606-368-6120.. 186 B
scottcornett@alc.edu
CORNETT, Vicki .... 785-227-3380.. 178 J
cornettv@bethanylb.edu
CORNIER, Wilfredo .... 787-841-2000.. 535 I
wcornier@pucpr.edu
CORNILLE, Keith, T .... 608-246-6464.. 523 F
kcornille@madisoncollege.edu
CORNISH, Charles .... 903-927-3253.. 479 K
chcornish@wileyc.edu
CORNISH, Irene, K .... 315-859-4999.. 315 D
icornish@hamilton.edu
CORNISH, John .... 505-224-4000.. 299 F
jcorn@cnm.edu
CORNISH, La Jerne .... 410-337-6210.. 207 H
lcornish@goucher.edu
CORNMAN, Thomas .... 847-317-7001.. 156 B
tcornman@tiu.edu
CORNNER, Ryan .... 323-265-8967.... 49 G
cornnerm@elac.edu
CORNNER, Ryan, M .... 213-891-2056.... 49 F
cornnerm@email.laccd.edu
CORNOG, Evan, W .... 516-463-5213.. 316 D
evan.cornog@hofstra.edu
CORNWELL, Grant, H .... 407-646-2120.. 107 O
president@rollins.edu
CORNWELL, Jennifer .... 417-667-8181.. 264 A
jcornwell@cottey.edu
CORNWELL, Julia .... 817-272-2194.. 476 A
cornwell@uta.edu
CORNWELL, Shirley, A .... 937-393-3431.. 377 F
scornwell@sscc.edu
CORONA, Guadalupe .... 619-482-6544.... 66 E
gcorona@swccd.edu
CORONA, Jamie .... 248-232-4513.. 239 E
jlcorona@oaklandcc.edu
CORONA, Lorena .... 909-652-7459.... 37 D
lorena.corona@chaffey.edu
CORONA, Nayeli .... 610-574-6909.... 55 G
ncorona@pacificcollege.edu
CORONA, Stacie .... 530-898-5103.... 32 C
scorona@csuchico.edu
CORONADO, Ricardo .... 817-515-5234.. 467 A
ricardo.coronado@tccd.edu
CORONADO, Roman .... 575-527-7694.. 301 C
rcorona@nmsu.edu
CORP, Cory .... 803-786-3886.. 429 A
bookstore@columbiasc.edu
CORP, Stephanie .... 518-587-2100.. 335 D
stephanie.corp@esc.edu
CORR, Daniel, P .... 928-344-7500.... 11 J
daniel.corr@azwestern.edu
CORR, Jane .... 508-793-2590.. 217 C
jcorr@holycross.edu
CORR, Marianne .... 574-631-6411.. 168 B
mcorr1@nd.edu
CORRADETTI, Arthur .... 718-631-6350.. 309 E
acorradetti@qcc.cuny.edu
CORRADO, Rebecca .... 212-217-4202.. 314 B
rebecca_corrado@fitnyc.edu
CORRAL, Jeff .... 562-902-8755.... 66 A
jeffcorral@scuhs.edu
CORRAL, Nohel .... 562-938-4268.... 49 D
ncorral@lbcc.edu
CORRAL-NAVA, Nita .... 915-831-2302.. 457 H
ncorraln@epcc.edu
CORREA, Arleen, E .... 787-765-1915.. 534 F
acorrea@opto.inter.edu
CORREA, Florinda .... 361-582-2516.. 478 F
florinda.correa@victoriacollege.edu
CORREA, Frank .... 714-966-8500.... 73 G
fcorrea@ves.edu
CORREA, Omar .... 402-554-2200.. 283 B
ogcorrea@unomaha.edu
CORREA, Peter .... 814-838-7673.. 403 G
pcorrea@fortisinstitute.edu
CORREA, Santy .... 787-284-1912.. 534 C
scorrea@ponce.inter.edu
CORREA, Sylvia .... 256-233-8116...... 1 F
sylvia.correa@athens.edu
CORREDERA, Enrique .... 802-656-2005.. 485 D
enrique.corredera@uvm.edu
CORRELL, Dennis, L .... 570-327-4761.. 413 O
dcorrell@pct.edu
CORRELL, Jen .... 717-728-2362.. 400 F
jencorrell@centralpenn.edu
CORRELL, Scott .... 701-777-2711.. 360 C
scott.correll@und.edu
CORRELL, Scott .... 715-232-2121.. 521 D
corrells@uwstout.edu
CORRELL-HUGHES, Larry 386-822-7201.. 113 B
lcorrell-hughes@stetson.edu
CORRENTI, Bill .... 718-368-5066.. 308 F
bcorrenti@kbcc.cuny.edu
CORRIE, Rosie .... 575-769-4021.. 299 G
rosie.corrie@clovis.edu
CORRIGAN, Boo .... 845-938-3701.. 529 C
boo.corrigan@usma.edu
CORRIGAN, Christopher .. 912-344-2516.. 116 E
christopher.corrigan@armstrong.edu
CORRIGAN, Kevin .... 404-727-6460.. 120 E
kcorrig@emory.edu
CORRIGAN, JR.,
Robert, F .... 713-798-6392.. 452 G
corrigan@bcm.edu
CORRIGLIANO, Paul .... 425-235-5555.. 506 F
pcorrigliano@rtc.edu
CORRINGAN, Terrance .... 713-718-7278.. 459 B
terrance.corrigan@hccs.edu
CORRISS, Mary Jean .... 540-362-6332.. 490 F
corrissmj@hollins.edu
CORRY, David, M .... 434-592-4008.. 491 D
dcorry@liberty.edu
CORSARO, Louis .... 412-392-6190.. 417 F
lcorsaro@pointpark.edu
CORSELLO, Christine, L .. 704-403-4336.. 342 E
christine.corsello@carolinashealthcare.org
CORSINI, Kevin, D .... 434-592-4691.. 491 D
kdcorsini@liberty.edu
CORSINO, Yvonne .... 787-798-3001.. 536 G
yvonne.corsino@uccaribe.edu
CORSO, Melody .... 386-752-1822.. 100 L
melody.corso@fgc.edu
CORSO, Michael .... 973-720-2202.. 298 G
corsom1@wpunj.edu
CORSO, Teri .... 973-290-4266.. 290 G
tcorso@cse.edu
CORSON-RIKERT,
Janet, L .... 607-255-3564.. 312 A
jlc18@cornell.edu
CORTELL, Sabrina .... 619-594-0336.... 35 A
scortell@mail.sdsu.edu
CORTES, Chris .... 559-638-0300.... 67 D
chris.cortes@reedleycollege.edu
CORTES, Edymariel .... 939-292-8918.. 539 A
edymariel.cortes@upr.edu
CORTES, Felix .... 787-841-2000.. 535 I
fcortes@pucpr.edu
CORTES, Frances .... 787-878-5475.. 533 H
fcortes@arecibo.inter.edu
CORTES, Gloria .... 787-891-0925.. 533 G
gcortes@aguadilla.inter.edu
CORTES, Maria .... 787-738-2161.. 538 A
maria.cortes1@upr.edu
CORTES, Tammy .... 831-813-6820.. 461 B
tammy.a.cortes@lonestar.edu
CORTESE, Joseph .... 570-504-9620.. 400 I
jcortese@tcmc.edu
CORTEZ, Carrie .... 985-448-7936.. 196 E
carrie.cortez@fletcher.edu
CORTEZ, Jack .... 973-748-9000.. 289 H
jack_cortez@bloomfield.edu
CORTEZ, Ray .... 956-721-5303.. 460 F
rcortez@laredo.edu
CORTEZ, Ronald, S .... 415-338-2521.... 35 B
rscortez@sfsu.edu
CORTEZ, Ruben .... 510-849-8931.... 55 I
rcortez@psr.edu
CORTEZ, Sandra, L .... 956-721-5374.. 460 F
sandra.cortez@laredo.edu
CORTEZ-FARAH, Terre ..... 619-684-8763.... 54 C
tcortez@newschoolarch.edu
CORTHELL, Ronald .... 219-989-2401.. 166 F
rcorthel@pnw.edu
CORTI, Tom .... 631-420-2264.. 335 E
tom.corti@farmingdale.edu
CORTILET-ALBRECHT,
Carol .... 773-821-2215.. 136 M
ccortile@csu.edu
CORTINAS, Debra .... 361-825-5743.. 468 E
debra.cortinas@tamucc.edu
CORTNER, Laquetta .... 614-837-4088.. 380 G
cortnerl@valorcollege.edu
CORUM, Amanda .... 719-549-3163.... 82 G
amanda.corum@pueblocc.edu
CORVEY, Barbara .... 903-886-5041.. 468 D
barbara.corvey@tamuc.edu
CORVEY, Rebecca, J .... 478-471-2734.. 124 E
rebecca.corvey@mga.edu
CORVIN, Clay, L .... 504-282-4455.. 198 H
claycor@wbsn.com
CORVINO, John .... 505-224-4639.. 299 F
jcorvino@cnm.edu
CORWIN, Courtney Lee ... 501-450-1352.... 20 F
corwin@hendrix.edu
CORY, Christopher .... 212-346-1117.. 325 J
ccory@pace.edu
CORYELL, Brett .... 815-753-2095.. 150 A
bcoryell@niu.edu
CORZO, Barbara .... 213-487-0110.... 42 H
financialaid@dula.edu
COSBY, Glen .... 509-533-7015.. 502 H
glen.cosby@scc.spokane.edu
COSBY, Glen .... 509-533-7015.. 502 I
glen.cosby@scc.spokane.edu
COSBY, Kevin, W .... 502-776-1443.. 192 C
srpastor1@aol.com
COSBY, Laura .... 268-488-4440.. 235 I
lcosby@kvcc.edu
COSBY, Sheliah .... 423-869-6353.. 441 E
sheliah.cosby@lmunet.edu
COSBY-GAITHER,
Christine .... 502-776-1443.. 192 C
ccosby@simmonscollegeky.edu
COSCIA, Paul .... 336-917-5577.. 355 E
paul.coscia@salem.edu
COSDEN, Julie .... 239-280-2544.... 95 Q
julie.cosden@avemaria.edu
COSDEN, Julie .... 239-280-2558.... 95 Q
julie.cosden@avemaria.edu
COSENTINO, Daniel .... 585-475-2411.. 327 E
COSENTINO, Joseph .... 914-323-5125.. 319 N
joseph.cosentino@mville.edu
COSENTINO, Lauren .... 310-506-6202.... 56 J
lauren.cosentino@pepperdine.edu
COSENTINO, Richard, E .. 864-388-8300.. 430 G
cosentino@lander.edu
COSEY, Arnel .... 504-671-5055.. 196 D
acosey@dcc.edu
COSGRIFF, Lawrence .... 202-462-2101.... 93 B
lcosgriff@iwp.edu
COSGROVE, John .... 570-662-4586.. 415 E
jcosgrov@mansfield.edu
COSGROVE, Mark .... 517-483-1345.. 237 A
cosgrom1@lcc.edu
COSIMO, Julie .... 630-829-6037.. 135 F
jcosimo@ben.edu
COSKY, Alicia, C .... 630-844-5116.. 135 E
acosky@aurora.edu
COSME-FERNANDEZ,
Yermarie .... 787-993-8898.. 537 G
yermarie.cosme@upr.edu
COSS, Ann .... 787-840-2575.. 535 H
anncoss@psm.edu
COSSAR, Nigel .... 215-898-8073.. 421 E
ncossar@upenn.edu
COSSICH, Marc .... 936-468-2608.. 466 H
mcossich@sfasu.edu
COSSICH, Monique .... 936-468-2504.. 466 H
cossichm@sfasu.edu
COSSITT, Brenda .... 307-755-2244.. 527 G
brenda.cossitt@zenith.org
COST, Timothy, P .... 904-256-7016.. 103 D
tcost@ju.edu
COSTA, Elizabeth, A .... 540-985-9701.. 491 A
eacosta@jchs.edu
COSTA, Guilherme .... 605-773-3455.. 436 L
guilherme.costa@sdbor.edu
COSTA, Linda, J .... 848-932-7743.. 296 B
linda.costa@rutgers.edu
COSTA, Maria, D .... 423-439-7737.. 444 F
costa@etsu.edu
COSTALAS, Georgia .... 570-408-7854.. 423 G
georgia.costalas@wilkes.edu
COSTANTINI, Camilla .... 203-332-5222.... 86 D
ccostantini@housatonic.edu
COSTANTINIDIS, Teresa .. 415-476-9887.... 70 D
teresa.costantinidis@ucsf.edu
COSTANTINO, Andrea .... 716-645-2171.. 331 C
costanti@buffalo.edu
COSTANTINO, Tracie .... 401-277-4946.. 426 A
tcostant@risd.edu
COSTANZA, Christine .... 909-621-8148.... 64 A
ccostanz@scrippscollege.edu
COSTANZA, Laina .... 334-387-3877...... 1 E
lainacostanza@amridgeuniversity.edu
COSTANZA, Laina, T .... 334-387-3878...... 1 E
lainacostanza@amridgeuniversity.edu
COSTANZA, Megan .... 979-209-7653.. 452 J
megan.costanza@blinn.edu
COSTANZO, Brian .... 570-961-7841.. 407 B
costanzob@lackawanna.edu
COSTAS, Carolyn .... 787-841-2000.. 535 I
ccostas@pucpr.edu
COSTAS, Edda .... 787-284-1912.. 534 C
ecostas@ponce.inter.edu
COSTAS, Pam .... 312-915-6239.. 146 G
pcostas@luc.edu
COSTE, Mike .... 303-914-6636.... 82 I
mike.coste@rrcc.edu
COSTELLO, Bernadette ..... 703-284-1554.. 492 A
bernadette.costello@marymount.edu
COSTELLO, Bernard .... 914-674-7569.. 320 G
bcostello@mercy.edu
COSTELLO, Cathy .... 585-345-6812.. 315 C
cecostello@genesee.edu
COSTELLO, Dana .... 410-225-2338.. 209 B
dcostello@mica.edu
COSTELLO, Dennis .... 586-445-7318.. 237 C
costellod@macomb.edu
COSTELLO, Eileen .... 978-632-6600.. 224 B
e_costello@mwcc.mass.edu
COSTELLO, Georgia .... 618-235-2700.. 155 C
georgia.costello@swic.edu
COSTELLO, Gregory, W ... 507-344-7305.. 244 K
gregory.costello@blc.edu
COSTELLO, Jamie .... 617-879-7703.. 222 A
jcostello@massart.edu
COSTELLO, Janice .... 860-727-6919.... 87 H
jcostello@goodwin.edu
COSTELLO, SJ, John .... 312-915-7535.. 146 G
jcoste2@luc.edu
COSTELLO, Ken .... 602-943-2311.... 18 C
ken.costello@west.edu
COSTELLO, Kevin .... 617-327-6777.. 229 H
kevin_costello@williamjames.edu
COSTELLO, Leon .... 406-994-4226.. 277 C
lcostello@msubobcats.com
COSTELLO,
Mary Elizabeth .... 973-761-9175.. 297 A
maryelizabeth.costello@shu.edu
COSTELLO, Richard, J .... 219-989-2540.. 166 F
rick@pnw.edu
COSTELLO STANIEC,
Andria .... 315-443-1899.. 337 A
costello@syr.edu
COSTELLO-SULLIVAN,
Kathleen, P .... 315-445-4310.. 318 E
sullivpk@lemoyne.edu
COSTIGAN, Harry .... 215-567-7080.. 397 H
hcostigan@edmc.edu
COSTIGAN, Harry .... 215-567-7080.. 397 H
hcostigan@aii.edu
COSTIGAN, Rosemary .... 401-825-2142.. 425 A
rcostigan@ccri.edu
COSTLEY, Lucien .... 830-895-7116.. 465 E
lrcostley@schreiner.edu
COSTNER, Carl .... 828-652-0614.. 351 C
carlc@mcdowelltech.edu
COSTON, Charlotte, M .... 716-851-1180.. 313 H
coston@ecc.edu
COSTON, Linda .... 229-430-2751.. 116 A
lcoston@albanytech.edu
COSTON, Robert, H .... 304-647-6574.. 512 C
rcoston@newriver.edu
COSTON, Todd .... 661-395-4601.... 47 J
tcoston@bakersfieldcollege.edu
COSTON, Yvonne .... 919-516-4096.. 355 D
ycoston@st-aug.edu

COSTON-MCHUGH, Rose 856-227-7200 .. 290 B
rcoston-mchugh@camdencc.edu
COT, Alea 504-280-6021 .. 198 D
acot@uno.edu
COTA, Marco 909-384-8630 .... 60 C
mcota@sbccd.cc.ca.us
COTE, Christine 509-453-0374 .. 506 A
COTE, Deborah 413-236-1022 .. 222 G
dcote@berkshirecc.edu
COTE, John, C 810-766-4191 .. 231 D
jcote01@baker.edu
COTE-BONANNO,
Joanne, F 973-655-6234 .. 293 A
bonannoj@mail.montclair.edu
COTGREAVE, Bruce 806-345-5565 .. 450 H
blcotgreave@actx.edu
COTHAM, Brian 559-278-2111 .... 32 F
bcotham@csufresno.edu
COTHAM, Rhonda 931-393-1719 .. 446 D
rcotham@mscc.edu
COTHRAN, Ginger 580-387-7112 .. 384 D
gcothran@mscok.edu
COTHRAN, Rick 864-646-1701 .. 433 C
rcothran@tctc.edu
COTNER, Dave, R 570-326-3761 .. 413 D
dcotner@pct.edu
COTNEY, Rachel 334-291-4979 ...... 2 H
rachel.cotney@cv.edu
COTO, Jennifer 714-628-4775 .... 58 H
coto_jennifer@sccollege.edu
COTREL, Jack, R 423-439-6900 .. 444 F
cotrel@etsu.edu
COTRONEO, Keith, J 304-710-3355 .. 512 B
cotroneo@mctc.edu
COTSONES, Rena 815-753-0834 .. 150 A
rcotsones@niu.edu
COTSONIS, Joachim 617-850-1243 .. 219 F
jcotsonis@hchc.edu
COTTAM, Michael 314-246-5972 .. 275 B
michaelcottam@webster.edu
COTTEN, Melinda 713-348-6200 .. 464 E
cotten@rice.edu
COTTEN-BROWN, Floya 919-572-1625 .. 341 M
fbrown@apexsot.edu
COTTER, Bob 513-487-1144 .. 378 E
bob.cotter@myunion.edu
COTTER, Dan, J 802-258-9297 .. 484 C
dcotter@marlboro.edu
COTTER, George 813-974-3305 .. 112 C
gcotter@usf.edu
COTTER, James, W 517-355-6532 .. 237 I
cotterj@msu.edu
COTTER, Mark, S 865-539-7266 .. 446 G
mscotter@pstcc.edu
COTTER, Michael 914-594-3675 .. 323 I
michael_cotter@nymc.edu
COTTER, Novelette 206-239-4500 .. 502 D
COTTINGHAM, Ryan, T 517-750-1200 .. 241 E
ryanc@arbor.edu
COTTO, Evelyn 787-746-1400 .. 532 M
ecoto@huertas.edu
COTTO, Marguerite, C 231-995-1775 .. 239 C
mcotto@nmc.edu
COTTO, Sugelenia 787-766-1717 .. 536 B
sucotto@suagm.edu
COTTON, Beverly 940-565-4098 .. 475 A
beverly.cotton@unt.edu
COTTON, Fran 806-894-9611 .. 465 G
fcotton@southplainscollege.edu
COTTON, George 850-599-3491 .. 110 J
george.cotton@famu.edu
COTTON, Joseph 803-535-5077 .. 428 B
jcotton@claflin.edu
COTTON, Michael 336-517-2299 .. 342 B
mcotton@bennett.edu
COTTON, Sabrina 256-726-7408 ...... 6 B
cotton@oakwood.edu
COTTON, Trae 336-750-3200 .. 359 B
cottontt@wssu.edu
COTTON KELLY,
Montique 860-486-2240 .... 89 D
montique.cotton.kelly@uconn.edu
COTTONE, John 607-753-2701 .. 333 A
john.cottone@cortland.edu
COTTONHAM, Patricia 337-482-6266 .. 201 D
patcottonham@louisiana.edu
COTTRAUX, Suzanne 817-515-1541 .. 467 A
suzanne.cottraux@tccd.edu
COTTRELL, Angela 816-235-1407 .. 273 F
cottrella@umkc.edu
COTTRELL, Debbie 830-372-8002 .. 470 C
dcottrell@tlu.edu
COTTRELL, Debbie 254-295-5059 .. 474 E
dcottrell@umhb.edu
COTTRELL, Janet 802-865-6492 .. 483 F
cottrell@champlain.edu
COTTRELL, Leslie 378-839-6452 .. 129 E
lcottrel@westga.edu
COTTRELL, Liesl 773-252-6464 .. 152 B
liesl.cottrell@resu.edu
COTTRELL, Rick 800-962-7682 .. 275 D
rcottrell@wma.edu
COTTRELL, Terrance, L 815-740-5041 .. 157 F
tcottrell@stfrancis.edu
COTTRILL, Chad 503-883-2506 .. 392 B
ccottril@linfield.edu
COTTRILL, F. Layton 304-696-6295 .. 513 D
cottrill@marshall.edu
COTY, Mark 941-782-5980 .. 407 D
mcoty@lecom.edu
COUCH, Alisha, M 740-368-3099 .. 376 B
amcouch@owu.edu
COUCH, Brian 239-280-1695 .... 95 Q
brian.couch@avemaria.edu
COUCH, Charlie 970-351-2231 .... 84 C
charlie.couch@unco.edu
COUCH, JR., Gene, C 276-739-2421 .. 499 A
gcouch@vhcc.edu
COUCH, Jennifer 208-562-3508 .. 133 F
jennifercouch@cwidaho.cc
COUCH, Lisa 760-384-6214 .... 47 K
lcouch@cerrocoso.edu
COUCH, Valerie 405-208-5440 .. 385 E
vcouch@okcu.edu
COUCHEY, Evangeline 845-675-4733 .. 325 C
evangeline.couchey@nyack.edu
COUGHENAIR, Russ 813-974-9718 .. 112 C
COUGHENOUR, Kevin 703-539-6890 .. 494 I
kcoughenour@stratford.edu
COUGHLIN, SJ,
Bernard, J 509-313-5520 .. 504 A
coughlin@gonzaga.edu
COUGHLIN, Cass 620-341-5264 .. 180 G
ccoughli@emporia.edu
COUGHLIN, Eileen, V 360-650-3839 .. 509 E
eileen.coughlin@wwu.edu
COUGHLIN, OFM,
F. Edward 518-783-2302 .. 330 E
ecoughlin@siena.edu
COUGHLIN, John 248-370-4618 .. 239 K
jcoughli@oakland.edu
COUGHLIN, Kathleen 210-829-6012 .. 474 D
coughlin@uiwtx.edu
COUGHLIN, Kevin 305-348-7347 .. 111 A
kevin.coughlin@fiu.edu
COUGHLIN, Mary Ann 413-748-3959 .. 228 E
mcoughlin@springfieldcollege.edu
COUGHLIN, Richard 660-785-4105 .. 273 B
coughlin@truman.edu
COULET DUGARD,
Caroline 856-351-2756 .. 296 L
ccoulet@salemcc.edu
COULIER, Laura 616-988-1000 .. 232 H
laura.c@compass.edu
COULLIETTE, Holly 904-808-7441 .. 108 B
hollycoulliette@sjrstate.edu
COULOMBE, Jennifer, E 336-734-7723 .. 349 G
jcoulombe@forsythtech.edu
COULON, Richard 949-824-6510 .... 69 C
rcoulon@uci.edu
COULOTTE, Clifford 718-997-5100 .. 309 D
clifford.coulotte@qc.cuny.edu
COULS, Lauren 803-641-2837 .. 433 G
laurenc@usca.edu
COULSTON, Susan 269-782-1396 .. 241 C
scoulston@swmich.edu
COULTER, Ann 641-782-1340 .. 177 B
coulter@swcciowa.edu
COULTER, Chris 719-389-6568 .... 77 J
chris.coulter@coloradocollege.edu
COULTER, Cindy 828-327-7000 .. 348 C
ccoulter@cvcc.edu
COULTER, Denise 609-343-5007 .. 288 H
dcoulter@atlantic.edu
COULTER, John, P 610-758-6310 .. 408 H
jc0i@lehigh.edu
COULTER, Kristin 512-313-3000 .. 455 F
kristin.coulter@concordia.edu
COULTER, Laurie 903-813-2900 .. 451 M
lcoulter@austincollege.edu
COULTER, Lisa 610-683-4072 .. 415 C
coulter@kutztown.edu
COULTER, Martha 802-468-1314 .. 485 H
martha.coulter@castleton.edu
COULTER, Seana 443-885-3110 .. 209 F
seana.coulter@morgan.edu
COUNCIL, Juanette 910-672-1208 .. 356 E
jcouncil@uncfsu.edu
COUNCIL, Mark 910-362-7009 .. 348 A
mcouncil@cfcc.edu
COUNSIL, Brian 620-365-5116 .. 178 A
counsil@allencc.edu
COUNTEE, Jerome 916-484-8202 .... 51 A
countej@arc.losrios.edu
COUNTS, LaNeta 404-471-6483 .. 115 J
lcounts@agnesscott.edu
COUPE, Maria 845-398-4038 .. 329 G
mcoupe@stac.edu
COURCHAINE, Jeff 714-892-7711 .... 39 F
jcourchaine@gwc.cccd.edu
COURET, Esther 845-431-8673 .. 312 G
esther.couret@sunydutchess.edu
COUREY, Scott 616-394-4287 .. 233 A
scott.courey@cornerstone.edu
COURSEY, Greg 706-437-6808 .. 117 C
gcoursey@augustatech.edu
COURTEMANCHE, Brian 978-927-2278 .. 218 D
bcourtem@endicott.edu
COURTEY, Susan 818-240-1000 .... 45 A
scourtey@glendale.edu
COURTLEY-TODD,
Laura, J 305-628-6677 .. 108 E
lcourtle@stu.edu
COURTNEY, Andalyn M 716-888-2780 .. 306 F
courtnea@canisius.edu
COURTNEY, Bonnie 717-262-2017 .. 424 A
bonnie.courtney@wilson.edu
COURTNEY, Hugh 617-373-3232 .. 227 B
COURTNEY, Justin 419-772-2145 .. 374 J
j-courtney@onu.edu
COURTNEY, Sharon, P 504-988-3390 .. 200 C
sharonc@tulane.edu
COURTRIGHT, Amy 209-954-5151 .... 61 F
acourtright@deltacollege.edu
COURTRIGHT, Caren 509-793-2038 .. 501 H
carenc@bigbend.edu
COURTWAY, Tom 501-450-5286 .... 24 G
tcourtway@uca.edu
COUSINS, Kathryn 212-484-1156 .. 308 E
kcousins@jjay.cuny.edu
COUSINS MELENDEZ,
Amirah 718-289-5155 .. 307 C
amirah.cousins@bcc.cuny.edu
COUTILISH, Theodore, G 734-487-2483 .. 233 J
ted.coutilish@emich.edu
COUTRIER, Karen 631-420-2723 .. 335 E
karen.coutrier@farmingdale.edu
COUTS, Suzann 325-793-4608 .. 461 F
couts.suzann@mcm.edu
COUTURE, Daniel, R 802-654-3243 .. 484 I
dcouture@smcvt.edu
COUTURIER, OFM,
David 716-375-2160 .. 328 B
dcoutur@sbu.edu
COVAL, Scott 610-282-1100 .. 402 B
scott.coval@desales.edu
COVAR, Tom 864-388-8305 .. 430 G
tcovar@lander.edu
COVAULT, Pamela 785-242-2067 .. 133 H
pcovault@neosho.edu
COVE, Lorraine, D 617-573-8160 .. 228 G
lcove@acad.suffolk.edu
COVER, Michael, S 570-577-3348 .. 398 L
mike.cover@bucknell.edu
COVERS, Beth, A 810-762-9925 .. 236 C
bcovers@kettering.edu
COVERT, Sarah 706-542-9389 .. 128 E
covert@uga.edu
COVERT, Sheree, S 319-352-8272 .. 177 G
sheree.covert@wartburg.edu
COVEY, Angie, E 540-674-3655 .. 497 G
acovey@nr.edu
COVEY, Bruce 404-727-6223 .. 120 E
bcovey@emory.edu
COVEY, David 518-861-2560 .. 320 A
dcovey@mariacollege.edu
COVEY, Douglass, F 404-413-1500 .. 122 D
dcovey@gsu.edu
COVINGTON, Adrienne 252-451-8236 .. 351 F
COVINGTON, Chatonda 919-530-7517 .. 357 A
cbcovington@nccu.edu
COVINGTON, Dan 606-546-1285 .. 193 E
dcovin@unionky.edu
COVINGTON, Dave, F 208-467-8060 .. 134 D
dcovington@nnu.edu
COVINGTON, Debra, F 828-262-2041 .. 356 B
covingtondf@appstate.edu
COVINGTON, Janet 713-348-6312 .. 464 E
jcov@rice.edu
COVINGTON, Mary 919-966-9176 .. 357 D
mary_covington@unc.edu
COVINGTON, Robert, D 501-450-5202 .... 24 G
COVINGTON, Sim 315-792-7165 .. 336 C
sim.covington@sunyit.edu
COVINGTON, Sirena 312-788-1146 .. 157 H
scovington@vandercook.edu
COVINGTON, Troy 757-823-9540 .. 492 F
tjcovington@nsu.edu
COVINGTON, Valerie, L 757-455-3108 .. 500 E
vcovington@vwc.edu
COVINO, Nicholas 617-327-6777 .. 229 H
nicholas_covino@williamjames.edu
COVINO, Paul, F 508-767-7057 .. 214 F
pf.covino@assumption.edu
COVINO, William, A 323-343-3030 .... 33 C
bill.covino@calstatela.edu
COVITZ, Bobby 513-487-3259 .. 315 F
rcovitz@huc.edu
COVONE, Michael 305-899-3551 .... 96 D
mcovone@barry.edu
COWAN, Anthony 901-435-1470 .. 441 C
anthony_cowan@loc.edu
COWAN, Cindy 864-977-2058 .. 431 G
cindy.cowan@ngu.edu
COWAN, Cristina 816-501-3756 .. 262 G
COWAN, David 507-389-2267 .. 250 E
david.cowan@mnsu.edu
COWAN, Judith 803-327-7402 .. 428 D
jcowan@clintoncollege.edu
COWAN, Kenneth, H 402-559-4238 .. 283 A
kcowan@unmc.edu
COWAN, Michelle 901-435-1000 .. 441 C
michelle_cowan@loc.edu
COWAN, Theresa 954-201-7554 .... 96 I
tcowan@broward.edu
COWAN, Vickie, M 718-862-7398 .. 319 L
vickie.cowan@manhattan.edu
COWARD, Darryl 410-617-2201 .. 208 G
COWARDIN, Anne 303-245-4633 .... 81 I
acowardin@naropa.edu
COWART, Lisa 803-323-2273 .. 435 B
cowartl@winthrop.edu
COWDEN, Clint 559-934-2701 .... 74 D
clintcowden@whccd.edu
COWDERY, Aaron 740-376-4452 .. 372 A
aaron.cowdery@marietta.edu
COWDIN, Terry 503-251-5727 .. 396 C
tcowdin@uws.edu
COWDREY, Scott 410-778-7894 .. 213 E
scowdrey2@washcoll.edu
COWELL, Elizabeth 831-459-2076 .... 70 F
mcowell@ucsc.edu
COWELL, JR., James, W 626-395-4464 .... 30 H
jcowell@caltech.edu
COWELL, Karen 661-722-6300 .... 27 B
kcowell@avc.edu
COWELL, Karen 803-778-7825 .. 427 G
cowellkw@cctech.edu
COWELL-OATES, June 314-454-8694 .. 265 E
jcowell-oates@bjc.org
COWEN, Rahmel 334-244-3668 ...... 2 A
rcowen@aum.edu
COWGER, John 701-594-8192 .. 361 E
john.cowger@lrsc.edu
COWGER, Melinda, K 303-722-5724 .... 81 E
mcowger@lincolntech.edu
COWGER, Tiffany 618-262-8641 .. 142 F
cowgert@iecc.edu
COWHERD, Mark 256-824-6480 ...... 8 F
mark.cowherd@uah.edu
COWHEY, Peter 858-534-2230 .... 70 C
evc@ucsd.edu
COWING, Michelle 503-493-6392 .. 391 A
mcowing@cu-portland.edu
COWLES, John 616-234-3673 .. 234 E
jcowles@grcc.edu
COWLEY, Dave 435-797-1146 .. 482 B
dave.cowley@usu.edu
COWLEY, Julie, A 512-863-1720 .. 466 G
cowleyj@southwestern.edu
COWLIN, Lynn 815-455-8688 .. 147 E
lcowlin@mchenry.edu
COWLING, Richard 630-353-8802 .. 136 G
rcowling@chamberlain.edu
COWSER, Erin, K 985-549-5861 .. 201 C
erin.moore@selu.edu
COX, Ann 212-875-4416 .. 304 E
acox@bankstreet.edu
COX, Anthony 706-778-8500 .. 125 J
acox@piedmont.edu
COX, Barbara 850-599-3796 .. 110 J
barbara.cox@famu.edu
COX, Barbara, J 619-239-0391 .... 36 A
bjc@cwsl.edu
COX, Bob 970-339-6509 .... 76 H
bob.cox@aims.edu
COX, Bobbie 704-406-4627 .. 344 E
bcox@gardner-webb.edu
COX, Brandy, A 479-575-2801 .... 22 I
brandyac@uark.edu
COX, Brant, M 757-446-5800 .. 489 B
coxbm@evms.edu
COX, Cameron 253-964-6598 .. 506 B
cmcox@pierce.ctc.edu
COX, Carolyn 304-384-5323 .. 513 A
ccox@concord.edu
COX, Carolyn, S 240-500-2000 .. 207 I
cscox@hagerstowncc.edu
COX, Cathy 706-379-3111 .. 130 B
ccox@yhc.edu
COX, Charlene 219-464-5093 .. 168 F
charlene.cox@valpo.edu
COX, Cheryl 864-592-4613 .. 432 H
coxc@sccsc.edu
COX, Christen 910-755-7300 .. 347 H
coxc@brunswickcc.edu
COX, Christopher, N 319-273-2737 .. 170 A
chris.cox@uni.edu
COX, Christopher, P 419-372-8932 .. 364 E
cpcox@bgsu.edu
COX, Colleen 978-656-3284 .. 224 A

COX, Dave .... 217-234-5376.. 145 D
dcox5612@lakeland.cc.il.us
COX, Dave .... 509-533-7179.. 502 I
dave.cox@scc.spokane.edu
COX, David, W .... 716-878-5336.. 332 F
coxdw@buffalostate.edu
COX, Deborah, M .... 270-824-8609.. 190 B
deborah.cox@kctcs.edu
COX, Dennis .... 949-214-3182.... 41 F
dennis.cox@cui.edu
COX, Dennis .... 727-376-6911.. 114 A
dcox@trinitycollege.edu
COX, Donna .... 870-543-5968.... 22 E
dcox@seark.edu
COX, Ed .... 845-431-8071.. 312 G
ecox@sunydutchess.edu
COX, Erika, M .... 210-458-4859.. 477 A
erika.cox@utsa.edu
COX, Fran .... 662-472-9035.. 258 B
fcox@holmescc.edu
COX, Gregg .... 561-237-7210.. 104 O
gcox@lynn.edu
COX, Helen .... 808-245-8210.. 132 B
helencox@hawaii.edu
COX, Jamie, S .... 256-766-6610...... 4 B
jcox@hcu.edu
COX, Jana .... 707-524-1579.... 63 G
jcox@santarosa.edu
COX, Janet .... 513-244-4466.. 373 C
janet.cox@msj.edu
COX, Janet, L .... 513-529-6724.. 372 K
coxjl@miamioh.edu
COX, Jeff, A .... 336-838-6112.. 354 C
jeff.cox@wilkescc.edu
COX, Jeffrey, W .... 585-475-7433.. 327 E
jwccst@rit.edu
COX, Jennifer .... 580-559-5714.. 383 H
jcox@ecok.edu
COX, Jennifer .... 503-228-6528.. 390 A
jcox@aii.edu
COX, Jesse .... 313-927-1404.. 237 E
jcox@marygrove.edu
COX, John .... 217-479-7047.. 147 C
john.cox@mac.edu
COX, John, L .... 508-362-2131.. 223 C
jcox@capecod.edu
COX, Kelli, S .... 785-532-2118.. 182 D
kellicox@ksu.edu
COX, Kenneth .... 540-831-7600.. 493 A
kcox3@radford.edu
COX, Kevin .... 214-887-5233.. 457 C
kcox@dts.edu
COX, Kevin, B .... 214-887-5233.. 457 C
kcox@dts.edu
COX, Kim .... 305-899-3189.... 96 D
kcox@barry.edu
COX, Lady, D .... 334-844-5672...... 1 G
ldc0006@auburn.edu
COX, Lane .... 205-348-8697...... 8 D
lcox@fa.ua.edu
COX, Larry .... 937-722-9280.. 380 E
larry.cox@urbana.edu
COX, Laurie .... 608-262-7890.. 519 K
cox@studentlife.wisc.edu
COX, Leah .... 540-654-1263.. 495 C
lcox@umw.edu
COX, Leana .... 970-675-3334.... 78 J
leana.cox@cncc.edu
COX, Lisa, B .... 423-869-6722.. 441 E
lisa.cox@lmunet.edu
COX, Lori .... 618-252-5400.. 154 G
lori.cox@sic.edu
COX, Lynne .... 541-917-4848.. 392 C
coxly@linnbenton.edu
COX, Mary .... 724-830-1027.. 419 D
cox@setonhill.edu
COX, Matthew .... 719-255-3375.... 83 L
mcox4@uccs.edu
COX, Megan, D .... 617-322-3568.. 219 H
megan_cox@laboure.edu
COX, Michele, D .... 804-289-8838.. 495 G
mcox@richmond.edu
COX, Miekka, M .... 812-464-1756.. 168 E
mmcox1@usi.edu
COX, Monte .... 501-279-4808.... 20 D
mcox@harding.edu
COX, Nancy, M .... 859-257-4772.. 193 G
ncox@email.uky.edu
COX, Paul .... 305-428-5700.. 105 E
pmcox@aii.edu
COX, Randall .... 903-785-7661.. 463 E
rcox@parisjc.edu
COX, Robert .... 360-736-9391.. 502 A
rcox@centralia.edu
COX, Robert .... 212-220-8041.. 307 B
rcox@bmcc.cuny.edu
COX, Ross .... 229-225-4098.. 127 G
rcox@southernregional.edu
COX, Ryan .... 916-568-3101.... 50 J
coxr@losrios.edu

COX, Sam .... 405-945-6789.. 386 C
coxjs@osuokc.edu
COX, Sandra .... 936-633-5211.. 451 D
scox@angelina.edu
COX, Sandy .... 309-796-5635.. 135 I
coxs@bhc.edu
COX, Sandy .... 920-424-2061.. 520 E
coxs@uwosh.edu
COX, Sarah .... 740-477-7816.. 374 G
scox4@ohiochristian.edu
COX, Sherry, P .... 336-838-6422.. 354 C
sherry.cox@wilkescc.edu
COX, Steven .... 918-595-7866.. 388 F
steven.cox@tulsacc.edu
COX, Steven, W .... 903-877-7456.. 477 E
steven.cox@uthct.edu
COX, Susan .... 559-453-2026.... 44 F
sue.cox@fresno.edu
COX, Susan, S .... 610-606-4609.. 400 E
sue@cedarcrest.edu
COX, Sylvia .... 910-642-7141.. 353 C
scox@sccnc.edu
COX, Terry .... 425-640-1489.. 503 E
terry.cox@edcc.edu
COX, Tiffa .... 615-963-7494.. 445 A
tcox9@tnstate.edu
COX, Traci, R .... 419-995-8040.. 370 G
cox.t@rhodesstate.edu
COX, Virgil .... 704-922-6295.. 350 A
cox.virgil@gaston.edu
COX, William .... 931-221-1400.. 444 E
coxw@apsu.edu
COX-KELLEY, Shannon ...... 903-434-8359.. 462 M
scoxkelley@ntcc.edu
COX-LANYON, Victoria ...... 508-793-7258.. 217 B
vcoxlanyon@clarku.edu
COX-THOMPSON,
Aleshia .... 731-410-6714.. 440 K
acox@lanecollege.edu
COY, Daniella .... 561-732-4424.. 108 F
COY, Katherine .... 847-925-6955.. 141 A
kcoy@harpercollege.edu
COY-OGAN, Lynne .... 207-973-1077.. 202 I
coyoganl@my.husson.edu
COYKENDALL, John, W ...... 785-833-4349.. 182 F
john.coykendall@kwu.edu
COYLE, James .... 714-997-7074...... 37 F
coyle@chapman.edu
COYLE, Jennifer .... 503-352-2770.. 394 C
coylej@pacificu.edu
COYLE, John .... 814-886-6465.. 411 C
jcoyle@mtaloy.edu
COYLE, Judi .... 903-233-3470.. 460 J
judicoyle@letu.edu
COYLE, Mark .... 612-624-4497.. 255 H
mcoyle@umn.edu
COYLE, Philip .... 903-233-3200.. 460 J
philipcoyle@letu.edu
COYNE, Ann, C .... 617-573-8239.. 228 G
aecoyne@suffolk.edu
COYNE, Colin, M .... 205-726-4037...... 6 E
ccoyne@samford.edu
COYNE, John, B .... 330-569-5284.. 369 J
coynejb@hiram.edu
COYNE, John, M .... 724-264-1328.. 404 F
jmcoyne@gcc.edu
COYNE, Michael .... 928-681-0800.. 225 B
coyne@mslaw.edu
COYNE, Michael .... 570-372-4128.. 419 H
coyne@susqu.edu
COYNE, Mildred .... 954-201-7811.... 96 I
mcoyne@broward.edu
COZART, Wayne .... 434-243-9041.. 495 H
wdc9q@virginia.edu
COZZENS, David .... 817-257-7926.. 469 G
d.s.cozzens@tcu.edu
COZZENS, Glenn .... 417-268-6022.. 262 H
gcozzens@gobbc.edu
COZZENS, Susan .... 404-894-5054.. 121 D
susan.cozzens@iac.gatech.edu
COZZOCREA, Rebecca .... 518-736-3622.. 315 A
rebecca.cozzocrea@fmcc.suny.edu
CRABB, Ann .... 208-467-8593.. 134 D
atcrabb@nnu.edu
CRABB, Jenna, S .... 505-277-2531.. 302 F
jennas@unm.edu
CRABB, John .... 407-923-1618.. 260 E
jcrabb@rts.edu
CRABBE, Kim .... 518-580-5790.. 330 F
kcrabbe@skidmore.edu
CRABILL, Casey .... 315-498-2211.. 325 G
president@sunyocc.edu
CRABREE, Troy .... 206-239-4500.. 502 D
troy.crabtree@cityu.edu
CRABTREE, April .... 415-422-5287...... 72 C
acrabtree@usfca.edu
CRABTREE, David .... 541-683-5141.. 391 E
dcrabtree@gutenberg.edu
CRABTREE, Davida Foy ..... 617-964-1100.. 214 D
dfcrabtree@ants.edu

CRABTREE, Diane .... 503-883-2507.. 392 B
dcrabtre@linfield.edu
CRABTREE, Gina, D .... 316-978-3672.. 185 J
gina.crabtree@wichita.edu
CRABTREE, Jerry .... 256-233-8222...... 1 F
jerry.crabtree@athens.edu
CRABTREE, JR., John, A . 317-789-8288.. 160 E
jcrabtree@crossroads.edu
CRABTREE, Kacy .... 828-898-8739.. 345 G
crabtree@lmc.edu
CRABTREE, Kay .... 402-481-8847.. 278 J
kay.crabtree@bryanhealthcollege.edu
CRABTREE, Peter .... 510-464-3218.... 57 D
pcrabtree@peralta.edu
CRABTREE, Robbin, D ..... 310-338-2716.... 51 E
robbin.crabtree@lmu.edu
CRABTREE, Shane .... 801-957-4571.. 483 A
shane.crabtree@slcc.edu
CRACCO, Elizabeth .... 860-486-4705.... 89 D
elizabeth.cracco@uconn.edu
CRACE, Robert, K .... 757-221-1236.. 488 F
rkcrac@wm.edu
CRACKENBERG, Peter ...... 503-554-2138.. 391 D
pcrackenberg@georgefox.edu
CRADDOCK, Alden .... 314-529-6687.. 267 B
acraddock@maryville.edu
CRADDOCK, Amanda, E .. 843-349-2979.. 428 E
acraddoc@coastal.edu
CRADDOCK, Chris .... 903-983-8181.. 460 D
ccraddock@kilgore.edu
CRADDOCK, Jackie .... 510-594-3612.... 29 K
jcraddock@cca.edu
CRADY, Thomas .... 406-243-5225.. 276 K
thomas.crady@umontana.edu
CRAFT, Edwin .... 662-846-4840.. 257 E
ecraft@deltastate.edu
CRAFT, Linda .... 214-638-0484.. 460 C
linda@kdstudio.com
CRAFT, Stephen .... 205-665-6540...... 9 B
scraft@montevallo.edu
CRAFT, Terri .... 229-732-5943.. 116 C
terricraft@andrewcollege.edu
CRAFT, Tonya .... 601-974-1200.. 258 H
craftte@millsaps.edu
CRAFT, William, J .... 218-299-3000.. 246 A
president@cord.edu
CRAFTON, Linda .... 262-595-2341.. 520 F
crafton@uwp.edu
CRAFTON, Michael .... 678-839-4875.. 129 E
mcrafton@westga.edu
CRAFTON, Teresa .... 478-274-7833.. 125 D
tcrafton@oftc.edu
CRAFTS, Deborah .... 617-236-5451.. 218 G
dcrafts@fisher.edu
CRAGAR, Beth .... 931-598-1312.. 443 O
bcragar@sewanee.edu
CRAGER, Cindy .... 609-626-3658.. 297 C
cindy.crager@stockton.edu
CRAGIN, Janet .... 415-575-6143.... 30 G
jcragin@ciis.edu
CRAGLE, Deb .... 570-586-2400.. 419 G
dcragle@summitu.edu
CRAGLE, Rachael, C .... 865-539-7219.. 446 G
rccragle@pstcc.edu
CRAGO, David, C .... 419-772-2034.. 374 J
d-crago@onu.edu
CRAHEN, Sherri, A .... 216-397-3010.. 370 H
scrahen@jcu.edu
CRAIG, Barbara .... 269-927-8147.. 236 G
craig@lakemichigancollege.edu
CRAIG, Catharine .... 641-784-5029.. 172 G
ceelliot@graceland.edu
CRAIG, Christopher, J ...... 417-836-5215.. 268 I
chriscraig@missouristate.edu
CRAIG, David .... 573-882-9570.. 273 E
davidcr@missouri.edu
CRAIG, David .... 406-657-2209.. 277 D
david.craig2@msubillings.edu
CRAIG, Dennis .... 914-251-6300.. 334 C
dennis.craig@purchase.edu
CRAIG, Erin .... 315-866-0300.. 316 A
CRAIG, James .... 520-206-6916...... 16 F
jcraig7@pima.edu
CRAIG, Jason .... 703-284-5988.. 492 A
jason.craig@marymount.edu
CRAIG, Jayne .... 575-769-4039.. 299 G
jayne.craig@clovis.edu
CRAIG, John .... 610-436-3133.. 416 C
jcraig@wcupa.edu
CRAIG, Johnny .... 773-602-5118.. 137 F
jcraig37@ccc.edu
CRAIG, Ken .... 828-898-8731.. 345 G
craig@lmc.edu
CRAIG, Kenneth .... 910-672-1151.. 356 E
kcraig@uncfsu.edu
CRAIG, Kim .... 651-603-6223.. 246 B
craig@csp.edu
CRAIG, La Saundra .... 513-569-1532.. 366 D
lasaundra.craig@cincinnatistate.edu
CRAIG, Martha, P .... 865-981-8167.. 441 H
mardi.craig@maryvillecollege.edu

CRAIG, Marva .... 212-220-8131.. 307 B
mcraig@bmcc.cuny.edu
CRAIG, Michael .... 816-501-4065.. 270 J
michael.craig@rockhurst.edu
CRAIG, Osubi .... 804-524-5247.. 499 G
ocraig@vsu.edu
CRAIG, Paige .... 708-209-3509.. 138 G
paige.craig@cuchicago.edu
CRAIG, Raymond .... 419-372-2340.. 364 E
racraig@bgsu.edu
CRAIG, Sandy .... 618-262-8641.. 142 F
craigs@iecc.edu
CRAIG, Stephanie, A .... 814-371-2090.. 420 H
scraig@triangle-tech.edu
CRAIG, Stephen .... 801-422-3013.. 132 J
stephen_craig@byu.edu
CRAIG, Steven .... 713-743-3812.. 473 F
scraig@uh.edu
CRAIG, Tammy .... 314-918-2624.. 265 A
tcraig@eden.edu
CRAIG, Thomas .... 903-877-7442.. 477 E
tom.craig@uthct.edu
CRAIG, Todd .... 404-261-1441.. 125 F
institutionalresearch@oglethorpe.edu
CRAIG, William, G .... 732-571-3427.. 292 F
craig@monmouth.edu
CRAIG KUNG, Pang-Jen . 919-301-6500.... 93 F
CRAIG-MARIUS, Renee .... 559-442-8218.... 67 C
renee.craig-marius@fresnocitycollege.edu
CRAIG-TAYLOR,
Phyliss, V .... 919-530-6112.. 357 A
pcraigtaylor@nccu.edu
CRAIGG, Dorenda .... 336-315-7800.... 93 F
CRAIGIE, Casey .... 541-485-1780.. 393 A
caseycraigie@newhope.edu
CRAIGMILES, Jan .... 859-858-3511.. 186 J
jan.craigmiles@asbury.edu
CRAIK, Rebecca, L .... 215-572-2143.. 397 G
craikr@arcadia.edu
CRAIN, BJ .... 940-898-3505.. 472 G
bcrain@twu.edu
CRAIN, John, L .... 985-549-2280.. 201 C
jcrain@selu.edu
CRAIN, R. David .... 972-883-6900.. 476 C
r.david.crain@utdallas.edu
CRAIN, Rick .... 678-717-3623.. 128 F
rick.crain@ung.edu
CRAIN, Terry .... 618-985-3741.. 143 F
terrycrain@jalc.edu
CRAINER, Bryan, E .... 989-964-4091.. 240 F
becraine@svsu.edu
CRAM, Stanley .... 920-924-6431.. 524 B
scram@morainepark.edu
CRAM-RAHLF, Shelly .... 563-288-6011.. 172 C
scramrahlf@eicc.edu
CRAMB, Alan .... 312-567-3106.. 142 I
president@iit.edu
CRAMER, Alicia .... 713-646-1808.. 459 A
acramer@hcl.edu
CRAMER, Gregory, D .... 630-889-6536.. 149 G
gcramer@nuhs.edu
CRAMER, Jane .... 718-951-5611.. 307 D
janec@brooklyn.cuny.edu
CRAMER, Janet .... 303-546-3588.... 81 I
jcramer@naropa.edu
CRAMER, Joel .... 317-738-8197.. 160 J
jcramer@franklincollege.edu
CRAMER, Judy .... 978-542-6139.. 222 D
judy.cramer@salemstate.edu
CRAMER, Robert, G .... 608-342-1226.. 521 A
cramerr@uwplatt.edu
CRAMER, Steven, M .... 608-262-5246.. 519 K
cramer@engr.wisc.edu
CRAMER, Walter .... 203-837-8547.... 85 I
cramerw@wcsu.edu
CRAMPTON, Anne-Marie . 719-336-1520.... 81 D
anne-marie.crampton@lamarcc.edu
CRAMPTON, Laraine .... 310-577-3000.... 75 H
lcrampton@yosan.edu
CRAMPTON, Roscoe .... 312-942-7165.. 153 B
roscoe_crampton@rush.edu
CRAMPTON, Scott .... 719-336-1681.... 81 D
scott.crampton@lamarcc.edu
CRAMPTON, Tom .... 810-762-0506.. 238 F
thomas.crampto@mcc.edu
CRAMPTON, Troy, D .... 515-574-1114.. 173 F
crampton@iowacentral.edu
CRAMSEY, Rachel .... 217-228-5520.. 136 A
rcramsey@brcn.edu
CRANCE, Gina-Lyn .... 610-921-7611.. 396 H
gcrance@albright.edu
CRANDALL, Donald, W ...... 479-524-7150.... 20 H
dcrandal@jbu.edu
CRANDALL, James .... 530-242-7989.... 64 D
jcrandall@shastacollege.edu
CRANDALL, Jordan .... 918-495-6010.. 386 H
jcrandall@oru.edu
CRANDALL, Julie .... 800-486-7049.. 378 E
julie.crandall@myunion.edu
CRANDALL, Larry .... 801-302-2800.. 480 L
larry.crandall@neumont.edu

CRANDALL, Laura .... 315-470-4865.. 334 E
ldcranda@esf.edu
CRANDALL, Paige .... 914-395-2575.. 329 K
pcrandall@sarahlawrence.edu
CRANDALL, Stephen, S .... 607-871-2987.. 303 F
fcrandall@alfred.edu
CRANDELL, Gale, M .... 989-386-6664.. 238 B
gcrandell@midmich.edu
CRANE, Amanda .... 972-580-7600.. 452 I
acrane@bhcarroll.edu
CRANE, Anne .... 316-295-5610.. 181 B
annec@friends.edu
CRANE, Daniel, R .... 651-631-5100.. 256 A
drcrane@unwsp.edu
CRANE, David .... 508-531-6145.. 221 C
dcrane@bridgew.edu
CRANE, Jeff .... 270-384-8150.. 191 E
cranej@lindsey.edu
CRANE, Jeff .... 360-438-4564.. 506 G
jcrane@stmartin.edu
CRANE, Malachi, D .... 517-750-1200.. 241 E
mcrane@arbor.edu
CRANE, Paul .... 810-762-9887.. 236 C
pcrane@kettering.edu
CRANE, Peter .... 203-432-5109.... 90 D
peter.crane@yale.edu
CRANE, Rob, M .... 913-288-7283.. 182 C
rcrane@kckcc.edu
CRANE, Robert .... 956-380-8100.. 464 F
rcrane@riogrande.edu
CRANE, Ron .... 972-825-4818.. 466 D
rcrane@sagu.edu
CRANE, Sarah, R .... 517-750-1200.. 241 E
scrane@arbor.edu
CRANE, Steven .... 415-561-6555.... 58 C
steven.crane@presidio.edu
CRANE, Susan .... 914-337-9300.. 311 F
susan.crane@concordia-ny.edu
CRANE, Susan, L .... 989-964-4350.. 240 F
scrane@svsu.edu
CRANFORD, Bill .... 601-925-3283.. 259 A
cranford@mc.edu
CRANFORD, Shannon ...... 580-628-6229.. 384 L
shannon.cranford@noc.edu
CRANFORD, Timothy .... 510-869-6610.... 59 L
tcranford@samuelmerritt.edu
CRANHAM, John, B .... 919-508-2336.. 359 G
jbcranham@peace.edu
CRANK, Robert .... 816-322-0110.. 262 N
bob.crank@calvary.edu
CRANMER, Wendy .... 585-395-2126.. 332 E
wcranmer@brockport.edu
CRANMORE, Jill, A .... 217-443-8756.. 139 B
jcranmore@dacc.edu
CRANSTON, Amy .... 215-951-1081.. 407 A
cranston@lasalle.edu
CRANSTON, Carey .... 708-444-4500.. 140 F
CRANSTON, Carolyn .... 412-924-1375.. 417 E
ccranston@pts.edu
CRANWELL, Mary .... 732-987-2285.. 292 A
mcranwell@georgian.edu
CRAPANZANO, Vincent ... 845-398-4019.. 329 G
vcrapanz@stac.edu
CRAREY, II, Patrick .... 301-891-4481.. 213 D
pcrarey@wau.edu
CRARY-STACHOWIAK,
Sage .... 413-205-3521.. 214 B
sage.stachowiak@aic.edu
CRASS, Sara, T .... 713-221-8679.. 474 B
crasss@uhd.edu
CRATER, Lucas .... 217-545-9362.. 154 H
lcrater@siumed.edu
CRATSLEY, Christopher ... 978-665-4716.. 221 D
ccratsley@fitchburgstate.edu
CRATTY, Frederic, W .... 203-837-8665.... 85 I
crattyf@wcsu.edu
CRAVEN, Bryan, C .... 850-718-2375.... 97 G
cravenb@chipola.edu
CRAVEN, Heather .... 973-328-5281.. 290 H
hcraven@ccm.edu
CRAVEN, Katherine .... 781-239-5955.. 214 G
kcraven@babson.edu
CRAVEN, Randy .... 423-236-2732.. 444 B
rlcraven@southern.edu
CRAVENS, Michael .... 419-824-3620.. 371 I
mcravens@sistersosf.org
CRAVENS, Sarah .... 330-972-2332.. 378 G
cravens@uakron.edu
CRAVER, Robert .... 303-369-5151.... 82 F
robert.craver@plattcolorado.edu
CRAVER, III, William .... 678-225-7509.. 416 F
williamcr@pcom.edu
CRAVO, Ana, M .... 201-761-6104.. 296 K
acravo@saintpeters.edu
CRAWFORD, Andrew, B .... 757-594-7663.. 488 E
andrew.crawford@cnu.edu
CRAWFORD, Anna .... 304-260-4380.. 511 L
acrawfor@blueridgectc.edu
CRAWFORD, Brian, L .... 304-336-8004.. 513 F
brian.crawford@westliberty.edu
CRAWFORD, Brittany .... 334-683-2382...... 5 G
bcrawford@marionmilitary.edu
CRAWFORD, Bruce .... 205-929-6312...... 5 D
bcrawford@lawsonstate.edu
CRAWFORD, Bryan .... 719-562-7002.... 82 G
bryan.crawford@pueblocc.edu
CRAWFORD, Cardon, B ..... 843-953-6966.. 428 A
cardon.crawford@citadel.edu
CRAWFORD, Charlie .... 425-640-1557.. 503 E
charlie.crawford@edcc.edu
CRAWFORD, Chemene, L .. 214-860-2170.. 456 E
chemene.crawford@dcccd.edu
CRAWFORD, Chris .... 605-642-6262.. 437 B
chris.crawford@bhsu.edu
CRAWFORD, Clinton .... 718-270-5140.. 309 B
crawford@mec.cuny.edu
CRAWFORD, Cynthia .... 909-537-5315.... 34 C
ccrawfor@csusb.edu
CRAWFORD, David .... 303-797-5762.... 76 J
david.crawford@arapahoe.edu
CRAWFORD, David .... 773-947-6250.. 147 D
dcrawford@mccormick.edu
CRAWFORD, David, S .... 202-526-3799.... 93 E
dcrawford@johnpaulii.edu
CRAWFORD, Debbie .... 970-945-8691.... 78 B
CRAWFORD, Deborah .... 703-993-2268.. 490 B
dcrawfo7@gmu.edu
CRAWFORD, Deena .... 601-266-4829.. 261 E
deena.crawford@usm.edu
CRAWFORD, Eboni .... 973-803-5000.. 294 B
ecrawford@pillar.edu
CRAWFORD, Galen .... 415-351-3509.... 61 B
gcrawford@sfai.edu
CRAWFORD, Gregory .... 513-529-2345.. 372 K
president@miamioh.edu
CRAWFORD, Holly .... 585-275-2800.. 338 K
hcrawford@admin.rochester.edu
CRAWFORD, Isiah .... 253-879-3201.. 508 D
president@pugetsound.edu
CRAWFORD, Jenny .... 410-777-1204.. 206 B
jlcrawford1@aacc.edu
CRAWFORD, John .... 330-672-2760.. 370 I
jcrawfor1@kent.edu
CRAWFORD, John, D .... 229-333-5939.. 129 G
jdcrawford@valdosta.edu
CRAWFORD, John, P .... 716-880-2879.. 320 D
jpc334@medaille.edu
CRAWFORD, Jonas .... 805-678-5870.... 73 E
jcrawford@vcccd.edu
CRAWFORD, Kevin .... 240-500-2000.. 207 I
klcrawford@hagerstowncc.edu
CRAWFORD, Kevin .... 803-641-3495.. 433 G
kevincr@usca.edu
CRAWFORD, Malinda .... 406-756-3828.. 276 E
mcrawfor@fvcc.edu
CRAWFORD, Matthew .... 612-659-6701.. 250 B
matthew.crawford@minneapolis.edu
CRAWFORD, Michael .... 773-838-7500.. 137 H
mcrawford34@ccc.edu
CRAWFORD, Mike .... 863-680-6211.. 101 E
mcrawford@flsouthern.edu
CRAWFORD, Missie .... 478-289-2172.. 120 C
mcrawford@ega.edu
CRAWFORD, R. Scott .... 765-361-6355.. 169 C
crawforr@wabash.edu
CRAWFORD, Ray Scott ...... 318-678-6000.. 195 I
rcrawford@bpcc.edu
CRAWFORD, Rhia, M .... 828-448-6048.. 354 B
rcrawford@wpcc.edu
CRAWFORD, Ronald, W ..... 804-204-1201.. 487 D
rcrawford@btsr.edu
CRAWFORD, Teresa .... 863-784-7061.. 109 G
teresa.crawford@southflorida.edu
CRAWFORD, Teri .... 281-998-6151.. 464 I
teri.crawford@sjcd.edu
CRAWFORD, Thomas, P ..... 412-624-5822.. 421 G
tom.crawford@ia.pitt.edu
CRAWFORD, Tim .... 254-295-4180.. 474 E
tcrawford@umhb.edu
CRAWFORD, Valerie .... 309-268-8150.. 141 C
val.crawford@heartland.edu
CRAWFORD, Virginia .... 601-266-5390.. 261 E
virginia.crawford@usm.edu
CRAWFORD, Wendy .... 870-733-6711.... 19 A
wcrawford@asumidsouth.edu
CRAWFORD, III,
William, H .... 480-732-7309.... 13 O
bill.crawford.iii@cgc.edu
CRAWFORD, Yashica .... 707-864-7112.... 65 A
yashica.crawford@solano.edu
CRAWFORD-FOWLER,
Sally .... 620-341-5221.. 180 G
scrowfo4@emporia.edu
CRAWLEY, Cathy .... 478-445-5149.. 121 A
cathy.crawley@gcsu.edu
CRAWLEY, William .... 850-474-2077.. 113 A
wcrawley@uwf.edu
CRAWSHAW, Taylor .... 620-331-4100.. 181 J
tcrawshaw@indycc.edu
CRAYS, Linda, L .... 713-500-2080.. 477 C
linda.l.crays@uth.tmc.edu
CRAYTON, D Onetta .... 617-253-5010.. 225 A
CREAGER, Carol .... 540-887-7310.. 491 G
ccreager@mbc.edu
CREAGH, Curtis, E .... 502-597-6735.. 191 B
curtis.creagh@kysu.edu
CREAGH, CM, Kevin .... 716-286-8400.. 324 E
kcreagh@niagara.edu
CREAHAN, Patricia, H ...... 716-888-2616.. 306 F
creahan@canisius.edu
CREAMER, Barry .... 214-818-1300.. 455 G
bcreamer@criswell.edu
CREAMER, David .... 513-529-4225.. 372 K
creamerd@miamioh.edu
CREAMER, Jenni .... 864-646-1615.. 433 C
jevans12@tctc.edu
CREAMER, Julie .... 507-222-4280.. 245 C
jcreamer@carleton.edu
CREAMER, Kelli .... 205-983-5242...... 5 B
kcreamer@jeffersstate.edu
CREAMER, Stephen .... 978-762-4000.. 224 C
screamer@northshore.edu
CREARY, Ferne .... 305-237-2222.. 105 D
fcreary@mdc.edu
CREASMAN, Alice .... 304-473-8440.. 515 B
creasman_aj@wvwc.edu
CREASMAN, Boyd .... 304-473-8042.. 515 B
creasman@wvwc.edu
CREASON, Paul .... 562-938-4171.... 49 D
pcreason@lbcc.edu
CREASON, Rita, A .... 270-789-5233.. 187 G
racreason@campbellsville.edu
CREASY, Rick .... 423-472-7141.. 445 E
rcreasy@clevelandstatecc.edu
CRECELIUS, Kathryn, J .... 443-997-2370.. 208 D
kcrecelius@jhu.edu
CREDILLE, John .... 417-328-1606.. 272 C
jcredille@sbuniv.edu
CREDLE, Sid, H .... 757-727-5361.. 490 E
sid.credle@hamptonu.edu
CREE, Robert A .... 315-364-3408.. 340 B
rcree@wells.edu
CREE, Sara .... 309-344-2518.. 136 C
scree@sandburg.edu
CREECH, Bill .... 918-595-7000.. 388 F
bill.creech@tulsacc.edu
CREECH, Jennifer, M .... 937-229-4141.. 379 D
jcreech1@udayton.edu
CREECH, Karlton, W .... 207-581-1052.. 204 H
karlton.creech@maine.edu
CREECH, Pat .... 918-540-6294.. 384 F
pcreech@neo.edu
CREECH, Tom .... 810-762-9616.. 236 C
tcreech@kettering.edu
CREECY, Scott .... 870-762-3159.... 18 G
screecy@smail.anc.edu
CREED, J. Bradley .... 910-893-1205.. 342 F
creed@campbell.edu
CREED-DIKEOGU, Gloria . 785-242-5200.. 183 M
creeddikeogu@ottawa.edu
CREEGER, Joan .... 704-216-3602.. 352 G
joan.creeger@rccc.edu
CREEHAN, Dennis, W .... 304-457-6404.. 510 B
creehandw@ab.edu
CREEK, Frederick .... 541-552-7672.. 395 A
creekf@sou.edu
CREEKMORE, Crystal .... 256-233-8174...... 1 F
crystal.creekmore@athens.edu
CREEKMORE, Paul, R .... 630-515-7217.. 148 C
rcreek@midwestern.edu
CREEL, Angie .... 928-344-7776.... 11 J
angela.creel-erb@azwestern.edu
CREEL, Ronnie .... 334-670-3496...... 7 H
rcreel@troy.edu
CREEL, Shane .... 361-593-2237.. 469 A
randolph.creel@tamuk.edu
CREELY, Hilliary .... 724-357-7730.. 415 B
hcreely@iup.edu
CREER, Andrew .... 801-863-8608.. 482 C
andrew.creer@uvu.edu
CREFT, Dawn, H .... 407-303-7894.... 95 C
dawn.creft@adu.edu
CREGER, LeAnn .... 517-607-2305.. 235 E
lcreger@hillsdale.edu
CREGGER, Crystal, Y .... 276-233-4762.. 499 C
ccregger@wcc.vccs.edu
CREIGHTON, Brenda .... 715-425-3926.. 521 E
brenda.creighton@uwrf.edu
CREIGHTON, Grace .... 914-674-7369.. 320 G
gcreighton@mercy.edu
CREMER, Douglas .... 818-767-0888.... 75 D
douglas.cremer@woodbury.edu
CREMER, Phyllis, A .... 818-767-0888.... 75 D
phyllis.cremer@woodbury.edu
CRENSHAW, Chris .... 601-266-4414.. 261 E
christopher.crenshaw@usm.edu
CRENSHAW, Christine .... 405-744-5358.. 385 G
christine.crenshaw@okstate.edu
CRENSHAW, Leticia .... 513-244-8447.. 366 E
hr@ccuniversity.edu
CRENSHAW, Pamela .... 714-556-3610.... 73 E
pcrenshaw@vanguard.edu
CRENSHAW, Sandra .... 215-572-2108.. 397 G
crenshaws@arcadia.edu
CREOLA, Thomas .... 561-697-9200.. 127 D
tcreola@southuniversity.edu
CRESCENZI, Nicole .... 415-351-3517.... 61 B
ncrescenzi@sfai.edu
CRESCENZO, Mario .... 212-650-5250.. 307 E
mcrescenzo@ccny.cuny.edu
CRESPIE, Nancie .... 301-891-4147.. 213 D
ncrespie@wau.edu
CRESPINO, Curt, J .... 816-235-1105.. 273 F
crespinocj@umkc.edu
CRESPO, Jorge .... 787-751-0178.. 535 N
ac_jcrespo@suagm.edu
CRESPO, Jorge, L .... 787-751-0178.. 535 N
ac_jcrespo@suagm.edu
CRESPO, Ricardo .... 787-751-1912.. 534 E
rcnevarez@juris.inter.edu
CRESPO-KEBLER,
Elizabeth .... 787-993-8864.. 537 G
elizabeth.crespo1@upr.edu
CRESPO-LOPEZ, Sylvia ...... 212-237-8897.. 308 E
sylopez@jjay.cuny.edu
CRESPO-MARTÍNEZ,
María, I .... 787-993-8886.. 537 G
maria.crespo@upr.edu
CRESPY, Charles, T .... 989-774-2481.. 232 D
cresp1ct@cmich.edu
CRESS, Pam .... 509-527-2421.. 508 G
pam.cress@wallawalla.edu
CRESSWELL, Timothy .... 860-297-2144.... 89 B
timothy.cresswell@trincoll.edu
CREVISTON, Thomas, E ... 913-684-3097.. 528 I
CREW, Dwayne .... 478-825-6200.. 120 F
crewd@fvsu.edu
CREW, Rudolph, F .... 718-270-5000.. 309 B
rcrew@mec.cuny.edu
CREWE, Sandra .... 202-806-7300.... 93 A
screwe@howard.edu
CREWELL, Don .... 626-395-6280.... 30 H
dcrewell@caltech.edu
CREWS, Amy .... 256-765-4437...... 9 C
aecrews@una.edu
CREWS, Angie .... 301-891-4134.. 213 D
acrews@wau.edu
CREWS, Bradford, W .... 561-297-2190.. 110 K
bcrews2@fau.edu
CREWS, Chris .... 812-941-2000.. 163 F
cmcrews@ius.edu
CREWS, Denise .... 217-875-7200.. 152 C
dcrews@richland.edu
CREWS, Kimberly .... 202-274-5857.... 94 B
kcrews@udc.edu
CREWS, Micah, R .... 423-652-4773.. 440 J
mrcrews@king.edu
CREWS, Michele .... 617-879-2114.. 229 G
mcrews@wheelock.edu
CREWS, Patricia, S .... 850-484-1000.. 106 H
pcrews@pensacolastate.edu
CREWS, Sharon .... 205-929-6307...... 5 D
sharon.crews@lawsonstate.edu
CREWS, William, O .... 360-882-2120.... 44 H
bcrews@nwbaptist.org
CREWSE, Valentina .... 602-242-6265.... 11 O
CRICK, James .... 502-451-0815.. 193 A
jcrick@sullivan.edu
CRICK, James .... 502-451-0815.. 193 B
jcrick@sullivan.edu
CRICKENBERGER, Leslie . 931-372-3034.. 445 B
lcrickenberger@tntech.edu
CRICKENBERGER,
Tamela .... 434-592-3508.. 491 D
tlcrickenberger@liberty.edu
CRICKMER, Janet .... 276-944-6658.. 489 I
jcrickme@ehc.edu
CRIDER, Scott .... 972-721-5218.. 473 D
crider@udallas.edu
CRIDER, Wayne .... 706-245-7226.. 120 D
wcrider@ec.edu
CRIGLER, Jeremy, T .... 504-865-5000.. 200 C
CRIHFIELD, Jud .... 610-921-7500.. 396 H
jcrihfield@albright.edu
CRILLEY, Bonnie .... 814-866-8144.. 407 D
bcrilley@lecom.edu
CRIMMIN, Nancy, P .... 774-354-0460.. 215 D
nancy.crimmin@becker.edu
CRIMMINS, Cindy .... 717-815-1216.. 424 F
ccrimmins@ycp.edu
CRIMMINS, Kate .... 410-837-6135.. 213 C
kcrimmins@ubalt.edu
CRIMMINS LECHOWICZ,
Catherine .... 860-685-2841.... 90 C
ccrimmins@wesleyan.edu
CRINO, Sally, E .... 563-333-6080.. 176 D
crinosallye@sau.edu
CRIPE, Stephen, A .... 989-837-4387.. 239 D
cripe@northwood.edu
CRIPPIN-HAAKE,
Tracy, L .... 515-574-1192.. 173 F
crippin@iowacentral.edu

CRIPPS, Kimberly 205-726-4180 6 E kcripps@samford.edu
CRISAFULLI, Susan 317-738-8240 160 J scrisafulli@franklincollege.edu
CRISER, III, Marshall, M 850-245-0466 110 I chancellor@flbog.edu
CRISLER, Pat 402-457-2759 280 J pcrisler@mccneb.edu
CRISLIP, Ann 518-262-9550 303 E crislia@mail.amc.edu
CRISLIP-TACY, Carolyn 304-367-4241 513 B crisliptacy@fairmontstate.edu
CRISMAN, Matthew 276-944-6491 489 I mcrisman@ehc.edu
CRISMAN, Steve 901-321-3278 439 E scrisman@cbu.edu
CRISMON, M. Lynn 512-471-3718 476 B lynn.crismon@austin.utexas.edu
CRISP, Brad 325-674-2503 449 J cbc06d@acu.edu
CRISP, JR., Delmas, S 910-630-7031 346 E dcrisp@methodist.edu
CRISP, Kathryn 615-898-2088 444 G kathy.crisp@mtsu.edu
CRISP, Michael, D 864-833-8308 432 B mdcrisp@presby.edu
CRISP, Whitney 229-931-2299 127 C wcrisp@southgatech.edu
CRISP, Winston, B 919-966-4045 357 D wbcrisp@email.unc.edu
CRISPELL, Brian, L 813-988-5131 100 F crispellb@floridacollege.edu
CRISS, Paul 901-888-3343 256 I pcriss@belhaven.edu
CRISS, Sarah 661-763-7711 67 F scriss@taftcollege.edu
CRISSINGER, Amy, S 605-256-5139 437 C amy.crissinger@dsu.edu
CRIST, Diane, G 651-962-6765 256 C dgcrist@stthomas.edu
CRIST, William, J 337-482-2001 201 D wjc4092@louisiana.edu
CRISTANCHO MERCADO, Oscar, J 407-582-3306 114 N ocristanchomercad@valenciacollege.edu
CRISTANTELLO, David 716-829-7582 313 A
CRISTE, Vince 800-877-5456 488 D alumni@christendom.edu
CRISTELLO, Justin 910-642-7141 353 C justin.cristello@sccnc.edu
CRISTOBAL, Remy, B 671-735-2218 530 B remybc@triton.uog.edu
CRISTOFARO, Theresa, R 856-225-6053 296 A terri.cristofaro@rutgers.edu
CRITE, Ken 815-802-8222 144 C kcrite@kcc.edu
CRITES, Randall 304-473-8030 515 B crites@wvwc.edu
CRITES, Tammy 304-473-8186 515 B crites_t@wvwc.edu
CRITTENDEN, Barbara, J 641-782-1425 177 B crittenden@swcciowa.edu
CRITTENDEN, Steve 763-433-1982 248 K steve.crittenden@anokaramsey.edu
CROCHET, Monique 985-448-4110 201 A monique.crochet@nicholls.edu
CROCITTO, Peter 954-776-4476 103 J peterc@keiseruniversity.edu
CROCKEM, Rajanel 713-313-1895 470 D crockemr@tsu.edu
CROCKER, Daniel 207-974-4623 203 J dcrocker@emcc.edu
CROCKER, Harold 201-684-7091 294 G hcrocker@ramapo.edu
CROCKER, Heidi 562-947-8755 66 A heidicrocker@scuhs.edu
CROCKER, Jack 575-538-6318 303 A jack.crocker@wnmu.edu
CROCKER, Jane, S 856-415-2250 295 D jcrocker@rcgc.edu
CROCKER, Leslie 804-330-0111 487 P bursarcrim@centura.edu
CROCKER, Marjorie 706-419-1544 119 G crocker@covenant.edu
CROCKER, Phyllis 313-596-0210 241 G pcrocker@udmercy.edu
CROCKER, Rhonda 575-624-7382 299 J rhonda.crocker@roswell.enmu.edu
CROCKETT, Bennie, R 601-318-6116 261 I crockett@wmcarey.edu
CROCKETT, Brian, S 540-464-7287 499 E briancrockett@vmiaa.org
CROCKETT, Charles, E 936-261-2653 467 E cecrockett@pvamu.edu
CROCKETT, Daniel, E 304-558-4618 512 O daniel.crockett@wvhepc.edu
CROCKETT, Deborah 207-947-4591 202 E dcrockett@bealcollege.edu
CROCKETT, Julie, E 309-794-7244 135 D juliecrockett@augustana.edu
CROCKETT, Michael 928-428-8215 13 B mike.crockett@eac.edu
CROCKETT, Nathan 864-242-5100 427 E
CROCKETT, Suzonne 409-882-3062 471 B suzonne.crockett@lsco.edu
CROCKETT, Vivian 239-304-7344 95 Q vivian.crockett@avemaria.edu
CROCKETT, William, P 410-706-3902 211 F bcrocket@umaryland.edu
CROCKETT-RAY, Sharon 210-486-2886 450 E scrockett-ray@alamo.edu
CROCKETT-RAY, Sharon 210-486-2887 450 E scrockett-ray@alamo.edu
CROCKROM, SR., Charles 205-929-1447 5 H ccrockrom@miles.edu
CROCQUET, Marc 954-262-8842 105 J crocquet@nsu.nova.edu
CROEKER, Jane 701-777-2097 360 C jane.croeker@und.edu
CROFF, Troy 503-581-8600 391 B tcroff@corban.edu
CROFT, Lucy, S 904-620-2525 112 B lcroft@unf.edu
CROFT, Maureen, G 832-842-8703 473 F mgcroft@uh.edu
CROFT, Nicole 866-680-2756 480 K academicdean@midwifery.edu
CROGAN, Evelyn 760-795-6610 52 K ecrogan@miracosta.edu
CROGHAN, Chris, M 605-336-6588 436 J
CROGHAN, David 301-846-2708 207 F dcroghan@frederick.edu
CROGHAN, John 315-859-4129 315 D jcroghan@hamilton.edu
CROKE, Ryan 217-206-7148 156 G rcroke@uis.edu
CROKE, Ryan 217-206-7795 156 G rcroke@uis.edu
CROLEY, Linda 386-752-1822 100 L linda.croley@fgc.edu
CROMARTIE, Anthony 973-877-1873 291 H cromartie@essex.edu
CROMARTY, Geoffrey 215-951-2970 416 G cromartyg@philau.edu
CROMBIE, Richard 651-635-8041 244 L r-crombie@bethel.edu
CROMIE, Carol 409-772-9795 478 A cacromie@utmb.edu
CROMLEY, Brenda 570-389-4674 414 D bcromley@bloomu.edu
CROMLEY, Robert 903-877-7455 477 E robert.cromley@uthct.edu
CRONAN, David 708-709-3585 151 C dcronan@prairiestate.edu
CRONAUER, Alan 315-866-0300 316 A cronaueab@herkimer.edu
CRONAUER, OSB, Patrick, T 724-805-2324 419 B patrick.cronauer@stvincent.edu
CRONE, Darren 972-883-4826 476 C darren.crone@utdallas.edu
CRONE, Kimberly 860-231-5360 90 B kcrone@usj.edu
CRONE, Marilyn 206-296-5841 507 E cronem@seattleu.edu
CRONIC, Sue 770-533-7007 123 L scronic@laniertech.edu
CRONIN, Charles 610-526-1458 397 E tip.cronin@theamericancollege.edu
CRONIN, Corey 978-542-6000 222 D corey.cronin@salemstate.edu
CRONIN, Kelly 956-665-3844 476 E kelly.cronin@utrgv.edu
CRONIN, Marta 772-462-7674 103 B mcronin@irsc.edu
CRONIN, Mary, A 713-348-4070 464 E cronin@rice.edu
CRONIN, Shawn 978-762-4000 224 C scronin@northshore.edu
CRONIN, Trish 508-793-7160 217 B tcronin@clarku.edu
CRONK, Keith 501-279-5700 20 D kcronk@harding.edu
CRONK, Nancy, L 765-285-1722 159 B ncronk@bsu.edu
CRONRATH, Daniel 386-752-1822 100 L daniel.cronrath@fgc.edu
CRONRATH, David 301-405-6287 211 E cronrath@umd.edu
CROOK, David 646-664-8102 306 M david.crook@cuny.edu
CROOK, Evonne 423-236-2830 444 B ercrook@southern.edu
CROOK, Linda 303-914-6256 82 I linda.crook@rrcc.edu
CROOK, Patricia 615-963-5280 445 A pcrook@tnstate.edu
CROOK, Rebecca 321-674-8099 100 M bcrook@fit.edu
CROOKENDALE, Humphrey 212-343-1234 321 B hcrookendale@mcny.edu
CROOKER, Benjamin 718-817-3048 314 G crooker@fordham.edu
CROOKS, John, R 440-365-5222 371 H
CROOM, Sally 318-675-8769 198 B scroom@lsuhsc.edu
CROONQUIST, Matt 641-673-2123 177 J croonquistm@wmpenn.edu
CROOP, Patricia 518-464-8642 314 A pcroop@excelsior.edu
CROOT, Rick 360-417-6553 505 I rcroot@pencol.edu
CROPPER, USMS, Thomas, A 707-654-1011 33 D tacropper@csum.edu
CROPSEY, Jeffrey 800-955-2527 181 D jcropsey@grantham.edu
CROSBIE, Jeff 435-797-1042 482 B jeff.crosbie@usu.edu
CROSBY, Anita, L 334-387-3877 1 E anitacrosby@amridgeuniversity.edu
CROSBY, Cheryl 352-854-2322 97 R crosbyc@cf.edu
CROSBY, Faye 831-459-5031 70 F fjcrosby@ucsc.edu
CROSBY, Gary 256-372-8164 1 A gary.crosby@aamu.edu
CROSBY, James 307-778-1340 526 K jcrosby@lccc.wy.edu
CROSBY, James, P 216-347-4282 370 H jcrosby@jcu.edu
CROSBY, Jean 765-285-7057 159 B jkcrosby@bsu.edu
CROSBY, Jesse 207-947-4591 202 E jcrosby@bealcollege.edu
CROSBY, John 740-284-5349 368 L jcrosby@franciscan.edu
CROSBY, Kim 870-307-7275 21 A kim.crosby@lyon.edu
CROSBY, Lynne 931-221-6240 444 E crosbyl@apsu.edu
CROSBY, Mark 207-859-5500 202 G mcrosby@colby.edu
CROSBY, Pamela 863-667-5279 109 L pscrosby@seu.edu
CROSBY, Susan, E 540-453-2363 496 F crosbys@brcc.edu
CROSBY LEHMANN, Carl 507-786-3894 254 P lehmann@stolaf.edu
CROSKERY, Patrick, T 419-772-2197 374 J p-croskery@onu.edu
CROSLIN, Joey 405-208-5075 385 E jcroslin@okcu.edu
CROSMAN, Karen 740-368-3104 376 B klcrosma@owu.edu
CROSON, Rachel 817-272-2881 476 A croson@uta.edu
CROSS, Berri, V 336-334-4822 350 B bvcross@gtcc.edu
CROSS, Charles, E 415-422-6522 72 C cross@usfca.edu
CROSS, Colette 281-649-3475 458 L ccross@hbu.edu
CROSS, Connie, S 417-268-1000 262 F crossc@evangel.edu
CROSS, David 603-862-2090 288 C counseling.center@unh.edu
CROSS, David 713-718-8636 459 B david.cross@hccs.edu
CROSS, Dean 916-577-2200 75 C dcross@jessup.edu
CROSS, Dennis, W 540-458-8232 500 F dcross@wlu.edu
CROSS, Dwight 802-225-6324 484 G dwight.cross@neci.edu
CROSS, Dwight 802-728-1250 486 D dcross@vtc.edu
CROSS, James 802-383-6633 483 F jcross@champlain.edu
CROSS, Jeffrey 248-476-1122 237 H jcross@mispp.edu
CROSS, Jeffrey, F 217-581-2121 139 H jfcross@eiu.edu
CROSS, Jesse 336-334-4822 350 B jlcross@gtcc.edu
CROSS, Joe 858-653-6740 47 G jcross@jpcatholic.com
CROSS, Kris 937-393-3431 377 F kcross@sscc.edu
CROSS, Kristen 870-612-2011 23 H kristen.cross@uaccb.edu
CROSS, Kristie 660-359-3948 269 I kcross@mail.ncmissouri.edu
CROSS, Logan 904-256-7137 103 D jcross3@ju.edu
CROSS, Mary, M 615-353-3301 446 E mary.cross@nscc.edu
CROSS, Myrna, J 580-477-7712 389 I myrna.cross@wosc.edu
CROSS, Neal 417-328-2055 272 C ncross@sbuniv.edu
CROSS, Penny 828-652-0645 351 C penncyc@mcdowelltech.edu
CROSS, Ray, W 608-262-2321 519 J rcross@uwsa.edu
CROSS, Roberta 724-503-1001 422 H rcross@washjeff.edu
CROSS, Stan 828-298-3325 359 F scross@warren-wilson.edu
CROSS, Stephanie 540-545-7245 494 B scross92@su.edu
CROSS, Stephen 404-894-8885 121 D cross@gatech.edu
CROSS, Teresa 660-359-3948 269 I tcross@mail.ncmissouri.edu
CROSS, Terry 423-614-8140 441 B tcross@leeuniversity.edu
CROSS, Tim, L 865-974-7114 448 E tlcross@utk.edu
CROSS, Timothy 740-826-6121 373 E
CROSS, Troy 330-941-3035 382 A tcross@ysu.edu
CROSSLAND, Elisa 713-226-5519 474 B crosslande@uhd.edu
CROSSLAND, Martin 913-971-3514 183 D mcrossland@mnu.edu
CROSSLEY, John 315-733-2300 338 L jcrossley@uscny.edu
CROSSLEY, John, L 315-733-2300 338 L jcrossley@uscny.edu
CROSSMAN, Herb 518-580-5819 330 F hcrossma@skidmore.edu
CROSSMAN, Linda 727-873-4143 112 D crossman@mail.usf.edu
CROSSMAN, Raymond, E 312-662-4001 134 I rec@adler.edu
CROSSON, Elaine 718-817-3111 314 G ecrosson@fordham.edu
CROSWELL, Katrina 510-549-4719 66 J kcroswell@sksm.edu
CROUCH, Alicia 859-256-3100 188 M alicia.crouch@kctcs.edu
CROUCH, Frank 610-861-1516 411 B crouchf@moravian.edu
CROUCH, Julia 918-335-6212 386 F jcrouch@okwu.edu
CROUCH, Michael, A 205-726-2820 6 E mcrouch@samford.edu
CROUCH, Mike 620-343-4600 180 H mcrouch@fhtc.edu
CROUCH, Nancy 910-775-4355 358 C nancy.crouch@uncp.edu
CROUCH, Peter, E 808-956-7727 131 F pcrouch@hawaii.edu
CROUCH, Steven 612-624-2006 255 H crouch@umn.edu
CROUCH, Tony 918-647-1320 382 I tacrouch@carlalbert.edu
CROUCHET, Cristeen 253-589-5895 502 F cristeen.crouchet@cptc.edu
CROUSE, Eileen 269-782-1369 241 C ecrouse@swmich.edu
CROUSE, JR., Francis, C 814-886-6383 411 C fcrouse@mtaloy.edu
CROUSE, Matt 575-646-3202 300 J mcrouse@nmsu.edu
CROUSE, Robert 573-592-5019 275 E rob.crouse@westminster-mo.edu
CROUSE, Steve 864-977-7016 431 G steve.crouse@ngu.edu
CROUTER, Ann, C 814-865-1420 412 F ac1@psu.edu
CROW, Angela 479-968-0271 19 F acrow@atu.edu
CROW, C. Robert 616-526-6165 232 A rcrow@calvin.edu
CROW, Carla 561-803-2155 106 C carla_crow@pba.edu
CROW, Donna, E 435-797-3588 482 B donna.crow@usu.edu
CROW, Len 909-652-6508 37 D leonard.crow@chaffey.edu
CROW, Macey 208-467-8523 134 D maceycrow@nnu.edu
CROW, Mandy 615-248-7782 447 F mmcrow@trevecca.edu
CROW, Mariesa, L 573-341-4154 274 B crow@mst.edu
CROW, Michael, G 912-358-4172 126 F crowm@savannahstate.edu
CROW, Michael, M 480-965-8972 11 H michael.crow@asu.edu
CROW, Scott 916-484-8647 51 A crows@arc.losrios.edu
CROW, Scott 419-824-3938 371 I scrow@lourdes.edu
CROW, Steven, L 831-646-4040 53 A scrow@mpc.edu
CROW, Tony, L 303-458-4161 82 L tcrow@regis.edu

CULLITON, Richard 860-685-2627 90 C rculliton@wesleyan.edu
CULLNANE, Chris 601-968-8505 256 I ccullnane@belhaven.edu
CULLO, Len 814-393-2240 414 G lcullo@clarion.edu
CULLUM, Douglas 585-594-6331 325 B cullumd@nes.edu
CULLUM, John, W 704-687-8003 358 A john.cullum@uncc.edu
CULLUM, Mary Clare 973-275-2589 297 A maryclare.cullum@shu.edu
CULORA, Thomas 401-841-2200 528 E
CULP, Kari 918-595-8845 388 F kari.culp@tulsacc.edu
CULP, Mark, K 610-861-5301 411 G mculp@northampton.edu
CULP, Shawn 412-291-6248 397 I sculp@aii.edu
CULPEPPER, Anthony 661-395-4487 47 J anthony.culpepper@bakersfieldcollege.edu
CULPEPPER, Suzann 229-430-3510 116 A sculpepper@albanytech.edu
CULSHAW, John, P 319-335-5867 169 H john-culshaw@uiowa.edu
CULVAHOUSE, Dallas 231-439-6321 239 A dculvahouse@ncmich.edu
CULVER, Gloria 585-273-5000 338 K gloria.culver@rochester.edu
CULVER, Jay 863-638-2914 115 D culverjr@webber.edu
CULVER, Randy 605-642-6245 437 B randy.culver@bhsu.edu
CULVER, Richard, W 410-543-6017 213 A rwculver@salisbury.edu
CULVER, Robert, E 706-225-5300 93 F
CULVER, Sandi 907-786-1007 10 F smculver@uaa.alaska.edu
CULVER, Steven 540-231-4581 499 F sculver@vt.edu
CULVERHOUSE, Robert 254-267-7040 463 K rculverhouse@rangercollege.edu
CUMBERLAND, Lyndsay 662-329-7295 259 E ldcumberland@muw.edu
CUMBIE, Donna, L 252-222-6161 348 B cumbied@carteret.edu
CUMBY, Rick 931-372-3973 445 B rcumby@tntech.edu
CUMENS, Chris 270-901-1113 190 F chris.cumens@kctcs.edu
CUMINGS, Victoria, R 503-517-1012 396 D vcumings@warnerpacific.edu
CUMMING, Carrie 269-387-4300 243 H carrie.cumming@wmich.edu
CUMMING, Tammie 718-260-5007 309 C tcumming@citytech.cuny.edu
CUMMINGS, Alison 404-270-5353 128 A acummin3@spelman.edu
CUMMINGS, Amanda 207-941-7875 202 I cummingsa@husson.edu
CUMMINGS, Andrew 503-845-3505 392 E andrew.cummings@mtangel.edu
CUMMINGS, Angela 404-297-9522 122 A cumminga@gptc.edu
CUMMINGS, SSE, Brian, J 802-654-2386 484 I bcummings@smcvt.edu
CUMMINGS, Carmen 850-599-3707 110 J carmen.cummings@famu.edu
CUMMINGS, Corlis 678-466-4270 119 A corliscummings@clayton.edu
CUMMINGS, Cynthia 508-910-6402 220 H ccumings2@umassd.edu
CUMMINGS, Edie 318-869-5191 194 I ecummings@centenary.edu
CUMMINGS, Edmond, M 504-286-5258 199 I ecumming@suno.edu
CUMMINGS, Evangeline 352-294-7158 112 A ecummings@ufl.edu
CUMMINGS, Glenn, T 207-780-4480 205 E glennc@maine.edu
CUMMINGS, Jeff 760-366-5289 41 K jcummings@cmccd.edu
CUMMINGS, Jim 270-745-2035 194 D jim.cummings@wku.edu
CUMMINGS, Joseph 718-489-5346 328 D jcummings@sfc.edu
CUMMINGS, Kevin, R 914-594-4536 323 I webmaster@nymc.edu
CUMMINGS, Kristin 651-690-6829 254 M kacummings@stkate.edu
CUMMINGS, Lawanda 706-396-7597 125 H lcummings@paine.edu
CUMMINGS, Leslie 205-387-0511 2 B leslie.cummings@bscc.edu
CUMMINGS, Lisa 802-635-1382 486 B lisa.cummings@jsc.edu
CUMMINGS, Marge 606-337-1407 187 I mcummings@ccbbc.edu
CUMMINGS, JR., McDuffie 910-521-6690 358 C mcduffie.cummings@uncp.edu
CUMMINGS, Monica 847-578-3431 153 A monica.cummings@rosalindfranklin.edu
CUMMINGS, Owen 503-845-3547 392 E owen.cummings@mtangel.edu
CUMMINGS, Robin, G 910-521-4471 358 C chancellor@uncp.edu
CUMMINGS, Steve 503-255-0332 392 G scummings@multnomah.edu
CUMMINGS, Twyla 585-475-5567 327 E tjcppr@rit.edu
CUMMINGS, Wm. Theodore 281-283-3100 474 A cummings@uhcl.edu
CUMMINS, Cheryl 662-846-4405 257 E ccummins@deltastate.edu
CUMMINS, David 440-365-5222 371 H
CUMMINS, Jim 810-766-4280 231 C jim.cummins@baker.edu
CUMMINS, Kendra 918-540-6224 384 F kendra.cummins@neo.edu
CUMMINS, Michelle 812-888-4573 169 A mcummins@vinu.edu
CUMMINS, Richard 509-542-4802 502 G rcummins@columbiabasin.edu
CUMMISKEY, Raymond, V 636-481-3100 266 C rcummisk@jeffco.edu
CUMPIANO, Barbarita 787-832-6000 532 O bcumpiano@icprjc.edu
CUNDALL, JR., Michael 336-285-2030 356 F mcundall@ncat.edu
CUNDARI, Alan 909-469-5670 74 K acundari@westernu.edu
CUNDIFF, Wendy 330-972-8907 378 H wcundif@uakron.edu
CUNION, Jessica 330-823-6051 379 F cunionjs@mountunion.edu
CUNION, William 216-987-2341 367 E william.cunion@tri-c.edu
CUNNINGHAM, Carl, G 251-460-6895 9 E ccunningham@southalabama.edu
CUNNINGHAM, Cecelia 616-632-2816 231 A cunnicec@aquinas.edu
CUNNINGHAM, Chad 619-201-8725 60 D chad.cunningham@sdcc.edu
CUNNINGHAM, Chad 330-684-8910 378 H chad6@uakron.edu
CUNNINGHAM, Damita 918-456-5511 384 G cunningh@nsuok.edu
CUNNINGHAM, Diane 270-707-3921 189 G diane.cunningham@kctcs.edu
CUNNINGHAM, Don 231-995-1705 239 C dcunningham@nmc.edu
CUNNINGHAM, Doreen 919-546-8476 355 F dcunningham@shawu.edu
CUNNINGHAM, Eric 573-875-7649 263 F ercunningham@ccis.edu
CUNNINGHAM, Gary 651-201-1749 248 I gary.cunningham@so.mnscu.edu
CUNNINGHAM, Jack, L 302-356-6921 91 I john.l.cunningham@wilmu.edu
CUNNINGHAM, James 315-279-5228 318 C jcunning@keuka.edu
CUNNINGHAM, Janet, L 580-327-8400 384 M jlcunningham@nwosu.edu
CUNNINGHAM, Jennifer, L 610-758-5799 408 H jlc516@lehigh.edu
CUNNINGHAM, Jim 660-596-7208 272 G jcunningham@sfccmo.edu
CUNNINGHAM, John 313-831-5200 233 K jcunningham@etseminary.edu
CUNNINGHAM, John 774-455-7601 220 E jcunningham@umassonline.net
CUNNINGHAM, Joi, M 248-370-3496 239 K cunning3@oakland.edu
CUNNINGHAM, Karla, K 317-940-9570 159 K kcunning@butler.edu
CUNNINGHAM, Kathleen 610-606-4635 400 E ksglass@cedarcrest.edu
CUNNINGHAM, Kay 901-321-3430 439 E kay.cunningham@cbu.edu
CUNNINGHAM, Kelly, L 734-936-2254 241 J kecunham@umich.edu
CUNNINGHAM, Kevin, A 563-884-5898 176 C kevin.cunningham@palmer.edu
CUNNINGHAM, Kima 937-376-6566 365 H kcunningham@centralstate.edu
CUNNINGHAM, Lawrence (Bubba), R 919-962-8200 357 D bubbac@email.unc.edu
CUNNINGHAM, Linda 402-559-7394 283 A lcunningham@unmc.edu
CUNNINGHAM, Mark 404-756-4654 116 I mcunningham@atlm.edu
CUNNINGHAM, Michael 504-865-5261 200 C mcunnin1@tulane.edu
CUNNINGHAM, Michael 201-684-7666 294 G mcunning@ramapo.edu
CUNNINGHAM, II, Michael, J 401-333-7121 425 A mjcunningham2@ccri.edu
CUNNINGHAM, Michael, M 570-326-3761 413 O mike.cunningham@pct.edu
CUNNINGHAM, Michael, R 858-642-8101 54 A mcunningham@nu.edu
CUNNINGHAM, Nancy 772-462-7275 103 B ncunning@irsc.edu
CUNNINGHAM, Pat 615-460-6617 438 J pat.cunningham@belmont.edu
CUNNINGHAM, Paul R, G 252-744-2201 356 C cunningham@ecu.edu
CUNNINGHAM, Philip, J 262-646-6518 518 G pcunningham@nashotah.edu
CUNNINGHAM, R. Michael 217-443-8831 139 B mcunningham@dacc.edu
CUNNINGHAM, Sarah 434-528-5276 500 C
CUNNINGHAM, Sean 512-463-4930 470 G sean.cunningham@tsus.edu
CUNNINGHAM, Shannon 405-744-2212 384 L shannon.cunningham@noc.edu
CUNNINGHAM, Shannon 918-540-6295 384 F scunningham@neo.edu
CUNNINGHAM, Sheree 740-753-7009 369 K cunninghams@hocking.edu
CUNNINGHAM, Steven 850-474-2210 113 A scunningham1@uwf.edu
CUNNINGHAM, Tamara 201-200-3454 293 C tcunningham@njcu.edu
CUNNINGHAM, Thomas 914-654-5714 311 A tcunningham@cnr.edu
CUNNINGHAM, Todd 724-357-7872 415 B todd.cunningham@iup.edu
CUNNINGHAM, Tom 513-861-6400 378 E tom.cunningham@myunion.edu
CUNNINGHAM, William, J 215-596-8535 422 A w.cunningham@usciences.edu
CUOMO, Robert 508-541-1791 217 G rcuomo@dean.edu
CUOZZO, Frank 201-200-3173 293 C fcuozzo@njcu.edu
CUOZZO, Jenifer 202-685-3785 528 B cuozzoj@ndu.edu
CUOZZO, Karen 201-216-5213 297 B karen.cuozzo@stevens.edu
CUP, Jo Beth 312-662-4101 134 I jcup@adler.edu
CUPICH, Blase 847-566-6401 157 G
CUPP, Dondi, L 734-647-6079 241 J dcupp@umich.edu
CUPP, Scott, A 432-837-8303 471 E
CURBO, Billy, D 254-659-7701 458 K bdcurbo@hillcollege.edu
CURCI, Roberto 708-524-6826 139 F rcurci@dom.edu
CURD, David 877-248-6724 13 K dcurd@hmu.edu
CURD, Francis 941-405-1507 407 D fcurd@lecom.edu
CURD, Michael 877-248-6724 13 K mcurd@hmu.edu
CURDIE, Stacey, L 603-535-2846 288 F scurdie@plymouth.edu
CURE, Douglas 256-830-2626 3 I dcure@faulkner.edu
CURE, Nancy 817-515-5392 467 A nancy.cure@tccd.edu
CURE, Reid 618-215-6485 148 I rcure@morthland.edu
CURETON, Alan, S 651-631-5250 256 A ascureton@unwsp.edu
CURFMAN, Mike 218-683-8565 251 C mike.curfman@northlandcollege.edu
CURIN, Donna, B 312-915-6404 146 G dcurin@luc.edu
CURL, John 801-581-8788 481 M jcurl@sa.utah.edu
CURLEY, Christine 608-262-0277 522 A christine.curley@uwex.uwc.edu
CURLEY, Greg, M 814-641-3521 406 F curleyg@juniata.edu
CURLEY, Lauren 781-239-2572 223 F lcurley@massbay.edu
CURLEY, Meredith 602-557-1217 17 L meredith.curley@phoenix.edu
CURLEY, Russell 989-686-9339 233 I russellcurley@delta.edu
CURLEY, Scott 815-224-0301 143 C scott_curley@ivcc.edu
CURLEY, William 814-768-3401 415 D wgc114@lhup.edu
CURLL, Steve 814-371-2090 420 H scurll@triangle-tech.edu
CURME, Michael, A 513-529-1877 372 K curmema@miamioh.edu
CURNUTT, Cindy 432-335-6601 463 B ccurnutt@odessa.edu
CURPHEY, Richena 805-525-4417 67 J rcurphey@thomasaquinas.edu
CURPHY, Kathleen 504-671-5420 196 D kcurph@dcc.edu
CURRALL, Steven, C 214-768-3219 465 J scc@smu.edu
CURRAN, Ericka 904-680-7650 100 E ecurran@fcsl.edu
CURRAN, Jack 718-862-7934 319 L jack.curran@manhattan.edu
CURRAN, James 941-359-4200 112 E
CURRAN, James, W 404-727-8720 120 E jcurran@sph.emory.edu
CURRAN, Jennifer 860-685-2008 90 C jcurran@wesleyan.edu
CURRAN, Katie 213-615-2700 37 I
CURRAN, Linda 303-678-3620 80 E linda.curran@frontrange.edu
CURRAN, Lizzy, E 402-280-2221 279 H lizzycurran@creighton.edu
CURRAN, Michael 914-968-6200 329 C
CURRAN, Sheri, L 309-794-8058 135 D shericurran@augustana.edu
CURRAN, Susan 401-232-6020 424 K scurran3@bryant.edu
CURRAN, Terrence, M 910-962-3876 358 D currant@uncw.edu
CURRAN, Thomas, B 816-501-4250 270 J thomas.curran@rockhurst.edu
CURRENT, Amy, L 563-589-0274 177 H acurrent@wartburgseminary.edu
CURRERI, Michelle 401-874-4462 426 D mcurreri@uri.edu
CURRIE, Catherine 401-232-6369 424 K ccurrie@bryant.edu
CURRIE, Cathleen 208-562-2008 133 F cathleencurrie@cwidaho.cc
CURRIE, Dave 978-468-7111 219 B dcurrie@gcts.edu
CURRIE, Eunice, M 817-272-5554 476 A currie@uta.edu
CURRIE, Jacqueline 205-366-8894 7 E jcurrie@stillman.edu
CURRIE, John 785-532-6912 182 D ksuad@ksu.edu
CURRIE, Lauren 518-562-4122 310 C lauren.currie@clinton.edu
CURRIE, Walter James 691-320-2480 529 F jimc@comfsm.fm
CURRIER, Camile 318-342-5215 201 E currier@ulm.edu
CURRIER, Chuck 630-942-2790 138 B currier@cod.edu
CURRIER, Michelle, L 315-386-7228 335 B curriermm@canton.edu
CURRIER, Nicole 301-891-4146 213 D ncurrier@wau.edu
CURRIER, Roxann 505-922-2886 299 K roxann.currier@eccu.edu
CURRIN, Alicia 903-886-5034 468 D alicia.currin@tamuc.edu
CURRIN, Bruce, A 402-472-3105 282 M bcurrin1@unl.edu
CURRIN, Thomas 678-915-7482 123 J tcurrin@kennesaw.edu
CURRISTINE, Eileen 609-343-6810 288 H ecurrist@atlantic.edu
CURRY, Amanda 302-622-8000 90 E acurry@dcad.edu
CURRY, Anne 205-226-4904 2 C acurry@bsc.edu
CURRY, Bonita, P 517-353-3243 237 I curryb@msu.edu
CURRY, Carolyn, S 240-895-4282 210 E cscurry@smcm.edu
CURRY, Chris 731-989-6349 440 D ccurry@fhu.edu
CURRY, JR., Chuck 336-316-2104 344 H curryrc@guilford.edu
CURRY, Cynthia 305-626-3619 101 A cynthia.curry@fmuniv.edu
CURRY, Cynthia, S 304-367-4386 513 B cindy.curry@fairmontstate.edu
CURRY, David, L 813-988-5131 100 F development@floridacollege.edu
CURRY, Dean, C 717-766-2511 410 J dcurry@messiah.edu
CURRY, Deborah 256-549-8321 3 M dcurry@gadsdenstate.edu
CURRY, Elizabeth, A 904-620-2615 112 B e.curry@unf.edu
CURRY, Evan 215-702-4863 399 E ecurry@cairn.edu
CURRY, Gina 916-278-5992 34 B curryg@skymail.csus.edu
CURRY, JR., H. Pete 717-337-6311 404 C pcurry@gettysburg.edu

CURRY, James .... 402-844-7063.. 282 B
jamesc@northeast.edu
CURRY, Janel .... 978-867-4063.. 219 A
janel.curry@gordon.edu
CURRY, Jason .... 615-329-8582.. 439 L
jcurry@fisk.edu
CURRY, Jason, R .... 615-329-8697.. 439 L
jcurry@fisk.edu
CURRY, Melissa .... 937-294-6155.. 364 H
CURRY, Molly .... 919-747-0007.. 353 I
mpcurry@waketech.edu
CURRY, Ralph .... 906-786-5802.. 231 O
curryr@baycollege.edu
CURRY, Reva .... 989-686-9298.. 233 I
revacurry@delta.edu
CURRY, Robert .... 607-587-3621.. 334 G
curryrl@alfredstate.edu
CURRY, Robert .... 662-252-8000.. 260 F
rcurry@rustcollege.edu
CURRY, Susan .... 601-318-6773.. 261 I
scurry@wmcarey.edu
CURRY, Susan .... 319-384-5452.. 169 H
sue-curry@uiowa.edu
CURRY, Susan .... 618-514-3110.. 151 E
susan.curry@principia.edu
CURRY, Terri, A .... 712-274-5257.. 175 C
curryte@morningside.edu
CURRY, II, Theodore, H .. 517-353-5300.. 237 I
thcurry@msu.edu
CURRY, Tim .... 606-546-1682.. 193 E
tcurry@unionky.edu
CURRY, William, N .... 601-318-6103.. 261 I
bill.curry@wmcarey.edu
CURTIN, Maria .... 508-565-1311.. 228 F
mcurtin@stonehill.edu
CURTIN, Shawn, P .... 717-867-6207.. 408 F
curtin@lvc.edu
CURTIN, Valerie .... 406-447-6913.. 277 B
valerie.curtin@umhelena.edu
CURTIN, William .... 773-508-8851.. 146 G
wcurtin@luc.edu
CURTIS, Amy .... 207-879-8757.. 203 A
acurtis@idsva.org
CURTIS, Carolyn, G .... 518-629-7204.. 316 G
c.curtis@hvcc.edu
CURTIS, Charles .... 903-813-2088.. 451 M
ccurtis@austincollege.edu
CURTIS, Chris .... 912-344-2919.. 116 E
chris.curtis@armstrong.edu
CURTIS, Christine .... 256-824-6335...... 8 F
provost@uah.edu
CURTIS, Danielle .... 203-432-4771.... 90 D
CURTIS, Danielle .... 828-898-3478.. 345 G
curtisd@lmc.edu
CURTIS, Deborah, J .... 660-543-4116.. 273 C
curtis@ucmo.edu
CURTIS, Elaine .... 931-540-2534.. 446 A
bcurtis@columbiastate.edu
CURTIS, III, Guy, E .... 540-868-4079.. 497 E
gcurtis@lfcc.edu
CURTIS, Jason .... 805-546-3125.... 41 L
jason_curtis@cuesta.edu
CURTIS, Jeanne, F .... 215-898-6300.. 421 E
curtis@isc.upenn.edu
CURTIS, Jennifer .... 760-384-6212.... 47 K
jennifer.curtis@cerrocoso.edu
CURTIS, Jerri .... 301-295-3638.. 528 G
jerri.curtis@usuhs.edu
CURTIS, K. Tyler .... 620-341-5440.. 180 G
kcurtis2@emporia.edu
CURTIS, Kelly .... 310-377-5501.... 51 G
kcurtis@marymountcalifornia.edu
CURTIS, Kelly, T .... 864-488-4601.. 430 H
kcurtis@limestone.edu
CURTIS, Linda, H .... 919-516-4297.. 355 D
lrhubbard@st-aug.edu
CURTIS, Mark .... 775-753-2265.. 284 I
mark.curtis@gbcnv.edu
CURTIS, Marvin .... 574-520-4170.. 163 E
mcurtis@iusb.edu
CURTIS, Matt .... 914-831-0313.. 311 C
mcurtis@cw.edu
CURTIS, Meg, K .... 719-884-5000.... 81 N
mkcurtis@nbc.edu
CURTIS, Michael .... 978-927-2300.. 219 A
michael.curtis@gordon.edu
CURTIS, Michelle .... 608-363-2663.. 515 G
CURTIS, Regina .... 413-775-1426.. 223 D
curtis@gcc.mass.edu
CURTIS, Rick .... 406-243-2122.. 276 K
richard.curtis@umontana.edu
CURTIS, Roxie .... 816-802-3437.. 266 D
rcurtis@kcai.edu
CURTIS, Tashana, M .... 315-684-6000.. 336 B
CURTIS, Timothy .... 928-428-8220.... 13 B
tim.curtis@eac.edu
CURTIS, Tommy .... 706-233-7358.. 127 A
tcurtis@shorter.edu
CURTIS, Trina .... 828-726-2303.. 347 I
tcurtis@cccti.edu
CURTIS, Yvonne .... 215-248-6393.. 409 D
hr@ltsp.edu
CURTIS POWELL
Melissa .... 614-235-4136.. 378 C
mcpowell@tlsohio.edu
CURTISS, Kathy .... 631-656-3121.. 314 F
kathy.curtiss@ftc.edu
CURTO, Stephen, A .... 732-224-2593.. 289 I
scurto@brookdalecc.edu
CUSACK, Emma .... 949-794-9090.... 66 H
ecusack@stanbridge.edu
CUSACK, Jacqueline, L ...... 973-596-6445.. 293 D
jacqueline.l.cusack@njit.edu
CUSACK, Kristen .... 303-360-4701.... 79 E
kristen.cusack@ccaurora.edu
CUSACK, Mary .... 810-762-0474.. 238 F
CUSATO, Brian .... 859-238-5205.. 187 H
b.cusato@centre.edu
CUSEO, Vincent .... 323-259-2700.... 55 A
vcuseo@oxy.edu
CUSHING, Katie .... 508-213-2111.. 227 A
katie.cushing@nichols.edu
CUSHING, Mark .... 865-545-5330.. 441 E
mark.cushing@lmunet.edu
CUSHING, Ryan .... 815-394-5047.. 152 G
rcushing@rockford.edu
CUSHMAN, Bob .... 509-527-2431.. 508 G
bob.cushman@wallawalla.edu
CUSHMAN, Jenifer .... 740-588-1435.. 375 H
cushmanj@ohio.edu
CUSHMAN, Ron .... 417-873-7323.. 264 H
rcushman@drury.edu
CUSICK, Dianna .... 612-659-6319.. 250 B
dianna.cusick@minneapolis.edu
CUSICK, Sherry .... 563-589-3721.. 177 C
scusick@dbq.edu
CUSICK, Susan .... 773-896-2400.. 137 A
scusick@ctschicago.edu
CUSSEN, Susan .... 845-451-1471.. 312 C
s_cussen@culinary.edu
CUSSON, Regina .... 860-486-5126.... 89 D
regina.cusson@uconn.edu
CUSTER, Carole, A .... 515-294-9624.. 169 G
cacuste@iastate.edu
CUSTER, Laura .... 859-344-3314.. 193 C
custerl@thomasmore.edu
CUSTODIA-LORA, Noemi .. 978-738-7401.. 224 D
ncustodialora@necc.mass.edu
CUTCHENS, Melinda .... 229-333-5952.. 129 G
cutchens@valdosta.edu
CUTCHIN, Claudine .... 812-749-1443.. 166 B
ccutchin@oak.edu
CUTCHIN, Jeff .... 618-395-7777.. 142 E
cutchinj@iecc.edu
CUTCHINS, Cathy .... 757-569-6712.. 498 B
ccutchins@pdc.edu
CUTHBERTSON, Mayhew .. 937-708-5496.. 381 B
mcuthbertson@wilberforce.edu
CUTHRELL, Patrick .... 252-335-0821.. 349 A
patrick_cuthrell@albemarle.edu
CUTIETTA, Robert, A .... 213-740-5389.... 72 D
musicdean@thornton.usc.edu
CUTLER, Brooke .... 310-506-4246.... 56 J
brooke.cutler@pepperdine.edu
CUTLER, Chris .... 315-268-6745.. 310 B
ccutler@clarkson.edu
CUTLER, Jerry, M .... 973-655-4227.. 293 A
cutlerje@mail.montclair.edu
CUTLER, Nancy .... 408-554-4915.... 63 E
ncutler@scu.edu
CUTLER, Stephen, J .... 803-777-8310.. 433 F
ashley@sccp.sc.edu
CUTONE, Joan .... 412-536-1079.. 406 K
joan.cutone@laroche.edu
CUTRELL, Kathy .... 336-821-2470.. 345 C
kcutrell@johnwesley.edu
CUTRELL, Lori .... 615-230-4834.. 447 C
lori.cutrell@volstate.edu
CUTRI, David .... 419-530-6294.. 380 D
david.cutri@utoledo.edu
CUTRIGHT, Patricia .... 509-963-1902.. 501 K
cutright@cwu.edu
CUTSHALL, Heather .... 620-223-2700.. 181 A
heatherc@fortscott.edu
CUTSHAW, Christy .... 620-365-5116.. 178 A
cutshaw@allencc.edu
CUTSHAW, Kathleen, D ...... 808-956-9190.. 131 F
cutshaw@hawaii.edu
CUTSHAW, Kyle .... 276-944-6529.. 489 I
kcutshaw@ehc.edu
CUTSHAW, Oliver .... 213-615-7211.... 37 I
ocutshaw@thechicagoschool.edu
CUTSPEC, John .... 828-251-6868.. 357 C
jcutspec@unca.edu
CUTTING, Jeff .... 617-928-4573.. 226 B
jcutting@mountida.edu
CUTTING, Judy .... 903-875-7573.. 462 J
judy.cutting@navarrocollege.edu
CUTTINO, Robert, E .... 770-538-4749.. 118 A
rcuttino@brenau.edu
CUTTONE, Carl .... 219-473-4295.. 159 L
ccuttone@ccsj.edu
CUZYDLO, Karen .... 517-787-0800.. 235 G
cuzydlokareni@jccmi.edu
CUZZOLINO, Robert, G ...... 215-871-6770.. 416 F
bob@pcom.edu
CVETIC, Mike .... 412-237-4146.. 401 B
mcvetic@ccac.edu
CVITKOVIC, Vicky .... 847-543-6504.. 138 C
vcvitkovic@clcillinois.edu
CYGAN, Brian, L .... 570-326-3761.. 413 D
brian.cygan@pct.edu
CYNAR, Deana .... 908-852-1400.. 290 D
cynard@centenarycollege.edu
CYPHERS, Christopher, J .. 212-752-1530.. 318 F
christopher.cyphers@limcollege.edu
CYPHERS, Russell .... 276-523-7473.. 497 F
rcyphers@mecc.edu
CYPHERS BENSON,
Laura .... 530-242-7649.... 64 D
lbenson@shastacollege.edu
CYPRESS, Sharen .... 731-989-6986.. 440 D
scypress@fhu.edu
CYR, Cheryl, A .... 860-253-3050.... 86 A
ccyr@asnuntuck.edu
CYREE, Kendall, B .... 662-915-1103.. 261 B
kbcyree@olemiss.edu
CYRUS, Cynthia, J .... 615-322-4474.. 449 A
cynthia.j.cyrus@vanderbilt.edu
CYRUS, Kasundra .... 225-771-4660.. 199 H
kasundra_cyrus@subr.edu
CZAJKIEWICZ, Zbigniew .. 281-283-3703.. 474 A
czajkiewicz@uhcl.edu
CZAPAR, George .... 217-333-5900.. 157 A
gfc@illinois.edu
CZARAPATA, Paul .... 859-256-3100.. 188 M
paul.czarapata@kctcs.edu
CZARDA, Lawrence, D .... 336-217-7221.. 344 G
lczarda@greensboro.edu
CZARNECKI, John .... 716-926-8800.. 316 B
jczarneck@hilbert.edu
CZEKANSKI, Kathleen .... 215-951-1432.. 407 A
czekanski@lasalle.edu
CZERWINSKI, Rick .... 540-887-7336.. 491 G
rczerwin@mbc.edu
CZUCHRY, Michael .... 830-372-6047.. 470 C
mczuchry@tlu.edu
CZULEGER, Cathy .... 805-893-3606.... 70 E
cz@essr.ucsb.edu

D

DA GRACA, John .... 956-968-2132.. 469 A
j-dagraca@tamuk.edu
DA SILVA, Jose .... 509-527-4300.. 508 F
jose.dasilva@wwcc.edu
DAAR, Judith .... 714-444-4141.... 75 B
jdaar@law.whittier.edu
DAAR, Karen .... 818-947-2378.... 50 D
daarkl@lavc.edu
DAAS, Mahesh .... 785-864-3114.. 185 D
mahesh@ku.edu
DABIRIAN, Amir .... 657-278-5000.... 33 A
adabirian@fullerton.edu
DABNEY, Emily, C .... 662-846-4052.. 257 E
edabney@deltastate.edu
DABNEY, Jerome .... 773-602-5252.. 137 F
jdabney@ccc.edu
DABOIN, Julie .... 718-261-5800.. 305 J
jdaboin@bramsonort.edu
DABOLL-LAVOIE,
Kathleen .... 585-389-2591.. 322 D
kdaboll9@naz.edu
DABOVAL, Jeanne, M .... 337-475-5508.. 200 H
jdaboval@mcneese.edu
DABROWSKI, Jan .... 503-699-6275.. 392 D
jdabrowski@marylhurst.edu
DACAL, Anita, S .... 412-578-6343.. 400 C
dacalas@carlow.edu
DACE, Karen, L .... 317-278-3820.. 163 D
kdace@iupui.edu
DACEY, Joe .... 508-565-1804.. 228 F
jdacey@stonehill.edu
DACEY, Susan .... 973-748-9000.. 289 H
susan_dacey@bloomfield.edu
DACHELET, Derek .... 608-822-2417.. 524 F
ddachelet@swtc.edu
DACHILLE, Nancy .... 215-248-7048.. 400 H
ndachill@chc.edu
DACOSTA, Herbert .... 309-694-5754.. 141 F
herbert.dacosta@icc.edu
DACOSTA, Tracy, M .... 401-254-3541.. 426 B
tdacosta@rwu.edu
DACUS, Kent .... 951-343-4687.... 29 H
kdacus@calbaptist.edu
DADABHOY,
Khushnur, Z .... 760-252-2411.... 28 B
kdadabhoy@barstow.edu
DADABHOY, Zavareh .... 661-395-4204.... 47 J
zav.dadabhoy@bakersfieldcollege.edu
DADARRIA, Nikki .... 908-835-9222.. 298 E
ndadarria@warren.edu
DADDONA, Sharon, N .... 860-727-6903.... 87 H
sdaddona@goodwin.edu
DADEY, Cheryl .... 702-254-7577.. 285 C
cheryl.dadey@northwestcareercollege.edu
DADEZ, Edward .... 352-588-8206.. 108 C
ed.dadez@saintleo.edu
DADEZ, Teresa .... 352-588-8347.. 108 C
teresa.dadez@saintleo.edu
DADIAN PEREZ, Sara .... 603-623-0313.. 287 D
saradadian@nhia.edu
DADY, Erin .... 612-624-9022.. 255 H
dady@umn.edu
DAFFER, Steve .... 405-733-7424.. 387 I
sdaffer@rose.edu
DAFFRON, Eric .... 201-684-7532.. 294 G
edaffron@ramapo.edu
DAFFRON, Jeanne .... 816-271-4234.. 269 C
daffron@missouriwestern.edu
DAFLER, James, E .... 724-946-7313.. 423 B
daflerje@westminster.edu
DAGANAAR, Mark .... 913-469-8500.. 182 A
mdaganaar@jccc.edu
DAGG, Joey .... 304-876-5395.. 513 E
jdagg@shepherd.edu
DAGGETT, Michael .... 518-243-4473.. 305 A
daggettm@ellismedicine.org
DAGGETT, Natalie .... 575-769-4956.. 299 G
natalie.daggett@clovis.edu
DAGGETT, Paula .... 210-486-0224.. 450 F
pdaggett@alamo.edu
DAGHER, Lisa, M .... 773-947-6320.. 147 D
ldagher@mccormick.edu
DAGLEY, Stephen .... 978-927-2300.. 219 A
stephen.dagley@gordon.edu
DAGUE, Saralyn .... 304-829-7835.. 510 G
sdague@bethanywv.edu
DAHER, Michael .... 313-845-6460.. 235 D
mdaher@hfcc.edu
DAHILL, Patricia .... 617-587-5632.. 226 E
dahillp@neco.edu
DAHILL, Rosemary .... 914-395-2202.. 329 K
rdahill@sarahlawrence.edu
DAHL, Barbara, A .... 219-981-4235.. 163 B
badahl@iun.edu
DAHL, Bonnie, L .... 701-355-8245.. 362 G
bldahl@umary.edu
DAHL, Katie .... 303-369-5151.... 82 F
katie.dahl@plattcolorado.edu
DAHL, Mark .... 503-768-7339.. 392 A
dahl@lclark.edu
DAHL, Nelson, D .... 715-422-5327.. 523 G
nelson.dahl@mstc.edu
DAHL, Noel .... 415-703-9537.... 29 K
ndahl@cca.edu
DAHL, Tracy .... 360-736-9391.. 502 A
tdahl@centralia.edu
DAHLBERG, Albert, A .... 401-863-1885.. 424 J
albert_a_dahlberg@brown.edu
DAHLBERG, James .... 715-468-2815.. 525 A
jim.dahlberg@witc.edu
DAHLBERG, Margaret .... 701-845-7200.. 361 B
margaret.dahlberg@vcsu.edu
DAHLBERG, Steve .... 218-935-0417.. 256 E
sdahlberg@wetcc.edu
DAHLBERG, Teresa .... 315-443-4341.. 337 A
dahlberg@syr.edu
DAHLE, Tammi .... 205-665-6262...... 9 B
dahlet@montevallo.edu
DAHLEN, David, L .... 507-284-2749.. 245 E
dahlen.david@mayo.edu
DAHLEN, David, L .... 507-284-4839.. 245 F
dahlen.david@mayo.edu
DAHLER, Nathan .... 513-721-7944.. 369 D
ndahler@gbs.edu
DAHLGREN, Jean .... 518-292-1704.. 327 H
scadean@sage.edu
DAHLGREN, Jerod, T .... 716-878-5569.. 332 F
dahlgrjt@buffalostate.edu
DAHLINGER MEANS,
Gretchen .... 213-740-5086.... 72 D
dahlinge@usc.edu
DAHLOR, Cara .... 816-415-5223.. 275 F
dahlorc@william.jewell.edu
DAHLQUIST, Kent, R .... 610-683-4027.. 415 C
dahlquis@kutztown.edu
DAHLQUIST, Sally .... 651-450-3567.. 249 F
sdahlqu@inverhills.edu
DAHLSTROM, Duane .... 320-308-5572.. 252 B
ddahlstrom@sctcc.edu
DAHLSTROM, Joe, F .... 361-570-4150.. 474 C
dahlstromj@uhv.edu
DAHLSTROM, Joe, F .... 361-570-4150.. 478 F
joe.dahlstrom@victoriacollege.edu
DAHLSTROM, Thomas .... 610-341-5898.. 412 C
tdahlstro@eastern.edu
DAHLSTROM, Thomas, A .... 610-341-5898.. 403 B
tdahlstr@eastern.edu
DAHLVANG, Donna, R .... 715-394-8393.. 521 E
ddahlva1@uwsuper.edu

DAHMES, Victoria 504-398-2237 200 D vdahmes@olhcc.edu
DAHMS, David, W 563-562-3263 175 F dahmsd@nicc.edu
DAHNERT, Stephen 845-437-5500 339 C stdahnert@vassar.edu
DAHULICH, Michael 570-561-1818 418 H bishop.michael@stots.edu
DAICHENDT, Jim 619-849-2412 57 M jimdaichendt@pointloma.edu
DAIEK, Deborah 734-462-4400 240 H ddaiek@schoolcraft.edu
DAIG, Bart 810-766-4280 231 C bart.daig@baker.edu
DAIGLE, Anna 337-421-6954 197 B anna.daigle@sowela.edu
DAIGLE, Claire 415-351-3573 61 B cdaigle@sfai.edu
DAIGLE, Darren 251-344-1203 3 J
DAIGLE, David 207-216-4410 204 B ddaigle@yccc.edu
DAIGLE, Dick 757-490-1241 486 E ddaigle@auto.edu
DAIGLER, David 207-629-4000 203 H ddaigler@mccs.me.edu
DAILEY, Bracken, J 951-827-3427 70 B bracken.dailey@ucr.edu
DAILEY, Brian 917-493-4469 319 M bdailey@msmnyc.edu
DAILEY, Brian 910-962-3711 358 D daileyb@uncw.edu
DAILEY, David 218-749-7772 249 I d.dailey@mesabirange.edu
DAILEY, Deborah 215-489-2915 402 A deborah.dailey@delval.edu
DAILEY, Janine 617-868-3450 218 E
DAILEY, Kathlyn, C 512-245-2208 471 F kd01@txstate.edu
DAILEY, Ronald 909-558-4683 49 C rdailey@llu.edu
DAILEY, Tim 541-888-7439 395 B tdailey@socc.edu
DAILY, Daniel, R 605-677-5371 437 A daniel.daily@usd.edu
DAILY, Hall, P 626-395-6256 30 H hdaily@caltech.edu
DAIN, Benny 580-349-1560 385 F bdain@opsu.edu
DAIN, Claudette, E 626-914-8886 38 D cdain@citruscollege.edu
DAINES, Cameron 928-724-6698 12 T ckdaines@dinecollege.edu
DAIRE, Andrew, P 804-827-2670 496 D apdaire@vcu.edu
DAIS, Olga 646-312-3320 307 A olga.dais@baruch.cuny.edu
DAISE, Abigail 215-887-5511 423 C adaise@wts.edu
DAISEY, Mary Beth, B 856-225-2825 296 A daisey@camden.rutgers.edu
DAISY, Jennifer 620-431-2820 183 H jdaisy@neosho.edu
DAISY, Joseph, M 691-320-2480 529 F jdaisy@comfsm.fm
DAITCH, Jonathan 562-977-6013 44 D jonathan.daitch@fremont.edu
DAKSHINAMURTHY, Raja 931-221-7414 444 E dakshinamurthyr@apsu.edu
DAKWAR, Mohammad 414-297-8087 524 A dakwarmm@matc.edu
DALAT-WARD, Yaprak 785-628-4756 180 I y_dalatward@fhsu.edu
DALBEY, Mark 314-434-4044 264 C presidentsoffice@covenantseminary.edu
DALBOW, Dawn, S 540-828-5310 487 H ddalbow@bridgewater.edu
DALE, Amie, G 757-594-7672 488 E amie.dale@cnu.edu
DALE, Cheryl 601-318-6199 261 I cheryl.dale@wmcarey.edu
DALE, Dianna, C 610-361-2448 411 E daled@neumann.edu
DALE, Elizabeth 215-503-5138 420 E elizabeth.dale@jefferson.edu
DALE, Karen 520-452-2621 12 L dalek@cochise.edu
DALE, Kimberly 954-776-4476 103 J kdale@keiseruniversity.edu
DALE, Kory, J 479-524-7116 20 H kdale@jbu.edu
DALE, Lynn, F 864-592-4833 432 H dalel@sccsc.edu
DALE, Marc 630-466-7900 157 K mdale@waubonsee.edu
DALE, Paul 602-787-6610 14 E paul.dale@paradisevalley.edu
DALE, Paul 480-731-8101 13 N
DALE-CARTER, April 909-384-8922 60 C acarter@sbccd.cc.ca.us
DALEKE, David 812-855-6902 162 F daleked@indiana.edu
DALENE, Jack 435-283-7130 482 E jack.dalene@snow.edu
DALES, Sandra 910-695-3789 353 A daless@sandhills.edu
DALEY, Ben 619-398-4902 46 D bdaley@hightechhigh.org
DALEY, Carol 540-338-2700 510 H cdaley@cdu.edu
DALEY, David 530-898-5844 32 C ddaley@csuchico.edu
DALEY, Elizabeth, M 213-740-2804 72 D edaley@cinema.usc.edu
DALEY, Karen 616-698-7111 233 C kdaley@davenport.edu
DALEY, Ken 641-472-1163 175 A kdaley@mum.edu
DALEY, Michael 802-387-6753 484 B michaeldaley@landmark.edu
DALEY, Michael, D 716-673-3434 331 D michael.daley@fredonia.edu
DALEY, Suzanne, L 518-564-2080 334 A daleysl@plattsburgh.edu
DALEY-WESTON, Marilyn 212-650-3995 308 D marilyn.daley-weston@hunter.cuny.edu
DALGARNO, Janice 307-268-2547 526 D dalgarno@caspercollege.edu
DALGLISH, Lucy, A 301-405-2383 211 E dalglish@umd.edu
DALLAM, Colleen, C 410-334-2864 213 G cdallam@worwic.edu
DALLAVALLE, Nancy 203-254-4000 87 G ndallavalle@fairfield.edu
DALLAVALLE, Til 732-906-2602 292 E tdallavalle@middlesexcc.edu
DALLMANN, Denise 503-552-1690 392 H ddallmann@nunm.edu
DALLY, Tammy 619-201-8670 60 D tammy.dally@sdcc.edu
DALONZO, Beth, A 740-826-8041 373 E bdalonzo@muskingum.edu
DALPE, Kyle 775-673-7812 284 K kdalpe@tmcc.edu
DALPE, Kyle, C 775-673-7025 284 K kdalpe@tmcc.edu
DALRYMPLE, Jim 417-626-1234 269 K dalrymple.jim@occ.edu
DALRYMPLE, Scott 573-875-8700 263 F sdalrymple@ccis.edu
DALSING, Deirdre, L 608-342-1865 521 A dalsingd@uwplatt.edu
DALSKE, James 707-654-1070 33 D jdalske@csum.edu
DALTO, Joseph 251-344-1203 3 J jdalto@fortiscollege.edu
DALTON, Amy 937-327-7457 381 F daltona@wittenberg.edu
DALTON, Ben 740-753-6516 369 K daltonb@hocking.edu
DALTON, Brenda 404-270-5245 128 A bdalton@spelman.edu
DALTON, Brenda 972-860-4677 456 B bdalton@dcccd.edu
DALTON, Brett, A 864-656-2444 428 C dbrett@clemson.edu
DALTON, Dana, L 336-734-7369 349 G ddalton@forsythtech.edu
DALTON, Dixie 434-736-2085 498 E dixie.dalton@southside.edu
DALTON, Dori 419-559-2342 377 M ddalton@terra.edu
DALTON, James 845-938-2050 529 C 8ord@usma.edu
DALTON, James, T 734-764-7312 241 J daltonjt@umich.edu
DALTON, Jill 207-699-5018 203 F jdalton@meca.edu
DALTON, John 765-973-8450 162 G jodalton@iue.edu
DALTON, Judith 215-572-4088 397 G daltonj@arcadia.edu
DALTON, Karen 909-447-2534 39 A kdalton@cst.edu
DALTON, Thomas 518-464-8632 314 A tdalton@excelsior.edu
DALTON, Valerie 404-215-2666 124 I valerie.dalton@morehouse.edu
DALTON, Walter, H 828-395-1300 350 E wdalton@isothermal.edu
DALTON-RUSSELL, Belinda 270-534-3081 190 H belinda.dalton-russell@kctcs.edu
DALY, Adrian 213-621-2200 39 I
DALY, Brian 619-239-0391 36 A bdaly@cwsl.edu
DALY, Cory 307-855-2186 526 E cdaly@cwc.edu
DALY, Erin 952-358-8834 251 A erin.daly@normandale.edu
DALY, Jillian 209-575-6149 76 A dalyj@mjc.edu
DALY, Jon 860-628-4751 88 C jdaly@lincolncollegene.edu
DALY, Jonathan, P 805-525-4417 67 J jdaly@thomasaquinas.edu
DALY, Kathleen 850-644-4453 111 C kdaly@fsu.edu
DALY, Kathleen, M 850-644-4453 111 C kdaly@fsu.edu
DALY, Lois, K 518-783-2306 330 E daly@siena.edu
DALY, Melissa 856-227-7200 290 B mdaly@camdencc.edu
DALY, Michael 718-429-6600 339 D michael.daly@vaughn.edu
DALY, Patrick 972-721-5145 473 D mpdaly@udallas.edu
DALY, Rebecca 906-487-7253 234 A rebecca.daly@finlandia.edu
DALY, Ross 914-251-6550 334 C ross.daly@purchase.edu
DALY EIMER, Anne, M 856-691-8600 290 I adaly@cccnj.edu
DALZELL, Douglas 410-951-3826 212 E ddalzell@coppin.edu
DALZIEL, Murray 410-837-4955 213 C mdalziel@ubalt.edu
DAMARI, David 231-591-3703 233 L daviddamari@ferris.edu
DAMAS, Tammi, L 202-806-4859 93 A tammi.damas@howard.edu
DAMAZO, Dennis, E 724-847-5678 404 B dedamazo@geneva.edu
DAMES, Christopher 314-516-6473 274 A cdames@umsl.edu
DAMES, Jeanine 203-432-0800 90 D jeanine.dames@yale.edu
DAMEWOOD, Tony, M 402-552-6109 279 D damewood@clarksoncollege.edu
DAMHOFF, Russ, K 815-835-6234 153 K russ.k.damhoff@svcc.edu
DAMIAN, Karen 802-387-6711 484 B registrar@landmark.edu
DAMIANI, Glenn 505-224-3223 299 F gdamiani@cnm.edu
DAMIANI, Joel, J 716-851-1405 313 H damiani@ecc.edu
DAMIANI, Susan, M 718-990-7562 328 F damianis@stjohns.edu
DAMIANO, Ann, E 717-867-6077 408 F damiano@lvc.edu
DAMIANO, Fred 315-781-3955 316 C damiano@hws.edu
DAMICI, Lindsay 802-654-2000 484 I
DAMICO, Debra, L 718-862-7213 319 L debra.damico@manhattan.edu
DAMICO, Paul 252-638-0156 349 B damicop@cravencc.edu
DAMINSKI, Sara, M 314-286-3658 270 G smdaninski@ranken.edu
DAMM, Richard, T 920-748-8322 519 E dammr@ripon.edu
DAMMER, Bob 310-434-4397 63 F dammer_bob@smc.edu
DAMMON, Robert 412-268-3696 400 D rd19@andrew.cmu.edu
DAMON, Brad 858-642-8318 54 A bdamon@nu.edu
DAMON, Jud 904-819-6252 99 M jdamon@flagler.edu
DAMONE, Bob 562-947-8755 66 A bobdamone@scuhs.edu
DAMORE, Gary 602-386-4188 11 D gary.damore@arizonachristian.edu
DAMPHOUSSE, Kelly, R 405-325-2077 389 B kdamp@ou.edu
DAMPIER, Paula 770-297-5896 118 A pland@brenau.edu
DAMRAUER, Robert 303-315-2131 84 A robert.damrauer@ucdenver.edu
DAMRON, Heather 318-342-1982 201 E ulm@campuscornerinc.com
DAMRON, Karla 214-860-2473 456 E kdamron@dcccd.edu
DAMRON, Nancy 913-971-3533 183 D nldamron@mnu.edu
DAMRON, Ronald 606-218-5276 194 C ronalddamron@upike.edu
DAMRON, Steve 254-968-9227 467 F sdamron@tarleton.edu
DAMRON, Toni 325-649-8097 459 E tdamron@hputx.edu
DAMROSE-MAHLMANN, Christine 757-822-1298 498 H cmahlmann@tcc.edu
DAMROW, Bobbi 715-675-3331 524 D damrow@ntc.edu
DAMS, Scott 610-861-1601 411 B damss@moravian.edu
DAMSCHRODER, Matthew 814-641-3151 406 F damschm@juniata.edu
DAN, Chong 704-216-6035 346 A cdan@livingstone.edu
DAN, Dale 214-329-4447 452 B dale.dan@bgu.edu
DANA, Robert, Q 207-581-1405 204 H rdana@maine.edu
DANAHAR, David 337-482-1000 201 D
DANAJOVITS, Joseph 860-738-6368 87 A jdanajovits@nwcc.edu
DANCE, Andrea 252-335-0821 349 A andrea_dance@albemarle.edu
DANCER, Erin 770-426-2974 124 B erin.dancer@life.edu
DANCKAERT, Seraphim 570-561-1818 418 H seraphim.danckaert@stots.edu
DANCY, Gerlinde 963-638-2941 115 D dancygl@webber.edu
DANCY, Regina, M 704-636-6454 345 B rdancy@hoodseminary.edu
DANDAPANI, Ramaswami 719-255-3551 83 L rdan@eas.uccs.edu
DANDELAKE, George 904-470-8150 98 N g.dandelake@ewc.edu
DANDO, Mary 303-492-2975 83 K mary.dando@colorado.edu
DANDORPH, Michael 312-942-5756 153 B michael_dandorph@rush.edu
DANDRIDGE, Horace 313-927-1555 237 E hdandridge@marygrove.edu
DANE, Francis, C 540-224-4515 491 A fcdane@jchs.edu
DANE, Jane, H 757-683-6702 492 G jhdane@odu.edu
DANEAU, Nancy, S 212-998-2121 324 C nancy.daneau@nyu.edu
DANEIL, Chris 813-974-2628 112 C cldaniel@usf.edu
DANEN, Todd 920-403-3943 519 G todd.danen@snc.edu
DANFORD, Richard, K 740-376-4736 372 A richard.danford@marietta.edu
DANFORD, Tom 615-366-4451 444 D tom.danford@tbr.edu
DANFORTH, Dave 218-281-8490 255 E danfo002@umn.edu
DANFORTH, Meridith 972-860-4823 456 B mdanforth@dcccd.edu
DANG, Kim 562-988-2278 26 N kdang@auhs.edu
DANG-WILLIAMS, Thao 314-246-8757 275 B thaodangwilliams@webster.edu
DANGERFIELD, Deneen 410-462-8311 206 D dedangerfield@bccc.edu
DANGLER, Steven 607-753-2111 333 A steven.dangler@cortland.edu
DANGOND, Edgardo 727-873-4040 112 D dangond@usfsp.edu
DANHAUSER, Susan 770-537-5353 129 M susan.danhauser@westgatech.edu
DANHEISER, Priscilla, R 478-301-2089 124 D danheiser_p@mercer.edu
DANICA, Kathleen 518-244-4552 327 H bouchk2@sage.edu
DANICKI, John, T 740-446-4367 369 C director@gallipoliscareercollege.edu
DANIEL, Andrea, D 706-369-5763 116 H adaniel@athenstech.edu
DANIEL, Brett 903-675-6393 473 B bdaniel@tvcc.edu
DANIEL, Chris 606-886-3863 189 A chris.daniel@kctcs.edu
DANIEL, David, E 512-499-4201 475 K ddaniel@utsystem.edu
DANIEL, Dean 940-855-4322 479 D danield@wbu.edu
DANIEL, Kathleen 305-809-3248 100 N kathleen.daniel@fkcc.edu
DANIEL, Kevin, S 719-587-7741 76 G ksdaniel@adams.edu
DANIEL, Larry 843-953-5097 428 A ldaniel@citadel.edu
DANIEL, Malinda 704-290-5261 353 B mdaniel@spcc.edu
DANIEL, Margaret 615-297-7545 438 F daniel@aquinascollege.edu
DANIEL, Meredith 864-941-8442 432 A meredith.d@ptc.edu
DANIEL, Nancy 828-448-3160 354 B ndaniel@wpcc.edu
DANIEL, Nancy, C 617-449-7068 229 B nancy.daniel@urbancollege.edu
DANIEL, Richard 915-747-8600 476 D rjdaniel@utep.edu
DANIEL, Robin, L 336-272-7102 344 G rdaniel@greensboro.edu
DANIEL, Sharlene 423-775-6596 443 H sdaniel@ogs.edu

DANIEL, Sherman .... 680-488-2471.. 530 E
shermand1961@yahoo.com
DANIEL, Steve, G .... 678-664-0530.. 129 M
steve.daniel@westgatech.edu
DANIEL, Tim .... 701-483-2100.. 360 D
tim.daniel@dickinsonstate.edu
DANIEL, W. John .... 205-934-3474...... 8 E
wdaniel@uab.edu
DANIEL-ROBINSON, Kim 973-720-3678.. 298 G
danielrobinsonk@wpunj.edu
DANIELL, Steven .... 817-531-4405.. 472 F
sdaniell@txwes.edu
DANIELS, Andrea .... 910-410-1724.. 352 C
asdaniels@richmondcc.edu
DANIELS, C. Wess .... 336-316-2445.. 344 H
danielscw@guilford.edu
DANIELS, Calvin .... 913-234-0710.. 179 M
calvin.daniels@cleveland.edu
DANIELS, Christy .... 252-328-6212.. 356 C
danielsc@ecu.edu
DANIELS, Clayton .... 912-279-5775.. 119 C
cdaniels@ccga.edu
DANIELS, Debra .... 661-763-7710.... 67 F
ddaniels@taftcollege.edu
DANIELS, Dennis, E .... 936-261-3085.. 467 E
dedaniels@pvamu.edu
DANIELS, Donna .... 617-243-2176.. 219 I
ddaniels@lasell.edu
DANIELS, Eric .... 732-255-0400.. 293 E
edaniels@ocean.edu
DANIELS, George, T .... 919-572-1625.. 341 M
gdaniels14@apexsot.edu
DANIELS, Gerri, L .... 906-227-2650.. 239 B
gdaniels@nmu.edu
DANIELS, Glynis, A .... 610-799-1936.. 408 G
gdaniels@lccc.edu
DANIELS, Greta .... 412-392-3999.. 417 F
gdaniels@pointpark.edu
DANIELS, Heather, M .... 608-263-1011.. 519 K
soas@soas.wisc.edu
DANIELS, III, Jack, E ...... 608-246-6676.. 523 F
jdanielsiii@madisoncollege.edu
DANIELS, Jim .... 508-678-2811.. 223 A
jim.daniels@bristolcc.edu
DANIELS, Julie .... 601-974-1443.. 258 H
julie.daniels@millsaps.edu
DANIELS, LaMetrius .... 615-248-1521.. 447 F
ldaniels@trevecca.edu
DANIELS, Linda .... 601-977-4462.. 261 A
ldaniels@tougaloo.edu
DANIELS, Lisa .... 518-608-8398.. 314 A
ldaniels@excelsior.edu
DANIELS, Mark .... 425-235-2352.. 506 F
mdaniels@rtc.edu
DANIELS, Martin .... 802-485-2969.. 484 H
mdaniel2@norwich.edu
DANIELS, Mary Sue .... 212-431-2162.. 323 H
marysue.daniels@nyls.edu
DANIELS, Matt .... 641-844-5708.. 173 L
matt.daniels@iavalley.edu
DANIELS, Maurice, C .... 706-542-5424.. 128 E
sswdean@uga.edu
DANIELS, Michael .... 617-585-0200.. 216 A
michael.daniels@the-bac.edu
DANIELS, Michael .... 828-448-3564.. 354 B
mdaniels@wpcc.edu
DANIELS, JR.,
Mitchell, E .... 765-494-4600.. 166 D
DANIELS, Monica .... 601-974-1000.. 258 H
monica.daniels@millsaps.edu
DANIELS, Nettie .... 608-342-7373.. 521 A
danielsne@uwplatt.edu
DANIELS, Orangel, J .... 910-362-7129.. 348 A
odaniels@cfcc.edu
DANIELS, Patti, J .... 618-537-6936.. 147 F
pjdaniels@mckendree.edu
DANIELS, Randell, W ...... 734-384-4224.. 238 C
rdaniels@monroeccc.edu
DANIELS, Rick .... 815-921-4284.. 152 E
s.daniels@rockvalleycollege.edu
DANIELS, Robert .... 631-656-2117.. 314 F
robert.daniels@ftc.edu
DANIELS, Ronald, J .... 410-516-4170.. 208 D
president@jhu.edu
DANIELS, Rowena .... 229-430-2799.. 115 K
rowena.daniels@asurams.edu
DANIELS, Shelia .... 407-823-2771.. 111 E
shelia.daniels@ucf.edu
DANIELS, Terri .... 407-708-2126.. 109 E
danielst@seminolestate.edu
DANIELS, Ursula .... 201-612-5355.. 289 E
udaniels@bergen.edu
DANIELS HERRON, Sally 612-330-1525.. 244 I
herron@augsburg.edu
DANIELSEN, Randy .... 480-219-6009.. 262 A
rdanielsen@atsu.edu
DANIELSON, David, D ...... 651-631-5329.. 256 A
dddanielson@unwsp.edu
DANIELSON, Lisa, M ...... 920-424-3007.. 520 E
danielsn@uwosh.edu

DANIELSON, Mary Ann ... 402-280-2535.. 279 H
maddam@creighton.edu
DANIELSON, Michelle ...... 507-285-7180.. 251 I
michelle.danielson@rctc.edu
DANIELSON, Timothy ..... 414-229-4463.. 520 D
danieltj@uwm.edu
DANIEU, Paul, F .... 716-851-1856.. 313 H
danieu@ecc.edu
DANIK, Steve .... 410-951-3575.. 212 E
sdanik@coppin.edu
DANILOWICZ, Bret .... 405-744-5663.. 385 G
bret.danilowicz@okstate.edu
DANKEL, Richard .... 401-232-6117.. 424 K
rdankel@bryant.edu
DANKO, James, M .... 317-940-9900.. 159 K
president@butler.edu
DANLEY, Charrita, D .... 757-727-5231.. 490 E
charrita.danley@hamptonu.edu
DANNA, Debra .... 504-864-7550.. 198 E
danna@loyno.edu
DANNA, John .... 716-851-1360.. 313 H
danna@ecc.edu
DANNA, Stephen .... 518-792-5425.. 334 A
dann1253@plattsburgh.edu
DANNECKER, Ronald .... 716-829-7600.. 313 A
dannecrh@dyc.edu
DANNEMILLER,
Stanley, D .... 330-325-6558.. 373 H
sdannemiller@neomed.edu
DANNEN, Troy .... 504-865-5500.. 200 C
tdannen@tulane.edu
DANNENBAUM,
Martha, C .... 979-458-8300.. 468 B
mdannenbaum@tamu.edu
DANNENBERG, Dave .... 907-786-4447.... 10 F
ddannenberg@uaa.alaska.edu
DANNER, Megan .... 512-863-1056.. 466 G
davidsom@southwestern.edu
DANOWITZ, Mary Ann ...... 919-515-5900.. 357 B
mdanowi@ncsu.edu
DANSBY, Bob .... 334-291-4965...... 2 H
bob.dansby@cv.edu
DANSER, Dolores A .... 717-245-1589.. 402 D
danserd@dickinson.edu
DANTLEY, Michael .... 513-529-6317.. 372 K
dantleme@miamioh.edu
DANUFF, Allan .... 352-854-2322..... 97 R
danuffa@cf.edu
DANZELL, Linda .... 508-678-2811.. 223 A
linda.danzell@bristolcc.edu
DANZEY, Ida .... 310-434-4792..... 63 F
danzey_ida@smc.edu
DANZI, SJ, Rocco .... 201-761-6014.. 296 K
rdanzi@saintpeters.edu
DAO, Chau .... 909-274-4450..... 53 C
cdao@mtsac.edu
DAOAS, Doman .... 691-320-2480.. 529 F
daoas@comfsm.fm
DAOOD, Christopher .... 262-691-5314.. 524 G
cdaood@wctc.edu
DAOUST, Carolyn .... 989-358-7211.. 230 G
daoust@alpenacc.edu
DAPICE-WONG,
Stephanie .... 631-665-1600.. 337 I
stephanie.wong@tcuro.edu
DAPP, Kelly .... 661-362-3983..... 40 A
kelly.dapp@canyons.edu
DAPRA, Joe .... 816-322-0110.. 262 N
joe.dapra@calvary.edu
DAQUILA, August .... 609-343-5116.. 288 H
adaquila@atlantic.edu
DARABI, Rachelle .... 417-836-8346.. 268 I
rachelledarabi@missouristate.edu
DARBEAU, Ron .... 479-788-7611..... 23 A
ron.darbeau@uafs.edu
DARBONE, Davidson .... 337-421-6940.. 197 B
david.darbone@sowela.edu
DARBUT, Jeff .... 480-461-7382..... 14 D
jeffrey.darbut@mesacc.edu
DARBY, Cindy .... 318-678-6000.. 195 I
cdarby@bpcc.edu
DARBY, Kadia .... 212-616-7263.. 315 G
kadia.darby@helenefuld.edu
DARBY, Mary, A .... 225-771-5923.. 199 H
magdarby@yahoo.com
DARCANGELO, Robin .... 415-485-9405..... 40 C
rdarcangelo@marin.edu
DARCY, Kip .... 810-762-7331.. 236 C
kdarcy@kettering.edu
DARDAR, Carmen .... 916-361-1660..... 36 E
cdardar@carrington.edu
DARDEN, Alyssa .... 614-947-6685.. 369 A
alyssa.darden@franklin.edu
DARDEN, Elbert .... 816-501-4275.. 270 J
elbert.darden@rockhurst.edu
DARDEN, Joanna .... 901-572-2448.. 438 I
joanna.darden@bchs.edu
DARDIS, Greg .... 503-675-3969.. 392 D
gdardis@marylhurst.edu
DARGA, Richard .... 773-995-2378.. 136 M
rdarga@csu.edu

DARIN, Jessica .... 805-756-6000..... 31 I
darin@calpoly.edu
DARING, William .... 508-854-4415.. 224 E
wdaring@qcc.mass.edu
DARK, Shawna .... 562-985-8854..... 33 B
shawna.dark@csulb.edu
DARK, Shawna .... 562-985-8115..... 33 B
shawna.dark@csulb.edu
DARLAND, Suzanne .... 270-706-8460.. 189 C
suzanne.darland@kctcs.edu
DARLAND, Zane .... 606-693-5000.. 191 A
zdarland@kmbc.edu
DARLING, Diane .... 215-612-6600.. 398 G
ddarling@chicareers.com
DARLING, Douglas, D .... 701-662-1506.. 361 E
doug.darling@lrsc.edu
DARLING, Hilary .... 661-253-7724..... 30 E
hdarling@calarts.edu
DARLINGTON, Carol .... 989-386-6625.. 238 B
cdarlington@midmich.edu
DARMON, Robin .... 619-260-4654..... 72 B
rdarmon@sandiego.edu
DARMSTAEDTER,
Nicholous .... 901-272-5177.. 442 B
ndarmstaedter@mca.edu
DARNALL BURKE, Randi 707-826-3361..... 34 F
darnall@humboldt.edu
DARNELL, Charles .... 435-797-1952.. 462 B
charles.darnell@usu.edu
DARNELL, Darrell, L .... 202-994-1000..... 92 D
ddarnell@gwu.edu
DARNELL, Meg .... 212-924-5900.. 336 I
mdarnell@swedishinstitute.edu
DARR, Eric, D .... 717-901-5111.. 405 H
edarr@harrisburgu.edu
DARR, Kristi .... 515-294-6458.. 169 G
kdarr@iastate.edu
DARR, Steven .... 863-638-7230.. 115 C
steven.darr@warner.edu
DARRELL, Bart .... 270-852-3104.. 191 C
bdarrell@kwc.edu
DARROW, David, W .... 937-229-4615.. 379 D
ddarrow1@udayton.edu
DARROW, Karen .... 406-756-3900.. 276 E
kdarrow@fvcc.edu
DARROW, Louis .... 330-490-7373.. 380 J
ldarrow@walsh.edu
DARST, Valerie .... 660-263-4100.. 269 D
valeried@macc.edu
DART, Lucas .... 308-698-5270.. 282 L
ldart@nufoundation.org
DARTY, Roxanne .... 210-690-9000.. 458 I
rdarty@hallmarkuniversity.edu
DARWIN, Mike .... 205-726-4241...... 6 E
mdarwin@samford.edu
DAS, Dilip .... 410-951-6102.. 212 E
ddas@coppin.edu
DAS, Pradeep, K .... 404-627-2681.. 117 G
pradeep.das@beulah.edu
DASBURG, Deanne .... 828-884-8129.. 342 C
dasburg@brevard.edu
DASENBROCK, Reed W ...... 808-956-8447.. 131 F
rdasenbr@hawaii.edu
DASEY-MORALES,
Maureen .... 316-978-3440.. 185 J
maureen.casey-morales@wichita.edu
DASGUPTA, Nandini .... 510-869-8711..... 59 L
ndasgupta@samuelmerritt.edu
DASHE, Alejandra .... 952-888-4777.. 253 Z
adashe@nwhealth.edu
DASHER, Leah .... 912-538-3186.. 127 E
ldasher@southeasterntech.edu
DASHIELD, Richeleen .... 908-526-1200.. 295 A
richeleen.dashield@raritanval.edu
DASHIELL, Christian .... 620-278-4341.. 185 A
cdashiell@sterling.edu
DASIGI, Venu .... 419-372-8719.. 364 E
vdasigi@bgsu.edu
DASILVA, Jose .... 940-872-5211.. 462 L
jdasilva@nctc.edu
DASILVA, Joseph .... 413-755-4889.. 224 G
jdasilva@stcc.edu
DASILVA, Kirsten .... 201-684-7621.. 294 G
kdasilv1@ramapo.edu
DASINGER, Hank .... 334-290-3265...... 4 G
hank.dasinger@istc.edu
DASTMOZD, Rassoul .... 651-846-1335.. 252 C
rassoul.dastmozd@saintpaul.edu
DATCHER, Dwight .... 617-879-2238.. 229 G
ddatcher@wheelock.edu
DATEMA, Betsy .... 574-232-2408.. 166 G
bdatema@rtuvt.com
DATHER, Julie .... 605-668-1525.. 436 D
jdather@mtmc.edu
DATTA, Asoke .... 808-544-1106.. 130 H
adatta@hpu.edu
DATTA, Sumana .... 979-845-6774.. 468 B
sumad@tamu.edu
DATTAGUPTA, Satya .... 504-865-5731.. 200 C
dattagupta@tulane.edu

DATTAGUPTA, Satyajit ..... 410-778-7700.. 213 E
sdattagupta2@washcoll.edu
DATUIN, Bonnie Mae, M 671-735-5616.. 529 G
bonniemae.datuin@guamcc.edu
DAUBERMAN, Barbara, A 804-752-7300.. 493 C
bdauberman@rmc.edu
DAUBMANN, Karl .... 248-204-2810.. 237 B
kdaubmann@ltu.edu
DAUDISTEL, Howard .... 915-747-8533.. 476 D
hdaudistel@utep.edu
DAUER, Eve .... 703-993-2446.. 490 B
edauer@gmu.edu
DAUGHERTY, Bob .... 858-513-9240..... 27 V
robert.daugherty@ashford.edu
DAUGHERTY, Carolyn ...... 719-549-2830..... 79 B
carolyn.daugherty@csupueblo.edu
DAUGHERTY, Caron .... 636-481-3300.. 266 C
cdaugherty@jeffco.edu
DAUGHERTY, Craig, A .... 740-427-5430.. 371 C
daugherty@kenyon.edu
DAUGHERTY, Debra .... 615-230-3526.. 447 C
debra.daugherty@volstate.edu
DAUGHERTY, Penny, J .... 541-346-2971.. 395 G
penny@uoregon.edu
DAUGHERTY, Robyn .... 479-524-7301..... 20 H
rdaugherty@jbu.edu
DAUGHERTY, Vernon, D . 828-398-7220.. 347 D
vdaugherty@abtech.edu
DAUGHETY, Kathy .... 252-399-6529.. 341 P
kdaughety@barton.edu
DAUGHT, Gary .... 423-461-8799.. 442 K
gfdaught@milligan.edu
DAUGHTRY, Dee Dee, D . 919-209-2066.. 350 G
dddaughtry@johnstoncc.edu
DAULTON, Jonathan, G ... 864-242-5100.. 427 E
DAUSEY, David .... 814-824-2268.. 410 H
ddausey@mercyhurst.edu
DAUSS, Jan .... 619-961-4247..... 68 A
jand@tjsl.edu
DAVAR, David .... 212-678-6161.. 317 I
dadavar@jtsa.edu
DAVAULT, Joey .... 405-736-0362.. 387 I
jdavault@rose.edu
DAVEE, Doug .... 949-376-6000..... 48 C
ddavee@lcad.edu
DAVENPORT, Beverly, J .. 513-556-2201.. 379 A
president@uc.edu
DAVENPORT,
Catherine, M .... 717-245-1231.. 402 D
davenpor@dickinson.edu
DAVENPORT, Cathy .... 860-215-9231..... 87 D
cdavenport@ttcc.commnet.edu
DAVENPORT, Daniel, D ... 208-885-6312.. 134 G
dand@uidaho.edu
DAVENPORT, Darrien ...... 717-815-1924.. 424 F
ddavenp2@ycp.edu
DAVENPORT, Darrien ...... 717-815-6663.. 424 F
ddavenp2@ycp.edu
DAVENPORT, Derek .... 412-924-1385.. 417 E
ddavenport@pts.edu
DAVENPORT, Doug .... 816-271-4534.. 269 C
ddavenport@missouriwestern.edu
DAVENPORT, Elizabeth .... 773-702-8282.. 156 D
ejld@uchicago.edu
DAVENPORT, Eric .... 215-991-2019.. 407 A
davenport@lasalle.edu
DAVENPORT, Fiona, E ..... 215-935-3868.. 423 C
fdavenport@wts.edu
DAVENPORT, Floyd .... 573-651-2217.. 272 B
fdavenport@semo.edu
DAVENPORT, Janet .... 508-373-9534.. 215 D
janet.davenport@becker.edu
DAVENPORT, John .... 309-438-2008.. 143 B
jmdaven@ilstu.edu
DAVENPORT, Kevin .... 256-306-2574...... 2 F
kevin.davenport@calhoun.edu
DAVENPORT, Kevin .... 804-524-5995.. 499 G
pdjackson@vsu.edu
DAVENPORT, Larry .... 860-215-9232..... 87 D
ldavenport@trcc.commnet.net
DAVENPORT, Lechelle, D 901-333-4195.. 447 B
ldavenport@southwest.tn.edu
DAVENPORT, Mary .... 507-433-0530.. 251 H
mary.davenport@riverland.edu
DAVENPORT, Mary .... 507-285-7215.. 251 I
mary.davenport@rctc.edu
DAVENPORT, Mike .... 270-824-8661.. 190 B
mike.davenport@kctcs.edu
DAVENPORT, Mona .... 217-581-6690.. 139 H
mydavenport@eiu.edu
DAVENPORT, Nancy .... 202-885-3237..... 91 J
davenpor@american.edu
DAVENPORT, Richard .... 507-389-1111.. 250 E
richard.davenport@mnsu.edu
DAVENPORT, Robert .... 405-585-5301.. 385 B
robert.davenport@okbu.edu
DAVENPORT, Robin .... 973-618-3905.. 290 A
rdavenport@caldwell.edu
DAVENPORT, Sharon, M . 508-849-3490.. 214 E
sdavenport@annamaria.edu

DAVENPORT, Shirley .... 636-481-3333.. 266 C
sdavenp1@jeffco.edu
DAVENPORT, Susan, C .... 609-652-4521.. 297 C
susan.davenport@stockton.edu
DAVENPORT, Thomas ..... 270-706-8699.. 189 C
tdavenport0008@kctcs.edu
DAVENPORT, Virginia ...... 937-502-3332.. 381 B
vdavenport@wilberforce.edu
DAVENPORT, Walter, C ... 919-516-4440.. 355 D
wcdavenport@st-aug.edu
DAVENPORT-RAMIREZ,
Keisha .... 212-229-8996.. 322 E
davenpok@newschool.edu
DAVENPORT TIGNOR,
Stephanie .... 804-828-0100.. 496 D
davenportse@vcu.edu
DAVEY, Cathleen .... 201-684-7612.. 294 G
cdavey@ramapo.edu
DAVEY, Daniel, K .... 757-479-3706.. 496 B
ddavey@vbts.edu
DAVEY, Patrick .... 202-319-6907.... 92 A
daveyp@cua.edu
DAVEY, Stephen .... 919-573-5350.. 355 G
DAVID, Emile .... 901-448-3246.. 448 H
edavid@uthsc.edu
DAVID, Garry .... 940-552-6291.. 478 D
gdavid@vernoncollege.edu
DAVID, Haven .... 940-552-6291.. 478 D
hdavid@vernoncollege.edu
DAVID, Jacob .... 212-563-6647.. 338 G
jacobdavid835@yahoo.com
DAVID, Kenneth .... 646-565-6000.. 337 I
kenneth.david@touro.edu
DAVID, Kevin, M .... 918-595-8100.. 388 F
kevin.david@tulsacc.edu
DAVID, Kim .... 478-553-2054.. 125 C
DAVID, Kimberly, C .... 713-798-1543.. 452 G
kcotner@bcm.edu
DAVID, Kyle .... 774-455-7560.. 220 E
kdavid@umassp.edu
DAVID, Marcella .... 850-599-3276.. 110 J
marcella.david@famu.edu
DAVID, Maureen .... 301-985-7047.. 212 C
maureen.david@umuc.edu
DAVID, Paula .... 508-793-7681.. 217 B
pdavid@clarku.edu
DAVID, Prabu .... 517-355-3410.. 237 I
pdavid@msu.edu
DAVID, Vivian .... 757-727-5331.. 490 E
vivian.david@hamptonu.edu
DAVIDHIZAR, Larry, J ..... 312-329-4005.. 148 F
larry.davidhizar@moody.edu
DAVIDOWITZ,
Menachem .... 585-473-2810.. 337 B
tiunyfax@gmail.com
DAVIDS, Cheryl .... 828-339-7018.. 353 D
c_davids@southwesterncc.edu
DAVIDSEN, Susanna .... 612-338-7224.. 256 D
susanna.davidsen@waldenu.edu
DAVIDSON, Anthony .... 914-323-5315.. 319 N
anthony.davidson@mville.edu
DAVIDSON, Anthony, R .... 718-817-4602.. 314 G
DAVIDSON, Bobbie .... 928-350-1113.... 16 P
bdavidson@prescott.edu
DAVIDSON, Camille .... 704-971-9393.. 343 E
cdavidson@charlottelaw.edu
DAVIDSON, Conrad .... 701-858-3159.. 360 F
conrad.davidson@minotstateu.edu
DAVIDSON, Debbie .... 262-564-3422.. 523 D
davidsond@gtc.edu
DAVIDSON, Don .... 719-389-6573.... 77 J
ddavidson@coloradocollege.edu
DAVIDSON, Donald .... 603-641-7287.. 287 G
ddavidson@anselm.edu
DAVIDSON, Dotti .... 757-352-4108.. 493 E
dorobur@regent.edu
DAVIDSON, Erin .... 817-598-6285.. 479 E
edavidson@wc.edu
DAVIDSON, Georglyn, L .. 215-968-8251.. 399 A
davidson@bucks.edu
DAVIDSON, JaCenda .... 615-329-8712.. 439 L
jdavidson@fisk.edu
DAVIDSON, Jack .... 858-642-8191.... 54 A
jdavidson@nu.edu
DAVIDSON, James, A ...... 410-827-5846.. 207 A
jdavidson@chesapeake.edu
DAVIDSON, Jamie .... 702-895-3627.. 284 L
jamie.davidson@unlv.edu
DAVIDSON, Janet .... 724-480-3395.. 401 F
janet.davidson@ccbc.edu
DAVIDSON, Jennifer .... 708-974-5633.. 148 G
davidsonj@morainevalley.edu
DAVIDSON, Jon .... 810-762-3300.. 242 B
jdavidso@umflint.edu
DAVIDSON, Joyce .... 515-294-0170.. 169 G
jad@iastate.edu
DAVIDSON, Katie .... 701-777-6438.. 360 C
DAVIDSON, Katrena, J .... 330-941-1712.. 382 A
katrena.davidson@ysu.edu
DAVIDSON, Keith, S .... 410-651-6496.. 212 B
kdavidson@umes.edu

DAVIDSON, Laura .... 919-760-8531.. 346 D
davidsonl@meredith.edu
DAVIDSON, Leslie .... 413-528-7245.. 214 H
leslied@simons-rock.edu
DAVIDSON, Michael, E .... 404-413-3156.. 122 D
mdavidson@gsu.edu
DAVIDSON, Mitch .... 260-481-6196.. 163 C
davidsom@ipfw.edu
DAVIDSON, Nancy .... 605-274-5516.. 435 E
nancy.davidson@augie.edu
DAVIDSON, Patricia .... 410-502-2361.. 208 D
pdavids3@jhu.edu
DAVIDSON, Randee .... 856-415-6632.. 295 D
rdavidso@rcgc.edu
DAVIDSON, Rob .... 512-492-3034.. 451 E
DAVIDSON, Roger .... 916-484-8216..... 51 A
davidsr@arc.losrios.edu
DAVIDSON, Shane .... 812-488-2829.. 167 I
sd10@evansville.edu
DAVIDSON, Sharon .... 718-262-2155.. 310 A
sdavid@york.cuny.edu
DAVIDSON, Stephanie ...... 405-692-3241.. 384 C
sdavidson@macu.edu
DAVIDSON, Steve .... 615-966-6280.. 441 F
steve.davidson@lipscomb.edu
DAVIDSON, Suellen .... 870-368-2059..... 21 F
sdavidson@ozarka.edu
DAVIDSON, Taja .... 812-888-4161.. 169 A
tdavidson@vinu.edu
DAVIDSON, Tracy .... 406-657-1015.. 278 D
tracy.davidson@rocky.edu
DAVIDSON, Valerie, J ..... 317-940-9281.. 159 K
vdavidso@butler.edu
DAVIE, Fred .... 212-280-1408.. 338 I
fdavie@uts.columbia.edu
DAVIE, Karen .... 845-675-4608.. 325 C
karen.davie@nyack.edu
DAVIE, Keith, A .... 845-675-4770.. 325 C
keith.davie@nyack.edu
DAVIES, Ann .... 608-363-2667.. 515 G
daviesa@beloit.edu
DAVIES, Anna .... 415-239-3000.... 38 E
adavies@ccsf.edu
DAVIES, Becky .... 972-721-5206.. 473 D
bdavies@udallas.edu
DAVIES, Bobby .... 201-327-8877.. 291 G
bdavies@eastwick.edu
DAVIES, Daniel .... 702-463-2122.. 285 J
DAVIES, Evan .... 757-221-2147.. 488 F
esdav2@wm.edu
DAVIES, H. Dele, O .... 402-559-5131.. 283 A
dele.davies@unmc.edu
DAVIES, Haldane .... 340-693-1004.. 539 C
hdavies@uvi.edu
DAVIES, Helen .... 603-645-9781.. 287 I
h.davies@snhu.edu
DAVIES, Mandy .... 916-660-7302.... 64 F
mdavies@sierracollege.edu
DAVIES, Marilyn, S .... 909-593-3511.... 71 B
mdavies@laverne.edu
DAVIES, Mark .... 405-208-5284.. 385 E
mdavies@okcu.edu
DAVIES, Mark, D .... 570-577-1019.. 398 L
mark.davies@bucknell.edu
DAVIES, Pamela, L .... 704-337-2216.. 355 A
daviesp@queens.edu
DAVIES, Patty .... 303-352-3037.... 79 F
patty.davies@ccd.edu
DAVIES, Paul .... 804-752-7399.. 493 C
pauldavies@rmc.edu
DAVIES, Robert, O .... 270-809-3763.. 192 A
rdavies@murraystate.edu
DAVIES, Robin, L .... 540-224-4515.. 491 A
rldavies@jchs.edu
DAVIES, Sharon .... 614-688-3389.. 375 A
davies.49@osu.edu
DAVIES, Susan .... 828-262-7244.. 356 B
daviess@appstate.edu
DAVIES, Susan .... 810-762-9927.. 236 C
sdavies@kettering.edu
DAVIES, William, E .... 301-447-5234.. 209 G
davies@msmary.edu
DAVILA, Alba .... 787-751-0160.. 531 M
adavila@cmpr.pr.gov
DAVILA, Alfonso, L .... 787-751-0178.. 535 N
adavila@suagm.edu
DAVILA, Annette .... 787-884-3838.. 530 G
adavila@atenascollege.edu
DAVILA, Cheyla .... 305-222-2812.... 99 S
cdavila@careercollege.edu
DAVILA, David .... 361-698-1561.. 457 D
ddavila23@delmar.edu
DAVILA, Grace .... 713-221-8633.. 474 B
davilag@uhd.edu
DAVILA, Ivan .... 787-841-2000.. 535 I
idavila@pucpr.edu
DAVILA, Jorge .... 787-850-9312.. 538 B
jorge.davila1@upr.edu
DAVILA, Michael .... 903-875-7414.. 462 J
michael.davila@navarrocollege.edu

DAVILA, Pilar .... 787-743-7979.. 536 A
pdavila6@suagm.edu
DAVIN, Donna .... 706-290-2163.. 117 F
ddavin@berry.edu
DAVINO, Richard .... 774-354-0451.. 215 D
rich.davino@becker.edu
DAVIS, A. Alex .... 323-953-4000.... 49 H
alexanal@lacitycollege.edu
DAVIS, Abigail .... 612-343-4450.. 253 Y
ahdavis@northcentral.edu
DAVIS, Adam .... 540-785-5440.. 496 A
adamdavis@vbc.edu
DAVIS, Adrienne, D .... 314-935-8583.. 274 N
adriennedavis@wustl.edu
DAVIS, Alan .... 870-235-5059..... 22 F
dadavis@saumag.edu
DAVIS, Alan, B .... 205-853-1200...... 5 B
adavis@jeffstateonline.com
DAVIS, Alana .... 804-752-7227.. 493 C
adavis@rmc.edu
DAVIS, Alex .... 919-760-8809.. 346 D
amdavis@meredith.edu
DAVIS, Andrew .... 334-347-2623....... 3 H
adavis@escc.edu
DAVIS, Andrew .... 541-383-7592.. 390 D
apdavis@cocc.edu
DAVIS, Barbara .... 614-222-4035.. 367 B
bdavis@ccad.edu
DAVIS, Becky .... 904-743-1122.. 103 G
bdavis@jones.edu
DAVIS, Becky .... 903-923-2136.. 457 G
bdavis@etbu.edu
DAVIS, Betsy .... 360-385-4948.. 505 D
betsy@nwswb.edu
DAVIS, Bill .... 203-596-4660.... 88 F
bdavis@post.edu
DAVIS, Brad .... 405-789-7661.. 388 B
brad.davis@swcu.edu
DAVIS, Bradley .... 408-741-2668.... 74 H
bradley.davis@wvm.edu
DAVIS, Bradley, W .... 941-752-5388.. 110 H
davisb@scf.edu
DAVIS, Bree .... 626-529-8204.... 55 H
bdavis@pacificoaks.edu
DAVIS, Brenda .... 251-442-2877....... 9 A
bdavis@umobile.edu
DAVIS, Brenda .... 601-928-6381.. 259 C
brenda.davis2@mgccc.edu
DAVIS, Brent .... 559-730-3912.... 40 E
brentd@cos.edu
DAVIS, Brett .... 406-994-4516.. 277 C
brett.davis2@montana.edu
DAVIS, Brian .... 803-778-6612.. 427 G
davisjb@cctech.edu
DAVIS, Brian, E .... 330-972-6084.. 378 G
bdavis@uakron.edu
DAVIS, Britt .... 910-893-1200.. 342 F
davisb@campbell.edu
DAVIS, Brittany .... 334-833-4428....... 4 D
finaid@hawks.huntingdon.edu
DAVIS, Brittany .... 850-245-0466.. 110 I
brittany.davis@flbog.edu
DAVIS, Bruce .... 801-626-6789.. 482 D
brucedavis@weber.edu
DAVIS, Bryan .... 951-343-4721.... 29 H
bdavis@calbaptist.edu
DAVIS, JR., C. Grant .... 334-844-4866....... 1 G
daviscg@auburn.edu
DAVIS, Carissa .... 708-974-5343.. 148 G
davisc274@morainevalley.edu
DAVIS, Carol .... 903-877-7450.. 477 E
carol.davis@uthct.edu
DAVIS, Carole .... 269-965-3931.. 236 A
davisc@kellogg.edu
DAVIS, Cassandra, E .... 973-761-7161.. 297 A
cassandra.davis@shu.edu
DAVIS, Catherine, C .... 609-497-7882.. 294 C
student.relations@ptsem.edu
DAVIS, Cathleen, M .... 937-775-5700.. 381 H
cathy.davis@wright.edu
DAVIS, Chanell .... 334-244-3602....... 2 A
cdavis34@aum.edu
DAVIS, Charles, N .... 706-542-1704.. 128 E
cndavis@uga.edu
DAVIS, Chase .... 314-367-8700.. 271 E
chase.davis@stlcop.edu
DAVIS, Cheryl .... 270-745-6733.. 194 D
cheryl.davis@wku.edu
DAVIS, Chris .... 706-385-1041.. 126 A
chris.davis@point.edu
DAVIS, Chris .... 501-450-3321..... 24 G
cdavis@uca.edu
DAVIS, Christine .... 479-619-3156..... 21 D
cdavis22@nwacc.edu
DAVIS, Christine .... 239-433-6950.. 101 F
christine.davis@fsw.edu
DAVIS, Christopher .... 602-943-2311..... 18 C
christopher.davis@west.edu
DAVIS, Christopher, A ..... 410-293-6381.. 529 D
cdavis@usna.edu

DAVIS, Chuck .... 206-934-4340.. 506 K
chuck.davis@seattlecolleges.edu
DAVIS, Cliff .... 708-344-4700.. 146 D
cdavis@lincolntech.edu
DAVIS, Cliff .... 417-447-2652.. 270 A
davisc@otc.edu
DAVIS, Colin .... 309-649-6395.. 155 G
colin.davis@src.edu
DAVIS, Connie .... 985-549-2094.. 201 C
cdavis@selu.edu
DAVIS, D. Scott .... 478-301-2110.. 124 D
davis_ds@mercer.edu
DAVIS, Dan .... 701-228-5451.. 361 D
danny.davis@dakotacollege.edu
DAVIS, Daniel .... 212-854-6939.. 304 I
ddavis@barnard.edu
DAVIS, Daniel .... 817-722-1614.. 460 E
daniel.davis@tku.edu
DAVIS, Danny .... 413-748-3532.. 228 E
ddavis@springfieldcollege.edu
DAVIS, Dave .... 218-855-8116.. 248 N
ddavis@clcmn.edu
DAVIS, David .... 601-974-1432.. 258 H
davisdc@millsaps.edu
DAVIS, David, H .... 828-694-1845.. 347 G
daviddav@blueridge.edu
DAVIS, Debra, C .... 251-445-9404...... 9 E
ddavis@southalabama.edu
DAVIS, Deidra .... 207-326-2138.. 204 C
deidra.davis@mma.edu
DAVIS, Dejon .... 714-556-3610.... 73 B
dejon.davis@vanguard.edu
DAVIS, Denise .... 314-264-1000.. 274 I
denise.davis@vatterott.edu
DAVIS, Derrick .... 301-860-3427.. 212 D
dldavis@bowiestate.edu
DAVIS, Dirk .... 951-343-3905.... 29 H
ddavis@calbaptist.edu
DAVIS, Don .... 626-815-3828.... 28 A
ddavis@apu.edu
DAVIS, Donald, L .... 972-883-6176.. 476 C
don.davis@utdallas.edu
DAVIS, Donna .... 760-757-2121.... 52 K
ddavis@miracosta.edu
DAVIS, Donna .... 636-922-8300.. 271 A
ddavis@stchas.edu
DAVIS, Donna, J .... 415-422-6822.... 72 C
davisdj@usfca.edu
DAVIS, Ed, L .... 404-880-8475.. 118 K
edavis@cau.edu
DAVIS, Eddie .... 972-825-4686.. 466 D
edavis@sagu.edu
DAVIS, Elizabeth .... 410-871-3376.. 209 D
emdavis@mcdaniel.edu
DAVIS, Elizabeth .... 864-294-2100.. 430 C
elizabeth.davis@furman.edu
DAVIS, Elizabeth, B .... 415-422-2508.... 72 C
ebdavis@usfca.edu
DAVIS, Ellen .... 254-298-8591.. 467 B
ellen.davis@templejc.edu
DAVIS, Eric .... 505-424-2351.. 299 L
eric.davis@iaia.edu
DAVIS, Erik .... 805-969-3626.... 56 B
edavis@pacifica.edu
DAVIS, Evelyn .... 423-624-0077.. 439 D
evelynd@chattanoogacollege.edu
DAVIS, Evett .... 706-771-4027.. 117 C
edavis@augustatech.edu
DAVIS, Faye .... 918-685-0724.. 382 D
davisf@bacone.edu
DAVIS, Fontaine .... 386-481-2005.... 96 H
davisf@cookman.edu
DAVIS, Forrest .... 814-824-2273.. 410 H
fdavis@mercyhurst.edu
DAVIS, Frances .... 478-471-2472.. 124 E
frances.davis@mga.edu
DAVIS, G. Scott .... 608-757-7754.. 523 A
sdavis40@blackhawk.edu
DAVIS, G. Todd .... 559-638-0300.... 67 D
todd.davis@reedleycollege.edu
DAVIS, Gayle, R .... 616-331-2400.. 234 F
davisgr@gvsu.edu
DAVIS, George .... 717-866-5775.. 403 F
george.davis@evangelical.edu
DAVIS, Gilda .... 504-286-5176.. 199 I
gdavis@suno.edu
DAVIS, Glenda .... 214-379-5526.. 463 G
gdavis@pqc.edu
DAVIS, Glenn .... 212-463-0400.. 337 I
glenn.davis2@touro.edu
DAVIS, Grant .... 610-647-4400.. 406 B
gdavis@immaculata.edu
DAVIS, Greg .... 360-438-8772.. 506 G
gdavis@stmartin.edu
DAVIS, Gregory .... 630-515-4554.. 139 D
gdavis@devrygroup.com
DAVIS, Gregory .... 920-465-2334.. 520 B
davisg@uwgb.edu
DAVIS, Guy .... 423-472-7141.. 445 E
gdavis08@clevelandstatecc.edu

DAVIS, Harriet, F .... 919-530-6151.. 357 A
hfdavis@nccu.edu
DAVIS, Hazel .... 480-517-8273.... 14 G
hazel.davis@riosalado.edu
DAVIS, Heather .... 336-750-3350.. 359 B
davish@wssu.edu
DAVIS, Heidi, L .... 504-865-3086.. 198 E
heidi@loyno.edu
DAVIS, Herbert, R .... 919-572-1625.. 341 M
hdavis@apexsot.edu
DAVIS, Houston .... 404-962-3060.. 129 F
houston.davis@usg.edu
DAVIS, Howard .... 248-204-2316.. 237 B
hdavis@ltu.edu
DAVIS, Jack .... 540-231-6416.. 499 F
davisa@vt.edu
DAVIS, Jackie .... 712-707-7114.. 176 B
jackie.davis@nwciowa.edu
DAVIS, James .... 310-206-0011.... 69 D
jdavis@conet.ucla.edu
DAVIS, James .... 804-819-4995.. 496 E
jdavis@vccs.edu
DAVIS, James .... 713-222-5382.. 474 B
davisjam@uhd.edu
DAVIS, James, F .... 308-865-8517.. 282 L
davisjf@unk.edu
DAVIS, James, J .... 202-806-6700.... 93 A
jdavis@howard.edu
DAVIS, Jamie .... 912-443-4162.. 126 G
jdavis@savannahtech.edu
DAVIS, Janis .... 949-794-9090.... 66 H
jdavis@stanbridge.edu
DAVIS, Jarred .... 214-860-8680.. 456 F
DAVIS, Jason .... 218-726-8782.. 255 D
jdavis@d.umn.edu
DAVIS, Jean .... 314-362-9180.. 265 E
jean.davis@bjc.org
DAVIS, Jeff .... 912-871-1640.. 125 E
jdavis@ogeecheetech.edu
DAVIS, Jeff .... 706-802-5105.. 121 C
jdavis@highlands.edu
DAVIS, Jeff .... 785-539-3571.. 183 B
mccweb@mccks.edu
DAVIS, Jeff .... 541-757-8944.. 392 C
jeff.davis@linnbenton.edu
DAVIS, Jeffrey .... 662-325-3444.. 259 D
jdavis@alumni.msstate.edu
DAVIS, Jenna .... 719-336-1589.... 81 D
jenna.davis@lamarcc.edu
DAVIS, Jennifer .... 252-246-1228.. 354 D
jdavis@wilsoncc.edu
DAVIS, Jennifer (J.J.) ...... 703-993-8750.. 490 B
jjdavis@gmu.edu
DAVIS, Jeremy .... 740-477-7485.. 374 G
jdavis@ohiochristian.edu
DAVIS, Jerold .... 212-592-2000.. 330 C
jdavis@sva.edu
DAVIS, Jerome .... 212-854-5017.. 311 E
jd2145@columbia.edu
DAVIS, Jerome .... 205-226-4848...... 2 C
jdavis@bsc.edu
DAVIS, Jerry, C .... 417-690-2470.. 263 E
pres@cofo.edu
DAVIS, Jerry, W .... 260-356-6000.. 161 O
DAVIS, Jim, L .... 701-477-7862.. 362 D
jdavis@tm.edu
DAVIS, Jimmy, H .... 731-661-5461.. 448 A
jdavis@uu.edu
DAVIS, Joan, Y .... 504-762-3000.. 196 D
jydavis@dcc.edu
DAVIS, Joanne .... 561-297-3015.. 110 K
joannedavis@fau.edu
DAVIS, Joe, D .... 641-422-4121.. 175 E
davisjoe@niacc.edu
DAVIS, Joel .... 973-803-5000.. 294 B
jdavis@pillar.edu
DAVIS, John .... 910-843-5304.. 347 A
DAVIS, John .... 626-873-2162.... 53 E
jdavis@mtsierra.edu
DAVIS, John .... 920-206-2332.. 517 G
john.davis@mbu.edu
DAVIS, John .... 920-206-2371.. 517 G
john.davis@mbu.edu
DAVIS, John .... 307-766-6225.. 527 B
jdavis71@uwyo.edu
DAVIS, John, M .... 540-423-9179.. 497 B
jdavis@germanna.edu
DAVIS, Jon .... 360-676-2772.. 505 C
jdavis@nwic.edu
DAVIS, Jon .... 843-863-7218.. 427 I
jdavis@csuniv.edu
DAVIS, Jonathan, M .... 802-626-6419.. 486 C
jonathan.davis@lyndonstate.edu
DAVIS, Jordan .... 214-333-6830.. 455 J
jordan@dbu.edu
DAVIS, Joy .... 970-207-4550.... 81 F
joyd@mckinleycollege.edu
DAVIS, Joy .... 970-207-4500.... 84 F
joyd@uscareerinstitute.edu
DAVIS, Joyce, E .... 404-270-5571.. 128 A
jdavis44@spelman.edu
DAVIS, Julia, T .... 478-301-2644.. 124 D
davis_jt@mercer.edu
DAVIS, Julie .... 478-934-3518.. 124 E
julie.davis3@mga.edu
DAVIS, Julie .... 630-752-5079.. 158 C
julie.davis@wheaton.edu
DAVIS, Julie .... 315-268-6713.. 310 B
davisju@clarkson.edu
DAVIS, Julie, A .... 207-778-7264.. 205 A
jadavis@maine.edu
DAVIS, June .... 910-296-2424.. 350 F
jdavis@jamessprunt.edu
DAVIS, Karan, P .... 850-718-2205.... 97 G
davisk@chipola.edu
DAVIS, Karen .... 805-493-3164.... 31 C
kdavis@callutheran.edu
DAVIS, Karen .... 401-863-3377.. 424 J
karen_davis@brown.edu
DAVIS, Kathleen, B .... 716-888-2500.. 306 F
daviskb@canisius.edu
DAVIS, Kathryn .... 501-370-5234.... 21 G
kdavis@philander.edu
DAVIS, Kathy .... 715-346-4193.. 521 C
kdavis@uwsp.edu
DAVIS, Kathy, K .... 207-768-9581.. 205 D
kathy.k.davis@umpi.edu
DAVIS, Katie .... 478-274-7775.. 125 D
kdavis@oftc.edu
DAVIS, Kelly .... 479-968-0242.... 19 F
kdavis@atu.edu
DAVIS, Kelly .... 817-272-2194.. 476 A
kdavis@uta.edu
DAVIS, Kelvin .... 662-846-4698.. 257 E
kddavis@deltastate.edu
DAVIS, Kelvin .... 803-376-5700.. 427 A
kdavis@allenuniversity.edu
DAVIS, Ken .... 803-536-7017.. 432 E
ken.davis@scsu.edu
DAVIS, Ken, R .... 423-478-7898.. 443 I
kdavis@ptseminary.edu
DAVIS, Kenneth, L .... 212-659-9003.. 317 A
DAVIS, JR., Kenneth, M .. 919-658-2502.. 355 K
kdavis@umo.edu
DAVIS, Kerry .... 904-819-6200.... 99 M
kdavis@flagler.edu
DAVIS, Kery .... 202-806-7141.... 93 A
kery.davis@howard.edu
DAVIS, Kevin, L .... 936-468-2011.. 466 H
DAVIS, Kim .... 843-661-1210.. 430 B
kdavis@fmarion.edu
DAVIS, Kristy .... 479-968-0329.... 19 F
kdavis51@atu.edu
DAVIS, Larry, D .... 501-977-2013.... 24 B
davis@uaccm.edu
DAVIS, Larry, E .... 412-624-6337.. 421 G
ledavis@pitt.edu
DAVIS, Larry, J .... 314-516-5606.. 274 A
ldavis@umsl.edu
DAVIS, LaTricia .... 870-235-4001.... 22 F
ldavis@saumag.edu
DAVIS, Leana .... 815-479-7661.. 147 E
ldavis@mchenry.edu
DAVIS, Leander .... 310-287-4314.... 50 E
davisl@wlac.edu
DAVIS, Lee .... 912-344-2535.. 116 E
lee.davis@armstrong.edu
DAVIS, LeeAnn .... 386-506-3404.... 98 E
davisl@daytonastate.edu
DAVIS, Len, L .... 516-876-3191.. 333 C
davisl@oldwestbury.edu
DAVIS, Lenny .... 941-377-4880.. 105 C
DAVIS, Linda .... 573-592-4382.. 275 G
linda.davis@williamwoods.edu
DAVIS, Linda .... 810-989-5765.. 240 G
ldavis@sc4.edu
DAVIS, Linda .... 617-879-2341.. 229 G
ldavis@wheelock.edu
DAVIS, Linda, P .... 386-822-7710.. 113 B
ldavis@stetson.edu
DAVIS, Lois .... 503-725-2320.. 394 G
loisd@pdx.edu
DAVIS, Loren .... 253-589-5771.. 502 F
loren.davis@cptc.edu
DAVIS, Lori, A .... 502-597-6414.. 191 B
lori.davis@kysu.edu
DAVIS, Lorna .... 559-934-2203.... 74 D
lornadavis@whccd.edu
DAVIS, Lowell, K .... 828-227-7495.. 359 A
lkdavis@wcu.edu
DAVIS, LuAnn .... 402-486-2503.. 282 I
ludavis@ucollege.edu
DAVIS, Lynne .... 508-270-4021.. 223 F
ldavis@massbay.edu
DAVIS, M. Andrew .... 919-572-1625.. 341 M
meandavis@gmail.com
DAVIS, MacArthur .... 336-744-0900.. 342 G
macarthur.davis@carolina.edu
DAVIS, Maggie .... 513-244-4630.. 373 C
maggie.davis@msj.edu
DAVIS, Malcolm .... 832-842-4719.. 473 F
mdavis@uh.edu
DAVIS, Margie .... 614-251-4567.. 374 I
davism8@ohiodominican.edu
DAVIS, Marie .... 269-749-7643.. 240 A
mdavis@olivetcollege.edu
DAVIS, Marilyn .... 404-880-8550.. 118 K
mdavis@cau.edu
DAVIS, Marilyn, S .... 217-424-6379.. 148 D
mdavis@millikin.edu
DAVIS, Marilynn, A .... 404-880-8502.. 118 K
mdavis@cau.edu
DAVIS, Marjorie .... 509-533-4152.. 503 A
marjorie.davis@sfcc.spokane.edu
DAVIS, Mark .... 706-880-8060.. 123 K
mdavis@lagrange.edu
DAVIS, Mark .... 310-506-4472.... 56 J
mark.davis@pepperdine.edu
DAVIS, Mark .... 205-652-5456...... 9 F
mdavis@uwa.edu
DAVIS, Mark .... 205-652-3570...... 9 F
mdavis@uwa.edu
DAVIS, Mark, L .... 515-964-0601.. 172 F
davism@faith.edu
DAVIS, Marsha .... 845-758-7433.. 304 F
davis@bard.edu
DAVIS, Marty .... 678-839-6614.. 129 E
gdavis@westga.edu
DAVIS, Marty .... 304-865-6033.. 511 C
marty.davis@ovu.edu
DAVIS, Mary .... 212-217-4300.. 314 B
mary_davis@fitnyc.edu
DAVIS, Mary .... 828-298-3325.. 359 F
mdavis@warren-wilson.edu
DAVIS, Matt .... 505-984-6000.. 301 I
DAVIS, Matthew .... 402-557-7232.. 278 I
matthew.davis@bellevue.edu
DAVIS, Matthew .... 920-206-2310.. 517 G
matthew.davis@mbu.edu
DAVIS, Matthew, D .... 812-877-8421.. 166 H
matthew.davis@rose-hulman.edu
DAVIS, Maureen .... 760-252-2411.... 28 B
mdavis3@barstow.edu
DAVIS, Meadow .... 207-725-3037.. 202 F
mdavis1@bowdoin.edu
DAVIS, Megan .... 478-757-3803.. 129 L
mdavis@wesleyancollege.edu
DAVIS, Megan, W .... 603-862-3894.. 288 C
megan.davis@unh.edu
DAVIS, Melissa .... 281-873-0262.. 455 B
library@commonwealth.edu
DAVIS, Melvin .... 601-979-1400.. 258 D
melvin.davis@jsums.edu
DAVIS, Melvin, D .... 256-765-4821...... 9 C
mdavis2@una.edu
DAVIS, Michael .... 770-381-7200.. 123 A
DAVIS, Michael .... 770-859-9779.. 123 B
mdavis@medtech.edu
DAVIS, Michael .... 318-342-5171.. 201 E
mdavis@ulm.edu
DAVIS, Michael .... 617-373-2121.. 227 B
DAVIS, Michele .... 770-394-8300.. 116 F
mrdavis@aii.edu
DAVIS, Michelle .... 404-527-7793.. 123 I
lmdavis@atc.edu
DAVIS, Michelle .... 781-292-2251.. 218 H
michelle.davis@olin.edu
DAVIS, Michelle .... 701-228-5670.. 361 D
michelle.r.davis@dakotacollege.edu
DAVIS, Michelle .... 434-544-8229.. 491 F
davis@lynchburg.edu
DAVIS, Mike .... 303-360-4754.... 79 E
mike.davis@ccaurora.edu
DAVIS, Mike .... 386-752-1822.. 100 L
mike.davis@fgc.edu
DAVIS, Mike .... 580-745-2392.. 387 M
mdavis@se.edu
DAVIS, Mike .... 215-489-2931.. 402 A
michael.davis@delval.edu
DAVIS, Miles .... 540-545-7253.. 494 B
mdavis3@su.edu
DAVIS, Mitch .... 970-247-7010.... 80 D
davis_m@fortlewis.edu
DAVIS, Mitch .... 251-442-2334...... 9 A
mdavis@umobile.edu
DAVIS, Mitchel, W .... 207-725-3930.. 202 F
mwdavis@bowdoin.edu
DAVIS, Myron .... 740-753-7020.. 369 K
davism@hocking.edu
DAVIS, Nan, M .... 903-813-3000.. 451 M
ndavis@austincollege.edu
DAVIS, Nancy .... 619-644-7000.... 45 J
nancy.davis@gcccd.edu
DAVIS, Natalie .... 601-643-8354.. 257 D
natalie.davis@colin.edu
DAVIS, Nelson .... 434-947-8315.. 493 B
ndavis@randolphcollege.edu
DAVIS, Nicole .... 262-650-4921.. 515 J
nluckett@carrollu.edu
DAVIS, Nolan .... 252-335-3271.. 356 D
dgbranch@ecsu.edu
DAVIS, Pam .... 772-546-5534.. 102 S
admissions@hsbc.edu
DAVIS, Pamela .... 919-760-8360.. 346 D
davisp@meredith.edu
DAVIS, Pamela, B .... 216-368-2825.. 365 B
pamela.davis@case.edu
DAVIS, Patricia .... 207-780-5911.. 205 E
patdavis@maine.edu
DAVIS, Patricia .... 972-860-8180.. 456 C
pdavis@dcccd.edu
DAVIS, Patricia .... 970-860-8180.. 456 C
pdavis@dcccd.edu
DAVIS, Patricia, A .... 251-380-3063...... 7 D
pdavis@shc.edu
DAVIS, Patti .... 410-386-8066.. 206 I
pdavis@carrollcc.edu
DAVIS, Paul .... 641-784-5138.. 172 G
padavis@graceland.edu
DAVIS, Paul .... 641-784-5422.. 172 G
pjdavis@graceland.edu
DAVIS, Paul .... 936-468-1111.. 466 H
pdavis@sfasu.edu
DAVIS, Paul, R .... 530-226-4719.... 64 H
pdavis@simpsonu.edu
DAVIS, Paula .... 419-372-9464.. 364 E
pmdavis@bgsu.edu
DAVIS, Paula .... 609-343-5091.. 288 H
pdavis@atlantic.edu
DAVIS, Peggy .... 804-524-5030.. 499 G
pdavis@vsu.edu
DAVIS, Pete, D .... 608-342-1155.. 521 A
davisp@uwplatt.edu
DAVIS, Rachelle .... 301-387-3044.. 207 G
rachelle.davis@garrettcollege.edu
DAVIS, Raeanne .... 212-237-8604.. 308 E
radavis@jjay.cuny.edu
DAVIS, Ralph, U .... 843-661-1110.. 430 B
rdavis@fmarion.edu
DAVIS, Rance .... 315-229-5551.. 329 D
rdavis@stlawu.edu
DAVIS, Randy .... 502-213-2122.. 190 A
randall.davis@kctcs.edu
DAVIS, Ray, J .... 410-651-6083.. 212 B
rjdavis@umes.edu
DAVIS, Rebecca, F .... 512-637-1949.. 464 G
rebeccad@stedwards.edu
DAVIS, Renee .... 334-386-7230...... 3 I
rdavis@faulkner.edu
DAVIS, Richard .... 863-667-5310.. 109 L
rbdavis@seu.edu
DAVIS, Richard .... 317-931-2391.. 160 B
ddavis@cts.edu
DAVIS, Richard, K .... 312-942-6909.. 153 B
richard_k_davis@rush.edu
DAVIS, Rick .... 850-973-9492.. 105 H
davisr@nfcc.edu
DAVIS, Rick .... 617-373-2134.. 227 B
DAVIS, Rick .... 703-993-8624.. 490 B
rdavi4@gmu.edu
DAVIS, Robert, H .... 303-492-7006.... 83 K
robert.davis@colorado.edu
DAVIS, JR., Robert, W .... 570-941-7500.. 422 B
robert.davis@scranton.edu
DAVIS, Roger .... 615-966-7161.. 441 F
roger.davis@lipscomb.edu
DAVIS, Roger, W .... 724-480-3471.. 401 F
roger.davis@ccbc.edu
DAVIS, Ronnie .... 919-530-7298.. 357 A
rdavis82@nccu.edu
DAVIS, Ryan .... 425-388-9212.. 503 F
rydavis@everettcc.edu
DAVIS, Sandie .... 706-295-6339.. 121 C
sdavis@highlands.edu
DAVIS, Sandra, S .... 803-535-1218.. 431 I
davisss@octech.edu
DAVIS, Shane .... 318-487-7305.. 195 F
shane.davis@lacollege.edu
DAVIS, Shannon .... 901-321-3545.. 439 E
0478mgr@follett.com
DAVIS, Shaqualyn .... 229-732-5932.. 116 C
shaqualyndavis@andrewcollege.edu
DAVIS, Shara .... 440-365-5222.. 371 H
DAVIS, Sharon .... 513-569-1475.. 366 D
sharon.davis@cincinnatistate.edu
DAVIS, Sharon .... 214-860-8705.. 456 F
sdavis1@dcccd.edu
DAVIS, Sharon .... 254-526-1346.. 454 A
sharon.davis@ctcd.edu
DAVIS, Shelly .... 207-893-7726.. 204 D
sdavis@sjcme.edu
DAVIS, Sherri .... 205-929-6357...... 5 D
sdavis@lawsonstate.edu
DAVIS, Sherri .... 828-254-1921.. 347 D
sherrijdavis@abtech.edu
DAVIS, Sherry .... 254-659-7818.. 458 K
sdavis@hillcollege.edu
DAVIS, Sherry .... 540-785-5440.. 496 A
sherrydavis@vbc.edu
DAVIS, Staci .... 765-285-5753.. 159 B
sldavis@bsu.edu
DAVIS, Stan .... 205-726-2366...... 6 E
csdavis@samford.edu

DAVIS, Stefan, S 317-274-8828 163 D ssdavis@iupui.edu
DAVIS, Stephanie 517-787-0800 235 G davisstephand@jccmi.edu
DAVIS, Steven 707-638-5270 68 C steven.davis@tu.edu
DAVIS, Steven, J 208-496-3305 132 J daviss@byui.edu
DAVIS, Stewart 256-549-8603 3 M sdavis@gadsdenstate.edu
DAVIS, Stormy, M 417-268-1000 262 F daviss@evangel.edu
DAVIS, Sue 225-768-1802 199 B sue.davis@ololcollege.edu
DAVIS, Sue, E 330-941-2000 382 A sedavis@ysu.edu
DAVIS, Sue, F 740-587-6667 368 B davissf@denison.edu
DAVIS, Suzanne 618-664-7004 140 I suzanne.davis@greenville.edu
DAVIS, Suzanne, E 315-268-6493 310 B sdavis@clarkson.edu
DAVIS, Tabitha 800-955-2527 181 D tdavis40@grantham.edu
DAVIS, Tamika 860-255-3510 87 E tdavis@txcc.commnet.edu
DAVIS, Tammy 325-574-7695 479 I tdavis@wtc.edu
DAVIS, Teresa 336-433-5570 356 F tmdavis4@ncat.edu
DAVIS, Theresa 657-278-7642 33 A thdavis@fullerton.edu
DAVIS, Theresa, A 626-395-4638 30 H theresa.davis@caltech.edu
DAVIS, Thom 661-654-2287 32 A tdavis31@csub.edu
DAVIS, Thomas 803-705-4687 427 D davist@benedict.edu
DAVIS, Thomas, J 317-274-8448 163 D iock100@iupui.edu
DAVIS, Tina 859-622-3876 188 F tina.davis@eku.edu
DAVIS, Tom 334-670-3981 7 H tomdavis@troy.edu
DAVIS, Tommye Lou 254-710-3750 452 H tommye_lou_davis@baylor.edu
DAVIS, Traci 309-796-5408 135 I davist@bhc.edu
DAVIS, Tracy 415-371-0002 55 D
DAVIS, Twyla 910-879-5516 347 F tdavis@bladencc.edu
DAVIS, Tyler 843-863-7523 427 I tdavis@csuniv.edu
DAVIS, Tyler 843-574-5505 427 I tdavis@csuniv.edu
DAVIS, Wain 618-393-2982 142 B davisw@iecc.edu
DAVIS, Wayne 865-974-5321 448 E wtdavis@utk.edu
DAVIS, Wayne 757-825-3513 498 G davisw@tncc.edu
DAVIS, Wendy 520-515-3623 12 L davisd@cochise.edu
DAVIS, Wendy 501-812-2273 21 H wdavis@pulaskitech.edu
DAVIS, Wesley 701-477-7862 362 D wdavis1@tm.edu
DAVIS, Wesley 701-477-7853 362 D wdavis1@tm.edu
DAVIS, Whitney 478-757-5170 129 L wdavis@wesleyancollege.edu
DAVIS, William 708-534-4105 140 H wdavis3@govst.edu
DAVIS, William 610-359-6500 401 L wdavis@dccc.edu
DAVIS, Zabe 662-562-3308 260 C
DAVIS-BLAKE, Alison 734-764-1363 241 J alisondb@umich.edu
DAVIS-DUKES, Janet 973-720-3096 298 G davisdukesj@wpunj.edu
DAVIS-EYENE, Mishawn 508-854-4576 224 E meyene@qcc.mass.edu
DAVIS-FREEMAN, Juana 803-934-3464 431 E jdavis@morris.edu
DAVIS FREEMAN, Louisa, M 413-755-4333 224 G ldavisfreeman@stcc.edu
DAVIS-JACKSON, Latacha 662-254-3579 260 A latacha.davis@mvsu.edu
DAVIS-JOHNSON, Max 208-426-3033 132 I maxdavisjohnson@boisestate.edu
DAVIS-JONES, Andrea 601-979-2245 258 D andrea.e.davis@jsums.edu
DAVIS JONES, Chrissy 509-533-3743 503 A chrissy.davis@sfcc.spokane.edu
DAVIS LITTLE, Shay 330-672-4050 370 I sdlittle@kent.edu
DAVIS-OCHI, Megan 219-989-2056 166 F megan.davis-ochi@pnw.edu
DAVIS-SAMUELS, Ivanetta 615-327-6141 442 A isamuel@mmc.edu
DAVIS-VAN ATTA, David 845-437-5276 339 C ddavisa@vassar.edu
DAVIS-VAN ATTA, David 845-437-5491 339 C ddavisva@vassar.edu
DAVISON, Colette 312-893-7173 140 D cdavison@erikson.edu
DAVISON, Don 513-721-7944 369 D ddavison@gbs.edu
DAVISON, Dorothy 718-420-4221 339 F ddavison@wagner.edu
DAVISON, Frieda, M 864-503-5610 434 G fdavison@uscupstate.edu
DAVISON, Ian, R 989-774-1870 232 D davis1ir@cmich.edu
DAVISON, Kimberly, K 972-985-3781 455 A kdavison@collin.edu
DAVISON, Michael, R 801-524-1991 480 J mrdavison@ldsbc.edu
DAVISON, Ruth, L 850-474-2463 113 A rdavison@uwf.edu
DAVISSON, Thomas, F 502-451-0815 193 A tdavisson@sullivan.edu
DAVISSON, Thomas, F 502-451-0815 193 B tdavisson@sullivan.edu
DAVITT, Jeffrey 904-819-6489 99 M jdavitt@flagler.edu
DAVITZ, Jeremy 614-875-1777 374 G jdavitz@bowshierdavitzlaw.com
DAVOLT, David 208-376-7731 132 H ddavolt@boisebible.edu
DAVOUD, Mohammad 912-478-7412 122 B mdavoud@georgiasouthern.edu
DAVROS, Harry 214-637-3530 479 C hdavros@wadecollege.edu
DAVY, Catherine, A 313-593-5030 242 A kdavy@umich.edu
DAW, Meredith 773-702-7040 156 D daw@uchicago.edu
DAW, Michael 415-442-6682 45 B mdaw@ggu.edu
DAWE, Lloyd, A 803-641-3338 433 G lloydd@usca.edu
DAWE, Richard, L 870-368-2006 21 F rdawe@ozarka.edu
DAWES, Arlene 406-638-3116 276 G dawesa@lbhc.edu
DAWES, Daniel 404-752-1833 125 A ddawes@msm.edu
DAWES, Douglas 209-667-3077 34 E ddawes@csustan.edu
DAWES, Stephen 864-294-3031 430 C steve.dawes@furman.edu
DAWKINS, E. Janyce 706-542-7912 128 E edawkins@uga.edu
DAWKINS, Lisa 304-357-4374 511 E lisadawkins@ucwv.edu
DAWKINS, Mark 904-620-2590 112 B mark.dawkins@unf.edu
DAWKINS, Norman 212-431-2142 323 H norman.dawkins@nyls.edu
DAWKINS, Phyllis 336-517-2154 342 B phyllis.dawkins@bennett.edu
DAWKINS, Rita 704-330-6862 348 E rita.dawkins@cpcc.edu
DAWKINS, Tom 213-763-7361 50 C dawkintl@lattc.edu
DAWKINS-FALTER, Amelia 256-551-3136 4 F amy.falter@drakestate.edu
DAWLEY, Anna Marie 315-268-6475 310 B adawley@clarkson.edu
DAWLEY, Lisa 310-954-4000 53 B ldawley@msmu.edu
DAWN-FISHER, Lisa 360-867-6185 503 G dawnl@evergreen.edu
DAWSEY, Tim 620-235-4365 184 C tdawsey@pittstate.edu
DAWSON, Allison, M 903-813-2192 451 M amdawson@austincollege.edu
DAWSON, B. James 423-869-6391 441 E james.dawson@lmunet.edu
DAWSON, Brandon, T 607-735-1816 313 F bdawson@elmira.edu
DAWSON, Brian 325-670-1253 458 J brian.r.dawson@hsutx.edu
DAWSON, Bridgette 304-336-8215 513 F bdawson@westliberty.edu
DAWSON, Darren, M 785-532-5590 182 D dmdawson@ksu.edu
DAWSON, Dave 479-575-5451 22 I daved@uark.edu
DAWSON, Frank 310-434-4585 63 F dawson_frank@smc.edu
DAWSON, Imara 765-285-5422 159 B ivdawson@bsu.edu
DAWSON, J. Lin 404-880-8123 118 K jldawson@cau.edu
DAWSON, Jim, T 615-353-3275 446 E jim.dawson@nscc.edu
DAWSON, John David 765-983-1211 160 G prexy@earlham.edu
DAWSON, Keith 574-520-4480 163 E khdawson@iusb.edu
DAWSON, L. Wayde 864-488-4522 430 H ldawson@limestone.edu
DAWSON, Patrick 410-455-2356 211 G pdawson@umbc.edu
DAWSON, Randall 210-486-2597 450 E rdawson@alamo.edu
DAWSON, Renita 919-735-5151 354 A rddawson@waynecc.edu
DAWSON, Royal 312-369-7514 138 F rdawson@colum.edu
DAWSON, Scott 805-756-2705 31 I scdawson@calpoly.edu
DAWSON, Teresa, U 256-765-4328 9 C tdawson2@una.edu
DAWSON, JR., Thomas, E 410-951-3792 212 E thdawson@coppin.edu
DAWSON, Timothy 717-901-5158 405 H tdawson@harrisburgu.edu
DAWSON, Yolanda 818-401-1041 40 G ydawson@columbiacollege.edu
DAWTON, Dennis 215-965-4073 411 A academic@moore.edu
DAY, Alexandra 212-799-5000 318 A
DAY, Barton 953-923-3201 470 F bart.day@tstc.edu
DAY, Dani, R 972-758-3804 455 A dday@collin.edu
DAY, Daniel, A 609-258-6108 294 D dday@princeton.edu
DAY, David 412-536-1070 406 K david.day@laroche.edu
DAY, Don 817-274-4284 452 I dday@bhcarroll.edu
DAY, Elaine 434-791-5696 487 C eday@averett.edu
DAY, Ian 508-999-8042 220 H iday@umassd.edu
DAY, John, R 404-413-2564 122 D jday@gsu.edu
DAY, Lawrence 315-792-3099 339 B lday@utica.edu
DAY, Leo 817-923-1921 466 E lday@swbts.edu
DAY, Marc 212-749-2802 319 M mday@msmnyc.edu
DAY, Mellani, J 303-963-3434 77 I mday@ccu.edu
DAY, Michael 812-941-2244 163 F micaday@ius.edu
DAY, Mitzi 231-591-3800 233 L mitziday@ferris.edu
DAY, Patricia 518-828-4181 311 D day@sunycgcc.edu
DAY, Patrick 209-946-2365 71 C pday@pacific.edu
DAY, Rebeckah, J 210-436-3727 464 H rday@stmarytx.edu
DAY, Rondall, H 470-578-6074 123 J rday9@kennesaw.edu
DAY, Terry 570-662-4000 415 E
DAY, Thelma 323-953-4000 49 H dayt@lacitycollege.edu
DAY, Valerie, I 865-471-3459 439 C vday@cn.edu
DAY-PERROOTS, Susan, D 304-293-3733 514 C sue.day-perroots@mail.wvu.edu
DAYHOFF, Brenda 301-846-2481 207 F bdayhoff@frederick.edu
DAYHOFF, Sharon, S 717-337-6276 404 C sdayhoff@gettysburg.edu
DAYLEY, Newell 801-863-7359 482 C newell.dayley@uvu.edu
DAYMON, Cynthia 215-368-5000 398 C cdaymon@biblical.edu
DAYNES, Gary 252-399-6343 341 P gdaynes@barton.edu
DAYOUB, Missy, H 770-720-5522 126 C mhd1@reinhardt.edu
DAYTON, Kay 615-230-3675 447 C kay.dayton@volstate.edu
DAYTON, Lynne 334-222-6591 5 F ldayton@lbwcc.edu
DAYTON-JOHNSON, Jeffrey 831-647-4647 484 F jdaytonjohnson@miis.edu
DE ANGELIS, John 212-678-3012 337 E deangelis@tc.edu
DE ANGULO, Bonnie 305-223-4561 108 A deangulo@sjvcs.edu
DE BAEZ SNYDER, Tracey 724-830-1125 419 D snyderdebaez@setonhill.edu
DE BARROS, Khym Isaac 508-767-7274 214 F ki.debarros@assumption.edu
DE BERRY, Ron 757-826-1883 487 E president@bcva.edu
DE BOER, David 616-451-3511 233 C ddeboer@davenport.edu
DE BONO, Chad 719-336-1517 81 D chad.debono@lamarcc.edu
DE BOTTON, Leonard 973-278-5400 305 B len@berkeleycollege.edu
DE BOTTON, Leonard 973-278-5400 289 F en@berkeleycollege.edu
DE CHANT, Richard 216-987-3193 367 E richard.dechant@tri-c.edu
DE DIOS, Paul 714-484-7335 54 G pdedios@cypresscollege.edu
DE DIOS UNANUE, Teresa 787-720-0596 531 A
DE FATIMA LIMA, Maria 615-327-6533 442 A mflima@mmc.edu
DE FAZIO, Alice 201-200-3317 293 C adefazio@njcu.edu
DE FILIPPIS, Daisy Cocco 203-575-8044 86 G ddefilippis@nv.edu
DE FINA, Allan 201-200-2101 293 C adefina@njcu.edu
DE FREITAS, Lisa, H 864-597-4203 435 C defreitaslh@wofford.edu
DE FRIES, Carol 215-496-6122 401 G cdefries@ccp.edu
DE GROAT, Arthur, S 785-532-0369 182 D degroata@ksu.edu
DE GUZMAN, Maria, I 787-257-7373 535 P ac_mguzman@suagm.edu
DE HARO, Oscar 707-256-7360 53 H odeharo@napavalley.edu
DE JESUS, Angela 787-864-2222 534 A angela.dejesus@guayama.inter.edu
DE JESUS, Eigna 787-257-7373 535 P eidejesus@suagm.edu
DE JESUS, Ramon 787-878-5475 533 H rdjesus@arecibo.inter.edu
DE JESUS, Victoria 787-751-0178 535 N ac_vdejesus@suagm.edu
DE JESÚS, Marcos 787-993-8953 537 G marcos.dejesus@upr.edu
DE JONG, Jinny 616-957-6046 232 B jinnydejong@calvinseminary.edu
DE JONG, Sven 304-829-7281 510 G sdejong@bethanywv.edu
DE KLUYVER, Cornelis, A 541-346-3843 395 G kees@uoregon.edu
DE KOKAL, Parrilla 801-626-8049 482 D mdekokal@weber.edu
DE LA CAMARA, Maria 630-829-6240 135 F mdelacamara@ben.edu
DE LA CERDA, Paul 323-267-3724 49 G delacep@elac.edu
DE LA FUENTE, Luciana 305-629-2929 108 G ldelafuente@sanignaciocollege.edu
DE LA GARZA, Marco 818-947-2324 50 D delagamj@lavc.edu
DE LA GARZA, Ricardo 956-872-3714 465 H rickdlg@southtexascollege.edu
DE LA GUARDIA, Teresa, S 305-284-2928 114 H tdelaguardia@miami.edu
DE LA ROSA, Carlos 202-806-2940 93 A carlos.delarosa@howard.edu
DE LA ROSA, Leticia 210-486-3000 450 D
DE LA ROSSA, Arnie 860-215-9236 87 D adelarossa@trcc.commnet.edu
DE LA TORRE, Jorge 425-640-1233 503 E jorge.delatorre@edcc.edu
DE LA TORRE, Susana 510-436-2598 57 E sdelatorre@peralta.edu
DE LA TORRE-BURMEISTER, Rosa 575-528-7009 301 C rosadela@nmsu.edu
DE LA VEGA, Kristina 818-677-2118 34 A kristina.delavega@csun.edu
DE LACEY, Lora 630-844-5510 135 E ldelacey@aurora.edu
DE LATORRE, Adela, I 530-752-2613 69 A vcstudentaffairs@ucdavis.edu
DE LEÓN, Beatriz 787-743-3038 535 L bdeleon@sanjuanbautista.edu
DE LEON, Daniel 956-872-5558 465 H ddeleon@southtexascollege.edu
DE LEON, Josephine 505-277-2611 302 F jdeleon@unm.edu
DE LEON, Lee 325-674-2353 449 J ldeleon5@acu.edu
DE LEONARDIS, David, J 614-885-5585 376 G ddeleon@pcj.edu
DE LONG, Linda 909-593-3511 71 B ldelong@laverne.edu

DECKER, John .... 417-268-6002.. 262 H
jdecker@gobbc.edu
DECKER, Kim .... 334-244-3255...... 2 A
kdecker@aum.edu
DECKER, Lisa .... 914-337-9300.. 311 F
lisa.decker@concordia-ny.edu
DECKER, Matthew, E .... 814-863-3746.. 412 F
med37@psu.edu
DECKER, Nancy .... 724-983-0700.. 408 E
ndecker@laurel.edu
DECKER, Nancy, M .... 724-439-4900.. 408 D
ndecker@laurel.edu
DECKER, Randy .... 903-586-2518.. 460 A
rdecker@jacksonville-college.edu
DECKER, Stephanie .... 973-684-6868.. 294 A
sdecker@pccc.edu
DECKER, Steven .... 715-468-2815.. 525 A
steven.decker@witc.edu
DECKER, Susan .... 812-535-5138.. 166 K
sdecker@smwc.edu
DECKER, Timothy .... 845-298-0755.. 312 G
tdecker@sunydutchess.edu
DECKER, William, C .... 501-569-3302.... 23 B
wcdecker@ualr.edu
DECKERT, Glenn .... 978-867-4736.. 219 A
glenn.deckert@gordon.edu
DECKINGA, Mike .... 219-864-2400.. 165 Q
mdeckinga@midamerica.edu
DECLEENE, Catherine .... 317-738-8090.. 160 J
cdecleene@franklincollege.edu
DECMAN, Mike .... 815-740-3427.. 157 F
mdecman@stfrancis.edu
DECOCINIS, Anthony .... 215-972-2007.. 413 L
adecocinis@pafa.edu
DECOCK, Murray .... 315-228-7489.. 310 G
mdecock@colgate.edu
DECONCILLIS, Pat .... 724-222-5330.. 412 E
pdeconcillis@penncommercial.edu
DECONINCK, Lori .... 603-668-2211.. 287 I
l.deconinck@snhu.edu
DECONNO, David .... 518-580-5719.. 330 F
ddeconno@skidmore.edu
DECOOKE, Peggy .... 914-251-6485.. 334 C
peggy.decooke@purchase.edu
DECORDOVA, Endia .... 860-512-2907.... 86 E
edecordova@manchestercc.edu
DECOSTA, Jean .... 805-756-5198.... 31 I
jdecosta@calpoly.edu
DECOSTER, Daisy .... 201-761-6465.. 296 K
ddecoster@saintpeters.edu
DECOTEAU, Katina .... 701-255-3285.. 362 E
kdecoteau@uttc.edu
DECOURSEY, Paul, A .... 515-574-1055.. 173 F
decoursey@iowacentral.edu
DECOUTEAU, Jolene .... 701-255-3285.. 362 E
jolene.decouteau@uttc.edu
DECRISTO, James .... 336-734-2862.. 358 E
decristoj@uncsa.edu
DECRISTOFORO,
Joesph, R .... 210-458-7070.. 477 A
joe.decristoforo@utsa.edu
DECUIR, Anthony .... 504-865-3039.. 198 E
decuir@loyno.edu
DECUIR, Bobbie .... 337-482-1000.. 201 D
bobbie@louisiana.edu
DEDDO, Gary .... 626-650-2306.... 45 E
DEDEAUX, Vanessa .... 601-928-6230.. 259 C
vanessa.dedeaux@mgccc.edu
DEDEO, Patrick .... 973-720-2224.. 298 G
dedeop@wpunj.edu
DEDIEMAR, Jeanette .... 317-788-3298.. 168 A
dediemarj@uindy.edu
DEDOMINICI, Peter .... 540-374-4300.... 93 F
DEDONATO, Joy .... 516-572-7943.. 322 C
joy.dedonato@ncc.edu
DEDWYLER, Jason .... 601-477-4075.. 258 E
jason.dedwyler@jcjc.edu
DEE, Edward .... 718-779-1499.. 326 D
edee@plazacollege.edu
DEE, Kay, C .... 812-877-8502.. 166 H
dee@rose-hulman.edu
DEE, Shawn, G .... 336-334-4822.. 350 B
sgdee@gtcc.edu
DEE, Tina .... 231-777-0660.. 238 G
tina.dee@muskegoncc.edu
DEEB, Bassam, M .... 716-826-1200.. 338 E
deebb@trocaire.edu
DEEB, Tiffni .... 612-659-6600.. 250 B
tiffni.deeb@minneapolis.edu
DEEDRICK, Gary, A .... 864-242-5100.. 427 E
DEEDS, Cher .... 330-684-8952.. 378 H
cher@uakron.edu
DEEDS, Sarene .... 417-873-7869.. 264 H
sdeeds@drury.edu
DEEDS, William, C .... 712-274-5103.. 175 C
deeds@morningside.edu
DEEGAN, Robert .... 619-421-6700.... 66 E
DEEGEN, Lynn .... 601-928-6212.. 259 C
lynn.deegen@mgccc.edu
DEEHR, Marylouise .... 440-449-4202.. 380 F
mdeehr@ursuline.edu
DEEK, Fadi, P .... 973-596-3220.. 293 D
fadi.deek@njit.edu
DEEL, Connie .... 785-594-8362.. 178 D
connie.deel@bakeru.edu
DEEL, Michael .... 276-498-5237.. 486 M
mdeel@acp.edu
DEEL, Susan, M .... 989-463-7176.. 230 F
deel@alma.edu
DEELY, Janet .... 630-829-6046.. 135 F
jdeely@ben.edu
DEEM, Marie .... 412-536-1128.. 406 K
marie.deem@laroche.edu
DEEN, Michael .... 903-813-2306.. 451 M
mdeen@austincollege.edu
DEEN, Robert .... 720-279-8990.... 80 I
bdeen@csl.org
DEEN, Stella .... 845-257-3280.. 331 E
provost@newpaltz.edu
DEER, Joe, W .... 308-635-6145.. 283 D
deerj234@wncc.edu
DEER, Susan .... 845-574-4280.. 327 G
sdeer@sunyrockland.edu
DEES, Charles .... 973-596-8293.. 293 D
charles.dees@njit.edu
DEES, Margaret .... 904-256-7885.. 103 D
mdees@ju.edu
DEES-BURNETT,
Keichanda .... 816-235-5628.. 273 F
deesk@umkc.edu
DEESE, Phyllis .... 903-823-3355.. 467 C
phyllis.deese@texarkanacollege.edu
DEESE, Todd .... 704-403-3218.. 342 E
todd.deese@carolinashealthcare.org
DEESS, Eugene, P .... 973-596-3110.. 293 D
deess@njit.edu
DEETER, Daniel, P .... 864-597-4232.. 435 C
deeterdp@wofford.edu
DEETZ, Kristi, R .... 812-888-4141.. 169 A
kdeetz@vinu.edu
DEFALCO, Ron, E .... 713-718-7586.. 459 B
ron.defalco@hccs.edu
DEFATTA, Jerry .... 601-266-5013.. 261 E
jerry.defatta@usm.edu
DEFAUW, Nikki, J .... 563-333-6345.. 176 D
defauwnikkij@sau.edu
DEFAZIO, Jeannie .... 330-490-7332.. 380 J
jdefazio@walsh.edu
DEFEDE, Kathryn .... 559-925-3145.... 74 C
kathryndefede@whccd.edu
DEFEIS, Evelyn .... 973-684-5900.. 294 A
edefeis@pccc.edu
DEFELICE, Robert .... 781-891-2256.. 215 F
rdefelice@bentley.edu
DEFELICE, Stacey .... 516-876-3009.. 333 C
defelices@oldwestbury.edu
DEFEO, Gregory .... 412-809-5100.. 417 D
defeo.greg@pti.edu
DEFFENBACHER, Mark ..... 559-453-2239.... 44 F
mark.deffenbacher@fresno.edu
DEFFENBAUGH,
Cynthia, B .... 804-289-8438.. 495 G
cdeffenb@richmond.edu
DEFLORIO, Melody .... 802-831-1037.. 485 F
mdeflorio@vermontlaw.edu
DEFOOR, Keith .... 706-379-3111.. 130 B
kdefoor@yhc.edu
DEFORD, Vicki .... 651-201-1664.. 248 I
victoria.deford@so.mnscu.edu
DEFORE, Jody .... 678-359-5990.. 122 E
jody@gordonstate.edu
DEFORE, Matt .... 205-726-4021...... 6 E
mdefore@samford.edu
DEFOREST, Kristin, A .... 607-746-4590.. 335 C
deforeka@delhi.edu
DEFRANCIS, Robert .... 304-214-8820.. 512 F
rdefrancis@wvncc.edu
DEFRANCO, Jeff .... 530-541-4660.... 48 D
defranco@ltcc.edu
DEFRATES, Bruce .... 509-359-6329.. 503 D
bdefrates@ewu.edu
DEFREECE, Michele, T ...... 607-746-4652.. 335 C
defreemt@delhi.edu
DEFREITAS, Jack .... 660-263-3900.. 263 A
jackdefreitas@cccb.edu
DEFRIES, Robert .... 320-762-4637.. 248 J
bobd@alextech.edu
DEGAIN, Sabrina .... 336-506-4161.. 347 C
sabrina.degain@alamancecc.edu
DEGAISH, Ann .... 361-825-2612.. 468 E
ann.degaish@tamucc.edu
DEGARMO, David .... 417-862-9533.. 265 D
ddegarmo@globaluniversity.edu
DEGARMO, Kristin .... 417-862-9533.. 265 D
kdegarmo@globaluniversity.edu
DEGAZON, Karen .... 212-938-5654.. 334 F
kdegazon@sunyopt.edu
DEGEARE, Christopher ...... 636-481-3467.. 266 C
cdegear1@jeffco.edu
DEGENHARDT, Brian .... 660-626-2397.. 262 A
bdegenhardt@atsu.edu
DEGENHART,
Mary Louise .... 314-367-8700.. 271 E
mary.degenhart@stlcop.edu
DEGEORGE, Christine, C . 941-359-7645.. 107 M
ccarnegi@ringling.edu
DEGEORGE, Steven .... 812-749-1399.. 166 B
sdegeorge@oak.edu
DEGER, Coquina, L .... 425-602-3006.. 501 D
cdeger@bastyr.edu
DEGERMAN, Roger .... 336-316-2123.. 344 H
degermanre@guilford.edu
DEGEUS, Marilyn, J .... 816-654-7262.. 266 E
mdegeus@kcumb.edu
DEGIACINTO, Jennifer ...... 808-455-0595.. 132 C
jdigiaci@hawaii.edu
DEGIOIA, John (Jack), J . 202-687-4134.... 92 E
president@georgetown.edu
DEGIOVANNI, Kim .... 301-387-3040.. 207 G
kim.degiovanni@garrettcollege.edu
DEGN, Jason .... 479-619-4337.... 21 D
jdegn@nwacc.edu
DEGNER, Katie .... 352-671-3391.. 108 C
katie.degner@saintleo.edu
DEGRAAF, Donald .... 616-526-6225.. 232 A
ddegraaf@calvin.edu
DEGRAFFENREID,
Pamela .... 828-227-7346.. 359 A
degraffen@wcu.edu
DEGRANGE, Karen, A .... 812-877-8285.. 166 H
karen.degrange@rose-hulman.edu
DEGRAW, Heather .... 425-739-8200.. 504 F
heather.degraw@lwtech.edu
DEGRAW, Julie .... 419-358-3248.. 364 D
degrawj@bluffton.edu
DEGRAW, Spencer .... 801-524-1947.. 480 J
sdegraw2@ldsbc.edu
DEGROAT, Kevin .... 718-405-3400.. 310 H
kevin.degroat@mountsaintvincent.edu
DEGROFT, Michael .... 717-391-3510.. 420 C
degroft@stevenscollege.edu
DEGROOT, Bridget .... 906-786-5802.. 231 O
bridget.degroot@baycollege.edu
DEGUZMAN, Pedro .... 239-939-4766.. 109 M
pdeguzman@southerntech.edu
DEGWECK, Benjamin, J ..... 205-358-1452...... 3 B
ben.degweck@ecacolleges.com
DEHAEMERS, Jennifer ...... 816-235-1143.. 273 F
dehaemersj@umkc.edu
DEHART, Carrick .... 805-375-8919.... 32 B
carrick.dehart@csuci.edu
DEHART, Doris .... 323-226-4911.... 50 F
ddehart@dhs.lacounty.gov
DEHART, Jennifer .... 207-509-7100.. 204 F
jdehart@unity.edu
DEHART, Joe .... 515-964-6279.. 171 B
jcdehart@dmacc.edu
DEHAVEN, Barbara .... 201-216-8762.. 297 B
bdehaven@stevens.edu
DEHAY, Galen .... 864-646-2037.. 433 C
gdehay@tctc.edu
DEHAYES, Donald, H .... 401-874-4410.. 426 D
donald_dehayes@uri.edu
DEHDOUH-BERG, Audrey 719-384-6997.... 82 A
audrey.dehdouh-berg@ojc.edu
DEHEN, Regina .... 503-552-1966.. 392 H
rdehen@nunm.edu
DEHGHANI, Mo .... 201-216-8911.. 297 B
mo.dehghani@stevens.edu
DEHMER, Mackenzie .... 402-449-2882.. 280 C
mdehmer8729@graceu.edu
DEHN, Paula .... 270-852-3117.. 191 C
pdehn@kwc.edu
DEHORN, Thomas .... 574-239-8383.. 161 N
tdehorn@hcc-nd.edu
DEHOYOS, Diane, N .... 915-747-5601.. 476 D
dndehoyos@utep.edu
DEI, Michael .... 281-649-3406.. 458 L
mdei@hbu.edu
DEIBERT, Glenn .... 912-287-5827.. 119 B
gdeibert@coastalpines.edu
DEIBERT, Renee .... 706-754-7700.. 125 B
rdeibert@northgatech.edu
DEIBLER, Lauren, C .... 717-361-1164.. 403 C
deiblerl@etown.edu
DEICHEN, Michael, G .... 407-823-2094.. 111 E
michael.deichen@ucf.edu
DEIFELL, Hope .... 828-669-8012.. 346 M
hdeifell@montreat.edu
DEIGHTON, Joseph .... 314-889-1410.. 265 C
jdeighton@fontbonne.edu
DEIGNAN, Kathleen .... 609-258-5431.. 294 D
kdeignan@princeton.edu
DEIKE, Randall, C .... 215-895-2901.. 402 G
rcd58@drexel.edu
DEIKE, Terri .... 903-233-3769.. 460 J
terrideike@letu.edu
DEIMAN-THORNTON,
Ann .... 651-450-3753.. 249 F
adeiman@inverhills.edu
DEINNOCENTIIS, Maria .... 212-517-0482.. 320 C
mdeinnocentiis@mmm.edu
DEITCH, Elaine, C .... 610-861-1340.. 411 B
deitche@moravian.edu
DEITCH, Marissa .... 215-572-2972.. 397 G
deitchm@arcadia.edu
DEITCHMAN, Jay .... 518-629-7567.. 316 G
j.deitchman@hvcc.edu
DEITEMEYER, Kandi, W .... 252-335-0821.. 349 A
kdeitemeyer@albemarle.edu
DEITRICK, Becky .... 570-372-4015.. 419 H
deitrick@susqu.edu
DEITTE, William .... 914-337-9300.. 311 F
william.deitte@concordia-ny.edu
DEJAGER, Brad .... 218-751-8670.. 254 A
braddejager@oakhills.edu
DEJAYNES, Lana .... 660-596-7295.. 272 G
ldejaynes@sfccmo.edu
DEJESUS, Jorge .... 212-650-3165.. 308 D
jd1339@hunter.cuny.edu
DEJESUS, Marian .... 787-765-3560.. 532 I
mjesus@edpuniversity.edu
DEJESUS-AVILES, Desire . 212-924-5900.. 336 I
ddejesusaviles@swedishinstitute.edu
DEJESUS-RUEFF, Richard 585-385-8229.. 328 E
rdejesus-rueff@sjfc.edu
DEJOICE, Mary Jo .... 304-637-1359.. 510 I
dejoicem@dewv.edu
DEJONG, Carol .... 616-395-7760.. 235 F
cdejong@hope.edu
DEJONG, David, N .... 412-624-4228.. 421 G
dejong@pitt.edu
DEJONG, E. Shawn .... 413-755-4260.. 224 G
esdejong@stcc.edu
DEJOY, Jennifer .... 207-326-2256.. 204 C
jennifer.dejoy@mma.edu
DEJTHAI, Eddie .... 239-280-2507.... 95 Q
eddie.dejthai@avemaria.edu
DEKAN, Doug, D .... 715-833-6238.. 523 B
ddekan@cvtc.edu
DEKAY, Amy .... 716-880-2177.. 320 D
adekay@medaille.edu
DEKAY, Amy, M .... 716-880-2224.. 320 D
amy.marie.dekay@medaille.edu
DEKENESSEY, Stefania ...... 212-229-8947.. 322 E
dekeness@newschool.edu
DEKETELAERE, Vicki .... 517-483-1478.. 237 A
deketelv@lcc.edu
DEKEYSER, Georgia .... 907-786-4048.... 10 F
gkdekeyser@uaa.alaska.edu
DEKKER, Jan .... 559-638-0300.... 67 D
jan.dekker@reedleycollege.edu
DEKKER NETTLEMAN,
Mary .... 605-357-1309.. 437 A
med@usd.edu
DEKLOTZ, Steve .... 503-493-6286.. 391 A
sdeklotz@cu-portland.edu
DEKOVEN, Aram .... 860-444-8444.. 529 A
aram.dekoven@uscg.mil
DEKREY, Susan .... 845-437-7400.. 339 C
sudekrey@vassar.edu
DEKRUIF, Kimberly .... 909-469-5342.... 74 K
kdekruif@westernu.edu
DEL BALZO, Mary Beth .. 914-831-0343.. 311 C
mbdelbalzo@cw.edu
DEL BELLO, Wendy .... 281-756-3600.. 450 G
wdebello@alvincollege.edu
DEL BELLO, Wendy .... 281-756-3600.. 450 G
wdelbello@alvincollege.edu
DEL C. RODRIGUEZ,
Maria .... 787-727-1515.. 539 B
mrodriguez@sagrado.edu
DEL CASINO, Vincent, J . 520-621-6688.... 17 I
vdelcasino@email.arizona.edu
DEL CERRO, Gerardo .... 212-353-4321.. 311 G
cerro@cooper.edu
DEL CONTE, Christopher . 817-257-7710.. 469 G
c.delconte@tcu.edu
DEL GIUDICE, Michale .... 303-724-0731.... 84 A
michael.delguidice@ucdenver.edu
DEL GIUDICE, Tristan, S . 814-641-3390.. 406 F
delgiut@juniata.edu
DEL MONTE, Kathleen ...... 218-723-6184.. 245 J
kdelmonte@css.edu
DEL PILAR BONNIN OROZCO,
Maria .... 787-848-5739.. 536 C
DEL PINO KLOQUES,
David .... 409-772-8423.. 478 A
dadelpin@utmb.edu
DEL RIO, Esteban .... 619-260-7455.... 72 B
edelrio@sandiego.edu
DEL RIO-MORALES,
Ricardo .... 787-725-6500.. 531 C
consejoactivo@gmail.com
DEL ROSARIO, Dativa ...... 510-434-3891.... 57 E
ddelrosario@peralta.edu
DEL ROSARIO, Diana .... 216-987-5027.. 367 E
diana.del-rosario@tri-c.edu
DEL TONDO, Bruce .... 719-587-7227.... 76 G
bdeltond@adams.edu
DEL TORO, Debra .... 210-829-6001.. 474 D
ddeltoro@uiwtx.edu

DEMENT, Jennifer .... 503-491-7385.. 392 F
jennifer.dement@mhcc.edu
DEMENT, Marilyn .... 281-756-3517.. 450 G
mdement@alvincollege.edu
DEMENT, Paul .... 732-263-5679.. 292 F
pdement@monmouth.edu
DEMENT, Sarah .... 573-518-2129.. 268 E
sdement@mineralarea.edu
DEMEO, Victor .... 609-497-7706.. 294 C
victor.demeo@ptsem.edu
DEMERITT, Daniel .... 207-621-3065.. 204 G
dan.demeritt@maine.edu
DEMERRITT, Stan .... 806-291-3415.. 479 D
demerritt@wbu.edu
DEMERS, Ben .... 323-241-5401.... 50 B
demersbk@lasc.edu
DEMERS, David, M .... 716-878-3694.. 332 F
demersdm@buffalostate.edu
DEMERS, Paul .... 603-897-8537.. 287 F
pdemers@rivier.edu
DEMERS, Susan, S .... 727-791-2501.. 108 D
demers.susan@spcollege.edu
DEMERS, Suzanne .... 863-784-7041.. 109 G
suzanne.demers@southflorida.edu
DEMERSSEMAN, Anne ..... 308-432-6224.. 281 H
ademersseman@csc.edu
DEMETRIOU, Sophia .... 212-925-6625.. 307 E
sdemetriou@ccny.cuny.edu
DEMETROS, John .... 315-568-3213.. 323 A
jdemetros@nycc.edu
DEMEYER, Fay .... 541-485-1780.. 393 A
faydemeyer@newhope.edu
DEMEZZO, Robert, C .... 203-392-5886.... 85 H
demezzor1@southernct.edu
DEMICHAEL, Mark .... 765-677-2317.. 164 B
mark.demichael@indwes.edu
DEMING, Els .... 253-840-8401.. 506 B
edeming@pierce.ctc.edu
DEMISHKEVICH, Maya .... 410-386-8157.. 206 I
mdemishkevich@carrollcc.edu
DEMITSAS, Yiani .... 260-422-5561.. 162 B
jdemitsas@indianatech.edu
DEMKO, Amy .... 513-244-4408.. 373 C
amy.demko@msj.edu
DEMMINGS, Elizabeth ...... 765-658-4220.. 160 F
betsydemmings@depauw.edu
DEMMITT, Kevin .... 678-466-4802.. 119 A
kevindemmitt@clayton.edu
DEMO, Tina .... 860-509-9549.... 88 A
tdemo@hartsem.edu
DEMORY, Yolanda, F .... 757-446-8498.. 489 B
demoryyf@evms.edu
DEMOTT, Robin .... 309-341-5221.. 136 C
rdemott@sandburg.edu
DEMPSEY, Connie .... 570-961-4692.... 16 C
connie.dempsey@pennfoster.edu
DEMPSEY, Ellen, E .... 330-569-5340.. 369 J
dempseyee@hiram.edu
DEMPSEY, Greg .... 206-934-5201.. 507 A
greg.dempsey@seattlecolleges.edu
DEMPSEY, Jamie .... 909-593-3511.... 71 B
jdempsey@laverne.edu
DEMPSEY, John, R .... 910-695-3700.. 353 A
dempseyj@sandhills.edu
DEMPSEY, Lawrence, S ... 706-542-6167.. 128 E
dempsey@uga.edu
DEMPSEY, Michael .... 845-848-4058.. 312 F
michael.dempsey@dc.edu
DEMPSEY, Patricia .... 410-972-4511.. 210 D
patricia.dempsey@sjc.edu
DEMPSEY, Richard .... 972-883-2141.. 476 C
rmdempsey@utdallas.edu
DEMPSEY, Ron .... 816-415-5034.. 275 F
dempseyr@william.jewell.edu
DEMPSEY, Ron .... 507-457-5020.. 252 G
rdempsey@winona.edu
DEMPSEY, Stephanie, C .. 512-223-7736.. 451 N
diina@austincc.edu
DEMPSEY, Van, O .... 910-962-3354.. 358 D
dempseyv@uncw.edu
DEMPSTER, Douglas, J ... 512-471-9601.. 476 B
ddempster@austin.utexas.edu
DEMSETZ, Laura .... 650-574-6581.... 62 H
demsetz@smccd.edu
DEMUTH, Paul .... 651-423-8370.. 249 B
paul.demuth@dctc.edu
DEMYER, Craig .... 219-980-6937.. 163 B
cdemyer@iun.edu
DEN BOER, Marten, L ..... 312-362-8610.. 139 C
DENARD, Carolyn .... 478-445-2361.. 121 A
carolyn.denard@gcsu.edu
DENARD, Jeffrey, D .... 630-637-5142.. 149 H
jddenard@noctrl.edu
DENARD, Letitia, J .... 404-270-5143.. 128 A
ldenard@spelman.edu
DENARDIS, Nick .... 313-577-4540.. 243 F
ndenardis@wayne.edu
DENBESTE, Michelle .... 559-278-3013.... 32 F
mdenbeste@csufresno.edu
DENBOBA, Rahel .... 410-706-2133.. 211 F
rdenboba@umaryland.edu
DENBY, Eric, N .... 434-924-4019.. 495 H
end@virginia.edu
DENBY, Karlene .... 281-487-1170.. 469 F
kdenby@txchiro.edu
DENEAULT, Henry .... 781-239-5700.. 214 G
deneault@babson.edu
DENEEN, Mary, C .... 757-683-3211.. 492 G
mdeneen@odu.edu
DENEEN, Tina .... 205-934-8152...... 8 E
tdeneen@uab.edu
DENEUI, Dan .... 541-552-6913.. 395 A
deneuid@sou.edu
DENG, Shery .... 718-261-5800.. 305 J
sdeng@bramsonort.edu
DENG, Yi .... 215-895-6824.. 402 G
yd362@drexel.edu
DENG, Yi .... 704-687-8450.. 358 A
yi.deng@uncc.edu
DENHAM, Cynthia .... 256-840-4133...... 6 H
cdenham@snead.edu
DENHAM, Mark .... 313-993-3250.. 241 G
denhamma@udmercy.edu
DENHEM, Sherri .... 940-696-8752.. 478 D
sdenhem@vernoncollege.edu
DENHOLM, Jack .... 712-749-2253.. 170 D
denholmj@bvu.edu
DENI, Lawrence .... 716-888-8362.. 306 F
deni@canisius.edu
DENIO, John .... 401-232-6140.. 424 K
jdenio@bryant.edu
DENISON, Bronda .... 334-670-5843...... 7 H
bdenison@troy.edu
DENISTON, Paul .... 719-255-4665.... 83 L
pdenisto@uccs.edu
DENKER, Audria .... 502-410-6200.. 188 H
adenker@galencollege.edu
DENKER, Lee .... 402-554-2444.. 283 B
ldenker@unomaha.edu
DENLEY, Tristan .... 615-366-4448.. 444 D
tristan.denley@tbr.edu
DENMAN, Jillian .... 210-297-9123.. 452 C
jldenman@baptisthealthsystem.com
DENN, Robert .... 423-697-2659.. 445 D
robert.denn@chattanoogastate.edu
DENNA, Eric .... 301-405-7700.. 211 E
edenna@umd.edu
DENNE, Cynthia, K .... 909-593-3511.... 71 B
cdenne@laverne.edu
DENNEHY, Michael .... 972-860-4607.. 456 B
mdennehy@dcccd.edu
DENNEY, Carolyn .... 509-527-2811.. 508 G
carolyn.denney@wallawalla.edu
DENNEY, James .... 662-329-7462.. 259 E
jldenney@muw.edu
DENNEY, Karen .... 828-627-4546.. 350 D
kdenney@haywood.edu
DENNEY, Martha .... 610-896-1232.. 405 I
mdenney@haverford.edu
DENNEY, Randy .... 520-515-5455.... 12 L
denneyr@cochise.edu
DENNEY, Tammy .... 903-670-2617.. 473 B
tdenney@tvcc.edu
DENNIE, Deidra .... 912-344-2669.. 116 E
deirdra.dennie@armstrong.edu
DENNIN, Michael .... 949-824-7761.... 69 C
mdennin@uci.edu
DENNING, CSC, John, F . 508-565-1301.. 228 F
jdenning@stonehill.edu
DENNING, Rusty .... 864-941-8417.. 432 A
denning.r@ptc.edu
DENNING, William .... 919-466-4400.... 93 F
DENNIS, Anne .... 515-643-6640.. 175 B
adennis@mercydesmoines.org
DENNIS, Christina, M ...... 610-399-2369.. 414 F
passhe-cdennis@cheyney.edu
DENNIS, Daryle .... 203-837-8549.... 85 I
dennisd@wcsu.edu
DENNIS, Dave .... 319-363-1323.. 175 D
ddennis@mtmercy.edu
DENNIS, Diana .... 815-753-2111.. 150 A
ddennis@niu.edu
DENNIS, Eliza .... 415-749-4536.... 61 B
edennis@sfai.edu
DENNIS, Geoff .... 502-897-4566.. 192 D
gdennis@sbts.edu
DENNIS, James, M .... 618-537-6936.. 147 F
jdennis@mckendree.edu
DENNIS, Jennifer .... 541-737-4881.. 393 H
DENNIS, Jill .... 229-226-1621.. 128 B
jdennis@thomasu.edu
DENNIS, Julia .... 843-525-8203.. 433 B
jdennis@tcl.edu
DENNIS, Larry .... 850-644-5804.. 111 C
ldennis@cci.fsu.edu
DENNIS, Lynn, M .... 863-680-4107.. 101 E
ldennis@flsouthern.edu
DENNIS, Marie .... 215-567-7080.. 397 H
mdennis@edmc.edu
DENNIS, Peggy .... 419-372-8495.. 364 E
fayed@bgsu.edu
DENNIS, Raymond .... 310-338-5994.... 51 E
raymond.dennis@lmu.edu
DENNIS, Roger, J .... 215-571-4755.. 402 G
rjd45@drexel.edu
DENNIS, Suzanne .... 718-780-0314.. 305 L
suzanne.dennis@brooklaw.edu
DENNIS, Tenique .... 614-508-7246.. 370 E
tdennis@hondros.edu
DENNIS, Terry .... 863-680-4148.. 101 E
vdennis@flsouthern.edu
DENNIS, Vicki .... 318-678-6000.. 195 I
vdennis@bpcc.edu
DENNIS, Yolanda .... 508-588-9100.. 223 G
DENNISON, Anne .... 207-699-5054.. 203 F
adennison@meca.edu
DENNISON, Corley .... 304-558-0261.. 512 O
corley.dennison@wvhepc.edu
DENNISON, Lori, R .... 315-859-4412.. 315 D
ldenniso@hamilton.edu
DENNISON, Patricia .... 330-672-9494.. 370 I
pdenniso@kent.edu
DENNISON, Sondra, R ...... 724-357-2696.. 415 B
sondra.dennison@iup.edu
DENNISON, Wayne .... 812-877-8858.. 166 H
dennison@rose-hulman.edu
DENNISTON, Marsha .... 605-331-6633.. 438 A
marsha.denniston@usiouxfalls.edu
DENNISTON, Terry .... 423-425-4203.. 448 F
terry-denniston@utc.edu
DENNY, Bryan .... 918-465-2361.. 383 I
bdenny@eosc.edu
DENNY, Christopher .... 734-462-4400.. 240 H
cdenny@schoolcraft.edu
DENNY, David .... 503-699-6313.. 392 D
ddenny@marylhurst.edu
DENNY, Richard .... 501-374-6305.... 22 C
DENON, Gregory .... 978-934-2418.. 221 A
gregory_denon@uml.edu
DENOR, Kathy .... 800-567-2344.. 516 B
kdenor@menominee.edu
DENSBERGER, Derek .... 714-556-3610.... 73 B
ddensberger@vanguard.edu
DENSBERGER, Janelle ...... 314-719-8057.. 265 C
jdensberger@fontbonne.edu
DENSE, Angela .... 417-865-2815.. 265 B
densea@evangel.edu
DENSLOW, Kathy .... 325-793-4903.. 461 F
kdenslow@mcm.edu
DENSMORE, Timothy .... 607-844-8222.. 337 G
tad@tc3.edu
DENSON, John .... 205-665-6235...... 9 B
jdenson1@montevallo.edu
DENSON, Michael .... 415-476-1414.... 70 D
mike.denson@ucsf.edu
DENSON, Rob .... 515-964-6638.. 171 B
rjdenson@dmacc.edu
DENT, Deborah, F .... 601-979-4299.. 258 D
deborah.f.dent@jsums.edu
DENT, Patricia .... 508-678-2811.. 223 A
patricia.dent@bristolcc.edu
DENT, Valeda .... 516-299-2307.. 319 B
valeda.dent@liu.edu
DENT, Valeda, F .... 718-990-2517.. 328 F
valedad@stjohns.edu
DENTE, Michael, A .... 802-626-6375.. 486 C
michael.dente@lyndonstate.edu
DENTINO, Daniel .... 913-758-6109.. 185 F
daniel.dentino@stmary.edu
DENTON, Andrew .... 612-343-4745.. 253 Y
adenton@northcentral.edu
DENTON, Brian .... 620-341-6374.. 180 G
bdenton1@emporia.edu
DENTON, Carol .... 704-922-6484.. 350 A
denton.carol@gaston.edu
DENTON, Christine .... 808-739-8597.. 130 F
christine.denton@chaminade.edu
DENTON, David .... 931-221-6380.. 444 E
dentond@apsu.edu
DENTON, Melissa .... 913-234-0750.. 179 M
melissa.denton@cleveland.edu
DENTON, Ray .... 601-484-8785.. 258 F
rdenton@meridiancc.edu
DENTON, Shelley .... 575-769-4910.. 299 G
shelley.denton@clovis.edu
DENVER, Genae .... 785-539-3571.. 183 B
gdenver@mccks.edu
DENYS, Mark .... 215-204-7500.. 420 B
mark.denys@temple.edu
DENZINE, Gypsy .... 304-293-5703.. 514 C
gypsy.denzine@mail.wvu.edu
DEOCAMPO, Erlinda, N ...... 323-415-4163.... 49 G
deocamen@elac.edu
DEOLALIKAR, Anil .... 951-827-1575.... 70 B
anil.deolalikar@ucr.edu
DEOLIVEIRA, Shushawna 718-270-2446.. 332 B
shushawna.deoliveira@downstate.edu
DEORIO, Frank, A .... 718-817-4910.. 314 G
deorio@fordham.edu
DEPACE, Paul .... 401-874-2725.. 426 D
pauldepace@uri.edu
DEPAOLA, John .... 518-262-6008.. 303 E
depaolj@mail.amc.edu
DEPAOLA, Natacha .... 312-567-3009.. 142 I
depaola@iit.edu
DEPAOLIS, Cheryl .... 412-924-1384.. 417 E
cdepaolis@pts.edu
DEPASS, Michelle .... 212-229-5400.. 322 E
michelle.depass@newschool.edu
DEPAUW, Karen, P .... 540-231-7581.. 499 F
kpdepauw@vt.edu
DEPEDER, Suzanne .... 312-362-8648.. 139 C
sdepeder@depaul.edu
DEPEDRO, Tracy .... 215-951-2738.. 416 G
depedrot@philau.edu
DEPERRO, Dennis, R .... 315-445-4685.. 318 E
deperrdr@lemoyne.edu
DEPEW, Chris .... 845-434-5750.. 336 H
cdepew@sullivan.suny.edu
DEPEW, Dennis, R .... 423-439-4289.. 444 F
depewd@etsu.edu
DEPEW, Dixie, A .... 937-328-6006.. 366 E
depewd@clarkstate.edu
DEPEW, Elizabeth .... 219-785-5239.. 166 F
ebabcock@pnw.edu
DEPEW, Sally .... 231-591-3823.. 233 L
sallydepew@ferris.edu
DEPIETRO, Laura, A .... 724-847-6590.. 404 B
ladepiet@geneva.edu
DEPINHO, Ronald .... 713-792-6000.. 477 F
DEPONTIER, Woodrow ...... 316-978-3447.. 185 J
woodrow.depontier@wichita.edu
DEPOO, Tilokie .... 212-343-1234.. 321 B
tdepoo@mcny.edu
DEPOUTOT, Al .... 727-376-6911.. 114 A
adepoutot@trinitycollege.edu
DEPOY, Bryan .... 440-375-7028.. 371 E
bdepoy@lec.edu
DEPPERT, Phillip .... 831-242-5200.. 527 K
DEPPONG, Greg .... 517-355-5020.. 237 I
deppong@msu.edu
DEPREY, Linda .... 207-834-7800.. 205 B
lindad@maine.edu
DEPRIEST, Doug .... 208-562-3505.. 133 F
dougdepriest@cwidaho.cc
DEPRIEST, Jon .... 619-201-8754.... 60 D
jon.depriest@sdcc.edu
DEPRIETO, Irma .... 509-865-8537.. 504 D
deprieto_i@heritage.edu
DEPUTY, Meghan .... 386-312-4169.. 108 B
meghandeputy@sjrstate.edu
DEPUTY, Paul .... 907-786-4413.... 10 F
pdeputy@uaa.alaska.edu
DEPUY, Rebecca .... 817-598-6388.. 479 E
rdepuy@wc.edu
DER KIUREGHIAN,
Armen .... 510-925-4282.... 26 M
adk@aua.am
DER SIMONIAN, Raffi .... 207-699-5010.. 203 F
rdersimonian@meca.edu
DERAMUS, Danny .... 501-279-4339.... 20 D
dderamus@harding.edu
DERANEK, Suzanne .... 507-457-1729.. 254 O
sderanek@smumn.edu
DERAVI, Fariba, S .... 334-244-3249...... 2 A
fderavi@aum.edu
DERBY, Dustin, C .... 563-884-5682.. 176 C
dustin.derby@palmer.edu
DERBYSHIRE, Lynne .... 401-874-4732.. 426 D
derbyshire@uri.edu
DERDEN, Wade .... 501-760-6390.... 21 B
mderden@np.edu
DERDERIAN, Todd .... 508-767-7392.. 214 F
tderderi@assumption.edu
DEREBERY, Britanny .... 903-813-2423.. 451 M
bderebery@austincollege.edu
DEREMER, Dennis .... 970-204-8255.... 80 E
dennis.deremer@frontrange.edu
DERICKSON, Christopher 919-962-8289.. 357 D
cderickson@unc.edu
DERICO, Amanda .... 513-244-8149.. 366 B
amanda.derico@ccuniversity.edu
DERITIS, Mark .... 315-268-6642.. 310 B
mderitis@clarkson.edu
DERK, Malcolm .... 570-372-4571.. 419 H
derk@susqu.edu
DERMISHYAN, Sima .... 916-484-7666.... 59 E
DERMODY, Sean, B .... 518-564-2539.. 334 A
dermodsb@plattsburgh.edu
DEROCHE, Jessica .... 940-899-8402.. 462 L
jderoche@nctc.edu
DEROCHI, Jack .... 803-323-2204.. 435 B
derochij@winthrop.edu
DEROSA, Mary Lou .... 203-396-8321.... 88 I
derosam@sacredheart.edu
DEROSA, Michael .... 510-869-6511.... 59 L
mderosa@samuelmerritt.edu
DEROSE, Angela .... 203-287-3032.... 88 E
paier.admin@snet.net
DEROSE, Angela .... 203-287-3033.... 88 E
paier.admin@snet.net

DEY, Anita ... 989-964-7094 .. 240 F
adey@svsu.edu
DEY, Farouk ... 650-723-1983 .... 66 I
fdey@stanford.edu
DEYOUNG, Jamie ... 903-233-3800 .. 460 J
jamiedeyoung@letu.edu
DEYOUNG, Michael ... 702-968-2006 .. 285 E
mdeyoung@roseman.edu
DEYOUNG, Paul, D ... 503-777-7290 .. 394 I
paul.deyoung@reed.edu
DEYOUNG, Renee ... 231-348-6618 .. 239 A
rdeyoung@ncmich.edu
DEZIEL, David ... 603-428-2417 .. 287 C
ddeziel@nec.edu
DEZIEL, Lisa ... 954-262-1387 .. 105 J
lisad@nova.edu
DEZURA, Mia, S ... 540-868-7087 .. 497 E
mleggettdezura@lfcc.edu
DHAKAR, Vandana ... 603-206-8152 .. 286 D
vdhakar@ccsnh.edu
DHALIWAL, Jasbir ... 901-678-5402 .. 445 C
jdhaliwl@memphis.edu
DHANIE, Julianna ... 312-944-0882 .. 145 F
jdhanie@chicago.chefs.edu
DHANKHER, Veena ... 413-552-2543 .. 223 E
vdhankher@hcc.edu
DHANWADA, Kavita, R ... 319-273-2518 .. 170 A
kavita.dhanwada@uni.edu
DHANWADA, Kavita, R ... 319-273-5976 .. 170 A
kavita.dhanwada@uni.edu
DHARMARAJ,
Premkumar ... 626-448-0023 .... 47 E
DHAWAN, Atam, P ... 973-596-8566 .. 293 D
atam.dhawan@njit.edu
DHILLON, Upinder, S ... 607-777-2314 .. 331 B
dhillon@binghamton.edu
DHILLON, Vineeta ... 707-654-1283 .... 33 D
vdhillon@csum.edu
DHIR, Krishna ... 808-932-7272 .. 131 E
kdhir@hawaii.edu
DI DIO, Stephen ... 718-631-6044 .. 309 E
sdidio@qcc.cuny.edu
DI DONATO, Ana ... 352-588-8992 .. 108 C
ana.didonato@saintleo.edu
DI FAVA, John ... 617-252-1703 .. 225 A
DI FRANCESCO, Gabriele 661-824-2977 .... 53 K
gdifrancesco@ntps.edu
DI IULIO, Tanya ... 773-697-2143 .. 139 E
diiulio@devry.edu
DI LELLO, Joseph ... 914-968-6200 .. 329 C
joseph.dilello@archny.org
DI LIBERTO, James, G ... 631-691-8733 .. 317 C
dilibertoj@idti.edu
DI LIBERTO, John, G ... 631-691-8733 .. 317 C
johng@idti.edu
DI LULLO, Trish ... 256-233-8184 ...... 1 F
trish.dilullo@athens.edu
DI MARE, Lesley ... 719-549-2951 .... 79 B
presidentsoffice@csupueblo.edu
DI MARIA, David ... 406-994-4031 .. 277 C
david.dimaria@montana.edu
DI NARDI, Jason ... 914-594-4668 .. 323 I
jason_dinardi@nymc.edu
DI NUCCI, Jo Ellen ... 208-426-1200 .. 132 I
jedinucc@boisestate.edu
DI PIERRO, John ... 269-965-3931 .. 236 A
dipierroj@kellogg.edu
DI SANTO, Dusty ... 630-752-5490 .. 158 C
dusty.disanto@wheaton.edu
DI STISO, Chris ... 860-628-4751 .... 88 C
cdistiso@lincolncollegene.edu
DIAB, Dorey ... 419-755-4811 .. 373 G
ddiab@ncstatecollege.edu
DIACHUN, Elizabeth ... 661-722-6300 .... 27 B
ediachun@avc.edu
DIACON, Todd ... 330-672-8529 .. 370 I
tdiacon@kent.edu
DIACONT, Matthew ... 954-731-8880 .... 98 A
mdiacont@concorde.edu
DIAH, Max ... 516-773-5000 .. 529 B
diahm@usmma.edu
DIAL, Bill ... 972-238-6386 .. 456 H
bdial@dcccd.edu
DIAL, Eugene, A ... 985-448-4021 .. 201 A
eugene.dial@nicholls.edu
DIAL, Janet, S ... 323-343-3060 .... 33 C
jdial@calstatela.edu
DIAL, Miqueas ... 408-741-4619 .... 74 H
miqueas.dial@westvalley.edu
DIALS, Julie ... 859-572-5487 .. 192 B
dialsj1@nku.edu
DIAMANDOPOULOS,
Kathy ... 610-282-1100 .. 402 B
kathy.diamandopoulos@desales.edu
DIAMOND, Alfreda ... 225-771-2552 .. 200 A
adiamond@sulc.edu
DIAMOND, Fred ... 626-914-8691 .... 38 D
fdiamond@citruscollege.edu
DIAMOND, Holly ... 313-845-9887 .. 235 D
hadiamond@hfcc.edu
DIAMOND, John, N ... 207-581-1138 .. 204 H
diamond@maine.edu
DIAMOND, Linda ... 336-517-2109 .. 342 B
ldiamond@bennett.edu
DIAMOND, Michael ... 706-721-6900 .. 117 D
mdiamond@augusta.edu
DIAMOND BURROWAY,
Sarah ... 606-326-2106 .. 188 N
sarah.diamondburroway@kctc.edu
DIAMOND-ROTHSTEIN,
Katherine ... 610-359-2791 .. 401 L
kdiamond@dccc.edu
DIANGELO, JR.,
Joseph, A ... 610-660-1645 .. 418 G
jodiange@sju.edu
DIAS, James ... 518-956-8170 .. 331 A
jdias@albany.edu
DIAS, Margaret, S ... 508-999-8791 .. 220 H
mdias@umassd.edu
DIAS, Orsete ... 212-247-3434 .. 319 K
odias@mandl.edu
DIAZ, Alfred ... 787-725-8120 .. 532 K
adiaz@eap.edu
DIAZ, Alphonso, V ... 703-284-3847 .. 492 A
al.diaz@marymount.edu
DIAZ, Andrea ... 814-332-2724 .. 397 A
adiaz@allegheny.edu
DIAZ, Arelis ... 787-753-6335 .. 532 O
adiaz@icprjc.edu
DIAZ, Armando ... 210-567-0372 .. 477 D
diaza@uthscsa.edu
DIAZ, Brett ... 787-844-8181 .. 538 E
brett.diaz@upr.edu
DIAZ, Daniel ... 336-316-2351 .. 344 H
diazdf@guilford.edu
DIAZ, Emma ... 909-384-8611 .... 60 C
ediaz@sbccd.cc.ca.us
DIAZ, Ester ... 219-473-4388 .. 159 L
ediaz@ccsj.edu
DIAZ, Francisco ... 973-720-3244 .. 298 G
diazf@wpunj.edu
DIAZ, Franco, L ... 787-284-1912 .. 534 C
fldiaz@ponce.inter.edu
DIAZ, Glenda ... 787-863-2390 .. 533 K
glenda.diaz@fajardo.inter.edu
DIAZ, Jackie ... 254-710-3805 .. 452 H
jackie_diaz@baylor.edu
DIAZ, Jillian ... 203-591-5619 .... 88 F
jdiaz@post.edu
DIAZ, Joel ... 805-678-5810 .... 73 E
jdiaz@vcccd.edu
DIAZ, Jorge, L ... 787-786-3030 .. 536 F
jdiaz@ucb.edu.pr
DIAZ, Josem ... 563-425-5231 .. 177 D
diazj93@uiu.edu
DIAZ, Kris ... 440-826-2900 .. 363 M
kdiaz@bw.edu
DIAZ, Leticia, M ... 321-206-5602 .... 96 D
ldiaz@barry.edu
DIAZ, Leyanis ... 305-821-3333 .. 101 B
idiazgil@fnu.edu
DIAZ, Luis, R ... 787-751-0160 .. 531 M
lrdiaz@cmpr.pr.gov
DIAZ, Maria, S ... 787-257-7373 .. 535 P
ue_mdiaz@suagm.edu
DIAZ, Mario ... 312-850-7492 .. 138 A
mdiaz103@ccc.edu
DIAZ, Mark ... 305-284-2862 .. 114 H
markdiaz@miami.edu
DIAZ, Mayra ... 787-993-8897 .. 537 G
mayra.diaz2@upr.edu
DIAZ, Mayra, E ... 787-725-8120 .. 532 K
mediaz@eap.edu
DIAZ, Minerva ... 787-738-2161 .. 538 A
minerva.diaz@upr.edu
DIAZ, Mischelle, R ... 512-448-8404 .. 464 G
mischeld@stedwards.edu
DIAZ, Paula ... 312-935-3131 .. 152 D
pdiaz@robertmorris.edu
DIAZ, Ramonita ... 787-878-5475 .. 533 H
rdiaz@arecibo.inter.edu
DIAZ, Ricardo ... 787-850-9375 .. 538 B
ricardo.diaz6@upr.edu
DIAZ, Robert ... 212-220-8305 .. 307 B
rdiaz@bmcc.cuny.edu
DIAZ, Roberto ... 215-717-3107 .. 401 J
roberto.diaz@curtis.edu
DIAZ, Russell ... 845-848-4048 .. 312 F
russell.diaz@dc.edu
DIAZ, Sam ... 570-504-9069 .. 400 I
sdiaz@tcmc.edu
DIAZ, Sharon, C ... 510-869-6512 .... 59 L
sdiaz@samuelmerritt.edu
DIAZ, Sonia ... 787-728-1515 .. 539 B
sdiaz@sagrado.edu
DIAZ, Sylvia ... 631-451-4486 .. 336 D
diazs@sunysuffolk.edu
DIAZ, Veronica ... 310-434-4224 .... 63 F
diaz_veronica@smc.edu
DIAZ, Walter ... 860-465-5000 .... 85 G
diazw@easternct.edu
DIAZ, Walter ... 956-665-3553 .. 476 E
walter.diaz@utrgv.edu
DIAZ, Zaida ... 787-257-0199 .. 537 H
zaida.diaz@upr.edu
DIAZ ALONSO, Herman .. 213-613-2200 .... 65 H
directors_office@sciarc.edu
DIAZ BONACQUISTI,
Judi ... 303-352-3074 .... 79 F
judi.diazbonacquisti@ccd.edu
DIAZ-DIAZ, Claribel ... 787-622-8000 .. 537 B
cladiaz@pupr.edu
DIAZ-HERRERA, Jorge, L 315-279-5201 .. 318 C
jdiazh@keuka.edu
DIAZ-RIOS, Erika ... 787-250-0000 .. 537 D
erika.diaz1@upr.edu
DIAZ-RODRIGUEZ,
Nereida ... 787-798-6732 .. 536 G
nereida.diaz@uccaribe.edu
DIAZ-RODRIGUEZ,
Victor ... 787-250-0000 .. 537 D
victor.diaz@upr.edu
DIAZ SEMPRIT, Ruth, M . 787-763-6700 .. 532 L
rmdiaz@se-pr.edu
DIAZ-TORRES, Marie ... 973-353-5089 .. 296 C
mdtorres@newark.rutgers.edu
DIAZ WREST, Alicia ... 559-323-2100 .... 61 E
awrest@sjcl.edu
DIAZPINEIRO, Odalys ... 718-997-5646 .. 309 D
odalys.diazpineiro@qc.edu
DIBARTOLO, Adraina ... 845-437-5315 .. 339 C
adbartolo@vassar.edu
DIBARTOLO, Gerard ... 410-546-4144 .. 213 A
grdibartolo@salisbury.edu
DIBARTOLOMEO,
Michael ... 973-720-2903 .. 298 G
dibartolomeom@wpunj.edu
DIBB, Andrew M, T ... 267-502-2582 .. 398 J
andrew.dibb@brynathyn.edu
DIBBERT, Douglas, S ... 919-962-7050 .. 357 D
doug_dibbert@unc.edu
DIBBLE, Deborah, A ... 716-673-3131 .. 331 D
deborah.dibble@fredonia.edu
DIBBLE, Rita ... 570-662-4000 .. 415 E
DIBELLA, Jeannette ... 603-206-8006 .. 286 D
jdibella@ccsnh.edu
DIBELLA, Sue ... 702-895-4317 .. 284 L
sue.dibella@unlv.edu
DIBENEDETTO, Eileen, M 212-854-7732 .. 304 I
edibened@barnard.edu
DIBENEDETTO, Steve ... 847-947-5409 .. 149 B
steve.dibenedetto@nl.edu
DIBERT, Cregg ... 814-262-3837 .. 413 P
cdibert@pennhighlands.edu
DIBIASIO, Daniel, A ... 419-772-2030 .. 374 J
d-dibiasio@onu.edu
DIBISCEGLIE, Lisa ... 732-255-0400 .. 293 E
ldibisceglie@ocean.edu
DIBLEY, Paula ... 704-216-3467 .. 352 G
paula.dibley@rccc.edu
DIBRIGIDA, Vladimir ... 303-329-6355 .... 78 O
director@cstcm.edu
DIBRITO, Kyle, J ... 717-736-4117 .. 405 C
kjdibrit@hacc.edu
DICAPRIO, Deborah, A ... 845-575-3000 .. 320 B
deborah.dicaprio@marist.edu
DICARLO, Joseph ... 508-929-8090 .. 222 F
jdicarlo1@worcester.edu
DICARO, David ... 585-385-8025 .. 328 E
ddicaro@sjfc.edu
DICARO, Kim ... 313-496-2625 .. 242 H
kdicaro1@wcccd.edu
DICE, Douglas ... 989-463-7162 .. 230 F
dice@alma.edu
DICENZO, Robert ... 540-665-1280 .. 494 B
dicenzo@su.edu
DICESARE, Deborah, A ... 818-778-5522 .... 50 D
dicesad@lavc.edu
DICHRISTINA, Joseph ... 860-297-2000 .... 89 B
DICK, Dan ... 847-628-2086 .. 144 B
daniel.dick@judsonu.edu
DICK, Melissa ... 724-357-2550 .. 415 B
m.l.dick@iup.edu
DICKENS, Brian ... 607-274-8000 .. 317 D
bdickens@ithaca.edu
DICKENS, Brian, K ... 713-313-1379 .. 470 D
dickensbk@tsu.edu
DICKENS, Linda, N ... 512-232-2646 .. 476 B
linda.dickens@austin.utexas.edu
DICKENS, Margaret, A ... 715-833-6419 .. 523 B
mdickens@cvtc.edu
DICKENS, Reginald ... 704-216-6025 .. 346 A
rdickens@livingstone.edu
DICKENS, Robert, I ... 210-458-4060 .. 477 A
robert.dickens@utsa.edu
DICKENS, Ross, N ... 731-881-7225 .. 448 G
rdicken2@utm.edu
DICKENSON, Henry, H ... 940-565-2662 .. 475 A
hank.dickenson@unt.edu
DICKER, James ... 215-204-1801 .. 420 B
james.dicker@temple.edu
DICKERMAN,
Christopher, M ... 610-359-5302 .. 401 L
cdickerman@dccc.edu
DICKERMAN, Robert ... 413-755-4606 .. 224 G
dickerman@stcc.edu
DICKERSON, Aerial ... 912-279-4514 .. 119 C
adickerson@ccga.edu
DICKERSON, Beverly ... 870-245-5299 .... 21 E
dickersonb@obu.edu
DICKERSON, Cathy, S ... 540-375-2262 .. 493 H
cdickerson@roanoke.edu
DICKERSON, Charlene ... 803-793-5134 .. 429 D
dickersonc@denmarktech.edu
DICKERSON, Darby ... 806-742-3990 .. 472 C
DICKERSON, Dee Ann ... 918-647-1300 .. 382 I
ddickerson@carlalbert.edu
DICKERSON, Glenn ... 334-727-8692 ...... 8 A
gdickerson@mytu.tuskegee.edu
DICKERSON, Hannah ... 704-233-8000 .. 359 H
h.dickerson@wingate.edu
DICKERSON, John ... 662-325-2663 .. 259 D
jdickerson@registrar.msstate.edu
DICKERSON, John, R ... 662-325-2663 .. 259 D
jdickerson@registrar.msstate.edu
DICKERSON, Larry ... 816-802-3363 .. 266 D
ldickerson@kcai.edu
DICKERSON, Leslie ... 406-496-4879 .. 277 G
ldickerson@mtech.edu
DICKERSON, Mark ... 626-387-5763 .... 28 A
mdickerson@apu.edu
DICKERSON, Mary Ann ... 913-469-8500 .. 182 A
mdkerson@jccc.edu
DICKERSON, Rochelle ... 973-290-4478 .. 290 G
rdickerson@cse.edu
DICKERSON, Shirley ... 936-468-4109 .. 466 H
sdickerson@sfasu.edu
DICKERT, Gerry ... 409-984-6342 .. 471 C
dickertgl@lamarpa.edu
DICKES, David ... 605-668-4020 .. 436 D
david.dickes@mtmc.edu
DICKEY, Daryl ... 678-839-6534 .. 129 E
ddickey@westga.edu
DICKEY, Janie ... 407-277-0311 .... 99 J
jdickey@evergladesuniversity.edu
DICKEY, JP ... 417-455-5466 .. 264 E
jamesdickey@crowder.edu
DICKEY, M. Thaxter ... 813-988-5131 .. 100 F
dickeyt@floridacollege.edu
DICKEY, Marilyn ... 850-201-6652 .. 113 E
dickeym@tcc.fl.edu
DICKEY, Matt ... 417-626-1234 .. 269 K
dickey.matt@occ.edu
DICKEY, Todd, R ... 213-740-8184 .... 72 D
svpadmin@usc.edu
DICKEY, Wanda ... 813-988-5131 .. 100 F
library@floridacollege.edu
DICKEY, Wyman ... 904-269-7086 .. 102 F
wdickey@fortiscollege.edu
DICKINSON, Carl ... 315-279-5204 .. 318 C
cdickinson@keuka.edu
DICKINSON, J. Barry ... 267-341-3373 .. 405 J
bdickinson@holyfamily.edu
DICKINSON, Marjorie, M 530-752-2619 .... 69 A
mmdickinson@ucdavis.edu
DICKINSON, Michele ... 718-518-4284 .. 308 C
mdickinson@hostos.cuny.edu
DICKINSON, Robyn ... 570-941-4178 .. 422 B
robyn.dickinson@scranton.edu
DICKINSON, Rosie, A ... 956-326-2202 .. 468 A
rosie@tamiu.edu
DICKINSON NEIL, Terri ... 509-527-2632 .. 508 G
rosa.jimenez@wallawalla.edu
DICKMAN, Brent ... 212-280-1402 .. 338 I
bdickman@uts.columbia.edu
DICKMAN, Tom ... 301-696-3494 .. 208 B
dickman@hood.edu
DICKMEYER, Nathan ... 718-482-6119 .. 309 A
ndickmeyer@lagcc.cuny.edu
DICKS, Karin ... 512-448-8405 .. 464 G
karind@stedwards.edu
DICKS, Nikasha ... 803-508-7477 .. 426 G
DICKSON, Brook, E ... 540-362-6287 .. 490 F
bdickson@hollins.edu
DICKSON, Carol ... 802-586-7711 .. 485 C
cdickson@sterlingcollege.edu
DICKSON, Chris, M ... 260-422-5561 .. 162 B
cmdickson@indianatech.edu
DICKSON, John ... 727-873-4350 .. 112 D
jdickson@mail.usf.edu
DICKSON, Kari ... 806-743-2946 .. 472 D
kari.dickson@ttuhsc.edu
DICKSON, Kevin ... 573-651-2513 .. 272 B
kdickson@semo.edu
DICKSON, Kristopher ... 760-384-6148 .... 47 K
kristopher.dickson@cerrocoso.edu
DICKSON, Laura, M ... 515-281-3939 .. 169 F
ldickson@iastate.edu
DICKSON, Risa, E ... 808-956-6897 .. 131 D
risad@hawaii.edu
DICKSON, Shannon ... 916-691-7738 .... 51 B
dicksos@crc.losrios.edu

DIMASI, Louis ... 802-654-2566 .. 484 I
ldimasi@smcvt.edu
DIMASI, William ... 973-278-5400 .. 289 F
wsd@berkeleycollege.edu
DIMASI, William ... 973-278-5400 .. 305 B
wsd@berkeleycollege.edu
DIMATTIA, Andrea ... 570-504-9634 .. 400 I
adimattia@tcmc.edu
DIMATTIO, David ... 610-819-2070 .. 410 L
ddimattio@mc3.edu
DIMAURO, JR., Alfred ... 508-831-6678 .. 230 C
fred@wpi.edu
DIMAURO, Giorgio, G ... 848-932-7787 .. 296 B
gdimauro@gaiacenters.rutgers.edu
DIMAURO, Michael ... 317-813-691 ... 316 C
dimauro@hws.edu
DIMENT, Gregory, S ... 269-337-7149 .. 235 H
greg.diment@kzoo.edu
DIMICK, Jeffrey, A ... 304-865-6131 .. 511 C
jeffrey.dimick@ovu.edu
DIMING, Mianta' ... 219-980-6620 .. 163 B
mdiming@iun.edu
DIMINO, John, L ... 215-204-7276 .. 420 B
john.dimino@temple.edu
DIMINO, Solweig ... 973-300-2215 .. 297 D
sdimino@sussex.edu
DIMITRIOU, Kathy ... 313-845-9650 .. 235 D
kdimitriou@hfcc.edu
DIMITROV, Danielle, E ... 718-982-2250 .. 307 F
danielle.dimitrov@csi.cuny.edu
DIMITROVA, Diana ... 604-274-3306 .. 317 D
ddimitrova@ithaca.edu
DIMKOVA, Dimitrina ... 703-323-5053 .. 497 H
ddimkova@nvcc.edu
DIMOLITSAS, Spiros ... 202-687-3730 .... 92 E
seniorvp@georgetown.edu
DIMON, Denise ... 619-260-6824 .... 72 B
dimon@sandiego.edu
DIMOND, David ... 914-632-5400 .. 321 I
ddimond@monroecollege.edu
DIMOS, Duane ... 817-272-1021 .. 476 A
ddimos@uta.edu
DINALLO, JR., Benjamin . 201-559-3507 .. 291 K
dinallob@felician.edu
DINARDO, N. John ... 215-895-2510 .. 402 G
dinardo@drexel.edu
DINDOFFER, Tamara, L ... 517-750-1200 .. 241 E
tammyd@arbor.edu
DINEEN-THACKERAY,
Lorrie ... 707-654-1086 .... 33 D
ldineen-thackeray@csum.edu
DINEGAR, Leonard ... 303-860-5600 .... 83 J
leonard.dinegar@cu.edu
DINEHART, Laura ... 305-348-3790 .. 111 A
laura.dinehart@fiu.edu
DINELLO, William, V ... 718-262-2350 .. 310 A
wdinello@york.cuny.edu
DINGER, Julie ... 918-463-2931 .. 383 F
julie.dinger@connorsstate.edu
DINGER, Tim ... 479-524-7234 .... 20 H
tdinger@jbu.edu
DINGES, Danielle ... 406-377-9410 .. 276 D
ddinges@dawson.edu
DINGESS, Debbie, C ... 304-896-7416 .. 512 E
debbie.dingess@southernwv.edu
DINGESS, Debbie, C ... 304-896-7408 .. 512 E
debbie.dingess@southernwv.edu
DINGFELDER, Diane ... 507-457-5138 .. 252 G
ddingfelder@winona.edu
DINGLE, Terry ... 843-661-8321 .. 429 J
terry.dingle@fdtc.edu
DINGLER, Mike ... 501-337-5000 .... 19 K
mdingler@coto.edu
DINGMAN, Brandie ... 518-381-1280 .. 330 B
dingmabm@sunysccc.edu
DINGMANN, Melissa ... 218-281-8576 .. 255 E
dingmann@umn.edu
DINKEL, Shirley ... 785-670-1470 .. 185 H
shirley.dinkel@washburn.edu
DINKINS, Sandy, E ... 904-264-2172 .. 107 N
sdinkins@iws.edu
DINNAN, Matthew, A ... 203-254-4000 .... 87 G
madinnan@fairfield.edu
DINNDORF, Elizabeth, A . 803-786-3178 .. 429 A
bdinndorf@columbiasc.edu
DINNO, Christopher ... 707-664-2870 .... 35 D
christopher.dinno@sonoma.edu
DINOVO, Carolyn ... 614-885-5585 .. 376 G
cdinovo@pcj.edu
DINSE, Jayne ... 507-389-7269 .. 252 D
jayne.dinse@southcentral.edu
DINWIDDIE, Ashley ... 417-328-1500 .. 272 C
adinwiddie@sbuniv.edu
DION, Danielle ... 913-758-6111 .. 185 F
danielle.dion@stmary.edu
DION, Susan ... 651-450-3568 .. 249 F
sdion@inverhills.edu
DIONISI, Lisa ... 216-987-2340 .. 367 E
lisa.dionisi@tri-c.edu
DIONISIO, Thomas ... 603-314-1494 .. 287 I
t.dionisio@snhu.edu

DIONNE, Elizabeth ... 508-793-3659 .. 217 C
edionne@holycross.edu
DIONNE, Trisha ... 603-271-6484 .. 286 F
tdionne@ccsnh.edu
DIONNE, Woody ... 802-635-1280 .. 486 B
woody.dionne@jsc.edu
DIORIETES, Chris ... 910-678-8443 .. 349 F
diorietc@faytechcc.edu
DIORIO, Annette ... 610-330-5082 .. 407 C
diorioa@lafayette.edu
DIORIO, Mary Ann ... 860-733-1404 .... 87 E
mdiorio@txcc.commnet.edu
DIORIO, Nicole ... 508-767-7078 .. 214 F
nm.diorio@assumption.edu
DIORIO, Richelle ... 918-587-6789 .. 388 K
richelle.diorio@twsweld.com
DIPADOVA-STOCKS,
Laurie ... 816-559-5617 .. 270 D
laurie.dipadovastocks@park.edu
DIPALMA, Kristy ... 212-410-8000 .. 323 C
kdipalma@nycpm.edu
DIPAOLA, Robert ... 859-323-5079 .. 193 G
rsdipaola@uky.edu
DIPAOLO, Lawrence ... 610-558-5507 .. 411 E
dipaolol@neumann.edu
DIPAOLO, Stephen, J ... 848-445-5012 .. 295 F
sdip@uco.rutgers.edu
DIPIERO, Thomas ... 214-768-3212 .. 465 J
tdipiero@smu.edu
DIPIETRO, Joe ... 865-974-2241 .. 448 D
utpresident@tennessee.edu
DIPIETRO, Mark ... 802-387-1632 .. 484 B
markdipietro@landmark.edu
DIPIETRO-STEWART,
Suze ... 609-652-4607 .. 297 C
suze.dipietro@stockton.edu
DIPIRO, Joseph, T ... 804-828-3000 .. 496 D
jtdipiro@vcu.edu
DIPLOCK, Peter ... 860-486-2915 .... 89 D
peter.diplock@uconn.edu
DIPPEL, Holger ... 508-999-9181 .. 220 H
hdippel@umassd.edu
DIPPMAN, Terry ... 419-473-2700 .. 367 J
tdippman@daviscollege.edu
DIRAIMO, Michael, J ... 814-865-6563 .. 412 F
mjd256@psu.edu
DIRE, James ... 808-245-8229 .. 132 B
dire@hawaii.edu
DIRIKER, Veronique, L ... 410-651-8142 .. 212 B
vdiriker@umes.edu
DIRINGER, Lissie ... 212-824-2212 .. 315 F
ldiringer@huc.edu
DIRK, Brian ... 440-375-7220 .. 371 E
bdirk@lec.edu
DIRKS, Kathleen, M ... 815-835-6386 .. 153 K
kathleen.m.dirks@svcc.edu
DIRKS, Nicholas, B ... 510-642-7464 .... 68 M
chancellor@berkeley.edu
DIRKS, Randy ... 952-829-1388 .. 244 J
randy.dirks@bethfel.org
DIRKSCHNEIDER, Carla ... 402-552-6295 .. 279 D
dirkschneider@clarksoncollege.edu
DIRKSE, John ... 661-654-6181 .... 32 A
jdirkse@csub.edu
DIRKSEN, Dawn ... 866-323-0233 .... 58 E
admin@providencecc.edu
DIRST, Eric ... 630-515-4510 .. 139 D
edirst@devry.edu
DISAIA, Kenneth, F ... 401-598-2346 .. 425 B
kdisaia@jwu.edu
DISALVIO, Philip ... 617-287-7925 .. 220 G
philip.disalvio@umb.edu
DISALVO, Anthony ... 909-652-6257 .... 37 D
anthony.disalvo@chaffey.edu
DISALVO, Stephen ... 314-529-9521 .. 267 B
sdisalvo@maryville.edu
DISALVO, Steven, R ... 603-641-7010 .. 287 G
sdisalvo@anselm.edu
DISANO, Maria ... 401-874-7078 .. 426 D
mdisano@uri.edu
DISANTI, Francis, J ... 610-660-1506 .. 418 G
disanti@sju.edu
DISATE, Nancy ... 303-861-1151 .... 79 G
ndisate@concorde.edu
DISBROW, Lynn ... 334-833-4366 ...... 4 D
ldisbrow@hawks.huntingdon.edu
DISCALA, Anthony ... 480-517-8411 .... 14 G
anthony.discale@riosalado.edu
DISCELLO, Michael ... 724-337-1000 .. 399 F
mdiscello@careerta.edu
DISCENZA, Tobias ... 239-489-9329 .. 101 F
tjdiscenza@fsw.edu
DISCHINO, Maureen ... 617-989-4009 .. 229 D
dischinom@wit.edu
DISHMAN, Leslie, B ... 985-448-4415 .. 201 A
leslie.dishman@nicholls.edu
DISHMAN, Marcie ... 919-718-7491 .. 348 D
mdishman@cccc.edu
DISHMAN, Mike ... 470-578-7588 .. 123 J
mdishma2@kennesaw.edu

DISION, Maria ... 691-320-2480 .. 529 F
mdison@comfsm.fm
DISKIN, Alan ... 702-651-7924 .. 284 H
alan.diskin@csn.edu
DISKIN, Becca, L ... 417-659-5422 .. 268 H
diskin-b@mssu.edu
DISLER, Heather ... 727-344-8065 .. 108 D
disler.heather@spcollege.edu
DISMUKES, David ... 225-578-4400 .. 197 I
dismukes@lsu.edu
DISNEW, Carolyn ... 212-752-1530 .. 318 F
carolyn.disnew@limcollege.edu
DISORBO, Brenda ... 301-696-3413 .. 208 B
disorbo@hood.edu
DISPIGNO, OFM,
Francis, J ... 716-375-2142 .. 328 B
fdispigno@sbu.edu
DISQUE, Carol ... 336-506-4138 .. 347 C
carol.disque@alamancecc.edu
DISTASI, Vincent, F ... 724-458-2116 .. 404 F
vfdistasi@gcc.edu
DISTEFANO, Ann, L ... 570-577-3200 .. 398 L
ann.distefano@bucknell.edu
DISTEFANO,
Jacqueline, S ... 585-385-8013 .. 328 E
jdistefano@sjfc.edu
DISTEFANO, Phillip, P ... 303-492-8908 .... 83 K
phil.distefano@colorado.edu
DISTISO, Christopher ... 860-628-4751 .... 88 C
cdistiso@lincolncollegene.edu
DITHOMAS, Deborah ... 760-252-2411 .... 28 B
ddithomas@barstow.edu
DITLEFSEN, Ed ... 208-732-6847 .. 133 E
editlefsen@csi.edu
DITMAN, Mark ... 713-348-5441 .. 464 E
mditman@rice.edu
DITOMASSO, Anthony ... 412-237-4413 .. 401 B
adtomasso@ccac.edu
DITORO, Tim ... 936-633-5204 .. 451 D
tditoro@angelina.edu
DITTEMORE, Nancy ... 951-785-2300 .... 48 A
ndittemo@lasierra.edu
DITTMAN, Jeff, L ... 605-256-5229 .. 437 C
jeff.dittman@dsu.edu
DITTMAN, Scott ... 540-458-8455 .. 500 F
sdittman@wlu.edu
DITTMER, Amy ... 573-592-4313 .. 275 G
amy.dittmer@williamwoods.edu
DITTMER,
Harold (Hal), E ... 916-447-5171 .. 280 D
hdittmer@wellhead.com
DITTMER, Michael ... 513-244-4619 .. 373 C
michael.dittmer@msj.edu
DITTO, John ... 979-230-3157 .. 453 A
john.ditto@brazosport.edu
DITTO, Liz ... 419-434-4510 .. 379 E
dittoe@findlay.edu
DITTRICH, Linda ... 315-786-2323 .. 317 H
ldittrich@sunyjefferson.edu
DITULIO, James, E ... 309-298-2453 .. 158 A
je-ditulio@wiu.edu
DITULLIO, Daniel, F ... 508-767-7321 .. 214 F
df.ditullio@assumption.edu
DITULLIO, James, A ... 315-267-2135 .. 334 B
ditullija@potsdam.edu
DITZLER, Mauri, A ... 517-629-0210 .. 230 E
mditzler@albion.edu
DIVALERIO, Thomas, J ... 856-225-6050 .. 296 A
tdivaler@camden.rutgers.edu
DIVELY, Mary Jo ... 412-268-9519 .. 400 D
mjdively@andrew.cmu.edu
DIVEN-BROWN, Laura ... 662-915-7175 .. 261 B
ldivenbr@olemiss.edu
DIVENS, Gary ... 856-338-1817 .. 290 B
gdivens@camdencc.edu
DIVINCENZO, Mark ... 617-452-2082 .. 225 A
DIVINE, Darren, D ... 307-268-2548 .. 526 D
darrendivine@caspercollege.edu
DIVINEY, Shelley ... 843-574-6350 .. 433 D
shelley.diviney@tridenttech.edu
DIVINO, Claudio, F ... 252-334-2049 .. 346 F
claudio.divino@macuniversity.edu
DIVITA, Brian ... 616-632-2929 .. 231 A
bjd002@aquinas.edu
DIVITO, Catherine ... 501-812-2206 .... 21 H
cdivito@pulaskitech.edu
DIVJAK, Robert ... 203-575-8235 .... 86 G
rdivjak@nv.edu
DIWARA, Patrica ... 719-502-2037 .... 82 B
patricia.diawar@ppcc.edu
DIXEY, Mary ... 413-552-2261 .. 223 E
mdixey@hcc.edu
DIXIE, Wendy, D ... 502-597-5725 .. 191 B
wendy.dixie@kysu.edu
DIXON, Brian ... 509-335-9711 .. 508 H
DIXON, Bruce, W ... 606-474-3215 .. 188 L
bdixon@kcu.edu
DIXON, Carol ... 757-352-4013 .. 493 E
carodix@regent.edu
DIXON, Catherine ... 509-359-4863 .. 503 D
cdixon@ewu.edu

DIXON, Catherine ... 410-626-2548 .. 210 D
cathy.dixon@sjc.edu
DIXON, Christopher ... 812-877-8460 .. 166 H
dixon1@rose-hulman.edu
DIXON, Clay-Edward ... 510-649-2540 .... 45 G
cedixon@gtu.edu
DIXON, David ... 216-649-8700 .. 370 I
ddixon@kent.edu
DIXON, Dawn, S ... 919-464-2373 .. 350 G
dsdixon@johnstoncc.edu
DIXON, Isaac ... 503-768-6239 .. 392 A
idixon@lclark.edu
DIXON, Jacqueline ... 727-553-3369 .. 112 C
jdixon@usf.edu
DIXON, Janet ... 701-224-5739 .. 361 C
janet.dixon@bismarckstate.edu
DIXON, Jenny ... 928-681-5656 .... 15 E
jdixon@mohave.edu
DIXON, Jeri, L ... 630-801-7900 .. 157 K
jdixon@waubonsee.edu
DIXON, Jesse ... 618-482-8326 .. 155 A
jessdix@siue.edu
DIXON, John ... 843-661-1335 .. 430 B
jdixon@fmarion.edu
DIXON, Joyce, A ... 662-254-3308 .. 260 A
jadixon@mvsu.edu
DIXON, Kathy ... 541-888-7408 .. 395 B
kathy.dixon@socc.edu
DIXON, Kevi ... 919-536-7200 .. 349 D
dixonk@durhamtech.edu
DIXON, Kristin ... 503-375-7080 .. 391 B
kdixon@corban.edu
DIXON, Lloyd, E ... 662-254-3335 .. 260 A
ldixon@mvsu.edu
DIXON, Lynn ... 512-223-1222 .. 451 N
cdixon@austincc.edu
DIXON, Margaret ... 662-621-4670 .. 257 B
mdixon@coahomacc.edu
DIXON, Melanie ... 916-608-6768 .... 51 C
dixonm@flc.losrios.edu
DIXON, Michael ... 770-394-8300 .. 116 F
midixon@aii.edu
DIXON, Michael, G ... 260-982-5000 .. 165 M
mgdixon@manchester.edu
DIXON, Patrick ... 870-972-2042 .... 18 J
pdixon@astate.edu
DIXON, Rick, L ... 660-543-4255 .. 273 C
dixon@ucmo.edu
DIXON, Robert ... 312-413-1878 .. 156 F
robd@uic.edu
DIXON, Robert ... 405-744-6512 .. 385 G
robert.dixon@okstate.edu
DIXON, Robert, M ... 610-399-2271 .. 414 F
DIXON, Roger ... 478-471-2720 .. 124 E
roger.dixon@mga.edu
DIXON, Samuel ... 678-466-4200 .. 119 A
samdixon@clayton.edu
DIXON, Terrance ... 404-954-6520 .. 124 I
terrance.dixon@morehouse.edu
DIXON, Tiffany ... 312-850-7000 .. 138 A
tdixon10@ccc.edu
DIXON, Todd ... 386-312-4190 .. 108 B
todddixon@sjrstate.edu
DIXON, Warlyn Kevi ... 919-546-8565 .. 355 F
kevi.dixon@shawu.edu
DIXON, William ... 270-831-9650 .. 189 F
bill.dixon@kctcs.edu
DIXON, Willie ... 334-229-4200 ...... 1 D
wdixon@alasu.edu
DIXON-PETERS, Earic ... 818-710-2911 .... 50 A
peterseb@piercecollege.edu
DIZAZZO, Laura ... 206-934-5492 .. 506 K
laura.dizazzo@seattlecolleges.edu
DIZINNO, Janet, B ... 210-436-3737 .. 464 H
jdizinno@stmarytx.edu
DIZON, Michael, M ... 773-442-4226 .. 149 J
m-dizon@neiu.edu
DJALALI, Chaden ... 319-335-2610 .. 169 H
chaden-djalali@uiowa.edu
DJUKIC, Stevan ... 918-876-2529 .. 386 F
sdjukic@okwu.edu
DJURIC, Teresa, A ... 540-887-7243 .. 491 G
tdjuric@mbc.edu
DLUGOS, James, S ... 207-893-7711 .. 204 D
jdlugos@sjcme.edu
DLUGOS, Joseph ... 252-399-6366 .. 341 P
jadlugos@barton.edu
DLUGOS, OSA, Raymond 978-837-5130 .. 225 E
raymond.dlugos@merrimack.edu
DMITROVSKY, Ethan ... 713-792-2121 .. 477 F
DO, Dao ... 714-484-7316 .... 54 G
ddo@cypresscollege.edu
DO, Teresa ... 312-427-2737 .. 143 G
tdo@jmls.edu
DOAK, Bryan, E ... 928-344-7617 .... 11 J
bryan.doak@azwestern.edu
DOAK, Greg ... 207-768-9571 .. 205 D
greg.doak@maine.edu
DOAK, Joshua, M ... 417-659-4460 .. 268 H
doak-j@mssu.edu

DOMINY, Robert .... 478-757-3579.. 118 G
rdominy@centralgatech.edu

DOMKE-DAMONTE,
Darla, J .... 843-349-2129.. 428 E
ddamonte@coastal.edu

DOMMER, David .... 919-658-7854.. 355 K
ddommer@umo.edu

DOMNICK, Krista, R .... 919-515-2866.. 357 B
krdomnic@ncsu.edu

DOMPE, Rudy .... 818-719-6440.... 50 A
domperf@piercecollege.edu

DOMPIERRE, Michael, B . 636-922-8355.. 271 A
mdompierre@stchas.edu

DOMZALSKI, Jim .... 570-740-0342.. 409 E
jdomzalski@luzerne.edu

DONA, David .... 541-383-7222.. 390 D
ddona@cocc.edu

DONAGHUE, Jennifer, H . 202-994-4477.... 92 D
iso@gwu.edu

DONAHOO, David .... 434-592-3084.. 491 D
ddonahoo@liberty.edu

DONAHUE, Amy .... 860-486-4037.... 89 D
amy.donahue@uconn.edu

DONAHUE, Bob .... 614-947-6010.. 369 A
robert.donahue@franklin.edu

DONAHUE, Colin .... 818-677-2333.... 34 A
colin.donahue@csun.edu

DONAHUE, David, A .... 802-443-3060.. 484 F
ddonahue@middlebury.edu

DONAHUE, Eileen, B .... 203-432-5850.... 90 D
eileen.donahue@yale.edu

DONAHUE, James, A ...... 925-631-4203.... 59 I
president@stmarys-ca.edu

DONAHUE, James, P .... 423-652-6002.. 440 J
jpd@king.edu

DONAHUE, Janice, M ..... 423-585-6921.. 447 D
janice.donahue@ws.edu

DONAHUE, Joseph .... 610-526-1867.. 405 B
jdonahue@harcum.edu

DONAHUE, Linda, V .... 802-654-2563.. 484 I
ldonahue@smcvt.edu

DONAHUE, Lorraine .... 814-262-3822.. 413 P
ldonahue@pennhighlands.edu

DONAHUE, Nancy .... 865-694-6541.. 446 G
ndonahue@pstcc.edu

DONAHUE, Patrick .... 812-855-3207.. 162 F
donahued@indiana.edu

DONAHUE, Robert .... 617-353-9515.. 216 E
rdonahue@bu.edu

DONAHUE, Sean .... 772-462-7751.. 103 B
sdonahue@irsc.edu

DONALD, Ryan, J .... 330-471-8195.. 371 J
rdonald@malone.edu

DONALDSON, Adam .... 334-386-7254...... 3 I
adonaldson@faulkner.edu

DONALDSON, Anthony .... 951-343-4841.... 29 H
adonaldson@calbaptist.edu

DONALDSON, Daniel .... 619-563-7211.... 54 A
ddonaldson@nu.edu

DONALDSON, Devlin .... 847-628-2087.. 144 B
devlin.donaldson@judsonu.edu

DONALDSON, Janice, W . 904-620-2476.. 112 B
jdonalds@unf.edu

DONALDSON, Jody .... 319-398-7186.. 174 I
jdonald@kirkwood.edu

DONALDSON, John, A .... 406-265-3520.. 277 E
jdonaldson@msun.edu

DONALDSON, Penny .... 785-442-6054.. 181 H
pdonaldson@highlandcc.edu

DONALDSON, Scott .... 510-780-4500.... 48 J
sdonaldson@lifewest.edu

DONALDSON, Stewart ..... 909-607-9013.... 38 I
stewart.donaldson@cgu.edu

DONALDSON, Terry .... 671-735-2187.. 530 B
tdonaldson@triton.uog.edu

DONALDSON, Tracey .... 732-255-0400.. 293 E
tdonaldson@ocean.edu

DONAT, Kim .... 920-424-3377.. 520 E
donatk@uwosh.edu

DONATH, Ben .... 712-749-2181.. 170 D
donath@bvu.edu

DONATHAN, David .... 859-336-1743.. 189 C
david.donathan@kctcs.edu

DONATI, Dana .... 724-480-3608.. 401 F
dana.donati@ccbc.edu

DONATO, CSC, John, J ... 503-943-8532.. 396 B
donato@up.edu

DONATO, Michelle .... 570-674-6265.. 410 K
mdonato@misericordia.edu

DONAVANT, Brian .... 731-881-3510.. 448 G
bdonavant@utm.edu

DONAVANT, Lori, A .... 731-881-7815.. 448 G
ldonavant@utm.edu

DONAVANT, Susan, H ..... 804-752-7222.. 493 C
sdonavan@rmc.edu

DONAVON, Annette .... 716-375-2234.. 328 B
amcgraw@sbu.edu

DONCEVIC, John, G .... 724-847-6692.. 404 B
jgdoncev@geneva.edu

DONCITS, Diane .... 651-641-3472.. 247 G
ddoncits@luthersem.edu

DONCSECZ, Joseph, J ..... 814-865-1355.. 412 F
jjd7@psu.edu

DONE, Karen .... 662-621-4153.. 257 B
kwdone@coahomacc.edu

DONE, Kenneth .... 662-254-3624.. 260 A
kennth.done@mvsu.edu

DONEGAN, Helen .... 407-235-3935.. 111 E
helen.donegan@ucf.edu

DONEGAN, John, P .... 734-487-3591.. 233 J
jdonega1@emich.edu

DONELAN, Pam .... 605-229-8401.. 436 H
pam.donelan@presentation.edu

DONELSON, Felecia .... 901-334-5823.. 442 C
fdonelson@memphisseminary.edu

DONELSON, Rollin .... 336-334-5963.. 358 B
rollin_donelson@uncg.edu

DONG, Suhua .... 717-337-6487.. 404 C
sdong@gettysburg.edu

DONHAM, Brent .... 903-886-5390.. 468 D
brent.donham@tamuc.edu

DONHAM, Marilyn .... 734-973-3630.. 242 G
mdonham@wccnet.edu

DONHARDT, Gary, L .... 901-678-2231.. 445 C
donhardt@memphis.edu

DONIN, Robert, B .... 603-646-0101.. 286 J
robert.b.donin@dartmouth.edu

DONINI, Joseph .... 845-398-4040.. 329 G
jdonini@stac.edu

DONIUS, Mary Alice .... 203-365-4508.... 88 I
doniusm@sacredheart.edu

DONKERSLOOT, Norman . 616-392-8555.. 244 A
norman@westernsem.edu

DONLAN, Michael, J .... 757-446-5890.. 489 B
donlanmj@evms.edu

DONLEY, Bob .... 515-281-3934.. 169 F
bdonley@iastate.edu

DONLEY, Michael .... 318-675-7765.. 198 B
mdonle@lsuhsc.edu

DONLEY, Michael .... 903-566-7284.. 477 B
mdonley@uttyler.edu

DONLEY, Steve .... 714-484-7233.... 54 G
sdonley@cypresscollege.edu

DONLEY, Steve .... 714-484-7345.... 54 G
sdonley@cypresscollege.edu

DONLIN, Linda .... 701-328-2962.. 360 B
linda.donlin@ndus.edu

DONLIN, Mary .... 507-453-1479.. 250 C
mdonlin@southeastmn.edu

DONNA, Jerry .... 863-784-7108.. 109 G
jerry.donna@southflorida.edu

DONNAY, Brent .... 320-308-3039.. 252 A
btdonnay@stcloudstate.edu

DONNELL, Kathy, S .... 951-487-3002.... 53 D
kdonnell@msjc.edu

DONNELL, Ramsey .... 312-427-2737.. 143 G
rdonnell@jmls.edu

DONNELL, Richard, H ..... 731-424-5883.. 440 K
rdonnell@lanecollege.edu

DONNELL, Robert .... 314-264-1000.. 274 I
robert.donnell@vatterott.edu

DONNELL, Shauna, H ...... 479-968-0343.... 19 F
sdonnell@atu.edu

DONNELLA, II,
Joseph, A .... 717-337-6280.. 404 C
donnella@gettysburg.edu

DONNELLI, Amber .... 775-753-2135.. 284 I
amber.donnelli@gbcnv.edu

DONNELLI-SALLEE,
Emily .... 816-584-6779.. 270 D
emily.donnelli@park.edu

DONNELLY, Cynthia .... 401-341-3160.. 426 C
cynthia.donnelly@salve.edu

DONNELLY, David .... 816-235-1333.. 273 F
donnellyd@umkc.edu

DONNELLY, David .... 914-654-5321.. 311 A
ddonnelly@cnr.edu

DONNELLY, Diane .... 262-595-2211.. 520 F
donnelly@uwp.edu

DONNELLY, Eileen, G ...... 302-356-6812.... 91 I
eileen.g.donnelly@wilmu.edu

DONNELLY, Jeffrey .... 732-987-2427.. 292 A
jdonnelly@georgian.edu

DONNELLY, Jilian .... 610-361-5261.. 411 E
donnellj@neumann.edu

DONNELLY, John .... 434-961-5205.. 498 C
jdonnelly@pvcc.edu

DONNELLY, JR., Joseph . 617-373-2520.. 227 B

DONNELLY, Sharon .... 215-489-2317.. 402 A
sharon.donnelly@delval.edu

DONNELLY, Sherri .... 518-445-2396.. 303 D
sdonn@albanylaw.edu

DONNELLY, William, H ... 740-376-4701.. 372 A
whdonnelly@sbcglobal.net

DONNELLY HAMILTON,
Ann .... 419-772-1022.. 374 J
a-donnelly@onu.edu

DONNER, Nancy .... 212-261-1572.. 323 G
nancy.donner@nyit.edu

DONNHAUSER, Marc ...... 909-384-8996.... 60 C
mdonnhau@sbccd.cc.ca.us

DONOFF, R. Bruce .... 617-432-1401.. 219 D

DONOFRIO, Jason .... 480-860-2700.... 13 G
jdonofrio@taliesin.edu

DONOFRIO, Joseph .... 864-578-8770.. 432 D
jdonofrio@sherman.edu

DONOGHUE, Daniel, J .... 858-822-5155.... 70 C
ddonoghue@ucsd.edu

DONOGHUE, Karen, A .... 203-254-4000.... 87 G
kdonoghue@fairfield.edu

DONOHOE, Janet .... 678-839-6636.. 129 E
jdonohoe@westga.edu

DONOHOE, Kerry .... 978-934-2542.. 221 A
kerry_donohoe@uml.edu

DONOHOE, Nancy .... 312-935-4804.. 152 D
ndonohoe@robertmorris.edu

DONOHOO, Daniel .... 650-325-5621.... 59 J
daniel.donohoo@stpatricksseminary.org

DONOHUE, Beth .... 315-568-3115.. 323 A
bdonohue@nycc.edu

DONOHUE, John .... 609-771-2393.. 290 F
jdonohue@tcnj.edu

DONOHUE, Mare .... 518-464-8636.. 314 A
mare@excelsior.edu

DONOHUE, Mary .... 518-736-3622.. 315 A
mdonohue@fmcc.suny.edu

DONOHUE, Michael .... 312-777-8582.. 142 G
mdonohue@aii.edu

DONOHUE, Michael, T .... 212-752-1530.. 318 F
michael.donohue@limcollege.edu

DONOHUE, Michelle .... 831-479-6525.... 29 G
midonohu@cabrillo.edu

DONOHUE, Patrick, R ..... 570-941-4072.. 422 B
patrick.donohue@scranton.edu

DONOHUE, OSA,
Peter, M .... 610-519-8881.. 422 G
peter.donohue@villanova.edu

DONOHUE, Terry .... 631-656-2121.. 314 F
theresa.donahue@ftc.edu

DONOHUE-GONZALEZ,
Kristen .... 914-323-7534.. 319 N
kristen.donohue-gonzalez@mville.edu

DONOTO, Chris .... 847-317-8113.. 156 B
cdonoto@tiu.edu

DONOVAN, Amy, E .... 978-468-7111.. 219 B
adonovan@gcts.edu

DONOVAN, SND, Anne ... 617-735-9822.. 218 C
donovan@emmanuel.edu

DONOVAN, Anthony .... 615-460-5802.. 438 J
anthony.donovan@belmont.edu

DONOVAN, Celeste .... 620-417-1016.. 184 I
celeste.donovan@sccc.edu

DONOVAN, Eileen .... 802-728-1325.. 486 D
ecd04180@vtc.edu

DONOVAN, Gary, L .... 320-589-6065.. 255 F
donovang@morris.umn.edu

DONOVAN, James .... 657-278-2777.... 33 A
jdonovan@fullerton.edu

DONOVAN, Joan .... 607-844-8222.. 337 G
donovaj@tc3.edu

DONOVAN, Joseph .... 978-542-6119.. 222 D
jdonovan@salemstate.edu

DONOVAN, Kevin .... 716-896-0700.. 339 E
kdonovan@villa.edu

DONOVAN, Mark .... 312-413-1401.. 156 F
mdonovan@uic.edu

DONOVAN, Michael .... 617-353-8630.. 216 E
donovanm@bu.edu

DONOVAN, R. Nowell ...... 817-257-7101.. 469 G
r.donovan@tcu.edu

DONOVAN, Susan .... 410-617-2842.. 208 G
sdonovan@loyola.edu

DONOVAN, Verna .... 312-362-6173.. 139 C
vdonovan@depaul.edu

DONOVAN, Veronica .... 913-758-4372.. 185 F
veronica.donovan@stmary.edu

DONOWAY, Troy .... 301-687-7003.. 212 F
dtdonoway@frostburg.edu

DONSBACH, Dave .... 217-351-2393.. 151 B
ddonsbach@parkland.edu

DONSBACH, James .... 585-343-0055.. 315 C
jadonsbach@genesee.edu

DONTES, Arnim .... 214-648-3572.. 478 C
arnim.dontes@utsouthwestern.edu

DOODY, Josh .... 650-508-3685.... 54 J
jdoody@ndnu.edu

DOOLEN, Toni .... 541-737-6400.. 393 H
toni.doolen@oregonstate.edu

DOOLEY, Chris .... 912-583-3221.. 118 B
cdooley@bpc.edu

DOOLEY, Dan .... 765-973-8348.. 162 G
dadooley@iue.edu

DOOLEY, David, M .... 401-874-2323.. 426 D
davedooley@ds.uri.edu

DOOLEY, Donna .... 603-271-6484.. 286 F
ddooley@ccsnh.edu

DOOLEY, Elizabeth, A ...... 407-823-2373.. 111 E
elizabeth.dooley@ucf.edu

DOOLEY, Frank, J .... 765-494-0615.. 166 D
dooleyf@purdue.edu

DOOLEY, John, E .... 540-231-2265.. 499 F
jdooley@vt.edu

DOOLEY, Joseph, M .... 203-392-5375.... 85 H
dooleyj1@southernct.edu

DOOLEY, Kathleen A, M .. 630-515-6078.. 148 C
kdoole@midwestern.edu

DOOLEY, Larry .... 864-656-3200.. 428 C
dooley@clemson.edu

DOOLEY, Lisa .... 701-858-3447.. 360 F
lisa.dooley@minotstateu.edu

DOOLEY, Marella .... 954-923-4440.. 104 G
mking@keycollege.edu

DOOLEY, Margaret .... 520-494-5215.... 12 J
margaret.dooley1@centralaz.edu

DOOLEY, Marietta .... 215-780-1260.. 419 C
mdooley@salus.edu

DOOLEY, Robert .... 423-425-4313.. 448 F
robert-dooley@utc.edu

DOOLEY, Ron .... 954-923-4440.. 104 G
admissions@keycollege.edu

DOOLEY, Ronald .... 954-923-4440.. 104 G
rdooley@keycollege.edu

DOOLEY, Sue .... 831-656-3023.. 528 D
sgdooley@nps.edu

DOOLIN, Bobbie .... 606-546-1263.. 193 E
bdoolin@unionky.edu

DOOLITTLE, Eric .... 630-637-5104.. 149 H
edoolittle@noctrl.edu

DOOLOS, Robert, K .... 225-578-1686.. 197 I
rdoolos@lsu.edu

DOORN, Dawn .... 760-480-8474.... 74 L
ddoorn@wscal.edu

DOOROS, Daniel, J .... 949-824-7475.... 69 C
djdooros@uci.edu

DOPF, Kevin, C .... 334-683-2321...... 5 G
kdopf@marionmilitary.edu

DOPP, Kristi .... 206-592-3504.. 504 E
kdopp@highline.edu

DOPP, Mary Jane .... 219-989-2915.. 166 F
dopp@pnw.edu

DOPSON, Brian .... 386-752-1822.. 100 L
brian.dopson@fgc.edu

DOPSON, Lea, R .... 909-869-3464.... 31 J
lrdopson@cpp.edu

DORADO, Luis .... 310-233-4031.... 49 I
doradol@lahc.edu

DORAN, Andrea .... 775-445-4265.. 285 B
andrea.doran@wnc.edu

DORAN, Brenda .... 401-232-6106.. 424 K
bdoran@bryant.edu

DORAN, Christine, M .... 315-267-3354.. 334 B
dorancm@potsdam.edu

DORAN, Douglas .... 772-462-7159.. 103 B
ddoran@irsc.edu

DORAN, Dru, A .... 810-762-3000.. 242 B
drudoran@umflint.edu

DORAN, Marcia .... 203-285-2389.... 86 C
mdoran@gwcc.commnet.edu

DORAN, Pam .... 803-777-2752.. 433 F
pdoran@mailbox.sc.edu

DORAN, Stacy .... 920-735-5698.. 523 C
doran@fvtc.edu

DORANTES, Andrew, R .... 909-621-8126.... 46 A
andrew_dorantes@hmc.edu

DORCEY, Penny, R .... 734-384-4311.. 238 C
pdorcey@monroeccc.edu

DORCHEUS, Greg .... 503-338-2489.. 390 G
gdorcheus@clatsopcc.edu

DORCHEUS, Stephanie .... 503-338-2425.. 390 G
sdorcheus@clatsopcc.edu

DORDICK, Jonathan, S .... 518-276-6000.. 327 B
dordij@rpi.edu

DORE, David .... 520-206-2111.... 16 F
ddore@pima.edu

DORE, David .... 520-206-7100.... 16 F
ddore@pima.edu

DORF, Laurie .... 718-997-3920.. 309 D
laurie.dorf@qc.cuny.edu

DORFF, Robert .... 470-578-6124.. 123 J
rdorff@kennesaw.edu

DORFMAN, Laura .... 310-377-5501.... 51 G
ldorfman@marymountcalifornia.edu

DORGAN, Mark, W .... 802-656-0518.. 485 D
mark.dorgan@uvm.edu

DORGAN, Sheila .... 508-910-6527.. 220 H
sdorgan@umassd.edu

DORHOUT, Peter, K .... 785-532-5110.. 182 D
dorhout@ksu.edu

DORIA, Joseph .... 201-761-6195.. 296 K
jdoria@saintpeters.edu

DORIANI, Daniel, M .... 314-434-4044.. 264 C
dan.doriani@covenantseminary.edu

DORINO, Hector .... 312-697-8045.. 141 B
hdorino@harrington.edu

DORIS, Eugene, P .... 203-254-4000.... 87 G
edoris@fairfield.edu

DORITY, Nancy .... 657-278-2350.... 33 A
ndority@fullerton.edu

DORMAN, Jay, A .... 334-833-4406...... 4 D
jdorman@hawks.huntingdon.edu

DORMAN, Jeremy .... 903-693-2009.. 463 D
jdorman@panola.edu

DOWELL, Tanya .... 620-417-1121.. 184 I
tanya.dowell@sccc.edu
DOWEN, Chris .... 303-315-2550.... 84 A
chris.dowen@ucdenver.edu
DOWER, David .... 202-885-3278.... 91 J
dower@american.edu
DOWER, Julia .... 603-542-7744.. 286 G
jdower@ccsnh.edu
DOWLAND, Pam .... 812-357-6515.. 167 B
pdowland@saintmeinrad.edu
DOWLESS, Donald, V ...... 706-233-7201.. 127 A
chimes@shorter.edu
DOWLING, Beth .... 603-428-2239.. 287 C
edowling@nec.edu
DOWLING, Earl .... 630-942-3416.. 138 B
dowlinge@cod.edu
DOWLING, Joseph, B ...... 714-895-8158.... 39 F
jdowling@gwc.cccd.edu
DOWLING, Timothy, F .... 302-831-3699.... 91 F
tdowling@udel.edu
DOWLING, Victoria, A ..... 618-537-2154.. 147 F
vadowling@mckendree.edu
DOWNES, Amanda .... 302-736-2318.... 91 G
amanda.downes@wesley.edu
DOWNES, Harry, W .... 302-857-7911.... 90 F
hdownes@desu.edu
DOWNES, John .... 770-426-2646.. 124 B
jdownes@life.edu
DOWNES, Kathy .... 316-978-3586.. 185 J
kathy.downes@wichita.edu
DOWNES, Kelly .... 618-437-5321.. 152 A
downes@rlc.edu
DOWNEY, Brenda .... 207-741-5500.. 203 M
bdowney@smccme.edu
DOWNEY, Christina .... 765-455-9385.. 163 A
downeyca@iuk.edu
DOWNEY, Diana .... 215-248-6309.. 409 D
ddowney@ltsp.edu
DOWNEY, James .... 412-924-1450.. 417 E
jdowney@pts.edu
DOWNEY, John, A .... 540-453-2200.. 496 F
downeyj@brcc.edu
DOWNEY, Liesl, V .... 773-442-4200.. 149 J
l-downey@neiu.edu
DOWNEY, Mechell .... 405-382-9260.. 387 L
m.downey@sscok.edu
DOWNEY, Nancy .... 207-859-4503.. 202 G
ndowney@colby.edu
DOWNEY, Nora .... 610-785-6582.. 418 E
ndowney@scs.edu
DOWNEY, Patricia .... 412-365-1199.. 400 G
downey@chatham.edu
DOWNEY, Paul .... 615-297-7545.. 438 F
downeyp@aquinascollege.edu
DOWNEY-SCHILLING,
JoAnna .... 562-463-3100.... 58 I
jschilling@riohondo.edu
DOWNING, Amy .... 617-730-7174.. 226 J
amy.downing@newbury.edu
DOWNING, Arthur .... 646-312-1020.. 307 A
arthur.downing@baruch.cuny.edu
DOWNING, Beverly .... 410-951-3010.. 212 E
bdowning@coppin.edu
DOWNING, Chris .... 404-894-7700.. 121 D
chris.downing@innovate.gatech.edu
DOWNING, Gerri .... 608-757-7759.. 523 A
gdowning1@blackhawk.edu
DOWNING, Irv .... 956-882-6577.. 476 E
irv.downing@utrgv.edu
DOWNING, Jay .... 432-837-8368.. 471 E
jdowning@sulross.edu
DOWNING, Jill .... 503-554-2121.. 391 D
jdowning@georgefox.edu
DOWNING, Kimberly .... 513-556-5028.. 379 A
kimberly.downing@uc.edu
DOWNING, Michael .... 508-336-8700.. 425 B
mdowning@jwu.edu
DOWNING, Rossann .... 816-604-4071.. 267 K
rossann.downing@mcckc.edu
DOWNING, Sherry .... 828-884-8437.. 342 C
downinsc@brevard.edu
DOWNING, Stacy, L .... 302-857-6300.... 90 F
sdowning@desu.edu
DOWNING, Steve .... 317-955-6351.. 165 N
sdowning@marian.edu
DOWNING, Tim .... 602-682-6800.... 11 I
tdowning@azsummitlaw.edu
DOWNS, Amy .... 717-815-1781.. 424 F
adowns@ycp.edu
DOWNS, Jesse, G .... 225-578-7180.. 197 I
jdowns@lsu.edu
DOWNS, Mary .... 920-735-5695.. 523 C
downsm@fvtc.edu
DOWNS, Sherry .... 740-593-4129.. 375 H
downs@ohio.edu
DOWNS, Timothy .... 605-626-2521.. 437 D
president@northern.edu
DOWNS, Wil .... 812-237-4114.. 162 A
wil.downs@indstate.edu
DOWNS, William .... 252-328-6249.. 356 C
downsw14@ecu.edu
DOWNS-BURNS, Kim ...... 802-443-5158.. 484 F
kdowns@middlebury.edu
DOWSEK, Richard .... 312-369-7060.. 138 F
rdowsek@colum.edu
DOWTY, Janet .... 317-738-8100.. 160 J
jdowty@franklincollege.edu
DOXEY, Tia, M .... 919-530-7269.. 357 A
tdoxey@nccu.edu
DOYLE, Adrian .... 310-338-1973.... 51 E
adrian.doyle@lmu.edu
DOYLE, Amanda .... 337-482-6730.. 201 D
amandad@louisiana.edu
DOYLE, Anne .... 617-663-7054.. 219 I
DOYLE, Barbara .... 805-765-9300.... 62 K
DOYLE, Catherine .... 585-389-2123.. 322 D
cdoyle0@naz.edu
DOYLE, Cathleen, H .... 410-777-2902.. 206 B
chdoyle@aacc.edu
DOYLE, Christy .... 208-769-3481.. 134 C
cadoyle@nic.edu
DOYLE, Clare .... 215-248-7071.. 400 H
doylec@chc.edu
DOYLE, David .... 315-792-7100.. 336 C
ddoyle@sunypoly.edu
DOYLE, Denise .... 210-829-3900.. 474 D
ddoyle@uiwtx.edu
DOYLE, Denise .... 210-283-6827.. 474 D
ddoyle@uiwtx.edu
DOYLE, Diana, M .... 303-797-5701.... 76 J
diana.doyle@arapahoe.edu
DOYLE, Eileen .... 914-633-2483.. 317 B
edoyle@iona.edu
DOYLE, Fiona, M .... 510-642-5472.... 68 M
graddean@berkeley.edu
DOYLE, Francis, J .... 617-495-1000.. 219 D
DOYLE, Fred .... 518-956-7942.. 331 A
fdoyle@albany.edu
DOYLE, Gerald .... 312-567-5203.. 142 I
doyle@iit.edu
DOYLE, J. Griffin .... 706-542-8096.. 128 E
gdoyle@uga.edu
DOYLE, Jamie .... 858-225-4301.... 30 F
DOYLE, Janice, B .... 301-445-1901.. 211 D
jdoyle@usmd.edu
DOYLE, Jeanette, M .... 413-748-3110.. 228 E
jdoyle2@springfieldcollege.edu
DOYLE, Jeff .... 254-710-1011.. 452 H
jeff_doyle@baylor.edu
DOYLE, Jillian .... 323-469-3300.... 26 A
jdoyle@amda.edu
DOYLE, Joy, E .... 724-847-6636.. 404 B
jedoyle@geneva.edu
DOYLE, Kevin .... 530-898-6222.... 32 C
kadoyle@csuchico.edu
DOYLE, Leslie .... 314-889-4503.. 265 C
ldoyle@fontbonne.edu
DOYLE, Lori, N .... 215-895-2613.. 402 G
lori.n.doyle@drexel.edu
DOYLE, Maria .... 678-839-4780.. 129 E
mdoyle@westga.edu
DOYLE, Mary .... 831-459-4906.... 70 F
mdoyle1@ucsc.edu
DOYLE, Michael, H .... 563-588-7823.. 174 K
mike.doyle@loras.edu
DOYLE, Sheila .... 607-777-3844.. 331 B
sdoyle@binghamton.edu
DOYLE, Susan .... 205-726-2375...... 6 E
sdoyle@samford.edu
DOYLE, Timothy .... 901-321-3548.. 439 E
tdoyle1@cbu.edu
DOYLE, William .... 804-758-6700.. 498 D
wdoyle@rappahannock.edu
DOYLEN, Michael .... 414-229-4781.. 520 D
doylenm@uwm.edu
DOZIER, Cheryl .... 912-358-4000.. 126 F
ssupresident@savannahstate.edu
DOZIER, John .... 803-777-9943.. 433 F
jdozier@mailbox.sc.edu
DOZIER, Ken .... 252-399-6596.. 341 P
kdozier@barton.edu
DOZIER, Kristine, L .... 317-788-3219.. 168 A
dozierk@uindy.edu
DOZIER, Luann, D .... 504-865-5794.. 200 C
ldozier@tulane.edu
DOZIER, Rodney .... 620-276-9603.. 181 C
rodney.dozier@gcccks.edu
DOZIER, Ronda .... 903-823-3088.. 467 C
ronda.dozier@texarkanacollege.edu
DRABIK, Joshua .... 954-545-4500.. 109 F
webmaster@sfbc.edu
DRABIK, Mary, A .... 954-545-4500.. 109 F
mdrabik@sfbc.edu
DRACHMAN, Annette, R .. 843-792-4063.. 431 A
drachmar@musc.edu
DRAEGER, James .... 262-691-5323.. 524 G
jdraeger5@wctc.edu
DRAEMEL, Ian .... 785-738-9031.. 183 J
idraemel@ncktc.edu
DRAGAN, Kimberly .... 860-738-6418.... 87 A
kdragan@nwcc.edu
DRAGON, Emily .... 207-602-2451.. 205 F
edragon@une.edu
DRAGOUN, Mary Beth .... 805-581-1233.... 43 B
mdragoun@eternitybiblecollege.com
DRAIN, Cecil, B .... 804-828-7247.. 496 D
cbdrain@vcu.edu
DRAIN, Jerome .... 713-718-7746.. 459 B
jerome.drain@hccs.edu
DRAIN, Timothy, S .... 903-510-2458.. 473 C
tdra@tjc.edu
DRAKE, Ann .... 315-787-4000.. 314 E
ann.drake@flhealth.org
DRAKE, Brian .... 713-221-2765.. 474 B
drakeb@uhd.edu
DRAKE, Brittney .... 714-816-0366.... 68 E
brittney.drake@trident.edu
DRAKE, Carlene .... 909-558-4581.... 49 C
cdrake@llu.edu
DRAKE, Christian .... 704-847-5600.. 355 J
cdrake@ses.edu
DRAKE, David .... 706-865-2134.. 128 D
ddrake@truett.edu
DRAKE, Dawn, M .... 608-342-1468.. 521 A
drake@uwplatt.edu
DRAKE, Edna .... 601-977-7876.. 261 A
edrake@tougaloo.edu
DRAKE, George .... 717-871-7333.. 415 F
george.drake@millersville.edu
DRAKE, Heather .... 334-876-9234...... 4 A
DRAKE, James .... 214-648-2088.. 478 C
james.drake@utsouthwestern.edu
DRAKE, Jennifer, A .... 317-791-5704.. 168 A
jdrake@uindy.edu
DRAKE, Kay, L .... 859-238-5467.. 187 H
kay.drake@centre.edu
DRAKE, Kourtney .... 816-279-7000.. 262 B
registrar@abtu.edu
DRAKE, Lynette .... 217-581-3221.. 139 H
ldrake@eiu.edu
DRAKE, Michael, V .... 614-292-2424.. 375 A
drake.379@osu.edu
DRAKE, Paul .... 671-734-1812.. 530 A
pdrake@piu.edu
DRAKE, Peter .... 212-966-0300.. 322 F
pdrake@nyaa.edu
DRAKE, Roger, D .... 660-248-6221.. 263 B
rdrake@centralmethodist.edu
DRAKE, Sheryl .... 217-351-2280.. 151 B
sdrake@parkland.edu
DRAKE, Steve .... 618-283-4170.. 145 D
DRAKE, Susan, K .... 217-245-3041.. 141 G
sdrake@mail.ic.edu
DRAKE, Tom .... 575-769-4994.. 299 G
tom.drake@clovis.edu
DRAKE, Tonya .... 425-640-1559.. 503 E
tonya.drake@edcc.edu
DRAKE, Tyler .... 480-212-1704.... 16 R
DRAKE-DEESE, Kent .... 603-358-2346.. 288 E
kdrakedeese@keene.edu
DRAKES, Gail .... 212-229-5600.. 322 E
drakesg@newschool.edu
DRAKSLER, Vicki .... 309-692-4092.. 147 I
vdraksler@midstate.edu
DRAMMEH, Lamin .... 803-793-5197.. 429 D
drammehl@denmarktech.edu
DRANSFIELD, Scott .... 540-261-4122.. 494 F
scott.dransfield@svu.edu
DRAPEAU, Guy .... 860-297-4210.... 89 B
guy.drapeau@trincoll.edu
DRAPER, David .... 310-377-5501.... 51 G
ddraper@marymountcalifornia.edu
DRAPER, Dennis .... 310-338-7504.... 51 E
dennis.draper@lmu.edu
DRAPER, Diana, M .... 203-254-4125.... 87 G
ddraper@fairfield.edu
DRAPER, Frances .... 303-492-7531.... 83 K
frances.draper@colorado.edu
DRAPER, Jeri .... 215-751-8199.. 401 G
jdraper@ccp.edu
DRAPER, Mark .... 717-866-5775.. 403 F
mdraper@evangelical.edu
DRAPER, Nancy, J .... 405-912-9024.. 387 D
ndraper@hc.edu
DRASGOW, Fritz .... 217-333-1480.. 157 A
fdrasgow@illinois.edu
DRASS, Mike .... 302-736-2545.... 91 G
michael.drass@wesley.edu
DRAUD, Matthew .... 517-264-7667.. 241 A
mdraud@sienaheights.edu
DRAUDE, Barbara, J .... 615-904-8383.. 444 G
barbara.draude@mtsu.edu
DRAUGHON,
Katherine, A .... 812-465-7107.. 168 E
kdraughon@usi.edu
DRAVES, Patricia, H .... 330-823-2690.. 379 F
dravesph@mountunion.edu
DRAWDY, Lester, W .... 770-720-5927.. 126 C
lwd@reinhardt.edu
DRAYER, Judy .... 602-274-1885.... 16 D
jdrayer@pihma.edu
DRAYFAHL, Perry, M .... 610-499-1291.. 423 E
pmdrayfahl@widener.edu
DRAYNA, Jonathan .... 414-425-8300.. 519 F
jdrayna@shsst.edu
DRAYTON, Paul .... 856-222-9311.. 295 C
DRAYTON, Ronald .... 803-738-7606.. 431 B
draytonr@midlandstech.edu
DREBIN, Diane .... 541-278-5796.. 390 C
ddrebin@bluecc.edu
DREES, Lynn .... 941-752-5428.. 110 H
dreesl@scf.edu
DREESSEN, Angela .... 309-694-5353.. 141 F
angela.dreessen@icc.edu
DREFFS, Daryl .... 603-668-2211.. 287 I
d.dreffs@snhu.edu
DREGER, Barb .... 920-735-4776.. 523 C
dreger@fvtc.edu
DREGIER, Denise, M .... 443-412-2428.. 208 A
ddregier@harford.edu
DREHER, H. Michael .... 914-654-5441.. 311 A
hdreher@cnr.edu
DREHER, Karolina .... 610-796-8218.. 397 D
karolina.dreher@alvernia.edu
DREIER, Alexander .... 203-432-4949.... 90 D
alexander.dreier@yale.edu
DREILING, Karolyn .... 913-758-6293.. 185 F
karolyn.dreiling@stmary.edu
DREISBACH, Joseph, H ... 570-941-4760.. 422 B
joseph.dreisbach@scranton.edu
DRELL, Persis .... 650-723-3938.... 66 I
DRENKOW, Daniel, D .... 605-274-5251.. 435 E
dan.drenkow@augie.edu
DRENNEN, Rebecca, J .... 212-986-4343.. 305 B
rjd@berkeleycollege.edu
DRENNEN, Rebecca, J .... 973-278-5400.. 289 F
rjd@berkeleycollege.edu
DRENNING, Caleb .... 814-472-3035.. 418 F
cdrenning@francis.edu
DRESCHER, Kurt, W .... 978-468-7111.. 219 B
kdrescher@gcts.edu
DRESS, Jennifer .... 410-455-2868.. 211 G
dress@umbc.edu
DRESSEN, Dan .... 507-786-3420.. 254 P
dressen@stolaf.edu
DRESSER, Charles .... 607-729-1581.. 312 E
cdresser@davisny.edu
DRESSER, Kathy .... 914-337-9300.. 311 F
kathy.dresser@concordia-ny.edu
DRESSER-RECKTENWALD,
Wendy .... 607-587-4025.. 334 G
dressews@alfredstate.edu
DRESSLER, Chris .... 563-588-8167.. 170 F
chris.dressler@clarke.edu
DRESSLER, Daniel .... 405-789-7661.. 388 B
daniel.dressler@swcu.edu
DREVON, Charles .... 574-239-8392.. 161 N
cdrevon@hcc-nd.edu
DREVS, John .... 312-915-6941.. 146 G
jdrevs@luc.edu
DREW, Daniel, J .... 716-888-2569.. 306 F
drewd@canisius.edu
DREW, John .... 617-827-6047.. 220 G
john.drew@umb.edu
DREW, Phil .... 405-425-1842.. 385 C
philip.drew@oc.edu
DREWELOW, Lonna .... 319-363-1323.. 175 D
ldrewelow@mtmercy.edu
DREWENSKI, Shirley .... 708-596-2000.. 154 E
sdrewenski@ssc.edu
DREWS, Dani .... 518-244-2274.. 327 H
drewsd@sage.edu
DREWS, David .... 517-265-5161.. 230 D
ddrews@adrian.edu
DREWS, Jennifer .... 715-425-4481.. 521 B
jennifer.drews@uwrf.edu
DREXEL, Penny, M .... 814-332-4311.. 397 A
pdrexel@allegheny.edu
DREXLER, Brad .... 610-796-8376.. 397 D
bradley.drexler@alvernia.edu
DREXLER, Jim .... 706-419-1427.. 119 G
jim.drexler@covenant.edu
DREXLER-HINES,
Elizabeth .... 508-767-7343.. 214 F
ea.drexlerhines@assumption.edu
DREYER, Allen, R .... 570-586-2400.. 419 G
adreyer@summitu.edu
DREYER, John, M .... 260-452-3139.. 160 D
john.dreyer@ctsfw.edu
DREYER, Thomas .... 978-934-4801.. 221 A
thomas_dreyer@uml.edu
DREYFUS, Mark, B .... 757-671-7171.. 489 C
president@ecpi.edu
DREYFUSS, Simeon .... 503-699-3961.. 392 D
sdreyfuss@marylhurst.edu
DREYFUSS, Teresa .... 562-908-3403.... 58 I
tdreyfuss@riohondo.edu
DRIEDGER, Derek .... 605-995-2635.. 435 F
dedriedg@dwu.edu
DRIER, Tracy, M .... 715-833-6498.. 523 B
tdrier@cvtc.edu

DUFFY, Brian .... 901-381-3939.. 449 F
brian@visible.edu
DUFFY, Cami .... 270-809-3155.. 192 A
cduffy@murraystate.edu
DUFFY, Chris .... 813-974-0658.. 112 C
cduffy@usf.edu
DUFFY, Dolly .... 574-631-2788.. 168 B
eduffy@nd.edu
DUFFY, James, P .... 717-337-6240.. 404 C
jpduffy@gettysburg.edu
DUFFY, James, P .... 757-683-3808.. 492 G
jduffy@odu.edu
DUFFY, Joan .... 805-546-3100.... 41 L
joan_duffy@cuesta.edu
DUFFY, Julia, A .... 203-254-4000.... 87 G
jduffy@fairfield.edu
DUFFY, Kristine .... 518-743-2237.. 335 A
duffyk@sunyacc.edu
DUFFY, Matthew .... 218-726-8829.. 255 D
duffy@d.umn.edu
DUFFY, Michael .... 517-265-5161.. 230 D
mduffy@adrian.edu
DUFFY, Michael .... 610-282-1100.. 402 B
michael.duffy@desales.edu
DUFFY, Pamela, A .... 619-239-0391.... 36 A
pduffy@cwsl.edu
DUFFY, Peter .... 508-999-9216.. 220 H
pduffy@umassd.edu
DUFFY, Rachelle, M .... 517-265-5161.. 230 D
rduffy@adrian.edu
DUFFY, Susan .... 781-239-6425.. 214 G
sduffy@babson.edu
DUFFY, II, William, R ..... 563-425-5221.. 177 D
duffyw@uiu.edu
DUFNER, Jessie .... 406-874-6226.. 276 H
dufnerj@milescc.edu
DUFOUR, Graciela .... 815-836-5270.. 145 H
dufourgr@lewisu.edu
DUFOUR, Jeff .... 518-694-7201.. 303 C
jeff.dufour@acphs.edu
DUFRENE, Uric .... 812-941-2208.. 163 F
udufrene@ius.edu
DUFRESNE-REYES, Alice . 408-848-4791.... 44 I
adufresnereyes@gavilan.edu
DUGAN, Brendan, J .... 718-489-5416.. 328 D
bdugan@sfc.edu
DUGAN, James .... 816-654-7219.. 266 E
jdugan@kcumb.edu
DUGAN, Mary .... 775-784-3941.. 285 A
mdugan@unr.edu
DUGAN, Melinda, E .... 215-887-5511.. 423 C
mdugan@wts.edu
DUGAN, Robert .... 850-474-2492.. 113 A
rdugan@uwf.edu
DUGAN, Suzanne .... 507-389-2111.. 250 E
suzanne.dugan@mnsu.edu
DUGAN-WOOD, Joyce ..... 205-929-1458....... 5 H
jduganwood@miles.edu
DUGATKIN, David .... 845-257-3802.. 331 E
dugatkind@newpaltz.edu
DUGGAN, Christina .... 781-768-7228.. 227 G
christina.duggan@regiscollege.edu
DUGGAN, David, B .... 315-464-9720.. 332 C
duggand@upstate.edu
DUGGAN, Kuris .... 937-327-6471.. 381 F
duggank@wittenberg.edu
DUGGAN, Sean .... 806-742-2661.. 472 C
s.duggan@ttu.edu
DUGGAN-GOLD, Lori ...... 516-877-3262.. 303 B
duggangold@adelphi.edu
DUGGAR, Michael .... 617-824-8268.. 218 B
michael_duggar@emerson.edu
DUGGER, Neil .... 214-333-5202.. 455 J
neil@dbu.edu
DUGUID, Stephanie .... 601-643-8341.. 257 D
stephanie.duguid@colin.edu
DUHAN, Julia .... 517-371-5140.. 243 I
duhan@cooley.edu
DUHE, Reginald .... 650-508-3500.... 54 J
rduhe@ndnu.edu
DUHL, Greg .... 651-290-6409.. 253 S
gregory.duhl@mitchellhamline.edu
DUHON, Gail .... 616-222-1431.. 233 A
gail.duhon@cornerstone.edu
DUIGNAN, Kevin .... 845-398-4017.. 329 G
kduignan@stac.edu
DUIN, Diane .... 406-896-5841.. 277 D
dduin@msubillings.edu
DUITCH, Suri .... 504-865-5555.. 200 C
sduitch@tulane.edu
DUKAKIS, Mary .... 603-668-2211.. 287 I
m.dukakis@snhu.edu
DUKE, Christopher .... 615-329-8505.. 439 L
cduke@fisk.edu
DUKE, Del, G .... 870-235-4171.... 22 F
dgduke@saumag.edu
DUKE, Lynda .... 309-556-3220.. 143 D
lduke@iwu.edu
DUKE, Phyllis .... 908-737-5000.. 292 C
pduke@kean.edu
DUKE, Robert .... 626-815-5441.... 28 A
rrduke@apu.edu
DUKE, Russell .... 626-650-2306.... 45 E
DUKE, Sean .... 206-533-6659.. 507 F
sduke@shoreline.edu
DUKE, Shalamon .... 310-287-4423.... 50 E
dukesa@wlac.edu
DUKE, Stacey .... 479-524-7371.... 20 H
sduke@jbu.edu
DUKE, Steven .... 336-758-5938.. 359 E
dukest@wfu.edu
DUKE, Steven, T .... 402-472-8845.. 282 K
sduke@nebraska.edu
DUKE, Todd .... 765-973-8611.. 162 G
mtduke@iue.edu
DUKERICH, Janet, M .... 512-232-3310.. 476 B
janet.dukerich@austin.utexas.edu
DUKES, Charlene, M .... 301-546-0400.. 210 C
dukescm@pgcc.edu
DUKES, Gary .... 503-838-8221.. 396 E
dukesg@wou.edu
DUKES, Jimmy .... 504-816-8092.. 198 H
jdukes@nobts.edu
DUKES, Mona, B .... 843-355-4121.. 435 A
dukesm@wiltech.edu
DULABAUM, Mary .... 847-628-2089.. 144 B
mdulabaum@judsonu.edu
DULANEY, Jeri .... 580-477-2000.. 389 I
jeri.dulaney@wosc.edu
DULANY, Ann .... 740-284-5254.. 368 L
adulany@franciscan.edu
DULAY, Sarah .... 708-237-5050.. 150 D
sdulay@nc.edu
DULEPSKI, Deborah, L .... 203-576-2388.... 89 C
ddulepsk@bridgeport.edu
DULEY, Louisa .... 303-273-3000.... 78 M
DULGAR, Laura .... 623-935-8808.... 14 A
laura.dulgar@estrellamountain.edu
DULIN, James .... 617-928-4554.. 226 B
jdulin@mountida.edu
DULL, Lindsay, N .... 607-733-7177.. 313 D
ldull@ebi-college.com
DULLEA, Robert .... 206-296-2590.. 507 E
dullea@seattleu.edu
DULSKI-BUCHOLZ,
Andi, L .... 701-788-4833.. 360 E
andrea.dulskibucholz@mayvillestate.edu
DUMANCELA, Fanny .... 718-518-4434.. 308 C
fdumancela@hostos.cuny.edu
DUMARCE, Harvey .... 605-698-3966.. 436 K
hmarce@swc.tc
DUMAS, Brandon .... 225-771-3922.. 199 H
brandon_dumas@subr.edu
DUMAS, Dan .... 502-897-4131.. 192 D
ddumas@sbts.edu
DUMAS, Doris .... 847-735-5039.. 145 B
dumas@lakeforest.edu
DUMAS, Maureen .... 401-598-2350.. 425 B
mdumas@jwu.edu
DUMAS, Roxanne .... 781-239-2751.. 223 F
rdumas@massbay.edu
DUMAS SERFES, Pamela . 860-439-5226.... 87 F
pamela.dumasserfes@conncoll.edu
DUMAUAL, Roberto .... 718-522-9073.. 304 D
rdumaual@asa.edu
DUMAY, Harry, E .... 603-641-7100.. 287 G
hdumay@anselm.edu
DUMBLETON, Eric .... 415-565-4616.... 69 B
dumbletoneric@uchastings.edu
DUMDEI, Mike .... 903-823-3107.. 467 C
michael.dumdei@texarkanacollege.edu
DUMIRE, William .... 724-852-3382.. 423 A
wdumire@waynesburg.edu
DUMM, Pamela .... 502-213-2109.. 190 A
pamela.dumm@kctcs.edu
DUMMER, Robin, K .... 530-226-4130.... 64 H
rdummer@simpsonu.edu
DUMONT, Elizabeth, R .... 413-545-2554.. 220 F
edumont@umass.edu
DUMONT, Greg .... 410-857-2762.. 209 D
gdumont@mcdaniel.edu
DUMONT, Judith, C .... 972-860-7026.. 456 D
jdumont@dcccd.edu
DUMONT, Ronald .... 201-692-2811.. 291 J
ronald_dumont@fdu.edu
DUMONT, Sara, E .... 202-885-1321.... 91 J
dumont@american.edu
DUMONT-SMITH, Cheryl . 860-343-5869.... 86 F
cdumont-smith@mxcc.edu
DUMONTELLE, Janine ..... 714-997-6553.... 37 F
jpdumont@chapman.edu
DUMPSON, Kimberly, C .. 410-651-7686.. 212 B
kdumpson@umes.edu
DUNAVIN, Callie .... 870-733-6840.... 19 A
cdunavin@asumidsouth.edu
DUNAWAY, Greg, A .... 804-594-1430.. 497 D
llclair@jtcc.edu
DUNAWAY, Gregory .... 304-293-4611.. 514 C
gregory.dunaway@mail.wvu.edu
DUNBAR, Brian .... 507-288-4563.. 246 C
bdunbar@crossroadscollege.edu
DUNBAR, Deirdre, M ...... 262-554-2010.. 518 B
midwestcollege@aol.com
DUNBAR, Dorlena .... 516-572-7759.. 322 C
dorlena.dunbar@ncc.edu
DUNBAR, Joan .... 313-577-5542.. 243 F
aj0824@wayne.edu
DUNBAR, Kristin .... 906-635-2625.. 236 J
kdunbar@lssu.edu
DUNBAR, Michelle .... 323-343-2730.... 33 C
mdunbar3@calstatela.edu
DUNBAR, Nathan .... 503-517-1206.. 396 D
ndunbar@warnerpacific.edu
DUNBAR, William, J .... 262-554-2010.. 518 B
dunbarphd@yahoo.com
DUNBAR-JACOB,
Jacqueline .... 412-624-2400.. 421 G
dunbar@pitt.edu
DUNCAN, C. Michael ...... 413-782-1240.. 229 E
cmichael.duncan@wne.edu
DUNCAN, Carolyn, W ...... 704-216-6195.. 346 A
cduncan@livingstone.edu
DUNCAN, Charles .... 919-508-2395.. 359 G
cduncan@peace.edu
DUNCAN, Christina .... 435-672-7753.. 482 A
duncan@dixie.edu
DUNCAN, Christopher ...... 314-977-2701.. 271 K
cmduncan@slu.edu
DUNCAN, Claudia .... 252-399-6521.. 341 P
cduncan@barton.edu
DUNCAN, Darrell .... 615-966-6166.. 441 F
darrell.duncan@lipscomb.edu
DUNCAN, Dennis, L .... 574-372-5100.. 161 B
duncandl@grace.edu
DUNCAN, JR., Eugene .... 717-299-7782.. 420 C
duncan@stevenscollege.edu
DUNCAN, Frances .... 850-484-2230.. 106 H
fduncan@pensacolastate.edu
DUNCAN, Geri .... 704-290-5221.. 353 B
gduncan@spcc.edu
DUNCAN, Issac .... 270-686-4324.. 187 C
issac.duncan@brescia.edu
DUNCAN, J. Ligon .... 601-923-1600.. 260 E
lduncan@rts.edu
DUNCAN, Jane .... 954-262-5382.. 105 J
janedunc@nova.edu
DUNCAN, Jenny .... 918-293-5488.. 386 B
jenny.duncan@okstate.edu
DUNCAN, Jerelyn .... 501-420-1237.... 18 F
jerelyn.duncan@arkansasbaptist.edu
DUNCAN, Jerelyn, L .... 501-420-1237.... 18 F
jerelyn.duncan@arkansasbaptist.edu
DUNCAN, Jim .... 901-843-3850.. 443 L
duncanjb@rhodes.edu
DUNCAN, Joan .... 470-578-3051.. 123 J
jduncan@kennesaw.edu
DUNCAN, John .... 740-377-2520.. 378 B
john.duncan@tsbc.edu
DUNCAN, John .... 313-883-8599.. 240 D
duncan.john@shms.edu
DUNCAN, John, B .... 843-863-7955.. 427 I
jduncan@csuniv.edu
DUNCAN, K. Michael .... 843-953-6356.. 428 G
duncanm@cofc.edu
DUNCAN, Kelly .... 605-626-2415.. 437 D
kelly.duncan@northern.edu
DUNCAN, Laura, H .... 334-833-4069....... 4 D
lduncan@hawks.huntingdon.edu
DUNCAN, Lee .... 661-362-2202.... 52 A
lduncan@masters.edu
DUNCAN, Lewis, M .... 401-841-7004.. 528 E
DUNCAN, Linda .... 773-244-5697.. 149 I
lduncan@northpark.edu
DUNCAN, Martina .... 207-725-3358.. 202 F
mduncan@bowdoin.edu
DUNCAN, Matthew .... 408-554-4583.... 63 E
mduncan@scu.edu
DUNCAN, Michael, W .... 724-847-6528.. 404 B
mwduncan@geneva.edu
DUNCAN, Nancy .... 503-399-2530.. 390 E
nancy.duncan@chemeketa.edu
DUNCAN, Randy .... 704-687-7323.. 358 A
rduncan@uncc.edu
DUNCAN, Renae .... 270-809-3744.. 192 A
rduncan@murraystate.edu
DUNCAN, Renae, D .... 270-809-3744.. 192 A
rduncan@murraystate.edu
DUNCAN, Robert .... 806-742-3904.. 472 C
robert.duncan@ttu.edu
DUNCAN, Robert, L .... 806-742-0012.. 472 C
chancellor@ttu.edu
DUNCAN, Robert, L .... 806-742-0012.. 472 A
DUNCAN, Steve .... 252-328-6105.. 356 C
duncans@ecu.edu
DUNCAN, Susan .... 502-852-6373.. 194 A
shdunc01@louisville.edu
DUNCAN, Suzanne .... 757-388-3693.. 494 A
sxduncan@sentara.com
DUNCAN, Teresa, S .... 865-882-4648.. 447 A
duncants@roanestate.edu
DUNCAN, Tim .... 678-466-4672.. 119 A
timduncan@clayton.edu
DUNCAN, Todd .... 513-556-6445.. 379 A
todd.duncan@uc.edu
DUNCAN, Wendy .... 559-325-3600.... 30 C
wduncan@chsu.org
DUNCAN, William, H .... 916-660-7000.... 64 F
DUNCAN, William, R .... 423-439-6000.. 444 F
duncanw@etsu.edu
DUNCAN-POITIER,
Johanna .... 518-320-1303.. 330 H
johanna.duncan-poitier@suny.edu
DUNCKLEE, Mary .... 508-565-3360.. 228 F
stonehillbkstr@fheg.follett.com
DUNDAS, Robert, G .... 559-278-3936.... 32 F
rdundas@csufresno.edu
DUNG, Peter .... 213-613-2200.... 65 H
peter_dung@sciarc.edu
DUNGAN, Bonnie, J .... 607-871-2612.. 303 F
dunganbj@alfred.edu
DUNGAN, Lynley .... 817-735-2000.. 475 C
lynley.dungan@unthsc.edu
DUNGEY, Deborah, J .... 936-361-1000.. 467 E
djdungey@pvamu.edu
DUNHAM, Andrew .... 517-629-0216.. 230 E
adunham@albion.edu
DUNHAM, Andrew, M ...... 517-629-0477.. 230 E
ddunham@albion.edu
DUNHAM, Anne .... 276-739-2456.. 499 A
adunham@vhcc.edu
DUNHAM, Anne, M .... 276-739-2456.. 499 A
adunham@vhcc.edu
DUNHAM, David .... 209-228-4264.... 70 A
ddunham@ucmerced.edu
DUNHAM, Dennis .... 405-974-2374.. 388 L
ddunham1@uco.edu
DUNHAM, Douglas, N ...... 816-501-4617.. 270 J
douglas.dunham@rockhurst.edu
DUNHAM, Elizabeth .... 802-447-4631.. 485 B
bdunham@svc.edu
DUNHAM, Mark, E .... 660-263-3900.. 263 A
markdunham@cccb.edu
DUNHAM, Rhonda, J .... 660-263-3900.. 263 A
rhondadunham@cccb.edu
DUNHAM, Stephen, S ...... 814-867-4088.. 412 F
ssd13@psu.edu
DUNHAM, Thomas .... 773-907-4477.. 137 E
tdunham@ccc.edu
DUNHAM, Wesley .... 508-849-3342.. 214 E
wdunham@annamaria.edu
DUNHAM HOWIE, Jules . 937-376-2946.. 376 F
juleshouse@payne.edu
DUNHAM STRAND, Amy 616-632-8900.. 231 A
stranamy@aquinas.edu
DUNIVAN, Daniel .... 812-749-1239.. 166 B
ddunivan@oak.edu
DUNIVAN, Daniel .... 812-749-1386.. 166 B
ddunivan@oak.edu
DUNIWAY, Robert .... 206-296-2105.. 507 E
rduniway@seattleu.edu
DUNKEL, Aaron .... 805-525-4417.... 67 J
adunkel@thomasaquinas.edu
DUNKEL, Norbert, W .... 352-392-2171.. 112 A
norbd@housing.ufl.edu
DUNKELMAN, James .... 562-907-4205.... 75 B
jdunkelman@whittier.edu
DUNKERTON, David, W .. 304-877-6428.. 510 F
david.dunkerton@abc.edu
DUNKLE, David .... 850-973-9440.. 105 H
dunkled@nfcc.edu
DUNKLE, John, H .... 847-491-2151.. 150 F
j-dunkle@northwestern.edu
DUNKLE, Kurt .... 646-717-9740.. 315 B
dunkle@gts.edu
DUNKLE, Mike .... 402-471-2505.. 281 G
mdunkle@nscs.edu
DUNKLEBERGER, Kay, E . 570-326-3761.. 413 O
kdunkleb@pct.edu
DUNKLEBERGER,
Robert, L .... 570-321-4278.. 409 F
dunkleberger@lycoming.edu
DUNKLEY, Eugene .... 618-664-6543.. 140 I
eugene.dunkley@greenville.edu
DUNKLIN, Ashley .... 251-380-3470....... 7 D
adunklin@shc.edu
DUNLAP, Doug .... 620-365-5116.. 178 A
ddunlap@allencc.edu
DUNLAP, James, H .... 517-355-2223.. 237 I
dunlap@msu.edu
DUNLAP, Marilyn .... 808-956-6151.. 131 F
mdunlap@hawaii.edu
DUNLAP, Merrilynn .... 814-393-2306.. 414 G
mdunlap@clarion.edu
DUNLAP, Scott .... 973-720-3232.. 298 G
dunlaps@wpunj.edu
DUNLAP, Susan, L .... 516-726-5816.. 529 B
dunlaps@usmma.edu
DUNLAP, Troneka .... 731-426-7526.. 440 K
DUNLAVY, Dustin .... 740-366-1351.. 365 D
ddunlavy@cotc.edu
DUNLAVY, Sean .... 317-940-9809.. 159 K
sdunlavy@butler.edu

DURR, Kimberly, H .... 618-650-2475.. 155 A
kdurr@siue.edu
DURRETT, Duane .... 817-598-6222.. 479 E
ddurrett@wc.edu
DURSI, Joseph, F .... 914-594-4234.. 323 I
joseph_dursi@nymc.edu
DURSI, Joseph, F .... 914-594-4487.. 323 I
joseph_dursi@nymc.edu
DURSI, Marcia .... 703-284-3839.. 492 A
marcia.dursi@marymount.edu
DURSO, Mary .... 215-568-9215.. 424 C
mdurso@phmc.org
DURSO, Thomas, W .... 610-921-7526.. 396 H
tdurso@albright.edu
DURST, Devoiry .... 732-414-2834.. 298 N
yeshivatoraschaim@gmail.com
DURST, Ellen .... 415-575-6153.... 30 G
edurst@ciis.edu
DURST, Lisa .... 440-525-7721.. 371 F
ldurst@lakelandcc.edu
DURST, Steve .... 231-591-2254.. 233 L
stevedurst@ferris.edu
DURYEA, David .... 607-753-2211.. 333 A
david.duryea@cortland.edu
DUSDIEKER, Carol .... 419-448-2080.. 369 G
cdusdiek@heidelberg.edu
DUSEK, Craig .... 620-417-1204.. 184 I
craig.dusek@sccc.edu
DUSENBURY, Renata .... 919-546-8252.. 355 F
rdusenbury@shawu.edu
DUSING, Roger .... 816-584-6386.. 270 D
roger.dusing@park.edu
DUSSEAU, Daniel .... 703-425-5369.. 497 H
ddusseau@nvcc.edu
DUSSOURD, Ellen, A .... 716-645-2258.. 331 C
dussourd@buffalo.edu
DUSTIN, Kevin, M .... 801-957-4083.. 483 A
kevin.dustin@slcc.edu
DUSZYNSKI, Aaron .... 920-686-6179.. 519 H
aaron.duszynski@sl.edu
DUTCH, Jennifer .... 402-363-5719.. 283 G
jdutch@york.edu
DUTCHER, Dave .... 315-733-2300.. 338 L
ddutcher@uscny.edu
DUTCHER, Debra .... 518-327-6082.. 326 B
ddutcher@paulsmiths.edu
DUTCHER, Donald .... 315-866-0300.. 316 A
dutcherdm@herkimer.edu
DUTCHER, James .... 518-255-5337.. 334 D
dutchejm@cobleskill.edu
DUTCHER, Victoria .... 603-862-4979.. 288 C
victoria.dutcher@unh.edu
DUTKO, Teresa .... 513-618-1307.. 366 C
tdutko@ccms.edu
DUTLER, Sue .... 312-935-2210.. 152 D
sdutler@robertmorris.edu
DUTMER, Brendan, C .... 815-599-3493.. 141 E
brendan.dutmer@highland.edu
DUTRA, Bruce .... 973-328-5400.. 290 H
bdutra@ccm.edu
DUTREMBLE, Kathy .... 850-484-2076.. 106 H
kdutremble@pensacolastate.edu
DUTRISAC, Gordon .... 425-352-8205.. 501 J
gdutrisac@cascadia.edu
DUTSCHKE, Jeremy, D .... 870-759-4120.... 24 J
jdutschke@wbcoll.edu
DUTTA, Debasish .... 765-494-9709.. 166 D
DUTTA, Mitra .... 312-996-6174.. 156 F
dutta@uic.edu
DUTTA, Soumitra .... 607-255-6418.. 312 A
sd599@cornell.edu
DUTTON, Ashley .... 860-231-5245.... 90 B
adutton@usj.edu
DUTTON, Colleen .... 972-883-2221.. 476 C
colleen.dutton@utdallas.edu
DUTTON, Dennis .... 620-278-4364.. 185 A
ddutton@sterling.edu
DUTTON, Timothy .... 937-752-2189.. 371 D
timothy.dutton@ketteringhealth.org
DUTTON COX, Deborah .. 603-862-1627.. 288 C
debbie.dutton@unh.edu
DUUS, Martin .... 212-280-1426.. 338 I
mduus@uts.columbia.edu
DUVAL, Amanda, L .... 920-923-8082.. 517 H
alduval92@marianuniversity.edu
DUVAL, Derethia .... 415-338-2208.... 35 B
derethia@sfsu.edu
DUVAL, John .... 804-828-0100.. 496 D
john.duval@vcuhealth.org
DUVALL, Staci .... 501-977-2087.... 24 B
duvall@uaccm.edu
DUVALL, Steve .... 740-389-4636.. 372 B
duvalls@mtc.edu
DUXBURY-EDWARDS,
Chris .... 303-329-6355.... 78 O
recruiting@cstcm.edu
DVIR, Arik .... 248-370-2762.. 239 K
dvir@oakland.edu
DVORACSEK, Joe .... 727-341-6108.. 108 D
dvoracsek.joe@spcollege.edu

DVORAK, Jerome .... 570-389-4995.. 414 D
jdvorak@bloomufdn.org
DVORAK, Leah, M .... 262-243-5700.. 516 E
leah.dvorak@cuw.edu
DVORAK, Robert .... 909-687-1560.... 44 H
robertdvorak@gs.edu
DVORAK, Sarah .... 574-284-4587.. 167 A
sdvorak@saintmarys.edu
DVORAK, Susan .... 414-464-9777.. 522 Q
dvorak.susan@wspp.edu
DVORKIN, Ariel .... 212-431-7959.. 323 H
ariel.dvorkin@nyls.edu
DWIGHT, Beverly, J .... 413-796-2210.. 229 E
beverly.dwight@wne.edu
DWIRE, Steven, W .... 518-454-5464.. 311 B
dwires@strose.edu
DWORACZYK, Bill .... 214-768-3140.. 465 J
billd@smu.edu
DWORKIN, Aaron, P .... 734-764-0584.. 241 J
aaronpau@umich.edu
DWORKIS, Paul, S .... 301-405-2589.. 211 E
pdworkis@umd.edu
DWORSCHAK, Mark .... 520-206-4558.... 16 F
mdworschak@pima.edu
DWYER, James, P .... 989-964-4287.. 240 F
jdwyer@svsu.edu
DWYER, Jeff .... 517-355-2308.. 237 I
dwyerje@msu.edu
DWYER, Johanna .... 360-596-5234.. 508 A
jdwyer@spscc.edu
DWYER, Katelyn .... 617-322-3524.. 219 H
katelyn_dwyer@laboure.edu
DWYER, Kathleen .... 502-410-6200.. 188 H
kdwyer@galencollege.edu
DWYER, Ken .... 508-854-4579.. 224 E
krd@qcc.mass.edu
DWYER, Susan, J .... 301-405-1102.. 211 E
dwyer@umd.edu
DWYER, Thomas .... 502-410-6200.. 188 H
tdwyer@galencollege.edu
DWYER, Thomas, L .... 401-598-1000.. 425 B
tom.dwyer@jwu.edu
DWYER, Thomas, P .... 804-752-7244.. 493 C
tdwyer@rmc.edu
DYAL, Donald .... 806-742-2261.. 472 C
donald.dyal@ttu.edu
DYBA, Chris .... 252-328-9565.. 356 C
dyba@ecu.edu
DYBA, Christopher .... 252-328-9565.. 356 C
dybac@ecu.edu
DYBICK, Thomas .... 413-205-3972.. 214 B
thomas.dybick@aic.edu
DYBWAD, Peter .... 510-841-9230.... 75 F
pdybwad@wi.edu
DYCKMAN, Gayle .... 585-245-5501.. 333 B
dyckman@geneseo.edu
DYE, Christine .... 910-755-7304.. 347 H
dyec@brunswickcc.edu
DYE, David .... 480-994-9244.... 17 C
davidd@swiha.edu
DYE, James .... 276-964-7278.. 498 F
james.dye@sw.edu
DYE, Jane .... 423-545-9572.. 440 F
dyejane@hiwassee.edu
DYE, Joanna .... 309-796-5442.. 135 I
dyej@bhc.edu
DYE, Larry .... 580-628-6217.. 384 L
larry.dye@noc.edu
DYE, Melissa .... 815-835-6253.. 153 K
melissa.m.dye@svcc.edu
DYE, Ryan, D .... 563-333-6389.. 176 D
dyeryand@sau.edu
DYE, Sheila .... 806-720-7233.. 461 C
sheila.dye@lcu.edu
DYER, Cheryl, A .... 414-955-8225.. 518 A
cdyer@mcw.edu
DYER, Cynthia, M .... 515-961-1519.. 176 H
cyd.dyer@simpson.edu
DYER, Esther, L .... 865-971-5216.. 446 G
eldyer@pstcc.edu
DYER, Jennifer .... 213-821-5002.... 72 D
jennifer.dyer@stevens.usc.edu
DYER, John, C .... 214-887-5141.. 457 C
jdyer@dts.edu
DYER, Karen .... 812-535-5101.. 166 K
kdyer@smwc.edu
DYER, Kent .... 484-664-3140.. 411 D
dyer@muhlenberg.edu
DYER, Kristyn, M .... 508-793-2418.. 217 C
kdyer@holycross.edu
DYER, Robin .... 704-669-4128.. 348 F
dyer@clevelandcc.edu
DYER, Ruth .... 785-532-6224.. 182 D
rdyer@ksu.edu
DYER, Tricia .... 207-621-3390.. 204 I
triciad@maine.edu
DYER, Una .... 340-693-1002.. 539 C
udyer@uvi.edu
DYER, Wayne, R .... 973-803-5000.. 294 B
wdyer@pillar.edu

DYERLY, Kevin, M .... 909-748-8026.... 71 K
kevin_dyerly@redlands.edu
DYESS, Hubert .... 601-426-6346.. 260 G
hdyess@southeasternbaptist.edu
DYKE, Gary .... 281-649-3335.. 458 L
gdyke@hbu.edu
DYKEMA, Ann, C .... 616-977-0599.. 240 B
ann.dykema@prts.edu
DYKES, Alllison, K .... 404-727-9895.. 120 E
allison.dykes@emory.edu
DYKES, Donald, E .... 860-444-8213.. 529 A
donald.e.dykes@uscga.edu
DYKES, Stephanie .... 206-934-3655.. 506 J
stephanie.dykes@seattlecolleges.edu
DYKHUIS, Pat .... 616-392-8555.. 244 A
pat.dykhuis@westernsem.edu
DYKSHOORN, Sharon .... 712-274-6400.. 177 I
sharon.dykshoorn@witcc.edu
DYKSTRA, Arlen, R .... 314-392-2201.. 268 F
adykstra@mobap.edu
DYKSTRA, Doug .... 808-235-7402.. 132 E
dykstra@hawaii.edu
DYKSTRA, Frank .... 520-515-5311.... 12 L
poncho@cochise.edu
DYKSTRA, Gail .... 972-708-7340.. 458 G
gail_dykstra@gial.edu
DYKSTRA, Joel .... 575-624-8203.. 300 I
dykstra@nmmi.edu
DYKSTRA, Kurt, D .... 708-239-4791.. 155 M
kurt.dykstra@trnty.edu
DYKSTRA, Philip .... 714-484-7311.... 54 G
pdykstra@cypresscollege.edu
DYLAK, Sandy .... 914-251-6953.. 334 C
sandy.dylak@purchase.edu
DYMCHENKO, Natalie ...... 909-667-4485.... 38 G
ndymchenko@claremontlincoln.edu
DYMENT, Christine .... 508-588-9100.. 223 G
DYMOWSKI, Tom .... 210-829-3131.. 474 D
dymowski@uiwtx.edu
DYMSKI, M, L .... 617-349-8208.. 220 B
mld@lesley.edu
DYNAN-DOBBERTIEN,
Lisa .... 904-620-2900.. 112 B
n00914995@unf.edu
DYRUD, Lars .... 218-683-8616.. 251 C
lars.dyrud@northlandcollege.edu
DYSARD, Nancy, J .... 443-412-2408.. 208 A
ndysard@harford.edu
DYSART, Charles .... 334-876-9248...... 4 A
charles.dysart@wccs.edu
DYSART, Sarah .... 773-508-7476.. 146 G
sdysart@luc.edu
DYSON, Keisha .... 708-534-4044.. 140 H
kdyson@govst.edu
DYSON, Melissa, J .... 217-245-3080.. 141 G
mdyson@mail.ic.edu
DZAPO, Kyle .... 309-677-2596.. 136 B
kdzapo@bradley.edu
DZIDZIENYO, Victor .... 202-806-7420.... 93 A
vdzidzienyo@howard.edu
DZIEDZIAK, Michael .... 610-341-1376.. 403 B
mdziedzi@eastern.edu
DZIEKAN, Rebecca .... 585-343-0055.. 315 C
rldziekan@genesee.edu
DZIERBICKI, Judie .... 248-689-8282.. 242 F
jdzierbi@walshcollege.edu
DZIESINSKI, Lori .... 989-356-9021.. 230 G
dziesinl@alpenacc.edu
DZIEWATKOSKI,
Julius, J .... 740-264-5591.. 368 D
jdziewatkoski@egcc.edu
DZINANKA, John, S .... 631-420-2017.. 335 E
john.dzinanka@farmingdale.edu
DZUREC, Laura, C .... 610-499-4214.. 423 E
lcdzurec@widener.edu
DZWONKOWSKI,
David, R .... 315-470-6641.. 334 E
drdzwonk@esf.edu
DÍAZ, Ángel .... 787-764-0000.. 538 F
angel.diaz10@upr.edu
DÍAZ, Tania .... 787-720-1022.. 531 A
recursos@atlanticu.edu
DÍAZ, Valerie .... 787-844-8181.. 538 E
valerie.diaz3@upr.edu
DÍAZ URBINA, Gloria .... 787-764-0000.. 538 F
gloria.diaz5@upr.edu
DÖANGELO, John .... 847-491-5120.. 150 F
johndangelo@northwestern.edu
D'ABROSCO, Lou .... 401-598-4621.. 425 B
louis.d'abrosca@jwu.edu
D'ADAMO-WEINSTEIN,
Lisa .... 518-587-2100.. 335 D
lisa.dadamo-weinstein@esc.edu
D'AGATI, Michael .... 973-684-5920.. 294 A
mdagati@pccc.edu
D'AGOSTINO, Alexis .... 914-674-7698.. 320 G
adagostino4@mercy.edu
D'AGOSTINO, Erica .... 610-330-5080.. 407 C
dagostie@lafayette.edu
D'AGOSTINO, Jennifer ...... 518-587-2100.. 335 D
jennifer.d'agostino@esc.edu

D'AGOSTINO, Jo Beth .... 773-508-7063.. 146 G
jdagost@luc.edu
D'AGOSTINO, Julie .... 847-925-6523.. 141 A
jdagosti@harpercollege.edu
D'AGOSTINO, Thomas .... 315-781-3307.. 316 C
tdagostino@hws.edu
D'AGOSTINO, Toni, J ..... 409-772-2138.. 478 A
todagost@utmb.edu
D'ALESSANDRO, Colleen 404-364-8319.. 125 F
cdalessandro@oglethorpe.edu
D'ALESSANDRO,
Enrico, L .... 315-684-6410.. 336 B
dalessel@morrisville.edu
D'ALESSIO, Edward .... 610-526-6025.. 405 B
edalessio@harcum.edu
D'ALLEGRO, Mary Lou ..... 518-783-2307.. 330 E
mdallegro@siena.edu
D'ALLEVA, Anne .... 860-486-3016.... 89 D
anne.dalleva@uconn.edu
D'AMATO, Anthony .... 312-567-8821.. 142 I
damato@iit.edu
D'AMATO, Christina .... 516-323-4835.. 321 H
cdamato@molloy.edu
D'AMBRA, Diane .... 401-598-1854.. 425 B
ddambra@jwu.edu
D'AMBROSE, Martin .... 312-987-2396.. 143 G
6dambrose@jmls.edu
D'AMBROSIO, Arnold ...... 313-993-1025.. 241 G
dambroaa1@udmercy.edu
D'AMBROSIO,
Christopher .... 914-337-9300.. 311 F
christopher.dambrosio@concordia-ny.edu
D'AMBROSIO, Rose .... 201-692-2706.. 291 J
rose_dambrosio@fdu.edu
D'AMBROSIO, Steve .... 856-227-7200.. 290 B
sdambrosio@camdencc.edu
D'AMBROSIO, Vincent ..... 352-588-8432.. 108 C
vincent.dambrosio@saintleo.edu
D'AMICO, Janna .... 517-265-5161.. 230 D
D'AMORE, Jonathan, L .... 802-654-2347.. 484 I
jdamore@smcvt.edu
D'AMOUR, Angela, L .... 805-565-6125.... 75 A
adamour@westmont.edu
D'ANDREA, Bill, J .... 864-231-2029.. 427 B
bdandrea@andersonuniversity.edu
D'ANGELO, Frank .... 928-771-4885.... 18 D
frank.dangelo@yc.edu
D'ANGELO, Kathryn, P .... 215-204-6545.. 420 B
kathryn.dangelo@temple.edu
D'ANGELO, Louann .... 413-572-5622.. 222 E
ldangelo@westfield.ma.edu
D'ANIERI, Paul .... 951-827-5034.... 70 B
provost@ucr.edu
D'ANJOU, Sara .... 617-730-7059.. 226 J
sara.danjou@newbury.edu
D'ANJOU TURNER,
Tamara .... 678-407-5000.. 121 B
tdanjout@ggc.edu
D'ANNA, Debora .... 828-884-8391.. 342 C
debora.danna@brevard.edu
D'ANTONIO, Louis, S ...... 203-285-2021.... 86 C
ldantonio@gwcc.commnet.edu
D'APOLITO, Kristine .... 609-771-2504.. 290 F
dapolito@tcnj.edu
D'APRIX, Kathleen .... 315-498-6088.. 325 G
k.a.daprix@sunyocc.edu
D'AQUILA, Michael .... 201-200-3191.. 293 C
md'aquila@njcu.edu
D'AQUINO, Erik .... 716-851-4681.. 313 H
daquino@ecc.edu
D'ARC CAMPBELL, Jean . 425-564-3160.. 501 F
jeandarc.campbell@bellevuecollege.edu
D'ARCY, Kelly .... 580-745-2948.. 387 M
kdarcy@se.edu
D'ARGENIO, John .... 518-783-2450.. 330 E
dargenio@siena.edu
D'ARGENT, Julie .... 765-658-4268.. 160 F
juliedargent@depauw.edu
D'ARRIGO, Diane .... 617-287-5052.. 220 G
diane.darrigo@umb.edu
D'ATTILIO, Michael .... 518-454-5115.. 311 B
dattilm@strose.edu
D'AVERSA, Robert .... 570-422-3324.. 414 H
rfdb@esu.edu
D'AVI, Ed .... 386-752-1822.. 100 L
edward.davi@fgc.edu
D'COSTA, Richard .... 787-761-0640.. 537 C
rdcostaofrey@utcpr.edu
D'EATH, Kelly .... 256-549-8266....... 3 M
kdeath@gadsdenstate.edu
D'ELIA, Christopher .... 225-578-8574.. 197 I
cdelia@lsu.edu
D'EMILIO, Deanne, H .... 412-578-6072.. 400 C
dhdemilio@carlow.edu
D'EMILIO, Matthew .... 412-628-4256.. 400 D
mdemilio@andrew.cmu.edu
D'ENTREMONT,
Mary Ann .... 203-596-4612.... 88 F
mdentremont@post.edu
D'IMPERIO, Pat .... 914-606-6846.. 340 C
pat.d'imperio@sunywcc.edu

ECK, Stephen 405-425-5118 385 C stephen.eck@oc.edu

ECK, Stephen, M 973-596-3306 293 D steven.eck@njit.edu

ECK, Tim 801-626-6352 482 D teck@weber.edu

ECKARDT, Chip, P 715-836-2381 520 A eckardpp@uwec.edu

ECKARDT, Jill 940-898-3676 472 G jeckardt@twu.edu

ECKEL, Todd 909-593-3511 71 B teckel@laverne.edu

ECKENRODE, Jeanine 315-498-2237 325 G j.a.eckenrode@sunyocc.edu

ECKER, Brian 717-262-2017 424 A brian.ecker@wilson.edu

ECKERT, Allison 928-226-4204 12 N allison.eckert@coconino.edu

ECKERT, Brian 540-458-8459 500 F beckert@wlu.edu

ECKERT, Jason, C 937-229-2045 379 D jeckert1@udayton.edu

ECKERT, Robin 610-372-4721 417 G reckert@racc.edu

ECKERT, Steve 928-314-9475 11 J steve.eckert@azwestern.edu

ECKERT, Wendy 423-439-6052 444 F research@etsu.edu

ECKLES, Blaine 208-885-6757 134 G beckles@uidaho.edu

ECKLES, Robert 212-410-8480 323 C reckles@nycpm.edu

ECKLEY, Amy 920-686-6175 519 H amy.eckley@sl.edu

ECKLEY, Catherine 304-357-4925 511 E catherineeckley@ucwv.edu

ECKLUND, Joe 402-280-5531 279 H josephecklund@creighton.edu

ECKLUND, Timothy 631-632-7320 332 A timothy.ecklund@stonybrook.edu

ECKMAN, Angela 715-738-3852 523 B aeckman@cvtc.edu

ECKMAN, Charles 305-284-1959 114 H ceckman@miami.edu

ECKMAN, Steven 386-506-3180 98 E eckmans@daytonastate.edu

ECKMAN, Steven, W 402-363-5621 283 G seckman@york.edu

ECKRICH, Steve, E 541-737-4323 393 H stevee@osubookstore.com

ECKSTEIN, Mark 716-829-8349 313 A eckstein@dyc.edu

ECKSTEIN, Melanie 704-461-6877 342 A melanieeckstein@bac.edu

EDAMALA, Charles 309-438-3618 143 B cmedama@ilstu.edu

EDBURG, Lisa 573-518-2294 268 E lisae@mineralarea.edu

EDDINGER, Pam, Y 617-228-2400 223 B peddinger@bhcc.mass.edu

EDDINGTON, Natalie, D 410-706-2176 211 F neddingt@rx.umaryland.edu

EDDINS, Trevell 815-280-2884 144 A teddins@jjc.edu

EDDS-ELLIS, Stacy 270-686-4573 190 D stacy.edds@kctcs.edu

EDDY, James, M 336-315-7317 358 B jmeddy@uncg.edu

EDDY, Laura, M 620-341-5465 180 G leddy@emporia.edu

EDDY, Libby 907-450-8000 10 E leddy@alaska.edu

EDDY, Rick 309-341-5234 136 C reddy@sandburg.edu

EDDY, Shayna 508-626-4506 221 E seddy@framingham.edu

EDDY, Tiana 719-384-6842 82 A tiana.eddy@ojc.edu

EDEL, Logan 515-961-1579 176 H logan.edel@simpson.edu

EDELBROCK, Craig 205-348-6331 8 D cedelbrock@ccs.ua.edu

EDELEN, Charles 812-941-2400 163 F cedelen@ius.edu

EDELMAN, Adam 406-994-5091 277 C aedelman@montana.edu

EDELMAN, Daniel 972-338-1400 475 B

EDELMAN, David 805-898-2926 43 K davidedelman@fielding.edu

EDELMAN, Debbie 618-468-2010 145 G dedelman@lc.edu

EDELMAYER, Kathleen 734-432-5300 237 D kodowd@madonna.edu

EDELSON, Jeffrey 510-642-5039 68 M swdean@berkeley.edu

EDELSON, Maurice, F 212-799-5000 318 A

EDELSTEIN, Ronald, A 323-563-4980 37 G ronaldedelstein@cdrewu.edu

EDEN, Bradford, L 219-464-5099 168 F brad.eden@valpo.edu

EDEN, Gene, F 610-799-1146 408 G geden@lccc.edu

EDEN, James, R 920-924-3317 524 B jeden@morainepark.edu

EDEN, James, V 262-335-5705 524 B jeden@morainepark.edu

EDEN, Peter, A 802-387-6730 484 B petereden@landmark.edu

EDEN, SM, Tim 210-436-3786 464 H teden@stmarytx.edu

EDENFIELD, Joe 757-569-6744 498 B jedenfield@pdc.edu

EDENS, Barb 423-236-2587 444 B barbedens@southern.edu

EDENS, Byron 423-308-9652 354 G edensb@piedmontu.edu

EDENS, Gary 915-747-7471 476 D gedens@utep.edu

EDENS, Mike 504-282-4455 198 H medens@nobts.edu

EDENS, Mike 903-693-2021 463 D medens@panola.edu

EDER, Jeff 847-628-2023 144 B jeffrey.eder@judsonu.edu

EDER, Robert 773-256-0784 147 A reder@lstc.edu

EDGAR, Kimberly, S 615-898-5825 444 G kimberly.edgar@mtsu.edu

EDGAR, Richard, J 240-895-3206 210 E rjedgar@smcm.edu

EDGAR, William, J 724-847-6610 404 B wjedgar@geneva.edu

EDGE, Johnnie 478-553-2124 125 C jedge@oftc.edu

EDGECOMBE, Nydia 718-518-4180 308 C nedgecombe@hostos.cuny.edu

EDGELL, Lauren 717-871-5156 415 F lauren.edgell@millersville.edu

EDGERTON, Gary 317-940-9825 159 K gedgerto@butler.edu

EDGERTON, Pam 402-354-7000 281 F pam.edgerton@methodistcollege.edu

EDGERTON, Teresa 402-486-2540 282 I teedgert@ucollege.edu

EDGEWORTH, Lori 419-251-1614 372 C lori.edgeworth@mercycollege.edu

EDGINGTON, Rick 580-628-6220 384 L rick.edgington@noc.edu

EDGINGTON, Steve 714-879-3901 46 F sedgington@hiu.edu

EDGINGTON, Thomas, J 574-372-5100 161 B edging@grace.edu

EDGMON, Angie 615-844-5049 449 H finaid@welch.edu

EDGREN, JR., Gerald 618-842-3711 142 C edgreng@iecc.edu

EDGREN, III, Gerald, R 920-924-3184 524 B gedgren@morainepark.edu

EDICK, Nancy 402-554-2719 283 B nedick@unomaha.edu

EDINGER, Joan, B 318-257-3036 200 G jedinger@latech.edu

EDINGTON, Julie 870-248-4000 19 H julie.edington@blackrivertech.edu

EDINGTON, Mary 253-833-9111 504 C medington@greenriver.edu

EDINGTON, Maurice 850-412-5978 110 J maurice.edington@famu.edu

EDINGTON, Pamela, R 845-431-8980 312 G pamela.edington@sunydutchess.edu

EDISON, Monica 616-632-2881 231 A edisomon@aquinas.edu

EDIZEL, Gerar 607-871-2412 303 F fedizel@alfred.edu

EDLER, Casey 985-867-2273 199 F cedler@sjasc.edu

EDLESTON, Brenda 785-243-1435 179 N bedleston@cloud.edu

EDLUND, Erin 651-423-8233 249 B erin.edlund@dctc.edu

EDLUND, Erin 651-450-3546 249 F eedlund@inverhills.edu

EDLUND, Matthew 651-361-3450 247 K medlund@mcnallysmith.edu

EDMAN, Neal, A 724-946-7110 423 B nedman@westminster.edu

EDMAN, Patricia 612-374-5800 246 F pedman@dunwoody.edu

EDMAN, Sally 712-707-7321 176 B sedman@nwciowa.edu

EDMINSTER, David 303-546-3514 81 I davee@naropa.edu

EDMINSTER, Warren 270-809-3166 192 A wedminster@murraystate.edu

EDMOND, Betty 512-492-3060 451 E

EDMOND, Beverly 406-243-4689 276 K beverly.edmond@umontana.edu

EDMOND, Cara 512-454-7001 451 E cedmond@aoma.edu

EDMOND, Georgia 478-289-2112 120 C gedmond@ega.edu

EDMONDS, Amy 262-472-4661 521 F edmondsa@uww.edu

EDMONDS, Charles, W 570-321-4347 409 F edmonds@lycoming.edu

EDMONDS, Jane 781-239-4998 214 G jedmonds@babson.edu

EDMONDS, John 540-785-5440 496 A johnedmonds@vbc.edu

EDMONDS, Kerry 540-362-6630 490 F kedmonds@hollins.edu

EDMONDS, Lawson, C 205-652-3545 9 F ledmonds@uwa.edu

EDMONDS, Lorna Jean 740-593-1889 375 H edmonds@ohio.edu

EDMONDS, Mabel 253-589-5510 502 F mabel.edmonds@cptc.edu

EDMONDS, Melody 931-393-1698 446 D medmonds@mscc.edu

EDMONDS, Michelle 434-949-1000 498 E michelle.edmonds@southside.edu

EDMONDS, Michelle, K 434-949-1006 498 E michelle.edmonds@southside.edu

EDMONDS, Mike 719-389-6684 77 J medmonds@coloradocollege.edu

EDMONDS, William 814-732-2761 415 A eup_admissions@edinboro.edu

EDMONDSON, Charles (Ricks) 817-515-7726 467 A charles.edmondson@tccd.edu

EDMONDSON, Jackie 256-549-8224 3 M jedmondson@gadsdenstate.edu

EDMONDSON, Lauren 417-873-7569 264 H ledmondson@drury.edu

EDMONDSON, Melanie, M 443-334-2272 211 A medmondson@stevenson.edu

EDMONDSON, William 814-871-7298 404 A edmondso002@gannon.edu

EDMONSON, Michele 661-362-3435 40 A michele.edmonson@canyons.edu

EDMONSON, Stacey 936-294-1101 471 D edu_sle01@shsu.edu

EDMUND, Devon 612-338-7224 256 D

EDMUNDSON, John 928-314-9500 11 J john.edmundson@azwestern.edu

EDONICK, Jessica 717-396-7833 413 M jedonick@pcad.edu

EDOUARD, Randall 607-777-6226 331 B redouard@binghamton.edu

EDRICH, Terri 972-860-4825 456 B tedrich@dcccd.edu

EDSALL, Denese 954-201-7502 96 I dedsall@broward.edu

EDSALL, Paul 724-838-4236 419 D edsall@setonhill.edu

EDSCORN, Steven 918-456-5511 384 G edscorn@nsuok.edu

EDSTROM, Julie 406-791-5271 278 G julie.edstrom@ugf.edu

EDUARDO, Marcelo 601-925-3214 259 A eduardo@mc.edu

EDWALDS-GILBERT, Gretchen 909-607-9100 64 A gedwalds@scrippscollege.edu

EDWARD, Alexander 229-430-0664 116 A ealexander@albanytech.edu

EDWARD, Paul 978-927-2300 219 A paul.edwards@gordon.edu

EDWARDS, Adele 928-344-7588 11 J adele.edwards@azwestern.edu

EDWARDS, Amy 217-333-3551 157 A aledward@illinois.edu

EDWARDS, Anne 856-222-9311 295 C aedwards@rcbc.edu

EDWARDS, Annette 757-789-1768 497 A aedwards@es.vccs.edu

EDWARDS, Bahola 432-685-4520 461 H bahola@midland.edu

EDWARDS, Bambi 252-638-7317 349 B edwardsb@cravencc.edu

EDWARDS, Barry 925-473-7391 41 J bedwards@losmedanos.edu

EDWARDS, Betty 334-420-4321 7 G bedwards@trenholmstate.edu

EDWARDS, Brad 703-993-3256 490 B bedwards@gmu.edu

EDWARDS, Bruce 808-356-5256 130 H bedwards@hpu.edu

EDWARDS, Byron 615-514-2787 443 F dredwards@nossi.edu

EDWARDS, Candace 410-386-8505 206 I cedwards@carrollcc.edu

EDWARDS, Carlton, G 804-257-5851 500 B cgedwards@vuu.edu

EDWARDS, Carmen 432-685-4589 461 H cedwards@midland.edu

EDWARDS, Carol 850-770-2100 111 C cdedwards@pc.fsu.edu

EDWARDS, Carol 806-742-0700 472 C carol.edwards@ttu.edu

EDWARDS, Cathy 214-860-8685 456 F cedwards@dcccd.edu

EDWARDS, Chris 601-481-1316 258 F cedwards@meridiancc.edu

EDWARDS, Christopher, J 513-558-5233 379 A christopher.edwards@uc.edu

EDWARDS, Cody 703-993-5287 490 B cedward7@gmu.edu

EDWARDS, Cynthia 404-297-9522 122 A edwardsc@gptc.edu

EDWARDS, David 330-941-3394 382 A dwedwards@ysu.edu

EDWARDS, David 609-586-4800 292 D edwardsd@mccc.edu

EDWARDS, Donald 828-689-1246 346 C dedwards@mhu.edu

EDWARDS, Doreen 607-871-2422 303 F dedwards@alfred.edu

EDWARDS, Doreen 585-475-2146 327 E ddeen@rit.edu

EDWARDS, Earl, W 858-534-8750 70 C ewedwards@ucsd.edu

EDWARDS, Elizabeth 662-862-8265 258 C etedwards@iccms.edu

EDWARDS, Ellen 207-947-4591 202 E eedwards@bealcollege.edu

EDWARDS, Emory 201-761-6108 296 K eedwards@saintpeters.edu

EDWARDS, Eugene 503-375-7010 391 B eedwards@corban.edu

EDWARDS, Frank 404-880-8672 118 K fedwards@cau.edu

EDWARDS, Gary 661-362-2291 52 A gedwards@masters.edu

EDWARDS, Geoffrey, M 812-488-1102 167 I ge21@evansville.edu

EDWARDS, Holly 336-838-6175 354 C holly.edwards@wilkescc.edu

EDWARDS, Ian, C 412-396-6204 403 A edwards181@duq.edu

EDWARDS, Ishmell, H 662-252-8000 260 F iedwards@rustcollege.edu

EDWARDS, Jakki 651-291-0177 247 K jakki.edwards@mcnallysmith.edu

EDWARDS, James 252-492-2061 353 H edwardsj@vgcc.edu

EDWARDS, James 202-865-6660 93 A

EDWARDS, James, E 757-822-5121 498 H jeedwards@tcc.edu

EDWARDS, Jamie 276-223-4829 499 C jedwards@wcc.vccs.edu

EDWARDS, Jan 719-227-8285 77 J jan.edwards@coloradocollege.edu

EDWARDS, Jan, M 719-884-5000 81 N jmedwards@nbc.edu

EDWARDS, Jane 203-432-8680 90 D jane.edwards@yale.edu

EDWARDS, Jason 252-985-5102 354 E jedwards@ncwc.edu

EDWARDS, Jeff 337-439-5765 195 A jeff@deltatech.edu

EDWARDS, Jennifer, T 254-968-9480 467 F jtedwards@tarleton.edu

EDWARDS, Jon 508-270-4102 223 F jedwards@massbay.edu

EDWARDS, Jonathan, P 843-661-1181 430 B jedwards@fmarion.edu

EDWARDS, Joyce, P 336-334-7755 356 F edwardsj@ncat.edu

EDWARDS, Judson 334-670-3989 7 H jcedwards@troy.edu

EDWARDS, Julie 417-447-8188 270 A edwardsj@otc.edu

EDWARDS, Karen 251-460-7092 9 E cedwards@southalabama.edu

EDWARDS, Karen 281-756-3639 450 G kedwards@alvincollege.edu

EDWARDS, Karen, K 641-269-3703 172 I edwardsk@grinnell.edu

EDWARDS, Karin 971-722-5302 394 F karin.edwards@pcc.edu

EDWARDS, Kelly 406-657-1006 278 D kelly.edwards@rocky.edu

EDWARDS, Kendra 816-604-1574 267 F kendra.edwards@mcckc.edu

EDWARDS, Kevin 740-477-7761 374 G kedwards@ohiochristian.edu

EDWARDS, Lance 641-673-1114 177 J edwardsl@wmpenn.edu

EDWARDS, Laurie, L 712-324-5061 175 G ledwards@nwicc.edu

EDWARDS, Lendozia 912-921-2900 93 F

EDWARDS, Lisa 646-660-6036 307 A lisa.edwards@baruch.cuny.edu

EDWARDS, Louis, W 713-313-6747 470 D edwards_lw@tsu.edu

EDWARDS, Mark, H 315-655-7334 306 H medwards@cazenovia.edu

EDWARDS, Mary, A 304-336-8000 513 F edwardsm@westliberty.edu

EDWARDS, Matthew 864-646-1474 433 C medward3@tctc.edu
EDWARDS, Melinda 256-352-8172 9 G melinda.edwards@wallacestate.edu
EDWARDS, Michael 641-673-2120 177 J edwardsml@wmpenn.edu
EDWARDS, Michelle 337-439-5765 195 A michelle@deltatech.edu
EDWARDS, Mike 615-844-5246 449 H mike.edwards@welch.edu
EDWARDS, Nigel 850-599-3183 110 J nigel.edwards@famu.edu
EDWARDS, Paul, S 502-597-5837 191 B paul.edwards@kysu.edu
EDWARDS, JR., Quinton, T 662-915-3784 261 B qtedward@olemiss.edu
EDWARDS, Randy 828-262-2090 356 B edwardsk@appstate.edu
EDWARDS, Richard 848-932-7821 295 F redwards@oldqueens.rutgers.edu
EDWARDS, Richard 848-932-7821 296 B redwards@oldqueens.rutgers.edu
EDWARDS, Richard 518-629-7356 316 G r.edwards@hvcc.edu
EDWARDS, Rick 828-395-1676 350 E redwards@isothermal.edu
EDWARDS, Rosie 334-514-5063 4 G rosie.edwards@istc.edu
EDWARDS, Sarah 270-706-8447 189 C sarah.edwards@kctcs.edu
EDWARDS, Shawn 843-953-6989 428 A shawn.edwards@citadel.edu
EDWARDS, Stacia 740-203-8011 367 C
EDWARDS, Stephanie 619-201-8713 60 D stephanie.edwards@sdcc.edu
EDWARDS, Steve 912-583-3218 118 B sedwards@bpc.edu
EDWARDS, TerCraig, D 336-734-7953 349 G tedwards@forsythtech.edu
EDWARDS, Thomas 207-859-1362 204 E edwardst@thomas.edu
EDWARDS, Tim 205-652-3457 9 F tedwards@uwa.edu
EDWARDS, Tim 205-652-3531 9 F tedwards@uwa.edu
EDWARDS, Timothy 208-882-1566 134 B timedwards@nsa.edu
EDWARDS, Tracy 405-945-3376 386 C tracyle@osuokc.edu
EDWARDS, Ulrica, S 318-274-6103 200 F edwardsu@gram.edu
EDWARDS, Valerie 802-635-1290 486 B valerie.edwards@jsc.edu
EDWARDS, Wanda 910-296-1812 350 F wedwards@jamessprunt.edu
EDWARDS, Wayne 516-876-3175 333 C edwardsw@oldwestbury.edu
EDWARDS-EVANS, Nicole 601-979-2244 258 D nicole.e.evans@jsums.edu
EDWARDS LANGE, Sheila 206-934-4144 506 K sheila.edwardslange@seattlecolleges.edu
EDWARDS LANGE, Sheila 206-934-4144 506 I sheila.edwardslange@seattlecolleges.edu
EELLS, Rachel 708-209-3255 138 G rachel.eells@cuchicago.edu
EERTWEGH, John 949-376-6000 48 C jeertwegh@lcad.edu
EFF, Ryan 517-265-5161 230 D reff@adrian.edu
EFFORD, Lelia 305-626-3180 101 A lefford@fmuniv.edu
EFTHIMIOU, Chris 718-289-5169 307 C chris.efthimiou@bcc.cuny.edu
EFTHYMIOU, Lampeto (Betty) 718-631-6611 309 E lefthymiou@qcc.cuny.edu
EFTINK, Maria 314-889-4533 265 C meftink@fontbonne.edu
EGAN, Beth-Anne 860-253-3030 86 A began@asnuntuck.edu
EGAN, Brian 973-684-5999 294 A began@pccc.edu
EGAN, Carolyn 850-644-4440 111 C cegan@admin.fsu.edu
EGAN, Eric 760-921-5520 56 E eegan@paloverde.edu
EGAN, Jonathon 562-947-8755 66 A jonathonegan@scuhs.edu
EGAN, Jonathon 315-568-3311 323 A jegan@nycc.edu
EGAN, Maryan 239-590-1234 110 L megan@fgcu.edu
EGAN, Russi 760-921-5524 56 E regan@paloverde.edu
EGAN, Thomas 215-572-2900 397 G egant@arcadia.edu
EGBE, Daniel 501-370-5268 21 G degbe@philander.edu
EGBE, Daniel 501-370-5259 21 G degbe@philander.edu
EGBE, Emmanuel 718-270-5170 309 B egbe@mec.cuny.edu
EGBE, Odey, P 478-289-2039 120 C oegbe@ega.edu
EGBERT, Jeb 949-783-4800 74 A jegbert@westcoastuniversity.edu
EGBERT, Jessica, D 801-375-5125 481 C jegbert@rmuohp.edu
EGDORF, Randall 217-641-4973 143 H regdorf@jwcc.edu
EGE, Daryle 309-467-6394 140 E dege@eureka.edu
EGE, Sybil 847-214-7034 140 A sege@elgin.edu
EGELER, William, G 207-768-2792 203 L wegeler@nmcc.edu
EGENESS, Cynthia 651-690-6864 254 M cnegeness@stkate.edu
EGENREIDER, Michael 740-420-5926 374 G megenreider@ohiochristian.edu
EGERER, Sarah 706-233-4065 117 F segerer@berry.edu
EGERSON, Veronica, V 414-464-9777 522 Q egerson.veronica@wspp.edu
EGERSTROM, Sarah 715-425-3500 521 B sarah.r.egerstrom@uwrf.edu
EGGEN, Tyler 907-564-8311 10 B teegen@alaskapacific.edu
EGGENSPERGER, Martin 870-508-6102 19 B meggensperger@asumh.edu
EGGERS, Daniel, W 512-245-1555 471 F dwe16@txstate.edu
EGGERS, John, M 320-308-0121 252 A jmeggers@stcloudstate.edu
EGGERS, Marilyn 909-558-7658 49 C meggers@llu.edu
EGGERS, Ron 252-399-6417 341 P reggers@barton.edu
EGGERS, Troy 212-854-5939 311 E te99@columbia.edu
EGGERSTEDT, Jane 318-675-6124 198 B jegger@lsuhsc.edu
EGGERT, Mary 414-847-3211 518 D maryeggert@miad.edu
EGGLESTON, Chadwick, L 334-833-4236 4 D provost@hawks.huntingdon.edu
EGGLESTON, Dana, S 302-356-6862 91 I dana.s.eggleston@wilmu.edu
EGGLESTON, Joseph 562-947-8755 66 A josepheggleston@scuhs.edu
EGGLESTON, Kathryn, K 972-238-6364 456 H keggleston@dcccd.edu
EGGLESTON, Meghan 276-656-0285 498 A meggleston@patrickhenry.edu
EGGLESTON, Tami 618-537-6926 147 F teggleston@mckendree.edu
EGGLESTON WILLIAMS, Latrice, E 773-995-2548 136 M egglest@csu.edu
EGITTO, Victor, T 323-259-2686 55 A egitto@oxy.edu
EGLE, Don 903-233-3290 460 J donegle@letu.edu
EGLSAER, Richard 936-294-1001 471 D eglsaer@shsu.edu
EGLY, Penny, J 260-422-5561 162 B pjegly@indianatech.edu
EGRESI, Chad 410-888-9048 209 C cegresi@muih.edu
EGUCHI, Amy 973-748-9000 289 H amy_eguchi@bloomfield.edu
EHASZ, Maribeth 407-823-4372 111 E maribeth.ehasz@ucf.edu
EHLER, Gina, M 262-524-7247 515 J gehler@carrollu.edu
EHLERS, Chris 918-781-7233 382 D ehlersc@bacone.edu
EHLERS, Kathleen 401-739-5000 425 C kehlers@neit.edu
EHLERS, Nancy, M 716-652-8900 306 K nehlers@cks.edu
EHLERS, Pam 405-744-2122 385 G pam.ehlers@okstate.edu
EHLERT, Alycia 386-506-3769 98 E alycia.ehlert@daytonastate.edu
EHLING, William 252-328-6387 356 C ehlingw16@ecu.edu
EHMANN, William 206-220-8214 507 E ehmannw@seattleu.edu
EHMEN, Stacy, L 217-443-8746 139 B stacy@dacc.edu
EHNAT, Karen 425-388-9272 503 F kehnat@everettcc.edu
EHRENREICH, Yaakov 718-941-8000 321 A
EHRESMAN, Terry 620-278-4264 185 A tehresman@sterling.edu
EHRHARDT, Tom 312-261-3165 149 B tom.ehrhardt@n[illegible].edu
EHRLICH, Anne, R 309-341-7221 145 A arehrlich@knox.edu
EHRLICH, Brian 321-674-8202 100 M behrlich@fit.edu
EHRLICH, Donna 617-928-4074 226 B dehrlich@mountida.edu
EHRLICH, Robert 660-626-2297 262 A rehrlich@atsu.edu
EHRLICH, Sam 830-372-8155 470 C sehrlich@tlu.edu
EHRLICH, Steven, M 314-935-4320 274 N ehrlich@wustl.edu
EHRMANTRAUT, Dominic 901-321-3286 439 E dehrmant@cbu.edu
EHST, Suzanne 574-535-7839 161 A sehst@goshen.edu
EIBECK, Pamela, A 209-946-2223 71 C president@pacific.edu
EICHELBERGER, Lisa 678-466-4900 119 A lisaeichelberger@clayton.edu
EICHELROTH, Kathleen 508-929-8098 222 F keichelroth@worcester.edu
EICHENBERGER, Julie 620-223-2700 181 A juliee@fortscott.edu
EICHENLAUB, Mark, P 618-235-2700 155 C mark.eichenlaub@swic.edu
EICHENSTEIN, Joseph 732-985-6533 294 E
EICHER, Michael 614-292-9858 375 A eicher@osu.edu
EICHFIELD, Tara 912-287-5809 119 B teichfield@coastalpines.edu
EICHHORN, Edward 201-559-1433 291 K eichhorne@felician.edu
EICHHORN, Gregory, E 203-582-8906 88 G gregory.eichhorn@quinnipiac.edu
EICHHORN, Gregory, E 610-921-7260 396 H geichhorn@albright.edu
EICHHORST, Amy 301-405-2102 211 E aeich@umd.edu
EICHHORST, Carly 507-786-3357 254 P eichho1@stolaf.edu
EICHLER, Barry 212-960-5214 341 G eichler@yu.edu
EICHLER, Richard 212-854-2878 311 E re1@columbia.edu
EICHNER, Kevin 785-242-5200 183 M kevin.eichner@ottawa.edu
EICHOLTZ, Kristin 610-282-1100 402 B kristin.eicholtz@desales.edu
EICHORST, Christopher 509-777-4780 509 H ceichorst@whitworth.edu
EICHORST, Shawn 402-472-3011 282 M seichorst@huskers.com
EICHTEN, Jonathan 320-308-5580 252 B jeichten@sctcc.edu
EICK, Christine, L 334-844-4870 1 G eickchr@auburn.edu
EICKEN, Hajo 907-474-7331 10 G heicken@alaska.edu
EICKHOFF, Jeffrey 402-643-4052 282 D sggs@stgregoryseminary.edu
EICKHOLT, Marcia 419-227-3141 380 A marcia@unoh.edu
EICKHORST, Lindsay 309-268-8031 141 C lindsay.eickhorst@heartland.edu
EICKMEIER, Valerie 317-920-2403 163 D veickmei@iupui.edu
EID, Haithum 504-286-5010 199 I heid@suno.edu
EIDE, Greg 503-375-7021 391 B geide@corban.edu
EIDENBERG, Julia 503-517-1816 396 F jeidenberg@westernseminary.edu
EIDGAHY, Saeid 619-388-2795 60 G seidgahy@sdccd.edu
EIDSON, Kristi 270-686-4216 187 C kristi.eidson@brescia.edu
EIDSON, Paul 714-841-6252 27 E dreidson@apollosuniversity.edu
EIDSON, Rebecca, W 864-646-1507 433 C reidson@tctc.edu
EIDSON, Scott 714-841-6252 27 E
EIERMANN, Jason 985-448-4521 201 A jason.eiermann@nicholls.edu
EIFERT, Robert 217-824-4004 145 D reifert@lakeland.cc.il.us
EIGENBROOD, Rick 206-281-2710 507 C eigend@spu.edu
EIGHMY, Taylor 865-974-8701 448 E vcresearch@utk.edu
EIKE, Claire 312-629-9379 154 A ceike@saic.edu
EIKENS, Anita 414-382-6343 515 D anita.eikens@alverno.edu
EIKNER, Megan, E 806-335-4352 450 H meeikner@actx.edu
EILAND, Victoria 229-430-4637 115 K victoria.eiland@asurams.edu
EILERING, Susan 217-479-7106 147 C susan.eilering@mac.edu
EIMER, Greg, A 217-732-3155 146 B geimer@lincolncollege.edu
EIMERS, Mardy, T 573-882-3412 273 E eimersm@missouri.edu
EINFELD, Aaron 616-957-7035 232 B aaron@calvinseminary.edu
EINHELLIG, Frank, E 417-836-5119 268 I frankeinhellig@missouristate.edu
EINOLF, Karl, W 301-447-5396 209 G einolf@msmary.edu
EINSPAHR, Kent 402-643-7315 279 F kent.einspahr@cune.edu
EINSTEIN, Heath 817-257-7490 469 G h.einstein@tcu.edu
EIOLA, William, T 419-772-2261 374 J w-eiola@onu.edu
EIS, Linda 417-625-3797 268 H eis-l@mssu.edu
EISELE, Chad 309-341-7280 145 A ceisele@knox.edu
EISEMAN, Margaret 412-396-6061 403 A eiseman@duq.edu
EISEN, Arnold, M 212-678-8072 317 I areisen@jtsa.edu
EISEN, Jeffrey, M 919-658-7759 355 K jeisen@umo.edu
EISEN, Karen 718-780-0343 305 L karen.eisen@brooklaw.edu
EISENBACH, Regina 760-750-4253 34 D regina@csusm.edu
EISENBACH, Theresa 203-332-5013 86 D teisenbach@hcc.commnet.edu
EISENBARTH, Jeffrey 407-646-2117 107 O jeisenbarth@rollins.edu
EISENBARTH, Kathryn, L 503-352-2705 394 C eisenbak@pacificu.edu
EISENBEISER, Colleen, K 410-777-1963 206 B ckeisenbeiser@aacc.edu
EISENBERG, Eric 813-974-2804 112 C eisenberg@usf.edu
EISENBERG, Jessica 617-559-8775 219 E jeisenberg@hebrewcollege.edu
EISENBERG, Larry, A 314-516-6469 274 A eisenbergl@umsl.edu
EISENBERGER, Israel 845-362-3053 304 J
EISENHARD, Craig 215-248-7381 409 D ceisenhard@ltsp.edu
EISENHART, Pamela 717-337-6010 404 C peisenha@gettysburg.edu
EISENHAUER, Jay 304-829-7465 510 G jeisenhauer@bethanywv.edu
EISENHAUER, Joseph 313-993-1204 241 G eisenhjg@udmercy.edu
EISENHAUER, Walt 570-484-2168 415 D weisenha@lhup.edu
EISENHUTH, Wayne 507-222-4427 245 C weisenhu@carleton.edu
EISENMAN, Ann 563-244-7040 172 B aeisenman@eicc.edu
EISENMAN, Elaine 781-239-4355 214 G eeisenman@babson.edu
EISENMENGER, Paul 847-317-7087 156 B peisenme@tiu.edu
EISENSTEIN, Laya 718-268-4700 326 L
EISENSTEIN, Paul 614-823-1609 376 C peisenstein@otterbein.edu
EISENTRAGER, Pete 816-235-2665 273 F eisentragerp@umkc.edu
EISGRUBER, Cristopher, L 609-258-3026 294 D eisgrube@princeton.edu
EISINGER, Robert 401-254-3043 426 B reisinger@rwu.edu
EISLER, David, L 231-591-2500 233 L davideisler@ferris.edu
EISNAUGLE, Eva 704-978-1344 351 D eeisnaugle@mitchellcc.edu
EISNER, SND, Janet 617-735-9825 218 C president@emmanuel.edu
EITEL, Keith 817-923-1921 466 E keitel@swbts.edu
EITEL, Norine 660-626-2391 262 A neitel@atsu.edu
EJIGIRI, Damien, D 225-771-5390 199 H damien_ejigiri@subr.edu
EKARIUS, John 215-503-5017 420 E john.ekarius@jefferson.edu
EKKER, David, A 757-822-7198 498 H dekker@tcc.edu
EKOUE-TOTOU, Patrick 415-883-2211 40 C pekouetotou@marin.edu
EKPO, NseAbasi 937-376-6411 365 H nekpo@centralstate.edu
EKSTROM, Rodney 603-535-2217 288 F raekstrom@plymouth.edu
EL-BERMAWY, Mohamed 573-288-6344 264 F melbermawy@culver.edu
EL FATTAL, David 805-652-5536 73 C delfattal@vcccd.edu

EL-HAGGAN, Ahmed .... 410-951-3850.. 212 E
elhaggan@coppin.edu

EL-KHOURY, Rodolphe .... 305-284-9092.. 114 H
rxe66@miami.edu

EL-REWINI, Hesham .... 701-777-3412.. 360 C
rewini@engr.und.edu

ELAM, Becky .... 951-487-3011.... 53 D
belam@msjc.edu

ELAM, Demar .... 334-387-3877...... 1 E
demarelam@amridgeuniversity.edu

ELAM, Harry, J .... 650-723-2300.... 66 I
helam@stanford.edu

ELAM, Joyce .... 305-348-2779.. 111 A
joyce.elam@fiu.edu

ELAM, Terry .... 434-592-3966.. 491 D
tlelam@liberty.edu

ELAM, Terry, D .... 706-771-4005.. 117 C
telam@augustatech.edu

ELAND, Tom .... 612-659-6286.. 250 B
thomas.eland@minneapolis.edu

ELARDE, Christopher .... 212-346-1200.. 325 J
celarde@pace.edu

ELBASSIOUNY, Samir ...... 908-835-9222.. 298 E
selbassiouny@warren.edu

ELBE, Michael .... 217-641-4101.. 143 H
melbe@jwcc.edu

ELBOW, Gary .... 806-742-2184.. 472 C
gary.elbow@ttu.edu

ELCHANANI, Matanya .... 203-576-4322.... 89 C
matanya@btidgeport.edu

ELDAYRIE, Elias, G .... 352-273-1788.. 112 A
eldayrie@ufl.edu

ELDEMIRE, Flavia .... 803-376-5700.. 427 A
feldemire@allenuniversity.edu

ELDER, Dana .... 509-359-6305.. 503 D
delder@ewu.edu

ELDER, Darla .... 814-732-2743.. 415 A
delder@edinboro.edu

ELDER, Jackie .... 903-223-3110.. 469 C
jackie.elder@tamut.edu

ELDER, Jill .... 605-718-2411.. 438 B
jill.elder@wdt.edu

ELDER, Keith .... 205-726-2011...... 6 E

ELDER, Matthew .... 502-585-9911.. 192 E
melder@spalding.edu

ELDER, Nanci .... 641-585-8143.. 177 F
nanci.elder@waldorf.edu

ELDER, Paul .... 269-471-3284.. 230 H
elderp@andrews.edu

ELDER, Steve .... 501-205-8893.... 19 J
selder@cbc.edu

ELDER, Thomas .... 903-510-2405.. 473 C
teld@tjc.edu

ELDER, Vivian .... 417-447-8114.. 270 A
elderv@otc.edu

ELDERS, Candice .... 269-927-8198.. 236 G
cedlers@lakemichigancollege.edu

ELDIN, III, Neil .... 713-743-4050.. 473 F
neldin@central.uh.edu

ELDREDGE, Brad .... 406-756-3894.. 276 E
beldredge@fvcc.edu

ELDRIDGE, Daryl .... 866-931-4300.. 270 I
daryl.eldridge@rockbridge.edu

ELDRIDGE, Jonathan .... 415-485-9619.... 40 C
jeldridge@marin.edu

ELDRIDGE, Karen .... 865-981-8207.. 441 H
karen.eldridge@maryvillecollege.edu

ELDRIDGE, Kim .... 202-884-9053.... 94 A
mortonk@trinitydc.edu

ELDRIDGE, Linda, P .... 859-846-5340.. 191 G
leldridge@midway.edu

ELDRIDGE, Marie .... 931-598-1111.. 443 O
police@sewanee.edu

ELDRIDGE, Paul .... 303-963-3093.... 77 I
peldridge@ccu.edu

ELDRIDGE, Randy .... 610-527-0200.. 418 D
reldridge@rosemont.edu

ELDRIDGE, Ray .... 615-966-5946.. 441 F
ray.eldridge@lipscomb.edu

ELEBARIO, Jessica .... 575-461-4413.. 300 A
jessicae@mesalands.edu

ELEFF, Zev .... 847-982-2500.. 141 D
eleff@htc.edu

ELENICH, Richard .... 906-487-2763.. 238 A
rjelenic@mtu.edu

ELENWO, Elizabeth .... 619-549-3974.... 65 J
elizabeth.elenwo@socalsem.edu

ELEY, Greg .... 765-998-5224.. 167 C
greley@taylor.edu

ELFRINK, Stephanie .... 314-529-9370.. 267 B
selfrink@maryville.edu

ELGARICO, Michael .... 805-493-3049.... 31 C
elgarico@callutheran.edu

ELGREN, Timothy .... 440-775-8410.. 374 C
tim.elgren@oberlin.edu

ELHINDI, Mohamed .... 608-785-8309.. 520 C
melhindi@uwlax.edu

ELI, Lauren .... 303-300-8740.... 77 F
lauren.eli@collegeamerica.com

ELIA, Anthony .... 317-937-2365.. 160 B
aelia@cts.edu

ELIADI, Carol .... 617-373-5680.. 225 C
carol.eliadi@mcphs.edu

ELIAS, Adam .... 502-262-1124.. 190 A
adam.elias@kctcs.edu

ELIAS, Charles .... 718-482-5052.. 309 A
celias@lagcc.cuny.edu

ELIAS, Jack .... 401-863-3330.. 424 J
jack_elias@brown.edu

ELIAS, Janelle .... 480-517-8767.... 14 G
janelle.elias@riosalado.edu

ELIAS, Stephanny, J .... 617-333-2010.. 217 F
selias0104@curry.edu

ELIASON, Eric, J .... 218-299-3001.. 246 A
vpaa@cord.edu

ELIASSEN, John .... 503-223-2245.. 391 H
jeliassen@portland.chefs.edu

ELIAV, Eli .... 585-275-5688.. 338 K
eli_eliav@urmc.rochester.edu

ELICK, Cynthia, M .... 260-481-6204.. 163 C
elick@ipfw.edu

ELICKER, Beth .... 207-699-5045.. 203 F
belicker@meca.edu

ELIJAH, Rhonda .... 219-866-6134.. 166 J
rhondae@saintjoe.edu

ELIPTICO, Frankie, M .... 670-237-6831.. 530 D
frankie.eliptico@marianas.edu

ELIQUE, Jose .... 702-895-3668.. 284 L
chiefofpolice@unlv.edu

ELISH-PIPER, Laurie .... 815-753-9055.. 150 A
laurieep@niu.edu

ELIZA, Lourdes .... 787-852-1430.. 532 N
leliza@hccpr.edu

ELIZANDRO, John .... 516-686-7605.. 323 G
jelizand@nyit.edu

ELIZONDO, Laura, M .... 956-326-2213.. 468 A
laura@tamiu.edu

ELIZONDO, Maria .... 956-664-4600.. 465 H
marye@southtexascollege.edu

ELIZONDO, Maria, G .... 956-872-3558.. 465 H
melizondo@southtexascollege.edu

ELKESHK, Abed .... 718-405-3300.. 310 H
abed.elkeshk@mountsaintvincent.edu

ELKINS, Becki .... 319-895-4595.. 171 A
belkins@cornellcollege.edu

ELKINS, Becki, S .... 319-895-4595.. 171 A
belkins@cornellcollege.edu

ELKINS, Germaine .... 910-695-3706.. 353 A
elkinsg@sandhills.edu

ELKINS, Julie, B .... 617-228-2436.. 223 B
jelkins@bhcc.mass.edu

ELKINS, Leah .... 513-241-4338.. 363 G
leah.elkins@antonellicollege.edu

ELKINS, Mark .... 904-596-2445.. 113 J
melkins@tbc.edu

ELKINS, Mary Jane .... 434-949-1051.. 498 E
maryjane.elkins@southside.edu

ELKINS, Paula, S .... 706-886-6831.. 128 C
pelkins@tfc.edu

ELKINS, Penny, L .... 478-301-2120.. 124 D
elkins_pl@mercer.edu

ELKINS, Susan .... 803-777-7695.. 433 F
selkins@mailbox.sc.edu

ELKS, Martha .... 404-752-1881.. 125 A
melks@msm.edu

ELLARD, Mark .... 334-291-4981...... 2 H
mark.ellard@cv.edu

ELLARD, Owen, H .... 210-567-2413.. 477 D
ellard@uthscsa.edu

ELLARD, Peter, C .... 518-783-2307.. 330 E
pellard@siena.edu

ELLENBERG, George, B ... 850-474-2035.. 113 A
gellenberg@uwf.edu

ELLENBERG, Todd, M ..... 305-284-6047.. 114 H
tellenberg@miami.edu

ELLENBERGER, Amy .... 818-333-3558.... 54 B

ELLENBERGER, Sheila, J . 740-826-8260.. 373 E
sheilaj@muskingum.edu

ELLENBURG, Aaron .... 434-200-7033.. 487 L
aaron.ellenburg@centrahealth.com

ELLENBURG, Phil .... 615-966-1000.. 441 F

ELLENS, S. Dean .... 630-617-3059.. 140 C
ellenss@elmhurst.edu

ELLENS, Timothy, L .... 616-526-6475.. 232 A
tje6@calvin.edu

ELLER, Greg .... 850-729-5332.. 105 I
eller@nwfsc.edu

ELLER, Greg .... 901-321-3307.. 439 E
geller@cbu.edu

ELLER, Jackie .... 615-898-2182.. 444 G
jackie.eller@mtsu.edu

ELLERBE, Laverne .... 757-822-1994.. 498 H
lellerbe@tcc.edu

ELLERKER, Charla .... 863-784-7176.. 109 G
charla.ellerker@southflorida.edu

ELLERSON, Patricia .... 760-245-4271.... 73 H
patricia.ellerson@vvc.edu

ELLERTSON, Chris .... 847-735-5011.. 145 B
ellertson@lakeforest.edu

ELLERTSON, Shari .... 208-426-1614.. 132 I
shariellerston@boisestate.edu

ELLIBEE, Margaret .... 501-812-2216.... 21 H
mellibee@pulaskitech.edu

ELLIE, Beth .... 715-675-3331.. 524 D
ellie@ntc.edu

ELLIFF POUND, Lee .... 417-625-9355.. 268 H
pound-l@mssu.edu

ELLIG, Tracy .... 406-994-5607.. 277 C
tellig@montana.edu

ELLIMAN, Don .... 303-315-7682.... 84 A
chancellor@ucdenver.edu

ELLIN, Nan .... 817-272-2801.. 476 A
nan.ellin@uta.edu

ELLING, Wayne, H .... 206-281-2599.. 507 C
elling@spu.edu

ELLINGER, Amanda, M .... 540-985-8206.. 491 A
amellinger@jchs.edu

ELLINGER, John, M .... 419-372-2006.. 364 E
johne@bgsu.edu

ELLINGHUYSEN, Scott ..... 507-457-5696.. 252 G
sellinghuysen@winona.edu

ELLINGSON, Mike .... 701-231-7307.. 361 A
michael.ellingson@ndsu.edu

ELLINGTON, Keri .... 317-738-8086.. 160 J
kellington@franklincollege.edu

ELLINGTON, Michael, A .. 304-293-2702.. 514 C
michael.ellington@mail.wvu.edu

ELLINGTON, Ross .... 850-645-6900.. 111 C
wellington@fsu.edu

ELLINOR, Ben .... 941-359-4200.. 112 E

ELLINWOOD, Dawn, M ... 802-654-2566.. 484 I
dellinwood@smcvt.edu

ELLIOT, Robert .... 646-717-9764.. 315 B
elliot@gts.edu

ELLIOT BROWN,
Karin, A .... 323-343-3820.... 33 C
kbrown5@calstatela.edu

ELLIOTT, Angela, P .... 563-333-6339.. 176 D
elliottangelap@sau.edu

ELLIOTT, Barbara .... 717-396-7833.. 413 M
belliott@pcad.edu

ELLIOTT, Brenda .... 402-399-2435.. 279 E
belliott@csm.edu

ELLIOTT, Brian .... 503-588-9207.. 391 B
belliott@corban.edu

ELLIOTT, Charles .... 304-384-5334.. 513 A
celliott@concord.edu

ELLIOTT, Clara .... 413-552-2219.. 223 E
celliott@hcc.edu

ELLIOTT, Clifton, R .... 843-355-4138.. 435 A
elliottr@wiltech.edu

ELLIOTT, Craig .... 510-869-6627.... 59 L
celliott@samuelmerritt.edu

ELLIOTT, Deborah, M ...... 315-786-2416.. 317 H

ELLIOTT, Doug .... 540-423-9073.. 497 B
delliott@germanna.edu

ELLIOTT, Erin .... 212-517-3929.. 330 G
e.elliott@sothebysinstitute.com

ELLIOTT, Fatina .... 318-670-9315.. 199 J
felliott@susla.edu

ELLIOTT, Holly .... 205-391-2211...... 6 G
helliott@sheltonstate.edu

ELLIOTT, Jacquelyn .... 520-494-5200.... 12 J
jackie.elliott@centralaz.edu

ELLIOTT, James .... 312-329-4166.. 148 F
jim.elliott@moody.edu

ELLIOTT, Jeffrey .... 402-885-8228.. 283 A
jeffrey.elliott@unmc.edu

ELLIOTT, John .... 860-486-1361.... 89 D
john.elliott@uconn.edu

ELLIOTT, John, P .... 412-624-6127.. 421 G
jelliott@cfo.pitt.edu

ELLIOTT, Kathy .... 405-744-4188.. 385 G
kathy.elliott@okstate.edu

ELLIOTT, Ken .... 601-709-0966.. 256 I
kelliott@belhaven.edu

ELLIOTT, Ken .... 828-327-7000.. 348 C
kelliott@cvcc.edu

ELLIOTT, Kenneth .... 337-550-1302.. 197 K
kelliott@lsue.edu

ELLIOTT, Kiersten .... 310-434-4173.... 63 F
elliott_kiersten@smc.edu

ELLIOTT, Lynn .... 276-944-6117.. 489 I
lelliott@ehc.edu

ELLIOTT, Marilyn .... 859-858-2033.. 186 I

ELLIOTT, Mark .... 615-248-1271.. 447 F
melliott@trevecca.edu

ELLIOTT, Marvin, L .... 606-474-3253.. 188 L
melliott@kcu.edu

ELLIOTT, Melissa .... 302-736-2586.... 91 G
melissa.elliott@wesley.edu

ELLIOTT, Melissa, J .... 940-552-6291.. 478 D
mjelliott@vernoncollege.edu

ELLIOTT, Michael .... 860-297-2000.... 89 B
michael.elliott@trincoll.edu

ELLIOTT, Michael, A .... 404-727-6817.. 120 E
mellio2@emory.edu

ELLIOTT, Michael, S .... 870-297-4261.... 89 B
michael.elliott@trincoll.edu

ELLIOTT, Myra .... 606-886-3863.. 189 A
myrat.elliott@kctcs.edu

ELLIOTT, Patrick .... 607-777-2043.. 331 B
pelliott@binghamton.edu

ELLIOTT, Peter .... 863-297-1081.. 106 I
pelliott@polk.edu

ELLIOTT, Rennae .... 256-726-7533...... 6 B
elliott@oakwood.edu

ELLIOTT, Richard, F .... 651-631-5118.. 256 A
rfelliott@unwsp.edu

ELLIOTT, Rita .... 815-226-3374.. 152 G
relliott@rockford.edu

ELLIOTT, Rob .... 715-675-3331.. 524 D
elliottr@ntc.edu

ELLIOTT, Scott .... 618-985-3741.. 143 F
scottelliott@jalc.edu

ELLIOTT, Scott, D .... 601-484-8619.. 258 F
selliott@meridiancc.edu

ELLIOTT, Sherman .... 602-639-7500.... 13 I

ELLIOTT, Stanley .... 919-719-1898.. 355 F
selliott@shawu.edu

ELLIOTT, Steven .... 402-375-7208.. 281 J
stellio1@wsc.edu

ELLIOTT, Tracy .... 408-808-2022.... 35 C
tracy.elliott@sjsu.edu

ELLIOTT CAIN, Pam .... 515-294-6218.. 169 G
pelliott@iastate.edu

ELLIOTT-NELSON, Linda .. 928-344-7516.... 11 J
linda.elliott-nelson@azwestern.edu

ELLIS, Brent .... 517-750-1200.. 241 E
bellis@arbor.edu

ELLIS, Bret, R .... 801-626-7660.. 482 D
bretellis@weber.edu

ELLIS, Brian, F .... 405-325-6211.. 389 B
be@ou.edu

ELLIS, Bridget .... 252-399-6371.. 341 P
bbellis@barton.edu

ELLIS, Christine .... 260-459-4501.. 164 C
cellis@ibcfortwayne.edu

ELLIS, Christopher, E ...... 515-964-0601.. 172 F
ellisc@faith.edu

ELLIS, Craig, D .... 717-764-9550.. 401 H
cellis@csb.edu

ELLIS, David .... 503-768-7691.. 392 A
dgellis@lclark.edu

ELLIS, David, A .... 513-529-3638.. 372 K
ellisda2@miamioh.edu

ELLIS, David, A .... 508-373-9464.. 215 D
david.ellis@becker.edu

ELLIS, David, A .... 513-529-3638.. 372 K
ellisda2@miamioh.edu

ELLIS, Dechelle .... 704-463-3411.. 354 F
dechelle.ellis@sodexo.com

ELLIS, Denise .... 402-826-8251.. 280 B
denise.ellis@doane.edu

ELLIS, Diane .... 870-307-7284.... 21 A
diane.ellis@lyon.edu

ELLIS, Donna .... 570-674-6266.. 410 K
dellis@misericordia.edu

ELLIS, Eric .... 617-322-3599.. 219 H
eric_ellis@laboure.edu

ELLIS, Evelynn .... 603-646-3197.. 286 J
evelynn.ellis@dartmouth.edu

ELLIS, Favor .... 802-586-7711.. 485 C
fellis@sterlingcollege.edu

ELLIS, George, W .... 813-974-5454.. 112 C
gellis@usf.edu

ELLIS, Graham .... 502-272-8218.. 187 A
gellis@bellarmine.edu

ELLIS, Heidi, B .... 903-813-2235.. 451 M
hellis@austincollege.edu

ELLIS, James, G .... 213-740-6422.... 72 D
dean@marshall.usc.edu

ELLIS, Jennifer .... 216-987-4236.. 367 E
jennifer.ellis@tri-c.edu

ELLIS, John .... 518-454-5166.. 311 B
ellisj@strose.edu

ELLIS, Kathy .... 863-680-4106.. 101 E
kellis@flsouthern.edu

ELLIS, Keats, L .... 910-521-6222.. 358 C
keats.ellis@uncp.edu

ELLIS, Kristie .... 505-566-3408.. 301 J
ellisk@sanjuancollege.edu

ELLIS, Larry .... 607-729-1581.. 312 E
lellis@davisny.edu

ELLIS, Leann .... 817-515-7701.. 467 A
leann.ellis@tccd.edu

ELLIS, Lee .... 618-374-5030.. 151 E
lee.ellis@principia.edu

ELLIS, Liz .... 575-646-2446.. 300 J
lellis@nmsu.edu

ELLIS, Machelle .... 580-387-7221.. 384 D
mellis@mscok.edu

ELLIS, Marjorie, N .... 254-710-8669.. 452 H
marjorie_ellis@baylor.edu

ELLIS, Pamela .... 828-395-1456.. 350 E
pellis@isothermal.edu

ELLIS, Pat .... 315-229-5392.. 329 D
pellis@stlawu.edu

ELLIS, R. Darin .... 313-577-0167.. 243 F
rdellis@wayne.edu

ELLIS, Reggie .... 310-434-3780.... 63 F
ellis_reggie@smc.edu

ELLIS, Rick 612-330-1581 244 I ellisr@augsburg.edu
ELLIS, Rodney 318-670-9312 199 J rellis@susla.edu
ELLIS, Roger 636-949-4839 266 J rellis@lindenwood.edu
ELLIS, Ronald, L 951-343-4210 29 H president@calbaptist.edu
ELLIS, Rose 541-463-3005 391 G ellisr@lanecc.edu
ELLIS, Sabrina 212-998-1205 324 C sabrina.ellis@nyu.edu
ELLIS, Samuel 207-216-4434 204 B sellis@yccc.edu
ELLIS, Shannon 775-784-6196 285 A elliss@admin.unr.edu
ELLIS, Susan 239-489-9234 101 F mellis3@fsw.edu
ELLIS, Susan 910-678-8372 349 F elliss@faytechcc.edu
ELLIS, Tom, M 423-425-4687 448 F tom-ellis@utc.edu
ELLIS, Tracie 301-387-3164 207 G tracie.ellis@garrettcollege.edu
ELLIS, Wade 408-848-4739 44 I wellis@gavsilan.edu
ELLIS, Wendy 802-287-8210 484 A ellisw@greenmtn.edu
ELLIS, William, N 325-649-8000 459 E hpupresident@hputx.edu
ELLIS-HILL, Ralonda 216-987-4624 367 E ralonda.ellis-hill@tri-c.edu
ELLIS KREAGER, Alexandra 260-399-7700 168 D aellis@sf.edu
ELLIS-PERRY, Barney 949-824-9741 69 C barney@uci.edu
ELLISON, Brian 209-384-6105 52 E brian.ellison@mccd.edu
ELLISON, David, R 202-231-3344 528 C david.ellison@dodiis.mil
ELLISON, Diane 585-475-7284 327 E dmeges@rit.edu
ELLISON, Doris, G 608-757-7678 523 A dellison2@blackhawk.edu
ELLISON, E. Christopher 614-292-2600 375 A ellison.2@osu.edu
ELLISON, Jimmy 325-674-2305 449 J jimmy.ellison@acu.edu
ELLISON, Kimberly 513-732-5221 379 C kimberly.ellison@uc.edu
ELLISON, Lori 239-513-1135 115 F lellison@wolford.edu
ELLISON, Maderia 928-532-6743 15 J maderia.ellison@npc.edu
ELLISON, Marjorie 573-288-6541 264 F mellison@culver.edu
ELLISON, Pamela 216-987-4459 367 E pamela.ellison@tri-c.edu
ELLISON, Rich 513-244-8427 366 B rich.ellison2@ccuniversity.edu
ELLISON, Rich 859-282-8989 123 F rellison@ict.edu
ELLISON, Ron 209-946-3042 71 C rellison1@pacific.edu
ELLISOR, Kimberly, M 843-661-1190 430 B kellisor@fmarion.edu
ELLMORE, Philip, T 609-626-3546 297 C philip.ellmore@stockton.edu
ELLSPERMANN, Sue, J 317-921-4980 164 E sellspermann@ivytech.edu
ELLSWORTH, Tim 731-661-5215 448 A tellsworth@uu.edu
ELLWANGER, Carolyn 712-279-5484 170 B carolyn.ellwanger@briarcliff.edu
ELLZEY, Janet, L 512-471-7020 476 B jellzey@mail.utexas.edu
ELMENDORF, Douglas 617-495-1000 219 D
ELMORE, Amy 270-534-3118 190 H amy.elmore@kctcs.edu
ELMORE, Cecilia 573-341-6798 274 B elmorec@mst.edu
ELMORE, Chris 336-272-7102 344 G chris.elmore@greensboro.edu
ELMORE, Dana 601-925-3371 259 A elmore@mc.edu
ELMORE, Diane 434-200-3070 487 L diane.elmore@centralhealth.com
ELMORE, Donna 803-535-1202 431 I elmored@octech.edu
ELMORE, Floyd 704-847-5600 355 J felmore@ses.edu
ELMORE, John 785-833-4340 182 F john.elmore@kwu.edu
ELMORE, Kenneth 617-353-4126 216 E kennmore@bu.edu
ELMORE, Rheena 251-580-2159 4 I rheena.elmore@faulknerstate.edu
ELMORE, Robert 513-875-3344 365 K robert.elmore@chatfield.edu
ELMORE, Ronald 336-841-9128 345 A relmore@highpoint.edu
ELMORE, Troy, A 270-384-8144 191 E elmoret@lindsey.edu
ELMORE, Wendy 903-675-6371 473 B welmore@tvcc.edu
ELMS, Duane 575-624-8110 300 I elms@nmmi.edu
ELNASHAI, Amr, S 814-865-7537 412 F ase2@psu.edu
ELNESS, Jodi, M 320-308-5087 252 B jelness@sctcc.edu
ELNICK, William 215-572-2172 397 G elnickb@arcadia.edu
ELNICKY, Rob 716-270-4621 313 H elnicky@ecc.edu
ELOFIR, Stacey 410-704-4414 213 B selofir@towson.edu
ELROD, David 706-272-4473 119 H delrod@daltonstate.edu
ELROD, Eileen, R 408-554-4136 63 E eelrod@scu.edu
ELROD, Roger 408-924-6112 35 C roger.elrod@sjsu.edu
ELROD, Susan 262-472-1918 521 F
ELSASS, Susan 603-577-6581 286 I elsass@dwc.edu
ELSBECK, George, J 607-431-4320 315 E elsbeckg@hartwick.edu
ELSBERRY, Meagan 561-237-7233 104 O melsberry@lynn.edu
ELSDEN, Anna 712-749-2155 170 D formichella@bvu.edu
ELSE, Iwalani 218-723-6583 245 J ielse@css.edu
ELSE, Robert 805-965-0581 63 D else@sbcc.edu
ELSEA, Kathy 660-785-4130 273 B kelsea@truman.edu
ELSENER, Daniel, J 317-955-6100 165 N delsener@marian.edu
ELSEROAD, Arleen 949-451-5220 65 E aelseroad@ivc.edu
ELSEROAD, Arleen 949-451-5409 65 F alseroad@ivc.edu
ELSHAYEB, Tarek, A 704-687-7781 358 A telshaye@uncc.edu
ELSHICK, Soha 201-216-9901 291 C soha.elshick@eicollege.edu
ELSLEY, Judy 801-626-6186 482 D jelsley@weber.edu
ELSTER, Janette 315-568-3053 323 A jelster@nycc.edu
ELSTON, Joseph, P 570-340-6024 409 H
ELSTON, Timothy, G 803-321-5197 431 F timothy.elston@newberry.edu
ELSWICK, Clark 575-562-4490 299 I clark.elswick@enmu.edu
ELTON, Nathan 302-831-8479 91 F nelton@udel.edu
ELVARD, Lesly 410-888-9048 209 C lelvard@muih.edu
ELVEY, William 608-262-3488 519 K belvey@fpm.wisc.edu
ELVIDGE, Janet 207-974-4606 203 J jelvidge@emcc.edu
ELWELL, SR., Daniel, P 201-200-3344 293 C delwell@njcu.edu
ELWELL, David 617-253-3795 225 A
ELWELL, Jan 518-255-5423 334 D elwellja@cobleskill.edu
ELWELL, Jan, A 607-746-4499 335 C elwellja@delhi.edu
ELWELL, Jeff 423-425-4635 448 F jeffery-elwell@utc.edu
ELWELL, Nancy 402-643-7337 279 F nancy.elwell@cune.edu
ELWOOD, Sharon 307-674-6446 526 M elwood@sheridan.edu
ELWORTH, Edyce 336-734-7296 349 G eelworth@forsythtech.edu
ELY, Janice 310-660-3109 42 J jely@elcamino.edu
ELY, SJ, Peter 206-296-6158 507 E ely@seattleu.edu
ELY, Tim 610-526-1862 405 B tely@harucm.edu
ELY, Tim 610-526-1862 405 B tely@harcum.edu
ELZARKA, Sammy 909-593-3511 71 B selzarka@laverne.edu
EMAMI, Azita 206-221-2472 508 E emamia@uw.edu
EMAMI, Morteza 801-626-6853 482 D memami@weber.edu
EMANUEL, Catherine, B 770-720-9232 126 C cbe@reinhardt.edu
EMANUEL, Rachel 225-771-2552 200 A remanuel@sulc.edu
EMBACHER, Barb 507-389-7493 252 D barb.embacher@southcentral.edu
EMBERTON, Sherilyn, R 260-359-4050 161 D semberton@huntington.edu
EMBLER, Marc 843-863-7131 427 I membler@csuniv.edu
EMBRY, Greg 205-665-6030 9 B embryg@montevallo.edu
EMBRY, Teresa 256-761-6211 7 F tembry@talladega.edu
EMDY, Jim 831-476-9424 43 M librarian@fivebranches.edu
EMENDORFER, Mike 608-342-1567 521 A emendorm@uwplatt.edu
EMENGER, Nancy, E 801-626-6017 482 D nemenger@weber.edu
EMERICK, Kenneth 301-687-4880 212 F kmemerick@frostburg.edu
EMERICK, Sandra, M 330-325-6759 373 H semerick@neomed.edu
EMERSON, Adam 413-236-2132 222 G aemerson@berkshirecc.edu
EMERSON, Brian 716-896-0700 339 E bemerson@villa.edu
EMERSON, Colleen 401-341-2908 426 C emersonc@salve.edu
EMERSON, Dana 714-241-6184 39 E
EMERSON, Dave 616-222-1426 233 A dave.emerson@cornerstone.edu
EMERSON, Jim 434-200-7026 487 L jim.emerson@centrahealth.com
EMERSON, Michael, D 773-244-5570 149 I moemerson@northpark.edu
EMERSON, Nate 507-453-2711 250 C nemerson@southeastmn.edu
EMERSON, Sally 608-789-6083 524 H emersons@westerntc.edu
EMERSON, Steve 951-343-4415 29 H semerson@calbaptist.edu
EMERSON, Tara 573-592-4251 275 G tara.emerson@williamwoods.edu
EMERSON, Tony 516-918-3675 305 K temerson@bcl.edu
EMERSON, Wendy, R 336-734-7540 349 G wemerson@forsythtech.edu
EMERSON, Yolanda 562-692-0921 58 I yemerson@riohondo.edu
EMERY, Hank 713-525-3111 475 J emeryh@stthom.edu
EMERZIAN, Janice 559-442-8237 67 C janice.emerzian@fresnocitycollege.edu
EMERZIAN, Janice 559-638-0300 67 D janice.emerzian@scccd.com
EMILIO, Linda 909-469-8421 74 K lemilio@westernu.edu
EMM, William, T 585-345-6811 315 C wtemm@genesee.edu
EMMANUEL-FRENEL, Rouseline 215-646-7300 404 G emmanuel.r@gmercyu.edu
EMMER, Karen 520-515-5417 12 L emmerk@cochise.edu
EMMERICH, Linda 443-518-3825 208 C lemmerich@howardcc.edu
EMMERT, Heather 321-693-5256 100 M hcudmore@fit.edu
EMMICK, Joseph, R 630-617-6422 140 C joseph.r.emmick@elmhurst.edu
EMMIL, Bruce 701-224-5758 361 C bruce.emmil@bismarckstate.edu
EMMONS, Carol-Ann 312-567-3827 142 I emmons@iit.edu
EMMONS, David 360-475-7120 505 F demmons@olympic.edu
EMMONS, Don 315-781-3559 316 C emmons@hws.edu
EMMONS, Ken 619-644-7653 45 J ken.emmons@gcccd.edu
EMMONS, Larry, K 989-964-2558 240 F lkemmons@svsu.edu
EMMONS, Luli 650-433-3845 56 D lemmons@paloaltou.edu
EMMONS, Scott 414-229-4762 520 D semm@uwm.edu
EMMONS, Todd, C 603-526-3076 285 L todd.emmons@colby-sawyer.edu
EMOND, Gean Ann 850-484-1728 106 H gemond@pensacolastate.edu
EMORY, Cynthia 301-696-3566 208 B emory@hood.edu
EMORY, Douglas, J 425-739-8311 504 F doug.emory@lwtech.edu
EMORY, Jerry 360-676-2772 505 C jbemory@nwic.edu
EMORY, Julie, W 252-398-6252 343 G emoryj@chowan.edu
EMRICH, Whitney 601-974-1105 258 H whitney.emrich@millsaps.edu
EMSWELLER, David, W 419-434-4578 379 E emsweller@findlay.edu
EMSWILER, Sue 717-299-7730 420 C emswiler@stevenscollege.edu
ENAMAIT, John 704-991-0220 353 E
ENAMAIT, John, D 252-823-5166 349 E enamaitj@edgecombe.edu
ENCARNACION, Jose, M 787-850-9375 538 B jose.encarnacion2@upr.edu
ENCARNACION, Mayra 787-257-0000 537 H mayra.encarnacion@upr.edu
ENCARNACION, Zaneta 619-216-6613 66 E zencarnacion@swccd.edu
ENCINA, Rosalinda 210-486-4609 450 C rencina@alamo.edu
ENDEAN, Kenneth, M 480-245-7969 13 L ken.endean@ibcs.edu
ENDER, Kenneth, L 847-925-6390 141 A kender@harpercollege.edu
ENDER, Steven, C 616-234-3901 234 E sender@grcc.edu
ENDERS, Naulayne, R 606-474-3276 188 L nenders@kcu.edu
ENDERS, Tom 323-343-3800 33 C thomas.enders@calstatela.edu
ENDICOTT, Daniel, D 904-620-2019 112 B dendicot@unf.edu
ENDICOTT, Jon 559-453-3484 44 F jon.endicott@fresno.edu
ENDICOTT, Patricia 812-749-1435 166 B pendicott@oak.edu
ENDRASKE, Mark 530-226-4108 64 H mendraske@simpsonu.edu
ENDRES, David 513-231-2223 363 K dendres@athenaeum.edu
ENDRESS, Wendy 360-867-6296 503 G endressw@evergreen.edu
ENDRIES, Jill, M 920-424-0228 520 E endries@uwosh.edu
ENDRIES, Mary 920-923-8937 517 H mendries@marianuniversity.edu
ENDRIJONAS, Erika, A 818-947-2600 50 D
ENDSLEY, Douglas 210-829-6004 474 D douge@uiwtx.edu
ENDY, Michael 817-598-6211 479 E mendy@wc.edu
ENEA, Marie, L 610-330-5200 407 C eneam@lafayette.edu
ENER, Sarah 970-330-8008 76 H sarah.ener@aims.edu
ENG, Carla 605-668-1514 436 D ceng@mtmc.edu
ENG, Dave 845-398-4084 329 G deng@stac.edu
ENG, Edwin 559-244-5910 67 A ed.eng@scccd.edu
ENGBROCK, M. Jeff 409-944-1215 458 D mengbroc@gc.edu
ENGEBRETSON, Pam 651-779-3994 249 A pam.engebretson@century.edu
ENGEL, Angela 309-438-3305 143 B akengel@ilstu.edu
ENGEL, Cristi, L 402-461-5177 280 H
ENGEL, Deidre 712-279-5448 170 B deidre.engel@briarcliff.edu
ENGEL, Heather 585-475-2627 327 E hcedar@rit.edu
ENGEL, Jennifer 773-508-3899 146 G jengel2@luc.edu
ENGEL, Michelle 414-382-6037 515 D michelle.engel@alverno.edu
ENGEL, Renata, S 814-863-6726 412 F rse1@psu.edu
ENGEL, Richard, R 530-752-9960 69 A rrengel@ucdavis.edu
ENGEL, Robert 718-997-4105 309 D robert.engel@qc.cuny.edu
ENGEL, Steven 912-478-0357 122 B sengel@georgiasouthern.edu
ENGELBACH, Karl, M 530-754-7237 69 A kmengelbach@ucdavis.edu
ENGELBOURG, Karen 617-638-4560 216 E engelbou@bu.edu
ENGELBRECHT, Laci 217-479-7043 147 C laci.engelbrecht@mac.edu
ENGELBRECHT, Sharon 417-626-1234 269 K engelbrecht.sharon@occ.edu
ENGELBRIDE, Ed 518-956-8140 331 A eengelbride@albany.edu
ENGELHARDT, Kelli 406-791-5237 278 G kelli.engelhardt@ugf.edu
ENGELHART, Brian, W 260-422-5561 162 B bwengelhart@indianatech.edu
ENGELHART, Rene 916-646-2774 59 L rengelhart@samuelmerritt.edu
ENGELKEMIER, John 312-329-2145 148 F john.engelkemier@moody.edu
ENGELKING, Heather 407-708-2103 109 E engelkingh@seminolestate.edu
ENGELLANT, Roxanne 406-683-7305 277 A roxanne.engellant@umwestern.edu
ENGELLS, Thomas 409-772-1503 478 A tengells@utmb.edu
ENGELMEYER, Renee 507-285-7183 251 I renee.engelmeyer@rctc.edu

ENGELS, Kristen 920-565-1102 517 D engelskl@lakeland.edu
ENGELSCHALL, Emily, D 951-827-3986 70 B emily.engelschall@ucr.edu
ENGELSEN, Karen 805-289-6153 73 F kengelsen@vcccd.edu
ENGELSMA, Chris 616-432-3406 240 B chris.engelsma@prts.edu
ENGEMANN, JR., Andrew, H 757-594-7053 488 E andrew.engemann@cnu.edu
ENGEN, Stuart 701-671-2446 361 F stuart.engen@ndscs.edu
ENGER, Lee 217-228-5432 151 F engerle@quincy.edu
ENGERT, Lara 312-752-2130 144 E lara.engert@kendall.edu
ENGFER, Tom 323-860-4349 53 G tengfer@mi.edu
ENGH, SJ, Michael, E 408-554-4100 63 E mengh@scu.edu
ENGH, Peter, M 508-213-2390 227 A peter.engh@nichols.edu
ENGISCH, Kathrin 937-775-2611 381 H kathrin.engisch@wright.edu
ENGLAND, A, W 313-593-5290 242 A england@umich.edu
ENGLAND, Amy 918-631-3288 389 E amy-england@utulsa.edu
ENGLAND, David 860-255-3500 87 E dengland@txcc.commnet.edu
ENGLAND, David 615-966-6210 441 F david.england@lipscomb.edu
ENGLAND, Richard 217-581-2017 139 H rengland@eiu.edu
ENGLAND, Robert 606-693-5000 191 A bengland@kmbc.edu
ENGLE, Chris 810-762-0242 238 F chris.engle@mcc.edu
ENGLE, Jason 509-544-4935 502 G jengle@columbiabasin.edu
ENGLE, Jenny 517-264-7143 241 A jengle@sienaheights.edu
ENGLE, Karen 937-484-1321 380 E kengle@urbana.edu
ENGLE, Kevin, E 330-972-8948 378 H kengle@uakron.edu
ENGLE, Marcia, J 540-432-4148 488 K marcy.engle@emu.edu
ENGLE, Patricia 517-483-1813 237 A englep@lcc.edu
ENGLEHARDT, Kirk 423-425-4363 448 F kirk-englehardt@utc.edu
ENGLEHARDT, Richard, E 606-693-5000 191 A registrar@kmbc.edu
ENGLERT, Anne 210-458-7228 477 A anne.englert@utsa.edu
ENGLERT, Bradley, G 512-232-1744 476 B b.englert@austin.utexas.edu
ENGLERT, Mark, G 307-686-0254 526 M menglert@sheridan.edu
ENGLERT, Patrick 502-272-8323 187 A penglert@bellarmine.edu
ENGLERT, Richard, M 215-204-7405 420 B president@temple.edu
ENGLERT, William, C 310-233-4301 49 I englerbc@lahc.edu
ENGLESTATTER, Pauline 301-447-5600 209 G englesta@msmary.edu
ENGLIN, Peter, D 515-294-5636 169 G penglin@iastate.edu
ENGLISH, Ana 928-317-6092 11 J ana.english@azwestern.edu
ENGLISH, Andrew 412-291-6423 397 I aenglish@aii.edu
ENGLISH, Andy 515-961-1547 176 H andy.english@simpson.edu
ENGLISH, Anna 770-537-5721 129 M anna.english@westgatech.edu
ENGLISH, Chris 828-694-1728 347 G chrise@blueridge.edu
ENGLISH, Claude 816-584-6492 270 D claude.english@park.edu
ENGLISH, David 336-770-3262 358 E englishd@uncsa.edu
ENGLISH, David, A 740-587-6262 368 B englishda@denison.edu
ENGLISH, Eva 406-353-2607 275 H eenglish@ancollege.edu
ENGLISH, John 479-575-3054 22 I jre@uark.edu
ENGLISH, John 267-295-2353 418 A jenglish@walnuthillcollege.edu
ENGLISH, La'Shea 619-684-8866 54 C lenglish@newschoolarch.edu
ENGLISH, Linda 970-945-8691 78 B
ENGLISH, Lindsay 216-987-3610 367 E lindsay.english@tri-c.edu
ENGLISH, Mechelle 850-412-6605 110 J mechelle.english@famu.edu
ENGLISH, Patricia 805-965-0581 63 D englishp@sbcc.edu
ENGLISH, Regina 757-823-8288 492 F renglish@nsu.edu
ENGLISH, Robert 812-237-3166 162 A robert.english@indstate.edu
ENGLISH, Sarah, H 845-575-3000 320 B sarah.english@marist.edu
ENGLISH, Susan 616-632-2045 231 A englisus@aquinas.edu
ENGLISH, Suzanne 724-805-2660 419 A suzanne.english@email.stvincent.edu
ENGLOT, Peter, T 973-353-5541 296 C peter.englot@rutgers.edu
ENGLOT, Peter, T 973-353-5541 295 F peter.englot@rutgers.edu
ENGLUND, Tim 509-963-1866 501 K tim.englund@cwu.edu
ENGSTROM, Dan, M 724-938-1523 414 E engstrom@calu.edu
ENGSTROM, Larry 775-784-6805 285 A engstrom@unr.edu
ENGSTROM, Larry 775-682-8803 285 A engstrom@unr.edu
ENGSTROM, Rick 425-889-6397 505 E rick.engstrom@northwestu.edu
ENGSTROM, Royce, C 406-243-2311 276 K royce.engstrom@umontana.edu
ENICKS, Charles 706-721-9660 117 D cenicks@augusta.edu
ENKE, Kathryn 320-363-5070 245 I kenke@csbsju.edu
ENKHBAYAR, Zolzaya 323-731-2383 55 J registrar@psuca.edu
ENLOE, Donald 303-871-2463 84 B denloe@du.edu
ENLOW, Grady 229-226-1621 128 B genlow@thomasu.edu
ENNEKING, Thomas 317-955-6014 165 N tenneking@marian.edu
ENNELLO-BUTLER, Deanna 518-694-7200 303 C
ENNIS, Daniel 843-349-2746 428 E dennis@coastal.edu
ENNIS, Daniel, G 410-516-2373 208 D danielgennis@jhu.edu
ENNIS, Jackie 252-399-6571 341 P jennis@barton.edu
ENNIS, Kim 205-387-0511 2 B kim.ennis@bscc.edu
ENNIS, Matt 941-752-5574 110 H ennism@scf.edu
ENNIS, Theresa 931-372-6124 445 B tennis@tntech.edu
ENNIST, Phyllis 937-529-2201 378 F pjennist@united.edu
ENNS-REMPEL, Kevin 559-453-2300 44 F kevin.enns.rempel@fresno.edu
ENO, Alisha 303-744-1287 80 M aeno@iliff.edu
ENO, Jerry 303-765-3186 80 M jeno@iliff.edu
ENOCH, Hollace, J 804-257-5841 500 B hjenoch@vuu.edu
ENOCKSON, Dustin 612-359-6491 244 I enocksd@augsburg.edu
ENOKAWA, Jerilyn 808-734-9899 131 I jilorenz@hawaii.edu
ENOS, Chris 785-670-1153 185 H chris.enos@washburn.edu
ENOS, Shon 330-684-8916 378 H shorlan@uakron.edu
ENOS, Stacey 828-771-3737 359 F senos@warren-wilson.edu
ENRIGHT, John 213-613-2200 65 H john_enright@sciarc.edu
ENRIGHT, Patrick 973-328-5700 290 H penright@ccm.edu
ENRIGHT, Sara 401-825-1084 425 A senright@ccri.edu
ENRIQUEZ, Anita, B 671-735-2994 530 B abe@triton.uog.edu
ENRIQUEZ, Igrí 787-765-3560 532 I enriquez@edpuniversity.edu
ENSER, Jason 518-743-2277 335 A enserj@sunyacc.edu
ENSER, Pamela 518-381-1271 330 B enserpe@sunysccc.edu
ENSING, Kim 805-922-6966 25 I kensing@hancockcollege.edu
ENSLEY, Cynthia 252-638-7201 349 B ensleyc@cravencc.edu
ENSLEY, Dana 706-379-3111 130 B ddensley@yhc.edu
ENSLEY, Kevin 817-923-1921 466 E kensley@swbts.edu
ENSLIN, Jonathan 262-472-1482 521 F enslinj@uww.edu
ENSMAN, JR., Richard, G 585-345-6809 315 C rgensman@genesee.edu
ENSMINGER, Michelle 806-743-9196 472 D michelle.ensminger@ttuhsc.edu
ENSOR, Pat 713-221-8011 474 B ensorp@uhd.edu
ENSTE, Joe 301-447-7436 209 G enste@msmary.edu
ENTERS, David, T 262-243-5700 516 E dave.enters@cuw.edu
ENTESSARI, Abbass 305-623-1441 101 A abbass.entessari@fmuniv.edu
ENTIN, Pauline 928-523-1580 15 H pauline.entin@nau.edu
ENTINGER, Julienne, N 651-628-3380 256 A jnentinger@unwsp.edu
ENTREKIN, Cindy 256-215-4251 2 G centrekin@cacc.edu
ENTRIKIN, Nicholas 574-631-5204 168 B entrikin.1@nd.edu
ENTRINGER, Chris, E 563-556-5110 175 F entringc@nicc.edu
ENTWISTLE, David, E 801-581-7480 481 M david.entwistle@hsc.utah.edu
ENTZ, Mary 515-791-1721 171 B mjentz@dmacc.edu
ENTZEROTH, Lyn 918-631-2400 389 E lyn-entzeroth@utulsa.edu
ENWEMEKA, Chukuka, S 619-594-6881 35 A enwemeka@mail.sdsu.edu
ENWRIGHT, Kelly 513-562-8743 363 H kenwright@artacademy.edu
ENYARD, Richard 847-214-7415 140 A renyard@elgin.edu
ENYEDI, Alex 707-826-3722 34 F alex.enyedi@humboldt.edu
ENZ, Jeff 760-355-6577 46 J jeff.enz@imperial.edu
ENZ FINKEN, Kathleen 805-756-2186 31 I kenzfink@calpoly.edu
ENZOR, Sharon, B 662-685-4771 257 A senzor@bmc.edu
ENZWEILER, Raymond, N 614-885-5585 376 G renzweiler@pcj.edu
EOFF, Shirley 325-942-2722 472 B shirley.eoff@angleo.edu
EOYANG, Thomas 617-682-1518 218 E teoyang@eds.edu
EPLING, Rob 513-569-1436 366 D rob.epling@cincinnatistate.edu
EPLION, David 812-941-2269 163 F deplion@ius.edu
EPP, Adam 425-889-5263 505 E adam.epp@northwestu.edu
EPP, Michelle 651-696-6062 247 I mepp@macalester.edu
EPPEHIMER, Trevor 704-636-6743 345 B teppehimer@hoodseminary.edu
EPPENSTEIN, Dillon 215-951-0263 416 G eppensteind@philau.edu
EPPER, Rhonda 303-556-3595 79 F
EPPERSON, Annissa 913-758-6172 185 F eppersona@stmary.edu
EPPERSON, Brenda 214-860-8678 456 F bepperson@dcccd.edu
EPPERSON, Brian 918-335-6207 386 F bepperson@okwu.edu
EPPERSON, Douglas 805-756-2706 31 I dleppers@calpoly.edu
EPPERSON, II, Richard, P 434-223-6153 490 D repperson@hsc.edu
EPPERSON, Shonte 903-927-3260 479 K sepperson@wileyc.edu
EPPERSON, Steve 360-416-7714 507 G steve.epperson@skagit.edu
EPPICH, David 505-566-3318 301 J eppichd@sanjuancollege.edu
EPPINETTE, Chance, W 318-342-5021 201 E eppinette@ulm.edu
EPPINGER, Beth 479-788-7334 23 A beth.eppinger@uafs.edu
EPPLER, Michelle 402-557-7010 278 I michelle.eppler@bellevue.edu
EPPLEY, Doug 814-472-3017 418 F deppley@francis.edu
EPPLING, Chris 706-865-2134 128 D ceppling@truett.edu
EPPLING, Marcie, T 256-824-6443 8 F marcie.eppling@uah.edu
EPPS, Angela, F 407-254-3268 110 J felecia.epps@famu.edu
EPPS, Bruce 614-236-6461 364 N bepps@capital.edu
EPPS, Charmica, D 804-342-3938 500 B cdepps@vuu.edu
EPPS, JoAnne, A 215-204-2742 420 B provost@temple.edu
EPPS, Patricia 717-358-4107 403 J patty.epps@fandm.edu
EPPS, Valerie 202-274-5210 94 B vepps@udc.edu
EPSTEIN, Adam 314-965-8363 268 A
EPSTEIN, Bonnie 212-678-8997 317 I boepstein@jtsa.edu
EPSTEIN, Catherine, A 413-542-2334 214 C cepstein@amherst.edu
EPSTEIN, Irving, R 781-736-2503 216 F irvingepstein@brandeis.edu
EPSTEIN, Joanne 352-335-2332 94 F
EPSTEIN, Keith 860-723-0062 85 E epsteink@ct.edu
EPSTEIN, Scott 616-554-5691 233 C sepstein1@davenport.edu
EPSTEIN, Shlomo, Z 718-438-1002 320 H
EPSTEIN, Warren 719-502-2666 82 B warren.epstein@ppcc.edu
EPTING, Kim 336-278-5595 344 D lepting@elon.edu
EQUINOA, Kim 805-893-3858 70 E kim.equinoa@sa.ucsb.edu
ERARDI, Lauren 203-582-3686 88 G lauren.erardi@quinnipiac.edu
ERARIO, Vince 678-264-8808 124 B vince.erario@life.edu
ERATO, Michael, J 414-425-8300 519 F merato@shsst.edu
ERB, Brian, I 706-236-2234 117 F berb@berry.edu
ERB, Daniel, E 336-841-4595 345 A derb@highpoint.edu
ERB, Jennifer, L 610-799-1034 408 G 0617mgr@sheg.follett.com
ERBELE, Cindy 706-865-2134 128 D cerbele@truett.edu
ERBERT, Daniel 785-442-6002 181 H derbert@highlandcc.edu
ERCKERT, Joseph 215-489-2397 402 A joseph.erckert@delval.edu
ERDEI, Diane 415-955-2100 25 J derdei@alliant.edu
ERDENGERG, Scott 630-620-2115 150 B serdenberg@seminary.edu
ERDICE, Stephanie 717-477-7447 416 A smerdice@ship.edu
ERDLE, Jennie 585-785-1263 314 D jennie.erdle@flcc.edu
ERDMAN, Al 813-253-7015 102 R aerdman2@hccfl.edu
ERDMAN, Amanda 612-330-1558 244 I erdmanam@augsburg.edu
ERDMAN, Anne, C 269-927-8127 236 G erdman@lakemichigancollege.edu
ERDMAN, Peg 928-532-6111 15 J peg.erdman@npc.edu
ERDMANN, Joel 251-460-7121 9 E jerdmann@southalabama.edu
ERDMANN, Paul 620-441-5264 180 D paul.erdmann@cowley.edu
ERDNER, Christine 215-885-2360 409 G cerdner@manor.edu
EREKSON, Homer 817-257-7527 469 G h.erekson@tcu.edu
EREKSON, Thomas 859-622-1409 188 F thomas.erekson@eku.edu
EREVELLES, Winston 210-436-3996 464 H werevelles@stmarytx.edu
ERFAN, Shahir 718-482-5501 309 A serfan@lagcc.cuny.edu
ERFFMEYER, Kenneth 616-526-6097 232 A kde2@calvin.edu
ERFORD, Dane 419-434-4524 379 E erford@findlay.edu
ERGIN, Laure 302-831-7364 91 F lbergin@udel.edu
ERHAN, Ali 616-632-2819 231 A erhanali@aquinas.edu
ERICKSEN, Donald, O 651-631-5249 256 A doericksen@unwsp.edu
ERICKSON, Chris 952-829-1919 244 J chris.erickson@bethfel.org
ERICKSON, Christine 831-582-4091 33 E cherickson@csumb.edu
ERICKSON, Colette 701-231-8788 361 A colette.erickson@ndsu.edu
ERICKSON, Craig 763-488-2518 249 D craig.erickson@hennepintech.edu
ERICKSON, Daryel 701-349-5788 362 C derickson@trinitybiblecollege.edu
ERICKSON, Deb 619-849-2323 57 M deberickson@pointloma.edu
ERICKSON, Elly 845-451-1468 312 C e_ericks@culinary.edu
ERICKSON, Ethan, E 785-532-6767 182 D eerickson@ksu.edu
ERICKSON, Fritz, J 906-227-2242 239 B fericksо@nmu.edu
ERICKSON, Gary 314-921-9290 274 F gerickson@ugst.edu
ERICKSON, Janell 480-994-9244 17 C janelle@swiha.edu
ERICKSON, Janet 303-546-5295 81 I jerickson@naropa.edu

ESTEP, Alison .... 206-378-5056.. 507 C
estep@spu.edu
ESTEP, Charles, R .... 864-379-8869.. 429 I
estep@erskine.edu
ESTEPP, J. Mark .... 276-964-7315.. 498 F
mark.estepp@sw.edu
ESTER, Joyce, C .... 952-358-8150.. 251 A
joyce.ester@normandale.edu
ESTERBERG, Kristin, G .... 315-267-2100.. 334 B
president@potsdam.edu
ESTERLINE, David, V .... 412-924-1366.. 417 E
desterline@pts.edu
ESTERS, Randy .... 870-743-3000.... 21 C
randy.esters@northark.edu
ESTES, Ashley .... 713-646-1793.. 459 A
aestes@hcl.edu
ESTES, Edward, R .... 757-479-3706.. 496 B
eestes@vbts.edu
ESTES, Eric .... 440-775-8462.. 374 C
eric.estes@oberlin.edu
ESTES, James .... 202-885-8696.... 94 E
jestes@wesleyseminary.edu
ESTES, Lane .... 205-226-4640...... 2 C
lestes@bsc.edu
ESTES, Wendy .... 678-717-3845.. 128 F
wendy.estes@ung.edu
ESTES, William .... 423-614-8175.. 441 B
bestes@leeuniversity.edu
ESTEVEZ, Edwin .... 618-664-7021.. 140 I
edwin.estevez@greenville.edu
ESTEVEZ, Francisco, A ...... 860-701-6728.. 529 A
fransisco.a.estevez@uscg.mil
ESTILL, Donna .... 256-306-2756...... 2 F
donna.estill@calhoun.edu
ESTILL, Sandi, L .... 606-759-7141.. 190 C
sandi.estill@kctcs.edu
ESTLACK, Ashlee .... 806-874-3571.. 454 F
estlack@clarendoncollege.edu
ESTLACK, Scarlet .... 806-874-3571.. 454 F
scarlet.estlack@clarendoncollege.edu
ESTLACK, Tom .... 412-809-5100.. 417 D
estlack.tom@pti.edu
ESTOCK, Steven .... 575-562-2632.. 299 I
steven.estock@enmu.edu
ESTRADA, Donna .... 985-448-7954.. 196 E
donna.estrada@fletcher.edu
ESTRADA, Ella Mae .... 212-431-2827.. 323 H
ellamae.estrada@nyls.edu
ESTRADA, George .... 203-576-4330.... 89 C
gestrada@bridgeport.edu
ESTRADA, George .... 530-242-7930.... 64 D
gestrada@shastacollege.edu
ESTRADA, Jeri .... 970-521-6730.... 81 O
jeri.estrada@njc.edu
ESTRADA, Maria .... 787-780-5134.. 535 C
mestrada@nuc.edu
ESTRADA, Rebecca .... 505-428-1604.. 301 K
rebecca.estrada@sfcc.edu
ESTRADA, Robert .... 925-473-7540.... 41 J
restrada@losmedanos.edu
ESTRADA-HAMBY, Lisa ... 940-397-4076.. 462 A
lisa.hamby@mwsu.edu
ESTRADA TORRES, Omar 516-876-3067.. 333 C
estradatorreso@oldwestbury.edu
ESTRELLA, Luz .... 787-882-2065.. 536 D
colocaciones@unitecpr.net
ESTRELLA, Luz .... 787-882-2065.. 536 D
recursoshumanos@unitecpr.net
ESTREMERA, Luis .... 787-758-2525.. 538 D
luis.estremera@upr.edu
ESTRIN, David .... 718-522-9073.. 304 D
david@asa.edu
ESTRY, Douglas .... 517-353-5380.. 237 I
estry@msu.edu
ETCHEMENDY, John, W .. 650-724-4074.... 66 I
provost@stanford.edu
ETE, Sonia .... 310-360-8888.... 25 C
ETE, Thierry .... 310-360-8888.... 25 C
ETHIER, Richard .... 802-224-3000.. 485 G
richard.ethier@vsc.edu
ETHINGTON, Caroline .... 810-762-9917.. 236 C
cethingt@kettering.edu
ETHINGTON, Robert .... 707-527-4573.... 63 G
rethington@santarosa.edu
ETIENNE, Guy .... 954-923-4440.. 104 G
registrar@keycollege.edu
ETIENNE, Sabrina .... 301-891-4177.. 213 D
setienne@wau.edu
ETINGE, Elias .... 706-821-8302.. 125 H
eetinge@paine.edu
ETSCHMAIER, Gale .... 619-594-1643.... 35 A
gale.etschmaier@sdsu.edu
ETTARO, Barbara .... 814-863-1030.. 412 F
bxm7@psu.edu
ETTER, Patricia .... 314-889-1419.. 265 C
petter@fontbonne.edu
ETTINGER, Sherri .... 617-521-2451.. 228 C
sherri.ettinger@simmons.edu
ETTLE, Violeta .... 202-885-2720.... 91 J
vi@american.edu
ETTLICH, Sherry .... 541-552-6576.. 395 A
ettlich@sou.edu
ETTLING, John .... 518-564-2010.. 334 A
president_office@plattsburgh.edu
ETTORE, JD .... 567-661-7974.. 376 D
johndavid_ettore@owens.edu
ETUALE, Mikaele .... 684-699-9155.. 529 E
m.etuale@amsamoa.edu
ETZEL, Brent .... 479-968-0417.... 19 F
betzel@atu.edu
EUBANK, Charlotte .... 573-840-9105.. 273 A
ceubank@trcc.edu
EUBANK, Chelsea .... 352-638-9747.... 96 F
ceubank@beaconcollege.edu
EUBANK, Jeff .... 215-702-4202.. 399 E
jeubank@cairn.edu
EUBANKS, David .... 864-294-2000.. 430 C
david.eubanks@furman.edu
EUBANKS, Gail .... 912-443-5443.. 126 G
geubanks@savannahtech.edu
EUBANKS, Jamie .... 252-399-6368.. 341 P
jceubanks@barton.edu
EUBANKS, Karen .... 904-256-1121.. 100 E
keubanks@fcsl.edu
EUBANKS, Karla .... 912-427-5899.. 119 B
keubanks@coastalpines.edu
EUBANKS, Kathleen, L .... 508-999-8086.. 220 H
keubanks@umassd.edu
EUBANKS, Nekita .... 704-216-3778.. 352 G
nekita.eubanks@rccc.edu
EULE, Ann .... 603-882-6923.. 286 E
aeule@ccsnh.edu
EUNICE, E, E .... 850-201-7000.. 113 E
eunicee@tcc.fl.edu
EURICH, David .... 610-526-1171.. 397 E
dave.eurich@theamericancollege.edu
EURY, Brian .... 610-902-8734.. 399 D
brian.eury@cabrini.edu
EUSEBIO, Zenda Gay, P .. 626-448-0023.... 47 E
EUSTROM, Jim .... 503-399-5144.. 390 E
jim.eustrom@chemeketa.edu
EVAN, Joseph .... 570-208-5895.. 406 J
josephevan@kings.edu
EVANGELISTA, Joleen, M 671-735-5540.. 529 G
materialsmanagement@guamcc.edu
EVANGELISTA, Nancy ...... 607-871-2649.. 303 F
fevangel@alfred.edu
EVANOSKY, Sonya .... 630-353-8708.. 136 G
sevanosky@chamberlain.edu
EVANOVICH, Dolan .... 614-292-8835.. 375 A
evanovich.1@osu.edu
EVANS, Aleia .... 216-201-9025.. 371 G
EVANS, Alice .... 314-434-4044.. 264 C
alice.evans@covenantseminary.edu
EVANS, Amy .... 903-463-8628.. 458 H
evansa@grayson.edu
EVANS, Andrea .... 708-534-8396.. 140 H
aevans6@govst.edu
EVANS, Angela .... 269-782-1323.. 241 C
aevans14@swmich.edu
EVANS, Angela, J .... 470-578-6300.. 123 J
aevans@kennesaw.edu
EVANS, Annette .... 706-542-7066.. 128 E
amevans@uga.edu
EVANS, April .... 765-998-4625.. 167 C
apevans@taylor.edu
EVANS, Ashley .... 478-934-3458.. 124 E
ashley.evans@mga.edu
EVANS, Barry, W .... 806-291-1028.. 479 D
evansb@wbu.edu
EVANS, Belinda .... 304-647-6401.. 514 A
bevans@osteo.wvsom.edu
EVANS, Beverly, A .... 717-815-1228.. 424 F
behinger@ycp.edu
EVANS, Brandt .... 216-987-4294.. 367 E
brandt.evans@tri-c.edu
EVANS, Brenda .... 978-934-5021.. 221 A
brenda_evans@uml.edu
EVANS, Brian .... 502-863-8223.. 188 I
brian_evans@georgetowncollege.edu
EVANS, Brian .... 423-697-2417.. 445 D
brian.evans@chattanoogastate.edu
EVANS, Brian, K .... 801-422-3760.. 480 C
brian_evans@byu.edu
EVANS, Carolyn, L .... 601-977-7764.. 261 A
cevans@tougaloo.edu
EVANS, Charlotte .... 402-554-2772.. 283 B
cevans@unomaha.edu
EVANS, Chas .... 601-635-2111.. 257 F
cevans@eccc.edu
EVANS, Cheryl .... 580-628-6201.. 384 L
cheryl.evans@noc.edu
EVANS, Cheryl, O .... 585-385-8015.. 328 E
cevans@sjfc.edu
EVANS, Chris .... 713-831-7863.. 475 J
evanscp@stthom.edu
EVANS, Craig, S .... 315-364-3200.. 340 B
cevans@wells.edu
EVANS, Damian .... 262-595-2540.. 520 F
damian.evans@uwp.edu
EVANS, Dana .... 501-708-0600.... 93 F
EVANS, Dana .... 601-718-5900.... 93 F
EVANS, Dave .... 619-388-2737.... 60 G
devans@sdccd.edu
EVANS, David .... 229-391-2609.. 127 G
devans@southernregional.edu
EVANS, David .... 406-756-3872.. 276 E
devans@fvcc.edu
EVANS, David .... 972-273-3561.. 456 G
devans@dcccd.edu
EVANS, David, R .... 802-447-6319.. 485 B
devans@svc.edu
EVANS, Diane, T .... 936-261-2202.. 467 E
dtevans@pvamu.edu
EVANS, Doreen .... 928-213-6060.... 12 Q
doreen.evans@collegeamerica.edu
EVANS, Edward .... 361-825-2693.. 468 E
edward.evans@tamucc.edu
EVANS, Emily .... 859-846-5815.. 191 G
eeevans@midway.edu
EVANS, Eric, D .... 781-981-7000.. 225 A
EVANS, Erik .... 570-389-4047.. 414 D
eevans@bloomu.edu
EVANS, Faye .... 404-225-4526.. 117 A
fevans@atlantatech.edu
EVANS, Frederick M, G ... 803-536-7133.. 432 E
fevans3@scsu.edu
EVANS, Gary .... 607-753-2302.. 333 A
gary.evans@cortland.edu
EVANS, George .... 618-545-3030.. 144 D
gevans@kaskaskia.edu
EVANS, JR., Gilbert, L .... 386-312-4127.. 108 B
gilbertevans@sjrstate.edu
EVANS, Ivan .... 858-534-2247.... 70 C
ercprovost@ucsd.edu
EVANS, J. David .... 470-578-6194.. 123 J
devans@kennesaw.edu
EVANS, Jack .... 706-721-3964.. 117 D
jaevans@augusta.edu
EVANS, JR., Jack .... 972-524-3341.. 466 F
EVANS, SR., Jack .... 972-524-3341.. 466 F
EVANS, Jacquie .... 757-481-5005.. 500 H
EVANS, Janet, D .... 412-392-3824.. 417 F
jevans@pointpark.edu
EVANS, Janie .... 802-287-8203.. 484 A
evansj@greenmtn.edu
EVANS, Jaylene .... 970-542-3168.... 81 H
jaylene.evans@morgancc.edu
EVANS, Jeannette, H .... 315-684-6067.. 336 B
evansjh@morrisville.edu
EVANS, Jeffrey, L .... 313-593-5110.. 242 A
jlevan@umich.edu
EVANS, Jennifer, M .... 717-867-6271.. 408 F
jevans@lvc.edu
EVANS, Jessica .... 254-968-9682.. 467 F
jevans@tarleton.edu
EVANS, Jill .... 208-496-9810.. 132 J
evansj@byui.edu
EVANS, Joseph .... 410-706-8501.. 211 F
jevans@umaryland.edu
EVANS, Joy .... 231-995-1084.. 239 C
jevans@nmc.edu
EVANS, Karen, V .... 610-921-7630.. 396 H
kevans@albright.edu
EVANS, Karyn .... 937-393-3431.. 377 F
kevans@sscc.edu
EVANS, Katherine .... 973-761-9500.. 297 A
katherine.evans@shu.edu
EVANS, Kathleen .... 315-312-2240.. 333 D
kathleen.evans@oswego.edu
EVANS, Kenne .... 214-860-3677.. 456 F
klevans@dcccd.edu
EVANS, Kenneth, R .... 409-880-8405.. 471 A
kenneth.evans@lamar.edu
EVANS, Kimberly .... 802-831-1225.. 485 F
kevans@vermontlaw.edu
EVANS, Laurie .... 313-664-1501.. 232 G
levans@collegeforcreativestudies.edu
EVANS, Layna .... 214-333-5275.. 455 J
layna@dbu.edu
EVANS, Lexie .... 206-934-3890.. 506 K
lexie.evans@seattlecolleges.edu
EVANS, Lisa .... 513-569-1564.. 366 D
lisa.evans@cincinnatistate.edu
EVANS, Liz .... 412-392-5945.. 417 F
eevans@pointpark.edu
EVANS, III, Louis, D .... 713-221-2766.. 474 B
evansl@uhd.edu
EVANS, Marcheta .... 210-434-6711.. 463 C
mevans@lake.ollusa.edu
EVANS, Marisa, L .... 814-886-6336.. 411 C
mevans@mtaloy.edu
EVANS, Mark .... 330-672-2972.. 370 I
mevans@kent.edu
EVANS, Mark .... 845-938-5502.. 529 C
mark.evans@usma.edu
EVANS, Maya .... 847-635-1973.. 150 G
mevans@oakton.edu
EVANS, Melissa .... 315-386-7123.. 335 B
evansm@canton.edu
EVANS, Mercedes .... 617-879-7060.. 222 A
msevans@massart.edu
EVANS, Michael .... 603-626-9100.. 287 I
m.evans@snhu.edu
EVANS, Michael, L .... 806-743-4282.. 472 D
michael.evans@ttuhsc.edu
EVANS, Oliver .... 540-887-7030.. 491 G
oevans@mbc.edu
EVANS, Piper .... 212-228-1888.. 327 A
EVANS, R. Gregory .... 912-478-2676.. 122 B
rgevans@georgiasouthern.edu
EVANS, JR., R. Lee .... 334-844-8348....... 1 G
evansrl@auburn.edu
EVANS, Rick .... 818-677-2906.... 34 A
rick.evans@csun.edu
EVANS, Robert .... 773-907-4817.. 137 E
revans@ccc.edu
EVANS, Roberta .... 406-243-4911.. 276 K
roberta.evans@umontana.edu
EVANS, Ronda .... 719-638-6580.... 80 B
revans@cci.edu
EVANS, Sam .... 270-745-4664.. 194 D
sam.evans@wku.edu
EVANS, Sarah .... 317-931-2303.. 160 B
sevans@cts.edu
EVANS, Sarah .... 336-342-4261.. 352 F
evanss@rockinghamcc.edu
EVANS, Scott .... 828-766-1305.. 351 B
sevans@mayland.edu
EVANS, Scott .... 440-375-7255.. 371 E
sevans@lec.edu
EVANS, Sharron .... 312-341-2004.. 152 H
sevans12@roosevelt.edu
EVANS, Sherry, L .... 405-325-3916.. 389 B
sevens@ou.edu
EVANS, Sidney .... 443-885-3144.. 209 F
sidney.evans@morgan.edu
EVANS, Sidney, S .... 540-458-8754.. 500 F
sevans@wlu.edu
EVANS, Steve .... 281-425-6887.. 460 I
sevans@lee.edu
EVANS, Susan .... 239-590-1057.. 110 L
sevans@fgcu.edu
EVANS, Thomas .... 406-447-4401.. 276 B
tevans@carroll.edu
EVANS, Tiffany .... 270-706-8406.. 189 C
tevans0138@kctcs.edu
EVANS, Tracy, L .... 304-929-5480.. 512 C
tevans@newriver.edu
EVANS, Virginia .... 434-982-2249.. 495 H
veb5u@virginia.edu
EVANS, W. Franklin .... 803-780-1019.. 434 M
fevans@voorhees.edu
EVANS, Zina .... 352-392-1365.. 112 A
zevans@ufl.edu
EVANS-DAME, Kimberly .. 315-792-5637.. 321 G
kevans-dame@mvcc.edu
EVANS JONES, Cheryl ..... 706-396-8102.. 125 H
cevansjones@paine.edu
EVANS-PLANTS, Penny .... 706-232-5374.. 117 F
peplants@berry.edu
EVANS TAYLOR,
Genevieve .... 805-437-8410.... 32 B
genevieve.evans-taylor@csuci.edu
EVASHEVSKI, Keith .... 307-766-2187.. 527 B
keski@uwyo.edu
EVE, Debra .... 406-353-2607.. 275 H
deve@ancollege.edu
EVE, Stacey .... 406-791-5307.. 278 G
stacey.eve@ugf.edu
EVELAND, Susan, M .... 541-346-3195.. 395 G
seveland@uoregon.edu
EVELER, Janet .... 915-831-5202.. 457 H
jeveler3@epcc.edu
EVELOFF, Vivian .... 314-516-6622.. 274 A
eveloffv@umsl.edu
EVELYN, Alan .... 516-299-2523.. 319 B
alan.evelyn@liu.edu
EVELYN, Tom .... 864-294-2151.. 430 C
tom.evelyn@furman.edu
EVEN, Susan, E .... 573-884-9388.. 273 E
evens@health.missouri.edu
EVENBECK, Scott .... 646-313-8000.. 309 F
president@guttman.cuny.edu
EVENSON, Brad .... 620-278-4221.. 185 A
bevenson@sterling.edu
EVENSON, Shane .... 715-468-2815.. 525 A
shane.evenson@witc.edu
EVENSON, Thomas, L .... 940-565-2239.. 475 A
evenson@unt.edu
EVENSON, Tresse .... 605-274-5520.. 435 E
tresse.evenson@augie.edu
EVENSVOLD, Marty .... 620-251-7700.. 180 B
martye@coffeyville.edu
EVERETT, Chris .... 301-784-5158.. 205 G
ceverett@allegany.edu
EVERETT, Daniel .... 781-891-2118.. 215 F
deverett@bentley.edu
EVERETT, David, D .... 330-569-5353.. 369 J
everettdd@hiram.edu
EVERETT, Dennis, F .... 850-718-2216.... 97 G
everettd@chipola.edu

F

FALCON-CHANDLER,
Carole 406-353-2607 275 H
cfalconchan@hotmail.com
FALCONE, Alice, A 978-867-4208 219 A
alice.falcone@gordon.edu
FALCONER, John 308-865-8702 282 L
falconerj@unk.edu
FALCONETTI, Angela, M 540-857-6020 499 B
afalconetti@virginiawestern.edu
FALDER, Mike 765-998-5538 167 C
mcfalder@taylor.edu
FALDUTO, Ellen 330-263-2230 367 A
efalduto@wooster.edu
FALE, Tauvela 684-699-9155 529 E
t.fale@amsamoa.edu
FALES, Michael, F 269-749-7624 240 A
mfales@olivetcollege.edu
FALESE, Joseph 815-836-5275 145 H
falesejo@lewisu.edu
FALEY, Heather 802-440-4423 483 E
hfaley@bennington.edu
FALGOUT, Katherine 985-380-2483 196 K
katherinefalgout@scl.edu
FALK, Adam, F 413-597-4233 230 A
adam.f.falk@williams.edu
FALK, Barry, L 804-828-1803 496 D
blfalk@vcu.edu
FALK, Dan 620-229-6267 184 J
dan.falk@sckans.edu
FALK, Israel 845-371-2481 340 L
FALK, Randy 541-917-4999 392 C
falkr@linnbenton.edu
FALK, Stephanie, A 717-867-6696 408 F
falk@lvc.edu
FALK-DAY, Tamie 262-595-2485 520 F
falkday@uwp.edu
FALKE, Steve, J 814-863-0205 412 F
sjf7@psu.edu
FALKENBERG, Janice 414-297-8718 524 A
falkenjm@matc.edu
FALKENHAGEN, Kim 715-682-1868 518 H
kfalkenhagen@northland.edu
FALKIEWICZ, Linda, K 313-577-3550 243 F
lfalkiewicz@wayne.edu
FALKNER, Tina 612-626-0302 255 H
rovic001@umn.edu
FALKS, Delisa, F 979-458-5311 468 B
delisa@tamu.edu
FALL, Matt 517-483-1953 237 A
fallm@lcc.edu
FALL, Stephany 850-599-3203 110 J
stephany.fall@famu.edu
FALLACARO, Anthony 603-645-9604 287 I
a.fallacaro@snhu.edu
FALLAVOLLITA, John 603-623-0313 287 D
johnfallavollita@nhia.edu
FALLDINE, Cory 620-341-5297 180 G
cfalldin@emporia.edu
FALLEN, Melissa 804-204-1210 487 D
mfallen@btsr.edu
FALLERT, Danelle 323-265-8797 49 G
fallerdj@elac.edu
FALLETA, David, A 304-457-6213 510 B
falletada@ab.edu
FALLETTA, Eva, R 480-732-7231 13 O
eva.falletta@cgc.edu
FALLING, Cary 405-425-5290 385 C
cary.falling@oc.edu
FALLING, Sali, K 765-285-5162 159 B
sfalling@bsu.edu
FALLIS, Drew 210-292-6258 528 G
drew.fallis@us.af.mil
FALLIS, Sue 925-631-4856 59 I
sfallis@stmarys-ca.edu
FALLON, Ann Marie 503-636-8141 392 D
provost@marylhurst.edu
FALLON, Anne Marie 508-830-6485 222 C
afallon@maritime.edu
FALLON, Greg 973-684-5895 294 A
gfallon@pccc.edu
FALLON, III, John, A 765-289-1241 159 B
jafallon@bsu.edu
FALLON, Kevin 410-543-6075 213 A
kcfallon@salisbury.edu
FALLON-KORB,
Melissa, A 607-436-3368 331 F
melissa.fallon@oneonta.edu
FALLONE, Deborah, A 914-323-5224 319 N
deborah.fallone@mville.edu
FALLOWS, Noel 706-542-2202 128 E
nfallows@uga.edu
FALLS, Meda 731-925-5722 446 C
mfalls@jscc.edu
FALLS, William, A 802-656-3166 485 D
william.falls@uvm.edu
FALVO, Amy 904-819-6305 99 M
afalvo@flagler.edu
FALWELL, JR., Jerry 434-582-2950 491 D
jlfjr@liberty.edu
FALWELL, Tyler 434-592-3095 491 D
twfalwell2@liberty.edu

FALZERANO, Christine, E 203-576-4566 89 C
cfalzera@bridgeport.edu
FALZONE, Kris 219-989-2217 166 F
kris.falzone@pnw.edu
FAMA, Melissa 978-632-6600 224 B
m_fama@mwcc.mass.edu
FAMBLE, JR., Freddie 325-793-4906 461 F
ffamble@mcm.edu
FAMULARE, Dominick, F 518-388-6532 338 H
famularn@union.edu
FAMULARE, Marybeth 717-264-4141 424 A
marybeth.famulare@wilson.edu
FAN, C. Cindy 310-825-4921 69 D
cfan@international.ucla.edu
FAN, Lori 417-836-5654 268 I
lfan@missouristate.edu
FANCHER, Janet 620-223-2700 181 A
janetf@fortscott.edu
FANCHER, Karen 503-255-0332 392 G
kfancher@multnomah.edu
FANCHER, Michael 315-792-7100 336 C
mfancher@sunypoly.edu
FANDOZZI, Melissa 518-828-4181 311 D
melissa.fandozzi@sunycgcc.edu
FANDRICH, Charisse 701-255-3285 362 E
cfandrich@uttc.edu
FANELLI, Sean, A 516-463-5740 316 D
sean.fanelli@hofstra.edu
FANEUFF, Ken 706-379-3111 130 B
kfaneuff@yhc.edu
FANGMEYER, Len, J 308-865-8555 282 L
fangmeyerlj@unk.edu
FANN, Erin 843-921-6916 431 H
efann@netc.edu
FANNAN, Lisa, L 816-604-2314 267 I
lisa.fannan@mcckc.edu
FANNIN, Larry 801-878-1053 285 E
lfannin@roseman.edu
FANNIN, Toni 925-969-2347 41 I
tfannin@dvc.edu
FANNING, Daniel 715-394-8213 521 E
dfanning@uwsuper.edu
FANNING, Lisa 617-879-5033 225 C
lisa.fanning@mcphs.edu
FANNING, Vivian 276-223-4777 499 C
vfanning@wcc.vccs.edu
FANNING, Will 208-562-2380 133 F
willfanning@cwidaho.cc
FANSHAW, Charles 202-685-3929 528 B
fanshawc@ndu.edu
FANSLAU, Michelle 239-489-9478 101 F
mfanslau@fsw.edu
FANSLER, A. Gigi 217-732-3155 146 B
gfansler@lincolncollege.edu
FANT, JR., Gene 561-803-2051 106 C
gene_fant@pba.edu
FANT, Greg 575-646-2127 300 J
gfant@nmsu.edu
FANT, Joshua, W 860-701-6727 529 A
joshua.w.fant@uscg.mil
FANTASIA, Bethany 617-262-5000 216 A
bethany.fantasia@the-bac.edu
FANTER, Jeff 317-921-4502 164 E
jfanter@ivytech.edu
FANTINI, Maria 856-351-2601 296 L
mfantini@salemcc.edu
FANTOZZI, Joseph 212-650-7865 307 E
jfantozzi@ccny.cuny.edu
FANUCCHI, Tina 773-577-8100 139 A
FANUZZI, Robert 718-390-4266 328 F
fanuzzir@stjohns.edu
FAONELUA, Lisa 808-675-3701 130 E
lisa.faonelua@byuh.edu
FAOUR, Sheila 318-675-6001 198 B
sfaour@lsuhsc.edu
FAOUR, William, G 423-624-0077 439 D
billf@chattanoogacollege.edu
FARAGALLA, Sameh 973-661-0600 291 F
FARAHANI, Gohar 301-846-2451 207 F
gfarahani@frederick.edu
FARAHI, Dawood 908-737-7000 292 C
dfarahi@kean.edu
FARAKISH, Negar 908-709-7550 298 A
FARANDA, Nick 617-928-4648 226 B
nfaranda@mountida.edu
FARANI, Heidi 425-640-1049 503 E
heidi.farani@edcc.edu
FARARA, Joseph 802-635-1272 486 B
joe.farara@jsc.edu
FARBANIEC, David 845-257-3196 331 E
farbanid@newpaltz.edu
FARE, Bridget, M 412-396-6052 403 A
fareb@duq.edu
FARES, Ted 575-562-2511 299 I
ted.fares@enmu.edu
FARFAN, Erika, M 740-427-5571 371 C
farfane@kenyon.edu
FARHA, Darron 219-464-6702 168 F
darron.farha@valpo.edu
FARHA, Darron, C 219-464-6702 168 F
darron.farha@valpo.edu

FARHANG, Ahad 718-951-5045 307 D
afarhang@brooklyn.cuny.edu
FARIA, Pamela 617-243-2221 219 I
pfaria@lasell.edu
FARIAS, Antonio 860-685-3927 90 C
afarias@wesleyan.edu
FARIAS, Isidro 707-654-1127 33 D
ifarias@csum.edu
FARIAS, Jaime 915-831-2394 457 H
jfarias@epcc.edu
FARIAS, Richard 210-486-0373 450 F
rfarias14@alamo.edu
FARINAS, Yenny 305-348-2621 111 A
yenny.diaz@fiu.edu
FARINELLI, Rob 301-934-7539 207 B
rfarinelli@csmd.edu
FARINO, Patricia 617-585-0200 216 A
patricia.farino@the-bac.edu
FARINOS, Jose 772-462-7235 103 B
jfarinos@irsc.edu
FARIS, Debbie 434-381-6324 494 M
dfaris@sbc.edu
FARISH, Donald, J 401-254-3201 426 B
dfarish@rwu.edu
FARISH, Guy, E 440-826-2478 363 M
gfarish@bw.edu
FARISH, Jennifer 662-846-4675 257 E
jfarish@deltastate.edu
FARKAS, Abraham 707-524-1508 63 G
afarkas@santarosa.edu
FARLAND, Lisa 310-338-7896 51 E
lisa.farland@lmu.edu
FARLESS, John, A 812-228-5157 168 E
jafarless@usi.edu
FARLEY, Andre 252-335-3669 356 D
afarley@ecsu.edu
FARLEY, Barbara, A 217-245-3001 141 G
barbara.farley@mail.ic.edu
FARLEY, Christy 602-728-9500 15 H
christy.farley@nau.edu
FARLEY, Dottie 972-241-3371 455 K
dfarley@dallas.edu
FARLEY, Dwayne 617-879-7805 222 A
dfarley@massart.edu
FARLEY, Emy 507-222-4289 245 C
efarley@carleton.edu
FARLEY, Erik, S 745-587-6605 368 B
farleye@denison.edu
FARLEY, Greg 785-628-4215 180 I
gfarley@fhsu.edu
FARLEY, Jeff 740-374-8716 381 A
jfarley1@wscc.edu
FARLEY, Jerry, B 785-670-1556 185 H
jerry.farley@washburn.edu
FARLEY, Karen 563-336-3323 172 A
kfarley@eicc.edu
FARLEY, Kim 307-382-1616 527 C
kfarley@westernwyoming.edu
FARLEY, Margaret 307-624-7010 526 G
margaret.farley@ewc.wy.edu
FARLEY, Mark 661-255-1050 30 E
FARLEY, Michael 704-971-2117 343 E
mfarley@charlottelaw.edu
FARLEY, Patrick 301-891-4551 213 D
pfarley@wau.edu
FARLEY, Penelope, L 410-778-7224 213 E
pfarley2@washcoll.edu
FARLEY, Susan 425-602-3354 501 D
sfarley@bastyr.edu
FARLEY, Tim 925-631-4830 59 I
tif5@stmarys-ca.edu
FARLEY, Troy 616-331-3311 234 F
farleytr@gvsu.edu
FARLOW, Carolyn 515-964-6520 171 B
cdfarlow@dmacc.edu
FARMBRY, Kyle, W 973-353-5834 296 C
kfarmbry@rutgers.edu
FARMELANT, Randie 508-373-9470 215 D
rfarmelant@follett.com
FARMER, Adam 765-677-2138 164 B
adam.farmer@indwes.edu
FARMER, Antoinette 602-639-7500 13 I
FARMER, Bradley 614-287-2787 367 C
bfarmer@cscc.edu
FARMER, Caleb 419-358-3376 364 D
farmerc@bluffton.edu
FARMER, Carla 417-667-8181 264 A
cfarmer@cottey.edu
FARMER, Carter 717-290-8701 408 B
president@lancasterseminary.edu
FARMER, David 910-695-3911 353 A
farmerdj@sandhills.edu
FARMER, John 714-432-5017 39 G
jfarmer@occ.cccd.edu
FARMER, Joyce 610-282-1100 402 B
joyce.farmer@desales.edu
FARMER, Larry, G 704-637-4227 343 B
lfarmer@catawba.edu
FARMER, Lindsey 910-695-3726 353 A
farmerl@sandhills.edu

FARMER, Lisa, D 775-673-7025 284 K
ldfarmer@tmcc.edu
FARMER, Lorna 908-852-1400 290 D
farmer@centenarycollege.edu
FARMER, Marcella 513-244-8132 366 B
marcella.farmer@ccuniversity.edu
FARMER, Melanie 304-384-6314 513 A
mfarmer@concord.edu
FARMER, Pam 864-977-7009 431 G
pam.farmer@ngu.edu
FARMER, Patricia J, B 315-229-5265 329 D
pfarmer@stlawu.edu
FARMER, Randy, L 901-448-7218 448 H
rfarme11@uthsc.edu
FARMER, Ricky 336-322-2107 351 H
rick.farmer@piedmontcc.edu
FARMER, Robert 518-891-2915 325 A
rfarmer@nccc.edu
FARMER, Scott 337-482-5393 201 D
sfarmer@louisiana.edu
FARMER, Stephen, M 919-966-3992 357 D
smfarmer@email.unc.edu
FARMER, Steve 601-968-5929 256 I
sfarmer@belhaven.edu
FARMER, Steve 419-227-3141 380 A
wfarmer@unoh.edu
FARMER-DIXON, Cherae 615-327-6207 442 A
cdixon@mmc.edu
FARMER-KAISER, Mary 337-482-6965 201 D
kaiser@louisiana.edu
FARMER-NEAL,
Rochonda 254-710-1453 452 H
rochonda_farmer-neal@baylor.edu
FARMER NOONAN, Erin 617-735-9991 218 C
farmer@emmanuel.edu
FARNER, Gabriele 618-634-3240 154 B
gabrielef@shawneecc.edu
FARNESKI, Anna 201-684-6844 294 G
afarnesk@ramapo.edu
FARNEY, Kirk 630-752-5016 158 C
kirk.farney@wheaton.edu
FARNHAM, Bruce 619-660-4347 45 I
bruce.farnham@gcccd.edu
FARNHAM, Margaret, L 614-235-4136 378 C
mfarnham@tlsohio.edu
FARNHAM, Robert 239-304-7093 95 Q
robert.farnham@avemaria.edu
FARNSWORTH, Scott 928-776-2234 18 D
scott.farnsworth@yc.edu
FARNSWORTH, Ward 512-232-1120 476 B
wf@law.utexas.edu
FAROL, Dorothy 714-997-6611 37 F
farol@chapman.edu
FARQUHARSON, Donald 816-523-9140 275 C
FARQUHARSON,
Janice, E 309-624-8980 153 F
janice.farquharson@osfhealthcare.org
FARR, Matthew 856-222-9311 295 C
mfarr@rcbc.edu
FARR, Myra 704-982-0121 353 E
FARR, Sharon 573-288-6633 264 F
sfarr@culver.edu
FARRAND, Karen 303-963-3283 77 I
kfarrand@ccu.edu
FARRAR, Carol 951-372-7017 59 B
carol.farrar@norcocollege.edu
FARRAR, James, D 540-458-8465 500 F
jdfarrar@wlu.edu
FARRAR, Jazaer 708-596-2000 154 E
jfouad-farrar@ssc.edu
FARRAR, Margaret, E 216-397-4215 370 H
mfarrar@jcu.edu
FARRAR, Rinalda 573-681-5528 266 I
farrarr@lincolnu.edu
FARRELL, Allison 315-445-4275 318 E
cudaal@lemoyne.edu
FARRELL, Christina 610-558-5638 411 E
farrellc@neumann.edu
FARRELL, Cynthia, H 724-589-2178 420 D
cfarrell@thiel.edu
FARRELL, Erin, P 317-788-2127 168 A
farrelle@uindy.edu
FARRELL, Gina 210-436-3517 464 H
gfarrell@stmarytx.edu
FARRELL, Gregory 212-220-1377 307 B
gfarrell@bmcc.cuny.edu
FARRELL, Jill 305-899-3649 96 D
jfarrell@barry.edu
FARRELL, Kathleen 914-251-6090 334 C
kathleen.farrell@purchase.edu
FARRELL, Lauren, M 724-925-4079 423 D
farrelll@wccc.edu
FARRELL, Lisa, M 636-584-6558 264 M
lisa.farrell@eastcentral.edu
FARRELL, Martin, F 610-660-1225 418 G
mfarrell@sju.edu
FARRELL, Mary, M 864-656-3026 428 C
maggie4@clemson.edu
FARRELL, Mary Ellen 973-275-2293 297 A
maryellen.farrell@shu.edu

FEHLER, Tim, G 864-294-3347 430 C tim.fehler@furman.edu
FEHN, Heather 609-771-2101 290 F hfehn@tcnj.edu
FEHNRICH, Jennifer 567-661-7101 376 D jennifer_fehnrich@owens.edu
FEHR, Joy 951-785-2982 48 A jfehr@lasierra.edu
FEHRENBACHER, Richard 206-220-8280 507 E fehrenbacher@seattleu.edu
FEIBEL, Ann 718-482-5642 309 A afeibel@lagcc.cuny.edu
FEICHTER, Kathryn 330-966-5452 377 J kfeichter@starkstate.edu
FEIER, Julie 970-943-3017 84 H jfeier@western.edu
FEIEREISEL, Mark 312-915-7625 146 G mfeiere@luc.edu
FEIERTAG, Jason 484-664-3140 411 D feiertag@muhlenberg.edu
FEIGELSTOCK, Yitzchok 516-225-4700 326 I rcli@mlb.edu
FEIGENBAUM, Peter 718-817-2243 314 G pfeigenbaum@fordham.edu
FEIGENSON, Neal, R 203-582-3213 88 G neal.feigenson@quinnipiac.edu
FEIGERT, Kendra, M 717-867-6126 408 F feigert@lvc.edu
FEIGH, Kim 847-735-6008 145 B weidnerfeigh@lakeforest.edu
FEIL, Hallie 308-635-6032 283 D feilh@wncc.edu
FEILEN, Bryan 317-632-5553 165 L bfeilen@lincolntech.edu
FEIN, Cheri 212-217-4700 314 B cheri_fein@fitnyc.edu
FEIN, Gene 718-817-3900 314 G fein@fordham.edu
FEIN, Jason 973-408-3648 291 B jfein@drew.edu
FEIN, Michael, T 434-832-7751 496 G feinm@cvcc.vccs.edu
FEINBERG, Diane 405-974-2658 388 L dfeinberg@uco.edu
FEINBERG, Elisha 718-268-4700 326 L
FEINGOLD, Ruth, P 503-370-6285 396 G feingold@willamette.edu
FEINMAN, Shannon 434-949-1012 498 E shannon.feinman@southside.edu
FEINSTEIN, Andrew 408-924-1000 35 C
FEINSTEIN, David 212-964-2830 320 I
FEINSTEIN, Lee 812-855-1646 162 F lafeinst@indiana.edu
FEINSTEIN, Sheryl, J 308-865-8265 282 L feinsteinsg@unk.edu
FEIST, K. Cameron 315-859-4413 315 D cfeist@hamilton.edu
FEISTHAMEL, Kevin, P 330-569-5952 369 J
FEITELBERG, Daniel 209-228-4400 70 A dfeitelberg@ucmerced.edu
FEITZ, David, A 801-321-7211 481 L dfeitz@ushe.edu
FEKARIS, Cynthia 212-594-4000 337 F cfekaris@tcicollege.edu
FEKE, Donald, L 216-368-4389 365 B dlf4@case.edu
FEKETE, Michael 815-836-5549 145 H feketemi@lewisu.edu
FEKULA, Michael 803-641-3340 433 G mickf@usca.edu
FELCH, Katrina 715-675-3331 524 D felch@ntc.edu
FELDBLUM, Miriam 909-621-8017 58 A miriam.feldblum@pomona.edu
FELDER, Bruce, B 304-696-3983 513 D felder1@marshall.edu
FELDER, JR., E. Lee 605-677-5671 437 A lee.felder@usd.edu
FELDER, Luther 706-821-8295 125 H lfelder@paine.edu
FELDER-DEAS, Altoya, A 803-934-3167 431 E afdeas@morris.edu
FELDHAUS, Joseph, H 513-745-3908 381 I feldhausjl@xavier.edu
FELDHEGE, Zach 916-649-8168 28 L zach.feldhege@brightwood.edu
FELDHUES, Nicole 412-396-5675 403 A feldhuesn@duq.edu
FELDHUS, Karima 949-451-5336 65 F kfeldhus@ivc.edu
FELDMAN, Aharon 410-484-7200 210 A raf@nirc.edu
FELDMAN, Andrew 541-917-4741 392 C feldmana@linnbenton.edu
FELDMAN, Barbara 508-531-1295 221 C barbara.feldman@bridgew.edu
FELDMAN, Dan 781-736-8405 216 F feldman@brandeis.edu
FELDMAN, Harriet, R 212-346-1200 325 J hfeldman@pace.edu
FELDMAN, James 518-225-5631 334 D feldmajs@cobleskill.edu
FELDMAN, Leonard, C 848-445-4524 295 F l.c.feldman@rutgers.edu
FELDMAN, Lori 219-989-2608 166 F feldman@pnw.edu
FELDMAN, Mary Jane 716-614-5926 324 D feldman@niagaracc.suny.edu
FELDMAN, Rachelle 510-642-7117 68 M
FELDMAN, Robert, S 413-545-2211 220 F feldman@chancellor.umass.edu
FELDMANN, Dorothy 781-891-2782 215 F dfeldmann@bentley.edu
FELDMANN, Jacob 718-645-0536 321 E
FELDMANN, Raymond, C 410-704-4672 213 B rfeldmann@towson.edu
FELDMEIER, Theresa 614-236-6813 364 N tfeldmei@capital.edu
FELDNER, Lisa 701-328-2960 360 B lisa.feldner@ndus.edu
FELDSTEIN, Andrew 785-628-4788 180 I apfeldstein@fhsu.edu
FELDSTEIN, Jay, S 215-871-6800 416 F jfeldstein@pcom.edu
FELDT, Tina 318-869-5424 194 I tfeldt@centenary.edu
FELIBERTY, Victor, A 787-284-1912 534 C vfeliber@ponce.inter.edu
FELICE, Susan 708-656-8000 149 A susan.felice@morton.edu
FELICIANA, Jerrye 301-736-3631 209 A jerrye.feliciana@msbbcs.edu
FELICIANO, Danilo 413-565-1000 215 A dfeliciano@baypath.edu
FELICIANO, Idali 517-265-5161 230 D ifeliciano@adrian.edu
FELICIANO, Patsy 813-974-3827 112 C pfelicia@admin.usf.edu
FELICIANO, Yelitza 787-783-0039 532 A yelitza.feliciano@dewey.edu
FELIO, John, R 518-783-2471 330 E jfelio@siena.edu
FELIU, Julio 787-841-2000 535 I jfeliu@pucpr.edu
FELIX, Hector 787-738-2161 538 A hector.felix1@upr.edu
FELIX, Jovany 850-561-2106 110 J jovany.felix@famu.edu
FELIX-MATA, Bertha 559-934-2217 74 D berthafelixmata@whccd.edu
FELKER, Sharon, M 303-963-3369 77 I sfelker@ccu.edu
FELKER, Steven 757-825-2716 498 G felkers@tncc.edu
FELKL, Roxy, J 907-796-6494 10 H rkfelkl@alaska.edu
FELL, Janet 732-923-4645 292 F jfell@monmouth.edu
FELL, Katherine, R 419-434-4510 379 E fell@findlay.edu
FELL, Stephanie 918-631-2241 389 E stephanie-fell@utulsa.edu
FELLEGY, Anna 218-879-0863 249 C afellegy@fdltcc.edu
FELLER, David, C 414-955-8424 518 A dfeller@mcw.edu
FELLER, Scott 765-361-6224 169 C fellers@wabash.edu
FELLINGER, Jennifer 616-395-7860 235 F fellinger@hope.edu
FELLOWS, Dawn 801-524-8156 480 J dfellows@ldsbc.edu
FELLOWS, Gail 610-436-3333 416 C gfellows@wcupa.edu
FELLOWS, Maureen, O 315-470-6621 334 E mfellows@esf.edu
FELSER, Francis, J 716-250-7500 306 A fjfelser@bryantstratton.edu
FELSKE, Eileen 973-618-3419 290 A efelske@caldwell.edu
FELSKE, Julie, L 989-837-4436 239 D felske@northwood.edu
FELSOVALYI, Erzsebet 973-748-9000 289 H elizabeth_felsovalyi@bloomfield.edu
FELT, K.C 208-282-3755 133 H feltkc@isu.edu
FELTES, Carol 212-327-8909 327 F cfeltes@rockvax.rockefeller.edu
FELTHOUSEN, Mat 216-421-7384 366 G mfelthousen@cia.edu
FELTHOUSEN, Robert 541-956-7147 394 J rfelthousen@roguecc.edu
FELTMAN, Richard 718-951-5693 307 D rfeltman@brooklyn.cuny.edu
FELTNER, Michael, E 310-506-4280 56 J michael.feltner@pepperdine.edu
FELTON, David, A 601-984-6000 261 C dafelton@umc.edu
FELTON, Herman 704-216-6044 346 A hfelton@livingstone.edu
FELTON, III, James, A 410-777-1472 206 B jafelton@aacc.edu
FELTON, Jennifer 712-749-2120 170 D feltonj@bvu.edu
FELTON, Pamela 312-322-1734 155 F pfelton@spertus.edu
FELTON, Rob 503-554-2129 391 D rfelton@georgefox.edu
FELTON, Shawn 607-255-5241 312 A admissions@cornell.edu
FELTON, Terence 630-466-7900 157 K tfelton@waubonsee.edu
FELTS, Renee 757-569-6760 498 B rfelts@pdc.edu
FELTS, Ronald 661-726-1911 68 K ron.felts@uav.edu
FELTY, Donna, H 423-652-4752 440 J dhfelty@king.edu
FEMINO, Charles 978-232-2221 218 D cfemino@endicott.edu
FEMINO, Donny 978-232-5201 218 D dfemino@endicott.edu
FENCSIK, Alissa 510-204-0727 38 C afencsik@cdsp.edu
FENDER, Samantha 828-689-1126 346 C sfender@mhu.edu
FENDERS, Nancy 207-941-7153 202 I fendersn@husson.edu
FENDRICH, Chris 719-549-2149 79 B chris.fendrich@csupueblo.edu
FENG, Phoenix 617-449-7067 229 B phoenix.feng@urbancollege.edu
FENLASON, Julie 320-762-4531 248 J julief@alextech.edu
FENLASON, Laurie 413-585-2170 228 D lfenlaso@smith.edu
FENN, Janice 812-877-8786 166 H fenn@rose-hulman.edu
FENN, Patricia 732-255-0400 293 E pfenn@ocean.edu
FENNELL, Angelia 903-593-8311 470 A afennell@texascollege.edu
FENNELL, Barbara 432-686-4250 461 H bfennell@midland.edu
FENNELL, Catherine 610-896-1221 405 I cfennell@haverford.edu
FENNELL, Catherine 610-527-0200 418 D fennell@roesmont.edu
FENNELL, Charles 901-333-4217 447 B cfennell1@southwest.tn.edu
FENNELL, Craig 215-204-8760 420 B craig.fennell@temple.edu
FENNELL, Dwight 903-593-8311 470 A dfennell@texascollege.edu
FENNELL, Lauren 214-333-8877 455 J bookstoremanager@dbu.edu
FENNELL, Sabrina 716-839-8228 312 D sfennell@daemen.edu
FENNER-LEINO, Patti 715-682-1230 518 H pfen-lei@northland.edu
FENNERN, Nicole 507-457-1638 254 O nfennern@smumn.edu
FENNING, Amy, E 731-881-7340 448 G
FENNING, Julie 218-793-2463 251 C julie.fenning@northlandcollege.edu
FENRICK, David, E 651-631-5229 256 A defenrick@unwsp.edu
FENSKE, Cynthia 734-995-7443 232 I cindy.fenske@cuaa.edu
FENSKE, Susanne 814-393-2351 414 G sfenske@clarion.edu
FENSTAD, Terry 413-572-5276 222 E tfenstad@westfield.ma.edu
FENTON, James, W 419-772-2070 374 J j-fenton.1@onu.edu
FENTON, Kimberly 716-286-8566 324 E kfenton@niagara.edu
FENTON, Lisa 708-802-6582 140 F lfenton@foxcollege.edu
FENTON, Patrick 408-741-2056 74 H pat.fenton@westvalley.edu
FENTON, William, E 502-272-8059 187 A wfenton@bellarmine.edu
FENTRESS, Craig, M 240-500-2000 207 I cmfentress@hagerstowncc.edu
FENVES, Gregory, L 512-471-1232 476 B president@utexas.edu
FENWICK, Garland 540-423-9046 497 B gfenwick@germanna.edu
FENWICK, Jim 818-947-2508 50 D fenwicjl@lavc.edu
FERALDI, Corey 803-641-3280 433 G coreyf@usca.edu
FERALDI, Patricia, A 716-673-3553 331 D patricia.feraldi@fredonia.edu
FERBER, Anna 212-431-2808 323 H anna.ferber@nyls.edu
FERBER, David 402-399-2319 279 E dferber@csm.edu
FERBER, Moshe 718-601-3523 341 F mosheferber1@gmail.com
FERBER, Stephen, M 412-624-8166 421 G smf200@pitt.edu
FERBRACHE, Jeanne 402-559-3937 283 A jferbrache@unmc.edu
FERCH, John 907-745-3201 9 H jferch@akbible.edu
FERCHLAND-PARELLA, Joanne 650-543-3704 52 D jferchland@menlo.edu
FERDAUS, Riaz 225-490-1662 199 B riaz.ferdaus@ololcollege.edu
FERDINAND, Amy, V 973-655-4367 293 A ferdinanda@mail.montclair.edu
FERDINAND, Jason 256-726-7277 6 B jferdinand@oakwood.edu
FERDOLAGE, Traci 707-826-4111 34 F traci.ferdolage@humboldt.edu
FEREBEE, Cheryl 404-872-3593 117 B cferebee@johnmarshall.edu
FEREBEE, Ryan, A 757-594-7553 488 E ryan.ferebee@cnu.edu
FEREDE, Mulugeta 512-475-6600 476 B mferede@utexas.edu
FEREIRA, James, A 864-231-2075 427 B jfereira@andersonuniversity.edu
FERGERSON, James 507-222-4292 245 C jfergers@carleton.edu
FERGERSON, Nicole 775-831-1314 285 G nfergerson@sierranevada.edu
FERGON, Elizabeth 661-654-3977 32 A efergon@csub.edu
FERGUSON, Angela 205-726-4841 6 E adfergus@samford.edu
FERGUSON, Brandi 620-225-0186 180 E bferguson@dc3.edu
FERGUSON, Brooke 540-857-6323 499 B bferguson@virginiawestern.edu
FERGUSON, Bruce 310-665-6935 55 E bferguson@otis.edu
FERGUSON, Buddy 864-379-8727 429 I ferguson@erskine.edu
FERGUSON, Charity, F 270-384-8100 191 E fergusonc@lindsey.edu
FERGUSON, Christy 716-286-8345 324 E clf@niagara.edu
FERGUSON, Colin 276-656-0349 498 A cferguson@patrickhenry.edu
FERGUSON, Cristie 903-693-2005 463 D cferguson@panola.edu
FERGUSON, Darla 321-433-7080 98 K fergusond@easternflorida.edu
FERGUSON, David 419-448-3584 378 A fergusonda@tiffin.edu
FERGUSON, Devin 972-825-4700 466 D dferguson@sagu.edu
FERGUSON, Douglas, J 610-359-7399 401 L dferguson@dccc.edu
FERGUSON, Hege 850-644-1389 111 C hferguson@admin.fsu.edu
FERGUSON, Jennifer 757-822-1913 498 H jferguson@tcc.edu
FERGUSON, Jessame, E 410-857-2741 209 D jferguson@mcdaniel.edu
FERGUSON, Joseph, S 361-570-4390 474 C fergusonj@uhv.edu
FERGUSON, Keith 256-233-8215 1 F keith.ferguson@athens.edu
FERGUSON, Kenlanna 269-337-7191 235 H kenlanna.feguson@kzoo.edu
FERGUSON, Kenneth, H 540-636-2900 488 D kferguson@christendom.edu
FERGUSON, Kevin 312-944-0882 145 F kferguson@chicago.chefs.edu
FERGUSON, Kevin 708-344-4700 146 D kferguson@lincolntech.edu
FERGUSON, Kimberly 814-332-4356 397 A kferguson@allegheny.edu
FERGUSON, Larry, A 205-387-0511 2 B larry.ferguson@bscc.edu
FERGUSON, La'Zarvius 815-965-7314 152 F lferguson@rockfordcareercollege.edu
FERGUSON, Lee 214-333-5460 455 J lee@dbu.edu
FERGUSON, Leonard 605-455-6057 436 G lferguson@olc.edu
FERGUSON, Lisa 270-789-5109 187 G lgferguson@campbellsville.edu
FERGUSON, Lisa, M 740-283-6450 368 L lferguson@franciscan.edu
FERGUSON, Lori 580-349-1566 385 F lorif@opsu.edu
FERGUSON, Lorrie 540-863-2823 496 H lwferguson@dslcc.edu
FERGUSON, Nicole 775-831-1314 285 G nferguson@sierranevada.edu
FERGUSON, Noreen 248-204-3106 237 B nferguson@ltu.edu
FERGUSON, Pamela 973-720-2615 298 G fergusonp4@wpunj.edu
FERGUSON, Rhonda 903-886-5014 468 D rhonda.ferguson@tamuc.edu

FICK, Katherine .... 507-786-3287.. 254 P
fick@stolaf.edu
FICK, Steve .... 512-313-3000.. 455 F
steve.fick@concordia.edu
FICK, Verlyn .... 520-515-5414.... 12 L
fickv@cochise.edu
FICKE, Joan, C .... 973-655-4368.. 293 A
fickej@mail.montclair.edu
FICKEN, Roger .... 970-675-3275.... 78 J
roger.ficken@cncc.edu
FICKENSCHER, II,
Carl, C .... 260-452-2131.. 160 D
carl.fickenscher@ctsfw.edu
FICKLER, Debra .... 610-519-7857.. 422 G
debra.fickler@villanova.edu
FIDATI, Brian .... 484-664-3110.. 411 D
bfidati@muhlenberg.edu
FIDELI, Baycan .... 631-451-4212.. 336 D
fidelib@sunysuffok.edu
FIDLER, Jane, P .... 617-333-2355.. 217 F
jfidler0803@curry.edu
FIDLER-SHEPPARD,
Rebecca .... 856-227-7200.. 290 B
rsheppard@camdencc.edu
FIEBELKORN, Donna .... 906-635-2728.. 236 J
dfiebelkorn@lssu.edu
FIEBIG, Andrea .... 847-925-6371.. 141 A
afiebig@harpercollege.edu
FIEDLER, Peter .... 617-353-6500.. 216 E
pfiedler@bu.edu
FIEDLER, Thomas .... 617-353-3488.. 216 E
tfiedler@bu.edu
FIEF, Gary .... 559-442-8277.... 67 C
gary.fief@fresnocitycollege.edu
FIEGE, William .... 804-594-1406.. 497 D
bfiege@jtcc.edu
FIEGEL, Gregg .... 805-756-7029.... 31 I
gfiegel@calpoly.edu
FIELD, Heather, M .... 415-565-4682.... 69 B
fieldh@uchastings.edu
FIELD, Jay .... 415-239-3993.... 38 E
jfield@ccsf.edu
FIELD, Jay .... 360-867-6000.. 503 G
fieldj@evergreen.edu
FIELD, Stephen, G .... 585-594-6150.. 327 D
fields@roberts.edu
FIELDER, Kala .... 931-221-1121.. 442 I
kala.fielder@miller-motte.com
FIELDER, Marsha .... 517-265-5161.. 230 D
mfielder@adrian.edu
FIELDHOUSE, Susan .... 615-898-5814.. 444 G
susan.fieldhouse@mtsu.edu
FIELDING, Ahn .... 707-476-4140.... 40 D
ahn-fielding@redwoods.edu
FIELDING, Chad .... 870-230-5420.... 20 E
fieldic@hsu.edu
FIELDING, Julie .... 607-735-1830.. 313 F
jfielding@elmira.edu
FIELDING, Ruby .... 803-376-5727.. 427 A
rfielding@allenuniversity.edu
FIELDING, William .... 256-782-5773...... 4 H
fielding@jsu.edu
FIELDS, Andy .... 530-529-8980.... 64 D
afields@shastacollege.edu
FIELDS, Ann, Z .... 901-722-3230.. 444 C
annfields@sco.edu
FIELDS, Bamby .... 509-359-6564.. 503 D
bfields@ewu.edu
FIELDS, Beverly .... 806-457-4200.. 458 B
bfields@fpctx.edu
FIELDS, Chad .... 479-394-7622.... 22 B
cfields@rmcc.edu
FIELDS, Cheryl .... 505-428-1238.. 301 K
cheryl.fields@sfcc.edu
FIELDS, Christine .... 276-739-2426.. 499 A
cfields@vhcc.edu
FIELDS, Darin .... 419-434-4553.. 379 E
fieldsd2@findlay.edu
FIELDS, Dave .... 646-664-9110.. 306 M
dave.fields@cuny.edu
FIELDS, Dennis .... 717-545-4747.. 406 I
FIELDS, Fonda .... 931-221-6279.. 444 E
fieldsf@apsu.edu
FIELDS, Gene .... 337-482-9246.. 201 D
gene.fields@louisiana.edu
FIELDS, Jeff .... 276-656-0222.. 498 A
jfields@patrickhenry.edu
FIELDS, Joe .... 864-488-8347.. 430 H
jfields@limestone.edu
FIELDS, John .... 229-430-4711.. 115 K
john.fields@asurams.edu
FIELDS, John .... 608-663-3407.. 516 F
jfields@edgewood.edu
FIELDS, Lee, M .... 252-334-2080.. 346 F
lee.fields@macuniversity.edu
FIELDS, Michael .... 707-668-5663.... 42 C
FIELDS, Michael .... 713-221-8179.. 474 B
fieldsm@uhd.edu
FIELDS, Mitch .... 315-312-6600.. 333 D
mitch.fields@oswego.edu
FIELDS, Petra .... 704-991-0231.. 353 E
pfields7679@stanly.edu
FIELDS, Richard .... 704-669-4243.. 348 F
fieldsr198@clevelandcc.edu
FIELDS, Russell .... 775-784-6987.. 285 A
rfields@unr.edu
FIELDS, Scott .... 603-897-8215.. 287 F
sfields@rivier.edu
FIELDS, Shawn .... 860-628-4751.... 88 C
sfields@lincolncollegene.edu
FIELDS, Stanley .... 708-656-8000.. 149 A
stanley.fields@morton.edu
FIELDS, Todd, E .... 972-881-5174.. 455 A
tfields@collin.edu
FIELDS, W. Bradley .... 859-238-5485.. 187 H
brad.fields@centre.edu
FIELER, Vickie, K .... 603-594-2567.. 287 H
vfieler@sjhnh.org
FIENE, Jay .... 909-537-5600.... 34 C
jfiene@csusb.edu
FIENSY, David, A .... 606-474-3263.. 188 L
dfiensy@kcu.edu
FIER, Luke .... 540-671-6981.. 488 D
luke.fier@christendom.edu
FIER, Sara .... 507-537-7150.. 252 E
sara.fier@smsu.edu
FIERKE, Kimberly .... 607-431-4000.. 315 E
fierkek@hartwick.edu
FIERO, Diane .... 661-362-3424.... 40 A
diane.fiero@canyons.edu
FIERRO, Jose, L .... 562-860-2451.... 36 P
jfierro@cerritos.edu
FIESE, Richard .... 325-646-2502.. 459 E
rfiese@hputx.edu
FIEZ, Terri .... 303-492-7401.... 83 K
terri.fiez@colorado.edu
FIFE, Linda, L .... 443-412-2377.. 208 A
lfife@harford.edu
FIFER, Susan .... 217-641-4201.. 143 H
sfifer@jwcc.edu
FIFER, Tom .... 660-831-4219.. 269 B
fifert@moval.edu
FIFRICK, Heather .... 608-822-2366.. 524 F
hfifrick@swtc.edu
FIGALLO, Jessica .... 559-737-5443.... 40 E
jessicaf@cos.edu
FIGARI, Carlos .... 619-421-6700.... 66 E
cfigari@swccd.edu
FIGARI, Charles, A .... 713-500-8400.. 477 C
charles.a.figari@uth.tmc.edu
FIGLER, Daniel, J .... 304-710-3495.. 512 B
figler@mctc.edu
FIGUEIREDO, Marianne ... 617-521-2270.. 228 C
marianne.figueiredo@simmons.edu
FIGUERA, Lilia .... 787-758-2525.. 538 D
ayudante-rector@upr.edu
FIGUEREDO, Ann, W .... 610-896-1142.. 405 I
afiguere@haverford.edu
FIGUEREDO, Danilo, H ... 973-748-9000.. 289 H
danilo_figueredo@bloomfield.edu
FIGUEREDO, Fernando ... 305-348-3829.. 111 A
figueref@fiu.edu
FIGUEROA, Arturo .... 787-728-1515.. 539 B
afigueroa@sagrado.edu
FIGUEROA, Aurea .... 787-884-3838.. 530 G
dir_rh@atenascollege.edu
FIGUEROA, Eduardo .... 787-882-2065.. 536 D
technoloa_industrial@unitecpr.net
FIGUEROA, Gema .... 787-738-2161.. 538 A
gema.figueroa@upr.edu
FIGUEROA, Ivan .... 802-447-4692.. 485 B
ifigueroa@svc.edu
FIGUEROA, Jennifer, E .... 570-577-1028.. 398 L
j.figueroa@bucknell.edu
FIGUEROA, Joel .... 787-884-3838.. 530 G
dir.admisiones@atenascollege.edu
FIGUEROA, Julio .... 787-257-7373.. 535 P
ue_jfigueroa@suagm.edu
FIGUEROA, Maria, V .... 787-743-7979.. 536 A
ut_mfigueroa@suagm.edu
FIGUEROA, Marilyn .... 787-728-1515.. 539 B
mfr@sagrado.edu
FIGUEROA, Mark .... 503-768-7676.. 392 A
figueroa@lclark.edu
FIGUEROA, Vitaliano .... 619-594-3557.... 35 A
vfigueroa@mail.sdsu.edu
FIGUEROA, William .... 787-758-2525.. 538 D
william.figueroa2@upr.edu
FIGUEROA-YOMARACHALIFF,
Luciano .... 787-265-3884.. 538 C
yomarachaliff-lucianofigueroa@uprm.edu
FIJAL, Amanda .... 773-702-7659.. 156 D
afijal@uchicago.edu
FIKE, David, J .... 415-442-7059.... 45 B
dfike@ggu.edu
FIKE, Janet .... 304-214-8837.. 512 F
jfike@wvncc.edu
FIKE, Jeffrey .... 540-828-5395.. 487 H
jfike@bridgewater.edu
FIKE, Linda, K .... 301-387-3049.. 207 G
linda.fike@garrettcollege.edu
FIKE-CURRY, Esther .... 407-831-9816.... 97 H
efike@citycollege.edu
FIKE-CURRY, Esther .... 954-492-5353.... 97 I
efike@citycollege.edu
FIKES, Gloria .... 713-942-9505.. 459 C
gfikes@hgst.edu
FIKSE, Peggy .... 209-575-7707.... 76 A
fiksep@mjc.edu
FILAN, Sonia .... 480-461-7446.... 14 D
sonia.filan@mesacc.edu
FILARDI, Salvatore .... 203-582-8800.... 88 G
salvatore.filardi@quinnipiac.edu
FILARDO, Amy .... 410-617-5576.. 208 G
afilardo@loyola.edu
FILBY, Ivan .... 618-664-7000.. 140 I
presidentfilby@greenville.edu
FILE, Carter .... 620-665-3505.. 181 I
filec@hutchcc.edu
FILEMYR, Ann .... 505-467-6823.. 302 D
annfilemyr@swc.edu
FILES, David .... 918-293-4987.. 386 B
dfiles@okstate.edu
FILIATREAU, Amy .... 561-237-7000.. 104 O
afiliatreau@lynn.edu
FILIP, Janet .... 517-586-3009.. 232 F
jfilip@cleary.edu
FILIPCHUK, Danielle .... 567-661-7970.. 376 D
danielle_filipchuk@owens.edu
FILIPP, Robert, B .... 773-442-5308.. 149 J
r-filipp@neiu.edu
FILIPPONE, Anne .... 610-902-8407.. 399 D
anne.filippone@cabrini.edu
FILIPPONE, Robin .... 716-270-5237.. 313 H
filippone@ecc.edu
FILLINGER, Barbara .... 734-973-3560.. 242 G
bfilling@wccnet.edu
FILLNER, Russ .... 406-447-6917.. 277 B
russ.fillner@umhelena.edu
FILLPOT, Jim .... 909-652-6460.... 37 D
jim.fillpot@chaffey.edu
FILORAMO, Dorothy .... 845-848-7400.. 312 F
dorothy.filoramo@dc.edu
FILOSA, Bruce .... 718-951-5366.. 307 D
bfilosa@brooklyn.cuny.edu
FILSON, Cori .... 518-580-5355.. 330 F
cfilson@skidmore.edu
FINAZZO, Susan .... 678-359-5680.. 122 E
sfinazzo@gordonstate.edu
FINCH, Aikyna .... 615-871-2260.... 93 F
FINCH, Aikyna .... 865-288-6000.... 93 F
FINCH, Amy .... 731-286-3347.. 446 B
finch@dscc.edu
FINCH, Christopher .... 201-559-6084.. 291 K
finchc@felician.edu
FINCH, Daniel .... 419-720-6670.. 376 I
dfinch@proskills.edu
FINCH, J. Howard .... 205-726-2364...... 6 E
hfinch@samford.edu
FINCH, Jack, R .... 740-377-2520.. 378 B
jfinch1@zoominternet.net
FINCH, Jeff .... 402-363-5651.. 283 G
jfinch@york.edu
FINCH, Joanna .... 636-529-0000.. 271 D
jfinch@slchcmail.com
FINCH, Jonathan .... 864-646-1853.. 433 C
jfinch1@tctc.edu
FINCH, Judy .... 503-768-7328.. 392 A
finchj@lclark.edu
FINCH, Kim .... 225-222-4251.. 196 G
FINCH, Manicia .... 386-481-2603.... 96 H
finchm@cookman.edu
FINCH, Mary Ellen .... 314-529-9400.. 267 B
mfinch@maryville.edu
FINCH, Thomas .... 315-786-2235.. 317 H
tfinch@sunyjefferson.edu
FINCH, Tony .... 662-720-7304.. 260 B
tfinch@nemcc.edu
FINCH, Tracy .... 870-972-2031.... 18 J
tfinch@astate.edu
FINCHAM, Brian, S .... 515-964-0601.. 172 F
finchamb@faith.edu
FINCHER, David, B .... 660-263-3900.. 263 A
president@cccb.edu
FINCK, David .... 802-258-3365.. 485 A
david.finck@worldlearning.org
FINDLEN, Sean, T .... 207-786-6328.. 202 D
sfindlen@bates.edu
FINDLEY, Brenda .... 575-538-6146.. 303 A
brenda.findley@wnmu.edu
FINDLEY, Caron .... 515-271-2424.. 171 K
caron.findley@drake.edu
FINDLEY, Pamela, L .... 256-782-5151...... 4 H
pfindley@jsu.edu
FINDT, William .... 910-879-5502.. 347 F
wfindt@bladencc.edu
FINDTNER, Rob .... 503-838-8000.. 396 E
findtnr@wou.edu
FINE, Ricka, K .... 410-777-1868.. 206 B
rkfine@aacc.edu
FINE, Susan .... 575-492-2781.. 300 H
sfine@nmjc.edu
FINEFROCK, Terry .... 440-375-7102.. 371 E
tfinefrock@lec.edu
FINEGAN, SC, Carol, M .. 718-405-3349.. 310 H
carol.finegan@mountsaintvincent.edu
FINEGAN, Kathleen .... 816-501-3621.. 262 G
kathleen.finegan@avila.edu
FINEGAN, Michael, J .... 570-961-4713.. 409 H
finegan@marywood.edu
FINEGOLD, David .... 412-365-1160.. 400 G
finegold@chatham.edu
FINEMAN, Barbara .... 401-232-6090.. 424 K
bfineman@bryant.edu
FINGADO, Marianne, B .... 619-876-4250.... 68 I
mfingado@usuniversity.edu
FINGAR, Melissa, A .... 585-292-2106.. 321 J
mfingar@monroecc.edu
FINGER, Eleanor .... 540-231-8893.. 499 F
efinger@vt.edu
FINGER, James .... 301-934-2251.. 207 B
jfinger@csmd.edu
FINGER, Mary .... 724-834-2200.. 419 D
mfinger@setonhill.edu
FINGERHUT, Randy .... 215-951-1284.. 407 A
fingerhut@lasalle.edu
FINK, Brenda .... 626-914-8830.... 38 D
bfink@citruscollege.edu
FINK, Ernest .... 718-409-7341.. 336 A
efink@sunymaritime.edu
FINK, Gayle, M .... 301-860-3403.. 212 D
gfink@bowiestate.edu
FINK, Heather .... 701-774-4281.. 361 G
heather.fink@willistonstate.edu
FINK, JoAnn, L .... 212-659-8888.. 317 A
joann.fink@mssm.edu
FINK, Kathrynn .... 479-248-7236.... 20 C
kathrynn.kennedy@gmail.com
FINK, Michael .... 909-652-6453.... 37 D
michael.fink@chaffey.edu
FINK, Michael .... 912-525-5000.. 126 E
mfink@scad.edu
FINK, Susan .... 917-493-4574.. 319 M
sfink@msmnyc.edu
FINKE, Michael .... 610-526-1000.. 397 E
michael.finke@theamericancollege.edu
FINKELSTEIN, Barbara ..... 207-216-4311.. 204 B
bfinkelstein@yccc.edu
FINKELSTEIN, Eric, M ..... 718-990-2417.. 328 F
finkelse@stjohns.edu
FINKELSTEIN, Jerry .... 212-229-1671.. 322 E
finkelsj@newschool.edu
FINKELSTEIN, Monte .... 850-201-8488.. 113 E
finkelsm@tcc.fl.edu
FINKELSTEIN, Richard ..... 540-654-1052.. 495 C
rfinkels@umw.edu
FINLAY, Cheryl, S .... 412-383-4473.. 421 G
cfinlay@pitt.edu
FINLAYSON, Al .... 218-733-7600.. 249 H
a.finlayson@lsc.edu
FINLAYSON,
Alexander (Sandy) .... 215-572-3823.. 423 C
sfinlayson@wts.edu
FINLAYSON, Deborah .... 806-742-0502.. 472 C
deborah.finlayson@ttu.edu
FINLAYSON, Jeanne .... 508-565-1337.. 228 F
jfinlayson@stonehill.edu
FINLEY, Adam .... 817-598-8831.. 479 E
aflinley@wc.edu
FINLEY, Becky .... 662-846-4051.. 257 E
becky@deltastate.edu
FINLEY, David .... 906-635-2211.. 236 J
dfinley@lssu.edu
FINLEY, David .... 906-635-2426.. 236 J
dfinley@lssu.edu
FINLEY, David .... 229-931-2068.. 127 C
dfinley@southgatech.edu
FINLEY, Jane .... 251-442-2219...... 9 A
jfinley@umobile.edu
FINLEY, Julius .... 360-779-9993.. 505 B
jfinley@ncad.edu
FINLEY, Lisa .... 276-656-0230.. 498 A
lfinley@patrickhenry.edu
FINLEY, Rebecca .... 215-503-9000.. 420 E
rebecca.finley@jefferson.edu
FINLEY, William .... 575-234-9200.. 301 B
wfinley@nmsu.edu
FINN, Alan .... 503-768-7827.. 392 A
afinn@lclark.edu
FINN, Alicia, A .... 603-641-7600.. 287 G
afinn@anselm.edu
FINN, Bob, D .... 509-313-6100.. 504 A
finn@gonzaga.edu
FINN, Donald .... 757-352-4278.. 493 E
dfinn@regent.edu
FINN, Erin, M .... 215-503-1040.. 420 E
erin.finn@jefferson.edu
FINN, Janice .... 267-620-4112.. 397 G
finn@arcadia.edu
FINN, John .... 330-263-2373.. 367 A
jfinn@wooster.edu
FINN, Kevin .... 248-204-4100.. 237 B
kfinn@ltu.edu

FINN, Louise .... 410-617-5252.. 208 G
lafinn@loyola.edu
FINN, Nathan .... 731-661-5082.. 448 A
nfinn@uu.edu
FINN, William .... 708-974-5727.. 148 G
finn@morainevalley.edu
FINN-SHERMAN, Miriam . 781-768-7222.. 227 G
miriam.sherman@regiscollege.edu
FINN-WELCH, Aliza .... 860-297-4054.... 89 B
aliza.finnwelch@trincoll.edu
FINNEGAN, Barry .... 636-949-4455.. 266 J
bfinnegan@lindenwood.edu
FINNEGAN, John .... 612-625-1179.. 255 H
finne001@umn.edu
FINNEGAN, Olya .... 414-443-8867.. 522 F
olya.finnegan@wlc.edu
FINNEGAN, Paul, J .... 617-495-1000.. 219 D
FINNEGAN, Robert .... 802-828-2800.. 486 A
robert.finnegan@ccv.edu
FINNEL, Kristin, M .... 920-922-8611.. 524 B
kfinnel@morainepark.edu
FINNELL, John .... 512-454-1188.. 451 E
jfinnell@aoma.edu
FINNELL, Karyn .... 928-350-3221.... 16 P
kfinnell@prescott.edu
FINNEN, Mary .... 646-660-6549.. 307 A
mary.finnen@baruch.cuny.edu
FINNERAN, Christina, M . 207-725-3897.. 202 F
cfinnera@bowdoin.edu
FINNERN, Julie .... 712-749-2065.. 170 D
finnern@bvu.edu
FINNERTY, Mary Beth ...... 518-782-6818.. 330 E
mfinnerty@siena.edu
FINNERTY, Robert .... 585-475-4733.. 327 E
bob.finnerty@rit.edu
FINNEY, Andy .... 208-769-3266.. 134 C
andy_finney@nic.edu
FINNEY, Gina .... 313-664-7650.. 232 G
gfinney@collegeforcreativestudies.edu
FINNEY, Jack .... 540-231-2350.. 499 F
jfinney@vt.edu
FINNEY, Lesley, M .... 717-361-1445.. 403 C
finneylm@etown.edu
FINNEY, Marc .... 252-536-7237.. 350 C
mfinney295@halifaxcc.edu
FINNEY, Maureen .... 716-829-7713.. 313 A
FINNEY, Sarah .... 206-296-6390.. 507 E
sfinney@seattleu.edu
FINNEY, Terry .... 870-972-2398.... 18 J
tfinney@astate.edu
FINNIE, David, A .... 937-775-2056.. 381 H
david.finnie@wright.edu
FINNIGAN, Kristia, H .... 803-777-6727.. 433 F
finnigan@sc.edu
FINNIN, Meredith .... 212-752-1530.. 318 F
meredith.finnin@limcollege.edu
FINNING, Shannon .... 413-748-3100.. 228 E
sfinning@springfieldcollege.edu
FINNKENNEY, Rebecca ... 610-796-8221.. 397 D
rebecca.finnkenney@alvernia.edu
FINO, Mike .... 760-757-2121.... 52 K
mfino@miracosta.edu
FINSETH, Karen .... 218-723-6104.. 245 J
kfinseth@css.edu
FINSTUEN, Andrew .... 208-426-1205.. 132 I
andrewfinstuen@boisestate.edu
FINTON, Stephan .... 860-215-9003.. 87 D
sfinton@trcc.commnet.edu
FINZEL, Bart .... 320-589-6015.. 255 F
finzelbd@morris.umn.edu
FIORAVANTI, Emil .... 508-999-8106.. 220 H
efioravanti@umassd.edu
FIORE, Doug .... 816-584-6445.. 270 D
doug.fiore@park.edu
FIORE, Francesca .... 718-482-5332.. 309 A
ffiore@lagcc.cuny.edu
FIORE, Laura .... 717-291-4278.. 403 J
laura.fiore@fandm.edu
FIORE CONTE, Johann ...... 607-777-2221.. 331 B
jmfconte@binghamton.edu
FIORELLA, Cynthia .... 270-686-4445.. 190 D
cindy.fiorella@kctcs.edu
FIORELLO, Christopher ..... 703-284-1615.. 492 A
chris.fiorello@marymount.edu
FIORENTINO, Chris .... 610-436-6973.. 416 C
cfiorentino@wcupa.edu
FIORENTINO, JR.,
Michael .... 570-484-2000.. 415 D
mfiorentino@lhup.edu
FIORENZA, Anthony .... 305-237-2867.. 105 D
afiorenz@mdc.edu
FIORESI, Rhonda .... 610-647-4400.. 406 B
rfioresi@immaculata.edu
FIORI, Christopher .... 781-280-3292.. 224 A
fioric@middlesex.mass.edu
FIORITO, Frank .... 312-567-7994.. 142 I
ffiorito@iit.edu
FIRESTONE, Bernard, J .... 516-463-5411.. 316 D
bernard.j.firestone@hofstra.edu
FIRESTONE, Elizabeth, E .. 865-694-6457.. 446 G
eefirestone@pstcc.edu

FIRMIN, Lisa, C .... 210-458-6097.. 477 A
lisa.firmin@utsa.edu
FIRMIN, Sally, E .... 254-710-3476.. 452 H
sally_firmin@baylor.edu
FIRTH, Ann, M .... 574-631-9164.. 168 B
firth.2@nd.edu
FISCHER, Aharon .... 732-367-7604.. 298 H
FISCHER, Andrew .... 734-384-4202.. 238 C
afischer@monroeccc.edu
FISCHER, Brock .... 815-455-8561.. 147 E
bfischer@mchenry.edu
FISCHER, Craig .... 914-606-6715.. 340 C
craig.fischer@sunywcc.edu
FISCHER, Donna .... 973-684-6333.. 294 A
dfischer@pccc.edu
FISCHER, Heidi .... 336-841-9636.. 345 A
hfischer@highpoint.edu
FISCHER, OSU, Helena ...... 270-686-4248.. 187 C
helena.fischer@brescia.edu
FISCHER, Howard .... 602-749-5120.. 183 M
howard.fischer@ottawa.edu
FISCHER, Jacqueline .... 660-263-4100.. 269 D
jackiefischer@macc.edu
FISCHER, John .... 419-372-5387.. 364 E
jfisch@bgsu.edu
FISCHER, Kelly .... 712-325-3413.. 174 B
kfischer@iwcc.edu
FISCHER, Lisa .... 309-467-6419.. 140 E
lfischer@eureka.edu
FISCHER, Mark, T .... 585-275-3340.. 338 K
mfische8@ur.rochester.edu
FISCHER, Marvin, J .... 631-420-2702.. 335 E
marvin.fischer@farmingdale.edu
FISCHER, Michael, R .... 210-999-8201.. 473 A
mfischer@trinity.edu
FISCHER, Paige, L .... 580-327-8545.. 384 M
plfischer@nwosu.edu
FISCHER, Pattie .... 360-417-6201.. 505 I
pfischer@pencol.edu
FISCHER, Patty .... 573-875-7260.. 263 F
pafischer@ccis.edu
FISCHER, Rachel .... 920-686-6278.. 519 H
rachel.fischer@sl.edu
FISCHER, JR., Robert, U . 615-898-2613.. 444 G
bud.fischer@mtsu.edu
FISCHER, Stacy .... 973-408-3047.. 291 B
sfischer@drew.edu
FISCHER, Susan .... 608-262-2087.. 519 K
susan.fischer@finaid.wisc.edu
FISCHER, Timothy .... 602-386-4105.... 11 D
tim.fischer@arizonachristian.edu
FISCHER, Tracy, A .... 414-410-4266.. 515 I
tafischer@stritch.edu
FISCHER, William, M .... 937-229-3311.. 379 D
wfischer1@udayton.edu
FISCHER-FREE, Todd .... 815-226-3385.. 152 G
tfree@rockford.edu
FISCHER-FREE, Todd .... 815-226-3385.. 152 G
tfischer-free@rockford.edu
FISCHLE, Helen .... 256-726-7000...... 6 B
hfischle@oakwood.edu
FISCHLER, Abraham .... 954-262-3827.. 105 J
fischler@nova.edu
FISCHLER, Mark, J .... 603-535-2240.. 288 F
mjfischler@plymouth.edu
FISCUS, Rosemarie .... 856-691-8600.. 290 I
rfiscus@cccnj.edu
FISER, Dawn, M .... 517-338-3327.. 232 F
dfiser@cleary.edu
FISH, Alan .... 443-997-8767.. 208 D
afish6@jhu.edu
FISH, Alicia .... 607-431-4021.. 315 E
fisha@hartwick.edu
FISH, David .... 417-626-1234.. 269 K
dfish@occ.edu
FISH, H. Woodrow .... 704-406-4254.. 344 E
hwfish@gardner-webb.edu
FISH, Jacqueline .... 843-863-7504.. 427 I
jfish@csuniv.edu
FISH, James, D .... 315-268-3859.. 310 B
jfish@clarkson.edu
FISH, Jennifer, N .... 757-683-4903.. 492 G
jfish@odu.edu
FISH, Mark .... 972-241-3371.. 455 K
mfish@dallas.edu
FISH, Nicole .... 800-567-2344.. 516 B
nfish@menominee.edu
FISH, Thomas, E .... 606-539-4214.. 193 F
tom.fish@ucumberlands.edu
FISHBACK, Bill .... 325-649-8012.. 459 E
bfishback@hputx.edu
FISHBACK, Jillian .... 714-533-1495.... 65 B
rosefish@southbaylo.edu
FISHBAUGH,
Mary Susan .... 406-657-2285.. 277 D
mfishbaugh@msubillings.edu
FISHBECK, Donna .... 701-224-5638.. 361 C
donna.fishbeck@bismarckstate.edu
FISHBEIN, Michael .... 508-541-1898.. 217 G
mfishbein@dean.edu

FISHBONE, Alexis .... 978-556-3615.. 224 D
afishbone@necc.mass.edu
FISHEL, Teresa .... 651-696-6343.. 247 I
fishel@macalester.edu
FISHER, Andrew .... 940-668-4234.. 462 L
afisher@nctc.edu
FISHER, Ann .... 313-993-1582.. 241 G
fisheram@udmercy.edu
FISHER, Anne, E .... 941-487-4254.. 111 D
fisher@ncf.edu
FISHER, Anthony .... 912-525-5000.. 126 E
afisher@scad.edu
FISHER, Barrett .... 651-638-6083.. 244 L
fisbar@bethel.edu
FISHER, Beth .... 901-722-3200.. 444 C
bfisher@sco.edu
FISHER, Brian .... 239-590-1786.. 110 L
bfisher@fgcu.edu
FISHER, Brock .... 815-455-8561.. 147 E
bfisher@mchenry.edu
FISHER, Christine .... 312-935-6696.. 152 D
cfisher@robertmorris.edu
FISHER, Courtney .... 870-762-3105.... 18 G
cfisher@smail.anc.edu
FISHER, Craig .... 325-674-2622.. 449 J
craig.fisher@acu.edu
FISHER, David .... 918-540-6233.. 384 F
dfisher@neo.edu
FISHER, David, A .... 864-242-5100.. 427 E
FISHER, Dawn .... 940-397-4787.. 462 A
dawn.fisher@mwsu.edu
FISHER, Denise .... 412-809-5100.. 417 D
fisher.denise@pti.edu
FISHER, Dianna, L .... 657-278-2586.... 33 A
difisher@fullerton.edu
FISHER, Donna, M .... 620-417-1111.. 184 I
donna.fisher@sccc.edu
FISHER, Edward .... 714-872-5692.... 51 F
efisher@ketchum.edu
FISHER, Elise .... 816-415-7641.. 275 F
fishere@william.jewell.edu
FISHER, Elizabeth, A .... 205-934-2974...... 8 E
FISHER, Ellen .... 212-472-1500.. 324 A
efisher@nysid.edu
FISHER, Glenn, R .... 570-577-1921.. 398
glenn.fisher@bucknell.edu
FISHER, Gloria .... 817-515-5777.. 467 A
gloria.fisher@tccd.edu
FISHER, Harry .... 212-817-7523.. 308 A
hfisher@gc.cuny.edu
FISHER, Hope .... 703-284-1538.. 492 A
hope.fisher@marymount.edu
FISHER, Howard .... 903-927-0183.. 479 K
hlfisher@wileyc.edu
FISHER, James, R .... 585-785-1208.. 314 D
james.fisher@flcc.edu
FISHER, Jane .... 516-877-3220.. 303 B
fisher2@adelphi.edu
FISHER, Jay .... 931-598-1142.. 443 O
jafisher@sewanee.edu
FISHER, Jeffrey, A .... 614-222-3277.. 367 B
jfisher@ccad.edu
FISHER, Jennifer, L .... 304-293-8531.. 514 C
jennifer.fisher@mail.wvu.edu
FISHER, Jeremy, M .... 402-280-3819.. 279 H
jfisher@creighton.edu
FISHER, Jim, J .... 843-792-4275.. 431 A
fisherj@musc.edu
FISHER, Joseph, B .... 210-690-9000.. 458 I
jfisher@hallmarkuniversity.edu
FISHER, Joy .... 310-233-4033.... 49 I
fisherjp@ahc.edu
FISHER, Judith .... 269-471-3470.. 230 H
jfisher@andrews.edu
FISHER, Julie .... 773-896-2400.. 137 A
julie.fisher@ctschicago.edu
FISHER, Karla .... 501-882-8956.... 18 I
FISHER, Katie .... 828-328-7247.. 345 H
katie.fisher@lr.edu
FISHER, Kelly .... 978-232-2328.. 218 D
kfisher@endicott.edu
FISHER, Laurie .... 406-243-6989.. 276 K
laurie.fisher@umontana.edu
FISHER, Lee .... 216-687-2300.. 366 I
l.fisher@law.csuohio.edu
FISHER, Linda .... 916-660-7605.... 64 F
lfisher@sierracollege.edu
FISHER, Lisa .... 405-682-7595.. 385 D
lisa.m.fisher@occc.edu
FISHER, Marc .... 805-893-3132.... 70 E
marc.fisher@vcadmin.ucsb.edu
FISHER, Mark .... 417-873-7294.. 264 H
mfisher005@drury.edu
FISHER, Michael .... 858-785-1458.. 314 D
michael.fisher@fcc.edu
FISHER, Michael .... 541-383-7238.. 390 D
mfisher@cocc.edu
FISHER, Myra .... 619-849-2388.... 57 M
myrafisher@pointloma.edu
FISHER, Nevan .... 585-389-2370.. 322 D
nfisher2@naz.edu

FISHER, Nicole .... 213-613-2200.... 65 H
nicole_fisher@sciarc.edu
FISHER, Ocie .... 903-593-8311.. 470 A
ofisher@texascollege.edu
FISHER, P. Brian .... 843-953-7532.. 428 G
fisherb@cofc.edu
FISHER, Patti, J .... 574-807-7625.. 159 D
patti.fisher@bethelcollege.edu
FISHER, Rebecca .... 877-248-6724.... 13 K
rfisher@hmu.edu
FISHER, Robert .... 507-457-6658.. 254 O
rfisher@smumn.edu
FISHER, Robert, C .... 615-460-6793.. 438 J
bob.fisher@belmont.edu
FISHER, Robert, H .... 773-298-3031.. 153 H
fisher@sxu.edu
FISHER, Scheiby, C .... 956-326-2780.. 468 A
sfisher@tamiu.edu
FISHER, Stephanie .... 704-991-0176.. 353 E
sfisher3774@stanly.edu
FISHER, Susan .... 814-262-3833.. 413 P
sfisher@pennhighlands.edu
FISHER, Tiffany .... 574-936-8898.. 158 I
tiffany.fisher@ancilla.edu
FISHER, Timothy .... 860-570-5127.... 89 D
timothy.fisher@uconn.edu
FISHER, Tom .... 505-323-9282.. 479 D
twfisher@wbu.edu
FISHER, William .... 508-793-7676.. 217 B
wfisher@clarku.edu
FISHER, Witney .... 864-596-9139.. 429 C
witney.fisher@converse.edu
FISHER-WILLIAMS, Nan .. 386-481-2098.... 96 H
williamsnan@cookman.edu
FISHMAN, Ariel .... 212-960-5400.. 341 G
afishma2@yu.edu
FISHMAN, David .... 845-406-4308.. 340 I
FISHMAN, Joan, R .... 212-431-2850.. 323 H
joan.fishman@nyls.edu
FISHMAN, Robert .... 734-764-1315.. 241 J
fishmanr@umich.edu
FISHMAN, Yisroel .... 718-645-0536.. 321 E
FISHSTEIN, Janet .... 781-239-5840.. 214 G
jfishstein@babson.edu
FISK, Cheryl .... 952-446-4172.. 246 D
fiskc@crown.edu
FISK, Francine, J .... 918-631-2495.. 389 E
francine-fisk@utulsa.edu
FISK, Robert .... 304-647-6361.. 514 A
rfisk@osteo.wvsom.edu
FISK, Sunshine .... 603-524-3207.. 286 C
sfisk@ccsnh.edu
FISK, Tammy .... 864-646-1812.. 433 C
tstout1@tctc.edu
FISKAA, Evelyn .... 845-848-4032.. 312 F
evelyn.fiskaa@dc.edu
FISKE, Jason .... 619-961-4217.... 68 A
jfiske@tjsl.edu
FISKE, Joshua, A .... 315-268-6718.. 310 B
jfiske@clarkson.edu
FISSINGER, Matthew, X ... 310-338-2750.... 51 E
mfissing@lmu.edu
FISTER, Cherie .... 314-529-9563.. 267 B
cfister@maryville.edu
FISTER, K. Renee .... 270-809-3763.. 192 A
kfister@murraystate.edu
FITCH, CD .... 620-862-5252.. 178 F
cd.fitch@barclaycollege.edu
FITCH, Gene .... 972-883-6236.. 476 C
gene.fitch@utdallas.edu
FITCH, James .... 814-332-2381.. 397 A
jfitch@allegheny.edu
FITCH, James .... 940-668-4271.. 462 L
jfitts@nctc.edu
FITCH, Jerome, H .... 803-535-5549.. 428 B
jfitch@claflin.edu
FITCH, Kim .... 618-664-7000.. 140 I
kim.fitch@greenville.edu
FITCH, Megan .... 610-896-2958.. 405 I
mfitch@haverford.edu
FITCH, Michelle .... 712-279-3503.. 176 E
michelle.fitch@stlukescollege.edu
FITCH, Peggy .... 641-628-5249.. 170 E
fitchp@central.edu
FITCH, Poppy .... 858-513-9240.... 27 V
poppy.fitch@ashford.edu
FITE-MORGAN, Amber ...... 256-765-4487...... 9 C
afitemorgan@una.edu
FITHEN, Debra .... 479-964-3245.... 19 F
dfithen@atu.edu
FITHIAN, David, B .... 773-702-2305.. 156 D
fithian@uchicago.edu
FITSIMMONS, Gary, N .... 423-775-7196.. 439 B
gary.fitsimmons@bryan.edu
FITTS, Alex .... 907-474-7980.... 10 G
affitts@alaska.edu
FITTS, Bev .... 503-517-1031.. 396 D
bfitts@warnerpacific.edu
FITTS, Michael, A .... 504-865-5201.. 200 C
maf@tulane.edu

FITZ, Craig, R .... 610-359-5288.. 401 L
cfitz@dccc.edu
FITZ, Franzetta .... 850-599-3460.. 110 J
franzetta.fitz@famu.edu
FITZ, Gregory .... 214-648-8712.. 478 C
greg.fitz@utsouthwestern.edu
FITZ, SM, James, F .... 937-229-2899.. 379 D
jfitz1@udayton.edu
FITZ-GERALD, Jim .... 251-580-2194...... 4 I
jim.fitz-gerald@faulknerstate.edu
FITZ-GERALD, Jim .... 251-580-2205...... 4 I
jim.fitz-gerald@faulknerstate.edu
FITZER, John .... 559-675-4800.... 67 D
john.fitzer@reedleycollege.edu
FITZGERALD, Ann .... 574-936-8898.. 158 I
ann.fitzgerald@ancilla.edu
FITZGERALD, Barrie, D .... 229-333-7836.. 129 G
bdfitzgerald@valdosta.edu
FITZGERALD, Darren .... 800-962-7682.. 275 D
dfitzgerald@wma.edu
FITZGERALD, Ed .... 618-252-5400.. 154 G
eddie.fitzgerald@sic.edu
FITZGERALD, Ed .... 765-973-8422.. 162 G
efitzger@iue.edu
FITZGERALD, Elizabeth .... 973-546-0123.. 305 B
eaf@berkeleycollege.edu
FITZGERALD, Elizabeth .... 973-546-0123.. 289 F
eaf@berkeleycollege.edu
FITZGERALD, Erin .... 860-723-0013.... 85 E
fitzgeralde@ct.edu
FITZGERALD, Erin .... 401-341-3108.. 426 C
erin.fitzgerald@salve.edu
FITZGERALD, Faith, M .... 757-823-8407.. 492 F
fmfitzgerald@nsu.edu
FITZGERALD, Francis, X .. 718-951-5504.. 307 D
fxfitzgerald@brooklyn.cuny.edu
FITZGERALD, Frank .... 540-231-1216.. 499 F
fitzgera@vt.edu
FITZGERALD, Glynis, A .... 860-832-2364.... 85 F
fitzgeraldg@ccsu.edu
FITZGERALD, Greg .... 503-594-3132.. 390 F
gregf@clackamas.edu
FITZGERALD, Gregory ..... 410-532-5109.. 210 B
gfitzgerald@ndm.edu
FITZGERALD, Hiram, E .... 517-353-8977.. 237 I
fitzger9@msu.edu
FITZGERALD, Ione .... 312-461-0600.. 134 K
ifitzgerald@aaart.edu
FITZGERALD, Jessica ..... 314-744-5301.. 268 F
fitzgerald@mobap.edu
FITZGERALD, Joanne .... 585-389-2070.. 322 D
jfitzge0@naz.edu
FITZGERALD, Larry, L ..... 434-924-5426.. 495 H
llf2n@virginia.edu
FITZGERALD, Lorraine, G 312-915-6411.. 146 G
lsnyde2@luc.edu
FITZGERALD, Marcia .... 518-828-4181.. 311 D
fitzgerald@sunycgcc.edu
FITZGERALD, Paul .... 814-868-9900.. 403 D
paulf@erieit.edu
FITZGERALD, SJ, Paul, J 415-422-6762.... 72 C
pjfitzgerald@usfca.edu
FITZGERALD, Robert, F .... 401-863-2500.. 424 J
robert_fitzgerald@brown.edu
FITZGERALD, Ryan .... 806-716-2175.. 465 G
rfitzgerald@southplainscollege.edu
FITZGERALD, Scott .... 614-823-0113.. 376 C
sfitzgerald@otterbein.edu
FITZGERALD, Sean, P ..... 419-372-0464.. 364 E
sfitzge@bgsu.edu
FITZGERALD, Shawn, M .. 610-499-4345.. 423 E
smfitzgerald@widener.edu
FITZGERALD, Susan .... 860-768-4011.... 89 G
fitzgeral@hartford.edu
FITZGERALD, Teresa .... 786-331-1000.. 105 G
tfitzgerald@maufl.edu
FITZGERALD MILLER,
Judith .... 573-882-0278.. 273 E
millerjud@missouri.edu
FITZGIBBON, Cecelia ...... 215-965-4000.. 411 A
cfitzgibbon@moore.edu
FITZGIBBON, Heather, M 330-263-2576.. 367 A
hfitzgibbon@wooster.edu
FITZGIBBON, John .... 831-582-3000.... 33 E
jfitzgibbon@csumb.edu
FITZGIBBONS, Courtney . 212-431-2859.. 323 H
courtney.fitzgibbons@nyls.edu
FITZGIBBONS, James ...... 510-231-5000.... 47 H
FITZGIBBONS, SJ,
John, P .... 303-458-4190.... 82 L
president@regis.edu
FITZHUGH, Keena .... 215-785-0111.. 413 K
FITZMAURICE, Patricia .... 212-752-1530.. 318 F
patricia.fitzmaurice@limcollege.edu
FITZPATRICK, Christiana . 706-419-1279.. 119 G
christiana.fitzpatrick@covenant.edu
FITZPATRICK, Christine .... 317-274-4417.. 163 D
FITZPATRICK, Craig .... 303-722-5724.... 81 E
cfitzpatrick@lincolntech.edu
FITZPATRICK, Daniel .... 304-384-5276.. 513 A
dfitzpatrick@concord.edu
FITZPATRICK, Holly .... 413-775-1813.. 223 D
fitzpatrickh@gcc.mass.edu
FITZPATRICK, James, D .. 203-254-4000.... 87 G
jfitzpatrick@fairfield.edu
FITZPATRICK, Jane .... 606-783-2053.. 191 H
j.fitzpatrick@moreheadstate.edu
FITZPATRICK, M. Louise . 610-519-4909.. 422 G
louise.fitzpatrick@villanova.edu
FITZPATRICK, SC,
Margaret, M .... 845-398-4013.. 329 G
mfitzpat@stac.edu
FITZPATRICK, Mark .... 212-229-5300.. 322 E
fitzpame@newschool.edu
FITZPATRICK, Mary Anne 803-777-7798.. 433 F
fitzpatm@mailbox.sc.edu
FITZPATRICK, Mary Anne 864-503-5200.. 434 G
maf@uscupstate.edu
FITZPATRICK, Michael ..... 620-672-5641.. 184 D
michaelf@prattcc.edu
FITZPATRICK, Pat .... 718-390-3131.. 339 F
pfitzpat@wagner.edu
FITZPATRICK, Scott, B .... 859-846-5300.. 191 G
sfitzpatrick@midway.edu
FITZPATRICK, Sharon ...... 405-945-3292.. 386 C
shfitzp@osuokc.edu
FITZPATRICK, Susan .... 906-635-2831.. 236 J
sfitzpatrick@lssu.edu
FITZPATRICK, Timothy, J 352-273-1325.. 112 A
timf@ufl.edu
FITZPATRICK,
Timothy, M .... 860-444-8603.. 529 A
timothy.m.fitzpatrick@uscga.edu
FITZPATRICK, Tracy .... 914-251-6105.. 334 C
tracy.fitzpatrick@purchase.edu
FITZSIMMONS, Joanne ... 518-445-2324.. 303 D
jfitz@albanylaw.edu
FITZSIMMONS, Peter .... 408-531-6130.... 62 C
peter.fitzsimmons@sjeccd.org
FITZSIMMONS,
Stephanie .... 732-224-2369.. 289 I
sfitzsimmons@brookdalecc.edu
FITZSIMMONS, Tracy ...... 540-665-4505.. 494 B
tfitzsim@su.edu
FITZSIMMONS, Verna, M 785-826-2601.. 182 D
vfitzsimmons@ksu.edu
FITZSIMONS, Connie .... 310-660-3715.... 42 J
cfitzsimons@elcamino.edu
FITZSIMONS, Debra .... 949-582-4665.... 65 E
dfitzsimons@socccd.edu
FIVECOAT, Frederick .... 610-892-1519.. 414 B
ffivecoat@pit.edu
FIXEN, Randall .... 701-662-1518.. 361 E
randy.fixen@lrsc.edu
FJORTOFT, Nancy, F .... 630-515-6072.. 148 C
nfjort@midwestern.edu
FLABIANO, Heather .... 314-446-8179.. 271 E
heather.flabiano@stlcop.edu
FLACK, Anna .... 631-451-4008.. 336 D
flacka@sunysuffolk.edu
FLACK, Felecia, J .... 906-227-1272.. 239 B
fflack@nmu.edu
FLACK, Lisa .... 217-228-5432.. 151 F
flackli@quincy.edu
FLACK, Tamala .... 315-228-7014.. 310 G
tflack@colgate.edu
FLACK, Toney .... 316-978-3919.. 185 J
toney.flack@wichita.edu
FLACK, Wayne, R .... 218-299-3362.. 246 A
flack@cord.edu
FLAD, Kiera .... 212-431-2164.. 323 H
kiera.flad@nyls.edu
FLAD-JESION, Ann, M .... 920-565-1104.. 517 D
flad-jesionad@lakeland.edu
FLADELAND, Diane .... 701-355-8140.. 362 G
dflade@umary.edu
FLADELAND, Sara .... 208-769-7750.. 134 C
sara_fladeland@nic.edu
FLADRY, Robert .... 303-753-6046.... 83 A
rfladry@rmcad.edu
FLAGEL, Andrew .... 781-736-2005.. 216 F
aflagel@brandeis.edu
FLAGG, Chuck, S .... 248-232-4811.. 239 E
csflagg@oaklandcc.edu
FLAGG, Mary .... 610-372-4721.. 417 G
mflagg@racc.edu
FLAGSTAD, Lois .... 605-642-6599.. 437 B
lois.flagstad@bhsu.edu
FLAGSTAD, Lois .... 605-642-6270.. 437 B
lois.flagstad@bhsu.edu
FLAGSTAD, Paul .... 952-446-4152.. 246 D
flagstadp@crown.edu
FLAHERTY, Anne .... 317-940-9570.. 159 K
aflahert@butler.edu
FLAHERTY, Anne, G .... 317-940-9470.. 159 K
aflahert@butler.edu
FLAHERTY, Jane .... 979-845-8588.. 468 B
jflaherty@tamu.edu
FLAHERTY, John .... 212-817-7769.. 308 A
jflaherty@gc.cuny.edu
FLAHERTY, Kathleen .... 914-337-9300.. 311 F
kathleen.flaherty@concordia-ny.edu
FLAHERTY, Mary Ellen .... 410-516-8404.. 208 D
mflaher8@jhu.edu
FLAHERTY, Michael .... 315-312-2106.. 333 D
michael.flaherty@oswego.edu
FLAHERTY, Pamela, B ..... 781-280-3631.. 224 A
flahertyp@middlesex.mass.edu
FLAHERTY, Richard, A ..... 617-746-5412.. 227 H
richard.flaherty@sjs.edu
FLAHIVE, Roger .... 973-328-5011.. 290 H
rflahive@ccm.edu
FLAKE, Forrest .... 801-422-3861.. 480 C
forrest_flake@byu.edu
FLAMER, Thelma .... 202-231-2768.. 528 C
thelma.flamer@dodiis.mil
FLAMM, Adele .... 302-736-2566.... 91 G
adele.flamm@wesley.edu
FLAMM, Andrew, R .... 574-372-5100.. 161 B
drew.flamm@grace.edu
FLANAGAN, Alyce .... 256-352-8295...... 9 G
alyce.malcolm@wallacestate.edu
FLANAGAN, Audra .... 218-733-7626.. 249 H
audra.flanagan@lsc.edu
FLANAGAN, Erin .... 619-388-3453.... 60 F
eflanaga@sdccd.edu
FLANAGAN, J. Kelly .... 801-422-3142.. 480 C
kelly_flanagan@byu.edu
FLANAGAN, James .... 407-582-5529.. 114 N
jflanagan@valenciacollege.edu
FLANAGAN, James .... 212-247-3434.. 319 K
jflanagan@mandl.edu
FLANAGAN, James, L .... 770-484-1204.. 124 C
lutherrice@lutherrice.edu
FLANAGAN, James, P .... 603-641-6025.. 287 G
jflanagan@anselm.edu
FLANAGAN, Jeanne .... 518-485-3902.. 311 B
flanagaj@strose.edu
FLANAGAN, John .... 510-642-3414.... 68 M
jgflanagan@berkeley.edu
FLANAGAN, Lori .... 314-516-5661.. 274 A
flanagamlo@umsl.edu
FLANAGAN, Mary Jane ... 989-774-3131.. 232 D
flana1mj@cmich.edu
FLANAGAN, Maureen, P . 215-574-9600.. 406 A
mflanagan@hussianart.edu
FLANAGAN, Melissa .... 770-962-7580.. 123 D
mflanagan@gwinnetttech.edu
FLANAGAN, Scott .... 608-663-2262.. 516 F
sflanagan@edgewood.edu
FLANDERS, Bruce .... 913-971-3568.. 183 D
blflanders@mnu.edu
FLANDERS, Lorene .... 678-839-6369.. 129 E
lflanders@westga.edu
FLANIGAN, Joanna .... 740-264-5591.. 368 D
jflanigan@egcc.edu
FLANIGAN, Marjie .... 304-384-6035.. 513 A
mflanigan@concord.edu
FLANIGAN, JR.,
Robert, D .... 404-270-5072.. 128 A
rflaniga@spelman.edu
FLANIK, Greg, G .... 440-826-2700.. 363 M
gflanik@bw.edu
FLANNAGAN, Larnell .... 318-274-3235.. 200 F
flannaganl@gram.edu
FLANNERY, Brenda .... 507-389-9423.. 250 E
brenda.flannery@mnsu.edu
FLANNERY, Chad .... 618-252-5400.. 154 G
chad.flannery@sic.edu
FLANNERY, Kathleen .... 620-235-4769.. 184 C
kflannery@pittstate.edu
FLANNERY, Kim .... 262-595-2301.. 520 F
bookstore@uwp.edu
FLANNERY, Maura, C .... 718-990-1860.. 328 F
flannerm@stjohns.edu
FLANNERY, Patrick .... 517-607-2239.. 235 E
pflannery@hillsdale.edu
FLANNERY,
Teresa (Terry) .... 202-885-2163.... 91 J
flannery@american.edu
FLASH, Kevin .... 916-558-2254.... 51 D
flashk@scc.losrios.edu
FLATEN, Mike .... 218-262-6749.. 249 E
mikeflaten@hibbing.edu
FLATLEY, Kate .... 314-889-1447.. 265 C
kflatley@fontbonne.edu
FLAUGHER, Amanda .... 989-775-4123.. 240 E
aflaugher@sagchip.edu
FLAUM, Leonard .... 210-458-4120.. 477 A
leonard.flaum@utsa.edu
FLAVIN, Stephen, P .... 508-831-5095.. 230 C
sflavin@wpi.edu
FLAX, Gale .... 252-335-0821.. 349 A
gale_flax@albemarle.edu
FLAX-HYMAN, Cheryl, L . 850-747-3215.. 102 M
cflax-hyman@gulfcoast.edu
FLEAGLE, Steven, R .... 319-384-0595.. 169 H
steve-fleagle@uiowa.edu
FLECHA, Gladys, E .... 787-852-1430.. 532 N
gflecha@hccpr.edu
FLECKINGER, Joe .... 405-878-5435.. 387 J
jmfleckinger@stgregorys.edu
FLEECE, David .... 937-722-9213.. 380 E
david.fleece@urbana.edu
FLEENOR, Leslie .... 724-938-4418.. 414 E
fleenor@calu.edu
FLEENOR, Rick .... 606-539-4154.. 193 F
rick.fleenor@ucumberlands.edu
FLEET, Frances .... 419-448-3326.. 378 A
ffleet@tiffin.edu
FLEETWOOD, Nick .... 619-596-2766.... 25 G
nfleetwood@advancedtraining.edu
FLEGE, Kelly, A .... 319-273-5885.. 170 A
kelly.flege@uni.edu
FLEISCHER, Sheila .... 516-239-9002.. 330 D
FLEISCHMAN, Linda .... 704-337-2543.. 355 A
fleischmanl@queens.edu
FLEISCHMAN, Robert .... 507-389-1333.. 250 E
robert.fleischman@mnsu.edu
FLEISCHMANN, Kenneth .. 314-367-8700.. 271 E
kenneth.fleischmann@stlcop.edu
FLEITAS, Dionisio .... 214-333-5481.. 455 J
dionisio@dbu.edu
FLEMING, A, L .... 803-536-7000.. 432 E
FLEMING, Allyson .... 615-327-6235.. 442 A
afleming@mmc.edu
FLEMING, Allyson, F .... 615-327-6111.. 442 A
FLEMING, Candace, C ..... 973-655-4040.. 293 A
flemingc@mail.montclair.edu
FLEMING, David .... 269-782-1201.. 241 C
dfleming@swmich.edu
FLEMING, Elizabeth .... 508-373-9537.. 215 D
elizabeth.corcoran@becker.edu
FLEMING, Elizabeth .... 413-565-1000.. 215 A
lfleming@baypath.edu
FLEMING, Erika .... 305-428-5700.. 105 E
efleming@aii.edu
FLEMING, J. Christopher 757-683-3685.. 492 G
jcflemin@odu.edu
FLEMING, James .... 503-352-1510.. 394 C
jfleming@pacificu.edu
FLEMING, SJ, James .... 304-243-2233.. 515 C
president@wju.edu
FLEMING, Jennifer .... 479-498-6020.... 19 F
jfleming@atu.edu
FLEMING, John .... 512-245-2308.. 471 F
jf18@txstate.edu
FLEMING, Joshua .... 518-736-3622.. 315 A
joshua.fleming@fmcc.suny.edu
FLEMING, Julie, C .... 770-720-5527.. 126 C
jcf@reinhardt.edu
FLEMING, Justin .... 507-786-3615.. 254 P
flemingj@stolaf.edu
FLEMING, Katherine .... 212-998-4568.. 324 C
kef1@nyu.edu
FLEMING, Kevin .... 951-739-7880.... 59 B
kevin.fleming@norcocollege.edu
FLEMING, Kirsten .... 909-537-5300.... 34 C
kfleming@csusb.edu
FLEMING, Latari .... 318-274-6100.. 200 F
flemingl@gram.edu
FLEMING, Leanna .... 603-623-0313.. 287 D
leannafleming@nhia.edu
FLEMING, Linda .... 814-871-7549.. 404 A
fleming006@gannon.edu
FLEMING, Mark .... 973-655-5225.. 293 A
flemingm@mail.montclair.edu
FLEMING, Mary Kay .... 513-244-4945.. 373 C
mary.kay.fleming@msj.edu
FLEMING, Michael, K .... 281-425-6231.. 460 I
mfleming@lee.edu
FLEMING, Mike, R .... 618-235-2700.. 155 C
mike.fleming@swic.edu
FLEMING, Patricia, A .... 574-284-4575.. 167 A
pfleming@saintmarys.edu
FLEMING, Paul, C .... 504-864-7490.. 198 E
pcflemin@loyno.edu
FLEMING, Richard .... 443-550-6021.. 207 B
rfleming@csmd.edu
FLEMING, Rita .... 501-686-2920.... 22 H
rfleming@uasys.edu
FLEMING, Robert .... 617-824-8670.. 218 B
robert_fleming@emerson.edu
FLEMING, Saundra, K ...... 773-878-4699.. 153 E
sfleming@staugustine.edu
FLEMING, Scott, S .... 202-687-3455.... 92 E
ssf2@georgetown.edu
FLEMING, Shezwae .... 301-624-2711.. 207 F
sfleming@frederick.edu
FLEMING, Siobhan .... 713-525-2112.. 475 J
sflemin@stthom.edu
FLEMING, Tom, O .... 310-338-2714.... 51 E
tfleming@lmu.edu
FLEMING, Trish .... 215-836-2222.. 397 F
tfleming@antonelli.edu
FLEMING, Wanda .... 757-873-1111.. 489 K
wanda.fleming@zenith.org
FLEMING, William, M .... 561-803-2001.. 106 C
william_fleming@pba.edu
FLEMING-WILLIS, Linda .. 614-825-6255.. 362 J
lfleming-willis@aiam.edu
FLEMMING, Sondra, G .... 214-860-2146.. 456 E
sflemming@dcccd.edu

FLENIKEN, Tracey ... 940-668-4207 .. 462 L tfleniken@nctc.edu

FLENNER, Ronald, W ... 757-446-5829 .. 489 B flennerw@evms.edu

FLESCHNER, Julius ... 712-279-5451 .. 170 B julius.fleschner@briarcliff.edu

FLESHLER, David ... 216-368-2399 .. 365 B david.fleshler@case.edu

FLESHNER, Amy ... 217-351-3818 .. 151 B afleshner@parkland.edu

FLESNER, Brian ... 402-826-8228 .. 280 B brian.flesner@doane.edu

FLETCHER, Bill ... 615-898-2500 .. 444 G bill.fletcher@mtsu.edu

FLETCHER, Carol ... 575-562-2611 .. 299 I carol.fletcher@enmu.edu

FLETCHER, Courtney ... 402-559-4333 .. 283 A cfletcher@unmc.edu

FLETCHER, Daryl ... 912-583-3230 .. 118 B dfletcher@bpc.edu

FLETCHER, David ... 706-649-1016 .. 119 F dfletcher@columbustech.edu

FLETCHER, James, A ... 208-282-3540 .. 133 H fletjame@isu.edu

FLETCHER, Janice ... 617-243-2145 .. 219 I jfletcher@lasell.edu

FLETCHER, John ... 252-328-5817 .. 356 C fletcherjo@ecu.edu

FLETCHER, Kathy ... 432-685-4526 .. 461 H kfletcher@midland.edu

FLETCHER, Kenneth Marty ... 808-969-8804 .. 131 J kmfletcher@hawaii.edu

FLETCHER, Lauronda ... 610-399-2224 .. 414 F lfletcher@cheyney.edu

FLETCHER, Leah ... 816-584-6407 .. 270 D leah.fletcher@park.edu

FLETCHER, Lynn ... 307-268-2211 .. 526 D lfletcher@caspercollege.edu

FLETCHER, Martha ... 615-844-5048 .. 449 H mfletcher@welch.edu

FLETCHER, Michael ... 229-333-2100 .. 130 A michael.fletcher@wiregrass.edu

FLETCHER, Randy ... 217-351-2236 .. 151 B rfletcher@parkland.edu

FLETCHER, Richard, L ... 440-826-2323 .. 363 M rfletche@bw.edu

FLETCHER, Scott ... 503-768-6001 .. 392 A graddean@lclark.edu

FLETCHER, Stephen ... 408-864-8642 .. 44 A fletcherstephen@deanza.edu

FLETCHER, Thomas ... 570-389-5161 .. 414 D tfletche@bloomu.edu

FLETCHER, Wanda ... 252-335-0821 .. 349 A wanda_fletcher@albemarle.edu

FLETCHER, William, A ... 843-953-5114 .. 428 A bill.fletcher@citadel.edu

FLEURISMOND, Jude ... 845-574-4224 .. 327 G jfleuri2@sunyrockland.edu

FLEURY, Karl ... 715-425-3133 .. 521 B karl.fleury@uwrf.edu

FLEURY, Traci ... 704-971-8538 .. 343 E tfleury@charlottelaw.edu

FLEWELLING, Colleen ... 570-372-4567 .. 419 H flewelling@susqu.edu

FLICK, Kay ... 508-849-3228 .. 214 E kflick@annamaria.edu

FLICK, Kenneth ... 843-525-8238 .. 433 B kflick@tcl.edu

FLICK, Larry ... 541-737-0123 .. 393 H larry.flick@oregonstate.edu

FLICK, Matt ... 937-294-0592 .. 377 B flick@saa.edu

FLICKER, John ... 928-350-4100 .. 16 P jflicker@prescott.edu

FLICKINGER, Catherine ... 516-686-7792 .. 323 G cflickin@nyit.edu

FLIEGE, Cheryl ... 309-694-5599 .. 141 F cfliege@icc.edu

FLING, Corey ... 619-849-2583 .. 57 M coreyfling@pointloma.edu

FLINN, Amy ... 254-298-8364 .. 467 B alflinn@templejc.edu

FLINN, Cara ... 479-979-1467 .. 24 I cflinn@ozarks.edu

FLINN, Randal ... 219-866-6165 .. 166 J rflinn@saintjoe.edu

FLINT, Aaron ... 603-645-9678 .. 287 I a.flint@snhu.edu

FLINT, Juanita ... 972-860-4694 .. 456 B juanitazf@dcccd.edu

FLINT, Laury ... 812-855-7621 .. 162 F lbarthol@indiana.edu

FLINT, Tora ... 310-577-3000 .. 75 H registrar@yosan.edu

FLINTOFT, Rebecca ... 303-273-3050 .. 78 M rflintof@mines.edu

FLIS, Denise ... 405-208-5848 .. 385 E dflis@okcu.edu

FLISS, Diana ... 507-223-1317 .. 250 G diana.fliss@mnwest.edu

FLLEMING, Kay ... 618-985-3741 .. 143 F kayfleming@jalc.edu

FLOCCHINI, Rancy ... 775-674-7688 .. 284 K rflocchini@tmcc.edu

FLOCK, Gretchen ... 724-805-2209 .. 419 A gretchen.flock@email.stvincent.edu

FLOCKEN, Lise ... 760-757-2121 .. 52 K lflocken@miracosta.edu

FLODEN, Robert ... 517-355-1734 .. 237 I floden@msu.edu

FLOHR, Robin ... 740-264-5591 .. 368 D rflohr@egcc.edu

FLOM, Sheldon ... 307-382-1609 .. 527 C sflom@westernwyoming.edu

FLOOD, Malia ... 619-482-6369 .. 66 E mflood@swccd.edu

FLOOD, Pierre ... 213-613-2200 .. 65 H pierre_flood@sciarc.edu

FLOOD, Thomas ... 718-489-5443 .. 328 D thomasflood@sfc.edu

FLOOD, Tim ... 619-421-6700 .. 66 E

FLOOD, Timothy, J ... 920-929-2136 .. 524 B tflood@morainepark.edu

FLOOD-WEINER, Christie ... 614-253-3502 .. 374 I weinerc@ohiodominican.edu

FLOOR, Gregory ... 617-850-1285 .. 219 F gfloor@hchc.edu

FLOR, Andrew, D ... 434-971-3304 .. 527 N andrew.d.flor.mil@mail.com

FLORA, Richard ... 727-302-6721 .. 108 D flora.richard@spcollege.edu

FLORCZAK, Joan, E ... 203-576-4665 .. 89 C joan@bridgeport.edu

FLOREN, Gillian ... 503-821-8888 .. 394 B gfloren@pnca.edu

FLORENCE, Bob, K ... 816-604-6546 .. 267 G bob.florence@mcckc.edu

FLORENCE, Brad ... 563-876-3353 .. 171 I bflorence@dwci.edu

FLORENCE, Christopher ... 314-434-4044 .. 264 C chris.florence@covenantseminary.edu

FLORENDO, Anthony ... 215-895-8737 .. 422 A a.florendo@usciences.edu

FLORENDO, Chava ... 541-552-6128 .. 395 A florendch@sou.edu

FLORENTINE, Dennis ... 908-835-2326 .. 298 E dflorentine@warren.edu

FLORES, Abraham ... 713-221-8685 .. 474 B floresa@uhd.edu

FLORES, Anna ... 480-517-8171 .. 14 G anna.flores@riosalado.edu

FLORES, Aron ... 559-325-3600 .. 30 C aflores@chsu.org

FLORES, Beatriz ... 787-753-6335 .. 532 O bflores@icprjc.edu

FLORES, Beatriz ... 787-753-6000 .. 532 O bflores@icprjc.edu

FLORES, Chio ... 509-682-6805 .. 509 D cflores@wvc.edu

FLORES, Deanna, L ... 407-303-1851 .. 95 C deanna.flores@adu.edu

FLORES, Eddie ... 575-538-6321 .. 303 A flores4@wnmu.edu

FLORES, Elizabeth ... 915-747-7872 .. 476 D lizaf@utep.edu

FLORES, Esmarelda ... 210-434-6711 .. 463 C emflores@lake.ollusa.edu

FLORES, Fernando ... 915-831-6391 .. 457 H fflore63@epcc.edu

FLORES, Gustavo ... 707-664-4388 .. 35 D gustavo.flores@sonoma.edu

FLORES, Hector ... 409-880-8305 .. 471 A hector.flores@lamar.edu

FLORES, Jaime ... 860-343-5805 .. 86 F jflores@mxcc.edu

FLORES, Javier ... 325-942-2047 .. 472 B javier.flores@angelo.edu

FLORES, Jayne, T ... 671-735-5638 .. 529 G pio@guamcc.edu

FLORES, Jennifer, L ... 520-626-9443 .. 17 I jenniferflores@email.arizona.edu

FLORES, John ... 214-637-3530 .. 479 C jflores@wadecollege.edu

FLORES, Juan ... 671-734-1812 .. 530 A jflores@piu.edu

FLORES, Kathy ... 253-680-7178 .. 501 E kflores@bates.ctc.edu

FLORES, Laureano ... 323-265-8640 .. 49 G floresl@elac.edu

FLORES, Lucinda ... 210-297-9638 .. 452 C lgflores@baptisthealthsystem.com

FLORES, Maria, E ... 787-743-7979 .. 536 A ut_mflores@suagm.edu

FLORES, Marilyn ... 714-628-5030 .. 58 H marilyn_flores@sccollege.edu

FLORES, Mary ... 208-792-2325 .. 134 A mflores@lcsc.edu

FLORES, Matt ... 512-245-2922 .. 471 F mgf20@txstate.edu

FLORES, Michael ... 210-486-3963 .. 450 A rflores@alamo.edu

FLORES, Michael ... 305-629-2929 .. 108 G mflores@sanignaciocollege.edu

FLORES, Michael ... 702-651-7336 .. 284 H michael.flores@csn.edu

FLORES, Mike ... 210-486-3960 .. 450 D rflores@alamo.edu

FLORES, Mildred ... 787-780-0070 .. 531 B mflores@caribbean.edu

FLORES, Minerva ... 707-468-3011 .. 52 C mflores@mendocino.edu

FLORES, Ricardo ... 787-701-5100 .. 532 H riflores@ediccollege.edu

FLORES, Robert, E ... 863-453-6661 .. 109 G robert.flores@southflorida.edu

FLORES, Waleska ... 787-184-1912 .. 534 C waflores@ponce.inter.edu

FLORES-CHURCH, Adriana ... 562-860-2451 .. 36 P achurch@cerritos.edu

FLORES GRIFFITH, Lisa ... 909-607-1887 .. 38 I lisa.griffith@cgu.edu

FLORES-LOPEZ, Brenda ... 423-236-2276 .. 444 B bfloreslopez@southern.edu

FLORES-MEDINA, Donna ... 505-454-5328 .. 299 M dflores@luna.edu

FLORES-SANTOS, Mayra, M ... 787-250-0000 .. 537 D mayra.flores@upr.edu

FLORESCA, Ann ... 270-745-6463 .. 194 D ann.floresca@wku.edu

FLOREY, Nancy ... 717-947-6098 .. 413 N neflorey@pacollege.edu

FLORIAN, Greg, E ... 217-875-7200 .. 152 C gflorian@richland.edu

FLORIAN, James, S ... 520-621-3680 .. 17 I florianj@email.arizona.edu

FLORIO, Laura, L ... 712-274-5381 .. 175 C floriol@morningside.edu

FLOROS, John ... 785-532-6147 .. 182 D floros@ksu.edu

FLORY, Julie, A ... 314-935-5408 .. 274 N julie.flory@wustl.edu

FLOT, Rob ... 847-735-5200 .. 145 B flot@lakeforest.edu

FLOTTE, Terence, R ... 508-856-8000 .. 221 B terry.flotte@umassmed.edu

FLOUHOUSE, Steve ... 606-326-2055 .. 188 N steve.flouhouse@kctcs.edu

FLOURNOY, Jacob, W ... 501-686-2901 .. 22 H jwflournoy@uasys.edu

FLOWER, Hannah ... 912-525-5000 .. 126 E hcrocket@scad.edu

FLOWER, Mark ... 212-621-3789 .. 308 E mflower@jjay.cuny.edu

FLOWER KIM, Laura ... 626-395-6330 .. 30 H laura.flowerkim@caltech.edu

FLOWERS, Carol, A ... 404-727-0833 .. 120 E caflowe@emory.edu

FLOWERS, Damon ... 734-677-5322 .. 242 G dflowers@wccnet.edu

FLOWERS, Daniel ... 574-284-4574 .. 167 A dflowers@saintmarys.edu

FLOWERS, Gayle ... 318-678-6000 .. 195 I gflowers@bpcc.edu

FLOWERS, Geni ... 843-521-4122 .. 434 A meflower@uscb.edu

FLOWERS, George ... 334-844-4700 .. 1 G flowegt@auburn.edu

FLOWERS, Juan ... 480-377-4561 .. 14 G juan.flowers@riosalado.edu

FLOWERS, Kathleen ... 315-781-3825 .. 316 C kflowers@hws.edu

FLOWERS, Ken ... 269-927-4103 .. 236 G flowers@lakemichigancollege.edu

FLOWERS, Laura ... 615-550-3168 .. 449 I laura@williamsoncc.edu

FLOWERS, Marshall ... 276-326-4355 .. 487 F mflowers@bluefield.edu

FLOWERS, Patricia, J ... 850-644-0415 .. 111 C pjflowers@fsu.edu

FLOWERS, Robert ... 315-781-3827 .. 316 C flowers@hws.edu

FLOYD, Andrew ... 229-430-3983 .. 115 K andrew.floyd@asurams.edu

FLOYD, Arlene ... 330-941-2333 .. 382 A afloyd@ysu.edu

FLOYD, Barbara ... 419-530-8549 .. 380 D barbara.floyd@utoledo.edu

FLOYD, Brian ... 304-367-4298 .. 512 D brian.floyd@pierpont.edu

FLOYD, Carey ... 580-371-2371 .. 384 D cfloyd@mscok.edu

FLOYD, Cindy ... 619-574-6909 .. 55 G cmfloyd@pacificcollege.edu

FLOYD, Daisy, H ... 478-301-2602 .. 124 D floyd_dh@law.mercer.edu

FLOYD, David ... 225-765-2437 .. 197 I dfloyd@su.edu

FLOYD, Dawn ... 828-328-7040 .. 345 H dawn.floyd@lr.edu

FLOYD, Deborah ... 561-297-4358 .. 110 K dfloyd@fau.edu

FLOYD, Donna ... 510-215-3804 .. 41 H dfloyd@contracosta.edu

FLOYD, India ... 215-612-6600 .. 398 G

FLOYD, James, J ... 909-621-8351 .. 38 J james.floyd@cmc.edu

FLOYD, Linda ... 706-233-7357 .. 127 A lfloyd@shorter.edu

FLOYD, Morris ... 316-942-4291 .. 183 I floydm@newmanu.edu

FLOYD, Polly, K ... 850-263-3261 .. 96 C pkfloyd@baptistcollege.edu

FLOYD, Shawnda ... 972-273-3482 .. 456 G shawndafloyd@dcccd.edu

FLOYD, Steven ... 405-585-5132 .. 385 B steven.floyd@okbu.edu

FLOYD, Tony ... 843-383-8175 .. 428 F tfloyd@coker.edu

FLUCKEY, Kari ... 402-461-7300 .. 280 D kfluckey@hastings.edu

FLUEGEMAN, Tere ... 949-582-4920 .. 65 E tfluegeman@socccd.edu

FLUGSTAD, Bjorn ... 928-523-4240 .. 15 H bjorn.flugstad@nau.edu

FLUGUM, Deborah ... 818-677-2301 .. 34 A deborah.flugum@csun.edu

FLUHARTY, Steven, J ... 215-898-7320 .. 421 E sasdean@sas.upenn.edu

FLUKE, Donald, W ... 574-372-5100 .. 161 B dwfluke@grace.edu

FLUKE, Gordon ... 505-428-1253 .. 301 K gordon.fluke@sfcc.edu

FLUKE, Lauri, A ... 405-585-5131 .. 385 B lauri.fluke@okbu.edu

FLUKER, Zillah ... 334-229-5679 .. 1 D zfluker@alasu.edu

FLUNDER, Urisonya ... 806-894-9611 .. 465 G uflunder@southplaincollege.edu

FLY, Chris ... 405-878-5142 .. 387 J cafly@stgregorys.edu

FLY, Pam ... 918-444-2060 .. 384 G fly@nsuok.edu

FLYER, Robert ... 440-365-5222 .. 371 H

FLYNN, JR., Charles, L ... 718-405-3232 .. 310 H charles.flynn@mountsaintvincent.edu

FLYNN, Chris ... 540-231-6557 .. 499 F flynnc@vt.edu

FLYNN, Christie ... 253-964-6553 .. 506 B cflynn@pierce.ctc.edu

FLYNN, Clif ... 864-503-5635 .. 434 G cflynn@uscupstate.edu

FLYNN, Daniel ... 561-297-0268 .. 110 K flynnd@fau.edu

FLYNN, Eric, F ... 203-285-2371 .. 86 C eflynn@gwcc.commnet.edu

FLYNN, Erin ... 503-725-8490 .. 394 G erin.flynn@pdx.edu

FLYNN, Gary ... 262-564-3218 .. 523 D flynng@gtc.edu

FLYNN, Jackie ... 412-391-7021 .. 422 F admissions@vettechinstitute.edu

FLYNN, Jeff ... 208-562-3220 .. 133 F jeffflynn@cwidaho.cc

FLYNN, Joan ... 410-617-5161 .. 208 G jflynn@loyola.edu

FLYNN, John ... 205-726-2732 .. 6 E jflynn@samford.edu

FLYNN, John, J ... 212-769-5055 .. 327 C

FLYNN, Karen ... 203-932-7317 .. 90 A kflynn@newhaven.edu

FLYNN, Kathy, A ... 319-296-4218 .. 173 B kathleen.flynn@hawkeyecollege.edu

FLYNN, Kevin ... 781-239-2549 .. 223 F kflynn@massbay.edu

FLYNN, Mari ... 570-945-8335 .. 406 H mari.flynn@keystone.edu

FLYNN, Marilyn, L ... 213-740-8311 .. 72 D mflynn@usc.edu

FLYNN, Mark ... 706-568-2080 .. 119 E flynn_mark@columbusstate.edu

FLYNN, Maura ... 716-926-8822 .. 316 B mflynn@hilbert.edu

FLYNN, Michael ... 716-685-9631 .. 323 A mflynn@nycc.edu

FLYNN, Seth, M ... 414-955-4780 .. 518 A sflynn@mcw.edu

FLYNN, Stuart, D ... 602-827-2066 .. 17 I flynns@email.arizona.edu

FLYNN, Thomas, F ... 610-796-8203 .. 397 D tom.flynn@alvernia.edu

FLYNN, Thomas, V ... 505-565-1413 .. 228 F tflynn@stonehill.edu

FOBBS, Shelia ... 318-274-3350 .. 200 F fobbshe@gram.edu

FOCARETO, Nicole ... 704-461-6665 .. 342 A nicolefocareto@bac.edu

FOCKLER, Debra ... 509-359-6348 .. 503 D dfockler@ewu.edu

FODNESS, Kacie, M ... 605-256-5100 .. 437 C kacie.fodness@dsu.edu

FOECKLER, Michael, S .... 540-636-2900.. 488 D
foeckler@christendom.edu
FOEHL, Brooks, L .... 413-597-4408.. 230 A
brooks.l.foehl@williams.edu
FOELSCH, Joseph .... 212-772-4540.. 308 D
jf1128@hunter.cuny.edu
FOERSTER, Amy, C .... 570-577-1954.. 398 L
amy.foerster@bucknell.edu
FOGARINO, Shirley .... 510-981-2852.... 57 B
sfogarino@peralta.edu
FOGARTY, John .... 850-644-1346.. 111 C
jfogarty@fsu.edu
FOGARTY, Raymond .... 401-232-6407.. 424 K
rfogarty@bryant.edu
FOGARTY, Timothy, P ..... 814-393-2235.. 414 G
tfogarty@clarion.edu
FOGARTY, William .... 413-552-2800.. 223 E
bfogarty@hcc.edu
FOGEL, Henry .... 312-341-3782.. 152 H
hfogel@roosevelt.edu
FOGEL, Kim .... 864-592-4600.. 432 H
FOGERSON, Linda .... 760-757-2121.... 52 K
lfogerson@miracosta.edu
FOGERTY, Jennifer .... 215-503-6335.. 420 E
jennifer.fogerty@jefferson.edu
FOGG, Davina, K .... 509-527-4201.. 508 F
davina.fogg@wwcc.edu
FOGG, Richard .... 785-320-4557.. 183 A
richardfogg@manhattantech.edu
FOGGS, Ranodore, M ...... 618-537-6911.. 147 F
rmfoggs@mckendree.edu
FOGLE, Laura .... 803-793-5129.. 429 D
foglel@denmarktech.edu
FOGLE, Leann .... 906-487-7276.. 234 A
leann.fogle@finlandia.edu
FOGLE, Shanda .... 803-780-1360.. 434 M
sruffin@voorhees.edu
FOGLEMAN, David .... 318-670-9590.. 199 J
dfogleman@susla.edu
FOGLIASSO, John .... 316-942-4291.. 183 I
fogliassoj@newmanu.edu
FOGT, James .... 314-340-3541.. 265 H
fogtj@hssu.edu
FOHRMAN, Jonathan .... 760-757-2121.... 52 K
jfohrman@miracosta.edu
FOIL WHITE, Quincy .... 704-330-6863.. 348 E
quincy.foil@cpcc.edu
FOISY, Brian, R .... 208-885-6174.. 134 G
brianfoisy@uidaho.edu
FOJTIK, Tom .... 920-424-3212.. 520 E
fojtik@uwosh.edu
FOK, Kristie .... 602-286-8062.... 14 B
kristie.fok@gatewaycc.edu
FOKUSORGBOR, Marlin .. 718-357-0500.. 329 E
mfokusorgbor@stpaulsschoolofnursing.edu
FOLBERG, Robert .... 248-370-3634.. 239 K
rfolberg@oakland.edu
FOLDA, Joe .... 719-549-2730.... 79 B
joe.folda@csupueblo.edu
FOLDEN, Tracey, Y .... 270-707-3825.. 189 G
tracey.folden@kctcs.edu
FOLDS-BENNETT, Trisha, H .... 843-953-5084.. 428 G
foldsbennettt@cofc.edu
FOLENSBEE, Michael .... 215-635-7300.. 404 D
mfolensbee@gratz.edu
FOLEY, Anne .... 312-369-7477.. 138 F
afoley@colum.edu
FOLEY, Beth .... 435-797-1437.. 482 B
beth.foley@usu.edu
FOLEY, Brad .... 541-346-5661.. 395 G
bfoley@uoregon.edu
FOLEY, Chris .... 844-948-4863.. 162 F
cfoley@iu.edu
FOLEY, Erin .... 410-532-3586.. 210 B
efoley@ndm.edu
FOLEY, Erin .... 541-885-1013.. 393 G
erin.foley@oit.edu
FOLEY, Gary, A .... 803-535-1264.. 431 I
foleyg@octech.edu
FOLEY, Henry (Hank), C .. 573-882-3387.. 273 E
foleyh@missouri.edu
FOLEY, Ian .... 919-658-7778.. 355 K
ifoley@umo.edu
FOLEY, Janice, A .... 336-841-9506.. 345 A
jfoley@highpoint.edu
FOLEY, Jeremy, N .... 352-375-4683.. 112 A
jeremy@gators.uaa.ufl.edu
FOLEY, John .... 508-793-7444.. 217 B
jfoley@clarku.edu
FOLEY, John .... 716-851-1114.. 313 H
foleyj@ecc.edu
FOLEY, Kathleen .... 570-674-6403.. 410 K
kfoley@misericordia.edu
FOLEY, Kevin .... 631-451-4380.. 336 D
foleyk@sunysuffolk.edu
FOLEY, Leslie Wu .... 617-585-1130.. 226 F
leslie.foley@necmusic.edu
FOLEY, Linda .... 402-354-7050.. 281 F
linda.foley@methodistcollege.edu
FOLEY, Lisa .... 530-541-4660.... 48 D
foley@ltcc.edu
FOLEY, Marie .... 973-761-9015.. 297 A
marie.foleyll@shu.edu
FOLEY, Mary .... 620-792-9278.. 178 G
foleym@bartonccc.edu
FOLEY, Nick .... 816-331-5700.. 270 E
nfoley@pcitraining.edu
FOLEY, Paul, J .... 563-333-6025.. 176 D
foleypaulj@sau.edu
FOLEY, Phyllis .... 615-230-4828.. 447 C
phyllis.foley@volstate.edu
FOLEY, Richard, T .... 304-457-6260.. 510 B
foleyrt@ab.edu
FOLEY, Rob .... 303-357-5838.... 79 I
rob.foley@denverseminary.edu
FOLEY, Ryan .... 912-688-6061.. 125 E
rfoley@ogeecheetech.edu
FOLEY, Thomas .... 413-265-2494.. 217 D
foleyt@elms.edu
FOLEY, Thomas, P .... 814-886-6411.. 411 C
tfoley@mtaloy.edu
FOLEY, Tim .... 503-943-8130.. 396 B
foleyt@up.edu
FOLGER, Pamela, M .... 217-424-6294.. 148 D
pmfolger@millikin.edu
FOLKESTAD, William .... 719-549-2865.... 79 B
william.folkestad@csupueblo.edu
FOLKS, Liesl .... 716-645-2771.. 331 C
seasdean@eng.buffalo.edu
FOLKS, Lonnie .... 609-652-4877.. 297 C
lonnie.folks@stockton.edu
FOLLICK, David .... 516-572-7210.. 322 C
david.follick@ncc.edu
FOLLICK, Edwin .... 714-533-1495.... 65 B
edfollick@southbaylo.edu
FOLLOWELL, Coleen .... 562-985-4121.... 33 B
coleen.followell@csulb.edu
FOLLOWELL, Wendell .... 859-256-3100.. 188 M
wendell.followell@kctcs.edu
FOLMER CLINTON, Leslie .... 717-477-1738.. 416 A
lfclin@ship.edu
FOLSE, Dick .... 309-556-3058.. 143 D
dfolse@iwu.edu
FOLSE, Victoria .... 309-556-3051.. 143 D
nursing@iwu.edu
FOLSOM, Michele .... 716-888-8367.. 306 F
folsom@canisius.edu
FOLT, Carol, L .... 919-962-1365.. 357 D
carol.folt@unc.edu
FOLTIN, Craig .... 216-987-4705.. 367 E
craig.foltin@tri-c.edu
FOLTZ, Amber .... 540-869-0799.. 497 E
afoltz@lfcc.edu
FOLTZ, Dyane .... 859-344-3531.. 193 C
foltzd@thomasmore.edu
FOLTZ, John .... 208-885-4159.. 134 G
jfoltz@uidaho.edu
FOLTZ, Kyla .... 307-268-2111.. 526 D
kfoltz@caspercollege.edu
FOLZ, James .... 518-828-4181.. 311 D
folz@sunycgcc.edu
FONDILLER, Jennifer .... 212-854-2817.. 304 I
jfondill@barnard.edu
FONG, Bruce, W .... 713-917-3941.. 457 C
bfong@dts.edu
FONG, Harry, M .... 408-554-4397.... 63 E
hfong@scu.edu
FONG, Lindy .... 323-780-6738.... 49 G
fonglw@elac.edu
FONG, Matt .... 402-461-7786.. 280 D
mfong@hastings.edu
FONG, Norman .... 916-686-8885.... 31 F
FONG, Steve .... 503-552-1584.. 392 H
sfong@nunm.edu
FONG, Wyman .... 952-485-5261.... 37 A
wfong@clpccd.org
FONG, Wyman .... 925-485-5261.... 37 B
wfong@clpccd.org
FONG, Yaa-Yin .... 808-956-7800.. 131 D
yaayin@hawaii.edu
FONGER, Ron .... 503-493-6510.. 391 A
rfonger@cu-portland.edu
FONJWENG, Godlove .... 607-431-4414.. 315 E
fonjwengg@hartwick.edu
FONOIMOANA, David ...... 808-675-3565.. 130 E
david.fonoimoana@byuh.edu
FONS, August .... 575-492-2721.. 300 H
afons@nmjc.edu
FONSECA, Anthony .... 413-265-2280.. 217 D
fonsecaa@elms.edu
FONSECA, Mimi .... 503-517-1100.. 396 D
mfonseca@warnerpacific.edu
FONT, Iris, J .... 787-740-4282.. 536 G
iris.font@uccaribe.edu
FONTAINE, Christopher, W .... 903-233-4071.. 460 J
chrisfontaine@letu.edu
FONTAINE, Dan .... 713-792-2121.. 477 F
FONTAINE, David .... 315-792-3050.. 339 B
dsfontaine@utica.edu
FONTAINE, Deborah .... 850-729-6451.. 105 I
fontaind@nwfsc.edu
FONTAINE, Deborah, C ... 757-823-8323.. 492 F
dcfontaine@nsu.edu
FONTAINE, Dorrie, K .... 434-924-0063.. 495 H
dkf2u@virginia.edu
FONTAINE, Kenneth .... 203-254-4000.... 87 G
kfontaine@fairfield.edu
FONTAINE, Linda .... 512-492-3014.. 451 E
FONTAINE, Paul, V .... 401-865-1575.. 425 D
FONTAINE, Sheryl .... 657-278-2024.... 33 A
sfontaine@fullerton.edu
FONTANAZZA, Angelo ..... 410-334-2933.. 213 G
afontanazza@worwic.edu
FONTANET-MALDONADO, Julio, E .... 787-751-1912.. 534 E
jfontane@juris.inter.edu
FONTANEZ, Eduardo .... 787-857-3600.. 533 I
efontanez@br.inter.edu
FONTANILLA, Linda .... 949-451-5214.... 65 F
lfontanilla@ivc.edu
FONTENETTE, Edward ...... 870-575-8000.... 23 E
fontenettee@uapb.edu
FONTENOT, Gwen .... 337-482-6491.. 201 D
fontenotg@louisiana.edu
FONTENOT, Janet, S .... 618-235-2700.. 155 C
janet.fontenot@swic.edu
FONTENOT, Karen .... 985-549-2101.. 201 C
kfontenot@selu.edu
FONTENOT, Olufunke ...... 229-430-4635.. 115 K
olufunke.fontenot@asurams.edu
FONTENOT, Patrick .... 210-486-4431.. 450 C
pfontenot@alamo.edu
FONTENOT, Roxane .... 337-475-5090.. 200 H
rfontenot@mcneese.edu
FONTES, Mary .... 218-793-2460.. 251 C
mary.fontes@northlandcollege.edu
FONTOURA, Ana .... 914-654-5456.. 311 A
afontoura@cnr.edu
FONTS, Raul, A .... 401-865-2754.. 425 D
rfonts@providence.edu
FONVILLE, John, A .... 252-638-7220.. 349 B
fonvillj@cravencc.edu
FOOSE, David .... 913-234-0650.. 179 M
david.foose@cleveland.edu
FOOTE, Bruce .... 815-740-3403.. 157 F
bfoote@stfrancis.edu
FOOTE, Chandra .... 716-286-8549.. 324 E
cjf@niagara.edu
FOOTE, Clarinda, L .... 870-307-7327.... 21 A
clarinda.foote@lyon.edu
FOOTE, Jeffrey, C .... 518-255-5300.. 334 D
footjc@cobleskill.edu
FOOTE, Monica, W .... 718-939-5100.. 319 A
mfoote@libi.edu
FOOTER, Nancy, S .... 214-752-5970.. 475 A
nancy.footer@untsystem.edu
FORAN, Fred .... 718-940-5346.. 328 G
fforan@sjcny.edu
FORBES, Beverly .... 757-683-4393.. 492 G
bforbes@odu.edu
FORBES, Cassie .... 828-766-1240.. 351 B
cforbes@mayland.edu
FORBES, Dan .... 503-494-6004.. 393 F
forbesd@ohsu.edu
FORBES, Gerald .... 580-559-5208.. 383 H
gforbes@ecok.edu
FORBES, J. Thomas .... 812-855-5394.. 162 E
jtforbes@indiana.edu
FORBES, J.T .... 812-855-5700.. 162 F
forbesjt@indiana.edu
FORBES, Karen, J .... 610-330-5005.. 407 C
forbesk@lafayette.edu
FORBES, Lindi, D .... 620-421-6700.. 182 G
lindif@labette.edu
FORBES, Scott .... 713-500-3289.. 477 C
scott.forbes@uth.tmc.edu
FORBES, Shawna .... 313-496-2587.. 242 H
sforbes1@wcccd.edu
FORBES, Suzetta, R .... 906-932-4231.. 234 C
suef@gogebic.edu
FORBES, Tonya .... 919-866-5595.. 353 I
tpforbes@waketech.edu
FORBES, Valery, E .... 612-624-2244.. 255 H
veforbes@umn.edu
FORBES ISAIS, Geraldine 505-277-2879.. 302 F
gforbes@unm.edu
FORBES MURPHY, Dawn 336-334-7595.. 356 F
dmurphy@ncat.edu
FORBESS, Tim .... 937-769-1825.. 363 E
tforbess@antioch.edu
FORCE, Bruce .... 918-293-5456.. 386 B
bruce.force@okstate.edu
FORCE, Darcy .... 817-202-6629.. 466 C
dforce@swau.edu
FORCINITO, Lorraine .... 262-524-7124.. 515 J
lforcini@carrollu.edu
FORD, Amy .... 580-559-5725.. 383 H
aford@ecok.edu
FORD, Beth .... 216-373-5351.. 374 B
bford@ndc.edu
FORD, Bob .... 509-963-2752.. 501 K
robert.ford@cwu.edu
FORD, Cathy .... 567-661-7398.. 376 D
catherine_ford@owens.edu
FORD, Charlene .... 912-443-4150.. 126 G
cford@savannahtech.edu
FORD, Chris .... 270-686-4291.. 187 C
chris.ford@brescia.edu
FORD, Clarice .... 217-206-6581.. 156 G
cford21@uis.edu
FORD, Deborah, L .... 262-595-2211.. 520 F
deborah.ford@uwp.edu
FORD, Dwedor .... 937-376-6657.. 365 H
dford@centralstate.edu
FORD, Felicia .... 334-347-2623...... 3 H
fford@escc.edu
FORD, Glenn .... 870-633-4480.... 20 B
gford@eacc.edu
FORD, Glenn, R .... 425-602-3040.. 501 D
gford@bastyr.edu
FORD, James .... 805-893-3174.... 70 E
j.ford@summer.ucsb.edu
FORD, Jean .... 734-384-4274.. 238 C
jford@monroeccc.edu
FORD, Jeff .... 417-690-3292.. 263 E
FORD, John .... 415-476-4998.... 70 D
jford@support.ucsf.edu
FORD, Kathy .... 909-469-5542.... 74 K
kford@westernu.edu
FORD, Kelli .... 317-917-5731.. 164 F
kford50@ivytech.edu
FORD, Kim, R .... 202-274-6726.... 94 B
kford@udc.edu
FORD, Kimberly .... 330-337-6403.. 362 I
college@awc.edu
FORD, Kristie, A .... 518-580-5425.. 330 F
kford@skidmore.edu
FORD, Lacy, K .... 803-777-2808.. 433 F
ford@mailbox.sc.edu
FORD, Laura, C .... 309-794-7452.. 135 D
lauraford@augustana.edu
FORD, Lynne, E .... 843-953-6531.. 428 G
fordl@cofc.edu
FORD, Madeline .... 718-518-4211.. 308 C
mford@hostos.cuny.edu
FORD, Mark, C .... 913-971-3614.. 183 D
mford@mnu.edu
FORD, Mary Beth .... 412-396-2061.. 403 A
fordmb@duq.edu
FORD, Michael .... 312-341-2322.. 152 H
mford@roosevelt.edu
FORD, Michelle .... 802-764-2139.. 484 G
michelle.ford@neci.edu
FORD, Nancy .... 620-365-5116.. 178 A
ford@allencc.edu
FORD, III, Obie .... 828-298-3325.. 359 F
oford@warren-wilson.edu
FORD, Pamela, R .... 318-257-3031.. 200 G
prford@latech.edu
FORD, Patrick .... 704-461-6545.. 342 A
patrickford@bac.edu
FORD, Ricky, G .... 662-720-7730.. 260 B
rgford@nemcc.edu
FORD, Robert .... 909-607-1554.... 38 I
robert.ford@cgu.edu
FORD, Shelly .... 601-928-6222.. 259 C
shelly.ford@mgccc.edu
FORD, Sherry .... 970-943-7052.... 84 H
sford@western.edu
FORD, Susan .... 618-453-5744.. 154 I
provost@siu.edu
FORD, Sylverna, V .... 901-678-2201.. 445 C
sford@memphis.edu
FORD, Wallace .... 718-270-5067.. 309 B
wford@mec.cuny.edu
FORD, Wanda .... 850-599-3527.. 110 J
wanda.ford@famu.edu
FORD FISHER, Margaret . 713-718-8010.. 459 B
margaret.fordfisher@hccs.edu
FORD-KEE, Dianthia .... 662-254-3550.. 260 A
dfkee@mvsu.edu
FORDE, Althea .... 718-960-8066.. 308 B
althea.forde@lehman.cuny.edu
FORDE, Christopher .... 617-544-8657.. 142 D
fordec@iecc.edu
FORDE, David, L .... 215-596-8719.. 422 A
d.forde@usciences.edu
FORDE, Dermot, M .... 419-372-9475.. 364 E
dforde@bgsu.edu
FORDE, Kevin .... 304-243-2053.. 515 C
kforde@wju.edu
FORDHAM, Traci .... 971-722-4667.. 394 F
traci.fordham@pcc.edu
FORDHAM, Tracy .... 941-377-4880.. 105 C
FORDIS, JR., C. Michael 713-798-8256.. 452 G
fordis@bcm.edu
FORE, Janet, S .... 574-284-5281.. 167 A
jfore@saintmarys.edu

FORE, Marilyn .... 843-349-5208.. 430 F
marilyn.fore@hgtc.edu
FORE, Taylor .... 208-769-7806.. 134 C
tlfore@nic.edu
FOREE, Amy .... 870-612-2144.... 23 H
amy.foree@uaccb.edu
FOREHAND, Cynthia, J ... 802-656-8060.. 485 D
cynthia.forehand@uvm.edu
FOREMAN, Adam .... 601-484-8615.. 258 F
tforeman@meridiancc.edu
FOREMAN, Artie .... 601-635-2111.. 257 F
aforeman@eccc.edu
FOREMAN, Hank, T .... 828-262-7525.. 356 B
foremanht@appstate.edu
FOREMAN, Karen, N .... 540-868-7109.. 497 E
kforeman@lfcc.edu
FOREMAN, Kyle .... 509-793-2299.. 501 H
kylef@bigbend.edu
FOREMAN, Margo .... 515-294-0123.. 169 G
mrforma@iastate.edu
FOREMAN, Marquis, D .... 312-942-7117.. 153 B
marquis_d_foreman@rush.edu
FOREMAN, Pamela, B .... 804-257-5821.. 500 B
pforeman@vuu.edu
FOREMAN, Todd, D .... 607-436-2081.. 331 F
todd.foreman@oneonta.edu
FOREST, John .... 918-270-6421.. 386 I
john.forest@ptstulsa.edu
FOREST, Laura Ann .... 334-844-6444...... 1 G
laf0009@auburn.edu
FOREST, Mark .... 609-771-2247.. 290 F
forestm@tcnj.edu
FOREST, Rebecca .... 978-632-6600.. 224 B
r_forest@mwcc.mass.edu
FOREST, Rebecca .... 978-630-9597.. 224 B
r_forest@mwcc.mass.edu
FOREST, Robert .... 610-647-4400.. 406 B
rforest@immaculata.edu
FORESTELL, Paul .... 315-279-5202.. 318 C
pforestell@keuka.edu
FORESTER, Lyn .... 402-826-8631.. 280 B
lyn.forester@doane.edu
FORESTER, Sherri, L .... 270-901-1115.. 190 F
sherri.forester@kctcs.edu
FORESYTH, Jan .... 432-264-5051.. 459 D
jforesyth@howardcollege.edu
FORGER, James .... 517-355-4583.. 237 I
forger@msu.edu
FORGET, Rob .... 507-537-6141.. 252 E
robert.forget@smsu.edu
FORGET, Robert, L .... 608-796-3012.. 522 O
rlforget@viterbo.edu
FORGETTE, Adrienne .... 505-566-3217.. 301 J
forgettea@sanjuancollege.edu
FORGEY, Laura .... 281-283-2180.. 474 A
forgey@uhcl.edu
FORHAN-MULCAHY,
Katie .... 513-558-5164.. 379 C
foranmkn@ucmail.uc.edu
FORINA, Olga .... 718-818-6470.. 329 F
FORK, Patricia, A .... 614-235-4136.. 378 C
pfork@tlsohio.edu
FORKNER, Peter .... 781-891-2274.. 215 F
pforkner@bentley.edu
FORLINES, Jon .... 615-844-5258.. 449 H
jforlines@welch.edu
FORLINES, Susan .... 615-844-5259.. 449 H
susan@welch.edu
FORMAN, Fran .... 417-690-3223.. 263 E
fforman@cofo.edu
FORMAN, Gary .... 415-476-5544.... 70 D
gary.forman@ucsf.edu
FORMAN, Kristi .... 901-321-4208.. 439 E
kforman@cbu.edu
FORMAN, Robert, J .... 718-990-7552.. 328 F
honors@stjohns.edu
FORMAN, Robin .... 504-865-5261.. 200 C
rforman@tulane.edu
FORMAN,
Scheherazade, W .... 301-546-0886.. 210 C
formansw@pgcc.edu
FORMAN, Tyrone, A .... 312-355-1308.. 156 F
tyforman@uic.edu
FORMICA, Melinda .... 203-582-3735.... 88 G
melinda.formica@quinnipiac.edu
FORNERIN, Miguel .... 787-738-2161.. 538 A
miguel.fornerin@upr.edu
FORNERIS, Glenda .... 815-802-8835.. 144 C
gforneris@kcc.edu
FORNEY, Heather .... 605-394-2373.. 437 E
heather.forney@sdsmt.edu
FORNEY, Judith .... 940-565-2436.. 475 A
judith.forney@unt.edu
FORNIERI, Diane, K .... 516-323-3000.. 321 H
dfornieri@molloy.edu
FORRAY, April .... 414-847-3233.. 518 D
aprilforray@miad.edu
FORRER, Janine .... 763-433-1216.. 248 K
janine.forrer@anokaramsey.edu
FORREST, Barbara .... 205-665-6055...... 9 B
forrestb@montevallo.edu
FORREST, Christian .... 248-204-2204.. 237 B
cforrest@ltu.edu
FORREST, Christy .... 336-249-8186.. 349 C
clforrest@davidsonccc.edu
FORREST, Danae .... 585-567-9200.. 316 F
danae.forrest@houghton.edu
FORREST, Seth .... 410-951-6183.. 212 E
sforrest@coppin.edu
FORRESTER, Cynthia .... 913-758-6114.. 185 F
cynthia.forrester@stmary.edu
FORRESTER, Don .... 540-785-5440.. 496 A
donforrester@vbc.edu
FORRESTER, Jill, M .... 717-245-1669.. 402 D
forrestj@dickinson.edu
FORRESTER, Julie .... 214-768-2574.. 465 J
jforrest@smu.edu
FORRESTER, Liane .... 406-683-7530.. 277 A
liane.forrester@umwestern.edu
FORRESTER, Lyndy, D .... 806-371-5044.. 450 H
lforrester@actx.edu
FORRESTER, Michael, P .. 864-592-4805.. 432 H
forresterm@sccsc.edu
FORRESTER, Risa .... 405-425-5954.. 385 C
risa.forrester@oc.edu
FORRESTER, Sallie .... 334-833-4527...... 4 D
sforrester@hawks.huntingdon.edu
FORRIDER, Holly .... 330-337-6403.. 362 I
college@awc.edu
FORRIDER, Timothy .... 330-337-6403.. 362 I
college@awc.edu
FORRY, Jennifer .... 617-713-5901.. 226 J
jennifer.forry@newbury.edu
FORSBERG, Peggy .... 785-442-6013.. 181 H
pforsberg@highlandcc.edu
FORSDICK, Emily .... 901-321-3461.. 439 E
emathis@cbu.edu
FORSETH, Eric, A .... 712-722-6004.. 171 J
eric.forseth@dordt.edu
FORSHEE, Scott .... 406-657-2298.. 277 D
sforshee@msubillings.edu
FORSHEY, Jennifer .... 906-932-4231.. 234 C
jennifer@gogebic.edu
FORSMAN, Carl .... 336-770-3236.. 358 E
forsmanc@uncsa.edu
FORSSTROM, Janice, M .. 978-762-4000.. 224 C
jforsstr@northshore.edu
FORSTER, Jerry .... 304-929-1478.. 511 E
jerryforster@ucwv.edu
FORSTER, Kathy .... 716-673-3341.. 331 D
kathy.forster@fredonia.edu
FORSTER, Michael .... 601-266-5253.. 261 E
michael.forster@usm.edu
FORSTER, Patrick .... 503-821-8912.. 394 B
pforster@pnca.edu
FORSTER, Sarah .... 507-222-4206.. 245 C
sforster@carleton.edu
FORSTER, Stefanie .... 207-216-4321.. 204 B
sforster@yccc.edu
FORSTMAN, Valerie .... 817-257-7513.. 453 O
v.forstman@tcu.edu
FORSYTH, Anne, S .... 805-525-4417.... 67 J
aforsyth@thomasaquinas.edu
FORSYTH, Nate .... 641-648-4611.. 173 K
nate.forsyth@iavalley.edu
FORSYTHE, Mary, E .... 910-962-3154.. 358 D
forsythem@uncw.edu
FORSYTHE, Robert, E .... 313-577-4501.. 243 F
robert.forsythe@wayne.edu
FORSYTHE, Ryan .... 508-929-8498.. 222 F
rforsythe@worcester.edu
FORT, Gregg .... 607-431-4026.. 315 E
fortg@hartwick.edu
FORT, Rebecca, L .... 330-471-8313.. 371 J
rfort@malone.edu
FORTE, Joe .... 603-456-2656.. 287 E
jforte@northeastcatholic.edu
FORTE, Mario .... 831-582-4796.... 33 E
mforte@csumb.edu
FORTE, Teresa (Terrie) .. 413-747-0204.. 217 A
teresa.forte@cambridgecollege.edu
FORTE-PARNELL,
Charlotte .... 661-722-6300.... 27 B
cforteparnell@avc.edu
FORTGANG, William .... 631-656-3189.. 314 F
william.fortgang@ftc.edu
FORTHMAN, Emily .... 618-634-3223.. 154 B
emilyf@shawneecc.edu
FORTHOFER, Scott .... 406-496-4500.. 277 G
sforthofer@mtech.edu
FORTI, Kevin .... 401-454-6651.. 426 A
kforti@risd.edu
FORTIN, Barbara .... 530-898-4113.... 32 C
bfortin@csuchico.edu
FORTIN, Maurice, G .... 325-942-2222.. 472 B
maurice.fortin@angelo.edu
FORTIN-WAVRA, Marion .. 402-554-4800.. 283 B
mfortin-wavra@unomaha.edu
FORTINI, Mary-Ellen .... 408-554-4806.... 63 E
mfortini@scu.edu
FORTINO, Matthew .... 212-924-5900.. 336 I
mfortino@swedishinstitute.edu
FORTMAN, Brian, J .... 864-833-8258.. 432 B
bjfortman@presby.edu
FORTMAN, Susan .... 516-323-4311.. 321 H
sfortman@molloy.edu
FORTNER, Beverly .... 785-832-6659.. 181 E
beverly.fortner@bie.edu
FORTNER, Everette .... 434-924-8900.. 495 H
ewf5db@virginia.edu
FORTNER, James .... 404-894-7894.. 121 D
james.fortner@business.gatech.edu
FORTNER, Martin .... 318-670-9322.. 199 J
mfortner@susla.edu
FORTNER, Melissa .... 706-865-2134.. 128 D
mfortner@truett.edu
FORTNEY, Jesse .... 615-297-7545.. 438 F
fortneyj@aquinascollege.edu
FORTOSIS, Robert .... 727-864-8252.... 98 L
fortoscr@eckerd.edu
FORTSCH, Peggy .... 319-226-2031.. 169 D
peggy.fortsch@allencollege.edu
FORTSON, Carolyn .... 803-793-5213.. 429 D
fortsonc@denmarktech.edu
FORTSON, Jill .... 325-674-2653.. 449 J
jill.fortson@acu.edu
FORTUNATO, Frank .... 904-264-2172.. 107 N
frank.fortunato@om.org
FORTUNE, Beth .... 615-322-4234.. 449 A
beth.fortune@vanderbilt.edu
FORTUNE, Diana .... 518-891-2915.. 325 A
dfortune@nccc.edu
FORTWENDEL, Kevin .... 412-365-1258.. 400 G
kfortwendel@chatham.edu
FOSCHIA, Christine .... 724-805-2524.. 419 A
chris.foschia@stvincent.edu
FOSDYCK, Rick .... 641-683-5117.. 173 C
rick.fosdyck@indianhills.edu
FOSHANG, Trevor .... 952-885-5462.. 253 Z
tfoshang@nwhealth.edu
FOSHEE, Brian, E .... 901-843-3870.. 443 L
foshee@rhodes.edu
FOSHEE, Kenneth, H .... 205-348-2857...... 8 D
ken.foshee@ua.edu
FOSKEY, Becky .... 478-289-2104.. 120 C
bfoskey@ega.edu
FOSS, Ben .... 941-487-4777.. 111 D
bfoss@ncf.edu
FOSS, Erica .... 620-278-4213.. 185 A
efoss@sterling.edu
FOSS, Jennifer, J .... 757-683-3132.. 492 G
jfoss@odu.edu
FOSS, Lisa .... 320-308-4028.. 252 A
lhfoss@stcloudstate.edu
FOSS, Michael, C .... 413-755-4510.. 224 G
mfoss@stcc.edu
FOSSEN, Linda .... 360-752-8440.. 501 G
lfossen@btc.edu
FOSSUM, Dallas .... 701-671-2314.. 361 F
dallas.fossum@ndscs.edu
FOSSUM, Scott .... 605-995-7178.. 436 C
scott.fossum@mitchelltech.edu
FOSSUM, Theresa, W .... 630-515-7663.. 148 C
tfossum@midwestern.edu
FOSTER, Adrienne .... 310-287-4589.... 50 E
fosteraa@wlac.edu
FOSTER, Alan .... 918-781-7285.. 382 D
fostera@bacone.edu
FOSTER, Andrew .... 203-773-8542.... 85 C
afoster@albertus.edu
FOSTER, Anne .... 513-569-1898.. 366 D
anne.foster@cincinnatistate.edu
FOSTER, Ben .... 972-524-3341.. 466 F
FOSTER, Cherie, A .... 248-341-2117.. 239 E
cafoster@oaklandcc.edu
FOSTER, Clark, M .... 518-564-3601.. 334 A
fostercm@plattsburgh.edu
FOSTER, Claybourne .... 901-435-1307.. 441 C
claybourne_foster@loc.edu
FOSTER, Connie .... 270-745-2904.. 194 D
connie.foster@wku.edu
FOSTER, Delbert, T .... 803-536-8191.. 432 E
dfoster@scsu.edu
FOSTER, Donna .... 864-941-8430.. 432 A
foster.d@ptc.edu
FOSTER, Dyrell .... 951-571-6384.... 59 A
dyrell.foster@mvc.edu
FOSTER, Gretchen, K .... 308-635-6183.. 283 D
fosterg2@wncc.edu
FOSTER, Isaac .... 646-378-6125.. 325 C
isaac.foster@nyack.edu
FOSTER, Jacqueline .... 910-362-7019.. 343 A
jfoster@cfcc.edu
FOSTER, James, E .... 503-554-2144.. 391 D
jfoster@georgefox.edu
FOSTER, Janet .... 562-985-5459.... 33 B
janet.foster@csulb.edu
FOSTER, Jennifer, M .... 937-775-3386.. 331 H
jennifer.foster@wright.edu
FOSTER, Joseph .... 703-284-1646.. 492 A
joseph.foster@marymount.edu
FOSTER, Karen .... 318-342-5236.. 201 E
kfoster@ulm.edu
FOSTER, Karen .... 208-535-5343.. 133 G
karen.foster@my.eitc.edu
FOSTER, Kathryn, A .... 207-778-7256.. 205 A
kfoster@maine.edu
FOSTER, Kathryn, V .... 512-232-3316.. 476 B
k.foster@austin.utexas.edu
FOSTER, Kristen .... 559-730-3921.... 40 E
kristenf@cos.edu
FOSTER, Lauren .... 828-898-2496.. 345 G
fosterlm@lmc.edu
FOSTER, Linda .... 904-470-8012.... 98 N
lefoster@ewc.edu
FOSTER, Mary Louise .... 402-844-7129.. 282 B
marylouise@northeast.edu
FOSTER, Meezie .... 302-225-6235.... 91 D
fosterm@gbc.edu
FOSTER, Meichele .... 573-876-7110.. 272 I
mfoster@stephens.edu
FOSTER, Michelle .... 319-208-5063.. 176 J
mfoster@scciowa.edu
FOSTER, Mike .... 641-673-1058.. 177 J
fostermik@wmpenn.edu
FOSTER, Mike .... 207-941-7063.. 202 I
fostermi@husson.edu
FOSTER, Morris, W .... 757-683-3460.. 492 G
mfoster@odu.edu
FOSTER, Nicola .... 212-346-1949.. 325 J
nfoster@pace.edu
FOSTER, Pam .... 785-670-1509.. 185 H
pam.foster@washburn.edu
FOSTER, Paul .... 406-657-1705.. 277 D
paul.foster4@msubillings.edu
FOSTER, Robert, W .... 304-647-6285.. 514 A
rfoster@osteo.wvsom.edu
FOSTER, Scot .... 510-869-6744.... 59 L
sfoster@samuelmerritt.edu
FOSTER, Shannon .... 907-834-1632.... 11 A
sfoster@pwscc.edu
FOSTER, Shelby .... 510-659-7369.... 55 B
sfoster@ohlone.edu
FOSTER, JR., Sidney, C .. 330-972-6102.. 378 G
sfoster@uakron.edu
FOSTER, Steve .... 281-998-6075.. 469 F
sfoster@txchiro.edu
FOSTER, Susan .... 402-472-3417.. 282 M
sfoster1@unl.edu
FOSTER, Tim .... 559-730-3902.... 40 E
timf@cos.edu
FOSTER, Tim .... 970-248-1498.... 77 L
tfoster@coloradomesa.edu
FOSTER, Timothy .... 717-757-1100.. 424 I
tim.foster@yti.edu
FOSTER, Timothy, W .... 207-725-3228.. 202 F
tfoster@bowdoin.edu
FOSTER, Traci, L .... 334-683-5190...... 5 C
tfoster@judson.edu
FOSTER, Tracy .... 920-206-2388.. 517 G
tracy.foster@mbu.edu
FOSTER CURTIS, Ellen .... 708-534-8046.. 140 H
efostercurtis@govst.edu
FOSTER ZSIGA, Erin .... 207-786-6215.. 202 D
efoster@bates.edu
FOSTNER, Jay, J .... 920-403-3169.. 519 G
jay.fostner@snc.edu
FOTH, Rod .... 336-334-4822.. 350 B
rsfoth@gtcc.edu
FOTI, Bill .... 603-526-3613.. 285 L
wfoti@colby-sawyer.edu
FOTIOO, Jamie .... 501-450-1373.... 20 F
fotioo@hendrix.edu
FOTOUHI, Farshad .... 313-577-3776.. 243 F
fotouhi@wayne.edu
FOUBERG, Andi .... 605-697-5198.. 437 F
andi.fouberg@statealum.com
FOUBERG, Erin .... 605-626-3456.. 437 D
erin.fouberg@northern.edu
FOUCART, Steve .... 417-836-4563.. 268 I
stevefoucart@missouristate.edu
FOUGERE, John .... 573-882-0601.. 273 D
fougerej@umsystem.edu
FOUGERES, Michel .... 727-864-7987.... 98 L
fougermw@eckerd.edu
FOUGHT, Rick .... 901-448-5694.. 448 H
rfought1@uthsc.edu
FOUGHT, Wendy .... 231-439-6349.. 239 A
wfought@ncmich.edu
FOULKROD, Marianna, K 317-788-3302.. 168 A
mfoulkrod@uindy.edu
FOUNTAIN, Barbara, L .... 512-505-3044.. 459 F
blfountain@htu.edu
FOUNTAIN, Cheryl, A .... 904-620-2496.. 112 B
fountain@unf.edu
FOUNTAIN, Jennifer .... 541-552-6234.. 395 A
fountainj@sou.edu
FOUNTAIN, Wesley .... 910-672-1685.. 356 E
wtfountain01@uncfsu.edu
FOUNTAINE, Cynthia .... 618-453-8761.. 154 I
fountaine@siu.edu
FOURMAN, Christopher .. 718-420-4164.. 339 F
christopher.fourman@wagner.edu

FOURMAN, Elizabeth .... 574-284-4584.. 167 A
efourman@saintmarys.edu
FOURMY CUTRER, Emily 903-223-3001.. 469 C
emily.cutrer@tamut.edu
FOURNIER, Jessica .... 303-644-4034.... 81 H
jessica.fournier@morgancc.edu
FOURNIER, Jody .... 614-236-6445.. 364 N
jfournier@capital.edu
FOURNIER, Nicole .... 207-768-9589.. 205 D
nicole.l.fournier@maine.edu
FOURNIER, Robert .... 313-577-4280.. 243 F
ai5611@wayne.edu
FOUST, Dane, R .... 410-543-6080.. 213 A
drfoust@salisbury.edu
FOUST, David .... 901-751-8453.. 442 E
dfoust@mabts.edu
FOUST, Jasper .... 706-646-6302.. 127 F
jfoust@sctech.edu
FOUST, Julia .... 708-239-4608.. 155 M
julia.foust@trnty.edu
FOUST, Karen, R .... 501-450-1362.... 20 F
foust@hendrix.edu
FOUST, Kevin .... 540-231-6512.. 499 F
foustk@vt.edu
FOUTS, Paul .... 415-442-7026.... 45 B
pfouts@ggu.edu
FOUTS, Susan .... 828-227-7397.. 359 A
sfouts@wcu.edu
FOUTY, Dennis .... 832-842-4603.. 473 E
dfouty@uh.edu
FOUTY, Dennis .... 832-842-4603.. 473 F
dfouty@uh.edu
FOWLE, Marilyn .... 940-397-4117.. 462 A
marilyn.fowle@mwsu.edu
FOWLER, Carlton .... 816-604-4101.. 267 K
carlton.fowler@mcckc.edu
FOWLER, Christopher ...... 419-358-3409.. 364 D
fowlerc@bluffton.edu
FOWLER, Craig .... 828-227-7282.. 359 A
cfowler@wcu.edu
FOWLER, Craig .... 715-234-7082.. 525 A
craig.fowler@witc.edu
FOWLER, George, J .... 757-683-4141.. 492 G
gfowler@odu.edu
FOWLER, Gregory, T .... 928-523-1186.... 15 H
gt.fowler@nau.edu
FOWLER, Heather, L .... 570-577-1188.. 398 L
h.fowler@bucknell.edu
FOWLER, James, R .... 401-341-2908.. 426 C
jim.fowler@salve.edu
FOWLER, Jason .... 919-761-2252.. 355 I
jfowler@sebts.edu
FOWLER, Jeffrey .... 314-977-2849.. 271 K
fowlerjl@slu.edu
FOWLER, Julie, H .... 903-983-8281.. 460 D
jfowler@kilgore.edu
FOWLER, Justin .... 503-552-1517.. 392 H
jfowler@nunm.edu
FOWLER, Kelly .... 559-325-5214.... 67 B
kelly.fowler@scccd.edu
FOWLER, Lee .... 864-503-5140.. 434 G
lfowler2@uscupstate.edu
FOWLER, Liesl, A .... 309-794-7211.. 135 D
lieslfowler@augustana.edu
FOWLER, Lisa .... 303-914-6302.... 82 I
lisa.fowler@rrcc.edu
FOWLER, Lisa Therese .... 212-962-0002.. 322 G
lfowler@nyci.edu
FOWLER, Logan .... 208-792-2200.. 134 A
ljfowler@lcsc.edu
FOWLER, Marc .... 616-222-1443.. 233 A
marc.fowler@cornerstone.edu
FOWLER, Mary .... 770-533-6918.. 123 L
mfowler@laniertech.edu
FOWLER, Matt .... 618-262-8641.. 142 F
fowlerm@iecc.edu
FOWLER, Matthew .... 913-288-7326.. 182 C
ffowler@kckcc.edu
FOWLER, Mike .... 502-451-0815.. 193 B
mfowler@sullivan.edu
FOWLER, Pamela, W .... 734-763-4119.. 241 J
pfowler@umich.edu
FOWLER, Paul .... 404-727-0512.. 120 E
pgfowle@emory.edu
FOWLER, Paul .... 337-550-1433.. 197 K
pfowler@lsue.edu
FOWLER, Perphelia .... 928-724-6950.... 12 T
pfowler@dinecollege.edu
FOWLER, Peter .... 617-989-4082.. 229 D
fowlerp@wit.edu
FOWLER, Ramsey .... 512-448-8736.. 464 G
ramseyf@stedwards.edu
FOWLER, Robert .... 315-866-0300.. 316 A
fowlerrc@herkimer.edu
FOWLER, S. Kevin .... 903-510-2419.. 473 C
kfow@tjc.edu
FOWLER, Sandra .... 229-931-2237.. 122 C
sandra.fowler@gsw.edu
FOWLER, Sandy .... 530-674-9199.... 36 B
sfowler@cambridge.edu
FOWLER, Tami .... 214-528-8600.. 463 L
FOWLER, Vivia, L .... 478-757-5229.. 129 L
vfowler@wesleyancollege.edu
FOWLER, Walter, B .... 412-365-1105.. 400 G
wfowler@chatham.edu
FOWLER-HILL, Sandra ..... 971-722-7305.. 394 F
sandra.fowlerhill@pcc.edu
FOWLER-YOUNG, Angela 410-706-7830.. 211 F
angela.fowleryoung@umaryland.edu
FOWLES, Erin .... 847-543-2375.. 138 C
efowles@clcillinois.edu
FOWLES, Gareth .... 561-237-7601.. 104 O
gfowles@lynn.edu
FOWLES, Michelle, R .... 818-947-2437.... 50 D
fowlesmr@lavc.edu
FOWLKES, Bruce, M .... 309-467-6423.. 140 E
bfowlkes@eureka.edu
FOWLKES, J. Brian .... 734-764-7516.. 241 J
fowlkes@umich.edu
FOWLKES, J. Keith .... 859-238-5572.. 187 H
keith.fowlkes@centre.edu
FOWLKES, Rodney .... 630-829-6584.. 135 F
rfowlkes@ben.edu
FOX, Alisha .... 423-472-7141.. 445 E
afox@clevelandstatecc.edu
FOX, Amanda .... 516-572-7436.. 322 C
amanda.fox@ncc.edu
FOX, Anthony .... 989-386-6622.. 238 B
aefox@midmich.edu
FOX, Carole, M .... 512-463-1808.. 470 G
carole.fox@tsus.edu
FOX, Chris .... 412-338-4770.. 398 H
cfox@brightwoodcareer.edu
FOX, Cindy, W .... 336-322-2101.. 351 H
cindy.fox@piedmontcc.edu
FOX, D. Jeff .... 208-732-6220.. 133 E
jfox@csi.edu
FOX, Dan .... 303-273-3231.... 78 M
dfox@mines.edu
FOX, Debbie .... 225-768-1727.. 199 B
deborah.fox@ololcollege.edu
FOX, Donnie, S .... 606-337-1530.. 187 I
dfox@ccbbc.edu
FOX, Douglas .... 325-942-2333.. 472 B
doug.fox@angelo.edu
FOX, Jeanne, E .... 574-807-7243.. 159 D
foxj@bethelcollege.edu
FOX, Jennifer .... 530-226-4763.... 64 H
jfox@simpsonu.edu
FOX, Jimmy .... 615-794-4254.. 443 G
jfox@omorecollege.edu
FOX, John .... 410-455-2591.. 211 G
johnfox@umbc.edu
FOX, Juliet .... 715-232-1151.. 521 D
foxj@uwstout.edu
FOX, Karen, L .... 717-560-8254.. 407 E
kfox@lbc.edu
FOX, Kelly, L .... 303-492-3224.... 83 K
kelly.fox@colorado.edu
FOX, Linda, K .... 706-542-4879.. 128 E
lkfox@uga.edu
FOX, Lori, E .... 212-678-3438.. 337 E
lfox@exchange.tc.columbia.edu
FOX, Lou .... 210-829-3869.. 474 D
lfox@uiwtx.edu
FOX, Lynn .... 209-946-2421.... 71 C
lfox@pacific.edu
FOX, Mac .... 360-779-9993.. 505 B
mfox@ncad.edu
FOX, Mark .... 423-461-8784.. 442 K
mpfox@milligan.edu
FOX, Mark .... 704-669-4175.. 348 F
foxm@clevelandcc.edu
FOX, II, Mark, O .... 864-833-8232.. 432 B
mfox@presby.edu
FOX, Mary David .... 864-503-5040.. 434 G
mdfox@uscupstate.edu
FOX, Melanie .... 828-251-6700.. 357 C
mrfox@unca.edu
FOX, Michael .... 912-478-1592.. 122 B
mfox@georgiasouthern.edu
FOX, Michael .... 716-851-1639.. 313 H
ascfoxm@ecc.edu
FOX, Michael, J .... 757-221-1693.. 488 F
mjfox1@wm.edu
FOX, Mike .... 712-749-2351.. 170 D
FOX, Miranda, D .... 802-626-6492.. 486 C
miranda.fox@lyndonstate.edu
FOX, Nicole .... 615-794-4254.. 443 G
nfox@omorecollege.edu
FOX, P. Michael .... 585-395-2504.. 332 E
mfox@brockport.edu
FOX, Pamela .... 540-887-7026.. 491 G
pfox@mbc.edu
FOX, Pamela, L .... 317-788-3231.. 168 A
foxp@uindy.edu
FOX, Pat .... 843-574-6307.. 433 D
pat.fox@tridenttech.edu
FOX, Paul .... 423-636-7300.. 447 G
pfox@tusculum.edu
FOX, Phyllis .... 423-461-8708.. 442 K
pfox@milligan.edu
FOX, Princess .... 541-684-7250.. 393 B
pfox@nwcu.edu
FOX, Richard .... 718-368-4799.. 308 F
rfox@kbcc.cuny.edu
FOX, Rob .... 804-204-1211.. 487 D
rfox@btsr.edu
FOX, Robert .... 502-852-6745.. 194 A
bob.fox@louisville.edu
FOX, BSG, Ronald, A .... 773-380-6781.. 135 H
rfox@bexleyseabury.edu
FOX, Sean .... 931-540-2762.. 446 A
sfox12@columbiastate.edu
FOX, Sidney .... 734-462-4400.. 240 H
sfox@schoolcraft.edu
FOX, Susan, E .... 804-278-4237.. 494 N
sfox@upsem.edu
FOX, Teresa .... 330-490-7503.. 380 J
tfox@walsh.edu
FOX, Thomas .... 909-706-3548.... 74 K
tfox@westernu.edu
FOX, Timothy .... 410-617-2863.. 208 G
tfox@loyola.edu
FOX, Toyin .... 618-985-2828.. 143 F
toyinfox@jalc.edu
FOX, Val .... 781-891-2810.. 215 F
vfox@bentley.edu
FOX, William .... 315-229-5892.. 329 D
wfox@stlawu.edu
FOX, William, A .... 740-587-6271.. 368 B
foxw@denison.edu
FOX-WILSON, Jessica ..... 608-363-2647.. 515 G
foxjs@beloit.edu
FOXMAN, Philip, R .... 814-332-5383.. 397 A
pfoxman@allegheny.edu
FOXWORTH, Derrick .... 971-722-4980.. 394 F
derrick.foxworth@pcc.edu
FOXWORTH, Jessica, L ... 601-877-6479.. 256 F
jfoxworth@alcorn.edu
FOY, Geoffrey, E .... 253-535-7126.. 505 G
foy@plu.edu
FOY, Joseph .... 608-263-7217.. 522 A
joseph.foy@uwc.edu
FOY, Morna, K .... 608-267-9066.. 522 R
president@wtcsystem.edu
FOYE, Shanen .... 949-675-4451.... 47 A
shanen@idi.edu
FOYLE, Kevin, J .... 713-500-4472.. 477 C
kevin.j.foyle@uth.tmc.edu
FOZARD, John, D .... 405-692-3176.. 384 C
ecox@macu.edu
FRABONI, Dave .... 678-839-6447.. 129 E
dfraboni@westga.edu
FRACASSA, Mike .... 740-420-2847.. 374 G
mfracassa@ohiochristian.edu
FRACASSO, Jack .... 860-297-2361.... 89 B
jack.fracasso@trincoll.edu
FRACTION, Lynette .... 651-290-6310.. 253 S
lynette.fraction@mitchellhamline.edu
FRADEN, Rena .... 209-946-2023.... 71 C
rfraden@pacific.edu
FRAGALE, Stephen .... 518-381-1339.. 330 B
fragalsa@sunysccc.edu
FRAGNOLI, Kristen, M ...... 585-785-1209.. 314 D
kristen.fragnoli@flcc.edu
FRAGOSO, Marcos .... 210-805-3014.. 474 D
fragoso@uiwtx.edu
FRAHM, Karyn .... 661-726-1911.... 68 K
karyn.frahm@uav.edu
FRAILE, Pedro .... 787-727-3583.. 539 B
pfraile@sagrado.edu
FRAINIER, Janine, L .... 317-940-9228.. 159 K
jfrainie@butler.edu
FRAIRE, John .... 503-725-5249.. 394 G
jfraire@pdx.edu
FRAIRE, Virginia .... 512-223-7053.. 451 N
vfraire@austincc.edu
FRAIZER, Bob .... 660-626-2380.. 262 A
rfraizer@atsu.edu
FRALEY, Bill .... 304-384-6334.. 513 A
bfraley@concord.edu
FRALEY, Paula .... 309-694-5432.. 141 F
pfraley@icc.edu
FRALEY, Paula .... 309-694-5520.. 141 F
pfraley@icc.edu
FRALEY, Priscilla .... 606-368-6045.. 186 B
priscillafrayley@alc.edu
FRALIC, Bradley .... 713-348-4927.. 464 E
bradley.w.fralic@rice.edu
FRAME, J. Davidson .... 703-516-0035.. 495 B
davidson.frame@umtweb.edu
FRANCAVILLA, Theodore . 914-337-9300.. 311 F
ted.francavilla@concordia-ny.edu
FRANCE, David, A .... 601-292-9852.. 417 I
dfrance@reseminary.edu
FRANCE, Lucy .... 406-243-4742.. 276 K
lucy.france@umontana.edu
FRANCE, Melissa, H .... 918-631-2516.. 389 E
melissa-france@utulsa.edu
FRANCIES, Karen .... 281-649-3450.. 458 L
kfrancies@hbu.edu
FRANCIOSI, Adrienne ...... 617-243-2214.. 219 I
afranciosi@lasell.edu
FRANCIS, Amy .... 419-783-2376.. 368 A
afrancis@defiance.edu
FRANCIS, Charles .... 559-324-6455.... 67 B
charles.francis@scccd.edu
FRANCIS, Consuela .... 843-953-7738.. 428 G
francisc@cofc.edu
FRANCIS, JR.,
D. Morgan .... 336-838-6102.. 354 C
morgan.francis@wilkescc.edu
FRANCIS, Diana .... 219-473-4211.. 159 L
dfrancis@ccsj.edu
FRANCIS, Heather .... 972-825-4627.. 466 D
hfrancis@sagu.edu
FRANCIS, Jeff .... 972-825-4731.. 466 D
jfrancis@sagu.edu
FRANCIS, Jeffrey .... 918-631-2084.. 389 E
jeffrey-francis@utulsa.edu
FRANCIS, Joshua, C .... 260-422-5561.. 162 B
jcfrancis@indianatech.edu
FRANCIS, Kathy .... 240-629-7804.. 207 F
kfrancis@frederick.edu
FRANCIS, Krista .... 360-417-6393.. 505 I
kfrancis@pencol.edu
FRANCIS, Lance .... 706-385-1062.. 126 A
lance.francis@point.edu
FRANCIS, Laurie, S .... 208-496-9510.. 132 J
francisl@byui.edu
FRANCIS, Leon .... 610-558-5584.. 411 E
francisl@neumann.edu
FRANCIS, CSV, Mark, R .. 773-371-5420.. 136 F
president@ctu.edu
FRANCIS, Melissa, A .... 252-940-6236.. 347 E
melissa.francis@beaufortccc.edu
FRANCIS, Monty, E .... 214-860-2178.. 456 E
mefrancis@dcccd.edu
FRANCIS, Nicola .... 425-602-3003.. 501 D
nfrancis@bastyr.edu
FRANCIS, Rebecca .... 270-852-3222.. 191 C
rfrancis@kwc.edu
FRANCIS, Robert, A .... 215-895-6966.. 402 G
raf47@drexel.edu
FRANCIS, Sean .... 410-617-5922.. 208 G
sefrancis@loyola.edu
FRANCIS, Terry .... 479-394-7622.... 22 B
tfrancis@rmcc.edu
FRANCIS-CONNOLLY,
Elizabeth .... 207-221-4523.. 205 F
efrancisconnolly@une.edu
FRANCISCHETTI, Jessica . 406-657-1041.. 278 D
francisj@rocky.edu
FRANCISCO, Eva Lynn .... 904-819-6460.... 99 M
efrancisco@flagler.edu
FRANCISCO, Joseph .... 402-472-6262.. 282 M
jfrancisco1@unl.edu
FRANCISCO, Michael .... 218-733-5976.. 249 H
m.francisco@lsc.edu
FRANCISCO, Renee .... 847-578-8810.. 153 A
renee.francisco@rosalindfranklin.edu
FRANCKO, David, A .... 205-348-8280...... 8 D
dfrancko@ua.edu
FRANCO, Barry .... 843-574-6796.. 433 D
barry.franco@tridenttech.edu
FRANCO, Darlery .... 201-360-4191.. 292 B
dfranco@hccc.edu
FRANCO, Juan .... 402-472-3755.. 282 M
jfranco2@unl.edu
FRANCO, Maria .... 386-226-6225.... 99 A
francom@erau.edu
FRANCO, Rita .... 209-478-0800.... 46 H
rfranco@humphreys.edu
FRANCO, Robert .... 808-734-9514.. 131 I
bfranco@hawaii.edu
FRANCO, Vilma .... 847-233-7700.. 150 D
vfranco@nc.edu
FRANCOIS, Dennis .... 509-963-1914.. 501 K
francoisd@cwu.edu
FRANCOIS, Jason .... 206-546-4514.. 507 F
jfrancois@shoreline.edu
FRANCOIS, Magda .... 212-217-7999.. 314 B
FRANCOIS-SEENY,
Denise .... 610-861-5066.. 411 G
dfrancois@northampton.edu
FRANCONE, Jennifer .... 212-229-5300.. 322 E
franconj@newschool.edu
FRANDSEN, Michael .... 440-775-6453.. 374 C
mfrandsen@oberlin.edu
FRANK, Anthony, A .... 970-491-6211.... 78 Q
presofc@colostate.edu
FRANK, April .... 713-221-8422.. 474 B
franka@uhd.edu
FRANK, Brian .... 727-341-4143.. 108 D
frank.brian@spcollege.edu
FRANK, Dawn .... 605-455-6035.. 436 G
dfrank@olc.edu
FRANK, Deborah .... 315-655-7122.. 306 H
dfrank@cazenovia.edu
FRANK, Donna .... 419-448-3508.. 378 A
frankd@tiffin.edu

FRANK, Gregory, P 757-822-7261 498 H gfrank@tcc.edu
FRANK, Jonathan 312-793-7150 140 D jfrank@erikson.edu
FRANK, Josh 919-508-2418 359 G josh.frank@peace.edu
FRANK, Katherine 509-963-1400 501 K katherine.frank@cwu.edu
FRANK, Larry 213-763-7052 50 C franklb@lattc.edu
FRANK, Linda 415-485-9528 40 C lfrank@marin.edu
FRANK, Marie 337-482-2148 201 D mcf3023@louisiana.edu
FRANK, Peter 704-233-8144 359 H pfrank@wingate.edu
FRANK, Robert 740-593-2850 375 H frank@ohio.edu
FRANK, Robert, G 505-277-2626 302 F unmpres@unm.edu
FRANK, Sandy, K 812-464-1762 168 E sfrank@usi.edu
FRANK, Shawn 828-328-7298 345 H shawn.frank@lr.edu
FRANK, Tony 303-534-6290 78 P chancellor@colostate.edu
FRANK, Vincent, P 717-901-5115 405 H vfrank@harrisburgu.edu
FRANK MAYS, Karen 978-665-3712 221 D kfrankmays@fitchburgstate.edu
FRANKBERRY, Constance 701-627-4738 361 H cfrank@nhsc.edu
FRANKE, James 660-263-3900 263 A jamiefranke@cccb.edu
FRANKEN, Kathy 563-425-5200 177 D frankenk@uiu.edu
FRANKEN, Kathy 563-425-5868 177 D frankenk@uiu.edu
FRANKEN, Lynn 724-589-2200 420 D lfranken@thiel.edu
FRANKER, Karen 608-663-3408 516 F kfranker@edgewood.edu
FRANKIEL, Tamar 310-824-1586 24 L tamar.frankiel@ajrca.org
FRANKILIN, Scott 806-291-1130 479 D franklins@wbu.edu
FRANKLAND, Phil 603-882-6923 286 E pfrankland@ccsnh.edu
FRANKLIN, Alison 315-792-3111 339 B ahfrannkl@utica.edu
FRANKLIN, Audrey 336-517-2247 342 B afranklin@bennett.edu
FRANKLIN, Beverly 202-274-6258 94 B bfranklin@udc.edu
FRANKLIN, Celeste 505-473-6318 302 A celeste.franklin@santafeuniversity.edu
FRANKLIN, Chris 205-387-0511 2 B chris.franklin@bscc.edu
FRANKLIN, David 202-274-6168 94 B david.franklin@udc.edu
FRANKLIN, Janice 334-229-4106 1 D franklin@alasu.edu
FRANKLIN, Joseph 575-835-5964 300 G jfranklin@admin.nmt.edu
FRANKLIN, Julie 801-422-2810 480 C julie_franklin@byu.edu
FRANKLIN, Karen 575-624-7138 299 J karen.franklin@roswell.enmu.edu
FRANKLIN, Kathy, C 434-528-5276 500 C kfranklin@vul.edu
FRANKLIN, Katrina, V 434-528-5276 500 C tfranklin@vul.edu
FRANKLIN, Laura 831-646-4816 53 A lfranklin@mpc.edu
FRANKLIN, Laura, A 608-342-1817 521 A franklinl@uwplatt.edu
FRANKLIN, Laurie 425-388-9035 503 F lfranklin@everettcc.edu
FRANKLIN, Marshall, E 864-242-5100 427 E
FRANKLIN, Mona 785-749-8448 181 E mona.franklin@bie.edu
FRANKLIN, Randall 434-832-7617 496 G franklinr@cvcc.vccs.edu
FRANKLIN, Roschoune 323-856-7621 26 rfranklin@afi.com
FRANKLIN, Shannon 541-278-5951 390 C sfranklin@bluecc.edu
FRANKLIN, Somer 936-294-1009 471 D somer@shsu.edu
FRANKLIN, Susan 402-461-7410 280 D sfranklin@hastings.edu
FRANKLIN, Timothy, V 973-596-5515 293 D timothy.v.franklin@njit.edu
FRANKLIN, Truitt 706-865-2134 128 D tfranklin@truett.edu
FRANKLIN, William 310-243-3784 32 D wfranklin@csudh.edu
FRANKMAN, Tom 573-592-1166 275 G tom.frankman@williamwoods.edu
FRANKOVICH, Lauren 917-493-4543 319 M lfrankovich@msmnyc.edu
FRANKS, Billie 606-589-3029 190 G billie.franks@kctcs.edu
FRANKS, Brian 817-531-4452 472 F bfranks@txwes.edu
FRANKS, Debra, J 864-388-8749 430 G jfranks@lander.edu
FRANKS, Dennis 336-278-5555 344 D dfranks3@elon.edu
FRANKS, Mark 920-498-6269 524 E mark.franks@nwtc.edu
FRANKS, Peter, J 215-895-0226 402 G pjf28@drexel.edu
FRANKS, Rita 318-257-2577 200 G rfranks@latech.edu
FRANKS, Tammy 228-497-7700 259 C tammy.franks@mgccc.edu
FRANKS, Tammy 228-497-7800 259 C tammy.franks@mgccc.edu
FRANKS, Tiffany, M 434-791-5670 487 C tfranks@averett.edu
FRANKS-HELWICH, Stephanie, L 724-938-4301 414 E franks@calu.edu
FRANQUI, Alicia 718-262-2137 310 A afranqui@york.cuny.edu
FRANQUIZ, Maria 801-581-5791 481 M maria.franquiz@utah.edu
FRANSON, Terry 626-812-3061 28 A tfranson@apu.edu
FRANTEL, Tracy, L 503-777-7508 394 I tracy.frantel@reed edu
FRANTZ, Michael 712-749-2140 170 D frantzm@bvu.edu
FRANTZ, Rita, A 319-335-7009 169 H rita-frantz@uiowa.edu
FRANZ, Chris 303-953-3415 77 I cfranz@ccu.edu
FRANZ, Janet 509-682-6400 509 D jfranz@wvc.edu
FRANZ, Jennifer 920-748-8108 519 E franzj@ripon.edu
FRANZ, Mark 314-889-1488 265 C mfranz@fontbonne.edu
FRANZ, Matt 937-328-6045 366 E franzm@clarkstate.edu
FRANZ, Sandra, L 802-626-4865 486 C sandra.franz@lyndonstate.edu
FRANZ, Scott 620-947-3121 185 B scottf@tabor.edu
FRANZ, William, T 804-752-7268 493 C wfranz@rmc.edu
FRANZA, Thomas 443-412-2489 208 A tfranza@harford.edu
FRANZBLAU, Alfred 734-763-1282 241 J afranz@umich.edu
FRANZEN, Kristine 563-387-1330 174 L frankr03@luther.edu
FRAONE, Kimberly 908-737-4600 292 C kfraone@kean.edu
FRASCA, Melissa Sue 617-873-0474 217 A melissasue.frasca@cambridgecollege.edu
FRASCO, Mark 970-542-3174 81 H mark.frasco@morgancc.edu
FRASER, Bruce 772-462-7691 103 B bfraser@irsc.edu
FRASER, Cathryn 507-284-9024 245 F fraser.cathryn@mayo.edu
FRASER, Donald, L 903-510-2371 473 C dfra@tjc.edu
FRASER, Dori 919-735-5151 354 A dori@waynecc.edu
FRASER, Greg 313-664-7660 232 G gfraser@collegeforcreativestudies.edu
FRASER, Heather 207-795-7166 203 G fraserhe@cmhc.org
FRASER, Jeanmarie 508-362-2131 223 C jfraser@capecod.edu
FRASER, Lynne 401-865-1534 425 D lfraser1@providence.edu
FRASER, Morrison 217-854-3231 135 K morrison.fraser@blackburn.edu
FRASER, Robin 845-368-7241 329 I robin.fraser@use.salvationarmy.org
FRASER, Sheri 207-621-3136 204 I fraser@maine.edu
FRASER, Sherry, J 914-337-9300 311 F sherry.fraser@concordia-ny.edu
FRASER, Tammy 937-481-2299 381 C tammy_fraser@wilmington.edu
FRASER, Wayne 603-366-5266 286 C wfraser@ccsnh.edu
FRASER-MOLINA, Maria 252-249-1851 351 G mfraser-molina@pamlicocc.edu
FRASHER, Kristy 765-973-8275 162 G sm628@bncollege.com
FRASIER, George 253-833-9111 504 C gfrasier@greenriver.edu
FRASIER, Tanisha 602-331-7500 11 K tfrasier@aii.edu
FRASSINELLI, David W 203-254-4254 87 G dfrassinelli@fairfield.edu
FRATELLA, Janet 541-552-6127 395 A fratellaj@sou.edu
FRATER, Joel, L 585-262-1610 321 J jfrater@monroecc.edu
FRAWLEY, Maria, H 202-242-6817 92 D mfrawley@gwu.edu
FRAZEE, David 336-506-4135 347 C david.frazee@alamancecc.edu
FRAZEE, David 216-987-5339 367 E david.frazee@tri-c.edu
FRAZEE, Sally, M 215-204-8611 420 B sally.frazee@temple.edu
FRAZELL, Mary 740-587-5717 368 B frazellm@denison.edu
FRAZER, Elmo 510-654-2934 43 D efrazer@expression.edu
FRAZER, Gael 850-484-1757 106 H gfrazer@pensacolastate.edu
FRAZER, Thomas, K 352-392-9230 112 A frazer@ufl.edu
FRAZIER, Al 501-279-4240 20 D afrazier@harding.edu
FRAZIER, III, Arthur E 404-270-5436 128 A aefrazier@spelman.edu
FRAZIER, Bryan 276-326-4272 487 F bfrazier@bluefield.edu
FRAZIER, Connie 701-777-4251 360 C connie.frazier@und.edu
FRAZIER, Dan 706-385-1017 126 A dan.frazier@point.edu
FRAZIER, David 918-540-6113 384 F david.frazier@neo.edu
FRAZIER, Deborah 360-417-6202 505 I dfrazier@pencol edu
FRAZIER, Deborah, J 870-612-2001 23 H debbie.frazier@uaccb.edu
FRAZIER, DeWayne 319-385-6205 174 A dewayne.frazier@iw.edu
FRAZIER, Doug 912-344-2818 116 E doug.frazier@armstrong.edu
FRAZIER, JR., Ernest, T 504-278-6421 196 I cfrazier@nunez.edu
FRAZIER, Fred 801-627-8471 481 A frazierf@owatc.edu
FRAZIER, Heli 619-684-8764 54 C hfrazier@newschoolarch.edu
FRAZIER, Herb 620-862-5252 178 F herb.frazier@barclaycollege.edu
FRAZIER, James 804-828-2787 496 D jfrazier@vcu.edu
FRAZIER, Jeanette 425-602-3043 501 D jfrazier@bastyr.edu
FRAZIER, Jenny 206-726-5085 503 B jfrazier@cornish edu
FRAZIER, John 330-823-2243 379 F fraziejl@mountunion.edu
FRAZIER, Judy 802-776-5236 433 G judy.frazier@csj.edu
FRAZIER, Julie 731-286-3204 446 B frazier@dscc.edu
FRAZIER, Kimberly 404-225-4608 117 A kfrazier@atlantatech.edu
FRAZIER, Larry 903-233-3951 460 J
FRAZIER, Larry 903-233-3951 460 J larryfrazier@letu edu
FRAZIER, Lisa 775-753-2147 234 I lisa.frazier@gbcnv.edu
FRAZIER, Lorraine 713-500-2001 477 C lorraine frazier@uth.tmc.edu
FRAZIER, Renae 864-941-8357 432 A frazier.r@ptc.edu
FRAZIER, Royce 620-862-5252 178 F president@barclaycollege.edu
FRAZIER, Sean 815-753-1000 150 A sfrazier@niu.edu
FRAZIER, Shanelle 662-621-4674 257 B sfrazier@coahomacc.edu
FRAZIER, Stephen, L 309-298-4500 158 A sl-frazier@wiu.edu
FRAZIER, Steven, R 860-738-6409 87 A sfrazier@nwcc.edu
FRAZIER-HELD, Jamie 912-650-5672 127 D jfrazier-held@southuniversity.edu
FRAZOR, Diane 210-826-7595 479 D frazord@wbu.edu
FRAZZA, Christian 406-447-4344 276 B cfrazza@carroll.edu
FREAD, Marilyn 630-889-6661 149 G mfread@nuhs.edu
FREAD, Susan, J 610-799-1072 408 G sfread@lccc.edu
FRECH, Leanne, C 717-736-4160 405 C lcfrech@hacc.edu
FRECHETTE, Carri 207-699-5073 203 F cfrechette@meca.edu
FRECHETTE, Michael, T 253-535-8725 505 G frechemt@plu.edu
FRED, Leota 406-586-3585 276 I leota.fred@montanabiblecollege.edu
FREDA, Kristin 212-875-4450 304 E kfreda@bankstreet.edu
FREDEEN, DonnaJean, A 609-896-5010 295 B dfredeen@rider.edu
FREDENBURGH, III, Paul, H 202-685-4342 528 B paul.h.fredenburgh@ndu.edu
FREDERICK, Athena, D 814-641-3171 406 F fredera@juniata.edu
FREDERICK, Brian 337-482-6480 201 D jdh7220@louisiana.edu
FREDERICK, David 513-721-7944 369 D dfrederick@gbs.edu
FREDERICK, Debra 605-274-5514 435 E deb.frederick@augie.edu
FREDERICK, G. Marcille, H 540-432-4170 488 K marci.frederick@emu.edu
FREDERICK, Heidi 615-248-1529 447 F hrfrederick@trevecca.edu
FREDERICK, Jeff 910-521-6439 358 C jeff.frederick@uncp.edu
FREDERICK, Julia 337-482-6700 201 D jcg0624@louisiana.edu
FREDERICK, Lesley, J 217-786-2597 146 E lesley.frederick@llcc.edu
FREDERICK, Linda, D 504-286-5106 199 I lfrederick@suno.edu
FREDERICK, Pam 540-423-9125 497 B pfrederick@germanna.edu
FREDERICK, Richard 662-252-8000 260 F rfrederick@rustcollege.edu
FREDERICK, Robert 256-824-7200 8 F robert.frederick@uah.edu
FREDERICK, Robert, J 319-273-6857 170 A robert.frederick@uni.edu
FREDERICK, Steven, G 518-562-4195 310 C steven.frederick@clinton.edu
FREDERICK, Thyssene 843-349-5246 430 F thyssene.frederick@hgtc.edu
FREDERICK, Tracy, H 620-229-6329 184 J tracy.frederick@sckans.edu
FREDERICK, Wayne 202-806-2500 93 A wfrederick@howard.edu
FREDERICKS, Dan 601-968-5977 256 I dfredericks@belhaven.edu
FREDERICKS, Kimberly 518-292-1782 327 H fredek1@sage.edu
FREDERICKSON, Joel 651-638-6317 244 L frejoe@bethel.edu
FREDERIKSEN, Jens 615-329-8762 439 L jfrederiksen@fisk.edu
FREDETTE, Emile 802-728-1292 486 D efredett@vtc.edu
FREDRICH, Dolores 516-463-1800 316 D dolores.fredrich@hofstra.edu
FREDRICK, Kay 605-626-2518 437 D kay.fredrick@northern.edu
FREDRICKSEN, Donovan 214-333-5405 455 J donovan@dbu.edu
FREDRICKSON, Angela 402-375-7220 281 J anfredr1@wsc.edu
FREDRICKSON, Kurt 626-584-5654 44 G kurtf@fuller.edu
FREDRICKSON, Maya 713-646-1801 459 A mfredrickson@hcl.edu
FREDS, Anthony 989-317-4602 238 B afreds@midmich.edu
FREDSON, Janice 509-682-6505 509 D jfredson@wvc.edu
FREE, Carolyn, G 803-536-8402 432 E cfree@scsu.edu
FREE, Rhona, C 860-231-5221 90 B rfree@usj.edu
FREE, Rikky, L 501-882-4445 18 I rlfree@asub.edu
FREEBOURN, Randal 937-327-7009 381 F freebournr@wittenberg.edu
FREEBURGH, Charles 225-216-8162 195 H freeburghc@mybrcc.edu
FREED, Carol 507-389-7211 252 D carol.freed@southcentral.edu
FREED, Curt 360-383-3230 509 F cfreed@whatcom.ctc.edu
FREED, Linda 817-257-7516 469 G linda.freed@tcu.edu
FREED, Mitchell 610-683-4175 415 C freed@kutztown.edu
FREED, Suzanne, K 518-242-6046 331 A sfreed@albany.edu
FREEDLAND, Gregory 717-871-5874 415 F gregory.freedland@millersville.edu
FREEDMAN, Cheryl 215-468-8800 406 D admissions@culinaryarts.edu
FREEDMAN, Daniel 845-257-3728 331 E freedmad@newpaltz.edu
FREEDMAN, Kimberly 617-588-1367 215 E kfreedman@bfit.edu
FREEDMAN, Michael 301-985-7200 212 C michael.freedman@umuc.edu

FREEDMAN, Phyllis, D .... 304-326-1390.. 511 D
pfreedman@salemu.edu
FREEDMAN, Stephen .... 718-817-3040.. 314 G
sfreedman@fordham.edu
FREEDMAN, Victoria .... 212-430-3179.. 341 G
vfreedman@aecom.yu.edu
FREEDMAN, Wendy, A ..... 845-437-5700.. 339 C
wefreedman@vassar.edu
FREEDMAN DOHERTY,
Elizabeth .... 617-287-5339.. 220 G
elizabeth.doherty@umb.edu
FREEH, Mary Beth .... 610-606-4605.. 400 E
mafreeh@cedarcrest.edu
FREEL, Lisa .... 301-846-2468.. 207 F
lfreel@frederick.edu
FREELAND, Kay .... 770-426-2944.. 124 B
freeland@life.edu
FREELANDER, Chichi .... 405-491-6396.. 388 A
cfreelan@snu.edu
FREELS, Cindy .... 573-288-6511.. 264 F
cfreels@culver.edu
FREELS, Ean .... 515-964-6514.. 171 B
enfreels@dmacc.edu
FREEMAN, Algeania, W ... 937-708-5704.. 381 B
afreeman@wilberforce.edu
FREEMAN, Alston .... 803-934-3179.. 431 E
afreeman@morris.edu
FREEMAN, Andrew .... 740-753-6079.. 369 K
freemana@hocking.edu
FREEMAN, Angela .... 404-752-1568.. 125 A
afreeman@msm.edu
FREEMAN, Angela .... 315-781-3339.. 316 C
freeman@hws.edu
FREEMAN, Carol Ann ...... 845-675-4794.. 325 C
carol_ann.freeman@nyack.edu
FREEMAN, Catharine ...... 319-296-4041.. 173 B
catharine.freeman@hawkeyecollege.edu
FREEMAN, Cecily .... 901-722-3200.. 444 C
cfreeman@sco.edu
FREEMAN, Craig .... 360-779-9993.. 505 B
cfreeman@ncad.edu
FREEMAN, Dennis .... 617-253-6056.. 225 A
FREEMAN, Donna, M .... 901-321-3251.. 439 E
dfreeman@cbu.edu
FREEMAN, Eddie .... 817-272-2106.. 476 A
efreeman@uta.edu
FREEMAN, Elijah, T .... 252-789-0276.. 351 A
efreeman@martincc.edu
FREEMAN, Everette .... 303-556-3786.... 79 F
FREEMAN, Gary .... 402-461-7752.. 280 D
gfreeman@hastings.edu
FREEMAN, Ginger, C .... 615-898-2922.. 444 G
ginger.freeman@mtsu.edu
FREEMAN, Irving .... 724-552-2880.. 407 D
ifreeman@lecom.edu
FREEMAN, Jackie .... 435-652-7612.. 482 A
freeman@dixie.edu
FREEMAN, Jerrid .... 918-456-5511.. 384 G
freema22@nsuok.edu
FREEMAN, Jim .... 417-690-3248.. 263 E
jfreeman@cofo.edu
FREEMAN, John, E .... 937-708-5611.. 381 B
jfreeman@wilberforce.edu
FREEMAN, Karen .... 315-786-2200.. 317 H
kfreeman@sunyjefferson.edu
FREEMAN, Karen, J .... 315-786-2234.. 317 H
kfreeman@sunyjefferson.edu
FREEMAN, Kenneth .... 314-246-5990.. 275 B
kennethfreeman@webster.edu
FREEMAN, Kenneth, W .... 617-353-6170.. 216 E
kfreeman@bu.edu
FREEMAN, Kevin .... 405-974-2446.. 388 L
kfreeman7@uco.edu
FREEMAN, Lisa .... 815-753-0493.. 150 A
lfreeman1@niu.edu
FREEMAN, Lisa .... 413-572-5204.. 222 E
lfreeman@westfield.ma.edu
FREEMAN, Mark .... 215-571-3608.. 402 G
maf375@drexel.edu
FREEMAN, Melanie, H ...... 662-329-7222.. 259 E
mhfreeman@muw.edu
FREEMAN, Michael .... 410-951-3000.. 212 E
mfreeman@coppin.edu
FREEMAN, Michael .... 615-963-5644.. 445 A
mfreeman@tnstate.edu
FREEMAN, Renee .... 616-331-3255.. 234 F
freemren@gvsu.edu
FREEMAN, Roger .... 763-576-4700.. 248 L
roger.freeman@anokaramsey.edu
FREEMAN, Roger .... 763-433-1378.. 248 K
roger.freeman@anokaramsey.edu
FREEMAN, Russell .... 404-876-1227.. 118 C
russell.freeman@bccr.edu
FREEMAN, Russell, T ...... 773-577-8100.. 139 A
FREEMAN, Sean, C .... 573-629-3269.. 265 G
sean.freeman@hlg.edu
FREEMAN, Sharon .... 662-254-3811.. 260 A
sharonf@mvsu.edu
FREEMAN, Sheila, D .... 662-685-4771.. 257 A
sfreeman@bmc.edu
FREEMAN, Stacy .... 912-538-3129.. 127 E
sfreeman@southeasterntech.edu
FREEMAN, Susan .... 863-680-4433.. 101 E
sfreeman@flsouthern.edu
FREEMAN, Tierra, M .... 502-597-5932.. 191 B
tierra.freeman@kysu.edu
FREEMAN, Tim .... 952-829-4691.. 244 J
tim.freeman@bethfel.org
FREEMAN, Tonya .... 225-771-2552.. 200 A
tfreeman@sulc.edu
FREEMAN, Yancy .... 423-425-4662.. 448 F
yancy-freeman@utc.edu
FREEMAN-GALLANT,
Corey .... 518-580-5727.. 330 F
cfreeman@skidmore.edu
FREEMAN-TAYLOR,
Rubye, A .... 903-730-4890.. 460 B
FREEMON, Yolanda .... 708-656-8000.. 149 A
yolanda.freemon@morton.edu
FREER, Doug .... 909-537-5130.... 34 C
dfreer@csusb.edu
FREER, Michael .... 763-424-0955.. 251 B
mfreer@nhcc.edu
FREER, Wayne .... 845-687-5053.. 338 F
freerw@sunyulster.edu
FREES-WILLIAMS,
Allison, L .... 217-581-6396.. 139 H
afreeswilliams@eiu.edu
FREESE, Rob .... 215-340-8401.. 399 A
earl.freese@bucks.edu
FREESTONE, Julie .... 801-832-2573.. 483 D
jfreestone@westminstercollege.edu
FREESTONE, Sarah .... 641-782-1455.. 177 B
freestone@swcciowa.edu
FREGIA, Olin .... 903-730-4890.. 460 B
ofregia@jarvis.edu
FREHSE, Sandra .... 518-454-5244.. 311 B
frehses@strose.edu
FREI, Jennifer .... 541-463-5306.. 391 G
freij@lanecc.edu
FREIBERGER, Amy, M ..... 918-631-3727.. 389 E
amy-freiberger@utulsa.edu
FREIBURGER, Chevy .... 641-628-7637.. 170 E
freiburgerc@central.edu
FREIBURGER, Lisa .... 616-234-4025.. 234 E
lfreiburger@grcc.edu
FREIDEL-NELSON, Kelsey 605-331-6632.. 438 A
kelsey.freidel.nelson@usiouxfalls.edu
FREIDENFELDS, Lauris .... 312-947-0001.. 153 B
lauris_freidenfelds@rush.edu
FREIJE, Brenda .... 317-931-2301.. 160 B
bfreije@cts.edu
FREIJE, Margaret .... 508-793-2541.. 217 C
mfreije@holycross.edu
FREILER, Dan .... 717-396-7833.. 413 M
dfreiler@pcad.edu
FREINKEL, Lisa .... 541-346-0825.. 395 G
freinkel@uoregon.edu
FREISCHLAG, Julie .... 916-734-3578.... 69 A
julie.freischlag@ucdmc.ucdavis.edu
FREMONT, Ronald .... 909-537-5004.... 34 C
rfremont@csusb.edu
FRENCH, Angie .... 870-248-4000.... 19 H
angie.french@blackrivertech.edu
FRENCH, Barbara .... 415-476-6296.... 70 D
bfrench@ucsf.edu
FRENCH, Brian .... 406-243-2565.. 276 K
brian.french@umontana.edu
FRENCH, Christopher ...... 860-297-5204.... 89 B
christopher.french@trincoll.edu
FRENCH, Daniel, J .... 315-443-9732.. 337 A
djfrench@syr.edu
FRENCH, Daphne .... 912-260-4232.. 127 B
daphne.french@sgsc.edu
FRENCH, JR., George, T . 205-929-1428...... 5 H
gtfrench@aol.com
FRENCH, Joy .... 303-724-2516.... 84 A
joy.french@ucdenver.edu
FRENCH, Kelly .... 859-344-3619.. 193 C
frenchk@thomasmore.edu
FRENCH, Marjorie, M ...... 210-458-4228.. 477 A
marjie.french@utsa.edu
FRENCH, Mark .... 614-287-2810.. 367 C
mfrench1@cscc.edu
FRENCH, Paige .... 540-515-3749.. 487 H
pfrench@bridgewater.edu
FRENCH, CSSP,
Raymond .... 412-396-5286.. 403 A
french@duq.edu
FRENCH, Steve .... 404-894-3380.. 121 D
steve.french@coa.gatech.edu
FRENCH, Sue .... 270-706-8611.. 189 C
sue.french@kctcs.edu
FRENCH, Vickie .... 870-248-4000.... 19 H
vickief@blackrivertech.edu
FRENCH, William .... 609-497-7789.. 294 C
bill.french@ptsem.edu
FRENCH-HART, Holly ...... 318-678-6000.. 195 I
ltaylordupre@bpcc.edu
FRENDEWEY, JR., James 906-487-2259.. 238 A
jimf@mtu.edu
FRENDIAN, Michel .... 312-893-7145.. 140 D
mfrendian@erikson.edu
FRENK, Julio .... 305-284-5155.. 114 H
jfrenk@miami.edu
FRENTZOS, Karla, W .... 734-462-4400.. 240 H
kfrentzo@schoolcraft.edu
FRENZEL, Michelle .... 218-755-2370.. 248 M
mfrenzel@bemidjistate.edu
FRERE, Leslie .... 540-828-5380.. 487 H
lfrere@bridgewater.edu
FRERICHS, Chris .... 515-961-1711.. 176 H
chris.frerichs@simpson.edu
FRERIDGE, Jenifer .... 601-928-6288.. 259 C
jenifer.freridge@mgccc.edu
FRESA, Kerin .... 215-871-6864.. 416 F
kerinf@pcom.edu
FRESCH, Cathy .... 814-871-5842.. 404 A
fresch001@gannon.edu
FRESE, Philip .... 814-393-2600.. 414 G
pfrese@clarion.edu
FRESHOUR, Brett .... 724-552-4372.. 419 D
bfreshour@setonhill.edu
FRESHWATER, Laurie, A .. 252-222-6281.. 348 B
freshwaterl@carteret.edu
FRESQUEZ, Julie .... 951-343-4302.... 29 H
jfresquez@calbaptist.edu
FRESSE, Daliana .... 787-815-0000.. 537 F
daliana.fresse@upr.edu
FRETWELL, Katharine, L .. 413-542-2328.. 214 C
admissions@amherst.edu
FREY, Aaron .... 309-341-5301.. 136 C
afrey@sandburg.edu
FREY, Alicia .... 740-695-9500.. 364 B
afrey@belmontcollege.edu
FREY, Angela .... 414-382-6206.. 515 D
angela.frey@alverno.edu
FREY, Donald, R .... 402-280-2300.. 279 H
donaldfrey@creighton.edu
FREY, Eva, R .... 253-535-7159.. 505 G
eva.frey@plu.edu
FREY, Frances .... 210-434-6711.. 463 C
ffrey@lake.ollusa.edu
FREY, Isabel, D .... 516-463-4779.. 316 D
isabel.d.frey@hofstra.edu
FREY, James .... 229-931-2039.. 127 C
jfrey@southgatech.edu
FREY, Joan, L .... 502-410-6200.. 188 H
jfrey@galencollege.edu
FREY, Len, T .... 870-972-3303.... 18 J
lfrey@astate.edu
FREY, Lori .... 717-262-2012.. 424 A
lfrey@wilson.edu
FREY, Margot .... 415-503-6265.... 61 C
mfrey@sfcm.edu
FREY, Melissa .... 503-589-7652.. 390 E
melissa.frey@chemeketa.edu
FREY, Paula .... 205-329-7870...... 3 B
paula.frey@ecacolleges.com
FREYBURGER, James .... 912-650-6251.. 127 D
jfreyburger@southuniversity.edu
FREYTAG, Peter .... 303-373-2008.... 83 B
pfreytag@rvu.edu
FREYTES, Celeste .... 787-759-6061.. 538 F
claribet.santana@upr.edu
FREYTES, Diana .... 787-523-6000.. 532 O
dfreytes@icprjc.edu
FREYTES, Liza .... 787-279-1912.. 533 J
lfreytes@bayamon.inter.edu
FRIAR, Tobyn, L .... 773-508-8636.. 146 G
tfriar@luc.edu
FRIAS, Frank .... 626-529-8064.... 55 H
ffrias@pacificoaks.edu
FRIAS, Mary Lou .... 508-531-1252.. 221 C
marylou.frias@bridgew.edu
FRICK, Caroline .... 770-533-7016.. 123 L
cfrick@laniertech.edu
FRICK, Don .... 301-934-2251.. 207 B
dfrick@csmd.edu
FRICK, Jeffrey .... 920-403-3001.. 519 G
jeff.frick@snc.edu
FRICK, Lillian, K .... 989-386-6605.. 238 B
lfrick@midmich.edu
FRICK, Richard, A .... 201-692-2001.. 291 J
rfrick@fdu.edu
FRICK, Wanda .... 910-576-6222.. 351 E
frickw@montgomery.edu
FRICK-RUPPERT,
Jennifer, E .... 828-884-8144.. 342 C
jefrick@brevard.edu
FRICKE, David .... 732-906-2519.. 292 E
dfricke@middlesexcc.edu
FRICKE, Erik .... 805-965-0581.... 63 D
fricke@sbcc.edu
FRICKS, Brad .... 256-228-6001...... 5 I
fricksb@nacc.edu
FRICKX, Gretchen .... 312-697-8002.. 141 B
gfrickx@harrington.edu
FRIDAY, Brenda .... 570-422-3455.. 414 H
bfriday@esu.edu
FRIDAY, Yolanda .... 909-652-7405.... 37 D
yolanda.fridayl@chaffey.edu
FRIDAY-STROUD,
Shawnta .... 850-599-3565.. 110 J
shawnta.fridaystroud@famu.edu
FRIDGE, Rob .... 417-873-7527.. 264 H
rfridge@drury.edu
FRIEBEL, Thomas .... 718-368-6646.. 308 F
tfriebel@kbcc.cuny.edu
FRIED, Barry, J .... 608-796-3811.. 522 O
bjfried@viterbo.edu
FRIED, David .... 814-866-6641.. 407 D
dfried@lecom.edu
FRIED, Linda, P .... 212-305-9300.. 311 E
lpfried@columbia.edu
FRIED, Marc .... 785-670-1712.. 185 H
marc.fried@washburn.edu
FRIEDBERG, Connie .... 412-809-5100.. 417 D
friedberg.connie@pti.edu
FRIEDEL, Kristin, M .... 315-859-4637.. 315 D
kfriedel@hamilton.edu
FRIEDER, Steven, W .... 414-288-7752.. 517 I
steven.frieder@marquette.edu
FRIEDERICHS, Michelle .... 972-686-7878.. 464 A
mfriederichs@remingtoncollege.edu
FRIEDHOFF, Scott .... 330-263-2118.. 367 A
sfriedhoff@wooster.edu
FRIEDKIN, Rebecca .... 212-851-2273.. 304 I
rfriedki@barnard.edu
FRIEDLAND, Susan .... 215-641-6543.. 410 L
sfriedla@mc3.edu
FRIEDLANDER, Jack .... 805-965-0581.... 63 D
friedlan@sbcc.edu
FRIEDLEN, Karen .... 414-930-3349.. 518 F
friedlek@mtmary.edu
FRIEDLEY, Margret .... 360-736-9391.. 502 A
mfriedley@centralia.edu
FRIEDLINE, Patrick .... 312-329-4414.. 148 F
patrick.friedline@moody.edu
FRIEDLING, Melissa .... 212-229-8903.. 322 E
friedlim@newschool.edu
FRIEDLY, Allison .... 253-833-9111.. 504 C
afriedly@greenriver.edu
FRIEDMAN, Al .... 425-388-9399.. 503 F
afriedman@everettcc.edu
FRIEDMAN, Avraham .... 847-982-2500.. 141 D
friedman@htc.edu
FRIEDMAN, Daniel, S ...... 808-956-3469.. 131 F
dsf4114@hawaii.edu
FRIEDMAN, David .... 410-484-7200.. 210 A
dfreidman@nirc.edu
FRIEDMAN, Elizabeth ...... 847-578-8482.. 153 A
elizabeth.friedman@rosalindfranklin.edu
FRIEDMAN, Elizabeth ...... 718-518-4314.. 308 C
efriedman@hostos.cuny.edu
FRIEDMAN, Eric .... 201-360-4012.. 292 B
efriedman@hccc.edu
FRIEDMAN, Frank .... 434-977-1620.. 498 C
ffriedman@pvcc.edu
FRIEDMAN, Jay, R .... 716-645-3313.. 331 C
jf5@buffalo.edu
FRIEDMAN, Jill, D .... 314-935-5261.. 274 N
jill.friedman@wustl.edu
FRIEDMAN, Joel, A .... 401-825-2003.. 425 A
jafriedman@ccri.edu
FRIEDMAN, Leora .... 323-259-2500.... 55 A
lfriedman@oxy.edu
FRIEDMAN, Lori .... 617-989-4233.. 229 D
friedmanl@wit.edu
FRIEDMAN, Melissa .... 212-280-6001.. 317 I
mefriedman@jtsa.edu
FRIEDMAN, Natalie .... 212-854-2024.. 304 I
nfriedma@barnard.edu
FRIEDMAN, Robert .... 212-960-5269.. 341 G
rfriedm2@yu.edu
FRIEDMAN, Robert, S .... 973-655-4228.. 293 A
friedmanro@mail.montclair.edu
FRIEDMAN, Scott .... 708-974-5359.. 148 G
friedmans5@morainevalley.edu
FRIEDMAN, Stephen, J ..... 212-346-1097.. 325 J
president@pace.edu
FRIEDMAN, William .... 312-369-7623.. 138 F
bfriedman@colum.edu
FRIEDMAN, Yaakov .... 847-982-2500.. 141 D
yfriedman@htc.edu
FRIEDMAN-LOMBARDO,
Jaclyn, J .... 973-655-7599.. 293 A
friedmanlj@mail.montclair.edu
FRIEDMANN, Mina .... 212-217-3560.. 314 B
mina_friedmann@fitnyc.edu
FRIEDMANN, Peggy, L ...... 913-288-7123.. 182 C
pfriedmann@kckcc.edu
FRIEDNER, Julia .... 602-429-4921.... 16 E
jfriedner@ps.edu
FRIEDRICH, Brian, L .... 402-643-7364.. 279 F
brian.friedrich@cune.edu
FRIEDRICH, Dan .... 605-256-5555.. 437 C
dan.friedrich@dsu.edu
FRIEDRICHSEN,
Steven, W .... 909-706-3911.... 74 K
sfriedrichsen@westernu.edu
FRIEL, Lydia .... 215-780-1251.. 419 C
lfriel@salus.edu

FRIEL, Wm. Jake .... 724-287-8711.. 399 B
jake.friel@bc3.edu
FRIELER, Callie .... 570-340-6016.. 409 H
frieler@marywood.edu
FRIEND, Dane .... 713-798-1544.. 452 G
dfriend@bcm.edu
FRIEND, David .... 402-457-2770.. 280 J
djfriend@mccneb.edu
FRIEND, Denise .... 301-387-3125.. 207 G
denise.friend@garrettcollege.edu
FRIEND, Gwyn .... 312-362-6961.. 139 C
gfriend@depaul.edu
FRIEND, Vivian, M .... 727-816-3427.. 106 F
friendv@phsc.edu
FRIERMAN, Rose .... 607-777-4863.. 331 B
frierman@binghamton.edu
FRIERSON, Henry, T .... 352-392-6622.. 112 A
hfrierson@ufl.edu
FRIERSON, Tobe .... 912-344-2503.. 116 E
tobe.frierson@armstrong.edu
FRIERSON, Tobe, R .... 864-379-6687.. 429 I
frierson@erskine.edu
FRIES, Jane .... 970-542-3106.... 81 H
jane.fries@morgancc.edu
FRIES, Katherine .... 203-857-7105.... 87 B
kfries@norwalk.edu
FRIESEN, Wilbert .... 847-628-1001.. 144 B
will.friesen@judsonu.edu
FRIESNER, Todd .... 989-463-7143.. 230 F
friesnertb@alma.edu
FRIGGE, Maria .... 334-808-6128...... 7 H
lfrigge@troy.edu
FRIGO, Sandy .... 213-613-2200.... 65 H
sandy_frigo@sciarc.edu
FRINK, Dorothy .... 219-980-6994.. 163 B
defrink@iun.edu
FRINK, Kandy .... 307-382-1602.. 527 C
kfrink@westernwyoming.edu
FRIONA, Joseph, M .... 260-399-7700.. 168 D
jfriona@sf.edu
FRISBEE, Holly .... 212-966-0300.. 322 F
hfrisbee@nyaa.edu
FRISBEE, Sean .... 304-293-4731.. 514 C
sean.frisbee@mail.wvu.edu
FRISBEE, Stephen .... 315-792-5399.. 321 G
sfrisbee@mvcc.edu
FRISBIE, Kathy .... 970-542-3240.... 81 H
kathy.frisbie@morgancc.edu
FRISBY, Anthony .... 215-503-4990.. 420 E
anthony.frisby@jefferson.edu
FRISBY, Bernard .... 703-212-7410.. 490 C
FRISCH, Kim .... 303-458-4909.... 82 L
kfrisch@regis.edu
FRISCH, Randy, C .... 858-642-8105.... 54 A
rfrisch@nu.edu
FRISCHMANN, John .... 320-308-2522.. 252 A
jmfrischmann@stcloudstate.edu
FRISENDA, Louis .... 703-247-8341.. 492 A
louis.frisenda@marymount.edu
FRISHMAN, Niki .... 760-872-2000.... 42 B
nikif@deepsprings.edu
FRISINA, Warren .... 516-463-4783.. 316 D
warren.frisina@hofstra.edu
FRISKICS, Scott .... 406-353-2607.. 275 H
friskics@hotmail.com
FRISKNEY, Paul .... 513-244-8128.. 366 B
paul.friskney@ccuniversity.edu
FRISQUE, Megan .... 512-863-1584.. 466 G
frisquem@southwestern.edu
FRIST, Matthew, J .... 412-396-6063.. 403 A
frist@duq.edu
FRITCH, John, E .... 319-273-2725.. 170 A
john.fritch@uni.edu
FRITCH, Margie .... 619-388-2789.... 60 G
mfritch@sdccd.edu
FRITSCH, Denise .... 859-442-4162.. 189 D
denise.fritsch@kctcs.edu
FRITSCHE, Teresa .... 570-422-3422.. 414 H
tfritsche@esu.edu
FRITSKY, Wren .... 570-389-4070.. 414 D
wfritsky@bloomu.edu
FRITTON, Sandra .... 540-654-1266.. 495 C
sfritton@umw.edu
FRITTS, Jack .... 630-829-6060.. 135 F
jfritts@ben.edu
FRITTS, Mary Lou, A .... 816-235-1107.. 273 F
frittsml@umkc.edu
FRITZ, Greg .... 402-399-2407.. 279 E
gfritz@csm.edu
FRITZ, John .... 410-455-6596.. 211 G
fritz@umbc.edu
FRITZ, Sarah .... 608-246-6559.. 523 F
fritz@madisoncollege.edu
FRITZ, Shelby .... 253-589-5533.. 502 F
shelby.fritz@cptc.edu
FRITZ, Stephen .... 806-742-1828.. 472 C
steve.fritz@ttu.edu
FRITZ, Stephen, J .... 651-962-5901.. 256 C
sjfritz@stthomas.edu
FRITZ, Susan, M .... 402-472-5242.. 282 K
smfritz@nebraska.edu
FRITZ, Ted, P .... 412-624-0072.. 421 G
tfritz@pitt.edu
FRITZ, Thomas, R .... 814-472-3006.. 418 F
tfritz@francis.edu
FRITZ, William, J .... 718-982-2400.. 307 F
president@csi.cuny.edu
FRITZE, Barbara, B .... 717-337-6582.. 404 C
bfritze@gettysburg.edu
FRITZE, Ronald .... 256-216-5524...... 1 F
ron.fritze@athens.edu
FRITZMAN, D. Jason .... 304-243-2043.. 515 C
jfritzman@wju.edu
FRIZZELL, Christine .... 508-999-8648.. 220 H
cfrizzell@umassd.edu
FRIZZELL, Douglas .... 412-396-3234.. 403 A
frizzelld@duq.edu
FRIZZELL, Robert .... 479-788-7205.... 23 A
robert.frizzell@uafs.edu
FROCK, Gemma .... 803-508-7277.. 426 G
frockg@atc.edu
FROEHLE, Mary .... 561-723-4424.. 108 F
mfroehle@svdp.edu
FROEHLE, Ryan .... 312-939-4975.. 141 B
rfroehle@harrington.edu
FROEHLICH-MUELLER,
Kerry, K .... 608-757-7654.. 523 A
kfroehlich-mueller@blackhawk.edu
FROHOFF, Katherine .... 816-501-4151.. 270 J
katherine.frohoff@rockhurst.edu
FROHRIB, Patti .... 920-735-5611.. 523 C
frohrib@fvtc.edu
FROLE, Angelo .... 614-287-5020.. 367 C
afrole@cscc.edu
FROMBGEN, Liz .... 402-461-7321.. 280 D
lfrombgen@hastings.edu
FROMING, William .... 650-433-3830.... 56 D
bfroming@paloaltou.edu
FROMMELT, Steve .... 309-796-5933.. 135 I
frommelts@bhc.edu
FRONCEK, Maureen .... 312-341-4167.. 152 H
mfroncek@roosevelt.edu
FRONCZEK, Andrew, F .... 216-397-4275.. 370 H
afronczek@jcu.edu
FRONCZEK, Walter .... 708-974-5372.. 148 G
fronczek@morainevalley.edu
FRONHEISER, Joey .... 405-945-3250.. 386 C
fronhei@osuokc.edu
FRONK, Michael, R .... 386-822-7523.. 113 B
mfronk@stetson.edu
FRONK, Peter .... 608-363-2375.. 515 G
fronkp@beloit.edu
FRONK, Suzette .... 828-898-8809.. 345 G
fronks@lmc.edu
FRONMUELLER, Michael .... 715-425-3335.. 521 B
michael.fronmueller@uwrf.edu
FRONRATH, Scott .... 727-341-4495.. 108 D
fronrath.scott@spcollege.edu
FRONTERA, Jose, A .... 787-841-2000.. 535 I
jose_frontera@pucpr.edu
FRONTIERA, Charlene .... 650-574-6312.... 62 H
frontierac@smccd.edu
FRONTIERA, Patrick .... 310-338-4489.... 51 E
pfrontiera@lmu.edu
FRONZONI, Susan .... 570-674-6249.. 410 K
sfronzon@misericordia.edu
FROSCH, Jeff .... 512-313-3000.. 455 F
jeff.frosch@concordia.edu
FROSLID JONES,
Karen, L .... 202-885-6155.... 91 J
kfroslid@american.edu
FROSSARD, RET.,
Margaret O'Mara .... 312-427-2737.. 143 G
mfrossar@jmls.edu
FROST, Brian .... 419-473-2700.. 367 J
bfrost@daviscollege.edu
FROST, Catherine .... 510-215-3928.... 41 H
cfrost@contracosta.edu
FROST, Dana, L .... 864-644-5004.. 432 G
dfrost@swu.edu
FROST, Eric .... 315-464-4393.. 332 C
froste@upstate.edu
FROST, James .... 830-303-0404.. 470 C
frost@frostlawoffice.com
FROST, Judith .... 207-755-5265.. 203 I
jfrost@cmcc.edu
FROST, Julia, H .... 479-979-1401.... 24 I
jfrost@ozarks.edu
FROST, Leanne .... 406-771-4372.. 277 F
leanne.frost@gfcmsu.edu
FROST, Linda .... 423-425-5922.. 448 F
linda-frost@utc.edu
FROST, Mark .... 518-783-4100.. 330 E
mfrost@siena.edu
FROST, Mark .... 518-276-8246.. 327 B
frostm@rpi.edu
FROST, Mike .... 406-243-4711.. 276 K
mike.frost@umontana.edu
FROST, Richard, A .... 616-395-7800.. 235 F
frost@hope.edu
FROST, Stacy .... 507-537-6483.. 252 E
stacy.frost@smsu.edu
FROST, Vivian .... 620-252-7199.. 180 B
vivianf@coffeyville.edu
FROUDE, Bill .... 859-572-5112.. 192 B
froudew1@nku.edu
FRUCHTHANDLER,
Abraham, H .... 718-377-0777.. 326 F
FRUEAN, Evelyn, V .... 684-699-9155.. 529 E
e.fruean@amsamoa.edu
FRUEH, Elizabeth .... 715-425-3737.. 521 B
elizabeth.frueh@uwrf.edu
FRUITTICHER, Lee .... 706-721-7928.. 117 D
lfruitticher@augusta.edu
FRUM, Jennifer, L .... 706-542-6126.. 128 E
jfrum@uga.edu
FRUMKIN, Howard .... 206-543-2100.. 508 E
frumkin@uw.edu
FRUMKIN, Jeffery, F .... 734-763-4551.. 241 J
jfrumkin@umich.edu
FRUMKIN, Michael .... 407-823-6424.. 111 E
michael.frumkin@ucf.edu
FRUMKIN, Steven .... 212-217-4330.. 314 B
steven_frumkin@fitnyc.edu
FRUTCHEY, Shelby .... 512-516-8703.. 127 D
sfrutchey@southuniversity.edu
FRUZZETTI, Armida .... 775-673-7135.. 284 K
afruzzetti@tmcc.edu
FRY, Angela .... 870-574-4523.... 22 G
afry@sautech.edu
FRY, Bobbye, G .... 210-829-6006.. 474 D
fry@uiwtx.edu
FRY, Donna .... 810-237-6503.. 242 B
donnafry@umflint.edu
FRY, Jacy .... 605-256-5267.. 437 C
jacy.fry@dsu.edu
FRY, John .... 708-239-4863.. 155 M
john.fry@trnty.edu
FRY, John, A .... 215-895-2100.. 402 G
jaf@drexel.edu
FRY, Pamela .... 405-744-5627.. 385 G
pamela.fry@okstate.edu
FRYDA, Kathleen .... 920-498-6288.. 524 E
kathleen.fryda@nwtc.edu
FRYE, Brandon .... 850-474-2384.. 113 A
bfrye@uwf.edu
FRYE, Harland .... 252-789-0225.. 351 A
hfrye@martincc.edu
FRYE, Holly .... 304-876-5402.. 513 E
hfrye@shepherd.edu
FRYE, Jeffrey .... 419-434-4501.. 379 E
frye@findlay.edu
FRYE, Joseph .... 502-272-3333.. 187 A
jfrye@bellarmine.edu
FRYE, Karen .... 910-576-6222.. 351 E
fryek@montgomery.edu
FRYE, Keener .... 307-766-4166.. 527 B
hfry1@uwyo.edu
FRYE, Lela .... 352-395-5420.. 109 C
lela.frye@sfcollege.edu
FRYE, Susan .... 307-766-3152.. 527 B
frye@uwyo.edu
FRYE, Todd .... 913-971-3617.. 183 D
tmfrye@mnu.edu
FRYER, Robert .... 570-484-2344.. 415 D
rcf138@lhup.edu
FRYLING, Michelle .... 724-357-2302.. 415 B
mfryling@iup.edu
FRYNS, Jennifer .... 352-854-2322.... 97 R
frynsj@cf.edu
FRYSON, David, M .... 304-293-3431.. 514 C
david.fryson@mail.wvu.edu
FU, Di .... 954-763-9840.... 95 N
fudi@atom.edu
FUCHKO, III, John, M .... 404-962-3025.. 129 F
john.fuchko@usg.edu
FUCHS, Catherine .... 615-327-7264.. 449 A
catherine.fuchs@vanderbilt.edu
FUCHS, Kyle .... 937-769-1366.. 363 F
kfuchs@antioch.edu
FUCHS, Monique .... 617-989-4513.. 229 D
fuchsm@wit.edu
FUCHS, Tina, M .... 503-838-8220.. 396 E
fuchst@wou.edu
FUCHS, W. Kent .... 352-392-1311.. 112 A
president@ufl.edu
FUDALLY, Steve .... 218-733-7600.. 249 H
steve.fudally@lsc.edu
FUDGE, Denise, G .... 270-384-8203.. 191 E
fudged@lindsey.edu
FUDGE, Melinda, F .... 229-333-5797.. 129 G
mffudge@valdosta.edu
FUDGE, Sara .... 513-244-8445.. 366 E
sara.fudge@ccuniversity.edu
FUENTES, Alan .... 718-289-5197.. 307 C
alan.fuentes@bcc.cuny.edu
FUENTES, Angeles .... 831-582-4136.... 33 E
afuentes@csumb.edu
FUENTES, Jaime .... 913-621-8771.. 180 F
jfuentes@donnelly.edu
FUENTES, Jose, A .... 787-279-1912.. 533 J
jfuentes@bayamon.inter.edu
FUENTES, Monsterrat .... 804-828-1674.. 496 D
mfuentes@vcu.edu
FUENTES, Ramonita .... 787-751-0178.. 535 N
ac_rfuentes@suagm.edu
FUENTES, Trisha, D .... 973-290-4130.. 290 G
tfuentes@cse.edu
FUENTES-AFFLICK, Elena .... 415-476-1977.... 70 D
elena.fuentes-afflick@ucsf.edu
FUENTEZ, Tammy .... 620-421-6700.. 182 G
tammyf@labette.edu
FUERST, Nathan .... 860-486-3137.... 89 D
nathan.fuerst@uconn.edu
FUERY, Patrick .... 714-997-6947.... 37 F
fuery@chapman.edu
FUEST, Melissa .... 201-216-3346.. 297 B
melissa.fuest@stevens.edu
FUEYO, Vivian .... 727-873-4010.. 112 D
vfueyo@usfsp.edu
FUGALE, Stephen .... 610-519-4400.. 422 G
stephen.fugale@villanova.edu
FUGATE, Amy .... 810-762-0237.. 238 F
amy.fugate@mcc.edu
FUGATE, Jessica .... 727-864-8404.... 98 L
fugatejb@eckerd.edu
FUGATE, Megan, A .... 620-421-6700.. 182 G
meganf@labette.edu
FUGATE, Stu .... 606-487-3196.. 189 E
stu.fugate@kctcs.edu
FUGATE, Wesley .... 434-947-8000.. 493 B
wfugate@randolphcollege.edu
FUGATE-ROBERTS,
Kimberly .... 352-395-5510.. 109 C
kimberly.fugate-roberts@sfcollege.edu
FUGAZZOTTO, Sam .... 212-678-4055.. 337 E
fugazzotto@tc.edu
FUGIEL, Lisa .... 413-755-4786.. 224 G
lfugiel@stcc.edu
FUGITT, Gilbert .... 949-214-3057.... 41 F
gilbert.fugitt@cui.edu
FUGLESTAD, Amy .... 701-845-7122.. 361 B
amy.fuglestad@vcsu.edu
FUGLIESE, Susan .... 617-731-7623.. 227 D
sfugliese@pmc.edu
FUHLER, Justin .... 217-479-7153.. 147 C
justin.fuhler@mac.edu
FUHRMAN, JR.,
L. Clifton .... 864-938-3907.. 432 B
lcfuhrman@presby.edu
FUHRMAN, Mary .... 864-592-4660.. 432 H
fuhrmanm@sccsc.edu
FUHRMAN, Susan, H .... 212-678-3131.. 337 E
susanf@tc.columbia.edu
FUHRMAN, Tim .... 509-793-2351.. 501 H
timf@bigbend.edu
FUHRMANN, Dave .... 805-652-5577.... 73 C
dfuhrmann@vcccd.edu
FUHRMANN, Donald, J .... 814-824-2104.. 410 H
dfuhrmann@mercyhurst.edu
FUITH, Leanne .... 651-290-7526.. 253 S
leanne.fuith@mitchellhamline.edu
FUJII, Marnie .... 952-829-4192.. 244 J
marnie.fujii@bethfel.org
FUJII, Stephanie .... 480-423-6300.... 14 H
stephanie.fujii@scottsdalecc.edu
FUJIYOSHI, Lois, M .... 808-932-7664.. 131 E
lfujiyos@hawaii.edu
FUKUMOTO, Erin .... 808-983-4115.. 130 I
efukumoto@tokai.edu
FULBRIGHT, Kyle .... 423-746-5327.. 447 E
kfulbright@twcnet.edu
FULCHER, D. Keith .... 662-846-4708.. 257 E
kfulcher@deltastate.edu
FULCHER, Kerry .... 619-849-2651.... 57 M
kerryfulcher@pointloma.edu
FULCOMER, Eric, W .... 815-226-4010.. 152 G
FULD, Kenneth .... 603-862-2062.. 288 C
ken.fuld@unh.edu
FULFORD, David .... 602-275-7133.... 16 Q
david.fulford@rsiaz.edu
FULFORD, Leroy .... 740-377-2520.. 378 B
lfulford@zoominternet.net
FULFORD, Lynda .... 805-493-3839.... 31 C
fulford@callutheran.edu
FULFORD, Sherri .... 334-242-2688...... 1 G
fulfosg@auburn.edu
FULFORD, William, J .... 251-460-7277...... 9 E
hfulford@southalabama.edu
FULIGNI, Paul .... 618-650-2560.. 155 A
pfulign@siue.edu
FULK, Scott .... 219-980-6792.. 163 B
sfulk@iun.edu
FULK, Sheryl, E .... 812-877-8344.. 166 H
sheryl.fulk@rose-hulman.edu
FULKERSON, Cathy .... 775-753-2108.. 284 I
cathy.fulkerson@gbcnv.edu
FULKERSON, Cathy .... 775-445-3219.. 285 B
cathy.fulkerson@wnc.edu
FULKERSON,
Christopher, D .... 336-278-5055.. 344 D
fulkers@elon.edu

FULKERSON, Diane .... 941-359-4316.. 112 E
dfulkerson@sar.usf.edu
FULL, Karen .... 239-280-2480.... 95 Q
karen.full@avemaria.edu
FULLEM, Wendy .... 973-300-2120.. 297 D
wfullem@sussex.edu
FULLER, Barbara, J .... 276-964-7200.. 498 F
barbara.fuller@sw.edu
FULLER, Belinda .... 304-766-3387.. 514 B
bfuller@wvstateu.edu
FULLER, Brian .... 806-874-3571.. 454 F
brian.fuller@clarendoncollege.edu
FULLER, Candy .... 361-354-2251.. 454 G
fuller_c@coastalbend.edu
FULLER, Cindy .... 217-424-3944.. 148 D
cfuller@millikin.edu
FULLER, Colleen .... 201-559-1454.. 291 K
fullerc@felician.edu
FULLER, David .... 478-757-2544.. 124 E
david.fuller@mga.edu
FULLER, JR., Henry, M ... 843-953-5185.. 428 A
hank.fuller@citadel.edu
FULLER, Howard .... 360-383-3295.. 509 F
hfuller@whatcom.ctc.edu
FULLER, Janet .... 336-278-7729.. 344 D
jfuller3@elon.edu
FULLER, Lori .... 661-654-2273.... 32 A
1250mgr@fheg.follett.com
FULLER, Mark .... 205-726-2711...... 6 E
dmfuller@samford.edu
FULLER, Mark, A .... 413-545-5583.. 220 F
dean@isenberg.umass.edu
FULLER, Max .... 937-529-2201.. 378 F
smfuller@united.edu
FULLER, Michael .... 541-684-7248.. 393 B
mfuller@nwcu.edu
FULLER, Michael .... 903-223-3060.. 469 C
michael.fuller@tamut.edu
FULLER, Mickey .... 405-945-8645.. 386 C
mickedf@osuokc.edu
FULLER, Mildred, K .... 757-823-2366.. 492 F
mkfuller@nsu.edu
FULLER, Norine .... 202-822-9633.... 43 J
nfuller@fidm.edu
FULLER, Peggy .... 318-678-6000.. 195 I
pfuller@bpcc.edu
FULLER, Rex .... 503-838-8888.. 396 E
rfuller@wou.edu
FULLER, Richard .... 315-792-7309.. 336 C
richard.fuller@sunyit.edu
FULLER, Roger, D .... 817-257-6122.. 469 G
r.fuller@tcu.edu
FULLER BEELER,
Rebecca .... 765-641-4337.. 158 J
rlbeeler@anderson.edu
FULLERTON, Adam .... 712-274-5247.. 175 C
fullertona@morningside.edu
FULLERTON, Darren, S ... 417-625-3135.. 268 H
fullerton-d@mssu.edu
FULLERTON, Fred, C .... 208-467-8530.. 134 D
ffullerton@nnu.edu
FULLMER, Paul .... 717-867-6135.. 408 F
fullmer@lvc.edu
FULMER, David .... 918-495-7480.. 386 H
dfulmer@oru.edu
FULMER, Deryl .... 252-536-7289.. 350 C
ddavisfulmer985@halifaxcc.edu
FULMER, Gregory, L .... 610-921-7749.. 396 H
gfulmer@albright.edu
FULMER, Hal .... 334-670-3112...... 7 H
hfulmer@troy.edu
FULMER, Judy .... 334-670-3102...... 7 H
jfulmer@troy.edu
FULMER-GARFIELD,
Dana .... 860-701-5047.... 88 D
fulmer_d@mitchell.edu
FULMORE, Robbin, S .... 757-683-4756.. 492 G
rfulmore@odu.edu
FULNECKY, Elizabeth .... 574-239-8404.. 161 N
efulnecky@hcc-nd.edu
FULOP, Timothy .... 434-791-5630.. 487 C
tfulop@averett.edu
FULP, Breean .... 602-331-7500.... 11 K
bfulp@aii.edu
FULTON, Andrew .... 914-323-5154.. 319 N
andrew.fulton@mville.edu
FULTON, Dean .... 360-752-8378.. 501 G
dfulton@btc.edu
FULTON, Deborah, M .... 540-231-0735.. 499 F
dfulton@vt.edu
FULTON, DoVeanna .... 713-221-8009.. 474 B
fultond@uhd.edu
FULTON, Erica .... 870-575-8491.... 23 E
fultone@uapb.edu
FULTON, Jodie .... 541-956-7200.. 394 J
jfulton@roguecc.edu
FULTON, Lori .... 509-452-5100.. 505 H
lfulton@pnwu.edu
FULTON, Richard .... 970-247-7150.... 80 D
fulton_r@fortlewis.edu
FULTON, Tara Lynn .... 603-862-1506.. 288 C
taralynn.fulton@unh.edu
FULTZ, Angela .... 606-759-7141.. 190 C
angela.fultz@kctcs.edu
FULTZ, Bob .... 502-863-8029.. 188 I
bob_fultz@georgetowncollege.edu
FULTZ, Larenda .... 731-286-3234.. 446 B
fultz@dscc.edu
FUNAI, Edmund, F .... 813-974-4531.. 112 C
funai@health.usf.edu
FUNAI, Gordy .... 425-739-8456.. 504 F
gordy.funai@lwtech.edu
FUNDERBURK,
Carolyn, W .... 336-599-0257.. 351 H
carolyn.funderburk@piedmontcc.edu
FUNICELLO, Lori .... 201-200-3489.. 293 C
lfunicello@njcu.edu
FUNIGIELLO, Tony .... 716-827-2481.. 338 E
funigielloa@trocaire.edu
FUNK, Carla .... 321-674-8921.. 100 M
cfunk@fit.edu
FUNK, Chad .... 916-484-8401.... 51 A
funkc@arc.losrios.edu
FUNK, David .... 503-255-0332.. 392 G
davefunk@multnomah.edu
FUNK, Ed .... 916-348-4689.... 43 A
efunk@epic.edu
FUNK, Nancy .... 530-938-5220.... 40 F
nfunk@siskiyous.edu
FUNK, Ruth .... 620-947-3121.. 185 B
ruthf@tabor.edu
FUNK, Tiger .... 435-586-7888.. 481 N
funk@suu.edu
FUNK, Tracy .... 317-921-4371.. 164 F
tfunk@ivytech.edu
FUNK-BAXTER, Kathryn ... 210-458-4201.. 477 A
kathryn.funk-baxter@utsa.edu
FUNKE, Rebecca .... 515-964-6328.. 171 B
rsfunke@dmacc.edu
FUNKE, Renata .... 831-386-7100.... 45 L
rfunke@hartnell.edu
FUNKE-LUFF, Libby .... 615-514-2787.. 443 F
lfunke@nossi.edu
FUQUA, Amy .... 605-642-6504.. 437 B
amy.fugua@bhsu.edu
FUQUA, Jacques .... 903-468-6041.. 468 D
jacques.fuqua@tamuc.edu
FUQUA, Jan, R .... 270-809-4049.. 192 A
jfuqua@murraystate.edu
FUQUAY, Melissa .... 757-352-4270.. 493 E
mfuquay@regent.edu
FURBECK, Lee .... 216-523-7417.. 366 I
l.furbeck@csuohio.edu
FURBEE, Thomas, V .... 304-829-7749.. 510 G
tfurbee@bethanywv.edu
FURBISH, Julie .... 781-239-2661.. 223 F
jfurbish@massbay.edu
FURDA, Eric, J .... 215-898-2886.. 421 E
furda@admissions.upenn.edu
FURDA, Mark .... 740-284-5326.. 368 L
mfurda@franciscan.edu
FURE-SLOCUM, Carolyn .. 507-222-4003.. 245 C
cfureslo@carleton.edu
FURGAL,
Charles (Chuck) .... 781-239-2694.. 223 F
cfurgal@massbay.edu
FURGE, Laura, L .... 269-337-7156.. 235 H
laura.furge@kzoo.edu
FURI-PERRY, Ursula .... 978-681-0800.. 225 B
furiperry@mslaw.edu
FURLAN, Rogerio .... 787-850-9006.. 538 B
rogerio.furlan@upr.edu
FURLER, Arthur .... 540-261-4094.. 494 F
arthur.furler@svu.edu
FURLONE, Jeffrey, C .... 603-535-2206.. 288 F
jfurlone@plymouth.edu
FURLONG, Deborah .... 920-465-2374.. 520 B
furlongd@uwgb.edu
FURLONG, Katherine .... 570-372-4320.. 419 H
kurlongk@susqu.edu
FURLONG, Matthew .... 409-772-5113.. 478 A
mfurlong@utmb.edu
FURLONG, Michael .... 805-893-3338.... 70 E
mfurlong@education.ucsb.edu
FURLONG, Scott .... 920-465-2336.. 520 B
furlongs@uwgb.edu
FURLONG, Vicki .... 315-312-3636.. 333 D
victoria.furlong@oswego.edu
FURMAN, John, A .... 360-650-3496.. 509 E
john.furman@wwu.edu
FURMAN, William, F .... 845-368-7202.. 329 I
william.furman@use.salvationarmy.org
FURNESS-FALLIN, Robyn 404-261-1441.. 125 F
rfurness@oglethorpe.edu
FURNISS, Rochel .... 740-392-6868.. 373 D
rochel.furniss@mvnu.edu
FURNO, Mike .... 303-871-2361.... 84 B
mike.furno@du.edu
FURR, James, H .... 713-942-9505.. 459 C
jfurr@hgst.edu
FURR, Jennifer .... 402-643-7341.. 279 F
alumni@cune.edu
FURR, Kathleen .... 214-768-2030.. 465 J
kfurr@smu.edu
FURR, Timothy, L .... 320-222-5735.. 251 G
tim.furr@ridgewater.edu
FURROW, Louise, S .... 206-281-2998.. 507 C
lfurrow@spu.edu
FURSE, Cynthia, M .... 801-581-7236.. 481 M
cfurse@ece.utah.edu
FURST-BOWE, Julie .... 715-858-1857.. 523 B
jfurstbowe@cvtc.edu
FURTON, Kenneth .... 305-348-2866.. 111 A
furtonk@fiu.edu
FURTWENGLER, Scott ..... 979-230-3256.. 453 A
scott.furtwengler@brazosport.edu
FURUI, Sadaoki .... 773-834-2493.. 155 K
furui@ttic.edu
FURUKAWA, Karen .... 707-527-4302.... 63 G
kfurukawa-schlereth@santarosa.edu
FURUKAWA-SCHLERETH,
Laurence .... 707-664-2310.... 35 D
laurence.furukawa-schlereth@sonoma.edu
FURUSETH, Laurie .... 701-774-4250.. 361 G
laurie.furuseth@willistonstate.edu
FURUSHIMA, Randall ...... 808-853-1040.. 131 B
randallfurushima@pacrim.edu
FURUTA, Lisa .... 808-739-4746.. 130 F
lisa.furuta@chaminade.edu
FURUTO, Brian .... 808-734-9572.. 131 I
bfuruto@hawaii.edu
FURUTO, Sandra, K .... 808-956-7487.. 131 D
yano@hawaii.edu
FURUYA, Dan .... 808-689-2545.. 131 G
dfuruya@hawaii.edu
FUSCHETTI, Deborah, M .. 863-784-7139.. 109 G
deborah.fuschetti@southflorida.edu
FUSCO, Joseph .... 610-902-8245.. 399 D
jf693@cabrini.edu
FUSCO, Valerie .... 315-792-7111.. 336 C
valerie.fusco@sunyit.edu
FUSCO, William, J .... 707-664-2639.... 35 D
bill.fusco@sonoma.edu
FUSE-HALL, Rosalind ...... 336-517-2225.. 342 B
rosalind.fuse-hall@bennett.edu
FUSILIER, LaDonna .... 870-574-4519.... 22 G
lfusilier@sautech.edu
FUSS, Kevin, J .... 815-825-9454.. 144 F
kevin.fuss@kishwaukeecollege.edu
FUSTE, Robert .... 269-471-6571.. 230 H
rfuste@andrews.edu
FUSTER, Luis .... 787-765-3560.. 532 I
lfuster@edpuniversity.edu
FUTHEY, Carol .... 970-248-1881.... 77 L
cfuthey@coloradomesa.edu
FUTHEY, Tracy .... 919-684-8111.. 343 J
futhey@duke.edu
FUTRELL, Michelle, G ...... 843-953-5674.. 428 G
futrellm@cofc.edu
FUTRELL, Tamara, Y .... 540-458-8766.. 500 F
tfutrell@wlu.edu
FUTTERER, Julie .... 815-740-3826.. 157 F
jfutterer@stfrancis.edu
FUZY, Robert .... 704-463-3076.. 354 F
robert.fuzy@pfeiffer.edu
FYDENKEVEZ,
Mary Ellen .... 413-775-1469.. 223 D
fydenkevez@gcc.mass.edu
FYE, Marty .... 402-826-8261.. 280 B
marty.fye@doane.edu
FYFE, Brenda, S .... 314-968-6913.. 275 B
fyfebv@webster.edu
FYFE, Dorothy .... 718-270-2726.. 332 B
dorothy.fyfe@downstate.edu
FYFE, John .... 415-442-6540.... 45 B
jfyfe@ggu.edu
FYFFE, Robert .... 937-775-3336.. 381 H
robert.fyffe@wright.edu
FYOCK, Debra, R .... 412-648-1458.. 421 G
dfyock@bc.pitt.edu

G

GÓMEZ, Sheila .... 787-751-1912.. 534 E
sgomez@juris.inter.edu
GAAL, John .... 215-276-6070.. 419 C
jgaal@salus.edu
GAALSWYK, Terry .... 507-372-3491.. 250 G
terry.gaalswyk@mnwest.edu
GAARDER, David .... 972-883-6374.. 476 C
dkg053000@utdallas.edu
GABA, Barbara .... 908-965-6091.. 298 A
gaba@ucc.edu
GABBARD, Clinton, E .... 815-455-8725.. 147 E
cgabbard@mchenry.edu
GABBARD, Kurt, A .... 609-497-7705.. 294 C
kurt.gabbard@ptsem.edu
GABBARD, Veronica .... 281-649-3747.. 458 L
vgabbard@hbu.edu
GABBERT, Jeri Pat .... 219-981-4242.. 163 B
jgabbert@iun.edu
GABBERT, Paula, S .... 864-294-2064.. 430 C
paula.gabbert@furman.edu
GABEHART, Luci .... 432-264-5074.. 459 D
lgabehart@howardcollege.edu
GABEL, Ann-Marie .... 562-938-4540.... 49 D
agabel@lbcc.edu
GABEL, Barb .... 419-448-2183.. 369 G
bgabel@heidelberg.edu
GABEL, Joan, T .... 803-777-2808.. 433 F
gabelj@mailbox.sc.edu
GABER, Sharon, L .... 419-530-2211.. 380 D
sharon.gaber@utoledo.edu
GABERT, Glen, E .... 201-360-4003.. 292 B
ggabert@hccc.edu
GABERT, Susan, S .... 603-641-7231.. 287 G
sgabert@anselm.edu
GABIANELLI, Barbara, A .. 203-576-4134.... 89 C
bag@bridgeport.edu
GABLE, Carol .... 315-229-5563.. 329 D
cgable@stlawu.edu
GABLE, Jill .... 252-335-3283.. 356 D
jegable@ecsu.edu
GABLE, Karla .... 314-539-5303.. 271 F
kgable4@stlcc.edu
GABLE, Nakita .... 251-344-1203...... 3 J
GABLE, Nicole .... 412-536-1022.. 406 K
nicole.gable@laroche.edu
GABOURY, John, D .... 517-355-5767.. 237 I
gaboury@msu.edu
GABOURY, Mario .... 203-932-7253.... 90 A
mgaboury@newhaven.edu
GABOVITCH, Rhonda .... 508-678-2811.. 223 A
rhonda.gabovitch@bristolcc.edu
GABRIEL, George, E .... 703-323-3129.. 497 H
ggabriel@nvcc.edu
GABRIEL, Lisa .... 281-283-3032.. 474 A
gabriel@uhcl.edu
GABRIEL, Mary .... 970-339-6248.... 76 H
mary.gabriel@aims.edu
GABRIEL, Robert .... 707-864-7000.... 65 A
robert.gabriel@solano.edu
GABRIELE, Gary, A .... 610-519-5860.. 422 G
gary.gabriele@villanova.edu
GABRIELSON, Kerry .... 719-846-5643.... 83 G
kerry.gabrielson@trinidadstate.edu
GACHETTE, Yves, M .... 716-878-4521.. 332 F
gachetym@buffalostate.edu
GACHUPIN, Allen (Ray) ... 505-346-7728.. 302 E
ray.gachupin@bie.edu
GACKENHEIMER,
Lois, M .... 561-683-1400.... 94 G
admin@anho.edu
GACKLE, Joel .... 714-556-3610.... 73 B
joel.gackle@vanguard.edu
GADBERRY, Brad .... 678-341-6615.. 123 L
bgadberry@laniertech.edu
GADDE, Sandee, A .... 989-463-7146.. 230 F
gadde@alma.edu
GADDIS, Glendi .... 210-999-7011.. 473 A
ggaddis@trinity.edu
GADDIS, Lydia .... 937-766-7886.. 365 C
lgaddis@cedarville.edu
GADE, Chris, W .... 507-284-2073.. 245 F
cgade@mayo.edu
GADE, Werner .... 608-263-6012.. 522 A
werner.gade@uwc.edu
GADE-JONES, Tish .... 402-465-2114.. 281 K
tgadejon@nebrwesleyan.edu
GADIKIAN,
Randolph Lee .... 716-673-3181.. 331 D
randolph.gadikian@fredonia.edu
GADSBY, Peter .... 845-758-7457.. 304 F
gadsby@bard.edu
GADSON, Mark, P .... 610-409-3164.. 422 D
mgadson@ursinus.edu
GADWOOD, Tyler .... 913-758-6331.. 185 F
tyler.gadwood@stmary.edu
GADZINSKI, James, G ...... 906-227-2971.. 239 B
jgadzins@nmu.edu
GAECKE, Lauren .... 920-403-3181.. 519 G
GAER-CARLTON, Kathy ..... 509-963-1211.. 501 K
katherine.gaer-carlton@cwu.edu
GAERTE, Phyllis .... 585-567-9620.. 316 F
phyllis.gaerte@houghton.edu
GAERTNER, Michelle .... 615-248-1463.. 447 F
mgaertner@trevecca.edu
GAETA, Alexa .... 404-471-6423.. 115 J
agaeta@agnesscott.edu
GAETA, James .... 512-863-1259.. 466 G
gaetaj@southwestern.edu
GAETA, Maria .... 805-482-2755.... 59 G
mgaeta@stjohnsem.edu
GAETANO, Davide .... 404-413-4469.. 122 D
davide@gsu.edu
GAETJENS, Stuart .... 931-393-1663.. 446 D
ssgaetjens@mscc.edu
GAFF, Crystal .... 603-535-2338.. 288 F
clgaff@plymouth.edu
GAFFEY, Donna .... 617-217-9887.. 215 B
dgaffey@baystate.edu

GAFFEY, Pat 480-947-6644 16 C
pat.gaffey@pennfoster.edu
GAFFNER, Lori 618-664-7120 140 I
lori.gaffner@greenville.edu
GAFFNEY, Eva 508-531-1337 221 C
egaffney@bridgew.edu
GAFFNEY, Kathryn 860-215-9266 87 D
kgaffney@trcc.commnet.edu
GAFFNEY, Kevin 775-445-4223 285 B
kevin.gaffney@wnc.edu
GAFFNEY, Lorita 920-686-6200 519 H
lorita.gaffney@sl.edu
GAFFNEY, Michelle 330-823-2496 379 F
gaffnemi@mountunion.edu
GAFFNEY, Phillip 706-204-2201 121 C
pgaffney@highlands.edu
GAFFNEY, Tiffany, D 401-865-2191 425 D
tgaffne1@providence.edu
GAFFORD, Brian 931-393-1576 446 D
bgafford@mscc.edu
GAGAN, Kelly 585-389-2411 322 D
kgagan8@naz.edu
GAGE, Adrian 508-929-8563 222 F
agage@worcester.edu
GAGE, Brent 319-335-1548 169 H
brent-gage@uiowa.edu
GAGE, Chris 812-866-7028 161 C
gage@hanover.edu
GAGE, David 315-781-3734 316 C
gage@hws.edu
GAGE, J. Scott 978-837-5468 225 E
j.scott.gage@merrimack.edu
GAGE, Jeannie 361-825-2332 468 E
jeannie.gage@tamucc.edu
GAGE, Julia 401-841-6535 528 E
julia.gage@usnwc.edu
GAGER, Sarah 203-575-8034 86 G
sgager@nv.edu
GAGLIARDI, Cathy 941-351-5100 107 M
cgagliardi@ringling.edu
GAGNE PENDLETON,
Lori 860-515-3858 85 D
lpendleton@charteroak.edu
GAGNON, Craig, L 920-832-6587 517 E
craig.l.gagnon@lawrence.edu
GAGNON, Jennifer 802-656-3360 485 D
jennifer.gagnon@uvm.edu
GAGNON, Karen 712-274-5159 175 C
gagnon@morningside.edu
GAGNON, Paula 207-216-4318 204 B
pgagnon@yccc.edu
GAGNON, Pauline 678-839-5450 129 E
pgagnon@westga.edu
GAGNON, Roberta 269-965-3931 236 A
gagnonr@kellogg.edu
GAGNOW, Robin, W 440-826-8153 363 M
rgagnow@bw.edu
GAHAGAN, Nicole 262-691-5240 524 G
ngahagan@wctc.edu
GAHAGANS, Steve 479-575-6626 22 I
steveg@uark.edu
GAHAN, Mick 402-457-2402 280 J
mgahan@mccneb.edu
GAHN, Sandra, W 515-294-5389 169 G
sgahn@iastate.edu
GAIA, Celeste 276-944-6917 489 I
cgaia@ehc.edu
GAIER, Mary 937-512-2163 377 D
mary.gaier@sinclair.edu
GAIKO, Sylvia 270-745-8985 194 D
sylvia.gaiko@wku.edu
GAIL, Keli, A 413-597-4233 230 A
kg8@williams.edu
GAILEY, Andrew 706-865-2134 128 D
agailey@truett.edu
GAILEY, Kim 970-943-3140 84 H
kgailey@western.edu
GAILLAT, Ana 508-678-2811 223 A
ana.gaillat@bristolcc.edu
GAILLIARD, Gary 817-735-2210 475 C
gary.gailliard@unthsc.edu
GAILOR, Kathleen 845-451-1302 312 C
k_gailor@culinary.edu
GAIMARO, Amy 516-323-3000 321 H
agaimaro@molloy.edu
GAINER, Nancy 610-436-4164 416 C
ngainer@wcupa.edu
GAINES, Adrienne, S 334-833-4480 4 D
againes@hawks.huntingdon.edu
GAINES, Angela 225-771-2552 200 A
againes@sulc.edu
GAINES, Anne 212-229-8908 322 E
gainesa@newschool.edu
GAINES, Chad 660-248-6197 263 B
cgaines@centralmethodist.edu
GAINES, Cliff 254-501-3101 454 A
cgaines@ctcd.edu
GAINES, Gina 914-606-7612 340 C
gina.gaines@sunywcc.edu
GAINES, Glynnis 254-299-8306 461 E
ggaines@mclennan.edu
GAINES, John 615-936-2811 449 A
john.gaines@vanderbilt.edu
GAINES, Justin 706-867-2781 128 F
justin.gaines@ung.edu
GAINES, Kim 256-306-2592 2 F
kim.gaines@calhoun.edu
GAINES, JR., Larry, R 856-225-6174 296 A
gaines@camden.rutgers.edu
GAINES, JR., Larry, R 856-225-6174 295 F
gaines@camden.rutgers.edu
GAINES, Randy 208-282-2872 133 H
gainrand@isu.edu
GAINES, Richard 559-442-8201 67 A
richard.gaines@scccd.edu
GAINES, Shawna 615-248-1378 447 F
ssgaines@trevecca.edu
GAINES, Shivaun, P 973-655-7648 293 A
gainess@mail.montclair.edu
GAINES, Steven, D 805-893-7363 70 E
gaines@ucsb.edu
GAINEY, John 601-366-8880 261 H
jgainey@wbs.edu
GAINEY, Karen, W 864-488-4504 430 H
kgainey@limestone.edu
GAINOUS, Chrissy 229-226-1621 128 B
cgainous@thomasu.edu
GAISER, J. Christopher 503-883-2308 392 B
cgaiser@linfield.edu
GAITAN, Deborah 210-486-4454 450 C
dgaitan@alamo.edu
GAITERS-JORDAN,
Jacquelyn 719-502-3078 82 B
jacquelyn.gaiters-jordan@ppcc.edu
GAITHER, Kimberly 573-288-6340 264 F
kgaither@culver.edu
GAITHER, Sonya 678-359-5078 122 E
sgaither@gordonstate.edu
GAITHER, Sophia 704-216-6222 346 A
sogaither@livingstone.edu
GAJDARDZISKA-JOSIFOVSKA,
Marija 414-229-5520 520 D
mgj@uwm.edu
GAJDOSIK, Olga 262-554-2010 518 B
GAJEWSKI, Jennifer 410-704-2356 213 B
jgajewski@towson.edu
GAJEWSKI, Linda 219-473-4217 159 L
lgajewski@ccsj.edu
GAJRIA, Meenakshi 845-398-4154 329 G
mgajria@stac.edu
GALADIMA, Bulus 562-903-4844 28 E
bulus.galadima@biola.edu
GALANES, Gloria 417-836-5247 268 I
gloriagalanes@missouristate.edu
GALANSKI, Kay, A 724-946-7218 423 B
galanska@westminster.edu
GALANSKY, Galia 212-772-4511 308 D
galia.galansky@hunter.cuny.edu
GALARD, Thomas, A 718-990-2966 328 F
galardt@stjohns.edu
GALARDI, Karen 215-504-2000 405 J
kgalardi@holyfamily.edu
GALARRAGA, Francesca 866-621-0124 84 E
francesca.galarraga@rockies.edu
GALATOLO, Ron, D 650-574-6550 62 F
galatolo@smccd.edu
GALAVIZ, Gina 541-962-3496 391 C
ggalaviz@eou.edu
GALBAVY, Tiffany 406-395-4875 278 F
tgalbavy@stonechild.edu
GALBIATI, Jacqueline 856-691-8600 290 I
jgalbiati@cccnj.edu
GALBIERZ, Todd 636-922-8359 271 A
tgalbierz@stchas.edu
GALBIERZ, Todd 636-922-8380 271 A
tgalbierz@stchas.edu
GALBRAITH, James, R 407-582-3420 114 N
jgalbraith1@valenciacollege.edu
GALBRAITH, Jennifer 909-274-4600 53 C
jgalbraith@mtsac.edu
GALBRAITH, Mark 619-849-2489 57 M
markgalbraith@pointloma.edu
GALBRAITH, OP,
Mary Sarah 615-297-7545 438 F
srmsarah@aquinascollege.edu
GALBRAITH, Richard, A 802-656-2918 485 D
richard.galbraith@uvm.edu
GALBRAITH, Thomas 530-226-4185 64 H
tgalbraith@simpsonu.edu
GALBREATH, Dodd 615-966-1771 441 F
dodd.galbreath@lipscomb.edu
GALBREATH, Susan, C 615-966-5952 441 F
susan.galbreath@lipscomb.edu
GALDEEN, Patricia 419-783-2523 368 A
pgaldeen@defiance.edu
GALDIERI, Virginia 908-852-1440 290 D
galdieriv@centenarycollege.edu
GALE, Andrea 909-607-1236 38 J
andrea.gale@cmc.edu
GALE, Jason 615-297-7545 438 F
galej@aquinascollege.edu
GALE, Jennifer, D 610-917-1488 422 C
jdgale@valleyforge.edu
GALE, Lewis 209-946-2466 71 C
lgale@pacific.edu
GALE, Mary 952-885-5437 253 Z
mgale@nwhealth.edu
GALE, Nicole, L 410-651-6458 212 B
nlgale@umes.edu
GALEA, Sandro 617-638-4644 216 E
sgalea@bu.edu
GALEA'I, Seth, P 684-699-9155 529 E
s.galeai@amsamoa.edu
GALEA'I-SCANLAN, Lina 684-699-9155 529 E
l.galeai-scanlan@amsamoa.edu
GALECKE, Robert, M 972-721-5203 473 D
galecke@udallas.edu
GALELEI, Scott 607-729-8915 313 D
sgalelei@ebi-college.com
GALEY, Franz, D 307-766-4133 527 B
fgaley@uwyo.edu
GALEY, Julie 716-652-8900 306 K
jgaley@cbts.edu
GALGANO, Mark 267-341-3545 405 J
mgalgano@holyfamily.edu
GALIANO, Carlos 787-850-9303 538 B
carlos.galiano@upr.edu
GALIK, Barbara 309-677-2850 136 B
barbara@bradley.edu
GALIL, Zvi 404-894-8357 121 D
galil@gatech.edu
GALINDO, Emily 530-752-0339 69 A
ecgalindo@ucdavis.edu
GALINDO, Gabriel 520-287-5583 12 L
galindog@cochise.edu
GALINDO, Vickie 575-527-7526 301 C
vigalind@nmsu.edu
GALINSKI, Bonnie 978-542-2532 222 D
bgalinski@salemstate.edu
GALIPEAU KONATE,
Bethany 540-542-6285 494 B
bgalipea@su.edu
GALKIN, Daphne 914-831-0413 311 C
dgalkin@cw.edu
GALL, Connie 405-692-3258 384 C
cgall@macu.edu
GALL, George 386-481-2043 96 H
gallg@cookman.edu
GALL, Jen 510-849-8241 55 I
jgall@psr.edu
GALL, Michael 212-594-4000 337 F
mgall@cicollege.edu
GALL RITCHIE, Amy, S 800-287-8822 159 C
ritcham@bethanyseminary.edu
GALLAGAN, Marilynn 978-656-3300 224 A
gallaganm@middlesex.mass.edu
GALLAGHER, Abisola 201-200-3165 293 C
agallagher@njcu.edu
GALLAGHER, Amber 909-384-8687 60 C
agallagher@sbccd.cc.ca.us
GALLAGHER, Amy 908-526-1200 295 A
amie.gallagher@raritanval.edu
GALLAGHER, Beth, E 805-756-2236 31 I
begallag@calpoly.edu
GALLAGHER, AA,
Dennis, M 508-767-7033 214 F
dgallagh@assumption.edu
GALLAGHER, Ed 256-766-6610 4 B
egallagher@hcu.edu
GALLAGHER, Elizabeth 925-631-4223 59 I
egallagh@stmarys-ca.edu
GALLAGHER,
Geraldine M, P 407-582-3155 114 N
ggallagher@valenciacollege.edu
GALLAGHER, Helen 256-215-4274 2 G
hgallagher@cacc.edu
GALLAGHER, CSC,
James, T 503-943-8011 396 B
gallaghe@up.edu
GALLAGHER, Joanna 215-572-2187 397 G
gallagher@arcadia.edu
GALLAGHER, Jody 814-732-1269 415 A
jgallagher@edinboro.edu
GALLAGHER, John 573-341-4286 274 B
gallagherjp@mst.edu
GALLAGHER, John 610-660-1164 418 G
jgalla02@sju.edu
GALLAGHER, Karen 607-753-4717 333 A
karen.gallagher@cortland.edu
GALLAGHER, Karen, S 213-740-5756 72 D
rsoedean@usc.edu
GALLAGHER, Kathleen 215-503-6959 420 E
kathleen.gallagher@jefferson.edu
GALLAGHER, Leslie, D 281-425-6301 460 I
lgallagher@lee.edu
GALLAGHER, Lori 713-525-3592 475 J
irishstudies@stthom.edu
GALLAGHER, Mary 213-763-7227 50 C
mgallagn@lattc.edu
GALLAGHER, Mary 213-763-7040 50 C
mgallagn@lattc.edu
GALLAGHER, Mary Beth 314-719-3554 265 C
mbgallagher@fontbonne.edu
GALLAGHER, Mary Beth 276-223-4765 499 C
mgallagher@wcc.vccs.edu
GALLAGHER, Matthew 310-665-6819 55 E
mgallagher@otis.edu
GALLAGHER, Maureen 914-395-2385 329 K
mgallagh@sarahlawrence.edu
GALLAGHER, Megan 717-396-7833 413 M
mgallagher@pcad.edu
GALLAGHER, Miles 717-871-7210 415 F
miles.gallagher@millersville.edu
GALLAGHER, Patricia 781-292-2416 218 H
patricia.gallagher@olin.edu
GALLAGHER, Patrick 412-624-4200 421 G
pdg@pitt.edu
GALLAGHER, Richard 914-968-6200 329 C
richard.gallagher@archny.org
GALLAGHER, Scott 573-592-4337 275 G
scott.gallagher@williamwoods.edu
GALLAGHER, Steve 336-631-1217 358 E
gallaghers@uncsa.edu
GALLAGHER, Susan, P 518-629-8138 316 G
s.gallagher@hvcc.edu
GALLAGHER, Suzanne 617-928-4026 226 B
sgallagher@mountida.edu
GALLAGHER, Tanya, M 217-333-2131 157 A
tmgallag@illinois.edu
GALLAHER, James 317-940-9249 159 K
jgallahe@butler.edu
GALLANT, Danny, R 936-468-2203 466 H
dgallant@sfasu.edu
GALLARDO, Ignacio 805-893-4412 70 E
ignacio.gallardo@ucsb.edu
GALLARDO, Mark 573-341-4981 274 B
gallardom@mst.edu
GALLARDO, Martin 858-309-3551 54 A
mgallardo@nu.edu
GALLARDO, Ruben, C 915-831-6306 457 H
rgalla16@epcc.edu
GALLART, Stephen 845-687-5187 338 F
gallarts@sunyulster.edu
GALLATIN, Cynthia 203-582-8521 88 G
cynthia.gallatin@quinnipiac.edu
GALLEGLY, Carolyn 628-985-3741 143 F
carolyngallegly@jalc.edu
GALLEGLY, Michael 973-300-2306 297 D
mgallegly@sussex.edu
GALLEGO, Hector, F 919-516-4929 355 D
hfgallego@st-aug.edu
GALLEGOS, Jeremy 316-295-5871 181 B
jeremy_gallegos@friends.edu
GALLEGOS, Joel, A 704-687-7755 358 A
jagalleg@uncc.edu
GALLEGOS, John 916-348-4689 43 A
jgallegos@epic.edu
GALLEGOS, Jose 303-937-4200 77 K
jgallegos@chu.edu
GALLEGOS, Jose Alfred 323-242-5511 50 B
gallegja@lasc.edu
GALLEGOS, Tommy 972-860-4799 456 B
tgallegos@dcccd.edu
GALLEN, Peter, C 864-592-4680 432 H
gallenp@sccsc.edu
GALLENBERG, Dale 715-425-3841 521 B
dale.gallenberg@uwrf.edu
GALLENTINE, Jerry, L 605-721-5225 436 E
jgallentine@national.edu
GALLEY, Amy 307-382-1645 527 C
agalley@westernwyoming.edu
GALLIANETTI, David, D 920-565-1119 517 D
gallianettidd@lakeland.edu
GALLIE, Alain 770-220-7908 120 G
agallie@gcuniv.edu
GALLIEN, Melissa, C 409-880-7011 471 A
melissa.gallien@lamar.edu
GALLIGAN, Chad 623-935-8075 14 A
chad.galligan@estrellamountain.edu
GALLIGAN, Chris 860-832-1764 85 F
galliganc@ccsu.edu
GALLIGAN, Gina 718-289-5562 307 C
gina.galligan@bcc.cuny.edu
GALLIGAN, Meghan 907-852-1763 10 D
registration@ilisagvik.edu
GALLIMORE, Anna 336-721-2852 355 E
anna.gallimore@ssalem.edu
GALLIMORE, Rebecca 269-965-3931 236 A
gallimorer@kellogg.edu
GALLIMORE, Sarah 717-815-6470 424 F
sgallimo@ycp.edu
GALLINGER, Dawn 406-447-5179 276 B
dgallinger@carroll.edu
GALLION, Melanie 843-525-8224 433 B
mgallion@tcl.edu
GALLIPEAU, Jean, B 315-443-3765 337 A
jbgallip@syr.edu
GALLISATH, Glenda 847-578-8787 153 A
GALLIVAN, Evan 617-262-5000 216 A
evan.gallivan@the-bac.edu
GALLIVAN, Patrick, J 802-654-2557 484 I
pgallivan@smcvt.edu

GALLIVAN, Thomas .... 562-860-2451.... 36 P tgallivan@cerritos.edu
GALLMAN, Kathleen .... 252-638-7233.. 349 B gallmank@cravencc.edu
GALLO, Eulogio .... 310-954-5080.... 29 D
GALLO, John, D .... 724-847-6796.. 404 B jdgallo@geneva.edu
GALLO, Kathleen .... 516-463-4074.. 316 D kathleen.gallo@hofstra.edu
GALLO, Kelly .... 562-902-3316.... 66 A kellygallo@scuhs.edu
GALLO, Liz .... 973-408-3097.. 291 B lgallo@drew.edu
GALLO, Maria .... 808-956-8234.. 131 F gallom@hawaii.edu
GALLO, Maria .... 215-489-2203.. 402 A president@delval.edu
GALLO, Patricia .... 732-224-2220.. 289 I pgallo@brookdalecc.edu
GALLONIO, Anthony .... 401-454-6636.. 426 A agalloni@risd.edu
GALLOUET, Catherine ...... 315-781-3467.. 316 C gallouet@hws.edu
GALLOWAY, Alison .... 831-459-3885.... 70 F cpevc@ucsc.edu
GALLOWAY, Carolina ...... 806-651-5309.. 469 D cgalloway@wtamu.edu
GALLOWAY, Curt .... 651-690-6980.. 254 M wcgalloway@stkate.edu
GALLOWAY, Cyndi .... 724-222-5330.. 412 E cmason@penncommercial.edu
GALLOWAY, Deborah, J .. 513-556-5054.. 379 A debi.galloway@uc.edu
GALLOWAY, Heather .... 512-245-2266.. 471 F hg02@txstate.edu
GALLOWAY, Merrill .... 606-589-3079.. 190 G merrill.galloway@kctcs.edu
GALLOWAY, Peter .... 610-436-3307.. 416 C pgalloway@wcupa.edu
GALLOWAY, Robin .... 319-296-4292.. 173 B robin.galloway@hawkeyecollege.edu
GALLOWAY, Sean .... 717-358-4210.. 403 J sean.galloway@fandm.edu
GALLOWAY, Sheila .... 910-755-7312.. 347 H galloways@brunswickcc.edu
GALLOWAY, Tami .... 740-389-4636.. 372 B gallowayt@mtc.edu
GALLOWAY-PERRY, Rulisa .... 212-237-8601.. 308 E rgalloway@jjay.cuny.edu
GALM, Molly, D .... 712-324-5061.. 175 G mgalm@nwicc.edu
GALM, Ruth .... 509-359-6567.. 503 D rgalm@ewu.edu
GALOYAN, Nazy .... 650-949-7772.... 44 B galoyannazy@foothill.edu
GALTNEY, Alfred .... 601-877-3965.. 256 F agaltney@alcorn.edu
GALUSKI, Bryan .... 336-272-7102.. 344 G bgaluski@greensboro.edu
GALVAN, Betty .... 210-434-6711.. 463 C bagalvan@lake.ollusa.edu
GALVAN, Dennis, C .... 541-346-5851.. 395 G dgalvan@uoregon.edu
GALVAN, Efren .... 714-432-5774.... 39 G egalvan@occ.cccd.edu
GALVAN, Margarita, M ..... 361-593-3209.. 469 A margarita.galvan@tamuk.edu
GALVAN, Michael .... 903-223-3013.. 469 C mgalvan@tamut.edu
GALVANONI, Mark .... 630-889-6661.. 149 G mgalvanoni@nuhs.edu
GALVIN, Carroll .... 410-532-5314.. 210 B cgalvin@ndm.edu
GALVIN, OFM, Garrett ..... 760-547-1800.... 44 C ggalvin@fst.edu
GALVIN, Jeanne .... 718-631-6226.. 309 E jgalvin@qcc.cuny.edu
GALVIN, Katherine .... 217-265-0340.. 157 A kagalvin@illinois.edu
GALVIN, Mary, E .... 574-631-6456.. 168 B mgalvin2@nd.edu
GALVIN, Michael .... 973-655-4199.. 293 A galvinm@mail.montclair.edu
GALVINHILL, Paul .... 508-793-3363.. 217 C pgalvin@holycross.edu
GALYEAN, Ann .... 325-574-7914.. 479 I agalyean@wtc.edu
GALYEAN, Michael .... 806-742-2808.. 472 C michael.galyean@ttu.edu
GALYEAN, Paul .... 903-586-2518.. 460 A pgalyean@jacksonville-college.edu
GAMACHE, Normand .... 401-454-6371.. 426 A ngamache@risd.edu
GAMBACINI, Michelle ..... 203-591-5615.... 88 F mgambacini@post.edu
GAMBILL, Todd .... 765-455-9360.. 163 A tgambill@iuk.edu
GAMBINO, Ellen, M .... 845-431-8954.. 312 G gambino@sunydutchess.edu
GAMBINO, Stephen .... 610-436-2133.. 416 C sgambino@wcupa.edu
GAMBLE, Brad .... 417-328-1823.. 272 C bgamble@sbuniv.edu
GAMBLE, Dee .... 850-599-3225.. 110 J santoras.gamble@famu.edu
GAMBLE, Gregory .... 856-225-3999.. 296 A gambleg@camden.rutgers.edu
GAMBLE, Jackie .... 760-547-1800.... 44 C jgamble@fst.edu
GAMBLE, Jim .... 616-538-2330.. 234 D jgamble@gbcol.edu
GAMBLE, John, E .... 361-825-6045.. 468 E john.gamble@tamucc.edu
GAMBLE, Kay .... 334-556-2397...... 3 N kgamble@wallace.edu
GAMBLE, Melanie .... 972-860-4269.. 456 B mgamble@dcccd.edu
GAMBLE, Mort .... 757-455-3217.. 500 E mgamble@vwc.edu
GAMBLE, Shawnia .... 505-786-4111.. 300 E sgamble@navajotech.edu
GAMBLE, Steven .... 575-562-2121.. 299 I steven.gamble@enmu.edu
GAMBLE, Thomas, J .... 518-438-3111.. 320 A tgamble@mariacollege.edu
GAMBLIN, Jeff .... 903-875-7355.. 462 J jeff.gamblin@navarrocollege.edu
GAMBOA, Anthony .... 773-481-8752.. 137 E agamboa@ccc.edu
GAMBOA, Anthony .... 773-481-8752.. 137 I agamboa@ccc.edu
GAMBOA, Larry .... 671-735-2359.. 530 B lgamboa@triton.uog.edu
GAMBOA, Noel .... 718-262-2372.. 310 A ngamboa@york.cuny.edu
GAMBRELL-BOONE, Letizia .... 804-524-5350.. 499 G lgambrell-boone@vsu.edu
GAMBRO, John, S .... 815-740-3829.. 157 F jgambro@stfrancis.edu
GAMER, Josh .... 608-785-9088.. 524 H gamerj@westerntc.edu
GAMEZ, Francisco .... 510-981-2881.... 57 B fgamez@peralta.edu
GAMMAGE, Laura, B .... 678-664-0506.. 129 M laura.gammage@westgatech.edu
GAMMELL, William .... 860-723-0054.... 85 E gammellw@ct.edu
GAMMON, Andrew .... 401-454-6420.. 426 A agammon@risd.edu
GAMMON, Jennifer .... 803-325-2874.. 435 D jgammon@yorktech.edu
GAMMON, Marcia, L .... 480-245-7918.... 13 L marcia.gammon@ibcs.edu
GAMMON, Steven .... 207-834-7510.. 205 B
GAMMON, Wiley .... 478-289-2090.. 120 C wgammon@ega.edu
GANAHL, Gina .... 636-949-4501.. 266 J gganahl@lindenwood.edu
GANAN, Frank .... 858-225-4301.... 30 F
GANAS, Sean .... 978-665-3599.. 221 D sganas@fitchburgstate.edu
GANCERES, Lupe .... 361-354-2712.. 454 G lupegg@coastalbend.edu
GANDHI, Jay .... 810-762-3476.. 242 B jgandhi@umflint.edu
GANDHI, Pratima, N .... 309-677-3123.. 136 B pratima@fsmail.bradley.edu
GANDRE, James .... 917-493-4438.. 319 M jgandre@msmnyc.edu
GANDU, Bobby .... 316-978-5675.. 185 J bobby.gandu@wichita.edu
GANDY, Beth .... 417-451-3223.. 264 E
GANDY, Fredrick .... 815-836-5125.. 145 H gandyfr@lewisu.edu
GANDY, Rex .... 931-221-7676.. 444 E gandyr@apsu.edu
GANEM, Lisa .... 619-684-8794.... 54 C lganem@newschoolarch.edu
GANESAN, Arasu .... 910-672-1477.. 356 E nganesan@uncfsu.edu
GANESH, Jaishankar .... 856-225-6217.. 296 A jganesh@camden.rutgers.edu
GANG, Martin (Marty) ..... 209-575-7979.... 75 I gangm@yosemite.edu
GANG, Tom .... 800-962-7682.. 275 D tgang@wma.edu
GANGER, Trisha .... 877-701-3800.. 135 A
GANGSTEAD, Sandra .... 478-445-4092.. 121 A sandra.gangstead@gcsu.edu
GANGWER, Val .... 540-665-4637.. 494 B vgangwer@su.edu
GANIO, Mary .... 619-482-6301.... 66 E mganio@swccd.edu
GANN, Alexander .... 516-367-6890.. 310 E ganna@cshl.edu
GANN, Brian .... 731-425-8820.. 446 C bgann1@jscc.edu
GANNAWAY, Anne, A .... 563-333-6283.. 176 D gannawayannem@sau.edu
GANNAWAY, Dale .... 575-492-4712.. 300 H dgannaway@nmjc.edu
GANNAWAY, Paula .... 806-720-7327.. 461 C paula.gannaway@lcu.edu
GANNETT-MALICK, Lynn . 205-970-9218...... 7 B lynngm@sebc.edu
GANNON, Debbie, K .... 515-263-6020.. 172 H dgannon@grandview.edu
GANNON, Kim .... 512-245-2371.. 471 F kg33@txstate.edu
GANNON, Marcy .... 301-934-7560.. 207 B marcyg@csmd.edu
GANNON, Susan .... 908-737-3461.. 292 C sgannon@kean.edu
GANNON, Violet .... 860-297-4033.... 89 B j.gannon@trincoll.edu
GANNT, Aubra, J .... 817-515-1450.. 467 A aubra.gantt@tccd.edu
GANO-PHILLIPS, Susan .. 810-762-3234.. 242 B sganop@umflint.edu
GANONG, Rick .... 207-725-3822.. 202 F rganong@bowdoin.edu
GANSCHOW, Darby .... 605-677-6623.. 437 A darby.ganschow@usd.edu
GANSERT, Heidi .... 775-784-4778.. 285 A hgansert@unr.edu
GANSZ, David .... 304-876-5179.. 513 E dgansz@shepherd.edu
GANT, Kim .... 828-726-2375.. 347 I kgant@cccti.edu
GANTMAN, Amy .... 310-665-6851.... 55 E agantman@otis.edu
GANTNER, Christine, M .. 920-424-3414.. 520 E gantner@uwosh.edu
GANTNER, Myrna .... 678-839-6445.. 129 E mgantner@westga.edu
GANTT, Bernard .... 718-289-5515.. 307 C bernard.gantt@bcc.cuny.edu
GANTT, Calvin .... 607-777-2791.. 331 B cgantt@binghamton.edu
GANTT, Dave .... 406-791-5926.. 278 G david.gantt@ugf.edu
GANTT, Kevin .... 913-758-6230.. 185 F ganttk@stmary.edu
GANTZ, Jennifer .... 316-942-4291.. 183 I gantzj@newmanu.edu
GANTZ, Katherine, L .... 240-895-4922.. 210 E klgantz@smcm.edu
GANUES, Jeffrey .... 567-661-7334.. 376 D jeffrey_ganues@owens.edu
GANYARD, Clifton .... 920-465-2033.. 520 B ganyardc@uwgb.edu
GANYARD, Paula .... 920-465-2537.. 520 B ganyardp@uwgb.edu
GANZEL, Toni .... 502-852-5192.. 194 A toni.ganzel@louisville.edu
GAO, Jing .... 215-646-7300.. 404 G gao.j@gmercyu.edu
GAO, Lan .... 617-521-2721.. 228 C lan.gao@simmons.edu
GAONA, Selin .... 816-604-4190.. 267 K selin.gaona@mcckc.edu
GAPASIN, Nando .... 408-498-5102.... 39 H ngapasin@cogswell.edu
GAPUZ, Joanne .... 510-780-4500.... 48 J jgapuz@lifewest.edu
GARAFOLO, Rich .... 252-527-6223.. 350 H rmgarafolo48@lenoircc.edu
GARAJEEAGHI, Reza .... 773-477-4822.... 55 G rgarajeeaghi@pacificcollege.edu
GARANZINI, Michael, J .. 773-274-3000.. 146 G mgaranz@luc.edu
GARANZINI, SJ, Michael, J .... 773-508-7301.. 146 G mgaranz@luc.edu
GARAVASO, Pieranno .... 320-589-6250.. 255 F garavapf@morris.umn.edu
GARAWITZ, Amy .... 212-229-5662.. 322 E garawita@newschool.edu
GARAY, Rufina .... 920-457-9050.. 523 E rufina.garay@gotoltc.edu
GARAYTA, Isabel .... 787-279-1912.. 533 J igarayta@bayamon.inter.edu
GARBADE, Henry .... 843-208-8910.. 434 A hgarbade@uscb.edu
GARBART, Hadley .... 410-225-2231.. 209 B hgarbart@mica.edu
GARBE, John .... 585-389-2038.. 322 D jgarbe6@naz.edu
GARBE, Theresa .... 423-461-8718.. 442 K tmgarbe@milligan.edu
GARBER, Alan .... 617-496-5100.. 219 D alan_garber@harvard.edu
GARBER, Barbara .... 415-351-3538.... 61 B bgarber@sfai.edu
GARBER, Kevin, S .... 913-971-3275.. 183 D ksgarber@mnu.edu
GARBER, Linda .... 408-551-1913.... 63 E lgarber@scu.edu
GARBER, Philip .... 847-214-7285.. 140 A pgarber@elgin.edu
GARBER BAX, Sharlene .. 660-543-4114.. 273 C bax@ucmo.edu
GARBINI, Dennis, J .... 973-761-9011.. 297 A dennis.garbini@shu.edu
GARBUTT, Keith .... 405-744-6799.. 385 G keith.garbutt@okstate.edu
GARCES, Brenda .... 703-891-1787.. 494 H financialaid@standardcollege.edu
GARCES, Fred .... 619-388-7750.... 60 H fgarces@sdccd.edu
GARCIA, Abigail .... 602-331-7500.... 11 K agarcia@aii.edu
GARCIA, Adam .... 775-784-4689.. 285 A adam_garcia@police.unr.edu
GARCIA, Aida .... 787-725-6500.. 531 C agarcia@sju.albizu.edu
GARCIA, Albert .... 916-558-2337.... 51 D garciaaj@scc.losrios.edu
GARCIA, Alberto .... 787-848-0810.. 538 E alberto.garcia3@upr.edu
GARCIA, Alfredo .... 305-474-2445.. 108 E agarcia@stu.edu
GARCIA, Andrea .... 707-638-5272.... 68 C andrea.garcia@tu.edu
GARCIA, Angelica .... 650-738-4333.... 62 I garciaa@smccd.edu
GARCIA, Ava, M .... 671-735-6013.. 529 G ava.garcia@guamcc.edu
GARCIA, Bo .... 517-483-9639.. 237 A garciab@lcc.edu
GARCIA, Bob .... 989-463-7299.. 230 F garciab@alma.edu
GARCIA, Bob .... 323-953-4000.... 49 H garciabj@lacitycollege.edu
GARCIA, Brenda, W .... 575-439-3697.. 301 A brgarcia@nmsu.edu
GARCIA, Brett .... 540-261-8401.. 494 F brett.garcia@svu.edu
GARCIA, Carlos .... 210-829-2717.. 474 D cagarci9@uiwtx.edu
GARCIA, Carol .... 718-779-1430.. 326 D cgarcia@plazacollege.edu
GARCIA, Carol .... 307-674-6446.. 526 M cgarcia@sheridan.edu
GARCIA, Carola .... 787-779-2500.. 531 I ccat@coqui.edu
GARCIA, Caroline, M .... 520-621-3900.... 17 I cmgarcia@email.arizona.edu
GARCIA, Cecilia .... 760-921-5478.... 56 E cecy.garcia@paloverde.edu
GARCIA, Christian .... 305-284-5451.. 114 H christian@miami.edu
GARCIA, Christina, M ...... 626-914-8825.... 38 D cmgarcia@citruscollege.edu
GARCIA, Daisy .... 940-668-3330.. 462 L dgarcia@nctc.edu
GARCIA, Dan, D .... 806-651-2031.. 469 D ddgarcia@mail.wtamu.edu
GARCIA, Daniel .... 810-762-9752.. 236 C dgarcia@kettering.edu
GARCIA, David .... 262-551-5850.. 516 A dgarcia@carthage.edu
GARCIA, David .... 509-777-4572.. 509 H dgarcia@whitworth.edu
GARCIA, David .... 330-672-1001.. 370 I tgarcia5@kent.edu
GARCIA, Donna .... 575-461-4413.. 300 A donnag@mesalands.edu
GARCIA, Elena .... 787-780-0070.. 531 B egarcia@caribbean.edu
GARCIA, Eliezer .... 787-786-3030.. 536 F egarcia@ucb.edu.pr
GARCIA, Florence .... 406-247-3010.. 277 D florence.garcia@msubillings.edu
GARCIA, Frances .... 787-786-2412.. 536 G frances.garcia@uccaribe.edu
GARCIA, Gilda .... 512-245-2539.. 471 F gg18@txstate.edu
GARCIA, Gladys .... 661-654-3485.... 32 A ggarcia32@csub.edu
GARCIA, Heather .... 305-809-3178.. 100 N heather.garcia@fkcc.edu
GARCIA, Helen .... 915-566-9621.. 479 H hgarcia@westerntech.edu
GARCIA, Herminia, C ...... 561-732-4424.. 108 F hgarcia@svdp.edu
GARCIA, Irma .... 718-489-5490.. 328 D igarcia@sfc.edu
GARCIA, Isabel .... 352-723-5800.. 112 A agarcia2@dental.ufl.edu
GARCIA, Ivonne .... 740-427-5114.. 371 C garciai@kenyon.edu
GARCIA, Jennifer .... 530-752-3113.... 69 A jlroth@ucdavis.edu
GARCIA, Jessica .... 239-513-1135.. 115 F jgarcia@wolford.edu
GARCIA, Jessica .... 325-670-1448.. 458 J jessica.garcia@hsutx.edu
GARCIA, Joann .... 760-252-2411.... 28 B jgarcia@barstow.edu

GARREN, Cynthia 863-784-7177 109 G cynthia.garren@southflorida.edu
GARREN, Kenneth, R 434-544-8200 491 F president@lynchburg.edu
GARREN, Mary Ann 870-762-3168 18 G mgarren@smail.anc.edu
GARREN, Steve 217-234-5459 145 D sgarren@lakeland.cc.il.us
GARRETSON, Angela, R 973-596-3108 293 D angela@njit.edu
GARRETSON, Charlie 601-477-4249 258 E charlie.garretson@jcjc.edu
GARRETSON, Janet 618-545-3333 144 D jgarretson@kaskaskia.edu
GARRETT, Allison 620-341-5551 180 G agarrett@emporia.edu
GARRETT, Bonnie, J 410-777-2503 206 B bjgarrett@aacc.edu
GARRETT, Charles 256-924-0511 5 E cgarrett@legacyu.net
GARRETT, Craig 402-844-7046 282 B craigg@northeast.edu
GARRETT, Dan, T 325-674-2508 449 J garrettd@acu.edu
GARRETT, Deborah, A 501-882-8986 18 I dagarrett@asub.edu
GARRETT, Don 325-674-2213 449 J dlg09a@acu.edu
GARRETT, Gaurachandra 803-376-5700 427 A
GARRETT, Geoffrey 215-898-4715 421 E ggarrett@wharton.upenn.edu
GARRETT, Gina 870-307-7557 21 A gina.garrett@lyon.edu
GARRETT, Glenda 214-860-8666 456 F ghall@dcccd.edu
GARRETT, Helen 206-685-2553 508 E helenbg@uw.edu
GARRETT, J. Craig 504-282-4455 198 H cgarrett@nobts.edu
GARRETT, James 412-268-5090 400 D garrett@cmu.edu
GARRETT, Jinnie 540-365-4370 489 M jrgarrett@ferrum.edu
GARRETT, Kara 509-793-2050 501 H karag@bigbend.edu
GARRETT, Kelly 713-623-2040 451 K kgarrett@aii.edu
GARRETT, Kevin 304-384-5340 513 A garrettad@concord.edu
GARRETT, Leonard 214-860-3697 456 F lgarrett@dcccd.edu
GARRETT, Lynn 407-404-6060 109 E garrettl@seminolestate.edu
GARRETT, Mark 270-901-1065 190 F mark.garrett@kctcs.edu
GARRETT, Natasha 412-536-1296 406 K natasha.garrett@laroche.edu
GARRETT, Nicole, L 919-658-7896 355 K ngarrett@umo.edu
GARRETT, P, B 202-994-0108 92 D pgarrett@gwu.edu
GARRETT, Paul 864-977-7035 431 G paul.garrett@ngu.edu
GARRETT, Paula, K 828-298-3325 359 F pgarrett@warren-wilson.edu
GARRETT, Rachele 936-468-2403 466 H nixonhr@sfasu.edu
GARRETT, Rick 765-641-4156 158 J ragarrett@anderson.edu
GARRETT, Robin 620-792-9303 178 G garrettr@bartonccc.edu
GARRETT, Sarah 301-387-3157 207 G sarah.garrett@garrettcollege.edu
GARRETT, Schnell, R 443-518-4766 208 C sgarrett@howardcc.edu
GARRETT, Shana 612-338-7224 256 D
GARRETT, Sonja 816-802-3445 266 D sgarrett@kcai.edu
GARRETT, Stacey 615-238-6350 439 L sgarrett@bonelaw.com
GARRETT, Susan, R 502-895-3411 191 F sgarrett@lpts.edu
GARRETT FINSTER, Susan 619-239-0391 36 A sgf@cwsl.edu
GARRICK DUHANEY, Laurel 845-257-3561 331 E duhaneyl@newpaltz.edu
GARRIGAN-DURANT, Michelle 215-965-8569 411 A mgarrigandurant@moore.edu
GARRIOCH, Shaynan 845-451-4365 312 C s_garrio@culinary.edu
GARRIS, Daffie, H 336-633-0290 352 B dhgarris@randolph.edu
GARRIS, Eric, L 843-661-1160 430 B egarris@fmarion.edu
GARRIS, Rick 303-963-3290 77 I rgarris@ccu.edu
GARRISON, Cindy 931-526-3660 440 A cynthia.stephenson@fortisinstitute.edu
GARRISON, David 706-880-8235 123 K dgarrison@lagrange.edu
GARRISON, Deborah 309-672-5513 147 H dgarrison@methodistcol.edu
GARRISON, Helene 949-376-6000 48 C hgarrison@lcad.edu
GARRISON, James, R 913-971-3296 183 D jgarriso@mnu.edu
GARRISON, Jayne, B 610-892-1002 414 B jgarrison@pit.edu
GARRISON, Joseph, L 989-774-5251 232 D garri2jl@cmich.edu
GARRISON, Julie, A 269-387-5202 243 H julie.garrison@wmich.edu
GARRISON, Mark 443-885-3185 209 F mark.garrison@morgan.edu
GARRISON, Michael 651-962-5187 256 C mgarrison@stthomas.edu
GARRISON, Rebecca 314-539-5154 271 F rgarrison@stlcc.edu
GARRISON, Ryan 828-652-6021 351 C rgarrison@mcdowelltech.edu
GARRISON, Scott 231-591-3729 233 L scottgarrison@ferris.edu
GARRISON, Walter, R 610-892-1001 414 B wgarrison@pit.edu
GARRITY, Christopher 413-205-3366 214 B christopher.garrity@aic.edu
GARRITY, Collette 212-343-1234 321 B cgarrity@mcny.edu
GARRITY, Kathleen, E 608-822-2471 524 F kgarrity@swtc.edu
GARRITY, Michael 708-456-0300 156 C michaelgarrity@triton.edu
GARRITY, Mitch 505-277-0111 302 F mgarrity@unm.edu
GARRITY, Patricia 608-897-8514 287 F pgarrity@rivier.edu
GARRITY, Robert 239-280-2581 95 Q robert.garrity@avemaria.edu
GARROW, Joy 517-264-7123 241 A jgarrow@sienaheights.edu
GARRY, Kirby 831-582-3534 33 E kgarry@csumb.edu
GARSTECKI, Marcus 605-256-5124 437 C marcus.garstecki@dsu.edu
GARTEN, Ann 310-660-3406 42 J agarten@elcamino.edu
GARTEN, Ann, M 310-660-3670 42 J agarten@elcamino.edu
GARTENMAYER, Charles 913-360-7583 178 I cgartenmayer@benedictine.edu
GARTHOFF, Jerry 207-621-3067 204 I garthoff@maine.edu
GARTHWAITE, Sharon 570-577-2000 398 L
GARTIN, Stanton 970-521-6650 81 O stanton.gartin@njc.edu
GARTNER, Lia 212-229-5192 322 E gartnerl@newschool.edu
GARTNER, Maggie 979-845-4427 468 B molona@tamu.edu
GARTON, Jilda 404-894-4819 121 D jilda.garton@gtrc.gatech.edu
GARTRELL, William 626-396-2316 27 L bill.gartrell@artcenter.edu
GARUS, Marcella Marie 716-896-0700 339 E smgarus@villa.edu
GARUS, Robert 716-826-1200 338 E garusr@trocaire.edu
GARVER, Beth 617-585-0200 216 A beth.garver@the-bac.edu
GARVER, Robert, A 419-866-0261 377 L ragarver@stautzenberger.com
GARVEY, Ann, L 612-330-1168 244 I garvey@augsburg.edu
GARVEY, Carol 712-274-5178 175 C garvey@morningside.edu
GARVEY, Hugh 217-786-2304 146 E hugh.garvey@llcc.edu
GARVEY, James 618-453-4550 154 I jgarvey@siu.edu
GARVEY, John, H 202-319-5100 92 A cua-president@cua.edu
GARVEY, Judy 714-241-6230 39 E jgarvey@coastline.edu
GARVEY, Kathleen, M 508-373-9455 215 D kathleen.garvey@becker.edu
GARVEY, Robert, F 610-799-1743 408 G rgarvey@lccc.edu
GARVIN, Maureen 912-525-5000 126 E mgarvin@scad.edu
GARVIN, William 417-873-7482 264 H wgarvin@drury.edu
GARVIN AQUILINO, Rose 240-567-4249 209 E rose.garvinaquilino@montgomerycollege.edu
GARVIN-LEIGHTON, Timothy 706-778-8500 125 J
GARWOOD, S. Lynn 336-757-3396 349 G sgarwood@forsythtech.edu
GARY, Aaron 201-216-5240 297 B aaron.gary@stevens.edu
GARY, Carole 865-539-7025 446 G cgary2@pstcc.edu
GARY, Cynthia 405-682-1611 385 D cynthia.d.gary@occc.edu
GARY, Kevin 610-527-0200 418 D kevin.gary@rosemont.edu
GARY, Marc 212-678-8080 317 I magary@jtsa.edu
GARY, William 216-987-3110 367 E william.gary@tri-c.edu
GARZA, Ana Lisa 512-245-2780 471 F ag02@txstate.edu
GARZA, Cynthia 713-718-7049 459 B cynthia.garza3@hccs.edu
GARZA, Edwardo 773-838-7500 137 H egarza20@ccc.edu
GARZA, Felipe 361-593-2611 469 A felipe.garza@tamuk.edu
GARZA, Javier 254-968-9104 467 F garza@tarleton.edu
GARZA, Jon 713-221-8950 474 B garzaj@uhd.edu
GARZA, Kim 509-793-2010 501 H kimg@bigbend.edu
GARZA, Lisa 940-898-2950 472 G lgarza10@twu.edu
GARZA, Noemi 956-872-2681 465 H ngarza24@southtexascollege.edu
GARZA, Nora, R 956-721-5868 460 F nrgarza@laredo.edu
GARZA, Rebecca, J 214-860-2618 456 E rgarza@dcccd.edu
GARZA, Richie 806-371-5022 450 H rrgarza@actx.edu
GARZA, Robert 214-860-8700 456 F robertgarza@dcccd.edu
GARZA, Roberto 305-223-4561 108 A rgarza@sjvcs.edu
GARZA, Roberto, A 956-326-2325 468 A facil@tamiu.edu
GARZA, JR., Victor 408-274-7900 62 D victor.garza@evc.edu
GARZA, Wanda 956-872-2770 465 H wgarza@southtexascollege.edu
GARZA-RODERICK, Jessie 209-833-7900 61 F jgarza-roderick@deltacollege.edu
GASAWAY, Debbie 870-460-1622 23 D gasaway@uamont.edu
GASBARRO, Dennis 716-614-5982 324 D dgasbarro@niagaracc.suny.edu
GASCHE, Currie 847-574-5158 145 C cgasche@lfgsm.edu
GASCHK, Kenneth, K 262-243-5700 516 E ken.gaschk@cuw.edu
GASCOIGNE, Carolyn 325-942-2162 472 B carolyn.gascoigne@angelo.edu
GASE, Chris 740-389-4636 372 B gasec@mtc.edu
GASH, Bill 678-717-2357 128 F william.gash@ung.edu
GASKELL, Carolyn 509-527-2133 508 G carolyn.gaskell@wallawalla.edu
GASKELL, Millicent 610-519-6371 422 G millicent.gaskell@villanova.edu
GASKIN, Elizabeth 772-462-5604 103 B egaskin@irsc.edu
GASKIN, Keith 901-334-5811 442 C kgaskin@memphisseminary.edu
GASKINS, Leebrian, E 956-326-2310 468 A lgaskins@tamiu.edu
GASOSKE, Betsy 314-434-4044 264 C registrar@covenantseminary.edu
GASPAR, Leigh 781-891-2874 215 F lgaspar@bentley.edu
GASPARD, Harold 504-671-6247 196 D hgaspa@dcc.edu
GASPARIAN, Albert 714-895-8334 39 F agasparian@gwc.cccd.edu
GASPARICH, Gail 978-542-6926 222 D ggasparich@salemstate.edu
GASPARRO, Paul 740-699-3037 364 B pgasparro@belmontcollege.edu
GASPER, Joseph 570-740-0372 409 E jgasper@luzerne.edu
GASPER, William 213-763-7043 50 C gasperw@lattc.edu
GASS, Melanie 704-403-1613 342 E melanie.gass@carolinashealthcare.org
GASS, Michael 828-232-5118 357 C mgass@unca.edu
GASSEAU, Michelle 617-243-2150 219 I mgaseau@lasell.edu
GASSIOT, Ken, W 706-886-6831 128 C kgassiot@tfc.edu
GASSMAN, Chad 847-628-1579 144 B chad.gassman@judsonu.edu
GASSNER, Sheila 573-681-5084 266 I gassners@lincolnu.edu
GAST, Brad 715-675-3331 524 D gast@ntc.edu
GAST, Kristen 307-674-6446 526 M kgast@sheridan.edu
GAST, Steve 712-279-1707 170 B steve.gast@briarcliff.edu
GAST, Tracy 716-270-5612 313 H gast@ecc.edu
GASTON, Aracelis 787-832-6000 532 O agaston@icprjc.edu
GASTON, David 785-864-3624 185 D adgaston@ku.edu
GASTON, Della, J 336-342-4261 352 F gastond@rockinghamcc.edu
GASTON, Kenneth 410-651-7550 212 B klgaston@umes.edu
GASTON, Lori 704-894-2208 343 I logaston@davidson.edu
GASTON, Neely 704-527-9909 219 B ngaston@gcts.edu
GASTON, Patricia 518-629-7292 316 G p.gaston@hvcc.edu
GASWICK, Kari 308-432-6487 281 H kgaswick@csc.edu
GATCH, Denise, D 941-752-5325 110 H gatchd@scf.edu
GATCHELL, Michael, D 864-294-2475 430 C mike.gatchell@furman.edu
GATELY, Kevin 603-897-8232 287 F kgately@rivier.edu
GATELY, Paul 401-841-7531 528 E
GATES, Amanda 617-585-1100 226 F amanda.gates@necmusic.edu
GATES, Anne 216-421-7463 366 G agates@cia.edu
GATES, Chris 907-745-3201 9 H cgates@akbible.edu
GATES, Cynthia, K 405-585-5255 385 B cynthia.gates@okbu.edu
GATES, Debra 315-279-5273 318 C dgates@keuka.edu
GATES, Dennis 513-751-1206 362 H dennis@aic-arts.edu
GATES, Glenn 973-618-3259 290 A ggates@caldwell.edu
GATES, Jane McBride 860-723-0058 85 E gatesj@ct.edu
GATES, Jeffrey 315-792-3006 339 B jtgates@utica.edu
GATES, Joan 859-572-5588 192 B
GATES, Joyce 503-253-3443 393 D joyce.gates@ocom.edu
GATES, Kathryn, F 662-915-7206 261 B kfg@olemiss.edu
GATES, Kristen 510-780-4500 48 J kgates@lifewest.edu
GATES, Leigh 312-697-3318 141 B lgates@harrington.edu
GATES, Pamela, S 989-774-3342 232 D gates1ps@cmich.edu
GATES, Reginald 817-515-5001 467 A reginald.gates@tccd.edu
GATES, Robert 570-389-4015 414 D rgates@bloomu.edu
GATES, William 409-880-1783 471 A william.gates@lamar.edu
GATES, William, R 831-656-2754 528 D bgates@nps.edu
GATES BLACK, L. Joy 817-515-5006 467 A linda.gates-black@tccd.edu
GATEWOOD, Algie, C 336-506-4150 347 C algie.gatewood@alamancecc.edu
GATEWOOD, David 714-895-8156 39 F dgatewood@gwc.cccd.edu
GATEWOOD, Dawn 434-381-6202 494 M dgatewood@sbc.edu
GATHERCOLE, Karen 321-674-7229 100 M kgathercole@fit.edu
GATHERS, Avis 803-793-5241 429 D gathersa@denmarktech.edu
GATHINGS, Cedric 304-696-4347 513 D studentaffairs@marshall.edu
GATHJE, Pete 901-334-5832 442 C pgathje@memphisseminary.edu
GATHMAN, Allen 573-651-2682 272 B agathman@semo.edu
GATLIN, Greg 617-573-8428 228 G ggatlin@suffolk.edu
GATLIN, Kenda 206-281-2569 507 C kgatlin@spu.edu
GATLING, Sharron 757-221-2617 488 F sggatl@wm.edu
GATO, Stacy 434-791-7110 487 C sgato@averett.edu
GATRELL, Jay, D 502-272-8259 187 A jgatrell@bellarmine.edu
GATTAS, Joyce, M 619-594-1343 35 A gattas@mail.sdsu.edu
GATTERDAM, Hans 817-272-3275 476 A hgatt@uta.edu

GATTI, Robert, M 614-823-1250 376 C rgatti@otterbein.edu
GATTIN, Tom 870-230-5135 20 E gattint@hsu.edu
GATTIS, Tom 614-222-3237 367 B tgattis@ccad.edu
GATTO, John 606-546-1728 193 E jgatto@unionky.edu
GATTO, Joseph, C 716-652-8900 306 K jgatto@cks.edu
GATTON, Pam 903-983-8207 460 D pgatton@kilgore.edu
GATZA, Camille 360-752-8549 501 G cgatza@btc.edu
GAU, Michael 608-342-1468 521 A gaum@uwplatt.edu
GAUBATZ, Noreen 205-226-4671 2 C ngaubatz@bsc.edu
GAUCHAT, Urs, P 973-596-3079 293 D urs.p.gauchat@njit.edu
GAUD, Angela 305-443-9170 107 P
GAUDIN, Wendy 504-520-7469 202 C wgaudin@xula.edu
GAUDINO, James, L 509-963-2111 501 K gaudino@cwu.edu
GAUDREAU, Alison, K 248-364-6117 239 K agaudreau@oakland.edu
GAUGH, Sherri 505-566-4007 301 J gaughs@sanjuancollege.edu
GAUGHAN, Cheryl 619-849-2499 57 M cherylgaughan@pointloma.edu
GAUL, Julie, M 412-578-6042 400 C gauljm@carlow.edu
GAUL, Volker 715-344-3063 523 G volker.gaul@mstc.edu
GAULT, Brian 407-923-1671 260 E bgault@rts.edu
GAULT, Brian, C 601-923-1671 260 E bgault@rts.edu
GAULT, Sandra 816-235-6234 273 F gaults@umkc.edu
GAUMER, Heather 515-643-6604 175 B hgaumer@mercydesmoines.org
GAUMER, Richard, K 276-944-6966 489 I rgaumer@ehc.edu
GAUNCE, Lori 606-759-7141 190 C lori.gaunce@kctcs.edu
GAUNDER, Alisa 512-863-1418 466 G gaundera@southwestern.edu
GAUNT, Victoria, F 410-864-4234 210 F vgaunt@stmarys.edu
GAURMER, Terry 303-458-1629 82 L tgaurmer@regis.edu
GAUS, Gregory, J 630-515-7307 148 C ggausx@midwestern.edu
GAUSS, Nancy 970-943-2053 84 H ngauss@western.edu
GAUSVIK, Tom 678-466-4000 119 A thomasgausvik@clayton.edu
GAUT, LaDonna 903-923-2477 479 K ldgaut@wileyc.edu
GAUTAM, Mridul 775-327-2363 285 A mgautam@unr.edu
GAUTHIER, Ana, M 607-871-2082 303 F gauthier@alfred.edu
GAUTHIER, Barry 920-424-1145 520 E gauthieb@uwosh.edu
GAUTHIER, Bev 315-229-5011 329 D
GAUTHIER, Laureen 802-225-3205 484 G laureen.gauthier@neci.edu
GAUTHIER, Theresa 585-785-1304 314 D theresa.gauthier@flcc.edu
GAUTNEY, Michael, B 256-765-4274 9 C mbgautney@una.edu
GAUVIN, Charles 508-289-2449 230 B cgauvin@whoi.edu
GAUVIN, Keith, R 203-837-9202 85 I gauvink@wcsu.edu
GAVALETZ, Tami 618-374-5187 151 E tami.gavaletz@principia.edu
GAVARRA-OH, Mary Anne 818-710-2234 50 A gavarrm@piercecollege.edu
GAVER, Bob 402-363-5721 283 G bagaver@york.edu
GAVIGAN, Lisa 508-286-3799 229 F gavigan_lisa@wheatoncollege.edu
GAVIN, Carrie 850-599-3076 110 J carrie.gavin@famu.edu
GAVIN, Jack 732-571-3536 292 F gavin@monmouth.edu
GAVIN, M. F. Chip 207-621-3173 204 G chip.gavin@maine.edu
GAVIN, Michael 414-297-6760 524 A gavinmj@matc.edu
GAVIN, Michael, H 410-777-2332 206 B mhgavin@aacc.edu
GAVIN, Mike 828-395-1295 350 E mgavin@isothermal.edu
GAVIN, Paul 319-363-1323 175 D pgavin@mtmercy.edu
GAVIN, Paula 386-752-1822 100 L paula.gavin@fgc.edu
GAVIN, Todd 803-822-3233 431 B gavint@midlandstech.edu
GAVLIK, Deborah 937-512-3999 377 D deborah.gavlik@sinclair.edu
GAWEL, Gary 616-331-2242 234 F gawelgar@gvsu.edu
GAWEL, Matthew 207-893-6601 204 D mgawel@sjcme.edu
GAWELEK, Mary Ann 419-824-3809 371 I mgawelek@lourdes.edu
GAWENDA, Matt 312-922-1884 147 B mgawenda@maccormac.edu
GAWRONSKI, JR., Michael 845-341-4284 325 H michael.gawronski@sunyorange.edu
GAWTHROP, Larry 610-762-0235 238 F larry.gawthrop@mcc.edu
GAXIOLA, Thomas 559-443-8612 67 C thom.gaxiola@fresnocitycollege.edu
GAXIOLA GAXIOLA, Tannya, R 520-621-4130 17 I tannya@email.arizona.edu
GAY, Bill 760-427-2314 46 J bill.gay@imperial.edu
GAY, Cliff 478-289-2025 120 C cgay@ega.edu
GAY, Gloria 919-536-7250 349 D gayg@durhamtech.edu
GAY, Jeff 315-684-6053 336 B
GAY, John 410-386-8434 206 I jgay@carrollcc.edu
GAY, Judith 215-751-8351 401 G jgay@ccp.edu
GAY, Michelle 704-403-1758 342 E michelle.gay@carolinashealthcare.org
GAY, Shirley 252-862-1307 352 D swgay6885@roanokechowan.edu
GAY, Thresa 404-270-5210 128 A tgay@spelman.edu
GAY, Tim 510-780-4500 48 J tgay@lifewest.edu
GAYESKI, Diane 607-274-3895 317 D gayeski@ithaca.edu
GAYLA, Shaffer 832-252-0750 454 H gayla.shaffer@cbshouston.edu
GAYLARD, Cindy, M 850-973-1618 105 H gaylardc@nfcc.edu
GAYLE, Robin 415-257-1305 42 G robin.gayle@dominican.edu
GAYLE, Ruth, R 215-965-4002 411 A rgayle@moore.edu
GAYLES, Jonathan 404-413-5638 122 D jgayles@gsu.edu
GAYLOR, IV, Charles 919-735-5151 354 A cpgaylor@waynecc.edu
GAYMER, Dawn, M 269-387-4207 243 H dawn.gaymer@wmich.edu
GAYMON, Denise 256-551-1710 4 F denise.gaymon@drakestate.edu
GAYMON, Joffery 850-474-3386 113 A jgaymon@uwf.edu
GAYNOR, Dona, E 321-674-8102 100 M dgaynor@fit.edu
GAYNOR, Julie 940-397-4353 462 A julie.gaynor@mwsu.edu
GAYNOR, Michael, M 610-519-4000 422 G michael.gaynor@villanova.edu
GAYNOR, Suzanne 607-431-4670 315 E gaynors@hartwick.edu
GAYS, Elizabeth 931-372-3034 445 B egays@tntech.edu
GAYTHORPE, John 425-602-3036 501 D johngaythorpe@bastyr.edu
GAYTON, Jeffrey 541-552-6833 395 A gaytonj@sou.edu
GAYTON, Linda 973-684-6104 294 A lgayton@pccc.edu
GAZAL, Mary 724-805-2627 419 A mary.gazal@stvincent.edu
GAZZALE, Bob 323-856-7600 26 I bgazzale@afi.com
GAZZARA HESS, Margaret 508-588-9100 223 G
GAZZILLO, Sara 201-684-7610 294 G sgazzill@ramapo.edu
GEAGHAN, Tom 216-687-4745 366 I t.geaghan@csuohio.edu
GEALT, Michael, A 989-774-3931 232 D gealt1ma@cmich.edu
GEANEY, Martha 610-683-4575 415 C geaney@kutztown.edu
GEAR, Jackie 215-968-8416 399 A jaclyn.gear@bucks.edu
GEAR, Lisa, L 213-738-6834 66 F admissions@swlaw.edu
GEARAN, Dan 603-428-2372 287 C dgearan@nec.edu
GEARAN, Mark, D 315-781-3309 316 C gearan@hws.edu
GEARHART, Gregory, L 717-691-6007 410 J gearhart@messiah.edu
GEARHART, Troy 610-917-1423 422 C tegearhart@valleyforge.edu
GEARHART TURNER, Patti 817-531-5820 472 F pturner@txwes.edu
GEARIN, Christopher, A 314-434-2212 266 B cgearin@hickeycollege.edu
GEARY, Colette 218-723-6033 245 J president@css.edu
GEARY, Gregg 562-903-4834 28 E gregg.geary@biola.edu
GEARY, Leslie, H 203-576-4625 89 C lgeary@bridgeport.edu
GEARY, Melanie 303-534-6290 78 P melanie.geary@colostate.edu
GEARY, Parrish 916-484-8172 51 A gearyp@arc.losrios.edu
GEARY, Ronald 815-921-2195 152 E r.geary@rockvalleycollege.edu
GEASEY, David, W 607-436-3314 331 F david.geasey@oneonta.edu
GEBEL, Karen 319-296-2320 173 B karen.gebel@hawkeyecollege.edu
GEBEL, Vicky 607-871-2186 303 F gebel@alfred.edu
GEBER, David 917-493-4516 319 M dgeber@msmnyc.edu
GEBERT, Gordon 212-650-7284 307 E ggebert@ccny.cuny.edu
GEBHARDT, Kristin 608-246-6902 523 F kgebhardt@madisoncollege.edu
GEBHARDT, Lynita 630-617-3020 140 C lynita.gebhardt@elmhurst.edu
GEBHARDT, Michael, B 215-204-6542 420 B michael.gebhardt@temple.edu
GEBHARDT, Virginia 660-263-4100 269 D virginig@macc.edu
GEBHART, Jennifer, L 937-775-5611 381 H jennifer.gebhart@wright.edu
GEBO, Kelly 410-516-5985 208 D kgebo@jhmi.edu
GEDDINGS, Scarlet 803-535-1243 431 I geddingss@octech.edu
GEDDIS, Catherine 212-854-2551 304 I cgeddis@barnard.edu
GEDDIS, Janet 610-558-5540 411 E geddisj@neumann.edu
GEDERS, Cindy, H 260-359-4068 161 O cgeders@huntington.edu
GEDNALSKE, Julie 605-331-6683 438 A julie.gednalske@usiouxfalls.edu
GEDRO, Julie 585-224-3222 335 D julie.gedro@esc.edu
GEE, Bradley, A 614-235-4136 378 C bgee@tlschio.edu
GEE, E. Gordon 304-293-5531 514 C gordon.gee@mail.wvu.edu
GEE, Henry 562-908-3489 58 I hgee@riohondo.edu
GEE, Terry 619-594-2853 35 A tgee@mail.sdsu.edu
GEEHAN, Margaret 518-629-7151 316 G m.geehan@hvcc.edu
GEENENS, Dave 913-360-7633 178 I dgeenens@benedictine.edu
GEER, John, G 615-322-2809 449 A john.geer@vanderbilt.edu
GEER, Nathan 503-375-7010 391 B ngeer@corban.edu
GEER, Robert, E 315-792-7400 336 C geerre@sunyit.edu
GEETER, Andy 229-732-5934 116 C andygeeter@andrewcollege.edu
GEETER, Candy 248-341-2138 239 E crgeeter@oaklandcc.edu
GEETTER, Erika 617-353-2326 216 E egeetter@bu.edu
GEFELL, Michele, D 315-786-2271 317 H mgefell@sunyjefferson.edu
GEFFERT, Bryn 413-542-2212 214 C bgeffert@amherst.edu
GEFFNER, Linda, O 860-231-5208 90 E lgeffner@usj.edu
GEGENHEIMER BALDASSARO, Sarah 202-994-5152 92 D sarahgb@gwu.edu
GEGG-LAPLUME, Tamara 314-968-6982 275 E laplume@webster.edu
GEGGIE, Steven 847-317-8178 156 E sgeggie@tiu.edu
GEHBAUER, Daryl 636-481-3120 266 C dgehbaue@jeffco.edu
GEHEBER, Leah 225-768-1746 199 E lgeheber@ololcollege.edu
GEHEN, Melanie 718-270-8590 332 E melanie.gehen@downstate.edu
GEHLER, Jan, L 480-423-6310 14 H jan.gehler@scottsdalecc.edu
GEHLER, Nick 619-388-7715 60 H ngehler@sdccd.edu
GEHLHAUSEN, Keith 812-488-2943 167 I kg77@evansville.edu
GEHRET, Steve 423-636-5096 447 G sgehret@tusculum.edu
GEHRICH, Michael, D 317-381-6000 169 A mgehrich@vinu.edu
GEHRIG, Stacy 309-694-5512 141 F sgehrig@icc.edu
GEHRING, Dale 701-483-2371 360 D
GEHRKE, Deb 651-793-1278 250 A deb.gehrke@metrostate.edu
GEHRKE, Sean 208-792-2456 134 A sjghrke@lcsc.edu
GEHRLS, Janet 563-355-3500 174 E jgehrls@kaplan.edu
GEHRMAN-ROTTIER, Laura 715-346-3811 521 C lgehrman@uwsp.edu
GEIB, Bethany 740-857-1311 376 L bgeib@rosedale.edu
GEIER, Doug 415-369-5275 45 B dgeier@ggu.edu
GEIER, Marisa 360-442-2391 504 G mgeier@lowercolumbia.edu
GEIER, Melissa 816-584-6273 270 D mgeier@park.edu
GEIER, Peter, E 614-292-2635 375 A geier.10@osu.edu
GEIGER, James 814-393-2572 414 G jgeiger@clarion.edu
GEIGER, Kimberly 423-775-6596 443 H
GEIGER, Kristen 814-393-2337 414 G kgeiger@clarion.edu
GEIGER, Martha 513-936-1691 379 B martha.geiger@uc.edu
GEIGER, William 903-565-5515 477 B wgeiger@uttyler.edu
GEIKEN, Jason 573-629-3124 265 G jason.geiken@hlg.edu
GEIL, Carol 641-844-5747 173 L carol.geil@iavalley.edu
GEILING, Bryan, K 610-989-1351 422 E bgeiling@vfmac.edu
GEIS, Scott 901-321-3349 439 E
GEISER, Laura 314-977-2543 271 K geiserla@slu.edu
GEISLER, Allison 218-322-2324 249 G allison.geisler@itascacc.edu
GEISLER, Michael 802-443-5275 484 F geisler@middlebury.edu
GEISLER, Michael, E 914-323-5230 319 N michael.geisler@mville.edu
GEISLER, Norman, L 714-966-8500 73 G info@ves.edu
GEIST, Alan 937-766-7768 365 C geista@cedarville.edu
GEIST, Amanda 630-466-7900 157 K ageist@waubonsee.edu
GEIST, Edward, V 203-576-4956 89 C edwgeist@bridgeport.edu
GELASCO, Andrew 843-792-5998 431 A gelascoa@musc.edu
GELASI, Frank 815-479-7583 147 E fgelasi@mchenry.edu
GELAYE, Enku 413-545-2684 220 F egelaye@stuaf.umass.edu
GELAYE, Enku 413-254-2300 220 F egelaye@stuaf.umass.edu
GELCH, Deborah 617-243-2390 219 I dgelch@lasell.edu
GELDENHUYS, Tammie 620-331-4100 181 J tgeldenhuys@indycc.edu
GELDER, Alvern 616-957-6045 232 B ag094@calvinseminary.edu
GELDER, Tom 661-395-4840 47 J tom.gelder@bakersfieldcollge.edu
GELDWORTH, Lipa 718-853-8500 337 H
GELDZAHLER, Daniel 718-633-4715 326 K collegeoy@gmail.com
GELERNTER, Mark 303-315-1020 84 A mark.gelernter@ucdenver.edu
GELFAND, M 732-364-1220 289 B
GELINAS, Cynthia, B 803-641-3609 433 G cindyg@usca.edu
GELINAS, David 704-894-2698 343 I dagelinas@davidson.edu
GELL, Barry 518-255-5440 334 D gellbf@cobleskill.edu
GELLE, Mark 507-786-3294 254 P gelle@stolaf.edu
GELLER, Jack, M 813-253-6262 114 M jgeller@ut.edu
GELLER, Laurie 701-858-3310 360 F laurie.geller@minotstateu.edu
GELLER, Mary, A 320-363-5601 245 I mgeller@csbsju.edu
GELLER, Steve 952-358-8954 251 A steve.geller@normandale.edu

GELO, Daniel, J .... 210-458-4359.. 477 A
daniel.gelo@utsa.edu
GELORMINI, John .... 617-745-3719.. 218 A
john.gelormini@enc.edu
GELPI-RODRÍGUEZ,
Phaedra .... 787-480-2430.. 531 J
pgelpi@sanjuanciudadpatria.com
GELY, Gilda .... 617-873-0232.. 217 A
gilda.gely@cambridgecollege.edu
GEMEDA, Mekbib, L .... 757-446-7151.. 489 B
gemedam@evms.edu
GEMME, Terese .... 203-392-5499.... 85 H
gemmet1@southernct.edu
GEMMER, Peter .... 513-936-1632.. 379 B
peter.gemmer@uc.edu
GEMPERLEIN, Monica, P 919-334-1520.. 353 I
mpgemperlein@waketech.edu
GEMPERLINE, Paul .... 252-328-6012.. 356 C
gemperlinep@ecu.edu
GEMPESAW, Conrado, M 718-990-6755.. 328 F
pres@stjohns.edu
GENANDT, Jim, J .... 785-320-4500.. 183 A
jimgenandt@manhattantech.edu
GENARD, Daniel, J .... 757-683-3090.. 492 G
dgenard@odu.edu
GENARD, Giovanna, M .... 757-683-3580.. 492 G
ggenard@odu.edu
GENARDO, Patricia .... 630-889-6597.. 149 G
pgenardo@nuhs.edu
GENDRON, Dennis .... 206-296-5556.. 507 E
gendron@seattleu.edu
GENDRON, Julie .... 603-428-2440.. 287 C
jgendron@nec.edu
GENECIN, Paul .... 203-432-0076.... 90 D
paul.genecin@yale.edu
GENERALS, Donald .... 215-751-8000.. 401 G
ggenerals@ccp.edu
GENES, Marna .... 408-924-2341.... 35 C
marna.genes@sjsu.edu
GENESE, Carol .... 914-632-5400.. 321 I
cgenese@monroecollege.edu
GENETTI, Carol .... 805-893-2013.... 70 E
cgenetti@graddiv.ucsb.edu
GENGLER, Charles .... 718-262-5310.. 310 A
cgengler@york.cuny.edu
GENIG, Dennis .... 734-462-4400.. 240 H
dgenig@schoolcraft.edu
GENNA, Angela .... 602-285-7357.... 14 F
angela.genna@phoenixcollege.edu
GENNARO, Gwen .... 719-255-3153.... 83 L
ggennaro@uccs.edu
GENNARO, Susan .... 617-552-1710.. 216 C
susan.gennaro@bc.edu
GENO, Rita, B .... 802-468-1203.. 485 H
rita.geno@castleton.edu
GENOUS, Zandra .... 847-543-2420.. 138 C
zgenous@clcillinois.edu
GENOVESE, Katherine ...... 518-292-1915.. 327 H
genovk@sage.edu
GENSHAFT, Judy, L .... 813-974-2791.. 112 C
jgensha@usf.edu
GENTALA, Luke .... 434-592-3470.. 491 D
GENTHNER, Patricia .... 585-389-2002.. 322 D
pgenthn5@naz.edu
GENTHON, Paulette .... 402-556-4456.. 282 J
paulettegenthon@ucha.edu
GENTILE, Jackie .... 415-485-3247.... 42 G
jacqueline.gentile@dominican.edu
GENTILE, Kathy, J .... 314-516-6383.. 274 A
gentilek@umsl.edu
GENTILE, Linda .... 412-268-5231.. 400 D
lgentile@cmu.edu
GENTILE, Lisa .... 801-832-2581.. 483 D
lgentile@westminstercollege.edu
GENTILE, Patricia, A .... 978-762-4000.. 224 C
pgentile@northshore.edu
GENTLEWARRIOR,
Sabrina .... 508-531-1429.. 221 C
sabrina.gentlewarrior@bridgew.edu
GENTRY, Bradley, D .... 217-786-2278.. 146 E
brad.gentry@llcc.edu
GENTRY, Eric, C .... 859-572-5129.. 192 B
egentry@nku.edu
GENTRY, Gisele .... 601-979-6938.. 258 D
gisele.n.gentry@jsums.edu
GENTRY, Helen .... 706-886-6831.. 128 C
hgentry@tfc.edu
GENTRY, Jerry .... 816-271-4417.. 269 C
jgentry7@missouriwestern.edu
GENTRY, Jerry, H .... 270-831-9622.. 189 F
jerry.gentry@kctcs.edu
GENTRY, Jodi, D .... 352-392-1075.. 112 A
jodi-gentry@ufl.edu
GENTRY, Keil .... 703-784-2105.. 528 A
keil.gentry@usmc.mil
GENTRY, Margaret .... 315-859-4607.. 315 D
mgentry@hamilton.edu
GENTRY, Marichal .... 931-598-1229.. 443 O
wmgentr@sewanee.edu
GENTRY, Susan .... 252-335-0821.. 349 A
susan_gentry@albemarle.edu
GENTRY, Vickie .... 318-357-5361.. 201 B
gentryv@nsula.edu
GENTRY, Vickie .... 318-357-6288.. 201 B
gentryv@nsula.edu
GENTRY-WRIGHT,
Susan, C .... 864-833-8100.. 432 B
sgentry-w@presby.edu
GENTSCH, James .... 205-652-3361...... 9 F
jgentsch@uwa.edu
GENTZLER, Randall .... 410-617-2345.. 208 G
rdgentzler@loyola.edu
GENUA, Kathy .... 516-918-3626.. 305 K
kgenua@bcl.edu
GEOCARIS, Diane, F .... 949-824-2880.... 69 C
dfgeocar@uci.edu
GEOFFRION-SCANNELL,
Kathryn .... 978-837-5211.. 225 E
geoffrionsck@merrimack.edu
GEOFFROY, Esther .... 603-882-6923.. 286 E
egeoffroy@ccsnh.edu
GEORGALLIS, Christine ... 352-588-8462.. 108 C
christine.georgallis@saintleo.edu
GEORGALLIS, Christine ... 352-588-8464.. 108 C
christine.georgallis@saintleo.edu
GEORGE, Abraham .... 706-507-8111.. 119 E
george_abraham@columbusstate.edu
GEORGE, Beena .... 713-525-5903.. 475 J
georgeb@stthom.edu
GEORGE, Bill .... 619-201-8959.... 65 J
bill.george@socalsem.edu
GEORGE, Charles .... 503-491-7131.. 392 F
charles.george@mhcc.edu
GEORGE, Chris .... 270-745-3978.. 194 D
chris.george@wku.edu
GEORGE, Chris .... 507-786-3775.. 254 P
georgec@stolaf.edu
GEORGE, Christi .... 205-652-3840...... 9 F
cjw@uwa.edu
GEORGE, Cynthia .... 229-317-6929.. 120 A
cynthia.george@darton.edu
GEORGE, Cynthia .... 229-430-4660.. 115 K
cynthia.george@asurams.edu
GEORGE, Dennis, K .... 270-745-3570.. 194 D
dennis.george@wku.edu
GEORGE, Ellen .... 309-999-4580.. 141 F
egeorge@icc.edu
GEORGE, Emily .... 605-995-2601.. 435 F
emgeorge@dwu.edu
GEORGE, Gene .... 316-322-3338.. 179 E
ggeorge@butlercc.edu
GEORGE, Jack, J .... 305-284-2858.. 114 H
jack.george@miami.edu
GEORGE, Janice, S .... 620-421-6700.. 182 G
janicec@labette.edu
GEORGE, Jennifer .... 719-255-3820.... 83 L
jennifer.george@uccs.edu
GEORGE, Karen .... 719-365-1038.... 83 I
karen.george@uchealth.org
GEORGE, Lee Ann .... 618-634-3228.. 154 B
leeanng@shawneecc.edu
GEORGE, Marie .... 570-945-8515.. 406 H
marie.george@keystone.edu
GEORGE, Mertha, V .... 601-877-6154.. 256 F
mgeorge@alcorn.edu
GEORGE, Michael .... 419-517-8990.. 371 I
mgeorge@lourdes.edu
GEORGE, Michel .... 503-768-7850.. 392 A
mgeorge@lclark.edu
GEORGE, Monique .... 646-660-6590.. 307 A
monique.george@baruch.cuny.edu
GEORGE, Pamela, L .... 216-397-1908.. 370 H
pgeorgemerrill@jcu.edu
GEORGE, Philip, J .... 315-445-4644.. 318 E
georgepj@lemoyne.edu
GEORGE, R. Dillard .... 757-683-4156.. 492 G
rdgeorge@odu.edu
GEORGE, Rick .... 303-492-6591.... 83 K
rick.george@colorado.edu
GEORGE, Robert .... 941-756-0690.. 407 D
rgeorge@lecom.edu
GEORGE, Russell .... 970-675-3201.... 78 J
russell.george@cncc.edu
GEORGE, Sarah, B .... 801-581-6927.. 481 M
sgeorge@umnh.utah.edu
GEORGE, Scott .... 816-604-1087.. 267 F
scott.george@mcckc.edu
GEORGE, Sheila .... 202-885-8657.... 94 E
sgeorge@wesleyseminary.edu
GEORGE, Simone, M .... 302-356-6898.... 91 I
simone.m.george@wilmu.edu
GEORGE, Stacy .... 513-529-1782.. 372 K
woodrus@miamioh.edu
GEORGE, Stacy .... 509-777-3851.. 509 H
sgeorge@whitworth.edu
GEORGE, Susan .... 304-473-8080.. 515 B
george@wvwc.edu
GEORGE, Tami, B .... 910-272-3541.. 352 E
tgeorge@robeson.edu
GEORGE, Thomas, F .... 314-516-5252.. 274 A
tfgeorge@umsl.edu
GEORGE, Timothy, F .... 205-726-2632...... 6 E
tfgeorge@samford.edu
GEORGE, William, D .... 570-577-1228.. 398 L
wdgeorge@bucknell.edu
GEORGE-WEINSTEIN,
Mindy .... 215-871-6654.. 416 F
GEORGES, Anthony, C ...... 314-516-5508.. 274 A
tony_georges@umsl.edu
GEORGIOPOULOS,
Michael .... 407-823-5338.. 111 E
michaelg@ucf.edu
GEORGIOU, Thales .... 972-238-6231.. 456 H
tgeorgiou@dcccd.edu
GEORGIOU, Tina .... 212-343-1234.. 321 B
tgeorgiou@mcny.edu
GEPHART, JR.,
George, W .... 215-299-1016.. 402 G
george.w.gephart@drexel.edu
GERA, Holly, P .... 973-655-5234.. 293 A
gerah@mail.montclair.edu
GERACE, Christopher .... 716-250-7500.. 306 A
cpgerace@bryantstratton.edu
GERACI, Luci .... 718-990-2023.. 328 F
geracil@stjohns.edu
GERAD, Mary, C .... 412-397-6410.. 418 B
gerad@rmu.edu
GERAGHTY, John .... 323-563-5929.... 37 G
johngeraghty@cdrewu.edu
GERAGHTY, Melissa .... 425-388-9572.. 503 F
mgeraghty@everettcc.edu
GERALD, Trudy .... 619-388-3522.... 60 F
tgerald@sdccd.edu
GERAMI, Keyvan .... 314-286-3670.. 270 G
kgerami@ranken.edu
GERARD, Debra .... 714-480-7450.... 58 F
gerard_debra@rsccd.edu
GERARD, Matthew, C .... 402-280-5746.. 279 H
mgerard@creighton.edu
GERARD, Pam .... 319-895-5267.. 171 A
pgerard@cornellcollege.edu
GERARD, Phil .... 864-242-5100.. 427 E
GERARD, Stacey .... 252-940-6241.. 347 E
stacey.gerard@beaufortccc.edu
GERARDO, Debbie .... 770-962-7580.. 123 D
dgerardo@gwinnetttech.edu
GERASSIMIDES, Gus .... 859-985-3158.. 187 B
gus_gerassimides@berea.edu
GERATY, Brent, G .... 909-748-8076.... 71 K
brent_geraty@redlands.edu
GERBACHT, Tonya, L .... 319-273-6520.. 170 A
tonya.gerbracht@uni.edu
GERBASI, Iris .... 714-997-6676.... 37 F
gerbasi@chapman.edu
GERBER, Andrew .... 404-894-2000.. 121 D
andrew.gerber@gtri.gatech.edu
GERBER, Brian, L .... 229-333-5950.. 129 G
blgerber@valdosta.edu
GERBER, Cheryl .... 724-946-6173.. 423 B
gerberca@westminster.edu
GERBER, Elizabeth, L .... 815-599-3421.. 141 E
liz.gerber@highland.edu
GERBER, Gary .... 870-245-5129.... 21 E
gerberg@obu.edu
GERBER, Molly .... 215-955-1061.. 420 E
molly.gerber@jefferson.edu
GERBER, Nathan .... 801-863-7973.. 482 C
nathan.gerber@uvu.edu
GERBER, Sue .... 201-200-3042.. 293 C
sgerber@njcu.edu
GERBERRY, Jeffrey .... 614-947-6007.. 369 A
jeffrey.gerberry@franklin.edu
GERBOTH, Karen .... 937-327-7894.. 381 F
kgerboth@wittenberg.edu
GERBSCH, Julie .... 912-344-2600.. 116 E
julie.gerbsch@armstrong.edu
GERBSCH, Reinhold .... 912-650-5682.. 127 D
rgerbsch@southuniversity.edu
GERDES, Darin .... 843-574-3220.. 427 I
dgerdes@csuniv.edu
GERDRUM, Kacie .... 541-684-7288.. 393 B
kgerdrum@nwcu.edu
GERE, Nicholas .... 207-602-2011.. 205 F
ngere@une.edu
GEREAUX, Teresa, T .... 540-375-2282.. 493 H
gereaux@roanoke.edu
GEREMIA, Kenneth .... 413-528-7291.. 214 H
kgeremia@simons-rock.edu
GERENZ, Eileen .... 781-239-2522.. 223 F
egerenz@massbay.edu
GERETY, RSM, Jane .... 401-341-2337.. 426 C
jane.gerety@salve.edu
GERGER, Rick .... 314-246-8708.. 275 B
rickgerger06@webster.edu
GERGES, Marilia .... 931-540-2618.. 446 A
mgerges@columbiastate.edu
GERHARDT, Cassie .... 701-777-4200.. 360 C
cassie.gerhardt@und.edu
GERHARDT, Winifred .... 440-826-2222.. 363 M
wgerhard@bw.edu
GERHARDT, Winifred, W . 440-826-8002.. 363 M
wgerhardt@bw.edu
GERHART, Phillip, M .... 812-488-2651.. 167 I
pg3@evansville.edu
GERHART, Robert .... 229-391-4850.. 115 I
rgerhart@abac.edu
GERHOFF, Sondra .... 866-251-3244.. 106 A
GERIG, Jill .... 912-478-5367.. 122 B
jgerig@georgiasouthern.edu
GERIGUIS, David .... 951-785-2002.... 48 A
dgerigui@lasierra.edu
GERIK, Debbie .... 254-659-7704.. 458 K
debgerik@hillcollege.edu
GERIN, Jean-Louis .... 802-225-3356.. 484 G
jean-louis.gerin@neci.edu
GERIS, Emily .... 651-255-6166.. 255 C
egeris@unitedseminary.edu
GERITY, Patrick, E .... 724-925-4219.. 423 D
gerityk@wccc.edu
GERKE, Mary Lu .... 608-796-3664.. 522 O
mlgerke@viterbo.edu
GERKEN, Keith .... 907-796-6496.... 10 H
wkgerken@alaska.edu
GERKEN, Stacey .... 715-346-3553.. 521 C
sgerken@uwsp.edu
GERKIN, Jeffrey, G .... 865-974-3131.. 448 E
jgerkin@utk.edu
GERKO, Danielle .... 814-262-3825.. 413 P
dgerko@pennhighlands.edu
GERL, Beth, R .... 410-857-2244.. 209 D
bgerl@mcdaniel.edu
GERLACH, Alysa .... 617-373-5144.. 227 B
GERLACH, David, M .... 217-732-3155.. 146 B
dgerlach@lincolncollege.edu
GERLACH, Karen .... 202-884-9203.... 94 A
gerlachk@trinitydc.edu
GERLACH, Peter .... 319-399-8843.. 170 G
pgerlachi@coe.edu
GERMAIN, George .... 989-328-1275.. 238 D
georgeg@montcalm.edu
GERMAN, Deborah .... 407-266-1000.. 111 E
deborah.german@ucf.edu
GERMAN, James, D .... 973-655-4382.. 293 A
germanj@mail.montclair.edu
GERMAN, Lisa .... 256-352-8306...... 9 G
lisa.german@wallacestate.edu
GERMAN, Lisa, A .... 713-743-0291.. 473 F
lagerman@uh.edu
GERMANO, William .... 212-353-4274.. 311 G
germano@cooper.edu
GERMANO, William .... 516-796-4800.. 323 A
wgermano@nycc.edu
GERMANY, Carole, H .... 601-635-6201.. 257 F
cgermany@eccc.edu
GERMANY, Debbie .... 803-754-4100.. 429 B
GERMERAAD, Stephanie .. 310-954-5080.... 29 D
GERMIC, Stephen, A .... 406-657-1020.. 278 D
stephen.germic@rocky.edu
GERMNO, Damien .... 914-654-5864.. 311 A
dgermino@cnr.edu
GERN, William, A .... 307-766-5353.. 527 B
willger@uwyo.edu
GERNER, Steven, W .... 262-243-5700.. 516 E
steven.gerner@cuw.edu
GERNES, Todd, S .... 508-565-1946.. 228 F
tgernes@stonehill.edu
GERODIMOS, Ashley .... 219-989-2414.. 166 F
ashley.geriodimos@pnw.edu
GEROSIMO, Veronica .... 516-876-3079.. 333 C
gerosimov@oldwestbury.edu
GEROW, Gary .... 207-941-7907.. 202 I
gerowg@husson.edu
GERRETSEN, Amy, L .... 920-748-8353.. 519 E
gerretsena@ripon.edu
GERRISH, James .... 973-290-4479.. 290 G
jgerrish@cse.edu
GERSEY, Martin, L .... 574-520-5522.. 163 E
mgersey@iusb.edu
GERSH, Geniene, M .... 269-387-1880.. 243 H
geniene.m.gersh@wmich.edu
GERSH, Sheila .... 914-674-7339.. 320 G
sgersh@mercy.edu
GERSHEN, Jay, A .... 330-325-6263.. 373 H
president@neomed.edu
GERSHMAN, Richard .... 615-383-4848.. 449 G
rgershman@watkins.edu
GERSICH, Frank .... 309-457-2119.. 148 E
fgersich@monmouthcollege.edu
GERSMAN, Kimberly .... 636-949-4366.. 266 J
kgersman@lindenwood.edu
GERST, Bernard .... 410-704-2505.. 213 B
bgerst@towson.edu
GERSTEIN, Dean .... 909-607-9406.... 38 I
dean.gerstein@cgu.edu
GERSTENBERGER, Julie ..... 806-716-2019.. 465 G
jgerstenberger@southplainscollege.edu
GERSTENBERGER, Shawn 702-895-1565.. 284 L
shawn.gerstenberger@unlv.edu
GERTH, Daniel .... 314-516-7197.. 274 A
gerthd@umsl.edu
GERTNER, Kimberly, A ...... 843-953-5758.. 428 G
gertnerka@cofc.edu
GERTSON, Katherine .... 212-799-5000.. 318 A

GERTZ, Genie .... 202-651-5653.... 92 C genie.gertz@gallaudet.edu
GERTZ, Tanya, M .... 563-387-1536.. 174 L gertta01@luther.edu
GERVAIS, Shayne .... 304-367-4658.. 513 B sgervais@fairmontstate.edu
GERVASI, Robert .... 217-228-5432.. 151 F gervasi@quincy.edu
GERZINA, Gretchen .... 413-577-3902.. 220 F dean@honors.umass.edu
GERZINA, Holly, A .... 330-325-6740.. 373 H hgerzina@neomed.edu
GESELE, G. Scott .... 757-594-7863.. 488 E scott.gesele@cnu.edu
GESO, Cristina .... 215-955-8164.. 420 E cristina.geso@jefferson.edu
GESSLER, Klaus .... 845-431-8939.. 312 G gessler@sunydutchess.edu
GESSNER, James, C .... 570-389-4105.. 414 D jgessner@bloomu.edu
GESSNER, James, R .... 218-722-4000.. 246 E jimg@dbumn.edu
GESSNER, Michael .... 270-706-8727.. 189 C bkselizabethtown@bnccollege.com
GESTOSO, Llloyd .... 215-702-4275.. 399 E lgestoso@cairn.edu
GESTRING, Sheila .... 605-677-5255.. 437 A sheila.gestring@usd.edu
GETCHELL, JR., Charles, M .... 603-641-7320.. 287 G cgetchell@anselm.edu
GETCHELL, Jeffrey .... 303-964-5429.... 82 L jgetchell@regis.edu
GETCHELL, Stephanie, L .. 919-530-7824.. 357 A getchells@nccu.edu
GETKIN, Ann .... 412-924-1369.. 417 E agetkin@pts.edu
GETMAN, Meghan .... 315-792-7264.. 336 C meghan.getman@sunyit.edu
GETSINGER, Joseph .... 856-415-6209.. 295 D jgetsinger@rcgc.edu
GETTINGS, Michael .... 540-362-6432.. 490 F mgettings@hollins.edu
GETTY, JacQui .... 651-523-2475.. 247 A jgetty01@hamline.edu
GETTY, Larry, R .... 785-628-4513.. 180 I lgetty@fhsu.edu
GETTY, Marc, D .... 304-326-1258.. 511 D mgetty@salemu.edu
GETZ, Karen .... 724-266-3838.. 421 C kgetz@tsm.edu
GETZ, Kathleen .... 410-617-2301.. 208 G kgetz@loyola.edu
GETZ, Rob .... 610-902-8147.. 399 D rag44@cabrini.edu
GETZ, Roger .... 207-768-9595.. 205 D roger.getz@maine.edu
GEU, Thomas .... 605-677-5443.. 437 A thomas.geu@usd.edu
GEUDER, Maridith .... 662-329-7119.. 259 E mgeuder@muw.edu
GEVITZ, Norman .... 660-626-2371.. 262 A ngevitz@atsu.edu
GEYE, Trina .... 254-968-9400.. 467 F geye@tarleton.edu
GEYER, Dennis .... 916-278-3625.... 34 B dgeyer@csus.edu
GEYER, Enid .... 518-262-5586.. 303 E geyere@mail.amc.edu
GEYER, Enid .... 518-262-6008.. 303 E geyere@mail.amc.edu
GEYER, Mariann, K .... 412-392-3805.. 417 F mgeyer@pointpark.edu
GFELLER, Josh .... 785-587-2800.. 183 A joshgfeller@manhattantech.edu
GHADIALI, Khushroo .... 575-234-9414.. 301 B khushroo@nmsu.edu
GHAHRAMANI, Saeed ...... 413-782-1218.. 229 E sghahram@wne.edu
GHALI, Ghali, E .... 318-675-5240.. 198 B gghali@lsuhsc.edu
GHAMMACHI, Gabe .... 502-456-6504.. 193 B gghammachi@sullivan.edu
GHAN, Mark .... 775-445-4468.. 285 B mark.ghan@wnc.edu
GHANEM, Salma .... 312-362-8610.. 139 C sghanem@depaul.edu
GHANNADIAN, F. Frank .. 813-253-6221.. 114 M fghannadian@ut.edu
GHAZARIAN, Esther, A .... 781-768-7280.. 227 G esther.ghazarian@regiscollege.edu
GHAZARYAN, Ashot .... 510-925-4282.... 26 M ashot.ghazaryan@aua.am
GHAZI-BIRRY, Hani .... 801-375-5125.. 481 C hsgbirry@rmuohp.edu
GHEE, Harry .... 910-323-5614.. 342 H dean@ccbs.edu
GHERKE, Amy .... 304-865-6034.. 511 C amy.gherke@ovu.edu
GHILANI, Mary .... 570-740-0456.. 409 E mghilani@luzerne.edu
GHILONI, Adam .... 212-749-2802.. 319 M aghiloni@msmnyc.edu
GHILONI, Adam .... 864-646-1583.. 433 C aghiloni@tctc.edu
GHIO, Frederick, W .... 401-456-8201.. 425 E fghio@ric.edu
GHITA, Florentin .... 423-478-7250.. 443 I fghita@ptseminary.edu
GHOLSON, Robert, D .... 601-266-4466.. 261 E robert.gholson@usm.edu
GHOLSON, Shari .... 270-534-3372.. 190 H shari.gholson@kctcs.edu
GHORASHI, Bahman .... 931-372-3224.. 445 B bghorashi@tntech.edu
GHORAYEB, Samir .... 409-984-6484.. 471 C samir.ghorayeb@lamarpa.edu
GHORI, Zaid .... 650-738-7088.... 62 I ghoriz@smccd.edu
GHORMOZ, Jacquelyn ..... 570-504-9073.. 400 I
GHOSAL, Bobby .... 601-923-6213.. 259 C bobby.ghosal@mgccc.edu
GHOSH, Avijit .... 312-355-5706.. 156 F ghosha@uic.edu
GHOSH, Guru .... 540-231-3205.. 499 F gghosh@vt.edu
GHOSH, Jayati .... 610-499-4300.. 423 E jghosh@widener.edu
GHOSH, Sibdas .... 914-633-2207.. 317 B sghosh@iona.edu
GHOSH, Soumitra .... 217-228-5432.. 151 F ghoshso@quincy.edu
GHYMN, Kyung-il .... 770-279-0507.. 120 G kyung.il.ghymn@gcuniv.edu
GIACOMINI, Michael .... 626-229-1300.... 48 H
GIACOMINI, Mike .... 626-300-5444.... 57 I
GIAMARTINO, Gary, A ..... 215-951-1040.. 407 A giamartino@lasalle.edu
GIAMBRA, Leonard, M ..... 860-701-6679.. 529 A leonard.m.giambra@uscg.mil
GIAMMARCO, Vicki .... 215-641-6688.. 410 L vgiammarco@mc3.edu
GIAMPAOLI, Michael, J ... 203-576-4168.... 89 C gmichael@bridgeport.edu
GIAMPIETRO, Michael ..... 413-565-1000.. 215 A mgiampietro@baypath.edu
GIANNESCHI, Matt .... 970-945-8691.... 78 B mgianneschi@coloradomtn.edu
GIANNET, Stanley, M .... 727-816-3490.. 106 F giannes@phsc.edu
GIANNINI, Gaetan .... 610-606-4666.. 400 E gtgianni@cedarcrest.edu
GIANNINI, Tula .... 718-636-3702.. 326 E tgiannin@pratt.edu
GIANNIOS, Paivi .... 816-501-4075.. 270 J paivi.giannios@rockhurst.edu
GIANNOTTI, Louis, J .... 410-293-1400.. 529 D giannott@usna.edu
GIANOTTI, Margaret .... 541-278-5775.. 390 C mgianotti@bluecc.edu
GIANOUSSOPOULOS, Denise .... 626-396-2298.... 27 L dgianou@artcenter.edu
GIARDULLO, Kelly .... 781-891-2014.. 215 F kgiardullo@bentley.edu
GIARRUSSO, John .... 518-956-8090.. 331 A jgiarrusso@albany.edu
GIAUQUE, Margie, T .... 218-755-2038.. 248 M mgiauque@bemidjistate.edu
GIBB, Julie .... 309-341-5242.. 136 C jgibb@sandburg.edu
GIBB, Katharine .... 864-503-5444.. 434 G kgibb@uscupstate.edu
GIBB, Randy .... 602-639-7500.... 13 I
GIBBEL, Mark .... 212-229-5662.. 322 E gibbelm@newschool.edu
GIBBENS, Charlie, E .... 915-747-5352.. 476 D cegibbens@utep.edu
GIBBISON, Godfrey .... 843-953-3596.. 428 G gibbisonga@lowcountrygraduatecenter.org
GIBBONS, Arthur .... 845-758-7442.. 304 F gibbons@bard.edu
GIBBONS, Dennis .... 315-792-5361.. 321 G dgibbons@mvcc.edu
GIBBONS, Earl, F .... 360-650-3308.. 509 E earl.gibbons@wwu.edu
GIBBONS, Kari .... 630-829-6306.. 135 F kgibbons@ben.edu
GIBBONS, Kristie .... 540-261-4100.. 494 F kristie.gibbons@svu.edu
GIBBONS, Michael .... 540-261-8470.. 494 F michael.gibbons@svu.edu
GIBBONS, Michael .... 478-471-2430.. 124 E michael.gibbons@mga.edu
GIBBONS, Michael, P .... 570-348-6221.. 409 H gibbons@marywood.edu
GIBBONS, Pete, W .... 304-724-3700.. 510 E pgibbons@apus.edu
GIBBONS, Susan .... 203-432-1818.... 90 D susan.gibbons@yale.edu
GIBBONS, Thomas, F .... 312-503-3011.. 150 F tgibbons@northwestern.edu
GIBBS, Beth B .... 207-859-1130.. 204 E gibbs@thomas.edu
GIBBS, Brad .... 800-955-2527.. 181 D bgibbs2@grantham.edu
GIBBS, Brian .... 503-494-5657.. 393 F cedma@ohsu.edu
GIBBS, Charles .... 202-238-2446.... 93 A charles.gibbs@howard.edu
GIBBS, Darry, C .... 865-882-4517.. 447 A gibbsdc@roanestate.edu
GIBBS, Donna .... 314-514-3101.. 151 E donna.gibbs@principia.edu
GIBBS, Donna, L .... 253-535-6023.. 505 G gibbsdl@plu.edu
GIBBS, Doug .... 314-514-3104.. 151 E doug.gibbs@principia.edu
GIBBS, Hilary, H .... 229-259-5503.. 129 G hhgibbs@valdosta.edu
GIBBS, J. D .... 252-527-6223.. 350 H jdgibbs27@lenoircc.edu
GIBBS, Jamie .... 252-249-1851.. 351 G jgibbs@pamlicocc.edu
GIBBS, Jeffery .... 863-674-6008.. 101 F jgibbs3@[illegible]sw.edu
GIBBS, Jeremiah .... 317-788-2058.. 168 A gibbsj@uindy.edu
GIBBS, Jim .... 806-651-3289.. 469 D jgibbs@mail.wtamu.edu
GIBBS, Kristen .... 660-248-6244.. 263 B kgibbs@centralmethodist.edu
GIBBS, Lisa .... 707-256-7170.... 53 H lgibbs@napavalley.edu
GIBBS, Lisa .... 707-256-7110.... 53 H lgibbs@napavalley.edu
GIBBS, Marilyn, Y .... 803-535-5309.. 428 B mgibbs@claflin.edu
GIBBS, Nicole .... 919-530-6096.. 357 A ngibbs2@nccu.edu
GIBBS, Patricia, M .... 478-757-5166.. 129 L pgibbs@wesleyancollege.edu
GIBBS, Patty .... 478-757-5260.. 129 L pgibbs@wesleyancollege.edu
GIBBS, Raymond .... 802-773-5900.. 483 G raymond.gibbs@csj.edu
GIBBS, Renisha, L .... 850-644-8082.. 111 C rgibbs@admin.fsu.edu
GIBBS, Ryan .... 806-716-2207.. 465 G rgibbs@southplainscollege.edu
GIBBS, Sarah .... 919-209-2086.. 350 G sfgibbs@johnstoncc.edu
GIBBS, Sarah, E .... 724-458-2183.. 404 F segibbs@gcc.edu
GIBBS, Shelby .... 325-793-3819.. 461 F gibbs.shelby@mcm.edu
GIBBS, Tricia .... 603-623-0313.. 287 D patriciagibbs@nhia.edu
GIBELLINO, Pamela .... 937-778-7856.. 368 E pgibellino@edisonohio.edu
GIBERT, Lisa .... 360-992-2677.. 502 E lgibert@clark.edu
GIBERTSON, Myrna .... 617-745-3724.. 218 A myrna.f.giberson@enc.edu
GIBLER, Linda .... 210-341-1366.. 463 A lgibler@ost.edu
GIBLER, Rhonda .... 573-882-2094.. 273 E giblerr@missouri.edu
GIBLIN, Frank .... 248-370-2395.. 239 K giblin@oakland.edu
GIBLIN, Patrick .... 314-246-7174.. 275 B patrickgiblin61@webster.edu
GIBLIN, Tara .... 714-432-5093.... 39 G tgiblin@occ.cccd.edu
GIBLIN, Tina .... 661-654-2241.... 32 A tgiblin@csub.edu
GIBNEY, Glenn .... 912-344-2563.. 116 E glenn.gibney@armstrong.edu
GIBONS, Penny .... 865-573-4517.. 440 I pgibons@johnsonu.edu
GIBRALTER, Jonathan ...... 315-364-3265.. 340 B president@wells.edu
GIBSON, Amy, B .... 630-515-7198.. 148 C agibso@midwestern.edu
GIBSON, Bernard .... 916-608-6780.... 51 G gibsonb@flc.losrios.edu
GIBSON, Bonnie, C .... 215-898-1135.. 421 E gibson@upenn.edu
GIBSON, Brandon, J .... 864-488-4371.. 430 H bgibson@limestone.edu
GIBSON, Brenda .... 503-255-0332.. 392 G bgibson@multnomah.edu
GIBSON, Cedrick .... 904-381-3534.. 101 G cedrick.gibson@fscj.edu
GIBSON, Christine .... 302-736-2571.... 91 G christine.gibson@wesley.edu
GIBSON, Chyvonne .... 708-209-3007.. 138 G chyvonne.gibson@cuchicago.edu
GIBSON, Clayton .... 256-372-5221...... 1 A clayton.gibson@aamu.edu
GIBSON, Colleen .... 901-435-1586.. 441 C colleen_gibson@loc.edu
GIBSON, Corinne, J .... 724-738-2700.. 416 B corinne.gibson@sru.edu
GIBSON, Dan .... 214-333-5340.. 455 J danielg@dbu.edu
GIBSON, David .... 413-559-6623.. 219 C djgcm@hampshire.edu
GIBSON, David, W .... 432-837-8702.. 471 E dgibson@sulross.edu
GIBSON, Dennis .... 301-387-3051.. 207 G dennis.gibson@garrettcollege.edu
GIBSON, Diana .... 304-327-4195.. 512 P dgibson@bluefieldstate.edu
GIBSON, Donald, E .... 203-254-4070.... 87 G dgibson@fairfield.edu
GIBSON, Donna, S .... 212-639-2109.. 319 I gibsond@mskcc.org
GIBSON, Edie, B .... 731-881-7508.. 448 G edgibson@utm.edu
GIBSON, Ginger .... 352-395-5211.. 109 C ginger.gibson@sfcollege.edu
GIBSON, Gloria .... 443-885-3350.. 209 F gloria.gibson@morgan.edu
GIBSON, J. Murray .... 850-410-6161.. 110 J jm.gibson@famu.edu
GIBSON, Jacqueline .... 662-254-3636.. 260 A jacqueline.gibson@mvsu.edu
GIBSON, James .... 662-476-5078.. 257 G jgibson@eastms.edu
GIBSON, Jane .... 901-375-4400.. 442 F janegibson@midsouthchristian.edu
GIBSON, Jeff .... 417-625-9727.. 268 H gibson-j@mssu.edu
GIBSON, Jeff .... 319-895-4357.. 171 A jgibson@cornellcollege.edu
GIBSON, Jeffrey .... 302-736-2420.... 91 G jeffrey.gibson@wesley.edu
GIBSON, Jencie .... 276-656-0202.. 498 A jgibson@patrickhenry.edu
GIBSON, Jeremy .... 978-837-5306.. 225 E gibsonj@merrimack.edu
GIBSON, John .... 918-595-7724.. 388 F john.gibson@tulsacc.edu
GIBSON, Joseph .... 843-574-6311.. 433 D joe.gibson@tridenttech.edu
GIBSON, Joyce .... 207-753-6594.. 205 E jgibson@maine.edu
GIBSON, Keith, E .... 540-464-7334.. 499 E gibsonke@vmi.edu
GIBSON, Kirk .... 541-956-7186.. 394 J kgibson@roguecc.edu
GIBSON, Kody .... 502-897-4617.. 192 D kgibson@sbts.edu
GIBSON, Lloyd, G .... 203-576-4385.... 89 C llgibson@bridgeport.edu
GIBSON, Lynn .... 662-685-4771.. 257 A lgibson@bmc.edu
GIBSON, Mandi .... 713-646-1702.. 459 A mgibson@hcl.edu
GIBSON, Marc .... 318-675-4928.. 198 B mgibso@lsuhsc.edu
GIBSON, Mark, T .... 919-866-5404.. 353 I mtgibson@waketech.edu
GIBSON, Melissa .... 904-596-2307.. 113 J mgibson@tbc.edu
GIBSON, Michael, A .... 434-924-8837.. 495 H mag3u@virginia.edu
GIBSON, Nola, R .... 601-974-1132.. 258 H gibsonk@millsaps.edu
GIBSON, Pamela .... 910-486-3930.. 349 F gibsonp@faytechcc.edu
GIBSON, Polly .... 480-990-3773.... 13 M
GIBSON, Rick .... 310-506-4125.... 56 J rick.gibson@pepperdine.edu
GIBSON, Rob .... 620-341-6694.. 180 G rgibson1@emporia.edu
GIBSON, Robert, L .... 301-405-5554.. 211 E rgibson@umd.edu
GIBSON, Ryan .... 606-368-6130.. 186 B ryangibson@alc.edu
GIBSON, Sally .... 816-271-4369.. 269 C sgibson14@missouriwestern.edu
GIBSON, Sandra, S .... 803-934-3419.. 431 E sangibson@morris.edu
GIBSON, Sheri .... 212-346-1619.. 325 J sgibson@pace.edu
GIBSON, Shonda .... 903-886-5743.. 468 D shonda.gibson@tamuc.edu
GIBSON, Stacey .... 208-282-3973.. 133 H gibssta2@isu.edu
GIBSON, Susan .... 404-880-8757.. 118 K sgibson@cau.edu
GIBSON, Tammy .... 706-379-3111.. 130 B tgibson@yhc.edu
GIBSON, Terry .... 972-923-6406.. 462 J terry.gibson@navarrocollege.edu
GIBSON, Tim .... 618-985-3741.. 143 F timgibson@jalc.edu
GIBSON, Tim .... 304-642-9997.. 510 I gibsont@dewv.edu

GIBSON, Todd, D .... 724-458-2147.. 404 F
tdgibson@gcc.edu
GIBSON, Tom .... 419-372-2211.. 364 E
GIBSON, Yolanda .... 703-284-1697.. 492 A
yolanda.gibson@marymount.edu
GIBSON-HAIGLER, Patricia .... 803-536-7104.. 432 E
phaigler@scsu.edu
GIBSON SHEFFIELD, Gail .... 802-387-6797.. 484 B
gailsheffield@landmark.edu
GIBSON-SHREVE, Lada ... 330-494-6170.. 377 J
lshreve@starkstate.edu
GIDDENS, Elizabeth .... 601-974-1123.. 258 H
giddeeo@millsaps.edu
GIDDENS, Jean .... 804-828-5174.. 496 D
jgiddens@vcu.edu
GIDDINGS, Andrew .... 480-461-7802.... 14 D
andrew.giddings@mesacc.edu
GIDDINGS, Geoffrey, J .... 937-376-6464.. 365 H
ggiddings@centralstate.edu
GIDDINGS, Meg, H .... 229-245-6490.. 129 G
mhgiddin@valdosta.edu
GIDDIS, Rayanne .... 352-854-2322.... 97 R
giddisr@cf.edu
GIDDY, Shawn .... 256-782-5781...... 4 H
sgiddy@jsu.edu
GIDEON, Amy, C .... 615-868-6503.. 442 G
amy@mtsa.edu
GIDLEY, James, S .... 724-847-6719.. 404 B
jsgidley@geneva.edu
GIE, Lori .... 504-520-5730.. 202 C
lgie@xula.edu
GIELISSE, Victor .... 845-451-1294.. 312 C
v_gielis@culinary.edu
GIELOW, Bob .... 617-559-8610.. 219 E
bgielow@hebrewcollege.edu
GIELOW, Curt .... 734-995-7331.. 232 I
curt.gielow@cuw.edu
GIERI, Joe .... 505-224-3037.. 299 F
jgieri@cnm.edu
GIEROK, Ed .... 503-554-2090.. 391 D
egierok@georgefox.edu
GIES, Jason .... 814-254-0564.. 401 A
jgies@pa.gov
GIESCHEN, Charles, A .... 260-452-2104.. 160 D
charles.gieschen@ctsfw.edu
GIESE, Melissa .... 816-604-1492.. 267 F
melissa.giese@mcckc.edu
GIESE, Ralph .... 719-255-4327.... 83 L
rgiese@uccs.edu
GIESE, Shane .... 406-243-2593.. 276 K
shane.giese@umontana.edu
GIESECKE, Marian, K .... 806-651-2055.. 469 D
mgiesecke@mail.wtamu.edu
GIESELMAN, Tammy .... 812-488-2260.. 167 I
tg85@evansville.edu
GIESEMAN, Mark .... 913-758-6526.. 185 F
giesemanm@stmary.edu
GIESSMAN, Michelle .... 636-949-4975.. 266 J
mgiessman@lindenwood.edu
GIFFIN, Ralph, G .... 201-216-8541.. 297 B
rgiffin@stevens.edu
GIFFIN, Thomas .... 678-466-4474.. 119 A
thomasgiffin@clayton.edu
GIFFORD, Darcy .... 734-487-5375.. 233 J
dgiffor2@emich.edu
GIFFORD, Denise, D .... 610-499-1265.. 423 E
ddgifford@widener.edu
GIFFORD, James .... 704-334-6882.. 343 D
jgifford@charlottechristian.edu
GIFFORD, Lyman .... 253-589-5782.. 502 F
lyman.gifford@cptc.edu
GIFFORD, Rachel .... 870-838-2902.... 18 G
rgifford@smail.anc.edu
GIFFORD, Rhonda .... 724-938-4413.. 414 E
gifford@calu.edu
GIFFROW, Tammy .... 281-756-3598.. 450 G
tgiffrow@alvincollege.edu
GIGER, Ann .... 662-846-4710.. 257 E
agiger@deltastate.edu
GIGER, Chris .... 662-846-4760.. 257 E
cgiger@deltastate.edu
GIGER, Lisa .... 662-846-4035.. 257 E
lgiger@deltastate.edu
GIGLIO, Elizabeth .... 845-758-7177.. 304 F
giglio@bard.edu
GIGLIOTTI, Chandra, M .. 410-827-5812.. 207 A
cgigliotti@chesapeake.edu
GIGLIOTTI, Lori, K .... 402-280-3517.. 279 H
lkg@creighton.edu
GIGOT, Jeremy .... 620-276-9570.. 181 C
jeremy.gigot@gcccks.edu
GIGUERE, Marlene .... 770-538-4722.. 118 A
mgiguere@brenau.edu
GIGUETTE, Marguerite ..... 504-520-7525.. 202 C
mgiguett@xula.edu
GIL, Andres .... 305-348-2494.. 111 A
andres.gil@fiu.edu
GIL, Betty .... 401-874-2310.. 426 D
bettyg@uri.edu

GILBERT, Aerin .... 410-923-4585.... 93 F
GILBERT, Alan .... 718-951-5102.. 307 D
agilbert@brooklyn.cuny.edu
GILBERT, Carl .... 580-559-5410.. 383 H
cgilbert@ecok.edu
GILBERT, Carol, S .... 703-330-5398.. 510 E
cgilbert@apus.edu
GILBERT, Cherryl .... 770-229-3409.. 127 F
cgilbert@sctech.edu
GILBERT, Clark, G .... 208-496-1111.. 132 J
gilbertc@byui.edu
GILBERT, Corynn .... 541-684-7222.. 393 B
cgilbert@nwcu.edu
GILBERT, David, H .... 414-906-4670.. 520 D
dhg@uwm.edu
GILBERT, Elinor .... 213-615-2700.... 37 I
GILBERT, Emily, R .... 806-371-5403.. 450 H
e0400185@actx.edu
GILBERT, Faye .... 601-266-4659.. 261 E
faye.gilbert@usm.edu
GILBERT, Fred .... 928-757-0854.... 15 E
fgilbert@mohave.edu
GILBERT, Glen, G .... 252-328-0038.. 356 C
gilbertg@ecu.edu
GILBERT, Jan .... 308-367-5252.. 283 C
jgilbert3@unl.edu
GILBERT, Jerome, A .... 304-696-3977.. 513 D
gilbert@marshall.edu
GILBERT, Joey .... 276-739-2473.. 499 A
jgilbert@vhcc.edu
GILBERT, Karen .... 404-471-6435.. 115 J
kgilbert@agnesscott.edu
GILBERT, Kat .... 414-382-6306.. 515 D
kat.gilbert@alverno.edu
GILBERT, Larry .... 916-278-7702.... 34 B
larry.gilbert@csus.edu
GILBERT, Larry .... 940-498-6282.. 462 L
lgilbert@nctc.edu
GILBERT, Lynda .... 205-348-4530...... 8 D
lgilbert@fa.ua.edu
GILBERT, Lynne .... 660-562-1110.. 269 J
lynneg@nwmissouri.edu
GILBERT, Michael .... 213-624-1200.... 43 J
mgilbert@fidm.edu
GILBERT, Michael .... 860-486-6137.... 89 D
michael.gilbert@uconn.edu
GILBERT, Michele .... 215-951-2562.. 416 G
gilbertm@philau.edu
GILBERT, Mindy .... 615-514-2787.. 443 F
mgilbert@nossi.edu
GILBERT, Nancy .... 419-448-3413.. 378 A
ngilbert@tiffin.edu
GILBERT, Peter, J .... 920-832-7353.. 517 E
peter.j.gilbert@lawrence.edu
GILBERT, Regina .... 615-383-4848.. 449 G
rgilbert@watkins.edu
GILBERT, Sharon .... 603-542-7744.. 286 G
sgilbert@ccsnh.edu
GILBERT, Susan, P .... 678-547-6438.. 124 D
gilbert_sp@mercer.edu
GILBERT, Teresa .... 423-478-7702.. 443 I
tgilbert@ptseminary.edu
GILBERT, Timothy .... 804-204-1221.. 487 D
tgilbert@btsr.edu
GILBERT, Trent .... 309-457-2210.. 148 E
tgilbert@monmouthcollege.edu
GILBERTSON, Sandi .... 701-671-2904.. 361 F
sandi.gilbertson@ndscs.edu
GILBERTSON, Troy .... 218-755-2965.. 248 M
tgilbertson@bemidjistate.edu
GILCHREST, Kendel .... 334-683-5108...... 5 C
kgilchrest@judson.edu
GILCHRIST, Cheryl, B ...... 502-852-8139.. 194 A
cbgilc01@louisville.edu
GILCHRIST, Debra .... 253-964-6584.. 506 B
dgilchrist@pierce.ctc.edu
GILCHRIST, Graham .... 386-481-2097.... 96 H
gilchrisstg@cookman.edu
GILCHRIST, James, A .... 269-387-2382.. 243 H
james.gilchrist@wmich.edu
GILCHRIST, Lou Ann .... 660-785-4111.. 273 B
lcg@truman.edu
GILCREASE, Kathy .... 936-294-1012.. 471 D
gilcrease@shsu.edu
GILCREAST, Emily .... 401-598-1000.. 425 B
egilcreastt@jwu.edu
GILDAWIE, Janice .... 413-528-7698.. 214 H
jgildawie@simons-rock.edu
GILDEN, Bruce, F .... 858-499-0202.... 39 J
bgilden@coleman.edu
GILDERSLEEVE, Elizabeth, T .... 781-283-2376.. 229 C
egilders@wellesley.edu
GILDERSLEEVE, Susan, M .... 402-472-3886.. 282 M
sgildersleeve1@unl.edu
GILDNER, Dan .... 937-529-2201.. 378 F
dgildner@united.edu
GILE, Jason .... 630-620-2105.. 150 B
jgile@seminary.edu

GILE, Joseph .... 316-942-4291.. 183 I
gilej@newmanu.edu
GILE, Shelby .... 802-485-2658.. 484 H
sgile@norwich.edu
GILES, Gordon .... 513-875-3344.. 365 K
gordon.giles@chatfield.edu
GILES, JR., Henry, C ...... 864-592-4616.. 432 H
gilesh@sccsc.edu
GILES, Marsha .... 617-537-6803.. 147 F
magiles@mckendree.edu
GILES, Pam .... 276-523-2400.. 497 F
pgiles@me.vccs.edu
GILES, Roger, W .... 870-235-4008.... 22 F
rwgiles@saumag.edu
GILES-HISER, Gina .... 614-287-2860.. 367 C
ggileshiser@cscc.edu
GILFERT, Christy .... 941-637-5678.. 101 F
cgilfert@fsw.edu
GILGOUR, Joe .... 660-596-7393.. 272 G
jgilgour@sfccmo.edu
GILKER, Bill .... 817-760-5504.. 458 K
wmgilker@hillcollege.edu
GILKERSON, Tammeil ..... 510-235-7800.... 41 H
tgilkerson@contracosta.edu
GILL, Allison .... 978-837-5174.. 225 E
gilla@merrimack.edu
GILL, Ann, M .... 970-491-5421.... 78 Q
ann.gill@colostate.edu
GILL, Anne, M .... 617-989-4193.. 229 D
gilla@wit.edu
GILL, Barbara, A .... 301-314-8350.. 211 E
bgill@umd.edu
GILL, Barbara, J .... 850-201-6570.. 113 E
gillb@tcc.fl.edu
GILL, Casey .... 937-327-7806.. 381 F
gillc@wittenberg.edu
GILL, Chris .... 515-271-3918.. 171 K
chris.gill@drake.edu
GILL, D. Christopher .... 573-288-6322.. 264 F
cgill@culver.edu
GILL, Dennis .... 541-881-5915.. 395 E
dgill@tvcc.cc
GILL, Elizabeth, A .... 716-888-2150.. 306 F
GILL, Gregory .... 219-866-6177.. 166 J
ggill@saintjoe.edu
GILL, Jackie .... 816-604-5250.. 267 H
jackie.gill@mcckc.edu
GILL, Janet .... 712-274-6400.. 177 I
janet.gill@witcc.edu
GILL, Janet .... 303-333-4224.... 77 A
GILL, Jason .... 847-866-3987.. 140 G
jason.gill@garrett.edu
GILL, Jeffery, A .... 574-372-5100.. 161 B
gillja@grace.edu
GILL, Keith .... 804-289-8345.. 495 G
kgill@richmond.edu
GILL, Lanae .... 313-993-1230.. 241 G
gilla@udmercy.edu
GILL, Lee, A .... 864-656-4238.. 428 C
lagill@clemson.edu
GILL, Mark .... 970-491-6211.... 78 Q
mark.gill@colostate.edu
GILL, Michele .... 402-844-7748.. 282 B
micheleg@northeast.edu
GILL, Nancy .... 805-437-8456.... 32 B
nancy.gill@csuci.edu
GILL, Nicholas .... 207-216-4467.. 204 B
ngill@yccc.edu
GILL, Paula .... 615-460-8637.. 438 J
paula.gill@belmont.edu
GILL, Russell .... 623-261-0009.. 139 D
rgill@devry.edu
GILL, Ruth .... 410-334-2928.. 213 G
rgill@worwic.edu
GILL, Sandra .... 630-829-6216.. 135 F
sgill@ben.edu
GILL, Sean .... 951-827-6063.... 70 B
sean.gill@ucr.edu
GILL, Steven .... 609-258-3466.. 294 D
sgill@princeton.edu
GILL, Tom .... 503-338-2368.. 390 G
tgill@clatsopcc.edu
GILLAHAN, Sheila .... 731-286-3316.. 446 B
gillahan@dscc.edu
GILLAM WEIR, Linda ...... 501-420-1200.... 18 F
linda.gillam@arkansasbaptist.edu
GILLAN, Maria .... 973-684-5904.. 294 A
mgillan@pccc.edu
GILLARD, Natalie .... 575-461-4413.. 300 A
natalieg@mesalands.edu
GILLARDI, Michael .... 401-598-1450.. 425 B
mgillardi@jwu.edu
GILLASPIE, Breanda .... 972-241-3371.. 455 K
bgillaspie@dallas.edu
GILLASPIE, Ray .... 270-824-8592.. 190 B
ray.gillaspie@kctcs.edu
GILLE, Chaudron .... 678-717-3835.. 128 F
chaudron.gille@ung.edu
GILLECE, Nancy, E .... 301-696-3710.. 208 B
gillece@hood.edu

GILLEN, Dan .... 319-296-4268.. 173 B
daniel.gillen@hawkeyecollege.edu
GILLENWATER, Jody .... 502-213-8803.. 193 A
jgillenwater@sullivan.edu
GILLES, Barbara, L .... 412-578-6123.. 400 C
gillesbl@carlow.edu
GILLESPIE, Adrienne, G .... 801-626-7243.. 482 D
adrienneandrews@weber.edu
GILLESPIE, Andrew, R ...... 334-844-5009...... 1 G
arg0014@auburn.edu
GILLESPIE, Anne Marie ... 740-351-3251.. 377 C
agillespie@shawnee.edu
GILLESPIE, Barbara .... 276-326-4237.. 487 F
bgillespie@bluefield.edu
GILLESPIE, Bart .... 678-839-6582.. 129 E
bgillesp@westga.edu
GILLESPIE, Christine .... 201-612-7488.. 289 E
cgillespie@bergen.edu
GILLESPIE, Dave .... 402-941-6545.. 280 N
gillespie@midlandu.edu
GILLESPIE, Denise .... 662-620-5368.. 258 C
dlgillespie@iccms.edu
GILLESPIE, Greg .... 805-289-6460.... 73 F
ggillespie@vcccd.edu
GILLESPIE, Griffin .... 701-777-2103.. 360 C
1120mgr@follett.com
GILLESPIE, Heather .... 605-256-5238.. 437 C
heather.gillespie@dsu.edu
GILLESPIE, Mary Ellen .... 920-465-2145.. 520 B
gillespm@uwgb.edu
GILLESPIE, Melanie .... 864-644-5504.. 432 G
mlgillespie@swu.edu
GILLESPIE, Michele, K ..... 336-758-5000.. 359 E
gillesmk@wfu.edu
GILLESPIE, Teresa .... 425-889-5290.. 505 E
teresa.gillespie@northwestu.edu
GILLESS, J. Keith .... 510-642-7171.... 68 M
gilless@berkeley.edu
GILLETT, Charisse, L .... 859-280-1230.. 191 D
cgillett@lextheo.edu
GILLETTE, Donna .... 207-947-4591.. 202 E
dgillette@bealcollege.edu
GILLETTE, Jack .... 617-349-8401.. 220 B
jgillett@lesley.edu
GILLETTE, John .... 406-657-1714.. 277 D
john.gillette2@msubillings.edu
GILLETTE, Kimberly .... 218-282-8442.. 255 E
gillette@umn.edu
GILLETTE, Lynn .... 985-448-4011.. 201 A
lynn.gillette@nicholls.edu
GILLETTE, Maureen .... 973-275-2725.. 297 A
GILLETTE, Susan .... 410-706-5353.. 211 F
sgillett@umaryland.edu
GILLEY, Amy .... 732-255-0400.. 293 E
agilley@ocean.edu
GILLEY, Janice .... 850-474-2218.. 113 A
jgilley@uwf.edu
GILLEY, Michael .... 276-523-2400.. 497 F
mgilley@me.vccs.edu
GILLIAM, Dara .... 405-273-5331.. 383 K
dgilliam@familyoffaithcollege.edu
GILLIAM, David .... 918-587-6789.. 388 K
david.gilliam@twsweld.com
GILLIAM, Franklin, D ...... 336-334-5266.. 358 B
fgilliam@uncg.edu
GILLIAM, Janice, H .... 423-323-0201.. 446 F
jhgilliam@northeaststate.edu
GILLIAM, Kevin, E .... 616-538-2330.. 234 D
kgilliam@gbcol.edu
GILLIAM, Melissa .... 773-834-0840.. 156 D
mgilliam@babies.bsd.uchicago.edu
GILLIAM, Nilse, F .... 662-252-8000.. 260 F
nfurtadogilliam@rustcollege.edu
GILLIAM, Rebecca .... 318-670-9353.. 199 J
rgilliam@susla.edu
GILLIAM, Thomas, J .... 850-484-1690.. 106 H
tgilliam@pensacolastate.edu
GILLIAM, Tom .... 850-484-1500.. 106 H
tgilliam@pensacolastate.edu
GILLIAM PHILLIPS, Ruth 919-530-7908.. 357 A
ruth.gilliam.phillips@nccu.edu
GILLIESPIE, Bailey .... 951-785-2041.... 48 A
bgillies@lasierra.edu
GILLIGAN, William .... 617-824-8190.. 218 B
william_gilligan@emerson.edu
GILLIHAN, Crystal .... 870-512-7747.... 19 C
crystal_gillihan@asun.edu
GILLILAN, Kevin .... 256-761-0949...... 7 F
kgillilan@talladega.edu
GILLILAND, Christie .... 253-833-9111.. 504 C
cgilliland@greenriver.edu
GILLILAND, Drew .... 541-552-6319.. 395 A
gilliland@sou.edu
GILLILAND, Jane, A .... 607-587-3979.. 334 G
gillilja@alfredstate.edu
GILLILAND, Mary, K .... 520-494-5210.... 12 J
marykay.gilliland@centralaz.edu
GILLILAND, William .... 301-295-9845.. 528 G
william.gilliland@usuhs.edu
GILLIN, Douglas, P .... 828-262-7781.. 356 B
gillindp@appstate.edu

GLASGOW, Michael .... 860-486-3619.... 89 D
michael.glasgow@uconn.edu
GLASGOW, Nicole .... 305-348-1925.. 111 A
nicole.kaufman@fiu.edu
GLASGOW, Sara .... 231-348-6604.. 239 A
sglasgow@ncmich.edu
GLASGOW, Terri .... 269-749-7623.. 240 A
tglasgow@olivetcollege.edu
GLASGOW, Wayne, C ...... 478-301-2024.. 124 D
glasgow_wc@mercer.edu
GLASIER, Jennifer .... 360-475-7128.. 505 F
GLASMAN, Yvonne .... 270-707-3722.. 189 G
yvonne.glasman@kctcs.edu
GLASOW, Vicki, W .... 304-457-6368.. 510 B
glasowvw@ab.edu
GLASPIE, Hank .... 352-854-2322.... 97 R
glaspieh@cf.edu
GLASPIE, Tamara .... 252-493-7339.. 352 A
tglaspie@email.pittcc.edu
GLASS, Alan, I .... 314-935-9626.. 274 N
aglass@wustl.edu
GLASS, AmyBeth .... 609-652-4298.. 297 C
amybeth.glass@stockton.edu
GLASS, Art .... 845-569-3210.. 322 B
art.glass@msmc.edu
GLASS, Carrie .... 504-865-3231.. 198 E
ceglass@loyno.edu
GLASS, Cheryl, A .... 651-631-5344.. 256 A
caglass@unwsp.edu
GLASS, Cynthia .... 313-845-9820.. 235 D
cmglass@hfcc.edu
GLASS, Fred .... 812-855-1966.. 162 F
iuad@indiana.edu
GLASS, Fred .... 812-856-1196.. 162 E
athldir@indiana.edu
GLASS, Jamie .... 205-929-3407...... 5 D
jglass@lawsonstate.edu
GLASS, Jennifer .... 731-352-4259.. 438 K
glassj@bethelu.edu
GLASS, John .... 630-752-5014.. 158 C
john.glass@wheaton.edu
GLASS, JR., Robert .... 706-776-0111.. 125 J
bglass@piedmont.edu
GLASS, Tony .... 309-467-6382.. 140 E
arglass@eureka.edu
GLASS, Wayne .... 618-453-4540.. 154 I
wglass@siu.edu
GLASS, Wendy, G .... 207-786-6096.. 202 D
wglass@bates.edu
GLASSCOCK, Darrell, R .... 210-434-6711.. 463 C
drglasscock@lake.ollusa.edu
GLASSER, Karen .... 406-756-3841.. 276 E
kglasser@fvcc.edu
GLASSMAN, Beth .... 610-499-4182.. 423 E
brglassman@widener.edu
GLASSMAN, David, M .... 217-581-2011.. 139 H
dglassman@eiu.edu
GLASSMAN, Jody .... 305-348-7596.. 111 A
jody.glassman@fiu.edu
GLASSMAN, Joel, N .... 314-516-5753.. 274 A
jglassman@umsl.edu
GLASSNER, Barry .... 503-768-7680.. 392 A
president@lclark.edu
GLASSON, Joseph .... 215-637-7700.. 405 J
jglasson@holyfamily.edu
GLATMAN, Elena .... 508-910-6958.. 220 H
eglatman@umassd.edu
GLATT, Camilla .... 509-542-5548.. 502 G
GLATT, Laura .... 970-248-1867.... 77 L
lglatt@coloradomesa.edu
GLATT, Robert .... 206-934-6790.. 507 A
robert.glatt@seattlecolleges.edu
GLATTER, Bryan .... 337-521-8994.. 197 A
bryan.glatter@solacc.edu
GLATTER, Jill .... 516-877-3321.. 303 B
registrar@adelphi.edu
GLAUS, Beth .... 573-651-5923.. 272 B
baglaus@semo.edu
GLAVIN, Anne, P .... 818-677-2201..... 34 A
anne.glavin@csun.edu
GLAVIN, JR., John, A ..... 610-359-5105.. 401 L
jglavin@dccc.edu
GLAZE, Doug .... 314-529-9606.. 267 B
dglaze@maryville.edu
GLAZER, Greer, L .... 513-558-5330.. 379 A
greer.glazer@uc.edu
GLAZER, Meir .... 718-268-4700.. 326 L
GLAZER, Randy .... 212-678-3724.. 337 E
glazer@tc.edu
GLAZIER, Steve .... 918-465-1811.. 383 I
sglazier@eosc.edu
GLAZIER, Steve, G .... 918-465-1811.. 383 I
sglazier@eosc.edu
GLAZIER-SMITH, Laura ... 718-368-6725.. 308 F
laura.glazier-smith@kbcc.cuny.edu
GLEAN, Randy .... 940-397-4568.. 462 A
randy.glean@mwsu.edu
GLEASON, Ann, C .... 919-760-8521.. 346 D
gleasona@meredith.edu
GLEASON, David .... 410-455-2709.. 211 G
gleason@umbc.edu
GLEASON, Joe .... 860-231-5700.... 90 B
jgleason@usj.edu
GLEASON, Josh .... 574-535-7000.. 161 A
joshag@goshen.edu
GLEASON, Karen .... 617-253-2029.. 225 A
GLEASON, Mark .... 507-222-4046.. 245 C
mgleason@carleton.edu
GLEASON, Nancy .... 402-461-7393.. 280 D
ngleason@hastings.edu
GLEASON, Paul .... 386-822-7464.. 113 B
pgleason@stetson.edu
GLEAVES, Scott .... 334-386-7154...... 3 I
sgleaves@faulkner.edu
GLEBA, James .... 212-772-4422.. 308 D
jg2123@hunter.cuny.edu
GLECKLER, Bryan .... 217-234-5224.. 145 D
bgleckler@lakeland.cc.il.us
GLEESON, Allison .... 610-359-5341.. 401 L
agleeson@dccc.edu
GLEIM, Jeffery, T .... 412-624-8277.. 421 G
jeff.gleim@ia.pitt.edu
GLEIMER, Steven .... 212-353-4151.. 311 G
sgleimer@cooper.edu
GLEIXNER, Stacy .... 408-924-1177.... 35 C
stacy.gleixner@sjsu.edu
GLEJZER, Richard .... 802-258-9234.. 484 C
rglejzer@marlboro.edu
GLEN, Will .... 949-451-5200.... 65 F
wglen@ivc.edu
GLENDE, Leah .... 860-512-3107.... 86 E
lglende@manchestercc.edu
GLENDENING, Andrew .... 909-748-8684.... 71 K
andrew_glendening@redlands.edu
GLENMAYE, Linnea .... 316-978-5054.. 185 J
linnea.glenmaye@wichita.edu
GLENN, Ashley .... 540-362-6609.. 490 F
cdc@hollins.edu
GLENN, Barbara, M .... 804-523-5263.. 497 C
bglenn@reynolds.edu
GLENN, Brian .... 806-651-2105.. 469 D
bglenn@mail.wtamu.edu
GLENN, Brooke .... 402-465-7518.. 281 K
bglenn@nebrwesleyan.edu
GLENN, Chance .... 256-372-5560...... 1 A
chance.glenn@aamu.edu
GLENN, Christy .... 931-393-1682.. 446 D
cglenn@mscc.edu
GLENN, Crystal .... 828-327-7000.. 348 C
cglenn@cvcc.edu
GLENN, Darrell .... 212-217-4075.. 314 B
darrell_glenn@fitnyc.edu
GLENN, Debra .... 610-526-1399.. 397 E
debra.glenn@theamericancollege.edu
GLENN, Dennis, E .... 706-385-1064.. 126 A
dennis.glenn@point.edu
GLENN, Jason, E .... 386-481-2361.... 96 H
glennj@cookman.edu
GLENN, Jenna .... 630-889-6620.. 149 G
jglenn@nuhs.edu
GLENN, Jonathan, A .... 501-450-3126.... 24 G
jona@uca.edu
GLENN, Lane, A .... 978-556-3855.. 224 D
lglenn@necc.mass.edu
GLENN, Mark, R .... 314-935-5514.. 274 N
mark_glenn@wustl.edu
GLENN, Robert .... 402-461-2422.. 278 K
rglenn@cccneb.edu
GLENN, Robert, K .... 256-233-8201...... 1 F
bob.glenn@athens.edu
GLENN, Susan .... 815-921-4503.. 152 E
s.glenn@rockvalleycollege.edu
GLENN, Thane .... 267-502-4844.. 398 J
thane.glenn@anc-gc.org
GLENN-SUMMITT, Peggy ... 918-456-5511.. 384 G
glennsum@nsuok.edu
GLENNEN, Debrah .... 701-777-3425.. 360 C
debrah.glennen@und.edu
GLENNON, Jennifer .... 410-857-2205.. 209 D
jglennon@mcdaniel.edu
GLETHEROW, Catherine .... 440-775-5547.. 374 C
catherine.gletherow@oberlin.edu
GLEW, Karen .... 207-453-5820.. 203 K
kglew@kvcc.me.edu
GLEZERMAN, David, R .... 215-204-7269.. 420 B
david.glezerman@temple.edu
GLICK, Carol .... 313-593-6751.. 242 A
cglick@umich.edu
GLICK, Steven .... 330-263-2590.. 367 A
sglick@wooster.edu
GLICKMAN, Gena .... 860-512-3100.... 86 E
gglickman@manchestercc.edu
GLICKMAN, Michael .... 516-299-3760.. 319 B
michael.glickman@liu.edu
GLICKSMAN, Martin .... 321-674-7318.. 100 M
mglicksman@fit.edu
GLIDDEN, Stacey, T .... 978-468-7111.. 219 B
sglidden@gcts.edu
GLIDEWELL, Chris .... 618-536-3345.. 154 H
cglide@siu.edu
GLIDWELL, Bob .... 417-328-1550.. 272 C
bglidwell@sbuniv.edu
GLIEM, Valerie .... 727-864-8408.... 98 L
gliemvm@eckerd.edu
GLIKSBERG, Gabriel .... 305-595-9500.... 95 A
GLIMCHER, Laurie .... 212-746-6005.. 312 A
glimche@med.cornell.edu
GLINDEMANN, Kent, E .... 276-223-4885.. 499 C
kglindemann@wcc.vccs.edu
GLINES, Carey .... 603-668-2211.. 287 I
c.glines@snhu.edu
GLINES, Carol, A .... 563-333-6328.. 176 D
glinescarola@sau.edu
GLINES, Carol, A .... 563-333-6329.. 176 D
glinescarola@sau.edu
GLINES, Lee .... 801-422-4147.. 480 C
lee.glines@byu.edu
GLINES, Neil .... 707-864-7000.... 65 A
neil.glines@solano.edu
GLINES, Ryan .... 508-856-8989.. 221 B
GLISCH, John .... 321-433-7017.... 98 K
glischj@easternflorida.edu
GLISSON, Micheal .... 337-521-8954.. 197 A
micheal.glisson@solacc.edu
GLISSON, Tony, L .... 270-745-5360.. 194 D
tony.glisson@wku.edu
GLOBIS, Roxanne .... 609-633-9658.. 297 F
rglobis@tesu.edu
GLOCK, Jon, W .... 563-588-8000.. 172 E
jglock@emmaus.edu
GLOD, Carol .... 978-837-5115.. 225 E
glodc@merrimack.edu
GLOGOWSKI,
Maryruth, F .... 716-878-4716.. 332 F
glogowmf@buffalostate.edu
GLORIA, Jackie .... 858-566-1200.... 42 D
jgloria@disd.edu
GLOS, Lindy .... 417-269-3083.. 264 D
lindy.glos@coxcollege.edu
GLOSE, Karen .... 610-861-4589.. 411 G
kglose@northampton.edu
GLOTZBACH, Philip, A .... 518-580-5700.. 330 F
pglotzba@skidmore.edu
GLOVEN, Greta .... 303-765-3109.... 80 M
ggloven@iliff.edu
GLOVER, David .... 501-812-2318.... 21 H
dglover@pulaskitech.edu
GLOVER, David .... 757-727-5259.. 490 E
david.glover@hamptonu.edu
GLOVER, Gail .... 585-245-5536.. 333 B
glover@geneseo.edu
GLOVER, Glenda .... 615-963-7401.. 445 A
president@tnstate.edu
GLOVER, Jennifer .... 804-425-5797.. 488 C
jglover@ccc-va.com
GLOVER, Joseph .... 352-392-2404.. 112 A
jglover@aa.ufl.edu
GLOVER, Joseph, M .... 812-941-2028.. 163 F
joglover@ius.edu
GLOVER, Katie .... 703-370-6600.. 492 I
GLOVER, Kerri .... 828-254-1921.. 347 D
kerriaglover@abtech.edu
GLOVER, Kofi .... 813-974-2010.. 112 C
glover@usf.edu
GLOVER, Larry .... 615-329-8826.. 439 L
lglover@fisk.edu
GLOVER, Laura .... 906-227-2244.. 239 B
lglover@nmu.edu
GLOVER, Nathaniel .... 904-470-8012.... 98 N
n.glover@ewc.edu
GLOVER, Paula .... 660-263-4100.. 269 D
paulag@macc.edu
GLOVER, Shirley .... 478-988-6890.. 118 H
sglover@centralgatech.edu
GLOWKA, Arthur, W .... 770-720-5628.. 126 C
awg@reinhardt.edu
GLUCKOWSKY,
Moshe, M .... 718-774-3430.. 306 J
GLYER-CULVER, Betty ...... 916-568-3068.... 50 J
glyercb@losrios.edu
GLYNN, Carol .... 248-689-8282.. 242 F
cglynn@walshcollege.edu
GLYNN, Graham .... 785-628-4241.. 180 I
geglynn@fhsu.edu
GLYNN, John, B .... 414-410-4313.. 515 I
jbglynn@stritch.edu
GLYNN, Terry, S .... 858-499-0202.... 39 J
tglynn@coleman.edu
GMEINER, Mary .... 810-762-0566.. 238 F
mary.gmeiner@mcc.edu
GMEINER, Rebecca .... 678-466-4145.. 119 A
rebeccagmeiner@clayton.edu
GNADE, Bruce .... 972-883-6636.. 476 C
gnade@utdallas.edu
GNAGE, Marie, F .... 904-632-5094.. 101 G
marie.gnage@fscj.edu
GNAN, Peter, D .... 708-209-3192.. 138 G
pete.gnan@cuchicago.edu
GNANDT, Brian .... 805-756-1400.... 31 I
bgnandt@calpoly.edu
GNASSO, Emil, A .... 610-758-3200.. 408 H
emg3@lehigh.edu
GNECCO, Donald .... 706-776-0117.. 125 J
dgnecco@piedmont.edu
GOAD, Philip .... 256-766-6610...... 4 B
pgoad@hcu.edu
GOAD, William .... 405-425-5180.. 385 C
bill.goad@oc.edu
GOALDER, Tiffany .... 573-876-7207.. 272 I
tgoalder@stephens.edu
GOAR, Michele .... 575-492-2161.. 302 M
mgoar@usw.edu
GOBEN, Allen .... 817-515-6200.. 467 A
allen.goben@tccd.edu
GOBEN, Jason .... 606-693-5000.. 191 A
jgoben@kmbc.edu
GOBER, Chris, G .... 636-922-8211.. 271 A
cgober@stchas.edu
GOBER, Jerome .... 423-697-4457.. 445 D
jerome.gober@chattanoogastate.edu
GOBER, Taylor, K .... 501-450-3197.... 24 G
kgober@uca.edu
GOBERISH, John, S .... 724-480-3450.. 401 F
john.goberish@ccbc.edu
GOBLE, Allison .... 606-326-2432.. 188 N
allison.goble@kctcs.edu
GOBLE, Bryen .... 606-886-3863.. 189 A
bryen.goble@kctcs.edu
GOBLE, David, S .... 843-953-1267.. 428 A
dgoble@citadel.edu
GOBLET, Lois .... 518-255-5524.. 334 D
gobletle@cobleskill.edu
GOCHENAUR, Heather, K 260-982-5873.. 165 M
hkgochenaur@manchester.edu
GOCHENAUR, Jack, A ..... 260-982-5245.. 165 M
jagochenaur@manchester.edu
GOCHIS, Cheryl .... 254-710-8562.. 452 H
cheryl_gochis@baylor.edu
GOCHIS, Sue .... 530-541-4660.... 48 D
gochis@ltcc.edu
GOCIAL, Tammy .... 314-529-6893.. 267 B
tgocial@maryville.edu
GOCKLEY, Daniel, L .... 214-458-6200.. 477 A
daniel.gockley@utsa.edu
GODARD, Mike .... 660-543-4811.. 273 C
godard@ucmo.edu
GODDARD, Amy .... 405-224-3140.. 389 D
GODDARD, Courtney .... 816-584-6559.. 270 D
courtney.goddard@park.edu
GODDARD, Deanna .... 507-457-2493.. 252 G
dgoddard@winona.edu
GODDARD, Diane, H .... 785-864-4904.. 185 D
dgoddard@ku.edu
GODDARD, Robert .... 802-776-5248.. 483 G
robert.goddard@csj.edu
GODDARD, Scott, D .... 304-637-1352.. 510 I
goddards@dewv.edu
GODDARD MCGUIRK,
Lisa .... 814-871-7664.. 404 A
GODDEN, Barb .... 712-325-3230.. 174 B
bgodden@iwcc.edu
GODDING, Jesse .... 972-825-4811.. 466 D
jgodding@sagu.edu
GODEK, Jim .... 949-376-6000.... 48 C
jgodek@lcad.edu
GODEL-GENGENBACH,
Kay .... 303-384-2120.... 78 M
kgengenb@mines.edu
GODES, Iris .... 508-541-1547.. 217 G
igodes@dean.edu
GODFREY, Christian .... 208-535-5387.. 133 G
christian.godfrey@my.eitc.edu
GODFREY, Kevin .... 805-482-2755.... 59 G
registrar-sjs@stjohnsem.edu
GODFREY, Lisa .... 919-777-7784.. 348 D
lgodfrey@cccc.edu
GODFREY, Rodney .... 662-241-7636.. 259 E
ragodfrey@muw.edu
GODFREY, W. Robert .... 760-480-8474.... 74 L
bvansolkema@wscal.edu
GODFREY-DAWSON,
Angela, R .... 252-335-0821.. 349 A
adawson@albemarle.edu
GODFRIAUX, Colleen .... 608-265-9807.. 522 A
colleen.godfriaux@uwc.edu
GODIN, Patricia, A .... 919-866-5170.. 353 I
pagodin@waketech.edu
GODLESKI, Kasha .... 315-445-4772.. 318 E
godleska@lemoyne.edu
GODLESKI, Mark, G .... 315-445-4520.. 318 E
godlesmg@lemoyne.edu
GODMAN, Anne .... 217-479-7141.. 147 C
anne.godman@mac.edu
GODO, James .... 630-637-5809.. 149 H
jwgodo@noctrl.edu
GODREAU, Susan, E .... 315-267-2162.. 334 B
godrease@potsdam.edu
GODSAVE, Sarah .... 580-699-7204.. 383 D
sgodsave@cnc.cc.ok.us
GODSEY, R. Kirby .... 478-330-5609.. 124 D
godsey_rk@mercer.edu
GODWIN, Angeline, D ...... 276-656-0201.. 498 A
agodwin@patrickhenry.edu

GOLTSER, Zhanna .... 410-857-2234.. 209 D
zgoltser@mcdaniel.edu
GOLUB, Andrew .... 207-602-2319.. 205 F
agolub@une.edu
GOMBERG, Barry, G .... 801-626-6240.. 482 D
bgomberg@weber.edu
GOMBOSKY, Brenda, B ... 502-852-5037.. 194 A
brenda.gombosky@louisville.edu
GOMES, Antoinette .... 401-456-8791.. 425 E
agomes@ric.edu
GOMES, David .... 508-999-8192.. 220 H
dgomes3@umassd.edu
GOMES, Farrah-Marie ...... 808-956-6897.. 131 D
fmgomes@hawaii.edu
GOMES, Farrahmarie .... 808-974-7664.. 131 E
fmgomes@hawaii.edu
GOMES, Lyle .... 661-632-6105.. 332 A
lyle.gomes@stonybrook.edu
GOMES, JR., Miguel .... 508-531-1207.. 221 C
mgomes@bridgew.edu
GOMES, Roxanne .... 401-874-2442.. 426 D
roxanne@uri.edu
GOMES, Stacy .... 619-574-6909.... 55 G
sgomes@pacificcollege.edu
GOMEZ, Alicia .... 956-872-5529.. 465 H
agomez@southtexascollege.edu
GOMEZ, Anita .... 937-708-5798.. 381 B
agomez@wilberforce.edu
GOMEZ, Bellegran .... 562-860-2451.... 36 P
bgomez@cerritos.edu
GOMEZ, Beth .... 951-372-7157.... 59 B
beth.gomez@norcocollege.edu
GOMEZ, Carlos, J .... 850-644-2003.. 111 C
cjgomez@fsu.edu
GOMEZ, Christina .... 312-899-7479.. 154 A
cgomez3@saic.edu
GOMEZ, David .... 718-518-4300.. 308 C
dgomez@hostos.cuny.edu
GOMEZ, Dax .... 615-514-2787.. 443 F
dgomez@nossi.edu
GOMEZ, Doris .... 757-352-4686.. 493 E
dorirop@regent.edu
GOMEZ, Elba .... 559-244-5973.... 67 A
elba.gomez@scccd.edu
GOMEZ, Elizabeth .... 213-252-5100.... 24 K
egomez@alu.edu
GOMEZ, Eva, C .... 805-437-3271.... 32 B
eva.gomez@csuci.edu
GOMEZ, Fernando, C .... 512-463-1808.. 470 G
fernando.gomez@tsus.edu
GOMEZ, Gabe .... 505-984-6102.. 301 I
gabe.gomez@sjc.edu
GOMEZ, Grace .... 787-279-1912.. 533 J
ggomez@bayamon.inter.edu
GOMEZ, Jaime, A .... 619-260-4886.... 72 B
jagomez@sandiego.edu
GOMEZ, Johanna .... 718-518-6556.. 308 C
jgomez@hostos.cuny.edu
GOMEZ, Jose, A .... 323-343-3030.... 33 C
jose.gomez@calstatela.edu
GOMEZ, Jose, D .... 787-834-9595.. 536 E
jgomez@uaa.edu
GOMEZ, Liz .... 850-484-1702.. 106 H
lgomez@pensacolastate.edu
GOMEZ, Mary .... 336-342-4261.. 352 F
gomezm@rockinghamcc.edu
GOMEZ, Petra .... 805-922-6966.... 25 I
petra.gomez@hancockcollege.edu
GOMEZ, Rebecca .... 312-915-8725.. 146 G
rgomez1@luc.edu
GOMEZ, Rowena .... 650-433-3823.... 56 D
rgomez@paloaltou.edu
GOMEZ-HEITZEBERG,
Nan .... 661-395-4305.... 47 J
ngomez@bakersfieldcollege.edu
GOMEZ-PALACIO, Dan .... 573-875-7421.. 263 F
edgomez@ccis.edu
GONCALVES, Andreia ...... 631-370-3300.. 330 A
agoncalves@sbmelville.edu
GONDEK, Gretchen .... 712-274-6400.. 177 I
gretchen.gondek@witcc.edu
GONG, Ann, M .... 212-752-1530.. 318 F
annmarie.gong@limcollege.edu
GONG, Changzhen .... 651-631-0204.. 244 E
tcmhealth@aol.com
GONG, Harry, S .... 716-286-8716.. 324 E
hgong@niagara.edu
GONNELLA, Chris .... 701-788-4807.. 360 E
christine.gonnella@mayvillestate.edu
GONSALVES, Michael ...... 404-364-8535.. 125 F
mgonsalves@oglethorpe.edu
GONSALVES-MCCABE,
Kristi .... 303-458-4153.... 82 L
kgonsalv@regis.edu
GONSIOR, Maura .... 575-538-6328.. 303 A
gonsiorm@wnmu.edu
GONSOULIN, Sid .... 601-266-5767.. 261 E
sidney.gonsoulin@usm.edu
GONTHIER, Sheri .... 603-271-6484.. 286 F
sgonthier@ccsnh.edu
GONYEA, David .... 207-755-5251.. 203 I
dgonyea@cmcc.edu
GONYEA, Nathan .... 518-587-2100.. 335 D
nathan.gonyea@esc.edu
GONZÁLEZ, Carlos .... 787-765-9695.. 538 F
carlos.gonzalez55@upr.edu
GONZÁLEZ, Celia .... 787-844-8181.. 538 E
celia.gonzalez@upr.edu
GONZÁLEZ, Lissette, V ... 787-265-3883.. 538 C
lissette.gonzalez1@upr.edu
GONZÁLEZ, Marisol .... 787-264-1912.. 534 D
mgonzale@intersg.edu
GONZÁLEZ, Terestella ..... 787-257-7373.. 535 P
tergonzalez@suagm.edu
GONZÁLEZ, Widalys .... 787-884-3838.. 530 G
wgonzalez@atenascollege.edu
GONZÁLEZ DE RESENDE,
María, A .... 787-993-8872.. 537 G
maria.gonzalez34@upr.edu
GONZÁLEZ TABOADA,
José, A .... 787-751-7410.. 538 F
jose.gonzalez63@upr.edu
GONZALES, Adrian .... 760-744-1150.... 56 F
adriangonzales@palomar.edu
GONZALES, Al .... 623-845-3035.... 14 C
al.gonzales@gccaz.edu
GONZALES, Alberto .... 615-460-8259.. 438 J
alberto.gonzales@belmont.edu
GONZALES, Ana .... 210-829-3937.. 474 D
anagonza@uiwtx.edu
GONZALES, Benito .... 575-562-2115.. 299 I
benito.gonzales@enmu.edu
GONZALES, Casey .... 817-272-2099.. 476 A
gonzales@uta.edu
GONZALES, Christina .... 303-492-8476.... 83 K
christina.gonzales@colorado.edu
GONZALES, Dianna .... 209-954-5059.... 61 F
dgonzales@deltacollege.edu
GONZALES, Frank .... 808-373-2849.. 132 G
GONZALES, Hector .... 830-591-7281.. 466 A
hegonzales@swtjc.edu
GONZALES, Jennifer .... 512-313-3000.. 455 F
jennifer.gonzales@concordia.edu
GONZALES, Joe .... 209-954-5139.... 61 F
jgonzales@deltacollege.edu
GONZALES, JR.,
Joseph, M .... 312-329-4202.. 148 F
joe.gonzales@moody.edu
GONZALES, Junius .... 919-843-8347.. 356 A
jjgonzales@northcarolina.edu
GONZALES, Leticia .... 432-837-8193.. 471 E
lgonzales@sulross.edu
GONZALES, Louis .... 432-335-6848.. 463 B
lgonzales@odessa.edu
GONZALES, Mario .... 559-638-0300.... 67 D
mario-gonzales@reedleycollege.edu
GONZALES, Mark .... 408-274-7900.... 62 D
mark.gonzales@evc.edu
GONZALES, Mary, J .... 401-874-2101.. 426 D
mjgonzales@uri.edu
GONZALES, Patrick .... 956-665-3110.. 476 E
patrick.gonzales@utrgv.edu
GONZALES, Philip .... 505-277-1092.. 302 F
gonzales@unm.edu
GONZALES, Ray, A .... 626-395-8115.... 30 H
rayg@caltech.edu
GONZALES, Rhonda .... 719-549-2315.... 79 B
rhonda.gonzales@csupueblo.edu
GONZALES, Richard .... 970-947-8428.... 78 B
rgonzales4@coloradomtn.edu
GONZALES, Robert .... 719-549-2943.... 79 B
robert.gonzales@csupueblo.edu
GONZALES, Roxanne .... 814-676-6591.. 414 G
rgonzales@clarion.edu
GONZALES, Samuel .... 210-458-4136.. 477 A
sam.gonzales@utsa.edu
GONZALES, Sonia .... 303-404-5558.... 80 E
sonia.gonzales@frontrange.edu
GONZALES, Veronica .... 956-665-7495.. 476 E
veronica.gonzales@utrgv.edu
GONZALES-TAPIA, Sarah 626-914-8556.... 38 D
sgonzales-tapia@citruscollege.edu
GONZALEZ, Alex .... 505-277-4792.. 302 F
agonzalez@unm.edu
GONZALEZ, Amilcar .... 939-292-2223.. 539 A
amilcar.gonzalez2@upr.edu
GONZALEZ, Anna .... 503-768-7110.. 392 A
annag@lclark.edu
GONZALEZ, Beatriz .... 909-593-3511.... 71 B
bgonzalez@laverne.edu
GONZALEZ, Bethaida .... 315-443-3259.. 337 A
bgonzale@syr.edu
GONZALEZ, Blanca, M .... 787-250-1912.. 534 B
bmgonzalez@metro.inter.edu
GONZALEZ, Carla .... 313-664-7431.. 232 G
cgonzalez@collegeforcreativestudies.edu
GONZALEZ, Carlos .... 915-831-3722.. 457 H
GONZALEZ, Carlos, J .... 787-622-8000.. 537 B
gonzalez@pupr.edu
GONZALEZ, Carlos, R ...... 818-364-7778.... 49 J
gonzalcr@lamission.edu
GONZALEZ, Caroline .... 787-786-3030.. 536 F
cagonzalez@ucb.edu.pr
GONZALEZ, Cheryl, N ..... 904-620-2507.. 112 B
cheryl.gonzalez@unf.edu
GONZALEZ, Claudia .... 305-348-2111.. 111 A
clgonzal@fiu.edu
GONZALEZ, Deena .... 310-338-1958.... 51 E
dgonzale@lmu.edu
GONZALEZ, Diana .... 515-242-6116.. 169 F
gonzalez@iastate.edu
GONZALEZ, Edith .... 212-817-7520.. 308 A
egonzalez@gc.cuny.edu
GONZALEZ, Eladio .... 787-664-0353.. 539 A
eladio.gonzalez1@upr.edu
GONZALEZ, Eliseo .... 805-678-5930.... 73 E
GONZALEZ, Elma, D .... 936-261-2124.. 467 E
edgonzalez@pvamu.edu
GONZALEZ, Fernando ...... 787-884-6000.. 532 O
fgonzalez@icprjc.edu
GONZALEZ, Francisco ...... 918-333-6151.. 386 F
francisco@gonzalezfirm.com
GONZALEZ, George .... 281-998-6177.. 464 I
george.gonzalez@sjcd.edu
GONZALEZ, Griselda .... 212-217-4000.. 314 B
griselda_gonzalez@fitnyc.edu
GONZALEZ, Griselda .... 212-217-3363.. 314 B
griselda_gonzalez@fitnyc.edu
GONZALEZ, Herman .... 602-787-6601.... 14 E
herman.gonzalez@paradisevalley.edu
GONZALEZ, Jaime .... 787-620-2040.. 530 F
carroyo@aupr.edu
GONZALEZ, Jaime .... 787-620-2958.. 530 F
jgonzalez@aupr.edu
GONZALEZ, Jean .... 714-867-5009.... 65 D
jgonzalez@southcoastcollege.com
GONZALEZ, Jenny .... 773-577-8100.. 139 A
GONZALEZ, Jorge, G .... 269-337-7220.. 235 H
jorge.gonzalez@kzoo.edu
GONZALEZ, Jose, N .... 787-850-9419.. 538 B
jose.gonzalez48@upr.edu
GONZALEZ, Juan .... 858-534-4370.... 70 C
vcsa@ucsd.edu
GONZALEZ, Juan, C .... 956-665-2124.. 476 E
juan.gonzalez@utrgv.edu
GONZALEZ, Julo .... 305-273-4499.... 97 M
julio.gonzalez@cbt.edu
GONZALEZ, Karen .... 787-766-1717.. 536 B
um_kgonzalez@suagm.edu
GONZALEZ, Kelly .... 214-648-3519.. 478 C
kelly.gonzalez@utsouthwestern.edu
GONZALEZ, Linda .... 915-831-2640.. 457 H
lgonz265@epcc.edu
GONZALEZ, Lizbeth .... 603-882-6923.. 286 E
lgonzalez@ccsnh.edu
GONZALEZ, Lori .... 901-448-4930.. 448 H
lsgonz01@uthsc.edu
GONZALEZ, Luis .... 724-357-2330.. 415 B
luis.gonzalez@iup.edu
GONZALEZ, Mari, G .... 787-743-7979.. 536 A
mggonzalez@suagm.edu
GONZALEZ, Maria .... 951-372-7137.... 59 B
maria.gonzalez@norcocollege.edu
GONZALEZ, Maria, M ...... 787-852-1430.. 532 N
mgonzalez@hccpr.edu
GONZALEZ,
Maria Teresa .... 787-758-2525.. 538 D
mariateresa.gonzalez@upr.edu
GONZALEZ, Marilyn .... 787-882-2065.. 536 D
secretaria_ejecutiva@unitecpr.net
GONZALEZ, Martha, O .... 956-326-2361.. 468 A
marthao.gonzalez@tamiu.edu
GONZALEZ, Mary .... 361-593-2494.. 469 A
kamlp00@tamuk.edu
GONZALEZ, Mauricio .... 904-620-2600.. 112 B
mgonzale@unf.edu
GONZALEZ, Megan .... 850-474-2658.. 113 A
megang@uwf.edu
GONZALEZ, Melissa .... 713-718-5053.. 459 B
melissa.gonzalez@hccs.edu
GONZALEZ, Mirna .... 956-665-2701.. 476 E
mirna.gonzalez@utrgv.edu
GONZALEZ, Monica, D ... 787-723-4481.. 531 D
mgonzalez@ceaprc.edu
GONZALEZ, Nichole .... 716-375-2572.. 328 B
ngonzalez@sbu.edu
GONZALEZ, Nicolas .... 956-872-2133.. 465 H
ngon@southtexascollege.edu
GONZALEZ, Norberto .... 787-250-0000.. 537 D
norberto.gonzalez4@upr.edu
GONZALEZ, Patricia .... 787-250-1912.. 534 B
pgonzalez@metro.inter.edu
GONZALEZ, Patricia .... 661-255-1050.... 30 E
gonzalez@calarts.edu
GONZALEZ, Paulette, B ... 718-990-6521.. 328 F
gonzalep@stjohns.edu
GONZALEZ, Ramon .... 787-758-2525.. 538 D
ramon.gonzalez5@upr.edu
GONZALEZ, Raymond ...... 718-289-5154.. 307 C
raymond.gonzalez@bcc.cuny.edu
GONZALEZ, Reinaldo .... 787-744-8519.. 532 H
rgonzalez@ediccollege.edu
GONZALEZ, Richard .... 239-992-4624.. 104 R
GONZALEZ, Rick .... 424-207-3727.... 55 E
rgonzalez@otis.edu
GONZALEZ, Roberto .... 310-434-4912.... 63 F
gonzalez_roberto@smc.edu
GONZALEZ, Rocelia, T .... 904-620-2870.. 112 B
rrgonz@unf.edu
GONZALEZ, Ruth .... 860-738-6315.... 87 A
rgonzalez@nwcc.edu
GONZALEZ, Samantha ...... 860-512-2674.... 86 E
sgonzalez@manchestercc.edu
GONZALEZ, Sandra .... 323-563-9375.... 37 G
sandragonzalez@cdrewu.edu
GONZALEZ, Sandra .... 787-882-2065.. 536 D
administracion_empresas@unitecpr.net
GONZALEZ, Saraliz .... 787-857-3600.. 533 I
sgonzalez@br.inter.edu
GONZALEZ, Sergio, M .... 305-284-4111.. 114 H
smgonzalez@miami.edu
GONZALEZ, Sophia .... 210-486-2247.. 450 E
fklein@alamo.edu
GONZALEZ, Stacy .... 515-244-2209.. 327 H
gonzas@sage.edu
GONZALEZ, Steven .... 602-286-8008.... 14 B
steven.gonalez@gatewaycc.edu
GONZALEZ, Thomasa .... 609-652-4724.. 297 C
t.gonzalez@stockton.edu
GONZALEZ, Tina .... 212-799-5000.. 318 A
GONZALEZ, Victor .... 956-872-2336.. 465 H
vgonzalez99@southtexascollege.edu
GONZALEZ, Yadira .... 541-278-5753.. 390 C
ygonzalez@bluecc.edu
GONZALEZ-CORTES,
Otilio .... 787-815-0000.. 537 D
otilio.gonzalez@upr.edu
GONZALEZ CORTES,
Otilio .... 787-815-0000.. 537 F
otilio.gonzalez@upr.edu
GONZALEZ-DE JESUS,
Naydeen .... 201-612-5467.. 289 E
ngonzalezdejesus@bergen.edu
GONZALEZ-GUERRA,
Migdalia .... 787-890-2681.. 537 E
migdalia.gonzalez2@upr.edu
GONZALEZ MEDINA, CMF,
Ruben, A .... 787-848-5265.. 535 I
ruben_gonzalez@pucpr.edu
GONZALEZ-SCARANO,
Francisco .... 210-567-4432.. 477 D
scarano@uthscsa.edu
GONZALEZ TORRES, Ali . 413-528-7647.. 214 H
agonzaleztorres@simons-rock.edu
GOOCH, Cheryl Renee ..... 484-365-7664.. 409 B
cgooch@lincoln.edu
GOOCH, Cynthia .... 402-457-2649.. 280 J
cgooch@mccneb.edu
GOOCH, Ellen .... 518-327-6225.. 326 B
egooch@paulsmiths.edu
GOOCH, Gene .... 254-299-8649.. 461 E
ggooch@mclennan.edu
GOOCH, Jackie .... 256-233-8211...... 1 F
jackie.gooch@athens.edu
GOOCH, Janet .... 660-785-4383.. 273 B
jquinzer@truman.edu
GOOCH, Janet .... 660-785-4248.. 273 B
jquinzer@truman.edu
GOOCH, Josh .... 620-665-3594.. 181 I
goochj@hutchcc.edu
GOOCH, Zanetta .... 615-963-7401.. 445 A
zgooch@tnstate.edu
GOOD, Claire .... 207-621-3000.. 204 I
claire.good@maine.edu
GOOD, Claire, E .... 561-297-3000.. 110 K
GOOD, Darrin .... 562-907-4204.... 75 B
dgood@whittier.edu
GOOD, Gayle, A .... 402-363-5621.. 283 G
gagood@york.edu
GOOD, Glenn .... 352-392-3261.. 112 A
ggood@coe.ufl.edu
GOOD, Jennifer .... 251-380-2278...... 7 D
jgood@shc.edu
GOOD, Kristin .... 734-973-3722.. 242 G
kgood@wccnet.edu
GOOD, Larry .... 402-363-5718.. 283 G
lbgood@york.edu
GOOD, Lee Anna .... 432-552-2800.. 478 B
good_l@utpb.edu
GOOD, Megan, R .... 334-844-6844...... 1 G
mrg0030@auburn.edu
GOOD, Michael, L .... 352-273-7500.. 112 A
mgood@ufl.edu
GOOD, Rhonda .... 717-337-6015.. 404 C
rgood@gettysburg.edu
GOOD, RT .... 561-237-7458.. 104 O
rgood@lynn.edu
GOOD FOX, Julia .... 785-830-2770.. 181 E
jgoodfox@haskell.edu
GOOD LUCK, Aldean .... 406-638-3118.. 276 G
goodluckav@lbhc.edu
GOODALE, Brian .... 518-587-2100.. 335 D
brian.goodale@esc.edu

GORHAM, Jayne .... 321-433-5282.... 98 K
gorhamj@easternflorida.edu
GORINI, Cathy .... 641-472-1161.. 175 A
dof@mum.edu
GORINSHTEYN, Dasha .... 718-368-4975.. 308 F
dasha.gorinshteyn@kbcc.cuny.edu
GORKA, Gary .... 415-482-3524.... 42 G
gary.gorka@dominican.edu
GORMAN, Bonnie, B .... 906-487-2212.. 238 A
bbgorman@mtu.edu
GORMAN, Deb .... 920-996-2813.. 523 C
gorman@fvtc.edu
GORMAN, Greg .... 818-654-1733.... 57 F
ggorman@pgu.edu
GORMAN, Keith .... 856-200-4638.. 290 I
kgorman@cccnj.edu
GORMAN, Kimberly .... 828-227-7469.. 359 A
ksgorman@wcu.edu
GORMAN, Lawrence, J .... 312-939-0111.. 139 G
larry@eastwest.edu
GORMAN, Leah .... 903-988-7521.. 460 D
lgorman@kilgore.edu
GORMAN, Luke .... 603-526-3797.. 285 L
luke.gorman@colby-sawyer.edu
GORMAN,
Margaret Mary .... 716-827-2480.. 338 E
gormanm@trocaire.edu
GORMAN, Mary .... 646-312-3315.. 307 A
mary.gorman@baruch.cuny.edu
GORMAN, Michael .... 856-351-2601.. 296 L
mgroman@salemcc.edu
GORMAN, Michael .... 312-980-9252.. 153 J
GORMAN, Robin .... 724-357-2410.. 415 B
rgorman@iup.edu
GORMAN, Susan, L .... 617-558-1788.. 226 I
sgorman@nesa.edu
GORMAN, Wil .... 573-651-2297.. 272 B
wgorman@semo.edu
GORMAN, William, P ...... 617-989-4147.. 229 D
gormanb@wit.edu
GORMLEY, Christina, L ... 717-337-6611.. 404 C
cgormley@gettysburg.edu
GORMLEY, Kenneth, G .... 412-396-6060.. 403 A
president@duq.edu
GORMLEY, Melissa, E ..... 608-342-1151.. 521 A
gormleym@uwplatt.edu
GORMLY, Richard .... 858-225-4301.... 30 F
GORNEAULT, Gregg .... 860-906-5127.... 86 B
ggorneault@ccc.commnet.edu
GORNICK, Frank, P .... 559-934-2107.... 74 C
frankgornick@whccd.edu
GORR, Nathan .... 612-330-1390.. 244 I
gorr@augsburg.edu
GORRELL, Cathy .... 303-458-4100.... 82 L
cgorrell@regis.edu
GORRELL, Cathy .... 303-458-4117.... 82 L
cgorrell@regis.edu
GORRELL, John .... 304-424-8269.. 514 D
john.gorrell@wvup.edu
GORRELL, Renee .... 314-454-8171.. 265 E
rgorrell@bjc.org
GORRILLA, Adele, N .... 740-587-8646.. 368 B
gorrilla@denison.edu
GORRY, Thomas .... 703-784-2105.. 528 A
thomas.gorry@usmc.mil
GORSKI, Holly .... 253-964-6519.. 506 B
hgorski@pierce.ctc.edu
GORSLINE, Denise, M ..... 218-477-2764.. 250 F
gorsline@mnstate.edu
GORSLINE, Michael .... 847-317-8145.. 156 B
mgorsline@tiu.edu
GORT, Amy .... 612-330-1041.. 244 I
gort@augsburg.edu
GORTI, Anantha .... 703-284-1488.. 492 A
anantha.gorti@marymount.edu
GORTON, Cynthia .... 484-365-7526.. 409 B
cgorton@lincoln.edu
GORTON, Holly, J .... 231-995-1012.. 239 C
hgorton@nmc.edu
GORZ, Christine .... 312-329-2016.. 148 F
christine.gorz@moody.edu
GOSA, Polly .... 520-515-8750.... 12 L
gosap@cochise.edu
GOSCH, Judy .... 865-539-7233.. 446 G
jagosch@pstcc.edu
GOSE, Becca .... 541-737-2474.. 393 H
GOSHORN, Ted .... 770-720-5634.. 126 C
tag2@reinhardt.edu
GOSNELL, Kelly, S .... 859-846-5788.. 191 G
ksgosnell@midway.edu
GOSNELL, Victor .... 434-947-8138.. 493 B
vgosnell@randolphcollege.edu
GOSPODARCZYK, Tom .... 715-346-3386.. 521 C
tom.gospodarczyk@uwsp.edu
GOSS, Barbara .... 205-853-1200...... 5 B
bgoss@jeffstateonline.com
GOSS, Jonathan, D .... 315-268-2290.. 310 B
jgoss@clarkson.edu
GOSS, Nathan, R .... 770-534-6162.. 118 A
ngoss@brenau.edu
GOSS, Ronald .... 541-956-7119.. 394 J
rgoss@roguecc.edu
GOSSARD, Paula .... 215-702-4264.. 399 E
pgossard@cairn.edu
GOSSELIN, Grant .... 508-286-3780.. 229 F
gosselin_grant@wheatoncollege.edu
GOSSELIN, Karen .... 603-623-0313.. 287 D
karengosselin@nhia.edu
GOSSEN, Douglas .... 920-693-1221.. 523 E
doug.gossen@gotoltc.edu
GOSSEN, Ronald, H .... 314-516-5776.. 274 A
ron@umsl.edu
GOSSEN, Tim .... 507-457-1597.. 254 O
tgossen@smumn.edu
GOSSETT, Betty .... 716-673-3321.. 331 D
betty.gossett@fredonia.edu
GOSSETT, Greg .... 615-333-3349.. 486 G
ggossett@an.edu
GOSSETT, John .... 828-652-0676.. 351 C
johngossett@mcdowelltech.edu
GOSSFELD-BENZING,
Sara .... 715-675-3331.. 524 D
gossfeld-benzing@ntc.edu
GOSWAMI, Jaya .... 361-593-4411.. 469 A
jaya.goswami@tamuk.edu
GOSWAMI, Utpal, K .... 816-604-3044.. 267 J
utpal.goswami@mcckc.edu
GOSWICK, Barbara .... 501-686-2500.... 22 H
bgoswic@uasys.edu
GOSZ, Mike .... 312-567-3198.. 142 I
gosz@iit.edu
GOTANDA, John .... 808-544-0201.. 130 H
jgotanda@hpu.edu
GOTAY, Susanne .... 787-725-8120.. 532 K
consejerasusanne@eap.edu
GOTCHER, David .... 615-904-8042.. 444 G
david.gotcher@mtsu.edu
GOTHAM, Kerry .... 585-395-2068.. 332 E
kgotham@brockport.edu
GOTHARD, Mathew, J ..... 303-963-3223.... 77 I
mgothard@ccu.edu
GOTSCH, Kenneth .... 847-543-2631.. 138 C
kgotsch@clcillinois.edu
GOTSCH, Sarah, A .... 574-631-3903.. 168 B
sgotsch@nd.edu
GOTSCHALL, Matt, R .... 402-562-1211.. 278 K
mgotschall@cccneb.edu
GOTSHALL, Kathy .... 812-535-5162.. 166 K
kgotshal@smwc.edu
GOTT, Jared .... 731-989-6649.. 440 D
jgott@fhu.edu
GOTTARDY, John .... 716-645-2450.. 331 C
johngott@buffalo.edu
GOTTDIENER, Yitzchok .... 718-941-8000.. 321 A
GOTTFRIED, Bradley .... 301-934-7625.. 207 B
bgottfried@csmd.edu
GOTTFRIED, Matt .... 719-389-6381.... 77 J
matt.gottfried@coloradocollege.edu
GOTTLIEB, Jane .... 212-799-5000.. 318 A
GOTTLIEB, Rachelle .... 904-620-2903.. 112 B
r.gottlieb@unf.edu
GOTTLIEB, Tracy, T .... 973-761-9074.. 297 A
tracy.gottlieb@shu.edu
GOTTSCHALK, Glenn, F .... 410-293-1911.. 529 D
gotts@usna.edu
GOTTSCHALK, Katherine .. 765-983-1267.. 160 G
gottska@earlham.edu
GOTTSCHALK, Sandy .... 785-623-6150.. 183 J
sgottschalk@ncktc.edu
GOTTSHALL, Lori .... 954-771-0376.. 104 H
lgottshall@knoxseminary.edu
GOTTULA, Todd .... 308-865-8454.. 282 L
gottulatm@unk.edu
GOTZON, Mary, A .... 610-282-1100.. 402 B
mary.gotzon@desales.edu
GOUCH, Shawn .... 724-805-2895.. 419 A
shawn.gouch@stvincent.edu
GOUDEAU, Arthur .... 281-487-1170.. 469 F
agoudeau@txchiro.edu
GOUDEAU, LaTasha .... 713-221-8162.. 474 B
goudeaul@uhd.edu
GOUDY, Senta .... 304-424-8341.. 514 D
senta.goudy@wvup.edu
GOUGH, Annette .... 732-571-3402.. 292 F
agough@monmouth.edu
GOUGH, Christopher .... 203-332-5022.... 86 D
cgough@hcc.commnet.edu
GOUGH, Darby .... 816-501-3660.. 262 G
darby.gough@avila.edu
GOUGH, Richard, J .... 843-525-8247.. 433 B
rgough@tcl.edu
GOUKER, Toby .... 301-654-7267.. 210 G
GOULD, Amanda .... 413-565-1000.. 215 A
agould@baypath.edu
GOULD, Brandon .... 478-757-5233.. 129 L
ltimms@wesleyancollege.edu
GOULD, Brandon .... 478-757-5272.. 129 L
bgould@wesleyancollege.edu
GOULD, Cassie .... 212-517-0687.. 320 C
cgould@mmm.edu
GOULD, Dean, J .... 702-889-8426.. 284 G
dean_gould@nshe.nevada.edu
GOULD, Jane .... 651-290-7522.. 253 S
jane.gould@mitchellhamline.edu
GOULD, Mark .... 978-837-5072.. 225 E
gouldm@merrimack.edu
GOULD, Robert, J .... 724-503-1001.. 422 H
rgould@washjeff.edu
GOULD, Stephanie .... 402-941-6048.. 280 N
gould@midlandu.edu
GOULD, Terri .... 989-686-9081.. 233 I
tlgould@delta.edu
GOULD, Thomas .... 252-493-7406.. 352 A
tgould@email.pittcc.edu
GOULD, Tim .... 253-566-5050.. 508 B
tgould@tacomacc.edu
GOULDING, Laurel .... 701-662-1513.. 361 E
laurel.goulding@lrsc.edu
GOULDING, Ruth .... 619-239-0391.... 36 A
rgoulding@cwsl.edu
GOULET, Bonnie .... 203-575-8234.... 86 G
bgoulet@nv.edu
GOULET, Caroline .... 210-283-6924.. 474 D
goulet@uiwtx.edu
GOULET, Stephen, P .... 508-793-7598.. 217 B
sgoulet@clarku.edu
GOULOS, Anastasios .... 312-935-4812.. 152 D
agoulous@robertmorris.edu
GOUNARD, Jean, F .... 716-878-5331.. 332 F
gounarjf@buffalostate.edu
GOUPIL, Sharon .... 951-781-2727.... 59 F
srgoupil@sagecollege.edu
GOURD, David .... 206-934-4349.. 506 K
david.gourd@seattlecolleges.edu
GOURDINE, Raji .... 334-876-9292...... 4 A
rgourdine@wccs.edu
GOURJI, Konstantin .... 650-685-6616.... 45 K
kgourji@gurnick.edu
GOURLAY, Charles .... 910-630-7156.. 346 E
sgourley@methodist.edu
GOURLEY, Kristin .... 865-981-8194.. 441 H
kristin.gourley@maryvillecollege.edu
GOURLEY, Pamela, L ...... 276-944-6122.. 489 I
pgourley@ehc.edu
GOURNEAU, Haven .... 406-768-6300.. 276 F
hgourneau@fpcc.edu
GOURNEAU, William .... 701-255-3285.. 362 E
wgourneau@uttc.edu
GOUSE, Richard, I .... 401-739-5000.. 425 C
rgouse@neit.edu
GOUVEA, Nicole, R .... 208-426-4362.. 132 I
nicolegouvea@boisestate.edu
GOUVEIA, Jan, N .... 808-956-6405.. 131 D
jgouveia@hawaii.edu
GOUVIN, Eric, J .... 413-796-2201.. 229 E
eric.gouvin@law.wne.edu
GOVAN, JR., Tom .... 708-596-2000.. 154 E
tgovan@ssc.edu
GOVE, Marilyn .... 949-480-4131.... 64 J
mgove@soka.edu
GOVE, Sue .... 573-897-5000.. 272 H
GOVEA, Sam .... 972-860-4216.. 456 B
sgovea@dcccd.edu
GOVENDER, Yogani .... 787-250-1912.. 534 B
ygovender@intermetro.onmicrosoft.com
GOVER, Bruce .... 606-679-8501.. 190 E
bruce.gover@kctcs.edu
GOVER, Kristie .... 904-256-7067.. 103 D
kgover1@ju.edu
GOVINDAN, Indira .... 201-692-2060.. 291 J
govindan@fdu.edu
GOVINDARAJU, Venu .... 716-645-3321.. 331 C
vpr@buffalo.edu
GOVITZ, Leanne .... 989-686-9490.. 233 I
leannegovitz@delta.edu
GOVITZ, Scott .... 989-386-6624.. 238 B
sgovitz@midmich.edu
GOW, Joe .... 608-785-8004.. 520 C
jgow@uwlax.edu
GOWAN, Mary .... 540-568-3254.. 490 J
gowanma@jmu.edu
GOWENS, Krystal .... 714-556-3610.... 73 B
krystal.gowens@vanguard.edu
GOWER, John, M .... 848-932-4300.. 295 F
michael.gower@rutgers.edu
GOWER, Paula .... 405-585-5410.. 385 B
paula.gower@okbu.edu
GOWER, Ryan .... 618-544-8657.. 142 D
gowerry@iecc.edu
GOWER, Stephanie .... 678-422-4100.... 93 F
GOYETTE, Barbara .... 410-295-5554.. 210 D
barbara.goyette@sjc.edu
GOYETTE, Sylvain .... 815-836-5974.. 145 H
goyettsy@lewisu.edu
GOYUNYAN, Gevorg .... 510-925-4282.... 26 M
gevorg@aua.am
GOZIK, Nick .... 617-552-3827.. 216 C
nick.gozik@bc.edu
GOZUM, Allan .... 937-769-1304.. 363 E
agozum@antioch.edu
GRABE, David .... 314-977-3923.. 271 K
dgrabe@slu.edu
GRABE, William .... 928-523-4340.... 15 H
william.grabe@nau.edu
GRABER, David .... 402-375-7257.. 281 J
dagrabe1@wsc.edu
GRABER, Doug .... 620-947-3121.. 185 B
dougg@tabor.edu
GRABER, Linda .... 866-931-4300.. 270 I
linda.graber@rockbridge.edu
GRABER, Thomas .... 570-208-5900.. 406 J
thomasgraber@kings.edu
GRABOWSKA, Lynette ...... 605-367-6122.. 437 G
lynette.grabowska@southeasttech.edu
GRABOWSKI, Janice, T ... 724-925-4123.. 423 D
grabowskij@wccc.edu
GRABOWSKI, John, F ...... 410-777-2231.. 206 B
jfgrabowski@aacc.edu
GRABOWSKI, Lisa .... 303-797-5746.... 76 J
lisa.grabowski@arapahoe.edu
GRABOWSKI, Mark .... 417-328-1556.. 272 C
mgrabowski@sbuniv.edu
GRABOWSKI, Rod, M ...... 513-556-6703.. 379 A
grabowrd@ucmail.uc.edu
GRABUS, Scott .... 215-572-8515.. 397 G
grabuss@arcadia.edu
GRACA, Michael .... 508-286-3503.. 229 F
graca_michael@wheatoncollege.edu
GRACE, Coy, F .... 870-633-4480.... 20 B
cgrace@eacc.edu
GRACE, Danielle .... 301-447-5330.. 209 G
grace@msmary.edu
GRACE, Dennis .... 239-304-7093.... 95 Q
dennis.grace@avemaria.edu
GRACE, Glenda .... 718-997-5725.. 309 D
glenda.grace@qc.cuny.edu
GRACE, John .... 517-264-7198.. 241 A
jgrace@sienaheights.edu
GRACE, Melissa, H .... 850-474-3423.. 113 A
mgrace@uwf.edu
GRACE, Michelle, M .... 847-543-2274.. 138 C
mgrace@clcillinois.edu
GRACE, Nabil, F .... 248-204-2500.. 237 B
ngrace@ltu.edu
GRACE, Selena .... 208-373-1874.. 133 H
gracsele@isu.edu
GRACE, Sherie .... 256-228-6001...... 5 I
graces@nacc.edu
GRACE, Ted, W .... 618-453-4485.. 154 I
tgrace@siu.edu
GRACEY, Marissa .... 814-506-8318.. 413 P
mgracey@pennhighlands.edu
GRACIA, Jessica, L .... 508-565-1301.. 228 F
jlgracia@stonehill.edu
GRACIANI, Ruben .... 412-392-6154.. 417 F
rgraciani@pointpark.edu
GRACIAS, Vincente, H ..... 732-235-6300.. 295 F
vincente.gracia@rutgers.edu
GRACYALNY, David .... 410-225-2220.. 209 B
dgracyal@mica.edu
GRACYK, June .... 440-684-6083.. 380 F
jgracyk@ursuline.edu
GRACZYK, Aaron .... 979-230-3443.. 453 A
aaron.graczyk@brazosport.edu
GRADDY, Elizabeth .... 213-740-6715.... 72 D
graddy@usc.edu
GRADOWSKI, Charles ...... 484-365-7404.. 409 B
cgradowski@lincoln.edu
GRADY, Amber, N .... 870-759-4188.... 24 J
agrady@wbcoll.edu
GRADY, Carole .... 453-879-4802.. 482 A
grady@dixie.edu
GRADY, David, L .... 205-348-6681...... 8 D
david.grady@ua.edu
GRADY, Dennis .... 540-831-5431.. 493 A
dgrady4@radford.edu
GRADY, Helene .... 443-997-3359.. 208 D
hgrady1@jhu.edu
GRADY, Jonathan .... 810-762-3085.. 242 B
jrgrady@umflint.edu
GRADY, Lynne .... 706-379-3111.. 130 B
lbgrady@yhc.edu
GRADY, Meghan .... 610-606-4612.. 400 E
megrady@cedarcrest.edu
GRADY, Sara .... 508-929-8130.. 222 F
sara.grady@worcester.edu
GRADY, Sarah .... 718-409-7262.. 336 A
sgrady@sunymaritime.edu
GRAEBER, Dennis .... 215-951-1300.. 407 A
graeber@lasalle.edu
GRAEBERT, James, K ...... 414-288-3048.. 517 I
james.graebert@marquette.edu
GRAEM, David .... 903-675-6364.. 473 B
dgraem@tvcc.edu
GRAETHER, Anna .... 816-654-7122.. 266 E
agraether@kcumb.edu
GRAF, Bob .... 651-696-6280.. 247 I
rgraf@macalester.edu
GRAF, Elizabeth .... 219-866-6195.. 166 J
bethg@saintjoe.edu

GRAF, Katie, M ... 716-839-8364 .. 312 D kgraf@daemen.edu
GRAF, Megan ... 713-646-2968 .. 459 A mgraf@hcl.edu
GRAFER, Maggie ... 516-877-3844 .. 303 B yoon@adelphi.edu
GRAFF, Eric, S ... 614-885-5585 .. 376 G egraff@pcj.edu
GRAFF, Irene ... 310-660-3670 .... 42 J igraff@elcamino.edu
GRAFF, Irene ... 310-660-3515 .... 42 J igraff@elcamino.edu
GRAFF, Jenna ... 920-424-0775 .. 520 E graff@uwosh.edu
GRAFF, Jonathan ... 575-624-8480 .. 300 I graff@nmmi.edu
GRAFF, Jonathan, K ... 575-624-8400 .. 300 I graff@nmmi.edu
GRAFF, Michael ... 440-525-7060 .. 371 F mgraff@laeklandcc.edu
GRAFF, Nadja ... 212-463-0400 .. 337 I nadja.graff@touro.edu
GRAFFIUS, Jeff ... 740-753-6336 .. 369 K graffiusj@hocking.edu
GRAFTON, Anthony ... 870-307-7315 .... 21 A anthony.grafton@lyon.edu
GRAFTON, David ... 215-248-7313 .. 409 D dgrafton@ltsp.edu
GRAFTON, Ken ... 701-231-7655 .. 361 A k.grafton@ndsu.edu
GRAFTON, Steve, C ... 734-763-9730 .. 241 J sgrafton@umich.edu
GRAGG, Derrick ... 918-631-2181 .. 389 E derrick-gragg@utulsa.edu
GRAGG, Philip, T ... 619-239-0391 .... 36 A pgragg@cwsl.edu
GRAHAM, Amy ... 315-470-7858 .. 305 H amygraham@crouse.org
GRAHAM, Angela ... 540-863-2806 .. 496 H agraham@dslcc.edu
GRAHAM, Annette ... 845-451-1610 .. 312 C a_graham@culinary.edu
GRAHAM, Anthony ... 336-334-7757 .. 356 F agraham@ncat.edu
GRAHAM, April ... 661-362-3248 .... 40 A april.graham@canyons.edu
GRAHAM, Archie ... 414-297-6870 .. 524 A grahama@matc.edu
GRAHAM, Arlean ... 240-567-7120 .. 209 E arlean.graham@montgomerycollege.edu
GRAHAM, Bernard ... 570-408-4280 .. 423 G bernard.graham@wilkes.edu
GRAHAM, Bobbi Jo ... 412-291-6286 .. 397 I bgraham@aii.edu
GRAHAM, Carole ... 540-857-6696 .. 499 B cgraham@virginiawestern.edu
GRAHAM, Chris ... 858-642-8076 .... 54 A cgraham2@nu.edu
GRAHAM, Christine ... 251-344-1203 ...... 3 J cgraham@fortiscollege.edu
GRAHAM, Christine ... 801-524-8168 .. 480 J cgraham@ldsbc.edu
GRAHAM, Christy ... 423-869-6314 .. 441 E christy.graham@lmunet.edu
GRAHAM, Chuck ... 352-335-2332 .... 94 F
GRAHAM, Cynthia ... 919-546-8333 .. 355 F cgraham@shawu.edu
GRAHAM, Darren ... 641-683-4273 .. 173 C darren.graham@indianhills.edu
GRAHAM, Donald Kim ... 706-233-7469 .. 127 A dgraham@shorter.edu
GRAHAM, Duncan ... 408-298-2181 .... 62 E duncan.graham@sjcc.edu
GRAHAM, Earl ... 203-332-5290 .... 86 D egraham@housatonic.edu
GRAHAM, Eva ... 661-255-1050 .... 30 E egraham@calarts.edu
GRAHAM, Greg ... 321-674-7707 .. 100 M ggraham@fit.edu
GRAHAM, Gwen ... 219-464-5115 .. 168 F gwen.graham@valpo.edu
GRAHAM, James, F ... 660-543-4279 .. 273 C graham@ucmo.edu
GRAHAM, Jean ... 251-580-2293 ...... 4 I jean.graham@faulknerstate.edu
GRAHAM, Jeanne ... 906-932-4231 .. 234 C jeanneg@gogebic.edu
GRAHAM, Jeffrey ... 956-665-2751 .. 476 E jeff.graham@utrgv.edu
GRAHAM, Jennifer ... 254-298-8592 .. 467 B jennifer.graham@templejc.edu
GRAHAM, Joan, E ... 585-475-6079 .. 327 E jegirp@rit.edu
GRAHAM, Joe ... 419-720-6670 .. 376 I
GRAHAM, John ... 845-938-5868 .. 529 C john.graham@usma.edu
GRAHAM, III, John ... 412-346-2100 .. 417 B jgrahamiii@pia.edu
GRAHAM, John, D ... 812-855-1432 .. 162 F grahamjd@indiana.edu
GRAHAM, John, M ... 512-471-4716 .. 476 B john.graham@athletics.utexas.edu
GRAHAM, John-Bauer ... 256-782-5255 ...... 4 H jgraham@jsu.edu
GRAHAM, Kathleen ... 570-577-3607 .. 398 L kathy.graham@bucknell.edu
GRAHAM, Keith ... 570-740-0307 .. 409 E kgraham@luzerne.edu
GRAHAM, Keith ... 901-375-4400 .. 442 F keithgraham@midsouthchristian.edu
GRAHAM, Kerwin ... 336-750-2078 .. 359 B grahamkw@wssu.edu
GRAHAM, Kevin ... 321-674-8111 .. 100 M kgraham@fit.edu
GRAHAM, Kevin, C ... 217-424-6360 .. 148 D kgraham@millikin.edu
GRAHAM, LeRoy ... 802-443-5669 .. 484 F leroyg@middlebury.edu
GRAHAM, JR., Lewis, P ... 803-934-3404 .. 431 E lgraham@morris.edu
GRAHAM, Lindsey ... 978-556-3621 .. 224 D lgraham@necc.mass.edu
GRAHAM, Lori ... 910-755-7325 .. 347 H grahaml@brunswickcc.edu
GRAHAM, JR., Louis, W ... 617-253-2808 .. 225 A
GRAHAM, MariAnn ... 651-962-5000 .. 256 C magraham@stthomas.edu
GRAHAM, Mark, R ... 276-944-6104 .. 489 I mgraham@ehc.edu
GRAHAM, Mary, H ... 317-940-8056 .. 159 K mandritz@butler.edu
GRAHAM, Mary, S ... 601-928-6280 .. 259 C mary.graham@mgccc.edu
GRAHAM, Michael ... 847-947-5333 .. 149 B michael.graham@nl.edu
GRAHAM, SJ, Michael, J 513-745-3502 .. 381 I
GRAHAM, Mickey ... 580-477-7782 .. 389 I mckey.graham@wosc.edu
GRAHAM, Nancy, D ... 724-847-6550 .. 404 B ngraham@geneva.edu
GRAHAM, Paula ... 914-964-4282 .. 310 D pgraham@riversidehealth.org
GRAHAM, Philip ... 858-795-5210 .... 62 J pgraham@shpdiscovery.org
GRAHAM, Randy ... 713-525-3813 .. 475 J grahamra@stthom.edu
GRAHAM, Robbie ... 907-450-8000 .... 10 E rgraham@alaska.edu
GRAHAM, Robert ... 773-602-5265 .. 137 F rgraham24@ccc.edu
GRAHAM, Robert ... 575-562-2125 .. 299 I robert.graham@enmu.edu
GRAHAM, Robert, J ... 724-458-2187 .. 404 F rjgraham@gcc.edu
GRAHAM, Robin ... 406-444-0360 .. 276 J rgraham@montana.edu
GRAHAM, Robin ... 914-282-6087 .. 338 G r.graham@uts.edu
GRAHAM, Ronald ... 760-245-4271 .... 73 H ronald.graham@vvc.edu
GRAHAM, Roy ... 803-934-3298 .. 431 E roygraham@morris.edu
GRAHAM, Sharon, D ... 785-864-4790 .. 185 D sgraham@ku.edu
GRAHAM, Stephanie ... 909-607-6722 .... 46 A stephanie_graham@hmc.edu
GRAHAM, Stephen, A ... 973-761-9011 .. 297 A stephen.graham@shu.edu
GRAHAM, Steve ... 252-492-2061 .. 353 H grahams@vgcc.edu
GRAHAM, Steven, W ... 573-884-3360 .. 273 D grahams@umsystem.edu
GRAHAM, Toby ... 706-542-0621 .. 128 E tgraham@uga.edu
GRAHAM-HILL, Stephen ... 502-597-6919 .. 191 B stephen.grahamhill@kysu.edu
GRAHAM-ROY, Anita ... 808-954-4935 .. 130 G
GRAHN, Lance ... 330-675-8820 .. 370 I lgrahn@kent.edu
GRAMELSPACHER, Dave ... 812-357-8429 .. 167 B dgramelspacher@saintmeinrad.edu
GRAMELSPACHER, Mike ... 812-357-8293 .. 167 B mgramelspacher@saintmeinrad.edu
GRAMENZ, Gary ... 559-453-2291 .... 44 F gary.gramenz@fresno.edu
GRAMLICH, Annalisa ... 816-501-4122 .. 270 J annalisa.gramlich@rockhurst.edu
GRAMLICH, Nicole ... 314-763-7806 .. 268 G ngramlich@missouricollege.com
GRAMLING, PJ ... 325-649-8406 .. 459 E pgramling@hputx.edu
GRAMLING, Tim ... 818-299-5500 .... 74 A tgramling@westcoastuniversity.edu
GRAMMER, Jody ... 918-293-4890 .. 386 B jody.grammer@okstate.edu
GRAMOPADHYE, Anand ... 864-656-5540 .. 428 C agramop@clemson.edu
GRAMPETRO, Beth ... 617-928-4599 .. 226 B bgrampetro@mountida.edu
GRAMS, Justin ... 701-671-2189 .. 361 F justin.grams@ndscs.edu
GRAN, Tracey ... 651-690-6566 .. 254 M tlgran@stkate.edu
GRANA, Joe ... 714-879-3901 .... 46 F jgrana@hiu.edu
GRANACHER, Mia ... 859-371-9393 .. 186 M
GRANADE, Ray ... 870-245-5121 .... 21 E granade@obu.edu
GRANADOS, Alexander ... 205-970-9214 ...... 7 B agranados@sebc.edu
GRANAHAN, Sonya ... 617-373-6963 .. 227 B
GRANART, Heather, ... 630-844-5448 .. 135 E hgranart@aurora.edu
GRANATA, Brian ... 215-572-2194 .. 397 G granatab@arcadia.edu
GRANATOWSKI, Doris ... 480-212-1704 .... 16 R
GRANBERRY, Jacqueline, M ... 601-857-3363 .. 258 A jgranberry@hinccc.edu
GRANBERRY-RUSSELL, Paulette ... 517-353-3922 .. 237 I prussell@msu.edu
GRANDALL, Jerolyn, R ... 608-785-9576 .. 524 H grandallj@westerntc.edu
GRANDCHAMP, Michael, N ... 401-341-2142 .. 426 C grandchm@salve.edu
GRANDGENETT, Laura ... 617-228-2293 .. 223 B lgrandge@bhcc.mass.edu
GRANDGEORGE, Cynthia 661-362-3420 .... 40 A cindy.grandgeorge@canyons.edu
GRANDILLO, Michael ... 734-432-5315 .. 237 D magrandillo@madonna.edu
GRANDINETTI, Margie ... 610-282-1100 .. 402 B margie.grandinetti@desales.edu
GRANDNER, Deborah, F ... 301-314-7343 .. 211 E dgrandre@umd.edu
GRANDO, Victoria ... 816-936-8715 .. 271 L vgrando@saintlukescollege.edu
GRANDY, Mike ... 231-591-2163 .. 233 L mikegrandy@ferris.edu
GRANER, Jessica, M ... 402-280-2972 .. 279 H jessicagraner@creighton.edu
GRANETO, John ... 816-654-7305 .. 266 E jgraneto@kcumb.edu
GRANFIELD, Cathy ... 414-955-8566 .. 518 A mcw@matthewsstores.com
GRANFIELD, Robert ... 716-645-2996 .. 331 C rgranfie@buffalo.edu
GRANGER, Daniel, M ... 318-675-6011 .. 198 B dgrang@lsuhsc.edu
GRANGER, Earl, T ... 757-221-1188 .. 488 F earl.granger@wm.edu
GRANGER, Gary ... 503-777-7379 .. 394 I grangerg@reed.edu
GRANGER, Jennifer ... 617-243-2475 .. 219 I jgranger@lasell.edu
GRANGER, Jill ... 828-227-7383 .. 359 A jngranger@wcu.edu
GRANGER, Joey ... 601-984-1199 .. 261 C jgranger@umc.edu
GRANGER, Ron ... 307-855-2025 .. 526 E rgranger@cwc.edu
GRANGER, Vern ... 614-247-6281 .. 375 A granger.74@osu.edu
GRANHOLD, Kevin, B ... 713-500-3624 .. 477 C kevin.b.granhold@uth.tmc.edu
GRANLUND, Shirley, M ... 952-446-4112 .. 246 D granlunds@crown.edu
GRANNAS, Amanda ... 610-519-5858 .. 422 G amanda.grannas@villanova.edu
GRANOT, Elad ... 419-289-5212 .. 363 J egranot@ashland.edu
GRANT, Alan ... 540-231-4152 .. 499 F algrant@vt.edu
GRANT, Alexandra ... 312-922-1884 .. 147 B agrant@maccormac.edu
GRANT, Amy ... 310-660-3350 .... 42 J agrant@elcamino.edu
GRANT, Andi ... 308-632-6933 .. 282 H
GRANT, Andrew ... 212-824-2294 .. 315 F agrant@huc.edu
GRANT, Andrew, D ... 419-372-3905 .. 364 E agrant@bgsu.edu
GRANT, Angela ... 617-824-8204 .. 218 B angela_grant@emerson.edu
GRANT, Anthony ... 317-805-1781 .. 511 D agrant@salemu.edu
GRANT, Armada ... 443-885-3195 .. 209 F armada.grant@morgan.edu
GRANT, Barry ... 860-512-3403 .... 86 E bgrant@manchestercc.edu
GRANT, Beth, A ... 813-988-5131 .. 100 F registrar@floridacollege.edu
GRANT, Bob ... 937-775-2771 .. 381 H bob.grant@wright.edu
GRANT, Brad ... 912-525-5000 .. 126 E bgrant@scad.edu
GRANT, Brian, T ... 315-268-6480 .. 310 B bgrant@clarkson.edu
GRANT, Caleb ... 518-255-5525 .. 334 D grantcr@cobleskill.edu
GRANT, Christa, J ... 518-783-2330 .. 330 E cgrant@siena.edu
GRANT, Christy ... 402-354-7077 .. 281 F christy.grant@methodistcollege.edu
GRANT, Dale, E ... 308-432-6202 .. 281 H dgrant@csc.edu
GRANT, Dana ... 434-200-3070 .. 487 L dana.grant@centralhealth.com
GRANT, Deborah, L ... 504-865-5210 .. 200 C dgrant@tulane.edu
GRANT, Diane ... 717-764-9550 .. 401 H dgrant@csb.edu
GRANT, Donald ... 626-529-8201 .... 55 H dgrant@pacificoaks.edu
GRANT, Donna ... 504-286-5040 .. 199 I dgrant@suno.edu
GRANT, G. Anthony ... 303-556-3939 .... 81 G ggrant5@msudenver.edu
GRANT, Gary, B ... 813-257-3006 .. 114 M ggrant@ut.edu
GRANT, George ... 616-331-6850 .. 234 F grantg@gvsu.edu
GRANT, Jamie ... 920-686-6206 .. 519 H jamie.grant@sl.edu
GRANT, Jeff ... 229-245-3852 .. 129 G jgrant@valdosta.edu
GRANT, Johnny ... 478-445-5852 .. 121 A johnny.grant@gcsu.edu
GRANT, Jordan, L ... 206-281-2469 .. 507 C grantj@spu.edu
GRANT, Karen ... 508-854-4275 .. 224 E kgrant@qcc.mass.edu
GRANT, Kathleen ... 513-556-3471 .. 379 A kathleen.grant@uc.edu
GRANT, Kathy ... 334-229-8448 ...... 1 D kathygrant@alasu.edu
GRANT, Keith ... 513-671-1920 .. 186 M kgrant@beckfield.edu
GRANT, Kenna ... 860-768-5433 .... 89 G mckenna@hartford.edu
GRANT, Kim ... 904-256-8000 .. 103 D kgrant7@ju.edu
GRANT, Kizuwanda ... 214-379-5500 .. 463 G kgrant@pqc.edu
GRANT, Linda ... 251-575-8204 ...... 1 C lgrant@ascc.edu
GRANT, Madeline ... 714-564-6750 .... 58 G grant_madeline@sac.edu
GRANT, Marvin ... 904-470-8892 .... 98 N marvin.grant@ewc.edu
GRANT, Mary, K ... 828-251-6500 .. 357 C chanoffi@unca.edu
GRANT, Michelle ... 219-989-2555 .. 166 F grantml@pnw.edu
GRANT, Nancy ... 907-852-1708 .... 10 D nancy.grant@ilisagvik.edu
GRANT, Nina ... 308-635-6104 .. 283 D grantel@wncc.edu
GRANT, Peter ... 580-774-7152 .. 388 C peter.grant@swosu.edu
GRANT, Ralph, T ... 973-803-5000 .. 294 B rgrant@pillar.edu
GRANT, Robert ... 816-501-4418 .. 270 J bob.grant@rockhurst.edu
GRANT, Sabrina ... 973-720-2754 .. 298 G grants@wpunj.edu
GRANT, Sharone, V ... 410-651-6597 .. 212 B svgrant@umes.edu
GRANT, Shaunette ... 305-899-4888 .... 96 D sgrant@barry.edu
GRANT, Terry ... 304-724-3700 .. 510 E tgrant@apus.edu
GRANT, Tina ... 518-464-8567 .. 314 A tgrant@excelsior.edu
GRANT, Velvet, L ... 757-683-3159 .. 492 G vlgrant2@odu.edu
GRANT BAHAN, Rebecca 314-889-4509 .. 265 C rgrantbahan@fontbonne.edu
GRANTHAM, Bill ... 334-670-3637 ...... 7 H bgranth@troy.edu
GRANTHAM, Rebecca ... 719-384-6912 .... 82 A rebecca.grantham@ojc.edu
GRANVILLE, Andrea, L ... 212-752-1530 .. 318 F andrea.granville@limcollege.edu
GRAPER, Dorothy ... 812-749-1303 .. 166 B dgraper@oak.edu
GRAPPO, Ann Marie ... 212-217-3900 .. 314 B ann_grappo@fitnyc.edu
GRASS-HEMMERT, Nancy 310-434-3493 .... 63 F grass_hemmert_nancy@smc.edu
GRASSADONIA, Jane, M ... 814-886-6472 .. 411 C jgrassadonia@mtaloy.edu
GRASSEL, OSB, Martin ... 503-845-3326 .. 392 E martin.grassel@mtangel.edu
GRASSETTI, J. Vincent ... 413-755-4061 .. 224 G vgrassetti@stcc.edu
GRASSI, Janel ... 417-447-2601 .. 270 A grassij@otc.edu
GRASSINI, Dennis, J ... 401-825-2151 .. 425 A dgrassini@ccri.edu

GRASSLER, Frank, P .... 214-648-8188.. 478 C
frank.grassler@utsouthwestern.edu

GRASSO, Domenico .... 302-831-2101.... 91 F
dg@udel.edu

GRASSO, Jennifer .... 216-421-8019.. 366 G
jgrasso@cia.edu

GRASSO, Maureen, G ...... 919-515-1983.. 357 B
mgrasso@ncsu.edu

GRASSO, Richard .... 718-489-3450.. 328 D
rgrasso@sfc.edu

GRATE, Cammy, D .... 803-516-4510.. 432 E
cgrate2@scsu.edu

GRATSON, Emily .... 616-949-5300.. 233 A
emily.gratson@cornerstone.edu

GRATTAN, Nancy .... 678-407-5000.. 121 B
ngrattan@ggc.edu

GRATTON, John .... 575-234-9200.. 300 J
jgratton@nmsu.edu

GRATTON, John .... 575-234-9210.. 301 B
jgratton@nmsu.edu

GRAU, Frances .... 787-720-1022.. 531 A
fgrau@atlanticu.edu

GRAU, Isidro .... 713-221-8494.. 474 B
graui@uhd.edu

GRAU, Leeann .... 740-389-4636.. 372 B
graul@mtc.edu

GRAU, Melissa .... 845-848-7602.. 312 F
melissa.grau@dc.edu

GRAU, Monica, C .... 607-436-2255.. 331 F
monica.grau@oneonta.edu

GRAUMAN, Greg .... 808-543-8061.. 130 H
ggrauman@hpu.edu

GRAUMLICH, Lisa .... 206-221-0907.. 508 E
graumlic@uw.edu

GRAUPE, Daniel .... 847-679-3135.. 144 G
dgraupe@ksi.edu

GRAVDAHL, Jeanette .... 605-698-3966.. 436 K
jgravdahl@swc.tc

GRAVEL, Matthew .... 413-755-4623.. 224 G
mgravel@stcc.edu

GRAVES, Becky .... 256-352-8159...... 9 G
becky.graves@wallacestate.edu

GRAVES, Devin .... 620-441-5595.. 180 D
devin.graves@cowley.edu

GRAVES, Diane, J .... 210-999-8121.. 473 A
diane.graves@trinity.edu

GRAVES, Estonia .... 903-983-8200.. 460 D
egraves@kilgore.edu

GRAVES, Finley .... 940-565-3952.. 475 A
finley.graves@unt.edu

GRAVES, Frank .... 254-299-8126.. 461 E
fgraves@mclennan.edu

GRAVES, Harold, B .... 719-884-5000.... 81 N
hbgraves@nbc.edu

GRAVES, James .... 207-780-5585.. 205 E
james.graves@maine.edu

GRAVES, Jeff .... 916-649-8168.... 28 L
jeff.graves@brightwood.edu

GRAVES, Kevin .... 504-280-6266.. 198 D
kgraves@uno.edu

GRAVES, Larry .... 608-262-9652.. 522 A
larry.graves@uwc.edu

GRAVES, Loreatha, D .... 336-334-7551.. 356 F
loretha@ncat.edu

GRAVES, Mallis .... 859-442-1608.. 189 D
mallis.graves@kctcs.edu

GRAVES, Matt .... 208-792-2247.. 134 A
mlgraves@lcsc.edu

GRAVES, Peter, E .... 512-463-1823.. 470 G
peter.graves@tsus.edu

GRAVES, Randy .... 918-647-1370.. 382 I
rggraves@carlalbert.edu

GRAVES, Randy, K .... 269-471-3854.. 230 H
gravesr@andrews.edu

GRAVES, Rita .... 318-357-5178.. 201 B
gravesr@nsula.edu

GRAVES, Robbie .... 731-661-5008.. 448 A
rgraves@uu.edu

GRAVES, Robert .... 413-528-7316.. 214 H
rgraves@simons-rock.edu

GRAVES, Romana .... 303-273-3746.... 78 M
rgraves@mines.edu

GRAVES, Sara .... 256-824-6868...... 8 F
sara.graves@uah.edu

GRAVES, Sara, J .... 256-824-6064...... 8 F
sara.graves@uah.edu

GRAVES, Scott .... 907-564-8342.... 10 B
sgraves@alaskapacific.edu

GRAVES, Susan .... 270-534-3155.. 190 H
susan.graves@kctcs.edu

GRAVES, Theresa, D .... 405-466-3201.. 383 M
tdgraves@langston.edu

GRAVES, William, T .... 318-342-1961.. 201 E
graves@ulm.edu

GRAVETT, Sharon, L .... 229-333-5950.. 129 G
sgravett@valdosta.edu

GRAVIETTE, Kimberly, K .. 402-461-7387.. 280 D
kgraviette@hastings.edu

GRAVLEY, John, W .... 913-667-5700.. 179 K
jgravley@cbts.edu

GRAY, Alicia .... 409-882-3343.. 471 B
alicia.gray@lsco.edu

GRAY, Amanda .... 816-995-2806.. 270 H
amanda.gray@researchcollege.edu

GRAY, Amy .... 630-844-5467.. 135 E
agray@aurora.edu

GRAY, Anita .... 260-359-4063.. 161 O
agray@huntington.edu

GRAY, Ashley .... 601-276-3732.. 260 H
sasser@smcc.edu

GRAY, Bart .... 641-585-8163.. 177 F
bart.gray@waldorf.edu

GRAY, Betty .... 252-940-6387.. 347 E

GRAY, Bill .... 517-607-2736.. 235 E
bgray@hillsdale.edu

GRAY, Bo .... 828-835-4222.. 353 G
bgray@tricountycc.edu

GRAY, Carol .... 254-526-1668.. 454 A
carol.gray@ctcd.edu

GRAY, Charlotte .... 417-967-5466.. 272 K

GRAY, Chris .... 812-482-3030.. 169 A
cgray@vinu.edu

GRAY, Chris .... 913-469-8500.. 182 A
chrisgray@jccc.edu

GRAY, Corey .... 402-643-3651.. 279 F
corey.gray@cune.edu

GRAY, Craig .... 205-665-6116...... 9 B
cgray2@montevallo.edu

GRAY, David .... 575-624-8078.. 300 I
david@nmmi.edu

GRAY, David .... 701-355-8180.. 362 G
dpgray@umary.edu

GRAY, David, J .... 814-865-6574.. 412 F
djg36@psu.edu

GRAY, David, R .... 540-868-7154.. 497 E
dgray@lfcc.edu

GRAY, Denise .... 502-418-5638.. 190 A
denise.gray@kctcs.edu

GRAY, Donna, L .... 312-777-8652.. 142 G
dlgray@aii.edu

GRAY, Douglass, P .... 410-827-5830.. 207 A
dgray@chesapeake.edu

GRAY, Gary .... 907-474-7780.... 10 G

GRAY, Gary, W .... 714-449-7481.... 51 F
ggray@ketchum.edu

GRAY, Glenn, P .... 319-273-2333.. 170 A
glenn.gray@uni.edu

GRAY, Gregory, S .... 334-727-8011...... 8 A
gsgray@tuskegee.edu

GRAY, Holly .... 662-620-5092.. 258 C
ehgray@iccms.edu

GRAY, Isabel .... 856-227-7200.. 290 B
igray@camdencc.edu

GRAY, James .... 781-736-4520.. 216 F
jwgray@brandeis.edu

GRAY, Jarrod .... 217-854-3231.. 135 K
jarrod.gray@blackburn.edu

GRAY, Jeff .... 478-387-4781.. 121 E
jgray@gmc.edu

GRAY, Jeffrey .... 515-271-1506.. 171 H
jeffrey.gray@dmu.edu

GRAY, Jeffrey, L .... 718-817-4750.. 314 G
gray@fordham.edu

GRAY, Joe .... 615-547-1255.. 439 H
jgray@cumberland.edu

GRAY, John .... 910-755-7434.. 347 H
grayj@brunswickcc.edu

GRAY, John, C .... 302-295-1139.... 91 I
john.c.gray@wilmu.edu

GRAY, Karen .... 614-251-4741.. 374 I
grayk4@ohiodominican.edu

GRAY, Karol .... 804-828-6116.. 496 D
kgray@vcu.edu

GRAY, Kelly .... 419-755-4823.. 373 G
kgray@ncstatecollege.edu

GRAY, Kelly .... 575-769-4179.. 299 G
kelly.gray@clovis.edu

GRAY, Kilen .... 502-895-3411.. 191 F
kgray@lpts.edu

GRAY, Kristen .... 706-778-0100.. 125 J
kgray@piedmont.edu

GRAY, Kristen .... 616-395-7945.. 235 F
gray@hope.edu

GRAY, Leslie .... 510-594-3705.... 29 K
lgray@cca.edu

GRAY, Lisa, G .... 410-546-6390.. 213 A
lggray@salisbury.edu

GRAY, Lloyd .... 601-974-1000.. 258 H
lloyd.gray@millsaps.edu

GRAY, Lydia, E .... 718-862-7231.. 319 L
lydia.gray@manhattan.edu

GRAY, Marisa .... 913-288-7284.. 182 C
mcgray@kckcc.edu

GRAY, Maryann, J .... 310-825-5573...... 69 D
mgray@conet.ucla.edu

GRAY, Michaelle .... 580-371-2371.. 384 D
mgray@mscok.edu

GRAY, Michelle .... 580-387-7131.. 384 D
mgray@mscok.edu

GRAY, Nancy .... 970-339-6392.... 76 H
nancy.gray@aims.edu

GRAY, Nancy, O .... 540-362-6321.. 490 F
presoffc@hollins.edu

GRAY, Rebecca .... 254-968-9473.. 467 F
rgray@tarleton.edu

GRAY, Robert, R .... 804-257-5842.. 500 B
rrgray@vuu.edu

GRAY, Sandra, C .... 859-858-3511.. 186 J
president@asbury.edu

GRAY, Sarah .... 309-649-6265.. 155 G
sarah.gray@src.edu

GRAY, Seneca .... 503-768-6781.. 392 A
seneca@lclark.edu

GRAY, Shashuna .... 540-891-3046.. 497 B
dgray@germanna.edu

GRAY, Shaun .... 207-741-5580.. 203 M
sgray@smccme.edu

GRAY, Shawn .... 409-880-8466.. 471 A
shawn.gray@lamar.edu

GRAY, Sheryl .... 865-471-3240.. 439 C
sgray@cn.edu

GRAY, Shonda .... 443-885-3430.. 209 F
shonda.gray@morgan.edu

GRAY, Simon .... 716-285-1212.. 324 E
sgray@niagara.edu

GRAY, Susan .... 207-602-2248.. 205 F
sgray@une.edu

GRAY, Susan .... 478-289-2028.. 120 C
sgray@ega.edu

GRAY, Tiffany .... 206-296-6070.. 507 E
grayt@seattleu.edu

GRAY, Tim .... 303-937-4420.... 77 B
tim.gray@augustineinstitute.org

GRAY, Tim .... 319-208-5022.. 176 J
tgray@scciowa.edu

GRAY, Toni, B .... 806-371-2912.. 450 H
tbgray@actx.edu

GRAY, Tracy .... 858-695-8587.... 46 G
tgray@horizonuniversity.edu

GRAY, Tuesday, A .... 225-216-8403.. 195 H
grayt@mybrcc.edu

GRAY, Vance .... 404-756-4033.. 116 I
vgray@atlm.edu

GRAY, Velma .... 901-435-1676.. 441 C
velma_gray@loc.edu

GRAY, Warren .... 606-589-3070.. 190 G
warren.gray@kctcs.edu

GRAY, Warren, S .... 401-865-1602.. 425 D
wgray@providence.edu

GRAY-DEVINE, Sherry ..... 580-387-7212.. 384 D
sgray@mscok.edu

GRAY KOGEN, Elizabeth . 212-472-1500.. 324 A
giving@nysid.edu

GRAY-LITTLE, Bernadette . 785-864-3131.. 185 D
graylittle@ku.edu

GRAY PAYTON, Pamela .. 619-260-4681.... 72 B
grayp@sandiego.edu

GRAY-ROBERTSON, Beth 252-536-7299.. 350 C
bgray-robertson498@halifaxcc.edu

GRAY-VICKREY, Peg .... 254-519-5447.. 468 C
gray-vickrey@tamuct.edu

GRAY WILSON,
Stephanie .... 614-236-6894.. 364 N
honors@capital.edu

GRAYBEAL, Jerry, G .... 801-626-8114.. 482 D
jgraybeal@weber.edu

GRAYBEAL, Susan, E .... 423-354-2471.. 446 F
segraybeal@northeaststate.edu

GRAYBILL, Jody, D .... 570-577-3351.. 398 L
jody.graybill@bucknell.edu

GRAYBOYS, James .... 334-229-4401...... 1 D
jgrayboys@alasu.edu

GRAYLEE, Laleh .... 657-278-4228.... 33 A
lgraylee@fullerton.edu

GRAYS, Rodney .... 301-447-7411.. 209 G
grays@msmary.edu

GRAYS, Shantay .... 713-718-7497.. 459 B
shanty.grays@hccs.edu

GRAYSON, Chinester .... 334-874-5700...... 3 A
cgrayson@ccal.edu

GRAYSON, Denise, R .... 605-256-5152.. 437 C
denise.grayson@dsu.edu

GRAYSON, Lorenzo .... 251-405-7170...... 2 D
lgrayson@bishop.edu

GRAYSON, Paul .... 212-774-0727.. 320 C
pgrayson@mmm.edu

GRAYSON, Shari .... 858-505-1100.... 47 B
sgrayson@ipsb.edu

GRAZIANO, Joanne .... 516-299-2999.. 319 C
joanne.graziano@liu.edu

GRAZIANO, Judith .... 651-793-1368.. 250 A
judith.graziano@metrostate.edu

GRAZIANO, Vincent, S .... 412-391-6710.. 398 E
vgraziano@bradfordpittsburgh.edu

GRAZZINI-OLSON,
Nancy .... 952-851-0066.. 244 C

GREAF, Eileen .... 304-829-7633.. 510 G
egreaf@bethanywv.edu

GREANEY, Bryan .... 917-493-4477.. 319 M
bgreaney@msmnyc.edu

GREANEY, KC .... 707-778-4188.... 63 G
kgreaney@santarosa.edu

GREASON, Jessica .... 816-584-6329.. 270 D
jessica.greason@park.edu

GREATHOUSE, Jo .... 979-230-3234.. 453 A
jo.greathouse@brazosport.edu

GREAVES, Christopher ..... 718-997-3930.. 309 D
christopher.greaves@qc.cuny.edu

GREAVES, Matthew, C ..... 202-687-3488.... 92 E
mcg3@georgetown.edu

GREB, Christine .... 215-951-2803.. 416 G
grebc@philau.edu

GREBEL, David, A .... 817-257-7130.. 469 G
d.grebel@tcu.edu

GREBERT, Robert .... 518-292-7702.. 327 H
greber@sage.edu

GREBIN, Kevin .... 605-331-6772.. 438 A
kevin.grebin@usiouxfalls.edu

GREBING, Karen .... 239-513-1122.. 102 T
kgrebing@hodges.edu

GREBING, Robin, E .... 314-539-5189.. 271 F
rgrebing2@stlcc.edu

GREBINOSKI, Jeff .... 920-498-7193.. 524 E
jeffrey.grebinoski@nwtc.edu

GRECO, Anne .... 215-751-8217.. 401 G
agreco@ccp.edu

GRECO, Frank, M .... 412-365-1133.. 400 G
greco@chatham.edu

GRECO, Juneann .... 570-340-6004.. 409 H
greco@marywood.edu

GRECO, Michelle .... 504-671-6001.. 196 D
mgreco@dcc.edu

GRECO, Peter .... 925-631-4747.... 59 I
peter.greco2@stmarys-ca.edu

GRECO, Tom .... 620-241-0723.. 179 L
tom.greco@centralchristian.edu

GREDEN, Leigh .... 734-487-8676.. 233 J
lgreden@emich.edu

GREDER, Darcy, L .... 309-556-3541.. 143 D
dgreder@iwu.edu

GREEAR, Amy .... 276-523-7480.. 497 F
agreear@mecc.edu

GREEN, Adam .... 304-558-0655.. 512 O
adam.green@wvhepc.edu

GREEN, Allen .... 914-395-2527.. 329 K
agreen@sarahlawrence.edu

GREEN, Andrew .... 516-726-6182.. 529 B
greena@usmma.edu

GREEN, Andy .... 256-782-5268...... 4 H
agreen@jsu.edu

GREEN, Anita .... 313-593-5190.. 242 A
ujima@umich.edu

GREEN, Ann, F .... 828-694-1709.. 347 G
anng@blueridge.edu

GREEN, Anne-Marie .... 815-825-9443.. 144 F
anne-marie.green@kishwaukeecollege.edu

GREEN, Ashley .... 817-722-1656.. 460 E
ashley.green@tku.edu

GREEN, Audrey .... 661-362-3424.... 40 A
audrey.green@canyons.edu

GREEN, Becky .... 806-874-3571.. 454 F
becky.green@clarendoncollege.edu

GREEN, Betti .... 315-781-3600.. 316 C
bgreen@hws.edu

GREEN, Beverly .... 909-607-7821.... 38 I
beverly.green@cgu.edu

GREEN, Bevley, W .... 251-460-6188...... 9 E
bwgreen@southalabama.edu

GREEN, Bichevia .... 803-536-0311.. 431 I

GREEN, Brenda .... 561-586-0121.. 102 N
bgreen@hci.edu

GREEN, Cheryl .... 703-526-6978.. 492 A
cheryl.green@marymount.edu

GREEN, Chris .... 805-546-3902.... 41 L
cgreen@cuesta.edu

GREEN, Chris .... 859-985-3727.. 187 B
greenchr@berea.edu

GREEN, Cindy .... 314-539-5227.. 271 F
cgreen2@stlcc.edu

GREEN, Clarence .... 660-562-1254.. 269 J
cgreen@nwmissouri.edu

GREEN, Constance, C ...... 503-842-8222.. 395 D
conniegreen@tillamookbaycc.edu

GREEN, David, A .... 217-786-2406.. 146 E
david.green@llcc.edu

GREEN, David, M .... 818-947-2679.... 50 D
greendm@lavc.edu

GREEN, Denise .... 334-670-5767...... 7 H
mbgreen@troy.edu

GREEN, Dennis .... 603-644-3194.. 287 I
d.green@snhu.edu

GREEN, Don .... 657-278-2413.... 33 A
dgreen@fullerton.edu

GREEN, Donald .... 217-732-3168.. 146 A
pres@lincolnchristian.edu

GREEN, Donald, J .... 706-295-6329.. 121 C
dgreen@highlands.edu

GREEN, Donna .... 562-985-5468.... 33 B
donna.green@csulb.edu

GREEN, Dwayne .... 320-629-5159.. 251 E
greend@pine.edu

GREEN, Elaine .... 215-248-7063.. 400 H
greene@chc.edu

GREEN, Eleanor, M .... 979-845-5051.. 468 B
emgreen@tamu.edu
GREEN, Elna .... 408-924-2450.... 35 C
elna.green@sjsu.edu
GREEN, Erik .... 512-313-3000.. 455 F
erik.green@concordia.edu
GREEN, Gary, M .... 336-734-7200.. 349 G
ggreen@forsythtech.edu
GREEN, Geoff .... 805-965-0581.... 63 D
green@sbccfoundation.org
GREEN, Greg .... 512-492-3017.. 451 E
ggreen@aoma.edu
GREEN, James .... 314-340-3502.. 265 H
greenj@hssu.edu
GREEN, James .... 843-574-6774.. 433 D
james.green@tridenttech.edu
GREEN, Janel .... 504-816-4447.. 195 B
jegreen@dillard.edu
GREEN, Jean .... 217-228-5432.. 151 F
greenje@quincy.edu
GREEN, Jeffrey .... 312-662-4401.. 134 I
jgreen@adler.edu
GREEN, Jennifer .... 909-621-8000.... 46 A
jgreen@hmc.edu
GREEN, Jennifer .... 860-932-4140.... 87 C
jgreen@qvcc.edu
GREEN, Jennifer .... 800-290-4226.. 440 G
jgreen@hchs.edu
GREEN, Jennifer, K .... 434-395-2944.. 491 E
greenjk@longwood.edu
GREEN, Jerry .... 718-817-4170.. 314 G
jgreen@fordham.edu
GREEN, Joel, B .... 626-584-5205.... 44 G
provost@fuller.edu
GREEN, Joel, B .... 626-584-5304.... 44 G
jbgreen@fuller.edu
GREEN, John .... 312-369-7291.. 138 F
jgreen@colum.edu
GREEN, John .... 620-276-9595.. 181 C
john.green@gcccks.edu
GREEN, John .... 252-222-6273.. 348 B
greenj@carteret.edu
GREEN, John .... 610-683-4000.. 415 C
GREEN, John, C .... 610-683-4114.. 415 C
jgreen@kutztown.edu
GREEN, John, C .... 330-972-1901.. 378 G
green@uakron.edu
GREEN, Jonathan, D .... 309-556-3101.. 143 D
provost@iwu.edu
GREEN, Judith .... 201-684-7523.. 294 G
jgreen2@ramapo.edu
GREEN, Julia .... 207-941-7129.. 202 I
greenj@husson.edu
GREEN, Karen .... 610-526-6008.. 405 B
kgreen@harcum.edu
GREEN, Karen .... 484-664-3182.. 411 D
green@muhlenberg.edu
GREEN, Kelly .... 360-596-5214.. 508 A
kgreen@spscc.edu
GREEN, Kerri .... 607-431-4162.. 315 E
greenk2@hartwick.edu
GREEN, Latrelle, A .... 804-257-5662.. 500 B
lagreen@vuu.edu
GREEN, Lillie, F .... 757-727-5057.. 490 E
lillie.green@hamptonu.edu
GREEN, Lina .... 757-455-2115.. 500 E
lgreen@vwc.edu
GREEN, Lisa .... 315-792-3736.. 339 B
lcgreen@utica.edu
GREEN, Lois .... 310-577-3000.... 75 H
lgreen@yosan.edu
GREEN, Lorry .... 864-977-7124.. 431 G
lorry.green@ngu.edu
GREEN, Lynette .... 920-403-3235.. 519 G
lynette.green@snc.edu
GREEN, Mariah .... 970-943-7122.... 84 H
mgreen@western.edu
GREEN, Mark, A .... 618-235-2700.. 155 C
mark.green@swic.edu
GREEN, Mary .... 269-965-3931.. 236 A
greenm@kellogg.edu
GREEN, Mary Jo .... 715-422-5504.. 523 G
maryjo.green@mstc.edu
GREEN, Matthew .... 805-546-3924.... 41 L
mgreen@cuesta.edu
GREEN, Matthew .... 845-688-1568.. 338 F
greenm@sunyulster.edu
GREEN, Matthew .... 423-869-6241.. 441 E
matthew.green@lmunet.edu
GREEN, Melanie, H .... 804-627-5300.. 487 G
melanie_green@bshsi.org
GREEN, Melissa .... 530-938-5374.... 40 F
mgreen8@siskiyous.edu
GREEN, Melissa .... 567-429-3535.. 376 D
melissa_green3@owens.edu
GREEN, III, Melvin .... 229-333-5954.. 129 G
GREEN, Michael, R .... 717-867-6208.. 408 F
mgreen@lvc.edu
GREEN, Michael, S .... 518-629-4554.. 316 G
m.green@hvcc.edu

GREEN, Mike .... 615-966-6000.. 441 F
mike.green@lipscomb.edu
GREEN, Mike .... 541-737-9275.. 393 H
GREEN, Mike .... 541-737-2447.. 393 H
GREEN, Moishe .... 845-352-5852.. 340 F
GREEN, Monica .... 951-372-7015.... 59 B
monica.green@norcocollege.edu
GREEN, Myrtes, D .... 205-929-6305...... 5 D
mdgreen@lawsonstate.edu
GREEN, Nancy .... 704-403-3599.. 342 E
nancy.green@carolinashealthcare.org
GREEN, Nicole .... 310-825-0768.... 69 D
ngreen@caps.ucla.edu
GREEN, O. Jerome .... 501-374-6305.... 22 C
GREEN, Paul .... 785-833-4387.. 182 F
green@kwu.edu
GREEN, Rachel .... 570-662-4815.. 415 E
rgreen@mansfield.edu
GREEN, Ragan .... 478-275-7865.. 125 D
rgreen@oftc.edu
GREEN, Ramona .... 903-223-3058.. 469 C
ramona.green@tamut.edu
GREEN, Ray .... 903-463-3005.. 468 D
raymond.green@tamuc.edu
GREEN, Rebecca .... 760-355-6499.... 46 J
becky.green@imperial.edu
GREEN, Remon, P .... 713-313-1814.. 470 D
greenrp@tsu.edu
GREEN, Richard .... 317-789-8271.. 160 E
rgreen@crossroads.edu
GREEN, Richard .... 484-365-7400.. 409 B
GREEN, Robert, L .... 540-464-7321.. 499 E
greenrl@vmi.edu
GREEN, Ronnie, D .... 402-472-2116.. 282 M
rgreen@unl.edu
GREEN, Rosalyn .... 405-744-9153.. 385 G
rosalyn.green@okstate.edu
GREEN, Rudolph, H .... 305-284-4636.. 114 H
r.green3@miami.edu
GREEN, Ruvain .... 845-352-5852.. 340 F
GREEN, Samantha .... 973-720-2107.. 298 G
greens19@wpunj.edu
GREEN, Sandy, B .... 864-488-8348.. 430 H
sgreen@limestone.edu
GREEN, Satasha .... 773-995-3764.. 136 M
sgreen34@csu.edu
GREEN, Sean-Michael .... 203-932-7157.... 90 A
smgreen@newhaven.edu
GREEN, Shawn .... 215-717-6415.. 421 D
sgreen@uarts.edu
GREEN, Shirley .... 602-787-6604.... 14 E
shirley.green@paradisevalley.edu
GREEN, Stacy .... 207-974-4679.. 203 J
sgreen@emcc.edu
GREEN, Susan .... 734-432-5595.. 237 D
sgreen@madonna.edu
GREEN, Susan .... 802-635-1308.. 486 B
susan.green@jsc.edu
GREEN, Teresa .... 806-716-2205.. 465 G
tgreen@southplainscollege.edu
GREEN, Teresa .... 806-894-9611.. 465 G
tgreen@southplainscollege.edu
GREEN, Tica, D .... 336-272-7102.. 344 G
tica.green@greensboro.edu
GREEN, Tiffany .... 256-539-8161...... 4 F
GREEN, Tim .... 256-549-8601...... 3 M
tgreen@gadsdenstate.edu
GREEN, Timothy, M .... 615-248-1378.. 447 F
tgreen@trevecca.edu
GREEN, Tom .... 216-421-7491.. 366 G
tgreen@cia.edu
GREEN, Tracey .... 315-498-2532.. 325 G
greent@sunyocc.edu
GREEN, Tracie .... 209-384-6000.... 52 E
tracie.green@mccd.edu
GREEN, Tracy, A .... 440-366-4073.. 371 H
GREEN, Tracy, S .... 804-523-5789.. 497 C
tgreen@reynolds.edu
GREEN, Vashba .... 813-880-8013.. 109 A
vgreen@sbtampa.com
GREEN, Walter .... 678-359-5733.. 122 E
walterg@gordonstate.edu
GREEN, Wayne .... 334-974-5700...... 3 A
wgreen@ccal.edu
GREEN, Wayne, A .... 845-938-3419.. 529 C
8sgs@usma.edu
GREEN, William .... 423-614-8240.. 441 B
wgreen@leeuniversity.edu.edu
GREEN, William, S .... 305-284-2006.. 114 H
wgreen@miami.edu
GREEN COWLES, Maria ... 610-647-4400.. 406 B
mcowles@immaculata.edu
GREEN-HAMANN,
Matthew .... 207-992-4951.. 202 I
green-hamannm@husson.edu
GREEN-QUARLES,
Ryanne .... 916-361-1660.... 36 E
rgreen@carrington.edu
GREEN-YOUNG, Brian ..... 405-208-5759.. 184 G
brian.green-young@spst.edu

GREENAN, Jennie .... 309-692-4092.. 147 I
jgreenan@midstate.edu
GREENBAUM, Yvonne ..... 856-415-2138.. 295 D
ygreenbaum@rcgc.edu
GREENBERG, Aaron .... 561-237-7915.. 104 O
agreenberg@lynn.edu
GREENBERG, David .... 212-854-4446.. 311 E
david.greenberg@columbia.edu
GREENBERG, Mark .... 360-650-3051.. 509 E
mark.greenberg@wwu.edu
GREENBERG,
Raymond S .... 512-499-4201.. 475 K
rgreenberg@utsystem.edu
GREENBERG, Roberta ...... 718-933-6700.. 321 I
rgreenbe@monroecollege.edu
GREENBERG, Scott, B ..... 508-626-4550.. 221 E
sgreenberg@framingham.edu
GREENBERG, Yeshaya ..... 305-534-7050.. 113 F
GREENBLATT,
Austria Jazmin .... 718-522-9073.. 304 D
agreenblatt@asa.edu
GREENE, Allen .... 716-645-3454.. 331 C
ub-athleticdirector@buffalo.edu
GREENE, Andrew, S .... 717-867-6200.. 408 F
greene@lvc.edu
GREENE, Brenda .... 718-270-4949.. 309 B
bgreene@mec.cuny.edu
GREENE, Cary .... 910-695-3781.. 353 A
greenec@sandhills.edu
GREENE, Christina .... 910-362-7074.. 348 A
cgreene@cfcc.edu
GREENE, Clark .... 401-456-8000.. 425 E
cgreene@ric.edu
GREENE, Clark, M .... 401-456-8000.. 425 E
cgreene@ric.edu
GREENE, Dale .... 706-542-4741.. 128 E
wdgreene@uga.edu
GREENE, David, A .... 207-859-4604.. 202 G
david.greene@colby.edu
GREENE, Doug .... 641-782-1324.. 177 B
greene@swcciowa.edu
GREENE, Dwaine .... 502-863-8030.. 188 I
president@georgetowncollege.edu
GREENE, Eric .... 269-965-3931.. 236 A
greenee@kellogg.edu
GREENE, Gayle .... 919-866-5143.. 353 I
dggreene@waketech.edu
GREENE, Gloria .... 256-824-6000..... 8 F
gloria.green@uah.edu
GREENE, Jason .... 256-824-6736..... 8 F
jason.greene@uah.edu
GREENE, Jeff W .... 606-474-3298.. 188 L
jgreene@kcu.edu
GREENE, Jessica, A .... 617-552-3111.. 216 C
jessica.greene.2@bc.edu
GREENE, Joseph, J .... 401-598-1038.. 425 B
jgreene@jwu.edu
GREENE, Julia .... 860-512-3372.... 86 E
jgreene@manchestercc.edu
GREENE, Karen, L .... 614-234-5685.. 373 B
kgreene@mccn.edu
GREENE, Ken, S .... 252-334-2019.. 346 F
ken.greene@macuniversity.edu
GREENE, Kimberly .... 714-556-3610.... 73 B
kimberly.greene@vanguard.edu
GREENE, Lori .... 317-940-6086.. 159 K
lgreene@butler.edu
GREENE, Michael .... 870-248-4000.... 19 H
mike.greene@blackrivertech.edu
GREENE, Michaelyn .... 936-633-5215.. 451 D
mgreene@angelina.edu
GREENE, Mike .... 480-732-7146.... 13 O
mike.greene@cgc.edu
GREENE, Myra .... 864-388-8351.. 430 G
mgreene@lander.edu
GREENE, Patricia .... 843-521-4117.. 434 A
pagreene@uscb.edu
GREENE, Peggy .... 503-399-6031.. 390 E
peggy.greene@chemeketa.edu
GREENE, Perry .... 516-877-4041.. 303 B
greene@adelphi.edu
GREENE, Richard .... 504-278-6418.. 196 I
rgreene@nunez.edu
GREENE, Ryan .... 206-296-6260.. 507 E
greener@seattleu.edu
GREENE, Sarah, E .... 717-867-6985.. 408 F
sgreene@lvc.edu
GREENE, Shelley, W .... 336-633-0174.. 352 B
swgreene@randolph.edu
GREENE, Tawana .... 870-460-1026.... 23 D
jonesta@uamont.edu
GREENE, Thomas, G .... 916-484-8211.... 51 A
greenet@arc.losrios.edu
GREENE, Thomas, G .... 503-943-7105.. 396 B
greene@up.edu
GREENE,
Thomas Christopher ..... 802-828-8613.. 485 E
thomas.greene@vcfa.edu
GREENE, Timothy, D .... 315-655-7377.. 306 H
tdgreene@cazenovia.edu

GREENE, Timothy, J .... 269-387-2378.. 243 H
tim.greene@wmich.edu
GREENE, Tom .... 718-636-3787.. 326 E
tgreene@pratt.edu
GREENE, Tracy .... 605-688-5248.. 437 F
tracy.greene@sdstate.edu
GREENE, Travis .... 661-255-1050.... 30 E
tgreene@calarts.edu
GREENE, Vanessa .... 616-395-7800.. 235 F
greene@hope.edu
GREENE-RAINEY, Velva ... 484-365-7335.. 409 B
vgrainey@lincoln.edu
GREENFELD, Shia .... 718-782-7070.. 338 J
swg@utsny.edu
GREENFIELD, Brenda, T .. 315-470-6683.. 334 E
bgreenfield@esf.edu
GREENFIELD, Helga .... 404-270-6425.. 128 A
hgreenfield@spelman.edu
GREENFIELD, Ilene .... 973-278-5400.. 305 B
igl@berkeleycollege.edu
GREENFIELD, Ilene .... 973-278-5400.. 289 F
igl@berkeleycollege.edu
GREENFIELD, Marriane .... 404-527-4520.. 118 F
mgreenfield@carver.edu
GREENFIELD, Meg .... 504-278-6424.. 196 I
mgreenfield@nunez.edu
GREENGART, Eli .... 410-484-7200.. 210 A
egreengart@nirc.edu
GREENHALGH, Jill .... 651-779-3338.. 249 A
jill.greenhalgh@century.edu
GREENHALGH, Mark .... 714-992-7042.... 54 H
mgreenhalgh@fullcoll.edu
GREENHAW, David, M .... 314-918-2620.. 265 A
dgreenhaw@eden.edu
GREENHAW, Eric .... 479-524-7285.... 20 H
egreenhaw@jbu.edu
GREENHOUSE, Jeremy .... 413-755-4524.. 224 G
jgreenhouse@stcc.edu
GREENING, Kris .... 870-743-3000.... 21 C
kgreening@northark.edu
GREENING, RK .... 920-686-6238.. 519 H
rk.greening@sl.edu
GREENLAND, Nicole .... 510-436-1462.... 46 E
greenland@hnu.edu
GREENLAND, William ...... 773-702-7433.. 156 D
greenland@uchicago.edu
GREENLAW, David, E ...... 407-303-7894.... 95 C
dave.greenlaw@adu.edu
GREENLEAF, Maxine .... 662-254-3577.. 260 A
max.greenleaf@mvsu.edu
GREENLEE, Carmen, M ... 207-725-3286.. 202 F
cgreenle@bowdoin.edu
GREENLEE, Lisa .... 580-477-7702.. 389 I
lisa.greenlee@wosc.edu
GREENLEE, Pam .... 815-939-5211.. 150 I
pgreenl@olivet.edu
GREENLEE, Zach .... 314-744-7639.. 268 F
greenleez@mobap.edu
GREENO, Darren .... 360-416-7729.. 507 G
darren.greeno@skagit.edu
GREENO, Jimmie .... 215-972-2303.. 413 L
jgreeno@pafa.edu
GREENO, John, G .... 412-396-6575.. 403 A
greenoj@duq.edu
GREENSLADE, Ernestine .. 978-556-3862.. 224 D
egreenslade@necc.mass.edu
GREENSLADE-SMITH,
Toni .... 614-292-8266.. 375 A
greenslade-smith.1@osu.edu
GREENSTEIN, Benjamin .. 319-895-4251.. 171 A
bgreenstein@cornellcollege.edu
GREENSTEIN, David .... 212-353-4198.. 311 G
davidg@cooper.edu
GREENSTEIN, Kerry .... 352-787-7660.... 96 F
kgreenstein@beaconcollege.edu
GREENSTREET, Robert, C 414-229-4016.. 520 D
bobg@uwm.edu
GREENTHAL, Joseph, T ... 607-587-3938.. 334 G
greentjt@alfredstate.edu
GREENUP, Troy .... 562-907-4287.... 75 B
greenup@whittier.edu
GREENWADE, Gabrielle ... 281-487-1170.. 469 F
ggreenwade@txchiro.edu
GREENWALD, J. Patrick .. 716-888-8216.. 306 F
greenwal@canisius.edu
GREENWALD, Lorraine .... 631-420-2479.. 335 E
lorraine.greenwald@farmingdale.edu
GREENWALD, Nicole .... 206-876-6100.. 507 D
ngreenwald@theseattleschool.edu
GREENWALD, Reesa .... 973-275-2828.. 297 A
reesa.greenwald@shu.edu
GREENWALD, Richard ..... 718-951-3136.. 307 D
greenwald@brooklyn.cuny.edu
GREENWALT, Riane, B .... 618-650-2852.. 155 A
rgreenw@siue.edu
GREENWAY, Adam .... 502-897-4043.. 192 D
agreenway@sbts.edu
GREENWAY, Doug .... 605-995-3056.. 436 C
doug.greenway@mitchelltech.edu
GREENWAY, Janet .... 605-995-7194.. 436 C
janet.greenway@mitchelltech.edu

GREENWAY, Kimberly ..... 256-765-4248...... 9 C
kagreenway@una.edu
GREENWAY, Lidell .... 229-468-2240.. 130 A
lidell.greenway@wiregrass.edu
GREENWELL, Brian .... 330-490-7282.. 380 J
bgreenwell@walsh.edu
GREENWELL, Joseph, D .. 510-642-6770.... 68 M
deanofstudents@berkeley.edu
GREENWOOD, Anita .... 978-934-4605.. 221 A
anita_greenwood@uml.edu
GREENWOOD, Brandon ... 501-370-5317..... 21 G
bgreenwood@philander.edu
GREENWOOD, Gail .... 423-472-7141.. 445 E
ggreenwood@clevelandstatecc.edu
GREENWOOD, Kevin .... 614-947-6095.. 369 A
kevin.greenwood@franklin.edu
GREENWOOD, Nichole .... 801-832-2027.. 483 D
nhg@westminstercollege.edu
GREENWOOD-BLACKSHEAR,
Sheila .... 410-706-2281.. 211 F
sheila.blackshear@umaryland.edu
GREER, Amy .... 585-292-3010.. 321 J
agreer@monroecc.edu
GREER, Bobby, T .... 864-488-8251.. 430 H
bgreer@limestone.edu
GREER, Charles .... 951-827-3093.... 70 B
charles.greer@ucr.edu
GREER, Chelsea .... 251-380-4195...... 7 D
cgreer@shc.edu
GREER, Christine, G .... 906-227-1700.. 239 B
cgreer@nmu.edu
GREER, Colleen .... 218-755-2988.. 248 M
cgreer@bemidjistate.edu
GREER, James .... 325-793-4882.. 461 F
jgreer@mcm.edu
GREER, Jennifer .... 205-348-4890...... 8 D
jdgreer@ua.edu
GREER, Jody .... 260-665-4105.. 167 E
greerj@trine.edu
GREER, Karla, J .... 972-860-7173.. 456 D
kgreer@dcccd.edu
GREER, Kevin .... 417-626-1234.. 269 K
greer.kevin@occ.edu
GREER, M. Bradley .... 864-429-8728.. 434 F
greerm@mailbox.sc.edu
GREER, Melodie .... 267-502-2407.. 398 J
melodie.greer@brynathyn.edu
GREER, Rebecca .... 914-360-6220.. 322 A
rgreer@montefiore.org
GREER, Sheree .... 606-474-3186.. 188 L
sgreer@kcu.edu
GREER, Sherman, D .... 901-333-4101.. 447 B
sdgreer@southwest.tn.edu
GREER, T. Richard .... 585-594-6160.. 327 D
greerr@roberts.edu
GREER, William, B .... 423-461-8710.. 442 K
bgreer@milligan.edu
GREGERSEN, Denise .... 707-545-3647.... 28 C
denise@berginu.edu
GREGERSON,
Robert (Bob) .... 239-590-7156.. 110 L
rgregerson@fgcu.edu
GREGG, Carla .... 712-274-5463.. 175 C
gregg@morningside.edu
GREGG, Chris, S .... 651-962-6390.. 256 C
csgregg@stthomas.edu
GREGG, Claire .... 864-455-8209.. 434 D
cgregg@ghs.org
GREGG, Cody .... 956-872-2528.. 465 H
cgregg@southtexascollege.edu
GREGG, Ellen .... 970-351-2877.... 84 C
ellen.gregg@unco.edu
GREGG, Gerald, A .... 503-943-7161.. 396 B
gregg@up.edu
GREGG, Karla .... 417-447-6966.. 270 A
greggk@otc.edu
GREGG, Kelly .... 954-262-4335.. 105 J
kgregg1@nova.edu
GREGG, Michael, J .... 817-552-3700.. 460 E
lpyun@tku.edu
GREGG, Phyllis .... 312-362-8850.. 139 C
pgregg@depaul.edu
GREGG, Robert, S .... 609-652-4542.. 297 C
robert.gregg@stockton.edu
GREGG, Virginia .... 518-276-6524.. 327 B
greggv@rpi.edu
GREGGS, Rob .... 405-682-7877.. 385 D
rgreggs@occc.edu
GREGOIRE, David, P .... 518-564-2090.. 334 A
gregoidp@plattsburgh.edu
GREGOIRE, JR., Paul, E . 504-282-4455.. 198 H
pgregoire@nobts.edu
GREGOIRE, Tom .... 614-292-9426.. 375 A
gregoire.5@osu.edu
GREGOR, Candy .... 919-497-3330.. 346 B
cgregor@louisburg.edu
GREGOR, Lynn, D .... 860-253-3163.... 86 A
lgregor@asnuntuck.edu
GREGORI-GAHAN, Heidi . 812-465-1248.. 168 E
gahan@usi.edu
GREGORIO, Kyle .... 918-293-5210.. 386 B
kylelg@okstate.edu
GREGOROWICZ, Stephen 609-586-4800.. 292 D
gregoros@mccc.edu
GREGORY, Alison .... 570-321-4082.. 409 F
gregory@lycoming.edu
GREGORY, Anne .... 260-982-5285.. 165 M
GREGORY, Brent .... 662-246-6302.. 259 B
bgregory@msdelta.edu
GREGORY, Carolyn .... 216-368-5276.. 365 B
carolyn.gregory@case.edu
GREGORY, Charles .... 630-829-6009.. 135 F
cgregory@ben.edu
GREGORY, Charles, J ...... 207-741-5643.. 203 M
cgregory@smccme.edu
GREGORY, Christine .... 212-517-0562.. 320 C
cgregory@mmm.edu
GREGORY, Christopher ... 508-626-4510.. 221 E
cgregory@framingham.edu
GREGORY, Dan .... 320-308-2192.. 252 A
ddgregory@stcloudstate.edu
GREGORY, Dan .... 512-313-3000.. 455 F
daniel.gregory@concordia.edu
GREGORY, Darlene .... 334-386-7108...... 3 I
dgregory@faulkner.edu
GREGORY, David .... 615-366-4403.. 444 D
david.gregory@tbr.edu
GREGORY, David, B .... 615-366-4430.. 444 D
david.gregory@tbr.edu
GREGORY, David, L .... 606-783-5100.. 191 H
d.gregory@moreheadstate.edu
GREGORY, Denise .... 205-726-2725...... 6 E
djgregor@samford.edu
GREGORY, Derek .... 570-961-7839.. 407 B
gregoryd@lackawanna.edu
GREGORY, Ellen, D .... 859-846-6046.. 191 G
egregory@midway.edu
GREGORY, Jeffery .... 570-961-7868.. 407 B
gregoryj@lackawanna.edu
GREGORY, Katherine .... 515-294-6162.. 169 G
gregoryk@iastate.edu
GREGORY, Lisa .... 217-875-7200.. 152 C
lgregory@richland.edu
GREGORY, Margot, L ...... 480-222-9207..... 17 B
m.gregory@scnm.edu
GREGORY, Melissa .... 240-567-5036.. 209 E
melissa.gregory@montgomerycollege.edu
GREGORY, Patrick .... 334-386-7259...... 3 I
pgregory@faulkner.edu
GREGORY, Paula .... 417-208-0632.. 266 E
pgregory@kcumb.edu
GREGORY, Rhonda .... 615-230-3668.. 447 C
rhonda.gregory@volstate.edu
GREGORY, Rich .... 818-909-5517..... 52 A
rgregory@tms.edu
GREGORY, Steve .... 906-635-2182.. 236 J
sgregory@lssu.edu
GREGORY, Tiffany .... 662-915-5026.. 261 B
tlgregor@olemiss.edu
GREGORY, Tom, F .... 570-326-3761.. 413 O
tgregory@pct.edu
GREGORY, Tony .... 864-424-8000.. 434 F
gregorga@mailbox.sc.edu
GREGORY, Travis .... 760-750-4954..... 34 D
tgregory@csusm.edu
GREGORY, Trisha .... 301-687-4201.. 212 F
tgregory@frostburg.edu
GREGORYK, Kerry .... 515-271-1665.. 171 H
kerry.gregoryk@dmu.edu
GREGORYK, Michael, D .. 909-274-4230..... 53 C
mgregoryk@mtsac.edu
GREGSON, Donald .... 210-690-9000.. 458 I
dgregson@hallmarkuniversity.edu
GREIFE, Alice, L .... 660-543-4450.. 273 C
greife@ucmo.edu
GREIFFENDORF, OP,
Mary Agnes .... 615-256-5486.. 438 F
smagreiffendorf@tn-op.org
GREIG, Carl .... 903-223-3062.. 469 C
carl.greig@tamut.edu
GREIG, Judith, M .... 650-508-3503..... 54 J
jgreig@ndnu.edu
GREIL, Stan .... 405-733-7488.. 387 I
sgreil@rose.edu
GREIM, Jeffrey .... 413-565-1000.. 215 A
jgreim@baypath.edu
GREIMAN, Judith .... 631-632-4418.. 332 A
judith.greiman@stonybrook.edu
GREINER, Cathleen .... 949-451-5565..... 65 F
cgreiner@ivc.edu
GREINER, Mary .... 641-269-4818.. 172 I
greinerm@grinnell.edu
GREINER, Melissa .... 262-595-2404.. 520 F
greinerm@uwp.edu
GREINER, Ruta .... 440-375-7224.. 371 E
rgreiner@lec.edu
GREINER, Stephanie .... 515-271-1386.. 171 H
stephanie.greiner@dmu.edu
GREINER, Stephen, G .... 304-336-8000.. 513 F
stephen.greiner@westliberty.edu
GREINER, Susan, L .... 336-322-2245.. 351 H
sue.greiner@piedmontcc.edu
GRELLSON, Mona, S .... 651-631-5390.. 256 A
msgrellson@unwsp.edu
GREMILLION, Henry .... 504-619-8500.. 198 A
hgremi@lsuhsc.edu
GREMMELS,
Gillian (Jill), S .... 704-894-2160.. 343 I
jigremmels@davidson.edu
GRENDER, Teresa .... 606-368-6044.. 186 B
teresagrender@alc.edu
GRENIER, Kyle .... 617-236-4446.. 218 G
kgrenier@fisher.edu
GRENIER, Tina .... 701-671-2612.. 361 F
tina.grenier@ndscs.edu
GRENNAN, Jon .... 845-451-1323.. 312 C
j_grenna@culinary.edu
GRENOT-SCHEYER,
Marquita .... 562-985-4513..... 33 B
marquita.grenot-scheyer@csulb.edu
GRENTZ, Jennifer .... 602-243-8030..... 14 I
jennifer.grentz@southmountaincc.edu
GRESCH, Mary .... 206-685-3710.. 508 E
mgresch@uw.edu
GRESH, Colleen .... 860-701-5030..... 88 D
gresh_c@mitchell.edu
GRESHAM, John .... 314-792-6308.. 266 F
gresham@kenrick.edu
GRESHAM, Jonathan .... 423-636-7300.. 447 G
jgresham@tusculum.edu
GRESHAM, Loren, P .... 405-491-6300.. 388 A
lgresham@snu.edu
GRESHAM, Susan .... 812-535-5121.. 166 K
sgresham@smwc.edu
GRESS, Lori .... 320-308-5937.. 252 B
lgress@sctcc.edu
GRESS, Michael .... 812-888-4176.. 169 A
mgress@vinu.edu
GRESS, Vicky .... 217-333-4493.. 157 A
gress@illinois.edu
GRESSLEY, Jerry, A .... 260-359-4052.. 161 O
jgressley@huntington.edu
GRETCH, Jim .... 406-791-5320.. 278 G
jim.gretch@ugf.edu
GRETZ, Dan .... 715-634-4790.. 517 C
dgretz@lco.edu
GRETZINGER, Jerry .... 315-792-7100.. 336 C
ggretzinger@sunypoly.edu
GREUFE, Sandra .... 641-648-4611.. 173 K
sandra.greufe@iavalley.edu
GREVE, Debbie .... 620-235-4206.. 184 C
dgreve@pittstate.edu
GREVE, Jennifer .... 402-844-7062.. 282 B
jenniferg@northeast.edu
GREVI, Laura .... 914-337-9300.. 311 F
laura.grevi@concordia-ny.edu
GREVING, John .... 402-465-2486.. 281 K
jgreving@nebrwesleyan.edu
GREW-GILLEN, Cheryl .... 701-777-4200.. 360 C
cheryl.grewgillen@und.edu
GREWAL, Daman .... 707-654-1727..... 33 D
dgrewal@csum.edu
GREWAL, Parwinder .... 956-882-6701.. 476 E
parwinder.grewal@utrgv.edu
GREY, Erin .... 307-382-1647.. 527 C
egrey@westernwyoming.edu
GREY, Kimberly .... 314-392-2241.. 268 F
grey@mobap.edu
GREY, Margaret .... 203-785-2393..... 90 D
margaret.grey@yale.edu
GREY, Pam .... 650-949-6193..... 44 A
greypam@fhda.edu
GREY, Thomasina .... 505-786-4186.. 300 E
tgrey@navajotech.edu
GREYDANUS, John .... 541-737-9099.. 393 H
john.greydanus@oregonstate.edu
GREYWATER, Brigitte .... 701-662-1546.. 361 E
brigitte.greywater@lrsc.edu
GRIBB, Molly .... 608-342-1561.. 521 A
gribbm@uwplatt.edu
GRIBBEN, Les .... 212-817-7470.. 308 A
lgribben@gc.cuny.edu
GRIBBIN, David .... 478-289-2047.. 120 C
dgribbin@ega.edu
GRIBBLE, Kari .... 608-663-2305.. 516 F
kgribble@edgewood.edu
GRIBBLE, Scott .... 308-632-6933.. 282 H
GRIBBLE, Shannon, L .... 301-687-7588.. 212 F
slgribble@frostburg.edu
GRIBBONS, Barry .... 661-362-5500..... 40 A
barry.gribbons@canyons.edu
GRIBLIN, Diana .... 316-942-4291.. 183 I
griblind@newmanu.edu
GRICE, Brittany .... 805-437-3608..... 32 B
brittany.grice@csuci.edu
GRICE, Ronnie, D .... 785-532-1131.. 182 D
raker@ksu.edu
GRICE, Vivian, D .... 803-641-3550.. 433 G
viviang@usca.edu
GRIDLEY, Lisa .... 310-577-3000..... 75 H
admissions@yosan.edu
GRIDLEY, Madison .... 206-592-3212.. 504 E
mgridley@highline.edu
GRIECO, Stephen .... 215-885-2360.. 409 G
sgrieco@manor.edu
GRIEGER, Mary .... 414-425-8300.. 519 F
mgrieger@shsst.edu
GRIEGO, Orlando .... 815-740-3452.. 157 F
ogriego@stfrancis.edu
GRIEP, Mary .... 507-786-3055.. 254 P
griep@stolaf.edu
GRIER, Douglas, L .... 630-466-7900.. 157 K
dgrier@waubonsee.edu
GRIER, Ed, A .... 804-827-1062.. 496 D
egrier@vcu.edu
GRIER, Frank, O .... 334-833-4005...... 4 D
fgrier@hawks.huntingdon.edu
GRIER, Judith .... 757-789-1753.. 497 A
jgrier@es.vccs.edu
GRIER, Lauri .... 909-748-8390..... 71 K
lauri_grier@redlands.edu
GRIESBACH, Scott .... 715-232-1334.. 521 D
griesbachs@uwstout.edu
GRIESHEIMER, Tina .... 303-797-5901..... 76 J
tina.griesheimer@arapahoe.edu
GRIESSE, Sarah .... 612-330-1489.. 244 I
griesse@augsburg.edu
GRIEVE, Cathy .... 303-871-2397..... 84 B
cgrieve@du.edu
GRIEVE, Kimberly .... 605-677-5331.. 437 A
kimberly.grieve@usd.edu
GRIFFEL, Michael, M .... 541-346-2667.. 395 G
mgriffel@uoregon.edu
GRIFFIIN-SOBEL, Joyce ... 315-464-3921.. 332 C
griffinj@upstate.edu
GRIFFIN, Adrian .... 718-260-5050.. 309 C
agriffin@citytech.cuny.edu
GRIFFIN, Bert .... 502-585-9911.. 192 E
bgriffin@spalding.edu
GRIFFIN, Cathy .... 908-526-1200.. 295 A
cathy.griffin@raritanval.edu
GRIFFIN, Clifton, P .... 410-677-0050.. 213 A
cpgriffin@salisbury.edu
GRIFFIN, Courtney, L .... 334-727-8011...... 8 A
GRIFFIN, Dale, M .... 405-585-5700.. 385 B
dale.griffin@okbu.edu
GRIFFIN, Dan .... 731-661-5120.. 448 A
dgriffin@uu.edu
GRIFFIN, Daniel .... 315-312-2250.. 333 D
daniel.griffin@oswego.edu
GRIFFIN, Deborah .... 510-659-6151..... 55 B
dgriffin@ohlone.edu
GRIFFIN, Donitha .... 334-876-9302...... 4 A
GRIFFIN, Donitha .... 334-876-9302...... 4 A
dgriffin@wccs.edu
GRIFFIN, Elaine .... 615-966-5818.. 441 F
elaine.griffin@lipscomb.edu
GRIFFIN, Ellen .... 973-655-3123.. 293 A
griffinel@mail.montclair.edu
GRIFFIN, SR., Ervin, V ..... 252-536-7217.. 350 C
egriffin518@halifaxcc.edu
GRIFFIN, Hayden .... 252-737-1026.. 356 C
griffino@ecu.edu
GRIFFIN, Heather .... 502-895-3411.. 191 F
hgriffin@lpts.edu
GRIFFIN, Jacquelyn, H ...... 864-977-7081.. 431 G
jackie.griffin@ngu.edu
GRIFFIN, Janie .... 503-491-6701.. 392 F
janie.griffin@mhcc.edu
GRIFFIN, Jason .... 567-661-2692.. 376 D
jason_griffin@owens.edu
GRIFFIN, Jean .... 704-216-6129.. 346 A
jgriffin@livingstone.edu
GRIFFIN, Jeff .... 765-455-9339.. 163 A
griffon0@purdue.edu
GRIFFIN, Jeff, D .... 504-816-8018.. 198 H
jgriffin@nobts.edu
GRIFFIN, Joan .... 805-493-3555..... 31 C
griffin@callutheran.edu
GRIFFIN, Joel .... 864-941-8446.. 432 A
griffin.j@ptc.edu
GRIFFIN, Jonathan .... 602-429-4912..... 16 E
jgriffin@ps.edu
GRIFFIN, Justin, D .... 804-524-3186.. 499 G
jdgriffin@vsu.edu
GRIFFIN, Karen .... 813-253-7002.. 102 R
kgriffin@hccfl.edu
GRIFFIN, Karen .... 636-584-6575.. 264 M
karen.griffin@eastcentral.edu
GRIFFIN, Kate .... 757-233-8785.. 500 E
agriffine@vwc.edu
GRIFFIN, Larry .... 252-399-6331.. 341 P
lcgriffin@barton.edu
GRIFFIN, Larry .... 901-375-4400.. 442 F
larrygriffin@midsouthchristian.edu
GRIFFIN, Leslie .... 662-846-4400.. 257 E
lgriffin@deltastate.edu
GRIFFIN, Lisa .... 229-217-4144.. 127 G
lgriffin@southernregional.edu
GRIFFIN, Lonnie .... 912-408-3024.. 126 G
lfgriffin@savannahtech.edu

GROOMS, David 808-984-3376 132 D grooms@hawaii.edu
GROOT, Joycelyn 714-241-6323 39 E jgroot@coastline.edu
GROPACK, Stacy 516-299-2486 319 C stacy.gropack@liu.edu
GROPEN, Laura 760-744-1150 56 F lgropen@palomar.edu
GROPP, Douglas, M 214-528-8600 463 L
GROPP, Jonathan 864-622-6014 427 B jgropp@andersonuniversity.edu
GROPPER, Daniel 561-297-3629 110 K dgropper@fau.edu
GRORUD, Kelley 608-663-2200 516 F kgrorud@edgewood.edu
GROS, Kathy, R 504-865-3237 198 E kgros@loyno.edu
GROSBY, Karen 954-262-5885 105 J grosby@nsu.nova.edu
GROSCH, Darren 310-665-6994 55 E dgrosch@otis.edu
GROSE, Kay 304-865-6230 511 C kay.grose@ovu.edu
GROSHANS, David, E 308-635-6105 283 D groshans@wncc.edu
GROSOVSKY, Andrew 617-287-5775 220 G andrew.grosovsky@umb.edu
GROSPITCH, Eric 785-670-2100 185 H eric.grospitch@washburn.edu
GROSS, Anne 303-871-3382 84 B agross@du.edu
GROSS, Bryan, J 413-782-1233 229 E bryan.gross@wne.edu
GROSS, Candace 870-512-7716 19 C candace_gross@asun.edu
GROSS, Carla, E 717-691-6027 410 J cgross@messiah.edu
GROSS, Cynthia, A 240-895-4382 210 E cagross@smcm.edu
GROSS, Dana 507-786-3624 254 P grossd@stolaf.edu
GROSS, Daryl, J 323-343-3080 33 C dgross4@calstatela.edu
GROSS, Dolores 915-831-6484 457 H dgross2@epcc.edu
GROSS, Erik 603-862-1584 288 C erik.gross@unh.edu
GROSS, Laura 518-255-5626 334 D grossll@cobleskill.edu
GROSS, Linda 517-884-1350 237 I grossl@msu.edu
GROSS, Michael 732-987-2373 292 A mgross@georgian.edu
GROSS, Michael 508-362-2131 223 C mgross@capecod.edu
GROSS, Michael, L 610-921-7672 396 H mgross@albright.edu
GROSS, Michelle 414-847-3262 518 D michellegross@miad.edu
GROSS, Michelle, R 410-951-3610 212 E mgross@coppin.edu
GROSS, Monika 301-860-4091 212 D mgross@bowiestate.edu
GROSS, Natalie 914-337-0700 329 K ngross@sarahlawrence.edu
GROSS, Peter 503-251-5709 396 C pgross@uws.edu
GROSS, Scott 606-487-3528 189 E scott.gross@kctcs.edu
GROSS, Susan 201-216-8142 297 B susan.gross@stevens.edu
GROSS, Tim 770-426-2658 124 B tgross@life.edu
GROSS-GRAY, Shelley, J 615-353-3259 446 E shelley.gross-gray@nscc.edu
GROSSE, Kerry 414-955-8874 518 A kegrosse@mcw.edu
GROSSE, Mike 502-451-0815 193 B mgrosse@sullivan.edu
GROSSI, OSB, Anthony 724-537-4554 419 A anthony.grossi@email.stvincent.edu
GROSSI, Deann 312-777-8665 142 G dgrossi@aii.edu
GROSSINGER, Harvey 202-651-5000 92 C harvey.grossinger@gallaudet.edu
GROSSKOPF, John 850-973-1601 105 H grosskopfj@nfcc.edu
GROSSMAN, David 714-992-7046 54 H dgrossman@fullcoll.edu
GROSSMAN, LuAnn 605-331-6738 438 A luann.grossman@usiouxfalls.edu
GROSSMAN, Miriam 845-425-1370 325 F
GROSSMAN, Pam 215-898-7014 421 E grossman@gse.upenn.edu
GROSSMAN, Richard, G 603-535-2425 288 F rggrossman@plymouth.edu
GROSSMAN, Ruth 732-414-2834 298 N ytcbks@gmail.com
GROSSMAN, Susan 312-915-7024 146 G sgrossm@luc.edu
GROSSO, Andrew 262-646-6510 518 G agrosso@nashotah.edu
GROSSO, Michael 626-571-8811 72 E michaelg@uwest.edu
GROSSO, Michael 360-486-8868 506 G michael.grosso@stmartin.edu
GROSZ, Julae 423-697-4721 445 D julae.grosz@chattanoogastate.edu
GROSZ, Ken 701-228-5403 361 D ken.grosz@dakotacollege.edu
GROSZ, Tanya, L 651-286-7453 256 A tlgrosz@unwsp.edu
GROTE, Lisa 605-626-2521 437 D lisa.grote@northern.edu
GROTH, Charlie 215-968-8285 399 A charlie.groth@bucks.edu
GROTH, Clayton 608-249-6611 516 M cgroth@herzing.edu
GROTH, Dennis 812-855-8783 162 F vpue@indiana.edu
GROTH, Kathy 219-464-5114 168 F kathy.groth@valpo.edu
GROTRIAN, James 402-457-2335 280 J jgrotrian@mccneb.edu
GROTTON, Nancy 503-253-3443 393 D ngrotton@ocom.edu
GROTZINGER, John, P 626-395-6005 30 H grotz@gps.caltech.edu
GROUNDS, Cynthia 785-749-8418 181 E cynthia.grounds@bie.edu
GROVE, Amber 208-376-7731 132 H agrove@boisebible.edu
GROVE, Dana 817-515-4506 467 A dana.grove@tccd.edu
GROVE, Daryl 563-425-5311 177 D groved@uiu.edu
GROVE, Doug 949-214-3434 41 F doug.grove@cui.edu
GROVE, Kathy, M 641-422-4382 175 E grovekat@niacc.edu
GROVE, Laurie 717-396-7188 420 C grove@stevenscollege.edu
GROVE, Luke, J 515-574-1062 173 F grove@iowacentral.edu
GROVE, Shannon, D 814-886-6391 411 C sgrove@mtaloy.edu
GROVE, Warren 513-244-4465 373 C warren.grove@msj.edu
GROVER, Barbara 801-957-4434 483 A barbara.grover@slcc.edu
GROVER, Carol, N 315-279-5252 318 C cgrover@keuka.edu
GROVER, Josh 352-638-9773 96 F jgrover@beaconcollege.edu
GROVER, Rajiv 901-678-3633 445 C rgrover@memphis.edu
GROVER, Susan, S 757-221-3846 488 F ssgrov@wm.edu
GROVER-BISKER, Edna 573-341-6170 274 B egroverb@mst.edu
GROVER-ROOSA, Janice 307-382-1701 527 C jgrover@westernwyoming.edu
GROVES, Allen, W 434-924-7429 495 H awg8vd@virginia.edu
GROVES, Christine 614-251-4613 374 I grovesc@ohiodominican.edu
GROVES, Danford, F 910-272-3335 352 E dgroves@robeson.edu
GROVES, Doris 309-438-7304 143 B dfgrove@ilstu.edu
GROVES, Jason 325-674-2646 449 J jason.groves@acu.edu
GROVES, Jay 309-438-5631 143 B jrgrove@ilstu.edu
GROVES, Jeffrey 909-621-8122 46 A groves@hmc.edu
GROVES, Kathleen, H 585-395-2317 332 E kgroves@brockport.edu
GROVES, Kathy 573-592-1106 275 G kathy.groves@williamwoods.edu
GROVES, Robert 517-884-1008 237 I grovesr@msu.edu
GROVES, Robert, M 202-687-6400 92 E provost@georgetown.edu
GROVES, William 937-769-1348 363 F bgroves@antioch.edu
GROVES, William 937-769-1348 363 E bgroves@antioch.edu
GROVES-SCOTT, Victoria 501-450-3175 24 G vickigs@uca.edu
GROW, David 801-274-3280 483 C dgrow@wgu.edu
GROW, Tamara, J 660-562-1146 269 J tammi@nwmissouri.edu
GROWNS, Richard, O 501-977-2024 24 B growns@uaccm.edu
GROZA, Adam 909-687-1450 44 H adamgroza@gs.edu
GRUBB, Dan 910-592-8081 352 H dgrubb@sampsoncc.edu
GRUBB, David 504-816-4024 195 B dgrubb@dillard.edu
GRUBB, Derek 970-542-3158 81 H derek.grubb@morgancc.edu
GRUBB, Geoffrey, J 419-824-3818 371 I ggrubb@lourdes.edu
GRUBB, Josh 276-326-4208 487 F jgrubb@bluefield.edu
GRUBB, Lillie 620-223-2700 181 A lillieg@fortscott.edu
GRUBBS, Steve 800-422-2418 96 E sgrubbs@baymedical.org
GRUBE, M. Marshall 423-439-4219 444 F grube@etsu.edu
GRUBE, Sean 816-235-8719 273 F grubes@umkc.edu
GRUBER, Carol 215-646-7300 404 G gruber.c@gmercyu.edu
GRUBER, Christopher, J 704-894-2710 343 I chgruber@davidson.edu
GRUBER, Darlene 610-917-1414 422 C d_gruber@valleyforge.edu
GRUBER, Jay 202-687-7014 92 E jg1502@georgetown.edu
GRUBER, Thomas 504-671-6480 196 D tgrube@dcc.edu
GRUBY, Elizabeth 773-878-3752 153 E egruby@staugustine.edu
GRUEN, Kris 802-322-1721 483 H kris.gruen@goddard.edu
GRUENDLER, Donny 323-860-1188 53 G donnyg@mi.edu
GRUENDLER, Donny 323-462-1384 53 G donnyg@mi.edu
GRUENIG, Gwendolyn 907-450-8190 10 E gdgruenig@alaska.edu
GRUENING, Kyle 715-365-4446 524 C gruening@nicoletcollege.edu
GRUESER, Suzanna 213-624-1200 43 J sgrueser@fidm.edu
GRUGAN, Megan, O 215-951-6841 416 G gruganm@philau.edu
GRUHLER, Sarah 360-992-2406 502 E sgruhler@clark.edu
GRUICHICH, Dawn 480-732-7050 13 O dawn.gruichich@cgc.edu
GRULKE, Kimmi 928-226-4343 12 N kimmi.grulke@coconino.edu
GRUNBLATT, Akiva 718-268-4700 326 L
GRUND, Faye 419-520-2602 363 J fgrund@ashland.edu
GRUNDEN, Jennifer, J 302-857-1040 91 C jgrunden@dtcc.edu
GRUNDER, Mark 989-358-7317 230 G grunderm@alpenacc.edu
GRUNDHAUSER, Tony 651-523-2219 247 A agrundhauser01@hamline.edu
GRUNDIG, John 863-680-6212 101 E jgrundig@flsouthern.edu
GRUNDY, Jeffrey, W 973-596-2451 293 D jeffrey.w.grundy@njit.edu
GRUNDY, Marc, A 423-236-2875 444 B magrundy@southern.edu
GRUNER, Celeste 704-878-4321 351 D cgruner@mitchellcc.edu
GRUNINGER, Sandra 212-686-9040 340 D sgruninger@woodtobecoburn.edu
GRUNKLEE, David 319-296-4042 173 B david.grunklee@hawkeyecollege.edu
GRUNLOH, Jean Anne 217-234-5329 145 D jgrunloh@lakeland.cc.il.us
GRUNOW, Tamie, L 513-556-1015 379 A grunowtl@ucmail.uc.edu
GRUNWALD, Gerald 215-503-8982 420 E gerald.grunwald@jefferson.edu
GRUNWALD, James, R 507-354-8221 247 J grunwajr@mlc-wels.edu
GRUS, Shannon, M 636-584-6505 264 M shannon.grus@eastcentral.edu
GRUSHINSKI, Alberta 570-945-8373 406 H alberta.grushinski@keystone.edu
GRUSKA, Julie 320-363-3395 254 N jgruska@csbsju.edu
GRUSKA, Julie, E 320-363-3395 245 I jgruska@csbsju.edu
GRUSKIN, Adrienne 212-463-0400 337 I adrienne.gruskin@touro.edu
GRUSKOS, Cynthia 732-224-2204 289 I cgruskos@brookdalecc.edu
GRUSZKA, Bill 678-466-4351 119 A billgruska@clayton.edu
GRUTKOWSKI, Marc 814-838-7673 403 G mgrutkowski@fortisinstitute.edu
GRUTZKUHN, Bill 301-846-2452 207 F wgrutzkuhn@frederick.edu
GRUVER, Wendy 903-886-5140 468 D wendy.gruver@tamuc.edu
GRZESIAK, Michael, P 724-503-1001 422 H mgrzesiak@washjeff.edu
GRZYBOWSKI, Mark, J 815-224-0393 143 C mark_grzybowski@ivcc.edu
GRZYWACZ, Norberto, M 202-687-5603 92 E norberto@georgetown.edu
GSCHWEND, Richard 217-875-7200 152 C rqschwend@richland.edu
GSTALDER, Steven 203-773-0129 85 C sgstalder@albertus.edu
GUADALUPE, Raúl 787-993-8867 537 G raul.guadalupe@upr.edu
GUADALUPE, Sarahi 787-276-0130 537 H sarahi.guadalupe@upr.edu
GUADALUPE, Yvonne 787-766-1717 536 B yguadalupe@suagm.edu
GUAJARDO, Dan 918-495-7707 386 H dguajardo@oru.edu
GUAJARDO, George 210-486-3736 450 D gguajardo41@alamo.edu
GUAJARDO, Nicole, R 757-594-8069 488 E nguajard@cnu.edu
GUAMAN, Luis 203-857-7025 87 B lguaman@norwalk.edu
GUAN, Sharon 773-325-7726 139 C xguan@depaul.edu
GUARASCI, Richard 718-390-3131 339 F guarasci@wagner.edu
GUARD, Louis 315-781-3309 316 C guard@hws.edu
GUARIGLIA, Carolyn, L 315-255-1743 306 G guarigliac@cayuga-cc.edu
GUARIGLIA, Daniel, M 716-286-8431 324 E dmg@niagara.edu
GUARIN-KLEIN, Natalia 718-951-5696 307 D nataliag@brooklyn.cuny.edu
GUARINO, Mindy 708-344-4700 146 D mguarino@lincolntech.edu
GUARNIERI, Reid 440-375-7480 371 E rguarnieri@lec.edu
GUASCONI, Joseph 973-378-2643 297 A joseph.guasconi@shu.edu
GUAY, Sheila 401-323-6324 424 K sguay@bryant.edu
GUBAN, Philip 440-943-7600 377 A pguban@dioceseofcleveland.org
GUBAN, Philip 440-943-7676 377 A pguban@dioceseofcleveland.org
GUBAN, Philip 440-943-7600 377 A pguban@dioceseofcleveland.org
GUBBINS, Jean, E 216-368-5557 365 B jeg2@case.edu
GUBKIN, Llora 661-654-2221 32 A lgubkin@csub.edu
GUBLER, Seth 435-652-7571 482 A sgubler@dixie.edu
GUCKAVAN, Joseph 215-489-2361 402 A joseph.guckavan@delval.edu
GUCKERT, Donald, J 319-335-1201 169 H don-guckert@uiowa.edu
GUDUR, Jaganmohan 303-458-4050 82 L jgudur@regis.edu
GUDVANGEN, John 860-685-2543 90 C jgudvangen@wesleyan.edu
GUDVANGEN, John, E 303-871-4857 84 B john.gudvangen@du.edu
GUECO, Allan 818-766-8151 41 C agueco@concorde.edu
GUELICH, Julie 952-358-8156 251 A julie.guelich@normandale.edu
GUENARD, Erik, M 906-932-4231 234 C erikg@gogebic.edu
GUENARD, Hayward 434-544-8168 491 F guenard_h@lynchburg.edu
GUENGERICH, Colleen 575-835-5525 300 G cguengerich@admin.nmt.edu
GUENTER-SCHLESINGER, Sue 360-650-3307 509 E sue.guenter-schlesinger@wwu.edu
GUENTHER, Thomas 847-543-2264 138 C tguenther@clcillinois.edu
GUENZLER-STEVENS, Marsha, A 301-314-8505 211 E mguenzle@umd.edu
GUERIN, David 318-257-4854 200 G dguerin@latech.edu
GUERIN, Donna 215-885-2360 409 G dguerin@manor.edu
GUERIN, Thomas, B 513-556-2389 379 A tom.guerin@uc.edu
GUERNSEY, Thomas, F 619-961-4272 68 A guernsey@tjsl.edu
GUERRA, Blanca 210-567-2621 477 D guerrabe@uthscsa.edu
GUERRA, Elizabeth 909-469-5418 74 K guerra@westernu.edu
GUERRA, Elizabeth 214-860-2202 456 E eguerra@dcccd.edu
GUERRA, Jennifer 903-586-2518 460 A jguerra@jacksonville-college.edu
GUERRA, JR., Juan, M 214-648-2400 478 C juan.guerra@utsouthwestern.edu
GUERRA, Luis 510-436-1516 46 E guerra@hnu.edu

GUERRA, Manuel .... 503-365-4684.. 390 E
manuel.guerra@chemeketa.edu
GUERRA, Michael .... 510-628-8031.... 49 A
mguerra@lincolnuca.edu
GUERRA, Nancy .... 949-824-6094.... 69 C
nguerra1@uci.edu
GUERRA, Olivia .... 972-860-8065.. 456 C
oguerra@dcccd.edu
GUERRA, Sabra .... 254-968-9770.. 467 F
sguerra@tarleton.edu
GUERRA, Yvonne .... 210-486-4339.. 450 C
yguerra6@alamo.edu
GUERRA GAIER, Norma .. 512-245-2645.. 471 F
ng14@txstate.edu
GUERRERO, Bertha, M ..... 671-735-5638.. 529 G
boardoftrustees@guamcc.edu
GUERRERO, Daniel .... 425-640-1058.. 503 E
daniel.guerrero@edcc.edu
GUERRERO, Daniel, G ..... 310-206-6382.... 69 D
dguerrero@athletics.ucla.edu
GUERRERO, Dolores .... 361-593-2717.. 469 A
dolores.guerrero@tamuk.edu
GUERRERO, Jennifer .... 609-984-1588.. 297 F
jguerrero@tesu.edu
GUERRERO, John .... 670-237-6805.. 530 D
john.guerrero@marianas.edu
GUERRERO, Ken .... 909-884-8891.... 41 D
GUERRERO, Larry .... 575-492-2107.. 302 M
lguerrero@usw.edu
GUERRERO, Omar .... 787-857-3600.. 533 I
oguerrero@br.inter.edu
GUERRERO, Philip, C .... 671-735-5640.. 529 G
philip.guerrero2@guamcc.edu
GUERRERO, Rico .... 559-324-6481.... 67 A
rico.guerrero@scccd.edu
GUERRERO, Roberto .... 210-509-8080.. 470 B
rguerrero@thsu.edu
GUERRERO, Tammy .... 219-989-2675.. 166 F
tsguerre@pnw.edu
GUERRERO, Tim .... 303-410-2429.... 82 K
tguerrero@redstone.edu
GUERRERO, Tracy .... 670-237-6714.. 530 D
tracy.guerrero@marianas.edu
GUERRERO, William, C ..... 203-773-8516.... 85 C
wguerrero@albertus.edu
GUERRERO-LONGORIA,
Marissa .... 956-721-5416.. 460 F
marissa.longoria@laredo.edu
GUERRETTE, Leslie .... 207-741-5715.. 203 M
lguerrette@smccme.edu
GUERRIERO, William .... 480-732-7012.... 13 O
william.guerriero@cgc.edu
GUERTIN, Donna .... 413-565-1000.. 215 A
dguertin@baypath.edu
GUESS, Melissa .... 310-660-3492.... 42 J
mguess@elcamino.edu
GUEST, Charles .... 251-460-6261...... 9 E
cguest@southalabama.edu
GUEST, Denise .... 540-891-3040.. 497 B
dguest@germanna.edu
GUEST, James .... 402-472-7488.. 282 M
jguest2@unl.edu
GUEST, James, H .... 845-368-7201.. 329 I
james.guest@use.salvationarmy.org
GUEST, Joshua .... 662-472-9023.. 258 B
jguest@holmescc.edu
GUEST, Lois, A .... 845-368-7220.. 329 I
lois.guest@use.salvationarmy.org
GUEST, Susan .... 870-633-4480.... 20 B
sguest@eacc.edu
GUETTI, Joan .... 973-761-9018.. 297 A
joan.guetti@shu.edu
GUEUERRA, Jonathan .... 305-809-3204.. 100 N
jonathan.gueuerra@fkcc.edu
GUEVARA, Christine .... 505-473-6652.. 302 A
christine.guevara@santafeuniversity.edu
GUFFEY, Larry, D .... 256-228-6001...... 5 I
ldguffey@nacc.edu
GUFFEY, Patti .... 828-669-8012.. 346 M
pguffey@montreat.edu
GUFFEY, Ryan .... 636-949-4475.. 266 J
rguffey@lindenwood.edu
GUGELCHUK, Gary .... 909-469-5381.... 74 K
gugelchuk@westernu.edu
GUGENHEIMER, Yirmiya . 718-853-8500.. 337 H
GUGGENHEIM, Joan .... 609-586-4800.. 292 D
guggenhj@mccc.edu
GUGLIELMO, B. Joseph ... 415-476-8010.... 70 D
guglielmoj@pharmacy.ucsf.edu
GUGLIELMO, David, R ..... 757-822-1177.. 498 H
dguglielmo@tcc.edu
GUGLIELMONI, Mark, J .. 203-254-4080.... 87 G
mguglielmoni@fairfield.edu
GUICE, Leslie, K .... 318-257-3785.. 200 G
guice@latech.edu
GUIDO, Deana .... 252-451-8244.. 351 F
dguido@nashcc.edu
GUIDO, Diane .... 626-812-3034.... 28 A
dguido@apu.edu
GUIDRY, Heather .... 504-821-5881.. 194 G
GUIGNI, Terry .... 707-256-7150.... 53 H
tguigni@napavalley.edu
GUILARTE, Tomas .... 305-348-2000.. 111 A
tomas.guilarte@fiu.edu
GUILBEAULT, Nancy, G .... 612-330-1169.. 244 I
guilbeau@augsburg.edu
GUILER, Douglas .... 352-365-3526.. 104 J
guilerd@lssc.edu
GUILES, Serena .... 802-287-8376.. 484 A
serena.guiles@greenmtn.edu
GUILFOILE, Patrick .... 715-232-2421.. 521 D
guilfoilep@uwstout.edu
GUILFORD, Renate, H ...... 703-993-2299.. 490 B
rguilfor@gmu.edu
GUILFOYLE, Michael, K .. 508-767-7331.. 214 F
mk.guilfoyle@assumption.edu
GUILIANO, Edward .... 516-686-7650.. 323 G
edwardg@nyit.edu
GUILLEN, Christian .... 707-826-3739.... 34 F
cg36@humboldt.edu
GUILLEN, George .... 281-283-3950.. 474 A
guillen@uhcl.edu
GUILLEN, Patrick, J .... 808-932-7348.. 131 E
GUILLETTE, Natalie, L ...... 802-656-4183.. 485 D
natalie.guillette@uvm.edu
GUILLIANI, Melissa .... 787-766-1717.. 536 B
mguilliani@suagm.edu
GUILLIOM, Allison .... 313-577-2230.. 243 F
dy9063@wayne.edu
GUILLORY, Abby .... 337-482-5811.. 201 D
abby@louisiana.edu
GUILLORY, Angela .... 225-578-2171.. 197 I
angelagu@lsu.edu
GUILLORY, Ann, V .... 201-559-6154.. 291 K
guillorya@felician.edu
GUILLORY, Christopher .... 225-771-4150.. 199 H
christopher_guillory@subr.edu
GUILLORY, Eli .... 225-771-2786.. 199 G
eli_guillory@subr.edu
GUILLORY, III, Eli, G .... 225-771-4741.. 199 H
eli_guillory@subr.edu
GUILLORY, Justin .... 360-676-2772.. 505 C
jguillory@nwic.edu
GUILLORY, Monique .... 973-290-4418.. 290 G
mguillory@cse.edu
GUILLORY, Tonya, L .... 202-806-5990.... 93 A
tguillory@howard.edu
GUILLOT, Sheila .... 409-984-6381.. 471 C
guillsr@lamarpa.edu
GUINAN, Mark, A .... 607-871-2909.. 303 F
guinan@alfred.edu
GUINARA, Angel .... 713-780-9777.. 451 A
info@acaom.edu
GUINEY, Julia .... 847-543-2218.. 138 C
jguiney@clcillinois.edu
GUINN, Lindsey .... 724-503-1001.. 422 H
lguinn@washjeff.edu
GUINN, Stephen .... 913-667-5700.. 179 K
sguinn@cbts.edu
GUINN, Traci, L .... 989-774-3945.. 232 D
guinn1tl@cmich.edu
GUION, John .... 916-278-7322.... 34 B
jguion@csus.edu
GUION, Kent .... 910-962-4084.. 358 D
guionw@uncw.edu
GUION-UTSLER, Judy .... 614-823-1409.. 376 C
jguionutsler@otterbein.edu
GUISER, Eric .... 724-938-4427.. 414 E
guiser@calu.edu
GUITERREZ-CALDWELL,
Jennifer, M .... 864-597-4043.. 435 C
guiterrezjm@wofford.edu
GUIZADO, Roy .... 909-469-5445.... 74 K
roygpac@westernu.edu
GUKICH, Doris, B .... 863-638-7261.. 115 C
doris.gukich@warner.edu
GULACHEK, Bernard .... 612-625-9867.. 255 H
bernard@umn.edu
GULARTE, Mary Anne .... 760-674-3777.... 40 B
mgularte@collegeofthedesert.edu
GULAS, Charles .... 314-529-9625.. 267 B
cgulas@maryville.edu
GULATI, Allison .... 484-664-3182.. 411 D
agulati@muhlenberg.edu
GULATI, Poonam .... 713-221-8066.. 474 B
gulatip@uhd.edu
GULEFF, Virginia .... 707-468-3068.... 52 C
vguleff@mendocino.edu
GULEMBO, Kathleen .... 616-331-2400.. 234 F
gulembok@gvsu.edu
GULINO, Tracy .... 858-566-1200.... 42 D
tgulino@disd.edu
GULIUZZA, Frank .... 540-338-1776.. 492 H
GULLATT, Yvette .... 510-987-9504.... 68 L
yvette.gullatt@ucop.edu
GULLEDGE, Jim, E .... 704-463-3366.. 354 F
jim.gulledge@pfeiffer.edu
GULLICKSON, Janet .... 509-533-3535.. 503 A
janet.gullickson@sfcc.spokane.edu
GULLICKSON, Janet .... 509-533-3535.. 502 H
janet.gullickson@spokanefalls.edu
GULLICKSON, Marcia, A . 563-387-1400.. 174 L
gullicma@luther.edu
GULLION, Kevin .... 304-877-6428.. 510 F
kevin.gullion@abc.edu
GULLIXSON, Amy .... 715-232-5269.. 521 D
gullixsona@uwstout.edu
GULLO, Safawo .... 507-285-7143.. 251 I
safawo.gullo@rctc.edu
GULMON-HURI, Joy .... 206-934-4386.. 506 K
joy.gulmonhuri@seattlecolleges.edu
GULSTAD, Rita .... 660-248-6211.. 263 B
rgulstad@centralmethodist.edu
GUMBRIS, Janet .... 508-531-1341.. 221 C
jgumbris@bridgew.edu
GUMERMAN, George .... 928-523-3498.... 15 H
george.gumerman@nau.edu
GUMM, Eric .... 325-674-2212.. 449 J
gummj@acu.edu
GUMMER, Rhonda .... 502-213-2182.. 190 A
rhonda.gummer@kctcs.edu
GUMP, James, O .... 619-260-7847.... 72 B
honors@sandiego.edu
GUMP, Jared .... 304-424-8226.. 514 D
jared.gump@wvup.edu
GUMPPER, Marianne, L .. 203-254-4184.... 87 G
mgumpper@fairfield.edu
GUMZ, Diane, B .... 503-777-7560.. 394 I
diane.gumz@reed.edu
GUNASEKARAN,
Angappa .... 508-999-9187.. 220 H
agunasekaran@umassd.edu
GUNASEKARAN, Suresh .. 214-633-1500.. 478 C
suresh.gunasekaran@utsouthwestern.edu
GUNDERMANN, Thomas . 651-641-8271.. 246 B
gundermann@csp.edu
GUNDERSON, Garth, M .. 208-496-3000.. 132 J
gundersong@byui.edu
GUNDERSON, Gayle, C ... 303-963-3252.... 77 I
ggunderson@ccu.edu
GUNDERSON, Greg .... 816-584-6202.. 270 D
greg.gunderson@park.edu
GUNDERSON, Wendy, A . 972-377-1536.. 455 A
wgunderson@collin.edu
GUNDRUM, Peggy .... 847-214-7122.. 140 A
pgundrum@elgin.edu
GUNDY, Shannon .... 301-314-8757.. 211 E
sgundy@umd.edu
GUNKEL, John .... 973-353-5541.. 295 F
jgunkel@rutgers.edu
GUNKEL, John .... 973-353-5213.. 296 C
jgunkel@andromeda.rutgers.edu
GUNN, E. Anthony .... 336-342-4261.. 352 F
gunnt@rockinghamcc.edu
GUNN, George, A .... 530-221-4275.... 64 C
ggunn@shasta.edu
GUNN, J. Martyn .... 209-664-6635.... 34 E
jgunn@csustan.edu
GUNN, Karen .... 334-229-4301...... 1 D
kgunn@alasu.edu
GUNN, Michael .... 671-735-2292.. 530 B
gunnm@triton.uog.edu
GUNN, Rae .... 701-255-3285.. 362 E
rgunn@uttc.edu
GUNN, Stanley, T .... 512-223-1200.. 451 N
sgunn@austincc.edu
GUNN, Susan .... 616-698-7111.. 233 C
sgunn3@davenport.edu
GUNNELL, Juanita .... 704-922-2254.. 350 A
gunnell.juanita@gaston.edu
GUNNELS, Amanda .... 256-840-4113...... 6 H
agunnels@snead.edu
GUNNELS, Robert .... 870-574-4541.... 22 G
rgunnels@sautech.edu
GUNNING, Mary Jo .... 570-961-4724.. 409 H
gunning@marywood.edu
GUNNING-FRANCIS,
Leah .... 317-931-2306.. 160 B
lgunningfrancis@cts.edu
GUNNINK, Brett .... 406-994-2111.. 277 C
bgunnink@montana.edu
GUNOVICH, David, E .... 253-535-7151.. 505 G
gunovich@plu.edu
GUNS, Michael .... 608-663-6714.. 516 F
mguns@edgewood.edu
GUNSALUS, Robert .... 818-677-4400.... 34 A
robert.gunsalus@csun.edu
GUNSAULS, Darline .... 510-659-6269.... 55 B
dgunsauls@ohlone.edu
GUNSELMAN, Ken, D .... 252-334-2046.. 346 F
ken.gunselman@macuniversity.edu
GUNTER, Kathy .... 334-244-3343...... 2 A
kgunter1@aum.edu
GUNTER, Mary .... 479-968-0398.... 19 F
mgunter@atu.edu
GUNTER, Mary .... 479-964-3217.... 19 F
mgunter@atu.edu
GUNTER, Ree .... 203-837-8691.... 85 I
gunterr@wcsu.edu
GUNTER, Robert, E .... 304-896-7439.. 512 E
bob.gunter@southernwv.edu
GUNTER, Steve .... 828-766-1320.. 351 B
sgunter@mayland.edu
GUNTER, Valerie .... 315-781-3467.. 316 C
gunter@hws.edu
GUNTER-SMITH,
Pamela, J .... 717-815-1221.. 424 F
collegepresident@ycp.edu
GUNTHER, Amanda .... 724-805-2933.. 419 A
amanda.gunther@email.stvincent.edu
GUNTHER, Elisabeth .... 209-228-2406.... 70 A
egunther@ucmerced.edu
GUNTHER, Janet .... 270-707-3833.. 189 G
janet.gunther@kctcs.edu
GUNTHER, Karah, L .... 804-828-6879.. 496 D
klgunther@vcu.edu
GUNTHER, Mike .... 661-362-3536.... 40 A
mike.gunther@canyons.edu
GUNTHORPE, Sydney, D . 505-224-4427.. 299 F
sydney@cnm.edu
GUNZENHAUSER,
Bonnie .... 312-341-3500.. 152 H
GUO, Lan .... 816-415-5032.. 275 F
guol@william.jewell.edu
GUPCHUP, Gireesh, V ...... 618-650-5153.. 155 A
ggupchu@siue.edu
GUPTA, Akhi .... 401-598-1954.. 425 B
agupta@jwu.edu
GUPTA, Amar .... 212-346-1810.. 325 J
agupta@pace.edu
GUPTA, Mahendra, R .... 314-935-6344.. 274 N
guptam@wustl.edu
GUPTA, Sanjay .... 517-355-8377.. 237 I
gupta@broad.msu.edu
GUPTA, Sunil .... 212-346-8449.. 307 B
sbgupta@bmcc.cuny.edu
GURA, Daniel, T .... 813-253-6277.. 114 M
dgura@ut.edu
GURA, Michelle .... 909-558-4567.... 49 C
sm8026@bncollege.com
GURANOWSKI, Vicki .... 212-217-4100.. 314 B
vicki_guranowski@fitnyc.edu
GUREK, Shannon .... 413-538-2040.. 226 A
sgurek@mtholyoke.edu
GURLAND, Suzanne .... 802-443-5323.. 484 F
sgurland@middlebury.edu
GURLER, Dan .... 415-575-6125.... 30 G
dgurler@ciis.edu
GURLEY, LaShonda .... 419-772-3145.. 374 J
l-gurley@onu.edu
GURNARI, Barbara .... 408-498-5106.... 39 H
bgurnari@cogswell.edu
GURNEY, James, G .... 901-678-4637.. 445 C
jggurney@memphis.edu
GURRERI, Joseph .... 717-337-6304.. 404 C
jgurreri@gettysburg.edu
GURROLA, Jeannette .... 909-607-8632.... 38 I
jeanette.gurrola@cgu.edu
GURSKIS, Daniel, A .... 973-655-5104.. 293 A
gurskisd@mail.montclair.edu
GURTATOWSKI, Jill .... 859-985-3968.. 187 B
gurtowskij@berea.edu
GUSKIEWICZ, Kevin .... 919-962-3082.. 357 D
gus@email.unc.edu
GUSLER, William .... 610-902-8257.. 399 D
william.j.gusler@cabrini.edu
GUSSIN, Louise .... 410-888-9048.. 209 C
lgussin@muih.edu
GUST, Jonathan .... 610-519-6508.. 422 G
jonathan.gust@villanova.edu
GUSTAFSON, Amanda .... 706-396-8112.. 125 H
agustafson@paine.edu
GUSTAFSON, Anita, O .... 478-301-2915.. 124 D
gustafson_ao@mercer.edu
GUSTAFSON, Crandon ..... 617-262-5000.. 216 A
crandon.gustafson@the-bac.edu
GUSTAFSON, Dale .... 847-635-1880.. 150 G
dgustafs@oakton.edu
GUSTAFSON, Eric .... 508-626-4012.. 221 E
egustafson1@framingham.edu
GUSTAFSON, Eric, T .... 704-847-5600.. 355 J
egustafson@ses.edu
GUSTAFSON, Jacqueline . 951-552-8372.... 29 H
jgustafson@calbaptist.edu
GUSTAFSON, Linda, M ..... 906-932-4231.. 234 C
lindag@gogebic.edu
GUSTAFSON, Michael .... 507-389-5566.. 250 E
michael.gustafson-1@mnsu.edu
GUSTAFSON, Ralph .... 651-638-6122.. 244 L
r-gustafson@bethel.edu
GUSTAFSON, Steve .... 620-242-0424.. 183 C
gustafs@mcpherson.edu
GUSTAFSON, Terri .... 231-995-1076.. 239 C
tgustafson@nmc.edu
GUSTAFSON, Thomas, J . 802-656-4450.. 485 D
thomas.gustafson@uvm.edu
GUSTAS, Sherrie, A .... 716-839-8209.. 312 D
sgustas@daemen.edu
GUSTAVSON, Leif .... 503-352-1431.. 394 C
gustavson@pacificu.edu
GUSTITUS, Carole, R .... 570-348-6247.. 409 H
gustitusc@marywood.edu

GUSTWILLER, Douglas ... 812-488-2678.. 167 I
dg57@evansville.edu
GUSZCZA, Susie, C ... 617-373-2101.. 227 B
GUTELIUS, Harry ... 610-341-1729.. 403 B
hguteliu@eastern.edu
GUTENBERGER,
Thomas, C ... 804-287-8052.. 495 G
tgutenbe@richmond.edu
GUTER, Donald, J ... 713-646-1819.. 459 A
dguter@hcl.edu
GUTERMAN, Neil ... 773-702-1420.. 156 D
nguterman@uchicago.edu
GUTFREUND, Dina ... 718-252-6333.. 341 E
GUTFREUND,
Meir Chaim ... 718-252-6333.. 341 E
GUTGESELL, Tara ... 215-637-7700.. 405 J
tgutgesell@holyfamily.edu
GUTH, Erin ... 608-363-2175.. 515 G
guthe@beloit.edu
GUTH, Lori ... 309-467-6312.. 140 E
lguth@eureka.edu
GUTH, Virginia ... 847-628-1151.. 144 B
gguth@judsonu.edu
GUTH, Wendee ... 309-999-4656.. 141 F
wguth@icc.edu
GUTHIER, Mark, C ... 608-262-4463.. 519 K
mcguthier@wisc.edu
GUTHMAN, John, C ... 516-463-6791.. 316 D
john.c.guthman@hofstra.edu
GUTHMILLER, Janet ... 402-472-1344.. 283 A
janet.guthmiller@unmc.edu
GUTHRIE, Belinda ... 408-554-4113.... 63 E
bguthrie@scu.edu
GUTHRIE, Charles ... 415-338-2218.... 35 B
charlesg@sfsu.edu
GUTHRIE, Chris ... 615-322-9800.. 449 A
chris.guthrie@vanderbilt.edu
GUTHRIE, Edward, L ... 302-356-6870.... 91 I
edward.l.guthrie@wilmu.edu
GUTHRIE, Frederica ... 713-718-2335.. 459 B
frederica.guthrie@hccs.edu
GUTHRIE, Grant ... 601-318-6193.. 261 I
grant.guthrie@wmcarey.edu
GUTHRIE, Gregory ... 641-472-1125.. 175 A
gguthrie@mum.edu
GUTHRIE, James ... 785-864-7546.. 185 D
jguthrie@ku.edu
GUTHRIE, Lauren ... 877-248-6724.... 13 K
lguthrie@hmu.edu
GUTHRIE, Mindy ... 713-646-1797.. 459 A
mguthrie@hcl.edu
GUTHRO, Clement, P ... 207-859-5104.. 202 G
cpguthro@colby.edu
GUTIERREZ, Andrea ... 909-607-3451.... 38 I
andrea.gutierrez@cgu.edu
GUTIERREZ, Ann, E ... 956-326-2346.. 468 A
ann.gutierrez@tamiu.edu
GUTIERREZ, Anthony ... 805-546-3289.... 41 L
agutierr@cuesta.edu
GUTIERREZ, Ben ... 434-592-4886.. 491 D
bgutierrez@liberty.edu
GUTIERREZ, Brian, G ... 817-257-7815.. 469 G
brian.gutierrez@tcu.edu
GUTIERREZ, Daniel ... 505-428-1203.. 301 K
daniel.gutierrez@sfcc.edu
GUTIERREZ, Derrick ... 717-396-7833.. 413 M
dgutierrez@pcad.edu
GUTIERREZ, Diana ... 989-686-9434.. 233 I
dianagutierrez@delta.edu
GUTIERREZ, Dionne, K ... 714-879-3901.... 46 F
dkgutierrezr@hiu.edu
GUTIERREZ, Edna, I ... 787-720-1022.. 531 A
registrador@atlanticu.edu
GUTIERREZ, Eduardo ... 305-271-6555.... 95 E
GUTIERREZ, Felipe ... 310-665-6810.... 55 E
fgutierrez@otis.edu
GUTIERREZ, Gloria ... 408-741-2668.... 74 H
gloria.gutierrez@westvalley.edu
GUTIERREZ, Jack ... 402-562-1234.. 278 K
jgutierrez@cccneb.edu
GUTIERREZ, Javier ... 651-523-3076.. 247 A
jgutierrez@hamline.edu
GUTIERREZ, Juan ... 714-432-5725.... 39 G
jgutierrez@occ.cccd.edu
GUTIERREZ, Katie ... 219-989-1234.. 166 F
kgtz@pnw.edu
GUTIERREZ, Luis ... 509-865-8505.. 504 D
gutierrez_l@heritage.edu
GUTIERREZ, Manuel ... 510-780-4500.... 48 J
mgutierrez@lifewest.edu
GUTIERREZ, Martin ... 530-741-6939.... 76 D
mgutierr@yccd.edu
GUTIERREZ, Mary ... 650-738-4343.... 62 I
gutierrezm@smccd.edu
GUTIERREZ, Mary ... 361-593-2601.. 469 A
sm698@bncollege.com
GUTIERREZ, Michael, J ... 972-860-7196.. 456 D
mgutierrez@dcccd.edu
GUTIERREZ, Nancy, A ... 704-687-0081.. 358 A
ngutierr@uncc.edu
GUTIERREZ, Roberto ... 305-348-2494.. 111 A
robert.gutierrez@fiu.edu
GUTIERREZ, Roberto ... 541-880-2210.. 391 F
gutierrezr@klamathcc.edu
GUTIERREZ, Susan ... 707-664-2287.... 35 D
susan.gutierrez@sonoma.edu
GUTIERREZ, Tiffany ... 518-694-7254.. 303 C
tiffany.gutierrez@acphs.edu
GUTIERREZ, Tim ... 505-277-0963.. 302 F
tguiterr@unm.edu
GUTIERREZ-LOPEZ,
Leticia ... 657-278-3040.... 33 A
lgutierrez-lopez@fullerton.edu
GUTIERREZ-SANDOVAL,
Yvonne ... 562-908-3411.... 58 I
ygutierrez-sandoval@riohondo.edu
GUTKIND, Susan ... 510-659-6266.... 55 B
sgutkind@ohlone.edu
GUTKNECHT, June ... 239-590-1227.. 110 L
jgutknec@fgcu.edu
GUTKNECHT, Leah, K ... 319-273-2846.. 170 A
leah.gutknecht@uni.edu
GUTMANN, Amy ... 215-898-7221.. 421 E
president@upenn.edu
GUTOSKEY, David, P ... 410-543-6040.. 213 A
dpgutoskey@salisbury.edu
GUTSTEIN, Daniel ... 410-225-4254.. 209 B
dgutstein@mica.edu
GUTTENTAG,
Christoph, O ... 919-684-2898.. 343 J
christoph.guttentag@duke.edu
GUTTERUD, Linda ... 909-537-5142.... 34 C
linda.gutterud@csusb.edu
GUTTMAN, Minerva ... 201-692-2890.. 291 J
minerva_guttman@fdu.edu
GUTTMAN, Stephen, J ... 610-758-4204.. 408 H
sjg2@lehigh.edu
GUVENDIREN, Ali ... 781-239-2557.. 223 F
aguvendiren@massbay.edu
GUY, Elmer ... 505-786-4112.. 300 E
eguy@navajotech.edu
GUY, Gary ... 812-357-8208.. 167 B
gguy@saintmeinrad.edu
GUY, Georgina ... 949-582-4738.... 65 G
gguy@saddleback.edu
GUY, Kristen ... 650-433-3878.... 56 D
kguy@paloaltou.edu
GUY, Shawn ... 336-517-2209.. 342 B
sguy@bennett.edu
GUY-ANDERSON, Adrian . 504-816-4325.. 195 B
aguy@dillard.edu
GUY-SHEFTALL, Beverly .. 404-270-5624.. 128 A
bsheftall@spelman.edu
GUYDEN, Janet ... 318-247-3811.. 200 F
guydenj@gram.edu
GUYER, Kim ... 402-898-1000.. 279 G
kim_g@creativecenter.edu
GUYETTE, Daniel ... 269-387-5810.. 243 H
daniel.guyette@wmich.edu
GUYETTE, Randy ... 828-835-4253.. 353 G
rguyette@tricountycc.edu
GUYNES, Del ... 972-923-5437.. 466 D
dguynes@sagu.edu
GUYOL, Kate ... 314-792-7435.. 266 F
guyol@kenrick.edu
GUYTON, Deirdre ... 304-327-4569.. 512 P
dguyton@bluefieldstate.edu
GUYTON, Don ... 713-743-8000.. 473 E
dguyton@uh.edu
GUYTON, Duffy ... 901-751-8453.. 442 E
dguyton@mabts.edu
GUYTON, Sondra ... 910-879-5634.. 347 F
sguyton@bladencc.edu
GUZAUSKAS, Lauren ... 206-934-5484.. 506 K
lauren.guzauskas@seattlecolleges.edu
GUZDAR, Farida, P ... 443-518-3823.. 208 C
fguzdar@howardcc.edu
GUZELIMIAN, Ara ... 212-799-5000.. 318 A
GUZICK, David, S ... 352-733-1700.. 112 A
dguzick@ufl.edu
GUZMAN, Alejandro ... 818-523-9026.... 49 J
guzmana4@lamission.edu
GUZMAN, Andrew ... 213-740-7331.... 72 D
andrewgu@usc.edu
GUZMAN, Debora ... 210-434-6711.. 463 C
daguzman@lake.ollusa.edu
GUZMAN, John ... 718-782-2200.. 305 I
jguzman@boricuacollege.edu
GUZMAN, Juan ... 308-865-8127.. 282 L
guzmanj@unk.edu
GUZMAN,
Juan Johnny, C ... 830-591-7264.. 466 A
jcguzman@swtjc.edu
GUZMAN, Leslie Ann ... 787-746-1400.. 532 M
lguzman@huertas.edu
GUZMAN, Margo ... 209-588-5222.... 75 J
guzmanm@yosemite.edu
GUZMAN, Ruben ... 949-451-5220.... 65 F
rguzman@ivc.edu
GUZMAN, Tobias ... 970-351-1944.... 84 C
tobias.guzman@unco.edu
GUZMAN-LOPEZ, Evelyn . 787-480-2410.. 531 J
eguzman@sanjuanciudadpatria.com
GUZOFSKY, Rosalie ... 215-635-7300.. 404 D
rguzofsky@gratz.edu
GUZZARDO, Joseph ... 609-777-3083.. 297 F
jguzzardo@tesu.edu
GUZZI, Martin ... 607-778-5245.. 332 D
guzzimj@sunybroome.edu
GUZZO, Linda ... 860-906-5132.... 86 B
lguzzo@ccc.commnet.edu
GWALTNEY, Darrell ... 615-460-5552.. 438 J
darrell.gwaltney@belmont.edu
GWARTNEY, Kurt ... 918-270-6470.. 386 I
kurt.gwartney@ptstulsa.edu
GWAZDA, Edward ... 609-586-4800.. 292 D
gwazdae@mccc.edu
GWINNER, Kevin, P ... 785-532-7227.. 182 D
kgwinner@ksu.edu
GYAPONG, Samuel ... 478-825-6732.. 120 F
gyapongs@fvsu.edu
GYERTSON, David ... 859-858-2335.. 186 I
GYLLIN, John ... 407-708-4722.. 109 E
gyllinj@seminolestate.edu
GYMZIAK, Paul ... 603-623-0313.. 287 D
paulgymziak@nhia.edu
GYORKE, Allan ... 305-284-6101.. 114 H
a.gyorke@miami.edu

H

HA, Kevin ... 760-328-5554.... 52 B
HA, Viet, X ... 864-833-8193.. 432 B
vxha@presby.edu
HAAB, Melissa ... 251-575-8227...... 1 C
mhaab@ascc.edu
HAACK, Julie, A ... 563-333-6314.. 176 D
haackjuliea@sau.edu
HAACK, Kristen ... 617-521-2917.. 228 C
kristen.haack@simmons.edu
HAAG, Brandon ... 678-717-3885.. 128 F
brandon.haag@ung.edu
HAAK, Robert ... 330-569-5125.. 369 J
haakrd@hiram.edu
HAAKE, Anne ... 585-475-4786.. 327 E
arhics@rit.edu
HAAKENSON, Thomas, O 510-594-3655.... 29 K
thaakenson@cca.edu
HAAKONSEN, Alexis ... 203-392-5644.... 85 H
haakonsena1@southernct.edu
HAAN, Andrea ... 563-884-5447.. 176 C
andrea.haan@palmer.edu
HAAN, Fred ... 712-722-6050.. 171 J
fred.haan@dordt.edu
HAAN, Stanley, L ... 616-526-6442.. 232 A
haan@calvin.edu
HAAR, Jean ... 507-389-5445.. 250 E
jean.haar@mnsu.edu
HAAR, Scott ... 417-862-5700.. 262 M
shaar@bryancolleges.edu
HAARSMA, Jill ... 712-707-7100.. 176 B
jhaarsma@nwciowa.edu
HAAS, Bob ... 740-389-4636.. 372 B
haasr@mtc.edu
HAAS, Brenda ... 740-351-3299.. 377 C
bhaas@shawnee.edu
HAAS, Evelyn ... 612-767-7044.. 244 D
ev@alfredadler.edu
HAAS, Fritz ... 610-358-4541.. 411 E
haasf@neumann.edu
HAAS, Jesse ... 575-528-7548.. 301 C
jhaas@nmsu.edu
HAAS, Mark ... 517-355-5014.. 237 I
hass@finance.msu.edu
HAAS, Mary Ann ... 207-992-4900.. 202 I
haasm@husson.edu
HAAS, Mitch ... 503-251-5728.. 396 C
mhaas@uws.edu
HAAS, Nate ... 970-351-1763.... 84 C
nate.haas@unco.edu
HAAS, Nicole ... 718-951-5671.. 307 D
nicole@brooklyn.cuny.edu
HAAS, Ocki ... 417-865-2815.. 265 B
haaso@evangel.edu
HAAS, Sarah ... 573-518-2307.. 268 E
shaas@mineralarea.edu
HAAS, Stephen ... 800-371-6105.... 15 F
shaas@nationalparalegal.edu
HAAS, Sue ... 434-961-5229.. 498 C
shaas@pvcc.edu
HAAS, Thomas, J ... 616-331-2100.. 234 F
president@gvsu.edu
HAASE, Ryan ... 620-862-5252.. 178 F
rhaase@barclaycollege.edu
HAATVEDT, Chad ... 218-322-2444.. 249 G
chad.haatvedt@itascacc.edu
HABA, Jerry ... 972-721-5018.. 473 D
dhaba@udallas.edu
HABACKER, Laura ... 508-849-3447.. 214 E
lhabacker@annamaria.edu
HABEGER, Christian, M .. 864-379-8813.. 429 I
habeger@erskine.edu
HABEGGER, Thomas ... 614-287-5422.. 367 C
thabegge@cscc.edu
HABEGGER, Toni ... 509-359-6373.. 503 D
thabegger@ewu.edu
HABEL, Leah ... 406-771-4327.. 277 F
lhabel@gfcmsu.edu
HABER, Carole ... 504-865-5225.. 200 C
chaber@tulane.edu
HABER, Jessica ... 914-674-7457.. 320 G
jhaber@mercy.edu
HABER, Melanie ... 860-512-2803.... 86 E
mhaber@manchestercc.edu
HABERER, Ronald, J ... 716-888-8527.. 306 F
habererr@canisius.edu
HABERLE, Charles, J ... 401-865-1154.. 425 D
chaberle@providence.edu
HABERMAN, Melissa ... 608-243-6320.. 523 F
mhaberman@madisoncollege.edu
HABETZ, Pauline, M ... 713-500-8425.. 477 C
pauline.m.habetz@uth.tmc.edu
HABIB, Bob ... 757-352-4840.. 493 E
robehab@regent.edu
HABIB, Claudia ... 559-638-0300.... 67 D
claudia.habib@reedleycollege.edu
HABROCK, Marty ... 402-554-3408.. 283 B
mhabrock@unomaha.edu
HABSCHMIDT, Cathy ... 765-983-1772.. 160 G
habscca@earlham.edu
HABUCHMAI, Joseph ... 691-320-2480.. 529 F
jhabuchmai@comfsm.fm
HABUKI, Daniel, Y ... 949-480-4005.... 64 J
habuki@soka.edu
HABURSKY, Mary Jo ... 304-243-2233.. 515 C
maryjoh@wju.edu
HABURSKY, Stephen ... 304-243-4453.. 515 C
habursky@wju.edu
HACHE, Jason ... 952-829-2405.. 244 J
jason.hache@bethfel.org
HACK, Mary, C ... 609-984-1661.. 297 F
mhack@tesu.edu
HACKBARTH, Wade ... 608-785-9123.. 524 H
hackbarthw@westerntc.edu
HACKENBERG, Caitlin ... 407-646-2268.. 107 O
chackenberg@rollins.edu
HACKER, Carol, J ... 781-239-4220.. 214 G
hackerc@babson.edu
HACKER, Cheryl ... 740-351-3283.. 377 C
chacker@shawnee.edu
HACKERT, Marvin, L ... 512-232-3604.. 476 B
m.hackert@austin.utexas.edu
HACKET, JR., William, C 863-667-5004.. 109 L
wchacket@seu.edu
HACKETT, Amy, E ... 253-879-3140.. 508 D
ahackett@pugetsound.edu
HACKETT, Gail ... 804-828-1345.. 496 D
ghackett@vcu.edu
HACKETT, Keith ... 907-786-1250.... 10 F
khackett2@uaa.alaska.edu
HACKETT, Lelia ... 254-526-1293.. 454 A
lelia.hackett@ctcd.edu
HACKETT, Mary ... 707-826-3311.... 34 F
mary.hackett@humboldt.edu
HACKETT, Matthew ... 859-572-5198.. 192 B
hackettm2@nku.edu
HACKETT, Royce ... 229-931-2074.. 122 C
royce.hackett@gsw.edu
HACKETT, Timothy ... 510-436-2464.... 57 E
thackett@peralta.edu
HACKLE, Dale ... 850-973-1616.. 105 H
hackled@nfcc.edu
HACKLER, Gwen ... 405-789-6400.. 388 A
ghackler@snu.edu
HACKLER, Yolanda ... 316-322-3104.. 179 E
yhackler@butlercc.edu
HACKNEY, Carrie, M ... 202-806-7234.... 93 A
hackney@howard.edu
HACKNEY, James ... 617-373-2101.. 227 B
HACKWORTH, Joe ... 256-331-5335...... 6 A
joehackworth@nwscc.edu
HADDAD, Abdallah ... 843-349-2938.. 428 E
abdallah@coastal.edu
HADDAD, Amy, M ... 402-280-2164.. 279 H
amyhaddad@creighton.edu
HADDAD, Emily, A ... 207-581-1954.. 204 H
emily.haddad@maine.edu
HADDAD, Kamel ... 760-750-8034.... 34 D
khaddad@csusm.edu
HADDELAND, Patricia ... 503-883-2259.. 392 B
phaddel@linfield.edu
HADDOCK, Gregory ... 660-562-1145.. 269 J
haddock@nwmissouri.edu
HADDOCK, Jennifer ... 870-743-3000.... 21 C
jhaddock@northark.edu
HADDOCK, Jorge ... 617-287-7700.. 220 G
jorge.haddock@umb.edu
HADDON, Phoebe, A ... 856-225-6095.. 295 F
chancellor@camden.rutgers.edu
HADDON, Phoebe, A ... 856-225-6095.. 296 A
chancellor@camden.rutgers.edu
HADDOW, Deborah, E ... 607-733-2300.. 338 L
dhaddow@uscny.edu

HALCUMB, Cambrea 573-840-9658 273 A
chalcumb@trcc.edu

HALDANE, Susan 828-398-7176 347 D
susanehaldane@abtech.edu

HALDEMAN, Pam 310-954-4366 53 B
phaldeman@msmu.edu

HALDER, Pradeep 315-792-7100 336 C
phalder@sunypoly.edu

HALE, Barry 903-923-2020 457 G
bhale@etbu.edu

HALE, Bill 801-333-8100 480 G
bill.hale@eaglegatecollege.edu

HALE, David, B 804-289-8150 495 G
dhale2@richmond.edu

HALE, Don 404-413-3025 122 D
dhale@gsu.edu

HALE, Donald 864-503-7417 434 G
dhale@uscupstate.edu

HALE, Georgia 479-788-7030 23 A
georgia.hale@uafs.edu

HALE, Jeffery, L 918-540-6201 384 F
jhale@neo.edu

HALE, Jeffrey 605-688-5148 437 F
jeffrey.hale@sdstate.edu

HALE, Jerold, L 843-953-0760 428 G
halejl@cofc.edu

HALE, Kandi 207-941-7138 202 I
halek@husson.edu

HALE, Kara 620-431-2820 183 H
khale@neosho.edu

HALE, Kenneth 216-987-4251 367 E
kenneth.hale@tri-c.edu

HALE, Latoya 443-394-3377 93 F

HALE, Lloyd 816-604-4062 267 K
lloyd.hale@mcckc.edu

HALE, Mark 214-333-5503 455 J
markh@dbu.edu

HALE, Melina 773-702-2102 156 D
mhale@uchicago.edu

HALE, Philip, P 312-915-6494 146 G
phale@luc.edu

HALE, Quinn 509-574-4702 510 A
qhale@yvcc.edu

HALE, Richard 401-253-1040 426 B
rhale@rwu.edu

HALE, Ryan 941-408-1405 110 H
haler@scf.edu

HALE, Sheri 540-545-7240 494 B
shale2@su.edu

HALE, Sheryl 918-293-5130 386 B
sheryl.hale@okstate.edu

HALE, Susie 863-784-7132 109 G
susie.hale@southflorida.edu

HALE, Ted 860-906-5053 86 B
thale@ccc.commnet.edu

HALE, Tricia, A 229-333-5940 129 G
tahale@valdosta.edu

HALEEM, Ali 312-427-2737 143 G
ahaleem@jmls.edu

HALES, Cassie 319-352-8553 177 G
cassie.hales@wartburg.edu

HALES, Christie, C 434-949-1068 498 E
christie.hales@southside.edu

HALES, Mike 859-572-5207 192 B
halesm1@nku.edu

HALEY, Christopher 207-326-2232 204 C
christopher.haley@mma.edu

HALEY, Donna 678-839-6438 129 E
dhaley@westga.edu

HALEY, SR., James, P 301-405-5837 211 E
jhaley@umd.edu

HALEY, John 315-445-4520 318 E
haleyjr@lemoyne.edu

HALEY, John, R 315-445-4689 318 E
haleyjr@lemoyne.edu

HALEY, Ken 903-785-7661 463 E
khaley@parisjc.edu

HALEY, Lynn 931-372-3232 445 B
lhaley@tntech.edu

HALEY, Ted 508-767-7215 214 F
thaley@assumption.edu

HALEY, Terence 256-824-6674 8 F
terence.haley@uah.edu

HALEY, Thomas 402-280-1862 279 H
toh00008@creighton.edu

HALEY-THOMSON, Lisa 518-454-5102 311 B
thomsonl@strose.edu

HALEY-THOMSON, Lisa 518-337-5239 311 B
thomsonl@strose.edu

HALFMANN, Tina 612-244-2800 247 D
thalfmann@ipr.edu

HALFORD, Sharon 602-285-7434 14 F
sharon.halford@phoenixcollege.edu

HALGERSON, Carolyn 605-688-4695 437 F
carolyn.halgerson@sdstate.edu

HALGREN, Cara 701-777-2664 360 C
cara.halgren@und.edu

HALIBURTON, Tori 731-426-7500 440 K

HALICKI, Sannon 304-336-8075 513 F
shalicki@westliberty.edu

HALICKI, Shannon, D 304-336-8075 513 F
shalicki@westliberty.edu

HALIEMUN, Cynthia 217-228-5432 151 F
haliecy@quincy.edu

HALL, Alfred 901-435-1201 441 C
alfred_hall@loc.edu

HALL, Allyson 860-465-5283 85 G
hallall@easternct.edu

HALL, Amber, L 501-450-5371 24 G
amberh@uca.edu

HALL, Amy, J 540-674-3600 497 G
ahall@nr.edu

HALL, Anders, W 615-322-2451 449 A
anders.hall@vanderbilt.edu

HALL, Andy 423-585-6801 447 D
robert.hall@ws.edu

HALL, Andy 425-889-5212 505 E
andy.hall@northwestu.edu

HALL, Andy 423-585-6801 447 D
andy.hall@ws.edu

HALL, Ann 989-463-7411 230 F
hall@alma.edu

HALL, Becky 404-364-8469 125 F
bhall1@oglethorpe.edu

HALL, Benjamin 740-362-3448 372 D
bhall@mtso.edu

HALL, Betty 864-592-4942 432 H
hallb@sccsc.edu

HALL, Bobbie 404-527-5264 123 I
bhall@itc.edu

HALL, Bobby, L 806-291-3400 479 D
hallb@wbu.edu

HALL, Brad, R 406-338-5441 276 A
brad@bfcc.edu

HALL, C. Rick 706-771-4020 117 C
chall@augustatech.edu

HALL, Carol 734-432-5447 237 D
clhall@madonna.edu

HALL, Carrie 510-430-2050 52 J
cmilliga@mills.edu

HALL, Cassie 406-447-4572 276 B
chall@carroll.edu

HALL, Cathy 605-229-8453 436 H
cathy.hall@presentation.edu

HALL, Charles 252-335-3961 356 D
crhall@ecsu.edu

HALL, Charles, F 310-506-4532 56 J
charles.hall@pepperdine.edu

HALL, Cheryl 985-549-5312 201 C
chall@selu.edu

HALL, Chris 618-537-6833 147 F
chall@mckendree.edu

HALL, Cynthia 530-283-0202 43 G
chall@frc.edu

HALL, Daniel 502-852-6026 194 A
daniel.hall@louisville.edu

HALL, Daniel 763-424-0817 251 B
dhall@nhcc.edu

HALL, Daniel, B 323-241-5467 50 B
halldb@lasc.edu

HALL, Dave, M 757-481-5005 500 H

HALL, David 340-693-1000 539 C
dhall@uvi.edu

HALL, Deborah, P 828-884-8262 342 C
dphall@brevard.edu

HALL, Delinda 617-745-3869 218 A
delinda.hall@enc.edu

HALL, Delores 216-421-7423 366 G
dhall@cia.edu

HALL, Dennis 817-531-4872 472 F
dhall@txwes.edu

HALL, Derek 906-227-2716 239 B
halld@nmu.edu

HALL, Don 508-854-4515 224 E
dhall@qcc.mass.edu

HALL, Donald 580-581-5577 382 G
dhall@cameron.edu

HALL, Donald, E 610-758-4570 408 H
deh211@lehigh.edu

HALL, Elizabeth 856-415-2228 295 D
ehall@rcgc.edu

HALL, Ellis, F 317-738-8080 160 J
ehall@franklincollege.edu

HALL, Eric 978-232-2294 218 D
ehall@endicott.edu

HALL, George 859-442-4188 189 D
george.hall@kctcs.edu

HALL, Gregory 860-444-8608 529 A
gregory.hall@uscga.edu

HALL, Gwen 304-724-3700 510 E
ghall@apus.edu

HALL, Heather 630-617-3576 140 C
heatherh@elmhurst.edu

HALL, Heather 616-632-2457 231 A
heather.hall@aquinas.edu

HALL, Hollie, M 607-587-4200 334 G
hallhm@alfredstate.edu

HALL, Jack, C 386-312-4293 108 B
jackhall@sjrstate.edu

HALL, Jackie 606-487-3180 189 E
jackie.hall@kctcs.edu

HALL, James 251-381-3491 7 D
jhall@shc.edu

HALL, James 520-515-5329 12 L
bohall@cochise.edu

HALL, James, R 864-597-4351 435 C
halljr@wofford.edu

HALL, Jami 706-272-4428 119 H
jhall@daltonstate.edu

HALL, Jason 910-893-1291 342 F
hallj@campbell.edu

HALL, Jean 785-227-3380 178 J
hallje@bethanylb.edu

HALL, Jeffrey, B 706-419-1121 119 G
hall@covenant.edu

HALL, Jennifer 330-829-6644 379 F
halljene@mountunion.edu

HALL, Jennifer, S 417-865-2815 262 F
hallj@evangel.edu

HALL, Jessica 910-521-6571 358 C
jessica.hall@uncp.edu

HALL, Jill 863-297-1072 106 I
jhall@polk.edu

HALL, Jim 479-619-4182 21 D
jhall@nwacc.edu

HALL, Jim 631-420-2457 335 E
jim.hall@farmingdale.edu

HALL, Jim 940-397-4278 462 A
jim.hall@mwsu.edu

HALL, III, Jim 405-325-1700 389 B
tripp@ou.edu

HALL, John, A 214-768-3518 465 J
jhall@smu.edu

HALL, John, D 817-272-2102 476 A
jhall@uta.edu

HALL, Jon Mark 812-464-1846 168 E
jmhall@usi.edu

HALL, Joy Lin 918-343-7541 387 F
jhall@rsu.edu

HALL, Juanita 805-493-3951 31 C
jahall@callutheran.edu

HALL, Jyl 435-652-7544 482 A
hall@dixie.edu

HALL, Karla 502-213-2507 190 A
karla.hall@kctcs.edu

HALL, Karyn 936-468-3806 466 H
khall@sfasu.edu

HALL, Kathleen 937-255-6234 527 H
kathleen.hall@afit.edu

HALL, Kathleen, K 937-255-6234 527 H
kathleen.hall@afit.edu

HALL, Kathy 319-398-7650 174 I
khall@kirkwood.edu

HALL, Katie 614-292-2424 375 A
hall.738@osu.edu

HALL, Kelli 606-886-3863 189 A
kelli.hall@kctcs.edu

HALL, Kellie 701-477-7862 362 D
kmhall@tm.edu

HALL, Kenneth, L 570-484-2598 415 D
khall@lhup.edu

HALL, Kevin 651-603-6165 246 B
khall@csp.edu

HALL, Kim 360-416-7601 507 G
kim.hall@skagit.edu

HALL, Kim, B 865-251-1800 444 A
khall@southcollegetn.edu

HALL, Kimberly 614-287-2408 367 C
khall46@cscc.edu

HALL, Kristin, E 845-758-7531 304 F
hall@bard.edu

HALL, Kristy 276-523-2400 497 F
khall@me.vccs.edu

HALL, Larretta 701-255-3285 362 E
lhall@uttc.edu

HALL, Larry 828-328-7112 345 H
larry.hall@lr.edu

HALL, Lataria 559-925-3338 74 E
latariahall@whccd.edu

HALL, Laurie 716-829-7640 313 A
halla@dyc.edu

HALL, Lawrence 860-832-2298 85 F
halllaw@ccsu.edu

HALL, JR., Lawrence 615-327-5732 442 A
lhall@mmc.edu

HALL, Les 803-545-5048 433 F
judith.johnson@uscmed.sc.edu

HALL, Linda, M 585-292-2103 321 J
lhall38@monroecc.edu

HALL, Lisa 423-236-2900 444 B
lhwoodcock@southern.edu

HALL, Lori 207-741-5501 203 M
lhall@smccme.edu

HALL, Lori 419-448-3433 378 A
halla@tiffin.edu

HALL, Lori 503-594-3162 390 F
lori.hall@clackamas.edu

HALL, Louis, J 662-254-3384 260 A
ljhall@mvsu.edu

HALL, Lydia 936-294-3608 471 D
lth003@shsu.edu

HALL, Lyndon 252-257-1900 353 H
halll@vgcc.edu

HALL, Lynn 812-866-7385 161 C
hall@hanover.edu

HALL, Mark 918-495-7742 386 H
mhall@oru.edu

HALL, Mark 919-545-8043 348 D
mhall@cccc.edu

HALL, Mark 734-384-4261 238 C
mhall@monroeccc.edu

HALL, Mark 615-297-7545 438 F
hallm@aquinascollege.edu

HALL, Marlon, R 530-251-8820 48 E
mhall@lassencollege.edu

HALL, Mary 828-232-5109 357 C
mhall7@unca.edu

HALL, Matthew 805-893-8989 70 E
matthall@ucsb.edu

HALL, Matthew 502-897-4555 192 D
mhall@sbts.edu

HALL, Michael 302-736-2483 91 G
j.michael.hall@wesley.edu

HALL, Michael, R 336-841-9235 345 A
mhall@highpoint.edu

HALL, Michael, W 540-654-1025 495 C
mhall2@umw.edu

HALL, Michelle 985-549-2077 201 C
mhall@selu.edu

HALL, Michelle 404-364-8336 125 F
mhall@oglethorpe.edu

HALL, Nancy 312-939-0111 139 G

HALL, Nicole 312-629-6100 154 A
nhall1@saic.edu

HALL, Norman, D 618-664-7119 140 I
norm.hall@greenville.edu

HALL, Pamela 313-845-6410 235 D
phall@hfcc.edu

HALL, Pat 620-862-5252 178 F
pat.hall@barclaycollege.edu

HALL, Patricia 479-394-7622 22 B
phall@rmcc.edu

HALL, Patty 402-465-2237 281 K
phall@nebrwesleyan.edu

HALL, Paulakay 423-775-7308 439 B
phall7036@bryan.edu

HALL, Philip, D 843-792-8979 431 A
hallpd@musc.edu

HALL, Randolph, W 213-740-6709 72 D
rwhall@usc.edu

HALL, Raymond, D 810-762-3335 242 B
raydhall@umflint.edu

HALL, Ricardo, D 305-284-5353 114 H
rdhall@miami.edu

HALL, Richard 307-674-6446 526 M
rhall@sheridan.edu

HALL, Rickey 206-685-0518 508 E
vpomad@uw.edu

HALL, Robert 716-829-7657 313 A
hallrm@dyc.edu

HALL, Rodney 804-524-2954 499 G
rhall@vsu.edu

HALL, Ron 865-251-1800 444 A
rhall@southcollegetn.edu

HALL, Sandy 325-674-2273 449 J
halls@acu.edu

HALL, Stacy 706-865-2134 128 D
shall@truett.edu

HALL, Steven 501-212-6608 19 J
shall@cbc.edu

HALL, Steven 309-341-7823 145 A
shall@knox.edu

HALL, Steven 304-236-7620 512 E
steven.hall@southernwv.edu

HALL, Steven, A 617-358-0476 216 E
sahall@bu.edu

HALL, Susan 214-378-1609 456 A
shall@dcccd.edu

HALL, Susan 856-415-2185 295 D
shall@rcgc.edu

HALL, Tami 870-307-7000 21 A
tami.hall@lyon.edu

HALL, Tammy 501-279-4018 20 D
thall@harding.edu

HALL, Teresa 410-704-2332 213 B
thall@towson.edu

HALL, Terry 225-771-2552 200 A
thall@sulc.edu

HALL, Terry 415-561-1908 38 E
thall@ccsf.edu

HALL, Tim 410-455-2207 211 G
halltw@umbc.edu

HALL, Tim 308-535-3612 280 M
hallt@mpcc.edu

HALL, Timothy 914-674-7307 320 G
thall@mercy.edu

HALL, Tom 904-256-7715 103 D
thall5@ju.edu

HALL, Tracy 845-434-5750 336 H
thall@sullivan.suny.edu

HALL, Tracy 360-867-6205 503 G
hallt@evergreen.edu

HAMILTON, Theresa .... 601-857-3250.. 258 A
thhamilton@hindscc.edu
HAMILTON, Tina .... 512-313-3000.. 455 F
tina.hamilton@concordia.edu
HAMILTON, W. Kent .... 210-567-5001.. 477 D
hamiltonw@uthscsa.edu
HAMILTON, Wallace, O ... 405-789-7661.. 388 B
wallace.hamilton@swcu.edu
HAMILTON, William .... 352-588-6610.. 108 C
william.hamilton02@saintleo.edu
HAMILTON-GOLDEN,
Barbara .... 201-447-7113.. 289 E
bagolden@bergen.edu
HAMILTON SLANE,
Sandra .... 530-242-7799.... 64 D
sslane@shastacollege.edu
HAMLET, Michael .... 931-221-7179.. 444 E
hamletm@apsu.edu
HAMLETT, Melvin, R .... 731-426-7539.. 440 K
hamlett@lanecollege.edu
HAMLETT, Rebecca .... 816-415-7620.. 275 F
hamlettr@william.jewell.edu
HAMLETT, Willie .... 626-815-3890.... 28 A
whamlett@apu.edu
HAMLIN, Jessica .... 907-786-1288.... 10 F
jdhamlin@uaa.alaska.edu
HAMLIN, John .... 337-550-1233.. 197 K
jhamlin@lsue.edu
HAMLIN, Kelly .... 828-652-0629.. 351 C
khamlin@mcdowelltech.edu
HAMLIN, Lindsey .... 605-688-4154.. 437 F
lindsey.hamlin@sdstate.edu
HAMLIN, Lyn .... 201-200-3525.. 293 C
lhamlin@njcu.edu
HAMLIN, Michael, D .... 323-822-9700.... 68 B
michael.hamlin@touro.edu
HAMLIN, Toby .... 518-608-8218.. 314 A
thamlin@excelsior.edu
HAMM, Bernard, C .... 804-828-1233.. 496 D
bchamm2@vcu.edu
HAMM, Bradley, J .... 847-491-2045.. 150 F
bradely.hamm@northwestern.edu
HAMM, Dede .... 479-899-6928.... 21 D
chamm@nwacc.edu
HAMM, Gavin .... 318-247-3811.. 200 F
HAMM, Harlisha .... 212-817-7150.. 308 A
hhamm@gc.cuny.edu
HAMM, Jennifer .... 828-327-7000.. 348 C
jhamm@cvcc.edu
HAMM, Jolene .... 434-961-5301.. 498 C
jhamm@pvcc.edu
HAMM, Joy .... 912-344-2514.. 116 E
joy.hamm@armstrong.edu
HAMM, L, L .... 504-988-5462.. 200 C
lhamm@tulane.edu
HAMM, Leonard .... 410-951-3906.. 212 E
lhamm@coppin.edu
HAMM, Rod .... 620-947-3121.. 185 B
rodneyhamm@tabor.edu
HAMM, Tammy, S .... 423-439-4457.. 444 F
hammt@etsu.edu
HAMMACK, Becky .... 325-674-2265.. 449 J
rsh12a@acu.edu
HAMMACK, Mike .... 325-670-1278.. 458 J
mhammack@hsutx.edu
HAMME, Gary .... 321-674-8832.. 100 M
gary@fit.edu
HAMMEKE, Curtis .... 785-628-4050.. 180 I
chammeke@fhsu.edu
HAMMEL, Nicole .... 484-664-3190.. 411 D
hammel@muhlenberg.edu
HAMMEL, Rachel .... 330-490-7452.. 380 J
rhammel@walsh.edu
HAMMELL, Rebecca, J ..... 717-245-1858.. 402 D
hammellr@dickinson.edu
HAMMER, Amanda .... 575-461-4413.. 300 A
amandah@mesalands.edu
HAMMER, Bradley, C ...... 419-434-6922.. 379 E
hammer@findlay.edu
HAMMER, Kimberley, A .. 412-397-6413.. 418 B
hammerk@rmu.edu
HAMMER, Larry .... 828-227-7232.. 359 A
hammer@wcu.edu
HAMMER, Lila, D .... 260-982-5234.. 165 M
ldhammer@manchester.edu
HAMMERMAN, Adam, D . 914-594-4570.. 323 I
adam_hammerman@nymc.edu
HAMMERSCHMIDT,
David .... 734-432-5441.. 237 D
dhammerschmidt@madonna.edu
HAMMERSEN, Frederick .. 202-231-6697.. 528 C
frederick.hammersen@dodiis.mil
HAMMES, Meg .... 563-387-1375.. 174 L
hammma01@luther.edu
HAMMETT, Amy, S .... 216-368-4318.. 365 B
registrar@case.edu
HAMMETT, Candi .... 325-674-2359.. 449 J
candi.hammett@acu.edu
HAMMETT, Fred .... 404-225-4016.. 117 A
fhammett@atlantatech.edu
HAMMETT, John .... 256-782-5445...... 4 H
jhammett@jsu.edu
HAMMETT, Maggie .... 406-994-2343.. 277 C
maggie.hammett@montana.edu
HAMMETT, Maria, A .... 478-301-2670.. 124 D
hammett_ma@mercer.edu
HAMMILL, Graham, L .... 716-645-3786.. 331 C
ghammill@buffalo.edu
HAMMILL, Viv .... 406-444-0325.. 276 J
vhammill@montana.edu
HAMMITT, Stephanie .... 218-879-0810.. 249 C
shammitt@fdltcc.edu
HAMMOCK, Susan .... 478-240-5162.. 125 C
shammock@oftc.edu
HAMMON, Darrel, L .... 801-863-7353.. 482 C
darrel.hammon@uvu.edu
HAMMON, Kyle .... 360-442-2551.. 504 G
khammon@lowercolumbia.edu
HAMMOND, Anna .... 904-470-8004.... 98 N
anna.hammond@ewc.edu
HAMMOND, Ben .... 781-283-2305.. 229 C
HAMMOND, Brad .... 307-754-6400.. 526 N
brad.hammond@nwc.edu
HAMMOND, Brian .... 301-934-7853.. 207 B
bhammond@csmd.edu
HAMMOND, Caroline ...... 870-864-7102.... 22 D
chammond@southark.edu
HAMMOND, Charles .... 646-378-6131.. 325 C
charles.hammond@nyack.edu
HAMMOND, Charles, A .... 302-225-6352.... 91 D
hammond@gbc.edu
HAMMOND,
Christine, M .... 989-386-6602.. 238 B
chammond@midmich.edu
HAMMOND, Dale, W .... 509-777-3730.. 509 H
dhammond@whitworth.edu
HAMMOND, Dave .... 425-602-3416.. 501 D
dhammond@bastyr.edu
HAMMOND, Debbie .... 843-953-5507.. 428 G
hammonddd@cofc.edu
HAMMOND, Denise .... 870-584-1118.... 23 F
dhammond@cccua.edu
HAMMOND, Dianne .... 352-245-4119.. 113 G
HAMMOND, Elizabeth, D 478-301-2964.. 124 D
hammond_bd@mercer.edu
HAMMOND, Erin .... 314-256-8808.. 262 D
hammond@ai.edu
HAMMOND, Jamie .... 203-575-8022.... 86 G
jhammond@nv.edu
HAMMOND, Jane, F .... 607-844-8222.. 337 G
hammonj@tc3.edu
HAMMOND, Jeff .... 601-266-5001.. 261 E
jeff.hammond@usm.edu
HAMMOND, Jerome .... 423-614-8310.. 441 B
jhammond@leeuniveristy.edu
HAMMOND, Karen, S ...... 240-500-2000.. 207 I
kshammond@hagerstowncc.edu
HAMMOND, Ken .... 573-876-7299.. 272 I
khammond@stephens.edu
HAMMOND, Mark .... 910-893-1211.. 342 F
hammond@campbell.edu
HAMMOND, Michael .... 765-998-5204.. 167 C
mchammond@taylor.edu
HAMMOND, Michelle ...... 620-341-5208.. 180 G
mhammon2@emporia.edu
HAMMOND, Mike .... 803-535-1267.. 431 I
hammondm@octech.edu
HAMMOND, Randy .... 717-477-1256.. 416 A
rphamm@ship.edu
HAMMOND, Russell .... 845-341-4007.. 325 H
russell.hammond@sunyorange.edu
HAMMOND, TeraKesha .... 773-291-6225.. 137 G
thammond12@ccc.edu
HAMMOND, Troy, D .... 630-637-5454.. 149 H
tdhammond@noctrl.edu
HAMMOND, Vanessa .... 423-614-8511.. 441 B
vhammond@leeuniversity.edu
HAMMOND NASS, Holly . 207-602-2306.. 205 F
hnass@une.edu
HAMMONDS, David .... 936-294-2709.. 471 D
david.hammonds@shsu.edu
HAMMONDS, Diane, M .... 610-526-1407.. 397 E
diane.hammonds@theamericancollege.edu
HAMMONDS, Luke .... 601-477-4058.. 258 E
luke.hammonds@jcjc.edu
HAMMONDS, MarTeze ..... 479-880-4358.... 19 F
mhammonds2@atu.edu
HAMMONS, Jamirae .... 606-539-4201.. 193 F
jamirae.hammons@ucumberlands.edu
HAMMONS, Stacy .... 765-677-3061.. 164 B
stacy.hammons@indwes.edu
HAMMONS, Steve .... 606-679-8501.. 190 E
steve.hammons@kctcs.edu
HAMMONTREE, Tonya ..... 501-205-8809.... 19 J
thammontree@cbc.edu
HAMNER, Elise .... 541-888-7211.. 395 B
elise.hamner@socc.edu
HAMNER, Mark, S .... 940-898-3013.. 472 G
mhamner@twu.edu
HAMP, Herlisa .... 408-741-4616.... 74 H
herlisa.hamp@westvalley.edu
HAMPSON, Bill .... 816-995-2818.. 270 H
bill.hampson@researchcollege.edu
HAMPSON, Nancy .... 970-207-4550.... 81 F
nancyh@mckinleycollege.edu
HAMPTON, Audrey .... 661-255-1050.... 30 E
HAMPTON, Diane .... 870-733-6880.... 19 A
dhampton@asumidsouth.edu
HAMPTON, Franki .... 540-453-2285.. 496 F
hamptonf@brcc.edu
HAMPTON, Iyisha .... 334-244-3674...... 2 A
ihampton@aum.edu
HAMPTON, Jarvis, D .... 806-651-3451.. 469 D
jhampton@mail.wtamu.edu
HAMPTON, Jennifer .... 630-752-5327.. 158 C
jennifer.hampton@wheaton.edu
HAMPTON, Joyce .... 413-265-2423.. 217 D
hamptonj@elms.edu
HAMPTON, Julie .... 309-649-6201.. 155 G
julie.hampton@src.edu
HAMPTON, Lacy .... 210-486-2178.. 450 E
lhampton14@alamo.edu
HAMPTON, Lee .... 517-787-0800.. 235 G
hamptonleem@jccmi.edu
HAMPTON, Logan, C .... 731-426-7595.. 440 K
lhampton@lanecollege.edu
HAMPTON, Mark, C .... 410-778-7264.. 213 E
mhampton2@washcoll.edu
HAMPTON, Michael .... 503-883-2442.. 392 B
mhampton@linfield.edu
HAMPTON, Mike .... 305-919-4018.. 111 A
mike.hampton@fiu.edu
HAMPTON, Renee .... 417-667-8181.. 264 A
rhampton@cottey.edu
HAMPTON, Tabatha .... 870-762-3121.... 18 G
thampton@smail.anc.edu
HAMPTON, Terri .... 951-222-8589.... 58 J
terri.hampton@rccd.edu
HAMPTON, Terri .... 626-585-7361.... 56 H
tlhampton@pasadena.edu
HAMPTON, Valerie, J ...... 607-777-4775.. 331 B
vhampton@binghamton.edu
HAMPTON, Vickie .... 404-507-8647.. 124 I
vickie.hampton@morehouse.edu
HAMPTON, Victoria .... 860-768-4296.... 89 G
vhampton@hartford.edu
HAMPTON, Wayne .... 219-844-0100.. 159 E
wayne.hampton@brightwood.edu
HAMPTON, William .... 386-226-4811.... 99 A
hamptonw@erau.edu
HAMPTON, William .... 903-730-4890.. 460 B
whampton@jarvis.edu
HAMPTON VANSANT,
Gwendolyn .... 413-528-7273.. 214 H
ghamptonvansant@simons-rock.edu
HAMRE, Lynne .... 218-723-5930.. 245 J
lhamre@css.edu
HAMRIC, Mark .... 540-231-1181.. 489 H
mhamric@vcom.vt.edu
HAMRICK, David, S .... 512-232-7604.. 476 B
dhamrick@utpress.utexas.edu
HAMRICK, Elizabeth .... 843-921-6912.. 431 H
ehamrick@netc.edu
HAMRICK, Howard, I .... 281-756-3700.. 450 G
hhamrick@alvincollege.edu
HAMRICK, James .... 410-857-2202.. 209 D
jhamrick@mcdaniel.edu
HAMRICK, Jeff .... 415-422-6136.... 72 C
jhamrick@usfca.edu
HAMRICK, Mike .... 304-696-5408.. 513 D
hamrickm@marshall.edu
HAMRICK, Robin, G .... 704-406-3996.. 344 E
rhamrick@gardner-webb.edu
HAMRICK, Sarah .... 202-651-5214.... 92 C
sarah.hamrick@gallaudet.edu
HAMSTRA, Brent .... 423-236-2203.. 444 B
bhamstra@southern.edu
HAMSTRA, Pete .... 602-386-4114.... 11 D
pete.hamstra@arizonachristian.edu
HAMZAVI, Maria .... 858-499-0202.... 39 J
mhamzavi@coleman.edu
HAN, David, S .... 423-478-7524.. 443 I
dhan@ptseminary.edu
HAN, Jenjen .... 407-888-8689.. 100 H
jhan@fcim.edu
HAN, Joseph .... 216-687-5343.. 366 I
joseph.han@csuohio.edu
HAN, Ki Won .... 714-527-0691.... 43 C
HAN, Larry, L .... 407-888-8689.. 100 H
lhan@fcim.edu
HAN, Peter .... 303-273-3131.... 78 M
phan@mines.edu
HAN, Yuan-Yuan .... 407-888-8689.. 100 H
y2han@fcim.edu
HANADA, Karen .... 808-984-3527.. 132 D
tkhanada@hawaii.edu
HANADA, Tamone Karen . 808-984-3527.. 132 D
tkhanada@hawaii.edu
HANASSAB, Shideh .... 310-825-1681.... 69 D
shanassa@saonet.ucla.edu
HANAVAN, Laura .... 816-415-7804.. 275 F
hanavanl@william.jewell.edu
HANBURY, II, George, L 954-262-7575.. 105 J
hanbury@nsu.nova.edu
HANBURY, John .... 276-656-0205.. 498 A
jhanbury@patrickhenry.edu
HANCE, JR., James, H .... 401-598-1000.. 425 B
HANCOCK, Anthony .... 713-718-6283.. 459 B
anthony.hancock@hccs.edu
HANCOCK, Barry .... 618-985-3741.. 143 F
barryhancock@jalc.edu
HANCOCK, JR., Ben, E .... 910-630-7000.. 346 E
bhancock@methodist.edu
HANCOCK, Blair .... 336-838-6128.. 354 C
blair.hancock@wilkescc.edu
HANCOCK, John .... 713-500-2401.. 477 C
john.hancock@uth.tmc.edu
HANCOCK, John .... 503-768-7160.. 392 A
hancock@lclark.edu
HANCOCK, Jory, L .... 520-626-8030.... 17 I
jory@email.arizona.edu
HANCOCK, Katrina .... 620-947-3121.. 185 B
katrinah@tabor.edu
HANCOCK, Lori .... 810-762-0321.. 238 F
lori.hancock@mcc.edu
HANCOCK, Lua .... 386-822-7343.. 113 B
lhancock@stetson.edu
HANCOCK, Mara .... 510-594-5080.... 29 K
mhancock@cca.edu
HANCOCK, Merodie .... 518-587-2100.. 335 D
president@esc.edu
HANCOCK, Richard, R ..... 501-450-5284.... 24 G
russh@mail.uca.edu
HANCOCK, Sean .... 760-921-5428.... 56 E
sean.hancock@paloverde.edu
HANCOCK, Wanda .... 229-225-5089.. 127 G
whancock@southernregional.edu
HANCOX, Robert, E .... 610-892-1578.. 414 B
rhancox@pit.edu
HAND, Christie .... 304-358-2000.. 510 J
christie@future.edu
HAND, Jeffrey .... 856-256-5186.. 295 E
handj@rowan.edu
HAND, Kelli .... 704-637-4416.. 343 B
kmhand@catawba.edu
HAND, Mary .... 518-743-2248.. 335 A
handm@sunyacc.edu
HAND, Natalie .... 484-664-3804.. 411 D
nhand@muhlenberg.edu
HAND, Theresa .... 518-244-4590.. 327 H
handt@sage.edu
HAND, Troy .... 757-569-6735.. 498 B
thand@pdc.edu
HANDCOX, Jenelle .... 910-521-6255.. 358 C
jenelle.handcox@uncp.edu
HANDEL, Greg .... 318-357-4330.. 201 B
handelg@nsula.edu
HANDEL, Greg .... 318-357-4522.. 201 B
handelg@nsula.edu
HANDFIELD, Sandy .... 321-433-5502.... 98 K
handfields@easternflorida.edu
HANDFORD, Ann .... 262-524-7211.. 515 J
ahandfor@carrollu.edu
HANDLER, Janet .... 319-363-1323.. 175 D
jhandler@mtmercy.edu
HANDLER, Jeffrey .... 201-761-7101.. 296 K
jhandler@saintpeters.edu
HANDLER, Lisa, M .... 414-410-4207.. 515 I
lmhandler@stritch.edu
HANDLEY, Cassandra .... 912-525-5000.. 126 E
chandley@scad.edu
HANDLEY, Robert, L .... 785-670-1878.. 185 H
bob.handley@washburn.edu
HANDOJO, Jeanne .... 626-584-5366.... 44 G
jeanne@fuller.edu
HANDS, Ashanti .... 619-388-2699.... 60 G
ahands@sdccd.edu
HANDS, Ashanti .... 619-388-2678.... 60 G
ahands@sdccd.edu
HANDS, Colette .... 847-635-1767.. 150 G
chands@oakton.edu
HANDS, Colette .... 847-635-2604.. 150 G
chands@oakton.edu
HANDWERK, Phil .... 336-758-5244.. 359 E
handwepg@wfu.edu
HANDY, Beth .... 410-888-9048.. 209 C
bhandy@muih.edu
HANDY, Cromwell .... 334-229-4309...... 1 D
chandy@alasu.edu
HANDY, Cynthia, H .... 404-752-1654.. 125 A
cynthia@msm.edu
HANDY, Linda, B .... 317-788-3349.. 168 A
handy@uindy.edu
HANDY, Maisha .... 404-527-7704.. 123 I
mhandy@itc.edu
HANDY, Summer, L .... 716-888-3145.. 306 F
HANDY, Ty, J .... 502-213-2121.. 190 A
ty.handy@kctcs.edu
HANDYSIDE, David .... 920-206-2341.. 517 G
david.handyside@mbu.edu
HANDZLIK, Diane, M .... 716-896-0700.. 339 E
dianeh@villa.edu

HANE, Jennifer .... 719-255-3180.... 83 L
jhane@uccs.edu

HANEBUTTE, Shema .... 253-566-5352.. 508 B
shanebutte@tacomacc.edu

HANEFIELD, Robert .... 580-581-2417.. 382 G
rhanefield@cameron.edu

HANELLY, William .... 570-484-2002.. 415 D
whanelly@lhup.edu

HANES, Barbara .... 484-840-4604.. 411 E
hanesb@neumann.edu

HANES, Billie .... 919-530-5086.. 357 A
bhanes@nccu.edu

HANES, Carol .... 903-875-7594.. 462 J
carol.hanes@navarrocollege.edu

HANES, Madlyn, L .... 814-863-0327.. 412 F
mqh3@psu.edu

HANES, Rick .... 937-778-8600.. 368 E
rhanes@edisonohio.edu

HANES-GOODLANDER,
Lisa .... 651-846-1383.. 252 C
lisa.hanes@saintpaul.edu

HANEWICH, Sheila, K .... 219-866-6157.. 166 J
sheilah@saintjoe.edu

HANEY, Cindy, M .... 610-799-1122.. 408 G
chaney1@lccc.edu

HANEY, David .... 908-852-1400.. 290 D
haneyd@centenarycollege.edu

HANEY, David, P .... 276-944-6168.. 489 I
dhaney@ehc.edu

HANEY, Frank .... 913-234-0788.. 179 M
frank.haney@cleveland.edu

HANEY, Jay .... 432-552-2764.. 478 B
haney_j@utpb.edu

HANEY, Joyce, A .... 814-863-0274.. 412 F
jzh8@psu.edu

HANEY, Kent .... 661-362-2844.... 52 A
khaney@masters.edu

HANEY, Lee Anna .... 828-694-1885.. 347 G
leeannah@blueridge.edu

HANEY, Michele .... 303-914-6215.... 82 I
michele.haney@rrcc.edu

HANEY, Monique .... 610-861-1340.. 411 B
haneym@moravian.edu

HANEY, Neil .... 512-476-2772.. 451 O

HANEY, Pamela .... 708-974-5204.. 148 G
haney@morainevalley.edu

HANEY, Regina .... 806-457-4200.. 458 B
rhaney@fpctx.edu

HANEY, Richard, J .... 847-543-2635.. 138 C
rhaney@clcillinois.edu

HANFORD, Thomas .... 607-753-4702.. 333 A
thomas.hanford@cortland.edu

HANG, Foua .... 920-693-1387.. 523 E
foua.hang@gotoltc.edu

HANIFIN, Martin .... 518-327-6226.. 326 B
mhanifin@paulsmiths.edu

HANIFIN, Sheila .... 413-782-1628.. 229 E
shanifin@wne.edu

HANIGAN, Sherri .... 402-826-8586.. 280 B
sherri.hanigan@doane.edu

HANINCIK, Amanda .... 610-921-7529.. 396 H
ahanincik@albright.edu

HANISH, Jan, M .... 319-273-2331.. 170 A
jan.hanish@uni.edu

HANK, Jack, L .... 210-434-6711.. 463 C
jlhank@lake.ollusa.edu

HANKE, Chris .... 864-503-5256.. 434 G
chanke@uscupstate.edu

HANKE, Robert .... 401-454-6599.. 426 A
rhanke@risd.edu

HANKERSON, Brian .... 954-486-7728.. 114 G
bhankersoncfo@uftl.edu

HANKES, Doug .... 334-844-5123...... 1 G
hankedm@auburn.edu

HANKINS, Jeff .... 501-660-1004.... 18 H
jhankins@asusystem.edu

HANKINS, Kim .... 815-455-8778.. 147 E
khankins@mchenry.edu

HANKINS, Lori .... 904-826-0084.... 72 A
lhankins@usa.edu

HANKINS, Orlando, E .... 919-516-4860.. 355 D
oehankins@st-aug.edu

HANKINS, Paul .... 479-788-7431.... 23 A
paul.hankins@uafs.edu

HANKINS, Stephen, J .... 864-242-5100.. 427 E

HANKS, Bob .... 928-541-7777.... 15 G
bhanks@ncu.edu

HANKS, Misty .... 606-783-5415.. 191 H
m.hanks@moreheadstate.edu

HANKS, Richard .... 970-339-6513.... 76 H
richard.hanks@aims.edu

HANKS, Robert .... 251-460-7051...... 9 E
rbhanks@southalabama.edu

HANKS, Sharon .... 928-757-0879.... 15 E
shanks@mohave.edu

HANLE, Donald .... 202-231-3335.. 528 C
donald.hanle@dodiis.mil

HANLEY, Darla, S .... 617-266-1400.. 215 G

HANLEY, Donna .... 417-873-7201.. 264 H
dhanley@drury.edu

HANLEY, Glenn .... 512-245-2392.. 471 F
gh18@txstate.edu

HANLEY, Paula .... 847-925-6337.. 141 A
phanley@harpercollege.edu

HANLEY, Peggy .... 318-274-6546.. 200 F
peggy@gram.edu

HANLEY, Rodney, S .... 615-329-8614.. 439 L
rshanley@fisk.edu

HANLEY, Theodore .... 713-718-8566.. 459 B
theodore.hanley@hccs.edu

HANLEY, William Lee .... 212-659-3604.. 318 D
wlhanley@tkc.edu

HANLIN, Shawn .... 541-888-1546.. 395 B
shanlin@socc.edu

HANLON, Christopher .... 610-921-7264.. 396 H
chanlon@albright.edu

HANLON, Erin .... 617-322-3552.. 219 H
erin_hanlon@laboure.edu

HANLON, Erin .... 617-322-3531.. 219 H
erin_hanlon@laboure.edu

HANLON, Joyce .... 617-730-7074.. 226 J
joyce.hanlon@newbury.edu

HANLON, Philip, J .... 603-646-2223.. 286 J
philip.j.hanlon@dartmouth.edu

HANNA, Aaron .... 210-431-3335.. 464 H
ahanna1@stmarytx.edu

HANNA, Bashar, W .... 215-489-2324.. 402 A
bashar.hanna@delval.edu

HANNA, C. Phil .... 270-384-8102.. 191 E
hannap@lindsey.edu

HANNA, Chris .... 616-432-3407.. 240 B
chris.hanna@prts.edu

HANNA, Kimberly .... 575-461-4413.. 300 A
kimberlyh@mesalands.edu

HANNA, Mae .... 513-732-5332.. 379 C
hannamh@email.uc.edu

HANNA, Michael .... 315-781-3574.. 316 C
hanna@hws.edu

HANNA, Patricia .... 610-861-7874.. 411 B
hannap@moravian.edu

HANNA, Sean .... 585-275-2354.. 338 K
sean.hanna@rochester.edu

HANNA, Tara .... 419-517-8908.. 371 I
thanna@lourdes.edu

HANNABAS, Liz .... 817-272-0777.. 476 A
hannabas@uta.edu

HANNABURY,
Stephen, P .... 781-292-2401.. 218 H
stephen.hannabury@olin.edu

HANNAFIN, Robert .... 203-254-4250.... 87 G
rhannafin@fairfield.edu

HANNAFORD, Bc, S .... 580-327-8406.. 384 M
bshannaford@nwosu.edu

HANNAFORD, Ron, G .... 562-903-6000.... 28 E
ron.hannaford@biola.edu

HANNAH, Marcus .... 334-876-9360...... 4 A
mhannah@wccs.edu

HANNAH, Roddy .... 570-586-2400.. 419 G
rhannah@summitu.edu

HANNAH, Russ .... 870-972-3303.... 18 J
rhannah@astate.edu

HANNAN,
Christopher, M .... 641-422-1521.. 175 E
chris.hannan@iwd.iowa.gov

HANNAN, Michael .... 814-732-2729.. 415 A
hannan@edinboro.edu

HANNAN, Steven, M .... 419-289-5007.. 363 J
shannan@ashland.edu

HANNAR, Christine .... 636-949-4965.. 266 J
channar@lindenwood.edu

HANNE, Benjamin, C .... 620-229-6371.. 184 J
ben.hanne@sckans.edu

HANNEMAN, Richard .... 402-457-2739.. 280 J
rhanneman@mccneb.edu

HANNER, Mary Beth .... 518-464-8500.. 314 A
mhanner@excelsior.edu

HANNES, Sarah .... 307-778-1178.. 526 K
shannes@lccc.wy.edu

HANNIGAN, Joseph .... 214-860-2232.. 456 E
joseph.hannigan@dcccd.edu

HANNIGAN, Terence .... 718-862-8000.. 319 L
terence.hannigan@manhattan.edu

HANNO, Dennis .... 508-286-8244.. 229 F
hanno_dennis@wheatoncollege.edu

HANNON, Bernard, M .... 765-285-1033.. 159 B
bmhannon@bsu.edu

HANNON, Jim, M .... 563-333-6359.. 176 D
hannonjamesm@ambrose.sau.edu

HANNON, Kristin .... 330-966-5459.. 377 J
khannon@starkstate.edu

HANNON, Kristina .... 626-914-8597.... 38 D
khannon@citruscollege.edu

HANNON, Ron .... 408-848-4895.... 44 I
rhannon@gavilan.edu

HANNUM, Judy, A .... 508-793-2431.. 217 C
jhannum@holycross.edu

HANNUM, Natalie .... 925-473-7403.... 41 J
nhannum@losmedanos.edu

HANOFEE, Rose .... 845-434-5750.. 336 H
rhanofee@sullivan.suny.edu

HANOLD, John, W .... 814-863-0768.. 412 F
jhh6@psu.edu

HANRAHAN, Chelsea .... 603-428-2291.. 287 C
chanrahan@nec.edu

HANRAHAN, Mark .... 740-284-5247.. 368 L
mhanrahan@franciscan.edu

HANRAHAN, Neil, S .... 212-998-4581.. 324 C
nsh2@nyu.edu

HANRAHAN, Susan, N .... 870-972-3112.... 18 J
hanrahan@astate.edu

HANRAHAN, Thomas .... 718-399-4308.. 326 E
hanrahan@pratt.edu

HANRAHAN, Thomas, M ...... 717-867-6030.. 408 F
hanrahan@lvc.edu

HANRAHAN, Tim .... 573-592-1107.. 275 G
tim.hanrahan@williamwoods.edu

HANS, John .... 651-905-3474.. 255 B
jhans@browncollege.edu

HANSBARGER, Tom .... 845-938-2715.. 529 C
tom.harsbarger@usma.edu

HANSBURG, David .... 303-273-3300.... 78 M
hansburg@mines.edu

HANSCOM, Marcus .... 401-254-3345.. 426 B
mhanscom@rwu.edu

HANSEL, Marie, C .... 708-709-3542.. 151 C
mhansel@prairiestate.edu

HANSEN, Anne, P .... 775-445-3235.. 235 B
anne.hansen@wnc.edu

HANSEN, Anne, W .... 518-564-2090.. 334 A
hansenaw@plattsburgh.edu

HANSEN, Elaine, J .... 828-898-8838.. 345 G
hansent@lmc.edu

HANSEN, Carl, F .... 707-826-3731.... 34 F
ch1@humboldt.edu

HANSEN, Chelsea .... 888-384-0849.... 25 P
chansen@allied.edu

HANSEN, Cheryl .... 402-494-2311.. 231 C

HANSEN, Chris .... 423-236-2915.. 444 B
chansen@southern.edu

HANSEN, Christian .... 203-576-4642.... 39 C
registrar@bridgeport.edu

HANSEN, Corinne .... 605-642-6215.. 437 B
corinne.hansen@bhsu.edu

HANSEN, Craig .... 651-793-1300.. 250 A
craig.hansen@metrostate.edu

HANSEN, Dan .... 619-201-8693.... 60 D
dan.hansen@sdcc.edu

HANSEN, David .... 605-367-7568.. 436 L
dave.hansen@sdbor.edu

HANSEN, David .... 843-574-6021.. 433 D
david.hansen@tridenttech.edu

HANSEN, David .... 435-797-1645.. 482 B
david.hansen@usu.edu

HANSEN, Douglas .... 801-957-4084.. 483 A
douglas.hansen@slcc.edu

HANSEN, Eric .... 619-594-2941.... 35 A
ehansen@mail.sdsu.edu

HANSEN, Eric .... 432-264-5046.. 459 D
ehansen@howardcollege.edu

HANSEN, Gregg .... 978-468-7111.. 219 B
ghansen@gcts.edu

HANSEN, Herbert .... 410-532-5340.. 210 B
hhansen@ndm.edu

HANSEN, Jennifer .... 315-229-5441.. 329 D
jhansen@stlawu.edu

HANSEN, Jessica .... 302-736-2444.... 91 G
jessica.warner@wesley.edu

HANSEN, John .... 307-532-8304.. 526 G
john.hansen@ewc.wy.edu

HANSEN, Jon .... 308-432-6231.. 281 H
jhansen@csc.edu

HANSEN, Julie .... 641-673-1096.. 177 J
hansenj@wmpenn.edu

HANSEN, Kathy .... 320-363-5307.. 245 I
kghansen@csbsju.edu

HANSEN, Kaylyn, L .... 580-327-8418.. 384 M
klhansen@nwosu.edu

HANSEN, Kenneth .... 402-559-5301.. 283 A
hansenk@unmc.edu

HANSEN, Kent, A .... 909-558-2644.... 49 C
khansen@claysonlaw.com

HANSEN, Kevin .... 319-398-5625.. 174 I
kevin.hansen@kirkwood.edu

HANSEN, Kevin .... 801-626-8022.. 482 D
khansen@weber.edu

HANSEN, Kristine .... 651-793-1300.. 250 A
kristine.hansen@metrostate.edu

HANSEN, Linda, L .... 406-768-6351.. 276 F
lhansen@fpcc.edu

HANSEN, Lynn .... 407-823-2362.. 111 E
lynn.hansen@ucf.edu

HANSEN, Marianne, W .... 509-777-4347.. 509 H
mhansen@whitworth.edu

HANSEN, Marie .... 207-973-1081.. 202 I
hansenm@my.husson.edu

HANSEN, Matt, B .... 563-333-6258.. 176 D
hansenmattb@sau.edu

HANSEN, Noah .... 619-594-4808.... 35 A
nhansen@mail.sdsu.edu

HANSEN, Patricia .... 417-865-2815.. 265 B
hansenp@evangel.edu

HANSEN, Peter .... 210-436-3324.. 464 H
phansen@stmarytx.edu

HANSEN, Richard .... 617-989-4485.. 229 D
hansenr1@wit.edu

HANSEN, Richard .... 913-971-3381.. 183 D
rdhanson@mnu.edu

HANSEN, Shelley .... 530-541-4660.... 48 D
hansen@ltcc.edu

HANSEN, Sherri .... 435-283-7251.. 482 E
sherri.hansen@snow.edu

HANSEN, Terry .... 432-264-5000.. 459 D
thansen@howardcollege.edu

HANSEN, Victor, M .... 617-422-7252.. 226 H
vhansen@nesl.edu

HANSEN-KIEFFER,
Kristin, M .... 717-796-5234.. 410 J
khansen@messiah.edu

HANSHEW, Daniel, S .... 304-877-6428.. 510 F
dan.hanshew@abc.edu

HANSHUMAKER, David ... 978-478-3400.. 227 C
dhanshumaker@northpoint.edu

HANSOM, Connie .... 615-297-7545.. 438 F
hansomc@aquinascollege.edu

HANSON, Andrew .... 208-792-2218.. 134 A
ahanson@lcsc.edu

HANSON, Andrew .... 845-938-2022.. 529 C
8gc@usma.edu

HANSON, Anna .... 630-829-1809.. 135 F
ahanson@ben.edu

HANSON, Brenda .... 406-756-3812.. 276 E
bhanson@fvcc.edu

HANSON, Catherine .... 979-230-3632.. 453 A
cathie.hanson@brazosport.edu

HANSON, Charlene .... 401-841-6541.. 528 E

HANSON, Charles, D .... 810-762-7812.. 236 C
chanson@kettering.edu

HANSON, Christina, R .... 717-766-2511.. 410 J
chanson@messiah.edu

HANSON, Daniel .... 402-872-2239.. 281 I
dhanson@peru.edu

HANSON, Danielle .... 312-915-7510.. 146 G
dhanson@luc.edu

HANSON, Denise .... 319-226-2012.. 169 D
denise.hanson@allencollege.edu

HANSON, Gail, S .... 202-885-3484.... 91 J
gsher@american.edu

HANSON, Gary, A .... 310-506-4405.... 56 J
gary.hanson@pepperdine.edu

HANSON, Glen .... 801-587-1208.. 481 M
glen.hanson@hsc.utah.edu

HANSON, Gordon .... 858-822-7523.... 70 C
ghanson@ucsd.edu

HANSON, Janet, K .... 507-786-3018.. 254 P
jhanson@stolaf.edu

HANSON, Karen .... 612-625-0051.. 255 H
karhan@umn.edu

HANSON, Kent .... 763-433-1179.. 248 K
kent.hanson@anokaramsey.edu

HANSON, Kent .... 763-576-4700.. 248 L

HANSON, Kirk, O .... 408-554-7898.... 63 E
kohanson@scu.edu

HANSON, Kristina .... 281-487-1170.. 469 F
khanson@txchiro.edu

HANSON, Linda .... 641-844-5731.. 173 L
linda.hanson@iavalley.edu

HANSON, Lisa .... 309-341-5212.. 136 C
lhanson@sandburg.edu

HANSON, Marilyn .... 847-578-3304.. 153 A
marilyn.hanson@rosalindfranklin.edu

HANSON, Mark .... 920-206-2373.. 517 G
mark.hanson@mbu.edu

HANSON, Megan .... 810-762-9781.. 236 C
mhanson@kettering.edu

HANSON, Melissa, S .... 901-321-3399.. 439 E
mhanson@cbu.edu

HANSON, Patricia .... 701-777-4228.. 360 C
pat.hanson@und.edu

HANSON, Paula .... 903-886-5890.. 468 D
paula.hanson@tamuc.edu

HANSON, Rhoda .... 503-842-8222.. 395 D
rhodahanson@tillamookbaycc.edu

HANSON, Richard .... 605-256-5136.. 437 C
richard.hanson@dsu.edu

HANSON, Richard .... 218-333-6600.. 251 D
rhanson@bemidjistate.edu

HANSON, Sara .... 402-399-2350.. 279 E
shanson@csm.edu

HANSON, Scott .... 701-483-2531.. 360 D
scott.hanson@dickinsonstate.edu

HANSON, Shirley, M .... 701-788-4767.. 360 E
shirley.m.hanson@mayvillestate.edu

HANSON, Stephen, E .... 757-221-3590.. 488 F
sehanson@wm.edu

HANSON, Steven, D .... 517-355-2350.. 237 I
ispdean@msu.edu

HANSON, Susan .... 909-469-5329.... 74 K
shanson@westernu.edu

HANSON, Susanah .... 724-266-3838.. 421 C
shanson@tsm.edu

HANSON, Tonya .... 952-358-8213.. 251 A
tonya.hanson@normandale.edu

HANSON, Travis .... 906-487-7234.. 234 A
travis.hanson@finlandia.edu
HANSON, Virginia .... 773-577-8100.. 139 A
HANSS, Patrick, G .... 315-386-7222.. 335 B
hanssp@canton.edu
HANSTAD, Kari .... 701-483-2326.. 360 D
kari.hanstad@dickinsonstate.edu
HANSTEIN, Andrea .... 650-949-7645.... 44 B
hansteinandrea@foothill.edu
HANTL, Bill .... 216-881-1700.. 375 G
bhantl@ohiotech.edu
HANTLA, Bryce, F .... 832-252-4615.. 454 H
bryce.hantla@cbshouston.edu
HANTZ, Joan .... 406-477-6215.. 276 C
jhantz@cdkc.edu
HANTZSCHEL, Linda, J ..... 516-463-6903.. 316 D
linda.j.hantzschel@hofstra.edu
HANUSA, Matt .... 206-239-4500.. 502 D
HANUSCIN, R. Douglas ... 419-755-4871.. 373 G
dhanusci@ncstatecollege.edu
HANYCZ, Colleen, M .... 215-951-1010.. 407 A
president@lasalle.edu
HANYPSIAK, Krista, L ..... 716-645-3020.. 331 C
klh5@buffalo.edu
HANZLIK, Gilbert .... 804-524-3698.. 499 G
ghanzik@vsu.edu
HANZLIK, Jodie, R .... 970-491-6817.... 78 Q
jodie.hanzlik@colostate.edu
HAO, Lan .... 626-914-8521.... 38 D
lhao@citruscollege.edu
HAPP, Judy, B .... 610-807-9488.. 406 C
judyhapp@iirp.edu
HAPPE, Doyle .... 713-529-2778.. 453 U
happe@paralegal.edu
HAPPOLD, Jennifer .... 402-844-7045.. 282 B
jennifer@northeast.edu
HAPSMITH, Linda, M ...... 907-474-1849.... 10 G
lhapsmith@alaska.edu
HARA, Lou .... 785-749-8440.. 181 E
lhara@haskell.edu
HARADA, Margaret .... 425-564-2064.. 501 F
maggie.harada@bellevuecollege.edu
HARARI-RAFUL, Joseph .. 347-394-1036.. 305 C
rjraful@ateret.net
HARBACH, Barbara .... 314-516-7776.. 274 A
bharbach@umsl.edu
HARBAUGH, Martha .... 314-529-9360.. 267 B
mharbaugh@maryville.edu
HARBAUGH, Melinda .... 360-442-2662.. 504 G
mharbaugh@lowercolumbia.edu
HARBER, Bruce .... 901-678-2121.. 445 C
bharber@memphis.edu
HARBER, Dan .... 507-433-0609.. 251 H
dharber@riverland.edu
HARBER, Linda .... 703-993-4181.. 490 B
lharber@gmu.edu
HARBER, Zachery .... 870-612-2081.... 23 H
zach.harber@uaccb.edu
HARBERT, Laura .... 626-584-5280.... 44 G
lauraharbert@fuller.edu
HARBERT, Robert, E .... 706-419-1116.. 119 G
harbert@covenant.edu
HARBIN, Averl .... 716-286-8406.. 324 E
aharbin@niagara.edu
HARBIN, Charles .... 904-646-9953.. 388 K
charles.harbin@twsweld.com
HARBIN, Suzanne .... 256-352-8144...... 9 G
suzanne.harbin@wallacestate.edu
HARBISON, Amanda .... 205-391-5878...... 6 G
aharbison@sheltonstate.edu
HARBOUK, Joseph .... 303-404-5546.... 80 E
joseph.harbouk@frontrange.edu
HARBOURT, Ellen, K .... 740-427-5121.. 371 C
harbourte@kenyon.edu
HARDASH, Peter .... 714-480-7340.... 58 F
hardash_peter@rsccd.edu
HARDASH, Peter .... 714-564-6000.... 58 G
hardash_peter@rsccd.edu
HARDAWAY, Rex .... 404-727-4332.. 120 E
rex.hardaway@emory.edu
HARDAWAY, Thelria .... 615-963-5137.. 445 A
thardaway@tnstate.edu
HARDCASTLE, Ben .... 918-444-2017.. 384 G
harrdcast@nsuok.edu
HARDCASTLE, Bob .... 610-359-5182.. 401 L
bhardcastle@dccc.edu
HARDCASTLE, Louis, B .... 770-484-1204.. 124 C
lutherrice@lutherrice.edu
HARDCASTLE, Sheri .... 517-264-7142.. 241 A
shardcas@sienaheights.edu
HARDEE, John .... 870-230-5320.... 20 E
hardeej@hsu.edu
HARDEE, Teresa .... 302-857-6200.... 90 F
thardee@desu.edu
HARDEE, Tim .... 803-778-6640.. 427 G
hardeebt@cctech.edu
HARDEMON, Rhonda .... 312-850-7894.. 138 A
rhardemon@ccc.edu
HARDEN, Daniel .... 916-348-4689.... 43 A
dharden@epic.edu
HARDEN, Derrick .... 847-543-2225.. 138 C
dharden@clcillinois.edu
HARDEN, Erica .... 478-553-2068.. 125 C
eharden@oftc.edu
HARDEN, Jim .... 906-487-7307.. 234 A
jim.harden@finlandia.edu
HARDEN, Kelly .... 731-661-5946.. 448 A
kharden@uu.edu
HARDEN, Kennith .... 360-596-5360.. 508 A
kharden@spscc.edu
HARDEN, Mark .... 617-427-7293.. 219 B
mharden@gcts.edu
HARDEN, Mark .... 419-289-5160.. 363 J
mharden@ashland.edu
HARDEN, Michelle .... 614-508-7219.. 370 E
mharden@hondros.edu
HARDEN, Robert .... 972-825-4814.. 466 D
rharden@sagu.edu
HARDEN, Ronald, W .... 916-348-4689.... 43 A
rharden@epic.edu
HARDEN, Sig .... 334-241-5473...... 7 H
sharden39277@troy.edu
HARDEN, Yoshiko .... 206-934-3842.. 506 K
yoshiko.harden@seattlecolleges.edu
HARDEN SMITH, Lisa ...... 336-770-3314.. 358 E
smithl@uncsa.edu
HARDER, James, M .... 419-358-3324.. 364 D
harderj@bluffton.edu
HARDER, Kenette .... 816-414-3730.. 268 D
kharder@mbts.edu
HARDER, Matthew .... 304-336-8006.. 513 F
mharder@westliberty.edu
HARDER, Natalie .... 337-521-8959.. 197 A
natalie.harder@solacc.edu
HARDERS, Lori .... 252-398-6246.. 343 G
hardel@chowan.edu
HARDERS, Michael .... 470-578-3007.. 123 J
mharders@kennesaw.edu
HARDESKI, Grace, L .... 215-955-6618.. 420 E
grace.hardeski@jefferson.edu
HARDESTY, Amy .... 806-720-7178.. 461 C
amy.hardesty@lcu.edu
HARDESTY, Jon, H .... 972-548-6803.. 455 A
jhardesty@collin.edu
HARDESTY, Karla .... 719-587-8124.... 76 G
karla_hardesty@adams.edu
HARDESTY, Larry, E .... 724-458-2700.. 404 F
lehardesty@gcc.edu
HARDGRAVE, Bill .... 334-844-4030...... 1 G
bch0014@auburn.edu
HARDGROVE, Mark .... 404-627-2681.. 117 G
mark.hardgrove@beulah.edu
HARDIE, Susan .... 909-652-6531.... 37 D
susan.hardie@chaffey.edu
HARDIGREE, Molly .... 787-766-1717.. 536 B
mhardigree@suagm.edu
HARDIN, Carlette .... 931-221-7511.. 444 E
hardinc@apsu.edu
HARDIN, Dan .... 575-492-2771.. 300 H
dhardin@nmjc.edu
HARDIN, David .... 910-362-7020.. 348 A
dhardin@cfcc.edu
HARDIN, David, M .... 910-362-7020.. 348 A
dhardin@cfcc.edu
HARDIN, Elizabeth, A ...... 704-687-5750.. 358 A
eahardin@uncc.edu
HARDIN, Fred .... 864-388-8340.. 430 G
fhardin@lander.edu
HARDIN, Karen .... 480-461-7584.... 14 D
karen.hardin@mesacc.edu
HARDIN, Marie .... 814-863-1484.. 412 F
mch208@psu.edu
HARDIN, Michael .... 205-726-2718...... 6 E
mhardin@samford.edu
HARDIN, Mike, W .... 704-406-4280.. 344 E
mhardin@gardner-webb.edu
HARDIN, Pam .... 828-627-4544.. 350 D
pahardin@haywood.edu
HARDIN, Phil .... 870-245-5400.... 21 E
hardinp@obu.edu
HARDIN, Philip, W .... 870-245-5400.... 21 E
hardinp@obu.edu
HARDIN, Richard, H .... 636-481-3130.. 266 C
rhardin@jeffco.edu
HARDIN, Sally, B .... 619-260-4550.... 72 B
shardin@sandiego.edu
HARDIN, Sandy .... 575-492-4735.. 300 H
shardin@nmjc.edu
HARDIN, Tammie .... 662-720-7594.. 260 B
twhardin@nemcc.edu
HARDIN, Walter, A .... 803-323-2261.. 435 B
hardinw@winthrop.edu
HARDIN, Wille .... 501-420-1252.... 18 F
willie.hardin@arkansasbaptist.edu
HARDING, Benjamin .... 215-702-4321.. 399 E
bharding@cairn.edu
HARDING, Hillary .... 518-608-8382.. 314 A
hharding@excelsior.edu
HARDING, James .... 802-287-8393.. 484 A
hardingj@greenmtn.edu
HARDING, Kelly .... 660-263-3900.. 263 A
bookstore@cccb.edu
HARDING, Marc, L .... 412-624-7175.. 421 G
mharding@pitt.edu
HARDING, Millicent .... 606-759-7141.. 190 C
millicent.harding@kctcs.edu
HARDING, Sally .... 212-431-2319.. 323 H
sally.harding@nyls.edu
HARDING, Sarah .... 612-874-3737.. 247 M
sharding@mcad.edu
HARDING, Shannan .... 218-235-2153.. 252 F
s.harding@vcc.edu
HARDING, Tayloe .... 803-777-4336.. 433 F
tharding@mozart.sc.edu
HARDING, Teresa .... 701-766-1309.. 360 A
teresa.harding@littlehoop.edu
HARDING, Terry, M .... 716-878-6112.. 332 F
hardintm@buffalostate.edu
HARDING, Timothy .... 813-258-7281.. 114 M
tharding@ut.edu
HARDISON, Al .... 910-893-1441.. 342 F
hardison@campbell.edu
HARDISON, John .... 910-296-2433.. 350 F
jhardison@jamessprunt.edu
HARDISON, R. Karol .... 270-809-4388.. 192 A
rhardison@murraystate.edu
HARDLEY, Michelle, M ..... 805-565-7263.... 75 A
mhardley@westmont.edu
HARDMAN, Alton (Tony) . 580-349-1542.. 385 F
ahardman@opsu.edu
HARDMAN, John .... 870-245-5189.... 21 E
hardmanj@obu.edu
HARDMAN, Michael, L ...... 801-581-7200.. 481 M
michael.hardman@utah.edu
HARDMAN, II, Robert, O 304-462-6181.. 513 C
robert.hardman@glenville.edu
HARDMON, Tamecka, C . 401-456-8213.. 425 E
thardmon@ric.edu
HARDRICK, Jaffus .... 305-348-2190.. 111 A
jaffus.hardrick@fiu.edu
HARDT, Jim .... 412-392-6186.. 417 F
jhardt@pointpark.edu
HARDT, John .... 708-327-9213.. 146 G
jhardt@lumc.edu
HARDT, John, P .... 570-577-1232.. 398 L
john.hardt@bucknell.edu
HARDT, William, M .... 609-258-3379.. 294 D
whardt@princeton.edu
HARDWICK, James .... 813-253-6209.. 114 M
jhardwick@ut.edu
HARDWICK, James, D ..... 406-447-4530.. 276 B
jhardwic@carroll.edu
HARDWICK, Karen, M ...... 202-274-5000.... 94 B
HARDWICK, Monica .... 719-549-3024.... 82 G
monica.hardwick@pueblocc.edu
HARDWOOD-ROM,
Melissa .... 479-575-2000.... 22 I
HARDWRICK, Vikita, B .... 870-230-5028.... 20 E
hardwrv@hsu.edu
HARDY, Anthony .... 334-556-2447...... 3 N
ahardy@wallace.edu
HARDY, Anthony .... 251-809-1531...... 5 A
anthony.hardy@jdcc.edu
HARDY, Anthony .... 251-809-1531...... 5 A
HARDY, Beatriz, B .... 410-543-6130.. 213 A
bbhardy@salisbury.edu
HARDY, Catherine .... 203-575-8080.... 86 G
chardy@nv.edu
HARDY, Charles .... 910-962-3460.. 358 D
hardyc@uncw.edu
HARDY, Daniel, R .... 330-337-6403.. 362 I
college@awc.edu
HARDY, SR., Daniel, R .... 330-337-6403.. 362 I
president@awc.edu
HARDY, Deborah, L .... 440-525-7828.. 371 F
dhardy@lakelandcc.edu
HARDY, Deborah, L .... 440-525-7446.. 371 F
dhardy@lakelandcc.edu
HARDY, Kacee .... 731-286-3238.. 446 B
hardy@dscc.edu
HARDY, Karen .... 760-245-4271.... 73 H
karen.hardy@vvc.edu
HARDY, Karin, S .... 801-585-6220.. 481 M
karin.hardy@utah.edu
HARDY, Kevin .... 207-947-4591.. 202 E
khardy@bealcollege.edu
HARDY, Lonza .... 870-575-8471.... 23 E
hardyl@uapb.edu
HARDY, Mark, G .... 615-963-5301.. 445 A
mhardy@tnstate.edu
HARDY, Pollye .... 205-348-3952...... 8 D
phardy@fa.ua.edu
HARDY, Randall .... 757-727-5640.. 490 E
randall.hardy@hamptonu.edu
HARDY, Rebekah, L .... 410-778-7865.. 213 E
rhardy2@washcoll.edu
HARDY, Richard, J .... 309-298-2228.. 158 A
rj-hardy@wiu.edu
HARDY, Rita .... 404-880-8566.. 118 K
rhardy@cau.edu
HARDY, Robert, M .... 203-396-8390.... 88 I
hardyr@sacredheart.edu
HARDY, Stacia .... 225-216-8247.. 195 H
hardys@mybrcc.edu
HARDY, Stephanie, K .... 540-261-4088.. 494 F
stephanie.hardy@svu.edu
HARDY, Steven .... 973-684-6036.. 294 A
shardy@pccc.edu
HARDY, Thomas .... 703-993-5890.. 490 B
thardy5@gmu.edu
HARDY, Thomas, P .... 312-996-3772.. 156 E
hardyt@uillinois.edu
HARDY, Tyrrell .... 505-786-4183.. 300 E
thardy@navajotech.edu
HARDY, Virginia .... 252-328-6541.. 356 C
hardyv@ecu.edu
HARDY-LUCAS, Faye .... 757-727-5233.. 490 E
faye.hardy-lucas@hamptonu.edu
HARE, Angela .... 717-766-2511.. 410 J
ahare@messiah.edu
HARE, Emily .... 919-718-7230.. 348 D
ehare@cccc.edu
HARE, Erica .... 802-828-8545.. 485 E
erica.hare@vcfa.edu
HARE, Michelle .... 803-323-2189.. 435 B
harem@winthrop.edu
HARE, Sara .... 605-256-7321.. 437 C
sara.hare@dsu.edu
HARE, Terri .... 309-298-2446.. 158 A
ta-hare@wiu.edu
HARE-PAYNTER, Jodi, M 262-472-1570.. 521 F
harej@uww.edu
HARELIK, Harry .... 254-299-8606.. 461 E
hharelik@mclennan.edu
HAREWOOD, Anita .... 410-837-4533.. 213 C
aharewood@ubalt.edu
HAREWOOD, Wayne, H .... 718-368-5681.. 308 F
wharewood@kbcc.cuny.edu
HAREZA, Dennis, F .... 216-397-1886.. 370 H
dhareza@jcu.edu
HARF, James .... 314-529-6851.. 267 B
jharf@maryville.edu
HARFORD, Ellen .... 207-216-4435.. 204 B
eharford@yccc.edu
HARFST, Terry .... 618-453-3102.. 154 I
terriw@siu.edu
HARGER, Kate .... 815-455-8695.. 147 E
kharger@mchenry.edu
HARGETT, Doug .... 256-331-5415...... 6 A
dhargett@nwscc.edu
HARGETT, Jack .... 901-321-3315.. 439 E
jhargett@cbu.edu
HARGIS, Joe .... 507-222-4327.. 245 C
jhargis@carleton.edu
HARGIS, Michael .... 501-450-3106.... 24 G
mhargis@uca.edu
HARGIS, Randall .... 318-487-7129.. 195 F
randall.hargis@lacollege.edu
HARGIS, V. Burns .... 405-744-6384.. 385 G
osupres@okstate.edu
HARGRAVE, Alan .... 765-285-8011.. 159 B
ahargrave@bsu.edu
HARGRAVE, Carolyn, H ... 225-578-6118.. 197 H
chargrave@lsu.edu
HARGRAVE, Gary .... 319-656-2447.. 176 F
HARGRAVE, Jaime .... 713-500-3476.. 477 C
jaime.n.hargrave@uth.tmc.edu
HARGRAVE, John, R .... 580-559-5213.. 383 H
hargrave@ecok.edu
HARGRAVE, Stephanie ...... 336-316-2499.. 344 H
hargravesj@gulford.edu
HARGRAVE MEISLAHN,
Nancy .... 860-685-2269.... 90 C
nmeislahn@wesleyan.edu
HARGRAVES, J. Stanley .. 804-278-4379.. 494 N
shargraves@upsem.edu
HARGROVE, Debra .... 717-245-1901.. 402 D
hargrove@dickinson.edu
HARGROVE, Demond .... 201-200-3507.. 293 C
dhargrove@njcu.edu
HARGROVE, Kristi .... 615-383-4848.. 449 G
khargrove@watkins.edu
HARGROVE, Kristy .... 615-383-4848.. 449 G
khargrove@watkins.edu
HARGROVE, S. Keith .... 615-963-5451.. 445 A
skhargrove@tnstate.edu
HARGROVE, Shannon .... 914-323-5484.. 319 N
shannon.hargrove@mville.edu
HARGROVE, Tony .... 870-584-1165.... 23 F
thargrove@cccua.edu
HARICHANDRAN, Ronald 203-932-7167.... 90 A
rharichandran@newhaven.edu
HARICOMBE, Lorraine, J . 512-495-4350.. 476 B
ljharic@austin.utexas.edu
HARING, Peter .... 402-399-2332.. 279 E
pharing@csm.edu
HARING-SMITH, Tori .... 724-503-1001.. 422 H
tharingsmith@washjeff.edu
HARKAVY, Ira .... 215-898-5351.. 421 E
harkavy@upenn.edu

HARRINGTON, Patricia .... 570-941-7673.. 422 B
patricia.harrington@scranton.edu
HARRINGTON, Robert ..... 417-625-3191.. 268 H
harrington-r@mssu.edu
HARRINGTON, Sean, P ... 540-464-7132.. 499 E
harringtonsp@vmi.edu
HARRINGTON,
Shawn, M .... 860-231-5314.... 90 B
sharrington@usj.edu
HARRINGTON,
Sherre Lee .... 706-236-2285.. 117 F
sharrington@berry.edu
HARRINGTON, Thomas ... 504-280-1154.. 198 D
trharrin@uno.edu
HARRINGTON-MARTIN,
Angela .... 317-543-3250.. 165 O
aharrington@martin.edu
HARRIOTT, Danielle .... 815-965-8616.. 152 F
dharriot@rockfordcareercollege.edu
HARRIS, Aaron .... 952-829-2411.. 244 J
aaron.harris@bethfel.org
HARRIS, Alex .... 302-292-6100.... 93 F
HARRIS, Alex .... 610-604-7700.... 93 F
HARRIS, Alex .... 208-769-7156.. 134 C
afharris@nic.edu
HARRIS, Alice .... 304-424-8224.. 514 D
alice.harris@wvup.edu
HARRIS, Allatia .... 281-459-7140.. 464 I
allatia.harris@sjcd.edu
HARRIS, Alvin .... 501-370-5284.... 21 G
aharris@philander.edu
HARRIS, Amelia, J .... 276-376-4557.. 495 I
ajh7a@uvawise.edu
HARRIS, Andrew .... 415-338-7692.... 35 B
a1harris@sfsu.edu
HARRIS, Angie .... 717-245-1556.. 402 D
harrisa@dickinson.edu
HARRIS, Anjour .... 804-828-2021.. 496 D
abharris@vcu.edu
HARRIS, Anne .... 415-338-6598.... 35 B
aharris@sfsu.edu
HARRIS, Anne .... 765-658-4359.. 160 F
aharris@depauw.edu
HARRIS, April .... 714-556-3610.... 73 B
april.harris@vanguard.edu
HARRIS, Bennie, L .... 404-752-1955.. 125 A
bharris@msm.edu
HARRIS, Bertha, L .... 404-962-3002.. 129 F
bertha.harris@usg.edu
HARRIS, Beth .... 203-287-3023.... 88 E
paierartlibrary@snet.net
HARRIS, Bethany .... 804-862-6100.. 493 F
bharris@rbc.edu
HARRIS, Bethany, W .... 434-949-1007.. 498 E
bethany.harris@southside.edu
HARRIS, Betsy, A .... 207-768-2791.. 203 L
bharris@nmcc.edu
HARRIS, Beverly .... 620-331-4100.. 181 J
bharris@indycc.edu
HARRIS, Beverly .... 757-823-2409.. 492 F
bbharris@nsu.edu
HARRIS, Brent .... 254-295-8642.. 474 E
bharris@umhb.edu
HARRIS, Brett .... 662-915-1537.. 261 B
beharris@olemiss.edu
HARRIS, JR., Calvin .... 410-209-6049.. 206 D
charris@bccc.edu
HARRIS, Camille .... 312-697-8035.. 141 B
charris@harrington.edu
HARRIS, Carol .... 605-342-0317.. 436 A
charris@johnwitherspooncollege.org
HARRIS, Carolyn .... 559-325-3600.... 30 C
charris@chsu.org
HARRIS, Chad .... 541-383-7283.. 390 D
charris7@cocc.edu
HARRIS, Charles .... 334-420-4232...... 7 G
charris@trenholmstate.edu
HARRIS, Charles, S .... 434-791-5701.. 487 C
csharris@averett.edu
HARRIS, Chelsy .... 719-502-3034.... 82 B
chelsy.harris@ppcc.edu
HARRIS, Chonnea .... 661-726-1911.... 68 K
chonnea.harris@uav.edu
HARRIS, Chris .... 949-214-3169.... 41 F
chris.harris@cui.edu
HARRIS, Chris .... 601-635-2111.. 257 F
charris@eccc.edu
HARRIS, Christopher .... 419-434-4347.. 379 E
harrisc1@findlay.edu
HARRIS, Clark .... 810-762-0500.. 238 F
clark.harris@mcc.edu
HARRIS, Clayton .... 216-987-4425.. 367 E
clayton.harris@tri-c.edu
HARRIS, Cliff .... 313-664-7403.. 232 G
charris@collegeforcreativestudies.edu
HARRIS, Craig .... 716-839-8212.. 312 D
charris@daemen.edu
HARRIS, Craig .... 540-857-7797.. 499 B
charris@virginiawestern.edu
HARRIS, Crystal .... 252-862-1246.. 352 D
cdharris6076@roanokechowan.edu
HARRIS, Dan, I .... 414-277-7230.. 518 E
harris@msoe.edu
HARRIS, Darrell, A .... 904-264-2172.. 107 N
dharris@iws.edu
HARRIS, David .... 805-756-1211.... 31 I
harris@calpoly.edu
HARRIS, David .... 320-308-4866.. 252 A
djharris@stcloudstate.edu
HARRIS, David .... 718-268-4700.. 326 L
HARRIS, David .... 843-574-6411.. 433 D
david.harris@tridenttech.edu
HARRIS, David, P .... 909-558-7600.... 49 C
dpharris@llu.edu
HARRIS, David, R .... 617-627-3310.. 228 H
david.harris@tufts.edu
HARRIS, David, W .... 505-277-7520.. 302 F
dwharris@unm.edu
HARRIS, David, W .... 319-273-2470.. 170 A
david.harris@uni.edu
HARRIS, Debbie .... 804-751-9191.. 488 C
dharris@ccc-va.com
HARRIS, Delana .... 601-403-1197.. 260 D
dharris@prcc.edu
HARRIS, Delphia .... 901-435-1380.. 441 C
delphia_harris@loc.edu
HARRIS, Delphine .... 205-247-8070...... 7 E
delphine.harris@stillman.edu
HARRIS, Denise .... 716-926-8727.. 316 B
dharris@hilbert.edu
HARRIS, Dennis .... 405-422-1283.. 387 E
harrisd@redlandscc.edu
HARRIS, Derrell .... 912-287-5855.. 119 B
dharris@coastalpines.edu
HARRIS, Dianne .... 801-581-8816.. 481 M
dianne.harris@hum.utah.edu
HARRIS, Dina .... 574-520-4131.. 163 E
dlharris@iusb.edu
HARRIS, Elizabeth .... 714-816-0366.... 68 E
elizabeth.harris@trident.edu
HARRIS, Emily .... 909-748-8047.... 71 K
emily_harris@redlands.edu
HARRIS, Eugenia .... 615-248-1268.. 447 F
eharris@trevecca.edu
HARRIS, SR., Forrest, E .. 615-256-1463.. 438 C
officeofthepresident@abcnash.edu
HARRIS, Fred .... 408-848-4715.... 44 I
fharris@gavilan.edu
HARRIS, Freda, J .... 608-262-6423.. 519 J
fharris@uwsa.edu
HARRIS, G. Duncan .... 860-512-3203.... 86 E
gharris@manchestercc.edu
HARRIS, Gail .... 423-746-5208.. 447 E
gharris@twcnet.edu
HARRIS, Gary, L .... 202-806-2550.... 93 A
gharris@howard.edu
HARRIS, Gary, L .... 202-806-6800.... 93 A
gharris@howard.edu
HARRIS, Greg .... 770-426-2836.. 124 B
gharris@life.edu
HARRIS, Greg .... 602-275-7133.... 16 Q
greg.harris@rsiaz.edu
HARRIS, Greg .... 503-584-7153.. 390 E
greg.harris@chemeketa.edu
HARRIS, Gregory .... 336-770-3349.. 358 E
harrisg@uncsa.edu
HARRIS, Helen .... 225-216-8287.. 195 H
harrish@mybrcc.edu
HARRIS, Hubert, D .... 804-524-1085.. 499 G
hharris@vsu.edu
HARRIS, Jacqueline .... 860-832-1945.... 85 F
jharris@ccsu.edu
HARRIS, James .... 903-593-8311.. 470 A
jharris@texascollege.edu
HARRIS, James, T .... 619-260-4520.... 72 B
president@sandiego.edu
HARRIS, Janette .... 530-938-5500.... 40 F
jharris6@siskiyous.edu
HARRIS, Jay, H .... 260-481-6785.. 163 C
harrishj@ipfw.edu
HARRIS, Jean .... 941-487-4570.. 111 D
jharris@ncf.edu
HARRIS, Jeff .... 912-525-5000.. 126 E
jeharris@scad.edu
HARRIS, Jeff .... 816-531-5223.. 263 H
jharris@concorde.edu
HARRIS, Jennifer, K .... 802-626-6458.. 486 C
jennifer.harris@lyndonstate.edu
HARRIS, Jesse .... 208-459-5222.. 133 D
jharris@collegeofidaho.edu
HARRIS, Jewell .... 601-979-1773.. 258 D
jewell.e.harris@jsums.edu
HARRIS, Jim, C .... 770-216-2960.. 123 F
jharris@ict.edu
HARRIS, John .... 515-961-1626.. 176 H
john.harris@simpson.edu
HARRIS, John .... 601-635-2111.. 257 F
jharris@eccc.edu
HARRIS, John .... 518-244-4582.. 327 H
harrisj8@sage.edu
HARRIS, John .... 903-923-2181.. 457 G
jharris@etbu.edu
HARRIS, Judy .... 760-744-1150.... 56 F
jharris@palomar.edu
HARRIS, Justin, L .... 615-353-3305.. 446 E
juustin.harris@nscc.edu
HARRIS, Kelly .... 309-467-6413.. 140 E
kharris@eureka.edu
HARRIS, Kendall, T .... 936-261-9900.. 467 E
ktharris@pvamu.edu
HARRIS, Kenneth, E .... 313-831-5200.. 233 K
kharris@etseminary.edu
HARRIS, Kim .... 662-720-7193.. 260 B
kkharris@nemcc.edu
HARRIS, Kim .... 865-882-4695.. 447 A
harriskb@roanestate.edu
HARRIS, Kip, B .... 208-496-9200.. 132 J
harrisk@byui.edu
HARRIS, Kristi .... 660-357-6203.. 269 I
kharris@mail.ncmissouri.edu
HARRIS, Kristin .... 940-855-2203.. 478 D
kharris@vernoncollege.edu
HARRIS, Lamel .... 408-288-3736.... 62 E
lamel.harris@sjcc.edu
HARRIS, Lesa, C .... 270-809-3750.. 192 A
lharris@murraystate.edu
HARRIS, Liesl, W .... 205-853-1200...... 5 B
lwharris@jeffstateonline.com
HARRIS, Lisa .... 763-433-1292.. 248 K
lisa.harris@anokaramsey.edu
HARRIS, Mark .... 609-586-4800.. 292 D
harrisma@mccc.edu
HARRIS, Mark .... 336-454-1126.. 350 B
meharris@gtcc.edu
HARRIS, Mark, T .... 414-229-8417.. 520 D
mtharris@uwm.edu
HARRIS, Martha .... 785-594-8338.. 178 D
martha.harris@bakeru.edu
HARRIS, Mary .... 317-931-4440.. 160 B
mharris@cts.edu
HARRIS, Mary, A .... 202-274-5498.... 94 B
mharris@udc.edu
HARRIS, Mary, E .... 512-223-7705.. 451 N
mharris3@austincc.edu
HARRIS, Mary, R .... 575-492-2162.. 302 M
mharris@usw.edu
HARRIS, Matthew .... 417-447-8290.. 270 A
harrism@otc.edu
HARRIS, Maurice, A .... 315-443-4734.. 337 A
maharr17@syr.edu
HARRIS, Mel .... 703-812-4757.. 491 B
mharris@leland.edu
HARRIS, Melissa, D .... 716-880-3368.. 320 D
melissa.d.harris@medaille.edu
HARRIS, Melvin .... 312-942-2030.. 153 B
melvin_harris@rush.edu
HARRIS, Melvin .... 256-726-7374...... 6 B
mharris@oakwood.edu
HARRIS, Michael .... 715-425-3774.. 521 B
michael.harris@uwrf.edu
HARRIS, Michael .... 918-595-8128.. 388 F
michael.harris284@tulsacc.edu
HARRIS, Michael, E .... 336-734-7764.. 349 G
mharris@forsythtech.edu
HARRIS, Nancy .... 323-856-7600.... 26 I
nharris@afi.com
HARRIS, Nick, L .... 504-816-4704.. 195 B
nharris@dillard.edu
HARRIS, Obadiah .... 323-663-2167.... 71 E
obadiahharris@uprs.edu
HARRIS, Patricia .... 662-252-8000.. 260 F
pharris@rustcollege.edu
HARRIS, Patricia, R .... 616-222-3000.. 236 F
pharris@kuyper.edu
HARRIS, Patrick .... 406-447-4380.. 276 B
pharris@carroll.edu
HARRIS, Patty .... 651-290-6358.. 253 S
patty.harris@mitchellhamline.edu
HARRIS, Paul .... 585-475-4992.. 327 E
pahdar@rit.edu
HARRIS, Peter .... 860-512-3213.... 86 E
pharris@manchestercc.edu
HARRIS, Peter, H .... 918-836-6886.. 388 E
peter.harris@spartan.edu
HARRIS, Philip, L .... 847-491-566 ... 150 F
phil.harris@northwestern.edu
HARRIS, Randy .... 814-866-8416.. 407 D
rharris@lecom.edu
HARRIS, Rhonda, L .... 757-683-4007.. 492 G
rlharris@odu.edu
HARRIS, Richard .... 479-508-3310.... 19 F
rharris1@atu.edu
HARRIS, Richard, C .... 516-671-2215.. 339 G
rharris@webb.edu
HARRIS, Rob .... 417-328-1827.. 272 C
rharris@sbuniv.edu
HARRIS, Robin .... 252-335-0821.. 349 A
robin_harris@albemarle.edu
HARRIS, Rotesha .... 404-880-6917.. 118 K
rharris@cau.edu
HARRIS, Scott .... 309-298-1949.. 158 A
sd-harris@wiu.edu
HARRIS, Sedgwick .... 815-825-9837.. 144 F
sedgwick.harris@kishwaukeecollege.edu
HARRIS, Shari .... 217-641-4532.. 143 H
sharris@jwcc.edu
HARRIS, Sharlene, J .... 340-693-1361.. 539 C
sharris@uvi.edu
HARRIS, Sheryl, O .... 817-515-5228.. 467 A
sheryl.harris@tccd.edu
HARRIS, Skip .... 802-651-5961.. 483 F
sharris@champlain.edu
HARRIS, Stephen, A .... 615-248-1245.. 447 F
sharris@trevecca.edu
HARRIS, Susan .... 901-381-3939.. 449 F
susan@visible.edu
HARRIS, Susan, G .... 434-924-7120.. 495 H
sgh4c@virginia.edu
HARRIS, Suzann .... 615-248-1201.. 447 F
sharris@trevecca.edu
HARRIS, Tara .... 864-941-8525.. 432 A
harris.t@ptc.edu
HARRIS, Terral .... 912-279-5726.. 119 C
tharris@ccga.edu
HARRIS, Terrance .... 805-756-2767.... 31 I
tharris@calpoly.edu
HARRIS, Terrance .... 936-294-1325.. 471 D
tjharris@shsu.edu
HARRIS, Terrence .... 315-786-2238.. 317 H
tharris@sunyjefferson.edu
HARRIS, Thomas, W .... 859-257-1933.. 193 G
tom.harris@uky.edu
HARRIS, Todd, D .... 910-630-7155.. 346 E
toharris@methodist.edu
HARRIS, Toi, B .... 713-798-3695.. 452 G
toih@bcm.edu
HARRIS, Tonya .... 870-838-2913.... 18 G
tharris@smail.anc.edu
HARRIS, Tosca .... 620-365-5116.. 178 A
harris@allencc.edu
HARRIS, Tracy .... 240-725-5300.. 207 B
tracy.harris@csmd.edu
HARRIS, Travaris .... 847-925-6673.. 141 A
tharris@harpercollege.edu
HARRIS, Wayne .... 757-727-5071.. 490 E
wayne.harris@hamptonu.edu
HARRIS, Wesley .... 314-516-7192.. 274 A
harriswr@umsl.edu
HARRIS, William, L .... 859-257-9101.. 193 G
wlharr2@email.uky.edu
HARRIS, Wilma, K .... 479-979-1215.... 24 I
wkharris@ozarks.edu
HARRIS, Yolanda .... 719-502-4689.... 82 B
yolanda.harris@ppcc.edu
HARRIS-CALDWELL,
Jeanne .... 949-582-4607.... 65 G
jharriscaldwell@saddleback.edu
HARRIS COHEN, David ... 626-264-8880.... 71 D
HARRIS-DUFF, Joanne ... 540-828-5749.. 487 H
jharris-duff@bridgewater.edu
HARRIS-HOOKER,
Sandra .... 404-752-1725.. 125 A
sharris-hooker@msm.edu
HARRIS-JOLLY,
Stephanie .... 229-903-3610.. 115 K
stephanie.harris-jolly@asurams.edu
HARRIS KISUNZU,
Cheryl .... 301-891-4116.. 213 D
charris@wau.edu
HARRIS-MATHEWS,
Colette .... 916-691-7170.... 51 B
harriscl@crc.losrios.edu
HARRIS PAOLILLO,
Linda .... 212-752-1530.. 318 F
linda.harris@limcollege.edu
HARRIS-SNYDER, April ... 570-459-1573.. 407 B
snydera@lackawanna.edu
HARRISON, Angela .... 757-823-2037.. 492 F
sm505@bncollege.com
HARRISON, Antione .... 518-381-1449.. 330 B
harrisaw@sunysccc.edu
HARRISON, B. Timothy ... 618-537-6962.. 147 F
btharrison@mckendree.edu
HARRISON, Bob .... 526-947-8755.... 66 A
bobharrison@scuhs.edu
HARRISON, Brian .... 334-683-2313...... 5 G
bharrison@marionmilitary.edu
HARRISON, Carol .... 301-934-7552.. 207 B
carolh@csmd.edu
HARRISON, Cheryl .... 718-862-7862.. 319 L
cheryl.harrison@manhattan.edu
HARRISON, Chris .... 615-230-3352.. 447 C
christopher.harrison@volstate.edu
HARRISON, Christopher .. 252-940-6444.. 347 E
chris.harrison@beaufortccc.edu
HARRISON, Crystal .... 920-498-5541.. 524 E
crystal.harrison@nwtc.edu
HARRISON, Cynthia, F ..... 914-968-6200.. 329 C
HARRISON, Darrel .... 619-388-7457.... 60 H
daharris@sdccd.edu
HARRISON, David .... 336-770-3273.. 358 E
harrisondl@uncsa.edu

HARTZ, Ronald, G .... 671-735-5555.. 529 G
ronald.hartz@guamcc.edu
HARTZ, Sandra, J .... 336-633-0156.. 352 B
sjhartz@randolph.edu
HARTZEL, Ruth Ann .... 724-847-5673.. 404 B
rhartzel@geneva.edu
HARTZELL, Jay, C .... 512-471-5058.. 476 B
dean.hartzell@mccombs.utexas.edu
HARTZLER, Christi .... 407-823-4663.. 111 E
christi.hartzler@ucf.edu
HARTZLER, Murray, G ...... 843-661-1237.. 430 B
mhartzler@fmarion.edu
HARTZOG, Art .... 864-587-4002.. 433 A
hartzoga@smcsc.edu
HARVEL, Kathryn .... 816-654-7285.. 266 E
kharvel@kcumb.edu
HARVEY, Addie .... 901-435-1704.. 441 C
addie_harvey@loc.edu
HARVEY, Amy .... 718-990-5076.. 328 F
goodmana@stjohns.edu
HARVEY, Barron, H .... 202-806-1500.... 93 A
bharvey@howard.edu
HARVEY, Bev .... 402-437-2554.. 282 F
bharvey@southeast.edu
HARVEY, Binti .... 909-607-9665.... 64 A
bharvey@scrippscollege.edu
HARVEY, Bryan, C .... 413-545-6238.. 220 F
harvey@chancellor.umass.edu
HARVEY, Cameron .... 901-381-3939.. 449 F
cameron@visible.edu
HARVEY, Diana .... 801-957-4278.. 483 A
diana.harvey@slcc.edu
HARVEY, George .... 919-761-2203.. 355 I
harvey@sebts.edu
HARVEY, John .... 803-754-4100.. 429 B
HARVEY, Kem .... 864-592-4795.. 432 H
harveyk@sccsc.edu
HARVEY, Kimberly .... 636-481-3200.. 266 C
kharvey@jeffco.edu
HARVEY, Kimberly .... 636-481-3207.. 266 C
kharvey@jeffco.edu
HARVEY, Laurie .... 516-686-7711.. 323 G
lharve05@nyit.edu
HARVEY, Lilia .... 404-471-6102.. 115 J
lharvey@agnesscott.edu
HARVEY, Linda .... 718-780-0382.. 305 L
linda.harvey@brooklaw.edu
HARVEY, Lydia .... 907-564-8218.... 10 B
lydiah@alaskapacific.edu
HARVEY, Marcus .... 816-604-4121.. 267 K
marcus.harvey@mcckc.edu
HARVEY, Melissa .... 715-682-1674.. 518 H
mharvey@northland.edu
HARVEY, Monica .... 712-279-3112.. 176 E
monica.harvey@stlukescollege.edu
HARVEY, Peter, W .... 509-527-5145.. 509 G
harvey@whitman.edu
HARVEY, Richard, C .... 304-367-4395.. 513 B
richard.harvey@fairmontstate.edu
HARVEY, Roberta .... 856-256-5140.. 295 E
harvey@rowan.edu
HARVEY, Ryan, D .... 740-826-8051.. 373 E
harvey@muskingum.edu
HARVEY, Sarah, J .... 260-359-4010.. 161 O
sharvey@huntington.edu
HARVEY, Scott .... 864-646-1556.. 433 C
sharvey@tctc.edu
HARVEY, Shannon, S ...... 717-339-3503.. 405 C
ssharvey@hacc.edu
HARVEY, Stephen .... 212-731-3419.. 317 A
stephen.harvey@mssm.edu
HARVEY, Stewart, A .... 207-581-2668.. 204 H
stewarth@maine.edu
HARVEY, Stu .... 405-682-7849.. 385 D
sharvey@occc.edu
HARVEY, William, R .... 757-727-5231.. 490 E
presidentsoffice@hamptonu.edu
HARVEY-LEE, Peggy, A .... 585-292-2252.. 321 J
pharvey-lee@monroecc.edu
HARVEY-LIVINGSTON,
Kim .... 903-566-7197.. 477 B
klivingston@uttyler.edu
HARVEY-SAHAK, Judy, B 909-621-8973.... 64 A
judy.sahak@scrippscollege.edu
HARVEY-SMITH,
Alicia, B .... 603-542-7744.. 286 G
aharveysmith@ccsnh.edu
HARVIN, Lillian .... 510-869-8785.... 59 L
lharvin@samuelmerritt.edu
HARVIN, Peter, B .... 864-231-2017.. 427 B
pharvin@andersonuniversity.edu
HARWARD, Brian .... 814-332-3027.. 397 A
bharward@allegheny.edu
HARWARD, Sherry .... 801-863-6813.. 482 C
sherry.harward@uvu.edu
HARWOOD, Debra .... 704-991-0206.. 353 E
dharwood5544@stanly.edu
HARWOOD, Gina .... 718-960-8245.. 308 B
gina.harwood@lehman.cuny.edu
HARWOOD, Scott .... 518-891-2915.. 325 A
sharwood@nccc.edu

HARYCKI, David .... 402-375-7389.. 281 J
daharyc1@wsc.edu
HASAN, Abul .... 918-293-4809.. 386 B
abul.hasan@okstate.edu
HASAN, Shah .... 937-484-1256.. 380 E
shah.hasan@urbana.edu
HASAN, Zia .... 803-535-5219.. 428 B
hasan@claflin.edu
HASBROUCK, Douglas .... 610-989-1451.. 422 E
dhasbrouck@vfmac.edu
HASELDEN, Gregory, W .. 864-379-8812.. 429 I
haselden@erskine.edu
HASELOFF, Gregory, K .... 859-858-3511.. 186 J
greg.haseloff@asbury.edu
HASENPFLUG, Cathy .... 406-994-4284.. 277 C
catherine.hasenpflug@montana.edu
HASH, Jennifer .... 303-722-5724.... 81 E
jhash@lincolntech.edu
HASH, Joseph .... 707-476-4213.... 40 D
joe-hash@redwoods.edu
HASHEMI-BOZARTH,
Monica .... 316-295-8701.. 181 B
monica_hashemi@friends.edu
HASHIM, Susanne .... 937-319-0163.. 363 D
shashim@antiochcollege.org
HASINGER, Guenther .... 808-956-8566.. 131 F
hasinger@hawaii.edu
HASKAMP, Misty .... 573-875-7582.. 263 F
mrhaskamp@ccis.edu
HASKETT, Tammy .... 828-227-7222.. 359 A
haskett@wcu.edu
HASKINS, Brenda .... 985-448-4518.. 201 A
brenda.haskins@nicholls.edu
HASKINS, Eileen, T .... 401-598-1035.. 425 B
ehaskins@jwu.edu
HASKINS, Jamie .... 573-592-5262.. 275 E
jamie.haskins@westminster-mo.edu
HASKINS, Michael .... 251-460-6211...... 9 E
mhaskins@southalabama.edu
HASLAG, Daniel .... 573-592-5240.. 275 E
dan.haslag@westminster-mo.edu
HASLAM, Kent .... 406-243-5348.. 276 K
kent.haslam@umontana.edu
HASLAM STRAUGHAN,
Hope .... 617-879-2330.. 229 G
hstraughan@wheelock.edu
HASLER, Paul .... 715-346-3059.. 521 C
phasler@uwsp.edu
HASLER, Susan .... 410-617-1619.. 208 G
sahasler@loyola.edu
HASLIM, Hue .... 602-943-2311.... 18 C
hue.haslim@west.edu
HASNAIN, Syed .... 850-729-6448.. 105 I
hasnains@nwfsc.edu
HASS, Marjorie .... 903-813-3001.. 451 M
mhass@austincollege.edu
HASS, Martha .... 518-694-7238.. 303 C
martha.hass@acphs.edu
HASS CORDOVA, Tracy .... 417-667-8181.. 264 A
tcordova@cottey.edu
HASSAN, Nidia .... 903-510-2883.. 473 C
nhas@tjc.edu
HASSANPOUR, Zinat .... 704-403-1698.. 342 E
zinat.hassanpour@carolinashealthcare.org
HASSEL, George, E .... 610-499-4182.. 423 E
gehassel.sr@widener.edu
HASSELL, Keith .... 203-576-4466.... 89 C
khassell@bridgeport.edu
HASSELL, Rusty .... 706-385-1503.. 126 A
rusty.hassell@point.edu
HASSEN, Marjorie .... 207-725-3281.. 202 F
mhassen@bowdoin.edu
HASSENZAHL, David, M . 530-898-6121.... 32 C
dhassenzahl@csuchico.edu
HASSENZAHL, Roger .... 765-285-1532.. 159 B
rahassenzahl@bsu.edu
HASSEVOORT, Darrin ...... 423-697-3383.. 445 D
darrin.hassevoort@chattanoogastate.edu
HASSIG, Kathleen, A .... 530-898-5201.... 32 C
khassig@csuchico.edu
HASSINGER, Steven .... 717-728-2262.. 400 F
stevehassinger@centralpenn.edu
HASSLER, Ardoth .... 202-687-1780.... 92 E
hasslera@georgetown.edu
HASSLER, Daniel, M .... 312-329-8913.. 148 F
daniel.hassler@moody.edu
HASSLER, Greg .... 252-744-6010.. 356 C
hasslerg@ecu.edu
HASSLER, Mark .... 757-479-3706.. 496 B
markhassler@vbts.edu
HASSLER, Mary Ellen ...... 856-351-2651.. 296 L
mhassler@salemcc.edu
HASSON, Amy, S .... 410-548-3316.. 213 A
ashasson@salisbury.edu
HASSUMANI, Sabrina .... 713-743-2755.. 473 F
shassumani@uh.edu
HASTAD, Doug, N .... 262-524-7246.. 515 J
dhastad@carrollu.edu
HASTED, Grigor .... 517-607-2620.. 235 E
ghasted@hillsdale.edu

HASTINGS, Adam .... 434-961-5348.. 498 C
ahastings@pvcc.edu
HASTINGS, Brian .... 402-458-1100.. 282 M
bhastings@nufoundation.org
HASTINGS, Dana, M .... 785-532-6221.. 182 D
dhasting@ksu.edu
HASTINGS, Jan .... 818-401-1298.... 40 G
jhastings@columbiacollege.edu
HASTINGS, Jennifer, D .... 253-879-2460.. 508 D
jhastings@pugetsound.edu
HASTINGS, Judeann .... 574-239-8372.. 161 N
jhastings@hcc-nd.edu
HASTINGS, Michael, M ... 207-581-1484.. 204 H
mhastings@maine.edu
HASTINGS, Michelle .... 314-367-8700.. 271 E
michelle.hastings@stlcop.edu
HASTINGS, Nancy .... 312-329-4415.. 148 F
nancy.hastings@moody.edu
HASTINGS, Paul, D .... 530-752-4663.... 69 A
pdhastings@ucdavis.edu
HASTINGS, Ron .... 909-384-8542.... 60 C
rhastings@sbccd.cc.ca.us
HASTY, Taylor .... 423-775-7568.. 439 B
jhasty6628@bryan.edu
HASZ, Dave .... 952-829-1896.. 244 J
dave.hasz@bethfel.org
HATANAKA, Janice .... 562-985-7878.... 33 B
janice.hatanaka@csulb.edu
HATCH, Donna, M .... 972-548-6884.. 455 A
dhatch@collin.edu
HATCH, SHCJ,
Jeanne Marie .... 610-527-0200.. 418 D
jhatch@rosemont.edu
HATCH, Joy .... 785-628-4488.. 180 I
jhatch@fhsu.edu
HATCH, Joyce .... 602-386-4115.... 11 D
joyce.hatch@arizonachristian.edu
HATCH, Mark .... 719-389-6805.... 77 J
mhatch@coloradocollege.edu
HATCH, Mary .... 847-214-7421.. 140 A
mhatch@elgin.edu
HATCH, Melanie .... 478-471-2730.. 124 E
melanie.hatch@mga.edu
HATCH, Nathan, O .... 336-758-5211.. 359 E
hatch@wfu.edu
HATCHER, Betty, K .... 252-638-3745.. 349 B
hatcherb@cravencc.edu
HATCHER, Brian .... 410-617-5026.. 208 G
bhatcher@loyola.edu
HATCHER, Doreen .... 909-537-5037.... 34 C
dhatcher@csusb.edu
HATCHER, Oeida .... 434-544-8344.. 491 F
hatcher@lynchburg.edu
HATCHER, Pam .... 859-246-6788.. 189 B
pam.hatcher@kctcs.edu
HATCHER, Robert .... 212-817-7020.. 308 A
rhatcher@gc.cuny.edu
HATCHER, Towana .... 804-330-0111.. 487 P
pnasstcrim@centura.edu
HATCHETT, Timothy, L .... 202-274-5000.... 94 B
HATFIELD, Amy .... 360-475-7555.. 505 F
ahatfield@olympic.edu
HATFIELD, Barbara, S .... 318-473-6446.. 197 J
bhatfield@lsua.edu
HATFIELD, Chad .... 914-961-8313.. 329 H
hatfield@svots.edu
HATFIELD, Jenna .... 252-335-0821.. 349 A
jenna_hatfield@albemarle.edu
HATFIELD, Karen .... 352-588-8460.. 108 C
karen.hatfield@saintleo.edu
HATFIELD, Mark .... 662-720-7270.. 260 B
mahatfield@nemcc.edu
HATFIELD, Misty .... 803-938-3728.. 434 E
hatfielm@uscsumter.edu
HATHAWAY, Brent, A .... 702-895-3362.. 284 L
brent.hathaway@unlv.edu
HATHAWAY, Charles, B .. 914-594-4480.. 323 I
charles_hathaway@nymc.edu
HATHAWAY, Gretchel, L .. 518-388-8327.. 338 H
hathawag@union.edu
HATHAWAY, Jeffrey .... 516-463-6750.. 316 D
jeffrey.hathaway@hofstra.edu
HATHAWAY, Joel .... 314-434-4044.. 264 C
joel.hathaway@covenantseminary.edu
HATHAWAY, Nicholas, S . 405-325-3916.. 389 B
nhathaway@ou.edu
HATHAWAY, Tom .... 513-569-1493.. 366 D
tom.hathaway@cincinnatistate.edu
HATHAWAY, William .... 757-352-4294.. 493 E
willhat@regent.edu
HATHAWAY-CLARK, Bill .... 303-458-4162.... 82 L
whathawa@regis.edu
HATHCOCK, Michele .... 828-398-7203.. 347 D
mhathcock@abtech.edu
HATHCOTE, Jan, M .... 706-542-6020.. 128 E
hathcote@uga.edu
HATHMAN, Laurie, E .... 816-501-4144.. 270 J
laurie.hathman@rockhurst.edu
HATHORN, Janine, M .... 540-458-8671.. 500 F
jhathorn@wlu.edu

HATHORN, Pamela .... 918-456-5511.. 384 G
hathorn@nsuok.edu
HATLEE, Mark .... 518-438-3111.. 320 A
mhatlee@mariacollege.edu
HATLEN, Mary, J .... 920-923-7161.. 517 H
mhatlen@marianuniversity.edu
HATRAK, Gregory .... 914-961-8313.. 329 H
ghatrak@svots.edu
HATT, Mark .... 207-255-1221.. 205 C
mark.hatt@maine.edu
HATTAWAY, Trey .... 903-983-8218.. 460 D
thattaway@kilgore.edu
HATTEBERG, Gregory, A .. 214-887-5101.. 457 C
alumni@dts.edu
HATTEN, Angie .... 309-692-4092.. 147 I
ahatten@midstate.edu
HATTENDORF, Lori .... 513-244-4230.. 373 C
lori.hattendorf@msj.edu
HATTO, Susan .... 989-328-1254.. 238 D
susanh@montcalm.edu
HATTON, Jay .... 703-784-2105.. 528 A
jay.hatton@usmc.mil
HATTON, John .... 314-577-8600.. 271 K
hattonjf@slu.edu
HATTON, Karl .... 618-664-7130.. 140 I
karl.hatton@greenville.edu
HATTON, Martin .... 662-329-7231.. 259 E
mlhatton@muw.edu
HATTON, Nora .... 620-235-4276.. 184 C
nhatton@pittstate.edu
HATTORI-UCHIMA,
Margaret .... 671-735-2653.. 530 B
muchima@uguam.uog.edu
HATZENBUEHLER, Linda . 208-282-4899.. 133 H
hatzlind@isu.edu
HAUB, Elaine .... 812-941-2284.. 163 F
ehaub@ius.edu
HAUBOLD, Glen .... 575-646-2101.. 300 J
ghaubold@nmsu.edu
HAUCK, Steven .... 605-882-5284.. 436 B
haucks@lakeareatech.edu
HAUCK, Tanya .... 510-885-4602.... 32 E
tanya.hauck@csueastbay.edu
HAUER, Donna .... 651-690-6827.. 254 M
dmhauer@stkate.edu
HAUF, Todd .... 701-483-2570.. 360 D
todd.hauf@dickinsonstate.edu
HAUFF, Brian .... 417-865-2815.. 265 B
hauffb@evangel.edu
HAUFF, Joel, S .... 520-621-0964.... 17 I
hauff@email.arizona.edu
HAUG, Amy .... 765-658-4181.. 160 F
amyhaug@depauw.edu
HAUG, Christopher .... 503-943-7205.. 396 B
haug@up.edu
HAUG, Marsha, L .... 610-436-3411.. 416 C
mhaug@wcupa.edu
HAUGABROOK,
Adrian, K .... 617-879-2008.. 229 G
ahaugabrook@wheelock.edu
HAUGABROOK, Brian, A . 229-333-7447.. 129 G
bahaugab@valdosta.edu
HAUGE, Todd, W .... 410-293-1600.. 529 D
hauge@usna.edu
HAUGEN, Daniel .... 612-861-7554.. 244 D
haugen@alfredadler.edu
HAUGEN, Dolores .... 253-566-6090.. 508 B
dhaugen@tacomacc.edu
HAUGEN, Donna, M .... 516-572-7809.. 322 C
donna.haugen@ncc.edu
HAUGEN, Doris .... 847-628-1510.. 144 B
dhaugen@judsonu.edu
HAUGEN, Doug .... 530-938-5295.... 40 F
haugen@siskiyous.edu
HAUGEN, Jay .... 314-977-2350.. 271 K
haugenjp@slu.edu
HAUGEN, Nancy .... 510-869-6511.... 59 L
nhaugen@samuelmerritt.edu
HAUGEN, Regina .... 270-384-8300.. 191 E
haugenr@lindsey.edu
HAUGH, Kevin .... 610-902-8258.. 399 D
kevin.o.haugh@cabrini.edu
HAUGHT, Kenneth .... 701-483-2149.. 360 D
ken.haught@dickinsonstate.edu
HAUGHT, Paul .... 901-321-3230.. 439 E
phaught@cbu.edu
HAUGO, Gary .... 218-477-2948.. 250 F
gary.haugo@mnstate.edu
HAUK, Gary, S .... 404-727-6021.. 120 E
gary.hauk@emory.edu
HAUK, Matthew .... 406-791-5224.. 278 G
matthew.hauk@ugf.edu
HAULOTTE, Erin .... 847-947-5491.. 149 B
erin.haulotte@nl.edu
HAUNERT, Bryan .... 410-617-5131.. 208 G
bthaunert@loyola.edu
HAUNGS, Megan .... 510-666-8248.... 25 D
mhaungs@aimc.edu
HAUPERT, Vincent, D ...... 260-359-4089.. 161 O
vhaupert@huntington.edu

HAYES, Michael .... 508-999-8058.. 220 H
mhayes@umassd.edu
HAYES, JR., Michael, F .. 716-888-2520.. 306 F
hayes28@canisius.edu
HAYES, Michelle .... 847-578-7124.. 152 D
mhayes@robertmorris.edu
HAYES, Mike .... 423-614-8406.. 441 B
mhayes@leeuniversity.edu
HAYES, Ray .... 205-348-9731...... 8 C
crhayes@uasystem.edu
HAYES, Richard, L .... 251-380-2738...... 9 E
rlhayes@southalabama.edu
HAYES, Rob .... 617-266-1400.. 215 G
HAYES, Robin, A .... 501-882-8936.... 18 I
rahayes@asub.edu
HAYES, Susan .... 859-246-6381.. 189 B
susan.hayes@kctcs.edu
HAYES, Susan .... 973-618-3553.. 290 A
shayes@caldwell.edu
HAYES, Terri .... 928-523-6608.... 15 H
terri.hayes@nau.edu
HAYES, Thomas .... 513-745-3528.. 381 I
hayes@xavier.edu
HAYES, Tony .... 217-228-5432.. 151 F
hayesto@quincy.edu
HAYES, Trent .... 937-529-2201.. 378 F
tdhayes@united.edu
HAYES, Valerie .... 609-652-4693.. 297 C
valerie.hayes@stockton.edu
HAYES, Valerie, O .... 814-732-2167.. 415 A
vhayes@edinboro.edu
HAYES, Wendy .... 937-376-6332.. 365 H
whayes@centralstate.edu
HAYES-MORRISON, Ruth 352-371-2833.... 98 I
admissions@dragonrises.edu
HAYGOOD, Courtney .... 870-574-4458.... 22 G
chaygood@sautech.edu
HAYGOOD, Jennifer .... 919-807-7021.. 347 B
haygoodj@nccommunitycolleges.edu
HAYHURST, David .... 601-266-4883.. 261 E
david.hayhurst@usm.edu
HAYHURST, Neil .... 225-216-8169.. 195 H
hayhurstn@mybrcc.edu
HAYMAN, Jerry .... 207-974-4685.. 203 J
jhayman@emcc.edu
HAYMORE, Teresa .... 706-865-2134.. 128 D
thaymore@truett.edu
HAYNER, Kate .... 510-869-4780.... 59 L
khayner@samuelmerritt.edu
HAYNER, Leon .... 407-646-2649.. 107 O
lhayner@rollins.edu
HAYNES, Amy, M .... 330-684-8932.. 378 H
hamy@uakron.edu
HAYNES, Anthony .... 615-741-8220.. 448 D
anthony.haynes@tennessee.edu
HAYNES, Brian, L .... 909-537-5185.... 34 C
bhaynes@csusb.edu
HAYNES, Carl, E .... 607-844-8222.. 337 G
haynesc@tc3.edu
HAYNES, Carolyn, A .... 513-529-6722.. 372 K
haynesca@miamioh.edu
HAYNES, David, A .... 540-985-4020.. 491 A
dahaynes@jchs.edu
HAYNES, Derrick .... 303-360-4721.... 79 E
derrick.haynes@ccaurora.edu
HAYNES, Douglas, M .... 949-824-1540.... 69 C
dhaynes@uci.edu
HAYNES, James .... 585-395-2651.. 332 E
jhaynes@brockport.edu
HAYNES, Jerry .... 301-846-2459.. 207 F
jhaynes@frederick.edu
HAYNES, John, G .... 806-743-7387.. 472 D
john.g.haynes@ttuhsc.edu
HAYNES, Karen, S .... 760-750-4040.... 34 D
pres@csusm.edu
HAYNES, Lamar .... 918-836-6886.. 388 E
lamar.haynes@spartan.edu
HAYNES, Leticia .... 413-597-4376.. 230 A
lseh1@williams.edu
HAYNES, Lisa .... 616-331-7204.. 234 F
haynesl@gvsu.edu
HAYNES, Martha, B .... 906-227-2610.. 239 B
haynes@nmu.edu
HAYNES, Mike .... 254-968-9354.. 467 F
rhaynes@tarleton.edu
HAYNES, Pamela, J .... 336-888-9055.. 345 A
phaynes@highpoint.edu
HAYNES, Patricia, A .... 636-922-8427.. 271 A
phaynes@stchas.edu
HAYNES, Penny, A .... 518-381-1374.. 330 B
haynespa@sunysccc.edu
HAYNES, Ryan .... 916-577-2200.... 75 C
dgluck@jessup.edu
HAYNES, Sandra .... 303-556-2978.... 81 G
hayness@msudenver.edu
HAYNES, Scott .... 870-245-5220.... 21 E
hayness@obu.edu
HAYNES, Stephanie, C ..... 304-637-1335.. 510 I
hayness@dewv.edu
HAYNES, Tiffany .... 559-791-2447.... 47 L
tduke@portervillecollege.edu
HAYNES, Tina .... 704-216-3461.. 352 G
tina.haynes@rccc.edu
HAYNES, Wendy .... 508-531-2809.. 221 C
whaynes@bridgew.edu
HAYNIE, Glenda, D .... 804-333-6719.. 498 D
ghaynie@rappahannock.edu
HAYNIE, Janice .... 910-672-1211.. 356 E
jhaynie@uncfsu.edu
HAYNIE, Stacia .... 225-578-8274.. 197 I
pohayn@lsu.edu
HAYNIE, Todd .... 928-428-8320.... 13 B
todd.haynie@eac.edu
HAYS, Antoinette, M .... 781-768-7122.. 227 G
antoinette.hays@regiscollege.edu
HAYS, Danny .... 870-245-5526.... 21 E
haysd@obu.edu
HAYS, Eric .... 785-594-8384.. 178 D
eric.hays@bakeru.edu
HAYS, Kristi .... 785-825-5422.. 179 C
khays@brownmackie.edu
HAYS, Kristin .... 603-577-6411.. 286 I
khays@dwc.edu
HAYS, Rex .... 913-469-8500.. 182 A
rhays@jccc.edu
HAYS, Richard .... 919-660-3411.. 343 J
richard.hays@duke.edu
HAYS, Ryan .... 513-556-2201.. 379 A
ryan.hays@uc.edu
HAYS, Samantha .... 270-852-3130.. 191 C
shays@kwc.edu
HAYS, Stacie .... 712-274-5254.. 175 C
hays@morningside.edu
HAYS, Wm. Randy .... 859-238-5471.. 187 H
randy.hays@centre.edu
HAYS-THOMAS, Helen .... 269-927-6874.. 236 G
hhays-thomas@lakemichigancollege.edu
HAYSBERT, JoAnn, W ...... 757-727-5693.. 490 E
joann.haysbert@hamptonu.edu
HAYTAS, Debra .... 304-263-6262.. 511 A
dhaytas@martinsburginstitute.edu
HAYTER, Christopher, A .. 614-823-1348.. 376 C
chayter@otterbein.edu
HAYTER, Richard .... 972-721-5227.. 473 D
rhayter@udallas.edu
HAYTER, Sonya .... 417-269-3469.. 264 D
sonya.hayter@coxcollege.edu
HAYTON, Heather .... 336-316-2397.. 344 H
hhayton@guilford.edu
HAYTON, James, C .... 848-445-4616.. 296 B
james.hayton@rutgers.edu
HAYWARD, Albert, G .... 803-516-4541.. 432 E
ahayward@scsu.edu
HAYWARD, Craig .... 949-451-5788.... 65 F
chayward@ivc.edu
HAYWARD, Dawn .... 215-646-7300.. 404 G
hayward.d@gmercyu.edu
HAYWARD, Maysa .... 732-255-0400.. 293 E
mhayward@ocean.edu
HAYWARD, Milian .... 540-857-6076.. 499 B
mhayward@virginiawestern.edu
HAYWARD, William, C .... 312-996-3254.. 156 F
whaywa2@uic.edu
HAYWOOD, Ben .... 903-233-3561.. 460 J
benhaywood@letu.edu
HAYWOOD, Carl .... 210-829-3935.. 474 D
carl@uiwtx.edu
HAYWOOD, Chanta .... 478-825-6118.. 120 F
haywoodc@fvsu.edu
HAYWOOD, Davida .... 334-229-4241...... 1 D
dhaywood@alasu.edu
HAYWOOD, Georgeann .... 302-857-6001.... 90 F
ghaywood@desu.edu
HAYWOOD, Michele .... 910-576-6222.. 351 E
haywoodm@montgomery.edu
HAYWOOD, Zina .... 262-564-3104.. 523 D
haywoodz@gtc.edu
HAYWORTH, Kimberly, K .. 517-750-1200.. 241 E
kimh@arbor.edu
HAZAM, Bruce .... 207-801-5645.. 202 H
bhazam@coa.edu
HAZARD, Laurie, L .... 401-232-6746.. 424 K
lhazard@bryant.edu
HAZARD, Terry .... 692-625-3291.. 530 C
thazard@cmi.edu
HAZARD, Victor, A .... 859-257-3754.. 193 G
vahaz@uky.edu
HAZEL, Julie .... 719-502-3005.... 82 B
julie.hazel@ppcc.edu
HAZEL, Stephanie .... 703-993-5106.. 490 B
shazel@gmu.edu
HAZELBAKER, Chato .... 360-992-2921.. 502 E
chazelbaker@clark.edu
HAZELBAKER, Nicole .... 406-683-7900.. 277 A
nicole.hazelbaker@umwestern.edu
HAZELKORN, Michael .... 912-279-5720.. 119 C
mhazelkorn@ccga.edu
HAZELTON, Janet .... 802-468-1208.. 485 H
janet.hazelton@castleton.edu
HAZELTON, Rahneeka .... 817-202-6733.. 466 C
rahneeka@swau.edu
HAZEN, Ian .... 315-268-7122.. 310 B
ihazen@clarkson.edu
HAZEN, Meghan .... 217-333-2034.. 157 A
registrar@illinois.edu
HAZEN, Ron .... 615-297-7545.. 438 F
hazenr@aquinascollege.edu
HAZLETT, Brian .... 717-871-5714.. 415 F
brian.hazlett@millersville.edu
HAZLETT, Laura .... 510-594-3688.... 29 K
lhazlett@cca.edu
HAZLETT, Margaret .... 717-358-5816.. 403 J
margaret.hazlett@fandm.edu
HAZLETT, Mia .... 508-362-2131.. 223 C
mhazlett@capecod.edu
HAZZARD, Mike .... 270-706-8686.. 189 C
mikew.hazzard@kctcs.edu
HAZZARD, Terry .... 251-405-7087...... 2 D
thazzard@bishop.edu
HA'O, Melanie .... 401-841-7367.. 528 E
HE, Phil .... 617-373-6817.. 227 B
HE, Yuxin .... 512-454-1188.. 451 E
info@aoma.edu
HEABERLIN, Robert .... 770-254-7280.. 129 E
rheaber@westga.edu
HEACOCK, Maureen .... 937-769-1351.. 363 E
mheacock@antioch.edu
HEACOCK, Maureen .... 937-769-1846.. 363 F
mheacock@antioch.edu
HEAD, Carolyn .... 901-321-3256.. 439 E
chead1@cbu.edu
HEAD, Daniel .... 251-575-8259...... 1 C
dhead@ascc.edu
HEAD, John .... 678-839-6423.. 129 E
jhead@westg.edu
HEAD, Judith .... 214-638-0484.. 460 C
jhead@kdstudio.com
HEAD, Rachel .... 610-328-8362.. 419 I
rhead1@swarthmore.edu
HEAD, Stephen .... 832-813-6515.. 461 B
steve.head@lonestar.edu
HEAD, Sue .... 417-690-2241.. 263 E
shead@cofo.edu
HEAD, Susan .... 315-792-7342.. 336 C
susan.head@sunyit.edu
HEADING-GRANT,
Wanda, R .... 802-656-8426.. 485 D
wanda.heading-grant@uvm.edu
HEADINGS, Ronald .... 419-358-3660.. 364 D
headingsr@bluffton.edu
HEADLEY, Scot .... 503-554-2836.. 391 D
sheadley@georgefox.edu
HEADRICK, Dennis .... 402-323-3427.. 282 F
dheadric@southeast.edu
HEADRICK, Robert .... 479-248-7236.... 20 C
bheadrick@ecollege.edu
HEADY, Emily .... 434-592-3232.. 491 D
eheady@liberty.edu
HEAFNER, Lori .... 843-349-7871.. 430 F
lori.heafner@hgtc.edu
HEAGLE, Leanne .... 937-255-6565.. 527 H
leanne.heagle@afit.edu
HEALD, Donna .... 518-244-3190.. 327 H
healdd@sage.edu
HEALEY, Dale .... 952-888-4777.. 253 Z
dhealey@nwhealth.edu
HEALEY, Maureen .... 219-866-6161.. 166 J
maureenh@saintjoe.edu
HEALEY, Stephen, E .... 203-576-4668.... 89 C
healey@bridgeport.edu
HEALEY, Tom .... 810-762-0417.. 238 F
thomas.healey@mcc.edu
HEALTON, Edward, B .... 202-877-1504.... 92 E
ebh4@georgetown.edu
HEALY, Amy .... 518-255-5118.. 334 D
healyak@cobleskill.edu
HEALY, David .... 904-256-7024.. 103 D
dhealy1@ju.edu
HEALY, Gayle .... 518-629-7326.. 316 G
g.healy@hvcc.edu
HEALY, Heidi .... 847-214-7006.. 140 A
hhealy@elgin.edu
HEALY, Joanne .... 313-664-1474.. 232 G
jhealy@collegeforcreativestudies.edu
HEALY, John (Jack) .... 218-477-2581.. 250 F
jack.healy@mnstate.edu
HEALY, Robert .... 716-286-8341.. 324 E
rhealy@niagara.edu
HEALY, Rose Mary .... 973-278-5400.. 305 B
rmh@berkeleycollege.edu
HEALY, Rose Mary .... 973-278-5400.. 289 F
rmh@berkeleycollege.edu
HEALY, William, L .... 863-680-4140.. 101 E
whealy@flsouthern.edu
HEAMES, Joyce .... 706-236-2233.. 117 F
jheames@berry.edu
HEANEY, Nicole .... 508-678-2811.. 223 A
nicole.heaney@bristolcc.edu
HEAP, Jeff .... 815-280-2401.. 144 A
jheap@jjc.edu
HEAP, Jeffrey .... 815-280-2401.. 144 A
jheap@jjc.edu
HEARD, Anissa .... 949-451-5364.... 65 F
aheard@ivc.edu
HEARD, Frederick .... 713-718-7757.. 459 B
frederick.heard@hccs.edu
HEARD, John .... 660-626-2397.. 262 A
jheard@atsu.edu
HEARD, Michael .... 404-756-4443.. 116 I
mheard@atlm.edu
HEARD, Michael .... 229-217-4207.. 127 G
mheard@southernregional.edu
HEARD, Sasha .... 888-384-0849.... 25 P
sheard@allied.edu
HEARD, Shalonda .... 229-317-6489.. 120 A
shalonda.heard@darton.edu
HEARN, Deyna .... 310-434-4435.... 63 F
hearn_deyna@smc.edu
HEARN, Greg, K .... 706-245-7226.. 120 D
ghearn@lifesprings.net
HEARN, Jessica .... 502-863-8000.. 188 I
jessica_hearn@georgetowncollege.edu
HEARN, Kevin .... 716-286-8405.. 324 E
khearn@niagara.edu
HEARN, Maribeth .... 815-740-3384.. 157 F
mhearn@stfrancis.edu
HEARN, Sabrina, B .... 205-934-9176...... 8 C
shearn@uasystem.edu
HEARNE, Chad .... 501-450-5015.... 24 G
HEARTLEIN, Karrie .... 309-341-7340.. 145 A
kheartle@knox.edu
HEARTS-GLASS, Angela ... 312-850-7168.. 138 A
aheartsglass@ccc.edu
HEASLEY, Ronald, P .... 717-361-1558.. 403 C
heasleyrp@etown.edu
HEASTON, Amy .... 912-344-2505.. 116 E
amy.heaston@armstrong.edu
HEATER, Margaret .... 585-343-0055.. 315 C
meheater@genesee.edu
HEATH, Aaron .... 816-322-0110.. 262 N
aaron.heath@calvary.edu
HEATH, Bill .... 863-638-2953.. 115 D
heathwl@webber.edu
HEATH, Bob .... 417-626-1234.. 269 K
heath.bob@occ.edu
HEATH, Cantey .... 803-777-2001.. 433 F
canteyh@mailbox.sc.edu
HEATH, Cassandra, A .... 530-226-4608.... 64 H
cheath@simpsonu.edu
HEATH, Cheryl, A .... 307-674-6446.. 526 M
cheath@sheridan.edu
HEATH, David, A .... 212-938-5650.. 334 F
dheath@sunyopt.edu
HEATH, Donna, R .... 336-334-5092.. 358 B
drheath@uncg.edu
HEATH, Hildy .... 415-405-4256.... 35 B
hheath@sfsu.edu
HEATH, Janie, H .... 859-257-9000.. 193 G
jheath@uky.edu
HEATH, Janine .... 573-840-9698.. 273 A
jheath@trcc.edu
HEATH, Jason .... 502-897-4106.. 192 D
jheath@sbts.edu
HEATH, Joan, L .... 512-245-2133.. 471 F
jh06@txstate.edu
HEATH, Judy .... 410-777-1177.. 206 B
jheath@aacc.edu
HEATH, Kathy .... 207-326-2339.. 204 C
kathy.heath@mma.edu
HEATH, Marie .... 904-470-8933.... 98 N
m.heath@ewc.edu
HEATH, Mary-Teresa .... 518-828-4181.. 311 D
mary-teresa.heath@sunycgcc.edu
HEATH, Rebekah, A .... 563-333-6447.. 176 D
heathrebekaha@sau.edu
HEATH, Richard, C .... 410-777-2204.. 206 B
rcheath@aacc.edu
HEATH, Robert .... 205-366-8851...... 7 E
rheath@stillman.edu
HEATHERLY, David, L .... 910-938-6789.. 348 G
heatherlyd@coastalcarolina.edu
HEATON, Dennis .... 641-472-7000.. 175 A
dheaton@mum.edu
HEATON, Haidee .... 573-288-6434.. 264 F
hheaton@culver.edu
HEATON, Karick .... 801-302-2879.. 480 L
karick.heaton@neumont.edu
HEATON, Mandy .... 503-777-7289.. 394 I
heatonm@reed.edu
HEATON, Scott .... 209-946-2541.... 71 C
sheaton@pacific.edu
HEATON, Tim .... 605-688-5117.. 437 F
tim.heaton@sdstate.edu
HEATOR, Martin .... 734-462-4400.. 240 H
mheator@schoolcraft.edu
HEATWOLE, Deirdre .... 617-287-5324.. 220 E
dheatwole@umassp.edu
HEATWOLE, Deirdre .... 774-455-7300.. 220 G
dheatwole@umassp.edu
HEAVENER, Mac .... 904-596-2400.. 113 J
macheavener@tbc.edu
HEAVENER, Matthew .... 904-596-2420.. 113 J
mheavener@tbc.org

HEIST, Daniel, P .... 814-865-1359.. 412 F dph3@psu.edu
HEIST, Richard .... 386-226-6216.... 99 A richard.heist@erau.edu
HEISTAD, Deirdre, A .... 319-273-2733.. 170 A d.heistad@uni.edu
HEITHAUS, Michael .... 305-348-2866.. 111 A michael.heithaus@fiu.edu
HEITKAMP, Andrew .... 701-858-4002.. 360 F andy.heitkamp@minotstateu.edu
HEITKAMP, Mike .... 701-252-3467.. 362 F mike.heitkamp@uj.edu
HEITKEMPER, Mary .... 509-313-4231.. 504 A heitkemper@gonzaga.edu
HEITMANN, Damen .... 402-461-7397.. 280 D dheitmann@hastings.edu
HEITNER, Douglas .... 570-586-2400.. 419 G dheitner@summitu.edu
HEITZ, Cheryl .... 928-523-3711.... 15 H cheryl.heitz@nau.edu
HEITZENRATER, Kim, D .... 931-598-1121.. 443 O kheitzen@sewanee.edu
HEITZMANN, Dennis, E ... 814-865-0966.. 412 F deh8@psu.edu
HEIZER NEWQUIST, Leslie .... 425-564-2191.. 501 F leslie.newquist@bellevuecollege.edu
HEJL, Cindy .... 303-556-4029.... 81 G hejlc@msudenver.edu
HEKKEL, Jerry .... 206-726-5151.. 503 B jhekkel@cornish.edu
HELBERG, Yvonne .... 314-539-5150.. 271 F yhelberg@stlcc.edu
HELBIG, Suzanne, C .... 949-824-7366.... 69 C shelbig@uci.edu
HELBIG, Tuesdi .... 270-745-3250.. 194 D tuesdi.helbig@wku.edu
HELBING, Shirley .... 570-702-8918.. 406 E shelbing@johnson.edu
HELBLE, Joseph .... 603-646-2238.. 286 J joseph.helble@dartmouth.edu
HELBLING, Brenda .... 208-885-9191.. 134 G brendah@uidaho.edu
HELD, Lynnette .... 805-756-5352.... 31 I lheld@calpoly.edu
HELDEROP, Sue .... 248-364-6135.. 239 K helderop@oakland.edu
HELDMAN, Lou .... 316-978-7114.. 185 J lou.heldman@wichita.edu
HELEKAR, Andrea, D .... 213-624-1200.... 43 J ahelekar@fidm.edu
HELENS, Joyce .... 320-308-5017.. 252 B jhelens@sctcc.edu
HELFENSTEIN, Patricia .... 610-372-4721.. 417 G phelfenstein@racc.edu
HELFRICH, Lori .... 314-719-3663.. 265 C lhelfrich@fontbonne.edu
HELGE, Kristyn, S .... 817-515-7463.. 467 A kristyn.helge@tccd.edu
HELGEN, Beth .... 612-330-1212.. 244 I helgen@augsburg.edu
HELGESEN, Paul .... 978-867-4730.. 219 A paul.helgesen@gordon.edu
HELGESEN, Pete .... 913-360-7476.. 178 I phelgesen@benedictine.edu
HELGESON, Grant .... 808-455-0645.. 132 C helgeson@hawaii.edu
HELGESON, Richard, J ..... 731-881-7380.. 448 G helgeson@utm.edu
HELGESTAD, Chris .... 612-861-7554.. 244 D chris.helgestad@alfredadler.edu
HELIEISAR, Jennifer .... 691-320-2480.. 529 F jenniferh@comfsm.fm
HELIS, James, A .... 516-726-5815.. 529 B helisj@usmma.edu
HELLA, Lori, L .... 989-774-7194.. 232 D hella1ll@cmich.edu
HELLAMS, Thomas .... 502-897-4121.. 192 D thellams@sbts.edu
HELLAND, Carol .... 218-749-7715.. 249 I c.helland@mesabirange.edu
HELLAND, Carol .... 218-285-7722.. 251 F carol.helland@rainyriver.edu
HELLDOBLER, Richard, J 773-442-5420.. 149 J r-helldobler@neiu.edu
HELLE, Laura .... 507-433-0664.. 251 H laura.helle@riverland.edu
HELLEMAN, Kathryn .... 419-434-4256.. 381 E khelleman@winebrenner.edu
HELLER, Adam .... 623-245-4600.... 17 G aheller@uti.edu
HELLER, Dana .... 757-683-3925.. 492 G dheller@odu.edu
HELLER, Donald .... 415-422-6136.... 72 C deheller@usfca.edu
HELLER, James .... 262-595-2455.. 520 F james.heller@uwp.edu
HELLER, Joshua, J .... 212-752-1530.. 318 F joshua.heller@limcollege.edu
HELLER, Joshua, W .... 585-785-1335.. 314 D joshua.heller@flcc.edu
HELLER, Laurent .... 608-263-2467.. 519 K lheller@vc.wisc.edu
HELLER, Mary .... 406-265-4198.. 277 E mary.heller@msun.edu
HELLER, Matt .... 847-945-8800.. 156 B mheller@tiu.edu
HELLER, Matthew, D .... 607-587-3992.. 334 G hellermd@alfredstate.edu
HELLER, Tracy .... 858-635-4535.... 25 J theller@alliant.edu
HELLER, Tracy .... 858-635-4535.... 25 K theller@alliant.edu
HELLER, William .... 727-873-4979.. 112 D heller@usfsp.edu
HELLER-ROSS, Holly, B .... 518-564-5180.. 334 A hellerhb@plattsburgh.edu
HELLERMANN, David .... 651-290-6457.. 253 S david.hellermann@mitchellhamline.edu
HELLERSTEIN, Laurel .... 978-232-2153.. 218 D lhellers@endicott.edu
HELLERUD, Nancy .... 314-246-7440.. 275 B nancyhellerud@webster.edu
HELLIE, Thomas .... 503-883-2408.. 392 B thellie@linfield.edu
HELLIGE, Joseph, B .... 310-338-2733.... 51 E jhellige@lmu.edu
HELLING, Mary Kay .... 605-688-4173.. 437 F mary.helling@sdstate.edu
HELLING, Nathan, M .... 605-336-6588.. 436 J nhelling@sfseminary.edu
HELLMAN, Frances .... 510-642-5872.... 68 M fhellman@berkeley.edu
HELLMAN, Joel .... 202-687-0100.... 92 E jhellman@georgetown.edu
HELLMICH, David, M .... 815-835-6303.. 153 K david.m.hellmich@svcc.edu
HELLMUND, Paul, C .... 413-369-4044.. 217 E hellmund@csld.edu
HELLRUNG, Scott, A .... 414-410-4697.. 515 I shellrung@stritch.edu
HELLUMS, Duane .... 502-410-6200.. 188 H dhellums@galencollege.edu
HELLUMS, Paula .... 337-421-6965.. 197 B paula.hellums@sowela.edu
HELLWIG, Beth, A .... 715-836-5992.. 520 A hellwiba@uwec.edu
HELLWIG, Brant, J .... 540-458-5352.. 500 F hellwig@wlu.edu
HELLYER, Brenda .... 281-998-6100.. 464 I brenda.hellyer@sjcd.edu
HELM, Hunt, C .... 502-272-8046.. 187 A hhelm@bellarmine.edu
HELM, Jonathan, C .... 254-710-8824.. 452 H jonathan_helm@baylor.edu
HELM, Lloyd .... 503-594-6793.. 390 F lloyd.helm@clackamas.edu
HELM, Peyton .... 508-999-8004.. 220 H chancellor@umassd.edu
HELM, Scott .... 641-782-1481.. 177 B helm@swcciowa.edu
HELM, Steven .... 540-831-5471.. 493 A shelm@radford.edu
HELM, Thomas .... 603-668-2211.. 287 I t.helm@snhu.edu
HELMBRECHT, Alex .... 308-432-6212.. 281 H ahlembrecht@csc.edu
HELMER, Robert, C .... 440-826-2424.. 363 M rhelmer@bw.edu
HELMER, Shannon .... 610-799-1857.. 408 G shelmer@lccc.edu
HELMICK, Mary .... 540-231-6221.. 499 F mhelmick@vt.edu
HELMICK, Michael, S .... 828-448-3102.. 354 B mhelmick@wpcc.edu
HELMICK, Tom .... 724-852-3210.. 423 A thelmick@waynesburg.edu
HELMING, Jay .... 202-685-3909.. 528 B jay.helming@ndu.edu
HELMREICH, Anne .... 817-257-2787.. 469 G a.helmreich@tcu.edu
HELMS, Chris .... 828-766-1291.. 351 B chelms@mayland.edu
HELMS, Clint .... 706-233-7265.. 127 A
HELMS, James, B .... 256-306-2545...... 2 F bryan.helms@calhoun.edu
HELMS, Lance .... 912-538-3207.. 127 E lhelms@southeasterntech.edu
HELMS, Mark .... 704-330-6127.. 348 E mark.helms@cpcc.edu
HELMS, Michael .... 334-347-2623...... 3 H mhelms@escc.edu
HELMS, Sherrie .... 478-289-2360.. 120 C shelms@ega.edu
HELMS, Steve .... 334-222-6591...... 5 F shelms@lbwcc.edu
HELMS, Wanda .... 505-224-4000.. 299 F whelms@cnm.edu
HELMS, Wanda .... 505-224-4551.. 299 F whelms@cnm.edu
HELMSING, Debra, F .... 260-665-4240.. 167 E helmsingd@trine.edu
HELMSTETTER, Ashley ...... 419-448-2231.. 369 G ahelmste@heidelberg.edu
HELMUS, Aimee .... 910-362-7012.. 348 A ahelmus@cfcc.edu
HELMUS, Mark .... 765-289-1241.. 159 B dmhelmus@bsu.edu
HELMUTH, Andrea, M .... 574-807-7351.. 159 D andrea.helmuth@bethelcollege.edu
HELOU, Ibrahim (Abe) ...... 909-593-3511.... 71 B ihelou@laverne.edu
HELSETH, Joe .... 423-697-2606.. 445 D joe.helseth@chattanoogastate.edu
HELSPER, Nancy .... 320-589-6012.. 255 F helsper@morris.umn.edu
HELSTON, Stephanie .... 212-757-1190.. 304 B shelston@funeraleducation.org
HELTON, Karen .... 903-927-3369.. 479 K khelton@wileyc.edu
HELTON, Patricia .... 727-873-4882.. 112 D phelton@mail.usf.edu
HELTON, Tom .... 706-507-8909.. 119 E helton_tom@columbusstate.edu
HELVERING, Christal .... 765-641-4205.. 158 J crhelvering@anderson.edu
HELVESTON, David .... 225-308-4420.. 195 G davidhelveston@lctcs.edu
HELVIE-MASON, Lora .... 254-968-9488.. 467 F helviemason@tarleton.edu
HELWIG, Christine, A .... 518-629-7343.. 316 G c.helwig@hvcc.edu
HELWIG, Daniel .... 717-867-6220.. 408 F helwig@lvc.edu
HELWIG, Denice .... 707-826-3300.... 34 F dh7003@humboldt.edu
HELWIG, Susan, M .... 570-674-6368.. 410 K shelwig@misericordia.edu
HELYER, Kella .... 503-838-8684.. 396 E helyerk@wou.edu
HEMANN, Patty .... 507-433-0816.. 251 H patty.hemann@riverland.edu
HEMANS, Peter .... 828-694-1723.. 347 G peterh@blueridge.edu
HEMBREE, Lois, D .... 620-421-6700.. 182 G loish@labette.edu
HEMBRICK, Donna, Y .... 919-530-6878.. 357 A dhembrick@nccu.edu
HEMENWAY, Jessica .... 920-693-1118.. 523 E jessica.hemenway@gotoltc.edu
HEMENWAY, Michael .... 303-765-3173.... 80 M mhemenway@iliff.edu
HEMESATH, Michael .... 320-363-2882.. 254 N sjpresident@csbsju.edu
HEMINGWAY, Wen .... 810-766-4105.. 231 D whemin01@baker.edu
HEMKER, Judy .... 618-545-3105.. 144 D jhemker@kaskaskia.edu
HEMLICK, Lisa, M .... 610-341-5830.. 403 B lhemlick@eastern.edu
HEMMASI, Harriette .... 401-863-2162.. 424 J harriette_hemmasi@brown.edu
HEMMENBACH, Jimmi .... 808-543-8083.. 130 H jhemmenbach@hpu.edu
HEMMER, Katie .... 212-966-0300.. 322 F khemmer@nyaa.edu
HEMMER, Laura .... 314-505-7203.. 263 I hemmerl@csl.edu
HEMMER, Michelle .... 919-508-2260.. 359 G michelle.hemmer@peace.edu
HEMMESCH, Michael .... 320-363-2595.. 254 N mhemmesch@csbsju.edu
HEMMESCH, Michael .... 320-363-2595.. 245 I mhemmesch@csbsju.edu
HEMMIG, Bill .... 215-504-8611.. 399 A bill.hemmig@bucks.edu
HEMMILA, Deanna .... 906-227-2637.. 239 B dhemmila@nmu.edu
HEMMING, Erik, G .... 414-229-4201.. 520 D hemmingc@aux.uwm.edu
HEMMINGSEN, Jens .... 614-236-6105.. 364 N jhemming@capital.edu
HEMMITT, Ernita .... 404-880-6128.. 118 K ehemmitt@cau.edu
HEMPEL, Lamont, C .... 909-748-8589.... 71 K monty_hempel@redlands.edu
HEMPEL-LAMER, Nele .... 562-985-4128.... 33 B nele.hempel-lamer@csulb.edu
HEMPHILL, F. Bruce .... 337-475-5563.. 200 H bhemphill@mcneese.edu
HEMPHILL, Teale .... 719-336-1591.... 81 D teale.hemphill@lamarcc.edu
HEMPILL, Geoffrey .... 718-420-4269.. 339 F geoffrey.hempill@wagner.edu
HEMPSEY, John Paul .... 928-524-7418.... 15 J paul.hempsey@npc.edu
HEMPTON, David, N .... 617-496-8026.. 219 D dhempton@hds.harvard.edu
HEMRICK, Robert, D .... 731-425-2636.. 446 C dhemrick@jscc.edu
HEMWALL, Lara .... 412-291-6315.. 397 I lhemwall@aii.edu
HEMWAY, Joseph .... 718-399-4293.. 326 E jhemway@pratt.edu
HENAHAN, David .... 518-587-2100.. 335 D david.henahan@esc.edu
HENAN, Carmen .... 505-424-2336.. 299 L chenan@iaia.edu
HENAO, Sandra .... 415-442-7833.... 45 B shenao@ggu.edu
HENARD, Kevin .... 254-298-8425.. 467 B kevin.henard@templejc.edu
HENCHEY, Russell .... 740-245-7231.. 380 C rhenchey@rio.edu
HENCHY, Alexandra .... 859-858-2049.. 186 I
HENCHY, Dolores .... 201-355-1133.. 291 K henchyd@felician.edu
HENCK, Anita .... 626-815-5348.... 28 A ahenck@apu.edu
HENDERSHOT, Debra ...... 256-306-2581...... 2 F debi.hendershot@calhoun.edu
HENDERSHOT, Jason ...... 814-393-2111.. 414 G jhendershot@clarion.edu
HENDERSHOT, Stephanie, N .... 412-262-6251.. 418 B hendershot@rmu.edu
HENDERSON, Aaron .... 559-453-2207.... 44 F aaron.henderson@fresno.edu
HENDERSON, Allan .... 314-773-0083.. 262 J allan.henderson@brookesbible.org
HENDERSON, Allen .... 817-531-4405.. 472 F ahenderson@txwes.edu
HENDERSON, Amanda ..... 210-410-9159.. 153 J ahenderson@careered.com
HENDERSON, Andrea .... 309-298-1977.. 158 A ad-henderson@wiu.edu
HENDERSON, Angela .... 773-995-2411.. 136 M ahende22@csu.edu
HENDERSON, Brad .... 620-331-4100.. 181 J bhenderson@indycc.edu
HENDERSON, Brian .... 276-656-0313.. 498 A bhenderson@patrickhenry.edu
HENDERSON, Carol .... 315-364-3356.. 340 B chenderson@wells.edu
HENDERSON, Carol, E ..... 302-831-2897.... 91 F ceh@udel.edu
HENDERSON, Carrie .... 904-632-3307.. 101 G carrie.henderson@fscj.edu
HENDERSON, Chad .... 763-488-0229.. 251 B chenderson@nhcc.edu
HENDERSON, Chiquita, A .... 727-816-3205.. 106 F henderc@phsc.edu
HENDERSON, Christina ... 515-271-1501.. 171 H christina.henderson@dmu.edu
HENDERSON, Christine ... 773-371-5450.. 136 F chenderson@ctu.edu
HENDERSON, Cynthia .... 903-223-3053.. 469 C cynthia.henderson@tamut.edu
HENDERSON, Darren .... 219-473-4346.. 159 L dhenderson@ccsj.edu
HENDERSON, Darwin, C . 505-786-4300.. 300 E chenderson@navajotech.edu
HENDERSON, Dave .... 541-917-4331.. 392 C henderd@linnbenton.edu
HENDERSON, Debbie .... 417-690-2222.. 263 E henderson@cofo.edu
HENDERSON, Dee .... 731-424-3520.. 446 C dhenderson@jscc.edu
HENDERSON, Eddie, W ... 806-651-2600.. 469 D ehenderson@mail.wtamu.edu
HENDERSON, Eric .... 928-524-7350.... 15 J eric.henderson@npc.edu
HENDERSON, Floyd .... 843-525-8271.. 433 B fhenderson@tcl.edu
HENDERSON, George .... 704-330-4806.. 348 E george.henderson@cpcc.edu
HENDERSON, Gregg .... 626-395-4701.... 30 H gregg.henderson@caltech.edu
HENDERSON, Howard .... 580-349-1380.. 385 F howardh@opsu.edu
HENDERSON, Idell .... 404-527-6356.. 123 I ihenderson@itc.edu
HENDERSON, James .... 856-256-4175.. 295 E henderson@rowan.edu
HENDERSON, James, B .... 318-357-6441.. 201 B jhenderson@nsula.edu
HENDERSON, James, P .... 608-262-3826.. 519 J jhenderson@uwsa.edu
HENDERSON, Janet .... 706-754-7833.. 125 B jhenderson@northgatech.edu
HENDERSON, Janice .... 850-729-5392.. 105 I hendersonj@nwfsc.edu
HENDERSON, Joe, T .... 731-881-3506.. 448 G jhende33@utm.edu
HENDERSON, Julie .... 510-987-9195.... 68 L julie.henderson@ucop.edu
HENDERSON, Kathy .... 408-855-5113.... 74 G kathy.henderson@missioncollege.edu
HENDERSON, Kenneth ..... 617-373-5089.. 227 B
HENDERSON, Kyle, W ...... 740-427-5729.. 371 C hendersonk@kenyon.edu

HENSLEY, Chiara .... 734-487-0074.. 233 J
emu_ombuds@emich.edu
HENSLEY, Linda .... 619-421-6700.... 66 E
lhensley@swccd.edu
HENSLEY, Mary .... 979-830-4112.. 452 J
president@blinn.edu
HENSLEY, Michele, R ...... 540-432-4139.. 488 K
michele.hensley@emu.edu
HENSLEY, Ron .... 417-255-7268.. 269 A
ronhensley@missouristate.edu
HENSLEY, Steve, L .... 864-242-5100.. 427 E
HENSON, Alexander, L .... 804-828-0138.. 496 D
alhenson@vcu.edu
HENSON, Chuck .... 573-882-2121.. 273 E
HENSON, Don .... 901-722-4719.. 444 C
dhenson@sco.edu
HENSON, Emily .... 618-252-5400.. 154 G
emily.henson@sic.edu
HENSON, Gregory, J .... 605-336-6588.. 436 J
ghenson@sfseminary.edu
HENSON, John, H .... 717-245-1363.. 402 D
henson@dickinson.edu
HENSON, Kevin .... 714-432-5796.... 39 G
khenson@occ.cccd.edu
HENSON, Michael, C .... 606-783-9080.. 191 H
m.henson@moreheadstate.edu
HENSON, Nicholas .... 937-395-8112.. 371 D
nicholas.henson@kc.edu
HENSON, Pamella, A .... 314-935-5277.. 274 N
hensonp@wustl.edu
HENSON, Travis .... 618-545-3177.. 144 D
thenson@kaskaskia.edu
HENSRUD, Faith, C .... 218-755-2011.. 248 M
fhensrud@bemidjistate.edu
HENTHORN, Becky .... 580-387-7181.. 384 D
bhenthorn@mscok.edu
HENTHORN, Janet .... 312-235-3507.. 154 C
j.henthorn@shimer.edu
HENTON, June, M .... 334-844-4790..... 1 G
hentoju@auburn.edu
HENTSCHEL, Alain, R ...... 386-312-4302.. 108 B
alainhentschel@sjrstate.edu
HENTZ, Paula .... 386-822-7012.. 113 B
phentz@stetson.edu
HENZE, George .... 920-693-1733.. 523 E
george.henze@gotoltc.edu
HENZEL, JR., John, R ..... 706-245-7226.. 120 D
jhenzel@ec.edu
HEOS, Pamela .... 517-371-5140.. 243 I
heosp@cooley.edu
HEPBURN, Deborah, G .... 814-371-2090.. 421 A
dhepburn@triangle-tech.edu
HEPBURN, Deborah, G .... 814-371-2090.. 421 B
dhepburn@triangle-tech.edu
HEPERI, Vernon, L .... 801-422-7254.. 480 C
vernon_heperi@byu.edu
HEPHNER LABANC,
Brandi .... 662-915-7705.. 261 B
bhl@olemiss.edu
HEPLER, Lisa, L .... 814-393-2229.. 414 G
lhepler@clarion.edu
HEPNER, Kevin .... 617-708-3501.. 224 F
khepner@rcc.mass.edu
HEPNER, Mickey .... 405-974-2809.. 388 L
mhepner@uco.edu
HEPPNER, Angela .... 817-554-5950.. 461 G
aheppner@messengercollege.edu
HEPPNER, Gloria .... 313-577-5600.. 243 F
heppnerg@wayne.edu
HEPPNER, Harold, H .... 406-353-2607.. 275 H
hheppner@ancollege.edu
HERALD, John .... 606-886-3863.. 189 A
john.herald@kctcs.edu
HERALD, Sara, B .... 305-899-3080.... 96 D
sherald@barry.edu
HERB, Amanda .... 740-374-8716.. 381 A
aherb@wscc.edu
HERB, Amanda, K .... 740-374-8716.. 381 A
aherb@wscc.edu
HERB, Martha .... 202-646-1337.... 93 C
HERB-SEPICH, Deb .... 605-331-6635.. 438 A
deb.sepich@usiouxfalls.edu
HERBERT, Eileen, C .... 716-888-2791.. 306 F
herberte@canisius.edu
HERBERT, George, E .... 319-335-3179.. 169 H
george-herbert@uiowa.edu
HERBERT, James, D .... 215-895-2285.. 402 G
jh49@drexel.edu
HERBERT, Jane .... 212-817-7100.. 308 A
jherbert@gc.cuny.edu
HERBERT, Julie .... 440-375-7000.. 371 E
jherbert@lec.edu
HERBERT, Loren .... 215-968-8638.. 399 A
loren.herbert@bucks.edu
HERBERT, Mike .... 541-888-7208.. 395 B
mherbert@socc.edu
HERBERT, Tom .... 513-529-4029.. 372 K
herbertw@miamioh.edu
HERBERT-ASHTON,
Marilyn, J .... 540-857-6372.. 499 B
mherbert-ashton@virginiawestern.edu

HERBOLD, Kirk .... 830-372-8150.. 470 C
kherbold@tlu.edu
HERBRAND, Laurie .... 209-228-2741.... 70 A
lherbrand@ucmerced.edu
HERBST, Adam .... 320-363-3819.. 254 N
aherbst@csbsju.edu
HERBST, Daniel .... 480-732-7120.... 13 O
daniel.herbst@cgc.edu
HERBST, Joel .... 561-297-3970.. 110 K
jherbst1@fau.edu
HERBST, John, H .... 859-257-5781.. 193 G
herbst@uky.edu
HERBST, Shea, A .... 563-556-5110.. 175 F
herbsts@nicc.edu
HERBST, Susan .... 860-486-2337.... 89 D
president@uconn.edu
HERBSTER, David .... 605-677-5309.. 437 A
david.herbster@usd.edu
HERBSTER, Jessica .... 334-347-2623....... 3 H
jherbster@escc.edu
HERCHMER, Janice .... 716-896-0700.. 339 E
jherchmer@villa.edu
HERCOD, Laura, H .... 603-646-0574.. 286 J
laura.h.hercod@dartmouth.edu
HERDLICK, Mike .... 419-448-3421.. 378 A
herdlickm@tiffin.edu
HEREDIA, Maria .... 619-398-4902..... 46 D
mheredia@hightechhigh.org
HEREFORD, Vicki .... 256-924-0511...... 5 E
vhereford@legacyu.net
HERENDEEN, Steve, A ..... 260-422-5561.. 162 B
saherendeen@indianatech.edu
HERESHKO, David .... 570-784-3123.. 414 D
hereshko@bloomu.edu
HERFEL, Amy .... 608-249-6611.. 516 M
amyherfel@herzing.edu
HERGAN, Mark, J .... 443-352-4400.. 211 A
mhergan@stevenson.edu
HERGERT, Erin .... 719-549-3226.... 82 G
erin.hergert@pueblocc.edu
HERGERT, Travis, J .... 641-422-4990.. 175 E
hergetra@niacc.edu
HERICH, Kirsten .... 616-222-3000.. 236 F
kherich@kuyper.edu
HERIGON, Amber .... 406-791-5248.. 278 G
amber.herigon@ugf.edu
HERINGER, David .... 325-793-4700.. 461 F
heringer.david@mcm.edu
HERLETH, Sally .... 660-785-4031.. 273 B
sallydet@truman.edu
HERLEY, Wade .... 402-844-7299.. 282 B
wade@northeast.edu
HERLIHY, Jim .... 334-244-3540...... 2 A
jherlihy@aum.edu
HERLIHY, Joseph, M .... 617-552-2855.. 216 C
joseph.herlihy@bc.edu
HERLOCKER, Linda, K ..... 407-582-1511.. 114 N
lherlocker@valenciacollege.edu
HERMAN, Amber .... 336-838-6292.. 354 C
amber.herman@wilkescc.edu
HERMAN, Anne .... 503-352-2777.. 394 C
hermana@pacificu.edu
HERMAN, Barbara, B .... 817-257-7855.. 469 G
b.herman@tcu.edu
HERMAN, Brian .... 612-624-5054.. 255 H
herman@umn.edu
HERMAN, Bruce .... 410-455-2472.. 211 G
bherman@umbc.edu
HERMAN, Bruce .... 410-455-2460.. 211 G
bherman@umbc.edu
HERMAN, Deborah .... 860-512-2872.... 86 E
dherman@manchestercc.edu
HERMAN, Harry .... 516-323-3503.. 321 H
hherman@molloy.edu
HERMAN, Harvey .... 605-856-5880.. 436 I
harvey.herman@sintegleska.edu
HERMAN, Jeanne .... 330-941-2264.. 382 A
jmherman@ysu.edu
HERMAN, Jeff .... 828-726-2294.. 347 I
jherman@cccti.edu
HERMAN, Jeffrey .... 619-849-2534..... 57 M
jeffreyherman@pointloma.edu
HERMAN, Nick .... 703-993-9515.. 490 B
nherman@gmu.edu
HERMAN, Stacie .... 330-490-7365.. 380 J
sherman@walsh.edu
HERMAN, Terry .... 740-588-1290.. 382 C
therman@zanestate.edu
HERMAN, Vanessa, J ...... 212-346-1025.. 325 J
vherman@pace.edu
HERMAN-BARLOW,
Janet .... 440-365-5222.. 371 H
HERMANN, David .... 815-802-8524.. 144 C
dhermann@kcc.edu
HERMANN, Michael .... 785-833-4410.. 182 F
mike.hermann@kwu.edu
HERMANN, Paula .... 785-833-4337.. 182 F
paula.hermann@kwu.edu
HERMANN-ARTIM, Diane 802-388-5371.. 486 A
diane.hermann-artim@ccv.edu

HERMANNY, Danielle, E . 503-943-8715.. 396 B
hermannd@up.edu
HERMANO, Mara .... 401-454-6336.. 426 A
mhermano@risd.edu
HERMANSEN, Beckie .... 435-283-7346.. 482 E
beckie.hermansen@snow.edu
HERMANSEN, Noreen, M 319-273-6078.. 170 A
noreen.hermansen@uni.edu
HERMANSTON, Fran .... 509-335-3942.. 508 H
HERMES, John .... 405-425-1815.. 385 C
john.hermes@oc.edu
HERMES, Joseph .... 312-996-3490.. 156 F
jhermes@uic.edu
HERMES, Wayne, J .... 970-247-7432.... 80 D
hermes_w@fortlewis.edu
HERMON, Vada .... 620-227-9213.. 180 E
vhermon@dc3.edu
HERMONSON, Eric .... 815-825-9810.. 144 F
eric.hermonson@kishwaukeecollege.edu
HERMS, Ron .... 559-453-2075.... 44 F
ron.herms@fresno.edu
HERMSEN, Al .... 239-433-8047.. 101 F
albert.hermsen@fsw.edu
HERMSEN, Cindy, L .... 248-370-3370.. 239 K
hermsen@oakland.edu
HERNÁNDEZ, Mariana, T 787-740-1611.. 536 G
mariana.hernandez@uccaribe.edu
HERNÁNDEZ, Nannette .... 787-265-3863.. 538 C
aeconomica@uprm.edu
HERNÁNDEZ, Olga .... 787-834-5151.. 535 I
olgan_hernandez@pucpr.edu
HERNÁNDEZ, Walitza .... 787-884-3838.. 530 G
dir_registra@atenascollege.edu
HERNÁNDEZ-AVEVEDO,
Brenda .... 787-884-3838.. 530 G
bacevedo@atenascollege.edu
HERNÁNDEZ NÚÑEZ,
Maria, L .... 787-884-3838.. 530 G
presidenta@atenascollege.edu
HERN, Marcia, J .... 502-852-8300.. 194 A
m.hern@louisville.edu
HERN, Marsha, L .... 716-338-1060.. 317 F
marshahern@mail.sunyjcc.edu
HERNANDEZ, Albert .... 303-765-3183.... 80 M
ahernandez@iliff.edu
HERNANDEZ, Alex .... 915-831-6383.. 457 H
aherna78@epcc.edu
HERNANDEZ, Alfredo ...... 561-732-4424.. 108 F
ahernandez@svdp.edu
HERNANDEZ, Ana .... 813-974-4262.. 112 C
ahernandez@usf.edu
HERNANDEZ, Anna .... 786-331-1000.. 105 G
ahernandez@maufl.edu
HERNANDEZ, Aracely, C . 956-326-2232.. 468 A
achernandez@tamiu.edu
HERNANDEZ, Arnold .... 208-459-5868.. 133 D
ahernandez@collegeofidaho.edu
HERNANDEZ, Arthur .... 361-825-2661.. 468 E
art.hernandez@tamucc.edu
HERNANDEZ, Axel, N .... 858-499-0202.... 39 J
ahernandez@coleman.edu
HERNANDEZ, Ayana, D ... 919-530-7266.. 357 A
ahernandez@nccu.edu
HERNANDEZ, Brian .... 787-284-1912.. 534 C
bhernand@ponce.inter.edu
HERNANDEZ, Caridad ...... 305-821-3333.. 101 B
csanchez@fnu.edu
HERNANDEZ, Carlos .... 936-294-2686.. 471 D
jch060@shsu.edu
HERNANDEZ, Carol .... 415-485-9506.... 40 C
chernandez@marin.edu
HERNANDEZ, Carolyn ..... 214-768-1979.. 465 J
hernandez@smu.edu
HERNANDEZ, Cathy .... 602-286-8028.... 14 B
cathleen.hernandez@gwmail.maricopa.edu
HERNANDEZ, Christine .... 916-558-2438.... 51 D
hernanc@scc.losrios.edu
HERNANDEZ, David .... 805-565-6164.... 75 A
dhernand@westmont.edu
HERNANDEZ, Deanne .... 713-500-3192.. 477 C
deanne.m.hernandez@uth.tmc.edu
HERNANDEZ, Dino .... 650-508-3512.... 54 J
dhernandez@ndnu.edu
HERNANDEZ, Edwin .... 407-303-5619.... 95 C
edwin.hernandez@adu.edu
HERNANDEZ, Edwin .... 787-881-1212.. 535 I
edwin_hernandez@pucpr.edu
HERNANDEZ, Eliza .... 210-486-4913.. 450 C
ehernandez716@alamo.edu
HERNANDEZ, Elizabeth .... 305-284-2777.. 105 B
elizabeth.hernandez@ncahealthcare.com
HERNANDEZ, Erika .... 281-459-7680.. 465 A
erika.hernandez@sjcd.edu
HERNANDEZ, Evelyn .... 360-475-7600.. 505 F
ehernandez@olympic.edu
HERNANDEZ, Felix .... 805-922-6966.... 25 I
fhernandez@hancockcollege.edu
HERNANDEZ, Grace .... 806-742-2121.. 472 C
grace.hernandez@ttu.edu
HERNANDEZ, Harry .... 787-738-2161.. 538 A
harry.hernandez2@upr.edu

HERNANDEZ, Hector .... 847-679-3135.. 144 G
hhernandez@ksi.edu
HERNANDEZ, Ilsama .... 787-751-0160.. 531 M
ihernandez@cmpr.pr.gov
HERNANDEZ, Isabel .... 787-725-6500.. 531 C
ihernandez@sju.albizu.edu
HERNANDEZ, Jean .... 425-640-1515.. 503 E
jean.hernandez@edcc.edu
HERNANDEZ, Jennifer ..... 787-753-6335.. 532 O
jhernandez@icprjc.edu
HERNANDEZ, Jessie .... 787-875-4150.. 536 B
jehernandez@suagm.edu
HERNANDEZ, John .... 714-628-4930.... 58 H
hernandez_john@sccollege.edu
HERNANDEZ, Jose .... 813-974-4373.. 112 C
jehernan@usf.edu
HERNANDEZ, Josephine . 973-341-1600.. 294 A
hernandez@pccc.edu
HERNANDEZ, Juan, C ..... 787-279-2250.. 533 J
jchernandez@bayamon.inter.edu
HERNANDEZ, Justin, J .... 660-944-2851.. 263 G
justin@conception.edu
HERNANDEZ, Karla .... 305-348-4163.. 111 A
karla.hernandez5@fiu.edu
HERNANDEZ, Kristan ...... 785-833-4332.. 182 F
kristan.hernandez@kwu.edu
HERNANDEZ, Kristi .... 701-662-1692.. 361 E
kristi.hernandez@lrsc.edu
HERNANDEZ, Lino .... 787-738-2161.. 538 A
lino.hernandez@upr.edu
HERNANDEZ, Luis .... 787-751-0160.. 531 M
lhernandez@cmpr.pr.gov
HERNANDEZ, Luz, S .... 787-620-2040.. 530 F
lhernandez@aupr.edu
HERNANDEZ, Madelline .. 818-364-7618.... 49 J
hernanm@lamission.edu
HERNANDEZ, Maria .... 715-422-5469.. 523 G
maria.hernandez@mstc.edu
HERNANDEZ, Mary Lou .. 520-494-5200.... 12 J
marylou.hernandez@centralaz.edu
HERNANDEZ, Michael ...... 757-352-4571.. 493 E
michher@regent.edu
HERNANDEZ, Michelle .... 212-616-7278.. 315 G
michelle.hernandez@helenefuld.edu
HERNANDEZ, Myrna .... 765-658-1087.. 160 F
myrnahernandez@depauw.edu
HERNANDEZ, Nancy .... 305-919-5813.. 111 A
nancy.hernandez@fiu.edu
HERNANDEZ, Nina .... 908-709-7127.. 298 A
hernandez@ucc.edu
HERNANDEZ, Noe .... 432-837-8603.. 471 E
noeh@sulross.edu
HERNANDEZ, Oscar .... 956-872-2522.. 465 H
oscarh@southtexascollege.edu
HERNANDEZ, Otto .... 609-343-4978.. 288 H
hernande@atlantic.edu
HERNANDEZ, JR., Pablo 956-872-2182.. 465 H
phernan@southtexascollege.edu
HERNANDEZ, Paul .... 517-483-1116.. 237 A
hernap@lcc.edu
HERNANDEZ, JR., Paul .. 956-872-8372.. 465 H
phernan@southtexascollege.edu
HERNANDEZ, Rachelle .... 612-625-2006.. 255 H
HERNANDEZ, Ramon .... 860-832-1619.... 85 F
hernandez@ccsu.edu
HERNANDEZ, Ramon ...... 787-841-2000.. 535 I
ramon_hernandezcruz@pucpr.edu
HERNANDEZ, Raul .... 787-284-1912.. 534 C
rhernand@ponce.inter.edu
HERNANDEZ, Raymond ... 650-738-4221.... 62 I
hernandezr@smccd.edu
HERNANDEZ, Rebecca ..... 503-554-2147.. 391 D
rhernandez@georgefox.edu
HERNANDEZ, Richard ...... 760-252-2411.... 28 B
rhernandez@barstow.edu
HERNANDEZ, Ricky .... 787-850-9367.. 538 B
ricky.hernandez@upr.edu
HERNANDEZ, Ruth, E ...... 787-279-1912.. 533 J
rehernandez@bayamon.inter.edu
HERNANDEZ, Samuel ...... 787-882-2065.. 536 D
asistencia_economica@unitecpr.net
HERNANDEZ, Sheila .... 831-582-3632.... 33 E
shernandez@csumb.edu
HERNANDEZ, Susan .... 214-645-5485.. 478 C
susan.hernandez@utsouthwestern.edu
HERNANDEZ, Thomas, J . 585-395-2510.. 332 E
thernand@brockport.edu
HERNANDEZ, Todd .... 419-267-1445.. 374 A
thernandez@northweststate.edu
HERNANDEZ, Victoria ...... 305-237-3221.. 105 D
vhernand@mdc.edu
HERNANDEZ, Wanda .... 646-565-6000.. 337 I
wandau@touro.edu
HERNANDEZ, West .... 307-754-6103.. 526 N
west.hernandez@nwc.edu
HERNANDEZ, Yvette .... 830-591-7318.. 466 A
yvetteh@swtjc.edu
HERNANDEZ-HUNTER,
Anna .... 503-838-8195.. 396 E
hernana@wou.edu

HETTLEMAN, Thomas ...... 410-617-1120.. 208 G
tdhettleman@loyola.edu
HETTON, Richard .... 937-327-7916.. 381 F
hettonr@wittenberg.edu
HETTRICK, Allyson .... 828-298-3325.. 359 F
ahettrick@warren-wilson.edu
HETZEL, Bob .... 608-785-6491.. 520 C
bhetzel@uwlax.edu
HETZEL, June .... 562-903-6000.... 28 E
june.hetzel@bioloa.edu
HETZEL, Lisa .... 815-226-3398.. 152 G
lhetzel@rockford.edu
HETZLER, Mark .... 816-501-4843.. 270 J
mark.hetzler@rockhurst.edu
HEUBLER, Deborah, T ..... 808-956-2980.. 131 F
dhuebler@hawaii.edu
HEUER, John, J .... 215-898-6884.. 421 E
heuer@upenn.edu
HEUER, Timothy .... 773-508-3254.. 146 G
theuer@luc.edu
HEUGEL, Jim .... 425-889-4098.. 505 E
jim.heugel@northwestu.edu
HEULITT, Ken .... 312-329-2070.. 148 F
ken.heulitt@moody.edu
HEUPEL, Dick .... 765-285-2894.. 159 B
dheupel@bsu.edu
HEURING, Curt .... 609-771-3269.. 290 F
heuring@tcnj.edu
HEUSCHELE, Joel .... 715-425-3265.. 521 B
joel.heuschele@uwrf.edu
HEUSER, Jacob .... 309-677-3159.. 136 B
jheuser@fsmail.bradley.edu
HEUSER, Kimberly .... 732-224-2268.. 289 I
kheuser@brookdalecc.edu
HEUSNER, Nadine .... 386-481-2272.... 96 H
heusnern@cookman.edu
HEUSNER, Scott .... 734-462-4400.. 240 H
sheusner@schoolcraft.edu
HEUSNER, Warren .... 386-481-2933.... 96 H
heusnerw@cookman.edu
HEUTON, Mary Ellen .... 304-696-6603.. 513 D
heuton@marshall.edu
HEWERDINE, Kevin, L ..... 812-877-8184.. 166 H
kevin.l.hewerdine@rose-hulman.edu
HEWES, Randy .... 405-325-3811.. 389 B
hewes@ou.edu
HEWETT, James, E .... 712-749-2248.. 170 D
hewettj@bvu.edu
HEWETT, Kelly .... 410-334-2908.. 213 G
khewett@worwic.edu
HEWETT, Lamar .... 803-549-6314.. 434 C
dlhewett@mailbox.sc.edu
HEWITT, Bradley, L .... 618-650-2871.. 155 A
bhewitt@siue.edu
HEWITT, Chris .... 602-943-2311.... 18 C
christopher.hewitt@west.edu
HEWITT, Dawn .... 718-262-2060.. 310 A
hewittd@york.cuny.edu
HEWITT, Emma .... 712-274-6400.. 177 I
emma.hewitt@witcc.edu
HEWITT, Gordon, J .... 315-859-4084.. 315 D
ghewitt@hamilton.edu
HEWITT, JR., Harold, W . 714-997-6815.... 37 F
hewitt@chapman.edu
HEWITT, Mark, S .... 781-736-2010.. 216 F
mhewitt@brandeis.edu
HEWITT, Michael, T .... 718-951-5000.. 307 D
HEWITT, Michele .... 518-831-8810.. 305 A
hewittm@ellismedicine.org
HEWITT, Russ .... 402-826-8295.. 280 B
russ.hewitt@doane.edu
HEWITT, Scott .... 657-278-2714.... 33 A
shewitt@fullerton.edu
HEWITT, Stephany .... 843-574-6922.. 433 D
stephany.hewitt@tridenttech.edu
HEWITT BOYD, Kimberly 612-624-9547.. 255 H
khewitt@umn.edu
HEWITT-CLARKE,
Gail-Selina .... 301-295-1667.. 528 G
gail-selina.hewitt-clarke@usuhs.edu
HEWITT WATKINS,
Sharon .... 718-990-3369.. 328 F
hewittws@stjohns.edu
HEWLETT, Rod .... 402-557-7125.. 278 I
rhewlett@bellevue.edu
HEXTER, Ralph, J .... 530-752-2065.... 69 A
chancellor@ucdavis.edu
HEY, Jeanne .... 207-602-2371.. 205 F
jhey@une.edu
HEYDARI, Shahryar .... 706-778-8500.. 125 J
sheydari@piedmont.edu
HEYE, Nick .... 858-653-6740.... 47 G
nheye@jpcatholic.com
HEYER, Cary, R .... 608-246-6443.. 523 F
cheyer@madisoncollege.edu
HEYER, Doreen, E .... 213-738-6801.... 66 F
academicadmin@swlaw.edu
HEYING, Lori .... 319-363-1323.. 175 D
lheying@mtmercy.edu
HEYING, Steve .... 210-829-6023.. 474 D
lindaw@uiwtx.edu
HEYLIGER, Wynton .... 404-527-4520.. 118 F
wheyliger@carver.edu
HEYMAN, George .... 585-271-3657.. 328 A
gheyman@stbernards.edu
HEYMAN, George, P .... 585-271-3657.. 328 A
gheyman@stbernards.edu
HEYMAN, Jeffrey .... 510-466-7369.... 57 E
jheyman@peralta.edu
HEYMAN, Jeffrey .... 510-466-7369.... 57 B
jheyman@peralta.edu
HEYMANN, Jody .... 310-825-6381.... 69 D
jody.heymann@ph.ucla.edu
HEYNDERICKX, Roy, F ..... 360-438-4307.. 506 G
president@stmartin.edu
HEYNING, Katharina, E ... 262-472-1101.. 521 F
heyningk@uww.edu
HEYWARD, ILene .... 340-693-1101.. 539 C
iheywar@uvi.edu
HEYWARD, Kerry, L .... 404-413-0500.. 122 D
kheyward@gsu.edu
HEYWARD, Loretta .... 912-358-3049.. 126 F
heywardl@savannahstate.edu
HEYWARD, Toyia .... 610-683-4102.. 415 C
heyward@kutztown.edu
HIATT, Aaron .... 510-485-7828.... 56 I
ahiatt@patten.edu
HIATT, Edwin, L .... 229-333-5886.. 129 G
elhiatt@valdosta.edu
HIATT, Elaine .... 614-825-6255.. 362 J
ehiatt@aiam.edu
HIATT, Jim .... 615-248-1613.. 447 F
jhiatt@trevecca.edu
HIATT, Jim .... 615-248-1256.. 447 F
jhiatt@trevecca.edu
HIATT, Jon .... 605-331-6636.. 438 A
jon.hiatt@usiouxfalls.edu
HIBBARD, J. Todd .... 313-993-1088.. 241 G
hibbarja@udmercy.edu
HIBBARD, Steven, V .... 262-243-5700.. 516 E
steve.hibbard@cuw.edu
HIBBARD, Susan .... 239-489-9013.. 101 F
shibbard@fsw.edu
HIBBERD, Charles .... 402-472-2966.. 282 M
hibberd@unl.edu
HIBBERT, Mary .... 405-491-6365.. 388 A
mhibbert@snu.edu
HIBBS, Randy .... 920-206-2318.. 517 G
randy.hibbs@mbu.edu
HIBBS, Roz .... 618-374-5153.. 151 E
roz.hibbs@principia.edu
HIBBS, Thomas, S .... 254-710-7689.. 452 H
thomas_hibbs@baylor.edu
HIBLER, Dirk .... 904-819-6336.... 99 M
dhibler@flagler.edu
HIBNER, Lisa .... 225-216-8244.. 195 H
hibnerl@mybrcc.edu
HICE, Muriel .... 269-488-4410.. 235 I
mhice@kvcc.edu
HICHWA, Richard, D .... 319-335-2106.. 169 H
richard-hichwa@uiowa.edu
HICKAM, Brian .... 937-481-2346.. 381 C
brian_hickam@wilmington.edu
HICKE, Linda, A .... 512-471-3285.. 476 B
cnsdean@austin.utexas.edu
HICKERSON, Amanda ...... 502-447-1000.. 192 G
ahickerson@spencerian.edu
HICKERSON, Jim .... 812-866-6741.. 161 C
hickerson@hanover.edu
HICKERSON, Keith, E .... 610-526-1000.. 397 E
keith.hickerson@theamericancollege.edu
HICKEY, Beverly .... 662-685-4771.. 257 A
bhickey@bmc.edu
HICKEY, David .... 513-569-1448.. 366 D
david.hickey@cincinnatistate.edu
HICKEY, Dean .... 617-243-2190.. 219 I
dhickey@lasell.edu
HICKEY, Jane .... 410-455-1517.. 211 G
jchickey@umbc.edu
HICKEY, Jay .... 401-841-6515.. 528 E
HICKEY, John, M .... 253-879-3203.. 508 D
hickey@pugetsound.edu
HICKEY, Lynn .... 210-458-4161.. 477 A
lynn.hickey@utsa.edu
HICKEY, Melissa .... 845-675-4424.. 325 C
melissa.hickey@nyack.edu
HICKEY, Michael, J .... 518-783-2355.. 330 E
mjhickey@siena.edu
HICKEY, JR., Robert, E .... 937-775-3326.. 381 H
robert.hickey@wright.edu
HICKMAN, Carla .... 314-889-1416.. 265 C
chickman@fontbonne.edu
HICKMAN, Gaby .... 803-786-3770.. 429 A
gahickman@columbiasc.edu
HICKMAN, George .... 518-262-8006.. 303 E
hickmag@mail.amc.edu
HICKMAN, Joseph .... 406-243-2412.. 276 K
joseph.hickman@umontana.edu
HICKMAN, Randall .... 586-445-7866.. 237 C
hickmanr@macomb.edu
HICKMAN, Saeedah .... 718-960-8357.. 308 B
saeedah.hickman@lehman.cuny.edu
HICKMAN, Tanner .... 901-751-8453.. 442 E
thickman@mabts.edu
HICKMAN, Tim .... 909-558-4532.... 49 C
thickman@llu.edu
HICKMAN, Tom .... 701-671-2354.. 361 F
tom.hickman@ndscs.edu
HICKMAN, Tynia .... 214-379-5542.. 463 G
thickman@pqc.edu
HICKMAN, Wesley .... 803-777-7440.. 433 F
whickman@mailbox.sc.edu
HICKMAN, Wesley, T .... 803-777-7440.. 433 F
whickman@mailbox.sc.edu
HICKMAN HOLLAND,
Heather .... 415-749-4540.... 61 B
hhickman@sfai.edu
HICKOX, Chad .... 406-447-6900.. 277 B
HICKS, Andrea .... 718-357-0500.. 329 E
ahicks@stpaulsschoolofnursing.edu
HICKS, Barbara .... 928-541-7777.... 15 G
bhicks@ncu.edu
HICKS, OSB, Boniface, N 724-532-6662.. 419 B
boniface.hicks@stvincent.edu
HICKS, Brenda, D .... 620-229-6387.. 184 J
brenda.hicks@sckans.edu
HICKS, Brian, A .... 336-734-7191.. 349 G
bhicks@forsythtech.edu
HICKS, Bruce .... 310-287-4307.... 50 E
hicksbr@wlac.edu
HICKS, Bruno .... 978-665-3239.. 221 D
HICKS, Bryan .... 256-372-4014...... 1 A
byran.hicks@aamu.edu
HICKS, Carlyle .... 718-522-9073.. 304 D
chicks@asa.edu
HICKS, JR., Cecil .... 402-554-2321.. 283 B
chicks@unomaha.edu
HICKS, Cliff .... 360-442-2441.. 504 G
chicks@lowercolumbia.edu
HICKS, David, L .... 610-292-9852.. 417 I
bishophicks@comcast.net
HICKS, Deanita .... 870-762-3146.... 18 G
dhicks@smail.anc.edu
HICKS, Debbie, L .... 757-455-3338.. 500 E
dlhicks@vwc.edu
HICKS, Dennis .... 765-973-8456.. 162 G
dehicks@iue.edu
HICKS, Doajo .... 435-652-7879.. 482 A
hicks@dixie.edu
HICKS, Douglas, A .... 404-784-8300.. 120 E
douglas.hicks@emory.edu
HICKS, Ed .... 334-386-7309...... 3 I
ehicks@faulkner.edu
HICKS, J. David .... 423-652-4782.. 440 J
jdhicks@king.edu
HICKS, Janet, K .... 570-586-2400.. 419 G
jhicks@summitu.edu
HICKS, Jim .... 423-425-4246.. 448 F
jim-hicks@utc.edu
HICKS, Jimmy .... 691-320-2480.. 529 F
jhicks@comfsm.fm
HICKS, Juanita .... 678-839-6424.. 129 E
jhicks@westga.edu
HICKS, Jud .... 806-457-4200.. 458 B
jhicks@fpctx.edu
HICKS, Julia .... 860-685-2100.... 90 C
jhicks@wesleyan.edu
HICKS, Julie .... 252-492-2061.. 353 H
hicksj@vgcc.edu
HICKS, Kathy .... 423-636-7320.. 447 G
khicks@tusculum.edu
HICKS, Kelly .... 918-343-7573.. 387 F
kellyhicks@rsu.edu
HICKS, Kristen .... 605-668-1270.. 436 D
kristen.hicks@mtmc.edu
HICKS, LaTanya, O .... 510-593-2991.... 63 H
lhicks@saybrook.edu
HICKS, Loretta .... 404-297-9522.. 122 A
hicksl@gptc.edu
HICKS, Marcelle .... 516-299-3102.. 319 C
marcelle.hicks@liu.edu
HICKS, Marcus .... 404-297-9522.. 122 A
hicksm@gptc.edu
HICKS, Maryruth .... 561-912-2166.... 99 J
mhicks@evergladesuniversity.edu
HICKS, Michael .... 706-821-8350.. 125 H
mhicks@paine.edu
HICKS, Michael, R .... 817-735-2000.. 475 C
michael.hicks@unthsc.edu
HICKS, Minora .... 803-327-7402.. 428 D
mhicks@clintoncollege.edu
HICKS, Mona, L .... 561-803-2174.. 106 C
mona_hicks@pba.edu
HICKS, Ramona .... 314-977-5028.. 271 K
rhicks1@slu.edu
HICKS, Renee, G .... 985-493-2556.. 201 A
renee.hicks@nicholls.edu
HICKS, Rickey, P .... 706-729-2260.. 117 D
rhicks@augusta.edu
HICKS, Scott, M .... 434-592-4808.. 491 D
smhicks@liberty.edu
HICKS, Shawn .... 415-422-5380.... 72 C
srhicks2@usfca.edu
HICKS, Terence .... 423-439-7616.. 444 F
hickstl1@etsu.edu
HICKS, Terri .... 205-226-4611...... 2 C
thicks@bsc.edu
HICKS, Timothy, J .... 315-859-4790.. 315 D
thicks@hamilton.edu
HICKS, Tom .... 319-399-8741.. 170 G
thicks@coe.edu
HICKS, Virginia .... 304-876-5712.. 513 E
vhicks@shepherd.edu
HICKS, Wanda .... 706-355-5160.. 116 H
whicks@athenstech.edu
HICKS, Willie .... 501-420-1232.... 18 F
willie.hicks@arkansasbaptist.edu
HICSWA, Stefani .... 307-754-6200.. 526 N
stefani.hicswa@nwc.edu
HIDALGO, Lisa .... 985-448-7939.. 196 E
lisa.hidalgo@fletcher.edu
HIDALGO, Rommel .... 657-278-5742.... 33 A
rhidalgo@fullerton.edu
HIEBERT, Theodore .... 773-947-6341.. 147 D
HIEDEMAN, Ann .... 218-477-2066.. 250 F
ann.hiedeman@mnstate.edu
HIEL, Edwin .... 619-388-3036.... 60 F
ehiel@sdccd.edu
HIELEMA, Leslie .... 407-629-7259.. 100 M
lhielema@fit.edu
HIEMENZ, Karen, A .... 320-308-5017.. 252 B
khiemenz@sctcc.edu
HIER, Cynthia .... 303-914-6298.... 82 I
HIERS, Richard .... 314-434-4044.. 264 C
richard.hiers@covenantseminary.edu
HIESIGER, Linda .... 413-585-2231.. 228 D
lhiesige@smith.edu
HIETALA, Robert .... 406-994-5523.. 277 C
robert.hietala@montana.edu
HIETAPELTO, Amy .... 218-726-7281.. 255 D
lsbe@d.umn.edu
HIETSCH, Stephen, C .... 717-245-1891.. 402 D
hietschs@dickinson.edu
HIGA, Pat .... 949-582-4585.... 65 G
phiga@saddleback.edu
HIGASHI, Lori .... 541-485-1780.. 393 A
lorihigashi@enewhope.edu
HIGBEE, Isabelle .... 601-974-1220.. 258 H
higbeie@millsaps.edu
HIGDEM, Julie .... 763-488-2453.. 249 D
julie.higdem@hennepintech.edu
HIGDON, Hal, L .... 417-447-2602.. 270 A
higdonh@otc.edu
HIGDON, Jo Ann .... 310-660-3107.... 42 J
jhigdon@elcamino.edu
HIGDON, Jo Ann .... 310-660-3670.... 42 J
jhigdon@elcamino.edu
HIGGINBOTHAM, Debra .. 940-397-4120.. 462 A
debra.higginbotham@mwsu.edu
HIGGINBOTHAM, Karen .. 212-472-1500.. 324 A
khigginbotham@nysid.edu
HIGGINBOTHAM, Ray ..... 931-393-1737.. 446 D
rhigginbotham@mscc.edu
HIGGINS, Bonnie .... 218-755-3732.. 248 M
bhiggins@bemidjistate.edu
HIGGINS, Brandon .... 903-823-3024.. 467 C
brandon.higgins@texarkanacollege.edu
HIGGINS, Brenda .... 660-785-4562.. 273 B
bhiggins@truman.edu
HIGGINS, Carla .... 419-783-2571.. 368 A
chiggins@defiance.edu
HIGGINS, Dalton .... 918-335-6865.. 386 F
dhiggins@okwu.edu
HIGGINS, Dawn .... 603-271-6484.. 286 F
dhiggins@ccsnh.edu
HIGGINS, Diana .... 309-341-5341.. 136 C
dhiggins@sandburg.edu
HIGGINS, Elizabeth .... 207-780-4632.. 205 E
bhiggins@maine.edu
HIGGINS, Kacey .... 325-670-1368.. 458 J
kacey.higgins@hsutx.edu
HIGGINS, Kerena .... 360-650-2040.. 509 E
kerena.higgins@wwu.edu
HIGGINS, Linda, A .... 803-641-3476.. 433 G
lindahi@usca.edu
HIGGINS, Lisa .... 716-829-7542.. 313 A
higginsl@dyc.edu
HIGGINS, Margaret .... 828-398-7302.. 347 D
margaretahiggins@abtech.edu
HIGGINS, Mark .... 314-977-3833.. 271 K
markhiggins@slu.edu
HIGGINS, Mark .... 802-387-1678.. 484 B
mhiggins@landmark.edu
HIGGINS, Michael .... 314-434-4044.. 264 C
mike.higgins@covenantseminary.edu
HIGGINS, TOR, Michael . 760-547-1800.... 44 C
mhiggins@fst.edu
HIGGINS, Michael, J .... 203-371-7902.... 88 I
higginsmw@sacredheart.edu
HIGGINS, Peter, J .... 678-359-5156.. 122 E
phiggins@gordonstate.edu
HIGGINS, Richard, J .... 518-564-2040.. 334 A
higginrj@plattsburgh.edu

HIGGINS, Ronnell, A .... 203-432-9455.... 90 D
ronnell.higgins@yale.edu
HIGGINS, Sandra .... 718-260-5700.. 309 C
shiggins@citytech.cuny.edu
HIGGINS, Shannon .... 909-448-4901.... 71 B
shiggins@laverne.edu
HIGGINS, Sharon .... 410-617-5025.. 208 G
sbhiggins@loyola.edu
HIGGINS, Tammy .... 620-235-4240.. 184 C
thiggins@pittstate.edu
HIGGINS, Terri .... 641-782-1431.. 177 B
thiggins@swcciowa.edu
HIGGINS, Thomas, J .... 518-564-3013.. 334 A
higgintj@plattsburgh.edu
HIGGS, David .... 601-643-8376.. 257 D
david.higgs@colin.edu
HIGGS, Jessica .... 309-677-2700.. 136 B
jhiggs@bradley.edu
HIGGS, Jessica .... 309-677-2700.. 136 B
bradleyhealthservices@fsmail.bradley.edu
HIGGS, John .... 724-480-3558.. 401 F
john.higgs@ccbc.edu
HIGGS, Ronnie .... 831-582-4363.... 33 E
rhiggs@csumb.edu
HIGGS, Toni .... 904-256-7954.. 103 D
thiggs@ju.edu
HIGH, Katherine, N .... 865-974-3843.. 448 D
khigh@tennessee.edu
HIGHAM, Pamela, S .... 814-332-3576.. 397 A
phigham@allegheny.edu
HIGHERS, Cami .... 918-444-4200.. 384 G
highersc@nsuok.edu
HIGHERS, Michael .... 408-270-6490.... 62 D
michael.highers@evc.edu
HIGHLEY, Melinda, C ...... 606-783-2033.. 191 H
m.highley@moreheadstate.edu
HIGHSMITH, Stephen ...... 610-902-1070.. 399 D
smh395@cabrini.edu
HIGHTOWER, Damara ...... 803-705-4438.. 427 D
hightowerd@benedict.edu
HIGHTOWER, Darlene ..... 405-744-3555.. 385 G
darlene.hightower@okstate.edu
HIGHTOWER, Jacqueline . 850-599-3225.. 110 J
jacqueline.hightower@famu.edu
HIGHTOWER, Tabitha ...... 773-947-6309.. 147 D
thightower@mccormick.edu
HIGINBOTHAM, Lynn, E . 212-998-4444.. 324 C
lynn.higinbotham@nyu.edu
HIGLE, Robin .... 978-468-7111.. 219 B
rhigle@gcts.edu
HIGLEY, Tony .... 509-434-5123.. 503 A
thigley@ccs.spokane.edu
HIGLEY, Tony .... 509-434-5123.. 502 I
tony.higley@ccs.spokane.edu
HIGLEY, Tony, D .... 509-434-5123.. 502 H
thigley@ccs.spokane.edu
HIGLEY, William, J .... 570-586-2400.. 419 G
whigley@summitu.edu
HIJLEH, Mark .... 212-659-7200.. 318 D
mhijleh@tkc.edu
HILARIO, Francis .... 787-704-1020.. 532 H
fhilario@ediccollege.edu
HILBERT, Diane .... 972-238-6250.. 456 H
dhilbert@dcccd.edu
HILBERT, Michael .... 814-732-1784.. 415 A
mhilbert@edinboro.edu
HILBERT, Pamela .... 703-323-3222.. 497 H
philbert@nvcc.edu
HILBORN, David .... 216-381-1680.. 374 B
dhilborn@ndc.edu
HILBRANDS, Steve .... 616-538-2330.. 234 D
shilbrands@gbcol.edu
HILBY, Jim .... 414-382-6327.. 515 D
jim.hilby@alverno.edu
HILD, Ann .... 307-766-4286.. 527 B
annhild@uwyo.edu
HILDAGO, Rommel .... 671-735-2645.. 530 B
rhildago@triton.uog.edu
HILDEBRAND, Carol .... 415-485-9306.... 40 C
childebrand@marin.edu
HILDEBRANDT,
Kristin, A .... 414-410-4007.. 515 I
kahildebrandt@stritch.edu
HILDERBRAND, Barbara .. 407-708-2114.. 109 E
hilderbrandb@seminolestate.edu
HILDERBRAND, Carey ...... 801-274-3280.. 483 C
carey.hilderbrand@wgu.edu
HILDRETH, Brandon .... 573-681-5205.. 266 I
hildrethb@lincolnu.edu
HILDRETH, James E.K ...... 615-327-6904.. 442 A
jhildreth@mmc.edu
HILEMAN, Jeffrey .... 814-732-1333.. 415 A
jhileman@edinboro.edu
HILES, Jason .... 602-639-7500.... 13 I
HILES, Tom .... 573-882-7703.. 273 E
hilest@missouri.edu
HILGENBRINK, Robert, J 618-235-2700.. 155 C
robert.hilgenbrink@swic.edu
HILKE, David .... 805-493-3960.... 31 C
dhilke@callutheran.edu
HILKE, Jurgen .... 301-846-2401.. 207 F
jhilke@frederic.edu
HILL, Alan .... 765-658-4199.. 160 F
alanhill@depauw.edu
HILL, Alan .... 765-361-6384.. 169 C
hilla@wabash.edu
HILL, Alan, P .... 765-361-6450.. 169 C
hilla@wabash.edu
HILL, Alan, P .... 765-658-4199.. 160 F
alanhill@depauw.edu
HILL, JR., Allen .... 281-283-2222.. 474 A
hilljr@uhcl.edu
HILL, Amber .... 928-524-7484.... 15 J
amber.hill@npc.edu
HILL, Angelina .... 707-476-4364.... 40 D
angelina-hill@redwoods.edu
HILL, B. Scott .... 540-985-4693.. 491 A
bshill@jchs.edu
HILL, Ben .... 319-384-3400.. 169 H
benjamin-hill-1@uiowa.edu
HILL, Brandi .... 931-372-3317.. 445 B
bhill@tntech.edu
HILL, Brandon .... 765-677-2200.. 164 B
brandon.hill@indwes.edu
HILL, Brian .... 412-268-1939.. 400 D
brianhill@cmu.edu
HILL, Brian, W .... 540-231-5107.. 489 H
bhill@vcom.vt.edu
HILL, Calvin, R .... 413-748-3552.. 228 E
chill@springfieldcollege.edu
HILL, Charles .... 920-424-1255.. 520 E
hill@uwosh.edu
HILL, Chris .... 301-581-5605.. 481 M
chill@huntsman.utah.edu
HILL, Chris .... 760-797-2121.... 52 K
chill@miracosta.edu
HILL, Christopher, D .... 404-413-2574.. 122 D
chill@gsu.edu
HILL, Christopher, J .... 412-392-4707.. 417 F
chill@pointpark.edu
HILL, Christopher, R .... 303-871-2539.... 84 B
christopher.r.hill@du.edu
HILL, Craig, C .... 214-768-2534.. 465 J
craighill@smu.edu
HILL, Craig, R .... 352-392-1336.. 112 A
craighill@ufl.edu
HILL, Curtis .... 435-865-8621.. 481 N
hillc@suu.edu
HILL, Dachea .... 269-387-2000.. 243 H
dachea.hill@wmich.edu
HILL, Deana .... 570-484-2014.. 415 D
dhill@lhup.edu
HILL, Deborah .... 843-746-5100.... 93 F
HILL, Deidra, W .... 212-650-5310.. 307 E
dhill@ccny.cuny.edu
HILL, Deidre, N .... 253-535-7101.. 505 G
hilldn@plu.edu
HILL, Dennis .... 479-394-7622.... 22 B
dhill@rmcc.edu
HILL, Diana .... 770-394-8300.. 116 F
diahill@aii.edu
HILL, Diane .... 973-353-1630.. 296 C
dianeh@andromeda.rutgers.edu
HILL, Doree .... 252-222-6282.. 348 B
hilld@carteret.edu
HILL, Doris .... 763-488-0129.. 251 B
dhill@nhcc.edu
HILL, Elizabeth .... 630-829-6664.. 135 F
ehill@ben.edu
HILL, Flo .... 229-430-4879.. 115 K
flo.hill@asurams.edu
HILL, G. Richard .... 801-626-7313.. 482 D
grhill@weber.edu
HILL, George, C .... 615-343-3112.. 449 A
george.c.hill@vanderbilt.edu
HILL, Gladys .... 205-391-2457...... 6 G
ghill@sheltonstate.edu
HILL, Holly, L .... 904-826-8636.... 99 M
hhill@flagler.edu
HILL, James .... 414-229-1122.. 520 D
jimhill@uwm.edu
HILL, Jamie .... 309-796-5284.. 135 I
hillj@bhc.edu
HILL, Janeen .... 714-628-7223.... 37 F
jhill@chapman.edu
HILL, Janice .... 973-290-4468.. 290 G
jhill01@cse.edu
HILL, Jean .... 505-454-3562.. 300 F
jlhill@nmhu.edu
HILL, Jennifer .... 256-352-8032...... 9 G
jennifer.hill@wallacestate.edu
HILL, Jessica .... 937-395-8006.. 371 D
jessica.hill@ketteringhealth.org
HILL, Jody .... 662-658-4771.. 257 A
jhill@bmc.edu
HILL, John .... 256-726-7353...... 6 B
jhill@oakwood.edu
HILL, Joseph .... 215-503-0033.. 420 E
joseph.hill@jefferson.edu
HILL, Joslyn .... 405-425-5476.. 385 C
joslyn.hill@oc.edu
HILL, Kady .... 336-821-2476.. 345 C
khill@johnwesley.edu
HILL, Katrina .... 937-298-3399.. 371 D
katrina.hill@kc.edu
HILL, Kelli .... 309-268-8100.. 141 C
kelli.hill@heartland.edu
HILL, Kelly .... 352-588-7560.. 108 C
kelly.hill02@saintleo.edu
HILL, Ken .... 207-801-5630.. 202 H
khill@coa.edu
HILL, Larry .... 773-702-2060.. 156 D
lhill@uchicago.edu
HILL, Leah .... 252-985-5291.. 354 E
lhill@ncwc.edu
HILL, Leia .... 662-476-5346.. 257 G
lhill@eastms.edu
HILL, Linda .... 504-286-5550.. 199 I
lhill@suno.edu
HILL, Lisa .... 252-940-6223.. 347 E
lisa.hill@beaufortccc.edu
HILL, Manda .... 907-564-8299.... 10 B
mhill@alaskapacific.edu
HILL, Marie .... 617-587-5678.. 226 E
hillm@neco.edu
HILL, Mark .... 651-641-8223.. 246 B
hill@csp.edu
HILL, Mark .... 574-239-8377.. 161 N
mhill1@hcc-nd.edu
HILL, Mark, J .... 315-470-6670.. 334 E
mjhill@esf.edu
HILL, Mary .... 202-806-2550.... 93 A
marhill@howard.edu
HILL, Mary, M .... 989-774-3331.. 232 D
hill1mm@cmich.edu
HILL, Mathew, B .... 651-631-5362.. 256 A
mbhill@unwsp.edu
HILL, Melissa .... 509-865-0411.. 504 D
hill_m@heritage.edu
HILL, Melissa, D .... 812-941-2359.. 163 F
mhill02@ius.edu
HILL, Michael .... 610-328-8067.. 419 I
mhill1@swarthmore.edu
HILL, Michelle .... 225-771-2350.. 199 G
michelle_hill@sus.edu
HILL, Michelle, D .... 757-823-8135.. 492 F
mdhill@nsu.edu
HILL, Miriam .... 651-638-6415.. 244 L
m-hill@bethel.edu
HILL, Nanyamka .... 619-660-4240.... 45 I
nanyamka.hill@gcccd.edu
HILL, Nelson, W .... 585-594-6944.. 327 D
hill_nelson@roberts.edu
HILL, Patrick .... 785-309-3107.. 184 H
patrick.hill@salinatech.edu
HILL, Paul, L .... 304-558-0699.. 512 D
paul.hill@wvhepc.edu
HILL, Reggie .... 352-588-8283.. 108 C
reggie.hill@saintleo.edu
HILL, Reinhold .... 708-534-4101.. 140 H
rhill@govst.edu
HILL, Reinhold, R .... 812-348-7226.. 163 D
HILL, Renee .... 514-287-5299.. 367 C
rhill39@cscc.edu
HILL, Rick .... 252-222-6153.. 348 B
hillr@carteret.edu
HILL, Robert .... 818-240-1000.... 45 A
rhill@glendale.edu
HILL, Robert, A .... 617-353-3560.. 216 E
rahill@bu.edu
HILL, Robert, W .... 936-468-3501.. 456 H
rhill@sfasu.edu
HILL, S. Trent .... 361-825-5749.. 458 E
trent.hill@tamucc.edu
HILL, Sam .... 703-878-5778.. 497 H
shill@nvcc.edu
HILL, Sean .... 618-468-6000.. 145 G
shill@lc.edu
HILL, Shannon .... 805-546-3279.... 41 L
shannon_hill@cuesta.edu
HILL, Shantey .... 631-687-1445.. 328 G
shill4@sjcny.edu
HILL, Sharon .... 781-891-2108.. 215 F
shill@bentley.edu
HILL, Sheila, M .... 706-771-4840.. 117 C
shill@augustatech.edu
HILL, Sherri .... 203-837-8200.... 85 I
HILL, Sherry .... 847-592-6600.. 151 D
shill@princeinstitute.edu
HILL, Shirley .... 901-435-1450.. 441 C
shirley_hill@loc.edu
HILL, Soni .... 513-569-1640.. 366 D
soni.hill@cincinnatistate.edu
HILL, Stanley .... 765-983-1380.. 160 G
hillst@earlham.edu
HILL, Stephen, E .... 801-422-4104.. 480 C
steve_hill@byu.edu
HILL, Steve .... 575-492-2643.. 300 H
shill@nmjc.edu
HILL, Tina .... 434-947-8537.. 493 B
thill@randolphcollege.edu
HILL, Travis, R .... 315-859-4023.. 315 D
thill@hamilton.edu
HILL, Valerie, D .... 512-505-3060.. 459 F
vdhill@htu.edu
HILL, W. Timothy .... 801-422-7011.. 480 C
wthill@byu.edu
HILL, Walter, A .... 334-727-8157...... 8 A
hillwa@mytu.tuskegee.edu
HILL, Wayne, R .... 330-972-2148.. 378 G
whill@uakron.edu
HILL, Wes .... 252-246-1339.. 354 D
whill@wilsoncc.edu
HILL, William .... 713-646-1764.. 459 A
whill@kennedywilson.com
HILL, William .... 732-571-3580.. 292 F
hill@monmouth.edu
HILL, II, William, L .... 215-965-4022.. 411 A
whill@moore.edu
HILL, JR., Willie, L .... 413-545-3517.. 220 F
drwhill@aol.com
HILL, Wynn, N .... 208-496-9200.. 132 J
hillw@byui.edu
HILL, Z. JoAnna .... 303-292-0015.... 79 H
z.hill@denverschoolofnursing.edu
HILL-CHEATOM, Petrina .. 716-851-1120.. 313 H
cheatom@ecc.edu
HILL-CLARKE, Kandi .... 812-237-2919.. 162 A
kandi.hill-clarke@indstate.edu
HILL-FLANAGAN,
LaVerne, M .... 202-274-6069.... 94 B
lflanagan@udc.edu
HILL HART, Erin .... 336-334-7965.. 356 F
ehhart@ncat.edu
HILL-HUBBARD, Marion . 214-333-5261.. 455 J
marion@dbu.edu
HILLARD, Cecilia, J .... 414-955-8493.. 518 A
jhillard@mcw.edu
HILLBERRY, Andrew .... 860-768-5574.... 89 G
hillberry@hartford.edu
HILLBERRY, Kai .... 303-477-7240.... 80 H
kais@heritage-education.com
HILLE, Jim .... 817-257-7031.. 469 G
j.hille@tcu.edu
HILLEBRAND, Kayli .... 714-556-3610.... 73 B
kayli.hillebrand@vanguard.edu
HILLEMEIER, A. Craig ..... 717-531-8323.. 412 F
ach10@psu.edu
HILLER, Jerry .... 315-279-5244.. 318 C
jhiller@keuka.edu
HILLER, Renee .... 906-487-2280.. 238 A
rlhiller@mtu.edu
HILLER-FREUND,
Darby, L .... 937-327-7930.. 381 F
hillerd@wittenberg.edu
HILLERMAN, Donnie .... 660-359-3948.. 269 I
dhillerman@mail.ncmissouri.edu
HILLERY, Barbara .... 516-876-3915.. 333 C
hilleryb@oldwestbury.edu
HILLES, Sharon .... 909-869-3261.... 31 J
shilles@cpp.edu
HILLESLAND, Michelle ..... 253-589-5586.. 502 F
michelle.hillesland@cptc.edu
HILLIAR, Mara, M .... 804-594-1570.. 497 D
mhilliar@jtcc.edu
HILLIARD, Aaron .... 425-564-2445.. 501 F
aaron.hilliard@bellevuecollege.edu
HILLIARD, Beth .... 859-256-3100.. 188 M
beth.hilliard@kctcs.edu
HILLIARD, Colette .... 903-675-6306.. 473 B
chilliard@tvcc.edu
HILLIARD, Dianne .... 775-445-3288.. 285 B
dianne.hilliard@wnc.edu
HILLIARD, Kristin .... 407-926-2000.... 93 F
HILLIARD, Kristina .... 904-538-1000.... 93 F
HILLIS, Greg .... 575-439-3624.. 301 A
ghillis@nmsu.edu
HILLIS, Michael .... 805-493-3422.... 31 C
mhillis@callutheran.edu
HILLMAN, Amy .... 480-965-3402.... 11 H
amy.hillman@asu.edu
HILLMAN, Brenda .... 925-631-4457.... 59 I
bhillman@stmarys-ca.edu
HILLMAN, Elizabeth, L ... 510-430-2094.... 52 J
bhillman@mills.edu
HILLMAN, Elizabeth, L .... 415-565-4682.... 69 B
hillmane@uchastings.edu
HILLMAN, Gracia .... 202-806-2530.... 93 A
gracia.hillman@howard.edu
HILLMAN, Melinda .... 865-481-2000.. 447 A
hillmanmk@roanestate.edu
HILLMAN, Michel .... 816-604-1070.. 267 F
michel.hillman@mcckc.edu
HILLMER, Paul .... 651-641-8215.. 246 B
hillmer@csp.edu
HILLS, Amy .... 616-988-1000.. 232 H
amy.h@compass.edu
HILLS, Fred .... 254-299-8661.. 461 E
fhills@mclennan.edu
HILLS, Michael, S .... 740-587-6627.. 368 B
hills@denison.edu

HILLS, Stacey .... 802-447-6359.. 485 B
shills@svc.edu
HILLS, Warren, L .... 269-387-3895.. 243 H
warren.l.hills@wmich.edu
HILLSTROM, Maury .... 310-377-5501.... 51 G
mhillstrom@marymountcalifornia.edu
HILLYER, Rebecca .... 503-399-8677.. 390 E
rebecca.hillyer@chemeketa.edu
HILMEY, David .... 716-375-2603.. 328 B
dhilmey@sbu.edu
HILSABECK, Alison .... 312-261-3149.. 149 B
ahilsabeck@nl.edu
HILSCHER, Ted .... 518-828-4181.. 311 D
ted.hilscher@sunycgcc.edu
HILT, Elizabeth .... 650-433-3818.... 56 D
ehilt@paloaltou.edu
HILTERBRAN, Stephen .... 870-543-5907.... 22 E
shilterbran@seark.edu
HILTON, Adriel .... 318-274-6103.. 200 F
chiefofstaff@gram.edu
HILTON, Carol .... 949-582-4872.... 65 G
chilton@saddleback.edu
HILTON, Don .... 254-647-3234.. 463 K
dhilton@rangercollege.edu
HILTON, III, Earl, M .... 336-334-7686.. 356 F
hiltone@ncat.edu
HILTON, Eric .... 215-968-8123.. 399 A
eric.hilton@bucks.edu
HILTON, James, L .... 734-764-9358.. 241 J
hilton@umich.edu
HILTON, Richard, H .... 315-697-2300.. 338 L
rhilton@uscny.edu
HILTON, Stacey .... 928-717-7775.... 18 D
stacey.hilton@yc.edu
HILTON, Warren .... 610-683-4327.. 415 C
hilton@kutztown.edu
HILTON-MORROW,
Wendy, S .... 309-794-7282.. 135 D
wendyhilton-morrow@augustana.edu
HILTS, Deb, B .... 607-431-4171.. 315 E
hiltsd@hartwick.edu
HILVO, Wendy .... 414-326-2337.. 516 D
wendy.hilvo@ccon.edu
HILYER, Billy, D .... 334-386-7414...... 3 I
bhilyer@faulkner.edu
HIMBEAULT-TAYLOR,
Simone .... 734-764-5132.. 241 J
shtaylor@umich.edu
HIMBER, David .... 212-960-5330.. 341 G
himber@yu.edu
HIMBER, Richard .... 985-549-2064.. 201 C
HIMES, A.C. (Buddy) .... 936-468-2801.. 466 H
himesac@sfasu.edu
HIMES, Christine .... 312-567-3933.. 142 I
chimes@iit.edu
HIMES, Shane, D .... 814-641-3141.. 406 F
himess@juniata.edu
HIMLEY, Margaret, R .... 315-443-1137.. 337 A
mrhimley@syr.edu
HIMMELBERGER, Jeffrey . 508-793-7374.. 217 B
jhimmelberger@clarku.edu
HIMMELBERGER,
Stacey, J .... 315-859-4416.. 315 D
shimmelb@hamilton.edu
HIMMELREICH, Ellen .... 607-735-1855.. 313 F
ehimmelreich@elmira.edu
HIMMELSTEIN, Amos ...... 323-259-1347.... 55 A
himmelstein@oxy.edu
HIMSEL, Christian, R .... 262-243-5700.. 516 E
christian.himsel@cuw.edu
HINCH, Virginia .... 509-359-2329.. 503 D
vhinch@ewu.edu
HINCHMAN, Mary .... 760-750-4520.... 34 D
mhinchmn@csusm.edu
HINCKLEY, Alicia, A .... 253-535-7447.. 505 G
hincklaa@plu.edu
HINCKLEY, Richard .... 702-651-7488.. 284 H
richard.hinckley@csn.edu
HINCKLEY, Shane .... 979-845-4621.. 468 B
shane.hinckley@tamu.edu
HIND, Jonathan, T .... 315-859-4116.. 315 D
jhind@hamilton.edu
HINDE, RJ .... 865-974-0684.. 448 E
rhinde@utk.edu
HINDERKS, Liz .... 309-556-3850.. 143 D
hinderks@iwu.edu
HINDES, Victoria .... 408-741-2020.... 74 H
victoria.hindes@westvalley.edu
HINDS, David .... 301-784-5000.. 205 G
dhinds@allegany.edu
HINDS, David .... 361-582-2560.. 478 F
david.hinds@victoriacollege.edu
HINDS, M. Ray .... 813-988-5131.. 100 F
hindsr@floridacollege.edu
HINDS, Steven .... 479-619-2220.... 21 D
schinds1@nwacc.edu
HINDSON, Ed .... 434-582-7711.. 491 D
ehindson@liberty.edu
HINDSON, Laurie .... 512-245-7952.. 471 F
lh35@txstate.edu

HINE, Christopher .... 661-336-5040.... 47 I
christopher.hine@kccd.edu
HINE, James .... 415-502-3037.... 70 D
jhine@finance.ucsf.edu
HINE, Laura .... 901-272-5115.. 442 B
lhine@mca.edu
HINE, Mark, L .... 434-592-3240.. 491 D
mhine@liberty.edu
HINE, Melissa .... 540-362-6281.. 490 F
hinemd@hollins.edu
HINE, Terry .... 203-576-5072.... 89 A
thine@stvincentscollege.edu
HINEMAN, Sheri .... 712-274-5335.. 175 C
hineman@morningside.edu
HINERMAN, Nate .... 415-442-6510.... 45 B
nhinerman@ggu.edu
HINES, Alexander .... 507-457-5597.. 252 G
ahines@winona.edu
HINES, Bonnie .... 318-473-6438.. 197 J
hines@lsua.edu
HINES, Clay, T .... 919-866-5699.. 353 I
cthines@waketech.edu
HINES, Cory .... 214-333-5628.. 455 J
coryh@dbu.edu
HINES, Craig .... 312-662-4111.. 134 I
chines@adler.edu
HINES, Deborah Harmon . 508-856-2444.. 221 B
deborah-harmon.hines@umassmed.edu
HINES, Florence, W .... 410-857-2273.. 209 D
fhines@mcdaniel.edu
HINES, Jean, C .... 804-289-8181.. 495 G
jhines@richmond.edu
HINES, Jillian .... 619-200-8993.... 65 J
jillian.hines@socalsem.edu
HINES, Joseph .... 908-497-4317.. 298 A
joseph.hines@ucc.edu
HINES, Joseph, D .... 724-847-6518.. 404 B
jdh@geneva.edu
HINES, Kenneth, D .... 919-658-7755.. 355 K
dhines@umo.edu
HINES, Lara .... 314-392-2242.. 268 F
robeyl@mobap.edu
HINES, Mark .... 978-934-3847.. 221 A
mark_hines@uml.edu
HINES, Melvin .... 334-229-4505...... 1 D
mhines@alasu.edu
HINES, Nancy, A .... 563-333-6377.. 176 D
hinesnancya@sau.edu
HINES, Nancy, G .... 509-777-4638.. 509 H
nhines@whitworth.edu
HINES, Odessa .... 919-546-8268.. 355 F
ohines@shawu.edu
HINES, Patrick .... 919-536-7220.. 349 D
hinesp@durhamtech.edu
HINES, Patti .... 619-574-6909.... 55 G
phines@pacificcollege.edu
HINES, Resche .... 386-822-7257.. 113 B
rhines@stetson.edu
HINES, Ruth .... 617-427-0600.. 224 F
rhines@rcc.mass.edu
HINES, Scott .... 650-433-3855.... 56 D
shines@paloaltou.edu
HINES, Susan .... 208-459-5826.. 133 D
shines@collegeofidaho.edu
HINES, Susan .... 434-395-2921.. 491 E
hinessr@longwood.edu
HINES, Tammy .... 434-395-2444.. 491 E
hinestm@longwood.edu
HINES, Teresa .... 919-658-7720.. 355 K
thines@umo.edu
HINES, Wendy .... 828-565-4069.. 350 D
whines@haywood.edu
HINEY, Delaine, S .... 712-362-0428.. 173 G
dhiney@iowalakes.edu
HINGA, Bethany .... 712-274-5388.. 175 C
hingab@morningside.edu
HINGA, Gilbert .... 308-865-8528.. 282 L
hingag2@unk.edu
HINGELBERG, Julie .... 313-664-7494.. 232 G
julieh@collegeforcreativestudies.edu
HINGSTON, Mariko .... 415-338-1761.... 35 B
mtodd@sfsu.edu
HINKEL, Nate .... 501-686-2951.... 22 H
nhinkel@uasys.edu
HINKES, Madeleine .... 619-388-2320.... 60 G
mhinkes@sdccd.edu
HINKIN, Sue .... 303-871-2525.... 84 B
sue.hinkin@du.edu
HINKLE, Adrian .... 405-789-7661.. 388 B
adrian.hinkle@swcu.edu
HINKLE, Ana .... 907-834-1612.... 11 A
ahinkle@pwscc.edu
HINKLE, Barbara .... 724-838-4206.. 419 D
hinkle@setonhill.edu
HINKLE, Barbara, C .... 724-838-4218.. 419 D
hinkle@setonhill.edu
HINKLE, Bernadette .... 479-968-0300.... 19 F
bhinkle@atu.edu
HINKLE, Christina .... 949-582-4605.... 65 G
chinkle@saddleback.edu

HINKLE, Craig .... 214-890-3837.. 456 H
chinkle@dcccd.edu
HINKLE, Keith .... 310-506-4898.... 56 J
keith.hinkle@pepperdine.edu
HINKLE, Lance .... 405-744-5237.. 385 G
lance.hinkle@okstate.edu
HINKLE, Robin .... 502-585-9911.. 192 E
rhinkle@spalding.edu
HINKLE, Sandy, L .... 573-651-2250.. 272 B
shinkle@semo.edu
HINKLE, Sara .... 610-436-3511.. 416 C
shinkle@wcupa.edu
HINKLEY, Lisa .... 847-735-5235.. 145 B
hinkley@lakeforest.edu
HINKLEY, Richard .... 434-592-3077.. 491 D
rdhinkle@liberty.edu
HINKS, David .... 919-515-6500.. 357 B
dhinks@ncsu.edu
HINKSMAN, Paul .... 407-277-0311.... 99 J
phinksman@evergladesuniversity.edu
HINKSON, Avis .... 212-854-3075.. 304 I
ahinkson@barnard.edu
HINNANT, Lori .... 704-233-8979.. 359 H
l.hinnant@wingate.edu
HINNEN, Marsha .... 251-981-3771...... 2 I
marsha.hinnen@columbiasouthern.edu
HINNERS, Gordon .... 828-689-1208.. 346 C
ghinners@mhu.edu
HINOJOSA, Felix .... 915-831-2623.. 457 H
fhinojo3@epcc.edu
HINOJOSA, Maggie .... 956-665-2321.. 476 E
maggie.hinojosa@utrgv.edu
HINOJOSA, Maria .... 210-486-2379.. 450 E
mhinojosa@alamo.edu
HINSHAW, Dana .... 620-665-3322.. 181 I
hinshawd@hutchcc.edu
HINSHAW, Garrett, D .... 828-327-7000.. 348 C
ghinshaw@cvcc.edu
HINSHAW, Jamie .... 719-549-2602.... 79 B
jamie.hinshaw@csupueblo.edu
HINSHAW, Lynn .... 828-898-3473.. 345 G
hinshaw@lmc.edu
HINSHAW, Stephanie .... 800-280-0307.. 158 E
stephanie.hinshaw@ace.edu
HINSON, Bobby .... 850-201-6071.. 113 E
hinsonb@tcc.fl.edu
HINSON, Brenda .... 251-460-6050...... 9 E
bhinson@southalabama.edu
HINTERLONG, James, E .. 804-828-1036.. 496 D
jehinterlong@vcu.edu
HINTON, Amy, E .... 601-426-6346.. 260 G
ahinton@southeasternbaptist.edu
HINTON, Billy, C .... 713-500-8444.. 477 C
william.c.hinton@uth.tmc.edu
HINTON, Eric .... 972-241-3371.. 455 K
ehinton@dallas.edu
HINTON, Jeff .... 903-223-3087.. 469 C
jhinton@tamut.edu
HINTON, John, A .... 252-398-6376.. 343 G
hintoj@chowan.edu
HINTON, Kisa .... 501-370-5367.... 21 G
khinton@philander.edu
HINTON, Mary .... 320-363-5505.. 245 I
csbpres@csbsju.edu
HINTON, Pat .... 919-497-3217.. 346 B
phinton@louisburg.edu
HINTON, Tim .... 205-391-2979...... 6 G
thinton@sheltonstate.edu
HINTON, Toby, R .... 770-534-6257.. 118 A
thinton@brenau.edu
HINTON, Wendy .... 570-955-1456.. 407 B
hintonw@lackawanna.edu
HINTY, Danny .... 614-222-3224.. 367 B
dhinty@ccad.edu
HINTZ, Carol .... 816-235-1621.. 273 F
hintzc@umkc.edu
HINTZ, Lynn .... 863-784-7105.. 109 G
lynn.hintz@southflorida.edu
HINTZ, Nancy, L .... 920-748-8346.. 519 E
hintzn@ripon.edu
HINTZ, Sharon .... 908-835-2356.. 298 E
hintz@warren.edu
HINZ, Laurence, A .... 505-473-6234.. 302 A
president@santafeuniversity.edu
HINZE, Jodey .... 281-649-3130.. 458 L
jhinze@hbu.edu
HINZMAN, Larry .... 907-474-5837.... 10 G
ldhinzman@alaska.edu
HIOCO, Barbara .... 559-324-6475.... 67 A
barbara.hioco@scccd.edu
HIONIDES, David .... 214-887-5201.. 457 C
dhionides@dts.edu
HIOTT, Connie .... 912-279-5965.. 119 C
chiott@ccga.edu
HIPES, Barrett .... 212-799-5000.. 318 A
HIPOLITO, Veronica .... 928-226-4334.... 12 N
veronica.hipolito@coconino.edu
HIPP, Joye, G .... 803-786-3178.. 429 A
joyehipp@columbiasc.edu
HIPP, Kathleen .... 603-577-6659.. 286 I
hipp@dwc.edu

HIPPEN, Kristi .... 309-457-2327.. 148 E
khippen@monmouthcollege.edu
HIPPLER, Stanley .... 337-562-4290.. 200 H
stan@mcneese.edu
HIPPOLITE WRIGHT,
Debbie .... 808-675-3799.. 130 E
debbie.hippolite.wright@byuh.edu
HIPPS, OSB, Norman, W 724-805-2271.. 419 A
norman.hipps@email.stvincent.edu
HIPPS, Suzanne .... 602-243-8153.... 14 I
suzanne.hipps@smcmail.maricopa.edu
HIPWELL, Jody .... 870-762-3191.... 18 G
jhipwell@smail.anc.edu
HIRAK, Joe .... 802-728-1238.. 486 D
jhirak@vtc.edu
HIRALDO, Rafael .... 787-863-2390.. 533 K
rafael.hiraldo@fajardo.inter.edu
HIRAMOTO, Patti .... 831-582-3366.... 33 E
phiramoto@csumb.edu
HIRASE-STACEY, Joanne . 208-282-3234.. 133 H
hirajoan@isu.edu
HIRATA, Heather .... 808-932-7369.. 131 E
hiratah@hawaii.edu
HIRATA, Ryen .... 559-325-5265.... 67 B
ryen.hirata@scccd.edu
HIRD, Lon .... 605-367-7284.. 437 G
lon.hird@southeasttech.edu
HIRDLER, Joy, L .... 707-965-6232.... 56 A
jhirdler@puc.edu
HIRE, Jack .... 740-587-5698.. 368 B
hire@denison.edu
HIRNEISEN, Deborah .... 610-917-2003.. 422 C
dghirneisen@valleyforge.edu
HIRNER, Leo, J .... 816-604-4501.. 267 F
leo.hirner@mcckc.edu
HIRONAKA-JUTEAU,
Jody .... 559-278-4004.... 32 F
jhironak@csufresno.edu
HIRSCH, Andrew .... 570-577-3698.. 398 L
andy.hirsch@bucknell.edu
HIRSCH, Andrew, H .... 570-577-3698.. 398 L
andy.hirsch@bucknell.edu
HIRSCH, Glenn .... 612-624-4390.. 255 H
ghirsch@umn.edu
HIRSCH, Linda, R .... 563-333-6296.. 176 D
hirschlindar@sau.edu
HIRSCH, Michele .... 718-489-5202.. 328 D
mhirsch@sfc.edu
HIRSCH, Samuel .... 215-751-8160.. 401 G
shirsch@ccp.edu
HIRSCHBECK, Denise, R . 314-935-5320.. 274 N
dhirschbeck@wustl.edu
HIRSCHFIELD,
Michael, T .... 262-472-1633.. 521 F
hirschfm@uww.edu
HIRSCHY, Margaret .... 419-434-4260.. 381 E
hirschym@findlay.edu
HIRSH, Erin .... 215-635-7300.. 404 D
ehirsh@gratz.edu
HIRSHMAN, Elliot .... 619-594-5201.... 35 A
presidents.office@sdsu.edu
HIRSHON, Arnold .... 216-368-5292.. 365 B
arnold.hirshon@case.edu
HIRST, Martha, K .... 718-817-3120.. 314 G
mhirst1@fordham.edu
HIRST, Thomas, M .... 845-451-1204.. 312 C
t_hirst@culinary.edu
HIRT, E. Jill .... 610-861-5421.. 411 G
jhirt@northampton.edu
HIRTLE, Christopher .... 413-572-5455.. 222 E
chris@westfield.ma.edu
HISCANO, Lisa .... 908-965-2358.. 298 A
hiscano@ucc.edu
HISE, Douglas .... 207-834-7844.. 205 B
douglas.hise@maine.edu
HISE, Douglas .... 207-949-0993.. 205 D
douglas.hise@maine.edu
HISE, Jeremy .... 580-628-6345.. 384 L
jeremy.hise@noc.edu
HISE, Paul .... 806-720-7279.. 461 C
paul.hise@lcu.edu
HISER, Larry, R .... 740-376-4665.. 372 A
larry.hiser@marietta.edu
HISEY, Richard, M .... 617-266-1400.. 215 G
HISKES, Anne .... 616-331-8655.. 234 F
hiskesa@gvsu.edu
HISLE, W. Lee .... 860-439-2650.... 87 F
wlhis@conncoll.edu
HISRICH, Matt .... 765-983-1523.. 160 G
hisrima@earlham.edu
HISS, Nancy .... 503-699-6242.. 392 D
nhiss@marylhurst.edu
HISSONG, Kimberly .... 315-229-5837.. 329 D
khissong@stlawu.edu
HISSONG, Wesley .... 315-786-6517.. 317 H
whissong@sunyjefferson.edu
HITCH, Elizabeth, J .... 801-321-7122.. 481 L
ehitch@ushe.edu
HITCHCOCK, Cheryl, Y .... 443-885-3535.. 209 F
cheryl.hitchcock@morgan.edu

HITCHCOCK, Claude, E ... 443-885-3938 .. 209 F
claude.hitchcock@morgan.edu

HITCHCOCK, Susan ... 607-255-9043 .. 312 A
sh54@cornell.edu

HITCHELL, Dan ... 860-297-4224 .... 89 B
dan.hitchell@trincoll.edu

HITE, Griffin ... 256-765-4400 ...... 9 C
una@bkstr.com

HITE, Joe ... 940-552-6291 .. 478 D
jhite@vernoncollege.edu

HITE, Robert, D ... 415-442-7058 .... 45 B
bhite@ggu.edu

HITE, Trudy, E ... 302-356-6965 .... 91 I
trudy.e.hite@wilmu.edu

HITES, Michael ... 217-244-0102 .. 156 E
hites@uillinois.edu

HITESMAN, Bill ... 402-461-2400 .. 278 K
bhitesman@cccneb.edu

HITT, Anisa ... 941-907-2262 .... 99 J
ahitt@evergladesuniversity.edu

HITT, John, C ... 407-823-1823 .. 111 E
john.hitt@ucf.edu

HITT, Richard, J ... 863-784-7036 .. 109 G
richard.hitt@southflorida.edu

HITTLE, Ann ... 509-452-5100 .. 505 H
ahittle@pnwu.edu

HITTLE, Ben ... 509-452-5100 .. 505 H
bhittle@pnwu.edu

HITZ, Randy ... 503-725-4697 .. 394 G
hitz@pdx.edu

HIX, Patty ... 803-754-4100 .. 429 B

HIX, Raymond, E ... 305-284-2270 .. 114 H
rnaulthix@miami.edu

HIXON, Carla ... 701-224-5580 .. 361 C
carla.hixson@bismarckstate.edu

HIXON, Sharon ... 706-272-4594 .. 119 H
shixon@daltonstate.edu

HIXSON, Carol ... 561-297-3165 .. 110 K
hixson@fau.edu

HIXSON, John ... 479-619-4341 .... 21 D
jhixson@nwacc.edu

HIXSON-WALLACE, Julie . 501-279-5205 .... 20 D
jahixson@harding.edu

HIYANE-BROWN, Kathi ... 360-383-3330 .. 509 F
presoffice@whatcom.ctc.edu

HJALTALIN, Lisa ... 509-434-5275 .. 502 H
lisa.hjaltalin@ccs.spokane.edu

HJALTALIN, Lisa ... 509-434-5210 .. 502 I
lisa.hjaltalin@ccs.spokane.edu

HJALTALIN, Lisa ... 509-434-5210 .. 503 A
lisa.hjaltalin@ccs.spokane.edu

HJELLUM, Wilma ... 402-457-2723 .. 280 J
whjellum@mccneb.edu

HJERPE, Karen ... 724-938-4351 .. 414 E
hjerpe@calu.edu

HLADEK, Thomas ... 718-482-5510 .. 309 A
tomhl@lagcc.cuny.edu

HLADIK, Barbara ... 215-489-2346 .. 402 A
barbara.hladik@delval.edu

HLADIS, Jirka ... 303-245-4702 .... 81 I
jirka@naropa.edu

HLASNY, Robert, G ... 603-535-2461 .. 288 F
rhlasny@plymouth.edu

HLAVENKA, Lawrence ... 201-689-7057 .. 289 E
lhlavenka@bergen.edu

HLAVIN, Karen ... 847-543-2384 .. 138 C
khlavin@clcillinois.edu

HLEBOWITSH, Peter ... 205-348-6052 ...... 8 D
peter.hleb@ua.edu

HLINAK, Matthew, J ... 708-524-6812 .. 139 F
mhlinak@dom.edu

HLINKA, Karen ... 270-534-3236 .. 190 H
karen.hlinka@kctcs.edu

HLUBB, Emma ... 931-424-7366 .. 441 G
ehlubb@martinmethodist.edu

HLUBB, James, R ... 931-424-7379 .. 441 G
jhlubb@martinmethodist.edu

HMIELESKI, Kristin ... 413-265-2340 .. 217 D
hmieleskik@elms.edu

HMIELEWSKI,
Christopher ... 507-537-7984 .. 252 E
christopher.hmielewski@smsu.edu

HO, Co ... 714-992-7020 .... 54 H
cho@fullcoll.edu

HO, Deanna ... 312-935-4860 .. 152 D
dho@robertmorris.edu

HO, Katy ... 808-845-9158 .. 132 A
katyho@hawaii.edu

HO, Sam ... 408-223-6798 .... 62 C
sam.ho@sjeccd.org

HO, Sandra ... 603-427-7614 .. 286 B
sho@ccsnh.edu

HO, Victor ... 415-565-4624 .... 69 B
hov@uchastings.edu

HOAG, David ... 847-317-7128 .. 156 B
dhoag@tiu.edu

HOAG, David, A ... 863-638-7209 .. 115 C
david.hoag@warner.edu

HOAG, Jamie, D ... 508-793-2011 .. 217 C
jhoag@holycross.edu

HOAG, William ... 617-541-5357 .. 224 F
whoag@rcc.mass.edu

HOANG, Andy ... 562-985-8201 .... 33 B
andy.hoang@csulb.edu

HOANG, Minh-Ha ... 619-260-4506 .... 72 B
hoangm@sandiego.edu

HOANG POE, Linh ... 808-734-9570 .. 131 I
lhoang@hawaii.edu

HOAR, Robert ... 406-657-2367 .. 277 D
rhoar@msubillings.edu

HOAR, Robert ... 608-785-8039 .. 520 C
rhoar@uwlax.edu

HOBAN, Elizabeth ... 973-328-5160 .. 290 H
ehoban@ccm.edu

HOBAN, Kristi, M ... 817-257-7803 .. 469 G
k.hoban@tcu.edu

HOBAN, Patricia, K ... 503-375-5477 .. 396 G
phoban@willamette.edu

HOBART, Will ... 361-825-2616 .. 468 E
will.hobart@tamucc.edu

HOBBIEBRUNKEN, Kayla 602-212-0501 .... 11 N

HOBBIEBRUNKEN, Kayla 602-212-0501 .... 16 B

HOBBS, Clinton, G ... 706-379-3111 .. 130 B
clinth@yhc.edu

HOBBS, Harriet ... 704-378-3572 .. 345 E
hhobbs@jcsu.edu

HOBBS, Jacy ... 570-558-1818 .. 403 I
jhobbs@fortisinstitute.edu

HOBBS, Jeanie ... 817-598-6267 .. 479 E
hobbs@wc.edu

HOBBS, Jeremy ... 415-351-3536 .... 61 B
jhobbs@sfai.edu

HOBBS, Marcia, B ... 270-809-2193 .. 192 A
mhobbs4@murraystate.edu

HOBBS, Nancy, A ... 734-764-7270 .. 241 J
hobbsn@umich.edu

HOBBS, Nicole ... 773-291-6100 .. 137 G
nhobbs3@ccc.edu

HOBBS, Pamelia, C ... 336-322-2120 .. 351 H
pam.hobbs@piedmontcc.edu

HOBBS, Patrick ... 732-445-8610 .. 295 F
ad@scarletknights.com

HOBBS, Patrick, E ... 732-445-7839 .. 296 B

HOBBS, Phillip, M ... 205-853-1200 ...... 5 B
mhobbs@jeffstateonline.com

HOBBS, Rick ... 408-855-5325 .... 74 G
rick.hobbs@missioncollege.edu

HOBBS, Tameka ... 305-626-3955 .. 101 A
tameka.hobbs@fmuniv.edu

HOBBY, Angela ... 229-333-2100 .. 130 A
angela.hobby@wiregrass.edu

HOBBY, Erett ... 713-221-5075 .. 474 B
hobbyb@uhd.edu

HOBBY-MEARS, Michelle 949-480-4134 .... 64 J
mhobby@soka.edu

HOBELMAN, Greg ... 317-896-9324 .. 167 H
ghobelman@ubca.org

HOBERMAN, Chaim ... 516-225-4700 .. 326 I

HOBIN, Caron, T ... 413-565-1333 .. 215 A
chobin@baypath.edu

HOBLER, Dean ... 419-998-3103 .. 380 A
dahobler@unoh.edu

HOBLET, Kent, H ... 662-325-1418 .. 259 D
hoblet@cvm.msstate.edu

HOBSON, Charles ... 219-980-6903 .. 163 B
chobson@iun.edu

HOBSON, Lynn, M ... 620-341-5267 .. 180 G
lhobson@emporia.edu

HOBSON, Paula, L ... 603-535-2212 .. 288 F
phobson@plymouth.edu

HOBSON, Sheila ... 301-860-3451 .. 212 D
shobson@bowiestate.edu

HOBSON, Tricia ... 405-422-1263 .. 387 E
hobsont@redlandscc.edu

HOBSON-PAPE, Karri ... 706-542-8090 .. 128 E
karrie@uga.edu

HOBY, Lori, L ... 503-370-6546 .. 396 G
lhoby@willamette.edu

HOBYAK, Michael, S ... 215-785-0111 .. 413 K

HOCHANADEL, Gary ... 972-438-6932 .. 463 F
ghochanadel@parker.edu

HOCHHALTER, Carol ... 616-222-3000 .. 236 F
chochhalter@kuyper.edu

HOCHMAN, Alex ... 415-422-2437 .... 72 C
ahochman@usfca.edu

HOCHRADEL, Ted ... 662-846-4745 .. 257 E
thochradel@deltastate.edu

HOCHSTEIN, Dale ... 212-774-0748 .. 320 C
phochstein@mmm.edu

HOCINE, Chabha ... 563-884-5442 .. 176 C
chabha.hocine@palmer.edu

HOCK, Amy ... 402-471-2505 .. 281 G
ahock@nscs.edu

HOCK, Joan ... 215-489-2975 .. 402 A
joan.hock@delval.edu

HOCK, Nathan ... 802-828-2800 .. 486 A
nathan.hock@ccv.edu

HOCKENBERRY,
Frederick ... 301-846-2544 .. 207 F
fhockenberry@frederick.edu

HOCKENHULL,
Benjamin, R ... 512-448-8688 .. 464 G
ben@stedwards.edu

HOCKMAN, Joan ... 814-371-2090 .. 420 H
jhockman@triangle-tech.edu

HOCKS, Jeffrey, T ... 606-886-3863 .. 139 A
jeffrey.hicks@kctcs.edu

HOCQUARD, Stephen, L . 989-964-4081 .. 240 F
shoc@svsu.edu

HOCUTT, Kirby ... 806-742-3355 .. 472 C
kirby.hocutt@ttu.edu

HODA-KEARSE, Rebecca . 315-498-2119 .. 325 G
r.a.hoda-kearse@sunyocc.edu

HODEL, Laura ... 607-778-5028 .. 332 D
hodellj@sunybroome.edu

HODGDEN, Jessica ... 401-454-6764 .. 426 A
jhodgden@risd.edu

HODGE, Andrea ... 213-740-4225 .... 72 D
ahodge@usc.edu

HODGE, Brad, K ... 215-670-9206 .. 412 D
bhodge@peirce.edu

HODGE, Brian ... 561-297-2774 .. 110 K
bhodge@fau.edu

HODGE, Charles ... 937-376-6007 .. 365 H
chodge@centralstate.edu

HODGE, David ... 334-291-4928 ...... 2 H
david.hodge@cv.edu

HODGE, Dena, S ... 864-379-8833 .. 429 I
hodge@erskine.edu

HODGE, Diane ... 937-328-6063 .. 366 E
dhodge@clarkstate.edu

HODGE, Evelyn ... 334-229-4139 ...... 1 D
ehodge@alasu.edu

HODGE, Gary, B ... 972-881-5897 .. 455 A
ghodge@collin.edu

HODGE, Jeremy ... 334-229-4156 ...... 1 D
jhodge@alasu.edu

HODGE, Jimmer ... 218-262-6705 .. 249 E
jimmerhodge@hibbing.edu

HODGE, Johnesa ... 313-496-2796 .. 242 H
jdimick1@wcccd.edu

HODGE, Margaret ... 706-385-1069 .. 126 A
margaret.hodge@point.edu

HODGE, Marilyn, R ... 757-822-7245 .. 498 H
mhodge@tcc.edu

HODGE, Michel ... 718-631-6351 .. 309 E
mhodge@qcc.cuny.edu

HODGE, Mildred ... 860-215-9252 .... 87 D
mhodge@trcc.commnet.edu

HODGE, Paula ... 661-362-5108 .... 40 A
paula.hodge@canyons.edu

HODGE, Rick ... 323-242-5388 .... 50 B
hodgerl@lasc.edu

HODGE, Ron ... 509-865-8521 .. 504 D
hodge_r@heritage.edu

HODGE, Sandra ... 601-979-2282 .. 258 D
sandra.hodge@jsums.edu

HODGE, Terrell, L ... 269-387-6000 .. 243 H
terrell.hodge@wmich.edu

HODGE, Tiffani ... 404-523-8520 .. 128 A
thodge3@spelman.edu

HODGEN, Danielle ... 509-527-4301 .. 508 F
danielle.hodgen@wwcc.edu

HODGES, Caryl ... 650-508-3621 .... 54 J
chodges@ndnu.edu

HODGES, Christophe ... 215-717-3117 .. 401 J
christopher.hodges@curtis.edu

HODGES, Courtney ... 434-395-2823 .. 491 E
hodgesmc@longwood.edu

HODGES, Daniel, K ... 540-365-4365 .. 489 M
dhodges@ferrum.edu

HODGES, Dawn ... 770-229-3293 .. 127 F
dhodges@sctech.edu

HODGES, Elizabeth, F ... 787-850-9337 .. 538 B
elizabeth.hodges@upr.edu

HODGES, Greg ... 276-656-0281 .. 498 A
ghodges@patrickhenry.edu

HODGES, Heath ... 918-463-2931 .. 383 F
heath.hodges@connorsstate.edu

HODGES, Jeff ... 540-362-6503 .. 490 F
jhodges@hollins.edu

HODGES, Jill ... 906-487-3310 .. 238 A
jhodges@mtu.edu

HODGES, Jimmy ... 256-352-8229 ...... 9 G
jimmy.hodges@wallacestate.edu

HODGES, Lorraine ... 973-803-5000 .. 294 B
lhodges@pillar.edu

HODGES, Mike ... 423-472-7141 .. 445 E
mhodges@clevelandstatecc.edu

HODGES, Mindy ... 859-371-9393 .. 186 M

HODGES, Omega ... 828-298-3325 .. 559 F
ohodges@warren-wilson.edu

HODGES, Rhonda ... 276-656-0256 .. 498 A
rhodges@patrickhenry.edu

HODGES, Richard ... 757-825-2868 .. 498 G
hodgesr@tncc.edu

HODGES, Ricky, C ... 336-734-7272 .. 349 G
rhodges@forsythtech.edu

HODGES, Stephen, J ... 617-746-1990 .. 219 G
stephen.hodges@hult.edu

HODGES, Tim ... 785-594-8365 .. 178 D
tim.hodges@bakeru.edu

HODGES, Tina ... 731-352-4032 .. 438 K
hodgest@bethelu.edu

HODGES, YLonne ... 912-688-6922 .. 125 E
yhodges@ogeecheetech.edu

HODGES, Zachary ... 713-718-5721 .. 459 B
zachary.hodges@hccs.edu

HODGES MOORE, Sue ... 859-572-5349 .. 192 B
moores4@nku.edu

HODGINS, Diane, W ... 850-729-6485 .. 105 I
hodginsd@nwfsc.edu

HODGINS, Ewart ... 919-573-5350 .. 355 G

HODGKISS, William, S ... 858-534-3131 .... 70 C
hodgkissavc@ucsd.edu

HODGSON, Bev ... 218-755-2020 .. 248 M
bhodgson@bemidjistate.edu

HODGSON, Jessica, J ... 863-680-4292 .. 101 E
jhodgson2@flsouthern.edu

HODGSON, Matt ... 707-826-3321 .... 34 F
matthodson@humboldt.edu

HODGSON, Robert ... 217-641-4349 .. 143 H
rhodgson@jwcc.edu

HODNETT, James ... 478-387-4715 .. 121 E
jhodnett@gmc.edu

HODNETT, Martin ... 256-726-7052 ...... 6 B
mhodnett@oakwood.edu

HODO, Tammy ... 904-256-1234 .. 100 E
thodo@fcsl.edu

HODOWANEC, Mary Kate 609-835-6000 .... 93 F

HODOWANEC, Mary Kate 856-482-4200 .... 93 F

HODOWANEC, Michael ... 610-372-4721 .. 417 G
mhodowanec@racc.edu

HODSDON, Roger ... 626-815-5080 .... 28 A
rhodsdon@apu.edu

HODSON, April ... 860-215-9007 .... 87 D
ahodson@trcc.commnet.edu

HODSON, Brad ... 417-625-9300 .. 268 H
hodson-b@mssu.edu

HODSON, Brad ... 417-625-3072 .. 268 H
hodson-b@mssu.edu

HODSON, Luke ... 859-985-3503 .. 187 B
hodsonl@berea.edu

HODUM, Robert ... 931-372-3888 .. 445 B
rhodum@tntech.edu

HOEBEE, John ... 602-386-4810 .... 11 D
john.hoebee@arizonachristian.edu

HOEBER, Mark, S ... 716-851-1413 .. 313 H
hoeber@ecc.edu

HOEF, Ted ... 314-968-6980 .. 275 B
hoeftl@webster.edu

HOEFFNER, Denise, R ... 785-309-3110 .. 184 H
denise.hoeffner@salinatech.edu

HOEFFNER, Lori ... 516-877-3232 .. 303 B
hoeffner@adelphi.edu

HOEG, Portia ... 814-332-3350 .. 397 A
phoeg@allegheny.edu

HOEH, Susan ... 407-888-8689 .. 100 H
shoeh@fcim.edu

HOEHN, Alex, J ... 718-990-2998 .. 328 F
hoehna@stjohns.edu

HOEHNKE, Diane ... 414-443-8627 .. 522 P
diane.hoehnke@wlc.edu

HOEKSEMA, Jim ... 641-673-1107 .. 177 J
hoeksemaj@wmpenn.edu

HOEKSTRA, Erik ... 712-722-6002 .. 171 J
erik.hoekstra@dordt.edu

HOEKSTRA, Jack ... 803-732-6716 .. 431 B
hoekstraj@midlandstech.edu

HOEKSTRA, Jonathan ... 254-867-4892 .. 470 F
jonathan.hoekstra@systems.tstc.edu

HOEL, Aaron ... 301-687-3101 .. 212 F
ahoel@frostburg.edu

HOEL, Monica, S ... 276-944-6126 .. 489 I
mshoel@ehc.edu

HOELLEN, Kathy, L ... 803-981-7150 .. 435 D
khoellen@yorktech.edu

HOELSCHER, Ronda ... 325-793-4857 .. 461 F
hoelscher.ronda@mcm.edu

HOERITZ, Kim ... 412-396-6213 .. 403 A
hoeritzk@duq.edu

HOERTH, Richard ... 920-693-1237 .. 523 E
rich.hoerth@gotoltc.edu

HOESING, Kristin ... 402-562-1296 .. 278 K
khoesing@cccneb.edu

HOESING, Paul ... 314-792-6136 .. 266 F
hoesing@kenrick.edu

HOEY, Danny ... 772-462-7606 .. 103 B
dhoey@irsc.edu

HOEY, John ... 508-999-8071 .. 220 H
jhoey@umassd.edu

HOFELDT, Kathryn ... 615-322-0344 .. 449 A
kathryn.hofeldt@vanderbilt.edu

HOFER, Glenn ... 651-638-6069 .. 244 L
glenn-hofer@bethel.edu

HOFER, Jared ... 605-995-3022 .. 436 C
jared.hofer@mitchelltech.edu

HOFER, Jeanie, H ... 573-341-6425 .. 274 B
jeanie@mst.edu

HOFER, Sean ... 512-568-3300 .... 93 F

HOFER, Sean ... 210-202-3700 .... 93 F

HOFF, Brad ..... 507-786-3310.. 254 P
hoff@stolaf.edu
HOFF, Dianne ..... 678-839-6570.. 129 E
dhoff@westga.edu
HOFF, Kevin ..... 541-956-7925.. 394 J
khoff@roguecc.edu
HOFF, Melissa ..... 336-272-7102.. 344 G
melissa.hoff@greensboro.edu
HOFF, Michael, B ..... 423-439-6593.. 444 F
hoffmb@etsu.edu
HOFFELT, Dana ..... 775-831-1314.. 285 G
dhoffelt@sierranevada.edu
HOFFHINES, Kristin ..... 847-925-6522.. 141 A
khoffhin@harpercollege.edu
HOFFLER, Undi, N ..... 919-530-5140.. 357 A
uhoffler@nccu.edu
HOFFMAN, A, P ..... 334-556-2225..... 3 N
ahoffman@wallace.edu
HOFFMAN, Barbara ..... 319-399-8540.. 170 G
bhoffman@coe.edu
HOFFMAN, Bart ..... 714-564-6800.... 58 G
hoffman_bart@sac.edu
HOFFMAN, Beth ..... 301-687-4101.. 212 F
bhoffman@frostburg.edu
HOFFMAN, Carolyn, F ..... 301-546-0561.. 210 C
hoffmacf@pgcc.edu
HOFFMAN, Charles, E ..... 314-516-6280.. 274 A
hoffmance@umsl.edu
HOFFMAN, Cierra ..... 678-331-4331.. 124 B
cierra.hoffman@life.edu
HOFFMAN, Emily, R ..... 716-839-8210.. 312 D
ehoffman@daemen.edu
HOFFMAN, Erin ..... 847-735-5207.. 145 B
hoffman@lakeforest.edu
HOFFMAN, H. John ..... 203-773-6678.... 85 C
hjhoffman@albertus.edu
HOFFMAN, Heather ..... 770-426-2780.. 124 B
hhoffman@life.edu
HOFFMAN, Holly ..... 419-559-2326.. 377 M
hhoffman01@terra.edu
HOFFMAN, Jaime ..... 323-259-2500.... 55 A
jhoffman@oxy.edu
HOFFMAN, James ..... 575-646-4083.. 300 J
jhoffman@nmsu.edu
HOFFMAN, Jeffrey, L ..... 315-255-1743.. 306 G
foundation@cayuga-cc.edu
HOFFMAN, John ..... 215-572-2900.. 397 G
hoffmanj@arcadia.edu
HOFFMAN, John, J ..... 848-932-7697.. 295 F
HOFFMAN, Joseph, M ..... 301-687-4120.. 212 F
jhoffman@frostburg.edu
HOFFMAN, Kyle, D ..... 209-228-4400.... 70 A
khoffman@ucmerced.edu
HOFFMAN, Larry ..... 914-395-2384.. 329 K
lhoffman@sarahlawrence.edu
HOFFMAN, Laura ..... 941-359-4237.. 112 E
hoffman@sar.usf.edu
HOFFMAN, Lawrence ..... 703-284-5716.. 492 A
lhoffman@marymount.edu
HOFFMAN, LeAnn ..... 712-274-6400.. 177 I
leann.hoffman@witcc.edu
HOFFMAN, Lorraine, B ..... 530-898-6231.... 32 C
lbhoffman@csuchico.edu
HOFFMAN, Louis ..... 410-484-7200.. 210 A
lhoffman@nirc.edu
HOFFMAN, Maria ..... 305-821-3333.. 101 B
mhoffman@fnu.edu
HOFFMAN, Marion, S ..... 850-488-2447.. 112 A
marionh@ufl.edu
HOFFMAN, Mark ..... 610-341-5935.. 403 B
hoffman@eastern.edu
HOFFMAN, SR.,
Martin, A ..... 856-222-9311.. 295 C
mhoffman@rcbc.edu
HOFFMAN, Mary ..... 719-587-7372.... 76 G
mchoffma@adams.edu
HOFFMAN, Mary, F ..... 715-836-4353.. 520 A
hoffmamf@uwec.edu
HOFFMAN, Michael ..... 515-965-7130.. 171 B
mjhoffman@dmacc.edu
HOFFMAN, Michael ..... 716-375-2530.. 328 B
mhoffman@sbu.edu
HOFFMAN, Michael, D ..... 414-410-4057.. 515 I
mdhoffman@stritch.edu
HOFFMAN, Molly ..... 740-362-3373.. 372 D
mhoffman@mtso.edu
HOFFMAN, Patricia ..... 410-706-7355.. 211 F
phoffman@umaryland.edu
HOFFMAN, Paula ..... 320-629-5180.. 251 E
hoffmanp@pine.edu
HOFFMAN, Peter ..... 912-344-2576.. 116 E
peter.hoffman@armstrong.edu
HOFFMAN, Phyllis ..... 510-642-6000.... 68 M
HOFFMAN, Sandra ..... 856-415-2220.. 295 D
shoffma2@rcgc.edu
HOFFMAN, Sharon, L ..... 802-287-8215.. 484 A
hoffmans@greenmtn.edu
HOFFMAN, Sharon, L ..... 802-287-8216.. 484 A
hoffmans2@greenmtn.edu
HOFFMAN, Sonia ..... 336-272-7102.. 344 G
sonia.hoffman@greensboro.edu
HOFFMAN, Steve ..... 765-361-6236.. 169 C
hoffmans@wabash.edu
HOFFMAN, Steven, A ..... 859-236-6688.. 187 H
steven.hoffman@centre.edu
HOFFMAN, Thomas ..... 507-453-2770.. 250 C
thoffman@southeastmn.edu
HOFFMANN, Donna ..... 909-389-3333.... 60 B
dhoffman@sbccd.edu
HOFFMANN,
Lowell (Bud) ..... 731-286-3307.. 446 B
hoffmann@dscc.edu
HOFFMANN, Mark ..... 701-777-2492.. 360 C
mark.hoffmann@und.edu
HOFFMANN, Pauline ..... 716-375-2578.. 328 B
hoffmann@sbu.edu
HOFFMANN, Stephanie ..... 314-367-8700.. 271 E
stephanie.hoffmann@stlcop.edu
HOFFMANN, Susie ..... 785-670-1643.. 185 H
susie.hoffmann@washburn.edu
HOFFMANN HARDING,
Erin ..... 574-631-7394.. 168 B
eharding@nd.edu
HOFFMANS, Kim ..... 805-289-6000.... 73 F
khoffmans@vcccd.edu
HOFFMEISTER, Chelsey ..... 952-829-1479.. 244 J
chelsey.hoffmeister@bethfel.org
HOFFMEYER, Tom ..... 254-710-1561.. 452 H
tom_hoffmeyer@baylor.edu
HOFHERR, Michael ..... 614-292-6553.. 375 A
hofherr3@osu.edu
HOFMANN, John ..... 650-508-3500.... 54 J
jmhofmann@ndnu.edu
HOFMANN, Karen ..... 407-823-2811.. 111 E
karen.hofmann@ucf.edu
HOFMANN, Paul ..... 916-278-6686.... 34 B
paul.hofmann@csus.edu
HOFMEISTER, David ..... 316-295-5685.. 181 B
david_hofmeister@friends.edu
HOFMEISTER, David ..... 316-295-5682.. 181 B
david_hofmeister@friends.edu
HOFMEISTER, Gretchen ..... 507-222-4301.. 245 C
ghofmeis@carleton.edu
HOFMEYER, Karna ..... 712-324-5061.. 175 G
khofmeyer@nwicc.edu
HOFRENNING, Ilene ..... 508-626-4900.. 221 E
ihofrenning@framingham.edu
HOFSTEDT, Petra ..... 715-682-1983.. 518 H
phofstedt@northland.edu
HOFSTETTER, Dale ..... 513-745-8308.. 379 B
hofsteda@uc.edu
HOFSTETTER, Shirley ..... 573-518-2190.. 268 E
shofstetter@mineralarea.edu
HOFSTETTER, Thomas ..... 410-706-2069.. 211 F
thofs001@umaryland.edu
HOFTIEZER, David ..... 609-984-1164.. 297 F
dhoftiezer@tesu.edu
HOGAN, Aaron ..... 479-968-0376.... 19 F
ahogan@atu.edu
HOGAN, Amy ..... 785-242-5200.. 183 M
amy.hogan@ottawa.edu
HOGAN, Andrea ..... 203-582-5215.... 88 G
andrea.hogan@quinnipiac.edu
HOGAN, Anne-Marie ..... 502-585-9911.. 192 E
ahogan02@spalding.edu
HOGAN, Barbara ..... 215-248-7120.. 400 H
hoganb@chc.edu
HOGAN, Beverly, W ..... 601-977-7730.. 261 A
bhogan@tougaloo.edu
HOGAN, Bill ..... 206-296-5451.. 507 E
hoganw@seattleu.edu
HOGAN, Brenda ..... 478-471-6684.. 124 E
brenda.hogan@mga.edu
HOGAN, Carrie ..... 518-783-2554.. 330 E
chogan@siena.edu
HOGAN, Cheryl ..... 231-843-5864.. 243 G
clhogan@westshore.edu
HOGAN, Christopher ..... 617-287-6800.. 220 G
christopher.hogan@umb.edu
HOGAN, Joan, P ..... 828-448-6041.. 354 B
jhogan@wpcc.edu
HOGAN, John ..... 501-760-4200.... 21 B
jhogan@np.edu
HOGAN, Judith ..... 781-280-3816.. 224 A
hoganj@middlesex.mass.edu
HOGAN, Kay ..... 850-973-1605.. 105 H
hogank@nfcc.edu
HOGAN, Kimberly ..... 860-343-5731.... 86 F
khogan@mxcc.edu
HOGAN, Lesley ..... 425-235-7872.. 506 F
lhogan@rtc.edu
HOGAN, Martha, A ..... 972-238-6210.. 456 H
mhogan@dcccd.edu
HOGAN, Matthew ..... 718-489-5447.. 328 D
mhogan@sfc.edu
HOGAN, Melissa ..... 847-330-4503.. 152 H
mhogan03@roosevelt.edu
HOGAN, Pashia ..... 423-354-2425.. 446 F
phhogan@northeaststate.edu
HOGAN, Pat ..... 910-362-7003.. 348 A
phogan@cfcc.edu
HOGAN, Patrick, D ..... 434-924-3252.. 495 H
pdh9t@virginia.edu
HOGAN, Patrick, N ..... 301-445-1927.. 211 D
phogan@usmd.edu
HOGAN, Paul ..... 603-271-6484.. 286 F
phogan@ccsnh.edu
HOGAN, Sean ..... 847-543-2419.. 138 C
shogan@clcillinois.edu
HOGAN, Sharon ..... 503-943-8677.. 396 B
hogans@up.edu
HOGAN, Susan, S ..... 413-597-4204.. 230 A
susan.s.hogan@williams.edu
HOGAN, Terrance, E ..... 305-474-6018.. 108 E
thogan@stu.edu
HOGAN, William ..... 907-786-4407.... 10 F
whhogan@uaa.alaska.edu
HOGARTY, Lisa ..... 603-646-0871.. 286 J
lisa.hogarty@dartmouth.edu
HOGENCAMP, Kelly ..... 909-607-2981.... 64 A
khogenca@scrippscollege.edu
HOGENSON, Liz ..... 763-424-0902.. 251 B
lhogenson@nhcc.edu
HOGG, Jake ..... 415-351-3556.... 61 B
jhogg@sfai.edu
HOGG, Steven ..... 706-855-8233.... 93 F
HOGG, Steven ..... 706-225-5300.... 93 F
HOGGE, Jane ..... 717-815-1410.. 424 F
jhogge@ycp.edu
HOGGLE, Layne ..... 334-683-5110..... 5 C
lhoggle@judson.edu
HOGLE, Paul ..... 216-791-5000.. 366 H
paul.hogle@cim.edu
HOGSETT, Denise ..... 304-696-2370.. 513 D
hogsettd@marshall.edu
HOGUE, Belinda ..... 334-727-8763..... 8 A
bahoque@mytu.tuskegee.edu
HOGUE, David ..... 814-393-2045.. 414 G
dhogue@clarion.edu
HOGUE, Eileen ..... 719-502-2419.... 82 B
eileen.hogue@ppcc.edu
HOGUE, Eric ..... 916-577-2200.... 75 C
ehogue@jessup.edu
HOGUE, Gina ..... 870-972-3057.... 18 J
ghogue@astate.edu
HOGUE, Gina ..... 870-972-2030.... 18 J
ghogue@astate.edu
HOGUE, Jarrod ..... 503-491-7019.. 392 F
jarrod.hogue@mhcc.edu
HOGUE, Jason ..... 402-872-2429.. 281 I
jhogue@peru.edu
HOGUE, Laurel ..... 660-543-4984.. 273 C
lhogue@ucmo.edu
HOGUE, Matthew, L ..... 843-349-2813.. 428 E
dhogue@coastal.edu
HOGUE, Stacey ..... 501-812-2299.... 21 H
shogue@pulaskitech.edu
HOGUE, William, F ..... 803-777-0707.. 433 F
wfhogue@mailbox.sc.edu
HOGYA, Tiffany ..... 330-823-2072.. 379 F
hogyata@mountunion.edu
HOHBERG, Tonian ..... 213-624-1200.... 43 J
thohberg@fidm.edu
HOHENSTEIN, Janet, M ..... 218-477-2956.. 250 F
hohenst@mnstate.edu
HOHERTZ, Cherie, L ..... 972-721-5040.. 473 D
chohertz@udallas.edu
HOHIEMER, Victoria ..... 270-686-4512.. 190 D
vickie.hohiemer@kctcs.edu
HOHL, Kathleen ..... 414-297-6208.. 524 A
hohlk@matc.edu
HOHMAN, Adam ..... 260-982-5228.. 165 M
arhohman@manchester.edu
HOHN, Daniel ..... 303-797-5753.... 76 J
daniel.hohn@arapahoe.edu
HOI, Samuel ..... 410-225-2237.. 209 B
president@mica.edu
HOIDA, Will ..... 775-881-1314.. 285 G
whoida@sierranevada.edu
HOILAND, Erin ..... 360-412-6149.. 506 G
ehoiland@stmartin.edu
HOILE, Linda ..... 209-575-6498.... 76 A
hoilel@yosemite.edu
HOILMAN, Sandra, K ..... 828-448-6020.. 354 B
shoilman@wpcc.edu
HOIT, Marc, I ..... 919-515-0141.. 357 B
mark_hoit@ncsu.edu
HOJAN, Elizabeth, M ..... 262-554-2010.. 518 B
mwcfinancialaid@aol.com
HOJAN-CLARK, Jane ..... 212-853-0469.. 311 E
jh3574@columbia.edu
HOJSACK, Dana ..... 619-849-2678.... 57 M
danahojsack@pointloma.edu
HOKE, Chris ..... 701-252-3467.. 362 F
choke@uj.edu
HOKE, Cynthia ..... 229-430-4605.. 115 K
cynthia.hoke@asurams.edu
HOKE, Mary ..... 210-829-3982.. 474 D
mhoke@uiwtx.edu
HOKOANA, Lui ..... 808-984-3636.. 132 D
lhokoana@hawaii.edu
HOLAHAN, Barbara ..... 516-686-7533.. 323 G
bholahan@nyit.edu
HOLAK, Susan, L ..... 718-982-2920.. 307 F
schoolofbusiness@csi.cuny.edu
HOLAWAY, Rick ..... 615-966-6133.. 441 F
rick.holaway@lipscomb.edu
HOLBERG, Connie ..... 315-786-2402.. 317 H
cholberg@sunyjefferson.edu
HOLBERG, John ..... 706-419-1565.. 119 G
john.holberg@covenant.edu
HOLBROOK, Carl ..... 334-347-2623..... 3 H
cholbrook@escc.edu
HOLBROOK,
Catherine, B ..... 413-662-5231.. 222 B
catherine.holbrook@mcla.edu
HOLBROOK, Christine ..... 413-552-2319.. 223 E
cholbrook@hcc.edu
HOLBROOK, Eddie ..... 704-669-4223.. 348 F
holbrook@clevelandcc.edu
HOLBROOK, Jennifer ..... 870-230-5275.... 20 E
holbroj@hsu.edu
HOLBROOK, Karen, A ..... 386-226-6203.... 99 A
holbrook@erau.edu
HOLBROOK, Kate ..... 719-389-7986.... 77 J
kate.holbrook@coloradocollege.edu
HOLBROOKS, Johnnie, L ..... 432-837-8100.. 471 E
johnnieh@sulross.edu
HOLCOMB, David ..... 254-295-4184.. 474 E
dholcomb@umhb.edu
HOLCOMB, Gay ..... 859-858-3511.. 186 J
gay.holcomb@asbury.edu
HOLCOMB, Glen ..... 405-789-6400.. 388 A
gholcomb@snu.edu
HOLCOMB, Mark ..... 815-939-5236.. 150 I
mholcomb@olivet.edu
HOLCOMB, Robert ..... 707-527-4615.... 63 G
rholcomb@santarosa.edu
HOLCOMB, Todd, R ..... 308-635-6101.. 283 D
holcombt@wncc.edu
HOLCOMB-MCCOY,
Cheryl ..... 410-516-8770.. 208 D
cholcomb@jhu.edu
HOLCOMBE, Annalisa ..... 801-832-2551.. 483 D
asteggell@westminstercollege.edu
HOLCOMBE, Annalisa ..... 801-832-2565.. 483 D
asteggell@westminstercollege.edu
HOLCOMBE, Bridget ..... 336-841-9470.. 345 A
bholcomb@highpoint.edu
HOLCOMBE, Robert ..... 864-429-8728.. 434 F
reholcom@mailbox.sc.edu
HOLDA, Heather ..... 860-509-9502.... 88 A
hholda@hartsem.edu
HOLDEMAN, David ..... 940-565-2497.. 475 A
david.holdeman@unt.edu
HOLDEMAN, Lisa, K ..... 713-743-8408.. 473 E
lkholdeman@uh.edu
HOLDEMAN, Lisa, K ..... 713-743-0945.. 473 F
lkholdeman@uh.edu
HOLDEN, Brad ..... 541-278-5783.. 390 C
bholden@bluecc.edu
HOLDEN, Bruce ..... 901-448-1830.. 448 H
bholden@uthsc.edu
HOLDEN, Dave ..... 618-664-6750.. 140 I
dave.holden@greenville.edu
HOLDEN, Eileen ..... 863-297-1098.. 106 I
eholden@polk.edu
HOLDEN, Elaine, P ..... 704-637-4402.. 343 B
epholden@catawba.edu
HOLDEN, Ginger ..... 209-954-5039.... 61 F
gholden@deltacollege.edu
HOLDEN, John ..... 973-408-3226.. 291 B
jholden@drew.edu
HOLDEN, Joseph, M ..... 714-966-8500.... 73 G
HOLDEN, Kimberly ..... 706-771-4019.. 117 C
kholden@augustatech.edu
HOLDEN, Larry ..... 615-327-6339.. 442 A
lholden@mmc.edu
HOLDEN, Nina ..... 313-664-7864.. 232 G
nholden@collegeforcreativestudies.edu
HOLDEN, Randy ..... 540-231-3171.. 499 F
rholden@vt.edu
HOLDEN, Ronald ..... 330-823-2138.. 379 F
holdenrf@mountunion.edu
HOLDEN, Scott, A ..... 212-799-5000.. 318 A
HOLDEN, Teresa ..... 618-664-6844.. 140 I
teresa.holden@greenville.edu
HOLDEN, Wesley ..... 772-546-5534.. 102 S
wesleyholden@hsbc.edu
HOLDEN-DUFFY, Cheryl ..... 410-651-6460.. 212 B
clduffy@umes.edu
HOLDER, Ann ..... 936-294-1613.. 471 D
lib_ahh@shsu.edu
HOLDER, Beth ..... 336-841-9279.. 345 A
bholder@highpoint.edu
HOLDER, Candace ..... 336-386-3382.. 353 F
holderc@surry.edu
HOLDER, Cheryl ..... 618-842-3711.. 142 C
holderc@iecc.edu
HOLDER, Dinelly ..... 718-429-6600.. 339 D
dinelly.holder@vaughn.edu

HOLMES, Gilbert .... 909-460-2000.... 71 B
gholmes@laverne.edu
HOLMES, Greg .... 541-463-5516.. 391 G
holmesg@lanecc.edu
HOLMES, Heather, W ...... 410-677-4850.. 213 A
hwholmes@salisbury.edu
HOLMES, Heidi .... 314-768-7808.. 268 G
hholmes@missouricollege.com
HOLMES, Joan .... 813-253-7043.. 102 R
jholmes16@hccfl.edu
HOLMES, John, D .... 402-449-2809.. 280 C
gupres@graceu.edu
HOLMES, Johnny, B .... 901-321-3445.. 439 E
jholmes@cbu.edu
HOLMES, Judy .... 785-825-5422.. 179 C
jholmes@brownmackie.edu
HOLMES, Kathryn .... 801-832-2565.. 483 D
kholmes@westminstercollege.edu
HOLMES, Kenneth, M ...... 202-806-2100.... 93 A
kenneth.holmes@howard.edu
HOLMES, Kimberly .... 912-358-4190.. 126 F
holmesk@savannahstate.edu
HOLMES, Kristen .... 256-352-8118...... 9 G
kristen.holmes@wallacestate.edu
HOLMES, Lisa .... 760-252-2411.... 28 B
lholmes@barstow.edu
HOLMES, Lloyd, A .... 585-292-2120.. 321 J
lholmes20@monroecc.edu
HOLMES, Lucina .... 508-362-2131.. 223 C
lholmes@capecod.edu
HOLMES, Malcolm .... 540-654-1617.. 495 C
mholmes3@umw.edu
HOLMES, Matthew .... 610-902-8228.. 399 D
matthew.holmes@cabrini.edu
HOLMES, Megan .... 314-529-6852.. 267 B
mholmes3@maryville.edu
HOLMES, Michael, S ...... 207-768-9477.. 205 D
michael.s.holmes@maine.edu
HOLMES, Michelle, M ...... 510-841-1905.... 26 C
mmholmes@absw.edu
HOLMES, Molly .... 651-635-8500.. 244 L
mp-holmes@bethel.edu
HOLMES, Myioshi, U ...... 972-860-8237.. 456 C
muh3310@dcccd.edu
HOLMES, Owen .... 657-278-5403.... 33 A
oholmes@fullerton.edu
HOLMES, O'Neal .... 334-683-2350...... 5 G
oholmes@marionmilitary.edu
HOLMES, Phillip, M .... 478-387-4905.. 121 E
mholmes@gmc.edu
HOLMES, IV, Richard ...... 805-493-3586.... 31 C
holmes@callutheran.edu
HOLMES, Robert .... 602-243-8062.... 14 I
bear.holmes@southmountaincc.edu
HOLMES, Robin, H .... 541-346-1137.. 395 G
rhholmes@uoregon.edu
HOLMES, Rodney .... 480-461-7325.... 14 D
rodney.holmes@mesacc.edu
HOLMES, Salanna, D ...... 919-866-5705.. 353 I
sdholmes1@waketech.edu
HOLMES, Shandria .... 773-602-5517.. 137 F
sholmes65@ccc.edu
HOLMES, Sharon, N .... 920-924-6326.. 524 B
sholmes@morainepark.edu
HOLMES, Stephanie .... 309-694-8420.. 141 F
stephanie.holmes@icc.edu
HOLMES, Terrell .... 302-857-6375.... 90 F
tholmes@desu.edu
HOLMES, Tiffany .... 850-561-2888.. 110 J
tiffany.holmes@famu.edu
HOLMES, Tiffany .... 312-759-1671.. 154 A
tholmes@saic.edu
HOLMES, Tori .... 248-476-1122.. 237 H
tholmes@mispp.edu
HOLMES, Wendy .... 845-341-4662.. 325 H
wendy.holmes@sunyorange.edu
HOLMES, William, A .... 989-774-4308.. 232 D
holme1wa@cmich.edu
HOLMES BACZKOWSKI,
Helene .... 215-951-1817.. 407 A
holmes@lasalle.edu
HOLMES-BUTLER, Layna . 610-399-2461.. 414 F
laynaholmes@cheyney.edu
HOLMES-LEOPOLD, RJ .... 319-895-4445.. 171 A
rholmes-leopold@cornellcollege.edu
HOLMGREN, Richard, A .. 814-332-2898.. 397 A
rholmgre@allegheny.edu
HOLMLUND, Eric .... 518-327-6272.. 326 B
eholmlund@paulsmiths.edu
HOLMOE, Tom .... 801-422-7649.. 480 C
tom_holmoe@byu.edu
HOLMQUIST, Eric .... 712-279-5435.. 170 B
eric.holmquist@briarcliff.edu
HOLMQUIST, Jake .... 718-862-7449.. 319 L
jake.holmquist@manhattan.edu
HOLOHAN-MOYER, Irene 716-839-8214.. 312 D
imoyer@daemen.edu
HOLOMAN, Christopher .. 318-869-5101.. 194 I
president@centenary.edu
HOLOWICKI, Linda .... 708-209-3170.. 138 G
linda.holowicki@cuchicago.edu

HOLS, Eric .... 703-284-1601.. 492 A
eric.hols@marymount.edu
HOLSAPPLE, Dawn .... 518-828-4181.. 311 D
holsapple@sunycgcc.edu
HOLSAPPLE, Matthew ...... 301-696-3569.. 208 B
holsapple@hood.edu
HOLSCLAW, Sheila, K ...... 859-846-5310.. 191 G
sholsclaw@midway.edu
HOLSENBECK, Daniel ...... 407-823-2387.. 111 E
daniel.holsenbeck@ucf.edu
HOLSER, Derek, P .... 757-481-5005.. 500 H
HOLSINGER, Kent .... 860-486-2182.... 89 D
kent.holsinger@uconn.edu
HOLSINGER-FUCHS,
Pamela .... 360-688-2101.. 506 G
pholsingerfuchs@stmartin.edu
HOLSOPPLE, Lee .... 202-885-3409.... 91 J
lee.holsopple@american.edu
HOLSTAD, Deb .... 320-308-3277.. 252 B
dholstad@sctcc.edu
HOLSTAD, Deb, A .... 320-308-3227.. 252 B
dholstad@sctcc.edu
HOLSTEGE, Christopher ... 434-924-5185.. 495 H
ch2fx@virginia.edu
HOLSTEIN, David .... 561-868-3004.. 106 D
holsteid@palmbeachstate.edu
HOLSTEIN, Michael, L ..... 317-788-3214.. 168 A
mholstein@uindy.edu
HOLSTEN, Robert .... 252-246-1254.. 354 D
rholsten@wilsoncc.edu
HOLSTEN, Robert, D .... 252-246-1254.. 354 D
rholsten@wilsoncc.edu
HOLSTER, Melissa .... 617-228-2271.. 223 B
mholster@bhcc.mass.edu
HOLSTON, Darnell .... 706-945-1362.. 125 H
dholston@paine.edu
HOLSTON, J.B .... 303-871-3773.... 84 B
jb.holston@du.edu
HOLSTON, Jo-Ann, M ...... 334-833-4410...... 4 D
jholston@hawks.huntingdon.edu
HOLSTON, Tavarez .... 770-533-6921.. 123 L
tholston@laniertech.edu
HOLSTON, William .... 336-841-9221.. 345 A
bookstor@highpoint.edu
HOLT, Anthony .... 313-577-2062.. 243 F
aa6479@wayne.edu
HOLT, Brooke .... 479-619-4298.... 21 D
bholt@nwacc.edu
HOLT, Bruce .... 865-981-8035.. 441 H
bruce.holt@maryvillecollege.edu
HOLT, Daniel .... 816-415-5977.. 275 F
holtd@william.jewell.edu
HOLT, Gail, W .... 413-542-2296.. 214 C
financialaid@amherst.edu
HOLT, Joseph .... 559-734-9000.... 61 G
josephh@sjvc.edu
HOLT, Joseph, L .... 410-778-7201.. 213 E
jholt2@washcoll.edu
HOLT, Lynda .... 518-608-8171.. 314 A
lholt@excelsior.edu
HOLT, Martee .... 336-316-2198.. 344 H
mholt@guilford.edu
HOLT, Mary Margaret ...... 405-325-7370.. 389 B
marymholt@ou.edu
HOLT, Raymond .... 229-931-2001.. 127 C
rholt@southgatech.edu
HOLT, Rosalind .... 770-216-2960.. 123 F
rholt@ict.edu
HOLT, Rosalyn, J .... 318-670-9436.. 199 J
rholt@susla.edu
HOLT, Russ .... 925-473-7375.... 41 J
rholt@losmedanos.edu
HOLT, Ryan, C .... 828-884-8217.. 342 C
holtrc@brevard.edu
HOLT, Ryan, J .... 724-847-6133.. 404 B
rjholt@geneva.edu
HOLT, Sam .... 580-387-7311.. 384 D
sholt@mscok.edu
HOLT, Shari .... 870-743-3000.... 21 C
sholt@northark.edu
HOLT, Shawn .... 269-749-7607.. 240 A
sholt@olivetcollege.edu
HOLT, Tina .... 706-419-1275.. 119 G
tina.holt@covenant.edu
HOLT, Wilford .... 334-420-4400...... 7 G
wholt@trenholmstate.edu
HOLTEN, Kathryn .... 828-884-8373.. 342 C
holtenki@brevard.edu
HOLTER, Joan .... 218-723-6041.. 245 J
jholter@css.edu
HOLTGRAVE, Lorie .... 410-617-2400.. 208 G
laholtgrave@loyola.edu
HOLTGREN, Shawn, M .... 574-807-7215.. 159 D
holtgrs@bethelcollege.edu
HOLTGRIEVE, Shaun .... 989-774-3111.. 232 D
holtg1s@cmich.edu
HOLTHAUS, Barbara .... 217-641-4104.. 143 H
bholthaus@jwcc.edu
HOLTHOUSER, David, M . 704-894-2220.. 343 I
daholthouser@davidson.edu

HOLTMYER-JONES,
Larissa .... 515-294-4077.. 169 G
larissah@foundation.iastate.edu
HOLTON, Carol .... 910-576-6222.. 351 E
holtonc@montgomery.edu
HOLTSCHNEIDER,
Dennis, H .... 312-362-8850.. 139 C
president@depaul.edu
HOLTSLAG, Shannon .... 315-801-4459.. 328 C
sholtslag@secon.edu
HOLTZ, Daniel, F .... 320-222-5205.. 251 G
daniel.holtz@ridgewater.edu
HOLTZ, Edwin .... 712-325-3227.. 174 B
eholtz@iwcc.edu
HOLTZ, Ryan .... 410-706-7481.. 211 F
rholtz@umaryland.edu
HOLTZCLAW, Rhonda ...... 239-590-1037.. 110 L
rholtzcl@wgcu.edu
HOLTZCLAW, Scott .... 732-743-3800.... 93 F
HOLTZCLAW, Scott .... 609-406-7600.... 93 F
HOLTZEN, Wende .... 714-879-3901.... 46 F
wholtzen@hiu.edu
HOLTZHAUSEN, Derina ... 409-880-8137.. 471 A
derina.holtzhausen@lamar.edu
HOLUBIK, Donna .... 734-487-0455.. 233 J
dholubik@emich.edu
HOLVEY BOWLES,
Joanna .... 315-228-7216.. 310 G
jholveybowles@colgate.edu
HOLWICK, Jana, W .... 770-426-2697.. 124 B
jana.holwick@life.edu
HOLYFIED, Patrick .... 704-991-0235.. 353 E
HOLZ, Doris .... 212-220-8021.. 307 B
dholz@bmcc.cuny.edu
HOLZ, Richard, C .... 414-288-7230.. 517 I
richard.holz@marquette.edu
HOLZ-CLAUSE, Mary .... 909-869-2200.... 31 J
msholzclause@cpp.edu
HOLZBERLEIN, Anne .... 405-974-2770.. 388 L
aholzberlein@uco.edu
HOLZCLAW, Mike .... 925-551-1822.... 41 I
mholzclaw@dvc.edu
HOLZEM, Madeline .... 608-785-8013.. 520 C
mholzem@uwlax.edu
HOLZEMER, William, L .... 973-353-5149.. 296 C
holzemer@andromeda.rutgers.edu
HOLZEMER, William, L .... 973-353-5149.. 296 B
holzemer@andromeda.rutgers.edu
HOLZENBURG, Andreas .. 956-665-2889.. 476 E
andreas.holzenburg@utrgv.edu
HOLZHEUSER, Christina .. 361-825-5975.. 468 E
christina.holzheuser@tamucc.edu
HOLZMAN, Terri, L .... 920-748-8351.. 519 E
holzmant@ripon.edu
HOLZMER, OSF,
M. Anita .... 260-399-7700.. 168 D
aholzmer@sf.edu
HOM, Kevin .... 718-260-5525.. 309 C
khom@citytech.cuny.edu
HOMAN, David .... 847-233-7700.. 150 D
dhoman@nc.edu
HOMAN, Elizabeth .... 443-518-4073.. 208 C
ehoman@howardcc.edu
HOMAN, Judi .... 901-375-4400.. 442 F
judihoman@midsouthchristian.edu
HOMAN, Patricia .... 513-875-3344.. 365 K
patricia.homan@chatfield.edu
HOMAN, Richard, V .... 757-446-5800.. 489 B
homanrv@evms.edu
HOMARD, Jennifer .... 352-395-5493.. 109 C
jen.homard@sfcollege.edu
HOMBURGER, John, R .... 518-564-2130.. 334 A
homburjr@plattsburgh.edu
HOMER, Cory .... 973-300-2116.. 297 D
chomer@sussex.edu
HOMESLEY, Diane .... 678-839-6582.. 129 E
dhomesle@westga.edu
HOMFELDT, Mike .... 541-880-2244.. 391 F
homfeldt@klamathcc.edu
HOMIAK, JR., Albert, J ... 302-831-7285.... 91 F
homiak@udel.edu
HOMICH, John .... 617-627-6333.. 228 H
john.homich@tufts.edu
HOMOLKA, Karen, K .... 217-245-3094.. 141 G
khomolk@mail.ic.edu
HOMSHER, Betsy, E .... 810-762-9540.. 236 C
bhomsher@kettering.edu
HOMZA, Lu Ann .... 757-221-2469.. 488 F
dean-ep@wm.edu
HONAKER, Lisa .... 609-652-4505.. 297 C
lisa.honaker@stockton.edu
HONDROS, Jack .... 610-526-1445.. 397 E
jack.hondros@theamericancollege.edu
HONEGAN, Rhonda .... 404-270-5075.. 128 A
rhonegan@spelman.edu
HONEGGER, Rose .... 337-482-6819.. 201 D
oia@louisiana.edu
HONEMAN, Donald .... 508-793-7419.. 217 B
dhoneman@clarku.edu
HONEYCUTT, Andrew, E .. 714-772-3330.... 26 O

HONEYCUTT, Tony, L ...... 606-679-8501.. 190 E
tony.honeycutt@kctcs.edu
HONG, E-Sing .... 408-260-0208.... 43 L
chinesedoctoral@fivebranches.edu
HONG, Luoluo .... 415-338-2032.... 35 B
luoluo@sfsu.edu
HONG, Rebecca .... 562-903-6000.... 28 E
rebecca.hong@biola.edu
HONG, Tran .... 951-343-3907.... 29 H
thong@calbaptist.edu
HONG, Z. George .... 718-817-1000.. 314 G
HONKE, Mary, J .... 402-844-7124.. 282 B
maryh@northeast.edu
HONNELL, Cherie .... 503-494-7878.. 393 F
acad@ohsu.edu
HONRATH, Marianne .... 414-847-3246.. 518 D
mariannehonrath@miad.edu
HONTS, Arlen .... 316-295-5800.. 181 B
ahonts@friends.edu
HOO, Karlene .... 406-994-5555.. 277 C
karlene.hoo@montana.edu
HOOD, Brent .... 919-735-5151.. 354 A
wbhood@waynecc.edu
HOOD, Carra .... 609-652-4514.. 297 C
carra.hood@stockton.edu
HOOD, Donna .... 828-395-1404.. 350 E
dhood@isothermal.edu
HOOD, Gwendolyn, D ...... 205-348-5855...... 8 D
ghood@aalan.ua.edu
HOOD, Jean .... 817-272-5554.. 476 A
jmhood@uta.edu
HOOD, Joshua, D .... 423-775-7574.. 439 B
jhood3724@bryan.edu
HOOD, Michael, J .... 724-357-2397.. 415 B
mhood@iup.edu
HOOD, Mike .... 903-233-4115.. 460 J
mikehood@letu.edu
HOOD, Patricia .... 706-649-1883.. 119 F
phood@columbustech.edu
HOOD, Philip .... 847-735-6003.. 145 B
hood@lakeforest.edu
HOOD, Robin .... 931-363-9800.. 441 G
rhood@martinmethodist.edu
HOOD, Scott, W .... 207-725-3256.. 202 F
shood@bowdoin.edu
HOOD, Sonya .... 931-393-1765.. 446 D
shood@mscc.edu
HOOD, Steven .... 435-283-7301.. 482 E
steve.hood@snow.edu
HOOD, Tim .... 815-599-3513.. 141 E
tim.hood@highland.edu
HOOD, W.C. (Chip) .... 864-656-3414.. 428 C
chip@clemson.edu
HOOGAKKER, John .... 540-458-8446.. 500 F
jhoogakker@wlu.edu
HOOK, Amy .... 617-353-2399.. 216 E
amyhook@bu.edu
HOOK, Beth .... 314-362-6590.. 265 E
beth.hook@bjc.org
HOOK, David .... 602-386-4131.... 11 D
david.hook@arizonachristian.edu
HOOK, Randall .... 540-828-5358.. 487 H
rhook@bridgewater.edu
HOOK, Rebecca .... 610-436-6973.. 416 C
rhook@wcupa.edu
HOOK, Samuel, S .... 864-592-4630.. 432 H
hooks@sccsc.edu
HOOKER, JR.,
Richard, D .... 202-685-3838.. 528 B
hookerr@ndu.edu
HOOKER-HARING,
Christopher .... 484-664-3245.. 411 D
hookerh@muhlenberg.edu
HOOKS, Alicia .... 913-288-7388.. 182 C
ahokks@kckcc.edu
HOOKS, Beth .... 919-735-5151.. 354 A
bhooks@waynecc.edu
HOOKS, Haley .... 229-317-6746.. 120 A
haley.hooks@darton.edu
HOOKS, Haley .... 229-243-3039.. 117 E
haley.hooks@bainbridge.edu
HOOKS, Rebecca .... 704-216-3488.. 352 G
rebecca.hooks@rccc.edu
HOOKS, Stephen, L .... 615-353-3232.. 446 E
stephen.hooks@nscc.edu
HOOLE, Thomas .... 978-934-3509.. 221 A
thomas_hoole@uml.edu
HOOPER, Celia, R .... 336-334-5744.. 358 B
crhooper@uncg.edu
HOOPER, Debra, A .... 919-488-8500.. 345 I
dhooper@living-arts-college.edu
HOOPER, Heath .... 706-292-3906.. 127 A
hhooper@shorter.edu
HOOPER, Ricardo .... 310-287-4513.... 50 E
hopperra@wlac.edu
HOOPER, Robert, D .... 740-427-5109.. 371 C
hooperr@kenyon.edu
HOOPER, Stephanie .... 304-336-8990.. 513 F
stephanie.hooper@westliberty.edu
HOOPES, Robbin .... 513-569-1511.. 366 D
robbin.hoopes@cincinnatistate.edu

HOOPES, Robbin .... 513-569-1616.. 366 D
robbin.hoopes@cincinnatistate.edu
HOOPES, Tom .... 913-360-7529.. 178 I
thoopes@benedictine.edu
HOOPS, Lisa .... 937-778-7955.. 368 E
lhoops@edisonohio.edu
HOORNBEEK, Corbin ...... 626-815-5328.... 28 A
choornbeek@apu.edu
HOOTEN, Michael .... 806-414-9683.. 472 D
michael.hooten@ttuhsc.edu
HOOTON, Linda, J .... 205-853-1200...... 5 B
lhooton@jeffstateonline.com
HOOTS, Cathy .... 336-750-2265.. 359 B
hoots@wssu.edu
HOOVER, Chris .... 620-341-5337.. 180 G
choover@emporia.edu
HOOVER, Christine .... 608-249-6611.. 516 M
choover@herzing.edu
HOOVER, Douglas .... 724-938-4096.. 414 E
hoover@calu.edu
HOOVER, James, W .... 214-887-5347.. 457 C
jhoover@dts.edu
HOOVER, Jean, B .... 717-262-2007.. 424 A
jhoover@wilson.edu
HOOVER, Jeffrey .... 717-560-8258.. 407 E
jhoover@lbc.edu
HOOVER, Josie .... 202-885-8601.... 94 E
jhoover@wesleyseminary.edu
HOOVER, Kathleen .... 610-558-5560.. 411 E
hooverk@neumann.edu
HOOVER, Kathy .... 360-596-5409.. 508 A
khoover@spscc.edu
HOOVER, Kelly .... 410-225-2422.. 209 B
khoover01@mica.edu
HOOVER, Kevin .... 559-325-3600.... 30 C
khoover@chsu.org
HOOVER, Kim .... 601-984-6200.. 261 C
khoover@umc.edu
HOOVER, Linda .... 806-742-3031.. 472 C
linda.hoover@ttu.edu
HOOVER, Lisa .... 214-637-3530.. 479 C
lhoover@wadecollege.edu
HOOVER, Lisa, D .... 570-577-3757.. 398 L
lisa.hoover@bucknell.edu
HOOVER, Lorette, M .... 706-649-1837.. 119 F
lhoover@columbustech.edu
HOOVER, Myrna .... 850-644-6089.. 111 C
mhoover@fsu.edu
HOOVER, Nancy .... 503-699-6261.. 392 D
nhoover@marylhurst.edu
HOOVER, Samantha .... 212-472-1500.. 324 A
shoover@nysid.edu
HOOVER, Sara .... 205-226-4989...... 2 C
shoover@bsc.edu
HOOVER, Steve .... 320-308-3023.. 252 A
smhoover@stcloudstate.edu
HOOVER, Tom .... 423-425-5300.. 448 F
tom-hoover@utc.edu
HOOVLER, David .... 216-987-4854.. 367 E
david.hoovler@tri-c.edu
HOPE, Deryle .... 864-503-5769.. 434 G
dhope@uscupstate.edu
HOPE, Henry .... 404-471-6355.. 115 J
hhope@agnesscott.edu
HOPE, John .... 251-981-3771...... 2 I
john.hope@columbiasouthern.edu
HOPE, Kelly .... 203-332-5973.... 86 D
khope@hcc.commnet.edu
HOPE, Laura .... 909-652-6113.... 37 D
laura.hope@chaffey.edu
HOPE, Oral .... 212-431-2300.. 323 H
oral.hope@nyls.edu
HOPE, Wilbert .... 718-270-6961.. 309 B
wilbert@mec.cuny.edu
HOPEWELL, JR.,
Woodson, H .... 757-727-5303.. 490 E
woodson.hopewell@hamptonu.edu
HOPEY, Christopher, E .... 978-837-5110.. 225 E
christopher.hopey@merrimack.edu
HOPIDA, Edgar .... 619-961-4314.... 68 A
ehopida@tjsl.edu
HOPIE, Linty .... 360-417-6504.. 505 I
lhopie@pencol.edu
HOPKINS, Alexander, M . 713-798-4262.. 452 G
ahopkins@bcm.edu
HOPKINS, Amanda .... 407-646-2124.. 107 O
ahopkins@rollins.edu
HOPKINS, Amanda, R ..... 407-646-2174.. 107 O
ahopkins@rollins.edu
HOPKINS, Becky .... 323-343-3200.... 33 C
bhopkins@cslanet.calstatela.edu
HOPKINS, Berta .... 864-592-4262.. 432 H
hopkinsb@sccsc.edu
HOPKINS, Bob .... 601-266-4947.. 261 E
bob.hopkins@usm.edu
HOPKINS, Boone .... 864-596-9183.. 429 C
boone.hopkins@converse.edu
HOPKINS, Bruce .... 229-430-2837.. 116 A
HOPKINS, Christi .... 620-242-0414.. 183 C
hopkinsc@mcpherson.edu

HOPKINS, Darlene .... 910-630-7150.. 346 E
dhopkins@methodist.edu
HOPKINS, David, R .... 937-775-2312.. 381 H
david.hopkins@wright.edu
HOPKINS, Dennis .... 828-726-2750.. 347 I
dhopkins@cccti.edu
HOPKINS, Drew, W .... 609-984-3430.. 297 F
dhopkins@tesu.edu
HOPKINS, Elijah .... 406-768-6371.. 276 F
ehopkins@fpcc.edu
HOPKINS, Gena .... 260-459-4500.. 164 C
ghopkins@ibcfortwayne.edu
HOPKINS, John .... 330-263-2082.. 367 A
jhopkins@wooster.edu
HOPKINS, John, L .... 203-596-4652.... 88 F
jhopkins@post.edu
HOPKINS, Joseph .... 205-726-2778...... 6 E
jhopkins@samford.edu
HOPKINS, Kathryn .... 870-777-5722.... 24 A
kathryn.hopkins@uacch.edu
HOPKINS, Kent .... 480-965-2408.... 11 H
kent.hopkins@asu.edu
HOPKINS, Kevin .... 785-594-8553.. 178 D
kevin.hopkins@bakeru.edu
HOPKINS, Laura .... 206-934-7798.. 506 J
laura.hopkins@seattlecolleges.edu
HOPKINS, Laurie, B .... 803-786-3669.. 429 A
lhopkins@columbiasc.edu
HOPKINS, OP, Maggie .. 608-663-3388.. 516 F
mhopkins@edgewood.edu
HOPKINS, Marilyn .... 707-638-5276.... 68 C
marilyn.hopkins@tu.edu
HOPKINS, Mark .... 706-236-2231.. 117 F
mhopkins@berry.edu
HOPKINS, Melissa .... 573-518-2177.. 268 E
mhopkins@mineralarea.edu
HOPKINS, Nicole .... 509-574-6870.. 510 A
nhopkins@yvcc.edu
HOPKINS, Paulette .... 619-388-7350.... 60 H
phopkins@sdccd.edu
HOPKINS, Randy .... 816-501-4659.. 270 J
randy.hopkins@rockhurst.edu
HOPKINS, Robert P .... 212-353-4350.. 311 G
bob@cooper.edu
HOPKINS, Robin .... 419-358-3661.. 364 D
hopkinsr@bluffton.edu
HOPKINS, Sara .... 615-248-1653.. 447 F
shopkins@trevecca.edu
HOPKINS, Sarah .... 707-527-4831.... 63 G
shopkins@santarosa.edu
HOPKINS, Shirley, L .... 804-523-5896.. 497 C
shopkins@reynolds.edu
HOPKINS, Stacy .... 724-357-2230.. 415 B
stacy.hopkins@iup.edu
HOPKINS, T. Hampton ...... 704-355-5585.. 343 A
hampton.hopkins@carolinascollege.edu
HOPKINS, Thomas, F .... 540-464-7228.. 499 E
hopkinstf@vmi.edu
HOPKINS, Tony .... 502-585-9911.. 192 E
thopkins@spalding.edu
HOPKINS, Willie .... 718-951-3166.. 307 D
whopkins@brooklyn.cuny.edu
HOPKINS-GROSS, Anne .. 518-255-5214.. 334 D
hopkinam@cobleskill.edu
HOPKINS-POSELLE,
Denise .... 914-637-2757.. 317 B
HOPMANS, Jan .... 530-752-7172.... 69 A
jwhopmans@ucdavis.edu
HOPP, Lisa .... 219-989-2818.. 166 F
ljhopp@pnw.edu
HOPP, Melissa .... 443-840-3176.. 207 C
mhopp@ccbcmd.edu
HOPP, Susan .... 503-883-2278.. 392 B
shopp@linfield.edu
HOPPE, Elizabeth .... 909-706-3497.... 74 K
shoppe@westernu.edu
HOPPE, James .... 617-824-8640.. 218 B
james_hoppe@emerson.edu
HOPPE, Ken .... 870-236-6901.... 20 A
khoppe@crc.edu
HOPPE, Marianne .... 406-265-3765.. 277 E
hoppe@msun.edu
HOPPER, Darla .... 812-535-5110.. 166 K
dhopper@smwc.edu
HOPPER, Gary .... 830-372-6309.. 470 C
ghopper@tlu.edu
HOPPER, George, M .... 662-325-2953.. 259 D
ghopper@cfr.msstate.edu
HOPPER, Jeffrey .... 501-279-4478.... 20 D
hopper@harding.edu
HOPPER, Karen, S .... 870-508-6110.... 19 B
khopper@asumh.edu
HOPPER, Lisa .... 501-760-4241.... 21 B
lhopper@np.edu
HOPPER, Lorrie .... 559-325-5246.... 67 B
lorrie.hopper@scccd.edu
HOPPER, Richard .... 207-453-5129.. 203 K
president@kvcc.me.edu
HOPPER, Rosita .... 401-598-1000.. 425 B
rhopper@jwu.edu

HOPPER, Susan .... 731-661-5078.. 448 A
shopper@uu.edu
HOPPER, William, E .... 305-626-3701.. 101 A
william.hopper@fmuniv.edu
HOPPLE, Marcella .... 574-936-8898.. 158 I
marcella.hopple@ancilla.edu
HOPSON, April .... 706-649-1858.. 119 F
ahopson@columbustech.edu
HOPSON, JR., George, A 864-977-2194.. 431 G
george.hopson@ngu.edu
HOPSON, Pamela, F .... 812-465-7188.. 168 E
pfhopson@usi.edu
HOPWOOD, Dennis, T .... 509-527-5172.. 509 G
hopwood@whitman.edu
HOPWOOD, Julie .... 765-285-1104.. 159 B
jhopwood@bsu.edu
HORADAN, Lloyd .... 478-553-2060.. 125 C
lhoradan@oftc.edu
HORADAN, Lloyd .... 478-553-2060.. 125 D
lhoradan@oftc.edu
HORAK, Janice .... 254-968-9857.. 467 F
jhorak@tarleton.edu
HORAK, Janice .... 254-968-9890.. 467 F
jhorak@tarleton.edu
HORAK, Maureen .... 413-662-5205.. 222 B
m.horak@mcla.edu
HORAN, Kevin .... 925-473-7401.... 41 J
khoran@losmedanos.edu
HORAN, Michael, D .... 614-236-6813.. 364 N
mhoran@capital.edu
HORAN, Sean .... 212-659-7200.. 318 D
shoran@tkc.edu
HORAN, Thomas .... 909-607-9302.... 38 I
thomas.horan@cgu.edu
HORAN, Thomas .... 909-607-3811.... 38 I
thomas.horan@cgu.edu
HORBACEWICZ, Jill .... 212-463-0400.. 337 I
jillh@touro.edu
HORBACK, Sachi .... 253-964-6531.. 506 B
shorback@pierce.ctc.edu
HORCH, Scott .... 574-936-8898.. 158 I
scott.horch@ancilla.edu
HORD, Lisa .... 937-393-3431.. 377 F
lhord@sscc.edu
HORGAN, Elizabeth .... 508-213-2289.. 227 A
elizabeth.horgan@nichols.edu
HORGAN, Joan .... 518-454-5296.. 311 B
horganj@strose.edu
HORGAN, Lynne .... 828-251-6417.. 357 C
lhorgan@unca.edu
HORGAN, Ralph, R .... 412-268-6156.. 400 D
rh44@andrew.cmu.edu
HORINEK, Charity .... 620-417-1133.. 184 I
charity.horinek@sccc.edu
HORINEK, Jon .... 580-581-2627.. 382 G
jhorinek@cameron.edu
HORISSIAN, Kevork, T .... 570-577-3623.. 398 L
kevork.horissian@bucknell.edu
HORN, Allison .... 503-883-2323.. 392 B
ahorn@linfield.edu
HORN, Brian, S .... 727-816-3458.. 106 F
hornb@phsc.edu
HORN, Cindy .... 231-591-5309.. 233 L
cindyhorn@ferris.edu
HORN, David, G .... 978-468-7111.. 219 B
dhorn@gcts.edu
HORN, Jamie .... 334-386-7168...... 3 I
jhorn@faulkner.edu
HORN, Jason .... 504-520-7330.. 202 C
jhorn1@xula.edu
HORN, Jay .... 817-272-2355.. 476 A
horn@uta.edu
HORN, John .... 608-890-0158.. 519 K
horn1@recsports.wisc.edu
HORN, John, F .... 215-898-7593.. 421 E
horn3@upenn.edu
HORN, Michael .... 704-330-5963.. 348 E
michael.horn@cpcc.edu
HORN, Paul, M .... 212-998-3228.. 324 C
paul.horn@nyu.edu
HORN, Samuel, E .... 864-242-5100.. 427 E
HORN, Sonya .... 530-741-6989.... 76 D
shorn@yccd.edu
HORN, Vincent .... 215-596-7532.. 422 A
v.horn@usciences.edu
HORN BUNK, Sheri .... 661-763-7936.... 67 F
shornbunk@taftcollege.edu
HORNBACHER, Noel .... 313-593-5410.. 242 A
noelhorn@umich.edu
HORNBECK, Billi .... 605-455-6037.. 436 G
bhornbeck@olc.edu
HORNBERGER, Lois .... 503-352-2240.. 394 C
lhornberger@pacificu.edu
HORNBERGER, Rob .... 417-836-6444.. 258 I
robhornberger@missouristate.edu
HORNBOSTEL, Rachael .... 303-369-5151.... 32 F
rachael.hornbostel@plattcolorado.edu
HORNBUCKLE, Delritta .... 617-243-2243.. 219 I
dhornbuckle@lasell.edu
HORNBUCKLE, Jami, M .. 606-783-2372.. 191 H
j.hornbuckle@moreheadstate.edu

HORNE, Arlene .... 903-886-5159.. 468 D
arlene.horne@tamuc.edu
HORNE, Bart .... 502-863-8182.. 188 I
bart_horne@georgetowncollege.edu
HORNE, Cathy .... 704-272-5337.. 353 B
chorne@spcc.edu
HORNE, David .... 410-704-4236.. 213 B
dhorne@towson.edu
HORNE, Derek .... 601-877-6500.. 256 F
djhorne@alcorn.edu
HORNE, Hadie, C .... 252-246-1221.. 354 D
hhorne@wilsoncc.edu
HORNE, Megan .... 606-326-2074.. 188 N
mhorne0001@kctcs.edu
HORNE, Pamela, T .... 765-494-9116.. 166 D
pamhorne@purdue.edu
HORNE, Valerie .... 601-403-1211.. 260 D
vhorne@prcc.edu
HORNER, Andrew, E .... 937-229-3736.. 379 D
ahorner1@udayton.edu
HORNER, Donnie .... 904-256-7030.. 103 D
dhorner3@ju.edu
HORNER, Ed .... 213-621-2200.... 39 I
HORNER, Jeff .... 719-502-2011.... 82 B
jeffrey.horner@ppcc.edu
HORNER, Jeffrey, T .... 423-798-7952.. 447 D
jeff.horner@ws.edu
HORNER, Jennifer .... 860-465-5775.... 85 G
hornerje@easternct.edu
HORNER, Jody .... 402-941-6000.. 280 N
president@midlandu.edu
HORNER, Kristin .... 620-251-7700.. 180 B
horner.kristin@coffeyville.edu
HORNER, Stacy .... 269-782-1220.. 241 C
shorner@swmich.edu
HORNER, Theresa .... 716-827-2485.. 338 E
hornert@trocaire.edu
HORNICK, Robert .... 510-567-6174.... 67 E
bhornick@sum.edu
HORNING, Kirsten .... 503-338-2341.. 390 G
khorning@clatsopcc.edu
HORNOR, Tara, F .... 843-953-5336.. 428 A
tara.mcnealy@citadel.edu
HORNS, Phyllis, N .... 252-744-2265.. 356 C
hornsp@ecu.edu
HORNSBY, Jake .... 415-518-5396.... 69 B
hornsbyj@uchastings.edu
HOROWITZ, Avery .... 718-252-7800.. 337 I
averymh@touro.edu
HOROWITZ,
Boruch Avrohom .... 718-438-2018.. 326 H
rcby26@aol.com
HOROWITZ, Elias .... 845-783-0833.. 339 A
HOROWITZ, Judy .... 716-673-3335.. 331 D
judy.horowitz@fredonia.edu
HOROWITZ, Samuel, L ... 904-264-2172.. 107 N
shorowitz@iws.edu
HOROWITZ, Sara .... 212-678-8838.. 317 I
sahorowitz@jtsa.edu
HORSCH, Ellen, S .... 906-487-1737.. 238 A
eshorsch@mtu.edu
HORSEY, Cheryl, L .... 215-641-5546.. 404 G
horsey.c@gmercyu.edu
HORSEY, Dwight, G .... 717-871-5100.. 415 F
dwight.horsey@millersville.edu
HORTON, Becky .... 478-825-6226.. 120 F
hortonb@fvsu.edu
HORTON, C, R .... 864-488-4586.. 430 H
chorton@limestone.edu
HORTON, Claudia .... 816-833-0524.. 172 G
horton@graceland.edu
HORTON, Connie .... 310-506-4210.... 56 J
connie.horton@pepperdine.edu
HORTON, Freeman .... 662-621-4231.. 257 B
fhorton@coahomacc.edu
HORTON, Howard, E .... 617-603-6900.. 226 D
howard.horton@necb.edu
HORTON, Jana .... 251-575-8252...... 1 C
jhorton@ascc.edu
HORTON, Jane, T .... 540-458-8401.. 500 F
jhorton@wlu.edu
HORTON, Jeff .... 270-707-3721.. 189 G
jeff.horton@kctcs.edu
HORTON, Johnna .... 507-389-7223.. 252 D
johnna.horton@southcentral.edu
HORTON, Joseph, M .... 603-641-7600.. 287 G
jhorton@anselm.edu
HORTON, Julian, K .... 240-500-2000.. 207 I
jkhorton@hagerstowncc.edu
HORTON, Kelley, R .... 910-775-4403.. 358 C
kelley.horton@uncp.edu
HORTON, Kimberly .... 937-778-7806.. 368 E
khorton@edisonohio.edu
HORTON, Leslie .... 508-854-2798.. 224 E
lhorton@qcc.mass.edu
HORTON, Lindsey .... 601-979-2580.. 258 D
lindsey.horton@jsums.edu
HORTON, Michele .... 850-471-4639.. 106 H
mhorton@pensacolastate.edu
HORTON, Monique .... 773-995-4424.. 136 M
m-horton@csu.edu

HORTON, Paul .... 772-462-7520.. 103 B phorton@irsc.edu
HORTON, Ray .... 513-244-8420.. 366 B ray.horton@ccuniversity.edu
HORTON, Rose .... 573-341-7685.. 274 B hortonrm@mst.edu
HORTON, Susan .... 845-434-5750.. 336 H shorton@sullivan.suny.edu
HORVATH, Fran .... 831-582-3878.... 33 E fhorvath@csumb.edu
HORVATH, Pamela .... 718-818-6470.. 329 F phorvath@edaff.com
HORVATH, Virginia, S ..... 716-673-3456.. 331 D virginia.horvath@fredonia.edu
HORVATH-PLYMAN, Melissa .... 201-684-7081.. 294 G mhorvath@ramapo.edu
HORWATH, Shannon ...... 908-835-9222.. 298 E shorwath@warren.edu
HOSACK, Susan, E .... 314-935-5567.. 274 N sue.hosack@wustl.edu
HOSCH, Braden, J .... 631-632-6210.. 332 A braden.hosch@stonybrook.edu
HOSCH, Jason .... 504-278-6281.. 196 I jhosch@nunez.edu
HOSEA, Walter .... 865-251-1800.. 444 A whosea@southcollegetn.edu
HOSEI, Huan .... 671-735-5558.. 529 G huan.hosei@guamcc.edu
HOSELTON, Steven, A ..... 312-341-2442.. 152 H shoselton@roosevelt.edu
HOSENEY, Jason .... 360-538-4066.. 504 B
HOSEY, Heidi .... 814-824-2336.. 410 H hhosey@mercyhurst.edu
HOSHIKO, Carol .... 808-734-9568.. 131 I hoshiko@hawaii.edu
HOSKEN, Dan .... 818-677-2246.... 34 A dan.hosken@csun.edu
HOSKEY, Lisa .... 607-274-3011.. 317 D
HOSKING, Amanda .... 215-567-7080.. 397 H ahosking@aii.edu
HOSKINS, Sheila .... 252-823-5166.. 349 E hoskinss@edgecombe.edu
HOSKINS, Steve .... 606-546-4151.. 193 E shoskins@unionky.edu
HOSKINSON, Heidi .... 918-343-7852.. 387 F hhoskinson@rsu.edu
HOSKOVEC, Victoria .... 402-399-2431.. 279 E vhoskovec@csm.edu
HOSKOWITZ, Joel, M ..... 410-386-8412.. 206 I jhoskowitz@carrollcc.edu
HOSLET, Charles .... 608-265-2822.. 519 K choslet@wisc.edu
HOSLEY, Robyn, L .... 315-267-2515.. 334 B hosleyrl@potsdam.edu
HOSMER, Kerri .... 706-295-6554.. 121 F khosmer@gntc.edu
HOSPEDALES, Rhonda ..... 215-572-2900.. 397 G
HOSS, Amy .... 785-227-3380.. 178 J hossaj@bethanylb.edu
HOSS, Cindy .... 620-665-3507.. 181 I hossc@hutchcc.edu
HOSS, Neal .... 760-750-4400.... 34 D nhoss@csusm.edu
HOSSAIN, Zakir .... 804-257-5606.. 500 B zhossain@vuu.edu
HOSSELTON, Crystal .... 618-985-3741.. 143 F crystalhosselton@jalc.edu
HOSSENLOPP, Jeanne, M .... 414-288-1532.. 517 I jeanne.hossenlopp@marquette.edu
HOSTALKA, Amanda .... 443-394-9549.. 211 A ahostalka@stevenson.edu
HOSTELLER, Mayme .... 212-228-1888.. 327 A
HOSTER, Robert, L .... 570-577-3342.. 398 L bob.hoster@bucknell.edu
HOSTETLER, Bumper, R ... 812-888-5333.. 169 A bhostetler@vinu.edu
HOSTETLER, Chad .... 304-457-6320.. 510 B hostetlercs@ab.edu
HOSTETLER, Lori, J .... 812-888-4121.. 169 A lhostetler@vinu.edu
HOSTETLER, Marna, M .... 812-464-1834.. 168 E mmhostetle@usi.edu
HOSTETLER, Theodore, J . 434-947-8133.. 493 B thostetler@randolphcollege.edu
HOSTETLER, Timothy, J ... 423-775-7262.. 439 B hostetti@bryan.edu
HOSTETTER, Julie, M ...... 800-287-8822.. 159 C hosteju@bethanyseminary.edu
HOSTETTER, Larry .... 270-686-4236.. 187 C larry.hostetter@brescia.edu
HOSTETTER, Sandy .... 215-884-8942.. 424 B librarian@woninstitute.edu
HOSTETTER, Steve, J .... 218-751-8670.. 254 A stevehostetter@oakhills.edu
HOSTINA, Michael .... 907-450-8080.... 10 E mike.hostina@alaska.edu
HOTALING, Diane, E .... 757-455-3216.. 500 E dhotaling@vwc.edu
HOTALING, Marcus, S ..... 518-388-6161.. 338 H hotalinm@union.edu
HOTCHKISS, Carolyn .... 781-239-5528.. 214 G hotchkiss@babson.edu
HOTCHKISS, Charles .... 617-989-4831.. 229 D hotchkissc@wit.edu
HOTCHKISS, Valerie .... 615-322-4782.. 449 A valerie.hotchkiss@vanderbilt.edu
HOTEZ, Peter, J .... 713-798-1199.. 452 G hotez@bcm.edu
HOTLE, C. Patrick .... 573-288-6394.. 264 F photle@culver.edu
HOTOVY, Steve .... 402-471-2505.. 281 G shotovy@nscs.edu
HOTTA, Tomoki .... 808-946-3773.. 130 D
HOTTEL, Haven .... 910-893-1421.. 342 F hottelh@campbell.edu
HOTTEL, Timothy, L .... 901-448-6202.. 448 H thottel@uthsc.edu
HOTTEL-COX, Anne .... 202-885-8694.... 94 E ahottelcox@wesleyseminary.edu
HOTTENSTEIN, Kristi .... 517-787-0800.. 235 G hottenskristin@jccmi.edu
HOTTINGER, Sara .... 603-358-2772.. 288 E shottinger@keene.edu
HOTZ, Lindsey .... 319-895-4244.. 171 A lhotz@cornellcollege.edu
HOTZFIELD, Brian .... 773-298-3096.. 153 H hotzfield@sxu.edu
HOTZLER, Russell, K .... 718-260-5400.. 309 C rhotzler@citytech.cuny.edu
HOUBECK, JR., Robert, L .... 810-762-3410.. 242 B rhoubeck@umflint.edu
HOUCHEN, David .... 785-594-8347.. 178 D david.houchen@bakeru.edu
HOUCHINS, Shelia, E .... 270-745-4493.. 194 D shelia.houchins@wku.edu
HOUCK, Beth .... 864-977-7200.. 431 G beth.houck@ngu.edu
HOUCK, Brenda .... 757-340-2121.. 488 A bshouck@centura.edu
HOUCK, Clarence, M .... 803-934-3235.. 431 E chouck@morris.edu
HOUCK, James, W .... 814-865-4294.. 412 F jwh32@psu.edu
HOUCK, Jancy .... 803-777-8315.. 433 F jancyh@mailbox.sc.edu
HOUCK, Laurie .... 330-263-2583.. 367 A lhouck@wooster.edu
HOUCK, Maureen, B .... 516-463-6745.. 316 D maureen.b.houck@hofstra.edu
HOUCK, Michelle .... 614-251-4603.. 374 I houckm@ohiodominican.edu
HOUDEK, Rob .... 605-642-6562.. 437 B robert.houdek@bhsu.edu
HOUDYSCHELL, Jendonnae .... 304-696-6704.. 513 D houdyschell2@marshall.edu
HOUDYSHELL, Michael ... 308-635-6123.. 283 D houdyshe@wncc.edu
HOUFER, Michael .... 651-747-4085.. 249 A michael.houfer@century.edu
HOUGH, Brad .... 636-227-2100.. 267 A
HOUGH, David .... 417-836-5254.. 268 I davidhough@missouristate.edu
HOUGH, John .... 304-724-3700.. 510 E jhough@apus.edu
HOUGH, John .... 571-633-9651.. 495 D
HOUGH, Melanie .... 419-772-2024.. 374 J m-hough@onu.edu
HOUGH, Tony .... 803-738-7695.. 431 B hought@midlandstech.edu
HOUGH, Twyla .... 210-999-8321.. 473 A twyla.hough@trinity.edu
HOUGHTON, David, C ...... 405-585-4400.. 385 B david.houghton@okbu.edu
HOUGHTON, James .... 212-799-5000.. 318 A
HOUGHTON, Susan .... 805-922-6966.... 25 I shoughton@hancockcollege.edu
HOUGLAND, Dawn .... 312-341-3531.. 152 H dhougland@roosevelt.edu
HOUK, Christopher .... 270-686-4241.. 187 C chris.houk@brescia.edu
HOUK, Suzanne, N .... 724-458-2208.. 404 F snhouk@gcc.edu
HOULIHAN, Janet, M ...... 714-895-8307.... 39 F jhoulihan@gwc.cccd.edu
HOULIHAN, Jill .... 501-337-5000.... 19 K jhoulihan@coto.edu
HOULIHAN, Robert .... 516-323-3457.. 321 H rhoulihan@molloy.edu
HOULIHAN, Timothy, J .... 718-489-5290.. 328 D thoulihan@sfc.edu
HOURANY, Lance .... 925-631-4767.... 59 I lph5@stmarys-ca.edu
HOURIGAN, Christopher, P .... 401-456-8998.. 425 E chourigan@ric.edu
HOURIGAN, Gerard .... 216-987-4706.. 367 E gerard.hourigan@tri-c.edu
HOUSE, Antionette, T ...... 804-257-5628.. 500 B athouse@vuu.edu
HOUSE, Brittany .... 574-284-4569.. 167 A bhouse@saintmarys.edu
HOUSE, DeAndre .... 601-857-3701.. 258 A deandre.house@hindscc.edu
HOUSE, H. Wayne .... 888-777-7675.. 503 H hwhouse@faithseminary.edu
HOUSE, J. Daniel .... 815-753-6002.. 150 A jhouse@niu.edu
HOUSE, Jacqueline .... 305-628-6727.. 108 E jhouse@stu.edu
HOUSE, Jess .... 203-837-9500.... 85 I housej@wcsu.edu
HOUSE, Kevin .... 509-244-6851.. 502 I kevin.house@scc.spokane.edu
HOUSE, Ron .... 618-985-2637.. 143 F ronhouse@jalc.edu
HOUSE, Seymour .... 503-845-3507.. 392 E seymour.house@mtangel.edu
HOUSE, Stephanie .... 208-769-3368.. 134 C stephanie.house@nic.edu
HOUSE, Steven, D .... 336-278-6647.. 344 D shouse@elon.edu
HOUSE, Vicki .... 325-670-1276.. 458 J vhouse@hsutx.edu
HOUSEKNECHT, Rick .... 215-338-5000.. 398 C rhouseknecht@biblical.edu
HOUSEKNECHT, Rick .... 215-368-5000.. 398 C rhouseknecht@biblical.edu
HOUSENICK, Joseph .... 570-408-4630.. 423 G joseph.housenick@wilkes.edu
HOUSER, Frieda .... 406-444-6570.. 276 J fhouser@montana.edu
HOUSER, Janet .... 303-458-4174.... 82 L jhouser@regis.edu
HOUSER, John .... 575-562-2123.. 299 I john.houser@enmu.edu
HOUSER, Kay .... 910-642-7141.. 353 C kay.houser@sccnc.edu
HOUSER, Robert .... 970-351-1759.... 84 C robert.houser@ucno.edu
HOUSER, Sue .... 302-736-2438.... 91 G susan.houser@wesley.edu
HOUSEWORTH, Julie .... 573-592-4260.. 275 G julie.houseworth@williamwoods.edu
HOUSHMAND, Ali, A .... 856-256-4100.. 295 E houshmand@rowan.edu
HOUSHOLDER, Suahil ..... 765-641-4131.. 158 J srhousholder@anderson.edu
HOUSHOWER, Hans .... 419-358-3234.. 364 D houshowerh@bluffton.edu
HOUSKA, Jeremy, A .... 908-852-1400.. 290 D houska@centenarycollege.edu
HOUSKA, Nila .... 712-749-2233.. 170 D houskan@bvu.edu
HOUSLEY, Brooks .... 334-387-3877...... 1 E brookshousley@amridgeuniversity.edu
HOUSLEY, Harold .... 903-875-7307.. 462 J harold.housley@navarrocollege.edu
HOUSLEY, Heather, L ...... 404-413-2070.. 122 D heatherh@gsu.edu
HOUSLEY, La Royce .... 310-954-4191...... 53 B ldodd@msmu.edu
HOUSTON, A. Glen .... 281-283-3000.. 474 A houston@uhcl.edu
HOUSTON, Adam .... 760-921-5463.... 56 E ahouston@paloverde.edu
HOUSTON, Bernard .... 334-229-4200...... 1 D bhouston@alasu.edu
HOUSTON, Chrystal .... 402-363-5607.. 283 G chrystal.houston@york.edu
HOUSTON, Don .... 408-855-5428.... 74 G don.houston@wvm.edu
HOUSTON, Doug .... 636-584-6732.. 264 M doug.houston@eastcentral.edu
HOUSTON, Douglas, B .... 530-741-6971.... 76 B dhouston@yccd.edu
HOUSTON, Glen .... 281-283-3000.. 474 A houston@uhcl.edu
HOUSTON, Jason .... 509-313-4220.. 504 A houston@gonzaga.edu
HOUSTON, Kim .... 731-352-6421.. 438 K houstonk@bethelu.edu
HOUSTON, Kristen .... 206-876-6100.. 507 D khouston@theseattleschool.edu
HOUSTON, Michael .... 662-621-4853.. 257 B mhouston@coahomacc.edu
HOUSTON, Nainsi .... 419-448-2108.. 369 G nhouston@heidelberg.edu
HOUSTON, Rachel .... 704-403-1228.. 342 E rachel.houston@carolinashealthcare.org
HOUSTON, Renee .... 253-879-3207.. 508 D rhouston@pugetsound.edu
HOUSTON, Richard .... 662-846-4694.. 257 E rhouston@deltastate.edu
HOUSTON, Rick .... 978-867-4130.. 219 A ric.houston@gordon.edu
HOUSTON, Teresa, L .... 601-635-6202.. 257 F thouston@eccc.edu
HOUSTON, Tim .... 740-695-9500.. 364 B thouston@belmontcollege.edu
HOUSTON, Tim .... 614-837-4088.. 380 G houstont@valorcollege.edu
HOUSTON, Vinson .... 256-782-5993...... 4 H vhouston@jsu.edu
HOUSTON-BROWN, Clive, K .... 909-593-3511.... 71 B chouston-brown@laverne.edu
HOUSTON-PHILPOT, Kimberly, R .... 989-774-2085.. 232 D houst1kr@cmich.edu
HOUTMAN, Anne .... 812-877-8956.. 166 H houtman@rose-hulman.edu
HOVATTER, Angela, L ...... 301-687-4301.. 212 F ahovatter@frostburg.edu
HOVEKAMP, Tina .... 541-383-7563.. 390 D thovekamp@cocc.edu
HOVELL, Mindy .... 251-380-2286...... 7 D mhovell@shc.edu
HOVESTOL, Dan .... 406-586-3585.. 276 I dan.hovestol@montanabiblecollege.edu
HOVEY, Ann .... 503-842-8222.. 395 D annhovey@tillamookbaycc.edu
HOVEY, Jeff .... 314-977-8375.. 271 K hoveyj@slu.edu
HOVEY, Mark .... 860-685-2337.... 90 C mhover@wesleyan.edu
HOVEY, Rebecca .... 413-585-2697.. 228 D rhovey@smith.edu
HOVEY, Roger, S .... 308-635-6012.. 283 D rhovey@wncc.edu
HOW, Christine .... 402-557-7002.. 278 I christine.doocy@bellevue.edu
HOWAR, Julie .... 309-694-5505.. 141 F julie.howar@icc.edu
HOWARD, Amy .... 314-529-6737.. 267 B ahoward@maryville.edu
HOWARD, Andrew .... 806-743-2870.. 472 D andrew.howard@ttuhsc.edu
HOWARD, Augustus .... 404-527-4520.. 118 F ahoward@caraver.edu
HOWARD, Bree .... 661-255-1050.... 30 E bhoward@calarts.edu
HOWARD, Bryan .... 734-487-2467.. 233 J bhowar22@emich.edu
HOWARD, Catherine .... 903-823-3285.. 467 C catherine.howard@texarkanacollege.edu
HOWARD, Catherine, W .. 804-828-8790.. 496 D choward@vcu.edu
HOWARD, Cecil, E .... 717-477-1161.. 416 A cehoward@ship.edu
HOWARD, Cedric, B .... 716-673-3271.. 331 D cedric.howard@fredonia.edu
HOWARD, Chad .... 479-248-7236.... 20 C choward@ecollege.edu
HOWARD, Charles, L .... 215-898-8457.. 421 E choward@pobox.upenn.edu
HOWARD, Cheryl .... 617-521-2131.. 228 C cheryl.howard@simmons.edu
HOWARD, Christie .... 903-593-8311.. 470 A choward@texascollege.edu
HOWARD, Christopher ...... 412-397-6403.. 418 B president@rmu.edu
HOWARD, Cindy .... 800-962-7682.. 275 D choward@wma.edu
HOWARD, Dale, S .... 330-490-7303.. 380 J dhoward@walsh.edu
HOWARD, Dan .... 575-646-1727.. 300 J provost@nmsu.edu
HOWARD, Dana, K .... 318-274-3133.. 200 F howardd@gram.edu
HOWARD, Daniel .... 318-473-6444.. 197 J dhoward@lsua.edu
HOWARD, Doris .... 415-503-6214.... 61 C finaid@sfcm.edu
HOWARD, Doug .... 615-460-6306.. 438 J doug.howard@belmont.edu
HOWARD, Douglas .... 603-888-1311.. 287 F dhoward@rivier.edu
HOWARD, JR., Eddie .... 330-941-2018.. 382 A ejhoward01@ysu.edu
HOWARD, Elizabeth .... 215-646-7300.. 404 G howard.e@gmercyu.edu
HOWARD, Elizabeth .... 817-531-6582.. 472 F ehoward@txwes.edu
HOWARD, Ezra .... 662-621-4083.. 257 B ehoward@coahomacc.edu
HOWARD, Gail .... 504-865-3849.. 198 E ghoward@loyno.edu
HOWARD, Gary, E .... 859-858-3511.. 186 J gary.howard@asbury.edu
HOWARD, Genevieve .... 360-992-2936.. 502 E ghoward@clark.edu
HOWARD, Gerard, L .... 601-979-1073.. 258 D gerard.l.howard@jsums.edu
HOWARD, Herman .... 803-705-4567.. 427 D howardh@benedict.edu
HOWARD, James .... 573-681-5275.. 266 I jhoward@nebook.com

HOWARD, Jane 620-792-9208 178 G
howardj@bartonccc.edu
HOWARD, Jane 317-738-8051 160 J
jhoward@franklincollege.edu
HOWARD, Jay, R 317-940-9874 159 K
jrhoward@butler.edu
HOWARD, Jeffery, S 423-439-4210 444 F
howardjs@etsu.edu
HOWARD, Jennifer, L 425-388-9232 503 F
jhoward@everettcc.edu
HOWARD, Jessica 971-722-6268 394 F
jessica.howard@pcc.edu
HOWARD, Joe 814-824-2829 410 H
jhoward@mercyhurst.edu
HOWARD, Jonathan 202-319-5232 92 A
howardjr@cua.edu
HOWARD, Kevin 937-708-5546 381 B
khoward@wilberforce.edu
HOWARD, Kimberly, A 802-656-4296 485 D
kimberly.howard@uvm.edu
HOWARD, Kristina 708-709-3556 151 C
khoward@prairiestate.edu
HOWARD, Lelia 267-502-2680 398 J
lelia.howard@brynathyn.edu
HOWARD, Leon 662-252-8000 260 F
lhoward@rustcollege.edu
HOWARD, Lonnie 409-880-8185 470 H
llhoward@lit.edu
HOWARD, Luke 662-621-4168 257 B
lhoward@coahomacc.edu
HOWARD, Martin, J 617-353-2290 216 E
mjhoward@bu.edu
HOWARD, Mary Ann 478-757-5137 129 L
mhoward@wesleyancollege.edu
HOWARD, Maureen 575-646-3221 300 J
mhoward@nmsu.edu
HOWARD, Megan 605-882-5284 436 B
megan.howard@lakeareatech.edu
HOWARD, Michael, P 518-564-3140 334 A
mhowa001@plattsburgh.edu
HOWARD, Michael, W 413-585-2200 228 D
mwhoward@smith.edu
HOWARD, Michelle, L 989-774-7506 232 D
howar1ml@cmich.edu
HOWARD, Patricia 913-345-8288 185 F
howardp@stmary.edu
HOWARD, Penny 804-862-6200 493 F
phoward@rbc.edu
HOWARD, Phil 847-214-7835 140 A
phoward@elgin.edu
HOWARD, Philip 706-721-4551 117 D
phoward@augusta.edu
HOWARD, Predita 478-934-3092 124 E
predita.howard@mga.edu
HOWARD, Rachel 415-451-2800 61 D
HOWARD, Randy, B 386-226-6000 99 A
randy.howard@erau.edu
HOWARD, Ronald 601-925-3203 259 A
howard@mc.edu
HOWARD, Sally 916-608-6643 51 C
howards@flc.losrios.edu
HOWARD, Sharon, L 304-647-6369 514 A
showard@osteo.wvsom.edu
HOWARD, Sherry 870-864-7193 22 D
showard@southark.edu
HOWARD, Steven 619-596-2766 25 G
showard@advancedtraining.edu
HOWARD, Susan 603-283-2367 363 E
showard@antioch.edu
HOWARD, Tim 717-755-2300 398 A
thoward@aii.edu
HOWARD, Trish 801-863-8440 482 C
howardpa@uvu.edu
HOWARD, Valerie, M 412-397-6801 418 B
howardv@rmu.edu
HOWARD, Vikki 218-335-4255 247 F
vikki.howard@lltc.edu
HOWARD, Yaffa 215-635-7300 404 D
yhoward@gratz.edu
HOWARD, Yelitza, M 956-326-2171 468 A
yelitza.howard@tamiu.edu
HOWARD-VITAL, Michelle 305-626-3186 101 A
mhoward-vital@fmuniv.edu
HOWARTH, James, R 860-465-4418 85 G
howarthj@easternct.edu
HOWARTH, Joan, W 517-432-6804 237 I
howarth@law.msu.edu
HOWATT-NAB, Summer 805-893-5752 70 E
showatt-nab@ltsc.ucsb.edu
HOWDEN, Norman 214-860-2176 456 E
norman@dcccd.edu
HOWDEN, Tonya 269-467-9945 234 B
thowden@glenoaks.edu
HOWDYSHELL, Cynthia, K 540-828-5314 487 H
chowdysh@bridgewater.edu
HOWDYSHELL, Linda 954-201-7426 96 I
lhowdysh@broward.edu
HOWE, Amanda 215-204-5578 420 B
amanda.howe@temple.edu
HOWE, Brian 620-792-9254 178 G
howeb@bartonccc.edu
HOWE, Deborah 503-253-3443 393 D
president@ocom.edu
HOWE, Derek 617-353-6500 216 E
dhowe@bu.edu
HOWE, Gregory 216-791-5000 366 H
gregory.howe@cim.edu
HOWE, Jennifer, L 937-229-2973 379 D
jhowe1@udayton.edu
HOWE, Jodi, L 607-871-2325 303 F
howe@alfred.edu
HOWE, Joseph 757-388-2604 494 A
jhowe@sentara.edu
HOWE, Kara 610-861-5494 411 G
khowe@northampton.edu
HOWE, Ken, D 985-549-2240 201 C
khowe@selu.edu
HOWE, Mark 951-343-4299 29 H
mhowe@calbaptist.edu
HOWE, Mark 518-464-8508 314 A
mhowe@excelsior.edu
HOWE, Melissa 317-266-1400 215 G
HOWE, Mic 503-352-2214 394 C
mic.howe@pacificu.edu
HOWE, Mike 507-433-0621 251 H
mike.howe@riverland.edu
HOWE, Nanci 650-725-3104 66 I
nanhowe@stanford.edu
HOWE, Terri 361-825-2629 468 E
terri.howe@tamucc.edu
HOWELL, Aaron 434-791-5651 487 C
ahowell@averett.edu
HOWELL, Allan 516-299-4225 319 B
allan.howell@liu.edu
HOWELL, Ann 208-282-7893 133 H
howeanna@isu.edu
HOWELL, Candice 402-465-2401 281 K
chowell@nebrwesleyan.edu
HOWELL, Carla 704-216-3452 352 G
carla.howell@rccc.edu
HOWELL, Charles 330-941-3265 382 A
clhowell01@ysu.edu
HOWELL, Daniel 978-478-3400 227 C
dhowell@northpoint.edu
HOWELL, David, B 540-365-4329 489 M
dhowell@ferrum.edu
HOWELL, Dianne, B 318-797-5190 198 C
dianne.howell@lsus.edu
HOWELL, Dustin 501-279-5776 20 D
dhowell@harding.edu
HOWELL, Ed 785-628-5304 180 I
ehowell@fhsu.edu
HOWELL, Elizabeth 520-206-4778 16 F
ehowell1@pima.edu
HOWELL, Hayes 870-759-4143 24 J
howell@wbcoll.edu
HOWELL, Helen 208-882-1566 134 B
hhowell@nsa.edu
HOWELL, James 806-716-2369 465 G
jhowell@southplainscollege.edu
HOWELL, James, R 252-398-6313 343 G
howelj@chowan.edu
HOWELL, Jay 409-747-9082 478 A
jhowell@utmb.edu
HOWELL, Jonathan 860-701-5161 88 D
howell_j@mitchell.edu
HOWELL, Karen 904-826-0084 72 A
khowell@usa.edu
HOWELL, Karen 262-551-5858 516 A
khowell@carthage.edu
HOWELL, Kathryn 414-410-4003 515 I
khowell@stritch.edu
HOWELL, Kevin, A 813-257-7777 114 M
khowell@ut.edu
HOWELL, La Donna 918-463-1753 383 I
lhowell@eosc.edu
HOWELL, Laura 662-846-4624 257 E
lhowell@deltastate.edu
HOWELL, Laurence, A 973-596-3686 293 D
laurence.a.howell@njit.edu
HOWELL, LaVerne, B 864-977-7013 431 G
laverne.howell@ngu.edu
HOWELL, Lee 229-317-6780 120 A
lee.howell@darton.edu
HOWELL, Lisa 760-773-2511 40 B
lihowell@collegeofthedesert.edu
HOWELL, Liz 501-279-4276 20 D
lhowell@harding.edu
HOWELL, Marie 803-535-1207 431 I
howellm@octech.edu
HOWELL, Martie 716-286-8300 324 E
meh@niagara.edu
HOWELL, Marya, L 704-894-2642 343 I
mahowell@davidson.edu
HOWELL, Rosemarie 916-348-4689 43 A
rhowell@epic.edu
HOWELL, Shelly 650-433-3858 56 D
showell@paloaltou.edu
HOWELL, Shirley 773-252-5125 152 B
shirley.howell@resu.edu
HOWELL, Stephen, C 419-289-5944 363 J
showell@ashland.edu
HOWELL, Steven 209-946-3066 71 C
showell@pacific.edu
HOWELL, Tirrell 803-754-4100 429 B
HOWELL, Verna, G 864-656-5444 428 C
howell@clemson.edu
HOWELL, Wendy 229-430-3816 116 A
whowell@albanytech.edu
HOWELL, Yolanda, M 914-606-6600 340 C
yolanda.howell@sunywcc.edu
HOWELLS, Jeffrey, C 318-675-8152 198 B
jhowel1@lsuhsc.edu
HOWERTER, Wendy, L 217-786-2283 146 E
wendy.howerter@llcc.edu
HOWERTON, Cheryl, L 217-424-6317 148 D
chowerton@millikin.edu
HOWERTON, Lisa, A 270-824-8582 190 B
lisa.howerton@kctcs.edu
HOWES, Jennifer 626-395-8331 30 H
jhowes@caltech.edu
HOWES, Meg 630-617-3781 140 C
howesm@elmhurst.edu
HOWEY, Debbie 573-334-6825 272 A
dhowey@sehealth.org
HOWIE, Dennis, J 248-204-2304 237 B
dhowie@ltu.edu
HOWIE, Douglas 972-524-3341 466 F
HOWIE, Michael 402-461-7743 280 D
mhowie@hastings.edu
HOWILER, Robert, W 864-833-8324 432 B
rhowiler@presby.edu
HOWLAND, Bonnie, J 413-662-5210 222 B
bonnie.howland@mcla.edu
HOWLAND, Kristine 210-999-8058 473 A
khowland@trinity.edu
HOWLAND, Susan 775-445-3249 285 B
susan.howland@wnc.edu
HOWLE, Jonathan 718-779-1499 326 D
jhowle@plazacollege.edu
HOWLE, Meg 843-574-6356 433 D
meg.howle@tridenttech.edu
HOWLETT, Bernadette 503-251-2812 396 C
bhowlett@uws.edu
HOWLETT, Beth 503-253-3443 393 D
bhowlett@ocom.edu
HOWLETT, Byron, E 909-869-3306 31 J
behowlett@cpp.edu
HOWLETT, Jeffrey 919-760-8828 346 D
howlettj@meredith.edu
HOWLETT, Lucy, J 540-674-3619 497 G
lhowlett@nr.edu
HOWLETT, Sophia 908-737-7030 292 C
sohowlet@kean.edu
HOWLEY, James 773-481-8460 137 I
jhowley@ccc.edu
HOWLEY, Kathleen 717-720-4200 414 C
khowley@passhe.edu
HOWLEY, Nicholas 410-888-9048 209 C
nhowley@muih.edu
HOWORTH, Aidan 773-244-6208 149 I
ahoworth@northpark.edu
HOWRIGAN, Penny 802-635-1219 436 B
penny.howrigan@jsc.edu
HOXIE, David, E 304-457-6306 510 B
hoxiede@ab.edu
HOXIE, Hal 620-241-0723 179 L
hal.hoxie@centralchristian.edu
HOXIE, Sandra, E 304-457-6278 510 B
hoxiese@ab.edu
HOXSIE, Patti, D 706-880-8327 123 K
phoxsie@lagrange.edu
HOXTER, Laney 410-287-1043 206 J
lhoxter@cecil.edu
HOY, Cliff 423-636-7307 447 G
choy@tusculum.edu
HOY, Leah 817-272-2185 476 A
hoy@uta.edu
HOY, Linda 575-538-6317 303 A
hoyl@wnmu.edu
HOY, Murray, K 410-334-2810 213 G
rhoy@worwic.edu
HOYACK, Chuck 520-417-4060 12 L
hoyackc@cochise.edu
HOYERT, Mark 219-980-6731 163 B
mhoyert@iun.edu
HOYLE, Ken, R 919-718-7436 348 D
khoyle@cccc.edu
HOYLE, Michael 617-243-2100 219 I
mhoyle@lasell.edu
HOYOS, Angel 787-758-2525 538 D
angel.hoyos@upr.edu
HOYOS, Denise 520-417-4148 12 L
hoyosd@cochise.edu
HOYT, Bill 717-764-9550 401 I
bhoyt@csb.edu
HOYT, Brad 217-641-4777 143 H
bhoyt@jwcc.edu
HOYT, Dana, G 936-294-1013 471 D
dghoyt@shsu.edu
HOYT, David, R 972-599-3133 455 A
dhoyt@collin.edu
HOYT, Debra 404-880-8773 118 K
dhoyt@cau.edu
HOYT, Jeffery 561-297-2719 110 K
hoytj@fau.edu
HOYT, William 717-394-6211 401 H
bhoyt@csb.edu
HOZDIK, Elaine 239-590-7931 110 L
ehozdik@fgcu.edu
HRABEC, Erika, J 734-764-6270 241 J
erikah@umich.edu
HRABOSKY, James, A 724-287-8711 399 B
james.hrabosky@bc3.edu
HRABOWSKI, Freeman, A 410-455-3880 211 G
hrabowski@umbc.edu
HRACZO, Rebecca 704-463-3368 354 F
rebecca.hraczo@pfeiffer.edu
HRADSKY, Robert 202-885-3318 91 J
hradsky@american.edu
HRANITZ, John, M 570-389-4208 414 D
jhranitz@bloomu.edu
HRDLICKA, Rick 909-384-8656 60 C
rhrdlicka@sbccd.cc.ca.us
HRENKO, Chris 864-225-7653 430 A
chrishrenko@forrestcollege.edu
HRIBAR, Frank, J 517-265-5161 230 D
fhribar@adrian.edu
HRISHENKO, Michael, S 330-941-3520 382 A
mshrishenko@ysu.edu
HRISTIS, Emilia 516-562-3405 313 C
ehristis@northwell.edu
HRITZAK, Susan, A 570-408-4850 423 G
susan.hritzak@wilkes.edu
HRNCIR, Charlie 979-458-7155 467 D
chrncir@tamus.edu
HROMISIN, Ronald, S 570-674-6312 410 K
rhromisi@misericordia.edu
HRON, Stacey 218-683-8584 251 C
stacey.hron@northlandcollege.edu
HRUBES, Julie 503-338-2429 390 G
jhrubes@clatsopcc.edu
HRUBY, Arlene 425-352-8630 501 J
ahruby@cascadia.edu
HRUBY, Nick 303-861-1151 79 G
nhruby@concorde.edu
HRUSKA, Amanda 920-924-3193 524 B
ahruska@morainepark.edu
HRUTKA, Mary Ellen 410-888-9048 209 C
mhrutka@muih.edu
HSIAO, Terrence 425-352-8870 501 J
thsiao@cascadia.edu
HSIEH, Cheng-Yuan 847-679-3135 144 G
cyhsieh@ksi.edu
HSIEH, Chialin 650-306-3145 62 G
hsiehc@smccd.edu
HSIEH, Jeanette 847-317-8138 156 B
jhsieh@tiu.edu
HSIEH, Patricia 619-388-7834 60 H
phsieh@sdccd.edu
HSIEH, Peter 510-592-9688 54 I
phsieh@npu.edu
HSIEH, Rosalia 562-868-6488 47 M
HSU, Andrew 419-530-2739 380 D
andrew.hsu@utoledo.edu
HSU, Becky 617-287-5152 220 G
becky.hsu@umb.edu
HSU, Kwei 979-532-6350 479 J
kweih@wcjc.edu
HSU, Ping 408-924-1000 35 C
HSU, Stephen 517-355-0306 237 I
hsu@msu.edu
HU, Jonathan 520-795-0787 11 G
ceo@asaom.edu
HU, Li 631-499-7100 319 A
lhu@libi.edu
HU, Mi 847-214-7137 140 A
mhu@elgin.edu
HU, S. Jack 734-764-1185 241 J
jackhu@umich.edu
HUA, Henry 909-384-8265 60 C
hhua@sbccd.cc.ca.us
HUA, Maggie 510-628-8029 49 A
maggiehua@lincolnuca.edu
HUA, Susan 818-677-2077 34 A
susan.hua@csun.edu
HUANG, Che-Tsao 718-262-2750 310 A
huang@york.cuny.edu
HUANG, Christopher 708-534-4503 140 H
chuang@govst.edu
HUANG, Gina 408-260-0208 43 L
sjstudentservices@fivebranches.edu
HUANG, Gina 408-260-0208 43 M
sjstudentservices@fivebranches.edu
HUANG, Guiyou 802-485-2025 484 H
vpaa@norwich.edu
HUANG, Jasmine 408-260-0208 43 L
jasmine@fivebranches.edu
HUANG, Jefferson 909-621-8114 38 J
jefferson.huang@cmc.edu

HUANG, Jerry .... 818-364-7836.... 49 J
huangjc@lamission.edu
HUANG, Lixin .... 415-575-6100.... 30 G
liximhuang@ciis.edu
HUANG, Roger, D .... 574-631-1691.. 168 B
huang.31@nd.edu
HUANG, Wen .... 713-780-9777.. 451 A
info@acaom.edu
HUARD, Jenny .... 660-944-2823.. 263 G
communications@conception.edu
HUARD, Ruth .... 408-924-2670.... 35 C
ruth.huard@sjsu.edu
HUARD, Susan, D .... 603-206-8002.. 286 D
shuard@ccsnh.edu
HUBAND, David, E .... 757-446-8474.. 489 B
hubandde@evms.edu
HUBBARD, Ann .... 772-462-7570.. 103 B
ahubbard@irsc.edu
HUBBARD, Betty .... 334-874-5700....... 3 A
b.hubbard@ccal.edu
HUBBARD, Daren .... 313-577-9489.. 243 F
daren@wayne.edu
HUBBARD, James .... 309-268-8452.. 141 C
jim.hubbard@heartland.edu
HUBBARD, Jeannette .... 726-946-7179.. 423 B
hubbarj@westminster.edu
HUBBARD, Joan .... 801-626-6403.. 482 D
jhubbard@weber.edu
HUBBARD, Laura, E .... 716-645-5124.. 331 C
laurahub@buffalo.edu
HUBBARD, Margaret .... 305-899-1156.... 96 D
mhubbard@barry.edu
HUBBARD, Michael .... 513-745-3741.. 381 I
0565mgr@fheg.follett.com
HUBBARD, Paul .... 617-850-1282.. 219 F
phubbard@hchc.edu
HUBBARD, R. Glenn .... 212-854-2888.. 311 E
rgh1@columbia.edu
HUBBARD, Ruth .... 443-334-2203.. 211 A
rhubbard@stevenson.edu
HUBBARD, Sandie .... 303-991-1575.... 76 I
sandie.hubbard@americansentinel.edu
HUBBARD, William .... 920-465-2510.. 520 B
hubbardw@uwgb.edu
HUBBELL, Kent, L .... 607-255-1115.. 312 A
dean_of_students@cornell.edu
HUBBELL, Lisa .... 510-485-7830.... 56 I
lhubbell@patten.edu
HUBBELL, Sarah .... 269-488-4207.. 235 I
HUBBERT, Daron .... 951-343-4229.... 29 H
dhubbert@calbaptist.edu
HUBBLE, Janelle .... 740-588-1408.. 382 C
hubblej@ohio.edu
HUBBS, Jocelyn .... 541-684-7291.. 393 B
jhubbs@nwcu.edu
HUBBS, Nicole .... 615-248-1237.. 447 F
nhubbs@trevecca.edu
HUBER, Amy .... 973-803-5000.. 294 B
ahuber@pillar.edu
HUBER, Chip .... 616-949-5300.. 233 A
chip.huber@cornerstone.edu
HUBER, E. Kim .... 303-315-2252.... 84 A
HUBER, Gary .... 309-796-5602.. 135 I
huberg@bhc.edu
HUBER, Jason .... 704-971-8381.. 343 E
jhuber@charlottelaw.edu
HUBER, Kristina .... 814-732-1669.. 415 A
khuber41@gmail.com
HUBER, Lane .... 701-224-5714.. 361 C
lane.huber@bismarckstate.edu
HUBER, Lydia .... 361-572-6461.. 478 F
lydia.huber@victoriacollege.edu
HUBER, Margaret .... 605-229-8405.. 436 H
margaret.huber@presentation.edu
HUBER, Mark, D .... 570-372-4247.. 419 H
huber@susqu.edu
HUBER, Michael .... 484-664-3150.. 411 D
huber@muhlenberg.edu
HUBER, Morgan .... 605-995-7250.. 436 C
morgan.huber@mitchelltech.edu
HUBER, Patricia, B .... 540-674-3631.. 497 G
phuber@nr.edu
HUBERMAN, Jeffrey, H ... 309-677-2360.. 136 B
huberman@bradley.edu
HUBERMAN, Steven .... 212-463-0400.. 337 I
stevenh@touro.edu
HUBERS, Todd, K .... 616-526-6495.. 232 A
thubers@calvin.edu
HUBERT, David .... 801-957-4280.. 483 A
david.hubert@slcc.edu
HUBERT, Lydia .... 229-468-2000.. 130 A
lydia.hubert@wiregrass.edu
HUBINGER, Amy, M .... 906-227-2626.. 239 B
ahubinge@nmu.edu
HUBLER, Barbara .... 415-338-2611.... 35 B
bhubler@sfsu.edu
HUBNER, Jamin .... 605-661-7262.. 436 A
jhubner@johnwitherspooncollege.org
HUBNER, Jessica .... 605-342-0317.. 436 A
jhubner@johnwitherspooncollege.org

HUBRIC, Kimberly, A ...... 610-921-7629.. 396 H
khubric@albright.edu
HUCH, Robert, E .... 540-261-4098.. 494 F
bob.huch@svu.edu
HUCK, Alysia .... 701-858-3065.. 360 F
alysia.huck@mnotstateu.edu
HUCKABA, Sam .... 850-644-4404.. 111 C
shuckaba@fsu.edu
HUCKABAY, Sonia .... 559-791-2403.... 47 L
shuckaba@portervillecollege.edu
HUCKABEE, Vicki .... 903-223-3025.. 469 C
vhuckabee@tamut.edu
HUCKABY, Henry, M .... 404-962-3000.. 129 F
chancellor@usg.edu
HUCKESTEIN, Jim .... 503-594-3010.. 390 F
jim.huckestein@clackamas.edu
HUCKESTEIN, Julie .... 503-399-6591.. 390 E
julie.huckestein@chemeketa.edu
HUCKS, Cheri, A .... 864-592-4931.. 432 H
hucksc@sccsc.edu
HUDACK, John, J .... 716-827-2512.. 338 E
hudackj@trocaire.edu
HUDAK, Jane, E .... 484-664-3300.. 411 D
hudak@muhlenberg.edu
HUDAK, Randy .... 304-293-7202.. 514 C
randy.hudak@mail.wvu.edu
HUDAK, Sharon .... 570-674-6295.. 410 K
shudak@misericordia.edu
HUDANICK, Richard .... 636-584-6500.. 264 M
richard.hudanick@eastcentral.edu
HUDDLESTON, Gwen .... 805-289-6388.... 73 F
ghuddleston@vcccd.edu
HUDDLESTON, Mark, W .. 603-862-2450.. 288 C
presidents.office@unh.edu
HUDDLESTON, Ryan .... 925-473-7328.... 41 J
rhuddleston@4cd.edu
HUDDLESTON, Sean .... 508-626-4515.. 221 E
shuddleston@framingham.edu
HUDGENS, Lisa .... 618-985-3741.. 143 F
lisahudgens@jalc.edu
HUDGIK, Mark .... 413-775-1810.. 223 D
hudgikm@gcc.mass.edu
HUDGIN, Denise .... 419-251-1324.. 372 C
denise.hudgin@mercycollege.edu
HUDGINS, John, L .... 410-951-3528.. 212 E
jhudgins@coppin.edu
HUDGINS, Karen .... 904-819-6252.... 99 M
khudgins@flagler.edu
HUDGINS, Tripp .... 510-841-1905.... 26 C
thudgins@absw.edu
HUDGINS, V. Lavoyed .... 859-985-3240.. 187 B
hudginsv@berea.edu
HUDLUN, Randy .... 417-862-9533.. 265 D
rhedlun@globaluniversity.edu
HUDMAN, Steve .... 936-633-5292.. 451 D
shudman@angelina.edu
HUDNELL, Jason .... 501-760-4374.... 21 B
jhudnell@np.edu
HUDSICK, Walter .... 360-752-8433.. 501 G
whudsick@btc.edu
HUDSON, Angela .... 501-686-2504.... 22 H
ahudson@uasys.edu
HUDSON, Bo .... 918-293-4912.. 386 B
steven.w.hudson@okstate.edu
HUDSON, Bobby .... 615-230-3445.. 447 C
bobby.hudson@volstate.edu
HUDSON, David, D .... 714-895-8907.... 39 F
dhudson@gwc.cccd.edu
HUDSON, Dean, P .... 843-349-2739.. 428 E
dhudson@coastal.edu
HUDSON, Donald, M .... 609-652-4883.. 297 C
donald.hudson@stockton.edu
HUDSON, Donna, P .... 888-760-2245.. 430 H
dhudson@limestone.edu
HUDSON, Earnest .... 828-227-7301.. 359 A
ehudson@wcu.edu
HUDSON, Elizabeth .... 417-690-2470.. 263 E
ehudson@cofo.edu
HUDSON, Elizabeth .... 617-373-2170.. 227 B
HUDSON, Garien, L .... 260-399-7700.. 168 D
ghudson@sf.edu
HUDSON, Greg .... 334-420-4332....... 7 G
ghudson@trenholmstate.edu
HUDSON, Harold .... 937-529-2201.. 378 F
hhudson@united.edu
HUDSON, Jackie .... 205-929-1401....... 5 H
jhudson@miles.edu
HUDSON, Jennifer, M .... 713-646-1899.. 459 A
jhudson@hcl.edu
HUDSON, John .... 713-221-8664.. 474 B
hudsonj@uhd.edu
HUDSON, Karen .... 615-550-3165.. 449 I
karen.hudson@williamsoncc.edu
HUDSON, Lea Ann .... 404-471-6402.. 115 J
lhudson@agnesscott.edu
HUDSON, Lyla .... 843-792-8721.. 431 A
hudsonly@musc.edu
HUDSON, Malinda, S .... 270-831-9626.. 189 F
malinda.hudson@kctcs.edu
HUDSON, Mark, A .... 217-581-3923.. 139 H
mahudson@eiu.edu

HUDSON, Matthew .... 417-447-8102.. 270 A
hudsonm@otc.edu
HUDSON, Maureen .... 781-280-3506.. 224 A
hudsonm@middlesex.mass.edu
HUDSON, Melissa, A .... 530-226-4974.... 64 H
mhudson@simpsonu.edu
HUDSON, Michael, J .... 630-637-5661.. 149 H
mjhudson@noctrl.edu
HUDSON, Patrick .... 816-414-3700.. 268 D
phudson@mbts.edu
HUDSON, Rachel .... 510-567-6174.... 67 E
rahudson@sum.edu
HUDSON, Rachel .... 615-297-7545.. 438 F
hudsonr@aquinascollege.edu
HUDSON, Raymond .... 510-567-6174.... 67 E
rhudson@sum.edu
HUDSON, Richard .... 502-585-9911.. 192 E
rhudson@spalding.edu
HUDSON, Rob .... 719-502-3193.... 82 B
rob.hudson@ppcc.edu
HUDSON, Robert .... 617-353-3710.. 216 E
rhudson@bu.edu
HUDSON, Rodeny, B .... 803-535-5470.. 428 B
rhudson@claflin.edu
HUDSON, Ronald .... 501-812-2232.... 21 H
rhudson@pulaskitech.edu
HUDSON, Sid .... 405-224-3140.. 389 D
HUDSON, Stacy .... 208-769-7819.. 134 C
stacy_hudson@nic.edu
HUDSON, Terri .... 601-974-5299.. 258 H
terri.hudson@millsaps.edu
HUDSON, Thomas .... 601-979-6883.. 258 D
thomas.k.hudson@jsums.edu
HUDSON, Tijuana, R .... 803-535-5197.. 428 B
thudson@claflin.edu
HUDSON, William .... 570-408-4600.. 423 G
william.hudson@wilkes.edu
HUDSON, JR., William .... 850-599-3183.. 110 J
william.hudson@famu.edu
HUDSPETH, Donald .... 585-475-7077.. 327 E
don.hudspeth@croatia.rit.edu
HUDSPETH, Philip .... 541-463-5898.. 391 G
hudspethp@lanecc.edu
HUDY, Karen .... 216-421-7320.. 366 G
khudy@cia.edu
HUEBER, Charlie .... 830-792-7277.. 465 E
cmhueber@schreiner.edu
HUEBNER, Janet .... 319-352-8227.. 177 G
janet.huebner@wartburg.edu
HUEBNER, JR.,
Thomas, M .... 662-476-8442.. 257 G
thuebner@eastms.edu
HUEBOTTER, Chris .... 573-288-6542.. 264 F
chuebotter@culver.edu
HUEG, Kurt .... 650-949-7394.... 44 B
huegkurt@foothill.edu
HUEGEL, Mary .... 978-232-2084.. 218 D
mhuegel@endicott.edu
HUELSBECK, David, R .... 253-535-7196.. 505 G
huelsdr@plu.edu
HUELSBECK, Tom, A .... 253-535-7200.. 505 G
tom.huelsbeck@plu.edu
HUELSMAN, Shelly .... 620-227-9285.. 180 E
shuelsman@dc3.edu
HUENEMANN, Kurt .... 419-448-2351.. 369 G
keh@heidelberg.edu
HUERTA, David .... 559-278-8400.... 32 F
davidhu@csufresno.edu
HUERTA, Patricia .... 312-362-8601.. 139 C
phuerta@depaul.edu
HUERTA, Paul .... 312-935-4569.. 152 D
phuerta@robertmorris.edu
HUERTAS, Belmarie .... 787-743-4041.. 531 K
bhuertas@columbiacentral.edu
HUERTAS, Carmelo, V .... 973-353-1670.. 296 C
huertacv@ca.rutgers.edu
HUERTAS, Felix, R .... 787-743-7979.. 536 A
fhuertas@suagm.edu
HUERTAS, Linda .... 773-481-8453.. 137 I
lhuertas@ccc.edu
HUERTAS SOLÁ, Mildred 787-257-7373.. 535 P
ue_mhuertas@suagm.edu
HUESER, Kyle .... 712-274-6400.. 177 I
kyle.hueser@witcc.edu
HUESTON, William, J .... 414-955-8220.. 518 A
whueston@mcw.edu
HUET, Yvette .... 704-687-8696.. 358 A
ymhuet@uncc.edu
HUETTEL, Patricia .... 412-291-5101.. 397 I
phuettel@aii.edu
HUEY, Emily .... 314-421-0949.. 272 J
ehuey@siba.edu
HUEY, Lindley .... 617-253-6162.. 225 A
HUFF, Eugene, C .... 925-229-6851.... 41 G
ehuff@4cd.edu
HUFF, Glenda .... 325-649-8014.. 459 E
ghuff@hputx.edu
HUFF, III, Joseph, E .... 409-944-1302.. 458 D
jhuff@gc.edu
HUFF, Kim .... 803-535-1210.. 431 I
huffk@octech.edu

HUFF, Lester .... 301-295-1210.. 528 G
lester.huff@usuhs.edu
HUFF, Liz .... 216-421-7957.. 366 G
lhuff@cia.edu
HUFF, Marie .... 419-372-8242.. 364 E
huffm@bgsu.edu
HUFF, Rick .... 772-546-5534.. 102 S
rickhuff@hsbc.edu
HUFF, Tim, T .... 405-744-5459.. 385 G
tim.huff@okstate.edu
HUFFAKER, John .... 806-742-2155.. 472 C
john.huffaker@ttu.edu
HUFFARD, Lorri .... 276-223-4794.. 499 C
lhuffard@wcc.vccs.edu
HUFFCUTT, Tom, G .... 715-833-6661.. 523 B
thuffcutt@cvtc.edu
HUFFLING, Brian .... 704-847-5600.. 355 J
bhuffling@ses.edu
HUFFMAN, Aaron, C .... 304-336-8200.. 513 F
ahuffman@westliberty.edu
HUFFMAN, Amanda .... 443-518-4773.. 208 C
ahuffman@howardcc.edu
HUFFMAN, Debbie .... 940-668-4475.. 462 L
dhuffman@nctc.edu
HUFFMAN, Don .... 312-662-4236.. 134 I
dhuffman@adler.edu
HUFFMAN, Gerald .... 206-296-5869.. 507 E
huffmanje@seattleu.edu
HUFFMAN, Jeff .... 865-981-8033.. 441 H
jeff.huffman@maryvillecollege.edu
HUFFMAN, Jeffery .... 419-559-2257.. 377 M
jhuffman01@terra.edu
HUFFMAN, Keith .... 740-362-3380.. 372 D
khuffman@mtso.edu
HUFFMAN, Lisa .... 580-581-2339.. 382 G
lhuffman@cameron.edu
HUFFMAN, Mari, L .... 419-866-0261.. 377 L
mlhuffman@stautzenberger.com
HUFFMAN, Monica, R .... 660-543-4106.. 273 C
mhuffman@ucmo.edu
HUFFMAN, Pat .... 425-640-1002.. 503 E
phuffman@edcc.edu
HUFFMAN, Rebecca .... 276-328-0139.. 495 I
reg5a@uvawise.edu
HUFFMAN, Robin .... 260-399-7700.. 168 D
rhuffman@sf.edu
HUFFMAN, Tammy, S .... 740-588-1212.. 382 C
thuffman@zanestate.edu
HUFFMAN, Virginia, A .... 212-327-8300.. 327 F
huffman@rockefeller.edu
HUFFORD, Adela .... 574-535-7706.. 161 A
ahufford@goshen.edu
HUFFORD, Chris .... 618-374-5135.. 151 E
chris.hufford@principia.edu
HUFFSTUTLER, Steven .... 618-650-5234.. 155 A
shuffst@siue.edu
HUFNAGEL, Michele .... 724-503-1001.. 422 H
mhufnagel@washjeff.edu
HUFSTETLER, Catrice .... 770-975-4000.. 118 J
HUFTALIN, Deneece .... 801-957-4226.. 483 A
deneece.huftalin@slcc.edu
HUG-ENGLISH, Cheryl .... 775-784-6122.. 285 A
cherylh@med.unr.edu
HUGANIR, Gail .... 717-815-1425.. 424 F
ghuganir@ycp.edu
HUGER, Sophia .... 386-481-2951.... 96 H
hugers@cookman.edu
HUGETZ, Edward .... 713-221-8003.. 474 B
hugetze@uhd.edu
HUGGETT, Monica .... 212-799-5000.. 318 A
HUGGINS, Brian .... 314-340-3335.. 265 H
hugginsb@hssu.edu
HUGGINS, Derrick, E .... 803-777-3150.. 433 F
dhuggins@mailbox.sc.edu
HUGGINS, Jonathan .... 706-236-2217.. 117 F
jhuggins@berry.edu
HUGGINS, Lance .... 816-654-7702.. 266 E
lhuggins@kcumb.edu
HUGGINS, Michael .... 850-474-2112.. 113 A
mhuggins@uwf.edu
HUGGINS, Michael .... 312-427-2737.. 143 G
mhuggins@jmls.edu
HUGGINS, Regina, M .... 919-866-5408.. 353 I
rmhuggins@waketech.edu
HUGHES, A. LeAnn .... 423-652-4706.. 440 J
lhughes@king.edu
HUGHES, Ally .... 912-525-5000.. 126 E
ahughes@scad.edu
HUGHES, Andrew .... 775-673-7240.. 284 K
ahughes@tmcc.edu
HUGHES, Angela .... 219-473-4227.. 159 L
ahughes2@ccsj.edu
HUGHES, B. Hilles .... 740-376-4645.. 372 A
hilles.hughes@marietta.edu
HUGHES, Bernice .... 229-391-5130.. 115 I
bhughes@abac.edu
HUGHES, Betsy .... 312-567-5045.. 142 I
hughes@iit.edu
HUGHES, Billy .... 205-665-6130...... 9 B
hugheswl@montevallo.edu

HUGHES, Blanche, M ... 970-491-1101 ... 78 Q
blanche.hughes@colostate.edu
HUGHES, Bobbi ... 208-885-5303 ... 134 G
bhughes@uidaho.edu
HUGHES, Bonnie ... 506-865-8588 ... 504 D
hughes_b@heritage.edu
HUGHES, C. Raymond ... 860-906-5012 ... 86 B
rhughes@ccc.commnet.edu
HUGHES, Carol ... 312-362-8592 ... 139 C
chughe23@depaul.edu
HUGHES, Charles, F ... 417-690-2211 ... 263 E
hughes@cofo.edu
HUGHES, Chris ... 870-236-6901 ... 20 A
chughes@crc.edu
HUGHES, Christine ... 617-824-8908 ... 218 B
christine_hughes@emerson.edu
HUGHES, Christy ... 812-866-7012 ... 161 C
hughes@hanover.edu
HUGHES, Cory ... 972-660-5701 ... 461 A
HUGHES, Cynthia ... 212-616-7200 ... 315 G
HUGHES, David ... 501-760-4311 ... 21 B
dhughes@np.edu
HUGHES, Dennis ... 864-596-9029 ... 429 C
dennis.hughes@converse.edu
HUGHES, DeVetta ... 843-574-6199 ... 433 D
devetta.hughes@tridenttech.edu
HUGHES, Donna, D ... 717-245-1577 ... 402 D
hughsdo@dickinson.edu
HUGHES, Dorothy ... 631-420-2166 ... 335 E
hughesd@farmingdale.edu
HUGHES, Erinn ... 281-649-3213 ... 458 L
erhughes@hbu.edu
HUGHES, Ernie ... 404-752-1734 ... 125 A
ehughes@msm.edu
HUGHES, Frank ... 605-274-4325 ... 435 E
frank.hughes@augie.edu
HUGHES, George ... 805-756-6650 ... 31 I
grhughes@calpoly.edu
HUGHES, Gerunda, B ... 202-865-0207 ... 93 A
ghughes@howard.edu
HUGHES, Glyn ... 804-484-1656 ... 495 G
ghughes@richmond.edu
HUGHES, Greg ... 301-369-2800 ... 206 H
ghughes@captechu.edu
HUGHES, Jacqueline ... 909-537-5029 ... 34 C
jacqueline.hughes@csusb.edu
HUGHES, James, J ... 860-297-2376 ... 89 B
james.hughes@trincoll.edu
HUGHES, James, J ... 617-287-5420 ... 220 G
jamesj.hughes@umb.edu
HUGHES, James, L ... 410-706-1935 ... 211 F
jhughes@umaryland.edu
HUGHES, James, W ... 848-932-2828 ... 296 B
jwhughes@ejb.rutgers.edu
HUGHES, Jay ... 870-460-1053 ... 23 D
hughesj@uamont.edu
HUGHES, Jennifer ... 650-574-6118 ... 62 H
hughesj@smccd.edu
HUGHES, Jerry, M ... 660-543-4250 ... 273 C
hughes@ucmo.edu
HUGHES, Jim ... 620-235-4154 ... 184 C
jhughes@pittstate.edu
HUGHES, John ... 661-362-2223 ... 52 A
jhughes@masters.edu
HUGHES, John ... 208-732-6549 ... 133 E
jhughes@csi.edu
HUGHES, Joseph ... 479-979-1228 ... 24 I
jhughes@ozarks.edu
HUGHES, Joseph, B ... 215-895-2210 ... 402 G
engineering@coe.drexel.edu
HUGHES, Joshua, A ... 419-289-5034 ... 363 J
jhughe11@ashland.edu
HUGHES, Karla ... 870-367-1020 ... 23 D
HUGHES, Kevin, M ... 757-594-7160 ... 488 E
kmhughes@cnu.edu
HUGHES, Korey ... 804-330-0111 ... 487 P
finaid2crim@centura.edu
HUGHES, Krisin ... 413-585-2701 ... 228 D
khughes@smith.edu
HUGHES, Laura ... 870-460-1454 ... 23 D
hughesl@uamont.edu
HUGHES, Laura ... 208-792-2224 ... 134 A
lhughes@lcsc.edu
HUGHES, LeAnn ... 423-636-7300 ... 447 G
lahughes@tusculum.edu
HUGHES, Lecia ... 325-793-4998 ... 461 F
hughes.lecia@mcm.edu
HUGHES, Leslie ... 601-635-2111 ... 257 F
lhughes@eccc.edu
HUGHES, Linda ... 402-354-7049 ... 281 F
linda.hughes@methodistcollege.edu
HUGHES, Louise ... 870-612-2013 ... 23 H
louise.hughes@uaccb.edu
HUGHES, Lucie ... 410-827-5879 ... 207 A
lhughes@chesapeake.edu
HUGHES, Mark ... 301-925-3800 ... 259 A
rmhughes@mc.edu
HUGHES, Mark ... 512-245-2501 ... 471 F
mh66@txstate.edu
HUGHES, Marshall ... 617-427-0600 ... 224 F
mhughes@rcc.mass.edu
HUGHES, Martha ... 972-273-3590 ... 456 G
mhughes@dcccd.edu
HUGHES, Matthew ... 850-718-2344 ... 97 G
hughesm@chipola.edu
HUGHES, Meghan ... 401-825-2188 ... 425 A
meghanhughes@ccri.edu
HUGHES, Melany ... 308-432-6415 ... 281 H
mhughes@csc.edu
HUGHES, Melissa ... 318-257-4205 ... 200 G
mhughes@latech.edu
HUGHES, Michael ... 415-422-2465 ... 72 C
hughesm@usfca.edu
HUGHES, Michele ... 508-588-9100 ... 223 G
HUGHES, Mike ... 231-591-2924 ... 233 L
mikehughes@ferris.edu
HUGHES, Mike, C ... 817-923-1921 ... 466 E
mhughes@swbts.edu
HUGHES, Nancy ... 405-224-3140 ... 389 D
nhughes@usao.edu
HUGHES, Nancy, B ... 607-746-4573 ... 335 C
hughesnb@delhi.edu
HUGHES, Pennie, D ... 864-488-4544 ... 430 H
phughes@limestone.edu
HUGHES, Perry ... 276-223-4757 ... 499 C
phughes@wcc.vccs.edu
HUGHES, Randy ... 361-593-3209 ... 469 A
j.hughes@tamuk.edu
HUGHES, Robert, A ... 402-398-5527 ... 279 C
robert.hughes@alegent.org
HUGHES, Robin, L ... 317-274-6862 ... 163 D
roblhugh@indiana.edu
HUGHES, Romana ... 817-257-7434 ... 469 G
r.hughes@tcu.edu
HUGHES, Samantha ... 740-427-5820 ... 371 C
hughess@kenyon.edu
HUGHES, Sandra ... 281-998-1170 ... 469 F
shughes@txchiro.edu
HUGHES, Sandra ... 843-863-7933 ... 427 I
shughes@csuniv.edu
HUGHES, Scott ... 610-861-1443 ... 411 B
hughess@moravian.edu
HUGHES, Sheila ... 925-631-4585 ... 59 I
smh21@stmarys-ca.edu
HUGHES, Stephen ... 315-228-7130 ... 310 G
shughes1@colgate.edu
HUGHES, Todd ... 508-588-9100 ... 223 G
HUGHES, Tom ... 928-776-2205 ... 18 D
tom.hughes@yc.edu
HUGHES HARRIS,
Cynthia ... 850-599-3818 ... 110 J
cynthia.hughesharris@famu.edu
HUGHES-MARION,
Dianna ... 662-252-8000 ... 260 F
dr_hughes@rustcollege.edu
HUGHEY, Andrew, C ... 713-313-7470 ... 470 D
hugheyac@tsu.edu
HUGHEY, Richard ... 831-459-1993 ... 70 F
vpdue@ucsc.edu
HUGHSTON, Patty ... 251-580-2101 ... 4 I
patty.hughston@faulknerstate.edu
HUGINE, JR., Andrew ... 256-372-5230 ... 1 A
andrew.hugine@aamu.edu
HUGLE, Shelbie ... 859-246-6216 ... 189 B
shelbie.hugle@kctcs.edu
HUGUENIN, Sanders ... 276-328-0120 ... 495 I
jsh4ew@uvawise.edu
HUGULEY, Wendy ... 706-864-1545 ... 128 F
wendy.huguley@ung.edu
HUH, Dong Hyun ... 714-525-0088 ... 45 F
HUHTA, Keith ... 480-245-7903 ... 13 L
khuhta@mgmi.org
HUI, Andrew ... 215-702-4203 ... 399 E
ahui@cairn.edu
HUI, Timothy, K ... 215-702-4377 ... 399 E
thui@cairn.edu
HUINDA, Jeff ... 417-865-2815 ... 265 B
huindaj@evangel.edu
HUISH, David ... 928-524-7888 ... 15 J
david.huish@npc.edu
HUISMAN, Brandon ... 712-722-6028 ... 171 J
brandon.huisman@dordt.edu
HUISMAN, Karen ... 231-591-2505 ... 233 L
karenhuisman@ferris.edu
HUISMAN, Rhonda ... 317-955-6223 ... 165 N
rhuisman@marian.edu
HUKE, Theresa ... 610-361-5249 ... 411 E
huket@neumann.edu
HUKILL, Lazlie ... 806-291-3446 ... 479 D
hukill@wbu.edu
HUKOWICZ, Elizabeth ... 413-265-2459 ... 217 D
hukowiczе@elms.edu
HULET, David ... 661-362-2832 ... 52 A
dhulet@masters.edu
HULETT, Kevin ... 918-293-5476 ... 386 B
kevin.hulett@okstate.edu
HULETT, Matt ... 505-277-0385 ... 302 F
mhulett@unm.edu
HULETT, Tom ... 816-604-3063 ... 267 J
tom.hulett@mcckc.edu
HULIN, Alicia ... 337-521-8920 ... 197 A
alicia.hulin@solacc.edu
HULIN, Christopher P ... 615-868-6503 ... 442 G
chris.hulin@mtsu.edu
HULKE, Carla, J ... 507-354-8221 ... 247 J
hulkecj@mlc-wels.edu
HULL, Anne ... 904-826-0084 ... 72 A
ahull@usa.edu
HULL, Edward, C ... 413-545-1964 ... 220 F
ehull@umass.edu
HULL, Hsiawen ... 661-362-3666 ... 40 A
hsiawen.hull@canyons.edu
HULL, James, L ... 419-755-4850 ... 373 G
jhull@ncstatecollege.edu
HULL, Jim ... 217-234-5225 ... 145 D
jhull17327@lakeland.cc.il.us
HULL, Joe ... 843-953-5546 ... 428 G
hulljj@cofc.edu
HULL, Judy, M ... 931-372-3491 ... 445 B
jmhull@tntech.edu
HULL, Justin ... 973-684-6741 ... 294 A
jhull@pccc.edu
HULL, Lynne ... 614-947-6046 ... 369 A
lynne.hull@franklin.edu
HULL, Robert ... 815-928-5429 ... 150 I
rehull@olivet.edu
HULL, Shawn ... 573-592-4220 ... 275 G
shawn.hull@williamwoods.edu
HULL, Stephen ... 863-297-1026 ... 106 I
shull@polk.edu
HULL, Teresa ... 909-652-7653 ... 37 D
teresa.hull@chaffey.edu
HULL, William ... 269-749-7535 ... 240 A
bjhull@olivetcollege.edu
HULLETT, Lisa ... 256-352-8267 ... 9 G
lisa.hullett@wallacestate.edu
HULMER, Matt ... 715-682-1824 ... 518 H
mhulmer@northland.edu
HULON, Jane ... 601-643-8310 ... 257 D
jane.hulon@colin.edu
HULS, Jack ... 360-417-6246 ... 505 I
jhuls@pencol.edu
HULS, Sean ... 218-726-8711 ... 255 D
shuls@d.umn.edu
HULSE, Debra ... 325-793-4761 ... 461 F
hulse.debra@mcm.edu
HULSEBOSCH, Patricia ... 202-448-7036 ... 92 C
patricia.hulsebosch@gallaudet.edu
HULSEBUS, John ... 269-927-6846 ... 236 G
jhulsebus@lakemichigancollege.edu
HULSEY, Amy ... 706-754-7852 ... 125 B
ahulsey@northgatech.edu
HULSEY, Janet ... 706-419-1262 ... 119 G
hulsey@covenant.edu
HULSEY, Janet ... 630-829-6347 ... 135 F
jhulsey@ben.edu
HULSEY, Tara ... 304-293-6521 ... 514 C
thulsey@hsc.wvu.edu
HULSMAN, J Patrick ... 716-878-3141 ... 332 F
hulsmjp@buffalostate.edu
HULST, Mary ... 616-526-7617 ... 232 A
msh4@calvin.edu
HULSTINE, Thomas ... 717-947-6095 ... 413 N
tjhulsti@pacollege.edu
HULT, Lori ... 219-757-6132 ... 166 I
lori.hult@franciscanalliance.org
HULT, Nicole ... 719-590-6708 ... 79 D
nhult@coloradotech.edu
HULTBERG, Jane ... 207-801-5660 ... 202 H
jhultberg@coa.edu
HULTBERG, Larry ... 503-375-7035 ... 391 B
lhutlberg@corban.edu
HULTIN, Steve, R ... 970-491-0006 ... 78 Q
steve.hultin@colostate.edu
HULVEY, Matt ... 931-393-1602 ... 446 D
mhulvey@mscc.edu
HUMBERGER, Laura ... 406-994-4361 ... 277 C
lhumberger@montana.edu
HUMBERT, Mark ... 315-312-2248 ... 333 D
mark.humbert@oswego.edu
HUMBLE, Dina ... 562-938-4446 ... 49 D
dhumble@lbcc.edu
HUMBLE, James ... 610-785-6275 ... 418 E
jhumble@scs.edu
HUMERICK, Rosalind, M ... 386-312-4212 ... 108 B
rosalindhumerick@sjrstate.edu
HUMES, Cynthia ... 909-607-8713 ... 38 J
cynthia.humes@cmc.edu
HUMESTON, Howard, D ... 305-899-3139 ... 96 D
dhumeston@barry.edu
HUMISTON, Dolores J ... 509-777-4320 ... 509 H
dhumiston@whitworth.edu
HUMKE, Amy ... 815-479-7518 ... 147 E
ahumke@mchenry.edu
HUMMEL, Alex ... 608-262-4463 ... 519 J
ahummel@uwsa.edu
HUMMEL, Beth ... 207-768-2739 ... 203 L
bhummel@nmcc.edu
HUMMEL, Kate ... 570-321-4246 ... 409 F
hummel@lycoming.edu
HUMMEL, Mandi ... 419-448-3422 ... 378 A
hummelas@tiffin.edu
HUMMEL, Sarah ... 757-481-5005 ... 500 H
HUMMEL, Scott ... 601-318-6497 ... 261 I
shummel@wmcarey.edu
HUMMEL, Scott, R ... 610-330-5403 ... 407 C
hummels@lafayette.edu
HUMMER, Alissa ... 805-893-4091 ... 70 E
alissa.hummer@planning.ucsb.edu
HUMMER, Jennifer ... 518-464-8750 ... 314 A
jennifer@excelsior.edu
HUMMER, Jim ... 760-773-2561 ... 40 B
jhummer@collegeofthedesert.edu
HUMMERT, Mary Lee ... 785-864-4904 ... 185 D
mlhummert@ku.edu
HUMMINGBIRD, Edward ... 505-922-6506 ... 302 E
edward.hummingbird@bie.edu
HUMMON, Diane ... 651-641-3520 ... 247 G
dhummon001@luthersem.edu
HUMMONS, Tina ... 937-512-3120 ... 377 D
tina.hummons@sinclair.edu
HUMPHREY, Bonnie ... 660-831-4108 ... 269 B
humphreyb@moval.edu
HUMPHREY, Dana, N ... 207-581-2217 ... 204 H
danah@maine.edu
HUMPHREY, David ... 541-552-6522 ... 395 A
humphred2@sou.edu
HUMPHREY, George ... 617-732-2292 ... 225 C
george.humphrey@mcphs.edu
HUMPHREY, George, D ... 520-626-7301 ... 17 I
ghumphre@email.arizona.edu
HUMPHREY, J. Timothy ... 217-786-2240 ... 146 E
tim.humphrey@llcc.edu
HUMPHREY, IV,
James, E ... 704-687-5732 ... 358 A
jesh.humphrey@uncc.edu
HUMPHREY, Kathy ... 412-624-4200 ... 421 G
kathyh@pitt.edu
HUMPHREY, Keith ... 805-756-1521 ... 31 I
humphrey@calpoly.edu
HUMPHREY, Kim ... 573-882-4018 ... 273 E
humphreyk@missouri.edu
HUMPHREY, Kim ... 919-761-2224 ... 355 I
khumphrey@sebts.edu
HUMPHREY, Lesley ... 949-582-4272 ... 65 G
lhumphrey@saddleback.edu
HUMPHREY, Marie ... 719-549-2100 ... 79 B
marie.humphrey@csupueblo.edu
HUMPHREY, Reed ... 460-243-2417 ... 276 K
reed.humphrey@umontana.edu
HUMPHREY, Roger ... 307-532-8346 ... 526 G
roger.humphrey@ewc.wy.edu
HUMPHREY, Scott ... 315-792-3835 ... 339 B
shumphrey@utica.edu
HUMPHREY, Twila ... 719-502-2052 ... 82 B
twila.humphrey@ppcc.edu
HUMPHREYS, Amy ... 309-268-8194 ... 141 C
amy.humphreys@heartland.edu
HUMPHREYS, Bryce ... 509-882-7049 ... 510 A
bhumphreys@yvcc.edu
HUMPHREYS, Carol, R ... 510-593-2920 ... 63 H
chumphreys@saybrook.edu
HUMPHREYS, Henry ... 215-951-2740 ... 416 G
humphreysh@philau.edu
HUMPHREYS, Jennifer ... 918-647-1200 ... 382 I
HUMPHREYS, Joe ... 361-485-4485 ... 474 C
humphreysj@uhv.edu
HUMPHREYS, John ... 903-886-5189 ... 468 D
john.humphreys@tamuc.edu
HUMPHREYS, Katie ... 702-895-0892 ... 284 L
katie.humphreys@unlv.edu
HUMPHREYS, JR.,
Robert, G ... 209-478-0800 ... 46 H
bhumphreys@humphreys.edu
HUMPHRIES, Brian, L ... 651-286-7620 ... 256 A
blhumphries@unwsp.edu
HUMPHRIES, Corey ... 706-233-7231 ... 127 A
chumphries@shorter.edu
HUMPHRIES, Gregory, G ... 704-406-4647 ... 344 E
ghumphries@gardner-webb.edu
HUMPHRIES, Karl ... 903-875-7600 ... 462 J
karl.humphries@navarrocollege.edu
HUMPHRIES, Tara ... 919-735-5151 ... 354 A
tarah@waynecc.edu
HUNCHBERGER, Mary ... 360-417-6535 ... 505 I
mhunchberger@pencol.edu
HUNDLEY, Christina ... 602-787-6622 ... 14 E
christina.hundley@paradisevalley.edu
HUNDLEY, Dawn ... 513-875-3344 ... 365 K
dawn.hundley@chatfield.edu
HUNDLEY, Stephen ... 317-278-0033 ... 163 D
HUNE, Raymond ... 573-592-1638 ... 275 G
raymond.hune@williamwoods.edu
HUNEYCUTT, Richy ... 252-527-6223 ... 350 H
rhuneycutt@lenoircc.edu
HUNG, Alex ... 626-571-5110 ... 49 B
alexhung@les.edu
HUNHOFF, Christian ... 605-668-5126 ... 436 D
christian.hunhoff@mtmc.edu
HUNKER, Kurt ... 619-684-8787 ... 54 C
khunker@newschoolarch.edu
HUNN, Martha, S ... 843-349-2962 ... 428 E
mhunn@coastal.edu

HUNN, II, Marvin, T .... 214-887-5281.. 457 C
mhunn@dts.edu
HUNNEWELL, Lila .... 617-358-4913.. 216 E
lilawell@bu.edu
HUNNICUTT, Marianne .... 630-942-4306.. 138 B
hunnicutt@cod.edu
HUNSADER, Patricia .... 941-359-4200.. 112 E
HUNSAKER, Charles .... 660-785-4133.. 273 B
hunsaker@truman.edu
HUNSAKER, Deanna .... 660-626-2356.. 262 A
dhunsaker@atsu.edu
HUNSAKER, Miles .... 801-524-8108.. 480 J
mhunsaker@ldsbc.edu
HUNSAKER, Wayne .... 801-622-1573.. 481 E
wayne.hunsaker@stevenhenager.edu
HUNSBERGER, Jill .... 734-481-2324.. 233 J
jhunsberg1@emich.edu
HUNSICKER, Donald .... 617-262-5000.. 216 A
don.hunsicker@the-bac.edu
HUNSINGER PATTEN,
Rachael .... 518-743-2255.. 335 A
pattenr@sunyacc.edu
HUNSINGER PATTEN,
Rachael .... 518-743-2243.. 335 A
pattenr@sunyacc.edu
HUNSPERGER, Susan ...... 208-459-5407.. 133 D
shunsperger@collegeofidaho.edu
HUNSUCKER, Jeremy ...... 847-467-2152.. 150 F
jhunsucker@northwestern.edu
HUNSUCKER, Scott, E ..... 704-233-8221.. 359 H
scotth@wingate.edu
HUNT, Alice .... 773-896-2400.. 137 A
ahunt@ctschicago.edu
HUNT, Ana .... 501-760-4213.... 21 B
ana.hunt@np.edu
HUNT, Brittany .... 919-497-3338.. 346 B
bhunt@louisburg.edu
HUNT, Cammie .... 910-521-6515.. 358 C
cammie.hunt@uncp.edu
HUNT, Chris .... 610-861-1503.. 411 B
huntc@moravian.edu
HUNT, Daphne .... 254-968-1852.. 467 F
djhunt@tarleton.edu
HUNT, Delores .... 704-406-4373.. 344 E
dhunt@gardner-webb.edu
HUNT, Denise .... 760-921-5510..... 56 E
dhunt@paloverde.edu
HUNT, Edward, L .... 212-870-1227.. 324 B
ehunt@nyts.edu
HUNT, Emily .... 806-651-5330.. 469 D
ehunt@mail.wtamu.edu
HUNT, Gerry .... 405-208-5582.. 385 E
ghunt@okcu.edu
HUNT, Gordon .... 407-265-8383.... 97 B
HUNT, James .... 325-793-3806.. 461 F
hunt.james@mcm.edu
HUNT, Jamie .... 336-750-3148.. 359 B
huntj@wssu.edu
HUNT, Janet .... 501-337-5000.... 19 K
jhunt@coto.edu
HUNT, Janette .... 727-341-3229.. 108 D
hunt.janette@spcollege.edu
HUNT, Jeff .... 864-592-4727.. 432 H
huntj@sccsc.edu
HUNT, Jeffrey .... 808-235-7442.. 132 E
jwhunt@hawaii.edu
HUNT, Jill .... 270-809-3763.. 192 A
thunt2@murraystate.edu
HUNT, Judith, L .... 973-655-4301.. 293 A
huntjl@mail.montclair.edu
HUNT, Karen .... 937-327-6377.. 381 F
khunt@wittenberg.edu
HUNT, Kathy .... 206-546-4741.. 507 F
khunt@shoreline.edu
HUNT, Lawrence .... 413-585-2260.. 228 D
lhunt@smith.edu
HUNT, Lisa, O .... 910-272-3501.. 352 E
lohunt@robeson.edu
HUNT, Lori .... 509-533-7378.. 502 I
lori.hunt@scc.spokane.edu
HUNT, Louis, D .... 919-515-1428.. 357 B
ldhunt@ncsu.edu
HUNT, Mark .... 334-386-7140...... 3 I
mhunt@faulkner.edu
HUNT, Morgan .... 910-521-6533.. 358 C
morgan.hunt@uncp.edu
HUNT, Patrick, G .... 240-895-4307.. 210 E
pghunt@smcm.edu
HUNT, Paul, M .... 517-432-4499.. 237 I
pmhunt@msu.edu
HUNT, Peter, G .... 434-949-1005.. 498 E
peter.hunt@southside.edu
HUNT, Roe .... 803-535-5000.. 428 B
rhunt@claflin.edu
HUNT, Roe, B .... 803-535-5471.. 428 B
rhunt@claflin.edu
HUNT, Rusty .... 336-249-8186.. 349 C
rthunt@davidsonccc.edu
HUNT, Sellestine .... 936-633-5290.. 451 D
shunt@angelina.edu
HUNT, Shane .... 870-972-3035.... 18 J
shunt@astate.edu
HUNT, Steve .... 828-327-7000.. 348 C
shunt@cvcc.edu
HUNT, Terry, L .... 541-346-8905.. 395 G
thunt@uoregon.edu
HUNT, Thomas .... 626-815-3004.... 28 A
thunt@apu.edu
HUNT, Todd, A .... 407-582-1463.. 114 N
thunt3@valenciacollege.edu
HUNT, Tolif, R .... 319-273-3217.. 170 A
tolif.hunt@uni.edu
HUNT-AHMED, Karen ...... 312-939-0111.. 139 G
HUNT-ALLEN, Altavese .... 803-327-7402.. 428 D
ahunt@clintoncollege.edu
HUNT-BULL, Nicholas ..... 518-327-6247.. 326 B
nhuntbull@paulsmiths.edu
HUNTER, Amelia .... 615-329-8537.. 439 L
ahunter@fisk.edu
HUNTER, Barbara .... 904-361-6352.. 101 G
barbara.hunter@fscj.edu
HUNTER, Ben, D .... 317-940-9982.. 159 K
bdhunter@butler.edu
HUNTER, Bill .... 850-973-9448.. 105 H
hunterb@nfcc.edu
HUNTER, Bill .... 850-201-6556.. 113 E
hunterb@tcc.fl.edu
HUNTER, Bonnie, L .... 219-464-5411.. 168 F
bonnie.hunter@valpo.edu
HUNTER, Carolyn, A .... 513-585-2068.. 366 A
carolyn.hunter@thechristcollege.edu
HUNTER, Chip .... 509-335-3596.. 508 H
chip.hunter@wsu.edu
HUNTER, David .... 208-562-2089.. 133 F
davidshunter@cwidaho.cc
HUNTER, Donna, L .... 304-766-4146.. 514 B
hunterdl@wvstateu.edu
HUNTER, Erin .... 607-735-1821.. 313 F
ehunter@elmira.edu
HUNTER, Gary .... 970-247-7224.... 80 D
ghunter@fortlewis.edu
HUNTER, Gayle .... 386-752-1822.. 100 L
gayle.hunter@fgc.edu
HUNTER, Gerald, E .... 757-823-8011.. 492 F
gehunter@nsu.edu
HUNTER, JR., Jairy, C .... 843-863-7500.. 427 I
jhunter@csuniv.edu
HUNTER, James, E .... 804-524-5997.. 499 G
jhunter@vsu.edu
HUNTER, Janet .... 563-387-2229.. 174 L
hunterja@luther.edu
HUNTER, Janice .... 760-872-2000.... 42 B
jhunter@deepsprings.edu
HUNTER, Jim .... 928-645-6681..... 12 N
jim.hunter@coconino.edu
HUNTER, John .... 417-626-1234.. 269 K
library@occ.edu
HUNTER, Kim .... 513-244-4248.. 373 C
kim.hunter@msj.edu
HUNTER, Kymm .... 803-705-4519.. 427 D
hunterk@benedict.edu
HUNTER, Lai-Monte .... 603-428-2298.. 287 C
lhunter@nec.edu
HUNTER, Larry, T .... 614-236-6641.. 364 N
lhunter2@capital.edu
HUNTER, Laura .... 800-495-7284.. 215 A
lhunter@baypath.edu
HUNTER, LeAnn .... 509-452-5100.. 505 H
lhunter@pnwu.edu
HUNTER, Lisa .... 716-673-3717.. 331 D
lisa.hunter@fredonia.edu
HUNTER, Lorna .... 208-459-5319.. 133 D
lhunter@collegeofidaho.edu
HUNTER, Lynn .... 781-239-3120.. 223 F
lhunter@massbay.edu
HUNTER, Marc .... 405-382-9950.. 387 L
m.hunter@sscok.edu
HUNTER, Melissa .... 931-221-7315.. 444 E
hunterm@apsu.edu
HUNTER, Pam .... 760-773-2508..... 40 B
phunter@collegeofthedesert.edu
HUNTER, Patricia .... 425-739-8361.. 504 F
patricia.hunter@lwtech.edu
HUNTER, Paul .... 410-386-8429.. 206 I
phunter@carrollcc.edu
HUNTER, Rathenia .... 847-947-5887.. 149 B
rhunter@nl.edu
HUNTER, Rebecca .... 508-793-7561.. 217 B
rhunter@clarku.edu
HUNTER, Richie, C .... 518-276-2815.. 327 B
hunter3@rpi.edu
HUNTER, Robert .... 432-837-8166.. 471 E
rhunter@sulross.edu
HUNTER, Steve .... 360-867-6310.. 503 G
hunters@evergreen.edu
HUNTER, Susan .... 503-552-1512.. 392 H
shunter@nunm.edu
HUNTER, Susan, J .... 207-581-1512.. 204 H
president@umaine.edu
HUNTER, Susan, S .... 804-523-5375.. 497 C
shunter@reynolds.edu
HUNTER, Teressa .... 405-466-3274.. 383 M
thunter@langston.edu
HUNTER, Tim, W .... 814-332-2755.. 397 A
thunter@allegheny.edu
HUNTER, Tracie .... 281-290-2722.. 461 B
tracie.n.hunter@lonestar.edu
HUNTER, W. Bingham ..... 602-429-4431..... 16 E
bhunter@ps.edu
HUNTER-CEVERA, Jenny . 301-447-5218.. 209 G
hunterce@msmary.edu
HUNTER-GOLDSWORTHY,
Heidi .... 540-654-2468.. 495 C
hhunterg@umw.edu
HUNTER HAYES, Tracy ... 732-247-5241.. 293 B
HUNTER-MCKINNEY,
Shaunna, E .... 434-223-6193.. 490 D
shunter@hsc.edu
HUNTER-RAINEY,
Sharron .... 918-877-8151.. 383 M
srainey@langston.edu
HUNTINGTON, Judith, A . 914-654-5430.. 311 A
president@cnr.edu
HUNTINGTON, Robert ..... 419-448-2202.. 369 G
president@heidelberg.edu
HUNTLEY, Deborah, R ..... 989-964-4296.. 240 F
huntley@svsu.edu
HUNTLEY, Julie .... 918-495-7040.. 386 H
jhuntley@oru.edu
HUNTLEY, Kristy .... 203-479-4559..... 90 A
khuntley@newhaven.edu
HUNTLEY, Richard .... 972-721-4142.. 473 D
rhuntley@udallas.edu
HUNTLEY, Steve, E .... 904-264-2172.. 107 N
steve.huntley@iws.edu
HUNTON, Ladonna, L ..... 270-745-6867.. 194 D
ladonna.hunton@wku.edu
HUNTOON, Ivan .... 785-594-8396.. 178 D
ivan.huntoon@bakeru.edu
HUNTOON, Jacqueline, E 906-487-2440.. 238 A
jeh@mtu.edu
HUNTSINGER, Trish .... 828-395-1297.. 350 E
thuntsing@isothermal.edu
HUNTSMAN, Deborah, C . 330-672-3237.. 370 I
dhuntsm1@kent.edu
HUNZER, Kathleen .... 715-425-3843.. 521 B
honors@uwrf.edu
HUNZIGER, Lucas .... 913-367-6204.. 181 H
lhunziger@highlandcc.edu
HUO, Xiaoming (Sharon) 931-372-3463.. 445 B
xhuo@tntech.edu
HUOPPI, Jennifer .... 860-465-4357..... 85 G
huoppij@easternct.edu
HUOPPI, Margie .... 860-932-4098..... 87 C
mhuoppi@qvcc.edu
HUOT, Anne, E .... 603-358-2000.. 288 E
ahuot@keene.edu
HUPFER, Mary, A .... 812-464-1627.. 168 E
mhupfer@usi.edu
HUPKE, Doug .... 415-405-3824..... 35 B
dhupke@sfsu.edu
HUPP, Mark .... 419-755-5665.. 373 G
mhupp@ncstatecollege.edu
HUPP, Stephen .... 304-424-8273.. 514 D
stephen.hupp@wvup.edu
HUPPE, Alicia, L .... 972-377-1749.. 455 A
ahuppe@collin.edu
HUPPERT, Susan .... 515-271-1384.. 171 H
susan.huppert@dmu.edu
HUPPON, Dana .... 561-433-2330.. 109 K
HURD, Anne, J .... 336-272-7102.. 344 G
anne.hurd@greensboro.edu
HURD, Brian, K .... 216-397-1974.. 370 H
bhurd@jcu.edu
HURD, Cathy .... 704-378-1181.. 345 E
churd@jcsu.edu
HURD, James, R .... 850-474-2214.. 113 A
jhurd@uwf.edu
HURD, Roy .... 707-546-4000..... 42 M
rhurd@empcol.edu
HURD, Sherie .... 707-546-4000..... 42 M
shurd@empcol.edu
HURD-CRANK, Cathy .... 606-886-3863.. 189 A
cathy.hurdcrank@kctcs.edu
HURDLE, Terri .... 513-244-4467.. 373 C
terri.hurdle@msj.edu
HURDLE-WINSLOW,
Lynn .... 252-335-0821.. 349 A
lynnhw@albermarle.edu
HURDT, Emily .... 704-669-4321.. 348 F
hurdte@clevelandcc.edu
HURLBURT, Linda .... 856-415-2106.. 295 D
lhurlbu2@rcgc.edu
HURLBUT, Jeffrey .... 949-451-5546..... 65 F
jhurlbut@ivc.edu
HURLBUT, L, E .... 540-464-7292.. 499 E
hurlbutle@vmi.edu
HURLBUT, Nancy .... 909-869-2319..... 31 J
nhurlbut@cpp.edu
HURLEY, Charles, T .... 574-631-7495.. 168 B
hurley.32@nd.edu
HURLEY, Deanne .... 440-646-8108.. 380 F
dhurley@ursuline.edu
HURLEY, Deanne .... 440-646-8320.. 380 F
dhurley@ursuline.edu
HURLEY, Deb, B .... 336-334-5946.. 358 B
dbhurley@uncg.edu
HURLEY, Elizabeth .... 212-799-5000.. 318 A
HURLEY, Gail, A .... 814-865-5423.. 412 F
gah5@psu.edu
HURLEY, James .... 423-869-6254.. 441 E
james.hurley@lmunet.edu
HURLEY, James, B .... 601-923-1630.. 260 E
jhurley@rts.edu
HURLEY, James, M .... 847-491-5114.. 150 F
j-hurley2@northwestern.edu
HURLEY, John .... 360-867-6500.. 503 G
hurleyj@evergreen.edu
HURLEY, John, J .... 716-888-2100.. 306 F
hurleyj@canisius.edu
HURLEY, Leah, A .... 214-648-7986.. 478 C
leah.hurley@utsouthwestern.edu
HURLEY, Rachel .... 937-529-2201.. 378 F
rehurley@united.edu
HURLEY, Ronald .... 201-200-3127.. 293 C
rhurley@njcu.edu
HURLEY, Sam .... 903-928-3288.. 473 B
shurley@tvcc.edu
HURLEY, Tracy .... 210-784-2300.. 469 B
thurley@tamusa.edu
HURLEY, Travis .... 417-626-1234.. 269 K
hurley.travis@occ.edu
HURLEY, Wanda .... 601-635-2111.. 257 F
whurley@eccc.edu
HURN, Jeffrey .... 785-442-6077.. 181 H
jhurn@highlandcc.edu
HURNS, Kimberly .... 734-973-3724.. 242 G
khurns@wccnt.edu
HURRELL, Rockie .... 719-502-2007..... 82 B
rockie.hurrell@ppcc.edu
HURREN, Lee .... 864-503-5577.. 434 G
blhurren@uscupstate.edu
HURSCHMANN, Michael . 510-780-4500..... 48 J
mhurschmann@lifewest.edu
HURSON, Abigail, S .... 443-352-4920.. 211 A
hurson@stevenson.edu
HURSSEY, Elizabeth .... 662-254-3531.. 260 A
ejhurssey@mvsu.edu
HURST, Andrew .... 719-590-6797..... 79 D
ahurst@coloradotech.edu
HURST, Jamie .... 303-556-8452..... 81 G
jhurst7@msudenver.edu
HURST, Jason .... 850-526-2761..... 97 G
hurstj@chipola.edu
HURST, Jeffrey, J .... 801-626-7256.. 482 D
jhurst@weber.edu
HURST, Larry .... 661-362-3875..... 40 A
larry.hurst@canyons.edu
HURST, Laura .... 610-660-1175.. 418 G
lannhurs@sju.edu
HURST, Mark .... 423-585-6876.. 447 D
mark.hurst@ws.edu
HURST, Mark .... 423-585-2629.. 447 D
mark.hurst@ws.edu
HURST, Richard, S .... 773-508-7465.. 146 G
rhurst@luc.edu
HURST, Roy .... 432-552-2120.. 478 B
HURST, Susan .... 870-245-5567..... 21 E
hursts@obu.edu
HURT, Amelia .... 405-208-5181.. 385 E
aehurt@okcu.edu
HURT, Chandra .... 773-777-4220.. 150 D
churt@nc.edu
HURTADO, Geoffrey .... 414-229-5390.. 520 D
ghurtado@uwm.edu
HURTADO, Jose .... 707-256-7333..... 53 H
thurtado@napavalley.edu
HURTADO, Wynn .... 801-622-1573.. 481 E
wynn.hurtado@stevenshenager.edu
HURTE, Vernon .... 757-221-2300.. 488 F
vjhurt@wm.edu
HURTIG, Juliet, K .... 419-772-2032.. 374 J
j-hurtig@onu.edu
HUSAIN, Naveed .... 212-678-3955.. 337 E
husain@tc.columbia.edu
HUSAK, William .... 310-338-5940..... 51 E
whusak@lmu.edu
HUSBAND, Eileen .... 313-845-6440.. 235 D
ekhusband@hfcc.edu
HUSBAND-ARDOIN,
Madeline .... 337-482-6826.. 201 D
msh9748@louisiana.edu
HUSCHLE, Brian .... 218-793-2592.. 251 C
brian.huschle@northlandcollege.edu
HUSEIN, Lori .... 909-607-9192..... 38 H
lori_husein@cuc.claremont.edu
HUSELTON, Ken .... 412-323-4000.. 398 D
khuselton@mcg-btc.org
HUSEMAN, Sue .... 207-255-1210.. 205 C
sue.huseman@maine.edu
HUSHON, Kate .... 814-868-9900.. 403 D
kateh@erieit.edu

HUSK, Mark, A ... 317-921-4723 .. 164 E
mhusk@ivytech.edu
HUSKEY, Jeffrey ... 605-688-6415 .. 437 F
jeffrey.huskey@sdstate.edu
HUSKEY, Melynda ... 509-335-5900 .. 508 H
melyndah@wsu.edu
HUSKINS, Steve ... 423-697-4466 .. 445 D
steve.huskins@chattanoogastate.edu
HUSLIG, Lori ... 940-898-3201 .. 472 G
lhuslig@twu.edu
HUSMANN, Calvin, D ... 920-832-6517 .. 517 E
calvin.d.husmann@lawrence.edu
HUSMANN, Mike ... 712-274-5310 .. 175 C
husmann@morningside.edu
HUSON, Lisa ... 309-438-8999 .. 143 B
lhuson@ilstu.edu
HUSPENI, Todd ... 715-346-4446 .. 521 C
todd.huspeni@uwsp.edu
HUSS, David ... 731-352-4001 .. 438 K
hussd@bethelu.edu
HUSS, Fenwick ... 646-312-3030 .. 307 A
fenwick.huss@baruch.cuny.edu
HUSSAIN, Asif ... 718-368-6674 .. 308 F
ahussain@kbcc.cuny.edu
HUSSAIN, Nayyer ... 845-574-4242 .. 327 G
rondell@sunyrockland.edu
HUSSEY, LeighAnn ... 601-928-6225 .. 259 C
leighann.hussey@mgccc.edu
HUSSEY, Mark, A ... 979-862-4384 .. 468 B
mhussey@tamu.edu
HUSSEY, Michael ... 207-786-6103 .. 202 D
mhussey@bates.edu
HUSSON, James, J ... 617-552-3441 .. 216 C
james.husson@bc.edu
HUSTED, Jean, L ... 203-582-8645 .... 88 G
jean.husted@quinnipiac.edu
HUSTOLES, Carol L, J ... 269-387-1900 .. 243 H
carol.hustoles@wmich.edu
HUSTON, Carole ... 619-260-4553 .... 72 B
huston@sandiego.edu
HUSTON, Robin, E ... 405-325-1974 .. 389 B
rhuston@ou.edu
HUSTON, Susan, A ... 716-645-5300 .. 331 C
huston@buffalo.edu
HUTCHCRAFT, Joy, D ... 309-438-8041 .. 143 B
jdhutch@ilstu.edu
HUTCHENS, David ... 606-218-5282 .. 194 C
davidhutchens@upike.edu
HUTCHENS, Sue ... 937-481-2214 .. 381 C
sue_hutchens@wilmington.edu
HUTCHERSON, Annette ... 863-297-1039 .. 106 I
ahutcherson@polk.edu
HUTCHERSON, Cecil, L ... 864-592-4693 .. 432 H
hutchersonc@sccsc.edu
HUTCHERSON, James ... 910-642-7141 .. 353 C
james.hutcherson@sccnc.edu
HUTCHERSON, Lindsay ... 251-575-8279 ...... 1 C
lhutcherson@ascc.edu
HUTCHERSON,
Patricia, J ... 318-274-3242 .. 200 F
jenkinsp@gram.edu
HUTCHESON, Donna, R ... 470-578-4421 .. 123 J
dhutches@kennesaw.edu
HUTCHESON, Philip ... 615-966-5850 .. 441 F
philip.hutcheson@lipscomb.edu
HUTCHINGS, Jessica ... 337-475-5512 .. 200 H
jhutchings@mcneese.edu
HUTCHINGS, Rachel ... 918-595-7846 .. 388 F
rachel.hutchings@tulsacc.edu
HUTCHINGS, Shawn ... 757-340-2121 .. 488 A
shutchings2@centura.edu
HUTCHINS, Carin ... 832-813-6737 .. 461 B
carin.a.hutchins@lonestar.edu
HUTCHINS, Christine ... 413-538-2899 .. 226 A
hutchins@mtholyoke.edu
HUTCHINS, Donald ... 870-307-7233 .... 21 A
donald.hutchins@lyon.edu
HUTCHINS, Frankie ... 334-872-2533 ...... 6 F
HUTCHINS, Jim ... 937-327-7307 .. 381 F
hutchinsj@wittenberg.edu
HUTCHINS, Paul, C ... 910-592-8081 .. 352 H
phutchins@sampsoncc.edu
HUTCHINS, Robin ... 918-444-2000 .. 384 G
hutchinr@nsuok.edu
HUTCHINS, Ronald ... 906-635-2446 .. 236 J
rhutchins@lssu.edu
HUTCHINS, Terrel, F ... 269-488-4244 .. 235 I
thutchins@kvcc.edu
HUTCHINS, Thelma, J ... 304-367-4122 .. 513 B
thelma.hutchins@fairmontstate.edu
HUTCHINS, Thomas ... 931-221-7456 .. 444 E
hutchinst@apsu.edu
HUTCHINS, Wesley, D ... 336-757-3053 .. 349 G
whutchins@forsythtech.edu
HUTCHINSON, Adriane ... 815-479-7829 .. 147 E
ahutchinson@mchenry.edu
HUTCHINSON, Alison ... 717-871-5005 .. 415 F
alison.hutchinson@millersville.edu
HUTCHINSON, Andre ... 503-943-7371 .. 396 B
hutchina@up.edu
HUTCHINSON, Brian, A ... 606-783-2088 .. 191 H
b.hutchinson@moreheadstate.edu
HUTCHINSON, Dana ... 802-860-2721 .. 483 F
dhutchinson@champlain.edu
HUTCHINSON, Diane, L ... 315-255-1743 .. 306 G
diane.hutchinson@cayuga-cc.edu
HUTCHINSON, Doug ... 714-556-3610 .... 73 B
doug.hutchinson@vanguard.edu
HUTCHINSON, Erica ... 207-509-7145 .. 204 F
ehutchinson@unity.edu
HUTCHINSON, Gayle, E ... 530-898-5201 .... 32 C
ghutchinson@csuchico.edu
HUTCHINSON, John, S ... 713-348-4996 .. 464 E
hutchinson@rice.edu
HUTCHINSON,
Kathryn, T ... 718-990-6820 .. 328 F
hutchink@stjohns.edu
HUTCHINSON, Laura ... 765-983-1317 .. 160 G
hutchla@earlham.edu
HUTCHINSON, Natalie ... 515-271-1430 .. 171 H
natalie.hutchinson@dmu.edu
HUTCHINSON, Natalie ... 503-760-3131 .. 390 B
natalie@birthingway.edu
HUTCHINSON, Paulette ... 610-527-0200 .. 418 D
phutchinson@rosemont.edu
HUTCHINSON, Ryan ... 919-761-2100 .. 355 I
rhutchinson@sebts.edu
HUTCHINSON, Steve ... 402-461-7339 .. 280 D
shutchinson@hastings.edu
HUTCHINSON, Tom ... 601-266-6407 .. 261 E
thomas.hutchinson@usm.edu
HUTCHINSON BELL,
Robin ... 614-234-1372 .. 373 B
rhutchinsonbell@mccn.edu
HUTCHISON, Adam, C ... 254-867-4834 .. 470 F
achutchison@tstc.edu
HUTCHISON, Chris ... 714-628-7321 .... 37 F
hutchiso@chapman.edu
HUTCHISON, David ... 660-248-6260 .. 263 B
drhutchi@centralmethodist.edu
HUTCHISON, Donna ... 217-732-3155 .. 146 B
dhutchison@lincolncollege.edu
HUTCHISON, Elizabeth ... 615-771-7821 .. 449 I
e.hutchison@williamsoncc.edu
HUTCHISON, Frances ... 409-747-2148 .. 478 A
fbhutchi@utmb.edu
HUTCHISON, James, R ... 928-344-7704 .... 11 J
james.hutchison@azwestern.edu
HUTCHISON, Karen ... 717-396-7833 .. 413 M
khutchison@pcad.edu
HUTCHISON, Kathleen ... 601-925-3870 .. 259 A
khutchis@mc.edu
HUTCHISON, Michael, V ... 479-968-0400 .... 19 F
mhutchison@atu.edu
HUTCHISON, Nancy ... 610-902-8305 .. 399 D
nancy.c.hutchison@cabrini.edu
HUTCHISON, Theresa, R ... 817-598-6271 .. 479 E
thutchison@wc.edu
HUTCHISON-CARAVEO,
Shannon ... 619-849-2549 .... 57 M
shannonhutchison@pointloma.edu
HUTCHISONS, Wendy ... 503-654-8000 .. 394 D
whutchisons@pioneerpacific.edu
HUTH, F. Robert ... 386-822-7015 .. 113 B
fhuth@stetson.edu
HUTH, Steven, K ... 412-268-1075 .. 400 D
huth@cmu.edu
HUTKIN, Samuel ... 727-298-8685 .. 114 D
HUTLEY, Mike ... 352-395-4177 .. 109 C
michael.hutley@sfcollege.edu
HUTSELL, Emily ... 574-936-8898 .. 158 I
emily.hutsell@ancilla.edu
HUTSELL, Richard ... 903-923-2048 .. 457 G
rhutsell@etbu.edu
HUTSON, Carol, A ... 903-510-3225 .. 473 C
chut@tjc.edu
HUTSON, Jerome ... 610-436-3273 .. 416 C
jhutson@wcupa.edu
HUTSON, Kristin, E ... 319-399-8546 .. 170 G
khutson@coe.edu
HUTSON, Mary Pope ... 434-381-6272 .. 494 M
mpmhutson@sbc.edu
HUTTENLOCHER,
Daniel, S ... 212-255-8587 .. 312 A
huttenlocher@cornell.edu
HUTTER, Jeffery, W ... 617-638-4780 .. 216 E
jhutter@bu.edu
HUTTI, Deb ... 217-234-5273 .. 145 D
dhutti@lakeland.cc.il.us
HUTTNER, Trinity ... 425-558-0299 .. 503 C
thuttner@digipen.edu
HUTTO, Dena ... 503-777-7572 .. 394 I
dhutto@reed.edu
HUTTO, J. Laurence ... 843-953-7696 .. 428 A
huttoj1@citadel.edu
HUTTO, Jimmy ... 334-493-3573 ...... 5 F
jhutto@lbwcc.edu
HUTTO, Kenneth ... 678-359-5010 .. 122 E
kennyh@gordonstate.edu
HUTTO, Kim, M ... 540-887-7216 .. 491 G
khutto@mbc.edu
HUTTO-HARRIS,
LaShanda ... 864-578-8770 .. 432 D
lhutto@sherman.edu
HUTTON, Debra ... 313-593-5430 .. 242 A
dghutton@umich.edu
HUTTON, James, D ... 317-447-6200 .. 161 I
james.hutton@harrison.edu
HUTTON, Ken ... 215-576-0800 .. 417 H
khutton@rc.edu
HUTTON, Nadine, L ... 240-895-3000 .. 210 E
nlhutton@smcm.edu
HUTTON, Tom ... 719-255-3439 .... 83 L
thutton@uccs.edu
HUTTON-LOPEZ, Karen ... 909-469-5650 .... 74 K
klopez@westernu.edu
HUTTON SISTARE, Sallie 843-792-3433 .. 431 A
hutton@musc.edu
HUTZLEY, Brian ... 315-228-7422 .. 310 G
bhutzley@colgate.edu
HUUS, Ken ... 803-786-3091 .. 429 A
khuus@columbiasc.edu
HUVAL, Barbara ... 409-984-6341 .. 471 C
barbara.huval@lamarpa.edu
HUVAL, Barbara ... 409-984-6330 .. 471 C
barbara.huval@lamarpa.edu
HUXEL, Mary, B ... 636-584-6613 .. 264 M
mary.huxel@eastcentral.edu
HUXFORD, Wye ... 706-385-1012 .. 126 A
wye.huxford@point.edu
HUYBRECHT, Melissa ... 612-874-3764 .. 247 M
mhubrecht@mcad.edu
HUYKE, Gretchen ... 787-832-6772 .. 538 C
asesorialegal@uprm.edu
HVIDSTEN, Lynne ... 651-450-3372 .. 249 F
lhvidst@inverhills.edu
HWANG, Amy ... 617-745-3855 .. 218 A
amy.hwang@enc.edu
HWANG, Delphine ... 510-649-8252 .... 55 I
dhwang@psr.edu
HWANG, Delphine ... 415-749-4535 .... 61 B
registrar@sfai.edu
HWANG, James ... 626-571-5110 .... 49 B
jhwang@les.edu
HWANG, Kathryn ... 816-584-6226 .. 270 D
kate.hwang@park.edu
HWANG, Leo ... 413-775-1221 .. 223 D
hwang@gcc.mass.edu
HWANG, Lily ... 678-407-5849 .. 121 B
lhwang@ggc.edu
HWU, Alex ... 707-826-3731 .... 34 F
sh1911@humboldt.edu
HYATT, Danny ... 903-463-8622 .. 458 H
hyattdan@grayson.edu
HYATT, Garey ... 410-951-3366 .. 212 E
ghyatt@coppin.edu
HYATT, Gwen ... 503-699-3316 .. 392 D
registrar@marylhurst.edu
HYATT, Katherine, E ... 770-720-5591 .. 126 C
keh@reinhardt.edu
HYATT, Regina ... 662-325-3045 .. 259 D
rhyatt@saffairs.msstate.edu
HYATT, Tom ... 410-225-2291 .. 209 E
thyatt@mica.edu
HYBL, Andrew ... 510-204-0718 .... 38 C
ahybl@cdsp.edu
HYDE, Clyanne ... 828-339-4000 .. 353 D
c_hyde@southwesterncc.edu
HYDE, Fred ... 931-424-9007 .. 441 G
fhyde@martinmethodist.edu
HYDE, Gerald ... 828-766-1220 .. 351 E
ghyde@mayland.edu
HYDE, Holly ... 828-835-4219 .. 353 G
hhyde@tricountycc.edu
HYDE, John ... 516-686-7527 .. 323 G
jmhyde@nyit.edu
HYDE, Katrina, A ... 304-336-8510 .. 513 F
katrina.hyde@westliberty.edu
HYDE, Matthew ... 610-330-5100 .. 407 C
hydem@lafayette.edu
HYDE, Richard, D ... 979-532-6346 .. 479 J
richardh@wcjc.edu
HYDE, Truell ... 254-710-3763 .. 452 H
truell_hyde@baylor.edu
HYDE-PINNER, Sarah ... 216-373-5290 .. 374 B
shydepinner@ndc.edu
HYDEN, John P ... 330-941-3235 .. 332 A
jphyden@ysu.edu
HYDER, Bret ... 651-638-6242 .. 244 L
bret-hyder@bethel.edu
HYDER, Mark ... 423-236-2155 .. 444 B
markhyder@southern.edu
HYDRO, Susan ... 609-771-2997 .. 290 F
berksus@tcnj.edu
HYELER, Maral ... 310-434-3551 .... 63 F
hyeler_maral@smc.edu
HYER, Cindy, T ... 727-376-6911 .. 114 A
cindy-hyer@trinitycollege.edu
HYER, Joel ... 308-432-6359 .. 281 H
jhyer@csc.edu
HYLAND, Cheryl ... 615-220-7801 .. 446 D
chyland@mscc.edu
HYLAND-MURR,
Mary Ann ... 502-213-2424 .. 190 A
mary.hyland-murr@kctcs.edu
HYLTON, Gary ... 304-384-5233 .. 513 A
ghylton@concord.edu
HYLTON, Katelin ... 606-368-6055 .. 186 B
katelinhylton@alc.edu
HYMAN, Cheryl, L ... 312-553-2500 .. 137 C
HYMAN, Susan ... 410-704-2097 .. 213 B
shyman@towson.edu
HYMANS, Diane, J ... 614-235-4136 .. 378 C
dhymans@tlsohio.edu
HYMES, Jacqueline, D ... 207-581-1226 .. 204 H
HYMON-PARKER, Shirley 336-334-7979 .. 356 F
sjhymonp@ncat.edu
HYND, George, W ... 248-370-3500 .. 239 K
hynd@oakland.edu
HYNDMAN, Steve ... 502-410-6200 .. 188 H
shyndman@galencollege.edu
HYNDMAN, III, William .. 850-599-3295 .. 110 J
william.hyndman@famu.edu
HYNDS, Andy ... 217-875-7200 .. 152 C
ahynds@richland.edu
HYNDS, Steve ... 417-873-7406 .. 264 H
shynds@drury.edu
HYNEK, Mary, T ... 913-360-7431 .. 178 I
mhynek@benedictine.edu
HYNES, Jeff ... 708-209-3444 .. 138 G
jeff.hynes@cuchicago.edu
HYNES, Kevin, P ... 630-515-6073 .. 148 C
khynes@midwestern.edu
HYNES, Peter ... 973-684-6602 .. 294 A
phynes@pccc.edu
HYNES, Robert ... 978-665-3152 .. 221 D
rhynes@fitchburgstate.edu
HYNES, Thomas ... 678-466-4300 .. 119 A
thomashynes@clayton.edu
HYNES-WILSON,
Mentha, A ... 410-543-6080 .. 213 A
mahynes-wilson@salisbury.edu
HYNICK, Karen ... 978-762-4000 .. 224 C
khynick@northshore.edu
HYNSON, Cassandra ... 302-736-2428 .... 91 G
cassandra.hynson@wesley.edu
HYSELL, Deborah ... 419-755-4894 .. 373 G
dhysell@ncstatecollege.edu
HYSELL, Jon ... 585-245-5626 .. 333 B
hysell@geneseo.edu
HYSON, Ronald ... 469-941-8300 .. 457 B
rhyson@dni.edu
HYUN, Byeong ... 770-279-0507 .. 120 G
drhyun@msn.com
HYUN, Eunsook ... 239-590-7791 .. 110 L
ehyun@fgcu.edu
HYUN, Timothy ... 253-752-2020 .. 503 H
librarian@faithseminary.edu

I

IACAMPO, Beth ... 860-297-2273 .... 89 B
beth.iacampo@trincoll.edu
IACOBUCCI, Richard, M .. 617-541-5394 .. 224 F
riacobucci@rcc.mass.edu
IACONO, Anthony ... 772-462-7215 .. 103 B
aiacono@irsc.edu
IACONO, Anthony, J ... 973-328-5031 .. 290 H
tiacono@ccm.edu
IACOVELLI, John ... 609-652-4833 .. 297 C
john.iacovelli@stockton.edu
IACOVOU, Charles ... 336-758-5110 .. 359 E
iacovou@wfu.edu
IACUESSA, Michelle, A ... 845-569-3217 .. 322 B
michelle.iacuessa@msmc.edu
IACULLO, Gerald ... 973-642-3888 .. 289 F
gji@berkeleycollege.edu
IACULLO, Gerald ... 973-642-3888 .. 305 B
gji@berkeleycollege.edu
IADAROLA, Michael ... 718-951-5065 .. 307 D
miadarola@brooklyn.cuny.edu
IADEVAIA, Norma ... 310-506-4149 .... 56 J
norma.iadevaia@pepperdine.edu
IALENTI, Vincent ... 978-632-6600 .. 224 B
v_ialenti@mwcc.mass.edu
IAMUNNO, Janine ... 910-962-2445 .. 358 D
iamunnoj@uncw.edu
IANELLO, Lisa, A ... 305-684-6020 .. 336 B
iannella@morrisville.edu
IANETTA, Catalina ... 617-585-0100 .. 216 A
catalina.ianetta@the-bac.edu
IANNACCONE, Judy ... 714-480-7503 .... 58 G
iannaccone_judy@rsccd.edu
IANNACCONE, Paul ... 510-659-6441 .... 55 B
piannaccone@ohlone.edu
IANNAZZI, Michael, L ... 203-371-7899 .... 88 I
iannazzim@sacredheart.edu
IANNELLI, Angela ... 973-290-4436 .. 290 G
aiannelli@cse.edu
IANNELLI, Clare ... 281-998-6150 .. 465 B
clare.iannelli@sjcd.edu
IANNELLI, Clare ... 281-998-6150 .. 465 A
clare.iannelli@sjcd.edu

IANNELLI, Clare .... 281-998-6150.. 464 J
clare.iannelli@sjcd.edu
IANNESSA, Katherine .... 512-499-4201.. 475 K
kiannessa@utsystem.edu
IANNO, Daniel .... 315-792-5356.. 321 G
dianno@mvcc.edu
IANNONE, Frank .... 732-255-0400.. 293 E
fiannone@ocean.edu
IANNUZZI, Maria Lise .... 909-447-2552.... 39 A
miannuzzi@cst.edu
IANNUZZI, Patricia .... 702-895-2226.. 284 L
patricia.iannuzzi@unlv.edu
IAPALUCCI, Philip .... 574-520-4218.. 163 E
IBARRA, Rudy .... 305-628-6633.. 108 E
ribarra@stu.edu
IBARRA, Teresita .... 787-766-1717.. 536 B
teibarra@suagm.edu
IBEANUSI, Victor .... 850-599-3550.. 110 J
victor.ibeanusi@famu.edu
IBEKIE, Oranu .... 219-769-2047.. 165 R
IBERT, Carissa .... 415-503-6251.... 61 C
cibert@sfcm.edu
IBSEN, Serenity .... 503-821-8970.. 394 B
sibsen@pnca.edu
ICASIANO, Arnold .... 415-703-9529.... 29 K
aicasiano@cca.edu
ICE, Jerry, T .... 860-215-9004.... 87 D
jice@trcc.commnet.edu
ICE, Richard .... 320-363-5503.. 254 N
rice@csbsju.edu
ICE, Richard .... 320-363-5088.. 245 I
rice@csbsju.edu
ICHON, Eric .... 310-287-4305.... 50 E
ichone@wlac.edu
ICHSAN, Tony .... 971-722-4338.. 394 F
tony.ichsan@pcc.edu
ICKES, Jessica, L .... 717-867-6205.. 408 F
ickes@lvc.edu
IDDINGS, R. Keith .... 610-341-4383.. 403 B
kiddings@eastern.edu
IDE, Susan .... 248-218-2059.. 240 C
side@rc.edu
IDELL, Steven .... 903-877-7674.. 477 E
steven.idell@uthct.edu
IDETA, Lori .... 808-956-3290.. 131 F
ideta@hawaii.edu
IERARDI, Kristina .... 508-362-2131.. 223 C
kierardi@capecod.edu
IERIEN, Kim .... 503-281-4181.. 390 J
IGHODARO, Osaro .... 602-243-8036.... 14 I
osaro.ighodaro@southmountaincc.edu
IGIEHON, Lisa .... 703-284-1618.. 492 A
lisa.igiehon@marymount.edu
IGNASH, Jan .... 850-245-0466.. 110 I
jan.ignash@flbog.edu
IGO, Mary .... 304-883-2424.. 512 C
migo@newriver.edu
IGOU, Daniel .... 619-388-7646.... 60 H
digou@sdccd.edu
IGWEBUIKE, John .... 601-877-6142.. 256 F
jigwe@alcorn.edu
IGWEBUIKE, John, L .... 601-877-6170.. 256 F
jigwe@alcorn.edu
IGWIKI, Richard .... 504-816-4830.. 195 B
rigwiki@dillard.edu
IGYARTO, Mia .... 630-942-3410.. 138 B
igyartom@cod.edu
IHDE, Rick .... 402-643-7422.. 279 F
rick.ihde@cune.edu
IHRER, Kenneth .... 212-650-7400.. 307 E
kihrer@ccny.cuny.edu
IHRKE, Barbara .... 765-677-1578.. 164 B
barbara.ihrke@indwes.edu
IJIRI, Lisa .... 617-349-8706.. 220 B
lijiri@lesley.edu
IKEDA, Kimi, M .... 805-756-2186.... 31 I
kikeda@calpoly.edu
IKEM, Fidelis, M .... 937-376-6441.. 365 H
fikem@centralstate.edu
IKEN, Mark .... 678-407-5400.. 121 B
miken@ggc.edu
IKEN, Stacie .... 701-224-5491.. 361 C
stacie.iken@bismarckstate.edu
IKENBERRY, David, L .... 303-492-1809.... 83 K
david.ikenberry@colorado.edu
IKHARO, Sadiq .... 510-466-7336.... 57 B
sikharo@peralta.edu
IKHARO, Sadiq .... 510-466-7336.... 57 E
sikharo@peralta.edu
ILDEFONSO, Chet .... 630-829-6431.. 135 F
cildefonso@ben.edu
ILER, Susan .... 216-791-5000.. 366 H
susan.iler@cim.edu
ILES, Linda .... 530-221-4275.... 64 C
finaid@shasta.edu
ILIAKIS-DOHERTY,
Sophia .... 360-417-6219.. 505 I
sdoherty@pencol.edu
ILICETO, Thomas .... 212-229-5101.. 322 E
ilicetot@newschool.edu
ILLICH, Paul .... 402-323-3415.. 282 F
pillich@southeast.edu
ILLIES, Diane .... 218-755-2448.. 248 M
dillies@bemidjistate.edu
ILLINGWORTH, Kendra .... 219-866-6428.. 166 J
kendra@saintjoe.edu
ILLINGWORTH,
Theresa, M .... 414-425-8300.. 519 F
tillingworth@shsst.edu
ILOVAR, Jasmin .... 304-243-2088.. 515 C
jilovar@wju.edu
ILSE, Thomas .... 304-327-4022.. 512 P
tilse@bluefieldstate.edu
ILYAS, Mohammad .... 561-297-3426.. 110 K
ilyas@fau.edu
ILYAS, Shazia .... 847-290-6425.. 150 C
silyas@nwsc.edu
IM, Manyul .... 203-576-4234.... 89 C
manyulim@bridgeport.edu
IMAI, Geri .... 808-235-7430.. 132 E
gerii@hawaii.edu
IMAI, Peggy, H .... 802-654-2222.. 484 I
pimai@smcvt.edu
IMASUEN, Edwin .... 810-762-9642.. 236 C
eimasuen@kettering.edu
IMBER, Margaret, A .... 207-786-6280.. 202 D
mimber@bates.edu
IMBIMBO, Patricia .... 646-312-4683.. 307 A
patricia.imbimbo@baruch.cuny.edu
IMBRAGULIO, Lisa .... 205-726-4172........ 6 E
lcimbrag@samford.edu
IMBRESCIA, Janelle .... 724-653-2192.. 402 F
janelle@dec.edu
IMBRESCIA, Jeffrey, D .... 724-653-2200.. 402 F
jimbrescia@dec.edu
IMBRESCIA, Julian .... 724-653-2213.. 402 F
julian@dec.edu
IMBRIALE, William .... 212-752-1530.. 318 F
william.imbriale@limcollege.edu
IMES, Melissa, J .... 717-262-2000.. 424 A
melissa.imes@wilson.edu
IMHOF, Howard .... 740-366-9379.. 365 D
himhof@cotc.edu
IMHOFF, Dan .... 608-822-2401.. 524 F
dimhoff@swtc.edu
IMHOFF, Donna .... 216-987-5125.. 367 E
IMHOFF, Maren, E .... 212-327-8682.. 327 F
imhoff@rockefeller.edu
IMLER, Mary Elizabeth .... 815-740-2274.. 157 F
mimler@stfrancis.edu
IMLER, Sylvia, J .... 330-941-3370.. 382 A
sjimler@ysu.edu
IMMERMAN, Stephen, D . 978-921-4242.. 225 G
steve.immerman@montserrat.edu
IMPELLIZZERI,
Melinda, A .... 502-597-7010.. 191 B
melinda.impellizzeri@kysu.edu
IMPERATO, Pamela .... 616-698-7111.. 233 C
pimperato@davenport.edu
IMWALLE, Todd, W .... 937-229-3299.. 379 D
timwalle1@udayton.edu
INABINET, Chad, E .... 231-843-5965.. 243 G
ceinabinet@westshore.edu
INAFUKU, Derek .... 808-845-9123.. 132 A
dinafuku@hawaii.edu
INBODY, Brian, L .... 620-431-2820.. 183 H
binbody@neosho.edu
INCANDELA, Joe .... 805-893-8270.... 70 E
incandela@research.ucsb.edu
INCANDELA, Marybeth .... 631-420-2107.. 335 E
marybeth.incandela@farmingdale.edu
INCH, Edward .... 510-885-3711.... 32 E
edward.inch@csueastbay.edu
INDELICATO, James .... 212-686-9040.. 340 D
jindelicato@woodtobecoburn.edu
INDIVERI-GANT,
Jeffrey, D .... 973-655-6911.. 293 A
gantj@mail.montclair.edu
INES, Caryn, L .... 603-535-2981.. 288 F
clines1@plymouth.edu
INFANTI, Steven, M .... 717-901-5146.. 405 H
sinfanti@harrisburgu.edu
INFINGER, Kim .... 425-739-8274.. 504 F
kim.infinger@lwtech.edu
INGALLS, Keith .... 413-748-3946.. 228 E
kingalls@springfieldcollege.edu
INGARGIOLA, Janet, M ... 217-443-8760.. 139 B
jingarg@dacc.edu
INGBER, Marc .... 303-556-2870.... 84 A
marc.ingber@ucdenver.edu
INGELSON, Jeannine .... 563-441-4046.. 172 D
jingleson@eicc.edu
INGERMAN, Bret .... 850-201-6082.. 113 E
ingermab@tcc.fl.edu
INGERSOLL, Christopher . 419-530-5453.. 380 D
christopher.ingersoll@utoledo.edu
INGERSOLL, Julia .... 610-526-6132.. 405 B
jingersoll@harcum.edu
INGERSOLL, Melinda .... 215-951-1374.. 407 A
ingersoll@lasalle.edu
INGERSOLL, Pat .... 616-234-3869.. 234 E
pingerso@grcc.edu
INGERSOLL, William .... 203-576-6024.... 89 A
william.ingersoll@stvincentscollege.edu
INGHAM, Joanne .... 212-431-2876.. 323 H
joanne.ingham@nyls.edu
INGHAM, Lester, A .... 661-824-2977.... 53 K
lingham@ntps.edu
INGLAND, Susan .... 620-417-1400.. 184 I
susan.ingland@sccc.edu
INGLE, Brooke .... 970-247-7421.... 80 D
bookstoremgr@fortlewis.edu
INGLE, Jeffery, S .... 865-981-8199.. 441 H
jeff.ingle@maryvillecollege.edu
INGLE, III, Kenneth, G .... 704-216-3577.. 352 G
ken.ingle@rccc.edu
INGLE, Kent .... 863-667-5002.. 109 L
kingle@seu.edu
INGLES, Roger, D .... 740-368-3738.. 376 B
rdingles@owu.edu
INGLES, Susan, L .... 414-410-4236.. 515 I
slingles@stritch.edu
INGLIS, Mark .... 216-421-7403.. 366 G
minglis@cia.edu
INGLISH, Darla .... 940-397-4321.. 462 A
darla.inglish@mwsu.edu
INGMIRE, Mac .... 706-886-6831.. 128 C
mingmire@tfc.edu
INGMIRE, Randall .... 217-732-3168.. 146 A
rlingmire@lincolnchristian.edu
INGOLDSBY, Lisa .... 213-252-5100.... 24 K
lingoldsby@alu.edu
INGOLFSLAND, Dennis ... 952-446-4239.. 246 D
ingolfsland@crown.edu
INGRAHAM, Barry .... 207-768-2706.. 203 L
bingraham@nmcc.edu
INGRAHAM, Jai .... 256-782-8565........ 4 H
jingraha@jsu.edu
INGRAHAM, Timothy .... 978-468-7111.. 219 B
tingraham@gcts.edu
INGRAM, Archinya .... 803-327-7402.. 428 D
aingram@clintoncollege.edu
INGRAM, Beth .... 701-231-7131.. 361 A
beth.ingram@ndsu.edu
INGRAM, Beverly .... 318-487-7694.. 195 F
beverly.ingram@lacollege.edu
INGRAM, Brian, C .... 731-881-7069.. 448 G
cingram@utm.edu
INGRAM, Charles, E .... 609-652-4381.. 297 C
charles.ingram@stockton.edu
INGRAM, David .... 817-461-8741.. 451 G
dingram@arlingtonbaptistcollege.edu
INGRAM, Earl .... 334-670-3104........ 7 H
ingram@troy.edu
INGRAM, Geoff .... 951-785-2000.... 48 A
gingram@lasierra.edu
INGRAM, Iris .... 310-287-4368.... 50 E
ingramii@wlac.edu
INGRAM, J. Kevin .... 785-539-3571.. 183 B
kingram@mccks.edu
INGRAM, Jamie .... 213-615-7231.... 37 I
presidentsassistant@thechicagoschool.edu
INGRAM, Jim .... 662-862-8047.. 258 C
jingram@iccms.edu
INGRAM, Joyce, A .... 850-599-3611.. 110 J
joyce.ingram@famu.edu
INGRAM, Kimberly .... 360-736-9391.. 502 A
kingram@centralia.edu
INGRAM, Lashawanda, T 315-386-7128.. 335 B
ingraml@canton.edu
INGRAM, Mark, T .... 205-934-0766........ 8 E
mingram@uab.edu
INGRAM, Mike .... 423-746-5316.. 447 E
mingram@twcnet.edu
INGRAM, SR.,
Roderick, L .... 330-325-6673.. 373 H
ringram@neomed.edu
INGRAM, Trent .... 870-248-4000.... 19 H
trent.ingram@blackrivertech.edu
INGRAM, Wanda Rhea .... 334-244-3476........ 2 A
wingram4@aum.edu
INGRAM, William .... 615-460-6568.. 438 J
william.ingram@belmont.edu
INGRAM, William, G .... 919-536-7250.. 349 D
ingramb@durhamtech.edu
INGRAM-WALLACE,
Brenda, J .... 610-921-7585.. 396 H
bingramwallace@albright.edu
INGS, Margaret Ann .... 617-824-8299.. 218 B
margaret_ann_ings@emerson.edu
INIGUEZ, Edmond .... 719-549-3206.... 82 G
edmond.iniguez@pueblocc.edu
INIGUEZ, Elizabeth .... 323-463-2500.... 67 I
lizm@toa.edu
INIGUEZ-JIMENEZ,
J. Alfredo .... 956-764-5798.. 460 F
ainiguez@laredo.edu
INKSTER, Kathy .... 606-546-4151.. 193 E
INKSTER, Larry .... 606-546-1233.. 193 E
linkster@unionky.edu
INKSTER, Whitney, M .... 304-336-8375.. 513 F
whitney.inkster@westliberty.edu
INLOW, Laura .... 618-468-3255.. 145 G
linlow@lc.edu
INMAN, Barbara, L .... 757-727-5264.. 490 E
barbara.inman@hamptonu.edu
INMAN, Dean .... 870-864-7142.... 22 D
dinman@southark.edu
INMAN, Gerald .... 617-989-4252.. 229 D
inmang@wit.edu
INMAN, James, P .... 540-464-7104.. 499 E
inmanjp@vmi.edu
INMAN, John, G .... 724-458-2176.. 404 F
jginman@gcc.edu
INMAN, Keith .... 502-852-6924.. 194 A
akinma01@louisville.edu
INMAN, Leigh .... 619-961-4278.... 68 A
glinman@tjsl.edu
INMAN, Linda, D .... 336-334-7708.. 356 F
ldinman@ncat.edu
INMAN, Lisa .... 919-536-7200.. 349 D
inmanl@durhamtech.edu
INMAN, Stan, D .... 801-585-5028.. 481 M
sinman@sa.utah.edu
INNIGER, Alyssa, K .... 507-344-7874.. 244 K
alyssa.inniger@blc.edu
INOA, Luis .... 845-437-5862.. 339 C
inoa@vassar.edu
INOCENCIO, Leticia .... 210-486-3117.. 450 D
linocencio@alamo.edu
INOUYE, Carolyn .... 805-678-5803.... 73 E
cinouye@vcccd.edu
INOUYE, Susan, K .... 808-956-8155.. 131 D
susani@hawaii.edu
INOWAY-RONNIE, Eden .. 608-265-5975.. 519 K
etinoway@wisc.edu
INSANALLI, Dawn .... 914-637-2726.. 317 B
dinsanalli@iona.edu
INSCH, Gary .... 419-530-5426.. 380 D
gary.insch@utoledo.edu
INSELL, Courtney .... 731-989-6011.. 440 D
cwilson@fhu.edu
INSERTO, Fathiah, E .... 714-542-8086.... 29 C
finserto@bristoluniversity.edu
INSKO, Celeste .... 541-278-5780.. 390 C
cinsko@bluecc.edu
INSKO, Thomas .... 541-962-3512.. 391 C
tinsko@eou.edu
INSLEY, Andrea .... 206-587-3899.. 506 K
ainsley@sccd.ctc.edu
INSLEY, Lynn .... 201-216-8927.. 297 B
lynn.insley@stevens.edu
INTILLE, Amy .... 617-989-4885.. 229 D
intillea@wit.edu
INTROCASO, CDP,
Candace .... 412-536-1204.. 406 K
cintrocaso@laroche.edu
INZER, Monica, C .... 315-859-4421.. 315 D
minzer@hamilton.edu
INZERILLA, Tina .... 925-424-1156.... 37 C
tinzerilla@laspositascollege.edu
IOANNIDES, Margaret .... 904-256-1158.. 100 E
mioannides@fcsl.edu
IOANNIDES, Vanessa .... 415-485-3235.... 42 G
vanessa.ioannides@dominican.edu
IOANNOU, Carin .... 336-770-3301.. 358 E
ioannouc@uncsa.edu
IOBST, William .... 570-504-7000.. 400 I
wiobst@tcmc.edu
IOLI, Christine .... 412-809-5100.. 417 D
ioli.christine@pti.edu
IORG, Jeff .... 909-687-1701.... 44 H
jeffiorg@gs.edu
IOVANNONE, Jeffry, J .... 716-673-4747.. 331 D
jeffry.iovannone@fredonia.edu
IPACH, Nichole .... 805-437-8893.... 32 B
nichole.ipach@csuci.edu
IPPOLITO, Andrew .... 201-692-2531.. 291 J
andrew_ippolito@fdu.edu
IRANI, Daraius .... 410-704-3780.. 213 B
dirani@towson.edu
IRBY, Adam, W .... 336-322-2253.. 351 H
adam.irby@piedmontcc.edu
IRBY, Bernice .... 803-934-3408.. 431 E
birby@morris.edu
IRBY, Matthew .... 714-241-6104.... 39 E
1180mgr@follett.com
IRBY, Michele .... 573-651-5120.. 272 B
mirby@semo.edu
IRBY, Sharon .... 770-229-3454.. 127 F
sirby@sctech.edu
IRELAND, Alan .... 336-750-2935.. 359 B
irelandag@wssu.edu
IRELAND, Asheley .... 270-809-5604.. 192 A
aireland@murraystate.edu
IRELAND, Jim, D .... 620-792-9339.. 178 G
irelandj@bartonccc.edu
IRELAND, Timothy .... 716-286-8342.. 324 E
toi@niagara.edu
IREY, Sayumi .... 425-564-2300.. 501 F
sayumi.irey@bellevuecollege.edu

J

JACKIEWICZ, Thomas, E . 323-442-9775.... 72 D
thomas.jackiewicz@med.usc.edu
JACKLOSKY, Robert .... 718-405-3301.. 310 H
robert.jacklosky@mountsaintvincent.edu
JACKMAN, Deborah .... 414-277-7154.. 518 E
JACKMAN, Diane, H .... 217-581-2524.. 139 H
dhjackman@eiu.edu
JACKO, Mariusz .... 787-250-1912.. 534 B
mjacko@intermetro.com
JACKS, Almeda .... 864-656-2161.. 428 C
arogers@clemson.edu
JACKS, Benjamin .... 404-527-4520.. 118 F
bjacks@carver.edu
JACKS, Olive .... 404-527-4520.. 118 F
ojacks@carver.edu
JACKSON, Addie, R .... 530-226-4788.... 64 H
ajackson@simpsonu.edu
JACKSON, Alexa .... 617-824-8133.. 218 B
alexa_jackson@emerson.edu
JACKSON, Alfred, B .... 601-979-2300.. 258 D
alfred.b.jackson@jsums.edu
JACKSON, Alicia .... 229-430-4014.. 115 K
alicia.jackson@asurams.edu
JACKSON, Amy .... 620-672-5641.. 184 D
amyj@prattcc.edu
JACKSON, Andrew .... 412-731-6000.. 417 J
ajackson@rpts.edu
JACKSON, Andrew .... 615-327-6894.. 442 A
aljackson@mmc.edu
JACKSON, Anthony .... 225-771-2430.. 199 H
anthony_jackson@subr.edu
JACKSON, Antonio .... 910-678-0058.. 349 F
jacksona@faytechcc.edu
JACKSON, Arrick .... 231-591-3648.. 233 L
arrickjackson@ferris.edu
JACKSON, Arthur, R .... 704-687-2206.. 358 A
ajacks90@uncc.edu
JACKSON, Athena .... 305-626-3782.. 101 A
athena.jackson@fmuniv.edu
JACKSON, Bradley, A ...... 513-585-0116.. 366 A
bradley.jackson@thechristcollege.edu
JACKSON, Brenda .... 251-578-1313...... 6 C
bjackson@rstc.edu
JACKSON, Brenda .... 910-695-3731.. 353 A
jacksonbr@sandhills.edu
JACKSON, Brenda, W .... 504-586-5274.. 199 I
bjackson@suno.edu
JACKSON, Brian, K .... 609-652-4900.. 297 C
brian.jackson@stockton.edu
JACKSON, Brittany .... 330-569-5380.. 369 J
jacksonb1@hiram.edu
JACKSON, Brooks .... 612-626-4949.. 255 H
jacksonb@umn.edu
JACKSON, Buddy .... 334-386-7293...... 3 I
bjackson@faulkner.edu
JACKSON, C. C .... 803-536-7000.. 432 E
JACKSON, Cameron .... 980-359-1039.. 359 H
c.jackson@wingate.edu
JACKSON, Candice .... 502-597-6395.. 191 B
JACKSON, Carla .... 803-793-5172.. 429 D
jacksonc@denmarktech.edu
JACKSON, Carol .... 212-517-0756.. 320 C
cjackson@mmm.edu
JACKSON, Charles, C ...... 240-895-4413.. 210 E
ccjackson@smcm.edu
JACKSON, Chauncey, J ... 405-466-2957.. 383 M
cjjackson@langston.edu
JACKSON, Chris .... 636-922-8271.. 271 A
chubbard@stchas.edu
JACKSON, Christine .... 402-472-4455.. 282 M
cjackson3@unl.edu
JACKSON, Christopher, J 518-564-4601.. 334 A
jacksocj@plattsburgh.edu
JACKSON, Claudia .... 361-698-1247.. 457 D
cjackson@delmar.edu
JACKSON, Clint .... 901-435-1233.. 441 C
clint_jackson@loc.edu
JACKSON, Courtney .... 508-270-4005.. 223 F
cjackson@massbay.edu
JACKSON, Craig .... 478-757-3508.. 118 H
cjackson@centralgatech.edu
JACKSON, Craig .... 478-757-3508.. 118 G
cjackson@centralgatech.edu
JACKSON, Craig .... 815-825-9526.. 144 F
craig.jackson@kishwaukeecollege.edu
JACKSON, Craig, R .... 909-558-4545.... 49 C
cjackson@llu.edu
JACKSON, Crystal .... 214-379-5518.. 463 G
cjackson@pqc.edu
JACKSON, Dalen, C .... 502-863-8300.. 186 L
dalen.jackson@bsky.org
JACKSON, Dan .... 513-244-8437.. 366 B
dan.jackson@ccuniversity.edu
JACKSON, Danielle .... 406-353-2607.. 275 H
djackson@ancollege.edu
JACKSON, Darlene .... 916-660-7800.... 64 F
djackson@sierracllege.edu
JACKSON, Darryl .... 256-372-4854...... 1 A
darryl.jackson1@aamu.edu
JACKSON, JR., David ...... 850-599-3505.. 110 J
david.jackson@famu.edu
JACKSON, David, H .... 941-351-5100.. 107 M
djackson@ringling.edu
JACKSON, David, H .... 941-309-0166.. 107 M
djackson@ringling.edu
JACKSON, Deanne .... 573-341-4362.. 274 B
registrar@mst.edu
JACKSON, Debbie .... 202-319-5044.... 92 A
jacksond@cua.edu
JACKSON, Deborah, C ..... 617-873-0112.. 217 A
deborah.jackson@cambridgecollege.edu
JACKSON, Debra .... 309-677-3085.. 136 B
dsjackson@bradley.edu
JACKSON, Derek, A .... 785-532-6453.. 182 D
derekaj@ksu.edu
JACKSON, Dexter .... 334-874-5700...... 3 A
djackson@ccal.edu
JACKSON, Dionne .... 501-450-3824.... 20 F
jackson@hendrix.edu
JACKSON, Donald .... 402-461-7326.. 280 D
djackson@hastings.edu
JACKSON, Edison, O .... 386-481-2001.... 96 H
jacksone@cookman.edu
JACKSON, Elizabeth .... 432-837-8145.. 471 E
ejackson@sulross.edu
JACKSON, Emily, S .... 302-225-6271.... 91 D
emily@gbc.edu
JACKSON, Equilla .... 936-261-1890.. 467 E
eqjackson@pvamu.edu
JACKSON, Eric .... 904-470-8216.... 98 N
eric.jackson@ewc.edu
JACKSON, Ericka .... 313-577-2100.. 243 F
emjackson@wayne.edu
JACKSON, Flossie .... 772-462-7467.. 103 B
fjackson@irsc.edu
JACKSON, Frances, L ...... 617-333-2970.. 217 F
fjackson@curry.edu
JACKSON, G. Smith .... 336-278-7220.. 344 D
jacksons@elon.edu
JACKSON, Gary .... 662-325-3036.. 259 D
gary@ext.msstate.edu
JACKSON, Gary .... 254-298-8456.. 467 B
gary.jackson@templejc.edu
JACKSON, Governor, E .... 940-898-3050.. 472 G
gjackson@twu.edu
JACKSON, Grace .... 713-623-2040.. 451 K
dgjackson@aii.edu
JACKSON, Gregory .... 508-626-4698.. 221 E
gjackson@framingham.edu
JACKSON, Gregory .... 256-372-8653...... 1 A
gregory.jackson@aamu.edu
JACKSON, H. Thomas ..... 336-256-0543.. 356 F
htjackson@ncat.edu
JACKSON, Harvey .... 973-328-5553.. 290 H
hjackson@ccm.edu
JACKSON, Heidi .... 308-635-6395.. 283 D
jacksonh@wncc.edu
JACKSON, Hollie .... 661-362-2209.... 52 A
hgjackson@masters.edu
JACKSON, Jackie .... 660-248-6239.. 263 B
jsjackson@centralmethodist.edu
JACKSON, Jacob .... 425-235-7863.. 506 F
jjackson@rtc.edu
JACKSON, Jacqueline, S . 410-777-2830.. 206 B
jsjackson6@aacc.edu
JACKSON, Jae .... 305-626-3762.. 101 A
jae.jackson@fmuniv.edu
JACKSON, JR., James, T 410-777-2529.. 206 B
jjackson@aacc.edu
JACKSON, Jane .... 615-963-7427.. 445 A
jjackson@tnstate.edu
JACKSON, Jannett, N ...... 925-485-5206.... 37 A
jjackson@clpccd.org
JACKSON, Jay .... 864-592-4723.. 432 H
jacksonj@sccsc.edu
JACKSON, Jean .... 919-760-8556.. 346 D
jacksonj@meredith.edu
JACKSON, Jeff .... 419-372-9487.. 364 E
jacksjl@bgsu.edu
JACKSON, Jerry .... 606-539-4250.. 193 F
jerry.jackson@ucumberlands.edu
JACKSON, Jim, C .... 580-581-2460.. 382 G
jjackson@cameron.edu
JACKSON, Jodie .... 304-293-6999.. 514 C
jjackson2@hsc.wvu.edu
JACKSON, John .... 916-577-2210.... 75 C
jjackson@jessup.edu
JACKSON, John .... 540-231-8508.. 499 F
johnj1@vt.edu
JACKSON, John, L .... 215-898-5511.. 421 E
jackson5@sp2.upenn.edu
JACKSON, Joseph, R .... 937-328-6003.. 366 E
jacksonj@clarkstate.edu
JACKSON, Judi .... 504-282-4455.. 198 H
jjackson@nobts.edu
JACKSON, Judy, T .... 256-765-4896...... 9 C
jtjackson@una.edu
JACKSON, Julie .... 662-846-4151.. 257 E
jjackson@deltastate.edu
JACKSON, Justin .... 973-408-3957.. 291 B
jjackson@drew.edu
JACKSON, Karen .... 212-787-5300.. 303 G
info@amda.edu
JACKSON, Karen .... 323-469-3300.... 26 A
info@amda.edu
JACKSON, Katherine .... 334-244-3704...... 2 A
kjackson@outreach.aum.edu
JACKSON, Kathleen .... 417-269-8316.. 264 D
kathleen.jackson@coxcollege.edu
JACKSON, Kathryn .... 773-508-7716.. 146 G
kjackson9@luc.edu
JACKSON, Keith .... 414-326-2335.. 516 D
kjackso4@ccon.edu
JACKSON, Kenneth .... 219-989-2366.. 166 F
kjackson@pnw.edu
JACKSON, Kevin .... 254-710-1314.. 452 H
kevin_jackson@baylor.edu
JACKSON, Kim .... 509-793-2067.. 501 H
kimj@bigbend.edu
JACKSON, Kimberly .... 252-940-6252.. 347 E
kimberly.jackson@beaufortccc.edu
JACKSON, Kristin .... 609-343-4916.. 288 H
kjackson@atlantic.edu
JACKSON, Lachanna .... 513-569-1515.. 366 D
lachanna.jackson@cincinnatistate.edu
JACKSON, LaTisha .... 501-370-5229.... 21 G
ljackson@philander.edu
JACKSON, LaToya .... 646-313-8000.. 309 F
latoya.jackson@guttman.cuny.edu
JACKSON, Laura .... 903-565-5936.. 477 B
laurajackson@uttyler.edu
JACKSON, Lauren .... 318-357-5961.. 201 B
potterl@nsula.edu
JACKSON, Leah .... 318-357-4553.. 201 B
jacksonl@nsula.edu
JACKSON, Lee, F .... 214-752-8585.. 475 A
chancellor@unt.edu
JACKSON, Linda, Y .... 512-505-3006.. 459 F
lyjackson@htu.edu
JACKSON, Lisa .... 225-743-8500.. 196 J
ljackson@rpcc.edu
JACKSON, Lisa .... 617-236-5423.. 218 G
ljackson@fisher.edu
JACKSON, Lorraine .... 516-323-3051.. 321 H
ljackson@molloy.edu
JACKSON, Manda .... 870-368-2045.... 21 F
manda.jackson@ozarka.edu
JACKSON, Marci .... 704-290-5833.. 353 B
mjackson@spcc.edu
JACKSON, Margaret, W ... 931-363-9836.. 441 G
mjackson@martinmethodist.edu
JACKSON, Marian, D .... 903-510-2759.. 473 C
mjac@tjc.edu
JACKSON, Mark .... 610-519-4110.. 422 G
m.w.jackson@villanova.edu
JACKSON, Martin .... 253-879-3207.. 508 D
mjackson@pugetsound.edu
JACKSON, Mary .... 901-375-4400.. 442 F
maryjackson@midsouthchristian.edu
JACKSON, Matthews .... 530-895-2547.... 29 F
jacksonma@butte.edu
JACKSON, Melanie, M ..... 863-784-7018.. 109 G
melanie.jackson@southflorida.edu
JACKSON, Melika .... 803-780-1259.. 434 M
mjackson@voorhees.edu
JACKSON, Melodie, R ..... 717-361-1404.. 403 C
jacksonmr@etown.edu
JACKSON, Michael .... 717-871-4292.. 415 F
michael.jackson@millersville.edu
JACKSON, Michael .... 256-766-6610...... 4 B
mjackson@hcu.edu
JACKSON, Michele, H ...... 757-221-2402.. 488 F
mhjackson@wm.edu
JACKSON, Mike .... 918-463-2931.. 383 F
mike.jackson@connorsstate.edu
JACKSON, Miles .... 360-992-2934.. 502 E
mjackson@clark.edu
JACKSON, Nicole, R .... 340-693-1404.. 539 C
nicole.wheatley@uvi.edu
JACKSON, Pamela .... 910-672-1818.. 356 E
pjackson@uncfsu.edu
JACKSON, Paul .... 603-880-8308.. 288 A
tmc@thomasmorecollege.edu
JACKSON, Paul .... 603-880-8308.. 288 A
pjackson@thomasmorecollege.edu
JACKSON, Paul .... 585-245-6128.. 333 B
jackson@geneseo.edu
JACKSON, Peggy .... 870-612-2030.... 23 H
peggy.jackson@uaccb.edu
JACKSON, Philip .... 870-972-3362.... 18 H
pjackson@asusystem.edu
JACKSON, R. Brooks .... 612-626-3700.. 255 H
jacksonb@umn.edu
JACKSON, Raymond, L .... 817-272-3186.. 476 A
jackson@uta.edu
JACKSON, Richard .... 615-687-6892.. 438 C
rjackson@abcnash.edu
JACKSON, Rickey .... 928-289-6530.... 15 J
rickey.jackson@npc.edu
JACKSON, Robert .... 270-809-6912.. 192 A
rjackson@murraystate.edu
JACKSON, Robert .... 901-678-8324.. 445 C
rjax@memphis.edu
JACKSON, Robert .... 715-682-1207.. 518 H
rjackson@northland.edu
JACKSON, Robert, D .... 847-578-3248.. 153 A
robert.jackson@rosalindfranklin.edu
JACKSON, Rodney .... 336-249-8186.. 349 C
rodney_jackson@davidsonccc.edu
JACKSON, Ron .... 864-592-4817.. 432 H
jacksonr@sccsc.edu
JACKSON, Ronald .... 718-951-5000.. 307 D
JACKSON, Ronald, c .... 718-951-5352.. 307 D
rcjackson@brooklyn.cuny.edu
JACKSON, Ruth .... 207-859-4753.. 202 G
ruth.jackson@colby.edu
JACKSON, Ruth .... 310-954-4371.... 53 B
rjackson@msmu.edu
JACKSON, Ruth, R .... 405-466-3265.. 383 M
rrjackson@langston.edu
JACKSON, Sally .... 509-533-3123.. 503 A
sally.jackson@sfcc.spokane.edu
JACKSON, Sarah .... 270-686-4285.. 187 C
sarah.jackson@brescia.edu
JACKSON, Shanna .... 615-790-4419.. 446 A
sjackson@columbiatate.edu
JACKSON, Sharon, S .... 804-752-3747.. 493 C
sjackson@rmc.edu
JACKSON, Sherry .... 904-256-7212.. 103 D
sjackso@ju.edu
JACKSON, Shirley, J .... 202-806-7565.... 93 A
sjackson@howard.edu
JACKSON, Shirley Ann .... 518-276-6211.. 327 B
president@rpi.edu
JACKSON, Stanley .... 410-455-1336.. 211 G
jackson@umbc.edu
JACKSON, Starlene .... 919-718-7216.. 348 D
sjackson@cccc.edu
JACKSON, Sue .... 509-777-4596.. 509 H
sjackson@whitworth.edu
JACKSON, Susan .... 406-586-3585.. 276 I
susan.jackson@montanabiblecollege.edu
JACKSON, Tamika .... 704-971-8500.. 343 E
tjackson@charlottelaw.edu
JACKSON, Tammi .... 415-458-3726.... 42 G
tammi.jackson@dominican.edu
JACKSON, Tanise .... 850-412-5246.. 110 J
tanise.jackson@famu.edu
JACKSON, Tekesha .... 229-732-5962.. 116 C
tekeshajackson@andrewcollege.edu
JACKSON, Teresa .... 636-529-0000.. 271 D
tburgess@slchcmail.com
JACKSON, Terilyn .... 949-214-3039.... 41 F
terilyn.jackson@cui.edu
JACKSON, Terrence .... 334-872-2533...... 6 F
JACKSON, Theron .... 318-670-6000.. 199 J
tjackson@susla.edu
JACKSON, Tiffany .... 941-359-4340.. 112 E
tjackson5@sar.usf.edu
JACKSON, Tim .... 512-448-8575.. 464 G
seubookstore@texasbook.com
JACKSON, Tom .... 918-456-5511.. 384 G
jacks009@nsuok.edu
JACKSON, JR., Tom .... 605-642-6111.. 437 B
tom.jackson@bhsu.edu
JACKSON, Tondaleya .... 803-705-4479.. 427 D
jacksont@benedict.edu
JACKSON, Tonishea .... 260-481-6147.. 163 C
jacksont@ipfw.edu
JACKSON, Twana .... 304-929-6716.. 512 C
tjackson@newriver.edu
JACKSON, Tyrone .... 601-857-3232.. 258 A
tyrone.jackson@hindscc.edu
JACKSON, Vanessa .... 312-777-8562.. 142 G
vjackson@aii.edu
JACKSON, Victor .... 214-649-4060.. 458 G
vic_jackson@gial.edu
JACKSON, Vincent .... 213-763-7035.... 50 C
vjackson@lattc.edu
JACKSON, Wayne .... 407-823-2716.. 111 E
wayne.jackson@ucf.edu
JACKSON, Weldon .... 301-860-3460.. 212 D
wjackson@bowiestate.edu
JACKSON, Wendy .... 704-216-6158.. 346 A
wjackso@livingstone.edu
JACKSON, William .... 301-891-4475.. 213 D
wjackson@wau.edu
JACKSON, William .... 217-234-5296.. 145 D
wjackson60312@lakeland.cc.il.us
JACKSON, Wilma .... 402-826-8620.. 280 B
wilma.jackson@doane.edu
JACKSON, Zena .... 817-515-3010.. 467 A
zena.jackson@tccd.edu
JACKSON-DAVIS,
Dorothy, G .... 601-877-6460.. 256 F
djdavis@alcorn.edu
JACKSON-ELMOORE,
Cynthia .... 517-355-2326.. 237 I
jacks174@msu.edu
JACKSON-HAMMOND,
Cynthia .... 937-376-6332.. 365 H
chammond@centralstate.edu

JAMES, Lisa 719-502-2056 82 B lisa.james@ppcc.edu
JAMES, Margaret 814-871-7238 404 A james015@gannon.edu
JAMES, Mark, S 816-604-1011 267 F mark.james@mcckc.edu
JAMES, Mary, B 503-777-7250 394 I mjames@reed.edu
JAMES, Matricia 716-375-2000 328 B mjames@sbu.edu
JAMES, Michael 360-676-2772 505 C mjames@nwic.edu
JAMES, Mike 501-279-4529 20 D james@harding.edu
JAMES, Mike 956-665-2451 476 E mike.james@utrgv.edu
JAMES, Monique 734-677-5327 242 G mdjames@wccnet.edu
JAMES, Pansy 212-594-4000 337 F pjames@tcicollege.edu
JAMES, Patricia 425-564-3152 501 F patricia.james@bellevuecollege.edu
JAMES, Patrick 256-824-6942 8 F patrick.james@uah.edu
JAMES, Patrick 312-629-6600 154 A pjames@saic.edu
JAMES, Paula 617-274-3331 225 C paula.james@mcphs.edu
JAMES, Peggy 262-595-2101 520 F james@uwp.edu
JAMES, Penny 402-354-7225 281 F penny.james@methodistcollege.edu
JAMES, Richard, L 801-585-5690 481 M rljames@usa.utah.edu
JAMES, Ronald 415-476-4181 70 D ron.james@ucsf.edu
JAMES, Ruby, F 217-420-6029 148 D rjames@millikin.edu
JAMES, Sarah, R 812-941-2020 163 F jamessr@ius.edu
JAMES, Scott 978-542-6243 222 D jscott@salemstate.edu
JAMES, Sean, P 661-336-5165 47 I sjames@kccd.edu
JAMES, Shauna 256-331-5368 6 A sjames@nwscc.edu
JAMES, Shauna 256-765-4279 9 C sljames@una.edu
JAMES, Skip 850-973-9477 105 H jamess@nfcc.edu
JAMES, Steven 865-981-8802 441 H steven.james@maryvillecollege.edu
JAMES, Susan, M 757-822-1084 498 H sjames@tcc.edu
JAMES, Sylvia 253-964-6715 506 B
JAMES, Thomas 212-678-3050 337 E james@tc.edu
JAMES, Timmy 256-331-6281 6 A timmy.james@nwscc.edu
JAMES, Tracy 636-481-3187 266 C tjames@jeffco.edu
JAMES, Vernon 706-880-8979 123 K vjames@lagrange.edu
JAMES, W. Brian 706-245-7226 120 D bjames@ec.edu
JAMES, Wayne 219-980-7222 163 B wljames@iun.edu
JAMES BLACKWELL, Leanna 413-565-1000 215 A ljamesblackwell@baypath.edu
JAMES-MOORE, Annette 901-272-5153 442 B amoore@mca.edu
JAMES PRYOR, Jennifer 914-323-5299 319 N jj.pryor@mville.edu
JAMESON, Deborah 603-577-6161 286 I djameson@dwc.edu
JAMESON, Dennis 916-577-2200 75 C djameson@jessup.edu
JAMESON, Gretchen, M 262-243-5700 516 E gretchen.jameson@cuw.edu
JAMESON, J, L 215-898-6796 421 E ljameson@mail.med.upenn.edu
JAMESON, Kim 405-682-1611 385 D kjameson@occc.edu
JAMESON, Maisha 510-464-3236 57 D mjameson@peralta.edu
JAMESON, Sean 914-395-2494 329 K sjameson@sarahlawrence.edu
JAMESON, Stacey 212-924-5900 336 I sjameson@swedishinstitute.edu
JAMIESON, Michelle, E 724-287-8711 399 B michelle.jamieson@bc3.edu
JAMIESON, Richard, J 216-368-3720 365 B rjj@case.edu
JAMIESON-DRAKE, David 919-684-0736 343 J david.jamieson.drake@duke.edu
JAMIL, Hasan 713-313-1953 470 D jamil_hx@tsu.edu
JAMISON, Calvin, D 972-883-2213 476 C cjamison@utdallas.edu
JAMISON, Charles 610-409-3607 422 D cjamison@ursinus.edu
JAMISON, David, L 412-397-6225 418 B jamison@rmu.edu
JAMISON, Kristin, E 217-245-3046 141 G kristin.jamison@mail.ic.edu
JAMISON, Leslie 609-343-5004 288 H ljamison@atlantic.edu
JAMISON, Matt 303-678-3845 80 E matt.jamison@frontrange.edu
JAMISON, Todd, M 740-587-5712 368 B jamisont@denison.edu
JAMROGOWICZ, John 843-574-6136 433 D john.jamrogowicz@tridenttech.edu
JAMROS, Brian 503-280-8554 391 A bjamros@cu-portland.edu
JANAIRO, Ed 920-693-1871 523 E ed.janairo@gotoltc.edu
JANAK, Bickram 443-885-3333 209 F bickram.janak@morgan.edu
JANAK, Kenneth 817-257-5712 469 G k.janak@tcu.edu
JANARO, Walter, A 540-636-2900 488 D walter@christendom.edu
JANCHENKO, Michael 312-329-4495 148 F michael.janchenko@moody.edu
JANDA, Kenneth, C 949-824-6022 69 C kcjanda@uci.edu
JANDHYALA, Vikram 206-543-0905 508 E vj@uw.edu
JANDRIS, Thomas 708-209-3597 138 G thomas.jandris@cuchicago.edu
JANELLE, William, P 603-862-2650 288 C william.janelle@unh.edu
JANES, Kristin 828-669-8012 346 M kjanes@montreat.edu
JANES, Michael, G 215-596-8697 422 A m.janes@usciences.edu
JANESCH, Cynthia, D 570-577-3763 398 L cindy.janesch@bucknell.edu
JANG, Michelle 714-533-1495 65 B michelle@southbaylo.edu
JANIK, Julie 972-721-4127 473 D jjanik@udallas.edu
JANIK, Mary Mark 716-896-0700 339 E janik@villa.edu
JANINI, Thom 330-287-1287 375 B janini.4@osu.edu
JANIS, Robert, J 312-362-8762 139 C bjanis@depaul.edu
JANIS, Roger 530-226-4758 64 H rjanis@simpsonu.edu
JANITZ, Suzanne 607-431-4244 315 E janitzs@hartwick.edu
JANKE, Louise, L 608-785-8604 520 C ljanke@uwlax.edu
JANKIEWICZ, Stacy 856-222-9311 295 C sjankiewicz@rcbc.edu
JANKO, Karen 312-777-8666 142 G kjanko@aii.edu
JANKOVIAK, Michael, W 989-386-6603 238 B mjankoviak@midmich.edu
JANKOWSKI, Cheryl 440-934-3101 374 F cjankowski@ohiobusinesscollege.edu
JANKOWSKI, Mark 518-587-2100 335 D mark.jankowski@esc.edu
JANKOWSKI, Phillip 219-989-2670 166 F phil.janskowski@pnw.edu
JANKOWSKI NIEMCZURA, Leslie 614-222-3225 367 B
JANNE, Rex 979-845-4570 468 B r-janne@tamu.edu
JANNEY, Cindy 507-389-1011 250 E cynthia.janney@mnsu.edu
JANNEY, Dell Ann 573-288-6388 264 F djanney@culver.edu
JANNEY, Suzanne 941-487-4110 111 D janney@ncf.edu
JANOSKY, Janine 313-593-5090 242 A jjanosky@umich.edu
JANOW, Merit, E 212-854-4604 311 E mj60@columbia.edu
JANOWSKI, Barbara 832-584-5122 127 D bjanowski@southuniversity.edu
JANOWSKI, Lori 212-650-3133 308 D lori.janowski@hunter.cuny.edu
JANSE, Korey 661-255-1050 30 E
JANSEN, James 208-562-2646 133 F jamesjansen@cwidaho.cc
JANSEN, James, S 402-280-1804 279 H jimjansen@creighton.edu
JANSEN, Mark 815-599-3455 141 E mark.jansen@highland.edu
JANSEN, Sandy 865-974-6611 448 D sjansen@utk.edu
JANSEN, Shelley 970-943-2101 84 H sjansen@western.edu
JANSMA, Dana 269-337-7210 235 H dana.jansma@kzoo.edu
JANSMA, Pamela 303-556-2557 84 A pamela.jansma@ucdenver.edu
JANSSEN, Jessica 402-941-6523 280 N janssen@midlandu.edu
JANSSEN, Jill, M 815-599-3412 141 E jill.janssen@highland.edu
JANSSEN, Michelle, L 765-361-6365 169 C janssenm@wabash.edu
JANSSON, Hilary 401-825-1122 425 A hjansson@ccri.edu
JANSSON, Jimilea 580-628-6771 384 L jimilea.jansson@noc.edu
JANUS, Cindy 808-739-4674 130 F cindy.janus@chaminade.edu
JANUSCH, Barry 360-475-7458 505 F bjanusch@olympic.edu
JANUTIS, Rachel 614-236-6383 364 N rjanutis@law.capital.edu
JANZ, Curtis 405-425-5358 385 C curtis.janz@oc.edu
JANZ, Jeff 414-288-7206 517 I jeff.janz@marquette.edu
JANZ, Kenneth 507-457-2299 252 G kjanz@winona.edu
JANZ, Mary 414-288-7208 517 I mary.janz@marquette.edu
JANZEN, Amy 405-425-5907 385 C amy.janzen@oc.edu
JANZEN, Scott 574-296-6213 158 H registrar@ambs.edu
JANZEN, Teresa 616-222-3000 236 F tjanzen@kuyper.edu
JAQUES, Kate 916-484-8654 51 A jaquesk@arc.losrios.edu
JAQUES, Kate 916-608-6653 51 C jaquesk@flc.losrios.edu
JAQUES, Richard 703-784-2105 528 A richard.jaques@usmc.mil
JAQUILLARD, Jenny 800-869-7223 126 E jjaquill@scad.edu
JARACZEWSKI, John 262-595-2591 520 F john.jaraczewski@uwp.edu
JARAMILLO, Brooke 229-333-2100 130 A brooke.jaramillo@wiregrass.edu
JARAMILLO, Ed 360-416-7719 507 G ed.jaramillo@skagit.edu
JARAMILLO, Jessica 505-454-3593 300 F jessica@nmhu.edu
JARAMILLO, John 949-582-4311 65 G jjaramillo@saddleback.edu
JARAMILLO, Justin 303-315-1845 84 A justin.jaramillo@ucdenver.edu
JARAMILLO FLEMING, Melissa 575-835-5880 300 G mjaramillo@admin.nmt.edu
JARBOE, Dan 870-245-5591 21 E jarboed@obu.edu
JARBOE, Marlena 540-453-2260 496 F jarboem@brcc.edu
JARBOE, Shannon, K 240-895-4309 210 E skjarboe@smcm.edu
JARDINE, Daniel, D 607-587-4036 334 G jardindd@alfredstate.edu
JARDINE, David 269-471-3965 230 H djardine@andrews.edu
JARETT, Sadie 334-874-5700 3 A sjarett@ccal.edu
JARICH, Amy 510-642-3175 68 M awjarich@berkeley.edu
JARLEY, Paul 407-823-2181 111 E pjarley@bus.ucf.edu
JARMIN MILLER, Catherine 503-883-2494 392 B cjarmin@linfield.edu
JARMULOWICZ, Linda, D 901-678-5800 445 C ljrmlwcz@memphis.edu
JARMUZ, Nick 312-935-6651 152 D njarmuz@robertmorris.edu
JARNAGIN, Lea, M 909-869-3310 31 J lmjarnagin@cpp.edu
JARNAGIN, Missy 805-437-3282 32 B missy.jarnagin@csuci.edu
JARONSKI, Ann 813-974-3598 112 C atj1@usf.edu
JAROSZ, John 402-354-7065 281 F john.jarosz@methodistcollege.edu
JAROT, Lisa 847-628-1572 144 B ljarot@judsonu.edu
JARR, William 770-426-2632 124 B wdjarr@life.edu
JARRATT, Frances, L 864-503-5195 434 G fjarratt@uscupstate.edu
JARRELL, Anne 850-729-6040 105 I southara@nwfsc.edu
JARRELL, Bruce, E 410-706-2304 211 F bjarrell@umaryland.edu
JARRELL, James 443-997-6393 208 D jjarrell@jhu.edu
JARRELL, Lacey 541-882-3521 391 F jarrell@klamathcc.edu
JARRELL, Michelle 205-391-2328 6 G mjarrell@sheltonstate.edu
JARRELL, Paul 805-965-0581 63 D pejarrell@sbcc.edu
JARRELL, Sasha 850-729-5360 105 I jarrells@nwfsc.edu
JARRELL, Sheila 928-776-2188 18 D sheila.jarrell@yc.edu
JARRET, Ronald 508-793-2541 217 C rjarret@holycross.edu
JARRETT, Amy 864-644-5000 432 G
JARRETT, Courtney 540-535-3461 494 B cjarrett1@su.edu
JARRETT, Dustin 304-243-2312 515 C djarrett@wju.edu
JARRETT, James 863-680-4459 101 E jjarrett@flsouthern.edu
JARRETT, Juan 706-542-2621 128 E jarrettj@uga.edu
JARRETT, Katrina 704-216-6004 346 A kjarrett@livingstone.edu
JARRY, Timothy 508-793-2515 217 C tjarry@holycross.edu
JARSTFER, Amiel 423-869-6203 441 E amiel.jarstfer@lmunet.edu
JARUSZEWICZ, Candace, L 843-953-5606 428 G jaruszewiczc@cofc.edu
JARVIS, Cliff 573-875-7300 263 F csjarvis@email.ccis.edu
JARVIS, Jeffrey, A 419-227-3141 380 A jjarvis@unoh.edu
JARVIS, Keith 307-532-8255 526 G keith.jarvis@ewc.wy.edu
JARZABSKI, Kerri, P 413-782-1312 229 E kerri.jarzabski@wne.edu
JARZYNA, Dave 260-665-4270 167 E jarzynad@trine.edu
JASCOR, Barb 715-422-5476 523 G barb.jascor@mstc.edu
JASEK, Michael, D 575-646-1722 300 J mjasek@nmsu.edu
JASHINSKI, Michelle, L 814-371-2090 420 H mjashinski@triangle-tech.edu
JASHO, Gay-linn 404-880-8892 118 K gjasho@cau.edu
JASINSKI, John 660-562-1110 269 J johnj@nwmissouri.edu
JASKEN, Julia 410-857-2247 209 D jjasken@mcdaniel.edu
JASKOVIAK, Paul 281-487-1170 469 F pjaskoviak@txchiro.edu
JASMAN, Troy 712-274-6400 177 I troy.jasman@witcc.edu
JASMIN, Reba 256-372-8692 1 A reba.jasmin@aamu.edu
JASON, Hoerr, U 610-921-7221 396 H jhoerr@albright.edu
JASON, Karen 508-531-2750 221 C kjason@bridgew.edu
JASPERSON, Steve 909-706-8661 74 K sjasperson@westernu.edu
JASS, Lori, K 503-517-1320 396 D ljass@warnerpacific.edu
JASSO, Sonia 210-805-5814 474 D sjasso@uiwtx.edu
JASTI, Bhaskara 209-946-3162 71 C bjasti@pacific.edu
JASTORFF, Mark, A 970-247-7074 80 D majastorff@fortlewis.edu
JASTORFF, Michael 605-642-6279 437 B michael.jastorff@bhsu.edu
JASUR, Angela 631-420-2717 335 E angela.jasur@farmingdale.edu
JASWAL, Faisal 425-564-6151 501 F fjaswal@bellevuecollege.edu
JASZKA, Michael, S 716-286-8343 324 E msj@niagara.edu
JATTKOWSKI-HUDSON, Anna, J 815-226-3392 152 G ajattkowski-hudson@rockford.edu
JAUNARAJS, Imants 740-593-2909 375 H jaunaraj@ohio.edu
JAURON, Lester 530-895-2266 29 F jauronle@butte.edu
JAVAHERIPOUR, G. H 530-741-6707 76 D gjavaher@yccd.edu
JAVARIZ, Gerardo 787-890-2681 537 E gerardo.javariz@upr.edu
JAVDEKAR, Chitra 781-239-2585 223 F cjavdekar@massbay.edu
JAVIER, Byron, A 312-850-7126 138 A
JAVOR, Seta 818-767-0888 75 D seta.javor@woodbury.edu
JAVOROSKI, Alan 715-422-5402 523 G al.javoroski@mstc.edu
JAWAHAR, Jim 309-438-7018 143 B jimoham@ilstu.edu
JAY, Carmen 619-388-7532 60 H cjay@sdccd.edu
JAY, Jodye 903-586-2518 460 A jjay@jacksonville-college.edu

JAYARAMAN, Ruki .... 224-293-5600.. 135 A
rjayaraman@aiuonline.edu
JAYASURIYA, Kumara ..... 304-766-3146.. 514 B
kjayasuriya@wvstateu.edu
JAYAWICKREMA, Arosha . 860-768-4276.... 89 G
jaya@hartford.edu
JAYE, Marilyn .... 617-559-8642.. 219 E
mjaye@hebrewcollege.edu
JAYNE, Bindu, K .... 828-262-2144.. 356 B
jaynebk@appstate.edu
JAYNE, Delaina .... 570-408-5000.. 423 G
JAYNE, Delaina .... 570-945-8130.. 406 H
delaina.jayne@keystone.edu
JAYNE, Joann .... 718-429-6600.. 339 D
joann.jayne@vaughn.edu
JAYNES, Kathy .... 406-265-4147.. 277 E
kjaynes@msun.edu
JAYNES, Lorene .... 406-771-4305.. 277 F
ljaynes@gfcmsu.edu
JAYNES, Tom .... 919-536-7250.. 349 D
jaynest@durhamtech.edu
JAZDZEWSKI, Richard, L 262-472-1305.. 521 F
jazdzewr@uww.edu
JAZWIECKI, Gabrielle, E .. 203-837-8281.... 85 I
jazwieckig@wcsu.edu
JAZZABI, Monica .... 323-343-3342.... 33 C
mjazzabi@cslanet.calstatela.edu
JBARA, Craig .... 269-353-1263.. 235 I
cjbara@kvcc.edu
JEAN, Libby .... 269-749-7655.. 240 A
ljean@olivetcollege.edu
JEAN, Marc .... 201-216-9901.. 291 C
marc.jean@eicollege.edu
JEAN, Martin, D .... 203-432-9681.... 90 D
martin.jean@yale.edu
JEAN, Paul .... 508-531-2660.. 221 C
paul.jean@bridgew.edu
JEAN-JACQUES, Alex ...... 617-427-0060.. 224 F
ajean-jacques@rcc.mass.edu
JEAN-LOUIS, Patrick .... 617-541-5388.. 224 F
pjeanlouis@rcc.mass.edu
JEAN-MARIE, Gaëtane ..... 319-273-2717.. 170 A
gaetane.jean-marie@uni.edu
JEANCAKE, Chris .... 912-427-1958.. 119 B
cjeancake@coastalpines.edu
JEANFREAU, Jennifer, N . 504-865-2282.. 198 E
jnjeanfr@loyno.edu
JEANOTTE, Leigh .... 701-777-4291.. 360 C
leigh.jeanotte@und.edu
JEBALI, Lisa .... 978-837-5109.. 225 E
lisa.jebali@merrimack.edu
JEBB, Cindy .... 845-938-2000.. 529 C
8dean@usma.edu
JECH, Sue .... 507-433-0610.. 251 H
sue.jech@riverland.edu
JECHURA, Kacey .... 303-300-8740.... 77 F
kacey.jechura@collegeamerica.com
JEDNAK, P. Michael .... 860-486-4741.... 89 D
michael.jednak@uconn.edu
JEELANI, Shaik .... 334-727-8970...... 8 A
jeelanis@mytu.tuskegee.edu
JEFFERIES-JACKSON,
Tamara .... 803-536-8103.. 432 E
thughes@scsu.edu
JEFFERS, Carrie .... 586-286-2187.. 237 C
jeffersc@macomb.edu
JEFFERS, Karen .... 918-595-7441.. 388 F
karen.jeffers@tulsacc.edu
JEFFERSON, Adriene .... 772-462-7156.. 103 B
ajeffers@irsc.edu
JEFFERSON, Barbie, F ..... 864-597-4237.. 435 C
jeffersonbf@wofford.edu
JEFFERSON, Donald .... 334-874-5700...... 3 A
djefferson@ccal.edu
JEFFERSON, Doug .... 817-598-6247.. 479 E
djefferson@wc.edu
JEFFERSON, Henry .... 606-759-7141.. 190 C
henry.jefferson@kctcs.edu
JEFFERSON, Jennifer .... 781-239-2625.. 223 F
jjefferson@massbay.edu
JEFFERSON, Joy, L .... 757-683-3097.. 492 G
jljeffer@odu.edu
JEFFERSON, Karl, E .... 301-937-8448.. 206 F
karl.jefferson@brightwood.edu
JEFFERSON, Lynda .... 803-780-1279.. 434 M
jefferson@voorhees.edu
JEFFERSON, Lynne, T ...... 919-516-4116.. 355 D
ltjefferson@st-aug.edu
JEFFERSON, Mara .... 919-890-7500.... 93 F
JEFFERSON, Michael .... 707-965-7080.... 56 A
mjeffereson@puc.edu
JEFFERSON, Patrick .... 713-221-8428.. 474 B
jeffersonpa@uhd.edu
JEFFERSON, Richard, P .... 617-552-3334.. 216 C
richard.jefferson@bc.edu
JEFFERSON, Shirley .... 802-831-1333.. 485 F
sjefferson@vermontlaw.edu
JEFFERSON, Venessa, F .. 803-934-3175.. 431 E
vjefferson@morris.edu
JEFFERSON, Willie .... 803-780-1049.. 434 M
williej@voorhees.edu

JEFFERY, Charles .... 623-845-3692.... 14 C
charles.jeffery@gccaz.edu
JEFFERY, John, A .... 610-660-1062.. 418 G
jjeffery@sju.edu
JEFFERY, Kathryn, E .... 310-434-4200.... 63 F
jeffery_kathryn@smc.edu
JEFFRESS, Conway, A ...... 734-462-4400.. 240 H
jeffress@schoolcraft.edu
JEFFREY, David, K .... 540-568-7044.. 490 J
jeffredk@jmu.edu
JEFFREY, Don .... 334-983-6556...... 7 H
djeffr@troy.edu
JEFFREY, Douglas .... 517-607-2518.. 235 E
djeffrey@hillsdale.edu
JEFFREY, Kim .... 806-874-3571.. 454 F
kim.jeffrey@clarendoncollege.edu
JEFFREY, Russell .... 512-313-3000.. 455 F
russell.jeffrey@concordia.edu
JEFFREYS, Wendell .... 903-566-7110.. 477 B
wjeffreys@uttyler.edu
JEFFRIES, Browning .... 404-872-3593.. 117 B
bjeffries@johnmarshall.edu
JEFFRIES, Christopher ...... 504-816-4662.. 195 B
cjeffries@dillard.edu
JEFFRIES, Frankie .... 901-435-1530.. 441 C
frankie_jeffries@loc.edu
JEFFRIES, Jolander .... 773-291-6413.. 137 G
jjeffries@ccc.edu
JEFFRIES, Michael .... 660-543-8203.. 273 C
jeffries@ucmo.edu
JEFFRIES, Pamela, R .... 202-994-8429.... 92 D
pjeffries@gwu.edu
JEFFRIES, Rick .... 863-669-2840.. 106 I
rjeffries@polk.edu
JEFFRIES, Shellie .... 616-632-2130.. 231 A
jeffrmic@aquinas.edu
JEFFRIES, Susan, K .... 580-327-8570.. 384 M
skjeffries@nwosu.edu
JEFFRIES, Terry .... 937-708-5544.. 381 B
tjeffries@wilberforce.edu
JEFFRION, William .... 504-520-6780.. 202 C
wjeffrio@xula.edu
JEFIMENKO, Otto .... 219-981-4291.. 163 B
ojefimen@iun.edu
JEFREMOW, George .... 212-217-4420.. 314 B
george_jefremow@fitnyc.edu
JEHNINGS, Marcia .... 860-512-2603.... 86 E
mjehnings@manchestercc.edu
JEKA, Mary, R .... 617-627-4220.. 228 H
mary.jeka@tufts.edu
JELINEK, John, A .... 312-329-4185.. 148 F
john.jelinek@moody.edu
JELINKOVA, Klara .... 713-348-2211.. 464 E
klara.jelinkova@rice.edu
JELLEMA, Kate .... 802-451-7510.. 484 C
katej@gradschool.marlboro.edu
JELLERSON, George .... 804-862-6212.. 493 F
gjellerson@rbc.edu
JELLISON, Rebecca .... 269-782-1241.. 241 C
rjellison@swmich.edu
JEMIOLA, Richard .... 757-352-4028.. 493 E
richjem@regent.edu
JEMISON, Jan .... 415-565-4723.... 69 B
jemisonj@uchastings.edu
JEMISON, William .... 315-268-6509.. 310 B
wjemison@clarkson.edu
JENAL, Robert, E .... 508-856-3892.. 221 B
robert.jenal@umassmed.edu
JENCKS, Doyle .... 580-477-7736.. 389 I
doyle.jencks@wosc.edu
JENDRASZAK, Stephen ...... 612-330-1182.. 244 I
jendra@augsburg.edu
JENE, Beverly .... 802-322-1650.. 483 H
beverly.jene@goddard.edu
JENERETTE, Kim .... 937-766-7866.. 365 C
kimjenerette@cedarville.edu
JENIK, Jeff .... 803-641-3258.. 433 G
jeffj@usca.edu
JENIOUS, Anita .... 615-322-4705.. 449 A
anita.jenious@vanderbilt.edu
JENKINS, Adam .... 660-248-6247.. 263 B
ajenkins@centralmethodist.edu
JENKINS, Allen .... 718-933-6700.. 321 I
ajenkins@monroecollege.edu
JENKINS, Amelia .... 504-520-7541.. 202 C
ajenki10@xula.edu
JENKINS, Anthony, L .... 304-766-3111.. 514 B
anthony.jenkins@wvstateu.edu
JENKINS, Bethany .... 212-659-7284.. 318 D
bjenkins@tkc.edu
JENKINS, Betty, A .... 803-705-4808.. 427 D
jenkinsb@benedict.edu
JENKINS, Bobby .... 580-349-1376.. 385 F
bjenkins@opsu.edu
JENKINS, Brandon .... 919-735-5151.. 354 A
bmjenkins@waynecc.edu
JENKINS, Brandon .... 919-739-6841.. 354 A
bmjenkins@waynecc.edu
JENKINS, Brian .... 301-687-3106.. 212 F
bjenkins@frostburg.edu

JENKINS, Briar .... 580-477-7700.. 389 I
briar.jenkins@wosc.edu
JENKINS, Bryan .... 919-807-7147.. 347 B
jenkinsb@nccommunitycolleges.edu
JENKINS, Cara .... 610-436-3513.. 416 C
cjenkins@wcupa.edu
JENKINS, Carri, P .... 801-422-1166.. 480 C
carri_jenkins@byu.edu
JENKINS, Cheryl, S .... 919-760-8338.. 346 D
jenkinsc@meredith.edu
JENKINS, Daniel .... 334-874-5700...... 3 A
djenkins@ccal.edu
JENKINS, Deborah, D .... 410-334-2904.. 213 G
djenkins@worwic.edu
JENKINS, Doug .... 417-865-2815.. 265 B
jenkinsd@evangel.edu
JENKINS, Drew .... 615-329-8690.. 439 L
djenkins@fisk.edu
JENKINS, Ernest .... 919-530-7639.. 357 A
ernest.jenkins@nccu.edu
JENKINS, Freddie .... 229-732-5919.. 116 C
freddiejenkins@andrewcollege.edu
JENKINS, G. Scott .... 336-334-7977.. 356 F
gsjenkin@ncat.edu
JENKINS, Garry .... 612-625-4841.. 255 H
JENKINS, Geraldine, M .... 440-646-8322.. 380 F
gerri.jenkins@ursuline.edu
JENKINS, Gloria .... 574-284-4723.. 167 A
gjenkins@saintmarys.edu
JENKINS, H.E .... 512-313-3000.. 455 F
he.jenkins@concordia.edu
JENKINS, J Marshall .... 706-236-2259.. 117 F
mjenkins@berry.edu
JENKINS, Jacqueline, M ...... 212-752-1530.. 318 F
jacqueline.jenkins@limcollege.edu
JENKINS, Jade .... 803-780-1019.. 434 M
jade@voorhees.edu
JENKINS, Jan .... 479-968-0456.... 19 F
ejenkins@atu.edu
JENKINS, Jeffrey, L .... 812-877-8209.. 166 H
jenkins@rose-hulman.edu
JENKINS, Jim .... 909-274-4570.... 53 C
jjenkins@mtsac.edu
JENKINS, SR., Jimmy, R ..... 704-216-6098.. 346 A
jjenkins@livingstone.edu
JENKINS, Jo Ann .... 708-608-4199.. 148 G
jenkinsj52@morainevalley.edu
JENKINS, John, A .... 404-527-4520.. 118 F
jjenkins@carver.edu
JENKINS, CSC, John I .... 574-631-3903.. 168 E
jenkins.1@nd.edu
JENKINS, Joyce, O .... 501-420-1242.... 18 F
joyce.jenkins@arkansasbaptist.edu
JENKINS, Kara .... 540-535-3572.. 494 B
kjenkins@su.edu
JENKINS, Katrina .... 407-646-2115.. 107 C
kejenkins@rollins.edu
JENKINS, Katrina, E .... 217-245-3060.. 141 G
katrina.jenkins@mail.ic.edu
JENKINS, Keith .... 585-475-7404.. 327 E
kbjgpt@rit.edu
JENKINS, Keith .... 936-294-1759.. 471 D
rca_kej@shsu.edu
JENKINS, Kevin .... 870-307-7220.... 21 A
kevin.jenkins@lyon.edu
JENKINS, Lucy .... 603-578-8991.. 286 E
ljenkins@ccsnh.edu
JENKINS, Malia .... 619-201-8728.... 60 D
malia.jenkins@sdcc.edu
JENKINS, Matt .... 304-263-0979.. 511 F
mjenkins@valley.edu
JENKINS, Melanie .... 617-573-5702.. 228 G
mjenkins@suffolk.edu
JENKINS, Mike .... 903-983-8189.. 460 D
mjenkins@kilgore.edu
JENKINS, Morris .... 573-651-2178.. 272 B
mjenkins@semo.edu
JENKINS, Nichelle .... 212-280-1317.. 333 I
njenkins@uts.columbia.edu
JENKINS, Nick .... 828-328-7356.. 345 H
nick.jenkins@lr.edu
JENKINS, Patsy .... 318-473-6474.. 197 J
pjenkins@lsua.edu
JENKINS, Paul .... 513-244-4351.. 373 C
paul.jenkins@msj.edu
JENKINS, Ramal .... 410-837-4821.. 213 C
rjenkins@ubalt.edu
JENKINS, Rebecca .... 419-434-5692.. 379 E
jenkinsr1@findlay.edu
JENKINS, Robert .... 909-384-8662.... 60 C
rjenkins@sbccd.cc.ca.us
JENKINS, Robert .... 903-877-7777.. 477 E
robert.jenkins@uth.tmc.edu
JENKINS, Robert .... 713-500-3334.. 477 C
robert.jenkins@uth.tmc.edu
JENKINS, Rod .... 972-708-7369.. 458 G
rod_jenkins@gial.edu
JENKINS, Rodney .... 570-484-2253.. 415 D
rj2253@lhup.edu
JENKINS, Sam .... 770-537-6012.. 129 M
sam.jenkins@westgatech.edu

JENKINS, Sharon .... 575-439-3806.. 301 A
djenkins@nmsu.edu
JENKINS, Sonja .... 478-988-6800.. 118 H
sjenkins@centralgatech.edu
JENKINS, Sonja .... 478-218-3308.. 118 G
sjenkins@centralgatech.edu
JENKINS, Stephen .... 678-466-4143.. 119 A
stephenjenkins@clayton.edu
JENKINS, Steve .... 619-201-8720.... 60 D
steve.jenkins@sdcc.edu
JENKINS, Steven .... 740-392-6868.. 373 D
steven.jenkins@mvnu.edu
JENKINS, Sylvia .... 708-974-5201.. 148 G
president@morainevalley.edu
JENKINS, Tara, F .... 508-854-4249.. 224 E
tjenkins@qcc.mass.edu
JENKINS, Timothy, S .... 219-464-5411.. 168 F
tim.jenkins@valpo.edu
JENKINS, Vanessa, C .... 757-823-8173.. 492 F
vcjenkins@nsu.edu
JENKS, Ann, M .... 269-337-7297.. 235 H
ann.jenks@kzoo.edu
JENKS, Catherine .... 678-839-6449.. 129 E
cjenks@westga.edu
JENKS, Dean .... 503-517-1093.. 396 D
djenks@warnerpacific.edu
JENKS, Debra .... 414-277-4516.. 518 E
jenks@msoe.edu
JENKS, Wayne .... 919-761-2277.. 355 I
wjenks@sebts.edu
JENNEMAN, Eugene, A .... 231-995-1572.. 239 C
ejenneman@nmc.edu
JENNETTE, Judy .... 252-789-0310.. 351 A
jjennette@martincc.edu
JENNETTEN, Tory .... 309-677-2259.. 136 B
tory@fsmail.bradley.edu
JENNINGS, Arbolina, L .... 713-313-7661.. 470 D
jennings_al@tsu.edu
JENNINGS, Barbara .... 641-844-5522.. 173 J
barb.jennings@iavalley.edu
JENNINGS, Bill .... 541-880-2247.. 391 F
jenningsb@klamathcc.edu
JENNINGS, Bret .... 256-765-4658...... 9 C
nmjennings@una.edu
JENNINGS, Carlette .... 404-876-1227.. 118 C
carlette.jennings@bccr.edu
JENNINGS, Charla .... 870-743-3000.... 21 C
charlam@northark.edu
JENNINGS, Charles .... 209-954-5040.... 61 F
cjennings@deltacollege.edu
JENNINGS, Chris .... 213-624-1200.... 43 J
cjennings@fidm.edu
JENNINGS, Christal .... 610-225-5102.. 403 B
cjenning@eastern.edu
JENNINGS, David, C .... 845-675-4616.. 325 C
david.jennings@nyack.edu
JENNINGS, Diana, E .... 508-531-1382.. 221 C
diana.jennings@bridgew.edu
JENNINGS, Donna .... 630-353-9069.. 139 D
djennings@devrygroup.com
JENNINGS, Hope .... 937-775-4818.. 381 H
hope.jennings@wright.edu
JENNINGS, Jamie .... 541-880-2228.. 391 F
jennings@klamathcc.edu
JENNINGS, John, L .... 903-813-2410.. 451 M
jjennings@austincollege.edu
JENNINGS, Lisa .... 603-645-9770.. 287 I
l.jennings@snhu.edu
JENNINGS, Liz .... 651-361-3411.. 247 K
liz.jennings@mcnallysmith.edu
JENNINGS, Lynn .... 252-335-0821.. 349 A
lynn_jennings@albemarle.edu
JENNINGS, Pamela .... 336-354-7358.. 358 E
jenningsp@uncsa.edu
JENNINGS, Patricia .... 203-596-4693.... 88 F
pjennings@post.edu
JENNINGS, Sarah, E .... 870-235-4040.... 22 F
sejennings@saumag.edu
JENNINGS, Susan .... 423-697-2576.. 445 D
susan.jennings@chattanoogastate.edu
JENNINGS, Thomas, W .... 850-645-9655.. 111 C
tjennings@fsu.edu
JENNINGS, Todd .... 909-537-5655.... 34 C
tjennin@csusb.edu
JENNISON, Barry .... 423-697-2614.. 445 D
barry.jennison@chattanoogastate.edu
JENNUM, Joe .... 909-274-4630.... 53 C
jjennum@mtsac.edu
JENOURE, Rita .... 202-651-5005.... 92 C
rita.jenoure@gallaudet.edu
JENSEN, Betty .... 850-201-8235.. 113 E
jensenb@tcc.fl.edu
JENSEN, Brenda .... 808-236-3533.. 130 H
bjensen@hpu.edu
JENSEN, Brian, C .... 724-847-6134.. 404 B
bcjensen@geneva.edu
JENSEN, Christopher .... 270-745-5065.. 194 D
christopher.jensen@wku.edu
JENSEN, Chuck .... 406-444-0319.. 276 J
cjensen@montana.edu

JENSEN, Dale 417-865-2815 265 B
jensend@evangel.edu
JENSEN, Dan 712-279-3734 176 E
dan.jensen@stlukescollege.edu
JENSEN, Dan 817-735-2500 475 C
danny.jensen@unthsc.edu
JENSEN, David, H 512-404-4821 452 A
djensen@austinseminary.edu
JENSEN, Doug 661-722-6300 27 B
djensen@avc.edu
JENSEN, Eric, R 309-556-3151 143 D
president@iwu.edu
JENSEN, Gail 210-458-4105 477 A
gail.jensen@utsa.edu
JENSEN, Gail, M 402-280-3727 279 H
gailjensen@creighton.edu
JENSEN, Genevieve, M 718-357-4522 329 E
gjensen@edaff.com
JENSEN, Jed 307-686-0254 526 M
jjensen@sheridan.edu
JENSEN, Jennifer, M 610-758-3705 408 H
jmj313@lehigh.edu
JENSEN, John, A 540-458-8604 500 F
jensenj@wlu.edu
JENSEN, Joshua 509-527-5768 509 G
jensenj@whitman.edu
JENSEN, Kae 208-562-3336 133 F
kaejensen@cwidaho.cc
JENSEN, Katie 425-388-9581 503 F
JENSEN, Kevin 607-436-2513 331 F
kevin.jensen@oneonta.edu
JENSEN, Larry 802-776-5236 483 G
larry.jensen@csj.edu
JENSEN, Laura 239-590-1155 110 L
ljensen@fgcu.edu
JENSEN, Laura 970-491-5939 78 Q
l.jensen@colostate.edu
JENSEN, Laurie 218-723-2380 249 H
laurie.jensen@lsc.edu
JENSEN, Leigh 662-325-2091 259 D
ljensen@saffairs.msstate.edu
JENSEN, Lori 507-433-0568 251 H
lori.jensen@riverland.edu
JENSEN, Malinda 319-363-1323 175 D
mjensen@mtmercy.edu
JENSEN, Melissa 319-398-5491 174 I
melissa.jensen@kirkwood.edu
JENSEN, Melissa 208-426-1093 132 I
melissajensen@boisestate.edu
JENSEN, Michael, E 801-422-4327 480 C
jensen@byu.edu
JENSEN, Nathan 714-432-5909 39 G
njensen@occ.cccd.edu
JENSEN, Patricia 414-382-6321 515 D
patricia.jensen@alverno.edu
JENSEN, Paul 708-456-0300 156 C
pauljensen@triton.edu
JENSEN, Pete 845-938-4379 529 C
pete.jensen@usma.edu
JENSEN, Peter, E 605-677-5341 437 A
pete.jensen@usd.edu
JENSEN, Robert 619-201-8698 60 D
robert.jensen@sdcc.edu
JENSEN, Sandra 319-234-5748 173 B
sandra.jensen@hawkeyecollege.edu
JENSEN, Scott 316-978-3693 185 J
scott.jensen@wichita.edu
JENSEN, Sol 701-777-3885 360 C
sol.jensen@und.edu
JENSEN, Stanley, C 313-845-9650 235 D
sjenson@hfcc.edu
JENSEN, Steve, M 563-588-8000 172 E
smjensen@emmaus.edu
JENSEN, Steven, M 330-471-8521 371 J
sjensen@malone.edu
JENSEN, Tom, P 618-537-6959 147 F
tpjensen@mckendree.edu
JENSEN, Tyler 307-674-6446 526 M
tjensen@sheridan.edu
JENSEN, Valerie 707-468-3280 52 C
vjensen@mendocino.edu
JENSON, Hal, B 269-337-4400 243 L
JENSON, Linda 817-515-4521 467 A
linda.jenson@tccd.edu
JENT, Laura 931-393-1544 446 D
ljent@mscc.edu
JEONG, Peter 973-748-9000 289 H
peter_jeong@bloomfield.edu
JEONG, Wooseob 620-341-5203 180 G
wjeong1@emporia.edu
JEPSON, Darla 815-802-8832 144 C
djepson@kcc.edu
JERALDS, Jeri Ann 314-837-6777 271 B
jjeralds@stlchristian.edu
JEREBKO, Peter, J 716-851-1221 313 H
jerebko@ecc.edu
JEREMIAH, David 619-201-8995 65 J
david.jeremiah@socalsem.edu
JERGOVIC, Diana 626-395-6214 30 H
jergovic@caltech.edu

JERICHO, Rosana 692-625-4803 530 C
rjericho@cmi.edu
JERIES, John 651-690-6533 254 M
jjeries@stkate.edu
JERMAN, Rita, H 919-866-5701 353 I
whjerman@waketech.edu
JERMAN LIGUORI, Denise 201-447-7480 289 E
djerman@bergen.edu
JERNBERG, Leslie 208-535-5353 133 G
leslie.jernberg@my.eitc.edu
JERNIEAN, Denise 615-361-7555 439 K
djernian@daymarinstitute.edu
JERNIGAN, Cliff 516-463-4680 316 D
cliff.jernigan@hofstra.edu
JERNIGAN, Cynthia 252-789-0253 351 A
cjernigan@martincc.edu
JERNIGAN, Ron 505-566-3035 301 J
jerniganr@sanjuancollege.edu
JERNIGAN, Tony 301-934-7715 207 B
tjernigan@csmd.edu
JERNIGAN, William 918-495-6723 386 H
wjernigan@oru.edu
JEROME, Allison 808-735-4852 130 F
ajerome@chaminade.edu
JEROME, Etido, S 504-520-7593 202 C
ejerome@xula.edu
JEROME, Leslie 914-632-5400 321 I
ljerome@monroecollege.edu
JEROME, Marc, M 914-632-5400 321 I
mjerome@monroecollege.edu
JEROME, Priya 619-482-6557 66 E
pjerome@swccd.edu
JEROME, Stephen, J 718-933-6700 321 I
sjerome@monroecollege.edu
JERRY, Lisa 516-726-5799 529 B
jerryl@usmma.edu
JERSKY, Brian 562-985-4128 33 B
brian.jersky@csulb.edu
JERUE, James, M 401-456-8262 425 E
jjerue@ric.edu
JERZAK, Page, A 407-582-3865 114 N
pjerzak@valenciacollege.edu
JESENSKY, Danielle 432-552-2100 478 B
jesensky_d@utpb.edu
JESIONOWSKI, Rosemary, K 540-654-2037 495 C
rjesiono@umw.edu
JESKA, Adam 952-446-4247 246 D
jeskaa@crown.edu
JESKO, Rhonda 575-769-4043 299 G
rhonda.jesko@clovis.edu
JESME, Shannon 218-683-8577 251 C
shannon.jesme@northlandcollege.edu
JESPERSEN, Christopher 706-864-1771 128 F
christopher.jespersen@ung.edu
JESSE, III, John, J 402-280-3835 279 H
johnjesse@creighton.edu
JESSEE, Pamela 815-836-5691 145 H
jesseepa@lewisu.edu
JESSELL, Kenneth 305-348-2101 111 A
kenneth.jessell@fiu.edu
JESSIE, Jason 334-222-6591 5 F
jjessie@lbwcc.edu
JESSOGNE, Cheryl 312-499-4186 154 A
cjessogne@saic.edu
JESSOP, Brad 580-559-5471 383 H
bjessop@ecok.edu
JESSOP, Craig 435-797-3046 482 B
craig.jessop@usu.edu
JESSUP, Jim 916-577-2200 75 C
jjessup@jessup.edu
JESSUP, Len 702-895-3201 284 L
len.jessup@unlv.edu
JESSUP, Rhonda, E 919-658-7754 355 K
rjessup@umo.edu
JESSUP, Tracy, C 704-406-4279 344 E
tjessup@gardner-webb.edu
JESTER, Christopher 302-736-2468 91 G
christopher.jester@wesley.edu
JESUS CESAREO, Lourdes 787-763-6700 532 L
ldjesus@se-pr.edu
JETER, Everett 704-922-6226 350 A
jeter.everett@gaston.edu
JETER, Jeff 817-272-2101 476 A
jeter@uta.edu
JETER, Kevin, D 213-891-2188 49 F
jeterk@email.laccd.edu
JETER-TWILLEY, Rhonda 301-860-3132 212 D
rjeter@bowiestate.edu
JETT, Andy 913-344-1247 178 D
andy.jett@bakeru.edu
JETT, Melissa 417-255-7955 269 A
melissajett@missouristate.edu
JETT, Susan, P 864-429-8728 434 F
jettsp@mailbox.sc.edu
JETT, Wendy 541-463-5803 391 G
jettw@lanecc.edu
JETTE, Tracey 406-265-3708 277 E
tracey.jette@msun.edu

JETTON, Kent 731-286-3250 446 B
jetton@dscc.edu
JEW, Carl 415-561-1875 38 E
cjew@ccsf.edu
JEWEL, Marion 210-297-9630 452 C
mtjewell@baptisthealthsystem.com
JEWELL, Christy 916-577-2200 75 C
cjewell@jessup.edu
JEWELL, Kirk 405-385-5100 385 G
kjewell@osugiving.com
JEWELL, Nikki 269-965-3931 236 A
jewelln@kellogg.edu
JEWELL, Scott 617-349-8714 220 B
sjewell@lesley.edu
JEWELL, Shelley 615-460-6643 438 J
shelley.jewell@elmont.edu
JEWETT, Darla 207-741-5584 203 M
djewett@smccme.edu
JEWETT, Jacqueline 860-701-5488 88 D
jewett_j@mitchell.edu
JEWETT, John 386-752-1822 100 L
john.jewett@fgc.edu
JEWSBURY, Evan 417-625-9805 268 H
jewsbury-e@mssu.edu
JEZAK, Patricia 567-661-2650 376 D
patricia_jezak@owens.edu
JEZEK, Kenda 918-495-6198 386 H
kjezek@oru.edu
JEZEK-TAUSSIG, Jennifer 314-516-5428 274 A
jezektaussig@umsl.edu
JEZIORSKI, Jennifer 847-735-5242 145 B
jeziorski@lakeforest.edu
JEZUIT, Deborah 847-543-2339 138 C
djezuit@clcillinois.edu
JHAJ, Sukhwant, S 503-725-2277 394 G
jhaj@pdx.edu
JHANJI, Andy, A 850-644-4747 111 C
ajhanji@foundation.fsu.edu
JHASHI, Tamara 914-674-7803 320 G
tjhashi@mercy.edu
JIAMBALVO, Jim 206-543-9132 508 E
jjiambal@uw.edu
JIANG, Jerome 626-289-7719 25 H
jjiang@amu.edu
JIANG, Jiao-sheng 512-444-8082 470 B
faid@thsu.edu
JIANG, Shaojie 608-796-3172 522 O
sjiang@viterbo.edu
JIE, Yiyun 334-229-6859 1 D
yjiek@alasu.edu
JIGA, Anthony 212-998-2278 324 C
anthony.jiga@nyu.edu
JILES, Michael 678-664-0534 129 M
michael.jiles@westgatech.edu
JIMÉNEZ, Mayra 787-250-8581 538 F
mayra.jimenez@upr.edu
JIMÉNEZ-PÉREZ, Nancy 787-993-8877 537 G
nancy.jimenez1@upr.edu
JIMENEZ, Allison 248-218-2268 240 C
ajimenez@rc.edu
JIMENEZ, Andre 707-654-1186 33 D
bookstore@csum.edu
JIMENEZ, Anna, A 480-732-7391 13 O
a.jimenez@cgc.edu
JIMENEZ, Araceli 661-726-1911 68 K
araceli.jimenez@uav.edu
JIMENEZ, Asdrubal 787-891-0925 533 G
ajimenez@aguadilla.inter.edu
JIMENEZ, Audra 706-754-7766 125 B
ajimenez@northgatech.edu
JIMENEZ, Elena 773-896-2400 137 A
ejimenez@ctschicago.edu
JIMENEZ, Eva 530-242-7560 64 D
ejimenez@shastacollege.edu
JIMENEZ, Irma 787-878-6000 532 O
ijimenez@icprjc.edu
JIMENEZ, Julie 719-549-3222 82 G
julie.jimenez@pueblocc.edu
JIMENEZ, Louis, E 512-245-3562 471 F
lej27@txstate.edu
JIMENEZ, Misael 787-834-9595 536 E
mjimenez@uaa.edu
JIMENEZ, Obed 787-834-9595 536 E
ojimenez@uaa.edu
JIMENEZ, Silverio 787-882-2065 536 D
dispensario@unitecpr.net
JIMENEZ, Tomas 787-766-1912 534 A
tjimenez@inter.edu
JIMENEZ, Zoe 787-850-9354 538 B
zoe.jimenez@upr.edu
JIMENEZ CHAFEY, Maria 787-764-0000 538 F
maria.jimenez16@upr.edu
JIMENEZ-SANDOVAL, Saul 559-278-3056 32 F
ssandoval@csufresno.edu
JIMISON, Nancy, M 804-706-5024 497 D
njiminson@jtcc.edu
JIMMERSON, Judy 229-430-3514 116 A
jjimmerson@albanytech.edu
JIN, Jiahe 512-444-8082 470 B
jjin@thsu.edu

JIN, Steve 916-577-2200 75 C
sjin@jessup.edu
JIN, Young Chung 213-381-0081 47 C
yjin@irus.edu
JINDRA, Barbara, A 972-985-3732 455 A
bjindra@collin.edu
JINGOZIAN, Sunshine 407-926-2000 93 F
JINGOZIAN, Sunshine 407-264-9400 93 F
JINGOZIAN, Sunshine 407-618-5900 93 F
JINKINS, Michael 502-895-3411 191 F
mjinkins@lpts.edu
JINOGOZIAN, Sunshine 904-538-1000 93 F
JINRIGHT, Dwight 205-358-8543 9 B
jinrightd@montevallo.edu
JIRAK, Randy 785-227-3380 178 J
jirakr@bethanylb.edu
JIROUSEK, Nancy 440-826-2298 363 M
njirouse@bw.edu
JIROVEC, Kelly 402-826-8265 280 B
kelly.jirovec@doane.edu
JIWANI, Nazleen 713-646-1869 459 A
njiwani@hcl.edu
JO, Hyun Seok 770-220-7918 120 G
chs@gcuniv.edu
JOACHIM KITZMAN, Patricia 641-628-5271 170 E
kitzmanp@central.edu
JOANIS, Jessica, L 920-748-8186 519 E
joanisj@ripon.edu
JOANIS, Pierre, D 570-577-1631 398 L
p.joanis@bucknell.edu
JOB, Raveen 501-370-5314 21 G
rjob@philander.edu
JOBE, Jarrett 405-974-2626 388 L
jjobe@uco.edu
JOBE, Nicholas 513-231-2223 363 K
njobe@athenaeum.edu
JOBE, Steve 812-866-7005 161 C
jobe@hanover.edu
JOBIN, Amy 650-508-3761 54 J
ajobin@ndnu.edu
JOBSON, John, E 616-395-7800 235 F
jobson@hope.edu
JOBST, Ken, B 502-776-1443 192 C
kjobst@simmonscollegeky.edu
JOCHEMS, Jeff 417-447-7932 270 A
jochemsj@otc.edu
JOCHEMS, Judith 303-837-0825 76 L
jochemsj@aii.edu
JODIS, Stephen, M 724-805-2358 419 A
stephen.jodis@email.stvincent.edu
JOEL, Harry 562-860-2451 36 P
hjoel@cerritos.edu
JOEL, Richard, M 212-960-5300 341 G
president@yu.edu
JOEL PEREZ, Joel 562-907-4233 75 B
jperez@whittier.edu
JOENSEN, William, M 563-588-7104 174 K
william.joensen@loras.edu
JOERSCHKE, Bonnie, C 706-542-8208 128 E
bonniej@uga.edu
JOFEN, Avraham 718-530-6934 306 I
JOFEN, Mordechai 718-530-6934 306 I
JOHANNES, Cheri 406-657-2158 277 D
cjohannes@msubillings.edu
JOHANNES, Stephen 706-886-6831 128 C
sjohannes@tfc.edu
JOHANNESEN, Christine 518-255-5522 334 D
johanncm@cobleskill.edu
JOHANNESEN, Glen 410-290-7100 208 F
JOHANNSEN, Danelle 712-279-3377 176 E
danelle.johannsen@stlukescollege.edu
JOHANNSEN, Danelle, D 712-279-3377 176 E
danelle.johannsen@stlukescollege.edu
JOHANSEN, Bob, L 626-815-4603 28 A
bjohansen@apu.edu
JOHANSEN, Paul 219-785-5344 166 F
johansen@pnw.edu
JOHANSON, Michael 808-675-3669 130 E
michael.johanson@byuh.edu
JOHANSON, Rod 503-517-1010 396 D
rjohanson@warnerpacific.edu
JOHANSSON, Theresa, C 540-231-8205 499 F
theresaj@vt.edu
JOHN, Adam 620-227-9422 180 E
ajohn@dc3.edu
JOHN, III, David, R 704-366-4853 260 E
djohn@rts.edu
JOHN, Jeremy 540-261-8598 494 F
jeremy.john@svu.edu
JOHN, JR., Leon, S 570-422-3659 414 H
JOHN, Mary 818-947-2313 50 D
johnms@lavc.edu
JOHN, Rebecca 612-330-1482 244 I
rjohn@augsburg.edu
JOHN, Rowan 219-989-2255 166 F
rowan@pnw.edu
JOHN, Samuel 201-447-7868 289 E
sjohn@bergen.edu
JOHN, Stephen, S 806-716-2217 465 G
sjohn@southplainscollege.edu

JOHNSON, Gordon, L ..... 270-745-2243.. 194 D
gordon.johnson@wku.edu
JOHNSON, Greg, L .... 612-343-3545.. 253 Y
JOHNSON, Gregg .... 412-392-3898.. 417 F
gjohnson@pointpark.edu
JOHNSON, Gregory, A .... 562-988-2278.... 26 N
gjohnson@auhs.edu
JOHNSON, Gregory, W .... 757-221-3952.. 488 F
gwjohnson@wm.edu
JOHNSON, H. Wayne ...... 847-317-8085.. 156 B
wjohnson@tiu.edu
JOHNSON, H. Wilson ...... 716-888-2301.. 306 F
johns273@canisius.edu
JOHNSON, Haley .... 615-269-8300.. 439 A
JOHNSON, Heidi .... 217-333-1676.. 157 A
johnso19@illinois.edu
JOHNSON, Henry .... 336-517-2137.. 342 B
hjohnson@bennett.edu
JOHNSON, Holly .... 319-296-4283.. 173 B
holly.johnson@hawkeyecollege.edu
JOHNSON, J. Lee .... 517-264-7108.. 241 A
ljohnson@sienaheights.edu
JOHNSON, J. Theodore .... 704-233-8105.. 359 H
tjohnson@wingate.edu
JOHNSON, Jacqueline ..... 320-589-6020.. 255 F
jrjohnso@morris.umn.edu
JOHNSON, James, F .... 215-898-2173.. 421 E
johnsonj@isc.upenn.edu
JOHNSON, James, K .... 651-286-7773.. 256 A
jkjohnson2@unwsp.edu
JOHNSON, James, M ...... 630-752-5113.. 158 C
james.johnson@wheaton.edu
JOHNSON, James, R .... 717-477-1373.. 416 A
jrjohnson@ship.edu
JOHNSON, Janet, L .... 812-464-1928.. 168 E
jljohnson@usi.edu
JOHNSON, Jason .... 580-628-6240.. 384 L
jason.johnson@noc.edu
JOHNSON, Jason, L .... 970-491-6270.... 78 Q
jason.johnson@colostate.edu
JOHNSON, Jay .... 314-889-1423.. 265 C
jjohnson@fontbonne.edu
JOHNSON, Jean .... 773-838-7544.. 137 H
jjohnson2@ccc.edu
JOHNSON, Jean, A .... 319-399-8561.. 170 G
jjohnson@coe.edu
JOHNSON, Jeff .... 318-628-4342.. 196 C
JOHNSON, Jeffrey .... 850-718-2237.... 97 G
johnsonj@chipola.edu
JOHNSON, Jeffrey, A ...... 757-446-6100.. 489 B
johnsonja@evms.edu
JOHNSON, Jeffrey, C ...... 561-237-7333.. 104 O
jjohnson@lynn.edu
JOHNSON, Jeffrey, W ...... 515-294-6561.. 169 G
jjohnsn@iastate.edu
JOHNSON, Jennifer .... 559-442-8281.... 67 C
jennifer.johnson@fresnocitycollege.edu
JOHNSON, Jennifer .... 503-768-6626.. 392 A
jjj@lclark.edu
JOHNSON, Jenny .... 731-989-6378.. 440 D
jjohnson@fhu.edu
JOHNSON, Jerry .... 812-866-7364.. 161 C
johnsonj@hanover.edu
JOHNSON, Jerry .... 713-221-2720.. 474 B
johnsonj@uhd.edu
JOHNSON, Jessica .... 918-335-6829.. 386 F
jjohnson@okwu.edu
JOHNSON, Jill .... 515-961-1595.. 176 H
jill.johnson@simpson.edu
JOHNSON, Jill .... 309-341-5320.. 136 C
jjohnson@sandburg.edu
JOHNSON, Jill .... 803-321-5136.. 431 F
jill.johnson@newberry.edu
JOHNSON, Jill, K .... 904-632-5016.. 101 G
jill.johnson@fscj.edu
JOHNSON, Jill, R .... 864-587-4232.. 433 A
johnsoj@smcsc.edu
JOHNSON, Jim .... 620-235-4389.. 184 C
jjohnson@pittstate.edu
JOHNSON, Jo Ann .... 580-559-5246.. 383 H
jajohnsn@ecok.edu
JOHNSON, JoAnna .... 254-526-1168.. 454 A
joanna.johnson@ctcd.edu
JOHNSON, Jodi, S .... 706-272-4475.. 119 H
jjohnson@daltonstate.edu
JOHNSON, Joel, T .... 651-631-5312.. 256 A
jtjohnson@unwsp.edu
JOHNSON, John, J .... 361-698-1269.. 457 D
jjohnson@delmar.edu
JOHNSON, JR., John, R . 704-406-4303.. 344 E
jrjohnson@gardner-webb.edu
JOHNSON, Joseph .... 619-594-1424.... 35 A
jjohnson@mail.sdsu.edu
JOHNSON, Joseph, F ...... 804-257-5835.. 500 B
JOHNSON, Joyce .... 229-430-4792.. 115 K
joyce.johnson@asurams.edu
JOHNSON, Joyce .... 951-639-5439.... 53 D
jajohnso@msjc.edu
JOHNSON, Joyce, B .... 336-322-2106.. 351 H
joyce.johnson@piedmontcc.edu

JOHNSON, Juanita .... 850-599-3491.. 110 J
juanita.johnson@famu.edu
JOHNSON, Judith .... 212-875-4512.. 304 E
jjohnson@bankstreet.edu
JOHNSON, Judy .... 309-438-7611.. 143 B
jjohns4@ilstu.edu
JOHNSON, Julia .... 608-785-8116.. 520 C
jjohnson2@uwlax.edu
JOHNSON, Julie .... 360-736-9391.. 502 A
jjohnson@centralia.edu
JOHNSON, Julie .... 309-556-3139.. 143 D
JOHNSON, Julie .... 605-455-6011.. 436 G
jjohnson@olc.edu
JOHNSON, Julie, A .... 352-273-6309.. 112 A
johnson@cop.ufl.edu
JOHNSON, Julie, A .... 209-667-3351.... 34 E
jjohnson34@csustan.edu
JOHNSON, Julie, H .... 920-748-8772.. 519 E
johnsonj@ripon.edu
JOHNSON, Juliet .... 615-329-8503.. 439 L
jjohnson@fisk.edu
JOHNSON, Karen .... 507-457-5300.. 252 G
kjohnson@winona.edu
JOHNSON, Karen .... 402-354-7038.. 281 F
karen.johnson@methodistcollege.edu
JOHNSON, Karen .... 918-495-7371.. 386 H
kjohnson@oru.edu
JOHNSON, Karen, A .... 574-284-4571.. 167 A
kjohnson@saintmarys.edu
JOHNSON, Karen, D .... 630-515-7268.. 148 C
kjohns@midwestern.edu
JOHNSON, Karen, E .... 832-826-6207.. 452 G
karenj@bcm.edu
JOHNSON, Karen, L .... 607-735-1827.. 313 F
kajohnson@elmira.edu
JOHNSON, Katharine ..... 602-787-7106.... 14 E
katharine.johnson@paradisevalley.edu
JOHNSON, Kathleen, L .... 404-215-2660.. 124 I
kathleen.johnson@morehouse.edu
JOHNSON, Kathryn, B ..... 315-268-5515.. 310 B
kjohnson@clarkson.edu
JOHNSON, Kathy .... 269-488-4223.. 235 I
kjohnson@kvcc.edu
JOHNSON, Kathy, E .... 317-274-4500.. 163 D
kjohnso@iupui.edu
JOHNSON, Kathy, J .... 605-642-6512.. 437 B
kathy.johnson@bhsu.edu
JOHNSON, Kay .... 936-468-2206.. 466 H
JOHNSON, Keesha .... 501-337-5000.... 19 K
kjohnson@coto.edu
JOHNSON, Keith .... 785-242-5200.. 183 M
keith.johnson@ottawa.edu
JOHNSON, Keith .... 270-706-8413.. 189 C
keith.johnson@kctcs.edu
JOHNSON, Keith .... 205-453-6300.... 93 F
JOHNSON, Keith .... 408-855-5457.... 74 G
keith.johnson@wvm.edu
JOHNSON, Keith .... 701-671-2218.. 361 F
keith.johnson@ndscs.edu
JOHNSON, Kelley .... 760-245-4271.... 73 H
kelley.johnson@vvc.edu
JOHNSON, Kellye .... 405-789-7661.. 388 B
kellye.johnson@swcu.edu
JOHNSON, Ken .... 505-566-4059.. 301 J
johnsonk@sanjuancollege.edu
JOHNSON, Kenneth .... 740-593-2247.. 375 H
johnsok9@ohio.edu
JOHNSON, Kenneth .... 850-644-9396.. 111 C
ken.johnson@fsu.edu
JOHNSON, Kent, M .... 319-273-2122.. 170 A
kent.johnson@uni.edu
JOHNSON, Kevin .... 620-341-5667.. 180 G
kjohnson@emporia.edu
JOHNSON, Kevin, R .... 530-752-7225.... 69 A
krjohnson@ucdavis.edu
JOHNSON, Kim .... 714-556-3610.... 73 B
officevpem@vanguard.edu
JOHNSON, Kim, M .... 773-896-2400.. 137 A
kjohnson@ctschicago.edu
JOHNSON, Kimberlee ...... 215-769-3128.. 403 B
kjohnso2@eastern.edu
JOHNSON, Kimberly .... 765-361-6209.. 169 C
johnsonk@wabash.edu
JOHNSON, Kirk .... 712-274-5116.. 175 C
johnson@morningside.edu
JOHNSON, Kristen .... 716-338-1056.. 317 F
kristenjohnson@mail.sunyjcc.edu
JOHNSON, Kristie .... 802-776-5234.. 483 G
kristie.johnson@csj.edu
JOHNSON, Kyle .... 808-739-8552.. 130 F
kyle.johnson@chaminade.edu
JOHNSON, LaKenya .... 229-931-2057.. 127 C
ljohnson@southgatech.edu
JOHNSON, Lakeshia .... 641-269-9801.. 172 I
johnsola@grinnell.edu
JOHNSON, Lakesia .... 641-269-9801.. 172 I
johnsola@grinnell.edu
JOHNSON, Landy, C .... 580-767-7666.. 214 F
lajohnson@assumption.edu
JOHNSON, Larry .... 706-272-4571.. 119 H
ljohnson@daltonstate.edu

JOHNSON, Larry .... 870-236-6901.... 20 A
ljohnson@crc.edu
JOHNSON, Larry .... 601-977-7758.. 261 A
ljohnson@tougaloo.edu
JOHNSON, Larry .... 202-685-2128.. 528 B
johnsonl@ndu.edu
JOHNSON, Latesha .... 757-822-1054.. 498 H
ldjohnson@tcc.edu
JOHNSON, Laura .... 906-217-4022.. 231 O
lauralee.johnson@baycollege.edu
JOHNSON, Laura .... 870-574-4513.... 22 G
ljohnson@sautech.edu
JOHNSON, Laura .... 502-863-7969.. 188 I
laura_johnson@georgetowncollege.edu
JOHNSON, Laura .... 704-216-6029.. 346 A
ljohnson@livingstone.edu
JOHNSON, Laura, T .... 520-621-3175.... 17 I
ltj@email.arizona.edu
JOHNSON, Lauren .... 716-488-3022.. 317 E
laurenjohnson@jbc.edu
JOHNSON, Lawrence, J .... 513-556-2322.. 379 A
lawrence.johnson@uc.edu
JOHNSON, Lawrence, P .. 413-572-8485.. 222 E
ljohnson@westfield.ma.edu
JOHNSON, Leda .... 623-935-8868.... 14 A
leda.johnson@estrellamountain.edu
JOHNSON, Lee Ann .... 229-333-5666.. 129 G
1493mgr@follett.com
JOHNSON, Les .... 218-281-8345.. 255 E
ljohnson@umn.edu
JOHNSON, Leslie .... 706-872-8072.. 121 C
ljohnson@highlands.edu
JOHNSON, Leslie .... 937-769-1345.. 363 E
lbates@antioch.edu
JOHNSON, Leslie, R .... 217-786-2848.. 146 E
leslie.johnson@llcc.edu
JOHNSON, Levester .... 309-438-5451.. 143 B
ljohn13@ilstu.edu
JOHNSON, Lisa .... 617-287-6020.. 220 G
lisa.johnson@umb.edu
JOHNSON, Lisa .... 407-646-2391.. 107 O
adjohnson@rollins.edu
JOHNSON, Lisa .... 701-858-3494.. 360 B
lisa.a.johnson@ndus.edu
JOHNSON, Lisa .... 423-636-7305.. 447 G
ljohnson@tusculum.edu
JOHNSON, Lisa, A .... 252-335-0821.. 349 A
lajohnson@albemarle.edu
JOHNSON, Lois, M .... 717-720-4122.. 414 C
ljohnson@passhe.edu
JOHNSON, Louise, N .... 563-589-0201.. 177 H
ljohnson@wartburgseminary.edu
JOHNSON, Lynda, K .... 470-578-6033.. 123 J
ljohnson@kennesaw.edu
JOHNSON, Lynn .... 216-791-5000.. 366 H
lynn.m.johnson@cim.edu
JOHNSON, Lynn .... 218-755-2068.. 248 M
ljohnson@bemidjistate.edu
JOHNSON, Lynn .... 631-632-6151.. 332 A
lynn.johnson@stonybrook.edu
JOHNSON, Lynn .... 970-491-1550.... 78 Q
lynn.johnson@colostate.edu
JOHNSON, Lynn .... 303-534-6290.... 78 P
lynn.johnson@colostate.edu
JOHNSON, Lynn .... 541-440-7690.. 395 F
lynn.johnson@umpqua.edu
JOHNSON, Lynne .... 907-796-6416.... 10 H
lejohnson@alaska.edu
JOHNSON, M. Eric .... 615-322-2534.. 449 A
eric.johnson@vanderbilt.edu
JOHNSON, Maggie, A .... 972-708-7573.. 458 G
admissions@gial.edu
JOHNSON, Malonda .... 740-351-3398.. 377 C
mjohnson@shawnee.edu
JOHNSON, Marc .... 775-784-4805.. 285 A
marc.johnson@unr.edu
JOHNSON, Marco .... 661-726-1911.... 68 K
marco.johnson@uav.edu
JOHNSON, Marcus .... 702-651-4148.. 284 H
marcus.johnson@csn.edu
JOHNSON, Marcus .... 701-228-5674.. 361 D
marcus.a.johnson@dakotacollege.edu
JOHNSON, Maren, A .... 701-788-4743.. 360 E
allison.johnson.3@mayvillestate.edu
JOHNSON, Margaret .... 208-282-3520.. 133 H
johnmarg@isu.edu
JOHNSON, Margaret .... 972-708-7616.. 458 G
financial-aid@gial.edu
JOHNSON, Marguerite ..... 617-274-3377.. 225 C
peg.johnson@mcphs.edu
JOHNSON, Maria .... 909-748-8333.... 71 K
maria_johnson@redlands.edu
JOHNSON, Marianne, H .. 215-699-5700.. 408 C
mjohnson@lsb.edu
JOHNSON, Marie, D .... 802-656-5700.. 485 D
marie.johnson@uvm.edu
JOHNSON, Mark .... 507-389-2555.. 250 E
mark.johnson@mnsu.edu
JOHNSON, Mark .... 248-218-2080.. 240 C
mjohnson@rc.edu

JOHNSON, Mark .... 314-889-1467.. 265 C
mjohnson@fontbonne.edu
JOHNSON, Mark .... 425-235-2352.. 506 F
mark.johnson@rtc.edu
JOHNSON, Mark, R .... 919-735-5151.. 354 A
mrjohnson@waynecc.edu
JOHNSON, Martha .... 252-473-5936.. 349 A
martha_johnson@albemarle.edu
JOHNSON, Mary .... 919-760-8535.. 346 D
mbjohnson@meredith.edu
JOHNSON, Mary .... 507-453-2745.. 250 C
mjohnson@southeastmn.edu
JOHNSON, Mary .... 402-494-2311.. 281 C
mjohnson@thenicc.edu
JOHNSON, Mary .... 618-262-8641.. 142 F
johnsonm@iecc.edu
JOHNSON, Mary .... 334-291-4973...... 2 H
mary.johnson@cv.edu
JOHNSON, Mary Jean ..... 419-358-3272.. 364 D
johnsonmj@bluffton.edu
JOHNSON, Mary Jo .... 307-674-6446.. 526 M
mjjohnson@sheridan.edu
JOHNSON, Matthew .... 701-349-5780.. 362 C
mjohnson@trinitybiblecollege.edu
JOHNSON, Matthew .... 413-205-3532.. 214 B
matthew.johnson@aic.edu
JOHNSON, Melinda .... 816-604-1000.. 267 J
melinda.johnson@mcckc.edu
JOHNSON, Melissa .... 701-671-2520.. 361 F
melissa.j.johnson@ndscs.edu
JOHNSON, Melvina .... 612-338-7224.. 256 D
melvina.johnson@laureate.net
JOHNSON, Meredith, G .... 404-814-8813.. 128 E
mgurley@uga.edu
JOHNSON, Merrill, L .... 503-554-2411.. 391 D
mjohnson@georgefox.edu
JOHNSON, Michael .... 660-562-1212.. 269 J
mikej@nwmissouri.edu
JOHNSON, Michael .... 256-372-5601...... 1 A
michael.johnson@aamu.edu
JOHNSON, Michael .... 615-248-7735.. 447 F
mjohnson@trevecca.edu
JOHNSON, Michael .... 713-743-8859.. 473 E
cmj@uh.edu
JOHNSON, Michael, C ...... 214-860-2167.. 456 E
mcjohnson@dcccd.edu
JOHNSON, Michael, D ...... 407-823-1911.. 111 E
michael.johnson@ucf.edu
JOHNSON, Michael, D ...... 607-255-5106.. 312 A
mdj27@cornell.edu
JOHNSON, Michael, L ...... 270-824-8567.. 190 B
michael.johnson@kctcs.edu
JOHNSON, Michele .... 253-864-3100.. 506 B
mjohnson@pierce.ctc.edu
JOHNSON, Michele .... 973-720-2397.. 298 G
johnsonm73j@wpunj.edu
JOHNSON, Michele .... 567-661-7545.. 376 D
michele_johnson@owens.edu
JOHNSON, Michelle .... 626-969-3434.... 28 A
mmjohnson@apu.edu
JOHNSON, Michelle .... 631-420-2369.. 335 E
michelle.johnson@farmingdale.edu
JOHNSON, Michelle .... 414-229-6444.. 520 D
john3453@uwm.edu
JOHNSON, Michelle, D ..... 719-333-4140.. 528 H
JOHNSON, Mike .... 479-575-6601.... 22 I
mrj03@uark.edu
JOHNSON, Mike .... 405-585-5130.. 385 B
mike.johnson@okbu.edu
JOHNSON, Mildred .... 540-231-6267.. 499 F
mildredj@vt.edu
JOHNSON, Mimi .... 334-420-4243...... 7 G
mjohnson@trenholmstate.edu
JOHNSON, Mindy .... 816-604-4339.. 267 K
mindy.johnson@mcckc.edu
JOHNSON, Mitchell .... 336-334-4822.. 350 B
mjohnson@gtcc.edu
JOHNSON, Molly, B .... 785-227-3380.. 178 J
johnsonm@bethanylb.edu
JOHNSON, Monika, L .... 901-333-5065.. 447 B
mljohnson@southwest.tn.edu
JOHNSON, Monty .... 218-631-7812.. 250 D
monty.johnson@minnesota.edu
JOHNSON, Nancy .... 607-962-9345.. 312 B
JOHNSON, Nancy .... 952-885-5428.. 253 Z
njohnson@nwhealth.edu
JOHNSON, Nancy .... 307-382-1757.. 527 C
njohnson@westernwyoming.edu
JOHNSON, Nancy, A .... 309-794-7475.. 135 D
nancyjohnson@augustana.edu
JOHNSON, Nancy, N .... 713-646-1751.. 459 A
njohnson@hcl.edu
JOHNSON, Nathan .... 707-664-4444.... 35 D
nate.johnson@sonoma.edu
JOHNSON, Nathan .... 616-538-2330.. 234 D
njohnson@gbcol.edu
JOHNSON, Nhadira .... 714-241-6186.... 39 E
JOHNSON, Nial, L .... 309-677-2333.. 136 B
nial@bradley.edu
JOHNSON, Odetta .... 919-530-5326.. 357 A
odetta.johnson@nccu.edu

JOHNSON, Pam .... 708-524-6562.. 139 F
pjohnson@dom.edu
JOHNSON, Pam .... 256-835-5456...... 3 M
pjohnson@gadsdenstate.edu
JOHNSON, Pamela .... 903-233-3140.. 460 J
pamjohnson@letu.edu
JOHNSON, Pamela, D ..... 937-766-7765.. 365 C
johnsonp@cedarville.edu
JOHNSON, Patricia, A ..... 610-758-3178.. 408 H
paj214@lehigh.edu
JOHNSON, Patrick .... 240-567-5288.. 209 E
patrick.johnson@montgomerycollege.edu
JOHNSON, Paul .... 404-727-7727.. 120 E
rpaul.johnson@emory.edu
JOHNSON, Paul, C .... 303-273-3280.... 78 M
presoffice@mines.edu
JOHNSON, Paula, A .... 781-283-2237.. 229 C
pjohnson@wellesley.edu
JOHNSON, CRM,
Paula, J .... 858-534-2552.... 70 C
pjjohnson@ucsd.edu
JOHNSON, Paulette .... 256-726-7250...... 6 B
pjohnson@oakwood.edu
JOHNSON, Peg .... 505-428-1352.. 301 K
peg.johnson@sfcc.edu
JOHNSON, Peter, B .... 701-777-4317.. 360 C
peter.johnson@und.edu
JOHNSON, Peter, B .... 701-777-2038.. 360 C
peter.johnson@und.edu
JOHNSON, Phil .... 334-244-3202...... 2 A
pjohns23@aum.edu
JOHNSON, Philip .... 906-487-7201.. 234 A
philip.johnson@finlandia.edu
JOHNSON, Philip, M .... 503-255-0332.. 392 G
pjohnson@multnomah.edu
JOHNSON, Phillip .... 205-391-2665...... 6 G
pjohnson@sheltonstate.edu
JOHNSON, Phillip, A .... 574-631-8338.. 168 B
johnson.30@nd.edu
JOHNSON, Quentin .... 363-334-4822.. 350 B
qrjohnson@gtcc.edu
JOHNSON, Ralph .... 301-891-4028.. 213 D
rejohnson@wau.edu
JOHNSON, Ralph .... 404-507-8697.. 124 I
ralph.johnson@morehouse.edu
JOHNSON, Ralph .... 504-520-7539.. 202 C
rjohns23@xula.edu
JOHNSON, Ralph .... 864-977-2077.. 431 G
ralph.johnson@ngu.edu
JOHNSON, Ralph, F .... 706-542-7369.. 128 E
rfj@uga.edu
JOHNSON, Raniyah .... 408-274-7900.... 62 D
raniyah.johnson@evc.edu
JOHNSON, Rebecca .... 770-467-6037.. 127 F
rajohnson@sctech.edu
JOHNSON, Rebecca .... 541-322-3100.. 393 H
rebecca.johnson@osucascades.edu
JOHNSON, Rebecca .... 414-930-3242.. 518 F
johnsonr@mtmary.edu
JOHNSON, Rebecca, D .... 203-932-7176.... 90 A
rjohnson@newhaven.edu
JOHNSON, Richard .... 870-236-6901.... 20 A
rjohnson@crc.edu
JOHNSON, Richard, A ..... 864-597-4090.. 435 C
johnsonra@wofford.edu
JOHNSON, Rick .... 919-684-3737.. 343 J
JOHNSON, Rick .... 602-682-6817.... 11 I
rjohnson@azsummitlaw.edu
JOHNSON, Rick .... 239-590-7072.. 110 L
rjohnson@wgcu.edu
JOHNSON, Rick .... 307-778-1281.. 526 K
rjohnson@lccc.wy.edu
JOHNSON, Rita .... 828-328-7235.. 345 H
rita.johnson@lr.edu
JOHNSON, Robert, E .... 508-373-1900.. 215 D
robert.johnson@becker.edu
JOHNSON, Robert, E .... 913-667-5700.. 179 K
rjohnson@cbts.edu
JOHNSON, Robert, E .... 704-687-8242.. 358 A
robejohn@uncc.edu
JOHNSON, JR.,
Robert, M .... 901-843-3745.. 443 L
johnsonb@rhodes.edu
JOHNSON, Robert, R .... 610-526-1301.. 397 E
bob.johnson@theamericancollege.edu
JOHNSON, Roberta, L ..... 515-294-0109.. 169 G
rljohns@iastate.edu
JOHNSON, Rod .... 503-699-6266.. 392 D
rjohnson@marylhurst.edu
JOHNSON, Rodney .... 937-766-4114.. 365 C
johnsnr@cedarville.edu
JOHNSON, Roger .... 870-248-4000.... 19 H
rogerj@blackrivertech.edu
JOHNSON, Ronald .... 714-432-5605.... 39 G
rgjohnson@occ.cccd.edu
JOHNSON, Ronald, A ...... 404-880-8566.. 118 K
rjohnson@cau.edu
JOHNSON, Ronald, A ...... 713-313-7922.. 470 D
johnsonra@tsu.edu
JOHNSON, Ronald, W ..... 310-206-0401.... 69 D
rojohnso@saonet.ucla.edu
JOHNSON, Rory .... 707-465-2300.... 40 D
rory-johnson@redwoods.edu
JOHNSON, Ruben .... 972-860-8160.. 456 C
rjohnson@dcccd.edu
JOHNSON, Rushton .... 404-225-4444.. 117 A
rjohnson@atlantatech.edu
JOHNSON, Ryan .... 501-205-8815.... 19 J
rjohnson@cbc.edu
JOHNSON, Ryan .... 254-442-5173.. 454 E
ryan.johnson@cisco.edu
JOHNSON, Sabrina, C ..... 540-654-1046.. 495 C
sjohnson@umw.edu
JOHNSON, Sandra .... 661-726-1911.... 68 K
sandra.johnson@uav.edu
JOHNSON, Sandra, S ...... 585-475-2267.. 327 E
ssjvsa@rit.edu
JOHNSON, Sara .... 517-787-0800.. 235 G
sjohnson@jccmi.edu
JOHNSON, Sara .... 315-265-9260.. 310 B
clarkson@bkstr.com
JOHNSON, Sarah .... 419-448-3039.. 378 A
depughst@tiffin.edu
JOHNSON, Scott .... 810-762-3160.. 242 B
scotjohn@umflint.edu
JOHNSON, Scott .... 336-833-6141.. 354 C
scott.johnson@wilkescc.edu
JOHNSON, Scott, L .... 716-873-5906.. 332 F
johnsosl@buffalostate.edu
JOHNSON, Sean .... 707-664-4032.... 35 D
sean.johnson@sonoma.edu
JOHNSON, Sean .... 701-252-3467.. 362 F
sean.johnson@uj.edu
JOHNSON, Seth .... 716-375-2382.. 328 B
sjohnson@sbu.edu
JOHNSON, Sharon .... 314-516-6817.. 274 A
sharon_johnson@umsl.edu
JOHNSON, Sharon .... 503-226-4391.. 394 B
sjohnson@pnca.edu
JOHNSON, Sharon .... 262-564-3164.. 523 D
johnsonsh@gtc.edu
JOHNSON, Shawn .... 608-663-2312.. 516 F
johnson@edgewood.edu
JOHNSON, Sheila, G .... 405-744-6321.. 385 G
sheila.johnson@okstate.edu
JOHNSON, Shelia .... 304-327-4040.. 512 P
sjohnson@bluefieldstate.edu
JOHNSON, Shemila .... 707-864-7000.... 65 A
shemila.johnson@solano.edu
JOHNSON, Sherie .... 410-951-3846.. 212 E
shejohnson@coppin.edu
JOHNSON, Sherrick, L ..... 706-771-4008.. 117 C
sjohnson@augustatech.edu
JOHNSON, Sonia .... 870-236-6901.... 20 A
sjohnson@crc.edu
JOHNSON, Stacey .... 718-939-5100.. 319 A
sjohnson@libi.edu
JOHNSON, Stacey, R .... 407-582-2216.. 114 N
srjohnson@valenciacollege.edu
JOHNSON, Stacy .... 248-689-8282.. 242 F
sjohnso6@walshcollege.edu
JOHNSON, Stephanie .... 573-875-7357.. 263 F
sgjohnson@ccis.edu
JOHNSON, Stephanie .... 704-379-6800.... 93 F
JOHNSON, Stephen .... 626-812-3020.... 28 A
sjohnson@apu.edu
JOHNSON, Stephen .... 560-860-2451.... 36 P
sjohnson@cerritos.edu
JOHNSON, Stephen .... 325-674-2751.. 449 J
scj98d@acu.edu
JOHNSON, Steve .... 913-360-7415.. 178 I
stevej@benedictine.edu
JOHNSON, Steve .... 504-280-6303.. 198 D
sgjohnso@uno.edu
JOHNSON, Steven .... 334-874-5700...... 3 A
sjohnson@ccal.edu
JOHNSON, Steven .... 212-346-1835.. 325 J
sjohnson@pace.edu
JOHNSON, Steven, D .... 816-604-6563.. 267 G
steven.johnson@mcckc.edu
JOHNSON, Steven, L .... 989-774-1169.. 232 D
johns1sl@cmich.edu
JOHNSON, Steven, L .... 973-655-7677.. 293 A
johnsonst@mail.montclair.edu
JOHNSON, Steven, L .... 937-512-2525.. 377 D
president@sinclair.edu
JOHNSON, Susan .... 775-831-1314.. 285 G
sjohnson@sierranevada.edu
JOHNSON, Susan, N .... 651-631-5333.. 256 A
snjohnson@unwsp.edu
JOHNSON, Suzanne .... 631-451-4245.. 336 D
johnsos@sunysuffolk.edu
JOHNSON, Sylvester, C .. 504-865-5300.. 200 C
sylj@tulane.edu
JOHNSON, Tammy .... 304-696-3161.. 513 D
johnson73@marshall.edu
JOHNSON, Tara .... 229-903-3622.. 115 K
tara.johnson@asurams.edu
JOHNSON, TaRita .... 616-526-6484.. 232 A
tdj4@calvin.edu
JOHNSON, Tasha .... 252-527-6223.. 350 H
tjohnson@lenoircc.edu
JOHNSON, Ted .... 858-822-5949.... 70 C
edjohnson@ucsd.edu
JOHNSON, Teisha .... 312-949-7407.. 142 A
tjohnson@ico.edu
JOHNSON, Teresa .... 573-840-9660.. 273 A
tjohnson@trcc.edu
JOHNSON, Terri .... 512-863-1342.. 466 G
tjohnson@southwestern.edu
JOHNSON, Terry, L .... 937-481-2222.. 381 C
terry_johnson@wilmington.edu
JOHNSON, Theodore .... 630-889-6512.. 149 G
tjohnson@nuhs.edu
JOHNSON, Theresa .... 301-934-2251.. 207 B
JOHNSON, Thomas .... 323-343-3488.... 33 C
tjohnson@cslanet.calstatela.edu
JOHNSON, Thomas .... 641-628-5276.. 170 E
johnsont@central.edu
JOHNSON, Thomas .... 314-246-7975.. 275 B
thomasjohnson18@webster.edu
JOHNSON, Thomas .... 417-836-5509.. 268 I
tomjohnson@missouristate.edu
JOHNSON, Thomas, A ...... 903-510-2950.. 473 C
tjoh@tjc.edu
JOHNSON, Thomasine ...... 202-319-6065.... 92 A
johnsotn@cua.edu
JOHNSON, Tianna .... 507-457-1635.. 254 O
tpjohnso@smumn.edu
JOHNSON, Tim, P .... 937-766-7777.. 365 C
johnsont@cedarville.edu
JOHNSON, Timothy .... 336-334-5636.. 358 B
tjjohns3@uncg.edu
JOHNSON, Todd, K .... 757-683-3415.. 492 G
tjohnso@odu.edu
JOHNSON, Tom .... 910-221-2224.. 344 F
tjohnson@gcd.edu
JOHNSON, Tonjanita .... 865-974-8184.. 448 D
tonjanita.johnson@tennessee.edu
JOHNSON, Tony .... 903-983-8102.. 460 D
tjohnson@kilgore.edu
JOHNSON, Tony .... 206-592-4320.. 504 E
tjohnson@highline.edu
JOHNSON, Toya .... 312-850-7267.. 138 A
tjohnson616@ccc.edu
JOHNSON, Tracci .... 757-451-7768.. 492 F
tkjohnson@nsu.edu
JOHNSON, Tracey .... 618-634-3271.. 154 B
traceyj@shawneecc.edu
JOHNSON, Tracie .... 615-383-4848.. 449 G
tjohnson@watkins.edu
JOHNSON, Troy .... 309-438-7018.. 143 B
tjohns3@ilstu.edu
JOHNSON, Trygve, D .... 616-395-7145.. 235 F
johnsont@hope.edu
JOHNSON, Ursa .... 540-365-4323.. 489 M
ujohnson@ferrum.edu
JOHNSON, Veronica .... 773-947-6319.. 147 D
vjohnson@mccormick.edu
JOHNSON, Vicki .... 731-989-6095.. 440 D
vjohnson@fhu.edu
JOHNSON, Victoria, D ...... 504-865-5591.. 200 C
victoria@tulane.edu
JOHNSON, Vince .... 717-569-7071.. 407 E
vjohnson@lbc.edu
JOHNSON, Vivian .... 937-529-2201.. 378 F
vjohnson@united.edu
JOHNSON, Wallace .... 909-384-8502.... 60 C
wjohnson@sbccd.cc.ca.us
JOHNSON, Walter .... 864-977-7068.. 431 G
walter.johnson@ngu.edu
JOHNSON, Wayne, E .... 704-406-4269.. 344 E
wjohnson@gardner-webb.edu
JOHNSON, Wendy .... 225-743-8500.. 196 J
wjohnson@rpcc.edu
JOHNSON, William .... 217-245-3046.. 141 G
william.johnson@mail.ic.edu
JOHNSON, William .... 864-596-9056.. 429 C
bill.johnson@converse.edu
JOHNSON, William .... 734-973-3490.. 242 G
billjohnson@wccnet.edu
JOHNSON, William, [illegible] ..... 203-254-4000.... 87 G
wjohnson@fairfield.edu
JOHNSON-BAILEY,
Juanita .... 706-542-2846.. 128 E
jjb@uga.edu
JOHNSON-CASSULO,
Nancy .... 208-459-5680.. 133 D
njohnsoncassulo@collegeofidaho.edu
JOHNSON-CRAMER,
Michael, E .... 570-577-1756.. 398 L
m.johnson-cramer@bucknell.edu
JOHNSON-FANNIN,
Arcelia .... 210-883-1015.. 474 D
johnsonf@uiwtx.edu
JOHNSON-HOUSTON,
Debbie, L .... 337-475-5716.. 200 H
djohnsonhouston@mcneese.edu
JOHNSON JONES,
Sylvia, M .... 847-543-2404.. 138 C
cps086@clcillinois.edu
JOHNSON RENVALL,
Poppy .... 505-224-4435.. 299 F
pjohnsonrenvall@cnm.edu
JOHNSON-ROULHAC,
Sheryl .... 313-993-1017.. 241 G
mcgrifsj@udmercy.edu
JOHNSON SHAHEED,
Karen .... 301-860-3555.. 212 D
kshaheed@bowiestate.edu
JOHNSON SUSKI,
Katharine .... 515-294-0815.. 169 G
ksuski@iastate.edu
JOHNSON-WEEKS,
Demetria .... 713-313-7940.. 470 D
weeks_dj@tsu.edu
JOHNSRUD, Jason .... 202-462-2101.... 93 B
johnsrud@iwp.edu
JOHNSRUD, Linda .... 817-272-2103.. 476 A
linda.johnsrud@uta.edu
JOHNSTEN, Christina ...... 215-248-6380.. 409 D
cjohnsten@ltsp.edu
JOHNSTON, Alysia .... 620-223-2700.. 181 A
alysiaj@fortscott.edu
JOHNSTON, Angela .... 330-263-2313.. 367 A
ajohnston@wooster.edu
JOHNSTON, Ann .... 218-262-6733.. 249 E
annjohnston@hibbing.edu
JOHNSTON, Brian .... 216-373-5252.. 374 B
bjohnston@ndc.edu
JOHNSTON, Brian, A .... 202-319-6425.... 92 A
johnston@cua.edu
JOHNSTON, Cheryl, L ..... 724-847-6577.. 404 B
cljohnst@geneva.edu
JOHNSTON, Cynthia .... 843-349-7835.. 430 F
cynthia.johnston@hgtc.edu
JOHNSTON, Deborah .... 907-564-8204.... 10 B
debj@alaskapacific.edu
JOHNSTON, Dusty, R ...... 940-552-6291.. 478 D
drj@vernoncollege.edu
JOHNSTON, Elizabeth ...... 214-637-3530.. 479 C
ejohnston@wadecollege.edu
JOHNSTON, Elizabeth ...... 412-237-8195.. 401 B
ejohnston@ccac.edu
JOHNSTON, Elliott .... 218-723-5939.. 245 J
ejohnston1@css.edu
JOHNSTON, Emily .... 251-460-6231...... 9 E
ejohnsto@southalabama.edu
JOHNSTON, J.V .... 316-942-4291.. 183 I
johnstonj@newmanu.edu
JOHNSTON, James .... 940-397-4594.. 462 A
james.johnston@mwsu.edu
JOHNSTON, Jan .... 314-529-9330.. 267 B
jjohnston@maryville.edu
JOHNSTON, Jed .... 402-466-4774.. 280 B
jed.johnston@doane.edu
JOHNSTON, Jessica .... 773-834-2500.. 155 K
JOHNSTON, Jobyna .... 319-226-2515.. 169 D
jobyna.johnston@allencollege.edu
JOHNSTON, John .... 212-217-3600.. 314 B
john_johnston@fitnyc.edu
JOHNSTON, Judy .... 912-279-5705.. 119 C
jjohnston@ccga.edu
JOHNSTON, Julie, L .... 530-251-8820.... 48 E
jjohnston@lassencollege.edu
JOHNSTON, Justin .... 716-839-8468.. 312 D
jjohnsto@daemen.edu
JOHNSTON, Kathryn, A ... 920-923-8745.. 517 H
kajohnston00@marianuniversity.edu
JOHNSTON, Kathy .... 636-481-3280.. 266 C
kjohnsto@jeffco.edu
JOHNSTON, Kathy .... 620-421-6700.. 182 G
kathyj@labette.edu
JOHNSTON, Ken .... 312-567-5850.. 142 I
johnston@iit.edu
JOHNSTON, Kerri .... 978-934-3948.. 221 A
kerri_johnston@uml.edu
JOHNSTON, Kimberly ...... 309-672-5583.. 147 H
kajohnston@methodistcol.edu
JOHNSTON, Kyle .... 218-736-1544.. 250 D
kyle.johnston@minnesota.edu
JOHNSTON, Laurel .... 510-204-0700.... 38 C
ljohnston@cdsp.edu
JOHNSTON, Lee .... 310-434-4549.... 63 F
johnston_lee@smc.edu
JOHNSTON, Lisa .... 727-864-8206.... 98 L
johnstln@eckerd.edu
JOHNSTON, Mary .... 618-842-3711.. 142 C
johnstonm@iecc.edu
JOHNSTON, Matt .... 714-338-1744.... 17 L
matt.johnston@phoenix.edu
JOHNSTON, Matthew .... 661-835-1111.... 62 L
JOHNSTON, Matthew .... 805-922-8256.... 63 A
JOHNSTON, Matthew .... 805-339-2999.... 63 B
JOHNSTON, Michael .... 850-484-1717.. 106 H
mjohnston@pensacolastate.edu
JOHNSTON, Michelle .... 203-392-6501.... 85 H
johnstonm2@southerct.edu
JOHNSTON, Michelle, R .. 740-245-7205.. 380 C
mjohnston@rio.edu
JOHNSTON, Mike .... 617-745-5704.. 218 A
michael.johnston@enc.edu

JOHNSTON, Mike .... 816-654-7338.. 266 E
gjohnston@kcumb.edu
JOHNSTON, Molly .... 218-235-2119.. 252 F
m.johnston@vcc.edu
JOHNSTON, Pamela .... 210-999-7507.. 473 A
pamela.johnston@trinity.edu
JOHNSTON, Peter .... 508-588-9100.. 223 G
JOHNSTON, Phil .... 615-460-6538.. 438 J
phil.johnston@belmont.edu
JOHNSTON, Robert, C ..... 315-445-4321.. 318 E
johnstrc@lemoyne.edu
JOHNSTON, Ronna .... 970-351-1848.... 84 C
ronna.johnston@unco.edu
JOHNSTON, Roxanne .... 706-233-7464.. 127 A
rjohnston@shorter.edu
JOHNSTON, S. Claiborne 512-495-5000.. 476 B
clay.johnston@utexas.edu
JOHNSTON, Sandra .... 386-752-1822.. 100 L
sandra.johnston@fgc.edu
JOHNSTON, Sandra .... 815-455-9793.. 147 E
sjohnston@mchenry.edu
JOHNSTON, Susan .... 903-823-3260.. 467 C
susan.johnston@texarkanacollege.edu
JOHNSTON, Susan .... 703-784-2884.. 528 A
susan.johnston@usmc.mil
JOHNSTON, Tim .... 269-749-7164.. 240 A
tjohnston@olivetcollege.edu
JOHNSTON, Timothy .... 530-242-7669.... 64 D
tjohnston@shastacollege.edu
JOHNSTON, William, S ... 406-243-5211.. 276 K
bill.johnston@umontana.edu
JOHNSTON-ORTIZ, Eric ... 575-624-7121.. 299 J
eric.johnston-ortiz@roswell.enmu.edu
JOHNSTONE, Jason, L ..... 936-468-1672.. 466 H
jljohnstone@sfasu.edu
JOICE, Chad .... 501-279-4442.... 20 D
cjoice@harding.edu
JOINER, Erin .... 502-897-4206.. 192 D
ejoiner@sbts.edu
JOINER, Haywood .... 318-473-6414.. 197 J
hjoiner@lsua.edu
JOINER, Haywood .... 318-473-6466.. 197 J
hjoiner@lsua.edu
JOINER, Jennie .... 315-279-5259.. 318 C
jjoiner@keuka.edu
JOINER, Karen .... 360-442-2861.. 504 G
kjoiner@lowercolumbia.edu
JOINER, Nina .... 361-593-5781.. 469 A
tamukcso@tamuk.edu
JOINER, Steve .... 615-966-7141.. 441 F
steve.joiner@lipscomb.edu
JOINES, Jacqueline .... 217-234-5354.. 145 D
jjoines@lakeland.cc.il.us
JOKELA, Roxana .... 402-559-4385.. 283 A
rjokela@unmc.edu
JOLER-LABBE, Michelle .. 207-859-1240.. 204 E
hr@thomas.edu
JOLLEY, JR., Edward, B .. 912-358-3000.. 126 F
jolleye@savannahstate.edu
JOLLEY, Kassandra .... 413-538-2756.. 226 A
kjolley@mtholyoke.edu
JOLLEY, Kate .... 707-527-4413.... 63 G
kjolley@santarosa.edu
JOLLEY, Renee, W .... 804-257-5756.. 500 B
rwjolley@vuu.edu
JOLLEY, Rick .... 864-596-9041.. 429 C
rick.jolley@converse.edu
JOLLIFFE, Vicki, M .... 724-439-4900.. 408 D
vjolliffe@laurel.edu
JOLLY, Connie .... 843-574-6150.. 433 D
connie.jolly@tridenttech.edu
JOLLY, Jim .... 248-204-2400.. 237 B
jjolly@ltu.edu
JOLLY, Julia, A .... 916-558-2407.... 51 D
jollyj@scc.losrios.edu
JOLLY, Laura .... 515-294-5380.. 169 G
ljolly@iastate.edu
JOLLY, Lawson .... 352-588-8354.. 108 C
lawson.jolly@saintleo.edu
JOLLY, Melody .... 714-850-4800.... 67 G
jolly@taftu.edu
JOLLY, Richard, C .... 432-685-4524.. 461 H
rjolly@midland.edu
JONAITIS, Aldona .... 907-474-6939.... 10 G
ajonaitis@alaska.edu
JONAS, Audrey .... 708-456-0300.. 156 C
audreyjonas@triton.edu
JONEN, Mike .... 520-626-5394.... 17 I
mjonen@email.arizona.edu
JONES, Aaron .... 417-873-7301.. 264 H
aaronjones@drury.edu
JONES, Adrianne .... 904-826-0084.... 72 A
ajones@usa.edu
JONES, Alan .... 574-239-8318.. 161 N
ajones1@hcc-nd.edu
JONES, Alesia, M .... 250-934-5321...... 8 E
amjones@uab.edu
JONES, Alex .... 765-641-4190.. 158 J
agjones@anderson.edu
JONES, Allison .... 323-953-4000.... 49 H
jonessa@lacitycollege.edu
JONES, Almarie .... 856-415-2154.. 295 D
ajones@rcgc.edu
JONES, Alonzo .... 434-791-4773.. 487 C
ajones@averett.edu
JONES, Alvena .... 903-927-3318.. 479 K
ajones@wileyc.edu
JONES, Amanda .... 641-269-4872.. 172 I
jonesama@grinnell.edu
JONES, Amy .... 734-462-4400.. 240 H
ajones2@schoolcraft.edu
JONES, Amy .... 425-889-7823.. 505 E
amy.jones@northwestu.edu
JONES, Amy, J .... 712-749-2101.. 170 D
jonesa@bvu.edu
JONES, Andrae .... 239-432-5206.. 101 F
ajones@fsw.edu
JONES, Andrea .... 404-413-1351.. 122 D
andreajones@gsu.edu
JONES, Andrea, R .... 434-223-6107.. 490 D
ajones@hsc.edu
JONES, Andrew .... 217-245-3010.. 141 G
andrew.jones@mail.ic.edu
JONES, Andrew .... 562-951-4455.... 31 H
JONES, Angela .... 850-474-2628.. 113 A
ajones1@uwf.edu
JONES, Angela, C .... 216-397-1531.. 370 H
acjones@jcu.edu
JONES, Annamarie .... 775-831-1314.. 285 G
ajones@sierranevada.edu
JONES, Anne .... 843-921-6994.. 431 H
ajones@netc.edu
JONES, Annie .... 603-862-2450.. 288 C
annie.jones@unh.edu
JONES, Anthony .... 765-658-4108.. 160 F
anthonyjones@depauw.edu
JONES, JR., Anthony, M . 256-761-6231...... 7 F
amjones@talladega.edu
JONES, April .... 704-330-6190.. 348 E
april.jones@cpcc.edu
JONES, Barbara .... 870-864-7107.... 22 D
brjones@southark.edu
JONES, Barbara .... 617-552-2052.. 216 C
barbara.jones@bc.edu
JONES, Barbara .... 601-484-8804.. 258 F
bjones@meridiancc.edu
JONES, Barbara, E .... 607-746-4440.. 335 C
jonesbe@delhi.edu
JONES, Ben .... 440-775-8624.. 374 C
ben.jones@oberlin.edu
JONES, Benjamin, F .... 605-256-5270.. 437 C
benjamin.jones@dsu.edu
JONES, Bert .... 804-819-4917.. 496 E
bjones@vccs.edu
JONES, Bill .... 209-543-7000.... 28 M
JONES, III, Bob .... 864-242-5100.. 427 E
JONES, Bonnie, J .... 941-359-4200.. 112 E
JONES, Bradley .... 317-738-8033.. 160 J
bjones@franklincollege.edu
JONES, Brenda .... 281-922-3403.. 465 B
brenda.jones@sjcd.edu
JONES, Brenda .... 414-847-3231.. 518 D
brendajones@miad.edu
JONES, Brian .... 310-544-6442.... 59 K
brian.jones@usw.salvationarmy.org
JONES, Brian .... 507-389-2422.. 250 E
brian.jones@mnsu.edu
JONES, Brian .... 704-378-1238.. 345 E
bjones@jcsu.edu
JONES, Brian, W .... 202-419-0400.... 93 F
JONES, Britt, E .... 325-670-1317.. 458 J
brittj@hsutx.edu
JONES, Bruce, A .... 713-743-2490.. 473 F
bajones@uh.edu
JONES, Bryan .... 757-825-2931.. 498 G
jonesb@tncc.edu
JONES, Bryan, H .... 206-281-2405.. 507 C
bryan@spu.edu
JONES, Byron .... 602-557-9322.... 17 L
byron.jones@phoenix.edu
JONES, C. Darryl .... 510-231-5000.... 47 H
JONES, Candice .... 404-297-9522.. 122 A
jonesc@gptc.edu
JONES, Carl .... 318-357-4254.. 201 B
jonesc@nsula.edu
JONES, Carnell .... 401-874-9500.. 426 D
carnell@uri.edu
JONES, Carol .... 706-272-4545.. 119 H
cjones@daltonstate.edu
JONES, Carol .... 478-218-3700.. 118 G
cjones@centralgatech.edu
JONES, Carol, F .... 478-988-6800.. 118 H
cjones@centralgatech.edu
JONES, Cassandra .... 706-419-1117.. 119 G
cassandra.jones@covenant.edu
JONES, Cassandra .... 240-567-4248.. 209 E
cassandra.jones@montgomerycollege.edu
JONES, Cassie .... 434-791-5684.. 487 C
cwjones@averett.edu
JONES, Cathy .... 704-330-1461.. 345 E
cjones2@jcsu.edu
JONES, Cecelia, K .... 903-927-3217.. 479 K
ckjones@wileyc.edu
JONES, Charles .... 478-825-6156.. 120 F
jonesc02@fvsu.edu
JONES, Charles .... 904-743-1122.. 103 G
cejones@jones.edu
JONES, Chris .... 641-472-7000.. 175 A
cjones@mum.edu
JONES, Chris .... 641-472-1219.. 175 A
cjones@mum.edu
JONES, Chris .... 405-585-4120.. 385 B
chris.jones@okbu.edu
JONES, Christa, K .... 972-860-7033.. 456 D
christaj@dcccd.edu
JONES, Christopher .... 978-867-4500.. 219 A
chris.jones@gordon.edu
JONES, Christopher .... 309-677-2380.. 136 B
cmjones@fsmail.bradley.edu
JONES, Cindy, M .... 417-873-7330.. 264 H
cjones@drury.edu
JONES, Clayton, H .... 662-915-1999.. 261 B
chj1@olemiss.edu
JONES, Cliff .... 870-733-6731.... 19 A
cejones@asumidsouth.edu
JONES, Clifton .... 254-519-5424.. 468 C
cwjones@tamuct.edu
JONES, Clifton .... 325-942-2337.. 472 B
clifton.jones@angelo.edu
JONES, Clifton .... 254-519-5424.. 468 C
cwjones@tamuct.edu
JONES, Courtney .... 405-382-9204.. 387 L
c.jones@sscok.edu
JONES, Cravor .... 304-327-4016.. 512 P
cjones@bluefieldstate.edu
JONES, Cristen .... 410-923-4500.... 93 F
JONES, Curtis .... 912-201-6123.. 127 D
cejones@southuniversity.edu
JONES, Dan .... 714-546-7600.... 39 E
djones@coastline.edu
JONES, Dan, L .... 828-262-3180.. 356 B
jonesdl@appstate.edu
JONES, Danson .... 979-532-6975.. 479 J
jonesd@wcjc.edu
JONES, Darci .... 814-824-2233.. 410 H
djones@mercyhurst.edu
JONES, Darnell .... 816-501-4117.. 270 J
darnell.jones@rockhurst.edu
JONES, Darren .... 501-977-2191.... 24 B
jones@uaccm.edu
JONES, Darren .... 301-736-3631.. 209 A
darren.jones@msbbcs.edu
JONES, Darrin .... 360-538-4234.. 504 B
djones@ghc.edu
JONES, David .... 573-592-5288.. 275 E
david.jones@westminster-mo.edu
JONES, David .... 706-542-8131.. 128 E
dsjones@uga.edu
JONES, David .... 931-363-9816.. 441 G
djones@martinmethodist.edu
JONES, David .... 507-389-2121.. 250 E
david.jones@mnsu.edu
JONES, David .... 251-809-1592...... 5 A
david.jones@jdcc.edu
JONES, David .... 307-766-4286.. 527 B
dljones@uwyo.edu
JONES, David, R .... 301-784-5000.. 205 G
djones@allegany.edu
JONES, Dawn .... 903-927-3203.. 479 K
dijones@wileyc.edu
JONES, Debra .... 229-430-3605.. 116 A
djones@albanytech.edu
JONES, Debra .... 618-374-5162.. 151 E
debra.jones@principia.edu
JONES, Dennis, H .... 256-766-6610...... 4 B
djones@hcu.edu
JONES, Diana .... 641-784-5412.. 172 G
dianaj@gracelend.edu
JONES, Dianna .... 781-768-7291.. 227 G
dianna.jones@regiscollege.edu
JONES, Dixie .... 318-675-5455.. 198 B
djon17@lsuhsc.edu
JONES, Don .... 312-341-2296.. 152 H
djones74@roosevelt.edu
JONES, Don .... 617-585-1154.. 226 F
don.jones@necmusic.edu
JONES, Donald .... 812-488-1209.. 167 I
dj29@evansville.edu
JONES, Donald .... 860-768-4751.... 89 G
djones@hartford.edu
JONES, Donald, A .... 502-371-8330.. 186 K
djones@ata.edu
JONES, Donald, E .... 803-754-4100.. 429 B
JONES, Dorothy, D .... 904-743-1122.. 103 G
vjones@jones.edu
JONES, Doug .... 423-636-7300.. 447 G
djones@tusculum.edu
JONES, Douglas, W .... 805-565-6048.... 75 A
vpfinance@westmont.edu
JONES, Duke .... 417-328-1714.. 272 C
djones@sbuniv.edu
JONES, Eddie, V .... 989-964-4228.. 240 F
evjones@svsu.edu
JONES, JR., Edward .... 202-274-7441.... 94 B
ejones@udc.edu
JONES, Eli .... 479-575-5949.... 22 I
ejones@walton.uark.edu
JONES, Eli .... 979-845-4712.. 468 B
elijones@tamu.edu
JONES, Elizabeth, R .... 404-413-3003.. 122 D
bethjones@gsu.edu
JONES, Elliot .... 318-247-3811.. 200 F
JONES, Elliot .... 248-218-2036.. 240 C
ejones@rc.edu
JONES, Elwin .... 251-981-3771...... 2 I
elwin.jones@columbiasouthern.edu
JONES, Eric .... 641-628-5420.. 170 E
jonese@central.edu
JONES, Eric .... 312-915-7452.. 146 G
ejones6@luc.edu
JONES, Ericka, D .... 512-505-3040.. 459 F
edjones@htu.edu
JONES, Eugene .... 352-365-3576.. 104 J
jonese@lssc.edu
JONES, Faye, M .... 615-353-3556.. 446 E
faye.jones@nscc.edu
JONES, Garry .... 407-679-0100.. 102 I
gjones@fullsail.com
JONES, Garry .... 662-243-2643.. 257 G
gjones@eastms.edu
JONES, Gary .... 618-252-5400.. 154 G
gary.jones@sic.edu
JONES, Gary .... 405-425-5904.. 385 C
gary.jones@oc.edu
JONES, Gayle .... 352-395-5226.. 109 C
gayle.jones@sfcollege.edu
JONES, Gena .... 806-743-2865.. 472 D
gena.jones@ttuhsc.edu
JONES, George, A .... 606-759-7141.. 190 C
george.jones@kctcs.edu
JONES, Gerald .... 334-386-7600...... 3 I
gjones@faulkner.edu
JONES, Geraldine .... 724-938-4400.. 414 E
jones_gm@calu.edu
JONES, Gina, G .... 803-323-2194.. 435 B
jonesgg@winthrop.edu
JONES, Gladys .... 601-977-7821.. 261 A
gjones@tougaloo.edu
JONES, Glendell .... 870-230-5091.... 20 E
president@hsu.edu
JONES, Glenn .... 973-720-2950.. 298 G
jonesg13@wpunj.edu
JONES, Glenna, S .... 815-224-0230.. 143 C
glenna_jones@ivcc.edu
JONES, Gloria .... 803-323-3900.. 435 B
jonesg@winthrop.edu
JONES, Gordon .... 208-426-2975.. 132 I
gojones@boisestate.edu
JONES, Grady, B .... 864-833-8006.. 432 B
gbjones@presby.edu
JONES, Greg .... 254-710-4772.. 452 H
greg_jones@baylor.edu
JONES, Greg .... 541-552-6758.. 395 A
gjones@sou.edu
JONES, Gwen .... 262-595-2151.. 520 F
gaines@uwp.edu
JONES, Harold .... 903-675-6256.. 473 B
hjones@tvcc.edu
JONES, Harold, P .... 205-934-5149...... 8 E
jonesh@uab.edu
JONES, Holly .... 319-385-6246.. 174 A
holly.jones@iw.edu
JONES, J. Pernell .... 610-341-5948.. 403 B
pjones1@eastern.edu
JONES, J. Preston .... 954-262-5127.. 105 J
prestonj@nova.edu
JONES, James .... 575-461-4413.. 300 A
jimj@mesalands.edu
JONES, James, M .... 812-888-5555.. 169 A
jjones@vinu.edu
JONES, Jane, M .... 423-439-4211.. 444 F
jonesj@etsu.edu
JONES, Janet .... 256-331-5310...... 6 A
janetj@nwscc.edu
JONES, Janice .... 270-707-3707.. 189 G
jjones0004@kctcs.edu
JONES, Jay .... 870-460-1022.... 23 D
jonesj@uamont.edu
JONES, Jay .... 870-460-1028.... 23 D
jonesj@uamont.edu
JONES, Jean .... 814-732-2981.. 415 A
jjones@edinboro.edu
JONES, Jeff .... 570-422-3833.. 414 H
jjones@esu.edu
JONES, Jeff .... 928-226-4297.... 12 N
jeff.jones@coconino.edu
JONES, Jeff .... 407-823-1582.. 111 E
jeffrey.jones@ucf.edu
JONES, Jeff .... 909-687-1750.... 44 H
jeffjones@gs.edu
JONES, Jen .... 254-295-8645.. 474 E
jen.jones@umhb.edu

JONES, Jennifer .... 201-200-3005.. 293 C
jjones@njcu.edu
JONES, Jennifer .... 815-455-8770.. 147 E
jjones@mchenry.edu
JONES, Jennifer .... 920-465-2111.. 520 B
jonesj@uwgb.edu
JONES, Jenny .... 704-687-7799.. 358 A
jenny.jones@uncc.edu
JONES, Jenny, L .... 404-880-8549.. 118 K
jjones@cau.edu
JONES, Jeremy .... 541-962-3553.. 391 G
jdjones1@eou.edu
JONES, Jerry .... 254-519-5446.. 468 G
jerry.jones@tamuct.edu
JONES, Jessica .... 815-921-4755.. 152 E
j.jones@rockvalleycollege.edu
JONES, Jessica, S .... 252-246-1216.. 354 D
jjones@wilsoncc.edu
JONES, Jessie .... 657-278-2620.... 33 A
jjones@fullerton.edu
JONES, Jill .... 309-438-3135.. 143 E
jajones2@ilstu.edu
JONES, Jill, D .... 208-467-8521.. 134 D
jdjones@nnu.edu
JONES, Jim .... 517-787-0800.. 235 G
jonesjamesl@jccmi.edu
JONES, Jim .... 325-670-1207.. 458 J
jjones@hsutx.edu
JONES, Jim .... 509-313-5926.. 504 A
jonesj@its.gonzaga.edu
JONES, John .... 316-978-7751.. 185 J
john.jones@wichita.edu
JONES, John .... 904-596-2304.. 113 J
jjones@tbc.edu
JONES, John .... 765-677-2387.. 164 B
john.jones@indwes.edu
JONES, John, D .... 870-307-7326.... 21 A
john.jones@lyon.edu
JONES, John, P .... 520-621-1112.... 17 I
jpjones@email.arizona.edu
JONES, III, John, R .... 205-934-4011...... 8 E
JONES, John, S .... 772-546-5534.. 102 S
johnjones@hsbc.edu
JONES, John Mark .... 903-468-8144.. 468 D
john.jones@tamuc.edu
JONES, Jon .... 417-268-6049.. 262 H
jjones@gobbc.edu
JONES, Joree .... 334-291-4913...... 2 H
joree.jones@cv.edu
JONES, Joseph .... 501-420-1202.... 18 F
joseph.jones@arkansasbaptist.edu
JONES, Joshua .... 785-864-3687.. 185 D
joshjones@ku.edu
JONES, Joshua .... 309-677-1000.. 136 B
jejones@bradley.edu
JONES, Joy .... 304-865-6102.. 511 C
joy.jones@ovu.edu
JONES, Joye .... 205-391-2283...... 6 G
jjones1@sheltonstate.edu
JONES, Judy .... 979-532-6561.. 479 J
judyj@wcjc.edu
JONES, Julia .... 801-581-5701.. 481 M
julia.jones@utah.edu
JONES, Justin, K .... 801-524-1921.. 480 J
jkjones@ldsbc.edu
JONES, Karen .... 419-448-2130.. 369 G
kjones9@heidelberg.edu
JONES, Karen .... 636-922-8258.. 271 A
kjones@stchas.edu
JONES, Karen .... 803-323-3708.. 435 B
jonesk@winthrop.edu
JONES, Karen, S .... 478-289-2012.. 120 C
kjones@ega.edu
JONES, Kate .... 952-446-4166.. 246 D
joneska@crown.edu
JONES, Kathleen .... 815-825-1709.. 144 F
kathleen.jones@kishwaukeecollege.edu
JONES, Kathryn, C .... 870-972-3027.... 18 J
kjones@astate.edu
JONES, Kathy .... 713-348-5460.. 464 E
kjones@rice.edu
JONES, Katie .... 413-565-1000.. 215 A
kjones@baypath.edu
JONES, Katie, P .... 864-488-4597.. 430 H
kjones@limestone.edu
JONES, Kelly .... 802-586-7711.. 485 C
kjones@sterlingcollege.edu
JONES, Kenneth .... 706-778-8500.. 125 J
kjones@piedmont.edu
JONES, Kenneth .... 904-743-1122.. 103 G
kjones@jones.edu
JONES, Kenneth .... 252-335-3858.. 356 D
kljones@ecsu.edu
JONES, JR., Kenneth .... 404-727-4144.. 120 E
kenneth.jones@emory.edu
JONES, Kent .... 256-228-6001...... 5 I
jonesk@nacc.edu
JONES, Kevin .... 863-638-7297.. 115 C
kevin.jones@warner.edu
JONES, Kevin .... 518-736-3622.. 315 A
kevin.jones@fmcc.suny.edu
JONES, Kim .... 903-823-3004.. 467 C
kim.jones@texarkanacollege.edu
JONES, Kim .... 361-593-2187.. 469 A
krkdy00@tamuk.edu
JONES, Kimberly .... 904-256-7048.. 103 D
kmarian@ju.edu
JONES, Kimberly, B .... 334-670-3113...... 7 H
kbrink@troy.edu
JONES, Kitty .... 360-867-6851.. 503 G
jonesk@evergreen.edu
JONES, Kona .... 217-875-7200.. 152 C
kona@richland.edu
JONES, Kristen .... 206-934-3701.. 506 J
kristen.jones@seattlecolleges.edu
JONES, Lance .... 307-268-2672.. 526 D
ljones@caspercollege.edu
JONES, Landon .... 816-415-6335.. 275 F
jonesl@william.jewell.edu
JONES, Laura .... 928-523-9084.... 15 H
laura.jones@nau.edu
JONES, Laura, B .... 734-764-7423.. 241 J
laurabj@umich.edu
JONES, Laurel .... 831-479-6302.... 29 G
lajones@cabrillo.edu
JONES, Laurene .... 609-586-4800.. 292 D
jonesl@mccc.edu
JONES, Laurie, S .... 706-568-2005.. 119 E
jones_laurie@columbusstate.edu
JONES, Leonard .... 360-650-2953.. 509 E
leonard.jones@wwu.edu
JONES, Leroy "Lee" .... 410-516-4612.. 208 D
JONES, II, Leroy .... 773-995-2965.. 136 M
ljones27@csu.edu
JONES, Leslie .... 985-448-4325.. 201 A
leslie.jones@nicholls.edu
JONES, Lewis .... 802-322-1676.. 483 H
JONES, Linda, E .... 413-782-1247.. 229 E
linda.jones@wne.edu
JONES, Linda, T .... 240-895-3246.. 210 E
ltjones1@smcm.edu
JONES, Lirse .... 973-720-2101.. 298 G
jonesl@wpunj.edu
JONES, Lisa .... 845-257-3216.. 331 E
jonesl@newpaltz.edu
JONES, Lisa .... 801-832-2237.. 483 D
ljones@westminstercollege.edu
JONES, Lisa .... 252-335-0821.. 349 A
lisa_jones@albemarle.edu
JONES, Loree, D .... 856-885-6095.. 296 A
loree.jones@rutgers.edu
JONES, Marcia .... 678-466-4250.. 119 A
marciajones@clayton.edu
JONES, Marcus .... 318-357-5701.. 201 B
marcusj@nsula.edu
JONES, Margaret .... 914-422-4043.. 325 J
mjones@pace.edu
JONES, Marian .... 704-378-1074.. 345 E
myjones@jcsu.edu
JONES, Marie .... 828-884-8248.. 342 C
jonesmf@brevard.edu
JONES, Marie .... 334-876-9284...... 4 A
marie.jones@wccs.edu
JONES, Mark .... 352-588-8367.. 108 C
mark.jones@saintleo.edu
JONES, Marvin, L .... 410-651-6144.. 212 B
mljones@umes.edu
JONES, Mary .... 913-971-3393.. 183 D
maryjones@mnu.edu
JONES, Mary .... 207-602-2096.. 205 F
bccareerservices@une.edu
JONES, Mary .... 805-289-6346.... 73 F
mjones@vcccd.edu
JONES, Matteel .... 864-250-8177.. 430 E
matteel.jones@gvltec.edu
JONES, Mautra .... 405-466-2937.. 383 M
mjones@langston.edu
JONES, Melanie, E .... 803-327-8012.. 435 D
mjones@yorktech.edu
JONES, Melinda, L .... 901-678-2690.. 445 C
mljones6@memphis.edu
JONES, Melissa .... 864-622-6011.. 427 B
melissajones@andersonuniversity.edu
JONES, Melissa .... 217-854-5514.. 135 K
melissa.k.jones@blackburn.edu
JONES, Melissa, A .... 910-678-8474.. 349 F
jonesma@faytechcc.edu
JONES, Melvin .... 304-766-3061.. 514 B
mjones55@wvstateu.edu
JONES, Meredith .... 580-559-5668.. 383 H
mjones@ecok.edu
JONES, Michael .... 909-607-7855.... 39 B
michael_jones@kgi.edu
JONES, Michael .... 814-886-6354.. 411 C
mjones@mtaloy.edu
JONES, Mike .... 601-925-3819.. 259 A
jones01@mc.edu
JONES, Mike .... 434-544-8538.. 491 F
jones.mj@lynchburg.edu
JONES, Mitchell .... 478-445-5800.. 121 A
mitchell.jones@gcsu.edu
JONES, Molly .... 513-618-1933.. 366 C
mjones@ccms.edu
JONES, Monica .... 859-985-3795.. 187 B
jonesmc@berea.edu
JONES, Nancy .... 714-241-6209.... 39 E
njones@coastline.edu
JONES, Natalie .... 207-780-4141.. 205 E
natalie.jones@maine.edu
JONES, Nathaniel .... 951-571-6341.... 59 A
nathaniel.jones@mvc.edu
JONES, Neil, J .... 518-783-2423.. 330 E
jones@siena.edu
JONES, Nicholas, P .... 814-865-2505.. 412 F
npj1@psu.edu
JONES, Nicole .... 619-660-4302.... 45 I
nicole.jones@gcccd.edu
JONES, Nina .... 662-915-7690.. 261 B
nina@olemiss.edu
JONES, Nolan .... 972-825-7970.. 466 D
nojones@sagu.edu
JONES, Norm .... 316-942-4291.. 183 I
jonesn@newmanu.edu
JONES, Norman .... 256-372-8653...... 1 A
norman.jones@aamu.edu
JONES, Olivia .... 919-530-7713.. 357 A
ojones@nccu.edu
JONES, Pam .... 909-621-8130.... 57 H
pam_jones@pitzer.edu
JONES, Pam, M .... 330-494-6170.. 377 J
pjones@starkstate.edu
JONES, Parago .... 303-329-6355.... 78 O
clinicdirector@cstcm.edu
JONES, Patricia .... 301-736-3631.. 209 A
patricia.jones@msbbcs.edu
JONES, Patricia .... 864-592-4634.. 432 H
jonesp@sccsc.edu
JONES, Patrick .... 904-256-7500.. 103 D
pjones15@ju.edu
JONES, Patrick .... 518-464-8500.. 314 A
pjones@excelsior.edu
JONES, Paul .... 478-825-6315.. 120 F
jonesp@fvsu.edu
JONES, Paulette .... 405-912-9020.. 387 D
pjones@hc.edu
JONES, Pernell .... 610-341-5948.. 412 C
pjones1@eastern.edu
JONES, Peter .... 215-204-2044.. 420 B
peter.jones@temple.edu
JONES, Phil .... 772-546-5534.. 102 S
philjones@hsbc.edu
JONES, Philip .... 717-245-1509.. 402 D
jonesph@dickinson.edu
JONES, JR. Philip, M .... 704-687-0514.. 358 A
pmjones@uncc.edu
JONES, R. Channing .... 910-272-3600.. 352 E
cjones@robeson.edu
JONES, Rachel .... 870-245-5593.... 21 E
jonesrm@obu.edu
JONES, Randy .... 805-565-7048.... 75 A
rjones@westmont.edu
JONES, Randy .... 302-857-6230.... 90 F
ljones@desu.edu
JONES, Randy .... 304-384-5385.. 513 A
rjones@concord.edu
JONES, Randy, P .... 214-768-2646.. 465 J
rpjones@smu.edu
JONES, Rauchelle .... 281-283-2536.. 474 A
jonesrau@uhcl.edu
JONES, Rene .... 870-733-6769.... 19 A
rjones@asumidsouth.edu
JONES, Renee .... 615-547-1359.. 439 H
rjones@cumberland.edu
JONES, Richard .... 856-256-4040.. 295 E
jonesri@rowan.edu
JONES, Rilla, C .... 662-720-7375.. 260 B
rcjones@nemcc.edu
JONES, Robert .... 303-762-6913.... 79 I
robert.jones@denverseminary.edu
JONES, Robert .... 239-732-3720.. 101 F
rrjones@fsw.edu
JONES, Robert .... 903-823-3154.. 467 C
robert.jones@texarkanacollege.edu
JONES, Robert .... 401-232-6027.. 424 K
rjones10@bryant.edu
JONES, Robert, A .... 317-788-3304.. 168 A
rjones@uindy.edu
JONES, Robert, H .... 864-656-3940.. 428 C
provost@clemson.edu
JONES, Robert, J .... 217-333-6677.. 157 A
JONES, Robert, J .... 217-333-6400.. 156 E
JONES, Robert, J .... 518-956-8010.. 331 A
presmail@albany.edu
JONES, Robert, P .... 915-831-3112.. 457 H
rjones35@epcc.edu
JONES, Robin .... 575-769-4921.. 299 G
robin.jones@clovis.edu
JONES, Rockwell, F .... 740-368-3000.. 376 B
rfjones@owu.edu
JONES, Roger .... 310-377-5501.... 51 G
rjones@marymountcalifornia.edu
JONES, Roger .... 434-544-8444.. 491 F
jones@lynchburg.edu
JONES, Ronald, L .... 901-272-5145.. 442 B
rjones@mca.edu
JONES, Rose .... 256-331-5313...... 6 A
jonesr@nwscc.edu
JONES, Rosemary .... 206-726-5169.. 503 B
rjones@cornish.edu
JONES, Rosetta .... 318-670-9315.. 199 J
rjones@susla.edu
JONES, Rythee .... 301-891-4542.. 213 D
eljones@wau.edu
JONES, Sam .... 850-729-4929.. 105 I
joness@nwfsc.edu
JONES, Sam .... 601-477-4038.. 258 E
sam.jones@jcjc.edu
JONES, Samuel .... 601-979-2260.. 258 D
samuel.jones@jsums.edu
JONES, Samuel, B .... 843-953-6367.. 428 G
jonessa@cofc.edu
JONES, Samuel, E .... 757-221-2565.. 488 F
sejone@wm.edu
JONES, Sarah, L .... 540-464-7667.. 499 E
jonessl10@vmi.edu
JONES, Scott .... 443-997-3715.. 208 D
scott.jonas@jhu.edu
JONES, Scott .... 765-455-9388.. 163 A
scotjone@iuk.edu
JONES, Serene .... 212-280-1403.. 338 I
sjones@uts.columbia.edu
JONES, Shannon .... 843-792-8839.. 431 A
joneshan@musc.edu
JONES, Sharon .... 575-646-2035.. 300 J
shjones@nmsu.edu
JONES, Sharon, A .... 503-943-7314.. 396 B
joness@up.edu
JONES, Shawn .... 870-230-5072.... 20 E
jonessh@hsu.edu
JONES, Shealeigh .... 940-552-6291.. 478 D
sjones@vernoncollege.edu
JONES, Sheba .... 312-662-4131.. 134 I
sjones@adler.edu
JONES, Sheila Dove .... 570-389-4027.. 414 D
sjones@bloomu.edu
JONES, Sheri .... 858-513-9240.... 27 V
sheri.jones@ashford.edu
JONES, Sheri .... 559-791-2459.... 47 L
sheri.jones@portervillecollege.edu
JONES, Sherry .... 781-762-1211.. 218 F
sjones@fmc.edu
JONES, Stacey .... 479-788-7302.... 23 A
stacey.jones@uafs.edu
JONES, Stanley .... 229-333-5732.. 129 G
sjones@valdosta.edu
JONES, Stephanie .... 313-993-1549.. 241 G
landerss@udmercy.edu
JONES, Steve .... 704-971-8500.. 343 E
sjones@charlottelaw.edu
JONES, Stuart .... 413-748-3757.. 228 E
sdjones@springfieldcollege.edu
JONES, Stuart .... 435-586-7775.. 481 N
jones@suu.edu
JONES, Sue .... 936-633-5291.. 451 D
sjones@angelina.edu
JONES, Susan .... 334-683-5108...... 5 C
sjones@judson.edu
JONES, Tara .... 251-380-4000...... 7 D
tjones@shc.edu
JONES, Teresa, A .... 225-216-8071.. 195 H
jonest@mybrcc.edu
JONES, Thomas, H .... 704-406-4369.. 344 E
tjones@gardner-webb.edu
JONES, Tiffane .... 708-596-2000.. 154 E
JONES, Tim .... 334-493-3573...... 5 F
twjones@lbwcc.edu
JONES, Tim .... 410-827-5704.. 207 A
tjones@chesapeake.edu
JONES, Tim .... 870-230-5117.... 20 E
jonest@hsu.edu
JONES, Tim .... 501-812-2760.... 21 H
thjones@pulaskitech.edu
JONES, Tim .... 850-245-0466.. 110 I
tim.jones@flbog.edu
JONES, Tim .... 412-536-1139.. 406 K
tim.jones@laroche.edu
JONES, Timothy Paul ...... 502-897-4347.. 192 D
tjones@sbts.edu
JONES, Tina, N .... 205-652-3497...... 9 F
tnj@uwa.edu
JONES, Todd .... 706-295-6339.. 121 C
tjones@highlands.edu
JONES, Todd .... 515-964-6242.. 171 B
tgjones@dmacc.edu
JONES, Todd .... 215-751-8167.. 401 G
tjones@ccp.edu
JONES, Tom, O .... 870-759-4101.... 24 J
tjones@wbcoll.edu
JONES, Tony .... 816-472-4852.. 266 D
tonyjones@kcai.edu
JONES, Tony .... 804-706-5235.. 497 D
tjones@jtcc.edu

JONES, Tracie .... 810-762-9536.. 236 C
tjones1@kettering.edu
JONES, Tracy, A .... 605-336-6588.. 436 J
tjones@sfseminary.edu
JONES, Trevor, H .... 410-334-2828.. 213 G
tjones@worwic.edu
JONES, Trina .... 757-569-6720.. 498 B
tjones@pdc.edu
JONES, Trish .... 859-846-5784.. 191 G
tjones@midway.edu
JONES, Tristan .... 785-242-2067.. 183 H
tjones@neosho.edu
JONES, Tyron .... 843-661-8324.. 429 J
tyron.jones@fdtc.edu
JONES, Ursula .... 802-383-6679.. 483 F
ujones@champlain.edu
JONES, V. Dale .... 434-223-6116.. 490 D
djones@hsc.edu
JONES, Valerie .... 740-477-7530.. 374 G
vjones3@ohiochristian.edu
JONES, Valorie .... 432-335-6477.. 463 B
vjones@odessa.edu
JONES, Verity .... 317-931-2327.. 160 B
vjones@cts.edu
JONES, Victor .... 937-708-5737.. 381 B
vjones@wilberforce.edu
JONES, Virginia .... 804-333-6781.. 498 D
vrjones@rappahannock.edu
JONES, Walter .... 310-287-4244.... 50 E
joneswc@wlac.edu
JONES, Wayne .... 405-733-7450.. 387 I
wzjones@rose.edu
JONES, Wendy .... 325-674-2359.. 449 J
jonesw@acu.edu
JONES, William .... 785-227-3380.. 178 J
president@bethanylb.edu
JONES, William, H .... 803-754-4100.. 429 B
JONES, Willie .... 504-284-5520.. 199 I
wijones@suno.edu
JONES, Wilma .... 718-982-4001.. 307 F
wilma.jones@csi.cuny.edu
JONES, Yasemin .... 212-217-4052.. 314 B
yasemin_jones@fitnyc.edu
JONES, Yolanda .... 622-254-3528.. 260 A
yjones@mvsu.edu
JONES-DULIN, Donna ..... 408-864-8209.... 44 A
jonesdulindonna@fhda.edu
JONES-JAMES, Kimberly . 225-490-1645.. 199 B
kimberly.jones-james@ololcollege.edu
JONES-JOHNSON,
Michelle .... 508-831-5473.. 230 C
mjonesjohnson@wpi.edu
JONES-MALONE, Dionne . 219-473-4305.. 159 L
djonesmalone@ccsj.edu
JONES-POPPE, Erin .... 802-443-2759.. 484 F
ejonespoppe@middlebury.edu
JONES ROSSI,
Meredythe .... 651-255-6162.. 255 C
mrossi@unitedseminary.edu
JONES-SCHENK, Jan .... 801-274-3280.. 483 C
jjonesschenk@wgu.edu
JONES SCHWEITZER,
Sharon .... 210-999-8406.. 473 A
sjones@trinity.edu
JONES-VARNELL,
Karla (Page) .... 252-638-7266.. 349 B
jonesp@cravencc.edu
JONES WATKINS,
Brenda .... 708-456-0300.. 156 C
brendawatkins@triton.edu
JONES-WILKINS, Brenda . 979-209-7264.. 452 J
brendawilkins@blinn.edu
JONG PARK, Tae .... 703-354-3533.. 491 C
JONGSMA KNAUSS,
Sonya .... 712-722-6024.. 171 J
sonya.knauss@dordt.edu
JONTE-PACE, Diane, E ..... 408-554-4751.... 63 E
djontepace@scu.edu
JOOF, Henan .... 213-763-7207.... 50 C
joofh@lattc.edu
JOOS DEKOVEN,
Chandra .... 413-528-7499.. 214 H
cdekoven@simons-rock.edu
JOPLIN, David .... 918-444-2885.. 384 G
joplind@nsuok.edu
JOPLING, James .... 318-345-9266.. 196 F
jamesjopling@ladelta.edu
JORDAHL, Ronald, I .... 704-847-5600.. 355 J
rjordahl@ses.edu
JORDAN, A. Dane .... 704-233-8026.. 359 H
djordan@wingate.edu
JORDAN, Amber .... 706-295-6768.. 121 F
ajordan@gntc.edu
JORDAN, Andy .... 803-508-7241.. 426 G
jordana@atc.edu
JORDAN, Angela .... 312-935-2002.. 152 D
ajordan@robertmorris.edu
JORDAN, Angelnique ...... 229-420-7030.. 115 K
angelnique.jordan@asurams.edu
JORDAN, Antonio .... 336-249-8186.. 349 C
antonio_jordan@davidsonccc.edu
JORDAN, Augustus .... 802-443-5141.. 484 F
jordan@middlebury.edu
JORDAN, Austina .... 706-245-7226.. 120 D
ajordan@ec.edu
JORDAN, Belva Brown .... 909-447-2527..... 39 A
bjordan@cst.edu
JORDAN, Ben .... 256-395-2211....... 7 C
benjordan@suscc.edu
JORDAN, Bill .... 715-346-2441.. 521 C
bjordan@uwsp.edu
JORDAN, Brett .... 734-432-5672.. 237 D
bjordan@madonna.edu
JORDAN, Brian .... 718-489-5493.. 328 D
bjordan@sfc.edu
JORDAN, Brian .... 252-335-3707.. 356 D
bnjordan@ecsu.edu
JORDAN, Brian, K .... 202-806-1100.... 93 A
brian.jordan@howard.edu
JORDAN, Cameron .... 706-368-6747.. 117 F
cjordan@berry.edu
JORDAN, Colin .... 941-487-4218.. 111 D
cjordan@ncf.edu
JORDAN, Cordell .... 405-682-1611.. 385 D
cjordan@occc.edu
JORDAN, Corey .... 315-386-7319.. 335 B
jordanc@canton.edu
JORDAN, Cyrenthia .... 507-389-2986.. 250 E
cyrenthia.jordan@mnsu.edu
JORDAN, Dave .... 443-518-3801.. 208 C
djordan@howardcc.edu
JORDAN, David, A .... 508-373-9594.. 215 D
david.jordan@becker.edu
JORDAN, Debi .... 281-425-6453.. 460 I
djordan@lee.edu
JORDAN, Donald, K .... 212-650-7278.. 307 E
djordan@aol.com
JORDAN, Edward, K .... 386-312-4151.. 108 B
edwardjordan@sjrstate.edu
JORDAN, Elizabeth, P ...... 302-295-1186.... 91 I
elizabeth.p.jordan@wilmu.edu
JORDAN, Eunice .... 802-225-3317.. 484 G
eunice.jordan@neci.edu
JORDAN, Holly .... 254-526-1128.. 454 A
holly.jordan@ctcd.edu
JORDAN, Jeanette .... 816-604-5444.. 267 H
jeanette.jordan@mcckc.edu
JORDAN, Jeffrey, C .... 206-281-2123.. 507 C
jordaj2@spu.edu
JORDAN, Jessica .... 415-422-5455.... 72 C
jgjordan@usfca.edu
JORDAN, John .... 425-889-7788.. 505 E
john.jordan@northwestu.edu
JORDAN, Judy, G .... 615-547-1249.. 439 H
jjordan@cumberland.edu
JORDAN, Katina .... 877-442-0505.... 84 E
katina.jordan@rockies.edu
JORDAN, Kelly .... 574-239-8355.. 161 N
kjordan@hcc-nd.edu
JORDAN, Kimberly .... 678-407-5000.. 121 B
kjordan@ggc.edu
JORDAN, Larry, W .... 301-736-3631.. 209 A
larry.jordan@msbbcs.edu
JORDAN, Lashanda .... 601-979-2477.. 258 D
lashanda.w.jordan@jsums.edu
JORDAN, Laurie .... 802-443-5626.. 484 F
ljordan@middlebury.edu
JORDAN, Lisa .... 619-239-0391.... 36 A
ljordan@cwsl.edu
JORDAN, Lisa .... 919-684-2424.. 343 J
lisa.jordan@duke.edu
JORDAN, Loretta .... 714-628-4933.... 58 H
jordan_lorrie@sccollege.edu
JORDAN, Lucille, A .... 603-882-6923.. 286 E
ljordan@ccsnh.edu
JORDAN, Marilyn, L .... 619-239-0391.... 36 A
mjordan@cwsl.edu
JORDAN, Mary, V .... 423-439-4445.. 444 F
jordanm@etsu.edu
JORDAN, Matthew .... 818-947-2316.... 50 D
jordanmt@lavc.edu
JORDAN, Megan, K .... 781-283-3795.. 229 C
mjordan@wellesley.edu
JORDAN, Michael .... 914-633-2206.. 317 B
mjordan@iona.edu
JORDAN, Michael .... 585-567-9228.. 316 F
michael.jordan@houghton.edu
JORDAN, Michael .... 864-977-7058.. 431 G
mike.jordan@ngu.edu
JORDAN, Michael, J .... 252-823-5166.. 349 E
jordanm@edgecombe.edu
JORDAN, Myron .... 510-748-2234.... 57 C
mjordan@peralta.edu
JORDAN, Nancy .... 603-623-0313.. 287 D
nancyjordan@nhia.edu
JORDAN, Nancy .... 903-223-3166.. 469 C
njordan@tamut.edu
JORDAN, Percy .... 409-984-6335.. 471 C
jordanpj@lamarpa.edu
JORDAN, Peter .... 817-515-4501.. 467 A
peter.jordan@tccd.edu
JORDAN, Richard .... 806-414-9648.. 472 D
richard.jordan@ttuhsc.edu
JORDAN, Ronald .... 714-997-6815.... 37 F
JORDAN, Sandra .... 803-641-3434.. 433 G
sandraj@usca.edu
JORDAN, Scott .... 860-486-3455.... 89 D
scott.jordan@uconn.edu
JORDAN, Stacy .... 501-205-8817.... 19 J
sjordan@cbc.edu
JORDAN, Stephen, M .... 303-556-3022.... 81 G
smjordan@msudenver.edu
JORDAN, Susan .... 870-862-8131.... 22 D
sjordan@southark.edu
JORDAN, Theresa .... 313-927-1261.. 237 E
tjordan@marygrove.edu
JORDAN, Tuajuanda, C ... 240-895-4410.. 210 E
tcjordan@smcm.edu
JORDAN, Vivian, R .... 240-895-2039.. 210 E
vrjordan@smcm.edu
JORDAN, Willis .... 312-980-9293.. 153 J
wjordan@iadtchicago.com
JORDAN-GOODEN,
Joyce .... 601-979-1591.. 258 D
joyce.m.jordan-gooden@jsums.edu
JORDAN-SMITH, Barbara 518-445-3398.. 303 D
bjord@albanylaw.edu
JORDANO, Mark .... 814-871-7438.. 404 A
jordan001@gannon.edu
JORDAY, Kindra, K .... 503-370-6055.. 396 G
kjordan@willamette.edu
JORDE, Sarah .... 507-288-4563.. 246 C
sjorde@crossroadscollege.edu
JORDEN, Rhonda .... 501-603-1401.... 23 C
jordenrhondal@uams.edu
JORDEN, Steven .... 660-626-2529.. 262 A
sjorden@atsu.edu
JORDON, Beth .... 512-472-4133.. 465 F
bjordon@ssw.edu
JORDON, Christina .... 863-638-2944.. 115 D
cmjordon@webber.edu
JORDON, Renee .... 617-603-6900.. 226 D
renee.jordon@necb.edu
JORDRE, Todd .... 605-626-3005.. 437 D
todd.jordre@northern.edu
JORE, Katie .... 715-346-3710.. 521 C
kjore@uwsp.edu
JORGENS, Amy, G .... 402-323-3414.. 282 F
ajorgens@southeast.edu
JORGENSEN, Harlan, R ... 712-707-7333.. 176 B
harlan@nwciowa.edu
JORGENSEN, Jerry .... 605-274-4045.. 435 E
jerry.jorgensen@augie.edu
JORGENSEN, Laurie .... 630-942-2755.. 138 B
jorgensenl@cod.edu
JORGENSEN, Michael ...... 435-283-7262.. 482 E
michael.jorgensen@snow.edu
JORGENSEN, Oona, A ..... 305-243-6501.. 114 H
a.jorgensen@med.miami.edu
JORGENSEN, Patti .... 920-735-5649.. 523 C
jorgensp@fvtc.edu
JORGENSEN, Ronald, A .. 712-274-5128.. 175 C
jorgensenr@morningside.edu
JORGENSON, Evelyn, E ... 479-619-4191.... 21 D
ejorgenson@nwacc.edu
JORGENSON, Jan .... 360-538-4243.. 504 B
jjorgens@ghc.edu
JORGENSON, Steve .... 651-696-6686.. 247 I
sjorgen2@macalester.edu
JORISSEN, Shari .... 612-338-7224.. 256 D
shari.jorissen@waldenu.edu
JOSAY ZULLO, Ashley .... 724-838-7832.. 419 D
josay@setonhill.edu
JOSCHKO, Brian .... 309-677-1002.. 136 B
bjoschko@bradley.edu
JOSE, Juana Clare .... 520-383-8401.... 17 E
jjose@tocc.edu
JOSE, Robert .... 617-373-7515.. 227 B
JOSE-EGUARAS, Agnes ... 661-763-7945.... 67 F
ajeguaras@taftcollege.edu
JOSEPH, Beatriz .... 210-486-3936.. 450 D
ijospeh@alamo.edu
JOSEPH, Cynthia .... 562-907-4830.... 75 B
cjoseph@whittier.edu
JOSEPH, Daniel, P .... 410-951-3549.. 212 E
djoseph@coppin.edu
JOSEPH, Darnell .... 713-313-1826.. 470 D
djoseph@tsu.edu
JOSEPH, Elizabeth .... 708-534-5000.. 140 H
ejoseph@govst.edu
JOSEPH, Eric .... 405-692-3106.. 384 C
ejoseph@macu.edu
JOSEPH, George .... 304-243-8160.. 515 C
gjosephwv@gmail.com
JOSEPH, James, E .... 315-445-4279.. 318 E
josepjae@lemoyne.edu
JOSEPH, Jann .... 574-520-4183.. 163 E
jljoseph@iusb.edu
JOSEPH, Jerry .... 217-206-6003.. 156 G
gjose1@uis.edu
JOSEPH, Joanne .... 315-792-7326.. 336 C
joanne.joseph@sunyit.edu
JOSEPH, John .... 810-766-4103.. 231 D
jjosep08@baker.edu
JOSEPH, Josh .... 212-960-0083.. 341 G
josh.joseph@yu.edu
JOSEPH, Laura .... 631-420-2003.. 335 E
laura.joseph@farmingdale.edu
JOSEPH, Laurel .... 281-756-3513.. 450 G
ljoseph@alvincollege.edu
JOSEPH, La'Vetta .... 510-485-7831.... 56 I
ljoseph@patten.edu
JOSEPH, Mark .... 740-284-5870.. 368 L
mjoseph@franciscan.edu
JOSEPH, Mary Ann .... 617-873-0227.. 217 A
maryann.joseph@cambridgecollege.edu
JOSEPH, Michael .... 219-464-6896.. 168 F
michael.joseph@valpo.edu
JOSEPH, Mitch .... 937-484-1262.. 380 E
jmjoseph@urbana.edu
JOSEPH, Noson .... 718-601-3523.. 341 F
njoseph@ytariverdale.com
JOSEPH, Patricia .... 484-365-7470.. 409 B
joseph@lincoln.edu
JOSEPH, Sonya, F .... 407-582-7734.. 114 N
sjoseph@valenciacollege.edu
JOSEPH, Stephen, M .... 724-287-8711.. 399 B
steve.joseph@bc3.edu
JOSEPH, Susan .... 423-697-3136.. 445 D
susan.joseph@chattanoogastate.edu
JOSEPH, Wendy .... 253-589-5822.. 502 F
wendy.joseph@cptc.edu
JOSEPH MATTISON, Sue 920-465-2050.. 520 B
mattisons@uwgb.edu
JOSEPH-SILVERSTEIN,
Jackie .... 920-459-6610.. 522 A
jackie.josephsilvers@uwc.edu
JOSEPHS, Nadine, W .... 412-291-6298.. 397 I
njosephs@aii.edu
JOSEPHSON, David .... 973-655-6956.. 293 A
josephsond@mail.montclair.edu
JOSEY, Peige .... 334-222-6591....... 5 F
pjosey@lbwcc.edu
JOSHEE, Jeet .... 562-985-8330.... 33 B
jeet.joshee@csulb.edu
JOSHEE, Jeet .... 562-985-4106.... 33 B
jeet.joshee@csulb.edu
JOSHI, Maulin .... 973-618-3519.. 290 A
mjoshi@caldwell.edu
JOSLIN, Dennis, A .... 402-354-7257.. 281 F
dennis.joslin@methodistcollege.edu
JOSLIN, Mike .... 661-362-3260.... 40 A
michael.joslin@canyons.edu
JOSLIN, Monica .... 413-662-5242.. 222 B
m.joslin@mcla.edu
JOSLIN, Randy .... 530-541-4660.... 48 D
joslin@ltcc.edu
JOSS, Jamie .... 304-637-1342.. 510 I
jossj@dewv.edu
JOSS, Liz .... 317-931-2316.. 160 B
ljoss@cts.edu
JOSSELL, Steven .... 662-621-4304.. 257 B
sjossell@coahomacc.edu
JOST, Steve, A .... 301-860-4212.. 212 D
sjost@bowiestate.edu
JOSVAI, Lisa .... 608-796-3913.. 522 O
lajosvai@viterbo.edu
JOTHEN, Karen, G .... 651-690-6666.. 254 M
kgjothen@stkate.edu
JOUGANATOS, Brandon .. 858-642-8066.... 54 A
bjouganatos@nu.edu
JOUGHIN, Sarah .... 207-581-3437.. 204 H
JOVANOVICH, Donna .... 804-594-1576.. 497 D
djovanovich@jtcc.edu
JOVELL, Kristi .... 802-865-5728.. 483 F
kjovell@champlain.edu
JOVEN, Robert .... 203-582-3468.... 88 G
robert.joven@quinnipiac.edu
JOWERS, Angel .... 205-652-3547...... 9 F
ajowers@uwa.edu
JOY, Darrell .... 314-290-0200.. 264 B
JOY, John .... 937-393-3431.. 377 F
jjoy@sscc.edu
JOYAUX, Aimee .... 804-862-6100.. 493 F
ajoyaux@rbc.edu
JOYCE, Colman .... 503-206-3205.. 396 C
cjoyce@uws.edu
JOYCE, Daniel .... 215-951-1539.. 407 A
joyced@lasalle.edu
JOYCE, David, C .... 828-884-8264.. 342 C
president@brevard.edu
JOYCE, Gerard .... 610-282-1100.. 402 B
gerard.joyce@desales.edu
JOYCE, Jane .... 617-349-8785.. 220 B
ajoyce5@lesley.edu
JOYCE, Jeffrey .... 816-654-7606.. 266 E
jjoyce@kcumb.edu
JOYCE, Kelly .... 812-866-7160.. 161 C
joyce@hanover.edu
JOYCE, Kevin .... 914-674-7775.. 320 G
kjoyce@mercy.edu
JOYCE, Mary .... 228-896-2517.. 259 C
mary.joyce@mgccc.edu

KAHLER, William .... 619-239-0391.... 36 A
wkahler@cwsl.edu
KAHLIG, Charla .... 254-295-5436.. 474 E
ckahlig@umhb.edu
KAHN, Amy, S .... 914-594-4529.. 323 I
amy_kahn@nymc.edu
KAHN, Avi .... 718-382-8702.. 340 J
KAHN, Carrie, W .... 716-270-5167.. 313 H
kahn@ecc.edu
KAHN, Jeannine .... 225-342-6950.. 200 E
jeannine.kahn@la.gov
KAHN, Patricia .... 718-982-2209.. 307 F
patricia.kahn@csi.cuny.edu
KAHOL, Pawan .... 620-235-4223.. 184 C
pkahol@pittstate.edu
KAHR, Audra, J .... 610-606-4630.. 400 E
ajhoffma@cedarcrest.edu
KAHWAJY-ANDERSON,
Joan .... 434-791-5624.. 487 C
jkahwajy@averett.edu
KAIDER-KOROL, Michele 585-340-9669.. 310 F
mkaider-korol@crcds.edu
KAIL, Pam .... 870-933-7903.... 18 H
pkail@asusystem.edu
KAIMINAAUAO, Colleen .. 808-245-8336.. 132 B
ckaimi@hawaii.edu
KAIN, Brian .... 610-526-1434.. 397 E
brian.kain@theamericancollege.edu
KAIN, Daniel .... 928-523-7122.... 15 H
daniel.kain@nau.edu
KAIN, Douglas .... 209-384-6344.... 52 E
kain.d@mccd.edu
KAIN, Gregory .... 708-709-3579.. 151 C
gkain@prairiestate.edu
KAINTH, Pritpal .... 516-876-3207.. 333 C
kainthp@oldwestbury.edu
KAIRO, Moses, T .... 410-651-6072.. 212 B
mkairo@umes.edu
KAISER, Carla .... 803-738-7610.. 431 B
kaiserc@midlandstech.edu
KAISER, Kenneth, H .... 215-204-6545.. 420 B
ken.kaiser@temple.edu
KAISER, Kim .... 720-496-1370.... 80 I
kim@cslsr.org
KAISER, Larry .... 215-707-8773.. 420 B
larry.kaiser@temple.edu
KAISER, Larry, R .... 215-707-8773.. 420 B
larry.kaiser@temple.edu
KAISER, Melissa, D .... 215-972-2002.. 413 L
mkaiser@pafa.edu
KAISER, Nancy .... 618-468-3315.. 145 G
nkaiser@lc.edu
KAISER, Sarah, J .... 805-525-4417.... 67 J
skaiser@thomasaquinas.edu
KAISER, Susan, B .... 530-752-3042.... 69 A
sbkaiser@ucdavis.edu
KAIVOLA, Karen .... 612-330-1024.. 244 I
kaivola@augsburg.edu
KAJIC, Martin .... 410-532-5855.. 210 B
mkajic@ndm.edu
KAJIWARA, Robert .... 808-245-8236.. 132 B
kajiwara@hawaii.edu
KAJSTURA, Alex .... 972-775-7250.. 462 J
alex.kajstura@navarocollege.edu
KAKAR, Casandra .... 602-285-7607.... 14 F
casandra.kakar@phoenixcollege.edu
KAKISH, William .... 770-729-8400.. 116 G
KAKIUCHI, Betty .... 760-355-6368.... 46 J
betty.kakiuchi@imperial.edu
KAKOULIDIS, Sofia .... 516-463-6810.. 316 D
sofia.kakoulidis@hofstra.edu
KAKUGAWA-LEONG,
Alyson, Y .... 808-932-7669.. 131 E
alyson@hawaii.edu
KALAFATIS, Lara, A .... 216-368-4244.. 365 B
lara.kalafatis@case.edu
KALAGORGEVICH, Mark .. 707-546-4000.... 42 M
mkal@empirecollege.com
KALANTZIS, Mary .... 217-333-0960.. 157 A
kalantzi@illinois.edu
KALB, Melanie, T .... 740-368-3377.. 376 B
mtkalb@owu.edu
KALBFLEISCH, Gary .... 206-546-5813.. 507 F
garyk@shoreline.edu
KALDIS, Paula .... 978-681-0800.. 225 B
paulad@mslaw.edu
KALDOR, Teresa .... 323-259-2966.... 55 A
tkaldor@oxy.edu
KALE, Kathy .... 408-554-5021.... 63 E
kkale@scu.edu
KALEMBA, Lena .... 815-455-8581.. 147 E
lkalemba@mchenry.edu
KALENDAE, Jeremiah .... 510-549-4704.... 66 J
jkalendae@sksm.edu
KALER, Eric, W .... 612-626-1616.. 255 H
upres@umn.edu
KALER, Robin .... 217-333-5010.. 157 A
rkaler@illinois.edu
KALERT, David .... 210-341-1366.. 463 A
dkalert@ost.edu
KALEVELA, Sylvester .... 719-549-2696.... 79 B
sylvester.kalevela@csupueblo.edu
KALEVITCH, Maria, V .... 412-397-4020.. 418 B
kalevitch@rmu.edu
KALFAYAN, Stephanie .... 650-725-2788.... 66 I
kalfayan@stanford.edu
KALFAYAN, Terry .... 619-260-5998.... 72 B
kalfayan@sandiego.edu
KALIAN, Heidi .... 703-658-4304.. 488 D
kalian@christendom.edu
KALICKI, Scott .... 603-524-3207.. 286 C
skalicki@ccsnh.edu
KALINA, Susan .... 907-786-1988.... 10 F
smkalina@uaa.alaska.edu
KALINOWSKI, Patricia .... 508-373-1901.. 215 D
patricia.kalinowski@becker.edu
KALINOWSKI, Teresa .... 716-270-5112.. 313 H
kalinowski@ecc.edu
KALIS, Michelle .... 860-231-5229.... 90 B
mkalis@usj.edu
KALISA, Marie-Chantal .... 402-472-3747.. 282 M
mkalisa2@unl.edu
KALISHMAN, Tony .... 352-338-1193.... 99 K
KALK, Jonathan .... 808-245-8272.. 132 B
kalk@hawaii.edu
KALKA, Alicia .... 304-367-4917.. 513 B
alicia.kalka@fairmontstate.edu
KALKBRENNER,
Suzanne, K .... 518-629-4530.. 316 G
s.kalkbrenner@hvcc.edu
KALLENBERGER, Melinda 414-382-6064.. 515 D
melinda.kallenberger@alverno.edu
KALLIERIS, Nick, C .... 847-543-2476.. 138 C
nkallieris@clcillinois.edu
KALLIN, Robert .... 717-337-6301.. 404 C
rkallin@gettysburg.edu
KALLIO, Kenneth .... 585-245-5531.. 333 B
kallio@geneseo.edu
KALLIS, John, A .... 724-938-4169.. 414 E
kallis@calu.edu
KALLUSKY, Barbara .... 651-227-9171.. 253 S
barbara.kallusky@mitchellhamline.edu
KALM, Stephen .... 406-243-4970.. 276 K
stephen.kalm@umontana.edu
KALMANOWITZ, Osher .... 718-645-0536.. 321 E
phecht@thejnet.com
KALMANSON, Dan, P .... 973-378-9856.. 297 A
daniel.kalmanson@shu.edu
KALMEY, Jon .... 814-866-8147.. 407 D
jkalmey@lecom.edu
KALOGIANNIS, Natalie .... 707-664-2874.... 35 D
natalie.kalogiannis@sonoma.edu
KALOOSTIAN, Damita .... 602-243-8021.... 14 I
damita.kaloostian@smcmail.maricopa.edu
KALOYEROS, Alain .... 518-956-7111.. 336 C
akaloyeros@sunypoly.edu
KALSBEEK, David, H .... 312-362-8706.. 139 C
dkalsbee@depaul.edu
KALSCHEUR, S.J.,
Gregory .... 617-552-2393.. 216 C
gregory.kalscheur@bc.edu
KALTCHEV, Matey .... 414-277-7544.. 518 E
kaltchev@msoe.edu
KALTEFLEITER, Caroline .. 607-753-4203.. 333 A
caroline.kaltefleiter@cortland.edu
KALTENMARK, Michael .... 317-940-9672.. 159 K
mkaltenm@butler.edu
KALTHOFF, Theodore, J .. 501-882-8830.... 18 I
tjkalthoff@asub.edu
KALU, Mma .... 919-546-8350.. 355 F
mkalu@shawu.edu
KALUSH, Paul .... 213-738-6818.... 66 F
accounting@swlaw.edu
KALWEIT, Clayton .... 847-970-4811.. 157 G
ckalweit@usml.edu
KALYAYEVA, Julia .... 510-845-0752.... 75 F
jkalyayeva@wi.edu
KALYN, Andrea .... 440-775-8200.. 374 C
andrea.kalyn@oberlin.edu
KALYNOVSKYI, Serhii .... 707-965-6218.... 56 A
skalynovskyi@puc.edu
KAM, Moshe .... 973-596-6506.. 293 D
moshe.kam@njit.edu
KAMAHELE, Ron .... 907-786-1419.... 10 F
rckamahale@uaa.alaska.edu
KAMARA, Sheku .... 414-277-7416.. 518 E
kamara@msoe.edu
KAMATH, Kiran .... 831-646-4034.... 53 A
kkamath@mpc.edu
KAMCIYAN, Jeanette .... 561-364-3064.... 96 G
KAMENETSKY, Shmuel .... 215-473-1212.. 420 A
talmudicalyeshiva@yahoo.com
KAMENETSKY, Sholom .... 215-477-1000.. 420 A
talmudicalyeshvia@yahoo.com
KAMIAB, Jane .... 336-770-3297.. 358 E
kamiabj@uncsa.edu
KAMIENIECKI, Sheldon .... 831-459-2919.... 70 F
sk1@ucsc.edu
KAMINSHINE, Steven, J .. 404-413-9040.. 122 D
skaminshine@gsu.edu
KAMINSKI, Crystal .... 312-752-2122.. 144 E
crystal.kaminski@kendall.edu
KAMINSKI, Don .... 304-243-8152.. 515 C
dkaminski@wju.edu
KAMINSKI, Janice, M .... 724-480-3423.. 401 F
jan.kaminski@ccbc.edu
KAMINSKI, Linda .... 509-574-4635.. 510 A
lkaminski@yvcc.edu
KAMINSKI, Marie .... 414-847-3334.. 518 D
mkaminski@miad.edu
KAMINSKI, Michael .... 213-624-1200.... 43 J
mkaminski@fidm.edu
KAMINSKY, Paul, A .... 615-353-3615.. 446 E
paul.kaminsky@nscc.edu
KAMLET, Lee .... 203-582-3641.... 88 G
lee.kamlet@quinnipiac.edu
KAMMER, Dan .... 573-876-7273.. 272 I
dkammer@stephens.edu
KAMMER, Roy .... 651-213-4863.. 247 B
rkammer@hazeldenbettyford.edu
KAMMERER, Joe .... 417-255-7240.. 269 A
joekammerer@missouristate.edu
KAMMERMAN, Amy .... 615-383-4848.. 449 G
akammerman@watkins.edu
KAMMERZELL, Joan .... 360-752-8436.. 501 G
jkammerzell@btc.edu
KAMOCHE, Njambi .... 847-925-6764.. 141 A
nkamoche@harpercollege.edu
KAMP, Cyndi .... 317-955-6103.. 165 N
ckamp@marian.edu
KAMPF, Stephen .... 419-372-7485.. 364 E
skampf@bgsu.edu
KAMPFSCHULTE, Darcy ... 616-632-2894.. 231 A
kampfdar@aquinas.edu
KAMPHAUS, Lisa .... 412-536-1526.. 406 K
lisa.kamphaus@laroche.edu
KAMPHAUS, Randy, W .... 541-346-1601.. 395 G
randyk@uoregon.edu
KAMPS, Anne .... 920-498-6367.. 524 E
anne.kamps@nwtc.edu
KAMPS, Larissa .... 866-323-0233.... 58 E
admissions@providencecc.edu
KAMPTNER, Elaine .... 231-591-2504.. 233 L
elainekamptner@ferris.edu
KAMWITHI, Gina .... 419-755-4711.. 373 G
gkamwithi@ncstatecollege.edu
KANACH, Nancy, A .... 609-258-5524.. 294 D
nkanach@princeton.edu
KANAK, Daniel .... 610-359-5135.. 401 L
dkanak@dccc.edu
KANANI, David .... 718-261-5800.. 305 J
dkanani@bramsonort.edu
KANAREK, Berel .... 914-736-1500.. 325 E
KANAREK, E .... 914-736-1500.. 325 E
KANAWADA, Christine .... 518-694-7355.. 303 C
christine.kanawada@acphs.edu
KANBAR, Hiam .... 831-242-5618.. 527 K
hiam.n.kanbar@dliflc.edu
KANDER, Ron .... 215-951-2106.. 416 G
kanderr@philau.edu
KANE, Andrew .... 609-258-3469.. 294 D
kane@princeton.edu
KANE, Barry, S .... 212-854-1458.. 311 E
barry@columbia.edu
KANE, Brian .... 610-785-6265.. 418 E
bkane@scs.edu
KANE, Candice .... 704-233-8631.. 359 H
c.kane@wingate.edu
KANE, Christopher .... 215-951-1585.. 407 A
kanec@lasalle.edu
KANE, Elizabeth .... 201-761-6046.. 296 K
ekane@saintpeters.edu
KANE, Jeffrey .... 516-299-2917.. 319 B
jeffrey.kane@liu.edu
KANE, Katherine, J .... 864-938-3913.. 432 B
kjkane@presby.edu
KANE, Kerri .... 413-755-4115.. 224 G
kpkane@stcc.edu
KANE, Kevin, M .... 610-660-3020.. 418 G
kevin.kane@sju.edu
KANE, Luanne .... 763-433-1297.. 248 K
luanne.kane@anokaramsey.edu
KANE, Michael .... 760-384-6258.... 47 K
michael.kane@cerrocoso.edu
KANE, Michael .... 859-858-3511.. 186 J
mike.kane@asbury.edu
KANE, Michael .... 281-476-1858.. 464 J
michael.kane@sjcd.edu
KANE, Robert, C .... 202-685-3927.. 528 B
galen.r.kane.mil@ndu.edu
KANE, Ryan, D .... 407-582-3421.. 114 N
rkane8@valenciacollege.edu
KANE, Sara, F .... 863-638-7602.. 115 C
sara.kane@warner.edu
KANE, Scott .... 401-456-8061.. 425 E
skane@ric.edu
KANE, Terrence .... 607-777-5014.. 331 B
tkane@binghamton.edu
KANE, Terrence .... 607-777-2131.. 331 B
tkane@binghamton.edu
KANE, Thomas .... 401-254-3531.. 426 B
tkane@rwu.edu
KANE, Thomas .... 781-891-2340.. 215 F
tkane@bentley.edu
KANE, Thomas, F .... 570-674-6223.. 410 K
tkane@misericordia.edu
KANE, Victor .... 626-571-8811.... 72 E
victork@uwest.edu
KANELLIS, Jennifer .... 908-737-7100.. 292 C
jkanelli@kean.edu
KANELOS, Gwen, E .... 708-209-3101.. 138 G
gwen.kanelos@cuchicago.edu
KANELOS, Peter .... 219-464-5022.. 168 F
peter.kanelos@valpo.edu
KANEVSKAYA, Svetlana ... 212-752-1530.. 318 F
svetlana.kanevskaya@limcollege.edu
KANG, David .... 303-492-4212.... 83 K
david.kang@colorado.edu
KANG, Hyo Jeong .... 714-535-3886.... 65 B
hjkang@southbaylo.edu
KANG, Jerry .... 310-825-3935.... 69 D
jkang@equity.ucla.edu
KANG, Mia .... 770-220-7906.. 120 G
academic@gcuniv.edu
KANG, Soohae .... 714-527-0691.... 43 C
KANG, Sung Do .... 213-386-0080.... 52 H
KANG, Woo Joong .... 562-926-1023.... 58 B
wookang78@ptsa.edu
KANG, Yunn, K .... 215-702-4461.. 399 E
ykang@cairn.edu
KANGAS, Michelle .... 218-855-8034.. 248 N
mkangas@clcmn.edu
KANGAS, Richard .... 218-322-2319.. 249 G
richard.kangas@itascacc.edu
KANIA, Edward, A .... 704-894-2125.. 343 I
edkania@davidson.edu
KANIKKEBERG, Dee Dee . 208-885-6571.. 134 G
deedeek@uidaho.edu
KANIPE, H. Dean .... 828-652-0634.. 351 C
deank@mcdowelltech.edu
KANIS, David .... 773-995-2497.. 136 M
dkanis@csu.edu
KANISS, John .... 253-589-5529.. 502 F
john.kaniss@cptc.edu
KANJIRATHINKAL,
Mathew .... 563-876-3353.. 171 I
mathewk@dwci.edu
KANLIOGLU, Osman .... 832-230-5555.. 462 K
osman@na.edu
KANN, Stephanie, J .... 847-808-8444.. 158 D
skann@worshamcollege.com
KANNAN, Gavindarajan ... 478-825-6320.. 120 F
kannang@fvsu.edu
KANNAN, Jack .... 919-735-5151.. 354 A
jek@waynecc.edu
KANNENBERG, Gregory .. 920-465-2239.. 520 B
kannenbg@uwgb.edu
KANNENWISCHER,
Susan, E .... 614-236-6511.. 364 N
skannenwischer@capital.edu
KANOTZ, Ashley .... 304-829-7411.. 510 G
akanotz@bethanywv.edu
KANOY, David .... 910-362-7695.. 348 A
dkanoy@cfcc.edu
KANPOL, Barry .... 616-331-6820.. 234 F
kanpolb@gvsu.edu
KANTARDJIEFF,
Katherine .... 760-750-7204.... 34 D
kkantard@csusm.edu
KANTER, Connie .... 206-296-6148.. 507 E
kanterc@seattleu.edu
KANTER, Steven .... 816-235-1803.. 273 F
kantersl@umkc.edu
KANTNER, Joanne .... 815-825-9450.. 144 F
joanne.kantner@kishwaukeecollege.edu
KANTNER, John .... 904-620-1360.. 112 B
j.kantner@unf.edu
KANTNER, John .... 904-620-2455.. 112 B
j.kantner@unf.edu
KANTNER, Michael .... 856-256-4566.. 295 E
kantner@rowan.edu
KANTO, Kind .... 691-330-2620.. 529 F
kank@comfsm.fm
KANTOR, Ali .... 617-521-1038.. 228 C
ali.kantor@simmons.edu
KANTOR, Rebecca .... 303-315-6343.... 84 A
rebecca.kantor@ucdenver.edu
KANU, Andrew .... 804-524-5930.. 499 G
akanu@vsu.edu
KANWISCHER, Charlie .... 419-372-9395.. 364 E
ckanwis@bgsu.edu
KANZ, Maryellen .... 507-453-2673.. 250 C
mkanz@southeastmn.edu
KAO, Chi-Chang .... 650-723-2300.... 66 I
KAO, Imin .... 631-632-7422.. 332 A
imin.kao@stonybrook.edu
KAO, Monica .... 628-448-0023.... 47 E
vp-admin@itsla.edu
KAO, Teresa .... 626-571-5110.... 49 B
teresakao@les.edu

KATZMAN, Carol 212-854-5768 304 I
ckatzman@barnard.edu
KAUCHER, Ellie 818-386-5627 57 F
ekaucher@pgu.edu
KAUFFMAN, Carol 301-784-5199 205 G
ckauffman@allegany.edu
KAUFFMAN, Dana 703-323-3750 497 H
tkauffman@nvcc.edu
KAUFFMAN, Jan 574-535-7515 161 A
jrkauffman@goshen.edu
KAUFFMAN, JR.,
John, M 910-893-1776 342 F
kauffmanj@campbell.edu
KAUFFMAN, Mark 814-868-2173 407 D
mkauffman@lecom.edu
KAUFFMAN, Steve 312-369-7383 138 F
skauffman@colum.edu
KAUFFMAN, Tina 502-272-8336 187 A
tkauffmann@bellarmine.edu
KAUFFMAN, Wendy 910-695-3814 353 A
kauffmanw@sandhills.edu
KAUFFMAN, William, R 314-977-3719 271 K
kauffman@slu.edu
KAUFMAN, Angela 817-257-7830 469 G
a.kaufman@tcu.edu
KAUFMAN, Cathryne 309-694-8504 141 F
cathryne.kaufman@icc.edu
KAUFMAN, Helena 507-222-4349 245 C
hkaufman@carleton.edu
KAUFMAN, Kris, A 716-878-3000 332 F
kaufmaka@buffalostate.edu
KAUFMAN, Lon 212-772-4150 308 D
lk506@hunter.cuny.edu
KAUFMAN, Lori 561-912-1211 99 J
lkaufman@evergladesuniversity.edu
KAUFMAN, Michael 303-384-3009 78 M
mkaufman@mines.edu
KAUFMAN, Michael, J 312-915-7143 146 G
mkaufma@luc.edu
KAUFMAN, Paulette 303-751-8700 77 C
kaufman@bel-rea.com
KAUFMAN, Steven 734-462-4400 240 H
skaufman@schoolcraft.edu
KAUFMANN, Marta 215-968-8242 399 A
kaufmann@bucks.edu
KAUFMANN, Sandra 516-876-2715 333 C
kaufmanns@oldwestbury.edu
KAUGARS, Karlis 607-436-3663 331 F
karlis.kaugars@oneonta.edu
KAUKUS, Arlene, F 716-645-2231 331 C
arleneks@buffalo.edu
KAUNITZ, Carol 516-876-3979 333 C
kaunitzc@oldwestbury.edu
KAUP, Joan 513-562-8745 363 H
jkaup@artacademy.edu
KAUR, Kuldeep 530-741-6723 76 D
kkaur@yccd.edu
KAUR, Kuldeep 530-741-6723 76 B
kkaur@yccd.edu
KAUR, Kuldeep 916-484-8484 51 A
kaurk@arc.losrios.edu
KAUS, Annette 402-375-7230 281 J
ankaus1@wsc.edu
KAUS, Cheryl 609-652-4512 297 C
cheryl.kaus@stockton.edu
KAUSHANSKY, Kenneth 631-444-9011 332 A
kenneth.kashansky@stonybrook.edu
KAUSHIK, Suresh, C 334-420-4244 7 G
skaushik@trenholmstate.edu
KAUSS, Bruce 541-278-5763 390 C
bkauss@bluecc.edu
KAUTZ, III, John 561-803-2084 106 C
john_kautz@pba.edu
KAUTZ, Kathy 203-932-7475 90 A
kkautz@newhaven.edu
KAUTZ, Rebecca 308-635-6062 283 D
kautzb2@wncc.edu
KAUTZ DE ARANGO,
Kathy 203-932-7000 90 A
KAUTZMAN, Amy 916-278-5679 34 B
kautzman@csus.edu
KAVAJECZ, Kenneth, A 315-443-9494 337 A
kakavaje@syr.edu
KAVALIERATOS,
Gerasimos (Jerry) 480-860-2700 13 G
gkavalieratos@taliesin.edu
KAVANAGH, Kathy, J 914-594-4487 323 I
kathy_johnston@nymc.edu
KAVANAGH, Kenneth 239-590-7007 110 L
kavanagh@fgcu.edu
KAVANAUGH, Gerard 508-999-8002 220 H
gkavanaugh@umassd.edu
KAVANAUGH, Maria, A 508-565-1331 228 F
mkavanaugh@stonehill.edu
KAVANAUGH, Michael 714-484-7108 54 G
mkavanaugh@cypresscollege.edu
KAVANAUGH, Steven 610-896-1141 405 I
skavanau@haverford.edu
KAVASCH, Kris 903-877-7399 477 E
kris.kavasch@uthct.edu
KAVCSAK, Lynn, E 919-866-5696 353 I
lekavcsak@waketech.edu
KAVENEY, Shannon 562-860-2451 36 P
skaveney@cerritos.edu
KAVOURIS, John 312-369-8646 138 F
jkavouris@colum.edu
KAVRAN, Elizabeth 440-646-8107 380 F
ekavran@ursuline.edu
KAWAI`AE`A, Keiki 808-932-7360 131 E
keiki@hawaii.edu
KAWAMOTO, Judy 401-232-6046 424 K
jkawamot@bryant.edu
KAWANNA, JR., Ronald 708-596-2000 154 E
rkawanna@ssc.edu
KAWAR, Ferris 310-434-3911 63 F
kawar_ferris@smc.edu
KAWAUCHI, John 970-943-2266 84 H
jkawauchi@western.edu
KAY, Audrey 603-623-0313 287 D
audreykay@nhia.edu
KAY, Carol 915-831-6725 457 H
ckay@epcc.edu
KAY, James, F 609-497-7815 294 C
academic.dean@ptsem.edu
KAY, Kent 314-539-5291 271 F
kentkay@stlcc.edu
KAY, R. David 570-327-4770 413 O
dkay@pct.edu
KAY, Sabrina 213-355-7777 44 D
sabrina.kay@fremont.edu
KAY, Steve, A 858-784-8469 64 B
kay@scripps.edu
KAY-WONG, Chelsea 808-932-7442 131 E
ckwong@hawaii.edu
KAYE, David 916-388-2803 36 D
dkaye@carrington.edu
KAYLOR, Alice, J 724-537-4566 419 A
alice.kaylor@email.stvincent.edu
KAYLOR, Debbie 208-426-4351 132 I
debbiekaylor@boisestate.edu
KAYLOR, Sean, P 845-575-3000 320 B
sean.kaylor@marist.edu
KAYLOR, Stacia 620-331-4100 181 J
skaylor@indycc.edu
KAYNAMA, Shohreh, A 410-704-3342 213 B
skaynama@towson.edu
KAYNARD, Meryl 718-982-2000 307 F
meryl.kaynard@csi.cuny.edu
KAYNE, Susan 908-737-0580 292 C
skayne@kean.edu
KAYS, Brenda, S 903-983-8100 460 D
bkays@kilgore.edu
KAYSEN-LUZBETAK,
Angie 815-280-6679 144 A
akaysen@jjc.edu
KAZAMA, Susan 808-734-9519 131 I
smurata@hawaii.edu
KAZANECKI-KEMPTER,
Diane 631-420-2065 335 E
diane.kazanecki-kempter@farmingdale.edu
KAZARIAN, Julie 508-929-8077 222 F
jkazarian@worcester.edu
KAZDA, Kathleen 262-691-5464 524 G
kkazda@wctc.edu
KAZEE, Thomas, A 812-488-2151 167 I
president@evansville.edu
KAZEN, James, D 210-567-0390 477 D
kazen@uthscsa.edu
KAZEN, Tom 708-239-4866 155 M
thomas.kazen@trnty.edu
KAZER, Meredith, W 203-254-4150 87 G
mkazer@fairfield.edu
KAZEROUNIAN, Kazem 860-486-2221 89 D
kazem.kazerounian@uconn.edu
KAZMAN, Nelly 909-593-3511 71 B
nkazman@laverne.edu
KAZMI, Saba 909-652-6193 37 D
saba.kazmi@chaffey.edu
KAZMIR, Darin 361-582-2417 478 F
darin.kazmir@victoriacollege.edu
KAZUMA, Clement 680-488-2471 530 E
KAZYAKA, Carrie 619-961-4324 68 A
ckazyaka@tjsl.edu
KEADY, Thomas, J 617-552-6795 216 C
thomas.keady@bc.edu
KEAGY, Thomas, A 215-951-1042 407 A
keagy@lasalle.edu
KEAIRNS, Kathy 303-871-4156 84 B
kathy.keairns@du.edu
KEAL, Aaron, J 620-421-6700 182 G
aaronk@labette.edu
KEALA, David 808-675-3572 130 E
david.keala@byuh.edu
KEALY, IHM,
Marie Hubert 610-647-4400 406 B
mkealy@immaculata.edu
KEAN, Linda 781-239-4284 214 G
kean@babson.edu
KEANE, Christopher 509-335-3574 508 H
chris.keane@vetmed.wsu.edu
KEANE, James 610-896-1023 405 I
jkeane@haverford.edu
KEANE, Nancyellen 434-381-6506 494 M
nkeane@sbc.edu
KEANE, Timothy 303-458-1844 82 L
keane@regis.edu
KEANE-DAWES,
Jennifer, M 410-651-6507 212 B
jmkeanedawes@umes.edu
KEARNEY, Anne, E 315-445-4195 318 E
kearneae@lemoyne.edu
KEARNEY, Janice 870-575-8000 23 E
kearneyj@uapb.edu
KEARNEY, Jeannie 507-433-0571 251 H
jeannie.kearney@riverland.edu
KEARNEY, Joseph, D 414-288-1955 517 I
joseph.kearney@marquette.edu
KEARNEY, Kimberly 540-261-8542 494 F
kim.kearney@svu.edu
KEARNEY, Margaret 585-275-9093 338 K
margaret.kearney@rochester.edu
KEARNEY, Matthew 314-889-4686 265 C
mkearney@fontbonne.edu
KEARNEY, Stephen 617-984-1734 227 F
skearney@quincycollege.edu
KEARNS, Chris 406-994-2828 277 C
chris.kearns@montana.edu
KEARNS, Gayle 405-470-2636 388 B
gayle.kearns@swcu.edu
KEARNS, Jane 802-728-1231 486 D
jkearns@vtc.edu
KEARNS, Joanne 973-328-5044 290 H
jkearns@ccm.edu
KEARNS, Kevin 716-673-3758 331 D
kevin.kearns@fredonia.edu
KEARNS, Lorna, R 412-624-6786 421 G
lrkearns@pitt.edu
KEARNS, Michael 928-757-0801 15 E
mkearns@mohave.edu
KEARNS, Michelle 801-863-8976 482 C
michelle.kearns@uvu.edu
KEARNS, Richard 918-631-2150 389 E
richard-kearns@utulsa.edu
KEARNS, Susan, L 512-475-7368 476 B
susan.kearns@austin.utexas.edu
KEARNS, Tom 765-983-1465 160 G
kearnto@earlham.edu
KEARNS-BARRETT,
Marybeth 508-793-2448 217 C
mkearns@holycross.edu
KEARY, Chris 785-864-5900 185 D
ckeary@ku.edu
KEAS, Lenora 361-698-1207 457 D
lkeas@delmar.edu
KEASLER, Robert, L 540-665-4533 494 B
rkeasler@su.edu
KEASLING, Diane 423-461-8968 442 K
dlkeasling@milligan.edu
KEAST, Cindy 620-665-3565 181 I
keastc@hutchcc.edu
KEATHLEY, Gwynne 410-225-5242 209 B
gkeathley@mica.edu
KEATING, Andrew 406-657-1104 278 D
andrew.keating@rocky.edu
KEATING, Brendan 312-915-6147 146 G
bkeating@luc.edu
KEATING, Clare 419-559-2383 377 M
ckeating01@terra.edu
KEATING, Frederick 856-415-2100 295 D
fkeating@rcgc.edu
KEATING, Jeff 909-469-5205 74 K
jkeating@westernu.edu
KEATING, Joseph 740-588-1396 382 C
jkeating@zanestate.edu
KEATING, Kathy 616-234-4953 234 E
kkeating@grcc.edu
KEATING, Lisa 518-454-2833 311 B
keatingl@strose.edu
KEATING, Richard, S 413-782-1473 229 E
richard.keating@wne.edu
KEATON, Alicia 407-823-2827 111 E
alicia.keaton@ucf.edu
KEATY, Anthony 781-899-5500 227 E
akeaty@psjs.edu
KEBABIAN, Helen 315-228-7451 310 G
hkebabian@colgate.edu
KEBISEK, Kris 503-297-5544 393 C
kkebisek@ocac.edu
KEBREAB, Ermia 530-754-9707 69 A
ekebreab@ucdavis.edu
KECHICHIAN,
Avedis (Avo) 909-593-3511 71 B
akechichian2@laverne.edu
KECK, Jenna 785-539-3571 183 B
jkeck@mccks.edu
KECK, Kathleen, A 518-327-6223 326 B
kkeck@paulsmiths.edu
KECK, Kay 269-965-3931 236 A
keckk@kellogg.edu
KECK, III, Ray, M 903-886-5011 468 D
ray.keck@tamuc.edu
KECKLEY, Kim 540-665-4841 494 B
kkeckley@su.edu
KECSKÉS, Gary 630-466-7900 157 K
gkecskes@waubonsee.edu
KEDDO, Dwain 239-489-9205 101 F
dkeddo@fsw.edu
KEDROSKI, Cristie 850-729-5357 105 I
kedroskc@nwfsc.edu
KEDROWSKI, Jeff 630-617-3042 140 C
jeffk@elmhurst.edu
KEDROWSKI, Karen 218-748-2418 249 G
kkedrowski@nhed.edu
KEDROWSKI, Karen 218-748-2418 249 I
kkedrowski@mesabirange.edu
KEDROWSKI, Karen, M 803-323-2160 435 B
kedrowskik@winthrop.edu
KEDSKI, Cathy 508-830-5042 222 C
ckedski@maritime.edu
KEE, Josh 870-235-4321 22 F
jrkee@saumag.edu
KEEBLER, David 805-289-6354 73 F
dkeebler@vcccd.edu
KEECH, Brian, T 215-895-2244 402 G
brian.keech@drexel.edu
KEECH, Renee 860-465-5348 85 G
keechr@easternct.edu
KEEDY, Thomas, E 765-361-6227 169 C
keedyt@wabash.edu
KEEFE, Kevin 973-328-5064 290 H
kkeefe@ccm.edu
KEEFE, Kristen, A 801-581-3402 481 M
k.keefe@utah.edu
KEEFE, Maureen 617-879-7705 222 A
mkeefe@massart.edu
KEEFE, Maureen 415-749-4577 61 B
mkeefe@sfai.edu
KEEFE, Phil 914-674-7782 320 G
pkeefe@mercy.edu
KEEFE, Terri, K 610-799-1580 408 G
tkeefe@lccc.edu
KEEFE, Thomas, W 972-721-5203 473 D
KEEFER, Elizabeth 216-368-4286 365 B
elizabeth.keefer@case.edu
KEEFER, Elizabeth, J 216-368-5555 365 B
elizabeth.keefer@case.edu
KEEFER, Matthew, W 618-453-7313 154 I
keefer@siu.edu
KEEFER, Maureen, H 412-397-6484 418 B
keefer@rmu.edu
KEEFER, Michael, R 814-393-1610 414 G
mkeefer@cuf-inc.org
KEEFER, Sue 719-384-6882 82 A
sue.keefer@ojc.edu
KEEGAN, Bridget, M 402-280-4015 279 H
bmkeegan@creighton.edu
KEEGAN, Joe 518-891-2915 325 A
jkeegan@nccc.edu
KEEGAN, Kim 603-206-8005 286 D
kkeegan@ccsnh.edu
KEEGAN, Michael 605-394-2336 437 E
michael.keegan@sdsmt.edu
KEEGAN, Thomas 360-416-7997 507 G
thomas.keegan@skagit.edu
KEEGAN, Vicki 608-262-3786 522 A
vicki.keegan@uwc.edu
KEEHLWETTER,
F. Stanley 724-458-2142 404 F
fskeehlwetter@gcc.edu
KEEHN, Jay 305-653-7141 378 E
jay.keehn@myunion.edu
KEEL, Brooks, A 706-721-2301 117 D
president@augusta.edu
KEEL, Dave 804-758-6731 498 D
dkeel@rappahannock.edu
KEELER, Anne, B 540-828-5386 487 H
akeeler@bridgewater.edu
KEELER, Bruce 714-241-6257 39 E
bkeeler@coastline.edu
KEELER, John, T 412-624-7605 421 G
keeler@pitt.edu
KEELER, Karen 603-206-8002 286 D
kkeeler@ccsnh.edu
KEELER-STROM, Michela 402-844-7122 282 B
michela@northeast.edu
KEELEY, Brian 360-383-3375 509 F
bkeeley@whatcom.ctc.edu
KEELEY, Dan 845-574-4452 327 G
dkeeley@sunyrockand.edu
KEELEY, Edward, J 608-663-2223 516 F
ekeeley@edgewood.edu
KEELEY, Eileen, M 704-894-2422 343 I
eikeeley@davidson.edu
KEELEY, Louise Carroll 508-767-7312 214 F
lkeeley@assumption.edu
KEELEY, Stephany 206-239-4500 502 D
KEELS, Carl 301-736-3631 209 A
genekeels@aol.com
KEEN, Cathy 352-395-5829 109 C
cathy.keen@sfcollege.edu
KEEN, Larry 910-678-8321 349 F
keenl@faytechcc.edu

KELLMAN, Jordan .... 337-482-6219.. 201 D
kellman@louisiana.edu
KELLOG, Torri .... 954-492-5353.... 97 I
tkellog@citycollege.edu
KELLOGG, Gary .... 530-221-4275.... 64 C
gkellogg@shasta.edu
KELLOGG, John .... 612-625-3387.. 255 H
j-kell@umn.edu
KELLOGG, Leslie .... 269-927-6748.. 236 G
lkellogg@lakemichigancollege.edu
KELLOGG, Magdalen .... 315-568-3067.. 323 A
mkellogg@nycc.edu
KELLOGG, Sandi .... 503-399-5041.. 390 E
sandi.kellogg@chemeketa.edu
KELLOGG, Tonia .... 405-585-5802.. 385 B
tonia.kellogg@okbu.edu
KELLY, Alan, J .... 516-463-5027.. 316 D
alan.j.kelly@hofstra.edu
KELLY, Amber .... 662-246-6263.. 259 B
akelly@msdelta.edu
KELLY, Anita .... 484-664-3178.. 411 D
akelly@muhlenberg.edu
KELLY, Anna .... 401-739-5000.. 425 C
akelly@neit.edu
KELLY, Audrey .... 908-737-7000.. 292 C
aukelly@kean.edu
KELLY, Barbara .... 334-386-7299...... 3 I
bkelly@faulkner.edu
KELLY, Benji .... 270-789-5211.. 187 G
jbkelly@campbellsville.edu
KELLY, Bonnie .... 229-468-2091.. 130 A
bonnie.kelly@wiregrass.edu
KELLY, Brenda, S .... 507-933-7541.. 246 J
bkelly@gustavus.edu
KELLY, Brendan .... 850-474-3306.. 113 A
bkelly@uwf.edu
KELLY, Brian .... 805-525-4417.... 67 J
bkelly@thomasaquinas.edu
KELLY, Brian .... 508-541-1622.. 217 G
bkelly@dean.edu
KELLY, Brian .... 510-780-4500.... 48 J
bkelly@lifewest.edu
KELLY, Brian .... 541-463-5310.. 391 G
kellyb@lanecc.edu
KELLY, Bryan .... 866-687-2258.... 30 I
KELLY, Calvin, A .... 512-448-8538.. 464 G
ckelly1@stedwards.edu
KELLY, Chassie .... 662-720-7239.. 260 B
cmkelly@nemcc.edu
KELLY, Chris .... 620-235-4122.. 184 C
ckelly@pittstate.edu
KELLY, Daniel .... 734-487-2031.. 233 J
dkelly20@emich.edu
KELLY, Darin .... 215-717-3108.. 401 J
darin.kelly@curtis.edu
KELLY, OSB, David .... 724-805-2644.. 419 A
david.kelly@email.stvincent.edu
KELLY, Debra .... 609-771-2161.. 290 F
dkelly@tcnj.edu
KELLY, Dennis .... 937-481-2555.. 381 C
dennis_kelly@wilmington.edu
KELLY, Donald .... 251-809-1521...... 5 A
don.kelly@jdcc.edu
KELLY, Donald .... 203-591-7394.... 88 F
dkelly@post.edu
KELLY, Drew .... 610-526-6669.. 405 B
dkelly@harcum.edu
KELLY, Edward, J .... 423-439-8550.. 444 F
kellye@etsu.edu
KELLY, Francis, E .... 845-575-3000.. 320 B
francis.kelly@marist.edu
KELLY, George, N .... 615-327-6800.. 442 A
gkelly@mmc.edu
KELLY, Grace, A .... 802-654-2568.. 484 I
gkelly@smcvt.edu
KELLY, Grayson .... 864-646-8361.. 433 C
KELLY, Hank .... 740-420-5924.. 374 G
hkelly@ohiochristian.edu
KELLY, Heather, A .... 302-831-2021.... 91 F
hkelly@udel.edu
KELLY, Inesha .... 773-481-8103.. 137 I
ikelly1@ccc.edu
KELLY, Jack .... 617-732-2143.. 225 C
jack.kelly@mcphs.edu
KELLY, Jack .... 717-262-2013.. 424 A
jkelly@wilson.edu
KELLY, Jacqueline .... 412-338-4770.. 398 H
jkelly@brightwoodcareer.edu
KELLY, James .... 401-841-3674.. 528 E
KELLY, Janet, H .... 478-988-6800.. 118 H
jkelly@centralgatech.edu
KELLY, Jeffrey, M .... 443-352-4012.. 211 A
jkelly@stevenson.edu
KELLY, Jennifer .... 412-338-4770.. 398 H
jkelly@brightwoodcareer.edu
KELLY, Jennifer .... 516-686-1254.. 323 G
jkelly16@nyit.edu
KELLY, John .... 617-735-9710.. 218 C
kellyjo@emmanuel.edu
KELLY, John .... 561-297-3450.. 110 K
president@fau.edu
KELLY, John, J .... 607-735-1981.. 313 F
jkelly@elmira.edu
KELLY, Karen .... 334-291-4938...... 2 H
karen.kelly@cv.edu
KELLY, Kathy .... 513-244-4418.. 373 C
kathy.kelly@msj.edu
KELLY, Kelly .... 608-822-2305.. 524 F
kkelly@swtc.edu
KELLY, Kevin, P .... 410-269-5087.. 211 F
kkelly@umaryland.edu
KELLY, Kevin, R .... 937-229-3557.. 379 D
kellyker@udayton.edu
KELLY, Kieran .... 617-254-2610.. 227 H
kieran.kelly@sjs.edu
KELLY, Kirk .... 503-725-6246.. 394 G
kkelly@pdx.edu
KELLY, Laura .... 315-312-3151.. 333 D
laura.kelly@oswego.edu
KELLY, Lee .... 516-299-3092.. 319 B
lee.kelly@liu.edu
KELLY, Leslie, E .... 207-834-7522.. 205 B
lesliek@maine.edu
KELLY, Lois, M .... 805-756-5893.... 31 I
lkelly@calpoly.edu
KELLY, Lori .... 305-809-3504.. 100 N
lori.kelly@fkcc.edu
KELLY, Lyn .... 585-475-2946.. 327 E
lyn.kelly@rit.edu
KELLY, Lynn .... 229-226-1621.. 128 B
lkelly@thomasu.edu
KELLY, Marcia, J .... 603-646-0445.. 286 J
marcia.j.kelly@dartmouth.edu
KELLY, Margaret, S .... 215-637-7700.. 405 J
mkelly@holyfamily.edu
KELLY, Marisa .... 617-573-8000.. 228 G
mjkelly@suffolk.edu
KELLY, Mark .... 269-927-8100.. 236 G
kelly@lakemichigancollege.edu
KELLY, Mark .... 312-369-7650.. 138 F
mkelly@colum.edu
KELLY, Mark .... 541-485-1780.. 393 A
markkelly@newhope.edu
KELLY, Matthew .... 740-364-9644.. 365 D
mkelly@cotc.edu
KELLY, Maureen .... 708-235-7556.. 140 H
mkelly7@govst.edu
KELLY, Mike .... 229-468-2034.. 130 A
mike.kelly@wiregrass.edu
KELLY, Mike .... 360-538-4011.. 504 B
mkelly@ghc.edu
KELLY, Paul .... 202-651-5075.... 92 C
paul.kelly@gallaudet.edu
KELLY, Paul .... 760-744-1150.... 56 F
pkelly@palomar.edu
KELLY, SCJ, Paul .... 414-425-8300.. 519 F
pkelly@shsst.edu
KELLY, Renee .... 518-608-8464.. 314 A
rkelly@excelsior.edu
KELLY, Richard .... 201-559-3510.. 291 K
kellyr@felician.edu
KELLY, Robert .... 620-665-3417.. 181 I
kellyr@hutchcc.edu
KELLY, Robert, D .... 518-388-6101.. 338 H
kellyrd@union.edu
KELLY, Rosemary .... 910-678-8325.. 349 F
kellyr@faytechcc.edu
KELLY, Roxanne .... 541-440-4662.. 395 F
roxanne.kelly@umpqua.edu
KELLY, Sara .... 585-395-2122.. 332 E
skelly@brockport.edu
KELLY, Sarah, M .... 802-654-3000.. 484 I
skelly@smcvt.edu
KELLY, Scott, A .... 979-458-6120.. 468 B
s-kelly@tamus.edu
KELLY, Stephanie .... 317-788-6099.. 168 A
spkelly@uindy.edu
KELLY, Stephen .... 212-220-8261.. 307 B
skelly@bmcc.cuny.edu
KELLY, Steve .... 757-481-5005.. 500 H
KELLY, Susan .... 617-287-7050.. 220 E
skelly@umassp.edu
KELLY, T. Liisa .... 910-843-5304.. 347 A
KELLY, Tami .... 281-459-7653.. 465 A
tami.kelly@sjcd.edu
KELLY, Thomas .... 607-431-4111.. 315 E
kellyt2@hartwick.edu
KELLY, Thomas, M .... 312-915-6400.. 146 G
tkelly4@luc.edu
KELLY, Todd .... 719-549-2380.... 79 B
todd.kelly@csupueblo.edu
KELLY, Tracy .... 716-338-1042.. 317 F
tracykelly@mail.sunyjcc.edu
KELLY, William .... 605-642-6371.. 437 B
william.kelly@bhsu.edu
KELLY, Yvan, J .... 904-819-6392.... 99 M
kellyyj@flagler.edu
KELLY-ALBERTSON,
Lynn, C .... 269-387-2745.. 243 H
lynn.kelly-albertson@wmich.edu
KELLY BATES, Martha .... 847-578-8582.. 153 A
martha.bates@rosalindfranklin.edu
KELLY-BOWRY, Tanya ..... 303-831-6192.... 83 J
tanya.kellybowry@cu.edu
KELLY KLEESE, Christine 919-536-7200.. 349 D
kleesec@durhamtech.edu
KELLY-VERGONA,
Barbara .... 973-957-0188.. 288 G
registrar@acs350.org
KELNHOFER, Jack .... 732-255-0400.. 293 E
jkelnhofer@ocean.edu
KELPSH, Len .... 602-387-2780.... 17 L
leonard.kelpsh@phoenix.edu
KELSCH, Anne .... 701-777-3325.. 360 C
anne.kelsch@und.edu
KELSCH, Tyler .... 970-521-6615.... 81 O
tyler.kelsch@njc.edu
KELSER, Sandra, B .... 334-833-4409...... 4 D
skelser@hawks.huntingdon.edu
KELSEY, Anita .... 765-285-8101.. 159 B
akelsey@bsu.edu
KELSEY, Jane .... 217-854-3231.. 135 K
jane.kelsey@blackburn.edu
KELSEY, Madelaine .... 203-596-4624.... 88 F
mkelsey@post.edu
KELSHEIMER, Bradley, A . 765-658-4161.. 160 F
bradkelsheimer@depauw.edu
KELSO, Linda, M .... 863-667-5010.. 109 L
lmkelso@seu.edu
KELSO, William .... 912-344-2541.. 116 E
william.kelso@armstrong.edu
KELSOE, Amanda .... 919-684-2174.. 343 J
amanda.kelso@duke.edu
KELTER, Paul .... 701-231-8692.. 361 A
paul.kelter@ndsu.edu
KELTING, Dan .... 518-327-6213.. 326 B
dkelting@paulsmiths.edu
KELTY, Ed .... 480-731-8246.... 13 N
edward.kelty@domail.maricopa.edu
KEMAH, Celestine .... 903-730-4890.. 460 B
ckemah@jarvis.edu
KEMBEL, Trisha .... 970-542-3126.... 81 H
trisha.kembel@morgancc.edu
KEMBER, Jerry .... 608-796-3000.. 522 O
jrkember@viterbo.edu
KEMERER, John, J .... 740-593-0465.. 375 H
kemerer@ohio.edu
KEMKER, Brett .... 504-280-6222.. 198 D
bkemker@uno.edu
KEMMY, Dave .... 401-254-3428.. 426 B
dkemmy@rwu.edu
KEMP, Ann .... 501-686-2500.... 22 H
pakemp@uasys.edu
KEMP, Arnold .... 312-899-1294.. 154 A
akemp@saic.edu
KEMP, Cathy .... 662-243-2623.. 257 G
ckemp@eastms.edu
KEMP, Dale, A .... 630-752-5085.. 158 C
dale.kemp@wheaton.edu
KEMP, Danny .... 540-831-7167.. 493 A
dmkemp@radford.edu
KEMP, Dawn .... 317-632-5553.. 165 L
dkemp@lincolntech.edu
KEMP, Gloria .... 501-686-6728.... 23 C
kempgloriad@uams.edu
KEMP, Jerylle .... 212-237-8964.. 308 E
jkemp@jjay.cuny.edu
KEMP, John .... 864-294-3717.. 430 C
john.kemp@furman.edu
KEMP, Josh .... 870-307-7398.... 21 A
josh.kemp@lyon.edu
KEMP, Karen, W .... 254-710-2519.. 452 H
karen_kemp@baylor.edu
KEMP, Katie .... 847-317-8177.. 156 B
katiek@tiu.edu
KEMP, Lisa .... 703-993-2660.. 490 B
lkemp@gmu.edu
KEMP, Rick .... 480-517-8508.... 14 G
rick.kemp@riosalado.edu
KEMP, Shirley .... 304-829-7485.. 510 G
skemp@bethanywv.edu
KEMP, Stephen .... 515-292-9694.. 169 E
stephen.kemp@antiochschool.edu
KEMP, Steve .... 760-366-5283.... 41 K
skemp@cmccd.edu
KEMP, Vandy .... 865-981-8111.. 441 H
vandy.kemp@maryvillecollege.edu
KEMPA, Richard .... 307-382-1731.. 527 C
rkempa@westernwyoming.edu
KEMPE, Michael, A .... 330-325-6481.. 373 H
mkempe@neomed.edu
KEMPEL, Leo .... 517-355-5133.. 237 I
kempel@egr.msu.edu
KEMPER, Brad .... 575-562-2425.. 299 I
brad.kemper@enmu.edu
KEMPER, James .... 740-588-1209.. 382 C
jkemper@zanestate.edu
KEMPER, Kenneth, B .... 616-538-2330.. 234 D
preskemper@gbcol.edu
KEMPER, Terry .... 262-695-3459.. 524 G
tkemper1@wctc.edu
KEMPER-PELLE, Cathy ..... 541-956-7000.. 394 J
ckemperpelle@roguecc.edu
KEMPF, Emily, J .... 816-501-3571.. 270 J
emily.kempf@rockhurst.edu
KEMPF, Gary .... 620-278-4469.. 185 A
gkempf@sterling.edu
KEMPF-LEONARD,
Kimberly .... 502-852-2234.. 194 A
asdean@louisville.edu
KEMPSON, Dorothy .... 912-877-1906.. 116 E
dorothy.kempson@armstrong.edu
KEMPTON, Daniel .... 740-283-6228.. 368 L
dkempton@franciscan.edu
KENAUSIS, Veronica .... 203-837-9109.... 85 I
kenausisv@wcsu.edu
KENBER, Tammy .... 707-664-3100.... 35 D
kenber@sonoma.edu
KENCH, Brian .... 203-932-7115.... 90 A
bkench@newhaven.edu
KENDALL, Chris .... 507-457-1640.. 254 O
ckendall@smumn.edu
KENDALL, Curtis, L .... 540-828-5476.. 487 H
ckendall@bridgewater.edu
KENDALL, Deborah .... 408-554-2717.... 63 E
dkendall@scu.edu
KENDALL, Donna .... 781-891-2913.. 215 F
dkendall@bentley.edu
KENDALL, Elizabeth .... 845-574-4269.. 327 G
ekendall@sunyrockland.edu
KENDALL, Justin .... 620-862-5252.. 178 F
justin.kendall@barclaycollege.edu
KENDALL, Kenny .... 315-470-7749.. 305 H
kennethkendall@crouse.org
KENDALL, Laura .... 717-871-7026.. 415 F
laura.kendall@millersville.edu
KENDALL, Matt .... 740-695-9500.. 364 B
mkendall@belmontcollege.edu
KENDALL, Peter .... 828-328-7100.. 345 H
peter.kendall@lr.edu
KENDALL, Rex .... 812-514-8446.. 162 A
rkendall@indstatefoundation.org
KENDALL, Stephanie .... 978-837-5321.. 225 E
kendalls@merrimack.edu
KENDALL, Susan .... 412-924-1421.. 417 E
skendall@pts.edu
KENDALL-DOMNICK,
Meitaka .... 692-625-3394.. 530 C
mkendall@cmi.edu
KENDIG, P. Tysen .... 860-486-6713.... 89 D
tysen.kendig@uconn.edu
KENDJORIA, Barrett .... 864-656-2354.. 428 C
bkendjo@clemson.edu
KENDREX, Bradley, S .... 480-732-7379.... 13 O
bradley.kendrex@cgc.edu
KENDRICK, Bethany .... 620-421-6700.. 182 G
bethanyk@labette.edu
KENDRICK, Catherine .... 978-934-2495.. 221 A
catherine_kendrick@uml.edu
KENDRICK, Curtis .... 607-777-4550.. 331 B
kendrick@binghamton.edu
KENDRICK, Dorsey, L .... 203-285-2060.... 86 C
dkendrick@gwcc.commnet.edu
KENDRICK, Haley .... 704-406-3957.. 344 E
KENDRICK, Lacy .... 804-204-1235.. 487 D
lkendrick@btsr.edu
KENDRICK, Mildred .... 706-945-1366.. 125 H
mkendrick@paine.edu
KENDRICK, R. Ryan .... 716-286-8708.. 324 E
rkendrick@niagara.edu
KENDZIERSKI, Christian .. 410-532-3191.. 210 B
ckendzierski@ndm.edu
KENERSON, Laura .... 401-874-5271.. 426 D
lkenerson@uri.edu
KENERSON, Murle .... 615-963-5203.. 445 A
mkenerson@tnstate.edu
KENESSON, Alexander .... 253-680-7150.. 501 E
akenesson@bates.ctc.edu
KENESSON, Summer .... 360-475-7108.. 505 F
skenesson@olympic.edu
KENIMER, Ann .... 979-845-3210.. 468 B
a-kenimer@tamu.edu
KENKEL, Kevin .... 605-995-2617.. 435 F
kekenkel@dwu.edu
KENKEL, Mary Beth .... 321-674-8142.. 100 M
mkenkel@fit.edu
KENMILLE, Cleo .... 406-275-4864.. 278 E
cleo_kenmille@skc.edu
KENNA-SCHENK, Becca ... 360-951-3733.. 509 E
becca.kenna-schenk@wwu.edu
KENNAMER, Mike .... 256-228-6001...... 5 I
kennamerm@nacc.edu
KENNARD, Douglas .... 304-876-5330.. 513 E
dkennard@shepherd.edu
KENNARD, Janet .... 713-942-9505.. 459 C
jkennard@hgst.edu
KENNARD, Mary, E .... 202-885-3285.... 91 J
mekesq@american.edu
KENNEDAY, Mark, A .... 501-686-5674.... 23 C
kennedaymark@uams.edu
KENNEDY, Aaron .... 575-461-4413.. 300 A
aaronk@mesalands.edu
KENNEDY, Alexis .... 708-534-7096.. 140 H
akennedy@govst.edu

KERSTEN, David, W .... 773-244-6235.. 149 I
dwkersten@northpark.edu
KERSTEN, James, B .... 515-574-1132.. 173 F
kersten@iowacentral.edu
KERSTETTER, Philip, P .... 919-658-7746.. 355 K
pkerstetter@umo.edu
KERTULIS-TARTAR, Gina . 706-272-4516.. 119 H
gkertulistartar@daltonstate.edu
KERTZ, Nancy .... 515-643-6615.. 175 B
nkertz@mercydesmoines.org
KERWIN, Cornelius, M .... 202-885-2121.... 91 J
president@american.edu
KERWIN, Courtney .... 315-792-7419.. 336 C
courtney.kerwin@sunyit.edu
KERWIN, Linda .... 716-827-2454.. 338 E
kerwinl@trocaire.edu
KERWITZ, Ann .... 815-921-4001.. 152 E
a.kerwitz@rockvalleycollege.edu
KERYLOW, Tiffany .... 802-387-6725.. 484 B
tiffanykerylow@landmark.edu
KESARIS, Thomas, L .... 610-660-1836.. 418 G
tkesaris@sju.edu
KESERAUSKIS, Beth .... 314-446-8207.. 271 E
beth.keserauskis@stlcop.edu
KESHNER, Larry .... 708-344-4700.. 146 D
lkeshner@lincolntech.edu
KESHVALA, Seelpa .... 281-290-3940.. 461 B
seelpa.h.keshvala@lonestar.edu
KESICKI, Michael .... 814-871-5873.. 404 A
kesicki001@gannon.edu
KESKULA, Douglas, R ..... 828-227-7271.. 359 A
drkeskula@wcu.edu
KESLER, Michael, W .... 802-776-5219.. 483 G
michael.kesler@csj.edu
KESNER, Idalene .... 812-855-8489.. 162 F
ikesner@indiana.edu
KESSEL, Christine .... 309-779-7708.. 156 A
christine.kessel@trinitycollegeqc.edu
KESSEL, Joyce .... 716-896-0700.. 339 E
jkessel@villa.edu
KESSELMAN, Harvey .... 609-652-4521.. 297 C
harvey.kesselman@stockton.edu
KESSIE, Michael .... 941-487-4212.. 111 D
mkessie@ncf.edu
KESSINGER, Steve .... 276-326-4603.. 487 F
skessinger@bluefield.edu
KESSLER, Gene .... 219-473-4299.. 159 L
gkessler@ccsj.edu
KESSLER, Jeffrey, A .... 516-877-3660.. 303 B
kessler@adelphi.edu
KESSLER, Karen .... 850-484-1673.. 106 H
kkessler@pensacolastate.edu
KESSLER, Kathleen .... 802-839-8317.. 484 G
kathleen.kessler@neci.edu
KESSLER, Lisa .... 512-313-3000.. 455 F
lisa.kessler@concordia.edu
KESSLER, Mary .... 812-488-2569.. 167 I
mk43@evansville.edu
KESSLER, Nevin, E .... 848-932-7890.. 295 F
nkessler@winants.rutgers.edu
KESSLER, Richard .... 212-580-0210.. 322 E
kesslerr@newschool.edu
KESSLER, Sheryl .... 215-972-7600.. 413 L
skessler@pafa.org
KESSLER, Susan, B .... 386-312-4021.. 108 B
susankessler@sjrstate.edu
KESSLER, Suzanne .... 914-251-6600.. 334 C
suzanne.kessler@purchase.edu
KESSLER-CLEARY,
Timothy .... 973-618-3484.. 290 A
tcleary@caldwell.edu
KESTEN, Philip, R .... 408-554-4311.... 63 E
pkesten@scu.edu
KESTER, Jennifer .... 623-845-3371.... 14 C
jennifer.kester@gccaz.edu
KESTER, John .... 910-410-1778.. 352 C
jikester@richmondcc.edu
KESTER, Kelly .... 360-383-3245.. 509 F
kkester@whatcom.ctc.edu
KESTER, Lori .... 303-352-4498.... 81 G
lkester@msudenver.edu
KESTERSON, Ronald, L ... 865-694-6608.. 446 G
rkesterson@pstcc.edu
KESTNER, Carly .... 276-326-4243.. 487 F
ckestner@bluefield.edu
KESTNER-RICKETTS,
Laura, F .... 414-288-7424.. 517 I
laura.kestner@marquette.edu
KETCHEN, John .... 865-573-4517.. 440 I
jketchen@johnsonu.edu
KETCHESON, Kathi, A ...... 503-725-3425.. 394 G
ketchesonk@pdx.edu
KETELS, Margo .... 563-589-3131.. 177 C
mketels@dbq.edu
KETELSEN, Scott, A .... 319-273-2761.. 170 A
scott.ketelsen@uni.edu
KETJEN, William .... 330-823-2293.. 379 F
ketjenwl@mountunion.edu
KETNER, Annette .... 619-260-2925.... 72 B
aketner@sandiego.edu

KETO, Stephen, W .... 218-726-7101.. 255 D
vcfo@d.umn.edu
KETO, Stephen, W .... 919-515-9224.. 357 B
steve_keto@ncsu.edu
KETTEMAN, Paul, G .... 615-844-5227.. 449 H
gketteman@welch.edu
KETTEN, Michelle .... 570-504-8094.. 407 B
kettenm@lackawanna.edu
KETTENBEIL, Kenneth ...... 313-593-5140.. 242 A
kketten@umich.edu
KETTERER, Patricia .... 212-772-4475.. 308 D
patricia.ketterer@hunter.cuny.edu
KETTERING, Juliane .... 801-627-8389.. 481 A
ketterij@owatc.edu
KETTERING, Rocky .... 706-507-8954.. 119 E
kettering_rocky@columbusstate.edu
KETTERING-LANE,
Denise .... 800-287-8822.. 159 C
kettede@bethanyseminary.edu
KETTERLING, Jayme .... 208-732-6552.. 133 E
jketterling@csi.edu
KETTERMAN, Beth .... 252-744-2212.. 356 C
kettermane@ecu.edu
KETTING-WELLER,
Ginger .... 951-785-2266.... 48 A
gketting@lasierra.edu
KETTINGER, Kevin .... 585-567-9350.. 316 F
kevin.kettinger@houghton.edu
KETTINGER, Kirk .... 585-594-6415.. 327 D
kettinger_kirk@roberts.edu
KETTLEWELL, Kelly .... 570-577-1604.. 398 L
kelly.kettlewell@bucknell.edu
KETTNER, Valrey, V .... 701-231-9608.. 361 A
val.kettner@ndsu.edu
KEUFFEL, Elizabeth .... 603-641-7203.. 287 G
ekeuffel@anselm.edu
KEUP, Mike .... 309-677-2677.. 136 B
mkeup@bradley.edu
KEUSS, Theresa .... 314-516-4602.. 274 A
keusst@umsl.edu
KEVARI, Jacob .... 760-366-5279.... 41 K
jkevari@cmccd.edu
KEVIL, Tim .... 903-875-7443.. 462 J
tim.kevil@navarrocollege.edu
KEVLIN, Dean .... 516-572-7771.. 322 C
dean.kevlin@ncc.edu
KEVORKIAN, Chris .... 206-726-5000.. 503 B
ckevorkian@cornish.edu
KEY, Dan .... 641-844-5741.. 173 L
dan.key@iavalley.edu
KEY, Dillon .... 864-977-7122.. 431 G
dillon.key@ngu.edu
KEY, Henry .... 908-709-7151.. 298 A
key@ucc.edu
KEY, Jonathan, C .... 504-282-4455.. 198 H
jkey@nobts.edu
KEY, Roby, V .... 817-257-7706.. 469 G
r.key@tcu.edu
KEY, Shelly .... 361-593-5991.. 469 A
shelly.key@tamuk.edu
KEY, Stacy .... 479-979-1360.... 24 I
skey@ozarks.edu
KEY, Stan, R .... 859-257-8907.. 193 G
stan.key@uky.edu
KEYES, Adam .... 508-793-7453.. 217 B
akeyes@clarku.edu
KEYES, Beth, H .... 937-229-3769.. 379 D
bkeyes@udayton.edu
KEYES, James, R .... 802-443-5523.. 484 F
jkeyes@middlebury.edu
KEYES, Judy .... 617-287-6300.. 220 G
judy.keyes@umb.edu
KEYES, Pat .... 401-841-3089.. 528 E
KEYO, Jenn .... 860-768-2417.... 89 G
keyo@hartford.edu
KEYS, Carolyn .... 909-274-4525.... 53 C
ckeys@mtsac.edu
KEYS, James, A .... 910-843-5304.. 347 A
KEYS, Margo, A .... 715-858-1825.. 523 B
mkeys@cvtc.edu
KEYS, Marina .... 503-845-3550.. 392 E
marina.keys@mtangel.edu
KEYS, Terrance .... 585-292-3432.. 321 J
tkeys@monroecc.edu
KEYSER, Kent .... 619-388-6939.... 60 E
kkeyser@sdccd.edu
KHACHATRYAN, Davit ..... 949-451-5326.... 65 F
dkhachatryan@ivc.edu
KHACHIKIAN, Crist .... 818-677-2138.... 34 A
crist.khachikian@csun.edu
KHADANGA, Dave .... 334-386-7113...... 3 I
dkhadanga@faulkner.edu
KHADEM, Farnaz .... 626-395-2240.... 30 H
fkhadem@caltech.edu
KHADKA, Chandni .... 256-782-8304...... 4 H
ckhadka@jsu.edu
KHALDEN, Jeff .... 817-598-6485.. 479 E
jkhalden@wc.edu
KHALEDI, Morteza .... 817-272-3491.. 476 A
morteza.khaledi@uta.edu

KHALILI, Kambiz .... 303-492-6494.... 83 K
kambiz.khalili@colorado.edu
KHALSA, Barbara .... 480-517-8778.... 14 G
barbara.khalsa@riosalado.edu
KHAMALAH, Joseph .... 260-481-6461.. 163 C
khamaljn@ipfw.edu
KHAMIS, Hanan .... 508-999-8845.. 220 H
admissions@umassd.edu
KHAMSAMRAN, Anna .... 575-758-8914.. 300 D
annak@midwiferycollege.edu
KHAN, Adil .... 636-227-2100.. 267 A
KHAN, Ali .... 402-559-4950.. 283 A
ali.khan@unmc.edu
KHAN, Jehana .... 320-222-5986.. 251 G
jehana.khan@ridgewater.edu
KHAN, M. Wasiullah .... 312-939-0111.. 139 G
chancellor@eastwest.edu
KHAN, Raza .... 410-386-8222.. 206 I
rkhan@carrollcc.edu
KHAN, Rehan .... 617-373-2752.. 227 B
KHAN, Sadya .... 708-974-5283.. 148 G
khans46@morainevalley.edu
KHAN-MARCUS, Zaveeni . 805-893-8411.... 70 E
zaveeni.khan-marcus@sa.ucsb.edu
KHANEJA, Gurvinder .... 201-684-7766.. 294 G
gkhaneja@ramapo.edu
KHANI, Anthony .... 646-717-9743.. 315 B
khani@gts.edu
KHANNA, Pradeep .... 217-333-9525.. 157 A
pkhanna@illinois.edu
KHANOYAN, Gayane .... 818-988-2300.... 53 I
KHARGONEKAR, Pramod 949-824-5796.... 69 C
KHARKOVYY, Andriy .... 269-471-3591.. 230 H
alumni@andrews.edu
KHARTABIL, Basim .... 312-935-6449.. 152 D
bkhartabil@robertmorris.edu
KHASAWNEH, Rami .... 815-836-5360.. 145 H
khasawra@lewisu.edu
KHATOR, Renu .... 713-743-8820.. 473 E
rkhator@uh.edu
KHATOR, Renu .... 713-743-8820.. 473 F
rkhator@uh.edu
KHATRI, Achal .... 617-873-0235.. 217 A
achal.khatri@cambridgecollege.edu
KHATTARI, Karen .... 610-606-4632.. 400 E
klkhatta@cedarcrest.edu
KHAVARI, Jenn .... 207-974-4673.. 203 J
jkhavari@emcc.edu
KHAWAR, Mariam .... 607-735-1932.. 313 F
mkhawar@elmira.edu
KHAYUM, Mohammed .... 812-464-1718.. 168 E
mkhayum@usi.edu
KHEHRA, Harry .... 281-290-6576.. 461 B
harry.khehra@lonestar.edu
KHLEIF, Samir .... 706-721-0570.. 117 D
skhleif@augusta.edu
KHODIER, Sayed .... 617-739-1700.. 226 G
skhodier@aii.edu
KHOJA, Faiza .... 713-221-8218.. 474 B
khojafai@uhd.edu
KHOO, Poh Lin .... 651-793-1828.. 250 A
pohlin.khoo@metrostate.edu
KHOSLA, Pradeep, K .... 858-534-3135.... 70 C
chancellor@ucsd.edu
KHOSRAVANI, Mariam .... 714-241-6159.... 39 E
mkhosravani@coastline.edu
KHOSROWPANAH,
Shahram .... 671-735-2694.. 530 B
khosrow@triton.uog.edu
KHOURY, Melik Peter .... 207-509-7221.. 204 F
mkhoury@unity.edu
KHOURY, Muna .... 313-496-2777.. 242 H
mkhoury1@wcccd.edu
KHOURY, Philip, S .... 617-253-0887.. 225 A
KHURANA, Nikki .... 909-607-2626.... 64 A
nkhurana@scrippscollege.edu
KHURANA, Rakesh .... 617-495-4137.. 219 D
rkhurana@fas.harvard.edu
KIA, Norman .... 575-769-4074.. 299 G
norman.kia@clovis.edu
KIAMAN, Matthew .... 626-585-3200.... 56 H
mxkiaman@pasadena.edu
KIAN, David .... 561-297-3007.. 110 K
dkian@fau.edu
KIBARDINA, Marina .... 708-709-7921.. 151 C
mkibardina@prairiestate.edu
KIBLER, Bill .... 432-837-8000.. 471 E
president@sulross.edu
KIBLER, David .... 864-941-8475.. 432 A
kibler.d@ptc.edu
KIBLER, Michele .... 614-222-4009.. 367 B
mkibler@ccad.edu
KICKLITER, Holly .... 727-873-4455.. 112 D
hkicklit@mail.usf.edu
KICKNER, Robert .... 253-833-9111.. 504 C
rkickner@greenriver.edu
KIDD, Anessa .... 334-876-9303...... 4 A
anessa.kidd@wccs.edu
KIDD, Beth Ann .... 903-675-6223.. 473 B
bkidd@tvcc.edu

KIDD, Jane .... 706-369-6833.. 125 J
jkidd@piedmont.edu
KIDD, Kevin .... 617-989-9095.. 229 D
kiddk@wit.edu
KIDD, Mary .... 615-514-2787.. 443 F
financialaid@nossi.edu
KIDD, Twyla .... 704-463-3067.. 354 F
twyla.kidd@pfeiffer.edu
KIDD, Windy .... 859-280-1237.. 191 D
wkidd@lextheo.edu
KIDDER, Paulette .... 206-296-5405.. 507 E
KIDDIE, Thomas .... 304-766-4116.. 514 B
tkiddie@wvstateu.edu
KIDDOO, Sandy .... 715-422-5525.. 523 G
sandy.kiddoo@mstc.edu
KIDESS LUCEY, Tamie .... 413-748-3161.. 228 E
tkidessl@springfieldcollege.edu
KIDNEY, Gary .... 203-432-6093.... 90 D
gary.kidney@yale.edu
KIDWELL, Debra .... 573-681-5418.. 266 I
purchasing@lincolnu.edu
KIDWELL, Eric, A .... 334-833-4420...... 4 D
ekidwell@hawks.huntingdon.edu
KIDWELL, John .... 870-460-1083.... 23 D
kidwell@uamont.edu
KIDWELL, Martin .... 503-253-3443.. 393 D
mkidwell@ocom.edu
KIEBA-TOLKSDORF,
Helen, C .... 248-689-8282.. 242 F
hkieba@walshcollege.edu
KIEC, Michael .... 216-373-5227.. 374 B
mkiec@ndc.edu
KIECKHAFER, David, S .... 608-342-1321.. 521 A
kieckhaferd@uwplatt.edu
KIEDA, David, B .... 801-581-8796.. 481 M
dave.kieda@utah.edu
KIEF, Bob .... 253-879-2820.. 508 D
bkief@pugetsound.edu
KIEFER, Cindy .... 406-756-3843.. 276 E
ckiefer@fvcc.edu
KIEFER, David, E .... 626-584-5409.... 44 G
dkiefer@fuller.edu
KIEFER, Irene .... 800-567-2344.. 516 B
ikiefer@menominee.edu
KIEFER, Mike .... 941-752-5000.. 110 H
KIEFER, William .... 412-809-5100.. 417 D
kiefer.william@pti.edu
KIEFFER, Barb .... 920-735-5734.. 523 C
kieffer@fvtc.edu
KIEFFER, Don .... 212-986-4343.. 305 B
dmk@berkeleycollege.edu
KIEFFER, Don .... 212-986-4343.. 289 F
dmk@berkeleycollege.edu
KIEFFER, Linda .... 509-359-6345.. 503 D
lkieffer@ewu.edu
KIEFFER, Shelly .... 318-473-6508.. 197 J
skieffer@lsua.edu
KIEFT, Thom .... 352-536-2150.. 104 J
kieftt@lssc.edu
KIEHL, Ermalynn .... 850-474-2405.. 113 A
ekiehl@uwf.edu
KIEHL, Gregg .... 607-844-8222.. 337 G
kiehlg@tc3.edu
KIEHNE, Rolfe, E .... 636-327-4645.. 268 C
sil@midwest.edu
KIEL, Annique .... 515-271-3039.. 171 K
annique.kiel@drake.edu
KIEL, Cindy, M .... 530-754-1184.... 69 A
cmkiel@ucdavis.edu
KIEL, Mark .... 847-376-7122.. 150 G
mkiel@oakton.edu
KIEL, Micah .... 563-333-6121.. 176 D
kielmicahd@sau.edu
KIELBASA, Jody, K .... 434-982-5326.. 495 H
jkk8j@virginia.edu
KIELHOFNER, Brad, B ..... 417-836-6865.. 268 I
bradkielhofner@missouristate.edu
KIELMEYER, David .... 419-372-8587.. 364 E
davidk@bgsu.edu
KIELT, Chris .... 919-962-3444.. 357 D
chris_kielt@unc.edu
KIELY, Ed .... 845-341-4934.. 325 H
ed.kiely@sunyorange.edu
KIELY, Maurice, J .... 804-412-2026.. 493 C
mkiely@rmc.edu
KIENER, Dan, W .... 412-397-5263.. 418 B
kiener@rmu.edu
KIENITZ, Kelli, S .... 320-222-5215.. 251 G
kelli.kienitz@ridgewater.edu
KIENLE-GRANZO,
Elizabeth, A .... 212-998-4407.. 324 C
ekg241@nyu.edu
KIENOW, Sharon .... 605-626-2640.. 437 D
sharon.kienow@northern.edu
KIENTOP, Margaret .... 815-836-5230.. 145 H
kientoma@lewisu.edu
KIERALDO, John .... 312-553-5761.. 137 D
jkieraldo@ccc.edu
KIERNAN, Catherine, A ... 973-761-9191.. 297 A
catherine.kiernan@shu.edu

KINCKERBOCKER, Troy 210-805-5818 474 D troyk@uiwtx.edu
KIND, Jule 765-677-2980 164 B jule.kind@indwes.edu
KIND-KEPPEL, Heather 262-595-2239 520 F kindkepp@uwp.edu
KINDER, Angie, M 304-260-4380 511 L akinder@blueridgectc.edu
KINDER, Jason 405-466-3359 383 M jason.kinder@sodexo.com
KINDER, L. Chad 580-774-7036 388 C chad.kinder@swosu.edu
KINDERS, Mark 405-974-5560 388 L mkinders@uco.edu
KINDL, Christine 724-938-5492 414 E kindl@calu.edu
KINDLE, Derek 608-262-0464 519 K derek.kindle@wisc.edu
KINDLE, Joan 563-336-3488 172 A jkindle@eicc.edu
KINDLER, Andreas 309-677-3107 136 B akindler@bradley.edu
KINDON, Victoria 434-395-4804 491 E kindonv@longwood.edu
KINEAVY, Jacqueline 973-684-6300 294 A jkineavy@pccc.edu
KINERSON, Sara 802-635-1257 486 B sara.kinerson@jsc.edu
KINES, James 864-231-2177 427 B jkines@andersonuniversity.edu
KINES, Teresa 336-249-8186 349 C tkines@davidsonccc.edu
KING, Adolf 865-354-3000 447 A kingaa@roanestate.edu
KING, Adrienne 270-809-4894 192 A aking20@murraystate.edu
KING, Ahyana 716-926-8835 316 B aking@hilbert.edu
KING, Albert 419-289-5959 363 J aking@ashland.edu
KING, Alicia, M 956-665-2118 476 E alicia.king@utrgv.edu
KING, Alissa 601-318-6474 261 I aking@wmcarey.edu
KING, Amy 303-871-7420 84 B amking@du.edu
KING, Amy, L 304-457-6354 510 B kingal@ab.edu
KING, Andrew 207-780-5670 205 E andrew.king@maine.edu
KING, Andrew, B 904-620-2602 112 B a.king@unf.edu
KING, Angella 859-246-6696 189 B angie.king@kctcs.edu
KING, Anthony 937-255-6565 527 H anthony.king@afit.edu
KING, Art 646-312-4570 307 A art.king@baruch.cuny.edu
KING, B, J 423-439-4414 444 F kingbj@etsu.edu
KING, Barbara 405-682-1611 385 D bking@occc.edu
KING, Becky, L 254-710-4566 452 H becky_king@baylor.edu
KING, Bob 210-999-7011 473 A bob.king@trinity.edu
KING, Brenda, M 304-336-8076 513 F kingbren@westliberty.edu
KING, Brian 916-568-3021 50 J kingb@losrios.edu
KING, Brian 814-866-6641 407 D bking@lecom.edu
KING, Bruce 510-235-7800 41 H bking@contracosta.edu
KING, Bruce 507-786-3334 254 P kingb@stolaf.edu
KING, Carol 302-736-2567 91 G carol.king@wesley.edu
KING, Carole 202-884-9125 94 A kingc@trinitydc.edu
KING, Carolee 409-772-1904 478 A caaking@utmb.edu
KING, Caroline 941-907-2262 99 J caking@evergladesuniversity.edu
KING, Charles 409-933-8404 454 O cking@com.edu
KING, Charles, W 540-568-6434 490 J kingcw@jmu.edu
KING, Cheryl 301-295-3045 528 G cheryl.king@usuhs.edu
KING, Christopher 956-665-2222 476 E chris.king@utrgv.edu
KING, Corey 561-297-3988 110 K cking14@fau.edu
KING, Corinna 515-263-2802 172 H cking@grandview.edu
KING, Craig 212-870-1238 324 B cking@nyts.edu
KING, Curt 413-662-5062 222 B curt.king@mcla.edu
KING, Cynthia, L 610-861-5510 411 G cking@northampton.edu
KING, D. Wayne 859-238-5550 187 H wayne.king@centre.edu
KING, Daniel, P 334-844-4810 1 G dpk0002@auburn.edu
KING, David, A 330-471-8121 371 J dking@malone.edu
KING, David, A 540-432-4440 488 K david.king@emu.edu
KING, David, A 541-737-2676 393 H ecampus@oregonstate.edu
KING, David, W 805-565-6036 75 A dking@westmont.edu
KING, Deborah 870-338-6474 23 G
KING, Del 404-727-7567 120 E dking2@emory.edu
KING, Denise 423-472-7141 445 E dking05@clevelandstatecc.edu
KING, Dennis 785-628-4276 180 I dking@fhsu.edu
KING, Dennis 828-398-7112 347 D dennisfking@abtech.edu
KING, Donald 508-999-8575 220 H dking@umassd.edu
KING, JR., Donald 765-285-1478 159 B jking@bsu.edu
KING, Donna 903-463-8735 458 H donnaking@grayson.edu
KING, Dottie 812-535-5296 166 K president@smwc.edu
KING, Duane 918-596-2710 389 E duane-king@utulsa.edu
KING, Ebony 712-749-2379 170 D kinge@bvu.edu
KING, Eddie 843-208-8135 434 A eking@uscb.edu
KING, Elizabeth, H 316-978-3510 185 J elizabeth.king@wichita.edu
KING, Eric 316-978-3106 185 J eric.king@wichita.edu
KING, Eric 903-730-4890 460 B
KING, Frances 704-463-3037 354 F frances.king@pfeiffer.edu
KING, Fred, L 304-293-3449 514 C fred.king@mail.wvu.edu
KING, Garrett 580-774-3267 388 C garrett.king@swosu.edu
KING, Glenda 662-252-8000 260 F gking@rustcollege.edu
KING, Gordon, B 617-557-1520 228 G gking@suffolk.edu
KING, Grace 909-537-5205 34 C gking@csusb.edu
KING, Greg 304-384-6305 513 A gking@concord.edu
KING, Greg 423-236-2983 444 B gking@southern.edu
KING, Gregory 330-823-2282 379 F kinggl@mountunion.edu
KING, JR., H. Lee 434-223-7258 490 D lking@hsc.edu
KING, Henry, D 260-422-5561 162 B hdking@indianatech.edu
KING, Herbert 651-793-1508 250 A herbert.king@metrostate.edu
KING, Irene 610-519-4080 422 G irene.king@villanova.edu
KING, Jackie, E 585-275-9900 338 K jking@admin.rochester.edu
KING, James 615-336-4460 444 D james.king@tbr.edu
KING, Janice 775-753-2361 284 I janice.king@gbcnv.edu
KING, Jean 508-856-4979 221 B jean.king@umassmed.edu
KING, Jennifer 413-559-5427 219 C
KING, Jeremy, R 864-656-4275 428 C jking2@clemson.edu
KING, Jerry 903-675-6211 473 B jking@tvcc.edu
KING, Jerry 903-675-6210 473 B jking@tvcc.edu
KING, Jim 570-585-9346 419 G jking@summitu.edu
KING, Jim, M 318-257-2445 200 G king@latech.edu
KING, Joan 509-335-9681 508 H joank@wsu.edu
KING, Jodie 215-248-7004 400 H kingj@chc.edu
KING, Joe, M 334-244-3600 2 A jmking@aum.edu
KING, Joel 308-398-7315 278 K joelking@cccneb.edu
KING, John 541-552-6261 395 A kingjo@sou.edu
KING, John, J 401-254-3042 426 B jjking@rwu.edu
KING, John, M 617-552-4445 216 C john.king.2@bc.edu
KING, John, W 423-652-4832 440 J jwking@king.edu
KING, Jonathan 619-482-6379 66 E jking@swccd.edu
KING, Jovanna, J 864-656-0663 428 C jovanna@clemson.edu
KING, Joy, S 512-505-3015 459 F jsking@htu.edu
KING, Julie, A 803-786-3871 429 A juking@columbiasc.edu
KING, Karen, D 423-439-5654 444 F kingk@etsu.edu
KING, Katherine 949-480-4161 64 J kking@soka.edu
KING, Katie 405-491-6350 388 A kking@snu.edu
KING, Kenneth 801-878-1419 285 E kking@roseman.edu
KING, Kimberly 239-280-2500 95 Q kimberly.king@avemaria.edu
KING, Kristyn 815-394-5061 152 G kking@rockford.edu
KING, Kwanna 918-463-2931 383 F kwanna.king@connorsstate.edu
KING, L. Dianne 864-231-2026 427 B ldking@andersonuniversity.edu
KING, Larry, J 936-468-1260 466 H lking@sfasu.edu
KING, Laura 870-512-7850 19 C laura_king@asun.edu
KING, Laura 651-846-1316 252 C laura.king@saintpaul.edu
KING, Laura, C 814-393-1926 414 G lking@clarion.edu
KING, Laura, M 651-201-1732 248 I laura.king@so.mnscu.edu
KING, Leslie 770-426-2713 124 B lesliek@life.edu
KING, Leslie 614-947-6132 369 A leslie.king@franklin.edu
KING, Libby 423-869-6358 441 E libby.king@lmunet.edu
KING, Linda 903-886-5013 468 D linda.king@tamuc.edu
KING, Lonnie 614-688-8749 375 A king.1518@osu.edu
KING, Lynn 910-879-5520 347 F lking@bladencc.edu
KING, Lynne, O 518-381-1240 330 B kinglo@sunysccc.edu
KING, Marlin 601-877-6471 256 F mbking@alcorn.edu
KING, Marsha, M 260-399-7700 168 D mking@sf.edu
KING, Martha 708-216-3354 146 G mking17@luc.edu
KING, Mary 641-472-1144 175 A registrar@mum.edu
KING, Mary 940-552-6291 478 D mking@vernoncollege.edu
KING, Mary, B 336-734-7901 349 G mking@forsythtech.edu
KING, Mary Jo 270-706-8530 189 C maryjo.king@kctcs.edu
KING, Maura 845-451-1429 312 C m_king@culinary.edu
KING, Melinda 205-348-4904 8 D
KING, Michael 706-754-7711 125 B mking@northgatech.edu
KING, Michael, A 540-432-4261 488 K michael.king@emu.edu
KING, Michelle 310-434-3323 63 F king_michelle@smc.edu
KING, Mike 812-535-5273 166 K mking2@smwc.edu
KING, Natalie 831-582-3609 33 E nmking@csumb.edu
KING, Natasha 912-287-5827 119 B nking@coastalpines.edu
KING, Nathaniel 702-992-2806 284 J nathaniel.king@nsc.edu
KING, Patricia, J 918-687-3299 382 D kingp@bacone.edu
KING, Paula Kay 765-973-8331 162 G pkayking@iue.edu
KING, Peggy 630-752-5246 158 C peggy.king@wheaton.edu
KING, Peter, D 843-661-1281 430 B pking@fmarion.edu
KING, Phillip 503-594-3430 390 F phillipk@clackamas.edu
KING, Phyllis 414-229-6175 520 D pking@wm.edu
KING, Rhonda 504-671-5051 196 D rking1@dcc.edu
KING, Rhonda 717-766-2511 410 J rking@messiah.edu
KING, Richard, A 858-784-8469 64 B
KING, Robert 707-654-1245 33 D rking@csum.edu
KING, Rodmon 859-238-5267 187 H rodmon.king@centre.edu
KING, Ronan 276-944-6125 489 I rking@ehc.edu
KING, Ryan 207-326-0136 204 C ryan.king@mma.edu
KING, S. Bruce 336-758-5774 359 E kingsb@wfu.edu
KING, Samuel 901-435-1509 441 C samuel_king@loc.edu
KING, Sasha 310-434-3404 63 F king_sasha@smc.edu
KING, Scott 916-649-8168 28 L scott.king@brightwood.edu
KING, Shawn 509-359-6878 503 D sking@ewu.edu
KING, Shelly 816-415-5963 275 F kings@william.jewell.edu
KING, Stacey 478-289-2145 120 C sking@ega.edu
KING, Stephanie 413-565-1000 215 A sking@baypath.edu
KING, Stephanie 716-851-1999 313 H kings@ecc.edu
KING, Steven 413-662-5410 222 B steven.king@mcla.edu
KING, Sue 816-501-3759 262 G sue.king@avila.edu
KING, Susan, L 207-780-4681 205 E susank@maine.edu
KING, Susan, R 919-962-1204 357 D susanking@unc.edu
KING, JR., Talmadge, E 415-476-2342 70 D talmadge.king@ucsf.edu
KING, Terry, S 765-285-5555 159 B tsking@bsu.edu
KING, Theresa 201-684-7800 294 G 0396mgr@fheg.follett.com
KING, Thomas 610-896-1111 405 I tking@haverford.edu
KING, Tiffany 708-239-4743 155 M tiffany.king@trnty.edu
KING, Tim 256-782-5020 4 H tbking@jsu.edu
KING, Tom 610-896-1111 398 K tking01@brynmawr.edu
KING, Tommy 601-318-6495 261 I pres@wmcarey.edu
KING, Venita 256-372-5248 1 A venita.king@aamu.edu
KING, Victor, I 323-343-3054 33 C vking@cslanet.calstatela.edu
KING, W. Cody 229-931-2045 122 C cody.king@gsw.edu
KING, Wayne 815-280-2210 144 A wking@jjc.edu
KING, Wendell, C 913-684-3280 528 I wendell.king@leavenworth.army.mil
KING, William 540-231-5992 489 H bking@vcom.vt.edu
KING, William, L 903-510-2252 473 C bkin@tjc.edu
KING, Yolanda, M 617-627-3248 228 H yolanda.king@tufts.edu
KING GASS, Sonia 803-780-1199 434 M kinggass@voorhees.edu
KING-LEROY, Cynthia, B 518-783-2420 330 E kingleroy@siena.edu
KING SANDERS, Nancy 361-593-3290 469 A nancy.kingsanders@tamuk.edu
KINGAN, Michael 817-272-2584 476 A mkkingan@uta.edu
KINGCADE, Fawn, M 580-327-8533 384 M fmkingcade@nwosu.edu
KINGHAM, Margaret, T 610-566-1776 423 H mkingham@williamson.edu
KINGKADE, H.K 502-863-8209 188 I hk_kingkade@georgetowncollege.edu
KINGREY, Daryl, L 540-887-7000 491 G
KINGRY, Kelly 912-486-7618 125 E kkingry@ogeecheetech.edu
KINGSBURY, Judy 507-285-7216 251 I judy.kingsbury@rctc.edu
KINGSFORD, Laura 562-985-5559 33 B laura.kingsford@csulb.edu
KINGSLEY, Lindsay 623-245-4600 17 G likingsley@uti.edu
KINGSLEY, Margery 580-581-6900 382 G margeryk@cameron.edu
KINGSOLVER, Robert 502-272-3628 187 A kingsolver@bellarmine.edu
KINGSTON, Laura 206-934-7959 507 A laura.kingston@seattlecolleges.edu
KINGSTON, Linda 651-846-1411 252 C linda.kingston@saintpaul.edu
KINGTON, Raynard, S 641-269-3000 172 I kington@grinnell.edu
KINIMAKA, Malia 562-985-4296 33 B malia.kinimaka@csulb.edu
KINKADE, Mike 870-584-1320 23 F mkinkade@cccua.edu

KITAGAWA, Susan 831-646-4014 53 A
skitagawa@mpc.edu
KITCH, Rhonda 701-231-7987 361 A
rhonda.k.kitch@ndsu.edu
KITCHEN, Augusta 803-780-1159 434 M
akitchen@voorhees.edu
KITCHEN, Barbara 859-846-5725 191 G
bkitchen@midway.edu
KITCHEN, Clifford 719-549-3121 82 G
clifford.kitchen@pueblocc.edu
KITCHEN, Herbert 510-466-7374 57 E
hkitchen@peralta.edu
KITCHEN, Janie 606-326-2163 188 N
janie.kitchen@kctcs.edu
KITCHEN, Mark 307-754-6405 526 N
mark.kitchen@nwc.edu
KITCHEN, Steve 650-949-6150 43 N
kitchensteve@fhda.edu
KITCHEN, Todd 479-619-4232 21 D
tkitchen@nwacc.edu
KITCHENS, Elizabeth 605-999-7136 436 C
elizabeth.kitchens@mitchelltech.edu
KITCHENS, Joann 701-662-1502 361 E
joann.kitchens@lrsc.edu
KITCHENS, Joseph, H 770-720-5966 126 C
jhk@reinhardt.edu
KITCHENS, Penny 478-553-2060 125 C
pkitchens@oftc.edu
KITCHENS, Ronnie 601-426-6346 260 G
rkitchens@southeasternbaptist.edu
KITCHENS, Tempie 770-233-6170 127 F
tkitchens@sctech.edu
KITCHENS, Willie 404-527-4520 118 F
wkitchens@carver.edu
KITCHIN, Steven, H 401-739-5000 425 C
skitchin@neit.edu
KITCHING, Aimee 662-846-4391 257 E
ahenderson@deltastate.edu
KITCHINGS, Maribeth 601-974-1002 258 H
kitchme@millsaps.edu
KITE, Joy, A 608-822-2319 524 F
jkite@swtc.edu
KITE, Michelle 269-782-1302 241 C
mkite@swmich.edu
KITE, Terry 636-481-3273 266 C
tkite@jeffco.edu
KITEI, Susan, C 610-758-3870 408 H
sck0@lehigh.edu
KITHCART, Jane 845-687-5111 338 F
kithcarj@sunyulster.edu
KITSON, Anna 502-410-6200 188 H
akitson@galencollege.edu
KITTINGER, Fred 407-823-1208 111 E
fred.kittinger@ucf.edu
KITTLE, Daniel 319-352-8745 177 G
daniel.kittle@wartburg.edu
KITTLE, Paul 336-841-9107 345 A
pkittle@highpoint.edu
KITTLESON, Mark 585-395-2350 332 E
mkittleson@brockport.edu
KITTNER, Missy 254-299-8514 461 E
mkittner@mclennan.edu
KITTO, Kathleen 360-650-5929 509 E
kathleen.kitto@wwu.edu
KITTREDGE,
Cynthia Briggs 512-472-4133 465 F
cynthia.kittredge@ssw.edu
KITTRELL-MIKELL,
Deborah 478-289-2161 120 C
dkittrell@ega.edu
KITTS, Justin 606-546-1232 193 E
jkitts@unionky.edu
KITTS, Kenneth 256-765-4211 9 C
kkitts@una.edu
KITZINGER, Denis 603-880-8308 288 A
dkitzinger@thomasmorecollege.edu
KITZINGER, Sara 603-880-8308 288 A
skitzinger@thomasmorecollege.edu
KIWUS, Christopher 540-231-6291 499 F
chkiwus@vt.edu
KIYOSHI, Jack, O 670-234-5498 530 D
KIZINA, Terrance 412-536-1275 406 K
terrance.kizina@laroche.edu
KJARTANSON, Mary 619-388-7968 60 H
mkjartan@sdccd.edu
KJELLEREN, Donald, J 413-597-2312 230 A
donald.f.kjelleren@williams.edu
KLAAS, Carlene 312-362-8146 139 C
cklaas@depaul.edu
KLAAS, Gerry 314-659-0816 266 F
klaas@kenrick.edu
KLAASSEN, Sara 816-322-0110 262 N
sara.klaassen@calvary.edu
KLABE, Kimberly 301-447-5377 209 G
klabe@msmary.edu
KLADIVKO, Deborah 803-641-3577 433 G
debk@usca.edu
KLAFFKE, David 360-383-3016 509 F
dklaffke@whatcom.ctc.edu
KLAG, Michael, J 410-955-3540 208 D
michaelj.klag@jhu.edu
KLAIBER, Beverly, G 530-226-4179 64 H
bklaiber@simpsonu.edu
KLAIBER, James, S 440-775-5603 374 C
jim.klaiber@oberlin.edu
KLAMEN, David 508-999-8010 220 H
dklamen@umassd.edu
KLAPATAUSKAS, Kyle, J 563-588-7829 174 K
kyle.klapatauskas@loras.edu
KLAPPER, Robert 770-729-8400 116 G
KLARUP, Doug 217-581-6227 139 H
dgklarup@eiu.edu
KLASEN, James 617-588-1344 215 E
jklasen@bfit.edu
KLASKO, Stephen, K 215-955-6617 420 E
stephen.klasko@jefferson.edu
KLASS, Stephen, P 413-597-3118 230 A
stephen.p.klass@williams.edu
KLATT, Sara 712-274-6400 177 I
sara.klatt@witcc.edu
KLAUBER, James, S 256-306-2555 2 F
jim.klauber@calhoun.edu
KLAUDER, Mark, J 802-447-6322 485 B
mklauder@svc.edu
KLAUS, Allen, R 210-434-6711 463 C
arklaus@lake.ollusa.edu
KLAUS, Byron, D 610-917-1402 422 C
bdklaus@valleyforge.edu
KLAUS, Carrie, F 765-658-6568 160 F
cklaus@depauw.edu
KLAUS, Chad, L 609-258-5498 294 D
klaus@princeton.edu
KLAUS, Dennis 801-957-4250 483 A
dennis.klaus@slcc.edu
KLAUSMEYER, Robert 573-875-7304 263 F
rklausmeyer@ccis.edu
KLAVER, Lenny 660-359-3948 269 I
lklaver@mail.ncmissouri.edu
KLAWE, Maria, M 909-921-8120 46 A
klawe@hmc.edu
KLAWITTER, Christina 608-363-2660 515 G
klawitterc@beloit.edu
KLAWUNN, Margaret 805-893-3651 70 E
margaret.klawunn@sa.ucsb.edu
KLAY, Kathy, A 937-328-6085 366 E
klayk@clarkstate.edu
KLEBE, Kelli 719-255-3779 83 L
kklebe@uccs.edu
KLEBESADEL, Shirley 715-232-2190 521 D
klebesadels@uwstout.edu
KLECKNER, Joan 610-902-8201 399 D
joan.d.kleckner@cabrini.edu
KLEDZIK, Eric 321-674-8107 100 M
ekledzik@fit.edu
KLEEMAN, Amy 407-582-1238 114 N
akleeman@valenciacollege.edu
KLEEMAN, Beverly, S 509-777-4548 509 H
bkleeman@whitworth.edu
KLEFFMAN, Terry, L 806-371-5111 450 H
tlkleffman@actx.edu
KLEICH, Tammie 308-635-6072 283 D
kleicht@wncc.edu
KLEIN, Andrew, O 508-849-3313 214 E
aklein@annamaria.edu
KLEIN, Andrew, R 317-274-2581 163 D
anrklein@iupui.edu
KLEIN, Barb 641-648-4611 173 K
barb.klein@iavalley.edu
KLEIN, Bridget 502-272-8423 187 A
bklein@bellarmine.edu
KLEIN, Cynthia 412-809-5100 417 D
klein.cynthia@pti.edu
KLEIN, David, A 434-223-6129 490 D
dklein@hsc.edu
KLEIN, Erin 701-252-3467 362 F
eklein@uj.edu
KLEIN, Gary 608-663-6713 516 F
garyklein@edgewood.edu
KLEIN, Jacob 248-689-8282 242 F
jklein@walshcollege.edu
KLEIN, Jacqueline 518-454-5111 311 B
KLEIN, Janie 925-631-4572 59 I
mminguill@stmarys-ca.edu
KLEIN, Jeff 909-652-6317 37 D
jeff.klein@chaffey.edu
KLEIN, Jennifer 949-582-4565 65 G
jklein26@saddleback.edu
KLEIN, Jim 502-456-6508 193 B
jklein@sullivan.edu
KLEIN, Judy 267-341-3615 405 J
jklein@holyfamily.edu
KLEIN, June 650-433-3849 56 D
jklein@paloaltou.edu
KLEIN, Karen 580-774-3268 388 C
karen.klein@swosu.edu
KLEIN, Lori 907-796-6036 10 H
laklein@alaska.edu
KLEIN, Marjorie, S 814-332-5910 397 A
mklein@allegheny.edu
KLEIN, Mendel 718-384-5460 341 A
KLEIN, Michael 718-368-5087 308 F
mklein@kbcc.cuny.edu
KLEIN, Michael 215-204-1927 420 B
mike.klein@temple.edu
KLEIN, Michelle, W 504-866-7426 199 A
finance@nds.edu
KLEIN, Paul 415-749-4589 61 B
paulklein@sfai.edu
KLEIN, Ray 812-941-2457 163 F
rayklein@ius.edu
KLEIN, Sara 718-420-4518 339 F
sara.klein@wagner.edu
KLEIN, Sara 201-216-3543 297 B
sara.klein@stevens.edu
KLEIN, Scott 812-866-7061 161 C
klein@hanover.edu
KLEIN, Shalin 785-539-3571 183 B
sklein@mccks.edu
KLEIN, Steve 503-352-2822 394 C
kleinsk@pacificu.edu
KLEIN, Steven 517-629-0321 230 E
sklein@albion.edu
KLEIN, Stuart 212-431-2170 323 H
stuart.klein@nyls.edu
KLEIN, Terry 715-468-2815 525 A
terry.klein@witc.edu
KLEINBERG, David, M 216-397-4357 370 H
dkleinberg@jcu.edu
KLEINDL, Brad 816-584-6308 270 D
brad.kleindl@park.edu
KLEINE, Patricia, A 715-836-2320 520 A
kleinepa@uwec.edu
KLEINER, Zev 347-394-1036 305 C
zkleiner@ateret.net
KLEINHANS, Randy 574-372-5100 161 B
kleinhrp@grace.edu
KLEINKAUFMAN, Dovid 718-327-7600 340 G
yfr1@verizon.net
KLEINKOPF, Karl 208-732-6201 133 E
csitrustees@csi.edu
KLEINLEIN, Tom 912-478-5047 122 B
tkleinlein@georgiasouthern.edu
KLEINMAN, Kent 607-255-9110 312 A
aapdean@cornell.edu
KLEINMAN, Kim 314-246-7768 275 B
kleinman@webster.edu
KLEINMAN, Yisroel 718-853-8500 337 H
KLEINPETER, Jennifer 225-743-8500 196 J
jkleinpeter@rpcc.edu
KLEINSCHMIDT, Robert 609-586-4800 292 D
kleinscr@mccc.edu
KLEINWORTH, Tom 713-798-6498 452 G
tklein@bcm.edu
KLEISER, Richele 559-325-3600 30 C
rkleiser@chsu.org
KLEMANN, M. Adam 330-471-8308 371 J
aklemann@malone.edu
KLEMENS, Kristina 262-595-2004 520 F
klemens@uwp.edu
KLEMENT, Emily 940-872-4002 462 L
eklement@nctc.edu
KLEMIUK, Christy 903-463-8650 458 H
klemiukc@grayson.edu
KLEMM, Dave 217-732-3155 146 B
dklemm@lincolncollege.edu
KLEMM, Jotisa 817-515-3083 467 A
jotisa.klemm@tccd.edu
KLEMPA, Richard, M 304-243-2394 515 C
rklempa@wju.edu
KLEMPNER, Mark, D 508-856-8000 221 B
mark.klempner@umassmed.edu
KLEN, Joseph, R 765-361-6052 169 C
klenj@wabash.edu
KLENIEWSKI, Nancy 607-436-2500 331 F
nancy.kleniewski@oneonta.edu
KLENKE, James, W 618-650-2020 155 A
jklenke@siue.edu
KLEPETAR, Adam 320-308-1060 252 A
asklepetar@stcloudstate.edu
KLEPITSCH, Heather, A 815-395-2446 153 D
heatherklepitsch@sacn.edu
KLEPONIS, Stephen 610-526-6017 405 B
skleponis@harcum.edu
KLESCHICK, Paul 413-205-3212 214 B
paul.kleschick@aic.edu
KLESNER, Joe, L 740-427-5114 371 C
klesner@kenyon.edu
KLETT, Breanna 562-903-4751 28 E
breanna.klett@biola.edu
KLETZER, Lori, G 207-859-4770 202 G
lori.kletzer@colby.edu
KLEVA, Barbara 609-984-1124 297 F
bkleva@tesu.edu
KLEVEN, Daniel 612-455-3420 245 A
daniel.kleven@bcsmn.edu
KLEVENO, Robert 951-222-8000 59 C
robert.kleveno@rcc.edu
KLEVER, Sunny 503-338-2306 390 G
sklever@clatsopcc.edu
KLEYN, Henk 616-977-0599 240 B
henk.kleyn@prts.edu
KLIER, Jody 701-845-7297 361 B
jody.klier@vcsu.edu
KLIER, Robert 323-953-4000 49 H
klierrm@lacitycollege.edu
KLIEWER, Lee 570-586-2400 419 G
lkliewer@summitu.edu
KLIEWONEIT, Chris 989-386-6652 238 B
ckliewon@midmich.edu
KLIGMAN, Linda 267-975-2254 406 C
lindakligman@iirp.edu
KLIKA, William 201-443-8972 291 J
helen_bajek@fdu.edu
KLIMA, Kris 785-670-1030 185 H
kris.klima@washburn.edu
KLIMCZYK, Karen 219-464-5015 168 F
karen.klimczyk@valpo.edu
KLIMITCHEK, Missy 361-572-6407 478 F
missy.klimitchek@victoriacollege.edu
KLIMKOWSKI,
Ann Francis 419-885-3211 371 I
aklimkowski@lourdes.edu
KLIMOFF, Dodi 215-635-7300 404 D
dklimoff@gratz.edu
KLIMPT, Kelly 409-944-1356 458 D
kklimpt@gc.edu
KLINE, Amy 212-875-4504 304 E
akline@bankstreet.edu
KLINE, Bob 251-626-3303 8 B
bkline@ussa.edu
KLINE, J 615-383-4848 449 G
jkline@watkins.edu
KLINE, John 847-585-0014 135 A
jkline@aiuonline.edu
KLINE, Julie 909-593-3511 71 B
jkline@laverne.edu
KLINE, Julie 651-523-2021 247 A
jkline04@hamline.edu
KLINE, Julie 507-933-7304 246 J
jkline@gustavus.edu
KLINE, Loni 570-321-4199 409 F
klinel@lycoming.edu
KLINE, Mae 407-328-2096 109 E
kline@seminolestate.edu
KLINE, Meredith 978-468-7111 219 B
mmkline@gcts.edu
KLINE, Patricia 701-671-2106 361 F
patty.kline@ndscs.edu
KLINE, Rebecca 573-876-7111 272 I
rkline@stephens.edu
KLINE, Richard 440-375-7512 371 E
rkline@lec.edu
KLINE, Ronald, J 610-861-1510 411 B
kliner@moravian.edu
KLINE, Thomas 262-551-6036 516 A
tkline@carthage.edu
KLINE, William 978-837-5134 225 E
klinew@merrimack.edu
KLINE, William 812-877-8136 166 H
william.kline@rose-hulman.edu
KLINEPETER, Pamela 606-326-2254 188 N
pamela.klinepeter@kctcs.edu
KLINESMITH, Jerry 740-264-5591 368 D
jklinesmith@egcc.edu
KLING, Deron 608-663-4420 516 F
dkling@edgewood.edu
KLING, Lenda 850-201-8660 113 E
klingl@tcc.fl.edu
KLINGBEIL, Nathan, W 937-775-5007 381 H
nathan.klingbeil@wright.edu
KLINGBERG, Jessica 708-209-3505 138 G
jessica.klingberg@cuchicago.edu
KLINGENBERG, Erin 701-845-7424 361 B
erin.klingenberg@vcsu.edu
KLINGENSMITH, John 972-860-4190 456 B
jklingensmith@dcccd.edu
KLINGENSMITH, Lynn 610-436-2513 416 C
lklingensmith@wcupa.edu
KLINGENSMITH, Ron, D 858-499-0202 39 J
rklingensmith@coleman.edu
KLINGER, Joe 708-456-0300 156 C
joeklinger@triton.edu
KLINGER, John 314-505-7384 263 I
klingerj@csl.edu
KLINGER, Michelle 602-285-7870 14 F
michelle.klinger@phoenixcollege.edu
KLINGERMAN, Trent 765-494-7395 166 D
klingert@purdue.edu
KLINGSHIRN, Connie 419-559-2228 377 M
cklingshirn01@terra.edu
KLINGSHIRN, Connie 419-267-1329 374 A
cklingshirn@northweststate.edu
KLINGSMITH, Libby 970-339-6431 76 H
libby.klingsmith@aims.edu
KLINK, Charles, J 804-828-7525 496 D
cjklink@vcu.edu
KLINKENBERG, Laurel 217-641-4500 143 H
lklinkenberg@jwcc.edu
KLINKHAMMER, Barbara 215-951-2828 416 G
klinkhammerb@philau.edu
KLINKNER, Melvin 262-595-2076 520 F
klinkner@uwp.edu
KLIPP, Todd L, C 617-353-9550 216 E
tklipp@bu.edu

KNOWLES, Harley 423-746-5201 447 E hknowles@twcnet.edu
KNOWLES, James, M 409-984-6432 471 C knowlejm@lamarpa.edu
KNOWLES, Lorelette 425-968-3400 63 H lknowles@saybrook.edu
KNOWLES, Melody, D 703-370-6600 492 I
KNOWLES, Monica 360-992-2904 502 E mknowles@clark.edu
KNOWLES, Susan 315-268-6633 310 B sknowles@clarkson.edu
KNOWLTON, Eloise 508-767-7487 214 F eknowlton@assumption.edu
KNOX, Chrisanne 925-969-2048 41 I cknox@dvc.edu
KNOX, Craig 850-201-8660 113 E
KNOX, David, K 864-656-0868 428 C knox2@clemson.edu
KNOX, George, C 620-421-6700 182 G georgek@labette.edu
KNOX, Ken 740-266-1670 368 D knox@egcc.edu
KNOX, Linda, B 219-989-3169 166 F lbknox@pnw.edu
KNOX, Linda, B 219-989-2337 166 F lbknox@pnw.edu
KNOX, Lindsay 503-554-2242 391 D lknox@georgefox.edu
KNOX, Michael, J 806-651-2050 469 D mknox@wtamu.edu
KNOX, Pamela 615-366-4482 444 D pamela.knox@tbr.edu
KNOX, Ruth, A 478-757-5212 129 L rknox@wesleyancollege.edu
KNOX, Ryan 309-248-8189 141 C ryan.knox@heartland.edu
KNOX, Teresa, L 918-610-0027 383 E tknox@communitycarecollege.edu
KNOX, Tracey 970-521-6643 81 O tracey.knox@njc.edu
KNOX, Wayne 512-505-3003 459 F wknox@htu.edu
KNUCKLES, Leator 410-238-9000 93 F
KNUDSEN, Alice, B 510-430-2350 52 J aknudsen@mills.edu
KNUDSEN, H. Peter 406-496-4395 277 G pknudsen@mtech.edu
KNUDSEN, J. Todd 562-902-3358 66 A toddknudsen@scuhs.edu
KNUDSEN, Ross 208-376-7731 132 H rknudsen@boisebible.edu
KNUDSON, Dan 218-299-6521 250 D dan.knudson@minnesota.edu
KNUDSON, Edward, T 661-722-6300 27 B eknudson@avc.edu
KNUDSON, Kari 701-224-5604 361 C kari.l.knudson@bismarckstate.edu
KNUDSON, Paula, M 608-785-8150 520 C pknudson@uwlax.edu
KNUDSON-CARL, Tara 402-399-2449 279 E tknudsoncarl@csm.edu
KNUEPFER, Peter 518-320-1376 330 H peter.knuepfer@suny.edu
KNUPPEL, Lisa 714-432-5575 39 G lknuppel@occ.cccd.edu
KNUTEL, Phillip 781-239-4225 214 G pknutel@babson.edu
KNUTH, Barbara, A 607-255-5864 312 A bak3@cornell.edu
KNUTH, Doug 775-784-6900 285 A dknuth@unr.edu
KNUTSEN, Mark 423-697-4785 445 D mark.knutsen@chattanoogastate.edu
KNUTSON, Jennifer 605-331-6611 438 A jennifer.knutson@usiouxfalls.edu
KNUTSON, Karen 320-363-5922 245 I kknutson@csbsju.edu
KNUTSON, Karen, G 320-363-5922 254 N kknutson@csbsju.edu
KNUTSON, Sherry 415-749-4571 61 B sknutson@sfai.edu
KNUTSON-KOLODZNE, Jim 320-308-5447 252 A jkolodzne@stcloudstate.edu
KNUTSON-MILLER, Kari 657-278-7511 33 A kkmiller@fullerton.edu
KO, Jeanne 212-472-1500 324 A jko@nysid.edu
KO, Shinsaeng 404-727-0825 120 E shinsaeng.ko@emory.edu
KO, Yoo, K 571-730-4750 268 C wdc@midwest.edu
KOAN, Mark 602-285-7855 14 F mark.koan@phoenixcollege.edu
KOBACK, Beth 704-971-2121 343 E bkoback@charlottelaw.edu
KOBALLA, Thomas 912-478-5648 122 B tkoballa@georgiasouthern.edu
KOBAYASHI, Frank 916-485-6028 51 A kobayaf@arc.losrios.edu
KOBERNA, Sharon 480-517-8220 14 G sharon.koberna@riosalado.edu
KOBES, Patricia 845-574-4280 327 G pkobes@sunyrockland.edu
KOBLER, Soheila 973-618-3724 290 A skobler@caldwell.edu
KOBLER, Wendy 937-327-7430 381 F koblerw@wittenberg.edu
KOBMAN, Lisa 513-244-4979 373 C lisa.kobman@msj.edu
KOBOLAKIS, Evan 516-876-3379 333 C kobolakise@oldwestbury.edu
KOBRIN, Jennifer 212-817-7209 308 A jkobrin@gc.cuny.edu
KOBRYN, Danielle 845-398-4016 329 G dkobryn@stac.edu
KOBUS, Gloria 330-941-3142 382 A gjkobus@ysu.edu
KOBYLSKI, Janet 570-408-4501 423 G janet.kobylski@wilkes.edu
KOCAR, Deb 617-349-8800 220 B ugadm@lesley.edu
KOCER, Ken 605-668-1589 436 D kkocer@mtmc.edu
KOCH, Bill 252-328-6166 356 C kochb@ecu.edu
KOCH, Bradley 610-902-8571 399 D bradley.r.koch@cabrini.edu
KOCH, Don 618-634-3289 154 B donk@shawneecc.edu
KOCH, Erec 646-660-6530 307 A erec.koch@baruch.cuny.edu
KOCH, Geraldine 201-559-3515 291 K kochg@felician.edu
KOCH, Greg 770-960-1298 123 F gkoch@ict.edu
KOCH, Kelly 989-386-6639 238 B kkoch@midmich.edu
KOCH, Kevin 781-762-1211 218 F kkoch@fmc.edu
KOCH, Malcolm 731-881-1017 448 G mkoch@utm.edu
KOCH, Paul 831-459-2931 70 F plkoch@ucsc.edu
KOCH, Paul 563-333-6212 176 D kochpaulc@sau.edu
KOCH, Susan 217-206-6634 156 E koch@uis.edu
KOCH, Susan 217-206-6634 156 G koch@uis.edu
KOCH, Thomas, L 520-621-2448 17 I tlkoch@email.arizona.edu
KOCH, Virginia, A 334-844-3466 1 G vak0001@auburn.edu
KOCHAN, Julie 518-454-5121 311 B kochanj@strose.edu
KOCHAN, Roman 562-985-4047 33 B roman.kochan@csulb.edu
KOCHANEK, Lea 210-341-1366 463 A lkochanek@ost.edu
KOCHARD, Lawrence, E 434-924-8976 495 H lek8e@virginia.edu
KOCHER, Andy, M 317-788-3493 168 A akocher@uindy.edu
KOCHER, Becky 419-372-2424 364 E rkocher@bgsu.edu
KOCHER, Craig, T 804-289-8500 495 G ckocher@richmond.edu
KOCHERA, Melissah 203-596-4652 88 F mkochera@post.edu
KOCHEVAR, Brenda 218-749-0314 249 I b.kochevar@mesabirange.edu
KOCHEVAR, Deborah 508-887-4700 228 H deborah.kochevar@tufts.edu
KOCHIEN, Kenneth, G 603-526-3627 285 L kkochien@colby-sawyer.edu
KOCHIS, Stephen, J 845-575-3000 320 B stephen.kochis@marist.edu
KOCHON, Barbara 413-565-1000 215 A bkochon@baypath.edu
KOCHUBA, Sara 724-503-1001 422 H skochuba@washjeff.edu
KOCIAN, Bryce 979-532-6315 479 J brycek@wcjc.edu
KOCIAN, Justin 402-494-2311 281 C jkocian@thenicc.edu
KOCIK, Piotr 718-518-6610 308 C pkocik@hostos.cuny.edu
KOCIOLEK, Patrick 303-492-8464 83 K patrick.kociolek@colorado.edu
KOCK, Timothy 670-234-3691 530 D tim.kock@marianas.edu
KOCOUR, Bruce 865-471-3240 439 C bkocour@cn.edu
KOCSIS, Katie, L 716-286-8669 324 E kkocsis@niagara.edu
KODAMA, Be-Jay 808-739-8526 130 F bkodama@chaminade.edu
KODAT, Catherine 503-768-7100 392 A kodat@lclark.edu
KODY, Hillary 617-682-1507 218 E hkody@eds.edu
KOEBEL, Dave 402-457-2391 280 J dkoebel@mccneb.edu
KOEGLER, Jason, W 304-336-8302 513 F jkoegler@westliberty.edu
KOEHLER, Al 636-922-8452 271 A alkoehler@stchas.edu
KOEHLER, David 308-635-6021 283 D koehlerd@wncc.edu
KOEHLER, David 541-881-5583 395 E dkoehler@tvcc.cc
KOEHLER, Donna 253-589-5588 502 F donna.koehler@cptc.edu
KOEHLER, John 406-791-5330 278 G john.koehler@ugf.edu
KOEHLER, Larry 810-232-8153 238 F larry.koehler@mcc.edu
KOEHLER, Laurie 202-994-1529 92 D koehler@gwu.edu
KOEHLER, Martha Kaye 813-253-7007 102 R mkoehler@hccfl.edu
KOEHLER, R. Brien 262-646-6545 518 G rkoehler@nashotah.edu
KOEHLER, Randy 513-244-8449 366 B randy.koehler@ccuniversity.edu
KOEHN, Effie, F 406-243-5580 276 K effie.koehn@umontana.edu
KOEHN, Jack 224-293-5961 79 D
KOEHN, Michelle 316-226-2002 169 D michelle.koehn@allencollege.edu
KOEHN, Sara 620-276-9574 181 C sara.koehn@gcccks.edu
KOEHNEKE, Mary, A 716-888-2300 306 F mkoehneke@canisius.edu
KOEHNKE, Paul 704-330-6121 348 E paul.koehnke@cpcc.edu
KOELBL, James 207-602-2678 205 F jkoelbl@une.edu
KOELKER, June 817-257-7106 469 G j.koelker@tcu.edu
KOELLER, Martin, E 973-761-9782 297 A martin.koeller@shu.edu
KOELTZOW, Dawn 309-677-2510 136 B dkoeltzow@fsmail.bradley.edu
KOENECKE, David 660-626-2410 262 A dkoenecke@atsu.edu
KOENIG, Gigi 715-394-8014 521 E gkoenig1@uwsuper.edu
KOENIG, Jason, T 864-833-8490 432 B jtkoenig@presby.edu
KOENIG, Jerry, L 317-921-4491 164 F jkoenig@ivytech.edu
KOENIG, Linda 740-351-3539 377 C lkoenig@shawnee.edu
KOEPKE, Andrea 419-434-4677 379 E koepke@findlay.edu
KOEPKE, Janelle 563-589-0712 177 H jkoepke@wartburgseminary.edu
KOEPKE, Mark 701-252-3467 362 F mkoepke@uj.edu
KOEPLIN, SJ, John 415-422-2563 72 C koeplin@usfca.edu
KOEPPEL, Edmund 516-572-7126 322 C edmund.koeppel@ncc.edu
KOEPPEN, Bruce 203-582-5301 88 G bruce.koeppen@quinnipiac.edu
KOERBER, Brent 614-236-7167 364 N bkoerber@capital.edu
KOERNER, Mari, E 602-543-6352 11 H mari.koerner@asu.edu
KOERNER, Melissa 801-832-2601 483 D mkoerner@westminstercollege.edu
KOERNERT, Andrew, H 757-594-8480 488 E andrew.koernert@cnu.edu
KOERSELMAN, Corky 712-707-7000 176 B corky.koerselman@nwciowa.edu
KOERWER, V. Scott 570-504-7000 400 I vkoerwer@tcmc.edu
KOESER, Bryan 920-693-1731 523 E bryan.koeser@gotoltc.edu
KOESTER, Craig 651-641-3471 247 G ckoester@luthersem.edu
KOETTING, Sandy 573-681-5071 266 I koettings@lincolnu.edu
KOETZNER, John 707-468-3000 52 C jkoetzne@mendocino.edu
KOEVEN, Gary, J 435-652-7770 482 A koeven@dixie.edu
KOFF, Gordon, D 603-646-2451 286 J gordon.d.koff@dartmouth.edu
KÖFFLER, Jeromy, A 503-943-7470 396 B koffler@up.edu
KOGA, Laura, A 815-740-3392 157 F lkoga@stfrancis.edu
KOGAN, Alexander 212-327-8001 327 F kogana@rockefeller.edu
KOGAN, Lilly 212-517-3929 330 G l.kogan@sothebysinstitute.com
KOGUT, Leonard 616-632-2885 231 A lvk001@aquinas.edu
KOH, Lee 781-239-2637 223 F lkoh@massbay.edu
KOHL, Bunny 856-227-7200 290 B bkohl@camdencc.edu
KOHL, James 978-934-2108 221 A james_kohl@uml.edu
KOHL, Marie 315-792-5340 321 G mkohl@mvcc.edu
KOHL, Troy 920-735-5766 523 C kohlt@fvtc.edu
KOHLER, Dave 360-867-6451 503 G kohlerd@evergreen.edu
KOHLER, David 806-651-2116 469 D dkohler@mail.wtamu.edu
KOHLER, Donald 712-325-3262 174 B dkohler@iwcc.edu
KOHLER, Elizabeth 734-462-4400 240 H bkohler@schoolcraft.edu
KOHLER, Patti 435-797-0174 482 B patti.kohler@usu.edu
KOHLER, Rebecca 315-866-0300 316 A kohlerrl@herkimer.edu
KOHLES, Paula, S 402-280-2731 279 H paulakohles@creighton.edu
KOHLHEPP, William, C 203-582-5226 88 G william.kohlhepp@quinnipiac.edu
KOHLI, Cathy, L 419-995-8060 370 G kohli.c@rhodesstate.edu
KOHLMAN, Bradley 316-284-5251 179 A bkohlman@bethelks.edu
KOHLMAN, Mark 740-427-5000 371 C kohlmanm@kenyon.edu
KOHLMEYER, Bill 503-399-6505 390 E bill.kohlmeyer@chemeketa.edu
KOHN, David 845-341-4388 325 H david.kohn@sunyorange.edu
KOHN, Gary 608-757-7769 523 A gkohn@blackhawk.edu
KOHN, Lorna 712-279-1705 170 B lorna.kohn@briarcliff.edu
KOHN, Melissa 920-236-6100 523 C kohn@fvtc.edu
KOHN, Paul 404-385-3708 121 D paul.kohn@ssc.gatech.edu
KOHN, Selina 706-821-8467 125 H skohn@paine.edu
KOHN, Shayeh 718-327-7600 340 G yfr1@verizon.net
KOHNEN-CAHALL, Nan 513-569-5807 366 D nan.cahall@cincinnatistate.edu
KOHNKE, Maria 805-493-3105 31 C kohnke@callutheran.edu
KOHR, Lesa, J 585-594-6966 327 D kohrl@roberts.edu
KOHRMAN, Robert 313-577-2001 243 F dt9443@wayne.edu
KOHRN, Lynn 203-932-7131 90 A lkohrn@newhaven.edu
KOHRS, Becky 402-471-2505 281 G bkohrs@nscs.edu
KOHSMANN, Laurie 703-561-1600 93 F laurie.kohsmann@strayer.edu
KOKAJKO, Hillary, C 336-841-9118 345 A hkokajko@highpoint.edu
KOKER, John, J 920-424-1210 520 E koker@uwosh.edu
KOKER, Michelle 612-624-2941 255 H koker@umn.edu
KOKILEPERSAUD, Premdat 443-885-3177 209 F prem.kokilepersaud@morgan.edu
KOKINOVA, Margarita, D 330-325-6333 373 H mkokinov@neomed.edu
KOKKALA, Irene 706-864-1862 128 F irene.kokkala@ung.edu
KOKOLUS, Cait 610-785-6280 418 E ckokolus@scs.edu
KOKOLUS, John 717-361-1291 403 C kokolusj@etown.edu
KOKONAS, Georgios 914-961-8313 329 H gkokonas@svots.edu
KOKX-TEMPLET, Ann 281-998-6103 464 I ann.kokx-templet@sjcd.edu
KOLACINSKI, John 213-484-8850 29 E
KOLANDER, John, D 414-443-8816 522 P john.kolander@wlc.edu
KOLB, Daniel 812-357-6566 167 B dkolb@saintmeinrad.edu
KOLB, Edward, W 773-702-7950 156 D rocky.kolb@uchicago.edu
KOLB, George, R 610-519-4580 422 G george.kolb@villanova.edu
KOLB, John, E 518-276-2122 327 B kolbj@rpi.edu
KOLBE, Donald, A 262-595-2228 520 F donald.kolbe@uwp.edu
KOLCHARNO, Julia 570-504-9614 400 I jkolcharno@tcmc.edu
KOLENBRANDER, Kirk, D 617-253-3365 225 A
KOLENDA, Richard 315-312-2246 333 D richard.kolenda@oswego.edu

KOSOKO-LASAKI, Sade ... 402-280-2332.. 279 H
sadekosoko-lasaki@creighton.edu
KOSOWSKY, Vicki .... 812-535-5216.. 166 K
vkosowsk@smwc.edu
KOSS, Michelle .... 586-286-2172.. 237 C
kossm26@macomb.edu
KOSSE, Glenn, F .... 502-272-8328.. 187 A
gkosse@bellarmine.edu
KOSSO, Cynthia .... 610-861-1348.. 411 B
kossoc@moravian.edu
KOSSUTH, Joanne .... 781-292-2431.. 218 H
joanne.kossuth@olin.edu
KOST, Patricia, L .... 216-368-2165.. 365 B
patricia.kost@case.edu
KOSTELL, Stacey, R .... 802-656-1394.. 485 D
stacey.kostell@uvm.edu
KOSTELNIK, Marjorie ...... 402-472-3751.. 282 M
mkostelnik2@unl.edu
KOSTEN, Linda .... 303-871-7922.... 84 B
linda.kosten@du.edu
KOSTER, Ed .... 402-761-8224.. 282 F
ekoster@southeast.edu
KOSTIHA-SMITH, Sarah ... 440-375-7504.. 371 E
skostihasmith@lec.edu
KOSTIHOVA, Marcela ...... 651-523-2252.. 247 A
mkostihova01@hamline.edu
KOSTRAB, Lynn, M .... 330-569-5109.. 369 J
kostrablm@hiram.edu
KOSTRZEWA, Waldemar .. 203-575-8297.... 86 G
wkostrzewa@nv.edu
KOSTYUKOV, Victoria ...... 718-522-9073.. 304 D
victoria_kostyukov@asa.edu
KOTAJARVI, Kathleen ...... 920-693-1163.. 523 E
kathleen.kotajarvi@gotoltc.edu
KOTCAMP, Butch .... 740-351-3429.. 377 C
bkotcamp@shawnee.edu
KOTECKI, Kathy .... 406-657-2087.. 277 D
kkotecki@msubillings.edu
KOTH, Jason .... 212-592-2000.. 330 C
jkoth@sva.edu
KOTLER, A. Malkiel .... 732-367-1060.. 289 G
KOTLER, Aaron .... 732-367-1060.. 289 G
akotler@bmg.edu
KOTLER, Yitzchok, S .... 732-367-1060.. 289 G
KOTLIKOFF, Michael, I .... 607-255-2364.. 312 A
provost@cornell.edu
KOTLINSKI, Michael, J .... 717-337-6363.. 404 C
mkotlinski@gettysburg.edu
KOTOISUVA, Agnes .... 692-625-3394.. 530 C
KOTORI, Chiaki .... 570-321-4029.. 409 F
kotori@lycoming.edu
KOTOWICZ, Keith, A .... 414-847-3301.. 518 D
keithkotowicz@miad.edu
KOTOWSKI, Kelli .... 740-597-1819.. 375 H
kotowskk@ohio.edu
KOTRBA, Darla .... 605-995-3023.. 436 C
darla.kotrba@mitchelltech.edu
KOTTAS, Kathy .... 620-792-9355.. 178 G
kottask@bartonccc.edu
KOTTER, David .... 303-963-3336.... 77 I
dkotter@ccu.edu
KOTTICH, Sarah .... 402-399-2427.. 279 E
skottich@csm.edu
KOTTON, Stevenson .... 692-625-4931.. 530 C
skotton@cmi.edu
KOTTOYIL, Joseph .... 305-223-4561.. 108 A
josephpothen@hotmail.com
KOTWICKI, Lee .... 941-363-7218.. 110 H
kotwicl@scf.edu
KOUA, Deb .... 515-965-7025.. 171 B
dkkoua@dmacc.edu
KOUBEK, Richard .... 225-578-1519.. 197 I
rkoubek@lsu.edu
KOUCOUMARIS, John, S 740-695-9500.. 364 B
jkoucoumaris@belmontcollege.edu
KOUDELIK-JONES,
Rachelle .... 540-857-6187.. 499 B
rkoudelikjones@virginiawestern.edu
KOUDOU, Nick .... 816-559-6182.. 270 D
nick.koudou@park.edu
KOUGH, Katherine .... 717-262-2006.. 424 A
kkough@wilson.edu
KOUKARI, Ray .... 262-619-6712.. 523 D
koukarir@gtc.edu
KOUKL, Shari .... 903-566-7214.. 477 B
skoukl@uttyler.edu
KOUKOL, June .... 617-333-2091.. 217 F
jkoukol@curry.edu
KOULIK, Chester .... 845-451-1347.. 312 C
c_koulik@culinary.edu
KOULOS, Elleni, R .... 909-593-3511.... 71 B
ekoulos@laverne.edu
KOUMARIANOS, Dee ...... 603-577-6570.. 286 I
ykoumarianos@dwc.edu
KOUMAS, Sokratis .... 508-999-8859.. 220 H
skoumas@umassd.edu
KOURIS, Demitris .... 605-394-2256.. 437 E
demitris.kouris@sdsmt.edu
KOURY, Kevin, A .... 724-938-4125.. 414 E
koury@calu.edu

KOUTSIDIS, Anastasia ..... 646-313-8000.. 309 F
anastasia.koutsidis@guttman.cuny.edu
KOUTSOUTIS, Kalli .... 718-429-6600.. 339 D
kalli.koutsoutis@vaughn.edu
KOVAC, Matt .... 724-287-8711.. 399 B
matt.kovac@bc3.edu
KOVACH, Karen, S .... 513-556-3483.. 379 A
karen.kovach@uc.edu
KOVACH-ALLEN,
Katharina, E .... 585-345-6831.. 315 C
kekovachallen@genesee.edu
KOVACICH, Christine, L .. 330-325-6551.. 373 H
ckovacich@neomed.edu
KOVACS, Anita .... 904-632-3218.. 101 G
anita.kovacs@fscj.edu
KOVACS, Charles .... 941-359-7650.. 107 M
ckovacs@ringling.edu
KOVACS, Gene .... 850-245-0466.. 110 I
gene.kovacs@flbog.edu
KOVACS, Mark, C .... 315-792-3025.. 339 B
mkovacs@utica.edu
KOVAL, Volga .... 707-826-4143.... 34 F
volga.koval@humboldt.edu
KOVALCHICK, Ann .... 209-228-4899.... 70 A
akovalchick@ucmerced.edu
KOVALCHICK, Mary .... 610-799-1957.. 408 G
mkovalchick@lccc.edu
KOVANES, Tera, D .... 540-654-1042.. 495 C
tkovanes@umw.edu
KOVATCH, Richard, A ...... 434-982-5166.. 495 H
rak3e@virginia.edu
KOVERMAN, Robert .... 312-369-6543.. 138 F
rkoverman@colum.edu
KOVEROLA, Catherine ...... 617-873-0607.. 217 A
catherine.koverola@cambridgecollege.edu
KOVLER, Allen .... 518-828-4181.. 311 D
kovler@sunycgcc.edu
KOWAL, Donna, M .... 585-395-5400.. 332 E
dkowal@brockport.edu
KOWAL, John .... 518-438-3111.. 320 A
jkowal@mariacollege.edu
KOWALESKI, Curt .... 920-403-3117.. 519 G
curt.kowaleski@snc.edu
KOWALEWSKI, John, L .... 801-626-7212.. 482 D
jkowalewski@weber.edu
KOWALEWSKY, Lyn .... 989-358-7280.. 230 G
kowalewl@alpenacc.edu
KOWALIK, Margaret .... 315-781-3695.. 316 C
kowalik@hws.edu
KOWALIK, Thomas .... 607-777-2792.. 331 B
kowalik@binghamton.edu
KOWALSKI, David .... 215-641-6674.. 410 L
dkowalsi@mc3.edu
KOWALSKI, Gerard, J ...... 706-542-8318.. 128 E
kowalski@uga.edu
KOWALSKI, Joann .... 607-735-1825.. 313 F
jkowalski@elmira.edu
KOWALSKI, Jonathan .... 414-277-4510.. 518 E
kowalski@msoe.edu
KOWALSKI, JR.,
Jonathan, V .... 414-277-4510.. 518 E
kowalski@msoe.edu
KOWALSKI, Karl .... 907-450-8383.... 10 G
karl.kowalski@alaska.edu
KOWALSKI, Karl .... 907-450-8383.... 10 E
kekowalski@alaska.edu
KOWALSKI, Marion .... 212-875-4475.. 304 E
mkowalski@bankstreet.edu
KOWALSKI, Melanie .... 570-504-1583.. 407 B
kowalskim@lackawanna.edu
KOWALSKI, Patrick, A ..... 513-556-1299.. 379 A
patrick.kowalski@uc.edu
KOWALSKI, Susan .... 717-338-3008.. 409 D
skowalski@ltsg.edu
KOWALSKI, Timothy, J ... 864-327-9800.. 489 H
KOWALSKI-BRAUN,
Marlene .... 616-331-3585.. 234 F
kowalskm@gvsu.edu
KOWALSKY, Margaret ..... 570-208-5986.. 406 J
margaretkowalsky@kings.edu
KOWCHECK, Tyler .... 724-503-1001.. 422 H
tkowcheck@washjeff.edu
KOWEEK, Joan .... 518-828-4181.. 311 D
joan.koweek@sunycgcc.edu
KOWICH, Colleen .... 816-271-5650.. 269 C
ckowich@missouriwestern.edu
KOWNACKI, James .... 570-484-2460.. 415 D
jkownack@lhup.edu
KOWTA, Mayumi .... 805-437-3107.... 32 B
mayumi.kowta@csuci.edu
KOZACHYN, Karen .... 610-359-5362.. 401 L
kkozachy@dccc.edu
KOZAK, Diane .... 907-786-4513.... 10 F
dhkozak@uaa.alaska.edu
KOZAK, Gregory .... 847-574-5194.. 145 C
gkozak@lfgsm.edu
KOZAK, Laura, A .... 410-706-8138.. 211 F
lkozak@umaryland.edu
KOZARIK, Greg .... 216-881-1700.. 375 G
gkozarik@ohiotech.edu

KOZDEMBA, Kathy .... 412-536-1047.. 406 K
kozdemba@verizon.net
KOZEL, Nikolas, G .... 215-951-5101.. 407 A
kozel@lasalle.edu
KOZERA, Mark .... 706-368-6945.. 117 F
mkozera@berry.edu
KOZERACKI, Carol .... 323-415-5374.... 49 G
kozeraca@elac.edu
KOZIATEK, Caroline .... 203-932-7479.... 90 A
ckoziatek@newhaven.edu
KOZIL, Cindy, T .... 508-541-1552.. 217 G
ckozil@dean.edu
KOZIMOR, Renee .... 847-635-1761.. 150 G
rkozimor@oakton.edu
KOZINSKI, Thaddeus ...... 307-332-2930.. 527 F
tkozinski@wyomingcatholiccollege.com
KOZIOL, Nicholas, J .... 716-880-2207.. 320 D
nicholas.j.koziol@medaille.edu
KOZISEK, Kelly, L .... 541-737-4261.. 393 H
kelly.kozisek@oregonstate.edu
KOZISEK, Sue .... 402-421-7410.. 281 A
KOZLOWSKI, Michael ..... 860-723-0261.... 85 E
kozlowskim@ct.edu
KOZLOWSKI, Michelle ...... 559-934-2240.... 74 C
michellekozlowski@whccd.edu
KOZOJED, Bob, J .... 701-788-4872.. 360 E
bob.kozojed@mayvillestate.edu
KOZUMA, Hikaru .... 215-898-6081.. 421 E
kozuma@upenn.edu
KOZY, Mallie .... 503-413-8080.. 392 B
mkozy@linfield.edu
KRABBENHOFT, Alan ...... 765-455-9275.. 163 A
agkrabbe@iupui.edu
KRAEMER, David .... 212-678-8075.. 317 I
dakraemer@jtsa.edu
KRAEMER, Laurence .... 516-465-8099.. 313 C
lkraemer@nshs.edu
KRAEMER, Ronald, D .... 574-631-9700.. 168 B
kraemer.5@nd.edu
KRAFT, Damon .... 785-833-4371.. 182 F
damon.kraft@kwu.edu
KRAFT, Deborah .... 443-334-2337.. 211 A
dkraft@stevenson.edu
KRAFT, Deborah .... 281-756-3509.. 450 G
dkraft@alvincollege.edu
KRAFT, Erin .... 847-851-5468.... 79 D
ekraft@coloradotech.edu
KRAFT, Gary, L .... 402-472-3609.. 282 M
gary.kraft@unl.edu
KRAFT, Jeff .... 773-371-5415.. 136 F
jkraft@ctu.edu
KRAFT, John .... 352-392-2398.. 112 A
john.kraft@warrington.ufl.edu
KRAFT, John .... 513-244-4426.. 373 C
john.kraft@msj.edu
KRAFT, Ronald, D .... 707-256-7160.... 53 H
rkraft@napavalley.edu
KRAFT, Thomas .... 405-682-1611.. 385 D
tkraft@occc.edu
KRAFT, Walter .... 734-487-6895.. 233 J
walter.kraft@emuch.edu
KRAFT-MEYER, Kelly .... 434-381-6425.. 494 M
kraft_meyer@sbc.edu
KRAFTICK, Chris .... 606-539-4540.. 193 F
KRAGT, Donna .... 616-234-4040.. 234 E
dkragt@grcc.edu
KRAGT, Nicole .... 269-337-7203.. 235 H
nicole.kragt@kzoo.edu
KRAGULJEVIC, Nev .... 401-598-1000.. 425 B
nkraguljevic@jwu.edu
KRAH, Stephanie .... 937-376-6493.. 365 H
skrah@centralstate.edu
KRAHE, Sharon, A .... 814-871-7670.. 404 A
krahe@gannon.edu
KRAHL, Tracy .... 312-362-5577.. 139 C
tkrahl@depaul.edu
KRAIMER, Paul .... 651-905-3509.. 255 B
pkraimer@browncollege.edu
KRAJEWSKI, Rex .... 978-762-4000.. 224 C
rkrajews@northshore.edu
KRAJEWSKI, Scott .... 612-330-1471.. 244 I
krajewsk@augsburg.edu
KRAJNIAK, Chris, A .... 262-554-2010.. 518 B
chriskrajn@aol.com
KRAKOFF, Steve, P .... 419-372-7127.. 364 E
skrakof@bgsu.edu
KRAKOW, Anne, Z .... 610-660-1905.. 418 G
akrakow@sju.edu
KRAL, Kathy .... 678-839-6585.. 129 E
kkral@westga.edu
KRAL, Luke .... 660-944-2886.. 263 G
admissions@conception.edu
KRAL, Martin, J .... 309-298-1838.. 158 A
mj-kral@wiu.edu
KRALL, Jason .... 412-578-6152.. 400 C
jkrall@carlow.edu
KRALL, Jessica .... 760-384-6362.... 47 K
jessica.krall@cerrocoso.edu
KRALL, Jim .... 479-524-7145.... 20 H
jkrall@jbu.edu

KRALL, Michael .... 832-813-6603.. 461 B
michael.j.krall@lonestar.edu
KRALLMAN, Denise, A .... 513-529-7095.. 372 K
krallmda@miamioh.edu
KRAMB, Jim .... 972-473-3416.. 465 J
jkramb@smu.edu
KRAMER, Alan .... 229-391-4928.. 115 I
akramer@abac.edu
KRAMER, Alan .... 860-913-2032.... 87 H
akramer@goodwin.edu
KRAMER, Art .... 617-373-4160.. 227 B
KRAMER, Cathy .... 828-298-3325.. 359 F
service@warren-wilson.edu
KRAMER, Christina .... 217-234-5475.. 145 D
ckramer@lakeland.cc.il.us
KRAMER, Esther .... 262-646-6530.. 518 G
ekramer@nashotah.edu
KRAMER, Jill .... 317-921-4569.. 164 E
jkramer5@ivytech.edu
KRAMER, Katrina .... 603-623-0313.. 287 D
katrinakramer@nhia.edu
KRAMER, Kirk, A .... 810-989-5503.. 240 G
kkramer@sc4.edu
KRAMER, Laurie .... 617-373-2333.. 227 B
KRAMER, Linda .... 507-354-8221.. 247 J
kramerlm@mlc-wels.edu
KRAMER, Lisa .... 415-442-7889.... 45 B
lkramer@ggu.edu
KRAMER, Mark .... 757-825-2815.. 498 G
kramerm@tncc.edu
KRAMER, SJ, Mark .... 314-792-6136.. 266 F
kramer@kenrick.edu
KRAMER, Matt .... 617-327-6777.. 229 H
matt_kramer@williamjames.edu
KRAMER, Monica .... 937-484-1247.. 380 E
mkramer@urbana.edu
KRAMER, Monte .... 605-773-3455.. 436 L
monte.kramer@sdbor.edu
KRAMER, Nancy .... 319-226-2040.. 169 D
nancy.kramer@allencollege.edu
KRAMER, Nikki, A .... 920-923-8142.. 517 H
nakramer22@marianuniversity.edu
KRAMER, Pamela .... 239-687-5305.... 95 P
pkramer@avemarialaw.edu
KRAMER, Scott, E .... 270-852-3122.. 191 C
scottkr@kwc.edu
KRAMER, Sue .... 610-902-8781.. 399 D
susan.m.kramer@cabrini.edu
KRAMER, Terry .... 781-239-2431.. 223 F
tkramer1@massbay.edu
KRAMER, Thomas, E .... 757-594-8671.. 488 E
tkramer@cnu.edu
KRAMER, William .... 401-454-6503.. 426 A
wkramer@risd.edu
KRAMER-JEFFERSON,
Kate .... 301-846-2409.. 207 F
kkramerjefferson@frederick.edu
KRAMKA, James, S .... 615-322-2591.. 449 A
jim.kramka@vanderbilt.edu
KRAMLICH, Carol .... 209-478-0800.... 46 H
ckramlich@humphreys.edu
KRANHOLD, Kathryn .... 310-825-4723.... 69 D
kkranhold@support.ucla.edu
KRANS, Gretchen .... 787-250-0000.. 537 D
gretchen.krans@upr.edu
KRANTZ, Margaret .... 812-866-7126.. 161 C
krantzm@hanover.edu
KRANTZ, Richard, N .... 843-953-6372.. 428 G
krantzr@cofc.edu
KRANZLER, Michael .... 212-960-5277.. 341 G
kranzler@yu.edu
KRAPF, Audrey .... 631-420-2009.. 335 E
audrey.krapf@farmingdale.edu
KRAPOHL, Robert, H .... 847-317-4004.. 156 B
rkrapohl@tiu.edu
KRAPPES, Frank .... 970-491-5105.... 78 Q
louis.krappes@colostate.edu
KRASNER, David .... 508-541-1610.. 217 G
dkrasner@dean.edu
KRATKY, Rita .... 406-874-6199.. 276 H
kratkyr@milescc.edu
KRATOCHVIL, Bob .... 925-473-7301.... 41 J
bkratochvil@losmedanos.edu
KRATOCHVIL,
Christopher .... 402-559-8490.. 283 A
ckrotoch@unmc.edu
KRATZ, JR., Charles, E .... 570-941-4008.. 422 B
charles.kratz@scranton.edu
KRATZ, David .... 212-966-0300.. 322 F
president@nyaa.edu
KRATZ, Dennis .... 972-883-2984.. 476 C
dkratz@utdallas.edu
KRATZ, Kee .... 501-337-5000.... 19 K
kkratz@coto.edu
KRATZ, Ken .... 504-568-4970.. 198 A
kkratz@lsuhsc.edu
KRATZER, Michelle .... 859-858-3511.. 186 J
michelle.kratzer@asbury.edu
KRAU WAYMIRE,
Kristina .... 615-383-4848.. 449 G
kwaymire@watkins.edu

KRUG, Cherie .... 301-387-3100.. 207 G
cherie.krug@garrettcollege.edu
KRUG, Christopher .... 858-642-8120.... 54 A
ckrug@nu.edu
KRUG, Jeffrey .... 570-389-4745.. 414 D
jakrug@bloomu.edu
KRUG, Sheila, R .... 620-229-6368.. 184 J
sheila.krug@sckans.edu
KRUG, Stefan .... 617-521-3929.. 228 C
stefan.krug@simmons.edu
KRUGER, Darrell, P .... 828-262-2070.. 356 B
krugerdp@appstate.edu
KRUGER, Jenny .... 712-325-3326.. 174 B
jkruger@iwcc.edu
KRUGER, Michael, J .... 704-366-5066.. 260 E
mkruger@rts.edu
KRUHLY, Leslie, L .... 215-898-7005.. 421 E
kruhly@upenn.edu
KRUIZENGA, Alicia .... 562-938-4083.... 49 D
akruizenga@lbcc.edu
KRUKONES, James, H ..... 216-397-4762.. 370 H
jkrukones@jcu.edu
KRULL, Kimberly .... 316-322-3100.. 179 E
kim.krull@butlercc.edu
KRULL, Lucille .... 503-251-6115.. 508 G
lucy.krull@wallawalla.edu
KRUMER, Walter .... 718-522-9073.. 304 D
vkrumer@asa.edu
KRUMHANSL, Ezra .... 502-585-9911.. 192 E
ekrumhansl@spalding.edu
KRUMI, Susan .... 402-941-6200.. 280 N
krumi@midlandu.edu
KRUMM, Beth .... 314-516-6604.. 274 A
krumme@umsl.edu
KRUMM, Brenda, L .... 620-431-2820.. 183 H
bkrumm@neosho.edu
KRUMM, Javier .... 951-785-2295.... 48 A
jkrumm@lasierra.edu
KRUMMEN SCHRAVEN,
Ginger, B .... 920-433-6631.. 515 F
ginger.krummen@bellincollege.edu
KRUMMRICH, Philip .... 606-783-2726.. 191 H
p.krummrich@moreheadstate.edu
KRUMPE, Keith .... 828-250-3880.. 357 C
kkrumpe@unca.edu
KRUPICA, Suzanne .... 217-854-3231.. 135 K
suzanne.krupica@blackburn.edu
KRUPIN, Maria .... 845-451-1385.. 312 C
m_krupin@culinary.edu
KRUPKA, Ben .... 413-528-7413.. 214 H
benkrupk@simons-rock.edu
KRUPKA, Moshe .... 646-565-6000.. 337 I
moshe.krupka@touro.edu
KRUPNICK, Kayla .... 415-442-7228.... 45 B
kkrupnick@ggu.edu
KRUPNIK, Malka Bracha . 718-252-6333.. 341 E
KRUPP, Jason .... 727-341-3339.. 108 D
krupp.jason@spcollege.edu
KRUPP, Robert, A .... 503-517-1838.. 396 F
rakrupp@westernseminary.edu
KRUPPS, Gina .... 309-341-5264.. 136 C
gkrupps@sandburg.edu
KRUPPSTADT, Tom .... 877-476-8674.. 458 F
KRUPSKI, Eric, A .... 617-422-7232.. 226 H
ekrupski@nesl.edu
KRUSE, Amy .... 320-629-5129.. 251 E
krusea@pine.edu
KRUSE, Beckie .... 262-243-5700.. 516 E
beckie.kruse@cuw.edu
KRUSE, Heather .... 602-285-7800..... 14 F
heather.kruse@phoenixcollege.edu
KRUSE, Janetta .... 817-598-6391.. 479 E
jkruse@wc.edu
KRUSE, Jerry, E .... 217-545-0200.. 154 I
jkruse@siumed.edu
KRUSE, Kate .... 651-290-6478.. 253 S
kate.kruse@mitchellhamline.edu
KRUSE, Mary .... 517-264-7112.. 241 A
mkruse@sienaheights.edu
KRUSE, Schoen .... 816-654-7641.. 266 E
skruse@kcumb.edu
KRUSE, Thomas, D .... 563-588-4948.. 174 K
tom.kruse@loras.edu
KRUSE, Tracy, L .... 402-844-7056.. 282 B
tracyk@northeast.edu
KRUSEE, Kelly .... 310-377-5501.... 51 G
kkrusee@marymountcalifornia.edu
KRUSEMARK, Stacy, L .... 605-256-5127.. 437 C
stacy.krusemark@dsu.edu
KRUSEMARK,
Stephanie, L .... 202-884-9401.... 94 A
krusemarks@trinitydc.edu
KRUSEN, Cynthia .... 978-840-0176.. 224 B
c_krusen@mwcc.mass.edu
KRUSLING, James .... 415-442-7248.... 45 B
jkrusling@ggu.edu
KRUSNIAK, Bryan .... 660-626-2364.. 262 A
bkrusniak@atsu.edu
KRUSSEL, John .... 503-768-7563.. 392 A
krussel@lclark.edu

KRUTKY, Judith, B .... 440-826-2257.. 363 M
jkrutky@bw.edu
KRUTZ, Ellen .... 610-519-4237.. 422 G
ellen.krutz@villanova.edu
KRUZANSKY, Charles ...... 518-434-4157.. 312 A
albany_office@cornell.edu
KRUZEL, Douglas .... 734-973-3497.. 242 G
kruzel@wccnet.edu
KRYCZKA, Susan .... 518-608-8150.. 314 A
skryczka@excelsior.edu
KRYGOWSKI, JeanMarie . 443-412-2102.. 208 A
jkrygowski@harford.edu
KRYLOWICZ, Brian .... 413-748-3345.. 228 E
bkrylowicz@springfieldcollege.edu
KRYSIAK, Richard .... 405-744-7147.. 385 G
rick.krysiak@okstate.edu
KRYSZAK, Alan .... 207-255-1237.. 205 C
alan.kryszak@maine.edu
KRYZHANOVSKAYA,
Tatyana .... 718-522-9073.. 304 D
tkryzhanovskaya@asa.edu
KRZAK, Chris .... 909-593-3511.... 71 B
ckrzak@laverne.edu
KRZANIK, Jacki .... 413-662-5421.. 222 B
j.krzanik@mcla.edu
KSEPKA, Matthew .... 612-330-1032.. 244 I
ksepka@augsburg.edu
KTUL, Kathy .... 252-492-2061.. 353 H
ktul@vgcc.edu
KUAN, Christine .... 212-517-3929.. 330 G
c.kuan@sothebysinstitute.com
KUAN, Jeffrey .... 909-447-2552.... 39 A
jkuan@cst.edu
KUANG, Connie .... 213-615-7269.... 37 I
ckuang@thechicagoschool.edu
KUBA, Jodie, M .... 808-956-7251.. 131 F
jodiek@hawaii.edu
KUBA, Shawn .... 304-473-8560.. 515 B
kuba_s@wvwc.edu
KUBACAK, James .... 254-299-8608.. 461 E
jkubacak@mclennan.edu
KUBASEK, Stephen .... 352-588-8355.. 108 C
stephen.kubasek@saintleo.edu
KUBAT, Robert, A .... 814-863-3681.. 412 F
rak28@psu.edu
KUBATZKE, Trevor .... 414-297-6279.. 524 A
kubatzkt@matc.edu
KUBEJA, Judy .... 814-732-1372.. 415 A
kubeja@edinboro.edu
KUBEK, Ron .... 717-560-8274.. 407 E
rkubek@lbc.edu
KUBERSKI, Chris .... 815-599-3417.. 141 E
chris.kuberski@highland.edu
KUBIK, Rachel .... 714-432-5834.... 39 G
rkubik@occ.cccd.edu
KUBILUS, Norbert, J .... 858-499-0202.... 39 J
nkubilus@coleman.edu
KUBINAK, Lois, A .... 610-921-7612.. 396 H
lkubinak@albright.edu
KUBO, Takeo .... 408-288-3733.... 62 E
takeo.kubo@sjcc.edu
KUBOW, Stephen .... 732-255-0356.. 292 C
skubow@kean.edu
KUCER, Peter .... 860-632-3001.... 88 B
pkucer@holyapostles.edu
KUCERA, Kevin .... 734-487-2390.. 233 J
kkucera@emich.edu
KUCERA, Victoria .... 402-461-2414.. 278 K
vkucera@cccneb.edu
KUCHARSKI HOWARD,
Janna .... 508-373-5872.. 225 C
janna.kucharskihoward@mcphs.edu
KUCIA, John, F .... 513-745-3997.. 381 I
kucia@xavier.edu
KUCIC, Terry .... 814-371-2090.. 421 B
tkucic@triangle-tech.edu
KUCIK, Maggie .... 317-955-6213.. 165 N
mkucik@marian.edu
KUCINSKI, Nancy .... 325-670-1298.. 458 J
nkicinski@hsutx.edu
KUCKER, Patricia .... 215-717-6388.. 421 D
pkucker@uarts.edu
KUCKO, Jane .... 817-257-7473.. 469 G
j.kucko@tcu.edu
KUCKUK, Robert .... 802-485-2185.. 484 H
rkuckuk@norwich.edu
KUDRAVETZ, Douglas ..... 202-885-3283.... 91 J
doug@american.edu
KUE, Mailee .... 401-232-6448.. 424 K
mkue@bryant.edu
KUEBLER, Alan, S .... 314-935-5727.. 274 N
alan_kuebler@wustl.edu
KUECKER, Aaron .... 708-239-4839.. 155 M
aaron.kuecker@trnty.edu
KUEHLER, Robert .... 303-837-2112.... 83 J
robert.kuehler@cu.edu
KUEHN, Martha .... 218-855-8221.. 248 N
mkuehn@clcmn.edu
KUEHN, Paul .... 808-455-0268.. 132 C
pkuehn@hawaii.edu

KUEHNER, Holly .... 850-872-3804.. 102 M
hkuehner@gulfcoast.edu
KUEHNER, Megan, R ...... 904-620-2523.. 112 B
mkuehner@unf.edu
KUENNEN, Connie .... 563-562-3263.. 175 F
kuennenc@nicc.edu
KUENTZEL, Jeffrey .... 313-577-2840.. 243 F
jkuentzel@wayne.edu
KUERZI, Kenneth .... 856-256-4138.. 295 E
kuerzi@rowan.edu
KUETER, Jeanne .... 847-574-5224.. 145 C
jkueter@lfgsm.edu
KUETER, Jeffrey, D .... 319-335-3294.. 169 H
jeff-kueter@uiowa.edu
KUETHER, Eva .... 414-297-6897.. 524 A
kuethere@matc.edu
KUFFEL, Lorne .... 205-348-7204...... 8 D
lkuffel@ua.edu
KUFFREY, Casey, W .... 770-484-1204.. 124 C
casey.kuffrey@lutherrice.edu
KUFUOR, Edward .... 718-522-9073.. 304 D
ekufuor@asa.edu
KUGLER, Adriana .... 202-687-5716..... 92 E
ak659@georgetown.edu
KUGLER, Angela .... 425-558-0299.. 503 C
akugler@digipen.edu
KUGLER, Anne .... 216-397-4770.. 370 H
akugler@jcu.edu
KUGLER, Sharon .... 203-432-1128.... 90 D
sharon.kugler@yale.edu
KUHAJDA, Kimberlee, A . 440-826-2251.. 363 M
kkuhajda@bw.edu
KUHAR, Marilyn .... 617-228-3290.. 223 B
mkkuhar@bhcc.mass.edu
KUHART, Mary Jeanne .... 541-463-5315.. 391 G
kuharmj@lanecc.edu
KUHL, Ryan .... 207-326-2479.. 204 C
ryan.kuhl@mma.edu
KUHL, Sara .... 262-472-1194.. 521 F
kuhls@uww.edu
KUHL, Susan .... 918-960-5255.. 388 K
sue.kuhl@twsweld.com
KUHLHORST, Michelle, L 260-399-7700.. 168 D
mkuhlhorst@sf.edu
KUHLMAN, Ann .... 203-432-2305.... 90 D
ann.kuhlman@yale.edu
KUHLMANN, Diana, E ...... 620-341-5304.. 180 G
dkuhlman@emporia.edu
KUHLMEIER, Sylvia .... 417-255-7949.. 269 A
sylviakuhlmeier@missouristate.edu
KUHN, Bill .... 952-446-4227.. 246 D
kuhnb@crown.edu
KUHN, Charles .... 301-447-5244.. 209 G
ckuhn@msmary.edu
KUHN, Helen .... 217-245-3013.. 141 G
registrar@mail.ic.edu
KUHN, Karen .... 630-942-2698.. 138 B
kuhnk36@cod.edu
KUHN, Kathryn, A .... 414-955-8217.. 518 A
kkuhn@mcw.edu
KUHN, Kevin .... 601-477-4108.. 258 E
kevin.kuhn@jcjc.edu
KUHN, Paul .... 732-247-5241.. 293 B
pkuhn@nbts.edu
KUHN, Sean .... 937-299-9450.. 486 G
sgkuhn@an.edu
KUHN, Sheila Jane .... 928-523-7732.... 15 H
jane.kuhn@nau.edu
KUHN, Shelly .... 262-691-5450.. 524 G
skuhn4@wctc.edu
KUHN, Stephen .... 262-524-7132.. 515 J
skuhn@carrollu.edu
KUHN, Wagner .... 269-471-3405.. 230 H
kuhn@andrews.edu
KUHN-SCHNELL, Tamara . 217-786-2353.. 146 E
tammy.schnell@llcc.edu
KUIPERS, David .... 229-931-2004.. 127 C
dkuipers@southgatech.edu
KUJAT, Marilee .... 989-386-6622.. 238 B
mkujat@midmich.edu
KUJAWA, Lisa, R .... 248-204-2403.. 237 B
lkujawa@ltu.edu
KUJAWA, Thomas .... 920-465-2300.. 520 B
kujawat@uwgb.edu
KUJAWA, Tricia, A .... 217-786-2211.. 146 E
tricia.kujawa@llcc.edu
KUJAWA-HOLBROOK,
Sheryl .... 909-447-2521.... 39 A
skujawa-holbrook@cst.edu
KUKAINIS, Maris .... 856-227-7200.. 290 B
mkukainis@camdencc.edu
KUKAY, Mike .... 406-496-4673.. 277 G
mkukay@mtech.edu
KUKER, Ronald .... 513-244-4711.. 373 C
ronald.kuker@msj.edu
KUKOR, Jerome, J .... 848-932-7275.. 296 B
kukor@aesop.rutgers.edu
KUKREJA, Anil .... 504-520-7652.. 202 C
akukreja@xula.edu
KUKREJA, Sunil .... 253-879-3207.. 508 D
skukreja@pugetsound.edu

KUKULIES, Emily Ann ..... 808-845-9219.. 132 A
kukulies@hawaii.edu
KULAGA, Jon, S .... 859-858-3511.. 186 J
jon.kulaga@asbury.edu
KULECK, Gary .... 313-993-1216.. 241 G
gary.kuleck@udmercy.edu
KULESZA, Darrell .... 508-541-1864.. 217 G
dkulesza@dean.edu
KULESZA, Randy .... 814-866-8423.. 407 D
rkulsza@lecom.edu
KULICK, Steven, W .... 315-445-4560.. 318 E
kulicksw@lemoyne.edu
KULIK, Dmitry .... 202-462-2101.... 93 B
kulik@iwp.edu
KULIS, Carol .... 858-653-3000.... 31 D
ckulis@calmu.edu
KULKARNI, Sanjeev .... 609-258-3035.. 294 D
kulkarni@princeton.edu
KULL, F. Jon .... 603-646-1552.. 286 J
f.jon.kull@dartmouth.edu
KULL, Michael .... 219-989-2231.. 166 F
mjkull@pnw.edu
KULMA, Michael .... 773-702-4664.. 156 D
mkulma@uchicago.edu
KULOW, Beth .... 641-782-1413.. 177 B
kulow@swcciowa.edu
KULPA, Brian .... 734-487-2390.. 233 J
bkulpa@emich.edu
KULSETH, Anna .... 312-662-4037.. 134 I
akulseth@adler.edu
KUMAR, Coleen .... 718-818-6470.. 329 F
ckumar@edaff.com
KUMAR, Neeraj .... 312-341-3587.. 152 H
neeraj.kumar@roosevelt.edu
KUMAR, Neeraj .... 432-703-5257.. 472 D
neeraj.kumar@ttuhsc.edu
KUMAR, Nikhil .... 914-323-5129.. 319 N
nikhil.kumar@mville.edu
KUMAR, Senthil .... 617-217-9733.. 215 B
skumar@baystate.edu
KUMAR, Sunil .... 773-702-1680.. 156 D
sunil.kumar@chicagobooth.edu
KUMAR, Sunil .... 410-516-8000.. 208 D
KUMAR, Thulasi .... 703-993-5883.. 490 B
traghura@gmu.edu
KUMAR, Vijay .... 215-898-7244.. 421 E
kumar@seas.upenn.edu
KUMARASAMY, Sundar ... 617-373-4810.. 227 B
KUMASHIRO, Kevin, K .... 415-422-2108.... 72 C
kkumashiro@usfca.edu
KUMASHIRO, Kristin .... 808-956-6451.. 131 F
kumashir@hawaii.edu
KUMLER, Kurt .... 412-268-2922.. 400 D
kkumler@andrew.cmu.edu
KUMM, Carol .... 620-227-9354.. 180 E
ckumm@dc3.edu
KUMM, David .... 402-643-7222.. 279 F
david.kumm@cune.edu
KUMM, James .... 620-227-9217.. 180 E
jkumm@dc3.edu
KUMMER, Maryann, S ...... 313-927-1373.. 237 E
mkummer@marygrove.edu
KUMMERMAN, Howard ... 562-908-3476.... 58 I
foundation@riohondo.edu
KUMMERMAN, Howard ... 562-908-3412.... 58 I
howard.kummerman@riohondo.edu
KUMP, Jessica .... 304-876-5378.. 513 E
jkump@shepherd.edu
KUMP, Melissa .... 406-496-4108.. 277 G
mkump@mtech.edu
KUMPF, Dan .... 805-289-6285.... 73 F
dkumpf@vcccd.edu
KUNA, Gerri .... 701-858-3497.. 360 F
gerri.kuna@minotstateu.edu
KUNCE, Kim, M .... 708-709-3684.. 151 C
kkunce@prairiestate.edu
KUNCL, Ralph, W .... 909-748-8390.... 71 K
ralph_kuncl@redlands.edu
KUNDELL, Ken .... 410-543-6112.. 213 A
kfkundell@salisblury.edu
KUNDINGER, Amy .... 920-403-4223.. 519 G
amy.kundinger@snc.edu
KUNE, Natacha, F .... 206-543-1240.. 508 E
fookune@uw.edu
KUNERT, Erin .... 219-464-5333.. 168 F
erin.kunert@valpo.edu
KUNG, Susanna .... 212-594-4000.. 337 F
skung@tcicollege.edu
KUNISUE, Yukari .... 808-983-4187.. 130 I
ykunisue@tokai.edu
KUNIYOSHI, Tammy .... 808-956-3028.. 131 F
tammyk@hawaii.edu
KUNKEL, Adam .... 970-521-6600.... 81 O
KUNKEL, Bruce .... 619-849-2571.... 57 M
brucekunkel@pointloma.edu
KUNKEL, Cheryl, A .... 859-371-9393.. 186 M
ckunkel@beckfield.edu
KUNKEL, Karl .... 573-651-2063.. 272 B
kkunkel@semo.edu
KUNKEL, Sharon, L .... 518-276-6233.. 327 B
kunkes@rpi.edu

L

LACIO, Erin .... 620-672-5641.. 184 D
erinl@prattcc.edu
LACK, Paul, D .... 443-334-2205.. 211 A
cvanrensselaer@stevenson.edu
LACKEY, Chad .... 704-878-3250.. 351 D
clackey@mitchellcc.edu
LACKEY, David, A .... 570-586-2400.. 419 G
dlackey@summitu.edu
LACKEY, Mary Lou .... 209-946-2011.... 71 C
mllackey@pacific.edu
LACKEY, Miles .... 515-294-2220.. 169 G
mlackey@iastate.edu
LACKEY, Polly, R .... 806-291-3702.. 479 D
lackeyp@wbu.edu
LACKEY, Russell, L .... 515-263-6004.. 172 H
rlackey@grandview.edu
LACKIE, Mary .... 479-788-7021.... 23 A
mary.lackie@uafs.edu
LACKLAND, Jonathan .... 309-438-5677.. 143 B
jwlackl@ilstu.edu
LACKNER, Andrew .... 985-871-6201.. 200 C
alackner@tulane.edu
LACKNER, Elisabeth .... 718-631-6279.. 309 E
elackner@qcc.cuny.edu
LACKNER, Sandra .... 252-246-1435.. 354 D
slackner@wilsoncc.edu
LACLAIR, Bethaney .... 802-258-3357.. 485 A
bethaney.laclair@worldlearning.org
LACOLA, Chris .... 803-786-3933.. 429 A
clacola@columbiasc.edu
LACOMBA, AJ .... 518-587-2100.. 335 D
aj.lacomba@esc.edu
LACOMBA, Todd .... 419-434-5184.. 379 E
lacomba@findlay.edu
LACOSTE-CAPUTO, Jenny 512-499-4363.. 475 K
jcaputo@utsystem.edu
LACOUR, Joseph .... 318-670-9378.. 199 J
jlacour@susla.edu
LACOURSE, Michael .... 435-652-7506.. 482 A
lacourse@dixie.edu
LACOURSE, Peter, W .... 231-995-1198.. 239 C
placourse@nmc.edu
LACOURSE, William .... 410-455-2598.. 211 G
lacourse@umbc.edu
LACOVARA, Vincent, A ...... 202-319-6735.... 92 A
lacovara@cua.edu
LACRO, Erika .... 808-845-9225.. 132 A
lacro@hawaii.edu
LACROIX, Mike .... 419-755-4048.. 373 G
lacroix.12@osu.edu
LACROIX, Mike .... 419-755-4313.. 373 G
lacroix.12@osu.edu
LACROIX, Nicole .... 303-914-6400.... 82 I
nicole.lacroix@rrcc.edu
LACROIX, Roland, J .... 207-581-4053.. 204 H
roland.j.lacroix@maine.edu
LACROIX, Suzy .... 323-259-2601.... 55 A
slacroix@oxy.edu
LACUEVA, Graciela .... 216-397-4625.. 370 H
glacueva@jcu.edu
LACY, Alan .... 309-438-8864.. 143 B
aclacy@ilstu.edu
LACY, Charles, F .... 702-968-2016.. 285 E
clacy@roseman.edu
LACY, Melanie .... 909-621-8129.... 57 H
melanie_lacy@pitzer.edu
LACY, Sherea .... 616-538-2330.. 234 D
slacy@gbcol.edu
LADAGE, Marcia .... 816-936-8716.. 271 L
mladage@saintlukescollege.edu
LADANY, Nicholas .... 619-260-4540.... 72 B
nladany@sandiego.edu
LADD, Cindy .... 952-358-8223.. 251 A
cindy.ladd@normandale.edu
LADD, Susan, K .... 515-271-3048.. 171 K
susan.ladd@drake.edu
LADE, Becky .... 515-271-1485.. 171 H
becky.lade@dmu.edu
LADER, Donald .... 816-279-7000.. 262 B
don.lader@abtu.edu
LADEWIG, Patricia, A .... 303-458-1843.... 82 L
pladewig@regis.edu
LADINO, Pedro .... 310-377-5501.... 51 G
pladino@marymountcalifornia.edu
LADITKA, Doug .... 330-263-2310.. 367 A
dladitka@wooster.edu
LADITKA, Robyn .... 330-263-2545.. 367 A
rladitka@wooster.edu
LADNER, Hilda .... 320-589-6095.. 255 F
hladner@morris.umn.edu
LADNER, Pam .... 228-497-7642.. 259 C
pamela.ladner@mgccc.edu
LADNER-MATHIS,
Jocelyn .... 216-987-4537.. 367 E
jocelyn.ladner-mathis@tri-c.edu
LADORE, Frank .... 203-392-5367.... 85 H
ladoref1@southernct.edu
LADUCER, Wanda .... 701-477-7822.. 362 D
wladucer@tm.edu
LADUE, Chad .... 518-891-2915.. 325 A
cladue@nccc.edu

LADUSAW, William .... 831-459-2115.... 70 F
artsdean@ucsc.edu
LADWIG, Laura .... 616-977-0599.. 240 B
laura.ladwig@prts.edu
LADY, David, E .... 970-410-0456.... 85 B
LAENEN, Carol .... 231-348-6839.. 239 A
claenen@ncmich.edu
LAFARGE, Vicki .... 781-891-2089.. 215 F
vlafarge@bentley.edu
LAFATA, Sandi .... 314-918-2691.. 265 A
slafata@eden.edu
LAFATA-JOHNSON,
Paulette .... 219-980-6769.. 163 B
plafataj@iun.edu
LAFAVE, Alan .... 605-626-2524.. 437 D
alan.lafave@northern.edu
LAFAVE, Joshua, J .... 315-267-2165.. 334 B
lafavejj@potsdam.edu
LAFAY, Tressie .... 518-743-2237.. 335 A
lafayt@sunyacc.edu
LAFAYETTE, Jack .... 610-921-6652.. 396 H
jlafayette@albright.edu
LAFERLA, Chris .... 712-325-3288.. 174 B
claferla@iwcc.edu
LAFERLA, Frank .... 949-824-5315.... 69 C
laferla@uci.edu
LAFEVOR, Kimberly .... 256-216-5359....... 1 F
kim.lafevor@athens.edu
LAFFERTY, T. Kevin .... 813-258-7456.. 114 M
klafferty@ut.edu
LAFFERTY, William, J .... 717-337-6912.. 404 C
wlaffert@gettysburg.edu
LAFFITTE, Ron .... 704-463-3401.. 354 F
ron.laffitte@pfeiffer.edu
LAFLAM, Stephanie .... 304-829-7131.. 510 G
slaflam@bethanywv.edu
LAFLAMME, Jacques .... 401-739-5000.. 425 C
jlaflamme@neit.edu
LAFLAMME, Martha .... 603-752-1113.. 286 H
mlaflamme@ccsnh.edu
LAFLASH, Debra, A .... 508-854-4551.. 224 E
dal@qcc.mass.edu
LAFONTAINE, Joni .... 701-477-7862.. 362 D
jlafontaine@tm.edu
LAFORGE, Daniel .... 207-509-7287.. 204 F
dlaforge@unity.edu
LAFORGE, William (Bill) .. 662-846-4000.. 257 E
wlaforge@deltastate.edu
LAFRANCE, Dawn .... 315-228-7385.. 310 G
dlafrance@colgate.edu
LAFRANCE, George .... 505-786-4311.. 300 E
glefrance@navajotech.edu
LAFRANCE, Mark .... 617-243-2178.. 219 I
mlafrance@lasell.edu
LAFRENZ, Todd .... 217-732-3155.. 146 B
tlafrenz@lincolncollege.edu
LAFROMEOISE, Tanya .... 605-698-3966.. 436 K
tlafromeoise@swc.tc
LAGANA, Brandon, T .... 815-753-4405.. 150 A
blagana@niu.edu
LAGATTA, James, J .... 518-629-4523.. 316 G
j.lagatta@hvcc.edu
LAGATTA, Regina .... 518-629-7736.. 316 G
r.lagatta@hvcc.edu
LAGEORGE, Lisa .... 661-362-2205.... 52 A
llageorge@masters.edu
LAGESON, David .... 541-962-3114.. 391 C
dlageson@eou.edu
LAGO, Baldomero .... 801-863-7301.. 482 C
lagoba@uvu.edu
LAGORIO, Grant .... 541-245-7873.. 394 J
glagorio@roguecc.edu
LAGRANGE, Janet .... 337-521-8900.. 197 A
janet.lagrange@solacc.edu
LAGRANGE, Teresa .... 216-687-4700.. 366 I
t.lagrange@csuohio.edu
LAGRASSA, Michael .... 508-999-9180.. 220 H
mlagrassa@umassd.edu
LAGUARDIA, Joseph .... 440-646-8120.. 380 F
jlaguardia@ursuline.edu
LAGUERRE, Jowel .... 510-466-7202.... 57 E
jlaguerre@peralta.edu
LAGUERRE, Jowel, C .... 510-466-7202.... 57 A
jlaguerre@peralta.edu
LAGUERRE-BROWN,
Caroline .... 410-516-8075.. 208 D
clbrown@jhu.edu
LAGUERRE-BROWN,
Caroline .... 202-994-1000.... 92 D
LAGUNA, Robert .... 512-492-3010.. 451 E
rlaguna@aoma.edu
LAHAIE, Ute .... 330-490-7453.. 380 J
ulahaie@walsh.edu
LAHART, Edward .... 570-504-7000.. 400 I
elahart@tcmc.edu
LAHER, Ron .... 307-532-8218.. 526 G
ron.laher@ewc.wy.edu
LAHEY, John, L .... 203-582-8700.... 88 G
john.lahey@quinnipiac.edu
LAHM, Chris .... 417-626-1234.. 269 K
lahm.chris@occ.edu

LAHM, Terry, D .... 614-236-6108.. 364 N
tlahm@capital.edu
LAHODA, Anne, L .... 412-397-5235.. 418 B
lahoda@rmu.edu
LAHR, Sheri, K .... 580-327-8550.. 384 M
sklahr@nwosu.edu
LAHTI, Michele .... 209-667-3131.... 34 E
mlahti@csustan.edu
LAI, Chun .... 215-887-5511.. 423 C
clai@wts.edu
LAI, James .... 386-481-2306.... 96 H
laij@cookman.edu
LAI, Mary, M .... 516-299-2502.. 319 B
mary.lai@liu.edu
LAI HING, Kenneth .... 256-726-7112....... 6 B
laihing@oakwood.edu
LAIDACKER, Crystal .... 972-241-3371.. 455 K
claidacker@dallas.edu
LAIDLAW, Katharine .... 336-770-3293.. 358 E
laidlawk@uncsa.edu
LAIN, Jill .... 214-860-8680.. 456 F
LAINE, Glen, A .... 979-845-8585.. 468 B
glaine@tamu.edu
LAINE, Vance .... 309-268-4355.. 146 B
vlaine@lincolncollege.edu
LAING, Steve .... 360-867-6189.. 503 G
laings@evergreen.edu
LAINO, Nicholas .... 315-866-0300.. 316 A
lainonf@herkimer.edu
LAIR, Patrick .... 651-423-8399.. 249 B
patrick.lair@dctc.edu
LAIRD, Allan .... 208-459-5454.. 133 D
alaird@collegeofidaho.edu
LAIRD, Richard .... 321-433-7090.... 98 K
lairdr@easternflorida.edu
LAIRD, Stephen .... 509-452-5100.. 505 H
slaird@pnwu.edu
LAIRMORE, Michael, D ...... 530-752-1361.... 69 A
mdlairmore@ucdavis.edu
LAJEUNESSE, Deb .... 419-824-3733.. 371 I
dlajeunesse@lourdes.edu
LAJINESS, Kim .... 912-583-3255.. 118 B
klajiness@bpc.edu
LAJINESS, Todd .... 313-883-8501.. 240 D
lajiness.todd@shms.edu
LAJUBUTU, Oyebanjo .... 573-341-4954.. 274 B
lajubutuo@mst.edu
LAKE, Claude .... 205-391-2996....... 6 G
clake@sheltonstate.edu
LAKE, Diana .... 360-475-7831.. 505 F
dlake@olympic.edu
LAKE, Doris, J .... 270-831-9617.. 189 F
doris.lake@kctcs.edu
LAKE, Kathryn .... 740-427-5113.. 371 C
lakek@kenyon.edu
LAKE, Kathy .... 231-591-2113.. 233 L
kathylake@ferris.edu
LAKE, Kathy .... 310-665-6860.... 55 E
klake@otis.edu
LAKE, Kathy .... 414-382-6084.. 515 D
kathy.lake@alverno.edu
LAKE, Lyndon, J .... 315-267-2573.. 334 B
lakelj@potsdam.edu
LAKE, Michael, P .... 850-644-2478.. 111 C
mlake@admin.fsu.edu
LAKE, Patti .... 406-683-7031.. 277 A
patricia.lake@umwestern.edu
LAKE, Rebecca .... 847-925-6633.. 141 A
rlake@harpercollege.edu
LAKE, Stephanie, S .... 919-866-5927.. 353 I
sslake@waketech.edu
LAKE, Todd .... 615-460-6628.. 438 J
todd.lake@belmont.edu
LAKE, Tracy .... 860-231-5447.... 90 B
tlake@usj.edu
LAKE-KING, Shirley, L ...... 340-693-1400.. 539 C
sking@uvi.edu
LAKEN, Michael, J .... 630-515-6148.. 148 C
mlaken@midwestern.edu
LAKER, Craig .... 260-665-4862.. 167 E
lakerc@trine.edu
LAKETA, Dave .... 815-740-3464.. 157 F
dlaketa@stfrancis.edu
LAKEY, David, L .... 903-877-5406.. 477 E
david.lakey@uthct.edu
LAKHANI, Vikash .... 661-654-2161.... 32 A
vlakhani@csub.edu
LAKHAVANI, Kumar .... 336-322-2215.. 351 H
kumar.lakhavani@piedmontcc.edu
LAKIS, James .... 570-321-4141.. 409 F
lakis@lycoming.edu
LAKOSIL, Jennifer .... 520-515-8750.... 12 L
lakosilj@cochise.edu
LALANDE, Emmanuel .... 314-340-5300.. 265 H
lalandee@hssu.edu
LALANDE, Emmanuel .... 314-340-5112.. 265 H
lalandee@hssu.edu
LALANNE, Bob .... 510-643-7384.... 68 M
vcre@berkeley.edu
LALCHANDANI, Atam .... 775-831-1314.. 285 G
kyoung@sierranevada.edu

LALIBERTE, Jean .... 334-670-3608....... 7 H
jlaliber@troy.edu
LALIBERTE, Michael, R ..... 607-746-4090.. 335 C
lalibemr@delhi.edu
LALJIANI, Karen .... 972-860-5295.. 456 C
laljiani@dcccd.edu
LALJIANI, Karen .... 972-860-8261.. 456 C
laljiani@dcccd.edu
LALLA, Sharon .... 505-454-5378.. 299 M
slalla@luna.edu
LALLEY, Joseph .... 740-566-7287.. 375 H
lalley@ohio.edu
LALLY, Jay .... 321-674-8225.. 100 M
jlally@fit.edu
LALLY, Kim, B .... 937-229-3902.. 379 D
klally1@udayton.edu
LALLY, Mary .... 617-573-8430.. 228 G
mlally@suffolk.edu
LALLY, Shiela .... 617-236-4422.. 218 G
slally@fisher.edu
LALLY-GREEN, Maureen .. 412-396-6281.. 403 A
LALOVIC-HAND, Mira .... 856-256-4146.. 295 E
lalovic-hand@rowan.edu
LALUZERNE, Joseph .... 651-638-6879.. 244 L
j-laluzerne@bethel.edu
LALUZERNE, Shannon, S 920-923-7661.. 517 H
slaluzerne@marianuniversity.edu
LAM, Edward .... 888-488-4968.... 47 D
edlam@itu.edu
LAM, Felix .... 212-650-8173.. 307 E
flam@ccny.cuny.edu
LAM, Hazzan Nathan .... 310-824-1586.... 24 L
LAM, Monica .... 215-951-2810.. 416 G
lamm@philau.edu
LAM, Simon, Y .... 415-338-2541.... 35 B
slam@sfsu.edu
LAM YUEN, Peteru, K .... 684-699-9155.. 529 E
p.lamyuen@amsamoa.edu
LAMADRID, Edward .... 773-477-4822.... 55 G
elamadrid@pacificcollege.edu
LAMADRID, Lucas .... 310-377-5501.... 51 G
llamadrid@marymountcalifornia.edu
LAMADRID, Lupe .... 225-578-1175.. 197 I
glamadrid@lsu.edu
LAMAGNA, Dan .... 570-961-1579.. 407 B
lamagnad@lackawanna.edu
LAMANA, Paul, A .... 716-851-1469.. 313 H
lamanna@ecc.edu
LAMANNA, Richard .... 718-289-5355.. 307 C
richard.lamanna@bcc.cuny.edu
LAMANQUE, Andrew .... 650-949-7179.... 44 B
lamanqueandrew@foothill.edu
LAMANTIA-WRIGHT,
Shelley .... 312-935-3037.. 152 D
slamantia@robertmorris.edu
LAMAR, Charlene .... 912-688-6039.. 125 E
clamar@ogeecheetech.edu
LAMAR, Kimberly .... 630-353-8711.. 136 G
klamar@chamberlain.edu
LAMAR, Melissa .... 860-773-1407.... 87 E
mlamar@txcc.commnet.edu
LAMAR, Sharmaine .... 610-690-5675.. 419 I
slamar1@swarthmore.edu
LAMARAND, Donita, M ...... 757-446-6009.. 489 B
lamaradm@evms.edu
LAMARCHE, Gilles .... 770-426-2674.. 124 B
gilles.lamarche@life.edu
LAMARCHE, Paul .... 609-258-4999.. 294 D
lamarche@princeton.edu
LAMARSH, Karen .... 678-466-5115.. 119 A
karenlamarsh@clayton.edu
LAMAS, Frank .... 559-278-2541.... 32 F
flamas@csufresno.edu
LAMASCUS, Scott .... 405-425-5469.. 385 C
scott.lamascus@oc.edu
LAMB, Bill .... 319-398-5509.. 174 I
blamb@kirkwood.edu
LAMB, Colin .... 620-276-9595.. 181 C
colin.lamb@gcccks.edu
LAMB, Craig .... 585-345-6969.. 315 C
crlamb@genesee.edu
LAMB, Craig .... 704-216-3500.. 352 G
craig.lamb@rccc.edu
LAMB, Curtis, S .... 864-488-8354.. 430 H
clamb@limestone.edu
LAMB, David .... 716-829-7652.. 313 A
kavinokytheater@dyc.edu
LAMB, Duane .... 205-348-8092....... 8 D
dlamb@fa.ua.edu
LAMB, Jason .... 540-261-8509.. 494 F
jason.lamb@svu.edu
LAMB, Jeffrey .... 510-436-2411.... 57 E
jlamb@peralta.edu
LAMB, Jennifer .... 276-326-4397.. 487 F
jlamb@bluefield.edu
LAMB, John, C .... 414-288-1671.. 517 I
john.lamb@marquette.edu
LAMB, Jon .... 734-462-4400.. 240 H
jlamb@schoolcraft.edu
LAMB, Keith .... 940-397-4291.. 462 A
keith.lamb@mwsu.edu

LANE, Jason .... 518-320-1448.. 330 H jason.lane@suny.edu
LANE, Jennifer .... 808-675-4971.. 130 E jennifer.lane@byuh.edu
LANE, Jeremy .... 405-466-3428.. 383 M jlane@langston.edu
LANE, Jill, L .... 678-466-4100.. 119 A jilllane@clayton.edu
LANE, John .... 713-221-8292.. 474 B lanej@uhd.edu
LANE, Jon .... 940-397-4241.. 462 A jon.lane@mwsu.edu
LANE, Kim .... 909-607-3778.... 38 H kiml@cuc.claremont.edu
LANE, Kristi .... 218-683-8631.. 251 C kristi.lane@northlandcollege.edu
LANE, Laura .... 248-476-1122.. 237 H llane@mispp.edu
LANE, Marguerite .... 516-323-4014.. 321 H mlane@molloy.edu
LANE, Mark .... 808-455-0213.. 132 C marklane@hawaii.edu
LANE, Michael .... 516-686-7723.. 323 G mlane@nyit.edu
LANE, Mike .... 816-271-4476.. 269 C lane@missouriwestern.edu
LANE, Natalie .... 307-382-1673.. 527 C nlane@westernwyoming.edu
LANE, Robert, J .... 515-961-1417.. 176 H bob.lane@simpson.edu
LANE, Russ .... 402-557-7452.. 278 I russ.lane@bellevue.edu
LANE, Shelese .... 404-270-5110.. 128 A sjlane@spelman.edu
LANE, Stephanie .... 707-826-3132.... 34 F sml19@humboldt.edu
LANE, Tracey, R .... 817-722-1621.. 460 E tracey.lane@tku.edu
LANE-MARTIN, Tanya ...... 585-345-6800.. 315 C tmlanemartin@genesee.edu
LANESSKOG, Stig .... 909-621-8026.... 38 H stig_lanesskog@cuc.claremont.edu
LANEY, Candy .... 406-874-6165.. 276 H laneyc@milescc.edu
LANEY, Mary, A .... 386-312-4069.. 108 B maryannelaney@sjrstate.edu
LANFEAR, Jeffery .... 773-325-8308.. 139 C jlanfear@depaul.edu
LANG, Ashley .... 319-352-8486.. 177 G ashley.lang@wartburg.edu
LANG, Chadra .... 773-602-5000.. 137 F clang@ccc.edu
LANG, Christine .... 843-574-6162.. 433 D chris.lang@tridenttech.edu
LANG, Christopher .... 304-865-6107.. 511 C christopher.lang@ovu.edu
LANG, Cyndi .... 574-520-4490.. 163 E clang@iusb.edu
LANG, JR., George, E ..... 410-293-1568.. 529 D lang@usna.edu
LANG, Heather .... 971-722-4532.. 394 F heather.lang@pcc.edu
LANG, Jean .... 808-544-0272.. 130 H jlang@hpu.edu
LANG, Jennifer, R .... 718-780-0679.. 305 L jennifer.lang@brooklaw.edu
LANG, Kathy, J .... 414-288-1782.. 517 I kathy.lang@marquette.edu
LANG, Krystal, P .... 314-516-6940.. 274 A langk@umsl.edu
LANG, Mandy .... 715-422-5446.. 523 G mandy.lang@mstc.edu
LANG, Marjorie .... 313-993-1802.. 241 G langma@udmercy.edu
LANG, Melissa, W .... 757-446-6054.. 489 B langmw@evms.edu
LANG, Michelle .... 503-517-1190.. 396 D mlang@warnerpacific.edu
LANG, Milton .... 530-752-8787.... 69 A lmlang@ucdavis.edu
LANG, Natasha .... 925-424-1634.... 37 C nlang@laspositascollege.edu
LANG, Stephen, W .... 432-837-8061.. 471 E slang@sulross.edu
LANG, Stuart .... 612-374-5800.. 246 F slang@dunwoody.edu
LANGAN, Nicole .... 570-945-8274.. 406 H nicole.langan@keystone.edu
LANGAN, Rikki .... 217-479-7030.. 147 C rikki.langan@mac.edu
LANGAN, Terrence, G ...... 651-962-6001.. 256 C tglangan@stthomas.edu
LANGDON, Deb .... 740-389-4636.. 372 B langdond@mtc.edu
LANGDON, Heather, H .... 828-262-2093.. 356 B langdonhh@appstate.edu
LANGDON, Rita .... 516-299-2334.. 319 C rita.langdon@liu.edu
LANGDON, Steven, D ...... 515-643-6716.. 175 B slangdon@mercydesmoines.org
LANGDON, Tennille .... 660-831-4157.. 269 B langdont@moval.edu
LANGE, Amy .... 785-243-1435.. 179 N alange@cloud.edu
LANGE, Andrea, G .... 410-778-7776.. 213 E alange2@washcoll.edu
LANGE, Douglas .... 843-661-8300.. 429 J douglas.lange@fdtc.edu
LANGE, Janet .... 309-677-2374.. 136 B lange@fsmail.bradley.edu
LANGE, Janet .... 309-677-2523.. 136 B lange@bradley.edu
LANGE, Jean .... 203-582-8444.... 88 G jean.lange@quinnipiac.edu
LANGE, Karen .... 307-778-1204.. 526 K klange@lccc.wy.edu
LANGE, Karen, M .... 651-962-6120.. 256 C kmlange@stthomas.edu
LANGE, Robert, J .... 757-594-7015.. 488 E robert.lange@cnu.edu
LANGE, Steven .... 320-629-5155.. 251 E langes@pine.edu
LANGE, Tom, J .... 715-831-7285.. 523 B tlange8@cvtc.edu
LANGE, Tyana .... 570-484-2087.. 415 D tsl400@lhup.edu
LANGEMAK, Elizabeth ..... 215-951-1145.. 407 A langemak@lasalle.edu
LANGEN, Jill .... 810-766-4374.. 231 C jill.langen@baker.edu
LANGENDORGER, Stephen, J .... 419-372-7234.. 364 E slangen@bgsu.edu
LANGER, Manfred .... 740-377-2520.. 378 B manfred.langer@tsbc.edu
LANGER, Nathan .... 218-723-6010.. 245 J nlanger@css.edu
LANGER, Patricia, M .... 651-696-6562.. 247 I planger@macalester.edu
LANGER, Peter .... 617-287-5611.. 220 G peter.langer@umb.edu
LANGERBEIN, Helmut .... 870-235-4200.... 22 F helmetlangerbein@saumag.edu
LANGERUD, Steve .... 641-472-7000.. 175 A slangerud@mum.edu
LANGEVIN, Duetta .... 909-274-4230.... 53 C dlangevin@mtsac.edu
LANGEVIN, John .... 207-602-2549.. 205 F jlangevin@une.edu
LANGFORD, Allison .... 417-328-2093.. 272 C alangford@sbuniv.edu
LANGFORD, David .... 201-692-9867.. 291 J david_langford@fdu.edu
LANGFORD, Debra .... 304-876-5216.. 513 E dlangfor@shepherd.edu
LANGFORD, Gabriel, J ...... 863-680-4316.. 101 E glangford@flsouthern.edu
LANGFORD, Joel, C .... 770-720-5585.. 126 C jcl@reinhardt.edu
LANGFORD, Marcus .... 516-745-5769.. 379 B marcus.langford@uc.edu
LANGFORD, Pamela .... 909-537-7454.... 34 C plangfor@csusb.edu
LANGFORD, Russ .... 417-862-9533.. 265 D rlangford@globaluniversity.edu
LANGHAM, Gay .... 601-643-8307.. 257 D gay.langham@colin.edu
LANGHAM, Julie .... 706-595-0166.. 117 C jlangham@augustatech.edu
LANGHAM, Lynda .... 936-468-2503.. 466 H llangham@sfasu.edu
LANGHAMMER, Paul .... 401-874-9500.. 426 D langhammer@uri.edu
LANGHAUSER, Derek .... 207-629-4000.. 203 H dlanghauser@mccs.me.edu
LANGHOUT, Regina .... 831-459-2769.... 70 F langhout@ucsc.edu
LANGKILDE, Jared .... 480-461-7396.... 14 D jared.langkilde@mesacc.edu
LANGLAND, Meg .... 573-592-5381.. 275 E meg.langland@westminster-mo.edu
LANGLEY, Amy .... 256-840-4185...... 6 H alangley@snead.edu
LANGLEY, Angie .... 662-720-7249.. 260 B alangle@nemcc.edu
LANGLEY, Goldie .... 937-722-9253.. 380 E goldie.langley@urbana.edu
LANGLEY, Goldie .... 614-947-6509.. 369 A goldie.langley@franklin.edu
LANGLEY, Jesse .... 252-985-5177.. 354 E jlangley@ncwc.edu
LANGLEY, Pamela .... 603-271-6484.. 286 F plangley@ccsnh.edu
LANGLEY, Winston .... 617-287-5600.. 220 G winston.langley@umb.edu
LANGLEY-TURNBAUGH, Samantha .... 859-572-7528.. 192 B langleys1@nku.edu
LANGLOIS, OP, John .... 202-495-3831.... 93 D president@dhs.edu
LANGLOIS, Judith, H .... 512-232-3300.. 476 B jlanglois@austin.utexas.edu
LANGLOIS, Mary Ann .... 716-888-2103.. 306 F langloim@canisius.edu
LANGOLF, Judi .... 810-766-8756.. 231 D jlango01@baker.edu
LANGONI, Kerri .... 505-566-3515.. 301 J langonik@sanjuancollege.edu
LANGRELL, Ron .... 253-680-7103.. 501 E rlangrell@bates.ctc.edu
LANGRIDGE, Nick .... 540-568-3197.. 490 J langrinl@jmu.edu
LANGSETH, Kay .... 319-895-4242.. 171 A klangseth@cornellcollege.edu
LANGSETH, Roger .... 507-535-3309.. 246 C rlangseth@crossroadscollege.edu
LANGSETH, Roger, W .... 507-288-4563.. 246 C rlangseth@crossroadscollege.edu
LANGSTON, II, Bill, C .... 863-680-4209.. 101 E blangston@flsouthern.edu
LANGSTON, Carol .... 903-334-6628.. 469 C carol.langston@tamut.edu
LANGSTON, Ginna, V .... 918-631-2641.. 389 E ruth-langston@utulsa.edu
LANGSTON, Louanne .... 601-857-3749.. 258 A louanne.langston@hindscc.edu
LANGSTON, Randall .... 585-395-2751.. 332 E rlangston@brockport.edu
LANGSTON, Randall .... 585-395-2772.. 332 E rlangsto@brockport.edu
LANGSTRAAT, Jim .... 971-722-4200.. 394 F jim.langstraat@pcc.edu
LANGSTRAAT, Nate .... 360-383-3350.. 509 F nlangstraat@whatcom.ctc.edu
LANGUTH, Christine .... 860-215-9260.... 87 D clanguth@trcc.commnet.edu
LANHAM, Allen, K .... 217-581-6061.. 139 H aklanham@eiu.edu
LANHAM, Heather .... 937-778-7803.. 368 E hlanham@edisonohio.edu
LANHAM, Jeff .... 740-245-7485.. 380 C jlanham@rio.edu
LANHAM, Terri .... 270-686-4548.. 190 D terri.lanham@kctcs.edu
LANIAK, Timothy, S .... 704-527-9909.. 219 B tlaniak@gcts.edu
LANIER, Annette .... 503-768-7685.. 392 A annette@lclark.edu
LANIER, Carolyn, D .... 330-325-6259.. 373 H clanier@neomed.edu
LANIER, Charity .... 281-201-3800.... 93 F
LANIER, Charity .... 281-619-9200.... 93 F
LANIER, Charity .... 281-949-1800.... 93 F
LANIER, Ginger .... 540-261-8469.. 494 F ginger.lanier@svu.edu
LANIER, Greg .... 850-474-3160.. 113 A glanier@uwf.edu
LANIER, John .... 706-385-1065.. 126 A john.lanier@point.edu
LANIER, Lisa .... 912-871-1606.. 125 E llanier@ogeecheetech.edu
LANIER, Mandy .... 334-556-2235...... 3 N mlanier@wallace.edu
LANIER, Marie .... 904-743-1122.. 103 G mlanier@jones.edu
LANIER, Percy .... 205-929-1663...... 5 H plani@mail.miles.edu
LANIER, Stephen, M .... 313-577-5600.. 243 F stephen.lanier@wayne.edu
LANIER, Walter .... 414-297-7710.. 524 A lanierw@matc.edu
LANIER WEYERS, Anna ... 316-978-3001.. 185 J anna.weyers@wichita.edu
LANK, Kristy .... 207-985-7976.. 203 E kristy@landingschool.edu
LANKES, Susan .... 716-652-8900.. 306 K slankes@buffalodiocese.org
LANN, Jennifer .... 802-387-6764.. 484 B jlann@landmark.edu
LANNERT, Mary .... 406-447-6944.. 277 B mary.lannert@umhelena.edu
LANNING, Brek .... 828-565-4027.. 350 D bwlanning@haywood.edu
LANNING, Crystal .... 715-425-3246.. 521 B crystal.lanning@uwrf.edu
LANNING, Gale .... 507-453-1443.. 250 C glanning@southeastmn.edu
LANNING, Paul .... 408-924-1120.... 35 C paul.lanning@sjsu.edu
LANNING, Stephanie .... 620-227-9370.. 180 E slg@dc3.edu
LANNUTTI, Pamela .... 215-951-1935.. 407 A lannuttip@lasalle.edu
LANOUE, David .... 870-235-4004.... 22 F davidlanoue@saumag.edu
LANPHER, Jim .... 803-754-4100.. 429 B
LANSER, Michael .... 920-693-1123.. 523 E michael.lanser@gotoltc.edu
LANSING, Sean, T .... 414-410-4583.. 515 I stlansing@stritch.edu
LANSIQUOT, Beverley, A . 340-692-4117.. 539 C beverley.lansiquot@uvi.edu
LANTAGNE, Douglas, O .. 802-656-2990.. 485 D doug.lantagne@uvm.edu
LANTAS, Kori .... 617-730-7034.. 226 J kori.lantas@newbury.edu
LANTHIER, Eric .... 617-243-2433.. 219 I elanthier@lasell.edu
LANTING, Mark .... 815-825-9453.. 144 F mark.lanting@kishwaukeecollege.edu
LANTIS, Glenda .... 541-318-3753.. 390 D glantis@cocc.edu
LANTZ, Donna .... 313-664-1495.. 232 G dlantz@collegeforcreativestudie.edu
LANTZ, Mary Jan .... 409-944-1281.. 458 D mlantz@gc.edu
LANTZ, Nicholas .... 302-736-2391.... 91 G nicholas.lantz@wesley.edu
LANTZKY-EATON, Kristina .... 716-926-8854.. 316 B
LANYON, Scott .... 612-625-2809.. 255 H slanyon@umn.edu
LANZA-GALINDO, Oscar . 610-499-4087.. 423 E
LANZI, Lesley .... 518-736-3622.. 315 A lesley.lanzi@fmcc.suny.edu
LAP, James .... 718-260-5565.. 309 C jlap@citytech.cuny.edu
LAPALOMBARA, Catherine .... 301-546-0414.. 210 C lapalocx@pgcc.edu
LAPAYOVER, Alan .... 215-576-0800.. 417 H alapayover@rrc.edu
LAPENTA, Thomas .... 302-831-8306.... 91 F lapenta@udel.edu
LAPERLE, Kimberly .... 508-856-8992.. 221 B kimberlymuri.laperle@umassmed.edu
LAPETINO, Kelly .... 708-709-3795.. 151 C klapetino@prairiestate.edu
LAPHAM, Steve .... 301-891-4161.. 213 D slapham@wau.edu
LAPIANA, William, P .... 212-431-2840.. 323 H william.lapiana@nyls.edu
LAPIDUS, Chaim, D .... 410-484-7200.. 210 A cdl@nirc.edu
LAPIDUS, Richard, S .... 978-665-3101.. 221 D rlapidus@fitchburgstate.edu
LAPIER, Terrance .... 407-265-8383.... 97 B
LAPIER, Terry .... 561-381-4990.... 97 A
LAPIERRE, Jonathan .... 617-879-2427.. 229 G jlapierre@wheelock.edu
LAPIKAS, Ken .... 814-724-0700.. 408 D klapikas@laurel.edu
LAPIKAS, Sonya, L .... 724-589-2172.. 420 D slapikas@thiel.edu
LAPINSKI, Scott .... 903-566-7181.. 477 B slapinski@uttyler.edu
LAPINSKY, David .... 610-379-8418.. 408 G dlapinsky@lccc.edu
LAPLANT, James, T .... 229-333-5694.. 129 G jtlaplant@valdosta.edu
LAPLANTE, Brian .... 518-445-2381.. 303 D blapl@albanylaw.edu
LAPLANTE, Kim .... 920-498-5487.. 524 E kim.laplante@nwtc.edu
LAPOINTE, Gregory .... 207-621-3240.. 204 I glapointe@maine.edu
LAPOINTE, Laurence .... 860-465-5113.... 85 G lapointel@easternct.edu
LAPOINTE, Michael .... 219-980-7106.. 163 B mslapoin@iun.edu
LAPOLLA, Anthony .... 315-792-7250.. 336 C anthony.lapolla@sunyit.edu
LAPOMARDO, Elaine .... 413-775-1804.. 223 D lapomardoe@gcc.mass.edu
LAPORTA, Jennifer .... 570-941-6645.. 422 B jennifer.laporta@scranton.edu
LAPORTE, Laura .... 518-736-3622.. 315 A llaporte@fmcc.suny.edu
LAPORTE, Sandra .... 312-567-5199.. 142 I laporte@iit.edu
LAPOS, Christopher .... 570-389-4740.. 414 D clapos@bloomu.edu
LAPP, Katherine, N .... 617-495-9877.. 219 D katie_lapp@harvard.edu
LAPPIN, Julie .... 909-869-4944.... 31 J
LAPPLE, James, H .... 212-327-8371.. 327 F james.lapple@rockefeller.edu
LAPRADE, Kimberly .... 602-639-7500.... 13 I
LAPRAY, Kim .... 208-732-6299.. 133 E klapray@csi.edu
LAPREZIOSA, Mark .... 215-572-2900.. 397 G laprezim@arcadia.edu
LAPRISE, John .... 423-585-2336.. 447 D john.laprise@ws.edu
LAQUEY, Karen .... 806-291-3526.. 479 D laqueyk@wbu.edu
LARA, Cynthia .... 210-999-8290.. 473 A clara@trinity.edu
LARA, Dan .... 928-692-3085.... 15 E dlara@mohave.edu

LARA, Ernest 623-935-8014 14 A ernie.lara@estrellamountain.edu
LARA, Javier 210-805-3572 474 D jdlara@uiwtx.edu
LARA, Jessika 214-379-5494 463 G jlara@pqc.edu
LARA, Larry 714-992-7025 54 H llara@fullcoll.edu
LARA, Matthew 575-538-6001 303 A laram@wnmu.edu
LARA, Rene 213-615-7243 37 I rlara@thechicagoschool.edu
LARACUENTE, Luis 787-815-0000 537 F luis.laracuente1@upr.edu
LARAMORE, Aimee 317-931-2315 160 B alaramore@cts.edu
LARANGE, Shannon 413-775-1410 223 D larange@gcc.mass.edu
LARAQUE-ARENA, Danielle, L 315-464-5540 332 C
LARCOM, Geoffrey 734-487-4401 233 J glarcom@emich.edu
LARDNER, Patrick 803-777-2036 433 F lardnerp@mailbox.sc.edu
LAREAU, Martin 708-596-2000 154 E mlareau@ssc.edu
LAREY, Keith, L 903-813-2431 451 M klarey@austincollege.edu
LARGE, JR., Donald, L 334-844-4650 1 G largedl@auburn.edu
LARGE, Kandice 703-284-1614 492 A bstore@marymount.edu
LARGE, Ron 509-313-6767 504 A large@gonzaga.edu
LARGEN, Kristin 717-334-6286 409 C klargen@ltsg.edu
LARGENT, Trudy 510-466-7252 57 B tlargent@peralta.edu
LARGENT, Trudy 510-466-7252 57 E tlargent@peralta.edu
LARIA, Miriam 201-200-3484 293 C mlaria@njcu.edu
LARIC, Katie 303-762-6948 79 katie.laric@denverseminary.edu
LARICK, Duane, K 919-515-2196 357 E duane_larick@ncsu.edu
LARIOS, Jose 828-669-8012 346 M jose.larios@montreat.edu
LARIOS, Liza 718-631-6356 309 E llarios@qcc.cuny.edu
LARK, Catherine 603-646-2442 286 catherine.lark@dartmouth.edu
LARKAN-SKINNER, Kara 210-434-6711 463 C klarkan-skinner@lake.ollusa.edu
LARKIN, Conal 203-575-8173 86 G clarkin@nv.edu
LARKIN, Earlene 334-876-9394 4 A earlene.larkin@wccs.edu
LARKIN, Josh 802-828-2835 486 A josh.larkin@ccv.edu
LARKIN, Linda 860-515-3841 85 D llarkin@charteroak.edu
LARKIN, SSJ, Mary Josephine 215-248-7055 400 H mjlarkin@chc.edu
LARKIN, Patti 619-482-6325 66 E plarkin@swccd.edu
LARKIN, Thomas, F 413-748-3458 228 E tlarkin@springfieldcollege.edu
LARKIN-BEENE, Bridgett 815-280-2476 144 A blarkin@jjc.edu
LARKINS, Mike 870-574-4516 22 G mlarkins@sautech.edu
LARMON, Natalie 661-255-1050 30 E
LARNER, Eve 914-606-6562 340 C eve.larner@sunywcc.edu
LAROBINA, Michael, D 203-371-7859 88 I larobinam@sacredheart.edu
LAROCCA, Sandy 402-898-1000 279 G sandy_l@creativecenter.edu
LAROCHELLE, Josee 408-924-1550 35 C josee.larochelle@sjsu.edu
LAROCQUE, Edward, A 260-399-7700 168 D elarocque@sf.edu
LAROCQUE, Monique, M 207-581-3143 204 H mlarocque@maine.edu
LAROCQUE, Sandra 701-477-7862 362 D salrocqu@tm.edu
LAROSA, George, P 631-420-2170 335 E larosa@farmingdale.edu
LAROSE, Eric 920-565-1039 517 D larosees@lakeland.edu
LAROSEE, Howie 617-879-7938 222 A hlarosee@massart.edu
LARRABEE, Ashley 361-825-3020 468 E ashley.larrabee@tamucc.edu
LARRAT, Paul 401-874-5011 426 D larrat@uri.edu
LARRIVEE, Linda 508-929-8333 222 F llarrivee@worcester.edu
LARRY, Latasha 773-291-6210 137 G llarry4@ccc.edu
LARSCHEID, Slade 605-274-4316 435 E slade.larscheid@augie.edu
LARSEN, Carl 423-636-7313 447 G clarsen@tusculum.edu
LARSEN, Cheryl 847-866-3995 140 G cheryl.larsen@garrett.edu
LARSEN, Chris 417-690-2373 263 E larsen@cofo.edu
LARSEN, Christian, P 404-727-5631 120 E clarsen@emory.edu
LARSEN, Daniel 630-466-7900 157 K dlarsen@waubonsee.edu
LARSEN, David 253-833-9111 504 C dlarsen@greenriver.edu
LARSEN, Geri 610-647-4400 406 B hr@immaculata.edu
LARSEN, Jacque 540-423-9050 497 B jlarsen@germanna.edu
LARSEN, Jennifer 402-559-4837 283 A jlarsen@unmc.edu
LARSEN, Jon-Erik 503-352-7221 394 C larsenj@pacificu.edu
LARSEN, Juliana, P 801-626-6459 482 D jlarsen@weber.edu
LARSEN, Katrina 715-425-4891 521 B katrina.larsen@uwrf.edu
LARSEN, Kerstin 609-258-9289 294 D klarsen@princeton.edu
LARSEN, Kevin, W 252-334-2044 346 F kevin.larsen@maccuniversity.edu
LARSEN, Kevin, W 252-334-2009 346 F kevin.larsen@maccuniversity.edu
LARSEN, Marci 435-283-7013 482 E marci.larsen@snow.edu
LARSEN, Matt 701-231-5614 361 A matt.larsen@ndsu.edu
LARSEN, Ron 406-994-4371 277 C ronl@montana.edu
LARSEN, Ronald, L 412-624-5139 421 G rlarsen@pitt.edu
LARSEN, Susan 575-562-2211 299 I susan.larsen@enmu.edu
LARSEN, Whitney, M 540-261-8530 494 F whitney.larsen@svu.edu
LARSON, Ann 502-852-6044 194 A ann.larson@louisville.edu
LARSON, Barb 308-398-7359 278 K blarson@cccneb.edu
LARSON, Barbara 913-469-8500 182 A blarson@jccc.edu
LARSON, Brittany 262-650-4887 515 J
LARSON, Cate 651-631-0204 244 E clarson@aaacm.edu
LARSON, Craig 763-424-0733 251 B clarson@nhcc.edu
LARSON, Dale, C 214-887-5021 457 C dlarson@dts.edu
LARSON, Dan 541-737-4771 393 H dan.larson@oregonstate.edu
LARSON, Debra 618-537-6816 147 F dlarson@mckendree.edu
LARSON, Debra 805-756-2131 31 I dslarson@calpoly.edu
LARSON, Doreen 937-778-7801 368 E
LARSON, Gary, N 630-752-5990 158 C gary.larson@wheaton.edu
LARSON, Gayle 651-423-8307 249 B gayle.larson@dctc.edu
LARSON, Gerry 509-527-2887 508 G gerry.larson@wallawalla.edu
LARSON, Gloria, C 781-891-2101 215 F glarson@bentley.edu
LARSON, Heidi 701-252-3467 362 F hlarson@uj.edu
LARSON, Jennifer 701-845-7401 361 B jennifer.larson@vcsu.edu
LARSON, Jon, H 732-255-0330 293 E jlarson@ocean.edu
LARSON, Joyce 603-535-2806 288 F jlarson@plymouth.edu
LARSON, Kalynn 435-652-7535 482 A larson@dixie.edu
LARSON, Kelly 815-280-2218 144 A klarson@jjc.edu
LARSON, Kristin 906-635-2453 236 J klarsen1@lssu.edu
LARSON, Lesley 570-321-4456 409 F larsonl@lycoming.edu
LARSON, Lisa 207-974-4691 203 J llarson@emcc.edu
LARSON, Lois 651-793-1411 250 A lois.larson@metrostate.edu
LARSON, Matthew 860-486-2616 89 D matthew.larson@uconn.edu
LARSON, Melinda 616-395-7070 235 F larson@hope.edu
LARSON, Paul, V 805-565-6286 75 A plarson@westmont.edu
LARSON, Rebecca 630-752-5566 158 C rebecca.a.larson@wheaton.edu
LARSON, Rick 952-446-4190 246 D larsonr@crown.edu
LARSON, Rob, K 563-387-1568 174 L larsro01@luther.edu
LARSON, Rodney 207-941-7122 202 I larsonr@husson.edu
LARSON, Ruth 315-470-4716 334 E rlarson@esf.edu
LARSON, Sandra 847-578-3400 153 A sandra.larson@rosalindfranklin.edu
LARSON, Sandy 229-931-2450 127 C slarson@southgatech.edu
LARSON, Shane 970-945-8691 78 B
LARSON, Shane 620-441-5246 180 D shane.larson@cowley.edu
LARSON, Steve 406-756-3821 276 E slarson@fvcc.edu
LARSON, Thomas 309-694-5225 141 F thomas.larson@icc.edu
LARSON, Thomas, F 423-652-4765 440 J trlarson@king.edu
LARSON, Vernon, C 607-436-3369 331 F vernon.larson@oneonta.edu
LARSON-COONEY, Kim 303-797-5723 76 J kim.larson-cooney@arapahoe.edu
LARSSON, E. Axel 973-408-3048 291 B elarsson@drew.edu
LARTEY, Charles, R 330-471-8469 371 J clartey@malone.edu
LARUE, Carol 830-591-7324 466 A cllarue@swtjc.edu
LARUE, Clint 405-425-5191 385 C clint.larue@oc.edu
LARUE, Rita, E 215-895-1534 402 G larue@drexel.edu
LARUE, Shanda 270-686-4252 187 C shanda.larue@brescia.edu
LARUSSO, Christopher 716-880-2377 320 D christopher.p.larusso@medaille.edu
LARVICK, Steve 541-552-6594 395 A larvick@sou.edu
LASAKOW, Paul, H 757-822-1452 498 H plasakow@tcc.edu
LASALA, Kathleen 540-678-4381 494 B klasala@su.edu
LASALDE-DOMINICCI, Jose, A 787-250-0000 537 D jose.lasalde@upr.edu
LASANEN, Raymond E 906-487-2510 238 A relasane@mtu.edu
LASCANO, Rey 432-552-2108 478 B lascano_r@utpb.edu
LASCEK-SPEAKMAN, Natalie 717-396-7833 413 M nlascek@pcad.edu
LASCH, Chris 480-860-2700 13 G clasch@taliesin.edu
LASCH, Jacqueline, D 407-582-3302 114 N jlasch@valenciacollege.edu
LASECKI, Matthew 410-706-3950 211 F matthew.lasecki@umaryland.edu
LASER KIGER, Amy 540-453-2211 496 F kigera@brcc.edu
LASEY, Brian 479-968-0261 19 F blasey@atu.edu
LASH, Jonathan 413-559-5521 219 C president@hampshire.edu
LASH, Julie 317-274-2548 163 D jlash@iupui.edu
LASH ESAU, Amy, M 316-866-3321 184 J amy.lashesau@sckans.edu
LASHBROOK, Jeffrey 585-395-5028 332 E jlashbro@brockport.edu
LASHBROOK, Jeffrey, T 585-395-5028 332 E jlashbro@brockport.edu
LASHER, Katherine, M 989-774-3253 232 D lashe1km@cmich.edu
LASHER, Marie 603-456-2656 287 E mlasher@northeastcatholic.edu
LASHER, Robert, W 603-646-3095 286 J robert.w.lasher@dartmouth.edu
LASHIN-CUREWITZ, Sandy 508-373-9529 215 D sandy.curewitz@becker.edu
LASHLEY, Bob 405-425-5120 385 C bob.lashley@oc.edu
LASHLEY, Brian, R 860-465-5306 85 G lashleyb@easternct.edu
LASHLEY, Edwin, L 410-543-6007 213 A ellashley@salisbury.edu
LASHLEY, Heather 212-616-7292 315 G heather.lashley@helenefuld.edu
LASHLEY, Jeffery 660-263-4100 269 D jeffl@macc.edu
LASHLEY, Kent 405-733-7306 387 I klashley@rose.edu
LASHLEY, Lynn 205-652-3417 9 F lsl@uwa.edu
LASHLEY, Marsha 660-831-4115 269 B lashleym@moval.edu
LASHLEY, Sarah, E 859-238-5573 187 H sarah.lashley@centre.edu
LASHURE, Faith 630-466-7900 157 K flashure@waubonsee.edu
LASICH, Deb 303-273-3097 78 M dlasich@mines.edu
LASIEWSKI, Doreen 401-739-5000 425 C dlasiewski@neit.edu
LASITER, Paul, B 310-506-4497 56 J paul.lasiter@pepperdine.edu
LASKA-NIXON, Diane 508-767-7239 214 F dlaska@assumption.edu
LASKARIS, Theodore 802-860-2757 483 F tlaskaris@champlain.edu
LASKE, Lori, L 719-587-7867 76 G lllaske@adams.edu
LASKER, Y. Mayer 718-377-0777 326 F
LASKIN, Emily 626-396-2455 27 L emily.laskin@artcenter.edu
LASKOFSKI, Mike 703-993-4573 490 B mlaskofs@gmu.edu
LASKY, Melodee, S 848-932-9064 295 F mlasky@echo.rutgers.edu
LASLEY, Steven, T 615-460-6404 438 J steve.lasley@belmont.edu
LASSEN, Gregg 504-280-6207 198 D glassen@uno.edu
LASSETTER, Jerry 919-761-2266 355 I jlassetter@sebts.edu
LASSIAL, Erin 315-386-7608 335 B lassiale@canton.edu
LASSITER, Carllos 662-252-8000 260 F classiter@rustcollege.edu
LASSITER, Colleen 706-233-7337 127 A classiter@shorter.edu
LASSITER, Donald, L 910-630-7081 346 E lassiter@methodist.edu
LASSITER, Elbert, J 336-633-0217 352 B ejlassiter@randolph.edu
LASSITER, John 706-295-6511 121 F jlassiter@gntc.edu
LASSITER, Joshua 252-335-3665 356 D jllassiter@ecsu.edu
LASSITER, Lisabeth 972-883-4715 476 C lisabeth.lassiter@utdallas.edu
LASSNER, David, K 808-956-8207 131 D david@hawaii.edu
LASSNER, Jennifer 319-335-2123 169 H jennifer-lassner@uiowa.edu
LAST, Brad 435-652-7858 482 A blast@dixie.edu
LAST, Brett, I 610-861-5460 411 G blast@northampton.edu
LASTER, Katherine 229-430-3848 115 K katherine.laster@asurams.edu
LASTINGER, Michael 304-293-6955 514 C michael.lastinger@mail.wvu.edu
LASTORIA, Cindy 585-567-9526 316 F cindy.lastoria@houghton.edu
LASTRA, Sarai 787-743-7979 536 A ut_slastra@suagm.edu
LATA, Fran 303-373-2008 83 B flata@rvu.edu
LATANE, Jane 520-383-8401 17 E jlatane@tocc.edu
LATCHAW HIRSH, Sharon 610-527-0200 418 D shirsh@rosemont.edu
LATCHUM, Lucy, L 757-594-7702 488 E llatchum@cnu.edu
LATCOVICH, Mark, A 440-943-7600 377 A mal@dioceseofcleveland.org
LATESSA, Kenneth 804-862-6237 493 F klatessa@rbc.edu
LATHAM, Adrienne 615-329-8632 439 L alatham@fisk.edu
LATHAM, Amy 662-562-3201 260 C a_latham@northwestms.edu
LATHAM, Brenda 209-381-6410 52 E latham.b@mccd.edu
LATHAM, Celeste 815-753-6525 150 A clatham@niu.edu
LATHAM, Clara 940-397-4757 462 A clara.latham@mwsu.edu
LATHAM, Heather 410-626-2511 210 D heather.latham@sjc.edu
LATHAM, JoAnne 518-608-8240 314 A jlatham@excelsior.edu
LATHAM, Linda, H 334-734-7582 349 G llatham@forsythtech.edu
LATHAM, Marilae 618-664-7110 140 I marilae.latham@greenville.edu
LATHAM, Mark 912-260-4300 127 B mark.latham@sgsc.edu
LATHAM, Michael 641-269-3100 172 I latham@grinnell.edu
LATHAM, Mike 252-443-4011 351 F mlatham@nashcc.edu

LATHAM, Paula, J .... 606-679-8501.. 190 E
paula.latham@kctcs.edu
LATHAM, Sarah .... 831-459-3778.... 70 F
sclatham@ucsc.edu
LATHAM, Sheila .... 701-858-4145.. 360 F
sheila.latham@minotstateu.edu
LATHAM, Tricia .... 580-477-7725.. 389 I
tricia.latham@wosc.edu
LATHEM, Lindsay, S .... 336-272-7102.. 344 G
lindsay.lathem@greensboro.edu
LATHIGARA, Rajesh .... 650-738-7076.... 62 I
lathigarar@smccd.edu
LATHROP, Sam .... 217-228-5432.. 151 F
lathrsa@quincy.edu
LATIF, Niaz .... 219-989-3251.. 166 F
nlatif@pnw.edu
LATIMER, Dewana .... 731-425-2624.. 446 C
dlatimer@jscc.edu
LATIMER, Maretta .... 904-470-8244.... 98 N
m.latimer@ewc.edu
LATIMER, Margaret .... 240-567-7711.. 209 E
margaret.latimer@montgomerycollege.edu
LATIMER, William .... 718-960-7306.. 308 B
william.latimer@lehman.cuny.edu
LATIMORE, Leatrice, D .... 504-284-5435.. 199 I
llatimor@suno.edu
LATIN, Quinton .... 903-730-4890.. 460 B
quinton.latin@jarvis.edu
LATINO, Jennifer, A .... 910-814-5577.. 342 F
latinoj@campbell.edu
LATINVILLE, Darlene .... 213-624-1200.... 43 J
dlatinville@fidm.edu
LATIOLAIS, Perry .... 281-487-1170.. 469 F
platiolais@txchiro.edu
LATIOLAIS, Scott .... 425-235-2409.. 506 F
slatiolais@rtc.edu
LATORELLA, Jacqueline .... 813-253-6219.. 114 M
jlatorella@ut.edu
LATORRACA, Dominic .... 732-224-2301.. 289 I
dlatorraca@brookdalecc.edu
LATORRE, Daria .... 610-796-8481.. 397 D
daria.latorre@alvernia.edu
LATOUF, Christina .... 646-660-6114.. 307 A
christina.latouf@baruch.cuny.edu
LATOUR, Bill .... 217-641-4290.. 143 H
blatour@jwcc.edu
LATOUR, Mickey, A .... 618-453-2469.. 154 I
mlatour@siu.edu
LATOUR, Terry, S .... 814-393-2343.. 414 G
tlatour@clarion.edu
LATSHAW, Todd, M .... 717-867-6330.. 408 F
latshaw@lvc.edu
LATTA, Bruce, J .... 410-293-1801.. 529 D
latta@usna.edu
LATTA, Mark, A .... 402-280-5061.. 279 H
marklatta@creighton.edu
LATTA, Michael .... 812-877-8975.. 166 H
michael.latta@rose-hulman.edu
LATTA KIRBY, Dawn .... 239-590-1094.. 110 L
dkirby@fgcu.edu
LATTER, Deborah .... 863-784-7251.. 109 G
latterd@southflorida.edu
LATTER, George .... 619-849-2317.... 57 M
georgelatter@pointloma.edu
LATTIMORE, Dan, L .... 901-678-2991.. 445 C
dlattimr@memphis.edu
LATTIMORE, John .... 704-669-4020.. 348 F
lattimorej@clevelandcc.edu
LATTIMORE, Mark .... 478-825-6296.. 120 F
lattimorem@fvsu.edu
LATTIMORE, Vergel, L .... 704-636-6823.. 345 B
vlattimore@hoodseminary.edu
LATTING, John .... 404-727-6036.. 120 E
john.latting@emory.edu
LATVIS, Mike .... 313-436-9152.. 242 A
latvism@umich.edu
LATZ, Gil .... 317-278-1265.. 163 D
glatz@iupui.edu
LAU, Allison .... 206-878-3710.. 504 E
alau@highline.edu
LAU, Bradley, A .... 503-554-2312.. 391 D
blau@georgefox.edu
LAU, John .... 760-355-6235.... 46 J
john.lau@imperial.edu
LAU, Lawrence .... 310-577-3000.... 75 H
lau@yosan.edu
LAU, Margaret .... 805-922-6966.... 25 I
mlau@hancockcollege.edu
LAU, Pam .... 217-351-2542.. 151 B
plau@parkland.edu
LAU, Serrine, S .... 313-577-1574.. 243 F
serrine.lau@wayne.edu
LAU, Stuart .... 808-956-8010.. 131 F
stuartl@hawaii.edu
LAUB, Jeffrey, W .... 434-832-7707.. 496 G
laubj@cvcc.vccs.edu
LAUB, Joe .... 212-484-1108.. 308 E
jlaub@jjay.cuny.edu
LAUBACH, Harold .... 954-262-1303.. 105 J
harold@nsu.nova.edu
LAUBE, Irene, H .... 919-536-7211.. 349 D
laubei@durhamtech.edu
LAUBE, Philip .... 740-826-8101.. 373 E
plaube@muskingum.edu
LAUBER, Jeremy .... 516-918-3628.. 305 K
jlauber@bcl.edu
LAUCHNER, Kathy .... 512-313-3000.. 455 F
kathy.lauchner@concordia.edu
LAUDE, David, A .... 512-232-3317.. 476 B
dalaude@austin.utexas.edu
LAUDENSLAGER, Kristin .. 610-282-1100.. 402 B
kristin.laudenslager@desales.edu
LAUDER, Frank .... 617-873-0137.. 217 A
finaid@cambridgecollege.edu
LAUDER, Sue, M .... 978-665-3313.. 221 D
slauder@fitchburgstate.edu
LAUDERBACK, Cindy .... 360-417-6341.. 505 I
clauderback@pencol.edu
LAUDERDALE, Tim, J .... 580-327-8530.. 384 M
tjlauderdale@nwosu.edu
LAUDERDALE, Wendy .... 985-549-5544.. 201 C
wlauderdale@selu.edu
LAUER, Andrew, J .... 212-960-0051.. 341 G
andrewlauer@yu.edu
LAUER, Bonnie .... 570-740-0734.. 409 E
blauer@luzerne.edu
LAUER, Brenda .... 719-502-2403.... 82 B
brenda.lauer@ppcc.edu
LAUER, Heather .... 304-205-6697.. 511 M
heather.lauer@bridgevalley.edu
LAUER, John .... 719-389-6618.... 77 J
jlauer@coloradocollege.edu
LAUER, Jonathan, D .... 717-766-2511.. 410 J
jlauer@messiah.edu
LAUER, Karla .... 941-752-5694.. 110 H
lauerk@scf.edu
LAUER, Theresa .... 909-607-2760.... 46 A
theresa_lauer@hmc.edu
LAUERMAN, Meg .... 402-472-0088.. 282 M
mlauerman1@unl.edu
LAUFER, Marilyn .... 334-844-1486...... 1 G
laufema@auburn.edu
LAUFFENBURGER,
Linda, M .... 937-327-7811.. 381 F
llauffenburger@wittenberg.edu
LAUG, Adam .... 641-269-3200.. 172 I
laugadam@grinnell.edu
LAUGHEAD, Ross .... 210-485-0060.. 450 A
rlaughead@alamo.edu
LAUGHHUNN, Seirra .... 217-234-5222.. 145 D
slaughhunn42647@lakeland.cc.il.us
LAUGHLIN, Frederick, L .. 231-995-1197.. 239 C
flaughlin@nmc.edu
LAUGHLIN, Karen, L .... 850-644-2740.. 111 C
klaughlin@admin.fsu.edu
LAUGHLIN, Lynn .... 217-732-3168.. 146 A
llaughli@lincolnchristian.edu
LAUGHLIN, Michelle, E .... 712-274-5493.. 175 C
laughlinm@morningside.edu
LAUGHLIN, Pat .... 312-567-3827.. 142 I
plaughli@iit.edu
LAUGHLIN, Ronda .... 360-752-8334.. 501 G
rlaughlin@btc.edu
LAUGHLIN, Russ .... 817-202-6462.. 466 C
laughlinr@swau.edu
LAUGHRAN, Patrick .... 508-626-4357.. 221 E
plaughran@framingham.edu
LAUGHTON, John .... 609-771-2278.. 290 F
jlaughto@tcnj.edu
LAUNDERVILLE, OSB,
Dale .... 320-363-3389.. 254 N
dlaunderville@csbsju.edu
LAUNEY, Lisa .... 225-752-4233.. 195 E
llauney@iticollege.edu
LAUNIUS, Katy .... 918-343-7707.. 387 F
klaunius@rsu.edu
LAUR, Dave .... 906-786-5802.. 231 O
dave.laur@baycollege.edu
LAURANZON,
Anne Marie .... 804-752-7317.. 493 C
alauranz@rmc.edu
LAURENCE, David .... 928-776-7666...... 18 D
david.laurence@yc.edu
LAURENS, Jay .... 704-463-3026.. 354 F
jay.laurens@pfeiffer.edu
LAURENT, Dianna .... 985-867-2415.. 199 F
dlaurent@sjasc.edu
LAURENT, Timothy .... 406-791-5302.. 278 G
tim.laurent@ugf.edu
LAURENZ, Jamie .... 575-562-2312.. 299 I
jamie.laurenz@enmu.edu
LAURENZI, Kellie, L .... 412-397-5201.. 418 B
laurenzi@rmu.edu
LAURETANO, Angela .... 914-632-5400.. 321 I
alauretano@monroecollege.edu
LAURIA, James .... 412-809-5100.. 417 D
lauria.james@pti.edu
LAURIE, Sean .... 516-323-4820.. 321 H
slaurie@molloy.edu
LAURINE, Robert .... 404-962-3300.. 129 F
bobby.laurine@usg.edu
LAURITA, Brandi .... 419-434-4663.. 379 E
ankney@findlay.edu
LAURITSEN, Jessica .... 763-488-2605.. 249 D
jessica.lauritsen@hennepintech.edu
LAURITZEN, Rhonda .... 801-627-8388.. 481 A
lauritzr@owatc.edu
LAURO, Reno .... 609-497-7948.. 294 C
reno.lauro@ptsem.edu
LAUSCH, Mark, C .... 608-243-4508.. 523 F
mlausch@madisoncollege.edu
LAUSELL, Ana, C .... 787-891-0925.. 533 G
amelon@aguadilla.inter.edu
LAUSIER, Patrick .... 864-578-8770.. 432 D
plausier@sherman.edu
LAUX, Carolyne .... 850-729-5360.. 105 I
lauxc@nwfsc.edu
LAUZON CLABO, Laurie .. 313-577-4082.. 243 F
laurie.lauzon.clabo@wayne.edu
LAVALLÉE-WELCH,
Catherine .... 608-785-8805.. 520 C
clavallee-welch@uwlax.edu
LAVALLEY, Ken .... 603-862-4343.. 288 C
ken.lavalley@unh.edu
LAVALLIERE, Pamela .... 608-663-3317.. 516 F
plavalliere@edgewood.edu
LAVANIA, Ambrish .... 803-793-5263.. 429 D
lavaniaa@denmarktech.edu
LAVELLI, Lucinda .... 352-392-0207.. 112 A
llavelli@arts.ufl.edu
LAVENDER, Bernadette .... 770-426-2633.. 124 B
bernadette.lavender@life.edu
LAVENDER, Julie .... 989-275-5000.. 236 E
julie.lavender@kirtland.edu
LAVENDER, Martha, G .... 256-549-8221...... 3 M
mlavender@gadsdenstate.edu
LAVENDER, Melissa .... 850-747-3211.. 102 M
mlavender@gulfcoast.edu
LAVENDER, Michael, K ... 828-652-0681.. 351 C
michaell@mcdowelltech.edu
LAVENDER, Randall .... 310-665-6963.... 55 E
rlavender@otis.edu
LAVERDIERE, Karen .... 904-256-7243.. 103 D
klaverd@ju.edu
LAVERGNE, Paul .... 718-429-6600.. 339 D
paul.lavergne@vaughn.edu
LAVERNIA, Enrique, J .... 949-824-5801.... 69 C
provost@uci.edu
LAVERY, Hugh, J .... 215-955-6834.. 420 E
hugh.lavery@jefferson.edu
LAVERY, Jim .... 740-389-4636.. 372 B
laveryj@mtc.edu
LAVERY, Roger .... 765-285-6000.. 159 B
rlavery@bsu.edu
LAVES, Beth .... 270-745-1900.. 194 D
beth.laves@wku.edu
LAVIAL, Pierre .... 772-466-4822.... 95 R
pierre.lavial@aviator.edu
LAVIGNA, Lisa .... 518-608-8252.. 314 A
llavigna@excelsior.edu
LAVIGNA, Robert .... 608-890-3888.. 519 K
rlavigna@ohr.wisc.edu
LAVIGNE, Robert, W .... 508-213-2217.. 227 A
robert.lavigne@nichols.edu
LAVIN, Gabrielle .... 215-965-4027.. 411 A
glavin@moore.edu
LAVIN, Thomas, J .... 401-456-8094.. 425 E
tlavin@ric.edu
LAVINE, Danielle .... 860-509-9511.... 88 A
dlavine@hartsem.edu
LAVINE, Steven, D .... 661-255-1050.... 30 E
slavine@calarts.edu
LAVIOLETTE, Marc .... 239-590-7891.. 110 L
mlaviole@fgcu.edu
LAVIT, Daniel, A .... 270-809-2160.. 192 A
dlavit@murraystate.edu
LAVNER, Lilly .... 610-896-1228.. 405 I
llavner@haverford.edu
LAVOIE, Chuck .... 802-468-1250.. 485 H
chuck.lavoie@castleton.edu
LAVOIE, Lisa .... 860-255-3786.... 87 E
llavoie@txcc.commnet.edu
LAVOIE, Rocky .... 541-888-7425.. 395 B
rlavoie@socc.edu
LAVORATA, Christina, M . 304-367-4101.. 513 B
chris.lavorata@fairmontstate.edu
LAVORGNA, Briana .... 304-434-8000.. 512 A
briana.lavorgna@easternwv.edu
LAW, Christy .... 516-918-3650.. 305 K
claw@bcl.edu
LAW, Danielle .... 503-552-1668.. 392 H
dlaw@nunm.edu
LAW, John .... 413-236-3001.. 222 G
jlaw@berkshirecc.edu
LAW, Nancy .... 903-983-8101.. 460 D
nlaw@kilgore.edu
LAW, Scott .... 515-271-3860.. 171 K
scott.law@drake.edu
LAW, Shirley .... 646-313-8000.. 309 F
shirley.law@guttman.cuny.edu
LAW, Theresa .... 505-454-3198.. 300 F
tlaw@nmhu.edu
LAW, William, D .... 727-341-3241.. 108 D
law.bill@spcollege.edu
LAWDERMILT, Sherry .... 701-777-6373.. 360 C
sherry.lawdermilt@und.edu
LAWERENCE, Gail .... 325-235-7333.. 470 F
gail.lawerence@sweetwater.tstc.edu
LAWHORN, Harry .... 937-778-7871.. 368 E
hlawhorn@edisonohio.edu
LAWHORN, Janice .... 928-428-8509.... 13 B
janice.lawhorn@eac.edu
LAWHORN, Paul .... 423-775-6596.. 443 H
plawhorn@ogs.edu
LAWHORN, Paul .... 423-775-6596.. 443 H
registrar@ogs.edu
LAWHORNE, Jeffrey, L .... 540-464-7215.. 499 E
lawhornejl@vmi.edu
LAWHORNE, Lectra .... 470-578-6620.. 123 J
llawhorn@kennesaw.edu
LAWLER, Brigid .... 802-258-9261.. 484 C
blawler@marlboro.edu
LAWLER, Hannah .... 310-434-3472.... 63 F
lawler_hannah@smc.edu
LAWLER, Marsha .... 915-566-9621.. 479 H
mlawler@westerntech.edu
LAWLESS, Daniel, M .... 843-349-2021.. 428 E
dan@coastal.edu
LAWLESS, J. Alan .... 918-343-7715.. 387 F
alawless@rsu.edu
LAWLESS, John .... 315-460-3161.. 335 D
john.lawless@esc.edu
LAWLESS, Richard .... 516-572-7317.. 322 C
richard.lawless@ncc.edu
LAWLOR, Andrew .... 928-226-4285.... 12 N
andrew.lawlor@coconino.edu
LAWLOR, Edward, F .... 314-935-6693.. 274 N
elawlor@wustl.edu
LAWLOR, Jayme .... 913-253-5055.. 184 G
jayme.lawlor@spst.edu
LAWLOR, Kevin, P .... 203-254-4000.... 87 G
klawlor@fairfield.edu
LAWLOR, Sarah .... 406-447-4515.. 276 B
slawlor@carroll.edu
LAWLOR, Susan .... 415-451-2853.... 61 D
slawlor@sfts.edu
LAWRENCE, Alexander .... 801-626-8940.. 482 D
alexanderlawrence@weber.edu
LAWRENCE, Alfred, C .... 915-831-4463.. 457 H
alawren4@epcc.edu
LAWRENCE, Alicia .... 212-854-5561.. 304 I
alawrenc@barnard.edu
LAWRENCE, Amanda .... 616-949-5300.. 233 A
amanda.lawrence@cornerstone.edu
LAWRENCE, Andrew .... 276-326-4477.. 487 F
alawrence@bluefield.edu
LAWRENCE, Barbara .... 336-316-2196.. 344 H
blawrenc@guilford.edu
LAWRENCE, Charles .... 206-296-6384.. 507 E
lawrence@seattleu.edu
LAWRENCE, Craig .... 205-929-3427...... 5 D
clawrence@lawsonstate.edu
LAWRENCE, Craig, D .... 205-929-3427...... 5 D
clawrence@lawsonstate.edu
LAWRENCE, Dana, J .... 563-884-5302.. 176 C
dana.lawrence@palmer.edu
LAWRENCE, Dave .... 707-965-6699.... 56 A
dlawrence@puc.edu
LAWRENCE, David .... 740-245-7182.. 380 C
lawrence@rio.edu
LAWRENCE, Deborah .... 317-955-6208.. 165 N
dlawrence@marian.edu
LAWRENCE, Deborah .... 518-244-2466.. 327 H
lawred@sage.edu
LAWRENCE, Derrick .... 605-698-3966.. 436 K
dlawrence@swc.tc
LAWRENCE, Diana .... 937-433-3410.. 368 H
dlawrence@fortiscollege.edu
LAWRENCE, Diana .... 937-433-3410.. 368 H
dlawrence@edaff.com
LAWRENCE, Frank .... 518-255-5317.. 334 D
lawrenfj@cobleskill.edu
LAWRENCE, Gary .... 805-893-3781.... 70 E
gary@ucen.ucsb.edu
LAWRENCE, Jason .... 870-368-2058.... 21 F
jason.lawrence@ozarka.edu
LAWRENCE, Jaye .... 507-222-4438.. 245 C
jlawrenc@carleton.edu
LAWRENCE, Jennifer .... 318-678-6000.. 195 I
jelawrence@bpcc.edu
LAWRENCE, Karen, R .... 914-395-2201.. 329 K
president@sarahlawrence.edu
LAWRENCE, Karl .... 518-608-8198.. 314 A
klawrence@excelsior.edu
LAWRENCE, JR.,
Kenneth .... 215-204-1976.. 420 B
kenneth.lawrence@temple.edu
LAWRENCE, Kevin .... 757-388-2862.. 494 A
klawrence@sentara.edu
LAWRENCE, Kim .... 903-434-8132.. 462 M
klawrence@ntcc.edu
LAWRENCE, Lara .... 660-263-3900.. 263 A
laralawrence@cccb.edu

LEAVITT, David .... 650-433-3839.... 56 D
support@paloaltou.edu

LEAVITT, David .... 617-228-3287.. 223 B
djleavit@bhcc.mass.edu

LEAVITT, Gabriel .... 503-517-7696.. 394 I
leavittg@reed.edu

LEAVITT, Stephen, C .... 518-388-6116.. 338 H
leavitts@union.edu

LEBAIL, Carolyn .... 802-387-6814.. 484 B
carolynlebail@landmark.edu

LEBAR, Peter, M .... 814-332-5369.. 397 A
plebar@allegheny.edu

LEBARRON, Lynne .... 203-837-8188.... 85 I
lebarronl@wcsu.edu

LEBBY, Kimberly .... 803-376-5700.. 427 A
klebby@allenuniversity.edu

LEBEAU, Bryan .... 913-758-6115.. 185 F
lebeau87@stmary.edu

LEBEAU, Mandie, A .... 617-422-7499.. 226 H
mlebeau@nesl.edu

LEBEAU, Michael .... 205-226-4719...... 2 C
mlebeau@bsc.edu

LEBEDEFF, Alex .... 510-659-6263.... 55 B
alebedeff@ohlone.edu

LEBER, Frank, W .... 312-329-4388.. 148 F
frank.leber@moody.edu

LEBER, Sally, S .... 740-368-3080.. 376 B
ssleber@owu.edu

LEBERT, Jeff .... 918-335-6842.. 386 F
jlebert@okwu.edu

LEBESCH, Anna, M .... 904-276-6783.. 108 B
annalebesch@sjrstate.edu

LEBESCO, Kathleen .... 212-517-0522.. 320 C
klebesco@mmm.edu

LEBHERZ, Joe .... 301-682-8316.. 209 G
lebherz@msmary.edu

LEBIODA, Ed .... 805-437-8547.... 32 B
ed.lebioda@csuci.edu

LEBLANC, Ann .... 757-352-4222.. 493 E
aleblanc@regent.edu

LEBLANC, AnnMarie, M .. 412-397-6460.. 418 B
leblanc@rmu.edu

LEBLANC, Corlin .... 225-216-8605.. 195 H
leblancc@mybrcc.edu

LEBLANC, David .... 601-635-2111.. 257 F
dleblanc@eccc.edu

LEBLANC, Elva, C .... 817-515-7750.. 467 A
elva.leblanc@tccd.edu

LEBLANC, Erica .... 310-434-4227.... 63 F
leblanc_erica@smc.edu

LEBLANC, Jacqueline .... 212-752-1530.. 318 F
jacqueline.leblanc@limcollege.edu

LEBLANC, Jerry, L .... 337-482-6235.. 201 D
jerrylukeleblanc@louisiana.edu

LEBLANC, Nina .... 337-439-5765.. 195 A
nina@deltatech.edu

LEBLANC, Paul .... 603-645-9631.. 287 I
p.leblanc@snhu.edu

LEBLANC, Thomas, J .... 305-284-3356.. 114 H
leblanc@miami.edu

LEBLANC, William .... 401-825-2225.. 425 A
leblanc@ccri.edu

LEBLEU BURNS, Michele 408-864-8218.... 44 A
lebleuburnsmichele@deanza.edu

LEBO, Cathy, J .... 443-997-4107.. 208 D
lebo@jhu.edu

LEBO, Maggie .... 717-728-2406.. 400 F
margeretlebo@centralpenn.edu

LEBO, Russ .... 559-734-9000.... 61 G
russl@sjvc.edu

LEBRECK, Paul .... 847-925-6647.. 141 A
plebreck@harpercollege.edu

LEBRETON, Ryan .... 570-577-3122.. 398 L
ryan.lebreton@bucknell.edu

LEBRON, Mayra .... 787-850-9392.. 538 B
mayra.lebron@upr.edu

LEBRON, Nestor, A .... 787-864-2222.. 534 A
nestor.lebron@guayama.inter.edu

LEBRUN, Kathy .... 512-472-4133.. 465 F
kathy.lebrun@ssw.edu

LEBSOCK, Gale .... 760-384-6230.... 47 K
glebsock@cerrocoso.edu

LECATO, William .... 757-789-1797.. 497 A
wlecato@es.vccs.edu

LECH, Jennifer .... 602-639-7500.... 13 I

LECHE, Adriane .... 252-536-7260.. 350 C
aleche096@halifaxcc.edu

LECHLER, Terry .... 254-299-8652.. 461 E
tlechler@mclennan.edu

LECHNER, David, E .... 402-472-2191.. 282 K
dlechner@nebraska.edu

LECHNER, JR., Jack, E .... 513-761-2020.. 366 C
jlechner@ccms.edu

LECHOWSKI, Piotr .... 773-929-8500.. 139 E
plechowski@devry.edu

LECHTENBERG, Melanie .. 217-641-4310.. 143 H
mlechtenberg@jwcc.edu

LECKONBY, Larry, W .... 704-637-4474.. 343 B
lleckonb14@catawba.edu

LECKRONE, Michael, J .... 260-982-5004.. 165 M
mjleckrone@manchester.edu

LECLAIR, Mary .... 315-781-3697.. 316 C
leclair@hws.edu

LECLERC, Robin .... 248-204-2203.. 237 B
rleclerc@ltu.edu

LECOUNT, Heidi .... 919-760-8633.. 346 D
lecounth@meredith.edu

LECOURT, Nancy .... 707-965-6234.... 56 A
nlecourt@puc.edu

LECRONE, Jeffrey, L .... 570-321-4112.. 409 F
lecrone@lycoming.edu

LEDBETTER, Beverly, E .... 401-863-9900.. 424 J
beverly_ledbetter@brown.edu

LEDBETTER, Brad .... 828-652-0674.. 351 C
bradl@mcdowelltech.edu

LEDBETTER, Bronson .... 602-387-4307.... 17 L
bronson.ledbetter@phoenix.edu

LEDBETTER, Kim, M .... 828-652-0602.. 351 C
kims@mcdowelltech.edu

LEDBETTER, Lisa .... 704-216-3620.. 352 G
lisa.ledbetter@rccc.edu

LEDBETTER, Mary, L .... 828-659-6001.. 351 C
maryl@mcdowelltech.edu

LEDBETTER, Neal .... 251-442-2429...... 9 A
nledbetter@umobile.edu

LEDBETTER, Sislena .... 202-274-5373.... 94 B
sledbetter@udc.edu

LEDDY, Michael .... 401-341-2195.. 426 C
mike.leddy@salve.edu

LEDERER, John .... 206-934-6075.. 506 J
john.lederer@seattlecolleges.edu

LEDERMAN, Bill .... 269-467-9945.. 234 B
blederman@glenoaks.edu

LEDERMANN, Sarah .... 518-255-5516.. 334 D
lederms@cobleskill.edu

LEDERMANN, Stacy, A .... 585-385-8142.. 328 E
sledermann@sjfc.edu

LEDESMA, Amadeo .... 575-527-7530.. 301 C
amadeol@nmsu.edu

LEDESMA, Joe .... 619-876-4266.... 68 I
jledesma@usuniversity.edu

LEDESMA, Mark .... 206-726-5028.. 503 B
mledesma@cornish.edu

LEDESMA, Rosalie .... 408-223-6782.... 62 C
rosalie.ledesma@sjeccd.org

LEDEZMA, Rosabla .... 336-750-2855.. 359 B
ledezmara@wssu.edu

LEDFORD, Catherine, M .. 858-534-3391.... 70 C
cledford@ucsd.edu

LEDFORD, Howard .... 770-535-6275.. 123 L
hledford@laniertech.edu

LEDFORD, Julia .... 270-686-4627.. 190 D
julia.ledford@kctcs.edu

LEDFORD, Julie .... 360-736-9391.. 502 A
jledford@centralia.edu

LEDFORD, Laura .... 217-362-6499.. 148 D
lledford@millikin.edu

LEDFORD, Patrick .... 706-754-7728.. 125 B
pledford@northgatech.edu

LEDFORD, Randy .... 828-766-1280.. 351 B
rledford@mayland.edu

LEDFORD, Terry .... 864-941-8568.. 432 A
ledford.t@ptc.edu

LEDFORD, Tommy, R .... 828-766-1190.. 351 B
tledford@mayland.edu

LEDING, Albert .... 479-979-1000.... 24 I

LEDLOW, Susan, E .... 407-582-3423.. 114 N
sledlow@valenciacollege.edu

LEDNICKY, Margaret .... 916-558-2544.... 51 D
lednicm@scc.losrios.edu

LEDONNE, Patricia, N ..... 540-375-2270.. 493 H
ledonne@roanoke.edu

LEDONNE, Peter .... 201-447-7159.. 289 E
pledonne@bergen.edu

LEDOUX, Debra .... 320-762-4482.. 248 J
debral@alextech.edu

LEDUC, Don .... 517-371-5140.. 243 I
leducd@cooley.edu

LEDUC, Laura .... 517-371-5140.. 243 I
leducl@cooley.edu

LEDUFF, Kimberly .... 850-474-2600.. 113 A
kleduff@uwf.edu

LEDVINA, Anne .... 205-226-7722...... 2 C
aledvina@bsc.edu

LEDYARD, Christopher, L 740-283-6437.. 368 L
cledyard@franciscan.edu

LEE, Abby .... 541-881-5582.. 395 E
alee@tvcc.cc

LEE, Allisha .... 270-707-3958.. 189 G
allisha.lee@kctcs.edu

LEE, Amanda .... 910-362-7555.. 348 A
alee@cfcc.edu

LEE, Amy .... 510-748-2288.... 57 C
ahlee@peralta.edu

LEE, Amy .... 207-741-5644.. 203 M
alee@smccme.edu

LEE, IHM, Andrea, J .... 414-382-6064.. 515 D
andrea.lee@alverno.edu

LEE, Annette .... 516-562-1108.. 313 C
alee@northwell.edu

LEE, Anthony .... 888-491-8686.... 74 I

LEE, Antwinett .... 425-739-8344.. 504 F
antwinett.lee@lwtech.edu

LEE, Asa .... 202-885-8614.... 94 E
alee@wesleyseminary.edu

LEE, Barbara, A .... 848-932-2600.. 295 F
blee@oldqueens.rutgers.edu

LEE, Bill .... 913-722-0272.. 182 B

LEE, Brandon, w .... 361-485-4400.. 474 C
leebw@uhv.edu

LEE, Brenda .... 419-530-7730.. 380 D
brenda.lee@utoledo.edu

LEE, Brian .... 310-577-3000.... 75 H
blee@yosan.edu

LEE, Brian, K .... 626-395-6307.... 30 H
brian.lee@caltech.edu

LEE, Bridgett, C .... 512-505-3074.. 459 F
bclee@htu.edu

LEE, Catherine .... 334-844-1350...... 1 G
leecath@auburn.edu

LEE, Catherine .... 910-362-7033.. 348 A
clee@cfcc.edu

LEE, Charley .... 714-527-0691.... 43 C

LEE, Chris .... 501-882-8887.... 18 I
cllee@asub.edu

LEE, Chris .... 270-706-8622.. 189 C
chris.lee@kctcs.edu

LEE, Christopher .... 785-460-5509.. 180 C
christopher.lee@colbycc.edu

LEE, Christopher .... 804-819-4685.. 496 E
clee@vccs.edu

LEE, Christopher .... 920-832-7694.. 517 E
christopher.lee@lawrence.edu

LEE, Chul .... 812-488-2155.. 167 I
cl162@evansville.edu

LEE, Chung-Shing .... 253-535-7251.. 505 G
clee@plu.edu

LEE, Cindy .... 352-588-8869.. 108 C
cindy.lee@saintleo.edu

LEE, Claire .... 858-225-4301.... 30 F

LEE, Crystal .... 225-743-8500.. 196 J
clee@rpcc.edu

LEE, Curtis .... 253-964-6595.. 506 B
clee@pierce.ctc.edu

LEE, Cynthia .... 713-313-7523.. 470 D
lee_cl@tsu.edu

LEE, Dana .... 914-594-4567.. 323 I
dana_lee@nymc.edu

LEE, Daniel, J .... 253-535-7177.. 505 G
daniel.lee@plu.edu

LEE, David .... 270-745-2297.. 194 D
david.lee@wku.edu

LEE, David .... 303-273-3155.... 78 M
dlee@mines.edu

LEE, David, C .... 706-542-5969.. 128 E
dclee@uga.edu

LEE, David, S .... 609-258-9548.. 294 D
davidlee@princeton.edu

LEE, David, Y .... 703-333-5904.. 500 G
dylee@wuv.edu

LEE, David Chang, S .... 714-525-0088.... 45 F

LEE, Deborah .... 949-214-3433.... 41 F
deborah.lee@cui.edu

LEE, Debra, A .... 330-471-8406.. 371 J
dlee@malone.edu

LEE, Delores .... 310-243-3189.... 32 D
dslee@csudh.edu

LEE, Dennis .... 229-227-2414.. 127 G
dlee@southernregional.edu

LEE, Dewain .... 907-786-1214.... 10 F
dllee@uaa.alaska.edu

LEE, Dewain .... 812-866-7078.. 161 C
lee@hanover.edu

LEE, Diane, M .... 410-455-2859.. 211 G
dlee@umbc.edu

LEE, Don .... 434-528-5276.. 500 C
dlee@vul.edu

LEE, Don .... 662-246-6441.. 259 B
dlee@msdelta.edu

LEE, Donna .... 651-696-6220.. 247 I
donnalee@macalester.edu

LEE, Donny .... 501-279-4187.... 20 D
dlee@harding.edu

LEE, Donzell .... 601-877-6142.. 256 F
dlee@alcorn.edu

LEE, Doug .... 724-852-3212.. 423 A
dlee@waynesburg.edu

LEE, Douglas .... 319-335-0444.. 169 H
douglas-lee@uiowa.edu

LEE, D'Andrea, J .... 225-771-2552.. 200 A
djlee@sulc.edu

LEE, E. Joseph .... 607-962-9264.. 312 B
elee2@corning-cc.edu

LEE, Ed .... 715-346-3612.. 521 C
ed.lee@uwsp.edu

LEE, El Cabrel .... 504-816-4713.. 195 B
eclee@dillard.edu

LEE, Eliot .... 562-926-1023.... 58 B
it@ptsa.edu

LEE, Elwyn, C .... 832-842-5090.. 473 F
eclee@uh.edu

LEE, Eun Moo .... 770-220-7929.. 120 G
emlee@gcuniv.edu

LEE, Eun Moo .... 770-222-0792.. 120 G
emlee@gcuniv.edu

LEE, Gloria .... 203-392-5200.... 85 H
leeg1@southernct.edu

LEE, Grayce .... 504-468-2900.. 200 B
drlee@southwest.edu

LEE, Hannah .... 213-381-0081.... 47 C
hlee@irus.edu

LEE, Harlan .... 425-564-4042.. 501 F
harlan.lee@bellevuecollege.edu

LEE, Hee, C .... 636-327-4645.. 268 C
hclee@midwest.edu

LEE, Helen Elaine .... 617-253-2642.. 225 A

LEE, Herbert .... 831-459-1349.... 70 F
vpaa@ucsc.edu

LEE, Ho Woo .... 770-279-0507.. 120 G
howlee21@gcuniv.edu

LEE, Holly .... 580-628-6274.. 384 L
holly.lee@noc.edu

LEE, Howoo .... 770-220-7920.. 120 G
howlee21@gcuniv.edu

LEE, Hubert .... 610-361-2499.. 411 E
leeh@neumann.edu

LEE, Humphrey .... 256-331-5214...... 6 A
hlee@nwscc.edu

LEE, Ilses-Mari .... 406-994-2452.. 277 C
ilselee@montana.edu

LEE, J. Brent .... 843-355-4144.. 435 A
leeb@wiltech.edu

LEE, Jaekyung .... 716-645-6640.. 331 C
jl224@buffalo.edu

LEE, James .... 760-252-2411.... 28 B
jlee@barstow.edu

LEE, James .... 617-873-0236.. 217 A
james.lee@cambridgecollege.edu

LEE, James, D .... 808-675-3289.. 130 E
james.lee@byuh.edu

LEE, James, S .... 626-448-0023.... 47 E
president@itsla.edu

LEE, Janet .... 303-458-3552.... 82 L
jlee@regis.edu

LEE, Jay .... 970-521-6607.... 81 O
jay.lee@njc.edu

LEE, Jay .... 507-537-7285.. 252 E
jay.lee@smsu.edu

LEE, Jeffrey .... 973-877-3000.. 291 H

LEE, John .... 651-255-6156.. 255 C
jlee@unitedseminary.edu

LEE, John .... 707-826-3961.... 34 F
john.lee@humboldt.edu

LEE, John .... 703-812-4757.. 491 B
jlee@leland.edu

LEE, Jonathan .... 310-233-4471.... 49 I
leej@lahc.edu

LEE, Jonathan .... 508-626-4697.. 221 E
jlee8@framingham.edu

LEE, Jonathan, E .... 540-375-2237.. 493 H
jelee@roanoke.edu

LEE, Judy .... 718-818-6470.. 329 F
jlee@edaff.com

LEE, Karen .... 619-849-2535.... 57 M
karenlee@pointloma.edu

LEE, Kathleen, F .... 317-917-5935.. 164 F
klee@ivytech.edu

LEE, Katrina, K .... 919-658-2502.. 355 K
klee@umo.edu

LEE, Kenya, N .... 646-312-3322.. 307 A
kenya.lee@baruch.cuny.edu

LEE, Keum Hee .... 213-385-2322.... 75 E
khlee@wmu.edu

LEE, Kevin, T .... 615-297-7545.. 438 F
leek@aquinascollege.edu

LEE, Kiama .... 601-923-1681.. 260 E
klee@rts.edu

LEE, Kimberly .... 229-420-1284.. 116 A
klee@albanytech.edu

LEE, Kwang Hoon .... 213-381-0081.... 47 C
khlee@irus.edu

LEE, Kyu, H .... 253-752-2020.. 503 H
klee@faithseminary.edu

LEE, Kyuboem .... 215-368-5000.. 398 C
klee@biblical.edu

LEE, Lenetta .... 484-365-7253.. 409 B
llee@lincoln.edu

LEE, Lily .... 240-567-5272.. 209 E
lily.lee@montgomerycollege.edu

LEE, Linda, S .... 657-725-7789.... 66 I
lslee@stanford.edu

LEE, Lisa .... 714-533-3946.... 35 E
lisa@calums.edu

LEE, Lisa .... 212-410-8007.. 323 C
llee@nycpm.edu

LEE, Lisa .... 610-328-8402.. 419 I
llee2@swarthmore.edu

LEE, Marsha .... 662-246-6314.. 259 B
mlee@msdelta.edu

LEE, Martin .... 707-524-1649.... 63 G
mlee@santarosa.edu

LEINAWEAVER, Justin ..... 417-873-7167.. 264 H
jleinaweaver@drury.edu
LEINBERRY, Beth .... 401-841-4448.. 528 E
LEINEN, Jared .... 402-363-5675.. 283 G
jaleinen@york.edu
LEINEN, Margaret .... 858-534-2827.... 70 C
mleinen@ucsd.edu
LEINGANG, Dan .... 701-224-5525.. 361 C
daniel.leingang@bismarckstate.edu
LEININGER, Earl .... 704-406-3522.. 344 E
eleininger@gardner-webb.edu
LEININGER, Jeffrey .... 708-209-3470.. 138 G
jeff.leininger@cuchicago.edu
LEIPOLD, Bil .... 973-353-5500.. 296 C
bil.leipold@rutgers.edu
LEISINGER, Scott, C .... 319-352-8495.. 177 G
scott.leisinger@wartburg.edu
LEIST, Terry .... 406-994-4361.. 277 C
tleist@montana.edu
LEITE, Pedro .... 913-621-8700.. 180 F
pleite@donnelly.edu
LEITE, Randy .... 740-593-9336.. 375 H
leite@ohio.edu
LEITER, Dena .... 908-709-7622.. 298 A
leiter@ucc.edu
LEITGEB, Robert .... 757-455-3114.. 500 E
rletgeib@vwc.edu
LEITHNER STAUFFER,
Andrea, C .... 570-577-1331.. 398 L
andrea.leithner.stauffer@bucknell.edu
LEITNER, Jennifer .... 603-882-6923.. 286 E
jleitner@ccsnh.edu
LEITSON, Cynthia .... 216-987-3510.. 367 E
cynthia.leitson@tri-c.edu
LEITZEL, Thomas, C .... 863-784-7110.. 109 G
leitzelt@southflorida.edu
LEIVA, Laurie .... 504-861-5419.. 198 E
laleiva@loyno.edu
LEJTER, Nelly .... 603-428-2217.. 287 C
nlejter@nec.edu
LEJUEZ, Carl, W .... 785-864-3661.. 185 D
clejuez@ku.edu
LELAND, Chris .... 405-733-7350.. 387 I
cleland@rose.edu
LELAND, Dorothy .... 209-228-4417.... 70 A
chancellor@ucmerced.edu
LELAND, John, E .... 937-229-2114.. 379 D
john.leland@udri.udayton.edu
LELAND, Melinda, T .... 276-739-2548.. 499 A
mleland@vhcc.edu
LELAND, Ted .... 209-946-2392.... 71 C
tleland@pacific.edu
LELCHOOK, Heather .... 970-667-4611.... 76 H
heather.lelchook@aims.edu
LELE, Pradeep .... 281-618-7123.. 461 B
pradeep.m.lele@lonestar.edu
LELFER, John .... 704-463-3039.. 354 F
john.lefler@pfeiffer.edu
LELIAERT, Deborah, S ..... 940-565-2108.. 475 A
deborah.leliaert@unt.edu
LELIK, Mary, K .... 919-515-6434.. 357 B
mklelik@ncsu.edu
LELONG, Kristine, D .... 504-865-3858.. 198 E
klelong@loyno.edu
LELOUDIS, James, L .... 919-966-5110.. 357 D
leloudis@unc.edu
LEMA, Barbara .... 508-286-3542.. 229 F
lema_barbara@wheatoncollege.edu
LEMAHIEU, Dan .... 847-735-5083.. 145 B
lemahieu@lakeforest.edu
LEMAHIEU, Keith .... 219-864-2400.. 165 Q
klemahieu@midamerica.edu
LEMAIRE, Renee .... 334-222-6591...... 5 F
rlemaire@lbwcc.edu
LEMARBE, Thomas, P ...... 248-370-2445.. 239 K
lemarbe@oakland.edu
LEMASTER, Charles .... 254-267-7060.. 463 K
clemaster@rangercollege.edu
LEMASTER, J. Michael ..... 937-258-8251.. 370 F
LEMASTERS, Michael .... 724-357-2696.. 415 B
michael.lemasters@iup.edu
LEMAY, Elaine .... 510-869-6739.... 59 L
elemay@samuelmerritt.edu
LEMAY, Jerret .... 315-312-2237.. 333 D
jerret.lemay@oswego.edu
LEMBKE, Roberta .... 507-786-3097.. 254 P
lembke@stolaf.edu
LEMBO, Vincent, J .... 617-373-2157.. 227 B
LEMBURG, Mary .... 713-718-8505.. 459 B
mary.lemburg@hccs.edu
LEMCOE, Diane .... 908-526-1200.. 295 A
diane.lemcoe@raritanval.edu
LEMELLE, Erica .... 757-352-4778.. 493 E
ericlem@regent.edu
LEMERE, Brian, J .... 864-597-4068.. 435 C
lemerebj@wofford.edu
LEMEROND, James .... 920-693-1840.. 523 E
james.lemerond@gototc.edu
LEMERY, Cynthia .... 518-327-6399.. 326 B
clemery@paulsmiths.edu
LEMEUNIER, Jennifer ...... 337-482-0900.. 201 D
jlemeunier@louisiana.edu
LEMIEN, Laura .... 603-524-3207.. 286 C
llemien@ccsnh.edu
LEMING, Heidi .... 615-366-3948.. 444 D
heidi.leming@tbr.edu
LEMIRE, Joseph .... 414-229-4627.. 520 D
lemire@uwm.edu
LEMIRE, Mark .... 315-792-7100.. 336 C
mark.lemire@sunypoly.edu
LEMISCH, Jamie .... 215-780-1391.. 419 C
jlemisch@salus.edu
LEMISH, Dafna, P .... 618-453-7708.. 154 I
dafnalemish@siu.edu
LEMKE, Chris .... 616-222-1360.. 233 A
chris.lemke@cornerstone.edu
LEMKE, Steve, W .... 504-282-4455.. 198 H
slemke@nobts.edu
LEMME, Daryl .... 605-718-2953.. 438 B
daryl.lemme@wdt.edu
LEMME, Gary, D .... 334-844-4444...... 1 G
gdl0003@aces.edu
LEMMON, John .... 650-508-3605.... 54 J
jlemmon@ndnu.edu
LEMMON, John .... 650-508-3494.... 54 J
jlemmon@ndnu.edu
LEMOINE, Patrice, A .... 860-297-2086.... 89 B
patrice.lemoine@trincoll.edu
LEMOINE, Sandra, M ...... 318-342-1235.. 201 E
slemoine@ulm.edu
LEMON, Cari .... 575-538-6675.. 303 A
lemonc@wnmu.edu
LEMON, Deborah, A .... 812-855-6783.. 162 F
dalemon@iu.edu
LEMON, Jason .... 619-260-4585.... 72 B
jasonlemon@sandiego.edu
LEMON, Ronald, E .... 304-896-7425.. 512 E
ronald.lemon@southernwv.edu
LEMON, William, J .... 314-516-4702.. 274 A
lemonj@umsl.edu
LEMONIS, Samuel .... 601-857-3204.. 258 A
splemonis@hindscc.edu
LEMONS, James .... 434-832-7680.. 496 G
lemonsj@cvcc.vccs.edu
LEMONS, L. Jay .... 570-372-4130.. 419 H
supres@susqu.edu
LEMUEL, Robert, L .... 989-964-4393.. 240 F
lemuel@svsu.edu
LEMURA, Linda, M .... 315-445-4120.. 318 E
president14@lemoyne.edu
LEMUS, Maria De Jesus .. 773-371-5453.. 136 F
mlemus@ctu.edu
LENA, III, Hugh, F .... 401-865-2155.. 425 D
hlena@providence.edu
LENAHAN, Robert .... 631-632-6350.. 332 A
robert.lenahan@stonybrook.edu
LENCHAK, Timothy, A ..... 563-876-3353.. 171 I
tlenchak@dwci.edu
LENCKE, Scott .... 901-381-3939.. 449 F
scott@visible.edu
LENCZOWSKI, John .... 202-462-2101.... 93 B
lenczowski@iwp.edu
LENFEST, Richard .... 413-572-5405.. 222 E
rlenfest@westfield.ma.edu
LENGA, Kirk .... 516-299-4209.. 319 B
kirk.lenga@liu.edu
LENHARDT, Andrew, R .... 812-464-1770.. 168 E
alenhardt@usi.edu
LENHART, Jeff .... 704-847-5600.. 355 J
jlenhart@ses.edu
LENIG, Joni, L .... 931-540-2752.. 446 A
jlenig@columbiastate.edu
LENIHAN, Bernard .... 908-709-7605.. 298 A
lenihan@ucc.edu
LENIHAN, David .... 787-840-2575.. 535 H
dlenihan@psm.edu
LENIHAN, Debra .... 515-309-9000.. 177 E
LENIO, Jim .... 612-338-7224.. 256 D
jim.lenio@waldenu.edu
LENITNI, James, P .... 248-370-2193.. 239 K
jlentini@oakland.edu
LENNEMAN, Marc .... 406-447-4336.. 276 B
mlenneman@carroll.edu
LENNERTON, Mark .... 718-289-5655.. 307 C
mark.lennerton@bcc.cuny.edu
LENNERTZ, Reid .... 239-590-7960.. 110 L
rlennert@fgcu.edu
LENNEY, Raina .... 202-885-5936.... 91 J
lenney@american.edu
LENNIE, Peter .... 585-273-5000.. 338 K
lennie@rochester.edu
LENNON, John .... 845-848-4061.. 312 F
john.lennon@dc.edu
LENNOX, JR., William, J 352-588-8242.. 108 C
bill.lennox@saintleo.edu
LENO, Melissa .... 218-733-5903.. 249 H
m.leno@lsc.edu
LENO, Tom .... 701-224-5497.. 361 C
thomas.leno@bismarckstate.edu
LENOIR, Nina .... 714-997-6622.... 37 F
lenoir@chapman.edu
LENON, Fe, L .... 773-442-5143.. 149 J
f-lenon@neiu.edu
LENORE-JENKINS, Shani . 314-529-9350.. 267 B
slenore@maryville.edu
LENOSKY, Charles, A ...... 402-280-2540.. 279 H
clenosky@creighton.edu
LENROW, Jon .... 215-670-9359.. 412 D
jlenrow@peirce.edu
LENSING, Peggy .... 563-387-1015.. 174 L
lensinpe@luther.edu
LENT, Tina .... 209-954-5151.... 61 F
tlent@deltacollege.edu
LENTINO, Nicholas .... 860-727-6765.... 87 H
nlentino@goodwin.edu
LENTNER, Nikolaus .... 914-251-6070.. 334 C
nikolaus.lentner@purchase.edu
LENTZ, Brannon .... 334-514-8607...... 4 G
brannon.lentz@istc.edu
LENTZ, Heather .... 605-995-7227.. 436 C
heather.lentz@mitchelltech.edu
LENTZ, Kristi, L .... 701-788-4772.. 360 E
kristi.lentz@mayvillestate.edu
LENTZ, Sherry .... 904-596-2443.. 113 J
slentz@tbc.edu
LENTZ, Victoria, A .... 410-543-6368.. 213 A
valentz@salisbury.edu
LENWAY, Stefanie, A .... 651-962-4201.. 256 C
lenw0002@stthomas.edu
LENZ, Christopher .... 323-343-3237.... 33 C
clenz@cslanet.calstatela.edu
LENZ, Craig, J .... 334-699-2266...... 1 B
LENZ, Joseph .... 515-271-4028.. 171 K
joseph.lenz@drake.edu
LENZ, Mary .... 320-762-4648.. 248 J
maryl@alextech.edu
LENZ, Patrick, J .... 510-987-9101.... 68 L
patrick.lenz@ucop.edu
LENZI, John .... 413-545-2313.. 220 F
jlenzi@registrar.umass.edu
LENZI, Patrick .... 610-436-1048.. 416 C
plenzi@wcupa.edu
LEO, Donald .... 706-542-1653.. 128 E
donleo@engr.uga.edu
LEO, Grace, D .... 787-279-1912.. 533 J
gdileo@bayamon.inter.edu
LEO, Jonathan .... 423-869-7094.. 441 E
jonathan.leo@lmunet.edu
LEO, Laurie .... 585-594-6861.. 325 B
leo_laurie@roberts.edu
LEO, Laurie .... 585-594-6861.. 327 D
leo_laurie@roberts.edu
LEO, Sydney, R .... 615-329-8663.. 439 L
sleo@fisk.edu
LEOMITI, Sonny, J .... 684-699-9155.. 529 E
s.leomiti@amsamoa.edu
LEON, Christine .... 714-564-6230.... 58 G
leon_christine@sac.edu
LEON, Gloria .... 914-606-6744.. 340 C
gloria.leon@sunywcc.edu
LEON, Juan, C .... 787-844-8812.. 538 E
juan.leon1@upr.edu
LEON, Kelly .... 513-745-3877.. 381 I
leon@xavier.edu
LEON, Linda, J .... 330-471-8442.. 371 J
lleon2@malone.edu
LEON, Nelson .... 212-752-1530.. 318 F
nelson.leon@limcollege.edu
LEON, Orlando .... 559-278-3923.... 32 F
oleon@csufresno.edu
LEON, Way .... 415-422-2868.... 72 C
leon@usfca.edu
LEON GUERRERO,
Ann S, A .... 671-735-2941.. 530 B
annsalg@uguam.uog.edu
LEON GUERRERO,
Barbara, B .... 671-735-5519.. 529 G
csi@guamcc.edu
LEON GUERRERO,
Deborah, D .... 671-735-2585.. 530 B
deborah@uguam.uog.edu
LEON-VICKS, Lilly .... 775-445-3324.. 285 B
lilly.leon-vicks@wnc.edu
LEONARD, Alan .... 315-228-7474.. 310 G
pleonard@colgate.edu
LEONARD, Bethany .... 262-695-6520.. 524 G
bleonard3@wctc.edu
LEONARD, Brenda .... 704-330-6626.. 348 E
brenda.leonard@cpcc.edu
LEONARD, Bryan .... 217-245-3048.. 141 G
bryan.leonard@mail.ic.edu
LEONARD, Charles .... 215-248-6340.. 409 D
cleaonard@ltsp.edu
LEONARD, David, M .... 540-458-8752.. 500 F
dleonard@wlu.edu
LEONARD, Debbie .... 305-809-3203.. 100 N
debbie.leonard@fkcc.edu
LEONARD, J. Rich .... 919-865-5878.. 342 F
leonardjr@campbell.edu
LEONARD, Jason .... 423-420-1211.. 440 F
LEONARD, Jesse, W .... 814-641-3162.. 406 F
leonarj@juniata.edu
LEONARD, Katie .... 570-702-8925.. 406 E
kleonard@johnson.edu
LEONARD, Marjolie .... 631-632-6280.. 332 A
marjolie.leonard@stonybrook.edu
LEONARD,
Mary Kathleen .... 814-871-7430.. 404 A
leonard010@gannon.edu
LEONARD, Pam .... 229-391-5050.. 115 I
pleonard@abac.edu
LEONARD, Patricia, L ...... 910-962-3117.. 358 D
leonard@uncw.edu
LEONARD, OSFS, Peter ... 610-282-1100.. 402 B
peter.leonard@desales.edu
LEONARD, Robert .... 256-824-2233...... 8 F
robert.leonard@uah.edu
LEONARD, Roberta .... 724-589-2842.. 420 D
rleonard@thiel.edu
LEONARD, Steve .... 317-738-8316.. 160 J
sleonard@franklincollege.edu
LEONARD, Thomas, C ...... 510-642-3773.... 68 M
toml@berkeley.edu
LEONARD, Timothy .... 410-704-3936.. 213 B
tleonard@towson.edu
LEONARD, Vee .... 239-590-1101.. 110 L
vleonard@fgcu.edu
LEONARD, William .... 617-735-9883.. 218 C
leonard@emmanuel.edu
LEONARD, William .... 610-361-5217.. 411 E
leonardw@neumann.edu
LEONARD-MARTIN, Peg .. 615-460-6856.. 438 J
peg.leonardmartin@belmont.edu
LEONE, Charles .... 215-204-7900.. 420 B
charles.leone@temple.edu
LEONE, John .... 518-828-4181.. 311 D
john.leone@sunycgcc.edu
LEONE, Loida .... 620-278-4202.. 185 A
lleone@sterling.edu
LEONETTI, Marc .... 401-254-3843.. 426 B
mleonetti@rwu.edu
LEONG, Helen .... 319-352-8220.. 177 G
helen.leong@wartburg.edu
LEONG, Nori .... 808-544-0292.. 130 H
nleong@hpu.edu
LEONI, Amy .... 740-695-9500.. 364 B
aleoni@belmontcollege.edu
LEONOR, JR., Samuel, E 951-785-2090.... 48 A
sleonor@lasierra.edu
LEOPALDI, Daniela .... 312-752-2198.. 144 E
daniel.leopaldi@kendall.edu
LEOPARD, David, R .... 770-720-5895.. 126 C
drl@reinhardt.edu
LEOPARD, Tim .... 205-348-8157...... 8 D
tleopard@fa.ua.edu
LEOPOLD, Emily .... 617-588-1347.. 215 E
eleopold@bfit.edu
LEOPOLD, Joseph .... 727-341-3719.. 108 D
LEOPOLD, Lillian .... 619-482-6564.... 66 E
lleopold@swccd.edu
LEOUSIS, Kim .... 251-442-2290...... 9 A
kleousis@umobile.edu
LEPAGE, Bob .... 413-755-4477.. 224 G
rglepage@stcc.edu
LEPAGE, Sharon .... 808-440-4263.. 130 F
slepage@chaminade.edu
LEPHART, Scott, M .... 859-323-1100.. 193 G
scott.lephart@uky.edu
LEPLEY, Pamela, D .... 804-828-6057.. 496 D
pdlepley@vcu.edu
LEPPANEN, Hannu .... 906-487-7285.. 234 A
hannu.leppanen@finlandia.edu
LEPPELLERE, Terry .... 312-777-8594.. 142 G
tleppellere@aii.edu
LEPPER, Charles .... 801-957-4285.. 483 A
charles.lepper@slcc.edu
LEPPER, David .... 231-591-3815.. 233 L
davidlepper@ferris.edu
LEPPERT, Glenn, W .... 620-862-5252.. 178 F
registrar@barclaycollege.edu
LEPPMANN, Erika .... 541-552-8484.. 395 A
leppmane@sou.edu
LEPSCIER, Crystal .... 800-567-2344.. 516 B
clepscier@menominee.edu
LERBINGER, Jan .... 617-585-1284.. 226 F
jan.lerbinger@necmusic.edu
LERCH, David .... 404-681-2800.. 124 I
david.lerch@morehouse.edu
LERCH, Derek .... 530-283-0202.... 43 G
dlerch@frc.edu
LERCH, Maureen, T .... 330-972-8951.. 378 H
mlerch@uakron.edu
LERER, Nava .... 516-877-3236.. 303 B
lerer@adelphi.edu
LERMA, Raul, H .... 915-831-2565.. 457 H
rlerma23@epcc.edu
LERMAN, Linda .... 203-857-7211.... 87 B
llerman@norwalk.edu
LERMAN, Steven, R .... 831-656-2371.. 528 D
slerman@nps.edu
LERNER, Sharon .... 212-817-7400.. 308 A
slerner@gc.cuny.edu

LEWIS, Beth .... 361-698-1205.. 457 D
bethlewis@delmar.edu
LEWIS, Beverly, N .... 336-734-7512.. 349 G
blewis@forsythtech.edu
LEWIS, Bill .... 505-566-3339.. 301 J
lewisb@sanjuancollege.edu
LEWIS, Bill, E .... 314-434-2212.. 266 B
blewis@hickeycollege.edu
LEWIS, Blaine, D .... 330-823-7365.. 379 F
lewisbd@mountunion.edu
LEWIS, Brenda .... 863-680-6285.. 101 E
blewis@flsouthern.edu
LEWIS, Brien .... 704-637-4414.. 343 B
wblewis@catawba.edu
LEWIS, Bruce .... 847-491-4933.. 150 F
balewis@northwestern.edu
LEWIS, Burt .... 919-658-7783.. 355 K
blewis@umo.edu
LEWIS, Byron, W .... 214-768-4354.. 465 J
lewisb@smu.edu
LEWIS, C. Jasper .... 870-235-4065.... 22 F
cjlewis@saumag.edu
LEWIS, Carmen .... 334-983-6556...... 7 H
cclewis@troy.edu
LEWIS, Carolyn .... 201-559-3560.. 291 K
lewisc@felician.edu
LEWIS, Cassandra, B .... 601-877-3905.. 256 F
cblewis@alcorn.edu
LEWIS, Charles, R .... 256-782-5003...... 4 H
crlewis@jsu.edu
LEWIS, Chet .... 281-998-6306.. 464 I
chet.lewis@sjcd.edu
LEWIS, Christine .... 847-543-2284.. 138 C
clewis2@clcillinois.edu
LEWIS, Christopher .... 517-371-5140.. 243 I
lewisch@cooley.edu
LEWIS, Chuck .... 918-647-1450.. 382 I
cllewis@carlalbert.edu
LEWIS, Cindy .... 805-493-3199.... 31 C
clewis@callutheran.edu
LEWIS, Cindy .... 865-573-4517.. 440 I
clewis@johnsonu.edu
LEWIS, Crissy .... 864-578-8770.. 432 D
clewis@sherman.edu
LEWIS, Cyndi .... 401-232-6000.. 424 K
clewis@bryant.edu
LEWIS, Cynthia .... 802-831-1444.. 485 F
clewis@vermontlaw.edu
LEWIS, Daniel, G .... 925-631-4616.... 59 I
dlewis@stmarys-ca.edu
LEWIS, David .... 501-370-5295.... 21 G
dlewis@philander.edu
LEWIS, David .... 405-974-2779.. 388 L
LEWIS, David, E .... 585-275-5240.. 338 K
david.lewis@rochester.edu
LEWIS, David, R .... 802-356-6824.... 91 I
david.r.lewis@wilmu.edu
LEWIS, David, W .... 317-274-0462.. 163 D
dlewis@iupui.edu
LEWIS, Dawanna .... 713-221-8974.. 474 B
lewisd@uhd.edu
LEWIS, Diane .... 530-541-4660.... 48 D
lewis@ltcc.edu
LEWIS, Don .... 763-433-1116.. 248 K
donald.lewis@anokaramsey.edu
LEWIS, Donald .... 763-433-1116.. 248 L
donald.lweis@anokaramsey.edu
LEWIS, Donna .... 601-925-3967.. 259 A
dlewis@mc.edu
LEWIS, E. Charles .... 817-202-6720.. 466 C
lewis@swau.edu
LEWIS, Edward .... 225-768-0804.. 199 B
edward.lewis@ololcollege.edu
LEWIS, Edward .... 336-770-3329.. 358 E
lewise@uncsa.edu
LEWIS, Emily, G .... 860-515-3860.... 85 D
elewis1@charteroak.edu
LEWIS, Felicia, Y .... 502-597-6286.. 191 B
felicia.lewis@kysu.edu
LEWIS, Fred .... 423-279-7665.. 446 F
fdlewis@northeaststate.edu
LEWIS, Georj .... 912-344-3562.. 116 E
georj.lewis@armstrong.edu
LEWIS, Gregory .... 804-257-5750.. 500 B
gelewis@vuu.edu
LEWIS, Gregory, V .... 661-824-2977.... 53 K
glewis@ntps.edu
LEWIS, Hal, M .... 312-322-1715.. 155 F
LEWIS, Jack .... 509-570-5926.. 148 F
jack.lewis@moody.edu
LEWIS, Jack, M .... 540-674-3601.. 497 G
jlewis@nr.edu
LEWIS, Jackie .... 252-985-5170.. 354 E
jlewis@ncwc.edu
LEWIS, James .... 302-736-2425.... 91 G
james.lewis@wesley.edu
LEWIS, James, E .... 206-934-5157.. 507 A
james.lewis@seattlecolleges.edu
LEWIS, Jan .... 252-328-2267.. 356 C
lewisja@ecu.edu
LEWIS, Jan, P .... 253-535-7283.. 505 G
lewisjp@plu.edu
LEWIS, Jan Ellen .... 973-353-5213.. 296 C
janlewis@andromeda.rutgers.edu
LEWIS, Jane .... 903-983-8620.. 460 D
jlewis@kilgore.edu
LEWIS, Jeanne .... 609-652-4201.. 297 C
jeanne.lewis@stockton.edu
LEWIS, Jeannie, M .... 559-323-2100.... 61 E
jlewis@sjcl.edu
LEWIS, Jeff .... 561-803-2702.. 106 C
jeff_lewis@pba.edu
LEWIS, Jerry .... 404-727-2793.. 120 E
jerrylewis@emory.edu
LEWIS, Jill .... 843-661-8003.. 429 J
jill.lewis@fdtc.edu
LEWIS, Jim .... 806-743-2530.. 472 D
jim.lewis@ttuhsc.edu
LEWIS, Jim .... 817-531-4404.. 472 F
jimlewis@txwes.edu
LEWIS, Jim .... 610-436-3200.. 416 C
jlewis@wcupa.edu
LEWIS, Jim, D .... 704-637-4720.. 343 B
jdlewis@catawba.edu
LEWIS, John .... 901-321-3227.. 439 E
john.lewis@cbu.edu
LEWIS, John .... 304-327-4191.. 512 P
jlewis@bluefieldstate.edu
LEWIS, Judith .... 716-829-7776.. 313 A
lewisj@dyc.edu
LEWIS, Katherine, P .... 570-340-6094.. 409 H
kplewis@marywood.edu
LEWIS, Kay .... 206-543-6107.. 508 E
sklewis@uw.edu
LEWIS, Keisha .... 205-929-1604...... 5 H
klewis@miles.edu
LEWIS, Kendrick, D .... 803-536-8227.. 432 E
klewis19@scsu.edu
LEWIS, Kenneth .... 803-536-8860.. 432 E
klewis31@scsu.edu
LEWIS, JR., Kenneth, A .. 252-492-2061.. 353 H
lewis@vgcc.edu
LEWIS, Keri .... 617-745-3774.. 218 A
keri.lewis@enc.edu
LEWIS, Lance .... 517-338-3431.. 232 F
llewis@cleary.edu
LEWIS, Larry .... 620-862-5252.. 178 F
larry.lewis@barclaycollege.edu
LEWIS, Laura .... 513-751-1206.. 362 H
laura@aic-arts.edu
LEWIS, Leslie, W .... 410-337-6044.. 207 H
leslie.lewis@goucher.edu
LEWIS, Lisa .... 805-898-4010.... 43 K
llewis@fielding.edu
LEWIS, Lisa .... 612-624-6142.. 255 H
lrlewis@umn.edu
LEWIS, Lori .... 828-227-7124.. 359 A
LEWIS, Luca .... 360-383-3076.. 509 F
llewis@whatcom.ctc.edu
LEWIS, Lynn .... 864-646-1437.. 433 C
llewis@tctc.edu
LEWIS, Lynn .... 434-381-6106.. 494 M
llewis@sbc.edu
LEWIS, Mark .... 952-358-8405.. 251 A
mark.lewis@normandale.edu
LEWIS, Mark .... 813-253-7017.. 102 R
mlewis73@hccfl.edu
LEWIS, Mark .... 325-674-2772.. 449 J
lewism@acu.edu
LEWIS, Marsha, L .... 716-829-2533.. 331 C
ubnursingdean@buffalo.edu
LEWIS, Mary .... 772-462-7444.. 103 B
mlewis@irsc.edu
LEWIS, Maryjo .... 937-376-2946.. 376 F
mlewis@payne.edu
LEWIS, Matthew .... 770-220-7925.. 120 G
mlewis@gcuniv.edu
LEWIS, Melissa .... 505-473-6404.. 302 A
melissa.lewis@santafeuniversity.edu
LEWIS, Melissa .... 931-526-3660.. 440 A
melissa.lewis@fortisinstitute.edu
LEWIS, Michael .... 614-251-4589.. 374 I
lewism2@ohiodominican.edu
LEWIS, Michelle .... 314-977-6063.. 271 K
lewisml@slu.edu
LEWIS, Mike .... 918-463-6358.. 383 F
mike.lewis@connorsstate.edu
LEWIS, Mildred .... 510-464-3413.... 57 D
mildredlewis@peralta.edu
LEWIS, Mitchell, R .... 607-735-1709.. 313 F
mlewis@elmira.edu
LEWIS, Monique .... 281-487-1170.. 469 F
mlewis@txchiro.edu
LEWIS, Nora, E .... 215-746-1172.. 421 E
nlewis@sas.upenn.edu
LEWIS, Orlando .... 704-216-6185.. 346 A
olewis@livingstone.edu
LEWIS, Pat .... 704-355-2029.. 343 A
pat.lewis@carolinascollege.edu
LEWIS, Paul, W .... 417-268-1000.. 262 F
lewisp@evangel.edu
LEWIS, Philip .... 701-627-4738.. 361 H
plewis@nhsc.edu
LEWIS, Rachael, L .... 202-231-4133.. 528 C
rachael.lewis@dodiis.mil
LEWIS, Raynold .... 508-929-8883.. 222 F
rlewis1@worcester.edu
LEWIS, Rebecca .... 585-245-5546.. 333 B
lewis@geneseo.edu
LEWIS, Rebecca, B .... 423-439-6155.. 444 F
bakerr@etsu.edu
LEWIS, Richard .... 928-350-1301.... 16 P
rlewis@prescott.edu
LEWIS, Richard, W .... 330-325-6344.. 373 H
rwl@neomed.edu
LEWIS, Rob .... 859-985-3323.. 187 B
lewisro@berea.edu
LEWIS, Rob .... 214-333-5821.. 455 J
robertl@dbu.edu
LEWIS, Robin .... 606-326-2423.. 188 N
robin.lewis@kctcs.edu
LEWIS, Ronald .... 605-342-0317.. 436 A
rlewis@johnwitherspooncollege.org
LEWIS, Russ .... 951-827-3009.... 70 B
russ.lewis@ucr.edu
LEWIS, Sally .... 832-476-8211.... 43 M
clinicqualitycontrol@fivebranches.edu
LEWIS, Shaun, M .... 504-286-5292.. 199 I
slewis@suno.edu
LEWIS, Shirley .... 707-864-7000.... 65 A
shirley.lewis@solano.edu
LEWIS, Stacy .... 415-422-5540.... 72 C
lewiss@usfca.edu
LEWIS, Susan .... 325-674-2024.. 449 J
lewiss@acu.edu
LEWIS, Susan, A .... 617-262-5000.. 216 A
susan.lewis@the-bac.edu
LEWIS, Suzanne .... 267-341-3481.. 405 J
slewis10@holyfamily.edu
LEWIS, Ted, A .... 865-694-6523.. 446 G
talewis@pstcc.edu
LEWIS, Terry, W .... 731-881-7890.. 448 G
tlewis@utm.edu
LEWIS, Thomas .... 443-287-9900.. 208 D
tomlewis@jhu.edu
LEWIS, Thomas, C .... 404-413-1404.. 122 D
tomlewis@gsu.edu
LEWIS, Tiffany .... 765-677-2102.. 164 B
tiffany.lewis@indwes.edu
LEWIS, Tracie, O .... 888-498-6752.. 356 F
tolewis@ncat.edu
LEWIS, Trevor .... 305-626-3750.. 101 A
trevor.lewis@fmuniv.edu
LEWIS, Trey .... 502-852-6701.. 194 A
trey.lewis@louisville.edu
LEWIS, Urick .... 610-526-6080.. 405 B
ulewis@harcum.edu
LEWIS, Victoria .... 831-479-6406.... 29 G
vilewis@cabrillo.edu
LEWIS, Vivian .... 585-273-2760.. 338 K
vivian.lewis@rochester.edu
LEWIS, Walter .... 518-587-2100.. 335 D
walter.lewis@esc.edu
LEWIS, Wendy .... 330-823-6596.. 379 F
lewisws@mountunion.edu
LEWIS, Whitney .... 404-364-8470.. 125 F
wlewis@oglethorpe.edu
LEWIS, William, A .... 601-403-1201.. 260 D
wlewis@prcc.edu
LEWIS-BOYD, Janice .... 313-593-5200.. 242 A
jckboyd@umich.edu
LEWIS-CHAMBERS, Terri . 937-376-6588.. 365 H
tlewis-chambers@centralstate.edu
LEWIS-JASPER, Vera .... 409-944-1496.. 458 D
vlewis@gc.edu
LEWIS LOGUE, Judith ..... 619-260-4720.... 72 B
jllogue@sandiego.edu
LEWIS MILLER, Andrea ... 901-435-1676.. 441 C
president@loc.edu
LEWIS SAULO, Mileva .... 650-292-5579.... 59 L
msaulo@samuelmerritt.edu
LEWIS-WHITE, Yasmin ..... 202-885-8552.... 94 E
ylwhite@wesleyseminary.edu
LEWIT, Jonathan, D .... 845-257-3130.. 331 E
lewit@newpaltz.edu
LEWKIEWICZ, Debra .... 845-434-5750.. 336 H
dlewkiew@sullivan.suny.edu
LEWLESS, Scott .... 989-686-9042.. 233 I
scottlewless@delta.edu
LEWTER, Andy .... 478-445-5169.. 121 A
andy.lewter@gcsu.edu
LEWY, MariLynn, J .... 941-752-5383.. 110 H
lewym@scf.edu
LEY, David .... 907-745-3201...... 9 H
dley@akbible.edu
LEYBA, Johanna .... 303-871-7661.... 84 B
johanna.leyba@du.edu
LEYBA-FRANK, Marylou .. 415-239-3291.... 38 E
mleyba@ccsf.edu
LEYBA RUIZ, Teresa .... 623-845-3010.... 14 C
teresa.leybaruiz@gccaz.edu
LEYDEN, John, J .... 401-865-2390.. 425 D
jleyden@providence.edu
LEYDON, John .... 919-962-4908.. 356 A
jleydon@northcarolina.edu
LEYKAM, Scott .... 503-943-7117.. 396 B
leykam@up.edu
LEZAK JANOW, Roseann 860-509-9501.... 88 A
rlezak@hartsem.edu
LE'I, Emilia .... 684-699-9155.. 529 E
e.lei@amsamoa.edu
LHOTKA, Kami .... 218-935-0417.. 256 E
kami.lhotka@wetcc.edu
LI, Dai .... 602-235-4179.. 184 C
dli@pittstate.edu
LI, Haipeng .... 209-228-2579.... 70 A
hli58@ucmerced.edu
LI, Joanne .... 937-775-4859.. 381 H
joanne.li@wright.edu
LI, Kanok .... 512-444-8082.. 470 B
admissions@thsu.edu
LI, Kevin .... 708-456-0300.. 156 C
kevinli@triton.edu
LI, Ming .... 269-387-2966.. 243 H
ming.li@wmich.edu
LI, Peter .... 361-593-4340.. 469 A
peter.li@tamuk.edu
LI, Qiaoyun (Liz) .... 650-493-4430.... 64 I
liz.li@sofia.edu
LI, Rui .... 610-430-4959.. 416 C
rli@wcupa.edu
LI, Sharon, F .... 415-422-2790.... 72 C
lis@usfca.edu
LI, Sheng .... 714-533-1495.... 65 B
sli@southbaylo.edu
LI, Yi .... 818-677-2957.... 34 A
yi.li@csun.edu
LI, Yongmei .... 864-596-9752.. 429 C
yongmei.li@converse.edu
LI, Zhan .... 925-631-4604.... 59 I
zgl1@stmarys-ca.edu
LI-BUGG, W. Cherry .... 714-808-4787.... 54 F
clibugg@nocccd.edu
LIANG, Bruce .... 860-679-2594.... 89 D
bliang@uchc.edu
LIANG, John Paul .... 713-780-9777.. 451 A
info@acaom.edu
LIANG, Mark .... 714-564-6040.... 58 G
liang_mark@sac.edu
LIANG, Sherry .... 510-628-8027.... 49 A
controller@lincolnuca.edu
LIAO-TROTH, Matthew ..... 808-544-0211.. 130 H
mliaotroth@hpu.edu
LIAS CLAFFEY, Renae ...... 508-929-8492.. 222 F
rliasclaffey@worcester.edu
LIAU, Yee .... 714-620-3700.... 27 I
LIAUTAUD, Danielle .... 973-720-2121.. 298 G
liautaudd@wpunj.edu
LIBBERTON, Larry .... 815-772-7218.. 148 H
llibberton@morrisontech.edu
LIBBIN, Jim .... 575-646-3748.. 300 J
jlibbin@nmsu.edu
LIBBY, Betsy .... 207-755-5250.. 203 I
blibby@cmcc.edu
LIBBY, Elizabeth .... 847-735-6011.. 145 B
libby@lakeforest.edu
LIBBY, John .... 240-567-7951.. 209 E
john.libby@montgomerycollege.edu
LIBBY, Wendy, B .... 386-822-7250.. 113 B
wlibby@stetson.edu
LIBERATI, Dennis .... 267-295-2314.. 418 A
dliberati@walnuthillcollege.edu
LIBERATORE, Anthony, F 217-424-6338.. 148 D
aliberatore@millikin.edu
LIBERATORI, Ellen, A ...... 607-746-4612.. 335 C
liberaem@delhi.edu
LIBERATOSCIOLI, Daniel . 267-295-2316.. 418 A
president@walnuthillcollege.edu
LIBERATOSCIOLI, Peggy . 267-295-2315.. 418 A
pl@walnuthillcollege.edu
LIBERMAN, Ira .... 718-438-1002.. 320 H
yliberman@yeshivanet.com
LIBERTELLI, Joseph .... 202-274-7338.... 94 B
jlibertelli@udc.edu
LIBERTO, Salvadore .... 617-730-7135.. 226 J
salvadore.liberto@newbury.edu
LIBERTO, Terri .... 412-536-1813.. 406 K
terri.liberto@laroche.edu
LIBERTY, Bob .... 254-526-1310.. 454 A
bob.liberty@ctcd.edu
LIBERTY, Cindy .... 336-770-3333.. 358 E
libertyc@uncsa.edu
LIBERTY, Paul .... 703-993-8860.. 490 B
pliberty@gmu.edu
LIBET, Alice, Q .... 843-792-4930.. 431 A
libeta@musc.edu
LIBHART, Bonnie .... 256-652-3752.. 443 H
drbonnie@me.com
LIBUTTI, Dean .... 401-874-4408.. 426 D
dean@uri.edu
LICARI, Frank .... 702-990-4433.. 285 E
flicari@roseman.edu

LICARI, Michael, J .... 812-237-2309 .. 162 A
mike.licari@indstate.edu
LICATA, Betty Jo .... 330-941-3064 .. 382 A
bjlicata@ysu.edu
LICATA, Christine, M .... 585-475-2953 .. 327 E
cmlnbt@rit.edu
LICHT, Daniel .... 914-395-2301 .. 329 K
dlicht@sarahlawrence.edu
LICHT, Jodi, N .... 212-752-1530 .. 318 F
jodi.licht@limcollege.edu
LICHT, William .... 920-206-2320 .. 517 G
william.licht@mbu.edu
LICHTBLAU, Jobey .... 710-231-7672 .. 361 A
jobey.lichtblau@ndsu.edu
LICHTENBERG, Anne, V .... 859-257-5068 .. 193 G
anne.lichtenberg@uky.edu
LICHTENBERGER, Lynn .... 856-691-8600 .. 290 I
llichtenberger@cccnj.edu
LICHTENSTEIN, Gregg .... 619-594-5281 .... 35 A
lichtens@mail.sdsu.edu
LICHTENSTEIN, Mark .... 315-470-4748 .. 334 E
malichte@esf.edu
LICHTLE, Richard .... 419-358-3314 .. 364 D
lichtler@bluffton.edu
LICHTMAN, Louis, J .... 607-871-2171 .. 303 F
flich@alfred.edu
LICHTSINN, Jill .... 260-982-5015 .. 165 M
jslichtsinn@manchester.edu
LIDDELL, Alan, C .... 908-526-1200 .. 295 A
alan.liddell@raritanval.edu
LIDDELL, Peter, E .... 315-294-8861 .. 306 G
liddell@cayuga-cc.edu
LIDDELL, Robert .... 352-588-8346 .. 108 C
robert.liddell@saintleo.edu
LIDDELL, Tammy .... 206-296-6052 .. 507 E
liddellt@seattleu.edu
LIDDICOAT, Al .... 805-756-2844 .... 31 I
aliddico@calpoly.edu
LIDDICOAT, Blair .... 480-517-8108 .... 14 G
blair.liddicoat@riosalado.edu
LIDDLE, Ken .... 713-348-2287 .. 464 E
kliddle@rice.edu
LIDDLE, Trevor, C .... 956-326-2380 .. 468 A
tliddle@tamiu.edu
LIDDY, Colette .... 973-618-3209 .. 290 A
cliddy@caldwell.edu
LIDDY, Elizabeth, D .... 315-443-2879 .. 337 A
liddy@syr.edu
LIDERS, Gunta .... 585-275-5373 .. 338 K
gliders@orpa.rochester.edu
LIDGUS, Jonathan, A .... 314-516-5537 .. 274 A
lidgusj@umsl.edu
LIDH, Todd .... 828-898-8712 .. 345 G
lidht@lmc.edu
LIDSTONE, Rhonda, W .... 478-301-2005 .. 124 D
lidstone_rw@mercer.edu
LIDSTONE, Sheila .... 409-772-9866 .. 478 A
shlidsto@utmb.edu
LIDSTROM, Mary, E .... 206-616-0804 .. 508 E
lidstrom@uw.edu
LIDY, Paul .... 217-362-6410 .. 148 D
plidy@millikin.edu
LIEBAU, Linda, B .... 513-244-4593 .. 373 C
linda.liebau@msj.edu
LIEBER, Barbara .... 217-641-4535 .. 143 H
blieber@jwcc.edu
LIEBER, Steve .... 480-461-7066 .... 14 D
steven.lieber@mesacc.edu
LIEBERMAN, Abraham .... 845-782-1380 .. 341 I
LIEBERMAN, Devorah, A . 909-593-3511 .... 71 B
dlieberman@laverne.edu
LIEBERMAN, Ilene .... 610-499-4275 .. 423 E
idlieberman@widener.edu
LIEBERMAN, Steven .... 956-296-1900 .. 476 E
steven.lieberman@utrgv.edu
LIEBERT, Jane .... 913-758-6126 .. 185 F
jane.liebert@stmary.edu
LIEBERTHAL, Susan .... 631-451-4539 .. 336 E
liebers@sunysuffolk.edu
LIEBESKIND, Lanny, S .... 404-727-6604 .. 120 E
chemll1@emory.edu
LIEBHABER, Karen .... 870-248-4000 .... 19 H
karenl@blackrivertech.edu
LIEBLING, Mark .... 231-995-1342 .. 239 C
mliebling@nmc.edu
LIEBOWITZ, Ronald, D .... 781-736-2000 .. 216 F
ronaldliebowi@brandeis.edu
LIEBRECHT, Alan .... 510-436-1198 .... 46 E
liebrecht@hnu.edu
LIEBROCK, Lorie .... 575-835-5481 .. 300 G
liebrock@cs.nmt.edu
LIEBSCHER, Kim, K .... 580-774-3776 .. 388 C
kim.liebscher@swosu.edu
LIECHTY, Dan .... 574-535-7563 .. 161 A
dankl@goshen.edu
LIECHTY, Jeanne, M .... 574-535-7401 .. 161 A
jeannem@goshen.edu
LIEDERBACH, Mark .... 919-761-2100 .. 355 I
mliederbach@sebts.edu
LIEDTKA, Theresa .... 423-425-4506 .. 448 F
theresa-liedtka@utc.edu
LIEDTKE, Richard, W .... 785-670-1812 .. 185 H
richard.liedtke@washburn.edu
LIEF, Charles, G .... 303-546-3517 .... 81 I
president@naropa.edu
LIEF, Nathan, P .... 651-696-6140 .. 247 I
nlief@macalester.edu
LIEGEL, Angela .... 312-915-6191 .. 146 G
aliegel@luc.edu
LIEHR, Michael .... 518-956-8685 .. 336 C
mliehr@sunypoly.edu
LIEN, Joelle .... 605-626-2558 .. 437 D
joelle.lien@northern.edu
LIEN, Joelle .... 605-626-7958 .. 437 D
joelle.lien@northern.edu
LIENHARD, Patrick .... 215-438-6503 .. 407 A
lienhard@lasalle.edu
LIERLEY, Mark .... 480-858-9100 .... 17 B
m.lierley@scnm.edu
LIERMAN, Michael .... 800-962-7682 .. 275 D
mlierman@wma.edu
LIERZ, Rachel .... 913-469-8500 .. 182 A
rachellierz@jccc.edu
LIES, CSC, James .... 508-565-1551 .. 228 F
jlies@stonehill.edu
LIES, CSC, William, M .... 574-631-9800 .. 168 B
lies.7@nd.edu
LIESE, Hank .... 801-581-6194 .. 481 M
hank.liese@socwk.utah.edu
LIESEN, Joseph .... 573-288-6480 .. 264 F
jliesen@culver.edu
LIESEN, Kristen .... 217-228-5432 .. 151 F
liesekr@quincy.edu
LIESKE, Barb .... 219-464-6717 .. 168 F
barb.lieske@valpo.edu
LIESKE, Brian .... 510-666-8248 .... 25 D
blieske@aimc.edu
LIESMAN, Laura .... 732-987-2685 .. 292 A
lliesman@georgian.edu
LIETO, Mary .... 914-923-2690 .. 325 J
mlieto@pace.edu
LIEU, Mark .... 510-659-6173 .... 55 B
mlieu@ohlone.edu
LIEURANCE, Lorissa .... 515-271-3781 .. 171 K
lorissa.lieurance@drake.edu
LIEVANOS, Destry .... 760-630-1555 .... 29 B
destry.lievanos@brightwood.edu
LIEWER, Chris .... 402-554-2200 .. 283 B
cliewer@unomaha.edu
LIFSEY, Britt .... 678-359-5108 .. 122 E
brittl@gordonstate.edu
LIGEIKIS, Kelli .... 607-778-5089 .. 332 D
ligeikiskh@sunybroome.edu
LIGHT, Brad .... 336-334-4355 .. 358 B
uncg@bkstore.com
LIGHT, Cathy .... 412-268-5345 .. 400 D
calight@andrew.cmu.edu
LIGHT, Cathy, A .... 412-268-5345 .. 400 D
calight@andrew.cmu.edu
LIGHT, Kathleen .... 210-829-3943 .. 474 D
light@uiwtx.edu
LIGHT, Margaret .... 717-262-2010 .. 424 A
margaret.light@wilson.edu
LIGHT, Steven .... 701-777-2167 .. 360 C
steven.light@und.edu
LIGHTCAP, Lisa .... 610-282-1100 .. 402 B
lisa.lightcap@desales.edu
LIGHTCAP, Rhonda .... 516-671-0379 .. 339 G
rlightcap@webb.edu
LIGHTCAP, Stephen .... 215-717-6375 .. 421 D
slightcap@uarts.edu
LIGHTFIELD, Nancy, R .... 608-757-7750 .. 523 A
nlightfield@blackhawk.edu
LIGHTFOOT, Carolyn, A .. 281-425-6455 .. 460 I
clightfo@lee.edu
LIGHTFOOT, Douglas .... 816-604-1061 .. 267 F
douglas.lightfoot@mcckc.edu
LIGHTFOOT, James, D .... 434-832-7643 .. 496 G
lightfootd@cvcc.vccs.edu
LIGHTHILL, M. Joyce .... 641-784-5222 .. 172 G
lighthil@graceland.edu
LIGHTNER, Michael .... 303-860-5726 .... 83 J
lightner@cu.edu
LIGHTNER, Robin .... 513-745-5660 .. 379 B
robin.lightner@uc.edu
LIGHTSEY, Marissa .... 405-585-5260 .. 385 B
marissa.lightsey@okbu.edu
LIGIOSO, Yulian .... 707-864-7000 .... 65 A
yulian.ligioso@solano.edu
LIGMAN, Scott .... 509-527-2395 .. 508 G
scott.ligman@wallawalla.edu
LIGNOWSKI, Beth .... 201-559-6027 .. 291 K
0267mgr@sheg.follett.com
LIGON, Eric .... 940-565-4003 .. 475 A
eric.ligon@unt.edu
LIGON, Theresa .... 713-780-9777 .. 451 A
LIKENS, Erin .... 601-643-8316 .. 257 D
erin.likens@colin.edu
LIKES, Wendy, M .... 901-448-6135 .. 448 H
wlikes@uthsc.edu
LIKNESS, Tabitha .... 605-668-1566 .. 436 D
tabitha.likness@mtmc.edu
LILES, Jeffrey, R .... 606-783-2000 .. 191 H
j.liles@moreheadstate.edu
LILES, Joel, D .... 740-389-4636 .. 372 B
lilesj@mtc.edu
LILES, Kevin .... 803-641-3319 .. 433 G
kevinl@usca.edu
LILES, Tammy .... 859-246-6449 .. 189 B
tammy.liles@kctcs.edu
LILFORD, Grant .... 912-583-2241 .. 118 B
glilford@bpc.edu
LILIENTHAL, Rhonda .... 615-248-1245 .. 447 F
rlilienthal@trevecca.edu
LILJEGREN, Donna .... 630-947-8914 .. 135 E
dliljegren@aurora.edu
LILJEGREN, Lisa .... 262-243-5700 .. 516 E
lisa.liljegren@cuw.edu
LILLBACK, Peter, A .... 215-572-3811 .. 423 C
plillback@wts.edu
LILLEBO, Troy .... 816-235-6585 .. 273 F
lillebot@umkc.edu
LILLEHAUGEN, Sandi .... 701-662-1543 .. 361 E
sandra.lillehaugen@lrsc.edu
LILLEMON, David .... 507-433-0543 .. 251 H
david.lillemon@riverland.edu
LILLES, Anthony .... 805-482-2755 .... 59 G
alilles@stjohnsem.edu
LILLESTON, Judith .... 914-831-0369 .. 311 C
jlilleston@cw.edu
LILLEY, Ben .... 252-985-5113 .. 354 E
blilley@ncwc.edu
LILLEY, Richard .... 443-840-4698 .. 207 C
rlilley@ccbcmd.edu
LILLGE, Crystal .... 608-796-3841 .. 522 C
clillge@viterbo.edu
LILLIBRIDGE, Fred .... 575-527-7728 .. 301 C
flillibr@nmsu.edu
LILLIE, Deb .... 319-385-6210 .. 174 A
deb.lillie@iw.edu
LILLIE, Sandra .... 720-890-8922 .... 80 C
president@itea.edu
LILLIS, John, R .... 574-372-5100 .. 161 E
lillisjr@grace.edu
LILLQUIST, Erik .... 973-275-4811 .. 297 A
erik.lillquist@shu.edu
LILLQUIST, Mark .... 863-297-1083 .. 106 I
mlilquist@polk.edu
LILLY, Bill .... 304-462-6052 .. 513 C
bill.lilly@glenville.edu
LILLY, Flavius, R .... 410-706-7767 .. 211 F
flilly@umaryland.edu
LILLY, Kenneth, E .... 304-877-6428 .. 510 F
ken.lilly@abc.edu
LILLY, Mary .... 617-732-2144 .. 225 C
mary.lilly@mcphs.edu
LILYARD-MITCHELL,
Corrine .... 757-822-1889 .. 498 H
cmitchell@tcc.edu
LIM, Adrienne, I .... 541-346-3056 .. 395 G
alim@uoregon.edu
LIM, Ben .... 620-229-6388 .. 184 J
ben.lim@sckans.edu
LIM, Bob .... 785-864-4999 .. 185 D
blim@ku.edu
LIM, Choong .... 808-735-4708 .. 130 F
clim@chaminade.edu
LIM, Colleen .... 650-723-2300 .... 66 I
LIM, Dan .... 407-303-9473 .... 95 C
dan.lim@adu.edu
LIM, Gim .... 215-751-8275 .. 401 G
glim@ccp.edu
LIM, Mercy .... 415-442-7080 .... 45 B
mlim@ggu.edu
LIM, Paul .... 213-385-2322 .... 75 E
paul1911@wmu.edu
LIM, Rosy .... 323-731-2383 .... 55 J
rosylim@psuca.edu
LIM, Sung Jin .... 213-385-2322 .... 75 E
sunglim@wmu.edu
LIM, Teik, C .... 513-556-4450 .. 379 A
teik.lim@uc.edu
LIM, Xieng .... 425-739-8264 .. 504 F
xieng.lim@lwtech.edu
LIM-THOMPSON,
Soo-Yin .... 218-281-8248 .. 255 E
slimthom@umn.edu
LIMA, Brad .... 508-830-5012 .. 222 C
blima@maritime.edu
LIMA, Judy, L .... 205-329-7904 ...... 3 B
judy.lima@ecacolleges.edu
LIMAS, Celestino .... 509-865-8580 .. 504 D
limas_c@heritage.edu
LIMAYEM, Moez .... 813-974-3229 .. 112 C
mlimayem@usf.edu
LIMBACH, Patrick, A .... 513-558-0026 .. 379 A
pat.limbach@uc.edu
LIMBIRD, Lee .... 615-329-1907 .. 439 L
llimbird@fisk.edu
LIMONCELLI, Jerry .... 516-686-7815 .. 323 G
jlimonce@nyit.edu
LIMPER, Leslie .... 503-352-2871 .. 394 C
limp5635@pacificu.edu
LIMTUATCO, Edwin, E .... 671-735-5560 .. 529 G
edwin.limtuatco@guamcc.edu
LIN, Anne .... 410-532-5545 .. 210 B
alin@ndm.edu
LIN, Chia-Yen .... 619-260-7692 .... 72 B
linc@sandiego.edu
LIN, Ellen .... 408-924-5910 .... 35 C
ellen.lin@sjsu.edu
LIN, Janice .... 219-464-5333 .. 168 F
janice.lin@valpo.edu
LIN, Kathleen .... 626-571-5110 .... 49 B
kathleenlin@les.edu
LIN, Kuo-Liang .... 626-571-5110 .... 49 B
klin@les.edu
LIN, Lisa (Ping-Hui) .... 512-444-8082 .. 470 B
lisalin@thsu.edu
LIN, Paul .... 512-444-8082 .. 470 B
thsu@thsu.edu
LIN, Susan, X .... 808-956-7161 .. 131 D
slin@hawaii.edu
LIN, Yi-Chun Tricia .... 203-392-6864 .... 85 H
lyny4@southernct.edu
LIN-COOK, Wendy .... 973-596-3309 .. 293 D
wendy.w.lin-cook@njit.edu
LINAKER, Kathleen .... 315-792-5376 .. 321 G
klinaker@mvcc.edu
LINAM, Alisha .... 251-575-8271 ...... 1 C
alinam@ascc.edu
LINAM, Gail .... 214-333-5372 .. 455 J
gaill@dbu.edu
LINAMEN, Larry .... 951-552-8744 .... 29 H
llinamen@calbaptist.edu
LINBACK, John .... 574-936-8898 .. 158 I
john.linback@ancilla.edu
LINC, Linda .... 330-490-7250 .. 380 J
llinc@walsh.edu
LINCKE, James .... 610-353-7630 .. 398 I
LINCOLN, Holly .... 636-481-3230 .. 266 C
hlincoln@jeffco.edu
LINCOLN, Jonathan .... 973-720-2580 .. 298 G
lincolnj@wpunj.edu
LINCOLN, Judy .... 314-837-6777 .. 271 B
jlincoln@stlchristian.edu
LINCOLN, Timothy .... 512-404-4873 .. 452 A
tlincoln@austinseminary.edu
LIND, Hanna .... 702-579-3548 .. 283 I
hlind@kaplan.edu
LIND, James, F .... 757-451-6200 .. 489 B
lindjf@evms.edu
LIND, Jan .... 812-877-8297 .. 166 H
lind@rose-hulman.edu
LIND, Kristen .... 218-322-2403 .. 249 G
kristen.lind@itascacc.edu
LIND, William .... 843-953-5011 .. 428 A
wlind@citadel.edu
LIND-GONZALEZ,
Patricia .... 631-420-2298 .. 335 E
patricia.lind-gonzalez@farmingdale.edu
LINDAHL, Roberta, D .... 503-943-7321 .. 396 B
lindahl@up.edu
LINDAHL, Susan .... 913-288-7645 .. 182 C
slindahl@kckcc.edu
LINDAHL, Susan .... 715-232-1184 .. 521 D
lindahls@uwstout.edu
LINDAHL, Wesley .... 773-244-5667 .. 149 I
wlindahl@northpark.edu
LINDBALD, Gary .... 562-903-4770 .... 28 E
gary.lindbald@biola.edu
LINDBERG, Brad .... 641-269-3250 .. 172 I
lindbergb@grinnell.edu
LINDBERG, Kevin, D .... 956-326-2601 .. 468 A
klindberg@tamiu.edu
LINDELL, Belinda, S .... 218-755-2043 .. 248 M
blindell@bemidjistate.edu
LINDELL, P. Griffith .... 503-375-7034 .. 391 B
glindell@corban.edu
LINDEMAN, Barbara .... 573-882-6007 .. 273 E
lindemanb@missouri.edu
LINDEMAN, Brian .... 651-696-6214 .. 247 I
lindeman@macalester.edu
LINDEMAN, Craig .... 316-978-7282 .. 185 J
craig.lindeman@wichita.edu
LINDEMUTH, Gregory, L . 610-566-1776 .. 423 H
glindemuth@williamson.edu
LINDEN, Eric .... 646-565-6000 .. 337 I
elinden@touro.edu
LINDEN, Erika .... 515-271-1526 .. 171 H
erika.linden@dmu.edu
LINDEN, Stephen, M .... 248-341-2192 .. 239 E
smlinden@oaklandcc.edu
LINDENBAUM, Sharon .... 816-235-2650 .. 273 F
lindenbaums@umkc.edu
LINDENBERG, David, A ... 802-447-6360 .. 485 B
dlindenberg@svc.edu
LINDENMAYER, Kathleen 203-837-8266 .... 85 I
lindenmayerk@wcsu.edu
LINDENMEYER, Kriste .... 856-225-2809 .. 296 A
kriste.lindenmeyer@camden.rutgers.edu
LINDENMEYER, Mark, L .. 410-617-2576 .. 208 G
lindenmeyer@loyola.edu

LINDENMEYR, Adele .... 610-519-4606.. 422 G
adele.lindenmeyr@villanova.edu
LINDER, Carol .... 505-454-3311.. 300 F
clinder@nmhu.edu
LINDER, Cynthia .... 912-287-4098.. 119 B
clinder@coastalpines.edu
LINDER, Kate .... 724-357-2455.. 415 B
krlinder@iup.edu
LINDER, Mark .... 256-765-4397..... 9 C
mdlinder@una.edu
LINDER, Roberta .... 937-327-6342.. 381 F
rlinder@wittenberg.edu
LINDGREN, Dianne .... 828-339-4269.. 353 D
diannel@southwesterncc.edu
LINDGREN, Rita .... 701-224-5427.. 361 C
rita.lindgren@bismarckstate.edu
LINDGREN, Robert, R .... 804-752-7211.. 493 C
rlindgren@rmc.edu
LINDGREN, Teresa, C ..... 606-783-2449.. 191 H
t.lindgren@moreheadstate.edu
LINDLEY, Carolyn, V ..... 847-491-8557.. 150 F
c-lindley@northwestern.edu
LINDLEY, Kelli .... 208-467-8825.. 134 D
klindley@nnu.edu
LINDLEY, Stu .... 314-744-7623.. 268 F
lindleys@mobap.edu
LINDMAN, Barbara, A ..... 651-631-5247.. 256 A
balindman@unwsp.edu
LINDNER, Angela .... 352-273-1102.. 112 A
alindner@aa.ufl.edu
LINDNER, Bill .... 850-644-7572.. 111 C
blindner@fsu.edu
LINDNER, Janet, E .... 203-432-2188.... 90 D
janet.lindner@yale.edu
LINDNER, JoEllen .... 605-626-2530.. 437 D
joellen.lindner@northern.edu
LINDNER, Rosalyn, A ..... 716-878-6939.. 332 F
lindera@buffalostate.edu
LINDO, Patricia .... 860-512-3613.... 86 E
plindo@manchestercc.edu
LINDO, Richanna .... 518-828-4181.. 311 D
richanna.lindo@sunycgcc.edu
LINDON, Jennifer .... 606-487-3136.. 189 E
jennifer.lindon@kctcs.edu
LINDON, Jennifer .... 606-487-3100.. 189 E
LINDOR, Keith, D .... 602-496-0789.... 11 H
keith.lindor@asu.edu
LINDQUIST, Brent .... 806-742-2566.. 472 C
brent.lindquist@ttu.edu
LINDQUIST, Cynthia, A ... 701-766-4055.. 360 A
president@littlehoop.edu
LINDQUIST, Joyce .... 970-207-4550.... 81 F
joycel@mckinleycollege.edu
LINDQUIST, Joyce .... 970-207-4500.... 84 F
joycel@uscareerinstitute.edu
LINDQUIST, Kathy .... 918-335-6234.. 386 F
klindquist@okwu.edu
LINDQUIST, Kimberly ...... 734-384-4101.. 238 C
klindquist@monroeccc.edu
LINDQUIST, Robert .... 256-824-2882...... 8 F
robert.lindquist@uah.edu
LINDQUIST, Robert .... 256-824-6100...... 8 F
robert.lindquist@uah.edu
LINDQUIST, Stefanie, A ... 706-542-2059.. 128 E
sl@uga.edu
LINDQUIST, Vern, L .... 804-862-6491.. 493 F
vllindquist@rbc.edu
LINDSAY, Barbara .... 303-360-4914.... 79 E
barbara.lindsay@ccaurora.edu
LINDSAY, Cecile .... 562-985-4128.... 33 B
cecile.lindsay@csulb.edu
LINDSAY, Charles, W ..... 607-735-1804.. 313 F
clindsay@elmira.edu
LINDSAY, Cheryl, A .... 315-255-1743.. 306 G
cheryl.lindsay@cayuga-cc.edu
LINDSAY, D. Michael ..... 978-867-4800.. 219 A
president@gordon.edu
LINDSAY, Dane .... 619-388-7823.... 60 H
dlindsay@sdccd.edu
LINDSAY, David .... 209-667-3288.... 34 E
dlindsay@csustan.edu
LINDSAY, Dawn, S .... 410-777-1177.. 206 B
dslindsay@aacc.edu
LINDSAY, Dennis .... 541-684-7253.. 393 B
dlindsay@nwcu.edu
LINDSAY, John .... 401-232-6154.. 424 K
jlindsay@bryant.edu
LINDSAY, Jonathan .... 603-623-0313.. 287 D
jonathanlindsay@nhia.edu
LINDSAY, Melissa .... 541-880-2392.. 391 F
lindsay@klamathcc.edu
LINDSAY, Nathan .... 406-243-4689.. 276 K
nathan.lindsay@umontana.edu
LINDSAY, Shawn .... 417-626-1234.. 269 K
lindsay.shawn@occ.edu
LINDSAY, Terry .... 518-327-6490.. 326 B
tlindsay@paulsmiths.edu
LINDSAY, Twila .... 301-548-5500.... 93 F
LINDSAY, Twila .... 202-722-8100.... 93 F
LINDSAY, Wanda .... 870-543-5950.... 22 E
wlindsay@seark.edu
LINDSAY-DENNIS,
LaShawnda .... 706-821-8726.. 125 H
llindsaydennis@paine.edu
LINDSETH, Lori .... 602-787-7102.... 14 E
lori.lindseth@paradisevalley.edu
LINDSETH, Paul .... 701-777-2791.. 360 C
lindseth@aero.und.edu
LINDSEY, April .... 336-821-2479.. 345 C
alindsey@johnwesley.edu
LINDSEY, Bethany .... 206-855-9559.. 506 E
bethany.lindsey@pinchot.edu
LINDSEY, Beverly .... 662-846-4009.. 257 E
blindsey@deltastate.edu
LINDSEY, Bruce, M .... 314-935-6200.. 274 N
blindsey@wustl.edu
LINDSEY, DeLois .... 860-768-5122.... 89 G
lindsey@hartford.edu
LINDSEY, Heidie .... 337-482-6272.. 201 D
hlindsey@louisiana.edu
LINDSEY, John .... 336-887-3000.. 345 C
jlindsey@johnwesley.edu
LINDSEY, Johnetta .... 601-977-4458.. 261 A
jlindsey@tougaloo.edu
LINDSEY, Kristin .... 810-424-5448.. 242 B
krislind@umflint.edu
LINDSEY, Lee .... 707-476-4100.... 40 D
lee-lindsey@redwoods.edu
LINDSEY, Ophelia .... 870-574-4480.... 22 G
olindsey@sautech.edu
LINDSEY, Pamela, L .... 217-424-6348.. 148 D
plindsey@millikin.edu
LINDSEY, Patrick, O .... 313-577-4228.. 243 F
patrick.lindsey@wayne.edu
LINDSEY, Shannon .... 785-628-4462.. 180 I
sdlindsey@fhsu.edu
LINDSEY, Terryl .... 918-293-4730.. 386 B
terryl.lindsey@okstate.edu
LINDSEY, Trumanue .... 651-779-3204.. 249 A
trumanue.lindsey@century.edu
LINDSTAEDT, William ...... 415-502-2422.... 70 D
bill.lindstaedt@ucsf.edu
LINDSTEDT, Monique .... 815-394-4376.. 152 G
mlindstedt@rockford.edu
LINDSTEN, Traci .... 605-331-6575.. 438 A
traci.lindsten@usiouxfalls.edu
LINDSTROM, David .... 509-527-2664.. 508 G
david.lindstrom@wallawalla.edu
LINDSTROM, Derrick .... 612-659-6030.. 250 B
derrick.lindstrom@minneapolis.edu
LINDSTROM, Lynne .... 563-884-5313.. 176 C
lynne.lindstrom@palmer.edu
LINDSTROM, Richard, W . 323-563-5832.... 37 G
richardlindstrom@cdrewu.edu
LINDSTROM, Ryan .... 801-863-8303.. 482 C
lindstry@uvu.edu
LINDSTROM, Yvonne .... 313-578-0328.. 241 G
lindstym@udmercy.edu
LINDTORTH, Scott, A ...... 919-684-0539.. 343 J
scott.lindroth@duke.edu
LINDUSKA, Kim .... 515-964-6628.. 171 B
kjlinduska@dmacc.edu
LINEBACK, Carla .... 802-258-3266.. 485 A
carla.lineback@worldlearning.org
LINEBERGER,
Susanne, B .... 386-312-4050.. 108 B
susannelineberger@sjrstate.edu
LINEBERRY, Gene, T .... 859-323-6589.. 193 G
gt.lineberry@uky.edu
LINEBERRY, Kevin .... 336-249-8186.. 349 C
kevin_lineberry@davidsonccc.edu
LINEBURG, Robert .... 540-831-5228.. 493 A
rlineburg@radford.edu
LINEHAN, Rob .... 765-998-4905.. 167 C
rblinehan@taylor.edu
LINEHAN, Sarah, J .... 518-743-2263.. 335 A
linehans@sunyacc.edu
LINER, Andrea .... 979-830-4413.. 452 J
andrea.liner@blinn.edu
LINFANTE, Patrick .... 973-761-9328.. 297 A
patrick.linfante@shu.edu
LINGEFELT, Jeff .... 803-938-3784.. 434 E
jdlingef@uscsumter.edu
LINGEN, Scott .... 701-224-5441.. 361 C
scott.lingen@bismarckstate.edu
LINGER, Frederick, S ..... 740-427-5250.. 371 C
lingerf@kenyon.edu
LINGER, Rob .... 304-367-4692.. 512 D
rob.linger@pierpont.edu
LINGLE, Richard .... 816-279-7000.. 262 B
richard.lingle@abtu.edu
LINGLE, Richard .... 213-252-5100.... 24 K
rlingle@alu.edu
LINGLE, Ronald, K .... 910-938-6211.. 348 G
lingler@coastalcarolina.edu
LINGRELL, Scott .... 678-839-6423.. 129 E
slingrel@westga.edu
LINGUA, Jan .... 314-256-8864.. 262 D
lingua@ai.edu
LINGUA, Jane .... 310-954-4132.... 53 B
jlingua@msmu.edu
LINHART, Steve .... 719-255-3838.... 83 L
slinhart@uccs.edu
LINING, Tina .... 440-684-6085.. 380 F
troan@ursuline.edu
LINIO, Rick, T .... 606-783-2066.. 191 H
r.linio@moreheadstate.edu
LINK, Christine, A .... 626-963-0323.... 38 D
clink@citruscollege.edu
LINK, Eric, C .... 260-481-5751.. 163 C
eric.link@ipfw.edu
LINK, Harvey .... 701-671-2112.. 361 F
harvey.link@ndscs.edu
LINK, Hilary, L .... 215-204-7000.. 420 B
hilary.link@temple.edu
LINK, Jane, J .... 316-978-3186.. 185 J
jane.link@wichita.edu
LINK, Johnson .... 864-656-7389.. 428 C
jwl@clemson.edu
LINK, Laura .... 612-874-3700.. 247 M
laura_link@mcad.edu
LINK, Laura, R .... 540-224-4668.. 491 A
lrlink@jchs.edu
LINK, Robert .... 419-434-4528.. 379 E
link@findlay.edu
LINK, Rosemary, J .... 515-961-1615.. 176 H
rosemary.link@simpson.edu
LINK, Stephen .... 202-687-1747.... 92 E
spl8@georgetown.edu
LINKER, Kari .... 970-542-3113.... 81 H
kari.linker@morgancc.edu
LINKER, Timothy, L .... 336-841-9313.. 345 A
tlinker@highpoint.edu
LINKHAUER, SC, Vivien .. 724-830-1052.. 419 D
linkhauer@setonhill.edu
LINKS, Jonathan .... 410-516-6880.. 208 D
jlinks1@jhu.edu
LINMAN, Eric .... 503-255-0332.. 392 G
elinman@multnomah.edu
LINN, Brent .... 901-375-4400.. 442 F
brentlinn@midsouthchristian.edu
LINN, Chad .... 501-205-8912.... 19 J
clinn@cbc.edu
LINN, Joseph, G .... 785-628-4277.. 180 I
jlinn@fhsu.edu
LINN, Richard, T .... 716-827-3451.. 338 E
linnr@trocaire.edu
LINN, Timon .... 410-626-6931.. 210 D
timon.linn@sjc.edu
LINNANE, SJ, Brian, F .... 410-617-2201.. 208 G
president@loyola.edu
LINNEHAN, Francis .... 215-895-2122.. 402 G
francis.linnehan@drexel.edu
LINNEMAN, Scott .... 360-650-7207.. 509 E
scott.linneman@wwu.edu
LINNEVERS, David .... 831-582-3094.... 33 E
dlinnevers@csumb.edu
LINNEWEBER, Travis, W . 765-658-4175.. 160 F
travislinneweber@depauw.edu
LINO, Paulette .... 510-723-2665.... 37 B
plino@chabotcollege.edu
LINOS, Megan, W .... 812-465-1061.. 168 E
mwlinos@usi.edu
LINSENMEYER, Machelle . 304-793-6871.. 514 A
alinsenmeyer@osteo.wvsom.edu
LINSEY, Carolyn, R .... 203-576-2374.... 89 C
clinsey@bridgeport.edu
LINSEY, Troy .... 678-513-5202.. 123 L
tlinsey@laniertech.edu
LINSIN, James .... 618-650-2842.. 155 A
jlinsin@siue.edu
LINSON, Marci .... 417-690-2636.. 263 E
linson@cofo.edu
LINSON, Robert .... 202-885-6013.... 91 J
rlinson@american.edu
LINSTRA, Ralph .... 434-582-2330.. 491 D
rlinstra@liberty.edu
LINTHICUM, Glen .... 615-248-1243.. 447 F
glinthicum@trevecca.edu
LINTNER, Tim .... 803-641-3564.. 433 G
tlintner@usca.edu
LINTON, Eugene .... 419-289-6995.. 363 J
elinton@ashland.edu
LINTON, Greg .... 865-573-4517.. 440 I
glinton@johnsonu.edu
LINTON, Leon, E .... 847-229-9595.. 154 D
LINTON, Pamela .... 212-752-1530.. 318 F
pamela.linton@limcollege.edu
LINTON, Peggy .... 334-493-3573...... 5 F
plinton@lbwcc.edu
LINTON, Richard, H .... 919-515-2668.. 357 B
richard_linton@ncsu.edu
LINTS, Richard .... 978-468-7111.. 219 B
rlints@gcts.edu
LINTZ, Amy .... 717-867-6161.. 408 F
lintz@lvc.edu
LINVILL, Christine .... 215-885-2360.. 409 G
clinvill@manor.edu
LINVILLE, Joann .... 225-216-8361.. 195 H
linvillej@mybrcc.edu
LINZER, Daniel, I .... 847-491-5117.. 150 F
dlinzer@northwestern.edu
LINZEY, Scott .... 912-525-5000.. 126 E
slinzey@scad.edu
LINZMEYER, Kathryn .... 510-723-6751.... 37 B
klinzmeyer@chabotcollege.edu
LION, Benjamin, C .... 407-582-1388.. 114 N
blion@valenciacollege.edu
LIOTTA, Sheila, A .... 401-865-2600.. 425 D
sadamus@providence.edu
LIPAN, Petruta .... 314-977-3571.. 271 K
lipanp@slu.edu
LIPE, Leslie .... 503-338-2450.. 390 G
llipe@clatsopcc.edu
LIPE, Lisa, M .... 207-834-7607.. 205 B
lisa.lipe@maine.edu
LIPHART, Jodi .... 904-826-0084.... 72 A
jliphart@usa.edu
LIPHART, Kristy .... 715-682-1496.. 518 H
kliphart@northland.edu
LIPINSKI, Tomas .... 414-229-4709.. 520 D
tlipinski@uwm.edu
LIPITZ, Jon .... 410-225-2516.. 209 B
jlipitz@mica.edu
LIPIZ GONZALEZ, Elaine 714-484-7277.... 54 G
egonzalez@cypresscollege.edu
LIPKIN, Michael .... 212-463-0400.. 337 I
michael.lipkin2@touro.edu
LIPMAN, Howard .... 305-348-6298.. 111 A
howard.lipman@fiu.edu
LIPOLD, Tony .... 949-582-4547.... 65 G
tlipold@saddleback.edu
LIPP, Evan, E .... 508-767-7285.. 214 F
elipp@assumption.edu
LIPP, Jacob .... 713-226-5585.. 474 B
lippp@uhd.edu
LIPPARD, Jed .... 212-875-4422.. 304 E
jlippard@bankstreet.edu
LIPPARD, Rodney .... 704-216-3686.. 352 G
rodney.lippard@rccc.edu
LIPPE, Diane .... 954-262-4932.. 105 J
lipped@nova.edu
LIPPENS, Susan, M .... 419-866-0261.. 377 L
smlippens@stautzenberger.com
LIPPERT, Patricia, A .... 812-488-2152.. 167 I
pl23@evansville.edu
LIPPERT, Rebecca .... 215-702-4241.. 399 E
blippert@cairn.edu
LIPPERT, Robert .... 559-453-2189.... 44 F
robert.lippert@fresno.edu
LIPPIELLO, Steve .... 724-925-4071.. 423 D
lippiellos@wccc.edu
LIPPINCOTT, Amanda, L .. 607-274-1574.. 317 D
alippincott@ithaca.edu
LIPPINCOTT, James .... 503-375-5304.. 396 G
jlippinc@willamette.edu
LIPPMAN, Fred .... 954-262-1508.. 105 J
flippman@nsu.nova.edu
LIPPMAN, Stuart .... 646-565-6000.. 337 I
stuartl@touro.edu
LIPSCHUTZ, Ronnie .... 831-459-3275.... 70 F
rligsch@ucsc.edu
LIPSCOMB, Benjamin ...... 585-567-9374.. 316 F
benjamin.lipscomb@houghton.edu
LIPSCOMB, Kimberly .... 212-616-7283.. 315 G
kimberly.lipscomb@helenefuld.edu
LIPSCOMB, Natasha .... 704-216-3622.. 352 G
natasha.lipscomb@rccc.edu
LIPSCOMB, Rodney .... 940-498-6445.. 462 L
rlipscomb@nctc.edu
LIPSCOMB, Sharon, M ..... 919-516-4203.. 355 D
smlipscomb@st-aug.edu
LIPSCOMB, Sharyon .... 225-578-8833.. 197 H
slipsc1@lsu.edu
LIPSCOMB, Tamra .... 540-863-2905.. 496 H
tlipscomb@dslcc.edu
LIPSETT, Teresa .... 787-743-7979.. 536 A
ut_tlipsett@suagm.edu
LIPSHITZ, Rita .... 773-973-0241.. 141 D
lipshitz@htc.edu
LIPSKIER, Hershel .... 973-267-9404.. 294 F
LIPSTREU, Tiffany .... 614-823-1414.. 376 C
tlipstreu@otterbein.edu
LIPTON, Mitchell .... 212-353-4126.. 311 G
lipton@cooper.edu
LIQUORI, Gary .... 401-874-1000.. 426 D
LIRA, Ken .... 949-451-5435.... 65 F
klira@ivc.edu
LIRLEY, Sean .... 719-336-1543.... 81 D
sean.lirley@lamarcc.edu
LISCHIN, Renee .... 973-408-3955.. 291 B
rlischin@drew.edu
LISCHKA, Rosemary, L ..... 913-288-7246.. 182 C
rlischka@kckcc.edu
LISCHWE, Sheila, T .... 864-656-1661.. 428 C
slischw@clemson.edu
LISCIO, Gina .... 315-792-7288.. 336 C
gina.liscio@sunyit.edu
LISENBY, Sadie .... 901-321-3527.. 439 E
slisenby@cbu.edu
LISENBY, Woods, B .... 334-833-4474...... 4 D
chaplain@hawks.huntingdon.edu

LISI, Claire ... 631-420-2239.. 335 E
claire.lisi@farmingdale.edu
LISI, Peter ... 860-768-2446.... 89 G
lisi@hartford.edu
LISK, Patti ... 540-423-9824.. 497 B
plisk@germanna.edu
LISKER, Donna ... 413-585-4900.. 228 D
dlisker@smith.edu
LISLE, Kristy ... 773-602-5020.. 137 F
clisle@ccc.edu
LISS, Donna ... 660-785-4163.. 273 B
dliss@truman.edu
LISS, Julia, E ... 909-607-3541.... 64 A
julia.liss@scrippscollege.edu
LISS, Ron ... 928-717-7778.... 18 D
ron.liss@yc.edu
LISS, Tony ... 212-650-7947.. 307 E
tliss@ccny.cuny.edu
LISSY, Barbara, G ... 215-576-0800.. 417 H
blissy@rrc.edu
LIST, Allison ... 631-687-5198.. 328 G
alist@sjcny.edu
LISTER, Basil ... 816-604-6748.. 267 G
basil.lister@mcckc.edu
LISTER, Carole, B ... 864-597-4230.. 435 C
listercb@wofford.edu
LISTER, Charlotte, T ... 302-857-1290.... 91 C
clister@dtcc.edu
LISTER, Kevin ... 314-367-8700.. 271 E
kevin.lister@stlcop.edu
LISTER, Tommy ... 626-584-5338.... 44 G
tommylister@fuller.edu
LISTI, Garnette ... 504-762-3032.. 196 D
glisti@dcc.edu
LISTON, Brenda ... 614-947-6532.. 369 A
brenda.liston@franklin.edu
LISTON, Sunny ... 503-534-4007.. 392 D
sliston@marylhurst.edu
LISTWAK, Jeffrey, A ... 412-397-5261.. 418 B
listwak@rmu.edu
LISZEWSKI, Stephen ... 410-293-1000.. 529 D
LISZKA, James, A ... 518-564-5402.. 334 A
jlisz001@plattsburgh.edu
LISZKA, Justin ... 336-272-7102.. 344 G
justin.liszka@greensboro.edu
LITCH, Mary ... 714-628-2753.... 37 F
litch@chapman.edu
LITCHMAN, Jennifer, B ... 410-706-3477.. 211 F
jlitchman@umaryland.edu
LITHERLAND, Steve, E ... 757-822-1944.. 498 H
slitherland@tcc.edu
LITMAN, Kay ... 610-372-4721.. 417 G
klitman@racc.edu
LITOLFF, Edwin ... 225-342-6950.. 200 E
edwin.litolff@la.gov
LITT, Eleni ... 212-229-8947.. 322 E
litte@newschool.edu
LITT, Jacquelyn, S ... 573-882-0647.. 273 E
littj@missouri.edu
LITT, Jacquelyn, S ... 848-932-2900.. 296 B
jacquelyn.litt@rutgers.edu
LITTERAL, David ... 973-300-2148.. 297 D
dlitteral@sussex.edu
LITTERAL, Samuel, M ... 304-896-7426.. 512 E
samuel.litteral@southernwv.edu
LITTLE, Albert ... 904-632-5167.. 101 G
al.little@fscj.edu
LITTLE, Andrew, P ... 410-777-2227.. 206 B
aplittle1@aacc.edu
LITTLE, Daniel ... 313-593-5500.. 242 A
delittle@umich.edu
LITTLE, Glenn, W ... 863-784-7218.. 109 G
glenn.little@southflorida.edu
LITTLE, Gloria ... 212-787-5300.. 303 G
LITTLE, Jennifer ... 864-592-4808.. 432 H
littlej@sccsc.edu
LITTLE, Kendall, G ... 601-977-7870.. 261 A
klittle@tougaloo.edu
LITTLE, Kevin, K ... 831-656-2508.. 528 D
klittle@nps.edu
LITTLE, Lara ... 704-463-3353.. 354 F
lara.little@pfeiffer.edu
LITTLE, Linda ... 559-325-5205.... 67 E
linda.little@scccd.edu
LITTLE, Nicole ... 302-622-8000.... 90 E
nlittle@dcad.edu
LITTLE, Rebecca, K ... 812-888-4220.. 169 A
rlittle@vinu.edu
LITTLE, Scott ... 601-968-5956.. 256
slittle@belhaven.edu
LITTLE, Shanon ... 415-257-1302.... 42 G
shanon.little@dominican.edu
LITTLE, Sylvester ... 863-292-3762.. 106
slittle@polk.edu
LITTLE, Verna, S ... 334-727-8503..... 8 A
little@mytu.tuskegee.edu
LITTLE, William ... 607-962-9458.. 312 E
wlittle@corning-cc.edu
LITTLE-BERRY, Teri ... 352-854-2322.... 97 F
berryt@cf.edu
LITTLE WHITEMAN, Iona ... 701-627-4738.. 361 H
ilittl@nhsc.edu
LITTLEBEAR, Richard ... 406-477-6215.. 276 C
rlbear@cdkc.edu
LITTLEFIELD, Elizabeth, S ... 804-523-5181.. 497 C
blittlefield@reynolds.edu
LITTLEFIELD, Julie ... 979-230-3576.. 453 A
julie.littlefield@brazosport.edu
LITTLEJOHN, Angela, F ... 864-294-2171.. 430 C
angela.littlejohn@furman.edu
LITTLEJOHN, Sylvia ... 803-738-7764.. 431 B
littlejohns@midlandstech.edu
LITTLEPAGE, Craig, K ... 434-982-5100.. 495 H
ckl9e@virginia.edu
LITTLETON, Denise ... 757-823-8701.. 492 F
LITTLETON, Robert, A ... 423-652-6022.. 440 J
ralittle@king.edu
LITTLETON-STEIB,
Larissa ... 504-671-6488.. 196 D
lsteib@dcc.edu
LITTMAN, Jared, E ... 718-990-2920.. 328 F
littmanj@stjohns.edu
LITTON, Freddie ... 361-570-4261.. 474 C
littonf@uhv.edu
LITTREL, Darla ... 972-923-6440.. 462 J
darla.littrel@navarrocollege.edu
LITTRELL, Beth ... 402-461-7372.. 280 D
blittrell@hastings.edu
LITTRELL, Johnny ... 931-540-2840.. 446 A
jlittrell@columbiastate.edu
LITTRELL, Meghann ... 513-244-4524.. 373 C
meghann.littrell@msj.edu
LITVINOV, Dimitri ... 713-743-4168.. 473 F
litvinov@central.uh.edu
LITWACK, Kim ... 414-229-4189.. 520 D
litwack@uwm.edu
LITWILLER, Eric ... 316-295-5820.. 181 B
eric_litwiller@friends.edu
LITWIN, Daveen, H ... 603-646-3780.. 286 J
daveen.h.litwin@dartmouth.edu
LITYNSKI, Daniel, M ... 269-387-8294.. 243 H
dan.litynski@wmich.edu
LITZ, Kerri ... 410-225-2277.. 209 B
klitz@mica.edu
LITZIN, Louise ... 928-724-6633.... 12 T
louise@dinecollege.edu
LITZMAN, Darcy ... 970-204-8375.... 80 E
darcy.litzman@frontrange.edu
LIU, Alan ... 626-289-7719.... 25 H
aliu@amu.edu
LIU, Lan ... 860-343-5833.... 86 F
lliu@mxcc.commnet.edu
LIU, Linyan ... 650-493-4430.... 64 I
linyan.liu@itp.edu
LIU, Monika ... 415-452-5730.... 38 E
mliu@ccsf.edu
LIU, Shuang ... 410-337-6062.. 207 H
shuang.liu@goucher.edu
LIU, Victor ... 734-973-3379.. 242 G
vliu@wccnet.edu
LIU, Ying ... 419-530-1248.. 380 D
ying.liu3@utoledo.edu
LIU, Ying ... 919-508-2048.. 359 G
ying.liu@peace.edu
LIU, Zhanjiang ... 334-844-4784..... 1 G
liuzhan@auburn.edu
LIVELY, Alisa ... 304-473-8441.. 515 B
lively_a@wvwc.edu
LIVELY, David ... 847-467-1829.. 150 F
david.lively@northwestern.edu
LIVELY, Lisa, A ... 304-293-8638.. 514 C
lisa.lively@mail.wvu.edu
LIVELY, Sam ... 951-343-4726.... 29 H
slively@calbaptist.edu
LIVELY, Shane ... 203-596-8507.... 88 F
slively@post.edu
LIVENGOOD, Lori ... 316-394-5227.. 179 A
llivengood@bethelks.edu
LIVENGOOD, Naomi ... 269-965-3931.. 236 A
livengoodn@kellogg.edu
LIVESAY, Dennis ... 316-978-3095.. 185 J
dennis.livesay@wichita.edu
LIVESAY, Stephen, D ... 423-775-7201.. 439 B
livesast@bryan.edu
LIVESAY, Wayne ... 410-386-8249.. 206 I
wlivesay@carrollcc.edu
LIVINGOOD,
Susannah, B ... 405-325-5065.. 389 B
slivingood@ou.edu
LIVINGSTON, Carolyn ... 507-222-4248.. 245 C
clivingston@carleton.edu
LIVINGSTON, David, J ... 815-836-5230.. 145 H
dlivingston@lewisu.edu
LIVINGSTON, Esther ... 859-985-3065.. 187 B
livginstone@berea.edu
LIVINGSTON, Geraldine ... 803-376-5700.. 427 A
glivingston@allenuniversity.edu
LIVINGSTON, Joe, A ... 407-582-8069.. 114 N
jlivingston@valenciacollege.edu
LIVINGSTON, Kathy ... 308-865-8204.. 282 L
livingstonke@unk.edu
LIVINGSTON, Lynette ... 715-858-1849.. 523 B
livingston3@cvtc.edu
LIVINGSTON, Randy ... 650-724-0213.... 66 I
livingston@stanford.edu
LIVINGSTON, Sarah, M ... 402-399-2430.. 279 E
slivingston@csm.edu
LIVINGSTON, Shannon ... 715-675-3331.. 524 D
livingst@ntc.edu
LIVINGSTON, Stan ... 601-477-4006.. 258 E
stan.livingston@jcjc.edu
LIVINGSTON, Tina ... 903-886-5667.. 468 D
tina.livingston@tamuc.edu
LIVINGSTONE, Linda, A ... 202-994-6380.... 92 D
llivings@gwu.edu
LIVIO, Michael, D ... 609-497-7805.. 294 C
michael.livio@ptsem.edu
LIWAG, Jonathan ... 670-237-6750.. 530 D
jonathan.liwag@marianas.edu
LIZAN, Rey ... 757-490-1241.. 486 E
rlizan@auto.edu
LIZARDI, David ... 787-738-2161.. 538 A
david.lizardi@upr.edu
LIZER, Shannon, K ... 815-227-2444.. 153 D
shannon.lizer@sacn.edu
LIZOTTE, Edmund ... 860-628-4751.... 88 C
elizotte@lincolncollegene.edu
LJUBICIC, Amanda ... 860-629-6115.... 88 D
ljubicic_a@mitchell.edu
LJUNGDAHL, Anders ... 617-746-1990.. 219 G
anders.ljungdahl@hult.edu
LLANA, James ... 212-237-8110.. 308 E
jllana@jjay.cuny.edu
LLANOS, Karen ... 787-620-2040.. 530 F
kllanos@aupr.edu
LLERANDI, Joanne, A ... 718-990-1487.. 328 F
llerandj@stjohns.edu
LLERANDI, Mariel ... 787-878-5475.. 533 H
mllerandi@arecibo.inter.edu
LLERENA, Fernando, N ... 305-273-4499.... 97 M
fllerena@cbt.edu
LLERENA, Gladys, P ... 305-273-4499.... 97 M
gladys@cbt.edu
LLERENA, Luis, E ... 305-273-4499.... 97 M
luis@cbt.edu
LLERENA, Monica ... 305-273-4499.... 97 M
monica@cbt.edu
LLOPIZ, Maria ... 773-481-8323.. 137 I
mllopiz@ccc.edu
LLORENS, Ashley, J ... 410-955-5107.. 208 D
ashley.llorens@jhuapl.edu
LLOSA, Talia ... 845-341-4090.. 325 H
talia.llosa@sunyorange.edu
LLOVIO, Kay ... 916-577-2200.... 75 C
kllovio@jessup.edu
LLOYD, Andrea ... 802-443-5735.. 484 F
lloyd@middlebury.edu
LLOYD, Celia, P ... 212-650-7859.. 307 E
clloyd@ccny.cuny.edu
LLOYD, Charles ... 603-271-6484.. 286 F
clloyd@ccsnh.edu
LLOYD, Charmaine, F ... 203-392-5250.... 85 H
lloydc1@southernct.edu
LLOYD, Chris ... 215-702-4339.. 399 E
clloyd@cairn.edu
LLOYD, Christine ... 239-590-1425.. 110 L
clloyd@fgcu.edu
LLOYD, Curtis ... 518-320-1192.. 330 H
curtis.lloyd@suny.edu
LLOYD, Daniel ... 630-942-2865.. 138 B
lloydd@cod.edu
LLOYD, David ... 985-543-4120.. 196 G
LLOYD, David ... 765-998-4634.. 167 C
dvlloyd@taylor.edu
LLOYD, Don ... 573-897-5000.. 272 H
LLOYD, Giovina ... 607-871-2966.. 303 F
lloydgm@alfred.edu
LLOYD, Glen, D ... 507-933-6517.. 246 J
glloyd@gustavus.edu
LLOYD, Gweneth ... 845-257-2920.. 331 E
lloydg@newpaltz.edu
LLOYD, James, W ... 352-392-2213.. 112 A
lloydjw@ufl.edu
LLOYD, Jan ... 407-708-2144.. 109 E
lloydj@seminolestate.edu
LLOYD, Jayson ... 208-732-6547.. 133 E
jlloyd@csi.edu
LLOYD, Mary, J ... 815-599-3418.. 141 E
mary.lloyd@highland.edu
LLOYD, Megan ... 207-699-5037.. 203 F
mlloyd@meca.edu
LLOYD, Patrick, M ... 614-292-9755.. 375 A
lloyd.256@osu.edu
LLOYD, Rachel ... 918-540-6971.. 384 F
rlloyd@neo.edu
LLOYD, Robert ... 561-803-2252.. 106 C
robert_lloyd@pba.edu
LLOYD, Rodie, F ... 207-725-3963.. 202 F
rlloyd@bowdoin.edu
LLOYD, Scott ... 513-244-8435.. 366 B
scott.lloyd@ccuniversity.edu
LLOYD, Sharon ... 678-359-5133.. 122 E
sharonl@gordonstate.edu
LLOYD, Sheila ... 909-748-8576.... 71 K
sheila_lloyd@redlands.edu
LLOYD, Willie, L ... 248-232-4142.. 239 E
wllloyd@oaklandcc.edu
LLOYD-DENNIS, Diann ... 617-217-9216.. 215 B
dlloyddennis@baystate.edu
LLOYD-DENNIS,
Diann, L ... 651-631-5330.. 256 A
dllloyd@unwsp.edu
LLYWELYN, SJ, Dorian ... 408-554-6917.... 63 E
dllywelyn@scu.edu
LO, Andrea, M ... 540-868-7088.. 497 E
alo@lfcc.edu
LO, Angie ... 888-488-4968.... 47 D
alo@itu.edu
LO, Deborah ... 907-796-6123.... 10 H
delo@alaska.edu
LO, Jasmine ... 304-243-8147.. 515 C
jlo@wju.edu
LOBASSO, Lisa, M ... 570-941-7459.. 422 B
lisa.lobasso@scranton.edu
LOBASSO, Thomas ... 386-506-3200.... 98 E
lobasst@daytonastate.edu
LOBATO, Ana ... 831-476-9424.... 43 M
studentservices@fivebranches.edu
LOBATO, Richard, L ... 915-831-7810.. 457 H
rlobato@epcc.edu
LOBB, Barry ... 434-544-8521.. 491 F
lobb@lynchburg.edu
LOBB, Monty ... 740-477-7707.. 374 G
mlobb@ohiochristian.edu
LOBB, William, K ... 414-288-7485.. 517 I
william.lobb@marquette.edu
LOBE, Robert ... 212-592-2661.. 330 C
rlobe@sva.edu
LOBERA, Kim ... 858-653-3000.... 31 D
klobera@calmu.edu
LOBERTINI, Jo ... 563-588-6432.. 170 F
jo.lobertini@clarke.edu
LOBIONDO, Mary ... 631-656-3137.. 314 F
mary.lobiondo@ftc.edu
LOBLAND, Brad ... 907-474-7700.... 10 G
balobland@alaska.edu
LOBO, Teri, A ... 610-409-3000.. 422 D
tlobo@ursinus.edu
LOBO-TORRES, Sally ... 219-473-4219.. 159 L
slobotorres@ccs.edu
LOBOA, Elizabeth, G ... 573-882-4371.. 273 E
egloboa@missouri.edu
LOCANDER, William ... 504-864-7946.. 198 E
locander@loyno.edu
LOCASCIO, Patti, P ... 352-395-5169.. 109 C
patti.locascio@sfcollege.edu
LOCATELLI, Dominic ... 914-633-2245.. 317 B
dlocatelli@iona.edu
LOCH, OSB, Killian ... 724-805-2350.. 419 A
killian.loch@email.stvincent.edu
LOCH, Robert ... 515-643-6732.. 175 B
rloch@mercydesmoines.org
LOCHBAUM, Doug ... 770-394-8300.. 116 F
dlochbaum@aii.edu
LOCHHEAD, Michael, J ... 617-552-3255.. 216 C
michael.lochhead@bc.edu
LOCHMANN, Steve ... 870-575-8165.... 23 E
assessment@uapb.edu
LOCHMUELLER, Stephen ... 859-622-2120.. 188 F
stephen.lochmueller@eku.edu
LOCHNER, Mary Ann ... 828-227-7116.. 359 A
lochner@wcu.edu
LOCHSTAMPFOR, Mike ... 770-534-6230.. 118 A
mlochstampfor@brenau.edu
LOCHTE, Lynne ... 410-337-6572.. 207 H
lynne.lochte@goucher.edu
LOCICERO, Jack ... 336-721-2625.. 355 E
jack.locicero@salem.edu
LOCK, Ben, W ... 806-742-0012.. 472 C
ben.lock@ttu.edu
LOCK, Cory ... 512-448-8720.. 464 G
julial@stedwards.edu
LOCK, Vickie ... 920-498-5447.. 524 E
victoria.lock@nwtc.edu
LOCKABY, Charlotte ... 606-589-3020.. 190 G
charlotte.lockaby@kctcs.edu
LOCKE, Andrew, G ... 262-243-5700.. 516 E
andrew.locke@cuw.edu
LOCKE, Bruce ... 850-410-6161.. 111 C
blocke@eng.fsu.edu
LOCKE, Don ... 601-925-3250.. 259 A
locke@mc.edu
LOCKE, Dot, M ... 662-685-4771.. 257 A
dlocke@bmc.edu
LOCKE, Heidi ... 503-821-8976.. 394 B
hlocke@pnca.edu
LOCKE, Jason ... 607-255-2000.. 312 A
jcl31@cornell.edu
LOCKE, Lisa ... 517-629-0206.. 230 E
llocke@albion.edu
LOCKE, Richard, M ... 401-863-2706.. 424 J
richard_locke@brown.edu

LOCKE, Samuel ... 860-509-9556 ... 88 A
slocke@hartsem.edu
LOCKE, Steven, S ... 781-736-3017 .. 216 F
slocke@brandeis.edu
LOCKE, Teb ... 717-358-4339 .. 403 J
teb.locke@fandm.edu
LOCKER, Rick ... 615-366-4417 .. 444 D
rick.locker@tbr.edu
LOCKETT, JR.,
Eugene, D ... 301-985-7330 .. 212 C
cfo@umuc.edu
LOCKETT, Rose ... 662-621-4287 .. 257 B
rlockett@coahomacc.edu
LOCKETT, Tom ... 217-224-0600 .. 157 J
tom.lockett@vatterott-college.edu
LOCKHART, Anne ... 318-342-5426 .. 201 E
LOCKHART, Bill ... 214-654-9075 .. 210 G
LOCKHART, Calandra ... 903-923-2429 .. 479 K
clockhart@wileyc.edu
LOCKHART, Elaine ... 828-726-2241 .. 347 I
elockhart@cccti.edu
LOCKHART, Felicia ... 818-299-5517 ... 74 A
felicia@westcoastuniversity.edu
LOCKHART, Janet ... 310-506-4301 ... 56 J
janet.lockhart@pepperdine.edu
LOCKHART, Janet, M ... 915-831-2676 .. 457 H
jlockha2@epcc.edu
LOCKHART, Michael ... 917-493-4460 .. 319 M
mlockhart@msmnyc.edu
LOCKHART, Teresa ... 606-218-5305 .. 194 C
teresalockhart@upike.edu
LOCKHART, Teresa ... 606-218-5306 .. 194 C
teresalockhart@upike.edu
LOCKLEAR, Amy ... 386-506-3079 ... 98 E
locklea@daytonastate.edu
LOCKLEAR, April ... 910-843-5304 .. 347 A
april@nativeamericanbiblecollege.org
LOCKLEAR, Chris ... 252-328-6105 .. 356 C
locklearc@ecu.edu
LOCKLEAR, Marla ... 910-521-6201 .. 358 C
marla.locklear@uncp.edu
LOCKLEAR, Ronnie ... 910-272-3347 .. 352 E
rlocklear@robeson.edu
LOCKLEAR, William, L ... 910-272-3304 .. 352 E
wlocklea@robeson.edu
LOCKLEAR, Zoe, W ... 910-521-6211 .. 358 C
zoe.locklear@uncp.edu
LOCKREM, Michael ... 605-688-6161 .. 437 F
michael.lockrem@sdstate.edu
LOCKWARD, Ana, C ... 516-323-4209 .. 321 H
alockward@molloy.edu
LOCKWOOD, Charles ... 813-974-0553 .. 112 C
cjlockwood@health.usf.edu
LOCKWOOD, James, A ... 517-321-0242 .. 235 C
jlockwood@glcc.edu
LOCKWOOD,
Lawrence, J ... 319-335-0217 .. 169 H
larry-lockwood@uiowa.edu
LOCKWOOD, Matthew, T . 313-577-9098 .. 243 F
mlockwood@wayne.edu
LOCKWOOD, Monica ... 203-576-2400 ... 89 C
monical@bridgeport.edu
LOCKWOOD, Sasha ... 517-321-0242 .. 235 C
slockwood@glcc.edu
LOCOCO, Nina ... 406-447-4388 .. 276 B
nlococo@carroll.edu
LOCURTO, Chuck ... 401-232-6196 .. 424 K
clocurto@bryant.edu
LOCUST, JR.,
Jonathan, E ... 419-207-5504 .. 363 J
jlocust@ashland.edu
LOCUST, Wayne ... 860-486-1463 ... 89 D
wayne.locust@uconn.edu
LODATO, A. Michelle ... 864-379-6606 .. 429 I
lodato@erskine.edu
LODEN, Kristin, B ... 215-893-5279 .. 401 J
kristin.loden@curtis.edu
LODEWYCK, Becky ... 602-557-3170 ... 17 L
becky.lodewyck@phoenix.edu
LODGE, Danielle ... 478-757-5161 .. 129 L
dlodge@wesleyancollege.edu
LODGE, Helen ... 417-667-8181 .. 264 A
hlodge@cottey.edu
LODGE, Jennifer, K ... 314-747-0515 .. 274 N
lodgejk@wustl.edu
LODGE, William ... 313-845-9615 .. 235 D
wclodge@hfcc.edu
LODOVICO, John ... 860-733-1321 ... 87 E
jlodovico@txcc.commnet.edu
LOE, Meika ... 315-228-7077 .. 310 G
mloe@colgate.edu
LOEDEL, Peter ... 610-738-0536 .. 416 C
ploedel@wcupa.edu
LOEFFEL, Linda, L ... 414-443-8842 .. 522 P
linda.loeffel@wlc.edu
LOEFFELHOLZ, Mary ... 617-373-2400 .. 227 B
LOEFFLER, Donald ... 231-995-1130 .. 239 C
dloeffler@nmc.edu
LOEFFLER, Lauren ... 215-968-8017 .. 399 A
loeffler@bucks.edu
LOEHFELM, Courtney ... 303-797-5914 ... 76 J
courtney.loehfelm@arapahoe.edu
LOERA, Daniel, L ... 909-593-3511 ... 71 B
dloera@laverne.edu
LOERZEL, Cathy ... 206-876-6100 .. 507 D
cloerzel@theseattleschool.edu
LOESCH, Richard ... 847-578-3225 .. 153 A
rick.loesch@rosalindfranklin.edu
LOESER, Diane ... 614-236-6159 .. 364 N
dloeser@capital.edu
LOESSIN, Bruce, A ... 216-368-4352 .. 365 B
bruce.loessin@case.edu
LOETHEN, Laurie ... 913-621-8765 .. 180 F
lloethen@donnelly.edu
LOETTERLE, Jon ... 402-461-7424 .. 280 D
jloetterle@hastings.edu
LOEW, Timothy ... 508-373-9460 .. 215 D
timothy.loew@becker.edu
LOEWEN, Sherrie ... 909-389-3362 ... 60 B
sloewen@craftonhills.edu
LOEWEN, Steve ... 620-343-4600 .. 180 H
sloewen@fhtc.edu
LOEWY-WELLISCH,
Peggy ... 310-233-4321 ... 49 I
loewywp@lahc.edu
LOFFLER, Alicia ... 847-491-4647 .. 150 F
a-loffler@kellogg.northwestern.edu
LOFFREDO, Joe ... 585-475-2829 .. 327 E
jjlrgr@rit.edu
LOFLIN, Gene ... 828-398-7240 .. 347 D
williamgloflin@abtech.edu
LOFMAN, Brian ... 831-755-6809 ... 45 L
blofman@hartnell.edu
LOFRANO, Bob ... 818-710-2823 ... 50 A
lofranrj@piercecollege.edu
LOFRUMENTO, Kristin ... 740-362-3126 .. 372 D
klofrumento@mtso.edu
LOFSTEAD, Rebecca, B ... 304-293-9358 .. 514 C
becky.lofstead@mail.wvu.edu
LOFT, Jan ... 507-537-6218 .. 252 E
jan.loft@smsu.edu
LOFTESNES, Teresa ... 701-858-3062 .. 360 F
teresa.loftesnes@minotstateu.edu
LOFTHOUSE, David, R ... 951-785-2938 ... 48 A
dlofthou@lasierra.edu
LOFTIN, Loren ... 903-223-3002 .. 469 C
lloftin@tamut.edu
LOFTIS, Elsa ... 503-297-5544 .. 393 C
eloftis@ocac.edu
LOFTON, Antwan ... 202-238-5960 ... 93 A
antwan.lofton@howard.edu
LOFTON, Lynn ... 580-559-5252 .. 383 H
llofton@ecok.edu
LOFTUS, Craig ... 207-221-4750 .. 205 F
cloftus1@une.edu
LOFTUS, Edward, J ... 570-577-1458 .. 398 L
edward.loftus@bucknell.edu
LOFTUS, James, K ... 412-624-4216 .. 421 G
ja1216@pitt.edu
LOFTUS, James, P ... 414-410-4003 .. 515 I
jploftus@stritch.edu
LOFTUS, Kate ... 262-472-1392 .. 521 F
loftusk@uww.edu
LOFTUS-BERLIN, Eileen ... 973-278-5400 .. 305 B
eml@berkeleycollege.edu
LOFTUS-BERLIN, Eileen ... 973-278-5400 .. 289 F
eml@berkeleycollege.edu
LOGAN, Barry ... 207-725-3290 .. 202 F
blogan@bowdoin.edu
LOGAN, Caleb ... 334-683-2304 ... 5 G
registrar@marionmilitary.edu
LOGAN, Cynthia ... 931-393-1588 .. 446 D
clogan@mscc.edu
LOGAN, Debra ... 785-833-4457 .. 182 F
debre.logan@kwu.edu
LOGAN, Doug ... 509-527-2074 .. 508 G
doug.logan@wallawalla.edu
LOGAN, Elaine ... 313-593-5400 .. 242 A
loganem@umich.edu
LOGAN, Erin ... 405-682-7821 .. 385 D
elogan@occc.edu
LOGAN, Erin ... 405-682-1611 .. 385 D
elogan@occc.edu
LOGAN, Ethan ... 806-742-1480 .. 472 C
ethan.logan@ttu.edu
LOGAN, Gary ... 210-999-7306 .. 473 A
glogan@trinity.edu
LOGAN, Jill, B ... 601-643-5101 .. 257 D
jill.logan@colin.edu
LOGAN, Katherine ... 706-272-4436 .. 119 H
klogan@daltonstate.edu
LOGAN, Kevin ... 703-632-1976 .. 528 C
kevin.logan@dodiis.mil
LOGAN, Linda ... 269-749-6669 .. 240 A
llogan@olivetcollege.edu
LOGAN, Mark ... 562-860-2451 ... 36 P
mlogan@cerritos.edu
LOGAN, Martin ... 206-934-7792 .. 506 J
martin.logan@seattlecolleges.edu
LOGAN, Matt ... 662-621-4050 .. 257 B
mlogan@coahomacc.edu
LOGAN, Michael, F ... 336-334-4104 .. 358 B
mflogan@uncg.edu
LOGAN, Mike ... 712-274-6400 .. 177 I
mike.logan@witcc.edu
LOGAN, Penny ... 870-512-7827 ... 19 C
penny_logan@asun.edu
LOGAN, Robin ... 210-829-3933 .. 474 D
rlogan@uiwtx.edu
LOGAN, Ruth ... 585-594-6260 .. 327 D
loganr@roberts.edu
LOGAN, Ruth ... 585-594-6408 .. 325 B
loganr@roberts.edu
LOGAN, Steven ... 386-323-8000 ... 99 A
logans4@erau.edu
LOGAN, Timothy, M ... 254-710-6665 .. 452 H
tim_logan@baylor.edu
LOGAN, Tonya ... 740-264-5591 .. 368 D
tlogan@egcc.edu
LOGAN, Traci ... 617-587-5711 .. 226 E
logant@neco.edu
LOGAN-BENNETT, Lorie .. 410-704-2386 .. 213 B
lloganbennett@towson.edu
LOGEL, Mark, J ... 812-488-2941 .. 167 I
ml44@evansville.edu
LOGGINS, Jeff ... 662-254-3325 .. 260 A
jloggins@mvsu.edu
LOGHIN, Sarah ... 512-313-3000 .. 455 F
sarah.loghin@concordia.edu
LOGLISCI, Marlene ... 856-415-2113 .. 295 D
mloglisc@rcgc.edu
LOGSDON, Michael ... 301-387-3333 .. 207 G
michael.logsdon@garrettcollege.edu
LOGSDON, Paul ... 417-865-2815 .. 265 B
logsdonp@evangel.edu
LOGUE, Mary ... 805-565-6251 ... 75 A
mlogue@westmont.edu
LOGUE, Melanie ... 602-639-7500 ... 13 I
LOH, Wallace, D ... 301-405-5803 .. 211 E
wdloh@umd.edu
LOHAN-BREMER,
Maureen ... 845-257-3250 .. 331 E
LOHDEN, Bethany, L ... 636-584-6503 .. 264 M
bethany.lohden@eastcentral.edu
LOHMANN, Courtney ... 925-631-4577 ... 59 I
ccarmign@stmarys-ca.edu
LOHNSON, Lance ... 406-791-5262 .. 278 G
lance.johnson@ugf.edu
LOHR, Joel ... 209-946-2325 ... 71 C
jlohr@pacific.edu
LOHRENZ, Steven ... 508-910-6550 .. 220 H
slohrenz@umassd.edu
LOHREY, Adam ... 937-481-2266 .. 381 C
adam_lohrey@wilmington.edu
LOHRMEYER, Robert ... 208-792-2225 .. 134 A
rlohrmey@lcsc.edu
LOHRUM, Kitty ... 314-889-4701 .. 265 C
clohrum@fontbonne.edu
LOHSANDT, Marie, A ... 605-256-5122 .. 437 C
marie.lohsandt@dsu.edu
LOHSE, MaryPat ... 617-349-8669 .. 220 B
mlohse@lesley.edu
LOHSTROH, Tracy ... 618-634-3203 .. 154 B
tracyl@shawneecc.edu
LOILAND, Sharon ... 701-777-3178 .. 360 C
sharon.loiland@und.edu
LOIS, Nancy ... 617-964-1100 .. 214 D
nlois@ants.edu
LOISEAU, Marvin ... 617-588-1337 .. 215 E
mloiseau@bfit.edu
LOIZEAUX, Elizabeth ... 617-353-2230 .. 216 E
ebloiz@bu.edu
LOIZZO, Joseph, A ... 740-284-7217 .. 368 L
jloizzo@franciscan.edu
LOJKO, Frank ... 435-652-7511 .. 482 A
lojko@dixie.edu
LOJOWSKY, MacAdam ... 707-468-3081 ... 52 C
mlojowsky@mendocino.edu
LOKER, William, M ... 530-898-6894 ... 32 C
wloker@csuchico.edu
LOKEY, Cheryl, P ... 318-323-2889 .. 198 F
cheryl.lokey@careertc.edu
LOKKEN, Pamela, S ... 314-935-5752 .. 274 N
lokken@wustl.edu
LOKMAN, Lawrence, H ... 814-863-1028 .. 412 F
lhl11@psu.edu
LOKUTA, Sharon ... 260-422-5561 .. 162 B
slokuta@indianatech.edu
LOLLAR, Cay ... 662-862-8032 .. 258 C
clollar@iccms.edu
LOLLARD, Sonja ... 530-741-6766 ... 76 D
slollard@yccd.edu
LOLLING, David ... 217-732-3155 .. 146 B
dlolling@lincolncollege.edu
LOLLINI, Thomas ... 415-405-3838 ... 35 B
LOMASTRO, Joseph, A ... 508-373-9546 .. 215 D
oseph.lomastro@becker.edu
LOMBARD, Anne, E ... 315-470-6658 .. 334 E
aelombard@esf.edu
LOMBARD, Karen, L ... 515-574-1140 .. 173 F
lombard@iowacentral.edu
LOMBARD-SIMS,
Danielle ... 504-568-3916 .. 198 A
dlomb3@lsuhsc.edu
LOMBARDI, Carol ... 617-873-0167 .. 217 A
carol.lombardi@cambridgecollege.edu
LOMBARDI, Mark ... 314-529-9330 .. 267 B
president@maryville.edu
LOMBARDI, Phillip ... 401-232-6374 .. 424 K
plombard@bryant.edu
LOMBARDI, Ryan, T ... 607-255-7595 .. 312 A
ryan.lombardi@cornell.edu
LOMBARDO, Joann ... 860-486-5519 ... 89 D
joann.lombardo@uconn.edu
LOMBARDO, John ... 631-851-6225 .. 336 D
lombarj@sunysuffolk.edu
LOMBARDO, Michael ... 503-777-7542 .. 394 I
lombardm@reed.edu
LOMBARDO, Natalie ... 814-944-5643 .. 424 G
natalie.lombardo@yti.edu
LOMBARDO, Natalie ... 814-944-5643 .. 424 I
natalie.lombardo@yti.edu
LOMBARDO, Paul ... 860-231-5396 ... 90 B
plombardo@usj.edu
LOMBARDO, Roberto ... 386-506-3159 ... 98 E
lombarr@daytonastate.edu
LOMBARDO, Tony ... 225-578-5603 .. 197 I
lombardo@lsu.edu
LOMBELLA, James, P ... 860-253-3001 ... 86 A
jlombella@asnuntuck.edu
LOMELI, Susan ... 213-252-5100 ... 24 K
slomeli@alu.edu
LOMENA, Sandra ... 305-821-3333 .. 101 B
slomena@fnu.edu
LOMIDZE, Kote ... 202-464-6973 .. 485 A
kote.lomidze@worldlearning.org
LOMMEN, Conrad ... 808-373-2849 .. 132 G
cjlommen88@gmail.com
LOMONACO, Barbara ... 401-341-2205 .. 426 C
barbara.lomonaco@salve.edu
LONABOCKER,
Louise, M ... 617-552-3300 .. 216 C
louise.lonabocker@bc.edu
LONBORG, David, W ... 808-956-8436 .. 131 D
dlonborg@hawaii.edu
LONDA, Ivan ... 212-962-0002 .. 322 G
ilonda@nyci.edu
LONDOIRO, Carol ... 631-632-6267 .. 332 A
carol.londoiro@stonybrook.edu
LONDON, Manuel ... 631-632-8304 .. 332 A
manuel.london@stonybrook.edu
LONDON, Michael ... 415-422-4400 ... 72 C
melondon@usfca.edu
LONDON, Samuel ... 256-726-7223 ... 6 B
slondon@oakwood.edu
LONDON-JONES, Emily ... 504-520-7517 .. 202 C
ejones@xula.edu
LONDONO, Hernan ... 305-899-4019 ... 96 D
hlondono@barry.edu
LONDRE, Tristan ... 816-604-1524 .. 267 F
tristan.londre@mcckc.edu
LONDRIGAN, Michael, P ... 212-752-1530 .. 318 F
michael.londrigan@limcollege.edu
LONE HILL, Karen ... 605-455-6100 .. 436 G
klonehill@olc.edu
LONEKER, Ronald ... 973-290-4229 .. 290 G
rloneker@cse.edu
LONERGAN, Dennis ... 718-862-7349 .. 319 L
dennis.lonergan@manhattan.edu
LONERGAN, Joel, C ... 256-824-6414 ... 8 F
joel.lonergan@uah.edu
LONEY, Teresa, A ... 816-604-1517 .. 267 F
teresa.loney@mcckc.edu
LONG, Andrew ... 308-345-8119 .. 280 M
longa@mpcc.edu
LONG, Antonio ... 404-756-4477 .. 116 I
along@atlm.edu
LONG, Aubrey ... 386-481-2801 ... 96 H
longa@cookman.edu
LONG, Beverly ... 706-864-1940 .. 128 F
beverly.long@ung.edu
LONG, Brenda, J ... 252-222-6151 .. 348 B
longb@carteret.edu
LONG, Brittney ... 402-399-2454 .. 279 E
blong@csm.edu
LONG, Bruce ... 972-241-3371 .. 455 K
blong@dallas.edu
LONG, Carol ... 310-434-4762 ... 63 F
long_carol@smc.edu
LONG, Carol ... 503-370-6300 .. 396 G
LONG, Carol, S ... 585-245-5531 .. 333 B
long@geneseo.edu
LONG, Catherine, E ... 607-255-2946 .. 312 A
cel3@cornell.edu
LONG, Christina ... 620-665-3521 .. 181 I
longc@hutchcc.edu
LONG, Christopher, P ... 517-355-4597 .. 237 I
cplong@msu.edu
LONG, Curt ... 563-588-6657 .. 170 F
curt.long@clarke.edu
LONG, Daniel ... 313-664-7675 .. 232 G
dlong@collegeforcreativestudies.edu

LONG, Deborah 336-278-5900 344 D
dlong@elon.edu

LONG, Donald 651-748-2626 249 A
donald.long@century.edu

LONG, Donald 515-964-0601 172 F
longd@faith.edu

LONG, Doreen 603-428-2303 287 C
dlong@nec.edu

LONG, Durwin 715-836-4899 520 A
longd@uwec.edu

LONG, Dustin 910-272-3566 352 E
dulong@robeson.edu

LONG, Faith, M 518-564-2090 334 A
long9194@plattsburgh.edu

LONG, Gerard, E 210-562-6285 477 D
longg@uthscsa.edu

LONG, Gladys 919-572-1625 341 M
doc_long@apexsot.edu

LONG, Jaime 815-825-9532 144 F
jaime.long@kishwaukeecollege.edu

LONG, Jeanine 229-227-2668 127 G
jlong@southernregional.edu

LONG, Jeff 575-562-2221 299 I
jeff.long@enmu.edu

LONG, Jeff 601-403-1041 260 D
jlong@prcc.edu

LONG, Jennifer 405-224-3140 389 D
jlong@usao.edu

LONG, Jesse 806-720-7657 461 C
jesse.long@lcu.edu

LONG, Jewel, B 757-727-5486 490 E
jewel.long@hamptonu.edu

LONG, Jim 573-592-4225 275 G
jim.long@williamwoods.edu

LONG, Jodi 352-395-5680 109 C
jodi.long@sfcollege.edu

LONG, John, W 813-974-3297 112 C
jwl@usf.edu

LONG, Jonathan 913-288-7691 182 C
jlong@kckcc.edu

LONG, Jonathan 913-288-7621 182 C
jlong@kckcc.edu

LONG, Joyce 704-290-5281 353 B
jlong@spcc.edu

LONG, Justin 239-985-8361 101 F
justin.long@fsw.edu

LONG, Karen, S 518-276-6000 327 B
longks@rpi.edu

LONG, Kelly 970-491-5932 78 Q
kelly.long@colostate.edu

LONG, Kenneth 231-777-0560 238 G
kenneth.long@muskegoncc.edu

LONG, Kenneth, A 570-422-3201 414 H
kenlong@esu.edu

LONG, Kim, C 903-923-1622 479 K
klong@wileyc.edu

LONG, Kimberly 870-358-8636 19 C
kimberly_long@asun.edu

LONG, Laurel 256-824-2259 8 F
laurel.long@uah.edu

LONG, Lauren 703-993-2909 490 B
llong3@gmu.edu

LONG, Leann 423-585-6772 447 D
leann.long@ws.edu

LONG, Lisa 265-761-6215 7 F
lelong@talladega.edu

LONG, Marcus 605-668-1514 436 D
marcus.long@mtmc.edu

LONG, Marilyn 405-631-3399 383 L

LONG, Matthew 336-272-7102 344 G
matt.long@greensboro.edu

LONG, Natalie 920-686-6134 519 H
natalie.long@sl.edu

LONG, Nathan 510-593-2910 63 H
nlong@saybrook.edu

LONG, Nigel 570-662-4000 415 E

LONG, Patricia, K 432-837-8696 471 E
plong@sulross.edu

LONG, Phil, D 512-475-6702 476 B
phil.long@austin.utexas.edu

LONG, Rebecca 770-528-4545 118 J

LONG, Rebecca 740-992-1880 380 C
rlong@rio.edu

LONG, Ronald, B 770-484-1204 124 C
lutherrice@lutherrice.edu

LONG, Sara 870-512-7874 19 C
sara_long@asun.edu

LONG, Shane 207-741-5544 203 M
slong@smccme.edu

LONG, Sheryl 336-721-2774 355 E
sheryl.long@salem.edu

LONG, Stephen 314-539-5311 271 F
slong@stlcc.edu

LONG, Susan 909-274-5200 53 C
slong@mtsac.edu

LONG, Tamara 325-674-2949 449 J
tnb99a@acu.edu

LONG, Terri 562-938-4127 49 D
tlong@lbcc.edu

LONG, Vicki 316-322-3152 179 E
vlong@butlercc.edu

LONG-COFFEE, Michelle 310-287-4597 50 E
longcofm@wlac.edu

LONG PORTER, Cindy 203-582-8722 88 G
cindy.porter@quinnipiac.edu

LONGACRE, Jeffrey 301-295-1917 528 G
jeffrey.longacre@usuhs.edu

LONGACRE, Teri, E 713-743-4669 473 F
elkins@central.uh.edu

LONGAKER, Frank, E 540-986-1800 486 G
frank@an.edu

LONGAZEL, Edward, G 215-255-7819 402 G
edward.longazel@drexel.edu

LONGBRAKE, John 773-702-0689 156 D
longbrake@uchicago.edu

LONGE, Ryan 802-287-8000 484 A
ryan.longe@greenmtn.edu

LONGENECKER, Penni 717-947-6093 413 N
pelongen@pacollege.edu

LONGFIELD, Bradley, J 563-599-3122 177 C
blongfie@dbq.edu

LONGHTA, Karie, L 217-786-2263 146 E
karie.longhta@llcc.edu

LONGIE, Candace 701-477-7862 362 D
clongie@tm.edu

LONGJOHN, Beth 616-222-1428 233 A
beth.longjohn@cornerstone.edu

LONGJOHN, Gerald 616-222-1423 233 A
gerald.longjohn@cornerstone.edu

LONGMAN, Tom 269-965-3931 236 A
longmant@kellogg.edu

LONGMIRE, Kolleen 615-514-2787 443 F
klongmire@nossi.edu

LONGMUIR, Marcus 212-229-5300 322 E
marcus.longmuir@newschool.edu

LONGO, Eugenio, A 787-622-8000 537 B
elongo@pupr.edu

LONGO, Laura 732-224-2259 289 I
llongo@brookdalecc.edu

LONGO, Rick 215-717-6618 421 D
rlongo@uarts.edu

LONGO, Thomas 703-993-4994 490 B
tlongo@gmu.edu

LONGSDORF, Brittany 207-753-6906 202 D
blongsdo@bates.edu

LONGSTON, Susan 203-285-2187 86 C
slogston@gwcc.commnet.edu

LONGSTRETH, Jason, S 813-988-5131 100 F
deanofstudents@floridacollege.edu

LONGUEVILLE, Lori 618-985-5980 143 F
lorilongueville@jalc.edu

LONGWELL, B. Thomas 812-461-1901 168 E
btlongwell@usi.edu

LONGWELL, Sarah 503-760-3131 390 B
sarah@birthingway.edu

LONGWORTH, Rhonda 734-487-3200 233 J
rkinney@emich.edu

LONGYEAR, JR.,
George, E 203-436-4899 90 D
george.longyear@yale.edu

LONIER, Terri 312-499-4135 154 A
tlonier@saic.edu

LONON, Justin 214-378-1816 456 A
justin.lonon@dcccd.edu

LONOWSKI, Jerrold 575-624-8421 300 I
lonowsk@nmmi.edu

LONSDALE Thorunn 607-274-3306 317 D
tlonsdale@ithaca.edu

LOO, Chih 256-824-2243 8 F
chih.loo@uah.edu

LOOBY, Lynn, S 508-213-2215 227 A
lynn.looby@nichols.edu

LOOCHTAN, Anne 703-822-6697 497 H
aloochtan@nvcc.edu

LOOMIS, Grace, H 585-785-1451 314 D
grace.loomis@flcc.edu

LOOMIS, Mary 478-825-6436 120 F
loomism@fvsu.edu

LOOMIS, Michael 530-226-4728 64 H
mloomis@simpsonu.edu

LOOMIS, Susan 951-639-5212 53 D
sloomis@msjc.edu

LOOMIS, Susan 207-326-2345 204 C
susan.loomis@mma.edu

LOOMIS HUBBELL,
Loren, W 802-626-6410 486 C
loren.loomishubbell@lyndonstate.edu

LOONAN, John, F 570-389-4115 414 D
jloonan@bloomu.edu

LOONEY, JoAnn 845-675-4542 325 C
joann.looney@nyack.edu

LOONEY, Joe 828-395-1443 350 E
jlooney@isothermal.edu

LOONEY, Joshua 570-422-3211 414 H
jlooney@esu.edu

LOONEY, Nita 770-426-2605 124 B
nlooney@life.edu

LOONEY, Susan, D 610-607-6271 417 G
slooney@racc.edu

LOONEY, CSC, Thomas 570-208-5900 406 J
thomaslooney@kings.edu

LOONEY, Todd 507-288-4563 246 C
tlooney@crossroadscollege.edu

LOOP, Quentin, C 405-912-9478 387 D
qloop@hc.edu

LOOPE, David, R 804-523-5547 497 C
dloope@reynolds.edu

LOOPER, William 850-729-5260 105 I
looperw@nwfsc.edu

LOOS, Christopher 320-308-6158 252 B
cloos@sctcc.edu

LOOS, Tal 912-443-4140 126 G
tloos@savannahtech.edu

LOOSE, Rich 605-642-6011 437 B
rich.loose@bhsu.edu

LOOSER, Jackie 269-749-7700 240 A
jlooser@olivetcollege.edu

LOOSMAN, Sharon 919-513-4206 357 B
sharon_loosman@ncsu.edu

LOPARDO, Gina 206-296-6460 507 E
glopardo@seattleu.edu

LOPCI, Kate 617-984-1654 227 F
klopci@quincycollege.edu

LOPDELL-LAWRENCE,
Murray 609-497-7756 294 C
m.lopdell lawrence@ptsem.edu

LOPER, Debra 970-945-8691 73 B

LOPER, Marianne 585-567-9328 316 F
marianne.loper@houghton.edu

LOPER, Shane 509-527-4571 503 F
shane.loper@wwcc.edu

LOPER, Thomas 413-565-1000 215 A
tloper@baypath.edu

LOPES, Anne 212-237-8423 303 E
alopes@jjay.cuny.edu

LOPES, Joyce 707-826-3351 34 F
joyce.lopes@humboldt.edu

LOPES, Zilma 919-718-7542 348 D
zlopes@cccc.edu

LOPEZ, Alberto 787-765-3560 532 I
lopeza@edpuniversity.edu

LOPEZ, Amarilis 787-746-1400 532 M
mlopez@huertas.edu

LOPEZ, Ana 787-758-2525 538 D
ana.lopez6@upr.edu

LOPEZ, Ana 504-865-5261 200 C
lopez@tulane.edu

LOPEZ, Andrea 956-721-5135 460 F
andrea.lopez@laredo.edu

LOPEZ, Antonio 202-526-3799 93 E
alopez@johnpaulii.edu

LOPEZ, Arthur 760-245-4271 73 H
arthur.lopez@vvc.edu

LOPEZ, Bernard 215-955-6844 420 E
bernard.lopez@jefferson.edu

LOPEZ, Beto 915-747-8244 476 D
alopez@utep.edu

LOPEZ, Boris 523-953-4000 49 H
lopezbv@lacitycollege.edu

LOPEZ, Carlos 714-564-6080 58 G
lopez_carlos@sac.edu

LOPEZ, Carmen, J 787-258-1501 531 K
clopez@columbiacentral.edu

LOPEZ, Chuck 509-359-2202 503 D
clopez17@ewu.edu

LOPEZ, Coral 775-445-4230 285 B
coral.lopez@wnc.edu

LOPEZ, Crystal 973-618-3472 290 A
cllopez@caldwell.edu

LOPEZ, Dana 310-954-4037 53 B
dlopez@msmu.edu

LOPEZ, JR., Daniel 773-442-4600 149 J
d-lopez@neiu.edu

LOPEZ, Derek 719-549-2535 79 B
derek.lopez@csupueblo.edu

LOPEZ, Desi 787-780-5134 535 C
dlopez@nuc.edu

LOPEZ, Don 559-489-2352 67 C
don.lopez@fresnocitycollege.edu

LOPEZ, Edgar 949-214-3073 41 F
edgar.lopez@cui.edu

LOPEZ, Edwin 337-521-8901 197 A
elopez@solacc.edu

LOPEZ, Elias, S 530-752-3619 69 A
eslopez@ucdavis.edu

LOPEZ, Eric 210-784-2500 469 B
elopez@tamusa.edu

LOPEZ, Francisco 313-664-7428 232 G
flopez@collegeforcreativestudies.edu

LOPEZ, Gabriel 787-766-1717 536 B
um_glopez@suagm.edu

LOPEZ, Gabriel, J 505-277-6128 302 F
vpr@unm.edu

LOPEZ, Gerardo 787-891-0925 533 G
glopez@aguadilla.inter.edu

LOPEZ, Gersom 914-632-5400 321 I
glopez@monroecollege.edu

LOPEZ, Gilma 909-621-8055 46 A
gilma_lopez@hmc.edu

LOPEZ, Gloria 610-861-5565 411 G
glopez@northampton.edu

LOPEZ, Heather 509-335-2001 508 H
hlopez@wsu.edu

LOPEZ, Hector, L 787-894-2828 539 A
hector.lopez975@upr.edu

LOPEZ, Ignacio 312-261-3468 149 B
ignacio.lopez@nl.edu

LOPEZ, Isis 956-665-2326 476 E
isis.lopez@utrgv.edu

LOPEZ, Ivan 505-747-2264 301 F
ilopez@nnmc.edu

LOPEZ, Jaime 787-834-9595 536 E
jlopez@uaa.edu

LOPEZ, Jane 757-221-3965 488 F
jalope@wm.edu

LOPEZ, Jarrod 502-863-8300 186 L
jarrod.lopez@bsky.org

LOPEZ, Jerry 415-439-2411 26 G
jlopez@act-sf.org

LOPEZ, Jilian 702-254-7577 285 C
jilian.lopez@northwestcareercollege.edu

LOPEZ, Jose 903-886-5623 468 D
jose.lopez@tamuc.edu

LOPEZ, Jose Israel 347-964-8600 305 I
jilopez@boricuacollege.edu

LOPEZ, Keila 787-882-2065 536 D
presidentutc@yahoo.com

LOPEZ, Kim 650-306-3236 62 G
lopezk@smccd.edu

LOPEZ, Kimberly 912-525-5000 126 E
klopez@scad.edu

LOPEZ, Lillian 712-274-5030 175 C
lopez@morningside.edu

LOPEZ, Lisa 503-251-5703 396 C
llopez@uws.edu

LOPEZ, Lorena 818-719-6449 50 A
lopezl6@piercecollege.edu

LOPEZ, Lorena 830-591-7352 466 A
lmlopez@swtjc.edu

LOPEZ, Luis 787-743-4041 531 K
llopez@columbiacentral.edu

LOPEZ, Lunill 787-848-1589 535 G

LOPEZ, Magdalis 787-786-3030 536 F
mlopez@ucb.edu.pr

LOPEZ, Manny 646-313-8000 309 F
manny.lopez@guttman.cuny.edu

LOPEZ, Maribel 203-285-2029 86 C
mlopez@gwcc.commnet.edu

LOPEZ, Mary 909-706-3860 74 K
mlopez@westernu.edu

LOPEZ, Matthew 801-585-9453 481 M
matthew.lopez@utah.edu

LOPEZ, Mayra, I 787-754-8000 537 B
mlopez@pupr.edu

LOPEZ, Melissa, H 203-576-4712 89 C
melissal@bridgeport.edu

LOPEZ, Myriam, D 787-841-2000 535 I
mdlopez@pucpr.edu

LOPEZ, Oscar 972-860-4837 456 B
olopez@dcccd.edu

LOPEZ, Paulette 509-574-4901 510 A
plopez@yvcc.edu

LOPEZ, Pete 805-765-9300 62 K

LOPEZ, Priscilla 310-233-4605 49 I
lopezpa@lahc.edu

LOPEZ, Robert 305-821-3333 101 B
rlopez@fnu.edu

LOPEZ, Robert 323-343-3050 33 C
robert.lopez@calstatela.edu

LOPEZ, Roberto 212-686-9244 304 A

LOPEZ, Ruben 787-746-1400 532 M
rublopez@huertas.edu

LOPEZ, Sam, M 213-740-1219 72 D
sam.lopez@usc.edu

LOPEZ, Sam, T 704-687-4759 358 A
slopez7@uncc.edu

LOPEZ, Santa, E 209-478-0800 46 H
selopez@humphreys.edu

LOPEZ, Silvia 305-629-2929 108 G
slopez@sanignaciocollege.edu

LOPEZ, Stacey, J 215-573-5836 421 E
staceylo@upenn.edu

LOPEZ, Sue Ann 806-716-2340 465 G
slopez@southplainscollege.edu

LOPEZ, Sylvia 787-725-6500 531 C
slopez@albizu.edu

LOPEZ, Tammy, L 719-587-7122 76 G
tllopez@adams.edu

LOPEZ, Teresa 787-725-8120 532 K
tlopez@eap.edu

LOPEZ, Theresa 562-860-2451 36 P
tmlopez@cerritos.edu

LOPEZ, Tom 818-947-2988 50 D
lopezt@lavc.edu

LOPEZ, Vanessa 210-829-3900 474 D
valopez1@uiwtx.edu

LOPEZ, Vanessa 718-779-1499 326 D
vlopez@plazacollege.edu

LOPEZ, Vince 323-343-6190 33 C
vlopez@cslanet.calstatela.edu

LOPEZ, Wilfredo 787-738-2161 538 A
wilfredo.lopez3@upr.edu

LOPEZ-AVILES, Maria del Mar ... 787-746-1400 .. 532 M
mlopez@huertas.edu

LOPEZ-CEPERO RAMOS, Maria, C ... 787-720-1022 .. 531 A
orientador@atlanticu.edu

LOPEZ-JORGE, Sylvia ... 787-725-6500 .. 531 C
slopez@albizu.edu

LOPEZ-MATTHEWS, Amy, L ... 937-229-3333 .. 379 D
amatthews1@udayton.edu

LOPEZ-MEDERO, Lilliana, M ... 787-765-4210 .. 531 H
llopez@cempr.edu

LOPEZ-PHILLIPS, Matthew ... 707-664-2838 .... 35 D
matthew.lopez-phillips@sonoma.edu

LOPEZ-ROSADO, Jorge ... 239-590-1210 .. 110 L
jlopez@fgcu.edu

LOPEZ-STRONG, Maria ... 806-894-9611 .. 465 G
mstrong@southplainscollege.edu

LOPEZ-WAGNER, Muriel . 909-537-3067 .... 34 C
mclopez@csusb.edu

LOPIAN, David ... 718-339-1090 .. 340 O

LOPIANSKY, Aaron ... 301-649-7077 .. 214 A
alopiansky@yeshiva.edu

LOPICCOLO, Joseph ... 831-656-2994 .. 528 D
jlopiccolo@nps.edu

LOPPNOW, Bruce ... 218-723-7033 .. 245 J
bloppnow@css.edu

LOPRESTI, James, M ... 724-458-3795 .. 404 F
jmlopresti@gcc.edu

LOPRESTI-GOODMAN, Stacy ... 703-284-1546 .. 492 A
stacy.lopresti-goodman@marymount.edu

LOR, Kia ... 262-243-5700 .. 516 E
kia.lor@cuw.edu

LORAINE, Donna ... 916-388-2800 .... 36 D
dloraine@carrington.edu

LORAN, James ... 406-338-5441 .. 276 A
jloran@bfcc.edu

LORAN, Roberto ... 787-743-7979 .. 536 A
rloran@suagm.edu

LORBER, Jeffrey, D ... 217-206-7822 .. 156 G
jlorber@uis.edu

LORCH, Teddi ... 949-582-4850 .... 65 G
tlorch@socccd.edu

LORD, Annette ... 702-651-5600 .. 284 H
annette.lord@csn.edu

LORD, Ashley ... 863-680-4186 .. 101 E
alord@flsouthern.edu

LORD, Blair, M ... 217-581-2121 .. 139 H
blord@eiu.edu

LORD, David ... 304-294-2010 .. 512 E
david.lord@southernwv.edu

LORD, Evelyn ... 510-464-3496 .... 57 D
elord@peralta.edu

LORD, Harold, W ... 585-567-9645 .. 316 F
harold.lord@houghton.edu

LORD, Jeanne, F ... 202-687-4056 .... 92 E
lordj@georgetown.edu

LORD, Jess ... 610-896-1350 .. 405 I
jlord@haverford.edu

LORD, Kenneth, R ... 818-677-2455 .... 34 A
kenneth.lord@csun.edu

LORD, Lisa ... 337-482-6863 .. 201 D
lisa@louisiana.edu

LORD, Mara ... 414-955-8298 .. 518 A
mlord@mcw.edu

LORD, Marianne, E ... 617-521-2328 .. 228 C
marianne.lord@simmons.edu

LORD, Patty, R ... 818-677-3776 .... 34 A
patty.lord@csun.edu

LORD, Resa ... 334-214-4818 ...... 2 H
resa.lord@cv.edu

LORDEN, Joan, F ... 704-687-5962 .. 358 A
jflorden@uncc.edu

LORE, Peggy ... 303-352-3526 .... 84 A
peggy.lore@ucdenver.edu

LORENSON, James, A ... 906-932-4231 .. 234 C

LORENTZEN, Marcia, H .. 203-576-4139 .... 89 C
marcia@bridgeport.edu

LORENZ, Aaron R, S ... 201-684-7624 .. 294 G
alorenz@ramapo.edu

LORENZ, Britt ... 605-626-2371 .. 437 D
britt.lorenz@northern.edu

LORENZ, Dan, P ... 701-788-4676 .. 360 E
daniel.lorenz@mayvillestate.edu

LORENZ, Georgia ... 310-434-4277 .... 63 F
lorenz_georgia@smc.edu

LORENZ, Gina ... 425-352-8880 .. 501 J
glorenz@cascadia.edu

LORENZ, Heather ... 603-668-2211 .. 287 I
h.lorenz@snhu.edu

LORENZ, Megan ... 304-205-6621 .. 511 M
megan.lorenz@bridgevalley.edu

LORENZ, Tracy ... 602-943-2311 .... 18 C
tracy.lorenz@west.edu

LORENZ, Tyler ... 414-326-1797 .. 516 D
tyler.lorenz@ccon.edu

LORENZA WHEELER, Edward ... 404-527-7702 .. 123 I
ewheeler@itc.edu

LORENZEN, Chris ... 307-268-3088 .. 526 D
chris.lorenzen@caspercollege.edu

LORENZEN, Michael ... 309-298-2762 .. 158 A
mg-lorenzen@wiu.edu

LORENZO, Bernice ... 619-388-3709 .... 60 F
blorenzo@sdccd.edu

LORENZO, JR., Joseph ... 303-797-5711 .... 76 J
joe.lorenzo@arapahoe.edu

LORENZO, Susan ... 650-738-4253 .... 62 I
lorenzo@smccd.edu

LORGAN, Jason ... 530-752-9075 .... 69 A
jplorgan@ucdavis.edu

LORGE-GROVER, Christina ... 715-422-5526 .. 523 G
christina.lorgegrover@mstc.edu

LORIA, Anne ... 616-250-7500 .. 306 A
alloria@bryantstratton.edu

LORIA, Annette ... 559-244-5977 .... 67 A
annette.loria@scccd.edu

LORIA, Sal ... 713-743-9092 .. 473 F
sloria@uh.edu

LORIA, Tonia ... 504-278-6278 .. 196 I
tloria@nunez.edu

LORICK, Piper ... 803-750-2510 .... 93 F

LORIMER, David, W ... 606-693-5000 .. 191 A
dlorimer@kmbc.edu

LORIMER, Steve, A ... 606-693-5000 .. 191 A
slorimer@kmbc.edu

LORIMER, Susan, L ... 916-568-3031 .... 50 J
lorimes@losrios.edu

LORIMER, Thomas, H ... 606-693-5000 .. 191 A
tlorimer@kmbc.edu

LORING, Christopher ... 413-585-2902 .. 228 D
cloring@smith.edu

LORING, Trish ... 603-271-6984 .. 286 F
tloring@ccsnh.edu

LORIUS, Billie Jo ... 701-328-4107 .. 360 B
billiejo.lorius@ndus.edu

LORKOVICH, Malinda ... 312-996-4366 .. 156 F
mlork@uic.edu

LORTON-ROWLAND, Julie ... 317-921-4715 .. 164 E
jlorton@ivytech.edu

LORTZ, Pete ... 206-934-6827 .. 507 A
peter.lortz@seattlecolleges.edu

LOSASSO, Joseph ... 609-652-4235 .. 297 C
joe.losasso@stockton.edu

LOSCHIAVO, Linda ... 718-817-3570 .. 314 G
loschiavo@fordham.edu

LOSE, David, J ... 215-248-6344 .. 409 D
dlose@ltsp.edu

LOSEY, Teri, L ... 616-331-2100 .. 234 F
loseyt@gvsu.edu

LOSHIN, David ... 954-262-1167 .. 105 J
loshin@nsu.nova.edu

LOSINGER, Regina ... 607-778-5040 .. 332 D
losingerr@sunybroome.edu

LOSS, Amy ... 618-842-3711 .. 142 C
lossa@iecc.edu

LOSSING, David, E ... 810-766-6647 .. 242 B
dalossin@umflint.edu

LOSTETTER, Ron ... 262-524-7200 .. 515 J
rlosett@carrollu.edu

LOTANO, Vincent ... 908-709-7046 .. 298 A

LOTFI, Vahid ... 810-762-3171 .. 242 B
vahid@umflint.edu

LOTH, Karen, M ... 616-331-6000 .. 234 F
lothk@gvsu.edu

LOTHAMER, Mary Ellen ... 615-383-4848 .. 449 G
mlothamer@watkins.edu

LOTHER, Nikki ... 413-662-5193 .. 222 B
n.lother@mcla.edu

LOTHRINGER, Bobby ... 940-898-3036 .. 472 G
rlothringer@twu.edu

LOTHRINGER, Rebecca ... 940-565-3793 .. 475 A
rebecca.lothringer@unt.edu

LOTITO, Larry, W ... 507-354-8221 .. 247 J
lotitolw@mlc-wels.edu

LOTITO, Tom ... 757-493-6000 .... 93 F

LOTKOWICTZ, Bob ... 315-464-4448 .. 332 C
lotkowir@upstate.edu

LOTRIONTE, John, D ... 901-321-3550 .. 439 E
jlotrion@cbu.edu

LOTT, Christine ... 815-967-7302 .. 152 F
clott@rockfordcareercollege.edu

LOTT, Christopher ... 607-431-4030 .. 315 E
lottc@hartwick.edu

LOTT, Ileo ... 847-214-7900 .. 140 A
ilott@elgin.edu

LOTT, Jesse ... 315-655-7161 .. 306 H
jlott@cazenovia.edu

LOTT, Patricia, D ... 850-474-3419 .. 113 A
plott@uwf.edu

LOTT, Theresa ... 904-633-8173 .. 101 G
theresa.lott@fscj.edu

LOTTIE, Jerry, W ... 518-564-2022 .. 334 A
lottiejw@plattsburgh.edu

LOTTO, Benjamin ... 845-437-5255 .. 339 C
lotto@vassar.edu

LOTURCO, Jennifer ... 518-320-1805 .. 330 H
jen.loturco@suny.edu

LOTYCZEWSKI, Halina ... 315-792-3087 .. 339 B
halotycz@utica.edu

LOU, Kris ... 503-370-5328 .. 396 G
klou@willamette.edu

LOUALLEN, Cheryl ... 937-481-2337 .. 381 C
cheryl_louallen@wilmington.edu

LOUBERT, Michelle ... 413-572-8574 .. 222 E
mloubert@westfield.ma.edu

LOUCH, Lesa ... 810-766-4183 .. 231 C

LOUCY, Brian, M ... 315-445-4174 .. 318 E
loucyb@lemoyne.edu

LOUDEN, Sandy ... 731-352-4095 .. 438 K
loudens@bethelu.edu

LOUDER, Corey ... 660-626-2203 .. 262 A
clouder@atsu.edu

LOUDIN, Rose Ellen ... 304-473-8600 .. 515 B
loudin_r@wvwc.edu

LOUDON, Tina ... 360-650-3240 .. 509 E
tina.loudon@wwu.edu

LOUFEK, Michelle ... 321-433-7765 .... 98 K
loufekm@easternflorida.edu

LOUGEE, Wendy, P ... 612-624-1807 .. 255 H
wlougee@umn.edu

LOUGHERY, James, F ... 215-968-8041 .. 399 A
loughery@bucks.edu

LOUGHMAN, Ann ... 518-262-5435 .. 303 E
loughma@mail.amc.edu

LOUGHRAN, Kristine ... 513-732-5218 .. 379 C
loughrke@ucmail.uc.edu

LOUGHRAN, Sean ... 203-837-9330 .... 85 I
loughrans@wcsu.edu

LOUIE, Larry ... 415-869-2900 .. 219 G
larry.louie@hult.edu

LOUIMA, Gariot ... 802-322-1676 .. 483 H
gariot.louima@goddard.edu

LOUIS, Michael ... 314-505-7301 .. 263 I
louism@csl.edu

LOUIS, Naomi ... 937-328-6031 .. 366 E
louisn@clarkstate.edu

LOUIS, Naomi ... 937-778-7814 .. 368 E
nlouis@edisonohio.edu

LOUIS, Tom ... 315-792-7100 .. 336 C
tlouis@sunypoly.edu

LOUISY, Heidi ... 256-782-5007 ...... 4 H
hlouisy@jsu.edu

LOULA, Karianne ... 651-423-8298 .. 249 B
karianne.loula@dctc.edu

LOUNSBERY, Monica ... 562-985-4691 .... 33 B
monica.lounsbery@csulb.edu

LOUREIRO, Rita, D ... 561-237-7035 .. 104 O
rloureiro@lynn.edu

LOURO, Jeffrey ... 508-999-8171 .. 220 H
jlouro@umassd.edu

LOUTHERBACK, George .. 254-295-4698 .. 474 E
gloutherback@umhb.edu

LOUTTIT, Julianne, E ... 724-287-8711 .. 399 B
julianne.louttit@bc3.edu

LOVATO, Jeremy ... 505-428-1767 .. 301 K
jeremy.lovato@sfcc.edu

LOVE, Andrea ... 225-771-2552 .. 200 A
alove@sulc.edu

LOVE, Anne ... 718-420-4212 .. 339 F
alove@wagner.edu

LOVE, Ceshia ... 713-221-8454 .. 474 B
lovec@uhd.edu

LOVE, Cindy ... 919-516-5082 .. 355 D
clove@st-aug.edu

LOVE, David ... 814-393-2334 .. 414 G
dlove@clarion.edu

LOVE, Deborah, A ... 757-221-1306 .. 488 F
dalove@wm.edu

LOVE, Deborah, E ... 504-862-8083 .. 200 C
dlove1@tulane.edu

LOVE, Edna ... 972-860-4806 .. 456 B
elove@dcccd.edu

LOVE, Eric ... 574-631-2859 .. 168 B
elove1@nd.edu

LOVE, Jan ... 404-727-6324 .. 120 E
jlove3@emory.edu

LOVE, Jane ... 864-294-2248 .. 430 C
jane.love@furman.edu

LOVE, Janice ... 714-564-6000 .... 58 G
love_janice@sac.edu

LOVE, Jim ... 917-493-4161 .. 319 M
jlove@msmnyc.edu

LOVE, Julie, B ... 800-431-8488 .... 27 F

LOVE, Julie, N ... 970-247-7503 .... 80 D
studenthousing@fortlewis.edu

LOVE, Kathryn ... 239-687-5430 .... 95 P
klove@avemarialaw.edu

LOVE, Kathy, S ... 912-443-3024 .. 126 G
klove@savannahtech.edu

LOVE, Kensey ... 740-753-7007 .. 369 K
love_k@hocking.edu

LOVE, Mark ... 616-538-2330 .. 234 D
mlove@gbcol.edu

LOVE, Monica ... 812-237-3837 .. 162 A
monica.love@indstate.edu

LOVE, Nikki ... 408-498-5107 .... 39 H
nlove@cogswell.edu

LOVE, Patrick ... 516-686-7882 .. 323 G
patrick.love@nyit.edu

LOVE, Tommy ... 503-838-8281 .. 396 E
lovet@wou.edu

LOVE, Tony ... 432-552-2633 .. 478 B
love_t@utpb.edu

LOVEDAY, Joyce ... 253-589-5500 .. 502 F
joyce.loveday@cptc.edu

LOVEDER, Alan ... 212-757-1190 .. 304 B
aloveder@funeraleducation.org

LOVEJOY, Mike ... 469-348-2500 .. 455 E

LOVEL, Stan ... 706-754-7868 .. 125 B
slovell@northgatech.edu

LOVELACE PETR, Carrie .. 402-826-8111 .. 280 B
carrie.petr@doane.edu

LOVELADY, III, Artis ... 832-252-4617 .. 454 H
artis@cbshouston.edu

LOVELAND, David, A ... 607-746-4013 .. 335 C
lovelada@delhi.edu

LOVELAND, George ... 252-399-6501 .. 341 P
gwloveland@barton.edu

LOVELESS, Cecelia ... 360-438-4366 .. 506 G
cloveless@stmartin.edu

LOVELESS, Debra ... 713-525-2150 .. 475 J
registrar@stthom.edu

LOVELIDGE, Robert ... 979-830-4194 .. 452 J
rlovelidge@blinn.edu

LOVELL, Ellen ... 719-336-1541 .... 81 D
library@lamarcc.edu

LOVELL, JR., Ernest, L ... 601-403-1183 .. 260 D
elovell@prcc.edu

LOVELL, Kim ... 706-778-3000 .. 125 J
klovell@piedmont.edu

LOVELL, Matthew ... 814-886-6388 .. 411 C
mlovell@mtaloy.edu

LOVELL, Michael, R ... 414-288-7223 .. 517 I
michael.lovell@marquette.edu

LOVELL, Rebecca ... 225-216-8031 .. 195 H
lovellr@mybrcc.edu

LOVELL, Sharon ... 540-568-2705 .. 490 J
lovellse@jmu.edu

LOVELL, William ... 856-227-7200 .. 290 B
wlovell@camdencc.edu

LOVELY, Christine, D ... 916-278-6078 .... 34 B
lovelyc@csus.edu

LOVERIDGE, Robert ... 801-863-8161 .. 482 C
loveriro@uvu.edu

LOVETT, Christopher, M .. 814-886-6400 .. 411 C
clovett@mtaloy.edu

LOVETT, Daniel ... 252-536-7275 .. 350 C
dlovett037@halifaxcc.edu

LOVETT, David, L ... 717-477-1164 .. 416 A
dllove@ship.edu

LOVETT, Leslie ... 304-367-4786 .. 512 D
leslie.lovett@pierpont.edu

LOVETT, Patricia ... 270-686-4336 .. 187 C
patricia.lovett@brescia.edu

LOVETT, Rod, M ... 217-351-2409 .. 151 B
rlovett@parkland.edu

LOVICK, Reed ... 252-527-6223 .. 350 H
rlovick@lenoircc.edu

LOVIK, Eric ... 540-831-5099 .. 493 A
elovik@radford.edu

LOVIN, Eddie ... 615-547-1231 .. 439 H
elovin@cumberland.edu

LOVINCE, Thomas ... 504-941-8504 .. 196 D
tlovin@dcc.edu

LOVINS, Greg ... 864-388-8305 .. 430 G
glovins@lander.edu

LOVINSKI, Kim ... 304-205-6622 .. 511 M
kimberly.lovinski@bridgevalley.edu

LOVITT, Carl, R ... 860-832-2228 .... 85 F
lovittcar@ccsu.edu

LOVSTUEN, Brenda, C ... 319-895-4292 .. 171 A
blovstuen@cornellcollege.edu

LOVVORN, Judi ... 229-217-4198 .. 127 G
jlovvorn@southernregional.edu

LOW, Catherine Yu-Ling . 808-371-5443 .. 131 A
cfo@orientalmedicine.edu

LOW, George ... 540-831-5187 .. 493 A
glow@radford.edu

LOW, Kathryn, G ... 207-786-6066 .. 202 D
klow@bates.edu

LOW, Ryan ... 207-581-1554 .. 204 H
ryan.low@maine.edu

LOW, Ryan ... 207-581-1554 .. 204 G
ryan.low@maine.edu

LOW, Wai Hoa ... 808-521-2288 .. 131 A
whlow@orientalmedicine.edu

LOWBRIDGE, John, D ... 270-824-1835 .. 190 B
john.lowbridge@kctcs.edu

LOWDEN, Paul ... 616-732-1194 .. 233 C
plowden@davenport.edu

LOWDER, Diane, M ... 804-752-7218 .. 493 C
dianelowder@rmc.edu

LOWDER, Michael ... 405-789-7661 .. 388 B
michael.lowder@swcu.edu

LUDLUM, Beth 202-885-8616 94 E
bludlum@wesleyseminary.edu

LUDWIG, Amy 479-394-7622 22 B
aludwig@rmcc.edu

LUDWIG, Amy 479-397-7622 22 B
aludwig@rmcc.edu

LUDWIG, Dean 419-824-3686 371 I
dludwig@lourdes.edu

LUDWIG, Deborah 785-628-4539 180 I
dmludwig@fhsu.edu

LUDWIG, Glenn 717-334-6286 409 C
gludwig@ltsg.edu

LUDWIG, James 513-875-3344 365 K
james.ludwig@chatfield.edu

LUDWIG, James, P 513-875-3344 365 K
james.ludwig@chatfield.edu

LUDWIG, Nancy 978-837-5947 225 E
ludwign@merrimack.edu

LUDWIG, Rebecca 727-341-4150 108 D
ludwig.rebecca@spcollege.edu

LUDWIG, Scott 408-741-2031 74 H
scott.ludwig@westvalley.edu

LUDWIG-JOHNSON, Stacey 801-274-3280 483 C
sludwig@wgu.edu

LUEBBERT, Paula, J 217-782-1086 146 E
paula.luebbert@llcc.edu

LUEBKE, Linda 804-706-5202 497 D
lluebke@jtcc.edu

LUEBKE, Miriam 651-651-8825 246 B
luebke@csp.edu

LUEBKE, Patricia 414-382-6368 515 D
patricia.luebke@alverno.edu

LUECK, Terrie 507-457-6921 254 O
tlueck@smumn.edu

LUECKE, Chris 435-797-2452 482 B
chris.luecke@usu.edu

LUEDER, Billie 808-845-9187 132 A
bktakaki@hawaii.edu

LUEDERS, Carol 847-735-6004 145 B
lueders@lakeforest.edu

LUEKEN, Paul, A 724-738-2021 416 B
paul.lueken@sru.edu

LUEKENGA, Chris 970-943-2616 84 H
cluekenga@western.edu

LUELLEN, Mark, M 434-243-2249 495 H
mml2r@virginia.edu

LUESING, Anne 415-451-2812 61 D
aluesing@sfts.edu

LUESSE, Amy 952-446-4122 246 D
luessea@crown.edu

LUETKEHANS, Lara 724-357-2482 415 B
lara.luetkehans@iup.edu

LUETSCHWAGER, Julie, A 920-923-8599 517 H
jaluetschwager25@marianuniversity.edu

LUETTGER, Michele 607-436-2514 331 F
michele.luettger@oneonta.edu

LUEVANOS, Aida 432-837-8000 471 E
aluevanos@sulross.edu

LUFF, Debra 916-558-2142 51 D
luffd@scc.losrios.edu

LUFF, Libby 615-514-2787 443 F
lfunke@nossi.edu

LUFF, Paula 312-362-8091 139 C
pluff@depaul.edu

LUFKIN, Daniel 757-825-3810 498 G
lufkind@tncc.edu

LUFKIN, Daniel, W 757-569-6712 498 B
dlufkin@pdc.edu

LUFKIN, MB 937-769-1323 363 E
mlufkin@antioch.edu

LUFT, John, P 717-766-2511 410 J
jluft@messiah.edu

LUGEMBE, Farida 310-453-8300 42 L
farida@emperors.edu

LUGO, Chantal 602-286-8330 14 B
chantal.lugo@gatewaycc.edu

LUGO, Daniel 207-859-4393 202 G
dan.lugo@colby.edu

LUGO, Efrain 787-620-2040 530 F
elugo@aupr.edu

LUGO, Eric 646-660-6095 307 A
eric.lugo@baruch.cuny.edu

LUGO, Francisco 787-841-2000 535 I
flugo@pucpr.edu

LUGO, Ivette 407-447-7300 102 D
ilugo@ftccollege.edu

LUGO, Javier 787-600-2819 539 A
opei.utuado@upr.edu

LUGO, María Inés 787-264-1912 534 D
milugo@intersg.edu

LUGO, Udeth 407-646-2573 107 O
ulugo@rollins.edu

LUGO, Victoria 805-289-6455 73 F
vlugo@vcccd.edu

LUHTA, Brad 440-375-7585 371 E
bluhta@lec.edu

LUHTALA, Erik 619-684-8801 54 C
eluhtala@newschoolarch.edu

LUI, Kat 612-659-7293 250 A
kat.lui@metrostate.edu

LUIKART, Nancy 563-288-6073 172 C
nluikart@eicc.edu

LUIKEN, Elizabeth 712-325-3445 174 B
eluiken@iwcc.edu

LUINENBURG, Amber 507-372-3499 250 G
amber.luinenburg@mnwest.edu

LUING, Kevin, L 973-278-5400 305 B
kevin@berkeleycollege.edu

LUING, Kevin, L 973-278-5400 289 F
kevin@berkeleycollege.edu

LUJAN, Annette 719-846-5679 83 G
annette.lujan@trinidadstate.edu

LUKAC, Dan 513-244-4617 373 C
dan.lukac@msj.edu

LUKACH, Matt 701-777-5930 360 C
matthew.lukach@und.edu

LUKACSKO, Debbie 201-684-7535 294 G
dlukacsk@ramapo.edu

LUKAS, Sofia 678-450-0550 123 F
slukas@ict.edu

LUKAS, Veronica 718-631-6367 309 E
vlukas@qcc.cuny.edu

LUKASZEWSKI, Patricia, L 919-508-2220 359 G
pllukaszewski@peace.edu

LUKE, Don, J 570-326-3761 413 O
dluke@pct.edu

LUKE, Gerri, F 570-326-3761 413 O
gluke@pct.edu

LUKE, Kristie 580-745-2176 387 M
kluke@se.edu

LUKE, Learie 803-533-3776 432 E
lluke@scsu.edu

LUKE, Learie, B 803-536-7180 432 E
lluke@scsu.edu

LUKE, Sarah 207-801-5670 202 H
sluke@coa.edu

LUKEHART, Debra 515-271-2169 171 K
debra.lukehart@drake.edu

LUKEN, James, O 843-349-2783 428 E
joluken@coastal.edu

LUKES, Don 812-855-4206 162 F
dlukes@iu.edu

LUKES, Don 812-855-4206 162 E
dlukes@iu.edu

LUKESH, Michelle 575-528-7245 301 C
mlukesh@nmsu.edu

LUKHAUP, Walter, P 724-480-3376 401 F
walter.lukhaup@ccbc.edu

LUKKEN, Jeff 706-880-8021 123 K
jlukken@lagrange.edu

LUKKES, Nathan 605-773-3455 436 L
nathan.lukkes@sdbor.edu

LUKMAN, Roy 407-303-8520 95 C
roy.lukman.phd@adu.edu

LUKOSHUS, Wes, K 219-989-2217 166 F
lukoshus@pnw.edu

LUKSA, Jennifer 570-674-6224 410 K
jsluzele@misericordia.edu

LULING, Jennifer 215-637-7700 405 J
jluling@holyfamily.edu

LULJAK, Thomas, L 414-229-4035 520 D
tluljak@uwm.edu

LULLI, Linda, S 401-232-6011 424 K
lslulli@bryant.edu

LUMAN, Karl 601-366-8880 261 H
kluman@wbs.edu

LUMETTA, Joanne 734-432-5689 237 D
jlumetta@madonna.edu

LUMM, Werner 920-390-2820 517 G
werner.lumm@mbu.edu

LUMM, Werner 920-206-2322 517 G
werner.lumm@mbu.edu

LUMM, Werner 920-206-2323 517 G
werner.lumm@mbu.edu

LUMPKIN, James 903-566-7346 477 B
jlumpkin@uttyler.edu

LUNA, Andrew, L 256-765-4221 9 C
alluna@una.edu

LUNA, Carmen 787-850-9394 538 B
carmen.luna@upr.edu

LUNA, Carmen, M 787-766-1717 536 B
cmluna@suagm.edu

LUNA, Edna 931-363-9824 441 G
eluna@martinmethodist.edu

LUNA, Jennifer 662-562-3271 260 C
jluna@northwestms.edu

LUNA, Leslie 520-383-8401 17 E
lluna@tocc.edu

LUNA, Mickey 314-977-3948 271 K
mluna@slu.edu

LUNA, Olga 787-766-1912 533 F
oluna@inter.edu

LUNA, Shirley, A 936-468-2605 466 H
sluna@sfasu.edu

LUNAN, Kathy 314-529-9332 267 B
klunan@maryville.edu

LUNARDI, Joseph, M 610-660-1221 418 G
jlunardi@sju.edu

LUNBECK, Jo 501-660-1030 18 H
jlunbeck@asusystem.edu

LUNCEFORD, Casey 772-462-2505 103 B
cluncefo@irsc.edu

LUND, Harold, E 530-226-4127 64 H
hlund@simpsonu.edu

LUND, James 760-480-8474 74 L
jlund@wscal.edu

LUND, Jon 563-387-1428 174 L
lundjon@luther.edu

LUND, Karla 406-874-6186 276 H
lundk@milescc.edu

LUND, Lisa 989-328-1219 238 D
lisal@montcalm.edu

LUND, Sarah 317-931-2311 160 B
slund@cts.edu

LUND, Stephen, R 608-263-5722 519 K
slund@ohr.wisc.edu

LUNDAHL, Deb 402-375-7209 281 J
delunda1@wsc.edu

LUNDAY, Bobbi, J 701-662-1501 361 E
bobbi.lunday@lrsc.edu

LUNDBERG, Alessandra 860-932-4170 87 C
alundberg@qvcc.edu

LUNDBERG, Barb 715-634-4790 517 C
blundberg@lco.edu

LUNDBERG, Cliff 805-565-7188 75 A
clundber@westmont.edu

LUNDBERG, Erik 734-615-4445 241 J
lerikl@umich.edu

LUNDBERG, Njal 303-964-5086 82 L
nlundber@regis.edu

LUNDBERG, Peter 410-287-1021 206 J
plundberg@cecil.edu

LUNDBERG, Todd 425-352-8168 501 J
tlundberg@cascadia.edu

LUNDBLAD, Jeffrey, K 773-244-5542 149 I
jlundblad@northpark.edu

LUNDBLAD, Tracey 302-736-2372 91 G
tracey.lundblad@wesley.edu

LUNDBURG, P. Wesley 631-451-4259 336 E
lundbuw@sunysuffolk.edu

LUNDE, Beth 757-822-1711 498 H
blunde@tcc.edu

LUNDEEN, Bruce 810-766-4018 231 C
bruce.lundeen@baker.edu

LUNDEEN, Kate 414-382-6103 515 D
kate.lundeen@alverno.edu

LUNDEN, Steve, M 509-313-5624 504 A
lunden@gonzaga.edu

LUNDERMAN, Dedria 850-729-5361 105 I
lundermand@nwfsc.edu

LUNDGREN, LaRae 951-827-2587 70 B
larae.lundgren@ucr.edu

LUNDGREN, LouAnne 505-224-4000 299 F
llundgren1@cnm.edu

LUNDQUIST, Donna 337-475-5493 200 H
dlundquist@mcneese.edu

LUNDQUIST, Lisa, M 678-547-6308 124 D
lundquist_lm@mercer.edu

LUNDQUIST, Sara 714-564-6085 58 G
lundquist_sara@sac.edu

LUNDSTREM, Karen 718-260-5140 309 C
klundstrem@citytech.cuny.edu

LUNDSTROM, Joel 712-792-8308 171 B
jtlundstrom@dmacc.edu

LUNDY, Constance, L 484-365-7785 409 B
lundy@lincoln.edu

LUNDY, Elizabeth 971-722-4005 394 F
elizabeth.lundy2@pcc.edu

LUNDY, Jennifer 412-365-1145 400 G
jlundy@chatham.edu

LUNN, Catherine 412-365-1255 400 G
clunn@chatham.edu

LUNN, D. Paul 919-513-6210 357 B
dplunn@ncsu.edu

LUNN, Francine 401-341-2231 426 C
monfettf@salve.edu

LUNNERMON, II, James, G 410-651-7606 212 B
jglunnermonii@umes.edu

LUNSFORD, Dale, A 903-233-3100 460 J
dalelunsford@letu.edu

LUNSFORD, Dan, G 828-689-1141 346 C
dlunsford@mhu.edu

LUNSFORD, Larry 305-348-2797 111 A
larry.lunsford@fiu.edu

LUO, Pengju George 864-578-8770 432 D
lpengju@sherman.edu

LUOMA, David, M 906-227-2355 239 B
daluoma@nmu.edu

LUONG, Carmen 718-482-5511 309 A
carmenl@lagcc.cuny.edu

LUONG, Huan 972-860-8102 456 C
hluong@dcccd.edu

LUPE, Mark 239-433-6948 101 F
mlupe@fsw.edu

LUPO, Bernadette 413-662-5203 222 B
bernadette.lupo@mcla.edu

LUPOLE, Barbara, H 610-799-1510 408 G
blupole@lccc.edu

LUPTON, Brendan 847-566-6401 157 G
blupton@usml.edu

LUPTON, Deborah 410-337-6135 207 H
dlupton@goucher.edu

LUQUETTE, Heidi 503-842-8222 395 D
heidiluquette@tillamookbaycc.edu

LURIA, J 845-731-3700 341 K
yv@ksrnet.com

LURSEN, Cara 704-403-1614 342 E
cara.lursen@carolinashealthcare.org

LUSHBAUGH, Jeffery 609-777-3083 297 F
jlushbaugh@tesu.edu

LUSK, D. Claude 806-291-3436 479 D
luskc@wbu.edu

LUSK, Jennifer 501-370-8525 21 G
jlusk@philander.edu

LUSK, Kent 312-553-5628 137 D
klusk1@ccc.edu

LUSKIN, Bernard 805-652-5502 73 C
bluskin@vcccd.edu

LUSNIA, Susann 504-314-7698 200 C
slusnia@tulane.edu

LUSSIER, Michel 207-741-5519 203 M
mlussier@smccme.edu

LUST, Jeff 325-793-4775 461 F
lust.jeff@mcm.edu

LUST, Kevin 217-789-1017 146 E
kevin.lust@llcc.edu

LUSTER, Pamela, T 619-388-2721 60 G
pluster@sdccd.edu

LUSTIG, Derek 315-781-3123 316 C
lustig@hws.edu

LUTCHEN, Kenneth, R 617-353-2800 216 E
klutch@bu.edu

LUTER, Gary, S 813-253-3333 114 M
gluter@ut.edu

LUTES, David 703-284-5993 492 A
david.lutes@marymount.edu

LUTGEN, Roxanne 715-675-3331 524 D
lugten@ntc.edu

LUTGRING, Ray 812-488-2589 167 I
rl5@evansville.edu

LUTHI, John, R 570-577-3332 398 L
john.luthi@bucknell.edu

LUTHJOHAN, Jeanne 269-783-2121 241 C
jluthjohan@swmich.edu

LUTON, Bill 888-384-0849 25 P
bluton@allied.edu

LUTON, Sally 315-498-2466 325 G
lutons@sunyocc.edu

LUTRICK, Candee 972-825-4612 466 D
clutrick@sagu.edu

LUTRICK, Donny 972-825-4824 466 D
dlutrick@sagu.edu

LUTTIG-KOMROSKY, Jennifer 773-702-3835 156 D
luttig@uchicago.edu

LUTTON, Margaret, K 817-515-5140 467 A
margaret.lutton@tccd.edu

LUTTRELL, Curt 760-776-7441 40 B
cluttrell@collegeofthedesert.edu

LUTY, Paul, J 503-943-8874 396 B
luty@up.edu

LUTZ, JR., Ben 865-573-4517 440 I
blutz@johnsonu.edu

LUTZ, Bob 561-803-2661 106 C
bob_lutz@pba.edu

LUTZ, Brock 517-607-2561 235 E
blutz@hillsdale.edu

LUTZ, Cathleen, A 570-321-4069 409 F
lutz@lycoming.edu

LUTZ, Cheryl 717-391-3595 420 C
lutz@stevenscollege.edu

LUTZ, Dan 765-285-8984 159 B
dlutz@bsu.edu

LUTZ, Debra, K 989-686-9386 233 I
dklutz@delta.edu

LUTZ, James 724-925-4185 423 D
lutzj@wccc.edu

LUTZ, John, M 615-875-8895 449 A
john.lutz@vanderbilt.edu

LUTZ, Nate, K 612-874-3780 247 M
nate_lutz@mcad.edu

LUTZ, Paula 307-766-4106 527 B
plutz@uwyo.edu

LUTZ, Susan 303-871-2118 84 B
susan.lutz@du.edu

LUTZ, Todd 254-519-5708 468 C
todd.lutz@tamuct.edu

LUTZ-DAVIDSON, Stacy 719-389-6953 77 J
sdavidson@coloradocollege.edu

LUTZKA, David 218-722-4000 246 E
davidl@dbumn.edu

LUUKKONEN, John 212-594-4000 337 F
jluukkonen@tcicollege.edu

LUVAAS, Linda 336-758-5000 359 E
luvaasls@wfu.edu

LUVERA, Michael 509-963-2959 501 K
luveram@cwu.edu

LUX, Jace, T 270-745-2551 194 D
jace.lux@wku.edu

LUXENBURG, Joan 405-974-5626 388 L
jluxenburg@uco.edu

MACADAM, Martha, P ..... 717-871-7520.. 415 F
martha.macadam@millersville.edu
MACALESTER, Tom .... 704-461-6721.. 342 A
tommacalester@bac.edu
MACALUSO, Anthony .... 718-990-2452.. 328 F
macalusa@stjohns.edu
MACALUSO, Daniel .... 909-621-8335.... 46 A
dmacaluso@hmc.edu
MACAN, Drew .... 386-822-7472.. 113 B
dmacan@stetson.edu
MACAPINLAC, Jonas, D .. 671-735-2944.. 530 B
jmac@triton.uog.edu
MACARI, Emir .... 504-280-7120.. 198 D
emacari@uno.edu
MACARTHUR, John .... 661-362-2220.... 52 A
sstaats@masters.edu
MACARTHUR, John .... 989-463-7241.. 230 F
macarthurjr@alma.edu
MACARTHUR, Josh .... 781-239-4528.. 214 G
wmacarthur@babson.edu
MACAULAY, Barbara .... 508-373-5897.. 225 C
barbara.macaulay@mcphs.edu
MACCARELLA, Kevin .... 610-361-2583.. 411 E
maccarek@neumann.edu
MACCARONE, Ellen, M .... 509-313-6136.. 504 A
maccarone@gonzaga.edu
MACCARTHY, Stephen, J . 215-898-8724.. 421 E
smaccar@upenn.edu
MACCHI, Thomas, J .... 215-572-2942.. 397 G
macchit@arcadia.edu
MACCHIAVELLI, Raul .... 787-265-3850.. 538 C
raul.macchiavelli@upr.edu
MACCLAREN, Jon, A .... 802-387-6721.. 484 B
jonmacclaren@landmark.edu
MACCORQUODALE,
Patricia .... 520-621-2848.... 17 I
pmac@email.arizona.edu
MACCUISH, Spencer .... 805-581-1233.... 43 B
smaccuish@eternitybiblecollege.com
MACCULLOCH, Heather ... 646-312-5045.. 307 A
heather.macculloch@baruch.cuny.edu
MACDONALD, Brian .... 802-654-2588.. 484 I
bmacdonald@smcvt.edu
MACDONALD, Brian .... 610-282-1100.. 402 B
brian.macdonald@desales.edu
MACDONALD, David .... 419-772-2200.. 374 J
d-macdonald@onu.edu
MACDONALD, Elizabeth .. 636-949-4396.. 266 J
emacdonald@lindenwood.edu
MACDONALD, Gail .... 802-225-3261.. 484 G
gail.macdonald@neci.edu
MACDONALD, Gordon .... 303-762-6890.... 79 I
gordon.macdonald@denverseminary.edu
MACDONALD, Gregory .... 540-868-7275.. 497 E
gmacdonald@lfcc.edu
MACDONALD, Gregory .... 610-330-5069.. 407 C
macdonag@lafayette.edu
MACDONALD, Lauren ...... 415-749-4557.... 61 B
lmacdonald@sfai.edu
MACDONALD, Lorri .... 313-578-0401.. 241 G
macdonlj@udmercy.edu
MACDONALD, Lyle, W .... 406-338-5441.. 276 A
lmacdonald@bfcc.edu
MACDONALD, Mark .... 808-675-3260.. 130 E
mark.macdonald@byuh.edu
MACDONALD, Nancy .... 518-454-2161.. 311 B
macdonan@strose.edu
MACDONALD, Nathan ..... 425-640-1423.. 503 E
nathan.macdonald@edcc.edu
MACDONALD,
Randall, M .... 863-680-4165.. 101 E
rmacdonald1@flsouthern.edu
MACDONALD, William .... 218-299-4358.. 246 A
macdonal@cord.edu
MACDONALD, William, L 740-366-3321.. 375 A
macdonald.24@osu.edu
MACDONALD-DENNIS,
Chris, A .... 651-696-6210.. 247 I
cmacdona@macalester.edu
MACDONELL, Chuck, C ... 402-552-2693.. 279 D
macdonell@clarksoncollege.edu
MACDONNELL, Frances ... 540-261-8538.. 494 F
frances.macdonnell@svu.edu
MACDONNELL, Lisa .... 313-993-1455.. 241 G
macdonnl@udmercy.edu
MACE, Chance .... 575-624-8214.. 300 I
mace@nmmi.edu
MACEO, Brenda, K .... 213-740-5371.... 72 D
maceo@usc.edu
MACEWAN, Bonnie .... 334-844-1714...... 1 G
macewbj@auburn.edu
MACFARLAND, Joseph ..... 410-626-2511.. 210 D
joseph.macfarland@sjc.edu
MACFARLAND,
Randolph, M .... 303-762-6900.... 79 I
provost@denverseminary.edu
MACFIE, Thomas, E .... 931-598-1274.. 443 O
tmacfie@sewanee.edu
MACGILLIVRAY, Derrick .. 865-251-1800.. 444 A
dmacgillivray@southcollegetn.edu
MACGILLIVRAY,
Diane, N .... 617-373-2520.. 227 B
MACH, Stella .... 312-935-4180.. 152 D
smach@robertmorris.edu
MACH, Thomas .... 937-766-7936.. 365 C
macht@cedarville.edu
MACHA, Barry .... 940-397-6225.. 462 A
barry.macha@mwsu.edu
MACHACEK, Jennifer .... 920-748-8185.. 519 E
machacekj@ripon.edu
MACHADO, Alyson .... 808-544-1126.. 130 H
amachado@hpu.edu
MACHADO, Fernando ...... 305-442-9223.. 105 F
fmachado@mrc.edu
MACHADO, Jorge, E .... 305-760-7500.. 104 K
MACHALSKI, Thomas .... 248-683-0311.. 241 F
tmachalski@sscms.edu
MACHAMER, Claire .... 336-770-3374.. 358 E
machamerc@uncsa.edu
MACHAN, Mark .... 937-376-6591.. 365 H
mmachan@centralstate.edu
MACHELL, James .... 405-974-5701.. 388 L
jmachell@uco.edu
MACHEN, Paul .... 210-486-2157.. 450 E
pmachen@alamo.edu
MACHI, Jeffrey .... 212-650-7125.. 307 E
jmachi@ccny.cuny.edu
MACHIA, Michael .... 580-628-6291.. 384 L
michael.machia@noc.edu
MACHIELSON, Allen, J .... 260-982-5052.. 165 M
ajmachielson@manchester.edu
MACHLIS, Gedelyah .... 718-232-7800.. 340 K
MACHNIK, Michael, E ..... 908-526-1200.. 295 A
mike.machnik@raritanval.edu
MACHOVSKY, Robert .... 660-562-1248.. 269 J
alumni@nwmissouri.edu
MACHT, Barbara, E .... 240-500-2000.. 207 I
bemacht@hagerstowncc.edu
MACHTLEY, Ronald, K ..... 401-232-6008.. 424 K
rmac@bryant.edu
MACHUCA, Elida .... 818-654-1704.... 57 F
emachuca@pgu.edu
MACHUSAK, Janice, M ... 313-927-1443.. 237 E
jmachusak@marygrove.edu
MACIAG, Clark .... 704-971-8500.. 343 E
cmaciag@charlottelaw.edu
MACIAS, Anita .... 412-563-6673.. 127 D
amacias@southuniversity.edu
MACIAS, Benjamin .... 626-914-8611.... 38 D
bmacias@citruscollege.edu
MACIAS, Joanne .... 361-593-3085.. 469 A
joanne.macias@tamuk.edu
MACIAS, Sandy .... 650-961-9300.... 56 D
smacias@paloaltou.edu
MACIAS, Tom .... 760-757-2121.... 52 K
tmacias@miracosta.edu
MACIAS-SILVERMAN,
Claudia .... 773-577-8100.. 139 A
MACIEJEWSKI, Felice, E .. 708-524-6873.. 139 F
fmaciejewski@dom.edu
MACIEJEWSKI, Kathryn ... 906-932-4231.. 234 C
kathrynm@gogebic.edu
MACIEL, Anthony .... 949-582-4882.... 65 G
amaciel@saddleback.edu
MACIEL, Rene .... 210-924-4338.. 452 F
rene.maciel@bua.edu
MACIK-FREY, Marilyn ...... 985-448-4170.. 201 A
marilyn.macik-frey@nicholls.edu
MACINNIS, Stewart, D ..... 540-464-7207.. 499 E
macinnissd@vmi.edu
MACINTYRE, Tamara .... 510-780-4500.... 48 J
tmacintyre@lifewest.edu
MACIULAITIS, Mark .... 631-632-6090.. 332 A
mark.maciulaitis@stonybrook.edu
MACK, Bruce .... 704-669-4115.. 348 F
mack@clevelandcc.edu
MACK, Carol .... 843-525-8250.. 433 B
cmack@tcl.edu
MACK, Cindy .... 716-614-6731.. 324 D
cmack@niagaracc.suny.edu
MACK, Craig .... 617-732-2929.. 225 C
craig.mack@mcphs.edu
MACK, Hailey .... 208-535-5337.. 133 G
hailey.mack@my.eitc.edu
MACK, Johnny .... 503-399-6243.. 390 E
johnny.mack@chemeketa.edu
MACK, Jon .... 610-917-1467.. 422 C
jmack@valleyforge.edu
MACK, Joseph .... 607-431-4209.. 315 E
mackj@hartwick.edu
MACK, Josh, C .... 641-422-4436.. 175 E
mackjosh@niacc.edu
MACK, Kari .... 845-687-5214.. 338 F
mackk@sunyulster.edu
MACK, Kimberly, J .... 252-536-6399.. 350 C
kmack219@halifaxcc.edu
MACK, Marva .... 973-877-3346.. 291 H
mack@essex.edu
MACK, Melvin .... 803-934-3401.. 431 E
mmack@morris.edu
MACK, Qing, L .... 860-253-3008.... 86 A
qmack@asnuntuck.edu
MACK, Sharon, K .... 207-255-1327.. 205 C
sharon.mack@maine.edu
MACK, Stephen, G .... 215-895-1910.. 402 G
stephen.g.mack@drexel.edu
MACK, Teresa .... 803-793-5106.. 429 D
mackt@denmarktech.edu
MACK, Tonya .... 530-741-6987.... 76 B
tmack@yccd.edu
MACK, Tracy .... 806-720-7380.. 461 C
tracy.mack@lcu.edu
MACK-HISGEN, Maura .... 518-262-5033.. 303 E
mmack@mail.amc.edu
MACKAY, Jeff .... 503-883-2436.. 392 B
jmackay@linfield.edu
MACKE, Charles .... 931-372-3414.. 445 B
cmacke@tntech.edu
MACKEITH, Peter .... 479-575-2702.... 22 I
mackeith@uark.edu
MACKEL, Thomas, J .... 678-839-6252.. 129 E
tmackel@westga.edu
MACKELWICH, Danielle .... 360-779-9993.. 505 B
dmackelwich@ncad.edu
MACKEN, Jennifer .... 303-914-6600.... 82 I
jen.macken@rrcc.edu
MACKENZIE, Lorie .... 315-229-5600.. 329 D
lmackenzie@stlawu.edu
MACKERETH, Anne .... 952-885-5417.. 253 Z
amackereth@nwhealth.edu
MACKERSIE, Chris .... 253-912-3655.. 506 B
cmackers@pierce.ctc.edu
MACKESY, Francis, J .... 904-620-2800.. 112 B
f.mackesy@unf.edu
MACKEY, Colin .... 315-386-7003.. 335 B
mackey@canton.edu
MACKEY, Geoffrey .... 724-266-3838.. 421 C
gmackey@tsm.edu
MACKEY, Jerry .... 562-903-4777.... 28 E
university.legalcounsel@biola.edu
MACKEY, Joshua .... 303-556-5034.... 81 G
jmackey@msudenver.edu
MACKEY, Peter, F .... 413-542-2321.. 214 C
comm@amherst.edu
MACKEY, Thomas .... 518-587-2100.. 335 D
thomas.mackey@esc.edu
MACKEY, Tonja .... 903-823-3028.. 467 C
tonja.mackey@texarkanacollege.edu
MACKIE, Jennifer .... 805-765-9300.... 62 K
MACKIE, Keith .... 828-327-7000.. 348 C
kmackie@cvcc.edu
MACKIE-MASON,
Jeffrey, K .... 734-647-3576.. 241 J
jmm@umich.edu
MACKILLOP, Jane .... 718-482-5302.. 309 A
jmackillop@lagcc.cuny.edu
MACKIN, James .... 607-436-2517.. 331 F
james.mackin@oneonta.edu
MACKIN, Jim .... 402-461-7482.. 280 D
jmackin@hastings.edu
MACKINNON, Fern .... 978-934-4660.. 221 A
fern_mackinnon@uml.edu
MACKINNON, George .... 414-955-2855.. 518 A
gmackinnon@mcw.edu
MACKINNON, Mary Jo .... 401-454-6625.. 426 A
mmackinn@risd.edu
MACKINNON, Neil, J ...... 513-558-3326.. 379 A
neil.mackinnon@uc.edu
MACKLER, Dan .... 818-333-3558.... 54 B
MACKLIN, James, F .... 518-629-7353.. 316 G
j.macklin@hvcc.edu
MACKLIN, Sharon .... 973-353-5541.. 296 C
sharon.macklin@rutgers.edu
MACKSEY, Jennifer .... 802-447-6310.. 485 B
jmacksey@svc.edu
MACLACHLAN, Scott .... 561-207-5325.. 106 D
maclachs@palmbeachstate.edu
MACLAINE, Julie, A .... 740-588-1201.. 382 C
jmaclaine@zanestate.edu
MACLAREN, James .... 504-865-5720.. 200 C
maclaren@tulane.edu
MACLAUGHLIN, Cordy ...... 808-984-3471.. 132 D
cordy.maclaughlin@uhfoundation.org
MACLEAN, Roger .... 406-243-2900.. 276 K
roger.maclean@umontana.edu
MACLEISH, Padraic .... 760-872-2000.... 42 B
padraicm@deepsprings.edu
MACLELLAND, Stuart .... 718-951-5000.. 307 D
MACLENNAN, Kevin, L ..... 303-492-6694.... 83 K
kevin.maclennan@colorado.edu
MACLENNAN, Richard ...... 301-387-3056.. 207 G
rick.maclennan@garrettcollege.edu
MACLENNAN, Richard, L . 208-769-3303.. 134 C
rmaclennan@nic.edu
MACLEOD, David, J .... 563-588-8000.. 172 E
dmacleod@emmaus.edu
MACLEOD, Ian .... 508-830-5269.. 222 C
imacleod@maritime.edu
MACLEOD, Kellye .... 952-851-0066.. 244 C
MACLEOD, Kimberly, M .. 607-746-4603.. 335 C
macleokm@delhi.edu
MACLEOD, Melissa, A ..... 724-458-2050.. 404 F
mamacleod@gcc.edu
MACLEOD, Robert .... 813-974-6015.. 112 C
rmacleod@usf.edu
MACLEOD WALLS,
Elizabeth .... 816-415-5026.. 275 F
macleodwallse@william.jewell.edu
MACMASTER, Donald ...... 989-358-7246.. 230 G
macmastd@alpenacc.edu
MACMENAMIE, Michael .. 310-377-5501.... 51 G
mmacmenamie@marymountcalifornia.edu
MACMILLAN, Cynthia ...... 609-984-1130.. 297 F
cmacmillan@tesu.edu
MACMILLAN FOX,
Rebecca .... 305-284-2648.. 114 H
rfox@miami.edu
MACMINN, Linda .... 305-809-3285.. 100 N
linda.macminn@fkcc.edu
MACNAMARA, Timothy ... 307-778-1256.. 526 K
tmacnama@lccc.wy.edu
MACNEIL, Jacqueline ...... 727-864-7856.... 98 L
macneijm@eckerd.edu
MACNEIL, M. A. J. Lex .... 630-515-7275.. 148 C
lmacne@midwestern.edu
MACNEIL, R. Lamont .... 860-679-2808.... 89 D
macneil@nso.uchc.edu
MACNEILL, Andrew, J ..... 619-388-2797.... 60 G
amacneil@sdccd.edu
MACNEILL, Lynn .... 863-784-7192.. 109 G
lynn.macneill@southflorida.edu
MACNEW, James .... 215-637-7700.. 405 J
jmacnew@holyfamily.edu
MACON, Kenneth .... 205-802-1200...... 3 C
kenneth.macon@vc.edu
MACONACHY, W. Vic .... 301-369-2800.. 206 H
wvmaconachy@captechul.edu
MACOPSON, Elmer, R ...... 828-652-0603.. 351 C
elmerm@mcdowelltech.edu
MACOSKO, Ron .... 830-792-7421.. 465 E
rpmacosko@schreiner.edu
MACPHERSON, Andrew ... 903-463-8768.. 458 H
macphersona@grayson.edu
MACPHERSON, Heidi, R .. 585-395-2361.. 332 E
hmacpherson@brockport.edu
MACPHERSON, Pamela ... 302-622-8000.... 90 E
pmacpherson@dcad.edu
MACQUEEN, William, J ... 248-341-2027.. 239 E
wjmacque@oaklandcc.edu
MACREYNOLDS,
William, K .... 336-727-7102.. 344 G
bill.macreynolds@greensboro.edu
MACRINA, Francis, L ...... 804-827-2262.. 496 D
macrina@vcu.edu
MACRISS, Bill .... 916-278-6348.... 34 B
bmacriss@csus.edu
MACRITCHIE, Andrea .... 508-854-4461.. 224 E
amacritchie@qcc.mass.edu
MACRO, Venessa .... 515-271-3710.. 171 K
venessa.macro@drake.edu
MACTAGGART, Julie .... 563-589-3619.. 177 C
jmactaggart@dbq.edu
MACUR, Kenneth, M .... 716-880-2202.. 320 D
kenneth.m.macur@medaille.edu
MACVARISH, Greg .... 312-662-4141.. 134 I
gmacvarish@adler.edu
MACVEY, Mark .... 760-480-8474.... 74 L
mmacvey@wscal.edu
MACWILLIAMS, David ...... 719-587-7800.... 76 G
dcmacwil@adams.edu
MACY, Dawn .... 657-278-3746.... 33 A
dmacy@fullerton.edu
MACZAK, Marie .... 409-747-4876.. 478 A
mmarczak@utmb.edu
MACZKA, Eric .... 402-941-6201.. 280 N
maczka@midlandu.edu
MADAIO-O'BRIEN,
Melanie .... 617-353-2256.. 216 E
asmelmad@bu.edu
MADAMA, Patrick .... 732-906-2551.. 292 E
pmadama@middlesexcc.edu
MADAMBA, Victor .... 510-780-4500.... 48 J
vmadamba@lifewest.edu
MADANIPOUR,
Manouche .... 617-928-7376.. 226 B
mmadanipour@mountida.edu
MADAUS, Joseph .... 860-405-9010.... 89 D
joseph.madaus@uconn.edu
MADDAHI,
Dariush (David) .... 323-728-9636.... 53 J
MADDALI, Ramesh .... 601-877-6146.. 256 F
rmaddali@alcorn.edu
MADDEN, Beverly .... 650-574-6538.... 62 H
maddenb@smccd.edu
MADDEN, Caitlin .... 213-624-1200.... 43 J
cmadden@fidm.edu
MADDEN, Carolyn .... 603-428-2386.. 287 C
cmadden@nec.edu
MADDEN, Christopher ..... 214-648-0702.. 478 C
christopher.madden@utsouthwestern.edu
MADDEN, Corey .... 336-770-1442.. 358 E
maddenc@uncsa.edu

MADDEN, Fred, H ... 856-415-2272.. 295 D
fmadden@rcgc.edu
MADDEN, John ... 575-624-7111.. 299 J
john.madden@roswell.enmu.edu
MADDEN, Kathleen ... 661-654-3450.... 32 A
kmadden@csub.edu
MADDEN, Margaret ... 518-783-2307.. 330 E
mmaden@siena.edu
MADDEN, Paul ... 740-351-3270.. 377 C
pmadden@shawnee.edu
MADDEN, Richard ... 931-363-9844.. 441 G
rmadden@martinmethodist.edu
MADDEN, Sally, J ... 847-578-3266.. 153 A
sally.madden@rosalindfranklin.edu
MADDEN, Susan ... 240-567-5274.. 209 E
susan.madden@montgomerycollege.edu
MADDEN, Tamara ... 405-682-7897.. 385 D
tamara.r.madden@occc.edu
MADDEN JOHNSON,
Anne ... 785-864-0306.. 185 D
amjohnson@ku.edu
MADDEX, Shelley ... 530-754-4138.... 69 A
sbmaddex@ucdavis.edu
MADDIGAN, Susan ... 508-362-2131.. 223 C
smaddigan@capecod.edu
MADDIN, Brent ... 212-228-1888.. 327 A
bmaddin@ttc.edu
MADDIRALA, James, S ... 340-693-1013.. 539 C
james.maddirala@uvi.edu
MADDOCK, Jay ... 979-436-9322.. 468 B
maddock@tamhsc.edu
MADDON, Jason ... 616-451-3511.. 233 C
jmaddon@davenport.edu
MADDOX, Gregory, H ... 713-313-7889.. 470 D
maddox_gh@tsu.edu
MADDOX, Kelley, L ... 770-534-6270.. 118 A
kmaddox@brenau.edu
MADDOX, Kenneth ... 256-372-4871...... 1 A
kenneth.maddox@aamu.edu
MADDOX, Nedra ... 704-669-4142.. 348 F
maddox@clevelandcc.edu
MADDOX, Tangella ... 312-341-3584.. 152 H
tmaddox@roosevelt.edu
MADDOX, Teri ... 731-286-3322.. 446 B
maddox@dscc.edu
MADDOX, Winston ... 609-586-4800.. 292 D
maddoxw@mccc.edu
MADDOX, Yvonne ... 301-295-3303.. 528 G
yvonne.maddox@usuhs.edu
MADDUX, Gary ... 256-824-2679...... 8 F
gary.maddux@us.army.mil
MADDUX, Pat ... 563-588-6366.. 170 F
pat.maddux@clarke.edu
MADDUX, Susan, A ... 864-833-8205.. 432 B
smaddux@presby.edu
MADDY, Angela, M ... 620-792-9322.. 178 G
maddya@bartonccc.edu
MADELONE LINCOLN,
Laura ... 607-436-2526.. 331 F
laura.madelone@oneonta.edu
MADER, Mary ... 978-542-6390.. 222 D
mary.mader@salemstate.edu
MADERE, Whit ... 804-819-4951.. 496 E
wmadere@vccs.edu
MADHAVA RAU, Leela ... 909-748-8285.... 71 K
leela_madhavarau@redlands.edu
MADIA, Sherrie ... 201-200-2472.. 293 C
smadia@njcu.edu
MADIGAN, David ... 212-854-8296.. 311 E
david.madigan@columbia.edu
MADIGAN, Dennis, J ... 617-603-6900.. 226 D
dennis.madigan@necb.edu
MADIGAN, Kay ... 330-652-9919.. 368 G
kaymadigan@eticollege.edu
MADIGAN, Kaye ... 320-762-4684.. 248 J
kayem@alextech.edu
MADIN, Laurence, P ... 508-289-2515.. 230 B
lmadin@whoi.edu
MADIOU-BEALE, Olga ... 410-888-9048.. 209 C
obeale@muih.edu
MADISON, Anna ... 617-287-7232.. 220 G
anna.madison@umb.edu
MADISON, Renee ... 765-658-4914.. 160 F
reneemadison@depauw.edu
MADISON, Stephen, S ... 817-515-1002.. 467 A
stephen.madison@tccd.edu
MADIX, Marcy ... 619-684-8813.... 54 C
mmadix@newschoolarch.edu
MADLOCK, Calvin ... 510-466-5398.... 57 E
cmadlock@peralta.edu
MADLOCK, Calvin ... 510-466-5398.... 57 A
cmadlock@peralta.edu
MADLOCK, Krystal ... 319-352-8434.. 177 G
krystal.madlock@wartburg.edu
MADONNA, Richard ... 860-439-2044.... 87 F
richard.madonna@conncoll.edu
MADORE, Keith ... 860-253-3041.... 86 A
kmadore@asnuntuck.edu
MADORIN, Jeanne, L ... 704-687-0659.. 358 A
jlmadori@uncc.edu
MADRAY, Van ... 704-216-3900.. 352 G
van.madray@rccc.edu
MADRID, Jered ... 949-794-9090.... 66 H
jmadrid@stanbridge.edu
MADRIGAL, Richard ... 856-687-2258.... 30 I
MADRIGAL-SHAFFER,
Maria ... 559-278-6715.... 32 F
mmadrigalshaffer@csufresno.edu
MADSEN, Alice ... 206-878-3710.. 504 E
amadsen@highline.edu
MADSEN, Christina ... 501-852-2659.... 24 G
christinam@uca.edu
MADSEN, Jenny, S ... 719-884-5000.... 81 N
jsmadsen@nbc.edu
MADSEN, Lois ... 785-833-4315.. 182 F
lois.madsen@kwu.edu
MADSEN, Patrick ... 704-687-0784.. 358 A
MADSEN, Ruthanne ... 617-824-8600.. 218 B
ruthanne_madsen@emerson.edu
MADSEN, Thor ... 816-414-3700.. 268 D
academicdean@mbts.edu
MADSEN-BROOKS,
Leslie ... 208-426-1700.. 132 I
lesliemadsen-brooks@boisestate.edu
MADSON, Gregory ... 406-791-5359.. 278 G
gregory.madson@ugf.edu
MADULI, Ed ... 408-741-2082.... 74 F
ed_maduli@wvm.edu
MADURA, Angela ... 303-245-4751.... 81 I
amadura@naropa.edu
MAEA, Cheri ... 540-834-1980.. 497 B
cmaea@germanna.edu
MAEDA, Sandy ... 808-455-0462.. 132 C
smaeda@hawaii.edu
MAENE, Sara ... 304-876-5112.. 513 E
smaene@shepherd.edu
MAES, Sue, C ... 785-532-5644.. 182 D
scmaes@ksu.edu
MAESTAS, Belen ... 719-587-7321.... 76 G
bmaestas@adams.edu
MAESTAS, Henrietta ... 505-454-2596.. 299 M
hmaestas@luna.edu
MAESTAS, Stacy ... 307-778-1240.. 526 K
smaestas@lccc.wy.edu
MAFFEI, Melody ... 209-667-3623.... 34 E
mmaffei@csustan.edu
MAFFEO, Angie ... 815-740-3711.. 157 F
amaffeo@stfrancis.edu
MAFFIA, Robert ... 201-216-3542.. 297 B
robert.maffia@stevens.edu
MAFFUCCI, Michael ... 704-290-5864.. 353 B
mmaffucci@spcc.edu
MAFREDI, Juan, J ... 412-624-0790.. 421 G
manfredi@pitt.edu
MAGALONG, Mariles ... 510-215-3847.... 41 H
mmagalong@contracosta.edu
MAGANA, Keri ... 828-898-8896.. 345 G
maganak@lmc.edu
MAGAZU, Daniel ... 508-626-4539.. 221 E
dmagazu@framingham.edu
MAGDALENO, Jose ... 718-960-8241.. 308 B
joseph.magdaleno@lehman.cuny.edu
MAGDZIARZ, Wayne ... 312-915-6403.. 146 G
wmagdzi@luc.edu
MAGEE, JR., David, E ... 423-439-4441.. 444 F
magee@etsu.edu
MAGEE, Edward ... 304-558-0281.. 512 O
ed.magee@wvhepc.edu
MAGEE, Erin ... 707-527-4431.... 63 G
emagee@santarosa.edu
MAGEE, Frances ... 508-793-7423.. 217 B
fmagee@clarku.edu
MAGEE, Gwen ... 601-477-4028.. 258 E
gwen.magee@jcjc.edu
MAGEE, Jeannette ... 323-953-4000.... 49 H
mageejm@lacitycollege.edu
MAGEE, Jennifer ... 214-637-3530.. 479 C
jmagee@wadecollege.edu
MAGEE, Jim ... 610-341-1720.. 403 B
jmagee@eastern.edu
MAGEE, John ... 734-432-5351.. 237 D
jmagee@madonna.edu
MAGEE, Kristy ... 814-886-6320.. 411 C
kmagee@mtaloy.edu
MAGEE, Maggie ... 207-947-4591.. 202 E
mmagee@bealcollege.edu
MAGEE-SAUER, Karen ... 856-256-4850.. 295 E
sauer@rowan.edu
MAGERS, Dwight, E ... 423-236-2992.. 444 B
magers@southern.edu
MAGET, Douglas ... 212-854-5204.. 304 I
dmaget@barnard.edu
MAGGARD, Shawn ... 615-383-4848.. 449 G
smaggard@watkins.edu
MAGGARD, Trent ... 620-862-5252.. 178 F
trent.maggard@barclaycollege.edu
MAGGELAKIS, Sophia ... 585-475-2483.. 327 E
sxmsma@rit.edu
MAGGERT, Jerry ... 800-962-7682.. 275 D
jmaggert@wma.edu
MAGGIO, Chirs ... 318-357-4250.. 201 B
maggioc@nsula.edu
MAGGIO, Cindy ... 318-676-7811.. 196 H
cindymaggio@nwltc.edu
MAGGIO, Evelyn ... 718-270-5103.. 309 B
emaggio@mec.cuny.edu
MAGGIO, Marielena ... 216-368-2519.. 365 B
mxm346@case.edu
MAGGIONI, Susan ... 781-239-2461.. 223 F
MAGGIORE, Fay ... 516-876-2031.. 333 C
maggiorer@oldwestbury.edu
MAGGIORE, Ronald ... 516-686-7925.. 323 G
ron.maggiore@nyit.edu
MAGGITTI, Patrick, G ... 610-519-4521.. 422 G
patrick.maggitti@villanova.edu
MAGGITTI, Sara ... 610-902-8561.. 399 D
sara.t.maggitti@cabrini.edu
MAGGS, Mark ... 814-234-7755.. 419 F
mmaggs@southhills.edu
MAGHSOODI, Amin ... 323-563-4842.... 37 G
aminmaghsoodi@cdrewu.edu
MAGHSOUD, Amanda F ... 803-323-4891.. 435 B
maghsouda@winthrop.edu
MAGIDA, David ... 802-485-2145.. 484 H
davem@norwich.edu
MAGIE, CM, Sandra, C ... 713-686-4345.. 475 J
smagie@stthom.edu
MAGIERA, Steve, L ... 239-590-1119.. 110 L
smagiera@fgcu.edu
MAGILL, Jim ... 828-298-3325.. 359 F
jmagill@warren-wilson.edu
MAGILL, M. Elizabeth ... 650-723-2300.... 66 I
MAGLIONE, Joyce ... 973-408-3631.. 291 B
jmaglion@drew.edu
MAGLISH, Mike ... 208-376-7731.. 132 H
mmaglish@boisebible.edu
MAGLIULO, Sabrina ... 201-360-4230.. 292 B
smagliulo@hccc.edu
MAGLOIRE, Yves, M ... 516-628-5007.. 333 C
magloirey@oldwestbury.edu
MAGNAN, Carolyn ... 860-832-3715.... 85 F
magnanc@ccsu.edu
MAGNER, Brent ... 402-363-5636.. 283 G
brent.magner@york.edu
MAGNER, Brent, N ... 402-363-5636.. 283 G
brent.magner@york.edu
MAGNER, Kevin ... 714-867-5009.... 65 D
kjmagner@southcoastcollege.com
MAGNER, Lois, B ... 620-417-1011.. 184 I
lois.magner@sccc.edu
MAGNER, Michael ... 978-837-5019.. 225 E
magnerm@merrimack.edu
MAGNER, Timothy ... 318-813-3543.. 198 B
tmagner@lsuhsc.edu
MAGNUS, Keith, B ... 317-940-9385.. 159 K
kmagnus@butler.edu
MAGNUSON, Audrey, J ... 210-458-6846.. 477 A
audrey.magnuson@utsa.edu
MAGNUSON, Dave ... 803-754-4100.. 429 B
MAGNUSON, Jacquelyn ... 651-641-8892.. 246 B
magnuson@csp.edu
MAGNUSON, Kelly, J ... 320-222-6094.. 251 G
kelly.magnuson@ridgewater.edu
MAGNUSON, Kendyl ... 760-744-1150.... 56 F
kmagnuson@palomar.edu
MAGNUSON, Matthew ... 559-934-2403.... 74 D
matthewmagnuson@whccd.edu
MAGNUSON, Nancy ... 410-337-6364.. 207 H
nmagnuson@goucher.edu
MAGNUSON, Nancy, M ... 314-516-5671.. 274 A
magnuson@umsl.edu
MAGNUSON, Terry ... 919-962-1319.. 357 D
tmagnuson@unc.edu
MAGNUSSON, Selena ... 706-295-6866.. 121 F
smagnusson@gntc.edu
MAGOON, Don ... 919-735-5151.. 354 A
djmagoon@waynecc.edu
MAGOON, Maggie ... 989-386-6622.. 238 B
mmagoon@midmich.edu
MAGOULIAS, Christine ... 217-424-6244.. 148 D
christiemagoulias@millikin.edu
MAGRETTA, Dawn ... 586-445-7302.. 237 C
magrettad@macomb.edu
MAGRO, Edward ... 401-232-6000.. 424 K
MAGUET, Kathryn, L ... 570-577-3700.. 398 L
kathryn.maguet@bucknell.edu
MAGUIRE, Eric, G ... 717-356-3953.. 403 J
eric.maguire@fandm.edu
MAGUIRE, Karen ... 212-355-1501.. 306 L
kmaguire@christies.edu
MAGUIRE, Ken ... 575-624-7160.. 299 J
ken.maguire@roswell.enmu.edu
MAGUIRE, Kenneth ... 575-624-7328.. 299 J
ken.maguire@roswell.enmu.edu
MAGUIRE, Kevin, C ... 617-627-3502.. 228 H
kevin.maguire@tufts.edu
MAGUIRE, Trish ... 575-562-2165.. 299 I
trish.maguire@enmu.edu
MAGUSIAK, Henry ... 724-738-4898.. 416 B
henry.magusiak@sru.edu
MAH, Al ... 323-241-5238.... 50 B
mahac@lasc.edu
MAHAFFEY, Angela ... 304-473-8100.. 515 B
mahaffey_a@wvwc.edu
MAHAFFEY, Danny ... 225-578-3962.. 197 H
dmahaf1@lsu.edu
MAHAFFEY, Rena ... 615-794-4254.. 443 G
rmahaffey@omorecollege.edu
MAHAFFY, Kevin ... 312-329-4134.. 148 F
kevin.mahaffy@moody.edu
MAHALINGAM, Shankar .. 256-824-6474...... 8 F
shankar.mahalingam@uah.edu
MAHAN, Amy, J ... 501-882-8880.... 18 I
ajmahan@asub.edu
MAHAN, Christine, P ... 610-341-1706.. 403 B
cmahan@eastern.edu
MAHAN, David ... 718-862-7597.. 319 L
david.mahan@manhattan.edu
MAHAN, Forest ... 843-921-6919.. 431 H
fmahan@netc.edu
MAHAN, Forest, E ... 803-508-7247.. 426 G
MAHAN, Karl ... 806-720-7122.. 461 C
karl.mahan@lcu.edu
MAHAN, Kim, B ... 806-371-5050.. 450 H
kbmahan@actx.edu
MAHAN, Lisa ... 317-738-8018.. 160 J
lmahan@franklincollege.edu
MAHAN, Marilyn ... 785-320-4501.. 183 A
marilynmahan@manhattantech.edu
MAHAN, Melissa ... 210-784-1350.. 469 B
melissa.mahan@tamusa.edu
MAHAN, Michael ... 678-359-5466.. 122 E
mmahan@gordonstate.edu
MAHAN, Mickie ... 417-455-5536.. 264 E
mickiemahan@crowder.edu
MAHAR, Kate ... 530-242-7769.... 64 D
kmahar@shastacollege.edu
MAHARAJ, Peter ... 714-241-6297.... 39 E
pmaharaj@coastline.edu
MAHARAJ,
Sandhya (Sandy), G ... 304-766-3236.. 514 B
smaharaj@wvstateu.edu
MAHARAS, Marian ... 303-404-5285.... 80 E
marian.maharas@frontrange.edu
MAHDI, Johnni, F ... 315-792-3209.. 339 B
jmahdi@utica.edu
MAHDI, Syed ... 803-705-4576.. 427 D
mahdis@benedict.edu
MAHER, Brian ... 973-278-5400.. 305 B
bdm@berkeleycollege.edu
MAHER, Brian ... 973-278-5400.. 289 F
bdm@berkeleycollege.edu
MAHER, Hannah ... 309-457-2286.. 148 E
hmaher@monmouthcollege.edu
MAHER, CM, James ... 716-286-8350.. 324 E
jjm@niagara.edu
MAHER, Jason ... 641-269-3450.. 172 I
maherjas@grinnell.edu
MAHER, Jerelyn ... 309-676-7611.. 136 B
jmaher2@fsmail.bradley.edu
MAHER, Jeremiah, J ... 530-752-7596.... 69 A
jeremiah.maher@ucdmc.ucdavis.edu
MAHER, John ... 304-696-4748.. 513 D
maherj@marshall.edu
MAHER, Judith ... 724-805-2900.. 419 A
judith.maher@email.stvincent.edu
MAHER, Mary ... 410-837-5392.. 213 C
mmaher@ubalt.edu
MAHER, Peter ... 314-246-8622.. 275 B
maherp@webster.edu
MAHER, Stella ... 908-737-2586.. 292 C
smaher@kean.edu
MAHER, Susan ... 218-726-8981.. 255 D
smaher@d.umn.edu
MAHER, Tracy ... 701-854-8039.. 362 B
tracym@sbci.edu
MAHER, Walter ... 210-829-3939.. 474 D
maher@uiwtx.edu
MAHER, William, J ... 716-888-2970.. 306 F
maherw@canisius.edu
MAHFOOD, Sebastian ... 860-632-3010.... 88 B
smahfood@holyapostles.edu
MAHFOUZ, Riham ... 757-825-2898.. 498 G
mahfouzr@tncc.edu
MAHINDRA, Ankush ... 310-665-6916.... 55 E
amahindra@otis.edu
MAHITAB, Frank ... 478-825-6754.. 120 F
mahitabf@fvsu.edu
MAHLBERG, James, A ... 712-325-3218.. 174 B
jmahlberg@iwcc.edu
MAHLBERG, Lynn, M ... 775-753-2282.. 284 I
lynn.mahlberg@gbcnv.edu
MAHLE, Krista ... 360-676-2772.. 505 C
kmahle@nwic.edu
MAHLER, Aaron ... 434-381-6387.. 494 M
amahler@sbc.edu
MAHLER, Craig ... 615-844-5292.. 449 H
cmahler@welch.edu
MAHLER, Greg ... 765-983-1318.. 160 G
gregm@earlham.edu
MAHLER, Stephen, J ... 337-482-6418.. 201 D
mahler@louisiana.edu

MAHLER, Steve .... 337-482-6780.. 201 D
mahler@louisiana.edu
MAHLMEISTER, Kenneth, J .... 718-990-5883.. 328 F
mahlmeik@stjohns.edu
MAHON, Edward, G .... 330-672-4704.. 370 I
emahon@kent.edu
MAHON, John .... 845-569-3287.. 322 B
john.mahon@msmc.edu
MAHON, Patricia, G .... 605-394-2416.. 437 E
patricia.mahon@sdsmt.edu
MAHONE, Reshunda .... 404-270-5126.. 128 A
rmahone@spelman.edu
MAHONE, Reshunda .... 804-524-5045.. 499 G
rmahone@vsu.edu
MAHONE-LEIWS, Gerald . 254-526-1166.. 454 A
gerald.mahone-lewis@ctcd.edu
MAHONEY, Jack .... 518-276-6790.. 327 B
mahonj@rpi.edu
MAHONEY, Jack, D .... 518-437-4928.. 331 A
jmahoney@albany.edu
MAHONEY, Janet .... 732-263-5271.. 292 F
jmahoney@monmouth.edu
MAHONEY, John .... 530-898-5749.... 32 C
jmahoney@csuchico.edu
MAHONEY, JR., John, L . 617-552-3100.. 216 C
john.mahoney.2@bc.edu
MAHONEY, Kathleen .... 603-899-4246.. 287 A
mahonek@franklinpierce.edu
MAHONEY, Kelly .... 401-874-5569.. 426 D
kellymahoney@uri.edu
MAHONEY, Lynn .... 323-343-3800.... 33 C
lynn.mahoney@calstatela.edu
MAHONEY, Paul, G .... 434-924-7343.. 495 H
pgm9h@virginia.edu
MAHONEY, Peter, E .... 724-805-2241.. 419 A
peter.mahoney@email.stvincent.edu
MAHONEY, Sharon, A ..... 508-767-7322.. 214 F
shmahone@assumption.edu
MAHONEY, Thomas .... 609-771-2734.. 290 F
tmahoney@tcnj.edu
MAHONEY, Trina .... 208-885-4387.. 134 G
tmahoney@uidaho.edu
MAHONY, Daniel, F .... 803-323-2225.. 435 B
mahonyd@winthrop.edu
MAHONY, James .... 517-264-3525.. 230 D
jmahony@adrian.edu
MAI, Bill .... 307-766-5766.. 527 B
william.mai@uwyo.edu
MAI, Brent .... 503-493-6560.. 391 A
bmai@cu-portland.edu
MAI, Brent, A .... 203-254-4000.... 87 G
bmai@fairfield.edu
MAI, Uyen .... 909-274-4121.... 53 C
umai@mtsac.edu
MAIDEN, Michael .... 732-263-5285.. 292 F
mmaiden@monmouth.edu
MAIDEN, Scott .... 617-364-3510.. 216 B
smaiden@boston.edu
MAIELLO, Gabriella .... 800-431-8488.... 27 F
MAIENSHEIN, Richard, W .... 215-887-5511.. 423 C
rmaienshein@wts.edu
MAIER, Kim .... 608-822-2463.. 524 F
kmaier@swtc.edu
MAIER, Mark .... 517-607-2445.. 235 E
mmaier@hillsdale.edu
MAIER, Richard, P .... 478-757-2083.. 129 L
rmaier@wesleyancollege.edu
MAIER-O'SHEA, Kathryn . 773-244-5582.. 149 I
kmaier@northpark.edu
MAIERHOFER, Jean .... 763-488-2633.. 249 D
jean.maierhofer@hennepintech.edu
MAIETTA, Heather .... 978-837-5038.. 225 E
maiettah@merrimack.edu
MAIGA, Harouna .... 218-281-8107.. 255 E
hmaiga@umn.edu
MAIGAARD, Brenda .... 785-864-4700.. 185 D
bmaigaard@ku.edu
MAILEN, Debbie .... 423-697-4487.. 445 D
deborah.mailen@chattanoogastate.edu
MAILHOT, John .... 413-748-3145.. 228 E
jmailhot@springfieldcollege.edu
MAILICK, Marsha, R .... 608-262-1044.. 519 K
mmailick@wisc.edu
MAILLET, Becky .... 504-278-6477.. 196 I
bmaillet@nunez.edu
MAILLET, Pierrette .... 470-578-4698.. 123 J
pmaillet@kennesaw.edu
MAILLOUX, Colin, C .... 904-632-3232.. 101 G
colin.mailloux@fscj.edu
MAIMON, Elaine, P .... 708-534-4130.. 140 H
emaimon@govst.edu
MAIMONE, Charles, A ..... 336-334-5200.. 358 B
camaimon@uncg.edu
MAIN, Mary, E .... 540-458-8920.. 500 F
mmain@wlu.edu
MAIN, Nathan .... 269-927-8169.. 236 G
nmain@lakemichigancollege.edu
MAIN, Sajid .... 708-534-4515.. 140 H
smain@govst.edu
MAINCA, Daniel .... 213-383-8999.... 25 F
MAINE, Kate .... 706-867-2550.. 128 F
kate.maine@ung.edu
MAINENTI, David .... 516-299-4212.. 319 B
david.mainenti@liu.edu
MAINS, Ashley .... 928-350-4501.... 16 P
amains@prescott.edu
MAIO, James .... 315-792-5401.. 321 G
jmaio@mvcc.edu
MAIORISI, Stephen, M .... 401-863-1297.. 424 J
stephen_maiorisi@brown.edu
MAIR, Bernard, A .... 202-806-6700.... 93 A
bernard.mair@howard.edu
MAIR, Dave .... 804-819-4929.. 496 E
dmair@vccs.edu
MAIRS, Rob .... 520-325-0123.... 17 D
rmairs@suva.edu
MAISEL, Jacqueline, M ... 410-543-6150.. 213 A
jmmaisel@salisbury.edu
MAISNIER, Stefan .... 773-481-8644.. 137 I
smaisnier@ccc.edu
MAISON, Amy .... 229-225-3977.. 127 G
amaison@southernregional.edu
MAISTER, Eric .... 215-568-9215.. 424 C
emaister@phmc.org
MAISTO, Jeremy, A .... 717-867-6215.. 408 F
maisto@lvc.edu
MAITINO, Jennifer .... 617-333-3165.. 217 F
jmaitino0615@curry.edu
MAITLAND, Jason, R .... 585-785-1437.. 314 D
jason.maitland@flcc.edu
MAITLAND, Tina, A .... 313-993-1005.. 241 G
maitlata@udmercy.edu
MAIURI, Geary .... 586-445-7579.. 237 C
maiurig@macomb.edu
MAIZE, Kay .... 402-481-8602.. 278 J
kay.maize@bryanhealthcollege.edu
MAJAK, Julieta .... 845-257-3295.. 331 E
majakj@newpaltz.edu
MAJCHROWSKI, Lauren .. 212-431-2829.. 323 H
lauren.majchrowski@nyls.edu
MAJEBE, Mary Cissy .... 828-225-3993.. 343 H
president@daoisttraditions.edu
MAJEROVIC, Chaim .... 516-239-9002.. 330 D
MAJERUS, Melissa .... 320-308-5922.. 252 B
mmajerus@sctcc.edu
MAJETTE, Yolanda .... 252-398-6249.. 343 G
majety@chowan.edu
MAJEWSKI, Deborah .... 508-999-9293.. 220 H
dmajewski@umassd.edu
MAJEWSKI, John .... 805-893-4327.... 70 E
majewski@ltsc.ucsb.edu
MAJEWSKI, Marc .... 415-338-2596.... 35 B
majewski@sfsu.edu
MAJEWSKIE, Michelle ..... 920-923-8083.. 517 H
mmajewski@marianuniversity.edu
MAJID, Anouar .... 206-221-4447.. 205 F
amajid@une.edu
MAJKA, David, R .... 412-397-5443.. 418 B
majka@rmu.edu
MAJKUT, Paul, S .... 417-255-7910.. 269 A
paulmajkut@missouristate.edu
MAJOR, Adrienne .... 802-387-7143.. 484 B
amajor@landmark.edu
MAJOR, Anthony .... 505-786-4327.. 300 E
amajor@navajotech.edu
MAJOR, JR., Anthony, W .... 505-786-4327.. 300 E
amajor@navajotech.edu
MAJOR, Carla .... 504-762-3003.. 196 D
cmajor@dcc.edu
MAJOR, Carrie .... 865-251-1800.. 444 A
cmajor@southcollegetn.edu
MAJOR, Michael, W .... 989-964-7130.. 240 F
mmajor@svsu.edu
MAJOR, Phillip .... 561-803-2034.. 106 C
phillip_major@pba.edu
MAJOR, Samantha .... 828-835-4203.. 353 G
smajor@tricountycc.edu
MAJOR, Tony .... 304-876-5287.. 513 E
tmajor@shepherd.edu
MAJOR, Wayne .... 785-272-0889.. 179 D
MAJOR-KELLY, Shanee ... 301-423-3600.... 93 F
MAJZNER, Kathy .... 903-233-4381.. 460 J
kathymajzner@letu.edu
MAKARECHI, Pejman ...... 215-503-7841.. 420 E
pejman.makarechi@jefferson.edu
MAKAROFF, JR., Christopher, A .... 513-529-4432.. 372 K
makaroca@miamioh.edu
MAKER, Caryn .... 412-268-1885.. 400 D
cmaker@andrew.cmu.edu
MAKER, Laurie .... 508-588-9100.. 223 G
MAKHIJA, Anil, K .... 614-292-7899.. 375 A
makhija.1@osu.edu
MAKI, Bill .... 218-471-0015.. 249 E
wmaki@nhed.edu
MAKI, David, W .... 906-227-1262.. 239 B
dmaki@nmu.edu
MAKI, Jackie .... 817-515-5379.. 467 A
jacqueline.maki@tccd.edu
MAKI, Kristen .... 508-856-1870.. 221 B
kristen.maki@umassmed.edu
MAKI, William .... 218-471-0015.. 249 I
wmaki@nhed.edu
MAKI, William, D .... 218-471-0015.. 249 G
wmaki@nhed.edu
MAKIN, Linda .... 801-863-8457.. 482 C
linda.makin@uvu.edu
MAKOFSKE, Rose .... 215-619-7383.. 410 L
rmakofske@mc3.edu
MAKREZ, Heather .... 978-934-4809.. 221 A
heather_makrez@uml.edu
MAKSYMEC, Jill .... 773-628-0131.. 150 D
jmaksymec@nc.edu
MAKSYMICZ, Kathy, E ..... 330-287-1283.. 375 B
maksymicz.1@osu.edu
MAKSYMIK, Michelle .... 814-262-3820.. 413 P
mmaksymik@pennhighlands.edu
MAKUAKANE-LUNDIN, Gail .... 808-932-7445.. 131 E
gailml@hawaii.edu
MAL, Mirlen .... 617-333-2193.. 217 F
mirlen.mal@curry.edu
MALAFA, Jeanette .... 217-652-6467.. 158 A
j-malafa@wiu.edu
MALANCA, Donna .... 630-617-3550.. 140 C
donnas@elmhurst.edu
MALANI, Upendra .... 703-284-1491.. 492 A
upendra.malani@marymount.edu
MALARA, Kathleen .... 718-817-4160.. 314 G
kmalara@fordham.edu
MALARET, Frank .... 530-747-5220.... 51 D
malarej@scc.losrios.edu
MALARTE-FELDMAN, Claire, L .... 603-862-1303.. 288 C
claire.malarte-feldman@unh.edu
MALASKA, Amy .... 330-490-7321.. 380 J
amalaska@walsh.edu
MALASKI, Donna .... 269-965-3931.. 236 A
malaskid@kellogg.edu
MALASPINA, Margaret ..... 860-906-5096.... 86 B
mmalaspina@ccc.commnet.edu
MALASRI, Pong .... 901-321-3419.. 439 E
pong@cbu.edu
MALAT, Heide .... 651-690-6805.. 254 M
hlmalat@stkate.edu
MALATESTA, Addy .... 570-408-4020.. 423 G
adelene.malatesta@wilkes.edu
MALATESTA, Matthew, J .. 518-388-6112.. 338 H
malatesm@union.edu
MALAVE, Cesar .... 979-845-2217.. 468 B
dean@qatar.tamu.edu
MALAVE-LASSO, Mara ..... 787-480-2418.. 531 J
mamalave@sanjuanciudadpatria.com
MALAVEZ, Jessica .... 718-260-5006.. 309 C
jmalavez@citytech.cuny.edu
MALAVOLTI, TOR, Nathan .... 740-283-6407.. 368 L
nmalavolti@franciscan.edu
MALBROUGH, Russell ..... 631-451-4630.. 336 D
malbror@sunysuffolk.edu
MALCHEFF, Jessica .... 309-796-5052.. 135 I
malcheffj@bhc.edu
MALCHOW, Larry, P .... 920-748-8347.. 519 E
malchowl@ripon.edu
MALCOLM, III, Everett, J 904-620-2600.. 112 B
emalcolm@unf.edu
MALCOLM, Jacquelyn ...... 202-319-6632.... 92 A
malcolmj@cua.edu
MALCOLM, Joshua .... 910-521-6201.. 358 C
joshua.malcolm@uncp.edu
MALCOLM, Kathy .... 309-796-5038.. 135 I
malcolmk@bhc.edu
MALCOLM, Kim .... 309-694-8815.. 141 F
kmalcolm@icc.edu
MALCOLM, Molly Beth .... 512-223-7683.. 451 N
mollybeth.malcolm@austincc.edu
MALCOLM, Thomas .... 863-638-3500.. 115 C
tom.malcolm@warner.edu
MALCONIAN, Sara .... 617-324-4538.. 225 A
MALDAR, Mustafa .... 832-230-5555.. 462 K
maldar@na.edu
MALDONADO, Amelia ..... 787-850-9327.. 538 B
amelia.maldonado1@upr.edu
MALDONADO, Angel .... 787-257-0000.. 537 H
angel.maldonado@upr.edu
MALDONADO, Candice ... 325-481-8300.. 459 D
MALDONADO, Cesar .... 713-718-5059.. 459 B
cesar.maldonado@hccs.edu
MALDONADO, Gilda .... 619-388-2817.... 60 G
gmaldona@sdccd.edu
MALDONADO, Ileana .... 787-725-8120.. 532 K
imaldonado@eap.edu
MALDONADO, Irving .... 787-743-3038.. 535 L
imaldonado@sanjuanbautista.edu
MALDONADO, Kenneth .... 787-751-0178.. 535 N
kenmaldona@suagm.edu
MALDONADO, Lourdes .... 787-766-1717.. 536 B
lmaldonado@suagm.edu
MALDONADO, Orlando .... 787-751-0160.. 531 M
omaldonado@cmpr.pr.gov
MALDONADO, Sarai .... 909-537-5250.... 34 C
smaldona@csusb.edu
MALDONADO, Theresa, A .... 956-665-8779.. 476 E
theresa.maldonado@utrgv.edu
MALDONADO, Victor .... 787-878-5475.. 533 H
vmaldonado@arecibo.inter.edu
MALDONADO, Wanda ...... 787-758-2525.. 538 D
wanda.maldonado1@upr.edu
MALDONADO FORTUNET, Francisco .... 787-265-3862.. 538 C
decano.estudiantes@uprm.edu
MALECHA, Marvin .... 619-684-8777.... 54 C
mmalecha@newschoolarch.edu
MALECHA, Marvin, J .... 919-515-8302.. 357 B
marvin_malecha@ncsu.edu
MALEK, Casey .... 620-227-9349.. 180 E
dcccgolf@dc3.edu
MALEK, Debby .... 620-227-9260.. 180 E
dmalek@dc3.edu
MALEKPOUR, Susan .... 773-291-6100.. 137 G
smalekpour@ccc.edu
MALEKZADEH, Ali .... 312-341-3800.. 152 H
amalekzadeh@roosevelt.edu
MALEPEAI, Alexis .... 606-487-3144.. 189 E
alexis.malepeai@kctcs.edu
MALESH, Rashmi .... 718-262-2916.. 310 A
rmalesh@york.cuny.edu
MALESZEWSKI, Joseph ... 850-245-0466.. 110 I
joseph.maleszewski@flbog.edu
MALEWICKI, Michael .... 202-884-9401.... 94 A
malewickim@trinitydc.edu
MALEWSKA, Sheila .... 248-675-0203.. 127 D
smalewska@southuniversity.edu
MALEWSKI, Erik .... 470-578-2614.. 123 J
emalewsk@kennesaw.edu
MALEY, Beth .... 859-344-3513.. 193 C
maleyb@thomasmore.edu
MALEY, Brian .... 513-745-3315.. 381 I
maley@xavier.edu
MALEY, Daniel .... 269-488-4298.. 235 I
dmaley@kvcc.edu
MALEY, David, C .... 607-274-3480.. 317 D
maley@ithaca.edu
MALEY, Robert .... 215-968-8116.. 399 A
robert.maley@bucks.edu
MALFITANO, Gregory, J .. 561-237-7277.. 104 O
gmalfitano@lynn.edu
MALHAS, Faris .... 860-832-1801.... 85 F
fm4241@ccsu.edu
MALHOTRA, Betine, A ..... 904-826-0084.... 72 A
bmalhotra@usa.edu
MALHOTRA, Rajiv .... 617-732-2791.. 225 C
rajiv.malhotra@mcphs.edu
MALHOTRA, Rishab .... 312-567-3909.. 142 I
rmalhot1@iit.edu
MALIA, Marcia .... 352-588-8242.. 108 C
marcia.malia@saintleo.edu
MALICZYSZYN, Amanda .. 609-406-7600.... 93 F
MALICZYSZYN, Amanda .. 732-743-3800.... 93 F
MALIEKAL, Jose .... 585-395-2394.. 332 E
jmalieka@brockport.edu
MALIG, Jannet .... 562-860-2451.... 36 P
jmalig@cerritos.edu
MALIGO, Pedro .... 816-501-4076.. 270 J
pedro.maligo@rockhurst.edu
MALIK, Christopher, P .... 716-839-8332.. 312 D
cmalik@daemen.edu
MALIK, Nish .... 415-405-4105.... 35 B
nish@sfsu.edu
MALIK, Rick .... 312-788-1188.. 157 H
rmalik@vandercook.edu
MALIK, Zafar, A .... 312-939-0111.. 139 G
zafar@eastwest.edu
MALIN, Burke .... 650-685-6616.... 45 K
bmalin@gurnick.edu
MALIN, John .... 217-854-5572.. 135 K
john.malin@blackburn.edu
MALINA, Joel, M .... 607-255-9029.. 312 A
vp-university@cornell.edu
MALINAK, Steven .... 724-503-1001.. 422 H
smalinak@washjeff.edu
MALINOWSKI, Frank .... 229-317-6832.. 120 A
frank.malinowski@darton.edu
MALINOWSKI-FERRARY, Sarah .... 201-761-6239.. 296 K
smalinowski@saintpeters.edu
MALISCH, Susan, M .... 773-508-7750.. 146 G
smalisc@luc.edu
MALIWESKY, Martin .... 614-287-3669.. 367 C
mmaliwes@cscc.edu
MALIZIA, Patricia .... 201-559-1425.. 291 K
maliziap@felician.edu
MALKEMES, Janet .... 704-330-4609.. 348 E
janet.malkemes@cpcc.edu
MALKOWSKI, Keith, J ..... 989-774-7226.. 232 D
malko1kj@cmich.edu
MALLARD, Jessica .... 806-651-2777.. 469 D
jmallard@mail.wtamu.edu
MALLARD, Kina, S .... 770-720-5502.. 126 C
ksm@reinhardt.edu

MANLEY-ROOK, Stephanie 252-493-7383.. 352 A
sgmrook@email.pittcc.edu
MANN, Brian 813-253-7022.. 102 R
bmann@hccfl.edu
MANN, Charles, G 301-696-3611.. 208 B
mann@hood.edu
MANN, Christy 870-512-7867.... 19 C
christy_mann@asun.edu
MANN, Daniel, R 217-333-0100.. 157 A
danmann@illinois.edu
MANN, Deanna 620-227-9253.. 180 E
dmann@dc3.edu
MANN, Doug 434-592-6190.. 491 D
dmann@liberty.edu
MANN, Douglas 410-225-2352.. 209 B
dmann@mica.edu
MANN, Gwendolyn 334-229-4436...... 1 D
gmann@alasu.edu
MANN, Henry, J 614-292-5711.. 375 A
mann.414@osu.edu
MANN, Janet 202-687-1307.... 92 E
mannj2@georgetown.edu
MANN, Jason 205-329-7875...... 3 B
jason.mann@ecacolleges.com
MANN, Judith 617-228-2027.. 223 B
jcmann@bhcc.mass.edu
MANN, Karen 502-585-9911.. 192 E
kmann@spalding.edu
MANN, Kevin, J 410-543-6202.. 213 A
kjmann@salisbury.edu
MANN, Lara, G 317-781-5760.. 168 A
mannlg@uindy.edu
MANN, Laura 507-457-5069.. 252 G
lmann@winona.edu
MANN, Lucretia 914-674-7492.. 320 G
lmann@mercy.edu
MANN, Lynde 256-228-6001...... 5 I
mannl@nacc.edu
MANN, Mark 619-849-2359.... 57 M
markmann@pointloma.edu
MANN, Randy 254-295-4618.. 474 E
rmann@umhb.edu
MANN, Suellen 561-868-3450.. 106 D
manns@palmbeachstate.edu
MANN, Warrenetta, C 757-221-3620.. 488 F
wcmann@wm.edu
MANN, FSC, William 507-457-1503.. 254 O
wmann@smumn.edu
MANNELLA, Stephen 610-436-2242.. 416 C
smannella@wcupa.edu
MANNERING, Susan, M .. 302-225-6232.... 91 D
manners@gbc.edu
MANNEY, Bill 218-262-6734.. 249 E
williammanney@hibbing.edu
MANNINEN, Kevin 906-487-7371.. 234 A
kevin.manninen@finlandia.edu
MANNING, Amelia 603-314-1416.. 287 I
a.manning@snhu.edu
MANNING, Beth 810-762-3150.. 242 B
bmanning@umflint.edu
MANNING, Carmen, K 715-836-3671.. 520 A
manninck@uwec.edu
MANNING, Colleen 713-646-1729.. 459 A
cmanning@hcl.edu
MANNING, Danielle 909-869-3020.... 31 J
dmanning@cpp.edu
MANNING, Dianne, M 413-662-5249.. 222 B
dianne.manning@mcla.edu
MANNING, Don 708-596-2000.. 154 E
dmanning@ssc.edu
MANNING, Gaye 870-574-4509.... 22 G
gmanning@sautech.edu
MANNING, Jason 518-458-5303.. 311 B
manningj@strose.edu
MANNING, Jean 501-374-6305.... 22 C
MANNING, Jean 513-569-1519.. 366 D
jean.manning@cincinnatistate.edu
MANNING, Jessica 325-674-2751.. 449 J
jxm15c@acu.edu
MANNING, Jessica 325-942-2021.. 472 B
jessica.manning@angelo.edu
MANNING, Joanne 617-682-1521.. 218 E
jmanning@eds.edu
MANNING, Joshau 870-307-7290.... 21 A
joshua.manning@lyon.edu
MANNING, Karen 910-695-3995.. 353 A
manningk@sandhills.edu
MANNING, Kevin, J 443-334-2203.. 211 A
rhubbard@stevenson.edu
MANNING, Kimberly, M .. 848-932-1769.. 295 F
kim.manning@rutgers.edu
MANNING, Kirk 845-398-4066.. 329 G
kmanning@stac.edu
MANNING, Linda 206-934-6415.. 507 A
linda.manning@seattlecolleges.edu
MANNING, Lynn Etta, G . 214-887-5366.. 457 C
lmanning@dts.edu
MANNING, Marcus 314-529-9313.. 267 B
mmanning@maryville.edu
MANNING, Mark 315-498-2268.. 325 G
m.r.manning@sunyocc.edu
MANNING, Noel, T 704-406-4631.. 344 E
ntmanning@gardner-webb.edu
MANNING, Patricia 850-201-8994.. 113 E
manningp@tcc.fl.edu
MANNING, Sandra, J 919-572-1625.. 341 M
smanning@apexsot.edu
MANNING, Scott 570-372-4256.. 419 H
manning@susqu.edu
MANNING, Sherron, K 580-928-5533.. 388 C
sherron.manning@swosu.edu
MANNING, Terri 704-330-6592.. 348 E
terri.manning@cpcc.edu
MANNING, Thomas 505-224-4000.. 299 F
tmanning@cnm.edu
MANNING, Tina 912-427-5814.. 119 B
tmanning@coastalpines.edu
MANNING, Vivian 360-992-2104.. 502 E
vmanning@clark.edu
MANNING-CLARK, Jean .. 303-273-3239.... 78 M
jeanmann@mines.edu
MANNING-MILLER, Donald 662-252-8000.. 260 F
manningmiller@rustcollege.edu
MANNINO, Jessica, L 315-445-4130.. 318 E
hammonjl@lemoyne.edu
MANNINO, Sam 502-459-3535.. 193 B
smannino@sullivan.edu
MANNINO, William 540-362-6435.. 490 F
bmannino@hollins.edu
MANNION, Joe 503-493-6233.. 391 A
jmannion@cu-portland.edu
MANNION, Tom, N 626-395-6174.... 30 H
mannion@caltech.edu
MANNISTO, Richard 414-443-8788.. 522 P
rich.mannisto@wlc.edu
MANNLE, Frank 212-346-1743.. 325 J
fmannle@pace.edu
MANNO, Anthony 517-607-2625.. 235 E
amanno@hillsdale.edu
MANNO, Mariann, M 508-856-2323.. 221 B
mariann.manno@umassmed.edu
MANNO, Mechele 707-967-2911.... 53 H
mmanno@napavalley.edu
MANNO, Vincent, P 781-292-2509.. 218 H
vincent.manno@olin.edu
MANNOLINI, III, Lawrence, P 570-321-4118.. 409 F
mannolin@lycoming.edu
MANNS, Derrick 985-448-5908.. 196 E
derrick.manns@fletcher.edu
MANNS, Jennifer 970-207-4500.... 84 F
jenniferm@uscareerinstitute.edu
MANNS, Jennifer 970-207-4550.... 81 F
MANOHAR, Aruna, S 410-323-6211.. 207 D
aruna.manohar@gmail.com
MANOHAR, John 410-323-6211.. 207 D
jmanohar@faiththeological.org
MANOHAR, Norman, J 410-323-6211.. 207 D
nmanohar@faiththeological.org
MANOLIS, Lilly 617-327-6777.. 229 H
lilly_manolis@williamjames.edu
MANOR, Scott 954-771-0376.. 104 H
smanor@knoxseminary.edu
MANORD, Wayne 256-352-8116...... 9 G
wayne.manord@wallacestate.edu
MANORE, David 315-792-7280.. 336 C
david.manore@sunyit.edu
MANORY, Joseph 315-229-5896.. 329 D
jmanory@stlawu.edu
MANOS, Dennis, M 757-871-9581.. 488 F
dmanos@wm.edu
MANOS, Steve 781-736-4404.. 216 F
ssmanos@brandeis.edu
MANOTTI, Ken 773-702-0686.. 156 D
kmanotti@uchicago.edu
MANOUSOS, Carol 713-221-8425.. 474 B
manousosc@uhd.edu
MANRIQUE, Santos 620-231-3690.. 181 A
santosm@fortscott.edu
MANRIQUEZ, Chris 310-243-3655.... 32 D
cmanriquez@csudh.edu
MANRY, J. Mark 248-218-2120.. 240 C
mmanry@rc.edu
MANSAPIT, Felix 671-482-8671.. 530 B
fmansapit@uguam.uog.edu
MANSDOERFER, Steve 866-621-0124.... 84 E
MANSER, Jacqueline, M .. 330-490-7117.. 380 J
jmanser@walsh.edu
MANSFIELD, Ashley 617-588-1354.. 215 E
amansfield@bfit.edu
MANSFIELD, Robin 908-737-4880.. 292 C
rmansfie@kean.edu
MANSFIELD, Tim 315-228-7433.. 310 G
tmansfield@colgate.edu
MANSFIELD-RICHARDSON, Virgina 315-781-3304.. 316 C
mansfieldrichardson@hws.edu
MANSHIP, James 651-690-8631.. 254 M
jlmanship@stkate.edu
MANSON, Daniel 325-793-4601.. 461 F
manson.daniel@mcm.edu
MANSON, Robert 714-564-6247.... 58 G
manson_robert@sac.edu
MANSOUR, Nick 602-222-9300.... 11 E
nmansour@arizonacollege.edu
MANSOUR, Ruchana 347-394-1036.. 305 C
rmansour@ateret.net
MANSOURIAN, Lida 562-408-6969.... 25 E
MANSPERGER, Thomas .. 419-755-4650.. 373 G
tmansperger@ncstatecollege.edu
MANSPERGER, Thomas .. 419-755-5650.. 373 G
tmansperger@ncstatecollege.edu
MANSTROM, Paul, W 269-337-7308.. 235 H
paul.manstrom@kzoo.edu
MANSUETO, Anthony 214-860-2693.. 456 E
anthony.mansueto@dcccd.edu
MANSUR, Jay 859-858-2305.. 186 I
MANTELLA, Philomena, V 617-373-4798.. 227 B
MANTELLI, Louis 719-846-5619.... 83 G
louis.mantelli@trinidadstate.edu
MANTERNACH, Dean 402-354-7058.. 281 F
dean.manternach@methodistcollege.edu
MANTHE, Theodore, E 507-344-7745.. 244 K
ted.manthe@blc.edu
MANTILLA, Tonya, M 414-410-4210.. 515 I
tmmantilla@stritch.edu
MANTLE, Judy 858-642-8340.... 54 A
jmantle@nu.edu
MANTLO, Ryan 910-362-7042.. 348 A
rmantlo@cfcc.edu
MANTONI, Thomas 610-282-1100.. 402 B
thomas.mantoni@desales.edu
MANTOOTH, Brooks, E 620-665-3497.. 181 I
mantoothb@hutchcc.edu
MANTOOTH, James, D 731-881-7053.. 448 G
jdmantooth@utm.edu
MANTOVANI, Theresa 407-265-8383.... 97 B
MANUEL, Amber Jo 415-439-2436.... 26 G
MANUEL, Barbara 718-262-2362.. 310 A
bmanuel@york.cuny.edu
MANUEL, Barbara 276-739-2432.. 499 A
bmanuel@vhcc.edu
MANUEL, Beulah 301-891-4184.. 213 D
bmanuel@wau.edu
MANUEL, Henry 662-246-6462.. 259 B
hmanuel@msdelta.edu
MANUEL, Janelle 337-521-9686.. 197 A
janelle.manuel@solacc.edu
MANUEL, Jeff 205-652-3682...... 9 F
jmanuel@uwa.edu
MANUEL, Kamran 323-822-9700.... 68 B
kamran.manuel@touro.edu
MANUEL, Keith 334-291-4950...... 2 H
keith.manuel@cv.edu
MANUEL, Marilyn, G 504-286-5020.. 199 I
mmanuel@suno.edu
MANUEL, Mark 859-246-6673.. 189 B
mark.manuel@kctcs.edu
MANUEL, Mary 661-362-3184.... 40 A
mary.manuel@canyons.edu
MANUEL, Robert, L 317-788-3211.. 168 A
rmanuel@uindy.edu
MANUEL, Shenethia 573-341-4241.. 274 B
manuels@mst.edu
MANUEL, Warde 734-764-9416.. 241 J
wardemanuelad@umich.edu
MANUEL-CORTEZ, Dorinna 808-934-2710.. 131 J
dorinna@hawaii.edu
MANUKYAN, Diana 510-925-4282.... 26 M
diana@aua.am
MANULI, Nunziatina, A ... 718-990-2401.. 328 F
manulin@stjohns.edu
MANZANARES, Lucy 828-328-7142.. 345 H
lucy.manzanares@lr.edu
MANZANARES, Magdaleno 575-538-6229.. 303 A
manzanaresm@wnmu.edu
MANZANO, Anna 310-665-6951.... 55 E
amanzano@otis.edu
MANZANO, Florentino 818-947-2691.... 50 D
manzanf@lavc.edu
MANZANO, Lynn 714-628-4930.... 58 H
manzano_lynn@sccollege.edu
MANZANO-BROWN, Yvonne 575-835-5533.. 300 G
ymanzano@admin.nmt.edu
MANZELLA, Shannon 931-553-0071.. 442 I
shannon.manzella@miller-motte.com
MANZIONE, Louis 860-768-5015.... 89 G
manzione@hartford.edu
MANZKE, Robert 715-346-3738.. 521 C
rmanzke@uwsp.edu
MANZO, Dennis 310-879-0554.... 66 G
MANZO, Pablo 916-856-3400.... 50 J
manzop@losrios.edu
MAO, Ruixuan 847-214-7440.. 140 A
rmao@elgin.edu
MAPES, Chris 270-789-5013.. 187 G
ctmapes@campbellsville.edu
MAPES, Kim 570-961-7810.. 407 B
mapesk@lackawanna.edu
MAPHUMULO, Peter 760-245-4271.... 73 H
peter.maphumulo@vvc.edu
MAPLE, Vicki 740-364-9565.. 365 D
vmaple@cotc.edu
MAPLES, James (Ron), R 865-974-1763.. 448 D
maples00@tennessee.edu
MAPLES, John 806-720-7476.. 461 C
john.maples@lcu.edu
MAPLES, Stephen 775-784-4700.. 285 A
smaples@unr.edu
MAPLEY, Gordon 816-271-4100.. 269 C
gmapley@missouriwestern.edu
MAPSTON, Austin 406-657-1024.. 278 D
mapstona@rocky.edu
MAPSTONE, David 315-781-3300.. 316 C
mapstone@hws.edu
MAR, Pansy 415-565-8902.... 69 B
marp@uchastings.edu
MARA, Mary 206-239-4500.. 502 D
mmara@cityu.edu
MARA, Stacy, J 920-832-6557.. 517 E
stacy.j.mara@lawrence.edu
MARABETI, Hilary, B 615-230-3355.. 447 C
hilary.marabeti@volstate.edu
MARABLE, Shelia 205-929-6437...... 5 D
smarable@lawsonstate.edu
MARAGAKIS, Emmanuel . 775-784-6925.. 285 A
maragaki@ce.unr.edu
MARAK, Randy 713-646-2912.. 459 A
rmarak@hcl.edu
MARANGONI, Daniel 918-343-7583.. 387 F
dmarangoni@rsu.edu
MARANO, Angie 413-597-3166.. 230 A
amm14@williams.edu
MARANO, Jeanne 973-655-5333.. 293 A
maranoj@mail.montclair.edu
MARANVILLE, Amy 978-478-3400.. 227 C
amaranville@northpoint.edu
MARASCO, Canio 716-829-7846.. 313 A
MARASKA, Monica 973-328-5340.. 290 H
mmaraska@ccm.edu
MARAVETZ, Sarah 410-225-2219.. 209 B
smaravetz@mica.edu
MARAVIGLIA, James, L ... 805-756-2311.... 31 I
jmaravig@calpoly.edu
MARAZITA, John 614-251-4687.. 374 I
marazitj@ohiodominican.edu
MARBACH, Joseph, R 732-987-2252.. 292 A
president@georgian.edu
MARBERT, Larry, D 305-284-5660.. 114 H
lmarbert@miami.edu
MARBLE, Alan 417-625-9501.. 268 H
marble-a@mssu.edu
MARBLE, Amanda, F 208-467-8402.. 134 D
afmarble@nnu.edu
MARBLE, Jan 507-389-5120.. 250 E
janice.marble@mnsu.edu
MARBRAY, Antionette 619-594-5211.... 35 A
amarbray@mail.sdsu.edu
MARBURY, Diane 516-562-0449.. 313 C
dmarbury@northwell.edu
MARBURY, Sonni 928-757-0879.... 15 E
smarbury@mohave.edu
MARBUT, Terry 256-782-5034...... 4 H
tmarbut@jsu.edu
MARCANO, Walbert 787-257-0000.. 537 H
walbert.marcano@upr.edu
MARCANO, Yoriel 312-850-7399.. 138 A
MARCANTONIO, Gina 203-575-8208.... 86 G
gmarcantonio@nv.edu
MARCANTONIO, James ... 573-681-5018.. 266 I
marcantonioj@lincolnu.edu
MARCEC, Paula 920-465-2207.. 520 B
marcecp@uwgb.edu
MARCEL, Gina 985-448-7929.. 196 E
gina.marcel@fletcher.edu
MARCEL, Yorgun 330-263-2262.. 367 A
ymarcel@wooster.edu
MARCELLA, Patricia 508-588-9100.. 223 G
MARCELLAIS, Alexsis 701-477-7862.. 362 D
amarcellais@tm.edu
MARCELLINO, Sara 510-215-3805.... 41 H
smarcellino@contracosta.edu
MARCH, Debra 706-379-3111.. 130 B
dbmarch@yhc.edu
MARCH, Peter 848-932-0990.. 296 B
peter.march@rutgers.edu
MARCHAL, Anne 845-434-5750.. 336 H
amarchal@sunysullivan.edu
MARCHAND, Nicole 612-861-7554.. 244 D
nicole.marchand@alfredadler.edu
MARCHAND, William 516-686-7904.. 323 G
wmarchan@nyit.edu
MARCHANT, Karen 605-626-7781.. 437 D
karen.marchant@northern.edu
MARCHANT, Linda 513-529-2021.. 372 K
marchalf@miamioh.edu

MARCHANT, Lloyd .... 660-263-4100.. 269 D
lloydm@macc.edu
MARCHANT, T. Eston ...... 919-718-7246.. 348 D
bmarchant@cccc.edu
MARCHASE, Richard, B ... 205-934-1294...... 8 E
marchase@uab.edu
MARCHBANKS, Pete .... 979-845-8423.. 468 B
pete-marchbanks@tamu.edu
MARCHELLETTA, Barbara . 207-947-4591.. 202 E
bmarchelletta@bealcollege.edu
MARCHELLO, Sara, L ...... 757-221-2801.. 488 F
slmarc@wm.edu
MARCHESCHI, Graziano .. 773-298-3419.. 153 H
marcheschi@sxu.edu
MARCHESE, Cynthia, C ... 212-687-3730.. 289 F
ccm@berkeleycollege.edu
MARCHESE, Cynthia, C ... 212-687-3730.. 305 B
ccm@berkeleycollege.edu
MARCHIONE,
Benjamin, D .... 716-286-8774.. 324 E
bmarchione@niagara.edu
MARCHIONE, Susan, M .. 716-839-8447.. 312 D
smarchio@daemen.edu
MARCHIONINI, Gary .... 919-962-8363.. 357 D
gary@ils.unc.edu
MARCHIORI, Dennis, M .. 563-884-5500.. 176 C
dennis.marchiori@palmer.edu
MARCHWICK, Colleen, C 715-836-4874.. 520 A
marchwcc@uwec.edu
MARCIAL, Carlos .... 787-725-8120.. 532 K
cmarcial@eap.edu
MARCIAL, Myriam .... 787-891-0925.. 533 G
mmarcial@aguadilla.inter.edu
MARCIAL-VEGA, Ivonne ... 787-993-8899.. 537 G
ivonne.marcial@upr.edu
MARCIANO, Jackie .... 610-902-8256.. 399 D
jmm745@cabrini.edu
MARCIN, Heidi, C .... 585-785-1609.. 314 D
heidi.marcin@flcc.edu
MARCINEK, Myron .... 570-961-4786.. 409 H
mmarcinek@marywood.edu
MARCINIAK, Joseph .... 706-880-8027.. 123 K
jmarciniak@lagrange.edu
MARCO SCANLON,
Cynthia, D .... 216-397-1699.. 370 H
cmarco@jcu.edu
MARCOCCIA, Louis, G ..... 315-443-3037.. 337 A
lmarcocc@syr.edu
MARCONE, Luigi .... 203-837-9314.... 85
marconel@wcsu.edu
MARCONI, Christopher .... 303-753-6046.... 83 A
cmarconi@rmcad.edu
MARCOTTE, Jeffrey .... 508-362-2131.. 223 C
jmarcotte@capecod.edu
MARCOTTE, Theresa .... 618-395-7777.. 142 E
marcottet@iecc.edu
MARCOU, William, L .... 414-410-4463.. 515 I
wlmarcou@stritch.edu
MARCOUX, Jamie .... 401-598-1000.. 425 E
jmarcoux@jwu.edu
MARCOUX, Mollie, D .... 609-258-3535.. 294 D
mmarcoux@princeton.edu
MARCUCCILLI,
Christine, M .... 260-481-6106.. 163 C
marcuccc@ipfw.edu
MARCUM, Jeff .... 708-444-4500.. 140 F
jmarcum@foxcollege.edu
MARCUS, Jamie .... 607-871-2660.. 303 F
marcus@alfred.edu
MARCUS, Lynn .... 978-762-4000.. 224 C
lmarcus@northshore.edu
MARCUS, Nancy .... 850-644-3500.. 111 C
nmarcus@fsu.edu
MARCUS, Robert, J .... 317-940-9910.. 159 K
rmarcus@butler.edu
MARCUS, Susan .... 773-907-4418.. 137 E
smarcus2@ccc.edu
MARCUS, W. Andrew .... 541-346-3902.. 395 G
marcus@uoregon.edu
MARCUS-NEWHALL, Amy 909-621-8148.... 64 A
president@scrippscollege.edu
MARCUSE, Adrian, G .... 212-752-1530.. 318 F
adrian.marcuse@limcollege.edu
MARCUSE, Elizabeth, S ... 212-752-1530.. 318 F
elizabeth.marcuse@limcollege.edu
MARCUSSEN, Thomas ...... 414-229-4537.. 520 D
marcusse@uwm.edu
MARCY, Mary, B .... 415-485-3200.... 42 G
president@dominican.edu
MARCZYNSKI, Jerry .... 775-784-4898.. 285 A
marczyns@unr.edu
MARDEN, Jennifer .... 661-395-4211.... 47 J
jmarden@bakersfieldcollege.edu
MARDEN, Rose .... 210-341-1366.. 463 A
rmarden@ost.edu
MARDER, Denise .... 617-868-3450.. 218 E
dmarder@lesley.edu
MARDIROSIAN, Haig .... 813-253-6100.. 114 M
hmardirosian@ut.edu
MARDIS, Michael .... 502-852-5787.. 194 A
mjmard01@louisville.edu

MARDIS, JR., Michael .... 502-852-5787.. 194 A
mjmard01@louisville.edu
MAREK, Amy .... 573-592-5195.. 275 E
amy.marek@westminster-mo.edu
MAREK, Diane .... 847-233-7700.. 150 D
dmarek@nc.edu
MAREK, Kate .... 708-524-6648.. 139 F
kmarek@dom.edu
MAREK, Robin .... 731-425-2654.. 446 C
rmarek@jscc.edu
MAREK, Sandra .... 660-263-4100.. 269 D
sandram@macc.edu
MAREKO, Joseph .... 808-689-2918.. 131 G
josephlm@hawaii.edu
MAREMONT-SILVER,
Ellen .... 707-527-4679.... 63 G
emaremontsilver@santarosa.edu
MARENTES, Henry .... 619-596-2766.... 25 G
hmarentes@advancedtraining.edu
MARES, Maria .... 787-864-2222.. 534 A
maria.mares@guayama.inter.edu
MARESH, Rachael .... 512-313-3000.. 455 F
rachael.maresh@concordia.edu
MARFELL, Julie .... 859-899-2512.. 188 G
julie.marfell@frontier.edu
MARFISE, Larry, J .... 813-253-6240.. 114 M
lmarfise@ut.edu
MARFOE, Tina .... 708-237-5050.. 150 D
tmarfoe@nc.edu
MARGERUM-LEYS, Jon .... 248-370-3087.. 239 K
jmargerumleys@oakland.edu
MARGETTS, James .... 308-432-6246.. 281 H
jmargetts@csc.edu
MARGHEIM, Jeffrey .... 386-822-7020.. 113 B
jmarghei@stetson.edu
MARGIOTTA, Frank .... 321-433-7515.... 98 K
margiottaf@easternflorida.edu
MARGOLIS, Liza .... 340-693-1053.. 539 C
lmargol@uvi.edu
MARGRAVE, Ann .... 563-884-5257.. 176 C
ann.margrave@palmer.edu
MARGRAVE, Carrie .... 207-326-0265.. 204 C
carrie.margrave@mma.edu
MARGULES, Gary, S .... 954-262-7507.. 105 J
margules@nsu.nova.edu
MARGULIES, Anne .... 617-495-9092.. 219 D
anne_margulies@harvard.edu
MARGULIES, L .... 718-853-8500.. 337 H
MARGULIES, Mordechai .. 718-854-2290.. 305 E
MARI, Mike .... 530-242-7590.... 64 D
mmari@shastacollege.edu
MARIANI, Elsa .... 787-257-7373.. 535 P
emariani@suagm.edu
MARIANI, William .... 716-829-7673.. 313 A
marianiw@dyc.edu
MARIANI, William .... 716-829-8194.. 313 A
marianiw@dyc.edu
MARIANO, Anthony, A ..... 802-485-2230.. 484 H
tmariano@norwich.edu
MARIANS, Kenneth, J ...... 646-888-6639.. 319 I
kmarians@sloankettering.edu
MARICHAL-LUGO, Carlos 787-993-8866.. 537 G
carlos.marichal@upr.edu
MARIN, Anthony, S .... 575-646-7207.. 300 J
amarin@nmsu.edu
MARIN, Elsa .... 787-764-0000.. 538 F
elsa.marin1@upr.edu
MARIN, Joseph, F .... 225-922-1635.. 195 G
jmarin@lctcs.edu
MARIN-HILL, Angelica ..... 214-648-3684.. 478 C
angelica.marin-hill@utsouthwestern.edu
MARINA, Joseph .... 315-445-4124.. 318 E
marinaj@lemoyne.edu
MARINACCIO, Jessica ...... 212-854-1222.. 311 E
jm996@columbia.edu
MARINACE, Betsy .... 973-684-6861.. 294 A
bmarinace@pccc.edu
MARINAN, Jerilyn .... 516-876-3158.. 333 C
marinanj@oldwestbury.edu
MARINCH, Maria .... 702-651-7546.. 284 H
maria.marinch@csn.edu
MARINELLI, Bryan, D ...... 401-865-1822.. 425 D
bmarinel@providence.edu
MARING, Bayta .... 206-546-6949.. 507 F
bmaring@shoreline.edu
MARINHO, Robson .... 269-471-3481.. 230 H
marinho@andrews.edu
MARINI, Janice .... 215-955-2244.. 420 E
janice.marini@jefferson.edu
MARINI, Mario .... 724-589-2022.. 420 D
mmarini@thiel.edu
MARINI, Stephen, T .... 508-854-4272.. 224 E
smarini@qcc.mass.edu
MARINIS, Jeremy .... 419-448-3301.. 378 A
marinisjj@tiffin.edu
MARINO, Chris .... 864-646-1836.. 433 C
cmarino@tctc.edu
MARINO, David .... 215-204-7663.. 420 B
david.marino0001@temple.edu
MARINO, Lucille .... 785-864-7431.. 185 D
lmarino@ku.edu

MARINUCCI, Dorothy ...... 718-817-3000.. 314 G
marinucci@fordham.edu
MARION, D. Keith .... 803-754-4100.. 429 B
MARION, Joseph .... 504-286-5389.. 199 I
jmarion@suno.edu
MARION, Lucy, N .... 706-721-3771.. 117 D
lumarion@augusta.edu
MARISCALCO, Michele .... 217-333-5465.. 157 A
mmmaris@illinois.edu
MARISOL, Cortes .... 646-313-8000.. 309 F
marisol.cortes@guttman.cuny.edu
MARIUCCI, Robert .... 805-546-3210.... 41 L
rmariucc@cuesta.edu
MARIX, Amy .... 225-578-3486.. 197 I
amarix@lsu.edu
MARK, Allen .... 704-461-6736.. 342 A
allanmark@bac.edu
MARK, Joy .... 620-947-3121.. 185 B
joym@tabor.edu
MARK, Kevin .... 208-732-6295.. 133 E
kmark@csi.edu
MARK, Marty, L .... 319-273-6258.. 170 A
marty.mark@uni.edu
MARKANTONAKIS,
Angelo .... 704-216-3710.. 352 G
angelo.markantonakis@rccc.edu
MARKEL, Mark, D .... 608-263-6716.. 519 K
markelm@svm.vetmed.wisc.edu
MARKELL, Dawn .... 517-338-3048.. 232 F
dmarkell@cleary.edu
MARKER, Brian .... 434-381-6144.. 494 M
bmarker@sbc.edu
MARKER, James .... 814-254-0404.. 401 A
jamarker@pa.gov
MARKEY, John .... 210-341-1366.. 463 A
jmarkey@ost.edu
MARKEY, Nanette .... 301-696-3620.. 208 B
markey@hood.edu
MARKEY-GRABILL,
Mindy .... 937-393-3431.. 377 F
mmarkey@sscc.edu
MARKHAM, Jan, S .... 703-370-6600.. 492 I
MARKIN, Karen .... 401-874-5971.. 426 D
markevicius@uri.edu
MARKIN, Rodney .... 402-559-7687.. 283 A
rmarkin@unmc.edu
MARKIN, Terence, C .... 202-231-4011.. 528 C
terrence.markin@dodiis.mil
MARKLAND, Scott .... 937-512-5502.. 377 D
scott.markland@sinclair.edu
MARKLE, Elizabeth .... 775-831-1314.. 285 G
emarkle@sierranevada.edu
MARKLE, Suzanne .... 412-346-2100.. 417 B
smarkle@pia.edu
MARKLEY, Bradley, A ...... 717-766-2511.. 410 J
bmarkley@messiah.edu
MARKLEY, John .... 954-771-0376.. 104 H
jmarkley@knoxseminary.edu
MARKLEY, Neil .... 707-664-4068.... 35 D
neil.markley@sonoma.edu
MARKOVITCH, Matthew ..... 707-524-1849.... 63 G
mmarkovitch@santarosa.edu
MARKOW, David .... 802-828-8535.. 485 E
david.markow@vcfa.edu
MARKOW, Joanne .... 617-746-1990.. 219 G
joanne.markow@hult.edu
MARKOWITT, Xenia .... 802-440-4390.. 483 E
xeniamarkowitt@bennington.edu
MARKOWITZ, Marianne .. 315-448-5040.. 329 B
MARKOWITZ, Michael ..... 215-637-7700.. 405 J
mmarkowitz@holyfamily.edu
MARKOWSKI, Vincent ...... 201-684-7432.. 294 G
vmarkows@ramapo.edu
MARKS, Alan .... 256-766-6610...... 4 B
amarks@hcu.edu
MARKS, Andrea, M .... 210-567-7020.. 477 D
marksa@uthscsa.edu
MARKS, Ellen .... 906-487-2500.. 238 A
ebmarks@mtu.edu
MARKS, Erica .... 845-257-3240.. 331 E
markse@newpaltz.edu
MARKS, Howard .... 432-552-2371.. 478 B
marks_h@utpb.edu
MARKS, Janice, L .... 443-518-4617.. 208 C
jmarks@howardcc.edu
MARKS, John .... 414-382-6360.. 515 D
john.marks@alverno.edu
MARKS, Lecta .... 913-288-7647.. 182 C
lmarks@kckcc.edu
MARKS, Lilly .... 303-724-5369.... 84 A
lilly.marks@ucdenver.edu
MARKS, Michelle .... 703-993-8705.. 490 B
mmarks@gmu.edu
MARKS, Nick .... 603-822-5434.. 233 D
nicholas.marks@granite.edu
MARKS, Patrice .... 908-526-1200.. 295 A
patrice.marks@raritanval.edu
MARKS, Sandra .... 562-860-2451.... 36 P
smarks@cerritos.edu
MARKS, Spider .... 602-557-9200.... 17 L
spider.marks@phoenix.edu

MARKS, Steven .... 718-780-7507.. 305 L
steven.marks@brooklaw.edu
MARKSON, Alison, W ...... 617-333-2120.. 217 F
amarkson1109@curry.edu
MARKULY, Mark .... 206-296-5330.. 507 E
markulym@seattleu.edu
MARKUM, Michael .... 254-298-8291.. 467 B
mmarkum@templejc.edu
MARKWOOD, Chris .... 706-507-8950.. 119 E
markwood_chris@columbusstate.edu
MARLAIRE, Natalyn, M .... 715-852-1399.. 523 B
nmarlaire@cvtc.edu
MARLAND, Jaime .... 401-427-6954.. 426 A
jmarland@risd.edu
MARLER, Dan .... 970-542-3157.... 81 H
dan.marler@morgancc.edu
MARLER, Eric .... 808-675-3708.. 130 E
eric.marler@byuh.edu
MARLER, Janet .... 609-343-4937.. 288 H
jmarler@atlantic.edu
MARLER, Kari .... 801-627-8392.. 481 A
marlerk@owatc.edu
MARLETT, Keith .... 607-729-1581.. 312 E
kmarlett@davisny.edu
MARLETTE, Marnie, S ...... 336-841-4683.. 345 A
mmarlett@highpoint.edu
MARLEY, Chad .... 307-778-1346.. 526 K
cmarley@lccc.wy.edu
MARLEY, Robert .... 573-341-4138.. 274 B
marleyr@mst.edu
MARLING, Garet .... 510-780-4500.... 48 J
gmarling@lifewest.edu
MARLING, Janet .... 706-864-1818.. 128 F
janet.marling@ung.edu
MARLOW, Amber .... 715-634-4790.. 517 C
marlowa@lco.edu
MARLOW, Dan .... 816-279-7000.. 262 B
dan@abtu.edu
MARLOW, Jean .... 859-622-1986.. 188 F
jean.marlow@eku.edu
MARLOW, Peter .... 619-260-7460.... 72 B
petermarlow@sandiego.edu
MARLOW-ORMSBY,
Sherry .... 423-697-3216.. 445 D
sherry.marlowormsby@chattanoogastate.
edu
MARLOWE, Bethany .... 803-323-4503.. 435 B
marloweb@winthrop.edu
MARLOWE, Channing, H . 205-391-2256...... 6 G
cmarlowe@sheltonstate.edu
MARLOWE, June .... 314-991-6245.. 136 G
jmarlowe@chamberlain.edu
MARLOWE, Monica .... 228-702-1775.. 261 I
mmarlowe@wmcarey.edu
MARLOWE, Robert, W ..... 843-953-2502.. 428 G
marlower@cofc.edu
MARLOWE, Sheree .... 508-793-7351.. 217 B
smarlowe@clarku.edu
MARMARELLI, Beth .... 313-593-5542.. 242 A
bethmar@umich.edu
MARMOLEJO,
Francisco, J .... 520-621-7761.... 17 I
fmarmole@email.arizona.edu
MARMOLEJO, William ...... 818-710-2955.... 50 A
marmolwa@piercecollege.edu
MARMUR, Michael .... 212-824-2215.. 315 F
mmarmur@huc.edu
MARNEN, Ted .... 814-871-7599.. 404 A
marnen001@gannon.edu
MARNEY, Katherine .... 573-288-6478.. 264 F
kmarney@culver.edu
MARNICH, Darlene .... 412-392-3474.. 417 F
dmarnich@pointpark.edu
MAROHL, Matthew .... 507-786-3092.. 254 P
marohl@stolaf.edu
MAROLDO, Brian .... 516-686-7449.. 323 G
bmaroldo@nyit.edu
MARONEY, Dustin .... 480-517-8418.... 14 G
dustin.maroney@riosalado.edu
MAROTTA, Marsha .... 413-572-5213.. 222 E
mmarotta@westfield.ma.edu
MARPE, Thomas .... 507-457-6963.. 254 O
tmarpe@smumn.edu
MARPLE, Bradley .... 214-648-2646.. 478 C
bradley.marple@utsouthwestern.edu
MARQUARDT, Brian .... 231-591-3745.. 233 L
brianmarquardt@ferris.edu
MARQUARDT,
Christopher .... 315-229-5250.. 329 D
cmarquardt@stlawu.edu
MARQUARDT, Clifford, L 740-377-2520.. 378 B
cmark@zoominternet.net
MARQUARDT, Richard .... 570-465-2344.. 407 B
marquardtr@lackawanna.edu
MARQUARDT, Shelly .... 714-547-9625.... 29 J
smarquardt@calcoast.edu
MARQUART, James, W ... 409-880-8398.. 471 A
james.marquart@lamar.edu
MARQUES, Javier .... 305-348-2111.. 111 A
javier.marques@fiu.edu

MARQUES, Jeffrey .... 413-775-1700.. 223 D
marquesj@gcc.mass.edu
MARQUES, Mike .... 201-327-8877.. 291 G
mmarques@eastwick.edu
MARQUEZ, Abigail .... 407-251-0007.. 106 B
amarquez@omi.edu
MARQUEZ, Dianne .... 575-492-2841.. 300 H
dmarquez@nmjc.edu
MARQUEZ, JR., Felix, J .. 407-251-0007.. 106 B
fmarquez@omi.edu
MARQUEZ, Ivan .... 914-337-9300.. 311 F
ivan.marquez@concordia-ny.edu
MARQUEZ, Kenneth, L .... 719-587-7227.... 76 G
klmarque@adams.edu
MARQUEZ, Krishna .... 787-746-1400.. 532 M
kmarquez@huertas.edu
MARQUEZ, Michelle .... 650-306-3403.... 62 G
marquezm@smccd.edu
MARQUEZ, Moses .... 505-454-5312.. 299 M
mmarquez@luna.edu
MARQUEZ, Myrna .... 505-224-4000.. 299 F
mmarquez43@cnm.edu
MARQUEZ, Nelson .... 863-734-1509.. 115 D
marqueznj@webber.edu
MARQUEZ, Nora .... 650-433-3865.... 56 D
nmarquez@paloaltou.edu
MARQUEZ, Patricia .... 619-260-7795.... 72 B
pmarquez@sandiego.edu
MARQUEZ, Walter .... 909-869-4947.... 31 J
wmmarquez@cpp.edu
MARQUEZ BELL, Mary ..... 516-876-3082.. 333 C
bellm@oldwestbury.edu
MARQUEZ-SCALLY,
Marline .... 505-984-6075.. 301 I
registrar@sjc.edu
MARQUIS, Jack .... 814-944-5643.. 424 G
john.marquis@yti.edu
MARQUIS, Kim .... 800-290-4226.. 440 G
kmarquis@hchs.edu
MARQUIS, Lauren .... 617-879-2328.. 229 G
lmarquis@wheelock.edu
MARQUIS, Susan .... 310-393-0411.... 56 G
smarquis@rand.org
MARQUSEE, Steven, J ..... 315-267-2231.. 334 B
marqussj@potsdam.edu
MARR, J, R .... 704-820-0726.. 342 A
jrmarr@bac.edu
MARR, Jay .... 502-456-6506.. 193 B
jmarr@sullivan.edu
MARR, Jena .... 405-422-1265.. 387 E
jena.marr@redlandscc.edu
MARR, John .... 216-987-2296.. 367 E
john.marr@tri-c.edu
MARR, JR., John, W .... 216-987-2296.. 367 E
john.marr-jr@tri-c.edu
MARR, Ronda .... 209-946-2206.... 71 C
rmarr@pacific.edu
MARRA, Angelina .... 718-261-5800.. 305 J
amarra@bramsonort.edu
MARRA, Joseph .... 845-574-4156.. 327 G
jmarra2@sunyrockland.edu
MARRA, Michele .... 740-376-4720.. 372 A
mm011@marietta.edu
MARRABLE, Laquana .... 678-839-6403.. 129 E
lmarrabl@westga.edu
MARRANT, Dale .... 913-234-0612.. 179 M
dale.marrant@cleveland.edu
MARRAPESE, Patricia ...... 607-777-2510.. 331 B
pmarra@binghamton.edu
MARRAPODI, Michael .... 617-984-1634.. 227 F
mmarrapodi@quincycollege.edu
MARRERO, Arelis .... 787-728-1515.. 539 B
amarrero@sagrado.edu
MARRERO, Argelio .... 860-906-5125.... 86 B
amarrero@ccc.commnet.edu
MARRERO, Christina .... 213-615-2700.... 37 I
cmarrero@thechicagoschool.edu
MARRERO, Kyle .... 678-839-6442.. 129 E
kmarrero@westga.edu
MARRERO, Lisette .... 787-894-2828.. 539 A
lisette.marrero@upr.edu
MARRERO, Petrina .... 814-824-2369.. 410 H
pwilliams@mercyhurst.edu
MARRERO, Rene .... 787-841-2000.. 535 I
rene_marrero@pucpr.edu
MARRERO, Wilma .... 787-765-1915.. 534 F
wmarrero@opto.inter.edu
MARRERO PEREZ, Rafael 787-780-0070.. 531 B
rmarrero@caribbean.edu
MARRETT, Clifford .... 860-465-5577.... 85 G
marrettc@easternct.edu
MARRIN, John .... 719-336-1511.... 81 D
john.marrin@lamarcc.edu
MARRINER, Nigel, R .... 716-878-4907.. 332 F
marrinnr@buffalostate.edu
MARRIOTT, Carol .... 585-343-0055.. 315 C
cmarriott@genesee.edu
MARRIOTT, Danny .... 760-480-8474.... 74 L
MARRIOTT, Donna .... 410-386-8032.. 206 I
dmarriott@carrollcc.edu
MARRIOTT, Jean .... 410-386-8121.. 206 I
jmarriott@carrollcc.edu
MARRIOTT, Karin .... 951-487-3060.... 53 D
kmarriott@msjc.edu
MARRIOTT, Martin .... 920-206-2310.. 517 G
marty.marriott@mbu.edu
MARRIOTT, Russell .... 214-818-1318.. 455 G
rmarriott@criswell.edu
MARROCCO, Susan .... 941-752-5201.. 110 H
marrocs@scf.edu
MARROCCO, Therese .... 203-857-7311.... 87 B
tmarrocco@norwalk.edu
MARROCHELLO, Drew ...... 617-353-7327.. 216 E
marroand@bu.edu
MARRON, Maria .... 402-472-3041.. 282 M
mmarron2@unl.edu
MARRON, Timothy .... 206-296-5990.. 507 E
marront@seattleu.edu
MARRONE-CREECH,
Tiana .... 541-463-5538.. 391 G
marrone-creecht@lanecc.edu
MARRONGELLE, Karen .... 503-725-5061.. 394 G
karen.marrongelle@pdx.edu
MARROTT, Ann .... 845-687-5070.. 338 F
marrotta@sunyulster.edu
MARROW, Cary .... 806-894-9611.. 465 G
cmarrow@southplainscollege.edu
MARROW, Sydne, M .... 508-531-1754.. 221 C
smarrow@bridgew.edu
MARRS, Rick .... 310-506-4261.... 56 J
rick.marrs@pepperdine.edu
MARRS, Sherrie .... 606-218-5261.. 194 C
sherriemarrs@upike.edu
MARS, Kandace .... 785-670-2270.. 185 H
kandace.mars@washburn.edu
MARSALEK, Lisa .... 419-783-2587.. 368 A
lmarsalek@defiance.edu
MARSALIS, Wynton .... 212-799-5000.. 318 A
MARSCH, Charlotte .... 417-328-1803.. 272 C
cmarsch@sbuniv.edu
MARSCHKE, Robyn .... 719-255-3640.... 83 L
rmarschk@uccs.edu
MARSDEN, Janet, L .... 802-440-4303.. 483 E
jmarsden@bennington.edu
MARSDEN, John, P .... 859-846-5310.. 191 G
jmarsden@midway.edu
MARSELIAN, Zareh .... 805-493-3119.... 31 C
marselia@callutheran.edu
MARSH, Anne .... 540-828-8024.. 487 H
atmarsh@bridgewater.edu
MARSH, Barry .... 843-349-7557.. 430 F
barry.marsh@hgtc.edu
MARSH, Bonnie .... 724-439-4900.. 408 D
bmarsh@laurel.edu
MARSH, Brent .... 918-343-7569.. 387 F
bmarsh@rsu.edu
MARSH, Cecilia .... 660-359-3948.. 269 I
cmarsh@mail.ncmissouri.edu
MARSH, Clay .... 304-293-1024.. 514 C
cbmarsh@hsc.wvu.edu
MARSH, Clay, B .... 304-293-1024.. 514 C
cbmarsh@hsc.wvu.edu
MARSH, David, F .... 989-837-4389.. 239 D
dmarsh@northwood.edu
MARSH, Dawn .... 517-265-5161.. 230 D
dmarsh@adrian.edu
MARSH, Donnita .... 509-865-8641.. 504 D
marsh_d@heritage.edu
MARSH, Douglas, K .... 574-631-4200.. 168 B
marsh.14@nd.edu
MARSH, Elinor .... 517-629-0247.. 230 E
emarsh@albion.edu
MARSH, Geoff .... 562-903-4742.... 28 E
geoff.marsh@biola.edu
MARSH, Gregory .... 409-880-2100.. 471 A
gregory.marsh@lamar.edu
MARSH, Heather, A .... 214-860-3611.. 456 F
hmarsh@dcccd.edu
MARSH, James, G .... 254-710-2467.. 452 H
jim_marsh@baylor.edu
MARSH, Janet .... 517-607-2341.. 235 E
jmarsh@hillsdale.edu
MARSH, Jed .... 609-258-7860.. 294 D
jmarsh@princeton.edu
MARSH, John .... 315-792-7125.. 336 C
john.marsh@sunyit.edu
MARSH, Jolee .... 910-678-8217.. 349 F
marshj@faytechcc.edu
MARSH, Kathleen .... 989-358-7458.. 230 G
marshk@alpenacc.edu
MARSH, Kent .... 970-248-1303.... 77 L
kmarsh@coloradomesa.edu
MARSH, Latonia, D .... 716-878-4618.. 332 F
marshld@buffalostate.edu
MARSH, MaToya .... 773-821-2601.. 136 M
mmarsh@csu.edu
MARSH, Nicole, Y .... 510-628-8011.... 49 A
librarian@lincolnuca.edu
MARSH, Robert .... 231-439-6353.. 239 A
rmarsh@ncmich.edu
MARSH-WILLIAMS,
Pamela, R .... 413-545-6493.. 220 F
marshwil@acad.umass.edu
MARSHAK, Helen Hopp .. 909-558-4578.... 49 C
hhoppmarshak@llu.edu
MARSHALL, Ave .... 404-270-5288.. 128 A
amarshall@spelman.edu
MARSHALL, Ben .... 813-253-7125.. 102 R
rmarshall10@hccfl.edu
MARSHALL, Bleuzette ...... 513-556-6262.. 379 A
bleuzette.marshall@uc.edu
MARSHALL, Bonnie .... 610-527-0200.. 418 D
bonnie.marshall@rosemont.edu
MARSHALL, Bryon .... 609-586-4800.. 292 D
marshalb@mccc.edu
MARSHALL, Charity .... 215-955-1861.. 420 E
charity.marshall@jefferson.edu
MARSHALL, Cheryl, A ..... 714-808-4797.... 54 F
cmarshall@nocccd.edu
MARSHALL, Connie .... 423-354-2533.. 446 F
cmarshall@northeaststate.edu
MARSHALL, Courtney ...... 316-978-3830.. 185 J
courtney.marshall@wichita.edu
MARSHALL, Darren .... 801-957-4782.. 483 A
darren.marshall@slcc.edu
MARSHALL, Darryl .... 850-644-5716.. 111 C
dmarshall@admin.fsu.edu
MARSHALL, Dave .... 218-235-2125.. 252 F
d.marshall@vcc.edu
MARSHALL, David .... 909-537-5032.... 34 C
dmarshall@csusb.edu
MARSHALL, David .... 979-230-3213.. 453 A
david.marshall@brazosport.edu
MARSHALL, David, B .... 805-893-2785.... 70 E
david.marshall@ucsb.edu
MARSHALL, Debbie .... 858-695-8587.... 46 G
MARSHALL, Deborah .... 504-520-5444.. 202 C
dmarsha2@xula.edu
MARSHALL, Elaine .... 864-503-5331.. 434 G
emarshall@uscupstate.edu
MARSHALL, Ernie .... 718-429-6600.. 339 D
ernie.marshall@vaughn.edu
MARSHALL, George .... 860-701-5182.... 88 D
marshall_g@mitchell.edu
MARSHALL, J, A .... 413-205-3263.. 214 B
ja.marshall@aic.edu
MARSHALL, JaNice .... 216-987-3287.. 367 E
janice.marshall@tri-c.edu
MARSHALL, Jay .... 765-983-1687.. 160 G
marshja@earlham.edu
MARSHALL, Jo .... 606-679-8501.. 190 E
jo.marshall@kctcs.edu
MARSHALL, Joan .... 732-247-5241.. 293 B
jmarshall@nbts.edu
MARSHALL, Joe .... 301-846-2824.. 207 F
jmarshall@frederick.edu
MARSHALL, John .... 970-248-1366.... 77 L
marshall@coloradomesa.edu
MARSHALL, Jon .... 620-365-5116.. 178 A
marshall@allencc.edu
MARSHALL, Joretta .... 817-257-7577.. 453 O
j.marshall@tcu.edu
MARSHALL, Juanita .... 731-426-7539.. 440 K
jmarshall@lanecollege.edu
MARSHALL, Judith .... 618-536-2626.. 154 I
jmarshal@siu.edu
MARSHALL, Justin, W ...... 989-837-4279.. 239 D
marshall@northwood.edu
MARSHALL, Katherine ..... 716-270-2661.. 313 H
marshallk@ecc.edu
MARSHALL, Keith .... 217-333-0302.. 157 A
keithmar@illinois.edu
MARSHALL, Kent .... 708-974-5390.. 148 G
marshallk34@morainevalley.edu
MARSHALL, Kimberly ...... 256-372-8481...... 1 A
kimberly.marshall@aamu.edu
MARSHALL, Larry .... 724-852-3230.. 423 A
lmarshal@waynesburg.edu
MARSHALL, Larry, W ...... 606-474-3277.. 188 L
lmarshall@kcu.edu
MARSHALL, Lori .... 856-256-4197.. 295 E
marshall@rowan.edu
MARSHALL, Lynette, L .... 319-335-3305.. 169 H
lynette-marshall@uiowa.edu
MARSHALL, Margaret, J .. 334-844-7474...... 1 G
mjm0030@auburn.edu
MARSHALL, Maura .... 603-641-7028.. 287 G
mmarshall@anselm.edu
MARSHALL, Michael .... 817-257-7808.. 469 G
m.marshall@tcu.edu
MARSHALL, Molly, T .... 913-667-5700.. 179 K
mtmarshall@cbts.edu
MARSHALL, Nancy .... 503-581-8600.. 391 B
nmarshall@corban.edu
MARSHALL, Peter .... 812-357-6280.. 167 B
pmarshall@saintmeinrad.edu
MARSHALL, Phillip .... 870-733-6810.... 19 A
pmarshall@asumidsouth.edu
MARSHALL, Phyllis .... 609-633-6460.. 297 F
pmarshall@tesu.edu
MARSHALL, Richard, A .... 309-457-2124.. 148 E
rmarshall@monmouthcollege.edu
MARSHALL, Rosita .... 606-693-5000.. 191 A
finaid@kmbc.edu
MARSHALL, Scott .... 503-725-5257.. 394 G
rsm@pdx.edu
MARSHALL, Steve .... 715-394-8365.. 521 E
smarsha8@uwsuper.edu
MARSHALL, Steven .... 610-282-1100.. 402 B
steven.marshall@desales.edu
MARSHALL, Susan .... 870-733-6716.... 19 A
smarshall@asumidsouth.edu
MARSHALL, Susan, D ...... 423-652-6006.. 440 J
sdmarsha@king.edu
MARSHALL, Tim .... 212-229-8947.. 322 E
provost@newschool.edu
MARSHALL, Tim .... 214-378-1856.. 456 A
tmarshall@dcccd.edu
MARSHALL, Toni .... 803-508-7242.. 426 G
marshalt@atc.edu
MARSHALL, William .... 218-322-2340.. 249 G
william.marshall@itascacc.edu
MARSHALL, William, G .... 956-296-1441.. 476 E
william.marshall@utrgv.edu
MARSHALL-BIGGINS,
Cynthia .... 903-593-8311.. 470 A
cmarshall-biggins@texascollege.edu
MARSHBURN, Roxann ..... 847-376-7099.. 150 G
rmarshbu@oakton.edu
MARSICANO, Leslie, M .... 704-894-2804.. 343 I
lemarsicano@davidson.edu
MARSICO, Richard, J ...... 330-941-3036.. 382 A
rjmarsico@ysu.edu
MARSILI, Amanda .... 401-254-3774.. 426 B
amarsili@rwu.edu
MARSON, Wendy .... 651-450-3392.. 249 F
wmarson@inverhills.edu
MARSOW, Mendel .... 718-774-5050.. 337 D
MARSTELLER, Diane .... 330-652-9919.. 368 G
dianemarsteller@eticollege.edu
MARSTELLER, Jill, A .... 610-409-3582.. 422 D
jmarsteller@ursinus.edu
MARSTON, Summer, S ..... 406-447-6927.. 277 B
summer.marston@umhelena.edu
MARSWILLO, Joseph, S .. 973-642-4568.. 293 D
joseph.s.marswillo@njit.edu
MARTAINDALE, Ward .... 281-283-2255.. 474 A
martaindale@uhcl.edu
MARTE, Benjamin .... 518-276-6287.. 327 B
marteb2@rpi.edu
MARTE, Maria .... 973-684-5993.. 294 A
mmarte@pccc.edu
MARTEL, Annette .... 701-224-5771.. 360 D
annette.martel@dickinsonstate.edu
MARTEL, David, W .... 434-924-7821.. 495 H
dwm5x@virginia.edu
MARTEL, Kristie, A .... 724-847-5751.. 404 B
kamartel@geneva.edu
MARTEL, Ronald .... 401-598-2848.. 425 B
rmartel@jwu.edu
MARTELL, Kathryn .... 509-963-1955.. 501 K
martellk@cwu.edu
MARTELLARO, John .... 816-235-1592.. 273 F
martellaroj@umkc.edu
MARTELLO, Michael .... 716-338-1030.. 317 F
michaelmartello@mail.sunyjcc.edu
MARTEN, Timothy .... 217-544-6464.. 153 G
timothy.marten@stjohnscollegespringfield.edu
MARTENS, Daniel, R .... 812-464-1799.. 168 E
dmartens@usi.edu
MARTENS, John .... 360-736-9391.. 502 A
jmartens@centralia.edu
MARTENS, Lisa .... 989-686-9826.. 233 I
lisamartens@delta.edu
MARTENS, Mum .... 847-635-1675.. 150 G
mmartens@oakton.edu
MARTENS, Mums .... 847-635-1675.. 150 G
mmartens@oakton.edu
MARTENSEN, Brian .... 507-389-5998.. 250 E
brian.martensen@mnsu.edu
MARTENSEN, Carsten, P . 607-274-3184.. 317 D
cmertensen@ithaca.edu
MARTERER, Aaron, C ...... 803-777-3333.. 433 F
marterer@sc.edu
MARTGIN, Anita .... 501-337-5000.... 19 K
amartin@coto.edu
MARTHERS, Paul .... 518-320-1672.. 330 H
paul.marthers@suny.edu
MARTI, Dennis .... 216-221-8584.. 380 I
dmarti@vmcad.edu
MARTI, Tammy, S .... 563-588-7142.. 174 K
tammy.marti@loras.edu
MARTI, Vionex .... 787-738-2161.. 538 A
vionex.marti@upr.edu
MARTICH, Luisa .... 718-289-5732.. 307 C
luisa.martich@bcc.cuny.edu
MARTICKE, Nathan .... 816-584-6844.. 270 D
nathan.marticke@park.edu
MARTIN, Aaron .... 337-482-6397.. 201 D
aaronmartin@louisiana.edu

MARTIN, Abigail .... 850-245-0466.. 110 I
abigail.martin@flbog.edu
MARTIN, Alan, B .... 304-293-7398.. 514 C
alan.martin@mail.wvu.edu
MARTIN, Allison .... 318-678-6000.. 195 I
amartin@bpcc.edu
MARTIN, Alvin .... 310-824-1586.... 24 L
amartin@ajrca.org
MARTIN, Ana .... 787-265-3800.. 538 C
business@uprm.edu
MARTIN, Andrew, D .... 734-764-0322.. 241 J
admart@umich.edu
MARTIN, Angela .... 785-227-3380.. 178 J
martinar@bethanylb.edu
MARTIN, Angela, A .... 515-574-1064.. 173 F
martin_a@iowacentral.edu
MARTIN, Angela, S .... 859-257-9830.. 193 G
angie.martin@uky.edu
MARTIN, Ann .... 303-964-5718.... 82 L
amartin@regis.edu
MARTIN, Ann .... 660-562-1570.. 269 J
amartin@nwmissouri.edu
MARTIN, Ann .... 330-972-8943.. 378 H
abmarti@uakron.edu
MARTIN, Anthony .... 281-649-3152.. 458 L
amartin@hbu.edu
MARTIN, Barbara .... 802-828-2800.. 486 A
martinb@ccv.edu
MARTIN, Barry .... 303-273-3900.... 78 M
bemartin@mines.edu
MARTIN, Bethany, A .... 315-386-7555.. 335 B
martinb@canton.edu
MARTIN, Billy .... 859-622-1515.. 188 F
billy.martin@eku.edu
MARTIN, Billy .... 859-622-3855.. 188 F
billy.martin@eku.edu
MARTIN, Bob .... 860-701-5178.... 88 D
martin_b@mitchell.edu
MARTIN, Bobby .... 405-491-6339.. 388 A
bgmartin@snu.edu
MARTIN, Bonnie .... 518-255-5402.. 334 D
martinbg@cobleskill.edu
MARTIN, Bonnie, G .... 607-746-4495.. 335 C
martinbg@delhi.edu
MARTIN, Brandon .... 818-677-3208.... 34 A
brandon.martin@csun.edu
MARTIN, Bridgit .... 920-403-3963.. 519 G
bridgit.martin@snc.edu
MARTIN, Brint .... 757-727-5425.. 490 E
alumni@hamptonu.edu
MARTIN, Byron .... 219-464-6760.. 168 F
byron.martin@vlapo.edu
MARTIN, JR., C. Vernon . 305-626-3714.. 101 A
vmartin@fmuniv.edu
MARTIN, Cameron, K ...... 801-863-8514.. 482 C
cameron.martin@uvu.edu
MARTIN, Carla, M .... 870-575-8873.... 23 E
martinm@uapb.edu
MARTIN, Carmella .... 904-470-8081.... 98 N
carmella.martin0906@ewc.edu
MARTIN, Carol .... 503-845-3555.. 392 E
carol.martin@mtangel.edu
MARTIN, Carolyn, R .... 804-289-8088.. 495 G
cmartin@richmond.edu
MARTIN,
Carolyn (Biddy), A .... 413-542-2234.. 214 C
president@amherst.edu
MARTIN, Cecelia .... 251-460-6591...... 9 E
cgmartin@southalabama.edu
MARTIN, Cecily .... 505-438-8884.. 302 B
admissions@acupuncturecollege.edu
MARTIN, Charles .... 340-693-1511.. 539 C
cmartin@uvi.edu
MARTIN, Charlie .... 727-376-6911.. 114 A
cmartin@trinitycollege.edu
MARTIN, Cheryl .... 617-427-0600.. 224 F
cmartin@rcc.mass.edu
MARTIN, Chicora .... 510-430-3189.... 52 J
chimartin@mills.edu
MARTIN, Chonte' .... 803-705-4539.. 427 D
cmartin@gcaservices.com
MARTIN, Chris .... 904-997-2924.. 101 G
chris.martin@fscj.edu
MARTIN, Chris .... 318-257-4526.. 200 G
cmartin@latech.edu
MARTIN, Chris .... 636-778-1058.. 272 B
cmartin@semo.edu
MARTIN, Christa, S .... 931-540-2644.. 446 A
cmartin@columbiastate.edu
MARTIN, Christina .... 617-236-8844.. 218 G
cmartin02@fisher.edu
MARTIN, Christopher ...... 208-769-3340.. 134 C
camartin@nic.edu
MARTIN, Christy .... 503-255-0332.. 392 G
cmartin@multnomah.edu
MARTIN, Clara .... 843-574-6326.. 433 D
clara.martin@tridenttech.edu
MARTIN, Cristina .... 909-537-5669.... 34 C
cristina.martin@csusb.edu
MARTIN, Curt .... 970-248-1396.... 77 L
cumartin@coloradomesa.edu
MARTIN, Curtis .... 256-372-5500...... 1 A
curtis.martin@aamu.edu
MARTIN, D. Michael .... 909-687-1600.... 44 H
michael.martin@gs.edu
MARTIN, Dale .... 318-357-4496.. 201 B
dale@nsula.edu
MARTIN, Dan .... 319-398-4984.. 174 I
dan.martin@kirkwood.edu
MARTIN, Dan, J .... 412-268-2349.. 400 D
djmartin@cmu.edu
MARTIN, Daniel, J .... 206-281-2114.. 507 C
dmartin@spu.edu
MARTIN, Dave .... 724-852-3463.. 423 A
dmartin@waynesburg.edu
MARTIN, David .... 414-847-3213.. 518 D
davidmartin@miad.edu
MARTIN, David .... 212-787-5300.. 303 G
MARTIN, David .... 423-636-7319.. 447 G
dmartin@tusculum.edu
MARTIN, David .... 415-241-2230.... 38 E
dmartin@ccsf.edu
MARTIN, David .... 502-852-4653.. 194 A
dcmart02@louisville.edu
MARTIN, David .... 352-365-3532.. 104 J
martind@lssc.edu
MARTIN, David .... 323-469-3300.... 26 A
dmartin@amda.edu
MARTIN, David .... 502-852-8220.. 194 A
dcmart02@louisville.edu
MARTIN, David .... 203-837-9600.... 85 I
martind@wcsu.edu
MARTIN, David .... 718-420-4341.. 339 F
dmartin@wagner.edu
MARTIN, David .... 570-674-6294.. 410 K
dmartin@misericordia.edu
MARTIN, David, J .... 979-845-0532.. 468 B
david-j-martin@tamu.edu
MARTIN, David, W .... 605-394-2400.. 437 E
david.martin@sdsmt.edu
MARTIN, Debbie .... 973-290-4208.. 290 G
dmartin@cse.edu
MARTIN, Debbie .... 910-296-1429.. 350 F
dmartin@jamessprunt.edu
MARTIN, Deborah .... 717-477-1121.. 416 A
dkmart@ship.edu
MARTIN, Deborah .... 312-629-6800.. 154 A
dmartin@saic.edu
MARTIN, Dewey .... 314-246-7560.. 275 B
deweymartin21@webster.edu
MARTIN, Diane, C .... 202-994-0513.... 92 D
dmartin@gwu.edu
MARTIN, Donald, L .... 706-233-7203.. 127 A
dmartin@shorter.edu
MARTIN, Donna .... 904-548-4414.. 101 G
donna.martin@fscj.edu
MARTIN, Dorothy .... 229-430-2804.. 115 K
dorothy.martin@asurams.edu
MARTIN, Dorothy .... 207-768-2806.. 203 L
dmartin@nmcc.edu
MARTIN, Doug .... 757-446-5035.. 489 B
martinsd@evms.edu
MARTIN, Dustin .... 765-641-4150.. 158 J
dlmartin@anderson.edu
MARTIN, Earl, F .... 515-271-2191.. 171 K
earl.martin@drake.edu
MARTIN, III, Earl Joe ..... 225-752-4230.. 195 E
jmartin@iticollege.edu
MARTIN, Edward .... 931-363-9832.. 441 G
emartin@martinmethodist.edu
MARTIN, Elaine, R .... 508-856-2399.. 221 B
elaine.martin@umassmed.edu
MARTIN, Eric .... 212-752-1530.. 318 F
eric.martin@limcollege.edu
MARTIN, Eric .... 814-393-2306.. 414 G
emartin@clarion.edu
MARTIN, Etienne .... 614-287-2491.. 367 C
emarti10@cscc.edu
MARTIN, Gale .... 610-526-6143.. 405 B
gmartin@harcum.edu
MARTIN, Gary .... 561-237-7157.. 104 O
gmartin@lynn.edu
MARTIN, Gary, D .... 651-696-6735.. 247 I
gmartin6@macalester.edu
MARTIN, George .... 603-526-3604.. 285 L
gmartin@colby-sawyer.edu
MARTIN, George, E .... 512-448-8411.. 464 G
georgem@stedwards.edu
MARTIN, Gerardina .... 610-738-0496.. 416 C
gmartin@wcupa.edu
MARTIN, Greg .... 515-964-6368.. 171 B
gcmartin@dmacc.edu
MARTIN, SR., Harold, L . 336-334-7940.. 356 F
hmartin@ncat.edu
MARTIN, Heath .... 419-559-2350.. 377 M
hmartin01@terra.edu
MARTIN, Irene .... 860-343-5740.... 86 F
imartin@mxcc.commnet.edu
MARTIN, Isis .... 530-226-2177.... 64 H
imartin@simpsonu.edu
MARTIN, Jackie, L .... 601-643-8322.. 257 D
jackie.martin@colin.edu
MARTIN, James .... 208-282-2341.. 133 H
martjame@isu.edu
MARTIN, James, J .... 501-882-8851.... 18 I
jjmartin@asub.edu
MARTIN, Jan .... 212-787-5300.. 303 G
MARTIN, Jana .... 918-293-5339.. 386 B
jana.s.martin@okstate.edu
MARTIN, Jeania .... 704-991-0114.. 353 E
jmartin8295@stanly.edu
MARTIN, Jeanne .... 210-366-2701.. 463 J
MARTIN, Jenni .... 509-533-7075.. 502 I
jenni.martin@scc.spokane.edu
MARTIN, Jennifer .... 940-898-3415.. 472 G
jmartin@twu.edu
MARTIN, Jerold .... 312-553-2500.. 137 C
jmartin46@ccc.edu
MARTIN, Jerry .... 334-387-3877...... 1 E
jerrymartin@amridgeuniversity.edu
MARTIN, Jill .... 571-633-9651.. 495 D
jill.martin@uona.edu
MARTIN, Jill .... 800-567-2344.. 516 B
jmartin@menominee.edu
MARTIN, Jim David .... 415-575-6165.... 30 G
jmartin@ciis.edu
MARTIN, Jimmy .... 832-813-6680.. 461 B
james.d.martin@lonestar.edu
MARTIN, Jimmy, D .... 864-488-4566.. 430 H
jmartin@limestone.edu
MARTIN, Jo Leda .... 303-963-3206.... 77 I
jomartin@ccu.edu
MARTIN, Joel .... 717-358-3986.. 403 J
joel.martin@fandm.edu
MARTIN, John .... 317-632-5553.. 165 L
johnmartin@lincolntech.edu
MARTIN, John .... 405-878-5293.. 387 J
jpmartin@stgregorys.edu
MARTIN, John, O .... 413-545-0361.. 220 F
jomartin@admin.umass.edu
MARTIN, John, U .... 941-487-4444.. 111 D
jmartin@ncf.edu
MARTIN, Joshua .... 972-825-4821.. 465 D
jmartin@sagu.edu
MARTIN, Joshua .... 508-854-7513.. 224 E
jmartin@qcc.mass.edu
MARTIN, Juanita, K .... 330-972-7082.. 378 G
juanita@uakron.edu
MARTIN, Karen, O .... 912-279-5750.. 119 C
kmartin@ccga.edu
MARTIN, Kari .... 859-622-1260.. 188 F
kari.martin@eku.edu
MARTIN, Kathleen .... 413-565-1000.. 215 A
kmartin@baypath.edu
MARTIN, Kathy .... 208-792-2282.. 134 A
kmartin@lcsc.edu
MARTIN, Kathy .... 704-406-4636.. 344 E
kmartin@gardner-webb.edu
MARTIN, Keith .... 918-343-7706.. 387 F
kmartin@rsu.edu
MARTIN, Keith .... 716-338-1261.. 317 F
keithmartin@mail.sunyjcc.edu
MARTIN, Kelley .... 316-295-5568.. 181 B
kelley_martin@friends.edu
MARTIN, Kelly .... 859-572-6565.. 192 B
martink29@nku.edu
MARTIN, Kelsey, C .... 310-794-9507.... 69 D
kcmartin@mednet.ucla.edu
MARTIN, Kenneth .... 972-937-7612.. 462 J
kenneth.martin@navarrocollege.edu
MARTIN, Kenneth, M ...... 717-815-1211.. 424 F
kmartin@ycp.edu
MARTIN, Kevin .... 302-225-6241.... 91 D
martink@gbc.edu
MARTIN, Kevin .... 618-650-2345.. 155 A
kemarti@siue.edu
MARTIN, Kevin .... 215-407-0584.. 413 L
kmartin@pafa.edu
MARTIN, Kim .... 949-794-9090.... 66 H
kmartin@stanbridge.edu
MARTIN, Kimberly .... 731-286-3346.. 446 B
martin@cscc.edu
MARTIN, Kyle, R .... 208-496-1010.. 132 J
martink@byui.edu
MARTIN, Lara .... 561-237-7459.. 104 O
lmartin@lynn.edu
MARTIN, Larry .... 657-278-6029.... 33 A
larrymartin@fullerton.edu
MARTIN, Larry .... 718-270-6405.. 309 B
lmartin@mec.cuny.edu
MARTIN, Laurel .... 859-246-6584.. 189 B
laurel.martin@kctcs.edu
MARTIN, Leandra .... 408-855-5182.... 74 G
leandra.martin@wvm.edu
MARTIN, Levi .... 503-255-0332.. 392 G
lmartin@multnomah.edu
MARTIN, Lisa .... 770-962-7580.. 123 D
lmartin@gwinnetttech.edu
MARTIN, Lisa .... 918-343-7614.. 387 F
lmartin@rsu.edu
MARTIN, Lizbeth, J .... 510-436-1040.... 46 E
martin@hnu.edu
MARTIN, Louisa, A .... 210-431-5005.. 464 H
lmartin@stmarytx.edu
MARTIN, Luke .... 619-298-1829.... 66 D
lmartin@ssu.edu
MARTIN, Lynn .... 734-973-3507.. 242 G
lgmartin@wccnet.edu
MARTIN, Maggie .... 229-391-5135.. 115 I
mmartin@abac.edu
MARTIN, Mallory .... 504-286-5329.. 199 I
mm@suno.edu
MARTIN, Marc .... 510-780-4500.... 48 J
mmartin@lifewest.edu
MARTIN, Marcus, L .... 434-243-2079.. 495 H
mlm8n@virginia.edu
MARTIN, Margo .... 904-632-3030.. 101 G
margo.martin@fscj.edu
MARTIN, Marian .... 256-378-2001...... 2 G
mmartin8@cacc.edu
MARTIN, Marie .... 651-604-4131.. 247 L
mmartin@minneapolisbusinesscollege.edu
MARTIN, Marie .... 803-780-1229.. 434 M
martin@voorhees.edu
MARTIN, Mariel .... 518-580-8212.. 330 F
mariel@skidmore.edu
MARTIN, Mark .... 704-357-2541.. 127 D
mmartin@southuniversity.edu
MARTIN, Mark, A .... 989-837-4497.. 239 D
martinm@northwood.edu
MARTIN, Marty .... 571-633-9651.. 495 D
marty.martin@uona.edu
MARTIN, Matthew, R ...... 478-757-5246.. 129 L
mmartin@wesleyancollege.edu
MARTIN, Michael .... 662-846-4638.. 257 E
mmartin@deltastate.edu
MARTIN, Michael .... 918-647-1360.. 382 I
mmartin@carlalbert.edu
MARTIN, Mike .... 619-702-9400.... 31 A
mike.martin@cibu.edu
MARTIN, Mirta, M .... 785-628-4231.. 180 I
m3martin@fhsu.edu
MARTIN, Nicola .... 904-826-0084.... 72 A
nmartin@usa.edu
MARTIN, Pat .... 610-328-8451.. 419 I
pmartin1@swarthmore.edu
MARTIN, Patrick .... 860-231-5311.... 90 B
pmartin@usj.edu
MARTIN, Paul .... 518-276-8711.. 327 B
martip@rpi.edu
MARTIN, Paul .... 617-730-7155.. 226 J
paul.martin@newbury.edu
MARTIN, Paula .... 907-747-7704.... 10 H
pjmartin2@alaska.edu
MARTIN, III, Quincy .... 708-456-0300.. 156 C
quincymartin@triton.edu
MARTIN, Rafael .... 972-883-4824.. 476 C
rafael.martin@utdallas.edu
MARTIN, II, Ralph, C ...... 617-373-2101.. 227 B
MARTIN, Randy .... 870-972-2093.... 18 J
rmartin@astate.edu
MARTIN, Randy .... 724-357-2244.. 415 B
rmartin@iup.edu
MARTIN, Ray .... 254-295-4590.. 474 E
rmartin@umhb.edu
MARTIN, Robert .... 202-885-8611.... 94 E
rmartin@wesleyseminary.edu
MARTIN, Robert .... 505-424-2301.. 299 L
MARTIN, Robert, E .... 303-233-4697.... 78 N
rm@schooloftrades.edu
MARTIN, Robert, K .... 989-774-7161.. 232 D
marti1rk@cmich.edu
MARTIN, Robyn .... 520-515-3688.... 12 L
martinrc@cochise.edu
MARTIN, Ronald .... 773-843-7553.. 137 H
rmartin@ccc.edu
MARTIN, Ronald, C .... 814-732-2743.. 415 A
martinr@edinboro.edu
MARTIN, Roneida .... 847-543-2641.. 138 C
rmartin@clcillinois.edu
MARTIN, Ronnie .... 434-592-6515.. 491 D
rbmartin@liberty.edu
MARTIN, Rosa, L .... 706-821-8365.. 125 H
rmartin@paine.edu
MARTIN, Rosalee, R .... 512-505-3098.. 459 F
rrmartin@htu.edu
MARTIN, Rosalynn .... 910-962-3712.. 358 D
martinr@uncw.edu
MARTIN, Roy, J .... 225-578-2284.. 197 I
rjmartin@lsu.edu
MARTIN, Russell .... 864-941-8669.. 432 A
martin.r@ptc.edu
MARTIN, Ruth .... 619-201-8685.... 60 D
ruth.martin@sdcc.edu
MARTIN, Ryan .... 201-360-4024.. 292 B
rmartin@hccc.edu
MARTIN, Sandra, E .... 870-235-4041.... 22 F
sandrasmith@saumag.edu
MARTIN, Sara .... 615-794-4254.. 443 G
smartin@omorecollege.edu
MARTIN, Sean .... 860-439-2058.... 87 F
sean.martin@conncoll.edu

MARTIN, Sean .... 314-256-8860.. 262 D
martin@ai.edu
MARTIN, Shane, P .... 310-338-7301..... 51 E
shane.martin@lmu.edu
MARTIN, Sharon, L .... 304-293-0111.. 514 C
shmartin@mail.wvu.edu
MARTIN, Staci .... 903-983-8200.. 460 D
smartin@kilgore.edu
MARTIN, Stephanie .... 219-464-5212.. 168 F
stephanie.martin1@valpo.edu
MARTIN, Steven, J .... 419-772-2277.. 374 J
s-martin.11@onu.edu
MARTIN, Susan, D .... 865-974-2445.. 448 E
sdmartin@utk.edu
MARTIN, Susan, M .... 630-942-3324.. 138 B
martinsu@cod.edu
MARTIN, Susie .... 310-377-5501.... 51 G
smartin@marymountcalifornia.edu
MARTIN, Terri .... 906-487-7225.. 234 A
terri.martin@finlandia.edu
MARTIN, Terry .... 318-487-7110.. 195 F
terry.martin@lacollege.edu
MARTIN, Terry .... 225-743-8500.. 196 J
tmartin@rpcc.edu
MARTIN, Thomas, K .... 972-758-3817.. 455 A
tmartin@collin.edu
MARTIN, Timothy, J .... 515-574-1097.. 173 F
martin@iowacentral.edu
MARTIN, Timothy, R .... 508-767-7373.. 214 F
timartin@assumption.edu
MARTIN, Tod .... 501-279-4403.... 20 D
registrar@harding.edu
MARTIN, Tom .... 361-593-3419.. 469 A
katdm00@tamuk.edu
MARTIN, Tony, L .... 336-386-3222.. 353 F
martint@surry.edu
MARTIN, Tracey .... 678-715-2200.... 93 F
MARTIN, Traci .... 410-337-6191.. 207 H
tmartin@goucher.edu
MARTIN, Traycee, F .... 229-333-5710.. 129 G
tmartin@valdosta.edu
MARTIN, Troy .... 716-375-2373.. 328 B
MARTIN, Valerie, G .... 570-372-4288.. 419 H
vmartin@susqu.edu
MARTIN, Vicki, J .... 414-297-6320.. 524 A
martinv@matc.edu
MARTIN, Victor .... 661-654-2161..... 32 A
vmartin4@csub.edu
MARTIN, Victor .... 661-654-2222..... 32 A
vmartin4@csub.edu
MARTIN, Walter .... 919-866-5385.. 353 I
wmartin@waketech.edu
MARTIN, Wayne .... 973-754-7192.. 294 A
wmartin@pccc.edu
MARTIN, Wayne .... 540-453-2347.. 496 F
martinw@brcc.edu
MARTIN, Willadean .... 972-860-4817.. 456 B
wmartin@dcccd.edu
MARTIN, William, J .... 614-292-8350.. 375 A
martin.3047@osu.edu
MARTIN-BROWN, Karen .. 352-371-2833..... 98 I
faa@dragonrises.edu
MARTIN-FEDICH, Laura ... 404-471-6054.. 115 J
lmartin@agnesscott.edu
MARTIN-HATCHER,
Dorothy .... 203-576-5756..... 89 A
dorothy.martin-hatcher@
stvincentscollege.edu
MARTIN LOPIT, Maribeth 206-281-2448.. 507 C
martinm3@spu.edu
MARTIN-OSORIO,
Carol, J .... 615-353-3268.. 446 E
carol.martin-osorio@nscc.edu
MARTIN PALMER,
Barbara .... 301-447-5371.. 209 G
palmer@msmary.edu
MARTIN-PARISIEN, Terri . 701-477-7862.. 362 D
tmartinparisien@tm.edu
MARTIN-REND, Jill .... 814-653-8265.. 399 B
jill.martin-rend@bc3.edu
MARTIN TSE, Jennifer ..... 315-464-4604.. 332 C
registrar@upstate.edu
MARTIN-VEGA, Louis, A . 919-515-2311.. 357 B
louis_martin-vega@ncsu.edu
MARTINDILL, Cindy .... 802-728-1586.. 486 D
cmartindill@vtc.edu
MARTINEAU, Jim .... 503-594-3271.. 390 F
jmartineau@clackamas.edu
MARTINEAU, Kevin .... 816-584-6225.. 270 D
kevin.martineau@park.edu
MARTINELLE, Lorraine ..... 508-213-2219.. 227 A
lorraine.martinelle@nichols.edu
MARTINELLI, Joseph, I ... 301-546-7422.. 210 C
jmartinelli@pgcc.edu
MARTINELLI, Joseph, L .. 301-546-0417.. 210 C
martinjl@pgcc.edu
MARTINELLI-FERNANDEZ,
Susan .... 309-298-1828.. 158 A
martinelli-fernandez@wiu.edu
MARTINELLO, Peter .... 614-882-2551.. 368 K

MARTINEZ, Abelardo .... 787-276-8240.. 537 H
abelardo.martinez@upr.edu
MARTINEZ, Albert, M ...... 973-596-3668.. 293 D
albert.martinez@njit.edu
MARTINEZ, Anthony .... 707-527-4568.... 63 G
amartinez@santarosa.edu
MARTINEZ, Auris .... 787-878-5475.. 533 H
amartinez@arecibo.inter.edu
MARTINEZ, Brenda .... 510-466-7203.... 57 E
bmartinez@peralta.edu
MARTINEZ, Carla .... 714-895-8705.... 39 F
cmartinez@gwc.cccd.edu
MARTINEZ, Carlos .... 361-593-2249.. 469 A
carlos.martinez@tamuk.edu
MARTINEZ, Carlos .... 817-531-4959.. 472 F
cmartinez@txwes.edu
MARTINEZ, Carlos, E ...... 512-471-6519.. 476 B
carlos.martinez@austin.utexas.edu
MARTINEZ, Carolina .... 505-454-3269.. 300 F
carolina@nmhu.edu
MARTINEZ, Chad .... 618-650-2333.. 155 A
cmartaa@siue.edu
MARTINEZ, Cristina .... 830-792-7281.. 465 E
cimartinez@schreiner.edu
MARTINEZ, Cristina .... 787-257-0000.. 537 H
cristina.martinezlebron@upr.edu
MARTINEZ, Debra .... 717-764-9550.. 401 I
dmartinez@csb.edu
MARTINEZ, Diana .... 630-942-3007.. 138 B
martinezd59@cod.edu
MARTINEZ, Diana .... 602-285-7800.... 14 F
dr.martinez@phoenixcollege.edu
MARTINEZ, Diana, S .... 210-458-8000.. 477 A
diana.martinez1@utsa.edu
MARTINEZ, Didit .... 806-743-2900.. 472 D
didit.martinez@ttuhsc.edu
MARTINEZ, Dolly .... 718-518-4300.. 308 C
dmartinez@hostos.cuny.edu
MARTINEZ, Edward .... 505-454-3366.. 300 F
eamartinez@nmhu.edu
MARTINEZ, Elena, M .... 956-326-2433.. 468 A
emartinez@tamiu.edu
MARTINEZ, Elizabeth .... 956-326-2335.. 468 A
elizabeth@tamiu.edu
MARTINEZ, Ernie .... 559-265-5711.... 67 C
ernie.martinez@fresnocitycollege.edu
MARTINEZ, Esther .... 361-354-2210.. 454 G
emartinez@coastalbend.edu
MARTINEZ, Everardo .... 928-314-9422.... 11 J
everardo.martinez@azwestern.edu
MARTINEZ, Freddie .... 787-841-2000.. 535 I
fmartinez@pucpr.edu
MARTINEZ, Geraldine ...... 575-527-7710.. 301 C
gerri66@nmsu.edu
MARTINEZ, German .... 609-497-7778.. 294 C
facilities-security@ptsem.edu
MARTINEZ, Heather .... 806-742-7017.. 472 C
heather.martinez@ttu.edu
MARTINEZ, Hector .... 787-284-1912.. 534 C
hmartin@ponce.inter.edu
MARTINEZ, Hector .... 787-284-1912.. 534 C
hemart@ponce.inter.edu
MARTINEZ, Henry .... 972-860-8142.. 456 C
hmartinez@dcccd.edu
MARTINEZ, Jacqueline .... 212-938-5500.. 334 F
jmartinez@sunyopt.edu
MARTINEZ, Janice, A ...... 787-850-9320.. 538 B
janice.martinez1@upr.edu
MARTINEZ, Javier .... 787-863-2390.. 533 K
javier.martinez@fajardo.inter.edu
MARTINEZ, Jeffrey .... 909-748-8400.... 71 K
jeff_martinez@redlands.edu
MARTINEZ, Jeremy .... 432-685-5523.. 461 H
jmartinez@midland.edu
MARTINEZ, Jesse .... 208-885-7716.. 134 G
jessem@uidaho.edu
MARTINEZ, Jesus .... 787-738-2161.. 538 A
jesus.martinez5@upr.edu
MARTINEZ, Jesus, J .... 830-591-7234.. 466 A
jjmartinez1060@swtjc.edu
MARTINEZ, Juan, F .... 787-279-2220.. 533 J
jmartinez@bayamon.inter.edu
MARTINEZ, Kara .... 806-716-4600.. 465 G
kmartinez@southplainscollege.edu
MARTINEZ, Kayla .... 619-961-4251.... 68 A
kmartinez@tjsl.edu
MARTINEZ, Kim .... 303-457-2757.... 80 C
kimberley.martinez@zenith.org
MARTINEZ, Kim .... 303-457-2757.... 80 C
kim.martinez@zenith.org
MARTINEZ, Kristen .... 617-236-5400.. 218 G
kmartinez@fisher.edu
MARTINEZ, Leticia .... 928-344-7644.... 11 J
leticia.martinez@azwestern.edu
MARTINEZ, Leticia .... 817-272-2099.. 476 A
martinezlc@uta.edu
MARTINEZ, Lisa .... 903-468-8175.. 468 D
lisa.martinez@tamuc.edu
MARTINEZ, Loretta, P ...... 303-556-3022.... 81 G
lpmartin@msudenver.edu

MARTINEZ, Lorna .... 787-766-1717.. 536 B
lomartinez@suagm.edu
MARTINEZ, Luis, E .... 786-331-1000.. 105 G
lmartinez@maufl.edu
MARTINEZ, Marco .... 915-532-3737.. 479 H
mmartinez@westerntech.edu
MARTINEZ, Maria .... 787-751-0178.. 535 N
ac_mmartinez@suagm.edu
MARTINEZ, Maria .... 407-646-2003.. 107 O
mmartinez@rollins.edu
MARTINEZ, Maria .... 361-593-2552.. 469 A
maria.martinez@tamuk.edu
MARTINEZ, Maria .... 918-465-1711.. 383 I
mmartinez@eosc.edu
MARTINEZ, Maria, D .... 860-486-4040.... 89 D
maria.d.martinez@uconn.edu
MARTINEZ, Maria, L .... 909-869-2373..... 31 J
mlmartinez@cpp.edu
MARTINEZ, Marilyn .... 787-863-2390.. 533 K
marilyn.martinez@fajardo.inter.edu
MARTINEZ, Mario .... 615-297-7545.. 438 F
martinezm@aquinascollege.edu
MARTINEZ, Marissa, M ... 909-869-3933..... 31 J
mmmartinez1@cpp.edu
MARTINEZ, Marvin .... 323-265-8662..... 49 G
martinmr@elac.edu
MARTINEZ, Michael .... 610-896-1293.. 405 I
mmartinez@haverford.edu
MARTINEZ, Mike .... 575-624-7116.. 299 J
mike.martinez@roswell.enmu.edu
MARTINEZ, Mildred .... 214-379-5438.. 463 G
mmartinez@pqc.edu
MARTINEZ, Miriam .... 787-284-1912.. 534 C
mmartine@ponce.inter.edu
MARTINEZ, Nina .... 502-456-6505.. 193 B
nmartinez@sullivan.edu
MARTINEZ, Patricia .... 815-753-9676.. 150 A
pmartinez2@niu.edu
MARTINEZ, Pedro .... 505-747-2112.. 301 F
pedro.martinez@nnmc.edu
MARTINEZ, Pedro, L .... 505-747-2112.. 301 F
pedro.martinez@nnmc.edu
MARTINEZ, Pedro, L .... 937-376-6636.. 365 H
pmartinez@centralstate.edu
MARTINEZ, Raul, J .... 972-985-3860.. 455 A
rjmartinez@collin.edu
MARTINEZ, Renee, D ...... 323-953-4000..... 49 H
martinrd@lacitycollege.edu
MARTINEZ, Richard .... 626-812-3002..... 28 A
rsmartinez@apu.edu
MARTINEZ, Rick .... 254-295-5030.. 474 E
rmartinez@umhb.edu
MARTINEZ, Robert .... 719-589-7035..... 83 G
robert.martinez@trinidadstate.edu
MARTINEZ, Rochellie ...... 787-738-2161.. 538 A
rochellie.martinez@upr.edu
MARTINEZ, Roman .... 305-237-0012.. 105 D
rmartin9@mdc.edu
MARTINEZ, Rosa, J .... 787-864-2222.. 534 A
rosa.martinez@guayama.inter.edu
MARTINEZ, Ruben, O ...... 407-303-9372..... 95 C
ruben.martinez@adu.edu
MARTINEZ, Sara .... 915-831-7792.. 457 H
smart237@epcc.edu
MARTINEZ, Sonia .... 303-300-8740..... 77 F
sonia.martinez@collegeamerica.com
MARTINEZ, Sonia, V .... 210-458-6887.. 477 A
sonia.martinez@utsa.edu
MARTINEZ, Stacey .... 209-384-6100..... 52 E
martinez.s@mccd.edu
MARTINEZ, Tara .... 612-659-6761.. 250 B
tara.martinez@minneapolis.edu
MARTINEZ, Vesta, M .... 817-515-7795.. 467 A
vesta.martinez@tccd.edu
MARTINEZ, Xochitl, E ..... 909-593-3511..... 71 B
xmartinez@laverne.edu
MARTINEZ, Yuli .... 619-201-8953..... 65 J
yuli.martinez@socalsem.edu
MARTINEZ, Yvonne .... 505-224-3232.. 299 F
ymartinez@cnm.edu
MARTINEZ-ABREU,
Heriberto .... 787-720-1022.. 531 A
martinezabreu@atlanticu.edu
MARTINEZ DE DIOS,
Heri .... 787-720-0596.. 531 A
hmartinez@atlanticu.edu
MARTINEZ-DOANE,
Karol .... 410-225-2284.. 209 B
kmartinez@mica.edu
MARTINEZ-GONZALEZ,
Liduvina .... 212-938-4030.. 334 F
lgonzalez@sunyopt.edu
MARTINEZ-LOPEZ,
Carmen Leonor .... 914-606-6795.. 340 C
carmen.martinez-lopez@sunywcc.edu
MARTINEZ-LUGO,
Miguel .... 787-725-6500.. 531 C
mmartinez@albizu.edu
MARTINEZ ORTIZ,
Daniel .... 787-725-6500.. 531 C
dmartinez@albizu.edu

MARTINEZ-QUILES,
Suzette .... 215-635-7300.. 404 D
smartinez@gratz.edu
MARTINEZ-SAENZ,
Miguel .... 614-823-1556.. 376 C
mmartinezsaenz@otterbein.edu
MARTINEZ STLUKA,
Rena .... 714-992-7077.... 54 H
rmartinezstluka@fullcoll.edu
MARTINEZ-WOODRUFF,
Regina .... 254-526-1397.. 454 A
regina.martinez-woodruff@ctcd.edu
MARTINEZ-YADEN,
Camille .... 520-383-8401.... 17 E
cmartinez@tocc.edu
MARTINI, Louis .... 609-777-5696.. 297 F
lmartini@tesu.edu
MARTINI, Ryan .... 650-508-3640.... 54 J
rmartini@ndnu.edu
MARTINI-HAUSNER,
Mary .... 315-279-5368.. 318 C
mmartini@keuka.edu
MARTINI-JOHNSON,
Lisa, A .... 610-799-1754.. 408 G
lmartinijohnson@lccc.edu
MARTINO, Andrew .... 603-668-2211.. 287 I
a.martino@snhu.edu
MARTINO, Bill .... 212-592-2000.. 330 C
wmartino@sva.edu
MARTINO, Gregory .... 215-972-2079.. 413 L
gmartino@pafa.edu
MARTINS, Sandra .... 630-942-2174.. 138 B
martinss14@cod.edu
MARTINSEN, Daniel .... 254-299-8333.. 461 E
dmartinsen@mclennan.edu
MARTINSON, Janis .... 617-349-8388.. 220 B
janis.martinson@lesley.edu
MARTIR, Jaime .... 787-753-0039.. 532 A
MARTIS, Pamela .... 352-588-8234.. 108 C
pamela.martis@saintleo.edu
MARTLAND, Paul .... 860-932-4124.... 87 C
pmartland@qvcc.edu
MARTLEW, Jeffrey .... 813-419-5100.. 243 I
martlewj@cooley.edu
MARTNER, James, E .... 630-942-2543.. 138 B
martner@cod.edu
MARTOCCI, Deanne .... 518-629-7154.. 316 G
d.martocci@hvcc.edu
MARTOCHE, Katie .... 716-926-8819.. 316 B
kmortoche@hilbert.edu
MARTOHUE, Kimberly ...... 860-832-2551..... 85 F
kmartohue@ccsu.edu
MARTON, Nathan .... 716-829-7583.. 313 A
MARTONE, Mark .... 225-768-1737.. 199 B
mark.martone@ololcollege.edu
MARTONI, Charles .... 724-325-6610.. 401 B
cmartoni@ccac.edu
MARTORANA,
Anne Marie .... 617-879-2231.. 229 G
amartorana@wheelock.edu
MARTORANA, Lorraine ..... 410-287-1030.. 206 J
lmartorana@cecil.edu
MARTOS, Jamie, D .... 510-883-2073..... 42 F
jmartos@dspt.edu
MARTS, Chad .... 757-490-1241.. 486 E
cmarts@auto.edu
MARTY, Angela, L .... 630-515-6120.. 148 C
amarty@midwestern.edu
MARTY, Patrick .... 570-321-4345.. 409 F
marty@lycoming.edu
MARTY-PEARSON, Julie .. 559-325-3600..... 30 C
jmarty-pearson@chsu.org
MARTYN, Margaret, J ...... 312-553-5901.. 137 D
mmartyn1@ccc.edu
MARTZEN, Mark .... 425-602-3162.. 501 D
mmartzen@bastyr.edu
MARTÍNEZ, Felipe .... 787-264-1912.. 534 D
felipe_martinez_arroyo@intersg.edu
MARTÍNEZ, Leticia .... 787-264-1912.. 534 D
letmarti@intersg.edu
MARTÍNEZ, Luz, E .... 787-894-2828.. 539 A
luz.martinez6@upr.edu
MARTÍNEZ, María Gil ...... 787-264-1912.. 534 D
mgmartin@intersg.edu
MARTÍNEZ, Sirimarie .... 787-765-1915.. 534 F
smartinez@opto.inter.edu
MARTÍNEZ, Vilma .... 787-892-4300.. 534 D
vilma_martinez_toro@intersg.edu
MARUCHA, Phillip, T ...... 503-494-8801.. 393 F
marucha@ohsu.edu
MARUGAN, Suresh .... 252-335-3339.. 356 D
sbmurugan@ecsu.edu
MARUGGI, Vincent .... 410-822-5400.. 207 A
vmaruggi@chesapeake.edu
MARUYAMA, Kenichi .... 480-461-7758..... 14 D
kenichi.maruyama@mesacc.edu
MARVI, Hassan .... 202-885-2799..... 91 J
hassan@american.edu
MARVIN, Benjamin .... 518-454-5102.. 311 B
marvinb@strose.edu

MATANYI, Eric .... 708-209-3255.. 138 G
eric.mantanyi@cuchicago.edu
MATARA, Ryan .... 715-394-8293.. 521 E
rmatara@uwsuper.edu
MATARESE, Amanda .... 617-236-8822.. 218 G
amatarese@fisher.edu
MATAS, Francine .... 805-969-3626.... 56 B
fmatas@pacifica.edu
MATASAR, Richard .... 504-314-7612.. 200 C
rmatasar@tulane.edu
MATASSINO, Dana .... 610-409-3188.. 422 D
dmatassino@ursinus.edu
MATCHAN, Steven .... 626-585-7489.... 56 H
sxmatchan@pasadena.edu
MATCHETT, Jill .... 715-634-4790.. 517 C
jmatchett@lco.edu
MATEJCIK, Mark, M .... 216-916-7515.. 370 I
mmatejci@kent.edu
MATEJKOVIC, Edward, M 610-436-3555.. 416 C
ematejkovic@wcupa.edu
MATEN, Lionel .... 662-915-7328.. 261 B
lmaten@olemiss.edu
MATEO, Aurorisa .... 787-743-7979.. 536 A
amateo@suagm.edu
MATEO, Frances .... 623-845-3147.... 14 C
frances.mateo@gccaz.edu
MATEO, Robin .... 407-646-2258.. 107 O
rmateo@rollins.edu
MATERN, Cindy .... 253-879-3369.. 508 D
cmatern@pugetsound.edu
MATES, Ilene .... 610-436-2128.. 416 C
emates@wcupa.edu
MATHAY, Patti, J .... 412-624-7512.. 421 G
mathay@pitt.edu
MATHENA, Cindy .... 904-826-0084.... 72 A
cmathena@usa.edu
MATHENEY, H. Scott .... 630-617-3025.. 140 C
hscottm@elmhurst.edu
MATHENEY, James .... 520-494-5446.... 12 J
james.matheney@centralaz.edu
MATHENY, Christopher ... 920-735-2401.. 523 C
matheny@fvtc.edu
MATHENY, Jacqueline ..... 716-827-2450.. 338 E
mathenyj@trocaire.edu
MATHENY, Kevin .... 503-493-6521.. 391 A
kmatheny@cu-portland.edu
MATHENY, Samuel .... 901-448-5568.. 448 H
samuel.matheny@uthsc.edu
MATHENY, Stephen .... 828-395-1293.. 350 E
smatheny@isothermal.edu
MATHER, Bruce, J .... 630-617-3178.. 140 C
brucem@elmhurst.edu
MATHER, Kim .... 978-867-4246.. 219 A
kim.mather@gordon.edu
MATHER, Patrick .... 570-577-3711.. 398 L
patrick.mather@bucknell.edu
MATHER, Peter .... 740-593-1935.. 375 H
matherp@ohio.edu
MATHERLY, Cheryl .... 918-631-3225.. 389 E
cheryl-matherly@utulsa.edu
MATHERLY, Cheryl, A ..... 610-758-2981.. 408 H
cam716@lehigh.edu
MATHERN, Rebecca .... 541-737-4331.. 393 H
rebecca.mathern@oregonstate.edu
MATHES, Cassie .... 417-625-9365.. 268 H
mathes-c@mssu.edu
MATHES, Dennis .... 717-477-1463.. 416 A
dhm@ship.edu
MATHES, Jonathan .... 606-693-5000.. 191 A
jmathes@kmbc.edu
MATHES, Leon .... 504-865-3148.. 198 E
mathes@loyno.edu
MATHESON, Linda, K .... 920-923-7668.. 517 H
lkmatheson85@marianuniversity.edu
MATHESON, Regina, M ... 563-333-5838.. 176 D
mathesonreginam@sau.edu
MATHEW, Bruce, E .... 608-785-9214.. 524 H
mathewb@westerntc.edu
MATHEW, Roy .... 915-747-5117.. 476 D
rmathew@utep.edu
MATHEW, Thomson .... 918-495-7016.. 386 H
tmathew@oru.edu
MATHEW, Usha .... 281-283-2135.. 474 A
mathew@uhcl.edu
MATHEWS, Angela .... 507-786-3231.. 254 P
mathews@stolaf.edu
MATHEWS, Audrey .... 850-201-6048.. 113 E
mathewsa@tcc.fl.edu
MATHEWS, Brendan .... 413-644-4281.. 214 H
bmathews@simons-rock.edu
MATHEWS, Bruce .... 808-932-7036.. 131 E
bmathews@hawaii.edu
MATHEWS, Chris .... 405-585-4300.. 385 B
chris.mathews@okbu.edu
MATHEWS, Darren .... 970-247-7428.... 80 D
mathews_d@fortlewis.edu
MATHEWS, David .... 269-782-1270.. 241 C
president@swmich.edu
MATHEWS, Jennifer .... 508-565-1915.. 228 F
jmathews@stonehill.edu
MATHEWS, John .... 215-968-8211.. 399 A
john.mathews@bucks.edu
MATHEWS, Karen .... 937-376-6076.. 365 H
kmathews@centralstate.edu
MATHEWS, Lakeisha .... 410-837-4030.. 213 C
lmathews@ubalt.edu
MATHEWS, Les .... 865-974-0367.. 448 D
lmathews@tennessee.edu
MATHEWS, Marc .... 859-233-8100.. 193 D
mmathews@transy.edu
MATHEWS, Michael .... 303-333-4224.... 77 A
MATHEWS, Michael .... 918-495-6812.. 386 H
mmathews@oru.edu
MATHEWS, Nancy, E .... 802-656-4280.. 485 D
nancy.mathews@uvm.edu
MATHEWS, Rita .... 336-249-8186.. 349 C
rita_mathews@davidsonccc.edu
MATHEWS, Robert .... 920-498-5701.. 524 E
robert.mathews@nwtc.edu
MATHEWS, Ruth .... 507-457-1481.. 254 O
rmathews@smumn.edu
MATHEWS, Shelly .... 501-279-4396.... 20 D
skmathews@harding.edu
MATHEWSON, Alfred .... 505-277-5820.. 302 F
mathewson@law.unm.edu
MATHIAS, Suzi .... 715-675-3331.. 524 D
mathias@ntc.edu
MATHIASEN, Rebecca ...... 402-354-7034.. 281 F
rebecca.mathiasen@methodistcollege.edu
MATHIE, Craig .... 435-893-2216.. 482 E
craig.mathie@snow.edu
MATHIE, SJ, Edward .... 414-288-1881.. 517 I
edward.mathie@marquette.edu
MATHIESEN, Gaylan .... 218-739-3375.. 247 H
gmathiesen@lbs.edu
MATHIEU, Dickens .... 860-297-5110.... 89 B
dickens.mathieu@trincoll.edu
MATHIEU, Richard .... 704-337-2234.. 355 A
shifflerr@queens.edu
MATHIOS, Alan, D .... 607-255-2138.. 312 A
adm5@cornell.edu
MATHIS, Carolyn .... 626-529-8437.... 55 H
cmathis@pacificoaks.edu
MATHIS, Clay, P .... 361-593-5401.. 469 A
clay.mathis@tamuk.edu
MATHIS, Elizabeth .... 215-965-4017.. 411 A
emathis@moore.edu
MATHIS, Jennifer, M .... 864-388-8307.. 430 G
jmathis@lander.edu
MATHIS, Jon .... 310-506-7586.... 56 J
jon.mathis@pepperdine.edu
MATHIS, Larry .... 864-977-7160.. 431 G
larry.mathis@ngu.edu
MATHIS, Malissa .... 501-569-3110.... 23 B
mktrantham@ualr.edu
MATHIS, Martha .... 802-485-2640.. 484 H
martham@norwich.edu
MATHIS, Maureen .... 610-660-1306.. 418 G
mmathis@sju.edu
MATHIS, Sharese .... 517-264-7606.. 241 A
smathis@sienaheights.edu
MATHIS, Shawn .... 501-450-1333.... 20 F
mathis@hendrix.edu
MATHIS, Teri .... 229-391-5045.. 115 I
tmathis@abac.edu
MATHISON, Jane .... 440-775-8400.. 374 C
jane.mathison@oberlin.edu
MATHOV, Sara .... 503-251-5739.. 396 C
smathov@uws.edu
MATHUES, Sabrina .... 732-255-0400.. 293 E
smathues@ocean.edu
MATHUR, Ambika .... 313-577-2170.. 243 F
ambika.mathur@wayne.edu
MATHUR, Guarav .... 202-651-5520.... 92 C
gaurav.mathur@gallaudet.edu
MATHWEG, Cathy, M ...... 920-923-8138.. 517 H
cmathweg@marianuniversity.edu
MATIAS, Barbara .... 561-868-3132.. 106 D
matiasb@palmbeachstate.edu
MATIER, Michael .... 254-710-2414.. 452 H
michael_matier@baylor.edu
MATIJEVIC, Patricia .... 970-339-6374.... 76 H
patricia.matijevic@aims.edu
MATILDA, Mecca .... 831-476-9424.... 43 M
finaid@fivebranches.edu
MATIS, Michelle, D .... 407-582-3130.. 114 N
mmatis@valenciacollege.edu
MATISON, Kim .... 253-566-5194.. 508 B
kmatison@tacomacc.edu
MATISTA, Theresa .... 916-568-3058.... 50 J
matistt@losrios.edu
MATITIA, Abraham .... 440-943-5300.. 376 J
MATKIN, Gary, W .... 949-824-5525.... 69 C
gmatkin@uci.edu
MATKIN, H. Neil .... 972-758-3800.. 455 A
nmatkin@collin.edu
MATLAK, Richard, E .... 508-793-2497.. 217 C
rmatlak@holycross.edu
MATLIN, David .... 808-956-7301.. 131 F
athdir@hawaii.edu
MATLOCK, Bianca .... 214-860-3670.. 456 F
bmatlock@dcccd.edu
MATLOCK, Bianca .... 615-329-8585.. 439 L
bmatlock@fisk.edu
MATLOCK, Debra .... 312-996-7084.. 156 F
mdebra@uic.edu
MATLOCK, Lydia .... 913-266-8619.. 183 M
lydia.matlock@ottawa.edu
MATLOCK, Mark .... 814-732-1301.. 415 A
mmatlock@edinboro.edu
MATLOCK, Maryann .... 973-290-4606.. 290 G
mmatlock@cse.edu
MATNEY, Bob .... 419-289-5777.. 363 J
bmatney@ashland.edu
MATNEY, Robin .... 816-584-6832.. 270 D
robin.matney@park.edu
MATOLA, Erich .... 719-549-2566.... 79 B
erich.matola@csupueblo.edu
MATON, Marjane .... 623-845-3059.... 14 C
marjane.maton@gccaz.edu
MATONAK, Andrew, J ..... 518-629-4530.. 316 G
a.matonak@hvcc.edu
MATONAK, Jessica, M .... 724-287-8711.. 399 B
jessica.matonak@bc3.edu
MATOS, Awilda .... 787-834-9595.. 536 E
amatos@uaa.edu
MATOS, Carol .... 917-493-4450.. 319 M
cmatos@msmnyc.edu
MATOS, Dalimary .... 787-894-2828.. 539 A
dalimary.matos@upr.edu
MATOS, Elsa .... 787-890-2681.. 537 E
elsa.matos@upr.edu
MATOS, Emily .... 787-844-8181.. 538 E
emily.matos@upr.edu
MATOS, Ilia .... 239-939-4766.. 109 M
imatos@southerntech.edu
MATOS, Jose, A .... 787-751-0160.. 531 M
jamatos@cmpr.pr.gov
MATOS, Juan Carlos .... 718-817-0664.. 314 G
jmatos6@fordham.edu
MATOS, Lillian .... 787-780-0070.. 531 B
lmatos@caribbean.edu
MATOS, Lorena .... 718-405-3338.. 310 H
lorena.matos@mountsaintvincent.edu
MATOS, Lynda .... 661-824-2977.... 53 K
lmatos@ntps.edu
MATOS, Yanira .... 787-890-2681.. 537 E
yanira.matos@upr.edu
MATOS RODRIGUEZ,
Felix, V .... 718-997-5550.. 309 D
qcpres@qc.cuny.edu
MATOSO, Michael .... 209-667-3566.... 34 E
mmatoso@csustan.edu
MATSCHERZ, Scott .... 714-966-8500.... 73 G
info@ves.edu
MATSDORF, Gary .... 541-485-1780.. 393 A
garymatsdorf@newhope.edu
MATSEN, Maureen .... 757-594-7585.. 488 E
maureen.matsen@cnu.edu
MATSON, Christine, B ..... 671-735-0231.. 529 G
christine.matson@guamcc.edu
MATSON, Jerry .... 435-652-7938.. 482 A
matson@dixie.edu
MATSON, Pamela, A .... 650-723-2750.... 66 I
pamela.matson@stanford.edu
MATSON, Ronald, R .... 316-978-6659.. 185 J
ron.matson@wichita.edu
MATSON, Steven, W .... 919-962-3251.. 357 D
smatson@bio.unc.edu
MATSUBARA, Melissa ..... 808-544-0288.. 130 H
mmatsubara@hpu.edu
MATSUDA, Matthew, K .... 848-932-2300.. 296 B
matt.matsuda@rutgers.edu
MATSUDA, Seiichi .... 713-348-4002.. 464 E
matsuda@rice.edu
MATSUMOTO, Mark .... 209-228-4021.... 70 A
MATSUMOTO, Rae .... 707-638-5926.... 68 C
rae.matsumoto@tu.edu
MATSUO, Monica .... 626-396-2268.... 27 L
monica.matsuo@artcenter.edu
MATT, Kathleen, S .... 302-831-8370.... 91 F
ksmatt@udel.edu
MATTEI, Vivien .... 787-284-1912.. 534 C
vmattei@ponce.inter.edu
MATTER, Rebecca .... 256-824-1997...... 8 F
rebecca.matter@uah.edu
MATTER, Shawn .... 765-677-2869.. 164 B
shawn.matter@indwes.edu
MATTERN, Carolyn .... 303-914-6372.... 82 I
carolyn.mattern@rrcc.edu
MATTES, Bili, S .... 717-901-5134.. 405 H
bmattes@harrisburgu.edu
MATTES, Marty .... 253-680-7156.. 501 E
mmattes@bates.ctc.edu
MATTESON, Bill .... 401-874-4275.. 426 D
wmatteson@uri.edu
MATTESON, Christi, G ..... 904-264-2172.. 107 N
christi.matteson@iws.edu
MATTESON, Ryan .... 805-756-7676.... 31 I
rmatteso@calpoly.edu
MATTESON, Stephen, J .... 574-807-7490.. 159 D
steve.matteson@bethelcollege.edu
MATTESON, Susan, A ...... 574-807-7824.. 159 D
sue.matteson@bethelcollege.edu
MATTEY, Melissa .... 443-518-4208.. 208 C
mmattey@howardcc.edu
MATTHEIS, Lacey .... 417-447-6903.. 270 A
mattheil@otc.edu
MATTHES, Bruce .... 619-684-8871.... 54 C
bmatthes@newschoolarch.edu
MATTHES, Peter .... 319-335-3714.. 169 H
peter-matthes@uiowa.edu
MATTHEWS, Adrienne .... 256-726-7398...... 6 B
amatthews@oakwood.edu
MATTHEWS, Al .... 740-753-6590.. 369 K
matthewsa11702@hocking.edu
MATTHEWS, Ann .... 573-840-9669.. 273 A
amatthews@trcc.edu
MATTHEWS, Anne .... 541-888-7612.. 395 B
amatthews@socc.edu
MATTHEWS, Beverly .... 903-785-7661.. 463 E
bmatthews@parisjc.edu
MATTHEWS, Brad .... 845-451-1309.. 312 C
b_matthews@culinary.edu
MATTHEWS, Bryan, L ...... 410-778-7231.. 213 E
bmatthews2@washcoll.edu
MATTHEWS, Caleb .... 585-594-6832.. 325 B
matthews_caleb@roberts.edu
MATTHEWS, Carolyn, E .... 510-841-1905.... 26 C
cmatthews@absw.edu
MATTHEWS, Cissy .... 409-944-1203.. 458 D
amatthew@gc.edu
MATTHEWS, Daniel .... 405-273-5331.. 383 K
dmatthews@familyoffaithcollege.edu
MATTHEWS, Daniel, J ..... 405-273-5331.. 383 K
dmatthews@familyoffaithcollege.edu
MATTHEWS, Dennis, W .... 215-968-8301.. 399 A
matthews@bucks.edu
MATTHEWS, Donnajean ... 714-449-7438.... 51 F
djmatthews@ketchum.edu
MATTHEWS, Douglas, K .. 859-858-2206.. 186 I
MATTHEWS, Ellen .... 903-510-2380.. 473 C
emat@tjc.edu
MATTHEWS, Elyse .... 212-875-4666.. 304 E
ematthews@bankstreet.edu
MATTHEWS, Gary, C .... 858-534-6820.... 70 C
gcmatthews@ucsd.edu
MATTHEWS, Greg .... 802-485-2001.. 484 H
gmatthe2@norwich.edu
MATTHEWS, Harold, P .... 812-488-2051.. 167 I
hm3@evansville.edu
MATTHEWS, Hazel .... 502-413-8880.. 193 B
hmatthews@sullivan.edu
MATTHEWS, Hazel .... 502-413-8880.. 193 A
hmatthews@sullivan.edu
MATTHEWS, Hewitt .... 678-547-6306.. 124 D
matthews_h@mercer.edu
MATTHEWS, Janet .... 828-328-7254.. 345 H
janet.matthews@lr.edu
MATTHEWS, Jeanne .... 703-284-1580.. 492 A
jeanne.matthews@marymount.edu
MATTHEWS, Jennifer .... 202-274-5449.... 94 B
jennifer.matthews@udc.edu
MATTHEWS, John .... 201-761-7431.. 296 K
jmatthews@saintpeters.edu
MATTHEWS, John, D .... 864-242-5100.. 427 E
MATTHEWS, Keith .... 937-376-6425.. 365 H
MATTHEWS, Kenneth .... 386-506-3810.... 98 E
matthek@daytonastate.edu
MATTHEWS, Kismet .... 252-789-0223.. 351 A
kmatthews@martincc.edu
MATTHEWS, Leon .... 704-330-6524.. 348 E
leon.matthews@cpcc.edu
MATTHEWS, Mary .... 907-474-5655.... 10 G
mcmatthews@alaska.edu
MATTHEWS, Matt .... 352-854-2322.... 97 R
matthewm@cf.edu
MATTHEWS, Pamela, R ... 979-845-5141.. 468 B
p-matthews@tamu.edu
MATTHEWS, Robert .... 810-232-2511.. 238 F
robert.matthews@mcc.edu
MATTHEWS, Robin .... 252-447-3818.. 349 B
matthewsr@cravencc.edu
MATTHEWS, Ron .... 704-378-1023.. 345 E
rmatthews@jcsu.edu
MATTHEWS, Ross, D .... 504-864-7914.. 198 E
rdmatthews@loyno.edu
MATTHEWS, Samuel, W .. 405-273-5331.. 383 K
MATTHEWS, Sasha .... 757-481-5005.. 500 H
MATTHEWS, Stephen, P .. 518-564-3824.. 334 A
matthesp@plattsburgh.edu
MATTHEWS, Thomas .... 216-368-4446.. 365 B
careers@case.edu
MATTHEWS, Valencia, E .. 850-599-3430.. 110 J
valencia.matthews@famu.edu
MATTHEWS, Victor .... 417-836-5529.. 268 I
victormatthews@missouristate.edu
MATTHEWS, Wesley .... 208-885-3478.. 134 G
wmatthews@uidaho.edu

MAYER, Patrick .... 606-679-8501.. 190 E
pmayer0003@kctcs.edu

MAYER, Russell .... 978-837-3499.. 225 E
mayerr@merrimack.edu

MAYER, Russell, K .... 920-923-7604.. 517 H
rkmayer@marianuniversity.edu

MAYERS, Darryl .... 617-287-5458.. 220 G
darryl.mayers@umb.edu

MAYERS, Ronnie .... 662-846-4300.. 257 E
rmayers@deltastate.edu

MAYERSKI, Christopher .. 610-558-5615.. 411 E
mayerskc@neumann.edu

MAYES, David, M .... 501-882-4420.... 18 I
dmmayes@asub.edu

MAYES, John, A .... 203-432-3503.... 90 D
john.mayes@yale.edu

MAYES, Kathleen .... 215-596-8970.. 422 A
president@usciences.edu

MAYES, Lakeisha, E .... 757-823-8396.. 492 F
lemayes@nsu.edu

MAYES, Larry, D .... 336-334-9876.. 358 B
ldmayes@uncg.edu

MAYES, Lisa .... 757-683-6746.. 492 G
lmayes@odu.edu

MAYES, Richard, A .... 336-272-7102.. 344 G
mayesr@greensboro.edu

MAYES, JR., Robert, G ..... 251-981-3771...... 2 I
robert@columbiasouthern.edu

MAYEUX, Teresa .... 225-752-4233.. 195 E
registrar@iticollege.edu

MAYEWSKI, Raymond ...... 585-275-4786.. 338 K
raymond_mayewski@urmc.rochester.edu

MAYFIELD, Amanda, B .... 860-439-2088.... 87 F
amanda.mayfield@conncoll.edu

MAYFIELD, Charles .... 660-562-1138.. 269 J
mayfield@nwmissouri.edu

MAYFIELD, Darrell .... 808-932-7644.. 131 E
darrell8@hawaii.edu

MAYFIELD, Donny .... 423-746-5253.. 447 E
dmayfield@twcnet.edu

MAYFIELD, Mike, W .... 828-262-7660.. 356 B
mayfldmw@appstate.edu

MAYHER, Michael, E .... 440-525-7255.. 371 F
mmayher@lakelandcc.edu

MAYHEW, Glen, R .... 540-985-8539.. 491 A
grmayhew@jchs.edu

MAYHEW, Kelly .... 619-388-3136.... 60 F
kmayhew@sdccd.edu

MAYHEW, Sally, A .... 618-537-6838.. 147 F
samayhew@mckendree.edu

MAYHEW, Sam .... 229-243-3025.. 117 E
sam.mayhew@bainbridge.edu

MAYHEW, Steven .... 620-231-7000.. 184 C
smayhew@pittstate.edu

MAYHEW, Susan, L .... 276-498-5201.. 486 M
slmayhew@acp.edu

MAYHORNE, John, F ...... 443-412-2382.. 208 A
jmayhorne@harford.edu

MAYLAND, Jason .... 215-968-8414.. 399 A
jason.mayland@bucks.edu

MAYLE, Teresa .... 252-536-7207.. 350 C
tmayle426@halifaxcc.edu

MAYNARD, Francyenne .... 972-273-3109.. 456 G
fmaynard@dcccd.edu

MAYNARD, Gene .... 916-348-4689.... 43 A
gmaynard@epic.edu

MAYNARD, Jennifer .... 937-769-1826.. 363 F
jmaynard@antioch.edu

MAYNARD, Kimberly, L .. 304-896-7345.. 512 E
kimberly.maynard@southernwv.edu

MAYNARD, Mae .... 513-562-6273.. 363 H
mmaynard@artacademy.edu

MAYNARD, Nelly .... 773-821-2453.. 136 M
nmaynard@csu.edu

MAYNARD, Pamela .... 973-877-3115.. 291 H
maynard@essex.edu

MAYNARD, Rebecca, A ... 207-768-2715.. 203 L
bmaynard@nmcc.edu

MAYNARD, Scott .... 662-325-3344.. 259 D
smaynard@career.msstate.edu

MAYNARD, Thurmond ..... 301-696-3546.. 208 B
maynard@hood.edu

MAYNARD NELSON,
Jeanette .... 612-767-7043.. 244 D
jeanette@alfredadler.edu

MAYNARD-REID, Pedrito 509-527-2028.. 508 G
pedrito.maynard-reid@wallawalla.edu

MAYNE, Deborah .... 651-779-4086.. 249 A
deborah.mayne@century.edu

MAYO, Amanda .... 712-279-5405.. 170 B
amanda.mayo@briarcliff.edu

MAYO, Cindy .... 870-743-3000.... 21 C
cmayo@northark.edu

MAYO, Dan .... 252-493-7304.. 352 A
dmayo@email.pittcc.edu

MAYO, Donna .... 706-864-1620.. 128 F
donna.mayo@ung.edu

MAYO, Jamaal .... 314-340-3534.. 265 H
mayoj@hssu.edu

MAYO, Jennifer .... 919-739-6721.. 354 A
jbmayo@waynecc.edu

MAYO, Karen .... 859-246-6525.. 189 B
karen.mayo@kctcs.edu

MAYO, Luis .... 787-257-7373.. 535 P
lmayo2@suagm.edu

MAYO, Michael .... 502-205-8826.... 19 J
mmayo@cbc.edu

MAYO, Michele .... 252-940-6233.. 347 E
michele.mayo@beaufortccc.edu

MAYO, Michelle, P .... 585-292-2370.. 321 J
mmayo@monroecc.edu

MAYO, Sandra .... 951-571-6160.... 58 J
sandra.mayo@mvc.edu

MAYO, Stephen, L .... 626-395-4951.... 30 H
steve@mayo.caltech.edu

MAYO, Tom .... 239-590-1520.. 110 L
tmayo@fgcu.edu

MAYO, William, E .... 337-421-6961.. 197 B
william.mayo@sowela.edu

MAYRAND, Leslie .... 325-486-6247.. 472 B
leslie.mayrand@angelo.edu

MAYRL, Matt .... 608-262-1165.. 519 K
matthew.maryl@wisc.edu

MAYROSE, James .... 716-878-4698.. 332 F
mayrosj@buffalostate.edu

MAYS, Allen .... 660-562-1307.. 269 J
ajmays@nwmissouri.edu

MAYS, Beth, A .... 410-777-2480.. 206 B
bamays@aacc.edu

MAYS, Cathy .... 434-381-6448.. 494 M
cdmays@sbc.edu

MAYS, Don .... 401-254-3764.. 426 B
dmays@rwu.edu

MAYS, Josh .... 619-594-7851.... 35 A
jmays@mail.sdsu.edu

MAYS, Justin .... 678-466-5544.. 119 A
justinmays@clayton.edu

MAYS, Marilyn .... 972-273-3501.. 456 G
mmays@dcccd.edu

MAYS, Nathaniel .... 617-349-8539.. 220 B
nmays@lesley.edu

MAYS, Shirley, L .... 602-682-6814.... 11 I
smays@azsummitlaw.edu

MAYS, Susan .... 615-550-3161.. 449 I
susan@williamsoncc.edu

MAYS, Theresa .... 205-856-7709...... 5 B
tmays@jeffersonstate.edu

MAYS, Vida .... 662-252-8000.. 260 F
vmays@rustcollege.edu

MAYS-JACKSON, Debra ... 601-885-7002.. 258 A
debra.mays-jackson@hindscc.edu

MAYSAMI, Raymin .... 601-979-2411.. 258 D
raymin.maysami@jsums.edu

MAYSE, Laura .... 302-736-2317.... 91 G
laura.mayse@wesley.edu

MAYSE, Tiffany .... 859-572-5806.. 192 B
masyset@nku.edu

MAYSILLES, Michael, E .... 973-596-5642.. 293 D
michael.maysilles@njit.edu

MAYTON, Dana, B .... 502-852-4876.. 194 A
dbmayt01@louisville.edu

MAZA, Jenice .... 786-331-1000.. 105 G
jmaza@maufl.edu

MAZA-DUERTO, Aristides 786-331-1000.. 105 G
amaza@maufl.edu

MAZACHEK, Juliann .... 785-670-4483.. 185 H
jmazachek@wufoundation.org

MAZACHEK, JuliAnn .... 785-670-1648.. 185 H
juli.mazachek@washburn.edu

MAZARIEGOS, John .... 847-947-5086.. 149 B
jmazariegos@nl.edu

MAZE, Mary, C .... 248-341-2051.. 239 E
mcmaze@oaklandcc.edu

MAZE, Tom .... 252-399-6533.. 341 P
tmaze@barton.edu

MAZER, Vickie .... 301-687-4595.. 212 F
vmmazer@frostburg.edu

MAZEY, Mary Ellen .... 419-372-2211.. 364 E
mmazey@bgsu.edu

MAZGULSKI, Judy .... 860-343-5868.... 86 F
jmazgulski@mxcc.commnet.edu

MAZIAR, Christine, M ...... 574-631-2749.. 168 B
maziar.1@nd.edu

MAZIAR, Lucia .... 860-444-8517.. 529 A
lucia.maziar@uscga.edu

MAZICH, OSB,
Edward, M .... 724-805-2592.. 419 B
edward.mazich@stvincent.edu

MAZLOFF, Nina .... 508-373-9770.. 215 D
nina.mazloff@becker.edu

MAZUK, Melody .... 609-497-7935.. 294 C
melody.mazuk@ptsem.edu

MAZUR, III, Francis, J ...... 352-873-5822.... 97 R
mazurf@cf.edu

MAZZA, Diane .... 203-392-5405.... 85 H
boutaughd1@southernct.edu

MAZZA, James, A .... 607-255-1989.. 312 A
jam16@cornell.edu

MAZZA, Jennifer .... 845-398-4034.. 329 G
jmazza@stac.edu

MAZZA, Joseph .... 760-757-2121.... 52 K
jmazza@miracosta.edu

MAZZA, Maralyn .... 814-234-7755.. 419 F

MAZZA, III, S. Paul .... 814-234-7755.. 419 F
pmazza@southhills.edu

MAZZA, Stephen, W .... 785-864-4550.. 185 D
smazza@ku.edu

MAZZARELLLI, Judi .... 419-995-8479.. 370 G
mazzarelli.j@rhodesstate.edu

MAZZEO, Erica .... 207-453-5117.. 203 K
emazzeo@kvcc.me.edu

MAZZEO, Michael, A .... 248-370-2957.. 239 K
mazzeo@oakland.edu

MAZZIOTTA, John .... 310-825-5687.... 69 D
jmazziotta@mednet.ucla.edu

MAZZOCCO, Lisa .... 213-740-6426.... 72 D
lisa.mazzocco@usc.edu

MAZZOLA, Frank .... 603-358-2242.. 288 E
fmazzola@keene.edu

MAZZOLA, Gregg .... 603-645-9635.. 287 I
g.mazzola@snhu.edu

MAZZUCA, Mary .... 717-358-5800.. 403 J
mary.mazzuca@fandm.edu

MAZZUCCA, Craig, M .... 704-334-6882.. 343 D
cmazzucca@charlottechristian.edu

MBAERI, Osmond .... 610-527-0200.. 418 D
osmond.mbaeri@rosemont.edu

MBOMEH, Gabriel, A .... 240-895-4305.. 210 E
gambomeh@smcm.edu

MBUWAYESANGO,
Dora, R .... 704-636-6077.. 345 B
dmbuwayesango@hoodseminary.edu

MBYIRUKIRA, James .... 256-726-7157...... 6 B
mbyirukira@oakwood.edu

MC CAIG, Robert .... 732-571-3413.. 292 F
rmccaig@monmouth.edu

MC COLLOUGH, Scott ...... 608-785-8711.. 520 C
smcclough@uwlax.edu

MC DONALD, Molly .... 408-554-6993.... 63 E
mmcdonald@scu.edu

MC ELROY, Chris .... 661-824-2977.... 53 K
cmcelroy@ntps.edu

MC GOVERN, Michael ...... 516-323-3030.. 321 H
mamcgovern@molloy.edu

MCABEE, Sarah .... 256-233-8102...... 1 F
sarah.mcabee@athens.edu

MCADAMS, Angie .... 434-791-5629.. 487 C
amcadams@averett.edu

MCADAMS, Beverly, R ..... 864-231-2100.. 427 B
bmcadams@andersonuniversity.edu

MCADAMS, Charles .... 662-846-4010.. 257 E
cmcadams@deltastate.edu

MCAFEE, Christy .... 714-620-3700.... 27 I

MCAFEE, Kurt .... 620-672-5641.. 184 D
kurtm@prattcc.edu

MCAFEE, Ouida .... 229-430-4767.. 115 K
ouida.mcafee@asurams.edu

MCAFEE, Stacy .... 209-946-2223.... 71 C
smcafee@pacific.edu

MCAFEE, Stacy .... 209-946-2311.... 71 C
smcafee@pacific.edu

MCALARY, Chris .... 310-954-4030.... 53 B
cmcalary@msmu.edu

MCALEER, Brenda .... 207-621-3425.. 204 I
mcaleer@maine.edu

MCALEER, Jessica .... 631-687-2667.. 328 G
jmcaleer@sjcny.edu

MCALEXANDER, Dan .... 706-880-8230.. 123 K
dmcalexander@lagrange.edu

MCALINEY, Peter .... 973-655-6824.. 293 A
mcalineyp@mail.montclair.edu

MCALISTER, George .... 208-769-3393.. 134 C
glmcalister@nic.edu

MCALISTER, Jean .... 609-343-4901.. 288 H
mcaliste@atlantic.edu

MCALISTER, Meree .... 803-778-6646.. 427 G
mcalistermm@cctech.edu

MCALISTER, Richie .... 601-484-8779.. 258 F
rmcalist@mcc.cc.ms.us

MCALLESTER, David .... 773-702-5562.. 155 K
mcallester@ttic.edu

MCALLISTER, Annemarie . 914-964-4282.. 310 D
amcallister@riversidehealth.org

MCALLISTER, Carol .... 760-750-4802.... 34 D
cmcallis@csusm.edu

MCALLISTER, Charles ...... 573-651-2062.. 272 B
cdmcallister@semo.edu

MCALLISTER, Charles ...... 573-651-2192.. 272 B
cdmcallister@semo.edu

MCALLISTER, Gary .... 501-205-8827.... 19 J
gmcallister@cbc.edu

MCALLISTER, Jean .... 303-871-7481.... 84 B
jean.mcallister@du.edu

MCALLISTER, Latrelle, P .. 704-378-1230.. 345 E
lmcallister@jcsu.edu

MCALLISTER, Mary, C ...... 607-871-2101.. 303 F
mcallister@alfred.edu

MCALLISTER, Michael ...... 704-272-5441.. 353 B
mmcallister@spcc.edu

MCALLISTER, Steven, G ... 540-458-8740.. 500 F
smcallister@wlu.edu

MCALLISTER-WILSON,
David .... 202-885-8601.... 94 E
president@wesleyseminary.edu

MCALMOND, Barb .... 406-447-6907.. 277 B
barb.mcalmond@umhelena.edu

MCALMONT, Shaun .... 801-302-2800.. 480 L
shaun.mcalmont@neumont.edu

MCALONAN, Jenny .... 313-993-3343.. 241 G
mcalonjl@udmercy.edu

MCALOOSE, Carl .... 239-489-9294.. 101 F
cmcaloose@fsw.edu

MCALPIN, Michael .... 925-631-4222.... 59 I
mdm5@stmarys-ca.edu

MCALPINE, Lynn .... 402-554-3514.. 283 B
lmcalpine@unomaha.edu

MCANALLY, David .... 903-675-6232.. 473 B
dmcanally@tvcc.edu

MCANALLY, Kent .... 785-670-1938.. 185 H
kent.mcanally@washburn.edu

MCANDREW, John .... 570-208-5958.. 406 J
johnmcandrew@kings.edu

MCANDREW, Kathleen ..... 217-353-2024.. 151 B
kmcandrew@parkland.edu

MCANDREW, Laura .... 202-885-6294.... 91 J
mcandrew@american.edu

MCANELLEY, Becky, J ..... 409-882-3318.. 471 B
becky.mcanelley@lsco.edu

MCANINCH, Amanda .... 502-456-6771.. 193 B
amcaninch@sullivan.edu

MCANIRLIN, Heather, A .. 207-509-7218.. 204 F
hmcanirlin@unity.edu

MCANNALLY, Linda, J ..... 864-833-8287.. 432 B
lmcannally@presby.edu

MCANUFF, Courtney .... 848-445-6601.. 295 F
courtney.mcanuff@rutgers.edu

MCANUFF, Courtney, O .... 848-445-6601.. 296 B
courtney.mcanuff@rutgers.edu

MCARDELL, James .... 218-855-8136.. 248 N
jmcardell@clcmn.edu

MCARDLE, Eliza .... 413-549-4600.. 219 C

MCARDLE, Karen .... 248-204-2000.. 237 B
kmcardle@ltu.edu

MCARDLE, Kate .... 818-401-1034.... 40 G
kmcardle@columbiacollege.edu

MCAREAVEY, Julie .... 605-331-6644.. 438 A
julie.mcareavey@usiouxfalls.edu

MCARTHUR, Bridgette ...... 863-616-6411.. 101 E
bmcarthur@flsouthern.edu

MCARTHUR, Deb .... 218-935-0417.. 256 E
dmcarthur@wetcc.edu

MCARTHUR, Douglas .... 517-607-2462.. 235 E
dmcarthur@hillsdale.edu

MCARTHUR, Jennifer .... 307-674-6446.. 526 M
jmcarthur@sheridan.edu

MCARTHUR, John, M .... 580-581-2201.. 382 G
jmcarthur@cameron.edu

MCARTHUR, Marcus .... 760-480-8474.... 74 L
mmcarthur@wscal.edu

MCARTHUR, Neil .... 478-757-3548.. 118 G
nmcarthur@centralgatech.edu

MCARTHUR, Phillip .... 808-675-3907.. 130 E
phillip.mcarthur@byuh.edu

MCARTHUR, Rachel, A ..... 859-371-9393.. 186 M
rmcarthur@beckfield.edu

MCASEY, Veronica .... 402-872-2218.. 281 I
vmcasey@peru.edu

MCATEE, Brooke .... 660-359-3948.. 269 I
bmcatee@mail.ncmissouri.edu

MCATEE, Christopher .... 847-566-6401.. 157 G
cmcatee@usml.edu

MCATEE, Jim .... 765-285-2420.. 159 B
jfmcatee@bsu.edu

MCAULEY, Patricia .... 541-552-6163.. 395 A
mcauleyp@sou.edu

MCAULIFF, Kimberly, B ... 315-445-4553.. 318 E
mcaulikb@lemoyne.edu

MCAULIFFE, Lynne .... 307-855-2206.. 526 E
lynne@cwc.edu

MCAULIFFE, Margaret ...... 718-997-5787.. 309 D
margaret.mcauliffe@qc.cuny.edu

MCAULIFFE, Richard, J .... 402-280-2104.. 279 H
rmcaulif@creighton.edu

MCAVOY, Eugene .... 425-388-9031.. 503 F

MCAVOY, John .... 304-876-5374.. 513 E
jmcavoy@shepherd.edu

MCAVOY, William, J .... 508-831-5337.. 230 C
wjmcavoy@wpi.edu

MCBEATH, Trish .... 918-465-1804.. 383 I
tmcbeath@eosc.edu

MCBEE, Barry .... 512-322-3715.. 475 K
bmcbee@utsystem.edu

MCBEE, Lori, A .... 479-979-1413.... 24 I
lamcbee@ozarks.edu

MCBEE, Misty .... 573-288-6507.. 264 F
mmcbee@culver.edu

MCBEE, Ronald .... 575-492-2116.. 302 M
rmcbee@usw.edu

MCBEE, Russ .... 620-227-9313.. 180 E
rmcbee@dc3.edu

MCBEE, Whitney .... 903-693-2067.. 463 D
wmcbee@panola.edu

MCBETH, Valerie .... 360-676-2772.. 505 C
vmcbeth@nwic.edu
MCBIRTH, Matthew .... 417-626-1234.. 269 K
mcbirth.matthew@occ.edu
MCBRAYER, Mike .... 903-463-8753.. 458 H
mmcbrayer@grayson.edu
MCBREEN, William .... 507-457-5122.. 252 G
wmcbreen@winona.edu
MCBRIDE, Ameerah .... 920-424-0330.. 520 E
mcbridea@uwosh.edu
MCBRIDE, Andrew, S ...... 804-289-8964.. 495 G
amcbride@richmond.edu
MCBRIDE, Becky .... 985-448-7924.. 196 E
becky.mcbride@fletcher.edu
MCBRIDE, Catherine .... 562-947-8755.... 66 A
catherinemcbride@scuhs.edu
MCBRIDE, Christy .... 618-985-3741.. 143 F
christymcbride@jalc.edu
MCBRIDE, Corinn .... 973-408-3560.. 291 B
cmcbride1@drew.edu
MCBRIDE, David .... 301-314-8117.. 211 E
dmcbrid2@umd.edu
MCBRIDE, David .... 731-661-5450.. 448 A
dmcbride@uu.edu
MCBRIDE, Dwight, A .... 847-491-8502.. 150 F
dwight-mcbride@northwestern.edu
MCBRIDE, Faith .... 218-322-2360.. 249 G
faith.mcbride@itascacc.edu
MCBRIDE, Jeanette .... 910-576-6222.. 351 E
mcbridej@montgomery.edu
MCBRIDE, Jennifer .... 910-362-7696.. 348 A
jmcbride@cfcc.edu
MCBRIDE, John, E .... 512-245-2557.. 471 F
jm05@txstate.edu
MCBRIDE, Joseph .... 267-341-3642.. 405 J
jmcbride@holyfamily.edu
MCBRIDE, Kristi, L .... 678-407-5874.. 121 B
kmcbride@ggc.edu
MCBRIDE, Lisa, M .... 215-871-6178.. 416 F
lisamcb@pcom.edu
MCBRIDE, Maria .... 504-865-2696.. 198 E
mmcbride@loyno.edu
MCBRIDE, Mark, F .... 585-292-2321.. 321 J
mmcbride17@monroecc.edu
MCBRIDE, Michael .... 276-739-2402.. 499 A
mmcbride@vhcc.edu
MCBRIDE, Nataly .... 949-794-9090.... 66 H
nmcbride@stanbridge.edu
MCBRIDE, Noel .... 206-934-3869.. 506 K
noel.mcbride@seattlecolleges.edu
MCBRIDE, Okang .... 201-692-7004.. 291 J
okang_mcbride@fdu.edu
MCBRIDE, Phil .... 928-428-8404.... 13 B
phil.mcbride@eac.edu
MCBRIDE, Regina .... 618-650-2712.. 155 A
rmcbrid@siue.edu
MCBRIDE, Robert .... 201-200-3057.. 293 C
rmcbride@njcu.edu
MCBRIDE, Robert, J .... 610-660-1351.. 418 G
rmcbride@sju.edu
MCBRIDE, Ron .... 910-221-2224.. 344 F
rmcbride@gcd.edu
MCBRIDE, Scott .... 606-783-2650.. 191 H
s.mcbride@moreheadstate.edu
MCBRIDE GATES, Jane .... 203-837-8400.... 85 I
gatesj@wcsu.edu
MCBRINE, Paul .... 617-236-8882.. 218 G
pmcbrine@fisher.edu
MCBROOM, Michael .... 806-651-4400.. 469 D
mmcbroom@mail.wtamu.edu
MCBRYDE, Tennie, S .... 334-420-4306........ 7 G
tmcbryde@trenholmstate.edu
MCBURNEY, Melissa .... 509-542-4832.. 502 G
mmcburney@columbiabasin.edu
MCCABE, Cynthia .... 814-262-6477.. 413 P
cmccabe@pennhighlands.edu
MCCABE, Daniel .... 516-877-4231.. 303 B
dmccabe@adelphi.edu
MCCABE, Eileen .... 718-405-3240.. 310 H
eileen.mccabe@mountsaintvincent.edu
MCCABE, John .... 315-464-4223.. 332 C
mccabej@upstate.edu
MCCABE, Kenneth, F ...... 401-825-2111.. 425 A
kfmccabe@ccri.edu
MCCABE, Kevin .... 505-277-2241.. 302 F
kmccab02@unm.edu
MCCABE, Philip, J .... 203-371-7934.... 88 I
mccabep@sacredheart.edu
MCCABE SMITH, Linda ...... 919-515-2191.. 357 B
MCCADDEN, Brian, M ...... 401-865-2503.. 425 D
bmccadde@providence.edu
MCCADDEN, Kevin .... 610-436-2223.. 416 C
kmccadden@wcupa.edu
MCCAFFERTY, Bridgit ...... 254-519-5484.. 468 C
bmccaffe@tamuct.edu
MCCAFFERTY, Coreen ...... 610-921-7274.. 396 H
cmccafferty@albright.edu
MCCAFFERTY, Frank .... 904-743-1122.. 103 G
fmccaffe@jones.edu
MCCAFFERTY, Patricia ...... 978-934-3238.. 221 A
patricia_mccafferty@uml.edu
MCCAFFREY, Dena .... 636-481-3400.. 266 C
dmccaffr@jeffco.edu
MCCAFFREY, Mary .... 610-558-5537.. 411 E
mccaffrm@neumann.edu
MCCAFFREY, Michael, H . 260-399-7700.. 168 D
mmccaffrey@sf.edu
MCCAGHREN, Chris .... 251-442-2218...... 9 A
cmccaghren@umobile.edu
MCCAIN, Gail, C .... 212-772-4000.. 308 D
gmccain@hunter.cuny.edu
MCCAIN, Lindy .... 662-472-9067.. 258 B
lmccain@holmescc.edu
MCCALEB, Cathy .... 972-721-5203.. 473 D
mccaleb@udallas.edu
MCCALEB, Colin .... 269-965-3931.. 236 A
mccalebc@kellogg.edu
MCCALEB, Gary, D .... 325-674-2156.. 449 J
mccalebg@acu.edu
MCCALEB, George .... 956-872-8396.. 465 H
gmccaleb@southtexascollege.edu
MCCALL, Amy Elizabeth ... 412-391-4100.. 417 F
amccall@pointpark.edu
MCCALL, Andy, K .... 865-981-8113.. 441 H
andy.mccall@maryvillecollege.edu
MCCALL, Ann .... 504-520-7470.. 202 C
amccall@xula.edu
MCCALL, Becky .... 530-242-7719.... 64 D
bmccall@shastacollege.edu
MCCALL, Brian .... 512-463-3280.. 470 G
brian.mccall@tsus.edu
MCCALL, Chris .... 713-221-8030.. 474 B
mccallc@uhd.edu
MCCALL, Devin .... 701-858-3993.. 360 F
devin.mccall@minotstateu.edu
MCCALL, Gloria .... 859-256-3100.. 188 M
gloria.mccall@kctcs.edu
MCCALL, John .... 334-670-3215...... 7 H
jmccall106692@troy.edu
MCCALL, John .... 205-652-3414...... 9 F
jmccall@uwa.edu
MCCALL, Kris .... 602-943-2311.... 18 C
kris.mccall@west.edu
MCCALL, Michele .... 660-263-4100.. 269 D
michelem@macc.edu
MCCALL, Mike .... 303-871-2562.... 84 B
mike.mccall@du.edu
MCCALL, Ryan .... 740-386-4199.. 372 B
mccallr@mtc.edu
MCCALL, Sam .... 850-644-6031.. 111 C
smmccall@fsu.edu
MCCALL, Sara .... 704-406-2118.. 344 E
smccall@gardner-webb.edu
MCCALLA, Connie, L ...... 610-359-5301.. 401 L
cmccalla@dccc.edu
MCCALLA, Justin .... 706-355-5008.. 116 H
jmccalla@athenstech.edu
MCCALLA, Kelly .... 507-433-0627.. 251 H
kelly.mccalla@riverland.edu
MCCALLA, Ray .... 870-307-7474.... 21 A
ray.mccalla@lyon.edu
MCCALLEY, Greg .... 651-779-3288.. 249 A
greg.mccalley@century.edu
MCCALLIE, Kathleen, D ... 918-270-6441.. 386 I
kathy.mccallie@ptstulsa.edu
MCCALLIN, Julia, M .... 626-395-3230.... 30 H
julia.mccallin@caltech.edu
MCCALLISTER, Ashley ...... 704-461-6717.. 342 A
ashleymccallister@bac.edu
MCCALLISTER, Emilie ...... 815-280-1321.. 144 A
emccalli@jjc.edu
MCCALLON, Melanie, C .. 270-809-4152.. 192 A
mmccallon@murraystate.edu
MCCALLUM, Arminda ...... 816-604-2631.. 267 I
mindy.mccallum@mcckc.edu
MCCALLUM, SJ,
David, C .... 315-445-6110.. 318 E
mccaldac@lemoyne.edu
MCCALLUM, Jeannie ...... 864-388-8053.. 430 G
jmccallum@lander.edu
MCCALLUM, Rex M .... 409-772-3639.. 478 A
remccall@utmb.edu
MCCALLUM, Richard ...... 229-732-5929.. 116 C
richardmccallum@andrewcollege.edu
MCCALLUM-BEATTY,
Krista .... 740-593-4330.. 375 H
mccallum@ohio.edu
MCCAMBRIDGE, Greg ...... 704-687-7683.. 358 A
gmccambr@uncc.edu
MCCAMPBELL,
Martha (Marty) .... 574-520-4524.. 163 E
mmccampb@iusb.edu
MCCANCE, John .... 575-492-2141.. 302 M
jmccance@usw.edu
MCCANDLESS, Amy, T ...... 843-953-1436.. 428 G
mccandlessa@cofc.edu
MCCANDLESS, Ann .... 724-287-8711.. 399 B
ann.mccandless@bc3.edu
MCCANDLESS, Beverly .... 270-686-4255.. 187 C
beverly.mccandless@brescia.edu
MCCANDLESS, John .... 513-529-2223.. 372 K
mccandjm@miamioh.edu
MCCANDLESS, Michael .... 209-384-6107.... 52 E
mccandless.m@mccd.edu
MCCANDLESS, N. Jane .... 678-839-5170.. 129 E
jmccandl@westga.edu
MCCANDLESS, Raymond . 419-434-4565.. 379 E
mccandless@findlay.edu
MCCANE, Latitia .... 251-405-7012...... 2 D
lmccane@bishop.edu
MCCANN, Bonnie .... 614-947-6017.. 369 A
bonnie.mccann@franklin.edu
MCCANN, Carrie .... 254-968-9007.. 467 F
cmccann@tarleton.edu
MCCANN, Elizabeth .... 562-938-4139.... 49 D
emccann@lbcc.edu
MCCANN, Erin .... 607-733-7177.. 313 D
emccann@ebi-college.com
MCCANN, Kevin .... 802-860-2754.. 483 F
kmccann@champlain.edu
MCCANN, Linda .... 215-968-8003.. 399 A
mccannl@bucks.edu
MCCANN, Paul, A .... 217-581-2921.. 139 H
pmccann@eiu.edu
MCCANN, Ralph, J .... 770-484-1204.. 124 C
lutherrice@lutherrice.edu
MCCANN, Shawn .... 713-221-2715.. 474 B
mccanns@uhd.edu
MCCANN, JR., Terence ... 410-337-6170.. 207 H
terence.mccann@goucher.edu
MCCANNON, Mindy .... 706-295-6846.. 121 F
mmccannon@gntc.edu
MCCARDELL JR.,
John, M .... 931-598-1101.. 443 O
jmmccard@sewanee.edu
MCCAREL, Lori .... 757-233-8786.. 500 E
lmccarel@vwc.edu
MCCAREY, Christine .... 508-362-2131.. 223 C
MCCARGO, Donovan .... 215-751-8876.. 401 G
dmccargo@ccp.edu
MCCARN, Sarah .... 912-525-5000.. 126 E
smccarn@scad.edu
MCCARRELL, Kyle .... 540-453-2269.. 496 F
mccarrellk@brcc.edu
MCCARRICK, Richard, G .. 914-594-4503.. 323 I
richard_mccarrick@nymc.edu
MCCARROLL, John, F ...... 515-294-6137.. 169 G
jmccarol@iastate.edu
MCCARRON, Anne .... 414-382-6068.. 515 D
anne.mccarron@alverno.edu
MCCARRON, Tom .... 619-594-5631.... 35 A
tmccarron@mail.sdsu.edu
MCCARRY, Tim .... 325-670-1434.. 458 J
facilities@hsutx.edu
MCCART, Robert .... 517-318-3330.. 232 C
MCCARTER, Debbie L ..... 423-585-6844.. 447 D
debbie.mccarter@ws.edu
MCCARTER, Safiya .... 425-602-3073.. 501 D
smcarter@bastyr.edu
MCCARTHEY, Piper .... 775-445-3270.. 285 B
piper.mccarthy@wnc.edu
MCCARTHY, Anne .... 651-523-2335.. 247 A
amccarthy02@hamline.edu
MCCARTHY, Anne, E .... 970-382-7463.... 80 D
MCCARTHY, Barbara .... 508-588-9100.. 223 G
MCCARTHY, Barbara .... 914-773-3741.. 325 J
bmccarthy@pace.edu
MCCARTHY, Casey, J ...... 218-755-3888.. 248 M
cmccarthy@bemidjistate.edu
MCCARTHY, Colby .... 973-408-3112.. 291 B
finaid@drew.edu
MCCARTHY, Daniel .... 985-549-2055.. 201 C
dmccarthy@selu.edu
MCCARTHY, David .... 301-447-5333.. 209 G
dmccarth@msmary.edu
MCCARTHY, Dominica ..... 972-860-4689.. 456 B
dmccarthy@dcccd.edu
MCCARTHY, Donna .... 414-288-3820.. 517 I
donnalee.mccarthy@marquette.edu
MCCARTHY, Douglas .... 602-285-7245.... 14 F
douglas.mccarthy@phoenixcollege.edu
MCCARTHY, Eileen .... 847-467-3622.. 150 F
eileen.mccarthy@northwestern.edu
MCCARTHY, Elizabeth, K . 508-678-2811.. 223 A
elizabeth.mccarthy@bristolcc.edu
MCCARTHY, Faith .... 530-221-4275.... 64 C
registrar@shasta.edu
MCCARTHY, Faith .... 530-221-4275.... 64 C
shastaonline@clearwire.net
MCCARTHY, Jack, H .... 617-373-2240.. 227 B
MCCARTHY, James .... 610-861-5506.. 411 G
jmccarthy@northampton.edu
MCCARTHY, Jeffrey, M .... 607-255-7120.. 312 A
jmm11@cornell.edu
MCCARTHY, John, C .... 202-319-5259.... 92 A
mccartjc@cua.edu
MCCARTHY, John, J .... 413-545-5271.. 220 F
jmccarthy@grad.umass.edu
MCCARTHY, Kate .... 802-635-1265.. 486 B
kathleen.mccarthy@jsc.edu
MCCARTHY, Katherine ..... 304-766-3039.. 514 B
kmccarthy@wvstateu.edu
MCCARTHY, Kelly .... 708-235-3966.. 140 H
kmccarthy@govst.edu
MCCARTHY, Kevin .... 315-568-3267.. 323 A
kmccarthy@nycc.edu
MCCARTHY, Kevin .... 518-255-5217.. 334 D
mccartk@cobleskill.edu
MCCARTHY, Kevin .... 704-330-6907.. 348 E
kevin.mccarthy@cpcc.edu
MCCARTHY, Kevin, D ...... 425-235-2235.. 506 F
kmccarthy@rtc.edu
MCCARTHY, Kristie .... 407-265-8383.... 97 B
MCCARTHY, Margaret ...... 716-888-2120.. 306 F
mmccarth@canisius.edu
MCCARTHY, Mark, D .... 216-397-4213.. 370 H
mmccarthy@jcu.edu
MCCARTHY, Marsha .... 908-737-7100.. 292 C
mmccarth@kean.edu
MCCARTHY, Mary .... 607-778-5210.. 332 D
mccarthyma@sunybroome.edu
MCCARTHY, Melissa .... 401-874-2599.. 426 D
mcmel@uri.edu
MCCARTHY, Michael .... 978-556-3924.. 224 D
mmccarthy@necc.mass.edu
MCCARTHY, SJ,
Michael, C .... 718-817-3013.. 314 G
mmccarthysj@fordham.edu
MCCARTHY, Michael, R ... 402-932-8600.. 279 H
mmccarthy@mccarthycapital.com
MCCARTHY, Pamela .... 413-585-2840.. 228 D
pmccarth@smith.edu
MCCARTHY, Patrice .... 216-373-5182.. 374 B
mpmccarthy@ndc.edu
MCCARTHY, Rosemary .... 412-536-1173.. 406 K
rosemary.mccarthy@laroche.edu
MCCARTHY, Sean .... 312-777-8726.. 142 G
smccarthy@aii.edu
MCCARTHY, Shannon ...... 617-730-7104.. 226 J
shannon.mccarthy@newbury.edu
MCCARTHY, Sherry .... 712-279-3158.. 176 E
sherry.mccarthy@stlukescollege.edu
MCCARTHY, Thomas .... 718-862-7977.. 319 L
thomas.mccarthy@manhattan.edu
MCCARTNEY, Cliff .... 865-573-4517.. 440 I
cmccartney@johnsonu.edu
MCCARTNEY, Jason .... 410-548-4085.. 213 A
MCCARTNEY, Jill .... 402-826-8583.. 280 B
jill.mccartney@doane.edu
MCCARTNEY, Kathleen ..... 413-585-2100.. 228 D
kmccartney@smith.edu
MCCARTNEY, Maureen .... 413-572-8801.. 222 E
mccartney@westfield.ma.edu
MCCARTNEY, William, G . 765-496-2270.. 166 D
mccart@purdue.edu
MCCARTNEY, JR.,
William, L .... 252-328-6050.. 356 C
mccartneyw@ecu.edu
MCCARTY, Dan .... 916-558-2198.... 51 D
mccartw@scc.losrios.edu
MCCARTY, Gerald .... 810-766-4206.. 231 C
MCCARTY, II, Gerald ...... 810-766-4206.. 231 D
gmccar01@baker.edu
MCCARTY, Lori .... 706-272-4462.. 119 H
lmccarty@daltonstate.edu
MCCARTY, Lori .... 276-656-0212.. 498 A
lmccarty@patrickhenry.edu
MCCARTY, Mike .... 570-585-9288.. 419 G
mmccarty@summitu.edu
MCCARTY, Shannon .... 480-517-8285.... 14 G
shannon.mccarty@riosalado.edu
MCCARTY, Susan .... 212-772-4850.. 308 D
susan.mccarty@hunter.cuny.edu
MCCARTY-HARRIS,
Yulanda .... 216-687-2223.. 366 I
y.mccartyharris@csuohio.edu
MCCARVEL, Thomas, J ..... 406-447-4409.. 276 B
tmccarve@carroll.edu
MCCARVER, Viva .... 419-372-8421.. 364 E
vivam@bgsu.edu
MCCARY, Jennifer, Q .... 717-337-6998.. 404 C
jmccary@gettysburg.edu
MCCASKILL, Sharrell .... 202-651-5642.... 92 C
sharrell.mccaskill@gallaudet.edu
MCCASLAND, Shannon .... 970-339-6563.... 76 H
shannon.mccasland@aims.edu
MCCASLIN, James, B ...... 270-901-1104.. 190 F
james.mccaslin@kctcs.edu
MCCASLIN, John .... 931-553-0071.. 442 I
john.mccaslin@miller-motte.com
MCCASLIN, Julie .... 423-746-5214.. 447 E
jmccaslin@twcnet.edu
MCCASLIN, Randall .... 814-732-1346.. 415 A
rmccaslin@edinboro.edu
MCCASLIN, Sharon .... 314-889-4567.. 265 C
smccaslin@fontbonne.edu
MCCAULEY, David, W ...... 304-473-8322.. 515 B
mccauley@wvwc.edu
MCCAULEY, Dennis .... 215-968-8394.. 399 A
mccauley@bucks.edu
MCCAULEY, Jeff .... 253-833-9111.. 504 C
jmccauley@greenriver.edu

MCCAULEY, Kathleen .... 610-647-4400.. 406 B
kmccauley@immaculata.edu
MCCAULEY, Laurie, K ...... 734-763-3311.. 241 J
mccauley@umich.edu
MCCAULEY, Linda .... 404-727-7976.. 120 E
linda.mccauley@emory.edu
MCCAULEY, Terry, L .... 248-232-4660.. 239 E
tlmccaul@oaklandcc.edu
MCCAULEY-JUGOVICH,
Shelly .... 218-748-2416.. 249 I
s.mccauley@mesabirange.edu
MCCAUSLAND, Bill .... 813-974-1868.. 112 C
mccausland@usf.edu
MCCAUSLIN, Lauren .... 617-243-2139.. 219 I
lmccauslin@lasell.edu
MCCAWLEY, Michael .... 831-459-2374.... 70 F
admissions@ucsc.edu
MCCAY, Patrick .... 603-623-0313.. 287 D
patrickmccay@nhia.edu
MCCAY, T. Dwayne .... 321-674-8099.. 100 M
tdmccay@fit.edu
MCCHURCH, Bob .... 309-796-5013.. 135 I
mcchurchb@bhc.edu
MCCINTY, Jill .... 312-935-3033.. 152 D
jmcginty@robertmorris.edu
MCCLAFFERTY, Joseph .... 406-496-4804.. 277 G
jmcclafferty@mtech.edu
MCCLAIN, Barbara, L ...... 304-326-1234.. 511 D
bmcclain@salemu.edu
MCCLAIN, Beth .... 309-694-5323.. 141 F
bmcclain@icc.edu
MCCLAIN, Dale .... 847-866-3920.. 140 G
dale.mcclain@garrett.edu
MCCLAIN, Elman .... 206-934-5437.. 506 K
elman.mcclain@seattlecolleges.edu
MCCLAIN, Gloria .... 404-756-4098.. 116 I
gmcclain@atlm.edu
MCCLAIN, James .... 626-914-8794.... 38 D
jmcclain@citruscollege.edu
MCCLAIN, James, W .... 870-838-2910.... 18 G
jmcclain@smail.anc.edu
MCCLAIN, Jason .... 304-829-7601.. 510 G
jmcclain@bethanywv.edu
MCCLAIN, Jeremy .... 334-670-3482...... 7 H
jamcclain@troy.edu
MCCLAIN, Mark .... 937-766-7933.. 365 C
mcclain@cedarville.edu
MCCLAIN, Paula, D .... 919-681-1560.. 343 J
pmmclain@duke.edu
MCCLAIN, Rebecca .... 281-756-3561.. 450 G
MCCLAIN, Rita .... 405-495-6300.. 388 A
rmcclain@snu.edu
MCCLAIN, Samantha, E .... 515-574-1080.. 173 F
mcclain@iowacentral.edu
MCCLAIN, Tamara .... 630-942-2422.. 138 B
mccalint57@cod.edu
MCCLAIN, Tammy, L .... 304-336-8023.. 513 F
tmcclain@westliberty.edu
MCCLAIN, Tim .... 360-486-8875.. 506 G
tmc@stmartin.edu
MCCLANAHAN, Ana .... 607-587-3101.. 334 G
mcclanam@alfredstate.edu
MCCLANAHAN, Ana, M ...... 919-513-2311.. 353 I
ammcclanahan@waketech.edu
MCCLANAHAN, Barry .... 717-477-1240.. 416 A
bkmcca@ship.edu
MCCLANAHAN, Danelle .... 301-934-2251.. 207 B
dmcclanahan1@csmd.edu
MCCLANAHAN, Denise ...... 434-961-5275.. 498 C
dmcclanahan@pvcc.edu
MCCLANAHAN, Keith .... 501-882-8811.... 18 I
mkmcclanahan@asub.edu
MCCLANAHAN, Keith .... 870-368-2004.... 21 F
keith.mcclanahan@ozarka.edu
MCCLANAHAN,
Thomas, H .... 559-278-0840.... 32 F
thomas_mcclanahan@csufresno.edu
MCCLATCHY, Anna .... 706-886-6831.. 128 C
amcclatchy@tfc.edu
MCCLAY, Diana, D .... 423-439-5890.. 444 F
mcclayd@etsu.edu
MCCLAY, Kelly .... 609-343-4939.. 288 H
mcclay@atlantic.edu
MCCLEARY, Caitlin .... 865-974-1000.. 448 E
MCCLEARY, Tim .... 406-638-3121.. 276 G
baaxpaa@lbhc.edu
MCCLELLAN, Craig, S ...... 304-326-1465.. 511 D
cmcclellan@salemu.edu
MCCLELLAN, Craig, S ...... 304-326-1247.. 511 D
cmcclellan@salemu.edu
MCCLELLAN, George, S .... 260-481-6844.. 163 C
mcclellg@ipfw.edu
MCCLELLAN, Jane .... 201-200-3196.. 293 C
jmcclellan@njcu.edu
MCCLELLAN, Laura .... 276-739-2425.. 499 A
lmcclellan@vhcc.edu
MCCLELLAN,
Meaghan, M .... 512-863-1454.. 466 G
mcclellme@southwestern.edu
MCCLELLAN, Mia, C .... 619-482-6542.... 66 E
mmcclellan@swccd.edu

MCCLELLAN, Patricia .... 828-251-6001.. 357 C
pmcclell@unca.edu
MCCLELLAN, Scott .... 206-220-8229.. 507 E
mcclells@seattleu.edu
MCCLELLAN, Steve, J .... 501-569-3202.... 23 B
sjmcclellan@ualr.edu
MCCLELLAND, Charles, F 713-313-7216.. 470 D
mcclellandcf@tsu.edu
MCCLELLAND, Jeremy ...... 214-860-2351.. 456 E
jmccleland@dcccd.edu
MCCLELLAND, Karin .... 925-631-4013.... 59 I
klm14@stmarys-ca.edu
MCCLELLAND, Theresa ..... 251-580-2120...... 4 I
theresa.mcclelland@faulknerstate.edu
MCCLELLAND, II,
Thomas, H .... 318-257-4827.. 200 G
tmcclelland@latech.edu
MCCLENAGAN, Cindy, M 806-291-1106.. 479 D
cindym@wbu.edu
MCCLENDON, Bev .... 479-788-7082.... 23 A
bev.mcclendon@uafs.edu
MCCLENDON, Jennifer ..... 918-456-5511.. 384 G
mcclendo@nsuok.edu
MCCLENDON, Karen .... 916-686-8602.... 31 F
MCCLENDON, Mark .... 940-397-4567.. 462 A
mark.mcclendon@mwsu.edu
MCCLENDON, Mark .... 817-515-5203.. 467 A
mark.mcclendon@tccd.edu
MCCLENDON, Rodney, P . 412-268-2056.. 400 D
rodneypm@andrew.cmu.edu
MCCLENDON, Vivienne ..... 425-564-3056.. 501 F
vivienne.mcclendon@bellevuecollege.edu
MCCLENNEY, Elizabeth .... 540-375-2293.. 493 H
mcclenney@roanoke.edu
MCCLIN, Raul .... 787-761-0640.. 537 C
admisiones1@utcpr.edu
MCCLINTOCK, Elizabeth ... 724-503-1001.. 422 H
emcclintock@washjeff.edu
MCCLINTOCK, Kate .... 707-527-4797.... 63 G
kmcclintock@santarosa.edu
MCCLINTOCK, Marta .... 724-938-4251.. 414 E
mcclintock@calu.edu
MCCLINTOCK, Melvin, A . 240-895-4309.. 210 E
mamcclintock@smcm.edu
MCCLINTOCK, Patty .... 812-237-2305.. 162 A
patty.mcclintock@indstate.edu
MCCLINTOCK, Stewart ..... 336-342-4261.. 352 F
mcclintocks@rockinghamcc.edu
MCCLINTON, Flandus .... 225-771-5550.. 199 G
flandus_mcclinton@sus.edu
MCCLINTON, Leon .... 405-744-9164.. 385 G
leon.mcclinton@okstate.edu
MCCLINTON, Martin .... 239-489-9229.. 101 F
mmcclinton1@fsw.edu
MCCLOSKEY, Brian .... 609-586-4800.. 292 D
mccloskb@mccc.edu
MCCLOSKEY, Erin, E .... 814-472-3100.. 418 F
emccloskey@francis.edu
MCCLOSKEY, James, M .... 302-356-6880.... 91 I
james.m.mccloskey@wilmu.edu
MCCLOSKEY, JR.,
John, R .... 610-796-3005.. 397 D
john.mccloskey@alvernia.edu
MCCLOUD, Alyssa .... 973-313-6146.. 297 A
alyssa.mccloud@shu.edu
MCCLOUD, Amber .... 806-291-3430.. 479 D
amber.mccloud@wbu.edu
MCCLOUD, Barbara, L ..... 630-515-7687.. 148 C
bmcclo@midwestern.edu
MCCLOUD, Bill .... 405-491-6602.. 388 A
bmccloud@snu.edu
MCCLOUD, Clarence .... 386-506-6301.... 98 E
mcclouc@daytonastate.edu
MCCLOUD, Jennifer .... 317-822-3489.. 165 O
jmccloud@martin.edu
MCCLOUD, Mickey .... 913-469-8500.. 182 A
MCCLOY, Eric .... 215-572-8521.. 397 G
mccloy@arcadia.edu
MCCLUNEY, Alice .... 828-395-1495.. 350 E
amccluney@isothermal.edu
MCCLUNG, Alan .... 423-614-8410.. 441 B
amcclung@leeuniversity.edu
MCCLUNG, Alex .... 973-408-3799.. 291 B
amcclung@drew.edu
MCCLUNG, Bruce, d .... 513-556-3737.. 379 A
bruce.mcclung@uc.edu
MCCLUNG, Leslie .... 808-932-7381.. 131 E
lmcclung@hawaii.edu
MCCLUNG, Philip, L .... 336-734-7212.. 349 G
pmcclung@forsythtech.edu
MCCLUNG, Shemeka .... 601-979-7030.. 258 D
shemeka.s.mcclung@jsums.edu
MCCLURE, A. Glenn .... 610-917-1453.. 422 C
agmcclure@valleyforge.edu
MCCLURE, Amber .... 575-461-4413.. 300 A
amberm@mesalands.edu
MCCLURE, Amy .... 740-368-3562.. 376 B
aamcclur@owu.edu
MCCLURE, Beverlee, J ..... 719-587-7341.... 76 G
bmcclure@adams.edu

MCCLURE, Erin .... 361-593-2795.. 469 A
erin.mcclure@tamuk.edu
MCCLURE, Guy .... 256-233-8296...... 1 F
guy.mcclure@athens.edu
MCCLURE, H. Lawrence ... 215-780-1331.. 419 C
larry@salus.edu
MCCLURE, Jennifer .... 847-214-7319.. 140 A
jmcclure@elgin.edu
MCCLURE, Judy .... 828-766-1272.. 351 B
jmmclure@mayland.edu
MCCLURE, Kelly .... 580-581-2255.. 382 G
kmcclure@cameron.edu
MCCLURE, Krista .... 801-426-8234.. 481 K
kmcclure@ucdh.edu
MCCLURE, Lawrence .... 215-780-1331.. 419 C
larry@salus.edu
MCCLURE, Mike .... 541-956-7237.. 394 J
mmclure@roguecc.edu
MCCLURE, Robert .... 845-446-1522.. 529 C
robert.mcclure@wpaog.org
MCCLURE, Shanna .... 765-641-4133.. 158 J
srmcclure@anderson.edu
MCCLURE, Tonya .... 478-757-3467.. 118 G
tmcclure@centralgatech.edu
MCCLURE, Tonya, L .... 478-757-3467.. 118 H
tmcclure@centralgatech.edu
MCCLURE, William .... 718-997-5790.. 309 D
william.mcclure@qc.cuny.edu
MCCLURE, William, S .... 413-545-2111.. 220 F
billmcclure@contined.umass.edu
MCCLUSKEY, Cindy .... 815-825-9333.. 144 F
cindy.mccluskey@kishwaukeecollege.edu
MCCLUSKEY, Eugene .... 207-768-2786.. 203 L
emccluskey@nmcc.edu
MCCLUSKEY, Jennifer .... 314-529-9561.. 267 B
jmccluskey@maryville.edu
MCCLUSKEY, Richard .... 978-665-3118.. 221 D
rmccluskey@fitchburgstate.edu
MCCLUSKEY, Steph .... 507-786-3885.. 254 P
mcclus1@stolaf.edu
MCCLUSKY, John .... 217-854-3231.. 135 K
john.mcclusky@blackburn.edu
MCCLYMONT, Jay, W .... 717-766-2511.. 410 J
jmcclymont@messiah.edu
MCCOEY, Margaret .... 215-951-1130.. 407 A
mccoey@lasalle.edu
MCCOLGIN, Cathleen, C .. 315-866-0300.. 316 A
mccolgicc@herkimer.edu
MCCOLLETT, Sherry .... 207-621-3141.. 204 I
umafa@maine.edu
MCCOLLOCH, Mark .... 443-840-1021.. 207 C
mmocolloch@ccbcmd.edu
MCCOLLOUGH, Laura, L . 907-474-1886.... 10 G
lcmccollough@alaska.edu
MCCOLLOUGH,
William, A .... 352-392-1202.. 112 A
amccollough@aa.ufl.edu
MCCOLLUM, Alonzo, L .... 516-876-3068.. 333 C
mccolluma@oldwestbury.edu
MCCOLLUM, Rick, L .... 501-450-3132.... 24 G
rickm@uca.edu
MCCOLLUM, Scott .... 937-512-3068.. 377 D
scott.mccullum@sinclair.edu
MCCOLLUM, Susan .... 334-291-4953...... 2 H
susan.mccollum@cv.edu
MCCOMAS, Pam .... 626-529-8033.... 55 H
pmccomas@pacificoaks.edu
MCCOMAS, Richard .... 580-581-2524.. 382 G
richardm@cameron.edu
MCCOMBS, Ed .... 928-724-6635.... 12 T
emccombs@dinecollege.edu
MCCOMBS, Gillian, M .... 214-768-2400.. 465 J
gmccombs@smu.edu
MCCOMBS, Laurie .... 216-687-3606.. 366 I
l.mccombs11@csuohio.edu
MCCONAHAY, Mark .... 812-855-0121.. 162 F
mcconaha@indiana.edu
MCCONATHY, Terry, M ... 318-257-4262.. 200 G
tmm@latech.edu
MCCONKEY, Susan .... 415-503-6285.... 61 C
smcconkey@sfcm.edu
MCCONNAUGHEY,
Scott, E .... 719-884-5000.... 81 N
semcconnaughey@nbc.edu
MCCONNELL, Blake .... 618-658-8331.. 145 D
james.mcconnell@doc.illinois.gov
MCCONNELL, Brian .... 607-733-7177.. 313 D
bmcconnell@ebi-college.com
MCCONNELL, Cary .... 617-573-8575.. 228 G
cmcconnell@suffolk.edu
MCCONNELL, Cheryl, M .. 816-501-4087.. 270 J
cheryl.mcconnell@rockhurst.edu
MCCONNELL, Frank, J ..... 706-864-1606.. 128 F
mac.mcconnell@ung.edu
MCCONNELL, Gaye .... 704-216-3600.. 352 G
gaye.mcconnell@rccc.edu
MCCONNELL, Glenn, F .... 843-953-5500.. 428 G
mcconnellgf@cofc.edu
MCCONNELL, Ilka .... 706-369-5763.. 116 H
imcconnell@athenstech.edu

MCCONNELL, Jason .... 423-869-6333.. 441 E
jason.mcconnell@lmunet.edu
MCCONNELL, John, D ...... 336-758-5000.. 359 E
MCCONNELL, Joyce .... 304-293-5701.. 514 C
joyce.mcconnell@mail.wvu.edu
MCCONNELL, Karl .... 856-227-7200.. 290 B
kmcconnell@camdencc.edu
MCCONNELL, Penny, J ..... 217-443-8747.. 139 B
pmcconn@dacc.edu
MCCONNELL, Will .... 818-767-0888.... 75 D
will.mcconnell@woodbury.edu
MCCONNELLOGUE, Ken .. 303-860-5600.... 83 J
ken.mcconnellogue@cu.edu
MCCONNICO, Kelly .... 336-758-5000.. 359 E
mcconnkm@wfu.edu
MCCONOUGHEY, Gina ...... 608-757-7723.. 523 A
gmcconoughey@blackhawk.edu
MCCONVILLE, Jennifer, A 308-367-5259.. 283 C
jmcconville2@unl.edu
MCCOOK, Sonya .... 336-506-4278.. 347 C
sonya.mccook@alamancecc.edu
MCCOOL, Bobby .... 606-886-3863.. 189 A
bobby.mccool@kctcs.edu
MCCOOL, Jeff .... 575-492-4711.. 300 H
jmccool@nmjc.edu
MCCOOL, Joan, L .... 716-878-4436.. 332 F
mccoolj l@buffalostate.edu
MCCORCLE, Michael .... 417-865-2815.. 265 B
mccorclem@evangel.edu
MCCORD, Christopher ...... 815-753-1061.. 150 A
mccord@niu.edu
MCCORD, Elizabeth .... 415-451-2832.... 61 D
emccord@sfts.edu
MCCORD, Jeff, D .... 423-354-5207.. 446 F
jdmccord@northeaststate.edu
MCCORD-FITHIAN,
Regina, L .... 812-888-5848.. 169 A
rmccord-fithian@vinu.edu
MCCORMACK, Amy .... 708-524-6770.. 139 F
amccormack@dom.edu
MCCORMACK, Beth .... 802-831-1327.. 485 F
bmccormack@vermontlaw.edu
MCCORMACK, Bridey .... 806-457-4200.. 458 B
bmccormack@fpctx.edu
MCCORMACK, Erin .... 801-302-2800.. 480 L
erin.mccormack@neumont.edu
MCCORMACK, Gary .... 713-942-3400.. 475 J
mccormack@stthom.edu
MCCORMACK, Jeff .... 405-425-1933.. 385 C
jeff.mccormack@oc.edu
MCCORMACK, Mike .... 205-726-2916...... 6 E
hmmccorm@samford.edu
MCCORMICK, Adrienne ..... 315-312-2285.. 333 D
adrienne.mccormick@oswego.edu
MCCORMICK, Brad .... 618-985-8340.. 143 F
bradmccormick@jalc.edu
MCCORMICK, Brad .... 423-697-3264.. 445 D
brad.mccormick@chattanoogastate.edu
MCCORMICK, Brian .... 319-296-4050.. 173 B
brian.mccormick@hawkeyecollege.edu
MCCORMICK, Charlie, T .. 830-792-7371.. 465 E
ctmccormick@schreiner.edu
MCCORMICK, Cheryl .... 816-654-7563.. 266 E
cmccormick@kcumb.edu
MCCORMICK,
Christine, B .... 413-545-2705.. 220 F
cmccormick@educ.umass.edu
MCCORMICK, David .... 312-567-4972.. 142 I
dmccormick@iitri.org
MCCORMICK, Dee .... 330-263-2321.. 367 A
dmccormick@wooster.edu
MCCORMICK, Gordon .... 831-656-2484.. 528 D
gmccormick@navy.edu
MCCORMICK, Heidi, A ..... 330-263-2533.. 367 A
hmccormick@wooster.edu
MCCORMICK, Heidi, A ..... 804-828-1645.. 496 D
hamccormick@vcu.edu
MCCORMICK,
Jennifer Higgins .... 716-827-2455.. 338 E
mccormickj@trocaire.edu
MCCORMICK, Jill .... 402-872-2257.. 281 I
jmccormick@peru.edu
MCCORMICK, Jim, S .... 303-963-3363.... 77 I
jimmccormick@ccu.edu
MCCORMICK, John .... 406-243-2532.. 276 K
john.mccormick@umontana.edu
MCCORMICK, John .... 801-957-4024.. 483 A
john.mccormick@slcc.edu
MCCORMICK, Joseph .... 303-797-5075.... 76 J
joseph.mccormick@arapahoe.edu
MCCORMICK, Karla, S ...... 334-844-4183...... 1 G
ksm0010@auburn.edu
MCCORMICK, Kelly, L ...... 303-765-3121.... 80 M
kmccormick@iliff.edu
MCCORMICK, Kevin, M .... 630-515-6053.. 148 C
kmccor@midwestern.edu
MCCORMICK, Kirsten, M . 714-879-3901.... 46 F
kmmccormick@hiu.edu
MCCORMICK, Mark .... 205-247-8831...... 7 E
mmccormick@stillman.edu

MCCORMICK, Mark .... 732-906-2515.. 292 E
mmccormick@middlesexcc.edu
MCCORMICK, OSU,
Mary .... 440-943-7600.. 377 A
mmccormick@dioceseofcleveland.org
MCCORMICK, Michael ...... 206-221-4344.. 508 E
mccorm50@uw.edu
MCCORMICK, Michael, R 315-386-7222.. 335 B
mccormic@canton.edu
MCCORMICK, Patrick, T .. 509-313-6715.. 504 A
mccormick@calvin.gonzaga.edu
MCCORMICK, Peter .... 970-247-7595.... 80 D
mccormick_p@fortlewis.edu
MCCORMICK, CSC,
Peter, M .... 574-631-7800.. 168 B
mccormick.23@nd.edu
MCCORMICK, Reenie ...... 410-334-2939.. 213 G
rmccormick@worwic.edu
MCCORMICK, Reid, W ..... 714-879-3901.... 46 F
rwmccormick@hiu.edu
MCCORMICK, Robert .... 312-362-6627.. 139 C
bmccormi@depaul.edu
MCCORMICK, Robert .... 734-995-7391.. 232 I
robert.mccormick@cuaa.edu
MCCORMICK, Silas .... 217-732-3168.. 146 A
smccormick@lincolnchristian.edu
MCCORMICK, Stanley ...... 229-420-7013.. 115 K
stanley.mccormick@asurams.edu
MCCORQUODALE,
Duncan, L .... 260-422-5561.. 162 B
dlmccorquodale@indianatech.edu
MCCORRY, Laurie, K ...... 617-228-2465.. 223 B
lkmccorry@bhcc.mass.edu
MCCORRY, Margaret .... 908-737-0580.. 292 C
mmccorry@kean.edu
MCCORRY, Wendy .... 845-688-1980.. 338 F
mccorryw@sunyulster.edu
MCCORRY-ANDALIS,
Catherine, M .... 915-747-5648.. 476 D
cmandalis@utep.edu
MCCORT, Tiffany .... 619-574-6909.... 55 G
thansen@pacificcollege.edu
MCCORY, Denise .... 216-987-5544.. 367 E
denise.mccory@tri-c.edu
MCCOULLUM, Valarie, S . 215-898-5337.. 421 E
cade@upenn.edu
MCCOURT, MaryFrances .. 215-898-1005.. 421 E
mfmccourt@upenn.edu
MCCOURT, Susan .... 508-678-2811.. 223 A
susan.mccourt@bristolcc.edu
MCCOWAN, Carla .... 217-333-3701.. 157 A
cmccowan@illinois.edu
MCCOWN, Amber .... 239-489-9226.. 101 F
amccown@fsw.edu
MCCOY, Avis, M .... 954-201-7401.... 96 I
amccoy@broward.edu
MCCOY, Carole, A .... 315-786-2230.. 317 H
cmccoy@sunyjefferson.edu
MCCOY, David, M .... 804-289-8718.. 495 G
dmccoy2@richmond.edu
MCCOY, Holly, M .... 724-738-2650.. 416 B
holly.mccoy@sru.edu
MCCOY, Janee .... 914-964-4282.. 310 D
MCCOY, John .... 423-236-2444.. 444 B
jmccoy@southern.edu
MCCOY, Julie .... 803-938-3753.. 434 E
jmccoy@uscsumter.edu
MCCOY, J'Neal .... 417-447-4817.. 270 A
mccoyj@otc.edu
MCCOY, Keith .... 773-838-7514.. 137 H
kmccoy@ccc.edu
MCCOY, Marilyn .... 847-491-4335.. 150 F
mmccoy@northwestern.edu
MCCOY, Mark .... 765-658-4220.. 160 F
president@depauw.edu
MCCOY, Martin .... 919-278-2669.. 355 F
martin.mccoy@shawu.edu
MCCOY, Mary .... 409-882-3080.. 471 B
mary.mccoy@lsco.edu
MCCOY, Matthew, J .... 541-383-7210.. 390 D
mmccoy@cocc.edu
MCCOY, Mike .... 256-216-3300...... 1 F
mike.mccoy@athens.edu
MCCOY, Paddy .... 509-527-2343.. 508 G
paddy.mccoy@wallawalla.edu
MCCOY, Patricia .... 602-212-0501.... 11 N
MCCOY, Peggy, S .... 406-496-4404.. 277 G
pmccoy@mtech.edu
MCCOY, Robert .... 907-474-7500.... 10 G
rpmccoy@alaska.edu
MCCOY, Ryan .... 303-404-5238.... 80 E
ryan.mccoy@frontrange.edu
MCCOY, Sue .... 916-484-8211.... 51 A
mccoys@arc.losrios.edu
MCCOY, Sue .... 212-353-4167.. 311 G
mccoy@cooper.edu
MCCOY, Thomas .... 678-717-3855.. 128 F
thomas.mccoy@ung.edu
MCCOY, Thomas, J .... 940-369-8249.. 475 A
thomas.mccoy@unt.edu
MCCOY, William, K .... 570-577-1609.. 398 L
bill.mccoy@bucknell.edu
MCCOY GRISSOM,
Shelly .... 419-251-1203.. 372 C
shelly.mccoy-grissom@mercycollege.edu
MCCOY-WILSON, Sonya .. 404-225-4672.. 117 A
smccoy-wilson@atlantatech.edu
MCCRACKEN, Carolyn ..... 423-354-2509.. 446 F
cgmccracken@northeaststate.edu
MCCRACKEN, Fawn .... 952-446-4325.. 246 D
mccrackenf@crown.edu
MCCRACKEN, Jeff, B .... 919-966-5730.. 357 D
jeff_mccracken@unc.edu
MCCRACKEN, Joann .... 610-989-1450.. 422 E
jbmiller@vfmac.edu
MCCRACKEN, Larry .... 503-517-1879.. 396 F
lmccracken@westernseminary.edu
MCCRACKEN, Mike .... 620-235-4624.. 184 C
mmccracken@pittstate.edu
MCCRAE, Bill .... 503-253-3443.. 393 D
bill.mccrae@ocom.edu
MCCRAE, Byron .... 413-559-5412.. 219 C
bmccrae@hampshire.edu
MCCRANEY, Lynn .... 912-260-4293.. 127 B
lynn.mccraney@sgsc.edu
MCCRARY, Brian .... 678-839-6619.. 129 E
bmccrary@westga.edu
MCCRARY, Cheryl .... 785-594-8327.. 178 D
cheryl.mccrary@bakeru.edu
MCCRARY, Kevin .... 386-506-3475.... 98 E
mccrark@daytonastate.edu
MCCRAW, Bethany, J .... 254-710-1715.. 452 H
bethany_mccraw@baylor.edu
MCCRAW, Liz .... 580-745-2080.. 387 M
lmccraw@se.edu
MCCRAW, Patti, H .... 864-488-4571.. 430 H
pmccraw@limestone.edu
MCCRAY, Carrie .... 573-592-4317.. 275 G
carrie.mccray@williamwoods.edu
MCCRAY, Corey, L .... 757-822-1184.. 498 H
cmccray@tcc.edu
MCCRAY, Jacquelyn .... 870-575-8475.... 23 E
mccrayj@uapb.edu
MCCRAY, Suzanne .... 479-575-4883.... 22 I
smccray@uark.edu
MCCRAY, Tammy .... 218-751-8670.. 254 A
registrar@oakhills.edu
MCCREA, Larry .... 816-604-6541.. 267 G
larry.mccrea@mcckc.edu
MCCREADY, Randall .... 412-624-7180.. 421 G
mccready@pitt.edu
MCCREARY, Jeff .... 573-518-2308.. 268 E
jmccreary@mineralarea.edu
MCCREARY, Lynn .... 940-565-2378.. 475 A
mccreary@unt.edu
MCCREARY, William .... 419-530-3990.. 380 D
william.mccreary@utoledo.edu
MCCREATH, Amy .... 617-682-1571.. 218 E
amccreath@eds.edu
MCCREE, Bernard, L .... 610-683-4032.. 415 C
mccree@kutztown.edu
MCCREE, Robin .... 704-991-0252.. 353 E
mmccree5540@stanly.edu
MCCREERY, Deborah, M .. 610-921-7501.. 396 H
dmccreery@albright.edu
MCCREERY, Shane .... 309-438-3383.. 143 B
msmccre@ilstu.edu
MCCROHAN, Betty, A .... 979-532-6304.. 479 J
bettym@wcjc.edu
MCCRORY, Cynthia .... 704-922-6406.. 350 A
mccrory.cynthia@gaston.edu
MCCRORY, Heidi, H .... 740-427-5154.. 371 C
mccroryh@kenyon.edu
MCCRORY, Martin .... 812-855-9308.. 162 F
mmccrory@indiana.edu
MCCRORY, Robert, L .... 585-275-4973.. 338 K
rmcc@lle.rochester.edu
MCCROSKEY, Lorie, L ...... 336-633-1118.. 352 B
llmccroskey@randolph.edu
MCCROW, Rich .... 661-720-2002.... 47 J
rmccrow@bakersfieldcollege.edu
MCCROY-HEINS,
Michelle .... 201-692-2190.. 291 J
michelle_mccroy@fdu.edu
MCCRYSTAL, Mary .... 216-373-5331.. 374 B
mmccrystal@ndc.edu
MCCUBBIN, Jeff .... 970-491-5841.... 78 Q
jeff.mccubbin@colostate.edu
MCCUBBIN, Todd, A .... 573-882-6017.. 273 E
mccubbint@missouri.edu
MCCUDDEN, Suzanne .... 253-833-9111.. 504 C
smccudden@greenriver.edu
MCCUE, Cindy .... 631-420-2319.. 335 E
cynthia.mccue@farmingdale.edu
MCCUE, Jennie .... 949-582-4320.... 65 G
jmccue@saddleback.edu
MCCUEN, Jan .... 714-997-6701.... 37 F
mccuen@chapman.edu
MCCUIEN-SMITH,
Cassandra .... 501-450-3173.... 24 G
cmccuien@uca.edu
MCCULLAR, Bryan, L .... 785-833-4339.. 182 F
bryan.mccullar@kwu.edu
MCCULLEN, Ann, S .... 904-620-2100.. 112 B
amccullen@unf.edu
MCCULLEY, Becky .... 214-645-5482.. 478 C
becky.mcculley@utsouthwestern.edu
MCCULLOCH, Dave .... 770-962-7580.. 123 D
dmcculloch@gwinnetttech.edu
MCCULLOCH, Greg .... 618-252-5400.. 154 G
greg.mcculloch@sic.edu
MCCULLOCH, Joseph .... 318-813-9201.. 198 B
jmccul@bsuhsc.edu
MCCULLOCH, Sonja .... 912-260-4402.. 127 B
sonja.mcculloch@sgsc.edu
MCCULLOH, Edna .... 330-490-7191.. 380 J
emcculloh@walsh.edu
MCCULLOH, Julie, A .... 509-313-6572.. 504 A
mcculloh@gonzaga.edu
MCCULLOH, Thayne, M ..... 509-313-6102.. 504 A
president@gonzaga.edu
MCCULLOUCH, Brandi .... 252-249-1851.. 351 G
bmccullough@pamlicocc.edu
MCCULLOUCH, Bryan .... 336-249-4688.. 349 C
bryan_mccullough@davidsonccc.edu
MCCULLOUCH, Catherine 802-728-1247.. 436 D
crm07130@vtc.vsc.edu
MCCULLOUCH,
Desiree, A .... 731-881-7014.. 448 G
dmccull1@utm.edu
MCCULLOUCH, Doreen ...... 802-776-5232.. 433 G
dmccullough@csj.edu
MCCULLOUCH, James .... 918-293-5068.. 336 B
james.mccullough@okstate.edu
MCCULLOUCH,
Jonathan, W .... 903-434-8115.. 462 M
jmccullough@ntcc.edu
MCCULLOUGH, Laura .... 912-478-5234.. 122 B
lmccullough@georgiasouthern.edu
MCCULLOUGH, Laura .... 304-205-6611.. 511 M
laura.mccullough@bridgevalley.edu
MCCULLOUGH, Lois, N ...... 419-783-2317.. 368 A
lmccullough@defiance.edu
MCCULLOUGH, Randy .... 419-559-2355.. 377 M
rmccullough01@terra.edu
MCCULLOUGH, Robbin ...... 415-451-2864.... 61 D
rmccullough@sfts.edu
MCCULLOUGH, Robert, R 216-368-5445.. 365 B
robert.mccullough@case.edu
MCCULLOUGH, Willie .... 606-326-2068.. 188 N
willie.mccullough@kctcs.edu
MCCULLY, Clare .... 617-730-7089.. 226 J
clare.mccully@newbury.edu
MCCUNE, Kate .... 562-947-8755.... 66 A
katmccune@scuhs.edu
MCCUNE, L.B .... 810-762-9629.. 236 C
lbmccune@kettering.edu
MCCUNE, Mary .... 315-312-3443.. 333 D
mary.mccune@oswego.edu
MCCUNE, Ryan .... 620-252-7180.. 180 B
ryanm@coffeyville.edu
MCCURDY, Clantha .... 617-727-9420.. 220 D
cmccurdy@osfa.mass.edu
MCCURDY, Debra, L .... 419-995-8200.. 370 G
mccurdy.d@rhodesstate.edu
MCCURDY, Eugene, M ...... 608-796-3921.. 522 O
emmccurdy@viterbo.edu
MCCURDY, Solynn .... 206-296-6116.. 507 E
mccurdys@seattleu.edu
MCCURREN, Cynthia .... 616-331-3558.. 234 F
mccurrec@gvsu.edu
MCCURRY, David .... 864-503-5509.. 434 G
dmccurry@uscupstate.edu
MCCURRY, Faith .... 803-536-0311.. 431 I
MCCURRY, Faith .... 803-535-1230.. 431 I
mccurryf@octech.edu
MCCURRY, Ricky, N .... 865-974-4531.. 448 D
rmccurry@tennessee.edu
MCCURTY, Kenyetta .... 334-387-3877...... 1 E
kenyettamccurty@amridgeuniversity.edu
MCCUTCHAN, Molly M .... 734-384-4245.. 238 C
mmccutchan@monroeccc.edu
MCCUTCHEN, Michael .... 731-989-6901.. 440 D
mmccutchen@fhu.edu
MCCUTCHEON, Bruce, E .. 610-330-5530.. 407 C
mccutchb@lafayette.edu
MCCUTCHEON, John .... 805-893-8320.... 70 E
jmccutch@athletics.ucsb.edu
MCDADE, Kate .... 216-987-4710.. 367 E
kate.mcdade@tri-c.edu
MCDADE, Linda .... 570-348-6249.. 409 H
lmcdade@marywood.edu
MCDADE, Lucinda .... 909-625-8767.... 38 I
lucinda.mcdade@cgu.edu
MCDADE-CLAY,
W. Thomas .... 585-340-9648.. 310 F
tmcdadeclay@crcds.edu
MCDAID, James .... 617-879-7960.. 222 A
jmcdaid@massart.edu
MCDANIEL, Anna, M .... 352-273-6324.. 112 A
annammcdaniel@ufl.edu
MCDANIEL, Cliff .... 817-461-8741.. 451 G
cmcdaniel@arlingtonbaptistcollege.edu
MCDANIEL, Diane .... 765-677-2436.. 164 B
diane.mcdaniel@indwes.edu
MCDANIEL, Donna .... 903-823-3220.. 467 C
donna.mcdaniel@texarkanacollege.edu
MCDANIEL, Elizabeth, A .. 806-742-3667.. 472 C
elizabeth.mcdaniel@ttu.edu
MCDANIEL, Gary, R .... 949-214-3055.... 41 F
gary.mcdaniel@cui.edu
MCDANIEL, Joy .... 580-371-2371.. 384 D
jmcdaniel@mscok.edu
MCDANIEL, Juley .... 620-223-2700.. 181 A
juleym@fortscott.edu
MCDANIEL, Julie .... 937-722-9316.. 380 E
julie.mcdaniel@urbana.edu
MCDANIEL, Kimberly .... 916-691-7487.... 51 B
mcdanik@crc.losrios.edu
MCDANIEL, Kristina, D .... 573-840-9695.. 273 A
kristinamcdaniel@trcc.edu
MCDANIEL, Lance .... 304-384-5258.. 513 A
mcdaniell26@mycu.concord.edu
MCDANIEL, Laura .... 701-231-8330.. 361 A
laura.mcdaniel@ndsu.edu
MCDANIEL, Lauren .... 505-473-6440.. 302 A
lauren.mcdaniel@santafeuniversity.edu
MCDANIEL, Lisa .... 662-329-7377.. 259 E
mcmcdaniel@muw.edu
MCDANIEL, Lucinda .... 870-933-7906.... 18 H
lmcdaniel@asusystem.edu
MCDANIEL, Mary .... 620-341-5223.. 180 G
mmcdanie@emporia.edu
MCDANIEL, Mary, W .... 864-388-8242.. 430 G
mmcdaniel@lander.edu
MCDANIEL, Mary Lee .... 601-857-3395.. 258 A
mlmcdaniel@hindscc.edu
MCDANIEL, Mick, R .... 607-844-8222.. 337 G
mcdanim@tc3.edu
MCDANIEL, Rose .... 336-249-8186.. 349 C
rose_mcdaniel@davidsonccc.edu
MCDANIEL, Stephen, L ..... 410-651-6676.. 212 B
slmcdaniel@umes.edu
MCDANIEL, Wendy .... 479-394-7622.... 22 B
wmcdaniel@rmcc.edu
MCDANIELS, Monique .... 803-786-3551.. 429 A
mmcdaniels@columbiasc.edu
MCDANIELS, Rob .... 573-882-4370.. 273 E
mcdanielsr@missouri.edu
MCDANIELS WILSON,
Cathy .... 614-236-6114.. 364 N
cmcdanielswilson@capital.edu
MCDAVID, Courtney .... 860-832-3003.... 85 F
mcdavidc@ccsu.edu
MCDAVIS, Roderick, J .... 740-593-1804.. 375 H
mcdavis@ohio.edu
MCDERMOTT, A. Keith ...... 617-541-2454.. 224 F
kmcderm@rcc.mass.edu
MCDERMOTT,
Anastacia, M .... 563-588-7056.. 174 K
anastacia.mcdermott@loras.edu
MCDERMOTT, Ann, B .... 508-793-2443.. 217 C
amcdermo@holycross.edu
MCDERMOTT, Anne .... 401-341-2140.. 426 C
anne.mcdermott@salve.edu
MCDERMOTT, Beth .... 617-552-4400.. 216 C
beth.mcdermott@bc.edu
MCDERMOTT, Brian .... 907-564-8248.... 10 B
bmcdermott@alaskapacific.edu
MCDERMOTT, Brian .... 308-398-7387.. 278 K
bmcdermott@cccneb.edu
MCDERMOTT, Christine ..... 315-568-3105.. 323 A
cmcdermott@nycc.edu
MCDERMOTT, Christine ..... 302-736-2491.... 91 G
christine.mcdermott@wesley.edu
MCDERMOTT, Colleen .... 816-531-5223.. 263 H
cmcdermott@concorde.edu
MCDERMOTT, David .... 617-287-7128.. 220 E
dmcdermott@umassp.edu
MCDERMOTT, Dennis .... 718-489-5362.. 328 D
dmcdermott@sfc.edu
MCDERMOTT, Erin .... 773-702-7684.. 156 D
erinmcd@uchicago.edu
MCDERMOTT, Harry .... 520-621-7428.... 17 I
mcdermot@email.arizona.edu
MCDERMOTT, John, R .... 563-588-7132.. 174 K
john.mcdermott@loras.edu
MCDERMOTT, Marty .... 231-777-0462.. 238 G
marty.mcdermott@muskegoncc.edu
MCDERMOTT, Patrice .... 410-455-3150.. 211 G
mcdermot@umbc.edu
MCDERMOTT, Patricia, L . 757-594-7222.. 488 E
mcdermot@cnu.edu
MCDERMOTT, Patrick .... 941-377-4880.. 105 C
pmcdermott@meridian.edu
MCDERMOTT, Randi .... 208-426-1493.. 132 I
randimcdermott@boisestate.edu
MCDERMOTT, Richard, L . 713-500-4963.. 477 C
richard.l.mcdermott@uth.tmc.edu
MCDERMOTT, Teresa .... 360-475-7480.. 505 F
tmcdermott@olympic.edu

MCDERMOTT, Walter, M . 434-223-6112.. 490 D
wmcdermott@hsc.edu
MCDEVITT, Brigid 206-934-6314.. 506 K
brigid.mcdevitt@seattlecolleges.edu
MCDEVITT, Jenna 740-587-6655.. 368 B
mcdevitts@denison.edu
MCDEVITT, Michelle 419-517-8953.. 371 I
mmcdevitt@lourdes.edu
MCDEVITT, Richard, K 704-406-2361.. 344 E
rmcdevitt@gardner-web.edu
MCDIARMID, Chris 620-331-0815.. 181 J
cmcdiarmid@indycc.edu
MCDILL, M. Augustus 843-661-1128.. 430 B
mmcdill@fmarion.edu
MCDILL, Sandy 602-787-7352.... 14 E
sandy.mcdill@paradisevalley.edu
MCDONAGH, David 212-749-2802.. 319 M
dmcdonagh@msmnyc.edu
MCDONALD, Amos 832-813-6621.. 461 B
amos.mcdonald@lonestar.edu
MCDONALD, Amy, L 561-868-3532.. 106 D
mcdonala@palmbeachstate.edu
MCDONALD, Aneisa, L 865-539-7378.. 446 G
almcdonald@pstcc.edu
MCDONALD, Ann, M 978-632-6600.. 224 B
a_mcdonald@mwcc.mass.edu
MCDONALD, Barbara 763-424-0820.. 251 B
bmcdonald@nhcc.edu
MCDONALD, Brian 845-341-4689.. 325 H
brian.mcdonald@sunyorange.edu
MCDONALD, Cathy 701-328-4111.. 360 B
cathy.mcdonald@ndus.edu
MCDONALD, Christopher 949-451-4823.... 65 F
cmcdonald@ivc.edu
MCDONALD, Christy 865-273-8851.. 441 H
christy.mcdonald@maryvillecollege.edu
MCDONALD, Clay 636-227-2100.. 267 A
MCDONALD, Dalene 620-229-6271.. 184 J
dalene.mcdonald@sckans.edu
MCDONALD, Dana 301-846-2458.. 207 F
dmcdonald@frederick.edu
MCDONALD, Danielle 813-974-6677.. 112 C
dmcdonald@usf.edu
MCDONALD, David 505-984-6082.. 301 I
gi@sjc.edu
MCDONALD, David 503-838-8211.. 396 E
mcdonald@wou.edu
MCDONALD, Debbie 626-966-4576.... 26 J
info@agu.edu
MCDONALD, Deborah 845-938-5706.. 529 C
admissions@usma.edu
MCDONALD, Dennis 417-865-2815.. 265 B
mcdonaldd@evangel.edu
MCDONALD, Dotty 337-550-1357.. 197 K
dmcdonal@lsue.edu
MCDONALD, Eric 864-587-4200.. 433 A
mcdonalde@smcsc.edu
MCDONALD, Francis, X 508-830-5001.. 222 C
fmcdonald@maritime.edu
MCDONALD, Frank 212-346-1800.. 325 J
fmcdonald@pace.edu
MCDONALD, Gary 415-422-2699.... 72 C
mcdonald@usfca.edu
MCDONALD, Ginger 978-478-3400.. 227 C
gmcdonald@northpoint.edu
MCDONALD, Jack 207-602-2562.. 205 F
jmcdonald10@une.edu
MCDONALD, James 612-374-5800.. 246 F
jmcdonald@dunwoody.edu
MCDONALD, James 435-586-7898.. 481 N
mcdonaldj@suu.edu
MCDONALD, James, L 415-451-2810.... 61 D
jmcdonald@sfts.edu
MCDONALD, Jan 864-977-7151.. 431 G
jan.mcdonald@ngu.edu
MCDONALD, Jason, S 503-943-7147.. 396 B
mcdonaja@up.edu
MCDONALD, Jennifer 714-241-6163.... 39 E
jmcdonald@coastline.edu
MCDONALD, Jestinah 740-753-7010.. 369 K
mcdonaldj21@hocking.edug.edu
MCDONALD, Joseph 239-590-1102.. 110 L
jmcdonald@fgcu.edu
MCDONALD, Joseph 256-761-6443...... 7 F
jmcdonald@talladega.edu
MCDONALD, Julia, J 270-745-4629.. 194 D
julia.mcdonald@wku.edu
MCDONALD, Kevin, G 573-882-0004.. 273 D
mcdonaldkg@umsystem.edu
MCDONALD, Kimberly 201-219-9901.. 291 C
kimberly.mcdonald@eicollege.edu
MCDONALD, Kurt 417-690-3200.. 263 E
purch@cofo.edu
MCDONALD, Latrice 601-928-6206.. 259 C
latrice.mcdonald@mgccc.edu
MCDONALD, Leander 701-255-3285.. 362 E
president@uttc.edu
MCDONALD, Lori 949-214-3074.... 41 F
lori.mcdonald@cui.edu
MCDONALD, Lori 801-581-7066.. 481 M
lmcdonald@sa.utah.edu

MCDONALD, Martha 626-914-8534.... 38 D
mmcdonald@citruscollege.edu
MCDONALD, Michael 567-661-7203.. 376 D
michael_mcdonald6@owens.edu
MCDONALD, Michael, A . 269-337-7162.. 235 H
michael.mcdonald@kzoo.edu
MCDONALD, Nancy, H 662-685-4771.. 257 A
nmcdonald@bmc.edu
MCDONALD, Nicholas 978-837-3597.. 225 E
mcdonaldn@merrimack.edu
MCDONALD, Patrick, S 716-880-2345.. 320 D
patrick.s.mcdonald@medaille.edu
MCDONALD, Paul, R 626-966-4576.... 26 J
paulmcdonald@agu.edu
MCDONALD, Pete 706-295-6928.. 121 F
pmcdonald@gntc.edu
MCDONALD, Pete 706-295-6960.. 121 F
pmcdonald@gntc.edu
MCDONALD, Peter 559-278-2403.... 32 F
pmcdonald@csufresno.edu
MCDONALD, Randy 936-468-1010.. 466 H
rmcdonald@sfasu.edu
MCDONALD, Robert 617-732-1605.. 218 C
mcdonaldr@emmanuel.edu
MCDONALD, Ryan 508-541-1664.. 217 G
rmcdonald@dean.edu
MCDONALD, Ryan 812-535-5263.. 166 K
rmcdonald@smwc.edu
MCDONALD, Sallie 671-735-2233.. 530 B
salliemcd@uguam.uog.edu
MCDONALD, Scott 979-458-0996.. 468 B
smcdonald@tamu.edu
MCDONALD, Sharon 309-268-8143.. 141 C
sharon.mcdonald@heartland.edu
MCDONALD, Steven 401-277-4955.. 426 A
smcdonal@risd.edu
MCDONALD, Tammy 361-698-1133.. 457 D
tmcdonal1@delmar.edu
MCDONALD, Thomas 212-752-1530.. 318 F
thomas.mcdonald@limcollege.edu
MCDONALD, Tim 770-533-6991.. 123 L
tmcdonal@laniertech.edu
MCDONALD, Todd 217-786-2253.. 146 E
todd.mcdonald@llcc.edu
MCDONALD, Tracie 406-275-4978.. 278 E
tracie_mcdonald@skc.edu
MCDONALD, William, A 973-748-9000.. 289 H
bill_mcdonald@bloomfield.edu
MCDONALD, William, M . 706-542-7774.. 128 E
bmcdonal@uga.edu
MCDONALD-RASH, Jean . 848-932-7057.. 295 F
jrash@rci.rutgers.edu
MCDONALD-RASH, Jean . 848-932-7057.. 296 B
jean.rash@ofa.rutgers.edu
MCDONALD-WILLEY,
Kristin, D 806-371-5420.. 450 H
k0369065@actx.edu
MCDONNELL, Brian, A 401-341-2185.. 426 C
mcdonneb@salve.edu
MCDONNELL,
Constance, F 570-941-7640.. 422 B
constance.mcdonnell@scranton.edu
MCDONNELL, John 773-481-8253.. 137 I
jmcdonnell@ccc.edu
MCDONNELL, Tom 402-457-2716.. 280 J
tjmcdonnell3@mccneb.edu
MCDONOUGH, Ann 702-774-4619.. 284 L
ann.mcdonough@unlv.edu
MCDONOUGH, David 207-786-6231.. 202 D
dmcdonou@bates.edu
MCDONOUGH, Eileen 305-899-3085.... 96 D
emcdonough@barry.edu
MCDONOUGH, Ellin 803-323-2141.. 435 B
mcdonoughe@winthrop.edu
MCDONOUGH, Michael 908-526-1200.. 295 A
michael.mcdonough@raritanval.edu
MCDONOUGH, Michael 802-447-4658.. 485 B
mmcdonough@svc.edu
MCDONOUGH, JR.,
Peter, J 848-932-7741.. 295 F
mcdonough@oldqueens.rutgers.edu
MCDORMAN, Heather 636-922-8277.. 271 A
hmcdorman@stchas.edu
MCDORMAN, Todd, F 765-361-6183.. 169 C
mcdormat@wabash.edu
MCDOUGAL, Bradley, N 540-464-7637.. 499 E
mcdougalbn@vmi.edu
MCDOUGAL, Doug 801-524-8165.. 480 J
dmcdougal@ldsbc.edu
MCDOUGALD, Sherlock 252-823-5166.. 349 E
mcdougalds@edgecombe.edu
MCDOUGALL, Gerald 573-651-2112.. 272 B
gmcdougall@semo.edu
MCDOUGALL, Gordon, A 804-828-8192.. 496 D
gamcdougall@vcu.edu
MCDOUGLE, James 304-205-6710.. 511 M
james.mcdougle@bridgevalley.edu
MCDOWALL, Douglass 785-460-5484.. 180 C
doug.mcdowall@colbycc.edu
MCDOWALL, Melissa 701-355-8181.. 362 G
mpmcdowall@umary.edu

MCDOWALL LONG,
Kimberly 316-942-4291.. 183 I
longk@newmanu.edu
MCDOWELL, Amy 802-763-7170.. 485 F
amcdowell@vermontlaw.edu
MCDOWELL, Denise 507-457-5300.. 252 G
dmcdowell@winona.edu
MCDOWELL, Jackie 706-236-2202.. 117 F
jmcdowell@berry.edu
MCDOWELL, James 860-512-3603.... 86 E
jmcdowell@manchestercc.edu
MCDOWELL, Jennifer 972-883-6301.. 476 C
jpazik@utdallas.edu
MCDOWELL, Jill 203-285-2007.... 86 C
jmcdowell@gwcc.commnet.edu
MCDOWELL, Katie 913-360-7578.. 178 I
kmcdowell@benedictine.edu
MCDOWELL, Laura, P 828-884-8112.. 342 C
mcdowell@brevard.edu
MCDOWELL, N. Renee 724-653-2212.. 402 F
rmcdowell@dec.edu
MCDOWELL, Pamela 507-786-3011.. 254 P
mcdowell@stolaf.edu
MCDOWELL, Ronald 903-593-8311.. 470 A
rmcdowell@texascollege.edu
MCDOWELL, Scott 615-966-5690.. 441 F
scott.mcdowell@lipscomb.edu
MCDOWELL, JR., T, J 402-465-2149.. 281 K
tmcdowe2@nebrwesleyan.edu
MCDOWELL, Travis 864-488-4615.. 430 H
tmcdowell@limestone.edu
MCDOWELL, Whitney 601-977-7821.. 261 A
wmcdowell@tougaloo.edu
MCDOWN, Linda 405-422-1203.. 387 E
mcdownl@redlandscc.edu
MCDUFFIE, Georgia 718-270-6222.. 309 B
gmcduffie@mec.cuny.edu
MCEACHERN, Daniel (JJ) 704-330-6395.. 348 E
jj.mceachern@cpcc.edu
MCELANEY-JOHNSON,
Ann 310-954-4011.... 53 B
amcelaney@msmu.edu
MCELHANEY, Patrick 706-233-7225.. 127 A
pmcelhaney@shorter.edu
MCELHANY, Ryan 972-825-4701.. 466 D
rmcelhany@sagu.edu
MCELHENY, Candi 225-768-1725.. 199 B
candi.mcelheny@ololcollege.edu
MCELHOE, Dennis 704-922-6476.. 350 A
mcelhoe.dennis@gaston.edu
MCELMURRY, Chauvette . 314-340-3600.. 265 H
mcelmurc@hssu.edu
MCELRATH, Ann 423-614-8105.. 441 B
amcelrath@leeuniversity.edu
MCELRATH, William 732-571-3488.. 292 F
wmcelrat@monmouth.edu
MCELROY, Annie, L 229-225-5200.. 127 G
amcelroy@southernregional.edu
MCELROY, Catherine, C 215-968-8213.. 399 A
mcelroyc@bucks.edu
MCELROY, Clint 704-330-6339.. 348 E
clint.mcelroy@cpcc.edu
MCELROY, Coleetta 408-924-6086.... 35 C
coleetta.mcelroy@sjsu.edu
MCELROY, Diana 909-537-5040.... 34 C
MCELROY, Doug 270-745-7009.. 194 D
doug.mcelroy@wku.edu
MCELROY, Edith 704-330-4386.. 348 E
edith.mcelroy@cpcc.edu
MCELROY, Emily, J 402-559-7078.. 283 A
emily.mcelroy@unmc.edu
MCELROY, Joe 714-966-8500.... 73 G
info@ves.edu
MCELROY, Kathleen 914-633-2201.. 317 B
kmcelroy@iona.edu
MCELROY, Kevin 650-949-6202.... 43 N
mcelroykevin@fhda.edu
MCELROY, Tim 918-683-0641.. 384 G
mcelroyt@nsuok.edu
MCELVEEN, John 706-507-5341.. 119 E
mcelveen_john@columbusstate.edu
MCELWAIN, Karen 708-344-4700.. 146 D
kmcelwain@lincolntech.edu
MCELWEE, Kay, E 217-581-5313.. 139 H
kemcelwee@eiu.edu
MCELWEE, Tim 260-992-5051.. 165 M
tamcelwee@manchester.edu
MCENEANY, Barbara 845-848-4031.. 312 F
barbara.mceneany@dc.edu
MCENEANY, Mary 413-559-5528.. 219 C
memtr@hampshire.edu
MCENTEE, Mary 413-775-1203.. 223 D
mcenteem@gcc.mass.edu
MCENTERGART, Rory 302-793-1101.... 91 E
MCENTIRE, David 801-863-7810.. 482 C
david.mcentire@uvu.edu
MCENTIRE, Tina, M 704-687-7019.. 358 A
tmmcenti@uncc.edu
MCEUEN, Brent 928-428-8201.... 13 B
brent.mceuen@eac.edu

MCEVOY, Ed, M 610-526-1286.. 397 E
ed.mcevoy@theamericancollege.edu
MCEVOY, Robert, T 910-630-7182.. 346 E
mcevoy@methodist.edu
MCEWAN, Anna, E 205-665-6360...... 9 B
mcewanae@montevallo.edu
MCEWEN, Beryl 336-334-7632.. 356 F
mcewenb@ncat.edu
MCEWEN, Ellen 413-265-2395.. 217 D
mcewene@elms.edu
MCEWEN, Ellen, J 512-505-3055.. 459 F
ejmcewen@htu.edu
MCEWEN, Jessie 312-939-4975.. 141 B
jmcewen@harrington.edu
MCEWEN, Jill 920-996-2847.. 523 C
mcewen@fvtc.edu
MCEWEN, Ruth 305-348-3264.. 111 A
ruthann.mcewen@fiu.edu
MCFADDEN, Calvin 203-857-7332.... 87 B
cmcfadden@norwalk.edu
MCFADDEN, David, F 260-982-5226.. 165 M
dfmcfadden@manchester.edu
MCFADDEN, John 305-899-3208.... 96 D
jmcfadden@barry.edu
MCFADDEN, Judy 970-521-6660.... 81 O
judy.mcfadden@njc.edu
MCFADDEN, Lisa 978-542-6000.. 222 D
lisa.mcfadden@salemstate.edu
MCFADDEN, Margaret, T . 207-859-4776.. 202 G
margaret.mcfadden@colby.edu
MCFADDEN, Mark 607-871-2164.. 303 F
mcfaddenm@alfred.edu
MCFADDEN, Mary 845-848-7809.. 312 F
mary.mcfadden@dc.edu
MCFADDEN, Mary Kay 208-885-4200.. 134 G
marykaymcfadden@uidaho.edu
MCFADDEN, Michael 202-806-1280.... 93 A
michael.mcfadden@howard.edu
MCFADDEN, Pam 817-735-2581.. 475 C
pam.mcfadden@unthsc.edu
MCFADDEN, Paul 870-236-6901.... 20 A
pmcfadden@crc.edu
MCFADDEN, Scott 509-527-2205.. 508 G
scott.mcfadden@wallawalla.edu
MCFADDEN, Susan 215-955-2867.. 420 E
susan.mcfadden@jefferson.edu
MCFADDEN, Tanya 517-483-1452.. 237 A
mcfaddet@lcc.edu
MCFADDEN, Thomas 540-636-2900.. 488 D
tmcfadden@christendom.edu
MCFADDEN, Toney, C 423-624-0077.. 439 D
tonym@chattanoogacollege.edu
MCFADDIN, David 859-622-6220.. 188 F
david.mcfaddin@eku.edu
MCFALL, Jan 763-488-0250.. 251 B
jmcfall@nhcc.edu
MCFALLS-SMITH, Tiffany . 270-706-8419.. 189 C
tmcfalls0001@kctcs.edu
MCFARLAND, F. Ozzie 252-398-6484.. 343 G
mcfarf@chowan.edu
MCFARLAND, James 412-731-1177.. 417 J
rptrustees@aol.com
MCFARLAND, Kathryn 813-226-4983.. 108 C
kathryn.mcfarland@saintleo.edu
MCFARLAND, Marielle 870-777-5722.... 24 A
marielle.mcfarland@uacch.edu
MCFARLAND, Michael, S 570-389-4050.. 414 D
mcfarland@bloomu.edu
MCFARLAND, Mike 919-962-2011.. 357 D
mike_mcfarland@unc.edu
MCFARLAND,
Reoungeneria 901-435-1213.. 441 C
reo_mcfarland@loc.edu
MCFARLAND, Robie 252-222-6021.. 348 B
mcfarlandr@carteret.edu
MCFARLAND, Ronald 661-362-3408.... 40 A
ronald.mcfarland@canyons.edu
MCFARLAND, Steven 630-844-5496.. 135 E
smcfarla@aurora.edu
MCFARLAND, Steven, W . 518-327-6436.. 326 B
smcfarland@paulsmiths.edu
MCFARLAND, Tracy 315-279-5215.. 318 C
tmcfarl@keuka.edu
MCFARLANE, Alison 801-957-4103.. 483 A
alison.mcfarlane@lscc.edu
MCFARLANE, Allen, M 212-998-4345.. 324 C
allen.mcfarlane@nyu.edu
MCFARLANE, Michele 208-732-6304.. 133 E
mmcfarlane@csi.edu
MCFARLIN, Dean, B 412-396-1372.. 403 A
mcfarlind@duq.edu
MCFARLIN, Diane, H 352-392-0466.. 112 A
dmcfarlin@ufl.edu
MCFARLIN, Leslie 706-754-8128.. 125 B
lmcfarlin@northgatech.edu
MCFARLING, Patricia, G . 270-852-3257.. 191 C
patmc@kwc.edu
MCFATRIDGE, Michael 310-954-4084.... 53 B
mmcfatridge@msmu.edu
MCFAYDEN, Andy 316-677-9400.. 185 I
amcfayden@watc.edu

MCGREAL, Paul, E .... 402-280-2874.. 279 H
paulmcgreal@creighton.edu
MCGREEVEY, Michael ...... 614-890-3000.. 376 C
mmcgreevey@otterbein.edu
MCGREEVEY, Sean .... 502-272-8426.. 187 A
kmcgreevey@bellarmine.edu
MCGREEVY, Bill .... 303-914-6634.... 82 I
bill.mcgreevy@rrcc.edu
MCGREEVY, Jeanette .... 515-643-6717.. 175 B
jmcgreevy@mercydesmoines.org
MCGREEVY, John, T .... 574-631-6642.. 168 B
mcgreevy.5@nd.edu
MCGREGOR, Kyle, W ...... 254-968-9890.. 467 F
mcgregor@tarleton.edu
MCGREGOR, Patricia .... 860-297-2120.... 89 B
patricia.mcgregor@trincoll.edu
MCGREGOR, Tiffany .... 610-361-2487.. 411 E
mcgregot@neumann.edu
MCGREGOR, Wilson, E .... 254-710-2663.. 452 H
bud_mcgregor@baylor.edu
MCGREGORY, Richard ...... 262-472-4985.. 521 F
mcgregor@uww.edu
MCGREW, Kevin .... 218-723-6198.. 245 J
kmcgrew@css.edu
MCGREW, Martha .... 505-272-2165.. 302 F
mmcgrew@salud.unm.edu
MCGREW, Paula .... 304-473-8461.. 515 B
mcgrew_p@wwc.edu
MCGREW, Shea .... 419-372-7706.. 364 E
smcgrew@bgsu.edu
MCGRIFF, Ilona .... 415-239-3677.... 38 E
imcgriff@ccsf.edu
MCGRIFF, Manuel .... 254-267-7010.. 463 K
mmcgriff@rangercollege.edu
MCGRISKEN, June .... 718-489-5352.. 328 D
jmcgrisken@sfc.edu
MCGUCKIN, Tammy .... 262-595-2571.. 520 F
mcguckin@uwp.edu
MCGUFFEY, Michael, J .... 304-696-3648.. 513 D
mcguffey@marshall.edu
MCGUFFIN, Kurt .... 816-271-5623.. 269 C
kmcguffin@missouriwestern.edu
MCGUIGAN, Bridget .... 610-341-5955.. 403 B
bmcguiga@eastern.edu
MCGUINESS, Ilona .... 845-569-3203.. 322 B
ilona.mcguiness@msmc.edu
MCGUINN, Ellen .... 215-248-7163.. 400 H
mcguinne@chc.edu
MCGUINNESS, Maureen .. 940-565-2648.. 475 A
moe@unt.edu
MCGUINNESS, Nina .... 425-602-3041.. 501 D
nmcguinness@bastyr.edu
MCGUINNESS, Paul .... 312-341-2006.. 152 H
pmcguinness01@roosevelt.edu
MCGUINNESS, Scott .... 724-503-1001.. 422 H
smcguinness@washjeff.edu
MCGUINNESS,
Thomas, P .... 617-552-3260.. 216 C
thomas.mcguinness@bc.edu
MCGUIRE, Brittany .... 256-766-6610...... 4 B
bmcguire@hcu.edu
MCGUIRE, Catherine .... 559-737-5410.... 40 E
catherinemc@cos.edu
MCGUIRE, Christine .... 617-353-4176.. 216 E
chmcguir@bu.edu
MCGUIRE, David, T .... 435-586-7755.. 481 N
mcguire@suu.edu
MCGUIRE, Ellen .... 570-504-7000.. 400 I
emcguire@tcmc.edu
MCGUIRE, Jamie .... 902-403-3166.. 519 G
jamie.mcguire@snc.edu
MCGUIRE, Jamie .... 336-838-6482.. 354 C
jamie.mcguire@wilkescc.edu
MCGUIRE, Jane .... 615-230-3204.. 447 C
jane.mcguire@volstate.edu
MCGUIRE, Kathleen .... 508-541-1615.. 217 G
kmcguire@dean.edu
MCGUIRE, Mark, T .... 740-284-5249.. 368 L
mmcguire@franciscan.edu
MCGUIRE, Maureen .... 509-313-6137.. 504 A
mcguirem@gonzaga.edu
MCGUIRE, Michael .... 303-871-3518.... 84 B
mmcguire@du.edu
MCGUIRE, Michael, J .... 785-670-1763.. 185 H
michael.mcguire@washburn.edu
MCGUIRE, Molly .... 205-726-4315...... 6 E
msmcguir@samford.edu
MCGUIRE, Nona, S .... 614-236-6908.. 364 N
nmcguire@capital.edu
MCGUIRE, Patricia, A ...... 202-884-9050.... 94 A
mcguirep@trinitydc.edu
MCGUIRE, Rachel, A .... 585-340-9596.. 310 F
rmcguire@crcds.edu
MCGUIRE, Rachel, L .... 641-422-4104.. 175 E
mcguirac@niacc.edu
MCGUIRE, Ruth, A .... 651-631-5343.. 256 A
ramcguire@unwsp.edu
MCGUIRE, Shirley .... 415-422-6136.... 72 C
mcguire@usfca.edu
MCGUIRE, Venus .... 903-463-8698.. 458 H
mcguirev@grayson.edu
MCGUIRL-HADLEY, Joy ... 386-822-7500.. 113 B
jhadley@stetson.edu
MCGURE, David .... 561-697-9200.. 127 D
ddmcguire@southuniversity.edu
MCGURGAN, Susan .... 513-231-2223.. 363 K
smcgurgan@athenaeum.edu
MCGURIMAN, Joseph .... 215-641-6605.. 410 L
jmcgurim@mc3.edu
MCGURK, Mark .... 432-552-2700.. 478 B
mcgurk_m@utpb.edu
MCGURN, Joseph, P .... 740-283-6278.. 368 L
jmcgurn@franciscan.edu
MCGURR, Paul .... 970-247-6737.... 80 D
mcgurr_p@fortlewis.edu
MCGURREN, Cynthia .... 978-542-7591.. 222 D
cmcgurren@salemstate.edu
MCGURTY, Thomas, S ..... 617-627-3264.. 228 H
thomas.mcgurty@tufts.edu
MCGUTHRY, John, W ...... 909-869-6442.... 31 J
jwmcguthry@cpp.edu
MCHALE, Barbara .... 215-641-5521.. 404 G
mchale.b@gmercyu.edu
MCHALE, JR., William .... 717-358-3870.. 403 J
william.mchale@fandm.edu
MCHAN, Elizabeth, C .... 218-299-3298.. 246 A
emchan@cord.edu
MCHANEY, Eric .... 251-981-3771...... 2 I
eric.mchaney@columbiasouthern.edu
MCHARGUE, Jackie .... 828-250-2370.. 357 C
jmchargu@unca.edu
MCHARRIS, Michael .... 315-792-5489.. 321 G
mmcharris@mvcc.edu
MCHATTON, Patricia, A .... 956-665-3627.. 476 E
patricia.mchatton@utrgv.edu
MCHENRY, Bart .... 949-582-4907.... 65 G
bmchenry@saddleback.edu
MCHENRY, Erin .... 949-582-4481.... 65 G
emchenry@saddleback.edu
MCHENRY, Lepaine .... 405-585-4450.. 385 B
lepaine.mchenry@okbu.edu
MCHENRY, Stephanie .... 216-687-3673.. 366 I
s.y.mchenry@csuohio.edu
MCHENRY, William .... 903-223-3015.. 469 C
william.mchenry@tamut.edu
MCHORNEY, Mark .... 630-829-6150.. 135 F
mmchorney@ben.edu
MCHUGH, Elizabeth .... 360-867-6808.. 503 G
mchughe@evergreen.edu
MCHUGH, John .... 704-748-5213.. 350 A
mchugh.john@gaston.edu
MCHUGH, Kevin .... 207-786-6341.. 202 D
kmchugh@bates.edu
MCHUGH, Mary .... 978-837-5125.. 225 E
mary.mchugh@merrimack.edu
MCHUGH, Mary .... 845-848-7407.. 312 F
mary.mchugh@dc.edu
MCHUGH, Shelley .... 402-465-2123.. 281 K
smchugh@nebrwesleyan.edu
MCHUGH, Tracy .... 630-889-6607.. 149 G
tmchugh@nuhs.edu
MCILHAGGA, Doug .... 618-650-3605.. 155 A
dmcilha@siue.edu
MCILHENNEY, Sharon ...... 717-299-7754.. 420 C
mcilhenney@stevenscollege.edu
MCILLECE, Michelle .... 319-399-8844.. 170 G
mmcillec@coe.edu
MCILNAY, Sandy .... 816-604-4616.. 267 K
sandy.mcilnay@mcckc.edu
MCILROY, Julia .... 208-885-6123.. 134 G
juliam@uidaho.edu
MCILVANE, Amy .... 770-426-2648.. 124 B
mcilvane@life.edu
MCINALLY, David, W .... 319-399-8686.. 170 G
dmcinally@coe.edu
MCINERNEY, Todd .... 203-932-7031.... 90 A
tmcinerney@newhaven.edu
MCINNES, Robert .... 704-334-6882.. 343 D
rmcinnes@charlottechristian.edu
MCINNIS, James, P .... 601-643-8488.. 257 D
jp.mcinnis@colin.edu
MCINNIS, Robert, L .... 704-216-6400.. 346 A
rmcinnis@livingstone.edu
MCINNIS, W. Dale .... 910-410-1806.. 352 C
wdmcinnis@richmondcc.edu
MCINTEE, Justin .... 714-556-3610.... 73 B
justin.mcintee@vanguard.edu
MCINTIRE, Mary .... 713-348-2599.. 464 E
maryb@rice.edu
MCINTIRE, OSFS,
Timothy .... 610-282-1100.. 402 B
timothy.mcintire@desales.edu
MCINTOSH, Cecilia, A ..... 423-439-4221.. 444 F
mcintosc@etsu.edu
MCINTOSH, Charles .... 352-854-2322.... 97 R
mcintosc@cf.edu
MCINTOSH, Craig .... 518-276-3992.. 327 B
mcintc@rpi.edu
MCINTOSH, Daniel .... 303-871-3712.... 84 B
daniel.mcintosh@du.edu
MCINTOSH, Gary .... 425-889-7790.. 505 E
gary.mcintosh@northwestu.edu
MCINTOSH, Gayle .... 253-879-3905.. 508 D
gmcintosh@pugetsound.edu
MCINTOSH, Glenn .... 248-370-4200.. 239 K
mcintosh@oakland.edu
MCINTOSH, Joe .... 817-515-5377.. 467 A
clifford.mcintosh@tccd.edu
MCINTOSH, Joe, E .... 336-734-7297.. 349 G
jmcintosh@forsythtech.edu
MCINTOSH, John .... 256-331-5323...... 6 A
jmcintosh@nwscc.edu
MCINTOSH, Joshua .... 207-786-6219.. 202 D
jmcintos@bates.edu
MCINTOSH, Julie .... 419-434-4062.. 379 E
mcintosh@findlay.edu
MCINTOSH, Kathy .... 858-635-4772.... 25 K
kmcintosh@alliant.edu
MCINTOSH, Katy .... 714-556-3610.... 73 B
katy.mcintosh@vanguard.edu
MCINTOSH, Keith .... 607-274-1530.. 317 D
kmcintosh@ithaca.edu
MCINTOSH, Keith, J .... 804-289-8467.. 495 G
kmcintosh@richmond.edu
MCINTOSH, Mark .... 573-882-9500.. 273 E
mcintoshm@umsystem.edu
MCINTOSH, Tanisha .... 734-432-5755.. 237 D
tmcintosh@madonna.edu
MCINTOSH, Tim .... 541-683-5141.. 391 E
tmcintosh@gutenberg.edu
MCINTOSH-DOTY, Mikail 512-313-3000.. 455 F
mikail.doty@concordia.edu
MCINTURF, Robert .... 940-565-4204.. 475 A
robert.mcinturf@unt.edu
MCINTYRE, Ellen, C .... 704-687-8722.. 358 A
ellen.mcintyre@uncc.edu
MCINTYRE, Faye, S .... 678-839-6467.. 129 E
fmcintyr@westga.edu
MCINTYRE, Helen, M ...... 205-934-8132...... 8 E
hmcintyre@uab.edu
MCINTYRE, Jacqueline .... 516-364-0808.. 323 B
jmcintyre@nycollege.edu
MCINTYRE, Janet .... 503-491-7589.. 392 F
janet.mcintyre@mhcc.edu
MCINTYRE, Karen, E .... 715-836-5171.. 520 A
mcintyke@uwec.edu
MCINTYRE, Kevin .... 217-424-6251.. 148 D
kmmcintyre@millikin.edu
MCINTYRE, Kevin .... 806-743-7425.. 472 D
kevin.mcintyre@ttuhsc.edu
MCINTYRE, Leonard .... 803-793-5101.. 429 D
mcintyrel@denmarktech.edu
MCINTYRE, Susan, H ...... 252-222-6230.. 348 B
mcintyres@carteret.edu
MCINTYRE, William, A .... 603-882-6923.. 286 E
bmcintyre@ccsnh.edu
MCINTYRE, Willie .... 910-672-1157.. 356 E
wmcintyre@uncfsu.edu
MCISAAC, Penny, J .... 561-868-3055.. 106 D
mcisaacp@palmbeachstate.edu
MCIVER, John .... 208-885-6651.. 134 G
jmciver@uidaho.edu
MCJANNET, Cathy .... 619-216-6762.... 66 E
cmcjannet@swccd.edu
MCJUNKIN, Gayle .... 507-222-4337.. 245 C
gmcjunki@carleton.edu
MCKAIN, Joshua .... 617-236-8854.. 218 G
jmckain@fisher.edu
MCKAMEY, Sheldon .... 406-994-6342.. 277 C
smckamey@montana.edu
MCKANN, Helen .... 804-594-1523.. 497 D
hmckann@jtcc.edu
MCKANNA, Nate .... 214-887-5041.. 457 C
nmckanna@dts.edu
MCKAY, Ashley, M .... 812-941-2075.. 163 F
atronc01@ius.edu
MCKAY, Bill .... 509-542-5531.. 502 G
bmckay@columbiabasin.edu
MCKAY, Cheryl, A .... 573-341-7060.. 274 B
cherylan@mst.edu
MCKAY, Janet .... 203-837-8460.... 85 I
mckayj@wcsu.edu
MCKAY, Jeffrey .... 207-778-7009.. 205 A
jeffrey.d.mckay@maine.edu
MCKAY, Kerri .... 313-664-7441.. 232 G
kmckay@collegeforcreativestudies.edu
MCKAY, Kevin .... 425-640-1547.. 503 E
kevin.mckay@edcc.edu
MCKAY, Kimberly .... 432-335-6683.. 463 B
kmckay@odessa.edu
MCKAY, Kimberly .... 956-872-2096.. 465 H
kjmckay@southtexascollege.edu
MCKAY, Michael, E .... 609-258-5491.. 294 D
mckay@princeton.edu
MCKAY, Michelle .... 541-881-5599.. 395 E
mmckay@tvcc.cc
MCKAY, Norman .... 404-364-8322.. 125 F
nmckay@oglethorpe.edu
MCKAY, Patricia .... 301-295-3185.. 528 G
patricia.mckay@usuhs.edu
MCKAY, Richard .... 281-998-6150.. 465 B
richard.mckay@sjcd.edu
MCKAY, Scott .... 870-235-4290.... 22 F
semckay@saumag.edu
MCKAY, Shaun, L .... 631-451-4736.. 336 D
mckays@sunysuffolk.edu
MCKAY, Tamara .... 810-762-3456.. 242 B
tamaramc@umflint.edu
MCKAYLE, Camille, A .... 340-693-1200.. 539 C
cmckayl@uvi.edu
MCKECHNIE, Dan .... 916-484-8320.... 51 A
mckechd@arc.losrios.edu
MCKECHNIE, Janna .... 701-858-3373.. 360 F
janna.mckechnie@minotstateu.edu
MCKECHNIE, Sally .... 225-578-2307.. 197 I
smckechnie@lsu.edu
MCKECHNIE, Susan, E ..... 410-706-7776.. 211 F
smckechnie@umaryland.edu
MCKEE, Andy .... 260-399-7700.. 168 D
amckee@sf.edu
MCKEE, Anne .... 865-981-8298.. 441 H
anne.mckee@maryvillecollege.edu
MCKEE, Bruce, G .... 641-422-4348.. 175 E
mckeebru@niacc.edu
MCKEE, Diann, E .... 812-237-2372.. 162 A
diann.mckee@indstate.edu
MCKEE, Eugenia .... 314-529-9509.. 267 B
gmckee@maryville.edu
MCKEE, J, P .... 803-323-2205.. 435 B
mckeej@winthrop.edu
MCKEE, John, C .... 409-747-9080.. 478 A
jcmckee@utmb.edu
MCKEE, Jonathon .... 808-984-3213.. 132 D
jvmckee@hawaii.edu
MCKEE, Joseph .... 662-621-4156.. 257 B
MCKEE, Kasey .... 636-922-8472.. 271 A
kmckee@stchas.edu
MCKEE, Larry .... 856-351-2605.. 296 L
lmckee@salemcc.edu
MCKEE, Lauren .... 408-274-7900.... 62 D
lauren.mckee@evc.edu
MCKEE, Lori .... 575-646-2172.. 300 J
lomckee@nmsu.edu
MCKEE, Lori .... 419-755-4828.. 373 G
lmckee@ncstatecollege.edu
MCKEE, Marites .... 808-687-7014.. 130 H
mmckee@hpu.edu
MCKEE, Mark .... 419-448-2194.. 369 G
mmckee@heidelberg.com
MCKEE, Michael .... 352-392-2402.. 112 A
mckee@ufl.edu
MCKEE, Mike .... 386-752-1822.. 100 L
mike.mckee@fgc.edu
MCKEE, Misty .... 740-366-9383.. 365 D
mckee.614@osu.edu
MCKEE, Richard .... 432-685-4734.. 461 H
rmckee@midland.edu
MCKEE, Sara .... 317-921-4607.. 164 F
smckee15@ivytech.edu
MCKEE, Suzanne .... 334-683-2347...... 5 G
smckee@marionmilitary.edu
MCKEE, William .... 615-547-1311.. 439 H
bmckee@cumberland.edu
MCKEE-LEONE, Virginia ... 951-222-8053.... 59 C
virginia.mckee-leone@rcc.edu
MCKEEGAN, John .... 503-883-2202.. 392 B
jmckeeg@linfield.edu
MCKEEN, Jerry .... 805-493-3139.... 31 C
jmckeen@callutheran.edu
MCKEEVER, Diane, M ...... 312-942-6830.. 153 B
diane_m_mckeever@rush.edu
MCKEEVER, Diane, M ...... 312-942-6950.. 153 B
diane_m_mckeever@rush.edu
MCKEEVER, Kerry .... 603-899-1130.. 287 A
mckeeverk@franklinpierce.edu
MCKEEVER, Matt .... 303-797-5859.... 76 J
matthew.mckeever@arapahoe.edu
MCKEEVER, Molly .... 530-226-4932.... 64 H
mmckeever@simpsonu.edu
MCKEEVER, William, P .... 716-829-7807.. 313 A
mckeever@dyc.edu
MCKELLIP, Mark .... 714-816-0366.... 68 E
mark.mckellip@trident.edu
MCKELLIPS, Stephen .... 901-678-5140.. 445 C
sjmckllp@memphis.edu
MCKELLIPS, Steve .... 901-678-5140.. 445 C
sjmckllp@memphis.edu
MCKELVEY, Kathryn .... 419-267-1327.. 374 A
kmckelvey@northweststate.edu
MCKELVEY, Steve .... 507-786-3421.. 254 P
mckelvey@stolaf.edu
MCKELVIE, OSF, Roberta 610-790-2876.. 397 D
roberta.mckelvie@alvernia.edu
MCKENDREE, Lynda .... 713-525-2151.. 475 J
mckendla@stthom.edu
MCKENDRICKS, John .... 775-849-4983.. 392 G
jmckendricks@multnomah.edu
MCKENNA, Catherine .... 718-405-3233.. 310 H
catherine.mckenna@mountsaintvincent.
edu
MCKENNA,
Charles (Doug) .... 202-885-2210.... 91 J
dmckenna@american.edu

MCKENNA, Corey .... 509-777-4269.. 509 H
cmckenna@whitworth.edu
MCKENNA, Crichton .... 207-453-5155.. 203 K
cmckenna@kvcc.me.edu
MCKENNA, David .... 903-886-5761.. 468 D
david.mckenna@sscserv.com
MCKENNA, Heidi .... 510-883-7160.... 42 F
hmckenna@dspt.edu
MCKENNA, Kevin .... 508-793-7468.. 217 B
kmckenna@clarku.edu
MCKENNA, Kevin .... 914-395-2510.. 329 K
kmckenna@sarahlawrence.edu
MCKENNA, Kristen .... 603-443-4200.. 286 G
kpmckenna@ccsnh.edu
MCKENNA, Megan .... 440-375-7508.. 371 E
mmckenna@lec.edu
MCKENNA, Megan .... 814-824-3355.. 410 H
mmckenna@mercyhurst.edu
MCKENNA, Patrick .... 404-894-6088.. 121 D
pat.mckenna@carnegie.gatech.edu
MCKENNA, Robert, E .... 860-444-8503.. 529 A
robert.e.mckenna@uscg.mil
MCKENNA, Sheila .... 412-392-3450.. 417 F
smckenna@pointpark.edu
MCKENNA, Timothy, J ..... 319-273-3241.. 170 A
tim.mckenna@uni.edu
MCKENNA FRAZIER,
Lynnette, M .... 260-399-7700.. 168 D
lfrazier@sf.edu
MCKENNA-JONES, Amy .. 573-518-2146.. 268 E
mjones@mineralarea.edu
MCKENNEY, William .... 574-239-8390.. 161 N
wmckenney@hcc-nd.edu
MCKENZIE, Amanda .... 478-289-2088.. 120 C
amckenzie@ega.edu
MCKENZIE, Andre, A .... 718-990-1892.. 328 F
mckenzia@stjohns.edu
MCKENZIE, Barbara, J ..... 724-847-6610.. 404 B
bmckenzi@geneva.edu
MCKENZIE, Bruce .... 937-778-7855.. 368 E
bmckenzie@edisonohio.edu
MCKENZIE, Connie, L ..... 757-965-8500.. 489 B
mckenzcl@evms.edu
MCKENZIE, Elizabeth .... 617-573-8705.. 228 G
emckenzi@suffolk.edu
MCKENZIE, Fred, R .... 630-947-8930.. 135 E
mckenzie@aurora.edu
MCKENZIE, JoAnn .... 404-727-6052.. 120 E
jmckenz@emory.edu
MCKENZIE, Joy .... 615-383-4848.. 449 G
jmckenzie@watkins.edu
MCKENZIE, Laura .... 208-282-2661.. 133 H
mckelaur@isu.edu
MCKENZIE, Lester .... 931-372-3073.. 445 B
lmckenzie@tetech.edu
MCKENZIE, Mark .... 651-603-6208.. 246 B
mckenzie@csp.edu
MCKENZIE, Natalie, E ...... 530-226-4103.... 64 H
nmckenzie@simpsonu.edu
MCKENZIE, Pia .... 919-807-6951.. 347 B
mckenziep@nccommunitycolleges.edu
MCKENZIE, Rene .... 541-956-7129.. 394 J
rmckenzie@roguecc.edu
MCKENZIE, Sheri .... 415-703-9535.... 29 K
smckenzie@cca.edu
MCKENZIE, Vandeen .... 575-439-3717.. 301 A
vmckenzi@nmsu.edu
MCKENZIE, Vandeen .... 575-439-3711.. 301 A
vmckenzi@nmsu.edu
MCKENZIE, W. Shelby ..... 225-578-4126.. 197 H
wmcken1@lsu.edu
MCKEON, Judith, O .... 540-985-9083.. 491 A
jomckeon@jchs.edu
MCKEON, Margaret, J ...... 336-334-3749.. 358 B
mjmckeon@uncg.edu
MCKEON, Michael .... 925-631-4552.... 59 I
mfm4@stmarys-ca.edu
MCKEOWN, Adrienne .... 605-274-5530.. 435 E
adrienne.mckeown@augie.edu
MCKEOWN, Anna .... 615-383-4848.. 449 G
amckeown@watkins.edu
MCKEOWN, Carol, M .... 585-292-2500.. 321 J
cmckeown2@monroecc.edu
MCKEOWN, Robert .... 716-614-6271.. 324 D
mckeown@niagaracc.suny.edu
MCKERNAN, Sarah .... 620-341-5551.. 180 G
smckerna@emporia.edu
MCKERNAN, Steve .... 505-272-2071.. 302 F
smckernan@salud.unm.edu
MCKESSON, Leslie .... 828-448-3156.. 354 B
lmckesson@wpcc.edu
MCKETHAN, Lisa, H .... 254-710-1011.. 452 H
lisa_mckethan@baylor.edu
MCKIBBEN, Nile .... 608-249-6611.. 516 M
nmckibben@herzing.edu
MCKIBBENS, Donna .... 617-879-2242.. 229 G
dmckibbens@wheelock.edu
MCKIBBIN, Barbara .... 704-669-4116.. 348 F
mckibbin@clevelandcc.edu
MCKIEL, Allen .... 503-838-8886.. 396 E
mckiela@wou.edu
MCKIERNAN, Jack .... 908-737-0600.. 292 C
jmckiern@kean.edu
MCKIM, Dana .... 704-463-3409.. 354 F
dana.mckim@pfeiffer.edu
MCKINLEY, Bob .... 817-598-6256.. 479 E
bmckinley@wc.edu
MCKINLEY, Elizabeth .... 816-501-3767.. 262 G
elizabeth.mckinley@avila.edu
MCKINLEY, Kathy .... 919-536-7244.. 349 D
mckinleyk@durhamtech.edu
MCKINLEY, Kristin, L .... 920-832-6532.. 517 E
kristin.l.mckinley@lawrence.edu
MCKINLEY, Patricia .... 713-525-3575.. 475 J
mckinley@stthom.edu
MCKINLEY, Rita .... 216-987-2044.. 367 E
rita.mckinley@tri-c.edu
MCKINLEY, Ronald, B ...... 409-772-2636.. 478 A
rbmckinl@utmb.edu
MCKINLEY, Scott .... 206-467-5481.. 227 B
MCKINNEY, Andre .... 404-880-6791.. 118 K
amckinney@cau.edu
MCKINNEY, Anya .... 865-251-1800.. 444 A
library@southcollegetn.edu
MCKINNEY, Bryan .... 870-245-5513.... 21 E
mckinneyb@obu.edu
MCKINNEY, Bryan .... 870-245-5250.... 21 E
mckinneyb@obu.edu
MCKINNEY, David, C .... 888-491-8686.... 74 I
MCKINNEY, David, C .... 828-398-7124.. 347 D
dmckinney@abtech.edu
MCKINNEY, Dee .... 478-289-2062.. 120 C
dmckinney@ega.edu
MCKINNEY, Donald, W ..... 252-334-2084.. 346 F
don.mckinney@macuniversity.edu
MCKINNEY, Frances, H .... 410-651-6668.. 212 B
fhmckinney@umes.edu
MCKINNEY, Gail .... 303-797-5647.... 76 J
gail.mckinney@arapahoe.edu
MCKINNEY, Jill .... 317-940-8312.. 159 K
jsmckinn@butler.edu
MCKINNEY, Joan, C .... 270-789-5214.. 187 G
jmckinney@campbellsville.edu
MCKINNEY, Joe .... 602-291-2237.. 388 K
joe.mckinney@stratatech.com
MCKINNEY, Marion .... 610-436-3307.. 416 C
mmckinney@wcupa.edu
MCKINNEY, Mica .... 435-797-1156.. 482 B
mica.mckinney@usu.edu
MCKINNEY, Michael .... 724-589-2600.. 420 D
mmckinney@thiel.edu
MCKINNEY, Michele .... 303-860-5600.... 83 J
michele.mckinney@cu.edu
MCKINNEY, Monica .... 919-760-8056.. 346 D
mckinneym@meredith.edu
MCKINNEY, Paul .... 662-325-7428.. 259 D
kpm137@msstate.edu
MCKINNEY, Rhonda .... 509-963-1391.. 501 K
rhonda.mckinney@cwu.edu
MCKINNEY, Richard, L ..... 785-864-3136.. 185 D
rlm@ku.edu
MCKINNEY, Robert .... 734-995-7328.. 232 I
robert.mckinney@cuaa.edu
MCKINNEY, Scott .... 828-298-3325.. 359 F
MCKINNEY, Shannon .... 813-988-5131.. 100 F
mckinney@floridacollege.edu
MCKINNEY, Shortie .... 978-934-4460.. 221 A
shortie_mckinney@uml.edu
MCKINNON, Brad .... 256-766-6610...... 4 B
bmckinnon@hcu.edu
MCKINNON, Keith .... 214-860-3633.. 456 F
kmckinnon@dcccd.edu
MCKINNON, Laura .... 972-238-6107.. 456 H
lauramckinnon@dcccd.edu
MCKINNON, Maureen .... 816-501-4831.. 270 J
maureen.mckinnon@rockhurst.edu
MCKINNON, Theresa .... 615-327-6185.. 442 A
tmckinnon@mmc.edu
MCKINNON, Will .... 301-863-8922.. 482 C
will.mckinnon@uvu.edu
MCKINNY, Charles .... 361-698-1794.. 457 D
cmckinn@delmar.edu
MCKINSEY-MABRY,
Kimberly .... 585-262-1616.. 321 J
kmckinseymabry@monroecc.edu
MCKINSTRIE, Natalie .... 845-569-3355.. 322 B
natalie.mckinstrie@msmc.edu
MCKINTYRE, Katherine .... 251-344-1203...... 3 J
MCKINZIE, Steve .... 704-637-4666.. 343 B
smckinzie@catawba.edu
MCKINZIE, Wes .... 405-425-5132.. 385 C
wes.mckinzie@oc.edu
MCKIRDY, Pam .... 434-791-5618.. 487 C
pmckirdy@averett.edu
MCKISIC, Bethaney .... 304-473-8017.. 515 B
mckisic_b@wvwc.edu
MCKISSON, Kevin .... 281-998-6150.. 464 J
kevin.mckisson@sjcd.edu
MCKISSON, Kevin .... 281-998-6150.. 465 A
kevin.mckisson@sjcd.edu
MCKISSON, Kevin .... 281-998-6150.. 465 B
kevin.mckisson@sjcd.edu
MCKITTRICK, Jerry .... 314-744-5345.. 268 F
mckittrickj@mobap.edu
MCKNIGHT, Carrie .... 650-508-3717.... 54 J
cmknight@ndnu.edu
MCKNIGHT, Cynthia .... 440-684-6102.. 380 F
cmcknight@ursuline.edu
MCKNIGHT, Frank .... 330-490-7226.. 380 J
fmcknight@walsh.edu
MCKNIGHT, Irby .... 972-825-4662.. 466 D
imcknight@sagu.edu
MCKNIGHT, Natalie .... 617-353-2852.. 216 E
njmck@bu.edu
MCKNIGHT, Oscar .... 419-289-5065.. 363 J
omcknight@ashland.edu
MCKNIGHT, Sandra .... 216-987-4832.. 367 E
sandra.mcknight@tri-c.edu
MCKNIGHT, Steven, H ..... 571-858-3002.. 499 F
shm@vt.edu
MCKNIGHT-TUTEIN,
Gillian .... 303-404-5497.... 80 E
gillian.mcknight-tutein@frontrange.edu
MCKONE, Kevin .... 601-643-8369.. 257 D
kevin.mckone@colin.edu
MCKOWN, Johnette .... 254-299-8601.. 461 E
jmckown@mclennan.edu
MCKOY, Cynthia .... 910-879-5566.. 347 F
cmckoy@bladencc.edu
MCLACKEN, Susan .... 401-232-6881.. 424 K
smcdonald@bryant.edu
MCLAIN, Chippy .... 423-585-6956.. 447 D
chippy.mclain@ws.edu
MCLAIN, Jeff, L .... 330-672-2222.. 370 I
jmclain3@kent.edu
MCLANE, Anne, P .... 214-648-5617.. 478 C
anne.mclane@utsouthwestern.edu
MCLANEY, Carl .... 323-563-4854.... 37 G
carlmclaney@cdrewu.edu
MCLARAN, Diane .... 503-316-3229.. 390 E
diane.mclaran@chemeketa.edu
MCLAREN, Donna .... 585-594-6114.. 327 D
mclaren_donna@roberts.edu
MCLAREN, Kate .... 508-531-6502.. 221 C
kate.mclaren@bridgew.edu
MCLARTY, Bruce, D .... 501-279-4274.... 20 D
president@harding.edu
MCLAUGHLIN, Allen .... 337-439-5765.. 195 A
allen@deltatech.edu
MCLAUGHLIN, Audrey .... 603-668-2211.. 287 I
a.mclaughlin1@snhu.edu
MCLAUGHLIN, Carl .... 315-470-7256.. 305 H
carlmclaughlin@crouse.org
MCLAUGHLIN, Chris .... 541-962-3516.. 391 C
cjmclaughlin@eou.edu
MCLAUGHLIN, David, B ..... 419-289-5555.. 363 J
dmclaugh@ashland.edu
MCLAUGHLIN,
Edward, K .... 804-828-6692.. 496 D
athleticsdir@vcu.edu
MCLAUGHLIN, Eric .... 626-350-1500.... 30 D
MCLAUGHLIN,
Francis, K .... 718-817-4300.. 314 G
mclaughlin@fordham.edu
MCLAUGHLIN, Gerald .... 215-641-5550.. 404 G
mclaughlin.g@gmercyu.edu
MCLAUGHLIN, Henry, J .... 646-660-6000.. 307 A
henry.mclaughlin@baruch.cuny.edu
MCLAUGHLIN, James .... 518-388-6284.. 338 H
mclaughj@union.edu
MCLAUGHLIN, Jane .... 714-432-5531.... 39 G
jmclaughlin@occ.cccd.edu
MCLAUGHLIN, John .... 401-456-8235.. 425 E
jmclaughlin@ric.edu
MCLAUGHLIN, Joyce .... 978-934-4237.. 221 A
joyce_mclaughlin@uml.edu
MCLAUGHLIN, Karen .... 603-862-2140.. 288 C
karen.mclaughlin@unh.edu
MCLAUGHLIN, Keith .... 708-656-8000.. 149 A
keith.mclaughlin@morton.edu
MCLAUGHLIN,
Kelly Anne .... 315-781-4357.. 316 C
mclaughlin@hws.edu
MCLAUGHLIN, Kevin .... 415-503-6253.... 61 C
kmclaughlin@sfcm.edu
MCLAUGHLIN, Kevin .... 401-863-9525.. 424 J
kevin_mclaughlin@brown.edu
MCLAUGHLIN, Laurie, L .. 612-626-1499.. 255 H
mclau001@umn.edu
MCLAUGHLIN, LaVerne ... 229-430-4799.. 115 K
laverne.mclaughlin@asurams.edu
MCLAUGHLIN, Margaret .. 386-752-1822.. 100 L
maggie.mclaughlin@fgc.edu
MCLAUGHLIN, Mary .... 513-745-3409.. 331 I
mclaughlin@xavier.edu
MCLAUGHLIN, Mary, W .... 860-832-0065.... 85 F
mclaughlinm@ccsu.edu
MCLAUGHLIN, Mary .... 603-526-3755.. 285 L
mmclaughlin@colby-sawyer.edu
MCLAUGHLIN, Mary, R ..... 518-454-5170.. 311 B
mclaughr@strose.edu
MCLAUGHLIN, Matt .... 207-974-4869.. 203 J
mmclaughlin@emcc.edu
MCLAUGHLIN, Maureen .. 215-248-7137.. 400 H
MCLAUGHLIN, Mike .... 319-398-4947.. 174 I
mclaug@kirkwood.edu
MCLAUGHLIN, Nora .... 503-777-7774.. 394 I
nora.mclaughlin@reed.edu
MCLAUGHLIN, Patrick, A 260-481-6128.. 163 C
mclaughp@ipfw.edu
MCLAUGHLIN, Robert ...... 713-798-4613.. 452 G
rmclaughlin@bcm.edu
MCLAUGHLIN, Robert, P . 973-761-9545.. 297 A
MCLAUGHLIN, Sandee ...... 805-546-3116.... 41 L
smclaugh@cuesta.edu
MCLAUGHLIN, Sean, M .. 614-823-1576.. 376 C
smclaughlin@otterbein.edu
MCLAUGHLIN, Steve .... 612-874-3759.. 247 M
smclaughlin@mcad.edu
MCLAURIN, Lisa, H .... 919-209-2178.. 350 G
lhmclaurin@johnstoncc.edu
MCLAWHORN, Toni, D .... 540-375-2303.. 493 H
mclawhorn@roanoke.edu
MCLAY, Deidre .... 831-656-2511.. 528 D
dmclay@nps.edu
MCLEAN, Amber .... 906-635-2382.. 236 J
amclean@lssu.edu
MCLEAN, Angela .... 406-444-0332.. 276 J
amclean@montana.edu
MCLEAN, Anita .... 609-258-3285.. 294 D
amclean@princeton.edu
MCLEAN, Brandon .... 402-844-7102.. 282 B
brandon@northeast.edu
MCLEAN, Connie .... 309-796-5369.. 135 I
mcleanc@bhc.edu
MCLEAN, David .... 970-491-3366.... 78 Q
david.mclean@colostate.edu
MCLEAN, Deborah .... 907-842-5109.... 10 G
dlmclean@alaska.edu
MCLEAN, Jack .... 773-508-3912.. 146 G
jmclean@luc.edu
MCLEAN, Janna .... 574-807-7191.. 159 D
janna.mclean@bethelcollege.edu
MCLEAN, Jennifer .... 570-326-3761.. 413 O
jmclean@pct.edu
MCLEAN, John .... 240-567-7360.. 209 E
john.mclean@montgomerycollege.edu
MCLEAN, Karen, P .... 515-271-1463.. 171 H
karen.mclean@dmu.edu
MCLEAN, Laura .... 704-378-1295.. 345 E
lmclean@jcsu.edu
MCLEAN, Liz .... 910-642-7141.. 353 C
liz.mclean@sccnc.edu
MCLEAN, Michael, F .... 805-525-4417.... 67 J
mmclean@thomasaquinas.edu
MCLEAN, Natalie .... 336-273-4431.. 342 B
nmclean@bennett.edu
MCLEAN, Pat .... 417-690-3441.. 263 E
mclean@cofo.edu
MCLEAN, William, H .... 847-491-7050.. 150 F
wmclean@northwestern.edu
MCLEAN-SCANLON,
Mary .... 585-785-1778.. 314 D
mary.mcleanscanlon@flcc.edu
MCLEANE, David .... 870-574-4504.... 22 G
dmcleane@sautech.edu
MCLEER, Karen .... 608-342-1615.. 521 A
mcleerk@uwplatt.edu
MCLELLAN, Holly, H .... 251-626-3303...... 8 B
hmclellan@ussa.edu
MCLELLAN, Katharyn .... 610-917-1431.. 422 C
kjmclellan@valleyforge.edu
MCLELLAN, Mark, R .... 435-797-1180.. 482 B
mark.mclellan@usu.edu
MCLELLAND, Brandy .... 310-243-3569.... 32 D
bmclelland@csudh.edu
MCLEMORE, Don .... 912-478-5465.. 122 B
dmclemore@georgiasouthern.edu
MCLEMORE, Larry, A .... 620-417-1651.. 184 I
rry.mclemore@sccc.edu
MCLEMORE, Maria, R .... 651-201-1745.. 248 I
maria.mclemore@so.mnscu.edu
MCLENDON, Catrenia .... 404-297-9522.. 122 A
mclendon@gptc.edu
MCLENDON, Kathi .... 704-330-6976.. 348 E
kathi.mclendon@cpcc.edu
MCLENDON, Michael .... 254-710-3111.. 452 H
michael_mclendon@baylor.edu
MCLENDON, Sandra .... 864-644-5354.. 432 G
smclendon@swu.edu
MCLENNAN, Dale .... 978-232-2101.. 218 D
dmclenna@endicott.edu
MCLEOD, Alisea .... 662-252-8000.. 260 F
amcleod@rustcollege.edu
MCLEOD, Allan .... 215-871-6826.. 416 F
allanm@pcom.edu
MCLEOD, Christa .... 601-266-5001.. 261 E
christa.mcleod@usm.edu
MCLEOD, Dale, a .... 571-553-8356.... 92 D
damcleod@gwu.edu
MCLEOD, Dwight .... 660-626-2842.. 262 A
dmcleod@atsu.edu
MCLEOD, Elizabeth .... 973-748-9000.. 289 H
barnes_noble@bloomfield.edu

MCLEOD, Judith .... 949-794-9090.... 66 H
jmcleod@stanbridge.edu
MCLEOD, Michael, J .... 516-877-3177.. 303 B
mcleod@adelphi.edu
MCLEOD, Renee .... 619-876-4250.... 68 I
rmcleod@usuniversity.edu
MCLEOD, Steve .... 706-864-1915.. 128 F
steve.mcleod@ung.edu
MCLESKEY, Stephanie ..... 828-689-1128.. 346 C
smcleskey@mhu.edu
MCLOGAN, Matthew, E ... 616-331-2190.. 234 F
mcloganm@gvsu.edu
MCLOUGHLIN, Eileen ...... 518-320-1193.. 330 H
eileen.mcloughlin@suny.edu
MCLOUGHLIN, II,
Paul, J .... 610-330-5082.. 407 C
mcloughp@lafayette.edu
MCLOUGHLIN, Suzanne .. 516-876-3109.. 333 C
mcloughlins@oldwestbury.edu
MCMAHAN, Carla .... 864-977-7090.. 431 G
carla.mcmahan@ngu.edu
MCMAHAN, Christopher .. 401-874-9742.. 426 D
cmcmahan@uri.edu
MCMAHAN, David .... 423-636-7315.. 447 G
dmcmahan@tusculum.edu
MCMAHAN, Kerrin .... 323-415-4135.... 49 G
mcmahakm@elac.edu
MCMAHAN, Maureen, E .. 260-399-7700.. 168 D
mmcmahan@sf.edu
MCMAHAN, Mendi .... 214-333-5119.. 455 J
mendi@dbu.edu
MCMAHAN, Oliver, L .... 423-478-7037.. 443 I
omcmahan@ptseminary.edu
MCMAHAN, Richard .... 304-647-6410.. 514 A
rmcmahan@osteo.wvsom.edu
MCMAHAN, Robert, K ..... 810-762-9864.. 236 C
mcmahan@kettering.edu
MCMAHAN, Shari .... 657-278-7000.... 33 A
smcmahan@fullerton.edu
MCMAHAN, Shari .... 909-537-5024.... 34 C
smcmahan@csusb.edu
MCMAHILL, Janet, M ...... 515-271-3726.. 171 K
janet.mcmahill@drake.edu
MCMAHON, Beth .... 641-628-5345.. 170 E
mcmahone@central.edu
MCMAHON, Charles, P ... 504-988-8555.. 200 C
cpm@tulane.edu
MCMAHON, Cindy .... 212-962-0002.. 322 G
cmcmahon@nyci.edu
MCMAHON, Dalton .... 701-788-4808.. 360 E
dalton.mcmahon@mayvillestate.edu
MCMAHON, David .... 413-748-3210.. 228 E
dmcmahon@springfieldcollege.edu
MCMAHON, Doug .... 727-864-8587.... 98 L
mcmahodh@eckerd.edu
MCMAHON, Jen .... 561-803-2629.. 106 C
jen_mcmahon@pba.edu
MCMAHON, Jessica .... 252-527-6223.. 350 H
jmcmahon@lenoircc.edu
MCMAHON, Julie .... 517-629-0224.. 230 E
MCMAHON, Kevin .... 213-613-2200.... 65 H
kevin_mcmahon@sciarc.edu
MCMAHON, Lori .... 704-687-5962.. 358 A
lorimcmahon@uncc.edu
MCMAHON, Lori, L .... 205-934-8227...... 8 E
mcmahon@uab.edu
MCMAHON, Mary Pat ...... 617-627-3158.. 228 H
mary.mcmahon@tufts.edu
MCMAHON, Melody, L .... 773-371-5460.. 136 F
mmcmahon@ctu.edu
MCMAHON, Michael .... 701-355-8336.. 362 G
msmcmahon@umary.edu
MCMAHON, Natalie .... 601-276-3865.. 260 H
nmcmahon@smcc.edu
MCMAHON, Patricia .... 513-862-2743.. 369 E
patricia_mcmahon@email.gscollege.edu
MCMAHON, Renee, M ..... 406-447-5501.. 276 B
rmcmahon@carroll.edu
MCMAHON, Roberta .... 708-524-6790.. 139 F
rmcmahon@dom.edu
MCMAHON, Shelly, A ...... 740-368-3201.. 376 B
samcmaho@owu.edu
MCMAHON, Stephen .... 802-654-2516.. 484 I
smcmahon@smcvt.edu
MCMAHON, Timothy, J .... 412-359-1000.. 421 A
tmcmahon@triangle-tech.edu
MCMAHON, Timothy, J .... 412-359-1000.. 421 B
tmcmahon@triangle-tech.edu
MCMAINS, III, Robert, E . 205-934-4427...... 8 E
mmains@uab.edu
MCMAKIN, Sandy .... 210-805-3005.. 474 D
mcmakin@uiwtx.edu
MCMANN, Daniel .... 716-286-8755.. 324 E
dmcmann@niagara.edu
MCMANNESS,
Matthew, S .... 718-862-7357.. 319 L
matthew.mcmanness@manhattan.edu
MCMANUS, Janet .... 816-501-3618.. 262 G
janet.mcmanus@avila.edu
MCMANUS, Jeffrey .... 239-348-4715.... 95 Q
jeff.mcmanus@avemaria.edu
MCMANUS, Kim .... 434-961-5208.. 498 C
kmcmanus@pvcc.edu
MCMANUS, Michael .... 303-797-5654.... 76 J
michael.mcmanus@arapahoe.edu
MCMANUS, Shirley .... 559-442-8215.... 67 C
shirley.mcmanus@fresnocitycollege.edu
MCMASTER, Dennis .... 724-503-1001.. 422 H
dmcmaster@washjeff.edu
MCMASTER, Pam .... 402-481-8718.. 278 J
pam.mcmaster@bryanhealthcollege.edu
MCMASTER, Robert .... 612-625-9883.. 255 H
mcmaster@umn.edu
MCMASTERS, Daniel .... 856-227-7200.. 290 B
dmcmasters@camdencc.edu
MCMEANS, Orlando, F .... 304-766-4300.. 514 B
mcmeanso@wvstateu.edu
MCMENAMIN,
Margaret, M .... 908-709-7100.. 298 A
mcmenamin@ucc.edu
MCMICKLE, Marvin, A ...... 585-340-9680.. 310 F
mmcmickle@crcds.edu
MCMILLAN, Byron .... 610-341-5906.. 403 B
bmcmilla@eastern.edu
MCMILLAN, D. Kevin .... 731-881-7660.. 448 G
kmcmillan@utm.edu
MCMILLAN, Denise .... 610-341-4365.. 403 B
dmcmill@eastern.edu
MCMILLAN, Karen .... 918-270-6402.. 386 I
karen.mcmillan@ptstulsa.edu
MCMILLAN, Karon .... 601-925-3212.. 259 A
kmcmilla@mc.edu
MCMILLAN, Katie .... 307-268-2488.. 526 D
kmcmillan@caspercollege.edu
MCMILLAN, Laura .... 470-578-3056.. 123 J
lmcmilla@kennesaw.edu
MCMILLAN, III, Lex, O .... 610-921-7600.. 396 H
lmcmillan@albright.edu
MCMILLAN, Michelle .... 918-495-6013.. 386 H
mmcmillan@oru.edu
MCMILLAN, Mike .... 501-812-2214.... 21 H
mmcillan@pulaskitech.edu
MCMILLAN, Minnie .... 334-874-5700...... 3 A
mmcmillan@ccal.edu
MCMILLAN, Sean .... 706-542-6128.. 128 E
smcmilla@uga.edu
MCMILLEN, Jeremy, P ..... 903-463-8600.. 458 H
mcmillenj@grayson.edu
MCMILLEN, Michelle .... 870-733-6782.... 19 A
mlmcmillen@asumidsouth.edu
MCMILLIAN, Anthony ...... 281-618-5524.. 461 B
anthony.mcmillian@lonestar.edu
MCMILLIAN, Carey .... 816-271-4582.. 269 C
mcmilli@missouriwestern.edu
MCMILLIAN, Josh .... 479-968-0222.... 19 F
jmcmillian1@atu.edu
MCMILLIN, Barbara, C .... 662-685-4771.. 257 A
bmcmillin@bmc.edu
MCMILLIN, David .... 417-626-1234.. 269 K
dmcmillin@occ.edu
MCMILLIN, Donna .... 870-972-3700.... 18 J
mcmillin@astate.edu
MCMILLIN, Jennifer .... 417-626-1234.. 269 K
jmcmillin@occ.edu
MCMILLIN, Linda, A .... 570-372-4127.. 419 H
mcmillin@susqu.edu
MCMILLIN, Lisa .... 601-635-2111.. 257 F
lmcmillan@eccc.edu
MCMILLIN, Nicole .... 208-562-3331.. 133 F
nicolemcmillin@cwidaho.cc
MCMILLIN, Nicole .... 605-367-4821.. 437 G
nicole.mcmillin@southeasttech.edu
MCMILLIN, Renee .... 303-292-0015.... 79 H
r.mcmillin@denverschoolofnursing.edu
MCMILLION, David .... 706-776-0114.. 125 J
dmcmillion@piedmont.edu
MCMILLION, Eric, C .... 859-858-3511.. 186 J
eric.mcmillion@asbury.edu
MCMILLON, Avis .... 732-224-2967.. 289 I
amcmillon@brookdalecc.edu
MCMILLON, Jeff .... 405-425-5919.. 385 C
jeff.mcmillon@oc.edu
MCMILLON, Kimberly ...... 813-253-7006.. 102 R
kmcmillon@hccfl.edu
MCMINIMY, Gisele .... 316-295-5809.. 181 B
mcminimy@friends.edu
MCMINN, Jamie, G .... 724-946-7121.. 423 B
mcminnjg@westminster.edu
MCMULLEN, Judith .... 216-987-4836.. 367 E
judith.mcmullen@tri-c.edu
MCMULLEN, Michael .... 315-498-2566.. 325 G
mcmullem@sunyocc.edu
MCMULLEN, Patricia .... 202-319-5403.... 92 A
mcmullep@cua.edu
MCMULLEN, Rebecca .... 478-825-6856.. 120 F
mcmullenr@fvsu.edu
MCMULLEN, William .... 817-515-1268.. 467 A
william.mcmullen@tccd.edu
MCMULLIN, Angeline .... 423-614-8357.. 441 B
amcmullin@leeuniversity.edu
MCMULLIN, Kyle, S .... 757-594-7420.. 488 E
kyle.mcmullin@cnu.edu
MCMULLIN, Sallie .... 706-867-2760.. 128 F
sallie.mcmullin@ung.edu
MCMURDOCK, Linda .... 703-284-1615.. 492 A
linda.mcmurdock@marymount.edu
MCMURPHY, Elizabeth .... 580-349-1564.. 385 F
liz@opsu.edu
MCMURPHY, Elizabeth .... 580-349-1566.. 385 F
liz@opsu.edu
MCMURRAY, Aaron .... 503-517-1220.. 396 D
amcmurray@warnerpacific.edu
MCMURRAY, Brock .... 661-763-7811.... 67 F
bmcmurray@taftcollege.edu
MCMURRAY, Kelly .... 301-934-7624.. 207 B
kmcmurray@csmd.edu
MCMURRAY, Tim .... 903-886-5568.. 468 D
timm@tamuc.edu
MCMURRY, Alice .... 717-871-7520.. 415 F
alice.mcmurry@millersville.edu
MCMURRY, Marna, R ...... 910-256-0255.. 355 K
mmcmurry@umo.edu
MCMURTRAY, Brian .... 270-831-9790.. 189 F
brian.mcmurtry@kctcs.edu
MCMURTRY, Craig .... 254-298-8524.. 467 B
craig.mcmurtry@templejc.edu
MCMURTRY, David .... 916-388-2885.... 36 D
dmcmurtry@carrington.edu
MCMURTY, Jerry .... 208-885-6244.. 134 G
mcmurtry@uidaho.edu
MCNABB, Ann, M .... 773-442-5110.. 149 J
a-mcnabb@neiu.edu
MCNABB, Deana, M .... 406-338-5441.. 276 A
deana_mcnabb@bfcc.edu
MCNABB, Diane .... 225-923-2524.. 194 E
MCNABB, Kathleen, J ...... 218-477-4321.. 250 F
mcnabb@mnstate.edu
MCNABB, Mark .... 509-865-8643.. 504 D
mcnabb_m@heritage.edu
MCNABOE, Dennis .... 304-326-1482.. 511 D
dmcnaboe@salemu.edu
MCNAIR, Christopher, L .. 325-670-1401.. 458 J
cmcnair@hsutx.edu
MCNAIR, Kala .... 706-355-5013.. 116 H
kmcnair@athenstech.edu
MCNAIR, Lily, D .... 718-390-3211.. 339 F
lily.mcnair@wagner.edu
MCNAIR, Ronna .... 216-987-4855.. 367 E
ronna.mcnair@tri-c.edu
MCNAIR, Sheila .... 804-524-6948.. 499 G
smcnair@vsu.edu
MCNAIRY, Joe .... 931-363-9800.. 441 G
MCNALL, Mike .... 309-457-2122.. 148 E
mike@monmouthcollege.edu
MCNALLY, Matthew .... 202-319-5373.... 92 A
mcnally@cua.edu
MCNALLY, Michael .... 480-423-6616.... 14 H
michael.mcnally@scottsdalecc.edu
MCNALLY, Minta, A .... 336-758-4237.. 359 E
mcnallma@wfu.edu
MCNALLY, Neal, P .... 330-941-2719.. 382 A
npmcnally@ysu.edu
MCNALLY, Patrick, J .... 313-496-2689.. 242 H
pmcnall1@wcccd.edu
MCNALLY, Robin .... 508-793-7467.. 217 B
rmcnally@clarku.edu
MCNALLY, Tom .... 803-777-3142.. 433 F
tom@mailbox.sc.edu
MCNAMARA, Bob, H .... 843-953-2072.. 428 A
bob.mcnamara@citadel.edu
MCNAMARA, Catherine ... 315-268-4394.. 310 B
cmcnamar@clarkson.edu
MCNAMARA, Connie .... 717-245-1813.. 402 D
mcnamarc@dickinson.edu
MCNAMARA, John .... 862-906-5102.... 86 B
jmcnamara@ccc.commnet.edu
MCNAMARA, John .... 815-394-5152.. 152 G
jmcnamara@rockford.edu
MCNAMARA, Kristine, E .. 401-598-1565.. 425 B
kmcnamara@jwu.edu
MCNAMARA, Nancy .... 704-334-6882.. 343 D
nmcnamara@charlottechristian.edu
MCNAMARA, Patrick .... 402-554-2389.. 283 B
pmcnamara@unomaha.edu
MCNAMARA, Paul .... 904-779-4141.. 101 G
paul.mcnamara@fscj.edu
MCNAMARA, Thomas .... 508-929-8033.. 222 F
tmcnamara@worcester.edu
MCNAMARA, Thomas .... 610-282-1100.. 402 B
tom.mcnamara@desales.edu
MCNAMEE, Anoush .... 305-237-0656.. 105 D
amcnamee@mdc.edu
MCNAMEE-SMITH, Chris . 215-955-0793.. 420 E
chris.smith@jefferson.edu
MCNANEY, Duane .... 903-983-8107.. 460 D
dmcnaney@kilgore.edu
MCNARY, Lisa .... 210-805-3596.. 474 D
lisas@uiwtx.edu
MCNATT, Rosemary Bray . 510-549-4724.... 66 J
rbraymcnatt@sksm.edu
MCNAUGHTON, Ethan ...... 717-569-7071.. 407 E
emcnaughton@lbc.edu
MCNAUGHTON, Jarrod .... 937-395-8165.. 371 D
jarrod.mcnaughton@ketteringhealth.org
MCNAUGHTON, Victor ..... 202-806-1106.... 93 A
vmcnaughton@howard.edu
MCNEAL, Deborah .... 662-621-4124.. 257 B
dmcneal@coahomacc.edu
MCNEAL, Gloria, J .... 858-309-3472.... 54 A
gmcneal@nu.edu
MCNEAL, Latanya, L .... 561-993-1156.. 106 D
mcneall@palmbeachstate.edu
MCNEAL, Lewatis .... 270-852-8607.. 190 D
lewatis.mcneal@kctcs.edu
MCNEAL, Lisa .... 912-279-4505.. 119 C
lmcneal@ccga.edu
MCNEAL, Nadine .... 731-989-6644.. 440 D
nmcneal@fhu.edu
MCNEAL, Scott .... 417-328-1499.. 272 C
smcneal@sbuniv.edu
MCNEALEY, Eloise .... 256-469-7333...... 4 E
MCNEAR, Marie .... 334-229-4200...... 1 D
mmcnear@alasu.edu
MCNEELEY, Wendy .... 325-649-8619.. 459 E
wmcneeley@hputx.edu
MCNEELY, Ann Marie .... 828-448-3509.. 354 B
amcneely@wpcc.edu
MCNEELY, Nate .... 847-628-2521.. 144 B
nmcneely@judsonu.edu
MCNEELY, Shelley .... 608-785-9880.. 524 H
mcneelys@westerntc.edu
MCNEELY, III, Stanton, F 504-671-5498.. 196 D
smcnee@dcc.edu
MCNEELY, Timothy, A ..... 304-367-4937.. 513 B
tim.mcneely@fairmontstate.edu
MCNEES MOSS, Shelley .. 662-329-7106.. 259 E
smmoss@muw.edu
MCNEESE, Margaret .... 713-500-5116.. 477 C
margaret.c.mcneese@uth.tmc.edu
MCNEESE, Tim, D .... 402-363-5683.. 283 G
tdmcnesse@york.edu
MCNEICE-STALLARD,
Barbara .... 909-274-4109.... 53 C
bmcneice-stallard@mtsac.edu
MCNEIL, Amanda .... 505-368-3524.... 12 T
amcneil@dinecollege.edu
MCNEIL, Carlene .... 407-708-2396.. 109 E
mcneilc@seminolestate.edu
MCNEIL, J. Derek .... 206-876-6105.. 507 D
dmcneil@theseattleschool.edu
MCNEIL, Jaquelyn .... 941-752-5231.. 110 H
mcneilj@scf.edu
MCNEIL, Jinawa, A .... 410-651-6411.. 212 B
jamcneil@umes.edu
MCNEIL, Marilyn .... 732-571-3414.. 292 F
mmcneil@monmouth.edu
MCNEIL, Mary, E .... 515-294-1443.. 169 G
mcneil@iastate.edu
MCNEIL, Paul, M .... 530-757-8601.... 69 A
mcneil@ucdavis.edu
MCNEIL, Ronald, D .... 217-206-6533.. 156 G
mcneil.ron@uis.edu
MCNEIL, Stephanie .... 704-216-6953.. 346 A
smcneil@livingstone.edu
MCNEIL, Wanda .... 314-340-3511.. 265 H
mcneilj@hssu.edu
MCNEILL, Denise .... 806-720-7527.. 461 C
denise.mcneill@lcu.edu
MCNEILL, Savonne .... 704-922-6420.. 350 A
mcneill.savonne@gaston.edu
MCNEILL, Warren .... 806-796-8800.. 461 C
MCNERNEY, David .... 515-271-1408.. 171 H
david.mcnerney@dmu.edu
MCNESBY, James .... 215-646-7300.. 404 G
mcnesby.j@gmercyu.edu
MCNEW, Regina .... 865-694-6650.. 446 G
rdmcnew@pstcc.edu
MCNICHOL, Danielle .... 610-358-4528.. 411 E
mcnichod@neumann.edu
MCNICHOLAS, Joseph .... 310-338-5119.... 51 E
jmcnich1@lmu.edu
MCNICHOLS, Amy .... 410-857-2461.. 209 D
amcnichols@mcdaniel.edu
MCNICOL, Greg, L .... 915-747-7182.. 476 D
gmcnicol@utep.edu
MCNIER, Michelle .... 989-463-7423.. 230 F
mcniermI@alma.edu
MCNIGHT, Jonathan .... 860-439-2035.... 87 F
john.mcnight@conncoll.edu
MCNITT, Zakary .... 517-787-0800.. 235 G
mcnittzakaryt@jccmi.edu
MCNULTY, Dan .... 412-268-3785.. 400 D
djmnulty@andrew.cmu.edu
MCNULTY, Donna, S .... 319-296-4201.. 173 B
donna.mcnulty@hawkeyecollege.edu
MCNULTY, George .... 785-460-5490.. 180 C
george.mcnulty@colbycc.edu
MCNULTY, Mary Kate .... 215-572-2877.. 397 G
mcnultym@arcadia.edu
MCNULTY, Patrick .... 312-942-6849.. 153 B
patrick_j_mnculty@rush.edu
MCNULTY, Paul, J .... 724-458-2500.. 404 F
pjmcnulty@gcc.edu

MEDEL, Michael 805-965-0581 63 D medel@sbcc.edu
MEDEMA, Pamela, S 815-835-6378 153 K pamela.s.medema@svcc.edu
MEDENBLIK, Julius, T 616-957-6024 232 B jmedenblik@calvinseminary.edu
MEDFORD, Adriane 215-567-7080 397 H amedford@aii.edu
MEDFORD, Kim 254-968-0515 467 F medford@tarleton.edu
MEDFORD, Mike 404-687-4576 119 D medfordm@ctsnet.edu
MEDINA, Cynthia 303-751-8700 77 C medina@bel-rea.com
MEDINA, Elizabeth 512-313-3000 455 F elizabeth.medina@concordia.edu
MEDINA, Gary 310-303-7302 51 G gmedina@marymountcalifornia.edu
MEDINA, Joseph 508-999-8801 220 H jmedina2@umassd.edu
MEDINA, Kelly 262-646-6506 518 G kmedina@nashotah.edu
MEDINA, Mara 787-780-0070 531 B mmedina@caribbean.edu
MEDINA, Mario 787-738-4660 538 A mario.medina@upr.edu
MEDINA, María, C 787-884-3838 530 G opdai@atenascollege.edu
MEDINA, Nancy 773-442-5240 149 J n-medina4@neiu.edu
MEDINA, Patricia 714-517-1945 28 D financialaid@buc.edu
MEDINA, Priscilla, G 956-721-5357 460 F pmedina@laredo.edu
MEDINA, Raúl 787-264-0406 534 D rimedina@intersg.edu
MEDINA, Reinalda 718-997-4455 309 D reinalda.medina@qc.cuny.edu
MEDINA, Ricco 262-646-6528 518 G rmedina@nashotah.edu
MEDINA, Widylia 787-890-2681 537 E widylia.medina@upr.edu
MEDINA-CABAN, Mario 787-738-2161 537 D mario.medina@upr.edu
MEDINA-ORTIZ, Roberto 787-622-8000 537 B rmedina@pupr.edu
MEDLEY, Lara 303-273-3200 78 M lmedley@mines.edu
MEDLEY, Mike 435-896-9714 482 E michael.medley@snow.edu
MEDLEY, Ticily 817-515-4742 467 A ticily.medley@tccd.edu
MEDLEY-WEEKS, Clarice 214-379-5565 463 G cweeks@pqc.edu
MEDLIN, Melissa, T 256-765-4276 9 C mtmedlin@una.edu
MEDLIN, Sherri 314-264-1000 274 I sherri.medlin@vatterott.edu
MEDRANO, Jennifer 801-832-2126 483 D jmedrano@westminstercollege.edu
MEDRO, Alfred 619-265-0107 57 L amedro@platt.edu
MEDVETZ, Betsy 603-428-2477 287 C bmedvetz@nec.edu
MEDWICK, Peter 215-972-2017 413 L pmedwick@pafa.edu
MEE, Christine, L 843-349-2091 428 E christin@coastal.edu
MEE, David 615-460-6785 438 J david.mee@belmont.edu
MEEAJANE, Natasha 312-922-1884 147 B nmeeajane@maccormac.edu
MEECE, Jeffrey 312-369-7151 138 F jmeece@colum.edu
MEECE, Jill, N 606-679-8501 190 E jill.meece@kctcs.edu
MEEHAN, Barbara 703-993-2380 490 B bmeehan@gmu.edu
MEEHAN, Barry 603-882-6923 286 E bmeehan@ccsnh.edu
MEEHAN, Gabriel 916-558-2097 51 D meehang@scc.losrios.edu
MEEHAN, Kathleen, F 718-990-6173 328 F meehank@stjohns.edu
MEEHAN, Linda, M 609-984-1105 297 F meehan@tesu.edu
MEEHAN, Martin, T 617-287-7050 220 E mmeehan@umassp.edu
MEEHAN, Paula, T 616-632-2852 231 A meehapau@aquinas.edu
MEEHAN, Sara 703-284-6815 492 A smeehan@marymount.edu
MEEK, Charles Ronald 340-693-1421 539 C charles.meek@uvi.edu
MEEK, Laura, E 740-587-6279 368 B meekl@denison.edu
MEEK, Michelle 606-886-3863 189 A michelle.meek@kctcs.edu
MEEK, Scott 602-787-7902 14 E scott.meek@paradisevalley.edu
MEEKER, April, M 605-642-6092 437 B april.meeker@bhsu.edu
MEEKER, Kimberly 660-359-3948 269 I kmeeker@mail.ncmissouri.edu
MEEKER, Steve, L 605-642-6385 437 B steve.meeker@bhsu.edu
MEEKMA, Glenn, A 269-471-3484 230 H meekma@andrews.edu
MEEKS, Andy 859-572-5575 192 B meeksa@nku.edu
MEEKS, Harry, L 812-888-4511 169 A hmeeks@vinu.edu
MEEKS, J. Duane 561-803-2610 106 C duane_meeks@pba.edu
MEEKS, Kimela, A 812-888-4377 169 A kmeeks@vinu.edu
MEEKS, Mark 478-445-5851 121 A mark.meeks@gcsu.edu
MEEKS, Matthew 972-241-3371 455 K mmeeks@dallas.edu
MEEKS, Ronald 662-685-4771 257 A rmeeks@bmc.edu
MEEKS, Susan 478-387-4801 121 E smeeks@gmc.edu
MEEKS, Tom 216-373-5206 374 B tmeeks@ndc.edu
MEENTS-DECAIGNY, Ellen 312-362-7298 139 C emeentsd@depaul.edu
MEER, Jonathan, D 609-896-5167 295 B jmeer@rider.edu
MEESE, Paul 303-678-3707 80 E paul.meese@frontrange.edu
MEESKE, Susan 402-461-7398 280 D smeeske@hastings.edu
MEGAHED, Nivine 312-261-3232 149 B nivine.megahed@nl.edu
MEGALE, Nicole 517-264-3850 230 D
MEGAW, Shelly 507-389-7289 252 D shelly.megaw@southcentral.edu
MEGGERT, Shannon 847-947-0575 149 B smeggert@nl.edu
MEGHREBLIAN, Caren 510-925-4282 26 M cmeghreblian@aua.am
MEHA, Arapata 808-675-3010 130 E ara.meha@byuh.edu
MEHAN, Uppinder 478-825-6211 120 F mehanu@fvsu.edu
MEHDIZADEH, Mojdeh 510-215-3801 41 H mojdeh@contracosta.edu
MEHLER, Mark 973-408-3309 291 B mmehler@drew.edu
MEHLHOFF, Monte 605-626-7781 437 D monte.mehlhoff@northern.edu
MEHLIG, Lisa 815-921-4070 152 E l.mehlig@rockvalleycollege.edu
MEHMERT, Rebecca 573-897-5000 272 H
MEHRABADI, Monte 619-594-6061 35 A mehrabadi@mail.sdsu.edu
MEHRHOFF, Jay 636-584-6585 264 M jay.mehrhoff@eastcentral.edu
MEHRING, Tes 785-594-8312 178 D tes.mehring@bakeru.edu
MEHTA, Neera 425-739-8211 504 F neera.mehta@lwtech.edu
MEHTA, Raj 513-556-6252 379 A raj.mehta@uc.edu
MEI, Jeffrey 617-731-7170 227 D jmei@pmc.edu
MEIDLINGER, Peter, K 417-873-7469 264 H pmeidlin@drury.edu
MEIER, Beth, A 919-760-8427 346 D meierb@meredith.edu
MEIER, Jared 970-248-1945 77 L jmeier@coloradomesa.edu
MEIER, Jay 701-224-5666 361 C jay.meier@bismarckstate.edu
MEIER, Karen, F 757-683-5026 492 G kmeier@odu.edu
MEIER, Lori 712-279-3518 176 E lori.meier@stlukescollege.edu
MEIER, Neal 513-487-1174 378 E neal.meier@myunion.edu
MEIER PFEIFER, Donna 620-672-2700 184 D donnamp@prattcc.edu
MEIERGERD, Joseph 314-792-6140 266 F meiergerd@kenrick.edu
MEIFERT, Janeen, M 920-923-8089 517 H jmmeifert82@marianuniversity.edu
MEIGHAN, Elizabeth, A 717-334-6286 409 C emeighan@ltsg.edu
MEIKSINS, Peter 216-687-5559 366 I p.meiksins@csuohio.edu
MEILMAN, Philip, W 202-687-6985 92 E pwm9@georgetown.edu
MEINDL, Lidia 212-463-0400 337 I lidia.meindl@touro.edu
MEINEKE, John 309-796-5053 135 I meinekej@bhc.edu
MEINERT, Anita 641-673-1063 177 J meinerta@wmpenn.edu
MEINERTS, Marita, K 651-631-5168 256 A mkmeinerts@unwsp.edu
MEINHARDT, Stephanie 972-881-5847 455 A smeinhardt@collin.edu
MEINZEN, David, L 260-399-7700 168 D dmeinzen@sf.edu
MEIR, Michael 212-594-4000 337 F mmeir@tcicollege.edu
MEIRICK, Craig, R 563-562-3263 175 F meirickc@nicc.edu
MEIS, Aaron 513-745-2941 381 I meisa@xavier.edu
MEIS, Darrell 719-587-7912 76 G djmeis@adams.edu
MEIS, Gail, N 404-471-6306 115 J gmeis@agnesscott.edu
MEISEL, Joseph, S 401-863-9499 424 J joseph_meisel@brown.edu
MEISEL, Seth 262-472-1013 521 F meisels@uww.edu
MEISENZAHL, Dan, T 808-956-5941 131 D dmeisenz@hawaii.edu
MEISNER, Delrita 352-323-3691 104 J meisnerd@lssc.edu
MEISNER, Jolene 570-662-4696 415 E jmeisner@mansfield.edu
MEISSNER, Ken 712-749-2111 170 D meissnerk@bvu.edu
MEISTER, Barbara 740-477-7858 374 G bmeister@ohiochristian.edu
MEISTER, Bobbi 712-274-5606 175 C meisterb@morningside.edu
MEISTER, Debra 312-915-7244 146 G dmeiste@luc.edu
MEISTER, Tony 660-944-2899 263 G tmeister@conception.edu
MEITZNER, June 507-285-7213 251 I june.meitzner@rctc.edu
MEIXSEL-CORDERO, Terri 623-245-4600 17 G tmeixsell@uti.edu
MEJIA, Gil 602-331-7500 11 K gmejia@aii.edu
MEJIA, Juan, E 903-510-2261 473 C jmej@tjc.edu
MEJIA, Laurie 626-966-4576 26 J lauriemejia@agu.edu
MEJIA KRUG, Miroslava 630-829-6418 135 F
MEJIA MARTINEZ, Marcela 714-997-6711 37 F mamartin@chapman.edu
MEJIAS, Ida, A 787-250-1912 534 B iamejias@metro.inter.edu
MEJIAS, Jackeline 787-765-1915 534 F jmejias@opto.inter.edu
MEJIAS, Luis 787-780-0070 531 B lmejias@caribbean.edu
MEJIAS, Nelson 787-753-6335 532 O nmejias@icprjc.edu
MEJIC, Tatiana 718-270-6016 309 B tmejic@mec.cuny.edu
MEKEEL, Naomi 518-255-5547 334 D mekeelnf@cobleskill.edu
MEKEMSON, Kristen, M 920-832-7449 517 E kristen.mekemson@lawrence.edu
MELÉNDEZ HERNÁNDEZ, Astrid, Y 787-884-3838 530 G dircontabilidad@atenascollege.edu
MELÉNDEZ RAMOS, Grisel, E 787-763-6299 538 F grisel.melendez@upr.edu
MELANCON, Kimberly 225-768-1710 199 B kimberly.melancon@ololcollege.edu
MELANSON, Chris 207-509-7141 204 F cmelanson@unity.edu
MELANSON, Leigh Anne 603-862-3292 288 C leigh-anne.melanson@unh.edu
MELARAGNI, Robert 617-670-4401 218 G rmelaragni@fisher.edu
MELARAGNO, Steven 401-254-3667 426 B smelaragno@rwu.edu
MELAVALIN, Robin 647-928-4624 226 B rmelavalin@mountida.edu
MELBY, Darlene 805-378-1550 73 D dmelby@vcccd.edu
MELBY, Diane 210-434-6711 463 C dmelby@ollusa.edu
MELBY, Laurie 714-241-6110 39 E lmelby@coastline.edu
MELCHER, Chris 706-721-4018 117 D cmelcher@augusta.edu
MELCHER, Mike 806-291-3425 479 D melcherp@wbu.edu
MELCHER, Rick, W 610-921-7748 396 H rmelcher@albright.edu
MELCHERT, Russell, B 816-235-1607 273 F melchertr@umkc.edu
MELCHIOR, Vonda 813-253-7107 102 R vmelchior@hccfl.edu
MELDER, Renee 318-487-7340 195 F renee.melder@lacollege.edu
MELDREM, Joyce, A 563-588-7164 174 K joyce.meldrem@loras.edu
MELEG, Mike 309-796-5002 135 I melegm@bhc.edu
MELEN, Pia 714-533-1495 65 B pmelen@southbaylo.edu
MELENDEZ, Georgianna 617-287-4818 220 G georgianna.melendez@umb.edu
MELENDEZ, Jennifer 212-472-1500 324 A jmelendez@nysid.edu
MELENDEZ, Martin 787-834-3718 538 C support@uprm.edu
MELENDEZ, Mercedes 212-343-1234 321 B mmelendez@mcny.edu
MELENDEZ, Nildalee 787-852-1430 532 N nmelendez@hccpr.edu
MELENDEZ, Nitza 787-725-8120 532 K nmelendez@eap.edu
MELENDEZ, Rafael 787-725-6500 531 C rmelendez@albizu.edu
MELENDEZ, Ruben 908-709-7085 298 A ruben.melendez@ucc.edu
MELENDEZ, Yahaira 787-620-2040 530 F melendezy@aupr.edu
MELENDEZ LEON, Leonardo 787-720-4476 537 A registraduria@mizpa.edu
MELENDY, Lisa, M 413-597-2477 230 A lisa.m.melendy@williams.edu
MELETIES, Panayiotis 718-262-2780 310 A pmeleties@york.cuny.edu
MELHART, Bonnie 817-257-7729 469 G b.melhart@tcu.edu
MELIAN, Carlos 773-442-4400 149 J c-melian@neiu.edu
MELIKOVA, Amy 785-460-4608 180 C amy.melikova@colbycc.edu
MELIN, Laurie, A 787-257-7373 535 P lamelin@suagm.edu
MELINE, Douglas 916-568-3017 50 J melined@losrios.edu
MELISI, Mary Ann 610-558-5611 411 E melisim@neumann.edu
MELISSARATOS, Aris 443-352-4140 211 A amelissaratos@stevenson.edu
MELKONIAN, Madeleine 718-405-3236 310 H madeleine.melkonian@mountsaintvincent.edu
MELL, Doug 715-232-1198 521 D melld@uwstout.edu
MELLAND, Helen 406-657-3784 277 C helen.melland@montana.edu
MELLE, Carl 541-278-5743 390 C cmelle@bluecc.edu
MELLEN, Brenda 215-702-4843 399 E bmellen@cairn.edu
MELLENKAMP, Kathleen 606-759-7141 190 C kathleen.mellenkamp@kctcs.edu
MELLER, Brenda 248-689-8282 242 F bmeller@walshcollege.edu
MELLER, Julie 312-935-4473 152 D jmeller@robertmorris.edu
MELLICHAMP, James, F 706-776-0100 125 J president@piedmont.edu
MELLING, Alice 206-934-3693 506 J alice.melling@seattlecolleges.edu
MELLINGER, Laurie, A 717-866-7581 403 F lmellinger@evangelical.edu
MELLO, James 740-283-3771 368 L jmello@franciscan.edu
MELLO, Jeffrey 401-456-8000 425 E
MELLO, Mary 559-934-2306 74 D marymello@whccd.edu
MELLO, Steven 401-874-2698 426 D smello@uri.edu
MELLO-GOLDNER, Diane 617-731-7106 227 D dmellogoldner@pmc.edu
MELLON, Edward, J 703-323-3083 497 H emellon@nvcc.edu
MELLON, James, P 808-932-7467 131 E mellon@hawaii.edu
MELLON, Suzanne, K 412-578-6123 400 C skmellon@carlow.edu
MELLON, Timothy 904-819-6459 99 M tmellon@flagler.edu
MELLONI, Suzanne 508-999-9299 220 H smelloni@umassd.edu
MELLOTT, David, M 717-290-8723 408 B rgawn@lancasterseminary.edu
MELLOTT, Ramona 928-523-6534 15 H ramona.mellott@nau.edu
MELLOW, Gail, O 718-482-5050 309 A gmellow@lagcc.cuny.edu
MELMED, Shlomo 310-423-8294 36 O
MELNICK, Julie 402-844-7123 282 B juliem@northeast.edu
MELNICK, Marie 215-637-7700 405 J mmelnick@holyfamily.edu
MELNICK, Patrick 216-221-8584 380 I pmelnick@vmcad.edu

MERIDITH, Pamela .... 870-759-4139.... 24 J
pmeridith@wbcoll.edu
MERILLAT, Jason, C .... 610-566-1776.. 423 H
jmerillat@williamson.edu
MERILLAT, Melinda .... 832-252-0745.. 454 H
melinda.merillat@cbshouston.edu
MERIMEE, Nancy, S .... 913-971-3427.. 183 D
nsmerimee@mnu.edu
MERINAR, Whitney, A ..... 570-321-4144.. 409 F
merinar@lycoming.edu
MERINGOLO,
Salvatore, M .... 540-654-1372.. 495 C
tmeringo@umw.edu
MERINO, Deanna .... 657-278-4498.... 33 A
dmarino@fullerton.edu
MERINO, Robert .... 281-998-6342.. 465 A
robert.merino@sjcd.edu
MERINO, Robert .... 281-998-6150.. 464 I
robert.merino@sjcd.edu
MERINO, Robert .... 281-998-6342.. 464 J
robert.merino@sjcd.edu
MERINO, Robert .... 281-998-6342.. 465 B
robert.merino@sjcd.edu
MERIWETHER, James, H . 805-437-3313.... 32 B
jim.meriwether@csuci.edu
MERIWETHER, Jan, Y ...... 252-399-6314.. 341 P
jymeriwether@barton.edu
MERIWETHER, Jason, L .. 812-941-2420.. 163 F
jlmeriwe@ius.edu
MERIWETHER, Mimi .... 803-786-3856.. 429 A
mmeriwether@columbiasc.edu
MERJIL, Mark .... 909-384-8900.... 60 C
mmerjil@sbccd.cc.ca.us
MERKEL, Diane, K .... 518-564-2195.. 334 A
dmerk001@plattsburgh.edu
MERKEL, Luz, I .... 509-777-4225.. 509 H
lmerkel@whitworth.edu
MERKIN, Yitzchok .... 301-962-5111.. 214 A
ymerkin@yeshiva.edu
MERKLE, Ben .... 208-882-1566.. 134 B
bmerkle@nsa.edu
MERKLE, Jean .... 563-425-5765.. 177 D
merklej@uiu.edu
MERKLE, Joseph, F .... 717-815-1460.. 424 F
jmerkle@ycp.edu
MERKLE, Karen, L .... 410-386-8107.. 206 I
kmerkle@carrollcc.edu
MERKLE, Patricia .... 315-568-3277.. 323 A
pmerkle@nycc.edu
MERKLIN, Lynn .... 269-471-6066.. 230 H
merklin@andrews.edu
MERKOUSKO, Wendy .... 912-358-4153.. 126 F
merkouskow@savannahstate.edu
MERKOW, Russ .... 425-739-8436.. 504 F
russ.merkow@lwtech.edu
MERKT, Dan .... 518-608-8371.. 314 A
dmerkt@excelsior.edu
MERKT, Mary Lou .... 864-294-2140.. 430 C
marylou.merkt@furman.edu
MERL, Jill .... 808-544-9364.. 130 H
jmerl@hpu.edu
MERLE, Dan .... 704-290-5219.. 353 B
dmerle@spcc.edu
MERLINO, Keith .... 412-809-5100.. 417 D
merlino.keith@pti.edu
MERLO, Antonio .... 713-348-3699.. 464 E
amerlo@rice.edu
MERLO, Barbara .... 254-526-1223.. 454 A
barbara.merlo@ctcd.edu
MERMANN-JOZWIAK,
Elisabeth .... 509-313-5522.. 504 A
mermann-jozwiak@gonzaga.edu
MERMELSTEIN, Joanne ... 978-837-5117.. 225 E
mermelsteinj@merrimack.edu
MERO, Neal, P .... 386-822-7406.. 113 B
nmero@stetson.edu
MERRELL, Melinda, M ..... 425-235-5846.. 506 F
mmerrell@rtc.edu
MERRELL, Sue .... 937-512-2917.. 377 D
sue.merrell@sinclair.edu
MERRICK, Robyn, M .... 225-771-4680.. 199 G
robyn_merrick@sus.edu
MERRICK, Vallyn .... 410-951-6300.. 212 E
vmerrick@coppin.edu
MERRIFIELD, Ann .... 573-875-7210.. 263 F
amerrifield@ccis.edu
MERRIFIELD, Mary .... 314-529-9510.. 267 B
mmerrifield@maryville.edu
MERRIGAN, Kathleen ...... 912-443-5500.. 126 G
kmerrigan@savannahtech.edu
MERRILL, Chad .... 828-694-1704.. 347 G
chadm@blueridge.edu
MERRILL, Dale .... 657-278-3256.... 33 A
dmerrill@fullerton.edu
MERRILL, H. Donald .... 704-233-8284.. 359 H
dmerrill@wingate.edu
MERRILL, Joanne .... 603-897-8257.. 287 F
jmerrill@rivier.edu
MERRILL, Katelyn .... 619-849-7082.... 57 M
katelynmerrill@pointloma.edu
MERRILL, Paul .... 256-331-5223...... 6 A
merrill@nwscc.edu
MERRILL, Scott, M .... 508-793-2438.. 217 C
smerrill@holycross.edu
MERRILL, Timothy .... 804-523-5131.. 497 C
tmerrill@reynolds.edu
MERRILL, Traci .... 619-260-7967.... 72 B
tmerrill@sandiego.edu
MERRILL-DOSS, Jean ...... 573-518-2154.. 268 E
jeanmer@mineralarea.edu
MERRILL-SANDS,
Deborah .... 603-862-1983.. 288 C
deborah.merrillsands@unh.edu
MERRIMAN, Gary .... 909-599-5433.... 48 K
gmerriman@lifepacific.edu
MERRIMAN, Karen .... 704-330-6796.. 348 E
karen.merriman@cpcc.edu
MERRIMAN, W, R .... 330-823-6050.. 379 F
merrimdr@mountunion.edu
MERRITT, Aaron .... 660-263-3900.. 263 A
aaronmerritt@cccb.edu
MERRITT, Bert .... 850-484-1140.. 106 H
bmerritt@pensacolastate.edu
MERRITT, Brandt .... 863-667-5777.. 109 L
bwmerritt@seu.edu
MERRITT, Brian .... 919-718-7426.. 348 D
bmerritt@cccc.edu
MERRITT, Cortina .... 254-519-5737.. 468 C
cortina.merritt@tamuct.edu
MERRITT, Debra .... 860-486-2337.... 89 D
debra.merritt@uconn.edu
MERRITT, Jaci, M .... 903-434-8103.. 462 M
jmerritt@ntcc.edu
MERRITT, James, A .... 608-246-6330.. 523 F
jamerritt1@madisoncollege.edu
MERRITT, Maribea .... 432-552-2809.. 478 B
merritt_m@utpb.edu
MERRITT, Nancy .... 412-268-1209.. 400 D
nmkm@andrew.cmu.edu
MERRITT, Nathan .... 626-584-5364.... 44 G
nathanmerritt@fuller.edu
MERRITT, Pearl, E .... 325-696-0503.. 472 D
pearl.merritt@ttuhsc.edu
MERRITT, Scott .... 318-869-5708.. 194 I
smerritt@centenary.edu
MERRITT, Stephen, R .... 610-519-7499.. 422 G
stephen.merritt@villanova.edu
MERRY, Nicholas .... 410-293-1010.. 529 D
nicholas.merry@navy.mil
MERRYMAN, Ed .... 408-554-5076.... 63 E
emerryman@scu.edu
MERRYMAN, Jon .... 870-245-5506.... 21 E
merrymanj@obu.edu
MERRYMAN, Marjorie ...... 917-493-4584.. 319 M
mmerryman@msmnyc.edu
MERSETH, Juel, O .... 507-344-7854.. 244 K
juel.merseth@blc.edu
MERSETH, Lynette, Y .... 507-344-7317.. 244 K
lynette.merseth@blc.edu
MERSMANN, Tina .... 513-244-4232.. 373 C
tina.mersmann@msj.edu
MERSON, Michael, H .... 919-681-7760.. 343 J
michael.merson@duke.edu
MERTENS, Daniel .... 701-662-1654.. 361 E
danial.mertens@lrsc.edu
MERTENS, Robert .... 262-472-1221.. 521 F
mertensr@uww.edu
MERTES, Michael .... 802-387-7179.. 484 B
michaelmertes@landmark.edu
MERTES, Scott .... 989-386-6622.. 238 B
smertes@midmich.edu
MERTH, Paula, B .... 651-290-6376.. 253 S
paula.merth@mitchellhamline.edu
MERTZ, Jennifer, L .... 610-758-3181.. 408 H
jlm207@lehigh.edu
MERTZ, Scot .... 936-294-1423.. 471 D
sdm007@shsu.edu
MERTZ-WEIGEL,
Dorothee .... 912-344-3128.. 116 E
dorothee.mertz-weigel@armstrong.edu
MERVINE, Ed .... 310-577-3000.... 75 H
financialaid@yosan.edu
MERVIUS, Sandra .... 516-463-4335.. 316 D
sandra.mervius@hofstra.edu
MERY, Pam .... 415-239-3227.... 38 E
pmery@ccsf.edu
MERYHEW, Barb .... 307-268-2249.. 526 D
bmeryhew@caspercollege.edu
MERZ, Marcie, L .... 215-898-6171.. 421 E
mmerz@dev.upenn.edu
MERZ, Nan .... 408-554-4007.... 63 E
nmerz@scu.edu
MERZ, Sarah .... 563-588-6307.. 170 F
sarah.merz@clarke.edu
MERZ, Soon, O .... 512-223-7035.. 451 N
smerz@austincc.edu
MESA, Tina .... 210-486-3901.. 450 D
tmesa@alamo.edu
MESARIS, Nikilos 'Nik' .... 951-487-3073.... 53 D
nmesaris@msjc.edu
MESCHA, Manal .... 973-300-2754.. 297 D
mmescha@sussex.edu
MESECAR, Christopher .... 919-317-3052.. 127 D
cjmesecar@southuniversity.edu
MESEROLE, Scott .... 618-842-3711.. 142 C
meseroles@iecc.edu
MESERVE, Mary .... 207-786-6097.. 202 D
mmeserve@bates.edu
MESERVEY, Patricia, M ... 978-542-6134.. 222 D
president@salemstate.edu
MESHCHERYAKOV, Nell ... 813-663-0100.... 93 F
MESHCHERYAKOV, Nell .. 813-882-0100.... 93 F
MESHKATY, Shahra .... 619-260-2298.... 72 B
meshkaty@sandiego.edu
MESICS, Linda, L .... 610-799-1585.. 408 G
lmesics@lccc.edu
MESINA, Irene .... 808-845-9195.. 132 A
imesina@hawaii.edu
MESKER, Bobby, S .... 432-837-8231.. 471 E
bmesker@sulross.edu
MESLER, Cecelia .... 616-632-2868.. 231 A
meslecec@aquinas.edu
MESLOH, Charles .... 906-227-2435.. 239 B
cmesloh@nmu.edu
MESONAS, Lenny .... 908-526-1200.. 295 A
lenny.mesonas@raritanval.edu
MESQUITA, Cezar .... 208-885-6163.. 134 G
cezarm@uidaho.edu
MESQUITA, Joseph .... 860-512-3215.... 86 E
jmesquita@manchestercc.edu
MESSA, Emily .... 832-842-8184.. 473 E
eamessa@uh.edu
MESSA, Emily .... 832-842-8184.. 473 F
eamessa@uh.edu
MESSAC, Achille .... 202-806-6565.... 93 A
messac@howard.edu
MESSAROS, Jean .... 570-674-6320.. 410 K
srjean@misericordia.edu
MESSER, Emily .... 706-233-7342.. 127 A
emesser@shorter.edu
MESSER, James .... 412-237-3108.. 401 B
jmesser@ccac.edu
MESSER, Kirk .... 414-930-3221.. 518 F
messerk@mtmary.edu
MESSER, Thomas, C .... 904-596-2411.. 113 J
tmesser@tbc.org
MESSERVY, Steven .... 256-824-6343...... 8 F
steven.messervy@uah.edu
MESSICK, Gary, A .... 260-422-5561.. 162 B
gamessick@indianatech.edu
MESSINA, John, A .... 330-972-6594.. 378 G
jam125@uakron.edu
MESSINA, John, A .... 330-972-7800.. 378 G
jam125@uakron.edu
MESSINA, Kimberlee .... 650-949-7209.... 44 B
messinekimberlee@foothill.edu
MESSINA, Rosalia .... 503-847-2555.. 396 C
rmessina@uws.edu
MESSINA, Susan, G .... 704-463-3040.. 354 F
susan.messina@pfeiffer.edu
MESSING, Robert, O .... 512-471-1735.. 476 B
romessing@austin.utexas.edu
MESSINGER, Jacquelyn .... 903-510-2305.. 473 C
jmes@tjc.edu
MESSITTE, Zachariah, P ... 920-748-8118.. 519 E
messittez@ripon.edu
MESSMAN-MANDICOTT,
Lea .... 301-687-4890.. 212 F
lmessman@frostburg.edu
MESSNER, Leonard, V ..... 312-949-7108.. 142 A
lmessner@ico.edu
MESSNER, Melody .... 816-936-8717.. 271 L
mmessner@saintlukescollege.edu
MESSNER, Robert, H .... 717-780-2333.. 405 C
rhmessne@hacc.edu
MESSNER, Stephanie .... 312-949-7013.. 142 A
smessner@ico.edu
MESSNER, Tom .... 904-646-2175.. 101 G
tom.messner@fscj.edu
MESSNER, William, F ...... 413-552-2700.. 223 E
wmessner@hcc.edu
MESTAN, Michael, A .... 315-568-3226.. 323 A
mmestan@nycc.edu
MESTAS, Richard .... 202-231-8650.. 528 C
richard.mestas@dodiis.mil
MESTETH, Leslie .... 605-455-6033.. 436 G
lmesteth@olc.edu
MESYEF, Whitney .... 866-680-2756.. 480 K
financialaid@midwifery.edu
METCALF, Christine .... 603-271-6484.. 286 F
cmetcalf@ccsnh.edu
METCALF, Courtney .... 620-223-2700.. 181 A
courtneym@fortscott.edu
METCALF, Dustin .... 208-467-8665.. 134 D
dmetcalf@nnu.edu
METCALF, Gary .... 559-453-2063.... 44 F
gary.metcalf@fresno.edu
METCALF, Jeff, K .... 606-474-3258.. 188 L
jmetcalf@kcu.edu
METCALF, Jonathan, G .... 240-500-2000.. 207 I
jgmetcalf@hagerstowncc.edu
METCALF, Kim, K .... 702-895-3375.. 284 L
kim.metcalf@unlv.edu
METCALF, Linda .... 817-531-7530.. 472 F
lmetcalf@txwes.edu
METCALF, Michael .... 937-769-1817.. 363 F
mmetcalf@antioch.edu
METCALF, Robert .... 907-443-8402.... 10 G
rgmetcalf@alaska.edu
METCALF, Shawn .... 435-722-6900.. 481 I
METCALF, Shirley, I .... 541-383-7201.. 390 D
METCALFE, Sharon .... 740-392-6868.. 373 D
sharon.metcalfe@mvnu.edu
METE, T.J .... 772-466-4822.... 95 R
tj.mete@aviator.edu
METEAU, Robert .... 661-763-7809.... 67 F
rmeteau@taftcollege.edu
METESH, John, J .... 406-496-4159.. 277 G
jmetesh@mtech.edu
METEVIER, Robert .... 602-787-7872.... 14 E
robert.metevier@paradisevalley.edu
METHVIN, Jennifer .... 417-455-5534.. 264 E
jennifermethvin@crowder.edu
METIANU, Mihaela .... 561-297-3049.. 110 K
mmetianu@fau.edu
METILLY, Paul .... 617-254-2610.. 227 H
paul.metilly@sjs.edu
METIVIER SCOTT, Shelly . 508-910-6402.. 220 H
sscott1@umassd.edu
METKE, L. Michael .... 903-510-2380.. 473 C
mmet@tjc.edu
METOYER, Waylon .... 501-975-8557.... 21 G
wmetoyer@philander.edu
METRESS, Chris .... 205-726-2192...... 6 E
cpmetres@samford.edu
METROPULOS,
Christopher, T .... 617-850-1280.. 219 F
pres_office@hchc.edu
METS, Lisa, A .... 727-864-8221.... 98 L
metsla@eckerd.edu
METTAUER, Janice, L ...... 608-246-6174.. 523 F
jmettauer@madisoncollege.edu
METTEE, Chris, J .... 330-325-6854.. 373 H
cmettee@neomed.edu
METTILLE, Teege .... 715-682-1224.. 518 H
tmettille@northland.edu
METTLEN, Susan .... 908-709-7538.. 298 A
susan.mettlen@ucc.edu
METTS, Amanda .... 252-399-6315.. 341 P
ahmetts@barton.edu
METTS, Deanna .... 931-372-3045.. 445 B
dmetts@tntech.edu
METZ, Catherine, A .... 765-361-6418.. 169 C
metzc@wabash.edu
METZ, Christine .... 516-562-3403.. 313 C
cmetz@northwell.edu
METZ, David .... 614-287-2617.. 367 C
dmetz@cscc.edu
METZ, George .... 843-863-7050.. 427 I
gmetz@csuniv.edu
METZ, Gregory .... 513-745-5720.. 379 B
gregory.metz@uc.edu
METZ, Linda, D .... 740-588-1386.. 382 C
lmetz@zanestate.edu
METZ, Matthew .... 716-829-7502.. 313 A
METZ, Perry .... 812-855-8000.. 162 F
metz@indiana.edu
METZ, Ray, E .... 313-593-5151.. 242 A
remetz@umich.edu
METZ, Robert, C .... 517-264-7117.. 241 A
rmetz@sienaheights.edu
METZ, Roxanne .... 949-582-4824.... 65 G
rmetz@saddleback.edu
METZ, Starla .... 727-341-4368.. 108 D
metz.starla@spcollege.edu
METZ, Susan .... 201-216-5245.. 297 B
susan.metz@stevens.edu
METZ, Terry .... 651-523-2160.. 247 A
tmetz01@hamline.edu
METZ, Tim .... 828-227-7239.. 359 A
tdmetz@wcu.edu
METZELAARS, Gretchen ... 614-688-8011.. 375 A
metzelaars.1@osu.edu
METZGAR, Johanna .... 415-254-6033.... 68 M
jmetzgar@berkeley.edu
METZGAR, Marlene .... 563-355-3500.. 174 E
mmetzgar@kaplan.edu
METZGAR, Michael .... 315-498-6061.. 325 G
m.c.metzgar@sunyocc.edu
METZGER, David, D .... 757-683-4865.. 492 G
dmetzger@odu.edu
METZGER, Elizabeth .... 505-277-3389.. 302 F
emetzger@unm.edu
METZGER, Nan .... 414-930-3338.. 518 F
metzgern@mtmary.edu
METZGER, Peggy .... 707-826-4321.... 34 F
mam7001@humboldt.edu
METZGER, Richard, A ...... 814-332-2755.. 397 A
rich.metzger@allegheny.edu
METZGER, Theresa .... 404-270-5232.. 128 A
tmetzger@spelman.edu

MICKOOL, Richard 937-525-3811 381 F rmickool@wittenberg.edu
MICKOOL, Richard 401-454-6390 426 A rmickool@risd.edu
MICUS, David 321-674-7400 100 M dmicus@fit.edu
MIDCAP, Richard, D 410-827-5858 207 A rmidcap@chesapeake.edu
MIDDEKER, Vicki 303-410-2438 82 K vmiddeker@westwood.edu
MIDDENDORF, Terry 651-523-2302 247 A tmiddendorf@hamline.edu
MIDDENDORF, Tom 615-248-1258 447 F tmiddendorf@trevecca.edu
MIDDLEKAUFF, Paul 212-659-0736 318 D pmiddlekauff@tkc.edu
MIDDLESWARTH, Jean, E 336-757-3288 349 G jmiddleswarth@forsythtech.edu
MIDDLESWARTH, Jean, E 336-734-7412 349 G jmiddleswarth@forsythtech.edu
MIDDLETON, Antoinette 212-220-1267 307 B amiddleton@bmcc.cuny.edu
MIDDLETON, Dewayne 601-849-0112 257 D dewayne.middleton@colin.edu
MIDDLETON, Jacqueline 330-263-2580 367 A jkmiddleton@wooster.edu
MIDDLETON, Kenna 859-622-1721 188 F kenna.middleton@eku.edu
MIDDLETON, Lyle 501-205-8830 19 J lmiddleton@cbc.edu
MIDDLETON, Melinda, L 812-877-8259 166 H melinda.l.middleton@rose-hulman.edu
MIDDLETON, Michael 617-287-7592 220 G michael.middleton@umb.edu
MIDDLETON, Michael, A 573-882-2011 273 D umpresident@umsystem.edu
MIDDLETON, Nigel, T 303-273-3327 78 M nmiddlet@mines.edu
MIDDLETON, Norma, L 336-316-2151 344 H nmiddlet@guilford.edu
MIDDLETON, Renee, A 740-593-4400 375 H middletr@ohio.edu
MIDDLETON, Rodney, C 989-328-1202 238 D rodm@montcalm.edu
MIDDLETON, Tracy 803-705-4594 427 D middletont@benedict.edu
MIDDLETON, Whittaker, V 803-535-5347 428 B wmiddleton@claflin.edu
MIDEI, Ron 954-262-5224 105 J ronmidei@nsu.nova.edu
MIDGETT, Pam 940-397-4182 462 A pam.midgett@mwsu.edu
MIDGETTE, Juanita 252-335-3586 356 D jmidgette@ecsu.edu
MIDGLEY, Michael, T 512-223-7579 451 N midgley@austincc.edu
MIDKIFF, Kittridge 270-686-4508 190 D kitt.midkiff@kctcs.edu
MIDKIFF, Lindsay 870-633-4480 20 B lindsay.midkiff@eacc.edu
MIDKIFF, Lori, A 304-929-5472 512 C lmidkiff@newriver.edu
MIDKIFF, JR., Robert, M 570-577-1547 398 L robert.midkiff@bucknell.edu
MIDKIFF, Scott, F 540-231-4227 499 F midkiff@vt.edu
MIDTHUN, Steve 414-277-7224 518 E midthun@msoe.edu
MIDURA, Matthew 310-506-4181 56 J matthew.midura@pepperdine.edu
MIDYETTE, Marilyn, W 757-221-1166 488 F mwmidyette01@wm.edu
MIEDEMA, Linda, L 321-433-7380 98 K miedemal@easternflorida.edu
MIELDEZIS, Cathie 618-937-2127 148 I cmieldezis@northland.edu
MIELISH, Julia 919-866-5649 353 I jcmielish@waketech.edu
MIELKE, Cindi 815-599-3491 141 E cindi.mielke@highland.edu
MIELKE, Dan 541-962-3833 391 C dmielke@eou.edu
MIELKE, John 262-595-3226 520 F mielke@uwp.edu
MIENE, Peter 507-457-5017 252 G pmiene@winona.edu
MIENIE, Edward 678-717-3410 128 F edward.mienie@ung.edu
MIERA, Joseph 505-277-2511 302 F jmiera@unm.edu
MIERES, Joann, B 570-372-4049 419 H antes@susqu.edu
MIERS, Michael 508-849-3326 214 E mmiers@annamaria.edu
MIERTSCHIN, Charla 507-457-5299 252 G cmiertschin@winona.edu
MIESS, Bob, D 701-788-4885 360 E robert.miess@mayvillestate.edu
MIGHTY, Hugh, E 202-806-5677 93 A hugh.mighty@howard.edu
MIGLAW, Kari, L 831-656-2077 528 D klmiglaw@nps.edu
MIGLER, Jerry 701-228-5431 360 F jerome.migler@dakotacollege.edu
MIGNARDOT, Henry 505-428-1225 301 K henry.mignardot@sfcc.edu
MIGNAULT, Richard 845-451-1369 312 C r_mignau@culinary.edu
MIGUEL, George 520-383-8401 17 E gmiguel@tocc.edu
MIGYANKO, Stephanie, M 724-439-4900 408 D smigyanko@laurel.edu
MIHAL, Deborah, F 843-953-1431 428 G mihaldf@cofc.edu
MIHAL, Matt 570-674-6336 410 K mmihal@misericordia.edu
MIHAL, Ruthie 704-609-1542 343 A ruthie.mihal@carolinascollege.edu
MIHALEVICH, Rick 573-897-5000 272 H
MIHALIC, Angela 214-648-2168 478 C angela.mihalic@utsouthwestern.edu
MIHALY, Christine 734-973-3477 242 G cmihaly@wccnet.edu
MIHALY, Marc 802-831-1237 485 F mmihaly@vermontlaw.edu
MIHALYOV, David 585-395-2577 332 E dmihalyo@brockport.edu
MIHEVC, Jake 315-792-5653 321 G jmihevc@mvcc.edu
MIHIR, Fnu 479-788-7456 23 A mihir@uafs.edu
MIHM-HEROLD, Wendy, A 563-562-3263 175 F mihm-heroldw@portal.nicc.edu
MIHO, Mariko 808-932-7692 131 E mariko.miho@uhfoundation.org
MIHOPULOS, Sheryl, L 516-877-3365 303 B mihopulos@adelphi.edu
MIKALSON, Joan 518-608-8144 314 A jmikalson@excelsior.edu
MIKE, James 717-477-1151 416 A jhmike@ship.edu
MIKE, Nena 691-370-3191 529 F nenam@comfsm.fm
MIKEMAN, Cindy 405-736-0315 387 I cmikeman@rose.edu
MIKESCH, Gregory 314-792-6119 266 F mikesch@kenrick.edu
MIKESELL, Brian 413-528-7274 214 H bmikesell@simons-rock.edu
MIKESELL, Leslie 530-283-0202 43 G lmikesell@frc.edu
MIKHAIL, Michael, B 312-996-2671 156 F mmikhail@uic.edu
MIKHAIL, Mona 626-812-3013 28 A mmikhail@apu.edu
MIKHAIL, Osama 915-747-8200 476 D omikhail@utep.edu
MIKHAIL, Osama, I 713-500-3047 477 C osama.i.mikhail@uth.tmc.edu
MIKHALEVSKY, Nina 540-654-1000 495 C nmik@umw.edu
MIKKELSEN, Carmelita 251-580-2213 4 I cormelita.mikkelsen@faulknerstate.edu
MIKLOVIC, Lauren 408-498-5158 39 H lmiklovic@cogswell.edu
MIKLUSAK, Courtney 619-239-0391 36 A cmiklusak@cwsl.edu
MIKNAVICH, Marie 315-792-3111 339 B mtmiknav@utica.edu
MIKOS, Shari 213-615-2700 37 I
MIKOWSKI, Thomas 616-632-2853 231 A mikowtho@aquinas.edu
MIKOYCHIK, Cindy 800-962-7682 275 D cmikoychik@wma.edu
MIKSA, Anthony, R 423-585-6770 447 D tony.miksa@ws.edu
MIKSCH, Joseph, T 412-624-4356 421 G jmiksch@pitt.edu
MIKTARIAN, Christine 559-244-5917 67 A christine.miktarian@scccd.edu
MIKULA, Susan 630-829-6274 135 F smikula@ben.edu
MIKULAY, Jennifer 414-382-6395 515 D jennifer.mikulay@alverno.edu
MIKUS, Robert, L 717-867-6234 408 F mikus@lvc.edu
MIKUSZEWSKI, Barbara 216-987-4497 367 E barbara.mikuszewski@tri-c.edu
MILAM, B. Hofler 336-758-3121 359 E bhm@wfu.edu
MILAM, John 540-868-7249 497 E jmilam@lfcc.edu
MILAM, Kathy, L 937-481-2336 381 C kathy_milam@wilmington.edu
MILAM, Linda 918-781-7247 382 D milaml@bacone.edu
MILAM, Rebecca 865-694-6560 446 G bmilam@pstcc.edu
MILANESI, Lou 612-338-7224 256 D
MILANI, Rachel 218-262-7258 249 E rachelmilani@hibbing.edu
MILAVETZ, Barry 701-777-4278 360 C barry.milavetz@und.edu
MILAZZO, Theresa 404-727-7404 120 E theresa.milazzo@emory.edu
MILBERG, Craig 503-370-6561 396 G cmilberg@willamette.edu
MILBERG, William 212-229-5901 322 E milbergw@newschool.edu
MILBOURNE, John, M 321-674-7160 100 M jmilbour@fit.edu
MILBRETT, Juanita 507-389-5860 250 E juanita.milbrett@mnsu.edu
MILBURN, John 661-362-3245 40 A john.milburn@canyons.edu
MILBURN, Trudy 914-251-6507 334 C trudy.milburn@purchase.edu
MILBY, Kevin, S 859-238-5534 187 H kevin.milby@centre.edu
MILBY, Megan, H 859-238-5516 187 H megan.milby@centre.edu
MILD, Robert, E 304-367-4219 513 B robert.mild@fairmontstate.edu
MILEHAM, Mardi 503-883-2217 392 B mmileham@linfield.edu
MILEK, Joseph 513-745-2000 381 I
MILEM, Jill 936-468-2401 466 H jmilem@sfasu.edu
MILES, Alicia, C 770-720-5542 126 C acm1@reinhardt.edu
MILES, Arletha 914-773-3856 325 J lmiles@pace.edu
MILES, Belinda, S 914-606-6707 340 C belinda.miles@sunywcc.edu
MILES, Cindy 619-644-7569 45 H cindy.miles@gcccd.edu
MILES, Daniel 740-283-3771 368 L dmiles@franciscan.edu
MILES, David 802-225-3240 484 G david.miles@neci.edu
MILES, David, A 201-692-2227 291 J dmiles@fdu.edu
MILES, Donald 814-472-3029 418 F dmiles@francis.edu
MILES, Jennifer 662-329-7129 259 E jmmiles@muw.edu
MILES, Jennifer, P 502-597-7023 191 B jennifer.miles@kysu.edu
MILES, John, D 864-597-4363 435 C milesjd@wofford.edu
MILES, Keith, D 202-238-2358 93 A kmiles@howard.edu
MILES, Kim 941-377-4880 105 C
MILES, Linda 386-506-3720 98 E milesl@daytonastate.edu
MILES, Linda 252-398-6505 343 G milesl@chowan.edu
MILES, Lloyd 301-985-7237 212 C lloyd.miles@umuc.edu
MILES, Lora 618-650-2020 155 A lflamm@siue.edu
MILES, Mark 651-635-8065 244 L m-miles@bethel.edu
MILES, Martin 757-727-5635 490 E martin.miles@hamptonu.edu
MILES, Mary, E 502-852-6688 194 A maryelizabeth.miles@louisville.edu
MILES, Ray 337-475-5192 200 H rmiles@mcneese.edu
MILES, Richard 513-721-7944 369 D rmiles@gbs.edu
MILES, Sarah, L 508-831-4180 230 C smiles@wpi.edu
MILES, Stephannie 704-461-6873 342 A stephanniemiles@bac.edu
MILES, Stephen 941-487-4200 111 D miles@ncf.edu
MILES, Thomas 773-702-4907 156 D tmiles@law.uchicago.edu
MILES, Tom 478-445-4027 121 A tom.miles@gcsu.edu
MILES, Vickie 334-670-3732 7 H vmiles@troy.edu
MILES-TRIBBLE, Valerie 510-841-1905 26 C
MILETTI, Linnette 787-743-4041 531 K lmiletti@columbiacentral.edu
MILEWICZ, Mark 910-521-6630 358 C mark.milewicz@uncp.edu
MILEY, Melinda 843-953-5426 428 G mileym@cofc.edu
MILEY, Tamara 812-749-1271 166 B tmiley@oak.edu
MILHAM, Donna 616-451-3511 233 C dmilham@davenport.edu
MILHAUSEN, Michael 503-399-6527 390 E michael.milhausen@chemeketa.edu
MILHOLLAND, Tom, A 325-674-2918 449 J milholland@acu.edu
MILICH, Marianne 219-980-6618 163 B mmilich@iun.edu
MILICI, JR., Roger, A 212-636-6545 314 G milici@fordham.edu
MILIONI, Mark, L 417-268-6008 262 H mmilioni@gobbc.edu
MILIONIS, Daren 503-375-7012 391 B dmilionis@corban.edu
MILJEVICH, Greg 715-365-4486 524 C gmiljevich@nicoletcollege.edu
MILKOVICH, Anne 920-424-4480 520 E milkovich@uwosh.edu
MILKOVICH, Patrice 619-575-6176 66 E pmilkovich@swccd.edu
MILKOWSKI, Rose 312-629-6182 154 A rmilkowski@saic.edu
MILKOWSKI, Tracy, L 920-923-8159 517 H tmilkowski@marianuniversity.edu
MILLA, Rosalinda 619-876-4250 68 I rmilla@usuniversity.edu
MILLAN, Iris 773-481-8765 137 I imillan3@ccc.edu
MILLANE, Maureen 716-839-8334 312 D mmillane@daemen.edu
MILLAR, Janet 661-654-3366 32 A jmillar@csub.edu
MILLAR, Jeremy 937-255-6565 527 H jeremy.millar@afit.edu
MILLARD, Cristi 801-957-4145 483 A cristi.millard@slcc.edu
MILLARD, James, R 252-638-7283 349 B millardj@cravencc.edu
MILLARD, Jill 704-290-5887 353 B jmillard@spcc.edu
MILLARD, Julia 702-579-3578 283 I jmillard@kaplan.edu
MILLARD, Kent 937-529-2201 378 F kmillard@united.edu
MILLARD, Rachel 859-233-8111 193 D rmillard@transy.edu
MILLARD, Robert, B 617-253-6700 225 A
MILLARD, Sandra 302-831-2231 91 F skm@udel.edu
MILLARD, Sandy 919-209-2011 350 G sbmillard@johnstoncc.edu
MILLARD, Stacey 313-228-7367 310 G smillard@colgate.edu
MILLARD, Tara 215-951-1013 407 A feeney@lasalle.edu
MILLARD, Timothy, R 540-985-9781 491 A trmillard@jchs.edu
MILLAS, Nikoletta 610-896-1032 405 I nmillas@haverford.edu
MILLEN, Jonathan 609-895-5789 295 B millen@rider.edu
MILLEN, Michelle 972-548-6677 455 A mmillen@collin.edu
MILLEN, Patricia 215-368-5000 398 C
MILLENBINE, Donnie 618-437-5321 152 A millenbined@rlc.edu
MILLENDER, Angelia, N 773-291-6313 137 G
MILLER, Adam 509-527-5778 509 G millera@whitman.edu
MILLER, Al 251-442-2357 9 A amiller@umobile.edu
MILLER, Alex 828-669-8012 346 M amiller@montreat.edu
MILLER, Allen 803-777-2930 433 F pamiller@sc.edu
MILLER, Amber 213-740-2531 72 D dean@dornsife.usc.edu
MILLER, Andrea 414-930-3343 518 F millera@mtmary.edu
MILLER, Andrew 863-667-5703 109 L aemiller@seu.edu
MILLER, Andrew, T 607-255-6384 312 A atmiller@cornell.edu
MILLER, Angela 601-718-5900 93 F
MILLER, Angela 501-708-0600 93 F
MILLER, Angela 865-981-8201 441 H angela.miller@maryvillecollege.edu
MILLER, Angela, M 608-342-1555 521 A millerang@uwplatt.edu
MILLER, Anita, L 814-871-5847 404 A miller064@gannon.edu
MILLER, Anna 812-888-6965 169 A amiller@vinu.edu
MILLER, Anne 212-217-4190 314 B anne_miller@fitnyc.edu
MILLER, Antoinette 216-791-5000 366 H antoinette.miller@cim.edu
MILLER, Ashley 270-384-8065 191 E millera@lindsey.edu
MILLER, Ave 770-962-7580 123 D amiller@gwinnetttech.edu
MILLER, Barbara 443-352-4369 211 A blmiller@stevenson.edu
MILLER, Baruch 718-530-6934 306 I

MILLER, Margaret, M ...... 609-258-5813.. 294 D
mmmiller@princeton.edu
MILLER, Mark ...... 417-447-2655.. 270 A
millerm@otc.edu
MILLER, Mark ...... 402-472-4823.. 282 M
mark.miller@unl.edu
MILLER, Mark ...... 318-869-5117.. 194 I
mmiller@centenary.edu
MILLER, Mark ...... 513-936-1567.. 379 B
mark.miller@uc.edu
MILLER, Marty, L ...... 757-823-9539.. 492 F
mlmiller@nsu.edu
MILLER, Martyn ...... 215-204-9579.. 420 B
martyn.miller@temple.edu
MILLER, Mary Anne ...... 617-928-4556.. 226 B
mamiller@mountida.edu
MILLER, Matt ...... 616-698-7111.. 233 C
MILLER, Matt ...... 989-386-6600.. 238 B
mmiller@midmich.edu
MILLER, Matthew ...... 903-875-7422.. 462 J
matt.miller@navarrocollege.edu
MILLER, Maureen ...... 810-766-8752.. 231 D
mparma02@baker.edu
MILLER, Megan ...... 410-225-2420.. 209 B
memiller@mica.edu
MILLER, Megan, M ...... 678-542-7537.. 222 D
mmiller@salemstate.edu
MILLER, Melanie ...... 904-633-8403.. 101 G
melanie.miller@fscj.edu
MILLER, Melinda ...... 615-248-1650.. 447 F
mmiller@trevecca.edu
MILLER, Melinda, A ...... 315-386-7085.. 335 B
millerm@canton.edu
MILLER, Melissa ...... 843-661-8104.. 429 J
melissa.miller@fdtc.edu
MILLER, Melissa, A ...... 585-785-1639.. 314 D
melissa.miller@flcc.edu
MILLER, Melissa, C ...... 386-312-4106.. 108 B
melissamiller@sjrstate.edu
MILLER, Melvin ...... 802-485-2134.. 484 H
miller@norwich.edu
MILLER, Merrill ...... 315-228-1000.. 310 G
mmiller@colgate.edu
MILLER, Michael ...... 805-893-2118.... 70 E
mike.miller@sa.ucsb.edu
MILLER, Michael ...... 937-376-2946.. 376 F
mmiller@payne.edu
MILLER, Michael ...... 715-682-1202.. 518 H
mmiller@northland.edu
MILLER, Michael, J ...... 718-289-5548.. 307 C
michael.miller@bcc.cuny.edu
MILLER, Michael, S ...... 510-436-1360.... 46 E
mmiller@hnu.edu
MILLER, Michael Patrick . 708-524-5921.. 139 F
mmiller@dom.edu
MILLER, Michelle ...... 802-860-2729.. 483 F
miller@champlain.edu
MILLER, Michelle, R ...... 757-727-5447.. 490 E
michelle.miller@hamptonu.edu
MILLER, Mike ...... 205-329-7950...... 3 B
mike.miller@ecacolleges.com
MILLER, Millie ...... 513-487-1191.. 378 E
mollie.miller@myunion.edu
MILLER, Mindy ...... 478-445-5771.. 121 A
mindy.miller@gcsu.edu
MILLER, Miryom, R ...... 845-434-5240.. 341 L
mmiller@ygzm.edu
MILLER, Morris ...... 253-589-5565.. 502 F
morris.miller@cptc.edu
MILLER, Nancy ...... 318-797-5383.. 198 C
nancy.miller@lsus.edu
MILLER, Natasha ...... 443-334-2831.. 211 A
nmiller5@stevenson.edu
MILLER, Ned ...... 515-964-6816.. 171 B
nlmiller4@dmacc.edu
MILLER, Nelson ...... 616-301-6800.. 243 I
millern@cooley.edu
MILLER, Nora, R ...... 662-329-7145.. 259 E
nrmiller@muw.edu
MILLER, Norm ...... 318-487-7194.. 195 F
norm.miller@lacollege.edu
MILLER, Pam ...... 985-380-2483.. 196 K
pamelamiller@scl.edu
MILLER, Pamela, B ...... 251-442-2360...... 9 A
pbuchanan@umobile.edu
MILLER, Pat ...... 517-629-0318.. 230 E
pmiller@albion.edu
MILLER, Pat ...... 405-912-9015.. 387 D
pmiller@hc.edu
MILLER, Paul ...... 662-243-1902.. 257 G
pmiller@eastms.edu
MILLER, Paul ...... 336-278-5882.. 344 D
millerp@elon.edu
MILLER, Peggy ...... 806-834-3850.. 472 C
peggy.miller@ttu.edu
MILLER, Peter ...... 516-671-7373.. 339 G
pmiller@webb.edu
MILLER, Peter, J ...... 508-849-3586.. 214 E
pmiller@annamaria.edu
MILLER, Peter, J ...... 215-596-8865.. 422 A
p.miller@usciences.edu

MILLER, Poppy ...... 815-939-5243.. 150 I
pmiller2@olivet.edu
MILLER, Rachel, S ...... 620-327-8213.. 181 G
rachelsm@hesston.edu
MILLER, Rebecca ...... 302-736-2495.... 91 G
rebecca.miller@wesley.edu
MILLER, Remy ...... 901-272-5107.. 442 B
rmiller@mca.edu
MILLER, Richard ...... 304-829-7516.. 510 G
rmiller@bethanywv.edu
MILLER, Richard, B ...... 417-625-9565.. 268 H
miller-r@mssu.edu
MILLER, Richard, C ...... 270-745-5468.. 194 D
richard.c.miller@wku.edu
MILLER, Richard, H ...... 307-766-4997.. 527 B
rmille@uwyo.edu
MILLER, Richard, K ...... 781-292-2301.. 218 H
richard.miller@olin.edu
MILLER, Richard, L ...... 713-500-3603.. 477 C
richard.l.miller@uth.tmc.edu
MILLER, Rob ...... 913-758-6160.. 185 F
millerr@stmary.edu
MILLER, Robert ...... 269-387-2073.. 243 H
bob.miller@wmich.edu
MILLER, Robert, B ...... 213-891-2152.... 49 F
millerrb@email.laccd.edu
MILLER, Robert, B ...... 626-585-7170.... 56 H
rbmiller@pasadena.edu
MILLER, Robert, G ...... 901-333-4368.. 447 B
rgmiller1@southwest.tn.edu
MILLER, Robert, H ...... 225-771-5170.. 199 H
rhmillerjr@aol.com
MILLER, Robert, L ...... 217-581-7249.. 139 H
rlmiller@eiu.edu
MILLER, JR., Robert, L ... 908-852-1400.. 290 D
millerr@centenarycollege.edu
MILLER, Robert, R ...... 540-828-5383.. 487 H
rmiller@bridgewater.edu
MILLER, Rodney, E ...... 316-978-3389.. 185 J
rodney.miller@wichita.edu
MILLER, Rodney, E ...... 706-419-1134.. 119 G
miller@covenant.edu
MILLER, Roger ...... 269-488-4257.. 235 I
rmiller@kvcc.edu
MILLER, Roger ...... 512-647-8792.. 470 F
roger.miller@tstc.edu
MILLER, Roland, G ...... 847-543-2551.. 138 C
com624@clcillinois.edu
MILLER, JR., Ronald, E ... 843-661-1678.. 430 B
rmiller@fmarion.edu
MILLER, Ruby ...... 480-517-8152.... 14 G
ruby.miller@riosalado.edu
MILLER, Ruth ...... 785-594-4530.. 178 D
ruth.miller@bakeru.edu
MILLER, Ruth ...... 650-306-3125.... 62 G
miller@smccd.edu
MILLER, Samuel, T ...... 229-928-1387.. 122 C
sam.miller@gsw.edu
MILLER, Sandra ...... 716-827-4348.. 338 E
millers@trocaire.edu
MILLER, Sandra ...... 973-720-2659.. 298 G
millers@wpunj.edu
MILLER, Scott ...... 308-398-7355.. 278 K
scottmiller@cccneb.edu
MILLER, Scott ...... 307-268-2025.. 526 D
smiller@caspercollege.edu
MILLER, Scott ...... 814-732-2400.. 415 A
millerse@edinboro.edu
MILLER, Scott ...... 814-732-2460.. 415 A
millerse@edinboro.edu
MILLER, Scott, D ...... 757-455-3215.. 500 E
smiller@vwc.edu
MILLER, Seth ...... 801-957-3448.. 483 A
seth.miller@slcc.edu
MILLER, Shari, K ...... 716-673-3438.. 331 D
shari.miller@fredonia.edu
MILLER, Sharri, K ...... 815-835-6345.. 153 K
sharri.k.miller@svcc.edu
MILLER, Shawn ...... 315-379-3820.. 335 B
millers@canton.edu
MILLER, Shawn ...... 425-352-8135.. 501 J
smiller@cascadia.edu
MILLER, Sherri ...... 757-352-4843.. 493 E
sstocks@regent.edu
MILLER, Stephanie ...... 256-782-5006...... 4 H
sdmiller@jsu.edu
MILLER, Stephanie ...... 317-632-5553.. 165 L
smiller@lincolntech.edu
MILLER, Stephen ...... 925-631-4970.... 59 I
scmiller@stmarys-ca.edu
MILLER, Stephen ...... 240-684-2037.. 212 C
stephen.miller@umuc.edu
MILLER, Steve ...... 912-871-1801.. 125 E
smiller@ogeecheetech.edu
MILLER, Steve ...... 573-288-6440.. 264 F
smiller@culver.edu
MILLER, Steve ...... 513-745-5736.. 379 B
steve.miller2@uc.edu
MILLER, Steven ...... 303-963-3353.... 77 I
stemiller@ccu.edu

MILLER, Steven, G ...... 228-865-4570.. 261 E
steven.g.miller@usm.edu
MILLER, Steven, P ...... 404-687-4568.. 119 D
millers@ctsnet.edu
MILLER, Stuart ...... 706-379-3111.. 130 B
samiller@yhc.edu
MILLER, Stuart, C ...... 626-395-6393.... 30 H
scmiller@caltech.edu
MILLER, Susan ...... 508-362-2131.. 223 C
smiller@capecod.edu
MILLER, Susan ...... 610-436-2442.. 416 C
smiller2@wcupa.edu
MILLER, Susan, A ...... 770-720-5543.. 126 C
sam1@reinhardt.edu
MILLER, Susan, S ...... 901-272-5152.. 442 B
smiller@mca.edu
MILLER, Svetlana ...... 516-629-6260.. 339 G
lmiller@webb.edu
MILLER, Tamara, D ...... 913-288-7136.. 182 C
tmiller@kckcc.edu
MILLER, Tamsin ...... 865-882-4730.. 447 A
miller@roanestate.edu
MILLER, Tana, J ...... 806-651-4911.. 469 D
tmiller@mail.wtamu.edu
MILLER, Tara ...... 641-648-4611.. 173 K
tara.miller@iavalley.edu
MILLER, Terence ...... 414-288-3208.. 517 I
terence.miller@marquette.edu
MILLER, Teresa, A ...... 716-645-6200.. 331 C
tmiller@buffalo.edu
MILLER, Thomas, D ...... 812-877-8210.. 166 H
thomas.miller@rose-hulman.edu
MILLER, Thomas, E ...... 813-974-9084.. 112 C
millert@usf.edu
MILLER, Thomas, K ...... 919-513-5006.. 357 B
tkm@ncsu.edu
MILLER, Thomas, P ...... 520-626-0202.... 17 I
tpm@email.arizona.edu
MILLER, Tina ...... 906-248-8437.. 231 N
tinamiller@bmcc.edu
MILLER, Tracy, L ...... 330-471-8238.. 371 J
tmiller@malone.edu
MILLER, Troy ...... 410-951-3580.. 212 E
trmiller@coppin.edu
MILLER, Troy ...... 301-860-4363.. 212 D
tmiller@bowiestate.edu
MILLER, Troy ...... 570-484-2625.. 415 D
troy.miller@lhufoundation.org
MILLER, Tyrus ...... 831-459-5905.... 70 F
vpdgs@ucsc.edu
MILLER, Valerie ...... 740-593-4141.. 375 H
millerv@ohio.edu
MILLER, Van ...... 309-556-3127.. 143 D
vmiller@iwu.edu
MILLER, Van ...... 254-298-8606.. 467 B
van.miller@templejc.edu
MILLER, Vanessa ...... 714-992-7094.... 54 H
vmiller@fullcoll.edu
MILLER, Vernease ...... 704-945-7313.. 354 F
vernease.miller@pfeiffer.edu
MILLER, Vince ...... 208-282-1045.. 133 H
millvince@isu.edu
MILLER, Vince ...... 229-333-5941.. 129 G
vincemiller@valdosta.edu
MILLER, Walter, C ...... 505-277-2331.. 302 F
wcmiller@unm.edu
MILLER, Wayne, C ...... 606-783-2158.. 191 H
w.miller@moreheadstate.edu
MILLER, Wendy ...... 847-214-7308.. 140 A
wmiller@elgin.edu
MILLER, Wendy, A ...... 570-326-3761.. 413 O
wendy.miller@pct.edu
MILLER, Will ...... 904-819-6322.... 99 M
wmiller@flagler.edu
MILLER, William, L ...... 724-287-8711.. 399 B
william.miller@bc3.edu
MILLER, Yolanda, D ...... 662-621-4101.. 257 B
ymiller@coahomacc.edu
MILLER-GILLILAND,
Sophie ...... 949-582-4722.... 65 G
smiller@saddleback.edu
MILLER-HERNANDEZ,
Leangela ...... 559-730-3795.... 40 E
leangelam@cos.edu
MILLER-REID, M. Susan . 925-631-4352.... 59 I
msm9@stmarys-ca.edu
MILLER-SCHUSTER,
Danielle ...... 309-438-5451.. 143 B
dnmille@ilstu.edu
MILLER-SUBER,
Evelyn, V ...... 516-463-6473.. 316 D
evelyn.v.miller-suber@hofstra.edu
MILLER-THORN, Jill ...... 631-656-2122.. 314 F
jill.millerthorn@ftc.edu
MILLER-WIETECHA, Lynn 248-204-2383.. 237 B
lmillerwi@ltu.edu
MILLER-YOW, Ronnie ...... 501-370-5297.... 21 G
rmiller-yow@philander.edu
MILLER-YOW, Ronnie ...... 501-370-5344.... 21 G
rmiller-yow@philander.edu

MILLERICK, Francis, E ...... 774-354-0481.. 215 D
frank.millerick@becker.edu
MILLERICK, Timothy, P ... 903-813-2228.. 451 M
tmillerick@austincollege.edu
MILLES, Michael ...... 240-567-6001.. 209 E
michael.mills@montgomerycollege.edu
MILLET, Matthew, B ...... 412-397-6406.. 418 B
millet@rmu.edu
MILLET, Michelle ...... 216-397-3053.. 370 H
mmillet@jcu.edu
MILLET, Peter ...... 205-366-8808...... 7 E
pmillet@stillman.edu
MILLETTE, Andrea ...... 513-241-4338.. 363 G
andrea.millette@antonellicollege.edu
MILLETTE, Paul ...... 802-287-8224.. 484 A
millettep@greenmtn.edu
MILLETTE, Paulette ...... 207-216-4342.. 204 B
pmillette@yccc.edu
MILLEY, Jane ...... 304-424-8242.. 514 D
jane.milley@wvup.edu
MILLHORN, David, E ...... 865-974-8913.. 448 D
millhorn@tennessee.edu
MILLHORN, David, E ...... 865-974-4048.. 448 D
millhorn@tennessee.edu
MILLICAN, Valorie ...... 816-654-7332.. 266 E
vmillican@kcumb.edu
MILLIGAN, Debra, A ...... 404-527-4520.. 118 F
dmilligan@carver.edu
MILLIGAN, Kristen ...... 760-776-7428.... 40 B
kmilligan@collegeofthedesert.edu
MILLIGAN, Laura ...... 573-840-9106.. 273 A
lmilligan@trcc.edu
MILLIGAN, Marty ...... 909-384-8949.... 60 C
mmilliga@sbccd.cc.ca.us
MILLIGAN, Pat ...... 713-646-1824.. 459 A
pmilligan@hcl.edu
MILLIGAN, Tom ...... 970-491-2359.... 78 Q
tom.milligan@colostate.edu
MILLIGAN, Troy ...... 405-422-1206.. 387 E
milligant@redlandscc.edu
MILLIGAN, Yuri Rodgers . 757-727-5253.. 490 E
yuri.milligan@hamptonu.edu
MILLIKEN, James, B ...... 646-664-9100.. 306 M
chancellor@cuny.edu
MILLIKEN, Roberta ...... 740-351-3550.. 377 C
rmilliken@shawnee.edu
MILLIKEN, Ronald, P ...... 207-778-7105.. 205 A
milliken@maine.edu
MILLIKEN, Stephanie ...... 270-534-3394.. 190 H
stephanie.milliken@kctcs.edu
MILLIKIN, Mary ...... 918-343-7615.. 387 F
mmillikin@rsu.edu
MILLIMAN, Robert, W ...... 316-284-5239.. 179 A
rmilliman@bethelks.edu
MILLION, Christina, C ...... 404-413-1430.. 122 D
cmillion@gsu.edu
MILLIOTIS, Dave ...... 507-457-1421.. 254 O
dmillioti@smumn.edu
MILLIRONS, Anna, S ...... 540-985-8530.. 491 A
asmillirons@jchs.edu
MILLIS, Jack ...... 714-532-6049.... 37 F
millis@chapman.edu
MILLISON, Jeffrey ...... 410-888-9048.. 209 C
jmillison@muih.edu
MILLLER, Susan ...... 219-989-2251.. 166 F
sue.miller@pnw.edu
MILLNER, Timothy ...... 410-225-4251.. 209 B
tmillner@mica.edu
MILLOY, Phyllis, F ...... 757-822-1063.. 498 H
pmilloy@tcc.edu
MILLS, Ashley ...... 864-250-7000.... 93 F
MILLS, Brian ...... 541-681-7304.. 393 B
bmills@nwcu.edu
MILLS, Chad ...... 573-518-2134.. 268 E
cmills@mineralarea.edu
MILLS, Cheryll ...... 757-789-1730.. 497 A
cmills@es.vccs.edu
MILLS, Chris ...... 610-896-1039.. 405 I
cmills@haverford.edu
MILLS, Dan ...... 616-222-1444.. 233 A
dan.mills@cornerstone.edu
MILLS, David ...... 617-587-8599.. 226 E
millsd@neco.edu
MILLS, Dora ...... 207-221-4621.. 205 F
dmills2@une.edu
MILLS, Edward ...... 916-278-6060.... 34 B
emills@csus.edu
MILLS, Edward, D ...... 912-478-1193.. 122 B
edmills@georgiasouthern.edu
MILLS, F. Joe ...... 931-221-7444.. 444 E
millsj@apsu.edu
MILLS, Frank ...... 340-693-1067.. 539 C
fmills@uvi.edu
MILLS, JR., Gordon, E ...... 251-460-7859...... 9 E
gmills@southalabama.edu
MILLS, Jacala ...... 802-387-6732.. 484 B
jacalamills@landmark.edu
MILLS, Janie ...... 319-363-1323.. 175 D
jmills@mtmercy.edu
MILLS, Jeffery, N ...... 207-581-5100.. 204 H
jeffmills@maine.edu

MILLS, Jessica .... 303-357-5891.... 79 I
jessica.mills@denverseminary.edu
MILLS, Jock, S .... 541-737-4514.. 393 H
jock.mills@oregonstate.edu
MILLS, John .... 606-368-6121.. 186 B
johnmills@alc.edu
MILLS, Kelly .... 863-638-7254.. 115 C
kelly.mills@warner.edu
MILLS, Kevin .... 209-932-3014.... 71 C
kmills@pacific.edu
MILLS, Kevin .... 828-398-7200.. 347 D
kevinsmills@abtech.edu
MILLS, Kimberly, A .... 410-651-8100.. 212 B
kamills@umes.edu
MILLS, Laura, J .... 912-344-3073.. 116 E
laura.mills@armstrong.edu
MILLS, Linda .... 212-992-9712.. 324 C
linda.mills@nyu.edu
MILLS, Linda, G .... 212-998-9712.. 324 C
linda.mills@nyu.edu
MILLS, Mark .... 215-898-1453.. 421 E
millsme@upenn.edu
MILLS, Martin .... 512-245-2501.. 471 F
mm79@txstate.edu
MILLS, Marvin .... 912-478-5558.. 122 B
mmills@georgiasouthern.edu
MILLS, Matthew .... 912-650-6218.. 127 D
mmills@southuniversity.edu
MILLS, Melissa .... 763-433-1332.. 248 K
melissa.mills@anokaramsey.edu
MILLS, Michael .... 918-631-2510.. 389 E
michael-mills@utulsa.edu
MILLS, Michael, E .... 847-491-4477.. 150 F
michael-mills@northwestern.edu
MILLS, Ossie .... 918-495-6384.. 386 H
omills@oru.edu
MILLS, Patti .... 201-692-2132.. 291 J
patti_mills@fdu.edu
MILLS, Priscilla, L .... 928-523-3312.... 15 H
priscilla.mills@nau.edu
MILLS, Randy, W .... 336-750-2706.. 359 B
millsrw@wssu.edu
MILLS, Richard, G .... 603-646-0459.. 286 J
richard.g.mills@dartmouth.edu
MILLS, Russell, S .... 530-898-5201.... 32 C
rmills@csuchico.edu
MILLS, Sandra, M .... 513-487-3206.. 315 F
smills@huc.edu
MILLS, Shirley, D .... 803-777-0980.. 433 F
smills@mailbox.sc.edu
MILLS, Tegan, C .... 207-947-4591.. 202 E
librarian@bealcollege.edu
MILLS, Terry, L .... 216-397-4455.. 370 H
tmills@jcu.edu
MILLS, Tom .... 405-382-9210.. 387 L
t.mills@sscok.edu
MILLS, William, R .... 617-552-8661.. 216 C
william.mills@bc.edu
MILLS-DICK, Melissa .... 413-549-4600.. 219 C
MILLSAP, B. Burr .... 405-325-5161.. 389 B
bmillsap@ou.edu
MILLSAP, Byron, B .... 405-325-5161.. 389 B
bmillsap@ou.edu
MILLSAP, Pam .... 409-933-8229.. 454 O
pmillsap@com.edu
MILLSAP, Pam .... 409-933-8192.. 454 O
pmillsap@com.edu
MILLSAPPS, Michael .... 970-339-6376.... 76 H
michael.millsapps@aims.edu
MILLSAPS, Brooke .... 828-298-3325.. 359 F
bmillsaps@warren-wilson.edu
MILLSON-MARTULA,
Christopher, A .... 434-544-8339.. 491 F
millsonmartula@lynchburg.edu
MILLUSH, Mary Ann .... 630-942-2269.. 138 B
millush@cod.edu
MILLWOOD, Kent, A .... 864-231-2049.. 427 B
kmillwood@andersonuniversity.edu
MILNE, Arryn .... 410-864-4000.. 210 F
amilne@stmarys.edu
MILNE, Dan .... 719-638-6580.... 80 B
dmilne@cci.edu
MILNE, Erin, M .... 413-662-5049.. 222 B
erin.milne@mcla.edu
MILNE, Sheila .... 252-399-6326.. 341 P
smilne@barton.edu
MILNER, Devika, M .... 305-284-6858.. 114 H
dmilner@miami.edu
MILNER, Eric .... 401-341-2218.. 426 C
eric.milner@salve.edu
MILNER, Jocelyn, L .... 608-263-5658.. 519 K
jlmilner@wisc.edu
MILNER, Laura .... 608-785-8095.. 520 C
lmilner@uwlax.edu
MILNER, Wesley .... 812-488-2686.. 167 I
wm23@evansville.edu
MILON, Ronald .... 212-217-4040.. 314 B
ronald_milon@fitnyc.edu
MILONE-NUZZO,
Paula, F .... 814-863-0245.. 412 F
pxm36@psu.edu

MILOWSKI, Nicholas, B .. 718-817-4975.. 314 G
nmilowski@fordham.edu
MILROY, James, B .... 585-245-5601.. 333 B
milroy@geneseo.edu
MILSO, Lisa .... 978-762-4000.. 224 C
lmilso@northshore.edu
MILSOM, Penny .... 443-840-5426.. 207 C
mmilsom@ccbcmd.edu
MILSTEIN, Mark .... 512-499-4246.. 475 K
mmilstein@utsystem.edu
MILSTONE, David, M .... 508-999-8640.. 220 H
dmilstone@umassd.edu
MILTENBERGER, Chad .... 509-758-1711.. 508 F
chad.miltenberger@wwcc.edu
MILTENBERGER, Susan .. 410-225-2201.. 209 B
smiltenb@mica.edu
MILTER, Rebecca .... 404-872-3593.. 117 B
rmilter@johnmarshall.edu
MILTON, Alice .... 205-929-6306...... 5 D
amilton@lawsonstate.edu
MILTON, Barbara, J .... 973-655-4349.. 293 A
miltonb@mail.montclair.edu
MILTON, Suzanne .... 509-359-7887.. 503 D
smilton@ewu.edu
MILTON, Theresa .... 602-386-4159.... 11 D
theresa.milton@arizonachristian.edu
MILTON, Vikki .... 850-718-2371.... 97 G
miltonv@chipola.edu
MILZ, George .... 713-646-1864.. 459 A
gmilz@hcl.edu
MIMMS, Jacqueline .... 661-654-2160.... 32 A
jmimms@csub.edu
MIMMS, Lee, S .... 817-552-3700.. 460 E
lmimms@tku.edu
MIMS, Christina .... 903-875-7419.. 462 J
christina.mims@navarrocollege.edu
MIMS, Dana, M .... 570-577-3171.. 398 L
dana.mims@bucknell.edu
MIMS, Jane .... 210-784-1000.. 469 B
jane.mims@tamusa.edu
MIMS, Janet .... 843-863-8004.. 427 I
jmims@csuniv.edu
MIMS, Lloyd .... 561-803-2400.. 106 C
lloyd_mims@pba.edu
MIMS, Yolanda, L .... 504-286-5335.. 199 I
ymims@suno.edu
MIMS-DEVEZIN, Lisa .... 504-286-5064.. 199 I
lmims@suno.edu
MIN, John .... 949-480-4171.... 64 J
min@soka.edu
MIN, Sangki .... 913-288-7686.. 182 C
smin@kckcc.edu
MIN, Sarah .... 323-731-2383.... 55 J
sarahmin@psuca.edu
MINA, Jean .... 847-578-3238.. 153 A
MINAR, Thomas, J .... 317-738-8010.. 160 J
president@franklincollege.edu
MINARD, Tiffany .... 859-815-7683.. 189 D
tiffany.minard@kctcs.edu
MINARDI, Coco .... 717-245-1571.. 402 D
minardin@dickinson.edu
MINASOVA, Irina .... 206-934-6432.. 507 A
irina.minasova@seattlecolleges.edu
MINATOYA, Lydia .... 206-934-3712.. 506 J
lydia.minatoya@seattlecolleges.edu
MINCH, Kevin .... 660-785-5384.. 273 B
kminch@truman.edu
MINCHEFF, Chris .... 303-753-6046.... 83 A
cmincheff@rmcad.edu
MINCHELLO, Brian .... 617-879-2205.. 229 G
bminchello@wheelock.edu
MINCKLER, Tye .... 254-968-9877.. 467 F
minckler@tarleton.edu
MINCKS, Kathy .... 907-564-8272.... 10 B
kmincks.akpacprop@gci.net
MINDEN, Courtney .... 781-239-5589.. 214 G
cminden@babson.edu
MINDRUM, Matthew, S ...... 317-940-9257.. 159 K
mmindrum@butler.edu
MINE, Jodi .... 808-934-2742.. 131 J
mine@hawaii.edu
MINEHAN, Cathy .... 617-521-3806.. 228 C
cathy.minehan@simmons.edu
MINEHART, Heather .... 760-252-2411.... 28 B
hminehart@barstow.edu
MINEHART, James .... 419-448-2160.. 369 G
jminehar@heidelberg.edu
MINEO, Michael .... 718-817-4931.. 314 G
mineo@fordham.edu
MINEO, Steve .... 912-525-5000.. 126 E
smineo@scad.edu
MINER, Anna, G .... 603-526-3702.. 285 L
anna.miner@colby-sawyer.edu
MINER, Brenda .... 479-394-7622.... 22 B
bminer@rmcc.edu
MINER, Judy, C .... 650-949-6100.... 43 N
minerjudy@fhda.edu
MINER, Madonne .... 801-626-6006.. 482 D
madonneminer@weber.edu

MINER ROMANOFF,
Karen .... 614-947-6241.. 369 A
karen.minerromanoff@franklin.edu
MINERVINI, Ron .... 617-730-7222.. 226 J
ron.minervini@newbury.edu
MINET, Jennifer, J .... 716-878-5335.. 332 F
siwulajj@buffalostate.edu
MINFORD, Joell .... 412-392-3422.. 417 F
jminford@pointpark.edu
MING, Amanda .... 248-476-1122.. 237 H
aming@mispp.edu
MINGEE, Sheila .... 217-709-0923.. 145 E
smingee@lakeviewcol.edu
MINGENBACK, Mary .... 620-341-5413.. 180 G
mmingenb@emporia.edu
MINGLE, James, J .... 607-255-3903.. 312 A
jjm19@cornell.edu
MINGO, Rhonda .... 864-596-9140.. 429 C
rhonda.mingo@converse.edu
MINGO, Susan .... 207-454-1032.. 204 A
smingo@wccc.me.edu
MINGO, Tracey .... 912-478-5413.. 122 B
tmingo@georgiasouthern.edu
MINHAS, Omer .... 419-772-2529.. 374 J
o-minhas@onu.edu
MINI, Susan .... 815-753-0495.. 150 A
smini@niu.edu
MINICK, Thomas .... 610-790-2862.. 397 D
thomas.minick@alvernia.edu
MINICOLA, Steven .... 215-573-0251.. 421 E
minicola@upenn.edu
MINIER, Matt .... 502-897-4205.. 132 D
mrminier@sbts.edu
MINIER-DELGADO,
Jesenia .... 718-289-5288.. 307 C
jesenia.minier-delgado@bcc.cuny.edu
MININGER, Marcus .... 219-864-2400.. 165 O
mmininger@midamerica.edu
MINIX, Jeannette .... 800-290-4226.. 440 G
jminix@hchs.edu
MINK, Randy, L .... 412-397-4901.. 418 B
mink@rmu.edu
MINK, Rose .... 901-751-8453.. 442 E
rmink@mabts.edu
MINKLER, James .... 360-538-4000.. 504 B
jim.minkler@ghc.edu
MINKLER, Steven .... 860-343-5706.... 86 F
sminkler@mxcc.commnet.edu
MINNE, Erin .... 312-362-8663.. 139 C
minne@depaul.edu
MINNEMA, Emily .... 614-825-6255.. 362 J
eminnema@aiam.edu
MINNER, Sam .... 505-454-3269.. 300 F
president_office@nmhu.edu
MINNETTE, Mitch .... 208-562-3516.. 133 F
mitchminnette@cwidaho.cc
MINNICH, Bryan, K .... 785-833-4428.. 182 F
bryan.minnich@kwu.edu
MINNICH, Dan .... 330-972-6476.. 378 G
dminnich@uakron.edu
MINNICH, Peggy .... 513-244-4531.. 373 C
peggy.minnich@msj.edu
MINNICH, William .... 650-738-4484.... 62 I
minnichw@smccd.edu
MINNICH KIESBO, Faith . 717-766-2511.. 410 J
fminnich@messiah.edu
MINNICH SPUHLER
Donna .... 973-720-3258.. 298 G
minnichspuhlerd@wpunj.edu
MINNICK, Ann, M .... 651-696-6036.. 247 I
aminnick@macalester.edu
MINNICK, William, C .... 712-707-7226.. 176 B
bminnick@nwciowa.edu
MINNIEFIELD, Angela, L . 323-563-4897.... 37 G
angelaminniefield@cdrewu.edu
MINNIS, Stephen, D .... 913-360-7400.. 178 I
sminnis@benedictine.edu
MINNIS, Tia .... 404-880-6294.. 118 K
tminnis@cau.edu
MINNITI, Lea .... 513-745-3711.. 381 I
minnitil@xavier.edu
MINOR, Diana, Y .... 909-869-3704.... 31 J
dyminor@cpp.edu
MINOR, Diane .... 312-553-2500.. 137 C
dminor1@ccc.edu
MINOR, Frankie, D .... 573-882-7275.. 273 E
minorf@missouri.edu
MINOR, Karen .... 770-533-7030.. 123 L
kminor@laniertech.edu
MINOR, Leslie .... 707-864-7000.... 65 A
leslie.minor@solano.edu
MINOR, Lloyd .... 650-723-2300.... 66 I
lminor@stanford.edu
MINOR, Lynn, C .... 229-333-5353.. 129 G
lcminor@valdosta.edu
MINOR, Scott .... 916-631-8108.... 31 F
MINOR, Tamra .... 518-956-8110.. 331 A
tminor@albany.edu
MINOW, Martha .... 617-495-4601.. 219 D
minow@law.harvard.edu

MINSON, Patrick .... 718-390-3304.. 339 F
patrick.minson@wagner.edu
MINTEN, Sam, L .... 615-868-6503.. 442 G
sam@mtsa.edu
MINTER, Doug, O .... 507-933-7527.. 246 J
dminter@gustavus.edu
MINTER, Douglas .... 309-268-8100.. 141 C
doug.minter@heartland.edu
MINTER, Michelle .... 609-258-6110.. 294 D
mminter@princeton.edu
MINTERN, Janet .... 252-493-7286.. 352 A
jmintern@email.pittcc.edu
MINTLE, Norm .... 434-582-2077.. 491 D
nmintle@liberty.edu
MINTO, Jean .... 215-702-4270.. 399 E
jminto@cairn.edu
MINTZ, Katrina, H .... 205-726-2896...... 6 E
kmintz@samford.edu
MINTZ, Zev .... 732-370-1560.. 289 C
MINTZER, Jen .... 610-358-4547.. 411 E
mintzerj@neumann.edu
MINUS, Daryl .... 910-362-7040.. 348 A
dminus@cfcc.edu
MINUS, Molly, E .... 512-448-8581.. 464 G
mollym@stedwards.edu
MINUS, Monica .... 252-633-1764.. 349 B
minusm@cravencc.edu
MIRABAL, Gloria .... 787-743-4041.. 531 K
gmirabal@columbiacentral.edu
MIRABAL, Larry .... 505-424-2316.. 299 L
lmirabal@iaia.edu
MIRABILE, Robert .... 608-363-2380.. 515 G
mirabiler@beloit.edu
MIRABITO, Michael .... 570-348-6209.. 409 H
mirabito@marywood.edu
MIRAMONTEZ, Daniel .... 619-388-7333.... 60 H
dmiramon@sdccd.edu
MIRANDA, Albert .... 714-484-7394.... 54 G
amiranda@cypresscollege.edu
MIRANDA, Alex .... 714-895-8107.... 39 F
amiranda42@gwc.cccd.edu
MIRANDA, Candida .... 312-567-3134.. 142 I
miranda@iit.edu
MIRANDA,
Edmund (Rick) .... 562-860-2451.... 36 P
ermiranda@cerritos.edu
MIRANDA, Elizabeth .... 787-250-1912.. 534 B
emiranda@metro.inter.edu
MIRANDA, Enid .... 787-841-2000.. 535 I
emiranda@pucpr.edu
MIRANDA, Gloria .... 310-660-3735.... 42 J
gmiranda@elcamino.edu
MIRANDA, Luis .... 252-639-7340.. 355 K
lmiranda@umo.edu
MIRANDA, Marie, L .... 734-764-2550.. 241 J
mlmirand@umich.edu
MIRANDA, Marie, L .... 713-348-4026.. 464 E
mlm@rice.edu
MIRANDA, Mark .... 732-571-3593.. 292 F
mmiranda@monmouth.edu
MIRANDA, Rick .... 970-491-6614.... 78 P
rick.miranda@colostate.edu
MIRANDA, Rick .... 970-491-6614.... 78 Q
rick.miranda@colostate.edu
MIRANDA, Rowan .... 773-702-4114.. 156 D
rmiranda@uchicago.edu
MIRANDA, Vivian .... 480-461-7246.... 14 D
vivian.miranda@mesacc.edu
MIRANDA, Yolanda .... 787-743-3038.. 535 L
ymiranda@sanjuanbautista.edu
MIRECKI, Julie .... 920-693-1193.. 523 E
julie.mirecki@gotoltc.edu
MIRELES, Melissa .... 575-492-2186.. 302 M
mmireles@usw.edu
MIRELES, Rod .... 936-261-1905.. 467 E
rmireles@pvamu.edu
MIRENBERG, Mark .... 718-261-5800.. 305 J
mmirenberg@ortopusa.org
MIRENBERG, Mark .... 718-261-5800.. 305 J
mmirenberg@ortopsusa.org
MIRENDA, Rosalie, M .... 610-558-5501.. 411 E
rmirenda@neumann.edu
MIRIZZI, Ray .... 859-572-6421.. 192 B
mirizzir1@nku.edu
MIRMIRAN, Amir .... 903-566-7104.. 477 B
amirmiran@uttyler.edu
MIRNICS, Karoly .... 402-559-5720.. 283 A
kmirnics@unmc.edu
MIRRETTI, Armaline .... 630-617-3239.. 140 C
amirretti@elmhurst.edu
MIRRO, Roberta .... 631-249-3048.. 335 E
sm711/bncollege@bncollege.com
MIRSHAB, Bahman .... 248-204-3050.. 237 B
bmirshab@ltu.edu
MIRTZ, Ruth .... 785-833-4396.. 182 F
ruth.mirtz@kwu.edu
MISAK, David .... 580-774-3275.. 388 C
david.misak@swosu.edu
MISCAVAGE, Denise .... 570-674-6248.. 410 K
dmiscava@misericordia.edu

MISCHE, Terri .... 320-308-6675.. 252 A tamische@stcloudstate.edu
MISCHKE, Carly .... 310-506-6738.... 56 J carly.mischke@pepperdine.edu
MISERENDINO, Peter ...... 203-287-3026.... 88 E paier.admin@snet.net
MISGEN, Sherry .... 312-899-5216.. 154 A smisgen@saic.edu
MISHEK, Mark .... 651-213-4006.. 247 B mmishek@hazeldenbettyford.org
MISHLER, Jeremy .... 231-591-2345.. 233 L jeremymishler@ferris.edu
MISHLER, Richard .... 814-886-6339.. 411 C rmishler@mtaloy.edu
MISHOE, Cindy .... 410-287-1901.. 206 J cmishoe@cecil.edu
MISHOE, Shelley, C .... 757-683-4960.. 492 G smishoe@odu.edu
MISHOU, Stephanie .... 207-947-4591.. 202 E smishou@bealcollege.edu
MISHRA, Sharda, D .... 615-327-6156.. 442 A smishra@mmc.edu
MISHRA, Tara .... 479-788-7002.... 23 A tara.mishra@uafs.edu
MISIANO, Chris .... 434-592-3144.. 491 D cjmisiano@liberty.edu
MISKELL, Anita .... 812-749-1240.. 166 B amiskell@oak.edu
MISKUS, Lynn .... 219-473-4310.. 159 L lmiskus@ccsj.edu
MISKY, Allison .... 860-727-2117.... 87 H amisky@goodwin.edu
MISNER, Sarah .... 210-486-3200.. 450 D syelland@alamo.edu
MISORI, Wanda .... 256-726-7000...... 6 B wmisori@oakwood.edu
MISRA, Hara, P .... 540-231-4000.. 489 H
MISRA, Kalpana .... 918-631-2547.. 389 E kalpana-misra@utulsa.edu
MISRA, Ravi, P .... 414-955-8778.. 518 A rmisra@mcw.edu
MISS, Stephen .... 704-461-6802.. 342 A stephenmiss@bac.edu
MISSEL, Thomas .... 716-375-2334.. 328 B
MISSURELLI, David, S ..... 630-637-5680.. 149 H dsmissurelli@noctrl.edu
MISTICK, Barbara, K .... 717-262-2000.. 424 A barbara.mistick@wilson.edu
MISTLER, Brian .... 707-826-3146.... 34 F bjm728@humboldt.edu
MISTO, RSM, Leona .... 401-341-2229.. 426 C mistol@salve.edu
MISTRIC, Amy .... 731-881-7040.. 448 G amistric@utm.edu
MITCHELL, Alan .... 256-331-5362...... 6 A mitchell@nwscc.edu
MITCHELL, Andrew, J .... 757-446-5199.. 489 B mitcheaj@evms.edu
MITCHELL, Annie, S .... 864-597-4199.. 435 C mitchellas1@wofford.edu
MITCHELL, Arden .... 863-680-4131.. 101 E amitchell@flsouthern.edu
MITCHELL, Asia .... 312-629-6115.. 154 A amitchell@saic.edu
MITCHELL, Bede .... 912-478-5116.. 122 B wbmitch@georgiasouthern.edu
MITCHELL, Belinda .... 205-934-4423...... 8 E bmitch1@uab.edu
MITCHELL, Betsy .... 626-395-6148.... 30 H betsy.mitchell@caltech.edu
MITCHELL, Bonnie .... 508-626-4651.. 221 E bmitchell@framingham.edu
MITCHELL, Bradley, J ...... 937-481-2231.. 381 C brad_mitchell@wilmington.edu
MITCHELL, Brenda .... 334-244-3464...... 2 A bmitche8@aum.edu
MITCHELL, Brenda, S ...... 301-546-0858.. 210 C bmitchell@pgcc.edu
MITCHELL, Brian .... 707-826-5788.... 34 F bam721@humboldt.edu
MITCHELL, Bryan .... 404-756-4025.. 116 I bmitchell@atlm.edu
MITCHELL, C. Ben .... 731-661-5355.. 448 A bmitchell@uu.edu
MITCHELL, Carl .... 910-678-8373.. 349 F mitchelc@faytechcc.edu
MITCHELL, Carlton .... 903-233-4451.. 460 J carltonmitchell@letu.edu
MITCHELL, Carrie .... 505-277-1758.. 302 F carriem@unm.edu
MITCHELL, Cassandra ..... 919-719-8880.. 355 F c.mitchell@shawu.edu
MITCHELL, Cathy .... 806-716-2360.. 465 G cmitchell@southplainscollege.edu
MITCHELL, Charles, E ..... 607-735-1804.. 313 F cmitchell@elmira.edu
MITCHELL, Chase .... 435-283-7340.. 482 E chase.mitchell@snow.edu
MITCHELL, Chris .... 501-205-8919.... 19 J cmitchell@cbc.edu
MITCHELL, Chrisie .... 845-431-8976.. 312 G chrisie.mitchell@sunydutchess.edu
MITCHELL, Cindy .... 207-581-1610.. 204 H cindy@maine.edu
MITCHELL, Cindy, J .... 207-859-4000.. 202 G cindy.mitchell@colby.edu
MITCHELL, Connie .... 803-754-4100.. 429 B
MITCHELL, Craig .... 206-517-4541.. 507 B cmitchell@siom.edu
MITCHELL, David .... 415-503-6218.... 61 C dlmitchell@sfcm.edu
MITCHELL, David, B .... 301-405-5726.. 211 E dmitche5@umd.edu
MITCHELL, David, C .... 360-475-7100.. 505 F dmitchell@olympic.edu
MITCHELL, Dawn, P .... 336-734-7207.. 349 G dmitchell@forsythtech.edu
MITCHELL, Debbie .... 734-432-4076.. 237 D doffman@madonna.edu
MITCHELL, Denise .... 843-953-5822.. 428 G mitchellda@cofc.edu
MITCHELL, Dennis .... 212-854-7161.. 311 E dmitchell@columbia.edu
MITCHELL, Donald .... 217-206-6690.. 156 G mitchell.donald@uis.edu
MITCHELL, Donna .... 740-245-7303.. 380 C mitchell@rio.edu
MITCHELL, III, Earnest, L .... 731-426-7604.. 440 K emitchell@lanecollege.edu
MITCHELL, Eleanor .... 717-245-1864.. 402 D mitchele@dickinson.edu
MITCHELL, Emanuel .... 770-537-6065.. 129 M emanuel.mitchell@westgatech.edu
MITCHELL, Gary .... 575-763-0535.. 479 D mitchellg@wbu.edu
MITCHELL, George .... 843-383-8300.. 428 F gmitchell@coker.edu
MITCHELL, Gregory .... 843-477-2032.. 430 F greg.mitchell@hgtc.edu
MITCHELL, Gregory .... 903-886-5719.. 468 D gregory.mitchell@tamuc.edu
MITCHELL, Gwendolyn, F 803-536-8212.. 432 E gmitche3@scsu.edu
MITCHELL, Heather .... 850-201-8580.. 113 E mitchelh@tcc.fl.edu
MITCHELL, Horace .... 661-654-2241.... 32 A hmitchell@csub.edu
MITCHELL, James, M .... 334-876-9231...... 4 A jmitchell@wccs.edu
MITCHELL, Joan .... 801-274-3280.. 483 C jmitchell@wgu.edu
MITCHELL, Joann .... 215-898-6630.. 421 E joannm@upenn.edu
MITCHELL, Joey .... 601-877-6380.. 256 F jmitchell@alcorn.edu
MITCHELL, Johnnie .... 501-337-5000.... 19 K jmitchell@coto.edu
MITCHELL, Juanita .... 870-574-4423.... 22 G jmitchel@sautech.edu
MITCHELL, Jud .... 870-574-4726.... 22 G jmitchel@sautech.edu
MITCHELL, Judy .... 815-280-2207.. 144 A jmitchel@jjc.edu
MITCHELL, Justin .... 706-233-7205.. 127 A jmitchell@shorter.edu
MITCHELL, Karen .... 615-230-3505.. 447 C karen.mitchell@volstate.edu
MITCHELL, Karrie .... 520-206-4973.... 16 F kdmitchell@pima.edu
MITCHELL, Kathy, J .... 276-739-2440.. 499 A kmitchell@vhcc.edu
MITCHELL, Kaylene .... 207-741-5571.. 203 M kmitchell@smccme.edu
MITCHELL, Keith .... 580-581-2211.. 382 G kmitchel@cameron.edu
MITCHELL, Kemper .... 650-433-3835.... 56 D kmitchell@paloaltou.edu
MITCHELL, Ken, H .... 919-209-2112.. 350 G khmitchell@johnstoncc.edu
MITCHELL, Kerrie .... 575-492-2560.. 300 H kmitchell@nmjc.edu
MITCHELL, Kim .... 502-456-6508.. 193 B kmitchell@sullivan.edu
MITCHELL, Kimberly, A .... 309-655-2230.. 153 F kimberly.a.mitchell@osfhealthcare.org
MITCHELL, Lorraine, C ..... 252-862-1272.. 352 D lcmitchell6878@roanokechowan.edu
MITCHELL, Marcia .... 413-552-2431.. 223 E mmitchell@hcc.edu
MITCHELL, Maria .... 610-372-4721.. 417 G mmitchell@racc.edu
MITCHELL, Marionette .... 713-525-3120.. 475 J marion@stthom.edu
MITCHELL, Melissa .... 308-432-6221.. 281 H mmitchell@csc.edu
MITCHELL, Michael .... 251-460-6172...... 9 E mmitchell@southalabama.edu
MITCHELL, Monique .... 252-862-1262.. 352 D memitchell6938@roanokechowan.edu
MITCHELL, Nancy, L .... 509-527-5168.. 509 G mitchenl@whitman.edu
MITCHELL, Natalie .... 703-284-6861.. 492 A natalie.mitchell@marymount.edu
MITCHELL, Neke .... 505-277-2611.. 302 F dmitchell@unm.edu
MITCHELL, Pablo .... 440-775-8410.. 374 C pmitchell@oberlin.edu
MITCHELL, Patrice .... 843-574-6010.. 433 D patrice.mitchell@tridenttech.edu
MITCHELL, Patricia .... 301-860-3416.. 212 D pmitchell@bowiestate.edu
MITCHELL, Paula .... 915-831-4030.. 457 H pmitche8@epcc.edu
MITCHELL, Peg, P .... 302-356-6810.... 91 I peg.p.mitchell@wilmu.edu
MITCHELL, Randolph .... 904-470-8150.... 98 N randolph.mitchell@ewc.edu
MITCHELL, Reavis .... 615-329-8610.. 439 L rmitchel@fisk.edu
MITCHELL, Renee, D .... 773-995-2040.. 136 M rmitch26@csu.edu
MITCHELL, Rick, L .... 330-287-1277.. 375 B mitchell.246@osu.edu
MITCHELL, Robert .... 502-456-6509.. 193 A rmitchell@sctd.edu
MITCHELL, JR., Robert .... 504-816-4864.. 195 B rvmitchell@dillard.edu
MITCHELL, Robin .... 563-288-6103.. 172 C rmitchell@eicc.edu
MITCHELL, Ronald, S .... 417-625-9531.. 268 H mitchell-r@mssu.edu
MITCHELL, Rose .... 973-748-9000.. 289 H rose_mitchell@bloomfield.edu
MITCHELL, Sandra .... 701-777-2167.. 360 C sandra.mitchell@und.edu
MITCHELL, Saralyn .... 256-233-8146...... 1 F saralyn.mitchell@athens.edu
MITCHELL, Seandra .... 414-277-6762.. 518 E
MITCHELL, Sharon, L ...... 716-645-2720.. 331 C smitch@buffalo.edu
MITCHELL, Sheila .... 731-661-5953.. 448 A smitchell@uu.edu
MITCHELL, Stephen .... 845-434-5750.. 336 H smitchell@sunysullivan.edu
MITCHELL, Stephen, R .... 202-687-3922.... 92 E mitchelr@georgetown.edu
MITCHELL, Steve .... 903-823-3065.. 467 C steven.mitchell@texarkanacollege.edu
MITCHELL, Tedd, L .... 806-743-2900.. 472 D tedd.mitchell@ttuhsc.edu
MITCHELL, Tee .... 229-333-5791.. 129 G rtmitchell@valdosta.edu
MITCHELL, Terrence .... 607-436-2830.. 331 F terrence.mitchell@oneonta.edu
MITCHELL, Thomas, J .... 352-392-5407.. 112 A tmitchell@uff.ufl.edu
MITCHELL, Thomas, R ..... 956-326-2240.. 468 A tmitchell@tamiu.edu
MITCHELL, Todd .... 270-534-3256.. 190 H todd.mitchell@kctcs.edu
MITCHELL, Tucker .... 843-661-1225.. 430 B cmitchell@fmarion.edu
MITCHELL, Venita .... 573-592-4239.. 275 G venita.mitchell@williamwoods.edu
MITCHELL, William .... 508-588-9100.. 223 G
MITCHELL, Zane, W .... 812-464-1701.. 168 E zwmitchell@usi.edu
MITCHELL BENAVENTE, Debra .... 562-902-3336.... 66 A debramitchell@scuhs.edu
MITCHELL-CRUMP, Pamela .... 860-512-2605.... 86 E pmitchell-crump@manchestercc.edu
MITCHELL WHEELER, Jennifer .... 919-497-3226.. 346 B jwheeler@louisburg.edu
MITCHELSON, Ron .... 252-328-5419.. 356 C mitchelsonr@ecu.edu
MITCHLER, Allan, M .... 414-410-4059.. 515 I admitchler@stritch.edu
MITCHLEY, Jill .... 570-484-2526.. 415 D jmitchle@lhup.edu
MITEZA, Ilir .... 313-593-5030.. 242 A imiteza@umich.edu
MITJANS, Dolores .... 787-882-2065.. 536 D compras@unitecpr.net
MITSUI, Mark .... 971-722-4365.. 394 F mark.mitsui@pcc.edu
MITTA, Ave, M .... 540-985-4097.. 491 A ammitta@jchs.edu
MITTELHAMMER, Ron .... 509-335-4561.. 508 H mittelha@wsu.edu
MITTEN, Richard .... 646-312-2076.. 307 A richard.mitten@baruch.cuny.edu
MITTERNDORFER, Sylvia . 757-221-3595.. 488 F smmitt@wm.edu
MITTLEMAN, Michael, H . 215-780-1280.. 419 C president@salus.edu
MITTMAN, Paul, A .... 480-858-9100.... 17 B p.mittman@scnm.edu
MITTON, Gregory, S .... 484-664-3175.. 411 D mitton@muhlenberg.edu
MITTUCH, Maggie, A .... 253-879-3673.. 508 D mmittuch@pugetsound.edu
MITZE, Marnie, D .... 310-506-4451.... 56 J marnie.mitze@pepperdine.edu
MITZEL, Thomas .... 701-483-2326.. 360 D thomas.mitzel@dickinsonstate.edu
MIULLI, Gail .... 425-388-9216.. 503 F gmiulli@everettcc.edu
MIX, Catherine .... 937-229-4311.. 379 D cmix01@udayton.edu
MIX, Kerry .... 281-459-7106.. 465 A kerry.mix@sjcd.edu
MIXNER, Mark, P .... 610-436-2731.. 416 C mmixner@wcupa.edu
MIXON, Bill .... 205-853-1200...... 5 B bmixon@jeffstateonline.com
MIXON, Lonnie .... 407-303-8192.... 95 C lonnie.mixon@adu.edu
MIXON, Melissa .... 206-934-7791.. 506 J melissa.mixon@seattlecolleges.edu
MIXON, Paul .... 870-972-2088.... 18 J pmixon@astate.edu
MIYAMOTO, Jack .... 951-487-3156.... 53 D jmiyamoto@msjc.edu
MIYAMOTO, Michael, H .. 563-589-3270.. 177 C mmiyamoto@dbq.edu
MIYARES, Javier .... 301-985-7077.. 212 C president-office@umuc.edu
MIYASAKI, Kevin, T .... 208-496-1155.. 132 J miyasakik@byui.edu
MIYASHIRO, Jane .... 310-665-6910.... 55 E jmiyashiro@otis.edu
MIYASHIRO, Ross .... 714-546-7600.... 39 E
MIZE, Charles .... 478-301-2951.. 124 D mize_c@mercer.edu
MIZE, Kyle, C .... 325-649-8049.. 459 E kmize@hputx.edu
MIZELL, Catherine, S ...... 865-974-3245.. 448 D cmizell@tennessee.edu
MIZELL, Paul .... 912-871-1645.. 125 E pmizell@ogeecheetech.edu
MIZELLE, Angela, J .... 919-866-5825.. 353 I ajmizelle@waketech.edu
MIZRAHI, Leah .... 323-822-9700.... 68 B leah.mizrahi@touro.edu
MLADENOVIC, Jeanette ... 503-494-4460.. 393 F provost@ohsu.edu
MLODZIK, Leigh, D .... 920-748-8704.. 519 E mlodzikl@ripon.edu
MMEJE, Kenechukwu .... 773-508-8840.. 146 G kmmeje@luc.edu
MNCUBE-BARNES, Fatima .... 615-327-5770.. 442 A fbarnes@mmc.edu
MNOOKIN, Jennifer, L .... 310-825-8202.... 69 D mnookin@law.ucla.edu
MOANANU, Letupu .... 684-699-9155.. 529 E l.moananu@amsamoa.edu
MOATS, Kyle .... 417-836-5244.. 268 I kylemoats@missouristate.edu
MOATS, Scott .... 952-446-4210.. 246 D moatss@crown.edu
MOBASSERI, Maria .... 217-403-4599.. 151 B mmobasseri@parkland.edu
MOBERG, Bret .... 847-578-8308.. 153 A bret.moberg@rosalindfranklin.edu
MOBERG, Kathleen .... 408-848-4732.... 44 I kmoberg@gavilan.edu
MOBERLY, Jonathon .... 402-643-7430.. 279 F jonathon.moberly@cune.edu
MOBERLY, Richard .... 402-472-6827.. 282 M moberly@unl.edu
MOBERLY, Tara .... 303-964-3640.... 82 L tmoberly@regis.edu
MOBLEY, Bob .... 863-638-7213.. 115 C bob.mobley@warner.edu
MOBLEY, Brandon .... 706-880-8052.. 123 K mmobley@lagrange.edu
MOBLEY, Cathryn, B .... 434-395-2759.. 491 E mobleycb@longwood.edu
MOBLEY, Karen .... 912-871-1638.. 125 E kmobley@ogeecheetech.edu
MOBLEY, Katie .... 802-654-0505.. 486 A katie.mobley@ccv.edu
MOBLEY, Marilyn, S .... 216-368-8877.. 365 B marilyn.mobley@case.edu
MOBLEY, Wade .... 763-544-9501.. 244 H
MOCABEE, Norma .... 626-815-4550.... 28 A nmocabee@apu.edu
MOCARSKI, Richard, A ..... 308-865-8496.. 282 L mocarskira@unk.edu
MOCCIA, Mario .... 575-646-7630.. 300 J moccia@nmsu.edu
MOCEK, Christian .... 812-357-6479.. 167 B cmocek@saintmeinrad.edu
MOCERI, Joane, T .... 503-943-7211.. 396 B moceri@up.edu
MOCK, Keith .... 334-386-7876...... 3 I kmock@faulkner.edu

MONETA, Larry .... 919-684-3737.. 343 J
studentaffairs@duke.edu
MONETTE, Marliss .... 575-835-5623.. 300 G
mmonette@admin.nmt.edu
MONEY, Ken .... 601-366-8880.. 261 H
kmoney@wbs.edu
MONEY, Royce .... 325-674-4974.. 449 J
moneyr@acu.edu
MONEYMAKER, Andrew .. 662-329-7127.. 259 E
amoneymaker@muw.edu
MONFETTE, Rachel .... 312-329-4189.. 148 F
rachel.monfette@moody.edu
MONG, Ronald .... 972-780-3601.. 475 B
president@untdallas.edu
MONGAN, Jason .... 800-444-1440.. 417 B
jmongan@pia.edu
MONGAN,
Jeremiah James .... 970-352-1181.... 76 F
MONGAR, Mark, J .... 402-280-2262.. 279 H
markmongar@creighton.edu
MONGE, Edwin .... 301-891-4008.. 213 D
emonge@wau.edu
MONGEON, Michael .... 508-373-9458.. 215 D
michael.mongeon@becker.edu
MONGEON-STEWART,
Karla .... 701-777-2015.. 360 C
karla.stewart@und.edu
MONGER, Todd .... 612-343-3513.. 253 Y
tjmonger@northcentral.edu
MONGERSON, John .... 815-939-5101.. 150 I
jmonger@olivet.edu
MONGILLO, Anne, M .... 516-463-6776.. 316 D
anne.mongillo@hofstra.edu
MONGO, Karen .... 214-860-2106.. 456 E
kmongo@dcccd.edu
MONHEIT, Yidel .... 718-853-2442.. 340 N
MONHOLLON, Michael ... 325-670-5870.. 458 J
mmonholl@hsutx.edu
MONIACI, Steve, C .... 281-649-3096.. 458 L
smoniaci@hbu.edu
MONIODIS, Paul .... 410-837-5270.. 213 C
pmoniodis@ubalt.edu
MONIT, Scott .... 724-480-3356.. 401 F
scott.monit@ccbc.edu
MONIZ, Jeffrey .... 808-689-2300.. 131 G
jmoniz@hawaii.edu
MONK, David, H .... 814-865-2526.. 412 F
dhm6@psu.edu
MONK, Matthew .... 802-828-8556.. 485 E
matthew.monk@vcfa.edu
MONK, Sam .... 256-782-5104...... 4 H
smonk@jsu.edu
MONK, Suzanne .... 662-476-5014.. 257 G
smonk@eastms.edu
MONKS, Birgit .... 909-652-6876.... 37 D
birgit.monks@chaffey.edu
MONNAT, Angela, B .... 585-385-8042.. 328 E
amonnat@sjfc.edu
MONNES, Mark, J .... 419-755-4824.. 373 G
mmonnes@ncstatecollege.edu
MONNIG, Amber .... 660-248-6280.. 263 B
armonnig@centralmethodist.edu
MONNOT, Charles .... 405-208-5295.. 385 E
cmonnot@okcu.edu
MONOD, Kelly .... 941-752-5491.. 110 H
monodk@scf.edu
MONOLO, Melissa .... 843-349-7883.. 430 F
melissa.monolo@hgtc.edu
MONROE, Alicia .... 856-256-4284.. 295 E
monroe@rowan.edu
MONROE, Alicia .... 713-798-2312.. 452 G
alicia.monroe@bcm.edu
MONROE, Jill .... 619-849-2298.... 57 M
jillmonroe@pointloma.edu
MONROE, Joseph, W ...... 859-257-5770.. 193 G
joe.monroe@uky.edu
MONROE, JP .... 541-346-2085.. 395 G
jpmonroe@uoregon.edu
MONROE, Maxine .... 845-569-3346.. 322 B
maxine.monroe@msmc.edu
MONROE, Randall, L .... 570-326-3761.. 413 O
rmonroe@pct.edu
MONROE, William .... 713-743-9007.. 473 F
wmonroe@uh.edu
MONROE-BAILLARGEON,
Ann .... 860-231-5322.... 90 B
annmonroe@usj.edu
MONROY, Isabel .... 626-873-2187.... 53 E
imonroy@mtsierra.edu
MONS, Marie .... 404-894-4582.. 121 D
marie.mons@finaid.gatech.edu
MONSANTO, Steve .... 951-372-7140.... 59 B
steve.monsanto@norcocollege.edu
MONTAG, Jerry .... 815-753-1747.. 150 A
jerry.montag@niu.edu
MONTAGNE, Michael ...... 617-732-2995.. 225 C
michael.montagne@mcphs.edu
MONTAGNINO, Chris ...... 518-608-8184.. 314 A
cmontagnino@excelsior.edu
MONTAGUE, Evan .... 734-973-3408.. 242 G
elmontague@wccnet.edu
MONTAGUE, Krista .... 406-657-2061.. 277 D
kmontague@msubillings.edu
MONTAGUE, Marlena, O . 671-735-5612.. 529 G
marlena.montague@guamcc.edu
MONTAGUE, Orinthia ...... 952-358-8283.. 251 A
orinthia.montague@normandale.edu
MONTALBAN, Silvia .... 646-557-4409.. 308 E
smontalban@jjay.cuny.edu
MONTALBANO, Ivonne .... 713-221-8060.. 474 B
montalbanoi@uhd.edu
MONTALTO, Karen .... 856-222-9311.. 295 C
kmontalto@rcbc.edu
MONTALVO, Carmen .... 787-878-5475.. 533 H
cmontalv@arecibo.inter.edu
MONTALVO, Cynthia .... 201-559-6036.. 291 K
montalvoc@felician.edu
MONTALVO, Devyn .... 863-638-2964.. 115 D
montalvods@webber.edu
MONTALVO, Luis .... 617-262-5000.. 216 A
luis.montalvo@the-bac.edu
MONTALVO, Provi .... 787-878-5475.. 533 H
pmontalvo@arecibo.inter.edu
MONTALVO-COLÓN,
Sonia, I .... 787-751-1912.. 534 E
smontalv@juris.inter.edu
MONTANA, Michael .... 717-262-2002.. 424 A
michael.montana@wilson.edu
MONTANARI, James .... 815-836-5222.. 145 H
montanja@lewisu.edu
MONTANARO,
Gregory, P .... 215-895-0541.. 402 G
gregory.p.montanaro@drexel.edu
MONTANEZ, John .... 212-220-8011.. 307 B
jmontanez@bmcc.cuny.edu
MONTANEZ-LOPEZ,
Nilda .... 787-740-3001.. 536 G
nilda.montanez@uccaribe.edu
MONTANO-CORDOVA,
Ruby, S .... 909-593-3511.... 71 B
rmontano-cordova@laverne.edu
MONTAÑEZ, Isabel .... 787-767-2040.. 538 F
isabel.montanez@upr.edu
MONTE, Renee .... 415-338-3982.... 35 B
rmonte@sfsu.edu
MONTEAGUDO, Rene ...... 305-284-5511.. 114 H
rxm981@miami.edu
MONTECALVO, Frank .... 814-472-3002.. 418 F
fmontecalvo@francis.edu
MONTEFUSCO, Anthony .. 401-254-3023.. 426 B
amontefusco@rwu.edu
MONTEFUSCO, Luis .... 609-343-5635.. 288 H
lmontefu@atlantic.edu
MONTEIRO, Beth .... 608-363-2699.. 515 G
monteirob@beloit.edu
MONTEIRO, Kenneth, P ... 415-338-1693.... 35 B
monteiro@sfsu.edu
MONTEIRO, Marconi .... 210-924-4338.. 452 F
marconi.monteiro@bua.edu
MONTEITH, Kellie .... 828-227-7147.. 359 A
monteith@wcu.edu
MONTELLA, Andrea .... 219-844-0100.. 159 E
andrea.m@brightwood.edu
MONTEMAYOR, Roland ..... 408-288-3146.... 62 E
roland.montemayor@sjcc.edu
MONTEMURRO,
Kimberly .... 914-633-2246.. 317 B
kmontemurro@iona.edu
MONTENEGRO, Luis .... 718-289-5939.. 307 C
luis.montenegro@bcc.cuny.edu
MONTERO, Grecia .... 609-771-3132.. 290 F
montero@tcnj.edu
MONTERO, Janina .... 310-825-1404.... 69 D
jmontero@saonet.ucla.edu
MONTERO, Joel .... 787-720-1022.. 531 A
admisiones@atlanticu.edu
MONTES, Aimee .... 406-395-4875.. 278 F
amontes@stonechild.edu
MONTES, Bruce, A .... 773-508-7601.. 146 G
bmontes@luc.edu
MONTES, Darlene .... 818-364-7758.... 49 J
montesd@lamission.edu
MONTES, Josefer .... 509-527-2615.. 508 G
josefer.montes@wallawalla.edu
MONTES, Luis .... 914-594-3723.. 323 I
luis_montes@nymc.edu
MONTES, Porfirio .... 787-863-2390.. 533 K
porfirio.montes@fajardo.inter.edu
MONTES, Rebecca .... 707-468-3009.... 52 C
rmontes@mendocino.edu
MONTES, Susan, R .... 305-284-6021.. 114 H
smontes@miami.edu
MONTES-BURGOS,
Carmen .... 787-993-8952.. 537 G
carmen.montes1@upr.edu
MONTES-HELU, Maria ...... 520-383-8401.... 17 E
mmontes@tocc.edu
MONTES-MORALES,
Maria .... 718-782-2200.. 305 I
mmontes@boricuacollege.edu
MONTESINO,
María del C .... 787-720-1022.. 531 A
recaudaciones@atlanticu.edu
MONTEVIRGEN,
Alexis, S .... 219-980-6824.. 163 B
amontevi@iun.edu
MONTEZ, Daniel .... 956-447-6635.. 465 H
dmontez@southtexascollege.edu
MONTEZ, Nicholas .... 619-482-6306.... 66 E
nmontez@swccd.edu
MONTGOMERY, Adrienne 978-837-5196.. 225 E
montgomerya@merrimack.edu
MONTGOMERY, Alan .... 772-462-7860.. 103 B
jmontgom@irsc.edu
MONTGOMERY, Alisa, L . 336-322-2213.. 351 H
alisa.montgomery@piedmontcc.edu
MONTGOMERY, Cathy ..... 912-427-6265.. 119 B
cmontgomery@coastalpines.edu
MONTGOMERY, Christy .. 985-543-4120.. 196 G
MONTGOMERY, Cindy .... 229-226-1621.. 128 B
cmontgomery@thomasu.edu
MONTGOMERY, JR.,
Clyde .... 405-466-3636.. 383 M
cmontgomery@langston.edu
MONTGOMERY, Dale .... 479-619-4234.... 21 D
dmontgom@nwacc.edu
MONTGOMERY, Daron .... 603-641-7107.. 287 G
dmontgomery@anselm.edu
MONTGOMERY, Daron .... 715-346-3688.. 521 C
dmontgom@uwsp.edu
MONTGOMERY,
Edward, B .... 202-687-6163.... 92 E
emb48@georgetown.edu
MONTGOMERY, Eric .... 620-331-4100.. 181 J
emontgomery@indycc.edu
MONTGOMERY, Francis .. 716-896-0700.. 339 E
franciscssf@villa.edu
MONTGOMERY, Grant ...... 800-962-7682.. 275 D
gmontgomery@wma.edu
MONTGOMERY, Isalene ... 386-506-3961.... 98 E
montgoi@daytonastate.edu
MONTGOMERY, Jeff .... 937-393-3431.. 377 F
jlmontgo@sscc.edu
MONTGOMERY, John ...... 951-343-4963.... 29 H
jmontgomery@calbaptist.edu
MONTGOMERY, John ...... 575-562-4002.. 299 I
john.montgomery@enmu.edu
MONTGOMERY,
Joseph, D .... 330-823-2295.. 379 F
montgojd@mountunion.edu
MONTGOMERY, Kara, H .. 724-946-7363.. 423 B
montgokh@westminster.edu
MONTGOMERY, Karen ..... 512-404-4816.. 452 A
kmontgomery@austinseminary.edu
MONTGOMERY, Kathryn .. 864-225-7653.. 430 A
kathrynmontgomery@forrestcollege.edu
MONTGOMERY, Keith ...... 715-261-6223.. 522 A
keith.montgomery@uwc.edu
MONTGOMERY, Kit .... 214-333-5209.. 455 J
kit@dbu.edu
MONTGOMERY,
Laura, M .... 630-752-5227.. 158 C
laura.montgomery@wheaton.edu
MONTGOMERY, Lisa .... 312-567-3777.. 142 I
montgomeryl@iit.edu
MONTGOMERY, Lisa .... 610-436-2568.. 416 C
lmontgomery@wcupa.edu
MONTGOMERY, Lisa, P ... 843-792-5050.. 431 A
montgoml@musc.edu
MONTGOMERY, Mark .... 315-733-2307.. 338 L
mmontgomery@uscny.edu
MONTGOMERY, Martha ... 254-442-5114.. 454 E
martha.montgomery@cisco.edu
MONTGOMERY, Melissa . 517-750-6426.. 241 E
melissa.montgomery@arbor.edu
MONTGOMERY, Mike .... 937-433-3410.. 368 H
mmontgomery@fortiscollege.edu
MONTGOMERY, Roark ..... 903-875-7487.. 462 J
roark.montgomery@navarrocollege.edu
MONTGOMERY, Robert ... 248-232-4808.. 239 E
rjmontgo@oaklandcc.edu
MONTGOMERY, Tammy .. 916-484-8408.... 51 A
montgot2@arc.losrios.edu
MONTGOMERY, Terri ...... 314-362-6255.. 265 E
txm9149@bjc.org
MONTGOMERY,
Toni-Marie .... 847-491-7552.. 150 F
t-montgomery@northwestern.edu
MONTGOMERY, Tony .... 662-476-5062.. 257 G
tmontgomery@eastms.edu
MONTGOMERY,
Tonya, Y .... 502-597-6434.. 191 B
tonya.montgomery@kysu.edu
MONTGOMERY,
Walter, C .... 336-322-2258.. 351 H
walter.montgomery@piedmontcc.edu
MONTGOMERY RICE,
Valerie .... 404-752-1740.. 125 A
vmontgomeryrice@msm.edu
MONTI, Joseph .... 407-644-1408.. 107 O
jmonti@rollins.edu
MONTIEL, Arthuro .... 956-488-5808.. 465 H
amontiel@southtexascollege.edu
MONTIJO, Minerva .... 716-896-0700.. 339 E
montijom@villa.edu
MONTIJO, River .... 503-768-6030.. 392 A
rmontijo@lclark.edu
MONTILEAUX, Kateri .... 605-455-6142.. 436 G
kmontileaux@olc.edu
MONTONE, Richard .... 413-644-4776.. 214 H
rmontone@simons-rock.edu
MONTOYA, Bernadette ..... 575-646-7607.. 300 J
bermonto@nmsu.edu
MONTOYA, Denise .... 505-454-2556.. 299 M
dmontoya@luna.edu
MONTOYA, Jimi .... 505-747-2139.. 301 F
jimi.montoya@nnmc.edu
MONTOYA, Michael .... 505-454-2534.. 299 M
mimontoya@luna.edu
MONTOYA, Michelle .... 510-780-4500.... 48 J
mmontoya@lifewest.edu
MONTOYA, Mitzi .... 541-737-6024.. 393 H
MONTOYA, Rolando .... 305-237-3872.. 105 D
rmontoya@mdc.edu
MONTOYA, Valerie .... 505-346-2330.. 302 E
valerie.montoya@bie.edu
MONTOYA, Victor .... 406-275-4974.. 278 E
victor_montoya@skc.edu
MONTREAL, Steven, R ...... 262-243-5700.. 516 E
steven.montreal@cuw.edu
MONTROSE, Lee .... 910-410-1813.. 352 C
ljmontrose@richmondcc.edu
MONTZ, Ruth .... 330-287-1247.. 375 B
montz.11@osu.edu
MOO, Deok Joo .... 770-220-7919.. 120 G
it@gcuniv.edu
MOO-YOUNG, Keith .... 509-372-7258.. 508 H
keith.mooyoung@wsu.edu
MOODY, Barbara .... 207-941-7000.. 202 I
moodyb@husson.edu
MOODY, Chip .... 602-429-4919.... 16 E
cmoody@ps.edu
MOODY, Chris .... 202-885-3370.... 91 J
moody@american.edu
MOODY, D. L .... 817-461-8741.. 451 G
dmoody@arlingtonbaptistcollege.edu
MOODY, Debra .... 334-222-6591...... 5 F
djmoody@lbwcc.edu
MOODY, Jan .... 601-928-6207.. 259 C
janet.moody@mgccc.edu
MOODY, Jeff, T .... 219-942-1459.. 160 C
jmoody@ccr.edu
MOODY, Kari .... 920-465-2226.. 520 B
moodyk@uwgb.edu
MOODY, Kay .... 219-942-1459.. 160 C
kay.moody@ccr.edu
MOODY, Krystal .... 903-927-3312.. 479 K
kmoody@wileyc.edu
MOODY, Linda .... 213-477-2560.... 53 B
lmoody@msmu.edu
MOODY, Marilyn .... 503-725-4616.. 394 G
marilynmoody@pdx.edu
MOODY, Marla .... 417-447-4842.. 270 A
moodym@otc.edu
MOODY, Mary .... 615-366-4438.. 444 D
mary.moody@tbr.edu
MOODY, Michelle, L .... 757-594-8819.. 488 E
mlmoody@cnu.edu
MOODY, Nancy, B .... 423-636-7301.. 447 G
nmoody@tusculum.edu
MOODY, Saundrette .... 229-430-4663.. 115 K
saundrette.moody@asurams.edu
MOODY, Timothy .... 912-344-2518.. 116 E
tim.moody@armstrong.edu
MOODY, Tonia .... 601-403-1214.. 260 D
tmoody@prcc.edu
MOOMAW, Jillian .... 724-847-6674.. 404 B
jgmoomau@geneva.edu
MOON, Beverly .... 662-846-4873.. 257 E
bmoon@deltastate.edu
MOON, Daniel, C .... 904-620-2261.. 112 B
dmoon@unf.edu
MOON, David .... 719-255-3566.... 83 L
cmoon@uccs.edu
MOON, Don .... 434-592-3235.. 491 D
donmoon@liberty.edu
MOON, Freddie, P .... 256-766-6610...... 4 B
pmoon@hcu.edu
MOON, Greg .... 503-517-1880.. 396 F
gmoon@westernseminary.edu
MOON, Greta .... 760-245-4271.... 73 H
greta.moon@vvc.edu
MOON, Hope .... 440-365-5222.. 371 H
MOON, Hyon, J .... 949-480-4139.... 64 J
hmoon@soka.edu
MOON, Jennifer .... 309-794-7208.. 135 D
jennifermoon@augustana.edu
MOON, Jessica .... 803-508-7262.. 426 G
moonj@atc.edu
MOON, Joshua .... 605-626-3336.. 437 D
joshua.moon@northern.edu

MOORE, Robin .... 402-323-3497.. 282 F
rmoore@southeast.edu
MOORE, Robin, S .... 757-822-1724.. 498 H
rmoore@tcc.edu
MOORE, Rochelle .... 954-201-7471.... 96 I
rmoore@broward.edu
MOORE, Rod .... 316-943-2241.. 186 A
MOORE, Rodney .... 936-261-9311.. 467 E
rvmoore@pvamu.edu
MOORE, Roger .... 501-882-8906.... 18 I
rlmoore@asub.edu
MOORE, Rudell .... 937-708-5734.. 381 B
rmoore@wilberforce.edu
MOORE, Russell .... 303-492-2890.... 83 K
rmoore@colorado.edu
MOORE, Sandra .... 803-535-1237.. 431 I
mooresj@octech.edu
MOORE, Sandy .... 620-227-9329.. 180 E
smoore@dc3.edu
MOORE, Sandy .... 620-365-5116.. 178 A
moore@allencc.edu
MOORE, Sara .... 212-517-3929.. 330 G
s.moore@sothebysinstitute.com
MOORE, Scott .... 559-278-0333.... 32 F
scottm@csufresno.edu
MOORE, Shamus .... 580-774-3001.. 388 C
shamus.moore@swosu.edu
MOORE, Shelly .... 724-480-3492.. 401 F
shelly.moore@ccbc.edu
MOORE, Shirley .... 937-778-7861.. 368 E
smoore@edisonohio.edu
MOORE, Stacey .... 803-327-8014.. 435 D
smoore@yorktech.edu
MOORE, Stan .... 817-274-4284.. 452 I
smoore@bhcarroll.edu
MOORE, Stephan, T .... 340-692-4188.. 539 C
stephan.moore@uvi.edu
MOORE, Stephany .... 575-835-5128.. 300 G
smoore@admin.nmt.edu
MOORE, Stephen, W .... 340-693-1582.. 539 C
stephen.moore@uvi.edu
MOORE, Steve .... 781-239-3938.. 214 G
scmoore@babson.edu
MOORE, Steve .... 214-648-7145.. 478 C
steve.moore@utsouthwestern.edu
MOORE, Steven, C .... 239-590-1919.. 110 L
cmoore@fgcu.edu
MOORE, Stuart .... 251-442-2203...... 9 A
smoore@umobile.edu
MOORE, Tammie, L .... 985-380-2957.. 196 K
tammiemoore1@scl.edu
MOORE, Tammy .... 320-363-5054.. 245 I
tmoore@csbsju.edu
MOORE, Tanya .... 217-228-5432.. 151 F
mooreta@quincy.edu
MOORE, Teresa .... 806-291-3753.. 479 D
teresam@wbu.edu
MOORE, Tessa .... 607-735-1900.. 313 F
tmoore@elmira.edu
MOORE, Theresa .... 608-796-3172.. 522 O
trmoore@viterbo.edu
MOORE, Thomas, F .... 304-457-6238.. 510 B
mooretf@ab.edu
MOORE, Timothy .... 518-255-5323.. 334 D
mooretw@cobleskill.edu
MOORE, Timothy .... 617-353-0750.. 216 E
mooretj@bu.edu
MOORE, Timothy .... 847-214-7651.. 140 A
tmoore@elgin.edu
MOORE, Timothy, E .... 850-412-5102.. 110 J
timothy.moore@famu.edu
MOORE, Timothy, J .... 919-530-7420.. 357 A
tmoore@nccu.edu
MOORE, Tina .... 217-234-5346.. 145 D
tmoore@lakeland.cc.il.us
MOORE, Tina .... 417-865-2815.. 265 B
mooret@evangel.edu
MOORE, Tomeka .... 601-877-6118.. 256 F
tmoore1@alcorn.edu
MOORE, Tony .... 504-520-7449.. 202 C
tmoore15@xula.edu
MOORE, Tonya .... 678-323-7700..... 93 F
MOORE, Virginia .... 304-357-4987.. 511 E
virginiamoore@ucwv.edu
MOORE, William (Joe) ..... 605-688-4692.. 437 F
william.moore@sdstate.edu
MOORE, Winifred, B .... 843-953-7477.. 428 A
bo.moore@citadel.edu
MOORE-COOPER, Robin ... 937-708-5685.. 381 B
rmoore-cooper@wilberforce.edu
MOORE-DAVIS, Feleccia .. 850-201-8680.. 113 E
mooredaf@tcc.fl.edu
MOORE-GARCIA, Beverly 305-237-2500.. 105 D
bmoorega@mdc.edu
MOORE-JONES,
Yolanda, V .... 919-536-7201.. 349 D
jonesym@durhamtech.edu
MOORER, Cassandra .... 205-366-8980....... 7 E
MOORER, Glynda, M .... 517-355-2488.. 237 I
moorerg@msu.edu
MOORES, Lisa .... 301-295-3185.. 528 G
lisa.moores@usuhs.edu
MOORHEAD, Tracey, A ... 219-299-3654.. 246 A
moorhead@cord.edu
MOORMAN, Annorrah ..... 309-556-3052.. 143 D
amoorman@iwu.edu
MOORMAN, Cathy .... 765-998-5123.. 167 C
ctmoorman@taylor.edu
MOORMAN, Jack, W .... 919-515-3000.. 357 B
jack_moorman@ncsu.edu
MOORMAN, Nate .... 706-245-7226.. 120 D
nmoorman@ec.edu
MOORMAN, Thomas .... 817-735-2505.. 475 C
thomas.moorman@unthsc.edu
MOORMON, Josh .... 818-333-3558.... 54 B
MOORS, Dean .... 402-462-4000.. 278 K
dmoors@cccneb.edu
MOORWOOD, Woody .... 626-815-3855..... 28 A
wmoorwood@apu.edu
MOOS, Chris .... 417-625-9703.. 268 H
moos-c@mssu.edu
MOOS, Michael .... 317-917-3623.. 165 O
mmoos@martin.edu
MOOS, William, H .... 509-335-0200.. 508 H
bill.moos@wsu.edu
MOOSBRUGGER, Bob ..... 419-372-7052.. 364 E
MOOSMAN, Lucas .... 916-660-8103.... 64 F
lmoosman@sierracollege.edu
MOOT, Bradley .... 212-678-8035.. 317 I
brmoot@jtsa.edu
MOOTHART, Kathy .... 319-385-6209.. 174 A
kathy.moothart@iw.edu
MOOTISPAW, Angel .... 937-393-3431.. 377 F
amootispaw@sscc.edu
MOOTZ, Allison, C .... 215-885-2360.. 409 G
amootz@manor.edu
MOOTZ, Jay .... 916-739-7151.... 71 C
jmootz@pacific.edu
MOPPERT, Jan .... 610-499-4177.. 423 E
jamoppert@widener.edu
MORA, Flora .... 808-984-3517.. 132 D
fmora@hawaii.edu
MORA, Isabelle .... 253-912-2290.. 506 B
MORA, Marc .... 760-872-2000.... 42 B
mmora@deepsprings.edu
MORA, Michelle .... 818-240-1000.... 45 A
mmora@glendale.edu
MORA, Nereida .... 787-765-4210.. 531 H
nmora@cempr.edu
MORA, Peter, L .... 609-343-4901.. 288 H
mora@atlantic.edu
MORADILLOS, Alicia .... 787-834-9595.. 536 E
amoradillos@uaa.edu
MORALE, Joseph, L .... 903-927-3232.. 479 K
jmorale@wileyc.edu
MORALE, Joseph, L .... 903-927-3233.. 479 K
jmorale@wileyc.edu
MORALE, Mary .... 706-821-8232.. 125 H
mmorale@paine.edu
MORALE, Sonja .... 903-566-7059.. 477 B
smorale@uttyler.edu
MORALES, Adelina, C ...... 325-942-2073.. 472 B
adelina.morales@angelo.edu
MORALES, Angelica, C .... 212-870-1251.. 324 B
amorales@nyts.edu
MORALES, Aurea .... 718-963-4112.. 305 I
amorales@boricuacollege.edu
MORALES, Betsy .... 787-832-4040.. 538 C
MORALES, Brenda, L .... 787-852-1430.. 532 N
bmorales@hccpr.edu
MORALES, Carlos .... 817-515-5021.. 467 A
carlos.morales@tccd.edu
MORALES, Cathy, A .... 212-870-1251.. 324 B
amorales@nyts.edu
MORALES, Denise .... 312-939-0111.. 139 G
MORALES, Edwin .... 787-786-3030.. 536 F
emorales@ucb.edu.pr
MORALES, Erica .... 713-221-8443.. 474 B
moralese@uhd.edu
MORALES, George .... 806-743-2952.. 472 D
george.morales@ttuhsc.edu
MORALES, George .... 336-917-5405.. 355 E
george.morales@salem.edu
MORALES, Hector .... 787-746-1400.. 532 M
hmorales@huertas.edu
MORALES, Ileana .... 787-878-5475.. 533 H
imorales@arecibo.inter.edu
MORALES, Irma .... 787-863-2390.. 533 K
irma.morales@fajardo.inter.edu
MORALES, Jackie .... 407-831-9816.... 97 H
jmorales@citycollege.edu
MORALES, James .... 435-797-1712.. 482 B
james.morales@usu.edu
MORALES, Jessica .... 575-538-6139.. 303 A
jessica.morales@wnmu.edu
MORALES, Jossue .... 787-891-0925.. 533 G
jomorales@aguadilla.inter.edu
MORALES, Julie .... 575-538-6238.. 303 A
moralesj@wnmu.edu
MORALES, Karen, G .... 787-841-2000.. 535 I
karen_morales@pucpr.edu
MORALES, Lindsay .... 909-621-8275.... 64 A
lindsay.morales@scrippscollege.edu
MORALES, Lorraine .... 520-206-7619.... 16 F
lomorales@pima.edu
MORALES, Lorraine .... 520-206-6577.... 16 F
lomorales@pima.edu
MORALES, Lupita .... 520-417-4047.... 12 L
moralesl@cochise.edu
MORALES, Marisol .... 909-593-3511.... 71 B
mmorales3@laverne.edu
MORALES, Milsa .... 787-264-1912.. 534 D
mmorale@intersg.edu
MORALES, Nancy .... 787-882-2065.. 536 D
controller@unitecpr.net
MORALES, Nora .... 361-354-2239.. 454 G
moralesn@coastlbend.edu
MORALES, Oscar .... 787-765-3560.. 532 I
oscarmorales@edpuniversity.edu
MORALES, Patricia .... 949-824-6701.... 69 C
patricia.morales@uci.edu
MORALES, Robert .... 805-965-0581.... 63 D
moralesr@sbcc.edu
MORALES, Rosa, M .... 787-884-3838.. 530 G
rmorales@atenascollege.edu
MORALES, Rosalia .... 787-864-2222.. 534 A
rosalia.morales@guayama.inter.edu
MORALES, Rosalie .... 787-780-0070.. 531 B
rmorales@caribbean.edu
MORALES, Sandra, M ...... 787-857-3600.. 533 I
smmorales@br.inter.edu
MORALES, Sulmarie .... 787-264-1912.. 534 D
smorales@intersg.edu
MORALES, Tomas .... 909-537-5002.... 34 C
tmorales@csusb.edu
MORALES MARTÍNEZ,
María .... 787-264-1912.. 534 D
marimo@intersg.edu
MORALES-TOMASSINI,
Leonardo .... 787-844-8181.. 537 D
leonardo.morales@upr.edu
MORALES TORRES, Nilsa 787-890-2681.. 537 E
nilsa.morales@upr.edu
MORAMARCO, Jacques ... 310-453-8300.... 42 L
jacques@emperors.edu
MORAN, Al .... 850-201-6079.. 113 E
morana@tcc.fl.edu
MORAN, Ashley .... 304-214-8852.. 512 F
amoran@wvncc.edu
MORAN, Bradley .... 907-474-7210.... 10 G
sbmoran@alaska.edu
MORAN, Carmella .... 630-844-5132.. 135 E
cmoran@aurora.edu
MORAN, Christyn .... 610-527-0200.. 418 D
christyn@rosemont.edu
MORAN, Demetria .... 401-456-8031.. 425 E
dmoran@ric.edu
MORAN, Eileen, P .... 940-565-2010.. 475 A
eileen.moran@unt.edu
MORAN, James .... 314-977-3873.. 271 K
jemoran@slu.edu
MORAN, III, James, D .... 605-677-6497.. 437 A
james.moran@usd.edu
MORAN, James, J .... 615-353-3249.. 446 E
josh.moran@nscc.edu
MORAN, Jason .... 603-535-2437.. 288 F
MORAN, Jay .... 203-392-6025.... 85 H
moranj1@southernct.edu
MORAN, Joseph .... 763-424-0772.. 251 B
jmoran@nhcc.edu
MORAN, Karen .... 610-921-7510.. 396 H
kmoran@albright.edu
MORAN, Kathryn, A .... 317-788-3367.. 168 A
kmoran@uindy.edu
MORAN, Kathy .... 518-464-8784.. 314 A
kmoran@excelsior.edu
MORAN, Ken .... 502-456-6504.. 193 B
kmoran@sullivan.edu
MORAN, Laura, P .... 615-353-3217.. 446 E
laura.moran@nscc.edu
MORAN, Maggie .... 662-562-3277.. 260 C
mmoran@northwestms.edu
MORAN, Matt .... 501-450-3814..... 20 F
moran@hendrix.edu
MORAN, Michael .... 413-565-1000.. 215 A
mmoran@baypath.edu
MORAN, Patricia .... 979-830-4157.. 452 J
pmoran@blinn.edu
MORAN, Patrick .... 307-766-4175.. 527 B
pmoran5@uwyo.edu
MORAN, Paul, J .... 570-208-5948.. 406 J
pjmoran@kings.edu
MORAN, Peter .... 206-685-4233.. 508 E
pkmoran@uw.edu
MORAN, Raymond .... 775-784-1641.. 285 A
rmoran@unr.edu
MORAN, Richard, A .... 650-543-3744..... 52 D
linda.teutschel@menlo.edu
MORAN, Timothy, R .... 610-921-7636.. 396 H
tmoran@albright.edu
MORAN, Virginia .... 760-245-4271.... 73 H
virginia.moran@vvc.edu
MORAN, Yvette .... 602-274-1885.... 16 D
ymoran@pihma.edu
MORANO, Lori .... 518-464-8648.. 314 A
lmorano@excelsior.edu
MORANO, Nancy .... 914-633-2046.. 317 B
nmorano@iona.edu
MORANSKI, Karen .... 217-206-7440.. 156 G
moranski.karen@uis.edu
MORANT, Blake, D .... 202-994-1000.... 92 D
morantbd@gwu.edu
MORAVEC, Todd, A .... 518-564-2072.. 334 A
moraveta@plattsburgh.edu
MORAVITZ, Judy .... 909-667-4411.... 38 G
jmoravitz@claremontlincoln.edu
MORAY, Yvonne .... 212-472-1500.. 324 A
ymoray@nysid.edu
MORAZ, Kristen, L .... 561-237-7602.. 104 O
kmoraz@lynn.edu
MORBER, Timothy, T .... 330-471-8279.. 371 J
tmorber@malone.edu
MORCOMB, Mike .... 952-829-2459.. 244 J
mike.morcomb@bethfel.org
MORDACH, John .... 312-942-5600.. 153 B
john_mordach@rush.edu
MORDEN, Erik .... 909-384-8671.... 60 C
emorden@sbccd.cc.ca.us
MOREA, John .... 757-822-1932.. 498 H
jmorea@tcc.edu
MOREAU, Donald .... 603-641-7350.. 287 G
dmoreau@anselm.edu
MOREAU, Joe .... 650-949-6120.... 44 A
moreaujoe@fhda.edu
MOREAU, Joseph .... 650-949-6119.... 43 N
moreaujoe@fhda.edu
MOREAU, Sandra, E .... 619-239-0391.... 36 A
sem@cwsl.edu
MOREAU, Suzanne .... 425-640-1246.. 503 E
suzanne.moreau@edcc.edu
MORECI, Rick .... 773-325-4283.. 139 C
rmoreci@depaul.edu
MOREFIELD, Bill, R .... 423-318-2735.. 447 D
bill.morefield@ws.edu
MOREHEAD, Jere, W .... 706-542-3000.. 128 E
MOREHEAD, Kaleybra ...... 870-543-5963.... 22 E
kmorehead@seark.edu
MOREIRA, Antonio, R ...... 410-455-6576.. 211 G
moreira@umbc.edu
MOREL, Derek .... 504-280-6102.. 198 D
dmorel@uno.edu
MOREL, Luis .... 917-493-4717.. 319 M
lmorel@msmnyc.edu
MOREL, Nina .... 615-966-2501.. 441 F
nina.morel@lipscomb.edu
MORELAND, Jeremy .... 866-621-0124.... 84 E
jeremy.moreland@rockies.edu
MORELAND, Kimberly .... 608-663-8334.. 516 F
kmoreland@edgewood.edu
MORELAND, Mark .... 503-821-8910.. 394 B
mmoreland@pnca.edu
MORELAND, Milton .... 901-843-3795.. 443 L
morelandm@rhodes.edu
MORELIUS, Michael, V .... 512-448-8452.. 464 G
mmoreliu@stedwards.edu
MORELL, Christina .... 434-924-3417.. 495 H
cm5c@virginia.edu
MORELLI, Brad .... 405-974-3573.. 388 L
bmorelli@uco.edu
MORELLO, Chanell .... 828-327-7000.. 348 C
cmorello@cvcc.edu
MORELLO, Debra .... 607-778-5199.. 332 D
morelloda@sunybroome.edu
MORELLO, John, T .... 540-654-1269.. 495 C
jmorello@umw.edu
MORELLO, JR., Joseph ... 650-738-4271.... 62 I
morelloj@smccd.edu
MORELOCK, Luann .... 309-655-7353.. 153 F
luann.morelock@osfhealthcare.org
MORELOCK, Tommy .... 352-854-2322.... 97 R
moreloct@cf.edu
MORELON, Carla .... 770-962-7580.. 123 D
cmorelon@gwinnetttech.edu
MOREMEN, Margaret .... 207-602-2708.. 205 F
mmoremen@une.edu
MOREMEN, Margy .... 207-221-4768.. 205 F
mmoremen@une.edu
MORENA, Pat .... 212-650-7997.. 307 E
MORENCY, Maurice .... 212-752-1530.. 318 F
maurice.morency@limcollege.edu
MORENO, Amy, R .... 717-358-3989.. 403 J
amy.moreno@fandm.edu
MORENO, Anthony .... 800-431-8488.... 27 F
amoreno@aptc.edu
MORENO, Ben .... 650-723-9406.... 66 I
MORENO, Francisco .... 787-738-2161.. 538 A
francisco.moreno@upr.edu
MORENO, Gettie .... 210-485-0374.. 450 A
gmoreno107@alamo.edu
MORENO, Linda .... 773-298-3379.. 153 H
moreno@sxu.edu
MORENO, Luis .... 309-796-5041.. 135 I
morenol@bhc.edu

- **MORRIS**, Ann 704-216-3542 352 G ann.morris@rccc.edu
- **MORRIS**, Barbara 970-247-7314 80 D morris_b@fortlewis.edu
- **MORRIS**, Barbara 410-532-5367 210 B bmorris@ndm.edu
- **MORRIS**, Ben 252-940-6374 347 E ben.morris@beaufortccc.edu
- **MORRIS**, Beth 828-766-1257 351 B bmorris@mayland.edu
- **MORRIS**, Bevan, H 641-472-8194 175 A president@mum.edu
- **MORRIS**, Brenda 870-584-1107 23 F bmorris@cccua.edu
- **MORRIS**, Brenda 903-468-3020 468 D brenda.morris@tamuc.edu
- **MORRIS**, Brett 859-622-3840 188 F admissions@eku.edu
- **MORRIS**, Brett 859-622-8835 188 F brett.morris@eku.edu
- **MORRIS**, Carlene 785-830-2702 181 E cmorris@haskell.edu
- **MORRIS**, Carlton, E 334-724-8784 8 A cmorris@mytu.tuskegee.edu
- **MORRIS**, Chad 661-654-3271 32 A cmorris@csub.edu
- **MORRIS**, Charles 214-860-2019 456 E cmorris@dcccd.edu
- **MORRIS**, Charlotte, P 334-727-8811 8 A
- **MORRIS**, Cheryl 970-245-8101 81 A cmorris@intelliteccollege.edu
- **MORRIS**, Clark 816-415-5997 275 F morrisc@william.jewell.edu
- **MORRIS**, Clark, W 816-415-5997 275 F morrisc@william.jewell.edu
- **MORRIS**, Claudia 352-365-3539 104 J morrisc@lssc.edu
- **MORRIS**, Connie 843-661-8315 429 J connie.morris@fdtc.edu
- **MORRIS**, Corinne 402-844-7361 282 B corinne@northeast.edu
- **MORRIS**, Craig 651-793-1272 250 A craig.morris@metrostate.edu
- **MORRIS**, Craig 541-552-6319 395 A cmorris@sou.edu
- **MORRIS**, Dan 702-651-5500 284 H dan.morris@csn.edu
- **MORRIS**, Daryl 334-244-3295 2 A dmorris@aum.edu
- **MORRIS**, Deborah 304-357-4849 511 E deborahmorris@ucwv.edu
- **MORRIS**, Delesa 561-803-2022 106 C delesa_morris@pba.edu
- **MORRIS**, Diana 800-567-2344 516 B dmorris@menominee.edu
- **MORRIS**, Don 314-968-7444 275 B morrisdo@webster.edu
- **MORRIS**, Dottie 603-358-2206 288 E dmorris@keene.edu
- **MORRIS**, Earl 808-675-3501 130 E earl.morris@byuh.edu
- **MORRIS**, Elizabeth 951-343-4507 29 H emorris@calbaptist.edu
- **MORRIS**, Gary 315-312-2255 333 D gary.morris@oswego.edu
- **MORRIS**, Gary 512-448-8731 464 G gmorris1@stedwards.edu
- **MORRIS**, Geri 419-998-3106 380 A geri@unoh.edu
- **MORRIS**, Glenn 352-335-2332 94 F
- **MORRIS**, Henry 507-389-1150 250 E henry.morris@mnsu.edu
- **MORRIS**, Jacqueline 205-366-8950 7 E jmorris@stillman.edu
- **MORRIS**, Jason 325-674-2830 449 J morrisj@acu.edu
- **MORRIS**, Jeff 620-252-7177 180 B jeffm@coffeyville.edu
- **MORRIS**, Jeffery, B 785-532-6415 182 D jbmorris@ksu.edu
- **MORRIS**, Jeremy 731-265-1703 440 K jkmorris@lanecollege.edu
- **MORRIS**, John 928-523-6187 15 H john.morris@nau.edu
- **MORRIS**, John 808-739-8555 130 F jmorris@chaminade.edu
- **MORRIS**, John 617-627-3232 228 H john.morris@tufts.edu
- **MORRIS**, Joseph 303-797-5801 76 J joseph.morris@arapahoe.edu
- **MORRIS**, Juanita 601-979-2914 258 D juanita.m.morris@jsums.edu
- **MORRIS**, Juanita 731-426-7533 440 K jmorris@lanecollege.edu
- **MORRIS**, Julia, M 304-457-6205 510 B auviljm@ab.edu
- **MORRIS**, Julie 404-876-1227 118 C
- **MORRIS**, Katherine, W 937-775-2809 381 H kathy.morris@wright.edu
- **MORRIS**, Kathryn 317-940-9903 159 K kmorris@butler.edu
- **MORRIS**, Kay 229-333-2120 130 A kay.morris@wiregrass.edu
- **MORRIS**, Kelli 256-306-2602 2 F kelli.morris@calhoun.edu
- **MORRIS**, Kelli 256-326-2602 2 F kelli.morris@calhoun.edu
- **MORRIS**, Kelly, M 770-720-5897 126 C km@reinhardt.edu
- **MORRIS**, Ken 570-586-2400 419 G kmorris@summitu.edu
- **MORRIS**, Kenielle, E 937-708-5760 381 B kmorris@wilberforce.edu
- **MORRIS**, Kevin 281-922-3479 465 B kevin.morris@sjcd.edu
- **MORRIS**, Kevin 936-294-1794 471 D kmorris@shsu.edu
- **MORRIS**, Kimberly 770-412-4005 127 F kmorris@sctech.edu
- **MORRIS**, Kizzy 570-422-2831 414 H registrar@esu.edu
- **MORRIS**, Kyle 307-755-2129 527 G kyle.morris@zenith.org
- **MORRIS**, Laura, M 302-295-1179 91 I laura.m.morris@wilmu.edu
- **MORRIS**, Lauren, N 248-204-2309 237 B lmorris2@ltu.edu
- **MORRIS**, Lawrence, J 202-319-5142 92 A morrisl@cua.edu
- **MORRIS**, Lela 817-598-6488 479 E morris@wc.edu
- **MORRIS**, Loren, L 620-665-3523 181 I morrisl@hutchcc.edu
- **MORRIS**, Malcolm, L 404-872-3593 117 B mmorris@johnmarshall.edu
- **MORRIS**, Marie 765-641-4020 158 J msmorris@anderson.edu
- **MORRIS**, Matt 661-654-6459 32 A morris-matt@aramark.com
- **MORRIS**, Matthew 417-836-5233 268 I mattmorris@missuristate.edu
- **MORRIS**, Melissa, M 334-844-7771 1 G morrimm@auburn.edu
- **MORRIS**, Nerissa, E 305-284-4476 114 H nmorris@miami.edu
- **MORRIS**, Nora 763-433-1632 248 K nora.morris@anokaramsey.edu
- **MORRIS**, Nora 763-433-1632 248 L nora.morris@anokaramsey.edu
- **MORRIS**, Paul 435-652-7504 482 A pmorris@dixie.edu
- **MORRIS**, Paul 401-456-8803 425 E pmorris1@ric.edu
- **MORRIS**, Reggie 323-241-5200 50 B morrisr@lasc.edu
- **MORRIS**, Regina 573-840-9606 273 A rmorris@trcc.edu
- **MORRIS**, Renea 740-593-2563 375 H morrisr@ohio.edu
- **MORRIS**, Rick 864-977-7777 431 G publicsafety@ngu.edu
- **MORRIS**, Robert 765-285-1333 159 B rmorris@bsu.edu
- **MORRIS**, Robert 724-287-8711 399 B robert.morris@bc3.edu
- **MORRIS**, Robert, D 404-413-2502 122 D robinmorris@gsu.edu
- **MORRIS**, Sandra, L 843-792-8720 431 A morriss@musc.edu
- **MORRIS**, Sara 716-888-2125 306 F morris@canisius.edu
- **MORRIS**, Sara, B 316-978-5520 185 J sara.morris@wichita.edu
- **MORRIS**, Scott 713-683-3817 465 D
- **MORRIS**, Steve 270-789-5017 187 G srmorris@campbellsville.edu
- **MORRIS**, Steve 217-854-5513 135 K steve.morris@blackburn.edu
- **MORRIS**, Tama 704-337-2363 355 A morrist@queens.edu
- **MORRIS**, Tammy, H 336-322-2150 351 H tammy.morris@piedmontcc.edu
- **MORRIS**, Todd 575-461-4413 300 A toddm@mesalands.edu
- **MORRIS**, Tommy 256-824-6576 8 F tommy.morris@uah.edu
- **MORRIS**, Tracy 309-694-8970 141 F tracy.morris@icc.edu
- **MORRIS**, Valerie, B 843-953-8222 428 G morrisv@cofc.edu
- **MORRIS**, Wanda 310-660-3281 42 J wmorris@elcamino.edu
- **MORRIS**, Wendi 478-296-6179 125 D wmorris@oftc.edu
- **MORRIS-DUEER**, Vicky 304-766-4189 514 B dueer@wvstateu.edu
- **MORRIS WOOD, JR.**, Dossie 910-843-5304 347 A
- **MORRISETT**, Greg 607-255-9188 312 A greg.morrisett@cornell.edu
- **MORRISETTE**, Joanna 919-735-5151 354 A jmmorrisette@waynecc.edu
- **MORRISON**, Allen 602-978-7203 11 H allen.morrison@asu.edu
- **MORRISON**, Angel 785-460-5418 180 C angel.morrison@colbycc.edu
- **MORRISON**, Barry, F 401-232-6017 424 K bmorriso@bryant.edu
- **MORRISON**, Betty, N 630-515-7600 148 C emorri@midwestern.edu
- **MORRISON**, Brenda, M 443-412-2409 208 A bmorrison@harford.edu
- **MORRISON**, Carberta, A 856-225-2949 296 A cammor@camden.rutgers.edu
- **MORRISON**, Carol 239-513-1122 102 T cmorrison@hodges.edu
- **MORRISON**, Cindi 352-854-2322 97 R morrisoc@cf.edu
- **MORRISON**, Darrell 210-784-2000 469 B drmorris@tamusa.edu
- **MORRISON**, David 770-534-6167 118 A dmorrison@brenau.edu
- **MORRISON**, Don 641-628-5280 170 E morrisond@central.edu
- **MORRISON**, Edwina 406-444-0326 276 J emorrison@montana.edu
- **MORRISON**, Gail 651-450-3512 249 F gmorris@inverhills.edu
- **MORRISON**, Jason 918-647-1230 382 I jlmorrison@carlalbert.edu
- **MORRISON**, Jean 617-353-2230 216 E morrison@bu.edu
- **MORRISON**, Jennifer 503-244-0726 389 J jennifermorrison@achs.edu
- **MORRISON**, Jennifer, K 508-767-7007 214 F jemorrison@assumption.edu
- **MORRISON**, John 856-351-2628 296 L jmorrison@salemcc.edu
- **MORRISON**, Joseph, B 508-767-7312 214 F jmorrison@assumption.edu
- **MORRISON**, Julie 734-973-5010 242 G jmorriso@wccnet.edu
- **MORRISON**, Karen 407-823-6479 111 E karen.morrison@ucf.edu
- **MORRISON**, Kim 510-723-6762 37 B kmorrison@chabotcollege.edu
- **MORRISON**, Kirk 858-513-9240 27 V kirk.morrison@ashford.edu
- **MORRISON**, Laura 252-335-0821 349 A laura_morrison@albemarle.edu
- **MORRISON**, Lolita 404-297-9522 122 A morrisonl@gptc.org
- **MORRISON**, Marty, G 540-654-2287 495 C mmorris3@umw.edu
- **MORRISON**, Michael 626-650-2363 45 E
- **MORRISON**, Michael, L 812-888-5736 169 A mmorrison@vinu.edu
- **MORRISON**, Nancy, J 212-998-4924 324 C nancy.morrison@nyu.edu
- **MORRISON**, Pamela 916-558-2088 51 D morrisp@scc.losrios.edu
- **MORRISON**, Rebecca, L 414-955-4949 518 A rmorriso@mcw.edu
- **MORRISON**, Regina 650-738-4350 62 I morrison@smccd.edu
- **MORRISON**, Robert 312-261-3372 149 B rob.morrison@nl.edu
- **MORRISON**, Rodney 631-632-6857 332 A rodney.morrison@stonybrook.edu
- **MORRISON**, Rodney 419-448-2391 369 G rmorriso@heidelberg.edu
- **MORRISON**, Roxanne 619-260-4749 72 B roxannemorrison@sandiego.edu
- **MORRISON**, Sarah, B 276-656-0322 498 A sbmorrison@patrickhenry.edu
- **MORRISON**, Scott 775-445-3000 285 B scott.morrison@wnc.edu
- **MORRISON**, Scott, D 540-828-5376 487 H smorriso@bridgewater.edu
- **MORRISON**, Sharon 580-745-3172 387 M smorrison@se.edu
- **MORRISON**, Thomas 812-855-6992 162 E morrison@indiana.edu
- **MORRISON**, Tom 812-855-6992 162 F morrisot@indiana.edu
- **MORRISON**, William 973-684-6741 294 A wmorrison@pccc.edu
- **MORRISON-BEEDY**, Dianne 813-974-2191 112 C dmbeedy@health.usf.edu
- **MORRISON-FRONCKOWIAK**, Lisa, T 716-878-4500 332 F morrislt@buffalostate.edu
- **MORRISON GOINGS**, Amy, M 425-739-8200 504 F amy.goings@lwtech.edu
- **MORRISON-SHETLAR**, Alison 828-227-7495 359 A aimorrison@wcu.edu
- **MORRISS**, Andrew, P 817-212-4100 468 B amorriss@tamu.edu
- **MORRISS-OLSON**, Melissa 413-565-1000 215 A mmolson@baypath.edu
- **MORRISSETTE**, Barbara 304-473-8162 515 B morrissette@wvwc.edu
- **MORRISSEY**, Ann, M 401-874-4402 426 D morrissey@uri.edu
- **MORRISSEY**, Barbara 925-424-1420 37 C bmorrissey@laspositascollege.edu
- **MORRISSEY**, Jeff, P 417-836-5770 268 I jeffmorrissey@missouristate.edu
- **MORRISSEY**, Sharon 804-819-4972 496 E smorrissey@vccs.edu
- **MORRISSEY**, Shawn 508-856-2265 221 B shawn.morrissey@umassmed.edu
- **MORRO**, Robert 610-519-4589 422 G robert.morro@villanova.edu
- **MORRONE**, Anastasia 317-274-3479 163 D amorrone@iupui.edu
- **MORRONE**, Anthony 702-992-2150 284 J finaid@nsc.edu
- **MORROW**, Andrea 567-661-7104 376 D andrea_morrow@owens.edu
- **MORROW**, Barbara, A 314-340-5763 265 H morrowb@hssu.edu
- **MORROW**, Bill, J 302-857-1245 91 C bmorrow@dtcc.edu
- **MORROW**, Carol, K 212-998-4798 324 C carol.morrow@nyu.edu
- **MORROW**, David 267-295-2357 418 A dmorrow@walnuthillcollege.edu
- **MORROW**, David, M 518-736-3622 315 A dmorrow@fmcc.suny.edu
- **MORROW**, Dorothy 402-557-7296 278 I dorothy.morrow@bellevue.edu
- **MORROW**, Erik 512-472-4133 465 F emorrow@ssw.edu
- **MORROW**, Frances 330-490-7312 380 J fmorrow@walsh.edu
- **MORROW**, Jeffrey, S 330-665-1084 374 H j.morrow@ocm.edu
- **MORROW**, Jessica 918-335-6268 386 F jmorrow@okwu.edu
- **MORROW**, Joyce 319-273-2701 170 A joyce.morrow@uni.edu
- **MORROW**, Kieran 646-312-4542 307 A kieran.morrow@baruch.cuny.edu
- **MORROW**, Laurie 318-357-3162 196 H lauriemorrow@nwltc.edu
- **MORROW**, Liz 573-681-5011 266 I morrowl@lincolnu.edu
- **MORROW**, Marjann 325-574-7608 479 I mmorrow@wtc.edu
- **MORROW**, Michael 651-523-1660 247 G mmorrow001@luthersem.edu
- **MORROW**, Monica 360-650-7731 509 E monica.morrow@wwu.edu
- **MORROW**, Rebecca 304-793-6591 514 A rmorrow@osteo.wvsom.edu
- **MORROW**, Rex 219-989-2335 166 F srmorrow@pnw.edu
- **MORROW**, Wanda 713-646-1825 459 A wmorrow@hcl.edu
- **MORROW**, Wes 425-388-9578 503 F wmorrow@everettcc.edu
- **MORROW-JENSEN**, Amanda 408-453-9900 46 B amorrow-jensen@henley-putnam.edu
- **MORROW RUETTEN**, Lydia 708-534-4110 140 H lruetten@govst.edu
- **MORSBERGER**, Michael, J 407-882-1250 111 E mike.mors@ucf.edu
- **MORSCHES**, Michael 708-974-5310 148 G morschesm@morainevalley.edu
- **MORSE**, Alicia 410-777-2587 206 B ammorse@aacc.edu
- **MORSE**, Austin 616-988-1000 232 H austin.m@compass.edu
- **MORSE**, Charles, C 508-831-5540 230 C cmorse@wpi.edu
- **MORSE**, Rachel 907-786-1278 10 F rlmorse@uaa.alaska.edu
- **MORSE**, Susan 740-427-5926 371 C morses@kenyon.edu
- **MORSE**, Weyland 818-766-8151 41 C wmorse@concorde.edu
- **MORSE**, William 909-607-9506 58 A william.morse@pomona.edu
- **MORSMAN**, Elaine 607-587-4061 334 G morsmaem@alfredstate.edu
- **MORSOVILLO**, Michael 708-524-6793 139 F morsomike@dom.edu
- **MORSS**, Susan 520-515-3662 12 L morsss@cochise.edu
- **MORT**, Dale 717-569-7071 407 E dmort@lbc.edu
- **MORT**, Jane 605-688-6197 437 F jane.mort@sdstate.edu

MORTALI, Jill, M .... 603-646-3007.. 286 J jill.m.mortali@dartmouth.edu
MORTELA, Cecilia .... 805-267-1690.... 48 F
MORTEN, Sally, C .... 540-231-6394.. 499 F scmorten@vt.edu
MORTENSEN, Brad .... 801-626-6002.. 482 D bmortensen@weber.edu
MORTENSEN, Daniel, W .. 610-917-1412.. 422 C dwmortensen@valleyforge.edu
MORTENSEN, John .... 435-797-1110.. 482 B john.mortensen@usu.edu
MORTENSEN, Larry .... 719-587-7402.... 76 G lsmorten@adams.edu
MORTENSEN, Norm .... 304-734-6680.. 511 M norm.mortensen@bridgevalley.edu
MORTENSON, Donald, W 206-281-2522.. 507 C dmort@spu.edu
MORTENSON, Gary .... 254-710-1221.. 452 H gary_mortenson@baylor.edu
MORTHLAND, Betsey ...... 309-796-5049.. 135 morthlandb@bhc.edu
MORTHLAND, Tim .... 618-937-2127.. 148 tmorthland@morthland.edu
MORTIMER, Gayle .... 620-862-5252.. 178 F gayle.mortimer@barclaycollege.edu
MORTIMER, Ian .... 585-389-2525.. 322 C imortim4@naz.edu
MORTIMER, Nathan, J ..... 330-972-6501.. 378 G njm9@uakron.edu
MORTIMER, Theresa .... 617-287-6800.. 220 G theresa.mortimer@umb.edu
MORTIMEYER, Jennifer .... 719-336-1572.... 81 D jennifer.mortimeyer@lamarcc.edu
MORTLAND, Stephen ...... 765-998-5206.. 167 C stmortlan@taylor.edu
MORTON, Amy, M .... 508-831-5874.. 230 C ammorton@wpi.edu
MORTON, Bradley .... 732-906-2601.. 292 E bmorton@middlesexcc.edu
MORTON, Cassandra .... 909-748-8391.... 71 K cassandra_morton@redlands.edu
MORTON, Christina .... 412-392-4207.. 417 F cmorton@pointpark.edu
MORTON, Clarresa .... 540-665-4517.. 494 B cmorton@su.edu
MORTON, Jim .... 910-362-7065.. 348 A jmorton@cfcc.edu
MORTON, John, F .... 808-956-7038.. 131 H jmorton@hawaii.edu
MORTON, John, F .... 808-956-7038.. 131 D jmorton@hawaii.edu
MORTON, Leo, E .... 816-235-1101.. 273 F mortonle@umkc.edu
MORTON, Linda .... 619-239-0391.... 36 A lm@cwsl.edu
MORTON, Lisa .... 414-276-5200.. 160 C lisa.morton@ccr.edu
MORTON, Lynn .... 704-337-2492.. 355 A mortonl@queens.edu
MORTON, Marcia .... 417-667-8181.. 264 A mmorton@cottey.edu
MORTON, Margaret .... 212-353-4208.. 311 G mortonnyc@cooper.edu
MORTON, Mary .... 518-587-2100.. 335 D mary.morton@esc.edu
MORTON, Matt .... 949-376-6000.... 48 C mmorton@lcad.edu
MORTON, Nina .... 304-357-4944.. 511 E ninamorton@ucwv.edu
MORTON, Patricia .... 801-581-8262.. 481 M patricia.morton@nurs.utah.edu
MORTON, Tonya, L .... 910-938-6211.. 348 G mortont@coastalcarolina.edu
MORTON, Wendy .... 918-495-6817.. 386 H wmorton@oru.edu
MORVICE, Michael .... 714-432-5741.... 39 G mmorvice@occ.cccd.edu
MORY, Scott .... 412-268-2135.. 400 D mory@cmu.edu
MORYAN, James .... 215-489-4889.. 402 A james.moryan@delval.edu
MOSBURG, Calleb, N .... 580-327-8415.. 384 M cnmosburg@nwosu.edu
MOSBY, David, C .... 301-546-0400.. 210 C mosbydc@pgcc.edu
MOSBY, John .... 408-855-5195.... 74 G john.mosby@missioncollege.edu
MOSBY-WILSON, Shatiqua, A .... 504-286-5030.. 199 I swilson@suno.edu
MOSCA, David .... 443-367-0035.. 211 D dmosca@usmd.edu
MOSCA, Joseph, L .... 330-941-3321.. 382 A jmosca@ysu.edu
MOSCARIELLO, Dawn, M 610-359-5298.. 401 L dmoscariello@dccc.edu
MOSCATO, Robin, A .... 609-258-3330.. 294 D moscato@princeton.edu
MOSCHELLA, Jayne .... 561-912-1211.... 99 J jmoschella@evergladesuniversity.edu
MOSCHENROSS, Sarah .... 641-269-3714.. 172 I moschenr@grinnell.edu
MOSELEY, John .... 573-681-5333.. 266 I moseleyj@lincolnu.edu
MOSELEY, Lynne .... 707-638-5223.... 68 C lynne.moseley@tu.edu
MOSELEY, Pope, H .... 501-526-4533.... 23 C pmoseley@uams.edu
MOSELEY-JONES, Vickie . 252-638-7225.. 349 B moseleyv@cravencc.edu
MOSELY-HAWKINS, Elizabeth .... 803-533-3681.. 432 E emosely@scsu.edu
MOSEMAN, Dennis .... 212-242-2692.. 338 D dennis.moseman@tsca.edu
MOSER, Drew .... 765-998-5384.. 167 C drmoser@taylor.edu
MOSER, Gary .... 707-654-1224.... 33 D gmoser@csum.edu
MOSER, Jack, T .... 662-685-4771.. 257 A jmoser@bmc.edu
MOSER, Jeremy .... 714-556-3610.... 73 B jeremy.moser@vanguard.edu
MOSER, Kristin, M .... 319-273-3050.. 170 A kristin.moser@uni.edu
MOSER, Mike .... 808-235-7361.. 132 E mikem@hawaii.edu
MOSER, Nina .... 802-447-4046.. 485 B nmoser@svc.edu
MOSER, Patrick .... 503-838-8063.. 396 E moserp@wou.edu
MOSER, Shelly .... 870-612-2034.... 23 H shelly.moser@uaccb.edu
MOSER, Steven .... 601-266-5002.. 261 E steven.moser@usm.edu
MOSER, Tina, L .... 724-738-2000.. 416 B tina.moser@sru.edu
MOSER, Tracy, S .... 662-685-4771.. 257 A tmoser@bmc.edu
MOSES, Bruce .... 520-206-4514.... 16 F bmoses3@pima.edu
MOSES, Carl .... 515-263-2835.. 172 H cmoses@grandview.edu
MOSES, Charles .... 931-221-7674.. 444 E mosesc@apsu.edu
MOSES, Darren .... 215-489-6370.. 402 A darren.moses@delval.edu
MOSES, David .... 316-978-6791.. 185 J david.moses@wichita.edu
MOSES, Henry .... 615-327-6266.. 442 A hmoses@mmc.edu
MOSES, Lola .... 229-732-5947.. 116 C lolamoses@andrewcollege.edu
MOSES, Orrin Douglas .... 831-656-3218.. 528 D dmoses@nps.edu
MOSES, Rhonda, M .... 512-505-3075.. 459 F rmmoses@htu.edu
MOSES, Robert, M .... 570-422-3138.. 414 H bmoses@esu.edu
MOSES-HOLMES, Jeanette .... 803-934-3989.. 431 E jholmes@morris.edu
MOSESSO, Lynn .... 479-575-5869.... 22 I mosesso@uark.edu
MOSEY, Douglas, L .... 860-632-3010.... 88 B rector@holyapostles.edu
MOSHER, Clifford, D .... 949-480-4235.... 64 J cmo@soka.edu
MOSHER, Craig .... 735-442-6019.. 181 H cmosher@highlandcc.edu
MOSHER, Craig .... 735-442-6017.. 181 H cmosher@highlandcc.edu
MOSHER, Craig, E .... 735-442-6019.. 181 H cmosher@highlandcc.edu
MOSHER, George .... 312-329-4268.. 148 F george.mosher@moody.edu
MOSHER, Michael .... 810-762-9583.. 236 C mmosher@kettering.edu
MOSHER, Sharon .... 512-471-6048.. 476 B smosher@jsg.utexas.edu
MOSHIER, Andrea .... 828-227-7212.. 359 A amoshier@wcu.edu
MOSHIER, Jeffrey .... 765-998-5203.. 167 C jfmoshier@taylor.edu
MOSIER, Greg .... 507-285-7256.. 251 I greg.mosier@rctc.edu
MOSIER, Gregory .... 775-784-4912.. 285 A greg.mosier@unr.edu
MOSIER, Roger .... 413-585-2400.. 228 D rmosier@smith.edu
MOSKALA, Jiri .... 269-471-3648.. 230 H moskala@andrews.edu
MOSKE, Amanda Kay .... 607-431-4997.. 315 E moskea@hartwick.edu
MOSKOVITZ, Joy .... 908-737-7030.. 292 C jmoskovi@kean.edu
MOSKOVITZ, Kristin .... 313-664-7496.. 232 G kmoskovitz@collegeforcreativestudies.edu
MOSKOWITZ, Roy, P .... 212-229-5432.. 322 E moskowir@newschool.edu
MOSKOWITZ, Seth .... 212-960-0863.. 341 G seth.maskowitz@yu.edu
MOSLEY, Ca[illegible] .... 320-363-3036.. 254 N cmosley@csbsju.edu
MOSLEY, Calvin .... 320-363-3036.. 245 I cmosley@csbsju.edu
MOSLEY, Carolyn .... 479-788-7856.... 23 A carolyn.mosley@uafs.edu
MOSLEY, Crystal .... 410-951-3579.. 212 E cmosley@coppin.edu
MOSLEY, David .... 409-880-2207.. 470 H dpmosley@lit.edu
MOSLEY, Debra .... 417-255-7900.. 269 A debbiemosley@missouristate.edu
MOSLEY, Eartha, J .... 803-536-7048.. 432 E emosely1@scsu.edu
MOSLEY, Gary .... 662-562-3216.. 260 C gtmosley@northwestms.edu
MOSLEY, Jennifer .... 561-237-7811.. 104 O jmosley@lynn.edu
MOSLEY, Juliana, M .... 484-365-7222.. 409 B jmosley2@lincoln.edu
MOSLEY, Julie .... 479-788-7404.... 23 A julie.mosley@uafs.edu
MOSLEY, Marvis .... 214-860-8758.. 456 F marvismosley@dcccd.edu
MOSLEY, Mary Lou .... 602-787-6607.... 14 E marylou.mosley@paradisevalley.edu
MOSLEY, Melissa .... 662-476-5074.. 257 G mmosley@eastms.edu
MOSLEY, Regina .... 734-462-4400.. 240 H rmosley@schoolcraft.edu
MOSLEY, Walter .... 903-593-8311.. 470 A wmosley@texascollege.edu
MOSLEY, Whitney .... 229-732-5950.. 116 C whitneymosley@andrewcollege.edu
MOSLEY, YoLunda .... 317-274-0838.. 163 D ymosley@iupui.edu
MOSQUEDA, Margarita .... 989-686-9512.. 233 I momosque@delta.edu
MOSQUEDA, Rolando ...... 702-651-4245.. 284 H rolando.mosqueda@csn.edu
MOSS, Aimi .... 810-762-3085.. 242 B aimi@umflint.edu
MOSS, Alan .... 918-465-1302.. 383 I amoss@eosc.edu
MOSS, Annie .... 318-670-9212.. 199 J amoss@susla.edu
MOSS, Ashley .... 303-333-4224.... 77 A registrar@aspen.edu
MOSS, Brendan .... 660-944-2928.. 263 G brendan@conception.edu
MOSS, Catherine .... 509-359-6362.. 503 D cmoss4@ewu.edu
MOSS, Edwin .... 718-390-3165.. 339 F edwin.moss@wagner.edu
MOSS, Elizabeth, H .... 443-518-4837.. 208 C emoss@howardcc.edu
MOSS, Kirsten .... 931-393-1764.. 446 D kmoss@mscc.edu
MOSS, Michael .... 704-330-6681.. 348 E michael.moss@cpcc.edu
MOSS, Orianna, M .... 786-331-1000.. 105 G omaza@maufl.edu
MOSS, Pamela .... 901-722-3318.. 444 C pmoss@sco.edu
MOSS, Renie .... 205-726-2116...... 6 E rmoss@samford.edu
MOSS, Sarah .... 712-722-6078.. 171 J sarah.moss@dordt.edu
MOSS, Tony .... 706-867-2712.. 128 F tony.moss@ung.edu
MOSSER, Daniel .... 301-934-7547.. 207 B dmosser@csmd.edu
MOSSETTE, Mary Beth ...... 559-442-8286.... 67 C marybeth.mossette@fresnocitycollege.edu
MOSSEY, Christophe .... 212-799-5000.. 318 A
MOSSHART, Marcia .... 405-491-6312.. 388 A mmosshar@snu.edu
MOSTAFAVI, Mosher .... 617-495-4364.. 219 D moshen_mostafavi@harvard.edu
MOSTARDI, CSA, Joseph .... 610-519-4080.. 422 G joseph.mostardi@villanova.edu
MOSTASHARI, Zary .... 703-284-1673.. 492 A zary.mostashari@marymount.edu
MOSTELLER, John .... 610-896-1376.. 405 I jmostell@haverford.edu
MOSTELLER, Kate .... 480-947-6644.... 16 C kate.mosteller@pennfoster.edu
MOSTILLER, Donna .... 716-286-8689.. 324 E dmostiller@niagara.edu
MOSTOV, Julie .... 215-895-6793.. 402 G julie.mostov@drexel.edu
MOTE, Jerry .... 724-266-3838.. 421 C jmote@tsm.edu
MOTE, Tanya .... 360-596-5229.. 508 A tmote@spscc.edu
MOTEN, Maria .... 847-925-6622.. 141 A mmoten@harpercollege.edu
MOTEN-TOLSON, Paula ... 919-546-8544.. 355 F pmotentolson@shawu.edu
MOTES, Caley .... 706-385-1458.. 126 A caley.motes@point.edu
MOTES, Kimberly, J .... 651-962-6949.. 256 C kjmotes@stthomas.edu
MOTHERWELL, Mary .... 734-487-2229.. 233 J mmotherwe@emich.edu
MOTL, Lori .... 870-245-5110.... 21 E motll@obu.edu
MOTLEY, Brittany .... 937-708-5251.. 381 B bmotley@wilberforce.edu
MOTLEY, Clay .... 239-590-7368.. 110 L cmotley@fgcu.edu
MOTLEY, J. Keith .... 617-287-6800.. 220 G keith.motley@umb.edu
MOTT, Jeanne .... 785-594-4595.. 178 D jeanne.mott@bakeru.edu
MOTT, Jeff .... 479-968-0332.... 19 F jmott@atu.edu
MOTT, Molly, A .... 315-386-7425.. 335 B mottma@canton.edu
MOTTE, Kristin .... 617-587-5658.. 226 E mottek@neco.edu
MOTTEN, Luisa .... 206-934-6782.. 507 A luisa.motten@seattlecolleges.edu
MOTTER, Kristi .... 256-824-4158...... 8 F kristi.motter@uah.edu
MOTTET, Timothy .... 660-562-1122.. 269 J tmottet@nwmissouri.edu
MOTTLEY, Darlene .... 412-365-2970.. 400 G dmottley@chatham.edu
MOTTLEY, Juanita, G .... 404-471-6443.. 115 J jgainousmottley@agnesscott.edu
MOTYL, Lynne, M .... 724-738-2070.. 416 B lynne.motyl@sru.edu
MOTZ, Arnell .... 651-582-5224.. 244 L a-motz@bethel.edu
MOTZER, Bill .... 402-465-2551.. 281 K wmotzer@nebrwesleyan.edu
MOU, Cai Ming .... 408-433-2280.... 38 B
MOUA, Pa Lee .... 920-832-7030.. 517 E palee.moua@lawrence.edu
MOUDGIL, Virinder, K ..... 248-204-2000.. 237 B president@ltu.edu
MOUDIAB, Jamilah .... 973-748-9000.. 289 H jamilah_moudiab@bloomfield.edu
MOUDY, Quentin, J .... 260-982-5267.. 165 M qjmoudy@manchester.edu
MOULD, Tom .... 336-278-5746.. 344 D tmould@elon.edu
MOULDS, Perry .... 615-460-6434.. 438 J perry.moulds@belmont.edu
MOULTON, Bob .... 775-784-4901.. 284 G bob_moulton@nshe.nevada.edu
MOULTON, David, A .... 202-419-0482.... 93 F dam@strayer.edu
MOULTON, Julie .... 951-343-4210.... 29 H jmoulton@calbaptist.edu
MOULTON, Paul .... 208-459-5217.. 133 D pmoulton@collegeofidaho.edu
MOULTRIE, Anne .... 301-445-2722.. 211 D amoultrie@usmd.edu
MOULTRIE, Gloria, B .... 504-286-5341.. 199 I gmoultrie@suno.edu
MOUNDS, Paul .... 860-512-3634.... 86 E pmounds@manchestercc.edu
MOUNFIELD, Gina .... 843-525-8257.. 433 B gmounfield@tcl.edu
MOUNT, Carole .... 330-490-7048.. 380 J cmount@walsh.edu
MOUNT, Judy .... 316-677-1619.. 185 I jmount@watc.edu
MOUNT, Marianne, E .... 540-338-2700.. 510 H mmount@cdu.edu
MOUNTAIN, Carel .... 916-558-2275.... 51 D mountac@scc.losrios.edu
MOUNTAIN, Mark .... 815-928-5794.. 150 I mcmountain@olivet.edu
MOUNTJOY, Loretta .... 520-515-5401.... 12 L mountjoyl@cochise.edu
MOUNTJOY, Shane .... 402-363-5614.. 283 G mountjoy@york.edu
MOUNTS, William .... 912-279-5851.. 119 C wmounts@ccga.edu
MOURACADE, John .... 907-786-1086.... 10 F jmmouracade@uaa.alaska.edu
MOURAD, Roger .... 734-677-5328.. 242 G mou@wccnet.edu
MOURING, Jane, A .... 563-588-7107.. 174 K jane.mouring@loras.edu
MOURN, Justin .... 620-241-0723.. 179 L justin.mourn@centralchristian.edu
MOURNIGHAN, Jim .... 401-341-2200.. 426 C
MOURTZANOS, Emmanuel .... 661-395-4406.... 47 J emmanuel.mourtzanos@bakersfieldcollege.edu
MOUSA, Shaker .... 518-694-7575.. 303 C shaker.mousa@acphs.edu

MOUSER, Debbie 615-844-5222 449 H debbie@welch.edu
MOUSER, Lisa 636-922-8319 271 A lmouser@stchas.edu
MOUSSALLI, Samir, R 334-833-4509 4 D samirm@hawks.huntingdon.edu
MOUTON, Jocelyn 707-864-7256 65 A jocelyn.mouton@solano.edu
MOUTOS, Don 503-654-8000 394 D dmoutos@pioneerpacific.edu
MOUTRAY, Tonya 518-244-2406 327 H moutrt@sage.edu
MOUTSATSON, Kelly 541-552-6411 395 A moutsatsk@sou.edu
MOUTTET, Nate 206-281-2652 507 C natem@spu.edu
MOVITZ, Michelle 847-324-5588 136 K mmovitz@ortchicagotech.edu
MOVSESIAN, David 858-279-4500 29 A
MOWBRAY, Nayeli 410-225-2493 209 B
MOWDER, William, J 610-683-4500 415 C mowder@kutztown.edu
MOWDY, Jennifer 281-998-6150 465 A jennifer.mowdy@sjcd.edu
MOWEN, Brenda 804-828-3361 496 D bmowen@vcu.edu
MOWEN, David 540-887-7370 491 G dmowen@mbc.edu
MOWERY, Chris 423-472-7141 445 E cmowery@clevelandstatecc.edu
MOWITZ, Marlane 828-251-6867 357 C mmowitz@unca.edu
MOWRY, Cynthia 253-589-5570 502 F cynthia.mowry@cptc.edu
MOY, James, S 813-974-7380 112 C moy@usf.edu
MOYA, Jacob 208-882-1566 134 B jmoya@nsa.edu
MOYANO, Angelica 954-607-4344 114 F
MOYD, Greg 910-670-1167 356 E gmoyd@uncfsu.edu
MOYE, Bobby 229-732-5946 116 C bobbymoye@andrewcollege.edu
MOYE, John, N 847-233-7700 150 D jnmoye@nc.edu
MOYE, Sara 541-956-7346 394 J smoye@roguecc.edu
MOYEN, Eric 423-614-8671 441 B emoyen@leeuniversity.edu
MOYER, Anna 618-545-3018 144 D amoyer@kaskaskia.edu
MOYER, Bonita 570-740-0379 409 E bmoyer@luzerne.edu
MOYER, Christina, L 610-799-1136 408 G cmoyer@lccc.edu
MOYER, James 616-331-3853 234 F moyerj@gvsu.edu
MOYER, James, G 863-638-7613 115 C james.moyer@warner.edu
MOYER, Monica 352-588-8646 108 C monica.moyer@saintleo.edu
MOYER, Paul 410-386-4660 209 D pmoyer@mcdaniel.edu
MOYER, Richard 323-265-8678 49 G moyerra@elac.edu
MOYERS, Penelope 651-690-6813 254 M pamoyers@stkate.edu
MOYLAN, Shannon 607-735-1782 313 F smoylan@elmira.edu
MOYNIHAN, Daniel 781-280-3625 224 A
MOZAFFARIAN, Dariush 617-636-3702 228 H dariush.mozaffarian@tufts.edu
MOZERSKY, Elisha 518-276-6000 327 B mozere@rpi.edu
MOZIE-ROSS, Yvette 410-455-3799 211 G mozie@umbc.edu
MOZLEY, Peter 575-835-5227 300 G vpaa@admin.nmt.edu
MOZLEY, Peter 575-835-5172 300 G pmozley@nmt.edu
MOZOLIK, Erik 414-464-9777 522 Q mozolik.erik@wspp.edu
MOZRALL, Jacqueline 585-475-7181 327 E jrmeie@rit.edu
MRASEK, Jean 817-257-5566 469 G j.mrasek@tcu.edu
MROZ, Donald, W 203-596-4666 88 F dmroz@post.edu
MROZ, Frank, D 610-799-1109 408 G fmroz@lccc.edu
MROZ, Glenn, D 906-487-2200 238 A gdmroz@mtu.edu
MROZEK, John 281-487-1170 469 F jmrozek@txchiro.edu
MROZIK, Jacek 701-858-3110 360 F jacek.mrozik@minotstateu.edu
MROZINSKI, Mark 847-925-6540 141 A mmrozins@harpercollege.edu
MRSNY, Jason 402-375-7195 281 J jamrsny1@wsc.edu

MRVOS, Dessa 412-396-1650 403 A mrvosds@duq.edu
MUCCINO, SJ, Keith 708-216-8763 146 G kmuccino@luc.edu
MUCH, Kari 507-389-1455 250 E karen.much@mnsu.edu
MUCHANE, Mary, W 704-894-2644 343 I mamuchane@davidson.edu
MUCHANE, Mur 336-758-4016 359 E mmuchane@wfu.edu
MUCHOW, Monica, M 612-343-4487 253 Y mmmuchow@northcentral.edu
MUDD, Bryan 941-359-4349 112 E bmudd@sar.usf.edu
MUDD, Kira 361-570-4869 474 C muddk@uhv.edu
MUDD, Michael, A 508-929-8746 222 F mmudd@worcester.edu
MUDD, Sara 864-231-6062 427 B smudd@andersonuniversity.edu
MUDD, Sarah, G 859-846-5390 191 G smudd@midway.edu
MUDRAK, Jeff 859-233-8701 193 D jmudrak@transy.edu
MUDROW, Dana, L 317-917-3249 165 O dmuldrow@martin.edu
MUECKE, Mary 718-409-7444 336 A mmuecke@sunymaritime.edu
MUECKE, Nancy 641-648-4611 173 K nancy.muecke@iavalley.edu
MUEGGE, Dave 417-836-4040 268 I davemuegge@missouristate.edu
MUEHSAM, Mitchell 936-294-1254 471 D mmuehsam@shsu.edu
MUELLER, Alan, C 336-316-2313 344 H muellerac@guilford.edu
MUELLER, II, Alfred, G 610-558-5508 411 E muellera@neumann.edu
MUELLER, Alicia 541-888-7465 395 B alicia.mueller@socc.edu
MUELLER, Beverley, D 757-594-7002 488 E bmueller@cnu.edu
MUELLER, Brian 602-639-7500 13 I
MUELLER, Chris 715-425-3505 521 B chris.mueller@uwrf.edu
MUELLER, Christie, L 864-833-8700 432 B clmueller@presby.edu
MUELLER, David 402-878-2380 280 G david.mueller@littlepriest.edu
MUELLER, Donna, G 585-292-2527 321 J dmueller@monroecc.edu
MUELLER, Edward, A 603-862-3272 288 C edward.mueller@unh.edu
MUELLER, Gregory 301-295-9474 528 G gregory.mueller@usuhs.edu
MUELLER, Jennifer 863-638-2918 115 D muellerjj@webber.edu
MUELLER, Joe, B 307-674-6446 526 M jbmueller@sheridan.edu
MUELLER, Julie 859-344-3386 193 C julie.mueller@thomasmore.edu
MUELLER, Lloyd 503-338-2412 390 G lmueller@clatsopcc.edu
MUELLER, Maggie 913-253-5097 184 G maggim@spst.edu
MUELLER, Martin 212-229-5896 322 E muellerm@newschool.edu
MUELLER, Michelle 734-477-8976 242 G mimueller@wccnet.edu
MUELLER, OSU, Pam 270-686-4319 187 C pam.mueller@brescia.edu
MUELLER, Ralph, O 219-989-2446 166 F rmueller@pnw.edu
MUELLER, Rita 715-634-4790 517 C rmueller@lco.edu
MUELLER, Shelia 412-536-1180 406 K sheila.mueller@laroche.edu
MUELLER, Steven, D 937-229-3141 379 D smueller1@udayton.edu
MUELLER, Steven, P 949-214-3386 41 F steve.mueller@cui.edu
MUELLER, Tom 319-296-4418 173 B thomas.mueller@hawkeyecollege.edu
MUELLER-ROEBKE, Jenny 402-643-7374 279 F jenny.roebke@cune.edu
MUENCH, Dean 510-845-5373 31 B
MUENCH, Kim 414-382-6091 515 D kim.muench@alverno.edu
MUERTZ, Julie, A 618-235-2700 155 C julie.muertz@swic.edu
MUESELER, Christine 724-838-4232 419 D mueseler@setonhill.edu
MUGANDA, Baraka 301-891-4112 213 D bmuganda@wau.edu
MUGG, Heather 404-727-9326 120 E hmugg@emory.edu
MUGGEO, Louis 845-398-4174 329 G lmuggeo@stac.edu
MUGGLETON, Mary 585-271-3657 328 A mmuggleton@stbernards.edu

MUGGLI, Darrin 913-360-7961 178 I dmuggli@benedictine.edu
MUGLIA, Kathleen 773-252-5368 152 B kathleen.muglia@resu.edu
MUGRIDGE, Philip 610-341-1721 403 B pmugridg@eastern.edu
MUGWANYA, Edmond, M 817-552-3700 460 E emugwanya@tku.edu
MUHA, Beth 202-885-2451 91 J bmuha@american.edu
MUHA, David 609-771-2132 290 F muhad@tcnj.edu
MUHA, Priscilla 707-654-1275 33 D pmuha@csum.edu
MUHAMMED, Robert 336-750-3299 359 B muhammedr@wssu.edu
MUHL, Erica 213-740-6267 72 D artdean@usc.edu
MUHLEMAN, Aimee 309-796-5505 135 I muhlemana@bhc.edu
MUHLFELDER, Leslie, F 610-330-5060 407 C muhlfell@lafayette.edu
MUHLIG, Eileen 315-801-8253 328 C emuhlig@secon.edu
MUHSIN, Karen 504-671-6138 196 D kmuhsi@dcc.edu
MUI, Eva Marie, L 671-735-8889 529 G evamarie.mui@guamcc.edu
MUIR, Bernard 650-723-2300 66 I
MUIR, Gary 507-786-3910 254 P muir@stolaf.edu
MUIR, Janette 703-993-5287 490 B jmuir@gmu.edu
MUIR, Julie 916-649-8168 28 L julie.muir@brightwood.edu
MUIR, Pete 616-949-5300 233 A pete.muir@cornerstone.edu
MUIR, Scott 856-256-4981 295 E muir@rowan.edu
MUIR, Thorton 770-426-2624 124 B tmuir@life.edu
MUIR, Troy 330-337-6403 362 I business@awc.edu
MUJAHID, Ihsan, R 484-365-7705 409 B rmujahid@lincon.edu
MUKASA, Samuel 603-862-1781 288 C sam.mukasa@unh.edu
MUKHARJI, Indrani 312-503-2903 150 F indrani@northwestern.edu
MUKHERJEE, Avinandan 678-466-4500 119 A avinandanmukherjee@clayton.edu
MULADORE, James, G 989-964-4045 240 F jgm@svsu.edu
MULANAX, Dennis, K 620-417-1181 184 I dennis.mulanax@sccc.edu
MULCAHY, Sean 913-360-7500 178 I smulcahy@benedictine.edu
MULDER, Lori 616-395-7811 235 F mulderl@hope.edu
MULDERICK, Thomas, J 610-799-1941 408 G tmulderick@lccc.edu
MULDOON, Kevin 215-572-4076 397 G muldoonk@arcadia.edu
MULDROW, Katrina 901-333-4462 447 B kmuldrow@southwest.tn.edu
MULERO, Daritza, R 787-258-1501 531 K dmulero@columbiacentral.edu
MULERO, Maria 787-850-9316 538 B maria.mulero2@upr.edu
MULERO, Minerva 787-864-2222 534 A minerva.mulero@guayama.inter.edu
MULERT, Terry 505-747-2147 301 F tmulert@nnmc.edu
MULET, Mariel 323-343-3040 33 C mariel.mulet@calstatela.edu
MULFORD, David, H 540-375-2215 493 H mulford@roanoke.edu
MULFORD, Joe 320-629-5120 251 E mulfordj@pine.edu
MULHALL, Lawrence, P 864-833-8300 432 B lmulhall@presby.edu
MULHERIN, April, C 207-778-7081 205 A april.mulherin@maine.edu
MULHERN, John 480-461-7627 14 D john.mulhern@mesacc.edu
MULHERN, Maureen 845-398-4067 329 G rmmulhern@stac.edu
MULHERN, Michelle, M 330-325-6263 373 H mmulhern@neomed.edu
MULHOLLAND, Angela, B 843-953-5502 428 G mulhollandab@cofc.edu
MULHOLLAND, William 413-236-2121 222 G wmulholl@berkshirecc.edu
MULICK, Patrick 870-307-7247 21 A patrick.mulick@lyon.edu
MULIK, James 425-640-1610 503 E james.mulik@edcc.edu
MULINEX, Stacy 614-287-5128 367 C smulinex@cscc.edu

MULKEY, Amelia 850-973-1621 105 H mulkeya@nfcc.edu
MULKIN, Alan 315-386-7777 335 B mulkina@canton.edu
MULKIN, Diana, M 607-871-2159 303 F mulkin@alfred.edu
MULL, Brenda 570-372-4451 419 H mullb@susqu.edu
MULL, Diane 803-754-4100 429 B
MULL, Jeff 541-737-9355 393 H jeff.mull@oregonstate.edu
MULL, Noah 304-243-8148 515 C nmull@wju.edu
MULLANE, William, S 512-223-1024 451 N wmullane@austincc.edu
MULLANEY, Kristin 603-228-3000 288 D kristin.mullaney@granite.edu
MULLANEY, Siri 928-226-4211 12 N siri.mullaney@coconino.edu
MULLANEY, William 201-447-7190 289 E wmullaney@bergen.edu
MULLEN, Adrienne, A 323-265-8613 49 G mullenaa@elac.edu
MULLEN, Courtney 501-450-5149 24 G cmullen@uca.edu
MULLEN, Deborah, F 404-378-8821 119 D mullend@ctsnet.edu
MULLEN, Denise 503-297-5544 393 C dmullen@ocac.edu
MULLEN, Eric 616-234-4164 234 E emullen@grcc.edu
MULLEN, Frank 508-541-1574 217 G fmullen@dean.edu
MULLEN, James, H 814-332-5380 397 A jmullen@allegheny.edu
MULLEN, Kate 518-327-6480 326 B kmullen@paulsmiths.edu
MULLEN, Ken 209-946-2345 71 C kmullen@pacific.edu
MULLEN, Laurie 410-704-2571 213 B lmullen@towson.edu
MULLEN, Megan 585-224-3222 335 D megan.mullen@esc.edu
MULLEN, Michael 610-361-5222 411 E mullenm@neumann.edu
MULLEN, Michael, D 919-515-2446 357 B mike.mullen@ncsu.edu
MULLEN, Robert 434-582-2651 491 D ramullen2@liberty.edu
MULLEN, Sally 618-650-3839 155 A smullen@siue.edu
MULLEN, Shirley, A 585-567-9310 316 F shirley.mullen@houghton.edu
MULLEN, Steve 214-333-5163 455 J stevem@dbu.edu
MULLEN, Steve, L 716-851-1294 313 H mullens@ecc.edu
MULLEN, William 612-330-1740 244 I mullen@augsburg.edu
MULLENIX, Elizabeth, R 513-529-6010 372 K mullener@miamioh.edu
MULLENIX, Joel 850-478-8496 106 G
MULLENS, Deborah, K 304-473-8181 515 B mullens_d@wvwc.edu
MULLENS, Liz 931-372-3149 445 B lmullens@tntech.edu
MULLENS, Rob, A 541-346-5455 395 G athleticdirector@uoregon.edu
MULLENS, Ward 517-586-3008 232 F wmullens@cleary.edu
MULLENS-SHAW, Christy, L 304-457-6324 510 B mullenscl@ab.edu
MULLER, Andrew 843-355-4150 435 A mullera@wiltech.edu
MULLER, Brook, W 541-346-3631 395 G bmuller@uoregon.edu
MULLER, David 212-241-8716 317 A
MULLER, Eugene, W 973-748-9000 289 H eugene_muller@bloomfield.edu
MULLER, Glen, C 607-255-5070 312 A gcm37@cornell.edu
MULLER, Jacquelyn, P 724-458-3302 404 F jpmuller@gcc.edu
MULLER, Joe 405-974-2502 388 L jmuller2@uco.edu
MULLER, Joseph 860-253-3055 86 A jmuller@asnuntuck.edu
MULLER, Katharine 310-434-3701 63 F muller_katharine@smc.edu
MULLER, Kathy 304-865-6127 511 C kathy.muller@ovu.edu
MULLER, Kathy, A 712-362-0433 173 G kmuller@iowalakes.edu
MULLER, Larry 304-424-8229 514 D larry.muller@wvup.edu
MULLER, Paul 218-755-2040 248 M pmuller@bemidjistate.edu
MULLER, Ralph, W 215-662-2203 421 E ralph.muller@uphs.upenn.edu

MULLER, Robert 847-947-5065 149 B
rmuller@nl.edu
MULLER, Stephen 352-638-9706 96 F
smuller@beaconcollege.edu
MULLER, Wade 541-278-5958 390 C
wmuller@bluecc.edu
MULLERY, Colleen 707-826-5086 34 F
cbm1@humboldt.edu
MULLIGAN, Bob 765-973-8337 162 G
rfmullig@iu.edu
MULLIGAN, Kate, A 620-417-2102 184 I
kate.mulligan@sccc.edu
MULLIGAN, Lucy 870-541-7850 20 G
MULLIGAN, Maura 617-989-4232 229 D
mulliganm@wit.edu
MULLIGAN, Rob 916-608-6736 51 C
mulligr@flc.losrios.edu
MULLIGAN, Zora, Z 573-882-2011 273 D
mulliganz@umsystem.edu
MULLIGAN-NGUYEN, Erin 513-244-4389 373 C
erin.mulligan-nguyen@msj.edu
MULLIKIN, Demeri 715-682-1307 518 H
dmullikin@northland.edu
MULLIKIN, Jane 419-473-2700 367 J
jmullikin@daviscollege.edu
MULLIKIN, Linka 808-235-7339 132 E
linka@hawaii.edu
MULLIN, Carol 610-359-5318 401 L
cmullin@dccc.edu
MULLIN, OSB, Douglas 320-363-2737 254 N
dmullin@csbsju.edu
MULLIN, Joan 716-896-0700 339 E
mullinj@villa.edu
MULLIN, John, C 972-377-1575 455 A
jmullin@collin.edu
MULLIN, Joseph 630-942-4278 138 B
mullin@cod.edu
MULLIN, Lucas 904-256-7532 103 D
lmullin2@ju.edu
MULLIN, Mark, E 573-341-4175 274 B
memullin@mst.edu
MULLIN, II, Miles, S 573-629-3092 265 G
miles.mullin@hlg.edu
MULLINAX, Kenneth 334-229-4104 1 D
kmullinax@alasu.edu
MULLINGS, Jennifer 904-363-6221 109 B
MULLINS, Brian 859-622-2821 188 F
brian.mullins@eku.edu
MULLINS, Cathy 802-258-3261 485 A
cathy.mullins@sit.edu
MULLINS, Cheryl 802-443-5542 484 F
cmullins@middlebury.edu
MULLINS, Gary 715-346-3906 521 C
gmullins@uwsp.edu
MULLINS, Greg 360-867-6243 503 G
mullinsg@evergreen.edu
MULLINS, James, L 765-494-2900 166 C
jmullins@purdue.edu
MULLINS, Jennifer 904-332-0910 102 F
MULLINS, Judy 660-785-4150 273 E
jmullins@truman.edu
MULLINS, Kathryn 616-234-4000 234 E
MULLINS, Kerry 908-852-1400 290 D
mullsk@centenarycollege.edu
MULLINS, Larry 803-327-7402 428 D
lmullins@clintoncollege.edu
MULLINS, Liza 904-256-7082 103 D
lmullin1@ju.edu
MULLINS, Michael 707-546-4000 42 M
mmullins@empirecollege.com
MULLINS, Rachel 501-977-2174 24 B
mullins@uaccm.edu
MULLINS, Stephanie, B 205-934-5121 8 E
smullins@uab.edu
MULLINS, Steve 479-968-0345 19 F
smullins@atu.edu
MULLINS, Steve 714-879-3901 46 F
smullins@hiu.edu
MULLINS, Turan 314-529-9434 267 B
tmullins@maryville.edu
MULLINS, William, E 740-826-8120 373 E
wmullins@muskingum.edu
MULLION, Carrie 760-921-5440 56 E
carrie.mullion@paloverde.edu
MULLIS, Charles 478-934-3064 124 E
charles.mullis@mga.edu
MULLIS, Jay 478-274-7879 125 D
jmullis@oftc.edu
MULLIS, Tres 540-458-8165 500 F
tmullis@wlu.edu
MULLISON, Mark 205-329-7942 3 B
mark.mullison@ecacolleges.com
MULLOWNEY, William, J 407-582-3411 114 N
bmullowney@valenciacollege.edu
MULRENAN, Holly 203-576-5518 89 A
hmulrenan@stvincentscollege.edu
MULROE, Michael 312-942-6214 153 B
mike_mulroe@rush.edu
MULROONEY, Bill 310-660-3593 42 J
bmulrooney@elcamino.edu
MULROONEY, Bill 310-660-3418 42 J
bmulrooney@elcamino.edu
MULROONEY, Debra 503-253-3443 393 D
dmulrooney@ocom.edu
MULROY, Kevin 909-621-8014 38 H
kevin_mulroy@cuc.claremont.edu
MULROY-BOWDEN, Linda 608-342-1845 521 A
mulroy@uwplatt.edu
MULROY-DEGENHART, Carmella 814-865-7611 412 F
qum11@psu.edu
MULRYAN, Michael 714-879-3901 46 F
mdmulryan@hiu.edu
MULSHINE, James, L 312-942-3589 153 B
james_l_mulshine@rush.edu
MULSO, Sara, K 651-641-8857 246 B
smulso@csp.edu
MULSO, William 507-537-6267 252 E
william.mulso@smsu.edu
MULTARI, James 516-323-3060 321 H
jmultari@molloy.edu
MULTOP, Kevin 541-383-7578 390 D
kmultop@cocc.edu
MULVEY, Colleen 415-351-3508 61 B
cmulvey@sfai.edu
MULVEY, Julie 508-588-9100 223 G
MULVEY, Kristin 815-280-2353 144 A
kmulvey@jjc.edu
MULVEY, Nick 262-551-5519 516 A
nmulvey@carthage.edu
MULVILLE, Matthew, H 716-888-2220 306 F
mulville@canisius.edu
MUMA, Richard, D 316-978-5761 185 J
richard.muma@wichita.edu
MUMFORD, Frank 657-278-2423 33 A
fmumford@fullerton.edu
MUMM, Michele 320-308-4066 252 A
michelem@stcloudstate.edu
MUMM-HILL, Deb 503-554-2332 391 D
dmummhill@georgefox.edu
MUMMERT, Kelly 304-243-2226 515 C
kmummert@wju.edu
MUMPER, Russ 706-542-0415 128 E
mumper@uga.edu
MUNA, Esther, A 671-735-5700 529 G
gccpresident@guamcc.edu
MUNA, Joann, W 671-735-5539 529 G
hr@guamcc.edu
MUNCH, Leah 718-405-3341 310 H
leah.munch@mountsaintvincent.edu
MUNCHEL, Christopher, T 765-285-5608 159 B
cmunchel@bsu.edu
MUNCHEL, Jeff 410-532-5324 210 B
jmunchel@ndm.edu
MUND, Barb 701-671-2204 361 F
barb.mund@ndscs.edu
MUND, Catherine 443-518-4781 208 C
cmund@howardcc.edu
MUNDAHL, Daniel, L 507-344-7739 244 K
daniel.mundahl@blc.edu
MUNDELL, Chris 614-222-4015 367 B
MUNDRANE, Michael 860-486-1777 89 D
michael.mundrane@uconn.edu
MUNDT, Jackie 620-672-5641 184 D
jackiem@prattcc.edu
MUNDY, Amy 361-582-2518 478 F
amy.mundy@victoriacollege.edu
MUNDY, Robert 574-631-7305 168 B
rmundy@nd.edu
MUNDY, Tiina 910-879-5556 347 F
tmundy@bladencc.edu
MUNFORD, Michael 507-537-7858 252 E
michael.munford@smsu.edu
MUNGAL, Godfrey 408-554-2375 63 E
mgmungal@scu.edu
MUNGER, James 208-426-4010 132 I
jmunger@boisestate.edu
MUNGER, Mary Lynn 816-604-3155 267 J
marylynn.munger@mcckc.edu
MUNGO, T. Rein 843-349-2577 428 E
tmungo@coastal.edu
MUNHOFEN, Troy 402-494-2311 281 C
tmunhofen@thenicc.edu
MUNIAK, Debby 330-684-8729 378 H
dmuniak@uakron.edu
MUNIER, Robert 508-289-3335 230 B
rmunier@whoi.edu
MUNIN, Eugene 312-553-2500 137 C
emunin@ccc.edu
MUNIZ, Amanda 361-593-3797 469 A
kaam003@tamuk.edu
MUNIZ, Hancy 787-891-0925 533 G
hrmuniz@aguadilla.inter.edu
MUNIZ, Herman 787-257-0744 537 H
herman.muniz@upr.edu
MUNIZ, Ivette 973-803-5000 294 B
imuniz@pillar.edu
MUNIZ, Maria 787-841-2000 535 I
mmuniz@pucpr.edu
MUNLEY, Almarie 757-727-5773 490 E
almarie.munley@hamptonu.edu
MUNN, James 208-732-6860 133 E
jmunn@csi.edu
MUNN, Janet, A 845-368-7210 329 I
janet.munn@use.salvationarmy.org
MUNN, Kathie, A 906-932-4231 234 C
kathiem@gogebic.edu
MUNNELL, Barbra, M 724-458-3824 404 F
bmmunnell@gcc.edu
MUNNERLYN, Sam 334-420-4216 7 G
smunnerlyn@trenholmstate.edu
MUNNS, Sarah 573-592-6050 275 E
sarah.munns@westminster-mo.edu
MUNOZ, Candelario 805-546-3147 41 L
cmunoz@cuesta.edu
MUNOZ, Carmen 818-401-1035 40 G
cmunoz@columbiacollege.edu
MUNOZ, Celia 954-763-9840 95 N
MUNOZ, Chris 713-348-6271 464 E
chris.munoz@rice.edu
MUNOZ, Deana 312-935-6657 152 D
dmiranda@robertmorris.edu
MUNOZ, Harry 787-720-4476 537 A
serviciocristiano@mizpa.edu
MUNOZ, Ivette 787-725-8120 532 K
imunoz@eap.edu
MUNOZ, Jesse 661-362-3155 40 A
jesse.munoz@canyons.edu
MUNOZ, Joe 325-942-2073 472 B
joe.munoz@angelo.edu
MUNOZ, Juan, S 806-742-7025 472 C
juan.munoz@ttu.edu
MUNOZ, Julio 787-284-1912 534 C
jcmunoz@ponce.inter.edu
MUNOZ, Justin 361-593-4338 469 A
justin.munoz@tamuk.edu
MUNOZ, Mike 562-908-3467 58 I
mrmunoz@riohondo.edu
MUNOZ, Raquel 323-357-3630 37 G
raquelmunoz@cdrewu.edu
MUNOZ, Rene 717-871-4457 415 F
rene.munoz@millersville.edu
MUNRO, Alex 717-295-9666 420 C
munro@stevenscollege.edu
MUNRO, Glenn 301-295-0064 528 G
glenn.munro@med.navy.mil
MUNRO, Sarah 801-972-3596 481 M
s.munro@partners.utah.edu
MUNRO, Stuart, J 508-767-7041 214 F
smunro@assumption.edu
MUNROE, Jane Ann 714-449-7446 51 F
jmunroe@ketchum.edu
MUNROE, Jeffrey 616-392-8555 244 A
jeff@westernsem.edu
MUNROE, Richard, A 574-807-7120 159 D
rick.munroe@bethelcollege.edu
MUNSCH, OSB, Nathan 724-805-2612 419 B
nathan.munsch@stvincent.edu
MUNSCHY, Karl 706-729-2179 117 D
kmunschy@augusta.edu
MUNSIL, Len 602-386-4102 11 D
len.munsil@arizonachristian.edu
MUNSON, David, C 734-647-7010 241 J
munson@umich.edu
MUNSON, Janet 309-649-6273 155 G
janet.munson@src.edu
MUNSON, Keith 612-330-1474 244 I
munsonk@augsburg.edu
MUNSON, Leo, W 817-257-7104 469 G
l.munson@tcu.edu
MUNSON, Robert, A 312-915-8703 146 G
rmunson@luc.edu
MUNSON, Scott 303-860-5600 83 J
scott.munson@cu.edu
MUNSON, Steve 703-284-6901 492 A
smunson@marymount.edu
MUNSON, Wanda 281-669-4711 464 I
wanda.munson@sjcd.edu
MUNSON, Wanda 281-669-4711 464 J
wanda.munson@sjcd.edu
MUNSON, Wanda 281-669-4711 465 B
wanda.munson@sjcd.edu
MUNSON, Wanda 281-669-4711 465 A
wanda.munson@sjcd.edu
MUNSON, William 713-743-5470 473 F
wfmunson@central.uh.edu
MUNSON-DRYER, Molly 309-556-3780 143 D
mmunsond@iwu.edu
MUNSTERMAN, Korin 904-680-7601 100 E
kmunsterman@fcsl.edu
MUNT, Glaca, C 512-863-1381 466 G
muntg@southwestern.edu
MUNTER, Judith 415-338-2687 35 B
jhmunter@sfsu.edu
MUNTZ, Donna 740-374-8716 381 A
dmuntz@wscc.edu
MUNZER, Pat 785-670-2111 185 H
pat.munzer@washburn.edu
MURACA, Paul 713-798-6617 452 G
muraca@bcm.edu
MURAKAWA, Janelle, L 808-956-6486 131 D
jmurakaw@hawaii.edu
MURALI, Viji 530-752-4998 69 A
vpiet-sup@ucdavis.edu
MURASKO, Donna 215-895-1892 402 G
dm37@drexel.edu
MURASSO, Thomas 914-323-5337 319 N
thomas.murasso@mville.edu
MURATA, Toshihiko 541-278-5856 390 C
tmurata@bluecc.edu
MURATORE, Lauren 717-334-6286 409 C
lmuratore@ltsg.edu
MURAVCHICK, Gregg 859-233-8135 193 D
gmuravchick@transy.edu
MURAWSKI, Pam 386-752-1822 100 L
pamela.murawski@fgc.edu
MURCH, Aimee 716-896-0700 339 E
murcha@villa.edu
MURCHISON, Joellle 860-486-2000 89 D
joelle.murchison@uconn.edu
MURDAUGH, Jim 850-201-8660 113 E
murdaugj@tcc.fl.edu
MURDEN MCCLURE, Tori 502-585-9911 192 E
tmcclure@spalding.edu
MURDEN-WOLDU, Romell 773-481-8451 137 I
rmurden@ccc.edu
MURDERS, Michael 479-667-1707 19 F
mmurders@atu.edu
MURDOCH, Jessica 978-665-3338 221 D
jmurdoch@fitchburgstate.edu
MURDOCH, William, G 909-558-6604 49 C
wmurdoch@llu.edu
MURDOCK, Alan, K 336-734-7757 349 G
amurdock@forsythtech.edu
MURDOCK, James, L 313-927-1226 237 E
jmurdock@marygrove.edu
MURDOCK, Rebecca 402-557-7136 278 I
rebecca.murdock@bellevue.edu
MURDZAK, Karen 814-732-1020 415 A
kmurdzak@edinboro.edu
MURGA, Margaret 252-536-7242 350 C
mmurga673@halifaxcc.edu
MURGA, Mario 617-327-6777 229 H
mario_murga@williamjames.edu
MURGOLO-POORE, Marie 775-337-5608 284 K
mmurgolo@tmcc.edu
MURGUIA, Stephanie 562-860-2451 36 P
smurguia@cerritos.edu
MURIANA, Joseph, P 718-817-3020 314 G
jmuriana@fordham.edu
MURIANKA, Luke 315-858-0940 316 E
lmurianka@hts.edu
MURILLO, Alice 617-228-2102 223 B
amurillo@bhcc.mass.edu
MURILLO, Kindred 530-541-4660 48 D
murillo@ltcc.edu
MURKA, Adam 937-512-2947 377 D
adam.murka@sinclair.edu
MURNANE, Ryan 757-352-4891 493 E
ryanmur@regent.edu
MURNEN, Tim 419-372-7983 364 E
tmurnen@bgsu.edu
MURPHEY, Diane 580-349-1402 385 F
diane@opsu.edu
MURPHREE, Danny, W 806-291-3635 479 D
murphree@wbu.edu
MURPHREE, David 806-291-3641 479 D
dmurphree@wbu.edu
MURPHREY, Hiram Todd 252-638-7263 349 B
murphret@cravencc.edu
MURPHY, Amy 508-793-3880 217 C
amurphy@holycross.edu
MURPHY, Amy 618-252-5400 154 G
amy.murphy@sic.edu
MURPHY, Ann, B 303-556-3245 81 G
murphann@msudenver.edu
MURPHY, Antoinette 309-341-5230 136 C
amurphy@sandburg.edu
MURPHY, Ashley, R 570-326-3761 413 O
MURPHY, Beverly, J 336-322-2117 351 H
beverly.murphy@piedmontcc.edu
MURPHY, Bobbie 320-308-2151 252 A
ramurphy@stcloudstate.edu
MURPHY, Brent, D 574-232-2408 166 G
bmurphy@rtuvt.com
MURPHY, Bret 775-753-2217 284 I
bret.murphy@gbcnv.edu
MURPHY, Brian 802-440-4335 483 E
bmurphy@bennington.edu
MURPHY, Brian 217-581-7618 139 H
blmurphy@eiu.edu
MURPHY, Brian 408-864-8705 44 A
murphybrian@deanza.edu
MURPHY, Brian 530-251-8836 48 E
bmurphy@lassencollege.edu
MURPHY, Brian 718-997-5910 309 D
brian.murphy@qc.cuny.edu
MURPHY, Brian 936-468-2803 466 H
murphybm1@sfasu.edu

MURPHY, Bridget .... 703-284-6478.. 492 A
bridget.murphy@marymount.edu
MURPHY, Britt Anne .... 501-450-1303.... 20 F
johnsen@hendrix.edu
MURPHY, Bruce, T .... 985-448-4003.. 201 A
bruce.murphy@nicholls.edu
MURPHY, Carolyn .... 402-471-2505.. 281 G
cmurphy@nscs.edu
MURPHY, Catherine .... 202-651-5019.... 92 C
catherine.murphy@gallaudet.edu
MURPHY, Catherine .... 615-460-6418.. 438 J
catherine.murphy@belmont.edu
MURPHY, Chad .... 309-649-6266.. 155 G
chad.murphy@src.edu
MURPHY, Charles, J .... 509-313-6139.. 504 A
murphyc@gonzaga.edu
MURPHY, Chris .... 805-756-5692.... 31 I
cmurph18@calpoly.edu
MURPHY, Chris .... 662-720-7280.. 260 B
cdmurphy@nemcc.edu
MURPHY, Christine .... 718-940-5800.. 328 G
cmurphy@sjcny.edu
MURPHY, Colleen .... 319-895-4215.. 171 A
cmurphy@cornellcollege.edu
MURPHY, Dan .... 803-705-4958.. 427 D
dan@benedict.edu
MURPHY, Darlene .... 802-654-0534.. 486 A
darlene.murphy@ccv.edu
MURPHY, David .... 414-288-4810.. 517 I
david.murphy@marquette.edu
MURPHY, David, L .... 773-702-9466.. 156 D
dlm@uchicago.edu
MURPHY, David, W .... 315-498-2530.. 325 G
murphydw@sunyocc.edu
MURPHY, Deanna .... 760-245-4271.... 73 H
deanna.murphy@vvc.edu
MURPHY, Denise .... 301-687-4457.. 212 F
dmurphy@frostburg.edu
MURPHY, Dennis, J .... 610-527-0200.. 418 D
dennis.murphy@rosemont.edu
MURPHY, Diane Lyden ... 315-443-3707.. 337 A
dlmurphy@syr.edu
MURPHY, Douglas, L .... 501-686-5730.... 23 C
dlmurphy@uams.edu
MURPHY, Eileen .... 845-398-4316.. 329 G
emurphy@stac.edu
MURPHY, Frank, J .... 815-835-6299.. 153 K
frank.j.murphy@svcc.edu
MURPHY, Frederick .... 704-378-1129.. 345 E
fmurphy@jcsu.edu
MURPHY, Gail .... 239-732-3953.. 101 F
gail.murphy@fsw.edu
MURPHY, Gaye .... 480-731-8638.... 13 N
gaye.murphy@domail.maricopa.edu
MURPHY, Gene .... 601-857-3330.. 258 A
temurphy@hindscc.edu
MURPHY, Gregory .... 215-751-8042.. 401 G
gmurphy@ccp.edu
MURPHY, OSB, Isaac .... 603-641-7150.. 287 G
imurphy@anselm.edu
MURPHY, Jack .... 773-481-8124.. 137 I
jmurphy@ccc.edu
MURPHY, III, James, E .. 704-894-2373.. 343 I
jamurphy@davidson.edu
MURPHY, James, H .... 573-341-4292.. 274 B
murphyj@mst.edu
MURPHY, Jan .... 309-438-7602.. 143 B
jshane@ilstu.edu
MURPHY, Janice .... 410-334-2808.. 213 G
jmurphy@worwic.edu
MURPHY, Jim .... 916-388-2812.... 36 D
jmurphy@carrington.edu
MURPHY, Jim .... 973-748-9000.. 289 H
jim_murphy@bloomfield.edu
MURPHY, John .... 317-921-4243.. 164 E
jmmurphy@ivytech.edu
MURPHY, John .... 203-837-8395.... 85 I
murphyj@wcsu.edu
MURPHY, John .... 210-458-3026.. 477 A
john.murphy@utsa.edu
MURPHY, John, D .... 207-834-7516.. 205 B
jdmurphy@maine.edu
MURPHY, Joseph, A .... 614-885-5585.. 376 G
jmurphy@pcj.edu
MURPHY, Joseph, M ...... 740-427-5120.. 371 C
murphyjm@kenyon.edu
MURPHY, Josephine .... 718-368-5144.. 308 F
jmurphy@kbcc.cuny.edu
MURPHY, Joshua .... 603-703-8484.. 286 D
jmurphy@ccsnh.edu
MURPHY, Joyce, A .... 508-856-4842.. 221 B
joyce.murphy@umassmed.edu
MURPHY, Kathleen .... 216-687-3613.. 366 I
kathleen.murphy@csuohio.edu
MURPHY, Kathleen, M .... 508-767-7110.. 214 F
kamurphy@assumption.edu
MURPHY, Keith .... 718-409-7349.. 336 A
kmurphy@sunymaritime.edu
MURPHY, Kenneth, E ...... 714-628-2876.... 37 F
MURPHY, Kenneth, R ...... 903-510-2547.. 473 C
kmur@tjc.edu
MURPHY, Kevin .... 607-735-1750.. 313 F
kmurphy@elmira.edu
MURPHY, Kristin .... 978-665-4141.. 221 D
kmurph72@fitchburgstate.edu
MURPHY, Lamar, R .... 585-276-3262.. 338 K
lamar.murphy@rochester.edu
MURPHY, Laura .... 508-929-8649.. 222 F
lmurphy@worcester.edu
MURPHY, Linda .... 802-651-5891.. 483 F
lmurphy@champlain.edu
MURPHY, Lisa .... 480-860-2700.... 13 G
lmurphy@taliesin.edu
MURPHY, Lisa .... 307-778-1110.. 526 K
lmurphy@lccc.wy.edu
MURPHY, Lisa, B .... 863-638-7690.. 115 C
lisa.murphy@warner.edu
MURPHY, Lynda .... 940-898-3405.. 472 G
lmurphy@twu.edu
MURPHY, M. Patrick .... 336-278-7640.. 344 D
murphyp@elon.edu
MURPHY, Maegan, K ...... 312-944-0882.. 145 F
mmurphy@chicago.chefs.edu
MURPHY, Margaret, L ..... 757-446-5828.. 489 B
murphyml@evms.edu
MURPHY, Marie .... 508-531-1338.. 221 C
mmurphy@bridgew.edu
MURPHY, Marilyn .... 319-363-1323.. 175 D
mmurphy@mtmercy.edu
MURPHY, Mark .... 402-465-2254.. 281 K
mam@nebrwesleyan.edu
MURPHY, Mary .... 612-343-4406.. 253 Y
mlmurphy@northcentral.edu
MURPHY, Mary, K .... 607-753-2303.. 333 A
maryk.murphy@cortland.edu
MURPHY, Mary Joan .... 212-854-2091.. 304 I
mmurphy@barnard.edu
MURPHY, Marybeth .... 201-615-3469.. 297 B
marybeth.murphy@stevens.edu
MURPHY, Maureen .... 732-224-2204.. 289 I
mmurphy@brookdalecc.edu
MURPHY, Maureen .... 617-824-8575.. 218 B
maureen_murphy@emerson.edu
MURPHY, Melanie .... 843-863-7765.. 427 I
mmurphy@csuniv.edu
MURPHY, Melissa .... 516-796-4800.. 323 A
mmurphy@nycc.edu
MURPHY, Michael .... 845-398-4118.. 329 G
mmurphy@stac.edu
MURPHY, Michael .... 303-762-6903.... 79 I
michael.murphy@denverseminary.edu
MURPHY, Mollie .... 202-685-3933.. 528 B
murphym@ndu.edu
MURPHY, Nancy .... 850-729-5365.. 105 I
murphyn@nwfsc.edu
MURPHY, Nelson .... 704-645-4535.. 343 B
namurphy14@catawba.edu
MURPHY, Patricia, B ...... 804-484-1581.. 495 G
pmurphy@richmond.edu
MURPHY, Paul .... 805-922-6966..... 25 I
pmurphy@hancockcollege.edu
MURPHY, Paul .... 781-768-7049.. 227 G
paul.murphy@regiscollege.edu
MURPHY, Pella .... 478-929-6744.. 124 E
pella.murphy@mga.edu
MURPHY, Peter, F .... 270-809-7064.. 192 A
pmurphy@murraystate.edu
MURPHY, Pollie .... 757-727-5201.. 490 E
pollie.muphy@hamptonu.edu
MURPHY, Pollie .... 757-727-5237.. 490 E
pollie.murphy@hamptonu.edu
MURPHY, Rebecca .... 330-672-8533.. 370 I
rmurph20@kent.edu
MURPHY, Richard .... 781-899-5500.. 227 E
dmurphy@psjs.edu
MURPHY, Robert .... 315-781-3622.. 316 C
murphy@hws.edu
MURPHY, Robert, P .... 716-829-8199.. 313 A
murphyrp@dyc.edu
MURPHY, Sean .... 661-255-1050..... 30 E
MURPHY, Seana .... 317-916-7974.. 164 E
smurphy45@ivytech.edu
MURPHY, Stephen .... 203-432-8094.... 90 D
stephen.murphy@yale.edu
MURPHY, Steve .... 781-821-2222.. 223 G
MURPHY, Susan, L .... 415-422-2620.... 72 C
murphy@usfca.edu
MURPHY, Suzanne .... 212-678-3755.. 337 E
smurphy@tc.columbia.edu
MURPHY, Suzanne, K ...... 215-596-8888.. 422 A
s.murphy@usciences.edu
MURPHY, Teresa .... 202-994-6510.... 92 D
tmurphy@gwu.edu
MURPHY, Thomas .... 516-876-3215.. 333 C
murphyt@oldwestbury.edu
MURPHY, Thomas, H .... 215-898-7581.. 421 E
tom.murphy@isc.upenn.edu
MURPHY, Tiffany .... 484-384-2986.. 403 B
tmurphy@eastern.edu
MURPHY, Tim .... 903-886-5550.. 468 D
tim.murphy@tamuc.edu
MURPHY, Todd .... 323-343-2500.... 33 C
tmurphy@cslanet.calstatela.edu
MURPHY, Todd .... 714-432-5896.... 39 G
todd.murphy@mail.cccd.edu
MURPHY, William .... 617-552-1272.. 216 C
william.murphy@bc.edu
MURPHY, William .... 845-574-4362.. 327 G
wmurphy@sunyrockland.edu
MURPHY ALEXANDER,
Coleen .... 845-758-7431.. 304 F
murphy@bard.edu
MURPHY HEALEY, Kerry . 781-239-4263.. 214 G
khealey@babson.edu
MURPHY-MORIARITY,
Kathy .... 802-485-2292.. 484 H
kmurphym@norwich.edu
MURPHY-NORRIS,
Carmel .... 540-453-2237.. 496 F
murphynorrisc@brcc.edu
MURPHY-STETZ,
Katherine .... 312-567-3080.. 142 I
murphy@iit.edu
MURR, Christopher .... 512-245-3975.. 471 F
cm18@txstate.edu
MURRAH, Matt .... 214-333-5160.. 455 J
matt@dbu.edu
MURRAY, Adam, A .... 540-568-3828.. 490 J
murrayal@jmu.edu
MURRAY, Ann .... 307-778-1113.. 526 K
amurray@lccc.wy.edu
MURRAY, Annette .... 219-769-2047.. 165 R
MURRAY, Barbara, M .... 909-748-8544.... 71 K
barbara_murray@redlands.edu
MURRAY, Ben .... 507-457-1443.. 254 O
bmurray@smumn.edu
MURRAY, Brian .... 972-721-5008.. 473 D
bmurray@udallas.edu
MURRAY, Carol .... 845-341-4700.. 325 H
carol.murray@sunyorange.edu
MURRAY, Carol .... 406-338-5441.. 276 A
c_murray@bfcc.edu
MURRAY, Christopher, D 406-994-2513.. 277 C
chris.murray@msuaf.org
MURRAY, Deborah .... 423-614-8118.. 441 B
debmurray@leeuniversity.edu
MURRAY, Delethia .... 713-221-8098.. 474 B
murrayd@uhd.edu
MURRAY, Derrick .... 336-750-2000.. 359 B
MURRAY, Douglas, J .... 575-624-8020.. 300 I
dmurray@nmmi.edu
MURRAY, Edwin .... 504-568-5135.. 198 A
emurray@lsuhsc.edu
MURRAY, Eric .... 425-352-8810.. 501 J
emurray@cascadia.edu
MURRAY, Frank .... 509-542-4835.. 502 G
fmurray@columbiabasin.edu
MURRAY, George, W .... 803-754-4100.. 429 B
MURRAY, Harris .... 803-535-1257.. 431 I
murrayh@octech.edu
MURRAY, Harris .... 803-535-1255.. 431 I
murrayh@octech.edu
MURRAY, Jamecia .... 903-927-3222.. 479 K
jlmurray@wileyc.edu
MURRAY, Jason .... 650-508-3525.... 54 J
jpmurray@ndnu.edu
MURRAY, Jay .... 203-837-8286.... 85 I
murrayj@wcsu.edu
MURRAY, Jill .... 570-504-1575.. 407 B
murrayj@lackawanna.edu
MURRAY, John, D .... 305-899-3021.... 96 D
MURRAY, Karen .... 254-968-9103.. 467 F
kmurray@tarleton.edu
MURRAY, Kate .... 516-572-0601.. 322 C
kathleen.murray@ncc.edu
MURRAY, Kathleen .... 509-527-5132.. 509 G
kmurry@whitman.edu
MURRAY, Kevin .... 434-799-5172.. 488 I
MURRAY, Lakisha .... 718-270-5000.. 309 B
lmurray@mec.cuny.edu
MURRAY, Louise .... 973-290-4430.. 290 G
lmurray@cse.edu
MURRAY, Lynne .... 785-594-8311.. 178 D
president@bakeru.edu
MURRAY, Mark, J .... 904-264-2172.. 107 N
mark.murray@iws.edu
MURRAY, Mary .... 307-332-2930.. 527 F
mmurray@wyomingcatholiccollege.com
MURRAY, Melissa .... 510-642-6483.... 68 M
mmurray@law.berkeley.edu
MURRAY, Melissa .... 814-262-6423.. 413 P
mmurray@pennhighlands.edu
MURRAY, Michael .... 814-838-7673.. 403 G
mmurray2@fortisinstitute.edu
MURRAY, Michele .... 206-296-6066.. 507 E
mmurray@seattleu.edu
MURRAY, Nancy .... 202-319-6916.... 92 A
murrayn@cua.edu
MURRAY, Nancy, K .... 219-464-5989.. 168 F
nancy.murray@valpo.edu
MURRAY, Patrick .... 208-769-5912.. 134 C
patrick.murray@nic.edu
MURRAY, Peter, J .... 410-706-2461.. 211 F
pmurray@umaryland.edu
MURRAY, Rhoda, R .... 540-985-8488.. 491 A
rrmurray@jchs.edu
MURRAY, Richard .... 914-633-2458.. 317 B
rmurray@iona.edu
MURRAY, Robert .... 845-398-4125.. 329 G
rmurray@stac.edu
MURRAY, Robert .... 309-556-3031.. 143 D
bmurray@iwu.edu
MURRAY, Robert .... 860-444-8520.. 529 A
robert.murray@uscga.edu
MURRAY, Rodney, B .... 215-596-8789.. 422 A
r.murray@usciences.edu
MURRAY, Sean .... 888-491-8686.... 74 I
MURRAY, Sharon .... 518-292-1753.. 327 H
murras2@sage.edu
MURRAY, Stephen, B .... 313-831-5200.. 233 K
smurray@etseminary.edu
MURRAY, Susan .... 770-229-3043.. 127 F
smurray@sctech.edu
MURRAY, Susan .... 503-399-5145.. 390 E
susan.murray@chemeketa.edu
MURRAY, Suzette .... 630-466-7900.. 157 K
smurray@waubonsee.edu
MURRAY, Tamsen .... 714-879-3901.... 46 F
tmurray@hiu.edu
MURRAY, Thomas .... 773-508-7030.. 146 G
tmurray3@luc.edu
MURRAY, Thomas .... 336-770-3277.. 358 E
murrayt@uncsa.edu
MURRAY, Thomas, F .... 402-280-2983.. 279 H
tfmurray@creighton.edu
MURRAY, Thomas, F .... 402-280-4076.. 279 H
tfmurray@creighton.edu
MURRAY, Timothy, S .... 845-575-3000.. 320 B
tim.murray@marist.edu
MURRAY, Tracey, L .... 410-951-3980.. 212 E
tmurray@coppin.edu
MURRAY, Trish .... 704-894-2099.. 343 I
trmurray@davidson.edu
MURRAY-JENSEN, Julie .. 541-880-2387.. 391 F
julie@klamathcc.edu
MURRAY-LAURY, Janice . 908-737-7080.. 292 C
jmurray@kean.edu
MURRAY-RUST,
Catherine .... 404-894-8914.. 121 D
catherine.rust@library.gatech.edu
MURRELL, Shana .... 508-531-2009.. 221 C
shana.murrell@bridgew.edu
MURRELL, Stephen .... 802-387-1689.. 484 B
stephenmurrell@landmark.edu
MURRELL, Terry .... 712-274-6400.. 177 I
terry.murrell@witcc.edu
MURRET, Patricia .... 504-865-5448.. 198 E
pmurret@loyno.edu
MURRIL, Antoinette .... 312-567-3012.. 142 I
amurril@iit.edu
MURRIN, Michael .... 716-926-8900.. 316 B
mmurrin@hilbert.edu
MURRY, Kim .... 620-365-5116.. 178 A
murry@allencc.edu
MURRY, Melanie .... 901-678-2155.. 445 C
mmurry@memphis.edu
MURTAGH, Michael .... 309-467-6315.. 140 E
mmurtagh@eureka.edu
MURTAUGH, Kelly .... 651-846-1363.. 252 C
kelly.murtaugh@saintpaul.edu
MURTAUGH, Peter, T .... 314-286-4813.. 270 G
ptmurtaugh@ranken.edu
MURTHY, Jayathi, Y .... 310-825-2938.... 69 D
jmurthy@seas.ucla.edu
MURTHY, Pushpalatha ..... 906-487-3007.. 238 A
ppmurthy@mtu.edu
MURTHY, Raj .... 520-206-4809.... 16 F
rmurthy@pima.edu
MURUAKO, Dominic .... 205-366-8854...... 7 E
dmuruako@stillman.edu
MURUGESAN, Hayley .... 619-398-4902.... 46 D
hmurugesan@hightechhigh.org
MURY, Hal .... 919-209-2000.. 350 G
hemury@johnstoncc.edu
MUSAL, Edward .... 914-251-6923.. 334 C
edward.musal@purchase.edu
MUSALINI, Laneika .... 864-646-1810.. 433 C
lmusalin@tctc.edu
MUSCARELLA, Joseph, V 516-572-0605.. 322 C
joseph.muscarella@ncc.edu
MUSCARELLA, Susan .... 510-845-5373.... 31 B
susan@cjc.edu
MUSCENTE, Catherine ..... 516-323-4710.. 321 H
cmuscente@molloy.edu
MUSCOLINO,
Mary Lin, L .... 815-740-3496.. 157 F
mmuscolino@stfrancis.edu
MUSE, Bill .... 830-792-7355.. 465 E
bmuse@schreiner.edu
MUSE, Bill .... 918-463-2931.. 383 F
wmuse@connorsstate.edu
MUSE, Charles .... 936-261-3860.. 467 E
cdmuse@pvamu.edu

NAIDU, Jay .... 650-543-3996.... 52 D
jnaidu@menlo.edu
NAIDU, Santhana .... 812-237-8764.. 162 A
santhana.naidu@indstate.edu
NAIFEH, Zeak .... 580-581-2217.. 382 G
znaifeh@cameron.edu
NAIL, Jordyn .... 706-729-2127.. 120 C
jdnail@ega.edu
NAIL, Lance .... 806-742-3171.. 472 C
lance.nail@ttu.edu
NAILLER, Katie .... 212-650-6507.. 307 E
knailler@ccny.cuny.edu
NAILS, Dana .... 731-425-2628.. 446 C
dnails@jscc.edu
NAIR, Ajay .... 404-727-4364.. 120 E
ajay.nair@emory.edu
NAIR, Murali .... 734-487-0077.. 233 J
mnair@emich.edu
NAIR, Sheila .... 928-523-0180.... 15 H
sheila.nair@nau.edu
NAIRN, Joseph .... 585-785-1464.. 314 D
joseph.nairn@flcc.edu
NAIRN, Roderick .... 303-315-2102.... 84 A
roderick.nairn@ucdenver.edu
NAJAM, Adil .... 617-358-7238.. 216 E
anajam@bu.edu
NAJIEB, Najla, F .... 713-313-6817.. 470 D
najieb_nf@tsu.edu
NAJJAR, Ghina .... 856-256-5747.. 295 E
najjar@rowan.edu
NAJJAR, Joe .... 229-430-6624.. 116 A
jnajjar@albanytech.edu
NAJJAR, Yasar .... 508-626-4769.. 221 E
ynajjar@framingham.edu
NAKAGAWA, Deborah ..... 808-956-0321.. 131 H
debn@hawaii.edu
NAKAI, Karen .... 562-985-4121.... 33 B
karen.nakai@csulb.edu
NAKAMA, Debra .... 808-984-3515.. 132 D
debran@hawaii.edu
NAKAMURA, Natalie .... 212-659-3601.. 318 D
nnakamura@tkc.edu
NAKAS, Victor .... 202-319-5244.... 92 A
nakas@cua.edu
NAKASONE, Nancy, K ..... 808-689-2525.. 131 G
nancynak@hawaii.edu
NAKASONE, Ron .... 818-240-1000.... 45 A
nakasone@glendale.edu
NAKHAI, Mandana .... 914-337-9300.. 311 F
mandana.nakhai@concordia-ny.edu
NALEPA, Laurie .... 818-947-2498.... 50 D
nalepal@lavc.edu
NALES PÉREZ, Nereida ... 787-884-3838.. 530 G
nnales@atenascollege.edu
NALLEY, Doug .... 919-761-2400.. 355 I
dnalley@sebts.edu
NALLY, Angela, D .... 765-658-4261.. 160 F
adnally@depauw.edu
NALLY, Harold, D .... 606-783-2097.. 191 H
h.nally@moreheadstate.edu
NALLY, Tracey .... 616-395-7316.. 235 F
nally@hope.edu
NAM, Jin Joo .... 213-385-2322.... 75 E
melody@wmu.edu
NAMIAN, Jeff .... 212-924-5900.. 336 I
registrar@swedishinstitute.edu
NAMUO, Clyne .... 520-515-3602.... 12 L
namuoc@cochise.edu
NAMYET, Jay .... 541-302-0308.. 395 G
jnamyet@uoregon.edu
NANCE, Agnieszka .... 504-862-3348.. 200 C
anance@tulane.edu
NANCE, Beverlee, S .... 910-642-7141.. 353 C
beverlee.nance@sccnc.edu
NANCE, Bill .... 731-661-5505.. 448 A
bnance@uu.edu
NANCE, Damon .... 951-372-7041.... 59 B
damon.nance@norcocollege.edu
NANCE, Donna .... 817-531-6579.. 472 F
dnance@txwes.edu
NANCE, Eva .... 574-631-1097.. 168 B
nance.1@nd.edu
NANCE, Melissa .... 620-421-6700.. 182 G
melissan@labette.edu
NANCE, Richard, E .... 757-683-3144.. 492 G
rnance@odu.edu
NANCE, Summer .... 704-406-4247.. 344 E
snance@gardner-webb.edu
NANCE, Teresa, A .... 610-519-4007.. 422 G
terry.nance@villanova.edu
NANNERY, Tracy .... 716-250-7500.. 306 A
tbnannery@bryantstratton.edu
NANNEY, Ana .... 985-448-7940.. 196 E
ana.nanney@fletcher.edu
NANNEY, Chris .... 704-669-4062.. 348 F
nanney@clevelandcc.edu
NANNI, Louis, M .... 574-631-6123.. 168 B
nanni.3@nd.edu
NAPIER, Anna .... 606-487-3090.. 189 E
anna.napier@kctcs.edu
NAPIER, Harold .... 260-982-5256.. 165 M
hnapier@manchester.edu
NAPIER, William .... 216-875-9970.. 366 I
w.napier@csuohio.edu
NAPOLEON, Nawa?a .... 808-734-9283.. 131 I
nawaa@hawaii.edu
NAPOLES, Gerald .... 832-813-6500.. 461 B
gerald.napoles@lonestar.edu
NAPOLI, Carianya .... 206-934-4591.. 506 J
carianya.napoli@seattlecolleges.edu
NAPOLI, Jason .... 319-895-4458.. 171 A
jnapoli@cornellcollege.edu
NAPOLI, Kathy .... 909-652-6102.... 37 D
kathy.napoli@chaffey.edu
NAPOLI, Ron .... 937-319-6139.. 363 D
rnapoli@antiochcollege.edu
NAPOLITANO, Daniel .... 607-871-2175.. 303 F
napolitano@alfred.edu
NAPOLITANO, Janet .... 510-987-9074.... 68 L
president@ucop.edu
NAPOLITANO, Ralph, E ... 515-294-9101.. 169 G
ren1@iastate.edu
NAPPER, Kathryn .... 415-422-4277.... 72 C
kmnapper@usfca.edu
NAQUIN, Rose .... 504-520-7301.. 202 C
xubooks@xula.edu
NARANJO, Adrian .... 509-963-3049.. 501 K
naranjoa@cwu.edu
NARANJO, Veronica .... 509-865-8617.. 504 D
naranjo_v@heritage.edu
NARCISSE, Margaretta, S 913-253-5097.. 184 G
margaretta.narcisse@spst.edu
NARCUM, Jeani, M .... 410-778-7214.. 213 E
jnarcum2@washcoll.edu
NARDI, Joanne .... 860-738-6329.... 87 A
jnardi@nwcc.edu
NARDI, Peter, A .... 410-293-1585.. 529 D
nardi@usna.edu
NARDIN, Gail .... 212-752-1530.. 318 F
gail.nardin@limcollege.edu
NARDONE, Leonard .... 617-236-4524.. 218 G
lnardone@fisher.edu
NARDONE, Mary, S .... 617-552-0346.. 216 C
mary.nardone@bc.edu
NARDONE, Paul .... 570-674-8144.. 410 K
pnardone@misericordia.edu
NARDUCCI, Julie .... 951-785-2578.... 48 A
jnarducc@lasierra.edu
NARIN, Michele .... 848-445-4636.. 295 F
michele.narin@rutgers.edu
NARMONTAS, Steven .... 413-782-1778.. 229 E
steven.narmontas@wne.edu
NARRA, Gavi .... 516-299-3794.. 319 B
gavi.narra@liu.edu
NARTAREZ, Chris .... 805-922-6966.... 25 I
cnartarez@hancockcollege.edu
NARVEKAR, Nirmal, P .... 212-851-2031.. 311 E
nn2017@columbia.edu
NARY, Thomas, I .... 617-552-3225.. 216 C
thomas.nary@bc.edu
NAS, Paula .... 810-424-5486.. 242 B
pnas@umflint.edu
NASCA, Philip .... 518-402-0281.. 331 A
pnasca@albany.edu
NASGOVITZ, Wendy .... 920-693-1277.. 523 E
wendy.nasgovitz@gotoltc.edu
NASH, Amy .... 724-938-4324.. 414 E
nash@calu.edu
NASH, Bob .... 714-241-6143.... 39 E
bnash@coastline.edu
NASH, Charles, R .... 205-348-8347...... 8 C
cnash@uasystem.edu
NASH, David .... 215-955-6969.. 420 E
david.nash@jefferson.edu
NASH, Dawn, P .... 478-757-5115.. 129 L
dnash@wesleyancollege.edu
NASH, Gail .... 731-989-6072.. 440 D
gnash@fhu.edu
NASH, Lauren .... 610-896-4984.. 405 I
lnash@haverford.edu
NASH, Mika .... 802-865-5488.. 483 F
nash@champlain.edu
NASH, Richard .... 812-866-7029.. 161 C
nash@hanover.edu
NASH, Robin .... 785-825-5422.. 179 C
rlnashi@brownmackie.edu
NASH, Timothy, G .... 989-837-4129.. 239 D
tgnash@northwood.edu
NASH, Victoria .... 262-691-5495.. 524 G
vnash@wcfc.edu
NASH-YORE, Kimberly .... 216-987-2173.. 367 E
kimberly.nash-yore@tri-c.edu
NASHUA, Lisa .... 909-652-6542.... 37 D
lisa.nashua@chaffey.edu
NASHUA, Loy .... 562-908-3405.... 58 I
lnashua@riohondo.edu
NASIMOVA, Angela .... 718-261-5800.. 305 J
anasimova@bramsonort.edu
NASIR, Na'ilah .... 510-642-7294.... 68 M
vcei@berkeley.edu
NASO, Mary Ann .... 717-262-2002.. 424 A
mnaso@wilson.edu
NASON, Bradley, A .... 406-657-1018.. 278 D
nasonb@rocky.edu
NASON, Stephen, S .... 207-509-7284.. 204 F
snason@unity.edu
NASR, Nabil .... 585-475-5106.. 327 E
nasr@rit.edu
NASR, Vali .... 202-663-5622.. 208 D
vnasr@jhu.edu
NASS, Allan .... 505-566-3447.. 301 J
nassa@sanjuancollege.edu
NASSAR, Anne, K .... 315-733-2300.. 338 L
anassar@uscny.edu
NASSAR, Sayed .... 248-370-2697.. 239 K
nassar@oakland.edu
NASSER, David .... 434-582-7731.. 491 D
davidnasser@liberty.edu
NASSER, Dawn, S .... 217-443-8755.. 139 B
dnasser@dacc.edu
NASSER, Edward, D .... 520-621-5449.... 17 I
enasser@email.arizona.edu
NASSER, Lisa .... 402-354-7000.. 281 F
lisa.nasser@methodistcollege.edu
NASSER, Ryn .... 919-613-5577.. 343 J
ryn.nasser@duke.edu
NASSON, Stephen .... 617-627-6540.. 228 H
stephen.nasson@tufts.edu
NAST, Paul .... 479-524-7296.... 20 H
pnast@jbu.edu
NASTANSKI, Michael .... 352-588-8244.. 108 C
michael.nastanski@saintleo.edu
NATAF, Daniel, D .... 410-777-2407.. 206 B
ddnataf@aacc.edu
NATALE, J. Peter .... 513-529-5322.. 372 K
natalejp@miamioh.edu
NATALE, Joel, A .... 610-558-5522.. 411 E
natalej@neumann.edu
NATALE, Vickie .... 859-572-6566.. 192 B
natalev1@nku.edu
NATALI, Glenn .... 724-480-3361.. 401 F
glenn.natali@ccbc.edu
NATALI, Jeanne, B .... 757-822-1669.. 498 H
jnatali@tcc.edu
NATALICIO, Diana, S .... 915-747-5555.. 476 D
dnatalicio@utep.edu
NATERA, Edmundo .... 432-837-8085.. 471 E
enatera@sulross.edu
NATHAN, Eileen .... 806-742-3671.. 472 C
eileen.nathan@ttu.edu
NATHAN, Vini .... 334-844-4285...... 1 G
vzn0007@auburn.edu
NATHANIEL, Shiran .... 712-274-5295.. 175 C
nathaniel@morningside.edu
NATHANSON, Mike .... 352-435-5027.. 104 J
nathansm@lssc.edu
NATION, Ramah .... 405-878-5634.. 387 J
rlnation@stgregorys.edu
NATION, Travis .... 206-296-2002.. 507 E
nationt@seattleu.edu
NATIVIDAD, Rory .... 310-660-3547.... 42 J
rnatividad@elcamino.edu
NATOCE, Russell .... 928-541-7777.... 15 G
rnatoce@ncu.edu
NATOLI, Joseph, T .... 305-284-3800.. 114 H
jnatoli@miami.edu
NATRIELLO, Gary .... 212-678-3087.. 337 E
gin6@tc.columbia.edu
NATTER, Gretchen .... 717-337-6490.. 404 C
gnatter@gettysburg.edu
NATTER, Wolfgang .... 215-248-7022.. 400 H
natterw@chc.edu
NATTINGER, Ann .... 414-955-8495.. 518 A
anatting@mcw.edu
NAUGHTON, Christine .... 413-662-5074.. 222 B
c.naughton@mcla.edu
NAUGHTON, Debbie .... 610-436-2813.. 416 C
dnaughton@wcupa.edu
NAUGHTON, Randy, L .... 623-935-8295.... 14 A
randy.naughton@estrellamountain.edu
NAUGLE, Deemie .... 214-333-5291.. 455 J
deemie@dbu.edu
NAUMANN, Cheryl .... 602-557-1742.... 17 L
cheryl.naumann@phoenix.edu
NAUSER, Julie .... 816-995-2855.. 270 H
julie.nauser@researchcollege.edu
NAUSER, Julie .... 816-995-2855.. 270 J
julie.nauser@researchcollege.edu
NAUTA, Cindy .... 858-505-1100.... 47 B
cindy@ipsb.edu
NAVA, Esmeralda .... 626-396-2267.... 27 L
esmeralda.nava@artcenter.edu
NAVA, Rachael .... 510-987-0500.... 68 L
rachael.nava@ucop.edu
NAVA, Robert, J .... 415-338-2517.... 35 B
rjnava@sfsu.edu
NAVA, Robert, J .... 415-338-2506.... 35 B
rjnava@sfsu.edu
NAVANT, Yves .... 303-753-6046.... 83 A
ynavant@rmcad.edu
NAVARI, Shelley .... 802-860-6405.. 483 F
navari@champlain.edu
NAVARRE, Michael .... 801-975-5094.. 483 A
michael.navarre@slcc.edu
NAVARRETE, Nancy .... 602-285-7392.... 14 F
nancy.navarrete@phoenixcollege.edu
NAVARRETTE, Jay .... 559-791-2365.... 47 L
jay.navarrette@portervillecollege.edu
NAVARRETTE, Ricardo .... 707-524-1647.... 63 G
rnavarrette@santarosa.edu
NAVARRO, JoAnn .... 607-777-3060.. 331 B
navarro@binghamton.edu
NAVARRO, Renee .... 415-476-7700.... 70 D
renee.navarro@ucsf.edu
NAVARRO, Yolanda .... 305-821-3333.. 101 B
ynavarro@fnu.edu
NAVARRO-CASTELLANOS,
Norma .... 520-206-4550.... 16 F
ngnavarro@pima.edu
NAVARRO-JUSINO,
Adam .... 830-372-8072.. 470 C
anavarro-jusino@tlu.edu
NAVARRO-NICOSIA,
Sylvia .... 631-420-2529.. 335 E
sylvia.nicosia@farmingdale.edu
NAVE, Felicia, M .... 926-261-2175.. 467 E
fmnave@pvamu.edu
NAVE, Jeffery, W .... 504-282-4455.. 198 H
jnave@nobts.edu
NAVIA, Pedro .... 269-471-3181.. 230 H
navia@andrews.edu
NAVIN, Tom .... 802-258-3173.. 485 A
tom.navin@worldlearning.org
NAVONEY, Sharon, M ..... 412-392-8097.. 417 F
snavoney@pointpark.edu
NAVROTSKY, Alexandra ... 530-754-8918.... 69 A
navdean@ucdavis.edu
NAWOICHIK, Michael .... 978-867-4500.. 219 A
mike.nawoichik@gordon.edu
NAWROCKI, Ann .... 610-796-8428.. 397 D
ann.nawrocki@alvernia.edu
NAYLER, Ronald .... 847-467-5810.. 150 F
r-nayler@northwestern.edu
NAYLON, Karen, C .... 336-888-6388.. 345 A
kcoffman@highpoint.edu
NAYLOR, Ben .... 845-574-4215.. 327 G
bnaylor@sunyrockland.edu
NAYLOR, Bob .... 435-722-6900.. 481 I
bob@ubatc.edu
NAYLOR, Edward .... 252-985-5404.. 354 E
enaylor@ncwc.edu
NAYLOR, Richard, N .... 508-373-9453.. 215 D
richard.naylor@becker.edu
NAYLOR, Suzette .... 816-802-3519.. 266 D
snaylor@kcai.edu
NAYLOR, Tere .... 816-936-8726.. 271 L
tnaylor@saintlukescollege.edu
NAYLOR, Tracy .... 270-686-9551.. 187 C
tracy.naylor@brescia.edu
NAYLOR-JOHNSON,
Darrell .... 912-525-5000.. 126 E
dnaylorj@scad.edu
NAYLOR MOORE,
Barbara .... 662-252-8000.. 260 F
bmoore@rustcollege.edu
NAYOR, Greg, J .... 716-839-8520.. 312 D
gnayor@daemen.edu
NAZARENKO, Larissa .... 714-432-5536.... 39 G
lnazarenko@occ.cccd.edu
NAZARENKO,
Nadezhda (Nadia) .... 281-756-3723.. 450 G
nnazarenko@alvincollege.edu
NAZARENKO, Tatiana .... 805-565-6070.... 75 A
tnazarenko@westmont.edu
NAZARIO-COLON,
Ricardo .... 606-783-9042.. 191 H
r.nazariocolon@moreheadstate.edu
NDIAYE, Momar .... 860-832-2050.... 85 F
mndiaye@ccsu.edu
NEAD, Kip .... 831-479-6213.... 29 G
kinead@cabrillo.edu
NEAD, Margaret, A .... 585-271-3778.. 310 F
mnead@crcds.edu
NEAD, Margaret, A .... 585-271-1320.. 310 F
mnead@crcds.edu
NEAGLE, Rebecca .... 919-866-5198.. 353 I
NEAL, Adam .... 614-251-4786.. 374 I
neala2@ohiodominican.edu
NEAL, Anthony .... 404-297-9522.. 122 A
nealwa@gptc.edu
NEAL, Brenda .... 304-260-4380.. 511 L
bneal@blueridgectc.edu
NEAL, Brigette .... 313-664-7470.. 232 G
bneal@collegeforcreativestudies.edu
NEAL, Charles, V .... 607-587-4019.. 334 G
nealcv@alfredstate.edu
NEAL, Donna, V .... 252-493-7309.. 352 A
dneal@email.pittcc.edu
NEAL, Gary, W .... 210-999-7411.. 473 A
gneal@trinity.edu

NELSON, Kris .... 251-442-2945...... 9 A
knelson@umobile.edu
NELSON, Kristy .... 989-686-9422.. 233 I
kristynelson@delta.edu
NELSON, Laura, M .... 701-788-4692.. 360 E
laura.m.nelson@mayvillestate.edu
NELSON, Lauren .... 770-426-2832.. 124 B
lauren.nielsen@life.edu
NELSON, Linda .... 816-604-2218.. 267 I
linda.nelson@mcckc.edu
NELSON, Linda, J .... 404-413-3300.. 122 D
lnelson@gsu.edu
NELSON, Linda, J .... 404-413-2567.. 122 D
lnelson@gsu.edu
NELSON, Lindsey .... 207-859-1405.. 204 E
registrar@thomas.edu
NELSON, Lisa .... 570-740-0732.. 409 E
lnelson@luzerne.edu
NELSON, Lisa .... 360-992-2488.. 502 E
lnelson@clark.edu
NELSON, Lynn .... 630-889-6702.. 149 G
lnelson@nuhs.edu
NELSON, Mark .... 205-348-4786...... 8 D
mnelson@ua.edu
NELSON, Mark .... 419-372-6067.. 364 E
nelsonm@bgsu.edu
NELSON, Mark .... 252-940-6213.. 347 E
mark.nelson@beaufortccc.edu
NELSON, Marshall .... 318-670-6000.. 199 J
mnelson@susla.edu
NELSON, Martha .... 870-248-4000.... 19 H
martha.nelson@blackrivertech.edu
NELSON, Mary .... 314-539-5330.. 271 F
mnelson178@stlcc.edu
NELSON, Merritt .... 402-941-6400.. 280 N
nelson@midlandu.edu
NELSON, Nadine .... 402-486-2504.. 282 I
nanelson@ucollege.edu
NELSON, Nancy, N .... 915-831-6631.. 457 H
nnelson2@epcc.edu
NELSON, Noah .... 903-886-5815.. 468 D
noah.nelson@tamuc.edu
NELSON, Peggy, L .... 208-535-5370.. 133 G
peggy.nelson@my.eitc.edu
NELSON, Peter, C .... 312-996-3259.. 156 F
nelson@uic.edu
NELSON, Phil .... 620-241-0723.. 179 L
phil.nelson@centralchristian.edu
NELSON, Phil .... 909-469-5661.... 74 K
pnelson@westernu.edu
NELSON, Randall .... 586-445-7119.. 237 C
nelsonr58@macomb.edu
NELSON, Randy .... 423-746-5271.. 447 E
rnelson@twcnet.edu
NELSON, Randy .... 605-575-6585.. 438 A
randy.nelson@usiouxfalls.edu
NELSON, Rebecca .... 773-244-5759.. 149 I
rnelson1@northpark.edu
NELSON, Rencelly .... 691-320-2480.. 529 F
rencelly@comfsm.fm
NELSON, Rhonda, L .... 701-788-4208.. 360 E
rhonda.nelson@mayvillestate.edu
NELSON, Richard, R .... 715-365-4415.. 524 C
nelson@nicoletcollege.edu
NELSON, Robert .... 504-865-2881.. 198 E
rjnelson@loyno.edu
NELSON, Robin .... 434-949-2092.. 498 E
robin.nelson@southside.edu
NELSON, Sarah .... 661-255-1050.... 30 E
NELSON, Sean .... 617-994-6918.. 220 D
snelson@bhe.mass.edu
NELSON, Shad .... 361-593-3712.. 469 A
shad.nelson@tamuk.edu
NELSON, Sharon .... 281-478-3656.. 464 J
sharon.nelson@sjcd.edu
NELSON, Shawn .... 402-941-6127.. 280 N
nelsons@midlandu.edu
NELSON, Sherri .... 401-863-3476.. 424 J
sherri_nelson@brown.edu
NELSON, Steve .... 504-568-4009.. 198 A
snelso1@lsuhsc.edu
NELSON, Steven, J .... 313-993-1524.. 241 G
nelsonsj@udmercy.edu
NELSON, Suzy .... 617-253-8566.. 225 A
NELSON, Tammy .... 207-768-2747.. 203 L
tnelson@nmcc.edu
NELSON, Theresa .... 510-436-1029.... 46 E
tnelson@hnu.edu
NELSON, Thomas .... 651-793-1466.. 250 A
thomas.nelson@metrostate.edu
NELSON, Tiffany .... 404-270-5195.. 128 A
tnelso15@spelman.edu
NELSON, Tim .... 510-723-6648.... 37 B
tnelson@chabotcollege.edu
NELSON, Tim .... 301-891-4045.. 213 D
tnelson@wau.edu
NELSON, Timothy .... 419-267-1226.. 374 A
tnelson@northweststate.edu
NELSON, Timothy, J .... 231-995-1010.. 239 C
tnelson@nmc.edu
NELSON, Tony .... 270-707-3771.. 189 G
tony.nelson@kctcs.edu
NELSON, Tony .... 931-372-3234.. 445 B
tnelson@tntech.edu
NELSON, Tonya .... 970-564-6222.... 82 G
tonya.nelson@pueblocc.edu
NELSON, Trevor .... 515-294-6792.. 169 G
tnelson@iastate.edu
NELSON, Troy .... 417-626-1234.. 269 K
nelson.troy@occ.edu
NELSON, Veronica .... 775-289-3589.. 284 I
veronica.nelson@gbcnv.edu
NELSON, Wilbert .... 602-285-7174.... 14 F
wilbert.nelson@phoenixcollege.edu
NELSON, William, L .... 800-867-2243.... 55 F
wnelson@pacific-college.edu
NELSON-BAILEY, Robin ... 781-736-4463.. 216 F
rnelsonbailey@brandeis.edu
NELSON MOELLER,
Rachel .... 610-330-5810.. 407 C
moellerr@lafayette.edu
NELSON NASH, Denise .... 909-607-7180.... 64 A
dnelnash@scrippscollege.edu
NELSON-RUSSOM,
Lynn, A .... 610-499-1183.. 423 E
lanelsonrussom@widener.edu
NELSON WINGER, Elyse . 309-556-3005.. 143 D
enelsonw@iwu.edu
NEMAN, Joseph .... 323-966-5444.... 50 H
NEMCIK, Henry .... 505-277-1586.. 302 F
hnemcik@unm.edu
NEMEC, Chellee .... 605-367-7464.. 437 G
chellee.nemec@southeasttech.edu
NEMEC, Mark, R .... 773-702-4950.. 156 D
mnemec@uchicago.edu
NEMETH, Kevin .... 406-896-5872.. 277 D
kevin.nemeth@msubillings.edu
NEMETI, Jami .... 417-862-9533.. 265 D
jnemeti@globaluniversity.edu
NEMITZ, James, W .... 304-647-6368.. 514 A
jnemitz@osteo.wvsom.edu
NENON, Thomas, J .... 901-678-4831.. 445 C
tnenon@memphis.edu
NENSTIEL, Greg .... 727-341-3026.. 108 D
nenstiel.greg@spcollege.edu
NEPA, Beth .... 315-781-3315.. 316 C
nepa@hws.edu
NEPHEW, Marvin .... 937-328-6125.. 366 E
nephewm@clarkstate.edu
NEPOMUCENO, Tina .... 708-209-3545.. 138 G
tina.nepomuceno@cuchicago.edu
NEPPER, Terry, S .... 806-651-2747.. 469 D
tnepper@mail.wtamu.edu
NEPPL, Susan .... 952-888-4777.. 253 Z
sneppl@nwhealth.edu
NEPTUNE, Vivian .... 787-999-9531.. 538 F
vneptune@law.upr.edu
NERE, Jeremy .... 843-383-8185.. 428 F
jnere@coker.edu
NERGER, Janice, L .... 970-491-6974.... 78 Q
janice.nerger@colostate.edu
NERIA, Angela .... 620-235-4603.. 184 C
aneria@pittstate.edu
NERIANI, Kelly .... 937-328-6075.. 366 E
nerianik@clarkstate.edu
NERO, Patrick .... 202-994-6650...... 92 D
NERONHA, Christopher .... 413-748-3628.. 228 E
cneronha@springfieldcollege.edu
NERY, Annebelle .... 760-776-7442.... 40 B
anery@collegeofthedesert.edu
NERY, Karen .... 910-893-1630.. 342 F
nery@campbell.edu
NERZAK, J. Peter .... 865-694-6517.. 446 G
pnerzak@pstcc.edu
NESBARY, Dale, K .... 231-777-0311.. 238 G
dale.nesbary@muskegoncc.edu
NESBIT, Jim .... 937-298-3399.. 371 D
jim.nesbit@kc.edu
NESBIT, Randy .... 865-882-4583.. 447 A
nesbitr@roanestate.edu
NESBIT, Ryan, A .... 706-542-1361.. 128 E
rnesbit@uga.edu
NESBITT, Joan, M .... 573-341-4111.. 274 B
nesbittj@mst.edu
NESBITT, Kathy .... 303-860-5600.... 83 J
kathy.nesbitt@cu.edu
NESBITT, Kristin .... 716-827-2433.. 338 E
nesbittk@trocaire.edu
NESBITT, Richard, L .... 413-597-2211.. 230 A
richard.l.nesbitt@williams.edu
NESBITT, Ryan .... 352-638-9723.... 96 F
rnesbitt@beaconcollege.edu
NESBITT, Shawna .... 214-648-2168.. 478 C
shawna.nesbitt@utsouthwestern.edu
NESBITT, Thomas, W .... 315-267-2180.. 334 B
nesbittw@potsdam.edu
NESCI, Anthony .... 716-851-1449.. 313 H
nesci@ecc.edu
NESEL, Gerard .... 413-528-7207.. 214 H
gnesel@simons-rock.edu
NESENJUK, Jennie .... 201-360-4221.. 292 B
jnesenjuk@hccc.edu
NESHEIM-KAUFFMAN,
Rhonda, K .... 641-422-4500.. 175 E
nesherho@niacc.edu
NESHIEM, Sheri .... 352-588-8023.. 108 C
sheri.neshiem@saintleo.edu
NESIN, Jeffrey .... 212-592-2000.. 330 C
jnesin@sva.edu
NESIUS, Elizabeth .... 201-360-4366.. 292 B
enesius@hccc.edu
NESLER, Mitchell, S .... 518-587-2100.. 335 D
mitchell.nesler@esc.edu
NESMITH, Dee .... 432-335-6429.. 463 B
dnesmith@odessa.edu
NESMITH, Robert, M .... 859-238-5356.. 187 H
bob.nesmith@centre.edu
NESMITH, Sylvia, L .... 843-953-6976.. 428 A
sylvia.nesmith@citadel.edu
NESPOR, Vana .... 413-565-1000.. 215 A
vnespor@baypath.edu
NESS, Claudia, L .... 509-527-5040.. 509 G
nesscl@whitman.edu
NESS, Deborah .... 708-209-3115.. 138 G
deb.ness@cuchicago.edu
NESS, Don .... 218-733-5934.. 249 H
don.ness@lsc.edu
NESS, E. Craig .... 713-313-1382.. 470 D
nessec@tsu.edu
NESS, Eric .... 570-389-4517.. 414 D
eness@bloomu.edu
NESS, Melvin, M .... 646-565-6000.. 337 I
meln@touro.edu
NESSAN, Craig, L .... 563-589-0207.. 177 H
cnessan@wartburgseminary.edu
NESSELRODE, Brian .... 904-819-6206...... 99 M
bness@flagler.edu
NESSET, Andrew .... 651-773-1705.. 249 A
andrew.nesset@century.edu
NESTER, Joel .... 434-791-5663.. 487 C
jnester@averett.edu
NESTER, Stefanie, E .... 610-799-1740.. 408 G
snester2@lccc.edu
NESTLEN, Charlianne .... 864-503-5240.. 434 G
cnestlen@uscupstate.edu
NESTLER, George .... 914-594-4470.. 323 I
george_nestler@nymc.edu
NESTOR, David, A .... 802-656-3380.. 485 D
david.nestor@uvm.edu
NESTOR, Mark .... 215-596-8910.. 422 A
m.nestor@usciences.edu
NETHERTON, James, S ... 478-301-2710.. 124 D
netherton_js@mercer.edu
NETLAND, John .... 731-661-5519.. 448 A
jnetland@uu.edu
NETTELL, Katie .... 701-662-1517.. 361 E
katie.nettell@lrsc.edu
NETTLES, Evelyn .... 615-963-7004.. 445 A
enettles1@tnstate.edu
NETTLES, Lafawn .... 270-384-8033.. 191 E
nettlesl@lindsey.edu
NETTLES, Ronald, E .... 601-643-8300.. 257 D
ronnie.nettles@colin.edu
NETTLES, Wanda .... 803-793-5196.. 429 D
nettlesw@denmark.edu
NETTLETON, Bridget .... 518-587-2100.. 335 D
bridget.nettleton@esc.edu
NETTLETON, Patricia, A ... 859-371-9393.. 186 M
panettleton@beckfield.edu
NETTLETON, Peter .... 859-371-9393.. 186 M
pnettleton@beckfield.edu
NETZER, Michael .... 304-724-3700.. 510 E
mnetzer@apus.edu
NETZHAMMER, Mel .... 360-546-9581.. 508 H
mel.netzhammer@vancouver.wsu.edu
NEU, Frances .... 727-341-3319.. 108 D
neu.frances@spcollege.edu
NEUBAUER, Jennifer .... 740-593-4300.. 375 H
neubauer@ohio.edu
NEUBAUER, Kirk .... 563-387-1434.. 174 L
neubauki@luther.edu
NEUBAUER, Lane, B .... 215-951-5157.. 407 A
neubauer@lasalle.edu
NEUBAUER, Michael .... 818-677-2957.... 34 A
michael.neubauer@csun.edu
NEUBAUER, Trish .... 563-387-1567.. 174 L
neubautr@luther.edu
NEUBERGER, Boruch .... 410-484-7200.. 210 A
byn@nirc.edu
NEUBERGER, Sheftel, M . 443-548-6059.. 210 A
sheftel@nirc.edu
NEUBRANDER, Judy .... 309-438-7400.. 143 B
jlneubr@ilstu.edu
NEUENSCHWANDER,
Pierre, F .... 903-877-7480.. 477 E
pierre.neuenschwander@uthct.edu
NEUERBURG, Kent .... 985-549-2135.. 201 C
kent.neuerburg@selu.edu
NEUFELD, Iris .... 419-358-3322.. 364 D
neufeldi@bluffton.edu
NEUFELD, Jane .... 773-508-3890.. 146 G
jneufe@luc.edu
NEUFELD, Kenley .... 805-965-0581.... 63 D
neufeld@sbcc.edu
NEUFELDT, Ellen, J .... 757-683-6085.. 492 G
eneufeld@odu.edu
NEUFIND, Nate .... 402-941-6009.. 280 N
neufind@midlandu.edu
NEUFVILLE, Janette .... 301-576-0123.. 213 D
jneufvil@wau.edu
NEUGEBAUER, Lisa .... 209-468-9192.... 67 H
lineugebauer@sjcoe.net
NEUHARD, Ian .... 904-646-2005.. 101 G
ineuhard@fscj.edu
NEUHAUSER, John, J .... 802-654-2212.. 484 I
jneuhauser@smcvt.edu
NEUHOLD, Patti .... 405-974-2560.. 388 L
pneuhold@uco.edu
NEUMAN, Yisroel .... 732-367-1060.. 289 G
NEUMANN, Bruce .... 262-691-5226.. 524 G
bneumann6@wctc.edu
NEUMANN, Edith .... 818-575-6800.... 68 B
edith.neumann@tuw.edu
NEUMANN, Edith .... 818-575-6800.... 68 D
edith.neumann@tuw.edu
NEUMANN, Gregory .... 716-645-6290.. 331 C
0405mgr@fheg.follette.com
NEUMANN, Kathleen .... 309-298-1066.. 158 A
k-neumann@wiu.edu
NEUMANN, Pam .... 214-333-5525.. 455 J
pamela@dbu.edu
NEUMANN, Pamela, R .... 716-839-8325.. 312 D
pneumann@daemen.edu
NEUMANN, Yoram .... 818-575-6800.... 68 B
yoram.neumann@tuw.edu
NEUMANN, Yoram .... 818-575-6800.... 68 D
yoram.neumann@tuw.edu
NEUN, Stephen .... 570-484-2133.. 415 D
spn207@lhup.edu
NEUPAUER, Nicholas, C . 724-287-8711.. 399 B
nicholas.neupauer@bc3.edu
NEUTENS, James, J .... 865-305-9290.. 448 H
jneutens@mc.utmck.edu
NEUVILLE, Jeff .... 828-327-7000.. 348 C
jneuville@cvcc.edu
NEVAREZ, Amy .... 909-652-6020.... 37 D
amy.nevarez@chaffey.edu
NEVAREZ, Augustine .... 831-755-6825.... 45 L
anevarez@hartnell.edu
NEVAREZ, Gerard .... 575-646-3635.. 300 J
gerardn@nmsu.edu
NEVE, Nancy .... 906-635-2080.. 236 J
nneve@lssu.edu
NEVELS, Lyle .... 510-642-4096...... 68 M
lnevels@berkeley.edu
NEVELS, Tiawanna, S .... 919-516-4150.. 355 D
tsnevels@st-aug.edu
NEVILLE, Frank .... 703-993-8700.. 490 B
fnevill2@gmu.edu
NEVILLE, Nancy .... 216-421-7427.. 366 G
nneville@cia.edu
NEVILLE, Tiffany .... 800-280-0307.. 158 E
tiffany.neville@ace.edu
NEVILLS, Landee .... 417-328-1826.. 272 C
lnevills@sbuniv.edu
NEVINS, Daniel .... 212-678-8067.. 317 I
danevins@jtsa.edu
NEVINS, Sherry, C .... 608-342-1854.. 521 A
nevinsm@uwplatt.edu
NEVOIS, Dana, A .... 636-481-3488.. 266 C
dnevois@jeffco.edu
NEW, Jim .... 775-856-5307.. 284 K
jnew@tmcc.edu
NEW, Lynn .... 903-923-2093.. 457 G
lnew@etbu.edu
NEW, Michael, J .... 802-654-2635.. 484 I
mnew@smcvt.edu
NEWBERG, Bella .... 760-750-4444.... 34 D
newberg@csusm.edu
NEWBERN, Judson .... 615-322-2715.. 449 A
judson.newbern@vanderbilt.edu
NEWBERRY, Beth .... 502-585-9911.. 192 E
bnewberry@spalding.edu
NEWBERRY, Byron .... 405-425-5428.. 385 C
byron.newberry@oc.edu
NEWBERRY, Robert .... 575-624-7180.. 299 J
robert.newberry@roswell.enmu.edu
NEWBOLD, Ken, F .... 574-535-7550.. 161 A
kfnewbold@goshen.edu
NEWBOLD, Martie .... 727-864-7675.... 98 L
newbolhm@eckerd.edu
NEWBOLD, Pamela .... 330-823-6555.. 379 F
newbolph@mountunion.edu
NEWBY, Jennifer .... 541-383-7530.. 390 D
jlnewby@cocc.edu
NEWBY, Stewart .... 903-675-6235.. 473 B
stewart.newby@tvcc.edu
NEWBY, Teresa .... 952-446-4484.. 246 D
newbyt@crown.edu
NEWCOMB, Bruce, C .... 208-426-1427.. 132 I
brucenewcomb@boisestate.edu

NICHOLS, Warren .... 615-366-4444.. 444 D
warren.nichols@tbr.edu
NICHOLS-ZONNO,
Belinda .... 719-590-6766.... 79 D
bnicholszonno@coloradotech.edu
NICHOLSON, Branden ..... 704-971-8500.. 343 E
NICHOLSON, Brian, W .... 254-710-8400.. 452 H
brian_nicholson@baylor.edu
NICHOLSON, Christena ... 913-234-0644.. 179 M
christena.nicholson@cleveland.edu
NICHOLSON, Cindy .... 810-989-5680.. 240 G
cnicholson@sc4.edu
NICHOLSON, Cindy .... 828-227-7203.. 359 A
nicholson@wcu.edu
NICHOLSON, Debra .... 620-276-9575.. 181 C
debra.nicholson@gcccks.edu
NICHOLSON, Denny .... 315-498-2912.. 325 G
nicholson.d@sunyocc.edu
NICHOLSON, Jane .... 651-779-3304.. 249 A
jane.nicholson@century.edu
NICHOLSON, Judd .... 202-687-4402.... 92 E
nicholsonj@georgetown.edu
NICHOLSON, Karen .... 718-862-7374.. 319 L
karen.nicholson@manhattan.edu
NICHOLSON, Kim .... 765-677-2131.. 164 B
kim.nicholson@indwes.edu
NICHOLSON, Kristal .... 903-875-7361.. 462 J
kristal.nicholson@navarrocollege.edu
NICHOLSON, JR.,
Malverse, A .... 301-546-0853.. 210 C
nicholma@pgcc.edu
NICHOLSON, Marie .... 828-689-1151.. 346 C
mnicholson@mhu.edu
NICHOLSON, Mary .... 850-872-3866.. 102 M
mnicholson@gulfcoast.edu
NICHOLSON, Nigel, J ...... 503-777-7257.. 394 I
nnichols@reed.edu
NICHOLSON, Robin .... 319-235-3516.. 169 D
robin.nicholson@unitypoint.org
NICHOLSON, Susie, S ..... 479-968-0402.... 19 F
snicholson@atu.edu
NICHOLSON, Tammy .... 706-295-6328.. 121 C
tnichols@highlands.edu
NICHOLSON, Tim .... 828-835-4261.. 353 G
tnicholson@tricountycc.edu
NICHOLSON, Vickie .... 251-578-1313...... 6 C
vickien@rstc.edu
NICHOLSON, II,
William, D .... 803-323-2275.. 435 B
nicholsond@winthrop.edu
NICHOLSON ANGLE,
Jan, C .... 540-365-4285.. 489 M
jcnicholson@ferrum.edu
NICHOLSON-PREUSS,
Mari .... 713-221-8236.. 474 B
nicholsonpreussm@uhd.edu
NICK, Sara, J .... 715-833-6275.. 523 B
snick1@cvtc.edu
NICKE, Glenda .... 309-796-4822.. 135 I
nickeg@bhc.edu
NICKEL, Kevin, A .... 419-358-3320.. 364 D
nickelk@bluffton.edu
NICKEL, Shelley, C .... 404-962-3241.. 129 F
shelley.nickel@usg.edu
NICKELL, Barbara, J .... 785-833-4390.. 182 F
bmarsh@kwu.edu
NICKELL, Chris .... 801-333-8100.. 480 G
chris.nickell@eaglegatecollege.edu
NICKELL, Jane Ellen .... 814-332-2800.. 397 A
jnickell@allegheny.edu
NICKELL, Julie .... 713-798-4951.. 452 G
jnickell@bcm.edu
NICKELS, Janet .... 410-386-8229.. 206 I
jnickels@carrollcc.edu
NICKELS, Jerrod .... 616-331-2450.. 234 F
nickelsj@gvsu.edu
NICKELS, Ken .... 309-796-5048.. 135 I
nickelsk@bhc.edu
NICKELS, Rosemerry .... 440-934-3101.. 374 F
rnickels@ohiobusinesscollege.edu
NICKENS, Tawanna .... 217-351-2390.. 151 B
tnickens@parkland.edu
NICKENS, Tawanna .... 217-353-2119.. 151 B
tnickens@parkland.edu
NICKERSON, Amanda ...... 817-257-7490.. 469 G
amanda.nickerson@tcu.edu
NICKERSON, Gary .... 405-585-5210.. 385 B
gary.nickerson@okbu.edu
NICKERSON, Lori .... 508-999-8004.. 220 H
lnickerson@umassd.edu
NICKERSON, Molly .... 660-284-4800.. 265 I
NICKERSON, Nate .... 617-258-5403.. 225 A
NICKERSON, Sherita .... 325-674-6802.. 449 J
sherita.nickerson@acu.edu
NICKLAS, Bill .... 815-825-9412.. 144 F
bill.nicklas@kishwaukeecollege.edu
NICKLAUS, Megan .... 719-389-6424.... 77 J
megan.nicklaus@coloradocollege.edu
NICKLAUS, Nick .... 608-785-8075.. 520 C
nnicklaus@uwlax.edu
NICKLE, Bonny .... 866-687-2258.... 30 I
NICKLE, Mary Anne .... 641-236-2202.. 173 J
maryanne.nickle@iavalley.edu
NICKLE, Stephen, R .... 210-999-7311.. 473 A
snickle@trinity.edu
NICKLESS, Kenneth .... 314-968-7146.. 275 B
nickleke@webster.edu
NICKLESS, Peter .... 315-568-3310.. 323 A
pnickless@nycc.edu
NICKLOW, John, W .... 504-280-5536.. 198 D
president@uno.edu
NICKOL, Kari .... 563-588-8137.. 170 F
kari.nickol@clarke.edu
NICKOSON, Carol .... 937-327-7800.. 381 F
nickosonc@wittenberg.edu
NICKSA, Gary, W .... 617-353-6500.. 216 E
nicksa@bu.edu
NICOL, David .... 231-591-2422.. 233 L
davidnicol@ferris.edu
NICOL, Patricia .... 617-824-8123.. 218 B
patricia_nicol@emerson.edu
NICOLAI, Camille .... 414-297-8875.. 524 A
nicolaic@matc.edu
NICOLAI, Michael .... 312-629-9411.. 154 A
mnicolai@saic.edu
NICOLAISEN, Megan .... 605-718-2418.. 438 B
megan.nicolaisen@wdt.edu
NICOLETTE, Guy .... 352-294-7439.. 112 A
gnic@ufl.edu
NICOLETTI, Katherine ...... 508-213-2238.. 227 A
katherine.nicoletti@nichols.edu
NICOLO, Anthony, J .... 540-674-3639.. 497 G
tnicolo@nr.edu
NICOTERA, Phillip .... 713-718-7628.. 459 B
phillip.nicotera@hccs.edu
NIEBO, Len .... 646-565-6000.. 337 I
leonard.niebo@touro.edu
NIEC-WILLIAMS, Derrek .. 202-806-6100.... 93 A
derrek.niecwilliams@howard.edu
NIEDENS, Rosemary .... 316-942-4291.. 183 I
niedensr@newmanu.edu
NIEDERHAUSER, Victoria 865-974-7584.. 448 E
vniederh@utk.edu
NIEDWIECKI, Anthony ..... 312-427-2737.. 143 G
aniedwie@jmls.edu
NIEDZWIECKI, Brian, E ... 419-866-0261.. 377 L
beniedzwiecki@stautzenberger.com
NIEDZWIECKI, Michael ... 718-933-6700.. 321 I
mniedzwiedi@monroecollege.edu
NIEHOFF, Brian, A .... 785-532-4797.. 182 D
niehoff@ksu.edu
NIEHOFF, SJ, Robert, L .. 216-397-4281.. 370 H
president@jcu.edu
NIEKRO, Cat, S .... 704-894-2533.. 343 I
NIELSEN, Brooke .... 775-784-4901.. 284 G
brooke_nielsen@nshe.nevada.edu
NIELSEN, David .... 860-512-3108.... 86 E
dnielsen@manchestercc.edu
NIELSEN, Erik .... 402-461-7738.. 280 D
enielsen@hastings.edu
NIELSEN, Kathryn .... 925-473-7628.... 41 J
knielsen@losmedanos.edu
NIELSEN, Leila .... 651-631-0204.. 244 E
lnielsen@aaaom.edu
NIELSEN, Lisa .... 831-459-4344.... 70 F
lmnielse@ucsc.edu
NIELSEN, Lori .... 334-244-3225...... 2 A
lneilsen@aum.edu
NIELSEN, Mark .... 208-885-0293.. 134 G
markn@uidaho.edu
NIELSEN, Mary .... 706-272-4403.. 119 H
mnielsen@daltonstate.edu
NIELSEN, Mary, F .... 414-277-7216.. 518 E
nielsen@msoe.edu
NIELSEN, Melore .... 206-296-2000.. 507 E
mnielsen@seattleu.edu
NIELSEN, Monty, E .... 785-532-6254.. 182 D
nielsen@ksu.edu
NIELSEN, Paul, D .... 412-268-7740.. 400 D
nielsen@sei.cmu.edu
NIELSEN, Richard, P .... 801-375-5125.. 481 C
rnielsen@rmuohp.edu
NIELSEN, Scott .... 775-753-2289.. 284 I
scott.nielsen@gbcnv.edu
NIELSEN, Tom .... 425-564-2442.. 501 F
tom.nielsen@bellevuecollege.edu
NIELSEN, Yasmin .... 732-571-3475.. 292 F
ynielsen@monmouth.edu
NIELSON, Eric .... 208-732-6267.. 133 E
enielson@csi.edu
NIELSON, Joel .... 330-672-3120.. 370 I
jnielson@kent.edu
NIELSON, Marian, J .... 315-733-2300.. 338 L
mnielson@uscny.edu
NIELSON, P. Douglas .... 808-675-3510.. 130 E
paul.nielson@byuh.edu
NIELSON, Robert .... 435-283-7037.. 482 E
rob.nielson@snow.edu
NIEMAN, Donald .... 607-777-2141.. 331 B
dnieman@binghamton.edu
NIEMAN, James .... 773-256-0728.. 147 A
jnieman@lstc.edu
NIEMAN, Larry .... 312-935-6448.. 152 D
lnieman@robertmorris.edu
NIEMAN, Paul .... 818-710-4121.... 50 A
niemanp@piercecollege.edu
NIEMANN, Kat .... 319-385-6262.. 174 A
kat.niemann@iw.edu
NIEMI, JR., Albert, W ..... 214-768-3012.. 465 J
aniemi@cox.smu.edu
NIEMI, Bill .... 970-943-3045.... 84 H
bniemi@western.edu
NIEMI, Cathy .... 906-227-2232.. 239 B
caniemi@nmu.edu
NIEMI, Jayne, L .... 651-696-6200.. 247 I
niemi@macalester.edu
NIEMIEC, Catherine .... 602-274-1885.... 16 D
cniemiec@pihma.edu
NIEMUTH, Brian .... 515-961-1670.. 176 H
brian.niemuth@simpson.edu
NIENABER, Steve .... 859-572-1366.. 192 B
nienabers1@nku.edu
NIENHUIS, Jeanne .... 616-526-6885.. 232 A
jeanen@calvin.edu
NIENHUIS, Nancy, E .... 617-964-1100.. 214 D
nnienhuis@ants.edu
NIES, Charles .... 209-228-7620.... 70 A
cnies@ucmerced.edu
NIESE, Vicki, J .... 419-772-2057.. 374 J
v-niese@onu.edu
NIESEL, David, W .... 409-772-0758.. 478 A
dniesel@utmb.edu
NIESEN DE ABRUNA,
Laura .... 717-815-1231.. 424 F
lniesen@ycp.edu
NIESPODZIANY, Aimee ...... 574-239-8314.. 161 N
aniespodziany@hcc-nd.edu
NIESSEN, Linda .... 954-262-7334.. 105 J
lniessen@nova.edu
NIETO, Javier .... 541-737-3220.. 393 H
NIETO, Leticia .... 773-508-8617.. 146 G
lnieto@luc.edu
NIETO-BRECHT, Erma, M 940-898-3270.. 472 G
enieto@twu.edu
NIEUWENHUIS, Michelle 520-206-2692.... 16 F
mnieuwenhuis@pima.edu
NIEUWKOOP, Ann, E .... 616-392-8555.. 244 A
ann@westernsem.edu
NIEUWSMA, Randal, G ..... 616-526-6334.. 232 A
nieuwr@calvin.edu
NIEVES, Beatriz .... 787-766-1717.. 536 B
um_bnieves@suagm.edu
NIEVES, Brenda .... 909-447-2504.... 39 A
bnieves@cst.edu
NIEVES, Danily .... 787-882-2065.. 536 D
NIEVES, Drusila, F .... 845-675-4564.. 325 C
drusila.nieves@nyack.edu
NIEVES, Gladys, T .... 787-765-3560.. 532 I
gnieves@edpuniversity.edu
NIEVES, Ivette .... 787-279-1912.. 533 J
inieves@bayamon.inter.edu
NIEVES, Lamberto, C .... 201-761-6085.. 296 K
lnieves@saintpeters.edu
NIEVES, Liliam .... 787-725-8120.. 532 K
programaextension@eap.edu
NIEVES, Lourdes .... 305-821-3333.. 101 B
lourdes@fnu.edu
NIEVES, Mayra .... 212-237-8918.. 308 E
mnieves@jjay.cuny.edu
NIEVES, Nancy .... 787-265-3858.. 538 C
placement@uprm.edu
NIEVES, Ruth .... 787-879-5270.. 537 F
ruth.nieves1@upr.edu
NIEVES, Wilfredo .... 860-906-5101.... 86 B
wnieves@ccc.commnet.edu
NIEWENHOUS, Susan .... 208-792-2396.. 134 A
sniewenh@lcsc.edu
NIEWIERSKI, Frank .... 210-436-4357.. 464 H
fniewierski@stmarytx.edu
NIGAGLIONI, Guillermo .. 787-754-7120.. 533 E
NIGGLI, Susan .... 585-275-7761.. 338 K
sniggli@admin.rochester.edu
NIGHSWONGER, Eve .... 707-527-4498.... 63 G
enighswonger@santarosa.edu
NIGHTINGALE, Charles .... 443-518-4615.. 208 C
cnightingale@howardcc.edu
NIGHTINGALE, Valerie ..... 860-932-4133.... 87 C
vnightingale@qvcc.edu
NIGLIAZZO, Marc, A .... 254-519-5720.. 468 C
marc.nigliazzo@tamuct.edu
NIGRO, Frank .... 530-242-7760.... 64 D
fnigro@shastacollege.edu
NIGRO, Nick .... 419-473-2700.. 367 J
nnigro@daviscollege.edu
NIGRO, Stephen, M .... 413-542-2101.. 214 C
smnigro@amherst.edu
NIGUIDULA, Amanda .... 305-348-3532.. 111 A
amanda.niguidula@fiu.edu
NIJLAND, Mark, J .... 210-567-0313.. 477 D
nijland@uthscsa.edu
NIKEL-ZUEGER, Manuel .. 510-883-2086.... 42 F
mnz@dspt.edu
NIKIAS, C. L, M .... 213-740-2111.... 72 D
president@usc.edu
NIKIRK, Sarah, F .... 859-218-3379.. 193 G
s.nikirk@uky.edu
NIKOLAEFF, Ivan .... 303-457-2757.... 80 C
ivan.nikolaeff@zenith.org
NIKOLAKIS, Michael .... 251-580-2122...... 4 I
mike.nikolakis@faulknerstate.edu
NIKOLOV, Victoria .... 561-912-1211.... 99 J
vnikolov@evergladesuniversity.edu
NIKOPOULOS, Beth .... 972-273-3171.. 456 G
bnikopoulos@dcccd.edu
NILAND, Bridget .... 716-839-8397.. 312 D
bniland@daemen.edu
NILAND, Eileen, A .... 716-888-2620.. 306 F
nilande@canisius.edu
NILAND, Joe .... 251-442-2288...... 9 A
jniland@umobile.edu
NILES, Maryann .... 781-280-3703.. 224 A
nilesm@middlesex.mass.edu
NILES, Spencer .... 757-221-2315.. 488 F
sgniles@wm.edu
NILES, Stefanie, D .... 717-245-1287.. 402 D
niles@dickinson.edu
NILES-HANSEN, Diana ..... 808-544-1102.. 130 H
dnileshansen@hpu.edu
NILKANT, Anita .... 412-397-5267.. 418 B
nilkant@rmu.edu
NILL, John (Jack) .... 417-862-9533.. 265 D
info@globaluniversity.edu
NILLES, Dawnita .... 701-777-3239.. 360 C
dawnita.nilles@und.edu
NILSEN, Cheryl .... 701-858-3150.. 360 F
cheryl.nilsen@minotstateu.edu
NILSEN, Kenneth .... 201-216-5699.. 297 B
kenneth.nilsen@stevens.edu
NILSON, Amy .... 209-588-5505.... 75 J
nilsona@yosemite.edu
NILSSON, Gary .... 253-680-7180.. 501 E
gnilsson@bates.ctc.edu
NIMES, Johnny .... 404-527-7782.. 123 I
jnimes@itc.edu
NIMMER, Carole .... 660-543-4919.. 273 C
cnimmer@ucmo.edu
NIMMO, Pam .... 615-732-7662.. 442 G
pam@mtsa.edu
NIMMO, Steven .... 706-776-0113.. 125 J
snimmo@piedmont.edu
NIMON, Opie .... 312-949-7610.. 142 A
onimon@ico.edu
NINAN, George .... 901-272-5125.. 442 B
gninan@mca.edu
NING, Bin .... 734-487-4924.. 233 J
bning@emich.edu
NINOS, Katherine .... 505-467-6819.. 302 D
katandall@aol.com
NIP, Kit .... 319-385-6250.. 174 A
knip@iw.edu
NIPP, Amanda .... 402-844-7733.. 282 B
amandan@northeast.edu
NIPP, Tim, J .... 731-881-7601.. 448 G
timnipp@utm.edu
NIPPERT, Jennifer .... 740-695-9500.. 364 B
jnippert@belmontcollege.edu
NIPPERT, Karen, F .... 901-333-4283.. 447 B
knippert@southwest.tn.edu
NIRENBERG, David .... 773-702-8799.. 156 D
nirenberg@uchicago.edu
NIROOMAND, Farhang .... 361-570-4230.. 474 C
niroomandf@uhv.edu
NIROUMAND, Madjid ..... 714-432-5765.... 39 G
mniroumand@occ.cccd.edu
NIROUMAND, Madjid ..... 714-432-5991.... 39 G
mniroumand@occ.cccd.edu
NISBET, Jane, A .... 603-862-0549.. 288 C
jan.nisbet@unh.edu
NISBET, Kenneth, J .... 734-763-0614.. 241 J
knisbet@umich.edu
NISHIME, Jeanie .... 310-660-3472.... 42 J
jnishime@elcamino.edu
NISHIZAWA, Yuichiro ...... 973-748-9000.. 289 H
yuichiro_nishizawa@bloomfield.edu
NISKA, Jennifer .... 651-638-6891.. 244 L
j-niska@bethel.edu
NISSEL, Chaim .... 646-685-0115.. 341 G
drnissel@yu.edu
NISSEN, Jill .... 314-367-8700.. 271 E
jill.nissen@stlcop.edu
NISSEN, Laura .... 503-725-3997.. 394 G
nissen@pdx.edu
NISSEN, Lindsey .... 319-296-4269.. 173 B
lindsey.nissen@hawkeyecollege.edu
NISSEN, Sarah .... 701-777-3579.. 360 C
sarah.nissen@und.edu
NISUN, Michelle, L .... 260-399-7700.. 168 D
mnisun@sf.edu
NISWANDER, Frederick ... 252-328-6975.. 356 C
niswanderf@ecu.edu
NITCH, Mindy .... 814-262-6433.. 413 P
mnitch@pennhighlands.edu

NORRIS, Darrell .... 517-787-0800.. 235 G
norrisdarrellr@jccmi.edu
NORRIS, Deb .... 937-512-5182.. 377 D
deb.norris@sinclair.edu
NORRIS, Debbie .... 601-925-3260.. 259 A
dnorris@mc.edu
NORRIS, Debbie .... 601-925-3225.. 259 A
dnorris@mc.edu
NORRIS, Dena .... 816-604-1527.. 267 F
dena.norris@mcckc.edu
NORRIS, Elissa .... 912-478-7288.. 122 B
enorris@georgiasouthern.edu
NORRIS, Emily .... 502-585-9911.. 192 E
enorris@spalding.edu
NORRIS, Gail .... 585-275-2758.. 338 K
gnorris@admin.rochester.edu
NORRIS, Heather .... 828-262-2058.. 356 B
hulburthm@appstate.edu
NORRIS, Helen .... 714-744-7848.... 37 F
hnorris@chapman.edu
NORRIS, Jeffery .... 901-843-3762.. 443 L
norrisj@rhodes.edu
NORRIS, John .... 704-330-1448.. 345 E
jnorris@jcsu.edu
NORRIS, Joye .... 417-836-4127.. 268 I
joyenorris@missouristate.edu
NORRIS, Kisha .... 256-726-7204...... 6 B
knorris@oakwood.edu
NORRIS, Lee .... 336-334-0398.. 358 B
clnorris@uncg.edu
NORRIS, Lesa .... 630-801-7900.. 157 K
lnorris@waubonsee.edu
NORRIS, Lisa .... 731-352-6437.. 438 K
norrisl@bethelu.edu
NORRIS, Mark, M .... 574-372-5100.. 161 B
norrismm@grace.edu
NORRIS, Marly, A .... 415-422-4162.... 72 C
manorris@usfca.edu
NORRIS, Mary .... 860-768-4716.... 89 G
norris@hartford.edu
NORRIS, Nancy, E .... 828-448-3150.. 354 B
nnorris@wpcc.edu
NORRIS, Patricia .... 910-296-2509.. 350 F
pnorris@jamessprunt.edu
NORRIS, Patricia, D .... 336-750-2900.. 359 B
norrispd@wssu.edu
NORRIS, Robert, F .... 630-752-5559.. 158 C
bob.norris@wheaton.edu
NORRIS, Sababu, C .... 716-888-2787.. 306 F
norris@canisius.edu
NORRIS, Shawn .... 225-752-4233.. 195 E
admissions@iticollege.edu
NORRIS, Steven .... 816-235-2672.. 273 F
norrissp@umkc.edu
NORRIS, Terry .... 702-651-5813.. 284 H
terry.norris@csn.edu
NORRIS, Todd .... 574-284-4560.. 167 A
tnorris@saintmarys.edu
NORRIS, Veta .... 810-766-4203.. 231 D
vnorri01@baker.edu
NORRIS, Will .... 541-506-6050.. 390 I
wnorris@cgcc.edu
NORRIS HALL, Sarah .... 206-543-6277.. 508 E
sahall@uw.edu
NORRIS-LANE, Virginia ..... 830-896-5411.. 465 E
vanorrislane@schreiner.edu
NORRIS-PAULISON,
Robin .... 828-694-1746.. 347 G
r_paulison@blueridge.edu
NORRIS-RAYNBIRD,
Carla .... 218-755-2828.. 248 M
cnorrisraynbird@bemidjistate.edu
NORSYM, Arlene .... 312-996-6569.. 156 F
afnorsym@uic.edu
NORTELL, Bruce .... 630-637-5214.. 149 H
bnortell@noctrl.edu
NORTH, Cecilia .... 802-635-1240.. 486 B
cecilia.north@jsc.edu
NORTH, Dana .... 765-983-1628.. 160 G
northda@earlham.edu
NORTH, Jane, D .... 717-337-6011.. 404 C
jnorth@gettysburg.edu
NORTH, Jon, D .... 913-971-3600.. 183 D
jonnorth@mnu.edu
NORTH, Joshua .... 785-442-6023.. 181 H
jnorth@highlandcc.edu
NORTH, Keith .... 503-552-1573.. 392 H
knorth@nunm.edu
NORTH, Linda .... 334-745-6437...... 7 C
lnorth@suscc.edu
NORTH, Matthew .... 412-396-4075.. 403 A
northm@duq.edu
NORTH, Mike .... 865-228-2303.. 446 G
mnorth@pstcc.edu
NORTH, Paula .... 918-293-5240.. 386 B
paula.north@okstate.edu
NORTH, Peter, C .... 717-337-6219.. 404 C
pnorth@gettysburg.edu
NORTHAM, Andrea .... 507-457-5024.. 252 G
anortham@winona.edu
NORTHAM, Mark .... 307-766-6897.. 527 B
mnortham@uwyo.edu
NORTHCUTT, David .... 706-419-1214.. 119 G
david.northcutt@covenant.edu
NORTHERN, Norma .... 502-213-2559.. 190 A
norma.northern@kctcs.edu
NORTHERN, Orathai .... 863-292-3645.. 106 I
onorthern@polk.edu
NORTHOVER, Michael ...... 971-722-8508.. 394 F
michael.northover@pcc.edu
NORTHROP, Cathy .... 607-844-8222.. 337 G
northrc@tc3.edu
NORTHUP, Bill .... 641-628-7645.. 170 E
northupb@central.edu
NORTHUP, Lesley .... 305-348-2099.. 111 A
lesley.northup@fiu.edu
NORTON, Alan .... 740-368-3351.. 376 B
ajnorton@owu.edu
NORTON, Amy .... 563-588-6338.. 170 F
amy.norton@clarke.edu
NORTON, Andrew .... 215-702-4318.. 399 E
anorton@cairn.edu
NORTON, Beth .... 865-694-6728.. 446 G
aenorton@pstcc.edu
NORTON, Cheryl .... 724-738-2000.. 416 B
cheryl.norton@sru.edu
NORTON, Clare .... 646-664-3620.. 306 M
clare.norton@cuny.edu
NORTON, Daniel .... 601-266-4344.. 261 E
daniel.norton@usm.edu
NORTON, Darryl, R .... 828-689-1248.. 346 C
dnorton@mhu.edu
NORTON, David .... 760-366-5249.... 41 K
dnorton@cmccd.edu
NORTON, David, P .... 352-392-9271.. 112 A
dpnorton@ufl.edu
NORTON, Greg .... 773-777-4220.. 150 D
gnorton@nc.edu
NORTON, H. Will .... 662-915-7146.. 261 B
hwnorton@olemiss.edu
NORTON, Hanna .... 479-880-4189.... 19 F
hnorton@atu.edu
NORTON, Holly .... 309-649-6050.. 155 G
holly.norton@src.edu
NORTON, James .... 860-439-2268.... 87 F
jwnor@conncoll.edu
NORTON, Jamie .... 260-665-4847.. 167 E
nortonj@trine.edu
NORTON, Karen .... 617-228-2177.. 223 B
kmnorton@bhcc.mass.edu
NORTON, Karen, M .... 617-228-2177.. 223 B
kmnorton@bhcc.mass.edu
NORTON, Kay .... 970-351-2121.... 84 C
kay.norton@unco.edu
NORTON, Lisa, M .... 812-877-8892.. 166 H
lisa.norton@rose-hulman.edu
NORTON, M. Grant .... 509-335-4505.. 508 H
mg_norton@wsu.edu
NORTON, Melanie .... 765-658-4212.. 160 F
melanienorton@depauw.edu
NORTON, Michael, E .... 515-294-5352.. 169 G
mnorton@iastate.edu
NORTON, Mitzi .... 312-662-4002.. 134 I
mnorton@adler.edu
NORTON, Noelle .... 619-260-4545.... 72 B
norton@sandiego.edu
NORTON, Patrick .... 504-862-8698.. 200 C
pjn@tulane.edu
NORTON, Patrick, J .... 802-443-5699.. 484 F
pnorton@middlebury.edu
NORTON, Ricky .... 903-223-3012.. 469 C
ricky.norton@tamut.edu
NORTON, Robert .... 517-607-2687.. 235 E
rnorton@hillsdale.edu
NORTON, Sheri, L .... 401-825-2311.. 425 A
slnorton@ccri.edu
NORTON, Steve .... 309-341-5227.. 136 C
snorton@sandburg.edu
NORTON, Susan .... 843-574-6211.. 433 D
susan.norton@tridenttech.edu
NORTON, Susan, A .... 706-721-3777.. 117 D
snorton@augusta.edu
NORTON, Timothy, A .... 770-720-5545.. 126 C
tan@reinhardt.edu
NORTON, Timothy, P .... 402-280-2355.. 279 H
timnorton@creighton.edu
NORVELL, Laura .... 202-885-8635.... 94 E
lnorvell@wesleyseminary.edu
NORWOOD, Aletia .... 308-635-3606.. 283 D
norwooda@wncc.edu
NORWOOD, Bertha .... 210-486-2212.. 450 E
bwebb@alamo.edu
NOSAL, Judith, S .... 860-723-0011.... 85 E
nosalj@ct.edu
NOSEGBE, Isibor, J .... 703-891-1787.. 494 H
NOSEL, Cathy .... 302-736-2410.... 91 G
cathy.nosel@wesle.edu
NOSEL, Erin .... 801-375-5125.. 481 C
enosel@rmuohp.edu
NOSEWORTHY, James, A 847-866-3952.. 140 G
jim.noseworthy@garrett.edu
NOSEWORTHY, John, H .. 507-266-4861.. 245 E
noseworthy.john@mayo.edu
NOSS, Rebecca .... 845-675-5767.. 325 C
rebecca.noss@nyack.edu
NOSSER, Mike, A .... 612-343-4178.. 253 Y
manosser@northcentral.edu
NOSTRAND, Dennis, L .... 813-253-6211.. 114 M
dnostrand@ut.edu
NOSTROM, Kim .... 607-436-2563.. 331 F
kim.nostrom@oneonta.edu
NOSTRUM, Rian .... 701-231-7890.. 361 A
rian.nostrum@ndsu.edu
NOTA, Michele .... 401-874-2242.. 426 D
mnota@uri.edu
NOTARESCHI, Rey, T .... 330-325-6796.. 373 H
rtn@neomed.edu
NOTCHICK, Thomas, K .... 570-348-6241.. 409 H
notchick@marywood.edu
NOTESTEIN, Mary .... 319-385-6204.. 174 A
mary.notestein@iw.edu
NOTIS, Chana .... 845-362-3053.. 304 J
cnotis@bytsem.org
NOTO, Lisa .... 707-664-3019.... 35 D
lisa.noto@sonoma.edu
NOTO, Robert, A .... 517-353-3530.. 237 I
notor@msu.edu
NOTSON, Jeanne .... 505-566-3209.. 301 J
notsonj@sanjuancollege.edu
NOTTKE, Janine .... 906-487-7267.. 234 A
janine.nottke@finlandia.edu
NOUEL, Gloria .... 215-884-8942.. 424 B
academicdean@woninstitute.edu
NOURI, Imad .... 313-845-9611.. 235 D
inouri@hfcc.edu
NOURSE, Chris .... 740-245-7228.. 380 C
cnourse@rio.edu
NOVAK, JR., Albert, J ..... 412-624-6800.. 421 G
nalbert@pitt.edu
NOVAK, Amy, C .... 605-995-2601.. 435 F
amnovak@dwu.edu
NOVAK, Bruce .... 972-883-2416.. 476 C
bxn111230@utdallas.edu
NOVAK, Christina .... 773-834-2216.. 155 K
cnovak@ttic.edu
NOVAK, David .... 219-464-6903.. 168 F
david.novak@valpo.edu
NOVAK, Debbie .... 970-945-8691.... 78 B
dnovak@coloradomtn.edu
NOVAK, Diane .... 832-813-6544.. 461 B
diane.novak@lonestar.edu
NOVAK, Greg .... 314-792-6221.. 266 F
gregnovak@kenrick.edu
NOVAK, Jackie .... 330-490-7319.. 380 J
jnovak@walsh.edu
NOVAK, Jeffrey .... 570-702-8920.. 406 E
jnovak@johnson.edu
NOVAK, Jeffrey .... 608-262-6982.. 519 K
novak4@wisc.edu
NOVAK, Jerry .... 734-995-7340.. 232 I
jerry.novak@cuaa.edu
NOVAK, John .... 219-980-6905.. 163 B
jmnovak@iun.edu
NOVAK, Joshua .... 724-287-8711.. 399 B
joshua.novak@bc3.edu
NOVAK, Linda .... 910-678-8225.. 349 F
novakl@faytechcc.edu
NOVAK, Mark .... 661-654-2441.... 32 A
mnovak@csub.edu
NOVAK, Mike .... 479-248-7236.... 20 C
mnovak@ecollege.edu
NOVAK, Paul .... 724-738-2465.. 416 B
paul.novak@sru.edu
NOVAK, Richard, J .... 848-932-0613.. 295 F
richard.novak@rutgers.edu
NOVAK, Ross .... 570-348-6236.. 409 H
rnovak@marywood.edu
NOVAK, Theresa, C .... 330-325-6755.. 373 H
tnovak@neomed.edu
NOVAK, Thomas .... 617-585-1308.. 226 F
tom.novak@necmusic.edu
NOVAK, Thomas .... 617-585-1200.. 226 F
tom.novak@necmusic.edu
NOVAK, Wendy .... 907-277-1000.... 10 C
contact@chartercollege.edu
NOVATON, Angela .... 561-391-1148.... 98 H
anovaton@dmac.edu
NOVICKI, Elizabeth .... 336-917-5421.. 355 E
elizabeth.novicki@salem.edu
NOVIELLO, Sheri, R .... 229-333-5959.. 129 G
srnoviello@valdosta.edu
NOVO, Frank .... 617-964-1111.. 214 D
fnovo@ants.edu
NOVO, Lizza .... 503-223-2245.. 391 H
lnovo@portland.chefs.edu
NOVOBILSKI, Andy .... 678-717-3698.. 128 F
andy.novobilski@ung.edu
NOVOTNY, Alicia .... 620-672-5641.. 184 D
alician@prattcc.edu
NOVOTNY, April .... 614-236-6565.. 364 N
anovotny@capital.edu
NOVOTNY, Dorene .... 650-949-6210.... 43 N
novotnydorene@fhda.edu
NOVOTNY, Jodi .... 425-235-2464.. 506 F
jnovotny@rtc.edu
NOVOTNY, Richard, J ..... 440-525-7358.. 371 F
rnovotny@lakelandcc.edu
NOWACZYK, Ronald .... 301-687-4111.. 212 F
rhnowaczyk@frostburg.edu
NOWAK, Janice .... 904-470-8192.... 98 N
janice.nowak@ewc.edu
NOWAK, Linda .... 978-542-6640.. 222 D
ctr_lnowak@salemstate.edu
NOWAK, Meg .... 607-431-4501.. 315 E
nowakm@hartwick.edu
NOWAK, Megan .... 213-624-1200.... 43 J
mnowak@fidm.edu
NOWAK, Patricia .... 219-989-2220.. 166 F
nowak28@pnw.edu
NOWAK, Peter .... 919-546-8272.. 355 F
peter.nowak@shawu.edu
NOWAK, Robert, J .... 262-243-5700.. 516 E
robert.nowak@cuw.edu
NOWAK, Thomas, S .... 845-848-4000.. 312 F
thomas.nowak@dc.edu
NOWAK, Tom .... 574-936-8898.. 158 I
tom.nowak@ancilla.edu
NOWAK, Tony, J .... 414-847-3240.. 518 D
tonynowak@miad.edu
NOWAKOWSKI,
Bernadette .... 413-265-2214.. 217 D
nowakowskib@elms.edu
NOWAR, Mariam .... 215-248-7311.. 409 D
mnowar@ltsp.edu
NOWEL, OP, Mark, D ...... 401-865-2649.. 425 D
mnowel@providence.edu
NOWELL, Cheryl .... 305-348-2434.. 111 A
nowell@fiu.edu
NOWELL, Jordan .... 701-349-5764.. 362 C
jnowell@trinitybiblecollege.edu
NOWICKI, Laura .... 740-593-1969.. 375 H
nowicki@ohio.edu
NOWICKI, Stacy, A .... 269-337-5750.. 235 H
stacy.nowicki@kzoo.edu
NOWICKI, Stephen .... 919-668-3420.. 343 J
snowicki@duke.edu
NOWICKI, Sue, A .... 989-837-4203.. 239 D
nowicki@northwood.edu
NOWIK, Christine, M ...... 717-736-4142.. 405 C
cmnowik@hacc.edu
NOWLAN, Marilyn, L .... 860-727-6782.... 87 H
mnowlan@goodwin.edu
NOWLIN, Brian .... 562-985-5537.... 33 B
brian.nowlin@csulb.edu
NOWLIN, Steve .... 626-396-2397.... 27 L
stephen.nowlin@artcenter.edu
NOWOGORSKI, Barbara .. 570-961-7835.. 407 B
nowogorskib@lackawanna.edu
NOWOSIELSKI, Lavinia .... 928-350-4204.... 16 P
lavinia.nowosielsk@prescott.edu
NOYES, Cynthia .... 269-749-7144.. 240 A
cnoyes@olivetcollege.edu
NOYES, Michelle .... 252-451-8258.. 351 F
NTOKO, Alfred .... 518-587-2100.. 335 D
alfred.ntoko@esc.edu
NUANES, Heather .... 904-256-1259.. 100 E
hnuanes@fcsl.edu
NUBEL, Anna .... 402-280-2222.. 279 H
annanubel@creighton.edu
NUCCI, John, A .... 617-973-1103.. 228 G
jnucci@suffolk.edu
NUCCIARONE, Mary, B .... 574-631-6436.. 168 B
nucciarone.2@nd.edu
NUCERA, Donna .... 201-216-9901.. 291 C
donna.nucera@eicollege.edu
NUCKOLS, Melanie, L ...... 336-734-7332.. 349 G
mnuckols@forsythtech.edu
NUDELMAN, Felice .... 937-769-1342.. 363 E
fnudelman@antioch.edu
NUESELL, Lisa, M .... 919-381-6912.. 355 K
lnuesell@umo.edu
NUFER, Ken .... 719-549-3474.... 82 G
ken.nufer@pueblocc.edu
NUGEN, Deb .... 402-399-2442.. 279 E
dnugen@csm.edu
NUGENT, Barli .... 212-799-5000.. 318 A
NUGENT, Joe .... 831-479-6140.... 29 G
jonugent@cabrillo.edu
NUGENT, John, D .... 860-439-5266.... 87 F
john.nugent@conncoll.edu
NUGENT, Kari .... 815-802-8256.. 144 C
knugent@kcc.edu
NUGENT, Katherine .... 601-266-5445.. 261 E
katherine.nugent@usm.edu
NUGENT, Kirk .... 256-726-7000...... 6 B
krnugent@oakwood.edu
NUGENT, Megan .... 503-251-2836.. 396 C
mnugent@uws.edu
NUGENT, Richard .... 574-284-5212.. 167 A
rnugent@saintmarys.edu
NUKAYA, Bruce .... 208-732-6352.. 133 E
bnukaya@csi.edu

NULL, David .... 608-265-1988.. 519 K
dnull@library.wisc.edu
NULL, Wesley .... 254-710-6120.. 452 H
wesley_null@baylor.edu
NUMRICH, Camille .... 401-825-2237.. 425 A
cnumrich@ccri.edu
NUNALEE, Carmen .... 252-823-5166.. 349 E
nunaleec@edgecombe.edu
NUNEMAKER, Christine .. 207-834-7593.. 205 E
christine.nunemaker@maine.edu
NUNES, Grafton, J .... 216-421-7410.. 366 G
gnunes@cia.edu
NUNES, John, A .... 914-337-9300.. 311 F
NUNES, Mary Louise .... 508-999-8233.. 220 H
mnunes2@umassd.edu
NUNES, Victoria .... 650-306-3274.... 62 G
nunes@smccd.edu
NUNEZ, Al .... 312-341-2187.. 152 H
anunez13@roosevelt.edu
NUNEZ, Awilda .... 787-769-2043.. 537 H
awilda.nunez@upr.edu
NUNEZ, Elaine .... 787-786-3030.. 536 F
enunez@ucb.edu.pr
NUNEZ, Elsa .... 860-465-5222.... 85 E
nuneze@easternct.edu
NUNEZ, Elsa, M .... 860-465-5222.... 85 G
nunez@easternct.edu
NUNEZ, Gabriel .... 718-522-9073.. 304 D
gnunez@asa.edu
NUNEZ, Ivon .... 973-596-3478.. 293 D
nunez@njit.edu
NUNEZ, Jordy, H .... 701-349-5405.. 362 C
jnunez@trinitybiblecollege.edu
NUNEZ, Jose .... 650-358-6836.... 62 F
nunezj@smccd.edu
NUNEZ, Jose Ramon .... 714-992-7030.... 54 H
jnunez@fullcoll.edu
NUNEZ, Juan .... 936-294-1910.. 471 D
jmn019@shsu.edu
NUNEZ, Lucia .... 608-246-6434.. 523 F
lnunez1@madisoncollege.edu
NUNEZ, Mayra .... 904-743-1122.. 103 G
mnunez@jones.edu
NUNEZ, Steve, C .... 815-835-6263.. 153 K
steve.c.nunez@svcc.edu
NUNEZ, William .... 402-472-2116.. 282 M
wnunez2@unl.edu
NUNEZ, William, J .... 402-472-2097.. 282 M
wnunez2@unl.edu
NUNEZ, Yancy .... 806-716-2338.. 465 G
ynunez@southplainscollege.edu
NUNLEY, Beth .... 815-802-8142.. 144 C
bnunley@kcc.edu
NUNLEY, Ernest, L .... 276-739-2510.. 499 A
enunley@vhcc.edu
NUNN, Dana .... 970-248-1868.... 77 L
dnunn@coloradomesa.edu
NUNN, Gaylene .... 254-519-5458.. 468 C
nunn@tamuct.edu
NUNN, Joshua .... 619-239-0391.... 36 A
jnunn@cwsl.edu
NUNN, Lori, A .... 540-674-3615.. 497 G
lnunn@nr.edu
NUNNA, Ramakrishna ...... 559-278-2500.... 32 F
rnunna@csufresno.edu
NUNNALLY, Delecia .... 209-954-5151.... 61 F
dnunnally@deltacollege.edu
NUNO, Karina .... 707-546-4000.... 42 M
knuno@empirecollege.com
NUOSCE, Mary .... 239-513-1122.. 102 T
mnuosce@hodges.edu
NURNBERGER,
Charles, A .... 757-825-2717.. 498 G
nurnbergerc@tncc.edu
NURSE, Learie .... 303-546-3506.... 81 I
lnurse@naropa.edu
NUSBAUM, Nancy .... 512-245-2244.. 471 F
nn01@txstate.edu
NUSS, Shelley .... 706-713-2188.. 128 E
snuss@uga.edu
NUSSBAUM, Daniel .... 860-231-5770.... 90 B
dnussbaum@usj.edu
NUSSBAUM, Irwin .... 860-768-7904.... 89 G
nussbaum@hartford.edu
NUSSBAUM, Renee .... 419-755-4772.. 373 G
rnussbau@ncstatecollege.edu
NUSSEL, Jay .... 810-424-5474.. 242 B
nusselj@umflint.edu
NUSSER, Sarah, M .... 515-294-6344.. 169 G
nusser@iastate.edu
NUSUM-SMITH, Michelle 301-846-2851.. 207 F
mnusumsmith@frederick.edu
NUTEFALL, Jennifer .... 408-554-6829.... 63 E
jnutefall@scu.edu
NUTI, Larry .... 925-631-4901.... 59 I
lnuti@stmarys-ca.edu
NUTT, Jill .... 616-395-7765.. 235 F
nutt@hope.edu
NUTT, Lee Ann .... 281-351-3644.. 461 B
leeann.nutt@lonestar.edu
NUTTER, Alberta .... 405-733-7979.. 387 I
anutter@rose.edu
NUTTER, April, H .... 606-783-9351.. 191 H
a.nutter@moreheadstate.edu
NUTTER, Jeff .... 740-389-4636.. 372 B
nutterj@mtc.edu
NUTTER, Mark .... 740-374-8716.. 381 A
mnutter@wscc.edu
NUTTER, Sarah .... 703-993-1807.. 490 B
snutter@gmu.edu
NUTTER, Shelly, J .... 740-368-3002.. 376 B
sjnutter@owu.edu
NUTTER, Susan, K .... 919-515-7188.. 357 B
susan_nutter@ncsu.edu
NUTTY, David .... 207-780-4276.. 205 E
david.nutty@maine.edu
NUZZO, Brittany .... 304-296-8282.. 514 I
bnuzzo@wvjc.edu
NUZZO, Jane .... 212-592-2000.. 330 C
jnuzzo@sva.edu
NUÑEZ, Cheryl .... 360-475-7740.. 505 F
cnunez@olympic.edu
NWAKEZE, Peter .... 718-933-6700.. 321 I
pnwakeze@monroecollege.edu
NWANGWU, Winifred ...... 401-874-1000.. 426 D
winny@uri.edu
NWANKWO, Charles .... 480-732-7020.... 13 O
charles.nwankwo@cgc.edu
NWANNE, Andrew, I .... 575-234-9215.. 301 B
anwanne@nmsu.edu
NWARIAKU, Fiemu, E ..... 214-648-9968.. 478 C
fiemu.nwariku@utsouthwestern.edu
NWOKEAFOR, Cosmos ..... 301-860-3232.. 212 D
cnwokeafor@bowiestate.edu
NWORIE, John .... 567-268-5123.. 378 A
nworiej@tiffin.edu
NWOSU, Peter .... 657-278-3602.... 33 A
pnwosu@fullerton.edu
NWOSU, Peter, O .... 404-880-8754.. 118 K
pnwosu@cau.edu
NYACHUBA, Daniel .... 903-927-3390.. 479 K
dnyachuba@wileyc.edu
NYBERG, Christopher, L .. 315-684-6083.. 336 B
nybergcl@morrisville.edu
NYBERG, Connie .... 307-855-2207.. 526 E
cnyberg@cwc.edu
NYE, Barney .... 801-863-7194.. 482 C
nyewi@uvu.edu
NYE, Jamey .... 916-563-3207.... 50 J
nyej@crc.losrios.edu
NYE, Judith .... 732-571-3637.. 292 F
nye@monmouth.edu
NYE, Ken .... 801-581-6510.. 481 M
ken.nye@fm.utah.edu
NYE, Robert .... 585-785-1201.. 314 D
robert.nye@flcc.edu
NYGAARD, Steven .... 310-258-5522.... 51 E
steven.nygaard@lmu.edu
NYGARD, Bonnie, K .... 907-786-6494.... 10 F
bknygard@uaa.alaska.edu
NYHAMMER, Diane .... 608-757-7737.. 523 A
dnyhammer@blackhawk.edu
NYHAN, Jeff .... 602-206-8220.. 286 D
jnyhan@ccsnh.edu
NYIRENDA, Stanley, M ... 410-651-6672.. 212 B
smnyirenda@umes.edu
NYLAND, Gerald .... 231-777-0315.. 238 G
gerald.nyland@muskegoncc.edu
NYLEN, John .... 847-578-3252.. 153 A
NYPAVER, David .... 330-972-6876.. 378 G
nypaver@uakron.edu
NYQUIST, J. Paul .... 312-329-4112.. 148 F
paul.nyquist@moody.edu
NYRE, Joseph, E .... 914-633-2203.. 317 B
jnyre@iona.edu
NYROP, Karin .... 206-543-4150.. 508 E
knyrop@uw.edu
NYSTROM, Ellen .... 210-567-2640.. 477 D
nystrom@uthscsa.edu
NYUL, Renata .... 617-373-7666.. 227 B
NZAMUTUMA, Issmael .... 951-785-2006.... 48 A
inzamutu@lasierra.edu
NZEH, Okoroafor .... 706-821-8331.. 125 H
onzeh@paine.edu
NZEOGWU, Okeleke .... 702-968-1659.. 285 E
onzeogwu@roseman.edu

O

O"BRIEN, Jennifer .... 412-291-6353.. 397 I
jlobrien@aii.edu
OAKES, Barbee .... 336-758-3106.. 359 E
oaks@wfu.edu
OAKES, Mary .... 312-369-6802.. 138 F
moakes@colum.edu
OAKES, Susan .... 504-865-2011.. 198 E
soakes@loyno.edu
OAKLEY, Christina .... 561-912-1211.... 99 J
coakley@evergladesuniversity.edu
OAKLEY, Danielle .... 608-262-8350.. 519 K
droakley@uhs.wisc.edu
OAKLEY, E[illegible] .... 562-938-4122.... 49 D
eoakley@bcc.edu
OAKLEY, Jennifer .... 201-360-4002.. 292 B
joakley@hccc.edu
OAKMAN, Tommy .... 828-694-1725.. 347 G
t_oakman@blueridge.edu
OAKS, Beth .... 605-642-6411.. 437 B
beth.oaks@bhsu.edu
OAKS, Diane, G .... 949-451-5277.... 65 F
doaks@ivc.edu
OAKS, Geneva .... 951-343-4702.... 29 H
gcooperoaks@calbaptist.edu
OAKS, Nick .... 605-642-6545.. 437 B
nicholas.oaks@bhsu.edu
OAKS SMITH, Tonya .... 870-230-5348.... 20 E
smithto@hsu.edu
OANES, Laura .... 507-457-6909.. 254 O
loanes@smumn.edu
OARD, Tasha .... 406-586-3585.. 276 I
tasha.oard@montanabiblecollege.edu
OATES, Andrea .... 229-931-2705.. 127 C
aoates@southgatech.edu
OATES, Bruce .... 847-635-1753.. 150 G
boates@oakton.edu
OATES, Bruce .... 847-635-1705.. 150 G
boates@oakton.edu
OATES, Justin .... 201-216-3495.. 297 B
justin.oates@stevens.edu
OATES, Nadine .... 716-652-8900.. 306 K
noates@cks.edu
OATES, Richard .... 678-717-3947.. 128 F
richard.oates@ung.edu
OATEY, J. Sue .... 218-299-3455.. 246 A
joatey@cord.edu
OATIS, Steve .... 479-979-1338.... 24 I
soatis@ozarks.edu
OATS, Evangela .... 845-434-5750.. 336 H
eoates@sunysullivan.edu
OBA, Saichi .... 907-450-8000.... 10 E
soba@alaska.edu
OBBINK, Kim .... 406-994-6550.. 277 C
kobbink@montana.edu
OBER, Jay .... 305-442-9223.. 105 F
jober@mrc.edu
OBEREM, Graham .... 760-750-4050.... 34 D
oberem@csusm.edu
OBERFELDT, Kathleen ...... 718-390-3435.. 339 F
koberfel@wagner.edu
OBERG, Beth .... 217-479-7130.. 147 C
beth.oberg@mac.edu
OBERGFELL, Ann .... 260-481-6100.. 153 C
obergfea@ipfw.edu
OBERHELMAN, Don .... 805-756-1407.... 31 I
obe@calpoly.edu
OBERHOLTZER, Brent ...... 717-867-6111.. 403 F
oberholt@hvc.edu
OBERHOLTZER, Curt .... 920-206-2372.. 517 G
curt.oberholtzer@mbu.edu
OBERLANDER, Cyril .... 707-826-3441.... 34 F
cyril.oberlander@humboldt.edu
OBERLANDER, Janel .... 970-824-1102.... 73 J
janell.oberlander@cncc.edu
OBERMAN, Anne .... 320-363-5999.. 245 I
aoberman@csbsju.edu
OBERMEISTER, Tuvia, M . 718-377-0777.. 326 F
OBERMEYER, Carole .... 316-295-5779.. 181 B
obermeyer@friends.edu
OBERMEYER, Carole .... 316-295-5628.. 181 B
obermeyer@friends.edu
OBERQUELL, Christian .... 406-265-3761.. 277 E
coberquell@msun.edu
OBERSTEIN, Leonard ...... 410-484-7200.. 210 A
loberstein@nirc.edu
OBERT, Brian .... 308-345-8109.. 280 M
obertb@mpcc.edu
OBI, Stacey .... 717-728-2248.. 400 F
staceyobi@centralpenn.edu
OBIELODAN, James, E .... 502-597-4723.. 191 B
james.obielodan@kysu.edu
OBILADE, Sandra, O .... 270-686-4209.. 187 C
sandra.obilade@brescia.edu
OBIN, Jason .... 773-508-8643.. 146 G
jobin@luc.edu
OBISESAN, Thomas, E .... 202-806-2550.... 93 A
tobisesan@howard.edu
OBLANDER, Douglas ...... 843-208-8256.. 434 A
oblander@uscb.edu
OBLANDER, Frances, W .. 912-650-5684.. 127 D
foblander@southuniversity.edu
OBLEY, Debora .... 510-987-9112.... 68 L
debora.obley@ucop.edu
OBLOY, Leonard .... 248-683-0446.. 241 F
lobloy@sscms.edu
OBRYCKI, Marybeth .... 973-290-4460.. 290 G
mobrycki@cse.edu
OBSNIUK, Karen .... 734-432-5648.. 237 D
kobsniuk@madonna.edu
OBST, Cheryl .... 619-201-8951.... 65 J
registrar@socalsem.edu
OBSTA, Kim .... 361-572-6410.. 478 F
kim.obsta@victoriacollege.edu
OBURN, Martha .... 713-718-8670.. 459 B
martha.oburn@hccs.edu
OCAMPO, Arturo .... 714-808-4830.... 54 F
OCAMPO, Carlota .... 202-884-9209.... 94 A
ocampoc@trinitydc.edu
OCAMPO, Kathy .... 928-314-9559.... 11 J
katheline.ocampo@azwestern.edu
OCASIO, Arcadio .... 787-257-0000.. 537 H
arcadio.ocasio@upr.edu
OCASIO, Joseph .... 610-917-1430.. 422 C
jaocasio@valleyforge.edu
OCASIO, Luz .... 787-765-1915.. 534 F
locasio@opto.inter.edu
OCASIO, Myra, D .... 610-917-1409.. 422 C
mdocasio@valleyforge.edu
OCCHIOGROSSO,
Gabrielle .... 718-405-3225.. 310 H
gabrielle.occhiogrosso@
mountsaintvincent.edu
OCCHIOGROSSO, Paul, F 212-650-8276.. 307 E
pocchiogrosso@ccny.cuny.edu
OCEGUERA, Gustavo .... 951-372-7885.... 59 B
gustavo.oceguera@norcocollege.edu
OCHOA, Daniel .... 210-829-2707.. 474 D
ochoa@uiwtx.edu
OCHOA, Eduardo, M .... 831-582-3532.... 33 E
emochoa@csumb.edu
OCHOA, Hector .... 505-277-7267.. 302 F
hectorochoa14@unm.edu
OCHOA, Laura .... 201-447-7184.. 289 E
lochoa@bergen.edu
OCHOA, Maria .... 510-723-6600.... 37 B
mochoa@chabotcollege.edu
OCHOA, Robert, L .... 956-721-5417.. 460 F
rochoa@laredo.edu
OCHRAN, Timothy, G ...... 903-877-8658.. 477 E
timothy.ochran@uthct.edu
OCHS, Joy .... 319-363-1323.. 175 D
jochs@mtmercy.edu
OCHS, Wayne, T .... 814-732-2757.. 415 A
wochs@edinboro.edu
OCHSENBEIN, Kim, D ...... 865-981-8121.. 441 H
kim.ochsenbein@maryvillecollege.edu
OCHSNER, Tom, J .... 402-465-2212.. 281 K
tjo@nebrwesleyan.edu
OCKEN, Scott .... 515-964-6364.. 171 B
sjocken@dmacc.edu
OCMAND, Lydia .... 504-468-2900.. 200 B
admissions@southwest.edu
OCONNELL KILLEN,
Patricia .... 509-313-6504.. 504 A
killen@gonzaga.edu
OCONNER, William .... 410-293-1000.. 529 D
william.oconner@usna.com
OCONNOR, Debra .... 516-323-4110.. 321 H
ODA, Donna Lee .... 310-665-6966.... 55 E
dleeoda@otis.edu
ODATO, David .... 415-353-4028.... 70 D
david.odato@hr.ucsf.edu
ODEGARD, Ilene .... 701-777-3904.. 360 C
ilene.odegard@und.edu
ODEH, Omar .... 478-445-6804.. 121 A
omar.odeh@gcsu.edu
ODELL, David .... 805-565-6010.... 75 A
dodell@westmont.edu
ODELL, Kara .... 970-339-6407.... 76 H
kara.odell@aims.edu
ODELL, Lynda .... 775-831-1314.. 285 G
lodell@sierranevada.edu
ODELL, Margaret .... 505-984-6066.. 301 I
careerservices@sjc.edu
ODELL, Michael .... 903-566-7132.. 477 B
modell@uttyler.edu
ODELL-CARLSON,
Kathleen .... 603-542-7744.. 286 G
kodellcarlson@ccsnh.edu
ODEM, Sharon .... 417-625-9300.. 268 H
odem-s@mssu.edu
ODEM, Sharon .... 417-625-9501.. 268 H
odem-s@mssu.edu
ODEN, Cassandra, L .... 412-397-6848.. 418 B
oden@rmu.edu
ODEN, JR., Joseph .... 304-766-3288.. 514 B
odenjr@wvstateu.edu
ODENBECK, Lisa .... 513-244-4475.. 373 C
lisa.odenbeck@msj.edu
ODHNER, Carroll, C .... 267-502-2547.. 398 J
carroll.odhner@brynathyn.edu
ODI, Henry, U .... 610-758-5923.. 408 H
huo0@lehigh.edu
ODIORNE, David, R .... 315-568-3146.. 323 A
dodiorne@nycc.edu
ODLE, Gary .... 785-738-9028.. 183 J
godle@ncktc.edu
ODOM, Amee, M .... 704-233-8096.. 359 H
ameeodom@wingate.edu
ODOM, Caitlin .... 575-492-2106.. 302 M
codom@usw.edu
ODOM, David .... 402-363-5732.. 283 G
dodom@york.edu

ODOM, Dexter .... 903-730-4890.. 460 B
dodom@jarvis.edu
ODOM, Don .... 601-318-6175.. 261 I
dodom@wmcarey.edu
ODOM, Evie .... 919-760-8424.. 346 D
registrar@meredith.edu
ODOM, Gale .... 318-869-5235.. 194 I
godom@centenary.edu
ODOM, James .... 870-762-3154.... 18 G
jodom@smail.anc.edu
ODOM, Julia .... 925-631-4529.... 59 I
jodom@stmarys-ca.edu
ODOM, Lorraine .... 206-592-4045.. 504 E
lodom@highline.edu
ODOM, Mark, R .... 325-793-4780.. 461 F
modom@mcm.edu
ODOM, Megan .... 530-898-5253.... 32 C
modom@csuchico.edu
ODOM, III, Olin, O .... 254-442-5130.. 454 E
olin.odom@cisco.edu
ODOM, III, Oscar .... 718-522-9073.. 304 D
oodom@asa.edu
ODOM, Tammy .... 479-394-7622.... 22 B
todom@rmcc.edu
ODOM, Troy .... 305-284-2667.. 114 H
t.odom@miami.edu
ODU, Michael .... 619-482-6344.... 66 E
modu@swccd.edu
ODUCADO, Joey .... 691-320-2480.. 529 F
joducado@comfsm.fm
ODVODY, Dwayne, E .... 828-262-4002.. 356 B
odvodyde@appstate.edu
OECHSLI, Kori, D .... 530-226-4941.... 64 H
koechsli@simpsonu.edu
OEFFLER, Kenneth, M ..... 215-503-6034.. 420 E
kenneth.oeffler@jefferson.edu
OEHLER, Bob .... 605-677-5341.. 437 A
bob.oehler@usd.edu
OEHLER, Candace .... 602-787-6606.... 14 E
candace.oehler@paradisevalley.edu
OEHLER, David .... 816-604-3048.. 267 J
david.oehler@mcckc.edu
OEHLERKING, Kelly .... 605-718-2931.. 438 B
kelly.oehlerking@wdt.edu
OEHME, Nacoma .... 620-687-4224.. 181 A
nacomao@fortscott.edu
OELSCHLAGER,
Sharon, G .... 412-396-5028.. 403 A
goedert@duq.edu
OEN-HOXIE, Tina .... 616-234-3925.. 234 E
thoxie@grcc.edu
OERLY-BENNETT,
Sandra, K .... 304-293-5242.. 514 C
sybennett@mail.wvu.edu
OERTEL, Barbara .... 507-457-5878.. 252 G
boertel@winona.edu
OERTEL, Christopher .... 518-244-2008.. 327 H
oertec@sage.edu
OERTLI, Gary .... 206-934-5311.. 506 I
gary.oertli@seattlecolleges.edu
OERTLI, Gary, L .... 206-934-5311.. 507 A
gary.oertli@seattlecolleges.edu
OESMANN, Jackie .... 908-737-4835.. 292 C
catholic@kean.edu
OESTER, Stephanie .... 541-881-5806.. 395 E
soester@tvcc.cc
OESTMANN, Deborah ...... 620-252-7075.. 180 B
debbio@coffeyville.edu
OESTREICHER, Edina, R .. 203-576-4392.... 89 C
edinao@bridgeport.edu
OESTREICHER, Paul .... 212-960-5285.. 341 G
paul.oestreicher@yu.edu
OETTING, Stephanie, J .... 260-399-7700.. 168 D
soetting@sf.edu
OETTINGER, Tony .... 704-463-3439.. 354 F
tony.oettinger@pfeiffer.edu
OFE, Suellen, S .... 334-833-4515...... 4 D
ofe@hawks.huntingdon.edu
OFFERMANN, Joseph ...... 815-729-9020.. 144 A
joffermann@jjc.edu
OFFICER, Danielle .... 212-237-8185.. 308 E
dofficer@jjay.cuny.edu
OFFORD, JR., Jerome ..... 573-681-5501.. 266 I
offordj@lincolnu.edu
OFODILE, Caroline .... 201-447-9242.. 289 E
cofodile@bergen.edu
OFORI, Terri .... 973-748-9000.. 289 H
terri_ofori@bloomfield.edu
OFORLEA, Veronica .... 714-564-6277.... 58 G
oforlea_veronica@sac.edu
OFOSU, Joseph .... 860-231-5538.... 90 B
jofosu@usj.edu
OFSTAD, Will .... 559-325-3600.... 30 C
wofstad@chsu.org
OGAWA, Kenneth .... 570-577-3015.. 398 L
ken.ogawa@bucknell.edu
OGAWA, Michael .... 419-372-0433.. 364 E
mogawa@bgsu.edu
OGAWA, Michael, Y .... 419-372-0433.. 364 E
mogawa@bgsu.edu
OGAWA, Timothy .... 617-262-5000.. 216 A
tim.ogawa@the-bac.edu
OGBAA, Clara .... 203-285-2058.... 86 C
cogbaa@gwcc.commnet.edu
OGBURN, Joyce, L .... 828-262-2000.. 356 B
ogburnjl@appstate.edu
OGBURN, Tamiko .... 313-927-1705.. 237 E
togburn@marygrove.edu
OGDEN, Bernie .... 559-278-2182.... 32 F
bogden@csufresno.edu
OGDEN, Denise .... 912-921-2900.... 93 F
OGDEN, Ervin .... 912-358-4350.. 126 F
ogdene@savannahstate.edu
OGDEN, Kristen .... 434-832-7016.. 496 G
ogdenk@cvcc.vccs.edu
OGDEN, Matt .... 414-847-3223.. 518 D
mattogden@miad.edu
OGDEN, Paul, E .... 979-436-0226.. 468 B
peogden78@tamu.edu
OGDEN, Rachel .... 814-860-5118.. 407 D
rogden@lecom.edu
OGDEN, Thomas, A .... 412-268-2328.. 400 D
togden@andrew.cmu.edu
OGEA, Reggie, R .... 504-282-4455.. 198 H
rogea@nobts.edu
OGEKA, Alex .... 610-683-4110.. 415 C
ogeka@kutztownufoundation.org
OGENE, Chidi .... 704-971-8515.. 343 E
cogene@charlottelaw.edu
OGG, E. Jerald .... 731-881-7010.. 448 G
jogg@utm.edu
OGG, Laurie .... 707-664-2036.... 35 D
laurie.ogg@sonoma.edu
OGLE, Christophor, M ..... 920-748-8111.. 519 E
oglec@ripon.edu
OGLE, Edward .... 201-559-6096.. 291 K
oglee@felician.edu
OGLE, Josh .... 541-956-7040.. 394 J
jogle@roguecc.edu
OGLE, Kaci .... 256-782-5405...... 4 H
kogle@jsu.edu
OGLES, Benjamin, M .... 801-422-2084.. 480 C
ben_ogles@byu.edu
OGLESBY, John .... 912-478-5629.. 122 B
joglesby@georgiasouthern.edu
OGLESBY, Joni .... 321-674-8700.. 100 M
joglesby@fit.edu
OGLESBY, Leisa .... 318-675-7629.. 198 B
logles@lsuhsc.edu
OGLESBY, Lindsay .... 888-384-0849.... 25 P
loglesby@allied.edu
OGONJI, Gilbert .... 410-951-4124.. 212 E
gogonji@coppin.edu
OGOREK, Richard, W ...... 813-253-6214.. 114 M
rogorek@ut.edu
OGREN, Kathy .... 909-748-8072.... 71 K
kathy_ogren@redlands.edu
OGRODNIK, Eugene, C ... 412-362-8500.. 417 C
pims5808@aol.com
OGRODNIK, Ryan .... 740-266-9656.. 368 D
rogrodnik@egcc.edu
OGULLUKIAN, Tania .... 212-924-5900.. 336 I
togullukian@swedishinstitute.edu
OGUNMAKIN, Dolapo .... 202-806-2864.... 93 A
dogunmakin@howard.edu
OGUNNAIKE,
Babatunde, A .... 302-831-8668.... 91 F
ogunnaik@udel.edu
OGUNSOLA, Elizabeth ..... 262-472-5669.. 521 F
ogunsole@uww.edu
OH, Haemoon .... 803-777-4290.. 433 F
oh@sc.edu
OH, Janet, S .... 818-677-3277.... 34 A
janetoh@csun.edu
OH, Jinny .... 323-563-4922.... 37 G
jinnyoh@cdrewu.edu
OH, Joha .... 213-381-0081.... 47 C
ojo@irus.com
OH, Judy .... 213-413-9500.... 66 B
president@scusoma.edu
OH, Myeong, H .... 636-327-4645.. 268 C
mhoh@midwest.edu
OHANESSIAN, Dawn .... 540-828-5685.. 487 H
dohaness@bridgewater.edu
OHL, Vicki .... 419-448-2216.. 369 G
vohl@heidelberg.edu
OHLANDT, George, W ..... 843-792-3281.. 431 A
ohlandtg@musc.edu
OHLEMACHER, Jan .... 410-386-8195.. 206 I
johlemacher@carrollcc.edu
OHLENDORF, Patricia, A . 512-471-1241.. 476 B
pohlendorf@austin.utexas.edu
OHLES, Frederik .... 402-465-2217.. 281 K
president@nebrwesleyan.edu
OHLES, Janet .... 610-861-1540.. 411 B
ohlesj@moravian.edu
OHLHOUS, Paula .... 518-381-1304.. 330 B
ohlhoup@sunysccc.edu
OHLMANN, Eric, H .... 904-264-2172.. 107 N
eohlmann@iws.edu
OHLSON, Vicky .... 334-347-2623...... 3 H
vohlson@escc.edu
OHMAN, Jessica .... 316-322-3231.. 179 E
johman@butlercc.edu
OHMAN, Paul .... 850-478-8496.. 106 G
pohman@pcci.edu
OHMER, Todd .... 734-487-4190.. 233 J
tohmer@emich.edu
OHOTNICKY, John .... 413-572-8971.. 222 E
johotnicky@westfield.ma.edu
OHOTNICKY, Julianne ..... 413-585-4940.. 228 D
johotnic@smith.edu
OIE, Svein .... 706-542-1914.. 128 E
soie@uga.edu
OIKELOME, Gloria .... 610-372-4721.. 417 G
goikelome@racc.edu
OISHI, Elaine .... 808-735-4728.. 130 F
eoishi@chaminade.edu
OJA, Christina .... 714-895-8101.... 39 F
coja@gwc.cccd.edu
OJAKIAN, Mark, E .... 860-723-0011.... 85 E
ojakainm@ct.edu
OJEDA, Daniel .... 415-338-2998.... 35 B
dojeda@sfsu.edu
OJEDA, Jessica .... 787-786-3030.. 536 F
jojeda@ucb.edu.pr
OJEDA, Jorge .... 626-568-8850.... 48 B
OJEDA FERNÁNDEZ,
Keila .... 787-884-3838.. 530 G
consejeria@atenascollege.edu
OJEISEKHOBA, John, O .. 562-903-4877.... 28 E
john.o.ojeisekhoba@biola.edu
OJETAYO, Abena .... 850-599-8231.. 110 J
abena.ojetayo@famu.edu
OJEZUA, Teresa .... 501-370-5306.... 21 G
tojezua@philander.edu
OJIBWAY, Michael .... 651-846-1722.. 252 C
michael.ojibway@saintpaul.edu
OJIKUTU, Kunle .... 360-650-2926.. 509 E
kunle.ojikutu@wwu.edu
OKADA, Daniel, T .... 671-735-5545.. 529 G
daniel.okada1@guamcc.edu
OKADA, David, S .... 671-735-2902.. 530 B
dsokada@triton.uog.edu
OKADA, Mary, Y .... 671-735-5700.. 529 G
gccpresident@guamcc.edu
OKAGAKI, Lynn .... 302-831-2147.... 91 F
okagaki@udel.edu
OKAMOTO, Mark, P .... 678-225-7340.. 416 F
mokamoto@pcom.edu
OKAMOTO LANE, Susan . 206-281-2598.. 507 C
solane@spu.edu
OKAMOTO-VAUGHN,
Wilma .... 209-478-0800.... 46 H
wvaughn@humphreys.edu
OKATY, George, J .... 757-822-1199.. 498 H
gokaty@tcc.edu
OKAY, Kathleen .... 973-300-2257.. 297 D
kokay@sussex.edu
OKEKE, Charles .... 702-651-7425.. 284 H
charles.okeke@csn.edu
OKERE, Erica .... 859-371-9393.. 186 M
OKEREKE, Augustine .... 718-270-5010.. 309 B
augokereke@mec.cuny.edu
OKESSON, Gregg .... 859-858-2261.. 186 I
OKESSON, Scott .... 630-752-7091.. 158 C
scott.okesson@wheaton.edu
OKINAGA, Carrie, K .... 808-956-2211.. 131 D
carrieok@hawaii.edu
OKKER, Patricia .... 573-882-6597.. 273 E
okkerp@missouri.edu
OKONKWO, Zephyrinus .. 229-430-1833.. 115 K
zephyrinus.oknkowo@asurams.edu
OKORONKWO,
Josephine .... 504-286-5361.. 199 I
jokoronkwo@suno.edu
OKOTIEURO, Gbubemi .... 212-986-4343.. 305 B
gbubemi-okotieur@berkeleycollege.edu
OKOTIEURO, Gbubemi .... 212-986-4343.. 289 F
gbubemi-okotieur@berkeleycollege.edu
OKUDA, Alex, H .... 949-480-4159.... 64 J
aokuda@soka.edu
OKUMA, Elizabeth, M ...... 330-569-5950.. 369 J
okumaem@hiram.edu
OKUMURA, Kelli .... 808-932-7614.. 131 E
ksugiyam@hawaii.edu
OKUN, Gail .... 973-278-5400.. 289 F
gso@berkeleycollege.edu
OKUN, Logan, L .... 252-222-6141.. 348 B
okunl@carteret.edu
OKWONNA, Alexander .... 281-922-3466.. 465 B
alexander.okwonna@sjcd.edu
OLADIPUPO, Adebisi .... 443-885-4431.. 209 F
adebisi.oladipup@morgan.edu
OLAN, David .... 212-817-7200.. 308 A
dolan@gc.cuny.edu
OLANDER, Renee, E .... 757-363-4108.. 492 G
rolander@odu.edu
OLATIDOYE,
Olugbemiga, O .... 404-880-6136.. 118 K
oolatidoye@cau.edu
OLATUNJI, Aderonke .... 925-473-7341.... 41 J
aolatunji@losmedanos.edu
OLAVE, Ricardo .... 312-777-8680.. 142 G
rolave@aii.edu
OLBERT, Doug .... 602-429-4971.... 16 E
dolbert@ps.edu
OLBRYSH, Marie .... 630-889-6723.. 149 G
molbrysh@nuhs.edu
OLCESE, Chuck .... 785-864-3617.. 185 D
colcese@ku.edu
OLCOTT, Sarah .... 507-453-2516.. 252 G
solcott@winona.edu
OLD BEAR, Te-Atta .... 406-638-3106.. 276 G
oldbeart@lbhc.edu
OLD COYOTE, Shaleen .... 406-638-3148.. 276 G
oldcoyotes@lbhc.edu
OLD CROW, William .... 406-638-3185.. 276 G
oldcrowb@lbhc.edu
OLDARCE, Cody .... 919-761-2285.. 355 I
registrar@sebts.edu
OLDENKAMP, Mike .... 712-324-5061.. 175 G
mikeo@nwicc.edu
OLDFIELD, Curt .... 309-649-6200.. 155 G
curt.oldfield@src.edu
OLDFIELD, Melody, K ..... 541-737-3871.. 393 H
university.marketing@oregonstate.edu
OLDHAM, Betty, A .... 208-496-1112.. 132 J
oldhamb@byui.edu
OLDHAM, Deborah .... 601-484-8636.. 258 F
doldham@meridiancc.edu
OLDHAM, Philip, B .... 931-372-3241.. 445 B
poldham@tntech.edu
OLDHAM, Robin .... 502-863-8031.. 188 I
robin_oldham@georgetowncollege.edu
OLDHAM, Todd, M .... 585-292-3057.. 321 J
toldham@monroecc.edu
OLDS, Carole .... 719-502-3249.... 82 B
carole.olds@ppcc.edu
OLDS, Scott .... 559-244-5957.... 67 A
scott.olds@scccd.edu
OLEGERIIL, Jay .... 680-488-2471.. 530 E
jayo@palau.edu
OLEJNICZAK, Sarah .... 414-930-3372.. 518 F
olejnics@mtmary.edu
OLEJNICZAK-CAUSHAJ,
Joanna .... 248-706-5363.. 241 F
jolejniczak@sscms.edu
OLEN, Simcha .... 718-252-6333.. 341 E
OLENIK-DORMAN, Lisa ... 334-833-4465...... 4 D
ldorman@hawks.huntingdon.edu
OLENS, Sam .... 470-578-6033.. 123 J
OLER, Gregory, S .... 302-831-8913.... 91 F
gregoler@udel.edu
OLES, Brian, M .... 508-565-1914.. 228 F
boles@stonehill.edu
OLESKA, Carla .... 413-265-2496.. 217 D
oleskac@elms.edu
OLESNAVAGE, John .... 414-425-8300.. 519 F
jolesnavage@shsst.edu
OLESON, Misty .... 918-781-7225.. 382 D
olesonm@bacone.edu
OLGUIN, Javier, E .... 972-860-5306.. 456 D
javiereolguin@dcccd.edu
OLGUIN-RYAN, Elizabeth 915-831-6325.. 457 H
eolguin@epcc.edu
OLIAN, Judy, D .... 310-825-7982.... 69 D
judy.olian@anderson.ucla.edu
OLIKONG, Deikola .... 680-488-2471.. 530 E
olikongd@gmail.com
OLIKONG, Deikola .... 680-488-2470.. 530 E
olikongd@gmail.com
OLIN, Jessica .... 302-736-2455.... 91 G
jessica.olin@wesley.edu
OLIN, Joanna .... 413-559-5521.. 219 C
OLIN, Robert, F .... 205-348-5972...... 8 D
olin@as.ua.edu
OLING-SISAY, Mary .... 415-955-2100.... 25 J
moling-sisay@alliant.edu
OLINGER, CSC, Gerard, J 503-943-7397.. 396 B
olinger@up.edu
OLINGER, Richard, P ...... 814-868-7767.. 407 D
rpolinger@mch1.org
OLINGER, Ronald, J .... 913-360-7413.. 178 I
rolinger@benedictine.edu
OLIPHINT, Melody .... 806-743-7382.. 472 D
melody.oliphint@ttuhsc.edu
OLIVA, Giacomo .... 212-217-4040.. 314 B
giacomo_oliva@fitnyc.edu
OLIVA, Joseph, E .... 718-990-6421.. 328 F
olivaj@stjohns.edu
OLIVA, Julia .... 718-289-5100.. 307 C
julia.oliva@bcc.cuny.edu
OLIVA, Mary .... 312-329-4112.. 148 F
mary.oliva@moody.edu
OLIVARES, Carlos, J .... 787-279-1912.. 533 J
colivares@bayamon.inter.edu
OLIVARES, Jose .... 201-360-4131.. 292 B
jolivares@hccc.edu
OLIVAREZ, Juan .... 616-632-2880.. 231 A
edisomon@aquinas.edu
OLIVAS, Isabel .... 713-692-0077.. 455 H

ONYEAGHALA, Raphael ... 507-537-6218.. 252 E
raphael.onyeaghala@smsu.edu
OOMS, Rhonda .... 907-786-1389.... 10 E
rhonda.ooms@alaska.edu
OORDT, Stan .... 712-722-6401.. 171 J
stan.oordt@dordt.edu
OPARAH, Chinyere .... 510-430-2096.... 52 J
jcoparah@mills.edu
OPAT, Misty .... 815-921-3807.. 152 E
m.opat@rockvalleycollege.edu
OPATZ, Patrick .... 651-779-3368.. 249 A
patrick.opatz@century.edu
OPAVA, William .... 617-731-7143.. 227 D
wopava@pmc.edu
OPDYCKE, Anita .... 312-567-7553.. 142 I
aopdycke@iit.edu
OPEL, Kathleen .... 574-631-9525.. 168 B
kopel@nd.edu
OPELKA, Frank .... 504-568-4769.. 197 H
fopelka@lsuhsc.edu
OPEM, Lisa .... 763-657-2401.. 249 D
lisa.opem@hennepintech.edu
OPHEIM, Cynthia, L .... 512-245-2205.. 471 F
co01@txstate.edu
OPITZ, Brian, R .... 724-287-8711.. 399 B
brian.opitz@bc3.edu
OPITZ, Donald .... 717-766-2511.. 410 J
dopitz@messiah.edu
OPP, Mike .... 651-423-8319.. 249 B
mike.opp@dctc.edu
OPP, Susan .... 707-654-1040.... 33 D
sopp@csum.edu
OPPENHEIMER, Ginette ... 787-620-2040.. 530 F
goppenheimer@aupr.edu
OPPENHEIMER, Martin ... 212-678-8804.. 317 I
maoppenheimer@jtsa.edu
OPPENHEIMER,
Phillip, R .... 209-946-2561.... 71 C
poppenhe@pacific.edu
OPPERMAN, John .... 806-742-0012.. 472 A
OPPERMAN, John .... 806-742-2121.. 472 C
john.opperman@ttu.edu
OPPERMAN,
Mary George, G .... 607-255-3621.. 312 A
mgo5@cornell.edu
OPPERMAN, Scott, R ...... 260-399-7700.. 168 D
sopperman@sf.edu
OPPERMANN, James .... 414-382-6120.. 515 D
jim.oppermann@alverno.edu
OPPMANN, Andrew .... 615-494-7800.. 444 G
andrew.oppmann@mtsu.edu
OPUNI, Kwame .... 713-223-7965.. 474 B
opunik@uhd.edu
OQUENDO, Carmen .... 787-250-1912.. 534 B
coquendo@metro.inter.edu
OQUENDO, Diane .... 646-660-6154.. 307 A
diane.oquendo@baruch.cuny.edu
OQUENDO, Migdalia .... 787-728-1515.. 539 B
moquendo@sagrado.edu
OQUENDO, Regina .... 787-894-2828.. 539 A
regina.oquendo@upr.edu
ORACION, Donna .... 575-624-7403.. 299 J
donna.oracion@roswell.enmu.edu
ORAMA, Carmen .... 787-850-9347.. 538 B
carmen.orama1@upr.edu
ORANGE, Taur, D .... 212-217-4170.. 314 B
taur_orange@fitnyc.edu
ORANSKY, Elissa .... 949-451-5472.... 65 F
eoransky@ivc.edu
ORANTE, Newin .... 925-969-2005.... 41 I
norante@dvc.edu
ORAVECZ, Joseph .... 406-657-2307.. 277 D
joe.oravecz@msubillings.edu
ORAVETZ, Teresa .... 203-332-5014.... 86 D
toravetz@hcc.commnet.edu
ORAVETZ, Teresa .... 203-332-5081.... 86 D
toravetz@hcc.commnet.edu
ORBAN, Joseph .... 318-670-9360.. 199 J
jorban@susla.edu
ORBE, Michelle .... 203-596-4516.... 88 F
morbe@post.edu
ORBINATI, Albert .... 518-292-1774.. 327 H
orbina@sage.edu
ORBITS, Elizabeth .... 734-677-5003.. 242 G
eorbits@wccnet.edu
ORCHARD, James, P .... 651-641-8705.. 246 B
orchard@csp.edu
ORCHARD, Sue .... 360-442-2301.. 504 G
sorchard@lowercolumbia.edu
ORCUTT, Jill .... 209-228-4785.... 70 A
jorcutt2@ucmerced.edu
ORCUTT, Jo-Ann .... 570-961-7873.. 407 B
orcuttj@lackawanna.edu
ORD, Kent, J .... 406-683-7301.. 277 A
kent.ord@umwestern.edu
ORDERS, Brenda .... 910-642-7141.. 353 C
brenda.orders@sccnc.edu
ORDONEZ-CAMPOS,
Christina .... 713-313-7197.. 470 D
aida.ordonez@tsu.edu
ORDOYNE, Charles, R ..... 985-448-4420.. 201 A
charles.ordoyne@nicholls.edu
ORDUNA, Aubray .... 402-552-3100.. 279 D
ORDUNA, Aubray, D .... 402-552-6118.. 279 D
orduna@clarksoncollege.edu
ORE, Dave .... 410-287-1947.. 206 J
dore@cecil.edu
ORE, Dwayne .... 305-222-2822.... 99 S
dore@careercollege.edu
OREDEIN, Adetokunbo .... 605-455-6044.. 436 G
aoredein@olc.edu
OREIRO, David .... 360-676-2772.. 505 C
doreiro@nwic.edu
ORELLANA, Darcy .... 978-656-3558.. 224 A
orellanad@middlesex.mass.edu
ORELLANA, Victoria .... 201-360-4121.. 292 B
vorellana@hccc.edu
OREM, Chris .... 540-863-2912.. 496 H
corem@dslcc.edu
OREN, Kim .... 989-386-6622.. 238 B
koren@midmich.edu
ORENDORFF, Jay .... 415-338-2862.... 35 B
jayo@sfsu.edu
ORENDORFF, Jay .... 415-338-2867.... 35 B
jayo@sfsu.edu
ORENDUFF, Lai, K .... 229-333-5950.. 129 G
lorenduff@valdosta.edu
ORENGO, Moises .... 787-276-0226.. 537 H
moises.orengo@upr.edu
ORENGO-AVILES, Moises 787-257-0000.. 537 D
moises.orengo@upr.edu
ORENGO-ORTEGA,
Orlando .... 787-993-0000.. 537 G
orlando.orengo@upr.edu
ORENSTEIN, David .... 718-270-4883.. 309 B
dorenstein@mec.cuny.edu
ORF, Michael .... 417-255-7272.. 269 A
michaelorf@missouristate.edu
ORFALI, Aline .... 703-526-6922.. 492 A
aline.orfali@marymount.edu
ORGAN, Regina .... 903-463-8714.. 458 H
organr@grayson.edu
ORGERON, Elizabeth .... 518-255-5842.. 334 D
orgeroed@cobleskill.edu
ORIAS, David .... 510-659-6105.... 55 B
dorias@ohlone.edu
ORICK, Ron .... 479-788-7019.... 23 A
ron.orick@uafs.edu
ORIDE, Leighton .... 808-245-8226.. 132 B
loride@hawaii.edu
ORIHUELA, Omar .... 619-482-6360.... 66 E
oorihuela@swccd.edu
ORIHUELA, Ruthanne ...... 303-556-3850.... 79 F
ruthanne.orihuela@ccd.edu
ORIO, Julie, J .... 415-422-2823.... 72 C
orioj@usfca.edu
ORIOLO, Michael .... 315-866-0300.. 316 A
orioloma@herkimer.edu
ORIS, James, T .... 513-529-3734.. 372 K
orisjt@miamioh.edu
ORITZ, Fernando .... 509-313-4054.. 504 A
oritz2@gonzaga.edu
ORKIN, Michael .... 510-466-7308.... 57 E
morkin@peralta.edu
ORKIN, Mike .... 510-466-7308.... 57 B
morkin@peralta.edu
ORLANDO, Clara .... 978-934-3567.. 221 A
clara_orlando@uml.edu
ORLANDO, Donald, A ..... 724-805-2010.. 419 A
don.orlando@stvincent.edu
ORLANDO, Matthew .... 207-725-3804.. 202 F
morlando@bowdoin.edu
ORLANDO, Michael .... 517-264-7601.. 241 A
morlando@sienaheights.edu
ORLANDO, Stephen, F .... 352-392-0186.. 112 A
sfo@ufl.edu
ORLAUSKI, Brian .... 951-639-5080.... 53 D
borlausk@msjc.edu
ORLOFF, Micah .... 951-639-5440.... 53 D
morloff@msjc.edu
ORLOWSKI, Martin, A ..... 248-232-4175.. 239 E
maorlows@oaklandcc.edu
ORLUCK, Gary .... 701-858-4016.. 360 F
gary.orluck@minotstateu.edu
ORME, James .... 517-321-0242.. 235 C
jorme@glcc.edu
ORME, Michael, R .... 801-422-3080.. 480 C
mike_orme@byu.edu
ORMEROD, Michelle .... 617-879-2270.. 229 G
mormerod@wheelock.edu
ORMISTON, Gayle, L .... 304-696-3716.. 513 D
ormiston@marshall.edu
ORMOND, Tom .... 706-864-1602.. 128 F
tom.ormond@ung.edu
ORMSBEE, Christine .... 405-744-1000.. 385 G
ormsbee@okstate.edu
ORMSBEE, David .... 937-722-9292.. 380 E
david.ormsbee@urbana.edu
ORMSBEE, David .... 937-484-1297.. 380 E
david.ormsbee@urbana.edu
ORMSBY, Colin .... 509-359-4217.. 503 D
cormsby@ewu.edu
ORNDORFF, Cathy .... 304-293-5305.. 514 C
cathy.orndorff@mail.wvu.edu
ORNDORFF, Robert, M .... 814-865-2377.. 412 F
rmo104@psu.edu
ORNE, Tracy .... 217-641-4106.. 143 H
torne@jwcc.edu
ORNELAS, Daniel .... 323-265-8751.... 49 G
ornelad@elac.edu
ORNELAS, Lynne .... 619-388-7392.... 60 H
lornelas@sdccd.edu
ORNELAS, Nohemy .... 805-735-6966.... 25 I
nornelas@hancockcollege.edu
ORNER, Lita, J .... 240-500-2000.. 207 I
ljorner@hagerstowncc.edu
ORNER, Randell .... 970-410-0456.... 85 B
ORNT, Bill .... 312-567-5104.. 142 I
ornt@iit.edu
ORNT, Daniel, B .... 585-475-4861.. 327 E
dboihst@rit.edu
OROK, Michael .... 804-257-5727.. 500 B
meorok@vuu.edu
ORONA, Frank .... 505-747-2111.. 301 F
forona@nnmc.edu
ORONA, Frank .... 505-747-2161.. 301 F
forona@nnmc.edu
ORONA, John .... 210-486-2510.. 450 E
jorona3@alamo.edu
OROZCO, Daniel .... 512-863-1346.. 466 G
orozcod@southwestern.edu
OROZCO, Lisa .... 843-863-8054.. 427 I
lorozco@csuniv.edu
OROZCO, Monica .... 505-277-2215.. 302 F
orozcom@unm.edu
ORR, Brenda, B .... 601-643-5101.. 257 D
brenda.orr@colin.edu
ORR, Deb .... 312-281-3145.. 152 H
dorr@roosevelt.edu
ORR, Debra .... 617-521-2180.. 228 C
debra.orr@simmons.edu
ORR, Ethan, R .... 520-621-0906.... 17 I
eorr@email.arizona.edu
ORR, Herb .... 785-242-5200.. 183 M
herb.orr@ottawa.edu
ORR, Jim .... 325-674-2659.. 449 J
jmo10a@acu.edu
ORR, Mark, C .... 925-631-4399.... 59 I
morr@stmarys-ca.edu
ORR, Michael .... 847-735-5021.. 145 B
morr@lakeforest.edu
ORR, Pattie .... 254-710-3200.. 452 H
pattie_orr@baylor.edu
ORR, Ray .... 253-535-7380.. 505 G
fama@plu.edu
ORR, Richard .... 860-486-5796.... 89 D
richard.orr@uconn.edu
ORR, Robert .... 478-445-1196.. 121 A
robert.orr@gcsu.edu
ORR, Robert, C .... 301-405-6355.. 211 E
rorr1@umd.edu
ORR, Shaun .... 208-496-9340.. 132 J
orrs@byui.edu
ORR, Stephanie, W .... 850-263-3261.... 96 C
sworr@baptistcollege.edu
ORR, Susan, L .... 603-513-1307.. 288 D
susan.orr@granite.edu
ORR, Sylvia .... 480-732-7014.... 13 O
sylvia.orr@cgc.edu
ORR, Sylvia .... 623-935-8413.... 14 A
sylvia.orr@estrellamountain.edu
ORR, Trina .... 828-227-7290.. 359 A
torr@wcu.edu
ORR, Wayne .... 859-985-3828.. 187 B
orrw@berea.edu
ORRILL, Landon .... 972-825-4636.. 466 D
lorrill@sagu.edu
ORRIS, Erika .... 301-985-7435.. 212 C
erika.orris@umuc.edu
ORRIS, Keith, A .... 215-571-4463.. 402 G
keith.a.orris@drexel.edu
ORRISON, Russell .... 423-236-2336.. 444 B
rorrison@southern.edu
ORSCHELN, Paul .... 816-271-3835.. 269 C
porscheln@missouriwestern.edu
ORSHANSKY, Mariya .... 510-628-8010.... 49 A
morshansky@lincolnuca.edu
ORSINI, Jamie .... 312-915-6424.. 146 G
jorsini@luc.edu
ORSINI, Jori .... 773-602-5333.. 137 F
jorsini@ccc.edu
ORSINI, SPHR, Teri .... 704-337-2297.. 355 A
orsinit@queens.edu
ORT, Shirley, A .... 919-962-2315.. 357 D
ort@email.unc.edu
ORTA, Edna .... 787-743-7979.. 536 A
ut_eorta@suagm.edu
ORTALE, Lynn .... 215-248-7030.. 400 H
ortalel@chc.edu
ORTALO-MAGNE',
Francois .... 608-262-7867.. 519 K
fom@bus.wisc.edu
ORTBERG, Jennifer, L ..... 714-895-8965.... 39 F
jortberg@gwc.cccd.edu
ORTEGA, Bonnie .... 719-589-7131.... 83 G
bonnie.ortega@trinidadstate.edu
ORTEGA, Carmen .... 787-257-7373.. 535 P
ue_cortega@suagm.edu
ORTEGA, David .... 210-486-1227.. 450 F
dortega@alamo.edu
ORTEGA, J. Martin .... 210-486-0721.. 450 F
jortega@alamo.edu
ORTEGA, Janet .... 602-243-8287.... 14 I
janet.ortega@southmountaincc.edu
ORTEGA, Noemi .... 909-447-2545.... 39 A
nortega@cst.edu
ORTEGA, Richard .... 210-784-1000.. 469 B
richard.ortega@tamusa.edu
ORTEGA, Vanessa .... 562-977-6020.... 44 D
vanessa.ortega@fremont.edu
ORTEGO, Carla .... 337-521-8922.. 197 A
carla.ortego@solacc.edu
ORTEGON, Beth .... 502-863-8034.. 188 I
beth_purdy@georgetowncollege.edu
ORTELLI, Tracy .... 502-410-6200.. 188 H
tortelli@galencollege.edu
ORTH, Linda .... 423-425-4669.. 448 F
linda-orth@utc.edu
ORTIKOV, Khudoyor, S .... 832-230-5555.. 462 K
khudoyor@na.edu
ORTIZ, Amy .... 505-747-2224.. 301 F
amyortiz@nnmc.edu
ORTIZ, Ann .... 910-893-1669.. 342 F
ortiz@campbell.edu
ORTIZ, Anthony .... 575-835-5424.. 300 G
tortiz@admin.nmt.edu
ORTIZ, Ariel .... 787-766-1717.. 536 B
um_aortiz@suagm.edu
ORTIZ, Arthur .... 713-525-3848.. 475 J
ortiza@stthom.edu
ORTIZ, Carlos .... 787-758-2525.. 538 D
carlos.ortiz33@upr.edu
ORTIZ, Carmen .... 787-257-0000.. 537 H
carmen.ortiz11@upr.edu
ORTIZ, Cruz .... 787-850-8380.. 538 B
museo.casaroig@upr.edu
ORTIZ, Daniel .... 617-287-5910.. 220 G
daniel.ortiz@umb.edu
ORTIZ, Edna .... 787-786-3030.. 536 F
eortiz@ucb.edu.pr
ORTIZ, Eduardo .... 787-250-1912.. 534 B
ehortiz@metro.inter.edu
ORTIZ, Eickel .... 212-616-7245.. 315 G
eickel.ortiz@helenefuld.edu
ORTIZ, Elizabeth, F .... 312-362-8588.. 139 C
eortiz4@depaul.edu
ORTIZ, Elvin, J .... 787-857-3600.. 533 I
ejortiz@br.inter.edu
ORTIZ, Francisco .... 787-761-0640.. 537 C
presidente@utcpr.edu
ORTIZ, Francisco .... 860-297-2054.... 89 B
francisco.ortiz@trincoll.edu
ORTIZ, Hilda, L .... 787-863-2390.. 533 K
hilda.ortiz@fajardo.inter.edu
ORTIZ, Jaime .... 713-743-7310.. 473 F
jortiz22@uh.edu
ORTIZ, John .... 856-415-2198.. 295 D
jortiz@rcgc.edu
ORTIZ, Juanita .... 405-733-7413.. 387 I
jrortiz@rose.edu
ORTIZ, Judy .... 714-449-7470.... 51 F
jortiz@ketchum.edu
ORTIZ, Kevin .... 910-221-2224.. 344 F
kortiz@gcd.edu
ORTIZ, Kristina .... 212-752-1530.. 318 F
kristina.ortiz@limcollege.edu
ORTIZ, Laura .... 630-466-7900.. 157 K
lortiz@waubonsee.edu
ORTIZ, Lillian, M .... 508-854-4232.. 224 E
lmortiz@qcc.mass.edu
ORTIZ, Luz .... 787-864-2222.. 534 A
luz.ortiz@guayama.inter.edu
ORTIZ, Luz, M .... 787-832-6000.. 532 O
mortiz@icprjc.edu
ORTIZ, Maribel .... 787-758-2525.. 538 D
maribel.ortiz5@upr.edu
ORTIZ, Mariely .... 787-815-0000.. 537 F
mariely.ortiz@upr.edu
ORTIZ, Mario .... 607-777-2311.. 331 B
mortiz@binghamton.edu
ORTIZ, Maritza .... 787-264-1912.. 534 D
maritza_ortiz_figueroa@intersg.edu
ORTIZ, Mary Lou .... 848-932-1990.. 296 B
marylou.ortiz@oldqueens.rutgers.edu
ORTIZ, María, C .... 787-766-1717.. 536 B
um_mortiz@suagm.edu
ORTIZ, Mati .... 716-286-8504.. 324 E
mortiz@niagara.edu
ORTIZ, Migdalia .... 787-279-1912.. 533 J
morti@bayamon.inter.edu

OUTLEY, Patrice ... 318-274-2288.. 200 F
outleyp@gram.edu
OUTON, Peggy, M ... 412-397-6000.. 418 B
outon@rmu.edu
OUTTEN, Donavan ... 314-246-6907.. 275 B
doutten@webster.edu
OVADIA, Zak ... 904-620-2016.. 112 B
zovadia@unf.edu
OVEDIA, Nicole, R ... 561-237-7237.. 104 O
novedia@lynn.edu
OVEL, Susan ... 319-398-5409.. 174 I
susan.ovel@kirkwood.edu
OVEN, Clare ... 858-653-6740.... 47 G
coven@jpcatholic.com
OVER, Lucinda ... 626-914-8538.... 38 D
lover@citruscollege.edu
OVERBY, David, B ... 605-256-5675.. 437 C
david.overby@dsu.edu
OVEREND, Gregory ... 203-932-7430.... 90 A
goverend@newhaven.edu
OVEREND, Wendy ... 425-278-9308.... 63 H
woverend@saybrook.edu
OVERFIELD, Denise ... 678-839-4759.. 129 E
doverfie@westga.edu
OVERLAND, Wanda ... 320-308-3111.. 252 A
wioverland@stcloudstate.edu
OVERMAN, Jodi ... 616-526-8915.. 232 A
jro24@calvin.edu
OVEROCKER, Josh ... 405-974-2709.. 388 L
joverocker@uco.edu
OVEROCKER, Quintin, M . 815-224-0437.. 143 C
quintin_overocker@ivcc.edu
OVERSHOWN, Jovan ... 818-722-1635.. 460 E
jovan.overshown@tku.edu
OVERSTREET, Al, W ... 540-985-8205.. 491 A
awoverstreet@jchs.edu
OVERSTREET, Darryl ... 580-559-5582.. 383 H
doverstt@ecok.edu
OVERSTREET, Mana ... 615-732-7893.. 442 G
m.overstreet@mtsa.edu
OVERTON, Chrystal ... 580-477-7831.. 389 I
chrystal.overton@wosc.edu
OVERTON, James ... 617-287-5800.. 220 G
james.overton@umb.edu
OVERTON, Lindi ... 573-876-7105.. 272 I
loverton@stephens.edu
OVERTON, Melanie, B ... 785-833-4336.. 182 F
melanie.overton@kwu.edu
OVERTON, Milton ... 850-599-3868.. 110 J
milton.overton@famu.edu
OVERTON, Reginald ... 412-788-7500.. 401 B
roverton@ccac.edu
OVERTON, Robert, A ... 864-488-4543.. 430 H
roverton@limestone.edu
OVERTON, Travis, E ... 843-349-4161.. 428 E
toverton@coastal.edu
OVERTON-HEALY, Julia ... 518-564-2071.. 334 A
jover004@plattsburgh.edu
OVERTURF, Kathy ... 318-487-7301.. 195 F
kathy.overturf@lacollege.edu
OVERTURF, Kellie ... 970-332-5755.... 81 H
kellie.overturf@morgancc.edu
OVERVOORDE, Paul ... 651-696-6581.. 247 I
overvoorde@macalester.edu
OVESON, Kip, R ... 320-222-6930.. 251 G
kip.oveson@ridgewater.edu
OVIEDO, Tara ... 912-525-5000.. 126 E
tpearsal@scad.edu
OVITT, Kimberly ... 503-494-0992.. 393 F
ovitt@ohsu.edu
OVWIGHO, Godfrey ... 330-972-6542.. 378 G
cio@uakron.edu
OWAN, Edna ... 808-675-3474.. 130 E
edna.owan@byuh.edu
OWAN, Robert ... 808-675-3916.. 130 E
robert.owan@byuh.edu
OWCZARCZAK, Kathleen . 716-884-9120.. 306 B
kowczarczak@bryantstratton.edu
OWCZAREK, Scott ... 608-262-3964.. 519 K
owczarek@em.wisc.edu
OWEN, Barbara ... 207-755-5233.. 203 I
bowen@cmcc.edu
OWEN, Bonnie ... 706-771-4163.. 117 C
bowen@augustatech.edu
OWEN, David, L ... 671-734-1812.. 530 A
dowen@piu.edu
OWEN, Erin ... 402-554-2762.. 283 B
eowen@unomaha.edu
OWEN, James (Chris) ... 863-667-5146.. 109 L
jcowen@seu.edu
OWEN, Jane, S ... 724-852-3225.. 423 A
jowen@waynesburg.edu
OWEN, Janet, D ... 904-620-2500.. 112 B
jowen@unf.edu
OWEN, Jimmy ... 706-379-3111.. 130 B
jpowen@yhc.edu
OWEN, Kelli, D ... 606-783-2700.. 191 H
k.owen@moreheadstate.edu
OWEN, Ken ... 765-658-4634.. 160 F
kowen@depauw.edu
OWEN, Kyle ... 940-397-4648.. 462 A
kyle.owen@mwsu.edu
OWEN, Laurinda, A ... 574-372-5100.. 161 B
owenla@grace.edu
OWEN, Pamela ... 501-450-1358.... 20 F
owen@hendrix.edu
OWEN, Ray ... 252-246-1239.. 354 D
rowen@wilsoncc.edu
OWEN, Robert ... 408-554-4581.... 63 E
rowen@scu.edu
OWEN, Robert ... 757-352-4569.. 493 E
rowen@regent.edu
OWEN, Rose Marie ... 804-819-4902.. 496 E
rmowen@vccs.edu
OWEN, Sherry, L ... 816-995-2815.. 270 H
sherry.owen@researchcollege.edu
OWEN, William ... 402-457-2715.. 280 J
bowen@mccneb.edu
OWENBY, Judy ... 828-835-4212.. 353 G
jowenby@tricountycc.edu
OWENBY, Stephanee ... 512-492-3021.. 451 E
sowenby@aoma.edu
OWENS, Anthony ... 512-223-1127.. 451 N
aowens@austincc.edu
OWENS, Bertha ... 501-370-5215.... 21 G
bowens@philander.edu
OWENS, Bettina ... 504-568-6130.. 198 A
bowens@lsuhsc.edu
OWENS, Candace ... 405-425-5961.. 385 C
candace.owens@oc.edu
OWENS, Colleen ... 207-941-7184.. 202 I
owensc@husson.edu
OWENS, Deborah ... 607-735-1819.. 313 F
dowens@elmira.edu
OWENS, Deborah, E ... 716-829-8198.. 313 A
owensde@dyc.edu
OWENS, Don ... 254-295-4691.. 474 E
dowens@umhb.edu
OWENS, Drake ... 318-357-4250.. 201 B
owensd@nsula.edu
OWENS, Esmeralda ... 831-755-6810.... 45 L
eowens@hartnell.edu
OWENS, Glenna ... 276-244-1303.. 486 N
gowens@asl.edu
OWENS, Ilona ... 336-506-4146.. 347 C
ilona.owens@alamancecc.edu
OWENS, Irene ... 919-530-6485.. 357 A
iowens@nccu.edu
OWENS, J, F ... 540-365-4255.. 489 M
jfowens@ferrum.edu
OWENS, James ... 609-633-9658.. 297 F
jowens@tesu.edu
OWENS, James, R ... 859-858-3511.. 186 J
jim.owens@asbury.edu
OWENS, Jamie ... 513-562-8754.. 363 H
jowens@artacademy.edu
OWENS, Jeremy ... 603-577-6612.. 286 I
jowens2@dwc.edu
OWENS, Josh ... 615-844-5288.. 449 H
jowens@welch.edu
OWENS, Karna ... 801-818-8900.. 481 B
OWENS, Kate ... 570-945-8222.. 406 H
kate.owens@keystone.edu
OWENS, Kathleen, C ... 215-641-5548.. 404 G
owens.k@gmercyu.edu
OWENS, Katrina ... 317-917-7165.. 164 F
kowens16@ivytech.edu
OWENS, Kelly ... 501-812-2233.... 21 H
kowens@pulaskitech.edu
OWENS, Kimberly ... 814-768-3430.. 415 D
kowens@lhup.edu
OWENS, Kristine ... 515-643-6659.. 175 B
kowens@mercydesmoines.org
OWENS, Laura ... 310-824-1586.... 24 L
laura.owens@ajrca.org
OWENS, Lillian ... 205-853-1200...... 5 B
lowens@jeffstateonline.com
OWENS, MacKubin ... 202-462-2101.... 93 B
mowens@iwp.edu
OWENS, Mark ... 618-664-6735.. 140 I
mark.owens@greenville.edu
OWENS, Michelle ... 972-481-7402.. 453 F
OWENS, Milton ... 312-553-3213.. 137 D
mowens63@ccc.edu
OWENS, Pamela ... 414-930-3380.. 518 F
owensp@mtmary.edu
OWENS, Patricia ... 724-805-2271.. 419 A
president@stvincent.edu
OWENS, Phillip ... 931-540-2572.. 446 A
powens5@columbiastate.edu
OWENS, R. Scott ... 859-238-5457.. 187 H
scott.owens@centre.edu
OWENS, Rick ... 252-493-7442.. 352 A
rowens@email.pittcc.edu
OWENS, Robert ... 931-372-3392.. 445 B
rowens@tntech.edu
OWENS, Sami ... 318-342-1885.. 201 E
saowens@ulm.edu
OWENS, Scott, D ... 856-225-6028.. 296 A
scott.owens@rutgers.edu
OWENS, Sharon ... 404-270-5082.. 128 A
sowens5@spelman.edu
OWENS, Sheila ... 662-720-7246.. 260 B
sbowens@nemcc.edu
OWENS, Stephen, J ... 573-882-3211.. 273 D
owenssj@umsystem.edu
OWENS, Susan ... 254-295-8686.. 474 E
sowens@umhb.edu
OWENS, Tara ... 410-462-8325.. 206 D
towens@bccc.edu
OWENS, Tracey ... 732-987-2287.. 292 A
towens@georgian.edu
OWENS, Valerie ... 304-876-5465.. 513 E
vowens@shepherd.edu
OWENS, Victoria, G ... 502-597-6033.. 191 B
victoria.owens@kysu.edu
OWENS, Waylan ... 817-923-1921.. 466 E
wowens@swbts.edu
OWENS-DELONG, Dana ... 405-470-2636.. 388 B
dana.owens-delong@swcu.edu
OWENS-SOUTHHALL,
Mary, E ... 410-951-3090.. 212 E
mowens@coppin.edu
OWENSKY, Fred ... 575-527-7543.. 301 C
fowensky@nmsu.edu
OWL, Diane ... 828-835-4220.. 353 G
dowl@tricountycc.edu
OWLES, Vicky ... 573-876-7212.. 272 I
vowles@stephens.edu
OWNBEY, Rita ... 620-278-4306.. 185 A
rownbey@sterling.edu
OWOLABI, Elizabeth ... 708-209-3020.. 138 G
elizabeth.owolabi@cuchicago.edu
OWSLEY, Laura ... 502-863-8007.. 188 I
laura_owsley@georgetowncollege.edu
OWSLEY, Stacy ... 520-383-8401.... 17 E
sowsley@tocc.edu
OWSTON, James, M ... 304-457-6222.. 510 B
owstonjb@ab.edu
OWUSU-ADUEMIRI,
Kwadwo ... 850-412-7469.. 110 J
kwadwo.owusuaduemiri@famu.edu
OWUSU-ANSAH, Edward . 973-720-3179.. 298 G
owusuansahe@wpunj.edu
OWUSU-SEKYERE,
Emmanuel ... 410-951-3862.. 212 E
manny@coppin.edu
OXENDINE, Derek ... 910-521-6401.. 358 C
derek.oxendine@uncp.edu
OXENREIDER, Tom ... 828-669-8012.. 346 M
toxenreider@montreat.edu
OXFORD,
Mary-Catherine ... 559-730-3826.... 40 E
marycat@cos.edu
OXFORD, Ron ... 559-925-3403.... 74 E
ronoxford@whccd.edu
OXFORD-PICKERAL,
Misti ... 352-335-2332.... 94 F
info@acupuncturist.edu
OXHOLM, III, Carl ... 856-256-4188.. 295 E
oxholm@rowan.edu
OXLEY, Timothy ... 304-367-4303.. 513 B
timothy.oxley@fairmontstate.edu
OXLEY, Timothy ... 304-367-4303.. 513 B
tiothy.oxley@fairmontstate.edu
OXTOBY, David, W ... 909-621-8131.... 58 A
david.oxtoby@pomona.edu
OYAMA, Jannine ... 808-845-9231.. 132 A
jannine@hawaii.edu
OYEKAN, Adebayo, O ... 713-313-4341.. 470 D
oyekan_ao@tsu.edu
OYMAN, Korhan ... 321-674-8971.. 100 M
koyman@fit.edu
OYOLA, Elias ... 212-694-1000.. 305 I
eoyola@boricuacollege.edu
OYOLA, Luaida ... 787-750-4405.. 537 H
luaida.oyola@upr.edu
OZAN, Randy ... 859-858-2210.. 186 I
OZAYSIN, Gokhan ... 912-525-5000.. 126 E
gozaysin@scad.edu
OZECHOSKI, Mary-Alice .. 610-606-4666.. 400 E
mozechos@cedarcrest.edu
OZEE, Nancy ... 815-802-8842.. 144 C
nozee@kcc.edu
OZMENT, Suzanne ... 205-665-6015...... 9 B
sozment@montevallo.edu
OZOLS, Ruta ... 315-229-5908.. 329 D
rozols@stlawu.edu
OZTURGUT, Osman ... 210-829-2759.. 474 D
ozturgut@uiwtx.edu
OZTURK, Mehmet ... 559-730-3790.... 40 E
mehmeto@cos.edu
OZUG, Steve ... 508-678-2811.. 223 A
steven.ozug@bristolcc.edu
OZUROVICH, John ... 949-582-4865.... 65 G
jozurovich@saddleback.edu
O'BANION, Rebecca ... 254-295-4603.. 474 E
robanion@umhb.edu
O'BANNER/JACKSON,
Marie ... 601-979-2127.. 258 D
marie.obanner-jackson@jsums.edu
O'BANNER-JACKSON,
Marie ... 601-979-7092.. 258 D
marie.obanner-jackson@jsums.edu
O'BANNON, Maia ... 405-789-6400.. 388 A
maiaobannon@snu.edu
O'BAR, Gary ... 210-485-0102.. 450 A
gobar@alamo.edu
O'BARR, Allen, H ... 919-966-3658.. 357 D
allen_obarr@unc.edu
O'BEIRNE, Kirsten ... 610-526-5041.. 398 K
kobeirne@brynmawr.edu
O'BEIRNE, OSF,
Marguerite ... 610-558-5511.. 411 E
mobeirne@neumann.edu
O'BERRY, V. Diane ... 803-780-1142.. 434 M
doberry@voorhees.edu
O'BOYLE, Andrew ... 206-296-6149.. 507 E
oboylea@seattleu.edu
O'BOYLE, Thomas ... 631-656-2126.. 314 F
thomas.oboyle@ftc.edu
O'BREIN, Catherine ... 713-718-2383.. 459 B
catherine.obrein2@hccs.edu
O'BRIAN, Jenni ... 406-546-3585.. 276 I
jenni.obrian@montanabiblecollege.edu
O'BRIANT, Hilliary ... 662-472-9134.. 258 B
hobriant@holmescc.edu
O'BRIEN, Alyssa ... 847-543-2409.. 138 C
aobrien@clcillinois.edu
O'BRIEN, Barry ... 910-522-5707.. 358 C
michael.o'brien@uncp.edu
O'BRIEN, Brad ... 309-649-6294.. 155 G
brad.obrien@src.edu
O'BRIEN, Casey ... 518-828-4181.. 311 D
casey.obrien@sunycgcc.edu
O'BRIEN, Corey ... 312-915-7451.. 146 G
cobrien@luc.edu
O'BRIEN, Courtney ... 312-553-6063.. 137 D
cobrien4@ccc.edu
O'BRIEN, Diane ... 805-893-8182.... 70 E
diane.obrien@ucsb.edu
O'BRIEN, Diane, E ... 570-408-4734.. 423 G
diane.obrien@wilkes.edu
O'BRIEN, Eddie ... 706-865-2134.. 128 D
eobrien@truett.edu
O'BRIEN, Eileen, M ... 978-542-7529.. 222 D
eobrien@salemstate.edu
O'BRIEN, Elizabeth ... 707-664-4023.... 35 D
elizabeth.obrien@sonoma.edu
O'BRIEN, Gregory ... 888-488-4968.... 47 D
gobrien@itu.edu
O'BRIEN, Gwen ... 574-284-4595.. 167 A
gobrien@saintmarys.edu
O'BRIEN, Heather ... 212-229-8947.. 322 E
obrienh@newschool.edu
O'BRIEN, Ian ... 701-349-5774.. 362 C
ianobrien@trinitybiblecollege.edu
O'BRIEN, Irene ... 973-353-5541.. 296 C
jobrien@andromeda.rutgers.edu
O'BRIEN, J. Randall ... 865-471-3200.. 439 C
robrien@cn.edu
O'BRIEN, Jim ... 480-965-9118.... 11 H
james.obrien@asu.edu
O'BRIEN, John, F ... 617-422-7221.. 226 H
jobrien@nesl.edu
O'BRIEN, Katie ... 315-655-7348.. 306 H
kobrien@cazenovia.edu
O'BRIEN, Kelly ... 860-297-2046.... 89 B
kelly.obrien@trincoll.edu
O'BRIEN, SJ, Kevin ... 202-687-1395.... 92 E
obrienkf@georgetown.edu
O'BRIEN, SJ, Kevin ... 510-549-5040.... 63 E
kobrien@jstb.edu
O'BRIEN, Kevin, J ... 253-535-7698.. 505 G
obrien@plu.edu
O'BRIEN, Martha ... 814-472-3217.. 418 F
mobrien@francis.edu
O'BRIEN, Mary ... 707-546-4000.... 42 M
mobrien@empirecollege.com
O'BRIEN, Mary Eileen ... 845-848-7801.. 312 F
mary.eileen.obrien@dc.edu
O'BRIEN, Mary Kate ... 802-258-3494.. 485 A
marykate.obrien@sit.edu
O'BRIEN, Maryellen ... 910-272-3324.. 352 E
mo'brien@robeson.edu
O'BRIEN, Maureen ... 724-830-1075.. 419 D
obrien@setonhill.edu
O'BRIEN, Michael ... 210-784-1200.. 469 B
michael.obrien@tamusa.edu
O'BRIEN, Michael, E ... 419-530-4987.. 380 D
michael.obrien6@utoledo.edu
O'BRIEN, Patricia ... 617-358-4944.. 216 E
pobrien@bu.edu
O'BRIEN, Paul ... 772-462-7376.. 103 B
pobrien@irsc.edu
O'BRIEN, Peg ... 708-209-3528.. 138 G
margaret.obrien@cuchicago.edu
O'BRIEN, Rachel ... 214-887-5368.. 457 C
robrien@dts.edu
O'BRIEN, Shannon ... 406-243-7852.. 276 K
shannon.obrien@umontana.edu

O'NEAL, Rene, S .... 202-994-9013.... 92 D
rstewartoneal@gwu.edu
O'NEAL, Sharon .... 478-553-2056.. 125 C
soneal@oftc.edu
O'NEAL, Tom .... 407-882-1120.. 111 E
oneal@ucf.edu
O'NEAL HOWARD, Erica . 323-259-2500.... 55 A
O'NEIL, Burton .... 864-656-4337.. 428 C
boneil@clemson.edu
O'NEIL, Christine .... 906-487-7328.. 234 A
christine.oneil@finlandia.edu
O'NEIL, Laura, L .... 607-777-2131.. 331 B
loneil@binghamton.edu
O'NEIL, Sally, C .... 402-280-1830.. 279 H
sallyoneill@creighton.edu
O'NEIL, Tabitha .... 773-602-5125.. 137 F
toneil@ccc.edu
O'NEIL, Tom .... 661-722-6300.... 27 B
loneil@avc.edu
O'NEIL KNIGHT,
Alicia, M .... 202-994-2371.... 92 D
aoknight@gwu.edu
O'NEILL, Amy, A .... 610-330-5000.. 407 C
oneilla@lafayette.edu
O'NEILL, Bettyann .... 706-236-2261.. 117 F
boneill@berry.edu
O'NEILL, Bill .... 435-879-4367.. 482 A
oneillb@dixie.edu
O'NEILL, Charles .... 724-830-1144.. 419 D
oneill@setonhill.edu
O'NEILL, Cheri, E .... 765-285-8314.. 159 B
ceoneill@bsu.edu
O'NEILL, Colin .... 612-874-3858.. 247 M
co5000@gmail.com
O'NEILL, Colleen .... 480-423-6177.... 14 H
colleen.oneill@scottsdalecc.edu
O'NEILL, Daniel .... 978-762-4000.. 224 C
daoneill@northshore.edu
O'NEILL, David .... 509-434-5425.. 502 H
david.o'neill@ccs.spokane.edu
O'NEILL, David .... 509-434-5425.. 503 A
david.oneill@ccs.spokane.edu
O'NEILL, David .... 509-434-5427.. 502 I
david.oneill@ccs.spokane.edu
O'NEILL, Denise .... 609-652-4332.. 297 C
denise.oneill@stockton.edu
O'NEILL, Dianne, M .... 301-369-2800.. 206 H
dmoneill@captechu.edu
O'NEILL, Ellizabeth .... 401-232-6000.. 424 K
O'NEILL, F. Shawn .... 201-684-7550.. 294 G
soneill@ramapo.edu
O'NEILL, Gayle .... 860-215-9276.... 87 D
goneill@trcc.commnet.edu
O'NEILL, Gerry, J .... 252-246-1337.. 354 D
goneill@wilsoncc.edu
O'NEILL, Jennifer .... 603-577-6000.. 286 I
joneill@dwc.edu
O'NEILL, Jerry, F .... 412-731-6000.. 417 J
joneill@rpts.edu
O'NEILL, Joan, E .... 203-432-5461.... 90 D
joan.oneill@yale.edu
O'NEILL, Keith .... 847-925-6225.. 141 A
koneill@harpercollege.edu
O'NEILL, Meggan .... 201-559-6022.. 291 K
oneillm@felician.edu
O'NEILL, Michael .... 610-519-7926.. 422 G
mike.oneill@villanova.edu
O'NEILL, Patrick .... 303-404-5400.... 80 E
patrick.o'neill@frontrange.edu
O'NEILL, Shannon .... 518-782-5830.. 330 E
soneill@siena.edu
O'NEILL, Stephen .... 507-786-3062.. 254 P
oneill@stolaf.edu
O'NEILL, Tess .... 504-398-2744.. 200 D
toneill@olhcc.edu
O'NEILL, Thomas .... 315-228-7418.. 310 G
toneill@colgate.edu
O'NEILL, Walter .... 616-554-5827.. 233 C
woneill1@davenport.edu
O'NEILL, William .... 402-559-1952.. 283 A
woneill@unmc.edu
O'NEILL, JR., William, J . 617-573-8300.. 228 G
woneill@suffolk.edu
O'NIELL, Claudia .... 720-890-8922.... 80 O
registrar@itea.edu
O'QUINN, Doretha .... 714-556-3610.... 73 B
officeoftheprovost@vanguard.edu
O'QUINN, Michael .... 979-845-2217.. 468 B
irishmike@tamu.edu
O'QUINN, Monica .... 912-427-5840.. 119 B
moquinn@coastalpines.edu
O'QUINN, Robin .... 918-463-2931.. 383 F
robin.oquinn@connorsstate.edu
O'REAR, Randy, G .... 254-295-4500.. 474 E
rorear@umhb.edu
O'REGAN, Danny .... 808-440-4226.. 130 F
daniel.oregan@chaminade.edu
O'REGGIO, Elizabeth .... 352-395-5486.. 109 C
elizabeth.oreggio@sfcollege.edu
O'REILLY, James, D .... 213-891-2366.... 49 F
jdoreilly@email.laccd.edu
O'REILLY, Kevin, P .... 914-968-6200.. 329 C
O'REILLY, Lillian .... 718-951-5114.. 307 D
loreilly@brooklyn.cuny.edu
O'REILLY, Maureen, A .... 603-641-7084.. 287 G
moreilly@anselm.edu
O'REILLY, Paul, J .... 805-525-4417.... 67 J
poreilly@thomasaquinas.edu
O'REILLY, Sharon .... 239-280-1654.... 95 Q
sharon.oreilly@avemaria.edu
O'REILLY, Thomas .... 617-731-7101.. 227 D
toreilly@pmc.edu
O'REILLY, Tricia .... 510-841-9230.... 75 F
toreilly@wi.edu
O'RILEY, Jane .... 318-670-9401.. 199 J
joriley@susla.edu
O'RILEY, Shawn .... 516-877-3404.. 303 B
oriley@adelphi.edu
O'RIORDAN, Steven .... 978-934-3463.. 221 A
steven_oriordan@uml.edu
O'RORKE, Kevin .... 530-242-7629.... 64 D
kororke@shastacollege.edu
O'ROURKE, Bernard, C ... 973-618-3409.. 290 A
borourke@caldwell.edu
O'ROURKE, Brian .... 908-526-1200.. 295 A
brian.o'rourke@raritanval.edu
O'ROURKE, Brian .... 213-477-2535.... 53 B
borourke@msmu.edu
O'ROURKE, Brian, J .... 864-656-4248.. 428 C
orourke@clemson.edu
O'ROURKE, Elizabeth ...... 401-874-9512.. 426 D
O'ROURKE, Kevin .... 718-489-5496.. 328 D
korourke@sfc.edu
O'ROURKE, Kim .... 540-231-6232.. 499 F
orourkek@vt.edu
O'ROURKE, Krysti .... 631-656-2163.. 314 F
krysti.orourke@ftc.edu
O'ROURKE, Maureen, A .. 617-353-3112.. 216 E
morourke@bu.edu
O'ROURKE, Pat .... 303-860-5600.... 83 J
patrick.orourke@cu.edu
O'ROURKE, Shawn .... 716-888-3164.. 306 F
orourke1@canisius.edu
O'ROURKE, Sheila, N ...... 973-618-3341.. 290 A
sorourke@caldwell.edu
O'ROURKE, Timothy, G .. 757-455-3210.. 500 E
torourke@vwc.edu
O'SABEN, Carol .... 928-523-2261.... 15 H
carol.osaben@nau.edu
O'SHAUGHNESSY,
Brian, J .... 413-205-3247.. 214 B
brian.oshaughnessy@aic.edu
O'SHEA, David .... 480-517-8689.... 14 G
david.oshea@riosalado.edu
O'SHEA, Dennis .... 443-287-9908.. 208 D
doshea@jhu.edu
O'SHEA, Donal, E .... 941-487-4100.. 111 D
doshea@ncf.edu
O'SHEA, Gregory, M .... 856-225-6475.. 296 A
osheag@camden.rutgers.edu
O'SHEA, Maureen .... 508-362-2131.. 223 C
moshea@capecod.edu
O'SHEA, Patrick, G .... 301-405-6499.. 211 E
poshea@umd.edu
O'SHEA, William .... 503-352-1419.. 394 C
osheawa@pacificu.edu
O'SHIELDS, Shannon .... 714-879-3901.... 46 F
soshields@hiu.edu
O'SULLIVAN, Eileen .... 508-531-2921.. 221 C
eosullivan@bridgew.edu
O'SULLIVAN, Gerard, P ... 201-761-6020.. 296 K
gosullivan@saintpeters.edu
O'SULLIVAN, Joseph .... 314-516-6800.. 274 A
osullivanj@umsl.edu
O'SULLIVAN, Leighton .... 404-880-8067.. 118 K
losullivan@cau.edu
O'SULLIVAN, Margaret .... 718-270-2487.. 332 B
margaret.o'sullivan@downstate.edu
O'SULLIVAN, Michael, J . 310-338-3015.... 51 E
michael.osullivan@lmu.edu
O'SULLIVAN, Patrick ...... 805-756-7244.... 31 I
posulliv@calpoly.edu
O'SULLIVAN, Patrick ...... 516-876-3135.. 333 C
osullivanp@oldwestbury.edu
O'SULLIVAN, Richard ...... 715-422-5325.. 523 G
richard.osullivan@mstc.edu
O'SULLIVAN, Trecia .... 646-717-9742.. 315 B
osullivan@gts.edu
O'TOOLE, Beth .... 605-331-6797.. 438 A
elisabeth.otoole@usiouxfalls.edu
O'TOOLE, Jason .... 620-441-5353.. 180 D
jason.otoole@cowley.edu
O'TOOLE, Lynne .... 978-232-2030.. 218 D
lynne@endicott.edu
O'TOOLE, Patty .... 540-362-6588.. 490 F
potoole@hollins.edu

P

PÉREZ, Alvaro .... 787-798-6732.. 536 G
alvaro.perez@uccaribe.edu
PÉREZ, Daisy .... 787-892-6442.. 534 D
dnperez@intersg.edu
PÉREZ, Jorge .... 470-578-3569.. 123 J
jperez@kennesaw.edu
PÉREZ, Norma .... 787-993-8858.. 537 G
norma.perez2@upr.edu
PÉREZ, Víctor .... 787-769-9965.. 537 H
victor.perez4@upr.edu
PÉREZ PACHECO,
Angél, F .... 787-265-3767.. 538 C
finanzaz@uprm.edu
PAAL, Christine .... 617-353-3608.. 216 E
cpaal@bu.edu
PAANANEN, Marian .... 425-640-1680.. 503 E
mpaanane@edcc.edu
PAAVOLA, Cindy, L .... 906-227-2720.. 239 B
cipaavol@nmu.edu
PABARCUS, Michael .... 314-837-6777.. 271 B
mpabarcus@stlchristian.edu
PABON, Jaqueline .... 787-765-1915.. 534 F
jpabon@opto.inter.edu
PABON-RODRIGUEZ,
Edith, C .... 787-751-1912.. 534 E
epabon@juris.inter.edu
PACACHA, Edith .... 772-462-7340.. 103 B
epacacha@irsc.edu
PACE, Christy .... 870-460-1121.... 23 D
pacec@uamont.edu
PACE, Derek .... 601-635-2111.. 257 F
dpace@eccc.edu
PACE, Donald, G .... 803-535-5679.. 428 B
dpace@claflin.edu
PACE, Duane .... 423-614-8104.. 441 B
dpace@leeuniversity.edu
PACE, JR., G. Michael .... 540-375-2047.. 493 H
gpace@roanoke.edu
PACE, Gay .... 870-460-1140.... 23 D
pace@uamont.edu
PACE, Harold .... 336-758-5206.. 359 E
hpace@wfu.edu
PACE, Jarrod .... 972-825-5469.. 466 D
japace@sagu.edu
PACE, Jessica .... 903-693-2044.. 463 D
jpace@panola.edu
PACE, Kris .... 816-501-4865.. 270 J
kristine.pace@rockhurst.edu
PACE, Lisa, L .... 843-953-4823.. 428 A
lisa.pace@citadel.edu
PACE, Meghan .... 325-942-2083.. 472 B
meghan.pace@angelo.edu
PACELLI, Catherine .... 575-439-3729.. 301 A
kpacelli@nmsu.edu
PACELLI, Kimberly, A ...... 207-725-3490.. 202 F
kpacelli@bowdoin.edu
PACENTI, Elena .... 619-684-8802.... 54 C
epacenti@newschoolarch.edu
PACHECO, Andrea .... 505-467-6809.. 302 D
registrar@swc.edu
PACHECO, Caryn, L .... 405-325-9627.. 389 B
cpacheco@ou.edu
PACHECO, Cathy .... 757-253-4900.. 488 F
cpacheco@wm.edu
PACHECO, Diane .... 816-604-1341.. 267 F
diane.pacheco@mcckc.edu
PACHECO, Edwin, R .... 401-456-8000.. 425 E
epacheco@ric.edu
PACHECO, Eric .... 303-410-2415.... 82 K
epacheco@redstone.edu
PACHECO, Jacob .... 505-747-2122.. 301 F
jpacheco@nnmc.edu
PACHECO, Jennifer .... 508-531-1221.. 221 C
jennifer.pacheco@bridgew.edu
PACHECO, Ken .... 360-992-2413.. 502 E
kpacheco@clark.edu
PACHECO, Manny .... 714-480-7333.... 58 F
pacheco_manny@rsccd.edu
PACHECO, Michael .... 606-218-5216.. 194 C
michaelpacheco@upike.edu
PACHECO, Philicia .... 508-678-2811.. 223 A
philicia.pacheco@bristolcc.edu
PACHECO, Richard, M ..... 913-971-3299.. 183 D
rmpacheco@mnu.edu
PACHECO, Sonia .... 787-840-2955.. 531 B
spacheco@ponce.caribbean.edu
PACHECO DUNN,
Tanhena .... 845-257-3172.. 331 E
pachecot@newpaltz.edu
PACHIS, Dimitrios, C ...... 860-465-4414.... 85 G
pachis@easternct.edu
PACHUAU, Lalsangkima .. 859-858-3581.. 186 I
PACIEJ-WOODRUFF,
Amy .... 570-340-6016.. 409 H
apaciej@marywood.edu
PACINI, Christine .... 313-993-1208.. 241 G
pacinicm@udmercy.edu
PACINI, Martha .... 404-297-9522.. 122 A
pacinim@gptc.edu
PACK, Daniel .... 423-425-2256.. 448 F
daniel-pack@utc.edu
PACK, Della .... 954-308-2524.... 95 K
dpack@aii.edu
PACK, Thomas, J .... 513-562-8779.. 363 H
tpack@artacademy.edu
PACK, W. Gary .... 513-585-1414.. 366 A
william.pack@thechristcollege.edu
PACKARD, James .... 573-341-4252.. 274 B
jpackard@mst.edu
PACKARD, Ryan .... 206-934-7804.. 506 J
ryan.packard@seattlecolleges.edu
PACKER, Ben .... 208-496-1411.. 132 J
PACKER, Mike .... 626-568-8850.... 48 B
PACKER-MUTI, Barbara ... 954-262-5398.. 105 J
packerb@nova.edu
PACKETT, Felicia, B .... 804-758-6742.. 498 D
fpackett@rappahannock.edu
PACKEY, Matthew .... 704-337-2375.. 355 A
packeym@queens.edu
PACKHAM, Larry .... 310-287-4424.... 50 E
packhald@wlac.edu
PACTOL, Brian .... 808-235-7403.. 132 E
pactol@hawaii.edu
PACTOL, Monica .... 916-608-6503.... 51 C
pactolm@flc.losrios.edu
PADASH, Ali .... 916-608-6648.... 51 C
padasha@flc.losrios.edu
PADDEN, Carol, A .... 858-534-6073.... 70 C
deansocsci@ucsd.edu
PADDOCK, Ericka .... 909-389-3457.... 60 B
epaddock@craftonhills.edu
PADDOCK, Jean .... 330-363-5205.. 363 L
jean.paddock@aultman.com
PADDOCK, John .... 315-498-2299.. 325 G
paddockj@sunyocc.edu
PADDOCK, Suzanne .... 315-866-0300.. 316 A
paddocksm@herkimer.edu
PADDOCK, Will .... 267-620-4834.. 397 G
paddockw@arcadia.edu
PADDOCK-O'REILLY,
Kimberly .... 636-227-2100.. 267 A
PADEN, Quincy .... 773-907-2474.. 137 E
qpaden@ccc.edu
PADEN, Russ .... 602-557-1723.... 17 L
russ.paden@phoenix.edu
PADGETT, Mila .... 803-641-3230.. 433 G
milap@usca.edu
PADILLA, Ailín, T .... 787-264-1912.. 534 D
ailin_padilla@intersg.edu
PADILLA, Alvin .... 616-392-8555.. 244 A
alvin.padilla@westernsem.edu
PADILLA, Edgar .... 254-799-3611.. 470 F
PADILLA, Elaine .... 212-870-1202.. 324 B
epadilla@nyts.edu
PADILLA, Eugene .... 505-224-4721.. 299 F
epadilla@cnm.edu
PADILLA, Frederick, M .... 202-685-3924.. 528 B
frederick.m.padilla.mil@ndu.edu
PADILLA, Jackie .... 850-484-1721.. 106 H
jpadilla@pensacolastate.edu
PADILLA, Jose .... 562-907-4211.... 75 B
jpadilla@whittier.edu
PADILLA, Jose, D .... 312-362-8590.. 139 C
jpadill7@depaul.edu
PADILLA, Mariwilda .... 787-766-1717.. 536 B
mpadilla19@suagm.edu
PADILLA, Mark .... 307-382-1690.. 527 C
mpadilla@westernwyoming.edu
PADILLA, Miriam .... 787-264-1912.. 534 D
miriam_padilla_camacho@intersg.edu
PADILLA, Ramon .... 651-201-1800.. 248 I
ramon.padilla@so.mnscu.edu
PADILLA, Rene .... 402-280-4745.. 279 H
renepadilla@creighton.edu
PADILLA, Sherrie .... 808-932-7451.. 131 E
sherriep@hawaii.edu
PADILLA-COTTO,
Lymaries .... 787-725-6500.. 531 C
lpadilla@sju.albizu.edu
PADIN, Carlos, M .... 787-766-1717.. 536 B
um_cpadin@suagm.edu
PADIN, Glenda .... 787-878-6000.. 532 O
onegron@icprjc.edu
PADMANABHAN, Anand . 212-229-5300.. 322 E
anand@newschool.edu
PADOVANI, John, J .... 607-746-4632.. 335 C
padovajj@delhi.edu
PADOW, Fran, A .... 816-604-1081.. 267 F
fran.padow@mcckc.edu
PADRON, Eduardo, J .... 305-237-3316.. 105 D
epadron@mdc.edu
PADRON, Margie .... 562-938-4947.... 49 D
mpadron@lbcc.edu
PADUAN, Jeffrey, D .... 831-656-3241.. 528 D
jdpaduan@nps.edu
PADULA, Fernando .... 915-747-5594.. 476 D
lfpadula@utep.edu
PAEPLOW, Randall, K .... 863-784-7083.. 109 G
randall.paeplow@southflorida.edu
PAESE, Paul .... 713-525-3540.. 475 J
PAEZ, Karen .... 971-722-4406.. 394 F
PAEZ-FIGUEROA, Jose .... 908-709-7084.. 298 A
paez@ucc.edu

PALMIERI, Rob 518-681-5601 335 A
palmierir@sunyacc.edu

PALMIERI, Tony 304-252-9547 511 F

PALMINI, JR., William 650-508-3502 54 J
safety@ndnu.edu

PALMITER, Lia Richards 570-961-4799 409 H
lpalmiter@marywood.edu

PALMOUR, Mack 843-208-8118 434 A
mpalmour@uscb.edu

PALOK, Debra 623-845-3536 14 C
debra.palok@gccaz.edu

PALOMBO, Ryan 615-361-7555 439 K
rpalombo@daymarinstitute.edu

PALOMBO, Tom, J 336-316-2290 344 H
tpalombo@guilford.edu

PALOMBO, Vince 216-373-6364 374 B
vpalombo@ndc.edu

PALOMBO, Vincent 216-373-5310 374 B
vpalombo@ndc.edu

PALSAK, Angela 269-782-1310 241 C
apalsak@swmich.edu

PALSER, Nicole 612-343-4453 253 Y
nmpalser@northcentral.edu

PALSER, Philip, V 715-833-6364 523 B
ppalser@cvtc.edu

PALTER-GILL, Dianne 978-762-4000 224 C
dpalterg@northshore.edu

PALUBNIAK, Dan 908-526-1200 295 A
daniel.palubniak@raritanval.edu

PALUMBO, Carmine 478-289-2046 120 C
cpalumbo@ega.edu

PALUMBO, John 602-275-7133 16 Q
john.palumbo@rsiaz.edu

PALUMBO, Katey 508-929-8835 222 F
kpalumbo2@worcester.edu

PALUMBO, Michelle 314-889-1492 265 C
mpalumbo@fontbonne.edu

PALUMBO-OLSZANSKI,
Linda 706-233-7409 127 A
lpalumbo@shorter.edu

PALUS, Christine 610-519-7093 422 G
christine.palus@villanova.edu

PALUSO, Eugene 843-953-3020 428 A
epaluso@citadel.edu

PALZER, Jon, A 585-785-1224 314 D
jon.palzer@flcc.edu

PAMINTUAN, Lisa 516-364-0808 323 B
pamintuan@nycollege.edu

PAMMER, Andrea, M 304-367-4686 513 B
andrea.pammer@fairmontstate.edu

PAMMIER, Darren 660-596-7232 272 G
dpannier@sfccmo.edu

PAMPE, Andie 618-395-7777 142 E
pampea@iecc.edu

PAN, Shouan 206-934-3872 506 I
shouan.pan@seattlecolleges.edu

PANAMA, Annie 684-699-9155 529 E
a.panama@amsamoa.edu

PANARELLA, Pamela 610-409-3163 422 D
ppanarella@ursinus.edu

PANAS, Voytek 703-821-8570 494 I
vpanas@stratford.edu

PANAYOTOVA, Evelina 610-790-1905 397 D
evelina.panayotova@alvernia.edu

PANCHAL, Praveen 718-270-6182 309 B
ppanchal@mec.cuny.edu

PANCHANA, Kimberly 770-394-8300 116 F
kpanchana@aii.edu

PANCIERA, Kathy 952-885-5465 253 Z
kpanciera@nwhealth.edu

PANCZA, Wayne 215-780-1402 419 C
wpancza@salus.edu

PANDE, Sameer 281-283-3008 474 A
pande@uhcl.edu

PANDEY, Bhuban, R 512-448-8442 464 G
bhubanp@stedwards.edu

PANDIT, Kavita 404-413-2613 122 D
kpandit@gsu.edu

PANDO, Paula 201-360-4021 292 B
ppando@hccc.edu

PANETTA, Carol 617-277-3915 216 D
panettac@bgsp.edu

PANFIL, Tim 630-617-6471 140 C
panfilt@elmhurst.edu

PANG, Alex 310-506-4561 56 J
alex.pang@pepperdine.edu

PANG, Eddie 808-735-4856 130 F
epang@chaminade.edu

PANG, John 510-981-2849 57 B
jpang@peralta.edu

PANG, Lily 310-506-4130 56 J
lily.pang@pepperdine.edu

PANG, Rebecca 760-384-6115 47 K
rebecca.pang@cerrocoso.edu

PANGBORN, Joseph 401-841-6555 528 E

PANGBORN, Robert, N 814-863-1864 412 F
rnp1@psu.edu

PANGELINAN, Leo 670-237-6766 530 D
leo.pangelinan@marianas.edu

PANGER, Brenda 218-723-6067 245 J
bpanger@css.edu

PANGONIS, Tricia 440-375-7100 371 E
tpangonis@lec.edu

PANI, Eric, A 318-342-1025 201 E
pani@ulm.edu

PANIGOT, Benjamin 269-471-3321 230 H
panigot@andrews.edu

PANKEN, Aaron 212-824-2219 315 F
apanken@huc.edu

PANKIEVICH, Michael 617-989-4575 229 D
pankievichm@wit.edu

PANKOW, Craig 808-853-1040 131 B
craigpankow@pacrim.edu

PANKRATZ, Terry 972-883-4802 476 C
terry.pankratz@utdallas.edu

PANLILIO, Carmen 219-989-2367 166 F
carmen.panlilio@pnw.edu

PANNEGGIANTE, John 201-559-6089 291 K
pane@felician.edu

PANNELL, Kerry, E 404-471-6361 115 J
kpannell@agnesscott.edu

PANNELL, Randall 864-977-7011 431 G
randall.pannell@ngu.edu

PANNELL, Randall, J 864-977-7018 431 G
randall.pannell@ngu.edu

PANNKUK, Matthew 620-417-1161 184 I
matthew.pannkuk@sccc.edu

PANOFF, Virginia 231-348-6698 239 A
vpanoff@ncmich.edu

PANTALEO, Josephine 718-631-6391 309 E
jpantaleo@qcc.cuny.edu

PANTEL, Braelin 303-352-4465 81 G
bpantel@msudenver.edu

PANTER, Deborah 415-422-4588 72 C
dpanter@usfca.edu

PANTIC, Zorica 617-989-4476 229 D
panticz@wit.edu

PANTLIK, Sandy 405-945-9196 386 C
spantli@osuokc.edu

PANTOJA, Antonio, L 787-279-1912 533 J
apantoja@bayamon.inter.edu

PANTOJA, Mirna 914-964-4282 310 D

PANTOJA, Veronica 818-785-2726 36 M
veronica.pantoja@casalomacollege.edu

PANTONE, Dirk 303-220-1200 77 D
dirk.pantone@cffp.edu

PANTULA, Sastry 541-737-4811 393 H
sastry.pantula@oregonstate.edu

PANU, Al, M 843-208-8242 434 A
apanu@uscb.edu

PANZARELLA, Amy 304-724-3700 510 E
apanzarella@apus.edu

PANZECA, Linda 513-244-4393 373 C
linda.panzeca@msj.edu

PAO, Roger 617-603-6900 226 D
roger.pao@necb.edu

PAOLINI, Francine 616-632-2131 231 A
paolifra@aquinas.edu

PAOLUCCI, Jeff 719-384-6833 82 A
jeff.paolucci@ojc.edu

PAPADIMITRIOU, Dimitri 914-758-7426 214 H
dpb@bard.edu

PAPADIMITRIOU,
Dimitri, B 845-758-7426 304 F
dbp@levy.bard.edu

PAPADIMITRIOU, K.P 434-381-6371 494 M
kp@sbc.edu

PAPADIMOS, Peter, J 419-530-8411 380 D
peter.papadimos@utoledo.edu

PAPADOPOULOS,
Michael 518-783-2376 330 E
mpapadopoulos@siena.edu

PAPAFIL, Drucie, A 757-446-6143 489 B
papafida@evms.edu

PAPAGEORGE, Anne 215-898-7241 421 E
fresvp@upenn.edu

PAPAJOHN, Michelle 631-687-5151 328 G
mpapajohn@sjcny.edu

PAPAKONSTANTINOU,
Karen 732-255-0400 293 E
karenp@ocean.edu

PAPALEO, Stefano 561-237-7831 104 O
spapaleo@lynn.edu

PAPALIA, Daria 845-451-1359 312 C
d_papalia@culinary.edu

PAPANIKOLAOU,
Constantia 617-994-6928 220 D
cpapanikolaou@bhe.mass.edu

PAPARIELLA, Justin 412-338-4770 398 H
jpapariella@brightwoodcareer.edu

PAPATHEOFANIS, Frank 760-471-1316 59 H

PAPATHOMAS,
Thomas, V 848-445-6533 296 B
papathom@rci.rutgers.edu

PAPAY, Dan 937-775-2587 381 H
daniel.papay@wright.edu

PAPAZIAN, Mary 408-924-1177 35 C
sjsupres@sjsu.edu

PAPAZIAN, Mary, A 203-392-5250 85 H
papazianm1@southernct.edu

PAPE, Jim 270-534-3370 190 H
jim.pape@kctcs.edu

PAPE, Randi 712-325-3428 174 B
rpape@iwcc.edu

PAPE, Sabrina 916-660-7202 64 F
spape@sierracollege.edu

PAPER, Teresa, A 563-441-4173 172 D
tapaper@eicc.edu

PAPESCH, Katherine 217-732-3155 146 B
kpapesch@lincolncollege.edu

PAPIA, Jeffrey 726-926-8924 316 B
jpapia@hilbert.edu

PAPILLON, Terry, L 931-598-1248 443 O
tlpapill@sewanee.edu

PAPINCHAK, John, R 412-268-7404 400 D
jp7p@andrew.cmu.edu

PAPINI, Dennis 605-688-4723 437 F
dennis.papini@sdstate.edu

PAPP, John 412-918-2614 127 D
jpapp@southuniversity.edu

PAPP, Justin 708-596-2000 154 E
jpapp@ssc.edu

PAPPAS, Amy 703-284-1681 492 A
amy.pappas@marymount.edu

PAPPAS, Domenica, G 312-567-3035 142 I
pappas@iit.edu

PAPPAS, Gregory, J 718-817-4350 314 G
pappas@fordham.edu

PAPPAS, James, P 405-325-6361 389 B
jpappas@ou.edu

PAPPAS, Jesse 304-358-2000 510 J

PAPPAS, Joanna 773-508-7429 146 G
jpappas@luc.edu

PAPPAS, Katherine 413-782-1327 229 E
katherine.pappas@wne.edu

PAPPAS, Richard, J 616-698-7111 233 C
rpappas@davenport.edu

PAPPAS, Tony, A 641-422-4350 175 E
pappaton@niacc.edu

PAPPATHAN, Matthew 802-828-8740 378 E
matt.pappathan@myunion.edu

PAPSON, Melissa 724-222-5330 412 E
mpapson@penncommercial.edu

PAPULI, Tina 212-247-3434 319 K
epapuli@mandl.edu

PAQUETTE, Ashley 906-932-4231 234 C
ashleyp@gogebic.edu

PAQUETTE, James 410-617-2283 208 G
jrpaquette1@loyola.edu

PAQUETTE, Kevin 207-893-7797 204 D
kpaquett@sjcme.edu

PAQUIN, Delbert 928-724-6772 12 T
dpaquin@dinecollege.edu

PARADEE, Melissa 802-776-5223 483 G
melissa.paradee@csj.edu

PARADIS, Ronald, S 541-383-7599 390 D
rparadis@cocc.edu

PARADIS, Thomas 317-940-8972 159 K
tparadis@butler.edu

PARADISE, Melanie, M 865-539-7130 446 G
mmparadise@pstcc.edu

PARADISE, Richard 321-433-7202 98 K
paradiser@easternflorida.edu

PARADKAR, Vish 719-389-6454 77 J
vparadkar@coloradocollege.edu

PARADKAR, Vishvas 719-389-6454 77 J
vishvas.paradkar@coloradocollege.edu

PARAMITHIOTTI,
Corrado 802-387-1611 484 B
cparamithiotti@landmark.edu

PARAMORE, Marcus 334-241-8622 7 H
marcus@troy.edu

PARAMORE, Pamela 757-455-3238 500 E
pparamore@vwc.edu

PARANDI, Tony 765-677-1566 164 B
tony.parandi@indwes.edu

PARCEL, Julie 636-922-8383 271 A
jparcel@stchas.edu

PARCELLS, Rex 254-659-7821 458 K
rparcells@hillcollege.edu

PARDALES, Michael 207-893-6643 204 D
mpardales@sjcme.edu

PARDEE, Joseph 860-701-5176 88 D
pardee_j@mitchell.edu

PARDO, Carlos 314-454-7547 265 E
cxp1679@bjc.org

PARDO, Carmen, L 973-353-5113 296 C
cpardo@newark.rutgers.edu

PARDO, Kathleen 314-246-7698 275 B
kpardo@webster.edu

PARDUE, Judi, D 817-531-4401 472 F
jpardue@txwes.edu

PARDUE, Karen 207-221-4361 205 F
kpardue@une.edu

PARDUE, Samuel 706-542-3924 128 E
slpcaes@uga.edu

PARE, Carroll 802-387-6885 484 B
cpare@landmark.edu

PARE, Judith 508-373-9784 215 D
judith.pare@becker.edu

PAREDES, Esteban 785-833-4307 182 F
esteban.paredes@kwu.edu

PAREKH, Purvi 201-684-7115 294 G
purvi@ramapo.edu

PARENS, Joshua, S 972-721-5241 473 D
parens@udallas.edu

PARENT, Cyrille 719-502-2975 82 B
cyrille.parent@ppcc.edu

PARENTI, Stefano 603-645-9695 287 I
s.parenti@snhu.edu

PARES-KANE, Nayda 585-292-3369 321 J
npares-kane@monroecc.edu

PARFITT, Richard 239-489-9339 101 F
richard.parfitt@fsw.edu

PARGE, Theodore, C 630-844-5262 135 E
tparge@aurora.edu

PARHAM, Loretta 404-978-2018 128 A
lparham@auctr.edu

PARHAM, Patricia 805-493-3185 31 C
pparham@callutheran.edu

PARHAM, Sandra 615-966-5837 441 F
sandra.parham@lipscomb.edu

PARHAM, Thomas, A 949-824-4804 69 C
taparham@uci.edu

PARHAM, Walter, H 803-777-7854 433 F
terry@mailbox.sc.edu

PARIANTE, Jody 212-431-2137 323 H
jody.pariante@nyls.edu

PARIGIAN, Debbie 503-244-0726 389 J
debbieparigian@achs.edu

PARIKH, Raj 413-205-3369 214 B
raj.parikh@aic.edu

PARINI, Shelly 503-594-3015 390 F
shellyp@clackamas.edu

PARIS, Chris 314-921-9290 274 F
dean@ugst.edu

PARIS, Lisa 215-670-9127 412 D
lparis@peirce.edu

PARIS, Mark, S 302-356-6829 91 I
mark.s.paris@wilmu.edu

PARIS, III, Oren 479-248-7236 20 C
oparis3@ecollege.edu

PARIS, Susan 919-536-7200 349 D
pariss@durhamtech.edu

PARISEAU, Anita 719-389-6772 77 J
anita.pariseau@coloradocollege.edu

PARISH, Michael, C 906-248-8400 231 N
mparish@bmcc.edu

PARISHER, Deborah 252-823-5166 349 E
parisherd@edgecombe.edu

PARISI, Anthony, J 831-656-2441 528 D
aparisi@nps.edu

PARISI, Dawn 352-588-8251 108 C
dawn.parisi@saintleo.edu

PARISI, Joe 636-949-4812 266 J
jparisi@lindenwood.edu

PARISI, Michael 410-293-1104 529 D
parisi@usna.edu

PARISI, Michael, J 860-444-8481 529 A
michael.j.parisi@uscg.mil

PARISI, Rob 805-922-6966 25 I
rparisi@hancockcollege.edu

PARISI, Robert 805-922-6966 25 I
rparisi@hancockcollege.edu

PARIZO, Daniel, C 920-923-8760 517 H
dcparizo94@marianuniversity.edu

PARK, Chan, J 561-237-7186 104 O
cpark@lynn.edu

PARK, Choong Gi 562-926-1023 58 B
choong.park@gmail.com

PARK, Christina 714-533-1495 65 B
christina@southbaylo.edu

PARK, Daniel, L 509-527-5999 509 G
park@whitman.edu

PARK, Daniel, W 858-822-1236 70 C
dwpark@ucsd.edu

PARK, Dave 213-413-9500 66 B
admin@scusoma.edu

PARK, David 714-533-3946 35 E
dpark@calums.edu

PARK, Doug, Y 541-346-3082 395 G
dougpark@uoregon.edu

PARK, Eun, K 470-578-5572 123 J
epark19@kennesaw.edu

PARK, George 310-453-8300 42 L
george@emperors.edu

PARK, Heerei 408-260-0208 43 L
korean@fivebranches.edu

PARK, Hojin 215-884-8942 424 B
hojin.park@woninstitute.edu

PARK, Hun Sung 213-381-0081 47 C
office@laopendoor.org

PARK, Hyung 213-252-5100 24 K
hpark@alu.edu

PARK, Jack, C 210-567-2020 477 D
parkjc@uthscsa.edu

PARK, James, S 540-464-7390 499 E
parkjs@vmi.edu

PARK, Jessica 213-252-5100 24 K
jpark@alu.edu

PARK, Jinsoo 973-877-3588 291 H
jpark@essex.edu

PARK, Joshua 770-232-2717 126 B

PARK, Joyce, G .... 703-333-5904.. 500 G
ghpark@wuv.edu
PARK, Kathryn .... 409-933-8201.. 454 O
kpark@com.edu
PARK, Kevin .... 404-687-4533.. 119 D
parkk@ctsnet.edu
PARK, Laura .... 801-649-5230.. 480 K
office@midwifery.edu
PARK, Linda .... 315-279-5208.. 318 C
lpark@keuka.edu
PARK, Matthew .... 940-397-4501.. 462 A
matthew.park@mwsu.edu
PARK, Mihyun .... 562-926-1023.... 58 B
mhpark@ptsa.edu
PARK, Mimi .... 714-533-1495.... 65 B
mimi@southbaylo.edu
PARK, Min .... 213-487-0110.... 42 H
officemanager@dula.edu
PARK, Myung .... 253-964-7327.. 506 B
mpark@pierce.ctc.edu
PARK, No Hee .... 310-206-6063.... 69 D
nhpark@dentistry.ucla.edu
PARK, Roger .... 317-632-5553.. 165 L
rpark@lincolntech.edu
PARK, Scott .... 309-341-7459.. 145 A
sapark@knox.edu
PARK, Steve .... 972-860-7771.. 456 A
spark@dcccd.edu
PARK, Sunny .... 806-720-7507.. 461 C
sunny.park@lcu.edu
PARK, Yong Hee .... 714-533-1495.... 65 B
yhpark@southbaylo.edu
PARK, Young, S .... 636-327-4645.. 268 C
dl@midwest.edu
PARK, Young Hae .... 202-559-0434.... 92 C
younghae.park@gallaudet.edu
PARK, Yung Won .... 610-917-1457.. 422 C
ywpark@valleyforge.edu
PARK ZERBEL, Jennifer .. 310-360-8888.... 25 C
PARKE, Lydia .... 215-780-1417.. 419 C
lparke@salus.edu
PARKE, Scott, J .... 972-599-3117.. 455 A
sparke@collin.edu
PARKER, Andrew .... 765-677-1989.. 164 B
andrew.parker@indwes.edu
PARKER, Annette .... 610-409-3141.. 422 D
aparker@ursinus.edu
PARKER, Annette .... 507-389-7211.. 252 D
annette.parker@southcentral.edu
PARKER, Anthony .... 718-270-2936.. 332 B
anthony.parker@downstate.edu
PARKER, Anthony .... 903-593-8311.. 470 A
aparker@texascollege.edu
PARKER, Anthony, O .... 229-430-0656.. 116 A
aparker@albanytech.edu
PARKER, Audrey .... 252-492-2061.. 353 H
parkera@vgcc.edu
PARKER, Ava, L .... 561-868-3501.. 106 D
parkera@palmbeachstate.edu
PARKER, Barbara .... 828-627-4515.. 350 D
bmparker@haywood.edu
PARKER, Barbara .... 315-268-6445.. 310 B
bparker@clarkson.edu
PARKER, Beverly, J .... 318-670-9571.. 199 J
bparker@susla.edu
PARKER, Brian .... 617-745-3864.. 218 A
brian.parker@enc.edu
PARKER, Bruce .... 406-657-1124.. 278 D
bruce.parker@rocky.edu
PARKER, Carol .... 505-277-2611.. 302 F
cparker@unm.edu
PARKER, Carol .... 617-824-8912.. 218 B
carol_parker@emerson.edu
PARKER, Carol, A .... 864-231-2120.. 427 B
cparker@andersonuniversity.edu
PARKER, Cassandra .... 202-274-5323.... 94 B
cparker@udc.edu
PARKER, Catherine .... 248-218-2154.. 240 C
cparker@rc.edu
PARKER, Cathy .... 601-484-8799.. 258 F
cparker@meridiancc.edu
PARKER, Charles, R .... 850-263-3261.... 96 C
crparker@baptistcollege.edu
PARKER, Chris .... 870-733-6047.... 19 A
crparker@asumidsouth.edu
PARKER, Christopher .... 704-463-3112.. 354 F
christopher.parker@pfeiffer.edu
PARKER, Collier, B .... 570-340-6000.. 409 H
cbparker@marywood.edu
PARKER, Corey .... 404-297-9522.. 122 A
parkerc@gptc.edu
PARKER, Craig .... 502-897-4142.. 192 D
cparker@sbts.edu
PARKER, Cynthia, L .... 401-598-1345.. 425 B
cparker@jwu.edu
PARKER, Cynthia Ann ...... 609-652-4378.. 297 C
cynthia.parker@stockton.edu
PARKER, Dana .... 513-558-9964.. 379 C
dana.parker@uc.edu
PARKER, Dana, C .... 610-436-2627.. 416 C
dparker@wcupa.edu
PARKER, Daniel .... 870-248-4000.... 19 H
daniel.parker@blackrivertech.edu
PARKER, Danny, M .... 864-231-2000.. 427 B
dparker@andersonuniversity.edu
PARKER, Darrell .... 828-227-7401.. 359 A
dfparker@wcu.edu
PARKER, David .... 336-506-4301.. 347 C
dave.parker@alamancecc.edu
PARKER, Deborah .... 870-762-3113.... 18 G
dparker@smail.anc.edu
PARKER, Debra .... 419-434-5478.. 379 E
parker@findlay.edu
PARKER, Debra, O .... 919-530-5269.. 357 A
dparker@nccu.edu
PARKER, Diane .... 617-243-2137.. 219 I
dparker@lasell.edu
PARKER, Fiona .... 817-554-5950.. 461 G
fparker@messengercollege.edu
PARKER, Frank .... 936-294-1786.. 471 D
fparker@shsu.edu
PARKER, Gail, C .... 318-342-1961.. 201 E
gparker@ulm.edu
PARKER, Heidi .... 641-673-1031.. 177 J
parkerh@wmpenn.edu
PARKER, Holly .... 518-327-6300.. 326 B
hparker@paulsmiths.edu
PARKER, Jack .... 321-433-7380.... 98 K
parkerj@easternflorida.edu
PARKER, James, T .... 801-581-6857.. 481 M
jparker@purchasing.utah.edu
PARKER, Janet .... 312-355-4565.. 156 F
japarker@uic.edu
PARKER, Janice, C .... 312-658-5100.. 155 I
janice.parker@tbiil.edu
PARKER, Jay .... 269-467-9945.. 234 B
jparker@glenoaks.edu
PARKER, Jeanette .... 270-789-5075.. 187 G
jjparker@campbellsville.edu
PARKER, Jerome, S .... 610-359-5100.. 401 L
jparker@dccc.edu
PARKER, Jill .... 530-752-2599.... 69 A
jblack@ucdavis.edu
PARKER, Jim, O .... 504-816-8592.. 198 H
jparker@nobts.edu
PARKER, Joe .... 970-491-3350.... 78 Q
joe.parker@colostate.edu
PARKER, Joyce, E .... 310-233-4551.... 49 I
parkerje@lahc.edu
PARKER, Juli .... 508-910-4582.. 220 H
jparker@umassd.edu
PARKER, Julia .... 601-643-8308.. 257 D
julia.parker@colin.edu
PARKER, Kathleen .... 320-363-2121.. 254 N
kparker@csbsju.edu
PARKER, Kathy .... 320-363-2121.. 245 I
kparker@csbsju.edu
PARKER, Keith .... 561-732-4424.. 108 F
kparker@svdp.edu
PARKER, Keith, S .... 310-794-6811.... 69 D
kparker@support.ucla.edu
PARKER, Kelly .... 312-487-4743.. 155 L
kelly.parker@tribecaflashpoint.edu
PARKER, Kevin .... 845-758-7511.. 304 F
parker@bard.edu
PARKER, Kim .... 214-637-3530.. 479 C
kparker@wadecollege.edu
PARKER, Kim .... 802-656-3434.. 485 D
kim.parker@uvm.edu
PARKER, Laura Lavado ..... 310-794-2304.... 69 D
lparker@support.ucla.edu
PARKER, III, Lee .... 804-289-8405.. 495 G
lparker@richmond.edu
PARKER, Linda .... 641-673-1327.. 177 J
parkerl@wmpenn.edu
PARKER, Linda, M .... 518-388-6123.. 338 H
parkerl@union.edu
PARKER, Mae .... 641-269-4631.. 172 I
parkerma@grinnell.edu
PARKER, Marcia .... 909-607-7855.... 39 B
marcia_parker@kgi.edu
PARKER, Maria .... 870-584-1121.... 23 F
mparker@cccua.edu
PARKER, Mark .... 405-208-5315.. 385 E
mparker@okcu.edu
PARKER, Mary .... 310-393-0411.... 56 G
mfparker@rand.org
PARKER, Mary, G .... 801-581-3490.. 481 M
mgparker@sa.utah.edu
PARKER, Mary Jo .... 713-221-8471.. 474 B
parkerm@uhd.edu
PARKER, Melanie, L .... 617-715-5329.. 225 A
PARKER, Micah .... 951-343-4381.... 29 H
miparker@calbaptist.edu
PARKER, Michael .... 210-341-1366.. 463 A
mparker@ost.edu
PARKER, Michelle .... 928-523-6500.... 15 H
michelle.parker@nau.edu
PARKER, Patsy .... 580-774-3284.. 388 C
patsy.parker@swosu.edu
PARKER, Pennie .... 407-646-2636.. 107 O
pparker@rollins.edu
PARKER, Philip, L .... 812-464-1865.. 168 E
plparker@usi.edu
PARKER, Pippin .... 212-229-5859.. 322 E
parkerp@newschool.edu
PARKER, Randy .... 336-334-4822.. 350 B
PARKER, Robert .... 707-256-7175.... 53 H
rparker@napavalley.edu
PARKER, Robin, L .... 513-529-6734.. 372 K
parkerrl@miamioh.edu
PARKER, Rodney .... 410-617-2310.. 208 G
rparker1@loyola.edu
PARKER, Ron .... 979-230-3480.. 453 A
ron.parker@brazosport.edu
PARKER, Shelly .... 678-839-6380.. 129 E
sparker@westga.edu
PARKER, Sonia .... 801-957-4446.. 483 A
sonia.parker@slcc.edu
PARKER, Sonya, L .... 270-824-8586.. 190 B
sonya.parker@kctcs.edu
PARKER, Tammie .... 541-278-5850.. 390 C
tparker@bluecc.edu
PARKER, Teresa .... 740-389-4636.. 372 B
parkert@mtc.edu
PARKER, Zoann, J .... 443-412-2170.. 208 A
zparker@harford.edu
PARKER AMES, Gwen ...... 845-675-4446.. 325 C
gwen.ames@nyack.edu
PARKER-BELL, Bernice .... 904-470-8261.... 98 N
bparkerbell@ewc.edu
PARKER-DER BOGHOSSIAN,
John .... 651-846-1757.. 252 C
john.parker@saintpaul.edu
PARKER-JEANNETTE,
Cyrus .... 562-985-4376.... 33 B
cyrus.parker-jeannette@csulb.edu
PARKER-KELLY, Darlene .. 323-563-9340.... 37 G
darleneparkerkelly@cdrewu.edu
PARKES, Martin, J .... 717-867-6038.. 408 F
parkes@ivc.edu
PARKHILL, Molly .... 828-694-1706.. 347 G
mollyp@blueridge.edu
PARKHURST, Abbie .... 540-828-5782.. 487 H
aparkhur@bridgewater.edu
PARKHURST, Cindy .... 951-785-2982.... 48 A
cparkhurst@lasierra.edu
PARKIN, Janice .... 312-341-4327.. 152 H
jparkin01@roosevelt.edu
PARKINSON, Curt .... 559-278-4062.... 32 F
cparkinson@csufresno.edu
PARKINSON, III,
Henry, C .... 978-665-3160.. 221 D
hparkinson@fitchburgstate.edu
PARKINSON, Michael .... 314-529-9553.. 267 B
mparkinson@maryville.edu
PARKINSON, Richard .... 815-772-7218.. 148 H
rcpark@morrisontech.edu
PARKINSON, Tracy .... 843-383-8012.. 428 F
tparkinson@coker.edu
PARKMAN, Julie .... 315-386-7119.. 335 B
parkmar@canton.edu
PARKS, Amy .... 216-987-6130.. 367 E
amy.parks@tri-c.edu
PARKS, Ann .... 660-263-4100.. 269 D
annp@macc.edu
PARKS, Cheri, S .... 303-963-3357.... 77 I
cparks@ccu.edu
PARKS, Cynthia .... 478-825-6605.. 120 F
parksc@fvsu.edu
PARKS, Cynthia .... 706-737-1431.. 117 D
cparks1@augusta.edu
PARKS, David .... 304-473-8011.. 515 B
parks.d@wvwc.edu
PARKS, Donald, K .... 850-201-8071.... 99 M
dparks@flagler.edu
PARKS, Earl .... 202-651-5494.... 92 C
earl.parks@gallaudet.edu
PARKS, Erik .... 312-487-4743.. 155 L
erik.parks@tribecaflashpoint.edu
PARKS, Jason .... 318-484-2184.. 201 B
parksj@nsula.edu
PARKS, Jeffrey .... 281-476-1806.. 464 J
jeffrey.parks@sjcd.edu
PARKS, Julie .... 616-234-3714.. 234 E
jparks@grcc.edu
PARKS, Marshall .... 970-351-1814.... 84 C
marshall.parks@unco.edu
PARKS, Michael .... 210-567-2791.. 477 D
parksm@uthscsa.edu
PARKS, Patricia .... 714-816-0366.... 68 E
patricia.parks@trident.edu
PARKS, Rodney .... 336-278-6677.. 344 D
rparks4@elon.edu
PARKS, Tammy .... 212-517-3929.. 330 G
t.parks@sothebysinstitute.com
PARKS, Thomas, N .... 801-581-7236.. 481 M
tom.parks@utah.edu
PARKS, Valerie .... 915-779-8031.. 478 J
vparks@computercareercenter.com
PARKS, Vanasia Corley .. 423-425-4467.. 448 F
vanasia-parks@utc.edu
PARKTON, Deanna .... 215-489-4728.. 402 A
deanna.parkton@delval.edu
PARKYN, David, L .... 773-244-5710.. 149 I
dparkyn@northpark.edu
PARLACOSKI, Julie .... 732-987-2219.. 292 A
jparlacoski@georgian.edu
PARLE, Joseph, D .... 713-785-5995.. 454 H
joe.parle@cbshouston.edu
PARLER, Branson .... 616-222-3000.. 236 F
bparler@kuyper.edu
PARLETT, Lynda, W .... 828-339-4265.. 353 D
l_parlett@southwesterncc.edu
PARLETT, Ray, M .... 585-567-9333.. 316 F
ray.parlett@houghton.edu
PARLETT-SWEENEY,
Mary, W .... 518-782-6988.. 330 E
mparlett-sweeney@siena.edu
PARLETTE, Jared .... 800-955-2527.. 181 D
jparlette@grantham.edu
PARMER, David .... 409-212-5724.. 452 D
PARMER, Marsha .... 503-223-2245.. 391 H
mparmer@portland.chefs.edu
PARNELL, Kathleen .... 410-617-2354.. 208 G
kmparnell@loyola.edu
PARNELL, Lauren .... 912-583-3211.. 118 B
lparnell@bpc.edu
PARNELL, Paul .... 559-244-5901.... 67 A
paul.parnell@scccd.edu
PARNELL, Philip .... 307-382-1639.. 527 C
pparnell@westernwyoming.edu
PARNELL, Rob Roy .... 512-463-2237.. 470 G
robroy.parnell@tsus.edu
PAROD, Daniel .... 406-657-1007.. 278 D
parodd@rocky.edu
PAROLINI, Roger, K .... 630-844-5489.. 135 E
rparolin@aurora.edu
PARR, Deidra, R .... 304-829-7033.. 510 G
dparr@bethanywv.edu
PARR, Josephine .... 212-229-5667.. 322 E
parrj@newschool.edu
PARR, Vanna .... 940-898-3525.. 472 G
vparr@twu.edu
PARR WALKER, Diane ...... 574-631-7790.. 168 B
diane.parr.walker@nd.edu
PARRA, Alicia, F .... 954-322-4460.. 103 H
aliciafernandaparra@jmvu.edu
PARRAMORE, Cheri .... 402-375-7241.. 281 J
chparra1@wsc.edu
PARRELLA, Michael .... 208-885-6681.. 134 G
mpp@uidaho.edu
PARRENT, Condoa .... 817-515-6532.. 467 A
condoa.parrent@tccd.edu
PARRENT, Jay, V .... 270-824-8571.. 190 B
jay.parrent@kctcs.edu
PARRENT, Rick .... 615-230-3321.. 447 C
rick.parrent@volstate.edu
PARRENT, Robert .... 314-246-7910.. 275 B
robertparrent@webster.edu
PARRETT, Brenda, J .... 601-643-8301.. 257 D
brenda.parrett@colin.edu
PARRILL, Jacqueline .... 740-366-9407.. 365 D
parrill.9@osu.edu
PARRILLA, Arlene .... 787-863-2390.. 533 K
arlene.parrilla@fajardo.inter.edu
PARRILLA, Margarita .... 787-850-9463.. 538 B
margarita.parrilla@upr.edu
PARRIOTT, Karen .... 307-532-8264.. 526 G
karen.parriott@ewc.wy.edu
PARRISH, Austen, L .... 812-855-8885.. 162 F
austparr@indiana.edu
PARRISH, Dave .... 770-533-7033.. 123 L
dparrish@laniertech.edu
PARRISH, David, K .... 308-632-6933.. 282 H
PARRISH, Debra, J .... 906-524-8414.. 236 D
dparrish@kbocc.edu
PARRISH, Gretchen .... 336-342-4261.. 352 F
parrishg@rockinghamcc.edu
PARRISH, J. Michael .... 408-924-4800.... 35 C
mparrish@science.sjsu.edu
PARRISH, John .... 336-342-4261.. 352 F
parrishj@rockinghamcc.edu
PARRISH, Kelly .... 617-989-4960.. 229 D
parrishk@wit.edu
PARRISH, Patricia .... 352-588-8417.. 108 C
trish.parrish@saintleo.edu
PARRISH, Phillip, A .... 434-243-4023.. 495 H
pap4n@virginia.edu
PARRISH, Rebecca .... 859-985-3524.. 187 B
parrishr@berea.edu
PARRISH, Sid .... 803-321-5263.. 431 F
sid.parrish@newberry.edu
PARROT, Autumn .... 615-383-4848.. 449 G
aparrot@watkins.edu
PARROTT, Aaron .... 509-682-6795.. 509 D
aparrott@wvc.edu
PARROTT, David .... 352-392-1265.. 112 A
davewp@ufl.edu
PARROTT, Mike .... 843-208-8040.. 434 A
rparrot@uscb.edu
PARROTT, Rebecca .... 606-242-0256.. 190 G
rebecca.parrott@kctcs.edu

- **PARROTT**, Roger 601-968-5919 256 I president@belhaven.edu
- **PARRY**, John 970-491-3939 78 Q john.parry@colostate.edu
- **PARRY**, John 216-687-4808 366 I john.parry@csuohio.edu
- **PARRY**, Joseph, D 801-422-3037 480 C joseph_parry@byu.edu
- **PARRY**, Karine 714-533-3946 35 E karine@calums.edu
- **PARRY**, Laura, S 518-783-8282 330 E lparry@siena.edu
- **PARRY**, Susan 845-341-4251 325 H susan.parry@sunyorange.edu
- **PARSELL RUMSEY**, Leah 317-738-8141 160 J lparsellrumsey@franklincollege.edu
- **PARSHALL**, William 215-204-8822 420 B william.parshall@temple.edu
- **PARSLEY**, Ashton 614-837-4088 380 G parsleya@valorcollege.edu
- **PARSLEY**, Nancy, L 847-578-8401 153 A nancy.parsley@rosalindfranklin.edu
- **PARSNIK**, Pamela 570-674-6310 410 K pparsnik@misericordia.edu
- **PARSON**, Mark 715-232-1151 521 D parsonm@uwstout.edu
- **PARSON**, Reginald 415-338-3068 35 B regg@sfsu.edu
- **PARSON**, Tara 417-328-1511 272 C tparson@sbuniv.edu
- **PARSONS**, Brian 405-208-5121 385 E pdparsons@okcu.edu
- **PARSONS**, Bruce 606-218-5273 194 C bruceparsons@upike.edu
- **PARSONS**, Cynthia 804-765-5800 494 G cynthia-parsons@chs.net
- **PARSONS**, Edy 319-363-1323 175 D eparsons@mtmercy.edu
- **PARSONS, JR.**, Frank, R 334-833-4294 4 D fparsons@hawks.huntingdon.edu
- **PARSONS**, Gayle 623-245-4600 17 G gparsons@uti.edu
- **PARSONS**, Geoffrey, J 843-349-2054 428 E parsons@coastal.edu
- **PARSONS**, James 207-859-1250 204 E maintenance@thomas.edu
- **PARSONS**, Kevin 910-410-1918 352 C ksparsons@richmondcc.edu
- **PARSONS**, Leland 231-348-6615 239 A lparsons@ncmich.edu
- **PARSONS**, Marty 831-755-6995 45 L mparsons@hartnell.edu
- **PARSONS**, Nancy, P 309-298-1066 158 A np-parsons@wiu.edu
- **PARSONS**, Pam 916-278-6446 34 B pparsons@csus.edu
- **PARSONS**, Paul, F 336-278-5724 344 D pparsons@elon.edu
- **PARSONS**, Philip 401-739-5000 425 C pparsons@neit.edu
- **PARSONS**, Priscilla 409-880-8489 471 A priscilla.parsons@lamar.edu
- **PARSONS**, Ray 302-857-1814 91 C rparson3@dtcc.edu
- **PARSONS**, Sue 562-860-2451 36 P parsons@cerritos.edu
- **PARSONS**, Teena 910-410-1810 352 C tlparsons@richmondcc.edu
- **PARSONS**, Timothy 570-558-1818 403 I tparsons@fortisinstitute.edu
- **PARSONS-ELLIS**, Sandy 530-898-6897 32 C skparsons@csuchico.edu
- **PARSONS-NIKOLIC**, Cathleen 215-951-1540 407 A parsonsnikolic@lasalle.edu
- **PARSONS-POLLARD**, Nicolle 732-571-3550 292 F nparsons@monmouth.edu
- **PARSONS-WELLS**, Rachel, E 864-833-7000 432 B reparsons@presby.edu
- **PARTAIN**, Julie 229-931-2249 127 C jpartain@southgatech.edu
- **PARTAIN**, Pam 706-272-2985 119 H ppartain@daltonstate.edu
- **PARTAIN**, Sandra 318-678-6000 195 I spartain@bpcc.edu
- **PARTCH**, Nancy 815-825-9365 144 F nancy.partch@kishwaukeecollege.edu
- **PARTEE**, Ben 805-965-0581 63 D partee@sbcc.edu
- **PARTELOW**, Kevin 815-967-7322 152 F kpartelow@rockfordcareercollege.edu
- **PARTEN**, Janice 559-278-2364 32 F jparten@csufresno.edu
- **PARTENZA**, Janet 914-674-7657 320 G jpartenza@mercy.edu
- **PARTIN**, Sherry 606-546-1625 193 E spartin2@unionky.edu
- **PARTOLAN-FRAY**, Liz 360-650-7970 509 E liz.partolan-fray@wwu.edu
- **PARTON**, Becky 217-786-2351 146 E becky.parton@llcc.edu
- **PARTON**, LeAnne 509-793-2004 501 H leannep@bigbend.edu
- **PARTON**, Stephanie 618-937-2127 148 I sparton@morthland.edu
- **PARTON**, Valerie 509-793-2371 501 H valeriep@bigbend.edu
- **PARTRIDGE**, Kristen, N 405-325-3163 389 B kpartridge@ou.edu
- **PARTRIDGE**, Patrick 801-274-3280 483 C ppartridge@wgu.edu
- **PARTRIDGE**, Richard 803-327-8031 435 D rpartridge@yorktech.edu
- **PARTRIDGE**, Steve 703-323-2383 497 H spartridge@nvcc.edu
- **PARVIZI**, Nasrin 607-753-5582 333 A nasrin.parvizi@cortland.edu
- **PARZIALE**, Anthony, J 401-825-2004 425 A ajparziale@ccri.edu
- **PARZY**, Robert 847-925-6649 141 A rparzy@harpercollege.edu
- **PASAG**, Maureen 415-338-2599 35 B mpasag@sfsu.edu
- **PASCAL**, Sandra, E 617-989-4478 229 D pascals@wit.edu
- **PASCALE**, Lynn 203-287-3031 88 E paier.admission@snet.net
- **PASCARELL**, Rose 703-993-8760 490 B rpascare@gmu.edu
- **PASCARELLA**, John 936-294-1458 471 D jbp014@shsu.edu
- **PASCARIELLO**, Jacqueline 631-632-6840 332 A jacqueline.pascariello@stonybrook.edu
- **PASCHAL**, Erin 814-641-3331 406 F paschae@juniata.edu
- **PASCHAL**, Linda, L 414-955-8208 518 A lpaschal@mcw.edu
- **PASCHALL**, Danny 562-903-4874 28 E danny.paschall@biola.edu
- **PASCHALL**, Kimberly, S 270-809-3809 192 A kpaschall@murraystate.edu
- **PASCHOLD**, Erika 402-465-7574 281 K epaschol@nebrwesleyan.edu
- **PASCO**, Leslie 315-228-7481 310 G lpasco@colgate.edu
- **PASCOE**, Frank, H 815-740-3216 157 F fpascoe@stfrancis.edu
- **PASCOE**, Tammie 903-983-8105 460 D tpascoe@kilgore.edu
- **PASCOE AGUILAR**, Daniel 541-346-6009 395 G dpascoe@uoregon.edu
- **PASCUA DEA**, Tracy 925-631-4165 59 I tjp2@stmarys-ca.edu
- **PASCUCCI**, Richard, A 215-871-6690 416 F richardp@pcom.edu
- **PASEK**, Heidi 406-771-4397 277 F hpasek@gfcmsu.edu
- **PASENELLI**, Rose 619-594-1630 35 A rpasenel@mail.sdsu.edu
- **PASHA**, Stephanie 508-831-6655 230 C spasha@wpi.edu
- **PASIC**, Amir 317-278-5652 163 D ampasic@iupui.edu
- **PASKEL**, Shanetta 410-462-8051 206 D spaskel@bccc.edu
- **PASKER**, Mark 563-876-3353 171 I mpasker@dwci.edu
- **PASKETT**, Lindy 307-855-2120 526 E lpaskett@cwc.edu
- **PASKEY**, Louise 712-279-5494 170 B louise.paskey@briarcliff.edu
- **PASKVAN**, Brian 567-661-7742 376 D brian_paskvan@owens.edu
- **PASKVAN**, Kevin, F 740-368-3052 376 B kfpaskva@owu.edu
- **PASQUARIELLO**, Gino 619-201-8970 65 J gino.pasquariello@socalsem.edu
- **PASQUARIELLO**, Robert 360-475-7835 505 F rpasquariello@olympic.edu
- **PASS-STERN**, Bernice 212-614-6176 326 C bstern@chpnet.org
- **PASSAFIUME**, Marisa 718-862-7796 319 L marisa.passafiume@manhattan. edumanhattan.edu
- **PASSARO**, Joanne 262-524-7364 515 J jpassaro@carrollu.edu
- **PASSARO**, Karen 973-275-2061 297 A karen.passaro@shu.edu
- **PASSAUER**, Bridgett, M 757-822-1536 498 H bpassauer@tcc.edu
- **PASSE**, Jeffrey 609-771-2100 290 F passej@tcnj.edu
- **PASSER**, Christine 269-782-1316 241 C cpasser@swmich.edu
- **PASSERINI**, Katia 973-642-7664 293 D katia.passerini@njit.edu
- **PASSERINI**, Katia 718-990-2773 328 F passerik@stjohns.edu
- **PASSEY**, Brent 239-513-1122 102 T bpassey@hodges.edu
- **PASTERIS**, Marc 309-467-6305 140 E mpasteris@eureka.edu
- **PASTERNAK**, Reuven 631-444-2701 332 A reuven.pasternak@stonybrookmedicine. edu
- **PASTIDES**, Harris 803-777-2001 433 F pastides@sc.edu
- **PASTIN**, John, R 856-256-4550 295 E pastin@rowan.edu
- **PASTOOR**, Robert, A 219-866-6157 166 J rpastoor@saintjoe.edu
- **PASTORELLA**, Mark, J 585-262-1509 321 J mpastorella@monroecc.edu
- **PASTORIZA**, Nelida 718-518-4412 308 C npastoriza@hostos.cuny.edu
- **PASTORRES-PALFFY**, Elizabeth 916-485-3276 378 E beth.pastorres-palffy@myunion.edu
- **PASTRANA**, Marie Luz 787-765-3560 532 I lpastrana@edpuniversity.edu
- **PASTRANA**, Marilyn 787-765-3560 532 I mpastrana@edpuniversity.edu
- **PASTVA**, Kimberlee, M 848-932-2457 295 F pastva@oldqueens.rutgers.edu
- **PASZKIEWICZ**, Wendy 312-662-4211 134 I paszk@adler.edu
- **PASZTOR**, Jim 303-220-1200 77 D jim.pasztor@cffp.edu
- **PATALANO**, Carla 617-603-6900 226 D carla.patalano@necb.edu
- **PATAWARAN**, Arrileen 773-995-2063 136 M apatawar@csu.edu
- **PATCHETT**, Heather 423-636-7303 447 G hpatchett@tusculum.edu
- **PATCHETT**, Margaret, B 704-403-3077 342 E meg.patchett@carolinashealthcare.org
- **PATCHIN**, Steve 906-487-2313 238 A shpatchi@mtu.edu
- **PATCHNER**, Michael 317-274-8362 163 D patchner@iupui.edu
- **PATE**, Herman 404-527-4520 118 F hpate@carver.edu
- **PATE**, Juston 606-759-7141 190 C juston.pate@kctcs.edu
- **PATE**, Kim 828-328-7128 345 H kim.pate@lr.edu
- **PATE**, Nino, T 671-734-1812 530 A npate@piu.edu
- **PATEE**, Carla 620-227-9378 180 E cpatee@dc3.edu
- **PATEGAS**, Dianna 203-582-8797 88 G dianna.pategas@quinnipiac.edu
- **PATEL**, Maqbool 410-951-3780 212 E mpatel@coppin.edu
- **PATEL**, Narendra, H 404-880-8064 118 K npatel@cau.edu
- **PATEL**, Prita 202-885-2177 91 J ppatel@american.edu
- **PATEL**, Rushika 810-424-5684 242 B rushika@umflint.edu
- **PATEL**, Sandip 203-582-3394 88 G sandip.patel@quinnipiac.edu
- **PATEL**, Tarun 518-694-7337 303 C tarun.patel@acphs.edu
- **PATENAUDE**, Craig 301-934-7643 207 B cpatenaude@csmd.edu
- **PATERSON**, John 802-728-1434 486 D jpaterson@vtc.edu
- **PATERSON**, Sharon 208-426-4062 132 I sharonpaterson@boisestate.edu
- **PATERSON**, Valerie 617-682-1593 218 E vpaterson@eds.edu
- **PATERSON**, Wendy, A 716-878-4214 332 F paterswa@buffalostate.edu
- **PATES**, Nancy 952-358-8200 251 A nancy.pates@normandale.edu
- **PATESTAS**, Maria 718-368-5597 308 F maria.patestas@kbcc.cuny.edu
- **PATH**, Bill 918-293-5256 386 B bpath@okstate.edu
- **PATHAK**, Dushyant 530-752-7309 69 A dpathak@ucdavis.edu
- **PATHAK**, Susanna 207-941-7187 202 I pathaks@husson.edu
- **PATHAK**, Susanna 414-425-8300 519 F spathak@shsst.edu
- **PATILLA**, Shane 770-394-8300 116 F spatilla@aii.edu
- **PATINO**, Beatriz 508-767-7100 214 F bpatino@assumption.edu
- **PATLOLLA**, Babu, P 601-877-6120 256 F bpatlolla@alcorn.edu
- **PATNAUDE**, Valerie 603-897-8533 287 F vpatnaude@rivier.edu
- **PATO**, Rosevonne 684-699-9155 529 E r.pato@amsamoa.edu
- **PATON**, Jeff 336-322-2237 351 H jeff.paton@piedmontcc.edu
- **PATON**, Nancy, E 716-645-6969 331 C nepaton@buffalo.edu
- **PATOSKY**, Julie 814-201-2733 413 P jpatosky@pennhighlands.edu
- **PATOUT**, Gerald 337-550-1380 197 K gpatout@lsue.edu
- **PATRIA**, Patricia, L 508-373-1981 215 D patty.patria@becker.edu
- **PATRIAS**, Marla 218-755-4147 248 M mpatrias@bemidjistate.edu
- **PATRICK**, Beth, G 606-783-2053 191 H b.patrick@moreheadstate.edu
- **PATRICK**, Brian 913-288-7362 182 C bpatrick@kckcc.edu
- **PATRICK**, Charles 817-923-1921 466 E cpatrick@swbts.edu
- **PATRICK**, Craig 914-632-6700 321 I cpatrick@monroecollege.edu
- **PATRICK**, Diane 616-234-4105 234 E dpatrick@grcc.edu
- **PATRICK**, Diane, D 616-234-4101 234 E dpatrick@grcc.edu
- **PATRICK**, Edward 803-536-7000 432 E
- **PATRICK**, Garry 707-476-4385 40 D garry-patrick@redwoods.edu
- **PATRICK**, Jamie 919-497-3245 346 B jpatrick@louisburg.edu
- **PATRICK**, Julietta 815-455-8613 147 E jpatrick@mchenry.edu
- **PATRICK**, Keeley 860-768-2441 89 G kpatrick@hartford.edu
- **PATRICK**, Kim 616-331-2280 234 F patricki@gvsu.edu
- **PATRICK**, Laura 949-376-6000 48 C lpatrick@lcad.edu
- **PATRICK**, Maggie 507-222-5568 245 C mpatrick@carleton.edu
- **PATRICK**, Michelle 610-436-2930 416 C mpatrick@wcupa.edu
- **PATRICK**, Nicole 662-329-7114 259 E jnpatrick@muw.edu
- **PATRICK**, Paul, D 843-953-0879 428 G patrickpd@cofc.edu
- **PATRICK**, Paul, G 864-379-6675 429 I ppatrick@erskine.edu
- **PATRICK**, Rochelle 914-633-2203 317 B rpatrick@iona.edu
- **PATRICK**, Ron 800-422-2418 96 E rpatrick@baymedical.org
- **PATRICK**, Roxann 937-294-0592 377 B roxann@saa.edu
- **PATRIDGE**, Emily 704-403-1798 342 E emily.patridge@carolinashealthcare.org
- **PATRIE**, Shannon 315-498-2802 325 G patries@sunyocc.edu
- **PATRY**, Roland 214-358-9042 472 D roland.patry@ttuhsc.edu
- **PATRYLA**, Trish 661-255-1050 30 E patryla@calarts.edu
- **PATSALIDES**, Eugene 270-831-9688 189 F eugenios.patsalides@kctcs.edu
- **PATTEE**, Bob 254-295-4524 474 E rpattee@umhb.edu
- **PATTEE**, Bonnie 801-274-3280 483 C bonnie.pattee@wgu.edu
- **PATTEN**, David, B 401-825-2194 425 A dpatten@ccri.edu
- **PATTEN**, Kaye 419-530-7963 380 D kaye.patten@utoledo.edu
- **PATTEN**, Shawn 941-752-5444 110 H pattens@scf.edu
- **PATTEN-LEMONS**, Rebecca 317-921-4667 164 F rpatten@ivytech.edu
- **PATTERSON**, Anthony 919-572-1625 341 M apatterson@apexsot.edu
- **PATTERSON**, Bart 702-992-2350 284 J president@nsc.edu
- **PATTERSON**, Becky 502-852-3385 194 A becky.patterson@louisville.edu
- **PATTERSON**, Ben 805-565-6210 75 A bpatters@westmont.edu
- **PATTERSON**, Bernie 715-346-2123 521 C
- **PATTERSON**, Blaike 251-380-3020 7 D bookstore@shc.edu
- **PATTERSON**, Carol 303-797-5701 76 J carol.patterson@arapahoe.edu
- **PATTERSON**, Charles, E 229-928-1360 122 C charles.patterson@gsw.edu
- **PATTERSON**, Charlotte 434-982-2961 495 H cjp@virginia.edu
- **PATTERSON**, Corey 325-674-6566 449 J pattersonc@acu.edu
- **PATTERSON**, Cynthia, A 252-638-7304 349 B pattersc@cravencc.edu
- **PATTERSON**, Dale 918-540-6319 384 F dale.patterson@neo.edu
- **PATTERSON**, Darrin 330-337-6403 362 I college@awc.edu
- **PATTERSON**, Donald, A 716-878-3447 332 F patterda@buffalostate.edu

PAYNE, Karen, E .... 937-529-2201.. 378 F
kepayne@united.edu
PAYNE, Kathryn .... 215-951-1000.. 407 A
paynek@lasalle.edu
PAYNE, Katie, W .... 270-809-3279.. 192 A
kpayne13@murraystate.edu
PAYNE, Kent .... 847-214-7552.. 140 A
kpayne@elgin.edu
PAYNE, Kevin .... 270-852-3207.. 191 C
kpayne@kwc.edu
PAYNE, Maribeth .... 573-840-9007.. 273 A
mpayne@trcc.edu
PAYNE, Mary .... 515-271-1452.. 171 H
mary.payne@dmu.edu
PAYNE, Melissa .... 319-398-5584.. 174 I
melissa.payne@kirkwood.edu
PAYNE, Molly .... 617-732-2218.. 225 C
molly.payne@mcphs.edu
PAYNE, Nikki .... 314-529-6864.. 267 B
npayne@maryville.edu
PAYNE, Penny .... 740-753-6472.. 369 K
paynep@hocking.edu
PAYNE, Rich .... 928-523-7618.... 15 H
rich.payne@nau.edu
PAYNE, Sherri .... 702-651-2678.. 284 H
sherri.payne@csn.edu
PAYNE, Stephen, D .... 269-471-6534.. 230 H
stephen@andrews.edu
PAYNE, Tamara .... 205-853-1200...... 5 B
tlpayne@jeffstateonline.com
PAYNE, Tara .... 603-513-1356.. 288 D
tara.payne@granite.edu
PAYNE, Tena .... 270-534-3342.. 190 H
tena.payne@kctcs.edu
PAYNE, Terry .... 828-298-3325.. 359 F
tpayne@warren-wilson.edu
PAYNE, Thomas .... 931-372-3372.. 445 B
tpayne@tntech.edu
PAYNE, Thomas, L .... 573-882-3846.. 273 E
paynet@missouri.edu
PAYNE, Tim .... 256-924-0511...... 5 E
tpayne@legacyu.net
PAYNE, Trent, D .... 864-379-8725.. 429 I
payne@erskine.edu
PAYNE, Tyler .... 740-477-7637.. 374 G
typayne@ohiochristian.edu
PAYNE, Vernon .... 269-387-2136.. 243 H
vernon.payne@wmich.edu
PAYNE, Wesley, A .... 573-840-9698.. 273 A
wpayne@trcc.edu
PAYNE, William .... 775-784-6604.. 285 A
bpayne@cabnr.unr.edu
PAYNE, William .... 218-726-7261.. 255 D
wpayne@d.umn.edu
PAYNTER, Chris .... 704-330-6531.. 348 E
chris.paynter@cpcc.edu
PAYNTER, Ronald .... 212-817-7650.. 308 A
rpaynter@gc.cuny.edu
PAYTON, Alvin .... 229-333-2123.. 130 A
alvin.payton@wiregrass.edu
PAYTON, Annie .... 256-372-4747...... 1 A
annie.payton@aamu.edu
PAYTON, Carol, A .... 478-757-5212.. 129 L
cpayton@wesleyancollege.edu
PAYTON, Janice, L .... 713-313-7885.. 470 D
janice.payton@tsu.edu
PAYTON, Janine .... 516-323-3458.. 321 H
jpayton@molloy.edu
PAYTON, Kari .... 502-736-0600.. 192 D
kpayton@sbts.edu
PAYTON, Kizzy .... 225-216-8404.. 195 H
paytonk2@mybrcc.edu
PAYTON, Shannon .... 304-214-8917.. 512 F
spayton@wvncc.edu
PAZ, Gabriel .... 717-867-6302.. 408 F
paz@lvc.edu
PAZZANI, Michael, J .... 951-827-5535.... 70 B
michael.pazzani@ucr.edu
PEABODY, William .... 845-437-7267.. 339 C
wipeabody@vassar.edu
PEACE, Derryle .... 903-886-5764.. 468 D
derryle.peace@tamuc.edu
PEACH, Jennifer .... 909-687-1465.... 44 H
jenniferpeach@gs.edu
PEACH, Kyle .... 618-262-8641.. 142 F
peachk@iecc.edu
PEACOCK, Caleb .... 423-478-7703.. 443 I
cpeacock@ptseminary.edu
PEACOCK, Joe .... 503-297-5544.. 393 C
jpeacock@ocac.edu
PEACOCK, Nelson .... 510-587-6050.... 68 L
nelson.peacock@ucop.edu
PEACOCK, Ross .... 440-775-6927.. 374 C
ross.peacock@oberlin.edu
PEACOCK, Steve .... 612-330-1583.. 244 I
peacock@augsburg.edu
PEACOCK-LANDRUM,
Linda, G .... 920-465-2163.. 520 B
peacockl@uwgb.edu
PEAK, Douglas, C .... 817-515-3076.. 467 A
douglas.peak@tccd.edu
PEAK, JR., James, F .... 804-204-1230.. 487 D
jpeak@btsr.edu
PEAK, Lisa .... 502-410-6200.. 188 H
lpeak@galencollege.edu
PEAK, Scott, S .... 414-229-6738.. 520 D
speak@uwm.edu
PEAKE, Jaklin .... 503-493-6545.. 391 A
jpeake@cu-portland.edu
PEAKS, Jason .... 757-352-4295.. 493 E
jasope1@regent.edu
PEALE, Kathy, O .... 502-597-6147.. 191 B
kathy.peale@kysu.edu
PEARCE, Arthur, B .... 229-333-5832.. 129 G
apearce@valdosta.edu
PEARCE, Chris .... 336-734-7570.. 349 G
cpearce@forsythtech.edu
PEARCE, Jared .... 641-673-2107.. 177 J
pearchj@wmpenn.edu
PEARCE, Jeff .... 505-473-6470.. 302 A
jeff.pearce@santafeuniversity.edu
PEARCE, Jennifer .... 614-823-1600.. 376 C
jpearce@otterbein.edu
PEARCE, Katheryn, P .... 386-822-7459.. 113 B
kpearce@stetson.edu
PEARCE, Melissa .... 662-846-4604.. 257 E
mpearce@deltastate.edu
PEARCE, Richard, R .... 540-654-1246.. 495 C
rpearce@umw.edu
PEARCE, Rick .... 309-268-8100.. 141 C
rick.pearce@heartland.edu
PEARCY, Shelly .... 231-591-3825.. 233 L
shellypearcy@ferris.edu
PEARIGEN, Rob .... 601-974-1001.. 258 H
rob.pearigen@millsaps.edu
PEARL, Melany .... 434-592-4020.. 491 D
mapearl@liberty.edu
PEARLE, Kathleen .... 508-678-2811.. 223 A
kathleen.pearle@bristolcc.edu
PEARLMAN, Lisa .... 617-243-2217.. 219 I
lpearlman@lasell.edu
PEARLMUTTER,
Roberta, S .... 401-456-8043.. 425 E
rpearlmutter@ric.edu
PEARMAN, Belinda .... 201-761-7302.. 296 K
bpearman@saintpeters.edu
PEARON, Jill, R .... 315-267-2108.. 334 B
pearonjr@potsdam.edu
PEARRING, Yu Yok .... 808-932-7672.. 131 E
yuyok@hawaii.edu
PEARROW, Angela .... 615-361-7555.. 439 K
apearrow@daymarinstitute.edu
PEARROW, Dorothy .... 409-772-8205.. 478 A
dapearro@utmb.edu
PEARSALL, Donald .... 919-546-8564.. 355 F
donald.pearsall@shawu.edu
PEARSALL, Joel, K .... 208-467-8521.. 134 D
president@nnu.edu
PEARSALL, Jonathan .... 617-824-8426.. 218 B
jonathan_pearsall@emerson.edu
PEARSON, Aimee .... 716-829-7803.. 313 A
pearsona@dyc.edu
PEARSON, Andrew, L .... 540-828-5410.. 487 H
apearson@bridgewater.edu
PEARSON, Ashton .... 662-915-1819.. 261 B
ashton@olemiss.edu
PEARSON, Barry .... 914-251-6020.. 334 C
barry.pearson@purchase.edu
PEARSON, Bob .... 580-477-7800.. 389 I
bob.pearson@wosc.edu
PEARSON, Bryan, J .... 814-886-6424.. 411 C
bpearson@mtaloy.edu
PEARSON, Craig .... 641-472-1186.. 175 A
cpearson@mum.edu
PEARSON, David .... 951-343-4298.... 29 H
dpearson@calbaptist.edu
PEARSON, David, L .... 515-574-1234.. 173 F
pearson@iowacentral.edu
PEARSON, Dawn .... 507-389-7219.. 252 D
dawn.pearson@southcentral.edu
PEARSON, Doug, R .... 478-301-2685.. 124 D
pearson_dr@mercer.edu
PEARSON, Elaine .... 713-221-8273.. 474 B
pearsone@uhd.edu
PEARSON, Elizabeth, R ..... 828-669-8012.. 346 M
epearson@montreat.edu
PEARSON, Geoff .... 410-857-2223.. 209 D
gpearson@mcdaniel.edu
PEARSON, Janice, L .... 559-323-2100.... 61 E
jpearson@sjcl.edu
PEARSON, John .... 412-392-3976.. 417 F
jpearson@pointpark.edu
PEARSON, Karen, L .... 208-467-8663.. 134 D
klpearson@nnu.edu
PEARSON, Lynn .... 626-815-6000.... 28 A
lpearson@apu.edu
PEARSON, Matt .... 707-778-3608.... 63 G
mpearson@santarosa.edu
PEARSON, Sam .... 503-581-8600.. 391 B
spearson@corban.edu
PEARSON, Sarah, R .... 207-786-6247.. 202 D
spearson@bates.edu
PEARSON, Sonya .... 480-461-7443.... 14 D
sonya.pearson@mesacc.edu
PEARSON, Stacy .... 208-426-1200.. 132 I
spearson@boisestate.edu
PEARSON, Steven, A .... 803-535-5434.. 428 B
spearson@claflin.edu
PEARSON, Theodore .... 812-749-1404.. 166 B
tpearson@oak.edu
PEARSON, Thomas .... 315-386-7448.. 335 B
pears105@canton.edu
PEARSON, Tracey .... 910-630-7122.. 346 E
tpearson@methodist.edu
PEARSON, Vanessa .... 207-768-9432.. 205 D
vanessa.pearson@maine.edu
PEARSON, Vonda .... 651-255-6115.. 255 C
vpearson@unitedseminary.edu
PEARSON, Walter .... 312-915-6501.. 146 G
wpearson@luc.edu
PEARSON-WHARTON,
Stacey .... 570-372-4238.. 419 H
pearsonwharton@susqu.edu
PEART, Sandra, J .... 804-289-6086.. 495 G
speart@richmond.edu
PEASE, Patrick, P .... 319-273-2221.. 170 A
patrick.pease@uni.edu
PEASE, Susan .... 860-832-3000.... 85 F
pease@ccsu.edu
PEASE, Susan .... 860-832-2605.... 85 F
pease@ccsu.edu
PEASLEE, Deidra .... 763-433-1829.. 248 K
deidra.peaslee@anokaramsey.edu
PEASTER, Carl, S .... 615-898-2424.. 444 G
buddy.peaster@mtsu.edu
PEAVEY, Donna, B .... 504-282-4455.. 198 H
dpeavey@nobts.edu
PEAVY, Kristi .... 478-757-5200.. 129 L
kpeavy@wesleyancollege.edu
PEAY, J. H. Binford .... 540-464-7311.. 499 E
peayjb@vmi.edu
PEAY, Steven, A .... 262-646-6512.. 518 G
speay@nashotah.edu
PECCHIA, John, P .... 845-575-3000.. 320 B
john.pecchia@marist.edu
PECEN, Reg, R .... 832-230-5540.. 462 K
regpecen@na.edu
PECENY, Mark .... 505-277-7381.. 302 F
markpec@unm.edu
PECHA, David, M .... 580-327-8528.. 384 M
dmpecha@nwosu.edu
PECK, Adam .... 936-468-7249.. 466 H
peckae@sfasu.edu
PECK, Barbara .... 864-379-6546.. 429 I
peck@erskine.edu
PECK, Cindy, J .... 217-443-8803.. 139 B
cpeck@dacc.edu
PECK, Daniel, A .... 408-855-5122.... 74 G
daniel.peck@wvm.edu
PECK, David .... 626-815-4503.... 28 A
dpeck@apu.edu
PECK, Edward, J .... 216-397-4218.. 370 H
epeck@jcu.edu
PECK, Jane .... 781-768-7307.. 227 G
jane.peck@regiscollege.edu
PECK, Jeanie .... 651-641-8709.. 246 B
peck@csp.edu
PECK, Kim .... 806-743-2297.. 472 D
kim.peck@ttuhsc.edu
PECK, Nan .... 563-876-3353.. 171 I
npeck@dwci.edu
PECK, Rebecca .... 816-936-8713.. 271 L
rpeck@saintlukescollege.edu
PECK, Robert .... 508-999-8539.. 220 H
rpeck@umassd.edu
PECK, Teresa, M .... 570-208-5895.. 406 J
tmpeck@kings.edu
PECKA, Kenneth, D .... 509-777-3292.. 509 H
kpecka@whitworth.edu
PECKHAM, Karissa, L .... 203-576-4552.... 89 C
kpeckham@bridgeport.edu
PECKHAM, Michael .... 920-403-3360.. 519 G
mike.peckham@snc.edu
PECKITT, JR., Carl, S .... 610-799-1114.. 408 G
cpeckitt@lccc.edu
PECOR, Sarah, A .... 262-243-5700.. 516 E
sarah.pecor@cuw.edu
PECORD, Melanie .... 608-985-2828.. 143 F
melaniepecord@jalc.edu
PECORONI, Deanna, L .... 314-434-2212.. 266 B
dpecoroni@hickeycollege.edu
PECOTA, Samuel .... 707-654-1164.... 33 D
specota@csum.edu
PECTOL, James, B .... 423-585-6823.. 447 D
james.pectol@ws.edu
PEDANO, Karen .... 610-896-1000.. 405 I
kpedano@haverford.edu
PEDE, Michael .... 315-792-5411.. 321 G
mpede@mvcc.edu
PEDE, Mike .... 713-743-9551.. 473 F
mlpede@uh.edu
PEDEN, Gary, S .... 315-470-6588.. 334 E
gspeden@esf.edu
PEDERSEN, Daniel, T .... 320-308-2166.. 252 A
dtpedersen@stcloudstate.edu
PEDERSEN, Eric .... 907-474-7500.... 10 G
PEDERSEN, Eric .... 360-867-6176.. 503 G
pedersee@evergreen.edu
PEDERSEN, Eric .... 435-652-7977.. 482 A
pedersen@dixie.edu
PEDERSEN, Eric, R .... 907-786-1266.... 10 F
erpedersen@uaa.alaska.edu
PEDERSEN, Ginger, L .... 561-967-7222.. 106 D
pederseg@palmbeachstate.edu
PEDERSEN, Jeffrey, M .... 631-451-4425.. 336 D
pedersj@sunysuffolk.edu
PEDERSEN, Jennifer, L .... 308-635-6078.. 283 D
pedersen@wncc.edu
PEDERSEN, Joel, D .... 402-472-1201.. 282 K
jdpedersen@nebraska.edu
PEDERSEN, Mary, E .... 805-756-2246.... 31 I
mdederse@calpoly.edu
PEDERSEN, Melissa .... 617-217-9036.. 215 B
mpedersen@baystate.edu
PEDERSEN, Patricia, E .... 203-436-8518.... 90 D
patty.pedersen@yale.edu
PEDERSEN, Phyllis .... 225-214-6979.. 199 B
phyllis.pedersen@ololcollege.edu
PEDERSON, Barb .... 701-231-7211.. 361 A
barbara.pederson@ndsu.edu
PEDERSON, Curtis .... 503-943-8046.. 396 B
pedersoc@up.edu
PEDERSON, Katie .... 303-220-1200.... 77 D
katie.pederson@cffp.edu
PEDERSON, Mark .... 765-677-2117.. 164 B
mark.pederson@indwes.edu
PEDERSON, Robert, A .... 207-778-7036.. 205 A
pederson@maine.edu
PEDESCLEAUX, Desiree .... 404-270-5696.. 128 A
dpedescl@spelman.edu
PEDIGO, Sue, H .... 615-230-3551.. 447 C
sue.pedigo@volstate.edu
PEDNEAU, Judy .... 276-326-4461.. 487 F
jpedneau@bluefield.edu
PEDRAZA, Jonathan, N .... 262-691-5308.. 524 G
jpedraza2@wctc.edu
PEDRICK, Andrea .... 315-786-2236.. 317 H
apedrick@sunyjefferson.edu
PEDRICK, Jim .... 319-385-6218.. 174 A
jim.pedrick@iw.edu
PEDRO, David .... 508-910-9070.. 220 H
dpedro@umassd.edu
PEDRONE, Dino, J .... 607-729-1581.. 312 E
dpedrone@davisny.edu
PEDROTTY, Kate .... 318-869-5715.. 194 I
kpedrotty@centenary.edu
PEDUTO, Michelle, A .... 412-578-6157.. 400 C
mapeduto@carlow.edu
PEE, Charles, M .... 803-934-3294.. 431 E
cpee@morris.edu
PEEBLES, Carolyn .... 919-572-1625.. 341 M
cpeebles@apexsot.edu
PEEBLES, Ethel .... 704-216-6111.. 346 A
epeebles@livingstone.edu
PEEBLES, Henry .... 321-674-7715.. 100 M
peebles@fit.edu
PEEBLES, Lee .... 401-739-5000.. 425 C
lpeebles@neit.edu
PEED, Stephen .... 207-326-2451.. 204 C
stephen.peed@mma.edu
PEEDIN, Pamela, L .... 603-646-2445.. 286 J
pamela.l.peedin@dartmouth.edu
PEEK, Brian .... 706-245-7226.. 120 D
bpeek@ec.edu
PEEK, Katherine .... 909-652-6333.... 37 D
kay.peek@chaffey.edu
PEEL, Bill .... 214-932-1112.. 460 J
billpeel@letu.edu
PEEL, Chermae .... 432-552-3744.. 478 B
peel_c@utpb.edu
PEEL, Claire .... 817-735-2762.. 475 C
claire.peel@unthsc.edu
PEEL, Henry .... 239-489-9011.. 101 F
hpeel@fsw.edu
PEEL, Michael, A .... 203-432-8362.... 90 D
mike.peel@yale.edu
PEELER, Chris Goff .... 704-461-6663.. 342 A
chrisgoff@bac.edu
PEELER, Jodi, S .... 919-508-2362.. 359 G
jspeeler@peace.edu
PEELER, Jody .... 740-283-3771.. 368 L
jpeeler@franciscan.edu
PEELER, Mark, L .... 864-379-8850.. 429 I
mlp@erskine.edu
PEELING, Rebecca .... 561-803-2024.. 106 C
becky_peeling@pba.edu
PEEPLES, Jim .... 706-778-8500.. 125 J
jpeeples@piedmont.edu
PEEPLES, Junelyn .... 909-607-3884.... 64 A
jpeeples@scrippscollege.edu
PEEPLES, Terry, G .... 870-245-5169.... 21 E
peeplest@obu.edu
PEEPLES, Tim .... 336-278-5613.. 344 D
peeples@elon.edu

PEER, Ronda .... 307-754-6123.. 526 N
ronda.peer@nwc.edu
PEERMAN, Carey, H .... 540-224-6973.. 491 A
chpeerman@jchs.edu
PEETZ, Ralf .... 718-982-2000.. 307 F
ralf.peetz@csi.cuny.edu
PEFFALL, Marianne .... 610-436-2705.. 416 C
mpeffall@wcupa.edu
PEFFER, Deb .... 313-593-5100.. 242 A
dkpeffer@umich.edu
PEGAH, Kris .... 941-359-7633.. 107 M
kpegah@ringling.edu
PEGG, Steven, M .... 410-777-2651.. 206 B
smpegg@aacc.edu
PEGGY, Allen .... 850-644-1841.. 111 C
mrallen@fsu.edu
PEGRAM, Mike .... 402-761-8270.. 282 F
mpegram@southeast.edu
PEGUES, Charlotte Fant ... 662-915-5974.. 261 B
cfant@olemiss.edu
PEGUES, Mollie .... 662-252-8000.. 260 F
mpegues@rustcollege.edu
PEGUES, Patricia .... 662-252-2491.. 260 F
ppegues@rustcollege.edu
PEGUES, Patricia .... 662-252-8000.. 260 F
ppegues@rustcollege.edu
PEHLMAN, Patricia, A ..... 717-245-1545.. 402 D
pehlman@dickinson.edu
PEHRSSON,
Dale-Elizabeth .... 989-774-6995.. 232 D
pehrs1d@cmich.edu
PEI, Alissa .... 573-876-7212.. 272 I
apei@stephens.edu
PEIFER, Bruce .... 301-891-4525.. 213 D
bpeifer@wau.edu
PEIFER, Michelle .... 704-991-0393.. 353 E
mpeifer7924@stanly.edu
PEIFFER, Cyndi .... 641-673-1040.. 177 J
peifferc@wmpenn.edu
PEIFFER, Kelly .... 215-885-2360.. 409 G
kpeiffer@manor.edu
PEIFFER, Mark, J .... 515-271-1475.. 171 H
mark.peiffer@dmu.edu
PEIRCE, Nathaniel .... 603-899-4320.. 287 A
peircen@franklinpierce.edu
PEISER, Andrew .... 212-615-3386.. 320 G
apeiser@mercy.edu
PEKRUL, William, A .... 507-354-8221.. 247 J
pekrulwa@mlc-wels.edu
PELAEZ, Michelle .... 813-253-6251.. 114 M
mpelaez@ut.edu
PELAK, Anne, C .... 914-654-5225.. 311 A
apelak@cnr.edu
PELAZZA, Todd, A .... 203-254-4090.... 87 G
tapelazza@fairfield.edu
PELC, Sharon .... 308-865-8523.. 282 L
pelcs@unk.edu
PELISSERO, John, P .... 773-508-7470.. 146 G
jpeliss@luc.edu
PELIZZA, John .... 518-244-2051.. 327 H
pelizj@sage.edu
PELKEY, David .... 360-596-5231.. 508 A
dpelkey@spscc.edu
PELLEGRIN, Amy, E .... 304-367-4135.. 513 B
amy.pellegrin@fairmontstate.edu
PELLEGRIN, Nathan .... 510-466-7210.... 57 E
npellegrin@peralta.edu
PELLEGRINI, Larry .... 570-674-6307.. 410 K
lpellegr@misericordia.edu
PELLEGRINI, Virginia .... 208-426-3236.. 132 I
virginiapellegrini@boisestate.edu
PELLEGRINO, Debra, A ..... 570-941-6305.. 422 B
debra.pellegrino@scranton.edu
PELLEGRINO, Diane .... 973-655-5460.. 293 A
pellegrinod@mail.montclair.edu
PELLEGRINO, Eric .... 856-351-2770.. 296 L
epellegrino@salemcc.edu
PELLEGRINO, Karen, A ..... 203-254-4100.... 87 G
kpellegrino@fairfield.edu
PELLEGRINO, Nicole .... 315-364-3240.. 340 B
npellegrino@wells.edu
PELLEGRINO, Thomas, C 203-254-4000.... 87 G
tpellegrino@fairfield.edu
PELLETIER, Corey .... 207-859-1106.. 204 E
pelletierc@thomas.edu
PELLETIER, Jo-Ann, M ...... 508-678-2811.. 223 A
jo-ann.pelletier@bristolcc.edu
PELLETIER, Kristan, M ...... 518-629-7328.. 316 G
k.pelletier@hvcc.edu
PELLETIER, Sherry .... 845-368-7215.. 329 I
sherry.pelletier@use.salvationarmy.org
PELLETT, Tracy .... 912-279-5960.. 119 C
tpellett@ccga.edu
PELLICANE, Patrick .... 657-278-2407.... 33 A
ppellicane@fullerton.edu
PELLICANO, Gregory, J ..... 215-898-7958.. 421 E
gpell@upenn.edu
PELLICO, Gary .... 317-921-4882.. 164 F
gpellico@ivytech.edu
PELLISH, Catherine .... 303-404-5022.... 80 E
catherine.pellish@frontrange.edu
PELLIZZI, Thomas .... 608-757-6328.. 523 A
tpellizzi@blackhawk.edu
PELLMAN, Samuel .... 315-859-4615.. 315 D
spellman@hamilton.edu
PELLOT, Robert .... 212-938-5720.. 334 F
rpellot@sunyopt.edu
PELLS, Ruth, R .... 509-777-4665.. 509 H
rpells@whitworth.edu
PELLY, Michael .... 714-997-6982.... 37 F
pelly@chapman.edu
PELOQUIN, Andy .... 503-517-1815.. 396 F
apeloquin@westernseminary.edu
PELOQUIN-DODD,
Mary, T .... 919-515-2143.. 357 B
mary_peloquin-dodd@ncsu.edu
PELOSI, Lisa .... 401-598-1000.. 425 B
lpelosi@jwu.edu
PELOSO, Elizabeth, D .... 215-746-0234.. 421 E
epeloso@upenn.edu
PELPHREY, Barry .... 606-546-1299.. 193 E
bpelphrey@unionky.edu
PELRINE, Edward .... 847-566-6401.. 157 G
epelrine@usml.edu
PELRINE, JR., John, P ...... 773-298-3121.. 153 H
pelrine@sxu.edu
PELTIER, Beverly .... 706-771-4023.. 117 C
bpeltier@augustatech.edu
PELTIER, Eileen .... 860-253-3032.... 86 A
epeltier@asnuntuck.edu
PELTIER, John .... 401-874-4530.. 426 D
jpeltier@uri.edu
PELTIER, Linda, M .... 937-778-7802.. 368 E
lpeltier@edisonohio.edu
PELTIER, Matthew, S .... 423-652-4740.. 440 J
mspeltie@king.edu
PELTO, William, L .... 828-262-3021.. 356 B
peltowl@appstate.edu
PELTON, Jack .... 208-426-4203.. 132 I
jpelton@boisestate.edu
PELTON, M. Lee .... 617-824-8525.. 218 B
lee_pelton@emerson.edu
PELTON, Mark .... 478-445-5075.. 121 A
mark.pelton@gcsu.edu
PELTON, Vanessa .... 805-965-0581.... 63 D
pelton@sbcc.edu
PELTON, Woody .... 336-278-6700.. 344 D
wpelton@elon.edu
PELTZ, Mark .... 641-269-4940.. 172 I
peltzm@grinnell.edu
PELUSI, Mario, J .... 309-556-3061.. 143 D
mpelusi@iwu.edu
PELUSO, Constance .... 718-631-6297.. 309 E
cpeluso@qcc.cuny.edu
PELUSO, Eileen .... 570-321-4135.. 409 F
pelusoem@lycoming.edu
PELUSO-VERDEND, Gary ..... 918-270-6405.. 386 I
gary.peluso@ptstulsa.edu
PELY, Laszlo .... 410-617-2421.. 208 G
lpely@loyola.edu
PELZEL, Kevin .... 314-719-3627.. 265 C
kpelzel@fontbonne.edu
PELZIER-GLAZE, Bernnel 713-313-7496.. 470 D
glazedm@tsu.edu
PEMBERTON, Barbara .... 870-245-5541.... 21 E
pembertonb@obu.edu
PEMBERTON, Cynthia .... 970-248-1881.... 77 L
cpemberton@coloradomesa.edu
PEMBERTON, Cynthia, L . 816-235-1107.. 273 F
pembertonc@umkc.edu
PEMBERTON, Loren .... 509-533-3503.. 503 A
loren.pemberton@sfcc.spokane.edu
PEMBERTON, Richard .... 573-897-5000.. 272 H
PEMBROOK, Randall, G .... 618-650-2481.. 155 A
rpembro@siue.edu
PEMSTEIN, Debra .... 845-758-7405.. 304 F
pemstein@bard.edu
PENA, Amy .... 505-747-2140.. 301 F
amy.pena@nnmc.edu
PENA, Andrew, M .... 575-646-1694.. 300 J
ampena@nmsu.edu
PENA, Damien, A .... 805-289-6113.... 73 F
dpena@vcccd.edu
PENA, Hector .... 787-725-6500.. 531 C
hpena@albizu.edu
PENA, Jesus .... 610-683-4700.. 415 C
pena@kutztown.edu
PENA, Maria .... 425-388-9979.. 503 F
mpena@everettcc.edu
PENA, Maria .... 360-417-6340.. 505 I
mpena@pencol.edu
PENA, Milagros .... 951-827-2762.... 70 B
milagros.pena@ucr.edu
PENA, Phil .... 636-584-6701.. 264 M
philip.pena@eastcentral.edu
PENA, Raquel, A .... 956-794-4988.. 460 F
rapena@laredo.edu
PENA, Rose .... 575-439-3700.. 301 A
rosep@nmsu.edu
PENALOZA, Carlos .... 518-381-1381.. 330 B
cpenaloza@sunysccc.edu
PENCE, Bill .... 540-868-7061.. 497 E
bpence@lfcc.edu
PENCE, Nadine, S .... 765-361-6434.. 169 C
pencen@wabash.edu
PENCE, Paula .... 541-880-2236.. 391 F
pence@klamathcc.edu
PENDAKUR,
Sumun (Sunni) .... 909-607-3470.... 46 A
spendakur@hmc.edu
PENDELTON, Alicia .... 313-577-2017.. 243 F
alicia.pendelton@wayne.edu
PENDERGAST, Kate .... 860-768-2403.... 89 G
pendergas@hartford.edu
PENDERGAST,
Katherine, M .... 617-373-2230.. 227 B
PENDERGAST, Linda .... 617-984-1695.. 227 F
lpendergast@quincycollege.edu
PENDERGRASS, Alice .... 850-718-2201.... 97 G
pendergrassa@chipola.edu
PENDERGRASS, Martha ..... 919-843-5048.. 357 D
mjpender@email.unc.edu
PENDERGRASS, Toni .... 505-566-3209.. 301 J
pendergrasst@sancollege.edu
PENDERGRAST, Runan .... 859-246-6305.. 189 B
runan.pendergrast@kctcs.edu
PENDERS, Brooke .... 860-528-4111.... 87 H
bpenders@goodwin.edu
PENDHARKAR, Daya .... 813-253-7091.. 102 R
dpendharkar@hccfl.edu
PENDLETON, Chris .... 540-261-8441.. 494 F
chris.pendleton@svu.edu
PENDLETON, Gail .... 510-981-2804.... 57 B
gpendleton@peralta.edu
PENDLETON, Janis, S .... 803-327-7402.. 428 D
jpendleton@clintoncollege.edu
PENDLETON, Laura .... 509-452-5100.. 505 H
lpendleton@pnwu.edu
PENDLETON, Laurence .... 615-963-7923.. 445 A
laurence.pendleton@tnstate.edu
PENDLETON, Mitch .... 801-524-1948.. 480 J
mpendleton@ldsbc.edu
PENDLETON, Patrick .... 928-541-7777.... 15 G
ppendleton@ncu.edu
PENDLETON, Penny .... 479-788-7121.... 23 A
penny.pendleton@uafs.edu
PENDLETON, Sally .... 502-895-3411.. 191 F
spendleton@lpts.edu
PENDSE, Ravindra .... 401-863-7250.. 424 J
ravi_pendse@brown.edu
PENFIELD, Randall, D .... 336-334-3944.. 358 B
rdpenfie@uncg.edu
PENGRA, Matt .... 407-679-0100.. 102 I
mpengra@fullsail.com
PENISTEN, Douglas .... 918-456-5511.. 384 G
penisten@nsuok.edu
PENIX, Doug .... 859-442-1634.. 189 D
doug.penix@kctcs.edu
PENIX, Kristine .... 501-882-3600.... 18 I
PENKALA, Robert .... 586-445-7636.. 237 C
penkalar@macomb.edu
PENKE, Ann K .... 920-565-1038.. 517 D
penkea@lakeland.edu
PENLAND, Joni, M .... 502-410-6200.. 188 H
jpenland@galencollege.edu
PENLAND, Nathan .... 417-328-1828.. 272 C
npenland@sbuniv.edu
PENLEY, Julie .... 915-831-7001.. 457 H
jpenley@epcc.edu
PENN, David .... 407-447-7300.. 102 D
dpenn@fccollege.edu
PENN, Deborah .... 620-947-3121.. 185 B
deborahp@tabor.edu
PENN, Jamie .... 570-484-2322.. 415 D
jks109@iup.edu
PENN, Jamilyn .... 425-739-8255.. 504 F
jamilyn.penn@lwtech.edu
PENN, Mark A .... 702-802-2837.. 285 E
mpenn@roseman.edu
PENN-HARGROVE,
Valencia .... 773-256-3000.. 147 G
vpennhargrove@meadville.edu
PENN-MARSHALL,
Michelle .... 757-727-5267.. 490 E
michelle.penn-marshall@hamptonu.edu
PENN-MARSHALL,
Michelle .... 757-637-2690.. 490 E
michelle.pennmarshall@hamptonu.edu
PENNA, Anthony .... 617-552-3475.. 216 C
anthony.penna@bc.edu
PENNACHIO, Michael .... 617-521-2190.. 228 C
michael.pennachio@simmons.edu
PENNARTZ-BROWNING,
Kathy .... 940-397-4214.. 462 A
kathy.pennartz@mwsu.edu
PENNER, Julie .... 815-836-5667.. 145 H
pennerju@lewisu.edu
PENNETTI, Dianna .... 212-854-3362.. 304 I
dpennetti@barnard.edu
PENNEY, Bill .... 352-395-5160.. 109 C
bill.penney@sfcollege.edu
PENNIMAN, Sarah .... 717-361-1428.. 403 C
pennimans@etown.edu
PENNINGS, Rhonda, R .... 712-324-5061.. 175 G
rpennings@nwicc.edu
PENNINGTON, Glenda, J 304-865-6141.. 511 C
jo.pennington@ovu.edu
PENNINGTON,
Josianne, E .... 410-704-3255.. 213 B
jpennington@towson.edu
PENNINGTON, Karen, L ..... 973-655-4311.. 293 A
penningtonk@mail.montclair.edu
PENNINGTON, Kevin .... 252-399-6467.. 341 P
knpennington@barton.edu
PENNINGTON, Kimberly .. 828-328-7473.. 345 H
kimberly.pennington@lr.edu
PENNINGTON, Laurie ...... 928-428-8231.... 13 B
laurie.pennington@eac.edu
PENNINGTON, Michael ..... 910-521-6637.. 358 C
michael.pennington@uncp.edu
PENNINGTON, Nicole ...... 740-533-4610.. 375 H
penningj@ohio.edu
PENNINGTON, Ronald, J 724-946-7014.. 423 B
rpenning@westminster.edu
PENNINGTON, Sandra ...... 801-375-5125.. 481 C
spennington@rmuohp.edu
PENNINGTON, Sherry, R . 417-667-8181.. 264 A
spennington@cottey.edu
PENNINGTON, Simon .... 650-949-7156.... 44 B
penningtonsimon@foothill.edu
PENNINGTON, Thomas ... 479-964-0824.... 19 F
tpennington@atu.edu
PENNINGTON, Wayne ..... 906-487-2005.. 238 A
wayne@mtu.edu
PENNINI, Susan, W .... 617-333-2165.. 217 F
spennini@curry.edu
PENNIPEDE, Barbara, S ... 914-923-2699.. 325 J
bpennipede@pace.edu
PENNIPIECE, Deirdre .... 718-960-8675.. 308 B
deirdre.pettipiece@lehman.cuny.edu
PENNISTON, Mary Ann ... 660-541-5127.. 269 J
mpenn@nwmissouri.edu
PENNIX, James .... 540-831-5371.. 493 A
jpennix@radford.edu
PENNOCK, Margaret .... 605-367-7667.. 437 G
margaret.pennock@southeasttech.edu
PENNY, Rick .... 440-525-7320.. 371 F
rpenny@lakelandcc.edu
PENNYMAN, Judy .... 706-419-1113.. 119 G
judy.pennyman@covenant.edu
PENROD, Donald .... 562-985-5091.... 33 B
don.penrod@csulb.edu
PENROSE, Betsy, S .... 315-786-2249.. 317 H
bpenrose@sunyjefferson.edu
PENROSE, John .... 513-875-3344.. 365 K
john.penrose@chatfield.edu
PENROSE, Leif .... 813-253-7370.. 102 R
lpenrose@hccfl.edu
PENRY, Jason .... 870-972-2060.... 18 J
jpenry@astate.edu
PENRY, Michael, A .... 919-866-5532.. 353 I
mapenry@waketech.edu
PENSE, Christine .... 610-861-5312.. 411 G
cpense@northampton.edu
PENSGARD, Sara, E .... 540-338-1776.. 492 H
library@phc.edu
PENSIS, Claude .... 602-639-7500.... 13 I
PENSON, Amy, M .... 828-395-1296.. 350 E
apenson@isothermal.edu
PENTZER, Scott .... 504-865-5339.. 200 C
cge@tulane.edu
PENWELL, Kelly .... 707-864-3382.... 65 A
kelly.penwell@solano.edu
PENZENSTADLER, SSND,
Joan .... 414-930-3388.. 518 F
penzenj@mtmary.edu
PENZIUL, Carl .... 607-844-8222.. 337 G
penziuc@tc3.edu
PEOPLE, Yasha .... 732-247-5241.. 293 B
ypeople@nbts.edu
PEOPLES, Frankie .... 334-874-5700...... 3 A
fpeoples@ccal.edu
PEOPLES, Peg .... 845-758-7432.. 304 F
peoples@bard.edu
PEOPLES, Shawn .... 217-581-3827.. 139 H
sdpeoples@eiu.edu
PEOPLES, Vanessa .... 312-996-2860.. 156 F
vpeoples@uic.edu
PEOPLES, Verjanis .... 225-771-2290.. 199 H
verjanis_peoples@subr.edu
PEPIN, Mark .... 918-495-7236.. 386 H
mpepin@oru.edu
PEPIN, Sean .... 408-741-2185.... 74 H
sean.pepin@westvalley.edu
PEPION, Kenneth .... 970-247-7334.... 80 D
pepion_k@fortlewis.edu
PEPITONE, Dianne .... 914-831-0367.. 311 C
dpepitone@cw.edu
PEPITONE, William .... 215-885-2360.. 409 G
wpepitone@manor.edu
PEPLINSKI, Michael .... 724-938-4950.. 414 E
peplinski@calu.edu

PEPLOW, Nena .... 309-677-3223.. 136 B
nena@bradley.edu
PEPPER, Evan .... 818-299-5727.... 74 A
epepper@westcoastuniversity.edu
PEPPER, Robert .... 717-766-2511.. 410 J
rpepper@messiah.edu
PEPPIN, Patricia .... 480-461-7456.... 14 D
pat.peppin@mesacc.edu
PEPPLE, Michael .... 913-621-8740.. 180 F
mpepple@donnelly.edu
PERAGALLO, Nilda, P ...... 305-284-2107.. 114 H
nperagallo@miami.edu
PERALES, Jose, J .... 585-385-8464.. 328 E
jperales@sjfc.edu
PERALES, Michelle .... 210-485-0031.. 450 A
mperales4@alamo.edu
PERANANAMGAM,
Reetha .... 313-593-5390.. 242 A
reetha@umich.edu
PERCHINSKY, Tessa, A .... 715-836-3887.. 520 A
perchita@uwec.edu
PERCIANTE, Linda, K .... 303-963-3237.... 77 I
lperciante@ccu.edu
PERCIVAL, Laura .... 989-275-5000.. 236 E
laura.percival@kirtland.edu
PERCONTI, Thomas .... 928-350-2100.... 16 P
thomas.perconti@prescott.edu
PERCUOCO, Robert, E ..... 563-884-5460.. 176 C
robert.percuoco@palmer.edu
PERCY, Paul .... 865-471-3219.. 439 C
ppercy@cn.edu
PERCY, Stephen .... 503-725-5143.. 394 G
spercy@pdx.edu
PERDOMO, Jose, A .... 425-235-2352.. 506 F
jperdomo@rtc.edu
PERDUE, Erika .... 941-752-5323.. 110 H
perduee@scf.edu
PERDUE, K. Alan .... 304-876-5009.. 513 E
aperdue@shepherd.edu
PERDUE, Laura .... 318-797-5257.. 198 C
laura.perdue@lsus.edu
PERDUE, Mark .... 859-858-3511.. 186 J
mark.perdue@asbury.edu
PERDUE, Penny .... 708-534-4130.. 140 H
pperdue@govst.edu
PERDUE, Rhonda .... 540-857-6325.. 499 B
rperdue@virginiawestern.edu
PERDUE, Robin, A .... 843-383-8025.. 428 F
rperdue@coker.edu
PERDUE, Tina, K .... 740-376-4730.. 372 A
tina.perdue@marietta.edu
PERDUE, Wendy, C .... 804-289-1779.. 495 G
wperdue@richmond.edu
PERDUYN, Ellen .... 330-972-6056.. 378 G
perduyn@uakron.edu
PEREA, Jennifer, R .... 312-362-1083.. 139 C
jrosato@depaul.edu
PEREBOOM, Maarten, L .. 410-543-6450.. 213 A
mlpereboom@salisbury.edu
PERECMAN, Dov .... 845-434-5240.. 341 L
dperecman@fallsburgyeshiva.com
PEREIRA, Freyja .... 707-527-4512.... 63 G
fpereira@santarosa.edu
PEREIRA, Greg .... 480-517-8376.... 14 G
greg.pereira@riosalado.edu
PEREIRA, Malin .... 704-687-7197.. 358 A
mpereira@uncc.edu
PEREIRA, Mary Ellen .... 541-485-1780.. 393 A
maryellenpereira@newhope.edu
PEREIRA, Sandra .... 508-849-3363.. 214 E
spereira@annamaria.edu
PEREKRESTOV, Michael ... 315-858-0945.. 316 E
library@hts.edu
PERELLI, Elizabeth .... 415-452-5466.... 38 E
eperelli@ccsf.edu
PERERA, Curtis .... 360-752-8330.. 501 G
cperera@btc.edu
PERETZ, Marc, H .... 989-964-4387.. 240 F
mhp@svsu.edu
PEREY, James .... 928-649-6513.... 18 D
james.perey@yc.edu
PEREYRA, Moises .... 212-694-1000.. 305 I
mpereyra@boricuacollege.edu
PEREZ, Alba .... 787-850-9109.. 538 B
alba.perez@upr.edu
PEREZ, Alice .... 805-965-0581.... 63 D
amperez17@sbcc.edu
PEREZ, Andrew .... 518-438-3111.. 320 A
andyp@mariacollege.edu
PEREZ, Angel, B .... 860-297-2000.... 89 B
PEREZ, Angeles .... 787-725-6500.. 531 C
aperez@albizu.edu
PEREZ, Antonio .... 212-220-1234.. 307 B
aperez@bmcc.cuny.edu
PEREZ, Arely .... 816-322-0110.. 262 N
arely.perez@calvary.edu
PEREZ, Awilda .... 787-766-1717.. 536 B
um_aperez@suagm.edu
PEREZ, Carlos .... 787-622-8000.. 537 B
cperez@pupr.edu
PEREZ, Carlos .... 787-754-8000.. 537 B
cperez@pupr.edu
PEREZ, Carmen, I .... 787-279-1912.. 533 J
cperez@bayamon.inter.edu
PEREZ, Cesar .... 208-732-6329.. 133 E
cperez@csi.edu
PEREZ, Cheryle .... 787-852-1430.. 532 N
cperez@hccpr.edu
PEREZ, Cristina .... 415-476-4753.... 70 D
cristina.perez@ucsf.edu
PEREZ, Diana .... 805-922-6966.... 25 I
dperez@hancockcollege.edu
PEREZ, Doris .... 787-891-0925.. 533 G
dperez@aguadilla.inter.edu
PEREZ, Doris, U .... 671-735-5517.. 529 G
doris.perez@guamcc.edu
PEREZ, Eduardo .... 787-279-1912.. 533 J
eperezd@bayamon.inter.edu
PEREZ, Enrique .... 714-480-7460.... 58 F
perez_enrique@rsccd.edu
PEREZ, Gay .... 434-243-3605.. 495 H
bgd2j@virginia.edu
PEREZ, JR., Gilberto .... 574-535-7775.. 161 A
gperez@goshen.edu
PEREZ, Heather, K .... 816-604-3007.. 267 J
heatherk.perez@mcckc.edu
PEREZ, Ivelisse .... 787-834-9595.. 536 E
iperez@uaa.edu
PEREZ, Jeffrey .... 803-323-2225.. 435 B
perezj@winthrop.edu
PEREZ, Jim .... 971-722-6111.. 394 F
jim.perez@pcc.edu
PEREZ, Joe .... 602-682-6841.... 11 I
jperez@azsummitlaw.edu
PEREZ, Jose .... 787-857-3600.. 533 I
japerez@br.inter.edu
PEREZ, Jose .... 915-566-9621.. 479 H
jperez@westerntech.edu
PEREZ, Lance, C .... 402-472-3751.. 282 M
lperez1@unl.edu
PEREZ, Luci .... 909-599-5433.... 48 K
lperez@lifepacific.edu
PEREZ, Lupe .... 509-542-4802.. 502 G
lperez@columbiabasin.edu
PEREZ, Lydia .... 646-565-6000.. 337 I
lydia.perez@touro.edu
PEREZ, Lynwood, C .... 407-366-9493.. 260 E
lperez@rts.edu
PEREZ, Magda .... 787-841-2000.. 535 I
magda_perez@pucpr.edu
PEREZ, Manuel .... 916-484-8925.... 51 A
perezm@arc.losrios.edu
PEREZ, Manuel .... 562-985-4151.... 33 B
manuel.perez@csulb.edu
PEREZ, Marciano .... 619-388-3498.... 60 F
mperez@sdccd.edu
PEREZ, Margarita .... 337-482-6272.. 201 D
mperez@louisiana.edu
PEREZ, Maria .... 787-891-0925.. 533 G
mperez@aguadilla.inter.edu
PEREZ, Maria del C .... 787-284-1912.. 534 C
mcperezr@ponce.inter.edu
PEREZ, Mario .... 323-343-3075.... 33 C
mario.perez@calstatela.edu
PEREZ, Michelle .... 717-871-5942.. 415 F
michelle.perez@millersville.edu
PEREZ, Mireya .... 708-656-8000.. 149 A
mireya.perez@morton.edu
PEREZ, Monica .... 413-552-2227.. 223 E
mperez@hcc.edu
PEREZ, Monica .... 864-644-5135.. 432 G
mperez@swu.edu
PEREZ, Monte, E .... 818-364-7796.... 49 J
perezme@lamission.edu
PEREZ, Myrna .... 787-786-3030.. 536 F
mperez@ucb.edu.pr
PEREZ, Natasha .... 316-295-5888.. 181 B
natasha_perez@friends.edu
PEREZ, Omar .... 787-740-1611.. 536 G
omar.perez@uccaribe.edu
PEREZ, Oscar .... 305-821-3333.. 101 B
operez@fnu.edu
PEREZ, Pablo .... 305-827-5452.... 95 B
PEREZ, Peter .... 203-254-4000.... 87 G
pperez1@fairfield.edu
PEREZ, Ricardo .... 818-240-1000.... 45 A
rperez@glendale.edu
PEREZ, Ron .... 760-744-1150.... 56 F
rperez@palomar.edu
PEREZ, Ronald .... 414-227-4128.. 520 D
perez@uwm.edu
PEREZ, Rowena Ellen ...... 671-735-5640.. 529 G
rowenaellen.perez@guamcc.edu
PEREZ, Ruperto .... 404-894-2575.. 121 D
ruperto.perez@vpss.gatech.edu
PEREZ, Scott, L .... 818-677-2901.... 34 A
scott.perez@csun.edu
PEREZ, Sonny, P .... 671-735-2372.. 530 B
sonnypz@uguam.uog.edu
PEREZ, Stephen .... 916-278-6331.... 34 B
sjperez@csus.edu
PEREZ, Suleyma .... 773-442-5400.. 149 J
s-perez6@neiu.edu
PEREZ, Vanessa .... 305-821-3333.. 101 B
vperez@fnu.edu
PEREZ, William .... 787-780-0070.. 531 B
wperez@caribbean.edu
PEREZ, Yolanda .... 787-834-9595.. 536 E
yperez@uaa.edu
PEREZ-CASANOVA,
María, T .... 787-480-2448.. 531 J
mperez02@sanjuanciudadpatria.com
PEREZ DE JESUS,
Margarita .... 787-848-5739.. 536 C
PEREZ DEL VALLE,
Lourdes .... 787-863-2390.. 533 K
lourdes.perez@fajardo.inter.edu
PEREZ-FRANCO, Mayte .... 619-260-2395.... 72 B
mpf@sandiego.edu
PEREZ-GONZALEZ,
Yariela .... 408-498-5145.... 39 H
yperez@cogswell.edu
PÉREZ-LÓPEZ, Antonio .... 787-878-5475.. 533 H
antperez@arecibo.inter.edu
PEREZ-LOPEZ,
Deborah, J .... 912-478-1566.. 122 B
dperezlopez@georgiasouthern.edu
PEREZ-LOPEZ, Myrna, E . 787-763-6700.. 532 L
meperez@se-pr.edu
PEREZ RIESTRA, Estela ... 787-764-0000.. 538 F
estela.perez@upr.edu
PEREZ-RODRIGUEZ,
Jose, F .... 787-723-4481.. 531 D
jperez@ceaprc.edu
PEREZ TOLEDO,
Elizabeth .... 787-848-5739.. 536 C
PERFECTO, Gerardo .... 787-257-0000.. 537 H
gerardo.perfecto@upr.edu
PERFETTI, Lisa, R .... 509-527-5187.. 509 G
perfetlr@whitman.edu
PERGI, Brenan .... 740-283-6445.. 368 L
bpergi@franciscan.edu
PERGOLA-RIVERA,
Maribelle .... 787-993-8951.. 537 G
maribelle.pergola@upr.edu
PERGOLIS, Robert .... 718-940-5419.. 328 G
rpergolis@sjcny.edu
PERGOLIZZI, Francis .... 207-973-1069.. 202 I
pergolizzif@husson.edu
PERGOLIZZI, Vanessa ..... 860-913-2160.... 87 H
vpergolizzi@goodwin.edu
PERHAC, Peter .... 702-567-1920.. 284 E
pperhac@cci.edu
PERI, Jonathan .... 215-885-2360.. 409 G
jperi@manor.edu
PERIGARD, Kim .... 360-779-9993.. 505 B
kperigard@ncad.edu
PERILLAT, Muriel .... 636-227-2100.. 267 A
PERILLO, Brian .... 212-998-6843.. 324 C
bperillo@nyu.edu
PERILLO, Patricia, A .... 540-231-6272.. 499 F
pperillo@vt.edu
PERIN, Thomas .... 540-891-3037.. 497 B
tperin@germanna.edu
PERISE, Julie .... 985-549-2150.. 201 C
julie.perise@selu.edu
PERKETT, Karen .... 734-973-3491.. 242 G
kperkett@wccnet.edu
PERKINS, Alisa .... 812-288-8878.. 165 P
aperkins@mid-america.edu
PERKINS, JR.,
Andrew, M .... 336-285-4551.. 356 F
perkins@ncat.edu
PERKINS, Anika, M .... 662-329-7119.. 259 E
amperkins@muw.edu
PERKINS, Bianca .... 309-796-8240.. 135 I
perkinsb@bhc.edu
PERKINS, Bruce .... 405-585-5120.. 385 B
bruce.perkins@okbu.edu
PERKINS, Charles .... 620-792-9245.. 178 G
perkinsc@bartonccc.edu
PERKINS, D. Clay .... 252-334-2004.. 346 F
president@macuniversity.edu
PERKINS, Eddie .... 606-539-4579.. 193 F
eddie.perkins@ucumberlands.edu
PERKINS, Elizabeth .... 229-317-6710.. 120 A
elizabeth.perkins@darton.edu
PERKINS, Faith .... 817-257-7790.. 469 G
faith.perkins@tcu.edu
PERKINS, Faye .... 715-425-3700.. 521 B
faye.perkins@uwrf.edu
PERKINS, Joseph, A .... 919-572-1625.. 341 M
jperk1987@apexsot.edu
PERKINS, Joseph, E .... 919-572-1625.. 341 M
jeperkins@apexsot.edu
PERKINS, Joyce, J .... 901-572-2585.. 438 I
joyce.perkins@bchs.edu
PERKINS, Julie .... 660-263-4100.. 269 D
juliep@macc.edu
PERKINS, Keith .... 937-376-6640.. 365 H
kperkins@centralstate.edu
PERKINS, Louis .... 302-857-6030.... 90 F
lperkins@desu.edu
PERKINS, Lynn .... 952-358-8507.. 251 A
lynn.perkins@normandale.edu
PERKINS, Mary .... 847-214-7414.. 140 A
mperkins@elgin.edu
PERKINS, Megan .... 315-279-5296.. 318 C
mryan1@keuka.edu
PERKINS, Michele, D .... 603-428-2222.. 287 C
mperkins@nec.edu
PERKINS, Myrna, L .... 620-792-9270.. 178 G
perkinsm@bartonccc.edu
PERKINS, Patricia .... 304-645-6336.. 514 A
pperkins@osteo.wvsom.edu
PERKINS, Peter .... 607-753-2518.. 333 A
peter.perkins@cortland.edu
PERKINS, Priscilla, L .... 413-782-1531.. 229 E
priscilla.perkins@wne.edu
PERKINS, Russell .... 913-758-6182.. 185 F
registrar@stmary.edu
PERKINS, Sarah, F .... 650-738-4321.... 62 I
perkinss@smccd.edu
PERKINS, Susan, K .... 732-906-2505.. 292 E
sperkins@middlesexcc.edu
PERKINS, Suzetta, M .... 910-672-1143.. 356 E
sperkins@uncfsu.edu
PERKINS, Will .... 503-352-2120.. 394 C
wperkins@pacificu.edu
PERKINS BROWN, Jayne 912-478-5218.. 122 B
jperkins@georgiasouthern.edu
PERKINSON, Ewa .... 330-867-1996.. 373 F
PERKINSON, JR.,
James, E .... 757-822-5159.. 498 H
jperkinson@tcc.edu
PERKINSON, Stephen .... 330-867-1996.. 373 F
PERKNER, Stanislav .... 209-478-0800.... 46 H
sperkner@humphreys.edu
PERKO, Janet, A .... 330-471-8340.. 371 J
jperko@malone.edu
PERKOWSKI, C, L .... 718-259-2525.. 305 F
PERKOWSKI, Henry .... 212-678-3016.. 337 E
hp2125@tc.columbia.edu
PERL, Emily .... 410-337-6122.. 207 H
eperl@goucher.edu
PERLADO, Ben .... 661-654-3381.... 32 A
bperlado@csub.edu
PERLICK, Nick .... 859-622-1583.. 188 F
nick.perlick@eku.edu
PERLIN, Jeremy .... 513-487-3215.. 315 F
jperlin@huc.edu
PERLMAN, Andrew .... 617-573-8157.. 228 G
aperlman@suffolk.edu
PERLMAN, Lynn .... 617-277-3915.. 216 D
perlmanl@bgsp.edu
PERLMUTTER, David .... 806-742-3385.. 472 C
david.perlmutter@ttu.edu
PERLMUTTER, David, H .... 314-362-6827.. 274 N
perlmutterd@wustl.edu
PERLMUTTER, Kathleen .... 805-756-0327.... 31 I
kmcmah02@calpoly.edu
PERLOFF, Carey .... 415-439-2422.... 26 G
cep@act-sf.org
PERLONGO, Chris .... 802-865-8740.. 483 F
cperlongo@champlain.edu
PERLOW, Yaakov .... 718-438-2727.. 341 J
PERLSTROM, Christine, L 847-574-5208.. 145 C
cperlstrom@lfgsm.edu
PERMAN, Jay, A .... 410-706-7002.. 211 F
jperman@umaryland.edu
PERMAR, Stephen .... 860-628-4751.... 88 C
spermar@lincolncollegene.edu
PERME, Connie .... 513-745-3992.. 381 I
perme@xavier.edu
PERMENTER, Andrew, H .. 863-667-5078.. 109 L
ahpermenter@seu.edu
PERNA, Michael .... 201-200-3542.. 293 C
mperna@njcu.edu
PERNICIARO, Richard ...... 609-343-5670.. 288 H
rpernici@atlantic.edu
PERNICK HUBER,
Maureen .... 716-827-2444.. 338 E
huberm@trocaire.edu
PERNOT, Laurent .... 312-553-2500.. 137 C
lpernot@ccc.edu
PEROLIO, Jessica .... 314-977-2154.. 271 K
jperolio@slu.edu
PERONE, Julie .... 610-436-2301.. 416 C
jperone@wcupa.edu
PERONI-CALLAHAN,
Kathy .... 617-521-2150.. 228 C
kathleen.peroni-callahan@simmons.edu
PEROO, Rama .... 620-441-5587.. 180 D
rama.peroo@cowley.edu
PEROW, Lauren, A .... 814-641-3302.. 406 F
perowl@juniata.edu
PEROZZI, Brett .... 801-626-6361.. 482 D
brettperozzi@weber.edu
PEROZZI, Thomas .... 847-574-5168.. 145 C
tperozzi@lfgsm.edu
PERR, Yechiel, I .... 718-327-7600.. 340 G
yfr1@verizon.net

PETERS, Suzanne .... 413-545-0356.. 220 F
sepeters@finaid.umass.edu
PETERS, Tara .... 732-263-5690.. 292 F
tpeters@monmouth.edu
PETERS, Teresa, A .... 570-348-6230.. 409 H
peters@marywood.edu
PETERS, Thomas, A .... 417-836-4525.. 268 I
tpeters@missouristate.edu
PETERS, Timothy, C .... 949-214-3363.... 41 F
tim.peters@cui.edu
PETERS, Tom .... 308-398-7365.. 278 K
tpeters@cccneb.edu
PETERS, Vincent .... 651-638-6124.. 244 L
v-peters@bethel.edu
PETERS-NGUYEN, Diane .. 808-735-4772.. 130 F
dpeters@chaminade.edu
PETERSEN, Aaron .... 517-607-2330.. 235 E
apetersen@hillsdale.edu
PETERSEN, Calvin .... 402-280-2796.. 279 H
creighton@bkstr.com
PETERSEN, Carol .... 309-341-5416.. 136 C
cpetersen@sandburg.edu
PETERSEN, Dana .... 207-216-4454.. 204 B
dpetersen@yccc.edu
PETERSEN, Donna .... 813-974-6603.. 112 C
dpeters@hsc.usf.edu
PETERSEN, Dorene .... 503-244-0726.. 389 J
dorenepetersen@achs.edu
PETERSEN, Karen, K .... 615-898-5580.. 444 G
karen.petersen@mtsu.edu
PETERSEN, Karl .... 314-768-7800.. 268 G
kpetersen@missouricollege.com
PETERSEN, Kenneth, J ..... 208-426-1135.. 132 I
kenpetersen@boisestate.edu
PETERSEN, Keri .... 336-517-2331.. 342 B
PETERSEN, Kevin .... 410-704-2487.. 213 B
kpetersen@towson.edu
PETERSEN, Kristin .... 402-471-2505.. 281 G
kpetersen@nscs.edu
PETERSEN, Linda .... 785-243-1435.. 179 N
lpetersen@cloud.edu
PETERSEN, Mark, A .... 336-758-6053.. 359 E
map@wfu.edu
PETERSEN, Marty .... 425-602-3027.. 501 D
mpetersen@bastyr.edu
PETERSEN, Mary, S .... 206-296-2043.. 507 E
marypete@seattleu.edu
PETERSEN, Molly .... 619-849-2463.... 57 M
mollypetersen@pointloma.edu
PETERSEN, Page .... 507-433-0650.. 251 H
ppeterse@riverland.edu
PETERSEN, Steve .... 847-925-6255.. 141 A
speterse@harpercollege.edu
PETERSEN, Tina .... 916-577-2200.... 75 C
tpetersen@jessup.edu
PETERSON, Al, L .... 661-824-2977.... 53 K
apeterson@ntps.edu
PETERSON, Alonzo .... 405-466-3419.. 383 M
afpeterson@langston.edu
PETERSON, Andrew .... 215-596-8877.. 422 A
a.peterson@usciences.edu
PETERSON, Andrew, T ..... 864-833-8486.. 432 B
atpeterso@presby.edu
PETERSON, Andy .... 503-517-1800.. 396 F
apeterson@westernseminary.edu
PETERSON, Angela .... 816-584-6510.. 270 D
angela.peterson@park.edu
PETERSON, Bill .... 413-585-3000.. 228 D
bpeterso@smith.edu
PETERSON, JR., Charles . 804-523-5821.. 497 C
cpeterson@reynolds.edu
PETERSON, Charles, D .... 701-231-7456.. 361 A
charles.peterson@ndsu.edu
PETERSON, Chris .... 405-491-6333.. 388 A
cpeterso@snu.edu
PETERSON, Christine ...... 443-423-1467.. 209 B
cpetersn@mica.edu
PETERSON, Cynthia .... 225-578-4201.. 197 I
cbpeterson@lsu.edu
PETERSON, Cynthia .... 903-923-2257.. 457 G
cpeterson@etbu.edu
PETERSON, Cynthia, L ..... 706-778-8500.. 125 J
cpeterson@piedmont.edu
PETERSON, Daniel .... 603-456-2656.. 287 E
dpeterson@northeastcatholic.edu
PETERSON, David .... 706-419-1189.. 119 G
david.peterson@covenant.edu
PETERSON, David .... 260-481-6130.. 163 C
petersod@ipfw.edu
PETERSON, Debra .... 218-755-4121.. 248 M
dpeterson@bemidjistate.edu
PETERSON, Derek .... 605-688-4163.. 437 F
derek.peterson@sdstate.edu
PETERSON, Dolores .... 610-372-4721.. 417 G
dpeterson@racc.edu
PETERSON, Donald .... 903-334-6650.. 469 C
donald.peterson@tamut.edu
PETERSON, Donn .... 707-826-5555.... 34 F
donn.peterson@humboldt.edu
PETERSON, Doug .... 312-322-1733.. 155 F
dpeterson@spertus.edu
PETERSON, Ellen .... 808-984-3582.. 132 D
epeterso@hawaii.edu
PETERSON, Ericka, K .... 218-299-3250.. 246 A
ekpeters@cord.edu
PETERSON, G. P. (Bud) .... 404-894-5051.. 121 D
president@gatech.edu
PETERSON, Gail .... 414-326-2303.. 516 D
gpeterso@ccon.edu
PETERSON, Greg .... 562-938-4140.... 49 D
gpeterson@lbcc.edu
PETERSON, Heath, J .... 785-864-4760.. 185 D
heathpeterson@kualumni.org
PETERSON, Heather .... 609-343-5008.. 288 H
hpeterso@atlantic.edu
PETERSON,
Jacqueline, D .... 508-793-2414.. 217 C
jpeterso@holycross.edu
PETERSON, James .... 510-540-7747.... 49 A
jamespeterson@lincolnuca.edu
PETERSON, Jennifer .... 904-632-3291.. 101 G
jennifer.peterson@fscj.edu
PETERSON, Jill .... 916-278-6940.... 34 B
jill.peteson@csus.edu
PETERSON, John, A .... 671-735-6912.. 530 B
jpeterson@uguam.uog.edu
PETERSON, Joyce, C .... 218-722-4000.. 246 E
joycep@dbumn.edu
PETERSON, Julie .... 470-578-3378.. 123 J
PETERSON, Kate, M .... 541-737-0759.. 393 H
kate.peterson@oregonstate.edu
PETERSON, Kathleen .... 973-300-2235.. 297 D
kpeterson@sussex.edu
PETERSON, Keith .... 479-936-5145.... 21 D
kpeterson2@nwacc.edu
PETERSON, Kellie .... 406-994-4570.. 277 C
kellie.peterson@montana.edu
PETERSON, Ken .... 864-294-2269.. 430 C
ken.peterson@furman.edu
PETERSON, Kent, A .... 414-277-7176.. 518 E
peterson@msoe.edu
PETERSON, Kevin .... 435-797-1223.. 482 B
kevin.peterson@usu.edu
PETERSON, Klay .... 864-503-5254.. 434 G
kpeterson@uscupstate.edu
PETERSON, Kristi .... 406-265-3536.. 277 E
kristi.peterson1@msun.edu
PETERSON, Larry .... 618-985-2828.. 143 F
larrypeterson@jalc.edu
PETERSON, Larry .... 701-231-8824.. 361 A
larry.r.peterson@ndsu.edu
PETERSON, Laura .... 940-397-4919.. 462 A
laura.peterson@mwsu.edu
PETERSON, Lori .... 406-447-5432.. 276 B
lpeterson@carroll.edu
PETERSON, Lori, W .... 512-448-8519.. 464 G
lorip@stedwards.edu
PETERSON, Maggie .... 406-496-4316.. 277 G
mpeterson@mtech.edu
PETERSON, Marc .... 214-768-3417.. 465 J
mpeterso@smu.edu
PETERSON, Margrette .... 510-869-6512.... 59 L
mpeterson@samuelmerritt.edu
PETERSON, Marie .... 206-296-6241.. 507 E
mpeters@seattleu.edu
PETERSON, Marika .... 434-949-1064.. 498 E
marika.peterson@southside.edu
PETERSON, Mark .... 651-450-3373.. 249 F
mpeters@inverhills.edu
PETERSON, Mark .... 715-682-1332.. 518 H
mpeterson@northland.edu
PETERSON, Megan .... 717-728-2398.. 400 F
meganpeterson@centralpenn.edu
PETERSON, Melissa .... 716-839-8477.. 312 D
mpeters2@daemen.edu
PETERSON, Michael, L ..... 510-215-3800.... 41 H
mpeterson@contracosta.edu
PETERSON, Michael, W .... 512-448-8788.. 464 G
michaelp@stedwards.edu
PETERSON, Michele .... 970-247-7435.... 80 D
peterson_m@fortlewis.edu
PETERSON, Michele .... 505-566-3363.. 301 J
petersonm@sanjuancollege.edu
PETERSON, Nell .... 813-974-6884.. 112 C
ncpeterson@usf.edu
PETERSON, Nichole .... 860-768-5365.... 89 G
npetersen@hartford.edu
PETERSON, Nicole .... 931-221-7979.. 444 E
petersonn@apsu.edu
PETERSON, Pamela .... 561-912-2166.... 99 J
ppeterson@evergladesuniversity.edu
PETERSON, Pamela .... 831-459-4300.... 70 F
pgpeters@ucsc.edu
PETERSON, Penelope, L .. 847-467-1190.. 150 F
p-peterson@northwestern.edu
PETERSON, Pete .... 310-506-7490.... 56 J
pete.n.peterson@pepperdine.edu
PETERSON, Phyllis, M ..... 815-740-3848.. 157 F
ppeterson@stfrancis.edu
PETERSON, Polly, J .... 701-252-3467.. 362 F
ppeterso@uj.edu
PETERSON, Randall .... 386-312-4022.. 108 B
randypeterson@sjrstate.edu
PETERSON, Randy .... 501-450-3826.... 20 F
peterson@hendrix.edu
PETERSON, Rebecca .... 802-865-6425.. 483 F
peterson@champlain.edu
PETERSON, Robert .... 435-722-6900.. 481 I
bobp@ubatc.edu
PETERSON, Robert .... 216-987-2836.. 367 E
robert.peterson@tri-c.edu
PETERSON, Roy .... 262-243-5700.. 516 E
roy.peterson@cuw.edu
PETERSON, Samantha ...... 918-335-6223.. 386 F
speterson@okwu.edu
PETERSON, Samuel .... 305-809-3179.. 100 N
samuel.peterson@fkcc.edu
PETERSON, Sandy .... 608-785-9207.. 524 H
petersons@westerntc.edu
PETERSON, Scott .... 740-392-6868.. 373 D
scott.peterson@mvnu.edu
PETERSON, Scott .... 864-225-7653.. 430 A
scottpeterson@forrestcollege.edu
PETERSON, Soo .... 703-284-1540.. 492 A
soo.peterson@marymount.edu
PETERSON, Stella .... 770-426-2930.. 124 B
peterson@life.edu
PETERSON, Stephanie ...... 785-442-6051.. 181 H
speterson@highlandcc.edu
PETERSON, Steve .... 434-592-5070.. 491 D
hberberich@liberty.edu
PETERSON, Susan, K .... 785-532-6221.. 182 D
skp@ksu.edu
PETERSON, Terry .... 312-942-7020.. 153 B
terry_peterson@rush.edu
PETERSON, Thomas .... 732-906-2512.. 292 E
tpeterson@middlesexcc.edu
PETERSON, Toby .... 301-696-3934.. 208 B
peterson@hood.edu
PETERSON, Tom .... 209-228-4439.... 70 A
twpeterson@ucmerced.edu
PETERSON, Travis .... 435-797-2836.. 482 B
travis.peterson@usu.edu
PETERSON, Tyler, M .... 205-934-8221...... 8 E
tpeterson@uab.edu
PETERSON, Val, L .... 801-863-8424.. 482 C
petersva@uvu.edu
PETERSON, Wendy .... 509-335-5586.. 508 H
wendyp@wsu.edu
PETERSON, Yvonne .... 503-228-6528.. 390 A
ypeterson@aii.edu
PETERSON-MILLER,
Connie .... 574-520-4591.. 163 E
copmiller@iusb.edu
PETERSON-SENIUK,
Peggy .... 419-473-2700.. 367 J
pseniuk@daviscollege.edu
PETERSON-VEATCH,
Ross .... 574-535-7503.. 161 A
rosspv@goshen.edu
PETERSSON, Arlette .... 561-912-1211.... 99 J
apetersson@evergladesuniversity.edu
PETHE-COOK, Marlyn ...... 813-253-6231.. 114 M
mpethe@ut.edu
PETHICK, Michael .... 231-591-3900.. 233 L
michaelpethick@ferris.edu
PETILLO, John, J .... 203-371-7900.... 88 I
petilloj@sacredheart.edu
PETIPRIN, Gary .... 502-272-8480.. 187 A
gpetiprin@bellarmine.edu
PETIT-FRERE, Yaruby ...... 908-737-0350.. 292 C
ypetitfr@kean.edu
PETITFILS, Brad .... 504-865-3080.. 198 E
bpetit@loyno.edu
PETITT, Becky, R .... 858-822-4783.... 70 C
bpetitt@ucsd.edu
PETITT, Bill .... 972-883-6166.. 476 C
bpetitt@utdallas.edu
PETITT, Charles, W .... 336-725-8344.. 354 G
petittc@piedmontu.edu
PETITTI, Mario .... 440-525-7328.. 371 F
mpetitti@lakelandcc.edu
PETKASH, John .... 607-778-5011.. 332 D
petkashjc@sunybroome.edu
PETKUS, Edward .... 201-684-7377.. 294 G
epetkus@ramapo.edu
PETLEY, Kathleen .... 518-629-4574.. 316 G
k.petley@hvcc.edu
PETOSKEY, Indira .... 860-465-5066.... 85 G
petoskeyi@easternct.edu
PETRAS, Donna .... 586-263-6266.. 237 C
petrasd@macomb.edu
PETREE, Dan .... 603-358-2104.. 288 E
daniel.petree@keene.edu
PETREN, Kenneth .... 513-556-5858.. 379 A
ken.petren@uc.edu
PETRESCU, Claudia, A ...... 248-370-3169.. 239 K
cpetrescu@oakland.edu
PETRI, Elizabeth .... 413-662-5219.. 222 B
e.petri@mcla.edu
PETRI, OP, Thomas .... 202-495-3832.... 93 D
dean@dhs.edu
PETRICCA, Joe .... 323-856-7721.... 26 I
jpetricca@afi.com
PETRICHENKO,
Kathleen, J .... 410-822-5400.. 207 A
kpetrichenko@chesapeake.edu
PETRICK, Joseph, E .... 802-287-8377.. 484 A
petrickj@greenmtn.edu
PETRIDIS, Heather .... 626-815-4570.... 28 A
hpetridis@apu.edu
PETRIE, Mark .... 315-279-5254.. 318 C
mpetrie@keuka.edu
PETRIE, Susan .... 518-608-8156.. 314 A
spetrie@excelsior.edu
PETRIKAT, Douglas .... 714-547-9625.... 29 J
dpetrikat@calcoast.edu
PETRILLO, Emilia, K .... 410-328-8404.. 211 F
epetr001@umaryland.edu
PETRIS, Raul .... 213-615-2700.... 37 I
PETRITES, Cindy .... 414-229-4519.. 520 D
petrites@uwm.edu
PETRITIS, Paul .... 603-427-7630.. 286 B
ppetritis@ccsnh.edu
PETRIZZO, Louis, S .... 631-451-4235.. 336 D
petrizl@sunysuffolk.edu
PETROFF, Les .... 317-738-8108.. 160 J
lpetroff@franklincollege.edu
PETROKA, Louise, A .... 203-285-2393.... 86 C
lpetroka@gwcc.commnet.edu
PETRONE, Eileen .... 412-536-1115.. 406 K
eileen.petrone@laroche.edu
PETROSIAN, Anahid .... 956-872-6790.. 465 H
anahid@southtexascollege.edu
PETROSIAN, Anahid .... 956-872-8339.. 465 H
anahid@southtexascollege.edu
PETROSINO, Chris .... 304-243-2165.. 515 C
cpetrosino@wju.edu
PETROSINO, Linda .... 607-274-3265.. 317 D
lpetrosino@ithaca.edu
PETROSKY, Joseph .... 586-498-4181.. 237 C
petroskyj@macomb.edu
PETROSYAN, Narine .... 510-925-4282.... 26 M
narinep@aua.am
PETROSYAN, Varduhi .... 510-925-4282.... 26 M
vpetrosi@aua.am
PETROV, John .... 301-985-7980.. 212 C
john.petrov@umuc.edu
PETROVICH, Tamberly .... 831-582-4137.... 33 E
tpetrovich@csumb.edu
PETROY, Anthony, R .... 573-341-4579.. 274 B
petroya@mst.edu
PETRUCCI, Michele .... 724-357-2295.. 415 B
michelep@iup.edu
PETRUCELLI, Amanda .... 574-936-8898.. 158 I
amanda.petrucelli@ancilla.edu
PETRUS, Robin .... 607-778-5201.. 332 D
petrusre@sunybroome.edu
PETRUSCH, Suzanne, M .... 864-833-8194.. 432 B
spetrusch@presby.edu
PETRUSO, Karl .... 817-272-7215.. 476 A
petruso@uta.edu
PETRUZZELLI,
Barbara, W .... 845-569-3601.. 322 B
barbara.petruzzelli@msmc.edu
PETRY, Ric .... 614-222-3227.. 367 B
rpetry@ccad.edu
PETRYSHAK, Bruce .... 615-898-5570.. 444 G
bruce.petryshak@mtsu.edu
PETRYSHYN, Laryssa .... 716-829-8119.. 313 A
petryshl@dyc.edu
PETSCHE, Carolyn .... 815-599-3577.. 141 E
carolyn.petsche@highland.edu
PETSCHE, Daniel .... 660-944-2875.. 263 G
daniel@conception.edu
PETSCHENKO, Lisa .... 630-953-3694.. 136 H
lpetschenko@chamberlain.edu
PETTA, Tim .... 360-992-2408.. 502 E
tpetta@clark.edu
PETTAZZONI, Jodi, E .... 336-334-5531.. 358 B
jepettaz@uncg.edu
PETTEGREW, Larry .... 919-573-5350.. 355 G
PETTENGER, Wade .... 417-862-9533.. 265 D
wpettenger@globaluniversity.edu
PETTERELLI, Mark, J .... 315-445-4444.. 318 E
pettermj@lemoyne.edu
PETTERSON, Jennifer .... 573-592-4280.. 275 G
jennie.petterson@williamwoods.edu
PETTEWAY, Venetia .... 810-762-7899.. 236 C
vpettewa@kettering.edu
PETTIGREW, Jason .... 605-229-8350.. 436 H
jason.pettigrew@presentation.edu
PETTIGREW, Yancey .... 731-661-5134.. 448 A
ypettigrew@uu.edu
PETTINGER, Brenda .... 208-562-3305.. 133 F
brendapettinger@cwidaho.cc
PETTINGER, Connie .... 708-209-3045.. 138 G
constance.pettinger@cuchicago.edu
PETTINGILL, Sara, Y .... 502-272-8401.. 187 A
spettingill@bellarmine.edu
PETTIS, Curtis .... 937-376-6207.. 365 H
cpettis@centralstate.edu

PETTIS, Stephanie .... 850-729-5362.. 105 I pettiss@nwfsc.edu
PETTIS-WALDEN, Karen, M .... 804-523-5029.. 497 C kpettis-walden@reynolds.edu
PETTIT, Cyndi .... 214-333-5235.. 455 J cyndi@dbu.edu
PETTIT, Emily .... 706-778-8500.. 125 J epettit@piedmont.edu
PETTIT, Frederick .... 570-208-5881.. 406 J frederickpettit@kings.edu
PETTIT, Jeanne .... 859-572-7544.. 192 B pettitje@nku.edu
PETTIT, Kathy .... 303-963-3327.... 77 I kpettit@ccu.edu
PETTIT, Martin, A .... 607-746-4702.. 335 C pettitma@delhi.edu
PETTIT, Paul, E .... 214-887-5102.. 457 C ppettit@dts.edu
PETTIT, Stephen, D .... 864-242-5100.. 427 E
PETTITT, Maureen .... 360-416-7919.. 507 G maureen.pettitt@skagit.edu
PETTY, Bradley .... 325-942-2191.. 472 B bradley.petty@angelo.edu
PETTY, Daniel, W .... 813-988-5131.. 100 F vpres@floridacollege.edu
PETTY, JoBeth .... 601-968-8901.. 256 I jbpetty@belhaven.edu
PETTY, Jonathan .... 806-291-3588.. 479 D pettyj@wbu.edu
PETTY, Leslie .... 734-462-4400.. 240 H lpetty@schoolcraft.edu
PETTY, Marcia, L .... 504-865-3030.. 198 E mlpetty@loyno.edu
PETTY, Mark .... 605-677-5434.. 437 A mark.petty@usd.edu
PETTY, Monica .... 202-885-8612.... 94 E mpetty@wesleyseminary.edu
PETTY, Nina .... 817-515-5433.. 467 A nina.petty@tccd.edu
PETTY, Philip .... 802-728-1533.. 486 D ppetty@vtc.edu
PETTY, Rachel .... 202-274-5072.... 94 B rpetty@udc.edu
PETTY, Tanjula .... 229-430-3511.. 116 A tpetty@albanytech.edu
PETULA, Eileen, E .... 610-328-8399.. 419 I epetula1@swarthmore.edu
PETZ, Dan .... 620-672-5641.. 184 D danp@prattcc.edu
PETZ, Thomas .... 248-689-8282.. 242 F tpetz@walshcollege.edu
PETZKE, Greg .... 704-378-1190.. 345 E gpetzke@jcsu.edu
PETZNICK, Michelle, L .... 641-422-4205.. 175 E petznmic@niacc.edu
PEUGH-WADE, Martha, A .... 415-422-2444.... 72 C peugh@usfca.edu
PEWE, Rich .... 517-607-2518.. 235 E rpewe@hillsdale.edu
PEYROUX, Elise .... 937-376-2946.. 376 F epeyroux@payne.edu
PEYTON, Elizabeth .... 949-794-9090.... 66 H epeyton@stanbridge.edu
PEYTON, Janice .... 936-270-7392.. 461 B janice.peyton@lonestar.edu
PEZOLD, Frank .... 361-825-2349.. 468 E frank.pezold@tamucc.edu
PEZZAROSSI, Alba .... 773-481-8059.. 137 I apezzarossi@ccc.edu
PEZZI, Eileen .... 315-464-7853.. 332 C pezzie@upstate.edu
PEZZOLI, Jeannie .... 808-984-3234.. 132 D pezzoli@hawaii.edu
PEÑALVER, Eduardo, M .. 607-255-3527.. 312 A eduardo.penalver@cornell.edu
PFANNENSTIEL, Myra .... 316-942-4291.. 183 I pfannenstielm@newmanu.edu
PFANNESTIEL, Todd .... 814-393-2223.. 414 G tpfannestiel@clarion.edu
PFEFER, Mark, T .... 913-234-0796.. 179 M mark.pfefer@cleveland.edu
PFEFFER, Carole .... 502-272-8184.. 187 A cpfeffer@bellarmine.edu
PFEIFER, Aimee .... 304-293-0169.. 514 C aimee.pfeifer@mail.wvu.edu
PFEIFER, Gene, R .... 507-344-7315.. 244 K gene.pfeifer@blc.edu
PFEIFER, Jane .... 419-473-2700.. 367 J jpfeifer@daviscollege.edu
PFEIFER, Joseph .... 503-251-5775.. 396 C jpfeifer@uws.edu
PFEIFER, Justin .... 316-677-1020.. 185 I jpfeifer@watc.edu
PFEIFER, Laura .... 701-228-5432.. 361 D laura.pfeifer@dakotacollege.edu
PFEIFER, Ron .... 920-465-2067.. 520 B pfeiferr@uwgb.edu
PFEIFER, Tad .... 308-535-3684.. 280 M pfeifert@mpcc.edu
PFEIFFER, Francine .... 202-220-1336.. 295 F francine@rutgers.edu
PFEIFFER, Glenn .... 714-997-6814.... 37 F pfeiffer@chapman.edu
PFEIFFER, Kelley .... 636-922-8544.. 271 A kpfeiffer@stchas.edu
PFEIFFER, Pattie .... 919-735-5151.. 354 A ppfeiffer@waynecc.edu
PFEIL, Christopher .... 858-566-1200.... 42 D pfeil@cisd.edu
PFLANZ, Mary .... 913-621-8764.. 180 F mpflanz@donnelly.edu
PFLEIGER, Kelly .... 215-368-5000.. 398 C kpfleiger@biblical.edu
PFLIPSEN, Andrew, J .... 701-788-4770.. 360 E andrew.pflipsen@mayvillestate.edu
PFOTENHAUER, George .. 708-709-7834.. 151 C gpfotenhauer@prairiestate.edu
PHAGAN, Kathy .... 770-533-6906.. 123 L kphagan@laniertech.edu
PHAIAH, Peter .... 218-281-8505.. 255 E phaiah@umn.edu
PHAKITTHONG, Rachelle . 920-693-1282.. 523 E rachelle.phakitthoong@gotoltc.edu
PHAM, Chinh .... 714-484-7464.... 54 G cpham@cypresscollege.edu
PHAM, Hue .... 714-432-5764.... 39 G hpham@occ.cccd.edu
PHAM, Michael .... 206-878-3701.. 504 E mpham@highline.edu
PHAM, Tom, C .... 617-984-1699.. 227 F tpham@quincycollege.edu
PHAM, Tosha .... 323-343-2700.... 33 C tosha.pham@calstatela.edu
PHAM, Trinh .... 323-343-5969.... 33 C tpham4@calstatela.edu
PHAN, Anh .... 619-961-4232.... 68 A aphan@tjsl.edu
PHAN, Nga .... 619-477-6310.... 68 I nphan@usuniversity.edu
PHANNENSTIEL, Matt .... 785-227-3380.. 178 J pfannenstielmm@bethanylb.edu
PHARO, SCN, Diane .... 812-357-6598.. 167 B dpharo@saintmeinrad.edu
PHARR, Christine .... 402-399-2419.. 279 E cpharr@csm.edu
PHARR, Julie .... 336-386-3452.. 353 F pharrj@surry.edu
PHARR, Kathy, R .... 706-542-0054.. 128 E pharr@uga.edu
PHARR, Zach .... 479-619-2664.... 21 D zpharr@nwacc.edu
PHARRIS, Heather .... 863-680-4754.. 101 E hpharris@flsouthern.edu
PHEASANT, Joel, C .... 814-641-5334.. 406 F pheasaj@juniata.edu
PHELAN, Carol .... 617-585-1139.. 226 F carol.phelan@necmusic.edu
PHELAN, Daniel, J .... 517-787-0800.. 235 G phelandanielj@jccmi.edu
PHELAN JOHNSON, Marcia .... 860-297-2041.... 89 B marcia.johnson@trincoll.edu
PHELPS, Bill .... 870-245-5567.... 21 E phelpswr@obu.edu
PHELPS, Carmen .... 928-523-9375.... 15 H carmen.phelps@nau.edu
PHELPS, Celeste .... 714-484-7107.... 54 G cphelps@cypresscollege.edu
PHELPS, Craig .... 660-626-2391.. 262 A cphelps@atsu.edu
PHELPS, Debbie .... 620-331-4100.. 181 J dphelps@indycc.edu
PHELPS, Dennis, L .... 504-282-4455.. 198 H dphelps@nobts.edu
PHELPS, Esther .... 330-337-6403.. 362 I depemp@raex.com
PHELPS, Gary, L .... 330-471-8127.. 371 J gphelps@malone.edu
PHELPS, Greg .... 636-627-2938.. 266 J gphelps@lindenwood.edu
PHELPS, Hilary .... 860-343-5856.... 86 F hphelps@mxcc.commnet.edu
PHELPS, Jean .... 718-262-2285.. 310 A phelps@york.cuny.edu
PHELPS, Jodi .... 910-521-6863.. 358 C jodi.phelps@uncp.edu
PHELPS, Joel .... 518-828-4181.. 311 D joel.phelps@sunycgcc.edu
PHELPS, Kathy .... 239-280-2500.... 95 Q kathy.phelps@avemaria.edu
PHELPS, Lena .... 863-784-7303.. 109 G lena.phelps@southflorida.edu
PHELPS, Martha .... 270-824-8591.. 190 B martha.phelps@kctcs.edu
PHELPS, Sherri .... 870-245-5410.... 21 E phelpss@obu.edu
PHENICIE, Christopher, N .... 864-488-4549.. 430 H cphenicie@limestone.edu
PHENIX, Amy .... 612-626-1616.. 255 H pheni001@umn.edu
PHIFER-MCGHEE, Kimberly, C .... 919-530-7593.. 357 A kpmcghee@nccu.edu
PHILBERT, Martin, A .... 734-763-5454.. 241 J philbert@umich.edu
PHILBIN, Catherine .... 617-322-3505.. 219 H catherine_philbin@laboure.edu
PHILIE, Lauren .... 802-635-1657.. 486 B lauren.philie@jsc.edu
PHILION, Thomas .... 312-853-4780.. 152 H tphilion@roosevelt.edu
PHILIPKOSKY, Thomas, G .... 843-953-5092.. 428 A tom.philipkosky@citadel.edu
PHILIPP, Diane .... 517-607-2333.. 235 E dphilipp@hillsdale.edu
PHILIPP, Jason .... 651-779-5834.. 249 A jason.philipp@century.edu
PHILIPP, Shirin .... 617-349-9600.. 220 B philipp@lesley.edu
PHILIPPA, Elaine .... 262-595-3215.. 520 F laine@uwp.edu
PHILIPPON, Roger .... 207-755-5357.. 203 I rphilippon@cmcc.edu
PHILIPS, JR., Billy, U .... 806-743-1338.. 472 D billy.philips@ttuhsc.edu
PHILIPSON, Randolph .... 504-314-7157.. 200 C rphilipson@tulane.edu
PHILLEY, Tim .... 918-495-6970.. 386 H tphilley@oru.edu
PHILLIIPS, Sarina .... 936-261-3600.. 467 E
PHILLIP, Thomas, G .... 262-243-5700.. 516 E thomas.phillip@cuw.edu
PHILLIPS, Alan .... 815-753-3400.. 150 A aphillips9@niu.edu
PHILLIPS, Allison .... 336-838-6491.. 354 C allison.phillips@wilkescc.edu
PHILLIPS, Amanda .... 724-653-2195.. 402 F aphillips@dec.edu
PHILLIPS, Andrew, T .... 410-293-1583.. 529 D aphillip@usna.edu
PHILLIPS, Annie .... 940-898-4114.. 472 G aphillips15@twu.edu
PHILLIPS, Anthony .... 856-222-9311.. 295 C aphillips@rcbc.edu
PHILLIPS, Antoinette .... 985-549-2258.. 201 C antoinette.phillips@selu.edu
PHILLIPS, Benet .... 603-641-7402.. 287 G bphillips@anselm.edu
PHILLIPS, Bob .... 909-687-1482.... 44 H bobphillips@gs.edu
PHILLIPS, Brad, C .... 607-733-7177.. 313 D bphillips@ebi-college.com
PHILLIPS, Brian .... 562-903-4897.... 28 E brian.phillips@biola.edu
PHILLIPS, Calvin .... 734-487-0035.. 233 J cphill34@emich.edu
PHILLIPS, Carme .... 205-970-9205...... 7 B cphillips@sebc.edu
PHILLIPS, Carol .... 910-938-6343.. 348 G phillipsc@coastalcarolina.edu
PHILLIPS, Chad .... 270-831-9614.. 189 F chad.phillips@kctcs.edu
PHILLIPS, Chelsea .... 405-224-3140.. 389 D cphillips@usao.edu
PHILLIPS, Christopher, G 410-706-2261.. 211 F cphillip@umaryland.edu
PHILLIPS, Clarenda .... 410-532-5321.. 210 B cphillips@ndm.edu
PHILLIPS, Clarenda, M .... 606-783-2434.. 191 H c.phillips@moreheadstate.edu
PHILLIPS, Danielle .... 717-337-6901.. 404 C dphillip@gettysburg.edu
PHILLIPS, Dave .... 870-777-5722.... 24 A dave.phillips@uacch.edu
PHILLIPS, Dave .... 619-849-2771.... 57 M davephillips@pointloma.edu
PHILLIPS, David .... 831-755-6729.... 45 L dphillips@hartnell.edu
PHILLIPS, David .... 410-516-8341.. 208 D dphillips@jhu.edu
PHILLIPS, Denise .... 972-721-5168.. 473 D dphilli@udallas.edu
PHILLIPS, Dianna, G .... 443-412-2475.. 208 A dphillips@harford.edu
PHILLIPS, Don .... 716-839-8222.. 312 D dphillip@daemen.edu
PHILLIPS, Douglas .... 585-275-3311.. 338 K dphillips@admin.rochester.edu
PHILLIPS, Earnest .... 206-934-4105.. 506 I earnest.phillips@seattlecolleges.edu
PHILLIPS, Eddie .... 773-602-5000.. 137 F tphillips@ccc.edu
PHILLIPS, Edward .... 504-520-6787.. 202 C ephillips@xula.edu
PHILLIPS, Elaine, W .... 405-273-5331.. 383 K ephillips@familyoffaithcollege.edu
PHILLIPS, El .... 205-226-4600...... 2 C ephillip@bsc.edu
PHILLIPS, Ellen .... 262-691-5257.. 524 G ephillips@wctc.edu
PHILLIPS, Faith .... 740-366-9492.. 365 D phillips.495@osu.edu
PHILLIPS, Farley .... 252-451-8287.. 351 F farley@nashcc.edu
PHILLIPS, Fred, R .... 719-884-5000.... 81 N frphillips@nbc.edu
PHILLIPS, Georgette, C ... 610-758-6725.. 408 H gcp214@lehigh.edu
PHILLIPS, Heather .... 218-477-4363.. 250 F phillipshe@mnstate.edu
PHILLIPS, Hilary .... 703-284-1598.. 492 A hilary.phillips@marymount.edu
PHILLIPS, Holli .... 540-665-4928.. 494 B hphillip@su.edu
PHILLIPS, J. Scot .... 910-893-1610.. 342 F phillipss@campbell.edu
PHILLIPS, Jacqueline .... 860-215-9279.... 87 D jphillips@trcc.commnet.edu
PHILLIPS, James .... 336-334-4822.. 350 B jkphillips@gtcc.edu
PHILLIPS, James, J .... 847-491-8880.. 150 F j-phillips@northwestern.edu
PHILLIPS, James, L .... 713-798-6598.. 452 G phillips@bcm.edu
PHILLIPS, Jay .... 207-786-6211.. 202 D jphilli2@bates.edu
PHILLIPS, Jennifer .... 315-859-4243.. 315 D jlphillips@hamilton.edu
PHILLIPS, Jerrett, D .... 337-550-1218.. 197 K jphillip@lsue.edu
PHILLIPS, Jim .... 815-599-3469.. 141 E jim.phillips@highland.edu
PHILLIPS, Jo, C .... 870-759-4101.... 24 J jphillips@wbcoll.edu
PHILLIPS, John .... 386-323-5020.... 99 A john.phillips@erau.edu
PHILLIPS, John, A .... 619-260-4523.... 72 B jphillips@sandiego.edu
PHILLIPS, Joseph, M .... 206-296-5700.. 507 E phillipsj@seattleu.edu
PHILLIPS, Karen .... 413-775-1305.. 223 D phillips@gcc.mass.edu
PHILLIPS, Kathryn .... 215-517-3093.. 397 G phillipsk@arcadia.edu
PHILLIPS, Kelly .... 419-383-5858.. 380 D kelly.phillips5@utoledo.edu
PHILLIPS, Kevin, J .... 203-932-7318.... 90 A kphillips@newhaven.edu
PHILLIPS, Kimberly .... 540-432-4131.. 488 K careerservices@emu.edu
PHILLIPS, Kristen .... 812-888-5421.. 169 A kphillips@vinu.edu
PHILLIPS, Kristopher .... 931-221-7127.. 444 E phillipsk@apsu.edu
PHILLIPS, Krystal .... 910-938-6234.. 348 G phillipsk@coastalcarolina.edu
PHILLIPS, Lauren .... 810-766-2190.. 231 D lphill03@baker.edu
PHILLIPS, Linda .... 580-581-2238.. 382 G lindap@cameron.edu
PHILLIPS, Lisa .... 740-376-4531.. 372 A pattersl@marietta.edu
PHILLIPS, Loraine .... 817-272-3365.. 476 A lorainep@uta.edu
PHILLIPS, Lori .... 307-766-3859.. 527 B lphil@uwyo.edu
PHILLIPS, Luke .... 562-902-3377.... 66 A lukephillips@scuhs.edu
PHILLIPS, Lynette .... 646-313-8000.. 309 F lphillips@cuny.edu
PHILLIPS, Lynette, M .... 212-817-7103.. 308 A lphillips2@gc.cuny.edu
PHILLIPS, Mari Anne .... 417-667-8181.. 264 A mphillips@cottey.edu
PHILLIPS, Marie .... 413-265-2365.. 217 D phillipsmarie@elms.edu
PHILLIPS, Mark .... 202-685-3140.. 528 B mark.phillips@ndu.edu
PHILLIPS, Mark .... 304-243-2232.. 515 C mphillips@wju.edu
PHILLIPS, Mary Lou .... 860-343-5751.... 86 F mphillips@mxcc.commnet.edu
PHILLIPS, Matthew .... 815-226-3372.. 152 G mphillips@rockford.edu
PHILLIPS, Maynard .... 918-343-7773.. 387 F mphillips@rsu.edu
PHILLIPS, Melissa, C .... 828-733-5883.. 351 B mphillips@mayland.edu
PHILLIPS, Mitsu .... 801-274-3280.. 483 C mitsu.phillips@wgu.edu
PHILLIPS, Monika .... 870-512-7703.... 19 C monika_phillips@asun.edu
PHILLIPS, Morgan .... 520-206-6752.... 16 F mphillips23@pima.edu
PHILLIPS, Morgan .... 520-206-5001.... 16 F mphillips23@pima.edu
PHILLIPS, Myra .... 804-524-5352.. 499 G mhphilli@vsu.edu

PHILLIPS, Nathan .... 503-699-6339.. 392 D
nphillips@marylhurst.edu
PHILLIPS, Patsy .... 505-428-5901.. 299 L
pphillips@iaia.edu
PHILLIPS, Patti .... 215-568-4012.. 411 A
pphillips@moore.edu
PHILLIPS, Phil, E .... 310-506-7227.... 56 J
phil.phillips@pepperdine.edu
PHILLIPS, Rachel .... 215-965-4025.. 411 A
rphillips@moore.edu
PHILLIPS, Richard, D ...... 404-413-7000.. 122 D
rphillips@gsu.edu
PHILLIPS, Rita, M .... 515-294-0231.. 169 G
rphillip@iastate.edu
PHILLIPS, Robert .... 304-243-2321.. 515 C
phillips@wju.edu
PHILLIPS, Sam .... 800-877-5456.. 488 D
sam.phillips@christendom.edu
PHILLIPS, Samanthia .... 252-823-5166.. 349 E
phillipss@edgecombe.edu
PHILLIPS, Sandi .... 404-756-5727.. 125 A
PHILLIPS, Sandy .... 724-222-5330.. 412 E
sphillips@penncommercial.edu
PHILLIPS, Sara, S .... 315-655-7225.. 306 H
ssphillips@cazenovia.edu
PHILLIPS, Sarah .... 785-320-4502.. 183 A
sarahphillips@manhattantech.edu
PHILLIPS, Sarah, L .... 704-894-2053.. 343 I
saphillips@davidson.edu
PHILLIPS, Shaina .... 562-908-3427.... 58 I
jphillips@riohondo.edu
PHILLIPS, Shannon .... 843-863-7035.. 427 I
sphillip@csuniv.edu
PHILLIPS, Sheri .... 417-865-2815.. 265 B
phillipss@evangel.edu
PHILLIPS, Sherry .... 215-641-6562.. 410 L
sphillips@mc3.edu
PHILLIPS, Staci .... 318-678-6000.. 195 I
sphillips@bpcc.edu
PHILLIPS, Stephen, S ...... 443-412-2286.. 208 A
sphillips@harford.edu
PHILLIPS, Steve .... 845-675-4741.. 325 C
steve.phillips@nyack.edu
PHILLIPS, Stuart .... 706-295-6868.. 121 F
sphillips@gntc.edu
PHILLIPS, Teddy .... 815-226-3387.. 152 G
tphillips@rockford.edu
PHILLIPS, Teri, P .... 253-535-7187.. 505 G
phillitp@plu.edu
PHILLIPS, Terri .... 406-243-2665.. 276 K
terri.phillips@umontana.edu
PHILLIPS, SR.,
Thomas, R .... 815-753-1811.. 150 A
tphillips3@niu.edu
PHILLIPS, Timothy .... 563-333-6259.. 176 D
phillipstimothy@sau.edu
PHILLIPS, Tina, A .... 610-499-1161.. 423 E
taphillips@widener.edu
PHILLIPS, Tom .... 909-447-2512.... 39 A
tphillips@cst.edu
PHILLIPS, Tom .... 570-389-4775.. 414 D
tphilli2@bloomu.edu
PHILLIPS, Valerie .... 619-596-2766.... 25 G
vphillips@advancedtraining.edu
PHILLIPS, Vicki .... 229-430-4766.. 115 K
vicki.phillips@asurams.edu
PHILLIPS, Virginia .... 619-684-8869.... 54 C
vphillips@newschoolarch.edu
PHILLIPS, Wendell, F ...... 919-530-5423.. 357 A
wendell.phillips@nccu.edu
PHILLIPS, William .... 401-232-6045.. 424 K
wphillip@bryant.edu
PHILLIPS, Wilma, D .... 334-386-7274...... 3 I
wphillips@faulkner.edu
PHILLIPS, Yancy .... 812-237-2100.. 162 A
yancy.phillips@indstate.edu
PHILLIPS-HAUSER,
Robin .... 336-838-6122.. 354 C
robin.phillips@wilkescc.edu
PHILLIPS-MADSON,
Robyn .... 210-283-6994.. 474 D
rmadson@uiwtx.edu
PHILLIS, Thomas, M .... 309-794-7279.. 135 D
tomphillis@augustana.edu
PHILO, Denise, M .... 518-564-2100.. 334 A
belldm@plattsburgh.edu
PHILO, Kathy .... 804-751-9191.. 488 C
kphilo@ccc-va.com
PHILPOTT, Sean .... 617-735-9937.. 218 C
philpotts@emmanuel.edu
PHINAZEE, Karen, B .... 919-532-5663.. 353 I
kbphinazee@waketech.edu
PHINNEY, D. Nathan .... 330-471-8119.. 371 J
nphinney@malone.edu
PHINNEY, James .... 419-755-4720.. 373 G
jphinney@ncstatecollege.edu
PHINNEY, Raymond, R ... 207-834-7562.. 205 B
rphinney@maine.edu
PHIPPS, Adam .... 301-784-5000.. 205 G
aphipps@allegany.edu
PHIPPS, Angela .... 606-368-6134.. 186 B
angelaphipps@alc.edu
PHIPPS, Heidi .... 602-943-2311.... 18 C
heidi.phipps@west.edu
PHIPPS, Jerry .... 760-366-5295.... 41 K
jphipps@cmccd.edu
PHIPPS, Kim, S .... 717-796-5085.. 410 J
kphipps@messiah.edu
PHIPPS, Kylene .... 406-874-6292.. 276 H
phippsk@milescc.edu
PHIPPS, Sam .... 336-841-4545.. 345 A
sphipps@highpoint.edu
PHIPPS, Sid .... 410-626-2545.. 210 D
sid.phipps@sjc.edu
PHIPPS, Terry .... 972-825-4802.. 466 D
tphipps@sagu.edu
PHIPPS, Wayne .... 706-233-4062.. 117 F
wphipps@berry.edu
PHIPPS-BOGER, Jayne .... 336-372-5061.. 354 C
jayne.boger@wilkescc.edu
PHIZACKLEA, Thomas ..... 410-857-2207.. 209 D
tphizacklea@mcdaniel.edu
PHLEGAR, Charles, D ...... 540-231-7676.. 499 F
cphlegar@vt.edu
PHOENIX, Dru .... 505-467-6815.. 302 D
druphoenix@swc.edu
PIANA, Cynthia .... 615-297-7545.. 438 F
pianac@aquinascollege.edu
PIANEZZOLA, Cristina ..... 801-863-8204.. 482 C
cristina.pianezzola@uvu.edu
PIANKA, Stephanie .... 212-998-2910.. 324 C
stephanie.pianka@nyu.edu
PIANTA, Robert, C .... 434-243-5483.. 495 H
rcp4p@virginia.edu
PIASKOWSKY, Robert ...... 201-200-2067.. 293 C
rpiaskowsky@njcu.edu
PIATT, Deidra .... 615-966-5881.. 441 F
deidra.piatt@lipscomb.edu
PIATT, James, B .... 336-278-7440.. 344 D
jpiatt@elon.edu
PIATT, Janet, M .... 423-775-7237.. 439 B
piattja@bryan.edu
PIATT, Ronda .... 217-732-3155.. 146 B
rpiatt@lincolncollege.edu
PIAZZA, Bradley .... 262-691-5594.. 524 G
bpiazza@wctc.edu
PIAZZA, Daniel .... 405-682-7891.. 385 D
daniel.c.piazza@occc.edu
PIAZZA, Rachel .... 815-939-5331.. 150 I
rpiazza@shet.follett.com
PIAZZA, Vincent .... 618-537-6500.. 147 F
vppiazzo@mckendree.edu
PIBURN, Mike .... 816-322-0110.. 262 N
mike.piburn@calvary.edu
PICARD, Ryan .... 863-638-2927.. 115 D
picardrp@webber.edu
PICARD, Sharon, A .... 401-825-2150.. 425 A
sapicard@ccri.edu
PICARDO, Calle .... 937-529-2201.. 378 F
kcpicardo@united.edu
PICCHI, Danielle .... 915-532-3737.. 479 H
dpicchi@westerntech.edu
PICCININNI, James .... 713-525-2192.. 475 J
jpicci@stthom.edu
PICCIRILLO, Tony .... 814-864-6666.. 404 E
tonyp@glit.edu
PICCOLI, Tracey .... 970-247-7464.... 80 D
piccoli_t@fortlewis.edu
PICCOLO, Joe .... 301-934-7822.. 207 B
jpiccolo@csmd.edu
PICCOLO, Nicholas, A ...... 989-463-7333.. 230 F
piccolo@alma.edu
PICCONE, James .... 856-691-8600.. 290 I
jpiccone@cccnj.edu
PICCORELLI, Tom .... 440-775-8445.. 374 C
tom.piccorelli@oberlin.edu
PICERNO, Nicholas, P ...... 540-828-5761.. 487 H
npicerno@bridgewater.edu
PICHA, Mike .... 847-317-7029.. 156 B
mikep@tiu.edu
PICHA, Patti .... 907-474-7596.... 10 G
plpicha@alaska.edu
PICHARDO, Jeannette .... 718-405-3255.. 310 H
jeannette.pichardo@mountsaintvincent.edu
PICINICH, Susan .... 410-704-3288.. 213 B
spicinich@towson.edu
PICKA, Chenek .... 757-490-1241.. 486 E
cpicka@auto.edu
PICKARD, Bert .... 601-928-6224.. 259 C
bert.pickard@mgccc.edu
PICKARD, Jennifer, M .... 520-626-8505.... 17 I
meyers@email.arizona.edu
PICKARD, Jeremy .... 563-288-6004.. 172 C
jpickard@eicc.edu
PICKARD, Larry .... 415-451-2803.... 61 D
lpickard@sfts.edu
PICKEL, Wendy .... 816-501-4824.. 270 J
wendy.pickel@rockhurst.edu
PICKELL, Barsha .... 706-233-7394.. 127 A
bpickell@shorter.edu
PICKEN, Conor, A .... 502-272-8188.. 187 A
cpicken@bellarmine.edu
PICKENS, Eva, K .... 713-313-4205.. 470 D
pickensek@tsu.edu
PICKENS, Joe .... 386-312-4111.. 108 B
joepickens@sjrstate.edu
PICKENS, Leo .... 410-295-6926.. 210 D
leo.pickens@sjc.edu
PICKER, Leah .... 412-365-1383.. 400 G
PICKERELL, Jennifer, K ... 618-537-6805.. 147 F
jkpickerell@mckendree.edu
PICKERILL, Ted, O .... 513-529-6225.. 372 K
ted.pickerill@miamioh.edu
PICKERING, Amanda .... 315-268-3994.. 310 B
apickeri@clarkson.edu
PICKERING, David .... 815-939-5240.. 150 I
dpickrng@olivet.edu
PICKERING, Jeff .... 252-789-0290.. 351 A
jpickering@martincc.edu
PICKERING, Jonathan ...... 815-939-5201.. 150 I
jmpickering@olivet.edu
PICKERING, Lora Lea ...... 580-477-2000.. 389 I
loralea.pickering@wosc.edu
PICKERING, Robert, P ...... 843-953-5096.. 428 A
robert.pickering@citadel.edu
PICKETT, Clyde .... 412-237-4436.. 401 B
cpickett@ccac.edu
PICKETT, Kareen .... 863-638-7248.. 115 C
kareen.pickett@warner.edu
PICKETT, Regina .... 281-283-2626.. 474 A
pickett@uhcl.edu
PICKETT, Todd .... 562-903-4754.... 28 E
todd.pickett@biola.edu
PICKLESIMER, Heith .... 704-334-6882.. 343 D
hpicklesimer@charlottechristian.edu
PICKMAN, Jerry .... 816-271-5647.. 269 C
pickman@missouriwestern.edu
PICKREN, Wade .... 607-274-3734.. 317 D
wpickren@ithaca.edu
PICKRON, Carlton .... 413-572-5400.. 222 E
cpickron@westfield.ma.edu
PICKRUM, Vita, C .... 302-857-6055.... 90 F
vpickrum@desu.edu
PICOLO MANZI,
Stephanie .... 401-254-3369.. 426 B
smanzi@rwu.edu
PICONE, Deborah .... 212-686-9244.. 304 A
PICONE, Gary .... 208-792-2275.. 134 A
gapicone@lcsc.edu
PICUS, Sharon, M .... 610-683-1353.. 415 C
picus@kutztown.edu
PIDDINGTON, Josh, R ..... 856-415-2270.. 295 D
jpiddington@rcgc.edu
PIECHOTA, Thomas, C .... 702-895-4412.. 284 L
thomas.piechota@unlv.edu
PIECZYNSKI, William, C .. 508-213-2162.. 227 A
william.pieczynski@nichols.edu
PIEDRAS, Alex, H .... 515-263-6017.. 172 H
apiedras@grandview.edu
PIEHL, Jon .... 909-667-4444.... 38 G
jpiehl@claremontlincoln.edu
PIEHL, Marnie .... 701-224-5748.. 361 C
marnie.piehl@bismarckstate.edu
PIEKARA, Lita .... 570-208-5962.. 406 J
litapiekara@kings.edu
PIEKUTOWSKI, Michelle . 864-656-4286.. 428 C
mtp@clemson.edu
PIEL, Duane .... 770-593-2257.. 122 F
dpiel@gupton-jones.edu
PIELLUSCH, Gina .... 410-857-2292.. 209 D
gpiellusch@mcdaniel.edu
PIELOCK, Stephen .... 413-545-5768.. 220 F
pielock@oit.umass.edu
PIENTA-LETTA, Diane .... 973-300-2226.. 297 D
dpienta-lett@sussex.edu
PIEPENBRING, Jack .... 865-981-8112.. 441 H
jack.piepenbring@maryvillecollege.edu
PIEPENBURG,
Marianne, B .... 214-768-3410.. 465 J
mpiepenb@smu.edu
PIEPER, John, A .... 314-367-8700.. 271 E
john.pieper@stlcop.edu
PIEPER, Michael .... 507-457-5039.. 252 G
mpieper@winona.edu
PIEPER, Sandi, J .... 515-574-1139.. 173 F
pieper@iowacentral.edu
PIEPER-OLSON, Heather .. 320-363-5964.. 245 I
hpieperolso@csbsju.edu
PIER, David .... 916-608-6809..... 51 C
pierd@flc.losrios.edu
PIER, Julie, H .... 605-677-5446.. 437 A
julie.pier@usd.edu
PIERCE, Amanda, K .... 757-594-8851.. 488 E
amanda.pierce@cnu.edu
PIERCE, Barb .... 800-962-7682.. 275 D
bpierce@wma.edu
PIERCE, Bill .... 479-788-7188.... 23 A
bill.pierce@uafs.edu
PIERCE, Bill .... 502-852-8372.. 194 A
wmpier01@louisville.edu
PIERCE, Brandon .... 316-295-5658.. 181 B
piercb@friends.edu
PIERCE, Brandon .... 334-347-2623...... 3 H
bpierce@escc.edu
PIERCE, Brynn .... 541-383-7402.. 390 D
bpierce@cocc.edu
PIERCE, Carl, G .... 610-499-4555.. 423 E
cgpierce@widener.edu
PIERCE, Carolyn .... 954-308-2101.... 95 K
cjpierce@aii.edu
PIERCE, Dee .... 630-752-5048.. 158 C
dee.pierce@wheaton.edu
PIERCE, Donald, E .... 864-294-2024.. 430 C
don.pierce@furman.edu
PIERCE, Donna, L .... 931-598-1880.. 443 O
dopierce@sewanee.edu
PIERCE, JR., Earl, E .... 607-871-2406.. 303 F
pierce@alfred.edu
PIERCE, Evan, F .... 716-286-8769.. 324 E
epierce@niagara.edu
PIERCE, Fred .... 608-785-8376.. 520 C
fpierce@uwlax.edu
PIERCE, Fred, M .... 608-785-8017.. 520 C
fpierce@uwlax.edu
PIERCE, Frederic .... 607-753-2518.. 333 A
fred.pierce@cortland.edu
PIERCE, Greg .... 601-266-5006.. 261 E
greg.pierce@usm.edu
PIERCE, Harold, J .... 802-656-4490.. 485 D
harold.pierce@uvm.edu
PIERCE, James .... 254-968-9781.. 467 F
jrpierce@tarleton.edu
PIERCE, Jason, A .... 828-689-1237.. 346 C
jpierce@mhu.edu
PIERCE, Jason, L .... 937-229-2601.. 379 D
jpierce2@udayton.edu
PIERCE, Jennifer .... 856-351-2642.. 296 L
jpierce@salemcc.edu
PIERCE, Jerry, D .... 318-357-6588.. 201 B
pierce@nsula.edu
PIERCE, Joan .... 608-785-9915.. 524 H
piercej@westerntc.edu
PIERCE, John .... 828-251-6742.. 357 C
jpierce@unca.edu
PIERCE, Jonathan .... 503-883-2490.. 392 B
jdpierce@linfield.edu
PIERCE, Joshua .... 573-629-3014.. 265 G
joshua.pierce@hlg.edu
PIERCE, Kathy .... 870-541-7850.... 20 G
PIERCE, Keith .... 803-641-3513.. 433 G
keithp@usca.edu
PIERCE, Kellee .... 406-657-1166.. 278 D
piercek@rocky.edu
PIERCE, Kenetta .... 803-786-3848.. 429 A
kpierce@columbiasc.edu
PIERCE, Kenneth .... 512-245-9650.. 471 F
krp91@txstate.edu
PIERCE, Kevin .... 941-355-9080.... 98 J
kpierce@ewcollege.org
PIERCE, Kristen .... 505-565-1075.. 228 F
kpierce1@stonehill.edu
PIERCE, LaRue, A .... 413-755-4868.. 224 G
lapierce@stcc.edu
PIERCE, Leighton .... 661-255-1050.... 30 E
lpierce@calarts.edu
PIERCE, Leslie .... 478-445-5596.. 121 A
leslie.pierce@gcsu.edu
PIERCE, Lori, J .... 734-764-0151.. 241 J
ljpierce@umich.edu
PIERCE, Malisa .... 918-270-6409.. 386 I
malisa.pierce@ptstulsa.edu
PIERCE, Marisa .... 425-640-1697.. 503 E
marisa.pierce@edcc.edu
PIERCE, Marisa, E .... 915-831-2864.. 457 H
mpierce6@epcc.edu
PIERCE, Mark .... 518-736-3622.. 315 A
mark.pierce@fmcc.suny.edu
PIERCE, Melody, C .... 336-334-7696.. 356 F
mcpierce@ncat.edu
PIERCE, Michael .... 562-903-4777.... 28 E
michael.pierce@biola.edu
PIERCE, Mike .... 941-487-4877.. 111 D
mpierce@ncf.edu
PIERCE, Misti .... 970-521-6619.... 81 O
misti.pierce@njc.edu
PIERCE, Peg .... 248-204-3143.. 237 B
mpierce@ltu.edu
PIERCE, Robert "Bob" .... 205-348-4767...... 8 D
bpierce@advance.ua.edu
PIERCE, Sharon .... 612-659-6300.. 250 B
sharon.pierce@minneapolis.edu
PIERCE, Susan .... 972-860-8058.. 456 C
spierce@dcccd.edu
PIERCE, Tom .... 708-656-8000.. 149 A
tom.pierce@morton.edu
PIERCE, Travis, L .... 906-487-2682.. 238 A
tlp@mtu.edu
PIERCE, Vicki, G .... 256-765-4311...... 9 C
vgpierce@una.edu

PISORS, Jesse, D .... 361-570-4829.. 474 C
pisorsj@uhv.edu
PISTILLI, Fran .... 352-323-3680.. 104 J
pistillf@lssc.edu
PISTILLO, Jason .... 602-383-8228.... 17 H
jay@uat.edu
PISTOLE, John .... 765-641-4010.. 158 J
jspistole@anderson.edu
PISTONO, Lita .... 573-876-7210.. 272 I
lpistono@stephens.edu
PISTOR, Sherry .... 410-287-1025.. 206 J
spistor@cecil.edu
PISTORINO, Thomas, G .. 781-768-7075.. 227 G
t.pistorino@regiscollege.edu
PISZKER, James .... 814-824-2429.. 410 H
jpiszker@mercyhurst.edu
PITARO, Teresa .... 781-239-4452.. 214 G
tpitaro@babson.edu
PITCHER, Carole, D .... 302-295-1133.... 91 I
carole.d.pitcher@wilmu.edu
PITCHER, Christopher, G . 302-295-1152.... 91 I
christopher.g.pitcher@wilmu.edu
PITCHER, Darren .... 509-533-3514.. 502 H
darren.pitcher@sfcc.spokane.edu
PITCHER, Darren .... 509-533-3514.. 503 A
darren.pitcher@sfcc.spokane.edu
PITCHER, John .... 617-228-2208.. 223 B
PITCHER, Katherine .... 585-245-5064.. 333 B
pitcher@geneseo.edu
PITCHER, Katherine, E ..... 240-895-4267.. 210 E
kepitcher@smcm.edu
PITCHER, Mark .... 918-293-5412.. 386 B
mark.pitcher@okstate.edu
PITCHER, Scott .... 641-585-8112.. 177 F
pitchers@waldorf.edu
PITCHFORD, Nicola .... 415-458-3759.... 42 G
nicola.pitchford@dominican.edu
PITCHFORD, Steven, L .... 662-254-3327.. 260 A
steven.pitchford@mvsu.edu
PITCOCK, Beth .... 559-323-2100.... 61 E
bpitcock@sjcl.edu
PITHIS, Nancy .... 617-236-8814.. 218 G
npithis@fisher.edu
PITMAN, Julia .... 716-614-6240.. 324 D
jpitman@niagaracc.suny.edu
PITONZO, Beth .... 336-334-4822.. 350 B
bjpitonzo@gtcc.edu
PITRUZZELLO, Carl .... 203-932-7047.... 90 A
cpitruzzello@newhaven.edu
PITT, Ronald, E .... 401-456-8003.. 425 E
rpitt@ric.edu
PITT, Sharon .... 607-777-6112.. 331 B
spitt@binghamton.edu
PITTENGER, David .... 304-696-2818.. 513 D
pittengerd@marshall.edu
PITTENGER, Susan, D ..... 315-568-3069.. 323 A
spittenger@nycc.edu
PITTER, Yeruchem .... 516-225-4700.. 326 I
PITTINGER, Teresa, L ...... 330-471-8121.. 371 J
tpittinger@malone.edu
PITTLE, Joseph .... 401-874-2170.. 426 D
joepittle@uri.edu
PITTMAN, Anthony .... 908-737-3750.. 292 C
apittman@kean.edu
PITTMAN, Crystal .... 864-941-8328.. 432 A
pittman.cg@ptc.edu
PITTMAN, Edward, L .... 845-437-5426.. 339 C
edpittman@vassar.edu
PITTMAN, James .... 315-268-2327.. 310 B
jpittman@clarkson.edu
PITTMAN, Jane, D .... 540-665-3489.. 494 B
jpittman@su.edu
PITTMAN, Jeff .... 314-539-5150.. 271 F
jeffpittman@stlcc.edu
PITTMAN, Jennifer .... 540-857-6807.. 499 B
jpittman@virginiawestern.edu
PITTMAN, Karan .... 229-732-5944.. 116 C
karanpittman@andrewcollege.edu
PITTMAN, L. Monique .... 269-471-3297.. 230 H
pittman@andrews.edu
PITTMAN, Lyndsay .... 405-945-3252.. 386 C
lyndsp@osuokc.edu
PITTMAN, Nancy Claire ... 918-610-8303.. 386 I
nancy.pittman@ptsulsa.edu
PITTMAN, Patrick .... 910-362-7043.. 348 A
ppittman@cfcc.edu
PITTMAN, Stanley, G .... 260-982-5270.. 165 M
sgpittman@manchester.edu
PITTMAN, Stephanie, M .. 262-554-2010.. 518 B
pittmanmwc@aol.com
PITTMAN, Suzanne .... 478-445-6283.. 121 A
suzanne.pittman@gcsu.edu
PITTMAN, Tiffany .... 314-918-2501.. 265 A
tpittman@eden.edu
PITTMAN, Trevor .... 864-596-9010.. 429 C
trevor.pittman@converse.edu
PITTMAN, W. Randall ...... 205-726-2331..... 6 E
rpittman@samford.edu
PITTMAN, Wayne .... 205-726-2020..... 6 E
rwpittma@samford.edu

PITTMAN-SCHULZ,
Kimberley .... 707-826-5139.... 34 F
kcp16@humboldt.edu
PITTS, Danny, C .... 601-426-6346.. 260 G
dpitts@southeasternbaptist.edu
PITTS, James, E .... 850-644-0538.. 111 C
jpitts@admin.fsu.edu
PITTS, John .... 510-841-9230.... 75 F
jpitts@wi.edu
PITTS, Laura .... 760-630-1555.... 29 B
laura.pitts@brightwood.edu
PITTS, Mark .... 619-849-2548.... 57 M
markpitts@pointloma.edu
PITTS, Mike .... 417-328-1412.. 272 C
mpitts@sbuniv.edu
PITTS, Mykeal .... 620-278-6247.. 185 A
mykeal.pitts@sterling.edu
PITTS, Otis .... 828-328-7179.. 345 H
otis.pitts@lr.edu
PITZNER, Alex, C .... 717-901-5124.. 405 H
apitzner@harrisburgu.edu
PIUROWSKI, Robert, C ... 607-746-4559.. 335 C
piurowrc@delhi.edu
PIVARNIK, OP,
R. Gabriel .... 401-865-2245.. 425 D
gpivarni@providence.edu
PIXLEY, Alan, D .... 972-758-3842.. 455 A
apixley@collin.edu
PIZAM, Abraham .... 407-903-8010.. 111 E
abraham.pizam@ucf.edu
PIZANA, Kathleen .... 574-520-4878.. 163 E
kpizana@iusb.edu
PIZER, Lori .... 518-292-7785.. 327 H
inst_res@sage.edu
PIZZANO, Patti .... 704-461-6573.. 342 A
pattipizzano@bac.edu
PIZZARDI, Frank .... 516-876-3013.. 333 C
pizzardif@oldwestbury.edu
PIZZOLA, Lorrie .... 518-454-5196.. 311 B
pizzolal@strose.edu
PIZZUTI, Linda, J .... 309-677-3153.. 136 B
lindap@fsmail.bradley.edu
PIZZUTO, Carmelo .... 212-353-4161.. 311 G
pizzut@cooper.edu
PIZZUTO, Phyllis .... 760-480-8474.... 74 L
ppizzuto@wscal.edu
PIZZUTO, William, J .... 203-236-9818.... 89 D
william.j.pizzuto@uconn.edu
PIÑERO, Hector .... 787-850-9104.. 538 B
hector.pinero@upr.edu
PIÑERO, Ileana .... 787-751-1912.. 534 E
ipinero@juris.inter.edu
PJATAK, Jennifer .... 203-932-7082.... 90 A
jpjatak@newhaven.edu
PLA-GOMEZ, Fernando .... 787-250-0000.. 537 D
fernando.pla1@upr.edu
PLACE, Linna, F .... 816-235-6230.. 273 F
placel@umkc.edu
PLACE, Nick, T .... 352-392-1761.. 112 A
nplace@ufl.edu
PLACEK, Kristen .... 863-680-4205.. 101 E
kplacek@flsouthern.edu
PLACER, Chandra .... 864-578-8770.. 432 D
cplacer@sherman.edu
PLACERES, Sonia .... 787-738-2161.. 538 A
sonia.placeres@upr.edu
PLACEY, David, L .... 603-526-3442.. 285 L
david.placey@colby-sawyer.edu
PLACIDI, Kathleen .... 434-381-6596.. 494 M
kplacidi@sbc.edu
PLACIDO, Rob .... 940-898-3980.. 472 G
rplacido@twu.edu
PLAEHN, Kris, H .... 253-535-7212.. 505 G
plaehnkh@plu.edu
PLAGGE, Sinead .... 360-416-7600.. 507 G
sinead.plagge@skagit.edu
PLAISANCE, DesLey .... 985-448-4191.. 201 A
desley.plaisance@nicholls.edu
PLANAS, Fernando .... 217-206-7949.. 156 G
fplanas@uis.edu
PLANDER, Kristy .... 402-481-8849.. 278 J
kristy.plander@bryanhealthcollege.edu
PLANEK, John .... 815-836-5937.. 145 H
planekjo@lewisu.edu
PLANK, Donna .... 254-295-4591.. 474 E
dplank@umhb.edu
PLANT, Jonathan .... 361-593-2599.. 469 A
jonathan.plant@tamuk.edu
PLANT, Maureen, C .... 301-443-5362.. 209 G
mplant@msmary.edu
PLANTE, Beverly .... 315-801-3034.. 328 C
bplante@secon.edu
PLANTE, Dawn, M .... 440-525-7327.. 371 F
dplante@lakelandcc.edu
PLANTE, Jacques .... 603-641-7380.. 287 G
jplante@anselm.edu
PLANTE, John, J .... 412-396-4937.. 403 A
plantej@duq.edu
PLANTEFABER, Lisa .... 413-572-5733.. 222 E
lplantefaber@westfield.ma.edu

PLANTENBERG, Diane ..... 262-646-6517.. 518 G
dplantenberg@nashotah.edu
PLANTY, Teresa .... 315-268-3852.. 310 B
tplanty@clarkson.edu
PLANTZ, Dorothy, B .... 443-518-4614.. 208 C
dplantz@howardcc.edu
PLANTZ-MASTERS, Shari . 303-458-4272.... 82 L
splantzmasters@regis.edu
PLASKER, Nancy .... 781-768-7019.. 227 G
nancy.plasker@regiscollege.edu
PLASKONOS, Melissa .... 619-260-4175.... 72 B
melissa@sandiego.edu
PLASTERS, Shana .... 336-272-7102.. 344 G
shana.plasters@greensboro.edu
PLATE, Jerrod .... 304-829-7717.. 510 G
jplate@bethanywv.edu
PLATE, William .... 843-349-4066.. 428 E
billplate@coastal.edu
PLATING, John .... 706-419-1663.. 119 G
john.plating@covenant.edu
PLATOVSKY, Jonathan ..... 718-268-4700.. 326 L
PLATSOUCAS, Chris .... 757-683-3277.. 492 G
cplatsoucas@odu.edu
PLATT, Jeffrey .... 716-829-7766.. 313 A
plattjh@dyc.edu
PLATT, Judy .... 617-353-5940.. 216 E
juplatt@bu.edu
PLATT, Kathleen .... 912-344-2576.. 116 E
kathy.platt@armstrong.edu
PLATT, Mark .... 318-675-5341.. 198 B
mplatt@lsuhsc.edu
PLATT, Mary .... 714-997-6607.... 37 F
platt@chapman.edu
PLATT, Sharon .... 412-536-1120.. 406 K
sharon.platt@laroche.edu
PLATT, Steven .... 401-456-8554.. 425 E
splatt@ric.edu
PLATTEN, Peter, G .... 920-565-1043.. 517 D
plattenpg@lakeland.edu
PLATUKUS, Graceann .... 570-740-0355.. 409 E
gplatukus@luzerne.edu
PLATZ, Matthew .... 808-932-7332.. 131 E
mplatz@hawaii.edu
PLATZEK, Russell .... 718-262-2140.. 310 A
rplatzek@york.cuny.edu
PLAYER, Kathleen, N .... 630-515-7664.. 148 C
kplayer@midwestern.edu
PLAZA, Claudia .... 562-985-4187.... 33 B
claudia.plaza@csulb.edu
PLAZA, Erica .... 920-498-6969.. 524 E
erica.plaza@nwtc.edu
PLAZA, Laurie .... 610-526-6038.. 405 B
lplaza@harcum.edu
PLAZA, Luis .... 917-493-4448.. 319 M
lplaza@msmnyc.edu
PLEAS, Dorothy, J .... 630-637-5156.. 149 H
djpleas@noctrl.edu
PLEAS-BAILEY, Dawn, E .. 620-229-6336.. 184 J
dawn.pleas-bailey@sckans.edu
PLEASANT, Klint .... 248-218-2058.. 240 C
kpleasant@rc.edu
PLEASANT, Lori .... 850-973-9469.. 105 H
pleasantl@nfcc.edu
PLEASANT-DOINE,
Sheia, I .... 904-819-6435.... 99 M
spleasant@flagler.edu
PLEASANTS, Jane .... 919-668-2565.. 343 J
jane.pleasants@duke.edu
PLEGER, Kimberly .... 253-680-7102.. 501 E
kpleger@bates.ctc.edu
PLEGER, Thomas, C .... 906-635-2202.. 236 J
tpleger@lssu.edu
PLEMMONS, Donna .... 501-450-1351.... 20 F
plemmons@hendrix.edu
PLEMMONS, Kim .... 704-403-1751.. 342 E
kim.plemmons@carolinashealthcare.org
PLETCHER, Ann .... 864-596-9086.. 429 C
ann.pletcher@converse.edu
PLETCHER, James, R .... 740-587-6469.. 368 B
pletcher@denison.edu
PLETCHER, Jill, M .... 316-978-3435.. 185 J
jill.pletcher@wichita.edu
PLETSCHER, Anthony, W . 215-368-5000.. 398 C
tpletscher@biblical.edu
PLEUSS, Carol, J .... 330-684-8928.. 378 H
cjpleus@uakron.edu
PLEVER, Steve .... 828-251-6526.. 357 C
splever@unca.edu
PLIML, Michelle .... 414-930-3397.. 518 F
plimlm@mtmary.edu
PLINER, Lauren .... 215-953-5999.... 93 F
PLINER, Lauren .... 484-809-7770.... 93 F
PLINER, Susan .... 315-781-3354.. 316 C
pliner@hws.edu
PLINSKE, Kathleen, A ...... 407-582-4975.. 114 N
kplinske@valenciacollege.edu
PLINSKE, Paul, M .... 308-865-8332.. 282 L
plinskep@unk.edu
PLINSKI, Christie .... 503-491-7295.. 392 F
christie.plinski@mhcc.edu

PLLOG, William .... 603-641-7174.. 287 G
wploog@anselm.edu
PLOECKELMAN, Erica .... 920-686-6127.. 519 H
erica.ploeckelman@sl.edu
PLOEGER, SM, Bernard ... 808-735-4741.. 130 F
bploeger@chaminade.edu
PLONSKY, Christine, A .... 512-471-4780.. 476 B
cp@utexas.edu
PLOTKIN, David .... 503-594-3020.. 390 F
david.plotkin@clackamas.edu
PLOTKIN, Helen .... 501-450-1225.... 20 F
plotkin@hendrix.edu
PLOTKOWSKI, Paul .... 616-331-6260.. 234 F
plotkowp@gvsu.edu
PLOTNER, Amy .... 315-312-3702.. 333 D
amy.plotner@oswego.edu
PLOTNICK, Tamra .... 212-346-1244.. 325 J
tplotnick@pace.edu
PLOTTS, Debra .... 334-214-4866...... 2 H
debra.plotts@cv.edu
PLOTTS, Douglas, J .... 610-861-1560.. 411 B
plottsd@moravian.edu
PLOTTS, John .... 972-721-5266.. 473 D
jplotts@udallas.edu
PLOUFF, Chris .... 616-331-2400.. 234 F
plouffc@gvsu.edu
PLOUFFE, Audrew .... 406-275-4969.. 278 E
audrew_plouffe@skc.edu
PLOUFFE, Jeffrey .... 401-874-4198.. 426 D
jeffplouffe@uri.edu
PLOURDE, Philip, D .... 319-273-2853.. 170 A
philip.plourde@uni.edu
PLOWFIELD, Lisa .... 410-704-2132.. 213 B
lplowfield@towson.edu
PLOWMAN, Donde .... 402-472-9500.. 282 M
dplowman2@unl.edu
PLUCHUTA, Alexander ...... 610-359-5057.. 401 L
apluchut@dccc.edu
PLUEMER, Julie .... 608-822-2369.. 524 F
jpluemer@swtc.edu
PLUHTA, Elizabeth, A .... 206-934-5141.. 507 A
elizabeth.pluhta@seattlecolleges.edu
PLUMB, Anne, M .... 901-572-2842.. 438 I
anne.plumb@bchs.edu
PLUMB, Richard, G .... 651-962-6720.. 256 C
rgplumb@stthomas.edu
PLUMB, Sylvia .... 802-626-6459.. 486 C
sylvia.plumb@lyndonstate.edu
PLUMLEY, Kelly .... 828-327-7000.. 348 C
kplumley@cvcc.edu
PLUMLY, Wayne, L .... 229-245-3825.. 129 G
lwplumly@valdosta.edu
PLUMMER, B. DaVida .... 757-727-6698.. 490 E
davida.plummer@hamptonu.edu
PLUMMER, Dale, H .... 610-566-1776.. 423 H
dplummer@williamson.edu
PLUMMER, David .... 956-872-5575.. 465 H
davidp@southtexascollege.edu
PLUMMER, Deborah, L ...... 508-856-2179.. 221 B
deborah.plummer@umassmed.edu
PLUMMER, Dianne .... 617-989-4036.. 229 D
plummerd@wit.edu
PLUMMER, Donna, M .... 859-238-5308.. 187 H
donna.plummer@centre.edu
PLUMMER, Eric .... 701-777-3391.. 360 C
eric.plummer@und.edu
PLUMMER, Laura .... 915-532-3737.. 479 H
lplummer@westerntech.edu
PLUMMER, Lisa .... 610-282-1100.. 402 B
lisa.plummer@desales.edu
PLUMMER, Meredith .... 760-366-5284.... 41 K
mplummer@cmccd.edu
PLUMMER, Robert, M .... 423-439-4218.. 444 F
plummerb@etsu.edu
PLUMMER, Troy, A .... 515-263-6050.. 172 H
tplummer@grandview.edu
PLUMMER, Vince .... 701-671-2319.. 361 F
vince.plummer@ndscs.edu
PLUMMER, Yhann .... 504-286-5191.. 199 I
yplummer@suno.edu
PLUNK, Kelly .... 870-584-1104.... 23 F
kplunk@cccua.edu
PLUNKETT, Cathy .... 540-769-8289.. 486 G
ceplunkett@an.edu
PLUNKETT, Chris .... 319-385-6206.. 174 A
chris.plunkett@iw.edu
PLUNKETT, James, C .... 215-951-1500.. 407 A
plunkett@lasalle.edu
PLUNKETT, Randy .... 505-922-2886.. 299 K
randy.plunkett@eccu.edu
PLUTA, Kate .... 661-395-4610.... 47 J
kpluta@bakersfieldcollege.edu
PLUTCHAK, Scott .... 205-934-5460...... 8 E
tscott@uab.edu
PLUTCHOK, Yisroel .... 718-438-5476.. 340 E
PLUTE, David .... 307-754-6025.. 526 N
david.plute@nwc.edu
PLYLER, Chris, P .... 803-777-7695.. 433 F
chrisp@mailbox.sc.edu
PLYLER, Jeffrey, B .... 704-463-3042.. 354 F
jeff.plyler@pfeiffer.edu

PLYMALE, Chad .... 585-567-9480.. 316 F
chad.plymale@houghton.edu
PLYMESSER, Jillian .... 402-354-7137.. 281 F
jillian.plymesser@methodistcollege.edu
PNACEK, Kevin .... 810-766-2240.. 231 D
kpnace01@baker.edu
POAGE, Alison .... 512-472-4133.. 465 F
alison.poage@ssw.edu
POARCH, Mark .... 828-726-2214.. 347 I
mpoarch@cccti.edu
POAT, Erica .... 618-634-3375.. 154 B
ericap@shawneecc.edu
POATS, Lillian, B .... 713-313-7978.. 470 D
poats_lb@tsu.edu
POBLENZ, Scott, B .... 978-468-7111.. 219 B
spoblenz@gcts.edu
POCAI, Rob .... 601-366-8880.. 261 H
rpocai@wbs.edu
POCHARD, Brad .... 864-294-3406.. 430 C
brad.pochard@furman.edu
POCHE, Paulette, M .... 985-549-5638.. 201 C
ppoche@selu.edu
POCK, Arnyce .... 301-295-9945.. 528 G
arnyce.pock@usuhs.edu
POCOCK, Beth .... 828-669-8012.. 346 M
beth.pocock@montreat.edu
PODANY, Jeremy .... 970-491-5709.... 78 Q
jeremy.podany@colostate.edu
PODELL, David .... 781-239-3101.. 223 F
dpodell@massbay.edu
PODESCHI, Amanda .... 217-424-3506.. 148 D
apodeschi@millikin.edu
PODESTÁ, Guido .... 608-262-9833.. 519 K
gpodesta@wisc.edu
PODLIN, Michael .... 206-296-6100.. 507 E
podlinm@seattleu.edu
PODOLSKY, Daniel, K ..... 214-648-2508.. 478 C
priscilla.alderman@utsouthwestern.edu
POE, JR., Donald .... 704-463-3041.. 354 F
don.poe@pfeiffer.edu
POE, Elmer .... 252-328-9066.. 356 C
poee@ecu.edu
POE, Scott .... 304-424-8212.. 514 D
scott.poe@wvup.edu
POE, Shawna .... 217-854-5506.. 135 K
shawna.poe@blackburn.edu
POEHLER, M.J .... 816-802-3393.. 266 D
mpoehler@kcai.edu
POEHLERT, Edward .... 760-757-2121.... 52 K
epoehlert@miracosta.edu
POELKER, Scott .... 843-574-6197.. 433 D
scott.poelker@tridenttech.edu
POELKING, Karen, L .... 216-373-5234.. 374 B
kpoelking@ndc.edu
POELVOORDE, Tracy, L ... 309-779-7710.. 156 A
tracy.poelvoorde@trinitycollegeqc.edu
POERTNER, Gary .... 949-582-4840.... 65 E
gpoertner@socccd.edu
POESE, Debra .... 240-567-7269.. 209 E
debra.poese@montgomerycollege.edu
POFF, G. Elaine, N .... 954-262-7261.. 105 J
poff@nova.edu
POFF, Robert, C .... 812-941-2331.. 163 F
rcpoff@ius.edu
POGGENDORF,
Brenda, P .... 540-375-2270.. 493 H
poggendorf@roanoke.edu
POGGENDORF,
Brenda, P .... 540-375-2235.. 493 H
bpoggendorf@roanoke.edu
POGGENDORF,
Richard, J .... 540-375-2043.. 493 H
rpoggendorf@roanoke.edu
POGONCHEFF, Elaine ...... 517-483-1016.. 237 A
pogonce@lcc.edu
POGORELC, Anthony .... 650-289-3344.... 59 J
anthony.pogorelc@stpatricksseminary.org
POGROSZEWSKI,
Donna, J .... 585-292-3202.. 321 J
dpogroszewski@monroecc.edu
POGUE, Frank .... 610-399-2220.. 414 F
president@cheyney.edu
POGUE, Gregory .... 609-771-3078.. 290 F
pogueg@tcnj.edu
POGUE, Roslynn .... 318-342-5327.. 201 E
pogue@ulm.edu
POHAS, Joanie .... 310-338-3068.... 51 E
jpohas@lmu.edu
POHERO, Mary Jane .... 973-596-3106.. 293 D
mary.j.pohero@njit.edu
POHIRA VIETH, Ann .... 407-264-9400.... 93 F
POHIRA VIETH, Ann .... 407-618-5900.... 93 F
POHL, Charles, A .... 215-503-6988.. 420 E
charles.pohl@jefferson.edu
POHL, Don .... 314-286-3653.. 270 G
dpohl@ranken.edu
POHL, Henry, S .... 518-262-5919.. 303 E
pohlh@mail.amc.edu
POHL, Jonathan .... 860-832-1945.... 85 F
pohlj@ccsu.edu

POHL, Laurie .... 617-353-9814.. 216 E
lpohl@bu.edu
POHL, Sara .... 815-825-9384.. 144 F
sara.pohl@kishwaukeecollege.edu
POHLGEERS, Linda .... 513-244-4824.. 373 C
linda.pohlgeers@msj.edu
POHLIG, Holly .... 407-646-2161.. 107 O
hpohlig@rollins.edu
POHLMAN, Jean .... 513-487-1126.. 378 E
jean.pohlman@myunion.edu
POHLSON, Scott .... 605-677-5759.. 437 A
scott.pohlson@usd.edu
POIGER, Uta .... 617-373-5173.. 227 B
POINDEXTER, Jeanne ...... 757-382-9900.... 93 F
POINDEXTER, Michael ..... 916-558-2101.... 51 D
poindem@scc.losrios.edu
POINT, Matthew .... 215-965-4035.. 411 A
mpoint@moore.edu
POINTS, Dan .... 405-733-7359.. 387 I
dpoints@rose.edu
POINTS, Emily .... 309-694-8501.. 141 F
emily.points@icc.edu
POIRIER, Dawn .... 508-541-1809.. 217 G
dpoirier@dean.edu
POIRIER, J. Nicolas .... 315-568-3197.. 323 A
npoirier@nycc.edu
POIRIER, Janet, L .... 603-641-7010.. 287 G
jpoirier@anselm.edu
POIRRIER, Gail, P .... 337-482-6808.. 201 D
poirrier@louisiana.edu
POISEL, Mark Allen .... 706-737-1411.. 117 D
mpoisel@augusta.edu
POISEL, Mark Allen .... 212-346-1200.. 325 J
mpoisel@pace.edu
POISION, Rebecca .... 843-863-7517.. 427 I
rpoision@csuniv.edu
POISSON, Craig .... 413-748-3333.. 228 E
cpoisson@springfieldcollege.edu
POITER, Emilia .... 410-532-5184.. 210 B
epoiter@ndm.edu
POITRA, Lyle .... 701-477-7862.. 362 D
lpoitra@tm.edu
POITRA, Peggy .... 218-879-0803.. 249 C
poitra@fdltcc.edu
POK, Shirley, M .... 209-667-3131.... 34 E
smpok@csustan.edu
POKHAREL, Padmanjali ... 571-633-9651.. 495 D
padmanjali.pokharel@uona.edu
POKORAK, Jeffrey .... 617-573-8000.. 228 G
jpokorak@suffolk.edu
POKORNOWSKI, Alex ...... 701-777-2664.. 360 C
alexander.pokornowski@und.edu
POKORNY, Anita, R .... 330-325-6760.. 373 H
app@neomed.edu
POKOT, Elena .... 262-472-1001.. 521 F
pokote@uww.edu
POL, Aileen .... 708-209-3237.. 138 G
aileen.pol@cuchicago.edu
POL, Lou .... 402-554-2303.. 283 B
lpol@unomaha.edu
POLAK, Benjamin .... 203-432-4444.... 90 D
benjamin.polak@yale.edu
POLAK, Debra .... 707-468-3605.... 52 C
dpolak@mendocino.edu
POLAKOW-SURANSKY,
Shael .... 212-875-4595.. 304 E
ssuransky@bankstreet.edu
POLAND, Caroline .... 765-998-5222.. 167 C
caroline_polland@taylor.edu
POLAND, D'Ann .... 361-698-2209.. 457 D
dpoland@delmar.edu
POLAND, Russell .... 615-327-6171.. 442 A
rpoland@mmc.edu
POLANIECKI, Andrew .... 574-239-8315.. 161 N
apolaniecki@hcc-nd.edu
POLANSKY, Thomas .... 323-259-2651.... 55 A
tpolansky@oxy.edu
POLASKI, Tamara, R .... 515-294-5225.. 169 G
tra@iastate.edu
POLATAJKO, Mark, M ..... 330-672-2422.. 370 I
mpolataj@kent.edu
POLCI, Andrea .... 718-780-7966.. 305 L
andrea.polci@brooklaw.edu
POLCYN, Steve .... 909-687-1550.... 44 H
stevepolycn@gs.edu
POLCZ, Becca .... 317-681-1776.. 162 F
rpolcz@iu.edu
POLCZYNSKI, Mimi .... 618-545-3363.. 144 D
mpolczynski@kaskaskia.edu
POLD, Ren, A .... 814-393-2166.. 414 G
rpold@clarion.edu
POLDING, Carl .... 651-793-1777.. 250 A
carl.polding@metrostate.edu
POLDING, John .... 973-720-2887.. 298 G
poldingj@wpunj.edu
POLESHEK, Jeffrey, A ...... 941-359-7635.. 107 M
jpoleshe@ringling.edu
POLETTI, Ed .... 215-972-2053.. 413 L
epoletti@pafa.edu
POLI-SMITH, Susie .... 248-204-2126.. 237 B
spolismit@ltu.edu

POLICASTRO, Mike .... 422-472-7141.. 445 E
mpolicastro@clevelandstatecc.edu
POLICASTRO, Stephanie .. 212-517-0658.. 320 C
spolicastro@mmm.edu
POLISHWALLA, Perzen .... 701-483-2340.. 360 D
perzen.polishwalla@dickinsonstate.edu
POLISI, Joseph, W .... 212-799-5000.. 318 A
POLITE-SOLOMON, Sue .. 229-430-4658.. 115 K
sue.solomon@asurams.edu
POLIVKA, Meg .... 540-785-5440.. 496 A
megpolivka@vbc.edu
POLIZZI, Dianne .... 617-243-2133.. 219 I
dpolizzi@lasell.edu
POLK, Ali .... 831-476-9424.... 43 M
marketing@fivebranches.edu
POLK, Alisa, L .... 540-636-2900.. 488 D
finaid@christendom.edu
POLK, Coreylon .... 951-343-4374.... 29 H
cpolk@calbaptist.edu
POLK, Laura .... 301-934-7506.. 207 B
laurap@csmd.edu
POLK, Molly .... 262-551-5819.. 516 A
mpolk@carthage.edu
POLKABLA-EYERS, Joy .... 330-941-2242.. 382 A
jlbyers@ysu.edu
POLL, Michael .... 970-248-1458.... 77 L
mpoll@coloradomesa.edu
POLL, Sherri L .... 563-588-8000.. 172 E
spopp@emmaus.edu
POLLACK, Ann, M .... 310-794-0387.... 69 D
apollack@resadmin.ucla.edu
POLLACK, Emanuel .... 312-413-9461.. 156 F
epollack@uic.edu
POLLACK, Gary .... 509-335-4750.. 508 H
gary.pollack@wsu.edu
POLLACK, Glenn .... 914-323-5158.. 319 N
glenn.pollack@mville.edu
POLLACK, Martha, E .... 734-764-9292.. 241 J
pollackm@umich.edu
POLLACK, Pamela .... 718-951-3118.. 307 D
pamela@brooklyn.cuny.edu
POLLACK, Reva .... 214-768-4202.. 465 J
reva@smu.edu
POLLACK, Susan .... 310-665-6981.... 55 E
spollack@otis.edu
POLLAK, Dianne .... 802-224-3000.. 485 G
dianne.pollak@vsc.edu
POLLARD, A .... 254-299-8669.. 461 E
apollard@mclennan.edu
POLLARD, III, Alton, B ... 202-806-0500.... 93 A
abpollard@howard.edu
POLLARD, Charles .... 479-524-7200.... 20 H
cpollard@jbu.edu
POLLARD, Cindy .... 940-898-3456.. 472 G
cpollard@twu.edu
POLLARD, Cindy .... 503-517-1018.. 396 D
cpollard@warnerpacific.edu
POLLARD, DeRionne, P ... 240-567-5264.. 209 E
president@montgomerycollege.edu
POLLARD, Diana .... 845-431-8403.. 312 G
pollard@sunydutchess.edu
POLLARD, James .... 781-239-4333.. 214 G
jpollard@babson.edu
POLLARD, Jamie, B .... 515-294-0123.. 169 G
jbp@iastate.edu
POLLARD, Jennie .... 214-860-2715.. 456 E
jpollard@dcccd.edu
POLLARD, Leslie .... 256-726-7000...... 6 B
lpollard@oakwood.edu
POLLARD, Mary Lee .... 518-464-8500.. 314 A
mpollard@excelsior.edu
POLLARD, Natalie, M .... 609-896-5340.. 295 B
pollardn@rider.edu
POLLARD, Norm .... 607-871-2132.. 303 F
pollard@alfred.edu
POLLARD, Pamela .... 914-606-6851.. 340 C
pamela.pollard@sunywcc.edu
POLLARD, Prudence, L ..... 256-726-7734...... 6 B
ppollard@oakwood.edu
POLLARD, Sherry .... 573-882-8420.. 273 E
pollards@missouri.edu
POLLARD, Simcha .... 800-375-9878.... 68 E
stephen pollard@trident.edu
POLLARD, Stephanie .... 503-255-0332.. 392 G
spollard@multnomah.edu
POLLASTRINI, Laura .... 847-233-7700.. 150 D
lpollastrini@nc.edu
POLLENZ, Hal .... 212-678-8000.. 317 I
hapollenz@jtsa.edu
POLLERT, Tim .... 708-596-2000.. 154 E
tpollert@ssc.edu
POLLEY, Debra Lee .... 518-454-2066.. 311 B
polleyd@strose.edu
POLLICINO MURPHY,
Elizabeth .... 631-687-2629.. 328 G
epollicinomurphy@sjcny.edu
POLLITZ, John, H .... 715-836-3715.. 520 A
pollitjh@uwec.edu
POLLMAN, Janeen .... 701-228-5458.. 361 D
bookcelt@dakotacollege.edu

POLLOCK, Diane .... 507-285-7229.. 251 I
diane.pollock@rctc.edu
POLLOCK, Holly, L .... 606-783-2000.. 191 H
h.pollock@moreheadstate.edu
POLLOCK, Judy .... 972-708-7547.. 458 G
judy_pollock@gial.edu
POLLOCK, Kevin .... 215-641-6500.. 410 L
kpollock@mc3.edu
POLLOCK, Shannon .... 229-333-2110.. 130 A
shannon.pollock@wiregrass.edu
POLLOI, Andrew .... 808-932-7464.. 131 E
polllia@hawaii.edu
POLLOM, Andrew .... 847-735-5202.. 145 B
pollom@lakeforest.edu
POLONSKY, Kenneth .... 773-702-9306.. 156 D
polonsky@bsd.uchicago.edu
POLOWCHAK, Michelle ... 315-279-5630.. 318 C
mpolowchak@keuka.edu
POLS, Birgit .... 207-725-3178.. 202 F
kbpols@bowdoin.edu
POLSDOFER, Duane .... 641-585-8121.. 177 F
polsdofed@waldorf.edu
POLSKY, Andrew .... 212-772-5195.. 308 D
apolsky@hunter.cuny.edu
POLTERSDORF, Todd .... 973-300-2253.. 297 D
tpoltersdorf@sussex.edu
POLTORAK, Jeff .... 310-243-3183.... 32 D
jpoltorak@csudh.edu
POLYARD, Brenda .... 417-255-7966.. 269 A
brendapolyard@missouristate.edu
POLYCHRONIS, Paul, D .. 660-543-4060.. 273 C
ppolychr@ucmo.edu
POLYDORE-SIMON,
Caroline .... 340-693-1109.. 539 C
cpolydo@uvi.edu
POLYNSKY, Helen .... 718-261-5800.. 305 J
hpolynsky@bramsonort.edu
POLYOT, Susan .... 207-947-4591.. 202 E
spolyot@bealcollege.edu
POLZIN, Elizabeth, A .... 262-243-5700.. 516 E
elizabeth.polzin@cuw.edu
POMA, John .... 757-221-3115.. 488 F
jmpoma@wm.edu
POMA, Lisa, M .... 810-762-0453.. 238 F
lisa.poma@mcc.edu
POMA, Mary Beth .... 804-862-6172.. 493 F
mbpoma@rbc.edu
POMALAZA-RAEZ,
Carlos .... 260-481-6839.. 163 C
raez@ipfw.edu
POMALES, Reinaldo .... 787-758-2525.. 538 D
reinaldo.pomales@upr.edu
POMALES, Robert .... 617-287-5666.. 220 G
robert.pomales@umb.edu
POMALES, Sandra .... 787-728-1515.. 539 B
spomales@sagrado.edu
POMATTO, Mary Carol ..... 620-235-4684.. 184 C
mpomatto@pittstate.edu
POMERENK, Julia .... 509-335-5511.. 508 H
pomerenk@wsu.edu
POMEROY, David .... 703-284-5941.. 492 A
david.pomeroy@marymount.edu
POMEROY, Sharon .... 919-301-6500.... 93 F
POMFRET, Margaret .... 419-289-5102.. 363 J
mpomfret@ashland.edu
POMMERER, Ron .... 701-845-7700.. 361 B
ron.pommerer@vcsu.edu
POMPA, Sara, A .... 956-764-5746.. 460 F
sara.pompa@laredo.edu
POMPER, Gwen, E .... 303-492-8223.... 83 K
gwen.pomper@colorado.edu
POMPER, Kirk, W .... 502-597-5942.. 191 B
kirk.pomper@kysu.edu
POMPEY, JR., Robert .... 336-334-7587.. 356 F
rpompey@ncat.edu
PONCE, Barbara .... 787-766-1717.. 536 B
beponce@mail.suagm.edu
PONCE, Christina .... 281-425-6302.. 460 I
cponce@lee.edu
PONCE, Gregorio .... 760-768-5659.... 35 A
gponce@mail.sdsu.edu
PONCE DE LEON,
Monica .... 609-258-3737.. 294 D
PONCELET, Jolene .... 651-385-6349.. 250 C
jponcelet@southeastmn.edu
POND, Eugene, W .... 214-887-5201.. 457 C
epond@dts.edu
POND, Lallon .... 540-887-7274.. 491 G
lpond@mbc.edu
PONDER, Anthony .... 937-512-2918.. 377 D
anthony.ponder@sinclair.edu
PONDER, Leslee .... 940-397-4350.. 462 A
leslee.ponder@mwsu.edu
PONDER, Nathan .... 318-473-6591.. 197 J
nponder@lsua.edu
PONIKVAR, Laura .... 216-421-7442.. 366 G
lponikvar@cia.edu
PONKO, Bill .... 352-365-3502.. 104 J
ponkow@lssc.edu
PONREMY, Sue .... 708-524-6965.. 139 F
sponremy@dom.edu

PONS, Jose, L 787-844-8181 538 E
jose.pons@upr.edu
PONSETTO, Jean 773-325-7503 139 C
jlentipo@depaul.edu
PONSFORD, Brenda, J 804-257-5697 500 B
bjponsford@vuu.edu
PONTELLI, Enrico 575-646-3500 300 J
epontell@nmsu.edu
PONTEP, Tanya 818-654-1721 57 F
tpontep@pgu.edu
PONTI, Marilyn, K 509-527-5986 509 G
pontimk@whitman.edu
PONTIFF STRINGER, Susie 904-256-1253 100 E
spontiff@fcsl.edu
PONTINEN, Jodi 218-749-7753 249 I
j.pontinen@mesabirange.edu
PONTIUS, JR., John, M 518-608-8384 314 A
jpontius@excelsior.edu
PONTIUS, Robert 906-786-5802 231 O
robert.pontius@baycollege.edu
PONTO, Thomas, M 920-748-8108 519 E
pontot@ripon.edu
PONTON, Cynthia, L 434-381-6136 494 M
cponton@sbc.edu
PONTON, JR., David, C 318-274-6115 200 F
pontond@gram.edu
PONTURO, Joseph 973-328-5500 290 H
jponturo@ccm.edu
POOL, Cleave 325-942-2555 472 B
cleave.pool@angelo.edu
POOL, Kim 585-567-9626 316 F
kim.pool@houghton.edu
POOL, Robert 585-567-9220 316 F
robert.pool@houghton.edu
POOLAW, Johnny 580-699-7205 383 D
jpoolaw@cnc.cc.ok.us
POOLE, Andrea 919-962-4592 356 A
arpoole@northcarolina.edu
POOLE, Angela 850-599-3211 110 J
angela.poole@famu.edu
POOLE, Bill 817-272-3571 476 A
bpoole@uta.edu
POOLE, Dan 800-287-8822 159 C
pooleda@bethanyseminary.edu
POOLE, David 951-343-3901 29 H
dpoole@calbaptist.edu
POOLE, Deborah 504-864-7051 198 E
poole@loyno.edu
POOLE, Heather 318-487-5443 196 B
heatherpoole@cltcc.edu
POOLE, James 215-572-2900 397 G
poolej@arcadia.edu
POOLE, Jason 501-205-8889 19 J
jpoole@cbc.edu
POOLE, Lakeshia 478-240-5143 125 C
lpoole@oftc.edu
POOLE, Lana 573-592-5313 275 E
lana.poole@westminster-mo.edu
POOLE, Leigh 803-323-2604 435 B
poolela@winthrop.edu
POOLE, Max, C 828-262-2130 356 B
poolemc1@appstate.edu
POOLE, Myra 252-862-1267 352 D
mpoole3943@roanokechowan.edu
POOLE, Paula 717-560-8257 407 E
ppoole@lbc.edu
POOLE, Penny 806-291-3414 479 D
poolep@wbu.edu
POOLE, Philip 205-726-2823 6 E
ppoole@samford.edu
POOLE, Rob 413-205-3547 214 B
rob.poole@aic.edu
POOLE, Russell 303-724-0425 84 A
russell.poole@ucdenver.edu
POOLE, Scott 865-974-5267 448 E
scott.poole@utk.edu
POOLE, Stan 870-245-5196 21 E
pooles@obu.edu
POOLE, Thomas, G 814-865-2507 412 F
tgp1@psu.edu
POOLE-ENDSLEY, Anita 405-878-5128 387 J
akpooleendsley@stgregorys.edu
POOLER, Traci, M 270-384-8100 191 E
poolert@lindsey.edu
POOLER, III, Willis 270-384-8070 191 E
poolerw@lindsey.edu
POOLEY, Ken 207-741-5548 203 M
kpooley@smccme.edu
POON, Thomas 909-621-8198 57 H
president@pitzer.edu
POOR, H. Vincent 609-258-1816 294 D
poor@princeton.edu
POORE, Scott 276-944-6890 489 I
pooresc@ehc.edu
POORE, Sharon 859-442-1175 189 D
sharon.poore@kctcs.edu
POORMAN, Brad 325-793-4910 461 F
bpoorman@mcm.edu
POORMAN, Julie 252-328-6373 356 C
poormanj@ecu.edu
POORMAN, CSC, Mark, L 503-943-7101 396 B
poorman@up.edu
POORT, Julianne 616-538-2330 234 D
jpoort@gbcol.edu
POOVEY, Gena, E 864-488-4509 430 H
gpoovey@limestone.edu
POPE, Christina 315-464-4582 332 C
popec@upstate.edu
POPE, Darryl 478-825-6211 120 F
POPE, Darryl 484-365-7391 409 B
dpope@lincoln.edu
POPE, Edward 843-953-8235 428 G
popeeb@cofc.edu
POPE, Jennifer 312-662-4142 134 I
jpope@adler.edu
POPE, John 562-938-4206 49 D
jpope@lbcc.edu
POPE, Justin 434-395-4805 491 E
popejn@longwood.edu
POPE, Kiesha, L 804-523-5137 497 C
kpope@reynolds.edu
POPE, Myron 405-974-2361 388 L
mpope5@uco.edu
POPE, Sarah 804-333-6705 498 D
spope@rappahannock.edu
POPE, Sharon 570-372-4018 419 H
popes@susqu.edu
POPE, Terri 216-987-3937 367 E
terri.pope@tri-c.edu
POPE-DAVIS, Don 575-646-5858 300 J
dpd@nmsu.edu
POPELKA, David, M 515-294-7007 169 G
dpopelka@iastate.edu
POPENFOOSE, G. Steve 217-732-3168 146 A
POPHAM, Heidi 706-295-6598 121 F
hpopham@gntc.edu
POPIELSKI, Michael 760-744-1150 56 F
mpopielski@palomar.edu
POPIOLEK, Marcus 313-664-7665 232 G
mpopiolek@collegeforcreativestudies.edu
POPKEY, Megan 920-498-7186 524 E
megan.popkey@nwtc.edu
POPKO, John, P 206-296-6222 507 E
jpopko@seattleu.edu
POPKO, Susan 408-554-3019 63 E
spopko@scu.edu
POPLAWSKI, Lisa 509-359-4555 503 D
lpoplawski@ewu.edu
POPLIN, Michelle 704-991-0208 353 E
mpoplin4375@stanly.edu
POPLOWSKI, Kira 973-408-3206 291 B
kpoplowski@drew.edu
POPOLOSKI, Tanya 603-623-0313 287 D
tpopoloski@nhia.edu
POPOOLA, Joseph, K 803-934-3290 431 E
jpopoola@morris.edu
POPOVICH, Donna, B 813-253-6237 114 M
dpopovich@ut.edu
POPOVICS, Alexander, J 518-629-7307 316 G
a.popovics@hvcc.edu
POPP, Connie 414-382-6352 515 D
connie.popp@alverno.edu
POPP, Melissa, D 636-584-6703 264 M
melissa.popp@eastcentral.edu
POPP, Tari 269-471-3613 230 H
tari@andrews.edu
POPP, William, C 770-720-5568 126 C
wcp@reinhardt.edu
POPPEN, Mark 616-392-8555 244 A
mark.poppen@westernsem.edu
POPPLEWELL, Venus 270-384-8189 191 E
popplewellv@lindsey.edu
POPPO, Kristin 607-587-3913 334 G
poppokr@alfredstate.edu
POPPRE, Beth 480-219-6026 262 A
bpoppre@atsu.edu
PORAT, Moshe 215-204-1836 420 B
moshe.porat@temple.edu
PORATH, Wiona 517-264-7613 241 A
wporath@sienaheights.edu
PORCARELLO, Irene 713-718-7071 459 B
irene.porcarello@hccs.edu
PORCARO, Mark, D 316-978-7787 185 J
mark.porcaro@wichita.edu
PORCELLI, Mary 973-748-9000 289 H
mary_porcelli@bloomfield.edu
PORCH, Alesia 601-857-3240 258 A
amporch@hindscc.edu
PORCHE, Demetrius 504-568-4106 198 A
dporch@lsuhsc.edu
PORCHE, JR., Francis 337-421-6916 197 B
francis.porche@sowela.edu
PORFIDO, Nancy 609-343-5095 288 H
porfido@atlantic.edu
POROCK, Davina 718-960-6932 308 B
davina.porock@lehman.cuny.edu
PORPILIA, Amy 585-594-6381 327 D
porpilaa@roberts.edu
PORRAS, Precious 785-864-4350 185 D
pporras@ku.edu
PORRAS, Ray 805-437-8434 32 B
ray.porras@csuci.edu
PORTEEN, Shana 906-487-7394 234 A
shana.porteen@finlandia.edu
PORTELA, Stanley 787-752-4540 537 H
stanley.portela@upr.edu
PORTELA IRIGOYEN, Celso, E 787-725-8120 532 K
cportela@centro.eap.edu
PORTELLEZ, Humberto 757-683-3626 492 G
hportell@odu.edu
PORTEOUS, Densil, R 614-222-3263 367 B
dporteous@ccad.edu
PORTER, Aaron 865-471-3229 439 C
aporter@cn.edu
PORTER, Adam 217-245-3010 141 G
aporter@mail.ic.edu
PORTER, Andrea 806-651-2037 469 D
aporter@wtamu.edu
PORTER, Ava, G 540-985-8531 491 A
agporter@jchs.edu
PORTER, Barbara 540-831-5408 493 A
bporter@radford.edu
PORTER, Barbara, A 202-994-3121 92 D
porter@gwu.edu
PORTER, Becky 317-278-1880 163 D
rporter@iupui.edu
PORTER, Brandi 540-365-4427 489 M
bporter@ferrum.edu
PORTER, Byron 540-261-4931 494 F
byron.porter@svu.edu
PORTER, Chad 304-865-6091 511 C
chad.porter@ovu.edu
PORTER, Charles 206-296-4490 507 E
porterc@seattleu.edu
PORTER, Chong, U 916-734-9402 69 A
chong.porter@ucdmc.ucdavis.edu
PORTER, Christine, M 540-654-1058 495 C
cjporter@umw.edu
PORTER, Christopher 540-857-6697 499 B
cporter@virginiawestern.edu
PORTER, Clifton 413-755-4026 224 G
ceporter@stcc.edu
PORTER, Clyde 972-860-7760 456 A
cporter@dcccd.edu
PORTER, Curtis, R 505-277-2611 302 F
cporter@unm.edu
PORTER, David 731-661-5343 448 A
dporter@uu.edu
PORTER, David, S 401-874-2370 426 D
dporter@uri.edu
PORTER, DeeDee 619-388-3976 60 F
dporter@sdccd.edu
PORTER, Fonda 919-497-3205 346 B
fporter@louisburg.edu
PORTER, Gerald 805-898-2940 43 K
gporter@fielding.edu
PORTER, Hugh, E 503-788-6604 394 I
hugh.porter@reed.edu
PORTER, J. Davidson 504-314-2188 200 C
jporter6@tulane.edu
PORTER, James, P 801-422-3963 480 C
james_porter@byu.edu
PORTER, Jefferson 313-577-5748 243 F
fy0624@wayne.edu
PORTER, Jeffry 615-898-5005 444 G
jeffry.porter@mtsu.edu
PORTER, Jennifer 973-278-5400 305 B
jnp@berkeleycollege.edu
PORTER, Jennifer 973-278-5400 289 F
jnp@berkeleycollege.edu
PORTER, Jennifer 617-735-9772 218 C
porterj@emmanuel.edu
PORTER, John, B 570-961-4772 409 H
porter@marywood.edu
PORTER, Jon, K 802-656-0123 485 D
jon.porter@uvm.edu
PORTER, Joseph 518-320-1344 330 H
joe.porter@suny.edu
PORTER, Kary 252-222-6224 348 B
porterk@carteret.edu
PORTER, Marc 510-485-7869 56 I
mporter@patten.edu
PORTER, Mario 210-341-1366 463 A
registrar@ost.edu
PORTER, Mark, J 401-863-3870 424 J
mark_porter@brown.edu
PORTER, Michael 651-962-4376 256 C
mporter@stthomas.edu
PORTER, Monica 313-583-6445 242 A
dmporte@umich.edu
PORTER, Nadine 240-567-5382 209 E
nadine.porter@montgomerycollege.edu
PORTER, Narda 276-328-0116 495 I
nnb3h@uvawise.edu
PORTER, Steve 620-665-3552 181 I
porters@hutchcc.edu
PORTER, Susie 801-581-8094 481 M
s.porter@utah.edu
PORTER, Thomas, R 540-261-8563 494 F
tr.porter@svu.edu
PORTER, Tracy 863-297-3743 106 I
tporter@polk.edu
PORTER, Vincent 210-829-2770 474 D
porterv@uiwtx.edu
PORTER, Wilma, B 248-341-2182 239 E
wbporter@oaklandcc.edu
PORTER-FRASER, Cyndi 916-686-8499 31 F
PORTER-UTLEY, Kristen 508-531-2418 221 C
PORTERFIELD, Ashley 386-481-2972 96 H
porterfielda@cookman.edu
PORTERFIELD, Daniel, R 717-358-3971 403 J
daniel.porterfield@fandm.edu
PORTERFIELD, Deana, L 585-594-6100 325 B
presidentsoffice@roberts.edu
PORTERFIELD, Deana, L 585-594-6100 327 D
presidentsoffice@roberts.edu
PORTERFIELD, Kent 314-977-2226 271 K
kporter6@slu.edu
PORTERFIELD, Rebecca 859-572-5551 192 B
porterfier1@nku.edu
PORTERVINT, Bernice 360-676-2772 505 C
bportervint@nwic.edu
PORTIER, Bonnie 301-447-5288 209 G
bportier@msmary.edu
PORTILLO, Cesar 909-537-5138 34 C
cportillo@csusb.edu
PORTIS-TURNER, Erica 334-290-3248 4 G
erica.turner@istc.edu
PORTLOCK, Caroline 815-280-1313 144 A
cportloc@jjc.edu
PORTLOCK, Jeremy 785-594-8415 178 D
jeremy.portlock@bakeru.edu
PORTMAN, Tarrell 507-457-2570 252 G
tportman@winona.edu
PORTMANN, Brooke 231-843-5866 243 G
bportmann@westshore.edu
PORTNOY, Robert, N 402-472-7450 282 M
rportnoy1@unl.edu
PORTWINE, Ronald, E 989-964-2064 240 F
report@svsu.edu
PORTWOOD, Amy 206-239-4500 502 D
alportwood@cityu.edu
PORTWOOD, Ryan 402-354-7848 281 F
ryan.portwood@methodistcollege.edu
PORTZ, Margaret, A 610-758-5794 408 H
mak5@lehigh.edu
PORTZEL, Curt 310-506-4893 56 J
curt.portzel@pepperdine.edu
POSEJPAL, Gigi 312-369-7458 138 F
gposejpal@colum.edu
POSER, Susan 312-413-3450 156 F
sposer@uic.edu
POSEY, Evan 770-484-1204 124 C
evan.posey@lutherrice.edu
POSEY, James, T 843-953-5708 428 G
poseyjt@cofc.edu
POSEY, Jamie 423-585-6894 447 D
jamie.posey@ws.edu
POSEY, Jeff 601-643-8411 257 D
jeff.posey@colin.edu
POSEY, Kathy 617-928-4003 226 B
kposey@mountida.edu
POSEY, Libby 601-857-3350 258 A
olivia.posey@hindscc.edu
POSEY, Monica 513-569-1515 366 D
monica.posey@cincinnatistate.edu
POSEY, Steven 505-473-6101 302 A
steven.posey@santafeuniversity.edu
POSHEK, Joseph 949-451-5650 65 F
jposhek@ivc.edu
POSILLICO, Joseph, J 973-618-3500 290 A
jposillico@caldwell.edu
POSING, Mary 815-802-8202 144 C
mposing@kcc.edu
POSKANZER, JR., Steven, G 507-222-4305 245 C
president@carleton.edu
POSKEY, Cindy 985-448-5914 196 E
cindy.poskey@fletcher.edu
POSKIN, Jill 630-829-6366 135 F
jposkin@ben.edu
POSLER, Brian 440-375-7200 371 E
president@lec.edu
POSLUSNY, Matthew 919-760-8514 346 D
mposlusny@meredith.edu
POSMAN, Jerald 718-270-5026 309 B
jposman@mec.cuny.edu
POSNER, Deborah 954-201-7482 96 I
dposner@broward.edu
POSNER, Kenneth 352-588-8992 108 C
kenneth.posner@saintleo.edu
POSNER, Marc 714-484-7006 54 G
mposner@cypresscollege.edu
POSNER, Mark 651-638-6383 244 L
m-posner@bethel.edu
POSNER, Sylvia 212-824-2211 315 F
sposner@huc.edu
POSS, Joe 509-313-6215 504 A
poss@gonzaga.edu
POSSIN, Sandra 206-780-6214 506 E
sandra.possin@pinchot.edu

POWERS, Shonda ... 606-539-4448.. 193 F
shonda.powers@ucumberlands.edu
POWERS, Susie ... 202-884-9000.... 94 A
powerss@trinitydc.edu
POWERS, Suzanne ... 417-328-1689.. 272 C
spowers@sbuniv.edu
POWERS, Tammy ... 575-528-7069.. 301 C
welchta@nmsu.edu
POWERS, Teri ... 619-574-6909.... 55 G
tpowers@pacificcollege.edu
POWERS, Tim ... 949-794-9090.... 66 H
tpowers@stanbridge.edu
POWERS, Tyrone ... 410-777-7496.. 206 B
tpowers@aacc.edu
POWERS, Wendy ... 414-382-6494.. 515 D
wendy.powers@alverno.edu
POWERS, William ... 617-989-4407.. 229 D
powersw2@wit.edu
POWERS, William, B ... 312-987-1435.. 143 G
6powers@jmls.edu
POWICKI, Mike ... 402-375-7520.. 281 J
mipowic1@wsc.edu
POWLEY, Mary, R ... 585-385-8057.. 328 E
mpowley@sjfc.edu
POYDRAS, Phebe, E ... 260-422-5561.. 162 B
pepoydras@indianatech.edu
POYNTER, Barry ... 859-622-5012.. 188 F
barry.poynter@eku.edu
POYNTER, Nelson ... 317-789-8266.. 160 E
npoynter@crossroads.edu
POZANC, Lisa ... 507-453-2402.. 250 C
lpozanc@southeastmn.edu
POZNACK, Virginia ... 845-431-8686.. 312 G
virginia.poznack@sunydutchess.edu
POZNANSKI, Brad ... 603-428-2390.. 287 C
bpoznanski@nec.edu
POZZI, Dave ... 626-568-8850.... 48 B
PRABHU, Vilas, A ... 717-871-7555.. 415 F
vilas.prabhu@millersville.edu
PRACHAND, Amit ... 847-467-5067.. 150 F
a-prachand@northwestern.edu
PRACHER, Mark ... 310-287-4467.... 50 E
prachem@wlac.edu
PRACJEK, Parker ... 212-343-1234.. 321 B
ppracjek@mcny.edu
PRADO, Guillermo ... 305-243-2748.. 114 H
gprado@miami.edu
PRADO, Lenore, M ... 305-628-6514.. 108 E
lprado@stu.edu
PRAET, Diane, M ... 313-993-3313.. 241 G
praetdm@udmercy.edu
PRALL, J. Andrew ... 260-399-7700.. 168 D
jprall@sf.edu
PRANGE, Raphaella ... 217-424-6395.. 148 D
rpalmer@millikin.edu
PRANGER, Henriette, M .. 860-727-6740.... 87 H
hpranger@goodwin.edu
PRANSKY, Devra ... 770-394-8300.. 116 F
djhenderson@edmc.edu
PRAPAVESSI, Despina ... 925-969-2689.... 41 I
dprapavessi@dvc.edu
PRASAD, Becky ... 954-545-4500.. 109 F
registrar@sfbc.edu
PRASAD, Kanti ... 414-229-3233.. 520 D
vkp@uwm.edu
PRASAD, Rashmi ... 907-786-4126.... 10 F
rprasad@uaa.alaska.edu
PRASIFKA, Matthew ... 713-525-3512.. 475 J
prasifm@stthom.edu
PRASLOVA, Ludmilla ... 714-556-3610.... 73 B
ludmilla.praslova@vanguard.edu
PRASSE, David, P ... 773-508-7470.. 146 G
dprasse@luc.edu
PRASTACOS, Gregory ... 201-216-8366.. 297 B
gregory.prastacos@stevens.edu
PRATER, Ann ... 971-722-4387.. 394 F
ann.prater@pcc.edu
PRATER, Chanda, F ... 270-852-3104.. 191 C
cprater@kwc.edu
PRATER, Kelly ... 806-371-5311.. 450 H
klprater@actx.edu
PRATER, Margaret ... 731-286-3585.. 446 B
prater@nwtnworks.org
PRATER, Mary Ann ... 801-422-3695.. 480 C
pregeant@byu.edu
PRATER, Michael ... 574-520-4319.. 163 E
maprater@iusb.edu
PRATER, Steve ... 580-477-7894.. 389 I
steve.prater@wosc.edu
PRATER, Susan ... 405-974-2300.. 388 L
sprater4@uco.edu
PRATER, Wendi ... 281-401-5349.. 461 B
wendi.c.prater@lonestar.edu
PRATHER, Curtis ... 703-370-6600.. 492 I
PRATHER, Faith ... 585-395-2504.. 332 E
fprather@brockport.edu
PRATHER, Kerry, N ... 317-738-8121.. 160 J
kprather@franklincollege.edu
PRATHER, Page ... 806-720-7125.. 461 C
page.prather@lcu.edu
PRATHER, Sean ... 925-424-1690.... 37 C
sprather@laspositascollege.edu
PRATSCHER, Valerie ... 618-936-2064.. 145 D
vpratscher@lakeland.cc.il.us
PRATT, Andrew, L ... 816-415-7557.. 275 F
pratta@william.jewell.edu
PRATT, Anne ... 802-251-7607.. 484 C
apratt@marlboro.edu
PRATT, Barbara ... 908-835-2355.. 298 E
pratt@warren.edu
PRATT, Denise ... 402-941-6135.. 280 N
pratt@midlandu.edu
PRATT, Edward, E ... 561-297-0567.. 110 K
epratt2@fau.edu
PRATT, Elizabeth ... 415-883-2211.... 40 C
epratt@marin.edu
PRATT, Eric ... 601-925-7652.. 259 A
epratt@mc.edu
PRATT, G. Michael ... 513-529-6721.. 372 K
prattgm@miamioh.edu
PRATT, Gary ... 509-359-2099.. 503 D
gpratt@ewu.edu
PRATT, H. Wes ... 417-836-3736.. 268 I
wpratt@missouristate.edu
PRATT, Janice ... 520-494-6602.... 12 J
janice.pratt@centralaz.edu
PRATT, Jonathan, R ... 763-417-8250.. 245 D
jpratt@centralseminary.edu
PRATT, Linda ... 951-571-6267.... 59 A
linda.pratt@mvc.edu
PRATT, Michael ... 205-652-3565...... 9 F
mpratt@uwa.edu
PRATT, Michele ... 989-686-9822.. 233 I
michelepratt@delta.edu
PRATT, Robert, C ... 517-750-1200.. 241 E
bpratt@arbor.edu
PRATT, Sarah ... 213-740-8867.... 72 D
pratt@usc.edu
PRATT, Scott, L ... 541-346-2800.. 395 G
spratt@uoregon.edu
PRATT, Tamara ... 405-733-7491.. 387 I
tpratt@rose.edu
PRATT, JR.,
Theodore, W ... 360-650-3450.. 509 E
ted.pratt@cc.wwu.edu
PRATT, Todd ... 678-372-2260.. 129 M
todd.pratt@westgatech.edu
PRATT-CLARKE, JR.,
Menah ... 540-231-7500.. 499 F
mcp@vt.edu
PRATT-COOK, Patricia ... 218-723-6602.. 245 J
pprattcook@css.edu
PRATTE, John ... 870-972-3079.... 18 J
jpratte@astate.edu
PRATTELLA, Todd ... 914-674-7844.. 320 G
tprattella@mercy.edu
PRATTS, Luis, N ... 787-780-0070.. 531 B
lpratts@caribbean.edu
PRAY, G. Jon ... 414-288-7532.. 517 I
jon.pray@marquette.edu
PRAY, Steve ... 770-484-1204.. 124 C
steve.pray@lutherrice.edu
PREAS, Derek ... 903-468-8781.. 468 D
derek.preas@tamuc.edu
PREAST, Lori ... 252-493-7224.. 352 A
lpreast@email.pittcc.edu
PREATHER, Gary ... 817-515-6742.. 467 A
gary.preather@tccd.edu
PRECHTER, Patricia ... 504-398-2213.. 200 D
pprechter@olhcc.edu
PRECHTL, Gregory, D ... 716-673-3101.. 331 D
gregory.prechtl@fredonia.edu
PRECISE, Leigh ... 740-362-3121.. 372 D
lprecise@mtso.edu
PRECZEWSKI, Stanley ... 678-407-5001.. 121 B
president@ggc.edu
PREDIC, Beba ... 303-937-4202.... 77 K
bpredic@chu.edu
PREDOEHL, Dan ... 949-582-4313.... 65 G
dpredoehl@saddleback.edu
PREECE, Barbara ... 410-617-6811.. 208 G
bpreece@loyola.edu
PREECE, Barbara ... 410-617-6811.. 210 B
bpreece@ndm.edu
PREGEANT, Gene, E ... 985-549-5888.. 201 C
gpregeant@selu.edu
PREGITZER, Kurt ... 208-885-6442.. 134 G
kpregitzer@uidaho.edu
PREISINGER, George, T .. 248-370-2127.. 239 K
preising@oakland.edu
PREISLER, Karen ... 979-532-6383.. 479 J
karenp@wcjc.edu
PRELLWITZ, Andrew, R ... 920-748-8175.. 519 E
prellwitza@ripon.edu
PRELOCK, Patricia, A ... 802-656-2216.. 485 D
patricia.prelock@uvm.edu
PRELOGER, Robert ... 605-274-4922.. 435 E
bob.preloger@augie.edu
PREMNATH,
Devadasan, N ... 585-271-3657.. 328 A
dnprem@stbernards.edu
PREMO, Brenda ... 909-469-5385.... 74 K
bpremo@westernu.edu
PREMO, Greg, V ... 253-535-8787.. 505 G
premogv@plu.edu
PRENDERGAST, Debra, L 708-709-3689.. 151 C
dprendergast@prairiestate.edu
PRENDERGAST, Nancy ... 847-635-1894.. 150 G
nprender@oakton.edu
PRENDERGAST, Precious 770-394-8300.. 116 F
pprendergast@aii.edu
PRENDERGAST,
Thomas, M ... 419-755-4712.. 373 G
tprendergast@ncstatecollege.edu
PRENEVOST, Jason ... 253-460-4462.. 508 B
jprenevost@tacomacc.edu
PRENGAMAN, Diane ... 410-225-2285.. 209 B
dprengam@mica.edu
PRENGAMAN, John, C ... 434-223-6161.. 490 D
jprengaman@hsc.edu
PRENGUBER, Marcia, A .. 203-576-4110.... 89 C
mprengub@bridgeport.edu
PRENTICE, Ann, E ... 205-348-4610...... 8 D
aeprentice@bama.ua.edu
PRENTICE, Deborah ... 609-258-3020.. 294 D
predebb@princeton.edu
PRENTICE, Ernest, D ... 402-559-6045.. 283 A
edprenti@unmc.edu
PRENTICE, Marilyn ... 847-214-7992.. 140 A
mprentice@elgin.edu
PREOCANIN, Shelley ... 812-866-7097.. 161 C
preocanins@hanover.edu
PRESCOD-CAESAR,
Pamela ... 610-328-8397.. 419 I
ppresco1@swarthmore.edu
PRESCOTT, Angel ... 785-738-9008.. 183 J
aprescott@ncktc.edu
PRESCOTT, Herman ... 202-274-5072.... 94 B
tprescott@udc.edu
PRESCOTT, Jay, B ... 515-263-2890.. 172 H
jprescott@grandview.edu
PRESCOTT, Loren, D ... 570-408-4000.. 423 G
loren.prescott@wilkes.edu
PRESCOTT, Patricia, M ... 516-671-0439.. 339 G
pprescot@webb.edu
PRESENT, Melissa ... 212-678-8820.. 317 I
mepresent@jtsa.edu
PRESENT, Wendy ... 716-338-1070.. 317 F
wendypresent@mail.sunyjcc.edu
PRESLAR, Andy ... 409-882-3357.. 471 B
andy.preslar@lsco.edu
PRESLEY, Alan ... 281-649-3446.. 458 L
apresley@hbu.edu
PRESLEY, Brian ... 276-244-1267.. 486 N
bpresley@asl.edu
PRESLEY, Doretha ... 601-977-4461.. 261 A
dpresley@tougaloo.edu
PRESLEY, Jody ... 662-720-7299.. 260 B
djpresleys@nemcc.edu
PRESNELL, Angela ... 317-788-3211.. 168 A
presnella@uindy.edu
PRESNELL, Deena ... 509-313-6803.. 504 A
presnell@gonzaga.edu
PRESNELL, Mark ... 847-491-3707.. 150 F
mark.presnell@northwestern.edu
PRESS, Andrew ... 714-533-3946.... 35 E
andrew@calums.edu
PRESSER, Art ... 800-290-4226.. 440 G
apresser@hchs.edu
PRESSEY, Natalie ... 212-229-5660.. 322 E
presseyn@newschool.edu
PRESSIMONE, J. Michael 314-889-1419.. 265 C
mpressimone@fontbonne.edu
PRESSLEY, Dan ... 706-754-7791.. 125 B
dpressley@northgatech.edu
PRESSLEY, Diana ... 713-500-2104.. 477 C
diana.j.pressley@uth.tmc.edu
PRESSLEY, Pamela ... 510-231-5000.... 47 H
PRESSMAN, Avraham ... 570-346-1747.. 424 E
PRESSON, Mark, A ... 563-588-8000.. 172 E
mpresson@emmaus.edu
PRESSWOOD, Theresa ... 281-283-2015.. 474 A
presswood@uhcl.edu
PREST, Stacy ... 509-527-4294.. 508 F
stacy.prest@wwcc.edu
PRESTAMO, Anne ... 305-348-5726.. 111 A
anne.prestamo@fiu.edu
PRESTBY, Tony ... 310-434-4271.... 63 F
prestby_tony@smc.edu
PRESTON, April ... 615-366-4404.. 444 D
april.preston@tbr.edu
PRESTON, Daniel ... 503-883-2294.. 392 B
dpreston@linfield.edu
PRESTON, James ... 312-329-4140.. 148 F
james.preston@moody.edu
PRESTON, James ... 559-925-3146.... 74 E
jamespreston@whccd.edu
PRESTON, Jeffrey, H ... 912-279-5751.. 119 C
jpreston@ccga.edu
PRESTON, Jennifer ... 270-831-9804.. 189 F
jennifer.preston@kctcs.edu
PRESTON, Joanne ... 541-552-7672.. 395 A
prestonj@sou.edu
PRESTON, Jon ... 470-578-3545.. 123 J
jprest20@kennesaw.edu
PRESTON, Karen ... 770-426-2688.. 124 B
kpreston@life.edu
PRESTON, Keely ... 303-546-5283.... 81 I
kpreston@naropa.edu
PRESTON, Kenneth, G ... 330-972-7845.. 378 G
kpreston@uakron.edu
PRESTON, Kenneth, G ... 330-972-8254.. 378 G
kpreston@uakron.edu
PRESTON, Laura, C ... 443-412-2438.. 208 A
lpreston@harford.edu
PRESTON, Lisa ... 212-229-5667.. 322 E
lisa.preston@newschool.edu
PRESTON, Mindy ... 903-823-3198.. 467 C
mindy.preston@texarkanacollege.edu
PRESTON, Robert ... 240-567-5327.. 209 E
robert.preston@montgomerycollege.edu
PRESTON, Sarah ... 440-684-6073.. 380 F
spreston@ursuline.edu
PRESTON, Travis ... 661-255-1050.... 30 E
tpreston@calarts.edu
PRESTWICH, Aaron ... 303-404-5332.... 80 E
aaron.prestwich@frontrange.edu
PRETTEJOHN, Amy ... 816-235-6210.. 273 F
prettejohna@umkc.edu
PRETTELT, Gordon ... 229-243-6030.. 117 E
gordon.prettelt@bainbridge.edu
PRETTI, Janet ... 541-888-1673.. 395 B
jpretti@socc.edu
PRETTO, Felix ... 212-594-4000.. 337 F
fpretto@tcicollege.edu
PRETTY, Keith, A ... 989-837-4203.. 239 D
pretty@northwood.edu
PRETZAT, Julie ... 315-312-2285.. 333 D
julie.pretzat@oswego.edu
PREUS, Camille ... 541-278-5950.. 390 C
cpreus@bluecc.edu
PREUSS, Timothy ... 949-214-3286.... 41 F
timothy.preuss@cui.edu
PREUSZ, Mike ... 864-644-5048.. 432 G
mpreusz@swu.edu
PREVATT, Doug ... 352-854-2322.... 97 R
prevattd@cf.edu
PREVATTE, David ... 336-506-4202.. 347 C
david.prevatte@alamancecc.edu
PREVAUX, Steven, D ... 813-974-7777.. 112 C
prevaux@usf.edu
PREVETT, Daniel ... 912-583-3178.. 118 B
dprevett@bpc.edu
PREVITA, Chris ... 617-739-1700.. 226 G
cprevita@aii.edu
PREVOST, Blair ... 903-923-2364.. 457 G
bprevost@etbu.edu
PREVOST, Emily ... 903-923-2074.. 457 G
eprevost@etbu.edu
PREVOST, Suzanne, S ... 205-348-1040...... 8 D
sprevost@ua.edu
PREVOST-SCHULTZ,
Justin ... 773-244-6263.. 149 I
jprevost@northpark.edu
PREWETT, Nick ... 573-882-6200.. 273 E
prewettn@missouri.edu
PREWITT, Michael ... 304-696-3765.. 513 D
prewitta@marshall.edu
PREWITT, Steve ... 615-966-5804.. 441 F
steve.prewitt@lipscomb.edu
PREWITT-FREILINO,
Polly ... 508-286-3621.. 229 F
ir@wheatoncollege.edu
PREZANT, Robert, S ... 973-655-5108.. 293 A
prezantr@mail.montclair.edu
PREZIOSI, Kristine ... 928-350-2306.... 16 P
kpreziosi@prescott.edu
PRIAL, Anne ... 845-341-4286.. 325 H
anne.prial@sunyorange.edu
PRIBBENOW, Dean ... 608-663-2200.. 516 F
dpribbenow@edgewood.edu
PRIBBENOW, Paul, C ... 612-330-1212.. 244 I
president@augsburg.edu
PRIBULSKY, Christopher . 814-262-3824.. 413 P
cpribulsky@pennhighlands.edu
PRIBYL, Kim ... 319-399-8000.. 170 G
kpribyl@coe.edu
PRICCI, Erica ... 570-955-1461.. 407 B
priccie@lackawanna.edu
PRICE, Adrienne ... 909-274-5417.... 53 C
aprice@mtsac.edu
PRICE, Alan ... 805-965-0581.... 63 D
aprice3@sbcc.edu
PRICE, Amy ... 920-832-7164.. 517 E
amy.price@lawrence.edu
PRICE, Amy, S ... 812-468-2334.. 168 E
asprice@usi.edu
PRICE, Angela ... 906-487-7231.. 234 A
angela.price@finlandia.edu
PRICE, Angie, C ... 423-775-7269.. 439 B
aprice6832@bryan.edu

PRICE, Annie ... 937-708-5813.. 381 B
aprice@wilberforce.edu
PRICE, Bill ... 540-231-4025.. 489 H
bprice@vcom.vt.edu
PRICE, Bryan ... 540-458-8184.. 500 F
bprice@wlu.edu
PRICE, Cecil, D ... 336-758-5218.. 359 E
price@wfu.edu
PRICE, Cynthia, J ... 206-281-2179.. 507 C
cprice@spu.edu
PRICE, Danny ... 706-368-5644.. 117 F
dprice@berry.edu
PRICE, David, E ... 706-778-8500.. 125 J
dprice2@piedmont.edu
PRICE, Dawne ... 402-494-2311.. 281 C
dprice@thenicc.edu
PRICE, Donna ... 931-221-7907.. 444 E
priced@apsu.edu
PRICE, Douglas ... 918-595-7853.. 388 F
douglas.price@tulsac.edu
PRICE, Elizabeth ... 254-267-7022.. 463 K
eprice@rangercollege.edu
PRICE, Gary ... 541-259-5808.. 392 C
priceg@linnbenton.edu
PRICE, Greg ... 334-670-3507...... 7 H
wgprice@troy.edu
PRICE, Irene, L ... 517-750-1200.. 241 E
iprice@arbor.edu
PRICE, James ... 706-771-4096.. 117 C
jprice@augustatech.edu
PRICE, James, B ... 610-436-3063.. 416 C
jprice@wcupa.edu
PRICE, Jason ... 806-457-4200.. 458 B
jprice@fpctx.edu
PRICE, Jennifer ... 386-752-1822.. 100 L
jennifer.price@fgc.edu
PRICE, Jennifer ... 717-358-2974.. 405 C
jmprice@hacc.edu
PRICE, Jennifer ... 518-262-5679.. 303 E
pricej@mail.amc.edu
PRICE, Jerry ... 714-997-6721.... 37 F
jprice@chapman.edu
PRICE, Jill ... 810-766-4348.. 231 D
jhovis02@baker.edu
PRICE, Jill ... 715-365-4461.. 524 C
jmrjenovich@nicoletcollege.edu
PRICE, June, M ... 269-471-3211.. 230 H
madrigal@andrews.edu
PRICE, Kendrick ... 252-493-7627.. 352 A
kprice@email.pittcc.edu
PRICE, Kevin, L ... 208-496-1705.. 132 J
priceke@byui.edu
PRICE, Laura ... 360-596-5227.. 508 A
PRICE, Leigh ... 912-478-5211.. 122 B
llprice@georgiasouthern.edu
PRICE, Linda, A ... 301-784-5000.. 205 G
lprice@allegany.edu
PRICE, Linda, L ... 812-877-8165.. 166 H
price@rose-hulman.edu
PRICE, Lisa ... 618-437-5321.. 152 A
price@rlc.edu
PRICE, JR., Major ... 419-755-9009.. 373 G
mprice@ncstatecollege.edu
PRICE, Marla ... 717-755-2300.. 398 A
maprice@aii.edu
PRICE, Megan ... 864-388-8019.. 430 G
mprice@lander.edu
PRICE, Nicole, G ... 617-973-1101.. 228 G
nprice@suffolk.edu
PRICE, Nikol ... 623-935-8087.... 14 A
nikol.price@estrellamountain.edu
PRICE, Pam ... 609-586-4800.. 292 D
pricep@mccc.edu
PRICE, Peggy ... 601-366-8880.. 261 H
pprice@wbs.edu
PRICE, Philip ... 919-718-7214.. 348 D
pprice@cccc.edu
PRICE, Robin ... 304-637-1243.. 510 I
pricer@dewv.edu
PRICE, Ron ... 770-975-4000.. 118 J
PRICE, Ronald, N ... 708-216-9949.. 146 G
rprice@lumc.edu
PRICE, Sarah ... 270-686-4501.. 190 D
sarah.price@kctcs.edu
PRICE, Vincent ... 215-898-7227.. 421 E
provost@upenn.edu
PRICE, W. Craig ... 504-282-4455.. 198 H
cprice@nobts.edu
PRICE, William ... 432-552-2170.. 478 B
price_w@utpb.edu
PRICE-PERRY,
Cassandra, F ... 901-334-5821.. 442 C
cfperry@memphisseminary.edu
PRICE-SEEGER, Marjorie .. 361-582-2587.. 478 F
marjorie.pseeger@victoriacollege.edu
PRICHARD, Patricia, A ... 503-517-1806.. 396 F
paprichard@westernseminary.edu
PRICHETT, Gordon ... 781-239-4428.. 214 G
prichett@babson.edu
PRICHETT, Robert ... 404-756-4714.. 116 I
rprichett@atlm.edu
PRICKEN, Stephanie ... 610-660-1379.. 418 G
spricken@sju.edu
PRIDA, Jonas ... 802-776-5215.. 483 G
jonas.prida@csj.edu
PRIDAL, Cathryn ... 816-501-3758.. 262 G
cathryn.pridal@avila.edu
PRIDDY, Don ... 618-985-3741.. 143 F
donpriddy@jalc.edu
PRIDDY, Michele ... 615-297-7545.. 438 F
priddym@aquinascollege.edu
PRIDE, Nicole ... 336-334-7940.. 356 F
npride@ncat.edu
PRIDE, Rachel ... 940-898-3207.. 472 G
rpride1@twu.edu
PRIDEAUX, Debra K ... 785-628-4430.. 180 I
dprideaux@fhsu.edu
PRIDEAUX, Leslie J ... 319-273-2355.. 170 A
leslie.prideaux@uni.edu
PRIDEMORE, William, A . 518-442-5214.. 331 A
wpridemore@albany.edu
PRIEB, Arnie ... 559-453-2128.... 44 F
arnie.prieb@fresno.edu
PRIES, Lonnie ... 734-995-7310.. 232 I
lonnie.pries@cuaa.edu
PRIESENGER, Nate ... 215-248-6321.. 409 D
npreisinger@ltsp.edu
PRIEST, Barry ... 910-879-5579.. 347 F
bpriest@bladencc.edu
PRIEST, Catherine ... 856-351-2624.. 296 L
cpriest@salemcc.edu
PRIEST, Jeff, M ... 803-641-3755.. 433 G
jeffp@usca.edu
PRIEST, Michelle ... 714-564-6606.... 58 G
priest_michelle@sac.edu
PRIETO, Beth ... 603-645-9724.. 287 I
b.prieto@snhu.edu
PRIETO, Diana ... 970-491-5836.... 78 Q
diana.prieto@colostate.edu
PRIETO, Diana ... 970-491-6947.... 78 Q
diana.prieto@colostate.edu
PRIETO, Eduardo ... 803-323-2191.. 435 B
prietoe@winthrop.edu
PRIETO-TSEREGOUNIS,
Emily ... 530-752-0946.... 69 A
eprieto@ucdavis.edu
PRIGAL, Helena ... 212-431-2318.. 323 H
helena.prigal@nyls.edu
PRIGG, Benson ... 256-726-7186...... 6 B
bprigg@oakwood.edu
PRIGGE, Amy ... 419-772-3961.. 374 J
a-prigge@onu.edu
PRIGGIE, Richard, W ... 309-794-7213.. 135 D
richardpriggie@augustana.edu
PRIHODA, Belinda ... 903-730-4890.. 460 B
bprihoda@jarvis.edu
PRILL, Kristina, L ... 518-244-6001.. 327 H
prillk@sage.edu
PRILLELTENSKY, Isaac ... 305-284-3505.. 114 H
isaacp@miami.edu
PRIMAS, Lamario ... 404-225-4714.. 117 A
lprimas@atlantatech.edu
PRIMAVERA, Louis, H ... 631-665-1600.. 337 I
louis.primavera@touro.edu
PRIMERANO, Jessica ... 704-971-8500.. 343 E
jprimerano@charlottelaw.edu
PRIMIANO, Leonard ... 610-902-8330.. 399 D
leonard.primiano@cabrini.edu
PRIMICH, Tracy ... 573-341-4011.. 274 B
primicht@mst.edu
PRIMM, Jenelle ... 501-370-5310.... 21 G
jprimm@philander.edu
PRIMO, John ... 405-733-7356.. 387 I
jprimo@rose.edu
PRIMOFF, Mark ... 845-758-7412.. 304 F
primoff@bard.edu
PRIMROSE, Bruce ... 909-599-5433.... 48 K
bprimrose@lifepacific.edu
PRIMUS, Joanna ... 641-844-5692.. 173 L
joanna.primus@iavalley.edu
PRIMUS, Lester ... 860-906-5050.... 86 B
lprimus@ccc.commnet.edu
PRINCE, Bobby, A ... 901-678-1335.. 445 C
baprince@memphis.edu
PRINCE, Christine B ... 215-885-2360.. 409 G
cprince@manor.edu
PRINCE, Iris ... 910-892-3178.. 344 I
iprince@heritagebiblecollege.edu
PRINCE, James, E ... 269-337-7225.. 235 H
james.prince@kzoo.edu
PRINCE, Jeff ... 510-642-9494.... 68 M
jprince@berkeley.edu
PRINCE, Joan, M ... 414-229-3101.. 520 D
jprince@uwm.edu
PRINCE, Judith ... 864-552-4243.. 434 G
jprince@uscupstate.edu
PRINCE, Ken ... 812-866-7051.. 161 C
princek@hanover.edu
PRINCE, Nate ... 661-362-2200.... 52 A
nprince@masters.edu
PRINCE, T. Greg ... 410-546-6938.. 213 A
tgprince@salisbury.edu
PRINEAS, Matthew ... 240-684-2830.. 212 C
matthew.prineas@umuc.edu
PRINGLE, Eboni ... 330-672-8700.. 370 I
epringle@kent.edu
PRINGLE, Ernest ... 803-641-3345.. 433 G
ernestp@usca.edu
PRINGLE, Nancy, E ... 607-274-3836.. 317 D
npringle@ithaca.edu
PRINGLE, Randy ... 903-923-2233.. 457 G
rpringle@etbu.edu
PRIOLEAU, Darwin ... 585-395-5806.. 332 E
dpriolea@brockport.edu
PRIOLEAU, Florence ... 202-806-2650.... 93 A
florence.prioleau@howard.edu
PRIOLEAU, Florence ... 202-806-2250.... 93 A
florence.prioleau@howard.edu
PRIOLO, Bob ... 616-949-5300.. 233 A
bob.priolo@cornerstone.edu
PRIOR, Roberta ... 203-285-2209.... 36 C
rprior@gwcc.commnet.edu
PRISCO, Anne ... 201-559-6022.. 291 K
priscoa@felician.edu
PRISELAC, Thomas ... 310-423-8294.... 36 O
PRISLIN, Radmila ... 619-594-5166.... 35 A
rprislin@mail.sdsu.edu
PRITCHARD, Alice ... 860-723-0016.... 35 E
pritcharda@ct.edu
PRITCHARD, Brett ... 256-215-4254...... 2 G
bpritchard@cacc.edu
PRITCHARD, Chanon ... 706-776-0105.. 125 J
cpritchard@piedmont.edu
PRITCHARD, Gary ... 562-860-2451.... 36 P
gpritchard@cerritos.edu
PRITCHARD, Lamar ... 713-743-1253.. 473 F
flpritchard@uh.edu
PRITCHARD, Lisa ... 636-481-3160.. 266 C
lpritcha@jeffco.edu
PRITCHARD, Michael ... 301-846-2417.. 207 F
mpritchard@frederick.edu
PRITCHARD, Rod ... 319-399-8605.. 170 G
rpritcha@coe.edu
PRITCHARD, Sarah, M ... 847-491-7640.. 150 F
spritchard@northwestern.edu
PRITCHETT, Alondrea, J .. 334-229-4737...... 1 D
apritchett@alasu.edu
PRITCHETT, Beth ... 304-327-4139.. 512 P
bpritchett@bluefieldstate.edu
PRITCHETT, Donald ... 518-262-5521.. 303 E
pritchd@mail.amc.edu
PRITCHETT, H. Franklin ... 678-839-6582.. 129 E
fpritche@westga.edu
PRITCHETT, Marie ... 586-445-7315.. 237 C
pritchettm@macomb.edu
PRITCHETT, Megan ... 601-925-3210.. 259 A
mpritchett@mc.edu
PRITCHETT, Terry ... 325-649-8608.. 459 E
tpritchett@hputx.edu
PRITTING, Shannon ... 315-792-7245.. 336 C
shannon.pritting@sunyit.edu
PRITTS, Barry ... 304-473-8040.. 515 B
pritts@wvwc.edu
PRITZ, Stephen, J ... 352-392-1374.. 112 A
spritz@ufl.edu
PRITZKER, Barry ... 518-580-5654.. 330 F
bpritzke@skidmore.edu
PRIVETT, SJ, Stephen, A . 415-422-6215.... 72 C
privett@usfca.edu
PRIVOTT, Ashley, E ... 540-568-6234.. 490 J
privotae@emu.edu
PROBST, Laura, K ... 218-299-4642.. 246 A
lprobst@cord.edu
PROBST, Robert ... 513-556-9808.. 379 A
robert.probst@uc.edu
PROBSTFELD, Carol, F ... 941-752-5201.. 110 H
probstc@scf.edu
PROBUS, Lawrence, K ... 509-777-4304.. 509 H
lprobus@whitworth.edu
PROCARIO-FOLEY, Carl ... 914-633-2632.. 317 B
cprocariofoley@iona.edu
PROCELL, Derrick ... 985-448-7941.. 196 E
derrick.procell@fletcher.edu
PROCH, Margaret, P ... 410-323-6211.. 207 D
mproch@faiththeological.org
PROCHNOW, Allen ... 262-243-4303.. 232 I
allen.prochnow@cuw.edu
PROCHNOW, Allen, J ... 262-243-5700.. 516 E
allen.prochnow@cuw.edu
PROCTER, Everett ... 949-794-9090.... 66 H
eprocter@stanbridge.edu
PROCTER, Ken ... 478-445-4441.. 121 A
ken.procter@gcsu.edu
PROCTER, Sharon ... 313-664-1487.. 232 G
sprocter@collegeforcreativestudies.edu
PROCTOR, Avis ... 954-201-2202.... 96 I
aproctor@broward.edu
PROCTOR, Catherine ... 732-247-5241.. 293 B
cproctor@nbts.edu
PROCTOR, Cynthia ... 724-925-4003.. 423 D
proctorc@wccc.edu
PROCTOR, Kelly ... 864-388-8398.. 430 G
kproctor@lander.edu
PROCTOR, Kristen ... 508-854-7552.. 224 E
kproctor@qcc.mass.edu
PROCTOR, Lee ... 910-576-6222.. 351 E
PROCTOR, Matt ... 417-626-1234.. 269 K
pres@occ.edu
PROCTOR, Michael, A ... 520-626-5531.... 17 I
mproctor@arizona.edu
PROCTOR, Ross ... 870-733-6875.... 19 A
prproctor@asumidsouth.edu
PROCTOR, William, L ... 904-819-6210.... 99 M
proctorw@flagler.edu
PROEHL, Erinn ... 815-939-5296.. 150 I
eproehl@olivet.edu
PROFETA, Patricia ... 772-462-7590.. 103 B
pprofeta@irsc.edu
PROFFITT, Beth ... 717-358-3871.. 403 J
beth.proffitt@fandm.edu
PROFITT, Aaron ... 513-721-7944.. 369 D
aprofitt@gbs.edu
PROHASKA, Thomas, R ... 703-993-1918.. 490 B
tprohask@gmu.edu
PROHN, Deborah, W ... 716-888-2919.. 306 F
prohnd@canisius.edu
PROISY, Alize ... 252-222-6240.. 348 B
proisya@carteret.edu
PROITE, Rosanne ... 512-245-2931.. 471 F
rp45@txstate.edu
PROKOP, Jessica ... 413-755-4529.. 224 G
japrokop@stcc.edu
PROKOP, Paul ... 530-754-8568.... 69 A
pjprokop@ucdavis.edu
PROKOVICH, Jeffrey, D ... 724-458-3846.. 404 F
jdprokovich@gcc.edu
PROMADES, Frederick, C 401-341-2117.. 426 C
promadef@salve.edu
PROPER, Sherry ... 808-689-2384.. 131 G
sproper@hawaii.edu
PROPST, Jennifer ... 828-448-6051.. 354 B
jpropst@wpcc.edu
PROPST, Joan, L ... 304-457-6201.. 510 B
propstjl@ab.edu
PROPST, Kent ... 660-248-6238.. 263 B
kpropst@centralmethodist.edu
PROPST, William, S ... 310-794-6027.... 69 D
wpropst@finance.ucla.edu
PROSCIA, Domenic ... 718-429-6600.. 339 D
domenic.procsia@vaughn.edu
PROSISE, Jodi, E ... 563-333-6485.. 176 D
prosisejodif@sau.edu
PROSPER, Yamilette ... 787-891-0925.. 533 G
yprosper@aguadilla.inter.edu
PROSSER, Deborah ... 678-717-3466.. 128 F
deborah.prosser@ung.edu
PROTAS, Elizabeth, J ... 409-772-3001.. 478 A
ejprotas@utmb.edu
PROTHERO, Charles, L ... 570-945-8015.. 406 H
charlie.prothero@keystone.edu
PROTHROW-STITH,
Deborah ... 323-563-6981.... 37 G
dprothrowstith@cdrewu.edu
PROTO, Matthew ... 207-859-4802.. 202 G
matthew.proto@colby.edu
PROUDFIT, Ann ... 216-987-5892.. 367 E
ann.proudfit@tri-c.edu
PROUDFOOT, Donald, W 903-510-2975.. 473 C
dpro@tjc.edu
PROUDFOOT, Michael, A 520-621-8747.... 17 I
tproudfoot@email.arizona.edu
PROULX, David, R ... 717-358-3993.. 403 J
dave.proulx@fandm.edu
PROULX, Dennis ... 802-468-1249.. 485 H
dennis.proulx@castleton.edu
PROUSE, Margaret, R ... 302-857-1065.... 91 C
mprouse@dtcc.edu
PROUT, Wilson ... 716-926-8910.. 316 B
wprout@hilbert.edu
PROUTY, Steve ... 941-752-5205.. 110 H
proutys@scf.edu
PROVAN, Amy ... 410-532-5379.. 210 B
aprovan@ndm.edu
PROVENCHER,
Catherine, A ... 603-862-1622.. 288 B
catherine.provencher@usnh.edu
PROVENCIO-VASQUEZ,
Elias ... 915-747-8217.. 476 D
eprovenciovasquez@utep.edu
PROVENZA, Joseph, S ... 904-819-6359.... 99 M
jprovenza@flagler.edu
PROVENZANO, Peter ... 248-341-2102.. 239 E
pmproven@oaklandcc.edu
PROVEZIS, Staci, J ... 217-333-1353.. 157 A
sprovez2@illinois.edu
PROVINE, Rick, E ... 765-658-4435.. 160 F
provine@depauw.edu
PROVOST, David, J ... 802-865-6400.. 483 F
djprovost@champlain.edu
PROVOST, Dawn ... 337-482-6391.. 201 D
dawn@louisiana.edu
PROVOST, Kathryn ... 802-485-2125.. 484 H
kathrynp@norwich.edu

PRUCE, Dora, J 216-397-4565 370 H dpruce@jcu.edu
PRUCHA, Christina 573-897-5000 272 H
PRUCHNICKI, Jennifer 580-581-2209 382 G jpruchni@cameron.edu
PRUCNAL, James, R 256-549-8242 3 M jprucnal@gadsdenstate.edu
PRUDE, Regina 615-256-1463 438 C rprude@abcnash.edu
PRUDEN, Elizabeth 513-487-1232 378 E elizabeth.pruden@myunion.edu
PRUDHOMME, Harvey, J 503-370-6348 396 G hprudhom@willamette.edu
PRUE, Stephen 785-832-6644 181 E stephen.prue@bie.edu
PRUEFER, Peter 218-723-5924 245 J ppruefer@css.edu
PRUETT, Karen 706-880-8977 123 K kpruett@lagrange.edu
PRUETT, Robert, R 919-658-7760 355 K rpruett@umo.edu
PRUETT, Tim 740-245-7358 380 C tpruett@rio.edu
PRUGH, JR., John, L 813-974-5437 112 C jprugh@usf.edu
PRUITT, Aaron 541-684-7217 393 B apruitt@nwcu.edu
PRUITT, Bart 806-720-7232 461 C bart.pruitt@lcu.edu
PRUITT, Betty 205-391-2251 6 G bpruitt@sheltonstate.edu
PRUITT, Beverly 305-284-2842 114 H b.pruitt@miami.edu
PRUITT, Chris 402-449-2917 280 C cpruitt9967@graceu.edu
PRUITT, Corey 480-517-8538 14 G corey.pruitt@riosalado.edu
PRUITT, Dennis, A 803-777-4172 433 F dpruitt@sc.edu
PRUITT, Elaine 336-631-1561 358 E pruitte@uncsa.edu
PRUITT, George, A 609-984-1105 297 F gpruitt@tesu.edu
PRUITT, Glenell 903-730-4890 460 B gpruitt@jarvis.edu
PRUITT, Jason 470-239-3103 128 F jason.pruitt@ung.edu
PRUITT, Jonathan 919-962-4600 356 A jpruitt@northcarolina.edu
PRUITT, Judy 612-343-4491 253 Y japruitt@northcentral.edu
PRUITT, Karl 205-929-6348 5 D kpruitt@lawsonstate.edu
PRUITT, Leah, L 864-587-4225 433 A pruittl@smcsc.edu
PRUITT, Samory, T 205-348-8376 8 D samory.pruitt@ua.edu
PRUITT, Steven 561-237-7834 104 O spruitt@lynn.edu
PRUNTY, Bonnie, S 607-274-3141 317 D bprunty@ithaca.edu
PRUNTY, Kathleen, A 909-869-3380 31 J kaprunty@cpp.edu
PRUS, Mark 607-753-2207 333 A mark.prus@cortland.edu
PRUSANK, Diane 413-572-5201 222 E dprusank@westfield.ma.edu
PRUSH, Nicholas 734-384-4103 238 C nprush@monroeccc.edu
PRUSHA, Tammy 641-269-4481 172 I prushatd@grinnell.edu
PRUSHA, Todd 319-398-5565 174 I tprusha@kirkwood.edu
PRUSHAN, Mike 610-526-1861 405 B mprushan@harcum.edu
PRUSKOWSKI, Nancy 717-871-4086 415 F nancy.pruskowski@millersville.edu
PRUSS, Julie, A 585-395-2361 332 E jpruss@brockport.edu
PRUSSIN, Shari 212-217-4000 314 B shari_prussin@fitnyc.edu
PRY, George 412-809-5100 417 D pry.georgel@pti.edu
PRYBUTOK, Victor 940-565-3946 475 A victor.prybutok@unt.edu
PRYJMAK, Myron 718-409-7311 336 A mpryjmak@sunymaritime.edu
PRYLES, Kathryn 508-588-9100 223 G
PRYLO, Caelynn 518-743-2238 335 A pryloc@sunyacc.edu
PRYOR, Christian 504-816-4696 195 B cpryor@dillard.edu
PRYOR, Douglas 305-809-3184 100 N douglas.pryor@fkcc.edu
PRYOR, Julie 205-453-6300 93 F
PRYOR, Kim, A 336-342-4261 352 F pryork@rockinghamcc.edu
PRYOR, Marcus 704-991-0278 353 E mpryor7642@stanly.edu
PRYOR, Raymond, G 570-208-5828 406 J rgpryor@kings.edu
PRYOR-HARRIS, Holli 312-567-3167 142 I pryor@iit.edu
PRYSOCK, James 614-823-1312 376 C jprysock@otterbein.edu
PRYSTOWSKY, Richard 517-483-1156 237 A prystowr@lcc.edu
PRZEKOP, Lisa 805-893-3641 70 E lisa.przekop@sa.ucsb.edu
PRZEKURAT, Paris 405-422-1442 387 E przekuratp@redlandscc.edu
PRZYBLYSKI, Jeannene 661-255-1050 30 E jeannene@calarts.edu
PRZYBOROKI, Carol 412-321-8383 399 C office@bcs.edu
PRZYGOCKI, Ginny 989-686-9276 233 I vlprzygo@delta.edu
PRZYGODA, Melitha, R 203-576-4588 89 C mprzygod@bridgeport.edu
PRZYWARA, Ann Marie 518-580-5765 330 F aprzywar@skidmore.edu
PRZYWARA, Richard, T 610-430-4156 416 C rprzywara@wcufoundation.org
PSAILA, Marisa 585-475-4932 327 E mxpdar@rit.edu
PSARRIS, Kleanthis 718-951-3170 307 D kpsarris@brooklyn.cuny.edu
PSEEKOS, Chantelle 508-373-9544 215 D chantelle.pseekos@becker.edu
PTACEK, Kelly, K 402-280-1485 279 H kellyptacek@creighton.edu
PTACHIK, Robert, A 646-664-9402 306 M robert.ptachik@cuny.edu
PUC, Gina 413-662-5416 222 B g.puc@mcla.edu
PUCCIARELLI, Matthew 718-990-7614 328 F pucciarm@stjohns.edu
PUCCIO O'BRIEN, Erica 617-879-7716 222 A erica.puccio@massart.edu
PUCINE, Richard 315-792-5309 321 G rpucine@mvcc.edu
PUCKETT, Christopher 303-315-6619 84 A chris.puckett@ucdenver.edu
PUCKETT, Jack 252-492-2061 353 H puckett@vgcc.edu
PUCKETT, Jackie, A 864-488-4585 430 H jpuckett@limestone.edu
PUCKETT, Jeffrey 616-395-7413 235 F puckett@hope.edu
PUCKETT, Joan 812-888-4480 169 A jpuckett@vinu.edu
PUCKETT-BOLER, Laura 864-503-5194 434 G lpuckett-boler@uscupstate.edu
PUDDESTER, Frederick, W 413-597-4421 230 A frederick.w.puddester@williams.edu
PUENTE, Jonathan 435-865-8726 481 N jonathanpuente@suu.edu
PUENTE, Maria, K 617-228-2032 223 B mkpuente@bhcc.mass.edu
PUETT, Debbie 828-395-1481 350 E dpuett@isothermal.edu
PUFFENBARGER, Jess 270-534-3504 190 H jess.puffenbarger@kctcs.edu
PUFHAL, Joy 207-780-5512 205 E joy.pufhal@maine.edu
PUGEL, Mary, E 336-758-3005 359 E mpugel@wfu.edu
PUGH, Benjamin 225-771-5021 199 H benjamin_pugh@subr.edu
PUGH, Crystal 252-789-0293 351 A cpugh@martincc.edu
PUGH, SR., Daniel, J 979-845-4728 468 B djpughsr@vpsa.tamu.edu
PUGH, David 912-525-5000 126 E dpugh@scad.edu
PUGH, Jason 601-928-6233 259 C jason.pugh@mgccc.edu
PUGH, Kendra, L 804-524-5845 499 G kpugh@vsu.edu
PUGH, Paul, F 610-519-4200 422 G paul.pugh@villanova.edu
PUGH, Vicki 561-803-2012 106 C viki_pugh@pba.edu
PUGLIESE, Beth 408-924-1116 35 C beth.pugliese@sjsu.edu
PUGLIESE, Stephen 814-886-6459 411 C spugliese@mtaloy.edu
PUGLIESI, Karen, L 928-523-9231 15 H karen.pugliesi@nau.edu
PUGLISI, Emma 978-921-4242 225 G emma.puglisi@montserrat.edu
PUGLISI, Michael, J 276-944-6662 489 I mpuglisi@ehc.edu
PUGNAIRE, Michele, P 508-856-4250 221 B michele.pugnaire@umassmed.edu
PUHALA, Kimberly 617-984-1727 227 F kpuhala@quincycollege.edu
PUHL, Dan 512-444-8082 470 B dpuhl@thsu.edu
PUHL WINKLER, Jenn 701-777-0729 360 C jennifer.puhlwinkler@und.edu
PUIG, Juan 787-815-0000 537 F juan.puig@upr.edu
PULAKOS, Joan 208-885-6716 134 G pulakos@uidaho.edu
PULCINI, Brad 740-755-7139 365 D bpulcini@cotc.edu
PULEIO, Samuel, T 814-393-2280 414 G spuleio@clarion.edu
PULIAFICO, Venus 216-368-4530 365 B venus.puliafico@case.edu
PULICE, Jon 814-732-1763 415 A jpulice@edinboro.edu
PULIDO, Jairo 787-250-1912 534 B jpulido@metro.inter.edu
PULLEN, Richard, L 806-354-6024 450 H rlpullen@actx.edu
PULLEN, Terri 513-862-7761 369 E terri.pullen@email.gscollege.edu
PULLEY, Brett 757-637-2018 490 E brett.pulley@hamptonu.edu
PULLEY, Eric 618-985-3741 143 F ericpulley@jalc.edu
PULLEY, Lawrence, B 757-221-2891 488 F larry.pulley@mason.wm.edu
PULLIAM, Camden 816-414-3700 268 D cpulliam@mbts.edu
PULLIAM, Cheryl 704-355-5043 343 A cheryl.pulliam@carolinashealthcare.org
PULLIAM, DeWayne 615-794-4254 443 G dpulliam@omorecollege.edu
PULLIAM, Joni, L 315-792-3344 339 B jpulliam@utica.edu
PULLIAM, Mark 252-249-1851 351 G mpulliam@pamlicocc.edu
PULLIN, Daniel, W 405-325-0100 389 B dpullin@ou.edu
PULLIN, Jennifer 651-730-5100 246 I jpullin@globeuniversity.edu
PULLIZA, Carmen 787-743-7979 536 A cpulliza@suagm.edu
PULS, Jonathan 562-903-4807 28 E jonathan.puls@biola.edu
PULSIPHER, Scott, D 801-274-3280 483 C spulsipher@wgu.edu
PULTRO, Judith 239-985-3477 101 F jpultro@fsw.edu
PULTZ, Stephen, F 619-260-4506 72 B spultz@sandiego.edu
PULVER, Chad, A 219-866-6154 166 J pulver@saintjoe.edu
PULVER, Patricia 315-279-5662 318 C ppulver@keuka.edu
PULVER, Shayne 615-226-3990 441 D spulver@lincolntech.edu
PUMA, Lynn, M 716-878-5509 332 F pumalm@buffalostate.edu
PUMPHREY, Dennis 970-351-2245 84 C dennis.pumphrey@unco.edu
PUNCHELLO-COBOS, Catharine 609-984-1180 297 F registrar@tesu.edu
PUNCHES, Kathy, M 419-783-2590 368 A kpunches@defiance.edu
PUNEKY, Warren 504-671-6100 196 D wpunek@dcc.edu
PUNG, Sha-Lene 512-444-8082 470 B administrator@thsu.edu
PUNT, David 916-577-2200 75 C dpunt@jessup.edu
PURA, Robert, L 413-775-1410 223 D pura@gcc.mass.edu
PURATICH, Kate 253-589-5846 502 F kate.puratich@cptc.edu
PURCELL, Anthony, B 205-934-2297 8 E bpurcell@uab.edu
PURCELL, Chris, A 405-325-4122 389 B regentspurcell@ou.edu
PURCELL, Jeanine 716-880-2259 320 D jp983@medaille.edu
PURCELL, Ladonna, M 606-783-2323 191 H l.purcell@moreheadstate.edu
PURCELL, Meredith 815-802-8512 144 C mpurcell@kcc.edu
PURCELL, Phillip 765-285-7070 159 B ppurcell@bsu.edu
PURCELL, Ruth 724-287-8711 399 B ruth.purcell@bc3.edu
PURCELL, Satch 949-794-9090 66 H spurcell@stanbridge.edu
PURCELL, Stacy, R 757-446-6002 489 B purcellsr@evms.edu
PURCELL, Terri 615-327-3927 440 H purcell@guptoncollege.edu
PURDOM, Kurt 662-915-7375 261 B kirk@olemiss.edu
PURDUE-LYNCH, Barbara 201-355-1122 291 K lynchb@felician.edu
PURDY, Brad 505-566-3301 301 J purdyb@sanjuancollege.edu
PURDY, G. Michael 212-854-1656 311 E gmp63@columbia.edu
PURDY, Jill 308-865-8421 282 L purdyj@unk.edu
PURDY, Judy 508-286-3785 229 F purdy_judy@wheatoncollege.edu
PURDY, Kim 479-619-4399 21 D kpurdy@nwacc.edu
PURDY, Ryan 308-535-3720 280 M purdyr@mpcc.edu
PURECE, Sarita 415-257-0137 42 G sarita.purece@dominican.edu
PURI, Anil 657-278-2592 33 A apuri@fullerton.edu
PURI, Anil 657-278-2614 33 A
PURI, Tribhuvan 570-422-3589 414 H
PURIFOY, Tangela 251-578-1313 6 C tpurifoy@rstc.edu
PURNELL, William 508-849-3482 214 E wpurnell@annamaria.edu
PUROHIT, Yasmin, S 412-397-5472 418 B purohit@rmu.edu
PURRINGTON, Kristen 603-524-3207 286 C kpurrington@ccsnh.edu
PURSER, Charles 252-335-0821 349 A charles_purser@albemarle.edu
PURSLEY, Linda 617-349-8563 220 B lpursley@lesley.edu
PURSOO, Eugene 718-270-5136 309 B pursoo@mec.cuny.edu
PURSWANI, Pavan 410-337-6403 207 H pavan.purswani@goucher.edu
PURTLE, Dorothy 913-722-0272 182 B dorothy.purtle@kansaschristian.edu
PURVIANCE, Chris 509-313-5858 504 A purviance@gonzaga.edu
PURVIS, Anne 678-359-5197 122 E a_purvis@gordonstate.edu
PURVIS, Donnie 817-598-6284 479 E dpurvis@wc.edu
PURVIS, Jonathan, D 812-855-7739 162 F jpurvis@indiana.edu
PURVIS, Kathy 254-968-9070 467 F kpurvis@tarleton.edu
PURVIS, Stephen 478-757-5167 129 L spurvis@wesleyancollege.edu
PURVIS-ROBERTS, Kathleen 909-621-8736 57 H kpurvis@jsd.claremont.edu
PURYEAR, Roberta (Robbi) 713-743-8780 473 E rdpuryea@uh.edu
PUSECKER, Kathleen, L 302-831-8537 91 F klp@udel.edu
PUSEY, Stephen, M 615-248-1258 447 F spusey@trevecca.edu
PUSICH, Ruth 630-617-3080 140 C ruthp@elmhurst.edu
PUSKA, Douglas, P 978-762-4000 224 C dpuska@northshore.edu
PUSTAY, Pamela, S 330-471-8159 371 J ppustay@malone.edu
PUSTEJOVSKY, Kathleen 254-659-7632 458 K kpustejovsky@hillcollege.edu
PUSTZ, Charles 815-836-5050 145 H pustzch@lewisu.edu
PUSZYNSKI, Jan, A 605-394-2493 437 E jan.puszynski@sdsmt.edu
PUTERBAUGH, Mark 336-249-8186 349 C mark_puterbaugh@davidsoncc.edu
PUTMAN, Jeffrey 718-270-2187 332 B jeffrey.putman@downstate.edu
PUTMAN, Paul 518-736-3622 315 A pputman@fmcc.suny.edu
PUTMAN, Stephen 256-765-4178 9 C jsputman@una.edu
PUTNAM, Diana 518-736-3622 315 A diana.putnam@fmcc.suny.edu
PUTNAM, Joshua 864-977-7669 431 G joshua.putnam@ngu.edu
PUTNAM, Mark 281-756-3584 450 G mputnam@alvincollege.edu
PUTNAM, Mark, L 641-628-5269 170 E president@central.edu
PUTNAM, Robin 701-328-2960 360 B robin.putnam@ndus.edu
PUTNAM, Timothy, J 641-422-4192 175 E putnatim@niacc.edu
PUTNEY, Luanna 209-228-4417 70 A lputney@ucmerced.edu
PUTO, Christopher 251-380-3865 7 D cputo@shc.edu
PUTREVU, Sanjay 307-766-4194 527 B sputrevu@uwyo.edu
PUTZKE, Robert 406-994-3220 277 C rputzke@montana.edu
PUTZOVA, Eva 928-523-7814 15 H eva.putzova@nau.edu
PYDO, Todd 715-682-1682 518 H tpydo@northland.edu
PYE, Barbara 313-831-5200 233 K registrar@etseminary.edu

PYE, Christopher .... 973-353-5679.. 296 C
cpye@rutgers.edu
PYE, Jennifer .... 318-371-3035.. 196 H
jenniferpye@nwltc.edu
PYEON, Yo Han .... 323-643-0301.... 26 H
PYER, Terri .... 831-755-6706.... 45 L
tpyer@hartnell.edu
PYFFEROEN, Michelle ..... 507-285-7425.. 251 I
michelle.pyfferoen@rctc.edu
PYLE, Allison .... 972-708-7552.. 458 G
gial_alumni@gial.edu
PYLE, Brenda .... 770-962-7580.. 123 D
bpyle@gwinnetttech.edu
PYLE, Carla, S .... 260-399-7700.. 168 D
cpyle@sf.edu
PYLE, Elizabeth .... 413-538-2000.. 226 A
epyle@mtholyoke.edu
PYLE, John .... 507-457-1743.. 254 O
jpyle@smumn.edu
PYLE, Marsha, A .... 816-235-2010.. 273 F
pylem@umkc.edu
PYLE, Ray .... 925-229-6842.... 41 G
rpyle@4cd.edu
PYLE, Thomas, C .... 724-847-5566.. 404 B
tcpyle@geneva.edu
PYLES, Gloria, D .... 803-536-8266.. 432 E
gpyles@scsu.edu
PYLES, Marvin .... 410-543-6050.. 213 A
mlpyles@salisbury.edu
PYLMAN, Maureen .... 773-907-4457.. 137 E
mpylman@ccc.edu
PYNCHON, Thomas .... 315-229-5583.. 329 D
tpynchon@stlawu.edu
PYNES, Penelope, J .... 336-334-5404.. 358 B
penelope_pynes@uncg.edu
PYNM, Paula .... 317-578-7353.. 158 F
PYO, Chang Sun .... 678-618-1158.. 120 G
changsun.pyo@gmail.com
PYO, George, F .... 814-472-3014.. 418 F
gpyo@francis.edu
PYRON, Susan .... 717-337-6542.. 404 C
spyron@gettysburg.edu

Q

QADER, Mirwais .... 608-246-6198.. 523 F
mqader@madisoncollege.edu
QAISSAUNEE, Laura, V ... 732-224-2756.. 289 I
lqaissaunee@brookdalecc.edu
QATU, Mohamad .... 734-487-0354.. 233 J
mqatu@emich.edu
QI, Feng .... 908-737-3737.. 292 C
fqi@kean.edu
QIN, Laura .... 860-215-9305.... 87 D
lqin@trcc.commnet.edu
QU, Jianmin .... 617-627-3237.. 228 H
jianmin.qu@tufts.edu
QUACH, Josephine .... 626-472-5121.... 42 I
jquach@esgvrop.org
QUACKENBUSH, Kent, B . 303-762-6923.... 79 I
kent.quackenbush@denverseminary.edu
QUACKENBUSH, Robert .. 509-359-2366.. 503 D
rquackenbush@ewu.edu
QUADE, Stephanie .... 414-288-1412.. 517 I
stephanie.quade@marquette.edu
QUAGLIANA, David .... 423-614-8415.. 441 B
dquagliana@leeuniversity.edu
QUAID, Randi .... 760-547-1800.... 44 C
rquaid@fst.edu
QUAID-MALTAGLIATI,
Marian .... 805-922-6966.... 25 I
marianqm@hancockcollege.edu
QUAINTANCE,
John (Jay) .... 845-434-5750.. 336 H
QUAKENBUSH, Win .... 910-893-1258.. 342 F
quakenbush@campbell.edu
QUALIA, Linda, R .... 972-881-5779.. 455 A
lqualia@collin.edu
QUALLS, Gena .... 989-775-4123.. 240 E
gqualls@sagchip.edu
QUALLS, Penny .... 606-326-2437.. 188 N
penny.qualls@kctcs.edu
QUALMANN, Tracy .... 920-923-8115.. 517 H
tqualmann@marianuniversity.edu
QUAM, Elaine .... 970-351-2222.... 84 C
elaine.quam@unco.edu
QUAM, Jean, K .... 612-626-5177.. 255 H
jquam@umn.edu
QUAN, Gamward .... 909-447-2560.... 39 A
gquan@cst.edu
QUAN, Ray .... 307-855-2113.. 526 E
rquan@cwc.edu
QUANBECK, Kirsten, K ..... 949-824-5594.... 69 C
quanbeck@uci.edu
QUANSTROM, Mark .... 815-939-5011.. 150 I
mquanstr@olivet.edu
QUARBERG, Brad, R .... 608-785-8572.. 520 C
bquarberg@uwlax.edu
QUARDERER, Kelly .... 715-634-4790.. 517 C
kquarderer@lco.edu
QUARLES, Markel .... 661-654-3033.... 32 A
mquarles@csub.edu
QUARLES, Robert .... 404-756-4010.. 116 I
rquarles@atlm.edu
QUARLES, Robert .... 304-473-8163.. 515 B
quarles_r@wvwc.edu
QUARTEY, Kojo .... 734-384-4166.. 238 C
kquartey@monroeccc.edu
QUAST, Debra .... 805-565-6182.... 75 A
dquast@westmont.edu
QUATHAMER, Mark .... 321-433-5364.... 98 K
quathamerm@easternflorida.edu
QUATTROCCHI, John .... 518-743-2394.. 335 A
quattrocchij@sunyacc.edu
QUAY, Sara .... 978-232-2200.. 218 D
squay@endicott.edu
QUAYE, Chandra .... 703-561-1600.... 93 F
chandra.quaye@strayer.edu
QUAYE, Sandra .... 608-899-4241.. 287 A
quayes@franklinpierce.edu
QUBBAJ, Ala .... 956-665-3229.. 476 E
ala.qubbaj@utrgv.edu
QUBEIN, Nido, R .... 336-841-9201.. 345 A
nqubein@highpoint.edu
QUDDUS, Munir .... 936-261-9200.. 467 E
muquddus@pvamu.edu
QUEEN, Harrell, W .... 706-245-7226.. 120 D
hqueen@ec.edu
QUEEN, Julie .... 907-474-5866.... 10 G
jmlarweth@alaska.edu
QUEEN, Scott .... 336-506-4154.. 347 C
scott.queen@alamancecc.edu
QUEEN, Scott .... 636-949-4920.. 266 J
squeen@lindenwood.edu
QUEEN, Todd .... 225-578-9959.. 197 I
tqueen@lsu.edu
QUEEN-HUBERT, Jody .... 212-346-1950.. 325 J
jqueenhubert@pace.edu
QUEENAN, Rosemary .... 518-445-3394.. 303 D
rquee@albanylaw.edu
QUEENAN, Theresa .... 410-651-6447.. 212 B
tqueenan@umes.edu
QUEHL-ENGEL,
Catherine, M .... 319-895-4402.. 171 A
cquehl-engel@cornellcollege.edu
QUEIROZ, William .... 770-220-7919.. 120 G
itsupport@gcuniv.edu
QUERO-MENDEZ, Doris .. 787-725-6500.. 531 C
dquero@albizu.edu
QUERRY, Michele .... 904-256-8000.. 103 D
mquerry1@ju.edu
QUESADA, Edmond .... 719-502-3352.... 82 B
edmond.quesada@ppcc.edu
QUEST, Karen .... 315-568-3060.. 323 A
kquest@nycc.edu
QUEST, Patrick .... 540-636-2900.. 488 D
patrick.quest@christendom.edu
QUESTELL, Alan .... 910-410-1916.. 352 C
ajquestell@richmondcc.edu
QUIATKOWSKI, Sandra .... 800-280-0307.. 158 E
sandra.quiatkowski@ace.edu
QUICK, Angela .... 865-981-8038.. 441 H
angela.quick@maryvillecollege.edu
QUICK, Beth .... 256-824-2325...... 8 F
beth.quick@uah.edu
QUICK, Debra .... 520-515-3640.... 12 L
quickd@cochise.edu
QUICK, Donna .... 803-786-3612.. 429 A
dquick@columbiasc.edu
QUICK, James, E .... 214-768-1115.. 465 J
jquick@smu.edu
QUICK, Matthew, D .... 816-501-4127.. 270 J
matt.quick@rockhurst.edu
QUICK, Michael .... 213-740-2101.... 72 D
uscprovost@usc.edu
QUIETT, Corey .... 405-382-9501.. 387 L
c.quiett@sscok.edu
QUIGGLE, Gregg .... 312-329-4059.. 148 F
gregg.quiggle@moody.edu
QUIGLEY, Brian .... 603-358-2438.. 288 E
bquigley1@keene.edu
QUIGLEY, David .... 617-552-3260.. 216 C
david.quigley@bc.edu
QUIGLEY, James M .... 252-451-8227.. 351 F
jquigley@nashcc.edu
QUIGLEY, JR.,
Kenneth, K .... 617-333-2236.. 217 F
kquigley@curry.edu
QUIGLEY, Kevin, F .... 802-258-9245.. 484 C
kevin@marlboro.edu
QUIGLEY, Lori .... 716-880-2240.. 320 D
lquigley@medaille.edu
QUIGLEY, Mark, R .... 978-542-6078.. 222 D
mquigley@salemstate.edu
QUIGLEY, Peter .... 808-956-3869.. 131 H
quigleyp@hawaii.edu
QUIGLEY, Susan .... 773-380-6785.. 135 H
squigley@seabury.edu
QUILES, Elisa .... 787-751-0178.. 535 N
ac_equiles@suagm.edu
QUILES, Elisa .... 787-257-7373.. 535 P
equiles@suagm.edu
QUILL, Robin .... 508-929-8013.. 222 F
rquill@worcester.edu
QUILLEN, Carol, E .... 704-894-2201.. 343 I
caquillen@davidson.edu
QUILLEN, David .... 630-466-7900.. 157 K
dquillen@waubonsee.edu
QUILLEN, Michael, D ...... 704-216-3475.. 352 G
michael.quillen@rccc.edu
QUIMBY, Kristyn .... 574-520-4154.. 163 E
krirhawk@iusb.edu
QUIMBY, Linda .... 603-899-4028.. 287 A
quimbyl@franklinpierce.edu
QUIMBY, T. Bart .... 907-786-1046.... 10 F
tbquimby@uaa.alaska.edu
QUINCY, Barbara, I .... 724-946-7340.. 423 B
quincyb@westminster.edu
QUINET, Bart, P .... 615-322-7712.. 449 A
bart.p.quinet@vanderbilt.edu
QUININE, Donte .... 509-682-6865.. 509 D
dquinine@wvc.edu
QUINLAN, Brian .... 508-213-2112.. 227 A
brian.quinlan@nichols.edu
QUINLAN, Catherine .... 213-821-2344.... 72 D
cquinlan@usc.edu
QUINLAN, Jeremiah .... 203-432-9321.... 90 D
jeremiah.quinlan@yale.edu
QUINLAN BEAME, Julie . 414-382-6371.. 515 D
julie.quinlan@alverno.edu
QUINLEY, Melissa .... 828-398-7633.. 347 D
mquinley@abtech.edu
QUINLIVAN, Gary .... 724-537-4597.. 419 A
gary.quinlivan@email.stvincent.edu
QUINN, Aaron, M .... 740-392-6868.. 373 D
aaron.quinn@mvnu.edu
QUINN, Anthony .... 734-384-4279.. 238 C
aquinn@monroeccc.edu
QUINN, Arthur .... 561-732-4424.. 108 F
aquinn@svdp.edu
QUINN, Bill .... 281-487-1170.. 469 F
bquinn@txchiro.edu
QUINN, Bonnie .... 781-768-7184.. 227 G
bonnie.quinn@regiscollege.edu
QUINN, Brian .... 215-951-1540.. 407 A
quinng@lasalle.edu
QUINN, Consuelo .... 706-821-8262.. 125 H
cquinn@paine.edu
QUINN, Cynthia, D .... 808-956-8213.. 131 D
bor@hawaii.edu
QUINN, Donna, M .... 302-356-6819.... 91 I
donna.m.quinn@wilmu.edu
QUINN, Edward, M .... 202-687-2627.... 92 E
quinne@georgetown.edu
QUINN, Erin .... 802-443-5253.. 484 F
quinn@middlebury.edu
QUINN, Frank .... 619-849-2338.... 57 M
frankquinn@pointloma.edu
QUINN, Gianna .... 215-641-5554.. 404 G
quinn.g@gmercyu.edu
QUINN, Gina .... 405-682-7502.. 385 D
gquinn@occc.edu
QUINN, Holli .... 484-809-7770.... 93 F
QUINN, Jack, F .... 716-851-1200.. 313 H
jquinn@ecc.edu
QUINN, Jeffery .... 845-675-4425.. 325 C
jeff.quinn@nyack.edu
QUINN, Kathy .... 314-529-9476.. 267 B
kquinn@maryville.edu
QUINN, Kenneth .... 901-435-1731.. 441 C
kenneth_quinn@loc.edu
QUINN, Kevin .... 610-647-4400.. 406 B
kquinn@immaculata.edu
QUINN, Kevin, C .... 315-443-8338.. 337 A
kcquinn@syr.edu
QUINN, SJ, Kevin, P ...... 570-941-7500.. 422 B
presidentquinn@scranton.edu
QUINN, Kimora .... 806-894-9611.. 465 G
kquinn@southplainscollege.edu
QUINN, Laurie .... 802-860-2729.. 483 F
lquinn@champlain.edu
QUINN, Leslie .... 913-469-8500.. 182 A
lquinn2@jccc.edu
QUINN, Linda .... 402-941-6280.. 280 N
quinn@midlandu.edu
QUINN, Margaret .... 609-652-4744.. 297 C
margaret.quinn@stockton.edu
QUINN, Marisa .... 615-297-7545.. 438 F
quinnm@aquinascollege.edu
QUINN, Michael .... 718-405-3334.. 310 H
michael.quinn@mountsaintvincent.edu
QUINN, Michael .... 206-296-5500.. 507 E
quinnm@seattleu.edu
QUINN, Michael, G .... 585-292-2151.. 321 J
mquinn@monroecc.edu
QUINN, Michael, J .... 434-947-8100.. 493 B
mjquinn@randolphcollege.edu
QUINN, Michael, P .... 401-598-2945.. 425 B
mquinn@jwu.edu
QUINN, Michelle .... 970-351-2773.... 84 C
michelle.quinn@unco.edu
QUINN, Molly .... 319-226-2001.. 169 D
molly.quinn@allencollege.edu
QUINN, Penny .... 618-545-3010.. 144 D
pquinn@kaskaskia.edu
QUINN, Randi .... 614-947-6543.. 369 A
randi.quinn@franklin.edu
QUINN, Robert .... 352-588-8351.. 108 C
robert.quinn@saintleo.edu
QUINN, SSJ, Roseann ..... 215-248-7031.. 400 H
quinnr@chc.edu
QUINN, Sarah, F .... 610-660-1230.. 418 G
squinn@sju.edu
QUINN, Shaman .... 307-754-6232.. 526 N
shaman.quinn@nwc.edu
QUINN, Sharon .... 410-455-2540.. 211 G
squinn@umbc.edu
QUINN, Stephen .... 973-618-3320.. 290 A
squinn@caldwell.edu
QUINN, Susan .... 585-389-2501.. 322 D
QUINN, Susan .... 707-524-1598.... 63 G
squinn@santarosa.edu
QUINN, Tania .... 914-654-5257.. 311 A
tquinn@cnr.edu
QUINN, Teresa .... 845-437-5370.. 339 C
tequinn@vassar.edu
QUINN, Thomas .... 989-275-5000.. 236 E
tom.quinn@kirtland.edu
QUINN, Thomas .... 309-556-3195.. 143 D
QUINN, Wade .... 910-362-7062.. 348 A
wquinn@cfcc.edu
QUINN, Wayne .... 229-243-6994.. 117 E
wayne.quinn@bainbridge.edu
QUINN, William, P .... 302-356-6775.... 91 I
william.p.quinn@wilmu.edu
QUINNAN, Tim .... 817-272-6080.. 476 A
quinnan@uta.edu
QUINNETT, Jim .... 325-793-4611.. 461 F
jquinnett@mcm.edu
QUINONES, Carlos, A ..... 787-753-0039.. 532 A
QUINONES, Irma .... 787-758-2525.. 538 D
irma.quinones1@upr.edu
QUINONES, Ivan, A .... 717-780-2455.. 405 C
iaquinon@hacc.edu
QUINONES, Jose Luis ..... 787-758-2525.. 538 D
jose.quinones9@upr.edu
QUINONES, Melinda .... 610-282-1100.. 402 B
melinda.quinones@desales.edu
QUINONES, Ray .... 787-265-3866.. 538 C
ray.quinones@upr.edu
QUINONES, Roberto .... 213-413-9500.... 66 B
robertoquinones@scusoma.edu
QUINONES, Rosa .... 787-257-0000.. 537 H
rosa.quinones1@upr.edu
QUINONES, Vicente .... 407-265-8383.... 97 B
QUINONEZ, Julie, R .... 419-530-6213.. 380 D
julie.quinonez@utoledo.edu
QUINT, Doug .... 620-242-0586.. 183 C
quintd@mcpherson.edu
QUINTAL, Jorge .... 336-334-5536.. 358 B
j_quinta@uncg.edu
QUINTAL, Rollande .... 508-849-3340.. 214 E
rquintal@annamaria.edu
QUINTANA, Pamela .... 561-912-1211.... 99 J
pquintana@evergladesuniversity.edu
QUINTANA, Rosaura .... 787-815-0000.. 537 F
rosaura.quintana@upr.edu
QUINTANA HESS,
Jessica, A .... 570-321-4318.. 409 F
hess@lycoming.edu
QUINTANILLA, Hector ..... 817-531-4840.. 472 F
hquintanilla@txwes.edu
QUINTANILLA, Kelly .... 361-825-2722.. 468 E
kelly.quintanilla@tamucc.edu
QUINTANS, Joel .... 817-272-2025.. 476 A
quintas@uta.edu
QUINTARA, Elena .... 312-662-4021.. 134 I
equintara@adler.edu
QUINTERO, Rebecca .... 787-728-1515.. 539 B
rquintero@sagrado.edu
QUINTERO-JIMENEZ,
Noel .... 787-725-6500.. 531 C
nquintero@albizu.edu
QUINTYNE, Renee .... 845-398-4207.. 329 G
rquintyn@stac.edu
QUIRE, Heather .... 802-447-6302.. 485 B
hquire@svc.edu
QUIRK, Donna .... 312-915-8723.. 146 G
dquirk@luc.edu
QUIRK-BAILEY, Sheila ..... 309-694-5520.. 141 F
sheila.quirk-bailey@icc.edu
QUIROLGICO, Ray .... 626-396-2325.... 27 L
ray.quirolgico@artcenter.edu
QUIROS, Kristi .... 830-372-8060.. 470 C
kquiros@tlu.edu
QUIROZ, Gloria .... 773-878-3606.. 153 E
gquiroz@staugustine.edu
QUIROZ, Saul .... 805-965-0581.... 63 D
squiroz@sbcc.edu
QUIS, Stephen .... 619-388-7876.... 60 H
squis@sdccd.edu

QUISENBERRY, Brian ...... 205-226-4670...... 2 C
bquisenb@bsc.edu
QUISENBERRY, JR.,
Henry, L .... 334-347-2623...... 3 H
cquisenberry@escc.edu
QUISTGARD, Fred .... 207-216-4406.. 204 B
fquistgard@yccc.edu
QUISTORF, Mark, W .... 414-410-4016.. 515 I
mwquistorf@stritch.edu
QUIÑONES, Angel .... 787-258-1501.. 531 K
alquinones@columbiacentral.edu
QUIÑONES, Yolanda .... 787-758-2525.. 538 D
yolanda.quinonez@upr.edu
QVARMSTROM, Jeanne ... 432-837-8585.. 471 E
jqvarmstrom@sulross.edu

R

RAAB, David .... 646-565-6000.. 337 I
david.raab@touro.edu
RAAB, Jennifer, J .... 212-772-4242.. 308 D
jennifer.raab@hunter.cuny.edu
RAAB, Lettie, M .... 936-261-5900.. 467 E
lmraab@pvamu.edu
RAAB, Maryrose .... 315-792-7215.. 336 C
maryrose.raab@sunyit.edu
RAASCH, Christopher ...... 734-995-7399.. 232 I
chris.raasch@cuaa.edu
RAATMA, Lucia .... 352-588-8572.. 108 C
lucia.raatma@saintleo.edu
RAATTAMA, Kristina .... 305-348-2103.. 111 A
maija.raattama@fiu.edu
RABAGO, Cristine .... 650-543-3782.... 52 D
crabago@menlo.edu
RABALAIS, Lawrence .... 225-578-3231.. 197 I
lrabal1@lsu.edu
RABB, Harriet .... 212-327-8070.. 327 F
harriet.rabb@rockefeller.edu
RABB, Sydni .... 254-442-5113.. 454 E
sydni.rabb@cisco.edu
RABBANY, Sina, Y .... 516-463-6672.. 316 D
sina.y.rabbany@hofstra.edu
RABBITT, Kara, M .... 973-720-2180.. 298 G
rabbittk@wpunj.edu
RABEK, Jeffrey .... 409-772-6026.. 478 A
jrabek@utmb.edu
RABEL, P, J .... 402-465-2102.. 281 K
prabel@nebrwesleyan.edu
RABEL, W. Huitt .... 770-720-9147.. 126 C
whr@reinhardt.edu
RABELO, Virginia .... 305-821-3333.. 101 B
vrabelo@fnu.edu
RABENOLD, Scott .... 865-974-9557.. 448 E
srabenol@utk.edu
RABER, II, Donald, R ...... 864-833-8233.. 432 B
draber@presby.edu
RABER, Rhonda, K .... 574-372-5100.. 161 B
raberrk@grace.edu
RABIDEAU, Shelly, S .... 317-940-8423.. 159 K
srabidea@butler.edu
RABIL, Alison .... 919-684-3501.. 343 J
alison.rabil@duke.edu
RABINEAU, Kevin .... 269-965-3931.. 236 A
rabineauk@kellogg.edu
RABINOVICH, Sheryl .... 213-624-1200.... 43 J
srabinovich@fidm.edu
RABINOWITZ, Celia, E ..... 603-358-2736.. 288 E
celia.rabinowitz@keene.edu
RABINOWITZ, David, B .... 973-290-4084.. 290 G
drabinowitz@cse.edu
RABINOWITZ, Eli .... 718-377-0777.. 326 F
RABINOWITZ, Stuart .... 516-463-6800.. 316 D
president@hofstra.edu
RABINOWITZ, Vita .... 664-646-8075.. 306 M
vita.rabinowitz@cuny.edu
RABITOY, Eric .... 626-914-8788.... 38 D
erabitoy@citruscollege.edu
RABITOY, Linda .... 909-667-4433.... 38 G
lrabitoy@claremontlincoln.edu
RABLE, Michelle .... 419-824-3816.. 371 I
mrable@lourdes.edu
RABLE, Michelle, A .... 419-824-3816.. 371 I
mrable@lourdes.edu
RABY, Domonic .... 601-877-6333.. 256 F
sm8053@bncollege.com
RABY, James .... 803-641-3569.. 433 G
jamesr@usca.edu
RABY, Sherry .... 252-249-1851.. 351 G
sraby@pamlicocc.edu
RABY, Susan .... 315-312-2260.. 333 D
susan.raby@oswego.edu
RACANSKY, Pam .... 206-934-3656.. 506 J
pam.racansky@seattlecolleges.edu
RACCANELLO, Paul .... 415-485-3223.... 42 G
paul.raccanello@dominican.edu
RACE, Debbie .... 828-262-2050.. 356 B
racedw@appstate.edu
RACE, Mary Jo .... 412-624-4200.. 421 G
mar6@pitt.edu
RACEHORSE, Brenda .... 785-749-8451.. 181 E
brenda.racehorse@bie.edu
RACETTE, Patrick .... 906-524-8301.. 236 D
patrick.racette@kbocc.edu
RACHAL, Bryan .... 256-765-4225...... 9 C
brachal@una.edu
RACHAL, Carol, E .... 256-233-8204...... 1 F
carol.rachal@athens.edu
RACHAL, Michael .... 504-865-2486.. 198 E
rachal@loyno.edu
RACHELL, Kelvin .... 803-536-7239.. 432 E
krachell@scsu.edu
RACHELL, Kelvin .... 804-524-5011.. 499 G
krachell@vsu.edu
RACHFORD, Jennifer .... 909-607-2201.... 58 A
jennifer.rachford@pomona.edu
RACHIS, Stefanie .... 919-546-8320.. 355 F
srachis@shawu.edu
RACHITA, David, A .... 281-283-2568.. 474 A
rachita@uhcl.edu
RACHOUH, Susan .... 201-216-3518.. 297 B
susan.rachouh@stevens.edu
RACHOWICZ, Nicholas ...... 516-726-5257.. 529 B
rachowiczn@usmma.edu
RACINE, Anne .... 406-338-5441.. 276 A
anne_racine@bfcc.edu
RACINE, Gail, M .... 508-767-7283.. 214 F
gracine@assumption.edu
RACINE, Leo .... 508-678-2811.. 223 A
leo.racine@bristolcc.edu
RACIOPPI, Jerry .... 402-461-2503.. 278 K
geraldracioppi@cccneb.edu
RACKAWAY, Chapman ..... 785-628-5391.. 180 I
crackawa@fhsu.edu
RACKLEY, Casey, C .... 865-688-9422.. 440 C
RACKLEY, J. Mike .... 662-325-9311.. 259 D
mike.rackley@msstate.edu
RACKLEY, Richard, W ...... 865-688-9422.. 440 C
info@fountainheadcollege.com
RACKLIFFE, Jerry, J .... 404-413-3000.. 122 D
jracklif@gsu.edu
RACZYNSKI, James, M ..... 501-526-6600.... 23 C
raczynskijamesm@uams.edu
RADAKOVICH, Dan .... 864-656-1935.. 428 C
danrad1@clemson.edu
RADCLIFFE, Shelby .... 503-370-6397.. 396 G
sradcliffe@willamette.edu
RADCLIFFE, Steve .... 513-244-4381.. 373 C
steve.radcliffe@msj.edu
RADDA, Hank .... 602-639-7500...... 13 I
RADDER, Shannon .... 716-839-8337.. 312 D
sradder@daemen.edu
RADEL, Marie .... 765-455-9468.. 163 A
meradel@iuk.edu
RADEL, Patti .... 585-594-6100.. 325 B
radelp@roberts.edu
RADEL, Patti .... 585-594-6100.. 327 D
radelp@roberts.edu
RADEMACHER, Eric .... 513-556-3304.. 379 A
eric.rademacher@uc.edu
RADER, Brian .... 503-399-8074.. 390 E
brian.rader@chemeketa.edu
RADER, Claude, K .... 410-951-3858.. 212 E
drader@coppin.edu
RADER, Sherri .... 309-649-6255.. 155 G
sherri.rader@src.edu
RADFORD, Brian .... 615-547-1240.. 439 H
bradford@cumberland.edu
RADFORD, Laurie .... 503-552-1617.. 392 H
lradford@nunm.edu
RADFORD, Marilyn .... 270-384-8022.. 191 E
radfordm@lindsey.edu
RADFORD, Ron .... 256-395-2211...... 7 C
rradford@suscc.edu
RADFORD, Russell .... 877-873-3481.. 140 B
rradford@ellis.edu
RADHAKRISHNAN,
Rashmi .... 610-921-7225.. 396 H
rradhakrishnan@albright.edu
RADIK, Amy .... 518-736-3622.. 315 A
amy.radik@fmcc.suny.edu
RADIONOFF, Kathleen, A 608-258-2309.. 523 F
kradionoff@madisoncollege.edu
RADISH, Ross .... 215-596-7573.. 422 A
r.radish@usciences.edu
RADKE, Cheryl .... 623-245-4600.... 17 G
cradke@uticuti.edu
RADKE, Suzette .... 712-749-2044.. 170 D
radkes@bvu.edu
RADLIFF, Mary .... 518-255-5211.. 334 D
radliffmd@cobleskill.edu
RADLOWSKI, Mark, E .... 315-792-5467.. 321 G
mradlowski@mvcc.edu
RADSON, Darrell, J .... 309-677-2255.. 136 B
radson@bradley.edu
RADT, Jennifer .... 513-732-8964.. 379 C
jennifer.radt@uc.edu
RADTKE, Elizabeth, L .... 651-523-2201.. 247 A
bradtke@hamline.edu
RADTKE, Scott, W .... 920-832-6574.. 517 E
scott.w.radtke@lawrence.edu
RADULESCU, Eugen .... 713-348-6725.. 464 E
eugen@rice.edu
RADVANSKY, Sandy, M .. 740-284-5357.. 368 L
sradvansky@franciscan.edu
RADWAN, Ann .... 509-963-3612.. 501 K
intlprog@cwu.edu
RADYCKI, Diane .... 610-861-1627.. 411 B
dradycki@moravian.edu
RAE, Jon .... 813-988-5131.. 100 F
raej@floridacollege.edu
RAE, Lisa .... 802-258-3149.. 485 A
lisa.rae@worldlearning.org
RAE, Mike, E .... 570-326-3761.. 413 O
mrae@pct.edu
RAE, Nicol .... 406-994-5023.. 277 C
nicol.rae@montana.edu
RAE, Rosemarie .... 510-642-5737.... 68 M
rrae@berkeley.edu
RAEBER, Michael .... 706-542-0006.. 128 E
mraeber@uga.edu
RAEFORD, James, E .... 540-828-5408.. 487 H
jraeford@bridgewater.edu
RAEHL, Cindy .... 325-696-0544.. 472 D
cynthia.raehl@ttuhsc.edu
RAEL, Sylvia .... 970-248-1029.... 77 L
srael@coloradomesa.edu
RAFATTI, Colleen .... 863-784-7411.. 109 G
colleen.rafatti@southflorida.edu
RAFELD, Jessica .... 920-403-3071.. 519 G
jessica.rafeld@snc.edu
RAFFAELLE, Ryne .... 585-475-2055.. 327 E
ryne.raffaelle@rit.edu
RAFFAELLI, Bethany, M ... 920-924-6431.. 524 B
braffaelli@morainepark.edu
RAFFENSPERGER,
Thomas .... 413-572-5233.. 222 E
traffensperger@westfield.ma.edu
RAFFETTO, William .... 281-998-6150.. 465 A
william.raffetto@sjcd.edu
RAFIEE, Farnoosh .... 606-326-2069.. 188 N
farnoosh.rafiee@kctcs.edu
RAFIEYMEHR, Ali .... 603-542-7744.. 286 G
arafieymehr@ccsnh.edu
RAFN, H. Jeffrey .... 920-498-5411.. 524 E
jeff.rafn@nwtc.edu
RAFOOL, Dawn, M .... 863-638-3818.. 115 C
dawn.rafool@warner.edu
RAFOTH, Mary Ann .... 412-397-6020.. 418 B
rafoth@rmu.edu
RAFTERY, OP, Paul .... 805-525-4417.... 67 J
praftery@thomasaquinas.edu
RAGAIN, Charles .... 281-649-3314.. 458 L
cragain@hbu.edu
RAGAN, Jody .... 515-961-1517.. 176 H
jody.ragan@simpson.edu
RAGAN, Kathleen, E .... 973-655-3450.. 293 A
ragank@mail.montclair.edu
RAGAN, McKenzie .... 229-732-5956.. 116 C
mckenzielragan@andrewcollege.edu
RAGAN, Nola .... 605-698-3966.. 436 K
nragan@swc.tc
RAGAN, Ronald, E .... 336-841-9193.. 345 A
rragan@highpoint.edu
RAGER, Michael .... 270-926-4040.. 188 E
mrager@daymarcollege.edu
RAGGO, Alan .... 812-888-5640.. 169 A
araggo@vinu.edu
RAGHAVAN, Padma .... 615-322-6067.. 449 A
padma.raghavan@vanderbilt.edu
RAGINS-RILEY, Anika ...... 856-222-9311.. 295 C
ariley@rcbc.edu
RAGLAND, Ethel .... 630-829-6583.. 135 F
eragland@ben.edu
RAGLAND, Heather .... 901-272-5124.. 442 B
hragland@mca.edu
RAGLAND, Janet .... 903-233-3815.. 460 J
janetragland@letu.edu
RAGLAND, Lori .... 618-437-5321.. 152 A
ragland@rlc.edu
RAGLAND, Matthew .... 334-244-3138...... 2 A
mragland@aum.edu
RAGNO, John .... 718-489-5364.. 328 D
jragno@sfc.edu
RAGNO, Kerry, S .... 757-822-1187.. 498 H
kragno@tcc.edu
RAGO, Jim .... 229-249-2672.. 130 A
jim.rago@wiregrass.edu
RAGSDALE, Chad .... 417-626-1234.. 269 K
ragsdale.chad@occ.edu
RAGSDALE, Jaime .... 978-478-3400.. 227 C
jaragsdale@northpoint.edu
RAGSDALE, Jennifer .... 201-761-6062.. 296 K
jragsdale@saintpeters.edu
RAGSDALE, Jonathan .... 978-478-3400.. 227 C
jragsdale@northpoint.edu
RAGSDALE, Lisa, B .... 704-233-8710.. 359 H
lisa.ragsdale@wingate.edu
RAGSDALE, JR., Roy Lee 704-233-8118.. 359 H
lragsdale@wingate.edu
RAGUSA, Sal .... 510-436-1008.... 46 E
ragusa@hnu.edu
RAH, Yumee .... 213-381-0081.... 47 C
yumeerah@irus.edu
RAHE, April .... 816-531-5223.. 263 H
arahe@concorde.edu
RAHM, Clare .... 216-687-5541.. 366 I
c.rahm@csuohio.edu
RAHMAN, Pervez .... 773-907-4452.. 137 E
prahman@ccc.edu
RAHMAN, Syedur .... 703-764-7384.. 497 H
syrahman@nvcc.edu
RAHMANI, Loretta .... 909-593-3511.... 71 B
lrahmani@laverne.edu
RAHMANN, Jack .... 512-245-2124.. 471 F
jcr140@txstate.edu
RAHMATIAN, Marteza ...... 657-278-1637.... 33 A
mrahmatian@fullerton.edu
RAHMLOW, Jeff .... 920-686-6166.. 519 H
jeff.rahmlow@sl.edu
RAHN, Adria .... 248-204-3030.. 237 B
bookstore@ltu.edu
RAHN, Daniel .... 501-686-5680.... 23 C
drahn@uams.edu
RAHN, Debra .... 618-235-2700.. 155 C
RAHN, Diane .... 419-251-1726.. 372 C
diane.rahn@mercycollege.edu
RAHN, Jason, M .... 651-641-8706.. 246 B
rahn@csp.edu
RAHN, Joel .... 512-313-3000.. 455 F
joel.rahn@concordia.edu
RAHNI, Michael .... 213-383-8999.... 25 F
RAHR, JR., Carl, H .... 607-587-3535.. 334 G
rahrch@alfredstate.edu
RAHUSEN, Jenifer .... 800-686-7022.... 88 C
jrahusen@lincolncollegene.edu
RAI, Mitali .... 937-484-1400.. 380 E
mitali.rai@urbana.edu
RAI, Sanjay .... 240-567-5006.. 209 E
sanjay.rai@montgomerycollege.edu
RAIBLEY, Jon .... 503-517-1899.. 396 F
jraibley@westernseminary.edu
RAICH, Michael .... 218-262-6702.. 249 E
michaelraich@hibbing.edu
RAICHE, Carol .... 978-232-2068.. 218 D
craiche@endicott.edu
RAICHE, Cheryl .... 617-217-9212.. 215 B
craiche@baystate.edu
RAICHIK, Shimon .... 323-937-2079.... 75 G
RAIKES, Mark, H .... 574-372-5100.. 161 B
raikesmh@grace.edu
RAIKES-COLBERT,
Deborah .... 845-575-3000.. 320 B
deborah.raikes-colbert@marist.edu
RAILEY, Clay .... 410-827-5806.. 207 A
crailey@chesapeake.edu
RAILEY, George, A .... 805-922-6966.... 25 I
grailey@hancockcollege.edu
RAILEY, James, H .... 417-268-1014.. 262 F
raileyj@evangel.edu
RAILEY, Kevin .... 585-385-8402.. 328 E
krailey@sjfc.edu
RAIMER, Ben, G .... 409-747-2789.. 478 A
bgraimer@utmb.edu
RAIMO, James .... 845-569-3227.. 322 B
james.raimo@msmc.edu
RAIMO, James .... 845-569-3202.. 322 B
james.raimo@msmc.edu
RAINBOW, Deanna .... 701-627-4738.. 361 H
drainb@nhsc.edu
RAINE, Meredith .... 713-500-3050.. 477 C
meredith.raine@uth.tmc.edu
RAINE, Michael .... 505-454-3405.. 300 F
mraine@nmhu.edu
RAINER, Art .... 919-761-2100.. 355 I
arainer@sebts.edu
RAINER, Don .... 205-652-3576...... 9 F
drainer@uwa.edu
RAINER, Kairyn .... 617-585-1100.. 226 F
kairyn.rainer@necmusic.edu
RAINES, Amanda .... 940-552-6291.. 478 D
araines@vernoncollege.edu
RAINES, Deborah .... 703-284-1530.. 492 A
debbie.raines@marymount.edu
RAINES, Jeremy .... 859-622-2977.. 188 F
jeremy.raines@eku.edu
RAINES, Jess, N .... 740-374-8716.. 381 A
jraines@wscc.edu
RAINES, Patrick .... 615-460-6000.. 438 J
pat.raines@belmont.edu
RAINES, Ruby .... 940-565-2026.. 475 A
ruby.raines@unt.edu
RAINEY, Christie .... 818-767-0888.... 75 D
christie.rainey@woodbury.edu
RAINEY, Jack, T .... 973-618-3230.. 290 A
jrainey@caldwell.edu
RAINEY, Jamie .... 325-481-9300.. 459 D
jrainey@howardcollege.edu
RAINEY, Kelli .... 704-378-3553.. 345 E
krainey@jcsu.edu
RAINEY, Nicole .... 785-623-6167.. 183 J
nrainey@ncktc.edu
RAINEY, Shawn .... 859-572-6532.. 192 B
raineys1@nku.edu

RAINFORD, William .... 202-319-5454.... 92 A
rainford@cua.edu

RAINONE, John, J .... 540-863-2827.. 496 H
rrainone@dslcc.edu

RAINS, Ben .... 501-812-2268.... 21 H
brains@pulaskitech.edu

RAINS, Brian .... 417-268-6036.. 262 H
brains@gobbc.edu

RAINS, Jerry .... 863-667-5197.. 109 L
jdrains@seu.edu

RAINS, TJ .... 636-949-4347.. 266 J
trains@lindenwood.edu

RAINS, Valerie .... 417-873-6965.. 264 H
vrains@drury.edu

RAINWATER, Jeanetta ...... 918-781-7263.. 382 D
rainwaterj@bacone.edu

RAIOLA, Lisa .... 401-254-3302.. 426 B
lraiola@rwu.edu

RAISANEN, Gregg .... 320-762-4618.. 248 J
greggr@alextech.edu

RAISH, Brad .... 618-468-3160.. 145 G
braish@lc.edu

RAISIAN, John .... 650-723-1198.... 66 I
raisian@hoover.stanford.edu

RAISOR, Jeremy .... 928-524-7462.... 15 J
jeremy.raisor@npc.edu

RAISOVICH, Andy .... 304-367-4682.. 513 B
andy.raisovich@fairmontstate.edu

RAISOVICH, Joanie .... 304-367-4131.. 513 B
joanie.raisovich@fairmontstate.edu

RAJA, Jay .... 704-687-5737.. 358 A
jraja@uncc.edu

RAJA, Tasleem .... 312-427-9580.. 139 G
tasleem@eastwest.edu

RAJAGOPALAN, Balaji ..... 815-753-1755.. 150 A
brajagopalan@niu.edu

RAJAGOPALAN, Hari, K .. 843-661-1420.. 430 B
hrajagopalan@fmarion.edu

RAJALA, Sarah .... 515-294-9988.. 169 G
rajala@iastate.edu

RAJAN, Altaf .... 415-442-7859.... 45 B
arajan@ggu.edu

RAJAN, Ravi .... 914-251-6750.. 334 C
ravi.rajan@purchase.edu

RAJASEKARAN,
Senthil, K .... 757-446-5630.. 489 B
rajasesk@evms.edu

RAJMAIRA, Christina .... 703-284-1615.. 492 A
christina.rajmaira@marymount.edu

RAJPUROHIT, Vikas .... 817-515-1254.. 467 A
vikas.rajpurohit@tccd.edu

RAJPUT, Hussein .... 651-523-2204.. 247 A
hrajput01@hamline.edu

RAKER, Keith .... 336-249-8186.. 349 C
kdraker@davidsonccc.edu

RAKES, Lee, L .... 540-464-7345.. 499 E
rakesel@vmi.edu

RAKES, Thomas, D .... 910-962-3174.. 358 D
rakest@uncw.edu

RAKESTRAW, Jennie .... 803-323-2151.. 435 B
rakestrawj@winthrop.edu

RAKHSHA, Deborah, B ..... 801-581-3325.. 481 M
debbie.rakhsha@utah.edu

RAKITA, Gordon, F .... 904-620-2820.. 112 B
grakita@unf.edu

RAKOW, Ernest, A .... 901-678-2399.. 445 C
erakow@memphis.edu

RALEY, Karen, C .... 240-895-3219.. 210 E
kcraley@smcm.edu

RALEY, Leonard, R .... 301-445-1941.. 211 D
raley@usmd.edu

RALL, John, P .... 270-809-3399.. 192 A
jrall@murraystate.edu

RALLIS, Jessica .... 203-576-4804.... 89 C
ubbookstore@bbasolutions.com

RALLS, Diana .... 559-278-4240.... 32 F
rallsd@csufresno.edu

RALLS, Diana .... 209-228-4306.... 70 A
dralls@ucmerced.edu

RALLS, Pam .... 314-837-6777.. 271 B
pralls@stlchristian.edu

RALLS, Scott .... 703-323-3101.. 497 H
sralls@nvcc.edu

RALPH, Brian, C .... 919-508-2220.. 359 G
officeofthepresident@peace.edu

RALPH, David .... 580-774-3191.. 388 C
david.ralph@swosu.edu

RALPH, Emily .... 973-408-3635.. 291 B
eralph@drew.edu

RALPH, James .... 802-443-5320.. 484 F
ralph@middlebury.edu

RALPH, Ken .... 719-389-6945.... 77 J
ken.ralph@coloradocollege.edu

RALPH, Lynette .... 504-520-7304.. 202 C
lralph@xula.edu

RALPH, Nicole, M .... 217-786-2342.. 146 E
nicole.ralph@llcc.edu

RALPH, Scott .... 317-955-6789.. 165 N
sralph@marian.edu

RALSTON, Craig .... 928-776-2311.... 18 D
craig.ralston@yc.edu

RALSTON, Nancy, M .... 402-552-2557.. 279 D
ralston@clarksoncollege.edu

RALSTON, Pamela .... 760-862-1340.... 40 B
pralston@collegeofthedesert.edu

RALSTON, Steven, M .... 606-783-2002.. 191 H
s.ralston@moreheadstate.edu

RALSTON, Tracy .... 203-596-4564.... 88 F
tralston@post.edu

RALSTON, Troy .... 804-727-6826.. 127 D
tralston@southuniversity.edu

RAM, Rosalind .... 808-675-3589.. 130 E
rose.ram@byuh.edu

RAMAEKERS, Eric .... 907-796-6255.... 10 H
esramaekers@alaska.edu

RAMAGE, Emily .... 217-234-5403.. 145 D
eramage@lakeland cc. l.us

RAMAGE, Sarah .... 323-259-2664.... 55 A
sramage@oxy.edu

RAMAGE, Thomas, R .... 217-351-2231.. 151 B
ramage@parkland.edu

RAMAKER, Dawn .... 641-585-8197.. 177 F
ramakerd@waldorf.edu

RAMAKER, Jason .... 641-585-8160.. 177 F
ramakerj@waldorf.edu

RAMAKRISHNAN, Jolly ... 610-399-2032.. 414 F
jramakrishnan@cheyney.edu

RAMALHO, Erika, A .... 814-871-5584.. 404 A
ramalho001@gannon.edu

RAMAN, Jaishankar .... 219-464-6880.. 168 F
jaishankar.raman@valpo.edu

RAMAN, Saravana .... 714-300-0300.... 65 I
sraman@scitech.edu

RAMANATHAN, Pamela ... 215-596-8891.. 422 A
p.ramanathan@usciences.edu

RAMARUI, Robert .... 680-488-2471.. 530 E
roramarui@gmail.com

RAMASWAMY, Nandini ..... 317-940-9032.. 159 K
nramaswa@butler.edu

RAMBEAU, Nadine .... 661-255-1050.... 30 E
nrambeau@calarts.edu

RAMBIKUR, Sara .... 512-892-2835.. 454 I

RAMBISH, Medea .... 630-466-7900.. 157 K
mrambish@waubonsee.edu

RAMBO, Bill .... 509-533-7038.. 502 I
bill.rambo@scc.spokane.edu

RAMBO, Helen .... 405-466-3260.. 383 M
hsrambo@langston.edu

RAMBO, Thomas, A .... 540-375-2310.. 493 H
rambo@roanoke.edu

RAMCHAND, Latha .... 713-743-4604.. 473 F
ramchand@uh.edu

RAMDATH, Danielle, D .... 413-585-3017.. 228 D
dramdath@smith.edu

RAMDATH, Sanjay .... 718-289-5705.. 307 C
sanjay.ramdath@bcc.cuny.edu

RAMER, Rod .... 509-434-5325.. 503 A
rod.ramer@ccs.spokane.edu

RAMER, Rod .... 509-434-5325.. 502 H
rramer@ccs.spokane.edu

RAMER, Rodney .... 509-434-5325.. 502 I
rod.ramer@ccs.spokane.edu

RAMES, Marysz .... 402-375-7200.. 281 J
marames1@wsc.edu

RAMESH, S, K .... 818-677-4501.... 34 A
s.ramesh@csun.edu

RAMET, Carlos .... 989-964-4042.. 240 F
ramet@svsu.edu

RAMEY, JR., Alfred, E .... 201-200-2039.. 293 C
aramey@njcu.edu

RAMEY, Diana, M .... 254-710-2005.. 452 H
diana_ramey@baylor.edu

RAMEY, Iris .... 757-723-6836.. 490 E
iris.ramey@hamptonu.edu

RAMEY, Lane .... 816-501-4633.. 270 J
lane.ramey@rockhurst.edu

RAMEY, Rob .... 336-334-4822.. 350 B
grramey@gtcc.edu

RAMEY, Teresa .... 843-661-1182.. 430 B
tramey@fmarion.edu

RAMEZANE, Marsha .... 650-574-6413.... 62 H
ramezanem@smccd.edu

RAMGOLAM, Geoffrey ...... 954-745-6960.... 93 F

RAMI, Janet .... 225-771-3266.. 199 H
janet_rami@subr.edu

RAMICONE, Arthur, G ...... 412-624-6576.. 421 G
aramicone@cfo.pitt.edu

RAMIG, JR., Steven, M .... 608-342-3961.. 521 A
ramigs@uwplatt.edu

RAMIN, Daniel .... 315-470-4933.. 334 E
dwramin@esf.edu

RAMIREZ, Alfred .... 818-240-1000.... 45 A
aramirez@glendale.edu

RAMIREZ, Amador .... 361-354-2554.. 454 G
aramirez@coastalbend.edu

RAMIREZ, Amy .... 410-706-7488.. 211 F
aramirez@umaryland.edu

RAMIREZ, Arnold .... 979-230-3235.. 453 A
arnold.ramirez@brazosport.edu

RAMIREZ, Arturo .... 309-438-5590.. 143 B
aramir@ilstu.edu

RAMIREZ, Aurelio .... 617-879-7847.. 222 A
aramirez@massart.edu

RAMIREZ, Cecilia .... 757-825-3525.. 498 G
ramirezc@tncc.edu

RAMIREZ, Daniel .... 956-872-2580.. 465 H
dramirez@southtexascollege.edu

RAMIREZ, David .... 610-328-8175.. 419 I
dramire1@swarthmore.edu

RAMIREZ, Desiree .... 404-756-8919.. 125 A
dramirez@msm.edu

RAMIREZ, Edward .... 614-837-4088.. 380 G
ramireze@valorcollege.com

RAMIREZ, Fausto .... 718-960-8593.. 308 B
fausto.ramirez@lehman.cuny.edu

RAMIREZ, Freddy .... 760-757-2121.... 52 K
framirez@miracosta.edu

RAMIREZ, Glenda .... 281-487-1170.. 469 F
gramirez@txchiro.edu

RAMIREZ, Irving .... 347-964-8600.. 305 I
iramirez@boricuacollege.edu

RAMIREZ, Jason .... 435-586-7700.. 481 N
jasonramirez@suu.edu

RAMIREZ, Jose .... 787-620-2040.. 530 F
jramirez@aupr.edu

RAMIREZ, Jose, L .... 915-831-2634.. 457 H
jramir20@epcc.edu

RAMIREZ, Juan .... 909-469-5622.... 74 K
jramirez@westernu.edu

RAMIREZ, Kathy .... 406-447-5185.. 276 B
kramirez@carroll.edu

RAMIREZ, Laura, M .... 323-265-8641.... 49 G
ramirelm@elac.edu

RAMIREZ, Lcida, R .... 787-704-1020.. 532 H
lramirez@edicccollege.edu

RAMIREZ, Maria Luisa .... 956-721-5394.. 460 F
mlramirez@laredo.edu

RAMIREZ, Mayra, I .... 787-723-4481.. 531 D
mramirez@ceaprc.edu

RAMIREZ, Miguel .... 305-899-3647.... 96 D
maramirez@barry.edu

RAMIREZ, Minita .... 956-326-2278.. 468 A
minita@tamiu.edu

RAMIREZ, Octavio .... 256-726-7340...... 6 B
oramirez@oakwood.edu

RAMIREZ, Patricia .... 561-912-1211.... 99 J
pramirez@evergladesuniversity.edu

RAMIREZ, Rosemary .... 520-494-5471.... 12 J
rosemary.ramirez@centralaz.edu

RAMIREZ, Sam .... 361-825-5826.. 468 E
samuel.ramirez@tamucc.edu

RAMIREZ, Sam .... 440-826-2908.. 363 M
sramirez@bw.edu

RAMIREZ, Sylvia .... 608-243-4587.. 523 F
sframirez@madisoncollege.edu

RAMIREZ, Yvonne .... 718-430-2544.. 341 G
yvonne.ramirez@aecom.yu.edu

RAMIREZ-CARLO, III
Bolivar .... 787-620-2040.. 530 F
bramirez@aupr.edu

RAMIREZ-FIGUEROA,
Jose .... 787-620-2040.. 530 F
jramirez@aupr.edu

RAMIREZ-GELPI, Sofia .... 805-922-6966.... 25 I
sgelpi@hancockcollege.edu

RAMIREZ-JASSO, Diana .. 617-262-5000.. 216 A
diana.ramirez-jasso@the-bac.edu

RAMIREZ-PEREZ, Felicia . 602-285-7558.... 14 F
felicia.a.ramirez-perez@phoenixcollege.edu

RAMIREZ-RIVERA, Rafael 787-878-5475.. 533 H
rramirez@arecibo.inter.edu

RAMKARAN, Arshaw .... 212-650-5824.. 307 E
aramkaran@ccny.cuny.edu

RAMKUMAR, S. Manian .. 585-475-5955.. 327 E
smrmet@rit.edu

RAMLER, Tom .... 903-434-8175.. 462 M
tramler@ntcc.edu

RAMM, Jennifer .... 254-295-5527.. 474 E
jramm@umhb.edu

RAMMING, Ron .... 918-463-2931.. 383 F
rronald@connorsstate.edu

RAMON, Deanna Rene .... 580-349-1556.. 385 F
rene.ramon@opsu.edu

RAMON, Luciano .... 956-721-5316.. 460 F
lramon@laredo.edu

RAMON, Ralph .... 325-574-7625.. 479 I
rramon@wtc.edu

RAMON, Scott .... 816-802-3473.. 266 D
sramon@kcai.edu

RAMONES, Eric .... 408-848-4753.... 44 I
eramones@gavilan.edu

RAMONT, John .... 760-346-8041.... 40 B
jramont@collegeofthedesert.edu

RAMOS, Ann .... 805-898-4018.... 43 K
aramos@fielding.edu

RAMOS, Angela .... 787-725-6500.. 531 C
aramos@albizu.edu

RAMOS, Anthony .... 210-805-1201.. 474 D
aramos@uiwtx.edu

RAMOS, Antonio .... 787-284-1912.. 534 C
aramos@ponce.inter.edu

RAMOS, Charlene .... 248-204-2334.. 237 B
cramos@ltu.edu

RAMOS, Chelsea .... 718-289-5153.. 307 C
chelsea.ayala@bcc.cuny.edu

RAMOS, Cynthia .... 602-285-7410.... 14 F
cynthia.ramos@phoenixcollege.edu

RAMOS, Daisy .... 787-738-2161.. 538 A
daisy.ramos@upr.edu

RAMOS, David, L .... 787-834-9595.. 536 E
dramos@uaa.edu

RAMOS, Derek .... 620-276-9559.. 181 C
derek.ramos@gcccks.edu

RAMOS, Edith .... 787-878-6000.. 532 O
eramos@icprjc.edu

RAMOS, Edwin .... 787-815-0000.. 537 F
edwin.ramos7@upr.edu

RAMOS, Gladys .... 787-738-2161.. 538 A
gladys.ramos@upr.edu

RAMOS, Irma .... 714-808-4810.... 54 F
iramos@nocccd.edu

RAMOS, Isamel .... 787-738-2161.. 538 A
ismael.ramos1@upr.edu

RAMOS, Josue .... 787-878-5475.. 533 H
jramos@arecibo.inter.edu

RAMOS, Kenneth .... 520-626-1197.... 17 I
ksramos@email.arizona.edu

RAMOS, Maria .... 903-886-5091.. 468 D
maria.ramos@tamuc.edu

RAMOS, Maria, A .... 787-863-2390.. 533 K
maria.ramos@fajardo.inter.edu

RAMOS, Nancy, L .... 401-254-3455.. 426 B
nramos@rwu.edu

RAMOS, Patricia .... 310-434-3311.... 63 F
ramos_patricia@smc.edu

RAMOS, Patricia, A .... 718-289-5896.. 307 C
patricia.ramos@bcc.cuny.edu

RAMOS, Remigio .... 406-656-9950.. 278 H

RAMOS, Richard, O .... 515-961-1536.. 176 H
rich.ramos@simpson.edu

RAMOS, Ronald .... 470-578-3013.. 123 J
rramos@kennesaw.edu

RAMOS, Sylvia .... 336-750-8759.. 359 B
ramossc@wssu.edu

RAMOS, Victor, E .... 717-358-2975.. 405 C
veramos@hacc.edu

RAMOS, Wilberto .... 256-761-8757...... 7 F
wramos@talladega.edu

RAMOS, Yolanda .... 432-685-4733.. 461 H
yramos@midland.edu

RAMOS MARTÍNEZ,
Diana, N .... 787-884-3838.. 530 G
profdg5@atenascollege.edu

RAMOS-WALKER,
Kristine .... 952-995-1406.. 249 D
kristine.ramoswalker@hennepintech.edu

RAMOSKA, John .... 518-861-2519.. 320 A
jramoska@mariacollege.edu

RAMPAUL, Andre .... 212-757-1190.. 304 B
arampaul@funeraleducation.org

RAMPERSAD, Dave .... 334-386-7100...... 3 I
drampersad@faulkner.edu

RAMPERSAD, Dave .... 334-386-7105...... 3 I
drampersad@faulkner.edu

RAMPINO, Tatiana .... 203-576-5990.... 89 A
trampino@stvincentscollege.edu

RAMPP, Carrie .... 717-358-4161.. 403 J
carrie.rampp@fandm.edu

RAMS, Richard .... 714-484-7355.... 54 G
rrams@cypresscollege.edu

RAMS, Richard .... 714-484-7374.... 54 G
rrams@cypresscollege.edu

RAMSAMMY, Jillian .... 352-854-2322.... 97 R
jillian.ramsammy@cf.edu

RAMSAMMY, Roger .... 305-237-8907.. 105 D
rramsamm@mdc.edu

RAMSARAN, Dave .... 570-372-4757.. 419 H
ramsaran@susqu.edu

RAMSAY, Darlene .... 573-341-4584.. 274 B
ramsayd@mst.edu

RAMSAY, John R, C .... 434-223-7154.. 490 D
jramsay@hsc.edu

RAMSAY, Kerr, C .... 336-841-9148.. 345 A
kramsay@highpoint.edu

RAMSAY, Kimberly .... 310-377-5501.... 51 G
kramsay@marymountcalifornia.edu

RAMSAY, Timothy, C ...... 305-284-4006.. 114 H
tramsay@miami.edu

RAMSDELL, Nancy, M ..... 508-929-8605.. 222 F
nramsdell@worcester.edu

RAMSDELL, Twyla .... 651-213-4180.. 247 B
tramsdell@hazeldenbettyford.edu

RAMSDEN-MEIER,
Joanna .... 319-226-2004.. 169 D
joanna.ramsden-meier@allencollege.edu

RAMSEY, Betty Jo .... 910-642-7141.. 353 C
bettyjo.ramsey@sccnc.edu

RAMSEY, David .... 813-253-6227.. 114 M
dramsey@ut.edu

RAMSEY, Gerald .... 619-388-7810.... 60 H
gramsey@sdccd.edu

RAMSEY, James, R .... 502-852-5417.. 194 A
jrrams02@louisville.edu
RAMSEY, Julie .... 865-981-8246.. 441 H
julie.ramsey@maryvillecollege.edu
RAMSEY, Julie, L .... 717-337-6921.. 404 C
ramsey@gettysburg.edu
RAMSEY, Katie .... 503-517-7904.. 394 I
kramsey@reed.edu
RAMSEY, Kimberly .... 310-377-5501.... 51 G
kramsey@marymountcalifornia.edu
RAMSEY, Kyle, H .... 630-515-6165.. 148 C
kramse@midwestern.edu
RAMSEY, Mae .... 540-362-6519.. 490 F
mramsey@hollins.edu
RAMSEY, Marleen .... 509-527-4289.. 508 F
marleen.ramsey@wwcc.edu
RAMSEY, Marty .... 828-227-7335.. 359 A
mramsey@wcu.edu
RAMSEY, Matthew .... 913-360-7387.. 178 I
mramsey@benedictine.edu
RAMSEY, Nancy, A .... 865-694-6526.. 446 G
naramsey@pstcc.edu
RAMSEY, Patricia .... 484-365-7436.. 409 B
RAMSEY, Paul, G .... 206-543-7718.. 508 E
pramsey@uw.edu
RAMSEY, Vickie .... 530-251-8852.... 48 E
vramsey@lassencollege.edu
RAMSEY-HAMACHER,
Paige .... 352-588-8489.. 108 C
paige.ramsey.hamacher@saintleo.edu
RAMSEYER, Larry, E .... 989-686-9234.. 233 I
larryramseyer@delta.edu
RAMSEYER, Rob .... 620-327-8279.. 181 G
rob.ramseyer@hesston.edu
RAMSIER, Rex .... 330-972-7593.. 378 G
provost@uakron.edu
RAMSOWER, Reagan .... 254-710-3554.. 452 H
reagan_ramsower@baylor.edu
RAMÍREZ, Manuel .... 787-884-3838.. 530 G
asisteco@atenascollege.edu
RAMÍREZ, Xenia .... 787-265-3813.. 538 C
registro@uprm.edu
RANA, Anniqua .... 650-306-3100.... 62 G
rana@smccd.edu
RANABARGAR, Kerry, D .. 620-431-2820.. 183 H
kranabargar@neosho.edu
RANALDI, Diane .... 413-565-1000.. 215 A
dranaldi@baypath.edu
RANALLI, Carlee, K .... 814-641-3103.. 406 F
ranallc@juniata.edu
RANALLI, Robert .... 518-464-8533.. 314 A
rranalli@excelsior.edu
RANCE, DeLonn, L .... 417-268-1000.. 262 F
ranced@evangel.edu
RANCE-RONEY, Judith ..... 610-282-1100.. 402 B
judith.rance-roney@desales.edu
RANCOURT, Chad .... 646-717-9765.. 315 B
rancourt@gts.edu
RANCOURT, Fran .... 603-752-1113.. 286 H
francourt@ccsnh.edu
RAND, Amy .... 417-455-5533.. 264 E
amyrand@crowder.edu
RAND, Benjamin .... 817-515-5034.. 467 A
benjamin.rand@tccd.edu
RAND, Jonathan .... 617-879-7263.. 222 A
jrand@massart.edu
RAND, Kathryn .... 701-777-2104.. 360 C
rand@law.und.edu
RAND, Valarie .... 312-280-3500.. 142 G
vrand@aii.edu
RANDALL, Caroline .... 830-792-7224.. 465 E
carandall@schreiner.edu
RANDALL, David .... 617-253-4861.. 225 A
RANDALL, Greg .... 256-840-4166....... 6 H
grandall@snead.edu
RANDALL, Greg .... 253-566-5207.. 508 B
grandall@tacomacc.edu
RANDALL, Jennifer .... 406-657-1660.. 277 D
jennifer.randall@msubillings.edu
RANDALL, Jennifer .... 570-674-6340.. 410 K
jrandall@misericordia.edu
RANDALL, Jeremy, C .... 202-238-2444.... 93 A
jcrandall@howard.edu
RANDALL, John .... 949-214-3358.... 41 F
john.randall@cui.edu
RANDALL, Meridith .... 909-652-6131.... 37 D
meridith.randall@chaffey.edu
RANDALL, Mike .... 618-468-3130.. 145 G
mrandall@lc.edu
RANDALL, Monica, E .... 410-951-3845.. 212 E
mrandall@coppin.edu
RANDALL, Monte .... 918-549-2800.. 383 C
mrandall@mcn-nsn.gov
RANDALL, Regina .... 614-287-5343.. 367 C
rrandal2@cscc.edu
RANDALL, Robin .... 508-286-8232.. 229 F
randall_robin@wheatoncollege.edu
RANDALL, Stacey .... 630-466-7900.. 157 K
srandall@waubonsee.edu
RANDALL, Taylor .... 801-587-3869.. 481 M
taylor.randall@utah.edu
RANDALL-LEE, Valerie, J . 410-543-6080.. 213 A
vjrandall-lee@salisbury.edu
RANDAZZA, Paula .... 603-897-8303.. 287 F
prandazza@rivier.edu
RANDAZZO, Maria .... 315-445-4195.. 318 E
randazmc@lemoyne.edu
RANDAZZO, Nino .... 312-935-4000.. 152 D
nrandazzo@robertmorris.edu
RANDERSON, Janet .... 312-329-4000.. 148 F
janet.randerson@moody.edu
RANDHAWA, Sabah .... 360-650-3480.. 509 E
president@wwu.edu
RANDLE, Benjamin .... 716-829-7836.. 313 A
randleb@dyc.edu
RANDLE, John .... 231-591-2892.. 233 L
johnrandle@ferris.edu
RANDLE, Jonathan .... 601-925-3849.. 259 A
randle@mc.edu
RANDLES,
Christopher, M .... 217-351-2513.. 151 B
crandles@parkland.edu
RANDLES, Jill, A .... 559-323-2100.... 61 E
jrandles@sjcl.edu
RANDO, Robert, A .... 937-775-3409.. 381 H
robert.rando@wright.edu
RANDOLPH, A.J .... 817-735-2336.. 475 C
a.j.randolph@unthsc.edu
RANDOLPH, Adrian .... 847-491-3276.. 150 F
RANDOLPH, Angela .... 252-536-7254.. 350 C
arandolph339@halifaxcc.edu
RANDOLPH, Brennan .... 812-535-1152.. 166 K
brennan.randolph@smwc.edu
RANDOLPH, Devin, L .... 803-535-5301.. 428 B
devin.randolph@claflin.edu
RANDOLPH, Robert, M .... 617-258-5484.. 225 A
RANDOLPH, Trent .... 256-331-5260...... 6 A
trentrandolph@nwscc.edu
RANDOLPH, William .... 937-376-6575.. 365 H
wrandolph@centralstate.edu
RANDOO, Jason, J .... 434-528-5276.. 500 C
jrandoo@vul.edu
RANDORF, Lori .... 330-672-5368.. 370 I
lrandorf@kent.edu
RANDY GREEN,
Jonathan .... 937-327-7321.. 381 F
jgreen@wittenberg.edu
RANE-SZOSTAK, Donna ... 949-582-4324.... 65 G
draneszostak@saddleback.edu
RANERO-RAMIREZ,
Jessica .... 910-938-6341.. 348 G
ranero-ramirezj@coastalcarolina.edu
RANES, Rodney .... 618-395-7777.. 142 E
ranesr@iecc.edu
RANES, Shannon, T .... 727-376-6911.. 114 A
shannon.ranes@trinitycollege.edu
RANESES, Jade .... 808-853-1040.. 131 B
jaderaneses@pacrim.edu
RANEY, Jonna, G .... 405-585-5020.. 385 B
jonna.raney@okbu.edu
RANGANATHAN, Dipti ...... 214-645-6461.. 478 C
dipti.rangananathan@utsouthwestern.edu
RANGE, Ronald .... 205-391-2644...... 6 G
rrange@sheltonstate.edu
RANGEL, Andrea .... 806-716-2370.. 465 G
arangel@southplainscollege.edu
RANGEL, Mario .... 765-677-2497.. 164 B
mario.rangel@indwes.edu
RANGUETTE, Renea, L ..... 608-757-7700.. 523 A
rranguette@blackhawk.edu
RANHEIM, John .... 314-434-4044.. 264 C
john.ranheim@covenantseminary.edu
RANIERI, Tracey, M .... 607-436-2446.. 331 F
tracey.ranieri@oneonta.edu
RANJEL, Mary .... 210-924-4338.. 452 F
mary.ranjel@bua.edu
RANK, Carin .... 413-559-5385.. 219 C
RANK, Heidi .... 415-485-9451.... 40 C
hrank@marin.edu
RANK, Mark .... 717-815-1218.. 424 F
mrank@ycp.edu
RANKIN, Donna .... 479-968-0394.... 19 F
drankin@atu.edu
RANKIN, James, M .... 479-575-5900.... 22 I
rankinj@uark.edu
RANKIN, James, W .... 330-325-6191.. 373 H
jwr@neomed.edu
RANKIN, Joni .... 620-229-6232.. 184 J
joni.rankin@sckans.edu
RANKIN, Mary Ann .... 301-405-5252.. 211 E
mrankin@umd.edu
RANKIN, Mona, G .... 516-876-3160.. 333 C
rankinm@oldwestbury.edu
RANKIN, Stephanie, A ..... 717-361-1569.. 403 C
rankins@etown.edu
RANKIN, Stephen .... 214-768-4502.. 465 J
rankins@smu.edu
RANKINS, JR., Alfred ...... 601-877-6111.. 256 F
arankins@alcorn.edu
RANSDELL, Gary, A .... 270-745-4346.. 194 D
gary.ransdell@wku.edu
RANSDELL, Junell, A .... 217-786-4506.. 146 E
junell.ransdell@llcc.edu
RANSLEM, Bradley .... 402-844-7717.. 282 B
bradleyr@northeast.edu
RANSOM, Glenda .... 662-254-3592.. 260 A
gran@mvsu.edu
RANSOM, Kimberly .... 304-793-6820.. 514 A
kransom@osteo.wvsom.edu
RANSOM, Lakeesha, K .... 330-972-7966.. 378 G
lransom@uakron.edu
RANSOM, Lakeesha, K .... 330-972-5365.. 378 G
ransom@uakron.edu
RANSOM, Portia .... 630-947-8913.. 135 E
pransom@aurora.edu
RANSOM, Tafaya .... 404-222-2588.. 124 I
tafaya.ransom@morehouse.edu
RANSON, Julie .... 804-706-5122.. 497 D
jranson@jtcc.edu
RANTA, Richard, R .... 901-678-2350.. 445 C
rranta@memphis.edu
RANTZ, Rick .... 805-735-3366.... 25 I
rrantz@hancockcollege.edu
RANUM, Brenda .... 563-387-1025.. 174 L
ranubr01@luther.edu
RAO, Julie, M .... 585-245-5553.. 333 B
rao@geneseo.edu
RAO, Michael .... 804-828-1200.. 496 D
president@vcu.edu
RAPACCIOLI, Donna .... 718-817-4100.. 314 G
rapaccioli@fordham.edu
RAPALA, Elise .... 708-456-0300.. 156 C
eliserapala@triton.edu
RAPAPORT, Ross, J .... 989-774-3381.. 232 D
rapap1rj@cmich.edu
RAPE, Bruce, M .... 217-443-8786.. 139 B
brape@dacc.edu
RAPELYE, Janet, L .... 609-258-6150.. 294 D
jrapelye@princeton.edu
RAPER, Bridgette .... 423-746-5301.. 447 E
braper@twcnet.edu
RAPER, Lorraine .... 252-399-6505.. 341 P
lhraper@barton.edu
RAPESS, Paul .... 516-299-2214.. 319 C
paul.rapess@liu.edu
RAPETTI, Mario .... 914-251-6320.. 334 C
mario.rapetti@purchase.edu
RAPHAEL, Joann .... 954-378-2400.... 93 F
RAPHAEL, Joann .... 561-904-3000.... 93 F
RAPHAEL, Valencia .... 562-860-2451.... 36 P
vraphael@cerritos.edu
RAPOPORT, Nancy, B ...... 702-895-5895.. 284 L
nancy.rapoport@unlv.edu
RAPOSA, Donna .... 781-239-2500.. 223 F
draposa@massbay.edu
RAPOSA, Kristina .... 781-292-2264.. 218 H
kristina.raposa@olin.edu
RAPOZA, Kaleihi'ikapoli .. 808-932-7626.. 131 E
kaleihii@hawaii.edu
RAPOZA, Mark, F .... 401-865-2064.. 425 D
mrapoza@providence.edu
RAPP, John .... 713-798-4517.. 452 G
jrapp@bcm.edu
RAPP, Norman .... 615-329-8848.. 439 L
nrapp@fisk.edu
RAPP, Peter .... 503-494-8744.. 393 F
hutching@ohsu.edu
RAPP, Ryan .... 573-882-6435.. 273 D
rappr@umsystem.edu
RAPP, Timothy .... 301-295-4231.. 528 G
timothy.rapp@usuhs.edu
RAPP, Tracy .... 828-627-4509.. 350 D
tkrapp@haywood.edu
RAPP, Virginia .... 310-660-3773.... 42 J
vrapp@elcamino.edu
RAPP, William, E .... 717-245-4400.. 528 J
RAPPE, Sylvia .... 936-294-3188.. 471 D
str017@shsu.edu
RAPPEL, Kevin .... 630-829-6404.. 135 F
krappel@ben.edu
RAPPLEY, Carol .... 616-234-5722.. 242 D
RAPPLEY, Marsha .... 804-828-0100.. 496 D
mdrappley@vcu.edu
RAQUEL, Lisa .... 707-654-1011.... 33 D
lraquel@csum.edu
RARIG, Jenny, M .... 610-359-5148.. 401 L
jrarig@dccc.edu
RARIG, Kris .... 757-825-2801.. 498 G
rarigk@tncc.edu
RASBERRY, Todd .... 502-863-8044.. 188 I
rasberry@georgetowncollege.edu
RASCH, J. Lee .... 608-785-9210.. 524 H
raschl@westerntc.edu
RASCH, Marvin .... 309-268-8423.. 141 C
marvin.rasch@heartland.edu
RASCH, Mike .... 218-751-8670.. 254 A
mikerasch@oakhills.edu
RASCH, Randolph .... 517-355-6527.. 237 I
randolph.rasch@hc.msu.edu
RASCOE, Fred .... 931-668-7010.. 446 D
frascoe@mscc.edu
RASCON, Tricia .... 805-893-4275.... 70 E
tricia.rascon@sa.ucsb.edu
RASH, Brian .... 225-214-6976.. 199 B
brian.rash@ololcollege.edu
RASH, R. Scott .... 814-871-7464.. 404 A
rash001@gannon.edu
RASHED, Jamal .... 513-244-4273.. 373 C
jamal.rashed@msj.edu
RASHEED, Waheed .... 510-356-4760.... 76 E
RASHID, Frank, D .... 313-927-1205.. 237 E
frashid@marygrove.edu
RASHID, John .... 218-726-8821.. 255 D
jrashid@d.umn.edu
RASK, Brenda .... 303-718-5907.... 76 H
brenda.rask@aims.edu
RASK, Kevin .... 719-389-6446.... 77 J
kevin.rask@coloradocollege.edu
RASKIND, Wayne .... 313-577-2519.. 243 F
raskind@wayne.edu
RASKOVICH, Linda .... 218-262-7370.. 249 E
lindaraskovich@hibbing.edu
RASMUSSEN, Allen .... 361-593-2809.. 469 A
allen.rasmussen@tamuk.edu
RASMUSSEN, Brock .... 612-874-3749.. 247 M
brock_rasmussen@mcad.edu
RASMUSSEN, Bruce, D .... 402-280-2487.. 279 H
bdrass@creighton.edu
RASMUSSEN, Carrie, M .. 209-667-3201.... 34 E
cmrasmussen@csustan.edu
RASMUSSEN, Cheryl .... 785-442-6021.. 181 H
crasmussen@highlandcc.edu
RASMUSSEN, Connie, A .. 308-432-6366.. 281 H
crasmussen@csc.edu
RASMUSSEN, Darin .... 360-650-3555.. 509 E
darin.rasmussen@wwu.edu
RASMUSSEN, David, W .... 850-644-5488.. 111 C
dwrasmussen@admin.fsu.edu
RASMUSSEN, Jack, L .... 801-626-6273.. 482 D
jrasmussen@weber.edu
RASMUSSEN, Karla, R ..... 757-455-3316.. 500 E
krasmussen@vwc.edu
RASMUSSEN, Laurel, R .... 563-588-8000.. 172 E
lrasmussen@emmaus.edu
RASMUSSEN, Linda .... 601-266-4050.. 261 E
linda.rasmussen@usm.edu
RASMUSSEN, Michele .... 773-702-7770.. 156 D
mrasmussen@uchicago.edu
RASMUSSEN, Phil .... 425-889-5271.. 505 E
phil.rasmussen@northwestu.edu
RASMUSSEN, Rob .... 815-479-7599.. 147 E
rrasmuss@mchenry.edu
RASMUSSEN, Robert, H ... 225-578-2154.. 197 H
rrasmus@lsu.edu
RASMUSSEN, Sarah .... 605-256-5048.. 437 C
sarah.rasmussen@dsu.edu
RASMUSSEN, Schauna ...... 608-243-4478.. 523 F
slrassmussen@madisoncollege.edu
RASMUSSEN, Scott .... 208-282-2507.. 133 H
rasmscot@isu.edu
RASMUSSON, Beth .... 605-626-2655.. 437 D
beth.rasmusson@northern.edu
RASNAKE, Martha, L .... 276-964-7389.. 498 F
martha.rasnake@sw.edu
RASNICK, Becky, D .... 501-450-5200.... 24 G
rebekahr@uca.edu
RASNICK, Natalie .... 417-690-2209.. 263 E
nrasnick@cofo.edu
RASNICK, JR.,
William, B .... 423-439-7900.. 444 F
rasnick@etsu.edu
RASOR, Mark .... 918-540-6213.. 384 F
mrasor@neo.edu
RASP, Allison, M .... 512-416-5888.. 464 G
allisonm@stedwards.edu
RASPILLER, Edward, E ..... 804-594-1571.. 497 D
traspiller@jtcc.edu
RASS, Heike .... 215-972-2031.. 413 L
hrass@pafa.org
RASSOUL, Hamid .... 321-674-7573.. 100 M
rassoul@fit.edu
RAST, Lawrence, R .... 260-452-2101.. 160 D
lawrence.rast@ctsfw.edu
RASZEWSKI, Thomas .... 410-864-3621.. 210 F
traszewski@stmarys.edu
RATAICZAK, Terry .... 740-374-8716.. 381 A
trataiczak@wscc.edu
RATCHFORD, Robert .... 423-425-4074.. 448 F
robert-ratchford@utc.edu
RATCLIFF, Chris .... 870-460-1058.... 23 D
ratcliff@uamont.edu
RATCLIFF, Christine, L ..... 662-252-8000.. 260 F
cratcliff@rustcollege.edu
RATCLIFF, Lance .... 417-269-3667.. 264 D
lance.ratcliff@coxcollege.edu
RATCLIFF, Stephen .... 903-923-2011.. 457 G
sratcliff@etbu.edu
RATCLIFF, Terry .... 208-855-4024.. 134 G
dee@uidaho.edu
RATCLIFF, Terry .... 626-529-8500.... 55 H
tratcliff@pacificoaks.edu

REASSO, Bob .... 704-463-3203.. 354 F
bob.reasso@pfeiffer.edu
REAT, Daniel, J .... 713-500-3278.. 477 C
daniel.j.reat@uth.tmc.edu
REAUME, Vicki .... 734-487-2410.. 233 J
vreaume@emich.edu
REAVES, Ken .... 678-872-8512.. 121 C
kreaves@highlands.edu
REAVES, Kenneth, M .... 863-680-3007.. 101 E
kreaves@flsouthern.edu
REAVES, Nicole .... 773-481-8182.. 137 I
nreaves2@ccc.edu
REAVES, Rita .... 252-328-1418.. 356 C
reavesr@ecu.edu
REAVIS, Bob .... 785-654-2416.. 178 A
breavis@allencc.edu
REBA, Kathleen .... 516-323-3952.. 321 H
kreba@molloy.edu
REBAR, Alan .... 919-515-2117.. 357 B
ahrebar@ncsu.edu
REBER, Christopher, M ... 724-480-3400.. 401 F
chris.reber@ccbc.edu
REBETA, Gail .... 330-672-3367.. 370 I
grebeta@kent.edu
REBHORN, Dale .... 317-738-8251.. 160 J
drebhorn@franklincollege.edu
REBIK, Clint .... 707-826-6205.... 34 F
clint@humboldt.edu
REBMAN, Brenda .... 530-752-3136.... 69 A
rebman@ucdavis.edu
REBRO, Jan .... 206-239-4500.. 502 D
jrebro@cityu.edu
RECA, Michael, F .... 609-896-5080.. 295 B
reca@rider.edu
RECCHIA, Karen .... 318-678-6000.. 195 I
krecchia@bpcc.edu
RECESSO, Art .... 478-471-5722.. 124 E
art.recesso@mga.edu
RECH, Tara .... 510-594-3670.... 29 K
trech@cca.edu
RECHTSCHAFFEN,
Joyce, A .... 202-220-1364.. 294 D
jrechtsc@princeton.edu
RECINOS, Alba .... 714-808-4796.... 54 F
arecinos@nocccd.edu
RECINOS, Diane .... 973-278-5400.. 289 F
dr@berkeleycollege.edu
RECINOS, Diane .... 973-278-5400.. 305 B
dr@berkeleycollege.edu
RECINOS, Jose .... 951-571-6113.... 59 A
jose.recinos@mvc.edu
RECK, Dawn .... 513-562-8773.. 363 H
dreck@artacademy.edu
RECKER, Edward, R .... 419-434-4791.. 379 E
reckere1@findlay.edu
RECKER, Mary, A .... 937-229-4354.. 379 D
mpoirier1@udayton.edu
RECKER, OSB, Ralph .... 503-845-3320.. 392 E
ralph.recker@mtangel.edu
RECKNER, Angela, T .... 215-489-2203.. 402 A
angela.reckner@delval.edu
RECKTENWALD, Kay .... 561-297-0026.. 110 K
kreckten@fau.edu
RECORD, James .... 847-578-3000.. 153 A
RECORD, Kim .... 336-334-5952.. 358 B
ksrecord@uncg.edu
RECORD, Victoria .... 315-787-4000.. 314 E
vicki.record@flhealth.org
RECTOR, Brenda .... 865-882-4526.. 447 A
rectorbw@roanestate.edu
RECTOR, David .... 660-785-7607.. 273 B
daverec@truman.edu
RECTOR, Dawn .... 480-858-9100.... 17 B
d.rector@scnm.edu
RECTOR, Lallene, J .... 847-866-3901.. 140 G
ljr@garrett.edu
RECTOR, Rob .... 417-447-4852.. 270 A
rectorr@otc.edu
RECZNIK, Joel, S .... 740-284-5236.. 368 L
jrecznik@franciscan.edu
RECZNIK, John .... 740-283-6497.. 368 L
jlrecznik@franciscan.edu
RECZNIK, Mark, E .... 740-284-5845.. 368 L
mrecznik@franciscan.edu
RED BEAR, Donnette .... 605-698-3966.. 436 K
dredbear@swc.tc
RED OWL, Sherry .... 605-856-5880.. 436 I
sherry.redowl@sintegleska.edu
REDD, Annie .... 804-524-5070.. 499 G
aredd@vsu.edu
REDD, Cliff .... 713-743-4921.. 473 F
rbredd@central.uh.edu
REDD, Randy .... 901-751-8453.. 442 E
rredd@mabts.edu
REDD, Rea .... 724-852-3254.. 423 A
rredd@waynesburg.edu
REDD, Scott .... 703-448-3393.. 260 E
sredd@rts.edu
REDDAY, Darlene .... 605-698-3966.. 436 K
dredday@swc.tc

REDDER, Vince .... 605-995-2631.. 435 F
viredder@dwu.edu
REDDERSON, Jeff, P .... 864-294-3262.. 430 C
jeff.redderson@furman.edu
REDDICK, Chenita, R .... 410-651-8045.. 212 B
crreddick@umes.edu
REDDICK, Don .... 815-939-5111.. 150 I
dreddick@olivet.edu
REDDICK, Laura, S .... 215-468-8100.. 420 B
laura.reddick@temple.edu
REDDICK, Rinardo .... 262-691-5295.. 524 G
rreddick@wctc.edu
REDDING, Michael .... 312-996-8153.. 156 F
reddingm@uic.edu
REDDING, Richard .... 714-628-2688.... 37 F
redding@chapman.edu
REDDING, Vic .... 775-784-4901.. 284 G
vic_redding@nshe.nevada.edu
REDDINGTON, Kathleen .. 575-527-7604.. 301 C
kredding@nmsu.edu
REDDITT, Megan .... 502-863-8066.. 188 I
megan_redditt@georgetowncollege.edu
REDDY, Chandra .... 615-963-7561.. 445 A
creddy@tnstate.edu
REDDY, Indra, K .... 979-458-7200.. 468 B
indrakreddy@tamu.edu
REDDY, Kirti .... 510-723-6641.... 37 B
kreddy@chabotcollege.edu
REDDY, Michael, S .... 205-934-4720...... 8 E
mreddy@uab.edu
REDDY, Narem .... 678-466-4100.. 119 A
naremreddy@clayton.edu
REDDY, JR., Robert, A .... 440-775-8142.. 374 C
rob.reddy@oberlin.edu
REDDY, Venkateshwar ..... 719-255-3113.... 83 L
vreddy@uccs.edu
REDDY, Venkateshwar ..... 719-255-3408.... 83 L
vreddy@uccs.edu
REDELL, Rebecca .... 541-440-4631.. 395 F
rebecca.redell@umpqua.edu
REDER-SCHOPP, Megan .. 605-394-6988.. 437 E
megan.reder-schopp@sdsmt.edu
REDFERN, Mark, S .... 412-624-9019.. 421 G
mredfern@pitt.edu
REDFERN, Paul, W .... 717-337-6829.. 404 C
predfern@gettysburg.edu
REDFIELD, Chaunta .... 317-921-4780.. 164 F
credfield@ivytech.edu
REDFIELD, Vanessa .... 802-258-9244.. 484 C
vredfield@marlboro.edu
REDING, Cheryl .... 913-360-7384.. 178 I
creding@benedictine.edu
REDING, Nichole .... 503-760-3131.. 390 B
nichole@birthingway.edu
REDING, Terrence .... 585-345-6850.. 315 C
tareding@genesee.edu
REDINGER, Matthew .... 406-657-2204.. 277 D
mredinger@msubillings.edu
REDINGTON, Joseph .... 570-674-6756.. 410 K
jredingt@misericordia.edu
REDINGTON, Lyn .... 319-335-1162.. 169 H
lyn-redington@uiowa.edu
REDLEAF, Betty .... 402-878-2380.. 280 G
bredleaf@littlepriest.edu
REDLER, Susan .... 212-431-2121.. 323 H
susan.redler@nyls.edu
REDLINGER, Lawrence, J 972-883-6188.. 476 C
redling@utdallas.edu
REDMAN, Donald, L .... 717-334-6286.. 409 C
dredman@ltsg.edu
REDMAN, Martin .... 215-898-3131.. 421 E
mredman@upenn.edu
REDMAN, JR., Robert, R 912-650-5649.. 127 D
roredman@southuniversity.edu
REDMAN, Thomas, J .... 978-232-2005.. 218 D
tredman@endicott.edu
REDMON, Charlie, L .... 859-233-8287.. 193 D
credmon@transy.edu
REDMON, Kelly .... 540-869-0758.. 497 E
kredmon@lfcc.edu
REDMOND, Angie .... 641-844-5712.. 173 L
angie.redmond@iavalley.edu
REDMOND, Jeff .... 805-267-1690.... 48 F
REDMOND, Johnny .... 617-262-5000.. 216 A
johnny.redmond@the-bac.edu
REDMOND, Katrina .... 845-848-4034.. 312 F
katrina.redmond@dc.edu
REDMOND, Michael, J ..... 303-458-4944.... 82 L
mredmond@regis.edu
REDMOND, Thomas, E .... 202-274-5935.... 94 B
tredmond@udc.edu
REDO, Keith .... 516-323-4853.. 321 H
kredo@molloy.edu
REDONNETT, Rosa .... 207-973-3231.. 204 G
rosar@maine.edu
REDWAY, Sandra .... 305-284-3584.. 114 H
sredway@miami.edu
REDWINE, Marian .... 405-491-6336.. 388 A
maredwin@snu.edu
REDWINE, Mike .... 405-491-6335.. 388 A
mredwine@snu.edu

REDWINE, William .... 606-783-2680.. 191 H
b.redwine@moreheadstate.edu
REECE, Bryan .... 909-389-3202.... 60 B
breece@craftonhills.edu
REECE, E. Albert .... 410-706-7410.. 211 F
deanmed@som.umaryland.edu
REECE, Jeremy .... 870-733-6786.... 19 A
jreece@asumidsouth.edu
REECE, Jonathan .... 910-962-3122.. 358 D
reecej@uncw.edu
REECE, Lenora .... 214-860-2700.. 456 E
lenora.reece@dcccd.edu
REECE, Ronda .... 405-945-8631.. 386 C
reecer@osuokc.edu
REECE, Sheila .... 903-785-7661.. 463 E
sreece@parisjc.edu
REECE, Terry .... 805-546-3283.... 41 L
treece@cuesta.edu
REECE, Victoria .... 352-588-8668.. 108 C
victoria.reece@saintleo.edu
REECK, Joanne .... 612-330-1111.. 244 I
reeck@augsburg.edu
REED, A. Diane .... 757-594-7202.. 488 E
dreed@cnu.edu
REED, Aaron .... 801-302-2800.. 480 L
aaron.reed@neumont.edu
REED, Adrienne .... 618-468-6030.. 145 G
ayreed@lc.edu
REED, Alexis .... 304-876-5157.. 513 E
apalladi@shepherd.edu
REED, Ann, M .... 304-462-6123.. 513 C
ann.reed@glenville.edu
REED, Annie, G .... 818-947-2320.... 50 D
reedag@lavc.edu
REED, Barrett .... 870-584-1462.... 23 F
breed@cccua.edu
REED, Beverly, S .... 301-546-0495.. 210 C
reedbs@pgcc.edu
REED, Brian, V .... 802-656-0903.. 485 D
brian.reed@uvm.edu
REED, Burton, J .... 402-554-2262.. 283 B
breed@unomaha.edu
REED, Carol .... 540-362-6610.. 490 F
creed@hollins.edu
REED, Charlene, K .... 330-672-2585.. 370 I
creed2@kent.edu
REED, Christine .... 805-922-6966.... 25 I
creed@hancockcollege.edu
REED, Cristina .... 810-762-9584.. 236 C
creed@kettering.edu
REED, Cynthia .... 859-572-6069.. 192 B
reedc11@nku.edu
REED, Cynthia .... 225-771-2552.. 200 A
creed@sulc.edu
REED, Dallas .... 973-278-5400.. 305 B
dfr@berkeleycollege.edu
REED, Dallas .... 973-278-5400.. 289 F
dfr@berkeleycollege.edu
REED, Dan .... 530-898-6451.... 32 C
dmreed@csuchico.edu
REED, Daniel .... 619-201-8727.... 60 D
daniel.reed@sdcc.edu
REED, Daniel .... 319-335-2132.. 169 H
dan-reed@uiowa.edu
REED, Daniel .... 319-335-2132.. 169 H
daniel-reed@uiowa.edu
REED, Darcy, A .... 507-284-3796.. 245 F
reed.darcy@mayo.edu
REED, David, D .... 906-487-3043.. 238 A
ddreed@mtu.edu
REED, Debra .... 903-813-2445.. 451 M
dreed@austincollege.edu
REED, Dee .... 812-535-5212.. 166 K
dreed@smwc.edu
REED, Donna .... 502-213-8245.. 193 A
dreed@sctd.edu
REED, Doug .... 870-245-5167.... 21 E
reedd@obu.edu
REED, Doug .... 405-744-4244.. 385 G
doug.reed@okstate.edu
REED, Elizabeth .... 215-884-8942.. 424 B
elizabeth.reed@woninstitute.edu
REED, Eric .... 270-745-2446.. 194 D
eric.reed@wku.edu
REED, Francesca .... 703-284-5906.. 492 A
francesca.reed@marymount.edu
REED, Gary .... 214-648-2631.. 478 C
gary.reed@utsouthwestern.edu
REED, George .... 719-255-4047.... 83 L
george.reed@uccs.edu
REED, Helen .... 970-351-2601.... 84 C
helen.reed@unco.edu
REED, James .... 979-830-4168.. 452 J
james.reed@blinn.edu
REED, Jeff .... 515-292-9694.. 169 E
jeff.reed@antiochschool.edu
REED, Jeffrey, G .... 920-923-8760.. 517 H
jreed@marianuniversity.edu
REED, Jeremy .... 262-472-1440.. 521 F
reedj@uww.edu

REED, Jerry .... 570-389-4040.. 414 D
jreed@bloomu.edu
REED, Jonathan .... 909-593-3511.... 71 B
jreed@laverne.edu
REED, Karen, A .... 419-755-4538.. 373 G
kreed@ncstatecollege.edu
REED, Kathy .... 310-338-4404.... 51 E
kathy.reed@lmu.edu
REED, Kevin .... 585-245-5571.. 333 B
reedk@geneseo.edu
REED, Kevin .... 541-346-3082.. 395 G
ksreed@uoregon.edu
REED, Kim .... 208-562-3114.. 133 F
kimreed@cwidaho.cc
REED, Kimberly .... 270-745-2242.. 194 D
kim.reed@wku.edu
REED, Kristen .... 217-245-3054.. 141 G
kristen.reed@mail.ic.edu
REED, LaTonya .... 870-574-4504.... 22 G
lreed@sautech.edu
REED, Lee .... 202-687-6513.... 92 E
athleticdirector@georgetown.edu
REED, Lori .... 507-457-5005.. 252 G
lreed@winona.edu
REED, Mark .... 603-646-9410.. 286 J
mark.reed@dartmouth.edu
REED, Mark, C .... 610-660-1200.. 418 G
reed@sju.edu
REED, Mark, F .... 610-861-1360.. 411 B
reedm@moravian.edu
REED, Martin .... 209-228-2977.... 70 A
mreed9@ucmerced.edu
REED, Maryanne .... 304-293-5746.. 514 C
maryanne.reed@mail.wvu.edu
REED, Matthew .... 732-224-2265.. 289 I
REED, Meredith .... 504-398-2236.. 200 D
mreed@olhcc.edu
REED, Michael, E .... 717-245-1159.. 402 D
reedme@dickinson.edu
REED, Michael, J .... 570-326-3761.. 413 O
mjr18@pct.edu
REED, Michelle .... 985-549-2241.. 201 C
mreed@selu.edu
REED, Mike .... 618-282-6682.. 155 C
mike.reed@swic.edu
REED, Nancy .... 901-572-2662.. 438 I
nancy.reed@bchs.edu
REED, Pamela .... 806-874-3571.. 454 F
pamela.reed@clarendoncollege.edu
REED, Rahim .... 530-752-2071.... 69 A
rreed@ucdavis.edu
REED, Randy .... 972-273-3301.. 456 G
randyreed@dcccd.edu
REED, Richard .... 216-687-4736.. 366 I
r.reed68@csuohio.edu
REED, Robert .... 443-334-2240.. 211 A
rreed1951@stevenson.edu
REED, Robert, A .... 504-865-3735.. 198 E
rareed@loyno.edu
REED, Rod .... 479-524-7134.... 20 H
rreed@jbu.edu
REED, Scott .... 541-737-2713.. 393 H
scott.reed@oregonstate.edu
REED, Sharon .... 614-251-4595.. 374 I
reeds@ohiodominican.edu
REED, Shawana .... 870-235-4015.... 22 F
sreed@saumag.edu
REED, Shelby .... 712-279-5239.. 170 B
shelby.reed@briarcliff.edu
REED, Shirley, A .... 956-872-8366.. 465 H
yolandao@southtexascollege.edu
REED, Stephanie .... 610-902-1061.. 399 D
stephanie.d.reed@cabrini.edu
REED, Stephen .... 651-793-1254.. 250 A
steve.reed@metrostate.edu
REED, Steve .... 620-241-0723.. 179 L
steve.reed@centralchristian.edu
REED, Steve, E .... 417-667-8181.. 264 A
sreed@cottey.edu
REED, Steven .... 615-460-6619.. 438 J
steven.reed@belmont.edu
REED, Stuart, C .... 205-329-7898...... 3 B
stu.reed@ecacolleges.com
REED, Sue .... 484-365-7929.. 409 B
sreed@lincoln.edu
REED, Tara .... 407-888-8689.. 100 H
treed@fcim.edu
REED, Tashena .... 513-241-4338.. 363 G
tashena.reed@antonellicollege.edu
REED, Terri .... 404-270-5002.. 128 A
treed15@spelman.edu
REED, Tita .... 440-775-6200.. 374 C
tita.reed@oberlin.edu
REED, Tom .... 251-575-8283...... 1 C
treed@ascc.edu
REED, Tracy .... 989-775-4123.. 240 E
treed@sagchip.edu
REED, Van .... 337-550-1211.. 197 K
vreed@lsue.edu
REED, William, O .... 503-943-7191.. 396 B
reed@up.edu

REILLY, John .... 303-724-0882 .... 84 A john.reilly@ucdenver.edu

REILLY, John, H .... 518-956-8050 .. 331 A jreilly@albany.edu

REILLY, Joseph, R .... 973-313-6233 .. 297 A joseph.reilly@shu.edu

REILLY, Karen .... 508-793-2372 .. 217 C kreilly@holycross.edu

REILLY, Kathryn .... 203-596-4630 .... 88 F kreilly@post.edu

REILLY, Kerin .... 212-686-9244 .. 304 A kreilly@aada.edu

REILLY, Kevin .... 540-365-4407 .. 489 M kpreilly@ferrum.edu

REILLY, Lenore .... 413-538-3438 .. 226 A lreilly@mtholyoke.edu

REILLY, Madelyn .... 412-396-5181 .. 403 A reillym@duq.edu

REILLY, Marianne .... 718-862-7891 .. 319 L mreilly01@manhattan.edu

REILLY, Mary Jane .... 516-323-4702 .. 321 H mreilly@molloy.edu

REILLY, MB .... 513-556-1824 .. 379 A reillymb@ucmail.uc.edu

REILLY, Patricia .... 617-627-2000 .. 228 H patricia.reilly@tufts.edu

REILLY, Seamus .... 217-353-2170 .. 151 B sereilly@parkland.edu

REILLY, William, T .... 704-894-2765 .. 343 I wireilly@davidson.edu

REILLY-KELLY, Tracy .... 360-992-2163 .. 502 E tkelly@clark.edu

REILLY-MYKLEBUST, Alice .... 715-425-9884 .. 521 B alice.m.reilly-myklebust@uwrf.edu

REIMAN, Brock .... 765-677-1569 .. 164 B brock.reiman@indwes.edu

REIMAN, Rick .... 912-260-4480 .. 127 B rick.reiman@sgsc.edu

REIMANN, Jan .... 573-334-9181 .. 267 C jan@metrobusinesscollege.edu

REIMANN, Rick .... 518-587-2100 .. 335 D rick.reimann@esc.edu

REIMER, Denise .... 608-243-4484 .. 523 F dmreimer@madisoncollege.edu

REIMER, Mark .... 978-762-4000 .. 224 C mreimer@northshore.edu

REIMER, Martin .... 641-844-8502 .. 173 J martin.reimer@iavalley.edu

REIMER, Michael .... 201-360-4158 .. 292 B mreimer@hccc.edu

REIMER, Rachel .... 515-271-1424 .. 171 H rachel.reimer@dmu.edu

REIMER, Robert .... 773-291-6740 .. 137 G rreimer@ccc.edu

REIMONDO, Sue .... 859-985-3212 .. 187 B sue_reimondo@berea.edu

REIN, Kim .... 303-914-6260 .... 82 I kim.rein@rrcc.edu

REIN, Laura .... 314-968-7152 .. 275 B lrein@webster.edu

REINA, Juana .... 212-650-5426 .. 307 E jreina@ccny.cuny.edu

REINCKE, Nancy .... 515-271-2161 .. 171 K nancy.reincke@drake.edu

REINDERS, Gretchen .... 608-785-8073 .. 520 C greinders@uwlax.edu

REINDL, Kay .... 209-478-0800 .... 46 H kreindl@humphreys.edu

REINECK, Marilyn .... 651-641-8730 .. 246 B reineck@csp.edu

REINEHR, Craig .... 918-456-5511 .. 384 G reinehr@nsuok.edu

REINELT, Douglas, A .... 214-768-3754 .. 465 J reinelt@smu.edu

REINER, Christian .... 435-586-7783 .. 481 N christianreiner@suu.edu

REINERS, Bradley, O .... 651-255-6164 .. 255 C breiners@unitedseminary.edu

REINERT, Duane .... 660-944-2852 .. 263 G dreinert@conception.edu

REING, Linda .... 212-875-4605 .. 304 E alumrel@bankstreet.edu

REINHARD, Herb .... 229-333-5462 .. 129 G hreinhar@valdosta.edu

REINHARDT, Alan, J .... 508-213-2201 .. 227 A alan.reinhardt@nichols.edu

REINHARDT, Kathleen .... 970-521-6603 .... 81 O kathleen.reinhardt@njc.edu

REINHART, Kellee, C .... 205-348-5938 .... 8 C kreinhart@uasystem.edu

REINHART, Rose .... 419-995-8310 .. 370 G reinhart.r@rhodesstate.edu

REINHOLD, David, S .... 269-387-4564 .. 243 H david.reinhold@wmich.edu

REINISCH, Sheryl .... 503-493-6233 .. 391 A sreinisch@cu-portland.edu

REINKE, Brenda .... 405-682-7510 .. 385 D breinke@occc.edu

REINKE, Mary, M .... 414-410-4202 .. 515 I mmreinke1@stritch.edu

REINKING, Jackie .... 212-686-9244 .. 304 A

REINL, Cindy, M .... 920-433-6660 .. 515 F cindy.reinl@bellincollege.edu

REINLAND, Jeffrey, E .... 509-527-4312 .. 508 F jeffrey.reinland@wwcc.edu

REINLIE, Carla .... 850-729-5357 .. 105 I reinliec@nwfsc.edu

REINOEHL, Jason, K .... 937-229-3725 .. 379 D jreinoehl@udayton.edu

REINSCH FRIESE, Ellen .... 937-775-2709 .. 381 H ellen.friese@wright.edu

REINSCHMIEDT, Lynn .... 662-325-3473 .. 259 D lynn.reinschmiedt@msstate.edu

REIS, Sally .... 860-486-4240 .... 89 D sally.reis@uconn.edu

REIS, Sally .... 860-486-4037 .... 89 D sally.reis@uconn.edu

REISBERG, Darren .... 773-702-7618 .. 156 D reisberg@uchicago.edu

REISBERG, Jeff .... 727-873-4552 .. 112 D reisberg@mail.usf.edu

REISECK, Carol, J .... 708-209-3262 .. 138 G carol.reiseck@cuchicago.edu

REISENAUER, Eric .... 803-938-3862 .. 434 E ericr@uscsumter.edu

REISENAUER, Janet .... 701-483-2532 .. 360 D janet.reisenauer@dickinsonstate.edu

REISER, Cyrill .... 818-785-2726 .... 36 M

REISER, Sharon .... 805-525-4417 .... 67 J sreiser@thomasaquinas.edu

REISETTER, Mary .... 641-585-8681 .. 177 F reisettem@waldorf.edu

REISETTER-HART, Judith .... 414-382-6431 .. 515 D judith.reisetter@alverno.edu

REISH, Brenda, J .... 800-287-8822 .. 159 C reishbr@bethanyseminary.edu

REISIG, Jerry .... 212-870-1213 .. 324 B jreisig@nyts.edu

REISING, Gregory .... 410-704-2512 .. 213 B greising@towson.edu

REISING, Paula .... 912-650-5687 .. 127 D preising@southuniversity.edu

REISINGER, Amanda, B .... 740-588-1275 .. 382 C amreisinger@zanestate.edu

REISINGER, Cynthia, E .... 717-815-1221 .. 424 F creising@ycp.edu

REISINGER, Tracy .... 503-699-6253 .. 392 D treisinger@marylhurst.edu

REISMAN, Lonn .... 254-968-9178 .. 467 F reisman@tarleton.edu

REISNER, Carrie .... 765-973-8404 .. 162 G hellerc@iue.edu

REISNER, Jeff .... 716-375-2000 .. 328 B jreisner@reisnerlawgroup.com

REISNER, John, A .... 937-255-3636 .. 527 H john.reisner@afit.edu

REISS, Michael, A .... 718-377-0777 .. 326 F

REISS, Richard .... 201-692-7003 .. 291 J reissr@fdu.edu

REISS, Yona .... 212-960-5347 .. 341 G yreiss@yu.edu

REISSENWEBER, Beth .... 612-330-1027 .. 244 I reissenw@augsburg.edu

REISSER, Peggy .... 901-448-4072 .. 448 H mreisser@uthsc.edu

REISSMAN, Sallie, A .... 302-356-6807 .... 91 I sallie.a.reissman@wilmu.edu

REIST, David .... 785-442-6010 .. 181 H dreist@highlandcc.edu

REITER, Angela .... 828-328-7109 .. 345 H angela.reiter@lr.edu

REITER, Lisa .... 773-508-2200 .. 146 G lreiter1@luc.edu

REITER, Sharon, L .... 909-869-3016 .... 31 J slreiter@cpp.edu

REITMAN, Meredith .... 212-396-6299 .. 308 D mr928@hunter.cuny.edu

REITMAN, Tzipora .... 845-574-4595 .. 327 G zreitman@sunyrockland.edu

REITTER, Kim .... 314-977-2828 .. 271 K reitterk@slu.edu

REITZ, Barbara .... 610-683-4132 .. 415 C reitz@kutztown.edu

REITZ, Chris .... 801-524-8109 .. 480 J creitz@ldsbc.edu

REITZ, S. Maggie .... 410-704-2131 .. 213 B mreitz@towson.edu

REITZ, Tiffany .... 352-638-9707 .... 96 F treitz@beaconcollege.edu

REJHOLEC, Taryn .... 212-217-4723 .. 314 B taryn_rejholec@fitnyc.edu

REKAU, Donna .... 630-353-9975 .. 139 D drekau@devry.edu

REKLAI, Hilda .... 680-488-3036 .. 530 E hildan@palau.edu

REKOWSKI, Lois, T .... 740-266-9654 .. 368 D lrekowski@egcc.edu

REL, Ricardo .... 575-646-5909 .. 300 J rrel@nmsu.edu

RELAY, Lynn .... 718-368-5034 .. 308 F lrelay@kbcc.cuny.edu

RELIHAN, Constance, C .... 334-844-4900 .... 1 G relihco@auburn.edu

RELLINGER, Brian .... 740-368-3656 .. 376 B

RELLINGER, Brian, A .... 740-368-3131 .. 376 B barellin@owu.edu

RELLINGER, Mackenzie .... 248-218-2057 .. 240 C mrellinger@rc.edu

RELLINGER, Tom .... 248-218-2049 .. 240 C trellinger@rc.edu

RELYEA, Michelle .... 212-229-5150 .. 322 E relyeam@newschool.edu

RELYEA, Steve .... 562-951-4600 .... 31 H srelyea@calstate.edu

REMBACZ, Mark .... 307-382-1899 .. 527 C mrembacz@westernwyoming.edu

REMBERT, Johnny .... 904-470-8277 .... 98 N johnny.rembert@ewc.edu

REMBOLD, Scott .... 202-319-6909 .... 92 A rembold@cua.edu

REMBOLT, Michelle .... 303-871-4478 .... 84 B mrembolt@du.edu

REMENDER, Kathleen, A .... 810-762-9794 .. 236 C kremende@kettering.edu

REMER, Rosalind .... 215-895-1203 .. 402 G rosalind.remer@drexel.edu

REMHOF, Tamara .... 540-891-3013 .. 497 B tremhof@germanna.edu

REMIAS, Roberta .... 586-498-4170 .. 237 C remiasr@macomb.edu

REMICE, Melba .... 212-517-3929 .. 330 G m.remice@sothebysinstitute.com

REMIERES-MORIN, Pamela .... 207-755-5224 .. 203 I premieres@cmcc.edu

REMILLARD, Bud .... 401-598-1900 .. 425 B bremillard@jwu.edu

REMILLARD, Theresa .... 413-755-4336 .. 224 G remillard@stcc.edu

REMINGTON, Brodie .... 201-216-5209 .. 297 B brodie.remington@stevens.edu

REMINGTON, Debra .... 440-375-7040 .. 371 E dremington@lec.edu

REMINGTON, Judith, V .... 847-491-8413 .. 150 F j-remington@northwestern.edu

REMLER, Nancy .... 912-344-2846 .. 116 E nancy.remler@armstrong.edu

REMLER, Nancy .... 912-344-3607 .. 116 E nancy.remler@armstrong.edu

REMLEY, Daniel, C .... 570-577-1195 .. 398 L dan.remley@bucknell.edu

REMMEL, Jeff .... 858-534-6882 .... 70 C jremmel@ucsd.edu

REMMERS, Dawn .... 903-813-2374 .. 451 M dremmers@austincollege.edu

REMOTTI, Melissa .... 805-437-8410 .... 32 B melissa.remotti@csuci.edu

REMSBURG, Barbara .... 801-587-0851 .. 481 M bremsburg@housing.utah.edu

REMSBURG, Robin, E .... 336-334-5016 .. 358 B reremsbu@uncg.edu

REMUND, Kathleen .... 651-255-6112 .. 255 C kremund@unitedseminary.edu

REN, Juan .... 504-671-5403 .. 196 D jren@dcc.edu

RENACIA, Victorina M, Y .... 671-735-2978 .. 530 B vrenacia@triton.uog.edu

RENADETTE, Magen, M .... 518-564-3246 .. 334 A mrena002@plattsburgh.edu

RENAGHAN, Dorothy .... 617-287-5450 .. 220 G dorothy.renaghan@umb.edu

RENAUD, Angela .... 401-598-1400 .. 425 B arenaud@jwu.edu

RENAUD, Robert, E .... 717-245-1072 .. 402 D renaudr@dickinson.edu

RENAULT, Tara, C .... 717-245-1390 .. 402 D renaultt@dickinson.edu

RENBARGER, Bridgette .... 402-399-2646 .. 279 E brenbarger@csm.edu

RENBARGER, Christopher .... 805-986-5826 .... 73 E crenbarger@vcccd.edu

RENCIS, Joseph .... 931-372-3172 .. 445 B jrencis@tntech.edu

RENDER, Philip .... 843-477-2171 .. 430 F philip.render@hgtc.edu

RENDON, James, E .... 860-444-8285 .. 529 A james.e.rendon@uscg.mil

RENDON, Michael .... 361-825-2414 .. 468 E michael.rendon@tamucc.edu

RENDON, Mindy, P .... 785-670-1065 .. 185 H mindy.rendon@washburn.edu

RENEAR, Allen, H .... 217-333-3280 .. 157 A renear@illinois.edu

RENEAU, Clint-Michael .... 512-245-2278 .. 471 F cr49669@txstate.edu

RENEAU, Daniel, D .... 225-342-6950 .. 200 E ulspresident@la.gov

RENEAU, Franz .... 850-599-5265 .. 110 J franz.reneau@famu.edu

RENEHAN, Colm .... 617-573-8444 .. 228 G crenehan@suffolk.edu

RENER, Christine .... 616-331-3498 .. 234 F renerc@gvsu.edu

RENEY, Richard .... 978-762-4000 .. 224 C rreney@northshore.edu

RENFREW, Michelle .... 907-474-5337 .... 10 G mmrenfrew@alaska.edu

RENFRO, Bryan .... 319-296-4427 .. 173 B bryan.renfro@hawkeyecollege.edu

RENFROE, Dennis .... 336-821-2475 .. 345 C drenfroe@johnwesley.edu

RENGIIL, Yoichi, K .... 671-735-3707 .. 530 B yoichi@uguam.uog.edu

RENICK, Larry .... 626-529-8098 .... 55 H lrenick@pacificoaks.edu

RENICK, Timothy, M .... 404-413-2580 .. 122 D trenick@gsu.edu

RENIFF, William, M .... 440-826-2212 .. 363 M breniff@bw.edu

RENKEMA, Teresa .... 616-222-3000 .. 236 F trenkema@kuyper.edu

RENN, Joanne, M .... 757-455-3303 .. 500 E jrenn@vwc.edu

RENNA, Kimberly .... 760-547-1800 .... 44 C krenna@fst.edu

RENNA, Matt .... 914-773-3813 .. 325 J mrenna@pace.edu

RENNER, Cynthia .... 215-489-2467 .. 402 A cynthia.renner@delval.edu

RENNER, Lance .... 417-447-8202 .. 270 A rennerl@otc.edu

RENNERT, Chaim .... 718-438-5476 .. 340 E

RENNIE, Christopher .... 810-989-5642 .. 240 G ccrennie@sc4.edu

RENNIE, John .... 318-678-6000 .. 195 I jrennie@bpcc.edu

RENNIE, Robert .... 203-392-5004 .... 85 H rennie@southernct.edu

RENNINGER, Laura .... 304-876-5461 .. 513 E lrenning@shepherd.edu

RENNIX, Louise .... 843-525-8318 .. 433 B lrennix@tcl.edu

RENO, Adam .... 301-846-2560 .. 207 F areno@frederick.edu

RENO, RET., Loren .... 937-766-7770 .. 365 C lreno@cedarville.edu

RENO-MUNRO, Jane .... 843-953-6378 .. 428 G munroj@cofc.edu

RENSBERGER, Jeffrey, L .... 713-646-1853 .. 459 A jrensberger@hcl.edu

RENSHAW, Paul .... 410-827-5870 .. 207 A prenshaw@chesapeake.edu

RENSHLER, E. Kevin .... 419-434-4439 .. 379 E renshler@findlay.edu

RENTHROPE, Jullin .... 504-286-5117 .. 199 I jrenthrope@suno.edu

RENTMEESTER, Matt, G .... 920-433-6657 .. 515 F matt.rentmeester@bellincollege.edu

RENTSCH, Janet, D .... 989-964-7120 .. 240 F jrentsch@svsu.edu

RENTSCH, Kathleen .... 508-854-2712 .. 224 E krentsch@qcc.mass.edu

RENTSCHLER, Gina .... 417-865-2815 .. 265 B rentschlerg@evangel.edu

RENTTO, Jessica .... 619-594-6018 .... 35 A jrentto@mail.sdsu.edu

RENTZ, Joyce, L .... 256-551-1712 .... 4 F joyce.rentz@drakestate.edu

RENTZ, Judy .... 916-577-2200 .... 75 C jrentz@jessup.edu

RENTZ, Linda, T .... 517-586-3010 .. 232 F lrentz@cleary.edu

RENVILLE, Allen .... 530-895-2239 .... 29 F renvilleal@butte.edu

RENWICK, Mairi .... 804-278-4222 .. 494 N mrenwick@upsem.edu

RENWICK, Michael, D .... 860-297-2055 .... 89 B michael.renwick@trincoll.edu

RENY, Denise .... 207-741-5568 .. 203 M dreny@smccme.edu

RENY, James .... 207-741-5888 .. 203 M jreny@smccme.edu

RENZ, Amy Button .... 785-532-5050 .. 182 D arenz@ksu.edu

RENZ, Christopher, M .... 510-883-2084 .... 42 F crenz@dspt.edu

RENZ, Dianna .... 307-382-1871 .. 527 C drenz@westernwyoming.edu

RENZULLI, Beth, W .... 603-526-3717 .. 285 L brenzull@colby-sawyer.edu

REPAC, Richard, A .... 301-687-4335 .. 212 F rrepac@frostburg.edu

REPALONE, Anthony .... 516-686-7791 .. 323 G arepalon@nyit.edu

REPENNING, Thomas .... 301-934-7630 .. 207 B tomr@csmd.edu

REPETSKI, Michael .... 330-941-1457 .. 382 A michael.repetski@cis.ysu.edu

REPETTO, Martha .... 212-812-4025 .. 323 E mrepetto@nycda.edu

REPETTO, Paul .... 212-431-2836 .. 323 H paul.repetto@nyls.edu

RHEA, Teresa, C 256-549-8230 3 M
trhea@gadsdenstate.edu
RHEAD, Lori 608-363-2630 515 G
rheadl@beloit.edu
RHEAULT, Wendy 847-578-8805 153 A
wendy.rheault@rosalindfranklin.edu
RHEAUME, Steve 603-535-2266 288 F
srheaume@plymouth.edu
RHEE, Elly 510-204-0731 38 C
erhee@cdsp.edu
RHEE, Elly 510-204-0731 38 C
erhee@gtu.edu
RHEE, Michael 212-431-2893 323 H
michael.rhee@nyls.edu
RHEIN, John 610-430-4163 416 C
jrhein@wcupa.edu
RHEINECKER, Matt 517-264-3109 230 D
mrheinecker@adrian.edu
RHEW, Steven, W 336-334-5806 358 B
steve_rhew@uncg.edu
RHEY, William 863-680-4277 101 E
wrhey@flsouthern.edu
RHI-KLEINERT, Susan 818-710-2289 50 A
rhiks@piercecollege.edu
RHIEL, Mary 603-862-0063 288 C
mary.rhiel@unh.edu
RHIM, Choonhee, L 323-265-8625 49 G
rhimcl@elac.edu
RHINE, Lisa, B 757-822-5201 498 H
lrhine@tcc.edu
RHINE, Randy 308-432-6201 281 H
rrhine@csc.edu
RHINEHART, YaKima 910-672-1287 356 E
yrhinehart@uncfsu.edu
RHINESMITH, Betsy 630-829-6018 135 F
brhinesmith@ben.edu
RHINEY, Lisa 205-348-8333 8 D
lisa.rhiney@ua.edu
RHOAD, Scott 660-543-4123 273 C
rhoad@ucmo.edu
RHOADES, Dianne 252-536-7239 350 C
dbarnes-rhoades128@halifaxcc.edu
RHOADES, Jeff 419-448-2977 369 G
jrhoade1@heidelberg.edu
RHOADES, Jeffrey 707-527-4811 63 G
jrhoades@santarosa.edu
RHOADES, Mack 573-882-2055 273 E
rhoadesma@missouri.edu
RHOADES, IV, Mack 254-710-1222 452 H
mack_rhoadesiv@baylor.edu
RHOADES, Margot 704-461-6733 342 A
margotrhoades@bac.edu
RHOADES, Matthew 575-835-7625 300 G
bureau@gis.nmt.edu
RHOADES, Samuel, T 804-257-5811 500 B
strhoades@vuu.edu
RHOADES, Valerie 719-346-9300 81 H
valerie.rhoades@morgancc.edu
RHOADS, Bill 620-768-2909 181 A
billr@fortscott.edu
RHOADS, Kay, M 803-934-3255 431 E
krhoads@morris.edu
RHODA, Christopher 207-859-1124 204 E
chris@thomas.edu
RHODE, Carolyn 336-506-4128 347 C
carolyn.rhode@alamancecc.edu
RHODE, Charles, G 404-894-4114 121 D
chuck.rhode@facilities.gatech.edu
RHODEN, Brenda 256-761-6204 7 F
brhoden@talladega.edu
RHODEN, Deborah 256-840-4137 6 H
drhoden@snead.edu
RHODEN, Joyce 334-727-8011 8 A
jrhoden@tuskegee.edu
RHODEN, Laura 336-744-0900 342 G
laura@carolina.edu
RHODEN, Richard, R 337-475-5887 200 H
rrhoden@mcneese.edu
RHODES, Angel 270-534-3426 190 H
angel.rhodes@kctcs.edu
RHODES, Angela 405-789-6400 388 A
arhodes@snu.edu
RHODES, Anthony, P 212-592-2000 330 C
arhodes@sva.edu
RHODES, Carla 706-880-8240 123 K
crhodes@lagrange.edu
RHODES, David 318-676-7811 196 H
davidrhodes@nwltc.edu
RHODES, David, J 251-578-1313 6 C
drhodes@rstc.edu
RHODES, David, J 212-592-2000 330 C
drhodes@sva.edu
RHODES, Dawn, M 410-706-2802 211 F
drhodes@umaryland.edu
RHODES, Eileen 860-906-5021 86 B
RHODES, Gale 502-852-5727 194 A
gale.rhodes@louisville.edu
RHODES, Gary, L 804-523-5200 497 C
grhodes@reynolds.edu
RHODES, Gina 704-290-5899 353 B
grhodes@spcc.edu

RHODES, Jack, W 843-953-3708 428 A
jack.rhodes@citadel.edu
RHODES, Jacqueline, G 973-596-3407 293 D
jacqueline.rhodes@njit.edu
RHODES, John 410-225-2201 209 B
jrhodes@mica.edu
RHODES, Karen 864-578-8770 432 D
RHODES, Kathleen, S 256-824-6775 8 F
kathleen.rhodes@uah.edu
RHODES, Kathryn 865-354-3000 447 A
rhodeskc@roanestate.edu
RHODES, Kathy 206-934-3796 506 J
kathy.rhodes@seattlecolleges.edu
RHODES, Kay 806-742-5170 472 C
kay.rhodes@ttu.edu
RHODES, Keith 203-582-7938 88 G
keith.rhodes@quinnipiac.edu
RHODES, Lawrence 212-799-5000 318 A
RHODES, Lisa, D 404-270-5728 128 A
lrhodes@spelman.edu
RHODES, Michelle 616-331-3234 234 F
rhodesmi@gvsu.edu
RHODES, Phil 254-299-8642 461 E
prhodes@mclennan.edu
RHODES, Randall 510-925-4282 26 M
randall.rhodes@aua.am
RHODES, Rebecca 509-533-7075 502 H
rebecca.rhodes@scc.spokane.edu
RHODES, Rhosetta, R 509-777-4238 509 H
rrhodes@whitworth.edu
RHODES, Richard, M 512-223-7598 451 N
rrhodes@austincc.edu
RHODES, Robert 325-674-2024 449 J
robert.rhodes@acu.edu
RHODES, Simon 317-274-7211 163 D
srhodes@iupui.edu
RHODES, Tasha 718-260-5800 309 C
trhodes@citytech.cuny.edu
RHODES, Vincent, A 757-446-7070 489 B
rhodesva@evms.edu
RHOM, Steven 918-595-7809 388 F
steve.rhom@tulsacc.edu
RHOTON, James, M 843-863-7050 427 I
jrhoton@csuniv.edu
RHUE, Monika 704-371-6741 345 E
mrhue@jcsu.edu
RHYNE, Teresa, L 757-455-3345 500 E
trhyne@vwc.edu
RHYNEER, Madeleine, E 570-372-4293 419 H
rhyneer@susqu.edu
RHYNER, Paula, M 414-227-3203 520 D
prhyner@uwm.edu
RHYNHART, Hans 860-486-4806 89 D
hans.rhynhart@uconn.edu
RHYS, Raji 818-677-2300 34 A
raji.rhys@csun.edu
RIAL, Scott 847-543-2652 138 C
srial@clcillinois.edu
RIANO, Kimberly, E 253-535-7337 505 G
riano@plu.edu
RIAS, Curtis 212-650-7073 307 E
curtis@ccny.cuny.edu
RIBAKOW, Larry 410-484-7200 210 A
lribakow@nirc.edu
RIBB, Bruce 301-369-2800 206 H
RIBORDY, J. Clark 785-242-5200 183 M
clark.ribordy@ottawa.edu
RICATTO, Pascal, J 201-493-3572 289 E
pjricatto@bergen.edu
RICAUD, Mary 225-248-1015 195 C
RICCA, Beth 201-684-7455 294 G
bricca@ramapo.edu
RICCARDI, JR., Louis, D 415-442-7224 45 B
lriccardi@ggu.edu
RICCARDI, Richard 203-392-5232 85 H
riccardir1@southernct.edu
RICCHEZZA, Lorraine 856-256-5130 295 E
ricchezza@rowan.edu
RICCI, Jose, L 787-727-7727 539 B
jricci@sagrado.edu
RICCI, Jose, L 787-728-1515 539 B
jricci@sagrado.edu
RICCIOTTI, MaryAnn 973-290-4475 290 G
mricciotti@cse.edu
RICE, Alaina, M 620-417-1061 184 I
alaina.rice@sccc.edu
RICE, Amy 281-649-3757 458 L
arice@hbu.edu
RICE, Angela 434-592-6327 491 D
amrice3@liberty.edu
RICE, Ann, M 916-734-0751 69 A
ann.rice@ucdmc.ucdavis.edu
RICE, Brian 937-393-3431 377 F
brice@sscc.edu
RICE, Carlton 205-929-6389 5 D
crice@lawsonstate.edu
RICE, Cynthia, E 410-706-3171 211 F
crice@umaryland.edu
RICE, Daniel, B 785-628-4260 180 I
drice@fhsu.edu

RICE, Edward 662-246-6442 259 B
erice@msdelta.edu
RICE, Gale 314-889-1479 265 C
grice@fontbonne.edu
RICE, Heather 256-228-6001 5 I
riceh@nacc.edu
RICE, Howard, T 270-809-2535 192 A
hrice@murraystate.edu
RICE, James, W 320-222-7474 251 G
jim.rice@ridgewater.edu
RICE, Jennifer 617-879-2233 229 G
jrice@wheelock.edu
RICE, Jonah 618-252-5400 154 G
jonah.rice@sic.edu
RICE, Julie 317-299-0333 167 D
julie@tcmi.org
RICE, Justin 505-454-3349 300 F
1258mgr@fheg.follett.com
RICE, Kyle 307-532-8336 526 G
kyle.rice@ewc.wy.edu
RICE, Larry 918-343-7612 387 F
lrice@rsu.edu
RICE, Laura 312-944-0882 145 F
lrice@careered.com
RICE, Leila 315-781-3700 316 C
rice@hws.edu
RICE, Malcolm 256-824-2555 8 F
malcolm.rice@uah.edu
RICE, Malcolm 256-824-6347 8 F
malcom.rice@uah.edu
RICE, Martin 765-677-2939 164 B
martin.rice@indwes.edu
RICE, Peggy 815-836-5350 145 H
ricepe@lewisu.edu
RICE, Peter 201-684-7601 294 G
price@ramapo.edu
RICE, Priscilla 215-968-8450 399 A
priscilla.rice@bucks.edu
RICE, Rachel 207-768-9447 205 D
rachel.rice@maine.edu
RICE, Raymond, J 207-768-9525 205 D
raymond.rice@maine.edu
RICE, Raymond, J 207-768-9518 205 D
raymond.rice@maine.edu
RICE, Scott 217-333-0560 157 A
serice@uillinois.edu
RICE, Sherwin 910-879-5646 347 F
srice@bladencc.edu
RICE, Stephen 201-684-7407 294 G
srice@ramapo.edu
RICE, Susan, I 336-633-0282 352 B
sirice@randolph.edu
RICE, Vance 662-325-6731 259 D
rice@safdfairs.msstate.edu
RICE AYALA, Maggie 773-907-4041 137 E
mrice19@ccc.edu
RICE-CARROLL, Cynthia 760-757-2121 52 K
crice@miracosta.edu
RICE-CLAYBORN, Kathy 501-450-3134 24 G
kathyc@uca.edu
RICE-MASON, Jenifer 870-972-3964 18 J
jrmason@astate.edu
RICE-SADDLER, Lori 404-880-8447 118 K
lrice@cau.edu
RICE-SPEARMAN, Lori 806-743-3223 472 D
lori.ricespearman@ttuhsc.edu
RICE-TUMA, Rachel 800-567-2344 516 B
rrice@menominee.edu
RICH, Arthur 402-457-2681 280 J
aarich@mccneb.edu
RICH, Forrest 912-583-3146 118 B
frich@bpc.edu
RICH, Frank 432-335-6507 463 B
frich@odessa.edu
RICH, Jack, W 325-674-2013 449 J
richj@acu.edu
RICH, Jeff 952-888-4777 253 Z
jrich@nwhealth.edu
RICH, Kathy 781-280-3501 224 A
richk@middlesex.mass.edu
RICH, Kim 860-932-4141 87 C
krich@qvcc.edu
RICH, Laura 910-893-4364 342 F
richl@campbell.edu
RICH, Marcus 252-985-5176 354 E
mritch@ncwc.edu
RICH, Scott 620-278-4213 185 A
srich@sterling.edu
RICH, Steven 617-236-8832 218 G
srich@fisher.edu
RICH, Steven, W 217-581-6616 139 H
swrich@eiu.edu
RICH, Timothy, A 651-631-5489 256 A
tarich@unwsp.edu
RICH-COATES, Robin 757-789-1748 497 A
rrich-coates@es.vccs.edu
RICHARD, Alison, A 570-372-4111 419 H
arichard@susqu.edu
RICHARD, Arthur 252-940-6210 347 E
arthur.richard@beaufortccc.edu

RICHARD, Cindy 978-998-7762 218 D
cirichar@endicott.edu
RICHARD, Dan 904-620-2700 112 B
drichard@unf.edu
RICHARD, David, C 407-646-2232 107 O
dcrichard@rollins.edu
RICHARD, Deborah 407-708-2487 109 E
richardd@seminolestate.edu
RICHARD, Delores 662-621-4205 257 B
RICHARD, Jasmine 985-448-7945 196 E
jasmine.richard@fletcher.edu
RICHARD, Mark 205-665-6600 9 B
mrichard11@montevallo.edu
RICHARD, Mark 256-840-4110 6 H
mrichard@snead.edu
RICHARD, Patricia 775-784-1110 285 A
prichard@unr.edu
RICHARD, Patricia 775-784-4805 285 A
prichard@unr.edu
RICHARD, Renee 216-987-4865 367 E
renee.richard@tri-c.edu
RICHARD, Robert 337-482-6923 201 D
bookstore@louisiana.edu
RICHARD, Thomas 603-358-2326 288 E
trichard@keene.edu
RICHARD, Trish 409-772-8221 478 A
plrichar@utmb.edu
RICHARD, Valerie 704-403-3507 342 E
valerie.richard@carolinashealthcare.org
RICHARDELLO, Denise 413-662-5201 222 B
denise.richardello@mcla.edu
RICHARDS, Belarmina 714-316-0366 68 E
belarmina.richards@trident.edu
RICHARDS, Char 262-524-6891 515 J
crichard@carrollu.edu
RICHARDS, Cheryl 980-224-8466 227 B
RICHARDS, Chris 715-346-3908 521 C
crichards@uwsp.edu
RICHARDS, Connie, L 229-333-5699 129 G
clrichards@valdosta.edu
RICHARDS, David 626-584-5458 44 G
richards@fuller.edu
RICHARDS, David, E 402-554-2640 283 B
derichards@unomaha.edu
RICHARDS, David, J 517-321-0242 235 C
drichards@glcc.edu
RICHARDS, Debbie 304-424-8201 514 D
debbie.richards@wvup.edu
RICHARDS, Elizabeth 603-668-2211 287 I
e.richards1@snhu.edu
RICHARDS, Faith 605-455-6029 436 G
frichards@olc.edu
RICHARDS, Ginger 317-805-1783 511 D
vrichards@salemu.edu
RICHARDS, Gordon 724-847-6718 404 B
grichard@geneva.edu
RICHARDS, Gwyn 812-855-2435 162 F
grichar@indiana.edu
RICHARDS, Harry, J 603-862-3009 288 C
harry.richards@unh.edu
RICHARDS, Jeni 949-376-6000 48 C
jrichards@lcad.edu
RICHARDS, Jerry 920-924-3184 524 B
jrichards2@morainepark.edu
RICHARDS, John 808-734-9518 131 I
john.richards@hawaii.edu
RICHARDS, Josh 816-936-8718 271 L
jmrichards@saintlukescollege.edu
RICHARDS, Kathi, S 937-778-7843 368 E
krichards@edisonohio.edu
RICHARDS, Kathy, A 906-227-1237 239 B
kathrich@nmu.edu
RICHARDS, Katie, J 701-788-4675 360 E
katie.richards.2@mayvillestate.edu
RICHARDS, Kent 218-733-5969 249 H
k.richards@lsc.edu
RICHARDS, Larry, J 801-524-8101 480 J
lrichards@ldsbc.edu
RICHARDS, Lawrence 610-399-2405 414 F
police@cheyney.edu
RICHARDS, Leah 603-668-2211 287 I
l.richards1@snhu.edu
RICHARDS, Lee 614-235-4136 378 C
lrichards@tlsohio.edu
RICHARDS, Letha 662-621-4126 257 B
lrichards@coahomacc.edu
RICHARDS, Marty 704-216-3459 352 G
marty.richards@rccc.edu
RICHARDS, Marvin 216-987-4883 367 E
marvin.richards@tri-c.edu
RICHARDS, Maryanne 508-830-5039 222 C
mrichards@maritime.edu
RICHARDS, Matthew 406-447-6900 277 B
RICHARDS, Matthew 207-741-5927 203 M
mrichards@smccme.edu
RICHARDS, Michael 212-752-1530 318 F
michael.richards@limcollege.edu
RICHARDS, Michael, D 702-651-5600 284 H
mike.richards@csn.edu
RICHARDS, Randy 561-803-2543 106 C
randy_richards@pba.edu

RIDDLE, Jennifer .... 208-459-5688.. 133 D
jriddle@collegeofidaho.edu
RIDDLE, Joyce, E .... 304-462-6184.. 513 C
joyce.riddle@glenville.edu
RIDDLE, Larry .... 770-426-2979.. 124 B
larry.riddle@life.edu
RIDDLE, Troy .... 312-427-2737.. 143 G
triddle@jmls.edu
RIDEAUX, Larry .... 817-515-4507.. 467 A
larry.rideaux@tccd.edu
RIDEL, Robert .... 503-228-6528.. 390 A
rridel@aii.edu
RIDENOUR, Nancy, A ...... 505-272-6284.. 302 F
nridenour@salud.unm.edu
RIDEOUT, Kathy .... 585-275-8902.. 338 K
kathy_rideout@urmc.rochester.edu
RIDER, Elizabeth (Betty) .. 717-361-1416.. 403 C
ridere@etown.edu
RIDER, Jeff .... 870-759-4194.... 24 J
jrider@wbcoll.edu
RIDER, Jonathan .... 703-812-4757.. 491 B
jrider@leland.edu
RIDER, Paul .... 515-263-2917.. 172 H
prider@grandview.edu
RIDER, Robert .... 865-974-2201.. 448 E
brider@utk.edu
RIDES HORSE, Curtis ...... 406-638-3111.. 276 G
rideshorsec@lbhc.edu
RIDGE, Terri .... 620-278-4220.. 185 A
tridge@sterling.edu
RIDGEDELL, Ken, W .... 985-549-2121.. 201 C
kridgedell@selu.edu
RIDGES, Jarvis .... 404-270-5003.. 128 A
jarvis.ridges@spelman.edu
RIDGEWAY, Gloria .... 229-317-6919.. 120 A
gloria.ridgeway@darton.edu
RIDGWAY, Dan .... 216-649-8900.. 370 I
dridgway@kent.edu
RIDGWAY, Lori .... 307-855-2103.. 526 E
lridgway@cwc.edu
RIDGWAY, Susan, M ...... 989-837-4219.. 239 D
ridgway@northwood.edu
RIDINGTON, M. Thomas . 610-341-4377.. 403 B
tridingt@eastern.edu
RIDLEY, Emmett, L .... 804-524-5068.. 499 G
eridley@vsu.edu
RIDLEY, Scott .... 806-742-1988.. 472 C
scott.ridley@ttu.edu
RIDLEY, Tim .... 661-654-2066.... 32 A
tridley@csub.edu
RIDLEY, JR., Wadell .... 610-660-1223.. 418 G
wridley@sju.edu
RIDOUT, Thomas, M .... 563-562-3263.. 175 F
ridoutt@nicc.edu
RIDPATH, Lance .... 304-647-6424.. 514 A
lridpath@osteo.wvsom.edu
RIDPATH, Lisa .... 540-857-7201.. 499 B
lridpath@virginiawestern.edu
RIDPATH, Tanya .... 540-375-2323.. 493 H
ridpath@roanoke.edu
RIEDEL, Eric .... 612-338-7224.. 256 D
eric.riedel@waldenu.edu
RIEDEL, Herbert, H .... 334-222-6591...... 5 F
hriedel@lbwcc.edu
RIEDEL CARNEY,
Elizabeth .... 651-690-6836.. 254 M
eacarney@stkate.edu
RIEDER, Rick .... 660-626-2555.. 262 A
rrieder@atsu.edu
RIEDL-FARREY, Cathy, J . 608-342-1435.. 521 A
riedlfac@uwplatt.edu
RIEDSTRA, Catherine .... 805-546-3130.... 41 L
cmachado@cuesta.edu
RIEDY, Joshua .... 701-777-4273.. 360 C
joshua.riedy@und.edu
RIEFKOHL, Jorge .... 787-780-0070.. 531 B
jriefkohl@caribbean.edu
RIEGER, Mark .... 302-831-2501.... 91 F
mrieger@udel.edu
RIEGLER, Alissa .... 563-588-6559.. 170 F
alissa.riegler@clarke.edu
RIEHL, Christine .... 503-338-2305.. 390 G
criehl@clatsopcc.edu
RIEHL, Gretchen, K .... 972-860-7297.. 456 D
griehl@dcccd.edu
RIEHL, Shelle .... 503-517-1814.. 396 F
sriehl@westernseminary.edu
RIEHLE, Douglas .... 937-778-7979.. 368 E
driehle@edisonohio.edu
RIEHN, Pamela .... 573-334-9181.. 267 C
pamela@metrobusinesscollege.edu
RIEHS, Steven .... 630-515-7702.. 139 D
sriehs@devrygroup.com
RIEKEMAN, Guy, F .... 770-426-2601.. 124 B
riekeman@life.edu
RIEKENBERG, Tim .... 620-227-9355.. 180 E
triekenberg@dc3.edu
RIEKERT, Jennifer .... 914-594-4536.. 323 I
jennifer_riekert@nymc.edu
RIEKS, Stephen, J .... 716-673-4670.. 331 D
stephen.rieks@fredonia.edu

RIELLO, Heidi, A .... 413-662-5331.. 222 B
heidi.riello@mcla.edu
RIEMAN, Jeff .... 419-772-3100.. 374 J
j-rieman@onu.edu
RIEN, Nate .... 209-588-5182.... 75 J
rienn@yosemite.edu
RIEPMA, Edward .... 949-794-9090.... 66 H
eriepma@stanbridge.edu
RIERA, José-Luis .... 302-831-8939.... 91 F
jriera@udel.edu
RIES, Barry .... 507-389-1242.. 250 E
barry.ries@mnsu.edu
RIES, Heidi, R .... 937-255-3633.. 527 H
heidi.ries@afit.edu
RIES, Kenneth .... 320-629-5195.. 251 E
riesk@pine.edu
RIES, Thomas Karl .... 651-641-8211.. 246 B
ries@csp.edu
RIESBERG, Anthony .... 507-389-7444.. 252 D
anthony.riesberg@southcentral.edu
RIESE, Sara .... 303-762-6995.... 79 I
sara.riese@denverseminary.edu
RIESER, Lori .... 812-855-4613.. 162 E
RIESGO, Andrea .... 760-366-5285.... 41 K
ariesgo@cmccd.edu
RIESINGER, Mick .... 701-483-2389.. 360 D
michael.riesinger@dickinsonstate.edu
RIESTER, Jon .... 812-866-7021.. 161 C
riester@hanover.edu
RIESTRA, Liza .... 787-841-2000.. 535 I
liza_riestra@pucpr.edu
RIESTRA, Miguel, A .... 787-622-8000.. 537 B
mriestra@pupr.edu
RIETHLE, Theresa .... 413-565-1000.. 215 A
triethle@baypath.edu
RIFE, Corie .... 276-935-4349.. 486 N
crife@asl.edu
RIFKIN, Benjamin .... 607-274-3113.. 317 D
brifkin@ithaca.edu
RIGALI, Mary .... 203-596-4504.... 88 F
mrigali@post.edu
RIGBY, Heather .... 248-689-8282.. 242 F
hrigby@walshcollege.edu
RIGGERT, Mark .... 402-557-7070.. 278 I
bubookstore@fheg.follett.com
RIGGINS, Darius .... 661-654-3277.... 32 A
driggins@csub.edu
RIGGINS, David, W .... 828-689-1219.. 346 C
driggins@mhu.edu
RIGGLE, Ron .... 217-786-2581.. 146 E
ron.riggle@llcc.edu
RIGGS, Alexia .... 325-649-8610.. 459 E
ariggs@hputx.edu
RIGGS, Allen .... 435-283-7125.. 482 E
allen.riggs@snow.edu
RIGGS, Bonnie .... 423-697-4465.. 445 D
bonnie.riggs@chattanoogastate.edu
RIGGS, Channing .... 612-624-6868.. 255 H
riggs035@umn.edu
RIGGS, David .... 765-677-2808.. 164 B
david.riggs@indwes.edu
RIGGS, Joyce .... 270-824-8581.. 190 B
joyce.riggs@kctcs.edu
RIGGS, Michelle .... 909-389-3391.... 60 B
mriggs@craftonhills.edu
RIGGS, Paul .... 570-408-4600.. 423 G
paul.riggs@wilkes.edu
RIGGS, Robert, F .... 214-887-5007.. 457 C
rriggs@dts.edu
RIGLER, Bill .... 303-546-3533.... 81 I
brigler@naropa.edu
RIGNEY, Doug .... 205-726-2032....... 6 E
drigney@samford.edu
RIGSBEE, Craig .... 530-895-2476.... 29 F
rigsbeecr@butte.edu
RIHA, James .... 618-235-2700.. 155 C
james.riha@swic.edu
RIHACEK, Robin .... 708-210-5754.. 154 E
rrihacek@ssc.edu
RIHL-LEWINSKY,
Elizabeth .... 215-572-2956.. 397 G
rihll@arcadia.edu
RIIS, Janet .... 406-447-5423.. 276 B
jriis@carroll.edu
RIKAKIS, Thanassis .... 540-231-6123.. 499 F
provost@vt.edu
RIKARD, Jennifer .... 619-594-5220.... 35 A
jrikard@mail.sdsu.edu
RIKEL, Randy .... 806-651-2092.. 469 D
rrikel@mail.wtamu.edu
RIKER, David, J .... 210-458-6143.. 477 A
dave.riker@utsa.edu
RIKOON,
James (Sandy), S .... 573-882-0861.. 273 E
rikoonsandy@missouri.edu
RILEY, Ann, C .... 573-882-1685.. 273 E
rileyac@missouri.edu
RILEY, Bruce .... 608-785-8218.. 520 C
briley@uwlax.edu
RILEY, Carla .... 320-589-6066.. 255 F
rileycj@morris.umn.edu

RILEY, Chris .... 325-674-6802.. 449 J
cmr97t@acu.edu
RILEY, Connie .... 409-984-6200.. 471 C
connie.riley@lamarpa.edu
RILEY, Dean .... 281-649-3182.. 458 L
driley@hbu.edu
RILEY, Doreen, K .... 216-397-4345.. 370 H
driley@jcu.edu
RILEY, Edward .... 617-254-2610.. 227 H
rev.edward.riley@sjs.edu
RILEY, Jan .... 334-222-6591...... 5 F
jriley@lbwcc.edu
RILEY, Jeannette .... 508-999-8352.. 220 H
j1riley@umassd.edu
RILEY, Jill .... 931-540-2573.. 446 A
jriley9@columbiastate.edu
RILEY, Karen .... 303-871-7874.... 84 B
kriley@du.edu
RILEY, Ken .... 432-685-4569.. 461 H
kriley@midland.edu
RILEY, Kimberly .... 816-604-4523.. 267 K
kim.riley@mcckc.edu
RILEY, Lisa .... 784-682-6017.. 285 A
lriley@unr.edu
RILEY, Lisa .... 608-822-2440.. 524 F
lriley@swtc.edu
RILEY, Matt .... 406-243-5455.. 276 K
matt.riley@umontana.edu
RILEY, Michael .... 312-944-0882.. 145 F
mriley@chicago.chefs.edu
RILEY, P. Thomas .... 703-654-1040.. 495 C
priley@umw.edu
RILEY, Patrick .... 440-684-6022.. 380 F
priley@ursuline.edu
RILEY, Rebecca .... 936-273-7222.. 461 B
rebecca.riley@lonestar.edu
RILEY, Robert .... 781-768-7147.. 227 G
robert.riley@regiscollege.edu
RILEY, Robert, J .... 651-962-6032.. 256 C
rjriley@stthomas.edu
RILEY, Sabrina .... 402-486-2514.. 282 I
sariley@ucollege.edu
RILEY, Sarah .... 900-652-6176.... 37 D
sarah.riley@chaffey.edu
RILEY, Sarah .... 305-899-3051.... 96 D
sriley@barry.edu
RILEY, Scott, T .... 218-285-2205.. 251 F
scott.riley@rainyriver.edu
RILEY, Shawn .... 610-292-9852.. 417 I
bookkeeping@reseminary.edu
RILEY, Stacy .... 262-564-3108.. 523 D
rileys@gtc.edu
RILEY, Susan .... 513-732-5324.. 379 C
rileysu@ucmail.uc.edu
RILEY, Tammy .... 409-984-6237.. 471 C
tammy.riley@lamarpa.edu
RILEY, Terisa .... 361-593-3612.. 469 A
terisa.riley@tamuk.edu
RILEY, Toni .... 312-567-5239.. 142 I
triley6@iit.edu
RILEY, Vicki .... 304-214-8800.. 512 F
vriley@wvncc.edu
RILEY, Whitney .... 513-529-1810.. 372 K
rileywc@miamioh.edu
RILING, Dean .... 702-579-3531.. 283 I
driling@kaplan.edu
RILL, Ann .... 540-785-5440.. 496 A
annmarierill@vbc.edu
RILL, Josef .... 941-752-5342.. 110 H
rillj@scf.edu
RILLEY, Karin .... 972-721-5363.. 473 D
krilley@udallas.edu
RILLORTA, Rhoda .... 704-355-3243.. 343 A
rhoda.rillorta@carolinashealthcare.org
RIMA, Kyle .... 801-832-2008.. 483 D
krima@westminstercollege.edu
RIMAI, Monica .... 503-370-6728.. 396 G
mrimai@willamette.edu
RIMAL, Sanjana .... 973-353-5940.. 296 C
srimal@andromeda.rutgers.edu
RIMANDO, Rosie .... 206-934-6763.. 507 A
rosie.rimando@seattlecolleges.edu
RIMAR, Mark .... 314-977-3529.. 271 K
rimarms@slu.edu
RIMBY, Susan .... 570-484-2073.. 415 D
ser1116@lhup.edu
RIMER, Barbara, K .... 919-966-3215.. 357 D
brimer@unc.edu
RIMIRCH, Bruce .... 680-488-2471.. 530 E
brucer@palau.edu
RIMKIS, Robert, C .... 540-224-6973.. 491 A
rcrimkis@jchs.edu
RIMMER, Jessica .... 405-692-3275.. 384 C
jrimmer@macu.edu
RINALDI WINN, Mary ..... 404-364-8476.. 125 F
mrinaldi@oglethorpe.edu
RINARD, Pat .... 727-341-3064.. 108 D
rinard.pat@spcollege.edu
RINAUDO, Brooke, H ...... 318-797-5108.. 198 C
brooke.rinaudo@lsus.edu

RINCON, Amilcar .... 787-279-1912.. 533 J
arincon@bayamon.inter.edu
RINCONES-GOMEZ,
Rigoberto, J .... 910-962-7638.. 358 D
rinconesr@uncw.edu
RINDE, Carla, M .... 610-409-3599.. 422 D
crinde@ursinus.edu
RINDERKNECHT, Bethany 319-363-1323.. 175 D
brinderknecht@mtmercy.edu
RINDO, Michael, J .... 715-836-4742.. 520 A
rindomj@uwec.edu
RINE, P. Jesse .... 724-264-4718.. 404 F
pjrine@gcc.edu
RINE, Veronica .... 740-755-7600.. 365 D
vrine@cotc.edu
RINEHART, John .... 304-877-6428.. 510 F
registrar@abc.edu
RINEHART, Kathleen, A ... 773-298-3344.. 153 H
rinehart@sxu.edu
RINEHART, Kenton, W ..... 845-575-3000.. 320 B
kent.rinehart@marist.edu
RINEHART, Melanie .... 405-382-9717.. 387 L
m.rinehart@sscok.edu
RINEHART, Robin, C .... 610-330-5070.. 407 C
rineharr@lafayette.edu
RINEHART, Shelley .... 281-998-6150.. 464 J
shelley.rinehart@sjcd.edu
RINEHART, Todd .... 303-871-3125.... 84 B
todd.rinehart@du.edu
RINEY, OSU, Judith, N .... 270-686-4288.. 187 C
judith.riney@brescia.edu
RING, Joshua .... 828-328-7927.. 345 H
joshua.ring@lr.edu
RING, Neal .... 864-242-5100.. 427 E
RING, Patricia .... 508-793-3459.. 217 C
pring@holycross.edu
RING, Ray .... 212-817-7394.. 308 A
rring@gc.cuny.edu
RINGA, Melanie .... 914-961-8313.. 329 H
finance@svots.edu
RINGENBERG, Ron .... 574-296-6212.. 158 H
rringenb@ambs.edu
RINGGOLD, Tonja .... 410-462-8001.. 206 D
tringgold@bccc.edu
RINGGOLD, Tonja .... 410-462-8302.. 206 D
tringgold@bccc.edu
RINGHAM, Rebecca .... 701-858-3126.. 360 F
rebecca.ringham@minotstateu.edu
RINGLE, John .... 217-206-6190.. 156 G
ringle.john@uis.edu
RINGLE, Martin, D .... 503-777-7254.. 394 I
martin.ringle@reed.edu
RINGLE, Suzanne .... 602-286-8110.... 14 B
suzanne.ringle@gwmail.maricopa.edu
RINGLER, Neil, H .... 315-470-6606.. 334 E
neilringler@esf.edu
RINGO, Teresa .... 936-294-1061.. 471 D
reg_tat@shsu.edu
RINGOLD, Debra .... 503-370-6440.. 396 G
dringold@willamette.edu
RINGWALD, Heather .... 603-899-4128.. 287 A
ringwaldh@franklinpierce.edu
RINGWOOD, Karen, K ...... 203-597-9036.... 89 C
klozada@bridgeport.edu
RINI, Anthony .... 617-373-4774.. 227 B
RINI, Bridget .... 216-397-4281.. 370 H
brini@jcu.edu
RINK, Darrell, C .... 479-788-7701.... 23 A
chris.rink@uafs.edu
RINK, Jonathan .... 828-328-7249.. 345 H
jonathan.rink@lr.edu
RINK, Susan .... 734-481-2310.. 233 J
srink@emich.edu
RINKENBAUGH, Bill .... 316-322-3297.. 179 E
brinkenb@butlercc.edu
RINKER, Craig .... 202-687-5867.... 92 E
cmr235@georgetown.edu
RINKER, Jonathan, A .... 304-877-6428.. 510 F
jon.rinker@abc.edu
RINKER, Linda .... 616-554-5183.. 233 C
lrinker@davenport.edu
RINKOFF, Carol .... 301-447-5840.. 209 G
rinkoff@msmary.edu
RINKUS, Michael, A .... 248-689-8282.. 242 F
mrinkus@walshcollege.edu
RINN, Martha .... 830-372-8110.. 470 C
mrinn@tlu.edu
RINN, Susan .... 830-372-8001.. 470 C
srinn@tlu.edu
RINNE, Henry .... 904-256-7926.. 103 D
hrinne@ju.edu
RINNE, Jason .... 660-831-4088.. 269 B
rinnej@moval.edu
RIO, Deborah .... 661-362-3298.... 40 A
debbie.rio@canyons.edu
RIOLA, Allison .... 303-871-4201.... 84 B
allison.riola@du.edu
RIOPEL, Becky .... 425-352-8545.. 501 J
briopel@cascadia.edu
RIORDAN, Charles .... 302-831-4007.... 91 F
riordan@udel.edu

RIVERA, Teresita .... 787-882-2065.. 536 D
admisiones@unitecpr.net
RIVERA, Teresita .... 787-780-0070.. 531 B
trivera@caribbean.edu
RIVERA, Wendy .... 818-364-7779.... 49 J
RIVERA, Yolanda .... 787-758-2525.. 538 D
yolanda.rivera3@upr.edu
RIVERA-ARROYO, Basilio 787-250-0000.. 537 D
basilio.rivera@upr.edu
RIVERA-CLAUDIO, Nelda . 787-764-1912.. 533 F
nerivera@inter.edu
RIVERA-DREYER, Ivette ... 860-512-3382.... 86 E
irivera-dreyer@manchestercc.edu
RIVERA LUGO, Yadira ..... 787-766-1717.. 536 B
um_yrivera@suagm.edu
RIVERA-MARQUEZ,
Annelis .... 787-480-2455.. 531 J
armarquez@sanjuanciudadpatria.com
RIVERA NEGRON,
Adrian, O .... 787-725-8120.. 532 K
actividadesculturales@eap.edu
RIVERA-OTERO, Milagros 787-621-2835.. 530 F
mrivera@aupr.edu
RIVERA PÉREZ,
Carlos, E .... 787-945-7010.. 532 K
rectoria@eap.edu
RIVERA VEGA,
Carmen, H .... 787-751-0500.. 538 F
decana.daa@upr.edu
RIVERO, Brenda .... 601-928-6380.. 259 C
brenda.rivero@mgccc.edu
RIVERO, David, A .... 305-284-1650.. 114 H
darivero@miami.edu
RIVERO, Estela .... 518-442-5800.. 331 A
erivero@albany.edu
RIVERO, Yaidany .... 305-474-6965.. 108 E
yrivero@stu.edu
RIVERS, Andrew .... 202-806-2550.... 93 A
andrew.rivers@howard.edu
RIVERS, Kyle .... 201-761-7102.. 296 K
krivers@saintpeters.edu
RIVERS, Nancy, A .... 434-982-2662.. 495 H
nan9k@virginia.edu
RIVERS, Verna, J .... 340-693-1121.. 539 C
vrivers@uvi.edu
RIVERS LANG,
Evangeline .... 256-726-7484...... 6 B
elang@oakwood.edu
RIVES, Joseph .... 309-762-8090.. 158 A
j-rives@wiu.edu
RIVETT, Donna .... 772-462-7656.. 103 B
drivett@irsc.edu
RIX, Charles .... 405-425-5379.. 385 C
charles.rix@oc.edu
RIX, Todd .... 843-383-8126.. 428 F
trix@coker.edu
RIXEN, Mary .... 580-387-7303.. 384 D
mrixen@mscok.edu
RIZA, Robert .... 806-874-4800.. 454 F
RIZK, Michelle .... 907-786-7711.... 10 E
mrizk@alaska.edu
RIZK, Michelle .... 907-450-8191.... 10 E
marizk@alaska.edu
RIZO, Sergio .... 417-626-1234.. 269 K
rizo.sergio@occ.edu
RIZVI, S. Abu Turab .... 610-330-5066.. 407 C
rizvia@lafayette.edu
RIZVI, Syed .... 714-628-4967.... 58 H
rizvi_syed@sccollege.edu
RIZZARDI, Bethany .... 707-826-4204.... 34 F
bethany.rizzardi@humboldt.edu
RIZZARDI, Morgan, M .... 724-287-8711.. 399 B
morgan.rizzardi@bc3.edu
RIZZI, Gino .... 518-828-4181.. 311 D
rizzi@sunycgcc.edu
RIZZO, Bryan .... 734-432-5604.. 237 D
brizzo@madonna.edu
RIZZO, Frank .... 949-508-2317.. 359 G
frank.rizzo@peace.edu
RIZZO, Mary .... 610-796-8379.. 397 D
mary.rizzo@alvernia.edu
RIZZO, Matt .... 802-440-4336.. 483 E
mattrizzo@bennington.edu
RIZZO, Pete .... 402-844-7151.. 282 B
pete@northeast.edu
RIZZO, Rosalina, B .... 716-880-2339.. 320 D
rosalina.b.rizzo@medaille.edu
RIZZUTO, James, T .... 719-384-6822.... 82 A
jim.rizzuto@ojc.edu
ROACH, H. William .... 864-833-8217.. 432 B
broach@presby.edu
ROACH, Kenneth .... 704-334-6882.. 343 D
kroach@charlottechristian.edu
ROACH, Kristin .... 651-962-6168.. 256 C
kagetting@stthomas.edu
ROACH, Mark .... 843-349-2964.. 428 E
mroach@coastal.edu
ROACH, Nicole .... 314-246-8250.. 275 B
nroach@webster.edu
ROACH, Steve .... 724-357-4295.. 415 B
sroach@iup.edu
ROACH, Virginia .... 212-636-6470.. 314 G
vroach@fordham.edu
ROACHE, Marshall .... 503-399-2339.. 390 E
marshall.roache@chemeketa.edu
ROADES, Nicole .... 937-393-3431.. 377 F
nroades@sscc.edu
ROAN, Anthony .... 651-793-1889.. 250 A
ROARK, Debbie .... 207-768-9755.. 205 D
deborah.roark@maine.edu
ROARK, Donna .... 606-487-3128.. 189 E
donnad.roark@kctcs.edu
ROARK, Ian .... 520-206-6424.... 16 F
iroark@pima.edu
ROARK, John, A .... 270-809-3536.. 192 A
jroark3@murraystate.edu
ROARK, Tony .... 208-426-2030.. 132 I
troark@boisestate.edu
ROATCH, Gay .... 910-576-6222.. 351 E
roatchg@montgomery.edu
ROBACK, Barbara, A .... 315-684-6615.. 336 B
robackba@morrisville.edu
ROBACK, Joseph, M .... 570-941-4385.. 422 B
joseph.roback@scranton.edu
ROBAIN LACAILLE,
Jemma .... 718-482-5077.. 309 A
jlacaille@lagcc.cuny.edu
ROBB, Annette, D .... 937-255-6800.. 527 H
annette.robb@afit.edu
ROBB, Cathy .... 812-749-1272.. 166 B
crobb@oake.edu
ROBB, Cathy .... 812-749-1272.. 166 B
crobb@oak.edu
ROBB, Daniel, J .... 803-641-3487.. 433 G
danr@usca.edu
ROBB, Hollie .... 661-362-2678.... 52 A
hrobb@masters.edu
ROBB, James .... 517-371-5140.. 243 I
robbj@cooley.edu
ROBB, Mercy .... 630-829-6095.. 135 F
mrobb@ben.edu
ROBB, Sarah .... 620-431-2820.. 183 H
sarah_robb@neosho.edu
ROBB, Susan, E .... 804-827-0479.. 496 D
sarobb@vcu.edu
ROBB SHIMKO, Molly .... 724-830-4620.. 419 D
shimko@setonhill.edu
ROBBEN, Richard, W ...... 734-763-9333.. 241 J
rrobben@umich.edu
ROBBIE, Kimberly .... 510-659-6165.... 55 B
krobbie@ohlone.edu
ROBBINS, Bradley .... 334-244-3345...... 2 A
brobbin2@aum.edu
ROBBINS, Brent .... 412-392-8183.. 417 F
brobbins@pointpark.edu
ROBBINS, Canty .... 901-678-3855.. 445 C
crobbns1@memphis.edu
ROBBINS, David .... 662-720-7302.. 260 B
wdrobbins@nemcc.edu
ROBBINS, Debbie .... 210-732-3000.. 453 S
ROBBINS, Donna .... 252-398-6280.. 343 G
robbid@chowan.edu
ROBBINS, Gayle, M .... 706-542-2124.. 128 E
grobbins@uga.edu
ROBBINS, Ian .... 850-644-9719.. 111 C
irobbins@fsu.edu
ROBBINS, Jill .... 478-387-4908.. 121 E
jrobbins@gmc.edu
ROBBINS, Kristine .... 614-823-1232.. 376 C
krobbins@otterbein.edu
ROBBINS, Kyle .... 570-558-1818.. 403 I
krobbins@fortisinstitute.edu
ROBBINS, Mark .... 260-399-7700.. 168 D
mrobbins@sf.edu
ROBBINS, Mary .... 936-294-1006.. 471 D
robbins@shsu.edu
ROBBINS, Michael .... 410-857-2242.. 209 D
mrobbins@mcdaniel.edu
ROBBINS, Nickey, L .... 870-508-6108.... 19 B
nrobbins@asumh.edu
ROBBINS, Patrica .... 719-587-7472.... 76 G
patrobbins@adams.edu
ROBBINS, Paul .... 608-265-5296.. 519 K
director@nelson.wisc.edu
ROBBINS, Rochelle .... 215-637-7700.. 405 J
robbins@holyfamily.edu
ROBBINS, Ruth .... 215-965-4038.. 411 A
rrobbins@moore.edu
ROBBINS, Sandra .... 617-735-9715.. 218 C
robbins@emmanuel.edu
ROBBINS, Scott, D .... 731-881-7775.. 448 G
sdrobbins@utm.edu
ROBBINS, Shawna, L ...... 760-252-2411.... 28 B
srobbins@barstow.edu
ROBBINS, Steve .... 662-685-4771.. 257 A
srobbins@bmc.edu
ROBBINS, Thomas, G ...... 617-353-5533.. 216 E
tqresq@bu.edu
ROBBINS, Thomas, J .... 563-589-3507.. 177 C
trobbins@dbq.edu
ROBBINS SMITH,
Patricia .... 562-860-2451.... 36 P
probbinssmith@cerritos.edu
ROBBINSON, Theresa ..... 212-924-5900.. 336 I
trobbinson@swedishinstitute.edu
ROBEAUU, Jim .... 985-867-2272.. 199 F
jrobeau@sjasc.edu
ROBECK, Mike .... 850-201-8546.. 113 E
robeckm@tcc.fl.edu
ROBEL, Kenneth .... 856-351-2704.. 296 L
krobel@salemcc.edu
ROBEL, Lauren .... 812-855-5752.. 162 E
provost@indiana.edu
ROBEL, Lauren .... 812-855-9011.. 162 F
provost@indiana.edu
ROBELOTTO, Vince .... 706-379-3111.. 130 B
vrobelotto@yhc.edu
ROBEN, Paul, W .... 858-246-0473.... 70 C
pwroben@ucsd.edu
ROBERSON, Alicia .... 229-245-4378.. 129 G
arroberson@valdosta.edu
ROBERSON, Carrie .... 870-230-5518.... 20 E
robersc@hsu.edu
ROBERSON, Cynthia .... 973-877-3259.. 291 H
crobers2@essex.edu
ROBERSON, Emily .... 903-923-2374.. 457 G
eroberson@etbu.edu
ROBERSON, Eric .... 617-850-1231.. 219 F
eroberson@hchc.edu
ROBERSON, James, A ..... 919-335-1020.. 353 I
jaroberson@waketech.edu
ROBERSON, Janet .... 434-791-5891.. 487 C
roberson@averett.edu
ROBERSON, John .... 910-893-1278.. 342 F
robersonj@campbell.edu
ROBERSON, John .... 910-893-1205.. 342 F
robersonj@campbell.edu
ROBERSON, John, A .... 713-798-4676.. 452 G
jarobers@bcm.edu
ROBERSON, Judith .... 225-768-1754.. 199 B
judith.vidrine@ololcollege.edu
ROBERSON, Kathleen .... 509-533-7042.. 502 I
kathleen.roberson@scc.spokane.edu
ROBERSON, Mark, A .... 951-552-8652.... 29 H
maroberson@calbaptist.edu
ROBERSON, Marla .... 864-646-1753.. 433 C
mrobers1@tctc.edu
ROBERSON, Miriam, C ..... 904-819-6204.... 99 M
registrar@flagler.edu
ROBERSON, Mo .... 949-214-3210.... 41 F
mo.roberson@cui.edu
ROBERSON, Richard, E ... 717-766-2511.. 410 J
rroberso@messiah.edu
ROBERSON, Rita, G .... 304-236-7648.. 512 E
rita.roberson@southernwv.edu
ROBERSON, Robin .... 580-559-5467.. 383 H
robrrob@ecok.edu
ROBERSON, TOR, Shawn 740-283-6463.. 368 L
sroberson@franciscan.edu
ROBERSON, Valerie, R .... 617-541-5301.. 224 F
vroberson@rcc.mass.edu
ROBERT, Bernadette .... 310-954-4099.... 53 B
brobert@msmu.edu
ROBERT, Cortney .... 718-522-2300.. 328 D
crobert@sfc.edu
ROBERTS, Aaron .... 402-643-7233.. 279 F
aaron.roberts@cune.edu
ROBERTS, Adam .... 706-880-8004.. 123 K
aroberts@lagrange.edu
ROBERTS, Al .... 434-949-1000.. 498 E
al.roberts@southside.edu
ROBERTS, Alan, P .... 845-687-5050.. 338 F
robertsal@sunyulster.edu
ROBERTS, III, Alvin .... 716-839-7699.. 312 D
aroberts@daemen.edu
ROBERTS, Amber .... 616-331-3266.. 234 F
roberamb@gvsu.edu
ROBERTS, Anita .... 954-308-2163.... 95 K
aroberts@aii.edu
ROBERTS, Ann .... 847-735-5188.. 145 B
roberts@lakeforest.edu
ROBERTS, Barbara .... 360-676-2772.. 505 C
broberts@nwic.edu
ROBERTS, Betty .... 914-654-5501.. 311 A
broberts@cnr.edu
ROBERTS, Bob, E .... 304-293-3136.. 514 C
bob.roberts@mail.wvu.edu
ROBERTS, Brent .... 406-657-2320.. 277 D
broberts@msubillings.edu
ROBERTS, Carmen .... 406-771-4392.. 277 F
carmen.roberts@gfcmsu.edu
ROBERTS, Carolyn .... 313-927-1474.. 237 E
croberts@marygrove.edu
ROBERTS, Carrie .... 630-829-6029.. 135 F
crobertsi@ben.edu
ROBERTS, Charles, H ...... 859-846-5750.. 191 G
chroberts@midway.edu
ROBERTS, Charlie .... 360-676-2772.. 505 C
chroberts@nwic.edu
ROBERTS, Chell .... 619-260-4627.... 72 B
croberts@sandiego.edu
ROBERTS, Cheryl .... 206-546-4551.. 507 F
cheryl.roberts@shoreline.edu
ROBERTS, Cheryl, A .... 340-692-4192.. 539 C
crobert@uvi.edu
ROBERTS, Christine .... 619-201-8760.... 60 D
chroberts@sdcc.edu
ROBERTS, Christopher, B 334-844-2308...... 1 G
robercr@auburn.edu
ROBERTS, Colleen .... 540-831-5500.. 493 A
ctroberts@radford.edu
ROBERTS, Daniel, M .... 804-524-6709.. 499 G
droberts@vsu.edu
ROBERTS, Dave .... 775-674-7100.. 284 K
droberts@tmcc.edu
ROBERTS, David, M .... 213-740-4577.... 72 D
dave.roberts@usc.edu
ROBERTS, Deborah .... 707-664-3236.... 35 D
deborah.roberts@sonoma.edu
ROBERTS, Dennis .... 530-938-5313.... 40 F
roberts@siskiyous.edu
ROBERTS, Doug .... 707-527-4421.... 63 G
droberts@santarosa.edu
ROBERTS, Douglas, P ..... 573-341-4300.. 274 B
robertsdp@mst.edu
ROBERTS, Dustin .... 870-584-1172.... 23 F
droberts@cccua.edu
ROBERTS, Gail .... 419-448-2013.. 369 G
groberts@heidelberg.edu
ROBERTS, Gary .... 269-927-8771.. 236 G
roberts@lakemichigancollege.edu
ROBERTS, Gary, A .... 501-450-3416.... 24 G
garyr@uca.edu
ROBERTS, Gary, O .... 607-871-2715.. 303 F
roberts@alfred.edu
ROBERTS, Gary, R .... 309-677-3167.. 136 B
groberts@fsmail.bradley.edu
ROBERTS, Gayla .... 765-641-4182.. 158 J
glroberts@anderson.edu
ROBERTS, Gayla .... 903-675-6212.. 473 B
groberts@tvcc.edu
ROBERTS, Glenda, V .... 607-746-4545.. 335 C
robertgv@delhi.edu
ROBERTS, Gregory .... 219-866-6429.. 166 J
groberts@saintjoe.edu
ROBERTS, Gregory, W ..... 434-982-3200.. 495 H
groberts@virginia.edu
ROBERTS, Howard, V .... 606-218-5019.. 194 C
howardroberts@upike.edu
ROBERTS, James .... 570-674-6758.. 410 K
jroberts@misericordia.edu
ROBERTS, James .... 843-863-8083.. 427 I
jroberts@csuniv.edu
ROBERTS, James, S .... 919-684-3501.. 343 J
james.roberts@duke.edu
ROBERTS, Janet .... 248-341-2020.. 239 E
jerobert@oaklandcc.edu
ROBERTS, Janet, E .... 248-341-2020.. 239 E
jerobert@oaklandcc.edu
ROBERTS, Jay .... 765-983-1269.. 160 G
roberja@earlham.edu
ROBERTS, Jayne .... 850-718-2209.... 97 G
robertsj@chipola.edu
ROBERTS, Jean .... 231-777-0519.. 238 G
jean.roberts@muskegoncc.edu
ROBERTS, Jeanne, M .... 813-253-6203.. 114 M
jroberts@ut.edu
ROBERTS, Jeri .... 207-509-7261.. 204 F
jroberts@unity.edu
ROBERTS, Jerilyn, C .... 605-394-2251.. 437 E
jerilyn.roberts@sdsmt.edu
ROBERTS, Jim, O .... 910-893-1240.. 342 F
roberts@campbell.edu
ROBERTS, Jimmy .... 254-298-8340.. 467 B
jdr@templejc.edu
ROBERTS, John .... 903-593-8311.. 470 A
jroberts@texascollege.edu
ROBERTS, Jonathan .... 912-344-2910.. 116 E
jonathan.roberts@armstrong.edu
ROBERTS, Jonathan .... 501-279-4257.... 20 D
jroberts@harding.edu
ROBERTS, Juanita .... 334-727-8894...... 8 A
jroberts@tuskegee.edu
ROBERTS, Juli .... 909-593-3511.... 71 B
jroberts@laverne.edu
ROBERTS, Julia .... 910-642-7141.. 353 C
julia.roberts@sccnc.edu
ROBERTS, Kathleen .... 859-572-6630.. 192 B
robertsk10@nku.edu
ROBERTS, Kay Lynn .... 580-745-2977.. 387 M
kroberts@se.edu
ROBERTS, Keith .... 909-748-8751.... 71 K
keith_roberts@redlands.edu
ROBERTS, Kelley .... 706-867-3280.. 128 F
kelley.roberts@ung.edu
ROBERTS, Kevin, J .... 325-674-2675.. 449 J
robertsk@acu.edu
ROBERTS, Kevin, W .... 518-564-5022.. 334 A
robertkw@plattsburgh.edu
ROBERTS, Leonard .... 973-748-9000.. 289 H
leonard_roberts@bloomfield.edu

ROBINSON, LaSandra ..... 803-536-7000.. 432 E
ROBINSON, Lesley, J ...... 512-428-1051.. 464 G
lrobinso@stedwards.edu
ROBINSON, Lois .... 251-578-1313...... 6 C
lrobinso@rstc.edu
ROBINSON, Lorne, T .... 651-696-6358.. 247 I
robinson@macalester.edu
ROBINSON, Louester .... 843-722-5556.. 433 D
lou.robinson@tridenttech.edu
ROBINSON, Luke .... 616-526-8686.. 232 A
lrobinso@calvin.edu
ROBINSON, Lynn .... 401-598-1405.. 425 B
lrobinson@jwu.edu
ROBINSON, Lynne .... 207-893-7841.. 204 D
lrobinson@sjcme.edu
ROBINSON, Lynne, P ...... 301-447-5296.. 209 G
lrobinso@msmary.edu
ROBINSON, M. Kevin ...... 334-844-4389...... 1 G
robinmk@auburn.edu
ROBINSON, Maria .... 979-458-6221.. 467 D
mrobinson@tamus.edu
ROBINSON, Marjorie .... 951-785-2167.... 48 A
mrobinso@lasierra.edu
ROBINSON, Mark .... 304-696-6773.. 513 D
robinsonma@marshall.edu
ROBINSON, Mary .... 716-896-0700.. 339 E
robinsonm@villa.edu
ROBINSON, Michael .... 901-435-1433.. 441 C
michael_robinson@loc.edu
ROBINSON, Michael .... 405-744-6523.. 385 G
michael.robinson@okstate.edu
ROBINSON, Mike .... 205-226-4935...... 2 C
mrobinso@bsc.edu
ROBINSON, Mike .... 858-513-9240.... 27 V
mike.robinson@ashford.edu
ROBINSON, Mike .... 541-776-9942.. 394 A
mike.r@pacificbible.com
ROBINSON, Mitch .... 931-221-7883.. 444 E
robinsonm@apsu.edu
ROBINSON, Monica .... 251-578-1313...... 6 C
mrobinson@rstc.edu
ROBINSON, Natalie .... 619-876-4261.... 68 I
nrobinson@usuniversity.edu
ROBINSON, Neal .... 802-654-2512.. 484 I
nrobinson@smcvt.edu
ROBINSON, Neil .... 214-768-7677.. 465 J
nrobinson@smu.edu
ROBINSON, Norm .... 615-248-1296.. 447 F
nrobinson@trevecca.edu
ROBINSON, Pam .... 405-585-4100.. 385 B
pam.robinson@okbu.edu
ROBINSON, Patricia .... 661-362-3992.... 40 A
patty.robinson@canyons.edu
ROBINSON, Paul, A .... 734-647-3502.. 241 J
probins@umich.edu
ROBINSON, Peter, J .... 585-275-4036.. 338 K
peter_robinson@urmc.rochester.edu
ROBINSON, Ralph .... 302-857-7381.... 90 F
rrobinson@desu.edu
ROBINSON, Regina .... 617-873-0470.. 217 A
regina.robinson@cambridgecollege.edu
ROBINSON, Regina .... 318-670-9617.. 199 J
rrobinson@susla.edu
ROBINSON, Robert .... 909-621-8136.... 58 A
robert.robinson@pomona.edu
ROBINSON, Robert .... 678-717-3654.. 128 F
robert.robinson@ung.edu
ROBINSON, Robert .... 802-654-2524.. 484 I
rrobinson@smcvt.edu
ROBINSON, Ronald, R .... 864-597-4051.. 435 C
robinsonrr1@wofford.edu
ROBINSON, Roy .... 253-879-3653.. 508 D
rrobinson@pugetsound.edu
ROBINSON, Rush .... 636-529-0000.. 271 D
rlrobinson@slchcmail.com
ROBINSON, Sandra .... 612-244-2800.. 247 D
srobinson@ipr.edu
ROBINSON, Sandra, T ..... 313-962-7150.. 242 H
srobins1@wcccd.edu
ROBINSON, Sandy .... 904-766-6551.. 101 G
sandy.robinson@fscj.edu
ROBINSON, Sara, C .... 207-941-7617.. 202 I
robinsons@husson.edu
ROBINSON, Sharon .... 704-233-8249.. 359 H
s.robinson@wingate.edu
ROBINSON, Shawn .... 813-253-7755.. 102 R
srobinson37@hccfl.edu
ROBINSON, Stanley, L .... 901-333-4737.. 447 B
srobinson@southwest.tn.edu
ROBINSON, Stephanie, R 559-442-4600.... 67 C
stephanie.robinson@fresnocitycollege.edu
ROBINSON, Steve .... 567-661-7101.. 376 D
steve_robinson@owens.edu
ROBINSON, Stuart .... 845-257-3910.. 331 E
robinsos@newpaltz.edu
ROBINSON, Sunnie .... 860-444-8508.. 529 A
sunnie.robinson@uscg.mil
ROBINSON, T. Hank .... 402-554-3750.. 283 B
trobinson@unomaha.edu
ROBINSON, Tammy .... 650-738-7099.... 62 I
robinsontammy@smccd.edu
ROBINSON, Tia, L .... 636-584-6601.. 264 M
tia.robinson@eastcentral.edu
ROBINSON, Tiffany .... 270-745-5432.. 194 D
tiffany.robinson@wku.edu
ROBINSON, Timothy .... 904-620-2657.. 112 B
trobinso@unf.edu
ROBINSON, Tony .... 276-523-2400.. 497 F
trobinson@mecc.edu
ROBINSON, Tray .... 530-898-4764.... 32 C
trobinson@csuchico.edu
ROBINSON, Varinia .... 610-917-3939.. 422 C
vcrobinson@valleyforge.edu
ROBINSON, Walter, A ...... 530-752-5589.... 69 A
uadirector@ucdavis.edu
ROBINSON, Warren .... 803-705-4662.. 427 D
robinson@benedict.edu
ROBINSON, Wayne .... 718-473-8960.. 309 C
wrobinson@citytech.cuny.edu
ROBINSON, Wayne .... 718-260-4900.. 309 C
wrobinson@citytech.cuny.edu
ROBINSON, Wayne .... 307-855-2104.. 526 E
wrobinson@cwc.edu
ROBINSON, Wendi .... 614-947-6768.. 369 A
wendi.robinson@franklin.edu
ROBINSON, Wendy .... 651-450-3692.. 249 F
wrobins@inverhills.edu
ROBINSON, Wendy .... 212-616-7250.. 315 G
wendy.robinson@heleneful d.edu
ROBINSON, Will .... 304-887-1795.. 487 F
wrobinson@bluefield.edu
ROBINSON, William .... 803-376-5700.. 427 A
wrobinson@allenuniversity.edu
ROBINSON, William .... 410-621-2355.. 212 B
wrobinson3@umes.edu
ROBINSON, Winston .... 903-927-3268.. 479 K
wrobinson@wileyc.edu
ROBINSON-ARMSTRONG,
Abbie .... 310-338-7598.... 51 E
arobinso@lmu.edu
ROBINSON-COOLIDGE,
Austin .... 507-222-5635.. 245 C
arobinso@carleton.edu
ROBINSON-GARDNER,
Dorris, R .... 601-979-2455.. 258 D
dorris.r.gardner@jsums.edu
ROBINSON GLOVER,
Maria .... 213-613-2200.... 65 H
maria_robinsonglover@sciarc.edu
ROBINSON KLOOS,
Jennifer .... 651-690-8831.. 254 M
jrkloos@stkate.edu
ROBINSON-LEWIS,
Denise .... 973-720-2885.. 298 G
lewisd@wpunj.edu
ROBINSON-PAUL, Ann ..... 701-231-8325.. 361 A
anne.robinson-paul@ndsu.edu
ROBISON, Daniel, J .... 304-293-2395.. 514 C
dan.robison@mail.wvu.edu
ROBISON, Deborah .... 858-745-2073.... 62 J
drobison@shpdiscovery.org
ROBISON, Elizabeth .... 661-253-7707.... 30 E
erobison@calarts.edu
ROBISON, Lori .... 419-267-1342.. 374 A
lrobison@northweststate.edu
ROBISON, Margaret .... 910-362-7101.. 348 A
mrobison@cfcc.edu
ROBISON, Mike .... 662-562-3438.. 260 C
jmrobison@northwestms.edu
ROBISON, Rick .... 925-969-2586.... 41 I
rrobisonl@dvc.edu
ROBISON, Timothy .... 617-349-8747.. 220 B
trobison@lesley.edu
ROBITAILLE, Marilyn .... 254-968-9632.. 467 F
robitaille@tarleton.edu
ROBLEDO, Marcelina .... 513-562-6267.. 363 H
mrobledo@artacademy.edu
ROBLEDO, Richard .... 563-589-0219.. 177 H
helpdesk@wartburgseminary.edu
ROBLES, Jonathan .... 623-935-8052.... 14 A
jonathan.robles@estrellamountain.edu
ROBLES, María, V .... 787-600-1070.. 539 A
maria.robles4@upr.edu
ROBLES, Pedro .... 787-786-3030.. 536 F
probles@ucb.edu.pr
ROBLES, Ray .... 787-864-2222.. 534 A
ray.robles@guayama.inter.edu
ROBLES JIMENEZ,
Elizabeth .... 213-477-2769.... 53 B
ejimenez@msmu.edu
ROBOMAN, Lourdes .... 691-350-2296.. 529 F
comfsmyap@comfsm.fm
ROBOTHAM, Tena .... 847-628-2002.. 144 B
trobotham@judsonu.edu
ROBSHAW, Jeff .... 262-564-3676.. 523 D
robshawj@gtc.edu
ROBSON, James, B .... 803-327-8047.. 435 D
jrobson@yorktech.edu
ROBUCK, Chris .... 503-594-3090.. 390 F
chrisr@clackamas.edu
ROBY, Latasha .... 708-344-4700.. 146 D
lroby@lincolntech.edu
ROBY, Mark .... 305-809-3165.. 100 N
mark.roby@fkcc.edu
ROBY, Mary .... 704-406-4298.. 344 E
mroby@gardner-webb.edu
ROBY, Peter, P .... 617-373-2672.. 227 B
ROBYN, Elisa .... 303-458-4081.... 82 L
erobyn@regis.edu
ROCA, Joan .... 507-389-5953.. 250 E
joan.roca@mnsu.edu
ROCAP, Donna .... 845-431-8066.. 312 G
rocap@sunydutchess.edu
ROCCIA, Miriam, I .... 314-516-5291.. 274 A
roccia@umsl.edu
ROCCO, Anne, L .... 718-990-2007.. 328 F
roccoa@stjohns.edu
ROCCO, Brian .... 212-774-4801.. 320 C
brocco@mmm.edu
ROCCO, Denine .... 508-531-1276.. 221 C
drocco@bridgew.edu
ROCCO, Karen, S .... 412-362-8500.. 417 C
krocco@pims.edu
ROCCONI, Christie .... 662-846-4670.. 257 E
chrcconi@deltastate.edu
ROCHAT, Angela .... 970-247-7695.... 80 D
rochat_a@fortlewis.edu
ROCHE, Daniel .... 973-655-4158.. 293 A
roched@mail.montclair.edu
ROCHE, Isabel .... 802-440-4406.. 483 E
iroche@bennington.edu
ROCHE, James .... 413-545-6330.. 220 F
jroche@provost.umass.edu
ROCHE, Keila, J .... 787-743-7979.. 536 A
keroche@suagm.edu
ROCHE, Mary Beth .... 570-504-1589.. 407 B
rochem@lackawanna.edu
ROCHE, Missy .... 618-235-2700.. 155 C
melissa.roche@swic.edu
ROCHE, Patrick .... 315-268-3734.. 310 B
proche@clarkson.edu
ROCHE, Sara .... 610-341-5854.. 403 B
sroche@eastern.edu
ROCHE, Stephen, H .... 407-303-8016.... 95 C
stephen.roche@adu.edu
ROCHELLE, Lori .... 903-823-3358.. 467 C
lori.rochelle@texarkanacollege.edu
ROCHELLE, Lugenia .... 803-780-1179.. 434 M
rochelle@voorhees.edu
ROCHESTER, Sylvia .... 410-462-8371.. 206 D
srochester@bccc.edu
ROCHETTE, Susan .... 802-447-6339.. 485 B
srochette@svc.edu
ROCHFORD, Rosemary .... 315-464-5468.. 332 C
rochforr@upstate.edu
ROCHLITZ, Mendel .... 718-853-8500.. 337 H
ROCHON, Ronald, S .... 812-465-1617.. 168 E
rochon@usi.edu
ROCHON, Sandra .... 978-762-4000.. 224 C
srochon@northshore.edu
ROCHON, Thomas, R ...... 607-274-3111.. 317 D
president@ithaca.edu
ROCK, Arlene, M .... 413-782-1538.. 229 E
arlene.rock@wne.edu
ROCK, David .... 662-915-7063.. 261 B
rock@olemiss.edu
ROCK, Jennifer .... 215-489-2917.. 402 A
jennifer.rock@delval.edu
ROCK, John .... 305-348-0570.. 111 A
john.rock@fiu.edu
ROCK, Kimberly .... 413-528-7229.. 214 H
krock@simons-rock.edu
ROCK, Stephen .... 845-437-5300.. 339 C
strock@vassar.edu
ROCK, Thomas .... 212-678-3083.. 337 E
tpr4@tc.columbia.edu
ROCKAFELLOW, Colleen . 708-456-0300.. 156 C
colleenrockafellow@triton.edu
ROCKAFELLOW, Mollie .... 815-740-3363.. 157 F
mrockafellow@stfrancis.edu
ROCKECHARLIE, Barbara . 704-372-0266.. 345 F
brockecharlie@kingscollegecharlotte.edu
ROCKETT, Jeri, M .... 651-962-6780.. 256 C
gmrockett@stthomas.edu
ROCKEY, Tim .... 210-486-0926.. 450 F
trockey@alamo.edu
ROCKHILL, Linda .... 718-779-1430.. 326 D
info@plazacollege.edu
ROCKHILL, Wendy .... 206-934-6921.. 506 K
wendy.rockhill@seattlecolleges.edu
ROCKLAND-MILLER,
Harry, S .... 413-545-2337.. 220 F
rockmill@uhs.umass.edu
ROCKLIN, Thomas, R ...... 319-335-3557.. 169 H
thomas-rocklin@uiowa.edu
ROCKMAN, Adam .... 718-997-5500.. 309 D
adam.rockman@qc.cuny.edu
ROCKOW, Amanda, O ...... 972-883-2106.. 476 C
arockow@utdallas.edu
ROCKWELL, Grant .... 530-760-5168.... 69 A
grockwell@ucdavis.edu
ROCKWELL, Jason .... 405-945-3315.. 386 C
jason.rockwell@osuokc.edu
ROCKWELL, Kelly .... 716-851-1198.. 313 H
rockwell@ecc.edu
ROCKWELL, Rick .... 314-246-8280.. 275 B
rickrockwell@webster.edu
ROCKWELL, Stephanie ..... 509-313-6404.. 504 A
rockwell@gonzaga.edu
ROCKWELL, Susan .... 408-924-6047.... 35 C
susan.rockwell@sjsu.edu
RODARTE, Susana .... 915-831-2018.. 457 H
srodart7@epcc.edu
RODAS, Mary .... 516-364-0808.. 323 B
rodas@nycollege.edu
RODDEN, Greg, A .... 863-638-7215.. 115 C
greg.rodden@warner.edu
RODDINI, Martin .... 516-572-7331.. 322 C
martin.roddini@ncc.edu
RODDY, Jackie .... 615-226-3990.. 441 D
jroddy@lincolntech.edu
RODDY, Marilyn .... 865-694-6529.. 446 G
mlroddy@pstcc.edu
RODE, Joe .... 817-515-7741.. 467 A
joe.rode@tccd.edu
RODECKER, Daniel .... 518-580-5860.. 330 F
drodecke@skidmore.edu
RODENBERG, Tamara, N . 304-829-7111.. 510 G
trodenberg@bethanywv.edu
RODENBORN, Steven, M 512-637-5618.. 464 G
stevero@stedwards.edu
RODERICK, Daniel .... 508-793-7578.. 217 B
droderick@clarku.edu
RODERICK, Gerald, K ...... 410-778-7810.. 213 E
jroderick2@washcoll.edu
RODERICK, Lori .... 309-794-7182.. 135 D
loriroderick@augustana.edu
RODGER, Doug .... 712-324-5061.. 175 G
drodger@nwicc.edu
RODGERS, Ardie .... 405-733-7434.. 387 I
arodgers@rose.edu
RODGERS, Barbara, J ..... 574-807-7209.. 159 D
rodgerb@bethelcollege.edu
RODGERS, Beverly .... 785-242-5200.. 183 M
beverly.rodgers@ottawa.edu
RODGERS, JR., Bob .... 404-835-6132.. 443 M
brodgers@richmont.edu
RODGERS, Chris, T .... 402-280-2455.. 279 H
chrisrodgers@creighton.edu
RODGERS, Christopher .... 718-817-4755.. 314 G
chrodgers@fordham.edu
RODGERS, Corey .... 310-233-4091.... 49 I
rodgercd@lahc.edu
RODGERS, Denise .... 973-972-3645.. 295 F
denise.rutgers@rutgers.edu
RODGERS, Harold, E .... 574-807-7751.. 159 D
rodgerh@bethelcollege.edu
RODGERS, Kenneth, G ..... 919-530-5079.. 357 A
krodgers@nccu.edu
RODGERS, Larry .... 541-737-4582.. 393 H
larry.rodgers@oregonstate.edu
RODGERS, Mark, E .... 570-340-6001.. 409 H
mrodgers@marywood.edu
RODGERS, Mike .... 270-686-4503.. 190 D
mike.rodgers@kctcs.edu
RODGERS, Mike .... 270-686-4481.. 190 D
mike.rodgers@kctcs.edu
RODGERS, Mike .... 325-649-8055.. 459 E
mrodgers@hputx.edu
RODGERS, Phillip .... 501-420-1249.... 18 F
phillip.rodgers@arkansasbaptist.edu
RODGERS, Ronald, F .... 603-862-0960.. 288 B
ron.rodgers@usnh.edu
RODGERS, Ronald, F .... 603-862-0960.. 288 C
ron.rodgers@usnh.edu
RODGERS, Ruby .... 270-534-3184.. 190 H
ruby.rodgers@kctcs.edu
RODGERS, Ruth .... 317-955-6321.. 165 N
rrodgers@marian.edu
RODGERS, Teresa, P .... 334-670-3221...... 7 H
trodgers@troy.edu
RODGERS, Victor .... 717-221-1361.. 405 C
vrodgers@hacc.edu
RODICIO, Lenore .... 305-237-3715.. 105 D
lrodicio@mdc.edu
RODKIN, Dan .... 352-395-4171.. 109 C
dan.rodkin@sfcollege.edu
RODLER, Trina .... 323-856-7699.... 26 I
trodler@afi.com
RODNE, Anne .... 561-912-1211.... 99 J
arodne@evergladesuniversity.edu
RODNEW, Faye .... 305-626-3132.. 101 A
faye.rodney@fmuniv.edu
RODNING, Janet, M .... 770-720-5954.. 126 C
jmr@reinhardt.edu
RODOCKER, Jason, L .... 540-458-8753.. 500 F
jrodocker@wlu.edu
RODOLF, Mark .... 405-974-3611.. 388 L
mrodolf@uco.edu
RODRGUEZ, Nemaris, C . 718-390-4351.. 328 F
rodrgun@stjohns.edu
RODRICK-SCHNAATH,
Heidi .... 215-248-6312.. 409 D
hrodrick-schnaath@ltsp.edu

RODRIGUE, Kelly, J .... 985-448-4154.. 201 A
kelly.rodrigue@nicholls.edu
RODRIGUE, Morris .... 530-242-7525.... 64 D
mrodrigue@shastacollege.edu
RODRIGUES-DOOLABH,
Lisa .... 203-596-2104.... 86 G
lrodrigues-doolabh@nv.edu
RODRIGUEZ, Abel .... 787-834-9595.. 536 E
arodriguez@uaa.edu
RODRIGUEZ, Abiezer .... 787-834-9595.. 536 E
abrodriguez@uaa.edu
RODRIGUEZ, Adrian .... 817-515-1007.. 467 A
adrian.rodriguez@tccd.edu
RODRIGUEZ, Aida, E .... 787-852-1430.. 532 N
arodriguez@hccpr.edu
RODRIGUEZ, Alba .... 352-365-3571.. 104 J
rodrigua@lssc.edu
RODRIGUEZ, Alfred .... 210-999-7206.. 473 A
alfred.rodriguez@trinity.edu
RODRIGUEZ, Alma .... 805-289-6360.... 73 F
arodriguez@vcccd.edu
RODRIGUEZ, Andy .... 970-248-1337.... 77 L
arodrigu@coloradomesa.edu
RODRIGUEZ, Angel .... 787-738-2161.. 538 A
angel.rodriguez40@upr.edu
RODRIGUEZ, Anita .... 402-449-2821.. 280 C
arodriguez@graceu.edu
RODRIGUEZ, Aristalia ...... 212-772-4804.. 308 D
aristalia.rodriguez@hunter.cuny.edu
RODRIGUEZ, Arlene .... 413-755-4440.. 224 G
arodriguez@stcc.edu
RODRIGUEZ, Armando .... 787-841-2000.. 535 I
armando_rodriguez@pucpr.edu
RODRIGUEZ, Art, D .... 845-437-7300.. 339 C
arodriguez@vassar.edu
RODRIGUEZ, Barbara .... 305-821-3333.. 101 B
bjrodriguez@fnu.edu
RODRIGUEZ, Barbara, J .. 305-821-3333.. 101 B
bjrodriguez@fnu.edu
RODRIGUEZ, Beatriz .... 908-709-7448.. 298 A
rodriguez@ucc.edu
RODRIGUEZ, Brenda .... 347-964-8600.. 305 I
brodriguez@boricuacollege.edu
RODRIGUEZ, Carlos .... 323-343-3929.... 33 C
carlos.rodriguez@calstatela.edu
RODRIGUEZ, Carlos .... 847-566-6401.. 157 G
crodriguez@usml.edu
RODRIGUEZ, Carlos .... 787-765-4210.. 531 H
crodriguez@cempr.edu
RODRIGUEZ, Carlos .... 787-725-6500.. 531 C
crodriguez@albizu.edu
RODRIGUEZ, Carmen ...... 787-878-5475.. 533 H
clrodri@arecibo.inter.edu
RODRIGUEZ, Carmen ...... 909-384-8592.... 60 C
marodrig@sbccd.cc.ca.us
RODRIGUEZ, Carmen, J .. 787-480-2436.. 531 J
crodriguez03@sanjuanciudadpatria.com
RODRIGUEZ, Claribel .... 787-621-2835.. 530 F
crodriguez@aupr.edu
RODRIGUEZ, Claribel .... 787-864-2222.. 534 A
claribel.rodriguez@guayama.inter.edu
RODRIGUEZ, Claribette ... 787-257-7373.. 535 P
clrodriguez@suagm.edu
RODRIGUEZ, Claudia .... 787-761-0640.. 537 C
asistenciaeconomica@utcpr.edu
RODRIGUEZ, Daniel, B .... 312-503-3460.. 150 F
daniel.rodriguez@law.northwestern.edu
RODRIGUEZ, Dawn, M .... 813-974-7297.. 112 C
dmrodriguez@usf.edu
RODRIGUEZ, Diana .... 909-384-4470.... 60 C
drodriguez@sbccd.cc.ca.us
RODRIGUEZ, Diana .... 787-852-1430.. 532 N
drodriguez@hccpr.edu
RODRIGUEZ, Diriee, Y .... 787-743-7979.. 536 A
dyrodriguez@suagm.edu
RODRIGUEZ, Ed .... 816-802-3436.. 266 D
erodriguez@kcai.edu
RODRIGUEZ, Edgar .... 787-841-2000.. 535 I
edrodrios@pucpr.edu
RODRIGUEZ, Edgar .... 203-582-3660.... 88 G
edgar.rodriguez@quinnipiac.edu
RODRIGUEZ, Edgar, D .... 787-257-7373.. 535 P
ue_erodrigue@suagm.edu
RODRIGUEZ, Elizabeth .... 561-683-1400.... 94 G
lrodriguez@anho.edu
RODRIGUEZ, Elsa .... 787-753-6335.. 532 O
e_rodriguez@icprjc.edu
RODRIGUEZ, Esaeas, J .... 260-422-5561.. 162 B
ejrodriguez@indianatech.edu
RODRIGUEZ,
Francisco, C .... 213-891-2201.... 49 F
mazarild@email.laccd.edu
RODRIGUEZ, Ginger .... 219-473-4305.. 159 L
grodriguez@ccsj.edu
RODRIGUEZ, Glorimar .... 787-780-5134.. 535 C
glrodriguez@nuc.edu
RODRIGUEZ, Guillermo ... 314-246-7881.. 275 B
rodriggu@webster.edu
RODRIGUEZ, Havidan ...... 956-665-2111.. 476 E
havidan@utrgv.edu
RODRIGUEZ, Irma, I .... 787-841-2000.. 535 I
irodriguez@pucpr.edu
RODRIGUEZ, Israel .... 787-780-0070.. 531 B
irodriguez@caribbean.edu
RODRIGUEZ, Jalibeth ...... 787-841-2000.. 535 I
jalibeth_rodriguez@pucpr.edu
RODRIGUEZ, Janeth .... 909-652-6541.... 37 D
janeth.rodriguez@chaffey.edu
RODRIGUEZ, Jesus .... 713-718-5222.. 459 B
jesus.rodriguez@hccs.edu
RODRIGUEZ, Jordan .... 208-459-5529.. 133 D
jrodriguez@collegeofidaho.edu
RODRIGUEZ, Jorge .... 787-766-1717.. 536 B
ac_jrodrigue@suagm.edu
RODRIGUEZ, Jorge .... 718-990-1485.. 328 F
rodriguj@stjohns.edu
RODRIGUEZ, Jose .... 305-237-2339.. 105 D
jrodri28@mdc.edu
RODRIGUEZ, Jose .... 787-279-1912.. 533 J
jarodriguez@bayamon.inter.edu
RODRIGUEZ, Jose .... 718-489-5315.. 328 D
jrodriguez@sfc.edu
RODRIGUEZ, Jose .... 214-860-8587.. 456 F
jcrodriguez@dcccd.edu
RODRIGUEZ, Jose Ginel . 787-798-6904.. 536 G
jose.ginel@uccaribe.edu
RODRIGUEZ, Jose Ginel . 787-269-4510.. 536 G
jose.ginel@uccaribe.edu
RODRIGUEZ, Juan .... 787-878-5475.. 533 H
jcrodrig@arecibo.inter.edu
RODRIGUEZ, Katrina .... 970-351-2796.... 84 C
katrina.rodriguez@unco.edu
RODRIGUEZ, Kristine ...... 785-833-4354.. 182 F
kristy.rodriguez@kwu.edu
RODRIGUEZ, Lee Ann ..... 941-487-4649.. 111 D
lrodriguez@ncf.edu
RODRIGUEZ, Lena .... 858-253-2157.... 54 A
lrodriguez@nu.edu
RODRIGUEZ, Leslie .... 847-233-7700.. 150 D
lrodriguez@nc.edu
RODRIGUEZ, Liliana .... 303-871-3080.... 84 B
liliana.rodriguez@du.edu
RODRIGUEZ, Lora .... 972-721-5322.. 473 D
lbrodriguez@udallas.edu
RODRIGUEZ, Lucia, M ..... 915-831-2848.. 457 H
lrodr258@epcc.edu
RODRIGUEZ, Luis .... 787-850-9305.. 538 B
luis.rodriguez39@upr.edu
RODRIGUEZ, Luis, R .... 787-850-9324.. 538 B
luis.rodriguez40@upr.edu
RODRIGUEZ, Magaly .... 787-850-9383.. 538 B
magaly.rodriguez1@upr.edu
RODRIGUEZ, Maggie .... 832-252-4623.. 454 H
maggie.rodriguez@cbshouston.edu
RODRIGUEZ, Maria .... 787-852-1430.. 532 N
ma.rodriguez.r@hccpr.edu
RODRIGUEZ, Maria .... 305-223-4561.. 108 A
rodriguez@sjvcs.edu
RODRIGUEZ,
Maria-Judith .... 413-542-2372.. 214 C
hr@amherst.edu
RODRIGUEZ, Marisela ..... 956-764-5798.. 460 F
marisela.rodriguez@laredo.edu
RODRIGUEZ, Mark .... 216-987-5459.. 367 E
mark.rodriguez@tri-c.edu
RODRIGUEZ, Marlene ...... 787-844-8181.. 538 E
marlene.rodriguez@upr.edu
RODRIGUEZ, Mary, J ...... 419-755-4767.. 373 G
mrodriguez@ncstatecollege.edu
RODRIGUEZ, Mary Ann ... 503-883-2458.. 392 B
mrodrigu1@linfield.edu
RODRIGUEZ, Mary Ann ... 361-582-2560.. 478 F
maryann.rodriguez@victoriacollege.edu
RODRIGUEZ, Mayra .... 787-743-7979.. 536 A
mrodrigu@suagm.edu
RODRIGUEZ, Melanie ...... 787-720-4476.. 537 A
biblioteca@mizpa.edu
RODRIGUEZ, Melba .... 812-866-7017.. 161 C
rodriguez@hanover.edu
RODRIGUEZ, Miguel .... 939-292-8915.. 539 A
miguel.rodriguez10@upr.edu
RODRIGUEZ, Miguel .... 973-748-9000.. 289 H
miguel_rodriguez@bloomfield.edu
RODRIGUEZ, Millie .... 330-941-1526.. 382 A
mjrodriguez02@ysu.edu
RODRIGUEZ, Moises .... 210-924-4338.. 452 F
moises.rodriguez@bua.edu
RODRIGUEZ, Monica .... 510-215-3958.... 41 H
mrodriguez@contracosta.edu
RODRIGUEZ, Narce .... 971-722-7249.. 394 F
nrodrigu@pcc.edu
RODRIGUEZ, Nilda .... 914-422-4213.. 325 J
nrodriguez@pace.edu
RODRIGUEZ, Nilda, E ..... 787-852-1430.. 532 N
nrodriguez@hccpr.edu
RODRIGUEZ, Norma .... 562-860-2451.... 36 P
nrodriguez@cerritos.edu
RODRIGUEZ, Olga .... 305-821-3333.. 101 B
ordriguez@fnu.edu
RODRIGUEZ, Oscar .... 252-639-7342.. 355 K
orodriguez@umo.edu
RODRIGUEZ, Peter .... 713-348-5928.. 464 E
RODRIGUEZ, Raquel .... 559-934-2218.... 74 D
raquelrodriguez@whccd.edu
RODRIGUEZ, Raul .... 714-480-7450.... 58 F
rodriguez_raul@rsccd.edu
RODRIGUEZ, Rene .... 512-232-2780.. 476 B
renerod@austin.utexas.edu
RODRIGUEZ, Reuban, B .. 804-828-8940.. 496 D
rbrodriguez@vcu.edu
RODRIGUEZ, Ricardo .... 787-751-0178.. 535 N
ricrodriguez@suagm.edu
RODRIGUEZ, Ricardo .... 817-531-4249.. 472 F
rrodriguez@txwes.edu
RODRIGUEZ, Ricardo .... 972-860-8325.. 456 D
ricardorodriguez@dcccd.edu
RODRIGUEZ, Richard .... 559-323-2100.... 61 E
rrodriguez@sjcl.edu
RODRIGUEZ, Ron .... 209-667-3709.... 34 E
rrodriguez36@csustan.edu
RODRIGUEZ, Rosa .... 860-832-1652.... 85 F
rosa.rodriguez@ccsu.edu
RODRIGUEZ, Salvador ...... 213-477-2697.... 53 B
srodriguez@msmu.edu
RODRIGUEZ, Shari, M ...... 574-284-4581.. 167 A
srodriguez@saintmarys.edu
RODRIGUEZ, Sherri .... 818-947-2726.... 50 D
rodrigsa@avc.edu
RODRIGUEZ, Silvio .... 305-237-7445.. 105 D
srodrig2@mdc.edu
RODRIGUEZ, Simon .... 641-472-1170.. 175 A
srodriguez@mum.edu
RODRIGUEZ, Sonia .... 585-475-2395.. 327 E
smrfa@rit.edu
RODRIGUEZ, Sonya, F ...... 575-624-8066.. 300 I
sonya@nmmi.edu
RODRIGUEZ, Steph .... 213-283-4253.... 37 I
srodriguez@thechicagoschool.edu
RODRIGUEZ, Stephanie ..... 310-660-3601.... 42 J
srodriguez@elcamino.edu
RODRIGUEZ, Steven .... 949-214-3003.... 41 F
steven.rodriguez@cui.edu
RODRIGUEZ, Sylvia .... 925-424-1542.... 37 C
srodriguez@laspositascollege.edu
RODRIGUEZ, Sylvia .... 925-424-1000.... 37 C
RODRIGUEZ, Sylvia, L .... 305-474-6871.. 108 E
srodriguez@stu.edu
RODRIGUEZ, Teresita .... 310-434-4774.... 63 F
rodriguez_teresita@smc.edu
RODRIGUEZ, Tiffany .... 619-684-8815.... 54 C
trodriguez@newschoolarch.edu
RODRIGUEZ, Velia .... 559-730-3775.... 40 E
veliar@cos.edu
RODRIGUEZ, Vince .... 714-241-6195.... 39 E
vrodriguez@coastline.edu
RODRIGUEZ, Vincent .... 210-283-5096.. 474 D
vincent@uiwtx.edu
RODRIGUEZ, Wanda .... 787-257-0000.. 537 H
wanda.rodriguez@upr.edu
RODRIGUEZ, Widilia .... 787-815-0000.. 537 F
widilia.rodriguez@upr.edu
RODRIGUEZ, Yanilda .... 787-766-1717.. 536 B
yrodriguez98@suagm.edu
RODRIGUEZ, Zulyn .... 787-764-0000.. 538 F
zulyn.rodriguez@upr.edu
RODRIGUEZ-CANCEL
Jaime, L .... 787-723-4481.. 531 D
jarodriguez@ceaprc.edu
RODRIGUEZ-CHARDAVOYNE,
Esther .... 718-518-4308.. 308 C
erodriguez@hostos.cuny.edu
RODRIGUEZ-DORESTANT,
Simone .... 718-804-8805.. 309 B
simone@mec.cuny.edu
RODRIGUEZ ESQUERDO,
Pedro, J .... 787-764-0000.. 538 F
pj.rodriguezesquerdo@upr.edu
RODRIGUEZ-FARRAR,
Hanna .... 415-482-1927.... 42 G
hrf@dominican.edu
RODRIGUEZ-GREGORY,
Lisa .... 732-906-2550.. 292 E
lgregory@middlesexcc.edu
RODRIGUEZ-HEFFNER,
Ermelinda .... 831-656-3054.. 528 D
erodriguez@nps.edu
RODRIGUEZ-HUMBERT,
Yojana .... 954-308-2601.... 95 K
yrodriguez@aii.edu
RODRIGUEZ-LOPEZ,
Miguel, A .... 787-723-4481.. 531 D
centro@ceaprc.edu
RODRIGUEZ-MOLINA,
Nilda, E .... 787-480-2439.. 531 J
nilrodriguez@sanjuanciudadpatria.com
RODRIGUEZ-PAZ, Maria . 787-620-2040.. 530 F
mrodriguez_paz@aupr.edu
RODRIGUEZ-QUINONES,
Jose .... 787-725-6500.. 531 C
jrodriguezq@albizu.edu
RODRIGUEZ SEGURA,
Kent .... 415-351-3522.... 61 B
krsegura@sfai.edu
RODRIGUEZ-VARGAS,
Claribel .... 787-261-2835.. 530 F
crodriguez@aupr.edu
RODRIGUEZ-VEGA,
Shirley .... 312-996-5563.. 156 F
srodri3@uic.edu
RODRIQUEZ, Camille ...... 303-329-6355.... 78 O
dean@cstcm.edu
RODRIQUEZ, Glendali ..... 715-232-2421.. 521 D
rodriquezg@uwstout.edu
RODRIQUEZ, Jason .... 503-883-2574.. 392 B
jrodriqu@linfield.edu
RODRIQUEZ, Mike .... 505-984-6058.. 301 I
RODRIQUEZ, Nicky, M .... 219-942-1459.. 160 C
nicky.rodriquez@ccr.edu
RODRÍGUEZ, Hector .... 787-743-7979.. 536 A
hrodriguez183@suagm.edu
RODRÍGUEZ, Israel .... 787-743-7979.. 536 A
ut_irodriguez@suagm.edu
RODRÍGUEZ, Ivette .... 787-725-8120.. 532 K
irodriguez@eap.edu
RODRÍGUEZ, Mayra .... 787-892-5115.. 534 D
mayra_rodriguez@sangerman.inter.edu
RODRÍGUEZ ALVARADO,
Diana .... 787-884-3838.. 530 G
drodriguez@atenascollege.edu
RODRÍGUEZ-BONANO,
Melysa .... 787-993-8896.. 537 G
melysa.rodriguez@upr.edu
RODRÍGUEZ-BONANO,
Melysa .... 787-993-8881.. 537 G
melysa.rodriguez@upr.edu
RODRÍGUEZ-ORTIZ,
Marcia .... 787-993-8856.. 537 G
marcia.rodriguez@upr.edu
RODRÍGUEZ-RIVERA,
Rafael, E .... 787-751-1600.. 534 E
rrodriguez@juris.inter.edu
RODRÍGUEZ-VALLÉS,
Nora .... 787-993-8868.. 537 G
nora.rodriguez1@upr.edu
RODUIN, Cheyenne .... 425-235-2235.. 506 F
croduin@rtc.edu
RODUIN, Cheyenne, M ... 425-739-8657.. 504 F
cheyenne.roduin@lwtech.edu
ROE, Aaron .... 309-649-6230.. 155 G
aaron.roe@src.edu
ROE, Michael .... 845-431-8018.. 312 G
michael.roe@sunydutchess.edu
ROE, Robert, M .... 989-774-3933.. 232 D
roe1rm@cmich.edu
ROE-BOSTON, Sheila ...... 708-237-5050.. 150 D
sroe-boston@nc.edu
ROEBUCK, Randy .... 316-677-9437.. 185 I
rroebuck@watc.edu
ROECKER-PHELPS,
Carolyn .... 937-229-3334.. 379 D
cphelps1@udayton.edu
ROECKS, Jan .... 650-574-6480.... 62 H
roecksj@smccd.edu
ROEDEL, Glenn .... 215-780-1296.. 419 C
groedel@salus.edu
ROEDER, Jerry .... 413-782-1386.. 229 E
gerard.roeder@wne.edu
ROEDER, Lynn, M .... 252-328-9297.. 356 C
roederl@ecu.edu
ROEHRICK, Randy .... 952-995-1525.. 249 D
randy.roehrick@hennepintech.edu
ROELFS, Melinda, A .... 620-235-4226.. 184 C
maroelfs@pittstate.edu
ROELFSEMA, Cheryl, E .... 815-224-0419.. 143 C
cheryl_roelfsema@ivcc.edu
ROELKE, Scott .... 651-423-8297.. 249 B
scott.roelke@dctc.edu
ROELLKE, Christopher ...... 845-437-5600.. 339 C
chroellke@vassar.edu
ROELOFS, Lyle, D .... 859-985-3522.. 187 B
roelofsl@berea.edu
ROEN, Duane .... 480-727-6513.... 11 H
duane.roen@asu.edu
ROEPKE, Tena .... 419-772-2130.. 374 J
t-roepke@onu.edu
ROERIG, Sandra, C .... 318-675-7618.. 198 B
sroeri@lsuhsc.edu
ROESCH, Adam .... 618-262-8641.. 142 F
roescha@iecc.edu
ROESTI, Bobette .... 785-738-9060.. 183 J
broesti@ncktc.edu
ROETHEMEYER,
Robert, V .... 260-452-2146.. 160 D
robert.roethemeyer@ctsfw.edu
ROETHER, Diane .... 940-668-4283.. 462 L
droether@nctc.edu
ROETHLER, Don .... 701-224-5485.. 361 C
donald.roethler@bismarckstate.edu
ROETTGER, Linda .... 219-464-5958.. 168 F
linda.roettger@valpo.edu

ROETTGER, Walter, B ...... 315-312-2290.. 333 D
walter.roettger@oswego.edu
ROEWER, Anita .... 815-455-8737.. 147 E
aroewer@mchenry.edu
ROFFEL, Linda .... 845-434-5750.. 336 H
lroffel@sunysullivan.edu
ROGALSKI, Kathryn .... 847-925-6221.. 141 A
krogalsk@harpercollege.edu
ROGALSKY, Amy .... 405-974-5376.. 388 L
arogalsky@uco.edu
ROGAN, Doreen .... 207-216-4320.. 204 B
drogan@yccc.edu
ROGAN, Fred, R .... 205-726-2837....... 6 E
cfrogan@samford.edu
ROGAN, Margaret .... 617-824-8590.. 218 B
margaret_rogan@emerson.edu
ROGAN, Mary, T .... 718-960-8559.. 308 B
mary.rogan@lehman.cuny.edu
ROGAN, William, D .... 615-230-3595.. 447 C
william.rogan@volstate.edu
ROGELSTAD, Todd .... 701-845-7209.. 361 B
todd.rogelstad@vcsu.edu
ROGENTINE, Linda .... 218-723-6022.. 245 J
lrogenti@css.edu
ROGER-GORDON,
A. Patrick .... 212-346-1295.. 325 J
arogergordon@pace.edu
ROGERS, Andria .... 970-339-6518.... 76 H
andria.rogers@aims.edu
ROGERS, Ann .... 203-857-7270.... 87 B
arogers@norwalk.edu
ROGERS, Beth .... 916-388-2889.... 36 D
brogers@carrington.edu
ROGERS, Blake .... 502-897-4720.. 192 D
brogers@sbts.edu
ROGERS, Brian .... 503-494-8362.. 393 F
cdrcadmin@ohsu.edu
ROGERS, Carl .... 770-533-6899.. 123 L
crogers@laniertech.edu
ROGERS, Cheryl .... 413-755-4454.. 224 G
carogers@stcc.edu
ROGERS, Cheryl, L .... 903-510-3217.. 473 C
crog@tjc.edu
ROGERS, Christina .... 212-659-7200.. 318 D
crogers@tkc.edu
ROGERS, Christopher ...... 803-777-5643.. 433 F
crogers@mailbox.sc.edu
ROGERS, Cindy, A .... 972-860-8186.. 456 C
car3810@dcccd.edu
ROGERS, Craig, L .... 270-789-5057.. 187 G
crogers@campbellsville.edu
ROGERS, Dana .... 409-882-3372.. 471 B
dana.rogers@lsco.edu
ROGERS, Dana, N .... 409-882-3397.. 471 B
dana.rogers@lsco.edu
ROGERS, David, E .... 315-684-6044.. 336 B
rogersde@morrisville.edu
ROGERS, Deborah .... 215-641-6506.. 410 L
drogers@mc3.edu
ROGERS, Demetrius .... 503-517-1809.. 396 F
drogers@westernseminary.edu
ROGERS, Donna .... 252-789-0290.. 351 A
drogers@martincc.edu
ROGERS, Donnita .... 405-466-3262.. 383 M
ddrogers@langston.edu
ROGERS, Duke .... 785-227-3380.. 178 J
rogersk@bethanylb.edu
ROGERS, Dwayne .... 318-473-6410.. 197 J
drogers@lsua.edu
ROGERS, Edwin .... 808-675-3544.. 130 E
edwin.rogers@byuh.edu
ROGERS, Elizabeth, A ...... 336-278-6350.. 344 D
rogers@elon.edu
ROGERS, Elsa .... 239-513-1122.. 102 T
erogers@hodges.edu
ROGERS, Emily .... 740-392-6868.. 373 D
emily.rogers@mvnu.edu
ROGERS, Fred, A .... 507-222-5411.. 245 C
frogers@carleton.edu
ROGERS, Frederick .... 803-508-7272.. 426 G
rogersf@atc.edu
ROGERS, Gail .... 423-746-5202.. 447 E
grogers@twcnet.edu
ROGERS, Glen .... 414-382-6269.. 515 D
glen.rogers@alverno.edu
ROGERS, Harry, C .... 215-898-7091.. 421 E
rogers@pobox.upenn.edu
ROGERS, Heather .... 270-901-1116.. 190 F
heather.rogers@kctcs.edu
ROGERS, Helen .... 808-932-7315.. 131 E
hrogers@hawaii.edu
ROGERS, J. Orion .... 540-831-5958.. 493 A
jorogers@radford.edu
ROGERS, Jacqueline .... 561-868-3414.. 106 D
rogersj@palmbeachstate.edu
ROGERS, James .... 212-517-0435.. 320 C
jrogers@mmm.edu
ROGERS, James .... 212-327-8506.. 327 F
jrogers@mail.rockefeller.edu
ROGERS, James .... 406-447-4536.. 276 B
jarogers@carroll.edu

ROGERS, Jan .... 931-393-1543.. 446 D
jrogers@mscc.edu
ROGERS, Janet .... 765-998-5330.. 167 C
jnrogers@taylor.edu
ROGERS, Jason .... 619-298-1829...... 66 D
jrogers@ssu.edu
ROGERS, Jason .... 615-460-6441.. 438 J
jason.rogers@belmont.edu
ROGERS, Jaye .... 765-641-4442.. 158 J
jlrogers2@anderson.edu
ROGERS, Jeff .... 304-457-6337.. 510 B
rogersja@ab.edu
ROGERS, Jeffrey .... 704-406-4724.. 344 E
jrogers3@gardner-webb.edu
ROGERS, Jenica, P .... 315-267-2482.. 334 B
rogersjp@potsdam.edu
ROGERS, Jennifer .... 308-635-6551.. 283 D
rogersj5@wncc.edu
ROGERS, Jessica .... 941-487-4900.. 111 D
ncalum@ncf.edu
ROGERS, Jevita .... 719-255-3460.... 83 L
jrogers3@uccs.edu
ROGERS, Jill .... 704-463-3406.. 354 F
jill.rogers@pfeiffer.edu
ROGERS, Johnell .... 803-934-3256.. 431 E
jrogers@morris.edu
ROGERS, Jolayne .... 816-322-0110.. 262 N
jolayne.rogers@calvary.edu
ROGERS, Jolene, R .... 712-362-0431.. 173 G
jrogers@iowalakes.edu
ROGERS, Jolynn .... 509-359-2383.. 503 D
jrogers@ewu.edu
ROGERS, Josh .... 928-536-6227.... 15 J
joshua.rogers@npc.edu
ROGERS, Judith, V .... 340-692-4132.. 539 C
jrogers@uvi.edu
ROGERS, Justin, P .... 716-888-2244.. 306 F
rogers44@canisius.edu
ROGERS, Kathleen, R ...... 617-521-2276.. 228 C
kathleen.rogers@simmons.edu
ROGERS, Katrina .... 805-898-2924.... 43 K
krogers@fielding.edu
ROGERS, Kim .... 580-559-5677.. 383 H
kimmrog@ecok.edu
ROGERS, Kiri .... 267-502-4890.. 398 J
kiri.rogers@brynathyn.edu
ROGERS, Lalita .... 318-670-9223.. 199 J
lrogers@susla.edu
ROGERS, Leslie .... 252-328-6212.. 356 C
rogersle@ecu.edu
ROGERS, Lisa, C .... 615-898-2150.. 444 G
lisa.rogers@mtsu.edu
ROGERS, Mark .... 478-274-7871.. 125 D
mwrogers@oftc.edu
ROGERS, Mary .... 619-388-6591...... 60 E
mrogers@sdccd.edu
ROGERS, Michael .... 202-274-5986...... 94 B
michael.rogers@udc.edu
ROGERS, Michael, B .... 607-735-1770.. 313 F
mrogers@elmira.edu
ROGERS, Michael, C .... 202-274-5000...... 94 B
ROGERS, Michael, C .... 202-274-5314...... 94 B
michael.rogers1@udc.edu
ROGERS, Michelle .... 909-748-8138...... 71 K
michelle_rogers@redlands.edu
ROGERS, Mike .... 209-946-2569...... 71 C
mrogers@pacific.edu
ROGERS, Nancy, B .... 812-237-7900.. 162 A
nancy.rogers@indstate.edu
ROGERS, Patricia .... 781-891-2622.. 215 F
progers@bentley.edu
ROGERS, Patricia .... 507-457-5010.. 252 G
progers@winona.edu
ROGERS, Patrick .... 802-635-1417.. 486 B
patrick.rogers@jsc.edu
ROGERS, Phil .... 208-459-5282.. 133 D
progers@collegeofidaho.edu
ROGERS, Phyllis .... 254-295-4501.. 474 E
progers@umhb.edu
ROGERS, Ralph, V .... 954-262-5796.. 105 J
rvrogers@nova.edu
ROGERS, Randy .... 660-626-2395.. 262 A
rrrogers@atsu.edu
ROGERS, Randy .... 336-386-3466.. 353 F
rogersrj@surry.edu
ROGERS, Raymond, C ..... 512-448-8532.. 464 G
rrogers1@stedwards.edu
ROGERS, Richard, L .... 313-664-7474.. 232 G
rrogers@collegeforcreativestudies.edu
ROGERS, Rodney, K .... 419-372-2915.. 364 E
rrogers@bgsu.edu
ROGERS, Rus .... 316-284-5273.. 179 A
rrogers@bethelks.edu
ROGERS, Russell .... 201-216-5688.. 297 B
russell.rogers@stevens.edu
ROGERS, Sandra .... 801-422-1801.. 480 C
sandra_rogers@byu.edu
ROGERS, Scott .... 828-726-2488.. 347 I
srogers@cccti.edu
ROGERS, Scott .... 509-542-4834.. 502 G
srogers@columbiabasin.edu

ROGERS, Scott, S .... 330-385-1070.. 376 A
ROGERS, Selwyn, O .... 409-772-5108.. 478 A
sorogers@utmb.edu
ROGERS, Stephanie .... 318-678-6000.. 195 I
srogers@bpcc.edu
ROGERS, Susan .... 845-434-5750.. 336 H
srogers@sunysulliivan.edu
ROGERS, Susan .... 412-624-2795.. 421 G
srogers@pitt.edu
ROGERS, Tamara .... 617-496-3069.. 219 D
tamara_rogers@harvard.edu
ROGERS, Tammy .... 706-880-8344.. 123 K
trogers@lagrange.edu
ROGERS, Tamy .... 214-333-5158.. 455 J
tamyr@dbu.edu
ROGERS, Terri .... 417-328-1520.. 272 C
tlrogers@sbuniv.edu
ROGERS, Terri .... 580-745-2510.. 387 M
trogers@se.edu
ROGERS, Thomas .... 502-213-7310.. 190 A
thomas.rogers@kctcs.edu
ROGERS, Tim .... 503-399-7506.. 390 E
tim.rogers@chemeketa.edu
ROGERS, Timothy .... 315-866-0300.. 316 A
rogerstd@herkimer.edu
ROGERS, Toby .... 806-720-7627.. 461 C
toby.rogers@lcu.edu
ROGERS, Tracy .... 719-587-7990.... 76 G
tracy_rogers@adams.edu
ROGERS-ADKINSON,
Diana .... 573-651-2408.. 272 B
drogersadkinson@semo.edu
ROGERSON, Andrew .... 707-664-2028.... 35 D
andrew.rogerson@sonoma.edu
ROGERSON, Joanie .... 360-736-9391.. 502 A
jrogerson@centralia.edu
ROGERSON, Sarah .... 518-445-3246.. 303 D
sroge@albanylaw.edu
ROGGE, Ann .... 302-736-2445.... 91 G
ann.rogge@wesley.edu
ROGGENSTEIN, Gary .... 661-722-6300.... 27 B
groggenstein@avc.edu
ROGGIE, Edie .... 315-786-2327.. 317 H
eroggie@sunyjefferson.edu
ROGNRUD, Carol .... 240-567-7493.. 209 E
carol.rognrud@montgomerycollege.edu
ROGOTZKE, Kathy, M ..... 641-422-4154.. 175 E
rogotkat@niacc.edu
ROGOVIN, Michael .... 914-594-4560.. 323 I
michael_rogovin@nymc.edu
ROGSTAD, Mark .... 509-574-4671.. 510 A
mrogstad@yvcc.edu
ROHAN, James, P .... 920-465-2075.. 520 B
rohanj@uwgb.edu
ROHANNA, Susan .... 610-902-8206.. 399 D
susan.rohanna@cabrini.edu
ROHDE, Ben, B .... 262-243-5700.. 516 E
benjamin.rohde@cuw.edu
ROHDE, Scott .... 860-685-2809...... 90 C
srohde@wesleyan.edu
ROHDER, Kelly .... 815-280-2915.. 144 A
krohder@jjc.edu
ROHDIN, Ben .... 973-353-5541.. 296 C
ben.rohdin@rutgers.edu
ROHDIN, Benjamin .... 201-200-3156.. 293 C
brohdin@njcu.edu
ROHENA, Ricardo .... 787-850-9328.. 538 B
ricardo.rohena@upr.edu
ROHLAND-HEINRICH,
Nancy .... 858-642-8824.... 54 A
nrohland@nu.edu
ROHLEDER, Ann .... 812-357-6610.. 167 B
arohleder@saintmeinrad.edu
ROHLEDER, John .... 651-779-3496.. 249 A
john.rohleder@century.edu
ROHLEDER-SOOK,
Wendy .... 785-628-4408.. 180 I
wmrohledersook@fhsu.edu
ROHMAN, Lynda .... 207-404-5651.. 202 I
rohmanl@husson.edu
ROHN, Marisa .... 330-494-6170.. 377 J
mrohn@starkstate.edu
ROHNER, Christy .... 270-686-4243.. 187 C
christy.rohner@brescia.edu
ROHR, Ann .... 970-207-4550.... 81 F
annr@mckinleycollege.edu
ROHR, Ann .... 970-207-4500.... 84 F
annr@uscareerinstitute.edu
ROHR, Launa .... 574-535-7543.. 161 A
launar@goshen.edu
ROHR, Margie .... 973-290-4054.. 290 G
mrohr@cse.edu
ROHRBACK, Jane, T .... 248-204-3160.. 237 B
jrohrback@ltu.edu
ROHRBAUGH,
Suzanne, Y .... 336-633-0218.. 352 B
syrohrbaugh@randolph.edu
ROHRBAUGH,
Suzanne, Y .... 336-342-4261.. 352 F
rohrbaughs8858@rockinghamcc.edu

ROHRER, Brad .... 305-284-1256.. 114 H
brohrer@miami.edu
ROHRER, Katherine .... 609-258-7800.. 294 D
krohrer@princeton.edu
ROIDT, Joseph .... 605-995-2625.. 435 F
joroidt@dwu.edu
ROIG, Katy .... 619-260-7404.... 72 B
kroig@sandiego.edu
ROIG, Lizzette .... 787-844-8181.. 538 E
lizzette.roig@upr.edu
ROJAS, Carlos .... 787-840-2575.. 535 H
crojas@psm.edu
ROJAS, Carmen, I .... 787-743-4041.. 531 K
crojas@columbiacentral.edu
ROJAS, Eddy, M .... 937-229-2306.. 379 D
erojas1@udayton.edu
ROJAS, Frank .... 406-377-9422.. 276 D
frojas@dawson.edu
ROJAS, Jason .... 860-297-4166...... 89 B
jason.rojas@trincoll.edu
ROJAS, Jesus .... 912-525-5000.. 126 E
jrojas@scad.edu
ROJAS, Pablo, E .... 787-891-0925.. 533 G
projas@aquadilla.inter.edu
ROJAS, Robyn, D .... 405-325-3337.. 389 B
rrojas@ou.edu
ROJAS, Rodney .... 213-613-2200...... 65 H
rodney_rojas@sciarc.edu
ROJAS ALVAREZ LOPEREN,
Clara .... 713-221-8179.. 474 B
rojasc@uhd.edu
ROJCEWICZ, Peter, M ..... 626-571-8811...... 72 E
peterr@uwest.edu
ROKICKY, Paul .... 216-987-5048.. 367 E
paul.rokicky@tri-c.edu
ROKOWSKY, Eli .... 845-425-1370.. 325 F
ROKOWSKY, Israel .... 845-425-1370.. 325 F
ROKSANDIC, Stevo .... 614-234-1644.. 373 B
sroksandic@mchs.com
ROKUSEK, Jim .... 605-367-6109.. 437 G
jim.rokusek@southeasttech.edu
ROLAND, Cheryl .... 269-387-8412.. 243 H
cheryl.roland@wmich.edu
ROLAND, David, E .... 706-233-7329.. 127 A
droland@shorter.edu
ROLAND, Harriet, A .... 803-533-3790.. 432 E
rolandha@scsu.edu
ROLAND, Kirc, J .... 360-442-2471.. 504 G
kroland@lowercolumbia.edu
ROLAND, Meg .... 503-699-3336.. 392 D
mroland@marylhurst.edu
ROLDAN, Marggi .... 864-578-8770.. 432 D
mroldan@sherman.edu
ROLEN, Scott .... 541-917-4420.. 392 C
rolens@linnbenton.edu
ROLEY, V. Vance .... 808-956-8377.. 131 F
vroley@hawaii.edu
ROLF, Joel .... 763-544-9501.. 244 H
ROLFE, Cynthia .... 405-974-2688.. 388 L
crolfe@uco.edu
ROLFE, Rial, D .... 806-743-2905.. 472 D
rial.rolfe@ttuhsc.edu
ROLFES, Katherine .... 337-521-8906.. 197 A
katherine.rolfes@solacc.edu
ROLFS, Trevor .... 620-792-9378.. 178 G
rolfst@bartonccc.edu
ROLHEISER, Ronald .... 210-341-1366.. 463 A
rrolheiser@ost.edu
ROLL, Debbie .... 907-564-8220...... 10 B
droll@alaskapacific.edu
ROLLACK, Nikesha .... 919-278-2672.. 355 F
nrollack@shawu.edu
ROLLAND, Erik .... 909-869-2400...... 31 J
erolland@cpp.edu
ROLLE, Jo-Ann .... 718-270-5070.. 309 B
jrolle@mec.cuny.edu
ROLLE, Kevin, A .... 256-372-5230........ 1 A
kevin.rolle@aamu.edu
ROLLER, Robert .... 626-812-3085...... 28 A
rroller@apu.edu
ROLLER, Robert .... 910-893-1326.. 342 F
roller@campbell.edu
ROLLER, Steven, A .... 617-228-2394.. 223 B
sroller@bhcc.mass.edu
ROLLESTON, George .... 440-826-2081.. 363 M
grollest@bw.edu
ROLLINO, Richard .... 307-332-2930.. 527 F
rrollino@wyomingcatholiccollege.com
ROLLINS, Cheryl .... 443-885-4429.. 209 F
cheryl.rollins@morgan.edu
ROLLINS, Dani .... 815-753-0446.. 150 A
drollins@niu.edu
ROLLINS, Elizabeth, J ...... 803-981-7122.. 435 D
erollins@yorktech.edu
ROLLINS, Judy .... 252-985-5111.. 354 E
jrollins@ncwc.edu
ROLLINS, Pam .... 334-420-4253...... 7 G
prollins@trenholmstate.edu
ROLLINS, Stephen, J .... 907-786-1825...... 10 F
srollins@uaa.alaska.edu

ROLLISON, Jeffrey 610-647-4400 406 B
jrollison@immaculata.edu
ROLLMAN, Catherine, A 804-752-7270 493 C
crollman@rmc.edu
ROLLO, Ann 315-364-3235 340 B
arollo@wells.edu
ROLLO, J. Michael 239-590-7910 110 L
jmrollo@fgcu.edu
ROLLOR, Michael 410-706-1875 211 F
mrollor@umaryland.edu
ROLLS, Dickie 620-252-7575 180 B
dickier@coffeyville.edu
ROLOFF, ReBecca, K 651-690-6525 254 M
broloff@stkate.edu
ROLON, John 641-269-3713 172 I
rolonjoe@grinnell.edu
ROLON, Liberty 787-750-4100 537 H
liberty.rolon@upr.edu
ROLON, Reynaldo 787-279-1912 533 J
rrolon@bayamon.inter.edu
ROLPH, Chris 606-539-3527 193 F
ROM, Kjetil 541-881-5746 395 E
krom@tvcc.cc
ROMA, Jennifer 305-273-4499 97 M
jennifer.roman@cbt.edu
ROMA, Lawrence, J 607-777-2224 331 B
lroma@binghamton.edu
ROMAGNI, Joanne 423-425-1743 448 F
joanne-romagni@utc.edu
ROMAGNOLI, Janice 615-655-7274 306 H
jaromagnoli@cazenovia.edu
ROMAIN, Pete 212-517-0414 320 C
promain@mmm.edu
ROMALI, Reagan, F 773-907-4450 137 E
rromali@ccc.edu
ROMAN, Albert, J 213-891-2173 49 F
romanaj@email.laccd.edu
ROMAN, Angela 231-591-2685 233 L
angelaroman@ferris.edu
ROMAN, Cynthia 248-942-3300 239 E
caroman@oaklandcc.edu
ROMAN, Jennifer 214-329-4447 452 B
jennifer.roman@bgu.edu
ROMAN, Juan, E 787-841-2000 535 I
jroman@pucpr.edu
ROMAN, Nilsa, M 787-891-0925 533 G
nroman@aguadilla.inter.edu
ROMAN, Vladimir 787-763-6425 533 F
vroman@inter.edu
ROMAN-VARGAS,
Madeline 773-878-3728 153 E
mroman02@staugustine.edu
ROMANCZUK, Jeffrey 704-886-6500 93 F
ROMANDINI, Russ 706-507-8898 119 E
romandini_russ@columbusstate.edu
ROMANDINI, Russ 513-618-1930 366 C
rromandini@ccms.edu
ROMANELLO, Mary 202-884-9677 94 A
romanellom@trinitydc.edu
ROMANO, C. Renee 217-333-1300 157 A
romano3@illinois.edu
ROMANO, Carol 301-295-9002 528 G
ROMANO, Cenia, K 787-884-3838 530 G
vpacademico@atenascollege.edu
ROMANO, Christopher 201-684-7309 294 G
cromano@ramapo.edu
ROMANO, Fred, D 630-515-6388 148 C
froman@midwestern.edu
ROMANO, Joan 401-254-3510 426 B
jromano@rwu.edu
ROMANO, Joseph 718-420-4599 339 F
joe.romano@wagner.edu
ROMANO, Joyce, C 407-582-3401 114 N
jromano@valenciacollege.edu
ROMANO, Judith, J 864-294-3470 430 C
judith.romano@furman.edu
ROMANO, Michael 623-245-4600 17 G
mromano@uti.edu
ROMANO, Nicole 302-356-6846 91 I
nicole.romano@wilmu.edu
ROMANO, Pam 910-272-3531 352 E
promano@robeson.edu
ROMANO, Sandra 340-693-1389 539 C
sromano@uvi.edu
ROMANO, Susan, M 585-785-1277 314 D
susan.romano@flcc.edu
ROMANO, Wendy, W 215-871-6300 416 F
wendyr@pcom.edu
ROMANS, John 405-744-3373 385 G
john.romans@okstate.edu
ROMANSKI, Beth, E 717-867-6336 408 F
romanski@lvc.edu
ROMANTIC, Thomas, W 607-255-8574 312 A
twr2@cornell.edu
ROMBALSKI, Patrick 617-792-3636 136 G
prombalski@chamberlain.edu
ROMBOUTS, Stephen, R 814-472-3009 418 F
srombouts@francis.edu
ROME, Alan, K 440-943-7600 377 A
akrome@dioceseofcleveland.org
ROME, Alan, K 440-943-7600 377 A
cpl@dioceseofcleveland.org
ROME, JoAnne 413-552-2259 223 E
jrome@hcc.edu
ROME, Kevin, D 573-681-5042 266 I
romek@lincolnu.edu
ROME, Michaela 212-229-8947 322 E
romem@newschool.edu
ROMELDA Simmons 478-825-6219 120 F
simmonsr@fvsu.edu
ROMEO, JR., Aldemaro 646-312-3870 307 A
aldemaro.romeo@baruch.cuny.edu
ROMER, Christine, E 636-922-8362 271 A
cromer@stchas.edu
ROMER, Mark 941-405-1519 407 D
mromer@lecom.edu
ROMERAO-ALDAZ,
Patrick 617-928-4073 226 B
promeroaldaz@mountida.edu
ROMERO, Andy 505-747-2166 301 F
andy@nnmc.edu
ROMERO, Angel 787-765-1915 534 F
aromero@opto.inter.edu
ROMERO, Bianca 909-593-3511 71 B
bromero@laverne.edu
ROMERO, Carol 305-821-3333 101 B
cromero@fnu.edu
ROMERO, Cecilia 505-747-5477 301 F
cromero@nnmc.edu
ROMERO, Christina 714-564-6091 58 G
romero_christina@sac.edu
ROMERO, Cynthia 757-446-7414 489 B
romerocc@evms.edu
ROMERO, Edward, W 903-886-5027 468 D
edward.romero@tamuc.edu
ROMERO, Georg 831-479-5771 29 G
geromero@cabrillo.edu
ROMERO, Herminio 787-622-8000 537 B
hromero@pupr.edu
ROMERO, Krystal 650-574-6440 62 H
romerok@smccd.edu
ROMERO, Lizbeth 787-878-5475 533 H
lromero@arecibo.inter.edu
ROMERO, Manuel 212-220-1238 307 B
mromero@bmcc.cuny.edu
ROMERO, Narda 914-674-7841 320 G
nromero@mercy.edu
ROMERO, Peter 505-473-6328 302 A
peter.romero@santafeuniversity.edu
ROMERO, Ramona, E 609-258-2511 294 D
ramonar@princeton.edu
ROMERO, Rebecca 970-521-6649 81 O
rebecca.romero@njc.edu
ROMERO, Reyna 713-221-8460 474 B
romeror@uhd.edu
ROMERO, Sally 970-943-2150 84 H
sromero@western.edu
ROMERO, Van, D 575-835-5646 300 G
vromero@nmt.edu
ROMERO, Victoria 909-621-8149 64 A
vromero@scrippscollege.edu
ROMERO-LEGGOTT,
Valerie 505-272-2728 302 F
vromero@salud.unm.edu
ROMERO-NIEVES,
Luis, E 787-751-1912 534 E
lromero@juris.inter.edu
ROMES, Lindsey 973-290-4322 290 G
lromes@cse.edu
ROMESBURG, Rosemarie 304-367-4284 512 D
rosemarie.romesburg@pierpont.edu
ROMIG, Kenneth, J 724-946-7141 423 B
romigkj@westminster.edu
ROMIG, Thomas, J 785-670-1662 185 H
thomas.romig@washburn.edu
ROMINGER, Anna 219-980-6636 163 B
arominge@iun.edu
ROMKEMA, Priscilla 605-642-6341 437 B
priscilla.romkema@bhsu.edu
ROMO, Nanette 520-515-5399 12 L
romon@cochise.edu
ROMO, Ricardo 210-458-4101 477 A
ricardo.romo@utsa.edu
ROMO, Wayne 210-436-3538 464 H
wromo@stmarytx.edu
ROMZEK, Barbara 202-885-6234 91 J
romzek@american.edu
RONAN, Donald 317-805-1791 511 D
dronan@salemu.edu
RONCA, Paul, L 804-523-5239 497 C
pronca@reynolds.edu
RONCHETTI, Michele 815-836-5498 145 H
ronchemi@lewisu.edu
RONCOLATO, David 814-332-5318 397 A
droncola@allegheny.edu
RONDA, René, S 787-743-7979 536 A
rsronda@suagm.edu
RONDEAU, Ann 630-942-2201 138 B
rondeaua@cod.edu
RONDINELLI, Diane 904-826-0084 72 A
drondinelli@usa.edu
RONEVICH, Nancy, S 740-284-5232 368 L
nronevich@franciscan.edu
RONEY, Linda 214-333-5147 455 J
linda@dbu.edu
RONIS, Sheila, R 248-689-8282 242 F
sronis@walshcollege.edu
RONK, Chris 336-725-8344 354 G
ronkc@piedmont.edu
RONKOSKI, Bob 636-922-8604 271 A
rronkoski@stchas.edu
RONNFELDT, Derek 253-833-9111 504 C
dronnfeldt@greenriver.edu
RONNING, Teresa 518-743-2261 335 A
ronningt@sunyacc.edu
RONNING LINDGREN,
Rachel 805-493-3690 31 C
rronning@callutheran.edu
RONVEAUX, Gail 951-343-5045 29 H
gronveaux@calbaptist.edu
ROOB, Sharon 414-930-3375 518 F
roobs@mtmary.edu
ROOB, Sharon, L 920-565-1327 517 D
roobsl@lakeland.edu
ROOCK, Mark 314-529-9673 267 B
mroock@maryville.edu
ROOD, Christi 208-562-2710 133 F
christirood@cwidaho.cc
ROOD, Dennis 262-691-5157 524 G
drood@wctc.edu
ROOD, Jessica 941-487-4150 111 D
jrood@ncf.edu
ROOD, Kathleen, C 617-262-5000 216 A
kathy.rood@the-bac.edu
ROOD, Robert 419-824-3730 371 I
rrood@lourdes.edu
ROODBEEN, Richard 508-373-9539 215 D
richard.roodbeen@becker.edu
ROODE, Dana, F 949-824-5173 69 C
dana.roode@uci.edu
ROOF, Karin 843-953-7526 428 G
roofk@cofc.edu
ROOFNER, Perry, F 412-397-5256 418 E
roofner@rmu.edu
ROOK, Steve 501-337-5000 19 K
srook@coto.edu
ROOK, Tony 252-823-5166 349 E
rookt@edgecombe.edu
ROOKARD, Crystal 803-822-3251 431 B
rookardc@midlandstech.edu
ROOKE, Michael 860-738-6300 87 A
mrooke@nwcc.edu
ROOKER, Allison 601-925-3310 259 A
abrooker@mc.edu
ROOKER, Darrin 315-568-3063 323 A
drooker@nycc.edu
ROOKER, Suzanne 580-477-7944 389 I
suzanne.rooker@wosc.edu
ROOKS, James 616-526-8694 232 A
jrooks@calvin.edu
ROOKS, Pamela, A 843-661-1526 430 B
prooks@fmarion.edu
ROOKS, Stephanie 770-962-7580 123 D
srooks@gwinnetttech.edu
ROONEY, Gail 217-333-0820 157 A
grooney@illinois.edu
ROONEY, Gerard, J 585-385-8010 328 E
grooney@sjfc.edu
ROONEY, Jo Ann 312-915-6400 146 G
jrooney@luc.edu
ROONEY, John, J 215-951-1282 407 A
rooney@lasalle.edu
ROONEY, Joseph, A 302-793-1101 91 E
ROONEY, L David 845-257-3260 331 E
rooneyd@newpaltz.edu
ROONEY, Paul 407-582-1100 114 N
prooney@valenciacollege.edu
ROONEY, Paula, M 508-541-1658 217 G
prooney@dean.edu
ROONEY, Thomas, J 507-933-7499 246 J
tomrooney@gustavus.edu
ROOPNARINE, Darshini 315-445-4661 318 E
roopnatd@lemoyne.edu
ROORBACH, Karen 765-677-2975 164 B
karen.roorbach@indwes.edu
ROOS, David 435-652-7704 482 A
roos@dixie.edu
ROOS, Johan 617-619-1900 219 G
johan.roos@hult.edu
ROOS, Matthew, R 561-237-7433 104 O
mroos@lynn.edu
ROOSA, Alexandra 310-506-6850 56 J
alexandra.roosa@pepperdine.edu
ROOSA, Mark, S 310-506-4252 56 J
mark.roosa@pepperdine.edu
ROOSE, Robert 989-358-7200 230 G
rooser@alpenacc.edu
ROOSEVELT, Mark 505-984-6098 301 I
president@sjc.edu
ROOT, David 606-539-4406 193 F
david.root@ucumberlands.edu
ROOT, Jeanne, V 802-287-8201 484 A
rootj@greenmtn.edu
ROOT, Jeff 870-245-4186 21 E
rootj@obu.edu
ROOT, Jeff 870-245-5154 21 E
rootj@obu.edu
ROOT, Larry 409-944-1208 458 D
lroot@gc.edu
ROOT, Mark, J 574-807-7219 159 D
rootm1@bethelcollege.edu
ROOT, Rennie, A 563-588-7775 174 K
rennie.root@loras.edu
ROOTES, Mary 334-285-5177 4 G
ROOTS, Keith, D 757-594-0581 488 E
keith.roots@cnu.edu
ROPELLA, Kristina 414-288-5460 517 I
kristina.ropella@marquette.edu
ROPER, Craig 618-545-3137 144 D
croper@kaskaskia.edu
ROPER, David 843-349-6532 428 E
droper@coastal.edu
ROPER, Gina 541-881-5577 395 E
groper@tvcc.cc
ROPER, Melinda 805-493-3553 31 C
mroper@callutheran.edu
ROPER, William, L 919-966-4161 357 D
william_roper@med.unc.edu
ROPER-DOTEN, Emily 781-292-2201 218 H
emily.roper-doten@olin.edu
ROQUEMORE, Glenn, R 949-451-5210 65 F
groquemore@ivc.edu
RORK, Jeannette 336-721-2618 355 E
jeannette.rork@salem.edu
ROSA, Carmen, J 787-780-0070 531 B
crosa@caribbean.edu
ROSA, Chris 646-664-8759 306 M
christopher.rosa@cuny.edu
ROSA, Jerry 718-518-6561 308 C
jrosa@hostos.cuny.edu
ROSA, John, W 843-953-5012 428 A
john.rosa@citadel.edu
ROSA, Luis 802-258-9238 484 C
luisr@marlboro.edu
ROSA, Maria 787-834-9595 536 E
mrosa@uaa.edu
ROSA, Maria, G 787-891-0925 533 G
mrosa@aquadilla.inter.edu
ROSA, Marta 617-879-2314 229 G
mrosa@wheelock.edu
ROSA, Peter 203-837-8376 85 I
rosap@wcsu.edu
ROSA, Ramonita 787-891-0925 533 G
rrosa@aguadilla.inter.edu
ROSA, Sandra 787-279-1912 533 J
srosa@bayamon.inter.edu
ROSA-NUÑEZ,
Waleska, Y 787-480-2458 531 J
wrosa01@sanjuanciudadpatria.com
ROSA VELEZ, Mariam, L 787-265-3879 538 C
prensa@uprm.edu
ROSAASEN, Orlynn 701-777-3823 360 C
orlynn.rosaasen@und.edu
ROSACCO, Claire 216-987-4804 367 E
claire.rosacco@tri-c.edu
ROSADO, Akilah 212-875-4596 304 E
arosado@bankstreet.edu
ROSADO, Carlos 787-764-0000 538 F
carlos.rosado13@upr.edu
ROSADO, Carmen 787-766-1717 536 B
um_crosado@suagm.edu
ROSADO, Judy 787-892-1365 534 D
judy.rosado@sodexo.com
ROSADO, Maria 787-279-1912 533 J
mrosado@bayamon.inter.edu
ROSADO, Martin 787-884-6000 532 O
mrosado@icprjc.edu
ROSADO, Nilda 787-257-7373 535 P
ue_nrosado@suagm.edu
ROSADO, Nilda, I 787-257-7373 535 P
ue_nrosado@suagm.edu
ROSADO, Reinaldo 787-284-1912 534 C
rrosado@ponce.inter.edu
ROSADO, Robert 787-815-0000 537 F
robert.rosado@upr.edu
ROSADO, Samuel 787-264-1912 534 D
samuel_rosado_nazario@intersg.edu
ROSALES, Elvia, H 512-471-3391 476 B
bd.elvia@austin.utexas.edu
ROSALES, Jerome 956-721-5148 460 F
jerome.rosales@laredo.edu
ROSALES, John 773-291-6776 137 G
jrosales57@ccc.edu
ROSANDICH, Thomas, J 251-626-3303 8 B
president@ussa.edu
ROSANDICH, Thomas, P 251-626-3303 8 B
tprosandich@ussa.edu
ROSANIA, Nick 641-472-1180 175 A
nrosania@mum.edu
ROSANIA, Sandra 641-472-1180 175 A
srosania@mum.edu

ROSARIO, Antonio, J ... 787-857-3600.. 533 I
arosario@br.inter.edu
ROSARIO, Daniel ... 787-850-9551.. 538 B
daniel.rosario4@upr.edu
ROSARIO, Enrique ... 787-780-0070.. 531 B
rel.publicas@caribbean.edu
ROSARIO, Glorivee ... 787-738-2161.. 538 A
glorivee.rosario@upr.edu
ROSARIO, Lisanette ... 718-518-4311.. 308 C
lrosario@hostos.cuny.edu
ROSARIO, Lucy ... 787-284-1912.. 534 C
lrsario@ponce.inter.edu
ROSARIO, Vera ... 914-594-4900.. 323 I
vera_rosario@nymc.edu
ROSARIO, Victoria ... 916-568-3150.... 50 J
rosariv@losrios.edu
ROSARIO, Yvette ... 718-960-8723.. 308 B
yvette.rosario@lehman.cuny.edu
ROSARIO-RODRIGUEZ,
Elizabeth ... 787-480-2444.. 531 J
erosario03@sanjuanciudadpatria.com
ROSARIO-ROSARIO,
Yolanda ... 787-725-6500.. 531 C
yrosario@sju.albizu.edu
ROSAS, Alisha ... 909-652-6115.... 37 D
alisha.rosas@chaffey.edu
ROSAS, Carla ... 925-473-7427.... 41 J
crosas@losmedanos.edu
ROSAS, Olivia ... 909-537-7577.... 34 C
orosas@csusb.edu
ROSATI, David, M ... 508-849-3420.. 214 E
drosati@annamaria.edu
ROSATI, David, M ... 617-422-7205.. 226 H
drosati@nesl.edu
ROSATI, Ron ... 308-367-5270.. 283 C
rosati@unl.edu
ROSATI, Ross ... 612-625-5516.. 255 H
rosat002@umn.edu
ROSATO, Michael ... 281-649-3633.. 458 L
mrosato@hbu.edu
ROSCOE, Brandy ... 864-225-7653.. 430 A
brandyroscoe@forrestcollege.edu
ROSDAIL, Lisa ... 803-938-3794.. 434 E
llrosdai@uscsumter.edu
ROSDAIL, Lisa ... 803-938-3794.. 434 E
lrosdai@uscsumter.edu
ROSDIL, Amy ... 303-404-5254.... 80 E
amy.rosdil@frontrange.edu
ROSE, Alisha, D ... 901-678-2230.. 445 C
arose3@memphis.edu
ROSE, Billy ... 256-352-8060...... 9 G
billy.rose@wallacestate.edu
ROSE, Brian ... 304-829-7292.. 510 G
brose@bethanywv.edu
ROSE, Brian, T ... 607-777-4788.. 331 B
brose@binghamton.edu
ROSE, Carey ... 254-298-8326.. 467 B
carey.rose@templejc.edu
ROSE, Carrie, J ... 724-458-2134.. 404 F
cjgault@gcc.edu
ROSE, Clayton ... 207-725-3221.. 202 F
crose@bowdoin.edu
ROSE, David ... 765-677-2075.. 164 B
david.rose@indwes.edu
ROSE, David, C ... 301-687-4335.. 212 F
drose@frostburg.edu
ROSE, David, S ... 858-534-4358.... 70 C
drose@ucsd.edu
ROSE, Deatrea ... 620-235-6556.. 184 C
drose@pittstate.edu
ROSE, Dennis ... 404-413-4510.. 122 D
drose@gsu.edu
ROSE, Don ... 620-665-3597.. 181 I
rosed@hutchcc.edu
ROSE, Douglas, N ... 608-263-3046.. 519 K
drose@fpm.wisc.edu
ROSE, E. Wayne ... 301-860-3957.. 212 D
cio@bowiestate.edu
ROSE, Gregory ... 816-584-6566.. 270 D
gregory.rose@park.edu
ROSE, Howard, A ... 713-525-6980.. 475 J
horo@stthom.edu
ROSE, Jane ... 941-359-4200.. 112 E
ROSE, John ... 212-772-4242.. 308 D
john.rose@hunter.cuny.edu
ROSE, Judy, W ... 704-687-6245.. 358 A
jwrose@uncc.edu
ROSE, Kathleen, A ... 408-848-4760.... 44 I
krose@gavilan.edu
ROSE, Kathleen, A ... 408-848-4712.... 44 I
krose@gavilan.edu
ROSE, Ken, G ... 580-774-3790.. 388 C
ken.rose@swosu.edu
ROSE, Keven, W ... 517-750-1200.. 241 E
kerose@arbor.edu
ROSE, Kevin ... 903-434-8223.. 462 M
krose@ntcc.edu
ROSE, Kristen ... 610-989-1301.. 422 E
krose@vfmac.edu
ROSE, Lawrence, D ... 909-537-3703.... 34 C
lrose@csusb.edu
ROSE, Lesa ... 207-333-7743.. 203 G
rosele@cmhc.org
ROSE, Linda, D ... 714-564-6975.... 58 G
rose_linda@sac.edu
ROSE, Lisa ... 310-434-4402.... 63 F
rose_lisa@smc.edu
ROSE, Louise ... 978-681-0800.. 225 B
lrose@mslaw.edu
ROSE, Margie ... 303-369-5151.... 82 F
margie.rose@plattcolorado.edu
ROSE, Maria, C ... 304-367-4151.. 513 B
maria.rose@fairmontstate.edu
ROSE, Matt, D ... 920-923-8954.. 517 H
mdrose86@marianuniversity.edu
ROSE, Melissa ... 315-792-7210.. 336 C
melissa.rose@sunyit.edu
ROSE, Melody ... 503-636-8141.. 392 D
president@marylhurst.edu
ROSE, Michael, J ... 215-898-5828.. 421 E
mjrose@pobox.upenn.edu
ROSE, Patricia, L ... 215-898-3208.. 421 E
prose@upenn.edu
ROSE, Rachel ... 276-376-4035.. 495 I
rlb7q@uvawise.edu
ROSE, Rebecca ... 315-498-2415.. 325 G
r.l.rose3@sunyocc.edu
ROSE, Rebecca ... 304-829-7221.. 510 G
rrose@bethanywv.edu
ROSE, Sarah ... 423-585-6752.. 447 D
sarah.rose@ws.edu
ROSE, Scott, H ... 312-935-4240.. 143 E
srose@icsw.edu
ROSE, Sharon ... 252-398-1229.. 343 G
rosesh@chowan.edu
ROSE, Shawn ... 970-521-6601.... 81 O
shawn.rose@njc.edu
ROSE, Steve ... 509-527-2402.. 508 G
steve.rose@wallawalla.edu
ROSE, Steven ... 973-684-5900.. 294 A
srose@pccc.edu
ROSE, Susan ... 713-525-6957.. 475 J
roses@stthom.edu
ROSE, Tara, A ... 859-257-6394.. 193 G
tara.rose@uky.edu
ROSEBERG, Nicole ... 208-282-2123.. 133 H
rosenico@isu.edu
ROSEBERRY, Lynn ... 614-236-6782.. 364 N
lroseber@capital.edu
ROSEBORO-BARNES,
Edwina ... 803-981-7162.. 435 D
eroseboro@yorktech.edu
ROSEBROUGH, Tom ... 731-661-5373.. 448 A
trosebro@uu.edu
ROSEDALE, Jeff ... 914-323-5277.. 319 N
jeff.rosedale@mville.edu
ROSEMEYER, Abbie ... 561-803-2180.. 106 C
abbie_rosemeyer@pba.edu
ROSEN, C. Martin ... 812-941-2262.. 163 F
crosen@ius.edu
ROSEN, David ... 615-794-4254.. 443 G
drosen@omorecollege.edu
ROSEN, Deborah ... 401-874-4393.. 426 D
drosen@uri.edu
ROSEN, Janet ... 218-723-6072.. 245 J
jrosen@css.edu
ROSEN, Janet, S ... 218-723-6072.. 245 J
jrosen@css.edu
ROSEN, Jeff ... 954-969-9771.. 100 K
jrosen@fcnh.com
ROSEN, Jonathan ... 518-262-5686.. 303 E
rosenj@mail.amc.edu
ROSEN, Mike, S ... 713-743-8155.. 473 F
msrosen@central.uh.edu
ROSEN, Sara ... 785-864-4904.. 185 D
rosen@ku.edu
ROSEN, Steven, T ... 626-256-4673.... 38 F
srosen@coh.org
ROSEN, Susan ... 415-476-1683.... 70 D
susan.rosen@ucsf.edu
ROSEN, Tal ... 312-322-1711.. 155 F
trosen@spertus.edu
ROSENBALM, Whitney ... 972-238-6023.. 456 H
wrosenbalm@dcccd.edu
ROSENBAUM, David, R ... 864-941-8377.. 432 A
rosenbaum.d@ptc.edu
ROSENBAUM, Irving ... 954-262-1507.. 105 J
irv@nova.edu
ROSENBAUM, Philip ... 610-896-1290.. 405 I
prosenba@haverford.edu
ROSENBAUM, Thomas, F 626-395-6301.... 30 H
tfr@caltech.edu
ROSENBERG, Alannah ... 949-582-4854.... 65 G
aorrison@saddleback.edu
ROSENBERG, Alex ... 312-235-3544.. 154 C
a.rosenberg@shimer.edu
ROSENBERG, Brian, C ... 651-696-6207.. 247 I
rosenbergb@macalester.edu
ROSENBERG, Chaim ... 718-854-2290.. 305 E
ROSENBERG, Eric ... 973-720-2303.. 298 G
rosenbergel@wpunj.edu
ROSENBERG, Jerry ... 408-864-8669.... 44 A
rosenbergjerry@deanza.edu
ROSENBERG, Lea ... 414-930-3422.. 518 F
rosenbel@mtmary.edu
ROSENBERG, Mark ... 305-348-2111.. 111 A
mark.rosenberg@fiu.edu
ROSENBERG, Michael ... 845-257-2800.. 331 E
rosenbem@newpaltz.edu
ROSENBERG, Naomi ... 617-636-2143.. 228 H
naomi.rosenberg@tufts.edu
ROSENBERG, Samuel ... 312-341-3697.. 152 H
srosenbe@roosevelt.edu
ROSENBERG, Sol ... 718-854-2290.. 305 E
ROSENBERG, Travis ... 435-652-7522.. 482 A
rosenberg@dixie.edu
ROSENBERG, Warren ... 914-831-0418.. 311 C
wrosenberg@cw.edu
ROSENBERGER,
Benjamin ... 610-372-4721.. 417 G
brosenberger@racc.edu
ROSENBERGER, Jeanne ... 408-554-4583.... 63 E
jrosenberger@scu.edu
ROSENBLATT, Roberta ... 646-565-6000.. 337 I
roberta.rosenblatt@touro.edu
ROSENBLOOM, Stuart ... 312-461-0600.. 134 K
srosenbloom@aaart.edu
ROSENBLUM, Charlie ... 254-519-8016.. 468 C
c.rosenblum@tamuct.edu
ROSENBLUM, Donald ... 954-262-8402.. 105 J
donr@nsu.nova.edu
ROSENBLUM, Yosef ... 718-854-2290.. 305 E
ROSENBOOM, David ... 661-255-1050.... 30 E
david@calarts.edu
ROSENBOOM, Sharon ... 712-722-6740.. 171 J
sharon.rosenboom@dordt.edu
ROSENBURY, Laura, A ... 352-273-0600.. 112 A
rosenbury@law.ufl.edu
ROSENDAHL, Matt ... 218-726-8130.. 255 D
lib@d.umn.edu
ROSENFELD, Renee ... 267-502-6038.. 398 J
renee.rosenfeld@brynathyn.edu
ROSENFELD, Sholom ... 718-774-5050.. 337 D
ohaleitorah@aol.com
ROSENFELDT, Mary ... 513-745-3022.. 381 I
rosenfeldt@xavier.edu
ROSENGARDEN, Jeffrey ... 646-565-6000.. 337 I
ROSENGART, Sharon ... 973-720-3019.. 298 G
rosengarts@wpunj.edu
ROSENGARTEN, Elaine ... 386-506-3075.... 98 E
rosenge@daytonastate.edu
ROSENGARTEN, Jayne ... 212-237-8624.. 308 E
jrosengarten@jjay.cuny.edu
ROSENGARTEN, Jeffrey ... 212-960-5239.. 341 G
rosengar@yu.edu
ROSENGARTEN, Lewis ... 607-753-4808.. 333 A
lewis.rosengarten@cortland.edu
ROSENGARTEN,
Richard, A ... 773-702-8221.. 156 D
raroseng@uchicago.edu
ROSENHEIN, Jonathan ... 973-655-5105.. 293 A
rosenheinj@mail.montclair.edu
ROSENKRANTZ, Laurie ... 817-531-4420.. 472 F
lerosenkrantz@txwes.edu
ROSENRAUCH, Yair ... 718-259-5300.. 305 J
yrosen@bramsonort.edu
ROSENSAFT, Jean, B ... 212-824-2209.. 315 F
jrosensaft@huc.edu
ROSENSTEIN, Arthur ... 858-566-1200.... 42 D
arthur@disd.edu
ROSENSTEIN, Ilena ... 860-768-4418.... 89 G
rosenstei@hartford.edu
ROSENSTEIN, Ilene ... 213-740-7711.... 72 D
irosenst@usc.edu
ROSENSTOCK, Jeffrey ... 718-997-4995.. 309 D
jeffrey.rosenstock@qc.cuny.edu
ROSENSTOCK, Larry ... 619-929-9748.... 46 D
lrosenstock@hightechhigh.org
ROSENSTONE, Steven, J ... 651-201-1696.. 248 I
steven.rosenstone@so.mnscu.edu
ROSENTHAL, Amy ... 817-202-6711.. 466 C
arosenthal@swau.edu
ROSENTHAL, Bruce ... 201-761-6475.. 296 K
brosenthal@saintpeters.edu
ROSENTHAL, Elizabeth ... 773-907-6833.. 137 E
erosenthal@ccc.edu
ROSENTHAL, Ellen ... 202-231-3354.. 528 C
ellen.rosenthal@dodiis.mil
ROSENTHAL, Eric ... 847-925-6677.. 141 A
erosenth@harpercollege.edu
ROSENTHAL,
Jean-Laurent ... 626-395-4068.... 30 H
rosentha@caltech.edu
ROSENTHAL, Jeffrey, E ... 315-255-1743.. 306 G
rosenthal@cayuga-cc.edu
ROSENTHAL, Julie ... 303-373-2008.... 83 B
jroesenthal@rvu.edu
ROSENTHAL, Ken ... 818-677-2561.... 34 A
ken.rosenthal@csun.edu
ROSENTHAL, Rachel ... 916-608-6572.... 51 C
rachel.rosenthal@flc.losrios.edu
ROSENTHAL, Susan ... 305-899-3050.... 96 D
srosenthal@barry.edu
ROSENWALD, Nancy ... 803-321-5229.. 431 F
nancy.rosenwald@newberry.edu
ROSETH, Lisa ... 218-723-6016.. 245 J
lroseth@css.edu
ROSEVEAR, Scott, G ... 570-577-3647.. 398 L
scott.rosevear@bucknell.edu
ROSEVEARE, Mark ... 864-592-4763.. 432 H
rosevearem@sccsc.edu
ROSEWALL, Michael ... 920-403-3272.. 519 G
michael.rosewall@snc.edu
ROSILEZ, Anthony ... 541-880-2203.. 391 F
rosilez@klamatcc.edu
ROSIN, Dallas ... 701-252-3467.. 362 F
dallas.rosin@uj.edu
ROSINE, Gregory, J ... 269-387-2071.. 243 H
greg.rosine@wmich.edu
ROSINSKI-KAUS, Donna . 732-255-0400.. 293 E
drosinski-kaus@ocean.edu
ROSKY, Bruce ... 818-610-6543.... 50 A
roskybr@piercecollege.edu
ROSMUS, Julie ... 802-776-5274.. 483 G
julie.rosmus@csj.edu
ROSOFF, Nancy ... 215-572-2921.. 397 G
rosoffn@arcadia.edu
ROSOVSKY, Leah ... 617-495-4193.. 219 D
leah_rosovsky@harvard.edu
ROSOWSKY, David, V ... 802-656-1417.. 485 D
david.rosowsky@uvm.edu
ROSPLOCK, Valerie, R ... 607-735-1174.. 313 F
vrosplock@elmira.edu
ROSS, Amy ... 423-585-6972.. 447 D
amy.ross@ws.edu
ROSS, Angela ... 304-710-3382.. 512 B
rossa@mctc.edu
ROSS, Anissa ... 870-460-1036.... 23 D
ross@uamont.edu
ROSS, Candice ... 520-494-5915.... 12 J
candice.ross@centralaz.edu
ROSS, Carla ... 510-869-6618.... 59 L
cross@samuelmerritt.edu
ROSS, Charles ... 470-578-7206.. 123 J
cross39@kennesaw.edu
ROSS, Cheryl ... 858-822-2797.... 70 C
caross@ucsd.edu
ROSS, Christine, C ... 434-223-6056.. 490 D
cross@hsc.edu
ROSS, Corey ... 605-331-6811.. 438 A
corey.ross@usiouxfalls.edu
ROSS, David ... 801-883-8336.. 480 M
dross@new.edu
ROSS, David ... 501-279-4930.... 20 D
dross@harding.edu
ROSS, David, A ... 972-708-7340.. 458 G
david_ross@gial.edu
ROSS, Dawn ... 508-626-4625.. 221 E
dross@framingham.edu
ROSS, Deborah ... 606-783-2572.. 191 H
d.ross@moreheadstate.edu
ROSS, Diane ... 541-383-7218.. 390 D
dross3@cocc.edu
ROSS, Donald, E ... 302-793-1101.... 91 E
ROSS, Donald, E ... 561-237-7782.. 104 O
dross@lynn.edu
ROSS, Elizabeth ... 617-735-9701.. 218 C
ross@emmanuel.edu
ROSS, Eric ... 660-263-4100.. 269 D
ericr@macc.edu
ROSS, III, Frank ... 518-276-6201.. 327 B
ROSS, Gary, L ... 315-228-7401.. 310 G
gross@colgate.edu
ROSS, George, E ... 989-774-3131.. 232 D
president@cmich.edu
ROSS, Gerald ... 410-225-2399.. 209 B
gross@mica.edu
ROSS, Gloria ... 662-254-3558.. 260 A
gloria.ross@mvsu.edu
ROSS, James, A ... 734-384-4259.. 238 C
jross@monroeccc.edu
ROSS, Jamison ... 952-446-4106.. 246 D
ROSS, Jason ... 864-977-7026.. 431 G
jason.ross@ngu.edu
ROSS, Jeffery ... 816-235-6212.. 273 F
umkccontracts@umkc.edu
ROSS, Jennifer, A ... 260-422-5561.. 162 B
jaross@indianatech.edu
ROSS, Jeremy, B ... 423-439-5353.. 444 F
rossjb@etsu.edu
ROSS, Jill, W ... 276-223-4880.. 499 C
jross@wcc.vccs.edu
ROSS, Jim ... 252-249-1851.. 351 G
jross@pamlicocc.edu
ROSS, JoAnn, L ... 304-766-4361.. 514 B
jross15@wvstateu.edu
ROSS, Julia ... 410-455-3400.. 211 G
jross@umbc.edu
ROSS, Julie, S ... 617-627-3360.. 228 H
j.ross@tufts.edu
ROSS, Karen ... 734-432-5529.. 237 D
kross@madonna.edu

ROUSSELL, Jeroid .... 503-699-6305.. 392 D
jroussell@marylhurst.edu
ROUTBORT, Julia, C .... 518-580-5555.. 330 F
jroutbor@skidmore.edu
ROUTE, Annie .... 907-786-1215..... 10 F
adroute@uaa.alaska.edu
ROUTE, RET., Ronald, A . 831-656-2511.. 528 D
raroute@nps.edu
ROUTH, Larry, R .... 402-472-8103.. 282 M
lrouth1@unl.edu
ROUTLEY, Jonathan, J ..... 563-588-8000.. 172 E
jjroutley@emmaus.edu
ROUX, Gayle .... 701-777-4555.. 360 C
gayle.roux@und.edu
ROUX, Sue .... 704-355-6676.. 343 A
sue.roux@carolinascollege.edu
ROUZAN-KAY, Renee ...... 310-954-4254..... 53 B
rkay@msmu.edu
ROVARIS, Dereck .... 225-578-5736.. 197 I
drovaris@lsu.edu
ROVARIS, Jill .... 408-554-4501.... 63 E
jrovaris@scu.edu
ROVEDA, Elizabeth .... 570-408-5000.. 423 G
elizabeth.roveda@wilkes.edu
ROVIG, Nicole .... 517-355-8700.. 237 I
rovig@msu.edu
ROVINELLI HELLER,
Nina .... 860-570-9141.... 89 D
nina.heller@uconn.edu
ROVINSKY-MAYER,
Michele, M .... 215-895-1403.. 402 G
mrovinsky@drexel.edu
ROWAN, Bernard .... 773-995-2439.. 136 M
trowanii@csu.edu
ROWAN, John Paul .... 912-525-5000.. 126 E
jprowan@scad.edu
ROWAN, Matthew, C .... 260-399-7700.. 168 D
mrowan@sf.edu
ROWAN, Melissa .... 515-294-0596.. 169 G
mrowan@foundation.iastate.edu
ROWAN, Paul .... 541-885-1720.. 393 G
paul.rowan@oit.edu
ROWAN, Robert, M .... 410-706-8200.. 211 F
rrowan@umaryland.edu
ROWDEN, Diana .... 479-788-7676..... 23 A
diana.rowden@uafs.edu
ROWE, Al .... 319-398-7611.. 174 I
arowe@kirkwood.edu
ROWE, Alan .... 229-333-7816.. 129 G
carowe@valdosta.edu
ROWE, Amy, W .... 814-866-8111.. 407 D
arowe@lecom.edu
ROWE, Christine .... 914-337-9300.. 311 F
christine.rowe@concordia-ny.edu
ROWE, Katherine .... 413-585-3000.. 228 D
karowe@smith.edu
ROWE, Nicole .... 906-932-4231.. 234 C
nicoler@gogebic.edu
ROWE, Philip .... 919-508-2329.. 359 G
prowe@peace.edu
ROWE, Theresa, M .... 248-370-4326.. 239 K
rowe@oakland.edu
ROWELL, Amy .... 251-275-8256..... 1 C
arowell@ascc.edu
ROWELL, Reda, K .... 229-931-2014.. 122 C
reda.rowell@gsw.edu
ROWELL, Sam, S .... 423-354-2582.. 446 F
ssrowell@northeaststate.edu
ROWEN, Cate .... 413-585-3021.. 228 D
crowen@smith.edu
ROWEN, Randall, C .... 803-777-2593.. 433 F
rowen@sccp.sc.edu
ROWH, Mark, C .... 540-674-3617.. 497 G
mrowh@nr.edu
ROWH, Mark, E .... 806-354-6070.. 450 H
merowh@actx.edu
ROWLAND, Bryan .... 423-425-4717.. 448 F
bryan-rowland@utc.edu
ROWLAND, Jenny .... 252-334-2020.. 346 F
jenny.rowland@macuniversity.edu
ROWLAND, Jim .... 918-540-6301.. 384 F
jrowland@neo.edu
ROWLAND, Leo .... 909-748-8717.... 71 K
leo_rowland@redlands.edu
ROWLAND, Linda .... 706-864-1358.. 128 F
linda.rowland@ung.edu
ROWLAND, Randy .... 913-360-7372.. 178 I
rrowland@benedictine.edu
ROWLAND, Rita, K .... 626-584-5484.... 44 G
rrowland@fuller.edu
ROWLAND, IV, Roy .... 863-667-5081.. 109 L
rrowland@seu.edu
ROWLAND, Sheri .... 850-201-8490.. 113 E
rowlands@tcc.fl.edu
ROWLAND, Sheri .... 478-471-2031.. 124 E
sheri.rowland@mga.edu
ROWLAND, Susie .... 434-239-5222.. 492 D
susie.rowland@miller-motte.edu
ROWLAND, Tania .... 801-818-8900.. 481 B
tania.rowland@provocollege.edu
ROWLAND, Theresa .... 415-239-3000.... 38 E
trowland@ccsf.edu
ROWLAND, Theresa .... 616-331-9530.. 234 F
rowlanth@gvsu.edu
ROWLANDS, Judith .... 856-227-7200.. 290 B
jrowlands@camdencc.edu
ROWLANDS, Steve .... 325-674-2626.. 449 J
rowlandss@acu.edu
ROWLES, Brian .... 863-638-7667.. 115 C
brian.rowles@warner.edu
ROWLETT, Carol .... 540-857-7277.. 499 B
crowlett@virginiawestern.edu
ROWLETT, Doug .... 713-718-6743.. 459 B
doug.rowlett@hccs.edu
ROWLETT, Sharron .... 603-888-1311.. 287 F
srowlett@rivier.edu
ROWLEY, Amanda, D .... 315-386-7559.. 335 B
rowleya@canton.edu
ROWLEY, Becky .... 575-769-4001.. 299 G
becky.rowley@clovis.edu
ROWLEY, Don .... 765-677-2313.. 164 B
don.rowley@indwes.edu
ROWLEY, Jill .... 409-880-8450.. 471 A
jill.rowley@lamar.edu
ROWLEY, Lisa .... 503-352-7252.. 394 C
lisajrowley@pacificu.edu
ROWLEY, Sarah, L .... 248-341-2081.. 239 E
slrowley@oaklandcc.edu
ROWNEY, Hillary .... 307-332-2930.. 527 F
hrowney@wyomingcatholiccollege.com
ROWSER, Mayola .... 812-465-7016.. 168 E
mrowser@usi.edu
ROXBURY, Peggy .... 256-761-6205...... 7 F
proxbury@talladega.edu
ROXWORTHY, Emily .... 858-534-1709.... 70 C
waprovost@ucsd.edu
ROY, Alisa .... 704-922-6202.. 350 A
roy.alisa@gaston.edu
ROY, Andy .... 209-667-3114.... 34 E
aroy@csustan.edu
ROY, Ashok .... 256-782-5820...... 4 H
aroy@jsu.edu
ROY, Gail .... 207-768-2700.. 203 L
groy@nmcc.edu
ROY, Judy, K .... 260-422-5561.. 162 B
jkroy@indianatech.edu
ROY, Justin .... 732-987-2764.. 292 A
jroy@georgian.edu
ROY, Lara .... 612-874-3778.. 247 M
lara_roy@mcad.edu
ROY, Lisa .... 207-326-4715.. 204 C
lisa.roy@mma.edu
ROY, Marc .... 856-351-2680.. 296 L
mroy@salemcc.edu
ROY, Marc .... 517-629-0221.. 230 E
mroy@albion.edu
ROY, Melissa .... 845-574-4758.. 327 G
mroy@sunyrockland.edu
ROY, Michael, D .... 802-443-5490.. 484 F
mdroy@middlebury.edu
ROY, Rani, R .... 718-862-7755.. 319 L
rani.roy@manhattan.edu
ROY, Rina .... 916-484-8108..... 51 A
royr@arc.losrios.edu
ROY, Tracey .... 218-322-2409.. 249 E
troy@itascacc.edu
ROY, Tracey .... 218-322-2409.. 249 I
tracey.roy@itascacc.edu
ROY, Tracey .... 218-322-2409.. 249 G
tracey.roy@itascacc.edu
ROY, Tracey .... 218-322-2409.. 252 F
t.roy@itascacc.edu
ROYAL, Angela .... 636-949-4983.. 266 J
aroyal@lindenwood.edu
ROYAL, Christina .... 651-450-3618.. 249 F
croyal@inverhills.edu
ROYAL, Karen, B .... 361-593-4758.. 469 A
karen.royal@tamuk.edu
ROYBAL, Juliane, M .... 480-726-4240..... 13 O
juliane.roybal@cgc.edu
ROYBAL, Phillip .... 575-492-2761.. 300 H
proybal@nmjc.edu
ROYBAL, Walter .... 719-587-8281..... 76 G
wsroybal@adams.edu
ROYCE, Kathy .... 530-339-3610..... 64 D
kroyce@shastacollege.edu
ROYCE, Lee, G .... 601-925-3200.. 259 A
lroyce@mc.edu
ROYCE, Richard, A .... 516-671-2356.. 339 G
rroyce@webb.edu
ROYCE, Rosa .... 909-274-4234..... 53 C
rroyce@mtsac.edu
ROYCE-DAVIS, Joanna, C 253-535-7191.. 505 G
roycedjc@plu.edu
ROYE, Shauna .... 202-495-3837..... 93 D
sroye@dhs.edu
ROYEEN, Charlotte .... 312-942-7120.. 153 B
charlotte_l_royeen@rush.edu
ROYER, James .... 504-671-5477.. 196 D
jroyer@dcc.edu
ROYER, Joseph .... 765-641-4000.. 158 J
jmroyer@anderson.edu
ROYER, Randy .... 913-288-7188.. 182 C
rroyer@kckcc.edu
ROYER, Roma .... 602-429-4947..... 16 E
rroyer@ps.edu
ROYKO, Barry .... 216-987-0205.. 367 E
barry.royko@tri-c.edu
ROYO, Sebastian .... 617-573-8120.. 228 G
sroyo@suffolk.edu
ROYOS, Andre .... 915-779-8031.. 478 J
aroyos@computercareercenter.com
ROYS, Cindy .... 631-730-2028.. 305 K
croys@bcl.edu
ROYSTER, Jacqueline, J .. 404-894-1728.. 121 D
jacqueline.royster@iac.gatech.edu
ROYSTER, Karen .... 214-860-2033.. 456 E
kstills@dcccd.edu
ROYSTER, Traci, D .... 828-262-6158.. 356 B
roystertd@appstate.edu
ROYSTON, Mimi .... 413-205-3448.. 214 B
mimi.royston@aic.edu
ROYSTON, Rosemary, R .. 706-379-3111.. 130 B
rosemary@yhc.edu
ROYUK, Brent .... 402-643-7304.. 279 F
brent.royuk@cune.edu
ROZ, Mugur .... 617-850-1545.. 219 F
mroz@hchc.edu
ROZ, Mugur .... 617-964-1100.. 214 D
mroz@ants.edu
ROZADA, Mayra .... 787-891-0925.. 533 G
mrozada@aguadilla.inter.edu
ROZAK, Edward .... 508-830-5030.. 222 C
erozak@maritime.edu
ROZANSKI, Kathy .... 856-256-5405.. 295 E
rozanski@rowan.edu
ROZEBOOM, Dave .... 325-671-2263.. 458 J
dave.rozeboom@hsutx.edu
ROZEK, Amy .... 808-235-7370.. 132 E
amyrozek@hawaii.edu
ROZEK, Charles, E .... 216-368-4390.. 365 B
cer2@case.edu
ROZEK, Richard, J .... 248-364-3562.. 239 K
rozek@oakland.edu
ROZELL, Laura .... 518-327-6291.. 326 B
lrozell@paulsmiths.edu
ROZELL, Liz .... 661-395-4231..... 47 J
mrozell@bakersfieldcollege.edu
ROZELL, Mark .... 703-993-4108.. 490 B
mrozell@gmu.edu
ROZEMA, Burton, J .... 708-239-4760.. 155 M
burt.rozema@trnty.edu
ROZEMBAJGIER, John ..... 614-885-5585.. 376 G
jrozembajgier@pcj.edu
ROZEWSKI, Mark .... 203-392-5456..... 85 H
rozewskim@southernct.edu
ROZIER, Nicholas .... 208-882-1566.. 134 B
nrozier@nsa.edu
RUANE, Beth .... 802-451-7577.. 484 C
bruane@marlboro.edu
RUANO, Norman .... 773-878-3894.. 153 E
nruano@iwe.staugustine.edu
RUBACK, Chad .... 847-578-8589.. 153 A
chad.ruback@rosalindfranlin.edu
RUBACK, Sally, A .... 920-929-2126.. 524 B
sruback@morainepark.edu
RUBALCABA, Ron .... 626-529-8224..... 55 H
rrubalcaba@pacificoaks.edu
RUBEL, Barbara, G .... 617-627-3780.. 228 H
barbara.rubel@tufts.edu
RUBEL, Carol .... 617-587-5650.. 226 E
rubelc@neco.edu
RUBEL, Tom .... 641-683-5252.. 173 C
tom.rubel@indianhills.edu
RUBEMEYER, Susan .... 636-922-8360.. 271 A
srubemeyer@stchas.edu
RUBENBAUER, Jason .... 229-243-6960.. 117 E
jason.rubenbauer@bainbridge.edu
RUBENS, Dave .... 330-684-8906.. 378 H
drubens@uakron.edu
RUBENSTEIN, David .... 202-687-1972..... 92 E
dr94@georgetown.edu
RUBENSTEIN, David .... 856-256-4222.. 295 E
rubenstein@rowan.edu
RUBERO, Maria, D .... 787-250-1912.. 534 B
mdrubero@metro.inter.edu
RUBIE, Jessica .... 979-845-2217.. 468 B
jrubie@tamu.edu
RUBIN, Beno .... 757-822-5077.. 498 H
brubin@tcc.edu
RUBIN, Beth .... 513-529-6069.. 372 K
rubinb@miamioh.edu
RUBIN, David .... 802-224-3000.. 485 G
david.rubin@vsc.edu
RUBIN, Gary, N .... 410-704-2358.. 213 B
grubin@towson.edu
RUBIN, Henry .... 646-565-6000.. 337 I
RUBIN, James .... 602-787-6546..... 14 E
james.rubin@paradisevalley.edu
RUBIN, Joshua .... 718-436-2122.. 337 C
RUBIN, Leona .... 573-884-1402.. 273 E
rubinl@missouri.edu
RUBIN, Lisa .... 770-426-2725.. 124 B
lrubin@life.edu
RUBIN, Lucas .... 212-966-4014.. 307 D
lrubin@brooklyn.cuny.edu
RUBIN, Moshe .... 515-239-9002.. 330 D
RUBIN, Rachel .... 860-486-2337..... 89 D
rachel.rubin@uconn.edu
RUBIN, Steve .... 719-219-9636..... 77 H
steverubindvm@att.net
RUBINO, Debra .... 410-225-2300.. 209 B
drubino@mica.edu
RUBINO, Joseph .... 410-293-1549.. 529 D
rubino@usna.edu
RUBINO, Karen, M .... 401-456-8849.. 425 E
krubino@ric.edu
RUBINO, Michael, H .... 508-767-7156.. 214 F
rubino@assumption.edu
RUBINSTEIN, Mark .... 603-513-1307.. 288 D
mark.rubinstein@granite.edu
RUBIO, Dave .... 909-384-8640..... 60 C
drubio@sbccd.cc.ca.us
RUBIO, Olga, D .... 956-721-5296.. 460 F
drubio@laredo.edu
RUBLE, Celeste .... 507-433-0666.. 251 H
celeste.ruble@riverland.edu
RUBLE, Joel .... 559-925-3127..... 74 E
joelruble@whccd.edu
RUBLE, Justin .... 304-260-4380.. 511 L
jruble@blueridgectc.edu
RUBLE, Michelle .... 301-934-4711.. 207 B
micheller@csmd.edu
RUBRITZ, Gerald .... 814-886-6460.. 411 C
grubritz@mtaloy.edu
RUBSAMEN, Rich .... 503-699-6252.. 392 D
rrubsamen@marylhurst.edu
RUCH, Adam .... 510-654-6932..... 43 D
aruch@expression.edu
RUCHALA, Patsy, L .... 775-784-6841.. 285 A
pruchala@unr.edu
RUCKER, Aithyni .... 704-971-8500.. 343 E
arucker@charlottelaw.edu
RUCKER, Cedric, B .... 540-654-1655.. 495 C
crucker@umw.edu
RUCKER, Jana .... 501-279-4316..... 20 D
jrucker@harding.edu
RUCKER, Marty, K .... 423-585-6983.. 447 D
marty.rucker@ws.edu
RUCKER, Nolan .... 800-950-8001..... 77 C
rucker@bel-rea.com
RUCKER, Paul .... 206-685-9223.. 508 E
uwalumni@uw.edu
RUCKER, Robert, E .... 662-685-4771.. 257 A
erucker@bmc.edu
RUCKER, Sherri, B .... 615-329-8555.. 439 L
srucker@fisk.edu
RUCKER, Sonia .... 573-651-2524.. 272 B
srucker@semo.edu
RUCKER-FRANKLIN,
Yvonne .... 870-633-4480..... 20 B
yrucker@eacc.edu
RUCKER-SHAMU, Marian 301-860-3849.. 212 D
mshamu@bowiestate.edu
RUDA, Ryan .... 620-276-9597.. 181 C
ryan.ruda@gcccks.edu
RUDASILL, Susann .... 850-644-1571.. 111 C
srudasill@fsu.edu
RUDATSIKIRA,
Emmanuel .... 269-471-6648.. 230 H
rudatsikira@andrews.edu
RUDAWITZ, Linda .... 503-517-1397.. 396 D
lrudawitz@warnerpacific.edu
RUDAWSKY, Donald, J ... 954-262-5392.. 105 J
rudawsky@nova.edu
RUDD, M. David .... 901-678-2234.. 445 C
mdrudd@memphis.edu
RUDD, Martin .... 920-832-2610.. 522 A
martin.rudd@uwc.edu
RUDDELL, Larry .... 281-579-9977.. 256 I
lruddell@belhaven.edu
RUDDEN, David .... 847-214-7925.. 140 A
drudden@elgin.edu
RUDE, Jen .... 253-535-7464.. 505 G
rudejl@plu.edu
RUDEAU, William .... 609-771-2187.. 290 F
rudeau@tcnj.edu
RUDECOFF, Christine, A . 315-684-6055.. 336 B
rudecoc@morrisville.edu
RUDEN, Becky .... 415-703-9360..... 29 K
becky@cca.edu
RUDEN, Lynne .... 989-275-5000.. 236 E
lynne.ruden@kirtland.edu
RUDER, Jackie .... 785-628-4326.. 180 I
jsruder@fhsu.edu
RUDGERS, Lisa, M .... 734-764-3526.. 241 J
rudgers@umich.edu
RUDIE, Scott .... 414-930-3555.. 518 F
rudies@mtmary.edu
RUDIGER, Brenda .... 906-487-2400.. 238 A
brudiger@mtu.edu

RUDIGER, Jennifer .... 715-232-1151.. 521 D rudigerj@uwstout.edu
RUDIN, Mark .... 208-426-5732.. 132 I markrudin@boisestate.edu
RUDISILL, Frank .... 864-503-5511.. 434 G frudisill@uscupstate.edu
RUDNEY, Gwen .... 320-589-6411.. 255 F rudneygl@morris.umn.edu
RUDNICK, Joseph .... 310-825-1042.... 69 D jrudnick@college.ucla.edu
RUDNICK, Virginia .... 607-962-9587.. 312 B vrudnick@corning-cc.edu
RUDNICKI, Rosemary .... 512-448-8540.. 464 G rosemars@stedwards.edu
RUDNITSKI, Rose .... 201-559-3551.. 291 K rudnitskir@felician.edu
RUDOLPH, Alan, S .... 970-491-7194.... 78 Q alan.rudolph@colostate.edu
RUDOLPH, Margaret .... 419-448-2111.. 369 G mrudolph@heidelberg.edu
RUDOLPH, Mary Kay .... 707-524-1516.... 63 G mrudolph@santarosa.edu
RUDOLPH, Meloni .... 303-556-8164.... 79 F meloni.rudolph@ccd.edu
RUDOVSKY, Michelle .... 650-378-6577.... 62 H rudovskym@smccd.edu
RUDOWSKY, Catherine ... 361-825-2643.. 468 E catherine.rudowsky@tamucc.edu
RUDY, Joel .... 276-739-2512.. 499 A jrudy@vhcc.edu
RUE, Cynthia .... 239-454-5000.. 107 D
RUE, Penny .... 336-758-5943.. 359 E rue@wfu.edu
RUEB, Jan, L .... 432-837-8178.. 471 E jrueb@sulross.edu
RUEB, Shirley .... 316-942-4291.. 183 I ruebs@newmanu.edu
RUEBEL, James, S .... 765-285-1024.. 159 B jruebel@bsu.edu
RUEDA, Isa .... 928-523-6504.... 15 H isa.rueda@nau.edu
RUEDAS, Lorena .... 916-558-2646.... 51 D ruedasl@scc.losrios.edu
RUEFF, Alicia .... 561-732-4424.. 108 F arueff@svdp.edu
RUEFLE, Colleen .... 412-536-1069.. 406 K colleen.ruefle@laroche.edu
RUEGG, Samuel (Tex) ...... 817-515-4591.. 467 A samuel.ruegg@tccd.edu
RUELAS, Patricia .... 510-485-7865.... 56 I pruelas@patten.edu
RUELLE, Joan .... 336-278-6572.. 344 D jruelle@elon.edu
RUELLE, Maggie .... 903-510-2490.. 473 C mrue@tjc.edu
RUESCH, Sherry .... 435-652-7551.. 482 A ruesch@dixie.edu
RUESCHMANN, Eva .... 413-559-5378.. 219 C erueschmann@hampshire.edu
RUESS, Trish .... 740-587-5620.. 368 B ruess@denison.edu
RUETER, Erik .... 724-503-1001.. 422 H erueter@washjeff.edu
RUETTEN, Amy .... 417-667-8181.. 264 A aruetten@cottey.edu
RUFF, Corey .... 325-674-2665.. 449 J clr06a@acu.edu
RUFF, Joy, C .... 305-237-2090.. 105 D jruff@mdc.edu
RUFF, Margaret .... 903-785-7661.. 463 E mruff@parisjc.edu
RUFF, Raymond, H .... 864-597-4171.. 435 C ruffrh@wofford.edu
RUFF, Rosemary, H .... 479-575-3845.... 22 I ruff@uark.edu
RUFFIN, Cynthia .... 919-572-1625.. 341 M cruffin@apexsot.edu
RUFFIN, Finee .... 601-477-4082.. 258 E finee.ruffin@jcjc.edu
RUFFIN, Gene .... 678-407-5000.. 121 B gruffin@ggc.edu
RUFFIN, Kimberly, N .... 312-341-2281.. 152 H kruffin@roosevelt.edu
RUFFING, Rebecca .... 315-866-0300.. 316 A ruffingrj@herkimer.edu
RUFFINO, John, J .... 703-323-3023.. 497 H jruffino@nvcc.edu
RUFFRAGE, Jo .... 315-792-7172.. 336 C ruffraj@sunyit.edu
RUFINO, Paul .... 856-415-2173.. 295 D prufino@rcgc.edu
RUFO, Joseph .... 315-470-6622.. 334 E jlrufo@esf.edu
RUGEMER, Ellen .... 410-857-2203.. 209 D erugemer@mcdaniel.edu
RUGER, Theodore, W ...... 215-898-7061.. 421 E deanruger@law.upenn.edu
RUGG, Marilyn .... 315-228-7288.. 310 G mrugg@colgate.edu
RUGG, Rebecca .... 914-251-6831.. 334 C rebecca.rugg@purchase.edu
RUGG, William .... 406-265-3726.. 277 E william.rugg@msun.edu
RUGGAR MARTIN, Jan ...... 323-469-3300.... 26 A jruggarmartin@amda.edu
RUGGIERI, David .... 407-447-7300.. 102 D druggieri@ftccollege.edu
RUGGIERO, Bruno .... 985-448-4262.. 201 A bruno.ruggiero@nicholls.edu
RUGGIRELLO, Frank .... 734-462-4400.. 240 H fruggire@schoolcraft.edu
RUGGLES, Jennifer .... 216-368-1723.. 365 B jor15@case.edu
RUGGLES, Matt .... 970-521-6611.... 81 O matthew.ruggles@njc.edu
RUGGLES, Shami .... 509-533-7085.. 502 I shami.ruggles@ccs.spokane.edu
RUGGLES, Shami, R .... 509-533-3567.. 502 H shami.ruggles@ccs.spokane.edu
RUHD, Jill .... 605-256-5650.. 437 C jill.ruhd@dsu.edu
RUHL, Austin .... 406-586-3585.. 276 I austin.ruhl@montanabiblecollege.edu
RUHL, Chris .... 317-921-4474.. 164 E cruhl@ivytech.edu
RUHL, Taylor .... 619-644-7390.... 45 J taylor.ruhl@gcccd.edu
RUHLAND, Gail .... 320-308-3081.. 252 A gmruhland@stcloudstate.edu
RUHLAND, Sheila .... 253-566-5100.. 508 B sruhland@tacomacc.edu
RUHLANDT, Karin .... 315-443-3949.. 337 A kruhland@syr.edu
RUIBAL, Pilar .... 787-751-0160.. 531 M pruibal@cmpr.pr.gov
RUITER, Kathy .... 217-854-5525.. 135 K kathleen.ruiter@blackburn.edu
RUIZ, Alberto .... 361-593-2837.. 469 A alberto.ruiz@tamuk.edu
RUIZ, Alfredo .... 269-471-6979.. 230 H jaruiz@andrews.edu
RUIZ, Andrew .... 806-894-9611.. 465 G aruiz@southplainscollege.edu
RUIZ, Angel, J .... 787-863-2390.. 533 K angel.ruiz@fajardo.inter.edu
RUIZ, Ediltrudys .... 718-960-8421.. 308 B ediltrudys.ruiz@lehman.cuny.edu
RUIZ, Emil .... 787-840-2575.. 535 H emilruiz@psm.edu
RUIZ, Encarnacion .... 209-228-4240.... 70 A eruiz@ucmerced.edu
RUIZ, Erick .... 503-251-2805.. 396 C eruiz@uws.edu
RUIZ, Israel .... 617-253-4495.. 225 A
RUIZ, Joaquin .... 520-621-4090.... 17 I jruiz@email.arizona.edu
RUIZ, OP, John Martin ... 202-495-3821.... 93 D jruiz@dhs.edu
RUIZ, Jose .... 787-863-2390.. 533 K jose.ruiz@fajardo.inter.edu
RUIZ, Kathleen .... 310-377-5501.... 51 G kruiz@marymountcalifornia.edu
RUIZ, Lucy .... 559-244-6137.... 67 A lucy.ruiz@scccd.edu
RUIZ, Luis, A .... 787-766-1717.. 536 B um_lruiz@suagm.edu
RUIZ, Luis, E .... 787-250-1912.. 534 B leruiz@metro.inter.edu
RUIZ, Maria-Luisa .... 718-270-6263.. 309 B mlruiz@mec.cuny.edu
RUIZ, Melanie .... 425-564-2710.. 501 F melanie.ruiz@bellevuecollege.edu
RUIZ, Miguel .... 713-221-8564.. 474 B ruizm@uhd.edu
RUIZ, Rachel .... 626-966-4576.... 26 J studentservices@agu.edu
RUIZ, Rafael .... 787-257-0000.. 537 H rafael.ruiz@upr.edu
RUIZ, Roseanna .... 909-537-7651.... 34 C rruiz@csusb.edu
RUIZ, Sacha, M .... 787-891-0925.. 533 G sruiz@aguadilla.inter.edu
RUIZ, Sina .... 903-875-7376.. 462 J sina.ruiz@navarrocollege.edu
RUIZ, Veronica .... 787-746-1400.. 532 M vruiz@huertas.edu
RUIZ, Wendy .... 661-362-3510.... 40 A wendy.ruiz@canyons.edu
RUIZ, Zaida .... 787-786-3030.. 536 F zrueiz@ucb.edu.pr
RUIZ-HUSTON, Ines .... 209-946-2132.... 71 C iruiz@pacific.edu
RUIZ-MATTEI, Enid .... 719-389-6699.... 77 J enid.ruizmattei@coloradocollege.edu
RUIZ-MORENO, Isabel ...... 818-364-7776.... 49 J
RUKSNAITIS, Diane .... 978-632-6600.. 224 B d_ruksnaitis@mwcc.mass.edu
RULAND, Heather, E .... 508-373-9430.. 215 D heather.ruland@becker.edu
RULAND, Judith, P .... 989-964-4145.. 240 F jruland@svsu.edu
RULAND, Michael .... 409-880-8108.. 471 A michael.ruland@lamar.edu
RULE, Anne .... 314-977-2495.. 271 K ruleam@slu.edu
RULE, David .... 425-564-2301.. 501 F dave.rule@bellevuecollege.edu
RULE, Kelli .... 503-847-2556.. 396 C krule@uws.edu
RULLÁN, Agustín .... 787-265-3822.. 538 C decano.ingenieria@upr.edu
RULLMAN, Loren, J .... 734-763-1291.. 241 J lrullman@umich.edu
RULLO, Michelle .... 718-779-1430.. 326 D mrullo@plazacollege.edu
RULOFSON, Eric .... 530-938-5851.... 40 F erulofson@siskiyous.edu
RUMBARGER, Josh .... 616-222-3000.. 236 F jrumbarger@kuyper.edu
RUMERY, Joyce, V .... 207-581-1655.. 204 H rumery@maine.edu
RUMIANO, Sara .... 530-898-5134.... 32 C srumiano@csuchico.edu
RUMLEY, Timothy .... 616-538-2330.. 234 D trumley@gbcol.edu
RUMMEL, J, D .... 402-280-1131.. 279 H rummel@creighton.edu
RUMMEL, Tina .... 903-675-6376.. 473 B trummel@tvcc.edu
RUMP, Rebecca .... 319-208-5065.. 176 J brump@scciowa.edu
RUMPZA, Matthew, D .... 651-696-6551.. 247 I mrumpza@macalester.edu
RUMSEY, Elizabeth .... 218-726-7471.. 255 D erumsey@d.umn.edu
RUND, James, A .... 480-965-2200.... 11 H james.rund@asu.edu
RUNDELL, Isabel .... 317-896-9324.. 167 H irundell@ubca.org
RUNDELL, Jay, A .... 740-362-3121.. 372 D jrundell@mtso.edu
RUNDSTROM, Amy, L .... 308-865-8501.. 282 L rundstromal@unk.edu
RUNESTAD, Eric .... 507-537-6220.. 252 E eric.runestad@smsu.edu
RUNESTAD, Eric .... 563-387-1507.. 174 L eric.runestad@luther.edu
RUNEY, Mimi, L .... 401-598-1000.. 425 B mruney@jwu.edu
RUNG, Paul .... 718-405-3722.. 310 H paul.rung@mountsaintvincent.edu
RUNGE, Carol .... 518-743-2313.. 335 A rungec@sunyacc.edu
RUNGE, Carol, E .... 315-255-1743.. 306 G crunge@cayuga-cc.edu
RUNGE, Mark, S .... 620-341-5331.. 180 G mrunge@emporia.edu
RUNGE, Marschall, S .... 734-647-9351.. 241 J
RUNGE, Steve .... 501-450-3126.... 24 G srunge@uca.edu
RUNIEWICZ, Michael, J ..... 314-935-8976.. 274 N michael_runiewicz@wustl.edu
RUNION, Kevin, L .... 812-237-8101.. 162 A kevin.runion@indstate.edu
RUNION, Robert .... 304-929-5026.. 512 C rrunion@newriver.edu
RUNKLE, Dan .... 563-589-3599.. 177 C drunkle@dbq.edu
RUNKLE, Gita .... 310-434-4370.... 63 F runkle_gita@smc.edu
RUNKSMEIER, Lori .... 860-465-4509.... 85 G runksmeierl@easternct.edu
RUNNELS, Greg .... 574-239-8312.. 161 N grunnels@hcc-nd.edu
RUNNELS, Marti, R .... 806-291-1086.. 479 D runnels@wbu.edu
RUNNING, Patrick .... 320-762-4483.. 248 J patrickr@alextech.edu
RUNNOE, Katie .... 920-686-6273.. 519 H katie.runnoe@sl.edu
RUNYAN, Andy .... 937-512-3140.. 377 D andy.runyan@sinclair.edu
RUNYAN, Laura .... 717-337-6505.. 404 C lrunyan@gettysburg.edu
RUNYON, David .... 717-901-5137.. 405 H drunyon@harrisburgu.edu
RUNYON, Jean .... 970-204-8100.... 80 E jean.runyon@frontrange.edu
RUNYON, Tim .... 417-626-1234.. 269 K runyon.tim@occ.edu
RUOCCO, Ann Michele .... 413-559-5411.. 219 C amrhr@hampshire.edu
RUPE, Jolene, K .... 785-539-3571.. 183 B jrupe@mccks.edu
RUPE, Manuel, R .... 989-774-3971.. 232 D rupe1mr@cmich.edu
RUPERT, Kimberly .... 517-750-1200.. 241 E krupert@arbor.edu
RUPERT, Mark .... 970-410-0456.... 85 B
RUPERT, Terry, A .... 937-481-2255.. 381 C terry_rupert@wilmington.edu
RUPIPER, Russ .... 402-557-7291.. 278 I russ.rupiper@bellevue.edu
RUPP, Sharon, L .... 864-429-8728.. 434 F ruppsl@mailbox.sc.edu
RUPP, Sheila .... 231-995-1058.. 239 C srupp@nmc.edu
RUPPERT, Becky, L .... 301-784-5000.. 205 G rruppert@allegany.edu
RUPRECHT, Rob .... 320-223-7507.. 254 D rob.ruprecht@rasmussen.edu
RURKA, Jessica .... 410-225-2573.. 209 B jrurka@mica.edu
RURSCH, Keri .... 309-794-7721.. 135 D kerirursch@augustana.edu
RUSCH, Kathleen, M .... 414-464-9777.. 522 Q rusch.kathleen@wspp.edu
RUSCH, Kelly .... 701-231-6542.. 361 A kelly.rusch@ndsu.edu
RUSCH-CURL, Kari .... 952-358-8776.. 251 A kari.rusch-curl@normandale.edu
RUSCHIVAL, Michael .... 303-292-0015.... 79 H m.ruschival@denverschoolofnursing.edu
RUSCHMAN, Doug .... 513-745-3185.. 381 I ruschman@xavier.edu
RUSCIO, Kenneth, P .... 540-458-8700.. 500 F president@wlu.edu
RUSE, Elaine .... 330-941-3505.. 382 A eruse@ysu.edu
RUSE, Michael .... 843-349-2548.. 428 E mruse@coastal.edu
RUSH, Amber .... 870-368-2008.... 21 F arush@ozarka.edu
RUSH, Bryan .... 812-464-1862.. 168 E rush@usi.edu
RUSH, Cherlyn, L .... 215-951-1948.. 407 A rush@lasalle.edu
RUSH, Dennis .... 845-569-3492.. 322 B dennis.rush@msmc.edu
RUSH, Elena .... 864-592-4627.. 432 H rushe@sccsc.edu
RUSH, James .... 662-476-5386.. 257 G jrush@eastms.edu
RUSH, JR., James .... 706-721-1626.. 117 D jrush@augusta.edu
RUSH, James, C .... 409-880-8354.. 471 A james.rush@lamar.edu
RUSH, Janet .... 402-363-5661.. 283 G jgrush@york.edu
RUSH, John .... 575-769-4030.. 299 G john.rush@clovis.edu
RUSH, John, H .... 563-588-8000.. 172 E jrush@emmaus.edu
RUSH, John, P .... 662-325-9306.. 259 D rush@devalumni.msstate.edu
RUSH, Keith .... 225-769-8820.. 197 G
RUSH, Mark, E .... 540-458-8904.. 500 F rushm@wlu.edu
RUSH, Maureen .... 215-898-7515.. 421 E mrush@publicsafety.upenn.edu
RUSH, Mike, G .... 605-773-3455.. 436 L mike.rush@sdbor.edu
RUSH, Nate .... 217-854-3231.. 135 K nate.rush@blackburn.edu
RUSH, Patrick .... 708-596-2000.. 154 E prush@ssc.edu
RUSH, III, Robert .... 610-861-1485.. 411 B rushr@moravian.edu
RUSH, Rosalee .... 570-389-4043.. 414 D rrush@bloomu.edu
RUSH, Tanya .... 443-885-3527.. 209 F tanya.rush@morgan.edu
RUSH WOODS, Dianne ...... 510-885-2809.... 32 E dianne.woods@csueastbay.edu
RUSHBROOK, Jill .... 860-253-3068.... 86 A jrushbrook@asnuntuck.edu
RUSHFORTH, Brenda .... 909-621-8175.... 58 A brenda.rushforth@pomona.edu
RUSHING, Beth .... 336-316-2205.. 344 H rushingb@guilford.edu
RUSHING, Cheri .... 618-437-5321.. 152 A rushing@rlc.edu
RUSHING, James Kenneth .... 904-264-2172.. 107 N krushing@iwsfla.org
RUSHING, Kevin .... 573-629-3240.. 265 G kevin.rushing@hlg.edu
RUSHING, Krysta .... 912-538-3157.. 127 E krushing@southeasterntech.edu
RUSHING, Linda .... 870-364-6414.... 23 D rushingl@uamont.edu
RUSHING, Natasha .... 573-629-3048.. 265 G natasha.rushing@hlg.edu
RUSHING, Ray .... 254-867-4893.. 470 F ray.rushing@tstc.edu
RUSHING, Wanda .... 601-923-1699.. 260 E wrushing@rts.edu
RUSHMER, Bernadette .... 570-674-8028.. 410 K brushmer@misericordia.edu
RUSHNAWITZ, P .... 248-968-3360.. 244 B
RUSHTON, Jeffery, A .... 502-852-6171.. 194 A jeff.rushton@louisville.edu

RUSILOSKI, Benjamin ..... 215-489-2911.. 402 A
benjamin.rusiloski@delval.edu
RUSINKIEWICZ, Marek, E ..... 973-596-5488.. 293 D
marek.rusinkiewicz@njit.edu
RUSKIN, Susan ..... 336-770-1333.. 358 E
ruskins@uncsa.edu
RUSNAK NOON, Anna .... 570-504-9695.. 400 I
anoon@tcmc.edu
RUSS, Larry ..... 201-216-5379.. 297 B
lruss@stevens.edu
RUSS-WILSON, Traci, L .. 704-894-2201.. 343 I
trruss@davidson.edu
RUSSE, Sarah, R ..... 630-844-4620.. 135 E
srusse@aurora.edu
RUSSEK, Lori ..... 361-593-4191.. 469 A
lori.russek@tamuk.edu
RUSSELL, Agnes, M ..... 616-222-3000.. 236 F
arussell@kuyper.edu
RUSSELL, Andrew ..... 315-792-7317.. 336 C
andrew.russell@sunyit.edu
RUSSELL, Andrew ..... 774-455-7590.. 220 E
arussell@umassp.edu
RUSSELL, Anne Marie, T . 207-786-8211.. 202 D
arussell@bates.edu
RUSSELL, Babs ..... 770-947-7260.. 129 M
babs.russell@westgatech.edu
RUSSELL, Barbara ..... 716-338-1210.. 317 F
barbararussell@mail.sunyjcc.edu
RUSSELL, Barry, A ..... 925-424-1001.... 37 C
brussell@laspositascollege.edu
RUSSELL, Bedelia ..... 931-372-6006.. 445 B
bhrussell@tntech.edu
RUSSELL, Brent ..... 803-778-6689.. 427 G
russellrd@cctech.edu
RUSSELL, Brian ..... 312-261-3912.. 149 B
brussell2@nl.edu
RUSSELL, Bruce ..... 724-287-8711.. 399 B
bruce.russell@bc3.edu
RUSSELL, Chris, A ..... 641-844-5716.. 173 L
chris.russell@iavalley.edu
RUSSELL, Christina, L .... 757-594-7278.. 488 E
christina.russell@cnu.edu
RUSSELL, Clifford ..... 404-527-5360.. 124 I
clifford.russell@morehouse.edu
RUSSELL, Craig ..... 501-279-5000.... 20 D
crussell@harding.edu
RUSSELL, Cynthia ..... 215-637-7700.. 405 J
crussell@holyfamily.edu
RUSSELL, Daniel ..... 860-515-3881.... 85 D
drussell@charteroak.edu
RUSSELL, Danny ..... 740-362-3322.. 372 D
drussell@mtso.edu
RUSSELL, David, W ..... 214-648-2695.. 478 C
david.russell@utsouthwestern.edu
RUSSELL, Denise ..... 614-236-6196.. 364 N
drussell@capital.edu
RUSSELL, Dororthy ..... 561-297-3134.. 110 K
druss@fau.edu
RUSSELL, Elizabeth ..... 207-974-4684.. 203 J
erussell@emcc.edu
RUSSELL, Elizabeth ..... 314-246-8298.. 275 B
russelmb@webster.edu
RUSSELL, Freda, R ..... 414-410-4735.. 515 I
frrussell@stritch.edu
RUSSELL, Gary, T ..... 941-752-5200.. 110 H
russelg@scf.edu
RUSSELL, James, H ..... 903-823-3198.. 467 C
jameshenry.russell@texarkanacollege.edu
RUSSELL, Jeff, D ..... 276-739-2491.. 499 A
jrussell@vhcc.edu
RUSSELL, Jeffrey ..... 608-262-5823.. 519 K
jrussell@dcs.wisc.edu
RUSSELL, Jennie ..... 314-921-9290.. 274 F
jrussell@ugst.edu
RUSSELL, Jennifer ..... 202-685-4094.. 528 B
jennifer.russell@ndu.edu
RUSSELL, Jill, T ..... 717-867-6076.. 408 F
russell@lvc.edu
RUSSELL, Joanna, S ..... 503-223-5100.. 395 C
jrussell@sumnercollege.edu
RUSSELL, Joanne ..... 718-368-5661.. 308 F
joanne.russell@kbcc.cuny.edu
RUSSELL, John ..... 808-544-1407.. 130 H
jrussell@hpu.edu
RUSSELL, Joyce ..... 610-519-4331.. 422 G
joyce.russell@villanova.edu
RUSSELL, Judith ..... 352-273-2505.. 112 A
jcrussell@ufl.edu
RUSSELL, Julia, H ..... 802-656-4063.. 485 D
julia.russell@uvm.edu
RUSSELL, Kathleen, M ..... 914-367-8208.. 329 C
kathleen.russell@archny.org
RUSSELL, Kelly ..... 785-670-1574.. 185 H
kelly.russell@washburn.edu
RUSSELL, Kevin ..... 601-968-8746.. 256 I
krussell@belhaven.edu
RUSSELL, Kimberly ..... 718-817-3085.. 314 G
krussell11@fordham.edu
RUSSELL, Kimberly, A ..... 337-550-1201.. 197 K
krussell@lsue.edu
RUSSELL, Kristie ..... 740-245-7191.. 380 C
krussell@rio.edu
RUSSELL, Leah, L ..... 540-375-2211.. 493 H
russell@roanoke.edu
RUSSELL, Leigh ..... 252-493-7354.. 352 A
lrussell@email.pittcc.edu
RUSSELL, Malcolm ..... 402-486-2501.. 282 I
marussel@ucollege.edu
RUSSELL, Mark ..... 419-772-2011.. 374 J
m-russell.7@onu.edu
RUSSELL, Mark ..... 847-578-8340.. 153 A
mark.rusell@rosalindfranklin.edu
RUSSELL, Michael ..... 785-833-4358.. 182 F
mike.russell@kwu.edu
RUSSELL, Michael ..... 415-955-2100.... 25 J
mrussell@alliant.edu
RUSSELL, Mindy ..... 620-223-2700.. 181 A
mindyr@fortscott.edu
RUSSELL, Nancy ..... 816-604-1326.. 267 F
nancy.russell@mcckc.edu
RUSSELL, Nancy ..... 816-604-5239.. 267 H
nancy.russell@mcckc.edu
RUSSELL, Patrice ..... 603-641-7202.. 287 G
prussell@anselm.edu
RUSSELL, Patrick, J ..... 414-425-8300.. 519 F
prussell@shsst.edu
RUSSELL, Robert ..... 605-626-7770.. 437 D
robert.russell@northern.edu
RUSSELL, Ronda ..... 406-994-5541.. 277 C
rrussell@montana.edu
RUSSELL, Ryan, M ..... 712-274-5148.. 175 C
russellr@morningside.edu
RUSSELL, Shannon ..... 252-399-6342.. 341 P
srussell@barton.edu
RUSSELL, Susan ..... 806-874-3571.. 454 F
susan.russell@clarendoncollege.edu
RUSSELL, Tammy ..... 269-467-9945.. 234 B
trussell@glenoaks.edu
RUSSELL, Terry ..... 636-949-4980.. 266 J
trussell@lindenwood.edu
RUSSELL, Thad ..... 559-688-3027.... 40 E
thadr@cos.edu
RUSSELL, Thomas ..... 312-369-7940.. 138 F
trussell@colum.edu
RUSSELL, Thomas ..... 580-581-6712.. 382 G
tomr@cameron.edu
RUSSELL, Tipton ..... 718-429-6600.. 339 D
tipton.russell@vaughn.edu
RUSSELL, Todd ..... 985-867-2266.. 199 F
trussell@sjasc.edu
RUSSELL, Traci ..... 206-934-5661.. 506 J
traci.russell@seattlecolleges.edu
RUSSELL, William ..... 860-632-3050.... 88 B
busoffice@holyapostles.edu
RUSSELL-EDWARDS, Juanita ..... 601-877-6191.. 256 F
juanita@alcorn.edu
RUSSIAKY, Rachel ..... 847-317-7033.. 156 B
rrussiak@tiu.edu
RUSSO, Betty, S ..... 812-941-2661.. 163 F
bsrusso@ius.edu
RUSSO, Cecelia, M ..... 718-990-6667.. 328 F
russoc@stjohns.edu
RUSSO, Cheri ..... 740-366-9420.. 365 D
russo.193@osu.edu
RUSSO, Frederic, J ..... 973-655-3219.. 293 A
russot@mail.montclair.edu
RUSSO, Greg ..... 619-574-6909.... 55 G
grusso@pacificcollege.edu
RUSSO, Kim ..... 310-665-6979.... 55 E
krusso@otis.edu
RUSSO, Lisa ..... 213-613-2200.... 65 H
lisarusso@sciarc.edu
RUSSO, Richard ..... 510-642-2700.... 68 M
russo@berkeley.edu
RUSSO, Robert, C ..... 203-254-4288.... 87 G
rcrusso@fairfield.edu
RUSSO, Ronald ..... 504-762-3066.. 196 D
rrusso@dcc.edu
RUSSO, Thomas ..... 417-873-7413.. 264 H
trusso@drury.edu
RUSSO, Tim ..... 202-685-3918.. 528 B
russot@ndu.edu
RUSSOM, Vaughn, N ..... 715-394-8327.. 521 E
vrussom@uwsuper.edu
RUSSOMANNO, David, J . 317-274-0802.. 163 D
drussoma@iupui.edu
RUSSOS, Milton, A ..... 904-442-2950.. 101 G
mrussos@fscjartistseries.org
RUST, Jodi ..... 715-852-1395.. 523 B
jrust5@cvtc.edu
RUST, Mark, M ..... 410-857-2503.. 209 D
mrust@mcdaniel.edu
RUST, Melissa ..... 501-686-2532.... 22 H
mrust@uasys.edu
RUSTAD, Dan ..... 507-222-7187.. 245 C
drustad@carleton.edu
RUSTAD, Melinda ..... 218-935-0417.. 256 E
melinda.rustad@wetcc.edu
RUTAN, Susan ..... 814-865-1412.. 412 F
smr9@psu.edu
RUTBERG, Barbara ..... 617-824-8275.. 218 B
barbara_rutberg@emerson.edu
RUTENBECK, Jeffrey ..... 202-885-2058.... 91 J
jeff@american.edu
RUTH, Chris ..... 310-453-8300.... 42 L
cruth@emperors.edu
RUTH, Matthew ..... 540-432-4118.. 488 K
matthew.ruth@emu.edu
RUTH, Rick ..... 717-477-1835.. 416 A
reruth@ship.edu
RUTHENBECK, Becky ..... 307-855-2254.. 526 E
rruthenbeck@cwc.edu
RUTHENBECK, Julie, J ..... 325-942-2255.. 472 B
julie.ruthenbeck@angelo.edu
RUTHER, Aisha ..... 312-850-7176.. 138 A
aruther@ccc.edu
RUTHER, Elliott ..... 513-569-1451.. 366 D
elliott.ruther@cincinnatistate.edu
RUTHERFORD, Greg, F ... 803-327-8050.. 435 D
grutherford@yorktech.edu
RUTHERFORD, Joan, M .. 419-251-1301.. 372 C
joan.rutherford@mercycollege.edu
RUTHERFORD, John, D ... 214-648-0400.. 478 C
john.rutherford@utsouthwestern.edu
RUTHERFORD, Karen, W . 803-705-4671.. 427 D
rutherk@benedict.edu
RUTHERFORD, Kimberly . 504-278-6421.. 196 I
krutherford@nunez.edu
RUTHERFORD, Lisa, H .... 413-542-5645.. 214 C
lrutherford@amherst.edu
RUTHERFORD, Marcella, M ..... 954-262-1963.. 105 J
rmarcell@nova.edu
RUTHERFORD, Marylyn ... 973-877-3408.. 291 H
rutherford@essex.edu
RUTHERFORD, Paul ..... 304-327-4403.. 512 P
prutherford@bluefieldstate.edu
RUTHERMAN, Kathy ..... 270-852-3143.. 191 C
krutherman@kwc.edu
RUTHKOSKY, Kathleen, O ..... 570-348-6203.. 409 H
ruthkosky@marywood.edu
RUTKOWSI, Leslie ..... 315-470-6655.. 334 E
larutkow@esf.edu
RUTKOWSKI, Sandra ..... 419-824-3762.. 371 I
srutkowski@lourdes.edu
RUTLEDGE, Beth ..... 610-341-5890.. 403 B
brutledg@eastern.edu
RUTLEDGE, Brian ..... 601-984-1010.. 261 C
brutledge@umc.edu
RUTLEDGE, Catherine ..... 484-365-8087.. 409 B
crutledge@lincoln.edu
RUTLEDGE, James ..... 662-846-4021.. 257 E
jrutledge@deltastate.edu
RUTLEDGE, Janet ..... 410-455-1781.. 211 G
jrutledge@umbc.edu
RUTLEDGE, Melissa, B .... 540-378-5120.. 493 H
rutledge@roanoke.edu
RUTLEDGE, Peter ..... 706-542-7140.. 128 E
borut@uga.edu
RUTLEDGE, Susan ..... 314-392-2355.. 268 F
rutledges@mobap.edu
RUTLEDGE, Todd ..... 417-269-3873.. 264 D
todd.rutledge@coxcollege.edu
RUTLEDGE, Valerie ..... 423-425-4249.. 448 F
valerie-rutledge@utc.edu
RUTT, Charles, D ..... 660-543-4370.. 273 C
rutt@ucmo.edu
RUTTEN, Chris ..... 402-844-7051.. 282 B
christopherr@northeast.edu
RUTTEN, Erich ..... 651-962-6561.. 256 C
erutten@stthomas.edu
RUTTER, Evan ..... 909-621-8153.... 38 J
evan.rutter@cmc.edu
RUTTER, Jeff ..... 602-386-4191.... 11 D
jeff.rutter@arizonachristian.edu
RUTTER, Jeff ..... 931-221-7213.. 444 E
rutterj@apsu.edu
RUTTER, John, P ..... 919-299-4818.. 355 K
jrutter@umo.edu
RUTTER, Ron ..... 503-821-8901.. 394 B
rrutter@pnca.edu
RUTTER, Sandy ..... 423-697-4475.. 445 D
sandy.rutter@chattanoogastate.edu
RUUD, William, N ..... 740-376-4701.. 372 A
wnr001@marietta.edu
RUXTON, Brooke ..... 815-753-1206.. 150 A
bruxton@niu.edu
RUYLE, Dianna ..... 217-854-3231.. 135 K
dianna.ruyle@blackburn.edu
RUYS, Jasmine ..... 661-362-3466.... 40 A
jasmine.ruys@canyons.edu
RUYS, Steve ..... 818-364-7886.... 49 J
ruyssc@lamission.edu
RUZICH, Steve ..... 708-596-2000.. 154 E
sruzich@ssc.edu
RUZICKA, James ..... 402-461-7337.. 280 D
jruzicka@hastings.edu
RUZZANO, Ethan ..... 303-360-4734.... 79 E
ethan.ruzzano@ccaurora.edu
RYALL, Patrick ..... 503-768-7294.. 392 A
ryall@lclark.edu
RYAN, Andrew ..... 718-862-8000.. 319 L
andrew.ryan@manhattan.edu
RYAN, Barry ..... 888-488-4968.... 47 D
RYAN, Bruce ..... 607-844-8222.. 337 G
ryanb@tc3.edu
RYAN, Cari ..... 808-853-1040.. 131 B
cariryan@pacrim.edu
RYAN, Caroll ..... 714-882-7800.... 31 G
cryan@calsouthern.edu
RYAN, Carrie ..... 336-278-5003.. 344 D
cryan2@elon.edu
RYAN, Casey ..... 215-596-8570.. 422 A
c.ryan@usciences.edu
RYAN, Catherine ..... 413-572-5218.. 222 E
cryan@westfield.ma.edu
RYAN, Christopher ..... 508-830-5003.. 222 C
cryan@maritime.edu
RYAN, Curtis, W ..... 801-832-2148.. 483 D
cryan@westminstercollege.edu
RYAN, Dennis ..... 757-340-2121.. 488 A
registrarcvab@centura.edu
RYAN, Dennis ..... 757-340-2121.. 488 A
adirectorcvab@centura.edu
RYAN, Diane, N ..... 757-822-5185.. 498 H
dryan@tcc.edu
RYAN, Dorothy ..... 217-732-3155.. 146 B
dryan@lincolncollege.edu
RYAN, Duane ..... 575-562-2112.. 299 I
duane.ryan@enmu.edu
RYAN, Ed ..... 408-554-5182.... 63 E
eryan@scu.edu
RYAN, Gail, L ..... 313-577-6595.. 243 F
gail.ryan@wayne.edu
RYAN, Greg ..... 714-992-7092.... 54 H
gryan@fullcoll.edu
RYAN, Helen, G ..... 502-272-8052.. 187 A
hryan@bellarmine.edu
RYAN, James ..... 617-262-5000.. 216 A
james.ryan@the-bac.edu
RYAN, James, E ..... 617-495-3401.. 219 D
james_ryan@gse.harvard.edu
RYAN, James, G ..... 336-217-5128.. 356 F
jgryan@ncat.edu
RYAN, James, G ..... 336-285-2805.. 358 B
jgryan@uncg.edu
RYAN, Jeanne-Marie, C .. 704-894-2492.. 343 I
jeryan@davidson.edu
RYAN, Jenny ..... 801-832-2502.. 483 D
jryan@westminstercollege.edu
RYAN, CSC, John ..... 570-208-5899.. 406 J
jjryan@kings.edu
RYAN, Joseph ..... 209-588-5087.... 75 J
ryanj@yosemite.edu
RYAN, Julie ..... 928-523-9658.... 15 H
julie.ryan@nau.edu
RYAN, Karen ..... 386-822-7515.. 113 B
kryan@stetson.edu
RYAN, Kathleen ..... 508-541-1515.. 217 G
kryan@dean.edu
RYAN, Kathleen ..... 617-732-5042.. 225 C
kathleen.ryan@mcphs.edu
RYAN, Kathleen ..... 614-823-1250.. 376 C
kryan@otterbein.edu
RYAN, Kelly, A ..... 812-941-2393.. 163 F
ryanka@ius.edu
RYAN, Kevin ..... 305-428-5700.. 105 E
kryan@aii.edu
RYAN, Kyle ..... 781-899-5500.. 227 E
kryan@psjs.edu
RYAN, Larry ..... 505-277-2847.. 302 F
larry@unm.edu
RYAN, Linda ..... 631-687-5143.. 328 G
lryan@sjcny.edu
RYAN, Mark, R ..... 573-882-0314.. 273 E
ryanmr@missouri.edu
RYAN, Mary, A ..... 651-962-6133.. 256 C
maryan@stthomas.edu
RYAN, Maura, A ..... 574-631-9488.. 168 B
mryan11@nd.edu
RYAN, Maureen ..... 601-266-4319.. 261 E
maureen.ryan@usm.edu
RYAN, Melissa ..... 904-725-0525.... 97 S
mryan@concorde.edu
RYAN, Michael ..... 617-585-1187.. 226 F
michael.ryan@necmusic.edu
RYAN, Molly ..... 661-255-1050.... 30 E
mryan@calarts.edu
RYAN, Pat ..... 503-842-8222.. 395 D
patryan@tillamookbaycc.edu
RYAN, Patricia ..... 540-674-3613.. 497 G
pryan@nr.edu
RYAN, Patrick ..... 973-720-3326.. 298 G
ryanp@wpunj.edu
RYAN, Patrick ..... 716-270-2869.. 313 H
ryan@ecc.edu
RYAN, Paula ..... 641-628-5198.. 170 E
ryanp@central.edu
RYAN, Peter ..... 662-325-3742.. 259 D
ryan@cvm.msstate.edu

S

ST. JAMES, Andrea .... 413-782-1775.. 229 E
andrea.stjames@wne.edu
ST. JAMES, Tim .... 860-253-3011.... 86 A
tstjames@asnuntuck.edu
ST. JEAN, Cyndie .... 909-389-3201.... 60 B
cstjean@craftonhills.edu
ST. JOHN, Jeffrey, E .... 207-581-1591.. 204 H
jeffrey.stjohn@maine.edu
ST. JOHN, Joy .... 781-283-2273.. 229 C
jstjohn@wellesley.edu
ST. JOHN, Meredith .... 617-558-1788.. 226 I
mstjohn@nesa.edu
ST. JOHN, Mike .... 405-382-9201.. 387 L
m.stjohn@sscok.edu
ST. LEDGER, Anne .... 717-720-4070.. 414 F
astledger@passhe.edu
ST. LEGER, Gabrielle .... 516-686-1488.. 323 G
gstleger@nyit.edu
ST. LOUIS, Daniel, C ...... 828-327-7000.. 348 C
dstlouis@cvcc.edu
ST. LOUIS, Moise .... 802-654-2663.. 484 I
mstlouis@smcvt.edu
ST. LOUIS, Shelly .... 518-891-2915.. 325 A
mstlouis@nccc.edu
ST. MARKS, Wanda .... 406-395-4875.. 278 F
wstmarks@stonecild.edu
ST. MAURO, Anne .... 609-258-3403.. 294 D
stmauro@princeton.edu
ST. MICHEL, Peter .... 207-621-3119.. 204 I
stmichel@maine.edu
ST. ONGE, Stephen .... 707-826-3451.... 34 F
srs706@humboldt.edu
ST. ONGE, Susan .... 321-674-6400.. 100 M
sstonge@fit.edu
ST. PIERRE, Gail, S .... 207-786-6120.. 202 D
gstpierr@bates.edu
ST. PIERRE, Nathaniel ...... 406-395-4875.. 278 F
nstpierre@stonechild.edu
ST. PIERRE, Traci .... 207-780-4771.. 205 E
tracy.st@maine.edu
SAINTJONES, Jerome .... 256-372-4863...... 1 A
jerome.saintjones@aamu.edu
SAINTSING, Tim .... 212-228-1888.. 327 A
SAINTVIL, Yamiley .... 718-409-7220.. 336 A
ysaintvil@sunymaritime.edu
SAIRS, Reuben .... 740-857-1311.. 376 L
rsairs@rosedale.edu
SAITTA, Tom .... 336-272-7102.. 344 G
thomas.saaita@greensboro.edu
SAJADIAN, Dalila, A .... 641-422-4103.. 175 E
sajaddal@niacc.edu
SAJDAK, Jeff .... 616-957-6042.. 232 B
js036@calvinseminary.edu
SAJJA, Prasada .... 770-484-1204.. 124 C
library@lutherrice.edu
SAJKO, Brian .... 402-354-7044.. 281 F
brian.sajko@methodistcollege.edu
SAKAGAWA, Tamara .... 863-292-3744.. 106 I
tsakagawa@polk.edu
SAKAGUCHI, Gary .... 559-325-5365.... 67 B
gary.sakaguchi@reedleycollege.edu
SAKAGUCHI, Gary .... 559-638-0300.... 67 D
gary.sakaguchi@reedleycollege.edu
SAKAI, Eric .... 802-828-2800.. 486 A
eric.sakai@ccv.edu
SAKAI, Eric .... 802-828-2800.. 486 A
sakaie@ccv.edu
SAKAI, Hiro .... 949-480-4008.... 64 J
sakai@soka.edu
SAKAI, Marcia .... 808-932-7650.. 131 E
marcias@hawaii.edu
SAKAKI, Judy, K .... 510-987-0158.... 68 L
judy.sakaki@ucop.edu
SAKAMOTO, June .... 415-703-8291.... 69 B
sakamotoj@uchastings.edu
SAKARYA, Mustafa .... 914-674-7258.. 320 G
msakarya@mercy.edu
SAKEY, Paula .... 617-989-4219.. 229 D
sakeyp@wit.edu
SAKOFS, Mitchell .... 718-405-3322.. 310 H
mitchell.sakofs@mountsaintvincent.edu
SAKS, Deborah .... 916-558-2582.... 51 D
saksd@scc.losrios.edu
SAKS, Greg .... 657-278-7030.... 33 A
gsaks@fullerton.edu
SALA, Anca .... 810-766-4111.. 231 D
asala01@baker.edu
SALA, Andrea .... 310-660-3593.... 42 J
asala@elcamino.edu
SALA, Andrea .... 310-660-3670.... 42 J
asala@elcamino.edu
SALADIN, Lisa .... 843-792-3031.. 431 A
saladinl@musc.edu
SALADINO, Susan .... 718-405-3376.. 310 H
susan.saladino@mountsaintvincent.edu
SALAHUDDIN, Mecca .... 253-566-5124.. 508 B
msalahuddin@tacomacc.edu
SALAK, Donna .... 513-745-3302.. 381 I
salakd@xavier.edu
SALAMONE, Vincent .... 201-360-4351.. 292 B
vsalamone@hccc.edu
SALAMY, James .... 315-866-0300.. 316 A
salamyjr@herkimer.edu
SALARI, Gholamereza ...... 717-394-6211.. 401 H
rsalari@csb.edu
SALAS, Alexandra .... 609-586-4800.. 292 D
salasa@mccc.edu
SALAS, Angela, M .... 812-941-2586.. 163 F
amsalas@ius.edu
SALAS, Charles, G .... 860-685-2002.... 90 C
csalas@wesleyan.edu
SALAS, Richard .... 515-271-1709.. 171 H
rich.salas@dmu.edu
SALASKI, Kori .... 608-796-3000.. 522 O
kfsalaski@viterbo.edu
SALATINO, Michael .... 630-829-6667.. 135 F
msalatino@ben.edu
SALAY, Lawrence .... 203-285-2046.... 86 C
lsalay@gwcc.commnet.edu
SALAZ, Eduardo .... 925-631-4212.... 59 I
els3@stmarys-ca.edu
SALAZ, Mark .... 520-494-5250.... 12 J
mark.salaz@centralaz.edu
SALAZAR, Andrea .... 530-541-4660.... 48 D
salazar@ltcc.edu
SALAZAR, Aracelly .... 425-602-3011.. 501 D
asalazar@bastyr.edu
SALAZAR, David .... 562-985-4131.... 33 B
david.salazar@csulb.edu
SALAZAR, Ed .... 928-541-7777.... 15 G
esalazar@ncu.edu
SALAZAR, SJ, Jose-Luis . 718-817-4503.. 314 G
jsalazar8@fordham.edu
SALAZAR, Leta .... 846-208-8263.. 434 A
lsalazar@uscb.edu
SALAZAR-VALENTINE,
Marcia .... 419-372-8183.. 364 E
marcias@bgsu.edu
SALAZAR-VALENTINE,
Marcia .... 419-372-8185.. 364 E
marcias@bgsu.edu
SALBATO, Mike .... 719-846-5653.... 83 G
mike.salbato@trinidadstate.edu
SALCIDO, Kevin, J .... 480-965-6608.... 11 H
kevin.j.salcido@asu.edu
SALCIDO, Steven .... 714-628-4836.... 58 H
salcido_steven@sccollege.edu
SALDANA-TALLEY, Jane .. 707-778-3931.... 63 G
lsaldana-talley@santarosa.edu
SALE, Gene .... 561-803-2352.. 106 C
gene_sale@pba.edu
SALE, Rachel .... 573-681-5442.. 266 I
saler@lincolnu.edu
SALEH, Bahaa .... 407-882-3326.. 111 E
besaleh@creol.ucf.edu
SALEH, Don .... 315-445-4707.. 318 E
salehda@lemoyne.edu
SALEM, Mike .... 610-647-4400.. 406 B
msalem@immaculata.edu
SALEM, Susan .... 310-954-4112.... 53 B
ssalem@msmu.edu
SALEMME, Brenda .... 716-488-3023.. 317 E
brendasalemme@jbc.edu
SALEMME, Kevin .... 978-837-5377.. 225 E
kevin.salemme@merrimack.edu
SALERNO, Dena .... 570-372-4302.. 419 H
salerno@susqu.edu
SALES, Laura .... 858-499-0202.... 39 J
lsales@coleman.edu
SALES, Vince .... 916-278-7043.... 34 B
vsales@csus.edu
SALESTROM, Charles .... 308-535-3636.. 280 M
salestromc@mpcc.edu
SALFITI, Mayer .... 303-937-4032.... 77 K
msalfiti@chu.edu
SALGUERO, Jossie .... 787-766-1912.. 533 F
jsalguer@inter.edu
SALII, Uroi, N .... 680-488-2471.. 530 E
usalii@palau.edu
SALIMAN, Todd .... 303-860-5600.... 83 J
todd.saliman@cu.edu
SALINAS, Antonio .... 575-439-3601.. 301 A
antsalin@nmsu.edu
SALINAS, Felix .... 210-486-4788.. 450 C
fsalinas26@alamo.edu
SALINAS, Francisco .... 208-426-5950.. 132 I
franciscosalinas@boisestate.edu
SALINAS, Joseph .... 602-331-7500.... 11 K
jsalinas@aii.edu
SALINAS, Lelia .... 956-872-7209.. 465 H
lelias1@southtexascollege.edu
SALINAS, Nick .... 914-395-2570.. 329 K
nsalinas@sarahlawrence.edu
SALINAS, Sallie .... 714-241-4901.... 39 E
ssalinas@coastline.edu
SALINAS, Stacy .... 845-848-7818.. 312 F
stacy.salinas@dc.edu
SALINAS-HOVAR, Marta .. 956-665-7304.. 476 E
marta.salinashovar@utrgv.edu
SALINE, Terrie .... 309-341-7436.. 145 A
tsaline@knox.edu
SALING MAYER, Marni ... 360-752-8325.. 501 G
msalingmayer@btc.edu
SALINGER, Mary, G .... 610-799-1165.. 408 G
msalinger@lccc.edu
SALISBURY, Jennifer .... 215-968-8461.. 399 A
jennifer.salisbury@bucks.edu
SALISBURY, Mark .... 309-794-7504.. 135 D
marksalisbury@augustana.edu
SALKIN, Patricia .... 631-761-7100.. 337 I
patricia.salkin@touro.edu
SALKOWSKI, Marita .... 859-344-3309.. 193 C
salkowm@thomasmore.edu
SALLAN, Veena .... 270-686-4639.. 190 D
veena.sallan@kctcs.edu
SALLEE-JUSTESEN, Dawn 541-506-6028.. 390 I
djustesen@cgcc.edu
SALLEH-BARONE,
Normah .... 708-974-5209.. 148 G
salleh-barone@morainevalley.edu
SALLER, Richard, P .... 650-723-9784.... 66 I
rsaller@stanford.edu
SALLIS, Archer .... 662-476-8414.. 257 G
jsallis@eastms.edu
SALM, Timothy .... 219-866-6187.. 166 J
tsalm@saintjoe.edu
SALMAN, Juli .... 505-426-2155.. 300 F
jesalman@nmhu.edu
SALMEIER, Michael .... 909-599-5433.... 48 K
msalmeier@lifepacific.edu
SALMERI, Patrice .... 612-330-1166.. 244 I
salmeri@augsburg.edu
SALMERON, Lois .... 405-208-5900.. 385 E
lsalmeron@okcu.edu
SALMO, Jim .... 618-453-7174.. 154 I
jims@foundation.siu.edu
SALMON, Garnett .... 239-489-9056.. 101 F
ggsalmon@fsw.edu
SALMON, Lorraine .... 845-687-5093.. 338 F
salmonl@sunyulster.edu
SALMON, Mark .... 334-670-3342...... 7 H
msalmon@troy.edu
SALMON, Orv .... 515-433-5050.. 171 B
ojsalmon@dmacc.edu
SALMON, Pamela .... 315-792-3011.. 339 B
pjsalmon@utica.edu
SALMON, Robert, O .... 801-524-8179.. 480 J
rsalmon@ldsbc.edu
SALOME, Joann .... 575-835-5955.. 300 G
jsalome@admin.nmt.edu
SALOMON, Carol .... 212-353-4187.. 311 G
salomo@cooper.edu
SALOMON, Mattisyahu .... 732-367-1060.. 289 G
SALOMON, Rachel .... 629-625-3291.. 530 C
rsalomon@cmi.edu
SALOMON-FERNANDEZ,
Yves .... 856-691-8600.. 290 I
ysalomonfernandez@cccnj.edu
SALOMONSON, Kristen ... 231-591-3801.. 233 L
kristensalomonson@ferris.edu
SALONEN, Neil Albert ..... 203-576-4665.... 89 C
nas@bridgeport.edu
SALONER, Garth .... 650-723-1940.... 66 I
saloner@stanford.edu
SALOUN, Pamela .... 414-930-3430.. 518 F
salounp@mtmary.edu
SALOVEY, Peter .... 203-432-2550.... 90 D
peter.salovey@yale.edu
SALOWITZ, Stewart, I ...... 309-556-3206.. 143 D
salowitz@iwu.edu
SALOWITZ, Susan .... 860-343-5724.... 86 F
ssalowitz@mxcc.commnet.edu
SALSBURY, Greg .... 970-943-2114.... 84 H
gsalsbury@western.edu
SALSBURY, Lysa .... 208-885-9358.. 134 G
lsalsbur@uidaho.edu
SALSGIVER, Amy .... 814-393-2109.. 414 G
asalsgiver@clarion.edu
SALT, Robert .... 715-232-1168.. 521 D
saltb@uwstout.edu
SALTALAMACHIA,
Joseph .... 207-509-7205.. 204 F
jsalty@unity.edu
SALTER, Anne .... 404-364-8514.. 125 F
asalter@oglethorpe.edu
SALTER, Les .... 770-533-6901.. 123 L
lsalter@laniertech.edu
SALTER, Sid .... 662-325-7454.. 259 D
ss51@msstate.edu
SALTER-SMITH,
Cassandra, L .... 716-839-8237.. 312 D
csalters@daemen.edu
SALTIEL, Henry .... 718-482-6120.. 309 A
hsaltiel@lagcc.cuny.edu
SALTON, Susan .... 814-332-4793.. 397 A
ssalton@allegheny.edu
SALTONSTALL,
Thomas, L .... 617-228-3311.. 223 B
tlsaltonstall@bhcc.mass.edu
SALTSMAN, Terry .... 931-372-3200.. 445 B
tsaltsman@tntech.edu
SALTSMAN, Terry .... 931-372-3387.. 445 B
tsaltsman@tntech.edu
SALTZBERG, Alex .... 510-593-2995.... 63 H
asaltzberg@saybrook.edu
SALVA, Miguel .... 787-894-2828.. 539 A
miguel.salva@upr.edu
SALVA, William, M .... 914-337-9300.. 311 F
william.salva@concordia-ny.edu
SALVADOR, Daniel .... 319-656-2447.. 176 F
SALVAGE, Lynn .... 718-818-6470.. 329 F
lsalvage@edaff.com
SALVAGGIO, Brian .... 508-531-1276.. 221 C
SALVAGGIO, Odette .... 909-387-1621.... 60 C
omcginnis@sbccd.cc.ca.us
SALVAGNE, Frank .... 502-213-8213.. 193 A
fsalvagne@sullivan.edu
SALVANTORIELLO,
Vincent .... 610-398-5300.. 408 I
vsalvantoriello@lincolntech.edu
SALVATO, Scott .... 516-323-3225.. 321 H
ssalvato@molloy.edu
SALVESEN, Guy .... 858-646-3114.... 62 J
gsalvesen@shpdiscovery.org
SALVINI, Tonia .... 785-830-2753.. 181 E
tsalvini@haskell.edu
SALVO, Robyn .... 732-263-5228.. 292 F
rsalvo@monmouth.edu
SALVUCCI, James .... 712-749-2243.. 170 D
salvuccij@bvu.edu
SALZBRUNN, Kimberly .... 630-637-5454.. 149 H
ksalzbrunn@noctrl.edu
SALZMAN, Christine .... 908-709-7485.. 298 A
SALZMANN, Nick .... 847-628-2492.. 144 B
nsalzmann@judsonu.edu
SAM, David .... 847-214-7374.. 140 A
dsam@elgin.edu
SAM, David, A .... 540-423-9039.. 497 B
dsam@germanna.edu
SAM, Mary .... 218-855-8159.. 248 N
msam@clcmn.edu
SAM, Penselyn .... 691-320-2480.. 529 F
petse@comfsm.fm
SAMAHA, Ahmed .... 803-641-3411.. 433 G
ahmeds@usca.edu
SAMALOT, Yamil .... 787-786-3030.. 536 F
ysamalot@ucb.edu.pr
SAMALOT-RIVERA, OP,
Yamil, A .... 787-786-4508.. 532 G
ysamalot@cedoc.edu
SAMAN, Sarmad .... 508-678-2811.. 223 A
sarmad.saman@bristolcc.edu
SAMANGO, Melissa .... 610-526-6196.. 405 B
msamango@harcum.edu
SAMANIEGO, Sue .... 719-384-6821.... 82 A
sue.samaniego@ojc.edu
SAMANT, Ajay .... 309-438-2251.. 143 B
asamant@ilstu.edu
SAMANTA, Shivaji .... 540-857-6335.. 499 B
ssamanta@virginiawestern.edu
SAMARKOS, Christy .... 619-594-5211.... 35 A
csamarko@mail.sdsu.edu
SAMBDMAN, Cory, W .... 563-333-6336.. 176 D
1312mgr@follett.com
SAMBERG, Wendy .... 203-285-2108.... 86 C
wsamberg@gwcc.commnet.edu
SAMBRANO, Richard .... 281-443-8900.. 453 I
richard.sambrano@brightwood.edu
SAMDAHL, JR.,
Donald, H .... 540-464-7228.. 499 E
samdahldh@vmi.edu
SAMEEI, Morteza .... 713-718-5251.. 459 B
morteza.sameei@hccs.edu
SAMEK, Linda .... 503-554-2871.. 391 D
lsamek@georgefox.edu
SAMENFINK, William, H . 978-232-2402.. 218 D
bsamenfi@endicott.edu
SAMHAT, Nayef, H .... 864-597-4010.. 435 C
president@wofford.edu
SAMM, Mary .... 812-535-5252.. 166 K
msamm@smwc.edu
SAMMAKIA, Bahgat .... 607-777-4818.. 331 B
bahgat@binghamton.edu
SAMMARCO, Erica, C .... 716-888-2100.. 306 F
sammarce@canisius.edu
SAMMARTINO, Kathleen .. 617-349-8515.. 220 B
ksammart@lesley.edu
SAMMIS, Robert, L .... 626-914-8550.... 38 D
rsammis@citruscollege.edu
SAMMONS, Gregory, S .... 607-587-3911.. 334 G
sammongs@alfredstate.edu
SAMMONS, Kenneth, R .... 509-313-6951.. 504 A
ksammons@plant.gonzaga.edu
SAMMONS, Sara .... 910-521-6629.. 358 C
sara.simmons@uncp.edu
SAMMONS, Steve .... 503-589-8145.. 391 B
ssammons@corban.edu
SAMO, Tia .... 641-782-1336.. 177 B
samo@swcciowa.edu
SAMOLEWSKI, Patrick, C 989-964-4221.. 240 F
pcs@svsu.edu

SANDERS, Sunny, M .... 630-515-3009.. 148 C
ssande@midwestern.edu
SANDERS, Thomas .... 903-923-2075.. 457 G
tsanders@etbu.edu
SANDERS, Tiffany .... 256-395-2211...... 7 C
tsanders@suscc.edu
SANDERS, Tom .... 330-337-6403.. 362 I
college@awc.edu
SANDERS, Tricia .... 218-281-8326.. 255 E
sand0803@umn.edu
SANDERS,
Wm Gerard (Gerry), Y .. 210-458-4313.. 477 A
gerry.sanders@utsa.edu
SANDERS-KELLEY, Kelly .. 731-352-4000.. 438 K
kelleyk@bethelu.edu
SANDERS-MCMURTRY,
Kijua .... 404-471-6391.. 115 J
ksanders-mcmurtry@agnesscott.edu
SANDERSON, Bruce .... 316-942-4291.. 183 I
sandersonb@newmanu.edu
SANDERSON, Francie, W 919-866-5944.. 353 I
fwsanderson@waketech.edu
SANDERSON, Janet .... 775-784-4805.. 285 A
jsanderson@unr.edu
SANDERSON, Karri .... 402-465-2411.. 281 K
ksanders@nebrwesleyan.edu
SANDERSON, Larry .... 575-492-2787.. 300 H
lsanderson@nmjc.edu
SANDERSON, Lex .... 818-401-1032.... 40 G
lsanderson@columbiacollege.edu
SANDFORD, Art .... 805-678-5800.... 73 E
SANDFORD, Gregory, W . 618-374-5507.. 151 E
greg.sandford@principia.edu
SANDHOFF, Diane .... 605-995-2119.. 435 F
disandho@dwu.edu
SANDHOFF, Jeff .... 706-419-1122.. 119 G
jeff.sandhoff@covenant.edu
SANDIDGE, Kyle .... 601-923-1700.. 260 E
ksandidge@rts.edu
SANDIDGE, William .... 434-832-7641.. 496 G
sandidgew@cvcc.vccs.edu
SANDIFAR, Mike .... 812-749-1290.. 166 B
msandifar@oak.edu
SANDIFER, Joyce .... 504-520-5230.. 202 C
jsandife@xula.edu
SANDIFER, William, A ..... 803-584-3446.. 434 C
sandifea@mailbox.sc.edu
SANDIFER, Willie .... 903-730-4890.. 460 B
wsandifer@jarvis.edu
SANDLER, David .... 206-934-5488.. 506 K
david.sandler@seattlecolleges.edu
SANDLER, Elysha .... 516-239-9002.. 330 D
SANDLES, Sherry .... 817-531-4401.. 472 F
slsandles@txwes.edu
SANDLIN, Rebecca, F ...... 540-375-2585.. 493 H
sandlin@roanoke.edu
SANDMANN, Warren .... 973-720-2122.. 298 G
sandmannw@wpunj.edu
SANDNER, Michael .... 860-509-9525.... 88 A
msandner@hartsem.edu
SANDNESS, Debra .... 701-224-5524.. 361 C
debra.sandness@bismarckstate.edu
SANDOE, Timothy .... 717-780-2300.. 405 C
SANDONE, Dawn .... 217-362-6428.. 148 D
dsandone@millikin.edu
SANDOS, Sunny .... 423-439-4242.. 444 F
sandoss@etsu.edu
SANDOVAL, April .... 928-226-4217.... 12 N
april.sandoval@coconino.edu
SANDOVAL, Barbara, A ... 360-650-7614.. 509 E
barbara.sandoval@wwu.edu
SANDOVAL, Derek, M ...... 830-703-1555.. 466 A
mdsandoval@swtjc.edu
SANDOVAL, James, W ..... 951-827-4641.... 70 B
james.sandoval@ucr.edu
SANDOVAL, Michael .... 818-333-3558.... 54 B
SANDOVAL, William .... 787-738-2161.. 538 A
william.sandoval@upr.edu
SANDOVAL-LUCERO,
Elena .... 303-360-4824.... 79 E
elena.sandoval-lucero@ccaurora.edu
SANDOVAL-ZAZUETA,
Belinda .... 909-748-8164.... 71 K
belinda_sandoval@redlands.edu
SANDQUIST, Rick, A .... 515-574-1347.. 173 F
sandquist@iowacentral.edu
SANDROCK, Jessica .... 503-584-7255.. 390 E
jessica.sandrock@chemeketa.edu
SANDS, Bryan, A .... 714-879-3901.... 46 F
basands@hiu.edu
SANDS, Charles .... 951-343-4213.... 29 H
csands@calbaptist.edu
SANDS, Deanna .... 206-296-5696.. 507 E
sandsd@seattleu.edu
SANDS, Harlan .... 502-852-6166.. 194 A
hmsand04@louisville.edu
SANDS, Timothy, D .... 540-231-6231.. 499 F
president@vt.edu
SANDS-VANKERK, Linda . 630-942-2621.. 138 B
sands-vankerkl@cod.edu
SANDS WISE, Jonathan .. 502-863-8009.. 188 I
jonathan_sandswise@georgetowncollege.edu
SANDSTROM, Karen .... 216-421-7417.. 366 G
ksandstrom@cia.edu
SANDSTROM, Kent .... 701-231-9588.. 361 A
kent.sandstrom@ndsu.edu
SANDSTROM, Marlene, J 413-597-4171.. 230 A
marlene.j.sandstrom@williams.edu
SANDT, Jennifer, A .... 410-334-2911.. 213 G
jsandt@worwic.edu
SANDU, Terri, B .... 440-365-5222.. 371 H
SANDUM TUNE, Rachel .. 937-327-7411.. 381 F
rtune@wittenberg.edu
SANDUSKY, Brian .... 989-837-4459.. 239 D
sandusky@northwood.edu
SANDVIG, Mark .... 314-434-4044.. 264 C
mark.sandvig@covenantseminary.edu
SANDY, Mark .... 765-285-5131.. 159 B
msandy@bsu.edu
SANDY, Michael .... 508-531-6183.. 221 C
michael.sandy@bridgew.edu
SANFILIPO, Michael .... 713-920-1120.. 459 G
SANFILIPPO, Rick .... 610-526-4600.. 405 B
rsanfilippo@harcum.edu
SANFILIPPO, Sarah .... 802-447-6312.. 485 B
ssanfilippo@svc.edu
SANFORD, David .... 503-581-8600.. 391 B
dsanford@corban.edu
SANFORD, Delacy .... 904-470-8290.... 98 N
dsanford@ewc.edu
SANFORD, Janell .... 757-826-1883.. 487 E
librarian@bcva.edu
SANFORD, Jennifer .... 707-826-3236.... 34 F
jls7003@humboldt.edu
SANFORD, Jessica .... 765-983-1432.. 160 G
SANFORD, Jonathan, J .... 972-721-5388.. 473 D
jsanford@udallas.edu
SANFORD, Larry .... 410-228-9250.. 212 A
SANFORD, Matthew .... 607-431-4460.. 315 E
sanfordm@hartwick.edu
SANFORD, Susan, H .... 315-470-6604.. 334 E
shsanfor@esf.edu
SANGER, Bryna .... 212-229-8947.. 322 E
sanger@newschool.edu
SANGER, Laurel, T .... 585-292-3398.. 321 J
lsanger@monroecc.edu
SANGER, Patrick .... 281-756-3663.. 450 G
psanger@alvincollege.edu
SANGER, Tchad .... 831-459-5604.... 70 F
cpsanger@ucsc.edu
SANGHVI, Kamlesh .... 708-974-5522.. 148 G
sanghvik@morainevalley.edu
SANGHVI, Pulin .... 609-258-0650.. 294 D
pulins@princeton.edu
SANGREY-BILLY, Cory .... 406-395-4875.. 278 F
csangrey@stonechild.edu
SANIDAD, Daniel .... 408-855-5139.... 74 G
daniel.sanidad@wvmccd.cc.ca.us
SANJANA, Espi .... 415-351-3550.... 61 B
esanjana@sfai.edu
SANKEY, Dean, A .... 715-232-2258.. 521 D
sankeyd@uwstout.edu
SANKO, Jerry .... 620-672-5641.. 184 D
jerrys@prattcc.edu
SANKS, Christer .... 334-291-4934...... 2 H
christer.sanks@cv.edu
SANKS GUIDRY, Beverly 909-469-5341.... 74 K
bguidry@westernu.edu
SANNI, Christine .... 617-627-3024.. 228 H
christine.sanni@tufts.edu
SANNS, Aaron, D .... 208-496-1610.. 132 J
sannsa@byui.edu
SANNUTO, Vicki .... 509-963-1921.. 501 K
career@cwu.edu
SANREGRET, Suzanne ..... 906-487-3070.. 238 A
srsangre@mtu.edu
SANSBURY, Timothy .... 954-771-0376.. 104 H
tsansbury@knoxseminary.edu
SANSEVIRO, Michael, L .. 470-578-6310.. 123 J
msansevi@kennesaw.edu
SANSING, Perry .... 662-915-7111.. 261 B
psansing@olemiss.edu
SANSOLA, Steve .... 845-575-3000.. 320 B
steve.sansola@marist.edu
SANSOM, Mel .... 501-279-4485.... 20 D
msansom@harding.edu
SANSON, Jerry .... 318-473-6470.. 197 J
jsanson@lsua.edu
SANSONE, Joseph .... 201-360-4006.. 292 B
jsansone@hccc.edu
SANT, Anne, M .... 508-565-1343.. 228 F
asant@stonehill.edu
SANTA, Sally .... 787-884-3838.. 530 G
dir_carreras@atenascollege.edu
SANTAMARIA, Anthony ... 973-290-4338.. 290 G
asantamaria@cse.edu
SANTAMARIA, Louis .... 413-775-1299.. 223 D
santamarial@gcc.mass.edu
SANTAMARIA-MAKANG,
Doris .... 301-687-7018.. 212 F
dsantamaria@frostburg.edu
SANTANA, Arleen .... 787-264-1912.. 534 D
asantana@intersg.edu
SANTANA, Evelyn .... 610-526-6006.. 405 B
esantana@harcum.edu
SANTANA, Lulu .... 408-554-4372.... 63 E
lsantana@scu.edu
SANTANA, Pedro .... 609-652-4601.. 297 C
pedro.santana@stockton.edu
SANTANA, Sylvia .... 305-595-9500.... 95 A
dean@amcollege.edu
SANTANA, Yara .... 312-427-2737.. 143 G
6santanay@jmls.edu
SANTANA-BRAVO,
Maydel .... 305-348-1555.. 111 A
santanam@fiu.edu
SANTANA MARINO,
Julio .... 787-725-6500.. 531 C
jsantana@albizu.edu
SANTANGELO,
Victoria, R .... 718-990-1363.. 328 F
santangv@stjohns.edu
SANTAW, Carrie .... 352-638-9705.... 96 F
csantaw@beaconcollege.edu
SANTEE, Wendi .... 864-379-8701.. 429 I
santee@erskine.edu
SANTELL, Candice .... 937-769-1343.. 363 E
csantell@antioch.edu
SANTELL, Ross .... 320-762-4404.. 248 J
rosss@alextech.edu
SANTESTEBAN, David ...... 340-692-4139.. 539 C
david.santesteban@uvi.edu
SANTIAGO, Alma, L .... 787-841-2000.. 535 I
alsantiago@pucpr.edu
SANTIAGO, Barbara .... 787-850-9386.. 538 B
barbara.santiago2@upr.edu
SANTIAGO, Cariluz .... 787-841-2000.. 535 I
cariluz_santiago@pucpr.edu
SANTIAGO, Carlos .... 617-994-6901.. 220 D
csantiago@mass.edu
SANTIAGO, Carol .... 787-620-2040.. 530 F
csantiago@aupr.edu
SANTIAGO, Castula .... 787-850-9361.. 538 B
castula.santiago@upr.edu
SANTIAGO, Christopher .. 508-286-8213.. 229 F
santiago_christoher@wheatoncollege.edu
SANTIAGO, Dalia .... 787-882-2065.. 536 D
orientacion@unitecpr.net
SANTIAGO, Delma .... 787-284-1912.. 534 C
dosantia@ponce.inter.edu
SANTIAGO, Edny .... 787-864-2222.. 534 A
edny.santiago@guayama.inter.edu
SANTIAGO, Eutimia .... 787-751-0160.. 531 M
esantiago@cmpr.pr.gov
SANTIAGO, Isaac .... 787-766-1912.. 533 F
isantiag@inter.edu
SANTIAGO, Jaime .... 787-250-1912.. 534 B
jaimesantiago@metro.inter.edu
SANTIAGO, Jamie .... 617-588-1358.. 215 E
jsantiago@bfit.edu
SANTIAGO, Joemille .... 215-572-2909.. 397 G
santiagoj@arcadia.edu
SANTIAGO, Jorge .... 787-764-0000.. 538 F
jorge.santiago21@upr.edu
SANTIAGO, Jose, G .... 787-279-1912.. 533 J
jsantiago@bayamon.inter.edu
SANTIAGO, Judith .... 212-343-1234.. 321 B
jsantiago@mcny.edu
SANTIAGO, Juliane .... 919-658-7769.. 355 K
jsantiago@umo.edu
SANTIAGO, Kenneth .... 773-481-8047.. 137 I
ksantiago6@ccc.edu
SANTIAGO, Maria .... 787-738-2161.. 538 A
maria.santiago25@upr.edu
SANTIAGO, Martha .... 863-297-1093.. 106 I
msantiago@polk.edu
SANTIAGO, Martha .... 863-292-3627.. 106 I
msantiago@polk.edu
SANTIAGO, Marya, Z .... 787-844-2318.. 538 E
marya.santiago@upr.edu
SANTIAGO, Miguel .... 787-764-0000.. 538 F
miguel.santiatgo16@upr.edu
SANTIAGO, Milton .... 718-960-8659.. 308 B
milton.santiago1i@lehman.cuny.edu
SANTIAGO, Rafael .... 787-780-0070.. 531 B
rsantiago@caribbean.edu
SANTIAGO, Rigoberto .... 787-834-9595.. 536 E
rsantiago@uaa.edu
SANTIAGO, Victor .... 787-857-3600.. 533 I
vsantiago@br.inter.edu
SANTIAGO, Viviana .... 787-720-1022.. 531 A
administracion@atlanticu.edu
SANTIAGO, Wanda .... 718-289-5352.. 307 C
wanda.santiago@bcc.cuny.edu
SANTIAGO, Yinaira .... 787-284-1912.. 534 C
yinsant@ponce.inter.edu
SANTIAGO ROSADO,
Lydia, E .... 787-863-2390.. 533 K
lydia.santiago@fajardo.inter.edu
SANTIAGO-TORO,
Clarissa .... 787-723-4481.. 531 D
centro@ceaprc.edu
SANTIAGO-TORO,
Clarissa .... 787-723-4481.. 531 D
csantiago@ceaprc.edu
SANTILLAN, Courtney ...... 208-562-3000.. 133 F
courtneysantillan@cwidaho.cc
SANTILLI, Nicholas, R ..... 216-397-4734.. 370 H
santilli@jcu.edu
SANTIN, Claudia .... 708-209-3228.. 138 G
claudia.santin@cuchicago.edu
SANTINI, Cathy .... 425-602-3107.. 501 D
media@bastyr.edu
SANTIROCCO,
Matthew, S .... 212-998-2197.. 324 C
matthew.santirocco@nyu.edu
SANTIVASCI, Joseph .... 610-436-3085.. 416 C
jsantivasci@wcupa.edu
SANTOMAURO,
Kristine, M .... 302-225-6233.... 91 D
santomk@gbc.edu
SANTORA, Anthony .... 908-737-6000.. 292 C
afs@kean.edu
SANTORE, JR., Chuck ..... 724-439-4900.. 408 D
csantore@laurel.edu
SANTORO, C. James .... 402-449-2910.. 280 C
jsantoro@graceu.edu
SANTOS, Annette, T .... 671-735-2553.. 530 B
atsantos@triton.uog.edu
SANTOS, Carmen, K .... 671-735-5548.. 529 G
carmen.kweksantos@guamcc.edu
SANTOS, Carol .... 508-999-8388.. 220 H
csantos1@umassd.edu
SANTOS, Catherine .... 315-312-4903.. 333 D
catherine.santos@oswego.edu
SANTOS, David, M .... 860-701-6787.. 529 A
david.m.santos@uscg.edu
SANTOS, Helena .... 617-243-2127.. 219 I
hsantos@lasell.edu
SANTOS, Joycette .... 787-841-4780.. 538 E
joycette.santos@upr.edu
SANTOS, Mae .... 323-343-3555.... 33 C
msantos@cslanet.calstatela.edu
SANTOS, Maggie .... 719-389-6707.... 77 J
maggie.santos@coloradocollege.edu
SANTOS, Maricarmen .... 787-743-7979.. 536 A
m_santos@suagm.edu
SANTOS, María del, C ..... 787-743-7979.. 536 A
ut_masantos@suagm.edu
SANTOS, Matthew .... 610-683-4113.. 415 C
santos@kutztown.edu
SANTOS, Nicole .... 413-265-2213.. 217 D
santosn@elms.edu
SANTOS, Paul .... 704-330-6689.. 348 E
paul.santos@cpcc.edu
SANTOS, Ramon .... 305-223-4561.. 108 A
santos@sjvcs.edu
SANTOS,
Roberto (Bobby), J .... 691-320-2480.. 529 F
rjsantas@comfsm.fm
SANTOS, Samuel .... 415-239-3762.... 38 E
ssantos@ccsf.edu
SANTOS, Shelly .... 718-261-5800.. 305 J
ssantos@bramsonort.edu
SANTOS, Susan .... 859-442-4165.. 189 D
susan.santos@kctcs.edu
SANTOS, Victor .... 302-857-6001.... 90 F
vsantos@desu.edu
SANTOS, Victor .... 508-362-2131.. 223 C
vsantos@capecod.edu
SANTOS-COY, Katie .... 714-449-7463.... 51 F
ksantoscoy@ketchum.edu
SANTOS-GEORGE, Arlene 847-543-2402.. 138 C
asgeorge@clcillinois.edu
SANTOS-GEORGE, Arlene 847-543-2310.. 138 C
asgeorge@clcillinois.edu
SANTOS-PEREZ,
Kennia, I .... 787-480-2463.. 531 J
kisantos@sanjuanciudadpatria.com
SANTOSTEFANO, Donald . 717-867-6341.. 408 F
dsantost@lvc.edu
SANTUCCI, George .... 412-392-3498.. 417 F
gsantucci@pointpark.edu
SANTUCCI, Wayne .... 212-517-0544.. 320 C
wsantucci@mmm.edu
SANYAL, Rajib, N .... 516-877-4661.. 303 B
rsanyal@adelphi.edu
SANYAL, Sabyasachi .... 972-721-5156.. 473 D
ssanyal@udallas.edu
SANZARI, Kelly .... 724-589-2014.. 420 D
ksanzari@thiel.edu
SAPARILAS, John, W .... 919-866-5450.. 353 I
jwsaparilas@waketech.edu
SAPERSTEIN, Shari .... 954-262-7201.. 105 J
ssaperst@nova.edu
SAPHIRE, Diane, G .... 210-999-8483.. 473 A
dsaphire@trinity.edu
SAPIENZA, Barb .... 314-977-7777.. 271 K
sapienzab@slu.edu

SAPIENZA, Christine .... 904-256-7626.. 103 D
csapien@ju.edu
SAPIENZA, Matthew .... 646-664-3014.. 306 M
matthew.sapienza@cuny.edu
SAPIENZA, Michael .... 803-754-4100.. 429 B
SAPP, Aimee .... 573-592-4368.. 275 G
aimee.sapp@williamwoods.edu
SAPP, Buddy .... 912-871-1634.. 125 E
bsapp@ogeecheetech.edu
SAPP, Fred .... 910-672-1204.. 356 E
fsapp@uncfsu.edu
SAPP, Judy .... 606-877-1421.. 190 E
judy.sapp@kctcs.edu
SAPP, Sarah .... 662-562-3274.. 260 C
ssapp@northwestms.edu
SAPPENFIELD, Elizabeth .. 317-738-8075.. 160 J
esappenfield@franklincollege.edu
SAPPENFIELD, George, O 336-386-3280.. 353 F
sappeng@surry.edu
SAPPINGTON, Eric .... 660-831-4168.. 269 B
sappingtone@moval.edu
SARAC, Isa .... 703-591-7042.. 499 D
isarac@viu.edu
SARACHICK, Daniel, T ...... 508-831-5000.. 230 C
dtsarachick@wpi.edu
SARAFIAN, Christopher ... 302-793-1101.... 91 E
SARAN, Rupa .... 714-432-5952.... 39 G
rsaran@occ.cccd.edu
SARANI, Saeed .... 405-692-3246.. 384 C
ssarani@macu.edu
SARANTAKOS, Paul .... 217-351-2385.. 151 B
psarantakos@parkland.edu
SARAO, Felix, G .... 562-908-3413.... 58 I
fsarao@riohondo.edu
SARAT, Austin, D .... 413-542-2308.. 214 C
adsarat@amherst.edu
SARATA, Andrew .... 708-974-5357.. 148 G
sarataa@morainevalley.edu
SARAVANAPAVAN,
Naomi .... 607-729-1581.. 312 E
nsaravanapavan@davisny.edu
SARBER, John .... 765-455-9505.. 163 A
jrsarber@iuk.edu
SARBER, Sarah .... 765-455-9204.. 163 A
shawkins@iuk.edu
SARDINAS, Maria .... 617-739-1700.. 226 G
msardinas@aii.edu
SARETSKY, Kelly .... 978-556-3866.. 224 D
ksaretsky@necc.mass.edu
SARFF, Michelle .... 614-251-4758.. 374 I
sarffm@ohiodominican.edu
SARGE, Sandy .... 661-726-1911.... 68 K
sandy.sarge@uav.edu
SARGEANT, Glenn .... 501-975-8536.... 21 G
gsargeant@philander.edu
SARGENT, Brent .... 802-879-2321.. 486 D
bsargent@vtc.edu
SARGENT, Daniel .... 315-866-0300.. 316 A
sargentda@herkimer.edu
SARGENT, Frank .... 617-730-7254.. 226 J
frank.sargent@newbury.edu
SARGENT, Gary .... 254-295-4242.. 474 E
gsargent@umhb.edu
SARGENT, Jenell .... 334-727-8350...... 8 A
jsargent@mytu.tuskegee.edu
SARGENT, Joe, E .... 423-585-6836.. 447 D
joe.sargent@ws.edu
SARGENT, John .... 903-923-2273.. 457 G
SARGENT, Madeline .... 215-568-9215.. 424 C
msargent@phmc.org
SARGENT, Mark, L .... 805-565-6007.... 75 A
msargent@westmont.edu
SARGENT, Peter, E .... 314-968-7006.. 275 B
sargenpe@webster.edu
SARGENT, Sheri .... 507-389-2015.. 250 E
sheri.sargent@mnsu.edu
SARGENT-MARTIN,
Shelia .... 304-327-4176.. 512 P
ssmartin@bluefieldstate.edu
SARHAN, Mostafa .... 912-358-3388.. 126 F
sarhanm@savannahstate.edu
SARIAN, Richard .... 216-421-7432.. 366 G
rsarian@cia.edu
SARIDAKIS, Dianne, I ...... 215-885-2360.. 409 G
dsaridakis@manor.edu
SARIEGO, Ivan .... 787-751-0160.. 531 M
isariego@cmpr.pr.gov
SARIN, Sanjiv .... 336-285-2371.. 356 F
sarin@ncat.edu
SARIN, Sanjiv .... 336-334-7920.. 356 F
sarin@ncat.edu
SARKIS, Hashim .... 617-253-4401.. 225 A
SARKISIAN, Jodi .... 215-898-7221.. 421 E
jodi@pobox.upenn.edu
SARLES, Harry .... 913-684-3097.. 528 I
harry.sarles@us.army.mil
SARMA, Sanjay .... 617-715-4532.. 225 A
SARMIENTO, Reine .... 718-960-8429.. 308 B
reine.sarmiento@lehman.cuny.edu
SARMIENTO, Steve .... 510-780-4500.... 48 J
ssarmiento@lifewest.edu

SARNA, Jason .... 847-543-2383.. 138 C
jsarna@clcillinois.edu
SARNA, Linda .... 310-825-9621.... 69 D
lsarna@sonnet.ucla.edu
SARNOVSKY, Joseph .... 407-708-2430.. 109 E
sarnovsj@seminolestate.edu
SARR, Akua .... 617-552-9144.. 216 C
akua.sarr@bc.edu
SARRAFIAN, Armen .... 312-553-5922.. 137 D
asarrafian@ccc.edu
SARRATORI, Peter .... 315-781-3647.. 316 C
sarrator@hws.edu
SARRETT, David, C .... 804-828-7235.. 496 D
dcsarrett@vcu.edu
SARRUBBO, Joseph, M ..... 407-582-2586.. 114 N
jsarrubbo@valenciacollege.edu
SARTAIN, Debra .... 303-837-0825.... 76 L
dsartain@aii.edu
SARTAIN, Karen .... 423-636-7376.. 447 G
ksartain@tusculum.edu
SARTARELLI, Jose, V .... 910-962-3030.. 358 D
sartarellij@uncw.edu
SARTINI, Chad .... 540-857-7731.. 499 B
csartini@virginiawestern.edu
SARTOR, Curtis .... 847-628-1017.. 144 B
csartor@judsonu.edu
SARTOR, Dan .... 708-239-4820.. 155 M
dan.sartor@trnty.edu
SARTORI, Lillian .... 212-229-5300.. 322 E
sartoril@newschool.edu
SARVER, Shawna .... 530-541-4660.... 48 D
sarver@ltcc.edu
SARVEY, Sharon .... 252-399-6401.. 341 P
sisarvey@barton.edu
SARVIS, Randall, F .... 937-481-2344.. 381 C
randy_sarvis@wilmington.edu
SASAKI, Charles .... 808-235-7371.. 132 E
sasakich@hawaii.edu
SASASKI, Hiroshi .... 626-571-8811.... 72 E
hiroshis@uwest.edu
SASS, Michael .... 314-367-8700.. 271 E
michael.sass@stlcop.edu
SASS, Terricita, E .... 203-392-9999.... 85 H
sass@southernct.edu
SASSAMAN, Margo, J ...... 717-871-7656.. 415 F
margo.sassaman@millersville.edu
SASSEL, Rachel .... 619-688-0800.... 41 E
rsassel@concorde.edu
SASSER, Jackson, N .... 352-395-5164.. 109 C
j.sasser@sfcollege.edu
SASSER, Jennifer .... 503-675-3964.. 392 D
jsasser@marylhurst.edu
SASSER, Mackey .... 334-556-2416...... 3 N
msasser@wallace.edu
SASSMAN, Jen, L .... 319-352-8262.. 177 G
jennifer.sassman@wartburg.edu
SASSO, Gary, M .... 610-758-3221.. 408 H
gms208@lehigh.edu
SASSO, Mary .... 702-651-5820.. 284 H
mary.sasso@csn.edu
SASSSER, Craig-Ellis .... 662-720-7411.. 260 B
cesasser@nemcc.edu
SASTRY, S. Shankar .... 510-642-5771.... 68 M
sastry@coe.berkeley.edu
SATA, Leigh .... 707-524-1704.... 63 G
lsata@santarosa.edu
SATCHWELL, Carol .... 315-655-7144.. 306 H
csatchwell@cazenovia.edu
SATELE, Arleen .... 714-628-4717.... 58 H
satele_arleen@sccollege.edu
SATHER, Greg .... 218-726-6137.. 255 D
gsather@d.umn.edu
SATHER, Steven, M .... 609-258-6479.. 294 D
sather@princeton.edu
SATKOWIAK, Ann, E .... 865-539-7153.. 446 G
asatkowiak@pstcc.edu
SATKOWSKI, John .... 313-845-9636.. 235 D
jssatkowski@hfcc.edu
SATO, Deirdre .... 212-217-5380.. 314 B
deirdre_sato@fitnyc.edu
SATO, Heidi .... 714-816-0366.... 68 E
heidi.sato@trident.edu
SATO, Kay .... 516-299-2584.. 319 C
kay.sato@liu.edu
SATO, Tami, A .... 714-449-7447.... 51 F
tsato@ketchum.edu
SATO, Toshiko .... 949-480-4364.... 64 J
tsato@soka.edu
SATRIANA, Dan .... 970-351-2399.... 84 C
dan.satriana@unco.edu
SATTAR, Mo .... 413-565-1000.. 215 A
msattar@baypath.edu
SATTERFIELD, Billy .... 281-283-2480.. 474 A
satterfield@uhcl.edu
SATTERFIELD, Derick .... 336-342-4261.. 352 F
satterfieldd@rockinghamcc.edu
SATTERFIELD, Jay .... 731-989-6058.. 440 D
jsatterfield@fhu.edu
SATTERFIELD, Lacey, L ... 770-720-5620.. 126 C
lls@reinhardt.edu

SATTERFIELD, Lisa .... 865-251-1800.. 444 A
lsatterfield@southcollegetn.edu
SATTERFIELD, Tanya .... 662-915-7692.. 261 B
tnsatter@olemiss.edu
SATTERLEE, Kevin .... 208-426-1203.. 132 I
ksatterl@boisestate.edu
SATTERLEE, Richard .... 718-862-7352.. 319 L
richard.satterlee@manhattan.edu
SATTERLUND,
Alysson, M .... 909-537-5185.... 34 C
asatterlund@csusb.edu
SATTERLY, Eric .... 502-272-8098.. 187 A
esatterly@bellarmine.edu
SATTERTHWAITE,
Shad, B .... 405-325-1931.. 389 B
shad@ou.edu
SATTERWHITE, Dawn ...... 919-761-2209.. 355 I
dsatterwhite@sebts.edu
SATTERWHITE, Robin ...... 806-716-2200.. 465 G
rsatterwhite@southplainscollege.edu
SATTLER, Brian .... 409-880-8396.. 471 A
brian.sattler@lamar.edu
SATTLER, Joan .... 309-677-3181.. 136 B
jls@fsmail.bradley.edu
SATZ, Michael .... 208-364-4041.. 134 G
msatz@uidaho.edu
SAUCEDA, James .... 509-793-2222.. 501 H
jamess@bigbend.edu
SAUCEDO, Joseph .... 773-508-3948.. 146 G
jsaucedo1@luc.edu
SAUCIER, Jason .... 207-780-5512.. 205 E
jason.saucier@maine.edu
SAUDER, Vinita .... 402-486-2500.. 282 I
visauder@ucollege.edu
SAUDERS, Charlette, F .... 574-372-5100.. 161 B
saudercr@grace.edu
SAUER, Carrie .... 405-208-5873.. 385 E
csauer@okcu.edu
SAUER, Greg .... 802-485-2170.. 484 H
gsauer@norwich.edu
SAUER, James .... 610-341-5957.. 412 C
jsauer@eastern.edu
SAUER, James, L .... 610-341-5957.. 403 B
jsauer@eastern.edu
SAUER, Jenni .... 215-489-6378.. 402 A
jenni.sauer@delval.edu
SAUER, Mary R .... 630-637-5801.. 149 H
mrsauer@noctrl.edu
SAUER, Melanie .... 626-529-8064.... 55 H
msauer@pacificoaks.edu
SAUER, Michael, L .... 702-895-1073.. 284 L
michael.sauer@unlv.edu
SAUER, Mike .... 702-895-1073.. 284 L
sauer@unlv.edu
SAUERBREI, Aaron .... 319-277-2490.. 173 B
aaron.sauerbrei@hawkeyecollege.edu
SAUERMAN, Gretchen ..... 321-674-7237.. 100 M
gsauerman@fit.edu
SAUERS, Darlene .... 724-838-4210.. 419 D
sauers@setonhill.edu
SAUERS, Gail .... 602-682-6800.... 11 I
gsauers@azsummitlaw.edu
SAUK, John .... 502-852-5295.. 194 A
john.sauk@louisville.edu
SAUL, Amy .... 610-861-1509.. 411 B
saula@moravian.edu
SAUL, J. Beau .... 607-844-8222.. 337 G
saulj@tc3.edu
SAUL, Sheryl .... 651-846-1384.. 252 C
sheryl.saul@saintpaul.edu
SAULE, Mara, R .... 802-656-2020.. 485 D
mara.saule@uvm.edu
SAULS, Jina M .... 276-244-1232.. 486 N
jsauls@asl.edu
SAULSBERRY, Keith .... 334-556-2470...... 3 N
ksaulsberry@wallace.edu
SAUM, Rob .... 386-506-3484.... 98 E
saumr@daytonastate.edu
SAUNDERS, Aleister .... 215-895-6203.. 402 G
aleister.j.saunders@drexel.edu
SAUNDERS, Amber .... 318-371-3035.. 196 H
ambersaunders@nwltc.edu
SAUNDERS, Bret .... 605-342-0317.. 436 A
bsaunders@johnwitherspooncollege.org
SAUNDERS, Brian .... 310-544-6487.... 59 K
brian.saunders@usw.salvationarmy.org
SAUNDERS, C. Tom .... 912-279-5757.. 119 C
tsaunders@ccga.edu
SAUNDERS, Clark .... 860-768-4504.... 89 G
clsaunder@hartford.edu
SAUNDERS, Dustin .... 757-340-2121.. 488 A
admdirectorcvab@centura.edu
SAUNDERS, Gary .... 336-506-4152.. 347 C
gary.saunders@alamancecc.edu
SAUNDERS, Greer .... 804-819-4906.. 496 E
gsaunders@vccs.edu
SAUNDERS, Joseph .... 304-766-3353.. 514 B
saundejs@wvstateu.edu
SAUNDERS, Kara, C .... 716-645-5725.. 331 C
kcs23@buffalo.edu

SAUNDERS, Kathleen .... 716-614-6848.. 324 D
ksaunders@niagaracc.suny.edu
SAUNDERS, Keith .... 319-335-0553.. 169 H
keith-saunders@uiowa.edu
SAUNDERS, Kenneth, K ... 516-572-7664.. 322 C
kenneth.saunders@ncc.edu
SAUNDERS, Kevin .... 515-271-1984.. 171 K
kevin.saunders@drake.edu
SAUNDERS, Kevin .... 831-582-3397.... 33 E
kesaunders@csumb.edu
SAUNDERS, Mark .... 405-878-5164.. 387 J
msaunders@stgregorys.edu
SAUNDERS, Martha, D ..... 850-474-2035.. 113 A
msaunders@uwf.edu
SAUNDERS, Melinda, D .. 304-896-7364.. 512 E
melinda.saunders@southernwv.edu
SAUNDERS, Richard .... 435-865-8392.. 481 N
rsaunders@suu.edu
SAUNDERS, Robert .... 334-983-6556...... 7 H
rsaunders@troy.edu
SAUNDERS, Ruth .... 860-701-5000.... 88 D
SAUNDERS, Scott, D .... 716-673-3171.. 331 D
scott.saunders@fredonia.edu
SAUNDERS, Sharon .... 336-517-2267.. 342 B
sharon.saunders@bennett.edu
SAUNDERS, Sharon .... 434-947-8114.. 493 B
ssaunders@randolphcollege.edu
SAUNDERS, Sharon .... 281-649-3206.. 458 L
ssaunders@hbu.edu
SAUNDERS, Sharon, E .... 281-649-3206.. 458 L
ssaunders@hbu.edu
SAUNDERS, Tanya, R ...... 607-274-3063.. 317 D
tsaunders@ithaca.edu
SAUNDERS, William, T .... 713-313-7846.. 470 D
saunders_wt@tsu.edu
SAUNDERS-WHITE,
Debra .... 919-530-6104.. 357 A
debra.saunders-white@nccu.edu
SAUNKEAH, Peggy .... 580-559-5890.. 383 H
saunkeah@ecok.edu
SAURBEK, Rhonda, R ...... 517-750-1200.. 241 E
rsaurbek@arbor.edu
SAURE, Debra, C .... 402-280-1277.. 279 H
debrasaure@creighton.edu
SAUTER, David, M .... 513-529-8781.. 372 K
sauterdm@miamioh.edu
SAUTER, Maranah .... 706-880-8201.. 123 K
msauter@lagrange.edu
SAUTER, Ramona .... 408-554-4397.... 63 E
rsauter@scu.edu
SAUVE, Stephanie, L .... 585-340-9588.. 310 F
ssauve@crcds.edu
SAUVIGNON, Carine .... 781-821-2222.. 223 G
SAVAGE, Ann .... 870-248-4000.... 19 H
annd@blackrivertech.edu
SAVAGE, Beth .... 619-961-4330.... 68 A
bsavage@tjsl.edu
SAVAGE, Carin .... 718-289-5184.. 307 C
carin.savage@bcc.cuny.edu
SAVAGE, Dean .... 718-997-5441.. 309 D
dean.savage@qc.cuny.edu
SAVAGE, Deana .... 432-685-4515.. 461 H
docsavage@midland.edu
SAVAGE, Donna .... 254-968-9246.. 467 F
dsavage@tarleton.edu
SAVAGE, Frederick .... 410-516-8128.. 208 D
fsavage@jhu.edu
SAVAGE, Jeffrey .... 435-283-7154.. 482 E
jeff.savage@snow.edu
SAVAGE, Mandara .... 618-453-4033.. 154 I
msavage@engr.siu.edu
SAVAGE, Martie .... 501-370-5333.... 21 G
msavage@philander.edu
SAVAGE, Mike .... 510-567-6174.... 67 E
msavage@sum.edu
SAVAGE, Monique, J .... 517-265-5161.. 230 D
msavage@adrian.edu
SAVAGE, Pam .... 314-744-5331.. 268 F
savagep@mobap.edu
SAVAGE, Suzanne .... 757-233-8736.. 500 E
ssavage@vwc.edu
SAVAGIAN, John .... 414-382-6358.. 515 D
john.savagian@alverno.edu
SAVASTA, Mark .... 508-849-3456.. 214 E
msavasta@annamaria.edu
SAVERANCE, R. Kyle .... 843-383-8017.. 428 F
ksaverance@coker.edu
SAVERESE, Lisa .... 508-849-3312.. 214 E
lsaverese@annamaria.edu
SAVIANESO, Michael .... 201-684-7402.. 294 G
msaviane@ramapo.edu
SAVICE, Candice .... 703-891-1787.. 494 H
admissions@standardcollege.edu
SAVICKY, Kim .... 402-399-2417.. 279 E
ksavicky@csm.edu
SAVIDGE, Lawrence .... 843-574-6051.. 433 D
lawrence.savidge@tridenttech.edu
SAVILLE, Vicki .... 704-330-6224.. 348 E
vicki.saville@cpcc.edu
SAVIN, Laura .... 651-846-1469.. 252 C
laura.savin@saintpaul.edu

SAVINO, Jeffrey .... 814-472-3006 .. 418 F jsavino@francis.edu
SAVINO, Stacey .... 360-538-4082 .. 504 B ssavino@ghc.edu
SAVIOR, Valerie .... 323-259-2623 .... 55 A vsavior@oxy.edu
SAVITZ, David .... 401-863-7408 .. 424 J david_savitz@brown.edu
SAVOCA, Marianna .... 631-632-6810 .. 332 A marianna.savoca@stonybrook.edu
SAVOIE, E. Joseph .... 337-482-6203 .. 201 D president@louisiana.edu
SAVOIE, Leslie, L .... 321-674-7362 .. 100 M lsavoie@fit.edu
SAVOIE, Michael .... 801-863-8237 .. 482 C msavoie@uvu.edu
SAVOIE, Michael, P .... 229-249-4894 .. 129 G mpsavoie@valdosta.edu
SAVOIT, Taina, J .... 337-475-5065 .. 200 H tsavoit@mcneese.edu
SAVRON, Doris .... 602-557-2433 .... 17 L doris.savron@phoenix.edu
SAVU, Vasemaca .... 692-625-3394 .. 530 C vsavu@cmi.edu
SAW, Kevin .... 718-357-0500 .. 329 E ksaw@stpaulsschoolofnursing.edu
SAWATZKY, Rachel, R .... 540-432-4133 .. 488 K rachel.sawatzky@emu.edu
SAWAY, Sabine .... 206-239-4500 .. 502 D ssaway@cityu.edu
SAWICKI, Gretchen .... 412-369-3610 .. 401 B gsawicki@ccac.edu
SAWICKI, Jerzy .... 216-687-9364 .. 366 I j.sawicki@csuohio.edu
SAWREY, Barbara .... 858-822-4358 .... 70 C avcdue@ucsd.edu
SAWTELLE, III, James (Jimmy), R .... 318-487-5443 .. 196 B jsawtelle@cltcc.edu
SAWYER, Cary, A .... 757-455-3310 .. 500 E casawyer@vwc.edu
SAWYER, Dana .... 816-802-3532 .. 266 D dsawyer@kcai.edu
SAWYER, Dana, L .... 302-857-1124 .... 91 C dsawyer1@dtcc.edu
SAWYER, Darrell, R .... 605-394-2667 .. 437 E darrell.sawyer@sdsmt.edu
SAWYER, Diane .... 410-295-5545 .. 210 D diane.sawyer@sjc.edu
SAWYER, Gretchen .... 775-673-7648 .. 284 K gsawyer@tmcc.edu
SAWYER, James .... 586-445-7196 .. 237 C sawyerj@macomb.edu
SAWYER, Jane .... 858-642-8091 .... 54 A jsawyer@nu.edu
SAWYER, Jenny, L .... 502-852-4957 .. 194 A jsawyer@louisville.edu
SAWYER, John .... 208-882-1566 .. 134 B jsawyer@nsa.edu
SAWYER, John, E .... 302-831-2021 .... 91 F sawyerj@udel.edu
SAWYER, Jonathan, C .... 202-319-5619 .... 92 A sawyerj@cua.edu
SAWYER, Julie .... 918-444-2210 .. 384 G sawjerjk@nsuok.edu
SAWYER, Katherine .... 847-214-7143 .. 140 A ksawyer@elgin.edu
SAWYER, Malcolm James .... 671-734-1812 .. 530 A mjsawyer@piu.edu
SAWYER, Michael .... 307-268-2492 .. 526 D msawyer@caspercollege.edu
SAWYER, Rebecca .... 410-532-5308 .. 210 B rsawyer@ndm.edu
SAWYER, Roger .... 803-777-0525 .. 433 F rhsawyer@mailbox.sc.edu
SAWYER, Shirley .... 863-774-3535 .... 96 B
SAWYER, Terrence .... 410-617-2290 .. 208 G tsawyer@loyola.edu
SAWYER, Wm. Gregory ... 805-437-8546 .... 32 B greg.sawyer@csuci.edu
SAWYERS, Cheryl .... 325-670-1091 .. 458 J cheryl.r.sawyers@hsutx.edu
SAWYERS, Dorret .... 305-348-2436 .. 111 A dorret.sawyers@fiu.edu
SAX, Christina .... 410-888-9048 .. 209 C csax@muih.edu
SAX, Joanna .... 619-239-0391 .... 36 A jsax@cwsl.edu
SAX, Richard .... 740-245-7214 .. 380 C rsax@rio.edu
SAXBY, William, R .... 303-963-3124 .... 77 I wsaxby@ccu.edu
SAXENA, Ashok .... 479-575-2151 .... 22 I asaxena@uark.edu
SAXENA, Pradeep .... 585-594-6430 .. 327 D saxenap@roberts.edu
SAXENIAN, AnnaLee .... 510-642-9980 .... 68 M anno@ischool.berkeley.edu
SAXON, Jackie .... 512-404-4885 .. 452 A jsaxon@austinseminary.edu
SAXON, Tina, M .... 714-850-4800 .... 67 G saxon@taftu.edu
SAXTON, Jane .... 425-602-3024 .. 501 D jsaxton@bastyr.edu
SAXTON, Susan .... 760-591-3012 .... 72 A ssaxton@usa.edu
SAY, Elizabeth, A .... 818-677-3301 .... 34 A elizabeth.say@csun.edu
SAYDSHOEV, Sally .... 765-973-8584 .. 162 G ssaydsho@iue.edu
SAYE, Shaydean .... 406-657-1051 .. 278 D shaydean.saye@rocky.edu
SAYEGH, John, J .... 716-376-7580 .. 317 F johnsayegh@mail.sunyjcc.edu
SAYEGH, Sharlene .... 562-985-5428 .... 33 B sharlene.sayegh@csulb.edu
SAYERS, Kimberly, J .... 330-287-0100 .. 375 B sayers.1@osu.edu
SAYLER, David, A .... 513-529-7286 .. 372 K saylerda@miamioh.edu
SAYLER, Michael .... 734-487-1414 .. 233 J msayler@emich.edu
SAYLES, Ellen .... 440-775-8540 .. 374 C ellen.sayles@oberlin.edu
SAYLES, Keith .... 270-831-9789 .. 189 F keith.sayles@kctcs.edu
SAYLES, Thomas .... 213-740-5371 .... 72 D sayles@usc.edu
SAYLOR, Danette .... 229-903-3604 .. 115 K danette.saylor@asurams.edu
SAYLOR, Danette .... 229-317-6728 .. 120 A
SAYLOR, Peggy .... 843-349-5269 .. 430 F peggy.saylor@hgtc.edu
SAYLORS, Tony .... 870-248-4000 .... 19 H tony.saylors@blackrivertech.edu
SAYRE, Jeff .... 304-214-8809 .. 512 F jsayre@wvncc.edu
SAYRE, Mary-Chris .... 214-528-8600 .. 463 L registrar@redeeme.edu
SAYRE, Matt .... 541-552-7672 .. 395 A sayrem@sou.edu
SAYRE, Richard .... 309-457-2190 .. 148 E rsayre@monmouthcollege.edu
SAYRE, William .... 505-424-2364 .. 299 L bsayre@iaia.edu
SAYRS, Elizabeth .... 740-593-1808 .. 375 H sayrs@ohio.edu
SAÑOSA, Joseph .... 657-278-2938 .... 33 A jsanosa@fullerton.edu
SBALBI, Tony .... 413-552-2391 .. 223 E tsbalbi@hcc.edu
SBRAGIA, Alberta, M .... 412-624-2137 .. 421 G sbragia@pitt.edu
SBREGA, John, J .... 508-678-2811 .. 223 A john.sbrega@bristolcc.edu
SBRISCIA, Amanda .... 413-565-1150 .. 215 A asbriscia@baypath.edu
SBRISCIA, Amanda .... 413-565-1000 .. 215 A asbriscia@baypath.edu
SCACCIA, Jeff .... 479-979-1310 .... 24 I jscaccia@ozarks.edu
SCADUTO, Dana, E .... 717-245-1013 .. 402 D scadutod@dickinson.edu
SCAFFIDI CLARKE, Nancy .... 845-569-3254 .. 322 B nancy.scaffidi@msmc.edu
SCAGGS, Randy .... 870-743-3000 .... 21 C rscaggs@northark.edu
SCAGLIONE, Kathy, L .... 515-271-1460 .. 171 H kathleen.scaglione@dmu.edu
SCALA, Kerry .... 603-862-1355 .. 288 C kerry.scala@unh.edu
SCALA, Natalie .... 440-375-7530 .. 371 E nscala@lec.edu
SCALBERG, Daniel .... 503-255-0332 .. 392 G dscalberg@multnomah.edu
SCALES, Andy .... 334-291-4960 .... 2 H andy.scales@cv.edu
SCALES, Michael, D .... 215-204-3121 .. 420 B michael.scales@temple.edu
SCALES, Michael, G .... 845-675-4777 .. 325 C president@nyack.edu
SCALES, Suzanne .... 303-300-8740 .... 77 F suzanne.scales@collegeamerica.edu
SCALESE, Mark .... 203-254-4000 .... 87 G mscalese@fairfield.edu
SCALISE, Julia .... 805-482-2755 .... 59 G julia@stjohnsem.edu
SCALISE-SMITH, Dale .... 859-572-5347 .. 192 B scalisemd1@nku.edu
SCALZO-MCNEIL, Anne ... 508-588-9100 .. 223 G
SCAMMELL, Richard, E .... 518-276-6281 .. 327 B scammr@rpi.edu
SCANDALIS, Thomas .... 509-452-5100 .. 505 H tscandalis@pnwu.edu
SCANDONE, Charles .... 215-641-6533 .. 410 L cscandon@mc3.edu
SCANDRETT, Clyde .... 831-656-2517 .. 528 D cscandrett@nps.edu
SCANDRETT, Nic .... 847-543-2477 .. 138 C nscandrett@clcillinois.edu
SCANGA, Diane .... 636-481-3420 .. 266 C dscanga@jeffco.edu
SCANLAN, Melissa .... 802-831-1066 .. 485 F mscanlan@vermontlaw.edu
SCANLAN, Peter .... 612-338-7224 .. 256 D
SCANLAN, Therese, A .... 773-252-5311 .. 152 B therese.scanlan@resu.edu
SCANLON, Jennifer .... 207-725-3578 .. 202 F jscanlon@bowdoin.edu
SCANLON, Tom .... 617-732-2775 .. 225 C tom.scanlon@mcphs.edu
SCANNELL, Janet .... 507-222-4077 .. 245 C jscannell@carleton.edu
SCANTLING, Edgar (Ed), L .... 308-865-8669 .. 282 L scantlinge@unk.edu
SCAPERLANDA, Michael .. 405-878-5100 .. 387 J mscaperlanda@stgregorys.edu
SCARANO, John, B .... 216-397-4717 .. 370 H jscarano@jcu.edu
SCARANO, Martin .... 603-862-2116 .. 288 C marty.scarano@unh.edu
SCARBERRY, Randy .... 606-218-5208 .. 194 C randalscarberry@upike.edu
SCARBORO, Donna .... 202-994-6360 .... 92 D scarboro@gwu.edu
SCARBORO, Kim .... 850-973-1613 .. 105 H scarborok@nfcc.edu
SCARBORO, Lynne, B .... 310-338-5236 .... 51 E lscarbor@lmu.edu
SCARBOROUGH, Edesa ... 813-253-3333 .. 114 M
SCARBOROUGH, John .... 702-651-7489 .. 284 H john.scarborough@csn.edu
SCARBOROUGH, Neil .... 317-274-7602 .. 163 D neilscar@iupui.edu
SCARCELLE, Ed .... 212-229-5598 .. 322 E scarcele@newschool.edu
SCARDINO, Janell .... 402-375-7553 .. 281 J jascard1@wsc.edu
SCARFF, Colleen .... 269-387-4281 .. 243 H colleen.scarff@wmich.edu
SCARINGE, John .... 562-902-3330 .... 66 A johnscaringe@scuhs.edu
SCARLESKI, Jordan .... 901-321-4036 .. 439 E jscarles@cbu.edu
SCARLETT, Barbara .... 607-777-4438 .. 331 B scarlett@binghamton.edu
SCARNIER, Marchelle .... 512-313-3000 .. 455 F marchelle.scarnier@concordia.edu
SCARPELLI, Geoff .... 817-735-5030 .. 475 C geoffrey.scarpelli@unthsc.edu
SCARPIELLO, Susan, M ... 215-699-5700 .. 408 C sscarpiello@lsb.edu
SCARPINO, John .... 407-708-2148 .. 109 E scarpinj@seminolestate.edu
SCARTELLI, Joseph .... 540-831-5404 .. 493 A jscartel@radford.edu
SCATES, LouAnn, P .... 704-406-4263 .. 344 E lscates@gardner-webb.edu
SCAVONE, Victoria, R .... 248-689-8282 .. 242 F vscavone@walshcollege.edu
SCAVUZZO, Connie, M ... 312-949-7079 .. 142 A cscavuzzo@ico.edu
SCEERY, Amy, L .... 203-576-4506 .... 89 C asceery@bridgeport.edu
SCEPANSKY, Patricia, S .. 610-359-7355 .. 401 L pscepansky@dccc.edu
SCHAAD, Dean .... 419-755-4855 .. 373 G dschaad@ncstatecollege.edu
SCHAAF, Laura .... 706-385-1122 .. 126 A laura.schaaf@point.edu
SCHAAKE, Vicki .... 518-587-2100 .. 335 D vicki.schaake@esc.edu
SCHAAL, Barbara, A .... 314-935-6820 .. 274 N schaal@wustl.edu
SCHAAL, Dave .... 641-784-5106 .. 172 G dschaal@graceland.edu
SCHAAL, Mary .... 928-344-7772 .... 11 J mary.schaal@azwestern.edu
SCHAAL, Michael, L .... 810-762-9733 .. 236 C mschaal@kettering.edu
SCHAB, Kristin .... 717-815-1285 .. 424 F kasummer@ycp.edu
SCHABERG, David .... 310-825-4856 .... 69 D dschaberg@college.ucla.edu
SCHABERT, Daniel .... 215-646-7300 .. 404 G schabert.d@gmercyu.edu
SCHACHT, Linda .... 615-966-6155 .. 441 F linda.schacht@lipscomb.edu
SCHACHTER, Shmuel .... 410-484-7200 .. 210 A finaid@nirc.edu
SCHACKMUTH, Kurt .... 815-836-5810 .. 145 H schackku@lewisu.edu
SCHACTLER, Linda .... 509-963-2111 .. 501 K linda.schactler@cwu.edu
SCHACTLER, Linda .... 509-963-2111 .. 501 K schactler@cwu.edu
SCHADE, Carrie .... 773-298-3123 .. 153 H schade@sxu.edu
SCHADEMAN, Emily .... 215-248-3648 .. 400 H schademane@chc.edu
SCHADING, Douglas .... 212-938-5880 .. 334 F dschading@sunyopt.edu
SCHAECHTER, Alexander . 718-854-8791 .. 319 J mh@thejnet.com
SCHAEFER, Joseph .... 516-299-2463 .. 319 B joseph.schaefer@liu.edu
SCHAEFER, K. C .... 540-458-8216 .. 500 F schaeferk@wlu.edu
SCHAEFER, Karen, D .... 575-646-2731 .. 300 J kschaefe@nmsu.edu
SCHAEFER, Karie .... 816-584-7401 .. 270 D karie.schaefer@park.edu
SCHAEFER, Karla .... 641-585-8159 .. 177 F schaeferk@waldorf.edu
SCHAEFER, Kelly .... 847-467-0301 .. 150 F kelly.schaefer@northwestern.edu
SCHAEFER, Lisa .... 970-521-6659 .... 81 O lisa.schaefer@njc.edu
SCHAEFER, Lynne .... 410-455-2939 .. 211 G lschaefer@umbc.edu
SCHAEFER, Mark .... 202-885-3304 .... 91 J schaef@american.edu
SCHAEFER, Maryann .... 312-629-6118 .. 154 A mschaefer@saic.edu
SCHAEFER, Rhonda .... 505-566-3087 .. 301 J schaeferr@sanjuancollege.edu
SCHAEFER, Sharon, P .... 813-253-6250 .. 114 M sschaefer@ut.edu
SCHAEFER, Thomas, G .... 412-536-1198 .. 406 K thomas.schaefer@laroche.edu
SCHAEFER, Verdell .... 909-558-4509 .... 49 C vschaefer@llu.edu
SCHAEFFER, Angela .... 860-297-2139 .... 89 B angela.schaeffer@trincoll.edu
SCHAEFFER, Angela, P .... 413-597-2025 .. 230 A aps1@williams.edu
SCHAEFFER, Lisa, L .... 910-521-6175 .. 358 C lisa.schaeffer@uncp.edu
SCHAEFFER, Scot .... 563-387-1287 .. 174 L schasc01@luther.edu
SCHAEFFER, William .... 310-665-6940 .... 55 E wschaeffer@otis.edu
SCHAEFFLER, Jan .... 203-332-5220 .... 86 D jschaeffler@hcc.commnet.edu
SCHAFER, Amy .... 724-589-2212 .. 420 D aschafer@thiel.edu
SCHAFER, Christine .... 651-793-1618 .. 250 A chris.schafer@metrostate.edu
SCHAFER, Clark .... 316-942-4291 .. 183 I schaferc@newmanu.edu
SCHAFER, Michael .... 419-772-2190 .. 374 J m-schafer@onu.edu
SCHAFER, Mike .... 239-936-5822 .. 102 O
SCHAFER, Stephen .... 914-395-2314 .. 329 K sschafer@sarahlawrence.edu
SCHAFER, William .... 304-293-5811 .. 514 C wschafer@mail.wvu.edu
SCHAFF, Monte .... 701-255-3285 .. 362 E mschaff@uttc.edu
SCHAFFELD, Linda .... 513-569-1601 .. 366 D linda.schaffeld@cincinnatistate.edu
SCHAFFER, Connie .... 567-661-7737 .. 376 D connie_schaffer@owens.edu
SCHAFFER, Doug .... 269-927-8120 .. 236 G dschaffer@lakemichigancollege.edu
SCHAFFER, Frederick, P .. 646-664-9210 .. 306 M frederick.schaffer@cuny.edu
SCHAFFER, James, P .... 610-330-5000 .. 407 C schaffej@lafayette.edu
SCHAFFER, Jeff .... 732-987-2600 .. 292 A jschaffer@georgian.edu
SCHAFFER, Joe .... 307-778-1102 .. 526 K jschaffer@lccc.wy.edu
SCHAFFER, Kerry .... 812-877-8172 .. 166 H schaffer@rose-hulman.edu
SCHAFFER, Mindy, M .... 410-822-5400 .. 207 A mschaffer@chesapeake.edu
SCHAFFER, Sandy .... 931-393-1536 .. 446 D sschaffer@mscc.edu
SCHAFFER, Shelley .... 858-513-9240 .... 27 V shelley.schaffer@ashford.edu
SCHAFFER, William .... 217-641-4314 .. 143 H bschaffer@jwcc.edu
SCHAFFNER, Barbara, H .. 614-823-1735 .. 376 C bschaffner@otterbein.edu
SCHAFFNER, Bradley .... 507-222-4267 .. 245 C bschaffner@carleton.edu
SCHAFRICK, James, A .... 203-773-8507 .... 85 C jschafrick@albertus.edu
SCHAKNOWSKI, Jennifer . 706-290-2167 .. 117 F jschaknowski@berry.edu
SCHALK, Heather .... 302-736-2306 .... 91 G heather.schalk@wesley.edu
SCHALK, Lawrence, E .... 269-471-3484 .. 230 H schalk@andrews.edu
SCHALL, Ellen .... 212-998-7438 .. 324 C ellen.schall@nyu.edu
SCHALL, Lawrence, M .... 404-364-8320 .. 125 F lschall@oglethorpe.edu
SCHALLER, Rhonda .... 718-636-5926 .. 326 E rshal20@pratt.edu

SCHALLOCK, Heather .... 715-365-4518.. 524 C
hschallock@nicoletcollege.edu
SCHAMANN, Matthew ...... 716-926-8925.. 316 B
mschamann@hilbert.edu
SCHAMING, Rachel .... 520-206-4646.... 16 F
raschaming@pima.edu
SCHANCK, Donald, S ...... 401-863-9570.. 424 J
donald_schanck@brown.edu
SCHANDEL, Kimberly, A .. 508-767-7312.. 214 F
kschande@assumption.edu
SCHANTZ, Janet, D .... 317-738-8009.. 160 J
jschantz@franklincollege.edu
SCHANTZ, Peter, K .... 740-368-3404.. 376 B
pkschant@owu.edu
SCHANZ, Jeff .... 518-276-6205.. 327 E
schanj@rpi.edu
SCHAPER, Nikki .... 760-757-2121.... 52 K
nschaper@miracosta.edu
SCHAPER, Sue .... 208-459-5837.. 133 D
sschaper@collegeofidaho.edu
SCHAPIRO, Chaim .... 973-455-9031.. 294 F
chaimschap@aol.com
SCHAPIRO, Mendel .... 323-937-3763.... 75 G
SCHAPIRO, Morton, O ..... 847-491-7456.. 150 F
nu-president@northwestern.edu
SCHAPIRO, Robert .... 404-712-8815.. 120 E
rschapi@emory.edu
SCHAPP, Rebecca, M .... 408-554-4528.... 63 E
rschapp@scu.edu
SCHAPPE, Mascheal .... 314-529-9670.. 267 E
mschappe@maryville.edu
SCHAPPERT, David, G ..... 570-961-4764.. 409 H
dschappert@marywood.edu
SCHARDT, Wendy, L .... 308-865-8047.. 282 L
schardtwl@unk.edu
SCHARER, Gregory .... 937-775-2620.. 381 H
greg.scharer@wright.edu
SCHARER, Lloyd, S .... 517-321-0242.. 235 C
lscharer@glcc.edu
SCHARER, Miriam .... 503-399-8486.. 390 E
miriam.rozin@chemeketa.edu
SCHARF, Michael, P .... 216-368-3283.. 365 B
michael.scharf@case.edu
SCHARF, Sara, A .... 515-574-1005.. 173 F
scharf@iowacentral.edu
SCHARFF, Virginia .... 505-277-2611.. 302 F
vscharff@unm.edu
SCHARLE, Joyce .... 215-646-7300.. 404 G
scharle.j@gmercyu.edu
SCHARLEMANN,
Linette, M .... 507-354-8221.. 247 J
scharllm@mlc-wels.edu
SCHARLOTT, Brooke .... 440-684-6129.. 380 F
brooke.scharlott@ursuline.edu
SCHARMAN, Janet, S .... 801-422-2387.. 480 C
jan_scharman@byu.edu
SCHARMER, Judy .... 575-624-8040.. 300 I
scharmer@nmmi.edu
SCHARN, Theresa .... 605-718-2402.. 438 B
theresa.scharn@wdt.edu
SCHARRE, Janice .... 215-780-1420.. 419 C
SCHARTMAN, Laura, A ..... 248-370-2387.. 239 K
schartma@oakland.edu
SCHATTMAN, Lisa .... 858-566-1200.... 42 D
lschattman@disd.edu
SCHATZ, Julianne .... 336-272-7102.. 344 G
julies@greensboro.edu
SCHATZBERG, Jeffrey, W 520-621-2238.... 17 I
jschatzb@email.arizona.edu
SCHATZEL, Kim .... 410-704-2356.. 213 B
presidentsoffice@towson.edu
SCHAUB, Linda .... 517-750-1200.. 241 E
lindas@arbor.edu
SCHAUB, Mark .... 616-331-3898.. 234 F
schaubm@gvsu.edu
SCHAUB, Mike .... 202-687-3493.... 92 E
jms46@georgetown.edu
SCHAUB, Rebekah .... 231-843-5568.. 243 G
rschaub@westshore.edu
SCHAUBHUT, Diana .... 504-398-2100.. 200 D
dschaubhut@olhcc.edu
SCHAUER, Anne, P .... 513-529-3735.. 372 K
schauerap@miamioh.edu
SCHAUER, Ariane .... 310-377-5501.... 51 G
aschauer@marymountcalifornia.edu
SCHAUFELBERGER, John 206-685-4440.. 508 E
jesbcon@u.washington.edu
SCHAUMANN, Neils .... 619-239-0391.... 36 A
nschaumann@cwsl.edu
SCHAURER, Susan .... 513-529-5040.. 372 K
susan.schaurer@miamioh.edu
SCHAUS, Jim .... 740-593-0982.. 375 H
schaus@ohio.edu
SCHEARS, Ben .... 785-890-3641.. 183 L
bschears@nwktc.edu
SCHECHTER, Aaron, M .... 718-377-0777.. 326 F
SCHECHTER, Mendel .... 718-377-0777.. 326 F
SCHECHTER, Richard .... 203-591-5042.... 88 F
rschechter@post.edu
SCHECHTER, Steven .... 718-951-5391.. 307 D
sschechter@brooklyn.cuny.edu

SCHECK, Stephen .... 503-838-8271.. 396 E
schecks@wou.edu
SCHECTER, David .... 661-654-6324.... 32 A
dschecter@csub.edu
SCHEDIN, Karen .... 603-897-8516.. 287 F
kschedin@rivier.edu
SCHEER, Cory .... 816-415-7872.. 275 F
scheerc@william.jewell.edu
SCHEER, RuthAnn .... 319-895-4324.. 171 A
rscheer@cornellcollege.edu
SCHEER, Sage, A .... 303-753-6046.... 83 A
sage@rmcad.edu
SCHEERER, Teresa .... 215-785-0111.. 413 K
SCHEESSELE, Marc .... 314-977-4132.. 271 K
mscheess@slu.edu
SCHEETZ, Anita, A .... 406-768-6341.. 276 F
ascheetz@fpcc.edu
SCHEETZ, Charles .... 570-662-4854.. 415 E
cscheetz@mansfield.edu
SCHEETZ, Christine .... 330-490-7102.. 380 J
cscheetz@walsh.edu
SCHEFF, Deborah, M .... 314-977-2802.. 271 K
scheff@slu.edu
SCHEFF, Julie .... 510-666-8248.... 25 D
admissions@aimc.edu
SCHEFFEL, Debora .... 303-963-3147.... 77 I
dscheffel@ccu.edu
SCHEFFEL, Kent .... 618-468-5000.. 145 G
kscheffe@lc.edu
SCHEFFER, James .... 713-529-2778.. 453 U
scheffer@paralegal.edu
SCHEHR, Terra .... 410-617-2271.. 208 G
tschehr@loyola.edu
SCHEIB, Roger .... 620-417-1240.. 184 I
roger.scheib@sccc.edu
SCHEIBEL, Cindy .... 562-902-3390.... 66 A
cindyscheibel@scuhs.edu
SCHEIBMEIR, Monica, S .. 785-670-1526.. 185 H
monica.scheibmeir@washburn.edu
SCHEIDT, Douglas .... 315-386-7202.. 335 B
scheidtd@canton.edu
SCHEIERN, Libby .... 618-374-5147.. 151 E
libby.scheiern@principia.edu
SCHEINBERG, Mark, E ..... 860-727-6757.... 87 H
mscheinberg@goodwin.edu
SCHEINES, Richard .... 412-268-2832.. 400 D
scheines@cmu.edu
SCHEINMAN, Steven, J .... 570-504-7000.. 400 I
sscheinman@tcmc.edu
SCHEIRER, Gwen .... 717-866-5775.. 403 F
gscheirer@evangelical.edu
SCHELCHER, Cindy .... 408-741-2165.... 74 H
cindy.schelcher@wvm.edu
SCHELCHER, Cindy .... 408-741-2165.... 74 H
cindy.schelcher@westvalley.edu
SCHELCHER, Cynthia .... 408-741-2165.... 74 F
cindy_schelcher@wvm.edu
SCHELIN, Kelly .... 510-215-3870.... 41 H
kschelin@contracosta.edu
SCHELINDER, Shawnda ... 320-629-5114.. 251 E
schelinders@pine.edu
SCHELL, John .... 407-823-5711.. 111 E
rick.schell@ucf.edu
SCHELL, Karen .... 518-292-1719.. 327 H
schelk@sage.edu
SCHELL, Michael, J .... 541-885-1452.. 393 G
michael.schell@oit.edu
SCHELL, Randa .... 830-591-2908.. 466 A
rschell@swtjc.edu
SCHELL, Shannon .... 507-453-2743.. 250 C
sschell@southeastmn.edu
SCHELLENBERGER,
Lauren .... 573-288-6429.. 264 F
lschellenberger@culver.edu
SCHELLER, William, L ...... 814-871-7912.. 404 A
scheller002@gannon.edu
SCHELLHASE, Cherea ...... 251-981-3771...... 2 I
cherea.schellhase@columbiasouthern.edu
SCHELLING, Jeffrey .... 815-226-4107.. 152 G
jschelling@rockford.edu
SCHEMENT, Jorge, R .... 848-932-2021.. 295 F
jr.schement@rutgers.edu
SCHEMENT, Jorge, R .... 848-932-2021.. 296 B
jr.schement@oldqueens.rutgers.edu
SCHEMPER, Lugene, L ...... 616-526-6121.. 232 B
lschempe@calvin.edu
SCHENA, Donna .... 240-567-3085.. 209 E
donna.schena@montgomerycollege.edu
SCHENCK, Merlin .... 706-886-6831.. 128 C
mschenck@tfc.edu
SCHENEWERK, Randal ..... 573-875-7256.. 263 F
raschenewerk@ccis.edu
SCHENK, Evelyn .... 989-275-5000.. 236 E
evelyn.schenk@kirtland.edu
SCHENK, Glenn .... 310-287-4579.... 50 E
schenkga@wlac.edu
SCHENK, Kimberely .... 925-969-2036.... 41 I
schenk@dvc.edu
SCHENK, Mark .... 207-834-8646.. 205 B
mark.schenk@maine.edu

SCHENK, Matthew, F .... 757-446-6043.. 489 B
schenkmr@evms.edu
SCHENK, Rebecca, J .... 716-878-4312.. 332 F
schenkrj@buffalostate.edu
SCHENK, Stacy, L .... 814-886-6357.. 411 C
sschenk@mtaloy.edu
SCHENKEL, Beverly, S ..... 660-562-1149.. 269 J
bevs@nwmissouri.edu
SCHENKER, Beth .... 312-922-9012.. 155 F
bschenker@spertus.edu
SCHEPEL, Bill .... 708-239-4805.. 155 M
bill.schepel@trnty.edu
SCHEPENS, Bennett .... 845-675-4543.. 325 G
bennett.schepens@nyack.edu
SCHEPENS, Dona, P .... 845-675-4618.. 325 G
dona.schepens@nyack.edu
SCHEPP, Robina, C .... 212-346-1281.. 325 J
rschepp@pace.edu
SCHER, Anne .... 510-869-6130.... 59 L
ascher@samuelmerritt.edu
SCHERBINSKE, Allen .... 208-732-6600.. 133 E
ascherbinske@csi.edu
SCHERCZINGER, Carol .... 704-216-3923.. 352 G
carol.scherczinger@rccc.edu
SCHERER, Amanda .... 612-330-1720.. 244 I
scherer@augsburg.edu
SCHERER, Dawn .... 310-825-2151.... 69 D
dscherer@conet.ucla.edu
SCHERER, Jean .... 715-346-2123.. 521 C
jscherer@uwsp.edu
SCHERER, Melanie, L ...... 410-777-2237.. 206 B
mlscherer@aacc.edu
SCHERER, Tim .... 989-275-5000.. 236 E
tim.scherer@kirtland.edu
SCHERGER, Celinda .... 419-448-3313.. 378 A
schergercm@tiffin.edu
SCHERI, Jennifer, C .... 815-224-0428.. 143 C
jennifer_scheri@ivcc.edu
SCHERLING, Sarah .... 303-963-3483.... 77 I
sscherling@ccu.edu
SCHERMERHORN,
Donald .... 251-343-8200...... 6 D
donald.schermerhorn@remingtoncollege.edu
SCHERRENS, Maurice, W 803-321-5102.. 431 F
mscherrens@newberry.edu
SCHERTZ, Mary, H .... 574-296-6218.. 158 H
mschertz@ambs.edu
SCHERTZ, Ronald, L .... 401-825-2179.. 425 A
rschertz@ccri.edu
SCHERZER, Karen .... 812-357-6522.. 167 B
kscherzer@saintmeinrad.edu
SCHETTER, Sheila .... 920-693-1238.. 523 E
sheila.schetter@gotoltc.edu
SCHETTINI-LYNCH,
Anne Marie .... 914-633-2480.. 317 B
aschettinilynch@iona.edu
SCHETTLER, Martha, A .... 330-569-5205.. 369 J
shettlerma@hiram.edu
SCHEUERMANN, Aimee ... 317-940-8123.. 159 K
arust@butler.edu
SCHEUERMANN, Joe .... 504-671-5452.. 196 D
jscheu@dcc.edu
SCHEUERMANN,
Rochelle .... 217-732-3168.. 146 A
rscheuermann@lincolnchristian.edu
SCHEULEN, Kathy .... 573-897-5000.. 272 H
SCHEUTZOW, Janice .... 585-389-2310.. 322 D
jscheut1@naz.edu
SCHEWE, Sharon, R .... 651-641-8228.. 246 B
schewe@csp.edu
SCHEXNEIDER, Martha, J 337-421-6925.. 197 B
jo.schexneider@sowela.edu
SCHEXNIDER-FIELDS
Ingenue, S .... 504-520-6209.. 202 C
itschexn@xula.edu
SCHEYETTE, Anna, M ...... 803-777-7886.. 433 F
anna.scheyette@sc.edu
SCHIAVELLI, Mel, D .... 703-323-4291.. 497 H
mschiavelli@nvcc.edu
SCHIAZZA, Douglas, J .... 413-597-3696.. 230 A
douglas.schiazza@williams.edu
SCHIBSTED, Leslie .... 619-594-7299.... 35 A
lschibsted@mail.sdsu.edu
SCHICK, Beth Ann .... 814-871-7659.. 404 A
shick001@gannon.edu
SCHICK, Marvin .... 732-985-6533.. 294 E
SCHICK, Wendell .... 419-227-3141.. 380 A
wschick@unoh.edu
SCHICKLING, William ...... 716-614-5931.. 324 D
bschickling@niagaracc.suny.edu
SCHIDLOW, Daniel, V ...... 215-762-3500.. 402 G
daniel.schidlow@drexelmed.edu
SCHIEBER, Amy, K .... 660-944-2847.. 263 G
aschieber@conception.edu
SCHIEBER, Craig .... 206-239-4500.. 502 D
cschieber@cityu.edu
SCHIEBER, Gary, W .... 816-604-1320.. 267 F
gary.schieber@mcckc.edu
SCHIEBER, Jeanette .... 660-944-2839.. 263 G
jschieber@conception.edu

SCHIEFEN, Kathleen .... 585-345-6975.. 315 C
kmschiefen@genesee.edu
SCHIELE, Evelyn, R .... 847-543-2622.. 138 C
eschiele@clcillinois.edu
SCHIELE, Jerome, H .... 301-860-3705.. 212 D
jschiele@bowiestate.edu
SCHIELKE, Philip .... 512-313-3000.. 455 F
philip.schielke@concordia.edu
SCHIER, DJ .... 716-896-0700.. 339 E
dschier@villa.edu
SCHIERBEEK, Hannah ...... 616-222-3000.. 236 F
hschierbeek@kuyper.edu
SCHIERER, John .... 858-795-5138.... 62 J
jschierer@shpdiscovery.org
SCHIERS, LaMont .... 520-417-4007.... 12 L
schiersl@cochise.edu
SCHIFF, Emanuel .... 845-356-1980.. 326 G
SCHIFF-ABRAMS,
Lindsey .... 661-255-1050.... 30 E
SCHIFFER, Peter, E .... 217-333-0034.. 157 A
pschiffe@illinois.edu
SCHIFFGENS, Hope .... 412-536-1266.. 406 K
hope.schiffgens@laroche.edu
SCHIFFMAN, Alyssa .... 212-879-2528.. 304 I
aschiffm@barnard.edu
SCHIFFMAN, Jeffrey .... 504-865-5000.. 200 C
jschiffm@tulane.edu
SCHIFFMAN, Robyn, L ..... 815-224-0433.. 143 C
robyn_schiffman@ivcc.edu
SCHIFFNER, Carli .... 509-682-6605.. 509 D
cschiffner@wvc.edu
SCHIFINO, Charlie .... 401-874-2611.. 426 D
cschifino@uri.edu
SCHILL, Michael, H .... 541-346-3036.. 395 G
pres@uoregon.edu
SCHILLER, Elizabeth, N .... 207-859-4622.. 202 G
enschill@colby.edu
SCHILLER, Teri .... 845-352-3431.. 341 D
tschiller@yst.edu
SCHILLER, Timothy .... 314-773-0083.. 262 J
SCHILLING, Denise .... 909-469-5294.... 74 K
dschilling@westernu.edu
SCHILLING, Michael .... 530-898-6209.... 32 C
mlschilling@csuchico.edu
SCHILLING, Steve .... 541-245-7802.. 394 J
sschilling@roguecc.edu
SCHILLINGER, Don, N ..... 318-257-3712.. 200 G
dschill@latech.edu
SCHILT, Louis, J .... 480-212-1704.... 16 R
SCHIMEK, Gwendolyn ...... 319-895-4234.. 171 A
gschimek@cornellcollege.edu
SCHIMELFINIG,
Marianne .... 610-660-3140.. 418 G
mschimel@sju.edu
SCHIMER, Maria, R .... 330-325-6354.. 373 H
maria@neomed.edu
SCHIMMEL, Kari .... 309-694-5590.. 141 F
kari.schimmel@icc.edu
SCHIMPF, Martin, E .... 208-426-1202.. 132 I
mschimpf@boisestate.edu
SCHINDLER, Gary .... 507-433-0829.. 251 H
gary.schindler@riverland.edu
SCHINDLER, Kerry .... 254-965-8875.. 463 K
kschindler@rangercollege.edu
SCHINDLER, Scott .... 706-419-1659.. 119 G
scott.schindler@covenant.edu
SCHION, Donna .... 409-984-6101.. 471 C
donna.schion@lamarpa.edu
SCHIPANI, Pamela .... 860-486-2926.... 89 D
p.schipani@uconn.edu
SCHIPPER, Chris .... 505-566-3449.. 301 J
schipperc@sanjuancollege.edu
SCHIPPER, William .... 703-942-6200.. 486 F
SCHIPPOREIT, Kim .... 308-865-8527.. 282 L
schipporeitk@unk.edu
SCHIRER-SUTER, Myron .. 978-867-4419.. 219 A
myron.schirer-suter@gordon.edu
SCHIRMER, Barbara .... 518-454-5160.. 311 B
schirmeb@strose.edu
SCHISSLER, John .... 330-490-7263.. 380 J
jschissler@walsh.edu
SCHISSLER, Kathy .... 303-914-6214.... 82 I
kathy.schissler@rrcc.edu
SCHISSLER, Stephen .... 419-530-5812.. 380 D
stephen.schissler@utoledo.edu
SCHIWIETZ, Michelle, B .. 214-887-5002.. 457 C
mschiwietz@dts.edu
SCHLABRA, Michael .... 914-337-9300.. 311 F
michael.schlabra@concordia-ny.edu
SCHLACHTER, John .... 812-357-6142.. 167 B
jschlachter@saintmeinrad.edu
SCHLACHTER, Stephany .. 815-836-5639.. 145 H
schlacst@lewisu.edu
SCHLACK, Marilyn, J .... 269-488-4200.. 235 I
mschlack@kvcc.edu
SCHLAG, Kevin .... 808-675-3735.. 130 E
kevin@byuh.edu
SCHLAGEL, Rosanna .... 360-736-9391.. 502 A
rschlagel@centralia.edu
SCHLAK, Timothy, M .... 412-397-6868.. 418 B
schlak@rmu.edu

SCHLAM, Elisheva 646-565-6000 337 I
elisheva.schlam@touro.edu
SCHLAPP, Andrew 316-978-3001 185 J
andy.schlapp@wichita.edu
SCHLARB, Mary 607-753-2209 333 A
mary.schlarb@cortland.edu
SCHLATER, Nicole 315-498-2581 325 G
schlaten@sunyocc.edu
SCHLATHER,
Mary Margaret 540-338-2700 510 H
srschlather@cdu.edu
SCHLATTER, Andy 802-440-4439 483 E
aschlatter@bennington.edu
SCHLATTER, Stephanie 818-710-4228 50 A
schleiss@piercecollege.edu
SCHLATTER, Thomas 732-247-5241 293 B
tschlatter@nbts.edu
SCHLAUCH, Erin 870-733-6790 19 A
egschlauch@asumidsouth.edu
SCHLECHTE, Dawn 217-234-5210 145 D
dschlechte@lakeland.cc.il.us
SCHLECT, Brenda 208-882-1566 134 B
bschlect@nsa.edu
SCHLECT, Christopher 208-882-1566 134 B
cschlect@nsa.edu
SCHLEGEL, Alice 509-542-4823 502 G
aschlegel@columbiabasin.edu
SCHLEGEL, Len 518-262-2929 303 E
schlegl@mail.amc.edu
SCHLEGEL, Natalie 781-891-3474 215 F
nschlegel@bentley.edu
SCHLEICH, David, J 503-552-1702 392 H
president@nunm.edu
SCHLEICH, Tamatha 309-649-6632 155 G
tamatha.schleich@src.edu
SCHLEICHER, Julie 781-239-3053 223 F
jschleicher@massbay.edu
SCHLEICHER, Rolf 818-710-4142 50 A
schleir@piercecollege.edu
SCHLEIFFER, Richard 214-698-0461 456 E
ecc5100@dcccd.edu
SCHLENBECKER, Darlene 847-925-6008 141 A
dschlenb@harpercollege.edu
SCHLENKER, Steven 215-702-4340 399 E
sschlenker@cairn.edu
SCHLESINGER, Ed 410-516-7134 208 D
tschles4@jhu.edu
SCHLESINGER, Kenneth 718-960-8000 308 B
kenneth.schlesinger@lehman.cuny.edu
SCHLESINGER, Patrick 510-642-2866 68 M
pschlesinger@berkeley.edu
SCHLESSELMAN, Beth 800-962-7682 275 D
bschlesselman@wma.edu
SCHLEY, Alisa, S 715-833-6266 523 B
ahoepner1@cvtc.edu
SCHLICHT, Terri 913-469-8500 182 A
tschlich@jccc.edu
SCHLICKMANN, Paul 860-832-3038 85 F
paulschlickmann@ccsu.edu
SCHLIENTZ, Matt 517-607-2745 235 E
mschlientz@hillsdale.edu
SCHLIMGEN, Matt 317-931-2382 160 B
mschlimgen@cts.edu
SCHLIMM, Katina 859-371-9393 186 M
SCHLIMPERT, Charles, E 503-280-8509 391 A
cschlimpert@cu-portland.edu
SCHLINGMANN, Dirk 864-503-5663 434 G
dschlingmann@uscupstate.edu
SCHLINSOG, Anthony 800-955-2527 181 D
aschlinsog@grantham.edu
SCHLISSEL, Mark, S 734-764-6270 241 J
presoff@umich.edu
SCHLOBOHM, Melissa 802-831-1339 485 F
mschlobohm@vermontlaw.edu
SCHLOEMANN, Carolyn 217-206-6724 156 G
ccima1@uis.edu
SCHLOER, Wolfgang 269-387-5890 243 H
wolfgang.schloer@wmich.edu
SCHLOESSER, Brad 507-389-7263 252 D
brad.schloesser@southcentral.edu
SCHLOESSER, Deann 507-389-7354 252 D
deann.schloesser@southcentral.edu
SCHLOSSER, David 610-225-5721 403 B
dschloss@eastern.edu
SCHLOSSER-BACON,
Angela 616-632-2860 231 A
schloang@aquinas.edu
SCHLOSSMAN, Paul 818-240-1000 45 A
pschloss@glendale.edu
SCHLOTTER, Pat 970-223-2669 80 K
pschlotter@ibmc.edu
SCHLOTTHAUER, Scott 405-744-5984 385 G
scott.schlotthauer@okstate.edu
SCHLUESSLER, Linnea 218-683-8560 251 C
linnea.schluessler@northlandcollege.edu
SCHLUETER, Amy 303-373-2008 83 B
aschlueter@rvu.edu
SCHLUETER, Carol, J 504-865-5722 200 C
cjs@tulane.edu
SCHLUETER, Margie 763-433-1119 248 K
margie.schlueter@anokaramsey.edu
SCHLUETER, Margie 763-433-1119 248 L
margie.schlueter@anokaramsey.edu
SCHLUGE, Daniel 317-738-8026 160 J
dschluge@franklincollege.edu
SCHLUTERMAN, Karen 479-979-1224 24 I
kschlut@ozarks.edu
SCHLUTT, Fred 907-474-7246 10 G
efschluttjr@alaska.edu
SCHMADER, Kelly, J 310-206-4181 69 D
kschmader@facnet.ucla.edu
SCHMAEF, Robert 800-290-4226 440 G
rschmaef@hchs.edu
SCHMAILZL, Randy 402-457-2415 280 J
rschmailzl@mccneb.edu
SCHMAL, Daniel 414-443-8875 522 P
dan.schmal@wlc.edu
SCHMALENBERG, Kate 218-793-2401 251 C
kate.schmalenberg@northlandcollege.edu
SCHMALL, Steve 507-285-7214 251 I
steve.schmall@rctc.edu
SCHMALTZ, John 860-768-7987 89 G
schmaltz@hartford.edu
SCHMALTZ, Michael 574-239-8362 161 N
mschmaltz@hcc-nd.edu
SCHMEER, Mary 318-342-5259 201 E
schmeer@ulm.edu
SCHMEISER, Monte 310-377-5501 51 G
mschmeiser@marymountcalifornia.edu
SCHMELCZER, Moshe 773-463-7738 155 J
menahel@telshe.edu
SCHMELZER, Judy 954-201-7458 96 I
jschmelzer@broward.edu
SCHMERSAL, Cindy 816-501-4303 270 J
cindy.schmersal@rockhurst.edu
SCHMID, Albertha 405-457-2354 280 J
acschmid@mccneb.edu
SCHMID, Gary 414-443-8821 522 P
gary.schmid@wlc.edu
SCHMID, Mark, A 312-595-1006 156 D
mschmid@inv.uchicago.edu
SCHMID, Patti, A 856-691-8600 290 I
paschmid@cccnj.edu
SCHMIDLI, Troy 517-265-5161 230 D
SCHMIDLKOFER,
Katherine 612-624-2854 255 H
kms@umn.edu
SCHMIDT, Amber 605-256-5079 437 C
amber.schmidt@dsu.edu
SCHMIDT, Amy 608-785-9139 524 H
schmidta@westerntc.edu
SCHMIDT, Andrew 678-407-5000 121 B
aschmidt@ggc.edu
SCHMIDT, Betsy 317-738-8054 160 J
bschmidt@franklincollege.edu
SCHMIDT, Brian 503-375-7199 391 B
brian@corban.edu
SCHMIDT, Christopher 270-384-8136 191 E
schmidtc@lindsey.edu
SCHMIDT, Chuck 509-542-4747 502 G
cschmidt@columbiabasin.edu
SCHMIDT, Craig, D 708-709-3953 151 C
cschmidt@prairiestate.edu
SCHMIDT, Curt 612-659-6902 250 B
curt.schmidt@minneapolis.edu
SCHMIDT, Dan 701-224-5735 361 C
daniel.j.schmidt@bismarckstate.edu
SCHMIDT, David 620-450-2188 184 D
davids@prattcc.edu
SCHMIDT, David, O 701-777-4151 360 C
david.schmidt@research.und.edu
SCHMIDT, Denise 973-328-5245 290 H
dschmidt@ccm.edu
SCHMIDT, Donald 815-479-7796 147 E
dschmidt@mchenry.edu
SCHMIDT, Douglas 845-574-4572 327 G
dschmidt@sunyrockland.edu
SCHMIDT, Ellen 217-373-3789 151 B
eschmidt@parkland.edu
SCHMIDT, Eric, R 608-796-3017 522 O
eschmidt@viterbo.edu
SCHMIDT, Harry, R 847-259-1840 137 B
hschmidt@christianlifecollege.edu
SCHMIDT, Jacqueline 815-836-5442 145 H
schmidjc@lewisu.edu
SCHMIDT, Jacqueline 212-799-5000 318 A
SCHMIDT, James, C 715-836-2327 520 A
jschmidt@uwec.edu
SCHMIDT, James, W 312-996-2695 156 F
jschmidt@uic.edu
SCHMIDT, Jane 316-284-5364 179 A
jschmidt@bethelks.edu
SCHMIDT, Janice 801-957-4227 483 A
janice.schmidt@slcc.edu
SCHMIDT, Jeffrey 410-704-3414 213 B
jschmidt@towson.edu
SCHMIDT, John 216-987-2942 367 E
john.schmidt@tri-c.edu
SCHMIDT, Jolene 515-271-3957 171 K
jolene.schmidt@drake.edu
SCHMIDT, Jona, M 605-256-5857 437 C
jona.schmidt@dsu.edu
SCHMIDT, Julie 402-826-8200 280 B
julie.schmidt@doane.edu
SCHMIDT, Karen 309-556-3834 143 D
kschmidt@iwu.edu
SCHMIDT, Karen 847-543-2640 138 C
kschmidtl@clcillinois.edu
SCHMIDT, Kaye 828-398-7113 347 D
kayenschmidt@abtech.edu
SCHMIDT, Keith, E 712-749-2230 170 D
schmidt@bvu.edu
SCHMIDT, Leslie 406-994-2381 277 C
lschmidt@montana.edu
SCHMIDT, Linda 856-222-9311 295 C
lschmidt@rcbc.edu
SCHMIDT, London 910-755-8393 347 H
schmidtl@brunswickcc.edu
SCHMIDT, Lynn 765-641-4388 158 J
lmschmidt@anderson.edu
SCHMIDT, Martin 617-253-4500 225 A
SCHMIDT, Maynard 845-341-4205 325 H
maynard.schmidt@sunyorange.edu
SCHMIDT, Paul 864-503-5036 434 G
pschmidt@uscupstate.edu
SCHMIDT, Penelope 229-293-6190 130 A
penelope.schmidt@wiregrass.edu
SCHMIDT, Rachel 216-687-5594 366 I
r.m.schmidt@csuohio.edu
SCHMIDT, Rachelle 651-846-1348 252 C
rachelle.schmidt@saintpaul.edu
SCHMIDT, Rachelle, M 651-846-1348 252 C
rachelle.schmidt@saintpaul.edu
SCHMIDT, Shana 715-833-6410 523 B
sschmidt42@cvtc.edu
SCHMIDT, Soren 906-487-7239 234 A
soren.schmidt@finlandia.edu
SCHMIDT, Susan 712-324-5061 175 G
sschmidt@nwicc.edu
SCHMIDT, Tania 507-457-2800 252 G
tschmidt@winona.edu
SCHMIDT CAMPBELL,
Mary 404-681-3643 128 A
mscampbell@spelman.edu
SCHMIDT-ROGERS,
Debrah 773-508-3300 146 G
dschmi6@luc.edu
SCHMIECHEN, Tim 608-363-2296 515 G
schmiech@beloit.edu
SCHMIEDE, Angela 800-556-3656 52 D
angela.schmiede@menlo.edu
SCHMIEDEL, Mary, E 202-687-3911 92 E
schmiedm@georgetown.edu
SCHMIEDL, Bruce 630-942-2972 138 B
schmiedlb@cod.edu
SCHMIEDL, Joe 808-544-1105 130 H
jschmiedl@hpu.edu
SCHMIEG, Rose, A 540-665-5534 494 B
rschmieg@su.edu
SCHMIESING, Ann 303-492-2890 83 K
ann.schmiesing@colorado.edu
SCHMIESING, David, A 740-284-6513 368 L
dschmiesing@franciscan.edu
SCHMILL, Stuart 617-258-5514 225 A
SCHMISEK, Brian 312-915-7400 146 G
bschmisek@luc.edu
SCHMIT, Harvey 734-995-7527 232 I
harvey.schmit@cuaa.edu
SCHMIT, Matt 563-336-3300 172 A
mschmit@eicc.edu
SCHMIT, Matt 563-441-4125 172 D
mschmit@eicc.edu
SCHMIT, Michaeline 920-498-7106 524 E
michaeline.schmit@nwtc.edu
SCHMIT, Shelly, M 641-422-4211 175 E
schmishe@niacc.edu
SCHMITT, Barbara, L 570-348-6225 409 H
schmitt@marywood.edu
SCHMITT, Deb 574-520-4398 163 E
dsschmit@iusb.edu
SCHMITT, Deborah 719-549-3175 82 G
deborah.schmitt@pueblocc.edu
SCHMITT, Deborah, F 716-851-1270 313 H
schmitt@ecc.edu
SCHMITT, Dorothy, M 718-990-6384 328 F
schmittd@stjohns.edu
SCHMITT, Karen 907-796-6531 10 H
kschmitt@alaska.edu
SCHMITT, Karen 907-796-6518 10 H
kschmitt@alaska.edu
SCHMITT, Linda 908-821-9701 294 B
lschmitt@pillar.edu
SCHMITT, Mark 315-464-4538 332 C
schmittm@upstate.edu
SCHMITT, Mark 520-515-5478 12 L
schmittm@cochise.edu
SCHMITT, Neal 517-355-6675 237 I
schmitt@msu.edu
SCHMITT, Patrick 408-741-2011 74 F
patrick.schmitt@wvm.edu
SCHMITT, Stacy, C 336-318-0025 352 B
scschmitt@randolph.edu
SCHMITTENDORF, Susan 716-270-5139 313 H
ascschmittendorfs@ecc.edu
SCHMITTLEIN, David, C 617-253-2804 225 A
SCHMITTMANN, Beate 515-294-3220 169 G
schmittb@iastate.edu
SCHMITTOU, Natasha 210-486-2339 450 E
nschmittou@alamo.edu
SCHMITZ, Chris 704-971-8500 343 E
cschmitz@charlottelaw.edu
SCHMITZ, Cody 740-284-5240 368 L
cschmitz@franciscan.edu
SCHMITZ, Donna 701-252-3467 362 F
dschmitz@uj.edu
SCHMITZ, Nancy, A 248-370-3352 239 K
schmitz@oakland.edu
SCHMITZ, Polly 516-877-3156 303 B
pschmitz@adelphi.edu
SCHMITZ, Stevie 406-657-1134 278 D
schmitzs@rocky.edu
SCHMITZ, Todd 812-856-1214 162 F
schmitz@iu.edu
SCHMITZ, William 718-636-3542 326 E
wschmitz@pratt.edu
SCHMOKE, Kurt, L 410-837-4866 213 C
president@ubalt.edu
SCHMOLL, Claire, B 207-786-6100 202 D
cschmoll@bates.edu
SCHMOLL, Kevin 618-650-3324 155 A
kschmol@siue.edu
SCHMOLL, Robert 724-589-2102 420 D
rschmoll@thiel.edu
SCHMOOCK, Allen 208-792-2215 134 A
atschmoock@lcsc.edu
SCHMOTZER, Mark 516-299-3547 319 B
mark.schmotzer@liu.edu
SCHMUCKER, Angie 248-364-6252 239 K
schmucke@oakland.edu
SCHMUDE, Michelle 570-504-9691 400 I
mschmude@tcmc.edu
SCHMUTTE, Gregory, T 413-205-3364 214 B
gregory.schmutte@aic.edu
SCHMUTZ, Betsy 314-968-6960 275 B
schmutz@webster.edu
SCHNABEL, William 907-474-6222 10 G
weschnabel@alaska.edu
SCHNABL, JC 413-545-5542 220 F
schnabl@admin.umass.edu
SCHNACK, Darcy 845-938-4379 529 C
8uscc@usma.edu
SCHNACK, Laura, L 309-794-7533 135 D
lauraschnack@augustana.edu
SCHNAIDMAN, Yaakov 570-346-1747 424 E
SCHNALL, David, J 212-340-7705 341 G
dschnall@yu.edu
SCHNAPP, Derek 217-206-7823 156 G
schnapp.derek@uis.edu
SCHNARR, Carmin, A 812-888-4332 169 A
cschnarr@vinu.edu
SCHNATZ, Kristofer 219-980-6793 163 B
kschnatz@iun.edu
SCHNEFKE, Emilee 314-421-0949 272 J
eschnefke@siba.edu
SCHNEID, Thomas, R 210-808-4492 528 G
thomas.schneid@usuhs.edu
SCHNEIDER, Amye 620-792-9302 178 G
schneidera@bartonccc.edu
SCHNEIDER, Andrew 251-981-3771 2 I
andrew.schneider@columbiasouthern.edu
SCHNEIDER, Angela 510-885-3000 32 E
SCHNEIDER, Brandt, L 806-743-2556 472 D
brandt.schneider@ttuhsc.edu
SCHNEIDER, Carrie 651-423-8244 249 B
carrie.schneider@dctc.edu
SCHNEIDER, Chad 740-389-4636 372 B
schneiderc@mtc.edu
SCHNEIDER, Colleen 785-841-9640 184 B
cschneider@pcitraining.edu
SCHNEIDER, David 614-823-1240 376 C
dschneider@otterbein.edu
SCHNEIDER, Deb 415-749-4587 61 B
dschneider@sfai.edu
SCHNEIDER, Debbie 314-531-7925 271 K
bksustlouis@bncollege.com
SCHNEIDER, Dona 848-932-2945 296 B
donas@rci.rutgers.edu
SCHNEIDER, Greg 913-288-7155 182 C
gschneid@kckcc.edu
SCHNEIDER, Helen 410-617-2995 208 G
hschneider@loyola.edu
SCHNEIDER, Howard 631-632-6265 332 A
howard.schneider@stonybrook.edu
SCHNEIDER, Jed, S 315-445-4500 318 E
schneij@lemoyne.edu
SCHNEIDER, Joan 660-562-1250 269 J
jschneider@nwmissouri.edu
SCHNEIDER, Joanne 315-228-7362 310 G
jschneider@colgate.edu
SCHNEIDER, Karen 707-664-4004 35 D
karen.schneider@sonoma.edu
SCHNEIDER, Kay 303-273-3087 78 M
kschnei@mines.edu

SCHROEDER, Stephanie ... 570-961-4161.... 16 C
stephanie.schroeder@pennfoster.edu
SCHROEDER, Stephanie ... 320-629-5126.. 251 E
schroeders@pine.edu
SCHROEDER, Stephen, C 727-816-3403.. 106 F
schroes@phsc.edu
SCHROEDER, Steven ... 414-443-8601.. 522 P
steve.schroeder@wlc.edu
SCHROEDER, Tracy ... 617-353-1150.. 216 E
tas@bu.edu
SCHROEDER-BIEK, Julie .. 574-284-4333.. 167 A
jsbiek@saintmarys.edu
SCHROER, Tara ... 785-460-5487.. 180 C
tara.schroer@colbycc.edu
SCHROER, Timothy ... 507-786-3615.. 254 P
schroert@stolaf.edu
SCHROTE, James, D ... 202-994-0543.... 92 D
jschrote@gwu.edu
SCHRUM, Jake, B ... 276-944-6107.. 489 I
jschrum@ehc.edu
SCHRUM, Lynne ... 954-262-8730.. 105 J
lschrum@nova.edu
SCHRUM, Mindi-Kim ... 505-566-3261.. 301 J
schrumm@sanjuancollege.edu
SCHUBERT, Donna ... 334-670-5830...... 7 H
schubert@troy.edu
SCHUBERT, Marianne, A . 336-758-5273.. 359 E
schubem@wfu.edu
SCHUBERT, Phil ... 325-674-2412.. 449 J
schubert@acu.edu
SCHUCH, Debra ... 717-299-7408.. 420 C
schuch@stevenscollege.edu
SCHUCHARDT, Bob ... 605-229-8406.. 436 H
bob.schuchardt@presentation.edu
SCHUCHARDT, Maureen .. 605-229-8427.. 436 H
maureen.schuchardt@presentation.edu
SCHUCHERT, Michael ... 703-284-3810.. 492 A
michael.schuchert@marymount.edu
SCHUCK, Emily, G ... 740-376-4712.. 372 A
schucke@marietta.edu
SCHUCKEL, Harry ... 410-837-4743.. 213 C
hschuckel@ubalt.edu
SCHUCKER, Julie ... 716-614-6251.. 324 D
jschucker@niagaracc.suny.edu
SCHUCKMAN, Amy ... 503-517-7834.. 394 I
schuckma@reed.edu
SCHUELKE, Mark ... 231-591-5916.. 233 L
markschuelke@ferris.edu
SCHUELKE, Nicholle ... 605-331-6765.. 438 A
nicholle.schuelke@usiouxfalls.edu
SCHUELLER, Kenneth ... 660-543-4721.. 273 C
schueller@ucmo.edu
SCHUEMANN, Kahler, B .. 269-387-2360.. 243 H
kahler.schuemann@wmich.edu
SCHUENAMAN, Bruce, R . 361-593-3528.. 469 A
brs@tamuk.edu
SCHUEREN, Monika ... 516-686-7615.. 323 G
mschuere@nyit.edu
SCHUERMER, David, A ... 270-824-8633.. 190 B
david.schuermer@kctcs.edu
SCHUESSLER, Jennifer ... 678-839-5640.. 129 E
jschuess@westga.edu
SCHUESSLER, Nicole ... 619-260-7408.... 72 B
nschuessler@sandiego.edu
SCHUETTE, Jan ... 323-856-7741.... 26 I
schuette@afi.com
SCHUETTE, Stefani, M ... 636-949-4900.. 266 J
sschuette@lindenwood.edu
SCHUETZ, Bill ... 541-463-3355.. 391 G
schuetzb@lanecc.edu
SCHUETZ, Gina ... 618-545-3099.. 144 D
gschuetz@kaskaskia.edu
SCHUH, Jane ... 701-231-8804.. 361 A
jane.schuh@ndsu.edu
SCHUH, Mary Paula ... 859-572-5122.. 192 B
schuh@nku.edu
SCHUHERT, Scott ... 607-778-5681.. 332 D
schuhertsm@sunybroome.edu
SCHUHMANN, Richard, J 207-985-7976.. 203 E
schuhmann@landingschool.edu
SCHUILING, Kerri ... 906-227-2920.. 239 B
kschuili@nmu.edu
SCHUKEI, Chris ... 402-461-7341.. 280 D
cschukei@hastings.edu
SCHULER, Jill ... 502-447-1000.. 192 G
jschuler@spencerian.edu
SCHULER, Nathan ... 513-875-3344.. 365 K
nathan.schuler@chatfield.edu
SCHULGASSER,
Binyomin ... 732-367-7604.. 298 H
SCHULGASSER, Nosson .. 732-367-7604.. 298 H
SCHULL, Gail ... 208-732-6232.. 133 E
gschull@csi.edu
SCHULLER, Aimee ... 330-823-2755.. 379 F
schullal@mountunion.edu
SCHULLER, Jennifer ... 330-569-5839.. 369 J
schullerjn@hiram.edu
SCHULMAN, Avrohom ... 908-354-6057.. 299 A
SCHULMAN, Jane ... 718-482-5302.. 309 A
janes@lagcc.cuny.edu
SCHULMAN, Jeffrey, L ... 802-656-3075.. 485 D
jeffrey.schulman@uvm.edu
SCHULMAN, Mark ... 415-561-6555.... 58 C
mark.schulman@presidio.edu
SCHULMAN, Sharon ... 609-626-3541.. 297 C
sharon.schulman@stockton.edu
SCHULT, Larry ... 231-591-2829.. 233 L
larryschult@ferris.edu
SCHULT, Richard ... 310-377-5501.... 51 G
mschult@marymountcalifornia.edu
SCHULT, Robert, W ... 909-621-8025.... 38 I
rwschult@cgu.edu
SCHULTE, Brandy ... 660-831-4108.. 269 B
schulteb@moval.edu
SCHULTE, Cynthia ... 641-844-5602.. 173 J
cindy.schulte@iavalley.edu
SCHULTE, David ... 636-922-8636.. 271 A
dschulte@stchas.edu
SCHULTE, Gerald ... 218-683-8557.. 251 C
gerald.schulte@northlandcollege.edu
SCHULTE, Kristi ... 940-397-4427.. 462 A
kristi.schulte@mwsu.edu
SCHULTE, Mary ... 618-468-3300.. 145 G
mschulte@lc.edu
SCHULTE, Nancy ... 540-665-4530.. 494 B
nschulte@su.edu
SCHULTE, Priscilla ... 907-228-4548.... 10 H
pmschulet@alaska.edu
SCHULTE, R. Gregg ... 706-886-6831.. 128 C
gschulte@tfc.edu
SCHULTE, Tim ... 660-831-4148.. 269 B
schultet@moval.edu
SCHULTE, Vickie ... 618-437-5321.. 152 A
schultev@rlc.edu
SCHULTE-SHOBERG, Kim 715-232-1285.. 521 D
schulteshobergk@uwstout.edu
SCHULTHEIS, Keri ... 904-256-7551.. 103 D
kschult5@ju.edu
SCHULTHEIS, Luke, D ... 804-827-8737.. 496 D
ldschultheis@vcu.edu
SCHULTHEIS, Stephen ... 678-466-4070.. 119 A
stephenschultheis@clayton.edu
SCHULTHEISS, Donna ... 216-687-9387.. 366 I
d.schultheiss@csuohio.edu
SCHULTINGKEMPER,
Kathy ... 910-323-5614.. 342 H
registrar@ccbs.edu
SCHULTIS, Ann ... 816-584-6704.. 270 D
ann.schultis@park.edu
SCHULTZ, Amber ... 320-308-3870.. 252 A
amschultz@stcloudstate.edu
SCHULTZ, Barb ... 563-425-5283.. 177 D
schultzb@uiu.edu
SCHULTZ, Barry ... 901-572-2500.. 438 I
barry.schultz@bchs.edu
SCHULTZ, Bruce ... 907-786-6108.... 10 F
brschultz@uaa.alaska.edu
SCHULTZ, Christina ... 480-731-8558.... 13 N
christina.schultz@domail.maricopa.edu
SCHULTZ, David ... 940-565-3940.. 475 A
david.schultz@unt.edu
SCHULTZ, Eric ... 605-882-5284.. 436 B
eric.schultz@lakeareatech.edu
SCHULTZ, Jennifer, A ... 815-835-6405.. 153 K
jennifer.a.schultz@svcc.edu
SCHULTZ, Jonathan ... 972-279-6511.. 450 I
jschultz@amberton.edu
SCHULTZ, Joseph, P ... 607-777-2187.. 331 B
jschultz@binghamton.edu
SCHULTZ, Justin ... 650-949-7200.... 44 B
schultzjustin@foothill.edu
SCHULTZ, Kelly ... 814-868-9900.. 403 D
schultzk@erieit.edu
SCHULTZ, Kevin, J ... 989-964-4049.. 240 F
kschultz@svsu.edu
SCHULTZ, Laura ... 845-257-3105.. 331 E
schultzl@newpaltz.edu
SCHULTZ, Linda ... 860-768-4169.... 89 G
schultz@hartford.edu
SCHULTZ, Michael ... 903-233-4441.. 460 J
michaelschultz@letu.edu
SCHULTZ, Michael, J ... 618-650-4628.. 155 A
mschult@siue.edu
SCHULTZ, Patrick ... 218-935-0417.. 256 E
patrick.schultz@wetcc.edu
SCHULTZ, Patty ... 218-935-0417.. 256 E
patty.schultz@wetcc.edu
SCHULTZ, Randy ... 661-952-5071.... 32 A
rschultz@csub.edu
SCHULTZ, Robert ... 845-434-5750.. 336 H
rschultz@sullivan.suny.edu
SCHULTZ, Roger, D ... 434-592-4030.. 491 D
rschultz@liberty.edu
SCHULTZ, Roger, W ... 951-487-3002.... 53 D
rschultz@msjc.edu
SCHULZ, Christa ... 360-416-7974.. 507 G
christa.schulz@skagit.edu
SCHULZ, Chuck ... 309-341-7205.. 145 A
cschulz@knox.edu
SCHULZ, Greg ... 714-992-7001.... 54 H
gschulz@fullcoll.edu
SCHULZ, Jack ... 701-483-1068.. 360 D
jack.schulz@dickinsonstate.edu
SCHULZ, Jerry ... 541-383-7275.. 390 D
jschulz@cocc.edu
SCHULZ, Karyn ... 410-837-4775.. 213 C
kschulz@ubalt.edu
SCHULZ, Kathy, L ... 201-216-5667.. 297 B
kathy.schulz@stevens.edu
SCHULZ, Kirk ... 509-335-4200.. 508 H
presidentsoffice@wsu.edu
SCHULZ, Michael ... 406-683-7492.. 277 A
mike.schulz@umwestern.edu
SCHULZ, Paul, A ... 914-337-9300.. 311 F
paul.schulz@concordia-ny.edu
SCHULZ, Phyllis ... 212-817-7460.. 308 A
pschulz@gc.cuny.edu
SCHULZ, Robert ... 619-594-5901.... 35 A
rschulz@mail.sdsu.edu
SCHULZ, Scott ... 623-845-3876.... 14 C
scott.schulz@gccaz.edu
SCHULZ, Scott ... 218-726-7171.. 255 D
sschulz1@d.umn.edu
SCHULZ, Scott ... 440-826-6970.. 363 M
saschulz@bw.edu
SCHULZ, Steven, D ... 641-422-4000.. 175 E
schulste@niacc.edu
SCHULZE, Edee ... 805-565-6028.... 75 A
eschulze@westmont.edu
SCHULZE, Lori, A ... 920-748-8310.. 519 E
schulzel@ripon.edu
SCHULZE, Louann, T ... 817-515-1280.. 467 A
louann.schulze@tccd.edu
SCHULZE, Robin, G ... 716-645-2711.. 331 C
cas-dean@buffalo.edu
SCHULZKE, Mario ... 406-243-2323.. 276 K
mario.schulzke@umontana.edu
SCHUM, Jennifer ... 919-530-6658.. 357 A
jschum@nccu.edu
SCHUMACHER, Bett ... 209-946-2314.... 71 C
bschumacher1@pacific.edu
SCHUMACHER, Betty, A .. 701-845-7412.. 361 B
betty.schumacher@vcsu.edu
SCHUMACHER, Bryan, J .. 605-394-2215.. 437 E
bryan.schumacher@sdsmt.edu
SCHUMACHER, Charlotte . 806-291-3549.. 479 D
schumacherc@wbu.edu
SCHUMACHER, Daniel, J . 715-836-5858.. 520 A
schumadj@uwec.edu
SCHUMACHER, Diane, E . 443-518-4522.. 208 C
dschumacher@howardcc.edu
SCHUMACHER, Frank ... 269-749-7668.. 240 A
fschumacher@olivetcollege.edu
SCHUMACHER, Gail ... 847-233-7700.. 150 D
gschumacher@nc.edu
SCHUMACHER, Janette ... 484-664-3180.. 411 D
schumach@muhlenberg.edu
SCHUMACHER, Lauren ... 847-233-7700.. 150 D
lwschumacher@nc.edu
SCHUMACHER, Lawrence 847-233-7700.. 150 D
lschumacher@nc.edu
SCHUMACHER, Lillian ... 419-448-3413.. 378 A
schumacherlb@tiffin.edu
SCHUMACHER,
Mary Jeanne ... 812-357-6501.. 167 B
mschumacher@saintmeinrad.edu
SCHUMACHER,
Mary Jeanne ... 812-357-6808.. 167 B
mschumacher@saintmeinrad.edu
SCHUMACHER, Michele .. 540-831-5434.. 493 A
bov@radford.edu
SCHUMACHER, Scott ... 979-830-4172.. 452 J
scott.schumacher@blinn.edu
SCHUMAKER, Terry, W ... 641-422-4170.. 175 E
schumter@niacc.edu
SCHUMAN, Alan, M ... 410-386-8495.. 206 I
aschuman@carrollcc.edu
SCHUMAN, John ... 205-329-7945...... 3 B
john.schuman@ecacolleges.com
SCHUMAN, Shmuel ... 847-982-2500.. 141 D
schuman@htc.edu
SCHUMANN, James ... 218-477-5869.. 250 F
james.schumann@mnstate.edu
SCHUMANN, Kenneth ... 503-352-2180.. 394 C
schumank@pacificu.edu
SCHUMANN, Patricia, J ... 304-766-3020.. 514 B
pschumann@wvstateu.edu
SCHUMANN, Renae ... 281-649-3300.. 458 L
rschumann@hbu.edu
SCHUMANN, Sherry, L ... 972-758-3880.. 455 A
sschumann@collin.edu
SCHUNK, Jill ... 812-855-5646.. 162 F
jschunk@iu.edu
SCHUPACK, Sara ... 773-481-8810.. 137 I
schupack1@ccc.edu
SCHUPPERT, Cindy ... 503-352-3191.. 394 C
schuppec@pacificu.edu
SCHUR, Jill ... 773-508-7392.. 146 G
jschur@luc.edu
SCHURMAN, Jane ... 610-957-5700.. 401 L
jschurman@dccc.edu
SCHURMAN, Ryan ... 402-552-3390.. 279 D
schurmanryan@clarksoncollege.edu
SCHUSTER, Danny ... 347-619-9074.. 341 H
SCHUSTER, Julian, Z ... 314-246-8242.. 275 B
julianschuster@webster.edu
SCHUSTER, Kristan ... 906-487-7391.. 234 A
kristan.schuster@finlandia.edu
SCHUSTER, Leslie ... 401-456-9723.. 425 E
lschuster@ric.edu
SCHUSTER, Sheldon, M .. 909-607-0108.... 39 B
sheldon_schuster@kgi.edu
SCHUSTER, Stacy ... 609-771-3214.. 290 F
schuster@tcnj.edu
SCHUSTER-MATLOCK,
Tracy ... 563-333-6049.. 176 D
schustertracy@sau.edu
SCHUSTER WEBB, Karen . 937-769-1826.. 363 F
kschusterwebb@antioch.edu
SCHUTH, Kristen ... 585-345-6898.. 315 C
keschuth@genesee.edu
SCHUTT, Michelle ... 208-732-6863.. 133 E
mschutt@csi.edu
SCHUTT, Stephen, D ... 847-735-5100.. 145 B
presiden@lakeforest.edu
SCHUTTE, Thomas, F ... 718-636-3647.. 326 E
tschutte@pratt.edu
SCHUTTEN, Mary ... 408-924-2915.... 35 C
mary.schutten@sjsu.edu
SCHUTZ, Christine ... 208-459-5524.. 133 D
cschutz@collegeofidaho.edu
SCHUTZLER, Lyndon ... 831-646-4221.... 53 A
lschutzler@mpc.edu
SCHUTZMAN, Carissa ... 859-442-1706.. 189 D
carissa.schutzman@kctcs.edu
SCHUYLER, Lori, G ... 804-289-8781.. 495 G
lschuyle@richmond.edu
SCHWAB, Brandon ... 828-227-7495.. 359 A
beschwab@wcu.edu
SCHWAB, Deb ... 715-425-3221.. 521 B
debra.schwab@uwrf.edu
SCHWAB, Mary, S ... 540-828-5487.. 487 H
mschwab@bridgewater.edu
SCHWAB, Nancy ... 916-660-7900.... 64 F
nschwab@sierracollege.edu
SCHWAB, Richard ... 860-486-3813.... 89 D
richard.schwab@uconn.edu
SCHWAB, Steve, J ... 901-448-4796.. 448 H
sschwab@uthsc.edu
SCHWAB, Victoria ... 952-358-8671.. 251 A
victoria.schwab@normandale.edu
SCHWABE, Jean, D ... 478-289-2464.. 120 C
jdschwabe@ega.edu
SCHWABROW, Lynsey ... 262-472-1801.. 521 F
schwabrl@uww.edu
SCHWAGER, Kathleen ... 860-773-1523.... 87 E
kschwager@txcc.commnet.edu
SCHWAIG, Kathy, S ... 470-578-6425.. 123 J
kschwaig@kennesaw.edu
SCHWAIGER, Patsy ... 513-244-4371.. 373 C
patsy.schwaiger@msj.edu
SCHWALBACH, Eileen ... 414-930-3430.. 518 F
schwale@mtmary.edu
SCHWANDT, Doug ... 573-882-6757.. 273 E
schwandtr@missouri.edu
SCHWANKE, Shellie ... 309-467-6316.. 140 E
sschwanke@eureka.edu
SCHWANTZ, Sara ... 217-732-3155.. 146 B
sschwantz@lincolncollege.edu
SCHWARTS, Brett ... 435-652-7593.. 482 A
bschwartz@dixie.edu
SCHWARTZ, Adam ... 515-294-2770.. 169 G
director@ameslab.gov
SCHWARTZ, Alycia ... 570-961-7845.. 407 B
schwartza@lackawanna.edu
SCHWARTZ, Beth ... 419-448-2216.. 369 G
bschwartz@heidelberg.edu
SCHWARTZ, Brian ... 303-373-2008.... 83 B
bschwartz@rvu.edu
SCHWARTZ, Celeste, M ... 215-641-6492.. 410 L
cschwartz@mc3.edu
SCHWARTZ, Corene ... 909-652-6242.... 37 D
cory.schwartz@chaffey.edu
SCHWARTZ, David ... 845-783-9901.. 339 A
utamds@gmail.com
SCHWARTZ, David, J ... 248-370-3465.. 239 K
schwart3@oakland.edu
SCHWARTZ, Doreen ... 847-635-1630.. 150 G
doreen@oakton.edu
SCHWARTZ, Eric ... 612-625-0669.. 255 H
eschwart@umn.edu
SCHWARTZ, Ernest ... 718-384-5460.. 341 A
SCHWARTZ, Gary ... 718-960-6093.. 308 B
gary.schwartz@lehman.cuny.edu
SCHWARTZ, Hayim ... 718-268-4700.. 326 L
SCHWARTZ, Janis ... 973-720-2175.. 298 G
schwartzj@wpunj.edu
SCHWARTZ, Jason ... 801-832-2262.. 483 D
jsj@westminstercollege.edu
SCHWARTZ, Jeff ... 941-351-5100.. 107 M
jschwartz@ringling.edu

SCHWARTZ, Jennifer .... 317-955-6056.. 165 N
jschwartz@marian.edu

SCHWARTZ, Jennifer .... 805-922-6966.... 25 I
jennifer.schwartz@hancockcollege.edu

SCHWARTZ, Jessica .... 715-833-6256.. 523 B
jschwartz31@cvtc.edu

SCHWARTZ, Joel, D .... 757-221-2460.. 488 F
jxschw@wm.edu

SCHWARTZ, Kenneth .... 504-865-5389.. 200 C
kschwartz@tulane.edu

SCHWARTZ, Lance, W ..... 507-344-7427.. 244 K
lance.schwartz@blc.edu

SCHWARTZ, Laura .... 707-638-5824.... 68 C
laura.schwartz@tu.edu

SCHWARTZ, Mark .... 610-359-5082.. 401 L
mschwartz@dccc.edu

SCHWARTZ, Mary, L .... 301-295-3013.. 528 G
mary.schwartz.ctr@usuhs.edu

SCHWARTZ, Mary Beth ... 803-327-8042.. 435 D
mbschwartz@yorktech.edu

SCHWARTZ, Matthew, J .. 812-888-5832.. 169 A
mschwartz@vinu.edu

SCHWARTZ, Rachel .... 912-478-0049.. 122 B
rschwartz@georgiasouthern.edu

SCHWARTZ, Randi, D ...... 914-594-4900.. 323 I
randi_schwartz@nymc.edu

SCHWARTZ, Robert .... 206-296-5831.. 507 E
schwartr@seattleu.edu

SCHWARTZ, Robert, W .... 573-882-2011.. 273 D
schwartzrob@umsystem.edu

SCHWARTZ, Sandor .... 718-963-1212.. 318 B
kyrs@thejnet.com

SCHWARTZ, Shari, P .... 404-413-2273.. 122 D
spiotrowski@gsu.edu

SCHWARTZ, Shuly .... 212-678-8826.. 317 I
shschwartz@jtsa.edu

SCHWARTZ, Steven .... 212-938-5712.. 334 F
sschwartz@sunyopt.edu

SCHWARTZ, Steven, J ..... 970-247-7196.... 80 D
schwartz_s@fortlewis.edu

SCHWARTZ, Teri .... 310-825-7891.... 69 D
tschwartz@tft.ucla.edu

SCHWARTZ, Terry .... 719-255-3121.... 83 L
tschwart@uccs.edu

SCHWARTZE, Derek .... 573-681-5515.. 266 I
schwartzed@lincolnu.edu

SCHWARTZE, Mary .... 432-837-8203.. 471 E
mschwartze@sulross.edu

SCHWARTZMAN,
Michael .... 215-596-8855.. 422 A
m.schwartman@usciences.edu

SCHWARZ, Felipe .... 978-837-5459.. 225 E
schwarzf@merrimack.edu

SCHWARZ, Marilyn .... 508-387-7231.. 384 D
mschwarz@mscok.edu

SCHWARZ, May, L .... 614-235-4136.. 378 C
mschwarz@tlsohio.edu

SCHWARZ, Steven .... 718-997-5903.. 309 D
steven.schwarz@qc.cuny.edu

SCHWARZ, Susan .... 619-644-7155.... 45 J
susan.schwarz@gcccd.edu

SCHWARZ, Thomas, J ...... 914-251-6010.. 334 C
thomas.schwarz@purchase.edu

SCHWARZ, Todd .... 208-732-6325.. 133 E
tschwarz@csi.edu

SCHWARZKOPF, David ..... 781-891-2783.. 215 F
dschwarzkopf@bentley.edu

SCHWEBEL, Lisa .... 718-951-4771.. 307 D
lisas@brooklyn.cuny.edu

SCHWEIBENZ, Donna .... 215-204-8106.. 420 B
donna.schweibenz@temple.edu

SCHWEIGER, Danielle .... 316-677-9400.. 185 I
dschweiger@watc.edu

SCHWEIGERT, Francis ...... 651-793-1300.. 250 A
francis.schweigert@metrostate.edu

SCHWEIGERT, Rich .... 303-534-6290.... 78 P
rich.schweigert@colostate.edu

SCHWEINFEST, Michael ... 513-569-1586.. 366 D
michael.schweinfest@cincinnatistate.edu

SCHWEITZER, Carrie .... 972-860-4848.. 456 B
cschweitzer@dcccd.edu

SCHWEITZER, Connie, J .. 989-964-4160.. 240 F
schw@svsu.edu

SCHWEITZER, Johanna .... 503-554-2235.. 391 D
jschweitzer@georgefox.edu

SCHWEITZER, Mike .... 210-999-8409.. 473 A
mschweit@trinity.edu

SCHWEITZER, Steven, J .. 800-287-8822.. 159 C
schwest@bethanyseminary.edu

SCHWENK, Monica .... 801-395-3781.. 481 A
schwenkm@owatc.edu

SCHWENK, Thomas, L ...... 775-784-6001.. 285 A
tschwenk@medicine.nevada.edu

SCHWENT, Margie .... 573-334-6825.. 272 A
mschwent@sehcollege.edu

SCHWERTNER, Melanie ... 325-574-6503.. 479 I
mschwertner@wtc.edu

SCHWIETERMAN, Jerry .... 219-473-4239.. 159 L
jschwieterman@ccsj.edu

SCHWINABART, Rhonda .. 301-387-3741.. 207 G
rhonda.schwinabart@garrettcollege.edu

SCHWINKE, Victoria .... 573-897-5000.. 272 H

SCHWIRZBIN, Brian .... 516-876-3242.. 333 C
schwirzbinb@oldwestbury.edu

SCIACCA, John .... 714-484-7285.... 54 G
jsciacca@cypresscollege.edu

SCIALABBA, Joseph, M ... 814-641-3114.. 406 F
scialaj@juniata.edu

SCIAME, Joseph, A .... 718-990-1941.. 328 F
sciamej@stjohns.edu

SCIAME-GIESECKE,
Susan .... 765-455-9221.. 163 A
sgiesec k@iuk.edu

SCIANNA, Dominic .... 718-990-6185.. 328 F
sciannad@stjohns.edu

SCIBETTA, Nicholas .... 631-632-6335.. 332 A
nicholas.scibetta@stonybrook.edu

SCICLUNA, Jon .... 260-452-2269.. 160 D
jon.scicluna@ctsfw.edu

SCIFO, Joe .... 309-794-7374.. 135 D
josephscifo@augustana.edu

SCIGLITANO, JR.,
Anthony, C .... 973-275-5847.. 297 A
anthony.sciglitano@shu.edu

SCIOLA, Michael .... 315-228-7380.. 310 G
msciola@colgate.edu

SCIOTTO, Page, C .... 401-598-2145.. 425 B
psciotto@jwu.edu

SCIPIO, Julius .... 912-358-3202.. 126 F
scipioj@savannahstate.edu

SCIPIO, Lisa .... 912-358-4000.. 126 F
scipiol@savannahstate.edu

SCIPLE, Melinda .... 662-476-5040.. 257 G
msciple@eastms.edu

SCISM, Bruce, R .... 434-797-8400.. 496 I
bscism@dcc.vccs.edu

SCISM, Darby, C .... 812-237-5000.. 162 A
darby.scism@indstate.edu

SCIUTO, Jim .... 925-631-8043.... 59 I
jsciuto@stmarys-ca.edu

SCLAFANI, Michael .... 302-831-2343.... 91 F
sclafani@udel.edu

SCOATES, Christopher .... 248-645-3301.. 233 B

SCOBEE, Georgia .... 225-216-8608.. 195 H
scobeeg@mybrcc.edu

SCOBLE, Kathleen .... 413-265-2204.. 217 D
scoblek@elms.edu

SCOBY, Jerry, L .... 231-591-2164.. 233 L
jerryscoby@ferris.edu

SCOBY, Rhonda .... 903-877-7077.. 477 E
rhonda.scoby@uthct.edu

SCODRO, Joseph, M .... 317-274-7460.. 163 D
jscodro@iu.edu

SCOFIELD, Dorie .... 913-722-0272.. 182 B

SCOFIELD, Elizabeth, A ... 215-951-1040.. 407 A
scofield@lasalle.edu

SCOFIELD, Jeff .... 206-296-5852.. 507 E
scofieldj@seattleu.edu

SCOGIN, James .... 903-223-3005.. 469 C
james.scogin@tamut.edu

SCOGNA, Bridget .... 610-282-1100.. 402 B
1269mgr@follett.com

SCOLA, Anthony .... 630-829-6319.. 135 F
ascola@ben.edu

SCOLARO, Diane .... 802-485-2358.. 484 H
dscolaro@norwich.edu

SCOLFORO, Karen .... 800-759-2727.. 400 F
karenscolforo@centralpenn.edu

SCONYERS, Ryan .... 912-260-4377.. 127 B
ryan.sconyers@sgsc.edu

SCOPAS, Constantine .... 212-686-9244.. 304 A

SCOPELLITI, Theresa .... 570-961-7840.. 407 B
scopellitit@lackawanna.edu

SCORDINO, Anthony .... 914-606-6521.. 340 C
anthony.scordino@sunywcc.edu

SCORSE, Bill .... 417-873-7200.. 264 H
bscorse@drury.edu

SCOTKA, Mary .... 210-434-6711.. 463 C
mscotka@lake.ollusa.edu

SCOTT, Adrian .... 205-247-8145...... 7 E
ascott@stillman.edu

SCOTT, Adrian, L .... 205-247-8145...... 7 E
ascott@stillman.edu

SCOTT, Adrienne .... 717-757-1100.. 424 I
adrienne.scott@yti.edu

SCOTT, Adrienne .... 717-767-4300.. 424 I
adrienne.scott@yti.edu

SCOTT, Alexander .... 973-290-4720.. 290 G
ascott@cse.edu

SCOTT, Amelia .... 508-999-8093.. 220 H
ascott4@umassd.edu

SCOTT, Amy .... 309-677-3538.. 136 B
alscott@fsmail.bradley.edu

SCOTT, Amy, M .... 563-333-6423.. 176 D
scottamym@sau.edu

SCOTT, Angela .... 305-899-3666.... 96 D
ascott@barry.edu

SCOTT, Anne .... 940-898-2586.. 472 G
ascott2@twu.edu

SCOTT, Annie .... 860-343-5767.... 86 F
ascott@mxcc.commnet.edu

SCOTT, Bart .... 530-938-5521.... 40 F
bscott6@siskiyous.edu

SCOTT, Billy .... 662-254-3319.. 260 A
bscott@mvsu.edu

SCOTT, Bob .... 580-349-1597.. 385 F
bobs@opsu.edu

SCOTT, Candice .... 830-792-7318.. 465 E
cscott@schreiner.edu

SCOTT, Carolyn .... 352-435-6308.. 104 J
scottc@lssc.edu

SCOTT, Cecelia .... 252-940-6264.. 347 E
cecelia.scott@beaufortccc.edu

SCOTT, Charles .... 212-817-7730.. 308 A
facilities@gc.cuny.edu

SCOTT, Charles .... 309-438-8851.. 143 B
cascott@ilstu.edu

SCOTT, Charles .... 817-722-1612.. 460 E
charles.scott@tku.edu

SCOTT, Charles .... 423-425-4463.. 448 F
charles-scott@utc.edu

SCOTT, Cheryl .... 971-722-7555.. 394 F
cscott@pcc.edu

SCOTT, Christopher .... 713-755-4961.. 224 G
cdscott@stcc.edu

SCOTT, Christopher .... 304-473-8007.. 515 B
scott.c@wvwc.edu

SCOTT, Christopher, D .... 815-772-7218.. 148 H
cdscott@morrisontech.edu

SCOTT, Clifford .... 617-266-2030.. 226 E
scottc@neco.edu

SCOTT, Connie, L .... 314-434-2212.. 266 B
cscott@hickeycollege.edu

SCOTT, Constance, E .... 260-422-5561.. 162 B
cescott@indianatech.edu

SCOTT, Corey .... 804-862-6100.. 493 F
cscott@rbc.edu

SCOTT, Dave .... 360-416-7751.. 507 G
dave.scott@skagit.edu

SCOTT, David, L .... 850-474-3117.. 113 A
dscott@uwf.edu

SCOTT, Dawn, M .... 262-524-7297.. 515 J
dscott@carrollu.edu

SCOTT, Deborah, C .... 508-831-6075.. 230 C
dscott@wpi.edu

SCOTT, Delbert, L .... 913-722-0272.. 182 B
delbert.scott@kansaschristian.edu

SCOTT, Deloria .... 270-707-3823.. 189 G
deloria.scott@kctcs.edu

SCOTT, Donna .... 512-404-4807.. 452 A
dscott@austinseminary.edu

SCOTT, Douglas .... 484-646-4250.. 415 C
dscott@kutztown.edu

SCOTT, Ed .... 412-392-6194.. 417 F
escott@pointpark.edu

SCOTT, Ed .... 850-263-3261.... 96 C
eescott@baptistcollege.edu

SCOTT, Eileen .... 856-256-4139.. 295 E
scotte@rowan.edu

SCOTT, Elijah .... 706-295-6318.. 121 C
escott@highlands.edu

SCOTT, Eric .... 907-796-6389.... 10 H
ewscott@alaska.edu

SCOTT, Eric .... 662-216-3429.. 260 F

SCOTT, Fionna .... 619-684-8800.... 54 C
fscott@newschoolarch.edu

SCOTT, Frank .... 615-966-1990.. 441 F
frank.scott@lipscomb.edu

SCOTT, Fred .... 979-230-3213.. 453 A
fred.scott@brazosport.edu

SCOTT, Gayanne .... 719-255-3388.... 83 L
gscott@uccs.edu

SCOTT, Greg .... 616-222-3000.. 236 F
gscott@kuyper.edu

SCOTT, Gregory, A .... 412-624-4247.. 421 G
gascott@pitt.edu

SCOTT, Hamilton .... 706-754-7890.. 125 B
hscott@northgatech.edu

SCOTT, Heather .... 605-626-2433.. 437 D
heather.scott@northern.edu

SCOTT, Heidi .... 618-468-5110.. 145 G
hscott@lc.edu

SCOTT, Henrietta .... 803-774-3339.. 427 G
scotth@cctech.edu

SCOTT, Jamal .... 630-466-7900.. 157 K
jscott@waubonsee.edu

SCOTT, James .... 305-899-3950.... 96 D
jscott@barry.edu

SCOTT, James .... 573-882-6008.. 273 E
scottj@missouri.edu

SCOTT, James, K .... 573-882-6008.. 273 E
scottj@missouri.edu

SCOTT, Janice, L .... 727-816-3424.. 106 F
cessnaj@phsc.edu

SCOTT, Jeff .... 216-373-5407.. 374 B
jscott@ndc.edu

SCOTT, Jeffrey .... 404-894-7444.. 121 D
jeff.scott@business.gatech.edu

SCOTT, Jillian .... 212-355-1501.. 306 L
jscott@christies.edu

SCOTT, Jo Ann .... 662-252-8000.. 260 F
jscott2@rustcollege.edu

SCOTT, Joseph .... 937-878-7985.. 527 H
scottjoseph@aafes.com

SCOTT, Josha .... 210-486-7280.. 450 E
jscott@alamo.edu

SCOTT, Joylynn .... 423-236-2801.. 444 B
jmichals@southern.edu

SCOTT, Julie .... 229-333-2100.. 130 A
julie.scott@wiregrass.edu

SCOTT, Karina .... 303-245-4686.... 81 I
kscott@naropa.edu

SCOTT, Kathleen, E .... 937-255-3636.. 527 H
kathleen.scott@afit.edu

SCOTT, Kathleen, J .... 410-543-6070.. 213 A
kjscott@salisbury.edu

SCOTT, Kelly .... 970-675-3273.... 78 J
kelly.scott@cncc.edu

SCOTT, Kenneth .... 518-458-5359.. 311 B
scottk@strose.edu

SCOTT, Lana .... 580-477-7719.. 389 I
lana.scott@wosc.edu

SCOTT, Laura .... 707-864-7000.... 65 A
laura.scott@solano.edu

SCOTT, Linda .... 309-692-4092.. 147 I

SCOTT, Linda .... 608-263-9725.. 519 K
ldscott@wisc.edu

SCOTT, Linda .... 804-524-5304.. 499 G
lscott@vsu.edu

SCOTT, Lisa, L .... 585-785-1454.. 314 D
lisa.scott@flcc.edu

SCOTT, Lisa, M .... 570-372-4415.. 419 H
scottl@susqu.edu

SCOTT, Louis, B .... 404-413-2400.. 122 D
lscott01@gsu.edu

SCOTT, Marcia .... 805-546-3119.... 41 L
mscott@cuesta.edu

SCOTT, CSA, Marie .... 920-923-7624.. 517 H
mscott@marianuniversity.edu

SCOTT, Mark .... 412-809-5100.. 417 D
scott.mark@pti.edu

SCOTT, Martha Lou .... 254-710-1761.. 452 H
martha_lou_scott@baylor.edu

SCOTT, Mary .... 617-984-1768.. 227 F
mscott@quincycollege.edu

SCOTT, Matthew .... 413-205-3015.. 214 B
matthew.scott@aic.edu

SCOTT, Megan .... 618-544-8657.. 142 D
scottm@iecc.edu

SCOTT, Megan .... 309-341-7948.. 145 A
mscott@knox.edu

SCOTT, Michael .... 415-405-3943.... 35 B
mjscott@sfsu.edu

SCOTT, Michael, H .... 817-257-7858.. 469 G
m.scott@tcu.edu

SCOTT, Michelle, T .... 240-567-5276.. 209 E
michelle.scott@montgomerycollege.edu

SCOTT, Monica .... 731-426-7500.. 440 K

SCOTT, Monica, R .... 843-953-5579.. 428 G
scottmr@cofc.edu

SCOTT, Neil .... 334-386-7200...... 3 I
nscott@faulkner.edu

SCOTT, Nicole .... 856-222-9311.. 295 C
nscott@rcbc.edu

SCOTT, Patricia, A .... 410-706-7347.. 211 F
pscott@umaryland.edu

SCOTT, Patty .... 541-888-7401.. 395 B
pscott@socc.edu

SCOTT, Phyllis .... 305-899-3900.... 96 D
pscott@barry.edu

SCOTT, Randa .... 512-313-3000.. 455 F
randa.scott@concordia.edu

SCOTT, Rebecca .... 707-256-7438.... 53 H
rscott@napavalley.edu

SCOTT, Renay .... 575-527-7500.. 300 J
rmscott@nmsu.edu

SCOTT, Renay, M .... 575-527-7510.. 301 C
daccpresident@dacc.nmsu.edu

SCOTT, Richard .... 269-965-3931.. 236 A
scottr@kellogg.edu

SCOTT, Richard .... 801-957-3334.. 483 A
richard.scott@slcc.edu

SCOTT, Richard, I .... 501-450-3198.... 24 G
ricks@uca.edu

SCOTT, Richard, M .... 352-365-3525.. 104 J
scottr@lssc.edu

SCOTT, Rob .... 770-426-2603.. 124 B
rob.scott@life.edu

SCOTT, Rob .... 207-509-7297.. 204 F
rscott@unity.edu

SCOTT, Ronald, B .... 513-529-0143.. 372 K
scottrb@miamioh.edu

SCOTT, Sandra, E .... 803-533-3721.. 432 E
sscott17@scsu.edu

SCOTT, Sharron .... 802-635-1208.. 486 B
sharon.scott@jsc.edu

SCOTT, Sharron, R .... 802-635-1208.. 486 B
sharron.scott@jsc.edu

SCOTT, Stephen, C .... 919-866-5141.. 353 I
scscott@waketech.edu

SCOTT, Steven, A .... 620-235-4100.. 184 C
sascott@pittstate.edu

SCOTT, Susan, W .... 601-266-5000.. 261 E
susan.w.scott@usm.edu
SCOTT, Tawana .... 864-877-1598.. 431 G
tawana.scott@ngu.edu
SCOTT, Teresa, M .... 209-575-6530.... 75 I
scottt@yosemite.edu
SCOTT, Thomas .... 208-769-5906.. 134 C
ttscott@nic.edu
SCOTT, Thomas, R .... 864-656-7551.. 428 C
trscott@clemson.edu
SCOTT, Todd .... 530-938-5201.... 40 F
tscott8@siskiyous.edu
SCOTT, Vann .... 256-840-4188..... 6 H
vscott@snead.edu
SCOTT, Wanda .... 570-849-8247.... 55 I
wscott@psr.edu
SCOTT, Wayne .... 731-989-6790.. 440 D
wscott@fhu.edu
SCOTT, Wayne .... 800-348-3481.. 440 D
wscott@fhu.edu
SCOTT, Wendy .... 601-925-7104.. 259 A
wbscott@mc.edu
SCOTT, William, J .... 260-399-7700.. 168 D
bscott@sf.edu
SCOTT, Winston .... 321-674-8000.. 100 M
wscott@fit.edu
SCOTT DUEX, Sandi .... 715-232-1181.. 521 D
duexs@uwstout.edu
SCOTT DUEX, Sandra ...... 715-232-2131.. 521 D
duexs@uwstout.edu
SCOTT-JOHNSON,
Pamela .... 323-343-2000.... 33 C
pscottj@calstatela.edu
SCOTT-JOHNSON,
Pamela .... 443-885-3509.. 209 F
pamela.scottjohnson@morgan.edu
SCOTT-KINNEY,
Wanda, A .... 803-705-4680.. 427 D
scottkinney@benedict.edu
SCOTT-LUNAU, Cynthia ... 903-877-7022.. 477 E
cindy.lunau@uthct.edu
SCOTT PAYNE, Moira ...... 206-726-5181.. 503 B
mpayne@cornish.edu
SCOTT PRICE, Charles ..... 318-371-3035.. 196 H
charlesprice@nwltc.edu
SCOTTI, Frank .... 714-879-3901.... 46 F
fscotti@hiu.edu
SCOUBES, Jim .... 530-283-0202.... 43 G
jscoubes@frc.edu
SCOVENS, Tarsha .... 215-751-8164.. 401 G
tscovens@ccp.edu
SCOVILLE, Jan .... 715-732-3888.. 524 E
jan.scoville@nwtc.edu
SCRAGG, Raymond .... 216-421-7312.. 366 G
rscragg@cia.edu
SCRANAGE, Kimberly ...... 859-572-7852.. 192 B
scranagek1@nku.edu
SCRANTON, Alec .... 319-335-5672.. 169 H
alec-scranton@uiowa.edu
SCREEN, Tommy .... 504-864-7082.. 198 E
tscreen@loyno.edu
SCREMENTI, Lori .... 773-244-5770.. 149 I
lmscrementi@northpark.edu
SCREWS, Doris .... 334-229-4250...... 1 D
dscrews@alasu.edu
SCREWS, Jacqueline, B ... 334-556-2485...... 3 N
jscrews@wallace.edu
SCRIBNER, Andrea .... 518-736-3622.. 315 A
andrea.scribner@fmcc.suny.edu
SCRIBNER, Douglas .... 575-527-7500.. 301 C
dscribner@nmsu.edu
SCRIMSHAW, Susan, C ... 518-244-2214.. 327 H
scrims@sage.edu
SCRIPPS, Jim .... 775-831-1314.. 285 G
jscripps@sierranevada.edu
SCRIVENER, Norma Jean . 601-857-3850.. 258 A
njscrivener@hindscc.edu
SCROGGINS, Anita .... 205-970-9213...... 7 B
ascroggins@sebc.edu
SCROGGINS, Don .... 580-477-7751.. 389 I
don.scroggins@wosc.edu
SCROGGINS, Melinda ...... 559-251-4215.... 29 I
financialaid@calchristiancollege.edu
SCROGGINS, Susan .... 219-464-6395.. 168 F
susan.scroggins@valpo.edu
SCROGGINS, William, T .. 909-274-4250.... 53 C
bscroggins@mtsac.edu
SCROGGS, Catherine, C .. 573-882-6776.. 273 E
scroggsc@missouri.edu
SCRUGGS, Jeffrey .... 478-218-3330.. 118 H
jscruggs@centralgatech.edu
SCULL, Alex, K .... 864-833-8228.. 432 B
akscull@presby.edu
SCULLY, Dale .... 712-749-2123.. 170 D
scullyd@bvu.edu
SCULLY, JR., Frank, E ..... 215-646-7300.. 404 G
scully.f@gmercyu.edu
SCULLY, Jonathan .... 413-205-3270.. 214 B
jonathan.scully@aic.edu
SCULLY, Joseph, F .... 856-256-4127.. 295 E
scullyj@rowan.edu
SCULLY, Pamela .... 910-678-8232.. 349 F
scullyp@faytechcc.edu
SCUTELLA, Clifford, M ..... 585-345-6832.. 315 C
cmscutella@genesee.edu
SCUTO, Donna, L .... 716-878-6700.. 332 F
scutodl@buffalostate.edu
SCUTTI, Diane .... 610-902-8415.. 399 D
diane.m.scutti@cabrini.edu
SEA, Karen .... 209-954-5151.... 61 F
ksea@deltacollege.edu
SEABERG, David, C .... 423-778-6956.. 448 H
dseaberg@uthsc.edu
SEABERG, Doug .... 570-372-4408.. 419 H
seaberg@susqu.edu
SEABERRY, Ben .... 408-531-6144.... 62 C
ben.seaberry@sjeccd.org
SEABERRY, Roosevelt ...... 318-675-8125.. 198 B
rseabe@lsuhsc.edu
SEABOY, Donna .... 701-854-8013.. 362 B
donnas@sbci.edu
SEABROOK WRIGHT,
Gloria .... 803-934-3192.. 431 E
gwright@morris.edu
SEACOTT, Damon, M .... 517-750-1200.. 241 E
dseacott@arbor.edu
SEACRIST, Ronald .... 806-742-3931.. 472 C
ronald.seacrist@ttu.edu
SEADLER, Alan, W .... 412-396-5168.. 403 A
seadlera@duq.edu
SEAGA, Andrew .... 305-237-7581.. 105 D
aseaga@mdc.edu
SEAGLE, Dennis .... 828-726-2705.. 347 I
dseagle@cccti.edu
SEAGO, Brenda .... 706-721-2856.. 117 D
bseago@augusta.edu
SEAGRAVES, John, R .... 606-474-3272.. 188 L
johnseagraves@kcu.edu
SEAGRAVES, Ronda .... 512-313-3000.. 455 F
ronda.seagraves@concordia.edu
SEAGULL, Amon .... 954-262-2048.. 105 J
amons@nova.edu
SEAL, Jennifer .... 601-403-1146.. 260 D
jseal@prcc.edu
SEAL, John .... 510-649-2462.... 45 G
jseal@gtu.edu
SEAL, Robert .... 973-720-2104.. 298 G
sealr@wpunj.edu
SEAL, Robert, A .... 773-508-2657.. 146 G
rseal@luc.edu
SEAL, Sherry .... 706-754-7730.. 125 B
sseal@northgatech.edu
SEAL, Timothy .... 901-751-8453.. 442 E
tseal@mabts.edu
SEALE, Danette .... 865-471-3248.. 439 C
dseale@cn.edu
SEALE, Francis Marie ..... 510-883-2068.... 42 F
sfmseale@dspt.edu
SEALINE, Alma .... 217-333-0610.. 157 A
asealine@illinois.edu
SEALS, Amanda .... 470-578-3880.. 123 J
aseals6@kennesaw.edu
SEALS, George .... 540-365-4211.. 489 M
gseals@ferrum.edu
SEALS, Jennifer .... 605-718-2909.. 438 B
jennifer.seals@wdt.edu
SEALS, Lisa .... 760-355-6257.... 46 J
lisa.seals@imperial.edu
SEALS, Nireata .... 718-482-5900.. 309 A
nseals@lagcc.cuny.edu
SEALS, Victoria .... 770-962-7580.. 123 D
vseals@gwinnetttech.edu
SEALY, Mondell .... 718-262-2305.. 310 A
msealy@york.cuny.edu
SEAMAN, Amanda .... 417-873-6956.. 264 H
mseaman@drury.edu
SEAMAN, Chuck .... 615-248-1240.. 447 F
cseaman@trevecca.edu
SEAMAN, Cynthia .... 610-372-4721.. 417 G
cseaman@racc.edu
SEAMAN, Daniel, B .... 315-229-5601.. 329 D
dseaman@stlawu.edu
SEAMAN, David .... 315-443-5533.. 337 A
dseaman@syr.edu
SEAMAN, Diane .... 937-328-6014.. 366 E
seamand@clarkstate.edu
SEAMAN, Jennifer .... 415-503-6230.... 61 C
jseaman@sfcm.edu
SEAMAN, Sara .... 501-760-4101.... 21 B
sseaman@np.edu
SEAMAN, Scott, H .... 740-593-2705.. 375 H
seaman@ohio.edu
SEAMAN, Shane .... 718-933-6700.. 321 I
sseaman@monroecollege.edu
SEAMONS, Ron .... 540-261-4095.. 494 F
ron.seamons@svu.edu
SEAMS, Jennifer .... 304-645-6383.. 514 A
jseams@osteo.wvsom.edu
SEANE, Oupa .... 904-620-2475.. 112 B
oseane@unf.edu
SEAQUIST, Carl .... 717-815-2084.. 424 F
cseaquis@ycp.edu
SEARA, Maira .... 212-647-7223.. 326 E
mseara@pratt.edu
SEARCY, Douglas, N .... 252-399-6309.. 341 P
dsearcy@barton.edu
SEARCY, Scott .... 785-890-1511.. 183 L
scott.searcy@nwktc.edu
SEARFOSS, Alexis .... 727-873-4519.. 112 D
asearfoss@usfsp.edu
SEARING, Linda .... 585-389-2870.. 322 D
lsearin9@naz.edu
SEARLE, Mark, S .... 480-965-1224.... 11 H
mark.searle@asu.edu
SEARLE, Natalie .... 802-786-5148.. 486 A
natalie.searle@ccv.edu
SEARS, Andrew .... 816-960-2008.. 263 D
asears@cityvision.edu
SEARS, Andrew, L .... 814-865-3528.. 412 F
aus67@psu.edu
SEARS, Courtney .... 912-260-4270.. 127 B
courtney.sears@sgsc.edu
SEARS, David .... 240-567-7492.. 209 E
david.sears@montgomerycollege.edu
SEARS, Douglas .... 617-358-4608.. 216 E
dsears@bu.edu
SEARS, Estella .... 512-492-3077.. 451 E
esears@aoma.edu
SEARS, J, W .... 252-985-5585.. 354 E
wsears@ncwc.edu
SEARS, John .... 303-220-1200.... 77 D
john.sears@cffp.edu
SEARS, John .... 401-874-7668.. 426 D
jsears@uri.edu
SEARS, Laura .... 402-826-6773.. 280 B
laura.sears@doane.edu
SEARS, Melissa .... 859-442-1156.. 189 D
melissa.sears@kctcs.edu
SEARS, Norward .... 504-816-4711.. 195 B
nsears@dillard.edu
SEARS, Richard .... 678-839-5353.. 129 E
rsears@westga.edu
SEARS, Ryan .... 502-213-8200.. 193 A
rsears@sctd.edu
SEARS, Steve, R .... 956-326-2480.. 468 A
steve.sears@tamiu.edu
SEARS, Steven, A .... 401-865-2425.. 425 D
ssears@providence.edu
SEARS, Suzanne .... 940-898-3748.. 472 G
SEARS, Tad .... 218-723-6017.. 245 J
tsears@css.edu
SEARSON, Robert .... 216-987-3943.. 367 E
robert.searson@tri-c.edu
SEASTEDT, Erik .... 716-375-2102.. 328 B
eseastedt@sbu.edu
SEASTEDT, Erik .... 907-450-8222.... 10 E
eseastedt@alaska.edu
SEATON, Ann .... 845-758-6822.. 304 F
aseaton@bard.edu
SEATON, William, J .... 609-984-1120.. 297 F
bseaton@tesu.edu
SEAVER, Catherine .... 413-775-1811.. 223 D
seaverc@gcc.mass.edu
SEAVER, Kent .... 972-273-3430.. 456 G
kseaver@dcccd.edu
SEAWORTH, Timothy .... 701-355-8150.. 362 G
seaworth@umary.edu
SEAY, Brooks .... 706-379-3111.. 130 B
cbseay@yhc.edu
SEAY, Gary .... 718-270-5031.. 309 B
garys@mec.cuny.edu
SEAY, Laodecea .... 334-214-4807...... 2 H
laodecea.seay@cv.edu
SEAY, Lonnie .... 530-242-7912.... 64 D
lseay@shastacollege.edu
SEBASTIAN, Chris .... 692-625-3291.. 530 C
csebastian@cmi.edu
SEBASTIAN, Denise .... 573-518-2249.. 268 E
denise@mineralarea.edu
SEBASTIAN, Donald, H ..... 973-596-8449.. 293 D
sebastian@njit.edu
SEBASTIAN, J. Jayakiran . 215-248-6306.. 409 D
jsebastian@ltsp.edu
SEBASTIAN, John .... 504-865-2304.. 198 E
jtsebast@loyno.edu
SEBASTIAN, Juliann .... 402-559-4000.. 283 A
julie.sebastian@unmc.edu
SEBASTIAN, Pam .... 660-831-4142.. 269 B
sebastianp@moval.edu
SEBASTIANI, Richard .... 713-221-8225.. 474 B
sebastianir@uhd.edu
SEBASTIEN, Anya .... 864-592-6207.. 432 H
sebastiena@sccsc.edu
SEBOLT, George, W .... 412-291-6210.. 397 I
gsebolt@aii.edu
SEBOLT, Kevin, G .... 740-284-5192.. 368 L
ksebolt@franciscan.edu
SEBRANEK, Lori, A .... 608-243-4185.. 523 F
lsebranek@madisoncollege.edu
SECHLER, Elizabeth .... 304-876-5172.. 513 E
esechler@shepherd.edu
SECHRIST, Ann .... 770-972-7580.. 123 D
asechrist@gwinnetttech.edu
SECHRIST, John .... 724-653-2184.. 402 F
jsechrist@dec.edu
SECHRIST, Shana .... 503-370-6210.. 396 G
ssechrist@willamette.edu
SECKER, Eric .... 847-628-2084.. 144 B
webmaster@judsonu.edu
SECOR, Dan .... 203-773-8506.... 85 C
dsecor@albertus.edu
SECORD, Anne-Marie ...... 858-541-7913.... 54 A
asecord@nu.edu
SECORD, Mark .... 361-354-2529.. 454 G
secordm@coastalbend.edu
SECORD, Paul .... 512-863-1211.. 466 G
secordp@southwestern.edu
SECREST, Karen .... 435-722-6900.. 481 I
SECREST, Kathy, L .... 330-471-8415.. 371 J
ksecrest@malone.edu
SECREST, Larry .... 415-451-2822.... 61 D
lsecrest@sfts.edu
SECRIST, Tammi .... 304-336-8281.. 513 F
tsecrist@westliberty.edu
SEDA, Iris .... 787-264-1912.. 534 D
iris_seda_rodriguez@intersg.edu
SEDANO, George .... 510-594-5033.... 29 K
gsedano@cca.edu
SEDDIKI, Mohamed .... 973-877-3080.. 291 H
seddiki@essex.edu
SEDDON, Tom, I .... 513-556-0831.. 379 A
seddontl@ucmail.uc.edu
SEDEN, John .... 415-749-4570.... 61 B
jseden@sfai.edu
SEDER, Diana .... 909-607-7785.... 38 J
diana.seder@cmc.edu
SEDILLO, Dacia .... 575-646-5690.. 300 J
dapachec@nmsu.edu
SEDILLO, Eileen .... 505-454-3430.. 300 F
sedillo_e@nmhu.edu
SEDLACEK, Bernard .... 402-457-2529.. 280 J
bsedlacek@mccneb.edu
SEDLACEK, Beverly .... 402-354-7249.. 281 F
bev.sedlacek@methodistcollege.edu
SEDLACEK, Paige .... 607-778-5213.. 332 D
sedlacekpm@sunybroome.edu
SEDLAK, John .... 570-740-0234.. 409 E
jsedlak@luzerne.edu
SEDLOCK, Chris .... 304-876-5378.. 513 E
csedlock@shepherd.edu
SEDNA, Jennifer .... 707-546-4000.... 42 M
jsedna@empirecollege.com
SEDRINE, Ben .... 904-363-6221.. 109 B
SEDUTTO, Dawn .... 603-668-2211.. 287 I
d.sedutto@snhu.edu
SEDYCIAS, Joao .... 201-200-3001.. 293 C
jsedycias@njcu.edu
SEDYCIAS, Joao .... 607-436-2520.. 331 F
joao.sedycias@oneonta.edu
SEE, David .... 501-337-5000.... 19 K
dsee@coto.edu
SEE, Joan .... 212-812-4050.. 323 E
jsee@nycda.edu
SEE, Jonathan .... 310-506-6256.... 56 J
jonathan.see@pepperdine.edu
SEE, Leslie, C .... 304-260-4380.. 511 L
lsee@blueridgectc.edu
SEEBO, Elane .... 806-291-3417.. 479 D
seeboe@wbu.edu
SEEGER, Daniel .... 828-298-3325.. 359 F
dseeger@warren-wilson.edu
SEEGER, Matthew .... 313-577-5342.. 243 F
matthew.seeger@wayne.edu
SEEGERT, Paul .... 206-616-3865.. 508 E
pseegert@uw.edu
SEEGMILLER, Jesse .... 540-261-8454.. 494 F
jesse.seegmiller@svu.edu
SEEK, Linda .... 301-846-2457.. 207 F
lseek@frederick.edu
SEEKINS, Travis, P .... 325-670-1589.. 458 J
seekins@hsutx.edu
SEEKLANDER, Marlene ..... 605-882-5284.. 436 B
seeklanm@lakeareatech.edu
SEELA, Joel .... 320-762-4635.. 248 J
joels@alextech.edu
SEELBACH, Brenda .... 540-636-2900.. 488 D
brendaseelbach@christendom.edu
SEELEY, Lisa .... 903-923-2175.. 457 G
SEELEY, Lisa .... 903-923-2175.. 457 G
lseeley@etbu.edu
SEELEY, Michael .... 321-674-8422.. 100 M
mseeley@fit.edu
SEELY, Bruce, E .... 906-487-2156.. 238 A
bseely@mtu.edu
SEELYE, Calvin, H .... 989-774-7526.. 232 D
seely1ch@cmich.edu
SEEMAN, Steve, C .... 563-588-8000.. 172 E
financialaid@emmaus.edu
SEEMANN, Jeffrey .... 860-486-3619.... 89 D
jeff.seemann@uconn.edu
SEERY, Denise .... 303-282-3414.... 83 C
denise.seery@archden.org
SEESSEL, Jessica .... 914-606-6963.. 340 C
jessica.seessel@sunywcc.edu

SERAFIMOV, Val .... 417-873-7262.. 264 H
vserafimov@drury.edu
SERAFIN, Renata .... 210-486-4689.. 450 C
rserafin@alamo.edu
SERAFINO, Candice, J .... 413-545-6253.. 220 F
serafino@acad.umass.edu
SERAICHICK, Laura .... 603-358-2526.. 288 E
lseraich@keene.edu
SERBALIK, James .... 518-783-2314.. 330 E
serbalik@siena.edu
SERBALIK, Sandy .... 518-783-2596.. 330 E
sserbalik@siena.edu
SERBAN, Andreea .... 714-438-4698.... 39 D
aserban@mail.cccd.edu
SERBER, Michael .... 214-648-9569.. 478 C
michael.serber@utsouthwestern.edu
SERDYUK, Yana, V .... 708-209-3053.. 138 G
yana.serdyuk@cuchicago.edu
SERENO, Jaime .... 253-680-7014.. 501 E
jsereno@bates.ctc.edu
SERGER, Carissa .... 303-457-2757.... 80 C
carissa.serger@zenith.org
SERGI, Joseph .... 603-645-9650.. 287 I
j.sergi@snhu.edu
SERHAL, Patty, J .... 606-474-3247.. 188 L
pserhal@kcu.edu
SERIO, Vincent .... 208-426-1459.. 132 I
vinceserio@boisestate.edu
SERJOIE, Ava .... 336-316-2178.. 344 H
SERLING, Kitty .... 816-276-4309.. 270 H
c.serling@researchcollege.edu
SERMONS, Debra .... 913-667-5700.. 179 K
SERMONS, Penny .... 252-940-6243.. 347 E
penny.sermons@beaufortccc.edu
SERNA, Edward .... 479-788-6925.... 23 A
edward.serna@uafs.edu
SERNAU, Scott .... 574-520-4429.. 163 E
ssernau@iusb.edu
SEROSHEK, Nichole .... 360-442-2371.. 504 G
nseroshek@lowercolumbia.edu
SEROTA COTE,
Pamela, A .... 540-375-2299.. 493 H
cote@roanoke.edu
SEROVICH, Julianne .... 813-974-7196.. 112 C
jserovich@usf.edu
SERPLISS, Ron .... 563-244-7021.. 172 B
rserpliss@eicc.edu
SERR, Jim .... 815-280-6641.. 144 A
jim.serr@jjc.edu
SERR, Roger, L .... 717-477-1308.. 416 A
rlserr@ship.edu
SERRA, Elena .... 201-761-6366.. 296 K
eserra@saintpeters.edu
SERRA, Neddie .... 973-748-9000.. 289 H
neddie_serra@bloomfield.edu
SERRA, Neuza, M .... 856-225-6005.. 296 A
nmserra@camden.rutgers.edu
SERRANO, Aixa .... 787-857-3600.. 533 I
aserrano@br.inter.edu
SERRANO, Alex .... 903-223-3114.. 469 C
alex.serrano@tamut.edu
SERRANO, Carlos .... 718-982-2460.. 307 F
carlos.serrano@csi.cuny.edu
SERRANO, Gladys .... 787-743-4041.. 531 K
gserrano@columbiacentral.edu
SERRANO, Iris .... 787-743-7979.. 536 A
iserrano@suagm.edu
SERRANO, Lucille .... 831-755-6900.... 45 L
lserrano@hartnell.edu
SERRANO, Luz, D .... 787-780-0070.. 531 B
lserrano@caribbean.edu
SERRANO, Mayra .... 787-798-3001.. 536 G
mayra.serrano@uccaribe.edu
SERRANO, Melba .... 787-890-2681.. 537 E
melba.serrano@upr.edu
SERRANO, Sandra, V .... 661-336-5104.... 47 I
sserrano@kccd.edu
SERRANO, Zaida .... 787-890-2681.. 537 E
zaida.serrano@upr.edu
SERRAO, Carlos .... 740-392-6868.. 373 D
carlos.serrao@mvnu.edu
SERRATA, William .... 915-831-6511.. 457 H
wserrata@epcc.edu
SERRAVILLO, JR., Lee ...... 518-442-3080.. 331 A
lserravillo@albany.edu
SERRECCHIA, Michael ..... 214-638-0484.. 460 C
mserrecchia@kdstudio.com
SERRETT, Marc .... 605-688-4128.. 437 F
marc.serrett@sdstate.edu
SERTSU, Neb .... 410-837-5069.. 213 C
nsertsu@ubalt.edu
SERVER, Timor .... 713-718-6453.. 459 B
timor.server@hccs.edu
SERVI, Angela, M .... 715-675-3331.. 524 D
servia@ntc.edu
SERVIDIO, Denise .... 718-990-6247.. 328 F
stjohns@bkstr.com
SERWATKA, Thomas, S ... 904-620-2500.. 112 B
tserwatk@unf.edu
SESSION, Norman .... 601-936-5555.. 258 A
norman.session@hindscc.edu
SESSIONS, Layne .... 775-831-1314.. 285 G
lsessions@sierranevada.edu
SESSIONS, Lisa, H .... 828-448-3126.. 354 B
lsessions@wpcc.edu
SESSIONS, Robin .... 251-809-1591...... 5 A
robin.sessions@jdcc.edu
SESSLER, April, L .... 806-371-5321.. 450 H
alsessler@actx.edu
SESSLER, Jeff .... 909-607-1225.... 64 A
jeff@scrippscollege.edu
SESSUMS, Cassandra ...... 601-925-3464.. 259 A
sessums@mc.edu
SESSUMS, Johnny .... 713-718-2093.. 459 B
johnny.sessums@hccs.edu
SESTAK, Brandi .... 402-465-7579.. 281 K
bsestak@nebrwesleyan.edu
SETAYESH, Flora, R .... 615-353-3394.. 446 E
flora.setayesh@nscc.edu
SETCHELL, Cara .... 765-658-4154.. 160 F
carasetchell@depauw.edu
SETCHELL, Steven, J .... 765-658-4215.. 160 F
ssetchell@depauw.edu
SETEK, Scott .... 315-445-4300.. 318 E
seteksl@lemoyne.edu
SETH, Niti .... 617-873-0208.. 217 A
niti.seth@cambridgecolleg.edu
SETHARES, Greg .... 508-678-2811.. 223 A
greg.sethares@bristolcc.edu
SETHRE-HOFSTAD, Lisa .. 218-299-3107.. 246 A
sethre@cord.edu
SETLAK, Tressa, A .... 240-895-4911.. 210 E
tasetlak@smcm.edu
SETLEY, David, M .... 717-867-6104.. 408 F
setley@lvc.edu
SETMEYER, Adam .... 317-955-6131.. 165 N
asetmeyer@marian.edu
SETTELE, Jim, D .... 207-581-1512.. 204 H
james.settele@maine.edu
SETTER, Paul, W .... 972-708-7321.. 458 G
accounting@gial.edu
SETTERGREN, Jennifer ..... 616-957-6675.. 232 B
jsetterg@calvinseminary.edu
SETTERLIND, Sharon .... 727-341-4677.. 108 D
setterlind.sharon@spcollege.edu
SETTLE, Jim, S .... 336-334-5099.. 358 B
jssettle@uncg.edu
SETTLES, Monica .... 406-756-3801.. 276 E
msettles@fvcc.edu
SETTOON, Paula .... 918-595-7728.. 388 F
paula.settoon@tulsacc.edu
SETZER, Jason .... 336-249-8186.. 349 C
jason_setzer@davidsonccc.edu
SETZER, Pat .... 619-660-4226.... 45 I
pat.setzer@gcccd.edu
SETZER, Patrick, K .... 828-262-3002.. 356 B
setzerpk@appstate.edu
SETZER, Tim, W .... 409-944-1365.. 458 D
tsetzer@gc.edu
SEUFERLING, Dale .... 785-832-7400.. 185 D
dseuferling@kuendowment.org
SEUFERT, Kyle .... 620-431-2820.. 183 H
kseufert@neosho.edu
SEUFFERLEIN, Catherine . 402-363-5614.. 283 G
cseufferlein@york.edu
SEUMANUTAFA, Loligi .... 684-699-9155.. 529 E
l.siaki@amsamoa.edu
SEUNARINE, Patricia .... 302-736-2385.... 91 G
patricia.seunarine@wesley.edu
SEVASTOS, Charlie, W ..... 386-323-8812.... 99 A
sevastoc@erau.edu
SEVER, Dennis .... 432-685-4690.. 461 H
dsever@midland.edu
SEVERANCE, Dana, A .... 301-687-4121.. 212 F
dseverance@frostburg.edu
SEVERANCE, Dianne .... 775-831-1314.. 285 G
dseverance@sierranevada.edu
SEVERANCE, Mary Ellen .. 508-793-7478.. 217 B
meseverance@clarku.edu
SEVERINO, Dan .... 215-596-8793.. 422 A
d.severino@usciences.edu
SEVERINO, Kristy .... 860-768-5403.... 89 G
kseverino@hartford.edu
SEVERINO-VALDEZ,
Carlos, E .... 787-764-0000.. 537 D
carlos.severino@upr.edu
SEVERNS, Mel .... 740-392-6868.. 373 D
mel.severns@mvnu.edu
SEVERS, Doug .... 541-737-2241.. 393 H
financial.aid@oregonstate.edu
SEVERSON, Christopher .. 715-675-3331.. 524 D
seversonc@ntc.edu
SEVERSON, Karen, J .... 402-844-7273.. 282 B
karens@northeast.edu
SEVERSON, Mark, W .... 716-878-6434.. 332 F
seversmw@buffalostate.edu
SEVERSON, Sheila .... 608-796-3001.. 522 O
smseverson@viterbo.edu
SEVERSON, Stacy .... 612-244-2800.. 247 D
sseverson@ipr.edu
SEVERTIS, JR., Ronald, E 812-941-2148.. 163 F
rseverti@ius.edu
SEVERY, Lisa .... 303-492-6541.... 83 K
lisa.severy@colorado.edu
SEVICK, Leona .... 540-828-5608.. 487 H
lsevick@bridgewater.edu
SEVIER, Karen .... 603-752-1060.. 286 H
ksevier@ccsnh.edu
SEVIER, Owen .... 405-692-3101.. 384 C
osevier@macu.edu
SEVIG, Todd, D .... 734-764-8312.. 241 J
tdsevig@umich.edu
SEVILLA, Henry .... 787-780-0070.. 531 B
hsevilla@caribbean.edu
SEVILLE, Scott .... 307-268-2713.. 527 B
sseville@uwyo.edu
SEWALL, Delmar .... 714-903-2762.... 68 G
SEWARD, Alison .... 603-526-3715.. 285 L
alison.seward@colby-sawyer.edu
SEWARD, David .... 415-565-4710.... 69 B
sewardd@uchastings.edu
SEWARD, David .... 479-788-7093.... 23 A
david.seward@uafs.edu
SEWARD, II, William .... 704-463-3066.. 354 F
bill.seward@pfeiffer.edu
SEWART, John, J .... 650-574-6196.... 62 H
sewart@smccd.edu
SEWELL, Devona .... 352-854-2322.... 97 R
sewelld@cf.edu
SEWELL, Gary .... 423-236-2700.. 444 B
garysewell@southern.edu
SEWELL, Holly .... 580-559-5203.. 383 H
hsewell@ecok.edu
SEWELL, Jason .... 423-472-7141.. 445 E
jsewell@clevelandstatecc.edu
SEWELL, John .... 601-974-1019.. 258 H
seweljl@millsaps.edu
SEWELL, Keli .... 864-977-7733.. 431 G
keli.sewell@ngu.edu
SEWELL, Kenneth .... 405-744-6501.. 385 G
kenneth.sewell@okstate.edu
SEWELL, Lisa .... 610-519-4646.. 422 G
lisa.sewell@villanova.edu
SEWELL, Robert .... 760-245-4271.... 73 H
robert.sewell@vvc.edu
SEWELL, Said .... 573-681-5074.. 266 I
sewells@lincolnu.edu
SEWELL, Sara .... 757-455-3237.. 500 E
ssewell@vwc.edu
SEWELL, Teresa .... 432-552-2600.. 478 B
sewell_t@utpb.edu
SEWELL, Thomas, R .... 423-585-2644.. 447 D
thomas.sewell@ws.edu
SEWELL, Zennabelle .... 212-261-1682.. 323 G
zsewell@nyit.edu
SEXTON, Ali .... 405-733-7459.. 387 I
asexton@rose.edu
SEXTON, Clarence .... 865-938-8186.. 439 G
SEXTON, Colleen .... 708-534-3958.. 140 H
csexton@govst.edu
SEXTON, Eric, L .... 316-978-3250.. 185 J
eric.sexton@wichita.edu
SEXTON, Gary .... 330-941-1778.. 382 A
sexton@wysu.org
SEXTON, Glenna, W .... 970-247-7331.... 80 D
sexton_g@fortlewis.edu
SEXTON, Michele, D .... 620-235-4187.. 184 C
msexton@pittstate.edu
SEXTON, Mike, B .... 408-554-5251.... 63 E
mbsexton@scu.edu
SEXTON, Steve .... 615-248-7792.. 447 F
ssexton@trevecca.edu
SEXTON, Susan .... 651-690-6565.. 254 M
swsexton@stkate.edu
SEXTON, Susan, K .... 937-229-4333.. 379 D
ssexton1@udayton.edu
SEXTON, Thelma .... 478-757-3947.. 129 L
tsexton@wesleyancollege.edu
SEXTON, Timothy, D .... 574-631-1785.. 168 B
sexton.30@nd.edu
SEXTON-JOHNSON, Sara 509-533-8486.. 502 H
ssexton-johnson@ccs.spokane.edu
SEYDEL, Tim .... 541-962-3740.. 391 C
tseydel@eou.edu
SEYERLE, Amy .... 626-529-8007.... 55 H
aseyerle@pacificoaks.edu
SEYMOUR, Avanti .... 617-449-7041.. 229 B
avanti.seymour@urbancollege.edu
SEYMOUR, Dennis .... 815-939-5302.. 150 I
dseymour@olivet.edu
SEYMOUR, Heather, B ...... 207-755-5100.. 203 I
SEYMOUR, Jodi, L .... 641-784-5112.. 172 G
seymour@graceland.edu
SEYMOUR, Mark .... 330-471-8100.. 371 J
mseymour@malone.edu
SEYMOUR, Michael .... 818-767-0888.... 75 D
michael.seymour@woodbury.edu
SEYMOUR, Michael .... 218-733-7600.. 249 H
michael.seymour@lsc.edu
SEYMOUR, Sharon .... 217-479-7025.. 147 C
sharon.seymour@mac.edu
SEYMOUR, William .... 423-478-6200.. 445 E
wseymour@clevelandstatecc.edu
SFRAGA, Mike .... 907-474-6533.... 10 G
msfraga@alaska.edu
SGANGA, Fred .... 631-444-8606.. 332 A
fred.sganga@stonybrook.edu
SGARLATA, Constance ..... 410-857-2280.. 209 D
csgarlata@mcdaniel.edu
SGRO, Michael .... 607-753-2517.. 333 A
michael.sgro@cortland.edu
SHAAB, Jane .... 410-706-8282.. 211 F
jshaab@umaryland.edu
SHAABAN-MAGANA,
Lamea .... 205-348-5040...... 8 D
lshaaban@sa.ua.edu
SHAAK, Melissa, J .... 781-239-4398.. 214 G
shaak@babson.edu
SHABAHANG, Homa .... 909-593-3511.... 71 B
hshabahang@laverne.edu
SHABAZ, Kwame, Z .... 601-979-2121.. 258 D
kwame.z.shabazz@jsums.edu
SHABAZZ, Ricky .... 909-384-8992.... 60 C
rshabazz@sbccd.cc.ca.us
SHABAZZI, Mohammad .. 601-979-8806.. 258 D
mohammad.shabazzi@jsums.edu
SHABLIA, Nataliia .... 215-572-2887.. 397 G
shablian@arcadia.edu
SHABLIN, Steven, J .... 248-370-3470.. 239 K
shablin@oakland.edu
SHABLOSKI, Regan .... 814-866-6641.. 407 D
rshabloski@lecom.edu
SHACHAR, Mickey .... 714-816-0366.... 68 E
mickey.shachar@trident.edu
SHACHTER, Amy, M .... 408-554-7041.... 63 E
ashachter@scu.edu
SHACKELFORD, Bonnie ... 614-825-6255.. 362 J
bshackelford@aiam.edu
SHACKELFORD, Carol ..... 601-635-2111.. 257 F
cshackelford@eccc.edu
SHACKELFORD, Harper ... 910-678-8413.. 349 F
shackelh@faytechcc.edu
SHACKELFORD, Peter, J .. 517-750-1200.. 241 E
pshackel@arbor.edu
SHACKELFORD, Philip .... 870-864-7116.... 22 D
pshackelford@southark.edu
SHACKLEFORD, Douglas . 919-962-1300.. 357 D
douglas_shackelford@kenan-flagler.unc.edu
SHACKLEFORD, Keith ...... 949-451-5398.... 65 F
kshackleford@ivc.edu
SHACKLEFORD, JR.,
Robert, S .... 336-633-0287.. 352 B
rsshackleford@randolph.edu
SHADDY, Deborah .... 913-758-6143.. 185 F
shaddy15@stmary.edu
SHADE-DAVISON,
Stephanie .... 580-745-2267.. 387 M
sdavison@se.edu
SHADELL, Vicki .... 501-977-2189.... 24 B
shadell@uaccm.edu
SHADER, Gail .... 518-828-4181.. 311 D
gail.shader@sunycgcc.edu
SHADICK, Richard .... 212-346-1526.. 325 J
rshadick@pace.edu
SHADLE, Joseph .... 513-745-3570.. 381 I
shadlej@xavier.edu
SHADLE, Julie .... 848-932-2207.. 295 F
jshadle@winants.rutgers.edu
SHADOIAN, Holly, L .... 401-456-8884.. 425 E
hshadoian@ric.edu
SHAFER, Barb .... 406-657-2301.. 277 D
bshafer@msubillings.edu
SHAFER, Jack, L .... 610-499-4454.. 423 E
jlshafer@widener.edu
SHAFER, Jesse .... 215-951-2850.. 416 G
shaferj@philau.edu
SHAFER, John, R .... 317-738-8080.. 160 J
jshafer@franklincollege.edu
SHAFER, Kathrynne, G .... 717-691-6003.. 410 J
kshafer@messiah.edu
SHAFER, Lisa .... 530-541-4660.... 48 D
shaferl@ltcc.edu
SHAFER, Lisa .... 610-328-8009.. 419 I
lshafer1@swarthmore.edu
SHAFER, Pamela .... 832-559-4217.. 461 B
pamela.n.shafer@lonestar.edu
SHAFER, Richard .... 214-768-1580.. 465 J
rashafer@smu.edu
SHAFER, Staci .... 618-985-3741.. 143 F
stacishafer@jalc.edu
SHAFER, Teresa .... 419-448-3309.. 378 A
tshafer@tiffin.edu
SHAFER, Trish .... 610-660-3101.. 418 G
tshafer@sju.edu
SHAFFER, Alan .... 740-392-6868.. 373 D
alan.shaffer@mvnu.edu
SHAFFER, Amy .... 912-443-5512.. 126 G
ashaffer@savannahtech.edu
SHAFFER, Brian, W .... 901-843-3976.. 443 L
shaffer@rhodes.edu
SHAFFER, Chris .... 334-670-3266...... 7 H
shafferc@troy.edu

SHARPLES, Stacey 941-752-5256 110 H
sharpls@scf.edu

SHARPNACK, Patricia 440-684-6032 380 F
psharpnack@ursuline.edu

SHARPS, Alonia, C 301-546-0170 210 C
sharpsac@pgcc.edu

SHARRAR, Jack 415-439-2412 26 G
jsharrar@act-sf.org

SHARRATT, Emily 541-962-3866 391 C
esharratt@eou.edu

SHASTEEN, C. Scott 931-393-1605 446 D
sshasteen@mscc.edu

SHATTUCK, Debra 605-342-0317 436 A
dshattuck@johnwitherspooncollege.org

SHATTUCK, Larry 410-532-5551 210 B
lshattuck@ndm.edu

SHATTUCK, R. Cooper 205-348-8345 8 C
cshattuck@uasystem.edu

SHATTUCK, Wendy 909-748-8447 71 K
wendy_shattuck@redlands.edu

SHAUB, Larry 610-796-8298 397 D
larry.shaub@alvernia.edu

SHAUGHNESSY, Anne 617-824-8525 218 B
anne_shaughnessy@emerson.edu

SHAUGHNESSY, Elizabeth 650-433-3806 56 D
eshaughnessy@paloaltou.edu

SHAUGHNESSY, Joseph 254-659-7821 458 K
jxs@hillcollege.edu

SHAUGHNESSY, Joseph 781-768-7133 227 G
joseph.shaughnessy@regiscollege.edu

SHAUGHNESSY, Josette 915-831-6330 457 H
jshaugh2@epcc.edu

SHAUGHNESSY, Mark 631-656-2147 314 F
mark.shaughnessy@ftc.edu

SHAUGHNESSY, Michael 724-503-1001 422 H
mshaughnessy@washjeff.edu

SHAUL, Lesa 205-652-3460 9 F
lcc@uwa.edu

SHAUNAK, Raj 662-243-1911 257 G
rshaunak@eastms.edu

SHAUNAK, Sudershan 760-757-2121 52 K
sshaunak@miracosta.edu

SHAVER, Deborah 208-885-4627 134 G
dshaver@uidaho.edu

SHAVER, Debra, D 413-585-2523 228 D
dshaver@smith.edu

SHAVER, Joan, L 520-626-6152 17 I
jshaver@email.arizona.edu

SHAVER, Joseph, E 304-326-1481 511 D
jshaver@salemu.edu

SHAW, Anne, C 910-938-6322 348 G
shawa@coastalcarolina.edu

SHAW, Barbara, L 209-946-2424 71 C
bshaw@pacific.edu

SHAW, Becky 413-585-4940 228 D
rshaw@smith.edu

SHAW, Benjamin 207-762-0146 205 D
benjamin.shaw@maine.edu

SHAW, Brandy 713-525-2124 475 J
shawb1@stthom.edu

SHAW, Brian, D 804-828-1200 496 D
bdshaw@vcu.edu

SHAW, Brian, R 202-231-8698 528 C
brian.shaw@dodiis.mil

SHAW, Carolyn 661-259-7800 40 A
carolyn.shaw@canyons.edu

SHAW, Carrie 970-943-7015 84 H
cshaw@western.edu

SHAW, Carrie 425-235-2415 506 F
cshaw@rtc.edu

SHAW, Chester 708-974-5360 148 G
schawc6@morainevalley.edu

SHAW, Chip 806-743-1500 472 D
chip.shaw@ttuhsc.edu

SHAW, Dameon 662-254-3901 260 A
dameon.shaw@mvsu.edu

SHAW, Dameon 662-254-3790 260 A
dameon.shaw@mvsu.edu

SHAW, Darlene, L 843-792-2228 431 A
shawd@musc.edu

SHAW, David 662-325-3570 259 D
dshaw@research.msstate.edu

SHAW, Deborah, L 256-765-5018 9 C
dshaw2@una.edu

SHAW, Douglas, B 202-994-0514 92 D
dbs@gwu.edu

SHAW, Gordon 580-581-2245 382 G
gshaw@cameron.edu

SHAW, J. Brandon 540-868-7000 497 E

SHAW, James, A 606-783-2599 191 H
j.shaw@moreheadstate.edu

SHAW, Jane 650-723-1762 66 I

SHAW, Jen, D 352-392-1261 112 A
jends@dso.ufl.edu

SHAW, Jerone 662-621-4085 257 B
jshaw@coahomacc.edu

SHAW, John 214-333-5870 455 J
johns@dbu.edu

SHAW, Karen 765-455-9216 163 A
kshaw28@iuk.edu

SHAW, Karen, A 585-262-1501 321 J
kshaw@monroecc.edu

SHAW, Kathleen 804-828-6683 496 D
kshaw5@vcu.edu

SHAW, Ken 817-202-6202 466 C
kshaw@swau.edu

SHAW, Kevin 909-469-5401 74 K
kshaw@westernu.edu

SHAW, Kristi 620-441-5206 180 D
kshaw@cowley.edu

SHAW, Linda 480-732-7307 13 O
linda.shaw@cgc.edu

SHAW, Linda 415-239-3303 38 E
lshaw@ccsf.edu

SHAW, Lori 620-331-2480 181 J
lshaw@indycc.edu

SHAW, Lorna, L 502-597-6443 191 B
lorna.shaw@kysu.edu

SHAW, Marc 646-664-3013 306 M
marc.shaw@cuny.edu

SHAW, Mary Ann 713-942-5036 475 J
shawme@sthom.edu

SHAW, Matthew 765-285-5277 159 B
mcshaw2@bsu.edu

SHAW, Nancy 802-224-3000 485 G
nancy.shaw@vsc.edu

SHAW, Pankaj 614-292-1486 375 A
pshah@oh-tech.org

SHAW, Penelope 707-826-3942 34 F
pjs25@humboldt.edu

SHAW, Rebecca 617-745-3714 218 A
rebecca.shaw@enc.edu

SHAW, Richard 806-291-1162 479 D
shawr@wbu.edu

SHAW, Rick 661-722-6300 27 B
rshaw@avc.edu

SHAW, Robert, S 570-348-6245 409 H
rsshaw@marywood.edu

SHAW, Russell 601-857-3961 258 A
rdshaw@hindscc.edu

SHAW, Stephen 937-769-1881 363 F
sshaw@antioch.edu

SHAW, Steve 937-769-1351 363 E
sshaw@antioch.edu

SHAW, Suzanne 417-836-5139 268 I
suzanneshaw@missouristate.edu

SHAW, Teresa 909-602-2505 58 A
teresa.shaw@pomona.edu

SHAW, Timothy 972-883-5291 476 C
tim.shaw@utdallas.edu

SHAW, Tom 269-965-3931 236 A
shawt@kellogg.edu

SHAW, Wade, H 478-301-2459 124 D
shaw_wh@mercer.edu

SHAW-BURNETT, Margaret, A 716-878-5907 332 F
shawma@buffalostate.edu

SHAW HORTON, Sheilah 410-617-2842 208 G
sshorton@loyola.edu

SHAWCROFT, Sally 970-542-3151 81 H
sally.shawcroft@morgancc.edu

SHAWN, Donna, S 913-627-4171 182 C
dshawn@kckcc.edu

SHAWNEY, Lisa, L 603-513-1335 288 D
lisa.shawney@granite.edu

SHAWVER, Jeffrey 304-647-6325 514 A
jshawver@osteo.wvsom.edu

SHAWVER, Rebecca 979-230-3313 453 A
rebecca.shawver@brazosport.edu

SHAWVER, William, G 513-529-9203 372 K
shawvewg@miamioh.edu

SHAY, Carla, E 231-843-5942 243 G
ceshay@westshore.edu

SHAY, Chris 408-554-4300 63 E
cshay@scu.edu

SHAY, Pamela 614-947-6135 369 A
pamela.shay@franklin.edu

SHAY, Patrick 612-436-7519 248 F
pshay@msbcollege.edu

SHAY, Robert 573-882-2606 273 E
shayr@missouri.edu

SHAY, Robert, S 303-492-7505 83 K
robert.shay@colorado.edu

SHAY, William 323-563-4840 37 G
williamshay@cdrewu.edu

SHCHEGOL, Alex 718-522-9073 304 D
ashchegol@asa.edu

SHCHEGOL, Alla 718-522-9073 304 D
allchik1@asa.edu

SHEA, Catherine 303-492-7896 83 K
catherine.shea@colorado.edu

SHEA, Claire 603-623-0313 287 D
claireshea@nhia.edu

SHEA, Diane 617-732-1604 218 C
shead@emmanuel.edu

SHEA, Donna 617-353-5124 216 E
dshea@bu.edu

SHEA, James, P 701-355-8100 362 G

SHEA, Jane 508-854-4358 224 E
jshea@qcc.mass.edu

SHEA, Kevin, J 617-552-3252 216 C
k.shea@bc.edu

SHEA, Missy 781-283-2335 229 C
mshea@wellesley.edu

SHEA, Rich, J 814-886-6474 411 C
rshea@mtaloy.edu

SHEAFF, Shannon 928-757-0817 15 E
ssheaff@mohave.edu

SHEAFFER, Andrea 510-649-2465 45 G
asheaffer@gtu.edu

SHEAFFER, Ellen 301-387-3003 207 G
ellen.sheaffer@garrettcollege.edu

SHEAFFER, Karen, M 570-321-4311 409 F
sheaffer@lycoming.edu

SHEAHAN, John 217-351-2555 151 B
jsheahan@parkland.edu

SHEAHAN, Mary 701-483-2883 360 D
mary.sheahan@dickinsonstate.edu

SHEALEY, Monika 856-256-4751 295 E
shealey@rowan.edu

SHEAR, Skip 660-944-2853 263 G
sshear@conception.edu

SHEAR, Stephen 813-253-7014 102 R
sshear2@hccfl.edu

SHEARD, Reed 805-565-7171 75 A
rsheard@westmont.edu

SHEARD, Reed, L 805-565-7171 75 A
rsheard@westmont.edu

SHEARER, Christine 406-657-2177 277 D
c.shearercremean@msubillings.edu

SHEARER, Erik 707-256-7150 53 H
eshearer@napavalley.edu

SHEARER, Jonathan, L 724-589-2700 420 D
jshearer@thiel.edu

SHEARER, Liz 410-704-2451 213 B
lshearer@towson.edu

SHEARER, Michelle 601-477-4039 258 E
michele.shearer@jcjc.edu

SHEARER, Pam 601-318-6561 261 I
pshearer@wmcarey.edu

SHEARIN, Lisa 252-246-1310 354 D
lshearin@wilsoncc.edu

SHEARIN, Wally, M 336-506-4279 347 C
wally.shearin@alamancecc.edu

SHEARON, James 910-892-3178 344 I
jshearon@heritagebiblecollege.edu

SHEARON, Randall 919-735-5151 354 A
shearon@waynecc.edu

SHEARRILL, Charmagne 661-255-1050 30 E
cshearrill@calarts.edu

SHEARS, III, George 704-334-6882 343 D
gshears@charlottechristian.edu

SHEBLE, Mary Ann 248-232-4512 239 E
masheble@oaklandcc.edu

SHEBLE, Mary Ann 248-942-3214 239 E
masheble@oaklandcc.edu

SHECKELLS, Sara 617-730-7072 226 J
sara.sheckells@newbury.edu

SHECKLER, Allyson 508-565-1724 228 F
asheckler@stonehill.edu

SHECTERLE, Ross, A 414-425-8300 519 F
rector@shsst.edu

SHEDD, Jean, E 847-491-8546 150 F
j-shedd@northwestern.edu

SHEDD, Louis 205-391-2359 6 G
lshedd@sheltonstate.edu

SHEDD, Sally 757-455-3283 500 E
sshedd@vwc.edu

SHEDEK, Lindsay 319-399-8617 170 G
lshedek@coe.edu

SHEDRICK, Karen, R 601-877-6111 256 F
karen@alcorn.edu

SHEEHAN, Bill 573-288-6395 264 F
wsheehan@culver.edu

SHEEHAN, Diep 781-768-7078 227 G
diep.sheehan@regiscollege.edu

SHEEHAN, Eugene 970-351-2817 84 C
eugene.sheehan@unco.edu

SHEEHAN, Heather 701-224-5465 361 C
heather.sheehan@bismarckstate.edu

SHEEHAN, James 508-999-8051 220 H
jsheehan4@umassd.edu

SHEEHAN, Jerry 406-994-2525 277 C
jsheehan@montana.edu

SHEEHAN, Robert, J 410-546-4127 213 A
rjsheehan@salisbury.edu

SHEEHAN, Ryan 803-323-3023 435 B
sheehanr@winthrop.edu

SHEEHAN, Tim 801-957-2001 483 A
tim.scheehan@slcc.edu

SHEEHAN, Timothy 651-213-4166 247 B
tsheehan@hazeldenbettyford.edu

SHEEHEY, John, D 802-654-2571 484 I
jsheehey@smcvt.edu

SHEEHY, Colette 434-924-3349 495 H
cc@virginia.edu

SHEEHY, Harry 603-646-2465 286 J
harry.sheehy@dartmouth.edu

SHEEHY, Matthew 781-736-4642 216 F
sheehy@brandeis.edu

SHEEKS, Gina 706-507-8730 119 E
sheeks_gina@columbusstate.edu

SHEELEY, Robert, G 203-392-6050 85 H
sheeleyr1@southernct.edu

SHEERAN, Kate 415-503-6251 61 C

SHEERAN, Robert, M 513-745-2072 381 I
sheeran@xavier.edu

SHEERAZI, Saji 718-281-5144 309 E
mgettingstraesser@qcc.cuny.edu

SHEERER, Marilyn 910-962-3389 358 D
sheererm@uncw.edu

SHEETS, Chad 651-423-8232 249 B
chad.sheets@dctc.edu

SHEETS, Christine 740-593-4094 375 H
sheetsch@ohio.edu

SHEETS, Helene 419-824-3965 371 I
hsheets@lourdes.edu

SHEETS, Julie 573-518-2206 268 E
jsheets@mineralarea.edu

SHEETS, Tami 740-245-7209 380 C
tsheets@rio.edu

SHEETZ, Ken 803-323-2275 435 B
sheetzk@winthrop.edu

SHEETZ, Tracey 724-938-4404 414 E
sheetz@calu.edu

SHEFF, Kimberly 207-509-7224 204 F
ksheff@unity.edu

SHEFFER, Ilene 574-520-4344 163 E
isheffer@iusb.edu

SHEFFIELD, Bethany, D 814-641-3101 406 F
sheffib@juniata.edu

SHEFFIELD, Christopher, R 716-286-8425 324 E
crs@niagara.edu

SHEFFIELD, Linda 434-736-2002 498 E
linda.sheffield@southside.edu

SHEFFIELD, Rori 512-245-2319 471 F
rp41@txstate.edu

SHEFFIELD, Roy, S 828-884-8312 342 C
scotts@brevard.edu

SHEFFIELD, Vonne 478-301-2500 124 D
sheffield_v@mercer.edu

SHEFFLETTE, Nancy, A 501-882-4581 18 I
nashefflette@asub.edu

SHEGAN, Christine 570-662-4900 415 E
cshegan@mansfield.edu

SHEHATA, Erika 610-399-2053 414 F
eshehata@cheyney.edu

SHEHEANE, Dene 404-894-1238 121 D
dene.sheheane@dev.gatech.edu

SHEHEE, Amy 859-985-3002 187 B
sheheea@berea.edu

SHEIBLEY, Thomas, J 610-660-1030 418 G
tsheible@sju.edu

SHEID, Christopher 307-382-1661 527 C
csheid@westernwyoming.edu

SHEIKH, Ammad 410-532-5393 210 B
asheikh@ndm.edu

SHEILLEY, Holly 859-233-8548 193 D
hsheilley@transy.edu

SHEILS, Cathleen 315-460-3150 335 D
cathleen.sheils@esc.edu

SHEIN, David 845-758-7454 304 F
shein@bard.edu

SHELBURNE, Stephanie 818-785-2726 36 M
stephanie.shelburne@casalomacollege.edu

SHELBY, Barbara 740-588-1315 382 C
bshelby@zanestate.edu

SHELBY, Jane 907-786-4708 10 F
njshelby@uaa.alaska.edu

SHELBY, Liz 541-552-6111 395 A
shelbyl@sou.edu

SHELBY, Nicole 318-869-5146 194 I
nshelby@centenary.edu

SHELDAHL, Tania 928-776-2128 18 D
tania.sheldahl@yc.edu

SHELDEN, Deborah, L 906-487-3112 238 A
dlassila@mtu.edu

SHELDON, Al 541-956-7440 394 J
asheldon@roguecc.edu

SHELDON, Jane 308-865-8427 282 L
sheldonj@unk.edu

SHELDON, Karen 859-371-9393 186 M

SHELDON, Todd 402-363-5601 283 G
tlsheldon@york.edu

SHELEK-FURBEE, Katherine 304-829-7189 510 G
kshelek-furbee@bethanywv.edu

SHELL, Cathy 828-898-8740 345 G
shell@lmc.edu

SHELL, Chandrea 423-461-8756 442 K
chshell@milligan.edu

SHELL, Christina 734-487-2382 233 J
cshell@emich.edu

SHELL, Deltha 870-368-2007 21 F
dshell@ozarka.edu

SHELL, Martin 650-723-4186 66 I
mshell@stanford.edu

SHELLABARGER, Roxanne 423-266-4574 443 M
rshellabarger@richmont.edu

SHERWOOD COOPER, Kristi ... 713-798-8685 .. 452 G kgc@bcm.edu
SHESKI, Harry ... 505-287-7981 .. 300 J hsheski@nmsu.edu
SHETLER, Clay, E ... 574-535-7351 .. 161 A clayes@goshen.edu
SHETTY, Devdas ... 202-274-5027 .. 94 B dshetty@udc.edu
SHEUCRAFT, Derrek, G ... 615-353-3272 .. 446 E derrek.sheucraft@nscc.edu
SHEVACH, Shirley ... 718-518-6655 .. 308 C sshevach@hostos.cuny.edu
SHEVEY, Wayne ... 414-443-8723 .. 522 P wayne.shevey@wlc.edu
SHEW, Rick ... 828-726-2704 .. 347 I rshew@cccti.edu
SHEWAN, Thomas, F ... 512-245-2148 .. 471 F tfs21@txstate.edu
SHEWMAKER, Jennifer ... 325-674-2459 .. 449 J jws02b@acu.edu
SHEWMAKER, Stephen ... 325-674-2710 .. 449 J sbs02a@acu.edu
SHIA, Mary ... 781-239-3123 .. 223 F mshia@massbay.edu
SHIAO, Jerry ... 408-435-8989 .... 64 G jshiao@svuca.edu
SHIBER, Cheryl ... 908-709-7511 .. 298 A cheryl.shiber@ucc.edu
SHIBLEY, Deborah ... 254-526-1331 .. 454 A deborah.shibley@ctcd.edu
SHIBLEY, Lisa, R ... 717-871-7871 .. 415 F lisa.shibley@millersville.edu
SHIBLEY, Robert ... 716-829-3981 .. 331 C rshibley@buffalo.edu
SHICK, Kourtney ... 570-945-8311 .. 406 H kourtney.shick@keystone.edu
SHIDE, Becky ... 219-866-6372 .. 166 J beckys@saintjoe.edu
SHIDELER, Lorri, P ... 814-641-3605 .. 406 F shidell@juniata.edu
SHIDLER, Linda ... 618-395-7777 .. 142 E shidlerl@iecc.edu
SHIEH, Charles ... 863-683-2975 .. 115 D shiehcs@webber.edu
SHIEL, Robert ... 630-889-6461 .. 149 G rshiel@nuhs.edu
SHIELDS, Brandt ... 816-271-4238 .. 269 C bshields4@missouriwestern.edu
SHIELDS, Brenda ... 610-399-2080 .. 414 F bshields@cheyney.edu
SHIELDS, Carmen ... 651-638-6233 .. 244 L c-shields@bethel.edu
SHIELDS, Chris ... 248-218-2114 .. 240 C cshields@rc.edu
SHIELDS, Chris ... 610-902-8366 .. 399 D cds28@drexel.edu
SHIELDS, JR., David, P .. 256-765-4223 ...... 9 C dpshields@una.edu
SHIELDS, Deanna, J ... 304-367-4775 .. 513 B deanna.shields@fairmontstate.edu
SHIELDS, Dennis, J ... 608-342-1234 .. 521 A shieldsd@uwplatt.edu
SHIELDS, Francis ... 860-439-2570 .... 87 F fjshi@conncoll.edu
SHIELDS, George, S ... 864-294-2007 .. 430 C george.shields@furman.edu
SHIELDS, Greg ... 937-294-6155 .. 364 H
SHIELDS, Jonathan ... 402-486-2897 .. 282 I joshield@ucollege.edu
SHIELDS, Joseph ... 740-593-0371 .. 375 H shieldj1@ohio.edu
SHIELDS, Loretta ... 330-672-2038 .. 370 I lshields@kent.edu
SHIELDS, Mathew ... 718-405-3215 .. 310 H mathew.shields@mountsaintvincent.edu
SHIELDS, Melany ... 716-896-0700 .. 339 E shieldsm@villa.edu
SHIELDS, Ronald ... 936-294-2771 .. 471 D rshield@shsu.edu
SHIELDS, Sally ... 309-649-6250 .. 155 G sally.shields@src.edu
SHIELDS, Theodosia, T ... 919-530-5233 .. 357 A tshields@nccu.edu
SHIELDS, Todd, G ... 479-575-4804 .... 22 I tshild@uark.edu
SHIELDS, Tonya ... 256-840-4165 ...... 6 H tshields@snead.edu
SHIELDS, Vickie ... 509-359-6081 .. 503 D vshields@ewu.edu
SHIELDS-GADSON, Alecia ... 410-951-3748 .. 212 E ashields-gadson@coppin.edu
SHIELL, Steve ... 907-834-1622 .... 11 A sshiell@pwscc.edu
SHIELL, William ... 630-620-2101 .. 150 B president@seminary.edu
SHIELS, Michael ... 262-691-7823 .. 524 G mshiels@wctc.edu
SHIER, Pat ... 907-786-4754 .... 10 F pshier1@uaa.alaska.edu
SHIFERRAW, Mahtem ... 310-665-6936 .... 55 E mshiferraw@otis.edu
SHIFFLETT, Lee, A ... 540-568-7926 .. 490 J shiffla@jmu.edu
SHIFFMAN, Paul ... 518-464-8803 .. 314 A pshiffman@excelsior.edu
SHIFLETT, Christopher ... 303-329-6355 .... 78 O assistantdean@cstcm.edu
SHIGEHARA, Deborah, S . 808-934-2516 .. 131 J deborahs@hawaii.edu
SHIGEMOTO, Steven ... 808-845-9166 .. 132 A sshigemo@hawaii.edu
SHIH, Alan ... 212-650-7909 .. 307 E ashih@ccny.cuny.edu
SHILL, Deb ... 641-269-3230 .. 172 I shilldeb@grinnell.edu
SHILLER, Barry ... 408-924-1141 .... 35 C barry.shiller@sjsu.edu
SHILLER, Barry ... 408-924-1000 .... 35 C barry.shiller@sjsu.edu
SHILLET, Gary ... 212-592-2000 .. 330 C gshillet@sva.edu
SHILLING, Chad ... 406-293-2721 .. 276 E cshilling@fvcc.edu
SHILLING, Corey ... 719-549-3195 .... 82 G corey.shilling@pueblocc.edu
SHILLING, Joseph ... 804-523-5230 .. 497 C jshilling@reynolds.edu
SHIM, Soyeon ... 608-262-4847 .. 519 K sshim7@wisc.edu
SHIMABUKURO, Julie ... 314-935-4893 .. 274 N jshimabukuro@wustl.edu
SHIMAZAKI, Leslie ... 619-388-2873 .... 60 G lshimaza@sdccd.edu
SHIMEK, Dennis, W ... 209-667-3351 .... 34 E dshimek@csustan.edu
SHIMEK, Gary, S ... 414-277-7181 .. 518 E shimek@msoe.edu
SHIMIZU, Jeff ... 310-434-4317 .... 63 F shimizu_jeffery@smc.edu
SHIMIZU, Stacey ... 309-556-3190 .. 143 D abroad@iwu.edu
SHIMOKAWA, Brandon ... 808-245-8230 .. 132 B shimokaw@hawaii.edu
SHIMOKAWA, Leila ... 808-689-2770 .. 131 G lwai@hawaii.edu
SHIN, David, H ... 714-527-0691 .... 43 C info@evangelia.edu
SHIN, Jason ... 714-533-3946 .... 35 E jshin@calums.edu
SHIN, Jason ... 714-533-1495 .... 65 B jshin@southbaylo.edu
SHIN, John ... 703-323-5690 .. 500 D
SHIN, Tia ... 213-387-4242 .... 48 I
SHIN LEE, Kyunglim ... 202-885-8620 .... 94 E kshinlee@wesleyseminary.edu
SHINAR, Tammera ... 530-895-2311 .... 29 F shinarta@butte.edu
SHINBERGER, Darcie, R .. 309-298-1993 .. 158 A dr-shinberger@wiu.edu
SHINDE, Prashant ... 773-995-2019 .. 136 M pshinde@csu.edu
SHINDLER, Kenda E, G ... 573-592-4216 .. 275 G kenda.shindler@williamwoods.edu
SHINE, Deanna ... 614-251-4645 .. 374 I shined@ohiodominican.edu
SHINER, Kimberly ... 909-537-7295 .... 34 C kshiner@csusb.edu
SHINER, Mark ... 315-228-7680 .. 310 G mshiner@colgate.edu
SHINEW, Dawn ... 419-372-7403 .. 364 E dshinew@bgsu.edu
SHINGLE, Barbara ... 814-472-3170 .. 418 F bshingle@francis.edu
SHINGLER, Jon ... 208-376-7731 .. 132 H jshingler@boisebible.edu
SHINGLETON, Jay ... 252-493-7777 .. 352 A jshingleton@email.pittcc.edu
SHINN, David ... 217-228-5432 .. 151 F shinnda@quincy.edu
SHINNERL, Clare ... 415-502-4457 .... 70 D clare.shinnerl@ucsf.edu
SHINVILLE, Padriac ... 309-268-8417 .. 141 C padriac.shinville@heartland.edu
SHINZATO, Noriko ... 415-338-1120 .... 35 B noriko@sfsu.edu
SHIPLEY, Aletha ... 614-287-2642 .. 367 C
SHIPLEY, Aletha ... 614-287-2640 .. 367 C ashipley@cscc.edu
SHIPLEY, Emily ... 513-745-4858 .. 381 I shipleye1@xavier.edu
SHIPLEY, Kip ... 802-287-8238 .. 484 A kip.shipley@greenmtn.edu
SHIPLEY, Robert ... 918-631-3092 .. 389 E robert-shipley@utulsa.edu
SHIPLEY, Robert, J ... 516-877-3452 .. 303 B shipley@adelphi.edu
SHIPLEY, Suzanne ... 940-397-4211 .. 462 A suzanne.shipley@mwsu.edu
SHIPMAN, Doug ... 618-395-7777 .. 142 E shipmand@iecc.edu
SHIPMAN, Jean, P ... 801-581-8771 .. 481 M jean.shipman@utah.edu
SHIPMAN, Richard ... 517-353-5940 .. 237 I shipmanr@msu.edu
SHIPMAN, Vicki ... 925-424-1355 .... 37 C vshipman@laspositascollege.edu
SHIPP, Brian ... 256-372-4276 ...... 1 A brian.shipp@aamu.edu
SHIPP, Daniel ... 402-554-2779 .. 283 B dshipp@unomaha.edu
SHIPP, Judith ... 217-206-7122 .. 156 G shipp.judy@uis.edu
SHIPP, Steve ... 940-397-4539 .. 462 A steve.shipp@mwsu.edu
SHIPPAM, Michael ... 912-478-6972 .. 122 B mshippam@georgiasouthern.edu
SHIPPEE, Ellen ... 603-535-2255 .. 288 F eshippee@plymouth.edu
SHIPWASH, Patrick ... 865-539-7401 .. 446 G jpshipwash@pstcc.edu
SHIPWAY, Ann, M ... 304-260-4380 .. 511 L ashipway@blueridgectc.edu
SHIRACHI, Susan ... 808-932-7623 .. 131 E shirachi@hawaii.edu
SHIRAH, Hank ... 850-484-2500 .. 106 H hshirah@pensacolastate.edu
SHIRAI, Calvin ... 808-245-8355 .. 132 B sharaic@hawaii.edu
SHIRAZI, Rhonda ... 251-380-2255 ...... 7 D rshirazi@shc.edu
SHIREMAN, Kimberly ... 336-342-4261 .. 352 F shiremank@rockinghamcc.edu
SHIREY, Benton ... 859-622-3311 .. 188 F benton.shirey@eku.edu
SHIREY, Jeanette ... 740-446-4367 .. 369 C jshirey@gallipoliscareercollege.edu
SHIREY, Jonathan ... 940-397-4324 .. 462 A jonathan.shirey@mwsu.edu
SHIREY, Kate, A ... 240-895-4203 .. 210 E kashirey@smcm.edu
SHIREY, JR., Robert, L ... 740-446-4367 .. 369 C rshirey@gallipoliscareercollege.edu
SHIREY NELSON, Linda .. 330-569-5441 .. 369 J shireylk@hiram.edu
SHIRING, Jennifer ... 724-852-3332 .. 423 A jshiring@waynesburg.edu
SHIRK, Jan, M ... 785-833-4302 .. 182 F jan@kwu.edu
SHIRLEY, John ... 607-753-7668 .. 333 A john.shirley@cortland.edu
SHIRLEY, Michele ... 706-754-7724 .. 125 B mshirley@northgatech.edu
SHIRLEY, Natalie ... 405-947-3200 .. 386 C natalie.shirley@osuokc.edu
SHIRLEY, Robert ... 334-387-3877 ...... 1 E robertshirley@amridgeuniversity.edu
SHIRLEY, Steven ... 701-858-3300 .. 360 F president@minotstateu.edu
SHIRLEY, JR., Thomas, R ... 215-951-2720 .. 416 G shirleyt@philau.edu
SHIRLEY, Vikki ... 850-245-0466 .. 110 I vikki.shirley@flbog.edu
SHIRVANI, Hamid, A ... 712-279-5400 .. 170 B hamid.shirvani@briarcliff.edu
SHISHOFF, John, W ... 937-778-7878 .. 368 E jshishoff@edisonohio.edu
SHISLER, Kirk, L ... 540-432-4203 .. 488 K kirk.shisler@emu.edu
SHISLER-RAPP, Susan, M ... 610-359-5040 .. 401 L srapp@dccc.edu
SHIVE, Hamp ... 601-857-3632 .. 258 A hfshive@hindscc.edu
SHIVELY, Bruce, L ... 775-784-6516 .. 285 A shively@unr.edu
SHIVELY, Debby, L ... 520-621-7151 .... 17 I dshively@email.arizona.edu
SHIVELY, Marnie ... 209-588-5105 .... 75 J shively@yosemite.edu
SHIVER, Michael ... 770-229-3044 .. 127 F mshiver@sctech.edu
SHIVERS, Melissa ... 865-974-7449 .. 448 E mshivers@utk.edu
SHIVLEY, Shane ... 620-341-5440 .. 180 G sshivley@emporia.edu
SHIVONE, Stephen ... 704-461-6831 .. 342 A stephenshivone@bac.edu
SHLAFER, David ... 352-395-5230 .. 109 C david.shlafer@sfcollege.edu
SHLESINGER, Ned ... 610-785-6284 .. 418 E nshlesinger@scs.edu
SHMIDMAN, Michael, A .. 212-463-0400 .. 337 I michaels@touro.edu
SHNEYDER, Mikhail ... 801-689-2160 .. 480 N mshneyder@nightingale.edu
SHNIDMAN, Avrohom ... 410-484-7200 .. 210 A
SHOALMIRE, Courtney ... 903-823-3142 .. 467 C courtney.shoalmire@texarkanacollege.edu
SHOBOWALE, Tokumbo .. 212-229-5600 .. 322 E shobowale@newschool.edu
SHOCK, Brent, L ... 513-529-8710 .. 372 K shockb@miamioh.edu
SHOCK, Stephanie ... 701-662-1655 .. 361 E stephanie.shock@lrsc.edu
SHOCKEY, Christina ... 740-446-4367 .. 369 C cshockey@gallipoliscareercollege.edu
SHOCKEY, James, W ... 520-626-2422 .... 17 I jshockey@email.arizona.edu
SHOCKEY, Ryan ... 269-749-7189 .. 240 A rshockey@olivetcollege.edu
SHOCKEY, Sherri, L ... 260-982-5237 .. 165 M slshockey@manchester.edu
SHOCKEY, Stacy ... 712-325-3269 .. 174 B sshockey@iwcc.edu
SHOCKEY, Susie ... 580-559-5219 .. 383 H sshockey@ecok.edu
SHOCKLEY, Charity ... 302-857-7801 .... 90 F cshockley@desu.edu
SHOCKLEY, Darlas ... 641-683-5174 .. 173 C darlas.shockley@indianhills.edu
SHOCKLEY, David, R ... 336-386-3213 .. 353 F shockleyd@surry.edu
SHOCKLEY, Erica ... 607-274-3222 .. 317 D eshockley@ithaca.edu
SHOCKLEY-ZALABAK, Pam ... 719-255-3436 .... 83 L chancellor@uccs.edu
SHODA, Gene ... 509-963-2777 .. 501 K gene.shoda@cwu.edu
SHOEMAKE, James, M ... 214-388-5466 .. 457 A difs@dallasinstitute.edu
SHOEMAKE, Kellie ... 910-695-3900 .. 353 A shoemakek@sandhills.edu
SHOEMAKE, Monte ... 417-626-1234 .. 269 K shoemake.monte@occ.edu
SHOEMAKER, Carol ... 417-328-1531 .. 272 C cshoemaker@sbuniv.edu
SHOEMAKER, Chris ... 276-326-4212 .. 487 F cshoemaker@bluefield.edu
SHOEMAKER, Cindy ... 717-262-2006 .. 424 A cshoemaker@wilson.edu
SHOEMAKER, Jamie ... 304-326-1540 .. 511 D jshoemaker@salemu.edu
SHOEMAKER, Peter ... 973-761-9022 .. 297 A
SHOEMAKER, Scott ... 619-849-2565 .... 57 M scottshoemaker@pointloma.edu
SHOEMAKER, Stowe ... 702-895-3308 .. 284 L stowe.shoemaker@unlv.edu
SHOEMAKER, Troy ... 850-478-8496 .. 106 G tshoemaker@pcci.edu
SHOEN, Eric ... 718-270-2075 .. 332 B eric.shoen@downstate.edu
SHOENBERGER, George .. 301-985-7576 .. 212 C george.shoenberger@umuc.edu
SHOENER, Gary ... 570-504-7949 .. 407 B shoenerg@lackawanna.edu
SHOENER, Pattie ... 504-282-4455 .. 198 H pshoener@nobts.edu
SHOFFNER, Dan ... 903-586-2518 .. 460 A dshoffner@jacksonville-college.edu
SHOGE, Ruth, C ... 410-778-7292 .. 213 E rshoge2@washcoll.edu
SHOGER, Diane, L ... 585-262-1504 .. 321 J dshoger@monroecc.edu
SHOGREN, Jana ... 218-855-8129 .. 248 N jshogren@clcmn.edu
SHOHO, Alan, R ... 414-229-4181 .. 520 D shoho@uwm.edu
SHOJAI, Siamack ... 973-720-2964 .. 298 G shojais@wpunj.edu
SHOKRALLA, Diana ... 281-998-6150 .. 465 B diana.shkralla@sjcd.edu
SHOLLENBERGER, Kevin . 410-516-8382 .. 208 D ksholle1@jhu.edu
SHOLLEY, Sonya ... 304-876-5107 .. 513 E ssholley@shepherd.edu
SHOLTEN, Bryan ... 303-963-3398 .... 77 I bsholten@ccu.edu
SHOLUND, Jennifer ... 205-226-4979 ...... 2 C jray@bsc.edu
SHOMAKER, Kelli ... 979-830-4459 .. 452 J kelli.shomaker@blinn.edu
SHOMAKER, Kelli, D ... 334-844-5588 ...... 1 G kds0053@auburn.edu
SHOMO, Thomas, H ... 434-223-6262 .. 490 D tshomo@hsc.edu
SHONBRUN, Anne ... 718-270-4551 .. 332 B anne.shonbrun@downstate.edu
SHONK, Brian ... 870-612-2003 .... 23 H brian.shonk@uaccb.edu
SHONROCK, Michael, D .. 636-949-4900 .. 266 J mshonrock@lindenwood.edu
SHONTZ, Susan, F ... 814-641-3304 .. 406 F shontzs@juniata.edu
SHOOK, Christopher ... 406-243-6195 .. 276 K christopher.shook@umontana.edu
SHOOK, Douglas ... 213-740-7197 .... 72 D shook@usc.edu
SHOOK, Mark ... 706-880-8976 .. 123 K mshook@lagrange.edu

SICO, Eileen ... 845-575-3000 .. 320 B
eileen.sico@marist.edu

SICONOLFI, Steven ... 570-662-4805 .. 415 E
ssiconol@mansfield.edu

SIDDARAJU, Raj ... 309-649-6387 .. 155 G
raj.siddaraju@src.edu

SIDDENS, Nancy ... 217-732-3168 .. 146 A
nsiddens@lincolnchristian.edu

SIDDENS, Nicole ... 806-457-4200 .. 458 B
nsiddens@fpctx.edu

SIDDIQI, Melanie ... 909-652-6780 .... 37 D
melanie.siddiqi@chaffey.edu

SIDDIQI, Muddassir ... 708-656-8000 .. 149 A
muddassir.siddiqi@morton.edu

SIDDIQUI, Wasim ... 808-947-4788 .. 132 G

SIDDOWAY, Mike ... 719-389-6681 .... 77 J
msiddoway@coloradocollege.edu

SIDEBOTTOM, Daniel ... 607-753-2501 .. 333 A
daniel.sidebottom@cortland.edu

SIDELI, Kathleen ... 812-855-9304 .. 162 F
sideli@iu.edu

SIDERAKIS, John ... 212-650-7226 .. 307 E
jsiderakis@ccny.cuny.edu

SIDERAS, John, F ... 216-368-4340 .. 365 B
john.sideras@case.edu

SIDERS, Angie ... 765-455-9515 .. 163 A
asiders@iuk.edu

SIDES, Courtney, M ... 361-570-4354 .. 474 C
sidesc@uhv.edu

SIDES, Diane, O ... 573-651-2256 .. 272 B
dosides@semo.edu

SIDHU, Elda ... 702-895-5185 .. 284 L
elda.sidhu@unlv.edu

SIDIO, Jerome ... 401-874-5488 .. 426 D
sidio@uri.edu

SIDLE, Meg ... 606-218-5290 .. 194 C
margaretsidle@upike.edu

SIDLE, Stuart ... 203-932-7339 .... 90 A
ssidle@newhaven.edu

SIDLER, Sherri ... 312-362-6727 .. 139 C
ssidler@depaul.edu

SIDOCK, Andrew ... 217-479-7066 .. 147 C
andrew.sidock@mac.edu

SIDOR, Stanley ... 352-365-3523 .. 104 J
sidors@lssc.edu

SIDWELL, Scott, A ... 415-422-2923 .... 72 C
sasidwell@usfca.edu

SIEBENMORGEN, Tom ... 501-450-1333 .... 20 F
siebenmorgen@hendrix.edu

SIEBENS, Libby ... 509-682-6436 .. 509 D
lsiebens@wvc.edu

SIEBERT, Alex ... 513-562-8749 .. 363 H
asiebert@artacademy.edu

SIEBERT, David, J ... 847-735-5040 .. 145 B
siebert@lakeforest.edu

SIEBERT, Mary Anne ... 501-450-1372 .... 20 F
siebert@hendrix.edu

SIEBERT, Scotti ... 417-873-7434 .. 264 H
ssiebert@drury.edu

SIECKE, Elizabeth ... 201-684-7318 .. 294 G
esiecke@ramapo.edu

SIEDZIK, Richard ... 401-232-6505 .. 424 K
rsiedzik@bryant.edu

SIEFERT, Ruth ... 507-285-7472 .. 251 I
ruth.siefert@rctc.edu

SIEFERT, Tom ... 773-291-6412 .. 137 G
tsiefert@ccc.edu

SIEFKEN, Rob ... 212-924-5900 .. 336 I
rsiefken@swedishinstitute.edu

SIEG, Judy ... 864-592-4051 .. 432 H
siegj@sccsc.edu

SIEGEL, Barb ... 847-574-5214 .. 145 C
bsiegel@lfgsm.edu

SIEGEL, Christine ... 203-254-4000 .... 87 G
csiegel@fairfield.edu

SIEGEL, Donald, S ... 518-442-4910 .. 331 A
dsiegel@albany.edu

SIEGEL, Edward ... 727-341-4772 .. 108 D

SIEGEL, Larry ... 978-934-2107 .. 221 A
laurence_siegel@uml.edu

SIEGEL, Lawrence, J ... 212-430-4204 .. 341 G
lsiegel@aecom.yu.edu

SIEGEL, Miriam ... 413-748-3118 .. 228 E
mjsiegel@springfieldcollege.edu

SIEGEL, Tavianna ... 210-297-9129 .. 452 C
tavianna.siegel@baptisthealthsystem.com

SIEGENTHALER, Kim ... 573-882-4808 .. 273 E
siegenthalerk@missouri.edu

SIEGER, Eric ... 507-222-4183 .. 245 C
esieger@carleton.edu

SIEGERT, Gerald, A ... 513-556-5006 .. 379 A
gerald.siegert@uc.edu

SIEGERT, Kara, O ... 410-543-6023 .. 213 A
kosiegert@salisbury.edu

SIEGFRIED, Jessica ... 435-283-7169 .. 482 E
jessica.siegfried@snow.edu

SIEGFRIED,
Kenneth (Ziggy) ... 661-654-2200 .... 32 A
ksiegfried@csub.edu

SIEGGREEN, Stephanie ... 270-745-4857 .. 194 D
stephanie.sieggreen@wku.edu

SIEGLE, Suzanne ... 734-995-7315 .. 232 I
suzanne.siegle@cuaa.edu

SIEGLER, Cynthia ... 413-572-8545 .. 222 E
csiegler@westfield.ma.edu

SIEGMANN, Starla, C ... 414-443-8862 .. 522 P
starla.siegmann@wlc.edu

SIEKER, Tina ... 636-922-8314 .. 271 A
tsieker@stchas.edu

SIEMINSKI, Randy, B ... 315-386-7335 .. 335 B
sieminski@canton.edu

SIEMSEN, Deanna ... 719-336-6646 .... 81 D
deanna.siemsen@lamarcc.edu

SIENA, Steven ... 516-628-5558 .. 333 C
sienas@oldwestbury.edu

SIENKIEWICZ, Janice ... 703-370-6600 .. 492 I

SIES, Susan ... 410-386-8325 .. 206 I
ssies@carrollcc.edu

SIESING, Gina ... 610-526-5272 .. 398 K
gsiesing@brynmawr.edu

SIETSEMA, Adriane ... 641-648-4611 .. 173 K
adriane.sietsema@iavalley.edu

SIEVERDING, John ... 605-770-0700 .. 436 C
john.sieverding@mitchelltech.edu

SIEVERS, Allison ... 303-963-3437 .... 77 I

SIEVERS, Debbie ... 708-974-5330 .. 148 G
sievers@morainevalley.edu

SIFERD, Sally, L ... 419-358-3324 .. 364 D
siferds@bluffton.edu

SIFFERLEN, Ned, J ... 937-512-2510 .. 377 D
ned.sifferlen@sinclair.edu

SIFRI, Tatiana ... 630-637-5161 .. 149 H
tsifri@noctrl.edu

SIFTAR, Michael ... 918-595-8123 .. 388 F
michael.siftar@tulsacc.edu

SIFUENTES, Alma ... 831-459-2347 .... 70 F
alma@ucsc.edu

SIFUENTES-JAUREGUI,
Ben ... 848-932-7865 .. 295 F
ben.sifuentes.jauregui@rutgers.edu

SIGALA, Al ... 503-491-7548 .. 392 F
al.sigala@mhcc.edu

SIGANOFF, Diana ... 714-620-3700 .... 27 I

SIGAUKE, Erica ... 417-667-8181 .. 264 A
esigauke@cottey.edu

SIGGERS, Julian, F ... 215-898-4052 .. 421 E
siggers@upenn.edu

SIGGERS, Lauretta ... 617-873-0170 .. 217 A
lauretta.siggers@cambridgecollege.edu

SIGISMOND, William, D .. 585-292-3220 .. 321 J
wsigismond@monroecc.edu

SIGLER, Jeffrey ... 718-270-4979 .. 309 B
jeffrey@mec.cuny.edu

SIGLER, Todd, D ... 704-894-2915 .. 343 I
tosigler@davidson.edu

SIGMAN, David ... 414-847-3263 .. 518 D
davidsigman@miad.edu

SIGMON, Judy ... 336-917-5471 .. 355 E
judy.sigmon@salem.edu

SIGNOR, Mary ... 212-998-2352 .. 324 C
mary.signor@nyu.edu

SIGNORELLO, John ... 973-761-9615 .. 297 A
john.signorello@shu.edu

SIGNORELLO, Rose ... 713-525-3162 .. 475 J
signorr@stthom.edu

SIGUAW, Judy ... 252-328-1098 .. 356 C
siguawj@ecu.edu

SIGURDSON, Chris, W ... 520-621-4608 .... 17 I
sig@email.arizona.edu

SIGWORTH, Steve ... 713-798-2500 .. 452 G
sigworth@bcm.edu

SIIMPSON, Lisa ... 330-287-1296 .. 375 B
simpson.613@osu.edu

SIKES, Bruce ... 479-667-4046 .... 19 F
bsikes1@atu.edu

SIKES, Genny ... 605-229-8536 .. 436 H
genny.sikes@presentation.edu

SIKES, Janine ... 352-846-3903 .. 112 A
jysikes@ufl.edu

SIKES, Pamela, J ... 619-260-4595 .... 72 B
psikes@sandiego.edu

SIKES, Steddon, L ... 402-363-5668 .. 283 G
slsikes@york.edu

SIKKA, Anjoo ... 585-245-5151 .. 333 B
sikka@geneseo.edu

SIKORA, Jen ... 415-749-4594 .... 61 B
jsikora@sfai.edu

SIKORSKI, Henry ... 631-420-2142 .. 335 E
henry.sikorski@farmingdale.edu

SIKORSKI, Lindsey ... 570-662-4000 .. 415 E

SIKOWITZ, Peter, R ... 212-346-1200 .. 325 J
psikowitz@pace.edu

SILAFAU-TOA, Emey ... 684-699-9155 .. 529 E
e.silafau@amsamoa.edu

SILAK, Cathy ... 503-955-1001 .. 391 A
csilak@cu-portland.edu

SILANDER, Liisa ... 401-454-6349 .. 426 A
lsilande@risd.edu

SILANSKIS, Theresa ... 410-837-6838 .. 213 C
tsilanskis@ubalt.edu

SILAS, Monique ... 205-929-6350 ...... 5 D
msilas@lawsonstate.edu

SILBER, Daniel, K ... 573-288-6325 .. 264 F
dsilber@culver.edu

SILBER, Jeffrey, A ... 607-255-2016 .. 312 A
jas9@cornell.edu

SILBER, Martin ... 516-739-1545 .. 323 D
clinicdirector@nyctcm.edu

SILBERLING, Rosanne ... 818-299-5500 .... 74 A
rsilberling@westcoastuniversity.edu

SILBERMAN, Gerald, L ... 610-683-4106 .. 415 C
silberma@kutztown.edu

SILBERNAGEL, Darin ... 503-838-8176 .. 396 E
silbernd@wou.edu

SILBERQUIT, Paul ... 732-255-0400 .. 293 E
psilberquit@ocean.edu

SILBERSTEIN, Dara, J ... 607-777-2815 .. 331 B
lael@binghamton.edu

SILBERSTEIN, Jeffrey ... 212-659-9091 .. 317 A

SILBERSTEIN, Lloyd ... 213-740-1638 .... 72 D
lloyd.silberstein@usc.edu

SILCOX, Steve ... 269-927-7060 .. 236 G
ssilcox@lakemichigancollege.edu

SILECCHIA, Lucia ... 202-319-5560 .... 92 A
silecchia@cua.edu

SILER, Cathy ... 317-955-6241 .. 165 N
csiler@marian.edu

SILER, Ginni ... 706-802-5136 .. 121 C
gsiler@highlands.edu

SILER, Linda, K ... 616-538-2330 .. 234 D
lsiler@gbcol.edu

SILES, Marcelo, E ... 757-683-5195 .. 492 G
msiles@odu.edu

SILICIANO, John, A ... 607-255-3062 .. 312 A
jas83@cornell.edu

SILK, Eleana ... 914-961-8313 .. 329 H
es@svots.edu

SILK, Elizabeth ... 708-524-6481 .. 139 F
esilk@dom.edu

SILK, Mary, L ... 692-625-4410 .. 530 C
msilk@cmi.edu

SILKWORTH, Sabina ... 410-209-6017 .. 206 D
ssilkworth@bccc.edu

SILLEN, Andrew ... 718-951-5074 .. 307 D
asillen@brooklyn.cuny.edu

SILLIMAN, Steve ... 509-313-3522 .. 504 A
silliman@gonzaga.edu

SILMAN, Shawn ... 281-459-7673 .. 465 A
shawn.silman@sjcd.edu

SILVA, Adelina ... 210-485-0153 .. 450 A
asilva@alamo.edu

SILVA, Alan ... 651-690-6500 .. 254 M
ajsilva@stkate.edu

SILVA, Alyson ... 954-262-5258 .. 105 J
asilva1@nova.edu

SILVA, David, J ... 978-542-6246 .. 222 D
provost@salemstate.edu

SILVA, Efrain ... 760-355-6249 .... 46 J
efrain.silva@imperial.edu

SILVA, Elizabeth ... 619-260-2888 .... 72 B
registrar@sandiego.edu

SILVA, Griselda ... 773-481-8186 .. 137 I
gsilva24@ccc.edu

SILVA, Jack ... 401-454-6480 .. 426 A
jsilva@risd.edu

SILVA, Jaime ... 503-838-8845 .. 396 E
silvaj@wou.edu

SILVA, Jennifer ... 904-632-3141 .. 101 G
jen.silva@fscj.edu

SILVA, Jessica ... 707-468-3012 .... 52 C
jsilva@mendocino.edu

SILVA, Jessica, L ... 401-456-8047 .. 425 E
jsilva@ric.edu

SILVA, Lourdes ... 910-521-6301 .. 358 C
lourdes.silva@uncp.edu

SILVA, Marcie ... 305-442-9223 .. 105 F
msilva@mrc.edu

SILVA, Mariza ... 312-922-1884 .. 147 B
msilva@maccormac.edu

SILVA, Maureen ... 540-828-5450 .. 487 H
msilva@bridgewater.edu

SILVA, Rebecca ... 575-234-9208 .. 301 B
rsilva75@nmsu.edu

SILVA, Rito ... 361-698-2250 .. 457 D
rsilva@delmar.edu

SILVA, Tammy, A ... 508-999-8486 .. 220 H
tsilva@umassd.edu

SILVANO, Brian ... 949-794-9090 .... 66 H
bsilvano@stanbridge.edu

SILVAS, Kassie ... 208-769-7783 .. 134 C
kmsilvas@nic.edu

SILVER, Bret ... 212-870-2530 .. 304 I
bsilver@barnard.edu

SILVER, Candace ... 828-898-2417 .. 345 G
silverc@lmc.edu

SILVER, Frank, D ... 828-659-7810 .. 351 C
franksil@mcdowelltech.edu

SILVER, Jonathan ... 646-717-9705 .. 315 B
silver@gts.edu

SILVER, Mariko ... 802-440-4300 .. 483 E
msilver@bennington.edu

SILVER, Paul ... 802-635-1347 .. 486 B
paul.silver@jsc.edu

SILVER, Paula ... 610-499-4352 .. 423 E
psilver@widener.edu

SILVER, Rhonda ... 828-652-0630 .. 351 C
rhonda@mcdowelltech.edu

SILVER, Steve ... 541-684-7235 .. 393 B
ssilver@nwcu.edu

SILVER, William ... 707-664-2220 .... 35 D
silverw@sonoma.edu

SILVERBLATT, Pamela, S . 646-664-2977 .. 306 M
pamela.silverblatt@cuny.edu

SILVERI, Annamaria ... 313-993-1170 .. 241 G
silveran@udmercy.edu

SILVERI, Don ... 716-896-0700 .. 339 E
dsilveri@villa.edu

SILVERIA, John ... 617-573-8320 .. 228 G
jsilveria@suffolk.edu

SILVERII, Glenda ... 601-643-8440 .. 257 D
glenda.silverii@colin.edu

SILVERII, Stan ... 985-448-4030 .. 201 A
stan.silverii@nicholls.edu

SILVERMAN, Ed ... 315-279-5120 .. 318 C

SILVERMAN, Edward ... 212-650-6480 .. 307 E
esilverman@ccny.cuny.edu

SILVERMAN, Lori ... 360-992-2077 .. 502 E
lsilverman@clark.edu

SILVERS, Liz ... 828-766-1273 .. 351 B
lsilvers@mayland.edu

SILVERSTEIN, Melinda ... 831-479-6338 .... 29 G
mesilver@cabrillo.edu

SILVERTHORN, Mike ... 989-463-7327 .. 230 F
silverthorn@alma.edu

SILVESTER, John ... 402-461-7477 .. 280 D
jsilvester@hastings.edu

SILVESTRI, Mary Ann ... 508-541-1602 .. 217 G
msilvestri@dean.edu

SILVESTRI, Sandro ... 313-845-9878 .. 235 D
sandro@hfcc.edu

SILVESTRINI, Maria ... 787-284-1912 .. 534 C
msilvest@ponce.inter.edu

SILVESTRO, Michael ... 973-761-9138 .. 297 A
michael.silvestro1@shu.edu

SILVEY, Greg ... 660-831-4183 .. 269 B
silveyg@moval.edu

SILVIS, Kathryn ... 412-536-1297 .. 406 K
kathryn.silvis@laroche.edu

SILVYN, Jeffrey ... 520-206-4678 .... 16 F
jsilvyn@pima.edu

SILWOSKI, Richard, F ... 804-828-9647 .. 496 D
rfsliwoski@vcu.edu

SILY, Michel ... 305-899-3781 .... 96 D
msily@barry.edu

SILZER, Peter ... 831-242-5828 .. 527 K
peter.silzer@dliflc.edu

SIMA, Andrea ... 909-274-5950 .... 53 C
asims@mtsac.edu

SIMALA, Jay ... 847-317-6507 .. 156 B
jsimala@tiu.edu

SIMAMA, Jabari ... 404-297-9522 .. 122 A
simamaj@gptc.edu

SIMAR, Gina, A ... 409-882-3311 .. 471 B
gina.simar@lsco.edu

SIMAS, Andrew ... 415-351-3537 .... 61 B
asimas@sfai.edu

SIMCOX, Mary Grace ... 717-947-6090 .. 413 N
mrsimcox@pacollege.edu

SIMEK, Kathy, M ... 503-943-7101 .. 396 B
simek@up.edu

SIMER, Lauren ... 864-250-8484 .. 430 E
lauren.simer@gvltec.edu

SIMERAL, RET., Robert ... 831-656-3276 .. 528 D
rlsimera@nps.edu

SIMERSON, Gordon ... 203-932-7290 .... 90 A
gsimerson@newhaven.edu

SIMES, Sharon ... 206-934-3615 .. 506 J
sharon.simes@seattlecolleges.edu

SIMFUKWE, David ... 904-470-8174 .... 98 N
dsimfukwe@ewc.edu

SIMHAI, Toofawn ... 701-662-1511 .. 361 E
toofawn.simhai@lrsc.edu

SIMIC, Laura ... 208-426-3236 .. 132 I
laurasimic@boisestate.edu

SIMILI, Sal ... 208-467-8365 .. 134 D
ssimili@nnu.edu

SIMINOE, Judith, P ... 320-308-2122 .. 252 A
jpsiminoe@stcloudstate.edu

SIMINOFF, Laura ... 215-204-8624 .. 420 B
lasiminoff@temple.edu

SIMION, Karen ... 691-320-2480 .. 529 F
ksimion@comfsm.fm

SIMISON, Kynan ... 765-641-4076 .. 158 J
klsimison@anderson.edu

SIMKIN, Breanne ... 973-748-9000 .. 289 H
breanne_simkin@bloomfield.edu

SIMMELINK, Scott, K ... 712-707-7170 .. 176 B
scotts@nwciowa.edu

SIMMERS, Susan ... 970-351-2109 .... 84 C
susan.simmers@unco.edu

SIMMONDS, Thomas ... 914-674-7473 .. 320 G
tsimmonds1@mercy.edu

SIMMONS, ADeidra ... 580-559-5239 .. 383 H
asimmons@ecok.edu

SINCLAIR, Ashley ... 847-735-5231 .. 145 B
sinclair@lakeforest.edu
SINCLAIR, Christian ... 610-625-7896 .. 411 B
sinclairc@moravian.edu
SINCLAIR, Kelli ... 630-466-7900 .. 157 K
ksinclair@waubonsee.edu
SINCLAIR, Lisa ... 617-373-2157 .. 227 B
SINCLAIR, Nancy ... 270-384-8001 .. 191 E
sinclairn@lindsey.edu
SINCLAIR, Robert, L ... 312-788-1144 .. 157 H
rsinclair@vandercook.edu
SINCLAIR, Shannon, E ... 804-287-6683 .. 495 G
ssinclai@richmond.edu
SINCLAIR, Sue ... 309-694-5429 .. 141 F
ssinclair@icc.edu
SINCLAIR, Tori ... 816-802-3379 .. 266 D
tsinclair@kcai.edu
SINCLAIR CURTIS,
Jennifer ... 530-752-0554 .... 69 A
jscurtis@ucdavis.edu
SINDELAR, Peggy ... 972-273-3283 .. 456 G
psindelar@dcccd.edu
SINDER, Janet ... 718-780-7975 .. 305 L
janet.sinder@brooklaw.edu
SINDT, Christopher ... 925-631-4088 .... 59 I
csindt@stmarys-ca.edu
SINDT, Christopher ... 925-631-4309 .... 59 I
csindt@stmarys-ca.edu
SINES, Robert, G ... 330-672-9780 .. 370 I
rsines@kent.edu
SINEWAY, Carla ... 989-775-4123 .. 240 E
csineway@sagchip.edu
SINGEL, David ... 406-994-4371 .. 277 C
dsingel@montana.edu
SINGELL, Larry ... 812-855-2392 .. 162 F
lsingell@indiana.edu
SINGER, David ... 518-445-3211 .. 303 D
dsing@albanylaw.edu
SINGER, Eric ... 410-337-6456 .. 207 H
eric.singer@goucher.edu
SINGER, Jefferson ... 860-439-2010 .... 87 F
jefferson.singer@conncoll.edu
SINGER, Lori ... 212-229-5662 .. 322 E
singerl@newschool.edu
SINGER, Lynn, T ... 216-368-4389 .. 365 B
lts5@case.edu
SINGER, Marc ... 609-984-1130 .. 297 F
msinger@tesu.edu
SINGER, Marjorie ... 212-237-8911 .. 308 E
msinger@jjay.cuny.edu
SINGER, Mark ... 914-493-1909 .. 323 I
mark_singer@nymc.edu
SINGER, Nancy ... 801-957-4186 .. 483 A
nancy.singer@slcc.edu
SINGER, Susan, R ... 407-646-2355 .. 107 O
srsinger@rollins.edu
SINGER, Terry, L ... 502-852-6402 .. 194 A
terry.singer@louisville.edu
SINGER, Timothy ... 315-498-2485 .. 325 G
singert@sunyocc.edu
SINGER, Toby ... 603-897-8630 .. 287 F
tsinger@rivier.edu
SINGER, Yossi ... 718-268-4700 .. 326 L
SINGH, Amit ... 937-328-6026 .. 366 E
singha@clarkstate.edu
SINGH, Amitabh ... 229-430-7845 .. 115 K
amitabh.singh@asurams.edu
SINGH, Avena ... 541-888-1583 .. 395 B
asingh@socc.edu
SINGH, Gangaram ... 858-642-8109 .... 54 A
gsingh@nu.edu
SINGH, Gurbhushan ... 816-604-2207 .. 267 I
gurbhushan.singh@mcckc.edu
SINGH, Hamwant (Neil) .. 718-429-6600 .. 339 D
neil.singh@vaughn.edu
SINGH, Joanne ... 859-985-3056 .. 187 B
singhj@berea.edu
SINGH, Kamla ... 201-761-6000 .. 296 K
SINGH, Kanwal ... 914-395-2303 .. 329 K
ksingh@sarahlawrence.edu
SINGH, Kulwant ... 408-864-8745 .... 44 A
singhkulwant@deanza.edu
SINGH, Lindsey ... 239-590-7992 .. 110 L
lsingh@fgcu.edu
SINGH, Meharvan ... 817-735-5429 .. 475 C
meharvan.singh@unthsc.edu
SINGH, Nancy ... 559-251-4215 .... 29 I
library@calchristiancollege.edu
SINGH, Raj ... 212-237-8512 .. 308 E
rsingh@jjay.cuny.edu
SINGH, Simran ... 805-893-8377 .... 70 E
singh-s@sa.ucsb.edu
SINGH, Sudhir ... 301-687-4019 .. 212 F
ssingh@frostburg.edu
SINGH, Tanuja ... 210-436-3706 .. 464 H
tsingh@stmarytx.edu
SINGH CHAUHAN,
Indrajeet ... 212-423-2769 .. 315 G
indrajeet.singh@helenefuld.edu
SINGH MOONILALL,
Seeta ... 561-912-1211 .... 99 J
seetas@evergladesuniversity.edu
SINGLER, Melissa ... 910-362-7329 .. 348 A
msingler@cfcc.edu
SINGLETARY, Chip ... 850-201-8544 .. 113 E
singlech@tcc.fl.edu
SINGLETARY, James, M .. 740-392-6868 .. 373 D
jim.singletary@mvnu.edu
SINGLETARY, Joshua ... 518-694-7896 .. 303 C
joshua.singletary@acphs.edu
SINGLETARY, Michael ... 360-383-3035 .. 509 F
msingletary@whatcom.ctc.edu
SINGLETARY, Shelia ... 985-732-6640 .. 196 G
SINGLETON, Andre ... 510-981-2877 .... 57 B
asingleton@peralta.edu
SINGLETON, Brian ... 313-496-2778 .. 242 H
bsingle1@wcccd.edu
SINGLETON, Dana, M ... 757-822-2181 .. 498 H
dsingleton@tcc.edu
SINGLETON, Daphne ... 903-730-4890 .. 460 B
dsingleton@jarvis.edu
SINGLETON, Derrick ... 859-985-3130 .. 187 B
singletonp@berea.edu
SINGLETON, Gena, L ... 713-646-1778 .. 459 A
gsingleton@hcl.edu
SINGLETON, Gregory ... 931-221-7005 .. 444 E
singletong@apsu.edu
SINGLETON, Heather ... 757-446-5870 .. 489 B
singleha@evms.edu
SINGLETON, J. Ron ... 864-488-8274 .. 430 H
rsingleton@limestone.edu
SINGLETON, Janet ... 404-880-8286 .. 118 K
jsingleton@cau.edu
SINGLETON, Jennie ... 252-940-6202 .. 347 E
jennie.singleton@beaufortccc.edu
SINGLETON, John, L ... 817-257-7871 .. 469 G
j.singleton@tcu.edu
SINGLETON, Robin ... 870-762-3161 .... 18 G
rsingleton@smail.anc.edu
SINGLETON, Shawn, T ... 859-233-8154 .. 193 D
ssingleton@transy.edu
SINGLETON-WALKER,
Catherine ... 662-254-3365 .. 260 A
cswalker@mvsu.edu
SINGLETON-YOUNG,
Patricia ... 843-349-2304 .. 428 E
psyoung@coastal.edu
SINGLEY, III, Charles ... 706-821-8320 .. 125 H
csingley@paine.edu
SINGLEY, Gail ... 801-524-8118 .. 480 J
gsingley@ldsbc.edu
SINGLEY, Jason ... 510-885-3441 .... 32 E
jason.singley@csueastbay.edu
SINIARD, Michelle ... 478-218-3330 .. 118 G
msiniard@centralgatech.edu
SINIARD, Michelle ... 478-218-3330 .. 118 H
msiniard@centralgatech.edu
SINIARI, Jayne ... 215-728-4700 .. 412 B
jayne.siniari@jevs.org
SINK, Joyce, A ... 540-375-2201 .. 493 H
sink@roanoke.edu
SINK, Susanna, C ... 724-357-2205 .. 415 B
scsink@iup.edu
SINK, Tom ... 567-661-7221 .. 376 D
thomas_sink@owens.edu
SINN, Brad ... 320-363-5211 .. 245 I
bsinn@csbsju.edu
SINN, Jeanna ... 203-591-5238 .... 88 F
jsinn@post.edu
SINNOT, Dawn ... 215-751-8085 .. 401 G
dsinnot@ccp.edu
SINUTKO, John ... 805-378-1454 .... 73 D
jsinutko@vcccd.edu
SIPE, Bryan ... 912-279-5819 .. 119 C
bsipe@ccga.edu
SIPE, Deborah ... 503-399-6045 .. 390 E
deborah.sipe@chemeketa.edu
SIPE, Rebecca ... 734-487-0341 .. 233 J
rsipe@emich.edu
SIPES, Jennifer, L ... 217-581-3221 .. 139 H
jlsipes@eiu.edu
SIPHER, Justin ... 315-229-5319 .. 329 D
jsipher@stlawu.edu
SIPP, Richard, G ... 419-372-3230 .. 364 E
rsipp@bgsu.edu
SIPPEL, Christopher ... 419-434-5467 .. 379 E
sippel@findlay.edu
SIPPEL, Len ... 336-316-2841 .. 344 H
sippellc@guilford.edu
SIPSER, Michael ... 617-253-8900 .. 225 A
SIPUSIC, David, J ... 216-397-6699 .. 370 H
dsipusic@jcu.edu
SIRANGELO-ELBADAWY,
Catherine ... 201-360-4261 .. 292 B
csirangelo@hccc.edu
SIRBU, Jerald, B ... 303-369-5151 .... 82 F
jbs@plattcolorado.edu
SIRCY, John, C ... 803-786-3966 .. 429 A
jsircy@columbiasc.edu
SIRIANNI, Frank ... 212-636-6265 .. 314 G
sirianni@fordham.edu
SIRILLA, Michael ... 740-283-6245 .. 368 L
msirilla@franciscan.edu
SIRIMANGKALA, Pawena 305-899-3453 .... 96 D
psirimangkala@barry.edu
SIRJU-JOHNSON, Nicole . 607-777-4472 .. 331 B
njohnson@binghamton.edu
SIRMON, John ... 850-973-9495 .. 105 H
sirmonj@nfcc.edu
SIRONEN, Jacqueline ... 419-448-2261 .. 369 G
jsironen@heidelberg.edu
SIRPILLA, Sharon, L ... 330-471-8411 .. 371 J
ssirpilla@malone.edu
SISCHO, Brian, C ... 919-515-9085 .. 357 B
bcsischo@ncsu.edu
SISCO, Craig ... 405-682-7568 .. 385 D
michael.c.sisco@occc.edu
SISCO, Rodney, K ... 630-752-5028 .. 158 C
rodney.sisco@wheaton.edu
SISCOE, Dee ... 417-836-5526 .. 268 I
dsiscoe@missouristate.edu
SISEMORE, John ... 417-455-5674 .. 264 E
johnsisemore@crowder.edu
SISK, Beth ... 402-399-2415 .. 279 E
bsisk@csm.edu
SISK, Grant ... 972-860-4788 .. 456 B
SISK, Grant ... 972-860-4788 .. 456 B
gsisk@dcccd.edu
SISK, Matthew ... 304-457-6247 .. 510 B
siskmr@ab.edu
SISKAR, John, F ... 716-878-3787 .. 332 F
siskarjf@buffalostate.edu
SISKO, John ... 704-337-2833 .. 355 A
SISLER, Kelli ... 301-387-3060 .. 207 G
kelli.sisler@garrettcollege.edu
SISNEROS, Caroline ... 818-386-5642 .... 57 F
csisneros@pgu.edu
SISNEROS, Kathy ... 970-491-6384 .... 78 Q
kathy.sisneros@colostate.edu
SISNEROS, Patrick ... 425-388-9026 .. 503 F
psisnero@everettcc.edu
SISSION, Amanda ... 843-863-7991 .. 427 I
asission@csuniv.edu
SISSON, Cindy, N ... 574-372-5100 .. 161 B
sissoncn@grace.edu
SISSON, Jeanne, M ... 518-580-5664 .. 330 F
jsisson@skidmore.edu
SISSON, Karen ... 909-621-8132 .... 58 A
karen.sisson@pomona.edu
SISSON, Karl ... 585-567-9340 .. 316 F
karl.sisson@houghton.edu
SISSON, Laura ... 205-226-4861 ...... 2 C
lsisson@bsc.edu
SISSON, Linda, G ... 248-370-3266 .. 239 K
lgsisson@oakland.edu
SISSON, Philip, J ... 978-322-8488 .. 224 A
sissonp@middlesex.mass.edu
SISSON, Russell ... 606-546-1321 .. 193 E
rsisson@unionky.edu
SITARSKI, Karen ... 856-415-2110 .. 295 D
ksitarski@rcgc.edu
SITES, John ... 954-776-4476 .. 103 J
jsites@keiseruniversity.edu
SITES, Linda, K ... 301-447-5306 .. 209 G
lsites@msmary.edu
SITHARAMAN, Sri ... 706-507-8963 .. 119 E
sri@columbusstate.edu
SITORIUS, Patty ... 402-461-7331 .. 280 D
psitorius@hastings.edu
SITTON, Michael, R ... 315-267-2812 .. 334 B
sittonmr@potsdam.edu
SIVERSON, Karen ... 510-430-3131 .... 52 J
ksiverson@mills.edu
SIVERT, Shayla ... 760-744-1150 .... 56 F
ssivert@palomar.edu
SIVILLO, Jeremy ... 814-866-8143 .. 407 D
jsivillo@lecom.edu
SIVLEY, Scott ... 310-577-3000 .... 75 H
ssivley@yosan.edu
SIX, Jonathan ... 919-761-2100 .. 355 I
jsix@sebts.edu
SIXTA, Jeff ... 913-288-7613 .. 182 C
jsixta@kckcc.edu
SIZEMORE, Amanda ... 636-922-8388 .. 271 A
asizemore@stchas.edu
SIZEMORE, Dorethea ... 434-736-2051 .. 498 E
dorethea.sizemore@southside.edu
SIZEMORE, Ella ... 404-225-4712 .. 117 A
esizemore@atlantatech.edu
SIZEMORE, Lisa ... 828-339-4000 .. 353 D
l_sizemore@southwesterncc.edu
SIZER, Judith ... 617-873-0171 .. 217 A
judith.sizer@cambridgecollege.edu
SJOGREN, Michelle ... 859-442-1172 .. 189 D
michelle.sjogren@kctcs.edu
SJOGREN, Roxie, L ... 785-227-3380 .. 178 J
sjogrenr@bethanylb.edu
SJOQUIST, Corey ... 608-785-8939 .. 520 C
csjoquist@uwlax.edu
SJOVOLD, Carl ... 916-558-2402 .... 51 D
sjovolc@scc.losrios.edu
SJUE, Jessie ... 575-624-7151 .. 299 J
jessie.sjue@roswell.enmu.edu
SJUTS, Joseph, H ... 816-501-3700 .. 262 G
joe.sjuts@avila.edu
SKABROUD, Ryan ... 920-693-1347 .. 523 E
ryan.skabroud@gotoltc.edu
SKACH, Peter ... 773-298-3548 .. 153 H
skach@sxu.edu
SKADBERG, Ingrid ... 508-854-7545 .. 224 E
iskadberg@qcc.mass.edu
SKAFF, Penny ... 949-582-4573 .... 65 G
pskaff@saddleback.edu
SKAFTADOTTIR, Margret . 727-864-8363 .... 98 L
skaftami@eckerd.edu
SKAGGS, Brandon ... 254-295-4599 .. 474 E
bskaggs@umhb.edu
SKAGGS, Derek, S ... 417-625-9378 .. 268 H
skaggs-d@mssu.edu
SKALLERUD, Ron ... 715-365-4416 .. 524 C
rskallerud@nicoletcollege.edu
SKALNIK, James ... 610-861-1435 .. 411 B
skalnikj@moravian.edu
SKAMRA, Brian ... 920-748-8174 .. 519 E
skamrab@ripon.edu
SKANTZ, Ingrid ... 423-236-2833 .. 444 B
ilskantz@southern.edu
SKARDA, Mary Jo ... 641-782-1425 .. 177 B
skarda@swcciowa.edu
SKARI, Lisa ... 206-878-3710 .. 504 E
lskari@highline.edu
SKARRO, Scott ... 701-255-3285 .. 362 E
sskaro@uttc.edu
SKARSTEN, Fawn ... 810-762-3327 .. 242 B
skarsten@umflint.edu
SKARUPPA, Cindy ... 216-687-5353 .. 366 I
c.skaruppa@csuohio.edu
SKATES, Kathy ... 229-430-3524 .. 116 A
kskates@albanytech.edu
SKEDROS, James ... 617-850-1212 .. 219 F
jskedros@hchc.edu
SKEENS, Randy ... 304-896-7366 .. 512 E
randy.skeens@southernwv.edu
SKELLON, Hilary ... 720-890-8922 .... 80 O
director@itea.edu
SKELLY, Theresa ... 978-921-4242 .. 225 G
theresa.skelly@montserrat.edu
SKELTON, Don ... 662-562-3354 .. 260 C
SKELTON, Lonnie ... 714-867-5009 .... 65 D
lskelton@southcoastcollege.com
SKENANDORE, George ... 920-498-5688 .. 524 E
george.skenadore@nwtc.edu
SKERIK, Maryellen ... 630-637-5678 .. 149 H
mjskerik@noctrl.edu
SKERRETT, Kahtleen, R ... 804-289-8128 .. 495 G
kskerrett@richmond.edu
SKERRETT-LLANOS,
Carmen ... 787-993-8860 .. 537 G
carmen.skerrett@upr.edu
SKEVAKIS, Anthony ... 201-761-7360 .. 296 K
askevakisp@saintpeters.edu
SKIDMORE, Alan ... 304-766-3261 .. 514 B
askidmore@wvstateu.edu
SKIDMORE, Charlene ... 515-271-2999 .. 171 K
charlene.skidmore@drake.edu
SKIDMORE, Daniel, L ... 315-445-4759 .. 318 E
skidmodl@lemoyne.edu
SKIDMORE, Heather ... 304-424-8210 .. 514 D
heather.skidmore@wvup.edu
SKIDMORE, Sue ... 423-461-8729 .. 442 K
shskidmore@milligan.edu
SKILES, Adam, L ... 260-359-4130 .. 161 O
askiles@huntington.edu
SKILL, Thomas, D ... 937-229-3511 .. 379 D
tskill1@udayton.edu
SKILLINGS, Laura ... 269-782-1312 .. 241 C
lskillings@swmich.edu
SKINKLE, Lee ... 417-328-1601 .. 272 C
lskinkle@sbuniv.edu
SKINNER, Adrienne ... 269-467-9945 .. 234 B
askinner@glenoaks.edu
SKINNER, Billie ... 727-569-1401 .. 114 A
bskinner@trinitycollege.edu
SKINNER, Bruce ... 573-651-5103 .. 272 B
bskinner@semo.edu
SKINNER, Celeste ... 310-265-6143 .... 59 K
celeste.skinner@usw.salvationarmy.org
SKINNER, Dana ... 978-934-2310 .. 221 A
dana_skinner@uml.edu
SKINNER, Daniel ... 973-748-9000 .. 289 H
daniel_skinner@bloomfield.edu
SKINNER, Dean ... 479-248-7236 .... 20 C
dskinner@ecollege.edu
SKINNER, Deb ... 641-784-5108 .. 172 G
dskinner@graceland.edu
SKINNER, Denese ... 806-651-2345 .. 469 D
dskinner@wtamu.edu
SKINNER, Katherine ... 615-460-6342 .. 438 J
kathryn.skinner@belmont.edu

SKINNER, Kendra .... 573-651-2274.. 272 B
ksskinner@semo.edu
SKINNER, Marc .... 208-282-7954.. 134 G
marcs@uidaho.edu
SKINNER, Patricia, A .... 704-922-6475.. 350 A
skinner.pat@gaston.edu
SKINNER, Randall .... 928-428-8252.... 13 B
randall.skinner@eac.edu
SKINNER, Rick .... 580-774-3788.. 388 C
rick.skinner@swosu.edu
SKINNER, Robert .... 304-473-8557.. 515 B
skinner_b@wvwc.edu
SKINNER, Sally .... 208-459-5770.. 133 D
sskinner@collegeofidaho.edu
SKINNER, Thomas .... 225-578-4713.. 197 I
tskinner@lsu.edu
SKINNER, Thomas .... 215-368-5000.. 398 C
tskinner@biblical.edu
SKIPP, Steven, I .... 904-819-6258.... 99 M
sskipp@flagler.edu
SKIPPER, Bob .... 270-745-4295.. 194 D
bob.skipper@wku.edu
SKIPPER, Curt .... 601-635-2111.. 257 F
cskipper@eccc.edu
SKIPPER, Eric .... 843-208-8000.. 434 A
SKIPPER, Tawana .... 215-728-4478.. 412 B
tawana.skipper@jevs.org
SKIPPER, Wray .... 229-931-2354.. 127 C
wskipper@southgatech.edu
SKIPWORTH, Stan .... 909-621-8033.... 38 H
stan_skipworth@cuc.claremont.edu
SKIVIAT, David, M .... 740-283-6223.. 368 L
dskiviat@franciscan.edu
SKLANDER, Linda .... 262-524-7288.. 515 J
sklander@carrollu.edu
SKLAR, David .... 914-347-3910.. 340 C
david.sklar@sunywcc.edu
SKLAR, Jay .... 314-434-4044.. 264 C
jay.sklar@covenantseminary.edu
SKLBA, Stephanie .... 262-564-2662.. 523 D
sklba@gtc.edu
SKLEDER, Anne .... 570-408-4200.. 423 G
anne.skleder@wilkes.edu
SKLUT, John .... 509-313-3175.. 504 A
sklut@gonzaga.edu
SKOBLA, Kristen .... 315-792-5321.. 321 G
kskobla@mvcc.edu
SKOFF, Robert, M .... 724-847-6581.. 404 B
rmskoff@geneva.edu
SKOGEN, Larry .... 701-224-5431.. 361 C
larry.skogen@bismarckstate.edu
SKOGEN, Larry, C .... 701-224-5431.. 361 C
larry.skogen@bismarckstate.edu
SKOGEN, Sherri .... 715-425-3201.. 521 B
sherri.skogen@uwrf.edu
SKOGLUND, Elizabeth, A . 410-543-6161.. 213 A
easkoglund@salisbury.edu
SKOLNIK, Richard, J .... 315-312-3168.. 333 D
richard.skolnik@oswego.edu
SKOLOS, Nancy .... 401-454-6280.. 426 A
nskolos@risd.edu
SKOMP, Elizabeth .... 931-598-1254.. 443 O
eskomp@sewanee.edu
SKONER, Peter, R .... 814-472-3085.. 418 F
pskoner@francis.edu
SKORACZEWSKI, Paul .... 715-682-1841.. 518 H
pskoraczewski@northland.edu
SKORTZ, Brian .... 270-686-6416.. 187 C
brian.skortz@brescia.edu
SKOWYRA, Jamie .... 508-213-2131.. 227 A
jamie.skowyra@nichols.edu
SKRABACZ, Shari .... 314-968-6996.. 275 B
shariskrabacz98@webster.edu
SKRAINER, Elizabeth .... 585-385-8427.. 328 E
eskrainer@sjfc.edu
SKRYD, Jackie .... 727-392-6809.. 108 D
skryd.jackie@spcollege.edu
SKUDZINSKAS, Al .... 518-454-5109.. 311 B
skudzina@strose.edu
SKURJA, Michael .... 801-375-5125.. 481 C
mskurja@rmuohp.edu
SKUTKA, Linda, L .... 240-895-4289.. 210 E
llskutka@smcm.edu
SKVARLA, Jennifer .... 815-836-5201.. 145 H
skvarlje@lewisu.edu
SKYLAND, Diane .... 406-756-3668.. 276 E
dskyland@fvcc.edu
SLAATS, Jacqueline .... 847-735-5285.. 145 E
slaats@lakeforest.edu
SLABACH, Donald .... 601-857-3751.. 258 A
donald.slabach@hindscc.edu
SLABACH, Frederick, G ..... 817-531-4401.. 472 F
fslabach@txwes.edu
SLABAUGH, David .... 864-644-5558.. 432 G
dslabaugh@swu.edu
SLABAUGH, Katie .... 765-285-1545.. 159 E
kslabaugh@bsu.edu
SLABODEN, Carolyn .... 781-283-2216.. 229 C
cslaboden@wellesley.edu
SLACK, Craig .... 301-314-7164.. 211 E
cslack@umd.edu

SLACK, David .... 785-227-3380.. 178 J
slackd@bethanylb.edu
SLACK, Elizabeth .... 304-357-4881.. 511 E
elizabethslack@ucwv.edu
SLACK, Gregory, C .... 315-268-6475.. 310 B
gslack@clarkson.edu
SLACK, Karen .... 320-762-4463.. 248 J
karens@alextech.edu
SLACK, Robert .... 626-914-8581.... 38 D
rslack@citruscollege.edu
SLADE, David .... 706-236-2229.. 117 F
dslade@berry.edu
SLADE, Kellie, W .... 856-691-8600.. 290 I
kslade@cccnj.edu
SLADE, Patricia .... 973-877-3209.. 291 H
slade@essex.edu
SLADE, Priscilla .... 601-979-1781.. 258 D
priscilla.d.slade@jsums.edu
SLADE, Rischa .... 707-864-7000.... 65 A
SLAFKOSKY, Mary, V .... 260-422-5561.. 162 B
mvslafkosky@indianatech.edu
SLAGELL, Jeff .... 662-846-4440.. 257 E
jslagell@deltastate.edu
SLAGELL-GOSSEN
Reonna .... 405-422-1253.. 387 E
gossenr@redlandscc.edu
SLAGER, Karen .... 815-802-8110.. 144 C
kslager@kcc.edu
SLAGLE, Judith, B .... 423-439-6076.. 444 F
slagle@etsu.edu
SLAICH, Lucy .... 410-704-2050.. 213 B
lslaich@towson.edu
SLANGER, Zvi Dov .... 410-486-0006.. 206 C
SLANN, Martin .... 903-566-7368.. 477 B
mslann@uttyler.edu
SLATER, Bernata .... 650-949-7364.... 44 B
slaterbernata@foothill.edu
SLATER, Emilee .... 559-442-8225.... 67 C
emilee.slater@fresnocitycollege.edu
SLATER, Richard .... 312-850-7016.. 138 A
rslater4@ccc.edu
SLATER, Robert .... 951-827-3658.... 70 B
bobsl@ucr.edu
SLATER, Ryan .... 412-291-6313.. 397 I
rslater@aii.edu
SLATER, Troy .... 231-348-6610.. 239 A
tslater@ncmich.edu
SLATER-DUFFY, Carrie ...... 715-682-1482.. 518 H
cslaterduffy@northland.edu
SLATON, Gwendolyn .... 973-877-3233.. 291 H
slaton@essex.edu
SLATON, Nate .... 270-534-3244.. 190 H
nathaniel.slaton@kctcs.edu
SLATTERY, Daniel .... 410-704-2364.. 213 B
dslattery@towson.edu
SLATTERY, Katheryn .... 815-836-5275.. 145 H
slatteka@lewisu.edu
SLATTERY, Kimberly .... 610-436-0043.. 416 C
kslattery@wcupa.edu
SLAUGHTER, Arnie .... 859-572-5538.. 192 B
slaughtera@nku.edu
SLAUGHTER, Barbara, R .. 713-798-6644.. 452 G
gayles@bcm.edu
SLAUGHTER, Craig, A .... 765-658-4030.. 160 F
craigslaughter@depauw.edu
SLAUGHTER, Dane, S .... 864-622-6001.. 427 B
dslaughter@andersonuniversity.edu
SLAUGHTER, John .... 254-647-3234.. 463 K
jslaughter@rangercollege.edu
SLAUGHTER, John .... 254-267-7023.. 463 K
jslaughter@rangercollege.edu
SLAUGHTER, Keith .... 404-614-6378.. 123 I
kslaughter@itc.edu
SLAUGHTER, Matthew, J . 603-646-2460.. 286 J
matthew.j.slaughter@dartmouth.edu
SLAUGHTER, Mildred .... 361-593-2834.. 469 A
mildred.slaughter@tamuk.edu
SLAUGHTER, Sabra, C ..... 843-792-2228.. 431 A
slaughsc@musc.edu
SLAUGHTER, Shirley .... 510-981-2840.... 57 B
sslaughter@peralta.edu
SLAUGHTER, Theresa .... 540-831-5582.. 493 A
tpslaught@radford.edu
SLAUGHTER ALLISON,
Michelle .... 619-961-4222.... 68 A
mallison@tjsl.edu
SLAUTA, Katherine .... 619-235-2049.... 43 J
kslauta@fidm.edu
SLAVIN, Dennis .... 646-660-6504.. 307 A
dennis.slavin@baruch.cuny.edu
SLAVIN, Joan, L .... 714-850-4800.... 67 G
slavin@taftu.edu
SLAVIN, Lisa .... 781-239-2501.. 223 F
lslavin@massbay.edu
SLAVINKAS, Brian, R .... 312-915-8787.. 146 G
bslavin@luc.edu
SLAWSON Linda .... 903-785-7661.. 463 E
lslawson@parisjc.edu
SLAYMAKER, Valerie .... 651-213-4746.. 247 B
vslaymaker@hazeldenbettyford.edu

SLAYTON, Deborah, L ..... 217-420-6774.. 148 D
dslayton@millikin.edu
SLEASMAN, Brent, C ...... 419-434-4201.. 331 E
president@winebrenner.edu
SLEDGE, Donald .... 205-929-6442...... 5 D
dsledge@lawsonstate.edu
SLEEMAN, Kerri .... 906-487-2303.. 238 A
kasleema@mtu.edu
SLEESMAN, George .... 419-772-2521.. 374 J
g-sleesman@onu.edu
SLEETH, Cathy .... 509-359-6582.. 503 D
csleeth1@ewu.edu
SLEIGH-LAYMAN, Staci ... 509-963-2205.. 501 K
staci@cwu.edu
SLEIGHT, Garth .... 406-874-6212.. 276 H
sleightg@milescc.edu
SLEJKO, Christa .... 972-273-3010.. 456 G
cslejko@dcccd.edu
SLEKAR, Timothy .... 608-663-2293.. 516 F
tslekar@edgewood.edu
SLENSKI, Amanda .... 989-463-7245.. 230 F
slenskiar@alma.edu
SLEPITZA, Ron .... 816-501-3750.. 252 G
ron.slepitza@avila.edu
SLESARANSKY-POE,
Graciela .... 215-572-4692.. 397 G
slesarag@arcadia.edu
SLESNICK, Daniel, T .... 512-471-4363.. 476 B
slesnick@austin.utexas.edu
SLETTEN, Sheryl, L .... 605-336-6588.. 436 J
ssletten@sfseminary.edu
SLEVA, Michael .... 616-451-3511.. 233 C
msleva@davenport.edu
SLIFE, Harry .... 315-792-3738.. 339 B
hfslife@utica.edu
SLIGO, Sarah .... 401-277-4863.. 426 A
ssligo@risd.edu
SLIMAN, David .... 601-266-6633.. 261 E
david.sliman@usm.edu
SLIMAN, George, S .... 412-578-8826.. 400 C
slimangs@carlow.edu
SLIMP, Mickey .... 903-877-1276.. 477 E
mickey.slimp@uthct.edu
SLINGER, Ron .... 303-914-6417.... 82 I
ron.slinger@rrcc.edu
SLINKARD, Tiffany .... 417-455-5636.. 264 E
tiffanyslinkard@crowder.edu
SLINKER, Bryan, K .... 509-335-9515.. 508 H
slinker@vetmed.wsu.edu
SLISZ, John, P .... 716-851-1851.. 313 H
slisz@ecc.edu
SLIZEWSKI, James .... 215-489-2220.. 402 A
james.slizewski@delval.edu
SLOAN, Barry .... 310-287-4278.... 50 E
sloanba@wlac.edu
SLOAN, Candice, Y .... 864-587-4282.. 433 A
sloanc@smcsc.edu
SLOAN, Damon, N .... 815-740-3398.. 157 F
dsloan@stfrancis.edu
SLOAN, Daniel .... 315-792-3282.. 339 E
drsloan@utica.edu
SLOAN, Justin, M .... 512-448-8545.. 464 G
jsloan@stedwards.edu
SLOAN, LaMonica .... 336-750-3240.. 359 E
singletonls@wssu.edu
SLOAN, Michael .... 530-242-7500.... 64 D
msloan@shastacollege.edu
SLOAN, Noel .... 806-742-4250.. 472 C
noel.a.sloan@ttu.edu
SLOAN, JR., Robert, B .... 281-649-3450.. 458 L
rsloan@hbu.edu
SLOAN, Susan .... 315-364-3264.. 340 E
ssloan@wells.edu
SLOAN LATTA, Marcia .... 419-434-5722.. 379 E
latta@findlay.edu
SLOANE, Raksha .... 847-233-7700.. 150 D
rsloane@[illegible]c.edu
SLOANE, Tomecca .... 919-760-8631.. 346 D
sloaneto@meredith.edu
SLOAS, Ike .... 901-843-3880.. 443 L
SLOATE, Steven .... 409-772-2664.. 478 A
sgsloate@utmb.edu
SLOBEN, Lisa .... 478-757-5171.. 129 L
lsloben@wesleyancollege.edu
SLOBERT, Yantee .... 585-385-8423.. 328 E
yslobert@sjfc.edu
SLOCUM, Cameron .... 214-648-6404.. 478 C
cameron.slocum@utsouthwestern.edu
SLOCUM, Jeff .... 315-655-7192.. 306 H
jslocum@cazenovia.edu
SLOCUM, Stacy, S .... 585-385-8388.. 328 E
sslocum@sjfc.edu
SLOKA, Sandra, L .... 815-740-5026.. 157 F
ssloka@stfrancis.edu
SLOMBIA, Sonia .... 937-376-6574.. 365 H
sslombia@centralstate.edu
SLOMOVITS, Mendel .... 732-414-2834.. 298 N
SLON, Dennis .... 310-338-5127.... 51 E
dslon@lmu.edu
SLONE, Tammy, L .... 937-766-7987.. 365 C
slonet@cedarville.edu

SLOOP, John, M .... 615-322-7360.. 449 A
john.m.sloop@vanderbilt.edu
SLOSS, Robert, E .... 401-232-6046.. 424 K
rsloss@bryant.edu
SLOT, William, J .... 407-582-1185.. 114 N
wslot@valenciacollege.edu
SLOTNICK, Ruth .... 508-531-2783.. 221 C
ruth.slotnick@bridgew.edu
SLOTTOW, Timothy .... 602-557-3211.... 17 L
tim.slottow@phoenix.edu
SLOUGH, Rebecca .... 574-296-6228.. 158 H
rslough@ambs.edu
SLOVAK, Jeffrey .... 708-534-4981.. 140 H
jslovak@govst.edu
SLOWENSKY, Joseph .... 714-744-7882.... 37 F
slowensky@chapman.edu
SLOWINSKI, Mandy .... 715-346-4771.. 521 C
mandy.slowinski@uwsp.edu
SLUDER, Brianna .... 913-360-7400.. 178 I
bsluder@benedictine.edu
SLUDER, Patrick .... 770-394-8300.. 116 F
psluder@aii.edu
SLUDER, Richard .... 615-898-2324.. 444 G
richard.sluder@mtsu.edu
SLUDER, Robin .... 423-478-7727.. 443 I
rsluder@ptseminary.edu
SLUIS, Kimberly .... 630-637-5152.. 149 H
kasluis@noctrl.edu
SLUSHER, Jennifer, J .... 540-985-8502.. 491 A
jjslusher@jchs.edu
SLUSSER, Karen, L .... 570-389-4055.. 414 D
kslusse2@bloomu.edu
SLUSSER, Kimberly .... 585-475-5911.. 327 E
rasdar@rit.edu
SLUSSER, Wayne .... 570-586-2400.. 419 G
wslusser@summitu.edu
SLUTSKY, Madeleine .... 630-515-4568.. 139 D
mslutsky@devry.edu
SMAIL, John .... 704-687-5630.. 358 A
jsmail@uncc.edu
SMAILAGIC, Aida .... 650-493-4430.... 64 I
aida.smailagic@sofia.edu
SMALE, Maura .... 718-260-5470.. 309 C
msmale@citytech.cuny.edu
SMALL, Allison .... 503-375-7193.. 391 B
asmall@corban.edu
SMALL, Brent .... 575-562-2194.. 299 I
brent.small@enmu.edu
SMALL, Christine .... 760-384-6376.... 47 K
christine.small@cerrocoso.edu
SMALL, Cindy .... 406-265-3787.. 277 E
csmall@msun.edu
SMALL, Daniel, E .... 202-994-6620.... 92 D
dsmall@gwu.edu
SMALL, Daphne .... 650-949-7218.... 44 B
smalldaphne@foothill.edu
SMALL, Darlene .... 843-383-8039.. 428 F
dsmall@coker.edu
SMALL, David .... 406-638-3110.. 276 G
smalld@lbhc.edu
SMALL, Elizabeth .... 508-793-3759.. 217 C
esmall@holycross.edu
SMALL, Gillian .... 201-692-2000.. 291 J
SMALL, Hank .... 843-863-7080.. 427 I
hsmall@csuniv.edu
SMALL, John, J .... 630-637-5701.. 149 H
jjsmall@noctrl.edu
SMALL, Josh .... 803-641-3719.. 433 G
joshs@usca.edu
SMALL, Justin .... 870-862-8131.... 22 D
jsmall@southark.edu
SMALL, Natissia .... 314-516-5128.. 274 A
smalln@umsl.edu
SMALLEN, David, L .... 315-859-4169.. 315 D
dsmallen@hamilton.edu
SMALLEY, Reid .... 585-345-6999.. 315 C
rjsmalley@genesee.edu
SMALLEY, Robin .... 727-864-7564.... 98 L
smallerm@eckerd.edu
SMALLS, Diondra .... 803-780-1023.. 434 M
dsmalls@voorhees.edu
SMALLS, Gerald .... 803-705-4694.. 427 D
smallsg@benedict.edu
SMALLWOOD, Pamela ..... 417-865-2815.. 265 B
smallwoodp@evangel.edu
SMALLWOOD, Will .... 405-878-2703.. 385 B
will.smallwood@okbu.edu
SMARKEL, James .... 419-434-4220.. 381 E
jsmarkel@winebrenner.edu
SMARRELLI, JR., John ..... 901-321-3250.. 439 E
jsmarrel@cbu.edu
SMART, Christopher .... 845-437-5742.. 339 C
chsmart@vassar.edu
SMART, III, Clifton, M .... 417-836-8500.. 268 I
president@missouristate.edu
SMART, Denise, T .... 512-245-2311.. 471 F
ds37@txstate.edu
SMART, James, G .... 305-284-4505.. 114 H
jsmart@miami.edu
SMART, Lucille .... 315-781-3449.. 316 C
smart@hws.edu

SMART, Robert .... 616-331-2281.. 234 F
smartr@gvsu.edu
SMART, Robert .... 203-582-3325.... 88 G
robert.smart@quinnipiac.edu
SMART, Scott .... 575-562-2611.. 299 I
scott.smart@enmu.edu
SMART, Stephanie .... 845-434-5750.. 336 H
ssmart@sunysullivan.edu
SMART, William .... 615-297-7545.. 438 F
smartb@aquinascollege.edu
SMATRESK, Neal .... 940-565-2026.. 475 A
president@unt.edu
SMAY, Kevin .... 412-237-3094.. 401 B
ksmay@ccac.edu
SMEATON, John, W .... 610-758-3890.. 408 H
jws2@lehigh.edu
SMEDLEY, Laduan .... 916-558-2120.... 51 D
smedlel3@scc.losrios.edu
SMEDLEY, Patricia .... 615-460-6403.. 438 J
patricia.smedley@belmont.edu
SMEDLEY, Susan .... 281-425-6336.. 460 I
ssmedley@lee.edu
SMEE, Sheryl .... 619-849-2509.... 57 M
sherylsmee@pointloma.edu
SMEED, Shane .... 816-584-6205.. 270 D
shane.smeed@park.edu
SMELSER, Dick .... 865-694-6565.. 446 G
rwsmelser@pstcc.edu
SMELTZ, Emily .... 724-357-5555.. 415 B
emily.smeltz@iup.edu
SMELTZER, Brian, K .... 717-815-1293.. 424 F
bksmeltzer@ycp.edu
SMELTZER, Deirdre .... 540-432-4141.. 488 K
deirdre.smeltzer@emu.edu
SMELTZER, Jill, M .... 276-944-6923.. 489 I
jsmeltzer@ehc.edu
SMELTZER, Paul .... 336-725-8344.. 354 G
smeltzerp@piedmontu.edu
SMETANKA, John .... 724-805-2227.. 419 A
john.smetanka@email.stvincent.edu
SMIALEK, William .... 903-730-4890.. 460 B
wsmialek@jarvis.edu
SMICK-ATTISANO, Regina, A .... 603-862-1025.. 288 C
regina.smick-attisano@unh.edu
SMID, Terry .... 563-425-5359.. 177 D
smidt@uiu.edu
SMIGIELSKI, Ben .... 312-915-8709.. 146 G
bsmigie@uc.edu
SMILEY, Brad .... 903-675-6218.. 473 B
bsmiley@tvcc.edu
SMILEY, Ellen .... 318-274-3228.. 200 F
smileye@gram.edu
SMILEY, Joseph .... 727-712-5851.. 108 D
smiley.joseph@spcollege.edu
SMILEY, Scott .... 432-552-2605.. 478 B
smiley_s@utpb.edu
SMILIE, Ethan .... 620-431-2820.. 183 H
esmilie@neosho.edu
SMITH, Adrian .... 212-343-1234.. 321 B
asmith@mcny.edu
SMITH, Adrienne .... 413-755-4561.. 224 G
asmith@stcc.edu
SMITH, Aidan .... 724-266-3838.. 421 C
asmith@tsm.edu
SMITH, Alastair .... 415-338-1759.... 35 B
aksmith@sfsu.edu
SMITH, Alexa .... 870-612-2165.... 23 H
alexa.smith@uaccb.edu
SMITH, Alexandra .... 610-861-1475.. 411 B
smithlexi@moravian.edu
SMITH, Amanda .... 972-883-6391.. 476 C
dos@utdallas.edu
SMITH, Amy .... 912-478-5391.. 122 B
amysmith@georgiasouthern.edu
SMITH, Amy .... 513-745-5615.. 379 B
amy.smith@uc.edu
SMITH, Amy, B .... 979-845-2217.. 468 B
amy.b.smith@tamu.edu
SMITH, Amy, E .... 716-926-8877.. 316 B
asmith@hilbert.edu
SMITH, Andrea, C .... 503-552-1692.. 392 H
acsmith@nunm.edu
SMITH, Andrew .... 817-202-6320.. 466 C
adsmith@swau.edu
SMITH, Andrew .... 865-471-3243.. 439 C
asmith@cn.edu
SMITH, Angela .... 765-455-9536.. 163 A
smith436@iuk.edu
SMITH, Angela .... 720-890-8922.... 80 O
finance@itea.edu
SMITH, Angi .... 706-379-3111.. 130 B
adsmith@yhc.edu
SMITH, Ann, T .... 859-238-5459.. 187 H
ann.smith@centre.edu
SMITH, Annabelle .... 254-526-1205.. 454 A
annabelle.smith@ctcd.edu
SMITH, Annie .... 864-429-7755.. 434 F
alsmith@mailbox.sc.edu
SMITH, April .... 731-410-6730.. 440 K
asmith@lanecollege.edu

SMITH, Art .... 870-236-6901.... 20 A
artsmith@crc.edu
SMITH, Ashley .... 252-493-7229.. 352 A
adsmith@email.pittcc.edu
SMITH, Ashley .... 704-991-0221.. 353 E
asmith1369@stanly.edu
SMITH, Audrey .... 215-780-1364.. 419 C
audrey@salus.edu
SMITH, Audrey, Y .... 413-585-4900.. 228 D
aysmith@smith.edu
SMITH, Barbara .... 205-366-8816...... 7 E
bsmith@stillman.edu
SMITH, Bea, W .... 864-503-5235.. 434 G
bwsmith@uscupstate.edu
SMITH, Beatrice .... 619-574-6909.... 55 G
bsmith@pacificcollege.edu
SMITH, Becky .... 435-652-7836.. 482 A
bsmith@dixie.edu
SMITH, Benjamin, J .... 620-431-2820.. 183 H
bsmith@neosho.edu
SMITH, Benny, R .... 828-398-7482.. 347 D
brsmith@abtech.edu
SMITH, Beth .... 910-576-6222.. 351 E
smithb@montgomery.edu
SMITH, Beth .... 870-972-2586.... 18 J
smitty@astate.edu
SMITH, Betsy .... 617-879-7761.. 222 A
betsy.smith@massart.edu
SMITH, Betty .... 610-917-1426.. 422 C
blsmith@valleyforge.edu
SMITH, Betty, J .... 910-678-8250.. 349 F
smithbj@faytechcc.edu
SMITH, Bill .... 401-232-6078.. 424 K
bsmith8@bryant.edu
SMITH, Bill .... 870-972-2169.... 18 J
billsmith@astate.edu
SMITH, Bill .... 818-345-7921.... 40 G
SMITH, Bill .... 213-763-3612.... 50 C
smithb@lattc.edu
SMITH, Bill .... 225-216-8588.. 195 H
smithb@mybrcc.edu
SMITH, Billy, R .... 731-989-6623.. 440 D
bsmith@fhu.edu
SMITH, Blake .... 865-981-8264.. 441 H
blake.smith@maryvillecollege.edu
SMITH, Bob .... 970-247-7525.... 80 D
SMITH, Bob .... 904-819-6332.... 99 M
bsmith@flagler.edu
SMITH, Brad .... 214-329-4447.. 452 B
brad.smith@bgu.edu
SMITH, Brad, D .... 937-766-7872.. 365 C
smthb@cedarville.edu
SMITH, Brad, K .... 608-743-4596.. 523 A
bsmith32@blackhawk.edu
SMITH, Bradley .... 215-461-1139.. 410 L
bsmith@mc3.edu
SMITH, Bradley, A .... 610-921-7529.. 396 H
bsmith@albright.edu
SMITH, Bradley, D .... 574-807-7232.. 159 D
smithb@bethelcollege.edu
SMITH, Brenda .... 601-643-8318.. 257 D
brenda.smith@colin.edu
SMITH, Brenda, A .... 585-292-2365.. 321 J
bsmith2@monroecc.edu
SMITH, Brenda, C .... 785-227-3380.. 178 J
bsmith@bethanylb.edu
SMITH, Brenda, J .... 212-217-3650.. 314 B
brenda_smith@fitnyc.edu
SMITH, Brian .... 716-888-2785.. 306 F
smith@canisius.edu
SMITH, Brian .... 701-858-3210.. 360 F
brian.smith@minotstateu.edu
SMITH, Brian, D .... 260-399-7700.. 168 D
bsmith@sf.edu
SMITH, Brian, D .... 972-241-3371.. 455 K
bsmith@dallas.edu
SMITH, Brian, K .... 864-379-6304.. 429 I
keith@erskine.edu
SMITH, Brien, N .... 812-237-2000.. 162 A
brien.smith@indstate.edu
SMITH, Bruce .... 303-871-6301.... 84 B
bruce.smith@du.edu
SMITH, Bruce .... 256-761-6225...... 7 F
bcsmith@talladega.edu
SMITH, Bruce .... 503-777-7521.. 394 I
smithb@reed.edu
SMITH, Bruce .... 814-393-2225.. 414 G
bsmith@clarion.edu
SMITH, Bryan .... 270-706-8616.. 189 C
bryan.smith@kctcs.edu
SMITH, Bryan, F .... 850-412-7907.. 110 J
bryanf.smith@famu.edu
SMITH, C. Mike .... 864-488-4609.. 430 H
csmith@limestone.edu
SMITH, Calvin .... 314-968-7138.. 275 B
smithca@webster.edu
SMITH, Cameron .... 978-837-5503.. 225 E
smithcr@merrimack.edu
SMITH, Candace, E .... 202-994-3566.... 92 D
cesmith@gwu.edu

SMITH, Carl .... 760-245-4271.... 73 H
carl.smith@vvc.edu
SMITH, Carlas .... 501-812-2366.... 21 H
crsmith@pulaskitech.edu
SMITH, Carlia, G .... 501-569-3492.... 23 B
cgsmith@ualr.edu
SMITH, Carol .... 719-587-7820.... 76 G
carolsmith@adams.edu
SMITH, Carol .... 970-247-7265.... 80 D
smith_carol@fortlewis.edu
SMITH, Carol .... 973-405-2111.. 305 B
crs@berkeleycollege.edu
SMITH, Carol .... 973-405-2111.. 289 F
crs@berkeleycollege.edu
SMITH, Carol, L .... 765-658-4580.. 160 F
clsmith@depauw.edu
SMITH, Carola .... 805-965-0581.... 63 D
smithc@sbcc.edu
SMITH, Carolyn .... 305-273-4499.... 97 M
carolyn@cbt.edu
SMITH, Carolyn .... 307-766-2376.. 527 B
csmith@uwyo.edu
SMITH, Carolyn, A .... 304-697-7550.. 510 K
csmith@huntingtonjuniorcollege.edu
SMITH, Carolyn, S .... 414-288-7184.. 517 I
carolyn.s.smith@marquette.edu
SMITH, Carter .... 502-410-6200.. 188 H
csmith2@galencollege.edu
SMITH, Caryn .... 847-947-5229.. 149 B
clsmith@nl.edu
SMITH, Catherine, E .... 585-292-2341.. 321 J
ksmith@monroecc.edu
SMITH, Caye .... 619-849-2313.... 57 M
cayesmith@pointloma.edu
SMITH, Ceil .... 856-351-2644.. 296 L
csmith@salemcc.edu
SMITH, Charlene .... 513-241-4338.. 363 G
charlene.smith@antonellicollege.edu
SMITH, Charles .... 816-414-3700.. 268 D
csmith@mbts.edu
SMITH, Charles .... 713-718-7564.. 459 B
charles.smith6@hccs.edu
SMITH, Charles, N .... 903-927-3387.. 479 K
cnsmith1@wileyc.edu
SMITH, Charmian .... 516-572-7376.. 322 C
charmian.smith@ncc.edu
SMITH, Cherie .... 816-415-5085.. 275 F
smithc@william.jewell.edu
SMITH, Cheryl .... 413-782-1542.. 229 E
cheryl.smith@wne.edu
SMITH, Chris .... 423-425-4646.. 448 F
chris-smith@utc.edu
SMITH, Chris .... 785-594-7890.. 178 D
chris.smith@bakeru.edu
SMITH, Chris .... 620-241-0723.. 179 L
chris.smith@centralchristian.edu
SMITH, Chris .... 303-986-2320.... 78 L
chris@csha.net
SMITH, Chris .... 610-499-1036.. 423 E
csmith@widener.edu
SMITH, Christala .... 580-745-3185.. 387 M
clsmith@se.edu
SMITH, Christine .... 678-466-5406.. 119 A
christinesmith@clayton.edu
SMITH, Christine .... 630-617-3050.. 140 C
chriss@elmhurst.edu
SMITH, Christine .... 518-762-7136.. 315 A
cmsmith@fmcc.suny.edu
SMITH, Christine, J .... 630-617-3150.. 140 C
chriss@elmhurst.edu
SMITH, Cindy .... 432-264-5034.. 459 D
csmith@howardcollege.edu
SMITH, Claire .... 210-999-8401.. 473 A
csmith9@trinity.edu
SMITH, Claire, L .... 410-777-2776.. 206 B
clsmith@aacc.edu
SMITH, Clarence, E .... 662-252-8000.. 260 F
csmith@rustcollege.edu
SMITH, Clark .... 530-741-6785.... 76 D
csmith@yccd.edu
SMITH, Cliff .... 913-627-4122.. 182 C
clsmith@kckcc.edu
SMITH, Cliff, L .... 864-379-8802.. 429 I
smith@erskine.edu
SMITH, Colleen .... 518-445-2336.. 303 D
csmit@albanylaw.edu
SMITH, Colleen, A .... 928-266-4217.... 12 N
colleen.smith@coconino.edu
SMITH, Connor .... 214-333-5365.. 455 J
connors@dbu.edu
SMITH, Corey .... 662-246-6405.. 259 B
csmith@msdelta.edu
SMITH, Craig .... 413-236-2186.. 222 G
csmith@berkshirecc.edu
SMITH, Craig .... 413-236-2188.. 222 G
csmith@berkshirecc.edu
SMITH, Craig .... 406-768-5555.. 276 F
csmith@fpcc.edu
SMITH, Crystal .... 903-877-7718.. 477 E
crystal.smith@uthct.edu

SMITH, Curtis .... 405-425-5931.. 385 C
curtis.smith@oc.edu
SMITH, Cynthia .... 301-687-4328.. 212 F
colsmith@frostburg.edu
SMITH, Cyrus .... 479-979-1425.... 24 I
csmith@ozarks.edu
SMITH, D. Gordon .... 801-422-6383.. 480 C
smithg@law.byu.edu
SMITH, Dale, T .... 914-831-0311.. 311 C
dsmith@cw.edu
SMITH, Dan .... 662-562-3305.. 260 C
dsmith@northwestms.edu
SMITH, Dan .... 812-855-6679.. 162 E
dansmith@indiana.edu
SMITH, Dana .... 760-944-4449.... 52 K
dsmith@miracosta.edu
SMITH, Daniel .... 562-860-2451.... 36 P
dsmith@cerritos.edu
SMITH, Daniel .... 864-242-5100.. 427 E
SMITH, Daniel, C .... 812-855-6679.. 162 F
dansmith@indiana.edu
SMITH, Daniel, C .... 252-334-2058.. 346 F
dan.smith@macuniversity.edu
SMITH, Daniel, P .... 802-728-1251.. 486 D
dsmith5@vtc.edu
SMITH, Darlene .... 301-687-4309.. 212 F
dcsmith@frostburg.edu
SMITH, Darlene, B .... 410-837-4996.. 213 C
dsmith@ubalt.edu
SMITH, Daryl .... 716-829-7623.. 313 A
smithd@dyc.edu
SMITH, Daryl .... 513-244-8686.. 366 B
daryl.smith@ccuniversity.edu
SMITH, Daryl .... 864-592-4600.. 432 H
smithd@sccsc.edu
SMITH, David .... 718-260-5345.. 309 C
dsmith@citytech.cuny.edu
SMITH, David .... 585-567-9321.. 316 F
david.smith@houghton.edu
SMITH, David .... 740-264-5591.. 368 D
dsmith@egcc.edu
SMITH, David .... 620-331-4100.. 181 J
dsmith@indycc.edu
SMITH, David .... 909-593-3511.... 71 B
dsmith3@laverne.edu
SMITH, David .... 765-677-2258.. 164 B
david.smith@indwes.edu
SMITH, David, B .... 518-783-2432.. 330 E
dsmith@siena.edu
SMITH, David, C .... 423-236-2801.. 444 B
davidavidsmith@southern.edu
SMITH, David, M .... 310-506-5689.... 56 J
david.smith@pepperdine.edu
SMITH, Dayle, M .... 315-268-2300.. 310 B
dsmith@clarkson.edu
SMITH, Dean .... 504-568-5960.. 198 A
dsmith@lsuhsc.edu
SMITH, Debbie .... 281-998-6150.. 465 B
deborah.smith@sjcd.edu
SMITH, Deborah .... 859-371-9393.. 186 M
SMITH, Deborah .... 409-212-5724.. 452 D
SMITH, Debra .... 931-668-7010.. 446 D
dsmith@mscc.edu
SMITH, Debra .... 252-536-7213.. 350 C
dsmith600@halifaxcc.edu
SMITH, Debra .... 252-536-7213.. 350 C
dsmith660@halifaxcc.edu
SMITH, Debra, M .... 330-665-1084.. 374 H
debbie@ocm.edu
SMITH, Del .... 256-372-5092...... 1 A
del.smith@aamu.edu
SMITH, Delois .... 256-824-4600...... 8 F
delois.smith@uah.edu
SMITH, Denise .... 567-661-7250.. 376 D
denise_smith4@owens.edu
SMITH, Denise, L .... 660-785-4133.. 273 B
dlsmith@truman.edu
SMITH, Denise, M .... 603-862-3396.. 288 C
denise.smith@unh.edu
SMITH, Dennis .... 530-226-4754.... 64 H
dsmith@simpsonu.edu
SMITH, Dennis .... 252-335-0821.. 349 A
dennis_smith@albemarle.edu
SMITH, Derek .... 215-489-2476.. 402 A
derek.smith@delval.edu
SMITH, Derrek .... 256-233-8274...... 1 F
derrek.smith@athens.edu
SMITH, Devin .... 402-643-7328.. 279 F
devin.smith@cune.edu
SMITH, Diana .... 303-762-6886.... 79 I
diana.smith@denverseminary.edu
SMITH, Dolores .... 951-639-5230.... 53 D
dolsmith@msjc.edu
SMITH, Don .... 229-931-2731.. 127 C
dsmith@southgatech.edu
SMITH, Don, N .... 362-570-4321.. 474 C
smithd@uhv.edu
SMITH, Donald .... 270-745-6256.. 194 D
donald.smith@wku.edu
SMITH, Donald .... 972-860-4808.. 456 B
dsmith@dcccd.edu

SMITH, Linda ... 650-543-3933 .. 52 D
lsmith@menlo.edu
SMITH, Linda ... 815-280-2660 .. 144 A
lsmith@jjc.edu
SMITH, Linda ... 340-692-4023 .. 539 C
lsmith@uvi.edu
SMITH, Linda, D ... 919-209-2024 .. 350 G
ldsmith@johnstoncc.edu
SMITH, Lisa ... 352-854-2322 .. 97 R
smithl@cf.edu
SMITH, Lisa ... 307-754-6292 .. 526 N
lisa.smith@nwc.edu
SMITH, Lisa ... 406-874-6181 .. 276 H
smithl@milescc.edu
SMITH, Lisa ... 931-438-0028 .. 446 D
lsmith@mscc.edu
SMITH, Lorenzo ... 916-278-6127 .. 34 B
lsmith@csus.edu
SMITH, Lorraine ... 559-244-2604 .. 67 C
lorraine.smith@fresnocitycollege.edu
SMITH, Lorraine ... 716-375-7873 .. 328 B
lsmith@sbu.edu
SMITH, LuAnn ... 801-863-8472 .. 482 C
smithlu@uvu.edu
SMITH, Luke ... 212-659-3615 .. 318 D
lsmith@tkc.edu
SMITH, Lura ... 978-656-3110 .. 224 A
smithlm@middlesex.mass.edu
SMITH, Lynn ... 606-546-1206 .. 193 E
tlsmith@unionky.edu
SMITH, Mable, H ... 912-650-5678 .. 127 D
mhsmith@southuniversity.edu
SMITH, Mable, H ... 702-968-2075 .. 285 E
msmith@roseman.edu
SMITH, MacKenzie ... 530-752-2110 .. 69 A
macsmith@ucdavis.edu
SMITH, Malinda ... 607-274-3222 .. 317 D
mbsmith@ithaca.edu
SMITH, Mandy ... 864-578-8770 .. 432 D
msmith@sherman.edu
SMITH, Marcus ... 575-769-4014 .. 299 G
marcus.smith@clovis.edu
SMITH, Margaret ... 412-392-3990 .. 417 F
msmith@pointpark.edu
SMITH, Margaret, D ... 931-540-2517 .. 446 A
margaret.smith@columbiastate.edu
SMITH, Marian ... 270-384-7351 .. 191 E
smithm@lindsey.edu
SMITH, Marianne ... 626-914-8701 .. 38 D
msmith@citruscollege.edu
SMITH, Marianne ... 610-896-1298 .. 405 I
msmith@haverford.edu
SMITH, Maribel ... 305-628-6704 .. 108 E
maribel.smith@stu.edu
SMITH, Marie ... 928-350-2100 .. 16 P
msmith@prescott.edu
SMITH, Marilyn ... 763-433-1306 .. 248 K
marilyn.smith@anokaramsey.edu
SMITH, Marilyn ... 703-993-8728 .. 490 B
mtsmith@gmu.edu
SMITH, Mark ... 607-871-2494 .. 303 F
msmith@alfred.edu
SMITH, Mark ... 518-276-6266 .. 327 B
smithm@rpi.edu
SMITH, Mark ... 615-327-6336 .. 442 A
msmith@mmc.edu
SMITH, Mark, A ... 254-298-8341 .. 467 B
mark.a.smith@templejc.edu
SMITH, Mark, A ... 740-477-7713 .. 374 G
mark.smith@ohiochristian.edu
SMITH, Mark, W ... 314-935-6489 .. 274 N
msmith@wustl.edu
SMITH, Marla ... 605-995-7157 .. 436 C
marla.smith@mitchelltech.edu
SMITH, Marla ... 317-955-6150 .. 165 N
msmith2@marian.edu
SMITH, Marlaine ... 561-297-3207 .. 110 K
msmit230@fau.edu
SMITH, Marsh-Allen ... 650-508-3459 .. 54 J
masmith@ndnu.edu
SMITH, Martha, J ... 260-359-4040 .. 161 O
msmith@huntington.edu
SMITH, Martha, J ... 757-352-4070 .. 493 E
martsmi@regent.edu
SMITH, Martha, L ... 601-403-1269 .. 260 D
mbyrd@prcc.edu
SMITH, Martin ... 859-233-8275 .. 193 D
msmith@transy.edu
SMITH, Marvin ... 563-288-6162 .. 172 C
msmith@eicc.edu
SMITH, Marvin ... 201-360-4054 .. 292 B
msmith@hccc.edu
SMITH, Marvin ... 304-766-3181 .. 514 B
smithm@wvstateu.edu
SMITH, Marvin, L ... 317-274-5924 .. 163 D
SMITH, Mary, A ... 713-500-9236 .. 477 C
mary.a.smith@uth.tmc.edu
SMITH, Mary, C ... 478-289-2165 .. 120 C
mcsmith@ega.edu
SMITH, Matthew ... 717-815-6579 .. 424 F
cmsmith@ycp.edu
SMITH, Matthew, B ... 919-866-5988 .. 353 I
mbsmith9@waketech.edu
SMITH, Matthew, J ... 269-399-7700 .. 168 D
msmith@sf.edu
SMITH, Matthew, J ... 253-535-7550 .. 505 G
smithmf@plu.edu
SMITH, Maureen, A ... 617-322-3568 .. 219 H
maureen_smith@laboure.edu
SMITH, Melissa ... 415-439-2413 .. 26 G
mysmith@act-sf.org
SMITH, Micah ... 731-989-6005 .. 440 D
msmith@fhu.edu
SMITH, Michael ... 212-966-0300 .. 322 F
msmith@nyaa.edu
SMITH, Michael ... 870-248-4000 .. 19 H
michael.smith@blackrivertech.edu
SMITH, Michael ... 410-706-4832 .. 211 F
msmith@umaryland.edu
SMITH, Michael ... 812-488-2958 .. 167 I
ms337@evansville.edu
SMITH, Michael ... 806-720-7521 .. 461 C
michael.smith@lcu.edu
SMITH, Michael, A ... 434-223-6219 .. 490 D
msmith@hsc.edu
SMITH, Michael, D ... 617-495-1566 .. 219 D
mike_smith@harvard.edu
SMITH, Michael, D ... 770-426-2039 .. 124 B
michael.smith@life.edu
SMITH, Michael, J ... 973-278-5400 .. 289 F
mj@berkeleycollege.edu
SMITH, Michael, J ... 212-986-4343 .. 305 B
mj@berkeleycollege.edu
SMITH, Michael, R ... 919-966-4107 .. 357 D
msmith@sog.unc.edu
SMITH, Michael, W ... 202-687-4640 .. 92 E
smithm4@georgetown.edu
SMITH, Michele ... 847-925-6427 .. 141 A
msmith@harpercollege.edu
SMITH, Michele, G ... 817-257-4739 .. 453 O
m.g.smith@tcu.edu
SMITH, Michelle ... 502-213-8240 .. 193 A
mbsmith@sctd.edu
SMITH, Mike ... 903-586-2518 .. 460 A
msmith@jacksonville-college.edu
SMITH, Mike ... 803-584-3446 .. 434 C
pmsmith@mailbox.sc.edu
SMITH, Missy ... 303-963-3337 .. 77 I
masmith@ccu.edu
SMITH, Misty ... 601-635-2111 .. 257 F
misty.smith@eccc.edu
SMITH, Molly, E ... 360-438-4310 .. 506 G
msmith@stmartin.edu
SMITH, Monica ... 510-780-4500 .. 48 J
msmith@lifewest.edu
SMITH, Monica, M ... 610-660-1015 .. 418 G
msmith@sju.edu
SMITH, Nancy ... 325-793-4667 .. 461 F
smith.nancy@mcm.edu
SMITH, Nancy ... 719-255-4411 .. 83 L
nsmith2@uccs.edu
SMITH, Nancy ... 484-365-7814 .. 409 B
nsmith@lincoln.edu
SMITH, Nancy, L ... 607-746-4665 .. 335 C
smithnl@delhi.edu
SMITH, Nate ... 954-745-6960 .. 93 F
SMITH, Nate ... 305-507-5700 .. 93 F
SMITH, Nate ... 305-507-5800 .. 93 F
SMITH, Nichloas, A ... 508-767-7416 .. 214 F
na.smith@assumption.edu
SMITH, Noreen ... 212-343-1234 .. 321 B
nsmith@mcny.edu
SMITH, Norma, M ... 207-768-2790 .. 203 L
nsmith@nmcc.edu
SMITH, Norman ... 727-864-8897 .. 98 L
smithnr@eckerd.edu
SMITH, Norman ... 256-228-6001 .. 5 I
smithn@nacc.edu
SMITH, Norman, R ... 607-735-1790 .. 313 F
nsmith@elmira.edu
SMITH, Ole, M ... 801-422-5500 .. 480 C
ole_smith@byu.edu
SMITH, Pam ... 727-341-3261 .. 108 D
smith.pam@spcollege.edu
SMITH, Pamela, A ... 918-631-2329 .. 389 E
pamela-smith@utulsa.edu
SMITH, Pat, A ... 559-323-2100 .. 61 E
psmith@sjcl.edu
SMITH, Patricia ... 931-372-3331 .. 445 B
plsmith@tntech.edu
SMITH, Patricia, A ... 516-876-3092 .. 333 C
smithp@oldwestbury.edu
SMITH, Patricia, T ... 407-582-5411 .. 114 N
psmith50@valenciacollege.edu
SMITH, Patty ... 540-231-6059 .. 489 H
psmith@vcom.vt.edu
SMITH, Paula ... 217-234-5252 .. 145 D
psmith12328@lakeland.cc.il.us
SMITH, Peggy ... 843-383-8178 .. 428 F
peggy.smith@coker.edu
SMITH, Peggy ... 340-693-1446 .. 539 C
psmith@uvi.edu
SMITH, Penny, L ... 814-871-7748 .. 404 A
smith006@gannon.edu
SMITH, Penny, R ... 330-325-6300 .. 373 H
psmith4@neomed.edu
SMITH, Pete ... 802-451-7588 .. 484 C
psmith@marlboro.edu
SMITH, Peter, L ... 563-589-3668 .. 177 C
plsmith@dbq.edu
SMITH, JR., Philip, L ... 225-216-8190 .. 195 H
smithp@mybrcc.edu
SMITH, Polly ... 315-792-3111 .. 339 B
psmith1@utica.edu
SMITH, Quentin, R ... 806-414-9277 .. 472 D
quentin.smith@ttuhsc.edu
SMITH, Rachel, E ... 814-865-7641 .. 412 F
rem4@psu.edu
SMITH, Raechell ... 816-802-3574 .. 266 D
raechell@earthlink.net
SMITH, Randy ... 434-592-5363 .. 491 D
rsmith108@liberty.edu
SMITH, Randy ... 920-498-5505 .. 524 E
randall.smith@nwtc.edu
SMITH, Randy, L ... 405-585-5810 .. 385 B
randy.smith@okbu.edu
SMITH, Rashad, E ... 812-465-7048 .. 168 E
resmith1@usi.edu
SMITH, Rebecca ... 619-849-2983 .. 57 M
rebeccasmith@pointloma.edu
SMITH, Rebecca, F ... 614-823-1400 .. 376 C
rsmith@otterbein.edu
SMITH, Regina ... 303-245-4662 .. 81 I
rsmith@naropa.edu
SMITH, Regina ... 323-953-4000 .. 49 H
smithrr2@lacitycollege.edu
SMITH, Regina ... 212-757-1190 .. 304 B
rtsmith@funeraleducation.org
SMITH, Reginald, B ... 662-252-8000 .. 260 F
rsmith@rustcollege.edu
SMITH, Renee, L ... 928-344-1723 .. 11 J
renee.smith@azwestern.edu
SMITH, Rhonda ... 205-391-2991 .. 6 G
rsmith@sheltonstate.edu
SMITH, Richard, A ... 540-375-2203 .. 493 H
rsmith@roanoke.edu
SMITH, Richard, S ... 718-409-7350 .. 336 A
rsmith@sunymaritime.edu
SMITH, Robert ... 601-979-2260 .. 258 D
robert.m.smith@jsums.edu
SMITH, Robert ... 612-728-5201 .. 254 O
rsmith@smunm.edu
SMITH, Robert ... 859-985-3330 .. 187 B
smithro@berea.edu
SMITH, Robert ... 305-626-3168 .. 101 A
robert.smith@fmuniv.edu
SMITH, Robert ... 205-929-6470 .. 5 D
rsmith@lawsonstate.edu
SMITH, Robert ... 912-344-2589 .. 116 E
robert.smith@armstrong.edu
SMITH, Robert ... 470-578-4935 .. 123 J
rsmit268@kennesaw.edu
SMITH, Robert ... 806-720-7111 .. 461 C
robert.smith@lcu.edu
SMITH, Robert, M ... 731-881-7500 .. 448 G
robert.smith@utm.edu
SMITH, Robert, R ... 520-621-7777 .. 17 I
rrsmith@u.arizona.edu
SMITH, Robert, W ... 252-334-2018 .. 346 F
bob.smith@macuniversity.edu
SMITH, Robin Ann ... 401-825-2096 .. 425 A
rasmith@ccri.edu
SMITH, Rochelle ... 256-782-8122 .. 4 H
rdsmith@jsu.edu
SMITH, Rodney ... 816-235-1167 .. 273 F
smithrodn@umkc.edu
SMITH, Roland, B ... 713-348-5688 .. 464 E
rbsmith@rice.edu
SMITH, Roland, K ... 512-463-1887 .. 470 G
roland.smith@tsus.edu
SMITH, Ron ... 904-997-2997 .. 101 G
ron.smith@fscj.edu
SMITH, Ron ... 408-741-2126 .. 74 F
ron_smith@wvm.edu
SMITH, Ronda, L ... 641-422-4001 .. 175 E
smithron@niacc.edu
SMITH, Rose Marie ... 405-422-1262 .. 387 E
rosemarie@smith@redlandscc.edu
SMITH, Roxie ... 626-264-8880 .. 71 D
SMITH, Roy ... 864-592-4905 .. 432 H
smithr@sccsc.edu
SMITH, Royce ... 406-994-4933 .. 277 C
royce.smith@montana.edu
SMITH, Rueben ... 626-585-7277 .. 56 H
rcsmith@pasadena.edu
SMITH, Russell, L ... 502-597-6805 .. 191 B
russell.smith@kysu.edu
SMITH, Ruth ... 618-634-3347 .. 154 B
ruths@shawneecc.edu
SMITH, Ruth ... 757-825-2807 .. 498 G
smithru@tncc.edu
SMITH, Ruth, S ... 407-582-1601 .. 114 N
rsmith257@valenciacollege.edu
SMITH, Ryan ... 309-438-2135 .. 143 B
rlsmith@ilstu.edu
SMITH, Ryan ... 916-649-8168 .. 28 L
ryan.smith@brightwood.edu
SMITH, Ryan, M ... 814-886-6373 .. 411 C
rsmith@mtaloy.edu
SMITH, Sacella ... 708-456-0300 .. 156 C
sacellasmith@triton.edu
SMITH, Sam ... 615-966-6056 .. 441 F
sam.smith@lipscomb.edu
SMITH, Sandra, B ... 540-674-3600 .. 497 G
ssmith@nr.edu
SMITH, Sandy ... 540-231-6231 .. 499 F
ssmith@vt.edu
SMITH, Sandy ... 760-366-5296 .. 41 K
ssmith@cmccd.edu
SMITH, Sarah ... 276-376-4514 .. 495 I
scs6p@uvawise.edu
SMITH, Sarah ... 615-230-3400 .. 447 C
sarah.smith@volstate.edu
SMITH, Sarah, A ... 304-293-4963 .. 514 C
sarah.smith@mail.wvu.edu
SMITH, Scott, A ... 803-786-3672 .. 429 A
scsmith@columbiasc.edu
SMITH, Scott, F ... 305-899-3085 .. 96 D
sfsmith@barry.edu
SMITH, Sean ... 805-565-6061 .. 75 A
sesmith@westmont.edu
SMITH, Sevealyn, V ... 919-516-4160 .. 355 D
svsmith@st-aug.edu
SMITH, Sha Duncan ... 610-690-5744 .. 419 I
sdsmith1@swarthmore.edu
SMITH, Sharon ... 202-495-3830 .. 93 D
secretary@dhs.edu
SMITH, Sharon ... 205-726-2247 .. 6 E
ssmith12@samford.edu
SMITH, Sharon ... 541-956-7187 .. 394 J
ssmith@roguecc.edu
SMITH, Sharon, E ... 616-632-2902 .. 231 A
smithsha@aquinas.edu
SMITH, Sharon, P ... 724-836-9911 .. 421 G
upgpres@pitt.edu
SMITH, Sharon, P ... 828-652-0697 .. 351 C
sharons@mcdowelltech.edu
SMITH, SharonAnn ... 618-374-5199 .. 151 E
sharonann.smith@principia.edu
SMITH, Shawn ... 217-732-3168 .. 146 A
ssmith@lincolnchristian.edu
SMITH, Shawn ... 816-604-5240 .. 267 H
shawn.smith@mcckc.edu
SMITH, Sheila ... 615-329-8710 .. 439 L
shsmith@fisk.edu
SMITH, Sheila, K ... 253-535-7674 .. 505 G
nurs@plu.edu
SMITH, Shelley ... 256-840-4128 .. 6 H
ssmith@snead.edu
SMITH, Shirley ... 714-484-7455 .. 54 G
ssmith@cypresscollege.edu
SMITH, Sommer ... 620-947-3121 .. 185 B
smiths@tabor.edu
SMITH, Sonya, G ... 901-448-5568 .. 448 H
ssmit209@uthsc.edu
SMITH, Stan ... 702-895-3197 .. 284 L
stan.smith@unlv.edu
SMITH, Stephanie ... 312-362-7552 .. 139 C
ssmit185@depaul.edu
SMITH, Stephanie ... 606-546-1259 .. 193 E
sasmith@unionky.edu
SMITH, Stephanie ... 304-696-2599 .. 513 D
smiths@marshall.edu
SMITH, Stephanie, M ... 800-782-2422 .. 31 E
smsmith@mail.cnuas.edu
SMITH, Stephen ... 206-546-4694 .. 507 F
spsmith@shoreline.edu
SMITH, Stephen, C ... 415-338-3879 .. 35 B
scsmith@sfsu.edu
SMITH, Stephen, E ... 918-465-1723 .. 383 I
ssmith@eosc.edu
SMITH, Steve ... 716-829-7600 .. 313 A
smith@dyc.edu
SMITH, Steve ... 626-584-5393 .. 44 G
stevensmith1@fuller.edu
SMITH, Steve ... 951-343-4261 .. 29 H
ssmith@calbaptist.edu
SMITH, Steve ... 915-831-6472 .. 457 H
ssmith54@epcc.edu
SMITH, Steve ... 512-837-2665 .. 460 G
jbrooks@tca.edu
SMITH, Steve ... 865-974-4127 .. 448 E
SMITH, Steve ... 432-264-5019 .. 459 D
sismith@howardcollege.edu
SMITH, Steve, A ... 801-422-6291 .. 480 C
steve_smith@byu.edu
SMITH, Steve, G ... 806-371-5008 .. 450 H
sgsmith@actx.edu
SMITH, Steven ... 970-521-6657 .. 81 O
steven.smith@njc.edu
SMITH, Steven ... 775-682-5613 .. 285 A
ssmith@unr.edu
SMITH, Steven ... 817-923-1921 .. 466 E
swsmith@swbts.edu

SNOWDEN, Bradley, C .... 540-665-5455.. 494 B
bsnowden@su.edu
SNOWDEN, Kent 334-241-9783...... 7 H
kesnowden@troy.edu
SNOWDEN, Michael, T .... 337-475-5428.. 200 H
msnowden@mcneese.edu
SNOWDEN, Monique, L .. 805-898-4154.... 43 K
msnowden@fielding.edu
SNOWDEN, Scott .... 908-737-5170.. 292 C
snowdens@kean.edu
SNOWDEN, Thelbert .... 202-462-2101.... 93 B
financialaid@iwp.edu
SNOWHITE, Mark .... 909-389-3205.... 60 B
msnowhite@craftonhills.edu
SNUFFIN, Gary .... 901-722-3260.. 444 C
gsnuffin@sco.edu
SNYDER, Alan, J .... 610-758-6964.. 408 H
ajs410@lehigh.edu
SNYDER, Alan, R .... 301-687-4242.. 212 F
arsnyder@frostburg.edu
SNYDER, Andrea .... 717-545-4747.. 406 I
SNYDER, Angie, P .... 479-248-7236.... 20 C
angie@ecollege.edu
SNYDER, Arlene, A .... 610-566-1776.. 423 H
asnyder@williamson.edu
SNYDER, Arthur, E .... 260-422-5561.. 162 B
aesnyder@indianatech.edu
SNYDER, Barbara, H .... 801-581-7793.. 481 M
bsnyder@sa.utah.edu
SNYDER, Barbara, R .... 216-368-4344.. 365 B
barbara.snyder@case.edu
SNYDER, Chris .... 724-830-1895.. 419 D
csnyder@setonhill.edu
SNYDER, Christopher ...... 662-325-2522.. 259 D
cas741@msstate.edu
SNYDER, Dan .... 303-217-4018.... 80 H
dans@heritage-education.com
SNYDER, Darla .... 217-641-4205.. 143 H
dsnyder@jwcc.edu
SNYDER, David .... 415-485-9506.... 40 C
dsnyder@marin.edu
SNYDER, David .... 903-813-3007.. 451 M
dsnyder@austincollege.edu
SNYDER, David, W .... 717-545-4747.. 406 I
SNYDER, Deborah .... 810-989-5545.. 240 G
dsnyder@sc4.edu
SNYDER, Dee Dee .... 330-287-1223.. 375 B
snyder.426@osu.edu
SNYDER, Diane, E .... 210-485-0010.. 450 A
dsnyder12@alamo.edu
SNYDER, Dianne, O .... 704-403-1558.. 342 E
dianne.snyder@carolinashealthcare.org
SNYDER, Donna .... 610-436-2955.. 416 C
dsnyder@wcupa.edu
SNYDER, Edward, A .... 203-432-6035.... 90 D
edward.snyder@yale.edu
SNYDER, Erin .... 563-336-3300.. 172 A
esnyder@eicc.edu
SNYDER, Gerry .... 718-636-3619.. 326 E
gsnyder@pratt.edu
SNYDER, Grant, S .... 610-359-5060.. 401 L
gsnyder@dccc.edu
SNYDER, Jacqueline .... 518-736-3622.. 315 A
jackie.snyder@fmcc.edu
SNYDER, Jan, E .... 712-324-5061.. 175 G
jsnyder@nwicc.edu
SNYDER, Jason .... 205-970-9235...... 7 B
jsnyder@sebc.edu
SNYDER, Jeff, B .... 651-631-5142.. 256 A
jbsnyder@unwsp.edu
SNYDER, Jenefer, D .... 757-822-2430.. 498 H
jsnyder@tcc.edu
SNYDER, John, F .... 724-738-2028.. 416 B
john.snyder@sru.edu
SNYDER, Josh .... 605-331-6895.. 438 A
josh.snyder@usiouxfalls.edu
SNYDER, Julie .... 810-762-5728.. 242 B
jusnyder@umflint.edu
SNYDER, Julie, A .... 419-372-9623.. 364 E
jmaiuri@bgsu.edu
SNYDER, Katherine .... 301-687-7487.. 212 F
ksnyder@frostburg.edu
SNYDER, Keith .... 423-236-2929.. 444 B
kasnyder@southern.edu
SNYDER, Kenneth .... 517-629-0213.. 230 E
ksnyder@albion.edu
SNYDER, Kimberly .... 828-395-1435.. 350 E
ksnyder@isothermal.edu
SNYDER, Ky, L .... 619-260-2930.... 72 B
kysnyder@sandiego.edu
SNYDER, JR., Larry .... 270-745-5208.. 194 D
lawrence.snyder@wku.edu
SNYDER, Lawrence .... 413-565-1000.. 215 A
lsnyder@baypath.edu
SNYDER, Lee, F .... 540-432-4100.. 488 K
lee.snyder@emu.edu
SNYDER, Linda .... 617-627-3334.. 228 H
linda.snyder@tufts.edu
SNYDER, Lisa, M .... 970-247-7543.... 80 D
lmsnyder@fortlewis.edu

SNYDER, Marcella, T .... 304-336-8345.. 513 F
msnyder@westliberty.edu
SNYDER, Marian, L .... 610-799-1734.. 408 G
msnyder@lccc.edu
SNYDER, Martin .... 215-968-8392.. 399 A
martin.snyder@bucks.edu
SNYDER, Matthew .... 315-792-5331.. 321 G
msnyder2@mvcc.edu
SNYDER, Michele .... 518-562-4334.. 310 C
michele.snyder@clinton.edu
SNYDER, Mike .... 217-245-3400.. 141 G
mike.snyder@mail.ic.edu
SNYDER, Noel .... 989-463-7231.. 230 F
snyderna@alma.edu
SNYDER, Pamela .... 440-775-8461.. 374 C
pamela.snyder@oberlin.edu
SNYDER, Paul .... 239-590-7050.. 110 L
psnyder@fgcu.edu
SNYDER, Randolph .... 614-947-6024.. 369 A
randy.snyder@franklin.edu
SNYDER, Rob, A .... 724-287-8711.. 399 B
rob.snyder@bc3.edu
SNYDER, Robert, J .... 610-282-1100.. 402 B
robert.snyder@desales.edu
SNYDER, Ryan .... 607-778-5407.. 332 D
1303mgr@fheg.follett.com
SNYDER, Sandra .... 503-552-1514.. 392 H
ssnyder@nunm.edu
SNYDER, Sheri .... 580-628-6208.. 384 L
sheri.snyder@noc.edu
SNYDER, Stephanie .... 270-852-3107.. 191 C
ssnyder@kwc.edu
SNYDER, Stephen .... 802-443-5979.. 484 F
ssnyder@middlebury.edu
SNYDER, Stephen, E .... 229-931-2037.. 122 C
stephen.snyder@gsw.edu
SNYDER, Susan, M .... 716-829-2476.. 331 C
smsnyder@buffalo.edu
SNYDER, Tamara .... 352-638-9764.... 96 F
tsnyder@beaconcollege.edu
SNYDER, Terry .... 610-896-1272.. 405 I
tsnyder@haverford.edu
SNYDER, Tim .... 904-256-7377.. 103 D
tsnyder2@ju.edu
SNYDER, Tim .... 414-443-8798.. 522 P
tim.snyder@wlc.edu
SNYDER, Timothy, L .... 310-338-2775.... 51 E
president@lmu.edu
SNYDER, Trina .... 717-477-1131.. 416 A
tmsnyd@ship.edu
SNYDER, Vanessa .... 404-233-3949.. 443 M
vsnyder@richmont.edu
SOARDS, Kathy .... 419-267-1314.. 374 A
ksoards@northweststate.edu
SOBA, Steven .... 610-861-1320.. 411 B
sobas@moravian.edu
SOBCZYK-BARRON,
Maggie .... 712-329-4753.. 174 B
msobczykbarron@iwcc.edu
SOBECKY, Patty .... 205-348-4890........ 8 D
psobecky@ua.edu
SOBEK, Christine, J .... 630-466-7900.. 157 K
csobek@waubonsee.edu
SOBEL, Jack .... 313-577-7574.. 243 F
jsobel@med.wayne.edu
SOBEL, Susan .... 501-450-3138.... 24 G
ssobel@uca.edu
SOBH, Tarek, M .... 203-576-4111.... 89 C
sobh@bridgeport.edu
SOBIERALSKI, Joe .... 803-641-3310.. 433 G
joes@usca.edu
SOBIESUO, Andrew, M .... 843-953-5537.. 428 G
sobiesuoa@cofc.edu
SOBIN, Rebecca .... 520-322-6330.... 13 J
rebecca@hanuniversity.edu
SOBLEY, Susan .... 662-329-7210.. 259 E
sasobley@muw.edu
SOBOLEWSKI, Rich .... 662-329-7119.. 259 E
resobolewski@muw.edu
SOBOLIK, Kristin .... 937-775-2225.. 381 H
kristin.sobolik@wright.edu
SOBOTTA, Sharon .... 925-631-4193.... 59 I
ssobotta@stmarys-ca.edu
SOCASH, Thomas .... 212-431-2825.. 323 H
thomas.socash@nyls.edu
SOCHA, Maureen .... 413-755-4460.. 224 G
mesocha@stcc.edu
SOCKWELL, Angela, A ..... 904-808-7492.. 108 B
angelasockwell@sjrstate.edu
SODEIKA, Lisa .... 630-353-3832.. 139 D
lsodeika@devrygroup.com
SODERGREN, Carl .... 570-389-4102.. 414 D
csodergr@bloomu.edu
SODERQUIST, Rich .... 815-802-8173.. 144 C
rsoderquist@kcc.edu
SODT, Jill .... 810-762-0415.. 238 F
jill.sodt@mcc.edu
SOE, Victor .... 719-587-8267.... 76 G
victorsoe@adams.edu
SOEFFING, William .... 605-331-6759.. 438 A
william.soeffing@usiouxfalls.edu

SOEFFKER-CULICERTO,
Heike, I .... 304-929-6731.. 512 C
hsoeffker@newriver.edu
SOFFA, Kari .... 661-362-5417.... 40 A
kari.soffa@canyons.edu
SOFIELD, Roy .... 423-697-2552.. 445 D
roy.sofield@chattanoogastate.edu
SOFISH, Marian .... 408-283-7500.... 35 C
marian.sofish@sjsu.edu
SOFRANKO, Greg .... 724-938-4274.. 414 E
sofranko@calu.edu
SOHAIL, Mohammad .... 517-371-5140.. 243 I
sohailm@cooley.edu
SOHAN, Donna .... 860-932-4153.... 87 C
dsohan@qvcc.edu
SOHL, Amanda .... 614-236-6574.. 364 N
asohl@capital.edu
SOHN, Christopher .... 937-766-2789.. 365 C
chrissohn@cedarville.edu
SOHN, David, Y .... 703-941-2020.. 490 G
SOHN, Eugene .... 718-518-4154.. 308 C
esohn@hostos.cuny.edu
SOHOLT, Pam, B .... 701-788-4823.. 360 E
pam.soholt@mayvillestate.edu
SOIFER, Aviam .... 808-956-6363.. 131 F
soifer@hawaii.edu
SOIFER, Yitzchok .... 845-362-3053.. 304 J
yitzchoks@bytsem.org
SOIFFER, Stephen .... 718-260-5400.. 309 C
ssoiffer@citytech.cuny.edu
SOIKA, Brian .... 713-348-4726.. 464 E
brian.soika@rice.edu
SOILEAU, Deidre .... 253-964-6232.. 506 B
dsoileau@pierce.ctc.edu
SOILEAU, M, J .... 407-823-5538.. 111 E
mj@ucf.edu
SOKOL, Bryan .... 314-977-2041.. 271 K
bsokol1@slu.edu
SOKOL, Moshe, Z .... 718-820-4800.. 337 I
sokolm@touro.edu
SOKOLL, Shane .... 512-313-3000.. 455 F
shane.sokoll@concordia.edu
SOLA, Peter, L .... 651-631-5349.. 256 A
plsola@unwsp.edu
SOLAN, George .... 252-399-6399.. 341 P
gsolan@barton.edu
SOLAND, Linda .... 602-285-7748.... 14 F
linda.soland@phoenixcollege.edu
SOLANDER, Sondra, K ...... 620-431-2820.. 183 H
ssolander@neosho.edu
SOLANO, Maria .... 213-477-2536.... 53 B
msolano@msmu.edu
SOLARES, Dennis .... 818-364-3355.... 49 J
solaredr@lamission.edu
SOLBACH, Robin .... 732-987-2681.. 292 A
rsolbach@georgian.edu
SOLBERG, Dale .... 916-348-4689.... 43 A
dsolberg@epic.edu
SOLBERG, Laura .... 352-588-8218.. 108 C
laura.solberg@saintleo.edu
SOLBERG, Lori .... 605-995-2805.. 435 F
losolber@dwu.edu
SOLBRIG, Ronald .... 208-282-2330.. 133 H
solbrona@isu.edu
SOLCHER, Iris .... 210-832-2110.. 474 D
isolcher@uiwtx.edu
SOLDWISCH, Sandie, S .... 815-395-5088.. 153 D
sandiesoldwisch@sacn.edu
SOLDZ, Stephen .... 617-277-3915.. 216 D
soldzs@bgsp.edu
SOLE, Mary, L .... 407-823-5496.. 111 E
mary.sole@ucf.edu
SOLECKI, Amanda .... 410-287-1003.. 206 J
asolecki@cecil.edu
SOLECKI, Jean .... 208-426-1979.. 132 I
jennifersolecki@boisestate.edu
SOLEIM, Heather, M .... 218-477-4060.. 250 F
heather.soleim@mnstate.edu
SOLEMSAAS, Rachel .... 775-673-7014.. 284 K
rsolemsaas@tmcc.edu
SOLEMSAAS, Rachel, H .... 808-934-2504.. 131 J
rsolems@hawaii.edu
SOLER, Adrienne .... 802-831-1059.. 485 F
asoler@vermontlaw.edu
SOLERNOU, Sheila .... 203-285-2393.... 86 C
ssolernou@gwcc.commnet.edu
SOLEY, Maryann .... 773-907-4755.. 137 E
msoley@ccc.edu
SOLFARO, Deb .... 570-662-4000.. 415 E
SOLHEIM, Derek, N .... 319-352-8330.. 177 G
derek.solheim@wartburg.edu
SOLIDAY, Rhett .... 714-556-3610.... 73 B
rhett.soliday@vanguard.edu
SOLIMINI, Karen .... 603-577-6585.. 286 I
ksolimini@dwc.edu
SOLIS, Amy .... 701-627-4738.. 361 H
asolis@nhsc.edu
SOLIS, Carlos .... 512-245-1799.. 471 F
crs218@txstate.edu
SOLIS, JR., Federico .... 956-794-4002.. 460 F
fsolis@laredo.edu

SOLIS, Gerard .... 813-974-1674.. 112 C
gsolis@usf.edu
SOLIS, Ricardo .... 956-721-5101.. 460 F
president@laredo.edu
SOLIS, Robert .... 774-455-7711.. 220 E
rsolis@umassp.edu
SOLIS, Vincent, R .... 956-764-5950.. 460 F
vincent.solis@laredo.edu
SOLIZ, Gina, M .... 315-228-7431.. 310 G
gsoliz@colgate.edu
SOLIZ, Sandra .... 713-525-3116.. 475 J
solizs@stthom.edu
SOLIZ, Ty .... 432-685-6467.. 461 H
asoliz@midland.edu
SOLLAND, Sara .... 715-425-4255.. 521 B
sara.m.solland@uwrf.edu
SOLLARS, David .... 785-670-2045.. 185 H
david.sollars@washburn.edu
SOLLENBERGER,
Donna, K .... 409-772-6116.. 478 A
dksoll@utmb.edu
SOLLENBERGER, Mitchel . 313-593-5353.. 242 A
msollenb@umich.edu
SOLLENBERGER, Mitchel . 313-593-5030.. 242 A
msollenb@umich.edu
SOLLIE, Donna, L .... 334-844-4396...... 1 G
sollidl@auburn.edu
SOLLOSI, Nancy, B .... 336-334-4822.. 350 B
nbsollosi@gtcc.edu
SOLMS, Daniel .... 260-356-6000.. 161 O
SOLNICK, Steven, L .... 828-298-3325.. 359 F
president@warren-wilson.edu
SOLO AQUINO, Limaris .. 787-725-8120.. 532 K
lsolo@eap.edu
SOLOCHEK, Arlen .... 480-731-8232.... 13 N
arlen.solochek@domail.maricopa.edu
SOLOMON, Daniel, L ...... 919-515-7277.. 357 B
solomon@ncsu.edu
SOLOMON, Debbie .... 425-235-2352.. 506 F
dsolomon@rtc.edu
SOLOMON, Ira .... 504-865-5422.. 200 C
isolomon@tulane.edu
SOLOMON, Jeffrey, S ...... 508-831-5288.. 230 C
solomon@wpi.edu
SOLOMON, Jerome .... 408-498-5154.... 39 H
jsolomon@cogswell.edu
SOLOMON, Joseph .... 718-851-8721.. 340 H
SOLOMON, Kimberly .... 803-780-1266.. 434 M
ksolomon@voorhees.edu
SOLOMON, Mary Ellen .... 412-396-6668.. 403 A
solomon3@duq.edu
SOLOMON, Mendel .... 973-267-9404.. 294 F
rabbisolo@aol.com
SOLOMON, Robert .... 912-754-2879.. 126 G
rsolomon@savannahtech.edu
SOLOMON, Ronald .... 225-216-8267.. 195 H
solomonr@mybrcc.edu
SOLOMON, Saige .... 318-869-5115.. 194 I
ssolomon@centenary.edu
SOLOMON, Samuel .... 401-454-6347.. 426 A
ssolomon@risd.edu
SOLOMON, Shoshana .... 973-267-9404.. 294 F
shoshanasolomon@rca.edu
SOLOMON, Sigrid, B .... 937-481-2270.. 381 C
sigrid_solomon@wilmington.edu
SOLOMON, Steven .... 850-201-6549.. 113 E
solomos@tcc.fl.edu
SOLOMON, William, G .... 478-301-2771.. 124 D
solomon_wg@mercer.edu
SOLOMONS, Mary, L .... 518-580-5619.. 330 F
msolomon@skidmore.edu
SOLOMONT, Alan .... 617-627-3453.. 228 H
alan.solomont@tufts.edu
SOLOMOU, Costas .... 202-994-6040.... 92 D
SOLORZANO, Fernando ... 562-985-4101.... 33 B
fernando.solorzano@csulb.edu
SOLORZANO, Jose .... 787-891-0925.. 533 G
jsolorza@aguadilla.inter.edu
SOLOWAY, Seth .... 914-251-6196.. 334 C
seth.soloway@purchase.edu
SOLSKI, Ed .... 661-824-2977.... 53 K
esolski@ntps.edu
SOLT, Karen .... 630-942-2292.. 138 B
soltka@cod.edu
SOLT, Michael .... 562-985-5306.... 33 B
michael.solt@csulb.edu
SOLTANIAN, Rita .... 661-255-1050.... 30 E
SOLTICE, Nathan .... 918-495-7473.. 386 H
nsoltice@oru.edu
SOLTIS, Corinne .... 206-934-6739.. 507 A
corinne.soltis@seattlecolleges.edu
SOLTMAN, Mary .... 360-596-5364.. 508 A
msoltman@spscc.edu
SOLTYS, Eugene .... 973-328-5096.. 290 H
esoltys@ccm.edu
SOLTZ, David, L .... 570-389-4526.. 414 D
dsoltz@bloomu.edu
SOLTZ-KNOWLTON,
Bonnie .... 860-528-4111.... 87 H
SOLUM, Catlin, E .... 701-788-4856.. 360 E
catlin.solum@mayvillestate.edu

SOLUM, Rachel ... 303-245-4804 ... 81 I
rsolum@naropa.edu
SOLVASON, Nanette ... 650-940-7730 ... 44 B
solvasonnanette@foothill.edu
SOLVERSON, Natalie ... 608-785-8006 .. 520 C
nsolverson@uwlax.edu
SOLVESON, Peg ... 707-654-1297 ... 33 D
psolveson@csum.edu
SOM, Andrew ... 707-654-1085 ... 33 D
asom@csum.edu
SOMAN, Sherril ... 616-331-3327 .. 234 F
somans@gvsu.edu
SOMERA, R. Ray, D ... 671-735-5528 .. 529 G
reneray.somera@guamcc.edu
SOMERLAD, Tracy ... 910-755-7422 .. 347 H
somerladt@brunswickcc.edu
SOMERO, Audrey ... 757-826-1883 .. 487 E
SOMERO, Marty ... 970-351-2502 ... 84 C
marty.somero@unco.edu
SOMERS, Christine ... 570-674-6314 .. 410 K
csomers@misericordia.edu
SOMERS, Cindy ... 303-797-5972 ... 76 J
cindy.somers@arapahoe.edu
SOMERS, John ... 520-533-2391 ... 12 L
somersj@cochise.edu
SOMERS, Kevin ... 870-743-3000 ... 21 C
ksomers@northark.edu
SOMERS, Michael ... 508-531-1255 .. 221 C
msomers@bridgew.edu
SOMERS, Micki ... 870-743-3000 ... 21 C
msomers@northark.edu
SOMERS, Robert, J ... 410-455-2695 .. 211 G
somers@umbc.edu
SOMERSET, Cheryl ... 864-587-4236 .. 433 A
somersetc@smcsc.edu
SOMERSON, Rosanne ... 401-454-6764 .. 426 A
president@risd.edu
SOMERVELL, Ronald ... 703-284-6941 .. 492 A
ronald.somervell@marymount.edu
SOMERVILLE, Charles ... 304-696-2424 .. 513 D
somervil@marshall.edu
SOMERVILLE, Dionne, D . 570-389-4062 .. 414 D
dsomervi@bloomu.edu
SOMERVILLE, Mary ... 303-556-4587 ... 84 A
mary.somerville@ucdenver.edu
SOMERVILLE, Tim ... 951-719-2994 ... 58 D
doc@golfcollege.edu
SOMMA, Ann Marie ... 518-743-2273 .. 335 A
sommam@sunyacc.edu
SOMMA, Lauren ... 951-781-2727 ... 59 F
lsomma@sagecollege.edu
SOMMA, Victor ... 508-425-1216 .. 224 E
vsomma@qcc.mass.edu
SOMMER, John ... 732-987-2416 .. 292 A
jsommer@georgian.edu
SOMMER, Pete, F ... 757-822-1783 .. 498 H
psommer@tcc.edu
SOMMER, Sally, W ... 419-358-3317 .. 364 D
sommers@bluffton.edu
SOMMER, Thomas ... 810-762-9525 .. 236 C
tsommer@kettering.edu
SOMMERER, Shaun ... 660-626-2395 .. 262 A
ssommerer@atsu.edu
SOMMERFELD, Curtis ... 541-956-7016 .. 394 J
curt@roguecc.edu
SOMMERFELD, Janee ... 253-833-9111 .. 504 C
jsommerfeld@greenriver.edu
SOMMERFELDT, Scott, D 801-422-2674 .. 480 C
scott_sommerfeldt@byu.edu
SOMMERS, Bill ... 304-876-5009 .. 513 E
wsommers@shepherd.edu
SOMMERS, Janet, B ... 651-631-5201 .. 256 A
jbsommers@unwsp.edu
SOMMERS, Kathleen, C ... 724-287-8711 .. 399 E
kathy.sommers@bc3.edu
SOMMERS, Mary ... 308-865-8520 .. 282 L
sommersm@unk.edu
SOMMERS, Rhoda ... 765-998-5108 .. 167 C
rhoda_sommers@taylor.edu
SOMMERVILLE, Jan ... 616-395-7780 .. 235 F
sommerville@hope.edu
SOMPOLSKI, Robert ... 847-635-1690 .. 150 G
somplski@oakton.edu
SONDEJ, Julia ... 510-278-9313 ... 63 H
SONDER, Henk, E ... 401-456-9577 .. 425 E
hsonder@ric.edu
SONDEY, Joann ... 914-831-0288 .. 311 C
jsondey@cw.edu
SONDEY, Stephen ... 201-684-7496 .. 294 G
ssondey@ramapo.edu
SONES, Rodney ... 740-477-7786 .. 374 G
rsones@ohiochristian.edu
SONEY, Ralph ... 336-334-4822 .. 350 B
rgsoney@gtcc.edu
SONG, A. Li ... 516-364-0808 .. 323 B
asong@nycollege.edu
SONG, Bok, H ... 636-327-4645 .. 268 C
dbo@midwest.edu
SONG, Connie ... 513-231-2223 .. 363 K
csong@athenaeum.edu
SONG, Hee Sook ... 770-220-7903 .. 120 G
joysong@gcuniv.edu
SONG, Hyongsig ... 770-220-7926 .. 120 G
libray@gcuniv.edu
SONG, Jae, M ... 636-327-4645 .. 268 C
vpson@midwest.edu
SONG, Jae, P ... 636-327-4645 .. 268 C
jp@midwest.edu
SONG, James ... 636-327-4645 .. 268 C
president@midwest.edu
SONG, John, M ... 213-385-2322 ... 75 E
president@wmu.edu
SONG, Sarah ... 818-947-2606 ... 50 D
songsj@lavc.edu
SONG, Sumie ... 773-244-5571 .. 149 I
ssong@northpark.edu
SONGER, Nancy, B ... 215-895-2167 .. 402 G
nancy.b.songer@drexel.edu
SONGSTER, Nora ... 707-546-4000 ... 42 M
nsongster@empirecollege.com
SONI, Bharat ... 931-372-3374 .. 445 B
bsoni@tntech.edu
SONI, Varun ... 213-740-6110 ... 72 D
vasoni@usc.edu
SONNEMA, Roy ... 509-359-2227 .. 503 D
rsonnema1@euw.edu
SONNENBERG, Jeff ... 602-557-1740 ... 17 L
jeff.sonnenberg@phoenix.edu
SONNENBERGER, David .. 630-829-6538 .. 135 F
dsonnenberger@ben.edu
SONNENBLICK, Carol ... 718-552-1170 .. 309 C
csonnenblick@citytech.cuny.edu
SONNENFELD, Gerald ... 401-874-4576 .. 426 D
gsonnenfeld@uri.edu
SONNENSCHEIN, Nurit ... 518-608-8307 .. 314 A
nsonnens@excelsior.edu
SONNENSTEIN, Mark ... 718-933-6700 .. 321 I
ssonnenstein@monroecollege.edu
SONNENSTRAHL, Samuel 202-651-5060 ... 92 C
samuel.sonnenstrahl@gallaudet.edu
SONNER, Mary ... 423-636-7345 .. 447 G
msonner@tusculum.edu
SONNIER-PLAISANCE,
Beverly ... 225-768-1797 .. 199 B
beverly.sonnierplaisance@ololcollege.edu
SONNTAG, Dave ... 509-313-6192 .. 504 A
sonntagd@gonzaga.edu
SONNTAG, Gabriela ... 909-748-8096 ... 71 K
gabriela_sonntag@redlands.edu
SONNTAG, Michael ... 803-938-3826 .. 434 E
sonntagm@uscsumter.edu
SONODA, Kazuhiro ... 509-865-8584 .. 504 D
sonoda_k@heritage.edu
SONQUIST, Eric, J ... 805-893-8585 ... 70 E
eric.sonquist@ucsb.edu
SONRICKER, Nicholas ... 716-851-1282 .. 313 H
sonrickern@ecc.edu
SONSTEBY, Jill ... 651-638-6254 .. 244 L
jks44888@bethel.edu
SONTAG, Michael ... 513-244-4766 .. 373 C
michael.sontag@msj.edu
SONTY, Vijay ... 352-588-8888 .. 108 C
vijay.sonty@saintleo.edu
SOO, Billy ... 617-552-3260 .. 216 C
billy.soo@bc.edu
SOODSMA, Heidi ... 920-693-1631 .. 523 E
heidi.soodsma@gotoltc.edu
SOOHOO-REFAEI, Sandy . 619-849-2783 ... 57 M
sandysoohoorefaei@pointloma.edu
SOOKDEO, David ... 718-429-6600 .. 339 D
david.sookdeo@vaughn.edu
SOONS, Peter, D ... 802-654-2374 .. 484 I
psoons@smcvt.edu
SOPCHAK, Elaine ... 802-224-3001 .. 485 G
elaine.sopchak@vsc.edu
SOPCICH, Joe ... 913-469-8500 .. 182 A
jsopcich@jccc.edu
SOPCZYK, Debbie ... 518-464-8728 .. 314 A
dsopczyk@excelsior.edu
SOPER, Jeff, D ... 712-362-0422 .. 173 G
jsoper@iowalakes.edu
SOPER, Sarah ... 765-973-8231 .. 162 G
saeaton@iue.edu
SOPHEA, So ... 646-313-8000 .. 309 F
sophea.so@guttman.cuny.edu
SOPKO, Jennifer ... 312-949-7412 .. 142 A
jsopko@ico.edu
SORA, Wendy ... 808-956-9264 .. 131 F
wendytak@hawaii.edu
SORBELLO, Barbara, C ... 804-627-5300 .. 487 G
barbara_sorbello@bshsi.org
SORBELLO, Janine ... 302-225-6261 ... 91 D
sorbello@gbc.edu
SORBER, Todd ... 973-684-5656 .. 294 A
tsorber@pccc.edu
SORCE, Tanya ... 973-290-4465 .. 290 G
tsorce@cse.edu
SORDELET, Teresa, A ... 260-399-7700 .. 168 D
tsordelet@sf.edu
SORELL, Rebecca ... 415-503-6287 ... 61 C
rsorell@sfcm.edu
SORELLE, Patrick ... 920-498-5753 .. 524 E
patrick.sorelle@nwtc.edu
SOREM, JR., James, R ... 918-631-2288 .. 389 E
james-sorem@utulsa.edu
SOREN, Vicki ... 605-688-4989 .. 437 F
vick.soren@sdstate.edu
SORENSEN, Carl, K ... 804-289-8166 .. 495 G
csorense@richmond.edu
SORENSEN, Dale ... 541-485-1780 .. 393 A
dalesorensen@newhope.edu
SORENSEN, Elisabeth ... 425-739-8134 .. 504 F
elisabeth.sorensen@lwtech.edu
SORENSEN, Gary ... 928-428-8247 ... 13 B
gary.sorensen@eac.edu
SORENSEN, Kathryn ... 916-691-7204 ... 51 B
sorensk@crc.losrios.edu
SORENSEN, Michael ... 503-552-1975 .. 392 H
msorensen@nunm.edu
SORENSEN, Miles, F ... 704-687-7201 .. 358 A
nfsorens@uncc.edu
SORENSEN, Robin ... 704-378-1048 .. 345 E
rsorensen@jcsu.edu
SORENSEN, Sarah ... 801-524-8149 .. 480 J
ssorenson@ldsbc.edu
SORENSEN, Teresa ... 651-846-1479 .. 252 C
teresa.sorensen@saintpaul.edu
SORENSEN, Zak ... 616-538-2330 .. 234 D
zsorensen@gbcol.edu
SORENSON, Amanda ... 573-288-6420 .. 264 F
asorenson@culver.edu
SORENSON, Amy ... 920-403-3165 .. 519 G
amy.sorenson@snc.edu
SORENSON, David ... 605-274-5223 .. 435 E
david.sorenson@augie.edu
SORENSON, Jennifer ... 909-537-5069 ... 34 C
jennifer.sorenson@csusb.edu
SORENSON, Nancee ... 813-253-7860 .. 102 F
csorenson@hccfl.edu
SORENSON, Nancy ... 651-523-2103 .. 247 A
nsorenson01@hamline.edu
SORENSON, Richard ... 847-947-5601 .. 149 E
rsorenson@nl.edu
SORENSON, Tanya ... 253-589-6090 .. 502 F
tanya.sorenson@cptc.edu
SOREY, Helaina ... 206-398-4627 .. 507 E
soreyh@seattleu.edu
SOREY, Kellie, C ... 757-822-1065 .. 498 H
ksorey@tcc.edu
SORG, Charlotte ... 843-574-6147 .. 433 D
charlotte.sorg@tridenttech.edu
SORIA, Deborah ... 559-925-3316 ... 74 E
deborahsoria@whccd.edu
SORIA, Richard ... 305-237-3310 .. 105 D
rsoria@mdc.edu
SORIANO, Brenda ... 212-962-0002 .. 322 G
bsoriano@nyci.edu
SORIERO, Julie ... 617-253-4499 .. 225 A
SORK, Victoria ... 310-825-7755 ... 69 D
vlsork@ucla.edu
SORRELL, Garry ... 660-596-7301 .. 272 G
gsorrell@sfccmo.edu
SORRELL, Michael, J ... 214-379-5550 .. 463 G
president@pqc.edu
SORRELLS, Glenn ... 972-279-6511 .. 450 I
gsorrells@amberton.edu
SORRELS, Paul ... 830-279-3013 .. 471 E
psorrels@sulross.edu
SORRENTINO,
Donna Marie ... 603-862-2930 .. 288 C
dms@unh.edu
SORRENTINO, Sebastian . 860-768-4034 ... 89 G
sorrentin@hartford.edu
SORROW, Russell, L ... 770-484-1204 .. 124 C
russell.sorrow@lutherrice.edu
SORTOR, Janet ... 207-629-4000 .. 203 H
jsortor@mccs.me.edu
SORTOR, Marci, J ... 507-786-3004 .. 254 P
sortor@stolaf.edu
SORVAAG, Scott ... 507-457-6612 .. 254 O
ssorvaag@smumn.edu
SOSA, David ... 516-726-5589 .. 529 B
sosad@usmma.edu
SOSA, Dona ... 212-343-1234 .. 321 B
dsosa@mcny.edu
SOSA, Horacio ... 856-256-4129 .. 295 E
sosa@rowan.edu
SOSA, Joe ... 619-684-8784 ... 54 C
jsosa@newschoolarch.edu
SOSA, Juan Carlos ... 787-743-7979 .. 536 A
SOSA, Robert ... 210-829-6077 .. 474 D
sosa@uiwtx.edu
SOSA, Velma Leticia ... 787-761-0640 .. 537 C
jefebiblioteca@uccpr.edu
SOSA, Victor ... 603-862-2001 .. 288 C
victor.sosa@unh.edu
SOSA-GUERRERO, Sandy 305-760-7500 .. 104 K
SOSA-HEGARTY, Dina ... 903-886-5101 .. 468 D
dina.sosa@tamuc.edu
SOSA PIERONI,
Alejandra ... 386-822-7082 .. 113 B
asosapieroni@stetson.edu
SOSCIA, Peter ... 845-341-9541 .. 325 H
peter.soscia@sunyorange.edu
SOSEBEE, JR., Hugh, D .. 478-301-2302 .. 124 D
sosebee_hd@mercer.edu
SOSEVSKY, Chana ... 800-950-4824 .. 337 I
chana.sosevsky@touro.edu
SOSHOWSKI, Donna ... 781-239-5264 .. 214 G
dsoshowski@babson.edu
SOSLAND, Steven, R ... 817-735-2000 .. 475 C
steven.sosland@unthsc.edu
SOSSEN, Nina ... 413-545-4741 .. 220 F
nsossen@admin.umass.edu
SOSULSKI, Michael, J ... 864-597-4020 .. 435 C
sosulskimj@wofford.edu
SOTA, Hai-Thom ... 510-869-6511 ... 59 L
ttran@samuelmerritt.edu
SOTHERDEN, James, J ... 717-691-6012 .. 410 J
jsotherd@messiah.edu
SOTIRIOU, Jessica ... 217-709-0945 .. 145 E
jsotiriou@lakeviewcol.edu
SOTO, Amilcar ... 787-878-5475 .. 533 H
asoto@arecibo.inter.edu
SOTO, Arlene ... 541-756-6445 .. 395 B
asoto@socc.edu
SOTO, Bobby ... 214-333-6894 .. 455 J
bobby@dbu.edu
SOTO, Cecilia ... 602-286-8290 ... 14 B
cecilia.soto@gatewaycc.edu
SOTO, Edgar ... 520-206-3260 ... 16 F
esoto@pima.edu
SOTO, Emilia ... 787-269-4510 .. 536 G
emilia.soto@uccaribe.edu
SOTO, Emilia ... 787-740-6631 .. 536 G
emilia.soto@uccaribe.edu
SOTO, Jose ... 402-323-3412 .. 282 F
jsoto@southeast.edu
SOTO, Juanita ... 920-686-6129 .. 519 H
juanita.soto@sl.edu
SOTO, Luis ... 787-250-1912 .. 534 B
lesotomieses@metro.inter.edu
SOTO, Luis, A ... 787-864-2222 .. 534 A
luis.soto@guayama.inter.edu
SOTO, Megan ... 619-388-3473 ... 60 F
msoto@sdccd.edu
SOTO, Nelson ... 513-861-6400 .. 378 E
nelson.soto@myunion.edu
SOTO, Yadirah ... 787-765-3560 .. 532 I
ysoto@edpuniversity.edu
SOTO, Zulay ... 787-884-3838 .. 530 G
dir_asociada@atenascollege.edu
SOTO AQUINO, Limaris .. 787-725-8120 .. 532 K
lisotoa@eap.edu
SOTO FULLER, Ineliz ... 206-281-2561 .. 507 C
ineliz@spu.edu
SOTO I COLON, Ana ... 787-848-5739 .. 536 C
SOTO-LÓPEZ, Heriberto ... 787-751-1912 .. 534 E
herisoto@juris.inter.edu
SOTO MALDONADO,
Ismael ... 787-720-4476 .. 537 A
decanatofinanzas@mizpa.edu
SOTTER, Trudy ... 724-964-8811 .. 411 F
tsotterfa@aol.com
SOTTILE, Christian ... 912-525-5000 .. 126 E
csottile@scad.edu
SOUBLET, Gia ... 504-520-7575 .. 202 C
gsoublet@xula.edu
SOUCIE, Evie ... 413-572-5637 .. 222 E
esoucie@westfield.ma.edu
SOUCIER, JoEllen ... 713-718-8891 .. 459 B
joellen.soucier@hccs.edu
SOUCY, Erin ... 207-834-7830 .. 205 B
esoucy@maine.edu
SOUCY, Ken, R ... 937-229-2641 .. 379 D
ksoucy1@udayton.edu
SOUCY, Matthew ... 920-686-6203 .. 519 H
matthew.soucy@sl.edu
SOUDAH, John, P ... 210-458-7531 .. 477 A
john.soudah@utsa.edu
SOUFLERIS, Dawn ... 585-475-2574 .. 327 E
dmsrhs@rit.edu
SOUL, Karen ... 318-869-5240 .. 194 I
ksoul@centenary.edu
SOULE, E.Whitney ... 207-725-3000 .. 202 F
SOULES, Robert, C ... 518-388-6176 .. 338 H
soulesr@union.edu
SOURBEER, Dan ... 760-744-1150 ... 56 F
dsourbeer@palomar.edu
SOURBEER, Daniel ... 760-744-1150 ... 56 F
SOURS, Lori ... 541-245-7803 .. 394 J
lsours@roguecc.edu
SOUSA, Antoni ... 845-575-3000 .. 320 B
antoni.sousa@marist.edu
SOUSA, Aron ... 517-353-1730 .. 237 I
sousaa@msu.edu
SOUSA, Camellia ... 603-924-2787 .. 287 D
camellia@sharonarts.org
SOUSA, Jennifer ... 573-288-6343 .. 264 F
jsousa@culver.edu
SOUSA, Marsha ... 907-474-7931 ... 10 G
mcsousa@alaska.edu

SOUSA, Mitsy 305-442-9223 105 F msousa@mrc.edu
SOUSA-PEOPLES, Kim 336-334-5231 358 B ksp@uncg.edu
SOUTER, Sharon 254-295-4667 474 E ssouter@umhb.edu
SOUTH, Gregory 530-938-5375 40 F gsouth@siskiyous.edu
SOUTH, James, D 580-774-3771 388 C james.south@swosu.edu
SOUTH, III, John, T 912-650-6200 127 D john.south@southuniversity.edu
SOUTH, Sandi 662-862-8956 258 C sssouth@iccms.edu
SOUTH, Stephen, A 865-251-1800 444 A ssouth@southcollegetn.edu
SOUTHALL, Ann 870-862-8131 22 D asouthall@southark.edu
SOUTHARD, Anne 850-729-6040 105 I southarda@nwfsc.edu
SOUTHARD, Brooke 479-968-0396 19 F bsouthard@atu.edu
SOUTHARD, Kristine 914-654-5522 311 A ksouthard@cnr.edu
SOUTHARD, Sonya 270-686-4526 190 D sonya.southard@kctcs.edu
SOUTHERLAND, Deana 412-338-4770 398 H dsoutherland@brightwoodcareer.edu
SOUTHERLAND, Johnnie 919-530-5321 357 A jsoutherland@nccu.edu
SOUTHERLAND, Nate 801-957-4542 483 A nate.southerland@slcc.edu
SOUTHERN, Debbie 309-341-7225 145 A dsouther@knox.edu
SOUTHERN, Jeff 620-276-9631 181 C jeff.southern@gcccks.edu
SOUTHERN, Keri 903-586-2501 452 E
SOUTHERN, Lori 254-299-8686 461 E lsouthern@mclennan.edu
SOUTHWELL, Michael 570-422-2871 414 H msouthwell@esu.edu
SOUTHWICK, Lacey 276-944-6240 489 I lsouthwick@ehc.edu
SOUTHWOOD, Lori 859-572-6383 192 B southwoodl1@nku.edu
SOUTHWORTH, Linda 978-934-2373 221 A linda_southworth@uml.edu
SOUTHWORTH, Pam 712-325-3441 174 B psouthworth@iwcc.edu
SOUTHWORTH-FISHER, Barbara 727-816-3116 106 F fisherb@phsc.edu
SOUTTER, Cathey 214-768-4795 465 J csoutter@smu.edu
SOUZA, David, E 215-699-5700 408 C dsouza@lsb.edu
SOUZA, Diana 231-348-6837 239 A dsouza@ncmich.edu
SOUZA, Jane Marie 585-273-2821 338 K janemarie.souza@rochester.edu
SOUZA, Nicole, L 212-346-1232 325 J nsouza@pace.edu
SOVA, Devin, A 336-318-7820 352 B dasova@randolph.edu
SOWELL, John, T 404-995-8484 260 E jsowell@rts.edu
SOWELL, Kathy 615-230-3476 447 C kathy.sowell@volstate.edu
SOWELL, Stacey 919-546-8271 355 F ssowell@shawu.edu
SOWER, Michelle 530-541-4660 48 D sower@ltcc.edu
SOWERS, Donna, S 301-846-2466 207 F dsowers@frederick.edu
SOWERS, Karen 865-974-3176 448 E kmsowers@utk.edu
SOWINSKI, Tomasz 212-472-1500 324 A tsowinski@nysid.edu
SOYER, Megan, M 817-257-5325 469 G m.m.soyer@tcu.edu
SOYRING, Mary 218-879-0811 249 C msoyring@fdltcc.edu
SOZZO, Anthony, M 914-594-4491 323 I tony_sozzo@nymc.edu
SPACH, Robert, C 704-894-2420 343 I rospach@davidson.edu
SPACK, Martha 870-972-2056 18 J mspack@astate.edu
SPADE, Douglas, R 713-798-7391 452 G dspade@bcm.edu
SPADEMAN, Robert 216-523-7284 366 I r.spademan@csuohio.edu
SPAETH, Jason 320-629-5100 251 E spaethj@pine.edu
SPAETH, Nick 309-457-2143 148 E nspaeth@monmouthcollege.edu
SPAETH, Paul, J 716-375-2327 328 B pspaeth@sbu.edu
SPAETH-BAUM, Barbara 701-671-2483 361 F barbara.baum@ndscs.edu
SPAGNA, Michael, E 818-677-2590 34 A michael.spagna@csun.edu
SPAGNOLO, Jean Paul 260-399-7700 168 D jspagnolo@sf.edu
SPAID, Darla 814-732-1364 415 A dspaid@edinboro.edu
SPAIN, Ashley 309-692-4092 147 I arspain@midstate.edu
SPAIN, Joanie 505-473-6676 302 A joanie.spain@santafeuniversity.edu
SPAIN, Tammy 252-249-1851 351 G tspain@pamlicocc.edu
SPAIN, William, R 401-841-3499 528 E
SPAK, Gale, T 973-596-8540 293 D gale.spak@njit.edu
SPAKE, Deborah, F 330-672-6317 370 I dspake@kent.edu
SPAKE, Ellen 816-501-4597 270 J ellen.spake@rockhurst.edu
SPALDING, Carol 704-216-3450 352 G carol.spalding@rccc.edu
SPALDING, David, P 515-294-2422 169 G spalding@iastate.edu
SPALDING, Jane 206-296-6118 507 E spalding@seattleu.edu
SPALDING, Richard, E 413-597-2483 230 A richard.e.spalding@williams.edu
SPALDING, Wendy 513-244-8492 366 B wendy.spalding@ccuniversity.edu
SPALLA, Tara 614-234-5950 373 B tspalla@mccn.edu
SPALTER, Mendel 323-937-3763 75 G mspalter@yoec.edu
SPALTER, Sholom 973-267-9404 294 F shspalter1@aol.com
SPANBAUER, John, K 716-286-8055 324 E jks@niagara.edu
SPANBAUER, Julie 312-427-2737 143 G 7spanbau@jmls.edu
SPANBAUER, Sharon 517-264-7190 241 A sspanbau@sienaheights.edu
SPANCAKE, Richard 229-391-4890 115 I rspancake@abac.edu
SPANG, David 856-222-9311 295 C ecasa@rcbc.edu
SPANG, Kimberly 610-330-5021 407 C spangk@lafayette.edu
SPANG, Zane 406-477-6215 276 C zspang@cdkc.edu
SPANGENBERG, Eric 949-824-8470 69 C ers@uci.edu
SPANGENBERG, Laurie 906-786-5802 231 O laurie.spangenberg@baycollege.edu
SPANGLER, Anthony 313-664-7462 232 G aspangler@collegeforcreativestudies.edu
SPANGLER, John, R 717-334-6286 409 C jspangler@ltsg.edu
SPANGLER, Michael 702-651-4959 284 H michael.spangler@csn.edu
SPANGLER, Stephanie 203-432-4446 90 D stephanie.spangler@yale.edu
SPANIOL, Lee 217-234-5263 145 D lspaniol@lakeland.cc.il.us
SPANJER, Pat 509-359-4557 503 D pspanjer@ewu.edu
SPANKROY, Mimi 661-362-3418 40 A mimi.spankroy@canyons.edu
SPANN, B. Steven 615-327-3927 440 H spann@guptoncollege.edu
SPANN, Chante 312-427-2737 143 G cspann@jmls.edu
SPANN, Sammy 419-530-5268 380 D sammy.spann@utoledo.edu
SPANN-PACK, Robin 601-979-2015 258 D robin.m.spann-pack@jsums.edu
SPANO, David, B 704-687-0311 358 A dspano@uncc.edu
SPAR, Debora, L 212-854-2021 304 I dspar@barnard.edu
SPARACINO, Debra 864-656-2171 428 C registrar@clemson.edu
SPARGEN, Dan 402-399-2600 279 E dspargen@csm.edu
SPARKES, Mike 281-425-6327 460 I msparkes@lee.edu
SPARKMAN, Calvin 951-343-4356 29 H csparkman@calbaptist.edu
SPARKMAN, Margo 606-368-6039 186 B margosparkman@alc.edu
SPARKMAN, Susan 205-652-3587 9 F sgt@uwa.edu
SPARKS, Brad 618-235-2700 155 C bradley.sparks@swic.edu
SPARKS, Carolyn, B 864-597-4160 435 C sparkscb@wofford.edu
SPARKS, Cheryl, T 432-264-5030 459 D csparks@howardcollege.edu
SPARKS, Doug 602-285-7254 14 F douglas.sparks@phoenixcollege.edu
SPARKS, George, E 540-568-7073 490 J sparksge@jmu.edu
SPARKS, Jane 760-757-2121 52 K jsparks@miracosta.edu
SPARKS, John 618-634-3230 154 B johns@shawneecc.edu
SPARKS, Karl 619-482-6328 66 E ksparks@swcc.edu
SPARKS, Kenton 610-341-5929 403 B ksparks@eastern.edu
SPARKS, Kim 606-759-7141 190 C kim.sparks@kctcs.edu
SPARKS, Larry, D 662-915-7200 261 B lsparks@olemiss.edu
SPARKS, Maria 518-464-8768 314 A msparks@excelsior.edu
SPARKS, Mark 410-455-2872 211 G sparks@umbc.edu
SPARKS, Michele 859-233-8236 193 D msparks@transy.edu
SPARKS, Rick 540-231-7951 499 F rasparks@vt.edu
SPARKS, Rick 509-793-2206 501 H ricks@bigbend.edu
SPARKS, Sonny 662-472-9015 258 B ssparks@holmescc.edu
SPARKS, Steve 252-222-6087 348 B sparkss@carteret.edu
SPARKS, Terrell 801-878-1494 285 E tsparks@roseman.edu
SPARKS, William, O 505-272-5849 302 F wsparks@salud.unm.edu
SPARLING, Steve 231-843-5824 243 G ssparling@westshor.edu
SPARR, Cynthia 630-466-7900 157 K csparr@waubonsee.edu
SPARROW, Anita 860-512-3223 86 E asparrow@manchestercc.edu
SPARROW, Rebecca, M 607-255-2723 312 A rms18@cornell.edu
SPARROW, Stephen 907-474-7083 10 G sdsparrow@alaska.edu
SPARROW, Suzanne 610-409-3600 422 D ssparrow@ursinus.edu
SPATAFORE, Marisa 408-864-8672 44 A spataforemarisa@deanza.edu
SPATARO, Keith 650-543-3853 52 D kspataro@menlo.edu
SPATARO-WILSON, Jennifer, A 540-665-5412 494 B jspataro@su.edu
SPATES, Gerald 336-334-7800 356 F gspates@ncat.edu
SPATZ, Dan 541-506-6110 390 I dspatz@cgcc.edu
SPAULDING, Angela 806-651-2730 469 D aspaulding@mail.wtamu.edu
SPAULDING, II, Henry, W 740-392-6868 373 D hspauldi@mvnu.edu
SPAULDING, Jeb 802-224-3000 485 G jeb.spaulding@vsc.edu
SPAULDING, Raymond 850-412-5843 110 J raymond.spaulding@famu.edu
SPAVENTA, Marilynn 805-965-0581 63 D spaventa@sbcc.edu
SPAYER, Roger 847-925-6360 141 A rspayer@harpercollege.edu
SPAZIANI, Gina 978-656-3145 224 A spazianig@middlesex.mass.edu
SPAZIANI, Rhonda 860-215-9293 87 D rspaziani@trcc.commnet.edu
SPEAKER, Cindy 315-364-3311 340 B cspeaker@wells.edu
SPEAKMAN, Thomas, W 989-774-1840 232 D speak1tw@cmich.edu
SPEAKS, Michael, A 315-443-0790 337 A maspeaks@syr.edu
SPEAKS, Tiffany 202-885-3651 91 J tspeaks@american.edu
SPEAR, Catherine 434-924-3200 495 H uvaeop@virginia.edu
SPEAR, Pamela 603-526-3621 285 L pspear@colby-sawyer.edu
SPEAR, Robert 208-885-0243 134 G rspear@uidaho.edu
SPEAREN, Charlene 803-376-5780 427 A cspearen@allenuniversity.edu
SPEARING, Mike 205-348-5490 8 D mspearing@uasystem.ua.edu
SPEARMAN, Howard 815-921-4109 152 E h.spearman@rockvalleycollege.edu
SPEARMAN, Leonard, H 713-313-1198 470 D lespearman@tmslaw.tsu.edu
SPEARMAN, Marilyn 229-430-1877 115 K marilyn.spearman@asurams.edu
SPEARS, Barbara Anne 256-215-4311 2 G bspears@cacc.edu
SPEARS, Eric 478-445-0874 121 A eric.spears@gcsu.edu
SPEARS, Gary Lee 662-562-3227 260 C glspears@northwestms.edu
SPEARS, James, W 304-462-6024 513 C james.spears@glenville.edu
SPEARS, Lanny 859-858-2298 186 I
SPEARS, Linda, C 615-963-5281 445 A lspears@tnstate.edu
SPEARS, Marty 501-279-4335 20 D mspears@harding.edu
SPEARS, Ron 806-894-9611 465 G rspears@southplainscollege.edu
SPEARS, Ronald 806-716-2341 465 G rspears@southplainscollege.edu
SPEARS, Sylvia 617-824-8500 218 B sylvia_spears@emerson.edu
SPEARS, Tim 802-443-5391 484 F spears@middlebury.edu
SPEARS-BOYD, Amy 931-540-2764 446 A aspears@columbiastate.edu
SPEAS, Philip, E 606-693-5000 191 A pspeas@kmbc.edu
SPEAS, Richard 218-683-8547 251 C richard.speas@northlandcollege.edu
SPECHLER, Julie 954-262-5348 105 J julies@nova.edu
SPECHT, Mark, A 610-566-1776 423 H mspecht@williamson.edu
SPECHT, Matthew, F 773-442-4600 149 J m-specht@neiu.edu
SPECHT, Nancy 585-275-5572 338 K nancy.specht@rochester.edu
SPECK, Anne 484-664-3165 411 D aspeck@muhlenberg.edu
SPECK, Christie 707-864-7000 65 A christie.speck@solano.edu
SPECTAR, Jem, M 814-269-2090 421 G spectar@pitt.edu
SPECTER, Robert, M 202-319-5606 92 A specter@cua.edu
SPECTOR, Carol 617-824-8586 218 B carol_spector@emerson.edu
SPECTOR, Harvey 212-678-3042 337 E spector@tc.edu
SPECTOR, Phillip 410-516-8068 208 D pspector@jhu.edu
SPEECH, Angela 903-593-8311 470 A amarshall@texascollege.edu
SPEED, Bonnie 404-727-6289 120 E baspeed@emory.edu
SPEED, Coleen 318-274-3338 200 F speedc@gram.edu
SPEED, Cynthia 800-782-2422 31 E cspeed@mail.cnuas.edu
SPEEDIE, Marilyn, K 612-624-1900 255 H speed001@umn.edu
SPEEDY, Nigel 661-824-2977 53 K nspeedy@ntps.edu
SPEEGLE, Charlotte 325-794-4411 454 E charlotte.speegle@cisco.edu
SPEEGLE, Diana 817-554-5950 461 G finaid@messengercollege.edu
SPEER, Brian 717-262-2607 424 A brian.speer@wilson.edu
SPEER, Brian 704-406-4269 344 E bspeer@gardner-webb.edu
SPEER, Jennifer 615-550-3170 449 I jennifer@earthlink.net
SPEHAR, John 708-596-2000 154 E jspehar@ssc.edu
SPEHN, Steven 507-222-4271 245 C sspehn@carleton.edu
SPEIDEL, Daniel 603-897-8576 287 F dspeidel@rivier.edu
SPEIDEL, III, William 724-357-5661 415 B william.speidel@iup.edu
SPEIGHT, LaCandance 828-398-7147 347 D lacandancespeight@abtech.edu
SPEIGHT, Ronald 803-535-5225 428 B rspeight@claflin.edu
SPEIGHT, Virginia 419-530-7262 380 D virginia.speight@utoledo.edu
SPEIR, Mary 540-828-5706 487 H mspeir@bridgewater.edu
SPEISER, Lynn 419-267-1312 374 A lspeiser@northweststate.edu
SPEISSER, Nancy 757-493-6946 127 D nspeisser@southuniversity.edu
SPELL, Donald, R 252-493-7211 352 A dspell@email.pittcc.edu
SPELL, Paul 601-477-4223 258 E paul.spell@jcjc.edu
SPELLINGS, Margaret 919-962-4622 356 A president@northcarolina.edu
SPELLMAN, Carlton 910-521-6326 358 C carlton.spellman@uncp.edu
SPELLMAN, Joseph 203-932-7134 90 A jspellman@newhaven.edu
SPELLMAN, Peter 617-266-1400 215 G
SPELLS, Bomani 334-727-8421 8 A bspells@mytu.tuskegee.edu
SPELLS, Doretha, J 757-727-5213 490 E doretha.spells@hamptonu.edu

SPELLS, Kaschia .... 252-246-1214.. 354 D
kspells@wilsoncc.edu
SPELMAN, Amy .... 309-298-1914.. 158 A
ae-spelman@wiu.edu
SPENCE, Bob, C .... 254-710-3731.. 452 H
bob_spence@baylor.edu
SPENCE, Charles .... 434-592-3503.. 491 D
cpspence@liberty.edu
SPENCE, Jeffery .... 215-572-2088.. 397 G
spencej@arcadia.edu
SPENCE, Jon, N .... 913-971-3279.. 183 D
jnspence@mnu.edu
SPENCE, Lisa .... 812-237-8439.. 162 A
lisa.spence@indstate.edu
SPENCE, Mary .... 716-829-7736.. 313 A
spencem@dyc.edu
SPENCE, Stan .... 817-461-8741.. 451 G
sspence@arlingtonbaptistcollege.edu
SPENCE, Thomas .... 615-460-6417.. 438 J
thom.spence@belmont.edu
SPENCE, Weymouth .... 301-891-4128.. 213 D
wspence@wau.edu
SPENCER, A. Clayton .... 207-786-6100.. 202 D
cspencer@bates.edu
SPENCER, Andrea, M .... 914-773-3870.. 325 J
aspencer@pace.edu
SPENCER, Andrew .... 405-585-4102.. 385 B
andrew.spencer@okbu.edu
SPENCER, Andrew, J .... 919-761-2234.. 355 I
aspencer@sebts.edu
SPENCER, Barbara .... 269-749-7642.. 240 A
bspencer@olivetcollege.edu
SPENCER, Brent .... 970-351-2396.... 84 C
brent.spencer@unco.edu
SPENCER, Carol .... 508-999-8705.. 220 H
cspencer@umassd.edu
SPENCER, Catherine .... 212-636-6522.. 314 G
caspencer@fordham.edu
SPENCER, Christine .... 410-837-6134.. 213 C
cspencer@ubalt.edu
SPENCER, Christine .... 312-341-3801.. 152 H
cspencer02@roosevelt.edu
SPENCER, Dan .... 254-298-8619.. 467 B
dan.spencer@templejc.edu
SPENCER, Deborah .... 860-231-5390.... 90 B
dspencer@usj.edu
SPENCER, DeLinda .... 254-267-7037.. 463 K
dspencer@rangercollege.edu
SPENCER, Delmy .... 530-741-6705.... 76 D
dspencer@yccd.edu
SPENCER, Dionyale .... 662-252-8000.. 260 F
dspencer@rustcollege.edu
SPENCER, Estelle, H .... 413-205-3461.. 214 B
estelle.spencer@aic.edu
SPENCER, Eugene .... 610-409-3789.. 422 D
gspencer@ursinus.edu
SPENCER, James, G .... 312-329-4070.. 148 F
james.spencer@moody.edu
SPENCER, Janett .... 256-306-2628...... 2 F
janet.spencer@calhoun.edu
SPENCER, Jay .... 434-592-3540.. 491 D
bjspencer@liberty.edu
SPENCER, Jed .... 801-626-6586.. 482 D
jedspencer@weber.edu
SPENCER, Jeremy .... 508-626-4500.. 221 E
jspencer1@framingham.edu
SPENCER, Joel .... 303-329-6355.... 78 O
finaid@cstcm.edu
SPENCER, SJ, John .... 617-735-9780.. 218 C
spencerj@emmanuel.edu
SPENCER, John, D .... 817-515-5079.. 467 A
john.spencer@tccd.edu
SPENCER, Judith .... 662-325-3713.. 259 D
jspencer@hrm.msstate.edu
SPENCER, Juliana .... 409-880-2292.. 470 H
jaspencer@lit.edu
SPENCER, Julie .... 424-207-3763.... 55 E
jspencer@otis.edu
SPENCER, Katrina .... 860-486-0930.... 89 D
katrina.spencer@uconn.edu
SPENCER, Keith, J .... 417-667-8181.. 264 A
kspencer@cottey.edu
SPENCER, Kenneth .... 513-875-3344.. 365 K
kenneth.spencer@chatfield.edu
SPENCER, Krystal, F .... 812-888-4587.. 169 A
kspencer@vinu.edu
SPENCER, Lisa .... 575-769-4115.. 299 G
lisa.spencer@clovis.edu
SPENCER, Lori .... 901-761-9494.. 439 F
lspencer@concorde.edu
SPENCER, Mark .... 812-488-2238.. 167 I
ms628@evansville.edu
SPENCER, Mary .... 414-277-4517.. 518 E
spencer@msoe.edu
SPENCER, Pamela .... 513-875-3344.. 365 K
pam.spencer@chatfield.edu
SPENCER, Richard .... 618-235-2700.. 155 C
richard.spencer@swic.edu
SPENCER, Rick, E .... 630-637-5209.. 149 H
respencer@noctrl.edu
SPENCER, Ruth .... 845-437-6820.. 339 C
ruspencer@vassar.edu
SPENCER, Sandra, L .... 217-353-2637.. 151 B
sspencer@parkland.edu
SPENCER, Scott, J .... 610-660-1018.. 418 G
sspencer@sju.edu
SPENCER, Shanan .... 304-876-5053.. 513 E
sspencer@shepherd.edu
SPENCER, Shannon .... 419-772-2036.. 374 J
s-spencer@onu.edu
SPENCER, Yvette .... 205-226-7720...... 2 C
yspencer@bsc.edu
SPENGLER, Gregory, C ...... 410-706-1264.. 211 F
gspengler@umaryland.edu
SPENNER, Anne .... 816-235-1576.. 273 F
spennerae@umkc.edu
SPERANZA, Dena, L .... 740-587-6526.. 368 B
speranzad@denison.edu
SPERGER, Herb .... 610-785-6525.. 418 E
hsperger@scs.edu
SPERLING, Chad .... 218-793-2436.. 251 C
chad.sperling@northlandcollege.edu
SPERLING, Michael .... 845-905-4616.. 312 C
m_sperli@culinary.edu
SPERLING, Susan S .... 510-723-6641.... 37 B
ssperling@chabotcollege.edu
SPEROS, Michael .... 916-278-5772.... 34 B
msperos@csus.edu
SPERRAZZA, Alex .... 570-408-4465.. 423 G
alexander.sperrazza@wilkes.edu
SPERRING, Tiffany .... 614-222-6183.. 367 B
tsperring@ccad.edu
SPERRY, Sarah .... 412-396-5894.. 403 A
sperrys@duq.edu
SPETKA, Rosemary, V .... 315-792-5495.. 321 G
rspetka@mvcc.edu
SPEWOCK, Kelly .... 412-291-6244.. 397 I
kspewock@aii.edu
SPEYER, Seth .... 202-885-3411.... 91 J
speyer@american.edu
SPEZIA, Robert .... 313-883-8576.. 240 D
spezia.robert@shms.edu
SPEZIALE, Michael .... 570-408-4679.. 423 G
michael.speziale@wilkes.edu
SPEZIANI, Humberto, M ..... 305-284-5450.. 114 H
hmspez@miami.edu
SPEZIO, Kim, E .... 423-746-5205.. 447 E
kespezio@twcnet.edu
SPEZZACATENA, Maricel .... 305-273-4499.... 97 M
maricel@cbt.edu
SPICER, Christopher .... 360-650-6144.. 509 E
kit.spicer@wwu.edu
SPICER, Donald, Z .... 301-445-2729.. 211 D
dspicer@usmd.edu
SPICER, Erin .... 850-484-1706.. 106 H
espicer@pensacolastate.edu
SPICER, Jacqueline .... 810-766-4273.. 231 C
jacqueline.spicer@baker.edu
SPICER, Michael .... 909-621-8142.... 58 A
michael.spicer@pomona.edu
SPICER, Udella .... 229-217-4159.. 127 G
uspicer@southernregional.edu
SPIECKER, Karl .... 719-549-2320.... 79 B
karl.spiecker@csupueblo.edu
SPIEGEL, Allen, M .... 212-430-2801.. 341 G
spiegel@aecom.yu.edu
SPIEGEL, Allen, M .... 212-960-3179.. 341 G
aspiegel@aecom.yu.edu
SPIEGEL, Benjamin .... 732-367-1060.. 289 G
SPIEGEL, Mary, K .... 205-348-8666...... 8 D
mary.spiegel@ua.edu
SPIEGEL, Sara .... 312-777-8616.. 142 G
sspiegel@aii.edu
SPIEGELMAN, Kathy .... 617-373-2226.. 227 B
SPIELBAUER, Brian .... 660-248-6390.. 263 B
bspielba@centralmethodist.edu
SPIERS, William .... 850-201-8399.. 113 E
spiersw@tcc.fl.edu
SPIES, Brent .... 314-889-4564.. 265 C
bspies@fontbonne.edu
SPIES, Carolyn, I .... 973-748-9000.. 289 H
carolyn_spies@bloomfield.edu
SPIES, Dennis .... 847-566-6401.. 157 G
dspies@usml.edu
SPIES, Don .... 281-459-7629.. 465 A
don.spies@sjcd.edu
SPIESMAN, John .... 440-375-7426.. 371 E
jspiesman@lec.edu
SPIGELMYER, Kathleen ...... 215-248-7025.. 400 H
spigelmyerk@chc.edu
SPIKEREIT, Damien .... 417-626-1234.. 269 K
spikereit.damien@occ.edu
SPILDE, Mary .... 541-463-5200.. 391 G
spildem@lanecc.edu
SPILKER, Christopher .... 313-883-8651.. 240 D
spilker.christopher@shms.edu
SPILLER, Elizabeth .... 540-231-6779.. 499 F
espiller@vt.edu
SPILLER, James .... 585-395-2525.. 332 E
jspiller@brockport.edu
SPILLER, Judith .... 603-862-2165.. 288 C
judy.spiller@unh.edu
SPILLER, Marwin .... 309-694-5361.. 141 F
marwin.spiller@icc.edu
SPILLERS, James .... 619-482-6551.... 66 E
jspillers@swccd.edu
SPILLING, Christopher ...... 314-516-5373.. 274 A
spillingc@umsl.edu
SPILLMAN, Tom .... 951-487-3945.... 53 D
tspillma@msjc.edu
SPILLUM, Carol .... 605-274-4090.. 435 E
carol.spillum@augie.edu
SPILOVOY, Tanya .... 701-224-2498.. 360 E
tanya.spilovoy@ndus.edu
SPINA, Anthony .... 716-829-7648.. 313 A
spinaaw@dyc.edu
SPINA, Eric, F .... 937-229-4122.. 379 D
president19@udayton.edu
SPINA, Matthew, R .... 609-497-7805.. 294 C
admissions@ptsem.edu
SPINA, Robert .... 409-880-8661.. 471 A
bob.spina@lamar.edu
SPINARD, John .... 617-873-0689.. 217 A
john.spinard@cambridgecollege.edu
SPINATO, Donna .... 903-886-5860.. 468 D
donna.spinato@tamuc.edu
SPINAZZA, Terri .... 208-426-2168.. 132 I
tspinazz@boisestate.edu
SPINDLE, Blair .... 405-491-6608.. 388 A
bspindle@snu.edu
SPINDLE, William .... 907-786-4622.... 10 F
whspindle@uaa.alaska.edu
SPINELLI, JR., Stephen ...... 215-951-2727.. 416 G
spinellis@philau.edu
SPINELLI-SEXTER, Eva .... 212-463-0400.. 337 I
espinelli@touro.edu
SPINILLO, Anthony .... 570-340-6057.. 409 H
spinillo@marywood.edu
SPINK, Nancy .... 907-450-8153.... 10 E
nkspink@alaska.edu
SPINK-FORMANSKI,
Christina .... 716-829-7775.. 313 A
SPINKS, Robert .... 337-475-5711.. 200 H
rspinks@mcneese.edu
SPINNATI, Jeannie .... 937-769-1324.. 363 E
jspinnati@antioch.edu
SPINNATO, Amy, R .... 443-412-2258.. 208 A
aspinnato@harford.edu
SPINNATO, Meredith .... 617-585-0200.. 216 A
meredith.spinnato@the-bac.edu
SPINNER, Arnold .... 212-463-0400.. 337 I
arnold.spinner@touro.edu
SPINNER, Bonita .... 405-682-1611.. 385 D
bonita.d.spinner@occc.edu
SPINO, Catherine, D .... 330-494-6170.. 377 J
cspino@starkstate.edu
SPINOSA, Tony .... 202-685-3946.. 528 B
spinosat@ndu.edu
SPINOSA DE VEGA,
Leah .... 612-330-1650.. 244 I
devega@augsburg.edu
SPIOTTI, Louis .... 585-475-2615.. 327 E
lxs4798@rit.edu
SPIRES, Chris .... 803-641-3463.. 433 G
chriss@usca.edu
SPIRES, Stuart .... 706-886-6831.. 128 C
sspires@tfc.edu
SPIRES, Tracy, M .... 864-379-8773.. 429 I
tspires@erskine.edu
SPIRO, Jonathan .... 802-468-1244.. 485 H
jonathan.spiro@castleton.edu
SPIROU, Costas .... 478-445-4715.. 121 A
costas.spirou@gcsu.edu
SPIRRISON, Hannah .... 937-319-0128.. 363 D
hspirrison@antiochcollege.org
SPISAK, Art, L .... 319-335-1681.. 169 H
art-spisak@uiowa.edu
SPISAK-CAMERON,
Jennifer .... 919-681-0417.. 343 J
jennifer.cameron@dev.duke.edu
SPISSO, Johnese Maria ...... 310-267-9315.... 69 D
jspisso@mednet.ucla.edu
SPITTAL, David, J .... 913-971-3392.. 183 D
president@mnu.edu
SPITTAL, Ryan .... 815-939-5452.. 150 I
rspittal@olivet.edu
SPITZ, Catherine .... 309-556-3120.. 143 D
cspitz@iwu.edu
SPITZ, Cody .... 575-562-2178.. 299 I
cody.spitz@enmu.edu
SPITZ, Laura, M .... 607-255-0157.. 312 A
lauraspitz@cornell.edu
SPITZER, Bruce .... 217-228-5432.. 151 F
spitzbr@quincy.edu
SPITZER, Linda .... 301-295-3357.. 528 G
linda.spitzer@usuhs.edu
SPIVAK, Michael .... 641-472-7000.. 175 A
mspivak@mum.edu
SPIVAK, Victoria .... 708-524-6950.. 139 F
vlamick@dom.edu
SPIVEY, Randy .... 615-966-2503.. 441 F
randy.spivey@lipscomb.edu
SPIVEY, Sheila, D .... 904-620-2528.. 112 B
sspivey@unf.edu
SPIVEY, Sheryl .... 404-215-2638.. 124 I
sheryl.spivey@morehouse.edu
SPIWAK, Doug .... 847-925-6969.. 141 A
dspiwak@harpercollege.edu
SPIZZIRRI, Erica .... 609-984-1588.. 297 F
espizzirri@tesu.edu
SPOERRI, Tamara, D .... 207-725-3837.. 202 F
tspoerri@bowdoin.edu
SPOFFORD, Kathy .... 657-278-2800.... 33 A
kspofford@fullerton.edu
SPOHN, Andrew .... 517-787-0800.. 235 G
spohnandrewb@jccmi.edu
SPOHR, Jean .... 513-562-8752.. 363 H
jspohr@artacademy.edu
SPOHR, Robert .... 989-328-1241.. 238 D
robs@montcalm.edu
SPOLTORE, Janet, D .... 860-439-2692.... 87 F
janet.spoltore@conncoll.edu
SPOMER, Michelle .... 412-924-1350.. 417 E
mspomer@pts.edu
SPONG, Mark, W .... 972-883-2974.. 476 C
mspong@utdallas.edu
SPONG, Melinda .... 859-572-1464.. 192 B
spongm1@nku.edu
SPONHOLZ, Karin .... 650-508-3714.... 54 J
ksponholz@ndnu.edu
SPONSELLER, Jared .... 740-392-6868.. 373 D
jared.sponseller@mvnu.edu
SPONSELLER, Kimberly .... 740-283-6855.. 368 L
ksponseller@franciscan.edu
SPOON, Adrea .... 419-372-7857.. 364 E
adrea@bgsu.edu
SPOONER, David .... 518-276-6890.. 327 B
spoond@rpi.edu
SPOONER, James .... 229-243-6859.. 117 E
james.spooner@bainbridge.edu
SPOONER, Joseph, C .... 540-365-4202.. 489 M
president@ferrum.edu
SPOOR, Suzanne, J .... 410-777-2448.. 206 B
sjspoor@aacc.edu
SPOR, Arvid .... 626-914-8881.... 38 D
aspor@citruscollege.edu
SPOR, Mary, W .... 502-597-6684.. 191 B
mary.spor@kysu.edu
SPORBERT, Derek .... 701-777-3809.. 360 C
derek.sporbert@und.edu
SPORE, MaryBeth .... 724-537-4567.. 419 A
marybeth.spore@email.stvincent.edu
SPORE, Robert, B .... 540-464-7322.. 499 E
sporerb@vmi.edu
SPORES, Jon .... 360-383-3440.. 509 F
jspores@whatcom.ctc.edu
SPOSILI, Michael .... 518-580-5610.. 330 F
msposili@skidmore.edu
SPOTO, Mary .... 352-588-8294.. 108 C
mary.spoto@saintleo.edu
SPOTSWOOD, James .... 620-341-5403.. 180 G
jspotswo@emporia.edu
SPOTTS, Cyndi .... 248-204-4109.. 237 B
cspotts@ltu.edu
SPOTTS, Deborah .... 602-285-7800.... 14 F
deborah.spotts@phoenixcollege.edu
SPRADLEY, Brandon .... 251-626-3303...... 8 B
bspradley@ussa.edu
SPRADLEY, Minou .... 619-388-3520.... 60 F
mdspradl@sdccd.edu
SPRADLEY, Wanda .... 434-381-6156.. 494 M
wspradley@sbc.edu
SPRADLIN, Chris .... 937-778-7887.. 368 E
cspradlin@edisonohio.edu
SPRADLIN, Michael, R .... 901-751-8453.. 442 E
mspradlin@mabts.edu
SPRADLING, Carol .... 304-357-4747.. 511 E
carolspradling@ucwv.edu
SPRADLING, John .... 903-785-7661.. 463 E
jspradling@parisjc.edu
SPRADLING, Steve .... 330-494-6170.. 377 J
sspradling@starkstate.edu
SPRAGINS, Robyn .... 610-436-2509.. 416 C
rspragins@wcupa.edu
SPRAGUE, Alice .... 503-399-2537.. 390 E
alice.sprague@chemeketa.edu
SPRAGUE, Carol .... 413-545-0698.. 220 F
sprague@research.umass.edu
SPRAGUE, Jamie .... 850-474-2156.. 113 A
jsprague@uwf.edu
SPRAGUE, Jennifer .... 505-984-6041.. 301 I
jsprague@sjc.edu
SPRAGUE, Kendra .... 360-442-2131.. 504 G
ksprague@lowercolumbia.edu
SPRAGUE, Kendra .... 360-442-2121.. 504 G
ksprague@lowercolumbia.edu
SPRAGUE, Lisa .... 614-251-4303.. 374 I
spraguel@ohiodominican.edu
SPRAGUE, Rhonda .... 715-346-4920.. 521 C
rhonda.sprague@uwsp.edu

SPRAGUE, Robert .... 310-287-4325.... 50 E
spragurl@wlac.edu
SPRAGUE, Viola .... 810-762-9668.. 236 C
vsprague@kettering.edu
SPRAKER, Matt .... 615-248-1245.. 447 F
mspraker@trevecca.edu
SPRANGEL, JR.,
Joseph, R .... 540-887-7067.. 491 G
jsprangel@mbc.edu
SPRATLIN, Steve .... 256-395-2211...... 7 C
sspratlin@suscc.edu
SPRATT, Bruce, R .... 404-413-3071.. 122 D
bspratt@gsu.edu
SPRATT, Sharon .... 270-706-8478.. 189 C
sharon.spratt@kctcs.edu
SPRAW, Deanna .... 419-434-4589.. 379 E
spraw@findlay.edu
SPRAW, William .... 419-434-4601.. 379 E
wspraw@findlay.edu
SPRECHER, Art .... 209-946-2011.... 71 C
asprecher@pacific.edu
SPRECHER, Becky .... 503-493-6454.. 391 A
bsprecher@cu-portland.edu
SPREER-ALBERT, Frances 518-262-5585.. 303 E
albertf@mail.amc.edu
SPREHE, Tara .... 503-594-3271.. 390 F
taras@clackamas.edu
SPREITZER, Mary, L .... 815-740-5038.. 157 F
mspreitzer@stfrancis.edu
SPRENGER, Cathy, J .... 717-477-1381.. 416 A
cjspre@ship.edu
SPRICK, David, W .... 715-836-2222.. 520 A
sprickdw@uwec.edu
SPRIGGS, Barry, A .... 315-684-6054.. 336 B
spriggbl@morrisville.edu
SPRIGGS, Barry, L .... 610-799-1634.. 408 G
bspriggs@lccc.edu
SPRIGGS, Janet .... 704-219-7165.. 352 G
janet.spriggs@rccc.edu
SPRING, Debra .... 601-304-4302.. 256 F
dspring@alcorn.edu
SPRING, SCC, Joseph ..... 973-957-0188.. 288 G
president@acs350.org
SPRINGALL, Robert, G .... 570-577-1446.. 398 L
r.springall@bucknell.edu
SPRINGER, Brianna .... 949-214-3046.... 41 F
brianna.springer@cui.edu
SPRINGER, Colleen .... 641-844-5523.. 173 J
colleen.springer@iavalley.edu
SPRINGER, Colleen .... 641-844-7106.. 173 L
colleen.springer@iavalley.edu
SPRINGER, Gabe .... 618-468-3700.. 145 G
gspringer@lc.edu
SPRINGER, John .... 877-701-3800.. 135 A
SPRINGER, Karen .... 215-612-6600.. 398 G
kspringer@chicareers.com
SPRINGER, Mark .... 320-308-3093.. 252 A
mspringer@stcloudstate.edu
SPRINGER, Molly .... 916-558-2194.... 51 D
springm@scc.losrios.edu
SPRINGER, Patrick .... 951-487-3590.... 53 D
pspringer@msjc.edu
SPRINGER, Robert, I .... 336-278-6644.. 344 D
springer@elon.edu
SPRINGER, Tracy .... 765-455-9356.. 163 A
tracylb@iuk.edu
SPRINGER-BALDWIN,
Nancy .... 512-472-4133.. 465 F
nancy.springer-baldwin@ssw.edu
SPRINGS, Andre .... 704-216-6012.. 346 A
asprings@livingstone.edu
SPRINKLE, Dean .... 276-223-4848.. 499 C
dsprinkle@wcc.vccs.edu
SPRINKLE, Stephen, D .... 619-260-4655.... 72 B
sdsprinkle@sandiego.edu
SPROLE, JoLynn, H .... 817-515-4563.. 467 A
jolynn.sprole@tccd.edu
SPROULS, David .... 212-472-1500.. 324 A
dsprouls@nysid.edu
SPROUSE, Clay .... 706-721-5632.. 117 D
csprouse@augusta.edugru.edu
SPROUSE, Judy .... 434-381-6323.. 494 M
jsprouse@sbc.edu
SPROUSE, Keith .... 435-722-6900.. 481 I
keiths@ubatc.edu
SPROUSE, Marlene .... 641-683-5104.. 173 C
marlene.sprouse@indianhills.edu
SPROWL, Don .... 765-677-3061.. 164 B
don.sprowl@indwes.edu
SPROWL, Dorenda .... 803-508-7283.. 426 G
sprowld@atc.edu
SPROWLS, Emily .... 706-886-6831.. 128 C
esprowls@tfc.edu
SPROWS, Sandra .... 631-451-4252.. 336 E
sprowss@sunysuffolk.edu
SPRUIELL, Vicki, P .... 205-652-3627...... 9 F
vspruiell@uwa.edu
SPRUILL, Juliet, A .... 304-457-6317.. 510 B
spruillj@ab.edu
SPRUILL, Wayne .... 615-844-5078.. 449 H
wspruill@welch.edu

SPRUNGER, Ben .... 620-327-8233.. 181 G
ben.sprunger@hesston.edu
SPRUNGER, Philip, W ..... 570-321-4038.. 409 F
sprunger@lycoming.edu
SPRUNK, Elizabeth .... 419-251-1524.. 372 C
elizabeth.sprunk@mercycollege.edu
SPRY, Maryjean .... 816-322-0110.. 262 N
maryjean.spry@calvary.edu
SPRY, Susan .... 570-740-0407.. 409 E
sspry@luzerne.edu
SPUCHES, Charles, M ..... 315-470-6817.. 334 E
cspuches@esf.edu
SPURGETIS, Greg .... 360-383-3000.. 509 F
SPURGIN, Hugh .... 845-752-3000.. 338 G
h.spurgin@uts.edu
SPURLING, John .... 817-722-1610.. 460 E
john.spurling@tku.edu
SPURLOCK, Chad .... 918-293-4622.. 386 B
chad.spurlock@okstate.edu
SPURLOCK, Jefferson ...... 334-670-3267...... 7 H
spurlock@troy.edu
SPURLOCK, Rhonda .... 918-343-7612.. 387 F
rspurlock@rsu.edu
SPURLOCK-EVANS, Karla 860-297-4234.... 89 B
karla.spurlockevans@trincoll.edu
SPYBEY, Joseph .... 614-222-3246.. 367 B
jspybey@ccad.edu
SQUARE, Chris .... 662-476-5347.. 257 G
csquare@eastms.edu
SQUARE, Marilyn, C .... 713-313-7859.. 470 D
squaremc@tsu.edu
SQUIER, Ragan, A .... 315-470-6681.. 334 E
rasquier@esf.edu
SQUILLA, Brian, N .... 215-503-0418.. 420 E
brian.squilla@jefferson.edu
SQUIRE, Craig .... 630-752-5128.. 158 C
craig.squire@wheaton.edu
SQUIRE, Frances .... 559-934-2134.... 74 C
francessquire@whccd.edu
SQUIRE, Roland .... 435-797-8380.. 482 B
roland.squire@usu.edu
SQUIRE, Wayne .... 435-283-7058.. 482 E
wayne.squire@snow.edu
SQUIRES, Catherine .... 815-753-7406.. 150 A
csquires@niu.edu
SQUIRES, Felicia .... 503-581-8600.. 391 B
fsquires@corban.edu
SQUIRES, Kyle .... 480-965-9235.... 11 H
kyle.squires@asu.edu
SQUIRES, Thomas .... 315-792-5445.. 321 G
tsquires@mvcc.edu
SQUIRES, Toni .... 651-641-8232.. 246 B
squires@csp.edu
SREENIVASAN,
Katepalli, R .... 212-992-7914.. 324 C
katepalli.sreenivasan@nyu.edu
SRIHARI, Hari .... 607-777-2336.. 331 B
srihari@binghamton.edu
SRIHARI, Hari .... 607-777-2871.. 331 B
srihari@binghamton.edu
SRIKANTH, Rajini .... 617-287-5520.. 220 G
rajini.srikanth@umb.edu
SRINIVAS, Shanthi, A ...... 909-869-2412.... 31 J
ssrinivas@cpp.edu
SRINIVASAN, Ganesan .... 707-527-4880.... 63 G
gsrinivasan@santarosa.edu
SRINIVASAN, Ganesan .... 559-675-4800.... 67 D
SRINIVASAN, Niruba .... 650-574-6573.... 62 H
srinivasann@smccd.edu
SRINIVASSAN, Asoka .... 601-977-7737.. 261 A
asrinnivasan@tougaloo.edu
SRITHARAN, Sivaguru, S 937-255-2321.. 527 H
sivaguru.sritharan@afit.edu
SRODA, Rebecca .... 863-784-7021.. 109 G
rebecca.sroda@southflorida.edu
SROF, Brenda .... 574-535-7376.. 161 A
brendajs@goshen.edu
SROKA, Anne, A .... 508-373-1905.. 215 D
anne.sroka@becker.edu
SROKA, Fred .... 415-442-5285.... 45 B
fsroka@ggu.edu
SRONCE, Robin .... 417-873-7438.. 264 H
rsronce@drury.edu
SROUFE, Darren .... 812-357-6501.. 167 B
dsroufe@saintmeinrad.edu
STAAB, Eric, P .... 269-337-7172.. 235 H
eric.staab@kzoo.edu
STAAK, OMI, John, M ..... 716-652-8900.. 306 K
jstaak@cks.edu
STAATS, Ray .... 252-638-7201.. 349 B
staatsr@cravencc.edu
STAATS, Sharon .... 661-362-2220.... 52 A
sstaats@masters.edu
STABB, Daniel .... 610-526-6118.. 405 B
dstabb@harcum.edu
STABEN, Chuck, A .... 208-885-6365.. 134 G
president@uidaho.edu
STABENOW, Max .... 909-687-1455.... 44 H
maxstabenow@gs.edu
STABILE, Donald, R .... 240-895-4388.. 210 E
drstabile@smcm.edu

STABILE, Steve .... 212-229-3500.. 322 E
stabiles@newschool.edu
STACE, Peter, A .... 718-817-3200.. 314 G
stace@fordham.edu
STACEY, Elizabeth .... 314-529-9364.. 267 B
estacey@maryville.edu
STACEY, John .... 910-695-3822.. 353 A
stacyj@sandhills.edu
STACEY, Lynn .... 810-766-4240.. 231 C
lynn.stacey@baker.edu
STACEY, Robert .... 206-221-3491.. 508 E
bstacey@u.washington.edu
STACEY, Simon .... 410-455-2164.. 211 G
spstacey@umbc.edu
STACHACZ, John .... 570-408-4254.. 423 G
john.stachaz@wilkes.edu
STACHOWIAK, Kris .... 610-359-5310.. 401 L
kstachowiak@dccc.edu
STACHOWSKI,
Mary Albertine .... 716-896-0700.. 339 E
smalbertine@villa.edu
STACK, Dana .... 619-388-7579.... 60 H
dstack@sdccd.edu
STACK, John .... 305-348-7266.. 111 A
john.stack@fiu.edu
STACK, OSA, John, P ...... 610-519-4550.. 422 G
john.stack@villanova.edu
STACK, Kim .... 401-874-4777.. 426 D
kstack@uri.edu
STACK, Lisa .... 617-984-1663.. 227 F
lstack@quincycollege.edu
STACK, Patrick .... 314-968-6921.. 275 B
stackpa@webster.edu
STACK, Rachel, C .... 618-650-2345.. 155 A
rstack@siue.edu
STACKHOUSE TAETZSCH,
Cindra .... 630-752-5049.. 158 C
cindra.taetzsch@wheaton.edu
STACKPOLE, Ronnie .... 813-988-5131.. 100 F
businessoffice@floridacollege.edu
STACKPOOLE, Roger, W .. 315-445-4174.. 318 E
stackprw@lemoyne.edu
STACKS, Pamela .... 408-924-2488.... 35 C
pstacks@jupiter.sjsu.edu
STACY, Brenda .... 580-371-2371.. 384 D
bstacy@mscok.edu
STACY, Jeanne .... 225-216-8591.. 195 H
stacyj@mybrcc.edu
STACY, Karin .... 847-214-7957.. 140 A
kstacy@elgin.edu
STACY, Mark, W .... 585-395-5149.. 332 E
mstacy@brockport.edu
STADICK, Anna .... 262-595-2077.. 520 F
stadick@uwp.edu
STADING, Gary .... 903-334-6678.. 469 C
gary.stading@tamut.edu
STADLER, Albert, E .... 417-625-9807.. 268 H
stadler-a@mssu.edu
STADLER, Lindsay .... 909-607-3373.... 38 I
lindsay.stadler@cgu.edu
STADLER, Rose .... 510-567-6174.... 67 E
rstadler@sum.edu
STADLER, Ueli .... 503-777-7758.. 394 I
ustadler@reed.edu
STADTLER, Walter .... 202-685-9082.. 528 B
walter.stadtler@ndu.edu
STAEBLER, Ned .... 313-577-2164.. 243 F
nedstaebler@wayne.edu
STAFFIER, Carol .... 781-239-2703.. 223 F
cstaffier@massbay.edu
STAFFORD, Alan .... 325-670-1486.. 458 J
stafford@hsutx.edu
STAFFORD, Ben .... 409-984-6354.. 471 C
staffordbk@lamarpa.edu
STAFFORD, Ingrid, S .... 847-491-7350.. 150 F
i-stafford@northwestern.edu
STAFFORD, James .... 254-295-4607.. 474 E
jstafford@umhb.edu
STAFFORD, Joanne .... 405-733-7373.. 387 I
joannestafford@rose.edu
STAFFORD, John .... 610-647-4400.. 406 B
jstafford@immaculata.edu
STAFFORD, Kulcey .... 843-921-6953.. 431 H
kcassidy@netc.edu
STAFFORD, Kyle .... 580-745-3079.. 387 M
kstafford@se.edu
STAFFORD, Laura .... 419-372-2079.. 364 E
llstaff@bgsu.edu
STAFFORD, Mary .... 503-251-5707.. 396 C
mstafford@uws.edu
STAFFORD, Matt .... 417-626-1234.. 269 K
stafford.matt@occ.edu
STAFFORD, Matthew, C ... 334-953-5613.. 527 I
matthew.stafford.6@us.af.mil
STAFFORD, Michael .... 281-290-5276.. 461 B
michael.d.stafford@lonestar.edu
STAFFORD, Michael Dale 713-780-9777.. 451 A
STAFFORD, Pam .... 606-759-7141.. 190 C
pam.stafford@kctcs.edu
STAFFORD, Tomas, L ...... 608-263-6105.. 519 J
tstafford@uwsa.edu

STAGE, Alan .... 320-222-5204.. 251 G
alan.stage@ridgewater.edu
STAGER, Helen, H .... 570-941-4330.. 422 B
helen.stager@scranton.edu
STAGER, Karl .... 281-756-3594.. 450 G
kstager@alvincollege.edu
STAGGERS, Leroy .... 803-934-3274.. 431 E
lstaggers@morris.edu
STAGGS, Robert .... 606-218-5357.. 194 C
robertstaggs@upike.edu
STAGNARO, Leta .... 510-659-6220.... 55 B
lstagnaro@ohlone.edu
STAGNER, Annessa .... 719-336-1519.... 81 D
annessa.stagner@lamarcc.edu
STAHL, C.J .... 215-972-2059.. 413 L
cstahl@pafa.edu
STAHL, Jason .... 989-686-9029.. 233 I
jfstahl@delta.edu
STAHL, Laurie Ann .... 716-829-7817.. 313 A
stahll@dyc.edu
STAHL, Stephen, D .... 440-826-2762.. 363 M
sstahl@bw.edu
STAHL, Timothy, W .... 724-925-4073.. 423 D
stahlt@wccc.edu
STAHLE, Noel .... 641-673-1010.. 177 J
stahlen@wmpenn.edu
STAHLEY-CUMMINGS,
Melissa .... 307-268-2349.. 526 D
cummings@caspercollege.edu
STAHURA, Kurt, A .... 716-286-8270.. 324 E
stahura@niagara.edu
STAIGER, Jennifer .... 301-447-5617.. 209 G
staiger@msmary.edu
STAINE, Kristin .... 617-217-9228.. 215 B
kstaine@baystate.edu
STAINES, Gail .... 660-543-4140.. 273 C
staines@ucmo.edu
STAKER, Julie .... 319-399-8500.. 170 G
jstaker@coe.edu
STAKES, Robert .... 915-747-5683.. 476 D
rlstakes@utep.edu
STAKES, Robert, L .... 915-747-5683.. 476 D
rlstakes@utep.edu
STALCUP, Susie .... 615-322-6673.. 449 A
susie.stalcup@vanderbilt.edu
STALDER, Michele .... 907-455-2850.... 10 G
mestalder@alaska.edu
STALEY, Marc .... 419-772-2462.. 374 J
m-staley@onu.edu
STALEY, Michael .... 407-708-2390.. 109 E
staleym@seminolestate.edu
STALEY, Priscilla, A .... 214-860-2038.. 456 E
pstaley@dcccd.edu
STALEY, Sally .... 216-368-4306.. 365 B
sjs29@case.edu
STALKER, Donna .... 630-617-3047.. 140 C
donna.stalker@elmhurst.edu
STALL, Beth .... 214-860-2392.. 456 E
sbstall@dcccd.edu
STALLINGS, Lynn .... 470-578-3550.. 123 J
lstallin@kennesaw.edu
STALLINGS, Samaria .... 617-682-1508.. 218 E
swilson@eds.edu
STALLINGS, Tamya .... 870-512-7822.... 19 C
tamya_stallings@asun.edu
STALLINGS, Undria .... 404-215-7748.. 124 I
undria.stallings@morehouse.edu
STALLKAMP, Melani .... 859-815-7797.. 189 D
melani.stallkamp@kctcs.edu
STALLMAN, Jeanne .... 541-552-6221.. 395 A
stallman@sou.edu
STALLMAN, Scott, R .... 217-287-7081.. 146 E
scott.stallman@llcc.edu
STALLMANN, Diane .... 773-298-3089.. 153 H
stallmann@sxu.edu
STALNAKER, Ron .... 912-478-1294.. 122 B
rstalnaker@georgiasouthern.edu
STALNAKER, Samantha ...... 817-515-1795.. 467 A
samantha.stalnaker@tccd.edu
STALTER, Catherine .... 217-351-2290.. 151 B
cstalter@parkland.edu
STALTER, Clifford .... 828-339-4250.. 353 D
c_stalter@southwesterncc.edu
STALVEY, John .... 907-786-1706.... 10 F
jstalvey@uaa.alaska.edu
STAM, Allan, C .... 434-924-0812.. 495 H
acs8tb@virginia.edu
STAM, Theodore, R .... 207-798-4282.. 202 F
tstam@bowdoin.edu
STAMBAUGH, Barbara .... 740-587-8575.. 368 B
stambaughb@denison.edu
STAMM, Paul .... 563-876-3353.. 171 I
pstamm@dwci.edu
STAMM, Timothy .... 504-671-5482.. 196 D
tstamm@dcc.edu
STAMMEL, Andrew .... 607-436-2830.. 331 F
andrew.stammel@oneonta.edu
STAMOS, Michael .... 949-824-1046.... 69 C
mstamos@uci.edu
STAMP, Diane, L .... 540-568-6495.. 490 J
stampdl@jmu.edu

STASSEN, Martha, L .... 413-545-5146.. 220 F
mstassen@acad.umass.edu
STASSIS, Bassel .... 973-684-6500.. 294 A
bstassis@pccc.edu
STASZAK, Patrick .... 920-693-1265.. 523 E
patrick.staszak@gotoltc.edu
STATEN, James .... 213-740-4611.... 72 D
svpfinance@usc.edu
STATEN, Michael .... 270-384-8106.. 191 E
statenm@lindsey.edu
STATEN, Shannon .... 850-644-3818.. 111 C
sstaten@fsu.edu
STATEN, Shannon, D .... 502-852-6636.. 194 A
sdstat01@louisville.edu
STATES, Hollyce .... 508-588-9100.. 223 G
STATHIS, Peter .... 818-240-1000.... 45 A
pstathis@glendale.edu
STATMORE, Kelly .... 215-646-7300.. 404 G
statmore.k@gmercyu.edu
STATMORE, Michael .... 203-591-5056.... 88 F
mstatmore@post.edu
STATON, Blanche, E .... 617-253-4860.. 225 A
STATON, Cecil, P .... 252-328-6212.. 356 C
chancellor@ecu.edu
STATON, Rae .... 419-358-3449.. 364 D
statonr@bluffton.edu
STATON, Robert, E .... 864-833-8222.. 432 B
bstaton@presby.edu
STATON, Trina, J .... 551-574-1312.. 173 F
staton@iowacentral.edu
STATON, Trish .... 404-627-2681.. 117 G
trish.staton@beulah.edu
STATON, Wendell .... 478-445-6341.. 121 A
wendell.staton@gcsu.edu
STATTON, Christine .... 559-730-3734.... 40 E
christines@cos.edu
STATZELL, Donna, S .... 952-995-1447.. 249 D
dstatzell@hennepintech.edu
STAUBLE, Jane .... 601-366-8880.. 261 H
jstauble@wbs.edu
STAUCHE, Ann .... 815-455-8710.. 147 E
astauche@mchenry.edu
STAUDERMAN, Elizabeth . 585-275-4124.. 338 K
elizabeth.stauderman@rochester.edu
STAUDT, Denise .... 210-829-2761.. 474 D
staudt@uiwtx.edu
STAUDT, Loretta .... 202-319-5744.... 92 A
staudt@cua.edu
STAUDT, Nancy .... 314-935-6420.. 274 N
nstaudt@wustl.edu
STAUFF, Jon .... 732-263-5843.. 292 F
jstauff@monmouth.edu
STAUFFER, Denise .... 314-918-2565.. 265 A
dstauffer@eden.edu
STAUFFER, Donald .... 757-455-3384.. 500 E
dstauffer@vwc.edu
STAUFFER, George, B ...... 848-932-5224.. 296 B
stauffer@masongross.rutgers.edu
STAUFFER, Gregory .... 801-321-7104.. 481 L
gstaufferr@ushe.edu
STAUFFER, Larry .... 208-885-6470.. 134 G
stauffer@uidaho.edu
STAUFFER, Lynn .... 707-664-2172.... 35 D
lynn.stauffer@sonoma.edu
STAUFFER, Patricia .... 978-478-3400.. 227 C
pstauffer@northpoint.edu
STAUFFER, Randy .... 818-767-0888.... 75 D
randy.stauffer@woodbury.edu
STAUFFER, II, Ronald, E . 570-577-3305.. 398 L
ron.stauffer@bucknell.edu
STAUSS, Michelle .... 973-618-3555.. 290 A
mstauss@caldwell.edu
STAUTZ, Shay, D .... 520-621-3108.... 17 I
stautzs@email.arizona.edu
STAVE, Kim .... 503-255-0332.. 392 G
kstave@multnomah.edu
STAVENGA, Mink .... 619-482-6569.... 66 E
mstavenga@swccd.edu
STAVITSKY, Alan .... 775-784-6656.. 285 A
ags@unr.edu
STAVOE, Laura .... 208-562-3449.. 133 F
laurastavoe@cwidaho.cc
STAVRIDIS, James .... 617-627-3050.. 228 H
james.stavridis@tufts.edu
STAYKOVA, Milena .... 540-985-8261.. 491 A
mpstaykova@jcsh.edu
STAYNER, Floyd .... 803-786-3007.. 429 A
fstayner@columbiasc.edu
STEAD, John .... 661-362-2626.... 52 A
jstead@masters.edu
STEADMAN, Charles .... 972-721-5305.. 473 D
cstead@udallas.edu
STEADMAN, Jacqui .... 423-461-8686.. 442 K
jrsteadman@milligan.edu
STEADMAN, John .... 251-460-6140...... 9 E
jsteadman@southalabama.edu
STEADMAN, Mimi, H .... 716-839-8567.. 312 D
msteadma@daemen.edu
STEADMAN, Sheryl .... 801-832-2168.. 483 D
ssteadman@westminstercollege.edu
STEADMAN, II,
William, A .... 914-594-4607.. 323 I
gus_steadman@nymc.edu
STEAGALL, Jeffrey .... 801-626-6063.. 482 D
jeffsteagall@weber.edu
STEANE, Joanne, E .... 307-766-2130.. 527 B
jesteane@uwyo.edu
STEARNS, Gail .... 714-628-7289.... 37 F
stearns@chapman.edu
STEARNS, Jill .... 209-575-6067.... 76 A
stearnsj@mjc.edu
STEARNS, Keith .... 805-546-3228.... 41 L
keith_stearns@cuesta.edu
STEARNS, Marc .... 215-503-0155.. 420 E
marc.stearns@jefferson.edu
STEARNS, Mary, F .... 513-732-5278.. 379 C
mary.stearns@uc.edu
STEARNS, Roger .... 470-578-6206.. 123 J
rstearns@kennesaw.edu
STEARNS, Sandra .... 262-691-5368.. 524 G
sstearns@wctc.edu
STEARNS, Stephanie, L ... 704-406-4236.. 344 E
sstearns@gardner-webb.edu
STEARNS, Susan, M .... 515-263-2955.. 172 H
sstearns@grandview.edu
STEARNS, Thaine .... 707-664-2146.... 35 D
stearnst@sonoma.edu
STEARNS MOORE, Kai ...... 714-808-4829.... 54 F
kstearnsmoore@nocccd.edu
STEARNS-SIMS, Elizabeth 406-447-6903.. 277 B
e.stearnssims@umhelena.edu
STEBBINS, Carla .... 515-271-1497.. 171 H
carla.stebbins@dmu.edu
STEBBINS, Chad .... 417-625-9736.. 268 H
stebbins-c@mssu.edu
STEBBINS, Gerald .... 304-829-7640.. 510 G
gstebbins@bethanywv.edu
STEBBINS, Tim .... 202-462-2101.... 93 B
tstebbins@iwp.edu
STEBBINS, Todd, H .... 608-246-6976.. 523 F
stebbins@madisoncollege.edu
STEBELTON, Jeanette .... 906-786-5802.. 231 O
stebeltj@baycollege.edu
STEC, Paul, T .... 518-783-2314.. 330 E
pstec@siena.edu
STECHSCHULTE,
Sharon, A .... 419-772-2030.. 374 J
s-stechschulte@onu.edu
STECK, Don .... 435-652-7641.. 482 A
steck@dixie.edu
STECKBAUER, Jill .... 715-422-5322.. 523 G
jill.steckbauer@mstc.edu
STECKER, Ann Page .... 603-526-3644.. 285 L
astecker@colby-sawyer.edu
STECKMAN, Rebecca .... 303-385-1070.. 376 A
STECKMANN, Chris .... 217-732-3155.. 146 B
csteckmann@lincolncollege.edu
STEED, Steve .... 254-968-9350.. 467 F
ssteed@tarleton.edu
STEEDLEY, Lorrie .... 863-638-7202.. 115 C
lorrie.steedley@warner.edu
STEEHLER, Jack, K .... 540-375-2540.. 493 H
jsteehler@roanoke.edu
STEEL, Ann, E .... 717-866-5775.. 403 F
asteel@evangelical.edu
STEEL, Diane, M .... 559-323-2100.... 61 E
dsteel@sjcl.edu
STEEL, Jaimie .... 814-472-3904.. 418 F
jsteel@francis.edu
STEEL, Virginia .... 310-825-1201.... 69 D
vsteel@library.ucla.edu
STEELANT, Wim, F .... 330-941-3009.. 382 A
wfsteelant@ysu.edu
STEELE, Cherie .... 253-589-6010.. 502 F
cherie.steele@cptc.edu
STEELE, Christopher .... 410-455-6841.. 211 G
csteele@umbc.edu
STEELE, Clover .... 212-247-3434.. 319 K
csteele@mandl.edu
STEELE, Diane .... 913-758-6102.. 185 F
steeled@stmary.edu
STEELE, Donna .... 731-989-6001.. 440 D
dsteele@fhu.edu
STEELE, E. Springs .... 610-660-1027.. 418 G
esteele@sju.edu
STEELE, Gail, T .... 340-693-1008.. 539 C
gsteele@uvi.edu
STEELE, Jessica .... 207-509-7293.. 204 F
jsteele@unity.edu
STEELE, Joanne .... 914-633-2691.. 317 B
jsteele@iona.edu
STEELE, Jonathan .... 727-791-5987.. 108 D
steele.jonathan@spcollege.edu
STEELE, Karen, B .... 718-631-6604.. 309 E
ksteele@qcc.cuny.edu
STEELE, Kemper .... 434-961-6585.. 498 C
ksteele@pvcc.edu
STEELE, Kevin .... 864-646-1858.. 433 C
ksteele@tctc.edu
STEELE, Kevin, L .... 913-971-3278.. 183 D
klsteele@mnu.edu
STEELE, Laura, L .... 714-879-3901.... 46 F
llsteele@hiu.edu
STEELE, Leslie .... 615-547-1268.. 439 H
lsteele@cumberland.edu
STEELE, Linda, M .... 614-947-6583.. 369 A
linda.steele@franklin.edu
STEELE, Lisa .... 615-966-5210.. 441 F
tenielle.buchanan@lipscomb.edu
STEELE, Michael .... 308-535-3723.. 280 M
steelem@mpcc.edu
STEELE, Misty .... 405-224-3140.. 389 D
msteele@usao.edu
STEELE, Mitzi, B .... 540-375-2249.. 493 H
steele@roanoke.edu
STEELE, Patrick, W .... 701-788-4794.. 360 E
patrick.steele@mayvillestate.edu
STEELE, Rachel .... 501-205-8873.... 19 J
rsteele@cbc.edu
STEELE, Richard .... 404-894-2803.. 121 D
rich.steele@gatech.edu
STEELE, Sarah, G .... 315-684-6038.. 336 B
steelesg@morrisville.edu
STEELE, Scott .... 859-985-3416.. 187 B
steeles@berea.edu
STEELE, Sharon .... 281-425-6389.. 460 I
ssteele@lee.edu
STEELE, Steven .... 970-223-2669.... 80 K
ssteele@ibmc.edu
STEELE, Valerie .... 212-217-4530.. 314 B
valerie_steele@fitnyc.edu
STEELE, Yolanda .... 706-385-1044.. 126 A
yolanda.steele@point.edu
STEELE-FIGUEREDO,
David, M .... 818-767-0888.... 75 D
president@woodbury.edu
STEELE-MARCELL, Lia ...... 501-370-5217.... 21 G
lsteele@philander.edu
STEELE-MIDDLETON,
Amanda .... 937-775-5200.. 381 H
amanda.steele-middleton@wright.edu
STEELEY, Jodie .... 559-489-2226.... 67 C
jodie.steeley@fresnocitycollege.edu
STEELY, Jeff .... 404-413-2000.. 122 D
STEELY, Kelly .... 208-562-2508.. 133 F
kellysteely@cwidaho.cc
STEELY, Wayne .... 860-231-5257.... 90 B
wsteely@usj.edu
STEEN, Carrie .... 417-255-7255.. 269 A
carriesteen@missouristate.edu
STEEN, Clayton .... 518-587-2100.. 335 D
clayton.steen@esc.edu
STEEN, Eric .... 206-934-6427.. 507 A
eric.steen@seattlecolleges.edu
STEEN, Franklin .... 646-565-6000.. 337 I
franklin.steen@touro.edu
STEEN, James .... 281-649-3208.. 458 L
jsteen@hbu.edu
STEEN, Kenneth, L .... 540-654-1159.. 495 C
ksteen@umw.edu
STEENBURGH, Chuck .... 888-980-9151.. 495 A
STEENHOEK, David .... 515-643-6680.. 175 B
dsteenhoek@mercydesmoines.edu
STEENIS, Paul, R .... 309-341-7145.. 145 A
psteenis@knox.edu
STEENSON, Greg .... 651-690-8825.. 254 M
gpsteenson@stkate.edu
STEENWYK, Thomas, L ...... 616-526-6549.. 232 A
steeto@calvin.edu
STEERMAN, Cindy .... 303-457-2757.... 80 C
cindy.steerman@zenith.org
STEEVES, Myron, R .... 714-836-7500.. 156 B
msteeves@tiu.edu
STEFANCO, Carolyn, J ..... 518-454-5120.. 311 B
stefancc@strose.edu
STEFANICK, Susan, A .... 609-896-5065.. 295 B
stefanic@rider.edu
STEFANKO, Lisa .... 412-392-4727.. 417 F
lstefanko@pointpark.edu
STEFANOWICZ, Michael .. 860-253-3102.... 86 A
mstefanowicz@asnuntuck.edu
STEFANOWICZ, Michael .. 802-654-3000.. 484 I
admissions@smcvt.edu
STEFANSKI, Kimberly .... 303-404-5481.... 80 E
kimberly.stefanski@frontrange.edu
STEFANSKY, Chaim .... 718-259-2525.. 305 F
STEFANUCA, Pamela .... 410-225-2506.. 209 B
pstefanuca@mica.edu
STEFFAN, Eileen .... 412-809-5100.. 417 D
steffan.eileen@pti.edu
STEFFEN, Joseph .... 912-358-4057.. 126 F
steffenj@savannahstate.edu
STEFFEN, Lloyd, H .... 610-758-3877.. 408 H
lhs1@lehigh.edu
STEFFEN, Penny .... 262-691-5471.. 524 G
psteffen4@wctc.edu
STEFFEN, Rebecca .... 269-927-8861.. 236 G
steffen@lakemichigancollege.edu
STEFFEN, Susan, S .... 630-617-3172.. 140 C
susanss@elmhurst.edu
STEFFEN, Wayne .... 559-453-2215.... 44 F
wayne.steffen@fresno.edu
STEFFENS, Kate .... 612-338-7224.. 256 D
kate.steffens@waldenu.edu
STEFFENS, Wayne .... 559-453-3677.... 44 F
wayne.steffens@fresno.edu
STEFFES, Gary .... 660-263-4100.. 269 D
garys@macc.edu
STEFFES, Thomas .... 765-983-1366.. 160 G
steffto@earlham.edu
STEGEMAN, Brittany .... 402-399-2422.. 279 E
bsstegemanr@csm.edu
STEGEMAN, Melanie .... 918-540-6188.. 384 F
melanie.stegeman@neo.edu
STEGER, Alicia .... 516-572-9634.. 322 C
alicia.steger@ncc.edu
STEGMAN, Margaret .... 816-604-4155.. 267 K
maggie.stegman@mcckc.edu
STEGMAN, Stephen, J ...... 518-629-7158.. 316 G
s.stegman@hvcc.edu
STEGNER, Joe .... 208-334-2315.. 134 G
jstegner@uidaho.edu
STEHOUWER, Kristin .... 989-837-4224.. 239 D
stehouwer@northwood.edu
STEIB, Summer .... 225-578-4807.. 197 I
summers@lsu.edu
STEIBE-PASALICH,
Susan, C .... 574-631-7336.. 168 B
steibe-pasalich.1@nd.edu
STEIDEL, Michael .... 412-268-2082.. 400 D
ms44@andrew.cmu.edu
STEIDL, Douglas .... 330-672-2917.. 370 I
dsteidl@kent.edu
STEIN, Anthony .... 818-299-5526.... 74 A
astein@westcoastuniversity.edu
STEIN, Beki .... 610-796-8202.. 397 D
beki.stein@alvernia.edu
STEIN, Bob .... 207-780-4200.. 205 E
rstein@maine.edu
STEIN, Carla .... 303-678-3755.... 80 E
carla.stein@frontrange.edu
STEIN, Cliff .... 503-517-1878.. 396 F
cstein@westernseminary.edu
STEIN, Cynthia .... 818-766-8151.... 41 C
cstein@concorde.edu
STEIN, David .... 718-232-7800.. 340 K
dstein@yks.edu
STEIN, Diane .... 818-364-7867.... 49 J
STEIN, Douglas .... 719-598-0200.... 79 D
dstein@coloradotech.edu
STEIN, Jeff .... 336-278-7304.. 344 D
jstein@elon.edu
STEIN, Jennifer .... 415-551-9313.... 29 K
jstein@cca.edu
STEIN, John .... 404-385-8772.. 121 D
john.stein@vpss.gatech.edu
STEIN, Karen P, Z .... 585-785-1298.. 314 D
karen.stein@flcc.edu
STEIN, Kathy .... 432-837-8770.. 471 E
kstein@sulross.edu
STEIN, Linda .... 610-917-1416.. 422 C
llstein@valleyforge.edu
STEIN, Lisa .... 308-432-6263.. 281 H
lstein@csc.edu
STEIN, Maria, K .... 617-373-2430.. 227 B
STEIN, Mark, A .... 507-354-8221.. 247 J
steinma@mlc-wels.edu
STEIN, Melanie .... 860-297-5244.... 89 B
melanie.stein@trincoll.edu
STEIN, N .... 732-364-1220.. 289 B
STEIN, Scott .... 802-447-6349.. 485 B
sstein@svc.edu
STEIN, Sonya .... 907-786-1517.... 10 F
sonya@uaa.alaska.edu
STEIN, Steve .... 408-420-2224.... 70 F
ststein@ucsc.edu
STEIN, Thomas, H .... 724-946-7105.. 423 B
steinth@westminster.edu
STEIN, Wayne .... 321-433-5150.... 98 K
steinw@easternflorida.edu
STEIN-SMITH, Kathy .... 201-692-2653.. 291 J
stein@fdu.edu
STEINACKER, Kathy .... 815-939-5359.. 150 I
ksteinac@olivet.edu
STEINBECK, Robin .... 951-571-6351.... 59 A
robin.steinbeck@mvc.edu
STEINBERG, Aaron .... 718-868-2300.. 304 K
STEINBERG, Bettie, M ..... 516-562-1159.. 313 C
bsteinbe@northwell.edu
STEINBERG, Bryan, E ...... 302-356-6858.... 91 I
bryan.e.steinberg@wilmu.edu
STEINBERG, Don .... 802-258-3357.. 485 A
donald.steinberg@worldlearning.org
STEINBERG, Kurt .... 617-879-7075.. 222 A
ksteinberg@massart.edu
STEINBERG, Leslie .... 213-738-6731.... 66 F
publicaffairs@swlaw.edu
STEINBERG, Scott .... 207-221-4208.. 205 F
ssteinberg@une.edu
STEINBERG, Stacey .... 414-847-3255.. 518 D
staceysteinberg@miad.edu
STEINBOCK, Valerie .... 928-541-7777.... 15 G
vsteinbock@ncu.edu

STEINER, Erika .... 860-723-0251.... 85 E
steinere@ct.edu

STEINER, Fred .... 313-845-9621.. 235 D
fred@hfcc.edu

STEINER, Frederick .... 215-898-3425.. 421 E
fsteiner@design.upenn.edu

STEINER, Frederick, R .... 512-471-1922.. 476 B
fsteiner@austin.utexas.edu

STEINER, Glen, D .... 708-209-3328.. 138 G
glen.steiner@cuchicago.edu

STEINER, Gregory, G .... 276-944-6763.. 489 I
gsteiner@ehc.edu

STEINER, James, D .... 563-589-3210.. 177 C
jsteiner@dbq.edu

STEINER, John .... 856-351-2638.. 296 L
jsteiner@salemcc.edu

STEINER, Joseph, F .... 307-766-6556.. 527 B
joe.steiner@uwyo.edu

STEINER, Karl, V .... 410-455-5827.. 211 G
steinerk@umbc.edu

STEINER, Kate .... 912-344-2504.. 116 E
kate.steiner@armstrong.edu

STEINER, Kim .... 276-944-6112.. 489 I
ksteiner@ehc.edu

STEINER, Lori .... 630-617-3034.. 140 C
lori.steiner@elmhurst.edu

STEINER, Lori .... 316-942-4291.. 183 I
steinerl@newmanu.edu

STEINER, Marcia .... 518-381-1442.. 330 B
steinemm@sunysccc.edu

STEINER, Melissa .... 410-626-2513.. 210 D
annapolis.registrar@sjc.edu

STEINER, Michael .... 660-562-1197.. 269 J
msteiner@nwmissouri.edu

STEINER, Michael .... 330-287-7504.. 375 B
steiner.255@osu.edu

STEINER, Rita, L .... 410-617-2504.. 208 G
rsteiner@loyola.edu

STEINER, Ted .... 216-373-5387.. 374 B
tsteiner@ndc.edu

STEINER-LANG, Kathy ..... 314-935-5910.. 274 N
ksteiner@wustl.edu

STEINERT, Brandon .... 620-792-9307.. 178 G
steinertb@bartonccc.edu

STEINFELD, Peter, K .... 712-749-2205.. 170 D
steinfeld@bvu.edu

STEINFELD, Trudy, G .... 212-998-4735.. 324 C
trudy.steinfeld@nyu.edu

STEINHARDT, Sydney ...... 212-650-6460.. 307 E
ssteinhardt@ccny.cuny.edu

STEINHILBER, Steven ...... 770-484-1204.. 124 C
steven.steinhilber@lutherrice.edu

STEINHOFF, Cynthia, K .... 410-777-2483.. 206 B
cksteinhoff@aacc.edu

STEINKE, Deana, B .... 304-877-6428.. 510 F
financialaid@abc.edu

STEINKE, Pamela, K .... 815-740-5099.. 157 F
psteinke@stfrancis.edu

STEINKE, Paul .... 206-876-6100.. 507 D

STEINKE, Robin .... 651-641-3211.. 247 G
rsteinke001@luthersem.edu

STEINKE, Scott .... 567-661-7575.. 376 D
scott_steinke@owens.edu

STEINKIRCHNER,
Linda, M .... 585-385-5242.. 328 E
lsteinkirchner@sjfc.edu

STEINMAN, Joan .... 775-673-7060.. 284 K
jsteinman@tmcc.edu

STEINMAYER, Janet .... 860-701-5027.... 88 D
steinmayer_j@mitchell.edu

STEINMETZ, JR.,
Edward, J .... 570-941-4289.. 422 B
edward.steinmetz@scranton.edu

STEINMETZ, Joseph, E .... 479-575-2000.... 22 I

STEINMETZ, Paul .... 203-837-9805.... 85 I
steinmetzp@wcsu.edu

STEINMETZ, Rob, R .... 717-736-4140.. 405 C
rrsteinm@hacc.edu

STEINNERD, Sarah .... 573-651-2588.. 272 B
ssteinnerd@semo.edu

STEINOUR, David .... 703-726-3602.... 92 D
steinour@gwu.edu

STEINWEDEL, Cheryl .... 419-227-3141.. 380 A
csteinwedel@unoh.edu

STEINWERT, Tiffany, L ..... 781-283-2656.. 229 C
tsteinwe@wellesley.edu

STEITZ, John, A .... 740-284-5177.. 368 L
jsteitz@franciscan.edu

STEJSKAL, Patricia .... 815-479-7530.. 147 E
pstejskal@mchenry.edu

STEKETEE, Gail .... 617-353-3760.. 216 E
steketee@bu.edu

STELLA, Hilda, V .... 787-284-1912.. 534 C
hstella@ponce.inter.edu

STELLA, Mark .... 304-384-5356.. 513 A
markstella@hotmail.com

STELLA, Steven .... 518-454-5139.. 311 B
stellas@strose.edu

STELLER, James, R .... 518-956-8045.. 331 A
jsteller@albany.edu

STELLO, Ncelle .... 503-552-1544.. 392 H
nstello@nunm.edu

STELTER, Caroline, W ...... 804-758-6728.. 498 D
cstelter@rappahannock.edu

STELZER, Stuart, P .... 479-979-1381.... 24 I
sstelzer@ozarks.edu

STEM, Elaine .... 252-492-2061.. 353 H
steme@vgcc.edu

STEMBRIDGE, Allen, F .... 269-471-3622.. 230 H
stem@andrews.edu

STEMKOSKI, Stephen .... 315-859-4301.. 315 D
sstemkos@hamilton.edu

STEMLEY, Edward .... 713-313-7777.. 470 D
stemleyec@tsu.edu

STEMMANN, Karsten .... 530-741-5564.... 76 D
kstemman@yccd.edu

STEMMER, John, K .... 502-272-8140.. 187 A
jstemmer@bellarmine.edu

STEMPEK, Thomas .... 563-884-5469.. 176 C
tom.stempek@palmer.edu

STEMPLE, JR.,
Frederick, E .... 757-822-7415.. 498 H
fstemple@tcc.edu

STENBERG, Josephine ..... 808-845-9119.. 132 A
jstenber@hawaii.edu

STENBERG, Steve .... 503-517-1238.. 396 D
sstenberg@warnerpacific.edu

STENCIL, Debra .... 715-675-3331.. 524 D
stencil@ntc.edu

STENDARDI, Deborah, M 585-475-5040.. 327 E
dmsgrl@rit.edu

STENDER, Julie .... 435-652-7703.. 482 A
stender@dixie.edu

STENEHJEM, Keith, A ...... 701-788-4711.. 360 E
keith.stenehjem@mayvillestate.edu

STENGEL, Mark .... 805-546-3159.... 41 L
mark_stengel@cuesta.edu

STENGER, JR.,
Harvey, G .... 607-777-2131.. 331 B
president@binghamton.edu

STENGER, Karen .... 440-826-2726.. 363 M
kstenger@bw.edu

STENGER, Tracy, L .... 716-673-3424.. 331 D
tracy.stenger@fredonia.edu

STENKO, Michael .... 860-465-4509.... 85 G
stenkom@easternct.edu

STENNES-SPIDAHL,
Naomi, R .... 608-796-3481.. 522 O
nrstennesspidahl@viterbo.edu

STENNETT, Debbie .... 806-291-3500.. 479 D
stennettd@wbu.edu

STENSLAND, Traci, L .... 509-777-4306.. 509 H
tstensland@whitworth.edu

STENSON, Charlene .... 701-845-7105.. 361 B
c.stenson@vcsu.edu

STENSON, Merry .... 602-429-4946.... 16 E
mstenson@ps.edu

STENZEL, Neal .... 918-495-6203.. 386 H
nstenzel@oru.edu

STEORTS, Ken .... 901-381-3939.. 449 F
ken@visible.edu

STEPAN-NORRIS, Judith .. 949-824-6043.... 69 C
jstepann@uci.edu

STEPANSKI, Lisa .... 617-735-9774.. 218 C
stepansk@emmanuel.edu

STEPANYAN, Anaida .... 916-484-7666.... 59 E

STEPEK, Agnes .... 847-735-5036.. 145 B
stepek@lakeforest.edu

STEPHAN, Andrew .... 330-494-6170.. 377 J
astephan@starkstate.edu

STEPHAN, Arline .... 215-641-6534.. 410 L
astephan@mc3.edu

STEPHAN, Deanna .... 954-545-4500.. 109 F
newsletter@sfbc.edu

STEPHAN, Josiah .... 954-545-4500.. 109 F
jstephan@sfbc.edu

STEPHAN, W. Karl .... 989-837-4211.. 239 D
stephan@northwood.edu

STEPHAN, William, B .... 317-274-2100.. 162 F
wstephan@iu.edu

STEPHAN, William, B .... 812-855-0850.. 162 E
wstephan@indiana.edu

STEPHAN HAINS,
Theresa, R .... 716-878-6711.. 332 F
stephatr@buffalostate.edu

STEPHEN, Cathleen .... 610-607-6205.. 417 G
cstephen@racc.edu

STEPHEN, Jomysha .... 212-854-2021.. 304 I
jstephen@barnard.edu

STEPHENOFF, Gail, C ...... 614-292-5648.. 375 A
stephenoff.1@osu.edu

STEPHENS, Alisa .... 478-387-4802.. 121 E
astephen@gmc.edu

STEPHENS, Amy, M .... 503-255-0332.. 392 G
astephens@multnomah.edu

STEPHENS, Andre .... 562-903-4752.... 28 E
andre.stephens@biola.edu

STEPHENS, Cathy .... 217-641-4515.. 143 H
cstephens@jwcc.edu

STEPHENS, Charlene .... 302-736-2505.... 91 G
charlene.stephens@wesley.edu

STEPHENS, Christina .... 207-326-2441.. 204 C
christina.stephens@mma.edu

STEPHENS, Crystal .... 661-726-1911.... 68 K
crystal.stephens@uav.edu

STEPHENS, David, J .... 931-363-9865.. 441 G
dstephens@martinmethodist.edu

STEPHENS, Denise .... 805-893-3256.... 70 E
dstephens@library.ucsb.edu

STEPHENS, Diane, S .... 818-677-5929.... 34 A
diane.stephens@csun.edu

STEPHENS, Edward .... 417-455-5596.. 264 E
edwardstephens@crowder.edu

STEPHENS, Elsa .... 415-274-2200.... 25 A

STEPHENS, Fred, W .... 407-303-5752.... 95 C
fred.stephens@a[illegible]u.edu

STEPHENS, Garry .... 706-771-4081.. 117 C
gstephens@augustatech.edu

STEPHENS, JR., Harvard . 773-256-0696.. 147 A
harvard.stephens@lstc.edu

STEPHENS, Hubert .... 575-624-8291.. 300 I
stephens@nmmi.edu

STEPHENS, Jay .... 208-426-4454.. 132 I
jaystephens@boisestate.edu

STEPHENS, Jenny .... 812-855-1053.. 162 E
stephejl@indiana.edu

STEPHENS, Jonavon .... 706-821-8463.. 125 H
jstephens@paine.edu

STEPHENS, Josh .... 806-720-7502.. 461 C
josh.stephens@lcu.edu

STEPHENS, Kevin, N .... 309-655-2291.. 153 F
kevin.n.stephens@osfhealthcare.org

STEPHENS, Kristie .... 530-226-4727.... 64 H
kstephens@simpsonu.edu

STEPHENS, Linda .... 334-347-2623...... 3 H
lstephens@escc.edu

STEPHENS, Lisa .... 760-379-5501.... 47 K
lisa.stephens@cerrocoso.edu

STEPHENS, Mark .... 931-372-3224.. 445 B
mstephens@tntech.edu

STEPHENS, Mark, R .... 701-355-8123.. 362 G

STEPHENS, Mary, E .... 562-985-1658.... 33 B
mary.stephens@csulb.edu

STEPHENS, Matthew .... 405-613-2536.. 388 B
matthew.stephens@swcu.edu

STEPHENS, Melinda, F .... 724-847-6605.. 404 B
mstephen@geneva.edu

STEPHENS, Melinda, F .... 724-847-5235.. 404 B
mstephen@geneva.edu

STEPHENS, Melissa .... 203-837-8582.... 85 I
stephensm@wcsu.edu

STEPHENS, Mika, K .... 717-290-8704.. 408 B
mkstephens@lancasterseminary.edu

STEPHENS, Paul .... 859-858-3511.. 186 J
paul.stephens@asbury.edu

STEPHENS, Ralph .... 361-593-3814.. 469 A
ralph.stephens@tamuk.edu

STEPHENS, Rick .... 607-871-2137.. 303 F
stephens@alfred.edu

STEPHENS, Robert .... 478-825-6092.. 120 F
stephensr@fvsu.edu

STEPHENS, Sandra .... 901-722-3220.. 444 C
sandra@sco.edu

STEPHENS, Sandra, S ...... 901-722-3220.. 444 C
sandra@sco.edu

STEPHENS, Sharon .... 215-968-8468.. 399 A
stephens@bucks.edu

STEPHENS, Shawna .... 541-888-7351.. 395 B
shawna.stephens@socc.edu

STEPHENS, Sonya .... 413-538-2500.. 226 A
stephens@mtholyoke.edu

STEPHENS, Steve .... 405-744-6494.. 385 G
steve.stephens@okstate.edu

STEPHENS, Toni .... 972-883-2693.. 476 C
tmesser@utdallas.edu

STEPHENS, Zena, A .... 936-261-1387.. 467 E
zastephens@pvamu.edu

STEPHENSON, Alan, H .... 828-694-1821.. 347 G
ah_stephenson@blueridge.edu

STEPHENSON, Andrea ..... 717-394-6211.. 401 H
astephenson@cst.edu

STEPHENSON, Cathy ...... 828-694-1807.. 347 G
ck_stephenson@blueridge.edu

STEPHENSON, Devin ...... 606-886-3863.. 189 A
devin.stephenson@kctcs.edu

STEPHENSON, E. Frank ... 252-398-6278.. 343 G
stephf@chowan.edu

STEPHENSON, James ...... 734-995-7502.. 232 I
security@cuaa.edu

STEPHENSON, Jeff .... 916-484-8376.... 51 A
stephej@arc.losrios.edu

STEPHENSON, Laura ...... 785-670-1561.. 185 H
laura.stephenson@washburn.edu

STEPHENSON,
Norman, J .... 308-635-6121.. 283 D
stephens@wncc.edu

STEPHENSON, Rod .... 206-878-3710.. 504 E
rstephenson@highline.edu

STEPHENSON, Susan .... 307-532-8325.. 526 G
susan.stephenson@ewc.wy.edu

STEPHENSON, Thomas .... 610-328-8319.. 419 I
tstephe1@swarthmore.edu

STEPHENSON, Zollie .... 501-370-8540.... 21 G
zstephenson@philander.edu

STEPINA, Karen .... 708-344-4700.. 146 D
kstepina@lincolntech.edu

STEPLIGHT JOHNSON,
S. Aisha .... 973-877-4447.. 291 H
ssteplig@essex.edu

STEPNEY, Ne'Keisha .... 630-466-7900.. 157 K
nstepney@waubonsee.edu

STEPNIAK, Michael, J ..... 540-665-4600.. 494 B
mstepnia@su.edu

STEPNOWSKI, OP,
Thomas More .... 615-297-7545.. 438 F
srtmore@aquinascollege.edu

STEPP, Gary .... 606-368-6105.. 186 B
garystepp@alc.edu

STEPP, James, D .... 207-768-9601.. 205 D
james.stepp@maine.edu

STEPP, Jim .... 606-368-6454.. 186 B
jamesstepp@alc.edu

STEPP, Joe, A .... 606-368-6027.. 186 B
joestepp@alc.edu

STEPP, Paul .... 606-539-4167.. 193 F
paul.stepp@ucumberlands.edu

STEPP, Perry .... 972-241-3371.. 455 K
pstepp@dallas.edu

STEPP, Terry .... 256-233-8243...... 1 F
terry.stepp@athens.edu

STEPTOE, David .... 478-289-2049.. 120 C
dsteptoe@ega.edu

STERK, Claire, E .... 404-727-6013.. 120 E
csterk@emory.edu

STERK, Jim .... 619-594-6357.... 35 A
adsdsu@mail.sdsu.edu

STERKOWITZ, Robert .... 708-974-5250.. 148 G
sterkowitz@morainevalley.edu

STERLING, Alan .... 972-721-5347.. 473 D
asterling@udallas.edu

STERLING, Carolin .... 937-376-6522.. 365 H
csterling@centralstate.edu

STERLING, Cheryl .... 713-718-5041.. 459 B
cheryl.sterling@hccs.edu

STERLING, Christa .... 860-832-2277.... 85 F
csterling@ccsu.edu

STERLING, Gregory, E ..... 203-432-5304.... 90 D
gregory.sterling@yale.edu

STERLING, Marcia .... 505-566-3588.. 301 J
sterlingm@sanjuancollege.edu

STERLING, Rose .... 210-486-2420.. 450 E
rspruill1@alamo.edu

STERN, Briendy .... 718-871-6187.. 337 I
briendy.stern@touro.edu

STERN, David .... 773-298-3350.. 153 H
stern@sxu.edu

STERN, David .... 813-258-7360.. 114 M
provost@ut.edu

STERN, David, M .... 901-448-5529.. 448 H
dstern@uthsc.edu

STERN, Elliot .... 425-739-8383.. 504 F
elliot.stern@lwtech.edu

STERN, Elsie .... 215-576-0800.. 417 H
estern@rrc.edu

STERN, Hal, S .... 949-824-7405.... 69 C
icsdean@uci.edu

STERN, Holly, C .... 973-596-6379.. 293 D
holly.stern@njit.edu

STERN, Joyce .... 641-269-3702.. 172 I
sternjm@grinnell.edu

STERN, Kevin, D .... 214-887-5111.. 457 C
kstern@dts.edu

STERN, Lorna .... 215-572-2901.. 397 G
sternl@arcadia.edu

STERN, Michael, J .... 773-442-6012.. 149 J
m-stern2@neiu.edu

STERN, Robert A, M .... 203-432-2279.... 90 D
robert.a.m.stern@yale.edu

STERN, Ronald .... 202-651-5346.... 92 C
ronald.stern@gallaudet.edu

STERN, Ross .... 301-405-6637.. 211 E
stern@umd.edu

STERN, Shannyn .... 928-541-7777.... 15 G
sstern@ncu.edu

STERN, Sharon .... 254-710-1010.. 452 H
sharon_stern@baylor.edu

STERN, Susan .... 262-695-3451.. 524 G
sstern1@wctc.edu

STERNER, Karl .... 602-386-4120.... 11 D
karl.sterner@arizonachristian.edu

STERNER, Sheri .... 714-432-5081.... 39 G
ssterner@occ.cccd.edu

STERNGOLD, James .... 646-664-9108.. 306 M
james.sterngold@cuny.edu

STERNKE, Timothy .... 414-930-3032.. 518 F
mmc-bookstore@mtmary.edu

STERNS, Teresa, G .... 304-462-6102.. 513 C
teresa.sterns@glenville.edu

STERRETT, Joseph, D ...... 610-758-4320.. 408 H
jds7@lehigh.edu

STERRETT, Myra .... 352-395-5150.. 109 C
myra.sterrett@sfcollege.edu

STERRITT, D. E. Lorraine 336-721-2603 355 E lorraine.sterritt@salem.edu
STERTZBACH, Rebecca, M 480-245-7971 13 L becky.stertzbach@ibcs.edu
STERTZBACH, Rebecca, M 480-245-7969 13 L becky.stertzbach@ibcs.edu
STETLER, Kent 513-721-7944 369 D kstetler@gbs.edu
STETLER, Maria 513-721-7944 369 D mstetler@gbs.edu
STETLER, P. Daniel 772-546-5534 102 S danstetler@hsbc.edu
STETLER, Paul 772-546-5534 102 S paulstetler@hsbc.edu
STETSON, Daniel 225-389-7200 197 I
STETTER, Mark 970-491-7051 78 Q mark.stetter@colostate.edu
STETTLER, Greg 618-985-3741 143 F gregstettler@jalc.edu
STETZER, Ed 630-752-5918 158 C ed.stetzer@wheaton.edu
STEUBER, Alicia 480-994-9244 17 C alicias@swiha.edu
STEUERWALD, Brian 317-917-3628 165 O bsteu@martin.edu
STEURBAUT, Margo 626-395-6275 30 H margo.steurbaut@caltech.edu
STEVENS, Adrian 909-607-8684 57 H adrian_stevens@pitzer.edu
STEVENS, Alison 206-546-4651 507 F amstevens@shoreline.edu
STEVENS, Andrea, N 662-329-7431 259 E anstevens@muw.edu
STEVENS, Anne, A 704-461-6718 342 A annestevens@bac.edu
STEVENS, Annie 802-656-3380 485 D annie.stevens@uvm.edu
STEVENS, Arshele 773-602-5016 137 F astevens11@ccc.edu
STEVENS, Bren 304-357-4911 511 E brenstevens@ucwv.edu
STEVENS, Brenda, D 330-471-8328 371 J bstevens@malone.edu
STEVENS, Carol 845-431-8974 312 G cstevens@sunydutchess.edu
STEVENS, Carrie 785-242-5200 183 M carrie.stevens@ottawa.edu
STEVENS, Carroll 909-621-8096 38 J carroll.stevens@cmc.edu
STEVENS, Cathleen, M 585-389-2001 322 D csteven9@naz.edu
STEVENS, Cheryl, L 270-745-4448 194 D cheryl.stevens@wku.edu
STEVENS, Daniel 540-785-5440 496 A danielstevens@vbc.edu
STEVENS, Darryl 406-771-4321 277 F darryl.stevens@gfcmsu.edu
STEVENS, Debbie 641-673-2173 177 J stevensd@wmpenn.edu
STEVENS, Dennis, G 434-223-6110 490 D dstevens@hsc.edu
STEVENS, Elizabeth 651-690-8600 254 M ejstevens@stkate.edu
STEVENS, Eric, A 660-263-3900 263 A academic@cccb.edu
STEVENS, Gladstone, H 650-325-5621 59 J gladstone.stevens@stpatricksseminary.org
STEVENS, Greg 509-434-5037 503 A greg.stevens@ccs.spokane.edu
STEVENS, Greg 509-434-5037 502 I greg.stevens@ccs.spokane.edu
STEVENS, Greg, L 509-434-5037 502 H gstevens@ccs.spokane.edu
STEVENS, Gwendolyn, M 412-578-8776 400 C gmstevens@carlow.edu
STEVENS, Jeffrey 215-503-7015 420 E jeffrey.stevens@jefferson.edu
STEVENS, John 435-283-7017 482 E john.stevens@snow.edu
STEVENS, Kevin 312-915-6115 146 G kstevens3@luc.edu
STEVENS, Laura 314-529-9252 267 B lstevens@maryville.edu
STEVENS, Mark 208-376-7731 132 H
STEVENS, Mark 818-677-4069 34 A mark.stevens@csun.edu
STEVENS, Mark, W 920-206-2314 517 G mark.stevens@mbu.edu
STEVENS, Marty 717-334-6286 409 C mstevens@ltsg.edu
STEVENS, RSM, Maryanne 402-399-2435 279 E mstevens@csm.edu
STEVENS, Matt 561-803-2200 106 C national@pba.edu
STEVENS, Michael 616-222-1430 233 A michael.stevens@cornerstone.edu
STEVENS, Michele 806-457-4200 458 B mstevens@fpctx.edu
STEVENS, Moira 207-699-5090 203 F mstevens@meca.edu
STEVENS, Peter 618-374-3530 151 E peter.stevens@principia.edu
STEVENS, Phil 207-699-5047 203 F pstevens@meca.edu
STEVENS, Randy 909-558-4558 49 C rstevens@llu.edu
STEVENS, Robert 203-932-7435 90 A rstevens@newhaven.edu
STEVENS, Roger, K 847-259-1840 137 B rstevens@christianlifecollege.edu
STEVENS, Ron 919-658-7834 355 K rstevens@umo.edu
STEVENS, Scott 802-860-2751 483 F stevens@champlain.edu
STEVENS, Sheri, R 207-621-3110 204 I sheri@maine.edu
STEVENS, Sylvia 513-481-2226 381 C sylvia_stevens@wilmington.edu
STEVENS, Timothy, S 847-491-7256 150 F tstevens@northwestern.edu
STEVENS, Victor 718-270-6069 309 B vstevens@mec.cuny.edu
STEVENS, Wayne 570-586-2400 419 G wstevens@summitu.edu
STEVENS HAYNES, Gale 718-488-1001 319 B gale.haynes@liu.edu
STEVENSON, Bill 479-524-7119 20 H wstevens@jbu.edu
STEVENSON, Daniel 406-994-2001 277 C daniel.stevenson1@montana.edu
STEVENSON, David 918-663-9000 387 B davidss@plattcollege.org
STEVENSON, Dena 402-891-6605 280 B dena.stevenson@doane.edu
STEVENSON, Duncan 253-964-6612 506 B dstevenson@pierce.ctc.edu
STEVENSON, Elizabeth 508-830-6683 222 C estevenson@maritime.edu
STEVENSON, Gwendolyn, A 937-778-7949 368 E gstevenson@edisonohio.edu
STEVENSON, James, E 904-632-3191 101 G james.stevenson@fscj.edu
STEVENSON, Jeanne, M 208-885-7941 134 G jeannec@uidaho.edu
STEVENSON, Jeff 404-297-9522 122 A stevensonj@gptc.edu
STEVENSON, John 954-545-4500 109 F academics@sfbc.edu
STEVENSON, Karen, L 615-353-3430 446 E karen.stevenson@nscc.edu
STEVENSON, Kim 252-335-3699 356 D knstevenson@ecsu.edu
STEVENSON, Leslie, W 804-289-8141 495 G lsteven2@richmond.edu
STEVENSON, Mark 724-266-3838 421 C mstevenson@tsm.edu
STEVENSON, Martha 205-226-4648 2 C mstevens@bsc.edu
STEVENSON, Martha 610-683-4484 415 C stevenson@kutztown.edu
STEVENSON, Melissa 270-707-3811 189 G melissa.stevenson@kctcs.edu
STEVENSON, Paula 954-545-4500 109 F library@sfbc.edu
STEVENSON, Sarah 718-405-3258 310 H sarah.stevenson@mountsaintvincent.edu
STEVENSON, Susan, G 334-683-2303 5 G sstevenson@marionmilitary.edu
STEVENSON, Tara 904-826-8508 99 M tstevenson@flagler.edu
STEVENSON, Terree, L 740-368-3151 376 B tlsteven@owu.edu
STEVENSON, Valerie, O 904-620-2920 112 B vstevens@unf.edu
STEVENSON-DUMAS, Laura 904-819-6205 99 M lstevenson@flagler.edu
STEVENSON MARSHALL, Brenda 509-313-3569 504 A stevenson-marshall@gonzaga.edu
STEVICK, David 585-567-9607 316 F david.stevick@houghton.edu
STEVINSON, Rebecca 218-749-7762 249 I b.stevinson@mesabirange.edu
STEWARD, Agnes 253-840-8403 506 B asteward@pierce.ctc.edu
STEWARD, Deborah 315-781-3500 316 C stewart@hws.edu
STEWARD, Gary 405-974-5528 388 L gsteward@uco.edu
STEWARD, Jerry, L 405-682-7502 385 D jsteward@occc.edu
STEWARD, Kyle 662-325-3221 259 D ksteward@pres.msstate.edu
STEWARD, Sarah 303-245-4863 81 I ssteward@naropa.edu
STEWARD, JR., Sterling 912-358-3449 126 F ssuathletics@savannahstate.edu
STEWART, Avis 765-983-1393 160 G aviss@earlham.edu
STEWART, Barbara 937-769-1863 363 F bstewart@antioch.edu
STEWART, Barbara, A 408-554-4396 63 E bstewart@scu.edu
STEWART, Barbara, E 608-785-5092 520 C bstewart@uwlax.edu
STEWART, Baxter 918-463-2931 383 F baxter.stewart@connorsstate.edu
STEWART, Ben 773-256-0769 147 A bstewart@lstc.edu
STEWART, Beth 828-398-7650 347 D bethstewart@abtech.edu
STEWART, Betsy 610-526-5632 398 K estewart@brynmawr.edu
STEWART, Betty 940-397-4226 462 A betty.stewart@mwsu.edu
STEWART, Billy, W 601-635-6200 257 F bstewart@eccc.edu
STEWART, Brad, J 240-567-1312 209 E brad.stewart@montgomerycollege.edu
STEWART, Brandon 937-376-2946 376 F bstewart@payne.edu
STEWART, Bryan 817-515-1011 467 A bryan.stewart@tccd.edu
STEWART, Carrie, E 310-243-3787 32 D cstewart@csudh.edu
STEWART, Charles 212-650-7271 307 E cstewart@ccny.cuny.edu
STEWART, Christy 618-985-2828 143 F christystewart@jalc.edu
STEWART, Concetta 914-674-7500 320 G cstewart@mercy.edu
STEWART, Connie 989-328-1249 238 D connies@montcalm.edu
STEWART, Dan 512-499-4616 475 K dstewart@utsystem.edu
STEWART, Daniel, P 904-818-6238 99 M stewartd@flagler.edu
STEWART, Danny 985-732-6640 196 G
STEWART, David 304-865-6089 511 C david.stewart@ovu.edu
STEWART, David, C 304-293-5811 514 C david.stewart@mail.wvu.edu
STEWART, David, R 651-638-6225 244 L d-stewart@bethel.edu
STEWART, Dawn 614-823-3529 376 C dstewart@otterbein.edu
STEWART, Dean 920-498-6995 524 E dean.stewart@nwtc.edu
STEWART, Deborah 802-828-2800 486 A das07200@ccv.vsc.edu
STEWART, Deborah, C 530-898-5241 32 C dcstewart@csuchico.edu
STEWART, Denise 251-809-1532 5 A
STEWART, DeShaunta 773-907-4044 137 E dstewart75@ccc.edu
STEWART, Diane 661-362-3503 40 A diane.stewart@canyons.edu
STEWART, Donette 864-503-5280 434 G dstewart@uscupstate.edu
STEWART, Dorothy 313-993-1028 241 G stewardm@udmercy.edu
STEWART, Doug 970-945-8691 78 B
STEWART, Douglas 601-877-2419 256 F stewartd@alcorn.edu
STEWART, Elizabeth, J 585-292-2536 321 J estewart@monroecc.edu
STEWART, H.D 828-898-8756 345 G stewarth@lmc.edu
STEWART, Jacqueline 606-368-6059 186 B jacquelinestewart@alc.edu
STEWART, James 410-951-2639 212 E jstewart@coppin.edu
STEWART, James 731-352-4093 438 K stewartj@bethelu.edu
STEWART, James 503-517-1898 396 F jstewart@westernseminary.edu
STEWART, Jane 313-664-1533 232 G jstewart@collegeforcreativestudies.edu
STEWART, Janeen, K 319-352-8331 177 G janeen.stewart@wartburg.edu
STEWART, Janie 810-766-4209 231 D jmouse01@baker.edu
STEWART, Jeff 239-489-9081 101 F jstewart10@fsw.edu
STEWART, Jellema 716-673-3398 331 D jellema.stewart@fredonia.edu
STEWART, Jennifer 314-968-7105 275 B jstewart15@webster.edu
STEWART, Jo Moore 404-270-5061 128 A jstewart@spelman.edu
STEWART, John, R 563-589-3642 177 C jstewart@dbq.edu
STEWART, III, John, W 205-665-6001 9 B presidentsoffice@montevallo.edu
STEWART, Josh 903-434-8242 462 M jstewart@ntcc.edu
STEWART, Juarine 256-372-5750 1 A juarine.stewart@aamu.edu
STEWART, June 864-225-7653 430 A junestewart@forrestcollege.edu
STEWART, Kara 830-372-8160 470 C kstewart@tlu.edu
STEWART, Larry 248-218-2023 240 C lstewart@rc.edu
STEWART, Lea, P 848-932-7127 296 B lstewart@rutgers.edu
STEWART, Leah 859-572-6437 192 B stewartl1@nku.edu
STEWART, Lisa 850-599-3730 110 J lisa.stewart@famu.edu
STEWART, Lisa 832-252-0758 454 H lisa.stewart@cbshouston.edu
STEWART, Lisa 434-791-7186 487 C lstewart@averett.edu
STEWART, Lynne 336-721-2600 355 E lynne.stewart@salem.edu
STEWART, Makena 704-290-5840 353 B mstewart@spcc.edu
STEWART, Marshall 573-882-2121 273 E
STEWART, Michael 478-471-2710 124 E michael.stewart@mga.edu
STEWART, Michael 404-233-3949 443 M mstewart@richmont.edu
STEWART, Michelle 731-426-7500 440 K
STEWART, Nathan 701-845-7160 361 B nathan.stewart@vcsu.edu
STEWART, Nora 956-721-5142 460 F nstewart@laredo.edu
STEWART, R. Wayne 580-349-1408 385 F rwstewart@opsu.edu
STEWART, Reginald, C 515-294-8840 169 G rstewart@iastate.edu
STEWART, Renee 615-366-4416 444 D renee.stewart@tbr.edu
STEWART, Rob 806-742-2184 472 C rob.stewart@ttu.edu
STEWART, Robert 251-380-3030 7 D rstewart@shc.edu
STEWART, Robert 617-552-2671 216 C bobstewart@theq.follett.com
STEWART, Robin 740-376-4683 372 A robin.stewart@marietta.edu
STEWART, Rod, S 517-750-1200 241 E rods@admin.arbor.edu
STEWART, Ross 206-281-2900 507 C rstewart@spu.edu
STEWART, Scott 616-222-1446 233 A scott.stewart@cornerstone.edu
STEWART, Sonja 931-221-7342 444 E stewarts@apsu.edu
STEWART, Spencer 229-243-3017 117 E sstewart@bainbridge.edu
STEWART, Stephanie 858-513-9240 27 V stephanie.stewart@ashford.edu
STEWART, Stephanie, M 920-433-6639 515 F stephanie.stewart@bellincollege.edu
STEWART, Terri 607-274-3758 317 D tastewart@ithaca.edu
STEWART, Thomas 510-485-7806 56 I tstewart@patten.edu
STEWART, Todd, I 937-255-2321 527 H todd.stewart@afit.edu
STEWART, Todd, M 270-745-5276 194 D todd.stewart@wku.edu
STEWART, Tommie, T 334-229-4232 1 D tstewart@alasu.edu
STEWART, Tommy 901-761-9494 439 F tstewart@concorde.edu
STEWART, Tracy 907-564-8261 10 B tstewart@alaskapacific.edu
STEWART, Tracy 717-545-4747 406 I
STEWART, Trevor 530-895-2421 29 F stewarttr@butte.edu
STEWART, Tynelle 585-275-7532 338 K tstewar4@ur.rochester.edu
STEWART, Vicki, L 717-815-1287 424 F vstewart@ycp.edu
STEWART, Walter, M 314-516-6377 274 A siewertw@umsl.edu
STEWART, Wendy 760-757-2121 52 K wstewart@miracosta.edu
STEWART, Wendy 253-833-9111 504 C wstewart@greenriver.edu
STEWART ALEXANDER, Mary 203-837-8839 85 I alexanderm@wcsu.edu
STEWART-JAMES, Joy 916-278-6461 34 B jsjames@csus.edu
STIBER, Greg, F 954-262-5381 105 J stiber@nova.edu
STICE, J. Michael 405-325-4687 389 B mstice@ou.edu
STICE, Mike 949-376-6000 48 C mstice@lcad.edu
STICHNOTE, Lynn 573-341-4075 274 B lks@mst.edu
STICHTER, Donald 518-262-7000 303 E stichtd@mail.amc.edu

STICK, Jim .... 515-964-6429.. 171 B
jwstick@dmacc.edu
STICKEL, Marianne .... 415-458-3722.... 42 G
mstickel@dominican.edu
STICKLES, Christopher ..... 541-880-2240.. 391 F
stickles@klamathcc.edu
STICKLEY, Ronald, G .... 540-665-4530.. 494 B
rstickle3@su.edu
STICKSEL, Lance .... 212-686-9244.. 304 A
STIEFEL, Joseph P, D ...... 630-889-6604.. 149 G
jstiefel@nuhs.edu
STIEFFEL, Deborah .... 313-993-1496.. 241 G
deborah.stieffel@udmercy.edu
STIEGLITZ, Matthew .... 201-200-3037.. 293 C
mstieglitz@njcu.edu
STIENBARGER,
Mary Ann .... 765-983-1346.. 160 G
stienma@earlham.edu
STIER, Mark .... 941-487-4504.. 111 D
mstier@ncf.edu
STIFF, Brenda .... 815-479-7529.. 147 E
bstiff@mchenry.edu
STIFF, Cindra, K .... 270-852-3113.. 191 C
cindrast@kwc.edu
STIFFIN, Rose Mary .... 305-626-3697.. 101 A
rose.stiffin@fmuniv.edu
STIFFLER, Daniel, J .... 314-367-8700.. 271 E
daniel.stiffler@stlcop.edu
STIFFLER, Faith .... 817-598-8874.. 479 E
fstiffler@wc.edu
STIFFLER, Gregory, S ...... 989-837-4320.. 239 D
stiffler@northwood.edu
STIFFLER, Jamee .... 919-718-7526.. 348 D
jstiffler@cccc.edu
STIFFLER, Sarah .... 509-279-6066.. 502 I
STIFTER, Michael, J .... 715-425-3827.. 521 B
michael.j.stifter@uwrf.edu
STIGNANI, Alicia .... 470-578-2337.. 123 J
STILES, Alyce .... 413-775-1607.. 223 D
stilesa@gcc.mass.edu
STILES, Andy .... 785-242-5200.. 183 M
andy.stiles@ottawa.edu
STILES, Angela .... 561-683-1400.... 94 G
astiles@anho.edu
STILES, Bill .... 610-796-3015.. 397 D
bill.stiles@alvernia.edu
STILES, Carl .... 207-941-7107.. 202 I
stilesc@husson.edu
STILES, Chip .... 207-893-7850.. 204 D
cstiles@sjcme.edu
STILES, Chip .... 978-837-5357.. 225 E
stilesc@merrimack.edu
STILES, Deborah .... 304-367-4111.. 513 B
deborah.stiles@fairmontstate.edu
STILES, Diane .... 605-882-5284.. 436 B
diane.stiles@lakeareatech.edu
STILES, John .... 513-732-5232.. 379 C
stilesjn@ucmail.uc.edu
STILES, Michael, D .... 712-279-3149.. 176 E
michael.stiles@stlukescollege.edu
STILES, Randall .... 641-269-4636.. 172 I
stilesr@grinnell.edu
STILES, Timothy .... 386-822-7315.. 113 B
tstiles@stetson.edu
STILL, George .... 434-797-8576.. 496 I
gstill@dcc.vccs.edu
STILL, Guy, M .... 856-225-2900.. 296 A
guystill@camden.rutgers.edu
STILL, Jill .... 936-468-5406.. 466 H
jstill@sfasu.edu
STILL, Kathy .... 276-376-0130.. 495 I
kls72d@uvawise.edu
STILL, Kennie, M .... 864-242-5100.. 427 E
STILL, Todd .... 254-710-3755.. 452 H
todd_still@baylor.edu
STILLE, Brand, R .... 864-597-4130.. 435 C
stillebr@wofford.edu
STILLE, Robyn, L .... 906-227-2661.. 239 B
rstille@nmu.edu
STILLE, Suzette .... 843-953-8148.. 428 G
stilles@cofc.edu
STILLERMAN, Harry .... 336-334-4822.. 350 B
hkstillerman@gtcc.edu
STILLEY, Dana .... 845-574-4224.. 327 G
dstilley@sunyrockland.edu
STILLEY, Kevin .... 214-818-1369.. 455 G
kstilley@criswell.edu
STILLMAN, Brian, C .... 208-467-8460.. 134 D
bcstillman@nnu.edu
STILLMAN, Bruce .... 516-367-8497.. 310 E
stillman@cshl.edu
STILLMAN, Cindy .... 760-773-7959.... 40 B
cstillman@alumni.collegeofthedesert.edu
STILLMAN, John, P .... 801-581-3655.. 481 M
john.stillman@hsc.utah.edu
STILLMAN, Matt .... 541-552-8535.. 395 A
stillmam@sou.edu
STILTS, Corey, E .... 607-735-1850.. 313 F
cstilts@elmira.edu
STILWELL, Jackie .... 951-343-4239.... 29 H
jstilwell@calbpatist.edu
STILWELL, Martha .... 269-965-3931.. 236 A
stilwellm@kellogg.edu
STIMAC, Robin .... 816-604-3071.. 267 J
robin.stimac@mcckc.edu
STIMELING, Kurt .... 603-897-8247.. 287 F
kstimeling@rivier.edu
STIMERS, Mitch .... 785-243-1435.. 179 N
mstimers@cloud.edu
STIMMEL, Glenn .... 323-442-1463.... 72 D
stimmel@usc.edu
STIMPERT, John, L .... 434-223-6110.. 490 D
kmariannino@hsc.edu
STIMPFL, Joseph .... 314-246-7160.. 275 B
jstimpfl@webster.edu
STIMPLE, Janet .... 216-687-3831.. 366 I
j.stimple@csuohio.edu
STIMPSON, Lee .... 208-535-5425.. 133 G
lee.stimpson@my.eitc.edu
STINE, Cory .... 419-559-2355.. 377 M
cstine@terra.edu
STINE, Terry, E .... 208-376-7731.. 132 H
tstine@boisebible.edu
STINEMETZ, Charles, L ... 740-368-3101.. 376 B
clstinem@owu.edu
STINER, Margaret .... 440-826-8061.. 363 M
mstiner@bw.edu
STINES, Marsha .... 828-627-4529.. 350 D
mstines@haywood.edu
STINIS, Jane .... 407-277-0311.... 99 J
jstinis@evergladesuniversity.edu
STINNER, Jerry .... 818-677-2004.... 34 A
jerry.stinner@csun.edu
STINNETT, Gary, W .... 704-687-0644.. 358 A
gwstinne@uncc.edu
STINNETT, Hester .... 215-777-9713.. 420 B
hesters@temple.edu
STINSON, Becky .... 573-592-4237.. 275 G
becky.stinson@williamwoods.edu
STINSON, Charlie .... 256-761-6301...... 7 F
cstinson@talladega.edu
STINSON, Claire .... 931-372-3311.. 445 B
cstinson@tntech.edu
STINSON, Greg .... 219-464-5212.. 168 F
greg.stinson@valpo.edu
STINSON, III, Harry, O ... 502-597-6922.. 191 B
harry.stinson@kysu.edu
STINSON, Lisa .... 860-701-5068.... 88 D
stinson_l@mitchell.edu
STINSON, Lori .... 208-792-2213.. 134 A
lstinson@lcsc.edu
STINSON, Matthew, P ..... 724-946-7368.. 423 B
stinsomp@westminster.edu
STINSON, Niki .... 706-245-7226.. 120 D
nstinson@ec.edu
STINSON, Pam .... 580-628-6210.. 384 L
pam.stinson@noc.edu
STINSON, Randy .... 502-897-4897.. 192 D
rstinson@sbts.edu
STINSON, Willette .... 304-766-3239.. 514 B
wstinson@wvstateu.edu
STINTON, Dale, A .... 855-786-6546.. 151 K
STINTON, Martha .... 808-853-1040.. 131 B
marthastinton@pacrim.edu
STIPCAK, Sondra, L .... 570-321-4322.. 409 F
stipcak@lycoming.edu
STIPE, Catie .... 937-328-8070.. 366 E
stipec@clarkstate.edu
STIPE, Richard .... 870-633-4480.... 20 B
rstipe@eacc.edu
STIPEK, Deborah .... 650-725-9090.... 66 I
STIPELMEAN, Brian .... 301-846-2646.. 207 F
bstipelman@frederick.edu
STIRBER-GAMELIN,
Donna .... 717-545-4747.. 406 I
dstirber-gamelin@hci.edu
STIRES, Elizabeth, M .... 570-348-6211.. 409 H
STIREWALT, Jesse .... 218-879-0708.. 249 C
housing@fdltcc.edu
STIRLING, Diane, S .... 704-894-2462.. 343 I
distirling@davidson.edu
STIRLING, Wynn, C .... 801-422-4465.. 480 C
wynn_stirling@byu.edu
STIRTON, Rob .... 517-787-0800.. 235 G
erstirton@jccmi.edu
STIRTZ, Michele, D .... 402-552-2543.. 279 D
stirtz@clarksoncollege.edu
STISO, Joseph .... 978-632-6600.. 224 B
j_stiso@mwcc.mass.edu
STITELER, Chad .... 360-752-8313.. 501 G
cstiteler@btc.edu
STITES, Ann .... 815-967-7306.. 152 F
astites@rockfordcareercollege.edu
STITES, Dorothy, D .... 785-749-8456.. 181 E
dstites@haskell.edu
STITES-DOE, Susan .... 585-395-2623.. 332 E
sstites@brockport.edu
STITHEM, Diana .... 928-757-0801.... 15 E
dstithem@mohave.edu
STITTS, Doria, K .... 336-750-2345.. 359 B
stittsd@wssu.edu
STIVEN, Janet, A .... 312-329-4123.. 148 F
janet.stiven@moody.edu
STIVER, Chris .... 517-264-3131.. 230 D
cstiver@adrian.edu
STIVERS, Laura .... 415-458-3734.... 42 G
laura.stivers@dominican.edu
STIVERS, Mary, E .... 859-846-5332.. 191 G
mestivers@midway.edu
ST JOHN, Meredith .... 617-558-1788.. 225 C
meredith.stjohn@mcphs.edu
STOAKS, Lindsay .... 641-782-1338.. 177 B
stoaks@swcciowa.edu
STOB, Barbara .... 410-337-6011.. 207 H
bstob@goucher.edu
STOB, Michael .... 616-526-7114.. 232 A
stob@calvin.edu
STOBER, Dan .... 650-723-7162.... 66 I
dan.stober@stanford.edu
STOBIE, Pete .... 816-654-7108.. 256 E
pstobie@kcumb.edu
STOBO, John D .... 510-987-9071.... 68 L
john.stobo@uco.edu
STOCCO, Jeff .... 712-749-2441.. 170 D
stoccoj@bvu.edu
STOCHAJ, Steven .... 575-646-2914.. 300 J
sstochaj@nmsu.edu
STOCK, Lawrence, E .... 724-287-8711.. 399 B
larry.stock@bc3.edu
STOCK, Lisa .... 612-330-1783.. 244 I
stock@augsburg.edu
STOCK, Lisa .... 641-648-4611.. 173 K
lisa.stock@iavalley.edu
STOCK, Renee .... 304-829-7572.. 510 G
rstock@bethanywv.edu
STOCK, Susan, R .... 773-442-4650.. 149 J
s-stock1@neiu.edu
STOCK-KUPPERMAN,
Gretel, L .... 608-796-3272.. 522 O
glstock@viterbo.edu
STOCKE, Mike .... 253-964-6534.. 506 B
mstocke@pierce.ctc.edu
STOCKER, Gary .... 573-592-5918.. 275 E
gary.stocker@westminster-mo.edu
STOCKER, Jane Ellen .... 708-596-2000.. 154 E
jstocker@ssc.edu
STOCKER, Scott .... 650-723-2300.... 66 I
STOCKERT, Brian .... 760-744-1150.... 56 F
bstockert@palomar.edu
STOCKERT, Patricia, A ..... 309-655-4124.. 153 F
patricia.a.stockert@osfhealthcare.org
STOCKING, Nancy .... 602-386-4138.... 11 D
nancy.stocking@arizonachristian.edu
STOCKLIN, Chris .... 620-241-0723.. 179 L
chris.stocklin@centralchristian.edu
STOCKMAN, Deb .... 316-295-5377.. 181 B
deb_stockman@friends.edu
STOCKS, Chad .... 601-857-3315.. 258 A
clstocks@hindscc.edu
STOCKS, Janet .... 202-884-9380.... 94 A
stocksj@trinitydc.edu
STOCKSLADER, Jon Jay .. 716-286-8189.. 324 E
js@niagara.edu
STOCKSTILL, Stephanie ... 281-756-3531.. 450 G
sstockstill@alvincollege.edu
STOCKTON, Dennis .... 770-533-7032.. 123 L
dstockton@laniertech.edu
STOCKTON, Hans .... 713-525-3530.. 475 J
stockton@stthom.edu
STOCKTON, Kathryn, B .... 801-581-7569.. 481 M
kathryn.stockton@utah.edu
STOCKTON, Nancy .... 812-855-5711.. 162 F
stocktnj@indiana.edu
STOCKTON, Shelli .... 909-748-8142.... 71 K
shelli_stockton@redlands.edu
STOCKTON, Thomas, B ... 336-841-4592.. 345 A
tstockto@highpoint.edu
STOCKTON, Ty .... 307-778-1170.. 526 K
tstockto@lccc.wy.edu
STOCKWELL, Dave .... 614-222-3216.. 367 B
dstockwell@ccad.edu
STODDARD, Eric .... 928-541-7777.... 15 G
estoddard@ncu.edu
STODDARD, Judith .... 845-575-3000.. 320 B
judith.stoddard@marist.edu
STODDARD, Kim .... 810-766-2296.. 231 D
kstodd01@baker.edu
STODDARD, Reed, J .... 208-496-9370.. 132 J
stoddardr@byui.edu
STODDARD, Sharon .... 336-750-3339.. 359 B
stoddards@wssu.edu
STODDARD, Troy .... 406-771-4387.. 277 F
troy.stoddard@gfcmsu.edu
STODDART, Jacqueline .... 561-912-1211.... 99 J
jstoddart@evergladesuniversity.edu
STODDART, Judith .... 517-353-3220.. 237 I
stoddart@grd.msu.edu
STOECKER, Judith .... 847-578-8694.. 153 A
judith.stoecker@rosalindfranklin.edu
STOECKER, Nancy .... 630-829-6000.. 135 F
nstoecker@ben.edu
STOECKLEIN, Amanda ..... 660-596-7379.. 272 G
astoecklein1@sfccmo.edu
STOECKLEIN, Denny .... 620-665-3526.. 181 I
stoecklein@hutchcc.edu
STOECKLIN, Dennis, J ..... 503-280-8503.. 391 A
dstoecklin@cu-portland.edu
STOEFFEL, Virginia .... 845-431-8908.. 312 G
virginia.stoeffel@sunydutchess.edu
STOELTING, Diane .... 716-286-8064.. 324 E
ds@niagara.edu
STOFAN, James .... 504-865-5901.. 200 C
jstofan@tulane.edu
STOFFA, Brenna .... 515-961-1543.. 176 H
brenna.stoffa@simpson.edu
STOFFEL, Larry, J .... 317-738-8148.. 160 J
lstoffel@franklincollege.edu
STOFFER, Brian, M .... 312-329-4359.. 148 F
brian.stoffer@moody.edu
STOFFT, Lori .... 928-314-9595.... 11 J
lorraine.stofft@azwestern.edu
STOGNER, Becky .... 806-651-2311.. 469 D
bstogner@mail.wtamu.edu
STOGNER, Brian .... 248-218-2112.. 240 C
bstogner@rc.edu
STOHLER, Christian, S .... 212-305-4511.. 311 E
cs3221@columbia.edu
STOICESCU, Dan .... 410-287-1923.. 206 J
dstoicescu@cecil.edu
STOJKOVIC, Stan .... 414-229-4400.. 520 D
stojkovi@uwm.edu
STOKAN, Matthew .... 724-852-3227.. 423 A
mstokan@waynesburg.edu
STOKELD, Keith .... 803-754-4100.. 429 B
STOKELY, Madlyn .... 212-772-4847.. 308 D
madlyn.stokely@hunter.cuny.edu
STOKELY, Sarah .... 717-477-1395.. 416 A
sestokely@ship.edu
STOKER, Daniel, J .... 260-422-5561.. 162 B
djstoker@indianatech.edu
STOKER, Michael .... 479-880-4040.... 19 F
mstoker@atu.edu
STOKES, Aaron .... 620-862-5252.. 178 F
STOKES, Brandon .... 919-760-8318.. 346 D
kbstokes@meredith.edu
STOKES, Douglas .... 803-535-1393.. 431 I
stokesd@octech.edu
STOKES, Garnett .... 573-882-6596.. 273 E
stokesg@missouri.edu
STOKES, Ginger, C .... 386-312-4074.. 108 B
gingerstokes@sjrstate.edu
STOKES, Jeannine .... 951-487-3151.... 53 D
jstokes@msjc.edu
STOKES, Jenny .... 336-917-5595.. 355 E
jenny.stokes@salem.edu
STOKES, Judi .... 845-431-8405.. 312 G
judi.stokes@sunydutchess.edu
STOKES, Ken .... 770-484-1204.. 124 C
ken.stokes@lutherrice.edu
STOKES, Kenneth .... 505-454-3080.. 300 F
kmstokes@nmhu.edu
STOKES, Madeline .... 251-405-4457...... 2 D
mstokes@bishop.edu
STOKES, Maureen .... 484-365-7250.. 409 B
mstokes@lincoln.edu
STOKES, Michael .... 423-478-6218.. 445 E
mstokes@clevelandstatecc.edu
STOKES, Mickey .... 662-476-5068.. 257 G
mstokes@eastms.edu
STOKES, Scott, M .... 712-362-0439.. 173 G
sstokes@iowalakes.edu
STOKES, Timothy .... 360-596-5206.. 508 A
tstokes@spscc.edu
STOKES-WILSON, Linda .. 708-596-2000.. 154 E
lwilson@ssc.edu
STOLL, Barbara, J .... 713-500-5010.. 477 C
barbara.j.stoll@uth.tmc.edu
STOLL, Kirby, R .... 651-631-5378.. 256 A
krstoll@unwsp.edu
STOLL, Laura, K .... 573-341-6292.. 274 B
lstoll@mst.edu
STOLL, Lisa .... 908-835-9222.. 298 E
lstoll@warren.edu
STOLL, Sherideen, S .... 419-372-8262.. 364 E
sstoll@bgsu.edu
STOLL, William, S .... 314-935-7574.. 274 N
stoll@wustl.edu
STOLLER, Brett .... 309-649-6211.. 155 G
brett.stoller@src.edu
STOLLSTEIMER, Terry ...... 248-370-2160.. 239 K
stollste@oakland.edu
STOLPER, Edward, M .... 626-395-6336.... 30 H
ems@caltech.edu
STOLPER, Lauren, B .... 626-395-2150.... 30 H
lstolper@caltech.edu
STOLTE, Scott .... 702-968-5944.. 285 E
sstolte@roseman.edu
STOLTMAN, Nate .... 507-536-5604.. 251 I
nate.stoltman@rctc.edu
STOLTZ, Adam .... 530-898-6322.... 32 C
astoltz@csuchico.edu

STOLTZ, Jacklyn, C 860-701-5040 88 D stoltz_j@mitchell.edu
STOLTZ, Marlene 406-756-3846 276 E mstoltz@fvcc.edu
STOLTZ-LOIKE, Marian 646-565-6000 337 I mstoltz-loike@touro.edu
STOLTZFUS, Ruth 574-535-7375 161 A ruthas@goshen.edu
STOLZE, Martha, A 630-637-5814 149 H mastolze@noctrl.edu
STOLZER, Donna 908-526-1200 295 A donna.stolzer@raritanval.edu
STOMBER, Richard 973-720-2277 298 G stomberr@wpunj.edu
STOMPER, Jeffrey 847-543-2531 138 C stomper@clcillinois.edu
STONE, Amy, E 803-777-3106 433 F astone@sc.edu
STONE, Audrey 540-362-6363 490 F stoneae@hollins.edu
STONE, Becka 406-265-3711 277 E becka.stone@msun.edu
STONE, Brett 479-979-1474 24 I bastone@ozarks.edu
STONE, Carolyn 561-803-2567 106 C carolyn_stone@pba.edu
STONE, David 815-753-9282 150 A dastone@niu.edu
STONE, David, M 212-854-9962 311 E dms2148@columbia.edu
STONE, Dawn 989-356-9021 230 G stoned@alpenacc.edu
STONE, Denise 503-255-0332 392 G dstone@multnomah.edu
STONE, Dennis 904-680-7703 100 E dstone@fcsl.edu
STONE, Derek 478-387-0386 121 E dstone@gmc.edu
STONE, Elizabeth 202-559-5079 92 C elizabeth.stone@gallaudet.edu
STONE, Emily 925-969-2113 41 I estone@dvc.edu
STONE, Glenice 662-720-7237 260 B gwstone@nemcc.edu
STONE, Greg 918-595-7224 388 F greg.stone@tulsacc.edu
STONE, Harold 312-235-3518 154 C h.stone@shimer.edu
STONE, James 325-670-1258 458 J jstone@hsutx.edu
STONE, Janice 806-720-7270 461 C janice.stone@lcu.edu
STONE, Jenna 315-268-3790 310 B jestone@clarkson.edu
STONE, John 661-362-2271 52 A jstone@masters.edu
STONE, Karen, J 904-620-2828 112 B kstone@unf.edu
STONE, Karin 216-791-5000 366 H karin.stone@cim.edu
STONE, Ken 773-896-2400 137 A kstone@ctschicago.edu
STONE, Kim 612-330-1173 244 I stonek@augsburg.edu
STONE, Mark 979-458-6450 467 D mstone@tamus.edu
STONE, Melissa 302-831-8189 91 F mstone@udel.edu
STONE, Paul 817-599-8324 479 E stone@wc.edu
STONE, Phillip, C 434-381-6210 494 M pstone@sbc.edu
STONE, Polly 601-923-1630 260 E pstone@rts.edu
STONE, Priscilla 802-258-3499 485 A priscilla.stone@sit.edu
STONE, Ralinda 817-598-6276 479 E rstone@wc.edu
STONE, Rhonda 870-248-4000 19 H rhonda.stone@blackrivertech.edu
STONE, Robert 626-256-4673 38 F rstone@coh.org
STONE, Sammy 229-931-2394 127 C sstone@southgatech.edu
STONE, Sandra 941-359-4200 112 E
STONE, Sandra 941-359-4340 112 C sandrastone@usf.edu
STONE, Sarah 919-515-9340 357 B
STONE, Scott 410-225-2398 209 B sstone@mica.edu
STONE, Shelly, T 336-694-8042 351 H shelly.stone@piedmontcc.edu
STONE, Squeak 802-258-3333 485 A squeak.stone@sit.edu
STONE, Staci 270-809-4717 192 A sstone@murraystate.edu
STONE, Steve 859-246-6387 189 B steve.stone@kctcs.edu
STONE, Sue 229-226-1621 128 B sstone@thomasu.edu
STONE, Susan 859-899-2510 188 G sstone@frontier.edu
STONE, Tia 256-331-5279 6 A tstone@nwscc.edu
STONE, Ty 937-512-3107 377 D ty.stone@sinclair.edu
STONECIPHER, Amanda, G 812-941-2674 163 F agstonec@ius.edu
STONECIPHER-FISHER, Kimberly 573-876-7106 272 I ksfisher@stephens.edu
STONEKING, Carole, B 336-841-9168 345 A stoneki@highpoint.edu
STONEKING, Dawn, M 812-464-1863 168 E dstoneking@usi.edu
STONEMAN, Marcia, L 828-694-1804 347 G marcias@blueridge.edu
STONER, Gayla, M 312-996-8586 156 F gayla@uic.edu
STONER, Joey 573-592-5225 275 E joey.stoner@westminster-mo.edu
STONER, Keith 419-755-4810 373 G kstoner@ncstatecollege.edu
STONER, Kevin 845-687-5092 338 F stonerk@sunyulster.edu
STONER, Melinda 402-280-4021 279 H registrar@creighton.edu
STONER, Melinda 402-354-7230 281 F melinda.stoner@methodistcollege.edu
STONESIFER, Cynthia 815-825-9806 144 F cynthia.stonesifer@kishwaukeecollege.edu
STOOKS, George, F 585-245-5663 333 B stooks@geneseo.edu
STOOKSBERRY, Robert 210-436-3301 464 H tstooksberry@stmarytx.edu
STOOPS, Charles 708-366-3288 139 F cstoops@dom.edu
STOOPS, Lynne 831-459-1376 70 F lstoops@ucsc.edu
STOOPS, Melinda, K 508-626-4596 221 E mstoops@framingham.edu
STOOPS, T.J 219-980-6832 163 B tkstoops@iun.edu
STOOS, Barbara 419-251-1702 372 C barbara.stoos@mercycollege.edu
STOPAK, Erin 712-325-3204 174 B estopak@iwcc.edu
STOPFORD, Michael, J 308-865-8246 282 L stopford@unk.edu
STOPPENBRINK, Ken 559-934-2160 74 C kenstoppenbrink@whccd.edu
STOPPENBRINK, Norm 614-837-4088 380 G stoppenbrinkn@valorcollege.edu
STOPPER, Suzanne, T 570-326-3761 413 O sstoppe2@pct.edu
STORCH, Judith 848-932-1689 296 B storch@aesop.rutgers.edu
STORCK, Christine, M 410-777-2219 206 B cmstorck@aacc.edu
STORCK, Eileen 772-462-7805 103 B estorck@irsc.edu
STORCK, Stephen 419-289-5012 363 J sstorck@ashland.edu
STOREY, Amy 315-279-5262 318 C astorey@keuka.edu
STOREY, Bruce 309-796-5129 135 I storeyb@bhc.edu
STOREY, G. Paul 909-869-2951 31 J gpstorey@cpp.edu
STOREY, Karen 906-635-2418 236 J kstorey@lssu.edu
STOREY GROVES, Margaret 802-443-5196 484 F mgroves@middlebury.edu
STORFA, Kristin 503-352-2883 394 C kstorfa@pacificu.edu
STORIE, Cheryl 240-582-5680 212 C financial-affairs@umuc.edu
STORIE, Monique 671-735-2333 530 B mstorie@uguam.uog.edu
STORIE, Monique, C 671-735-2162 530 B mstorie@uguam.uog.edu
STORK, Gilbert, H 805-546-3118 41 L gstork@cuesta.edu
STORLAZZI, Caesar, T 203-432-0371 90 D caesar.storlazzi@yale.edu
STORM, Kathleen, H 509-777-4535 509 H kstorm@whitworth.edu
STORM, Maryam 818-708-9232 49 E
STORMS, Curtis 318-371-3035 196 H curtisstorms@nwltc.edu
STORMS, Joyce, A 616-538-2330 234 D jstorms@gbcol.edu
STORMS, Melanie 352-588-7805 108 C melanie.storms@saintleo.edu
STORR, Robert 203-432-2606 90 D robert.storr@yale.edu
STORRS, Debbie 701-777-2749 360 C debbie.storrs@und.edu
STORRS, Helen 415-405-4343 35 B hstorrs@sfsu.edu
STORRS, Regina, M 313-593-5020 242 A rstorrs@umich.edu
STORY, Adam 509-452-5100 505 H astory@pnwu.edu
STORY, JR., John, H 315-733-4764 338 L jstory@uscny.edu
STORY, Lisa, L 712-324-5061 175 G lstory@nwicc.edu
STORY, Megan 757-631-8101 487 B megan.story@atlanticuniv.edu
STORY, Rick 706-754-7736 125 B rstory@northgatech.edu
STORY, Sarah 830-372-8023 470 C sstory@tlu.edu
STORY-HUFFMAN, Ru 229-931-2259 122 C ru.story-huffman@gsw.edu
STOSBERG, Tobey 816-276-4740 270 H tobey.stosberg@researchcollege.edu
STOSKOPF, Janna, M 701-231-6537 361 A janna.stoskopf@ndsu.edu
STOSS, Kate 765-285-1847 159 B kpstoss@bsu.edu
STOSS, Kate 513-529-3131 372 K stossk@miamioh.edu
STOTHART, Natalie 413-565-1000 215 A nstothart@baypath.edu
STOTLER, Doug 618-468-6200 145 G
STOTO, Robert 609-896-5140 295 B stoto@rider.edu
STOTT, Andrew, M 716-645-5001 331 C vpue@buffalo.edu
STOTT, Larry 801-422-2383 480 C larry_stott@byu.edu
STOTT, Roger, F 443-518-4463 208 C rstott@howardcc.edu
STOTTER, Jennifer 808-932-7641 131 E jstotter@hawaii.edu
STOTTLEMEYER, Rebecca 304-876-5287 513 E bstottle@shepherd.edu
STOTTS, Bob 270-789-5017 187 G restotts@campbellsville.edu
STOTTS, James 404-880-8992 118 K jstotts@cau.edu
STOTTS, Keith 304-865-6005 511 C keith.stotts@ovu.edu
STOTTS, Melissa 701-662-1538 361 E melissa.stotts@lrsc.edu
STOUDENMIRE, Phyllis 803-536-0311 431 I
STOUFFER, Wendy, D 479-575-2711 22 I wstouff@uark.edu
STOUT, Allen 909-593-3511 71 B astout@laverne.edu
STOUT, Chris 248-689-8282 242 F cstout@walshcollege.edu
STOUT, David 732-224-2215 289 I dstout@brookdalecc.edu
STOUT, Keith 612-330-1616 244 I stoutk@augsburg.edu
STOUT, Michael 336-334-4822 350 B mcstout@gtcc.edu
STOUT, Ross 503-370-6911 396 G rstout@willamette.edu
STOUT, Thomas, B 757-822-5230 498 H tstout@tcc.edu
STOVALL, Alfred, J 662-252-8000 260 F ajstovall@rustcollege.edu
STOVALL, Chris 940-397-4273 462 A chris.stovall@mwsu.edu
STOVALL, Jerry 229-931-2562 127 C jstovall@southgatech.edu
STOVALL, Michael 410-386-8206 206 I mstovall@carrollcc.edu
STOVALL, Terri 817-923-1921 466 E tstovall@swbts.edu
STOVALL, Tina 217-234-5250 145 D tstovall@lakeland.cc.il.us
STOVALL, Trena 304-384-6292 513 A tstovall@concord.edu
STOVALL, Tyler 831-459-2696 70 F humanities@ucsc.edu
STOVALL, Vincent 703-284-1612 492 A vstovall@marymount.edu
STOVER, Cheryln 425-602-3093 501 D cstover@bastyr.edu
STOVER, Dennis 877-954-1500 442 D
STOVER, Dennis, L 941-359-4200 112 E
STOVER, Janice 620-441-5247 180 D janice.stover@cowley.edu
STOVER, Kathy, J 402-844-7268 282 B kathy@northeast.edu
STOVER, Lois 703-284-1620 492 A lois.stover@marymount.edu
STOVER, Mark 818-677-2271 34 A mark.stover@csun.edu
STOVER, Mary 207-255-1223 205 C mstover@maine.edu
STOVER, Paul, A 714-449-7461 51 F pstover@ketchum.edu
STOVER, Ronalda, S 803-778-6688 427 G stoverrs@cctech.edu
STOVER, Stacey 734-462-4400 240 H sstover@schoolcraft.edu
STOVER, Teri 903-223-3088 469 C teri.stover@tamut.edu
STOVERINK, Al 870-972-2066 18 J astoverink@astate.edu
STOW, George, B 215-951-1097 407 A stow@lasalle.edu
STOWASSER, Melissa 843-574-6312 433 D melissa.stowasser@tridenttech.edu
STOWE, Brook 718-522-9073 304 D bstowe@asa.edu
STOWE, Cindy 502-456-6504 193 B cstowe@sullivan.edu
STOWE, Gwendolyn 641-472-1110 175 A admissions@mum.edu
STOWE, Lentz 252-940-6306 347 E lentz.stowe@beaufortccc.edu
STOWE, Melissa 205-387-0511 2 B melissa.stowe@bscc.edu
STOWELL, Dale 541-917-4214 392 C stowelld@linnbenton.edu
STOWELL, Joseph, M 616-222-1428 233 A joe.stowell@cornerstone.edu
STOWELL, Michael, B 913-971-3294 183 D mstowell@mnu.edu
STOWERS, Marian 269-337-7192 235 H marian.stowers@kzoo.edu
STOWERS, Rebecca 937-766-7872 365 C stowersr@cedarville.edu
STOWIK, Stanley 401-232-6240 424 K
STRACK, Freda 816-654-7196 266 E fstrack@kcumb.edu
STRADA, Samuel, J 251-460-7189 9 E sstrada@southalabama.edu
STRADER, Bob 325-674-2784 449 J straderb@acu.edu
STRADER, Cynthia 979-230-3119 453 A cynthia.strader@brazosport.edu
STRADER, Scott, C 727-864-8421 98 L stradesc@eckerd.edu
STRAHN-KOLLER, Brooke 319-398-4911 174 I bstrahn@kirkwood.edu
STRAIT, LuAnn 605-882-5284 436 B straitl@lakeareatech.edu
STRAIT, Micah 435-283-7145 482 E micah.strait@snow.edu
STRAITS, Jeffrey 202-885-8684 94 E jstraits@wesleyseminary.edu
STRAKA, Richard 507-389-6621 250 E richard.straka@mnsu.edu
STRAKA, Ronald 952-446-4127 246 D strakar@crown.edu
STRALEY, Leah 619-961-4220 68 A lstraley@tjsl.edu
STRAMPEL, William, D 517-355-9616 237 I strampe3@msu.edu
STRAND, Robert 715-394-8101 521 E
STRANEY, Donald, O 808-932-7348 131 E dstraney@hawaii.edu
STRANG, Bryce, B 503-943-8009 396 B strang@up.edu
STRANGE, Alan 219-864-2400 165 Q astrange@midamerica.edu
STRANGE, Kendra 864-587-4298 433 A strangek@smcsc.edu
STRANGE, Thomas 423-585-2668 447 D thomas.strange@ws.edu
STRANIAK, Kimberly 330-369-3200 378 D kastraniak32@trumbull.edu
STRANO, Kimberly 845-257-3215 331 E lavoiek@newpaltz.edu
STRASENBURGH, David, R 585-395-2385 332 E dstrasen@brockport.edu
STRASNER, Sam 479-498-6045 19 F sstrasner@atu.edu
STRASSER, Nora 316-295-5818 181 B strasser@friends.edu
STRATMAN, Debbie 931-553-0071 442 I debbie.stratman@miller-motte.com
STRATMAN, Jason, L 308-635-6740 283 D stratman@wncc.edu
STRATMAN, Victoria, D 626-395-5940 30 H victoria.stratman@caltech.edu
STRATMANN, Charles, M 904-632-3299 101 G charles.stratmann@fscj.edu
STRATTON, Chris 706-886-6831 128 C cstratton@tfc.edu
STRATTON, Jacob 606-218-5293 194 C jacobstratton@upike.edu
STRATTON, Jonathan 772-546-5534 102 S jonstratton@hsbc.edu
STRATTON, Michael 518-454-5456 311 B strattom@mail.strose.edu
STRAUB, Bernie 843-574-6994 433 D bernie.straub@tridenttech.edu
STRAUB, Dahnja 707-546-4000 42 M dstraub@empirecollege.com

STRUDWICK, Daniel .... 217-228-5432.. 151 F strudda@quincy.edu
STRUEBEL, Philip .... 716-851-1588.. 313 H struebel@ecc.edu
STRULOEFF, Mark .... 503-699-6252.. 392 D mstruloeff@marylhurst.edu
STRUM, Leanne .... 757-352-4172.. 493 E leangar@regent.edu
STRUNK, Brian .... 606-546-1249.. 193 E bstrunk@unionky.edu
STRUNK, Jeffrey .... 859-572-6448.. 192 B strunk@nku.edu
STRUNK, Mary, C .... 518-783-2314.. 330 E strunk@siena.edu
STRUPP, Kindra .... 812-464-1902.. 168 E ksstrupp@usi.edu
STRUPPA, Daniele, C .... 714-997-6611.... 37 F struppa@chapman.edu
STRUSOWSKI, Lisa, S ..... 302-857-1400.... 91 C lstrusow@dtcc.edu
STRUTHERS, Hap .... 757-423-2095.. 489 L
STRYBOS, John .... 210-485-0701.. 450 A jstrybos@alamo.edu
STRYKER, H. Ford .... 814-865-4402.. 412 F hfs2@psu.edu
STRYKER, Joann .... 406-247-5752.. 277 D joann.stryker@msubillings.edu
STRYKER, Joanne .... 401-454-6177.. 426 A jstryker@risd.edu
STRYKER, Marcy .... 518-464-8527.. 314 A mstryker@excelsior.edu
STRYSICK, Michael, P ..... 859-238-5710.. 187 H michael.strysick@centre.edu
STRZEPEK, Katy, A .... 563-333-6113.. 176 D strzepekkatya@sau.edu
STUARD, Avis .... 504-520-7583.. 202 C astuard@xula.edu
STUART, Alesia, K .... 251-578-1313..... 6 C akstuart@rstc.edu
STUART, Barbara .... 802-586-7711.. 485 C bstuart@sterlingcollege.edu
STUART, Carol, M .... 252-334-2010.. 346 F carol.stuart@macuniversity.edu
STUART, Cheryl .... 937-775-2556.. 381 H cheryl.stuart@wright.edu
STUART, Cledis, D .... 870-235-4046.... 22 F cdstuart@sauniag.edu
STUART, Dana .... 765-641-4114.. 158 J dsstuart@anderson.edu
STUART, Diana .... 573-518-2100.. 268 E diana@mineralarea.edu
STUART, D'Anne .... 575-646-2431.. 300 J dstuart@nmsu.edu
STUART, Eddie .... 910-962-3626.. 358 D stuarte@uncw.edu
STUART, Forrest, M .... 864-294-2204.. 430 C forrest.stuart@furman.edu
STUART, G. Rob .... 216-987-4757.. 367 E g.rob.stuart@tri-c.edu
STUART, Gail, W .... 843-792-3941.. 431 A stuartg@musc.edu
STUART, James .... 630-617-3456.. 140 C james.stuart@elmhurst.edu
STUART, John, G .... 903-927-3326.. 479 K jstuart@wileyc.edu
STUART, Kathryn .... 440-775-6789.. 374 C kathryn.stuart@oberlin.edu
STUART, Lofton, K .... 865-974-2508.. 448 D jstuart@tennessee.edu
STUART, Nancy, M .... 860-768-5135.... 89 G nstuart@hartford.edu
STUART, Ramon .... 478-825-6330.. 120 F stuartt@fvsu.edu
STUART, Roberta, P .... 413-559-5724.. 219 C
STUART, Susan .... 913-288-7265.. 182 C sstuart@kckcc.edu
STUBAUS, Karen, R .... 848-932-4889.. 296 B stubaus@oldqueens.rutgers.edu
STUBAUS, Karen, R .... 848-932-4889.. 295 F stubaus@oldqueens.rutgers.edu
STUBBE, Alethea, F .... 712-324-5061.. 175 G aletheas@nwicc.edu
STUBBEMAN, Nancy .... 513-569-1501.. 366 D nancy.stubbeman@cincinnatistate.edu
STUBBINGS, Donald .... 913-758-6196.. 185 F donald.stubbingsr@stmary.edu
STUBBLEFIELD, Jay .... 912-650-6215.. 127 D rstubblefield@southuniversity.edu
STUBBLEFIELD, Kellyanne .... 803-786-3723.. 429 A kstubblefield@columbiasc.edu
STUBBLEFIELD, Michael, A .... 225-771-3890.. 199 H michael_stubblefield@subr.edu
STUBBS, Brent .... 912-443-5827.. 126 G bstubbs@savannahtech.edu
STUBBS, Gail .... 617-287-5500.. 220 G gail.stubbs@umb.edu
STUBBS, Loretta .... 901-435-1680.. 441 C loretta_stubbs@loc.edu
STUBBS, Michelle .... 912-486-7865.. 125 E mstubbs@ogeecheetech.edu
STUBBS, Robert .... 303-492-8631.... 83 K robert.stubbsd@colorado.edu
STUBBS, Sandra .... 256-372-5230....... 1 A sandra.stubbs@aamu.edu
STUBBS, Sidney, J .... 334-833-4354...... 4 D sstubbs@hawks.huntingdon.edu
STUBBS, Steve .... 706-864-1798.. 128 F steven.stubbs@ung.edu
STUCHELL, Tina .... 330-823-2844.. 379 F stuchetm@mountunion.edu
STUCK, Helen .... 315-568-3133.. 323 A hstuck@nycc.edu
STUCK, Kelley .... 573-882-2011.. 273 D fuemmelert@umsystem.edu
STUCK, Shelly .... 315-568-3111.. 323 A sstuck@nycc.edu
STUCKENBRUCK, Emily ... 715-365-4481.. 524 C estuckenbruck@nicoletcollege.edu
STUCKEY, Dennis .... 612-330-1713.. 244 I stuckey@augsburg.edu
STUCKEY, Jon, C .... 717-766-2511.. 410 J jstuckey@messiah.edu
STUCKEY, Julie .... 210-434-6711.. 463 C jstuckey@lake.ollusa.edu
STUCKEY, Mike .... 816-501-2414.. 262 G mike.stuckey@avila.edu
STUCKEY, Mike .... 740-389-4636.. 372 B stuckeym@mtc.edu
STUCKEY, Sheila, A .... 502-597-6852.. 191 B sheila.stuckey@kysu.edu
STUCKEY, Thomas, L ...... 419-267-1310.. 374 A tstuckey@northweststate.edu
STUCKLY, JR., Elton, E ... 254-867-3963.. 470 F elton.stuckly@tstc.edu
STUCKY, Amy .... 765-998-5314.. 167 C amstucky@taylor.edu
STUCKY, Duane .... 618-536-3475.. 154 H dustucky@siu.edu
STUCKY, Gail .... 316-284-5363.. 179 A gstucky@bethelks.edu
STUCKY, Kent, D .... 260-665-4311.. 167 E stuckyk@trine.edu
STUDDS, Susan, M .... 202-231-3322.. 528 C susan.studds@dodiis.mil
STUDEBAKER, Eric .... 208-562-3247.. 133 F ericstudebaker@cwidaho.cc
STUDENC, Bill .... 828-227-7122.. 359 A bstudenc@wcu.edu
STUDER, Mary Ann .... 419-783-2553.. 368 A mstuder@defiance.edu
STUDER, Nancy .... 219-866-6150.. 166 J nancys@saintjoe.edu
STUDWELL, II, Raymond, W .... 540-828-5660.. 487 H cstudwel@bridgewater.edu
STUEBNER, Susan, D ...... 603-526-3451.. 285 L sue.stuebner@colby-sawyer.edu
STUFANO, Thomas .... 865-882-4512.. 447 A stufanotj@roanestate.edu
STUFF, Jerry .... 903-566-7431.. 477 B jstuff@uttyler.edu
STUFFLEBEAN, Ernie .... 816-415-5969.. 275 F stuffle@william.jewell.edu
STUFFLICK, William .... 217-641-4956.. 143 H wstufflick@jwcc.edu
STUGELMAYER, Lesley, A .... 608-796-3808.. 522 O lastugelmayer@viterbo.edu
STUHR, Eloise, D .... 713-743-8165.. 473 E edstuhr@central.uh.edu
STUHR, Eloise, D .... 713-743-8165.. 473 F edstuhr@central.uh.edu
STUIFBERGEN, Alexa, M . 512-471-4100.. 476 B astuifbergen@mail.utexas.edu
STUKANE, Edward .... 201-216-3472.. 297 B edward.stukane@stevens.edu
STULL, David .... 415-503-6230.... 61 C jseaman@sfcm.edu
STULL, Megan .... 563-588-6377.. 170 F megan.stull@clarke.edu
STULL, Robert, W .... 915-747-5347.. 476 D rstull@utep.edu
STULL, William .... 215-204-5022.. 420 B
STULTS, Karen .... 410-225-2438.. 209 B kstults@mica.edu
STULTS, Randy .... 205-387-0511...... 2 B randy.stults@bscc.edu
STUMB, Paul .... 615-547-1234.. 439 H pstumb@cumberland.edu
STUMBO, Christine .... 606-368-6125.. 186 B christinestumbo@alc.edu
STUMBRIS, Steven, V ...... 570-577-3791.. 398 L steven.stumbris@bucknell.edu
STUMNE, James .... 651-779-3918.. 249 A james.stumne@century.edu
STUMO, Karl, A .... 218-299-3004.. 246 A kstumo@cord.edu
STUMP, Chellye .... 334-347-2623....... 3 H cstump@escc.edu
STUMP, Colleen .... 301-687-3171.. 212 F cstump@frostburg.edu
STUMP, Doug .... 540-665-5445.. 494 B jstump14@su.edu
STUMP, Linda, J .... 352-392-5445.. 112 A lstump@ufl.edu
STUMP, Mark .... 912-443-5706.. 126 G mstump@savannahtech.edu
STUMP, Sandra .... 610-921-7205.. 396 H stump@albright.edu
STUMP, Tom .... 406-994-2661.. 277 C stump@montana.edu
STUMPF, Michelle .... 814-262-6436.. 413 P mstumpf@pennhighlands.edu
STUNTZ, Jane .... 419-251-1314.. 372 C jane.stuntz@mercycollege.edu
STUOPIS, Cecilia Warpinski .... 617-253-1774.. 225 A
STUPAR, Eric, H .... 202-231-2767.. 528 C eric.stupar@dodiis.mil
STURCH, Patty, J .... 740-264-5591.. 368 D psturch@egcc.edu
STURDEVANT, Peggy .... 641-784-5125.. 172 G peggys@graceland.edu
STURDIVANT, Alvin .... 206-296-6066.. 507 E sturdial@seattleu.edu
STURDY, Ryan .... 785-460-5548.. 180 C ryan.sturdy@colbycc.edu
STURE, Linda .... 907-563-7575.... 10 A
STURGEON, Kathy, R ...... 217-443-8805.. 139 B ksturgeon@dacc.edu
STURGEON, Paul .... 270-706-8639.. 189 C paul.sturgeon@kctcs.edu
STURGEON, Stacy .... 435-797-1266.. 482 B stacy.sturgeon@usu.edu
STURGEON, Timothy, A .. 502-272-8131.. 187 A tsturgeon@bellarmine.edu
STURGILL, David .... 859-246-6896.. 189 B david.sturgill@kctcs.edu
STURGIS, Maureen .... 603-899-4165.. 287 A sturgism@franklinpierce.edu
STURGIS, Paul .... 573-592-4463.. 275 G paul.sturgis@williamwoods.edu
STURGIS, Thomas, C ...... 601-877-6138.. 256 F tsturgis@alcorn.edu
STURM, James, P .... 716-926-8935.. 316 B jsturm@hilbert.edu
STURM, Joel .... 212-410-8047.. 323 C jsturm@nycpm.edu
STURM, Joey .... 337-482-6449.. 201 D joey.sturm@louisiana.edu
STURM, Neal, M .... 973-443-8689.. 291 J sturm@fdu.edu
STURM-SMITH, Melissa .. 515-271-2835.. 171 K melissa.sturm-smith@drake.edu
STURRUP, Daniel, H .... 207-581-1799.. 204 H dsturrup@maine.edu
STURRUS, Teresa .... 231-777-0251.. 238 G teresa.sturrus@muskegoncc.edu
STURTZ, Alan, J .... 860-913-2034...... 87 H asturtz@goodwin.edu
STURTZ, Carma .... 641-628-5269.. 170 E sturtzc@central.edu
STURZENBECKER, Diane . 716-488-3021.. 317 E financialaid@jamestownbusinesscollege.edu
STUTES, Ann, B .... 806-291-1066.. 479 D stutesa@wbu.edu
STUTEVILLE, Rebekkah .... 816-584-6597.. 270 D rebekkah.stuteville@park.edu
STUTTS, Rosie .... 805-289-6313.... 73 F rstutts@vcccd.edu
STUTZMAN, Dallas .... 620-327-8110.. 181 G dallass@hesston.edu
STUTZMAN, Karl .... 574-296-6233.. 158 H
STUTZMAN, Timothy .... 540-432-4197.. 488 K timothy.stutzman@emu.edu
STYER, Daniel .... 916-558-2201.... 51 D styerd@scc.losrios.edu
STYLES, Elise .... 864-977-7018.. 431 G elise.styles@ngu.edu
STYLES, Julie .... 864-977-1246.. 431 G julie.styles@ngu.edu
STYRON, Kelli .... 254-968-9141.. 467 F styron@tarleton.edu
SU, John, J .... 414-288-3476.. 517 I john.su@marquette.edu
SU, Nancy .... 212-217-3640.. 314 B nancy_su@fitnyc.edu
SU, Ren Jeng .... 503-725-8393.. 394 G renjengs@pdx.edu
SU, Susan .... 516-739-1545.. 323 D records@nyctcm.edu
SUAREZ, Angelica .... 619-482-6315.... 66 E asuarez@swccd.edu
SUAREZ, Carmen .... 503-725-5969.. 394 G csuarez@pdx.edu
SUAREZ, Doris, L .... 646-664-9109.. 306 M doris.suarez@cuny.edu
SUAREZ, Enrique .... 787-850-9107.. 538 B enrique.suarez@upr.edu
SUAREZ, Jeri, L .... 540-362-6000.. 490 F jsuarez@hollins.edu
SUAREZ, Michelle .... 618-453-5855.. 154 I msuarez@siu.edu
SUAREZ-ESPINAL, Cynthia .... 718-289-5914.. 307 C cynthia.suarez-espinal@bcc.cuny.edu
SUAREZ-HERRERO, Ismael .... 787-863-2390.. 533 K ismael.suarez@fajardo.inter.edu
SUAREZ-OROZCO, Marcelo, M .... 310-825-8308.... 69 D mms-o@gseis.ucla.edu
SUBBASWAMY, Kumble, R .... 413-545-2211.. 220 F chancellor@umass.edu
SUBBIONDO, Joseph, L .. 415-575-6105.... 30 G jsubbiondo@ciis.edu
SUBE, Bob .... 805-678-5821.... 73 E bsube@vcccd.edu
SUBER, Jennifer .... 601-477-4040.. 258 E jennifer.suber@jcjc.edu
SUBER, Megan .... 704-878-4395.. 351 D msuber@mitchellcc.edu
SUBLETT, Roger, H .... 513-861-6400.. 378 E roger.sublett@myunion.edu
SUBLETTE, Gaylah .... 660-626-2860.. 262 A gsublette@atsu.edu
SUBRAMANIAN, Ashok ... 479-788-7807.... 23 A ashok.subramanian@uafs.edu
SUBRAMANIAN, Sandhya .... 440-775-8401.. 374 C sandhya.subramanian@oberlin.edu
SUCH, Tami, L .... 701-788-4716.. 360 E tami.such@mayvillestate.edu
SUCHANIC, Angela, C ..... 302-356-6924.... 91 I angela.c.suchanic@wilmu.edu
SUCHON, Donnetta .... 281-425-6400.. 460 I dsuchon@lee.edu
SUCY, Alison, P .... 207-530-3003.. 204 G alison.sucy@maine.edu
SUDAK, Sarah .... 615-898-5342.. 444 G sarah.sudak@mtsu.edu
SUDDICK, Lori .... 920-498-5401.. 524 E lori.suddick@nwtc.edu
SUDDUTH, David .... 864-455-8213.. 434 D dsudduth@greenvillemed.sc.edu
SUDEIKIS, Barbara .... 269-965-3931.. 236 A sudeikisb@kellogg.edu
SUDELA, Tiffany .... 360-779-9993.. 505 B tsudela@ncad.edu
SUDERMAN, Bonnie .... 661-722-6300.... 27 B bsuderman@avc.edu
SUDHAKAR, Rama .... 212-237-8628.. 308 E rsudhakar@jjay.cuny.edu
SUDHAKAR, Samuel .... 909-537-5100.... 34 C ssudhakar@csusb.edu
SUDKAMP, Thomas, A .... 937-775-3035.. 381 H thomas.sudkamp@wright.edu
SUDLER, Kimberly, R ...... 302-857-7036.... 90 F krsudler@desu.edu
SUDLOW, Jennifer .... 215-572-4483.. 397 G sudlowj@arcadia.edu
SUDOL, Mary .... 845-434-5750.. 336 H msudol@sullivan.suny.edu
SUDTELGTE, Beau .... 712-279-1633.. 170 B beau.sudtelgte@briarcliff.edu
SUEBERT, Jack .... 305-809-3195.. 100 N jack.seubert@fkcc.edu
SUELFLOW, Sara, C .... 651-696-6307.. 247 I suelflow@macalester.edu
SUERTH, Matthew, P .... 815-224-0550.. 143 C matt_suerth@ivcc.edu
SUESS, Jack, J .... 410-455-2582.. 211 G jack@umbc.edu
SUESSER, John, P .... 724-346-2073.. 399 B john.suesser@bc3.edu
SUFFEL, Charles .... 201-216-8031.. 297 B csuffel@stevens.edu
SUGALSKI, Mark .... 315-279-5267.. 318 C
SUGALSKI, Noelle .... 302-857-1072.... 91 C nsugalsk@dtcc.edu
SUGARMAN, Roger, P ..... 859-257-7989.. 193 G rpsuga0@email.uky.edu
SUGG, Donald .... 870-743-3000.... 21 C dsugg@northark.edu
SUGG, Jason .... 252-328-6787.. 356 C suggj@ecu.edu
SUGGS, Amber .... 618-634-3236.. 154 B ambers@shawneecc.edu
SUGGS, Benny .... 919-515-3375.. 357 B benny_suggs@ncsu.edu
SUGGS, Sheena .... 252-862-1316.. 352 D srsuggs9932@roanokechowan.edu
SUGIMOTO, Lara .... 808-845-9235.. 132 A larahs@hawaii.edu
SUGRUE, Seana .... 239-280-1625.... 95 Q seana.sugrue@avemaria.edu
SUH, Duckin .... 262-554-2010.. 518 B duckin_suh@yahoo.com
SUH, Eun Ja .... 714-525-0088.... 45 F

SUNDARAM, Sridhar .... 727-873-4700.. 112 D
sundarams@usf.edu
SUNDAY, Diana .... 209-588-5389.... 75 J
SUNDBERG, Lori .... 847-735-5034.. 145 B
lsundber@lakeforest.edu
SUNDBERG, Lori, H .... 847-735-5034.. 145 B
lsundber@lakeforest.edu
SUNDBERG, Lori, L .... 309-341-5214.. 136 C
lsundberg@sandburg.edu
SUNDBORG, SJ,
Stephen, V .... 206-296-1891.. 507 E
sundborg@seattleu.edu
SUNDBY-THORP, Valerie . 360-596-5451.. 508 A
vsundby-thorp@spscc.edu
SUNDERLAND, JR.,
Richard .... 304-724-3700.. 510 E
rsunderland@apus.edu
SUNDERMAN, Rick .... 614-947-6605.. 369 A
rick.sunderman@franklin.edu
SUNDERMEIER, Elisabeth 816-472-4852.. 266 D
SUNDGREN, Donald, E ... 434-982-5834.. 495 H
des5j@virginia.edu
SUNDQUIST, Mike .... 209-575-6081.... 76 A
sundquistm@mjc.edu
SUNDSETH, Robin .... 541-880-2273.. 391 F
sundseth@klamathcc.edu
SUNDSMO, Alecia, D ...... 717-245-1663.. 402 D
sundsmoa@dickinson.edu
SUNDSTEDT, Bernard ...... 815-226-3371.. 152 G
bsunstedt@rockford.edu
SUNDSTEDT, Casey .... 847-628-1561.. 144 B
csundstedt@judsonu.edu
SUNDSTROM, Michelle ... 330-823-2568.. 379 F
sundstme@mountunion.edu
SUNDSTROM, Sandy .... 503-777-7224.. 394 I
sundstrom@reed.edu
SUNDY, Carolyn .... 606-589-3052.. 190 G
carolyn.sundy@kctcs.edu
SUNG, Donghyun .... 714-533-3946.... 35 E
davidit@calums.edu
SUNG, Joshua .... 213-252-5100.... 24 K
jsung@alu.edu
SUNGJI KIM, Howard ..... 562-622-3368.... 45 C
SUNI, Ellen, Y .... 816-235-1007.. 273 F
sunie@umkc.edu
SUNLEAF, Arthur, W .... 563-588-7959.. 174 K
arthur.sunleaf@loras.edu
SUNNYGARD, John .... 303-807-9956.... 84 A
john.sunnygard@ucdenver.edu
SUNQUIST, Scott, W .... 626-584-5265.... 44 G
sunquist@fuller.edu
SUNSER, James .... 585-345-6812.. 315 C
jmsunser@genesee.edu
SUNSHINE, Brian .... 254-526-7161.. 454 A
brian.sunshine@ctcd.edu
SUNSHINE, Phyllis .... 410-337-6046.. 207 H
psunshine@goucher.edu
SUOMI, Sue .... 864-977-2094.. 431 G
susan.suomi@ngu.edu
SUOREZ, Paula .... 760-384-6298.... 47 K
psuorez@cerrocoso.edu
SUPAK, Brian .... 254-298-8609.. 467 B
brian.supak@templejc.edu
SUPER, Joseph, F .... 304-457-6484.. 510 B
superjf@ab.edu
SUPERNAW, Robert, B .... 704-233-8015.. 359 H
supernaw@wingate.edu
SUPINSKI, Jessica .... 425-235-2352.. 506 F
jsupinski@rtc.edu
SUPLER, Robin .... 954-262-4349.. 105 J
rsupler@nsu.nova.edu
SUPOWITZ, Paul, A .... 412-624-2901.. 421 G
psupowit@pitt.edu
SUPPELSA, Robert, E .... 310-233-4051.... 49 I
suppelre@lahc.edu
SUPPLEE, JR., Jack .... 859-257-8288.. 193 G
supplee@uky.edu
SUPPLEE, Janice .... 937-766-8319.. 365 C
suppleej@cedarville.edu
SUPURGECI, Jonna .... 605-668-1515.. 436 D
jsupurgeci@mtmc.edu
SUR, Sarah Gilman .... 808-235-7435.. 132 E
sgilman@hawaii.edu
SURATY-CLARKE,
Mercedes .... 713-743-1185.. 473 F
msclarke@uh.edu
SURBAUGH, Joyce .... 304-734-6603.. 511 M
joyce.surbaugh@bridgevalley.edu
SURBECK, III, Carlton, E 410-337-6127.. 207 H
carlton.surbeck@goucher.edu
SURBROOK, Will .... 619-388-6589.... 60 E
wsurbroo@sdccd.edu
SURDOVEL, Grace .... 570-408-3102.. 423 G
grace.surdovel@wilkes.edu
SURENDER, Sheelu, M .... 316-978-5337.. 185 J
sheelu.surender@wichita.edu
SURESH, Subra .... 412-268-2201.. 400 D
suresh@andrew.cmu.edu
SURGALA, David, J .... 570-577-3811.. 398 L
dsurgala@bucknell.edu

SURGEONER, James, W .. 610-799-1658.. 408 G
jsurgeoner@lccc.edu
SURGES, Rebecca .... 414-930-3472.. 518 F
surgesr@mtmary.edu
SURLS, Courtney .... 202-885-1334.... 91 J
surls@american.edu
SURMA, Barry .... 814-472-3200.. 418 F
bsurma@francis.edu
SUROWIEC, Barbara .... 203-332-5049.... 86 D
bsurowiec@hcc.commnet.edu
SURRATT, Jacob .... 276-223-4729.. 499 C
jsurratt@wcc.vccs.edu
SURRELL, Matt .... 662-472-9178.. 258 B
msurrell@holmescc.edu
SURRETT, Caron .... 828-884-8261.. 342 C
caron@brevard.edu
SURRIDGE, Jack, F .... 773-244-5676.. 149 I
jsurridge@northpark.edu
SURRIDGE, Mary, K .... 773-244-6264.. 149 I
msurridge@northpark.edu
SURRUSCO, Anet .... 203-576-5675.... 89 A
asurrusco@stvincentscollege.edu
SUSANA, Gil .... 619-961-4316.... 68 A
gsusana@tjsl.edu
SUSANKA, Thomas, J ..... 805-525-4417.... 67 J
tsusanka@thomasaquinas.edu
SUSANTO, Yuliana .... 502-597-7014.. 191 B
yuliana.susanto@kysu.edu
SUSHINSKY, David, M .... 240-895-4282.. 210 E
dmsushinksy@smcm.edu
SUSICK, Timothy .... 724-938-4056.. 414 E
susick@calu.edu
SUSKI-LENCZEWSKI,
Anna .... 860-832-1757.... 85 F
lenczewskia@mail.ccsu.edu
SUSMAN, Catherine, D .... 541-346-1255.. 395 G
susman@uoregon.edu
SUSMAN, Jeffrey, L .... 330-325-6122.. 373 H
jsusman@neomed.edu
SUSMANN, Phillip .... 802-485-2213.. 484 H
susmann@norwich.edu
SUSMARSKI, Aaron .... 814-860-5101.. 407 D
asusmarski@lecom.edu
SUSSENBACH, Michelle ... 618-664-7025.. 140 I
michelle.sussenbach@greenville.edu
SUSSKIND, Gary .... 718-953-5889.. 337 D
ohaleitorah@optonline.net
SUSSMAN, David .... 503-491-7258.. 392 F
david.sussman@mhcc.edu
SUSSMAN, Nan, M .... 718-982-2315.. 307 F
nan.sussman@csi.cuny.edu
SUSSMAN, Ronny .... 818-883-9002.... 73 A
SUSSWEIN, Gary, J .... 512-471-4945.. 476 B
susswein@austin.utexas.edu
SUSTAIRE, Karan .... 903-923-2296.. 457 G
ksustaire@etbu.edu
SUSTICH, Andrew .... 870-972-2025.... 18 J
sustich@astate.edu
SUTCH, Laurie .... 781-891-2103.. 215 F
lsutch@bentley.edu
SUTER, Cindy .... 419-448-2090.. 369 G
csuter@heidelberg.edu
SUTER, Vicki .... 541-552-8290.. 395 A
suterv@sou.edu
SUTERA, Paul, J .... 914-637-2710.. 317 B
psutera@iona.edu
SUTERA, Tom .... 360-538-4207.. 504 B
tom.sutera@ghc.edu
SUTHERLAND, David .... 218-879-0816.. 249 C
dsutherland@fdltcc.edu
SUTHERLAND, David .... 501-450-1254.... 20 F
sutherlandd@hendrix.edu
SUTHERLAND, Diane .... 864-231-2000.. 427 B
dsutherland@andersonuniversity.edu
SUTHERLAND, Jim .... 678-839-6410.. 129 E
sutherla@westga.edu
SUTHERLAND, Kathleen .. 973-408-3000.. 291 B
ksutherl@drew.edu
SUTHERLAND, Richard .... 989-358-7368.. 230 G
sutherlr@alpenacc.edu
SUTHERLAND, Richard .... 740-392-6868.. 373 D
richard.sutherland@mvnu.edu
SUTHERLAND, Ronald ...... 765-998-5118.. 167 C
rnsutherl@taylor.edu
SUTHERLAND, Shari .... 319-363-1323.. 175 D
ssutherland@mtmercy.edu
SUTHERLAND, Timothy ... 219-980-6946.. 163 B
sutherla@iun.edu
SUTHERLAND, Tricia .... 712-274-6400.. 177 I
tricia.sutherland@witcc.edu
SUTHERLIN, Lea .... 314-340-3383.. 265 H
sutherlinl@hssu.edu
SUTKOWSKI, Ernest, H ... 914-831-0343.. 311 C
SUTKUS, Janel .... 412-268-8729.. 400 D
jsutkus@cmu.edu
SUTLIFF, Danielle .... 912-260-4419.. 127 B
dani.sutliff@sgsc.edu
SUTLIFF, Michael .... 714-432-5122.... 39 G
msutliff@occ.cccd.edu
SUTLIFF, Michael .... 714-432-0202.... 39 G
msutliff@occ.cccd.edu

SUTLIVE, Charles .... 404-962-3053.. 129 F
charles.sutlive@usg.edu
SUTPHEN, Debra .... 916-660-7502.... 64 F
dsutphen@sierracollege.edu
SUTTER, Brian .... 712-325-3328.. 174 B
bsutter@iwcc.edu
SUTTER, Crystal .... 217-228-5432.. 151 F
suttecr@quincy.edu
SUTTER, Frankie, K .... 910-592-8081.. 352 H
fsutter@sampsoncc.edu
SUTTER, Thaddeus .... 309-556-3059.. 143 D
tsutter@iwu.edu
SUTTERFIELD, Shirley ...... 251-442-2414...... 9 A
ssutterfield@umobile.edu
SUTTLE, J. Lloyd .... 203-432-4453.... 90 D
j.suttle@yale.edu
SUTTMEIER, Bruce .... 503-768-7174.. 392 A
bruces@lclark.edu
SUTTON, Barbara .... 773-298-3504.. 153 H
sutton@sxu.edu
SUTTON, Barbara, B .... 252-335-3224.. 356 D
bbsutton@ecsu.edu
SUTTON, Bob .... 847-866-3921.. 140 G
bob.sutton@garrett.edu
SUTTON, Cynthia .... 314-392-2291.. 268 F
suttonc@mobap.edu
SUTTON, David .... 254-968-9510.. 467 F
sutton@tarleton.edu
SUTTON, Deborah .... 252-527-6223.. 350 H
dsutton@lenoircc.edu
SUTTON, Deborah, S .... 252-527-6223.. 350 H
dsutton@lenoircc.edu
SUTTON, Dennis .... 910-296-2575.. 350 F
dsutton@jamessprunt.edu
SUTTON, Ellen .... 630-942-2353.. 138 B
suttone@cod.edu
SUTTON, Gentry .... 918-335-6285.. 386 F
gsutton@okwu.edu
SUTTON, Jama .... 865-774-5800.. 447 D
jama.sutton@ws.edu
SUTTON, Judith .... 304-485-5487.. 511 B
jsutton@msc.edu
SUTTON, Kay .... 309-690-6886.. 141 F
ksutton@icc.edu
SUTTON, Kenneth, W ...... 410-778-7269.. 213 E
ksutton2@washcoll.edu
SUTTON, Lawrence .... 724-805-2402.. 419 B
lawrence.sutton@stvincent.edu
SUTTON, Lynn .... 336-758-5480.. 359 E
suttonls@wfu.edu
SUTTON, Melinda .... 662-915-7705.. 261 B
mjsutton@olemiss.edu
SUTTON, Michael .... 909-607-3562.... 38 J
mike.sutton@cms.claremont.edu
SUTTON, Nancy .... 217-351-2402.. 151 B
nsutton@parkland.edu
SUTTON, R. Anderson ...... 808-956-8818.. 131 F
rasutton@hawaii.edu
SUTTON, Rick .... 334-699-2266...... 1 B
SUTTON, Robert, E .... 509-452-5100.. 505 H
rsutton@pnwu.edu
SUTTON, Ronald .... 813-419-5100.. 243 I
suttonr@cooley.edu
SUTTON, Rosemary .... 425-352-8255.. 501 J
rsutton@cascadia.edu
SUTTON, Stephanie .... 440-365-5222.. 371 H
SUTTON, Ty .... 317-940-9620.. 159 K
tlsutton@butler.edu
SUTTON-COLLIER, Kayla . 910-892-3178.. 344 I
ksutton@heritagebiblecollege.edu
SUTTON GERBER,
Ronette .... 910-521-6268.. 358 C
ronette.gerber@uncp.edu
SUTTON-HAYWOOD,
Marilyn .... 704-463-1360.. 354 F
marilyn.sutton-haywood@pfeiffer.edu
SUTTON-SMITH, Leslie .... 973-655-4376.. 293 A
suttonsmithl@mail.montclair.edu
SUTTON-WALLACE,
Pamela, M .... 434-924-9308.. 495 H
ps5gb@virginia.edu
SUTTON-YOUNG,
Tasheka .... 718-368-5109.. 308 F
tasheka.sutton-young@kbcc.cuny.edu
SUTYAK, John .... 508-286-3987.. 229 F
sutyak_john@wheatoncollege.edu
SUTZKO, Christopher ...... 570-208-5874.. 406 J
christophersutzko@kings.edu
SUZOR, Michael, J .... 413-755-4044.. 224 G
msuzor@stcc.edu
SUZOW, Bo .... 213-738-6762.... 66 F
mis@swlaw.edu
SUZUKI, Joyce .... 707-664-4470.... 35 D
joyce.suzuki@sonoma.edu
SUZUKI, Takeo .... 423-425-4759.. 448 F
takeo-suzuki@utc.edu
SU'ESU'E, Jessie .... 684-699-9155.. 529 E
j.suesue@amsamoa.edu
SVACINA, Jean, M .... 443-518-4807.. 208 C
jsvacina@howardcc.edu

SVANDA, Gary .... 402-559-4432.. 283 A
gsvanda@unmc.edu
SVEC, Andrew .... 218-281-8438.. 255 E
asvec@umn.edu
SVEI, Yehuda .... 215-477-1000.. 420 A
talmudicalyeshiva@yahoo.com
SVERID, Julie .... 517-338-3322.. 232 F
SVETE, Lee, J .... 574-631-5200.. 168 B
svete.1@nd.edu
SVETLIK, Brenda .... 361-570-4823.. 474 C
svetlikb@uhv.edu
SVILAR, Kendra, E .... 216-397-6630.. 370 H
ksvilar@jcu.edu
SVOBODA, Angela, M .... 512-448-8622.. 464 G
asvoboda@stedwards.edu
SWAFFORD, Denise .... 239-489-9358.. 101 F
denise.swafford@fsw.edu
SWAFFORD, Jeanna, C ..... 731-881-7629.. 448 G
jswafford@utm.edu
SWAGER, Kendra .... 804-752-7374.. 493 C
kendraswager@rmc.edu
SWAGER, Sarah .... 509-963-1515.. 501 K
swagers@cwu.edu
SWAID, Samar .... 501-370-5335.... 21 G
sswaid@philander.edu
SWAIDAN, Christina .... 413-572-5374.. 222 E
cswaidan@westfield.ma.edu
SWAILS, Joel .... 706-245-7226.. 120 D
jswails@ec.edu
SWAIM, Charles .... 757-825-2952.. 498 G
swaimc@tncc.edu
SWAIM, Kevin, C .... 765-361-6252.. 169 C
swaimk@wabash.edu
SWAIN, Carole .... 925-631-4695.... 59 I
cswain@stmarys-ca.edu
SWAIN, Chalimar, L .... 801-581-8876.. 481 M
c.swain@ic.utah.edu
SWAIN, Corliss .... 507-786-3277.. 254 P
swain@stolaf.edu
SWAIN, Cristal .... 970-351-1142.... 84 C
cristal.wain@unco.edu
SWAIN, Edgar .... 443-518-4974.. 208 C
eswain@howardcc.edu
SWAIN, Emily, L .... 304-367-4015.. 513 B
emily.swain@fairmontstate.edu
SWAIN, Eric .... 559-443-8523.... 67 C
eric.swain@fresnocitycollege.edu
SWAIN, Heather, C .... 517-355-2262.. 237 I
heather.swain@cabs.msu.edu
SWAIN, Jackie .... 406-275-4755.. 278 E
jackie_swain@skc.edu
SWAIN, Jeffrey, D .... 305-626-3674.. 101 A
jeffrey.swain@fmuniv.edu
SWAIN, Robert .... 813-881-0007.. 109 A
rswain@sbtampa.com
SWAIN, Rodney .... 414-229-5895.. 520 D
rswain@uwm.edu
SWAIN, Sarah .... 910-893-1236.. 342 F
swain@campbell.edu
SWAIN, Stuart, G .... 207-255-1342.. 205 C
sswain@maine.edu
SWAIN, Valerie, T .... 443-412-2344.. 208 A
vswain@harford.edu
SWALGA, Dan .... 412-392-3911.. 417 F
dswalga@pointpark.edu
SWALLOW, John, R .... 931-598-1101.. 443 O
jrswallo@sewanee.edu
SWALLOW, Steven .... 937-529-2201.. 378 F
slswallow@united.edu
SWALWELL, Joe .... 405-682-1611.. 385 D
jswalwell@occc.edu
SWAN, Beth Ann .... 215-503-8057.. 420 E
bethann.swan@jefferson.edu
SWAN, Bobi .... 503-493-6526.. 391 A
bswan@cu-portland.edu
SWAN, Deba .... 254-526-1237.. 454 A
deborah.swan@ctcd.edu
SWAN, III, George, W ..... 313-496-2344.. 242 H
gswan1@wcccd.edu
SWAN, John .... 916-577-2200.... 75 C
jswan@jessup.edu
SWAN, Kevin .... 573-840-9682.. 273 A
kswan@trcc.edu
SWAN, Lynn .... 213-740-4154.... 72 D
lynnswan@usc.edu
SWAN, Rhonda .... 817-598-6283.. 479 E
rswan@wc.edu
SWAN, S. Tomeka .... 410-287-1892.. 206 J
tswan@cecil.edu
SWAN, Steve .... 360-650-3482.. 509 E
steve.swan@wwu.edu
SWAN, Terry, W .... 270-384-8148.. 191 E
swant@lindsey.edu
SWAN, William .... 718-636-3518.. 326 E
wswan@pratt.edu
SWANAGAN, Diana .... 706-233-7301.. 127 A
dswanagan@shorter.edu
SWANBERG, Jeff .... 815-967-7321.. 152 F
jswanberg@rockfordcareercollege.edu
SWANER, James .... 786-331-1000.. 105 G
jwaner@maufl.edu

SYLER-JONES, Tracy .... 817-257-7811.. 469 G
t.syler-jones@tcu.edu
SYLVESTER, Cynthia .... 603-577-6514.. 286 I
csylvester@dwc.edu
SYLVESTER, Douglas .... 480-965-6188.... 11 H
douglas.sylvester@asu.edu
SYLVESTER, Jason .... 239-280-2525.... 95 Q
jason.sylvester@avemaria.edu
SYLVESTER, Kenneth .... 810-766-3383.. 242 B
kenms@umflint.edu
SYLVESTER-CAESAR, Jemma .... 713-221-8006.. 474 B
caesarj@uhd.edu
SYMS, Deirdre .... 586-445-7862.. 237 C
symsd@macomb.edu
SYNDER, Brittany .... 305-809-3233.. 100 N
brittany.snyder@fkcc.edu
SYNDER, Jake .... 978-921-4242.. 225 G
jake.synder@montserrat.edu
SYNDER, Jane .... 617-277-3915.. 216 D
synderj@bgsp.edu
SYNDER, Tamara .... 352-638-9764.... 96 F
tsnyder@beaconcollege.edu
SYNER, Alicia .... 304-205-6746.. 511 M
alicia.syner@bridgevalley.edu
SYNODI, George, S .... 203-832-7273.... 90 A
gsynodi@newhaven.edu
SYRMOS, Vassilis, L .... 808-956-5006.. 131 D
syrmos@hawaii.edu
SYSYN, Nicola .... 503-699-6309.. 392 D
nsysyn@marylhurst.edu
SYVERUD, Kent .... 315-443-2235.. 337 A
ksyverud@syr.edu
SZABADOS, Anna .... 707-524-1519.... 63 G
aszabados@santarosa.edu
SZABO, Julia .... 419-358-3245.. 364 D
szaboj@bluffton.edu
SZABO, Mihaela, A .... 304-336-8270.. 513 F
mszabo@westliberty.edu
SZADOKIERSKI, Cindy .... 804-752-3103.. 493 C
cindyszadokierski@rmc.edu
SZAFRAN, Zvi .... 315-386-7204.. 335 B
president@canton.edu
SZAJ, Christine .... 651-290-6362.. 253 S
christine.szajv@mitchellhamline.edu
SZAKALY, CSC, Anthony . 508-565-1343.. 228 F
aszakaly@stonehill.edu
SZAKAS, Joe, S .... 207-621-3198.. 204 I
szakas@maine.edu
SZALANKIEWICZ, Linda .. 413-552-2155.. 223 E
lszalankiewicz@hcc.edu
SZALAY, Annette .... 216-373-7139.. 374 B
aszalay@ndc.edu
SZALKOWSKI, Denise, M 716-673-3456.. 331 D
denise.szalkowski@fredonia.edu
SZANI, Phyllis .... 201-200-3350.. 293 C
pszani@njcu.edu
SZAREK, Michael .... 201-559-6047.. 291 K
szarekm@felician.edu
SZARLETA, Ellen .... 219-980-6698.. 163 B
eszarlet@iun.edu
SZATARAY, Balint .... 209-946-2654.... 71 C
bsztaray@pacific.edu
SZCZERBACKI, David .... 617-333-2233.. 217 F
dszczerbacki@curry.edu
SZEJKO, Thomas .... 724-503-1001.. 422 H
tszejko@washjeff.edu
SZELEST, Bruce .... 518-437-4928.. 331 A
bszelest@albany.edu
SZELISTOWSKI, Warren ... 410-532-5110.. 210 B
wszelistowski@ndm.edu
SZENTMIKLOSI, Jillian, M .... 407-582-4142.. 114 N
jszentmiklosi@valenciacollege.edu
SZEP, Chris Ann .... 410-287-8327.. 206 J
caszep@cecil.edu
SZESZYCKI, Donald, J ..... 319-335-3565.. 169 H
donald-szeszycki@uiowa.edu
SZKODNEY, Robert .... 908-526-1200.. 295 A
bob.szkodny@raritanval.edu
SZKOTAK, Michael .... 415-575-6120.... 30 G
mszkotak@ciis.edu
SZPARAGOWSKI, George 610-785-6205.. 418 E
gszparagowski@scs.edu
SZPRYNGEL, Christopher 203-591-7375.... 88 F
cszpryngel@post.edu
SZPYRKA, Susan .... 719-255-3678.... 83 L
sszpyrka@uccs.edu
SZROMBA, Mathew, P ..... 920-923-8505.. 517 H
mpszromba93@marianuniversity.edu
SZUKALSKI, SVD, John .. 563-876-3353.. 171 I
jszukalski@dwci.edu
SZUR, Katalin .... 212-237-8041.. 308 E
kszur@jjay.cuny.edu
SZURGOT, Tricia .... 610-790-1938.. 397 D
tricia.szurgot@alvernia.edu
SZWEDKO, Emmalee .... 801-832-2550.. 483 D
eszwedko@westminstercollege.edu
SZYBALA, Jamie .... 520-322-6330.... 13 J
jamie@hanuniversity.edu
SZYMANSKI, David, M .... 513-556-7001.. 379 A
david.szymanski@uc.edu
SZYMANSKI, Heidi .... 201-559-6004.. 291 K
szymanskih@felician.edu
SZYMKOWICZ, Caitlin, B 413-585-4944.. 228 D
cszymkowicz@smith.edu
SZYMURSKI, Patricia .... 404-471-6382.. 115 J
pszymurski@agnesscott.edu

T

TA, Jennie .... 626-350-1500.... 30 D
TA, Minh-Hoa .... 415-561-1850.... 38 E
mhta@ccsf.edu
TA, Minh-Hoa .... 415-239-3363.... 38 E
mhta@ccsf.edu
TABARELLA-REED, Cheryl .... 319-363-8213.. 175 D
credd@mtmercy.edu
TABAREZ, Mirasol .... 956-326-1303.. 468 A
mtabarez@tamiu.edu
TABATABAI, Habib .... 405-974-2865.. 388 L
htabatabai@uco.edu
TABB, Brian .... 612-455-3420.. 245 A
brian.tabb@bcsmn.edu
TABB, Winston, G .... 410-516-8328.. 208 D
wtabb@jhu.edu
TABBACK, George .... 201-684-6842.. 294 G
gtabback@ramapo.edu
TABBUTT, Ken .... 360-867-6400.. 503 G
tabbuttk@evergreen.edu
TABER, Charles .... 631-632-4360.. 332 A
charles.taber@stonybrook.edu
TABER, Charles .... 631-632-7035.. 332 A
charles.taber@stonybrook.edu
TABER, K. Celeste .... 405-744-6876.. 385 G
celeste.taber@okstate.edu
TABER, Ralph .... 717-358-4390.. 403 J
ralph.taber@fandm.edu
TABERNER, Ian .... 617-262-5000.. 216 A
ian.taberner@the-bac.edu
TABING, Karla .... 618-985-3741.. 143 F
karlatabing@jalc.edu
TABOADA, Luz, E .... 915-831-7796.. 457 H
ltaboad2@epcc.edu
TABOL, Tim .... 614-234-2682.. 373 B
ttabol@mccn.edu
TABOR, Anne .... 207-973-1090.. 202 I
tabora@husson.edu
TABOR, Pamela .... 615-687-6896.. 438 C
registrar@abcnash.edu
TABOR, Susan .... 405-682-1611.. 385 D
stabor@occc.edu
TABOR, Tammy .... 620-276-9508.. 181 C
tammy.tabor@gcccks.edu
TABRON, Jasmine .... 570-208-5898.. 406 J
jasminetabron@kings.edu
TABRON, Judith, L .... 516-463-6316.. 316 D
judith.t.tabron@hofstra.edu
TACCONE, Al .... 760-757-2121.... 52 K
ataccone@miracosta.edu
TACEA, Christopher .... 518-891-2915.. 325 A
ctacea@nccc.edu
TACHA, Deanell .... 310-506-4621.... 56 J
deanell.tacha@pepperdine.edu
TACK, Eric .... 678-466-4085.. 119 A
erictack@clayton.edu
TACKET, Karen .... 805-546-3100.... 41 L
ktacket@cuesta.edu
TACKETT, Kelli .... 740-593-1804.. 375 H
tackettk@ohio.edu
TACKETT, Larry .... 304-510-8760.. 512 F
ltackett@wvncc.edu
TACKETT, Lisa, K .... 740-368-3398.. 376 B
lktacket@owu.edu
TADAMY, Everett, L .... 412-268-1018.. 400 D
et19@andrew.cmu.edu
TADAO, Tzuchie .... 680-488-2471.. 530 E
tzuchiet@gmail.com
TADEO, Joseph .... 352-588-8244.. 108 C
joseph.tadeo@saintleo.edu
TADEPALLI, Raghu .... 336-278-6000.. 344 D
rtadepalli@elon.edu
TADESSE, Asmare .... 408-855-5021.... 74 G
asmare.tadesse@wvm.edu
TADESSE, Berhanu .... 657-278-8748.... 33 A
btadesse@fullerton.edu
TADLOCK, Brett .... 931-526-3660.. 440 A
btadlock@fortisinstitute.edu
TADLOCK, Katherine .... 740-597-2577.. 375 H
tadlockk@ohio.edu
TADLOCK, Martin .... 727-873-4324.. 112 D
mtadlock@usfsp.edu
TAETZSCH, Blixy, K .... 607-844-8222.. 337 G
taetzsb@tc3.edu
TAFARO, John, P .... 513-875-3344.. 365 K
john.tafaro@chatfield.edu
TAFAWA, Weusi, A .... 617-228-2115.. 223 B
wtafawa@bhcc.mass.edu
TAFFORA, Raymond, P .... 608-263-7400.. 519 K
rtaffora@vc.wisc.edu
TAFOYA, Christina .... 805-678-5824.... 73 E
ctafoya@vcccd.edu
TAFOYA, Yvette .... 562-860-2451.... 36 P
ytafoya@cerritos.edu
TAGGART, Bruce, M .... 610-758-3025.. 408 H
bmt2@lehigh.edu
TAGGART, James .... 205-247-8927...... 7 E
jtaggart@stillman.edu
TAGGART, James, R .... 801-627-8306.. 481 A
taggartj@owatc.edu
TAGGART, Julie .... 614-222-4025.. 367 B
jtaggart@ccad.edu
TAGGART, Tom .... 904-256-7663.. 103 D
ttaggar@ju.edu
TAGGART, William .... 404-215-2659.. 124 I
william.taggart@morehouse.edu
TAGGETT, Glenn .... 207-551-5765.. 203 L
gtaggett@nmcc.edu
TAGLIARENI, James .... 409-933-8989.. 454 O
jtagliareni@com.edu
TAGLIATELA, Gayle, S ..... 203-932-7455.... 90 A
gtagliatela@newhaven.edu
TAGYE, Jim .... 515-643-6678.. 175 B
jtagye@mercydesmoines.org
TAHA, Dianne .... 516-726-5837.. 529 B
tahad@usmma.edu
TAHA, Sipel .... 760-630-1555.... 29 B
sipel.taha@brightwood.edu
TAHERI, Reza .... 818-299-5500.... 74 A
rtaheri@westcoastuniversity.edu
TAHMASSEBI, Debbie ...... 408-554-4455.... 63 E
dtahmassebi@scu.edu
TAI WANG, Yong .... 903-566-7043.. 477 B
ywang@uttyler.edu
TAILLON, Gretchen .... 603-342-3003.. 286 H
gtaillon@ccsnh.edu
TAILOR, Bhavna .... 973-661-0600.. 291 F
TAIT, Erica .... 509-865-0420.. 504 D
tait_e@heritage.edu
TAIT, Lane, H .... 830-792-7462.. 465 E
ltait@schreiner.edu
TAIT, Melissa .... 847-214-7365.. 140 A
mtait@elgin.edu
TAITANO, Carlos .... 671-735-2600.. 530 B
ctaitano@uguam.uog.edu
TAKACS, Audrey .... 586-445-7314.. 237 C
takacsa@macomb.edu
TAKAHASHI, Jack .... 800-754-1009.. 518 C
TAKAHASHI, Lois .... 310-206-3487.... 69 D
takahashi@luskin.ucla.edu
TAKAHASHI, Tomoko ...... 949-480-4047.... 64 J
ttakahashi@soka.edu
TAKAMI, Andrew, B .... 812-590-9185.. 163 F
atakami@purdue.edu
TAKAMURA, Jeanette, C .. 212-851-2288.. 311 E
jct8@columbia.edu
TAKAO, Carol .... 415-502-3233.... 70 D
carol.takao@ucsf.edu
TAKATA, Kacie .... 480-461-7300.... 14 D
kacie.takata@mesacc.edu
TAKATORI, Alyssa .... 404-627-2681.. 117 G
alyssa.takatori@beulah.edu
TAKEDA-TINKER, Becky .. 800-462-7845.... 79 A
becky.takeda-tinker@csuglobal.edu
TAKEMOTO, Mary Ann ..... 562-985-5146.... 33 B
maryann.takemoto@csulb.edu
TAKES, Faith, A .... 518-786-0855.. 321 C
faith.takes@mildred-elley.edu
TAKIGUCHI, Amy .... 808-735-4707.. 130 F
ahigashi@chaminade.edu
TAKSAR, Stephen .... 413-572-8424.. 222 E
staksar@westfield.ma.edu
TALABER, Matthew .... 845-938-3415.. 529 C
matthew.talaber@usma.edu
TALAMANTEZ, Frank .... 415-575-6283.... 30 G
ftalamantez@ciis.edu
TALAVERA, Karla .... 661-255-1050.... 30 E
talavera@calarts.edu
TALAVINIA, Phillip .... 419-358-3226.. 364 D
talaviniap@bluffton.edu
TALBERT, Kelly .... 208-426-1156.. 132 I
kellytalbert@boisestate.edu
TALBOOM, Scott .... 928-226-4374.... 12 N
scott.talboom@coconino.edu
TALBOT, A. Scott .... 435-652-7601.. 482 A
talbot@dixie.edu
TALBOT, Sandra .... 413-265-2293.. 217 D
talbots@elms.edu
TALBOT, Sandra, C .... 413-265-2293.. 217 D
talbots@elms.edu
TALBOT, William .... 212-594-4000.. 337 F
btalbot@tcicollege.edu
TALBOTT, Jeffrey .... 909-748-8888.... 71 K
jeff_talbott@redlands.edu
TALBOTT, Linda .... 406-243-4215.. 276 K
linda.talbott@umontana.edu
TALBOTT, Richard .... 251-445-9254...... 9 E
rtalbott@southalabama.edu
TALBOTT, Robert .... 650-543-3714.... 52 D
rtalbott@menlo.edu
TALBOTT, Sherry .... 540-828-5369.. 487 H
stalbott@bridgewater.edu
TALDO, Tom .... 785-242-5200.. 183 M
tom.taldo@ottawa.edu
TALENTINO, Andrea .... 802-485-2410.. 484 H
atalenti@norwich.edu
TALENTINO, Karen, A ...... 802-654-2216.. 484 I
ktalentino@smcvt.edu
TALENTINO, Mary .... 928-226-4283.... 12 N
mary.talentinow@coconino.edu
TALERICO, Katie .... 412-291-6247.. 397 I
ktalerico@aii.edu
TALESH, Rameen, A .... 949-824-5590.... 69 C
rtalesh@uci.edu
TALIAFERRO, Beth .... 702-434-6599.. 285 G
btaliaferro@sierranevada.edu
TALIAFERRO, Kevin .... 813-529-2640.. 528 C
kevin.c.taliaferro@centcom.mil
TALIENTO, Tamela, K ...... 931-431-9700.. 443 E
ttaliento@nci.edu
TALKINGTON, Barbara ..... 206-592-4319.. 504 E
btalkington@highline.edu
TALL CHIEF, Russ .... 405-208-6288.. 385 E
trtallchief@okcu.edu
TALLAKSEN, Kevin .... 318-274-2419.. 200 F
tallaksenk@gram.edu
TALLANT, Pat, L .... 903-434-8102.. 462 M
ptallant@ntcc.edu
TALLANT, Steven, H .... 361-593-3209.. 469 A
steven.tallant@tamuk.edu
TALLARIDA, Ronald, J ...... 856-256-5413.. 295 E
tallarida@rowan.edu
TALLENT, Judy .... 606-679-8501.. 190 E
judy.tallent@kctcs.edu
TALLERICO, Betty, L .... 724-458-3790.. 404 F
bltallerico@gcc.edu
TALLEY, Braque .... 662-252-8000.. 260 F
braquetalley@rustcollege.edu
TALLEY, Chestley .... 903-730-4890.. 460 B
ctalley@jarvis.edu
TALLEY, Frederico, J .... 240-895-2185.. 210 E
fjtalley@smcm.edu
TALLEY, Kathryn .... 800-280-0307.. 158 E
kathryn.talley@ace.edu
TALLEY, Lillian .... 208-562-3229.. 133 F
lilliantalley@cwidaho.cc
TALLMAN, Doug .... 402-486-2534.. 282 I
dotallma@ucollege.edu
TALLMAN, Lawrence, J .... 304-457-6247.. 510 B
tallmanlj@ab.edu
TALLON, Brooke .... 405-425-5104.. 385 C
brooke.tallon@oc.edu
TALMADGE, Rosemary ...... 718-482-5059.. 309 A
rtalmadge@lagcc.cuny.edu
TALMAN, Martha, A .... 970-247-7315.... 80 D
matalman@fortlewis.edu
TALMO, Richard .... 760-744-1150.... 56 F
rtalmo@palomar.edu
TAM, Stanley .... 607-871-2300.. 303 F
tam@alfred.edu
TAM, Victor .... 707-527-4246.... 63 G
vtam@santarosa.edu
TAMADA, Mike .... 503-788-6613.. 394 I
tamadam@reed.edu
TAMANAHA, David .... 808-984-3253.. 132 D
davidt@hawaii.edu
TAMANAHA, Stephen .... 714-432-5809.... 39 G
stamanaha@occ.cccd.edu
TAMANDL, Salisha .... 480-994-9244.... 17 C
salishat@swiha.edu
TAMASCO, Mary .... 973-353-5541.. 296 C
tamasco@rutgers.edu
TAMAYO, Daniel .... 559-934-2432.... 74 D
danieltamayo@whccd.edu
TAMBERT, John .... 703-284-5946.. 492 A
john.tambert@marymount.edu
TAMBOUE, Helene .... 803-705-4573.. 427 D
tamboueh@benedict.edu
TAMEO, John .... 401-254-3859.. 426 B
jtameo@rwu.edu
TAMERIUS, Travis .... 573-592-4241.. 275 G
travis.tamerius@williamwoods.edu
TAMES, Kirk .... 512-499-4517.. 475 K
ktames@utsystem.edu
TAMEZ, Meritza .... 713-226-5227.. 474 B
tamezm@uhd.edu
TAMIM, Tanya .... 303-837-0825.... 76 L
ttamim@aii.edu
TAMMEUS, Lisen .... 816-235-5613.. 273 F
tammeusl@umkc.edu
TAMPIO, Michael, W .... 716-888-2503.. 306 F
tampiom@canisius.edu
TAMPKE, Dale .... 773-508-7067.. 146 G
dtampke@luc.edu
TAMROWSKI, Nina .... 518-320-1256.. 330 H
TAMTE-HORAN, Deborah 484-664-3190.. 411 D
tamte-horan@muhlenberg.edu
TAN, Amy .... 713-718-7814.. 459 B
amy.tan@hccs.edu
TAN, Finian .... 949-359-0045.... 30 I

TAYLOR, Cameron .... 404-727-5311.. 120 E cameron.taylor@emory.edu
TAYLOR, Carol, A .... 417-865-2815.. 265 B taylorc@evangel.edu
TAYLOR, Carol, R .... 864-488-4510.. 430 H ctaylor@limestone.edu
TAYLOR, Cathy .... 618-650-5176.. 155 A cattayl@siue.edu
TAYLOR, Cathy .... 615-460-6781.. 438 J cathy.taylor@belmont.edu
TAYLOR, Caughman .... 803-545-5036.. 433 F caughman.taylor@uscmed.sc.edu
TAYLOR, Charles, T .... 330-325-6461.. 373 H ctaylor@neomed.edu
TAYLOR, Chelsa .... 276-739-2423.. 499 A ctaylor@vhcc.edu
TAYLOR, Cheryl, A .... 417-268-1000.. 262 F taylorch@evangel.edu
TAYLOR, Chris .... 801-863-8484.. 482 C taylorch@uvu.edu
TAYLOR, Christopher .... 973-408-3495.. 291 B ctaylor@drew.edu
TAYLOR, Christopher .... 973-408-3321.. 291 B ctaylor@drew.edu
TAYLOR, Craig .... 541-463-5364.. 391 G taylorc@lanecc.edu
TAYLOR, Craig, B .... 503-554-2911.. 391 D ctaylor@georgefox.edu
TAYLOR, Cyrus, C .... 216-368-4437.. 365 B casdean@case.edu
TAYLOR, Daniel .... 304-358-2000.. 510 J dtaylor@future.edu
TAYLOR, Danille, K .... 404-880-6774.. 118 K dtaylor3@cau.edu
TAYLOR, Danny, H .... 615-966-7650.. 441 F danny.taylor@lipscomb.edu
TAYLOR, Darrell .... 304-896-7432.. 512 E darrell.taylor@southernwv.edu
TAYLOR, David .... 828-669-8012.. 346 M dtaylor@montreat.edu
TAYLOR, David, A .... 718-289-5598.. 307 C david.taylor@bcc.cuny.edu
TAYLOR, David, B .... 716-286-8087.. 324 E dtaylor@niagara.edu
TAYLOR, David, E .... 202-885-2121.... 91 J taylor@american.edu
TAYLOR, David, F .... 336-758-5000.. 359 E taylordf@wfu.edu
TAYLOR, David, R .... 540-568-3720.. 490 J taylordr@jmu.edu
TAYLOR, Deb, A .... 864-622-6063.. 427 B dtaylor@andersonuniversity.edu
TAYLOR, Debora, W .... 512-448-8450.. 464 G deboraw@stedwards.edu
TAYLOR, Deborah .... 562-903-4703.... 28 E deborah.taylor@biola.edu
TAYLOR, Deborah, A .... 757-446-6031.. 489 B taylorta@evms.edu
TAYLOR, Denise .... 760-921-5415.... 56 E denise.taylor@paloverde.edu
TAYLOR, Dennis, D .... 740-392-6868.. 373 D denny.taylor@mvnu.edu
TAYLOR, Denny .... 740-392-6868.. 373 D denny.taylor@mvnu.edu
TAYLOR, Donald .... 610-902-8200.. 399 D donald.taylor@cabrini.edu
TAYLOR, Donald, R .... 870-307-7204.... 21 A donald.taylor@lyon.edu
TAYLOR, Donald, W .... 561-868-3280.. 106 D taylord@palmbeachstate.edu
TAYLOR, Ed .... 206-616-7175.. 508 E edtaylor@uw.edu
TAYLOR, Edward .... 608-663-2333.. 516 F edtaylor@edgewood.edu
TAYLOR, Edward .... 706-778-8500.. 125 J etaylor@piedmont.edu
TAYLOR, Ella .... 503-838-8757.. 396 E taylore@wou.edu
TAYLOR, Faye .... 732-247-5241.. 293 B ftaylor@nbts.edu
TAYLOR, Francis, H .... 334-833-4407...... 4 D ftaylor@hawks.huntingdon.edu
TAYLOR, Frederick .... 662-252-8000.. 260 F ftaylor@rustcollege.edu
TAYLOR, G. Don .... 540-231-9752.. 499 F don.taylor@vt.edu
TAYLOR, Gary .... 865-251-1800.. 444 A gtaylor@southcollegetn.edu
TAYLOR, Geraldine .... 781-891-2222.. 215 F gtaylor@bentley.edu
TAYLOR, Gia .... 480-423-6300.... 14 H gia.taylor@scottsdalecc.edu
TAYLOR, Gregory .... 559-244-5909.... 67 A gregory.taylor@scccd.edu
TAYLOR, Gwen .... 706-771-4180.. 117 C gtaylor@augustatech.edu
TAYLOR, Heather .... 312-915-8903.. 146 G htaylor1@luc.edu
TAYLOR, Heather .... 304-829-7408.. 510 G htaylor@bethanywv.edu
TAYLOR, Heather, H .... 757-822-1738.. 498 H htaylor@tcc.edu
TAYLOR, Helene .... 610-660-1202.. 418 G htaylor@sju.edu
TAYLOR, Hunter .... 252-536-7228.. 350 C htaylor397@halifaxcc.edu
TAYLOR, J. Kevin .... 805-756-1503.... 31 I jktaylor@calpoly.edu
TAYLOR, Jackie .... 731-661-5302.. 448 A jtaylor@uu.edu
TAYLOR, Jacqueline .... 609-771-3032.. 290 F taylorj@tcnj.edu
TAYLOR, Jaime .... 931-221-7971.. 444 E taylorjr@apsu.edu
TAYLOR, James .... 410-777-2318.. 206 B jmtaylor@aacc.edu
TAYLOR, James .... 502-456-6504.. 193 B jtaylor@sullivan.edu
TAYLOR, James .... 801-626-6055.. 482 D jamestaylor8@weber.edu
TAYLOR, Jan .... 304-558-4128.. 512 O jan.taylor@wvhepc.edu
TAYLOR, Janet .... 619-482-6309.... 66 E jtaylor@swccd.edu
TAYLOR, Janice .... 617-521-2360.. 228 C janice.taylor@simmons.edu
TAYLOR, Janie .... 817-461-8741.. 451 G jtaylor@arlingtonbaptistcollege.edu
TAYLOR, Jason .... 609-586-4800.. 292 D taylorj@mccc.edu
TAYLOR, Jay, P .... 417-268-1000.. 262 F taylorj@evangel.edu
TAYLOR, Jazmin .... 414-229-5923.. 520 D jazmin@uwm.edu
TAYLOR, Jeffrey, D .... 315-268-6477.. 310 B jdtaylor@clarkson.edu
TAYLOR, Jeffrey, S .... 814-871-7213.. 404 A taylor030@gannon.edu
TAYLOR, Jennifer .... 805-565-6085.... 75 A jmtaylor@westmont.edu
TAYLOR, Jim .... 253-964-6589.. 506 B jtaylor@pierce.ctc.edu
TAYLOR, Joe .... 208-496-7010.. 132 J taylorj@byui.edu
TAYLOR, John .... 530-257-6181.... 48 E jtaylor@lassencollege.edu
TAYLOR, John .... 585-785-1300.. 314 D john.taylor@flcc.edu
TAYLOR, Joseph .... 804-342-1264.. 500 B jdtaylor@vuu.edu
TAYLOR, Joseph, P .... 276-944-6124.. 489 I jptaylor@ehc.edu
TAYLOR, Joyce, K .... 540-674-3600.. 497 G jtaylor@nr.edu
TAYLOR, Juanyce .... 601-984-1010.. 261 C jdtaylor@umc.edu
TAYLOR, Judith, M .... 240-567-7337.. 209 E judith.taylor@montgomerycollege.edu
TAYLOR, Julie, Y .... 256-765-4680...... 9 C jayates@una.edu
TAYLOR, Katherine, A .... 217-245-3035.. 141 G katatylor@mail.ic.edu
TAYLOR, Kathy .... 504-816-4304.. 195 B ktaylor@dillard.edu
TAYLOR, Kathy .... 870-230-5103.... 20 E taylork@hsu.edu
TAYLOR, Kay-lynne .... 816-271-4206.. 269 C ktaylor19@missouriwestern.edu
TAYLOR, Kayla .... 907-277-1000.... 10 C contact@chartercollege.edu
TAYLOR, Keith .... 814-871-7609.. 404 A ktaylor@gannon.edu
TAYLOR, Kelley, G .... 334-844-4794...... 1 G taylokg@auburn.edu
TAYLOR, Kelli .... 910-630-7157.. 346 E ktaylor@methodist.edu
TAYLOR, Kenneth .... 870-230-5214.... 20 E taylork@hsu.edu
TAYLOR, Kent .... 575-624-8235.. 300 I kent@nmmi.edu
TAYLOR, Kenya, S .... 308-865-8843.. 282 L taylorks@unk.edu
TAYLOR, Kevin .... 864-242-5100.. 427 E
TAYLOR, Kim .... 773-702-7749.. 156 D kimtaylor@uchicago.edu
TAYLOR, Kristen .... 817-257-4161.. 469 G kristen.taylor@tcu.edu
TAYLOR, Kyle .... 706-419-1516.. 119 G kyle.taylor@covenant.edu
TAYLOR, Ladd .... 601-928-6299.. 259 C ladd.taylor@mgccc.edu
TAYLOR, LaTonya .... 630-752-5015.. 158 C media.relations@wheaton.edu
TAYLOR, Lauren, M .... 205-726-2956...... 6 E lmtaylor@samford.edu
TAYLOR, Laurna .... 615-361-7555.. 439 K ltaylor@daymarinstitute.edu
TAYLOR, Leah, A .... 304-929-6701.. 512 C ltaylor@newriver.edu
TAYLOR, Lee .... 334-387-3877...... 1 E leetaylor@amridgeuniversity.edu
TAYLOR, Leslie, W .... 501-686-8998.... 23 C taylorlesliew@uams.edu
TAYLOR, Linda .... 610-499-1039.. 423 E lmtaylor@widener.edu
TAYLOR, Linda .... 580-387-7261.. 384 D lrobins@mscok.edu
TAYLOR, Lindsey .... 706-236-2207.. 117 F ltaylor@berry.edu
TAYLOR, Loren, R .... 217-333-1478.. 156 E lrtaylor@uillinois.edu
TAYLOR, Lori .... 740-245-7204.. 380 C ltaylor@rio.edu
TAYLOR, Malcolm .... 256-726-7356...... 6 B mgtaylor@oakwood.edu
TAYLOR, Marcia .... 918-781-7271.. 382 D taylorm@bacone.edu
TAYLOR, Marcie .... 765-641-4495.. 158 J mjtaylor@anderson.edu
TAYLOR, Margaret .... 870-575-8733.... 23 E taylorm@uapb.edu
TAYLOR, Maria .... 704-233-8126.. 359 H m.taylor@wingate.edu
TAYLOR, Marilyn .... 520-621-3876.... 17 I taylorm@email.arizona.edu
TAYLOR, Martha, M .... 334-844-4438...... 1 G taylomm@auburn.edu
TAYLOR, Mary, A .... 334-683-5248...... 5 C mtaylor@judson.edu
TAYLOR, Matthew, A .... 601-979-3950.. 258 D matthew.a.taylor@jsums.edu
TAYLOR, Maurice .... 443-885-4075.. 209 F maurice.taylor@morgan.edu
TAYLOR, Melanie .... 562-903-4800.... 28 E melanie.taylor@biola.edu
TAYLOR, Melinda .... 714-992-7001.... 54 H mtaylor1@fullcoll.edu
TAYLOR, Melody .... 843-574-6225.. 433 D melody.taylor@tridenttech.edu
TAYLOR, Mervin, V .... 340-693-1560.. 539 C mtaylor2@uvi.edu
TAYLOR, Mia .... 617-449-7428.. 229 B taylor@urbancollege.edu
TAYLOR, Michael .... 617-449-7037.. 229 B michael.taylor@urbancollege.edu
TAYLOR, Michael .... 253-589-6085.. 502 F michael.taylor@cptc.edu
TAYLOR, Michael, A .... 812-877-8145.. 166 H michael.a.taylor@rose-hulman.edu
TAYLOR, Michelle .... 918-495-6581.. 386 H mtaylor@oru.edu
TAYLOR, Michelle .... 215-635-7300.. 404 D mtaylor@gratz.edu
TAYLOR, Michelle, O .... 801-863-6158.. 482 C taylormo@uvu.edu
TAYLOR, Misty .... 386-752-1822.. 100 L misty.taylor@fgc.edu
TAYLOR, Nancy, K .... 716-375-2017.. 328 B nktaylor@sbu.edu
TAYLOR, Orlando .... 805-898-4038.... 43 K otaylor@fielding.edu
TAYLOR, Pamela, L .... 781-283-3694.. 229 C
TAYLOR, Pat .... 417-328-1500.. 272 C ptaylor@sbuniv.edu
TAYLOR, Pat .... 253-680-7080.. 501 E ptaylor@bates.ctc.edu
TAYLOR, Patty, L .... 920-565-1032.. 517 D taylorpl@lakeland.edu
TAYLOR, OSB, Paul .... 724-805-2527.. 419 A paul.taylor@email.stvincent.edu
TAYLOR, Quintin .... 225-922-2391.. 195 G quintintaylor@lctcs.edu
TAYLOR, R .... 503-399-6566.. 390 E r.taylor@chemeketa.edu
TAYLOR, Ramona, L .... 804-524-5326.. 499 G rtaylor@vsu.edu
TAYLOR, Renee .... 312-413-2411.. 156 F rtaylor@uic.edu
TAYLOR, Richard .... 513-529-7135.. 372 K taylorrt@miamioh.edu
TAYLOR, Richard, A .... 214-887-5316.. 457 C rtaylor@dts.edu
TAYLOR, Rickie .... 417-447-4802.. 270 A taylorrd@otc.edu
TAYLOR, Robbie .... 910-410-1705.. 352 C rltaylor@richmondcc.edu
TAYLOR, Robbin, M .... 270-745-4586.. 194 D robbin.taylor@wku.edu
TAYLOR, Robert .... 530-938-5512.... 40 F rtaylor18@siskiyous.edu
TAYLOR, Robert .... 712-722-6077.. 171 J robert.taylor@dordt.edu
TAYLOR, Robert .... 850-561-2644.. 110 J robert.taylor@famu.edu
TAYLOR, Robert .... 806-874-3571.. 454 F robert.taylor@clarendoncollege.edu
TAYLOR, Robert .... 401-598-2900.. 425 B rtaylor@jwu.edu
TAYLOR, Robert, F .... 860-701-6194.. 529 A robert.f.taylor@uscg.mil
TAYLOR, Rochelle .... 313-317-4138.. 235 D rtaylor33@hfcc.edu
TAYLOR, Ronald, K .... 304-462-6451.. 513 C ronald.taylor@glenville.edu
TAYLOR, Russell .... 828-254-1921.. 347 D russellgtaylor@abtech.edu
TAYLOR, Sandi .... 661-395-4266.... 47 J staylor@bakersfieldcollege.edu
TAYLOR, Sandi .... 909-748-8428.... 71 K sandi_taylor@redlands.edu
TAYLOR, Sharon .... 562-985-4162.... 33 B sharon.taylor@csulb.edu
TAYLOR, Sharon .... 724-503-1001.. 422 H staylor@washjeff.edu
TAYLOR, Shawn .... 863-638-7655.. 115 C shawn.taylor@warner.edu
TAYLOR, Shawn .... 510-986-6941.... 57 D staylor@peralta.edu
TAYLOR, Shawn .... 805-765-9300.... 62 K
TAYLOR, Sherri .... 256-215-4273...... 2 G staylor@cacc.edu
TAYLOR, Sherri .... 417-667-8181.. 264 A
TAYLOR, Sherry .... 417-447-8801.. 270 A taylorst@otc.edu
TAYLOR, Stacey .... 617-732-2800.. 225 C stacey.taylor@mcphs.edu
TAYLOR, Stan .... 214-648-7518.. 478 C stan.taylor@utsouthwestern.edu
TAYLOR, Stephanie .... 704-637-4470.. 343 B sataylor@catawba.edu
TAYLOR, Stephanie .... 412-291-6200.. 397 I staylor@aii.edu
TAYLOR, Stephanie .... 423-614-8600.. 441 B staylor@leeuniversity.edu
TAYLOR, Stephanie, A .... 270-824-1743.. 190 B stephanie.taylor@kctcs.edu
TAYLOR, Steve .... 252-789-0225.. 351 A staylor@martincc.edu
TAYLOR, Steven .... 334-670-3399...... 7 H sltaylor@troy.edu
TAYLOR, Steven, P .... 262-243-5700.. 516 E steve.taylor@cuw.edu
TAYLOR, Steven, T .... 303-963-3138.... 77 I staylor@ccu.edu
TAYLOR, Susan .... 541-440-7678.. 395 F susan.taylor@umpqua.edu
TAYLOR, Suzanne .... 806-742-2121.. 472 C suzanne.taylor@ttu.edu
TAYLOR, T. A .... 214-638-0484.. 460 C tataylor@kdstudio.com
TAYLOR, Tammy .... 903-927-3300.. 479 K ttaylor@wileyc.edu
TAYLOR, Tamra .... 801-524-8105.. 480 J ttaylor@ldsbc.edu
TAYLOR, Tawny .... 918-631-2315.. 389 E tawny-taylor@utulsa.edu
TAYLOR, Terri .... 931-372-3554.. 445 B ttaylor@tntech.edu
TAYLOR, Theresa .... 719-365-5087.... 83 I theresa.taylor@uchealth.org
TAYLOR, Thomas .... 205-391-2617...... 6 G ttaylor@sheltonstate.edu
TAYLOR, Thomas .... 978-934-3933.. 221 A thomas_taylor@uml.edu
TAYLOR, Timothy .... 803-376-5766.. 427 A ttaylor@allenuniversity.edu
TAYLOR, Timothy, L .... 248-232-4500.. 239 E tltaylor@oaklandcc.edu
TAYLOR, Todd .... 503-280-8535.. 391 A totaylor@cu-portland.edu
TAYLOR, Tracy .... 605-668-1518.. 436 D tracy.taylor@mtmc.edu
TAYLOR, Traki, L .... 850-561-2989.. 110 J traki.taylor@famu.edu
TAYLOR, Vernon .... 540-442-0395.... 54 A vtaylor@nu.edu
TAYLOR, Virginia .... 585-345-6886.. 315 C vmtaylor@genesee.edu
TAYLOR, Vorley .... 740-366-9443.. 365 D taylor.1051@osu.edu
TAYLOR, JR., Walter, F .... 614-235-4136.. 378 C wtaylor@tlsohio.edu
TAYLOR, William .... 505-454-3163.. 300 F btaylor@nmhu.edu
TAYLOR, William, F .... 972-881-5579.. 455 A wtaylor@collin.edu
TAYLOR, William, F .... 804-706-5016.. 497 D ftaylor@jtcc.edu
TAYLOR, William, R .... 626-395-3727.... 30 H bill.taylor@caltech.edu
TAYLOR, Yolanda, D .... 918-631-2327.. 389 E yolanda-taylor@utulsa.edu
TAYLOR-ALLEYNE, Dian .. 215-572-2932.. 397 G taylor-alleyne@arcadia.edu
TAYLOR-ARCHER, Mordean .... 502-852-6153.. 194 A motayl01@louisville.edu
TAYLOR-BENNS, Kimberly .... 484-365-7218.. 409 B ktaylorbenns@lincoln.edu
TAYLOR-BROWNE, Wintlett .... 563-387-1486.. 174 L brownewi@luther.edu

TERRY, Penelope .... 718-951-5924.. 307 D
pterry@brooklyn.cuny.edu
TERRY, Robert .... 602-386-4127.... 11 D
bob.terry@arizonachristian.edu
TERRY, Rondale .... 510-567-6174.... 67 E
rterry@sum.edu
TERRY, Scott .... 304-357-4363.. 511 E
scottterry@ucwv.edu
TERRY, Steven .... 804-330-0111.. 487 P
careercrim@centura.edu
TERRY, Susan .... 206-543-0535.. 508 E
nahe@uw.edu
TERRY, Tina .... 606-886-3863.. 189 A
tterry0025@kctcs.edu
TERRY, Troy, M .... 864-294-2213.. 430 C
troy.terry@furman.edu
TERRY, Willa .... 662-252-2491.. 260 F
wterry@rustcollege.edu
TERRY-JACKSON,
Tonishea .... 847-578-8489.. 153 A
tonishea.terry-jackson@rosalindfranklin.edu
TERTYCHNY, Gerard, A .... 610-989-1276.. 422 E
gtertychny@vfmac.edu
TERVALA, Debra .... 505-473-6292.. 302 A
debra.tervala@santafeuniversity.edu
TERWILLIGER, Linda .... 845-451-1342.. 312 C
l_terwil@culinary.edu
TERZAGHI, Vanessa .... 202-885-8649.... 94 E
vterzaghi@wesleyseminary.edu
TESCHNER, Pam .... 503-375-7180.. 391 B
pteschner@corban.edu
TESFAMARIAM, Biniam ... 574-520-4104.. 163 E
biktesfa@iusb.edu
TESFAY, Isaac .... 508-929-8784.. 222 F
itesfay@worcester.edu
TESH, J. Michael .... 210-567-2590.. 477 D
tesh@uthscsa.edu
TESKE, Paul .... 303-315-2805.... 84 A
paul.teske@ucdenver.edu
TESKE, Yolanda, K .... 252-334-2029.. 346 F
yolanda.teske@macuniversity.edu
TESLUK, Paul, E .... 716-645-3221.. 331 C
ptesluk@buffalo.edu
TESS, Dan, E .... 570-484-2238.. 415 D
dtess@lhup.edu
TESS, Paul, A .... 507-354-8221.. 247 J
tesspa@mlc-wels.edu
TESSIER, Dorita .... 509-527-2646.. 508 G
dorita.tessier@wallawalla.edu
TESSIER, Michael, A .... 812-488-2956.. 167 I
mt28@evansville.edu
TESSIER, Nanci .... 617-552-2805.. 216 C
nanci.tessier@bc.edu
TESSIER-LAVIGNE, Marc .. 650-723-2481.... 66 I
president@stanford.edu
TESSIER-LAVIGNE, Marc .. 212-327-8080.. 327 F
marctl@rockefeller.edu
TESSITORE, Amy .... 518-243-1577.. 305 A
tessitorea@ellismedicine.org
TESSLER, Faith .... 310-824-1586.... 24 L
ftessler@ajrca.org
TESSLER, Lisa .... 845-437-5438.. 339 C
litessler@vassar.edu
TESSMAN, Brock .... 406-243-2541.. 276 K
brock.tessman@umontana.edu
TESSMANN, Cary, A .... 262-691-5214.. 524 G
ctessmann@wctc.edu
TESTA, Michael .... 610-892-1548.. 414 B
mtesta@pit.edu
TESTA, Noelle .... 785-242-5200.. 183 M
noelle.testa@ottawa.edu
TESTA, Phil .... 607-778-5575.. 332 D
testapf@sunybroome.edu
TESTA-BUZZEE, Kristina .. 203-857-7220.... 87 B
ktesta-buzzee@norwalk.edu
TESTANI, Joe .... 585-275-2366.. 338 K
j.testani@rochester.edu
TESTERMAN, Misty .... 304-425-2323.. 511 H
TESTI, Andrea .... 541-881-5761.. 395 E
atesti@tvcc.cc
TESTY, Kellye, Y .... 206-543-2586.. 508 E
lawdean@uw.edu
TETERS, Charlene .... 505-424-2354.. 299 L
cteters@iaia.edu
TETI, Polly .... 215-242-7777.. 400 H
tetip@chc.edu
TETLOW, Tania .... 504-865-5201.. 200 C
ttelow@tulane.edu
TETRAULT, Martha, R .... 413-597-2681.. 230 A
martha.r.tetrault@williams.edu
TETREAU, Jerry, C .... 480-245-7944.... 13 L
jerry.tetreau@ibcs.edu
TETREAU, Jerry, C .... 480-245-7969.... 13 L
jerry.tetreau@ibcs.edu
TETREAULT, Jules .... 203-392-5556.... 85 H
tetreaultj4@southernct.edu
TETREAULT, Patricia, L .... 570-941-7767.. 422 B
patricia.tetreault@scranton.edu
TETTEH, Edem .... 856-222-9311.. 295 C
etetteh@rcbc.edu

TETZLOFF, Jason .... 989-275-5000.. 236 E
jason.tetzloff@kirtland.edu
TETZLOFF, Lisa .... 920-465-2200.. 520 B
tetzlofl@uwgb.edu
TEURNER, Mary .... 660-596-7249.. 272 G
mteurner@sfccmo.edu
TEUTSCH, David .... 215-576-0800.. 417 H
dteutsch@rrc.edu
TEUTSCHMANN, Susan ... 402-461-7725.. 280 D
steutschmann@hastings.edu
TEW, Keith .... 252-399-6361.. 341 P
ktew@barton.edu
TEW, Mark .... 325-649-8002.. 459 E
mtew@hputx.edu
TEXIDOR, Migdalia .... 787-250-1912.. 534 B
mtexidor@metro.inter.edu
TEXTOR, Laurie .... 920-424-1037.. 520 E
textorl@uwosh.edu
TEYMOURTASH, Janet, L . 415-422-5898.... 72 C
janet@usfca.edu
TEZENO, Albert .... 972-599-3151.. 455 A
atezeno@collin.edu
TEZUKA, Hiroko .... 574-239-8341.. 161 N
htezuka@hcc-nd.edu
THACKER, Allison .... 713-348-4818.. 464 E
invest@rice.edu
THACKER, Karen, S .... 610-796-8306.. 397 D
karen.thacker@alvernia.edu
THACKER, Linda .... 314-529-9308.. 267 B
lthacker@maryville.edu
THACKER, Strom .... 518-388-6102.. 338 H
thackers@union.edu
THACKER, Tiffany .... 606-218-5953.. 194 C
tiffanythacker@upike.edu
THADANI, Indra .... 510-464-3516.... 57 D
ithadani@peralta.edu
THADEN, Mark .... 540-654-2160.. 495 C
mthad2zw@umw.edu
THAKKAR, Monica .... 212-799-5000.. 318 A
THAMES, Brenda .... 209-575-6058.... 76 A
thamesb@mjc.edu
THAMES, James, H .... 214-887-5013.. 457 C
jthames@dts.edu
THAMES, Jamie .... 478-757-4024.. 129 L
jthames@wesleyancollege.edu
THAMES, Kathleen, A ...... 337-482-6397.. 201 D
kat@louisiana.edu
THANKI, Sandip .... 702-992-2992.. 284 J
sandip.thanki@nsc.edu
THAO, Maisee .... 805-898-2927.... 43 K
mthao@fielding.edu
THAO, PaHnia .... 715-675-3331.. 524 D
thaop@ntc.edu
THARAKUNNEL, Kurian ... 708-456-0300.. 156 C
kuriantharakunnel@triton.edu
THARP, Brent .... 912-478-5444.. 122 B
btharp@georgiasouthern.edu
THARP, Carla .... 978-542-6401.. 222 D
ctharp@salemstate.edu
THARP, Karen .... 931-598-1270.. 443 O
kmtharp@sewanee.edu
THARPE, Barbara .... 615-327-6827.. 442 A
btharpe@mmc.edu
THARPE, Brad .... 909-621-8519.... 57 H
brad_tharpe@pitzer.edu
THARRINGTON, Sally ...... 434-949-1061.. 498 E
sally.tharrington@southside.edu
THARRINGTON, Sterling . 910-892-3178.. 344 I
stharrington@heritagebiblecollege.edu
THATCHER, Debra .... 541-440-4622.. 395 F
debra.thatcher@umpqua.edu
THATCHER, Derek .... 740-366-9453.. 365 D
dthatche@cotc.edu
THATCHER, Paula .... 503-352-1556.. 394 C
thatchep@pacificu.edu
THATCHER, Tom .... 513-244-8172.. 366 B
tom.thatcher@ccuniversity.edu
THAXTON, Deron .... 318-473-6409.. 197 J
dthaxton@lsua.edu
THAXTON, Deron .... 318-473-6574.. 197 J
dthaxton@lsua.edu
THAYER, Scott .... 619-660-4301.... 45 I
scott.thayer@gcccd.edu
THAYER, Scott .... 304-829-7138.. 510 G
sthayer@bethanywv.edu
THAYER, Tammy .... 608-246-6451.. 523 F
tthayer2@madisoncollege.edu
THAYER-MENCKE, Laura . 712-325-3287.. 174 B
lthayermencke@iwcc.edu
THAYNE, Lewis, E .... 717-867-6211.. 408 F
thayne@lvc.edu
THE, James .... 817-202-6719.. 466 C
jthe@swau.edu
THEEUWES, Jim .... 251-580-2154...... 4 I
jim.theeuwes@faulknerstate.edu
THEIMER, Donna .... 970-824-1111.... 78 J
donna.theimer@cncc.edu
THEINERT, Amber .... 405-878-5171.. 387 J
adtheinert@stgregorys.edu
THEIS, Ann .... 567-661-7270.. 376 D
ann_theis@owens.edu

THEIS, Cindy .... 612-874-3777.. 247 M
ctheis@mcad.edu
THEIS, Gabriela .... 715-394-8297.. 521 E
gtheis@uwsuper.edu
THEIS, Lori, C .... 318-257-2238.. 200 G
ltheis@latech.edu
THEISEN, Darlene, A .... 814-871-7609.. 404 A
theisen001@gannon.edu
THEISEN, Jason .... 320-308-6012.. 252 B
jtheisen@sctcc.edu
THEISSEN, Craig .... 330-325-6758.. 373 H
ctheissen@neomed.edu
THEKKUMKARA, Thomas 806-414-9268.. 472 D
thomas.thekkumkara@ttuhsc.edu
THELANDER, Laura .... 651-641-3216.. 247 G
lthelander001@luthersem.edu
THELEN, Cindy .... 715-675-3331.. 524 D
thelen@ntc.edu
THELEN, Craig .... 616-395-7833.. 235 F
thelen@hope.edu
THELEN, James, B .... 207-621-3452.. 204 G
university.counsel@maine.edu
THELEN, Kevin .... 724-357-2141.. 415 B
kthelen@iup.edu
THEMISTOCLEOUS,
Ann-Margaret, J .... 864-231-2185.. 427 B
athemistocleous@andersonuniversity.edu
THEOBALD, Brent .... 714-556-3610.... 73 B
brent.theobald@vanguard.edu
THEOBALD, Michael, J .... 816-501-4061.. 270 J
mike.theobald@rockhurst.edu
THEODORA, Dawn, S .... 805-756-5529.... 31 I
theodora@calpoly.edu
THEODORE, Leslie .... 415-422-4055.... 72 C
latheodore@usfca.edu
THEODORE, Renelle .... 570-586-2400.. 419 G
rtheodore@summitu.edu
THEODORE, Steve .... 254-295-4500.. 474 E
stheodore@umhb.edu
THEODOROPOULOS,
Christine .... 805-756-1414.... 31 I
ctheodor@calpoly.edu
THEODOSIOU,
Constantine .... 718-862-7948.. 319 L
constantine.theodosiou@manhattan.edu
THEODOULOU, Stella, Z . 818-677-3317.... 34 A
stella.theodoulou@csun.edu
THEOLBALD, Brent .... 714-556-3610.... 73 B
brent.theobald@vanguard.edu
THEONUGRAHA, Felix ..... 847-317-4061.. 156 B
ftheonug@tiu.edu
THEONUGRAHA, Feliy ...... 847-317-4062.. 156 B
ftheonug@tiu.edu
THEORET, Julie .... 802-635-1333.. 486 B
julie.theoret@jsc.edu
THERIAULT, Monique .... 206-726-5013.. 503 B
mtheriault@cornish.edu
THERIOT, Clifton .... 985-448-4621.. 201 A
clifton.theriot@nicholls.edu
THERMER, Clifford .... 860-913-2058.... 87 H
cthermer@goodwin.edu
THEROULDE, Leslie .... 305-428-5700.. 105 E
theroulde@aii.edu
THEROUX, Robert, R .... 401-739-5000.. 425 C
btheroux@neit.edu
THESENVITZ, Michael, D . 918-631-2583.. 389 E
michael-thesenvitz@utulsa.edu
THESING-RITTER,
Jodi, M .... 715-836-3015.. 520 A
thesinjm@uwec.edu
THETFORD, Byron .... 205-652-3435...... 9 F
behetford@uwa.edu
THEULE, Ryan .... 661-362-5930.... 40 A
ryan.theule@canyons.edu
THEULEN, Michael .... 413-782-1377.. 229 E
michael.theulen@wne.edu
THIBADEAU, Suzette .... 920-424-0200.. 520 E
thibadea@uwosh.edu
THIBEAULT, Alan .... 207-602-2253.. 205 F
athibeault@une.edu
THIBEAULT, Nancy .... 937-512-2926.. 377 D
nancy.thibeault@sinclair.edu
THIBEDEAU, Dawn .... 414-277-7126.. 518 E
thibedeau@msoe.edu
THIBODEAU, Adam .... 207-780-4546.. 205 E
adam.l.thibodeau@maine.edu
THIBODEAU, Jim .... 402-457-2428.. 280 J
jrthibodeau@mccneb.edu
THIBODEAU, John .... 262-564-3050.. 523 D
thibodeauj@gtc.edu
THIBODEAU, Marianne .... 207-255-1254.. 205 C
mthibod@maine.edu
THIBODEAU, Wayne, J .... 248-370-4240.. 239 K
thibodea@oakland.edu
THIBODEAUX, Chad .... 337-475-5523.. 200 H
cthibodeaux@mcneese.edu
THIBODEAUX, Corrie .... 903-988-7517.. 460 D
cthibodeaux@kilgore.edu
THIBODEAUX, Ramie .... 337-475-5136.. 200 H
rthibodeaux@mcneese.edu

THIBOUTOT, Paul .... 507-222-4190.. 245 C
pthibout@carleton.edu
THIE, Susan .... 605-331-6592.. 438 A
susan.thie@usiouxfalls.edu
THIEDE, Jaci .... 317-940-9913.. 159 K
jthiede@butler.edu
THIEL, Becky .... 740-351-3017.. 377 C
bthiel@shawnee.edu
THIEL, Janet .... 732-987-2200.. 292 A
jthiel@georgian.edu
THIEL, John, E .... 203-254-4000.... 87 G
jthiel@fairfield.edu
THIELE, Dianna .... 206-878-3710.. 504 E
dthiele@highline.edu
THIELE, Dwain, L .... 214-648-8711.. 478 C
dwain.thiele@utsouthwestern.edu
THIELE, Nicholas .... 573-276-4577.. 272 B
njthiele@semo.edu
THIELEMANN, Heather .... 936-294-1345.. 471 D
thielemann@shsu.edu
THIELER, George .... 724-832-1050.. 421 A
gthieler@triangle-tech.edu
THIEME, Sacha .... 812-855-9770.. 162 F
sthieme@indiana.edu
THIENEL, Molly .... 508-213-2218.. 227 A
molly.thienel@nichols.edu
THIERFELDER,
William, K .... 704-461-6726.. 342 A
billthierfelder@bac.edu
THIERSTEIN, Joel .... 513-244-4301.. 373 C
joel.thierstein@msj.edu
THIES, Nate .... 785-833-4327.. 182 F
nate.thies@kwu.edu
THIESEN, Lynn .... 707-476-4183.... 40 D
lynn-thiesen@redwoods.edu
THIESFELDT, Steven, R .... 507-354-8221.. 247 J
thiesfsr@mlc-wels.edu
THIESSEN, Bradley .... 941-487-4104.. 111 D
bthiessen@ncf.edu
THIESSEN, Melissa .... 509-527-4675.. 508 F
melissa.thiessen@wwcc.edu
THIGPEN, Buck .... 912-287-5813.. 119 B
bthigpen@coastalpines.edu
THIGPEN, Paula, M .... 410-864-3605.. 210 F
pthigpen@stmarys.edu
THIGPEN, Suzanne .... 615-460-6474.. 438 J
suzanne.thigpen@belmont.edu
THILL, Jesse .... 501-450-3130.... 24 G
jthill@uca.edu
THILL, Jonathan .... 910-576-6222.. 351 E
THILL, Robert .... 212-353-4348.. 311 G
thill@cooper.edu
THILLMAN, Peter .... 920-693-1119.. 523 E
peter.thillman@gotoltc.edu
THIMBA, Evelyn .... 215-895-6712.. 402 G
evelyn.k.thimba@drexel.edu
THIMMESCH, Timothy ..... 616-331-3845.. 234 F
thimmest@gvsu.edu
THIROS, Pauline .... 208-282-3470.. 133 H
thirpaul@isu.edu
THIRSK, William, T .... 845-575-3000.. 320 B
william.thirsk@marist.edu
THIS, Craig .... 937-775-4296.. 381 H
craig.this@wright.edu
THISS, Ramona, H .... 540-985-9828.. 491 A
rhthiss@jchs.edu
THISSEN, Sally, L .... 863-680-4127.. 101 E
sthissen@flsouthern.edu
THISTLE, Dawn, M .... 508-767-7095.. 214 F
dthistle@assumption.edu
THISTLETHWAITE, Polly .. 212-817-7060.. 308 A
pthistlethwaite@gc.cuny.edu
THIVIERGE, Michelle .... 518-861-2536.. 320 A
mthivierge@mariacollege.edu
THOBABEN, James .... 859-858-2369.. 186 I
THODE, Arnold .... 563-441-4131.. 172 D
athode@eicc.edu
THOENNES, Karla .... 715-425-4555.. 521 B
karla.thoennes@uwrf.edu
THOLEN, Robin .... 937-393-3431.. 377 F
rtholen@sscc.edu
THOM-KALEY, Marcia ...... 434-381-6331.. 494 M
mthomkaley@sbc.edu
THOMA, Katy .... 530-898-3406.... 32 C
cthoma@csuchico.edu
THOMAN, Richard, C .... 651-631-5100.. 256 A
rcthoman@unwsp.edu
THOMAS, Adam .... 334-214-4880...... 2 H
adam.thomas@cv.edu
THOMAS, Alan, R .... 615-898-2852.. 444 G
alan.thomas@mtsu.edu
THOMAS, Alvetta, P .... 404-225-4601.. 117 A
athomas@atlantatech.edu
THOMAS, Amanda .... 410-617-2327.. 208 G
atthomas@loyola.edu
THOMAS, Amy .... 614-251-4690.. 374 I
thomasa3@ohiodominican.edu
THOMAS, Andrew, J .... 716-888-2336.. 306 F
thomas97@canisius.edu
THOMAS, Andrine .... 212-616-7253.. 315 G
andrine.thomas@helenefuld.edu

THOMAS, Angela .... 409-880-8878.. 471 A
angela.thomas@lamar.edu
THOMAS, Anice .... 973-353-5805.. 296 C
anice.thomas@rutgers.edu
THOMAS, Anita, J .... 317-788-6126.. 168 A
ajthomas@uindy.edu
THOMAS, Anne .... 479-788-7033.... 23 A
anne.thomas@uafs.edu
THOMAS, Anne, C .... 317-788-3543.. 168 A
athomas@uindy.edu
THOMAS, Auden .... 518-580-5590.. 330 F
athomas@skidmore.edu
THOMAS, Barbara, J .... 415-422-6352.... 72 C
thomasb@admin.usfca.edu
THOMAS, Becky .... 949-451-5484.... 65 F
bthomas@ivc.edu
THOMAS, Bill .... 425-739-8164.. 504 F
bill.thomas@lwtech.edu
THOMAS, Billy, R .... 501-296-1397.... 23 C
billyrthomas@uams.edu
THOMAS, Bonnie .... 443-334-2260.. 211 A
blthomas@stevenson.edu
THOMAS, Brad .... 425-640-1884.. 503 E
brad.thomas@edcc.edu
THOMAS, Brenna .... 503-493-6456.. 391 A
bthomas@cu-portland.edu
THOMAS, Brent .... 828-898-8777.. 345 G
thomasb@lmc.edu
THOMAS, Brice .... 937-769-1664.. 363 E
bthomas6@antioch.edu
THOMAS, Bridgett .... 217-732-3155.. 146 B
bthomas@lincolncollege.edu
THOMAS, Brodrick .... 615-248-1426.. 447 F
bthomas1@trevecca.edu
THOMAS, Carei .... 212-220-8085.. 307 B
cthomas@bmcc.edu
THOMAS, Carl .... 541-885-1151.. 393 G
carl.thomas@oit.edu
THOMAS, Carol .... 626-914-8592.... 38 D
cthomas@citruscollege.edu
THOMAS, Carol .... 603-428-2481.. 287 C
cthomas@nec.edu
THOMAS, Carol .... 614-508-7233.. 370 E
cthomas@hondros.edu
THOMAS, Carolyn .... 530-752-6068.... 69 A
ccthomas@ucdavis.edu
THOMAS, Carolyn, D .... 504-520-7364.. 202 C
cthomas@xula.edu
THOMAS, Carrie .... 603-526-3686.. 285 L
cathomas@colby-sawyer.edu
THOMAS, Charles .... 248-341-2305.. 239 E
ccthomas@oaklandcc.edu
THOMAS, JR.,
Charles, E .... 404-527-7711.. 123 I
cthomas@itc.edu
THOMAS, Christine .... 916-484-8452.... 51 A
thomasc2@arc.losrios.edu
THOMAS, Christine .... 217-732-3168.. 146 A
csthomas@lincolnchristian.edu
THOMAS, Christine, C ...... 334-229-4327...... 1 D
ccthomas@alasu.edu
THOMAS, Christine, L ...... 715-346-4617.. 521 C
cthomas@uwsp.edu
THOMAS, Christopher ...... 337-475-5613.. 200 H
thomas@mcneese.edu
THOMAS, Clancy .... 229-430-0548.. 115 K
clancy.thomas@asurams.edu
THOMAS, Claudine .... 215-965-4061.. 411 A
cthomas@moore.edu
THOMAS, Clyde, G .... 503-554-2013.. 391 D
cthomas@georgefox.edu
THOMAS, Corlisse .... 973-353-5541.. 296 C
corlisse.thomas@rutgers.edu
THOMAS, Damani .... 718-368-5696.. 308 F
dthomas@kbcc.cuny.edu
THOMAS, Dana, L .... 907-474-7112.... 10 G
uaf.chancellor@alaska.edu
THOMAS, Daphne, J .... 901-435-1539.. 441 C
daphne_thomas@loc.edu
THOMAS, David .... 509-527-2194.. 508 G
dave.thomas@wallawalla.edu
THOMAS, David, A .... 202-687-3883.... 92 E
dathomas@georgetown.edu
THOMAS, David, E .... 215-751-8000.. 401 G
dthomas@ccp.edu
THOMAS, Debbie .... 860-906-5010.... 86 B
dthomas@ccc.commnet.edu
THOMAS, Debera .... 928-523-2656.... 15 H
debera.thomas@nau.edu
THOMAS, Deborah .... 502-776-1443.. 192 C
dthomas@simmonscollegeky.edu
THOMAS, Deborah .... 402-559-5245.. 283 A
thomasd@unmc.edu
THOMAS, Deborah .... 402-559-6301.. 283 A
thomasd@unmc.edu
THOMAS, Debra, K .... 865-974-3265.. 448 E
dthomas@utk.edu
THOMAS, Dene Kay .... 970-247-7100.... 80 D
thomas_d@fortlewis.edu
THOMAS, Denee .... 361-570-4149.. 474 C
thomasd@uhv.edu
THOMAS, Donna .... 301-369-2800.. 206 H
dgthomas@captechu.edu
THOMAS, Dorian .... 773-291-6384.. 137 G
dthomas236@ccc.edu
THOMAS, Doug .... 978-665-4095.. 221 D
dthoma27@fitchburgstate.edu
THOMAS, Downing .... 319-335-0370.. 169 H
downing-thomas@uiowa.edu
THOMAS, III, E. Nathan .. 785-864-4932.. 185 D
nathomas@ku.edu
THOMAS, Eddie, B .... 205-366-8848...... 7 E
ebthomas@stillman.edu
THOMAS, Elizabeth .... 910-695-4971.. 353 A
thomase@sandhills.edu
THOMAS, Fitzroy .... 301-891-4115.. 213 D
fthomas@wau.edu
THOMAS, Flecia .... 815-479-7620.. 147 E
fthomas@mchenry.edu
THOMAS, Fredel .... 605-995-2652.. 435 F
frthomas@dwu.edu
THOMAS, Frederick, A ...... 207-768-9580.. 205 D
frederick.thomas@maine.edu
THOMAS, Gayla .... 509-359-6874.. 503 D
gthomas@ewu.edu
THOMAS, Gregory, A .... 708-709-3501.. 151 C
gthomas2@prairiestate.edu
THOMAS, Helen .... 912-538-3126.. 127 E
hthomas@southeasterntech.edu
THOMAS, Huw, F .... 617-636-6636.. 228 H
huw.thomas@tufts.edu
THOMAS, Isaiah .... 610-957-6113.. 419 I
ithomas1@swarthmore.edu
THOMAS, J. Matthew .... 770-534-6174.. 118 A
mthomas@brenau.edu
THOMAS, Jack .... 309-298-1824.. 158 A
j-thomas2@wiu.edu
THOMAS, James .... 301-696-3545.. 208 B
thomasj@hood.edu
THOMAS, James .... 269-387-8785.. 243 H
jim.thomas@wmich.edu
THOMAS, James .... 910-296-1974.. 350 F
jthomas@jamessprunt.edu
THOMAS, Jan .... 742-427-5114.. 371 C
thomasj@kenyon.edu
THOMAS, Jane .... 410-827-5802.. 207 A
jthomas@chesapeake.edu
THOMAS, Janell, D .... 701-355-8244.. 362 G
jdthomas@umary.edu
THOMAS, Janette, B .... 607-587-4122.. 334 G
thomasj@alfredstate.edu
THOMAS, Janice .... 732-224-2174.. 289 I
jthomas@brookdalecc.edu
THOMAS, Jeanne .... 954-763-9840.... 95 N
library@atom.edu
THOMAS, Jeremy .... 979-209-7214.. 452 J
jeremy.thomas@blinn.edu
THOMAS, Jerry .... 501-760-4202.... 21 B
jerry.thomas@np.edu
THOMAS, Jessica .... 361-593-2174.. 469 A
jessica.thomas@tamuk.edu
THOMAS, Jim .... 209-468-4807.... 67 H
jthomas@sjcoe.net
THOMAS, Jim .... 615-966-5828.. 441 F
jim.thomas@lipscomb.edu
THOMAS, Joan .... 413-755-4817.. 224 G
jthomas@stcc.edu
THOMAS, Joe .... 541-888-7399.. 395 B
jthomas@socc.edu
THOMAS, John .... 661-255-1050.... 30 E
THOMAS, John .... 951-785-2064.... 48 A
jthomas@lasierra.edu
THOMAS, JR., John .... 918-270-6455.. 386 I
john.thomas@ptstulsa.edu
THOMAS, John, L .... 863-680-6215.. 101 E
jthomas@flsouthern.edu
THOMAS, Joseph .... 610-921-7643.. 396 H
jthomas@albright.edu
THOMAS, Joseph .... 212-752-1530.. 318 F
joseph.thomas@limcollege.edu
THOMAS, Joseph .... 317-788-6179.. 168 A
jodthomas@uindy.edu
THOMAS, Joseph .... 803-536-7033.. 432 E
jthomas@scsu.edu
THOMAS, Julia, M .... 585-385-8015.. 328 E
jthomas@sjfc.edu
THOMAS, Julie .... 319-296-4275.. 173 B
julie.thomas@hawkeyecollege.edu
THOMAS, Julie, B .... 252-823-5166.. 349 E
thomasj@edgecombe.edu
THOMAS, K. B .... 318-487-7389.. 195 F
kb.thomas@lacollege.edu
THOMAS, Kanet .... 310-506-4264.... 56 J
kanet.thomas@pepperdine.edu
THOMAS, Karen .... 706-649-1854.. 119 F
kthomas@columbustech.edu
THOMAS, Karen .... 386-312-4037.. 108 B
karenthomas@sjrstate.edu
THOMAS, Karla .... 773-298-3937.. 153 H
kthomas@sxu.edu
THOMAS, Kathryn S .... 706-355-5116.. 116 H
kthomas@athenstech.edu
THOMAS, Ka[illegible] .... 601-484-8689.. 258 F
kthomas@meridiancc.edu
THOMAS, Ka[illegible], M .... 252-398-6226.. 343 G
thomak@chowan.edu
THOMAS, Kelland .... 201-216-3728.. 297 E
kelland.thomas@stevens.edu
THOMAS, Kevin .... 973-803-5000.. 294 E
kthomas@pillar.edu
THOMAS, Kendall .... 412-359-1000.. 421 E
kthomas@triangle-tech.edu
THOMAS, Kenneth .... 334-229-4200...... 1 D
kthomas@alasu.edu
THOMAS, Kerry .... 601-977-4463.. 261 A
kthomas@tougaloo.edu
THOMAS, Laurita, E .... 734-647-5574.. 241 J
laurita@umich.edu
THOMAS, LaVona .... 818-401-1031.... 40 G
lthomas@columbiacollege.edu
THOMAS, Latell .... 912-871-1624.. 125 E
lthomas@ogeecheetech.edu
THOMAS, Linda .... 559-325-5356.... 67 E
linda.thomas@scccd.edu
THOMAS, Linda, V .... 340-693-1324.. 539 C
lthomas2@uvi.edu
THOMAS, Lisa .... 231-995-1043.. 239 C
lthomas@nmc.edu
THOMAS, Lisa .... 651-905-3490.. 255 E
lthomas@browncollege.edu
THOMAS, L[illegible] .... 765-983-1211.. 160 G
thomaly@earlham.edu
THOMAS, Mandy .... 714-628-7337.... 37 F
mthomas@chapman.edu
THOMAS, Marcia, R .... 312-460-0600.. 134 K
mthomas@aaart.edu
THOMAS, Maria .... 601-977-7769.. 261 A
mthomas@tougaloo.edu
THOMAS, Marjorie .... 757-221-2510.. 488 F
mthomas@wm.edu
THOMAS, Mark .... 863-638-2345.. 115 C
mark.thomas@warner.edu
THOMAS, Mark .... 608-246-6301.. 523 F
mthomasjr@madisoncollege.edu
THOMAS, Mary Beth .... 617-735-9766.. 218 C
thomasmb@emmanuel.edu
THOMAS, Mary Jean .... 859-846-5306.. 191 G
mjthomas@midway.edu
THOMAS, Maurice .... 856-691-8600.. 290 I
mthomas@cccnj.edu
THOMAS, Melissa .... 503-554-2214.. 391 D
mthomas@georgefox.edu
THOMAS, Melissa, M .... 843-953-8178.. 428 G
thomasmm1@cofc.edu
THOMAS, Michael .... 610-341-5800.. 403 B
mthoma[illegible]@eastern.edu
THOMAS, Michael .... 618-985-3741.. 142 B
thomasm@iecc.edu
THOMAS, Michael, A .... 706-880-8911.. 123 K
mathomas@lagrange.edu
THOMAS, Mike, R .... 618-235-2700.. 155 C
michael.thomas@swic.edu
THOMAS, Nancy .... 248-204-3203.. 237 B
nthomas@ltu.edu
THOMAS, Nathan .... 309-677-3140.. 136 B
nthomas@fsmail.bradley.edu
THOMAS, Ne[illegible] .... 713-348-4009.. 464 E
elt@rice.edu
THOMAS, Nishanth .... 973-803-5000.. 294 B
nthomas@pillar.edu
THOMAS, Patricia, A .... 202-274-6314.... 94 B
pthomas@udc.edu
THOMAS, Patti .... 425-889-6376.. 505 E
patti.thomas@northwestu.edu
THOMAS, Paul .... 337-482-2976.. 201 D
pdt2867@louisiana.edu
THOMAS, Peter, A .... 508-831-6074.. 230 C
pthomas@wpi.edu
THOMAS, Philemon .... 404-752-1663.. 125 A
pthomas@msm.edu
THOMAS, R. Brent .... 620-341-5278.. 180 G
rthomas2@emporia.edu
THOMAS, Randi Malcolm 513-529-4151.. 372 K
randi.thomas@miamioh.edu
THOMAS, Rebecca .... 845-758-7421.. 304 F
rthomas@bard.edu
THOMAS, Renard .... 661-362-3469.... 40 A
renard.thomas@canyons.edu
THOMAS, Renee .... 276-223-4752.. 499 C
rthomas@wcc.vccs.edu
THOMAS, Richard, W .... 301-295-3013.. 528 G
charles.thomas@usuhs.edu
THOMAS, Rikki .... 757-727-5250.. 490 E
rikki.thomas@hamptonu.edu
THOMAS, Roberta .... 864-578-8770.. 432 D
rthomas@sherman.edu
THOMAS, Robin .... 334-872-2533...... 6 F
THOMAS, Ronald, C .... 718-262-2332.. 310 A
rthomas@york.cuny.edu
THOMAS, Ryan .... 801-626-7931.. 482 D
ryanthomas2@weber.edu
THOMAS, Sam .... 901-383-6750.... 93 F
THOMAS, Sam .... 901-369-0835.... 93 F
THOMAS, Sam .... 303-360-4738.... 79 E
sam.thomas@ccaurora.edu
THOMAS, Samantha .... 214-768-3603.. 465 J
thomassa@smu.edu
THOMAS, Sandi .... 760-252-2411.... 28 B
sthomas@barstow.edu
THOMAS, Sarah, E .... 617-496-1295.. 219 D
sarah_e_thomas@harvard.edu
THOMAS, Scott .... 802-656-3424.. 485 D
scott.thomas@uvm.edu
THOMAS, Shannon .... 404-225-4634.. 117 A
sthomas@atlantatech.edu
THOMAS, Shira .... 850-599-3591.. 110 J
shira.thomas@famu.edu
THOMAS, Stacey .... 765-455-9391.. 163 A
stathoma@iuk.edu
THOMAS, Stacy .... 276-739-2401.. 499 A
sthomas@vhcc.edu
THOMAS, Steve .... 432-685-4520.. 461 H
steve@midland.edu
THOMAS, Steven .... 206-934-3791.. 506 J
steven.thomas@seattlecolleges.edu
THOMAS, Stuart .... 970-339-6232.... 76 H
stuart.thomas@aims.edu
THOMAS, Susan, L .... 660-785-4100.. 273 B
suethomas@truman.edu
THOMAS, Tammi, L .... 301-860-3506.. 212 D
tlthomas@bowiestate.edu
THOMAS, Teresa, W .... 615-898-2603.. 444 G
teresa.thomas@mtsu.edu
THOMAS, Terri .... 502-410-6200.. 188 H
tthomas@galencollege.edu
THOMAS, Terri .... 607-436-3388.. 331 F
terri.thomas@oneonta.edu
THOMAS, Tiffany .... 806-457-4200.. 458 B
tthomas@fpctx.edu
THOMAS, Timothy .... 315-792-5611.. 321 G
tthomas@mvcc.edu
THOMAS, Todd .... 423-652-6045.. 440 J
tthomas@king.edu
THOMAS, Todd, S .... 518-464-8526.. 314 A
tthomas@excelsior.edu
THOMAS, Tony .... 509-682-6705.. 509 D
tthomas@wvc.edu
THOMAS, Tony, G .... 229-333-5351.. 129 G
tgthomas@valdosta.edu
THOMAS, Tyrone .... 843-355-4152.. 435 A
thomast@wiltech.edu
THOMAS, Valerie, A .... 410-455-3142.. 211 G
valerie.thomas@umbc.edu
THOMAS, Vincent .... 612-659-6438.. 250 B
vincent.thomas@minneapolis.edu
THOMAS, W. Eric .... 252-862-1308.. 352 D
thomase@roanokechowan.edu
THOMAS, Wade .... 607-436-3333.. 331 F
wade.thomas@oneonta.edu
THOMAS, Wayne .... 423-636-7300.. 447 G
wthomas@tusculum.edu
THOMAS, Wendell, C .... 502-597-6707.. 191 B
wendell.thomas@kysu.edu
THOMAS, Wilbert, L .... 757-727-5356.. 490 E
bill.thomas@hamptonu.edu
THOMAS, William, A .... 713-313-6816.. 470 D
thomaswa@tsu.edu
THOMAS-ANDERSON,
Tricia .... 972-860-7396.. 456 D
triciathomas-anderson@dcccd.edu
THOMAS-GLOVER, Linda . 757-789-1775.. 497 A
lglover@es.vccs.edu
THOMAS-LARUE, Kim ...... 865-694-6681.. 446 G
kthomas@pstcc.edu
THOMAS-LITTLE, Jill, M .. 586-445-7576.. 237 C
littlej@macomb.edu
THOMAS-WILLIAMS,
Regina .... 912-443-5708.. 126 G
rthomas@savannahtech.edu
THOMASES, Josh .... 212-875-4519.. 304 E
jthomases@bankstreet.edu
THOMASON, Brian .... 310-506-4497.... 56 J
brian.thomason@pepperdine.edu
THOMASON, Chris .... 870-777-5722.... 24 A
chris.thomason@uacch.edu
THOMASON, Chris .... 205-652-3533...... 9 F
cthomason@uwa.edu
THOMASON, Chris .... 205-652-5467...... 9 F
cthomason@uwa.edu
THOMASON, Donald, B ... 901-448-5538.. 448 H
dthomaso@uthsc.edu
THOMASON, Jonathan ...... 918-781-7218.. 382 D
thomasonj@bacone.edu
THOMASON, Laura .... 478-471-5765.. 124 E
laura.thomason@mga.edu
THOMASON, Mary .... 817-554-5950.. 461 G
mthomason@messengercollege.edu
THOMASON, Scotty .... 530-938-5200.... 40 F
sthomason1@siskiyous.edu
THOMASON, Tommy .... 713-221-8056.. 474 B
thomasont@uhd.edu
THOMASSON, Susan .... 704-355-3921.. 343 A
susan.thomasson@carolinas.org

THOMES, Christopher, P . 850-747-3250.. 102 M
cthomes@gulfcoast.edu
THOMEY, Bane .... 262-564-3096.. 523 D
thomeyb@gtc.edu
THOMMEN, Bettsy .... 610-527-0200.. 418 D
bettsy.thommen@rosemont.edu
THOMPSOM, Cathy .... 423-614-8200.. 441 B
cthompson@leeuniversity.edu
THOMPSON, Adam .... 503-223-2245.. 391 H
athompson@portland.chefs.edu
THOMPSON, Adelia, P .... 757-594-8759.. 488 E
adelia.thompson@cnu.edu
THOMPSON, Al .... 715-346-2481.. 521 C
al.thompson@uwsp.edu
THOMPSON, Alan .... 406-447-6941.. 277 B
thompsona@umhelena.edu
THOMPSON, Alanna .... 256-306-2601...... 2 F
alanna.thompson@calhoun.edu
THOMPSON, Allison, L .... 318-342-6917.. 201 E
althompson@ulm.edu
THOMPSON, Alton .... 410-651-2200.. 212 B
THOMPSON, Amanda .... 937-393-3431.. 377 F
athompson@sscc.edu
THOMPSON, Amber .... 719-336-1592.... 81 D
amber.thompson@lamarcc.edu
THOMPSON, Amy .... 718-940-5713.. 328 G
althompson@sjcny.edu
THOMPSON, Andy .... 319-656-2447.. 176 F
admissions@shilohuniversity.edu
THOMPSON, Ann .... 270-706-8444.. 189 C
ann.thompson@kctcs.edu
THOMPSON, Ann .... 734-487-1280.. 233 J
athomp51@emich.edu
THOMPSON, Annette .... 210-283-5091.. 474 D
athompson@uiwtx.edu
THOMPSON, April .... 607-777-2804.. 331 B
athompso@binghamton.edu
THOMPSON, Arlene .... 334-229-4406...... 1 D
athompson@alasu.edu
THOMPSON, Barbara .... 334-556-2629...... 3 N
bthompson@wallace.edu
THOMPSON, Bill .... 317-632-5553.. 165 L
bthompson@lincolntech.edu
THOMPSON, Blake .... 614-292-6359.. 375 A
thompson.2061@osu.edu
THOMPSON, Blake .... 614-297-8468.. 375 A
thompson.2601@osu.edu
THOMPSON, Bob .... 405-912-9453.. 387 D
bthompson@hc.edu
THOMPSON, Bradley .... 901-751-8453.. 442 E
bthompson@mabts.edu
THOMPSON, Brenda .... 512-863-1956.. 466 G
thompso2@southwestern.edu
THOMPSON, Brian, L .... 904-819-6249.... 99 M
bthompson@flagler.edu
THOMPSON, Caitlyn .... 662-846-4020.. 257 E
ccthompson@deltastate.edu
THOMPSON, Carey .... 901-843-3000.. 443 L
thompsonc@rhodes.edu
THOMPSON, Carlene, M . 317-274-7617.. 163 D
hra@iupui.edu
THOMPSON, Carmela .... 716-878-5519.. 332 F
thompsc@buffalostate.edu
THOMPSON, Carrie .... 615-966-5250.. 441 F
carrie.thompson@lipscomb.edu
THOMPSON, Cesarina ..... 413-205-3056.. 214 B
cesarina.thompson@aic.edu
THOMPSON, Chad .... 650-738-7035.... 62 I
thompsonc@smccd.edu
THOMPSON, Charles, G .. 413-542-2221.. 214 C
cgthompson@amherst.edu
THOMPSON, Charles, S .. 423-652-4742.. 440 J
csthomps@king.edu
THOMPSON, Chaundra ..... 334-244-3106...... 2 A
cthompson23@aum.edu
THOMPSON, Cheryl .... 928-724-6679.... 12 T
cthompson@dinecollege.edu
THOMPSON,
Christopher, J .... 651-962-5771.. 256 C
cjthompson@stthomas.edu
THOMPSON, Corinne, B .. 802-656-7898.. 485 D
corinne.thompson@uvm.edu
THOMPSON, Craig .... 208-282-2120.. 133 H
thomcra2@isu.edu
THOMPSON, Craig, B ...... 646-888-6639.. 319 I
thompsonc@mskcc.org
THOMPSON, Cynthia .... 217-206-6665.. 156 G
thompson.cynthia@uis.edu
THOMPSON, Daniel .... 410-287-1027.. 206 J
dthompson@cecil.edu
THOMPSON, Daniel .... 651-690-6285.. 254 M
djthompson@stkate.edu
THOMPSON, David .... 256-782-5455...... 4 H
dthompston@jsu.edu
THOMPSON, Dawn, G ...... 503-777-7502.. 394 I
dthomp@reed.edu
THOMPSON, Dawn, M ..... 302-831-3266.... 91 F
dawnt@udel.edu
THOMPSON, Deanna .... 815-802-8552.. 144 C
drthompson@kcc.edu
THOMPSON, Debbi, N ...... 864-597-4208.. 435 C
thompsondn@wofford.edu
THOMPSON, Deborah, L . 904-819-6302.... 99 M
dthompson@flagler.edu
THOMPSON, Deborah, L . 269-337-7318.. 235 H
debbie.roberts@kzoo.edu
THOMPSON, Debra .... 480-731-8510...... 13 N
debra.thompson@domail.maricopa.edu
THOMPSON, Delores .... 575-492-2519.. 300 H
dthompson@nmjc.edu
THOMPSON, Desiree .... 207-454-1021.. 204 A
dthompson@wccc.me.edu
THOMPSON, Dhyia .... 312-850-7344.. 138 A
dthompson143@ccc.edu
THOMPSON, Diane .... 559-791-2278.... 47 L
dithomps@portervillecollege.edu
THOMPSON, Dianne .... 410-617-2901.. 208 G
dcthompson1@loyola.edu
THOMPSON, Dick .... 207-621-3417.. 204 G
dick.thompson@maine.edu
THOMPSON, Dixie .... 865-974-2475.. 448 E
dixielee@utk.edu
THOMPSON, Edward, J .... 516-323-4600.. 321 H
ethompson@molloy.edu
THOMPSON, Eileen .... 617-879-2413.. 229 G
ethompson@wheelock.edu
THOMPSON, Emily .... 816-604-3022.. 267 J
emily.thompson@mcckc.edu
THOMPSON, Erik .... 202-274-5000.... 94 B
THOMPSON, Fannie, G .... 301-736-3631.. 209 A
fannie.thompson@msbbcs.edu
THOMPSON, Formon .... 928-724-6857.... 12 T
fthompson@dinecollege.edu
THOMPSON, Gary .... 518-783-2550.. 330 E
thompson@siena.edu
THOMPSON, Gary .... 701-845-7197.. 361 B
gary.thompson@vcsu.edu
THOMPSON, Geoffrey, B . 507-284-3268.. 245 F
thompson.geoffrey@mayo.edu
THOMPSON, Gerene .... 863-669-2886.. 106 I
gthompson@polk.edu
THOMPSON, Gina .... 662-243-2623.. 257 G
gthompson@eastms.edu
THOMPSON, III,
H. Lawrence .... 724-266-3838.. 421 C
lthompson@tsm.edu
THOMPSON, H. Paul .... 864-977-7768.. 431 G
paul.thompson@ngu.edu
THOMPSON, Herbert .... 386-481-2661.... 96 H
thompsoh@cookman.edu
THOMPSON, Houston ...... 815-939-5051.. 150 I
hthompson@olivet.edu
THOMPSON, Howard .... 563-425-5307.. 177 D
thompsonh@uiu.edu
THOMPSON, Ingrid .... 408-288-3131.... 62 E
ingrid.thompson@sjcc.edu
THOMPSON, Isabella .... 504-520-5441.. 202 C
ithompso@xula.edu
THOMPSON, Ivan .... 214-648-7101.. 478 C
ivan.thompson@utsouthwestern.edu
THOMPSON, J. Michael .. 209-946-2011.... 71 C
jmthompson@pacific.edu
THOMPSON, Jack .... 479-619-4140.... 21 D
jthompson19@nwacc.edu
THOMPSON,
Jacquelyn, F .... 407-582-5062.. 114 N
jthompson147@valenciacollege.edu
THOMPSON, James, P ..... 865-974-7262.. 448 E
jthompson@utk.edu
THOMPSON, Jamie .... 210-999-7547.. 473 A
jamie.thompson@trinity.edu
THOMPSON, Jana .... 701-777-2126.. 360 C
jana.k.thompson@und.edu
THOMPSON, Janet .... 908-526-1200.. 295 A
janet.thompson@raritanval.edu
THOMPSON, Jayne, M ..... 724-589-2130.. 420 D
pjthompson@thiel.edu
THOMPSON, Jean-Noel ... 334-386-7300...... 3 I
jthompson@faulkner.edu
THOMPSON, Jeanine, M . 845-575-3000.. 320 B
jeanine.thompson@marist.edu
THOMPSON, Jeanne, E ... 715-394-8598.. 521 E
jthomp51@uwsuper.edu
THOMPSON, Jeffrey, S .... 775-784-4591.. 285 A
thompson@physics.unr.edu
THOMPSON, Jennifer .... 802-443-5917.. 484 F
jenthompson@middlebury.edu
THOMPSON, Jennifer, L .. 804-752-7315.. 493 C
jenniferthompson@rmc.edu
THOMPSON, Jennifer, M . 605-677-5339.. 437 A
jennifer.m.thompson@usd.edu
THOMPSON, Jeremiah ...... 847-628-2016.. 144 B
jeremiah.thompson@judsonu.edu
THOMPSON, Jerry .... 252-536-7265.. 350 C
gthompson605@halifaxcc.edu
THOMPSON, Jerry, L .... 501-882-4523...... 18 I
jthompson@asub.edu
THOMPSON, Joan .... 478-218-3298.. 118 G
jthompson@centralgatech.edu
THOMPSON, Joanna .... 304-327-4050.. 512 P
jthompson@bluefieldstate.edu
THOMPSON, Joanne .... 507-453-2725.. 250 C
jthompson@southeastmn.edu
THOMPSON, John .... 562-938-4102.... 49 D
jthompson@lbcc.edu
THOMPSON, John .... 252-985-5218.. 354 E
jthompson@ncwc.edu
THOMPSON, John .... 517-629-0244.. 230 E
jthompson@albion.edu
THOMPSON, John .... 817-257-7860.. 469 G
j.thompson@tcu.edu
THOMPSON, Julie, G .... 828-694-1752.. 347 G
juliet@blueridge.edu
THOMPSON, Karen .... 970-207-4550.... 81 F
karent@mckinleycollege.edu
THOMPSON, Kathryn, S .. 770-533-6968.. 123 L
ksummey@laniertech.edu
THOMPSON, Kathy .... 641-628-5186.. 170 E
thompsonk@central.edu
THOMPSON, Kathy .... 703-764-0896.. 497 H
kthompson@nvcc.edu
THOMPSON, Kelly, M ...... 573-288-6323.. 264 F
kthompson@culver.edu
THOMPSON, Kelsel .... 214-379-5532.. 463 G
kthompson@pqc.edu
THOMPSON, Ken .... 601-974-1502.. 258 H
ken.thompson@millsaps.edu
THOMPSON, Kerry .... 323-259-2634.... 55 A
kthompson@oxy.edu
THOMPSON, Kevin .... 218-281-8254.. 255 E
thom2358@umn.edu
THOMPSON, Kevin, A ...... 270-384-8400.. 191 E
thompsonk@lindsey.edu
THOMPSON, Kim .... 206-546-6910.. 507 F
kthompson@shoreline.edu
THOMPSON, Kirsten .... 617-603-6900.. 226 D
kirsten.thompson@necb.edu
THOMPSON, Larry .... 501-786-7353.... 18 F
larry.thompson@arkansasbaptist.edu
THOMPSON, Larry, R ...... 941-359-7601.. 107 M
lthompson@ringling.edu
THOMPSON, Leroy .... 918-360-9694.. 382 D
thompsol@bacone.edu
THOMPSON, Lisa .... 425-640-1148.. 503 E
lthompson@edcc.edu
THOMPSON, Lonnie .... 386-506-3824.... 98 E
thompsl@daytonastate.edu
THOMPSON, Lori .... 304-473-8090.. 515 B
thompson_l@wvwc.edu
THOMPSON, Lynda .... 508-588-9100.. 223 G
THOMPSON, Lynn .... 386-481-2216.... 96 H
thompsol@cookman.edu
THOMPSON, Marcy .... 847-214-7486.. 140 A
mthompson@elgin.edu
THOMPSON, Maria .... 410-951-3838.. 212 E
THOMPSON, Mark .... 706-737-1418.. 117 D
mthompson@augusta.edu
THOMPSON, Mark .... 641-683-5306.. 173 C
mark.thompson@indianhills.edu
THOMPSON, Mark .... 315-228-7425.. 310 G
mthompson@colgate.edu
THOMPSON, Mark, A .... 203-582-8914.... 88 G
mark.thompson@quinnipiac.edu
THOMPSON, Mary .... 626-585-7202.... 56 H
mhthompson@pasadena.edu
THOMPSON, Matt .... 641-683-5185.. 173 C
matt.thompson@indianhills.edu
THOMPSON, Matthew, R . 785-833-4302.. 182 F
matt.thompson@kwu.edu
THOMPSON, Maxine .... 315-464-5234.. 332 C
thompsms@upstate.edu
THOMPSON, Michael .... 601-484-8700.. 258 F
mthompso@meridiancc.edu
THOMPSON, Michael .... 850-599-3301.. 110 J
michael.thompson@famu.edu
THOMPSON, Michael .... 309-556-1041.. 143 D
mthomps4@iwu.edu
THOMPSON, Michael .... 404-687-4530.. 119 D
thompsonm@ctsnet.edu
THOMPSON, Michael .... 808-853-1040.. 131 B
michaelthompson@pacrim.edu
THOMPSON, Mikah .... 816-235-6910.. 273 F
thompsonmikah@umkc.edu
THOMPSON, Mitch .... 719-596-7400.... 80 J
mthompson@intellitecmedical.edu
THOMPSON, Nancy .... 916-577-2200.... 75 C
nthompson@jessup.edu
THOMPSON, Nancy .... 620-343-4600.. 180 H
nthompson@fhtc.edu
THOMPSON, Nancy, R ..... 315-859-4020.. 315 D
nthompso@hamilton.edu
THOMPSON, Naomi .... 401-874-7077.. 426 D
naomi@uri.edu
THOMPSON, Natalie .... 201-200-2016.. 293 C
nthompson@njcu.edu
THOMPSON, Nigel .... 718-270-6136.. 309 B
nigel@mec.cuny.edu
THOMPSON, Pat .... 972-825-4670.. 466 D
pthompson@sagu.edu
THOMPSON, Patricia, A .. 607-735-1730.. 313 F
pthompson@elmira.edu
THOMPSON, III, Paul ...... 312-553-5963.. 137 D
pthompson40@ccc.edu
THOMPSON, Peter .... 315-568-3123.. 323 A
pthompson@nycc.edu
THOMPSON, Phyllis .... 803-705-4720.. 427 D
thompsop@benedict.edu
THOMPSON, Phyllis, A .... 423-439-4125.. 444 F
thompsop@etsu.edu
THOMPSON, PJ .... 618-537-6813.. 147 F
pbthompson@mckendree.edu
THOMPSON, Priscilla, C . 301-546-0462.. 210 C
thompspc@pgcc.edu
THOMPSON, R. Renee ..... 609-835-6000.... 93 F
THOMPSON, R. Renee ..... 856-482-4200.... 93 F
THOMPSON, Rachael, G .. 540-863-2837.. 496 H
rthompson@dslcc.edu
THOMPSON, Raymond ...... 252-985-5169.. 354 E
rthompson@ncwc.edu
THOMPSON, Remy, J ...... 804-342-3812.. 500 B
rjthompson@vuu.edu
THOMPSON, Rhonda .... 281-283-2021.. 474 A
thompsonr@uhcl.edu
THOMPSON, Richard, P ... 989-964-4166.. 240 F
thompson@svsu.edu
THOMPSON, Robert .... 229-243-3016.. 117 E
robert.thompson@bainbridge.edu
THOMPSON, Robert .... 920-206-2377.. 517 G
rob.thompson@mbu.edu
THOMPSON, Robert, J .... 301-295-3013.. 528 G
robert.thompson@usuhs.edu
THOMPSON, Robin .... 909-607-3822.... 57 H
robin_thompson@pitzer.edu
THOMPSON, Roger, J ..... 541-346-2542.. 395 G
rjt@uoregon.edu
THOMPSON, Ronald, C .... 864-294-2092.. 430 C
ron.thompson@furman.edu
THOMPSON, Ronelle .... 605-274-4921.. 435 E
ronelle.thompson@augie.edu
THOMPSON, Ryan .... 515-263-6149.. 172 H
rthompson@grandview.edu
THOMPSON, Sara .... 303-492-5148.... 83 K
sara.thompson@colorado.edu
THOMPSON, Sarah .... 303-724-1679.... 84 A
sarah.thompson@ucdenver.edu
THOMPSON, Sarah .... 352-335-2332.... 94 F
THOMPSON, Scott .... 530-242-7512.... 64 D
sthompson@shastacollege.edu
THOMPSON, Seth .... 607-844-8222.. 337 G
thompss@tc3.edu
THOMPSON, Sharling .... 803-705-4721.. 427 D
thompsons@benedict.edu
THOMPSON, Sheila .... 517-586-3013.. 232 F
sthompson@cleary.edu
THOMPSON, Sherwood .... 859-622-6587.. 188 F
sherwood.thompson@eku.edu
THOMPSON, Stacy .... 510-723-6627.... 37 B
sthompson@chabotcollege.edu
THOMPSON, Steve .... 309-467-6377.. 140 E
sthompson@eureka.edu
THOMPSON, Stuart .... 509-963-1004.. 501 K
stuart.thompson@cwu.edu
THOMPSON, Susan .... 843-349-7818.. 430 F
susan.thompson@hgtc.edu
THOMPSON, Tahmeka ...... 913-253-5026.. 184 G
tahmeka.thompson@spst.edu
THOMPSON, Teresa .... 912-478-1863.. 122 B
thompson@georgiasouthern.edu
THOMPSON, Teresa .... 520-621-6266.... 17 I
tlthompson@email.arizona.edu
THOMPSON, Terry .... 304-327-4062.. 512 P
tthompson@bluefieldstate.edu
THOMPSON, Thomas .... 928-428-8376.... 13 B
thomas.thompson@eac.edu
THOMPSON, Thomas .... 229-430-1718.. 115 K
thomas.thompson@asurams.edu
THOMPSON, Tola .... 850-599-3413.. 110 J
tola.thompson@famu.edu
THOMPSON, Tracey .... 610-683-4112.. 415 C
thompson@kutztownufoundation.org
THOMPSON, Traci .... 719-219-9636.... 77 H
tthompson@cavt.edu
THOMPSON, Travis .... 501-279-4464.... 20 D
thompson@harding.edu
THOMPSON, Troy, J .... 336-841-9404.. 345 A
tthompso@highpoint.edu
THOMPSON, Valerie .... 601-877-6385.. 256 F
valerie@alcorn.edu
THOMPSON, Venesia .... 415-405-4061.... 35 B
venesia@sfsu.edu
THOMPSON, Vinton .... 212-343-1234.. 321 B
vthompson@mcny.edu
THOMPSON, Virginia .... 918-781-7275.. 382 D
thompsonv@bacone.edu
THOMPSON, Walter .... 603-880-8308.. 288 A
jthompson@thomasmorecollege.edu
THOMPSON, Will .... 806-874-3571.. 454 F
will.thompson@clarendoncollege.edu
THOMPSON, William .... 717-299-7793.. 420 C
thompson@stevenscollege.edu
THOMPSON, William, G ... 386-226-7457.... 99 A
thompsb@erau.edu

TILLIS, Antonio, D .... 843-953-5770.. 428 G
tillisad@cofc.edu
TILLMAN, Harry, J .... 757-446-7073.. 489 B
tillmahj@evms.edu
TILLMAN, Henry .... 225-771-5497.. 199 H
henry_tillman@sus.edu
TILLMAN, Henry, J .... 225-771-5497.. 199 G
henry_tillman@sus.edu
TILLMAN, Keith .... 815-280-2385.. 144 A
ktillman@jjc.edu
TILLMAN, Mark .... 470-578-6565.. 123 J
mtillm@kennesaw.edu
TILLMAN, Rosalyn, P ...... 865-329-3101.. 446 G
rtillman@pstcc.edu
TILLMAN, Shalita .... 909-384-8659.... 60 C
scunningh@sbccd.cc.ca.us
TILLOTSON, Christina ...... 720-496-1370.... 80 I
christi999@roadrunner.com
TILLOTSON, James, R ..... 515-964-0601.. 172 F
tillotsonj@faith.edu
TILLOTSON, Jeanette .... 607-778-5195.. 332 D
tillotsonjo@sunybroome.edu
TILOT, Mary Jo .... 920-498-5409.. 524 E
maryjo.tilot@nwtc.edu
TILSON, E. Vincent ...... 704-233-8115.. 359 H
tilson@wingate.edu
TILSON, Linda .... 864-656-4542.. 428 C
nilson@clemson.edu
TILTON, Abigail .... 940-898-3326.. 472 G
atilton@twu.edu
TILTON, Brent .... 715-232-2346.. 521 D
tiltonb@uwstout.edu
TILTON, James .... 401-863-2721.. 424 J
james_tilton@brown.edu
TIMBERLAKE, Gregory ...... 419-755-4740.. 373 G
gtimberlake@ncstatecollege.edu
TIMBY, Tracy .... 215-968-8225.. 399 A
tracy.timby@bucks.edu
TIMKO, Michael, A .... 724-503-1001.. 422 H
mtimko@washjeff.edu
TIMLIN, Kevin .... 573-986-6863.. 272 B
TIMLIN, Kevin, J .... 906-227-2428.. 239 B
ktimlin@nmu.edu
TIMLIN, Laynee, H .... 757-455-2137.. 500 E
etimlin@vwc.edu
TIMM, Robert .... 480-212-1704.... 16 R
TIMMANN, David .... 610-436-2984.. 416 C
dtimmann@wcupa.edu
TIMMER, Amy .... 517-371-5140.. 243 I
timmera@cooley.edu
TIMMER, JR., James .... 616-526-6037.. 232 A
jrt3@calvin.edu
TIMMER, Jeff .... 708-293-4597.. 155 M
jeff.timmer@trnty.edu
TIMMERMAN, Candace ... 402-375-7034.. 281 J
catimme1@wsc.edu
TIMMERMAN, David, M .. 309-457-2325.. 148 E
dtimmerman@monmouthcollege.edu
TIMMERMAN, Melanie .... 740-392-6868.. 373 D
mtimmerman@mvnu.edu
TIMMINS, Alan, P .... 503-943-7507.. 396 B
timmins@up.edu
TIMMONS, George .... 518-464-8830.. 314 A
gtimmons@excelsior.edu
TIMMONS, Joseph, F ...... 918-631-2710.. 389 E
joseph-timmons@utulsa.edu
TIMMONS, Lora .... 312-935-6436.. 152 D
lotimmons@robertmorris.edu
TIMMONS, Tim .... 708-239-4787.. 155 M
tim.timmons@trnty.edu
TIMPONE, Peter .... 802-828-8554.. 485 E
peter.timpone@vcfa.edu
TIMPSON, Brigham .... 707-654-1788.... 33 D
btimpson@csum.edu
TIMS, Michael .... 410-888-9048.. 209 C
mtims@muih.edu
TIMS, Ray, L .... 919-532-5523.. 353 I
rltims@waketech.edu
TIMSON, Joe .... 816-802-3419.. 266 D
jtimson@kcai.edu
TIMUR, Aysegul .... 239-513-1122.. 102 T
atimur@hodges.edu
TINCHER, Lee .... 800-280-0307.. 158 E
lee.tincher@ace.edu
TINCHER, Steven .... 317-921-4882.. 164 E
stincher@ivytech.edu
TINDALL, Amanda .... 502-213-2255.. 190 A
amanda.tindall@kctcs.edu
TINDALL, Carolyn .... 262-691-5566.. 524 G
ctindall@wctc.edu
TINDALL, David, W .... 206-281-2982.. 507 C
dtindall@spu.edu
TING, Helen .... 650-520-3451.... 56 D
hting@paloaltou.edu
TING, John .... 978-934-2215.. 221 A
john_ting@uml.edu
TINGELSTAD, Erik .... 425-352-8162.. 501 J
etingelstad@cascadia.edu
TINGEY, Jeff .... 208-282-4064.. 133 H
tingjeff@isu.edu
TINGEY, Kent, M .... 208-282-3198.. 133 H
tingkent@isu.edu
TINGKANG, Monique ...... 808-844-2398.. 132 A
monique4@hawaii.edu
TINGLE, Caroline, D .... 386-312-4270.. 108 B
carolinetingle@sjrstate.edu
TINGLE, Chris .... 615-366-4449.. 444 D
chris.tingle@tbr.edu
TINGLEFF, Brian, P .... 515-643-6663.. 175 B
btingleff@mercydesmoines.org
TINGSON-GATUZ,
Connie .... 734-432-5883.. 237 D
ctingson-gatuz@madonna.edu
TINKEY, Danya .... 412-536-1029.. 406 K
dayna.tinkey@laroche.edu
TINKEY, Jim .... 412-536-1011.. 406 K
jim.tinkey@laroche.edu
TINKHAM, Shelley .... 413-572-5713.. 222 E
stinkham@westfield.ma.edu
TINLEY, Jeffrey .... 773-481-8830.. 137 I
jtinley@ccc.edu
TINLING, Walter .... 301-295-3083.. 528 G
walter.tinling@usuhs.edu
TINNEMEYER, James .... 724-852-3271.. 423 A
jtinneme@waynesburg.edu
TINNEY, Tina .... 985-893-7237.. 196 G
TINNY, Nicole .... 352-536-2145.. 104 J
tinnyn@lssc.edu
TINSLEY, Joseph .... 205-247-8885...... 7 E
jtinsley@stillman.edu
TINTERA, Judith, E .... 321-674-6303.. 100 M
jtintera@fit.edu
TINTLE, Nathan .... 712-722-6264.. 171 J
nathan.tintle@dordt.edu
TIONGSON, Stacie .... 212-817-7200.. 308 A
stiongson@gc.cuny.edu
TIPMORE, Barbara .... 270-686-4530.. 190 D
barbara.tipmore@kctcs.edu
TIPPIN, Mark .... 405-733-7343.. 387 I
mtippin@rose.edu
TIPPING, Christopher ...... 215-489-4190.. 402 A
christopher.tipping@delval.edu
TIPPINS, Kira .... 559-442-4600.... 67 C
kira.tippins@fresnocitycollege.edu
TIPPINS, Sharon .... 937-708-5626.. 381 B
stippins@wilberforce.edu
TIPPS, Jane .... 615-898-2670.. 444 G
jane.tipps@mtsu.edu
TIPTON, Alzada .... 509-527-5398.. 509 G
tiptona@whitman.edu
TIPTON, David, K .... 859-985-3728.. 187 B
tiptond@berea.edu
TIPTON, Joellen .... 936-294-1810.. 471 D
joellen@shsu.edu
TIPTON, Linda .... 812-749-1237.. 166 B
ttipton@oak.edu
TIPTON, Ryan .... 575-492-2137.. 302 M
rtipton@usw.edu
TIPTON-ROGERS, Donna . 828-835-4204.. 353 G
dtipton@tricounty.edu
TIRADO, Betty, M .... 607-436-2081.. 331 F
elizabeth.tirado@oneonta.edu
TIRELLA, Joseph .... 718-960-8013.. 308 B
joseph.tirella@lehman.cuny.edu
TIRONE, Shannon .... 330-941-3732.. 382 A
stirone@ysu.edu
TIRRELL, Matthew .... 773-834-2001.. 156 D
mtirrell@uchicago.edu
TISCH, Kate .... 414-382-6036.. 515 D
kate.tisch@alverno.edu
TISDALE, Bradley .... 601-923-1600.. 260 E
btisdale@rts.edu
TISDALE, Henry, N .... 803-535-5412.. 428 B
tisdale@claflin.edu
TISDALE, James .... 843-208-8050.. 434 A
jtisdale@mailbox.sc.edu
TISDALE, Jilo .... 404-270-5305.. 128 A
jtisdale@spelman.edu
TISDALE, Verlie, A .... 803-535-5433.. 428 B
vtisdale@claflin.edu
TISON, Jennifer, S .... 606-783-9507.. 191 H
j.tison@moreheadstate.edu
TITERA, Will .... 619-876-4252.... 68 I
wtitera@usuniversity.edu
TITHERADGE, Inge-Lise ... 626-584-5464.... 44 G
ititheradge@fuller.edu
TITSWORTH, Scott .... 740-593-4828.. 375 H
titswort@ohio.edu
TITTLE, Brandon .... 501-279-4442.... 20 D
btittle@harding.edu
TITTLE, Katelyn .... 918-343-6816.. 387 F
ktittle@rsu.edu
TITTMANN, Frederick .... 703-323-4220.. 497 H
ftittmann@nvcc.edu
TITUS, Charlie .... 617-287-7895.. 220 G
charlie.titus@umb.edu
TITUS, Elizabeth .... 575-646-1508.. 300 J
etitus@nmsu.edu
TITUS, Lisa .... 610-341-1955.. 403 B
ltitus@eastern.edu
TITUS, Sherry .... 760-744-1150.... 56 F
stitus@palomar.edu
TITUS, Steven, E .... 319-385-6204.. 174 A
stitus@iw.edu
TITUS, Varkey, K .... 478-471-2724.. 124 E
varkey.titus@mga.edu
TIU, Carla .... 605-394-2649.. 437 E
carla.tiu@sdsmt.edu
TIVEY, Margaret, K .... 508-289-3362.. 230 B
mktivey@whoi.edu
TIWARI, Suresh .... 843-661-8101.. 429 J
suresh.tiwari@fdtc.edu
TIZOL, Iris .... 787-258-1502.. 531 K
itizol@columbiacentral.edu
TJEERDSMA, Mel .... 660-562-1212.. 269 J
mtjeerdsma@nwmissouri.edu
TKACH, Christopher .... 281-655-3719.. 461 B
christopher.t.tkach@lonestar.edu
TO, Dai, L .... 925-631-4362.... 59 I
dlt4@stmarys-ca.edu
TO, Karen .... 719-389-6144.... 77 J
kto@coloradocollege.edu
TO, Tom .... 714-484-7097.... 54 G
tto@cypresscollege.edu
TOADER, Andreea .... 843-863-7826.. 427 I
atoader@csuniv.edu
TOAL, Erin .... 607-431-4547.. 315 E
toale@hartwick.edu
TOAY, Taun .... 845-758-7745.. 304 F
toay@bard.edu
TOBAKOS, Leslie .... 248-645-3360.. 233 B
ltobakos@cranbrook.edu
TOBEK, Alexandra, C .... 626-395-6594.... 30 H
atobeck@caltech.edu
TOBEN, Bradley J, B .... 254-710-1911.. 452 H
brad_toben@baylor.edu
TOBIAS, Barbara, A .... 330-325-6726.. 373 H
btobias@neomed.edu
TOBIAS, David .... 610-409-3316.. 422 D
dtobias@ursinus.edu
TOBIAS-JOHNSON,
Jaynn .... 708-239-4759.. 155 M
jaynn.tobias-johnson@trnty.edu
TOBIN, Christopher .... 843-953-3694.. 428 G
tobinc@cofc.edu
TOBIN, Donald .... 410-706-2041.. 211 F
dtobin@law.umaryland.edu
TOBIN, Doreen .... 570-422-3463.. 414 H
dtobin@esu.edu
TOBIN, Jeanette .... 712-279-5433.. 170 B
jeanette.tobin@briarcliff.edu
TOBIN, Jim .... 516-773-5993.. 529 B
jim.tobin@alumni.usmma.edu
TOBIN, John, M .... 617-373-7666.. 227 B
TOBIN, Kristen .... 617-266-2030.. 226 E
TOBIN, JR., Walt .... 803-535-1201.. 431 I
tobinw@octech.edu
TOBIN, William, M .... 765-658-4156.. 160 F
wtobin@depauw.edu
TOBROCKE, Toby .... 518-587-2100.. 335 D
toby.tobrocke@esc.edu
TODA, Frank .... 541-506-6103.. 390 I
ftoda@cgcc.edu
TODARO, Julie .... 512-223-3071.. 451 N
jtodaro@austincc.edu
TODD, Allysen .... 614-287-3820.. 367 C
atodd12@cscc.edu
TODD, JR., Billy, R .... 214-887-5351.. 457 C
btodd@dts.edu
TODD, Christine .... 212-799-5000.. 318 A
TODD, Christine .... 440-934-3101.. 374 F
ctodd@ohiobusinesscollege.edu
TODD, Christopher .... 670-237-6797.. 530 D
christopher.todd@marianas.edu
TODD, Dwayne, K .... 740-368-3135.. 376 B
dktodd@owu.edu
TODD, Greg .... 248-689-8282.. 242 F
gtodd@walshcollege.edu
TODD, Harold .... 985-549-2222.. 201 C
TODD, James .... 209-575-6060.... 76 A
toddj@mjc.edu
TODD, Jason, L .... 417-268-6005.. 262 H
jtodd@gobbc.edu
TODD, Joan .... 765-285-5953.. 159 B
jtodd@bsu.edu
TODD, Mark .... 213-740-2101.... 72 D
mtodd@usc.edu
TODD, Nicole .... 812-855-0454.. 162 E
stodd@iu.edu
TODD, Patricia, A .... 315-386-7333.. 335 B
toddpa@canton.edu
TODD, Sarah .... 610-341-5384.. 403 B
stodd@eastern.edu
TODD, Sarah, E .... 315-379-3975.. 335 B
todds@canton.edu
TODD, Sharon, K .... 773-442-4670.. 149 J
s-todd4@neiu.edu
TODD, Sharon, O .... 850-872-3891.. 102 M
stodd@gulfcoast.edu
TODD, Timothey .... 270-809-4181.. 192 A
ttodd@murraystate.edu
TODD ROSKA, Kiely .... 651-255-6121.. 255 C
ktoddroska@unitedseminary.edu
TODD SPRAGUE,
Diane, C .... 512-475-6203.. 476 B
dtsprague@austin.utexas.edu
TODERO, Catherine, M .... 402-280-2004.. 279 H
catherinetodero@creighton.edu
TODESCHI, Kevin .... 757-631-8101.. 487 B
ktodeschi@atlanticuniv.edu
TODHUNTER, Jody .... 903-886-5072.. 468 D
jody.todhunter@tamuc.edu
TODISH, Marian .... 616-632-2959.. 231 A
todismar@aquinas.edu
TODOKI, Gayle .... 808-373-2849.. 132 G
g.todoki@wmi.edu
TODT, David .... 641-472-7000.. 175 A
dtodt@mum.edu
TOEBBEN, Martha, A .... 636-922-8243.. 271 A
mtoebben@stchas.edu
TOENISKOETTER, Richard 812-464-1899.. 168 E
rtoeniskoe@usi.edu
TOEPFER, Brandon .... 760-773-2552.... 40 B
btoepfer@collegeofthedesert.edu
TOEPPNER, Robert .... 267-341-3335.. 405 J
rtoeppner@holyfamily.edu
TOEWS, Brian, G .... 215-702-4227.. 399 E
provost@cairn.edu
TOGLIA, Joan .... 914-674-7813.. 320 G
jtoglia@mercy.edu
TOGONON, Roselle .... 691-320-2480.. 529 F
rbtogonon@comfsm.fm
TOKAR, Stephen, A .... 317-788-4905.. 168 A
tokarsa@uindy.edu
TOKPAH, Christopher ...... 610-359-5106.. 401 L
TOKUNAGA, Susan .... 808-984-3380.. 132 D
suetoku@hawaii.edu
TOLAN, Beth .... 972-883-4037.. 476 C
bnt031000@utdallas.edu
TOLANO-LEVEQUE,
Maryann .... 626-914-8602.... 38 D
mtolano-leveque@citruscollege.edu
TOLAR, Allison .... 205-726-2762...... 6 E
aplemons@samford.edu
TOLBERT, Arnold, J .... 305-623-1440.. 101 A
arnold.tolbert@fmuniv.edu
TOLBERT, Blair .... 706-379-3111.. 130 B
betolbert@yhc.edu
TOLBERT, Dawn, C .... 706-233-7215.. 127 A
dtolbert@shorter.edu
TOLBERT, Jason .... 870-245-5410.... 21 E
tolbertj@obu.edu
TOLBERT, Kit .... 270-745-2037.. 194 D
kit.tolbert@wku.edu
TOLBERT, Michael .... 848-932-4371.. 296 B
mtolbert@rci.rutgers.edu
TOLBERT, Stephanie, B .. 919-497-3233.. 346 B
stolbert@louisburg.edu
TOLBERT, Tom .... 802-258-3134.. 485 A
tom.tolbert@worldlearning.org
TOLCHER, Edward, A .... 989-774-1441.. 232 D
tolch1e@cmich.edu
TOLD, Thomas .... 303-373-2008.... 83 B
ttold@rvu.edu
TOLEDO, Angelica .... 323-267-3746.... 49 G
toledoa@elac.edu
TOLEDO, Armando .... 787-751-0160.. 531 M
mtoledo@cmpr.pr.gov
TOLEDO, Diana .... 360-596-5206.. 508 A
dtoledo@spscc.edu
TOLER, Paul .... 816-942-8400.. 262 G
paul.toler@avila.edu
TOLER, Terry .... 405-491-6314.. 388 A
ttoler@snu.edu
TOLER, Whiting .... 252-940-6334.. 347 E
whiting.toler@beaufortccc.edu
TOLES, Mellanie .... 937-328-6002.. 366 E
tolesm@clarkstate.edu
TOLES, Sharon, M .... 313-927-1341.. 237 E
stoles@marygrove.edu
TOLFA, Jill .... 415-749-4530.... 61 B
jtolfa@sfai.edu
TOLFREE, Timothy .... 910-938-6323.. 348 G
tolfreet@coastalcarolina.edu
TOLIA, Sam .... 708-456-0300.. 156 C
stolia@triton.edu
TOLISANO, Joseph .... 860-723-0125.... 85 E
tolidanoj@ct.edu
TOLIVER, Felicia .... 270-706-8438.. 189 C
felicia.toliver@kctcs.edu
TOLIVER-ROBERTS,
Rita, J .... 215-670-9265.. 412 D
rjtoliver@peirce.edu
TOLL, Ronald, B .... 239-590-7035.. 110 L
rtoll@fgcu.edu
TOLL, William .... 765-998-4931.. 167 C
btoll@cse.taylor.edu
TOLLADAY, Debra .... 615-333-3344.. 443 D
dtolladay@national-college.edu
TOLLEFSON, Allen .... 530-752-5418.... 69 A
jatollefson@ucdavis.edu

TOLLEFSON, Deborah ...... 336-334-5702.. 358 B
ddtollef@uncg.edu
TOLLEFSON, Leah .... 218-879-0813.. 249 C
leah@fdltcc.edu
TOLLESON, Jennifer .... 312-935-4244.. 143 E
jtolleson@icsw.edu
TOLLESON, Joanne, P ..... 678-341-6640.. 123 L
jtolleso@laniertech.edu
TOLLEY, April .... 540-863-2808.. 496 H
atolley@dslcc.edu
TOLLISON, Scott .... 662-329-7152.. 259 E
cstollison@muw.edu
TOLLIVER, Joseph .... 315-229-5311.. 329 D
jtolliver@stlawu.edu
TOLLIVER, Ona .... 903-565-5645.. 477 B
otolliver@uttyler.edu
TOLSMA, Robert .... 303-315-3701.... 84 A
robert.tolsma@ucdenver.edu
TOLSON, Stephanie .... 636-922-8512.. 271 A
stolson@stchas.edu
TOM, Marlene, K .... 415-422-2350.... 72 C
mktom@usfca.edu
TOM, Vicki .... 510-436-1520.... 46 E
tom@hnu.edu
TOMAN, Janelle .... 605-773-3455.. 436 L
janelle.toman@sdbor.edu
TOMANEK, Debra, J .... 520-621-7380.... 17 I
dtomanek@email.arizona.edu
TOMANEK, Jody .... 308-535-3624.. 280 M
tomanekj@mpcc.edu
TOMANENG, Rowena, M . 510-981-2850.... 57 B
rtomaneng@peralta.edu
TOMANIO, David .... 561-297-3076.. 110 K
TOMAS, Don, L .... 828-339-4242.. 353 D
d_tomas@southwesterncc.edu
TOMASELLO, Nicole .... 716-827-4352.. 338 E
tomasellon@trocaire.edu
TOMASIK, Paula, J .... 304-336-8340.. 513 F
ptomasik@westliberty.edu
TOMASZKIEWICZ, Teri .... 630-844-5511.. 135 E
ttomaszk@aurora.edu
TOMBARGE, Chuck .... 612-625-8510.. 255 H
tombarge@umn.edu
TOMBARGE, John .... 540-458-8134.. 500 F
tombargej@wlu.edu
TOMBERLIN, Lisa .... 229-468-2078.. 130 A
lisa.tomberlin@wiregrass.edu
TOMBLIN, John, S .... 316-978-5234.. 185 J
john.tomblin@wichita.edu
TOMBLIN-BYRD, Terri, L . 304-710-3472.. 512 B
tomblin@mctc.edu
TOMCZAK, Patricia .... 217-228-5432.. 151 F
tomczpa@quincy.edu
TOMCZYK, Christie, L ..... 304-243-2304.. 515 C
ctomczyk@wju.edu
TOMEI, Lawrence, A .... 412-397-6229.. 418 B
tomei@rmu.edu
TOMEK, Deb .... 402-552-3395.. 279 D
tomekdeb@clarksoncollege.edu
TOMENENDAL, Robert, J . 757-479-3706.. 496 B
rtomenendal@vbts.edu
TOMESCU, Cosmin .... 212-592-2000.. 330 C
ctomescu@sva.edu
TOMETSKO, Jim .... 814-824-2279.. 410 H
jtometsko@mercyhurst.edu
TOMFOHRDE, Tammy ..... 423-869-6465.. 441 E
tammy.tomfohrde@lmunet.edu
TOMHAVE, Brad .... 253-879-3529.. 508 D
btomhave@pugetsound.edu
TOMHAVE, Brian .... 909-599-5433.... 48 K
btomhave@lifepacific.edu
TOMHAVE, Daniel, P .... 507-344-7451.. 244 K
dan.tomhave@blc.edu
TOMKINS, Patrick .... 757-825-2799.. 498 G
tomkinsp@tncc.edu
TOMLIN, Elisabeth .... 719-587-7746.... 76 G
listomlin@adams.edu
TOMLIN, George .... 253-879-3522.. 508 D
tomlin@pugetsound.edu
TOMLIN, Kathy, H .... 540-464-7323.. 499 E
tomlinkh@vmi.edu
TOMLIN, Ross .... 541-888-7417.. 395 B
rtomlin@socc.edu
TOMLINSON, Ann .... 323-265-8669.... 49 G
tomlina@elac.edu
TOMLINSON, Bill .... 518-580-5177.. 330 F
wtomlins@skidmore.edu
TOMLINSON, Elise .... 907-796-6300.... 10 H
emtomlinson@alaska.edu
TOMLINSON, Jan .... 740-364-9510.. 365 D
jtomlins@cotc.edu
TOMLINSON, Jessica .... 207-699-5016.. 203 F
jtomlinson@meca.edu
TOMLINSON, Karen .... 706-864-1948.. 128 F
karen.tomlinson@ung.edu
TOMLINSON, Keith .... 727-736-5082.. 109 D
ktomlinson@schiller.edu
TOMLINSON, Rob .... 573-840-9649.. 273 A
rtomlinson@trcc.edu
TOMLINSON, Tim .... 865-938-8186.. 439 G
TOMLINSON, Timothy ..... 612-455-3420.. 245 A
tim.tomlinson@bcsmn.edu
TOMLINSON, Virginia ..... 503-883-2575.. 392 B
vtomlins@linfield.edu
TOMLINSON, Virginia ..... 509-542-4881.. 502 G
vtomlinson@columbiabasin.edu
TOMMASINO, Joseph ..... 631-665-1600.. 337 I
tpaphd@aol.com
TOMMEY, Dale .... 870-574-4512.... 22 G
dtommey@sautech.edu
TOMPKINS,
Anthony (Tony) .... 913-288-7150.. 182 C
atompkins@kckcc.edu
TOMPKINS, OSB,
John-Mary .... 724-805-2845.. 419 B
johnmary.tompkins@stvincent.edu
TOMPKINS, OSB,
John-Mary .... 724-805-2771.. 419 B
johnmary.tompkins@stvincent.edu
TOMPKINS, Karen .... 978-232-2131.. 218 D
ktompkin@endicott.edu
TOMPKINS, Michael .... 845-758-7523.. 304 F
tompkins@bard.edu
TOMPKINS, Perry .... 417-328-1488.. 272 C
ptompkins@sbuniv.edu
TOMPKINS, Ricky .... 479-619-4325.... 21 D
rtompkins1@nwacc.edu
TOMPKINS, Terrence ...... 503-845-3569.. 392 E
terry.tompkins@mtangel.edu
TOMPKINS, JR., Wendell 912-478-2586.. 122 B
wtompkins@georgiasouthern.edu
TOMPOS, Betty .... 717-391-6947.. 420 C
tomposb@stevenscollege.edu
TOMS, Debbie .... 605-718-2958.. 438 B
deborah.toms@wdt.edu
TOMS, Lisa, C .... 870-235-4300.... 22 F
lctoms@saumag.edu
TOMSIC, Frank .... 312-942-6832.. 153 B
frank_tomsic@rush.edu
TOMSIC, Margie .... 253-589-4520.. 502 F
margie.tomsic@cptc.edu
TOMSON, Kent .... 620-365-5116.. 178 A
tomson@allencc.edu
TONCHE, JR., Carlos ..... 845-569-3249.. 322 B
carlos.tonche@msmc.edu
TONCIC, JR., Andrew, A . 724-458-2170.. 404 F
aatoncic@gcc.edu
TONDER, Rick .... 701-777-4270.. 360 B
rick.tonder@ndus.edu
TONDI, Greg .... 973-290-4470.. 290 G
gtondi@cse.edu
TONELLI, Laura .... 978-921-4242.. 225 G
laura.tonelli@montserrat.edu
TONELLI-BROWN, Judith 508-373-9719.. 215 D
judith.tonellibrown@becker.edu
TONER, James, D .... 207-778-7494.. 205 A
james.d.toner@maine.edu
TONEY, Eileen .... 269-782-1301.. 241 C
etoney01@swmich.edu
TONEY, Glenn .... 706-245-7226.. 120 D
gtoney@ec.edu
TONEY, Jeffrey .... 908-737-7030.. 292 C
jetoney@kean.edu
TONEY, Patricia, A .... 508-854-4425.. 224 E
ptoney@qcc.mass.edu
TONG, Vincent, P .... 203-285-2415.... 86 C
vtong@gwcc.commnet.edu
TONI, Keith .... 508-678-2811.. 223 A
keith.toni@bristolcc.edu
TONIONI, Renee .... 630-466-7900.. 157 K
rtonioni@waubonsee.edu
TONKOWICH, Jonathan ... 307-332-2930.. 527 F
jtonkowich@wyomingcatholiccollege.com
TONN, Anke .... 985-448-4633.. 201 A
anke.tonn@nicholls.edu
TONN BOOKER,
Paulette, L .... 507-344-7840.. 244 K
paulette.tonnbooker@blc.edu
TONNESON, Julie, A .... 612-625-4517.. 255 H
tonne001@umn.edu
TONNOUS, Tracey .... 740-588-1377.. 382 C
ttonnous@zanestate.edu
TONONO, Hiroko .... 949-480-4116.... 64 J
htononc@soka.edu
TONREY, Donna, A .... 215-991-3726.. 407 A
tonrey@lasalle.edu
TOOEY, Mary, J .... 410-706-2693.. 211 F
mjtooey@hshsl.umaryland.edu
TOOKE-RAWLINS, Dixie .. 540-231-6059.. 489 H
dtrawlins@vcom.vt.edu
TOOKE-RAWLINS, Dixie .. 540-231-4000.. 489 H
dtrawlins@vcom.vt.edu
TOOLE, Raymond, L .... 610-359-5330.. 401 L
rtoole@dccc.edu
TOOLEY, Gary .... 901-321-4122.. 439 E
gtooley@cbu.edu
TOOMBS, Jean .... 216-791-5000.. 366 H
jean.toombs@cim.edu
TOOMER, Victoria, E .... 856-225-6104.. 296 A
vikki.toomer@camden.rutgers.edu
TOOMEY, Elaine .... 617-323-6662.. 229 H
elaine_toomey@williamjames.edu
TOOMEY, Marcia, D .... 978-232-2060.. 218 D
mtoomey@endicott.edu
TOOMEY, Richard, J .... 812-237-2510.. 152 A
richard.toomey@indstate.edu
TOOMEY, Summer .... 312-777-8513.. 142 G
stoomey@aii.edu
TOOMSEN, Corbett .... 414-847-3335.. 518 D
corbetttoomsen@miad.edu
TOON, Kellie .... 865-539-7245.. 446 G
kltoon@pstcc.edu
TOON, Rhonda .... 678-359-5124.. 122 E
rhondat@gordonstate.edu
TOON, Rhonda .... 518-454-5111.. 311 B
TOONE, Darlette .... 785-243-1435.. 179 N
dtoone@cloud.edu
TOONE, Eric .... 919-681-3484.. 343 J
eric.toone@duke.edu
TOOTOONCHI, Ahmad ..... 301-687-4436.. 212 F
tootoonchi@frostburg.edu
TOP, Brent .... 801-422-2736.. 430 C
tbltop@byu.edu
TOPHAM, Susan .... 619-388-2896.... 60 G
stopham@sdccd.edu
TOPIC, Milos .... 201-761-7827.. 296 K
mtopic@saintpeters.edu
TOPLIFF, Donald, R .... 325-942-2165.. 472 B
don.topliff@angelo.edu
TOPOLSKI, Virginia .... 201-559-6055.. 291 K
topolskiv@felician.edu
TOPOREK, Bob .... 847-317-6400.. 156 B
btopore@tiu.edu
TOPOUSIS, Dana .... 530-752-9841.... 69 A
dtopousis@ucdavis.edu
TOPP, Joelle .... 517-371-5140.. 243 I
toppj@cooley.edu
TOPPE, Michele .... 503-725-4422.. 394 G
toppem@pdx.edu
TOPPER, David .... 717-477-1124.. 416 A
datopp@ship.edu
TOPPER, Maria, L .... 301-447-5211.. 209 G
mtopper@msmary.edu
TOPPING, Ann, V .... 585-262-1676.. 321 J
atopping@monroecc.edu
TOPPING, Scott .... 269-782-1249.. 241 C
stopping@swmich.edu
TOPPLE, Dianne .... 518-828-4181.. 311 D
dianne.topple@sunycgcc.edu
TOPSHE, Joyce .... 860-685-3757.... 90 C
jtopshe@wesleyan.edu
TOPUZ, John, C .... 832-230-5350.. 462 K
john@na.edu
TORABI, Mohammed .... 812-855-1250.. 162 F
torabi@indiana.edu
TORAIN, Martarash, M .... 919-516-4118.. 355 D
mmtorain@st-aug.edu
TORCHIA, Richard .... 215-572-2131.. 397 G
torchia@arcadia.edu
TORCZON, Virginia .... 757-221-3460.. 488 F
vjtorc@wm.edu
TORDENTI, Laura .... 860-832-1605.... 85 F
tordentilau@ccsu.edu
TORGERSON, Adam .... 503-370-6274.. 396 G
atorgers@willamette.edu
TORGERSON, Jane .... 817-257-7940.. 469 G
j.torgerson@tcu.edu
TORGESEN, Stafford .... 410-857-2714.. 209 D
TORIAN, Aquia .... 251-344-1203...... 3 J
atorian@fortiscollege.edu
TORICK, Marc .... 717-396-7833.. 413 M
mtorick@pcad.edu
TORINO, Frank .... 212-659-7200.. 318 D
ftorino@tkc.edu
TORKELSON, Rick .... 310-954-4348.... 53 B
rtorkelson@msmu.edu
TORLONE, Daniel, J .... 260-399-7700.. 168 D
dtorlone@sf.edu
TORMEY, Jessica .... 608-265-5953.. 519 J
jtormey@uwsa.edu
TORMEY, Susan .... 315-498-2764.. 325 G
tormeys@sunyocc.edu
TORNETTA, Effie .... 510-628-8023.... 49 A
studentservices@lincolnuca.edu
TORNO, Keith .... 616-222-3000.. 236 F
itdirector@kuyper.edu
TORNQUIST, Kristi .... 605-688-5106.. 437 F
kristi.tornquist@sdstate.edu
TORNQUIST, Susan .... 541-737-6943.. 393 H
susan.tornquist@oregonstate.edu
TORNQUIST, Wade .... 734-487-0042.. 233 J
wtornquis@emich.edu
TORO, Dan .... 714-556-3610.... 73 B
daniel.toro@vanguard.edu
TORO, Elba .... 787-878-5475.. 533 H
etoro@arecibo.inter.edu
TORO, Sofia .... 909-607-7855.... 39 B
sofia_toro@kgi.edu
TORO, Zulma, R .... 501-569-3204.... 23 B
zrtoro@ualr.edu
TORO-CAMACHO,
Catherine .... 787-993-8870.. 537 G
catherine.toro@upr.edu
TORO-ZAPATA, Rogelio ... 787-264-1912.. 534 D
rtoro@intersg.edu
TOROK, Kate, M .... 585-385-3801.. 328 E
ktorok@sjfc.edu
TOROSYAN, Roben .... 508-531-2435.. 221 C
roben.torosyan@bridgew.edu
TORPEY, Stacey .... 860-701-7787.... 88 D
torpey_s@mitchell.edu
TORPEY GARGANTA,
Kathleen .... 508-678-2811.. 223 A
kathy.garganta@bristolcc.edu
TORRACA MONDRIGUEZ,
Jose, G .... 787-720-4476.. 537 A
decanatoacademico@mizpa.edu
TORRANCE, Peggy, L ...... 218-299-3339.. 246 A
torrance@cord.edu
TORRE, Patrick .... 203-932-7224.... 90 A
ptorre@newhaven.edu
TORRE, Scott .... 201-761-7403.. 296 K
storre@saintpeters.edu
TORRECILHA, Ramon, S .. 413-572-5201.. 222 E
president@westfield.ma.edu
TORREGROSSA, Tom .... 318-342-5353.. 201 E
torregrossa@ulm.edu
TORRENCE, Michael .... 615-230-3350.. 447 C
michael.torrence@volstate.edu
TORRENS, Michael .... 435-797-0220.. 482 B
michael.torrens@usu.edu
TORRES, Abigail .... 787-878-5475.. 533 H
atorres@arecibo.inter.edu
TORRES, Ana, D .... 787-834-9595.. 536 E
atorres@uaa.edu
TORRES, Angela .... 787-751-1912.. 534 E
atorres@juris.inter.edu
TORRES, Angelica .... 787-850-0000.. 538 B
angelica.torres3@upr.edu
TORRES, Anna .... 330-941-3675.. 382 A
amtorres@ysu.edu
TORRES, Arlene .... 914-337-9300.. 311 F
arlene.torres@concordia-ny.edu
TORRES, Betania .... 863-667-5463.. 109 L
btorres@seu.edu
TORRES, Cari .... 415-485-9505.... 40 C
ctorres@marin.edu
TORRES, Carmen .... 787-864-2222.. 534 A
carmen.torres@guayama.inter.edu
TORRES, Carmen .... 787-878-4146.. 537 F
carmen.torres6@upr.edu
TORRES, Carmen, Z .... 787-841-2000.. 535 I
cl_torres@pucpr.edu
TORRES, Cathy .... 305-809-3250.. 100 N
cathy.torres@fkcc.edu
TORRES, Christine .... 281-998-6150.. 464 J
christine.torres@sjcd.edu
TORRES, Cristobal .... 305-899-3836.... 96 D
ctorres@barry.edu
TORRES, Darlin .... 787-250-1912.. 534 B
djtorres@metro.inter.edu
TORRES, Doris, S .... 787-844-8181.. 538 E
doris.torres3@upr.edu
TORRES, Eliseo, S .... 505-277-0952.. 302 F
cheo@unm.edu
TORRES, Elsie, M .... 787-258-1501.. 531 K
etorres@columbiacentral.edu
TORRES, Enrique .... 219-473-7770.. 159 L
TORRES, Evelyn .... 787-264-1912.. 534 D
evetorre@intersg.edu
TORRES, Evelyn .... 787-882-2065.. 536 D
directora_planificacion@unitecpr.net
TORRES, Frank .... 623-845-3904.... 14 C
frank.torres@gccaz.edu
TORRES, Gaile .... 406-395-4875.. 278 F
gtorres@stonechild.edu
TORRES, Gema, C .... 787-279-1912.. 533 J
gtorres@bayamon.inter.edu
TORRES, Gloria .... 405-682-1611.. 385 D
gloria.torres@occc.edu
TORRES, Greg .... 325-574-7640.. 479 I
gtorres@wtc.edu
TORRES, Henry .... 870-972-3033.... 18 J
htorres@astate.edu
TORRES, Joan .... 670-237-6777.. 530 D
joan.torres@marianas.edu
TORRES, Jorge, A .... 787-257-7373.. 535 P
jotorres@suagm.edu
TORRES, Jose .... 909-382-4021.... 60 A
jtorres@sbccd.cc.ca.us
TORRES, Juan, C .... 817-515-3055.. 467 A
juan.torres@tccd.edu
TORRES, Judith .... 787-786-3030.. 536 F
jtorres@ucb.edu.pr
TORRES, Kareen .... 954-201-7493.... 96 I
ktorres@broward.edu
TORRES, Leticia .... 949-753-4774.... 28 F
lespinoz@brandman.edu
TORRES, Louis .... 773-291-6245.. 137 G
ltorres@ccc.edu

TORRES, Lourdes .... 718-518-4151.. 308 C
ltorres@hostos.cuny.edu

TORRES, Luis .... 787-257-0000.. 537 H
luis.torres3@upr.edu

TORRES, Maribel .... 787-884-6000.. 532 O
mtorres@icprjc.edu

TORRES, Mariela .... 914-654-5568.. 311 A
martorres@cnr.edu

TORRES, Mary .... 713-221-8611.. 474 B
torresm@uhd.edu

TORRES, Michael .... 516-323-4834.. 321 H
mtorres@molloy.edu

TORRES, Migdalia .... 787-288-1118.. 535 O

TORRES, Miguel .... 787-664-0352.. 539 A
miguel.torres10@upr.edu

TORRES, Miriam .... 215-489-2267.. 402 A
miriam.torres@delval.edu

TORRES, Monica .... 574-527-7521.. 301 C
dacc-vpaa@dacc.nmsu.edu

TORRES, Nancy .... 562-985-4031.... 33 B
nancy.torres@csulb.edu

TORRES, Omar .... 661-362-3135.... 40 A
omar.torres@canyons.edu

TORRES, Rhonda .... 817-598-6212.. 479 E
rtorres@wc.edu

TORRES, Roamé .... 787-754-2744.. 538 F
roametorres@gmail.com

TORRES, Roberto, D .... 312-922-1884.. 147 B
rtorres@maccormac.edu

TORRES, Robin .... 559-443-8604.... 67 C
robin.torres@fresnocitycollege.edu

TORRES, Rosa del C .... 787-738-2161.. 538 A
rosadelc.torres@upr.edu

TORRES, Rosalie .... 818-364-7612.... 49 J

TORRES, Rosie .... 787-832-4040.. 538 C
servmed@uprm.edu

TORRES, Sarey .... 310-360-8888.... 25 C

TORRES, Sulynet .... 787-753-6000.. 532 O
storres@icprjc.edu

TORRES, Sylka .... 787-815-0000.. 537 F
sylka.torres@upr.edu

TORRES, Vanessa .... 210-486-0881.. 450 F
vtorres120@alamo.edu

TORRES, Viviana .... 787-884-6000.. 532 O
vtorres@icprjc.edu

TORRES, Wilmarie .... 787-743-4041.. 531 K
wtorres@columbiacentral.edu

TORRES-BATISTA,
Nelliud .... 787-993-8862.. 537 G
nelliud.torres@upr.edu

TORRES CAMPOS,
Cidhinnia .... 617-989-4366.. 229 D
torrescamposc@wit.edu

TORRES-DIAZ, Madeline . 845-341-4537.. 325 H
madeline.torresdiaz@sunyorange.edu

TORRES-ELLIS, Regina ..... 562-902-3343.... 66 A
reginatorres@scuhs.edu

TORRES-LUGO,
Irmannette .... 787-738-2161.. 538 A
irmannette.torres@upr.edu

TORRES-PETRILLI, Diana . 212-678-8011.. 317 I
dipetrilli@jtsa.edu

TORRES-PETRILLI, Diana . 212-678-8014.. 338 I
dipetrilli@uts.columbia.edu

TORRES-RUIZ, Jose .... 787-840-2575.. 535 H
jtorres@psm.edu

TORREY, William .... 781-891-2377.. 215 F
wtorrey@bentley.edu

TORREZ, Nasha .... 505-277-3361.. 302 F
nashatorrez@unm.edu

TORREZ, Veronica .... 575-492-2146.. 302 M
vtorrez@usw.edu

TORRY, Phyllis .... 901-435-1555.. 441 C
phyllis_torry@loc.edu

TORTELLI, John .... 216-373-5308.. 374 B
jtortelli@ndc.edu

TORTI, Sylvia .... 801-581-7339.. 481 M
sylvia.torti@utah.edu

TORTORA, Michael .... 203-254-4000.... 87 G
mtortora@fairfield.edu

TOS, Angela .... 209-384-6192.... 52 E
angela.tos@mccd.edu

TOSCANO, James, P .... 757-822-1015.. 498 H
jtoscano@tcc.edu

TOSCHKOFF, Marisa, L ... 989-837-4337.. 239 D
toschkof@northwood.edu

TOSTADO, Francisco .... 831-646-3043.... 53 A
ftostado@mpc.edu

TOSTEN, Lori .... 717-262-2017.. 424 A
ltosten@wilson.edu

TOSTEN, Rod .... 717-337-6601.. 404 C
rtosten@gettysburg.edu

TOSTENSON, Wendi .... 229-217-4142.. 127 G
wtostenson@southernregional.edu

TOSTON, Margaret, Y ...... 731-881-7710.. 448 G
mtoston@utm.edu

TOTH, Jason .... 419-530-1420.. 380 D
jason.toth@utoledo.edu

TOTH, Joseph .... 609-652-4895.. 297 C
joseph.toth@stockton.edu

TOTH, Maria .... 215-497-8717.. 399 A
maria.toth@bucks.edu

TOTINO, Robert .... 617-989-4325.. 229 D
totinor@wit.edu

TOTTEN, Willette .... 870-575-4713.... 23 E
tottenw@uapb.edu

TOTTY, Angela .... 417-255-7225.. 269 A
angelatotty@missouristate.edu

TOU, Phillip .... 510-763-7787.... 25 B
ktou@acchs.edu

TOUCHSTONE, Lea .... 601-276-3726.. 260 H
ltouchstone@smcc.edu

TOUHY, Jack .... 773-298-3540.. 153 H
jtouhy@sxu.edu

TOUNEY, Shawn .... 270-809-4437.. 192 A
stouney@murraystate.edu

TOUPS, David, L .... 561-732-4424.. 108 F
dtoups@svdp.edu

TOURE, Kathleen .... 252-862-1282.. 352 D
krtoure5066@roanokechowan.edu

TOURGEMAN, Rachel ...... 305-821-3333.. 101 B
rtourgeman@fnu.edu

TOUSSAINT, Jess .... 630-466-7900.. 157 K
jtoussaint@waubonsee.edu

TOUTANJI, Houssam .... 269-276-3253.. 243 H
houssam.toutanji@wmich.edu

TOUTGES, Greg, A .... 218-477-2131.. 250 F
toutges@mnstate.edu

TOUZEAU, Leigh, A .... 865-539-7013.. 446 G
latouzeau@pstcc.edu

TOVAR, Cindy .... 312-788-1122.. 157 H
ctovar@vandercook.edu

TOVAR, Rina .... 386-822-7773.. 113 B
rtovar@stetson.edu

TOVARES, Carlos .... 951-487-3410.... 53 D
ctovares@msjc.edu

TOVES, Louise, M .... 671-735-2995.. 530 B
lmtoves@triton.uog.edu

TOVMASYAN, Anna .... 818-988-2300.... 53 I
atovmas@nccusa.edu

TOW, Sharon .... 817-554-5950.. 461 G
stow@messengercollege.edu

TOWAL, Patricia .... 340-692-4187.. 539 C
ptowal@uvi.edu

TOWARD, Ron .... 301-934-7728.. 207 B
rtoward@csmd.edu

TOWERS, Jason .... 540-769-8261.. 486 G
jtowers@an.edu

TOWERS, Joel .... 212-229-8950.. 322 E
towersj@newschool.edu

TOWEY, James .... 239-280-2511.... 95 Q
jim.towey@avemaria.edu

TOWLE, David, C .... 319-273-2676.. 170 A
david.towle@uni.edu

TOWLE, Elizabeth .... 410-857-2241.. 209 D
etowle@mcdaniel.edu

TOWLE, Roger, K .... 724-458-3355.. 404 F
rktowle@gcc.edu

TOWLE, Thomas .... 603-271-6484.. 286 F
ttowle@ccsnh.edu

TOWLES WILHELM,
Regina .... 423-478-7725.. 443 I
rwilhelm@ptseminary.edu

TOWNE, Becky, L .... 713-942-9505.. 459 C
btowne@hgst.edu

TOWNE, Melanie .... 541-684-7326.. 393 B
mtowne@nwcu.edu

TOWNER, Mark .... 978-232-2255.. 218 D
mtowner@endicott.edu

TOWNER, Valmadge, T .... 662-621-4130.. 257 B
vtowner@coahomacc.edu

TOWNES, Emilie, M .... 615-343-3966.. 449 A
emilie.m.townes@vanderbilt.edu

TOWNS, Gail .... 732-987-2266.. 292 A
gtowns@georgian.edu

TOWNSEND, Alan .... 919-613-8004.. 343 J
alan.townsend@duke.edu

TOWNSEND, Anitra, L ..... 208-459-5502.. 133 D
atownsend@collegeofidaho.edu

TOWNSEND, Bill .... 601-925-3257.. 259 A
btownsen@mc.edu

TOWNSEND, Candace, V . 337-475-5635.. 200 H
ctownsend@mcneese.edu

TOWNSEND, Debra .... 518-580-5733.. 330 F
dtownsen@skidmore.edu

TOWNSEND, Elizabeth, R 336-322-2104.. 351 H
elizabeth.townsend@piedmontcc.edu

TOWNSEND, Gayle .... 509-527-5183.. 509 G
townsegv@whitman.edu

TOWNSEND, George .... 913-667-5700.. 179 K
gtownsend@cbts.edu

TOWNSEND, Gregory ...... 540-636-2900.. 488 D
gtownsend@christendom.edu

TOWNSEND, Heidi .... 360-475-7160.. 505 F
htownsend@olympic.edu

TOWNSEND, JoAnn .... 727-864-8223.... 98 L
townsej@eckerd.edu

TOWNSEND, Joshua, W .. 410-334-2958.. 213 G
jtownsend@worwic.edu

TOWNSEND, Kenneth .... 601-974-1000.. 258 H
kenneth.townsend@millsaps.edu

TOWNSEND, Lori .... 516-726-5637.. 529 B
mcdonnelll@usmma.edu

TOWNSEND, Lori, A .... 828-262-2190.. 356 B
townsendla@appstate.edu

TOWNSEND, P, J .... 434-223-6144.. 490 D
pjtownsend@hsc.edu

TOWNSEND, Sonia .... 281-998-6150.. 465 A
sonia.townsend@sjcd.edu

TOWNSLEY, R. Michael ... 260-422-5561.. 162 B
rmtownsley@indianatech.edu

TOWSLEY, Scott .... 507-574-4929.. 510 A
stowsley@yvcc.edu

TOY, Charles .... 517-371-5140.. 243 I
toyc@cooley.edu

TOY, Matthew .... 615-248-1380.. 447 F
mtoy@trevecca.edu

TOY, Tasha .... 706-368-6985.. 117 F
ttoy@berry.edu

TOYA, Gregory .... 310-660-3504.... 42 J
gtoya@elcamino.edu

TOYADA, Maria .... 617-573-8265.. 228 G
mtoyoda@suffolk.edu

TOYAMA, Gordon, K .... 503-370-6265.. 396 G
gtoyama@willamette.edu

TOYE-HALE, Bernadette ... 270-686-4506.. 190 D
bernie.hale@kctcs.edu

TRABKA, Ellen .... 505-747-2209.. 301 F
etrabka@nnmc.edu

TRACEY, CM, Bernard, M 718-990-6570.. 328 F
traceyb@stjohns.edu

TRACEY, SC, Kathleen ..... 718-405-3775.. 310 H
kathleen.tracey@mountsaintvincent.edu

TRACEY, Kevin, J .... 516-562-3467.. 313 C

TRACEY, Patrick .... 401-739-5000.. 425 C
ptracey@neit.edu

TRACEY, Timothy .... 239-687-5303.... 95 P
ttracey@avemarialaw.edu

TRACHIAN, Barkev .... 336-725-8344.. 354 G
trachianb@piedmontu.edu

TRACHIER, Steven .... 817-531-4874.. 472 F
strachier@txwes.edu

TRACHTE, Kent, C .... 570-321-4101.. 409 F
trachte@lycoming.edu

TRACIA, Michele .... 617-582-4498.. 226 G
mtracia@aii.edu

TRACIA, Michele .... 603-623-0313.. 287 D
micheletracia@nhia.edu

TRACY, Carla, B .... 309-794-7266.. 135 D
carlatracy@augustana.edu

TRACY, Christine .... 217-228-5432.. 151 F
tracych@quincy.edu

TRACY, Danielle .... 567-661-7401.. 376 D
danielle_tracy@owens.edu

TRACY, David .... 508-588-9100.. 223 G

TRACY, II, Edward .... 313-993-1554.. 241 G
tracyeg@udmercy.edu

TRACY, Emily .... 315-733-2300.. 338 L
etracy@uscny.edu

TRACY, Emmett .... 617-746-1990.. 219 G
emmett.tracy@hult.edu

TRACY, Geofrey, L .... 419-372-8262.. 364 E
gtracy@bgsu.edu

TRACY, Heidi .... 940-898-3863.. 472 G
htracy@twu.edu

TRACY, James, W .... 785-864-7298.. 185 D
james.tracy@ku.edu

TRACY, Michael .... 229-931-2245.. 122 C
michael.tracy@gsw.edu

TRACY, Morgan, A .... 859-858-3511.. 186 J
morgan.tracy@asbury.edu

TRACY, Rhonda .... 859-256-3100.. 188 M
rhonda.tracy@kctcs.edu

TRACY, Sandra, G .... 901-843-3800.. 443 L
tracy@rhodes.edu

TRACY, Susan .... 641-472-7000.. 175 A
stracy@mum.edu

TRACY, Tim, S .... 859-257-5290.. 193 G
tim.tracy@uky.edu

TRACZYK, Joyce .... 763-433-1243.. 248 K
joyce.traczyk@anokaramsey.edu

TRAFECANTE, Michael ...... 203-254-4000.... 87 G
mtrafecante@fairfield.edu

TRAGNI, Carolyn .... 845-451-1615.. 312 C
c_tragni@culinary.edu

TRAHAN, Shelia .... 409-984-6239.. 471 C
trahansc@lamarpa.edu

TRAIGER, Jeff .... 816-235-5660.. 273 F
traigerj@umkc.edu

TRAIN, Larissa .... 480-423-6300.... 14 H
larissa.train@scottsdalecc.edu

TRAINA, Joyce .... 201-327-8877.. 291 G
jtraina@eastwick.edu

TRAINA, Lou .... 239-489-9215.. 101 F
ltraina@fsw.edu

TRAINA, Samuel .... 209-228-2857.... 70 A
straina@ucmerced.edu

TRAINER, James, F .... 610-519-7578.. 422 G
james.trainer@villanova.edu

TRAINER, Jason .... 701-777-3791.. 360 C
jason.trainer@und.edu

TRAINER, Jill .... 916-278-4655.... 34 B
jill.trainer@csus.edu

TRAINER, Karin .... 609-258-3170.. 294 D
ktrainer@princeton.edu

TRAINOR, David, P .... 617-552-3335.. 216 C
david.trainor.2@bc.edu

TRAINOR, Hope .... 563-425-5264.. 177 D
trainorh@uiu.edu

TRAINOR, Judith, L .... 508-831-5423.. 230 C
jtrainor@wpi.edu

TRAINOR, Kelly .... 704-330-4409.. 348 E
kelly.trainor@cpcc.edu

TRAINOR, Timothy, W ..... 301-447-5600.. 209 G
president@msmary.edu

TRAKTMAN, Paula .... 843-876-2405.. 431 A
traktman@musc.edu

TRAME, Michael .... 217-351-2433.. 151 B
mtrame@parkland.edu

TRAME, Mike .... 217-351-2551.. 151 B
mtrame@parkland.edu

TRAMEL, Caitlin .... 646-745-8310.. 304 I
ctramel@barnard.edu

TRAMMEL, Sheila .... 318-257-2235.. 200 G
strammel@latech.edu

TRAMMELL, C. David .... 859-858-3511.. 186 J
david.trammell@asbury.edu

TRAMONTANA, Joseph ... 803-641-3388.. 433 G
josepht@usca.edu

TRAMONTANO,
William, A .... 718-951-5864.. 307 D
tramontano@brooklyn.cuny.edu

TRAMONTE, Michael .... 713-500-3158.. 477 C
michael.tramonte@uth.tmc.edu

TRAMPF, Judith, M .... 262-472-4672.. 521 F
trampfj@uww.edu

TRAMUTA, Daniel, M ...... 716-673-3181.. 331 D
daniel.tramuta@fredonia.edu

TRAMUTA, Daniel, M ...... 716-673-3253.. 331 D
daniel.tramuta@fredonia.edu

TRAN, Bang .... 563-876-3353.. 171 I
btran@dwci.edu

TRAN, Binh .... 202-319-5244.... 92 A
tran@cua.edu

TRAN, Christy .... 415-371-0002.... 55 D

TRAN, Deborah .... 415-565-4740.... 69 B
trand@uchastings.edu

TRAN, Hanh .... 818-778-5959.... 50 D
tranh@lavc.edu

TRAN, Hieu .... 916-686-8484.... 31 F

TRAN, Lena .... 408-270-6434.... 62 D
lena.tran@evc.edu

TRAN, My Linh .... 773-907-4770.. 137 E
mtran@ccc.edu

TRAN, Nathanael .... 415-371-0002.... 55 D

TRANEL, Angela .... 817-722-1711.. 460 E
angela.tranel@tku.edu

TRANEL, Mark .... 314-516-5273.. 274 A
mtranel@umsl.edu

TRANG, Thuy .... 408-855-5081.... 74 G
thuy.trang@wvm.edu

TRANQUADA, Jim .... 323-259-2990.... 55 A
jtranqua@oxy.edu

TRANSUE, Mary .... 706-802-5457.. 121 C
mtransue@highlands.edu

TRANT, Meg .... 617-217-9046.. 215 B
mtrant@baystate.edu

TRANT, Rachel .... 508-626-4523.. 221 E
rtrant@framingham.edu

TRAPANICK, Benjamin, J 508-626-4505.. 221 E
btrapanick@framingham.edu

TRAPASSO, Kristen, P ..... 315-445-4265.. 318 E
trapaskp@lemoyne.edu

TRAPP, Daniel .... 313-883-8540.. 240 D
trapp.daniel@shms.edu

TRAPP, Lori .... 734-973-3529.. 242 G
lori@wccnet.edu

TRAQUAIR, Brianna .... 651-641-8866.. 246 B
traquair@csp.edu

TRASK, III, Tallman .... 919-684-6600.. 343 J
t3@duke.edu

TRASVINA, John, D .... 415-422-6304.... 72 C
jdtrasvina@usfca.edu

TRAUB, Gilbert .... 718-409-7385.. 336 A
gtraub@sunymaritime.edu

TRAUBE, David .... 304-357-0014.. 511 E
davidtraube@ucwv.edu

TRAUBE, Eve .... 212-410-8006.. 323 C
etraube@nycpm.edu

TRAUGH, Cecelia .... 212-875-4668.. 304 E
ctraugh@bankstreet.edu

TRAUPMAN-CARR, Carol . 610-861-1348.. 411 B
traupman-carrc@moravian.edu

TRAUSCH, Diane, M .... 312-261-3230.. 149 B
diane.trausch@nl.edu

TRAUTH, Denise, M .... 512-245-2121.. 471 F
president@txstate.edu

TRAUTMAN, Karla .... 605-688-4792.. 437 F
karla.trautman@sdstate.edu

TRAUTMANN, Roger .... 503-255-0332.. 392 G
rtrautmann@multnomah.edu

TROTT CLARK, Beth 717-796-5066 410 J bclark@messiah.edu
TROTTA, Carianne 518-381-1176 330 B trottac@sunysccc.edu
TROTTA, Neil 617-236-8867 218 G ntrotta@fisher.edu
TROTTER, Cheryl 704-461-6714 342 A cheryltrotter@bac.edu
TROTTER, David 913-360-7656 178 I dtrotter@benedictine.edu
TROTTER, Dennis 215-248-7304 409 D dtrotter@ltsp.edu
TROTTIER, Sheila 701-477-7862 362 D strottier@tm.edu
TROTTIER, Tracey 413-755-4057 224 G tatrottier@stcc.edu
TROTTY, Willie, F 936-261-3500 467 E wftrotty@pvamu.edu
TROUP, James 203-575-8220 86 G jtroup@nv.edu
TROUP, Pat 251-981-3771 2 I pat.troup@columbiasouthern.edu
TROUP, Patrick 612-659-6707 250 B patrick.troup@minneapolis.edu
TROUPE, Bonnie, L 508-565-1069 228 F btroupe@stonehill.edu
TROUSDELL, Roy 218-748-2413 249 I r.trousdell@mesabirange.edu
TROUT, Darice 847-925-6070 141 A dtrout@harpercollege.edu
TROUT, Margaret 503-943-7134 396 B troutma@up.edu
TROUTH, Catherine 303-361-7365 79 E catherine.trouth@ccaurora.edu
TROUTMAN, Linda 850-478-8496 106 G ltroutman@pcci.edu
TROUTMAN, Marcus 312-922-1884 147 B mtroutman@maccormac.edu
TROUTMAN, Matthew 301-696-3577 208 B troutman@hood.edu
TROUTMAN, Todd 810-762-0409 238 F todd.troutman@mcc.edu
TROUTT, Amy 618-545-3048 144 D atroutt@kaskaskia.edu
TROUTT, William, E 901-843-3730 443 L trouttw@rhodes.edu
TROUTWINE, Jason 765-973-8444 162 G jtroutwi@iue.edu
TROVALL, Carl 512-313-3000 455 F carl.trovall@concordia.edu
TROVER, Clay 706-721-4854 117 D ctrover@augusta.edu
TROW, Virginia, M 607-746-4635 335 C trowvm@delhi.edu
TROWBRIDGE, Christian, A 302-295-1151 91 I christian.a.trowbridge@wilmu.edu
TROWBRIDGE, Cory, D 316-322-0110 262 N cory.trowbridge@calvary.edu
TROXELL, Jeffrey, E 610-330-5330 407 C troxellj@lafayette.edu
TROY, Dan 805-546-3120 41 L daniel_troy1@cuesta.edu
TROY, Randy, D 260-399-7700 168 D rtroy@sf.edu
TROY, Robert 212-237-8118 308 E rtroy@jjay.cuny.edu
TROY, Shawn 989-386-6658 238 B stroy@midmich.edu
TROY SMYSER, Kathleen 717-396-7833 413 M ksmyser@pcad.edu
TROYER, Cindy 903-566-7461 477 B ctroyer@uttyler.edu
TROYER, Mark, J 859-858-3511 186 J mark.troyer@asbury.edu
TROYER, Melissa 402-437-2619 282 F mtroyer@southeast.edu
TRUBACZ, Joseph 727-873-4287 112 D trubacz@usfsp.edu
TRUBE, Julie 248-370-3915 239 K dichtel@oakland.edu
TRUBOVITZ, Dan 619-388-7495 60 H dtrubovi@sdccd.edu
TRUCKENMILLER, Greg 518-736-3622 315 A gtrucken@fmcc.suny.edu
TRUDEAU, Marc, V 805-482-2755 59 G rector@stjohnsem.edu
TRUDEAU, Mary, L 701-788-4754 360 E mary.trudeau@mayvillestate.edu
TRUDEAU, Sara, L 202-526-3799 93 E strudeau@johnpaulii.edu
TRUDEAU, Scott 248-204-3852 237 B strudeau@ltu.edu
TRUDEAU, Skip 765-998-5368 167 C sktrudeau@taylor.edu
TRUDEL, OP, Albert 202-495-3836 93 D registrar@dhs.edu
TRUDEL, Jeannie 864-644-5486 432 G jtrudel@swu.edu
TRUDO, Glenn 740-695-9500 364 B gtrudo@belmontcollege.edu
TRUE, Christopher, J 240-895-4317 210 E cjtrue@smcm.edu
TRUE, Don 803-508-7491 426 G trued@atc.edu
TRUE, Elizabeth 207-326-2251 204 C elizabeth.true@mma.edu
TRUE, Robert, L 317-274-4860 163 D rtrue@iupui.edu
TRUE, Shannon, M 850-245-0466 110 I shannon.mcdermott@flbog.edu
TRUEBLOOD-GAMBLE, Marjorie 541-552-6459 395 A truebloom@sou.edu
TRUELOVE, Bobby 205-652-3601 9 F bjt@uwa.edu
TRUESDELL, Cheryl, B 260-481-6506 163 C truesdel@ipfw.edu
TRUESDELL, Joanne 503-594-3000 390 F joannet@clackamas.edu
TRUESDELL, Nancy, D 920-832-6596 517 E nancy.d.truesdell@lawrence.edu
TRUESDELL, Nicole 608-363-2120 515 G truesdellnd@beloit.edu
TRUETT, William, M 704-272-5363 353 B wtruett@spcc.edu
TRUFANT, Nicole 207-602-2157 205 F ntrufant@une.edu
TRUHLAR, Mary, R 631-632-8950 332 A mary.truhlar@stonybrookmedicine.edu
TRUITT, Bettie 309-796-5001 135 I truittb@bhc.edu
TRUITT, Jennifer 217-228-5432 151 F truitje@quincy.edu
TRUITT, Terry 765-641-4354 158 J tctruitt@anderson.edu
TRUJILLO, Adrian 415-351-3515 61 B atrujillo@sfai.edu
TRUJILLO, Daniel 914-395-2252 329 K dtrujillo@sarahlawrence.edu
TRUJILLO, George 301-985-7283 212 C george.trujillo@umuc.edu
TRUJILLO, Henrietta 505-747-2134 301 F henri@nnmc.edu
TRUJILLO, Julie 801-818-8900 481 B julia.tetrick@provocollege.edu
TRUJILLO, Patricia 505-747-5448 301 F patriciatrujillo@nnmc.edu
TRUJILLO, Tamara 707-638-5317 68 C tamara.trujillo@tu.edu
TRUJILLO, Wendy 661-362-3447 40 A wendy.trujillo@canyons.edu
TRULL, Gregory 503-588-2722 391 B gtrull@corban.edu
TRULL, Jason 334-347-2623 3 H jtrull@escc.edu
TRULOVE, Milyon 503-777-7510 394 I milyon.trulove@reed.edu
TRULSON, Gary 608-743-4526 523 A gtrulson@blackhawk.edu
TRUMAN, Grace, H 561-868-3122 106 D trumang@palmbeachstate.edu
TRUMAN, Kevin, Z 816-235-2399 273 F trumank@umkc.edu
TRUMBLE, Jeremy 315-781-3806 316 C trumble@hws.edu
TRUMBO, Joelle 478-387-4775 121 E jtrumbo@gmc.edu
TRUMBULL, William, N 843-953-7416 428 A wtrumbul@citadel.edu
TRUMPOWER, Peter 330-494-6170 377 J ptrumpower@starkstate.edu
TRUONG, Chris 714-564-6043 58 G truong_chris@sac.edu
TRUONG, Lan 650-949-7823 44 B truonglan@foothill.edu
TRUONG, Susan 510-981-2937 57 B struong@peralta.edu
TRUSCH, Robert 413-755-4039 224 G rbtrusch@stcc.edu
TRUSCHKE, Michael 818-767-0888 75 D michael.truschke@woodbury.edu
TRUSDELL, James 267-341-3329 405 J jtrusdell@holyfamily.edu
TRUSHEIM, Dale 215-596-7291 422 A d.trusheim@usciences.edu
TRUSKEY, George 919-660-5389 343 J george.truskey@duke.edu
TRUSS, B. Donta 478-825-6291 120 F trussd@fvsu.edu
TRUSS, B. Donta 478-827-7594 120 F trussd@fvsu.edu
TRUSSELL, Jay 828-884-8340 342 C trusselljj@brevard.edu
TRUSTY, Denise, M 606-783-2000 191 H dmtrusty@moreheadstate.edu
TRUSTY, Steve 501-760-4240 21 B strusty@np.edu
TRUSZ, Bob 740-351-3267 377 C btrusz@shawnee.edu
TRUTNA, Kevin 530-283-0202 43 G ktrutna@frc.edu
TRUXAL, Randy 903-463-8717 458 H truxalr@grayson.edu
TRUXILLO, Betty, D 225-923-2524 194 E director@brsc.edu
TRYON, Sandy 515-964-6408 171 B sbtryon@dmacc.edu
TRYTTEN, Julie 563-387-1865 174 L julie.trytten@luther.edu
TRZASKA, Ken, J 620-417-1010 184 I ken.trzaska@sccc.edu
TRZEBIATOWSKI, Brian 773-481-8287 137 I btrzebiatowski@ccc.edu
TRZECIAK, Jeffrey, G 314-935-5415 274 N jeffrey.trzeciak@wustl.edu
TRZEPACZ, Angie 270-809-6861 192 A atrzepacz@murraystate.edu
TSAFFARAS, Peter, H 617-984-1776 227 F ptsaffaras@quincycollege.edu
TSAI, Patty 866-323-0233 58 E tsai@providencecc.edu
TSATSOULIS, Costas 940-565-4300 475 A costas.tsatsoulis@unt.edu
TSCHEPIKOW, Kyle 706-542-0054 128 E kyletsch@uga.edu
TSCHERTER, Andrea, G 812-888-5794 169 A atscherter@vinu.edu
TSCHETTER, Randall, C 605-336-6588 436 J rtschetter@sfseminary.edu
TSCHETTER, Wesley, G 605-688-4920 437 F wesley.tschetter@sdstate.edu
TSE, Waiyi 336-334-4244 358 B waiyi.tse@uncg.edu
TSEGAI, Adiam 716-884-9120 306 B aktsegai@bryantstratton.edu
TSEGAYE, Teferi, D 502-597-6310 191 B teferi.tsegaye@kysu.edu
TSO, Jay 212-757-1190 304 B jtso@funeraleducation.org
TSOLAKIS, Alkis 225-578-5863 197 I atsolakis@lsu.edu
TSURUMI, Tsuyoshi 808-983-4155 130 I yoshi.tsurumi@tokai.edu
TSUTSUI, William, M 501-450-1351 20 F tsutsui@hendrix.edu
TUAN, Mia 206-543-2353 508 E mtuan@uw.edu
TUBB, Joe 806-894-9611 465 G jtubb@southplainscollege.edu
TUBBS, Jeffrey, L 704-406-4253 344 E jtubbs@gardner-webb.edu
TUBBS, Richard, E 941-351-4742 107 M rtubbs@ringling.edu
TUBBS, Teresa 910-272-3662 352 E ttubbs@robeson.edu
TUBENS, Sylvia 787-738-2161 538 A sylvia.tubens@upr.edu
TUBMAN, Jonathan, G 202-885-3778 91 J jtubman@american.edu
TUBMAN, Lynn 215-248-7046 400 H tubmanl@chc.edu
TUCCI, Barbara 505-428-1264 301 K barbara.tucci@sfcc.edu
TUCHINSKY, Adam 207-780-4347 205 E adam.tuchinsky@maine.edu
TUCHMAN, Nancy 773-508-2475 146 G ntuchma@luc.edu
TUCHTEN, Ashley 773-577-8100 139 A
TUCK, Amy 662-325-3221 259 D at25@msstate.edu
TUCK, Martin 740-774-7200 375 H tuck@ohio.edu
TUCKER, Adam 704-847-5600 355 J atucker@ses.edu
TUCKER, Archie 256-372-8344 1 A archie.tucker@aamu.edu
TUCKER, Archie 256-372-5230 1 A archie.tucker@aamu.edu
TUCKER, Arlene, C 337-550-1288 197 K atucker@lsue.edu
TUCKER, Barbara 608-822-2456 524 F btucker@swtc.edu
TUCKER, Brandon 734-677-5087 242 G brtucker@wccnet.edu
TUCKER, Carey 870-864-7147 22 D ctucker@southark.edu
TUCKER, Carol, M 713-221-8269 474 B tuckerca@uhd.edu
TUCKER, Carolyn 360-416-7600 507 G carolyn.tucker@skagit.edu
TUCKER, Cecelia, T 757-683-5210 492 G ctucker@odu.edu
TUCKER, Charles, L 217-333-6677 157 A ctucker@illinois.edu
TUCKER, Cheryl 707-476-4293 40 D cheryl-tucker@redwoods.edu
TUCKER, David, A 812-888-4266 169 A dtucker@vinu.edu
TUCKER, Dawn 919-718-7437 348 D dmtucker@cccc.edu
TUCKER, Dayton 914-251-6915 334 C dayton.tucker@purchase.edu
TUCKER, Destin 731-881-7020 448 G
TUCKER, Diane, P 617-358-6887 216 E dtucker@bu.edu
TUCKER, Don, L 612-343-4162 253 Y dltucker@northcentral.edu
TUCKER, Eileen 610-660-1346 418 G tucker@sju.edu
TUCKER, G.L 218-846-3765 250 D gl.tucker@minnesota.edu
TUCKER, Gary, R 517-750-1200 241 E garyt@arbor.edu
TUCKER, Geraldine 512-223-7572 451 N gtucker@austincc.edu
TUCKER, Gretchen, G 704-406-4491 344 E gtucker1@gardner-webb.edu
TUCKER, Herman, V 254-299-8660 461 E htucker@mclennan.edu
TUCKER, Irene 775-445-4234 285 B irene.tucker@wnc.edu
TUCKER, Jameel 610-526-6092 405 B jtucker@harcum.edu
TUCKER, James 518-327-6286 326 B jtucker@paulsmiths.edu
TUCKER, Jean 251-460-6294 9 E jtucker@southalabama.edu
TUCKER, Jim 785-749-8460 181 E jtucker@haskell.edu
TUCKER, John 501-760-4229 21 B jtucker@np.edu
TUCKER, John, D 619-298-1829 66 D jtucker@ssu.edu
TUCKER, Karen 630-752-5060 158 C karen.tucker@wheaton.edu
TUCKER, Ken 205-652-3527 9 F ktucker@uwa.edu
TUCKER, Mark 336-386-3217 353 F tuckerm@surry.edu
TUCKER, Mark 513-244-8102 366 B mark.tucker@ccuniversity.edu
TUCKER, Mary, E 520-621-9438 17 I mtucker@email.arizona.edu
TUCKER, Melanie 701-483-2560 360 D melanie.tucker@dickinsonstate.edu
TUCKER, Michael 765-641-4295 158 J matucker@anderson.edu
TUCKER, Murl 714-547-9625 29 J mtucker@calcoast.edu
TUCKER, Nate 423-473-1190 441 B ntucker@leeuniversity.edu
TUCKER, Ned 402-826-8601 280 B ned.tucker@doane.edu
TUCKER, Patrick 860-832-1786 85 F ptucker@ccsu.edu
TUCKER, Richard 504-486-7411 202 C rtucker@xula.edu
TUCKER, Robert 325-670-1427 458 J robert.tucker@hsutx.edu
TUCKER, Sandra 386-481-2106 96 H tuckers@cookman.edu
TUCKER, Sarah 304-558-0265 512 O tucker@wvctcs.org
TUCKER, Sarah, A 304-558-0265 511 K tucker@wvctcs.org
TUCKER, Seth 315-498-2123 325 G tuckers@sunyocc.edu
TUCKER, Sheryl 405-744-6368 385 G sheryl.tucker@okstate.edu
TUCKER, Stacey 423-614-8637 441 B stucker@leeuniversity.edu
TUCKER, Stacy 913-288-7239 182 C stucker@kckcc.edu
TUCKER, Tom, T 304-367-4110 513 B tom.tucker@fairmontstate.edu
TUCKER, Tommy 870-307-7324 21 A thomas.tucker@lyon.edu
TUCKER, William 510-587-6037 68 L william.tucker@ucop.edu
TUCKER, William, T 631-451-4760 336 D tuckerw@sunysuffolk.edu
TUCKER-MCCLOUD, Janice, L 740-826-8024 373 E jtucker@muskingum.edu
TUDELA, Virginia, C 671-735-5590 529 G virginia.tudela@guamcc.edu
TUDGE, Christopher 202-885-2033 91 J ctudge@american.edu
TUDOR, Amanda 859-985-3316 187 B tudora@berea.edu
TUDOR, Donna, K 615-248-7703 447 F dtudor@trevecca.edu
TUDOR, Gail 207-941-7039 202 I tudorg@husson.edu
TUDOR, Jarrod 330-684-8940 378 H
TUDOR, jarrod 330-972-8940 378 G grt2@uakron.edu
TUDOR, Jeremiah 502-863-8727 188 I jeremiah_tudor@georgetowncollege.edu
TUDOR, Lisa 239-489-9350 101 F ltudor@fsw.edu
TUDRYN, Jonathan 413-755-4420 224 G jtudryn@stcc.edu

TUEDIO, James, A ... 209-667-3531 ... 34 E
jtuedio@csustan.edu
TUEL, Alexander ... 301-387-3028 ... 207 G
alexander.tuel@garrettcollege.edu
TUELL, David ... 865-471-2020 ... 439 C
TUELLER, Steven ... 808-675-3935 ... 130 E
steve.tueller@byuh.edu
TUESCHER-GILLE, Heidi ... 608-342-1125 ... 521 A
tuescheh@uwplatt.edu
TUFANO, Joseph, J ... 718-990-5800 ... 328 F
tufanoj@stjohns.edu
TUFANO, Tony ... 315-279-5251 ... 318 C
atufano@keuka.edu
TUFAU-AFRIYIE, Michelle ... 508-854-7568 ... 224 E
mtufau@qcc.mass.edu
TUFEL, Peter ... 212-686-9244 ... 304 A
TUGGLE, Joseph ... 601-477-4277 ... 258 E
joseph.tuggle@jcjc.edu
TUIA, Jennifer ... 360-596-5369 ... 508 A
jtuia@spscc.edu
TUITASI, Michael ... 310-434-4389 ... 63 F
tuitasi_michael@smc.edu
TUITASI, Sifagatogo ... 684-699-9155 ... 529 E
s.tuitasi@amsamoa.edu
TUITE, Kathleen ... 973-618-3534 ... 290 A
ktuite@caldwell.edu
TUITT, Frank ... 303-871-2591 ... 84 B
ftuitt@du.edu
TULAFONO, Grace ... 684-699-9155 ... 529 E
g.tulafono@amsamoa.edu
TULAK, William ... 318-487-5443 ... 196 B
williamtulak@cltcc.edu
TULL, Ashley ... 254-968-9080 ... 467 F
tull@tarleton.edu
TULLEY, Nickolas, B ... 240-895-4336 ... 210 E
nbtulley@smcm.edu
TULLEY, Ronald ... 419-434-4445 ... 379 E
rtulley@findlay.edu
TULLIER, Michelle ... 404-385-7344 ... 121 D
michelle.tullier@gatech.edu
TULLIO, Ann ... 718-631-6215 ... 309 E
atullio@qcc.cuny.edu
TULLOCH, Helen (Meg) ... 202-685-3948 ... 528 B
tullochh@ndu.edu
TULLOS, Charlotte ... 225-578-3113 ... 197 I
ctullos2@lsu.edu
TULLY, Greg, J ... 815-772-7218 ... 148 H
gtully@morrisontech.edu
TULLY, Sarah ... 414-229-4523 ... 520 D
swtully@uwm.edu
TULLY-DARTEZ, Stephanie ... 870-862-8131 ... 22 D
stully-dartez@southark.edu
TUMELTY, Susanne, M ... 718-960-1190 ... 308 B
susanne.tumelty@lehman.cuny.edu
TUMEO, Mark, A ... 904-620-1350 ... 112 B
m.tumeo@unf.edu
TUMEO, Michael, D ... 214-768-2808 ... 465 J
mtumeo@smu.edu
TUMER, Lisa, L ... 540-568-7820 ... 490 J
tumerll@jmu.edu
TUMIEL, John ... 207-221-4628 ... 205 F
jtumiel@une.edu
TUMLINSON, Karen, L ... 520-621-2516 ... 17 I
kdenman@email.arizona.edu
TUMMINO, Pauline ... 718-990-6106 ... 328 F
tumminop@stjohns.edu
TUMMOLO, Paul ... 212-353-4100 ... 311 G
pault@cooper.edu
TUNE, Kathie ... 434-791-7106 ... 487 C
ktune@averett.edu
TUNG, Lisa ... 617-879-7335 ... 222 A
ltung@massart.edu
TUNGSETH, Margaret ... 651-523-2203 ... 247 A
mtungseth01@hamline.edu
TUNNING, Michael ... 563-884-5865 ... 176 C
michael.tunning@palmer.edu
TUNSTALL, Denise, S ... 804-523-5029 ... 497 C
dtunstall@reynolds.edu
TUNSTILL, Hilda ... 931-393-1573 ... 446 D
htunstill@mscc.edu
TUOHEY, Christina ... 413-755-4475 ... 224 G
cctuohey@stcc.edu
TUOMEY, Lianne, M ... 802-656-2027 ... 485 D
lianne.tuomey@uvm.edu
TUPALA, Kay ... 920-498-5482 ... 524 E
kay.tupala@nwtc.edu
TUPPER, Barb ... 319-399-8000 ... 170 G
btupper@coe.edu
TUPPER, Rick ... 605-274-4499 ... 435 E
rick.tupper@augie.edu
TUPUOLA, Tafaimamao ... 684-699-9155 ... 529 E
t.tupuola@amsamoa.edu
TURANO, Rosemary ... 617-964-1100 ... 214 D
rturano@ants.edu
TURANSKY, June, S ... 302-857-1126 ... 91 C
june.turansky@dtcc.edu
TURAY, Abdul, M ... 502-597-6916 ... 191 B
abdul.turay@kysu.edu
TURBEVILLE, Donna ... 910-642-7141 ... 353 C
donna.turbeville@sccnc.edu
TURBEVILLE, John ... 315-470-6660 ... 334 E
jturbev@esf.edu
TURBIDE, Gerard ... 607-274-3124 ... 317 D
gturbide@ithaca.edu
TURCIOS, Mirna ... 661-726-1911 ... 68 K
mirna.turcios@uav.edu
TURCOTT, Frances ... 410-777-2340 ... 206 B
fmturcott@aacc.edu
TURCOTTE, Colleen, D ... 401-825-2159 ... 425 A
cdturcotte@ccri.edu
TURCOTTE, Jim ... 601-925-3809 ... 259 A
turcotte@mc.edu
TURCOTTE, Kristen ... 508-286-3561 ... 229 F
turcotte_kristen@wheatoncollege.edu
TURCOTTE, Paul ... 254-501-5817 ... 468 C
paul.turcotte@tamuct.edu
TUREK, John, G ... 714-879-3901 ... 46 F
jgturek@hiu.edu
TUREK, Joseph ... 434-544-8651 ... 491 F
turek@lynchburg.edu
TUREK, Lara ... 314-968-5944 ... 275 B
tureklar@webster.edu
TURELL, Susan ... 607-436-2125 ... 331 F
susan.turell@oneonta.edu
TUREN, Chris ... 323-663-7555 ... 26 D
TURGEON, Marla ... 309-649-6603 ... 155 G
marla.turgeon@src.edu
TURGEON, Paul ... 714-556-3610 ... 73 B
paul.turgeon@vanguard.edu
TURGEON, Pennie ... 508-421-3813 ... 217 B
pturgeon@clarku.edu
TURICO, Michael ... 602-538-9396 ... 11 B
TURK, David, F ... 845-675-4422 ... 325 C
david.turk@nyack.edu
TURK, Don ... 815-753-1088 ... 150 A
dtuck@niu.edu
TURK, Laura ... 540-831-5248 ... 493 A
lturk@radford.edu
TURK, Michael, W ... 334-833-4322 ... 4 D
mturk@hawks.huntingdon.edu
TURK FIECOAT, Heather ... 775-784-1110 ... 285 A
TURKS, Stacie ... 209-946-2225 ... 71 C
sturks@pacific.edu
TURLETES, Christopher ... 907-786-1110 ... 10 F
cmturletes@uaa.alaska.edu
TURLEY, Alicestyne ... 859-985-3783 ... 187 B
turlleya@berea.edu
TURLEY, Niki, W ... 229-333-5920 ... 129 G
nwturley@valdosta.edu
TURLEY-AMES, Kandi ... 208-282-3204 ... 133 H
turlkand@isu.edu
TURLINGTON, Ashley ... 410-778-7710 ... 213 E
aturlington2@washcoll.edu
TURLINGTON, Lisa ... 910-592-8081 ... 352 H
lturlington@sampsoncc.edu
TURMAN, Kevan ... 484-365-7441 ... 409 B
kturman@lincoln.edu
TURMAN, Paul ... 605-773-3455 ... 436 L
paul.turman@sdbor.edu
TURMAN, Thad ... 918-456-5511 ... 384 G
turman@nsuok.edu
TURNAGE, Craig, A ... 936-468-3407 ... 466 H
turnagecraig@sfasu.edu
TURNBO, Doreen, B ... 302-295-1192 ... 91 I
doreen.b.turnbo@wilmu.edu
TURNER, Aimee, L ... 607-255-6243 ... 312 A
alt82@cornell.edu
TURNER, Amanda ... 708-456-0300 ... 156 C
amandaturner@triton.edu
TURNER, Ann ... 315-279-5615 ... 318 C
aturner@keuka.edu
TURNER, Anthony ... 312-329-2022 ... 148 F
anthony.turner@moody.edu
TURNER, B, P ... 334-387-3877 ... 1 E
businessoffice@amridgeuniversity.edu
TURNER, Barbara, J ... 870-759-4112 ... 24 J
bturner@wbcoll.edu
TURNER, Barry ... 912-681-2758 ... 125 E
bturner@ogeecheetech.edu
TURNER, Brian ... 504-520-7515 ... 202 C
bturner7@xula.edu
TURNER, Caroline ... 916-278-6639 ... 34 B
csturner@csus.edu
TURNER, Carolyn ... 870-946-3506 ... 23 G
TURNER, Christine ... 503-699-3381 ... 392 D
cturner@marylhurst.edu
TURNER, Dale ... 205-802-1594 ... 3 C
dale.turner@vc.edu
TURNER, Darron ... 817-257-5566 ... 469 G
d.turner@tcu.edu
TURNER, David ... 734-487-9733 ... 233 J
dturne27@emich.edu
TURNER, Deb ... 419-358-3343 ... 364 D
turnerd@bluffton.edu
TURNER, Debra ... 304-384-5338 ... 513 A
turner@concord.edu
TURNER, Donna, A ... 252-246-1240 ... 354 D
daturner@wilsoncc.edu
TURNER, Eric ... 870-248-4000 ... 19 H
eric.turner@blackrivertech.edu
TURNER, Eric ... 870-759-4220 ... 24 J
eturner@wbcoll.edu
TURNER, Gary ... 615-844-5276 ... 449 H
gturner@welch.edu
TURNER, Gredon ... 402-465-2256 ... 281 K
gpt@nebrwesleyan.edu
TURNER, J Leigh ... 979-845-7725 ... 468 B
jl-turner@tamu.edu
TURNER, James ... 607-844-8222 ... 337 G
turnerj@tc3.edu
TURNER, James ... 601-318-6610 ... 261 I
jturner@wmcarey.edu
TURNER, Janet, K ... 503-943-7311 ... 396 B
turnerj@up.edu
TURNER, Jere ... 603-206-8165 ... 286 D
jturner@ccsnh.edu
TURNER, III, Joel, L ... 936-468-6315 ... 466 H
turnertrey@sfasu.edu
TURNER, John ... 318-345-9145 ... 196 F
johnturner@ladelta.edu
TURNER, Joseph ... 239-489-9015 ... 101 F
joseph.turner@fsw.edu
TURNER, Joseph ... 252-335-0821 ... 349 A
joseph_turner@albemarle.edu
TURNER, Julie, D ... 616-234-5708 ... 242 D
TURNER, June ... 760-921-5558 ... 56 E
june.turner@paloverde.edu
TURNER, Kandy ... 610-499-4498 ... 423 E
kkturner@widener.edu
TURNER, Kara ... 443-885-3350 ... 209 F
kara.turner@morgan.edu
TURNER, Karen ... 970-351-1216 ... 84 C
karen.turner@unco.edu
TURNER, Kathy, A ... 928-213-6060 ... 12 Q
kathy.turner@collegeamerica.edu
TURNER, Keith ... 218-879-0805 ... 249 C
kturner@fdltcc.edu
TURNER, Larry ... 704-355-7577 ... 343 A
larry.turner@carolinashealthcare.org
TURNER, Lathan ... 252-328-6495 ... 356 C
turnerla@ecu.edu
TURNER, Lauren ... 978-934-1804 ... 221 A
lauren_turner@uml.edu
TURNER, Laurie, L ... 253-535-7361 ... 505 G
turnerll@plu.edu
TURNER, Leslie ... 561-803-2473 ... 106 C
leslie_turner@pba.edu
TURNER, Lisa ... 937-708-5532 ... 381 B
lturner@wilberforce.edu
TURNER, Louise ... 406-586-3585 ... 276 I
louise.turner@montanabiblecollege.edu
TURNER, Marcia ... 702-889-8426 ... 284 G
marcia_turner@nshe.nevada.edu
TURNER, Marcia ... 239-513-1122 ... 102 T
mturner@hodges.edu
TURNER, Marietta ... 217-351-2505 ... 151 B
mturner@parkland.edu
TURNER, Mark, P ... 402-280-4073 ... 279 H
markturner@creighton.edu
TURNER, Marlene ... 408-924-1000 ... 35 C
TURNER, Mary Donovan ... 510-849-8209 ... 55 I
mdturner@psr.edu
TURNER, Matt ... 304-558-4016 ... 512 O
matt.turner@wvhepc.edu
TURNER, Michael ... 218-723-6387 ... 245 J
mturner@css.edu
TURNER, Michael, G ... 334-387-3877 ... 1 E
mcturner@amridgeuniversity.edu
TURNER, Patricia, A ... 310-206-3961 ... 69 D
pturner@college.ucla.edu
TURNER, Patrick ... 734-462-4400 ... 240 H
pturner@schoolcraft.edu
TURNER, Peter ... 315-268-6544 ... 310 B
pturner@clarkson.edu
TURNER, Phyllis ... 903-233-4170 ... 460 J
phyllisturner@letu.edu
TURNER, R. Elaine ... 352-392-1961 ... 112 A
returner@ufl.edu
TURNER, R. Gerald ... 214-768-3300 ... 465 J
mjj@smu.edu
TURNER, Rachel ... 305-626-3605 ... 101 A
ra.turner@fmuniv.edu
TURNER, Rebecca ... 727-341-3241 ... 108 D
turner.rebecca@spcollege.edu
TURNER, Rebecca ... 812-941-2547 ... 163 F
rebeturn@ius.edu
TURNER, Rebecca, E ... 256-782-5485 ... 4 H
bturner@jsu.edu
TURNER, Rebecca, O ... 256-782-5540 ... 4 H
rturner@jsu.edu
TURNER, Rich ... 904-632-5112 ... 101 G
rich.turner@fscj.edu
TURNER, Rick ... 714-997-6658 ... 37 F
raturner@chapman.edu
TURNER, Robert ... 910-362-7050 ... 348 A
wrturner72@cfcc.edu
TURNER, Robert, L ... 757-823-8670 ... 492 F
rlturner@nsu.edu
TURNER, Sandra ... 212-242-5499 ... 338 D
sandra.turner@tsca.edu
TURNER, Sarah ... 304-384-5348 ... 513 A
slturner@concord.edu
TURNER, Savonda ... 706-754-7870 ... 125 B
savonda@northgatech.edu
TURNER, Sharisse ... 850-201-8582 ... 113 E
turners@tcc.fl.edu
TURNER, Steve ... 219-989-2232 ... 166 F
sturner@pnw.edu
TURNER, Steve ... 918-456-5511 ... 384 G
turner@nsuok.edu
TURNER, Sue, Z ... 912-443-5485 ... 126 G
sturner@savannahtech.edu
TURNER, Susan ... 812-535-5143 ... 166 K
sturner3@smwc.edu
TURNER, Susan ... 203-932-7478 ... 90 A
sturner@newhaven.edu
TURNER, Sylvia ... 209-953-2119 ... 67 H
syturner@sjcoe.net
TURNER, Tara ... 410-951-3812 ... 212 E
tturner@coppin.edu
TURNER, Toi ... 830-372-8019 ... 470 C
tturner@tlu.edu
TURNER, Walter ... 404-627-2681 ... 117 G
walter.turner@beulah.org
TURNER, Wilson ... 304-243-2090 ... 515 C
wturner@wju.edu
TURNER, Windell ... 276-964-7342 ... 498 F
windell.turner@sw.edu
TURNER, Zoa Ann ... 972-524-3341 ... 466 F
TURNER-WATTS, Sheryl ... 864-503-5490 ... 434 G
sturner-watts@uscupstate.edu
TURNEY, Ann ... 870-307-7208 ... 21 A
ann.turney@lyon.edu
TURNIPSEED, Brandi ... 208-732-6378 ... 133 E
bturnipseed@csi.edu
TURNIS, Jane ... 719-389-6138 ... 77 J
jturnis@coloradocollege.edu
TURNOCK, Madeline ... 503-493-8550 ... 391 A
mturnock@cu-portland.edu
TURNQUIST, David, C ... 303-724-1100 ... 84 A
david.turnquist@ucdenver.edu
TURNQUIST, Sandra ... 906-487-7240 ... 234 A
sandra.turnquist@finlandia.edu
TURNSKY, Josh ... 909-794-1084 ... 40 H
jturnsky@communitychristiancollege.com
TURNTINE, John ... 817-598-6482 ... 479 E
jturntine@wc.edu
TUROCY, Paula, S ... 412-396-6652 ... 403 A
turocyp@duq.edu
TURPEN, James ... 402-559-4288 ... 283 A
jturpen@unmc.edu
TURPIN, Craig ... 502-213-2110 ... 190 A
craig.turpin@kctcs.edu
TURPIN, John, C ... 336-841-9000 ... 345 A
jturpin@highpoint.edu
TURPIN, Michael, H ... 903-983-8207 ... 460 D
mturpin@kilgore.edu
TURPIN, Randy ... 614-837-4088 ... 380 G
turpinr@valorcollege.edu
TURPIN, Tyler ... 715-634-4790 ... 517 C
tturpin@lco.edu
TURRENS, Julio ... 251-460-6312 ... 9 E
jturrens@southalabama.edu
TURRENTINE, Cathryn ... 603-358-2117 ... 288 E
cturrentine@keene.edu
TURRENTINE, Michael ... 304-336-8152 ... 513 F
mturrent@westliberty.edu
TURRIETTA, Anthony ... 915-747-6127 ... 476 D
aturrietta@utep.edu
TURTELTAUB, Rhea ... 310-794-5567 ... 69 D
rheat@support.ucla.edu
TUSACK, Donna ... 619-594-7500 ... 35 A
donna.tusack@sdsu.edu
TUSCHAK, Mark ... 830-792-7215 ... 465 E
mctuschak@schreiner.edu
TUSCHEN, Marc, A ... 863-680-3908 ... 101 E
mtuschen@flsouthern.edu
TUSCHMAN, Keli ... 620-331-4100 ... 181 J
ktuschman@indycc.edu
TUSKI, Don ... 503-821-8881 ... 394 B
presidentsoffice@pnca.edu
TUSKI, Donald ... 207-699-5011 ... 203 F
dtuski@meca.edu
TUTEN, Jennifer ... 212-772-4622 ... 308 D
jtuten@hunter.cuny.edu
TUTHILL, John ... 406-477-6215 ... 276 C
jtuthill@cdkc.edu
TUTON, Ginger ... 910-938-6225 ... 348 G
tutong@coastalcarolina.edu
TUTSOCK, Robert, J ... 989-964-4082 ... 240 F
tutsock@svsu.edu
TUTT, Betsy ... 573-592-4354 ... 275 G
betsy.tutt@williamwoods.edu
TUTT, Larry ... 270-831-9783 ... 189 F
larry.tutt@kctcs.edu
TUTTLE, Ann ... 315-279-5286 ... 318 C
TUTTLE, Cheryl, R ... 843-661-1360 ... 430 B
ctuttle@fmarion.edu

TUTTLE, David, M ... 210-999-8843 .. 473 A dtuttle@trinity.edu

TUTTLE, Gail ... 315-792-3016 .. 339 B gtuttle@utica.edu

TUTTLE, Gail, C ... 336-841-9120 .. 345 A gtuttle@highpoint.edu

TUTTLE, Heather ... 517-327-6253 .. 326 B htuttle@paulsmiths.edu

TUTTLE, Jane ... 803-786-3701 .. 429 A jtuttle@columbiasc.edu

TUTTLE, Lori ... 803-323-2145 .. 435 B tuttlel@winthrop.edu

TUTTLE, Nick ... 580-349-1353 .. 385 F nick.tuttle@opsu.edu

TUTTLE, Ronald ... 914-968-6200 .. 329 C ronald.tuttle@archny.org

TUTTLE, Stephen ... 212-217-4030 .. 314 B

TUXHORN, Rick ... 620-242-0468 .. 183 C tuxhornr@mcpherson.edu

TVARKUNAS, Michael ... 662-476-5059 .. 257 G mtvar@eastms.edu

TVRDY, Peggy ... 402-826-8260 .. 280 B peggy.tvrdy@doane.edu

TWADDELL, Gerald, E ... 859-344-3307 .. 193 C twaddeg@thomasmore.edu

TWARDOCK, Rob ... 847-543-2499 .. 138 C eng491@clcillinois.edu

TWEED, Brittany ... 763-433-1399 .. 248 L brittany.tweed@anokaramsey.edu

TWEED, Brittany ... 763-433-1399 .. 248 K brittany.tweed@anokaramsey.edu

TWEED, Emily ... 952-888-4777 .. 253 Z etweed@nwhealth.edu

TWEED, James ... 617-243-2225 .. 219 I jtweed@lasell.edu

TWEEDELL, Cynthia ... 740-420-7799 .. 374 G ctweedell@ohiochristian.edu

TWEEDIE, Frank ... 401-598-2503 .. 425 B ftweedie@jwu.edu

TWEEDY, Alison ... 214-768-1909 .. 465 J atweedy@smu.edu

TWELLMAN, David ... 313-883-8512 .. 240 D twellman.david@shms.edu

TWENTYMAN, Craig ... 808-521-2288 .. 131 A

TWERSKI, Boruch ... 718-438-2727 .. 341 J btwerski@novominsk.com

TWIGG, Sharon ... 802-635-1351 .. 486 B sharon.twigg@jsc.edu

TWINING, Hillary ... 802-451-7588 .. 484 C htwining@marlboro.edu

TWINING, Katie ... 912-344-3275 .. 116 E katie.twining@armstrong.edu

TWIST, Tony ... 317-299-0333 .. 167 D tony@tcmi.org

TWITTY, Brian ... 951-487-3103 .... 53 D btwitty@msjc.edu

TWITTY, Jennifer ... 256-352-8479 ...... 9 G jennifer.twitty@wallacestate.edu

TWITTY, Pamela, E ... 919-516-4127 .. 355 D ptwitty@st-aug.edu

TWO BULLS, Wayne ... 406-768-6312 .. 276 F wtwobulls@fpcc.edu

TWOMBLY, Jim ... 607-735-1702 .. 313 F jtwombly@elmira.edu

TWOMBLY, Meredith ... 413-559-5890 .. 219 C

TWOMBLY, Meredith ... 413-559-5471 .. 219 C admissions@hampshire.edu

TWOMEY, Dan ... 845-569-3591 .. 322 B dan.twomey@msmc.edu

TWOMEY, Maryanne, H ... 718-990-5743 .. 328 F twomeym@stjohns.edu

TWYMAN, Anthony ... 610-359-2816 .. 401 L atwyman1@dccc.edu

TYACK, Justin ... 212-875-4518 .. 304 E jtyack@bankstreet.edu

TYBURSKI, Kevin, R ... 336-322-2184 .. 351 H kevin.tyburski@piedmontcc.edu

TYBURSKI, Robert, L ... 315-228-7445 .. 310 G rtyburski@colgate.edu

TYDINGS, Flora ... 423-697-4455 .. 445 D flora.tydings@chattanoogastate.edu

TYDLASKA, Faye, F ... 407-646-2161 .. 107 O ftydlaska@rollins.edu

TYEHIMBA, Hope ... 919-530-6105 .. 357 A hope.tyehimba@nccu.edu

TYKOCINSKI, Mark, L ... 215-955-1628 .. 420 E mark.tykocinski@jefferson.edu

TYKSINSKI, Deborah, J ... 610-519-4300 .. 422 G deborah.tyksinski@villanova.edu

TYKWINSKI, Joseph ... 701-845-7330 .. 361 B joe.tykwinski@vcsu.edu

TYLEE, Katrina ... 308-635-6026 .. 283 D tyleek@wncc.edu

TYLER, Aaron ... 210-436-3716 .. 464 H atyler@stmarytx.edu

TYLER, Aesha ... 502-852-6585 .. 194 A altyle04@louisville.edu

TYLER, Barry ... 210-924-4338 .. 452 F barry.tyler@bua.edu

TYLER, Carol ... 304-829-7567 .. 510 G ctyler@bethanywv.edu

TYLER, Diane ... 210-297-9630 .. 452 C dtyler@baptisthealthsystem.com

TYLER, Indira, D ... 502-597-6964 .. 191 B indira.tyler@kysu.edu

TYLER, Jeanie ... 619-388-3414 .... 60 F jtyler@sdccd.edu

TYLER, Karlene ... 620-242-0400 .. 183 C tylerk@mcpherson.edu

TYLER, Katie ... 701-858-4363 .. 360 F katie.tyler@minotstateu.edu

TYLER, Ken, D ... 540-654-1876 .. 495 C ktyler2@umw.edu

TYLER, Lauren ... 903-510-2611 .. 473 C ltyl@tjc.edu

TYLER, Littleton ... 802-728-1252 .. 486 D jxt12280@vtc.edu

TYLER, Melvin, C ... 816-235-1141 .. 273 F tylerm@umkc.edu

TYLER, Michael ... 410-857-2500 .. 209 D mtyler@mcdaniel.edu

TYLER, Nathan ... 256-306-2817 ...... 2 F nathan.tyler@calhoun.edu

TYLER, Rico ... 773-325-4680 .. 139 C rtyler@depaul.edu

TYLER, Victoria ... 914-455-3515 .. 320 G vtyler@mercy.edu

TYLER-SIMPSON, Decla ... 816-501-4250 .. 270 J decla.tyler-simpson@rockhurst.edu

TYMANN, Daniel ... 978-867-4260 .. 219 A dan.tymann@gordon.edu

TYMANN, Jon ... 978-867-4039 .. 219 A jon.tymann@gordon.edu

TYMAS-JONES, Raymond 801-581-3887 .. 481 M r.tymasjones@finearts.utah.edu

TYMMS, Magaly ... 727-341-3195 .. 108 D tymms.magaly@spcollege.edu

TYMOCZKO, Michelle ... 303-477-7240 .... 80 H michellet@heritage-education.com

TYMUS, Peter ... 516-299-3370 .. 319 B peter.tymus@liu.edu

TYNAN, Craig ... 518-454-5111 .. 311 B

TYNDALL, Brad ... 307-855-2111 .. 526 E btyndall@cwc.edu

TYNER, Dennis ... 785-242-5200 .. 183 M dennis.tyner@ottawa.edu

TYNER, JR., Gary ... 214-638-0484 .. 460 C tynerjr1@yahoo.com

TYNER, Jennifer ... 707-965-6311 .... 56 A jtyner@puc.edu

TYNER, Kathy ... 619-482-6337 .... 66 E ktyner@swccd.edu

TYNER, Kathy ... 214-638-0484 .. 460 C ktyner@kdstudio.com

TYNER, Lee ... 662-915-7014 .. 261 B ltyner@olemiss.edu

TYNES, Craig ... 601-403-1155 .. 260 D ctynes@prcc.edu

TYNES, Sheryl, R ... 210-999-8201 .. 473 A stynes@trinity.edu

TYNON, Kathy ... 402-872-2365 .. 281 I ktynon@peru.edu

TYO, Keith, D ... 518-564-3930 .. 334 A tyokd@plattsburgh.edu

TYRA, Patti ... 213-615-7272 .... 37 I ptyra@thechicagoschool.edu

TYREE, Jonathan ... 434-947-8112 .. 493 B jtyree@randolphcollege.edu

TYREE, Tracy ... 203-392-5550 .... 85 H tyreet1@southernct.edu

TYRELL, Steve, J ... 518-891-2915 .. 325 A president@nccc.edu

TYRNAUER, Yitzchok ... 845-782-1380 .. 341 I

TYRRELL, Elizabeth ... 408-270-6453 .... 62 D elizabeth.tyrrell@evc.edu

TYRRELL, Wil ... 914-323-7178 .. 319 N wil.tyrrell@mville.edu

TYSON, AJ ... 252-789-0232 .. 351 A atyson@martincc.edu

TYSON, Daquiri ... 229-732-5958 .. 116 C daquirityson@andrewcollege.edu

TYSON, Jennifer ... 859-246-6507 .. 189 B jennifer.tyson@kctcs.edu

TYSON, John ... 334-386-7257 ...... 3 I jtyson@faulkner.edu

TYSON, John, N ... 248-218-2011 .. 240 C jtyson@rc.edu

TYSON, LaTanya, V ... 336-744-0900 .. 342 G latanya@carolina.edu

TYSON, Linda ... 252-399-6330 .. 341 P ltyson@barton.edu

TYSON, Shannon ... 570-484-3131 .. 415 D styson@lhup.edu

TYSON, Thayer ... 336-744-0900 .. 342 G tyrone@carolina.edu

TYSON, Thomas, N ... 410-334-2913 .. 213 G ttyson@worwic.edu

TYSON, William, R ... 919-893-9101 .. 348 D btyson@cccc.edu

TYUS, Bing ... 863-297-1004 .. 106 I btyus@polk.edu

TZENG, Fei-Ing ... 408-260-0208 .... 43 L daom@fivebranches.edu

TZENG, Huey-Ming ... 931-372-3651 .. 445 B htzeng@tntech.edu

TZENG, Walker ... 415-371-0002 .... 55 D

TZIMBAL, Tootie ... 831-479-5730 .... 29 G totzimba@cabrillo.edu

U

UBAGO, Maria ... 323-343-2586 .... 33 C mubago@cslanet.calstatela.edu

UCCI, Anthony ... 508-678-2811 .. 223 A anthony.ucci@bristolcc.edu

UCCI, Mary ... 859-572-5768 .. 192 B uccim@nku.edu

UDALL, David ... 928-428-8295 .... 13 B david.udall@eac.edu

UDD, Kris, J ... 402-449-2811 .. 280 C registrar@graceu.edu

UDDIN, Rita ... 718-260-5610 .. 309 C ruddin@citytech.cuny.edu

UDEH, Igwe, E ... 504-286-5331 .. 199 I iudeh@suno.edu

UDELHOFEN, Angela, M . 608-342-1125 .. 521 A rulea@uwplatt.edu

UDELHOFEN, Denise, A .. 563-588-7742 .. 174 K denise.udelhofen@loras.edu

UDEN, Jayme ... 816-584-6595 .. 270 D jayme.uden@park.edu

UDEN, Michael, D ... 262-243-5700 .. 516 E michael.uden@cuw.edu

UDEOGALANYA, Anthony 718-270-6213 .. 309 B anthonyu@mec.cuny.edu

UDERMANN, Brian ... 608-785-8181 .. 520 C budermann@uwlax.edu

UDIS-KESSLER, Amanda .. 719-227-8177 .... 77 J audiskessler@coloradocollege.edu

UDOH, Emmanuel ... 502-456-6504 .. 193 B eudoh@sullivan.edu

UDOVIC, Edward, R ... 312-362-8042 .. 139 C eudovic@depaul.edu

UDOVIC, CM, Edward, R . 312-362-8042 .. 139 C eudovic@depaul.edu

UDPA, Satish, S ... 517-355-5014 .. 237 I udpa@adminsv.msu.edu

UDUMA, Letitia ... 313-943-4058 .. 242 H luduma1@wcccd.edu

UDVARDY, Yolonda ... 215-489-4966 .. 402 A yolonda.udvardy@delval.edu

UEDA, Rikklyn, S ... 619-239-0391 .... 36 A rueda@cwsl.edu

UEHARA, Edwina ... 206-685-2480 .. 508 E eddi@uw.edu

UEKI, Omdasu, T ... 680-488-2471 .. 530 E oueki@palau.edu

UESUGI, Koji ... 951-372-7877 .... 59 B koji.uesugi@norcocollege.edu

UETRECHT, Dan ... 573-341-6418 .. 274 B uetrecht@mst.edu

UFERT FAIRLESS, Nancy, J ... 618-650-3187 .. 155 A nufert@siue.edu

UFFORD, Brian, K ... 207-778-7334 .. 205 A brian.ufford@maine.edu

UFFORD, Lori ... 541-506-6025 .. 390 I lufford@cgcc.edu

UFOMATA, Titilayo ... 315-781-3304 .. 316 C ufomata@hws.edu

UGALDE, Aileen, M ... 305-284-2700 .. 114 H augalde@miami.edu

UGOCHUKWU, Chioma, R ... 417-667-8181 .. 264 A cugochukwu@cottey.edu

UGORJI, Lauren, D ... 973-596-5695 .. 293 D lauren.d.ugorji@njit.edu

UGUCCIONI, Dominick ... 413-265-2461 .. 217 D uguccionid@elms.edu

UHAL, Len ... 563-876-3353 .. 171 I luhal@dwci.edu

UHAZY, Les ... 661-722-6300 .... 27 B luhazy@avc.edu

UHDE, Alicia ... 701-224-5764 .. 361 C alicia.uhde@bismarckstate.edu

UHER, Bill ... 505-277-5598 .. 302 F wuher@salud.unm.edu

UHLENKAMP, James ... 641-784-5221 .. 172 G jim.uhlenkamp@graceland.edu

UHLER, Jill ... 803-508-7247 .. 426 G uhlerj@atc.edu

UHLINGER, Eleanor, S ... 831-656-2342 .. 528 D euhlinger@nps.edu

UHLIR, James ... 715-232-2188 .. 521 D uhlirj@uwstout.edu

UHRICH, James ... 323-259-2500 .... 55 A juhrich@oxy.edu

UHRICH, Kathryn ... 951-827-3101 .... 70 B

UHUAD, Betsy ... 207-780-4714 .. 205 E betsy.uhuad@maine.edu

UJLAKI, Stephen, G ... 310-338-5800 .... 51 E sujlaki@lmu.edu

ULBRICH, Casandra ... 586-445-7244 .. 237 C ulbrichc@macomb.edu

ULETT, Phyllis ... 716-614-6895 .. 324 D pulett@niagaracc.suny.edu

ULIANA, Maria ... 818-364-7729 .... 49 J ulianamr@lamission.edu

ULIBARRI, Katherine ... 505-224-4413 .. 299 F kulibarri8@cnm.edu

ULLIMAN, Jeff ... 937-775-3154 .. 381 H jeff.ulliman@wright.edu

ULLMAN, David, F ... 973-596-2915 .. 293 D david.ullman@njit.edu

ULLMAN, Greg ... 323-473-5673 .... 74 A gullman@westcoastuniversity.edu

ULLMAN, Julie ... 414-382-6053 .. 515 D julie.ullman@alverno.edu

ULLMANN, Brian ... 301-314-6650 .. 211 E ullmann@umd.edu

ULLMANN, Timothy ... 334-683-2241 ...... 5 G tullmann@marionmilitary.edu

ULLOA, Emilio ... 619-594-6298 .... 35 A emilio.ulloa@mail.sdsu.edu

ULLOA-HEATH, Julie ... 671-735-5595 .. 529 G julie.ulloaheath@guamcc.edu

ULMAN, Cynthia ... 510-869-6511 .... 59 L culman@samuelmerritt.edu

ULMEN, Dan ... 406-265-3755 .. 277 E dulmen@msun.edu

ULMER, Jeffrey ... 386-822-7738 .. 113 B julmer@stetson.edu

ULMER, L. Ward ... 612-338-7224 .. 256 D ward.ulmer@waldenu.edu

ULMER, Rhonda, S ... 407-582-3861 .. 114 N rulmer@valenciacollege.edu

ULMER, Robert, R ... 702-895-0628 .. 284 L robert.ulmer@unlv.edu

ULMSCHNEIDER, John, E 804-828-1105 .. 496 D jeulmsch@vcu.edu

ULOZAS, Catherine, B ... 215-895-6685 .. 402 G catherine.b.ulozas@drexel.edu

ULREY, Burke ... 828-884-8282 .. 342 C ulreydb@brevard.edu

ULRICH, Carlea ... 432-264-5027 .. 459 D culrich@howardcollege.edu

ULRICH, Gail, L ... 814-641-3194 .. 406 F ulrichg@juniata.edu

ULRICH, James ... 312-235-3523 .. 154 C j.ulrich@shimer.edu

ULRICH, James ... 312-235-3511 .. 154 C j.ulrich@shimer.edu

ULRICH, Tina, J ... 231-995-1063 .. 239 C tulrich@nmc.edu

ULRICH, Trey, P ... 215-951-1671 .. 407 A ulrich@lasalle.edu

ULSES, Randy ... 513-556-3511 .. 379 A ulsesrj@ucmail.uc.edu

ULSETH, Julie, A ... 810-762-9844 .. 236 C julseth@kettering.edu

ULSHAFER, Kevin, L ... 478-757-5125 .. 129 L kulshafer@wesleyancollege.edu

ULZ, Mary Ann ... 847-566-6401 .. 157 G mulz@usml.edu

UMBLE, Diane ... 717-871-7160 .. 415 F diane.umble@millersville.edu

UMEHIRA, Ron ... 808-455-0228 .. 132 C umehira@hawaii.edu

UMFRESS, Jason, W ... 912-279-5970 .. 119 C jumfress@ccga.edu

UMHOLTZ, Lynn ... 316-322-3144 .. 179 E lumholtz@butlercc.edu

UMIDI, Joseph ... 757-352-4404 .. 493 E joseumi@regent.edu

UMLAND, Jeanne, M ... 718-990-6776 .. 328 F umlandj@stjohns.edu

UMMER, Christopher, T .. 802-626-6477 .. 486 C christopher.ummer@lyndonstate.edu

UMPHRES, James ... 360-538-4085 .. 504 B james.umphres@ghc.edu

UMSTATTD, Rustin ... 816-414-3700 .. 268 D rumstattd@mbts.edu

UNBEHAGEN, Leonard ... 504-278-6438 .. 196 I lunbehagen@nunez.edu

UNDERCOFFER, Anita ... 909-652-6032 .... 37 D anita.undercoffer@chaffey.edu

UNDERCOFLER, James ... 914-251-6707 .. 334 C james.undercofler@purchase.edu

UNDERHILL, Terri ... 304-357-4980 .. 511 E terriunderhill@ucwv.edu

UNDERWOOD, Allen ... 419-893-1986 .. 369 G aunderwo@heidelberg.edu

UNDERWOOD, Anita ... 845-675-4476 .. 325 C anita.underwood@nyack.edu

UNDERWOOD, Ann ... 806-651-2121 .. 469 D aunderwood@wtamu.edu

UNDERWOOD, Anthony ... 304-424-8209 .. 514 D anthony.underwood@wvup.edu

UNDERWOOD, Brenetta ... 314-264-1000 .. 274 I brenetta.underwood@vatterott.edu

UNDERWOOD, Carrie ... 817-554-5950 .. 461 G cunderwood@messengercollege.edu

VALENTIN, Marjorie .... 860-215-9006.... 87 D
mvalentin@trcc.commnet.edu
VALENTIN, Norberto .... 312-553-6048.. 137 D
nvalentin1@ccc.edu
VALENTINE, Ann .... 319-887-3614.. 174 I
ann.valentine@kirkwood.edu
VALENTINE, Anne, P .... 317-921-4882.. 164 F
VALENTINE, Anne, P .... 317-921-4882.. 164 E
apennyvalentine@ivytech.edu
VALENTINE, Bryan .... 505-984-6096.. 301 I
bvalentine@sjc.edu
VALENTINE, Carey, G ...... 248-204-3800.. 237 B
campfac@ltu.edu
VALENTINE, Carole .... 407-601-0411.. 100 G
VALENTINE, David .... 617-928-4710.. 226 B
dvalentine@mountida.edu
VALENTINE, Erick .... 318-274-2275.. 200 F
valentinee@gram.edu
VALENTINE, Jared .... 503-517-1008.. 396 D
jvalentine@warnerpacific.edu
VALENTINE, Leanne .... 712-749-2164.. 170 D
valentinel@bvu.edu
VALENTINE, Maureen .... 724-503-1001.. 422 H
mvalentine@washjeff.edu
VALENTINE, Peggy .... 336-750-2570.. 359 B
valentinepe@wssu.edu
VALENTINE, Sidney .... 863-784-7120.. 109 G
sid.valentine@southflorida.edu
VALENTINI, James, J .... 212-854-2443.. 311 E
jjv1@columbia.edu
VALENTINO, Christina ...... 401-874-2433.. 426 D
clvalentino@uri.edu
VALENTINO, Teresa .... 828-652-0657.. 351 C
teresavalentino@mcdowelltech.edu
VALENTO, Bernard .... 716-375-2128.. 328 B
bvalento@sbu.edu
VALENZA, John, A .... 713-486-4021.. 477 C
john.a.valenza@uth.tmc.edu
VALENZUELA, Angelica ... 480-994-9244.... 17 C
angelicav@swiha.edu
VALENZUELA, Cesario, E 432-837-8076.. 471 E
cesariov@sulross.edu
VALENZUELA, Eileen .... 925-473-7406.... 41 J
evalenzuela@losmedanos.edu
VALENZUELA, Ernesto ...... 520-494-5459.... 12 J
ernesto.valenzuela@centralaz.edu
VALERA, Luis .... 702-895-2389.. 284 L
luis.valera@unlv.edu
VALERA, Marco .... 718-817-3842.. 314 G
valera@fordham.edu
VALERIO, Brett .... 414-443-8785.. 522 P
brett.valerio@wlc.edu
VALERY, Suzanne .... 805-922-6966.... 25 I
svalery@hancockcollege.edu
VALINES, Francisco .... 305-348-2347.. 111 A
valinesf@fiu.edu
VALINTIS, Michelle .... 503-777-7705.. 394 I
mvalintis@reed.edu
VALIS, Ashley, R .... 410-706-5179.. 211 F
avalis@umaryland.edu
VALITSKY, Susan .... 440-646-8312.. 380 F
susan.valitsky@ursuline.edu
VALKENBURG, Stephen ... 201-612-5499.. 289 E
svalkenburg@bergen.edu
VALLANCE, Brenda, J ...... 512-448-8550.. 464 G
brendav@stedwards.edu
VALLEJO, Jesus, G .... 832-824-4204.. 452 G
jvallejo@bcm.edu
VALLEJO, Maria, M .... 561-993-1128.. 106 D
vallejom@palmbeachstate.edu
VALLELLANES, Luz, N ..... 787-786-3030.. 536 F
nereidav@ucb.edu.pr
VALLER, Thomas .... 970-945-8691.... 78 B
VALLEREUX, Alison .... 617-732-1655.. 218 C
vallereuxa@emmanuel.edu
VALLES, Arleen .... 575-835-5162.. 300 G
avalles@admin.nmt.edu
VALLEY, Timothy .... 414-277-7150.. 518 E
valley@msoe.edu
VALLI, Robert .... 516-299-4000.. 319 C
rob.valli@liu.edu
VALLS, Ophelia .... 305-442-9223.. 105 F
ovalls@mrc.edu
VALOSKY, Kenneth, G ..... 610-519-4530.. 422 G
ken.valosky@villanova.edu
VALSARAJ, Kalliat, T ...... 225-578-7696.. 197 I
valsaraj@lsu.edu
VALTOS, Jennifer .... 770-426-2762.. 124 B
jvaltos@life.edu
VALUCK, Angela .... 217-245-3002.. 141 G
angela.valuck@mail.ic.edu
VALVERDE, Shannon .... 508-541-1841.. 217 G
svalverde@dean.edu
VAN ALLEN, George, H ... 615-353-3236.. 446 E
george.vanallen@nscc.edu
VAN ALSBURG,
Teresa, D .... 304-457-6380.. 510 B
vanalsburgtd@ab.edu
VAN ALSTINE, Tim, M .... 414-410-4839.. 515 I
tvanalstine@stritch.edu

VAN ARNAM, Sherrie ...... 718-940-5754.. 328 G
svanarnam@sjcny.edu
VAN AUKEN, James .... 757-631-8101.. 487 B
james.vanauken@atlanticuniv.edu
VAN AUKEN, Sharon ...... 518-327-6242.. 326 B
svanauken100@paulsmiths.edu
VAN BLARCOM, Ronald .. 949-214-3135.... 41 F
ron.vanblarcom@cui.edu
VAN BROEKHOVEN,
Rollin .... 704-243-0737.. 443 H
rvanbroekhoven@futurelead.org
VAN BRUNT, Mary .... 610-902-8765.. 399 D
VAN BRUNT, Troy, G ...... 956-721-5326.. 460 F
troyvb@laredo.edu
VAN BUREN, Jason .... 610-409-3249.. 422 D
afeick@ursinus.edu
VAN CLEAVE, Rachel ...... 415-442-6601.... 45 B
rvancleave@ggu.edu
VAN CLEAVE, Robb .... 541-506-6150.. 390 I
rvancleave@cgcc.edu
VAN CLEAVE, Samuel, J . 480-423-6003.... 14 H
samuel.vancleave@scottsdalecc.edu
VAN CLEAVE, William ...... 504-865-5767.. 200 C
wvanclea@tulane.edu
VAN CLEEF, Robert .... 978-867-4610.. 219 A
robert.vancleef@gordon.edu
VAN CLEEF, Sarah, E ...... 903-510-2033.. 473 C
svan@tjc.edu
VAN COTT, Margret, G .... 860-253-3003.... 86 A
mvancott@asnuntuck.edu
VAN DAM, Dale .... 530-642-5615.... 51 C
vandamd@flc.losrios.edu
VAN DAME, Tiffany .... 620-862-5252.. 178 F
VAN DE LOO, John .... 715-365-4553.. 524 C
vandeloo@nicoletcollege.edu
VAN DE MOORTELL,
Raymond .... 617-254-2610.. 227 H
rev.vandemoortell@sjs.edu
VAN DE VOORDE, Peter . 239-280-2500.... 95 Q
peter.vandevoorde@avemaria.edu
VAN DEKKER, Angela ..... 718-817-3800.. 314 G
avandekker@fordham.edu
VAN DELFT, Leo .... 918-293-5394.. 386 B
leo.vandelft@okstate.edu
VAN DEN ABBEELE,
Georges .... 949-824-5133.... 69 C
gvandena@uci.edu
VAN DEN HEEVER,
Nicolaas .... 949-783-4800.... 74 A
nvandenheever@westcoastuniversity.edu
VAN DEN HEUVEL,
Nicole .... 713-348-4055.. 464 E
nvdh@rice.edu
VAN DEN HUL,
Richard, D .... 360-650-3182.. 509 E
rich.vandenhul@wwu.edu
VAN DENEND,
Michael, J .... 616-526-6142.. 232 A
vanden@calvin.edu
VAN DER AA, Jan .... 901-448-2500.. 448 H
jvandera@uthsc.edu
VAN DER BURG, Anna ... 860-685-2810.... 90 C
avanderburg@wesleyan.edu
VAN DER KAAY,
Christopher .... 863-784-7413.. 109 G
christopher.vanderkaay@southflorida.edu
VAN DER KARR, Carol ... 607-753-2206.. 333 A
carol.vanderkarr@cortland.edu
VAN DER KLEY, Jan .... 269-387-2365.. 243 H
jan.vanderkley@wmich.edu
VAN DER MERWE,
Derek .... 931-221-6206.. 444 E
vandermerwed@apsu.edu
VAN DER POL, Willem .... 657-278-3133.... 33 A
wvanderpol@fullerton.edu
VAN DER SCHYF,
Cornelis .... 208-282-3134.. 133 H
vandcorn@isu.edu
VAN DER SCHYF,
Cornelis .... 208-282-2490.. 133 H
vandcorn@isu.edu
VAN DER VEER,
Mary Caroline .... 518-587-2100.. 335 D
marycaroline.powers@esc.edu
VAN DER VELDEN,
Andre .... 530-283-0202.... 43 G
avandervelden@frc.edu
VAN DER WALL,
Melissa .... 201-684-7457.. 294 G
mvanderw@ramapo.edu
VAN DEREN, Jessica ...... 802-728-1244.. 486 D
jvanderen@vtc.edu
VAN DERVEER,
Rachael, E .... 724-847-6596.. 404 B
revander@geneva.edu
VAN DEVEN, Randy .... 903-468-8181.. 468 D
randy.vandeven@tamuc.edu
VAN DONSELAAR, Brian . 712-722-6299.. 171 J
brian.vandonselaar@dordt.edu
VAN DUSEN, Michael ..... 561-912-2166.... 99 J
mvandusen@evergladesuniversity.edu

VAN DUYNE, Patrick .... 815-280-6696.. 144 A
pvanduyn@jjc.edu
VAN DUZER, Jeffrey, B ... 206-281-2508.. 507 C
vandj@spu.edu
VAN DYK, Leanne .... 404-687-4514.. 119 D
vandykl@ctsnet.edu
VAN DYK, Vanessa .... 406-496-4322.. 277 G
vvandyk@mtech.edu
VAN DYKE, Greg .... 712-722-6083.. 171 J
greg.vandyke@dordt.edu
VAN DYKE, Jon .... 217-234-5378.. 145 D
jvandyke@lakeland.cc.il.us
VAN DYKE, Karin .... 906-487-7344.. 234 A
karin.vandyke@finlandia.edu
VAN DYKEN, Douglas ..... 616-395-7810.. 235 F
vandyken@hope.edu
VAN DYNE, Karen .... 617-619-1900.. 219 G
karen.vandyne@hult.edu
VAN ECK, Thomas, A ...... 616-526-8553.. 232 A
tveck@calvin.edu
VAN ESS, Jami .... 928-226-4209.... 12 N
jami.vaness@coconino.edu
VAN-ESS, Michelle .... 212-217-4132.. 314 B
michelle_vaness@fitnyc.edu
VAN ETTEN, Mark .... 570-674-6272.. 410 K
mvanette@misericordia.edu
VAN FOSSEN, Dell Jean . 951-785-2088.... 48 A
dvanfoss@lasierra.edu
VAN FOSSEN, Drew .... 920-403-4427.. 519 G
drew.vanfossen@snc.edu
VAN FOSSEN, JR.,
Richard .... 215-951-1540.. 407 A
vanfossen88@lasalle.edu
VAN GAALEN, Joseph ..... 239-433-6965.. 101 F
jfvangaalen@fsw.edu
VAN GALEN, Dean, A ..... 715-425-3201.. 521 B
dean.vangalen@uwrf.edu
VAN GENDEREN, Eric ..... 510-925-4282.... 26 M
eric.vangenderen@aua.am
VAN GILDER, Holly .... 330-490-7146.. 380 J
hvangilder@walsh.edu
VAN GILS-PIERCE,
Adriane .... 508-793-7587.. 217 B
avangils@clarku.edu
VAN GINHOVEN, Lee, H . 269-927-8611.. 236 G
vanginhoven@lakemichigancollege.edu
VAN GORDON, Beth .... 219-981-4282.. 163 B
vgordon@iun.edu
VAN GORDON, Elizabeth 574-520-4463.. 163 E
vgordon@iusb.edu
VAN GORDON, Elizabeth 317-274-3022.. 163 F
vgordon@iu.edu
VAN GRONINGEN, Willis 708-239-4880.. 155 M
bill.vangroningen@trnty.edu
VAN GRUENSVEN,
Sheryl .... 920-465-2210.. 520 B
vangrues@uwgb.edu
VAN GUILDER, Connie ... 707-545-3647.... 28 C
admissions@berginu.edu
VAN GUILDER, Sean ...... 352-588-8268.. 108 C
sean.vanguilder@saintleo.edu
VAN GUNDY, Douglas .... 304-473-8243.. 515 B
vangundy@wvwc.edu
VAN HAMERSVELD, Pete 310-243-3825.... 32 D
pvanhamersveld@csudh.edu
VAN HARPEN, Robin, L .. 414-229-4461.. 520 D
rvanharp@uwm.edu
VAN HEMERT, John, L .... 540-674-3660.. 497 G
jvanhemert@nr.edu
VAN HOECK, Michele ...... 707-654-1097.... 33 D
mvanhoeck@csum.edu
VAN HOLLAND,
Phyllis, L .... 360-417-6291.. 505 I
pvanholland@pencol.edu
VAN HOOK, Dianne, G ... 661-362-3400.... 40 A
dianne.vanhook@canyons.edu
VAN HORN, Brian, W ...... 270-809-4159.. 192 A
bvanhorn@murraystate.edu
VAN HORN, Donald, L .... 304-696-6433.. 513 D
vanhorn@marshall.edu
VAN HORN, Drew .... 828-328-7108.. 345 H
drew.vanhorn@lr.edu
VAN HORN, Leigh .... 713-221-8991.. 474 B
vanhornl@uhd.edu
VAN HORN, Megan .... 231-348-6667.. 239 A
mvanhorn1@ncmich.edu
VAN HORN, Stuart .... 559-934-2131.... 74 C
stuartvanhorn@whccd.edu
VAN HORN, Wayne .... 601-925-3297.. 259 A
wvanhorn@mc.edu
VAN HOUTEN, Carol .... 201-360-4722.. 292 B
cvanhouten@hccc.edu
VAN HOUTEN, Michael ... 517-629-0567.. 230 E
mvanhouten@albion.edu
VAN HUIS, Bill .... 312-487-4743.. 155 L
bill.vanhuis@tribecaflashpoint.edu
VAN KEULEN, Michael .... 507-223-7252.. 250 G
michael.vankeulen@mnwest.edu
VAN KEUREN, Karen, A .. 585-785-1206.. 314 D
karen.vankeuren@flcc.edu

VAN KLEY, Eric .... 641-628-5422.. 170 E
vankleye@central.edu
VAN KLEY, Sandy .... 712-707-7145.. 176 B
svankley@nwciowa.edu
VAN KLOMPENBERG,
Brian .... 312-862-3217.... 68 E
brian.vanklompenberg@kirkland.com
VAN KOOY, Samantha .... 856-415-2276.. 295 D
svankooy@rcgc.edu
VAN LANINGHAM,
Kathy, M .... 479-575-5910.... 22 I
kvl@uark.edu
VAN LEAR, Eryn .... 804-355-8135.. 487 D
evanlear@btsr.edu
VAN LEAR, Michael .... 808-544-9339.. 130 H
mvanlear@hpu.edu
VAN LEER, Sharon .... 651-290-6416.. 253 S
sharon.vanleer@mitchellhamline.edu
VAN LEIDEN, Melissa ..... 785-594-8306.. 178 D
melissa.vanleiden@bakeru.edu
VAN LIERE, Lori .... 419-866-0261.. 377 L
lori.vanliere@sctoday.edu
VAN LIEW, Fred .... 303-937-4035.... 77 K
fvanliew@chu.edu
VAN LOO, Scott, D .... 419-289-5088.. 363 J
svanloo@ashland.edu
VAN METER, Eric .... 605-995-2919.. 435 F
ervanmet@dwu.edu
VAN METER, Linda, L ..... 570-422-3277.. 414 H
lvanmeter@esu.edu
VAN NESS, Forrest, L ..... 314-516-6680.. 274 A
vannessf@umsl.edu
VAN NOORT, Kim .... 919-961-2000.. 356 A
kpvannoort@northcarolina.edu
VAN NORMAN, Karen ...... 973-761-9076.. 297 A
karen.vannorman@shu.edu
VAN OMMEREN, Andrew 712-707-7000.. 176 B
andrew.vanommeren@nwciowa.edu
VAN OMMEREN, Ryan ...... 805-493-3211.... 31 C
rvommere@callutheran.edu
VAN OOT, Amy .... 860-701-5019.... 88 D
vanoot_a@mitchell.edu
VAN ORMAN, Kit .... 315-364-3317.. 340 B
kit@wells.edu
VAN ORMAN, Sarah, A ... 608-262-1885.. 519 K
svanorman@uhs.wisc.edu
VAN ORSDEL, Lee .... 616-331-2621.. 234 F
vanorsdl@gvsu.edu
VAN OSTERN, Kristyn ..... 603-230-3509.. 286 A
kvanostern@ccsnh.edu
VAN PELT, Donna .... 515-294-1280.. 169 G
dvanpelt@foundation.iastate.edu
VAN RIJN, Paul .... 215-885-2360.. 409 G
pvanrijn@manor.edu
VAN RYZIN, Gregg, G ..... 973-353-3985.. 296 C
vanryzin@newark.rutgers.edu
VAN SCHARREL,
Mark, H .... 773-256-0676.. 147 A
mvanscha@lstc.edu
VAN SCOTT, Michael ...... 252-328-9479.. 356 C
vanscottm@ecu.edu
VAN SLYKE, Craig .... 928-523-7345.... 15 H
craig.vanslyke@nau.edu
VAN SOELEN, Timothy .... 712-722-6228.. 171 J
timothy.vansoelen@dcrdt.edu
VAN STAVERN, Becky ...... 417-328-1815.. 272 C
bvanstavern@sbuniv.edu
VAN STENSEL, James ...... 864-379-8820.. 429 I
vanstensel@erskine.edu
VAN STRATEN, Amy .... 920-831-4355.. 523 C
vanstrat@fvtc.edu
VAN TASSEL, Kristin .... 785-227-3380.. 178 J
vantasselk@bethanylb.edu
VAN TASSEL, Sherri .... 740-264-5591.. 368 D
svantassel@egcc.edu
VAN TASSELL, TOR,
Malachi .... 814-472-3001.. 418 F
mvantassell@francis.edu
VAN TIL, Seth, J .... 724-458-3887.. 404 F
sjvantil@gcc.edu
VAN UUM, Elizabeth .... 314-516-5774.. 274 A
vanuum@umsl.edu
VAN VLECK, Thomas .... 660-626-2138.. 262 A
tvanvleck@atsu.edu
VAN VLERAH, Abagail ..... 516-299-2255.. 319 C
abby.vanvlerah@liu.edu
VAN VOORHIS, Amanda . 508-999-9114.. 220 H
avanvoorhis@umassd.edu
VAN VOORHIS, Sue, N .... 612-625-8098.. 255 H
vanvo002@umn.edu
VAN VOORST, James ...... 518-956-8120.. 331 A
VAN WAGNER, Thomas .. 202-231-4193.. 528 C
thomas.vanwagner@dodiis.mil
VAN WAGONER,
Randall, J .... 315-792-5333.. 321 G
rvanwagoner@mvcc.edu
VAN WIE, Lisa .... 518-629-8143.. 316 G
l.vanwie@hvcc.edu
VAN WINKLE, Ken .... 575-439-3640.. 301 A
kvanwink@nmsu.edu

VARGAS-GOMEZ, Raquel, G ... 787-894-2828 .. 537 D raquel.vargas@upr.edu

VARGAS GOMEZ, Raquel, G ... 787-894-2828 .. 539 A raquel.vargas@upr.edu

VARGO, Deborah ... 734-432-5465 .. 237 D dvargo@madonna.edu

VARGO, Michael ... 616-234-4690 .. 234 E mvargo@grcc.edu

VARHOLAK, Mark ... 203-582-8613 .... 88 G mark.varholak@quinnipiac.edu

VARHUS, Sara ... 585-389-2011 .. 322 D svarhus0@naz.edu

VARI, April ... 215-489-2413 .. 402 A april.vari@delval.edu

VARI, Patty, M ... 540-985-8532 .. 491 A pmvari@jchs.edu

VARKONYI, Istvan, L ... 215-204-2855 .. 420 B istvan.varkonyi@temple.edu

VARLOTTA, Lori, E ... 330-569-5120 .. 369 J varlottale@hiram.edu

VARMA, Mrinal Mugdh ... 281-283-3020 .. 474 A varma@uhcl.edu

VARMA, Rohit ... 323-442-6411 .... 72 D deanksom@usc.edu

VARMECKY, Richard ... 717-728-2275 .. 400 F richardvarmecky@centralpenn.edu

VARN, James, S ... 603-862-3290 .. 288 C jim.varn@unh.edu

VARNAVA, Penelope ... 773-907-2472 .. 137 E pvarnava@ccc.edu

VARNELL, Jon ... 219-464-5917 .. 168 F jon.varnell@valpo.edu

VARNER, Donna, A ... 757-594-8816 .. 488 E dvarner@cnu.edu

VARNER, Jenny, M ... 336-249-8186 .. 349 C jmvarner@davidsonccc.edu

VARNER, Julie ... 334-290-3265 ...... 4 G julie.varner@istc.edu

VARNER, Mary, C ... 610-526-1302 .. 397 E mary.varner@theamericancollege.edu

VARNER, Monica ... 580-774-3252 .. 388 C monica.varner@swosu.edu

VARNER, Robin ... 859-280-1242 .. 191 D rvarner@lextheo.edu

VARNER, Stuart ... 731-989-6073 .. 440 D svarner@fhu.edu

VARNER, Tiffany ... 318-670-9692 .. 199 J twilliams@susla.edu

VARNEY, Rhonda ... 207-326-2220 .. 204 C rhonda.varney@mma.edu

VARNEY, Ruth ... 804-594-1559 .. 497 D rvarney@jtcc.edu

VARNUM, Linda, J ... 603-526-3738 .. 285 L lindav@colby-sawyer.edu

VARSALONA, Jack, P ... 302-356-6818 .... 91 I donna.m.quinn@wilmu.edu

VARSALONA, Jacque, R .. 302-295-1168 .... 91 I jacqueline.r.varsalona@wilmu.edu

VARSEK, Tamara, B ... 814-393-2240 .. 414 G tvarsek@clarion.edu

VARSO, Shawn, V ... 330-941-3527 .. 382 A svvarso@ysu.edu

VARTABEDIAN, Robert, A 816-271-4237 .. 269 C president@missouriwestern.edu

VARTANIAN, Heather ... 414-326-2333 .. 516 D heather.vartanian@ccon.edu

VARVILLE, Paul ... 956-872-2330 .. 465 H pbvarvil@southtexascollege.edu

VARWIG, Jana ... 410-704-2270 .. 213 B jvarwig@towson.edu

VARY KEELE, Renee ... 404-364-8868 .. 125 F rvary@oglethorpe.edu

VASARHELYI, Marina ... 914-323-5139 .. 319 N marina.vasarhelyi@mville.edu

VASCONCELLOS, Tina ... 510-748-2205 .... 57 C tvasconcellos@peralta.edu

VASCURA, Jacquelyn, L .. 740-826-8084 .. 373 E jkent@muskingum.edu

VASEY, Todd, A ... 508-541-1815 .. 217 G tvasey@dean.edu

VASICA, Christine ... 910-296-2400 .. 350 F cvasica@jamessprunt.edu

VASILAS, Darcy ... 828-898-8785 .. 345 G vasilasd@lmc.edu

VASILATOS-YOUNKEN, Regina ... 814-865-2516 .. 412 F rxv@psu.edu

VASKELIS, Frank, M ... 650-358-6720 .... 62 F vaskelis@smccd.edu

VASKO, Genevieve ... 908-835-9222 .. 298 E vasko@warren.edu

VASQUEZ, Albert ... 310-434-4302 .... 63 F vasquez_albert@smc.edu

VASQUEZ, Albert ... 209-228-7865 .... 70 A avasquez39@ucmerced.edu

VASQUEZ, Amanda ... 915-747-5544 .. 476 D avasquez6@utep.edu

VASQUEZ, Becky, L ... 386-226-6948 .... 99 A vasquezb@erau.edu

VASQUEZ, Graciela ... 562-860-2451 .... 36 P gvasquez@cerritos.edu

VASQUEZ, James ... 718-260-5244 .. 309 C jvazquez@citytech.cuny.edu

VASQUEZ, Jeffrey ... 206-934-3643 .. 506 J jeffrey.vasquez@seattlecolleges.edu

VASQUEZ, Jessika ... 310-665-6898 .... 55 E jvasquez@otis.edu

VASQUEZ, Lisa, R ... 972-758-3894 .. 455 A lvasquez@collin.edu

VASQUEZ, Patricia ... 617-745-3851 .. 218 A patty.vasquez@enc.edu

VASQUEZ, Rojelio ... 559-442-8558 .... 67 A rojelio.vasquez@fresnocitycollege.edu

VASQUEZ, Rojelio ... 559-442-4600 .... 67 C rojelio.vasquez@fresnocitycollege.edu

VASQUEZ, Sandy ... 915-747-7873 .. 476 D svasquez@utep.edu

VASQUEZ DE VELASCO, Guillermo ... 773-325-1858 .. 139 C gvv@depaul.edu

VASQUEZ-LEVY, David ... 510-849-8223 .... 55 I president@psr.edu

VASQUEZ-PORITZ, Justin 718-260-5008 .. 309 C jvazquez-poritz@citytech.cuny.edu

VASS, Robert ... 203-576-4228 .... 89 C rvass@bridgeport.edu

VASSALLO, Donna ... 609-343-4972 .. 288 H dvassall@atlantic.edu

VASSAR, John, S ... 318-797-5326 .. 198 C john.s.vassar@lsus.edu

VASSAR, Pam ... 913-469-8500 .. 182 A pvassar@jccc.edu

VASSELLI, John ... 713-718-5690 .. 459 B john.vasselli@hccs.edu

VASUDEVAN, Palligarnai, T ... 603-862-3290 .. 288 C vasu@unh.edu

VATANDOOST, Cyrus ... 615-514-2787 .. 443 F cyrus@nossi.edu

VATANDOOST, Nossi ... 615-514-2787 .. 443 F nossi@nossi.edu

VATER, Ruth ... 608-363-2606 .. 515 G vaterr@beloit.edu

VATTER, Hilary, F ... 262-243-5700 .. 516 E hilary.vatter@cuw.edu

VATTIMO, Casey ... 518-320-1311 .. 330 H

VAUGHAN, Anthony ... 212-678-8816 .. 317 I anvaughan@jtsa.edu

VAUGHAN, Bruce, F ... 757-455-3309 .. 500 E bvaughan@vwc.edu

VAUGHAN, Cathy, A ... 270-824-1705 .. 190 B cathy.vaughan@kctcs.edu

VAUGHAN, Chris ... 309-794-7292 .. 135 D chrisvaughan@augustana.edu

VAUGHAN, Greg ... 562-903-4752 .... 28 E greg.vaughan@biola.edu

VAUGHAN, Icer ... 316-942-4291 .. 183 I vaughani@newmanu.edu

VAUGHAN, Jesse ... 804-524-5877 .. 499 G jvaughan@vsu.edu

VAUGHAN, Joseph ... 909-621-8613 .... 46 A joseph_vaughan@hmc.edu

VAUGHAN, Karen ... 908-526-1200 .. 295 A karen.vaughan@raritanval.edu

VAUGHAN, Larry, F ... 615-547-1222 .. 439 H lvaughan@cumberland.edu

VAUGHAN, Leslie ... 617-989-4510 .. 229 D vaughanl@wit.edu

VAUGHAN, Sally, J ... 585-385-8196 .. 328 E svaughan@sjfc.edu

VAUGHAN, Terri ... 515-271-2871 .. 171 K terri.vaughan@drake.edu

VAUGHAN, Timothy, S ... 715-836-2500 .. 520 A vaughats@uwec.edu

VAUGHN, Andy ... 415-955-2001 .... 25 J

VAUGHN, Deborah, S ... 662-915-1687 .. 261 B dvaughn@olemiss.edu

VAUGHN, Denise ... 334-229-8450 ...... 1 D dvaughn@alasu.edu

VAUGHN, Erin ... 601-979-2326 .. 258 D erin.c.vaughn@jsums.edu

VAUGHN, Katherine ... 870-743-3000 .... 21 C kvaughn@northark.edu

VAUGHN, Kellie ... 270-789-5001 .. 187 G kpvaughn@campbellsville.edu

VAUGHN, Lori ... 413-565-1000 .. 215 A lvaughn@baypath.edu

VAUGHN, Patti ... 617-262-5000 .. 216 A patti.vaughn@the-bac.edu

VAUGHN, Ray ... 256-824-6100 ...... 8 F ray.vaughn@uah.edu

VAUGHN, Robert ... 323-856-7661 .... 26 I rvaughn@afi.com

VAUGHN, Ronald, L ... 813-253-6201 .. 114 M president@ut.edu

VAUGHN, Sandra, C ... 662-252-8000 .. 260 F svaughn@rustcollege.edu

VAUGHN, Suzanne, A ... 661-395-4301 .... 47 J svaughn@bakersfieldcollege.edu

VAUGHN, Woodrow ... 256-726-7306 ...... 6 B wvaughn@oakwood.edu

VAUGHT, Mike ... 602-639-7500 .... 13 I

VAUGHT, Wayne ... 816-235-2815 .. 273 F vaughtw@umkc.edu

VAUPEL, Christian ... 516-877-3258 .. 303 B cpvaupel@adelphi.edu

VAUPEL, Richard ... 229-226-1621 .. 128 B rvaupel@thomasu.edu

VAUX-MICHEL, Teresa ... 570-561-1818 .. 418 H teresa.vauxmichel@stots.edu

VAVASOUR, JoEllen, L ... 914-654-5541 .. 311 A jvavasour@cnr.edu

VAVOLIZZA, Ann ... 845-848-4001 .. 312 F ann.vavolizza@dc.edu

VAVREK, Milan, C ... 304-462-6110 .. 513 C milan.vavrek@glenville.edu

VAVRICKA, Janda ... 414-277-2234 .. 518 E vavricka@msoe.edu

VAWTER, Charles ... 503-841-2890 .. 394 B cvawter@pnca.edu

VAWTER, Cheryl, D ... 509-777-4518 .. 509 H cvawter@whitworth.edu

VAYDA, Michael, E ... 479-575-2034 .... 22 I mvayda@uark.edu

VAYDA, Michael, E ... 978-934-2168 .. 221 A michael_vayda@uml.edu

VAZ, Maria, J ... 248-204-2400 .. 237 B provost@ltu.edu

VAZQUEZ, Adela ... 787-620-2040 .. 530 F avazquez@aupr.edu

VAZQUEZ, Airlyn ... 787-882-2065 .. 536 D biblioteca@unitecpr.net

VAZQUEZ, Carlos ... 787-738-2161 .. 538 A carlos.vazquez5@upr.edu

VAZQUEZ, Carmen, M ... 619-260-4588 .... 72 B carmenvazquez@sandiego.edu

VAZQUEZ, David ... 714-556-3610 .... 73 B david.vazquez@vanguard.edu

VAZQUEZ, David ... 239-590-1123 .. 110 L dvazquez@fgcu.edu

VAZQUEZ, Felice ... 908-737-7000 .. 292 C fvazquez@kean.edu

VAZQUEZ, Frank ... 888-384-0849 .... 25 P fvazquez@allied.edu

VAZQUEZ, Guillermo ... 787-766-1717 .. 536 B gvazquez93@suagm.edu

VAZQUEZ, Heber ... 787-834-9595 .. 536 E heberv@uaa.edu

VAZQUEZ, Hector ... 787-765-3560 .. 532 I hvazquez@edpuniversity.edu

VAZQUEZ, Javier ... 787-780-0070 .. 531 B asistenciaeconomica@caribbean.edu

VAZQUEZ, Lucia ... 217-206-6512 .. 156 G lvazq1@uis.edu

VAZQUEZ, Maria ... 787-864-2222 .. 534 A maria.vazquez@guayama.inter.edu

VAZQUEZ, Maria ... 787-725-8120 .. 532 K mvazquez0060@eap.edu

VAZQUEZ, Marie ... 402-457-2430 .. 280 J mvazquez@mccneb.edu

VAZQUEZ, Obed ... 925-969-2423 .... 41 I ovazquez@dvc.edu

VAZQUEZ, Rosabel ... 787-620-2040 .. 530 F rvazquez@aupr.edu

VAZQUEZ, Silvio ... 805-565-6200 .... 75 A svazquez@westmont.edu

VAZQUEZ, Vilmaris ... 787-878-5475 .. 533 H vvazquez@arecibo.inter.edu

VAZQUEZ-BARQUET, Ernesto ... 787-754-8000 .. 537 B evazquez@pupr.edu

VAZQUEZ-CALLE, Fernando ... 787-738-2161 .. 538 A fernando.vazquezcalle@upr.edu

VAZQUEZ-LONG, Mitzi ... 216-687-3968 .. 366 I m.vazquezlong@csuohio.edu

VAZQUEZ-MARTINEZ, Ernesto ... 787-622-8000 .. 537 B evazquezjr@pupr.edu

VAZQUEZ MEDINA, Edwin ... 787-890-2681 .. 537 E edwin.vazquez7@upr.edu

VAZQUEZ-SKILLINGS, Rebecca, D ... 614-823-1354 .. 376 C rvazquez-skillings@otterbein.edu

VAZQUEZ-VERA, Efrain ... 787-850-0000 .. 537 D rectoria.uprh@upr.edu

VAZQUEZCALLE, Fernando ... 787-738-2161 .. 538 A fernando.vazquezcalle@upr.edu

VEACH, Grace ... 863-667-5061 .. 109 L gveach@seu.edu

VEAL, Don-Terry ... 443-885-3035 .. 209 F don-terry.veal@morgan.edu

VEALE, Keith ... 740-392-6868 .. 373 D keith.veale@mvnu.edu

VEAZ, María, G ... 787-257-7373 .. 535 P m_veaz@suagm.edu

VEAZEY, Barbara ... 270-534-3082 .. 190 H barbara.veazey@kctcs.edu

VEAZEY, David, A ... 253-535-8145 .. 505 G veazeyda@plu.edu

VECCHIO, Maria ... 201-559-6017 .. 291 K vecchiom@felician.edu

VECCHIO, Paul ... 607-871-2193 .. 303 F vecchio@alfred.edu

VECCHIONE, Tom ... 209-946-2365 .... 71 C

VECHINI, Jose, A ... 787-864-2222 .. 534 A jose.vechini@guayama.inter.edu

VEDDER, Lori ... 810-762-3444 .. 242 B lvedder@umflint.edu

VEECH, Guthrie ... 314-837-6777 .. 271 B gveech@stlchristian.edu

VEEDER, Samantha ... 585-275-3226 .. 338 K sveeder2@finaid.rochester.edu

VEENSTRA, Tim ... 517-586-3014 .. 232 F tveenstra@cleary.edu

VEER, Chelly ... 701-766-1302 .. 360 A chelly.veer@littlehoop.edu

VEGA, Aixa ... 787-834-9595 .. 536 E avega@uaa.edu

VEGA, Annette ... 787-878-5475 .. 533 H avega@arecibo.inter.edu

VEGA, Barbara ... 432-837-8810 .. 471 E bvega@sulross.edu

VEGA, Cheni ... 312-487-4743 .. 155 L cheni.vega@tribecaflashpoint.edu

VEGA, Erlinda ... 787-264-1912 .. 534 D linvega@intersg.edu

VEGA, Eva ... 787-746-1400 .. 532 M evega@huertas.edu

VEGA, Evelyn ... 787-250-1912 .. 534 B evega@metro.inter.edu

VEGA, Francesca ... 818-677-2123 .... 34 A francesca.vega@csun.edu

VEGA, Fredrick ... 787-250-1912 .. 534 B fredrickvega@metro.inter.edu

VEGA, Javier ... 212-592-2000 .. 330 C jvega@sva.edu

VEGA, Juan ... 787-844-8181 .. 538 E juan.vegavega@upr.edu

VEGA, Kennethia, J ... 714-564-6975 .... 58 G vega_kennethia@sac.edu

VEGA, Manfredo ... 787-620-2040 .. 530 F mvega@aupr.edu

VEGA, Matt ... 731-989-6310 .. 440 D mvega@fhu.edu

VEGA, Patricia ... 773-878-7837 .. 153 E pvega@staugustine.edu

VEGA, Pete ... 708-239-4770 .. 155 M pete.vega@trnty.edu

VEGA, Zaida ... 787-766-1717 .. 536 B zvega@suagm.edu

VEGA-GONZALEZ, Melvin ... 787-480-2429 .. 531 J melvega@sanjuanciudadpatria.com

VEGA-GUTIERREZ, Guadalupe ... 787-993-8958 .. 537 G guadalupe.vega@upr.edu

VEGA-LA SERNA, Jennifer ... 559-730-3823 .... 40 E jenniferl@cos.edu

VEHR, Gregory, J ... 513-556-3028 .. 379 A greg.vehr@uc.edu

VEILLEUX, John ... 817-531-4269 .. 472 F jveilleux@txwes.edu

VEIT, Kathy ... 650-723-2300 .... 66 I

VEIT, Kenneth, J ... 215-871-6770 .. 416 F kenv@pcom.edu

VEITCH, Dionne ... 814-824-3315 .. 410 H dveitch@mercyhurst.edu

VEITCH, Jonathan ... 323-259-2691 .... 55 A

VELA, Alicia, L ... 512-448-8515 .. 464 G aliciav@stedwards.edu

VELA, JR., Cesar, E ... 956-721-5370 .. 460 F cvela@laredo.edu

VELA, Eddie ... 530-898-6262 .... 32 C evela@csuchico.edu

VELA, Jason ... 307-674-6446 .. 526 M jvela@sheridan.edu

VELA, Robert ... 210-486-0961 .. 450 A rvela63@alamo.edu

VELA, Robert, H ... 210-486-0959 .. 450 F rvela63@alamo.edu

VELAR-PRIETO, Jorge ... 787-993-8869 .. 537 G jorge.velar@upr.edu

VELASCO, Amy ... 805-756-2982 .... 31 I aevelasc@calpoly.edu

VELASCO, Debbie ... 612-767-7064 .. 244 D debbie.velasco@alfredadler.edu

VELASCO, Steven, C ... 805-893-2434 .... 70 E steven.velasco@ucsb.edu

VELASCO, Ulises ... 707-468-3110 .... 52 C uvelasco@mendocino.edu

VELASQUEZ, Lorrie ... 719-846-5534 .... 83 G lorrie.velasquez@trinidadstate.edu

VELASQUEZ, Marisol ... 708-656-8000 .. 149 A marisol.velasquez@morton.edu

VELASQUEZ, Tom ... 661-654-2211 .... 32 A tvelasquez2@csub.edu

VICTOR, Jan 847-317-7121 156 B
jvictor@tiu.edu
VICTOR, Michael, T 814-824-2311 410 H
mvictor@mercyhurst.edu
VICTORIN-VANGERUD,
Nancy, M 651-523-2878 247 A
nvictorinvangerud01@hamline.edu
VICTORINE, Jon 978-934-5060 221 A
jon_victorine@uml.edu
VICTORY, Darrell, D 785-833-4321 182 F
victory@kwu.edu
VICTORY, Gregory, J 617-627-0813 228 H
gregory.victory@tufts.edu
VIDAL, Andy 978-232-2384 218 D
avidal@endicott.edu
VIDAL, Betsy 787-704-1020 532 H
bvidal@ediccollege.edu
VIDAL, Karyn 561-202-6333 103 C
VIDAL, Lili, C 818-677-2085 34 A
lili.vidal@csun.edu
VIDAL, Molly 608-890-0181 522 A
molly.vidal@uwex.uwc.edu
VIDAL, Terry 914-337-9300 311 F
terry.vidal@concordia-ny.edu
VIDAL-KENDALL, Olive 706-649-1442 119 F
ovidal-kendall@columbustech.edu
VIDMAR, Anthony 940-397-4782 462 A
anthony.vidmar@mwsu.edu
VIDRINE, Christopher 504-568-5976 198 A
cvidri@lsuhsc.edu
VIECK, Jana, L 812-888-5090 169 A
jvieck@vinu.edu
VIEFHUES-BAILEY,
Ludger 315-445-5427 318 E
viefhulh@lemoyne.edu
VIEHMAN, David 215-368-5000 398 C
dviehmans@biblical.edu
VIEIRA, Elvira 973-877-3062 291 H
vieira@essex.edu
VIEIRA, Margarida 508-531-2877 221 C
mvieira@bridgew.edu
VIEIRA, Michele 903-886-5025 468 D
michele.vieira@tamuc.edu
VIELBIG, Matthew 425-235-7836 506 F
mvielbig@rtc.edu
VIELE, Dan 314-529-9671 267 B
dan.viele@maryville.edu
VIEMEISTER, Sara 541-506-6029 390 I
financialaid@cgcc.edu
VIEN, Michele 518-694-7216 303 C
michele.vien@acphs.edu
VIENNA, Michael 404-727-2834 120 E
michael.vienna@emory.edu
VIENNE, Charlie 936-294-1840 471 D
cvienne@shsu.edu
VIERA, Eddie 561-868-3390 106 D
vierae@palmbeachstate.edu
VIERA, Javier 973-408-3258 291 B
jviera@drew.edu
VIERECK, Shannon 605-668-1467 436 D
shannon.viereck@mtmc.edu
VIEREGGE, Van 217-206-6002 156 G
vvier2@uis.edu
VIERS, Christopher 812-855-9086 162 F
cviers@iu.edu
VIERTEL, Cynthia, S 920-748-8312 519 E
viertelc@ripon.edu
VIEWEG, Bruce, W 218-299-4737 246 A
bvieweg@cord.edu
VIEWEG, Johannes 954-262-0510 105 J
jvieweg@nova.edu
VIGDOR, Corey 908-737-4782 292 C
cvigdor@kean.edu
VIGEANT, Paul 508-678-2811 223 A
paul.vigeant@bristolcc.edu
VIGESAA, Linda 503-491-6928 392 F
linda.vigesaa@mhcc.edu
VIGIL, Cynthia 509-533-3405 503 A
cynthia.vigil@sfcc.spokane.edu
VIGIL, James 304-876-5219 513 E
jvigil@shepherd.edu
VIGIL, Renee 719-587-7526 76 G
reneevigil@adams.edu
VIGNA, Natan 951-785-2100 48 A
nvigna@lasierra.edu
VIGNERON, David 978-232-2376 218 D
dvignero@endicott.edu
VIGO VERESTÍN, Milka 787-763-6700 532 L
milkavigo@gmail.com
VIGOREAUX, Jim 802-656-4627 485 D
jim.vigoreaux@uvm.edu
VIJITHA-KUMARA,
Kanaka 309-467-6434 140 E
kumara@eureka.edu
VIKANDER, David 507-537-6281 252 E
david.vikander@smsu.edu
VILA, Cherly, T 692-625-3394 530 C
cvila@cmi.edu
VILA, Dendy 787-765-3560 532 I
dmvila@edpuniversity.edu

VILA, Joaquin 505-747-2194 301 F
joaquin.vila@nnmc.edu
VILACRUZ, Geraldo, G 608-246-6442 523 F
gvilacruz@madisoncollege.edu
VILE, John, R 615-898-2596 444 G
john.vile@mtsu.edu
VILEGI PAYNE, Deborah 570-740-0232 409 E
dvilegi@luzerne.edu
VILELLE, Luke 540-362-6592 490 F
lvilelle@hollins.edu
VILES, Vickery 541-383-7258 390 D
vviles@cocc.edu
VILIC, Boris 609-896-5033 295 B
bvilic@rider.edu
VILKINA, Galina 212-616-7270 315 G
galina.vilkina@helenefuld.edu
VILLA, Christopher 818-364-7642 49 J
villachr@lamission.edu
VILLA, Cynthia 805-756-2171 31 I
cvvilla@calpoly.edu
VILLA, William 808-739-4695 130 F
william.villa@chaminade.edu
VILLAGRANA, Ana, L 530-661-5711 76 C
avillagr@yccd.edu
VILLAGRANA, George 559-638-0300 67 D
george.villagrana@reedleycollege.edu
VILLAIZAN, Sonia 787-878-5475 533 H
svillaiz@arecibo.inter.edu
VILLALOBOS, Alex 559-934-2373 74 D
alexjvillalobos@whccd.edu
VILLALOBOS, Bobbi 310-233-4028 49 I
villalb@lahc.edu
VILLAMARIA, Paul 303-282-3318 83 C
paul.villamaria@archden.org
VILLAMIL-TORRES,
Margarita, E 787-250-0000 537 D
margarita.villamil@upr.edu
VILLANELLA, Michael 212-752-1530 318 F
michael.villanella@limcollege.edu
VILLANTI, Athony 315-792-3053 339 B
avillanti@utica.edu
VILLANUEVA, Celeste 510-869-6744 59 L
cvillanueva@samuelmerritt.edu
VILLANUEVA, Christina 210-431-6789 464 H
cvillanueva@stmarytx.edu
VILLANUEVA, Daniel, G 818-364-7772 49 J
villand@lamission.edu
VILLANUEVA,
Donna-Mae 818-719-6444 50 A
villandm@piercecollege.edu
VILLANUEVA, Gil 804-289-8640 495 G
gvillanu@richmond.edu
VILLANUEVA, Ismael 787-890-2681 537 E
ismael.villanueva@upr.edu
VILLANUEVA, Lynda 979-230-3422 453 A
lynda.villanueva@brazosport.edu
VILLANUEVA, Rebecca 432-264-5190 459 D
rvillanueva@howardcollege.edu
VILLANUEVA, Sumaya 212-484-1346 308 E
svillanueva@jjjay.cuny.edu
VILLAR, Jeremy 323-953-4000 49 H
villarjv@lacitycollege.edu
VILLARE, Kathryn 978-681-0800 225 B
kvillare@mslaw.edu
VILLAREAL, Henry 650-574-6590 62 H
henry.villareal@smccd.edu
VILLAROSE, Lesley 434-791-5627 487 C
lvillarose@averett.edu
VILLARREAL, Abe 575-538-6336 303 A
news@wnmu.edu
VILLARREAL, Carlos 713-743-5688 473 F
cvillarr@central.uh.edu
VILLARREAL, Elisabeth 210-829-2736 474 D
villaret@uiwtx.edu
VILLARREAL, James 210-431-4312 464 H
jvillarreal12@stmarytx.edu
VILLARREAL, Luis 713-313-1089 470 D
luis.villarreal@tsu.edu
VILLARREAL, Oscar 559-925-3347 74 E
oscarvillarreal@whccd.edu
VILLARREAL, Pete 530-749-3879 76 D
pvillarre@yccd.edu
VILLARREAL, Velda 210-485-0735 450 A
vvillarreal@alamo.edu
VILLARROEL, Gratzia 920-403-3887 519 G
gratzia.villarroel@snc.edu
VILLARRUEL, Antonia 215-898-8283 421 E
nursingdean@nursing.upenn.edu
VILLEGAS, Gregorio 787-766-1717 536 B
um_gvillegas@suagm.edu
VILLEGAS, Kevin, J 717-766-2511 410 J
kvillega@messiah.edu
VILLEGAS, Lucille 310-954-4010 53 B
lvillegas@msmu.edu
VILLEGAS-VIDAL, Ludi 818-364-7643 49 J
villegl@lamission.edu
VILLELLA, John 610-436-3111 416 C
jvillella@wcupa.edu
VILLELLA, Theresa 814-732-1297 415 A
tvillella@edinboro.edu

VILLENEUVE, Martha 603-897-8260 287 F
mvilleneuve@rivier.edu
VILLETT, Stephen, H 207-947-4591 202 E
svillett@bealcollege.edu
VILLINES, Trish 870-743-3000 21 C
tvillines@northark.edu
VILLOLDO, Sergio 787-754-8000 537 B
svilloldo@pupr.edu
VINAL, Alicia 978-232-2271 218 D
avinal@endicott.edu
VINBERG, Dawn 206-546-6955 507 F
dvinberg@shoreline.edu
VINCENT, Alisha 605-995-2937 435 F
alvincen@dwu.edu
VINCENT, Andrew 502-897-4785 192 D
avincent@sbts.edu
VINCENT, Angela 814-732-2921 415 A
vincent@edinboro.edu
VINCENT, Danny, E 740-826-8110 373 E
dvincent@muskingum.edu
VINCENT, Deborah, S 708-239-4793 155 M
deborah.vincent@trnty.edu
VINCENT, Gregory, J 512-471-3212 476 B
gvincent@mail.utexas.edu
VINCENT, Kitt 909-593-3511 71 B
kvincent@laverne.edu
VINCENT, Nelson, C 513-556-2323 379 A
nelson.vincent@uc.edu
VINCENT, Sara 860-512-3100 86 E
svincent@manchestercc.edu
VINCENT, Vincent 256-306-2773 2 F
vincent.vincent@calhoun.edu
VINCENT, William, K 951-639-5201 53 D
bvincent@msjc.edu
VINE, Scott 717-358-3843 403 J
scott.vine@fandm.edu
VINES, Erin, E 661-722-6300 27 B
evines@avc.edu
VINES, Robert 239-590-7044 110 L
rvines@fgcu.edu
VINET, Mary Christine 251-460-6185 9 E
cvinet@southalabama.edu
VINEYARD, Ed 580-548-2207 384 L
edwin.vineyard@noc.edu
VINEYARD, George 314-367-8700 271 E
george.vineyard@stlcop.edu
VINEYARD, Julie 785-242-2067 183 H
jvineyard@neosho.edu
VINGER, Christopher 212-472-1500 324 A
cvinger@nysid.edu
VINIAR, Barbara, A 410-827-5802 207 A
bviniar@chesapeake.edu
VINK, Cher 715-468-2815 525 A
cher.vink@witc.edu
VINOVRSKI, Bernie 559-278-2061 32 F
bernard_vinovrski@csufresno.edu
VINROE, Richard 316-295-5911 181 B
vinroer@friends.edu
VINSON, Ben 202-994-6130 92 D
bvinson3@gwu.edu
VINSON, John, N 206-543-0521 508 E
vinso1jn@uw.edu
VINSON, Richard 336-721-2619 355 E
richard.vinson@salem.edu
VINSON, Terence 318-670-9426 199 J
tvinson@susla.edu
VINSON, Wendy 706-245-7226 120 D
wvinson@ec.edu
VINSON, William 608-249-6611 516 M
wvinson@msn.herzing.edu
VINYARD, Lisa 636-481-3101 266 C
lvinyard@jeffco.edu
VINZANT, Becky 601-266-5000 261 E
rebecca.vinzant@usm.edu
VINZANT, Douglas 601-266-5005 261 E
douglas.vinzant@usm.edu
VINZANT, Jeffrey, P 334-244-3576 2 A
jvinzant@aum.edu
VIOLA, Anthony 617-730-7255 226 J
anthony.viola@newbury.edu
VIOLA, Joe 541-383-7776 390 D
jviola@cocc.edu
VIOLA, Judah 312-261-3527 149 B
judah.viola@nl.edu
VIOLANTI, Karen 410-857-2750 209 D
kviolanti@mcdaniel.edu
VIOLET, Matt 510-845-6232 66 J
mviolet@sksm.edu
VIOLETT, Edward 225-768-1711 199 B
edward.violett@ololcollege.edu
VIOLETTE, Mike 706-771-4037 117 C
mviolette@augustatech.edu
VIOLLT, Kathleen 312-935-6444 152 D
kviollt@robertmorris.edu
VIOLLT, Michael, P 312-935-6600 152 D
mviollt@robertmorris.edu
VIRASAWMI, Errol 516-364-0808 323 B
errol@nycollege.edu
VIRAY, Sydnee 802-656-3874 485 D
sydnee.viray@uvm.edu

VIRCKS, Andrea 651-523-2100 247 A
avircks01@hamline.edu
VIRDEN, Rebecka 501-977-2033 24 B
virden@uaccm.edu
VIRELLO, Mark 617-322-3502 219 H
mark_virello@laboure.edu
VIRES, Charles 731-989-6171 440 D
cvires@fhu.edu
VIRGIN, Richard, P 402-280-2741 279 H
richardvirgin@creighton.edu
VIRJEE, Framroze, M 562-951-4500 31 H
fvirjee@calstate.edu
VIRK, Surinder 718-997-5760 309 D
surinder.virk@qc.cuny.edu
VIRKLER, Lyndon 802-225-3258 484 G
lyndon.virkler@neci.edu
VIRTS, Paul, H 651-631-5096 256 A
phvirts@unwsp.edu
VIRTUE, Alicia 707-524-1664 63 G
avirtue@santarosa.edu
VIRZI, Amanda 262-741-8392 523 D
virzia@gtc.edu
VISCHER, Robert 651-962-4838 256 C
rkvischer@stthomas.edu
VISCO, JR., Donald, P 330-972-7930 378 G
dviscoj@uakron.edu
VISCOMI, Susan 315-312-3056 333 D
susan.viscomi@oswego.edu
VISCONAGE, Elizabeth, L 410-864-4261 210 F
bvisconage@stmarys.edu
VISCUSI, Nicolette 518-264-2524 303 E
viscusn@mail.amc.edu
VISCUSI, Peter 304-384-5241 513 A
pviscusi@concord.edu
VISCUSI, Raymond 610-359-5070 401 L
rviscusi@dccc.edu
VISEL, OSB, Jeana 812-357-6721 167 B
jvisel@saintmeinrad.edu
VISENTIN, Peter 203-837-8680 85 I
visentinp@wcsu.edu
VISIN, David 319-335-5026 169 H
david-visin@uiowa.edu
VISKER, Thomas 574-807-7259 159 D
viskert@bethelcollege.edu
VISKOZKI, Lynette 318-869-5137 194 I
lviskozk@centenary.edu
VISOT, Cynthia, S 813-974-1678 112 C
cvisot@usf.edu
VISSER, Erik 707-864-7000 65 A
erik.visser@solano.edu
VISSER, Jen 319-895-4167 171 A
jvisser@cornellcollege.edu
VISSER, Sarah 616-526-6453 232 A
sav36@calvin.edu
VISTOCCO, Valerie 315-781-3309 316 C
vistocco@hws.edu
VISUANO, Denise 503-838-8349 396 E
visuanod@wou.edu
VITA, Claudine 610-526-6012 405 B
cvita@harcum.edu
VITA, Paul 314-977-2500 271 K
vitap@slu.edu
VITAL, Allen 256-372-5230 1 A
allen.vital@aamu.edu
VITALE, Bob 319-385-6270 174 A
bob.vitale@iw.edu
VITALE, Frank 410-888-9048 209 C
fvitale@muih.edu
VITALE, Joseph 973-328-5060 290 H
jvitale@ccm.edu
VITALE, JR., Joseph 440-775-5573 374 C
jvitale@oberlin.edu
VITALE, Michael 913-288-7689 182 C
mvitale@kckcc.edu
VITALE, Tim 435-797-1351 482 B
tim.vitale@usu.edu
VITALI, John 973-408-3501 291 B
jvitali@drew.edu
VITALOS, Mark 610-606-4642 400 E
mavitalo@cedarcrest.edu
VITANGCOL REGOSO,
Aimee 269-471-3375 230 H
aimeev@andrews.edu
VITANGELI, Kory, M 317-788-3485 168 A
kvitangeli@uindy.edu
VITATOE, David, A 216-397-1984 370 H
dvitatoe@jcu.edu
VITATOE, Steven, P 216-397-4277 370 H
svitatoe@jcu.edu
VITEK, Melissa 215-780-1527 419 C
mvitek@salus.edu
VITELLI, Chris 209-384-6185 52 E
chris.vitelli@mccd.edu
VITELLI, Kelly 814-732-1965 415 A
kvitelli@edinboro.edu
VITELLI, Mary 407-628-6303 107 O
mvitelli@rollins.edu
VITELLO, Joan 508-856-5081 221 B
joan.vitello@umassmed.edu
VITO, Christine 704-886-6500 93 F

W

WADA-MCKEE, Nancy ...... 323-343-6076.... 33 C
n.wadamckee@calstatela.edu
WADDELL, Barbara .... 419-372-5312.. 364 E
bwaddel@bgsu.edu
WADDELL, Edwin, B .... 336-734-7326.. 349 G
ewaddell@forsythtech.edu
WADDELL, Jenetta .... 662-685-4771.. 257 A
jwaddell@bmc.edu
WADDELL, Sandy .... 816-501-4689.. 270 J
sandy.waddell@rockhurst.edu
WADDELL, Stacy .... 865-251-1800.. 444 A
swaddell@southcollegetn.edu
WADDLE, Chris .... 308-398-7325.. 278 K
cwaddle@cccneb.edu
WADDY, Jeff .... 708-596-2000.. 154 E
jwaddy@ssc.edu
WADE, Aletha, R .... 301-369-2800.. 206 H
arwade@captechu.edu
WADE, Alton .... 901-321-4102.. 439 E
awade2@cbu.edu
WADE, Andrea, C .... 585-292-2170.. 321 J
awade13@monroecc.edu
WADE, Bernadette .... 914-674-7473.. 320 G
bwade@mercy.edu
WADE, Chandra .... 773-947-6285.. 147 D
cwade@mccormick.edu
WADE, Connie, H .... 678-359-5053.. 122 E
connie_w@gordonstate.edu
WADE, Courtney .... 413-597-4139.. 230 A
courtney.wade@williams.edu
WADE, Damon, R .... 318-274-7701.. 200 F
waded@gram.edu
WADE, Douglas .... 661-654-2251.... 32 A
dwade3@csub.edu
WADE, Gary .... 865-545-5313.. 441 E
gary.wade@lmunet.edu
WADE, Gourdine .... 334-229-6810...... 1 D
gwade@alasu.edu
WADE, Gwen .... 404-880-8290.. 118 K
gwade@cau.edu
WADE, H. Keith .... 863-638-2940.. 115 D
wadehk@webber.edu
WADE, James, E .... 256-782-5649...... 4 H
jwade@jsu.edu
WADE, Jennifer, G .... 901-843-3850.. 443 L
goodloe@rhodes.edu
WADE, Jerrel .... 281-998-6150.. 465 A
jerrel.wade@sjcd.edu
WADE, John .... 510-215-3804.... 41 H
jwade@contracosta.edu
WADE, John .... 847-635-2602.. 150 G
jwade@oakton.edu
WADE, John .... 859-622-1405.. 188 F
john.wade@eku.edu
WADE, Kaleb .... 214-638-0484.. 460 C
kalebwade@kdstudio.com
WADE, Ken .... 404-526-7366.. 126 D
k.wade@sae.edu
WADE, Kevin .... 510-834-5740.... 57 D
kwade@peralta.edu
WADE, Lara .... 813-974-9060.. 112 C
larawade@usf.edu
WADE, Marcia .... 310-434-4010.... 63 F
wade_marcia@smc.edu
WADE, Margaret .... 432-685-4615.. 461 H
mwade@midland.edu
WADE, Melissa .... 954-969-9771.. 100 K
mwade@fcnh.com
WADE, Noreen .... 516-572-3559.. 322 C
noreen.wade@ncc.edu
WADE, Randy .... 541-956-7076.. 394 J
rwade@roguecc.edu
WADE, Scott .... 509-963-2160.. 501 K
wades@cwu.edu
WADE, Susan .... 785-594-8382.. 178 D
susan.wade@bakeru.edu
WADE, Veronica .... 206-934-5216.. 507 A
veronica.wade@seattlecolleges.edu
WADE, Virginia .... 310-377-5501.... 51 G
vwade@marymountcalifornia.edu
WADHOLM, Rick .... 701-349-5959.. 362 C
rwadholm@trinitybiblecollege.edu
WADIAN, Becky .... 563-425-5270.. 177 D
wadianb@uiu.edu
WADKINS, Jesse, E .... 479-248-7236.... 20 C
jwadkins@ecollege.edu
WADLEIGH, Jackie .... 817-722-1731.. 460 E
jackie.wadleigh@tku.edu
WAECHTER, James .... 727-341-3267.. 108 D
jwaechter@spcollege.edu
WAECHTER, Julie .... 719-587-7165.... 76 G
jmwaecht@adams.edu
WAELCHLI, Paul .... 319-895-4260.. 171 A
pwaelchli@cornellcollege.edu
WAGAR, Hayden .... 504-398-2167.. 200 D
hwagar@olhcc.edu
WAGEMESTER, Doug .... 319-398-4909.. 174 I
dwageme@kirkwood.edu
WAGENER, Mark .... 973-278-5400.. 305 B
maw@berkeleycollege.edu

WAGENER, Mark .... 973-278-5400.. 289 F
maw@berkeleycollege.edu
WAGENER, William, C .... 304-336-8177.. 513 F
wagenerw@westliberty.edu
WAGENSONNER, Eric ...... 510-485-7832.... 56 I
ewagensonner@patten.edu
WAGER, Lisa .... 212-217-4700.. 314 B
lisa_wager@fitnyc.edu
WAGERS, Karen, C .... 859-280-1236.. 191 D
kwagers@lextheo.edu
WAGES, Charlene .... 843-661-1140.. 430 B
cwages@fmarion.edu
WAGES, Heather .... 701-777-6345.. 360 C
hwages@nd.gov
WAGES, Sam .... 210-805-5836.. 474 D
wages@uiwtx.edu
WAGGENER, Anna .... 251-981-3771........ 2 I
anna.waggener@columbiasouthern.edu
WAGGONER, David .... 757-455-3201.. 500 E
dwaggoner@vwc.edu
WAGGONER, Earl .... 303-963-3485.... 77 I
ewaggoner@ccu.edu
WAGGONER, George .... 603-206-8081.. 286 D
gwaggoner@ccsnh.edu
WAGGONER, Greg .... 575-562-2153.. 299 I
greg.waggoner@enmu.edu
WAGGONER, Julia .... 715-682-1302.. 518 H
jwaggoner@northland.edu
WAGGONER, Karen .... 432-685-5540.. 461 H
kwaggoner@midland.edu
WAGGONER, Reneau .... 502-213-2620.. 190 A
reneau.waggoner@kctcs.edu
WAGGONER, Todd .... 417-862-9533.. 265 D
twaggoner@globaluniversity.edu
WAGGONER, Wes, K .... 214-768-2110.. 465 J
wwaggoner@smu.edu
WAGLEY, Spencer .... 620-278-4262.. 185 A
swagley@sterling.edu
WAGNER, Alex .... 617-236-8879.. 218 G
awagner@fisher.edu
WAGNER, Anne Marie ..... 513-244-4810.. 373 C
anne.marie.wagner@msj.edu
WAGNER, Anthony, E ...... 706-721-2901.. 117 D
awagner@augusta.edu
WAGNER, Ashley .... 619-684-8825.... 54 C
awagner@newschoolarch.edu
WAGNER, Claire, M .... 513-529-7592.. 372 K
wagnercm@miamioh.edu
WAGNER, Craig .... 641-472-1177.. 175 A
wagner-craig@aramark.com
WAGNER, Daniel .... 419-755-4817.. 373 G
dwagner@ncstatecollge.edu
WAGNER, Danielle .... 610-558-5502.. 411 E
wagnerd@neumann.edu
WAGNER, Dave .... 615-966-5683.. 441 F
dave.wagner@lipscomb.edu
WAGNER, David, H .... 336-334-7880.. 356 F
dhwagner@ncat.edu
WAGNER, Deanna .... 614-236-6904.. 364 N
dwagner1453@capital.edu
WAGNER, Donna .... 575-646-2810.. 300 J
dlwagner@nmsu.edu
WAGNER, James, M .... 214-648-2168.. 478 C
james.wagner@utsouthwestern.edu
WAGNER, Jane .... 617-682-1511.. 218 E
jwagner@eds.edu
WAGNER, Janet, M .... 609-652-4534.. 297 C
janet.wagner@stockton.edu
WAGNER, Jean .... 503-491-6113.. 392 F
jean.wagner@mhcc.edu
WAGNER, Jeanne, A .... 717-901-5117.. 405 H
jwagner@harrisburgu.edu
WAGNER, Jeff .... 320-308-2286.. 252 A
jswagner@stcloudstate.edu
WAGNER, Jodi .... 509-527-2772.. 508 G
jodi.wagner@wallawalla.edu
WAGNER, Joseph .... 413-592-3189.. 217 D
wagnerj@elms.edu
WAGNER, Ken .... 808-675-3760.. 130 E
ken.wagner@byuh.edu
WAGNER, Kevin, J .... 740-826-6129.. 373 E
kevinw@muskingum.edu
WAGNER, Kimberly .... 260-481-6103.. 163 C
wagnerk@ipfw.edu
WAGNER, Kurt .... 732-571-4401.. 292 F
kwagner@monmouth.edu
WAGNER, Lana .... 325-649-8076.. 459 E
lwagner@hputx.edu
WAGNER, Laura .... 219-866-6116.. 166 J
lwagner@saintjoe.edu
WAGNER, Linda, L .... 814-871-7423.. 404 A
wagner001@gannon.edu
WAGNER, Marci, K .... 724-450-4089.. 404 F
mkwagner@gcc.edu
WAGNER, Maria .... 971-722-4497.. 394 F
maria.wagner@pcc.edu
WAGNER, Marilyn, D .... 940-565-3487.. 475 A
mwagner@unt.edu
WAGNER, Mary .... 803-777-7700.. 433 F
mary.wagner@sc.edu

WAGNER, Mervin .... 816-322-0110.. 262 N
merv.wagner@calvary.edu
WAGNER, Michael, F .... 603-646-0459.. 286 J
michael.f.wagner@dartmouth.edu
WAGNER, Michelle, L ...... 262-243-5700.. 516 E
michelle.wagner@cuw.edu
WAGNER, Mike .... 309-556-3561.. 143 D
mwagner@iwu.edu
WAGNER, Patrick, W .... 704-406-4250.. 344 E
pwagner@gardner-webb.edu
WAGNER, Rich .... 612-374-5800.. 246 F
rwagner@dunwoody.edu
WAGNER, Richard, A .... 413-796-2306.. 229 E
richard.wagner@wne.edu
WAGNER, Richard, T .... 240-895-3421.. 210 E
rtwagner@smcm.edu
WAGNER, Robert .... 212-563-6647.. 338 G
r.wagner@uts.edu
WAGNER, Robert, A .... 971-722-4696.. 394 F
robert.wagner3@pcc.edu
WAGNER, Robin .... 717-337-7000.. 404 C
rowagner@gettysburg.edu
WAGNER, Roger, W .... 760-245-4271.... 73 H
roger.wagner@vvc.edu
WAGNER, Sandra .... 620-672-5641.. 184 D
pamd@prattcc.edu
WAGNER, Susan .... 520-795-0787.... 11 G
registrar@asaom.edu
WAGNER, Teresa, J .... 315-464-4252.. 332 C
wagnert@upstate.edu
WAGNER, Tina .... 651-690-8890.. 254 M
tmwagner@stkate.edu
WAGNER, Tracy, A .... 941-359-7511.. 107 M
twagner@ringling.edu
WAGNER-FOSSEN, Dena . 406-771-4312.. 277 F
dfossen@gfcmsu.edu
WAGNER-LIND, Wendy ... 954-308-2620.... 95 K
wwagner@aii.edu
WAGNITZ, Jeff .... 206-878-3711.. 504 E
jwagnitz@highline.edu
WAGNON, Bill .... 601-635-6242.. 257 F
bwagnon@eccc.edu
WAGNON, Shelley .... 313-993-1588.. 241 G
wagnonsm@udmercy.edu
WAGONER, Jessica .... 657-278-2570.... 33 A
jwagoner@fullerton.edu
WAGONER, Natalie, M ..... 260-399-7700.. 168 D
nwagoner@sf.edu
WAGONER, Zandra, L ...... 909-593-3511.... 71 B
zwagoner@laverne.edu
WAGSTAFF, Grayson .... 202-319-5417.... 92 A
wagstaff@cua.edu
WAGSTAFF, Robert .... 617-603-6900.. 226 D
robert.wagstaff@necb.edu
WAGSTAFFE, Paul .... 916-686-8816.... 31 F
WAGUESPACK, Bruce ...... 225-675-5397.. 196 J
bwaguespack@rpcc.edu
WAGUESPACK, Cathy ...... 504-398-2111.. 200 D
cwaguespack@olhcc.edu
WAHL, Chris .... 201-360-4030.. 292 B
cwahl@hccc.edu
WAHL, Doug, J .... 715-232-2501.. 521 D
wahld@uwstout.edu
WAHL, Katherine .... 585-271-3657.. 328 A
kwahl@stbernards.edu
WAHL, Lynette .... 651-523-3000.. 247 A
lwahl@hamline.edu
WAHL, Robert .... 860-255-3472.... 87 E
rwahl@txcc.commnet.edu
WAHLBERG, David, C ..... 218-477-2175.. 250 F
david.wahlberg@mnstate.edu
WAHLERS, Mark, E .... 503-280-8578.. 391 A
mwahlers@cu-portland.edu
WAHLFELDT, Tracy, D ...... 217-443-8772.. 139 B
twahlfeldt@dacc.edu
WAHLROOS-RITTER,
Ingalill .... 818-767-0888.... 75 D
ingalill.wahlroos-ritter@woodbury.edu
WAHLSTROM, David, A ... 617-989-4552.. 229 D
wahlstromd@wit.edu
WAHNEE, Robbie .... 580-591-0203.. 383 D
rwahnee@cnc.cc.ok.us
WAHR, Linda .... 312-329-2213.. 148 F
linda.wahr@moody.edu
WAHRHAFTIG, Matt .... 937-481-2263.. 381 C
matt_wahrhaftig@wilmington.edu
WAID, Landon .... 205-348-7287...... 8 D
landon.waid@ua.edu
WAID, Monica, K .... 941-359-7511.. 107 M
mwaid@ringling.edu
WAID, Patti, W .... 209-228-4483.... 70 A
pwaid@ucmerced.edu
WAINWRIGHT, Lisa .... 312-629-1236.. 154 A
lwainwright@saic.edu
WAINWRIGHT, Philip ...... 404-727-7504.. 120 E
pwainwr@emory.edu
WAINWRIGHT,
William, S .... 985-732-6640.. 196 G
WAIS, Marc, L .... 212-998-4401.. 324 C
marc.wais@nyu.edu

WAIT, Julianna, M .... 757-594-7385.. 488 E
julianna.wait@cnu.edu
WAIT, Mark .... 615-322-7660.. 449 A
mark.wait@vanderbilt.edu
WAITE, Boyd, A .... 410-293-1582.. 529 D
waite@usna.edu
WAITE, Dan .... 949-214-3472.... 41 F
dan.waite@cui.edu
WAITE, Joann .... 509-313-5870.. 504 A
waite@gonzaga.edu
WAITE, Megan .... 504-398-2130.. 200 D
mwaite@olhcc.edu
WAITE, Michelle .... 402-472-2116.. 282 M
mwaite1@unl.edu
WAITE, Zauyah .... 412-365-2794.. 400 G
zwaite@chatham.edu
WAITERS, Destinee .... 940-898-3250.. 472 G
dwaiters@twu.edu
WAITERS, Ernest .... 301-860-4040.. 212 D
ewaiters@bowiestate.edu
WAITES, Cheryl, E .... 313-577-4400.. 243 F
deanssw@wayne.edu
WAITLEY, Erin .... 970-521-6662.... 81 O
erin.waitley@njc.edu
WAITS, David .... 405-744-2325.. 385 G
david.waits@okstate.edu
WAITS, Lisa .... 707-638-5270.... 68 C
lisa.waits@tu.edu
WAITZ, Ian, A .... 617-253-0218.. 225 A
WAJDA, Phillip, J .... 518-388-8394.. 338 H
wajdap@union.edu
WAJERT, Susan .... 419-251-1314.. 372 C
susan.wajert@mercycollege.edu
WAKE, Sarah .... 773-702-5671.. 156 D
swake@uchicago.edu
WAKEFIELD, Donna .... 513-751-1206.. 362 H
donna@aic-arts.edu
WAKEFIELD, Sandra .... 563-355-3500.. 174 E
swakefield@kaplan.edu
WAKEFIELD, Sarah .... 425-235-2285.. 506 F
swakefield@rtc.edu
WAKELEE, Daniel, W .... 805-437-8542.... 32 B
dan.wakelee@csuci.edu
WAKELING, William, M ... 617-373-5001.. 227 B
WAKEMAN, Joe .... 740-753-6098.. 369 K
wakemanj@hocking.edu
WAKEMAN, Rebecca .... 740-477-7549.. 374 G
rwakeman@ohiochristian.edu
WAKSDAHL, Robert, B ..... 715-394-8017.. 521 E
rwaksdah@uwsuper.edu
WALBERT, Mark .... 309-438-7018.. 143 B
mswalber@ilstu.edu
WALBORN, Ronald .... 845-770-5716.. 325 C
ronald.walborn@nyack.edu
WALBORN, Wanda, F ...... 845-675-4457.. 325 C
wanda.walborn@nyack.edu
WALCHER, Sheldon .... 630-942-3628.. 138 B
walchers@cod.edu
WALCHESKI, Michael .... 651-603-6184.. 246 B
walcheski@csp.edu
WALCHLE, John .... 740-392-6868.. 373 D
john.walchle@mvnu.edu
WALCK, Barbara .... 716-614-5902.. 324 D
bwalck@niagaracc.suny.edu
WALCROFT, Marie, B .... 215-699-5700.. 408 C
mwalcroft@lsb.edu
WALCZAK, Mary .... 507-786-3498.. 254 P
walczak@stolaf.edu
WALD, Cara .... 651-638-6400.. 244 L
c-wald@bethel.edu
WALD, Donna .... 972-438-6932.. 463 F
dwald@parker.edu
WALD, Frederica, N .... 212-346-1200.. 325 J
fwald@pace.edu
WALDBILLIG, Amy .... 513-569-1414.. 366 D
amy.waldbillig@cincinnatistate.edu
WALDECK, Steve .... 661-362-2767.... 52 A
swaldeck@masters.edu
WALDEN, Bernadine .... 919-516-4140.. 355 D
bwalden@st-aug.edu
WALDEN, Dan .... 323-953-4000.... 49 H
waldendw@lacitycollege.edu
WALDEN, David .... 315-859-4340.. 315 D
dwalden@hamilton.edu
WALDEN, Shawn .... 785-243-1435.. 179 N
swalden@cloud.edu
WALDEN, Valerie .... 361-570-4815.. 474 C
waldenv@uhv.edu
WALDHOF, Kenneth .... 718-862-7362.. 319 L
kenneth.waldhof@manhattan.edu
WALDMAN, Chaim, A .... 718-259-5600.. 313 G
WALDMANN, Robert, G ... 718-429-6600.. 339 D
robert.waldmann@vaughn.edu
WALDNER, Joanne, L ...... 978-232-2013.. 218 D
jwaldner@endicott.edu
WALDNER, Louann .... 559-688-3027.... 40 E
louannw@cos.edu
WALDO, Hilary .... 404-872-3593.. 117 B
hwaldo@johnmarshall.edu
WALDON, James, G .... 802-447-4004.. 485 B
jwaldon@svc.edu

WALL, Laurie .... 417-255-7976.. 269 A
lauriewall@missouristate.edu
WALL, Letitia, C .... 336-750-2132.. 359 B
cornishl@wssu.edu
WALL, Mark .... 918-540-6451.. 384 F
mark.wall@neo.edu
WALL, Matthew, R .... 229-333-5705.. 129 G
mrwall@valdosta.edu
WALL, Michael, A .... 973-596-5629.. 293 D
michael.a.wall@njit.edu
WALL, Mike .... 636-949-4880.. 266 J
mwall@lindenwood.edu
WALL, Rich .... 760-701-5380.... 88 D
wall_r@mitchell.edu
WALL, Richard .... 973-290-4290.. 290 G
rwall@cse.edu
WALL, Rick .... 323-343-3700.... 33 C
rwall2@calstatela.edu
WALL, Seth, P .... 603-314-1705.. 225 C
seth.wall@mcphs.edu
WALL, Thomas .... 617-552-4470.. 216 C
thomas.wall.2@bc.edu
WALL, Timothy .... 660-562-1179.. 269 J
timwall@nwmissouri.edu
WALL, Vanessa .... 229-931-2713.. 127 C
vwall@southgatech.edu
WALL, Yvette .... 718-270-4894.. 309 B
ywall@mec.cuny.edu
WALLACE, Amy .... 805-437-8911.... 32 B
amy.wallace@csuci.edu
WALLACE, Andrea .... 912-279-5931.. 119 C
awallace@ccga.edu
WALLACE, Antonio .... 770-593-2257.. 122 F
awallace@gupton-jones.edu
WALLACE, Auguster .... 662-254-3425.. 260 A
akeys@mvsu.edu
WALLACE, Bentley .... 501-907-6670.... 21 H
bwallace@pulaskitech.edu
WALLACE, Beth, D .... 864-597-4370.. 435 C
wallacebd@wofford.edu
WALLACE, Brent .... 318-795-4215.. 198 C
brent.wallace@lsus.edu
WALLACE, Chad .... 765-641-4374.. 158 J
cewallace@anderson.edu
WALLACE, Chris .... 804-524-5070.. 499 G
cwallace@vsu.edu
WALLACE, Christina .... 718-780-0305.. 305 L
christina.wallace@brooklaw.edu
WALLACE, Christine .... 810-762-9575.. 236 C
cwallace@kettering.edu
WALLACE, Cindy .... 704-406-4103.. 344 E
cwallace@gardner-webb.edu
WALLACE, Dave .... 972-800-4616.... 67 E
dwallace@sum.edu
WALLACE, David .... 562-985-5381.... 33 B
david.wallace@csulb.edu
WALLACE, David .... 270-534-3859.. 190 H
david.wallace@kctcs.edu
WALLACE, David .... 573-882-6601.. 273 E
wallaced@missouri.edu
WALLACE, Debbie .... 870-543-5996.... 22 E
dwallace@seark.edu
WALLACE, Deborah .... 818-677-2305.... 34 A
deborah.wallace@csun.edu
WALLACE, Debra, S .... 919-866-5920.. 353 I
dswallace@waketech.edu
WALLACE, Denise .... 504-816-4546.. 195 B
dwallace@dillard.edu
WALLACE, Don .... 509-527-2147.. 508 G
don.wallace@wallawalla.edu
WALLACE, Donald .... 760-921-5499.... 56 E
donald.wallace@paloverde.edu
WALLACE, Douglas, J .... 864-833-8312.. 432 B
dwallace@presby.edu
WALLACE, Effie .... 540-261-8492.. 494 F
effie.wallace@svu.edu
WALLACE, Elaine .... 954-262-1407.. 105 J
ewallace@nova.edu
WALLACE, Eric, C .... 806-356-3682.. 450 H
ecwallace@actx.edu
WALLACE, G. Brent .... 940-668-4230.. 462 L
bwallace@nctc.edu
WALLACE, Gillian .... 650-508-3718.... 54 J
gwallace@ndnu.edu
WALLACE, JR., Glenn, E . 912-525-5000.. 126 E
gwallace@scad.edu
WALLACE, JR., James ..... 219-980-6601.. 163 B
jamewall@iun.edu
WALLACE, James, A .... 405-466-6765.. 383 M
jawallace@langston.edu
WALLACE, Jamey .... 206-834-4100.. 501 D
jwallace@bastyr.edu
WALLACE, Jason .... 303-282-3423.... 83 C
father.wallace@archden.org
WALLACE, Jeff .... 765-998-5395.. 167 C
jfwallace@taylor.edu
WALLACE, Jerry .... 910-893-1205.. 342 F
wallace@campbell.edu
WALLACE, Joel .... 817-202-6333.. 466 C
jwallace@swau.edu
WALLACE, Jon, R .... 626-812-3075.... 28 A
jwallace@apu.edu
WALLACE, Joyce .... 214-333-5229.. 455 J
joycew@dbu.edu
WALLACE, Kim .... 303-404-5316.... 81 D
kim.wallace@frontrange.edu
WALLACE, Kim .... 303-404-5671.... 80 E
kim.wallace@frontrange.edu
WALLACE, Kimberly .... 239-590-1087.. 110 L
kwilliam@fgcu.edu
WALLACE, Laura, J .... 434-592-7330.. 491 D
jwallac@liberty.edu
WALLACE, Leigh .... 229-217-4143.. 127 G
lwallace@southernregional.edu
WALLACE, Linda .... 765-455-9288.. 163 A
lwallace@iuk.edu
WALLACE, Lynn .... 215-702-4337.. 399 E
lwallace@cairn.edu
WALLACE, Lynn, C .... 304-724-3700.. 510 E
WALLACE, Margaret .... 610-526-6001.. 405 B
mwallace@harcum.edu
WALLACE, Margaret, T ..... 610-526-6001.. 405 B
mwallace@harcum.edu
WALLACE, Mark, T .... 615-936-6709.. 449 A
mark.wallace@vanderbilt.edu
WALLACE, Michael .... 512-313-3000.. 455 F
michael.wallace@concordia.edu
WALLACE, Mike, J .... 408-554-4981.... 63 E
mjwallace@scu.edu
WALLACE, Miriam .... 941-487-4360.. 111 D
mwallace@ncf.edu
WALLACE, Molly .... 252-536-4221.. 350 C
WALLACE, Paula .... 912-525-5000.. 126 E
pwallace@scad.edu
WALLACE, Paula, J .... 434-947-8126.. 493 B
pwallace@randolphcollege.edu
WALLACE, Randy .... 512-499-4527.. 475 K
rwallace@utsystem.edu
WALLACE, Ray .... 812-941-2200.. 163 F
raywall@ius.edu
WALLACE, Renee, L .... 512-471-9266.. 476 B
rlwallace@austin.utexas.edu
WALLACE, Robert .... 304-766-3190.. 514 B
wallacer@wvstateu.edu
WALLACE, Sam, G .... 318-257-2769.. 200 G
wallace@latech.edu
WALLACE, Sherrie .... 330-823-7803.. 379 F
wallacsj@mountunion.edu
WALLACE, Tami .... 615-230-3573.. 447 C
tami.wallace@volstate.edu
WALLACE, Teresa .... 307-268-2621.. 526 D
twallace@caspercollege.edu
WALLACE, Terry .... 501-370-5224.... 21 G
twallace@philander.edu
WALLACE, Thomas .... 661-654-2161.... 32 A
twallace4@csub.edu
WALLACE, Tiffany .... 662-254-3440.. 260 A
trwallace@mvsu.edu
WALLACE, Tim .... 864-587-4267.. 433 A
wallacet@smcsc.edu
WALLACE, Tom .... 615-898-2137.. 444 G
tom.wallace@mtsu.edu
WALLACE, Tony .... 606-783-1538.. 190 C
tony.wallace@kctcs.edu
WALLANDER, Marcia, M . 412-578-8772.. 400 C
mmwallander@carlow.edu
WALLEN, Esther .... 773-252-5133.. 152 B
esther.wallen@resu.edu
WALLER, Art .... 801-774-9900.. 479 B
awaller@vistacollege.edu
WALLER, Caroline .... 870-235-4006.... 22 F
acwaller@saumag.edu
WALLER, Christine .... 315-792-7100.. 336 C
cwaller@sunypoly.edu
WALLER, Cynthia, G .... 615-353-3645.. 446 E
cynthia.waller@nscc.edu
WALLER, Frank .... 301-860-3813.. 212 D
fwaller@bowiestate.edu
WALLER, J.J .... 912-525-5000.. 126 E
jwaller@scad.edu
WALLER, Janet .... 256-824-6282...... 8 F
janet.waller@uah.edu
WALLER, Jason .... 903-510-2507.. 473 C
jwal@tjc.edu
WALLER, Jennifer .... 662-645-3555.. 257 E
jwaller@deltastate.edu
WALLER, Lorie .... 919-735-5151.. 354 A
loriew@waynecc.edu
WALLER, Melinda .... 941-907-2262.... 99 J
mwaller@evergladesuniversity.edu
WALLER, Peter .... 970-945-8691.... 78 B
WALLER, Steve .... 225-578-5388.. 197 I
swaller@lsu.edu
WALLER, Steven .... 402-472-2201.. 282 M
swaller1@unl.edu
WALLER, Wanda, M .... 318-670-9248.. 199 J
wmwaller@susla.edu
WALLERSTEIN,
Mitchel, B .... 646-312-3310.. 307 A
president@baruch.cuny.edu
WALLESHAUSER,
Linda, M .... 716-888-2244.. 306 F
walleshl@canisius.edu
WALLET, Robert, M .... 717-361-1524.. 403 C
walletrm@etown.edu
WALLEY, Anna-Jean .... 559-251-4215.... 29 I
bookkeeper@calchristiancollege.edu
WALLEY, Jennifer .... 559-251-4215.... 29 I
jwalley@calchristiancollege.edu
WALLEY, Trent .... 559-251-4215.... 29 I
admissions@calchristiancollege.edu
WALLEY, Wendell, L .... 559-251-4215.... 29 I
wwalley@calchristiancollege.edu
WALLIN, Celeste .... 212-616-7273.. 315 G
celeste.wallin@helenefuld.edu
WALLIN, William .... 303-329-6355.... 78 O
registrar@cstcm.edu
WALLING, Lisa .... 931-526-3660.. 440 A
lisaq.walling@fortisinstitute.edu
WALLING, Ray .... 785-594-8389.. 178 D
ray.walling@bakeru.edu
WALLINGA, Michael .... 712-707-7108.. 176 B
mwalling@nwciowa.edu
WALLIS, OSB, Jonathan .. 985-867-2249.. 199 F
WALLIS, Madeline .... 978-762-4000.. 224 C
mwallis@northshore.edu
WALLIS, Matthew .... 817-257-5808.. 469 G
matthew.wallis@tcu.edu
WALLIS, Sarah .... 937-769-1862.. 363 F
swallis@antioch.edu
WALLIS, Sherry, L .... 660-263-3900.. 263 A
sherrywallis@cccb.edu
WALLMAN, Marc .... 701-231-8640.. 361 A
marc.wallman@ndsu.edu
WALLNER, Heidi .... 715-346-2926.. 521 C
hwallner@uwsp.edu
WALLNER, Steve .... 262-595-2451.. 520 F
steve.wallner@uwp.edu
WALLS, Arnita .... 651-641-3599.. 247 G
hr@luthersem.edu
WALLS, Eric, R .... 210-562-6201.. 477 D
wallse@uthscsa.edu
WALLS, George, H .... 301-369-2800.. 206 H
ghwalls@captechu.edu
WALLS, Lesley .... 617-732-2800.. 225 C
lesley.walls@mcphs.edu
WALLS, Maryanna .... 301-962-5111.. 214 A
mwalls@yeshiva.edu
WALLS, Melinda .... 304-293-2067.. 514 C
mfwalls@mail.wvu.edu
WALLS, Skip .... 972-686-7878.. 464 A
swalls@remingtoncollege.edu
WALLS-MCKAY,
Maureen, J .... 434-395-2409.. 491 E
wallsmckaymj@longwood.edu
WALLY, William .... 680-488-6223.. 530 E
willyw@palau.edu
WALN, Ursula .... 505-224-4000.. 299 F
uwaln@cnm.edu
WALPOLE, Tommy .... 318-342-5419.. 201 E
walpole@ulm.edu
WALROND, Helena .... 386-481-2349.... 96 H
walrondh@cookman.edu
WALSH, Bernadette .... 215-646-7300.. 404 G
walsh.b@gmercyu.edu
WALSH, Brendan .... 845-451-1616.. 312 C
b_walsh@culinary.edu
WALSH, Clifton .... 915-747-6636.. 476 D
cwalsh@utep.edu
WALSH, CSSP, Daniel ...... 412-396-4827.. 403 A
walshd@duq.edu
WALSH, Debra .... 715-852-1353.. 523 B
dwalsh7@cvtc.edu
WALSH, Frannie .... 480-994-9244.... 17 C
franniew@swiha.edu
WALSH, James, V .... 831-656-3658.. 528 D
jvwalsh@nps.edu
WALSH, Jeffrey .... 813-226-4901.. 108 C
jeffrey.walsh@saintleo.edu
WALSH, Jennifer .... 626-815-6000.... 28 A
jwalsh@apu.edu
WALSH, Joe .... 256-782-5616...... 4 H
ejwalsh@jsu.edu
WALSH, John .... 520-417-4081.... 12 L
walshd@cochise.edu
WALSH, John .... 978-632-6600.. 224 B
j_walsh@mwcc.mass.edu
WALSH, John, T .... 909-748-8368.... 71 K
john_walsh@redlands.edu
WALSH, Joseph, T .... 847-491-3485.. 150 F
vp-research@northwestern.edu
WALSH, Julie .... 845-257-2632.. 331 E
walshj@newpaltz.edu
WALSH, Kimberly, A .... 563-588-7417.. 174 K
kimberly.walsh@loras.edu
WALSH, Lenore, J .... 516-876-4974.. 333 C
walshle@oldwestbury.edu
WALSH, Mariellen .... 570-945-8162.. 406 H
mariellen.walsh@keystone.edu
WALSH, Mark .... 813-974-2660.. 112 C
mwalsh@usf.edu
WALSH, Mary, T .... 504-314-2537.. 200 C
mary@tulane.edu
WALSH, Mary Lee .... 434-961-6540.. 498 C
mwalsh@pvcc.edu
WALSH, Melissa .... 610-526-6197.. 405 B
mwalsh@harcum.edu
WALSH, Michael .... 414-297-6246.. 524 A
walshm@matc.edu
WALSH, Michael, D .... 540-568-5681.. 490 J
walshmd@jmu.edu
WALSH, Michele .... 781-891-2070.. 215 F
mwalsh1@bentley.edu
WALSH, Michelle .... 845-437-7750.. 339 C
miwalsh@vassar.edu
WALSH, Nancy .... 217-333-6677.. 157 A
njwalsh@illinois.edu
WALSH, Patricia .... 773-995-3862.. 136 M
pwalsh@csu.edu
WALSH, Patricia, J .... 913-971-3453.. 183 D
pwalsh@mnu.edu
WALSH, Patrick .... 608-363-2174.. 515 G
walshpj@beloit.edu
WALSH, Patrick .... 541-684-7244.. 393 B
pwalsh@nwcu.edu
WALSH, Peter, J .... 512-448-8441.. 464 G
peterjw@stedwards.edu
WALSH, Rosalie, K .... 406-447-5440.. 276 B
rwalsh@carroll.edu
WALSH, Susan .... 541-552-6114.. 395 A
walsh@sou.edu
WALSH, Susan .... 209-384-6101.... 52 E
walsh.s@mccd.edu
WALSH, Tammy, S .... 941-359-7505.. 107 M
twalsh@ringling.edu
WALSH, Teresa .... 732-255-0400.. 293 E
twalsh@ocean.edu
WALSH, Timothy .... 919-684-5055.. 343 J
tim.walsh@duke.edu
WALSH, Timothy, J .... 716-878-4201.. 332 F
walshtj@buffalostate.edu
WALSH FITZPATRICK,
Mary .... 518-445-2377.. 303 D
mfitz@albanylaw.edu
WALSHOK, Mary, L .... 858-534-3411.... 70 C
mwalshok@ucsd.edu
WALSKI, Don .... 507-457-5555.. 252 G
dwalski@winona.edu
WALSTEAD, Brenda .... 360-992-2474.. 502 E
bwalstead@clark.edu
WALSTER, Jane .... 360-992-2447.. 502 E
jwalster@clark.edu
WALSTON, Angie .... 252-399-6313.. 341 P
amwalston@barton.edu
WALSTROM, Katherine ..... 941-487-4493.. 111 D
walstrom@ncf.edu
WALTER, B. Kaye .... 201-447-7237.. 289 E
president@bergen.edu
WALTER, Blakely .... 630-942-2353.. 138 B
walterb@cod.edu
WALTER, Carla .... 510-723-6618.... 37 B
cwalter@chabotcollege.edu
WALTER, Cory .... 516-364-0808.. 323 B
cwalter@nycollege.edu
WALTER, Hank .... 812-855-3562.. 162 F
walterh@indiana.edu
WALTER, Jaclyn .... 812-535-5236.. 166 K
jaclyn.walter@smwc.edu
WALTER, Jim .... 706-355-5120.. 116 H
jwalter@athenstech.edu
WALTER, John, M .... 661-362-2239.... 52 A
jwalter@masters.edu
WALTER, Kelly .... 617-353-3530.. 216 E
kwalter@bu.edu
WALTER, Kenneth .... 503-768-7921.. 392 A
jwalter@lclark.edu
WALTER, Kristy .... 617-243-2147.. 219 I
kwalter@lasell.edu
WALTER, Lisa, A .... 715-232-2266.. 521 D
walterl@uwstout.edu
WALTER, Rachel .... 419-434-4570.. 379 E
walterr@findlay.edu
WALTER, Robyn, C .... 636-584-6617.. 264 M
robyn.walter@eastcentral.edu
WALTER, Scott .... 773-325-8023.. 139 C
swalte11@depaul.edu
WALTER, Shulem .... 718-855-4092.. 326 J
swalter@rcosy.org
WALTER, Toni .... 660-596-7222.. 272 G
awalter@sfccmo.edu
WALTER, Willis .... 386-481-2087.... 96 H
walterw@cookman.edu
WALTER-MACK, Kathy ...... 816-604-1587.. 267 F
kathy.walter-mack@mcckc.edu
WALTERREIT, Jay .... 989-358-7215.. 230 G
walterrj@alpenacc.edu
WALTERS, Almar .... 614-236-6011.. 364 N
awalters@capital.edu
WALTERS, Carmen .... 601-928-6205.. 259 C
carmen.walters@mgccc.edu
WALTERS, Carolyn .... 812-855-3403.. 162 F
cwalters@indiana.edu

WARD, Robert, A 585-385-8310 328 E bward@sjfc.edu
WARD, Roger, J 410-706-2477 211 F rward@umaryland.edu
WARD, Rose Marie 513-529-9266 372 K wardrm1@miamioh.edu
WARD, Ryan 406-586-3585 276 I ryan.ward@montanabiblecollege.edu
WARD, Scott 231-845-6211 243 G scward@westshore.edu
WARD, Stephen, P 704-687-7225 358 A stephen.ward@uncc.edu
WARD, Steve 605-677-5307 437 A steve.ward@usd.edu
WARD, Steve 360-736-9391 502 A sward@centralia.edu
WARD, Susan 864-455-7902 434 D wardse@mailbox.sc.edu
WARD, Susie 402-354-7063 281 F susie.ward@methodistcollege.edu
WARD, Tamika 408-864-8292 44 A wardtamica@deanza.edu
WARD, Terry 336-334-7750 356 F tdward@ncat.edu
WARD, Thomas, J 203-576-4966 89 C ward@bridgeport.edu
WARD, Thomas, J 516-877-3131 303 B tward@adelphi.edu
WARD, Tim 718-862-7307 319 L tim.ward@manhattan.edu
WARD, Timothy, J 601-974-1405 258 H wardtj@millsaps.edu
WARD, Tony 334-727-8364 8 A tward@tuskegee.edu
WARD, Tracy 951-343-4552 29 H tward@calbaptist.edu
WARD, Tracy 910-296-2503 350 F tward@jamessprunt.edu
WARD, Vicki 352-323-3697 104 J wardv@lssc.edu
WARD, Zachary 989-686-9590 233 I zacharyward2@delta.edu
WARD-ROOF, Jeanine 231-591-3578 233 L jeaninewardroof@ferris.edu
WARD-ROOF, Jeanine 850-644-2428 111 C jwardroof@admin.fsu.edu
WARDALL, Scott 909-218-3253 26 E
WARDE, Robin, T 401-232-6253 424 K rwarde@bryant.edu
WARDELL, Lisa 630-725-1930 139 D lwardell@devrygroup.com
WARDELL-GHIRARDUZZI, Mary, J 415-422-2821 72 C mjwardell@usfca.edu
WARDEN, Catherine 212-355-1501 306 L cwarden@christies.edu
WARDEN, Chris 510-659-6044 55 B cwarden@ohlone.edu
WARDEN, Ken 479-788-7218 23 A ken.warden@uafs.edu
WARDEN, Margo 802-635-1260 486 B margo.warden@jsc.edu
WARDEN, Michael, L 404-894-0870 121 D michael.warden@gatech.edu
WARDINSKY, Ken 208-769-3377 134 C kmwardinsky@nic.edu
WARDLAW, Theodore, J 512-404-4824 452 A twardlaw@austinseminary.edu
WARDLEY, Lloyd 914-337-9300 311 F lloyd.wardley@concordia-ny.edu
WARDLOW, Rebecca 928-541-7777 15 G rwardlow@ncu.edu
WARE, A. Charles 317-789-8247 160 E president@crossroads.edu
WARE, Amy 901-321-3331 439 E aware1@cbu.edu
WARE, Bob 870-222-5360 23 D wareb@uamont.edu
WARE, Helen, B 337-475-5126 200 H hware@mcneese.edu
WARE, Kate 859-846-5304 191 G kware@midway.edu
WARE, Larry 304-647-6220 514 A lware@osteo.wvsom.edu
WARE, Lisa 864-587-4295 433 A warel@smcsc.edu
WARE, Paige, D 214-768-4242 465 J pware@smu.edu
WARE, Peggy, J 309-341-7211 145 A pjware@knox.edu
WARE, Stacy 713-348-4966 464 E ware@rice.edu
WARE, Steven, J 218-751-8670 254 A stevenware@oakhills.edu
WARE, Thomas 662-476-5087 257 G tware@eastms.edu
WARE JOSEPH, Caran 303-765-3111 80 M cwarejoseph@iliff.edu
WARFIELD, Aimee, S 518-381-1207 330 B warfieas@sunysccc.edu
WARFIELD, Martha, B 269-387-6313 243 H martha.warfield@wmich.edu
WARFIELD, Rodney, E 610-921-7766 396 H rwarfield@albright.edu
WARFIELD, Tasha 517-787-0800 235 G warfieltashac@jccmi.edu
WARFORD, Jill 620-223-2700 181 A jillw@fortscott.edu
WARFORD, Kimberly 630-787-7800 152 D kwarford@robertmorris.edu
WARFORD, Lindsey 212-229-5600 322 E warfordl@newschool.edu
WARFORD, Pam 281-425-6361 460 I pwarford@lee.edu
WARGO, Gerald 610-647-4400 406 B gwargo@immaculata.edu
WARGO, Lisa 318-678-6000 195 I lwargo@bpcc.edu
WARGO, Melissa 828-227-7100 359 A wargo@wcu.edu
WARING, Stacie 646-717-9761 315 B registrar@gts.edu
WARK, Maureen 978-921-4242 225 G maureen.wark@montserrat.edu
WARMA, Karl 217-228-5432 151 F warmaka@quincy.edu
WARMACK, Dwaun 314-340-3380 265 H president@hssu.edu
WARMAN, Cassie 503-352-3096 394 C warman@pacificu.edu
WARMANN, Cheryl 847-635-1719 150 G cwarmann@oakton.edu
WARMOTH, Kristin 701-858-3822 360 F kris.warmoth@minotstateu.edu
WARNAS, Jennifer 801-524-1965 480 J jwarnas@ldsbc.edu
WARNE, Janie 573-334-9181 267 C janie@metrobusinesscollege.edu
WARNER, Amy, C 317-274-7400 163 D awarner@iupui.edu
WARNER, Andre 484-365-7345 409 B akwarner@lincoln.edu
WARNER, Charles 610-436-2117 416 C cwarner@wcupa.edu
WARNER, Charles 740-351-3468 377 C cwarner@shawnee.edu
WARNER, Dan 713-348-2875 464 E dan.warner@rice.edu
WARNER, Dave 509-452-5100 505 H dwarner@pnwu.edu
WARNER, David 240-500-2000 207 I cdwarner@hagerstowncc.edu
WARNER, Donald, D 406-874-6201 276 H warnerd@milescc.edu
WARNER, Emily 410-532-5395 210 B ewarner@ndm.edu
WARNER, Isiah, M 225-578-7230 197 I iwarner@lsu.edu
WARNER, Janice 732-987-2662 292 A jwarner@georgian.edu
WARNER, John 214-645-5476 478 C john.warner@utsouthwestern.edu
WARNER, Karen, R 330-471-8120 371 J kwarner@malone.edu
WARNER, Kathleen 410-888-9048 209 C kwarner@muih.edu
WARNER, Kee 719-255-3203 83 L kwarner@uccs.edu
WARNER, Linda 913-288-7194 182 C lwarner@kckcc.edu
WARNER, Mark, J 540-568-3685 490 J warnermj@jmu.edu
WARNER, Mark, S 319-335-3127 169 H mark-warner@uiowa.edu
WARNER, Martin, O 610-328-8299 419 I mwarner1@swarthmore.edu
WARNER, Meredith 602-285-7856 14 F meredith.warner@phoenixcollege.edu
WARNER, Ryan 740-351-3127 377 C rwarner@shawnee.edu
WARNER, Sandra 913-469-8500 182 A swarner@jccc.edu
WARNER, Susan, T 440-826-2476 363 M swarner@bw.edu
WARNER, Thomas, R 504-278-6468 196 I twarner@nunez.edu
WARNER, Timothy, R 650-723-4567 66 I trw@stanford.edu
WARNICK, Lorin, D 607-253-3030 312 A ldw3@cornell.edu
WARNICK, Mark 870-236-6901 20 A mwarnick@crc.edu
WARNKE, Kelly 419-448-2517 369 G kwarnke@heidelberg.edu
WARNOCK, Brenda 928-317-7601 11 J brenda.warnock@azwestern.edu
WARR, Annie 831-582-3595 33 E awarr@csumb.edu
WARR, Fred 208-459-5006 133 D fwarr@collegeofidaho.edu
WARREN, Aileen 402-559-8992 283 A aileen.warren@unmc.edu
WARREN, Ann 310-233-4247 49 I warrenal@lahc.edu
WARREN, Becky 870-612-2048 23 H becky.warren@uaccb.edu
WARREN, Beverly 619-388-3246 60 F bewarren@sdccd.edu
WARREN, Beverly, J 330-672-2210 370 I beverlywarren@kent.edu
WARREN, Briele 619-388-7834 60 H bwarren@sdccd.edu
WARREN, Carol 901-572-2640 438 I carol.warren@bchs.edu
WARREN, Carolyn 662-562-3205 260 C cwarren@northwestms.edu
WARREN, Charlotte, J 217-786-2273 146 E charlotte.warren@llcc.edu
WARREN, Cher 601-484-8614 258 F cwarren@meridiancc.edu
WARREN, Chris 601-643-8306 257 D chris.warren@colin.edu
WARREN, Cleve 904-357-8896 101 G clwarren@fscj.edu
WARREN, David 717-464-7050 408 A
WARREN, Debra, P 260-422-5561 162 B dpwarren@indianatech.edu
WARREN, Diana 812-535-5284 166 K dwarren@smwc.edu
WARREN, Doris, C 281-649-3013 458 L dcwarren@hbu.edu
WARREN, E.J 405-682-7569 385 D ejwarren@occc.edu
WARREN, Earl 256-782-5306 4 H ewarren@jsu.edu
WARREN, Helen 507-786-3009 254 P warren1@stolaf.edu
WARREN, JR., James 212-410-8063 323 C jwarren@nycpm.edu
WARREN, Jason, D 270-707-3801 189 G jason.warren@kctcs.edu
WARREN, Jo 619-596-2766 25 G jwarren@advancedtraining.edu
WARREN, Joan 636-481-3110 266 C jwarren@jeffco.edu
WARREN, Joan, D 212-779-5000 318 A
WARREN, John, S 850-474-2415 113 A jwarren@uwf.edu
WARREN, Katie 507-786-2222 254 P
WARREN, Kim 913-253-5050 184 G kim.warren@spst.edu
WARREN, Leslie, A 906-227-2117 239 B lwarren@nmu.edu
WARREN, Mike 601-925-3204 259 A mjwarren@mc.edu
WARREN, Pamela 920-923-7614 517 H pwarren@marianuniversity.edu
WARREN, Richard, A 610-660-1282 418 G warren@sju.edu
WARREN, Robert 401-739-5000 425 C bwarren@neit.edu
WARREN, Sara 410-225-2264 209 B swarren@mica.edu
WARREN, Shannon 304-645-6382 514 A swarren@osteo.wvsom.edu
WARREN, Shauna 773-896-2400 137 A shauna.warren@ctschicago.edu
WARREN, Sydney 270-686-6415 187 C sydney.warren@brescia.edu
WARREN, Teresa 479-936-5171 21 D twarren4@nwacc.edu
WARREN, Thomas 207-941-7786 202 I warrent@husson.edu
WARREN, Todd 251-380-3095 7 D twarren@shc.edu
WARREN, William 202-319-6925 92 A warrenw@cua.edu
WARREN, William, J 801-581-6773 481 M william.warren@utah.edu
WARREN-MARLATT, Rebeccah 909-389-3355 60 B rmarla@craftonhills.edu
WARRICK, JR., Douglas, R 803-641-3406 433 G randyw@usca.edu
WARRINGTON, Adam 802-654-0505 486 A adam.warrington@ccv.edu
WARRINGTON, Myrna 800-567-2344 516 B mwarrington@menominee.edu
WARRINGTON, Sarah, G 802-656-2925 485 D sarah.warrington@uvm.edu
WARSHEL, Chad 315-568-3297 323 A cwarshel@nycc.edu
WARTERS, Alissa 843-661-1616 430 B twarters@fmarion.edu
WARTHAN, Eric 928-350-4406 16 P eric.warthan@prescott.edu
WARTHMAN, Susan 401-739-5000 425 C swarthman@neit.edu
WARTMAN, Bruce 215-728-4422 412 B bruce.wartman@jevs.org
WARWICK, Ann 212-938-5600 334 F awarwick@sunyopt.edu
WARWICK, Jay 334-953-1303 527 I jay.warwick@us.af.mil
WARWICK, John, J 618-453-4321 154 I warwick@siu.edu
WARYCK, Susan, H 740-826-8086 373 E shoglund@muskingum.edu
WASAN, Darsh, T 312-567-3001 142 I wasan@iit.edu
WASCHULL, Stefanie 352-395-5175 109 C stefanie.waschull@sfcollege.edu
WASDEN, Mitch 573-884-8738 273 D wasdenm@health.missouri.edu
WASDIN, Angela 912-260-4428 127 B angela.wasdin@sgsc.edu
WASESCHA, Anna 860-343-5703 86 F awasescha@mxcc.commnet.edu
WASHAM, Ronnie 606-337-1722 187 I rwasham@ccbbc.edu
WASHBURN, Curtis 808-455-0260 132 C cwashbur@hawaii.edu
WASHINGTON, A. Eugene 919-684-2255 343 J eugene.washington@duke.edu
WASHINGTON, Adrienne, J 610-758-5834 408 H ajw416@lehigh.edu
WASHINGTON, Amona 706-855-8233 93 F
WASHINGTON, Andre 859-442-4176 189 D andre.washington@kctcs.edu
WASHINGTON, August, J 615-343-9750 449 A august.j.washington@vanderbilt.edu
WASHINGTON, Brandon 239-745-4367 110 L bwashington@fgcu.edu
WASHINGTON, Chad 803-376-5700 427 A cwashington@allenuniversity.edu
WASHINGTON, Cheryl 803-793-5192 429 D washingtonc@denmarktech.edu
WASHINGTON, Cheryl 334-874-5700 3 A cwashington@ccal.edu
WASHINGTON, Christopher, L 614-947-6129 369 A christopher.washington@franklin.edu
WASHINGTON, Crystal 773-838-7535 137 H cwashington59@ccc.edu
WASHINGTON, Dana 815-802-8962 144 C dwashington@kcc.edu
WASHINGTON, Dennis, C 804-342-5203 500 B dcwashington@vuu.edu
WASHINGTON, DeSandra 910-678-0037 349 F washingd@faytechcc.edu
WASHINGTON, Earlie 269-387-2638 243 H earlie.washington@wmich.edu
WASHINGTON, Eddie, L 734-763-8391 241 J washine@umich.edu
WASHINGTON, Edwina 901-678-2307 445 C etwshngt@memphis.edu
WASHINGTON, Eric 718-960-8181 308 B eric.washington@lehman.cuny.edu
WASHINGTON, Erin 864-587-4249 433 A washingtone@smcsc.edu
WASHINGTON, Fred, E 936-261-2140 467 E fewashington@pvamu.edu
WASHINGTON, George 405-789-7661 388 B george.washington@swcu.edu
WASHINGTON, Geovette 412-624-4747 421 G gew@pitt.edu
WASHINGTON, Gregory 949-824-6002 69 C gregory.washington@uci.edu
WASHINGTON, Ingrid 859-442-1148 189 D ingrid.washington@kctcs.edu
WASHINGTON, J. Leon 610-758-3100 408 H jnw207@lehigh.edu
WASHINGTON, James Bernard 252-536-7220 350 C jwashington660@halifaxcc.edu
WASHINGTON, Jennifer 860-515-3820 85 D jwashington@charteroak.edu
WASHINGTON, Jewel 301-405-5648 211 E jmwashin@umd.edu
WASHINGTON, Kaye, L 318-670-9474 199 J kwashington@susla.edu
WASHINGTON, Kheysia, H 318-670-9417 199 J kwashington@susla.edu
WASHINGTON, L. Marshall 304-929-5472 512 C lmwashington@newriver.edu
WASHINGTON, Leila 410-951-3660 212 E lwashington@coppin.edu
WASHINGTON, Lonnie 312-850-7154 138 A lewashington@ccc.edu
WASHINGTON, Mary 229-317-6761 120 A mary.washington@darton.edu
WASHINGTON, Maurice 404-653-7857 124 I maurice.washington@morehouse.edu
WASHINGTON, Michael, S 901-678-2713 445 C mswshng1@memphis.edu

WATTS, Jon, C .... 308-865-8205.. 282 L
wattsjc@unk.edu
WATTS, Jonathan .... 256-840-4125...... 6 H
djwatts@snead.edu
WATTS, Karen .... 256-840-4193...... 6 H
kwatts@snead.edu
WATTS, Katherine, K ...... 336-917-5563.. 355 E
katherine.watts@salem.edu
WATTS, Laurie, S .... 504-816-8180.. 198 H
lawatts@nobts.edu
WATTS, Lynwood .... 803-938-3724.. 434 E
lynwoodw@uscsumter.edu
WATTS, Peggy .... 254-298-8362.. 467 B
peggy.watts@templejc.edu
WATTS, Ray .... 909-748-8358.... 71 K
ray_watts@redlands.edu
WATTS, Ray, L .... 205-934-4636...... 8 E
rlwatts@uab.edu
WATTS, Rhonda .... 252-335-0821.. 349 A
rhonda_watts@albemarle.edu
WATTS, Robert .... 601-979-2522.. 258 D
robert.d.watts@jsums.edu
WATTS, Ruby, W .... 803-705-4738.. 427 D
watts@benedict.edu
WATTS, Sherry .... 304-434-8000.. 512 A
sherry.watts@easternwv.edu
WATTS, Timothy .... 214-333-5810.. 455 J
timothyw@dbu.edu
WATTS, Tyler .... 864-644-5000.. 432 G
twatts@swu.edu
WATTS, W. David .... 432-552-2100.. 478 B
watts_d@utpb.edu
WATTS, Wendy .... 843-349-2544.. 428 E
wwatts@coastal.edu
WATTS, Whitney .... 843-383-8360.. 428 F
wwatts@coker.edu
WATTS-MARTINEZ,
Evanda .... 804-862-6263.. 493 F
ewatts@rbc.edu
WATWOOD, Maribeth ...... 928-523-9322.... 15 H
maribeth.watwood@nau.edu
WATZIN, Mary .... 919-515-2883.. 357 B
mary_watzin@ncsu.edu
WATZKE, John, L .... 503-943-7135.. 396 B
watzke@up.edu
WAUGH, Edith .... 316-322-3227.. 179 E
ewaugh@butlercc.edu
WAUGH, Linda .... 513-244-8451.. 366 B
linda.waugh@ccuniversity.edu
WAUGH, OSB, Luke .... 812-357-6422.. 167 B
lwaugh@saintmeinrad.edu
WAUGH, Margaret .... 978-921-4242.. 225 G
margaret.waugh@montserrat.edu
WAUGH, Russell .... 609-343-6815.. 288 H
rwaugh@atlantic.edu
WAUGH, Scott .... 310-825-2052.... 69 D
evc@conet.ucla.edu
WAUKAU, Susan .... 800-567-2344.. 516 B
swaukau@menominee.edu
WAUKECHON, Chad .... 800-567-2344.. 516 B
cwaukechon@menominee.edu
WAVE, Shelby .... 903-233-4070.. 460 J
shelbywave@letu.edu
WAVLE, Dana, C .... 812-941-2202.. 163 F
dwavle@ius.edu
WAVLE-BROWN,
Elizabeth, M .... 607-735-1865.. 313 F
ewavlebrown@elmira.edu
WAWRZASZEK, Susan, V 508-286-8225.. 229 F
wawrzaszek_susan@wheatoncollege.edu
WAWRZUSIN, Andrea ...... 513-745-3009.. 381 I
wawrzusin@xavier.edu
WAXLER, Mel .... 979-830-4335.. 452 J
mel.waxler@blinn.edu
WAXMAN, Deborah .... 215-576-0800.. 417 H
officeofthepresident@rrc.edu
WAY, Joshua .... 845-675-4416.. 325 C
joshua.way@nyack.edu
WAY, Kimera, K .... 715-836-5180.. 520 A
waykk@uwec.edu
WAY, Philip .... 724-738-2170.. 416 B
philip.way@sru.edu
WAY, Phillip .... 928-524-7400.... 15 J
phillip.way@npc.edu
WAY, Sheila .... 202-885-3586.... 91 J
way@american.edu
WAY BOLT, Mary .... 410-287-1025.. 206 J
mbolt@cecil.edu
WAYE, Holly Anne .... 315-568-3055.. 323 A
hwaye@nycc.edu
WAYE, Kathy .... 315-279-5602.. 318 C
kwaye@keuka.edu
WAYLAND, Debra, C .... 740-376-4835.. 372 A
debra.wayland@marietta.edu
WAYLAND, Marilina, L .... 787-250-1912.. 534 B
mwayland@metro.inter.edu
WAYMAN, Abby .... 217-228-5432.. 151 F
waymaab@quincy.edu
WAYMAN, Susan .... 508-213-2230.. 227 A
susan.wayman@nichols.edu

WAYMAN-GORDON,
Ellen .... 201-200-3426.. 293 C
ewaymangordo@njcu.edu
WAYNE, William .... 315-568-3025.. 323 A
bwayne@nycc.edu
WAYNE, William, R .... 405-325-2700.. 389 B
wwayne@ou.edu
WAYT, Missy .... 304-865-6003.. 511 C
missy.wayt@ovu.edu
WEARDEN, Stanley .... 312-369-7495.. 138 F
swearden@colum.edu
WEARN, Mary .... 478-471-2730.. 124 E
mary.wearn@mga.edu
WEASENFORTH,
Donald, L .... 972-881-5794.. 455 A
dweasenforth@collin.edu
WEATHERALL, Maureen .. 310-338-1949.... 51 E
maureen.weatherall@lmu.edu
WEATHERBY, Beth .... 406-683-7151.. 277 A
beth.weatherby@umwestern.edu
WEATHERBY, Susan .... 315-364-3208.. 340 B
sweatherby@wells.edu
WEATHERFORD, Tess ...... 870-368-2006.... 21 F
tess.weatherford@ozarka.edu
WEATHERINGTON,
Elsie, S .... 804-524-5040.. 499 G
eweatherington@vsu.edu
WEATHERLY, Alice .... 870-850-8629.... 22 E
aweatherly@seark.edu
WEATHERMAN,
Donald, V .... 870-307-7201.... 21 A
president@lyon.edu
WEATHERMAN, Tammy .... 559-934-2117.... 74 C
tammyweatherman@whccd.edu
WEATHERS, Diane .... 718-289-5770.. 307 C
diane.weathers@bcc.cuny.edu
WEATHERS, Madonna, B . 606-783-2070.. 191 H
m.weathers@moreheadstate.edu
WEATHERS, Melonie ...... 336-386-3207.. 353 F
weathersm@surry.edu
WEATHERSBEE, Byron ..... 254-295-4150.. 474 E
bweathersbee@umhb.edu
WEATHERSPOON, David . 847-543-2138.. 138 C
dweatherspoon@clcillinois.edu
WEATHERWAX, Alan .... 978-837-5234.. 225 E
weatherwaxa@merrimack.edu
WEAVER, Angela .... 618-468-5300.. 145 G
aweaver@lc.edu
WEAVER, Beckie .... 501-279-4640.... 20 D
bweaver@harding.edu
WEAVER, Bradley, K ...... 765-361-6308.. 169 C
weaverb@wabash.edu
WEAVER, Candace .... 601-477-4075.. 258 E
candace.weaver@jcjc.edu
WEAVER, Carol .... 304-457-6331.. 510 B
weaverc@ab.edu
WEAVER, Carolyn .... 515-271-1426.. 171 H
carolyn.weaver@dmu.edu
WEAVER, Dan .... 970-351-2032.... 84 C
dan.weaver@unco.edu
WEAVER, Danielle .... 716-839-8200.. 312 D
dweaver2@daemen.edu
WEAVER, David .... 907-786-7212.... 10 F
dweaver@uaa.alaska.edu
WEAVER, Deirdre .... 310-434-4791.... 63 F
weaver_deirdre@smc.edu
WEAVER, Devon .... 215-965-4042.. 411 A
dweaver@moore.edu
WEAVER, Donna .... 530-895-2568.... 29 F
weaverdo@butte.edu
WEAVER, Ernestine .... 860-723-0114.... 85 E
weavere@ct.edu
WEAVER, Gina .... 585-345-6808.. 315 C
gmweaver@genesee.edu
WEAVER, Harry .... 909-687-1520.... 44 H
harryweaver@gs.edu
WEAVER, James, S .... 740-376-4611.. 372 A
jim.weaver@marietta.edu
WEAVER, Jeff .... 501-760-4113.... 21 B
jeff.weaver@np.edu
WEAVER, John .... 325-674-2476.. 449 J
jbw11a@acu.edu
WEAVER, Joseph .... 229-245-3737.. 129 G
jgweaver@valdosta.edu
WEAVER, JR., Joseph, B 405-744-2690.. 385 G
joe.weaver@okstate.edu
WEAVER, Julie .... 231-439-6306.. 239 A
jweaver@ncmich.edu
WEAVER, Karin, F .... 615-353-3604.. 446 E
karin.weaver@nscc.edu
WEAVER, Karyn .... 870-733-6722.... 19 A
kweaver@asumidsouth.edu
WEAVER, Kathleen .... 909-593-3511.... 71 B
kweaver@laverne.edu
WEAVER, Kenneth .... 620-341-5367.. 180 G
kweaver@emporia.edu
WEAVER, Laura .... 510-659-6518.... 55 B
lweaver@ohlone.edu
WEAVER, Marianne .... 541-962-3524.. 391 C
mweaver@eou.edu

WEAVER, Matthew .... 717-867-6228.. 408 F
mweaver@lvc.edu
WEAVER, Melanie .... 419-772-2272.. 374 J
m-weaver@onu.edu
WEAVER, Monica .... 609-586-4800.. 292 D
weaverm@mccc.edu
WEAVER, Neal .... 985-448-4134.. 201 A
neal.weaver@nicholls.edu
WEAVER, Paula .... 518-736-3622.. 315 A
paula.weaver@fmcc.suny.edu
WEAVER, Rhonda .... 704-403-1756.. 342 E
rhonda.weaver@carolinashealthcare.org
WEAVER, Sandie .... 562-903-4760.... 28 E
sandie.weaver@biola.edu
WEAVER, Sean .... 505-545-3380.. 300 F
slweaver@nmhu.edu
WEAVER, Sean, F .... 412-396-2560.. 403 A
weavers2@duq.edu
WEAVER, Steven .... 479-979-1448.... 24 I
sweaver@ozarks.edu
WEAVER, Tammy .... 479-968-0272.... 19 F
tweaver@atu.edu
WEAVER, Terri, E .... 312-996-7808.. 156 F
teweaver@uic.edu
WEAVER, Theresa .... 906-635-2733.. 236 J
tweaver@lssu.edu
WEAVER, Vickie, L .... 609-896-5029.. 295 B
weaver@rider.edu
WEAVER, Wendy .... 414-930-3335.. 518 F
weaverw@mtmary.edu
WEAVER-GRIGGS, Linda . 803-327-8024.. 435 D
lwgriggs@yorktech.edu
WEAVER HART, Ann .... 520-621-5511.... 17 I
president@email.arizona.edu
WEAVIL, Vicki .... 336-770-3266.. 358 E
weavilv@uncsa.edu
WEBB, Amy .... 530-242-7628.... 64 D
awebb@shastacollege.edu
WEBB, Anda, L .... 434-924-0999.. 495 H
al6b@virginia.edu
WEBB, Angela, P .... 336-322-2160.. 351 H
angela.webb@piedmontcc.edu
WEBB, Barbara .... 989-686-9228.. 233 I
brwebb@delta.edu
WEBB, Brent, W .... 801-422-6201.. 480 C
webb@byu.edu
WEBB, Burton, J .... 606-218-5261.. 194 C
burtonwebb@upike.edu
WEBB, Candice .... 919-760-2255.. 346 D
webbcan@meredith.edu
WEBB, Carol .... 281-487-1170.. 469 F
cwebb@txchiro.edu
WEBB, Cheryl, A .... 803-327-7402.. 428 D
cwebb@clintoncollege.edu
WEBB, Dann .... 478-988-6800.. 118 H
dwebb@centralgatech.edu
WEBB, Deborah .... 870-733-6701.... 19 A
dwebb@asumidsouth.edu
WEBB, Dixie .... 931-221-6346.. 444 E
webbd@apsu.edu
WEBB, Donna .... 229-391-5001.. 115 I
dwebb@abac.edu
WEBB, Donnetta .... 916-558-2408.... 51 D
webbd@scc.losrios.edu
WEBB, Duncan .... 312-461-0600.. 134 K
dwebb@aaart.edu
WEBB, Eric .... 307-766-3059.. 527 B
ewebb1@uwyo.edu
WEBB, Eric, C .... 484-365-7451.. 409 B
ewebb@lincoln.edu
WEBB, II, Ernest, R .... 915-831-5051.. 457 H
ewebb1@epcc.edu
WEBB, Farrell .... 818-677-3001.... 34 A
farrell.webb@csun.edu
WEBB, Gwen .... 919-546-8223.. 355 F
gwebb@shawu.edu
WEBB, Jac .... 208-562-2063.. 133 F
jacwebb@cwidaho.cc
WEBB, James, D .... 806-651-1240.. 469 D
jwebb@mail.wtamu.edu
WEBB, Jay, K .... 434-544-8218.. 491 F
webb@lynchburg.edu
WEBB, Jeanie .... 405-733-7300.. 387 I
jwebb@rose.edu
WEBB, Jen .... 715-675-2775.. 177 D
webbj@uiu.edu
WEBB, Jennifer .... 254-295-4526.. 474 E
jwebb@umhb.edu
WEBB, Jerrad .... 620-276-9521.. 181 C
jerrad.webb@gcccks.edu
WEBB, Jodi .... 419-372-9348.. 364 E
jwebb@bgsu.edu
WEBB, Joshua, M .... 989-964-4359.. 240 F
jmwebb@svsu.edu
WEBB, Katheryn .... 812-749-1392.. 166 B
kwebb@oak.edu
WEBB, Kathleen, M .... 937-229-4263.. 379 D
kwebb1@udayton.edu
WEBB, Keith .... 404-270-5279.. 128 A
kwebb5@spelman.edu

WEBB, Ken .... 619-680-4430.... 30 A
ken.webb@cc-sd.edu
WEBB, Kenneth .... 903-785-7661.. 463 E
kwebb@parisjc.edu
WEBB, Kyle .... 901-843-3760.. 443 L
webb@rhodes.edu
WEBB, Lee .... 870-512-7849.... 19 C
lee_webb@asun.edu
WEBB, Leslie .... 208-426-4208.. 132 I
lesliewebb@boisestate.edu
WEBB, Lezley, A .... 901-333-5560.. 447 B
lcurrin@southwest.tn.edu
WEBB, Lisa .... 650-543-3976.... 52 D
lisa.webb@menlo.edu
WEBB, Lynda .... 432-685-6884.. 461 H
lwebb@midland.edu
WEBB, Mark, F .... 931-598-1284.. 443 O
mwebb@sewanee.edu
WEBB, Melessia, D .... 423-354-5106.. 446 F
mdwebb@northeaststate.edu
WEBB, Michael .... 815-921-2151.. 152 E
m.webb@rockvalleycollege.edu
WEBB, Michelle .... 207-453-5020.. 203 K
mwebb@kvcc.me.edu
WEBB, Molly .... 606-326-2231.. 188 N
molly.webb@kctcs.edu
WEBB, Nick .... 530-242-7739.... 64 D
nwebb@shastacollege.edu
WEBB, Pat .... 214-860-8789.. 456 F
pwebb@dcccd.edu
WEBB, R. Brian .... 254-710-8797.. 452 H
brian_webb@baylor.edu
WEBB, Randy .... 870-733-6750.... 19 A
rwebb@asumidsouth.edu
WEBB, Reggie .... 540-828-8014.. 487 H
rwebb@bridgewater.edu
WEBB, Reginal .... 863-298-6828.. 106 I
rwebb@polk.edu
WEBB, Sam .... 830-792-7428.. 465 E
swebb@schreiner.edu
WEBB, Sandy .... 641-782-1422.. 177 B
webb@swcciowa.edu
WEBB, Tom .... 937-775-5680.. 381 H
thomas.webb@wright.edu
WEBB, Toya .... 847-214-7769.. 140 A
twebb@elgin.edu
WEBB, Travis .... 414-805-8622.. 518 A
trwebb@mcw.edu
WEBB, Troycia .... 229-430-3396.. 116 A
WEBB, Walter, W .... 815-939-5333.. 150 I
wwebb@olivet.edu
WEBB-CURTIS, Susan .... 423-472-7141.. 445 E
susanwebb-curtis@clevelandstatecc.edu
WEBB SHARPE, Lisa .... 517-483-1106.. 237 A
sharpel@lcc.edu
WEBBER, Adrienne .... 410-651-6621.. 212 B
WEBBER, Adrienne, C ..... 803-536-8638.. 432 E
awebber@scsu.edu
WEBBER, Diane .... 202-685-7375.. 528 B
diane.webber@ndu.edu
WEBBER, Henry, S .... 314-935-7877.. 274 N
hwebber@wustl.edu
WEBBER, Leah .... 617-928-4513.. 226 B
lwebber@mountida.edu
WEBBER, Louise .... 909-621-8265.... 38 I
louise.webber@cgu.edu
WEBBER, Meg .... 803-323-2220.. 435 B
webberm@winthrop.edu
WEBBER, Robert .... 802-831-1209.. 485 F
rwebber@vermontlaw.edu
WEBBER, Rochelle .... 716-851-1169.. 313 H
webberr@ecc.edu
WEBBER MCLEAN,
Kalynda .... 818-610-6567.... 50 A
mcleankw@piercecollege.edu
WEBER, A. Scott .... 716-645-6029.. 331 C
sweber@buffalo.edu
WEBER, Brad .... 620-252-7076.. 180 B
bradw@coffeyville.edu
WEBER, Bruce, W .... 302-831-1211.... 91 F
bweber@udel.edu
WEBER, Chris .... 301-447-5114.. 209 G
cweber@msmary.edu
WEBER, Daniel, R .... 773-442-4000.. 149 J
d-weber3@neiu.edu
WEBER, Dave .... 352-365-3530.. 104 J
weberd@lssc.edu
WEBER, Dawn .... 419-289-4142.. 363 J
dweber1@ashland.edu
WEBER, Debra .... 262-695-7842.. 524 G
dweber28@wctc.edu
WEBER, Ellen .... 631-420-2744.. 335 E
ellen.weber@farmingdale.edu
WEBER, Eric .... 801-957-4136.. 483 A
eric.weber@slcc.edu
WEBER, Jacqueline, J .... 573-592-5307.. 275 E
jackie.weber@westminster-mo.edu
WEBER, Janet .... 419-473-2700.. 367 J
jweber@daviscollege.edu
WEBER, Jennifer .... 701-224-2540.. 360 B
jennifer.weber@ndus.edu

WEINMAN, Geoffrey .... 201-443-8750.. 291 J
weinman@fdu.edu
WEINMAN, Kevin, C .... 413-542-2325.. 214 C
kweinman@amherst.edu
WEINMAN, Tammy .... 518-445-3210.. 303 D
twein@albanylaw.edu
WEINMAN, Todd, N .... 802-656-3340.. 485 D
todd.weinman@uvm.edu
WEINREICH,
Christine, M .... 901-722-3311.. 444 C
cweinreich@sco.edu
WEINS, Sean, A .... 918-595-7916.. 388 F
sean.weins@tulsacc.edu
WEINS, W. Jesse .... 605-995-2686.. 435 F
jeweins@dwu.edu
WEINSHEIM, Leslie .... 970-521-6714.... 81 O
leslie.weinsheim@njc.edu
WEINSHEL, Seth, D .... 202-994-2552.... 92 D
sdweingw@gwu.edu
WEINSTEIN, Cindy, A ...... 626-395-6249.... 30 H
caw@hss.caltech.edu
WEINSTEIN, David, A ...... 973-972-7525.. 295 F
weinstein@oldqueens.rutgers.edu
WEINSTEIN, Heather .... 802-828-2800.. 486 A
heather.weinstein@ccv.edu
WEINSTEIN, John .... 843-953-7796.. 428 A
WEINSTEIN, Mark .... 937-766-8800.. 365 C
mweinstein@cedarville.edu
WEINSTEIN, Randy .... 610-519-4520.. 422 G
randy.weinstein@villanova.edu
WEINSTEIN, Steve .... 856-256-5106.. 295 E
weinsteins@rowan.edu
WEINSTEIN, Susan, L ...... 650-724-3658.... 66 I
susan.weinstein@stanford.edu
WEINTRAUB, Seth .... 213-621-2200.... 39 I
WEINTRAUB, Susan .... 603-641-7600.. 287 G
sweintraub@anselm.edu
WEINTRAUB, Yitzchok ..... 732-985-6533.. 294 E
WEINTROP, Joseph .... 646-312-3092.. 307 A
joseph.weintrop@baruch.cuny.edu
WEIPPERT, Linda .... 620-229-6175.. 184 J
linda.weippert@sckans.edu
WEIR, Amy .... 765-361-6078.. 169 C
weira@wabash.edu
WEIR, Ashley .... 304-204-4340.. 514 B
ashley.weir@wvstateu.edu
WEIR, Dennis .... 434-961-5447.. 498 C
dweir@pvcc.edu
WEIR, James .... 304-232-0361.. 511 J
jweir@wvbc.edu
WEIR, Karissa, L .... 704-406-4732.. 344 E
kweir@gardner-webb.edu
WEIR, Laura .... 239-433-6941.. 101 F
lweir2@fsw.edu
WEIR, Lljuna .... 601-877-6700.. 256 F
weir@alcorn.edu
WEIR, Robert .... 617-287-5240.. 220 G
bob.weir@umb.edu
WEIR, Roseanne, N .... 315-786-2408.. 317 H
rweir@sunyjefferson.edu
WEIR, Walter, G .... 402-472-2862.. 282 K
wweir@nebraska.edu
WEIRICK, Chad .... 740-755-7327.. 365 D
cweirick@cotc.edu
WEIS, Bob, M .... 863-638-2920.. 115 D
weisrm@webber.edu
WEIS, Charlene .... 701-255-3285.. 362 E
cweis@uttc.edu
WEIS, Dallas .... 509-527-2608.. 508 G
dallas.weis@wallawalla.edu
WEIS, Ed .... 914-674-7632.. 320 G
eweis@mercy.edu
WEIS, Lisa, K .... 918-877-8116.. 383 M
lkweis@langston.edu
WEIS, Mary .... 630-844-3866.. 135 E
mweis@aurora.edu
WEIS, Richard .... 859-280-1256.. 191 D
rweis@lextheo.edu
WEIS, Tim .... 217-228-5432.. 151 F
weisti@quincy.edu
WEISBERG, Bradley .... 408-741-4012.... 74 H
bradley.weisberg@westvalley.edu
WEISBORD, Beryl .... 410-484-7200.. 210 A
WEISBROD, Angela .... 507-457-1493.. 254 O
aweisbro@smumn.edu
WEISEN, Jan, G .... 617-745-3705.. 218 A
jan.weisen@enc.edu
WEISEN, Sheryl .... 317-745-3703.. 218 A
sheryl.weisen@enc.edu
WEISENBURGER, Earl ...... 605-626-2529.. 437 D
earl.weisenburger@northern.edu
WEISENBURGER, Leigh ... 207-786-6000.. 202 D
lweisenb@bates.edu
WEISENBURGER, Perk ..... 231-591-2863.. 233 L
perkweisenburger@ferris.edu
WEISER, Bridget, R .... 785-833-4325.. 182 F
bridget@kwu.edu
WEISER, Kent, L .... 620-341-5350.. 180 G
kweiser@emporia.edu
WEISER, Sharon .... 660-357-6300.. 269 I
sweiser@mail.ncmissouri.edu
WEISGERBER,
James (Chip) .... 423-869-7758.. 441 E
james.weisgerber@lmunet.edu
WEISGERBER,
James (Chip), E .... 412-536-1765.. 406 K
chip.weisgerber@laroche.edu
WEISGRAM, Molly .... 605-773-3455.. 436 L
molly.weisgram@sdbor.edu
WEISHAAR, Mary .... 618-650-3785.. 155 A
mweisha@siue.edu
WEISHAR, Peter .... 850-644-5244.. 111 C
pweishar@fsu.edu
WEISKOPF, Lee .... 662-325-1008.. 259 D
lee.weiskopf@pres.msstate.edu
WEISKOPFF, Jacqueline .. 973-290-4393.. 290 G
jeiskopff@cse.edu
WEISMAN, Iris .... 937-769-1890.. 363 E
iweisman@antioch.edu
WEISMAN, Sarah .... 607-962-9385.. 312 B
sweismal@corning-cc.edu
WEISMAN, Susan, E .... 718-489-5242.. 328 D
sweisman@sfc.edu
WEISNER, Andrew .... 828-328-7248.. 345 H
andrew.weisner@lr.edu
WEISPFENNING, John ..... 714-438-4888.... 39 D
johnw@cccd.edu
WEISS, David .... 210-567-3709.. 477 D
weissd@uthscsa.edu
WEISS, H .... 732-364-1220.. 289 B
WEISS, Ira, R .... 919-515-5560.. 357 B
ira_weiss@ncsu.edu
WEISS, Janet, A .... 734-764-4401.. 241 J
janetw@umich.edu
WEISS, Jason .... 323-463-2500.... 67 I
jasonw@toa.edu
WEISS, Jeff, A .... 617-349-8500.. 220 B
jweiss@lesley.edu
WEISS, Jeffery, I .... 718-990-6357.. 328 F
weissj@stjohns.edu
WEISS, Johanna .... 804-594-1500.. 497 D
jweiss@jtcc.edu
WEISS, Karen .... 618-252-5400.. 154 G
karen.weiss@sic.edu
WEISS, Kay .... 909-384-8535.... 60 C
kweiss@sbccd.cc.ca.us
WEISS, Nicolas .... 303-245-4664.... 81 I
nweiss@naropa.edu
WEISS, Rod, P .... 858-499-0202.... 39 J
rweiss@coleman.edu
WEISS, Stephanie .... 612-330-1476.. 244 I
weisss@augsburg.edu
WEISS, Suzanne .... 920-686-6196.. 519 H
suzanne.weiss@sl.edu
WEISS, Valerie .... 313-664-7852.. 232 G
vweiss@collegeforcreativestudies.edu
WEISS-COOK, Laura .... 785-320-4541.. 183 A
lauraweiss-cook@manhattantech.edu
WEISSENBURGER, David .. 254-968-9464.. 467 F
weissenburger@tarleton.edu
WEISSENBURGER, Jackie 715-394-8449.. 521 E
jweissen@uwsuper.edu
WEISSENFLUH, Anji .... 541-962-3236.. 391 C
aweissen@eou.edu
WEISSMAN, Neil, B .... 717-245-1322.. 402 D
weissmne@dickinson.edu
WEITER, Stephen, P .... 248-370-2459.. 239 K
spweiter@oakland.edu
WEITMAN, Catheryn, J ..... 956-326-2801.. 468 A
catheryn.weitman@tamiu.edu
WEITZ, Anna, D .... 610-607-6210.. 417 G
aweitz@racc.edu
WEITZEL, Jann .... 417-667-8181.. 264 A
jweitzel@cottey.edu
WEITZER, Joseph .... 262-695-7824.. 524 G
jweitzer@wctc.edu
WEITZMAN, Lauren .... 801-581-6826.. 481 M
lweitzman@sa.utah.edu
WEKESA, Kennedy .... 334-229-4316...... 1 D
wekesai@alasu.edu
WELAGE, Lynda, S .... 505-272-0906.. 302 F
lswelage@salude.unm.edu
WELBORN, Ruth, B .... 512-245-3300.. 471 F
rw01@txstate.edu
WELBURN, Janice .... 414-288-7214.. 517 I
janice.welburn@marquette.edu
WELBURN, William .... 414-288-8028.. 517 I
william.welburn@marquette.edu
WELCH, Aaron, P .... 660-263-3900.. 263 A
aaronwelch@cccb.edu
WELCH, Alexis .... 252-527-6223.. 350 H
awelch@lenoircc.edu
WELCH, April .... 312-567-3196.. 142 I
welcha@iit.edu
WELCH, Ba-Shen, T .... 205-929-1574...... 5 H
bwelch@miles.edu
WELCH, Becky .... 253-680-7100.. 501 E
bwelch@bates.ctc.edu
WELCH, Charles, L .... 501-660-1000.... 18 H
president@asusystem.edu
WELCH, Dan .... 814-866-8151.. 407 D
dwelch@lecom.edu
WELCH, Denise .... 903-693-1121.. 463 D
dwelch@panola.edu
WELCH, Dirk .... 940-397-4972.. 462 A
dirk.welch@mwsu.edu
WELCH, Edwin .... 765-998-5523.. 167 C
edwelch@taylor.edu
WELCH, Edwin, H .... 304-357-4713.. 511 E
edwinwelch@ucwv.edu
WELCH, Frances, C .... 943-953-5613.. 428 G
welchf@cofc.edu
WELCH, George .... 619-684-8826.... 54 C
gwelch@newschoolarch.edu
WELCH, James .... 405-224-3140.. 389 D
jwelch@usao.edu
WELCH, Jennifer, C .... 315-464-4570.. 332 C
welchj@upstate.edu
WELCH, Jim .... 570-662-4000.. 415 E
WELCH, Joel .... 336-734-7182.. 349 G
jwelch@forsythtech.edu
WELCH, John .... 412-924-1401.. 417 E
jwelch@pts.edu
WELCH, Julia .... 707-638-5425.... 68 C
julia.perhac@tu.edu
WELCH, Julie .... 843-953-5254.. 428 A
jwelch3@citadel.edu
WELCH, Kathleen .... 831-479-5076.... 29 G
kawelch@cabrillo.edu
WELCH, Lena .... 615-248-1393.. 447 F
lwelch@trevecca.edu
WELCH, Leo .... 970-351-2515.... 84 C
leo.welch@unco.edu
WELCH, Lynne .... 908-709-7167.. 298 A
welch@ucc.edu
WELCH, Marc .... 765-361-6480.. 169 C
welchm@wabash.edu
WELCH, Marjorie .... 712-325-3202.. 174 B
mwelch@iwcc.edu
WELCH, Marolyn .... 903-586-2518.. 460 A
acadean@jacksonville-college.edu
WELCH, Matt .... 254-968-9002.. 467 F
welch@tarleton.edu
WELCH, Michael .... 847-578-3238.. 153 A
michael.welch@rosalindfranklin.edu
WELCH, Mike .... 847-543-2247.. 138 C
mwelch1@clcillinois.edu
WELCH, Mike .... 269-927-1000.. 236 G
WELCH, Nick .... 740-588-1224.. 382 C
nwelch@zanestate.edu
WELCH, Patricia .... 443-885-3385.. 209 F
patricia.welch@morgan.edu
WELCH, Paul .... 508-626-4640.. 221 E
pwelch@framingham.edu
WELCH, Paul .... 415-955-2100.... 25 J
pwelch@alliant.edu
WELCH, Regina, E .... 804-627-5350.. 487 G
regina_welch2@bshsi.org
WELCH, Renee .... 970-351-2127.... 84 C
renee.welch@unco.edu
WELCH, Ronald, W .... 843-953-6499.. 428 A
rwelch1@citadel.edu
WELCH, Sally .... 313-927-1211.. 237 E
swelch@marygrove.edu
WELCH, Sam .... 315-859-4668.. 315 D
rwelch@hamilton.edu
WELCH, Sandra, T .... 210-458-4706.. 477 A
sandra.welch@utsa.edu
WELCH, Sharon .... 773-256-3000.. 147 G
swelch@meadville.edu
WELCH, Sherri, L .... 856-691-8600.. 290 I
swelch@cccnj.edu
WELCH, Susan .... 814-865-7691.. 412 F
sxw11@psu.edu
WELCH, Susan, T .... 518-564-5062.. 334 A
welchst@plattsburgh.edu
WELCH, Teresa .... 417-626-1234.. 269 K
welch.teresa@occ.edu
WELCH, Terry .... 828-227-7100.. 359 A
welcht@wcu.edu
WELCH, Thomas .... 843-661-1136.. 430 B
rwelch@fmarion.edu
WELCH, Thomas .... 919-497-3230.. 346 B
twelch@louisburg.edu
WELD, Jeff .... 802-468-1241.. 485 H
jeff.weld@castleton.edu
WELDEN, David .... 770-962-7580.. 123 D
dwelden@gwinnetttech.edu
WELDEN, Jonathan .... 901-272-5121.. 442 B
jwelden@mca.edu
WELDEN, Soraya .... 601-484-8628.. 258 F
swelden@meridiancc.edu
WELDON, James .... 803-780-1119.. 434 M
jweldon@voorhees.edu
WELDON, Leslie .... 406-377-9412.. 276 D
lweldon@dawson.edu
WELDON, Leslie .... 618-634-3337.. 154 B
lesliew@shawneecc.edu
WELDON, Rich .... 803-508-7382.. 426 G
weldonr@atc.edu
WELDON, Scott .... 251-460-8018...... 9 E
sweldon@southalabama.edu
WELDON, Sherrie .... 561-237-7788.. 104 O
sweldon@lynn.edu
WELDON, Stephanie, J ...... 603-206-8111.. 286 D
sjweldon@ccsnh.edu
WELDON, Wray .... 972-883-6994.. 476 C
wray.weldon@utdallas.edu
WELDY, Eric .... 815-753-1573.. 150 A
eweldy@niu.edu
WELKER, Amanda .... 573-288-6450.. 264 F
awelker@culver.edu
WELKER, Dan .... 928-428-8300.... 13 B
dan.welker@eac.edu
WELKER, Heston .... 928-428-8225.... 13 B
heston.welker@eac.edu
WELKER, Josh .... 217-641-4110.. 143 H
jwelker2@jwcc.edu
WELKER, Kristen .... 605-668-1577.. 436 D
kristen.welker@mtmc.edu
WELKER, Mark, A .... 309-341-7255.. 145 A
mawelker@knox.edu
WELKER, Sharon, L .... 919-866-5611.. 353 I
sfwelker@waketech.edu
WELKEY, Sharon .... 210-832-2115.. 474 D
welkey@uiwtx.edu
WELLBORN, Linda .... 417-865-2815.. 265 B
wellbornl@evangel.edu
WELLE, David .... 760-920-6432.... 42 B
dwelle@deepsprings.edu
WELLER, Eddie .... 281-998-6150.. 465 B
eddie.weller@sjcd.edu
WELLER, Eddie .... 281-998-6150.. 465 A
eddie.weller@sjcd.edu
WELLER, Eddie .... 281-998-6150.. 464 J
eddie.weller@sjcd.edu
WELLER, Julie .... 231-777-0461.. 238 G
julie.weller@muskegoncc.edu
WELLER, Lisa .... 610-225-5007.. 403 B
lweller2@eastern.edu
WELLER-DENGEL,
Pamela .... 507-389-6061.. 250 E
pamela.weller-dengel@mnsu.edu
WELLES, Julia .... 816-802-3302.. 266 D
jwelles@kcai.edu
WELLINGS, Keith .... 304-724-3700.. 510 E
kwellings@apus.edu
WELLINGTON, Eric, R .... 610-359-5394.. 401 L
ewellington@dccc.edu
WELLINGTON, Katie .... 580-559-5651.. 383 H
katmwel@ecok.edu
WELLINGTON, Susan .... 607-778-5187.. 332 D
wellingtonsl@sunybroome.edu
WELLINGTON-BAKER,
Kristi .... 509-527-4263.. 508 F
kristi.wellington-baker@wwcc.edu
WELLMAN, Andrea, G .... 540-985-8491.. 491 A
agwellman@jchs.edu
WELLMAN, Barbara .... 217-228-5432.. 151 F
wellmba@quincy.edu
WELLMAN, Chris .... 941-752-5443.. 110 H
wellmac@scf.edu
WELLMAN, Debra .... 407-646-2175.. 107 O
dwellman@rollins.edu
WELLMAN, Ronald, D .... 336-758-5616.. 359 E
wellmanr@wfu.edu
WELLNER, Justin .... 805-756-7003.... 31 I
jwellner@calpoly.edu
WELLOCK, Barbara .... 530-221-4275.... 64 C
bwellock12@shasta.edu
WELLS, Alison .... 225-768-1713.. 199 B
alison.wells@ololcollege.edu
WELLS, Barbara .... 901-333-4259.. 447 B
bwells@southwest.tn.edu
WELLS, Barbara .... 865-981-8278.. 441 H
barbara.wells@maryvillecollege.edu
WELLS, Beth .... 503-845-3243.. 392 E
beth.wells@mtangel.edu
WELLS, Billy .... 706-864-1630.. 128 F
billy.wells@ung.edu
WELLS, Bonnie .... 860-439-5001.... 87 F
bonnie.wells@conncoll.edu
WELLS, Brian, J .... 502-776-1443.. 192 C
bwells@simmonscollegeky.edu
WELLS, C. Gene .... 812-488-2664.. 167 I
gw5@evansville.edu
WELLS, C. Richard .... 605-342-0317.. 436 A
president@johnwitherspooncollege.org
WELLS, Carol .... 909-384-8925.... 60 C
cwells@sbccd.cc.ca.us
WELLS, Carole .... 610-683-4212.. 415 C
wells@kutztown.edu
WELLS, Clinton .... 505-224-4000.. 299 F
cwells21@cnm.edu
WELLS, Dan .... 713-743-2619.. 473 F
dwells2@uh.edu
WELLS, Douglas .... 605-394-1763.. 437 E
douglas.wells@sdsmt.edu
WELLS, Earl .... 716-880-2524.. 320 D
ewells@medaille.edu
WELLS, Elaine .... 212-938-5690.. 334 F
ewells@sunyopt.edu

WEST, Michael .... 919-546-8542.. 355 F michael.west@shawu.edu
WEST, Michael, D .... 518-580-5810.. 330 F mwest@skidmore.edu
WEST, Mickey .... 615-329-8680.. 439 L mwest@fisk.edu
WEST, Mike .... 913-469-8500.. 182 A mikewest@jccc.edu
WEST, Mike .... 817-272-5988.. 476 A mpwest@uta.edu
WEST, Monica .... 301-445-1937.. 211 D mwest@usmd.edu
WEST, Olivia .... 801-524-1992.. 480 J toodiew@idsbc.edu
WEST, Patricia .... 617-541-5386.. 224 F pwest@rcc.mass.edu
WEST, Ryan .... 760-471-1316.... 59 H
WEST, Stephanie .... 606-886-3863.. 189 A stephanie.west@kctcs.edu
WEST, Susan, H .... 615-460-6435.. 438 J susan.west@belmont.edu
WEST, Tom .... 323-856-7680.... 26 I twest@afi.com
WEST, Tom .... 954-262-4994.. 105 J twest@nova.edu
WEST, Vicki .... 806-742-2166.. 472 C vicki.west@ttu.edu
WEST-DAVIS, Angela .... 518-381-1279.. 330 B westaa@sunysccc.edu
WEST ENGELKEMEYER, Susan .... 508-213-2215.. 227 A president@nichols.edu
WESTACOTT, Vicky .... 607-871-2269.. 303 F fcobb@alfred.edu
WESTARY, Kenneth .... 443-840-3213.. 207 C kwestary@ccbcmd.edu
WESTAWAY, Shawn .... 248-218-2064.. 240 C swestaway@rc.edu
WESTBERRY, Becky .... 386-752-1822.. 100 L becky.westberry@fgc.edu
WESTBROOK, Ashley .... 706-245-7226.. 120 D adenny@ec.edu
WESTBROOK, Denise, Z .. 302-356-6915.... 91 I denise.z.westbrook@wilmu.edu
WESTBROOK, Diane .... 716-884-9120.. 306 B dwestbrook@bryantstratton.edu
WESTBROOK, Gail, L ...... 304-462-6161.. 513 C gail.westbrook@glenville.edu
WESTBROOK, Steve .... 936-468-2701.. 466 H swestbrook@sfasu.edu
WESTBROOK, Velma, S ... 985-448-4687.. 201 A sue.westbrook@nicholls.edu
WESTBY, Kim .... 562-860-2451.... 36 P westby@cerritos.edu
WESTCOTT, James .... 605-367-5675.. 437 G james.westcott@southeasttech.edu
WESTCOTT, III, S. Wickes .... 864-656-0161.. 428 C westc@clemson.edu
WESTENBROEK, Steve ..... 402-399-2465.. 279 E swestenbroek@csm.edu
WESTER, Ken .... 479-968-0218.... 19 F kwester@atu.edu
WESTERBERG PRAGER, Susan .... 213-738-6710.... 66 F deansoffice@swlaw.edu
WESTERFIELD, Mary Ann, K .... 302-356-6936.... 91 I maryann.k.westerfield@wilmu.edu
WESTERFIELD, Michael, W .... 573-592-4383.. 275 G michael.westerfield@williamwoods.edu
WESTERHOUSE, Joni, L .. 314-286-0120.. 274 N westerhousej@wustl.edu
WESTERIK, Robin .... 714-841-6252.... 27 E
WESTERMAN, III, W. Scott .... 517-355-8314.. 237 I wsw@msu.edu
WESTERMEYER, Lawrence, W .... 314-516-4010.. 274 A larry_westermeyer@umsl.edu
WESTERMEYER, Susan, M .... 317-940-9135.. 159 K swesterm@butler.edu
WESTERN, Jon .... 413-538-2372.. 226 A jwestern@mtholyoke.edu
WESTERN, Lindajean, H .. 330-569-5174.. 369 J westernlh@hiram.edu
WESTERVELT, Robert, K ... 503-554-2136.. 391 D rwestervelt@georgefox.edu
WESTFALL, Andrew .... 410-337-6095.. 207 H andrew.westfall@goucher.edu
WESTFALL, Michael .... 509-359-7099.. 503 D mwestfall@ewu.edu
WESTFALL, Sarah, B .... 269-337-7209.. 235 H sarah.westfall@kzoo.edu
WESTHOFF, James .... 207-992-4909.. 202 I westhoffj@husson.edu
WESTHOFF, Randall .... 218-755-2016.. 248 M rwesthoff@bemidjistate.edu
WESTLAKE, Christopher, J .... 850-872-3212.. 102 M cwestlake@gulfcoast.edu
WESTLAKE, Rachel .... 925-969-2003.... 41 I rwestlake@dvc.edu
WESTLEY, Elizabeth, K ..... 757-594-7345.. 488 E elizabeth.westley@cnu.edu
WESTLUND, Julie, A .... 218-726-7985.. 255 D jwestlun@d.umn.edu
WESTMAN, Craig .... 856-225-6510.. 296 A craig.westman@rutgers.edu
WESTMAN, Dennis .... 580-371-7121.. 384 D dwestman@mscok.edu
WESTMAN, Dennis .... 580-745-2148.. 387 M dwestman@se.edu
WESTMAN, Hans .... 412-291-6409.. 397 I hwestman@aii.edu
WESTMORELAND, T. Andrew .... 205-726-2727...... 6 E tawestmo@samford.edu
WESTON, Brian .... 661-362-3102.... 40 A brian.weston@canyons.edu
WESTON, JR., Donald, E 609-258-3407.. 294 D donw@princeton.edu
WESTON, Jeff .... 916-278-3901.... 34 B jweston@csus.edu
WESTON, John, H .... 507-284-2073.. 245 E weston.john@mayo.edu
WESTOVER, Kristin .... 276-656-0315.. 498 A kwestover@patrickhenry.edu
WESTPHAL, Arthur, P .... 507-344-7375.. 244 K art.westphal@blc.edu
WESTPHAL, Donald, M .... 507-344-7320.. 244 K don.westphal@blc.edu
WESTPHAL, Kristianne, R 507-933-7495.. 246 J kristi@gustavus.edu
WESTPHAL, Lorraine, M .. 757-594-7608.. 488 E lwestpha@cnu.edu
WESTPHAL, Matt .... 918-540-6249.. 384 F mwestphal@neo.edu
WESTRA, Jeff .... 608-249-6611.. 516 M careers@msn.herzing.edu
WESTRA, Kayla .... 507-372-3435.. 250 G kayla.westra@mnwest.edu
WESTRICK, Karyn, J .... 419-434-4758.. 379 E westrick@findlay.edu
WESTWATER, Julia .... 508-289-3379.. 230 B jwestwater@whoi.edu
WETHERELL, Dale, R .... 401-825-2109.. 425 A drwetherell@ccri.edu
WETHERILL, Elsbeth .... 510-204-0733.... 38 C ewetherill@cdsp.edu
WETHERINGTON, Lee ...... 252-527-6223.. 350 H lwetherington@lenoircc.edu
WETHERINGTON, Nicole . 310-453-8300.... 42 L nicole@emperors.edu
WETHINGTON, Charles ... 252-638-7350.. 349 B
WETMORE, David .... 620-227-9201.. 180 E dwetmore@dc3.edu
WETSELL, Linda, S .... 814-332-4790.. 397 A lwetsell@allegheny.edu
WETSTEIN, Matt .... 209-954-5047.... 61 F mwetstein@deltacollege.edu
WETTER, Kevin .... 808-356-5261.. 130 H kvetter@hpu.edu
WETTSTEIN, Deena .... 608-757-7716.. 523 A dwettstein@blackhawk.edu
WETZEL, Derrick .... 610-282-1100.. 402 B derrick.wetzel@desales.edu
WETZEL, Kathryn .... 972-860-4751.. 456 B kwetzel@dcccd.edu
WETZEL, Mary, E .... 717-728-2260.. 400 F marywetzel@centralpenn.edu
WETZEL, Mike .... 717-358-4759.. 403 J mike.wetzel@fandm.edu
WETZEL, Shelby .... 307-754-6110.. 526 N shelby.wetzel@nwc.edu
WETZEL, Suzanne, M ...... 734-384-4206.. 238 C swetzel@monroeccc.edu
WETZEL HARDER, Wendy .... 949-480-4081.... 64 J wwharder@soka.edu
WETZSTEIN, James .... 219-464-5096.. 168 F james.wetzstein@valpo.edu
WEVODAU, Clint, D .... 570-577-7439.. 398 L clint.wevodau@bucknell.edu
WEXLER, Joan, G .... 718-780-7900.. 305 L joan.wexler@brooklaw.edu
WEXLER, Jonathan, D ...... 518-276-6143.. 327 B
WEXLER, Judie .... 415-575-6104.... 30 G jwexler@ciis.edu
WEXLER, Robert .... 310-476-9777.... 26 K
WEY, Lora .... 309-438-2592.. 143 B lwey@ilstu.edu
WEYAND, Andy .... 330-490-7320.. 380 J aweyand@walsh.edu
WEYAND, Joel .... 402-826-8242.. 280 B joel.weyand@doane.edu
WEYANDT, Anne .... 651-690-7701.. 254 M afweyandt@stkate.edu
WEYERS, Lori, A .... 715-675-3331.. 524 D weyers@ntc.edu
WEYGANT, Susan .... 914-923-2397.. 325 J sweygant@pace.edu
WEYHAUPT, Adam .... 314-889-1460.. 265 C aweyhaupt@fontbonne.edu
WEYHENMEYER, James, A .... 404-413-3516.. 122 D jweyhenmeyer@gsu.edu
WEYL, Ronnie .... 908-526-1200.. 295 A ronnie.weyl@raritanval.edu
WEYLER, Megan, E .... 215-895-6383.. 402 G m.weyler@drexel.edu
WEZNER, Kelley, C .... 270-809-3340.. 192 A kwezner@murraystate.edu
WHALEN, Alice .... 636-584-6532.. 264 M alice.whalen@eastcentral.edu
WHALEN, David .... 845-451-1406.. 312 C d_whalen@culinary.edu
WHALEN, David .... 517-607-2321.. 235 E dwhalen@hillsdale.edu
WHALEN, James, L .... 513-556-4930.. 379 A james.whalen@uc.edu
WHALEN, Jeff .... 209-588-5126.... 75 J whalenj@yosemite.edu
WHALEN, Lynn .... 217-786-2219.. 146 E lynn.whalen@llcc.edu
WHALEN, Melissa .... 913-253-5091.. 184 G melissa.whalen@spst.edu
WHALEN, Michael .... 860-685-2908.... 90 C mwhalen@wesleyan.edu
WHALEN, Michael .... 419-251-1824.. 372 C michael.whalen@mercycollege.edu
WHALEN, Scott, M .... 315-255-1743.. 306 G scott.whalen@cayuga-cc.edu
WHALEN, Thomas .... 212-229-5456.. 322 E whalent@newschool.edu
WHALEN, Tina .... 513-558-7485.. 379 A tina.whalen@uc.edu
WHALEN, Toni .... 502-213-2118.. 190 A toni.whalen@kctcs.edu
WHALEN-SMITH, Heather, C .... 315-655-7132.. 306 H hcwhalensmith@cazenovia.edu
WHALEY, Chris .... 865-882-4501.. 447 A whaleycl@roanestate.edu
WHALEY, David .... 270-809-6849.. 192 A dwhaley2@murraystate.edu
WHALEY, David, J .... 802-485-2300.. 484 H davew@norwich.edu
WHALEY, Deonne .... 843-208-8723.. 434 A dwhaley@mailbox.sc.edu
WHALEY, Frances, A .... 815-224-0263.. 143 C frances_whaley@ivcc.edu
WHALEY, Melanie, A .... 814-871-7470.. 404 A whaley003@gannon.edu
WHALEY, Michael .... 636-949-4561.. 266 J mwhaley@lindenwood.edu
WHALEY, Michael, J .... 860-685-3160.... 90 C mwhaley@wesleyan.edu
WHALEY, Mitchell .... 765-285-5816.. 159 B mwhaley@bsu.edu
WHALEY, Sheree .... 530-242-7667.... 64 D swhaley@shastacollege.edu
WHALEY, Vernon .... 434-582-2562.. 491 D vwhaley@liberty.edu
WHAM, Ben .... 843-953-5088.. 428 A ben.wham@citadel.edu
WHANG, Christine .... 909-447-6741.... 39 A cwhang@cst.edu
WHANG, Kyu-Jung .... 607-255-4394.. 312 A kw253@cornell.edu
WHANN, Christopher ...... 646-230-1207.. 335 D christopher.whann@esc.edu
WHAPHAM, Ted .... 972-721-4068.. 473 D twhapham@udallas.edu
WHARTON, Barbara .... 740-593-1059.. 375 H whartonb@ohio.edu
WHARTON, Kristin .... 704-233-8366.. 359 H kwharton@wingate.edu
WHARTON, Martha, L ...... 410-617-2988.. 208 G mwharton1@loyola.edu
WHARTON, Randy .... 740-588-1379.. 382 C rwharton@zanestate.edu
WHATELY, Lorrie .... 253-752-2020.. 503 H admissions@faithseminary.edu
WHATLEY, Melissa .... 657-278-2380.... 33 A mkwhatley@fullerton.edu
WHATLEY, Melissa, L ...... 205-934-4324...... 8 E mwhatley@uab.edu
WHATLEY, Sherri .... 903-566-7247.. 477 B swhatley@uttyler.edu
WHEAT, Gary .... 417-626-1234.. 269 K gwheat@occ.edu
WHEATLEY, Joyce .... 215-641-6573.. 410 L jwheatley@mc3.edu
WHEATLEY, Michelle, M . 509-313-4238.. 504 A wheatleym@gonzaga.edu
WHEATLY, Michele .... 315-443-2494.. 337 A mwheatly@syr.edu
WHEATLY, Stephen .... 805-493-3828.... 31 C wheatly@callutheran.edu
WHEATON, David, M .... 651-696-6211.. 247 I wheaton@macalester.edu
WHEATON, Katie .... 970-943-3216.... 84 H kwheaton@western.edu
WHEATON, Michele .... 814-824-2086.. 410 H mwheaton@mercyhurst.edu
WHEATON, Timothy, W .... 207-859-4904.. 202 G tim.wheaton@colby.edu
WHEATON, Tom .... 605-642-6446.. 437 B tom.wheaton@bhsu.edu
WHEELAND, Craig .... 610-519-4520.. 422 G craig.wheeland@villanova.edu
WHEELAND, Todd .... 815-455-8564.. 147 E twheeland@mchenry.edu
WHEELDON, Tim, T .... 515-263-6152.. 172 H twheeldon@grandview.edu
WHEELER, Alfred .... 864-646-1425.. 433 C awheele4@tctc.edu
WHEELER, Amy .... 603-206-8131.. 286 D awheeler@ccsnh.edu
WHEELER, Brad .... 812-855-5802.. 162 F bwheeler@indiana.edu
WHEELER, Brad, C .... 812-855-3478.. 162 E bwheeler@indiana.edu
WHEELER, Bruce, W .... 612-343-4417.. 253 Y bwwheele@northcentral.edu
WHEELER, Cassandra, L . 956-326-4473.. 468 A cwheeler@tamiu.edu
WHEELER, Cecilia, B .... 919-528-4737.. 353 H wheelerc@vgcc.edu
WHEELER, Dawn, A .... 910-521-6270.. 358 C dawn.wheeler@uncp.edu
WHEELER, Frank, E .... 402-363-5646.. 283 G fwheeler@york.edu
WHEELER, H. William ..... 434-592-3003.. 491 D hwwheeler@liberty.edu
WHEELER, Ike .... 870-512-7865.... 19 C ike_wheeler@asun.edu
WHEELER, Jacklyn, G ...... 215-699-5700.. 408 C jwheeler@lsb.edu
WHEELER, Jessica .... 213-613-2200.... 65 H jessica_wheeler@sciarc.edu
WHEELER, John .... 253-752-2020.. 503 H registrar@faithseminary.edu
WHEELER, Kara .... 620-331-4100.. 181 J kwheeler@indycc.edu
WHEELER, Laurie .... 707-965-7200.... 56 A lwheeler@puc.edu
WHEELER, Lisa .... 952-358-8286.. 251 A lisa.wheeler@normandale.edu
WHEELER, Mark .... 714-564-6319.... 58 G wheeler_mark@sac.edu
WHEELER, Mark .... 208-426-1140.. 132 I mwheeler@boisestate.edu
WHEELER, Mark .... 208-467-8772.. 134 D mwheeler@nnu.edu
WHEELER, Mary .... 254-526-1200.. 454 A mary.wheeler@ctcd.edu
WHEELER, Michelle .... 907-564-8210.... 10 B mwheeler@alaskapacific.edu
WHEELER, Michelle .... 248-476-1122.. 237 H mwheeler@mispp.edu
WHEELER, Nolan .... 360-442-2201.. 504 G nwheeler@lowercolumbia.edu
WHEELER, Paul .... 541-383-7588.. 390 D pwheeler@cocc.edu
WHEELER, Quentin, D ..... 315-470-6681.. 334 E qwheeler@esf.edu
WHEELER, Rosemary, L .. 336-721-2600.. 355 E rosemary.wheeler@salem.edu
WHEELER, Sharon .... 434-582-3036.. 491 D swheeler@liberty.edu
WHEELER, Sherrell .... 575-439-3668.. 301 A swheeler@nmsu.edu
WHEELER, Susan, L .... 540-568-3727.. 490 J wheel2sl@jmu.edu
WHEELER, Tim .... 425-739-8252.. 504 F tim.wheeler@lwtech.edu
WHEELER, Tony .... 401-232-6707.. 424 K awheeler2@bryant.edu
WHEELER, Walter .... 252-789-0259.. 351 A wwheeler@martincc.edu
WHEELING, Barbara .... 406-657-1651.. 277 D barbara.wheeling@msubillings.edu
WHEELIS, Tina .... 870-368-2008.... 21 F twheelis@ozarka.edu
WHEELOCK, Pam .... 612-624-3557.. 255 H wheelock@umn.edu
WHELAN, JR., Donald, J 817-257-7785.. 469 G d.whelan@tcu.edu
WHELAN, Janet .... 410-837-4779.. 213 C jwhelan@ubalt.edu
WHELAN, John .... 812-855-2239.. 162 F whelanj@iu.edu
WHELAN, Lara .... 706-238-5876.. 117 F lwhelan@berry.edu
WHELAN, Matthew .... 631-632-6833.. 332 A matthew.whelan@stonybrook.edu

WHITE, Renée, T .... 508-286-8212.. 229 F
white_renee@wheatoncollege.edu
WHITE, Renee .... 617-521-2079.. 228 C
renee.white@simmons.edu
WHITE, Rex .... 713-221-8505.. 474 B
whiter@uhd.edu
WHITE, Richard, D .... 225-578-2848.. 197 I
rwhit12@lsu.edu
WHITE, Robert .... 816-654-7616.. 266 E
rwhite@kcumb.edu
WHITE, Roederick .... 225-771-2552.. 200 A
rwhite@sulc.edu
WHITE, Roederick, C .... 225-771-2552.. 200 A
rwhite@sulc.edu
WHITE, Roger .... 504-865-2427.. 198 E
rwhite@loyno.edu
WHITE, Ronald .... 706-245-7226.. 120 D
rwhite@ec.edu
WHITE, Ryan .... 309-796-5194.. 135 I
whitery@bhc.edu
WHITE, Ryan .... 972-883-5561.. 476 C
ryan.white@utdallas.edu
WHITE, Sandra .... 559-278-2061.... 32 F
sandraw@csufresno.edu
WHITE, Sarah .... 603-428-2906.. 287 C
swhite@nec.edu
WHITE, Scott .... 718-482-5421.. 309 A
WHITE, Shelley .... 828-398-7937.. 347 D
swhite@abtech.edu
WHITE, Stephanie, M ...... 804-257-5745.. 500 B
swhite@vuu.edu
WHITE, Stephen .... 718-862-7548.. 319 L
stephen.white@manhattan.edu
WHITE, Stephen, E .... 401-254-3681.. 426 B
swhite@rwu.edu
WHITE, Stephen, F .... 615-898-2422.. 444 G
stephen.white@mtsu.edu
WHITE, Stephone .... 336-334-7600.. 356 F
oswhite@ncat.edu
WHITE, Steven .... 316-978-3782.. 185 J
steven.white@wichita.edu
WHITE, Steven .... 859-246-6326.. 189 B
steven.white@kctcs.edu
WHITE, Susan, K .... 913-627-4125.. 182 C
swhite@kckcc.edu
WHITE, Tamara .... 303-360-4703.... 79 E
tamara.white@ccaurora.edu
WHITE, Tamisia .... 212-870-1229.. 324 B
finaid@nyts.edu
WHITE, Tammy, S .... 205-652-3651...... 9 F
thw@uwa.edu
WHITE, Tasia, Y .... 814-641-3520.. 406 F
whitet@juniata.edu
WHITE, Thelma .... 270-706-8409.. 189 C
thelma.white@kctcs.edu
WHITE, Theodore .... 816-235-1330.. 273 F
whitetc@umkc.edu
WHITE, Thomas .... 775-784-4832.. 285 A
thomaswhite@unr.edu
WHITE, Thomas, R .... 508-929-8023.. 222 F
twhite@worcester.edu
WHITE, Timothy, L .... 352-846-0850.. 112 A
tlwhite@ufl.edu
WHITE, Timothy, P .... 562-951-4700.... 31 H
twhite@calstate.edu
WHITE, W. Scott .... 704-406-4259.. 344 E
swhite@gardner-webb.edu
WHITE, Wayman .... 252-335-0821.. 349 A
waywhite@albemarle.edu
WHITE, Wendy, S .... 215-746-5240.. 421 E
wendy.white@ogc.upenn.edu
WHITE BULL, David .... 605-455-6076.. 436 G
dwhitebull@olc.edu
WHITE-DANIELS, Sheila .. 408-864-8945.... 44 A
whitedanielssheila@deanza.edu
WHITE-HURST, Elizabeth . 541-880-2282.. 391 F
elizabeth@klamathcc.edu
WHITE-SMITH, Kimberly .. 909-593-3511.... 71 B
kwhite-smith@laverne.edu
WHITE-ZOLLMAN, Casey 541-278-5839.. 390 C
cwhitezollman@bluecc.edu
WHITECAVAGE, Michele .. 714-449-7404.... 51 F
mwhitecavage@ketchum.edu
WHITED, Frances, P .... 330-287-1216.. 375 B
whited.16@osu.edu
WHITED, Jimmy, R .... 540-375-2308.. 493 H
whited@roanoke.edu
WHITEFIELD, Joe .... 615-904-8375.. 444 G
joe.whitefield@mtsu.edu
WHITEFORD, Aaron .... 503-768-7944.. 392 A
ahw@lclark.edu
WHITEFORD, Craig .... 410-287-1914.. 206 J
cwhiteford@cecil.edu
WHITEFORD, Marion .... 802-447-6388.. 485 B
mwhitfrd@svc.edu
WHITEHEAD, Debbie .... 503-255-0332.. 392 G
debbiew@multnomah.edu
WHITEHEAD, Doug .... 435-652-7500.. 482 A
dkw@dixie.edu
WHITEHEAD, Gwen .... 409-882-3926.. 471 B
gwen.whitehead@lsco.edu
WHITEHEAD, Heidi, M .... 812-888-4313.. 169 A
hwhitehead@vinu.edu
WHITEHEAD, JaRenae ..... 305-626-3631.. 101 A
jarenae.whitehead@fmuniv.edu
WHITEHEAD, JR., Joe, B 336-334-7965.. 356 F
jbwhiteh@ncat.edu
WHITEHEAD, Johnny .... 713-348-6000.. 464 E
johnny.whitehead@rice.edu
WHITEHEAD, Kim .... 662-241-6850.. 259 E
kmwhitehead@muw.edu
WHITEHEAD,
Kimberly, D .... 410-651-3553.. 212 B
kdwhitehead@umes.edu
WHITEHEAD, Nicole .... 434-381-6510.. 494 M
nwhitehead@sbc.edu
WHITEHEAD, Richard, G . 540-261-4095.. 494 F
richard.whitehead@svu.edu
WHITEHEAD, Susan .... 617-984-1721.. 227 F
swhitehead@quincycollege.edu
WHITEHEAD, Teresa .... 575-769-4066.. 299 G
teresa.whitehead@clovis.edu
WHITEHOUSE, Deborah .... 859-622-1523.. 188 F
deborah.whitehouse@eku.edu
WHITEHOUSE, Jennifer ... 985-867-2240.. 199 F
jwhitehouse@sjasc.edu
WHITEHOUSE, Steve, M .. 253-535-7119.. 505 G
whitehsm@plu.edu
WHITEHURST, Alan .... 540-261-8598.. 494 F
alan.whitehurst@svu.edu
WHITEHURST, Marcus, A 814-865-5906.. 412 F
maw163@psu.edu
WHITEHURST-MCLEAN,
Makitta .... 252-335-3355.. 356 D
mmmclean@ecsu.edu
WHITEING, Kelli .... 605-256-5112.. 437 C
kelli.whiteing@dsu.edu
WHITELAW, Kenneth .... 603-513-1375.. 288 D
kenneth.whitelaw@granite.edu
WHITELAW, Lydia .... 610-896-1177.. 405 I
lwhitela@haverford.edu
WHITELEY, Janell .... 360-475-7504.. 505 F
jwhiteley@olympic.edu
WHITELY, Patricia, A ...... 305-284-4922.. 114 H
pwhitely@miami.edu
WHITEMAN, Betty .... 386-822-8869.. 113 B
bwhiteman@stetson.edu
WHITEMAN, Charles, H .. 814-863-0448.. 412 F
chw17@psu.edu
WHITEMAN, Michael .... 704-330-6706.. 348 E
mike.whiteman@cpcc.edu
WHITEMAN, Raymond, E 574-807-7139.. 159 D
ray.whiteman@bethelcollege.edu
WHITEMORE, Alan, T .... 617-989-4307.. 229 D
whitemorea@wit.edu
WHITER, Kimberly .... 540-985-8106.. 491 A
kawhiter@jchs.edu
WHITESELL, Melissa .... 706-272-4527.. 119 H
mwhitesell@daltonstate.edu
WHITESIDE, Harold, D .... 615-898-2900.. 444 G
harold.whiteside@mtsu.edu
WHITEY, Jeff .... 541-888-7634.. 395 B
jwhitey@socc.edu
WHITFIELD, Aleczander ... 704-378-3501.. 345 E
awhitfield@jcsu.edu
WHITFIELD, Candis .... 912-352-8331.. 108 C
candis.whitfield@saintleo.edu
WHITFIELD, Henry .... 478-934-3167.. 124 E
henry.whitfield@mga.edu
WHITFIELD, Jacques .... 530-741-6976.... 76 B
jwhitfie@yccd.edu
WHITFIELD, Jacques .... 530-741-6976.... 76 D
jwhitfie@yccd.edu
WHITFIELD, Keith .... 919-761-2127.. 355 I
kwhitfield@sebts.edu
WHITFIELD, Keith .... 313-577-2433.. 243 F
keith.whitfield@wayne.edu
WHITFIELD, Meredith ...... 828-227-7059.. 359 A
mcwhitfield@wcu.edu
WHITFIELD, Rick .... 910-962-3383.. 358 D
whitfieldr@uncw.edu
WHITFIELD, Rick, N .... 910-962-3383.. 358 D
whitfieldr@uncw.edu
WHITFILL, Gene .... 806-291-1045.. 479 D
whitfillg@wbu.edu
WHITFILL, Jill .... 731-352-4083.. 438 K
whitfillj@bethelu.edu
WHITFORD, Betty Lou ..... 334-844-4448...... 1 G
blw0017@auburn.edu
WHITFORD, Daryl .... 808-675-3730.. 130 E
daryl.whitford@byuh.edu
WHITFORD, Jewel, L .... 406-395-4875.. 278 F
jewelwhitford@hotmail.com
WHITHAM, John, H .... 610-526-1308.. 397 E
john.whitham@theamericancollege.edu
WHITHAUS, Becky .... 573-897-5000.. 272 H
WHITING, Alison .... 808-675-3551.. 130 E
alison.whiting@byuh.edu
WHITING, J. Scott .... 334-874-5700...... 3 A
swhiting@ccal.edu
WHITING, Sarah, M .... 713-348-4044.. 464 E
sarah.whiting@rice.edu
WHITING, Shari, K .... 315-859-4313.. 315 D
swhiting@hamilton.edu
WHITIS, Andrew .... 419-434-4767.. 379 E
whitis@findlay.edu
WHITIS, Harold .... 210-485-0605.. 450 A
hwhitis2@alamo.edu
WHITIS, Matt .... 815-939-5350.. 150 I
mwhitis@olivet.edu
WHITLATCH, Frank .... 707-826-5101.... 34 F
frank@humboldt.edu
WHITLEDGE, Terry .... 907-474-7229.... 10 G
terry@ims.uaf.edu
WHITLEY, Darrell, S .... 252-985-5105.. 354 E
dwhitley@ncwc.edu
WHITLEY, Norm .... 504-280-6723.. 198 D
provost@uno.edu
WHITLEY, Rebecca .... 575-492-2546.. 300 H
rwhitley@nmjc.edu
WHITLING, Jacqueline .... 570-484-3045.. 415 D
jwhitlin@lhup.edu
WHITLOCK, David, W ...... 405-585-5801.. 385 B
david.whitlock@okbu.edu
WHITLOCK, Doug .... 870-972-3030.... 18 J
dwhitlock@astate.edu
WHITLOCK, Eugene .... 650-358-6883.... 62 F
whitlocke@smccd.edu
WHITLOCK, Kevin .... 320-308-2038.. 252 A
kcwhitlock@stcloudstate.edu
WHITLOCK, Monica .... 509-777-4216.. 509 H
mwhitlock@whitworth.edu
WHITLOCK, Shawna .... 216-373-5335.. 374 B
swhitlock@ndc.edu
WHITLOCK, Stephen .... 678-839-6426.. 129 E
swhitlock@westga.edu
WHITLOCK, Tonya, F .... 678-664-0532.. 129 M
tonya.whitlock@westgatech.edu
WHITMAN, Carl, E .... 240-567-3146.. 209 E
carl.whitman@montgomerycollege.edu
WHITMAN, David .... 651-604-4118.. 247 L
dwhitman@minneapolisbusinesscollege.edu
WHITMAN, Deirdre .... 914-674-7316.. 320 G
dwhitman@mercy.edu
WHITMAN, Josh .... 217-333-3631.. 157 A
illiniad@illinois.edu
WHITMAN, Joshua, H .... 314-935-5288.. 274 N
whitman@wustl.edu
WHITMAN, Melissa .... 252-249-1851.. 351 G
mwhitman@pamlicocc.edu
WHITMAN, Paul .... 803-321-5600.. 431 F
paul.whitman@newberry.edu
WHITMAN, R. Douglas ...... 313-577-1625.. 243 F
dwhitman@wayne.edu
WHITMAN, Rebecca, R ..... 616-234-4010.. 234 E
rwhitman@grcc.edu
WHITMAN, Richard .... 910-296-2487.. 350 F
rwhitman@jamessprunt.edu
WHITMAN, William, D ...... 989-386-6696.. 238 B
wwhitman@midmich.edu
WHITMER, Ann .... 517-629-0440.. 230 E
awhitmer@albion.edu
WHITMEYER, Antoinette ... 301-295-6013.. 528 G
antoinette.whitmeyer@usuhs.edu
WHITMIRE, Teresa .... 479-619-4175.... 21 D
twhitmire@nwacc.edu
WHITMORE, Joe .... 256-782-5777...... 4 H
whitmore@jsu.edu
WHITMORE, Kimberly, N ... 515-574-1138.. 173 F
whitmore@iowacentral.edu
WHITMORE, Lee .... 617-266-1400.. 215 G
WHITMORE, Michele .... 802-635-1452.. 486 B
michele.whitmore@jsc.edu
WHITMORE, Petia .... 781-239-4543.. 214 G
pwhitmore1@babson.edu
WHITMORE, Vincent .... 410-462-8594.. 206 D
vwhitmore@bccc.edu
WHITNEY, Candice .... 408-848-4754.... 44 I
cwhitney@gavilan.edu
WHITNEY, Cynthia .... 605-229-8381.. 436 H
cynthia.whitney@presentation.edu
WHITNEY, Gleaves .... 616-331-2770.. 234 F
whitneyg@gvsu.edu
WHITNEY, Glenda .... 573-897-5000.. 272 H
WHITNEY, Heather .... 518-743-2342.. 335 A
charpentierh@sunyacc.edu
WHITNEY, J.J .... 501-450-1263.... 20 F
whitney@hendrix.edu
WHITNEY, Jarrid .... 626-395-6341.... 30 H
jwhitney@caltech.edu
WHITNEY, Joan, G .... 610-519-4050.. 422 G
joan.whitney@villanova.edu
WHITNEY, Karen .... 928-541-7777.... 15 G
kwhitney@ncu.edu
WHITNEY, Karen, M .... 814-393-2220.. 414 G
president@clarion.edu
WHITNEY, Laura .... 860-768-5691.... 89 G
lwhitney@hartford.edu
WHITNEY, Majid .... 973-313-6008.. 297 A
majid.whitney@shu.edu
WHITNEY, Marian, D .... 315-684-6010.. 336 B
whitnemd@morrisville.edu
WHITNEY, Patricia .... 603-645-9609.. 287 I
p.whitney@snhu.edu
WHITNEY, Patrick, F .... 312-595-4900.. 142 I
whitney@id.iit.edu
WHITNEY, Paul .... 401-874-5224.. 426 D
pwhitney@uri.edu
WHITNEY, Richard .... 641-269-3300.. 172 I
whitney@grinnell.edu
WHITNEY, Roger .... 650-723-2300.... 66 I
WHITSON, Brian .... 757-221-7876.. 488 F
bwwhit@wm.edu
WHITSON, Edelweiss .... 509-777-4563.. 509 H
ewhitson@whitworth.edu
WHITSON, Janet .... 512-313-3000.. 455 F
janet.whitson@concordia.edu
WHITSON, Jennifer .... 507-786-3000.. 254 P
whitson@stolaf.edu
WHITSON, Tony .... 901-435-1733.. 441 C
tony_whitson@loc.edu
WHITT, Cynthia, L .... 423-869-6394.. 441 E
cindy.whitt@lmunet.edu
WHITT, David, T .... 205-726-2386...... 6 E
dtwhitt@samford.edu
WHITT, Elizabeth .... 209-228-2317.... 70 A
ewhitt@ucmerced.edu
WHITT, Ellen .... 317-955-6597.. 165 N
ewhitt@marian.edu
WHITT, Julie .... 817-257-6571.. 469 G
j.whitt@tcu.edu
WHITT, Zack .... 706-886-6831.. 128 C
zwhitt@tfc.edu
WHITTAKER, A. Dale .... 407-823-2303.. 111 E
dale.whittaker@ucf.edu
WHITTAKER, David .... 816-584-6710.. 270 D
dave.whittaker@park.edu
WHITTAKER, Lori .... 757-240-2200.. 493 G
lori.whittaker@rivhs.com
WHITTAKER, Nancy, H ..... 205-348-6690...... 8 D
nwhittaker@fa.ua.edu
WHITTAKER-DAVIS,
Sharon .... 205-366-8838...... 7 E
swhittaker@stillman.edu
WHITTED, Tenial .... 708-596-2000.. 154 E
WHITTEMORE, Steve .... 508-626-4923.. 221 E
swhittemore@framingham.edu
WHITTEN, James .... 207-844-2103.. 203 M
jwhitten@smccme.edu
WHITTEN, Mandy .... 864-503-5420.. 434 G
mwhitten@uscupstaet.edu
WHITTEN, Pamela .... 706-583-0506.. 128 E
pwhitten@uga.edu
WHITTEN, Patrice .... 850-484-1714.. 106 H
pswhitten@pensacolastate.edu
WHITTENBURG, Nashia ... 912-344-2514.. 116 E
nashia.whittenburg@armstrong.edu
WHITTENBURG, Scott ...... 406-243-6670.. 276 K
scott.whittenburg@umontana.edu
WHITTENTON, Kathy .... 870-307-7505.... 21 A
kathy.whittenton@lyon.edu
WHITTEY, Chris .... 216-421-7455.. 366 G
cwhittey@cia.edu
WHITTINGHAM, Michelle 831-459-1453.... 70 F
michelle@ucsc.edu
WHITTINGHAM, Rachel .... 501-205-8876.... 19 J
rwhittingham@cbc.edu
WHITTINGTON, Connie ... 318-869-5101.. 194 I
cwhitt@centenary.edu
WHITTINGTON, Donna .... 225-743-8500.. 196 J
dwhittington@rpcc.edu
WHITTINGTON, Elizabeth 713-623-2040.. 451 K
ewhittington@aii.edu
WHITTINGTON,
Gerald, O .... 336-278-5434.. 344 D
whitting@elon.edu
WHITTINGTON, Lee .... 828-766-1196.. 351 B
lwhittington@mayland.edu
WHITTINGTON, Ray .... 312-362-6781.. 139 C
rwhittin@depaul.edu
WHITTLESEY, Valerie, D .. 470-578-6023.. 123 J
vwhittle@kennesaw.edu
WHITTUM, Terry .... 410-532-5105.. 210 B
twhittum@ndm.edu
WHITTUM, Timothy .... 603-645-9709.. 287 I
t.whittum@snhu.edu
WHITWELL, Jeff .... 615-898-2700.. 444 G
jeff.whitwell@mtsu.edu
WHITWORTH, Amy, F ..... 210-486-4097.. 450 C
awhitworth@alamo.edu
WHITWORTH, Bruce .... 559-278-2795.... 32 F
bwhitwor@csufresno.edu
WHITWORTH, Jerry .... 940-898-2202.. 472 G
jwhitworth@twu.edu
WHOLEBEN, Belinda .... 815-226-4065.. 152 G
bwholeben@rockford.edu
WHORLEY, William .... 517-607-2454.. 235 E
wwhorley@hillsdale.edu
WHORTON, Susan .... 864-656-6256.. 428 C
whorton@clemson.edu
WHTYE, William .... 262-564-3228.. 523 D
whytew@gtc.edu

WHYNOTT, Anne ... 262-564-2758.. 523 D
whynotta@gtc.edu
WHYTE, Novia, P ... 516-463-6928.. 316 D
novia.p.whyte@hofstra.edu
WHYTE, William ... 262-564-3228.. 523 D
whytew@gtc.edu
WIBBELS, Alan ... 954-771-0376.. 104 H
awibbels@knoxseminary.edu
WIBBENMEYER, Kana ... 773-508-3489.. 146 G
kwibben@luc.edu
WIBLE, Doug ... 949-214-3029.... 41 F
doug.wible@cui.edu
WICHERN, Adam ... 718-405-3776.. 310 H
adam.wichern@mountsaintvincent.edu
WICHERT, Jerome, L ... 580-774-3786.. 388 C
jerome.wichert@swosu.edu
WICHROSKI, Pamela, J ... 207-786-6207.. 202 D
pwichros@bates.edu
WICHSER, John ... 301-846-2674.. 207 F
jwichser@frederick.edu
WICK, Martha ... 641-683-5231.. 173 C
martha.wick@indianhills.edu
WICK, Michael, R ... 240-895-4389.. 210 E
mrwick@smcm.edu
WICKEHAM, Daniel ... 414-955-8826.. 518 A
dwickeha@mcw.edu
WICKER, Jeff ... 803-321-5676.. 431 F
jeffrey.wicker@newberry.edu
WICKER-MCCREE,
Ingrid, L ... 919-530-7057.. 357 A
iwicker@nccu.edu
WICKERING, Deborah ... 616-632-2075.. 231 A
wickedeb@aquinas.edu
WICKERSHAM, Cassie ... 608-663-6715.. 516 F
cwickersham@edgewood.edu
WICKERSHAM, Walter ... 617-358-0300.. 216 E
wnw@bu.edu
WICKERT, Jonathan, A ... 515-294-0070.. 169 G
wickert@iastate.edu
WICKETT, Brenda, K ... 515-961-1611.. 176 H
brenda.wickett@simpson.edu
WICKHAM, Gerald ... 563-441-4201.. 172 D
gwickham@eicc.edu
WICKLAND, Mary ... 409-984-6125.. 471 C
mary.wickland@lamarpa.edu
WICKLESS, Megan ... 402-552-6119.. 279 D
wicklessmegan@clarksoncollege.edu
WICKLIFFE, Cari, S ... 314-977-2350.. 271 K
wicklics@slu.edu
WICKLIFFE-CAMPBELL,
Carol ... 631-451-4169.. 336 D
wicklic@sunysuffolk.edu
WICKLINE, Jason ... 217-424-6217.. 148 D
jwickline@millikin.edu
WICKLUND, Greg, A ... 817-202-6743.. 466 C
wicklund@swau.edu
WICKS, Donna ... 810-762-7853.. 236 C
dwicks@kettering.edu
WICKSTROM, Brian ... 318-342-5361.. 201 E
wickstrom@ulm.edu
WICKSTROM, Sherry ... 763-576-4874.. 248 L
swickstrom@anokatech.edu
WIDDOWS, Daniella ... 434-223-6311.. 490 D
dwiddows@hsc.edu
WIDELL, Mike ... 405-945-3284.. 386 C
mike@okstate.edu
WIDEMAN, Ben ... 920-686-6141.. 519 H
ben.wideman@sl.edu
WIDEMAN, Gene ... 918-595-7262.. 388 F
gene.wideman@tulsacc.edu
WIDEMAN, Ramon ... 803-793-5248.. 429 D
widemanr@denmarktech.edu
WIDENER, J, J ... 620-417-1202.. 184 I
jj.widener@sccc.edu
WIDENHOFER,
Stephen, B ... 217-424-6300.. 148 D
swidenhofer@millikin.edu
WIDENMANN, Sally ... 541-917-4534.. 392 C
widenms@linnbenton.edu
WIDGER, Mari Jo ... 308-345-8106.. 280 M
widgerm@mpcc.edu
WIDING, II, Robert, E ... 216-368-1156.. 365 B
WIDMER, Robert, D ... 309-268-8106.. 141 C
rob.widmer@heartland.edu
WIDNER, Kenneth ... 662-329-7021.. 259 E
kwidner@muw.edu
WIDNER, Melissa ... 229-420-4070.. 115 K
melisa.widner@asurams.edu
WIECHMAN, Jeffery, P ... 507-354-8221.. 247 J
wiechmjp@mlc-wels.edu
WIECKI, Lisa ... 864-388-8035.. 430 G
lwiecki@lander.edu
WIECKOWSKI, Ellen, G ... 412-397-6901.. 418 B
wieckowski@rmu.edu
WIED, Christine ... 979-830-4224.. 452 J
cwied@blinn.edu
WIEDEFELD, Kimberley ... 585-594-6199.. 327 D
wiedefeld_kimberley@roberts.edu
WIEDEFELD, Kimberly ... 626-812-3016.... 28 A
kwiedefeld@apu.edu

WIEDEN, Ted ... 925-969-2001.... 41 I
twieden@dvc.edu
WIEDENHOEFT, Margaret ... 269-337-7133.. 235 H
margaret.wiedenoeft@kzoo.edu
WIEGAND, Joe ... 706-865-2134.. 128 D
jwiegand@truett.edu
WIEGAND, Mark ... 502-272-8368.. 187 A
mwiegand@bellarmine.edu
WIEGAND, Randall, V ... 671-735-2905.. 530 B
wiegandr@triton.uog.edu
WIEGANDT, Scott, P ... 502-272-8496.. 187 A
swiegandt@bellarmine.edu
WIEGEL, Lisa ... 563-288-6003.. 172 C
lwiegel@eicc.edu
WIEGMAN, Karen, D ... 913-971-3698.. 183 D
kdwiegman@mnu.edu
WIELEBINSKI, Daria ... 570-422-3282.. 414 H
dwielebinski@esu.edu
WIELENGA, Jay ... 712-707-7111.. 176 B
jayw@nwciowa.edu
WIELGUS, Jeanne ... 707-826-4206.... 34 F
jw7001@humboldt.edu
WIELHORSKI, Karen ... 281-283-3930.. 474 A
wielhorski@uhcl.edu
WIELINSKI, Peter ... 218-631-7810.. 250 D
peter.wielinski@minnesota.edu
WIELK, John ... 212-396-6434.. 308 D
jw2157@hunter.cuny.edu
WIENCEK, John, M ... 208-885-6448.. 134 G
provost@uidaho.edu
WIERBICKI ABRAHAMS,
Jill ... 617-928-4633.. 226 B
jwabrahams@mountida.edu
WIERDA, Bruce ... 231-777-0657.. 238 G
bruce.wierda@muskegoncc.edu
WIERDA, Kire ... 989-328-1286.. 238 D
kire.wierda@montcalm.edu
WIERENGA, Sue ... 415-955-2100.... 25 J
swierenga@alliant.edu
WIERS, Alison ... 336-334-4822.. 350 B
ajwiers@gtcc.edu
WIERSMA, Noelle ... 509-777-4874.. 509 H
nwiersma@whitworth.edu
WIERTEL, Anthony ... 716-926-8818.. 316 B
twiertel@hilbert.edu
WIERZBICKI, Andrzej ... 251-460-6280..... 9 E
awierzbicki@southalabama.edu
WIESCAMP, Cheryl ... 970-247-7364.... 80 D
wiescamp_c@fortlewis.edu
WIESE, Joelle, D ... 202-687-7150.... 92 E
jdw237@georgetown.edu
WIESEHAN, Terry ... 765-973-8221.. 162 G
twieseha@iue.edu
WIESEMANN, Lois ... 801-957-4255.. 483 A
lois.wiesemann@slcc.edu
WIESENBERG, Mark ... 801-863-8740.. 482 C
mwiesenberg@uvu.edu
WIESEPAPE, Craig ... 979-830-4195.. 452 J
craig.wiesepape@blinn.edu
WIESNER, Bob ... 803-641-3522.. 433 G
bobw@usca.edu
WIESS, Renee ... 361-593-3991.. 469 A
rennee.wiess@tamuk.edu
WIEWEL, Christine ... 217-641-4517.. 143 H
cwiewel@jwcc.edu
WIEWEL, Wim ... 503-725-4411.. 394 G
president@pdx.edu
WIGBOLDY, Kyle ... 616-222-3000.. 236 F
kwigboldy@kuyper.edu
WIGFALL, Arthur ... 212-463-0400.. 337 I
arthur.wigfall@touro.edu
WIGGINS, Amy, F ... 252-862-1225.. 352 D
afwiggins7415@roanokechowan.edu
WIGGINS, Charles ... 828-395-1306.. 350 E
cpwiggins@isothermal.edu
WIGGINS, David, J ... 952-446-4112.. 246 D
wigginsj@crown.edu
WIGGINS, Devon ... 903-510-2385.. 473 C
dwig@tjc.edu
WIGGINS, Donnell ... 937-722-9239.. 380 E
admissions@urbana.edu
WIGGINS, Jack ... 409-839-2014.. 470 H
jowiggins@lit.edu
WIGGINS, Jill ... 417-836-5636.. 268 I
jillwiggins@missouristate.edu
WIGGINS, Michaele ... 336-334-7593.. 356 F
sm8093@bncollege.com
WIGGINS, Nimmi, K ... 859-257-6547.. 193 G
nwiggin@uky.edu
WIGGINS, Rob ... 503-517-1876.. 396 F
rwiggins@westernseminary.edu
WIGGINS, Roy ... 781-891-2249.. 215 F
wwiggins@bentley.edu
WIGGINS, Roy ... 781-891-3166.. 215 F
rwiggins@bentley.edu
WIGGINS, Sarah ... 954-201-6455.... 96 I
swiggins@broward.edu
WIGGINS, Shelia ... 252-527-6223.. 350 H
swiggins@lenoircc.edu
WIGGINS, Symphoni ... 706-396-7594.. 125 H
swiggins@paine.edu

WIGGINTON, Van, A ... 281-542-2000.. 464 J
van.wigginton@sjcd.edu
WIGHT, Charles, A ... 801-626-6001.. 482 D
president@weber.edu
WIGHT, Laura ... 406-771-4318.. 277 F
laura.wight@gfcmsu.edu
WIGHT, Randall ... 870-245-5107.... 21 E
wight@cbu.edu
WIGHTKIN, Steven, P ... 312-942-5947.. 153 B
steven_wightkin@rush.edu
WIGHTMAN, Beth, A ... 818-677-2969.... 34 A
beth.wightman@csun.edu
WIGHTMAN, Todd ... 208-535-5440.. 133 G
todd.wightman@my.eitc.edu
WIGINTON, Chad ... 580-477-7918.. 389
chad.wiginton@wosc.edu
WIGINTON, Melissa ... 512-404-4862.. 452 A
mwiginton@austinseminary.edu
WIGLEY, Kimberly ... 404-627-2681.. 117 G
kimberly.wigley@beulah.edu
WIGNALL, Eric ... 574-936-8898.. 158
eric.wignall@ancilla.edu
WIGNALL, Scott, D ... 724-946-7135.. 423 B
wignalsc@westminster.edu
WIGNER, Dee ... 620-276-9577.. 181 C
dee.wigner@gcccks.edu
WIGNES, David, R ... 608-785-9140.. 524 H
wignesd@westerntc.edu
WIGTIL, Brad ... 254-710-2222.. 452 H
brad_wigtil@baylor.edu
WIHBEY, Jean ... 561-868-3400.. 106 D
wihbeyj@palmbeachstate.edu
WIILKINSON, Joann, F ... 314-516-5301.. 274 A
wilkinsonj@umsl.edu
WILBANKS, Cynthia, H ... 734-763-5554.. 241 J
wilbanks@umich.edu
WILBANKS, Jennifer ... 660-596-7229.. 272 G
jwilbanks@sfccmo.edu
WILBANKS, Jennifer ... 803-276-9000.. 432 A
wilbanksj@ptc.edu
WILBANKS, Laura ... 734-481-2318.. 233 J
laura.wilbanks@emich.edu
WILBORN, Colin ... 254-295-8642.. 474 E
cwilborn@umhb.edu
WILBUR, Gregg ... 518-736-3622.. 315 A
gregg.wilbur@fmcc.suny.edu
WILBUR, Janice ... 508-849-3406.. 214 E
jwilbur@annamaria.edu
WILBUR, Kathleen, M ... 989-774-3871.. 232 D
wilbu1km@cmich.edu
WILBUR, Peter, B ... 401-254-3365.. 426 B
pwilbur@rwu.edu
WILBUR, Roy, A ... 215-965-8561.. 411 A
rwilbur@moore.edu
WILBUR, Shelley ... 941-487-4100.. 111 D
mwilbur@ncf.edu
WILBURN, Howard, L ... 336-725-8344.. 354 G
piedmontu@piedmontu.edu
WILBURN, Kevin ... 251-442-2223...... 9 A
kwilburn@umobile.edu
WILBURN, Roberta ... 509-777-4603.. 509 H
rwilburn@whitworth.edu
WILCH, Peter, J ... 415-422-6423.... 72 C
pwilch@usfca.edu
WILCOTS, Barbara ... 303-871-2706.... 84 B
bwilcots@du.edu
WILCOX, Anthony ... 978-665-3482.. 221 D
awilcox@fitchburgstate.edu
WILCOX, Bonnie ... 417-873-7811.. 264 H
bwilcox@drury.edu
WILCOX, Cordelia, A ... 919-658-7494.. 355 K
cwilcox@umo.edu
WILCOX, Dan ... 910-362-7676.. 348 A
dwilcox@cfcc.edu
WILCOX, Dean ... 336-770-3243.. 358 E
wilcoxd@uncsa.edu
WILCOX, Denise ... 909-469-5393.... 74 K
dwilcox@westernu.edu
WILCOX, Heather ... 303-797-5674.... 76 J
heather.wilcox@arapahoe.edu
WILCOX, Jerry ... 203-837-8242.... 85
wilcoxj@wcsu.edu
WILCOX, Kathleen, J ... 937-328-6060.. 366 E
wilcoxk@clarkstate.edu
WILCOX, Kenneth ... 718-522-9073.. 304 D
coachwilcox@asa.edu
WILCOX, Kevin ... 518-956-8120.. 331 A
kwilcox@albany.edu
WILCOX, Kim ... 970-351-2496.... 84 C
kim.wilcox@unco.edu
WILCOX, Kim, A ... 951-827-5201.... 70 B
chancellor@ucr.edu
WILCOX, Mark ... 412-536-1104.. 406 K
mark.wilcox@laroche.edu
WILCOX, Nancy ... 228-896-3809.. 259 C
nancy.wilcox@mgccc.edu
WILCOX, Ralph ... 813-974-8347.. 112 C
rcwilcox@usf.edu
WILCOX, Reed, N ... 540-261-4100.. 494 F
reed.wilcox@svu.edu

WILCOX, Robbin ... 419-267-1460.. 374 A
rwilcox@northweststate.edu
WILCOX, Robert, M ... 803-777-6857.. 433 F
wilcoxrm@law.sc.edu
WILCOX, Stan ... 850-644-2525.. 111 C
swilcox2@fsu.edu
WILCOX, Tamera ... 785-309-3183.. 184 H
tamera.wilcox@salinatech.edu
WILCOXEN, Andrica ... 913-288-7652.. 182 C
awilcoxen@kckcc.edu
WILCOXSON, Douglas, A ... 517-750-1200.. 241 E
dwilcoxs@arbor.edu
WILCZEK, Amity ... 760-572-2000.... 42 B
awilczek@deepsprings.edu
WILD, Larry ... 847-628-2036.. 144 B
lwild@judsonu.edu
WILD, Lorie ... 206-281-2608.. 507 C
wildl@spu.edu
WILD, Lynn, A ... 585-475-6543.. 327 E
lawctc@rit.edu
WILD, Robert, M ... 314-935-8081.. 274 N
rob.wild@wustl.edu
WILDA, Christine ... 774-455-7549.. 220 E
cwilda@umassp.edu
WILDE, Jerry ... 765-973-8554.. 162 G
jwilde@iue.edu
WILDECK, Steve, C ... 608-265-3040.. 522 A
steve.wildeck@uwex.uwc.edu
WILDENTHAL,
B. Hobson ... 972-883-2271.. 476 C
wildenbh@utdallas.edu
WILDER, Aliza ... 860-486-4038.... 89 D
aliza.wilder@uconn.edu
WILDER, Carmen, C ... 704-216-6009.. 346 A
cwilder@livingstone.edu
WILDER, Carol ... 212-229-8903.. 322 E
wilderc@newschool.edu
WILDER, Carrie ... 229-931-2351.. 127 C
cwilder@southgatech.edu
WILDER, Diane ... 610-896-1209.. 405 I
dwilder@haverford.edu
WILDER, Kristie ... 423-236-2206.. 444 B
kwilder@southern.edu
WILDER, Linda ... 860-515-3862.... 85 D
lwilder@charteroak.edu
WILDER, Martin, A ... 540-654-1301.. 495 C
mwilder@umw.edu
WILDER, Michael ... 630-752-5818.. 158 C
michael.wilder@wheaton.edu
WILDER, Paul, J ... 812-888-5131.. 169 A
pwilder@vinu.edu
WILDER, Richard, D ... 352-294-3220.. 112 A
rwilder@ufl.edu
WILDER, Robert ... 774-354-0500.. 215 D
robert.wilder@becker.edu
WILDER, Stanley ... 225-578-2217.. 197 I
wilder@lsu.edu
WILDER, Sterly ... 919-684-5114.. 343 J
sterly.wilder@daa.duke.edu
WILDER, W. Mark ... 662-915-5756.. 261 B
acwilder@olemiss.edu
WILDER-BYRD, Ellen, M ... 803-323-2236.. 435 B
wilderbyrde@winthrop.edu
WILDERMUTH, Amy ... 801-581-8763.. 481 M
amy.wildermuth@utah.edu
WILDES, SJ, Kevin, W ... 504-865-3847.. 198 E
wildesk@loyno.edu
WILDEY, Diane ... 518-743-2337.. 335 A
daltod@sunyacc.edu
WILDING, Michael ... 661-362-3498.... 40 A
michael.wilding@canyons.edu
WILDING, Tim ... 205-226-4643...... 2 C
trwildin@bsc.edu
WILDING-FARRELL, Jody ... 281-649-3070.. 458 L
jwilding@hbu.edu
WILDMAN, Katie ... 605-642-6270.. 437 B
katherine.wildman@bhsu.edu
WILDNER-BASSETT,
Mary, E ... 520-621-9294.... 17 I
wildnerb@email.arizona.edu
WILEBSKI, Jason ... 563-355-3500.. 174 E
jwilebski@kaplan.edu
WILENSKY, Heather ... 410-857-2289.. 209 D
hwilensky@mcdaniel.edu
WILES, Jan ... 618-842-3711.. 142 C
wilesj@iecc.edu
WILES, Mari, E ... 252-398-6268.. 343 G
wilesm@chowan.edu
WILES, Patrick, J ... 716-851-1901.. 313 H
wiles@ecc.edu
WILEY, Byron, A ... 864-656-3553.. 428 C
bwiley@clemson.edu
WILEY, Casey ... 864-455-8204.. 434 D
wileyc@greenvillemed.sc.edu
WILEY, Ellen ... 717-947-6089.. 413 N
ewiley@pacollege.edu
WILEY, Fran, K ... 864-941-8351.. 432 A
wiley.f@ptc.edu
WILEY, Jeanelle ... 314-968-7123.. 275 B
jeanellewiley10@webster.edu

WILEY, Jeffrey .... 315-786-2200.. 317 H
jwiley@sunyjefferson.edu
WILEY, Joe .... 731-989-6001.. 440 D
jwiley@fhu.edu
WILEY, Karen .... 815-455-8547.. 147 E
kwiley@mchenry.edu
WILEY, Louise .... 903-983-8242.. 460 D
lwiley@kilgore.edu
WILEY, LuSharon .... 850-474-2161.. 113 A
lwiley@uwf.edu
WILEY, Marilyn .... 940-565-3097.. 475 A
marilyn.wiley@unt.edu
WILEY, Mark .... 562-985-4128.... 33 B
mark.wiley@csulb.edu
WILEY, Nina .... 937-328-7936.. 366 E
wileyn@clarkstate.edu
WILEY, Paul, G .... 931-598-1731.. 443 O
pwiley@sewanee.edu
WILEY, Stacey .... 585-245-5721.. 333 B
wileys@geneseo.edu
WILEY, Stacey .... 814-824-2311.. 410 H
swiley@mercyhurst.edu
WILEY, Zelia, Z .... 785-532-6276.. 182 D
zwiley@ksu.edu
WILEY-HARRIS, Courtney 212-870-1253.. 324 B
cwiley@nyts.edu
WILFAHRT, Dannette, C .. 651-631-5190.. 256 A
dcwilfahrt@unwsp.edu
WILFONG, Barry .... 573-518-3806.. 268 E
bwilfong@mineralarea.edu
WILFONG, Earl .... 563-884-5684.. 176 C
earl.wilfong@palmer.edu
WILGA, Dave .... 907-564-8259.... 10 B
dwilga@alaskapacific.edu
WILGENBUSCH, Sandy .... 563-876-3353.. 171 I
wilgenbu@dwci.edu
WILGUS, Robynne .... 541-440-4623.. 395 F
robynne.wilgus@umpqua.edu
WILHEIM, Michael .... 910-962-2736.. 358 D
wilhelmm@uncw.edu
WILHELM, Jane .... 608-663-2203.. 516 F
jwilhelm@edgewood.edu
WILHELM, John, L .... 402-280-2762.. 279 H
johnwilhelm@creighton.edu
WILHELM, Laura .... 773-256-0741.. 147 A
lwilhelm@lstc.edu
WILHELM, Robert, W .... 704-687-8428.. 358 A
rgwilhel@uncc.edu
WILHELMI, Lisa .... 254-299-8640.. 461 E
lwilhelmi@mclennan.edu
WILHELMS, Angela .... 541-346-5561.. 395 G
wilhelms@uoregon.edu
WILHELMSON, Paul .... 608-796-3040.. 522 O
pjwilhelmson@viterbo.edu
WILHEMI, Jeremy .... 479-979-1307.... 24 I
jwilhemi@ozarks.edu
WILHITE, Christa .... 601-635-2111.. 257 F
cwilhite@eccc.edu
WILHITE, David .... 502-863-8016.. 188 I
david_wilhite@georgetowncollege.edu
WILHITE, Lee .... 562-903-4079..... 28 E
lee.wilhite@biola.edu
WILHITE, Stephen, C .... 610-499-4105.. 423 E
scwilhite@widener.edu
WILHOUR, Reo .... 217-351-2558.. 151 B
rwilhour@parkland.edu
WILJANEN, Mark .... 502-456-6504.. 193 B
mwiljanen@sullivan.edu
WILK, Thomas .... 586-445-7135.. 237 C
wilkt@macomb.edu
WILKE, Dennis, F .... 412-521-6200.. 418 C
dennis.wilke@rosedaletech.org
WILKE, Ekkehard, T .... 312-939-0111.. 139 G
wil3t@eastwest.edu
WILKE, Janet, S .... 308-865-8595.. 282 L
wilkej@unk.edu
WILKE, Stephen, K .... 620-229-6277.. 184 J
steve.wilke@sckans.edu
WILKEN, Danielle .... 860-727-6714.... 87 H
dwilken@goodwin.edu
WILKEN, Danielle, S .... 860-727-6780.... 87 H
dwilken@goodwin.edu
WILKERSON, Aimee, J .... 270-824-8696.. 190 B
aimee.wilkerson@kctcs.edu
WILKERSON, Ame .... 912-260-4407.. 127 B
ame.wilkerson@sgsc.edu
WILKERSON, Charles ...... 931-372-3634.. 445 B
cwilkerson@tntech.edu
WILKERSON, Jeffrey .... 563-387-1005.. 174 L
wilkerje@luther.edu
WILKERSON, Jon .... 303-937-4273.... 77 K
jwilkerson@chu.edu
WILKERSON, Karen, D .... 816-235-2757.. 273 F
wilkersonkd@umkc.edu
WILKERSON, Lindsey, S . 318-342-1530.. 201 E
lwilkerson@ulm.edu
WILKERSON, Lois .... 714-241-6160.... 39 E
lwilkerson@coastline.edu
WILKERSON, Mathew, C . 540-654-1048.. 495 C
mwilkers@umw.edu
WILKERSON, Sharon, A .. 979-436-0111.. 468 B
swilkerson44@tamu.edu
WILKERSON, Tanya .... 443-885-3170.. 209 F
tanya.wilkerson@morgan.edu
WILKERSON, Terry .... 618-437-5321.. 152 A
wilkersont@rlc.edu
WILKERSON, William ...... 256-824-2339...... 8 F
william.wilkerson@uah.edu
WILKERSON, Zeda .... 870-368-2028.... 21 F
zwilkerson@ozarka.edu
WILKES, Barrie, J .... 989-774-3334.. 232 D
wilke1bj@cmich.edu
WILKES, C. Gene .... 817-274-4284.. 452 I
gwilkes@bhcarroll.edu
WILKES, David, S .... 434-982-4050.. 495 H
dsw4n@virginia.edu
WILKES, Deborah .... 706-886-6831.. 128 C
dwilkes@tfc.edu
WILKES, Eileen .... 850-872-3801.. 102 M
ewilkes@gulfcoast.edu
WILKES, Jeanna .... 662-846-4666.. 257 E
jdwilkes@deltastate.edu
WILKES, Jeremy .... 901-572-2670.. 438 I
jeremy.wilkes@bchs.edu
WILKES, Lisa .... 540-231-5706.. 499 F
lwilkes@vt.edu
WILKES, Yvette .... 505-454-3197.. 300 F
ydwilkes@nmhu.edu
WILKEY, Jill, J .... 701-231-8466.. 361 A
jill.wilkey@ndsu.edu
WILKIE, Marilyn, L .... 212-517-0453.. 320 C
mwilkie@mmm.edu
WILKIN, John .... 814-641-3707.. 406 F
wilkinj@juniata.edu
WILKIN, John, P .... 217-333-0790.. 157 A
jpwilkin@illinois.edu
WILKIN, Noel, E .... 662-915-5317.. 261 B
nwilkin@olemiss.edu
WILKINS, Ashli .... 334-556-2226...... 3 N
awilkins@wallace.edu
WILKINS, Deborah, T ...... 270-745-5398.. 194 D
deborah.wilkins@wku.edu
WILKINS, Derrick .... 252-335-3324.. 356 D
dlwilkins@ecsu.edu
WILKINS, Harry, T .... 614-508-7277.. 370 E
hwilkins@hondros.edu
WILKINS, Ken .... 702-968-5568.. 285 E
kwilkins@roseman.edu
WILKINS, Linda .... 317-632-5553.. 165 L
lindawilkins@lincolntech.edu
WILKINS, Lorinda .... 575-624-7345.. 299 J
lorinda.wilkins@roswell.enmu.edu
WILKINS, Mardell .... 775-753-2265.. 284 I
mardell.wilkins@gbcnv.edu
WILKINS, Marianne .... 251-380-2261...... 7 D
mwilkins@shc.edu
WILKINS, Patricia, A .... 512-505-3081.. 459 F
pawilkins@htu.edu
WILKINS, Pyeper .... 214-378-1538.. 456 A
pwilkins@dcccd.edu
WILKINS, Vickie .... 419-448-3595.. 378 A
galaskavm@tiffin.edu
WILKINS GREEN, Clair ... 504-520-5251.. 202 C
cwilkins@xula.edu
WILKINSON, Christine, K 480-965-7782.... 11 H
c.wilkinson@asu.edu
WILKINSON, Jay .... 515-961-1288.. 176 H
jay.wilkinson@simpson.edu
WILKINSON, John .... 704-878-3202.. 351 D
jwilkinson@mitchellcc.edu
WILKINSON, Joni .... 601-276-3708.. 260 H
jwilkinson@smcc.edu
WILKINSON, Julie .... 941-782-5678.. 407 D
jwilkinson@lecom.edu
WILKINSON, Linda .... 312-341-3659.. 152 H
lpwilkinson@roosevelt.edu
WILKINSON, Lonnie .... 225-771-3015.. 199 H
lonnie_wilkinson@subr.edu
WILKINSON, Melissa .... 309-647-4645.. 155 G
WILKINSON, Michael .... 361-485-4409.. 474 C
wilkinsonmr@uhv.edu
WILKINSON, Mike .... 817-923-1921.. 466 E
mwilkinson@swbts.edu
WILKINSON, Mike .... 405-692-3132.. 384 C
mwilkinson@macu.edu
WILKINSON, Missy .... 309-649-6305.. 155 G
missy.wilkinson@src.edu
WILKINSON, Patrick, J ..... 920-424-2147.. 520 E
wilkinso@uwosh.edu
WILKINSON, Robert .... 386-506-3656.... 98 E
wilkinr@daytonastate.edu
WILKINSON, Timothy, J .. 509-777-4585.. 509 H
twilkinson@whitworth.edu
WILKINSON, Todd .... 252-399-6552.. 341 P
twilkinson@barton.edu
WILKINSON, William, J ... 215-204-0564.. 420 B
william.wilkinson@temple.edu
WILKOS-GREENBERG,
Janice .... 617-585-0200.. 216 A
janice.greenberg@the-bac.edu
WILKOSKI, Donna, M ...... 215-698-8203.. 399 A
wilkoski@bucks.edu
WILKOW, Beth .... 516-299-2589.. 319 B
beth.wilkow@liu.edu
WILKS, Karrin .... 212-220-8321.. 307 B
kwilks@bmcc.cuny.edu
WILKS, Preston .... 509-793-2194.. 501 H
prestonw@bigbend.edu
WILKS, Ronald, W .... 317-788-3517.. 168 A
wilks@uindy.edu
WILKSON, Nancy .... 575-439-3798.. 301 A
nmontgom@nmsu.edu
WILKYMACKY, Eric .... 859-344-3321.. 193 C
wilkyme@thomasmore.edu
WILL, Christina .... 386-312-4152.. 108 B
christinawill@sjrstate.edu
WILL, Eleanor .... 828-771-2082.. 359 F
ewill@warren-wilson.edu
WILL, John .... 715-468-2815.. 525 A
john.will@witc.edu
WILL, Kris .... 303-986-2320.... 78 L
kris@csha.net
WILL, Lee .... 480-245-7937.... 13 L
lee.will@ibcs.edu
WILLAMON, Nancy, R .... 217-351-2533.. 151 B
nwillamon@parkland.edu
WILLAN, Dawn, E .... 843-953-5997.. 428 G
willande@cofc.edu
WILLAN, William .... 740-593-2551.. 375 H
willanw@ohio.edu
WILLARD, Joseph .... 215-991-3586.. 407 A
willard@lasalle.edu
WILLARD, Paul, S .... 727-376-6911.. 114 A
paul.willard@trintycollege.edu
WILLBANKS, Stephanie ... 802-831-1277.. 485 F
swillbanks@vermontlaw.edu
WILLBORG, Erik .... 406-657-1032.. 278 D
erik.willborg@rocky.edu
WILLCOX, Abby .... 239-489-9059.. 101 F
awillcox@fsw.edu
WILLCOX, Jan, M .... 540-231-0920.. 489 H
WILLCOX, Wayne .... 912-344-2689.. 116 E
wayne.willcox@armstrong.edu
WILLE, Diane, E .... 812-941-2300.. 163 F
dwille@ius.edu
WILLEKENS, Rene, G .... 623-935-8069.... 14 A
rene.willekens@estrellamountain.edu
WILLEMAN-BUCKELEW,
Diana, L .... 540-224-4491.. 491 A
dlwilleman@jchs.edu
WILLEMS, Greg .... 785-532-6266.. 182 D
gregw@found.ksu.edu
WILLEMSEN, David, W ...... 972-825-4630.. 466 D
dwillemsen@sagu.edu
WILLENBERG, Lisa .... 501-977-2025.... 24 B
willenberg@uaccm.edu
WILLENBORG, Andy, B ... 563-589-0217.. 177 H
awillenborg@wartburgseminary.edu
WILLENBRINK, Bob .... 816-271-4575.. 269 C
rwillenbrink@missouriwestern.edu
WILLENSKY, Violet, J ...... 908-526-1200.. 295 A
violet.willensky@raritanval.edu
WILLER, Anthony .... 701-483-2215.. 360 D
anthony.willer@dickinsonstate.edu
WILLETT, Dana .... 512-245-2322.. 471 F
drw134@txstate.edu
WILLETT, Terrence .... 831-477-5656.... 29 G
terrence@cabrillo.edu
WILLETTS, Jeffrey, G .... 678-547-6495.. 124 D
willetts_jg@mercer.edu
WILLEY, Edward, W .... 561-207-5411.. 106 D
willeye@palmbeachstate.edu
WILLEY, Kevin .... 570-577-3208.. 398 L
kevin.willey@bucknell.edu
WILLEY, Leslie .... 573-876-7213.. 272 I
lwilley@stephens.edu
WILLEY, Sharon .... 408-924-7096.... 35 C
sharon.willey@sjsu.edu
WILLEY, Sue, C .... 317-788-3412.. 168 A
swilley@uindy.edu
WILLGING, Gregory, A ..... 563-556-5110.. 175 F
willging@nicc.edu
WILLGING, Pete .... 815-599-3421.. 141 E
pete.willging@highland.edu
WILLIAMS, Adam .... 757-352-4894.. 493 E
awilliams@regent.edu
WILLIAMS, Adelia .... 212-346-1555.. 325 J
awilliams@pace.edu
WILLIAMS, Alex .... 402-363-5689.. 283 G
aawilliams@york.edu
WILLIAMS, Alfred .... 860-932-4172.... 87 C
awilliams@qvcc.edu
WILLIAMS, Alison, P .... 740-587-6469.. 368 B
williamsa@denison.edu
WILLIAMS, Allison .... 617-277-3915.. 216 D
williamsa@bgsp.edu
WILLIAMS, Alonda .... 425-564-2810.. 501 F
alonda.williams@bellevuecollege.edu
WILLIAMS, Alvin .... 208-769-3348.. 134 C
al_williams@nic.edu
WILLIAMS, Amanda .... 913-288-7218.. 182 C
awilliams@kckcc.edu
WILLIAMS, Amber, S .... 402-472-0671.. 282 M
amber.williams@unl.edu
WILLIAMS, Amy, H .... 704-637-4414.. 343 B
ahwillia@catawba.edu
WILLIAMS, Andre .... 252-331-4881.. 349 A
andre_williams@albemarle.edu
WILLIAMS, Andy .... 847-543-2210.. 138 C
wwilliams@clcillinois.edu
WILLIAMS, Andy .... 847-635-1600.. 150 G
WILLIAMS, Angela .... 678-422-4100.... 93 F
WILLIAMS, Angela .... 303-797-5715.... 76 J
angela.williams@arapahoe.edu
WILLIAMS, Angela .... 405-585-5801.. 385 B
angela.williams@okbu.edu
WILLIAMS, Angela .... 803-738-7691.. 431 B
williamsa@midlandstech.edu
WILLIAMS, Angela, L .... 410-651-8420.. 212 B
alwilliams@umes.edu
WILLIAMS, Angela, S .... 479-575-2806.... 22 I
angelaw@uark.edu
WILLIAMS, Ann, L .... 570-961-4725.. 409 H
awilliams@marywood.edu
WILLIAMS, Annette .... 540-453-2332.. 496 F
williamsa@brcc.edu
WILLIAMS, Annie .... 501-370-8506.... 21 G
amwilliams@philander.edu
WILLIAMS, Annie .... 719-549-2116.... 79 B
annie.williams@csupueblo.edu
WILLIAMS, Anthony .... 312-980-9255.. 153 J
awilliams@iadtchicago.edu
WILLIAMS, Anthony .... 425-388-9282.. 503 F
anwilliams@everettcc.edu
WILLIAMS, Anthony .... 212-343-1234.. 321 B
awilliams@mcny.edu
WILLIAMS, Anthony, T ..... 325-674-5288.. 449 J
williamsa@acu.edu
WILLIAMS, Antonio .... 410-706-7032.. 211 F
awilliams@police.umaryland.edu
WILLIAMS, Archie .... 478-825-6832.. 120 F
williamsa01@fvsu.edu
WILLIAMS, Arlene .... 406-683-7511.. 277 A
arlene.williams@umwestern.edu
WILLIAMS, Arley .... 307-766-4839.. 527 B
arley.williams@uwyo.edu
WILLIAMS, Audrey .... 352-365-3510.. 104 J
williama@lssc.edu
WILLIAMS, Audrey, J .... 865-539-7198.. 446 G
ajwilliams@pstcc.edu
WILLIAMS, Barry .... 570-208-5932.. 406 J
barrywilliams@kings.edu
WILLIAMS, Bert .... 478-387-4782.. 121 E
bwilliams@gmc.edu
WILLIAMS, Beth .... 513-618-1309.. 366 C
ewilliams@ccms.edu
WILLIAMS, Betty, B .... 843-383-8055.. 428 F
bwilliams@coker.edu
WILLIAMS, BJ .... 907-834-1649.... 11 A
bjwilliams@pwscc.edu
WILLIAMS, Blake .... 229-732-5951.. 116 C
blakewilliams@andrewcollege.edu
WILLIAMS, Bobby .... 936-294-4205.. 471 D
ath_brw@shsu.edu
WILLIAMS, Brad .... 954-262-7282.. 105 J
bradwill@nsu.nova.edu
WILLIAMS, Brad .... 405-945-3204.. 386 C
bradford.williams@osuokc.edu
WILLIAMS, Bradley, E ...... 530-226-4172.... 64 H
bwilliams@simpsonu.edu
WILLIAMS, Brandon .... 859-622-5094.. 188 F
brandon.williams@eku.edu
WILLIAMS, Brandy .... 662-329-7293.. 259 E
bmwilliams@muw.edu
WILLIAMS, Bre .... 760-471-1316.... 59 H
WILLIAMS, Brenda, D .... 609-497-7820.. 294 C
registrar@ptsem.edu
WILLIAMS, Brenda, K .... 256-372-5254...... 1 A
brenda.williams@aamu.edu
WILLIAMS, Brett .... 763-417-8250.. 245 D
bwilliams@centralseminary.edu
WILLIAMS, Brian .... 503-223-2245.. 391 H
bwilliams@portland.chefs.edu
WILLIAMS, Brian, G .... 216-397-4252.. 370 H
bwilliams@jcu.edu
WILLIAMS, Brockton .... 615-343-4411.. 449 A
brock.williams@vanderbilt.edu
WILLIAMS, Bruce .... 601-877-4713.. 256 F
bwilliams@alcorn.edu
WILLIAMS, Bryon .... 850-599-3090.. 110 J
bryon.williams@famu.edu
WILLIAMS, Byron .... 513-244-8462.. 366 B
byron.williams@ccuniversity.edu
WILLIAMS, Calvin .... 813-974-2612.. 112 C
williams374@usf.edu
WILLIAMS, Calvin .... 607-962-9233.. 312 B
williams@corning-cc.edu
WILLIAMS, Calvin, H .... 717-815-1226.. 424 F
cwilliam@ycp.edu
WILLIAMS, Camelia .... 816-995-2808.. 270 H
camelia.williams@researchcollege.edu

WILLIAMS, Lynne .... 218-726-6141.. 255 D
lwilliam@d.umn.edu
WILLIAMS, Lyrae .... 719-389-6699.... 77 J
lyrae.williams@coloradocollege.edu
WILLIAMS, Mandy .... 303-963-3365.... 77 I
aewilliams@ccu.edu
WILLIAMS, Marcellette .... 617-287-7050.. 220 E
mwilliams@umassp.edu
WILLIAMS, Marchetta, L .. 803-938-3721.. 434 E
mlwillia@uscsumter.edu
WILLIAMS, Margaret .... 701-777-5963.. 360 C
margaret.williams@und.edu
WILLIAMS, Marianne, R .. 518-262-5422.. 303 E
willimr@mail.amc.edu
WILLIAMS, Marie .... 919-515-2191.. 357 B
WILLIAMS, Mark .... 661-763-7871.... 67 F
mwilliams@taftcollege.edu
WILLIAMS, Mark .... 352-588-8614.. 108 C
mark.williams05@saintleo.edu
WILLIAMS, Martinique ..... 336-334-7555.. 356 F
mcwilli2@ncat.edu
WILLIAMS, Mary .... 501-374-6305.... 22 C
WILLIAMS, Mary, E .... 724-357-2560.. 415 B
mary.e.williams@iup.edu
WILLIAMS, Mary Beth ...... 717-262-2006.. 424 A
marybeth.williams@wilson.edu
WILLIAMS, Matt .... 919-536-7201.. 349 D
williamsm@durhamtech.edu
WILLIAMS, Max, E .... 423-585-6861.. 447 D
max.williams@ws.edu
WILLIAMS, Melanie, K .... 269-337-7220.. 235 H
williams@kzoo.edu
WILLIAMS, Melissa .... 916-608-6585.... 51 C
william@flc.losrios.edu
WILLIAMS, Melissa .... 706-292-3900.. 127 A
mwilliams@shorter.edu
WILLIAMS, Melissa .... 254-295-4020.. 474 E
mford@umhb.edu
WILLIAMS, Melva .... 318-670-9314.. 199 J
mwilliams@susla.edu
WILLIAMS, Melvenia .... 803-535-5412.. 428 B
mwilliams@claflin.edu
WILLIAMS, Melvin .... 386-481-2900.... 96 H
wiliamsm@cookman.edu
WILLIAMS, Michael .... 207-768-2712.. 203 L
mwilliams@nmcc.edu
WILLIAMS, Michael .... 510-642-5316..... 68 M
athletic.director@berkeley.edu
WILLIAMS, Michael .... 817-735-2509.. 475 C
WILLIAMS, Michael .... 609-984-1130.. 297 F
mwilliams@tesu.edu
WILLIAMS, Michael, D .... 334-386-7103...... 3 I
mwilliams@faulkner.edu
WILLIAMS, Michelle, D ... 978-468-7111.. 219 B
mwilliams@gcts.edu
WILLIAMS, Michelle, L .... 314-286-4863.. 270 G
mlwilliams@ranken.edu
WILLIAMS, Michelle, M .. 724-458-2216.. 404 F
mmwilliams@gcc.edu
WILLIAMS, Miriam .... 612-436-7541.. 248 F
mwilliams@msbcollege.edu
WILLIAMS, Miriam .... 612-436-7524.. 248 F
mwilliams@msbcollege.edu
WILLIAMS, Monica .... 313-993-1028.. 241 G
leonarmj@udmercy.edu
WILLIAMS, Murray .... 404-225-4545.. 117 A
mwilliams@atlantatech.edu
WILLIAMS, Myles .... 803-778-6643.. 427 G
williamsmh@cctech.edu
WILLIAMS, Nate .... 254-295-4696.. 474 E
nwilliams@umhb.edu
WILLIAMS, Nichelle .... 661-722-6300.... 27 B
nwilliams@avc.edu
WILLIAMS, Nicole .... 508-999-9208.. 220 H
nwilliams2@umassd.edu
WILLIAMS, Nicole .... 910-755-7391.. 347 H
williamsn@brunswickcc.edu
WILLIAMS, Nikisha .... 212-752-1530.. 318 F
nikisha.williams@limcollege.edu
WILLIAMS, Nikki .... 540-362-6639.. 490 F
nwilliams@hollins.edu
WILLIAMS, Owen .... 218-281-8395.. 255 E
owilliam@umn.edu
WILLIAMS, Pat .... 410-293-1881.. 529 D
pwilliam@usna.edu
WILLIAMS, Patricia .... 585-395-5118.. 332 E
pwilliam@brockport.edu
WILLIAMS, Patricia, A ..... 515-263-2912.. 172 H
pwilliams@grandview.edu
WILLIAMS, Patricia, R ..... 585-292-3026.. 321 J
pwilliams@monroecc.edu
WILLIAMS, Patti .... 912-583-3156.. 118 B
pwilliams@bpc.edu
WILLIAMS, Paul .... 229-391-4900.. 115 I
pwwilliams@abac.edu
WILLIAMS, Paul .... 804-330-0111.. 487 P
admdircrim@centura.edu
WILLIAMS, Paulita, N ...... 336-322-2170.. 351 H
tasha.williams@piedmontcc.edu
WILLIAMS, Peter .... 317-940-9700.. 159 K
williams@butler.edu
WILLIAMS, Philip, C .... 337-475-5556.. 200 H
pwilliams@mcneese.edu
WILLIAMS, Philip, M .... 315-733-2300.. 338 L
pwilliams@uscny.edu
WILLIAMS, Phillip, L .... 706-542-0939.. 128 E
pwilliam@uga.edu
WILLIAMS, Pilar .... 671-735-5590.. 529 G
pilar.williams@guamcc.edu
WILLIAMS, Priscilla .... 912-358-3132.. 126 F
williamsp@savannahstate.edu
WILLIAMS, Ramona, A .... 423-439-4219.. 444 F
ramona@etsu.edu
WILLIAMS, Randy .... 336-278-7243.. 344 D
rwilliams32@elon.edu
WILLIAMS, Rayanne .... 619-594-1686.... 35 A
william7@mail.sdsu.edu
WILLIAMS, Rich .... 775-674-7979.. 284 K
rwilliams@tmcc.edu
WILLIAMS, Richard .... 508-270-4013.. 223 F
rwilliams@massbay.edu
WILLIAMS, Richard .... 229-430-4754.. 115 K
richard.williams@asurams.edu
WILLIAMS, Richard .... 724-805-2084.. 419 A
richard.williams@stvincent.edu
WILLIAMS, Richard, B ..... 435-652-7502.. 482 A
president@dixie.edu
WILLIAMS, Rick .... 870-743-3000.... 21 C
rickw@northark.edu
WILLIAMS, Rick .... 336-316-2134.. 344 H
williamsrl@guilford.edu
WILLIAMS, Rick, E .... 909-558-4510.... 49 C
rwilliams@llu.edu
WILLIAMS, Rob .... 870-236-6901.... 20 A
rwilliams@crc.edu
WILLIAMS, Robert .... 310-825-8011.... 69 D
bwilliams@asucla.ucla.edu
WILLIAMS, Robert, F .... 920-832-6528.. 517 E
robert.f.williams@lawrence.edu
WILLIAMS, Robin .... 661-362-3240.... 40 A
robin.williams@canyons.edu
WILLIAMS, Ron .... 478-471-2490.. 124 E
ron.williams@mga.edu
WILLIAMS, Ron .... 575-562-2108.. 299 I
ron.williams@enmu.edu
WILLIAMS, Ron .... 915-747-7390.. 476 D
rwilliams@utep.edu
WILLIAMS, Ronald .... 309-298-1066.. 158 A
rc-williams@wiu.edu
WILLIAMS, Ronald, C ...... 309-298-1814.. 158 A
rc-williams@wiu.edu
WILLIAMS, Ronda, L .... 304-462-6430.. 513 C
ronda.williams@glenville.edu
WILLIAMS, Ronnie, D ...... 501-450-3416.... 24 G
ronniew@uca.edu
WILLIAMS, Rosemary .... 718-270-5104.. 309 B
rosemary@mec.cuny.edu
WILLIAMS, Russ .... 478-445-5650.. 121 A
russ.williams@gcsu.edu
WILLIAMS, Ruth .... 847-635-1686.. 150 G
rwilliams@oakton.edu
WILLIAMS, Ryan .... 845-569-3105.. 322 B
ryan.williams@msmc.edu
WILLIAMS, Ryan, A .... 309-624-9268.. 153 F
ryan.a.williams@osfhealthcare.org
WILLIAMS, Sabrina .... 252-335-3969.. 356 D
srwilliams@ecsu.edu
WILLIAMS, Sage .... 703-891-1787.. 494 H
WILLIAMS, Sanchia .... 954-492-5353.... 97 I
sawilliams@citycollege.edu
WILLIAMS, Sara .... 402-399-2467.. 279 E
swilliams@csm.edu
WILLIAMS, Sarah .... 540-868-7086.. 497 E
swilliams@lfcc.edu
WILLIAMS, Scott .... 270-686-4508.. 190 D
scott.willliams@kctcs.edu
WILLIAMS, Scott, E .... 276-944-6242.. 489 I
swilliams@ehc.edu
WILLIAMS, Scott, E .... 434-223-6164.. 490 D
swilliams@hsc.edu
WILLIAMS, Scott, K .... 315-733-2300.. 338 L
swilliams@uscny.edu
WILLIAMS, Scott, T .... 706-542-3375.. 128 E
scottw@uga.edu
WILLIAMS, Selase, W ...... 617-349-8518.. 220 B
williams@lesley.edu
WILLIAMS, Shane .... 601-484-8620.. 258 F
swilliam@meridiancc.edu
WILLIAMS, Shaun .... 817-515-5154.. 467 A
shaun.williams@tccd.edu
WILLIAMS, Shaundria .... 307-382-1832.. 527 C
slwilliams@westernwyoming.edu
WILLIAMS, Sheila .... 404-526-9366.. 126 D
s.williams@sae.edu
WILLIAMS, Shelitha .... 585-262-1665.. 321 J
swilliams@monroecc.edu
WILLIAMS, Sheree .... 502-213-2156.. 190 A
sheree.williams@kctcs.edu
WILLIAMS, Sherry .... 828-327-7000.. 348 C
swilliams@cvcc.edu
WILLIAMS, Shirley, J .... 610-796-8340.. 397 D
shirley.williams@alvernia.edu
WILLIAMS, Sonya .... 315-781-3312.. 316 C
swilliams@hws.edu
WILLIAMS, Sonya .... 405-682-1611.. 385 D
swilliams@occc.edu
WILLIAMS, Sophia .... 414-297-6288.. 524 A
wills12@matc.edu
WILLIAMS, Stelfanie .... 252-492-2061.. 353 H
swilliams@vgcc.edu
WILLIAMS, Stephen .... 414-277-7114.. 518 E
williams@msoe.edu
WILLIAMS, Stephen, R .... 419-755-4811.. 373 G
swilliam@ncstatecollege.edu
WILLIAMS, Steve .... 256-840-4174...... 6 H
swilliams@snead.edu
WILLIAMS, Sue .... 360-992-2619.. 502 E
swilliams@clark.edu
WILLIAMS, Susan .... 304-255-0793.. 513 A
swilliams@concord.edu
WILLIAMS, Susan .... 626-650-2306.... 45 E
WILLIAMS, Susan .... 828-448-3178.. 354 B
swilliams@wpcc.edu
WILLIAMS, Susan .... 919-760-8262.. 346 D
williams@meredith.edu
WILLIAMS, Susan, D .... 828-694-1824.. 347 G
susanw@blueridge.edu
WILLIAMS, Susan, D .... 203-576-4651.... 89 C
swilliams@bridgeport.edu
WILLIAMS, Susan, L .... 302-831-8436.... 91 F
susanlyn@udel.edu
WILLIAMS, Suzanne .... 213-477-2861.... 53 B
swilliams@msmu.edu
WILLIAMS, Sylvia, R .... 843-953-5333.. 428 A
swilli22@citadel.edu
WILLIAMS, Tamara .... 704-330-4119.. 348 E
tamara.williams@cpcc.edu
WILLIAMS, Tamara, R ...... 253-531-7203.. 505 G
williatr@plu.edu
WILLIAMS, Tara, A .... 336-633-0279.. 352 B
tawil@randolph.edu
WILLIAMS, Tasha .... 312-850-7120.. 138 A
tholmes@ccc.edu
WILLIAMS, Teresa .... 615-966-1788.. 441 F
teresa.williams@lipscomb.edu
WILLIAMS, Teresa, G ...... 704-233-8210.. 359 H
tgwilliams@wingate.edu
WILLIAMS, Terrence .... 610-409-3719.. 422 D
twilliams@ursinus.edu
WILLIAMS, Terria, C .... 803-535-5720.. 428 B
twilliams@claflin.edu
WILLIAMS, Teyanna .... 818-240-1000.... 45 A
twilliams@glendale.edu
WILLIAMS, Thomas .... 630-512-8867.. 136 G
twilliams@devrygroup.com
WILLIAMS, Tiffany .... 757-455-3242.. 500 E
twilliams2@vwc.edu
WILLIAMS, Tiffany, S ...... 816-235-5599.. 273 F
williamsti@umkc.edu
WILLIAMS, Tim .... 618-985-3741.. 143 F
timwilliams@jalc.edu
WILLIAMS, Tim .... 502-895-3411.. 191 F
twilliams@lpts.edu
WILLIAMS, Todd, J .... 215-702-4861.. 399 E
president@cairn.edu
WILLIAMS, Tom .... 318-678-6000.. 195 I
twilliams@bpcc.edu
WILLIAMS, Tommy .... 979-458-6040.. 467 D
twilliams@tamus.edu
WILLIAMS, Tonjua, L .... 727-341-3344.. 108 D
williams.tonjua@spcollege.edu
WILLIAMS, Tonya .... 706-396-7591.. 125 H
tjwilliams@paine.edu
WILLIAMS, Traci, N .... 423-746-5213.. 447 E
twilliams@twcnet.edu
WILLIAMS, Tracy .... 651-523-2651.. 247 A
twilliams05@hamline.edu
WILLIAMS, Tracy, S .... 229-430-4654.. 115 K
tracy.williams@asurams.edu
WILLIAMS, Travis .... 707-826-5038.... 34 F
tjw17@humboldt.edu
WILLIAMS, Trayce .... 302-857-6050.... 90 F
twilliams@desu.edu
WILLIAMS, Treby .... 609-258-7097.. 294 D
trebyw@princeton.edu
WILLIAMS, Trudy .... 412-392-8085.. 417 F
twilliams@pointpark.edu
WILLIAMS, Trysta .... 785-320-4565.. 183 A
trystawilliams@manhattantech.edu
WILLIAMS, Tyler, R .... 208-496-1301.. 132 J
williamst@byui.edu
WILLIAMS, Valerie .... 229-430-3867.. 116 A
vwilliams@albanytech.edu
WILLIAMS, Vaughn, A ...... 470-578-6284.. 123 J
vwilliam@kennesaw.edu
WILLIAMS, Vernon .... 703-284-5796.. 492 A
vernon.williams@marymount.edu
WILLIAMS, Vicki .... 501-492-0570.... 18 F
vicki.williams@arkansasbaptist.edu
WILLIAMS, Vickie .... 907-796-6363.... 10 H
vlwilliams@alaska.edu
WILLIAMS, Vickie .... 334-214-4803...... 2 H
vickie.williams@cv.edu
WILLIAMS, Victoria .... 870-972-2054.... 18 J
vrwilliams@astate.edu
WILLIAMS, Victoria .... 610-796-5511.. 397 D
victoria.williams@alvernia.edu
WILLIAMS, Virginia, M .... 530-221-4275.... 64 C
vwilliams@shasta.edu
WILLIAMS, Walter .... 518-587-2100.. 335 D
walter.williams@esc.edu
WILLIAMS, Wendi .... 212-875-4547.. 304 E
WILLIAMS, Wendy, E .... 843-953-5506.. 428 G
williamsw@cofc.edu
WILLIAMS, Willie .... 402-449-2924.. 280 C
wwilliams4931@graceu.edu
WILLIAMS, Winifred .... 312-915-6175.. 146 G
wwilliams5@luc.edu
WILLIAMS, Yolanda .... 763-488-2731.. 249 D
yolanda.williams@hennepintech.edu
WILLIAMS DANDRIDGE,
Gwen .... 804-524-5583.. 499 G
gdandridge@vsu.edu
WILLIAMS-DYER,
Sharon, M .... 781-891-2000.. 215 F
swilliamsdyer@bentley.edu
WILLIAMS-GOLDSTEIN,
Brittany, A .... 201-684-7609.. 294 G
bwilla1@ramapo.edu
WILLIAMS-HARMON,
Arlitha .... 559-791-2374.... 47 L
arlitha.williams@portervillecollege.edu
WILLIAMS LESSANE,
Patricia .... 843-953-7234.. 428 G
lessanepw@cofc.edu
WILLIAMS LOSTON,
Adena .... 210-486-2900.. 450 E
aloston@alamo.edu
WILLIAMS LOSTON,
Adena .... 210-486-2900.. 450 A
aloston@alamo.edu
WILLIAMS-PEREZ,
Kendra .... 319-226-2040.. 169 D
kendra.williams-perez@allencollege.edu
WILLIAMS RUSHIN,
Palisa .... 859-246-6522.. 189 B
palisa.rushin@kctcs.edu
WILLIAMS-SOWERS,
Kelly .... 334-291-4921...... 2 H
kelly.williams@cv.edu
WILLIAMS-THOMAS,
Tafflyn .... 503-552-1625.. 392 H
twiliams-thomas@nunm.edu
WILLIAMS-THOMPSON,
Phyllis .... 413-265-2262.. 217 D
williamsthompsonp@elms.edu
WILLIAMSON, Angela .... 417-690-2208.. 263 E
awilliamson@cofo.edu
WILLIAMSON, Betty .... 860-215-9260.... 87 D
bwilliamson@trcc.commnet.edu
WILLIAMSON, Bob .... 360-992-2123.. 502 E
bwilliamson@clark.edu
WILLIAMSON, Brad .... 757-443-6200.. 528 B
brad.williamson@ndu.edu
WILLIAMSON, Carla .... 919-658-7749.. 355 K
cwilliamson@umo.edu
WILLIAMSON, Carol .... 641-628-7667.. 170 E
williamsonc@central.edu
WILLIAMSON, Cathy .... 641-673-1700.. 177 J
williamsonc@wmpenn.edu
WILLIAMSON, Celia .... 940-565-4961.. 475 A
celia@unt.edu
WILLIAMSON, David .... 601-266-1000.. 261 E
david.williamson@usm.edu
WILLIAMSON, Dean .... 936-261-2188.. 467 E
cdwilliamson@pvamu.edu
WILLIAMSON, Emily .... 406-657-2188.. 277 D
emily.williamson@msubillings.edu
WILLIAMSON, George .... 619-849-2610..... 57 M
georgewilliamson@pointloma.edu
WILLIAMSON, JR.,
Harold, A .... 573-882-5606.. 273 E
williamsonh@health.missouri.edu
WILLIAMSON, Heather ...... 866-931-4300.. 270 I
heather.williamson@rockbridge.edu
WILLIAMSON, Hilda .... 757-727-5251.. 490 E
hilda.williamson@hamptonu.edu
WILLIAMSON, James .... 919-807-6951.. 347 B
williamsonj@nccommunitycolleges.edu
WILLIAMSON, James, E .. 706-542-5813.. 128 E
jwilliamson@police.uga.edu
WILLIAMSON, James, R .. 858-784-8469.... 64 B
gradprgm@scripps.edu
WILLIAMSON, Jane, K .... 901-334-5812.. 442 C
jwilliamson@memphisseminary.edu
WILLIAMSON, Jeff .... 507-372-3408.. 250 G
jeff.williamson@mnwest.edu
WILLIAMSON, Jennifer ..... 610-921-7700.. 396 H
jwilliamson@albright.edu
WILLIAMSON, Joann .... 803-641-3473.. 433 G
joannw@usca.edu
WILLIAMSON, Jon .... 214-648-1500.. 478 C
jon.williamson@utsouthwestern.edu

WILSON, Jamelle .... 804-289-8428.. 495 G
jwilson9@richmond.edu
WILSON, JR., James, D .. 302-295-1194.... 91 I
jim.d.wilson@wilmu.edu
WILSON, JR., James, J .. 936-261-2175.. 467 E
jjwilson@pvamu.edu
WILSON, JR., James, J .. 936-261-5256.. 467 E
jjwilson@pvamu.edu
WILSON, Jamie, B .... 601-974-1070.. 258 H
wilsojb@millsaps.edu
WILSON, Jan .... 316-295-5824.. 181 B
jan_wilson@friends.edu
WILSON, JD .... 901-381-3939.. 449 F
jd@visible.edu
WILSON, Jeff .... 615-966-7617.. 441 F
jeff.wilson@lipscomb.edu
WILSON, Jeffrey, G .... 512-505-3030.. 459 F
jwilson@htu.edu
WILSON, Jim .... 641-844-5550.. 173 J
jim.wilson@iavalley.edu
WILSON, Jo .... 252-577-6223.. 350 H
djwilson45@lenoircc.edu
WILSON, Jocelyn, M .... 516-671-2215.. 339 G
WILSON, Jocelyn, M .... 516-671-2215.. 339 G
jwilson@webb.edu
WILSON, John .... 504-816-4723.. 195 B
jwilson@dillard.edu
WILSON, John .... 254-710-3457.. 452 H
john_wilson@baylor.edu
WILSON, John .... 212-217-4200.. 314 B
john_wilsonn@fitnyc.edu
WILSON, John .... 706-867-2844.. 128 F
john.wilson@ung.edu
WILSON, John .... 843-863-7102.. 427 I
jewilson@csuniv.edu
WILSON, John, R .... 804-278-4330.. 494 N
jwilson@upsem.edu
WILSON, JR., John, S .... 404-215-2645.. 124 I
WILSON, Jonathan .... 601-984-1010.. 261 C
jwilson5@umc.edu
WILSON, Josh .... 706-272-2473.. 119 H
jwilson@daltonstate.edu
WILSON, Josh .... 870-368-2027.... 21 F
josh.wilson@ozarka.edu
WILSON, Joshua .... 641-472-1190.. 175 A
alumni@mum.edu
WILSON, Judge .... 859-985-3131.. 187 B
judge_wilson@berea.edu
WILSON, Julie .... 307-778-1218.. 526 K
jwilson@lccc.wy.edu
WILSON, Karen .... 213-615-7231.... 37 I
karenwilson@thechicagoschool.edu
WILSON, Kathi .... 865-981-8211.. 441 H
kathi.wilson@maryvillecollege.edu
WILSON, Kathryn .... 585-395-2137.. 332 E
kwilson@brockport.edu
WILSON, Kathy, A .... 863-638-2930.. 115 D
wilsonka@webber.edu
WILSON, Katie .... 864-225-7653.. 430 A
katiewilson@forrestcollege.edu
WILSON, Keisha .... 704-330-1455.. 345 E
kwilson@jcsu.edu
WILSON, Kelly .... 417-625-9363.. 268 H
wilson-k@mssu.edu
WILSON, Kelly .... 740-264-5591.. 368 D
kwilson@egcc.edu
WILSON, Kenneth .... 912-358-4166.. 126 F
wilsonk@savannahstate.edu
WILSON, Kenny .... 636-481-3356.. 266 C
kwilso20@jeffco.edu
WILSON, Kevin .... 570-945-8376.. 406 H
kevin.wilson@keystone.edu
WILSON, Kimberly, M ..... 540-224-4313.. 491 A
kmwilson@jchs.edu
WILSON, Kimberly, P ...... 859-257-4751.. 193 G
kwilson@email.uky.edu
WILSON, Kristina .... 956-872-5583.. 465 H
kmwilson@southtexascollege.edu
WILSON, Kyla .... 773-907-4443.. 137 E
kwilson@ccc.edu
WILSON, LaDrina .... 563-441-4016.. 172 D
lnwilson@eicc.edu
WILSON, Larry, L .... 972-860-7218.. 456 D
larrywilson@dcccd.edu
WILSON, Laura, J .... 410-778-7849.. 213 E
lwilson3@washcoll.edu
WILSON, Laura, L .... 650-723-9633.... 66 I
laura.wilson@stanford.edu
WILSON, Leon, C .... 334-229-5176...... 1 D
lwilson@alasu.edu
WILSON, Leslie, K .... 319-273-6240.. 170 A
leslie.wilson@uni.edu
WILSON, LeVon, E .... 404-880-6042.. 118 K
lwilson@cau.edu
WILSON, Lisa .... 478-825-6253.. 120 F
wilsonl@fvsu.edu
WILSON, Lizabeth, A .... 206-543-1760.. 508 E
betsyw@uw.edu
WILSON, Lori, J .... 570-577-3334.. 398 L
lwilson@bucknell.edu
WILSON, Lucy, P .... 478-301-2460.. 124 D
wilson_l@mercer.edu
WILSON, Lynn .... 863-669-2898.. 106 I
lwilson@polk.edu
WILSON, Lynn, Y .... 715-836-5521.. 520 A
wilsonly@uwec.edu
WILSON, M. Roy .... 313-577-2230.. 243 F
president@wayne.edu
WILSON, Maleta .... 504-865-3262.. 198 E
mawilson@loyno.edu
WILSON, Marcus .... 806-743-6443.. 472 D
marcus.wilson@ttuhsc.edu
WILSON, Mardell .... 314-977-8500.. 271 K
wilsonma@slu.edu
WILSON, Margaret .... 660-626-2354.. 262 A
mwilson@atsu.edu
WILSON, Mark .... 605-995-3024.. 436 C
mark.wilson@mitchelltech.edu
WILSON, Mark .... 931-372-3961.. 445 B
mwilson@tntech.edu
WILSON, Mark .... 423-472-7141.. 445 E
mwilson@clevelandstatecc.edu
WILSON, Martha .... 207-221-4514.. 205 F
mwilson13@une.edu
WILSON, Mary .... 931-598-1381.. 443 O
mewilson@sewanee.edu
WILSON, Maryrose .... 301-846-2436.. 207 F
mwilson@frederick.edu
WILSON, Matthew .... 734-462-4400.. 240 H
mwilson@schoolcraft.edu
WILSON, Matthew, J .... 330-972-7869.. 378 G
mjwilson@uakron.edu
WILSON, Megan .... 307-754-6031.. 526 N
megan.wilson@nwc.edu
WILSON, Melanie .... 218-335-4280.. 247 F
melanie.wilson@lltc.edu
WILSON, Melanie .... 865-974-2521.. 448 E
WILSON, Michael, D .... 714-556-3610.... 73 B
mdwilson@vanguard.edu
WILSON, Michele .... 304-424-8355.. 514 D
michele.wilson@wvup.edu
WILSON, Michelle .... 870-633-4480.... 20 B
rwilson@eacc.edu
WILSON, Mike .... 864-294-3464.. 430 C
mike.wilsont@furman.edu
WILSON, Mindy .... 518-743-2252.. 335 A
wilsonm@sunyacc.edu
WILSON, Monett .... 207-453-5123.. 203 K
mwilson@kvcc.me.edu
WILSON, Monica .... 304-434-8000.. 512 A
monica.wilson@easternwv.edu
WILSON, Natalie, L .... 412-578-6171.. 400 C
wilsonnl@carlow.edu
WILSON, Neyle .... 843-349-5201.. 430 F
neyle.wilson@hgtc.edu
WILSON, Pam .... 940-898-3503.. 472 G
pwilson@twu.edu
WILSON, Pamala, P .... 270-831-9649.. 189 F
pamala.wilson@kctcs.edu
WILSON, Patricia .... 205-391-2290...... 6 G
pwilson@sheltonstate.edu
WILSON, Patricia .... 256-306-2743...... 2 F
patricia.wilson@calhoun.edu
WILSON, Patrick .... 615-366-3917.. 444 D
patrick.wilson@tbr.edu
WILSON, Patrick .... 931-372-3224.. 445 B
pwilson@tntech.edu
WILSON, Paul, S .... 434-971-3301.. 527 N
paul.s.wilson4.mil@mail.mil
WILSON, Peggy, M .... 865-694-6403.. 446 G
pwilson@pstcc.edu
WILSON, Perry, T .... 843-661-1486.. 430 B
pwilson@fmarion.edu
WILSON, Phillip .... 479-394-7622.... 22 B
pwilson@rmcc.edu
WILSON, Piper .... 417-477-7428.. 270 A
wilsonp@otc.edu
WILSON, Qiana .... 478-445-2037.. 121 A
qiana.wilson@gcsu.edu
WILSON, Regina .... 574-284-5382.. 167 A
rwilson@saintmarys.edu
WILSON, Robert, H .... 512-471-8947.. 476 B
rwilson@austin.utexas.edu
WILSON, Roger .... 425-889-5336.. 505 E
roger.wilson@northwestu.edu
WILSON, Ronalyn .... 518-736-3622.. 315 A
rwilson@fmcc.suny.edu
WILSON, Rowena, G .... 757-823-8668.. 492 F
rgwilson@nsu.edu
WILSON, Ryan .... 989-328-1245.. 238 D
ryan.wilson@montcalm.edu
WILSON, Sandra .... 313-664-7471.. 232 G
sandra@collegeforcreativestudies.edu
WILSON, Scott .... 651-846-1694.. 252 C
scott.wilson@saintpaul.edu
WILSON, Scott .... 931-598-1173.. 443 O
swilson@sewanee.edu
WILSON, Scott, L .... 641-269-3500.. 172 I
wilsons@grinnell.edu
WILSON, Shain .... 205-853-1200...... 5 B
swilson@jeffstateonline.com
WILSON, Shawn .... 989-964-7090.. 240 F
swilson@svsu.edu
WILSON, Sheila .... 252-399-6309.. 341 P
spwilson@barton.edu
WILSON, Shelli .... 843-383-8082.. 428 F
swilson@coker.edu
WILSON, Sherry .... 828-726-2306.. 347 I
swilson@cccti.edu
WILSON, Sherwood, G .... 540-231-4416.. 499 F
sgwilson@vt.edu
WILSON, Shirley .... 213-624-1200.... 43 J
swilson@fidm.edu
WILSON, Sonali, B .... 216-687-3860.. 366 I
s.b.wilson@csuohio.edu
WILSON, Stacey .... 704-403-1639.. 342 E
stacey.wilson@carolinashealthcare.org
WILSON, Stanley .... 954-262-1266.. 105 J
swilson@nova.edu
WILSON, Stephan, M ...... 405-744-9805.. 385 G
stephan.m.wilson@okstate.edu
WILSON, Stephen .... 478-445-5331.. 121 A
steve.wilson@gcsu.edu
WILSON, Susan .... 816-235-6704.. 273 F
wilsonsb2@umkc.edu
WILSON, Susan, A .... 802-322-1641.. 483 H
susan.wilson@goddard.edu
WILSON, Sylvia .... 573-681-6107.. 266 I
wilsons@lincolnu.edu
WILSON, Ted, H .... 270-707-3865.. 189 G
ted.wilson@kctcs.edu
WILSON, Terez .... 901-321-3254.. 439 E
twilso22@cbu.edu
WILSON, Thalia .... 901-333-5112.. 447 B
twilson@southwest.tn.edu
WILSON, Tiffany .... 803-778-6668.. 427 G
wilsontd@cctech.edu
WILSON, Timothy, B .... 805-565-6038.... 75 A
twilson@westmont.edu
WILSON, Tommy .... 706-649-1894.. 119 F
twilson@columbustech.edu
WILSON, Tony .... 336-725-8344.. 354 G
wilsont@piedmontu.edu
WILSON, Tracy .... 651-403-4118.. 252 C
tracy.wilson@saintpaul.edu
WILSON, Travis .... 606-539-4002.. 193 F
WILSON, Tressey, D .... 936-361-1700.. 467 E
tdwilson@pvamu.edu
WILSON, Valeri .... 619-660-4221.... 45 I
valeri.wilson@gcccd.edu
WILSON, Valerie .... 870-574-4514.... 22 G
vwilson@sautech.edu
WILSON, Valvia .... 601-977-7844.. 261 A
vwilson@tougaloo.edu
WILSON, Vicki .... 724-852-3375.. 423 A
vwilson@waynesburg.edu
WILSON, Victor, K .... 706-542-3564.. 128 E
wilsonv@uga.edu
WILSON, W. Chandler ..... 503-255-0332.. 392 G
chandlerwilson@multnomah.edu
WILSON, Warren .... 605-642-6930.. 437 B
warren.wilson@bhsu.edu
WILSON, Wendy .... 229-430-5217.. 115 K
wendy.wilson@asurams.edu
WILSON, Wendy .... 713-221-8568.. 474 B
wilsonwe@uhd.edu
WILSON, Wes .... 404-627-2681.. 117 G
wes.wilson@beulah.edu
WILSON, William .... 859-341-4867.. 193 C
wilsonw@thomasmore.edu
WILSON, William .... 423-354-2541.. 446 F
wrwilson@northeaststate.edu
WILSON, William .... 216-687-4686.. 366 I
william.wilson@csuohio.edu
WILSON, William, M .... 918-495-6175.. 386 H
president@oru.edu
WILSON, Yolanda .... 803-327-8021.. 435 D
ywilson@yorktech.edu
WILSON, Zaphon .... 919-516-4280.. 355 D
zrwilson@st-aug.edu
WILSON-BARNES, Yvette . 212-280-1396.. 338 I
ywilson@uts.columbia.edu
WILSON-FENNELL,
Nicole .... 734-462-4400.. 240 H
nwilson@schoolcraft.edu
WILSON-PORTER, Cyndi . 210-829-2706.. 474 D
porter@uiwtx.edu
WILSON-TAYLOR,
Sharon .... 312-369-7221.. 138 F
swilson-taylor@colum.edu
WILT, Darrell .... 717-815-1288.. 424 F
dwilt1@ycp.edu
WILT, Jason .... 269-783-2159.. 241 C
jwilt@swmich.edu
WILT, Richard, W .... 610-799-1164.. 408 G
rwilt@lccc.edu
WILT, Valerie .... 386-481-2004.... 96 H
collmanv@cookman.edu
WILTENMUTH, III,
John, P .... 540-654-1047.. 495 C
jwiltenm@umw.edu
WILTGEN, JR., Jim .... 501-450-1222.... 20 F
wiltgen@hendrix.edu
WILTROUT, Deborah .... 239-590-1089.. 110 L
dwiltrout@fgcu.edu
WILTSCHEK, Walt .... 260-982-5243.. 165 M
wjwiltschek@manchester.edu
WILTSE, Mary Alane .... 518-828-4181.. 311 D
wiltse@sunycgcc.edu
WILTSHIRE, Rolly .... 718-289-5186.. 307 C
rolly.wiltshire@bcc.cuny.edu
WILTZIUS, Pierre .... 805-893-5024.... 70 E
mlpsdean@ltsc.ucsb.edu
WIMBERLEY,
Bernadette, H .... 302-225-6312.... 91 D
wimberlb@gbc.edu
WIMBERLEY, Carrie .... 478-471-2712.. 124 E
carrie.wimberley@mga.edu
WIMBERLY, Chuck .... 478-289-2036.. 120 C
cwimberly@ega.edu
WIMBERLY, Frances .... 706-396-7596.. 125 H
fwimberly@paine.edu
WIMBERLY, Joan, M .... 805-565-6055.... 75 A
jwimberly@westmont.edu
WIMBERLY, Yvette .... 501-420-1249.... 18 F
yvette.wimberly@arkansasbaptist.edu
WIMBISH, Jennifer, L ...... 972-860-8251.. 456 C
jwimbish@dcccd.edu
WIMBUSH, James .... 812-856-5700.. 162 E
jwimbush@indiana.edu
WIMBUSH, James .... 812-855-2739.. 162 F
jwimbush@iu.edu
WIMBUSH, James .... 812-855-2739.. 162 F
jwimbush@indiana.edu
WIMER, Jodie .... 304-358-2000.. 510 J
jwimer@future.edu
WIMER, Valinda .... 386-822-8850.. 113 B
vwimer@stetson.edu
WIMS, Daniel, K .... 256-372-5275...... 1 A
daniel.wims@aamu.edu
WIMS, Lois, A .... 508-929-8038.. 222 F
lwims@worcester.edu
WINANS, Bill .... 940-668-3353.. 462 L
bwinans@nctc.edu
WINANT, Richard .... 718-270-7411.. 332 B
richard.winant@downstate.edu
WINBORNE, Malverne ..... 734-487-2086.. 233 J
mwinborne@emich.edu
WINCHELL, Barbara .... 845-569-3298.. 322 B
barbara.winchell@msmc.edu
WINCHESTER, Linda .... 207-454-1033.. 204 A
lwinchester@wccc.me.edu
WINCHESTER, Paul .... 316-295-5836.. 181 B
winchp@friends.edu
WINCHESTER, Samuel ...... 919-573-5350.. 355 G
WINCHESTER, Sara .... 732-255-0400.. 293 E
swinchester@ocean.edu
WINCKELMAN, Stephen .. 952-358-8597.. 251 A
stephen.winckelman@normandale.edu
WINCOWSKI, Joel .... 207-581-1619.. 204 H
joel.wincowski@maine.edu
WINDER, Katie .... 541-917-4547.. 392 C
winderk@linnbenton.edu
WINDER, Mark .... 319-895-4518.. 171 A
mwinder@cornellcollege.edu
WINDERL, James .... 845-434-5750.. 336 H
jwinderl@sullivan.suny.edu
WINDERS, Tim .... 219-989-2417.. 166 F
winders@pnw.edu
WINDHAM, Ana, M .... 210-999-7306.. 473 A
awindham@trinity.edu
WINDHAM, Don .... 772-462-7357.. 103 B
dwindham@irsc.edu
WINDHAM, Greg .... 662-720-7210.. 260 B
jgwindham@nemcc.edu
WINDHAM, Jameka .... 216-373-5287.. 374 B
jwindham@ndc.edu
WINDHAM, John .... 731-661-5006.. 448 A
jwindham@uu.edu
WINDHOLZ, Kevin .... 405-208-5600.. 385 E
kwindholz@okcu.edu
WINDHOLZ, Mindy .... 405-208-7902.. 385 E
mbwindholz@okcu.edu
WINDLE, Frank, H .... 215-871-6750.. 416 F
frankwi@pcom.edu
WINDLE, Lawrence, B ...... 956-380-8100.. 464 F
lwindle@riogrande.edu
WINDLE, Ruth .... 956-380-8183.. 464 F
psecretary@riogrande.edu
WINDROW, Vincent .... 615-898-2338.. 444 G
vincent.windrow@mtsu.edu
WINE IMBLER, Toni .... 918-270-6412.. 386 I
toni.imbler@ptstulsa.edu
WINEBRAKE, James, J ...... 585-475-2447.. 327 E
jjwgpt@rit.edu
WINEGARD, Kathryn .... 660-248-6210.. 263 B
kwinegar@centralmethodist.edu
WINEGARD, Tanya, C .... 402-280-2775.. 279 H
tanyawinegard@creighton.edu
WINEGARDEN, Daniel, J . 641-422-4191.. 175 E
winegdan@niacc.edu

WITHERS, Stacie ... 816-995-2832.. 270 H
stacie.withers@researchcollege.edu

WITHERSPOON, Alanna, S ... 312-850-7031.. 138 A
awitherspoon5@ccc.edu

WITHERSPOON, Collin, C ... 806-371-5142.. 450 H
ccwitherspoon@actx.edu

WITHERSPOON, Everette, L ... 336-750-2131.. 359 B
witherspoone@wssu.edu

WITHERSPOON, Karen ... 212-650-6400.. 307 E
kwitherspoon@ccny.cuny.edu

WITHERSPOON, Patricia .. 915-747-7018.. 476 D
withersp@utep.edu

WITHERUP, Philip ... 570-321-4220.. 409 F
witherup@lycoming.edu

WITHROW, Amy, S ... 717-221-1303.. 405 C
aswithro@hacc.edu

WITHROW, Lisa ... 740-362-3343.. 372 D
lwithrow@mtso.edu

WITHUS, George ... 701-858-4444.. 360 F
george.withus@minotstateu.edu

WITKEN, David ... 708-209-3625.. 138 G
david.witken@cuchicago.edu

WITKOVSKY, Lowell, D ... 814-641-3360.. 406 F
witkovl@juniata.edu

WITMER, Kenneth, D ... 610-436-2321.. 416 C
kwitmer@wcupa.edu

WITMER, Timothy, Z ... 215-572-3831.. 423 C
twitmer@wts.edu

WITRYK, Ted ... 610-683-4822.. 415 C
witryk@kutztown.edu

WITT, Allen ... 813-259-6151.. 102 R
awitt3@hccfl.edu

WITT, Betsy, A ... 864-488-8288.. 430 H
bwitt@limestone.edu

WITT, Don, E ... 859-257-3458.. 193 G
dwitt@email.uky.edu

WITT, Jack ... 567-661-7314.. 376 D
fjwitt@owens.edu

WITT, Karla ... 605-455-6001.. 436 G
kwitt@olc.edu

WITT, Linda ... 615-327-6724.. 442 A
lwitt@mmc.edu

WITT, Marie, D ... 215-898-1199.. 421 E
witt@upenn.edu

WITT, Ron, A ... 304-336-8844.. 513 F
wittron@westliberty.edu

WITT, Tiffanie ... 270-824-8575.. 190 B
tiffanie.witt@kctcs.edu

WITTE, Bob ... 417-626-1234.. 269 K
witte.bob@occ.edu

WITTE, Dennis, E ... 708-209-3205.. 138 G
dennis.witte@cuchicago.edu

WITTE, John ... 616-526-6547.. 232 A
jwitte@calvin.edu

WITTE, Kevin ... 360-992-2356.. 502 E
kwitte@clark.edu

WITTE, Lois, J ... 417-667-8181.. 264 A
lwitte@cottey.edu

WITTE, III, Paul, R ... 616-526-7920.. 232 A
prw3@calvin.edu

WITTE, Peter, T ... 816-235-2731.. 273 F
wittep@umkc.edu

WITTE, Sandra ... 559-278-2448.... 32 F

WITTE, Sarah ... 541-962-3511.. 391 C
switte@eou.edu

WITTENBERG, Diane ... 626-396-2326.... 27 L
diane.wittenberg@artcenter.edu

WITTENMYER, Kathryn ... 415-503-6223.... 61 C
klw@sfcm.edu

WITTER, Kevin, G ... 540-857-7341.. 499 B
kwitter@virginiawestern.edu

WITTER, Pamela ... 716-827-4344.. 338 E
witterp@trocaire.edu

WITTER, Terry ... 903-877-7704.. 477 E
terry.witter@uthct.edu

WITTGENFELD, Tania ... 773-291-6359.. 137 G
twittgenfeld@ccc.edu

WITTHOFT, Andrea ... 618-437-5321.. 152 A
witthoft@rlc.edu

WITTIE, Roger ... 254-968-0526.. 467 F
wittie@tarleton.edu

WITTIG, William ... 313-993-1532.. 241 G
wittigw@udmercy.edu

WITTLER, Kim ... 301-369-2800.. 206 H
kwittler@captechu.edu

WITTLER, Michele, A ... 920-748-8119.. 519 E
wittlerm@ripon.edu

WITTMAN, William ... 301-295-3185.. 528 G
william.wittman@usuhs.edu

WITTMANN-PRICE, Ruth, A ... 843-661-4625.. 430 B
rwittmannprice@fmarion.edu

WITTNER, Charity ... 251-442-2507...... 9 A
cwittner@umobile.edu

WITTROCK, David, A ... 701-231-7033.. 361 A
david.wittrock@ndsu.edu

WITTROCK, Monica ... 920-403-3146.. 519 G
monica.wittrock@snc.edu

WITTSTEIN, Bob ... 781-891-2005.. 215 F
bwittstein@bentley.edu

WITTSTRUCK, Clifford ... 307-382-1714.. 527 C
cwittstruck@westernwyoming.edu

WITTY, Janeen ... 803-705-4761.. 427 D
wittyj@benedict.edu

WITZ, MaryJo, A ... 585-292-2188.. 321 J
mwitz@monroecc.edu

WITZEL, Stephanie ... 707-668-5663.... 42 C

WIXSOM, Richard ... 413-236-3003.. 222 G
rwixsom@berkshirecc.edu

WNUK, Beth ... 414-930-3332.. 518 F
wnukb@mtmary.edu

WOBBE, Michelle ... 314-918-2599.. 265 A
mwobbe@eden.edu

WOBBY, Lauren ... 802-485-2040.. 484 H
laurenw@norwich.edu

WOBIG, Jayne ... 507-457-1438.. 254 O
jwobig@smumn.edu

WOBSCHALL, Rachel, A .. 651-962-6992.. 256 C
rawobschall@stthomas.edu

WOCHOK, Lauren ... 610-989-1257.. 422 E
lwochok@vfmac.edu

WODKA, Chris ... 520-494-5230.... 12 J
chris.wodka@centralaz.edu

WOEBKENBERG, Eric ... 610-499-4090.. 423 E
eewoebkenberg@widener.edu

WOEF, Paul ... 317-578-7353.. 158 F

WOELKERS, Joseph, F ... 903-877-7750.. 477 E
joseph.woelkers@uthct.edu

WOELL, John ... 517-629-0222.. 230 E
jwoell@albion.edu

WOERDEHOFF, Valorie, A ... 563-588-7565.. 174 K
valorie.woerdehoff@loras.edu

WOGAN, Maureen ... 773-298-3010.. 153 H
wogan@sxu.edu

WOGEN, Brian, M ... 641-422-4177.. 175 E
wogenbri@niacc.edu

WOHL, David ... 803-323-2323.. 435 B
wohld@winthrop.edu

WOHL, James ... 860-486-5143.... 89 D
jim.wohl@uconn.edu

WOHLERT, Amy ... 505-277-1092.. 302 F
awohlert@unm.edu

WOHLETZ, Dale ... 318-357-5581.. 201 B
wohletz@nsula.edu

WOHLFORD, Corinne ... 314-889-1401.. 265 C
cwohlford@fontbonne.edu

WOHLMAN, Jason, L ... 530-752-9793.... 69 A
jlwohlman@ucdavis.edu

WOHLMAN, Katie ... 828-328-7699.. 345 H
katie.wohlman@lr.edu

WOHLPART, A. James ... 319-273-2566.. 170 A
jim.wohlpart@uni.edu

WOHLSTEIN, Melissa ... 540-831-5407.. 493 A
mwohlstein@radford.edu

WOIKE, David ... 734-487-0076.. 233 J
dwoike@emich.edu

WOITOWITZ, Chris ... 417-455-5712.. 264 E
cwoitowitz@crowder.edu

WOIWODE, Kristin ... 309-672-5513.. 147 H
kwoiwode@methodistcol.edu

WOJAK, Angie ... 212-592-2000.. 330 C
awojak@sva.edu

WOJCIECHOWSKI, Keli ... 708-524-6827.. 139 F
kallen@dom.edu

WOJCIECHOWSKI, Thomas ... 716-839-8585.. 312 D
twoj@daemen.edu

WOJCIK, Alketa ... 760-757-2121.... 52 K
awojcik@miracosta.edu

WOJKE, Katie ... 360-491-4700.. 506 G
kwojke@stmartin.edu

WOJNAS, Sherry ... 315-801-8206.. 328 C
swojnas@secon.edu

WOJNOWSKI, Jeffrey ... 414-456-7106.. 518 A
jwojnows@mcw.edu

WOJNOWSKI, Mark, E ... 716-286-9718.. 324 E
mew@niagara.edu

WOJTAL, Steve ... 440-775-8410.. 374 C
swojtal@oberlin.edu

WOJTALEWICZ, Jeanette .. 402-572-3650.. 279 C

WOJTOWICZ, Robert ... 757-683-4885.. 492 G
rwojtowi@odu.edu

WOLANIN, Monique ... 860-932-4174.... 87 C
mwolanin@qvcc.edu

WOLANSKYJ, Alexandra, P ... 507-284-3627.. 245 F
wolanskyj.alexandra@mayo.edu

WOLBERT, Jodi ... 603-513-1302.. 288 D
jodi.wolbert@granite.edu

WOLCH, Jennifer ... 510-642-0831.... 68 M
wolch@berkeley.edu

WOLCOFF, Elana ... 617-327-6777.. 229 H
elana_wolcoff@williamjames.edu

WOLCOWITZ, Jeffrey ... 216-368-2928.. 365 B
jeffrey.wolcowitz@case.edu

WOLD, Kayleigh ... 206-934-5338.. 507 A
keyleigh.wold@seattlecolleges.edu

WOLD, Lisa ... 503-255-0332.. 392 G
lwold@multnomah.edu

WOLD, Mark, C ... 608-363-2359.. 515 G
woldm@beloit.edu

WOLD, Paul, G ... 507-344-7346.. 244 K
paul.wold@blc.edu

WOLD-MCCORMICK, Kristi ... 303-492-6970.... 83 K
kristi.woldmccormick@colorado.edu

WOLDU, Feseha ... 202-865-4806.... 93 A
feseha.woldu@howard.edu

WOLEVER, Jack ... 805-893-4581.... 70 E
jack.wolever@dcs.ucsb.edu

WOLF, Andrea ... 617-521-2488.. 228 C
andrea.wolf@simmons.edu

WOLF, Andreas ... 650-574-6461.... 62 H
wolfa@smccd.edu

WOLF, Bill ... 865-573-4517.. 440 I
bwolf@johnsonu.edu

WOLF, Elyse ... 603-577-6209.. 286 I
ewolf@dwc.edu

WOLF, George ... 517-264-7177.. 241 A
gwolf@sienaheights.edu

WOLF, Greg ... 508-856-4296.. 221 B
greg.wolf@umassmed.edu

WOLF, Howard, E ... 650-724-5992.... 66 I
howardwolf@stanford.edu

WOLF, Jay, D ... 812-888-4172.. 169 A
jwolf@vinu.edu

WOLF, Jeffery, M ... 812-488-2183.. 167 I
jw268@evansville.edu

WOLF, Kelly, B ... 541-346-3165.. 395 G
kbwolf@uoregon.edu

WOLF, Kenneth ... 973-720-2432.. 298 G
wolfk@wpunj.edu

WOLF, Laurie ... 515-964-6437.. 171 B
lawolf@dmacc.edu

WOLF, Linda ... 614-251-4715.. 374 I
wolfl2@ohiodominican.edu

WOLF, Margaret ... 815-802-8302.. 144 C
mwolf@kcc.edu

WOLF, Nick ... 619-849-2384.... 57 M
nickwolf@pointloma.edu

WOLF, Paul ... 317-578-7353.. 486 G
pwwolf@an.edu

WOLF, Paul, J ... 937-255-3636.. 527 H
paul.wolf@afit.edu

WOLF, Rachel, B ... 972-860-7358.. 456 D
rwolf@dcccd.edu

WOLF, Rebecca, E ... 501-882-8867.... 18 I
rewolf@asub.edu

WOLF, Rob ... 352-854-2322.... 97 R
wolfr@cf.edu

WOLF, JR., Thomas ... 269-387-5473.. 243 H
tom.wolf@wmich.edu

WOLFARTH, Ariel ... 718-268-4700.. 326 L

WOLFE, Agata ... 973-313-6128.. 297 A
agata.wolfe@shu.edu

WOLFE, Andrew ... 315-792-7234.. 336 C
andrew.wolfe@sunyit.edu

WOLFE, Barbara, E ... 401-874-5339.. 426 D
bwolfe@uri.edu

WOLFE, Bill ... 318-797-5279.. 198 C
bill.wolfe@lsus.edu

WOLFE, Clarissa ... 509-574-4651.. 510 A
cwolfe@yvcc.edu

WOLFE, Deidre ... 540-863-2807.. 496 H
dwolfe@dslcc.edu

WOLFE, Elizabeth ... 304-696-6007.. 513 D
mccormi8@marshall.edu

WOLFE, Erin, M ... 570-372-4314.. 419 H
wolfeerin@susqu.edu

WOLFE, Gregory ... 508-565-1357.. 228 F
gwolfe@stonehill.edu

WOLFE, James, E ... 812-464-1782.. 168 E
jwolfe2@usi.edu

WOLFE, Joel ... 205-970-9253...... 7 B
jwolfe@sebc.edu

WOLFE, Johanna ... 713-221-8909.. 474 B
wolfej@uhd.edu

WOLFE, John, S ... 812-877-8590.. 166 H
john.s.wolfe@rose-hulman.edu

WOLFE, Ken ... 727-864-8835.... 98 L
wolfefk@eckerd.edu

WOLFE, Lori ... 816-802-3434.. 266 D
lwolfe@kcai.edu

WOLFE, Michael ... 419-267-1322.. 374 A
mwolfe@northweststate.edu

WOLFE, Peggy, L ... 337-475-5820.. 200 H
pwolfe@mcneese.edu

WOLFE, Thomas, V ... 303-765-3102.... 80 M
tvwolfe@iliff.edu

WOLFE, Tim, A ... 757-221-3980.. 488 F
tawolfe@wm.edu

WOLFE, Timothy ... 775-784-4666.. 285 A
tawolfe@unr.edu

WOLFE, Todd ... 818-677-3700.... 34 A
todd.wolfe@csun.edu

WOLFE, Vicki ... 205-970-9245...... 7 B
vwolfe@sebc.edu

WOLFE-LEE, Chyerl ... 360-650-3774.. 509 E
chyerl.wolfe-lee@wwu.edu

WOLFE-LYGA, Katherine .. 315-312-4416.. 333 D
katherine.wolfelyga@oswego.edu

WOLFE-STEPRO, Charlene ... 603-206-8072.. 286 D
cwolfe@ccsnh.edu

WOLFER, Diane, G ... 859-371-9393.. 186 M
dwolfer@beckfield.edu

WOLFERSBERGER, Mark .. 808-675-3628.. 130 E
mark.wolfersberger@byuh.edu

WOLFERT, Kelly ... 920-693-1171.. 523 E
ltc.bookstore@gotoltc.edu

WOLFF, Diane ... 617-928-4515.. 226 B
dwolff@mountida.edu

WOLFF, Donald ... 541-962-3359.. 391 C
dwolff@eou.edu

WOLFF, Holly, D ... 563-425-5221.. 177 D
wolffh@uiu.edu

WOLFF, Jennifer ... 210-434-6711.. 463 C
jswolff@follett.com

WOLFF, Michael, A ... 314-977-2774.. 271 K
mwolff3@slu.edu

WOLFF, Peg, A ... 308-635-6064.. 283 D
pwolff@wncc.edu

WOLFF, Susan ... 815-939-5203.. 150 I
swolff@olivet.edu

WOLFF, Susan, J ... 406-771-4305.. 277 F
susan.wolff@gfcmsu.edu

WOLFGRAMM, Jolynn, T 801-524-8106.. 480 J
jwolfgramm@ldsbc.edu

WOLFKILL, John ... 303-360-4833.... 79 E
john.wolfkill@ccaurora.edu

WOLFSON, Amy ... 410-617-2495.. 208 G
awolfson@loyola.edu

WOLFSON, Hannah ... 205-226-4922...... 2 C
hwolfson@bsc.edu

WOLIN, Richard, R ... 231-995-2003.. 239 C
rwolin@nmc.edu

WOLINSKY, Lawrence, E . 214-828-8300.. 468 B
wolinsky@tamu.edu

WOLK, David, S ... 802-468-1201.. 485 H
dave.wolk@castleton.edu

WOLK, Joseph ... 508-531-1229.. 221 C
joseph.wolk@bridgew.edu

WOLKEN, James ... 603-899-4343.. 287 A
wolkenj@franklinpierce.edu

WOLKING, Daryl ... 540-338-1776.. 492 H

WOLLENBERG, Chad ... 434-949-1033.. 498 E
chad.wollenberg@southside.edu

WOLLENBURG, Doug ... 912-525-5000.. 126 E
dwollenbu@scad.edu

WOLLER, Eric, K ... 507-344-7790.. 244 K
eric.woller@blc.edu

WOLLMAN, Julie, E ... 610-499-4101.. 423 E
jewollman@widener.edu

WOLLMAN, Rick, G ... 712-274-5320.. 175 C
wollman@morningside.edu

WOLLMERING, Jerry ... 660-785-4235.. 273 B
jerryw@truman.edu

WOLMARK, Adrienne ... 503-552-1605.. 392 H
awolmark@nunm.edu

WOLPERN, Kevin ... 952-888-4777.. 253 Z
kwolpern@nwhealth.edu

WOLPIN, Aryeh ... 718-232-7800.. 340 K

WOLPIN, Chaim ... 718-232-7800.. 340 K

WOLPIN, Ken ... 908-737-3290.. 292 C
wolpin@kean.edu

WOLSEY, Timothy ... 480-732-7125.... 13 O
timothy.wolsey@cgc.edu

WOLSZON, Linda ... 817-257-7863.. 469 G
l.wolszon@tcu.edu

WOLTERS, Daniel ... 406-657-1161.. 278 D
woltersd@rocky.edu

WOLTJERS, Gavin ... 918-335-6285.. 386 F
gwoltjers@okwu.edu

WOLZ, Jay ... 573-651-2930.. 272 B
jwolz@semo.edu

WOMACK, Cindy ... 541-278-5965.. 390 C
cwomack@bluecc.edu

WOMACK, Donna ... 318-678-6000.. 195 I
dwomack@bpcc.edu

WOMACK, Joseph ... 541-684-7241.. 393 B
jwomack@nwcu.edu

WOMACK, Juanita ... 301-891-4485.. 213 D
jwomack@wau.edu

WOMACK, Juanita ... 215-951-2990.. 416 G
womackj@philau.edu

WOMACK, Kenneth ... 732-571-3419.. 292 F
kwomack@monmouth.edu

WOMACK, Veronica ... 478-445-4233.. 121 A
veronica.womack@gcsu.edu

WOMACK, Wayne ... 479-788-7407.... 23 A
wayne.womack@uafs.edu

WOMACK, William ... 918-495-7088.. 386 H
wwomack@oru.edu

WOMBLE, Haley ... 314-837-6777.. 271 B
hwomble@stlchristian.edu

WOMBLE, Jeff ... 910-672-1474.. 356 E
jwomble@uncfsu.edu

WOODS, Debra ... 714-449-7434 ... 51 F
danderson@ketchum.edu
WOODS, Debra, D ... 724-925-4083 .. 423 D
woodsde@wccc.edu
WOODS, Dexter, A ... 202-865-6100 ... 93 A
dexter.woods@howard.edu
WOODS, Donovan ... 405-945-6705 .. 386 C
dwoods@osugiving.com
WOODS, Douglas ... 414-288-0327 .. 517 I
douglas.woods@marquette.edu
WOODS, Ed ... 214-870-3772 .. 463 G
ewoods@pqc.edu
WOODS, Ed ... 503-589-7746 .. 390 E
ed.woods@chemeketa.edu
WOODS, Elizabeth ... 508-854-4294 .. 224 E
ewoods@qcc.mass.edu
WOODS, Erin ... 806-743-4569 .. 472 D
erin.woodws@ttuhsc.edu
WOODS, James, M ... 630-515-6173 .. 148 C
jwoods@midwestern.edu
WOODS, Jami ... 336-386-3266 .. 353 F
woodsj@surry.edu
WOODS, Jann ... 928-505-3300 ... 15 E
WOODS, Jeffrey ... 479-968-0274 ... 19 F
jwoods@atu.edu
WOODS, John ... 205-552-1284 ... 3 B
john.woods@ecacolleges.com
WOODS, Kimberly, J ... 830-792-7282 .. 465 E
kjwoods@schreiner.edu
WOODS, Kristin, J ... 804-289-8026 .. 495 G
kwoods@richmond.edu
WOODS, Kristin, L ... 319-273-2332 .. 170 A
kristin.woods@uni.edu
WOODS, Kristy, F ... 202-865-7470 ... 93 A
kristy.woods@howard.edu
WOODS, Lauren ... 312-567-5167 .. 142 I
lwoods1@iit.edu
WOODS, Marty ... 864-587-4044 .. 433 A
woodsm@smcsc.edu
WOODS, Mary Lou ... 909-621-8000 ... 58 A
marylou.woods@pomona.edu
WOODS, Maura, A ... 718-990-1985 .. 328 F
woodsm@stjohns.edu
WOODS, Phillip ... 423-478-7993 .. 443 I
pwoods@ptseminary.edu
WOODS, Rebekah ... 517-787-0800 .. 235 G
woodsrebekahs@jccmi.edu
WOODS, Richard, G ... 765-361-6188 .. 169 C
woodsr@wabash.edu
WOODS, Rochelle ... 657-278-2738 ... 33 A
rwoods@fullerton.edu
WOODS, Serrita ... 815-395-5089 .. 153 D
serritawoods@sacn.edu
WOODS, Sharmon ... 520-325-0123 ... 17 D
WOODS, Sharon ... 864-503-5354 .. 434 G
swoods@uscupstate.edu
WOODS, Susan ... 781-280-3200 .. 224 A
woodss@middlesex.mass.edu
WOODS, Tim ... 559-265-5700 ... 67 C
tim.woods@fresnocitycollege.edu
WOODS, Tony ... 406-395-4875 .. 278 F
twoods@stonechild.edu
WOODS, Tracie, J ... 225-771-4680 .. 199 G
traice_woods@sus.edu
WOODS, Tracy ... 478-289-2035 .. 120 C
twoods@ega.edu
WOODS, Tracy ... 304-724-3700 .. 510 E
WOODSBY, Wendy ... 864-503-5199 .. 434 G
wwoodsby@uscupstate.edu
WOODSIDE, Christina, S . 704-847-5600 .. 355 J
cwoodside@ses.edu
WOODSON, Corliss, B ... 804-523-5877 .. 497 C
cwoodson@reynolds.edu
WOODSON, Heather ... 704-922-6310 .. 350 A
woodson.heather@gaston.edu
WOODSON, Kendra, B ... 864-833-8220 .. 432 B
kbwoodson@presby.edu
WOODSON, Lenee ... 973-290-4227 .. 290 G
lwoodson@cse.edu
WOODSON, Lovisa ... 215-635-7300 .. 404 D
lwoodson@gratz.edu
WOODSON, Rosalind ... 248-942-3337 .. 239 E
rdwoodso@oaklandcc.edu
WOODSON, Sandra ... 916-577-2200 ... 75 C
swoodson@jessup.edu
WOODSON, Terrance, S .. 214-887-5371 .. 457 C
twoodson@dts.edu
WOODSON, William ... 937-708-5711 .. 381 B
wwoodson@wilberforce.edu
WOODSON,
William Randy ... 919-515-2191 .. 357 B
randy_woodson@ncsu.edu
WOODSON DAY, Beverly 210-458-4536 .. 477 A
beverly.woodsonday@utsa.edu
WOODWARD, Angus ... 225-768-1704 .. 199 B
angus.woodward@ololcollege.edu
WOODWARD, Beth ... 503-534-4023 .. 392 D
bwoodward@marylhurst.edu
WOODWARD, Clifford ... 973-290-4345 .. 290 G
cwoodward@cse.edu

WOODWARD, David, B ... 920-748-8101 .. 519 E
woodwardd@ripon.edu
WOODWARD,
Elisabeth, M ... 610-660-1242 .. 418 G
ewoodwar@sju.edu
WOODWARD, Gregory, S 262-551-5858 .. 516 A
president@carthage.edu
WOODWARD, Holleigh ... 828-669-8012 .. 346 M
holleigh.woodward@montreat.edu
WOODWARD, John ... 253-879-3375 .. 508 D
woodward@pugetsound.edu
WOODWARD, Jonathan ... 228-896-2519 .. 259 C
jonathan.woodward@mgccc.edu
WOODWARD, LouAnn ... 601-984-1010 .. 261 C
lawoodward@umc.edu
WOODWARD, Scott ... 210-341-1366 .. 463 A
rsw@ost.edu
WOODWARD, Scott ... 979-845-5129 .. 468 B
feedback@athletics.tamu.edu
WOODWARD, Sheryl ... 530-898-6771 ... 32 C
swoodward@csuchico.edu
WOODWARD, Travis ... 432-552-2806 .. 478 B
woodward_t@utpb.edu
WOODWARD, Wade ... 864-596-9072 .. 429 C
wade.woodward@converse.edu
WOODWARD, Wendy ... 630-752-5656 .. 158 C
wendy.woodward@wheaton.edu
WOODWORTH, Jody ... 402-354-7000 .. 281 F
jody.woodworth@methodistcollege.edu
WOODWORTH, Judith ... 215-965-4059 .. 411 A
jwoodworth@moore.edu
WOODWORTH-NEY,
Laura ... 208-282-2171 .. 133 H
woodlaur@isu.edu
WOODY, Clay ... 864-294-3609 .. 430 C
clay.woody@furman.edu
WOODY, Craig ... 303-871-3588 ... 84 B
cwoody@du.edu
WOODY, Jaime ... 512-863-1624 .. 466 G
woodyj@southwestern.edu
WOODY, Jeannine, H ... 336-249-8186 .. 349 C
jwoody@davidsonccc.edu
WOODY, Keith, W ... 425-602-3045 .. 501 D
kwoody@bastyr.edu
WOODY, Pam ... 865-882-4501 .. 447 A
woodypm@roanestate.edu
WOODY, Tammie ... 585-785-1274 .. 314 D
tammie.woody@flcc.edu
WOODYARD, Steve ... 714-241-6240 ... 39 E
WOOLARD, Emily ... 252-940-6204 .. 347 E
emily.woolard@beaufortccc.edu
WOOLARD, Jo ... 252-940-6327 .. 347 E
jo.woolard@beaufortccc.edu
WOOLARD, Larry ... 217-732-3168 .. 146 A
lwoolard@lincolnchristian.edu
WOOLBERT, Stephanie ... 617-277-3915 .. 216 D
woolberts@bgsp.edu
WOOLDRIDGE,
Deborah, G ... 419-372-7851 .. 364 E
dgwoold@bgsu.edu
WOOLDRIDGE, Heath ... 870-612-2039 ... 23 H
heath.wooldridge@uaccb.edu
WOOLDRIDGE, James ... 951-222-8420 ... 59 C
jim.wooldridge@rcc.edu
WOOLDRIDGE, Peter ... 919-536-7200 .. 349 D
wooldridgep@durhamtech.edu
WOOLEY, Christine, A ... 240-895-4441 .. 210 E
cawooley@smcm.edu
WOOLEY, Travis ... 407-303-9440 ... 95 C
travis.wooley@adu.edu
WOOLF, Neil ... 509-359-6584 .. 503 D
nwoolf@ewu.edu
WOOLF, Sarah ... 617-731-7083 .. 227 D
woolfsar@pmc.edu
WOOLFOLK, Alan ... 904-819-6248 ... 99 M
awoolfolk@flagler.edu
WOOLFOLK, Jerald ... 315-312-3214 .. 333 D
jerald.woolfolk@oswego.edu
WOOLIVER, Matt ... 918-293-4888 .. 386 B
matt.wooliver@okstate.edu
WOOLLEN, Elizabeth, G ... 405-325-5141 .. 389 B
lwoollen@ou.edu
WOOLLEY, Craig ... 937-775-4008 .. 381 H
craig.woolley@wright.edu
WOOLLEY, Mark ... 718-409-3224 .. 336 A
mwoolley@sunymaritime.edu
WOOLLEY, Mark ... 718-409-7200 .. 336 A
mwoolley@sunymaritime.edu
WOOLLEY, Peter ... 973-443-8084 .. 291 J
woolley@fdu.edu
WOOLLEY, Rose, M ... 412-578-6274 .. 400 C
rmwoolley@carlow.edu
WOOLLISCROFT,
James, O ... 734-764-8175 .. 241 J
woolli@umich.edu
WOOLRIDGE, Cindy, B ... 910-938-6145 .. 348 G
burkhartc@coastalcarolina.edu
WOOLSCHLAGER, John ... 239-590-1897 .. 110 L
jwoolschlager@fgcu.edu
WOOLSEY, Andrew ... 949-480-4112 ... 64 J
awoolsey@soka.edu

WOOLSEY, Clint ... 812-749-1440 .. 166 B
cwoolsey@oak.edu
WOOLSEY, Roger, W ... 603-646-2215 .. 286 J
roger.w.woolsey@dartmouth.edu
WOOLSTON, Paul (PJ) ... 317-955-6307 .. 165 N
pwoolston@marian.edu
WOOLWINE, Lora ... 304-384-5224 .. 513 A
lwoolwine@concord.edu
WOOST, Michael, G ... 440-943-7600 .. 377 A
mgwoost@yahoo.com
WOOSTER, Ginger ... 979-230-3210 .. 453 A
ginger.wooster@brazosport.edu
WOOSTER, Phyllis, L ... 973-655-4212 .. 293 A
woosterp@mail.montclair.edu
WOOSTER, Timothy, T ... 617-745-3707 .. 218 A
timothy.t.wooster@enc.edu
WOOTEN, Bradley ... 847-635-1912 .. 150 G
bwooten@oakton.edu
WOOTEN, Cornelius ... 724-357-2202 .. 415 B
cornelius.wooten@iup.edu
WOOTEN, Dean, A ... 757-352-4062 .. 493 E
deanwoo@regent.edu
WOOTEN, Dolores ... 662-560-1105 .. 260 C
dbwooten@northwestms.edu
WOOTEN, Manat ... 413-528-7203 .. 214 H
mwooten@simons-rock.edu
WOOTEN, Maria ... 901-751-8453 .. 442 E
mwooten@mabts.edu
WOOTEN, Pam ... 662-562-3349 .. 260 C
pwooten@northwestms.edu
WOOTEN, Randall ... 832-447-1461 .. 470 F
randall.wooten@marshall.tstc.edu
WOOTEN, Rodney ... 252-335-0821 .. 349 A
rodney_wooten91@albemarle.edu
WOOTEN, Sheila ... 973-748-9000 .. 289 H
sheila_wooten@bloomfield.edu
WOOTEN, Susan ... 828-726-2233 .. 347 I
swooten@cccti.edu
WOOTEN, Susan, B ... 864-231-2151 .. 427 B
swooten@andersonuniversity.edu
WOOTON, Chris ... 502-895-3411 .. 191 F
cwooton@lpts.edu
WOOTTERS, Adrienne ... 413-662-5526 .. 222 B
adrienne.wootters@mcla.edu
WOOTTON, Katie ... 304-424-8203 .. 514 D
katie.wootton@wvup.edu
WOOTTON, Tim ... 562-938-4072 ... 49 D
twootton@lbcc.edu
WORD, John ... 559-791-2254 ... 47 L
jword@portervillecollege.edu
WORDELL, Kathleen, A ... 508-678-2811 .. 223 A
kathleen.wordell@bristolcc.edu
WORDEN, Jeannie, M ... 715-675-3331 .. 524 D
worden@ntc.edu
WORDEN, Jennifer ... 208-459-5307 .. 133 D
jworden@collegeofidaho.edu
WORDEN, Jodi ... 509-527-4561 .. 508 F
jodi.worden@wwcc.edu
WORDEN, Michael ... 845-341-4901 .. 325 H
michael.worden@sunyorange.edu
WORDEN, Natalia ... 858-566-1200 ... 42 D
nworden@disd.edu
WORDEN, Randy ... 559-453-7154 ... 44 F
randy.worden@fresno.edu
WORDEN, Richard, B ... 315-568-3095 .. 323 A
rworden@nycc.edu
WORDEN, Sylvia ... 714-432-5026 ... 39 G
sworden@occ.cccd.edu
WORK, Christine ... 845-341-4763 .. 325 H
christine.work@sunyorange.edu
WORK, Denise ... 402-552-2796 .. 279 D
workdenise@clarksoncollege.edu
WORK, Galen, J ... 848-445-1747 .. 296 C
gwork@rutgers.edu
WORK, Patricia ... 202-495-3835 ... 93 D
assistant@dhs.edu
WORKMAN, Andrew, A ... 401-254-3030 .. 426 B
aworkman@rwu.edu
WORKMAN, Christine ... 410-857-2267 .. 209 D
cworkman@mcdaniel.edu
WORKMAN, Cindy, R ... 402-280-2969 .. 279 H
cworkman@creighton.edu
WORKMAN, Greg ... 336-821-2478 .. 345 C
gworkman@johnwesley.edu
WORKMAN, Mary ... 954-201-7324 ... 96 I
mworkman@broward.edu
WORKMAN, Sue, B ... 216-368-2000 .. 365 B
sue.workman@case.edu
WORKMAN, Tamara ... 618-453-2903 .. 154 I
tworkman@siu.edu
WORKU, Adu ... 707-965-6242 ... 56 A
aworku@puc.edu
WORLAND, Brooke, A ... 317-738-8167 .. 160 J
bworland@franklincollege.edu
WORLEY, David ... 303-765-3107 ... 80 M
dworley@iliff.edu
WORLEY, Elizabeth, J ... 325-670-1229 .. 458 J
eworley@hsutx.edu
WORLEY, John ... 713-646-1863 .. 459 A
jworley@hcl.edu

WORLEY, John ... 510-659-6111 ... 55 B
jworley@ohlone.edu
WORLEY, Louise ... 717-815-1446 .. 424 F
lworley@ycp.edu
WORLEY, Mark ... 972-241-3371 .. 455 K
mworley@dallas.edu
WORLEY, Michael, J ... 404-413-3405 .. 122 D
mworley@gsu.edu
WORLEY, Paul ... 828-835-9564 .. 353 G
pworley@tricountycc.edu
WORLEY, Tim ... 561-803-2116 .. 106 C
tim_worley@pba.edu
WORM, Lori ... 920-424-3033 .. 520 E
worm@uwosh.edu
WORM, Lori, M ... 920-424-3033 .. 520 E
worm@uwosh.edu
WORMACK, Janet ... 240-567-1744 .. 209 E
janet.wormack@montgomerycollege.edu
WORMAN, Ernie ... 803-947-2052 .. 431 F
ernie.worman@newberry.edu
WORMLEY, Lonnie ... 229-434-8440 .. 115 K
lonnie.wormley@asurams.edu
WORMSER, Jennifer ... 949-376-6000 ... 48 C
jwormser@lcad.edu
WORNALL, Robyn ... 707-256-7192 ... 53 H
rwornall@napavalley.edu
WORNAT, Judy ... 225-578-5255 .. 197 I
mjwornat@lsu.edu
WOROBEC, Sophia ... 312-942-6857 .. 153 B
sophia_worobec@rush.edu
WORONER, Desiree ... 727-302-6823 .. 108 D
woroner.desiree@spcollege.edu
WORRALL, Jay ... 610-796-8371 .. 397 D
jay.worrall@alvernia.edu
WORSHAM, Charleen ... 903-983-3700 .. 460 D
cworsham@kilgore.edu
WORSHAM, Thomas ... 318-487-7498 .. 195 F
thomas.worsham@lacollege.edu
WORSLEY, Christine ... 925-969-2747 ... 41 I
cworsley@dvc.edu
WORSTER, Kathy ... 803-321-3353 .. 431 F
kathy.worster@newberry.edu
WORTH, Benjamin ... 540-863-2933 .. 496 H
bworth@dslcc.edu
WORTHAM, Donald ... 239-513-1122 .. 102 T
dwortham@hodges.edu
WORTHAM, Stanton ... 617-552-4030 .. 216 C
stanton.wortham@bc.edu
WORTHAM, Trudy ... 361-570-4110 .. 474 C
worthamt@uhv.edu
WORTHEN, Kevin ... 585-389-2880 .. 322 D
kworthe6@naz.edu
WORTHEN, Kevin, J ... 801-422-2521 .. 480 C
kevin_worthen@byu.edu
WORTHINGTON, Jennifer 308-398-0800 .. 280 B
jennifer.worthington@doane.edu
WORTHINGTON, Joni ... 919-962-4929 .. 356 A
worthj@northcarolina.edu
WORTHINGTON, Leslie ... 256-549-8256 ... 3 M
lworthington@gadsdenstate.edu
WORTHINGTON, Melissa 920-924-6326 .. 524 B
mworthington@morainepark.edu
WORTHY, Mark ... 225-752-4233 .. 195 E
mworthy@iticollege.edu
WOSSUM, Doris, F ... 931-363-9895 .. 441 G
dwossum@martinmethodist.edu
WOTTON, Heather ... 203-773-8558 ... 85 C
hwotton@albertus.edu
WOUDENBERG, Robert ... 315-866-0300 .. 316 A
woudenbra@herkimer.edu
WOUDSTRA, Earl ... 712-707-7292 .. 176 B
earl@nwciowa.edu
WOUGHTER, Kathy ... 607-871-2132 .. 303 F
woughter@alfred.edu
WOULFE, Rebecca ... 303-797-5822 ... 76 J
rebecca.woulfe@arapahoe.edu
WOUNG, Simone ... 703-284-1520 .. 492 A
simone.woung@marymount.edu
WOYAK, Amber ... 847-578-8354 .. 153 A
amber.woyak@rosalindfranklin.edu
WOZNIAK, Andrew ... 630-889-6878 .. 149 G
awozniak@nuhs.edu
WOZNIAK, Robert, A ... 716-652-8900 .. 306 K
rwozniak@cks.edu
WOZNICKI, John ... 609-984-1130 .. 297 F
jwoznicki@tesu.edu
WRAGE, Rebecca ... 308-535-3679 .. 280 M
wrager@mpcc.edu
WRAITH, Jon, M ... 603-862-1453 .. 288 C
jon.wraith@unh.edu
WRAY, Donald, W ... 318-795-2392 .. 198 C
donald.wray@lsus.edu
WRAY, John, W ... 330-325-6728 .. 373 H
jwray@neomed.edu
WRAY, Kyle ... 405-744-4366 .. 385 G
kyle.wray@okstate.edu
WRAY, Lois ... 804-862-6206 .. 493 F
lwray@rbc.edu
WRAY, Rachel ... 207-786-6240 .. 202 D
rwray@bates.edu

WURTZ, Keith 909-389-3206 60 B
kwurtz@craftonhills.edu
WURTZEL, Barbara 413-755-4816 224 G
bwurtzel@stcc.edu
WURTZEL, Julie, A 563-562-3263 175 F
wurtzelj@nicc.edu
WURZER, Christine 916-608-6645 51 C
wurzerc@flc.losrios.edu
WUSSOW, Helen 916-278-4433 34 B
WUTHRICH, Chris 208-426-1484 132 I
chriswuthrich@boisestate.edu
WUTHRICH, Philip 979-532-6305 479 J
philipw@wcjc.edu
WUTOH, Anthony, K 202-806-2550 93 A
awutoh@howard.edu
WUTOH, Rita 301-860-4170 212 D
rwutoh@bowiestate.edu
WYANDOTTE, Annette, M 812-941-2208 163 F
awyandot@ius.edu
WYANDT, Christy, M 662-915-7474 261 B
cwyandt@olemiss.edu
WYATT, Ben 859-280-1246 191 D
bwyatt@lextheo.edu
WYATT, Bill, J 540-568-4908 490 J
wyattwj@jmu.edu
WYATT, Charles, W 864-488-4603 430 H
cwyatt@limestone.edu
WYATT, Clarence, R 309-457-2127 148 E
cwyatt@monmouthcollege.edu
WYATT, Danny 808-696-0714 132 C
dwyatt@hawaii.edu
WYATT, Gary 620-341-5254 180 G
gwyatt@emporia.edu
WYATT, Jimmy 865-471-7164 439 C
jwyatt@cn.edu
WYATT, Joy, D 440-826-2180 363 M
jwyatt@bw.edu
WYATT, Julie 870-972-3670 18 J
jwyatt@astate.edu
WYATT, Jymmyca 770-962-7580 123 D
jwyatt@gwinnetttech.edu
WYATT, Mark, A 951-343-4474 29 H
mwyatt@calbaptist.edu
WYATT, Molly 252-985-5194 354 E
mwyatt@ncwc.edu
WYATT, Robert, L 843-383-8010 428 F
rwyatt@coker.edu
WYATT, Scott, L 435-586-7700 481 N
wyatt@suu.edu
WYATT, Shay 801-832-2344 483 D
swyatt@westminstercollege.edu
WYATT, Terri 804-257-5726 500 B
vuu@bkstr.com
WYBAN, Bruce 310-434-4376 63 F
wyban_bruce@smc.edu
WYBLE, Shannon 410-778-7200 213 E
swyble2@washcoll.edu
WYBOURNE, Martin, N 603-646-4091 286 J
martin.n.wybourne@dartmouth.edu
WYCHE, Lynn 850-973-9404 105 H
wychel@nfcc.edu
WYCHE, Sandy 972-860-4282 456 B
swyche@dcccd.edu
WYCKOFF, Harold 910-678-8287 349 F
wyckoffh@faytechcc.edu
WYCKOFF, Steven 718-960-8720 308 B
steven.wyckoff@lehman.cuny.edu
WYCO, Jeff 304-205-6611 511 M
jeff.wyco@bridgevalley.edu
WYCOFF-HORN, Marcie 608-785-8127 520 C
mwycoff-horn@uwlax.edu
WYDEN, JR., Leon 419-434-4521 379 E
wyden@findlay.edu
WYDER, Bruce 330-494-6170 377 J
bwyder@starkstate.edu
WYETT, Megan 315-792-7530 336 C
megan.wyett@sunyit.edu
WYKES, Paul 508-793-7385 217 B
pwykes@clarku.edu
WYKOFF, Dan 706-410-1129 119 G
dan.wykoff@covenant.edu
WYKOFF, Randolph, F 423-439-4243 444 F
wykoff@etsu.edu
WYLIE, Amy 859-344-4069 193 C
wyliea@thomasmore.edu
WYLIE, Brian 978-232-2440 218 D
bwylie@endicott.edu
WYLIE, Kathrine 707-962-2662 40 D
katherine-wylie@redwoods.edu
WYLIE, Michael 513-569-1492 366 D
michael.wylie@cincinnatistate.edu
WYLIE, Richard, E 978-232-2001 218 D
rwylie@endicott.edu
WYLIE, Rick 770-454-9270 93 F
WYMAN, J. Vernon 401-874-2501 426 D
jvernonwyman@uri.edu
WYMAN, Tracey 763-493-0546 251 B
twyman@nhcc.edu
WYMER, Cindy 423-461-8415 442 K
clwymer@milligan.edu
WYMER, Douglas, A 352-365-3522 104 J
wymerd@lssc.edu
WYMER, Greg 605-688-4482 437 F
greg.wymer@sdstate.edu
WYND, Christine, A 614-234-5800 373 B
cwynd@mccn.edu
WYNDER, Robin 301-687-4050 212 F
rwynder@frostburg.edu
WYNEGAR, Robert 775-445-4431 285 B
robert.wynegar@wnc.edu
WYNES, David, L 404-727-3889 120 E
david.wynes@emory.edu
WYNES, Tim 651-423-8213 249 B
tim.wyes@dctc.edu
WYNES, Timothy 651-450-3641 249 F
twynes@inverhills.edu
WYNN, Amanda 757-352-4148 493 E
amanwyn@regent.edu
WYNN, Bobby, C 910-672-1232 356 E
bwynn@uncfsu.edu
WYNN, Curt, J 757-822-1460 498 H
cjwynn@tcc.edu
WYNN, Denise, Y 919-530-7331 357 A
dwynn3@nccu.edu
WYNN, Hal 334-386-7285 3 I
hwynn@faulkner.edu
WYNN, Keren 229-333-2103 130 A
keren.wynn@wiregrass.edu
WYNN, Sandra 304-327-4213 512 P
swynn@bluefieldstate.edu
WYNN, Steve 617-746-1990 219 G
steve.wynn@hult.edu
WYNN, Tor 316-295-5451 181 B
tor_wynn@friends.edu
WYNNE, Jeremy 509-777-4277 509 H
jwynne@whitworth.edu
WYNNE, Joe 713-221-2799 474 B
wynnejo@uhd.edu
WYNNE, Joshua 701-777-2516 360 C
joshua.wynne@med.und.edu
WYNNE, Joshua 701-777-2514 360 C
joshua.wynne@med.und.edu
WYNTER, Cadence 949-582-4958 65 G
cwynter@saddleback.edu
WYONT, Kimberly 704-922-6482 350 A
wyont.kimberly@gaston.edu
WYPISZYNSKI, Gregory 920-424-0007 520 E
wypiszyn@uwosh.edu
WYRICK, Chris 479-575-6800 22 I
cwyrick1@uark.edu
WYRICK, Kathleen 907-564-8265 10 B
kwyrick@alaskapacific.edu
WYSE, Joe 530-242-7510 64 D
jwyse@shastacollege.edu
WYSOCKI, Barbara 630-515-6321 148 C
bwysoc@midwestern.edu
WYSOCKI, Charlene 610-921-7667 396 H
cwysocki@albright.edu
WYSOCKI, Joseph, T 815-740-2274 157 F
jwysocki@stfrancis.edu
WYSOGLAD, Anne 773-481-8634 137 I
awysoglad@ccc.edu
WYSONG, James 813-253-7236 102 R
rwysong@hccfl.edu
WYSTEPEK, Christopher 413-782-1794 229 E
christopher.wystepek@wne.edu

X

XANTHOS, Christopher 619-594-6018 35 A
cxanthos@mail.sdsu.edu
XIA, Jingfeng 845-574-4408 327 G
jxia@sunyrockland.edu
XIA, Jingfeng 570-422-3467 414 H
XIANG, Yun 603-862-2081 288 C
yun.xiang@unh.edu
XIE, Jin Hua 262-554-2010 518 B
drj-xie@yahoo.com
XIE, Ping 718-405-3733 310 H
ping.xie@mountsaintvincent.edu
XIE, Yan 909-748-8187 71 K
yan_xie@redlands.edu
XIMENEZ, David 817-515-5354 467 A
david.ximenez@tccd.edu
XIMINES, Sheryl, H 919-516-4343 355 D
sximines@st-aug.edu
XIONG, Brian 218-299-6505 250 D
brian.xiong@minnesota.edu
XIONG, Shoua 916-686-7400 31 F
XIONG-CHAN, Mai Nhia 651-523-2440 247 A
mxiongchan01@hamline.edu
XIPPOLITOS, Lee 631-444-3549 332 A
lee.xippolitos@stonybrook.edu
XIRINACHS, Susan 207-947-4591 202 E
sxirinachs@bealcollege.edu
XU, Amanda 707-468-3096 52 C
axu@mendocino.edu
XU, Jackie 202-274-5545 94 B
jxu@udc.edu

Y

YABUR, Lupe 562-947-8755 66 A
lupeyabur@scuhs.edu
YACAVONE, Mark 607-753-4711 333 A
mark.yacavone@cortland.edu
YACKEE, Grace, B 734-384-4221 238 C
gyackee@monroeccc.edu
YACYNYCH, Holly 610-799-1718 408 G
hyacynych@lccc.edu
YADAMA, Gautam, N 617-552-4020 216 C
gautam.yadama@bc.edu
YADEGAR, Mahvash 310-662-2101 54 A
myadegar@nu.edu
YAEAGER, Mona 312-944-0882 145 F
ryaeger@chicago.chefs.edu
YAEGER, Evelyn 810-762-9782 236 C
eyaeger@kettering.edu
YAEGER, John, W 202-685-0080 528 B
yaegerj@ndu.edu
YAEGER, Lisa 802-485-2075 484 H
lyaeger@norwich.edu
YAGER, David 215-717-6000 421 D
dyager@uarts.edu
YAHNG, Charles 314-529-9312 267 B
cyahng@maryville.edu
YAHNKE, Eric 503-838-8459 396 E
yahnkee@wou.edu
YAHYAZADEH, Bizhan 802-485-2145 484 H
bizhan@norwich.edu
YAKLICH, Richard 305-430-1167 101 A
richard.yaklich@fmuniv.edu
YAKOWICZ, William 201-612-5253 289 E
wyakowicz@bergen.edu
YAKSHE, Patti, L 412-281-2600 417 A
YALE, Amanda, A 724-738-2011 416 B
amanda.yale@sru.edu
YALE, Jacob 716-926-8785 316 B
jyale@hilbert.edu
YALE, Jake 775-831-1314 285 G
jyale@sierranevada.edu
YALE, Janet 402-557-7095 278 I
janet.yale@bellevue.edu
YAM, Marylou 410-532-5300 210 B
YAMADA, Emiko 650-508-3749 54 J
eyamada@ndnu.edu
YAMADA, Frank, M 773-947-6301 147 D
fyamada@mccormick.edu
YAMAGATA-NOJI,
Audrey 909-274-4505 53 C
ayamagat@mtsac.edu
YAMAGUCHI, Steve 626-584-5370 44 G
steveyamaguchi@fuller.edu
YAMAKAWA, Lynn 310-233-4387 49 I
yamakalm@lahc.edu
YAMAMOTO, Catherine 402-472-7749 282 M
cyamamoto1@unl.edu
YAMAMOTO, Cindy 808-984-3288 132 D
cindy@hawaii.edu
YAMAMOTO, Donald 202-685-3924 528 B
donald.yamamoto@ndu.edu
YAMAMOTO, June, Y 909-389-3216 60 B
jyamamoto@craftonhills.edu
YAMAMOTO, Kayoko 831-476-9424 43 M
studentaccounts@fivebranches.edu
YAMAMOTO, Keith 415-476-3128 70 D
yamamoto@ucsf.edu
YAMAMOTO, Lance 808-956-5148 131 H
lance@hawaii.edu
YAMAMURA, Whitney 916-691-7326 51 B
yamamuw@crc.losrios.edu
YAMASE, Universe 691-320-2480 529 F
uyamase@comfsm.fm
YAMAUCHI, Kent 626-585-7995 56 H
ktyamauchi@pasadena.edu
YAMBA, A. Zachary 973-877-4462 291 H
yamba@essex.edu
YAMBA, A. Zachary 973-877-3022 291 H
yamba@essex.edu
YAMBA, Mohamed 724-938-4240 414 E
yamba@calu.edu
YAMBO, Marc 630-889-6517 149 G
myambo@nuhs.edu
YAMEEN, Deanna 508-588-9100 223 G
YAMILKOSKI, Vince, J 770-534-6134 118 A
vyamilkoski@brenau.edu
YAMPOLSKY, Chana 212-964-2830 320 I
cpy145@aol.com
YAMRICK, Emmalyn 212-774-0740 320 C
eyamrick@mmm.edu
YAN, Ruth 319-226-2080 169 D
ruth.yan@allencollege.edu
YAN, Song 313-577-0633 243 F
ej7020@wayne.edu
YANAI, Carolyn 702-463-2122 285 J
YANCEY, Deborah 540-857-7986 499 B
dyancey@virginiawestern.edu
YANCEY, Jennifer, L 361-582-2519 478 F
jennifer.yancey@victoriacollege.edu
YANCEY, John, E 904-620-5176 112 B
jyancey@unf.edu
YANCEY, Laurica 919-658-7750 355 K
lyancey@umo.edu
YANCHAK, Frank 614-947-6723 369 A
frank.yanchak@franklin.edu
YANCKELLO, Robert 407-823-2711 111 E
bob.yanckello@ucf.edu
YANCY, Chad 205-929-3497 5 D
cyancy@lawsonstate.edu
YANDA, Wayne 619-482-6414 66 E
wyanda@swccd.edu
YANES, Kenneth 212-484-1339 308 E
kyanes@jjay.cuny.edu
YANEZ, Mercedes 310-233-4127 49 I
yanezm@lahc.edu
YANG, Alice 831-459-2328 70 F
ayang@ucsc.edu
YANG, Anna 559-325-3600 30 C
ayang@chsu.org
YANG, Chuayi 715-425-3531 521 B
chuayi.yang@uwrf.edu
YANG, Dang 715-831-7229 523 B
dyang19@cvtc.edu
YANG, Faxian 908-526-1200 295 A
faxian.yang@raritanval.edu
YANG, Henry, T 805-893-2231 70 E
henry.yang@ucsb.edu
YANG, Hong 401-232-6885 424 K
hyang@bryant.edu
YANG, Honggang 954-262-3016 105 J
yangh@nsu.nova.edu
YANG, Neng 503-838-8590 396 E
yangn@wou.edu
YANG, Nicole 920-693-1120 523 E
nicole.yang@gotoltc.edu
YANG, Olivia 509-335-5571 508 H
olivia.yang@wsu.edu
YANG, Olivia 509-335-5524 508 H
olivia.yang@wsu.edu
YANG, Paul 626-448-0023 47 E
YANG, Peter 612-244-2800 247 D
pyang@ipr.edu
YANG, Philip 408-532-5567 54 D
YANG, Sixian 719-549-2110 79 B
sixian.yang@csupueblo.edu
YANG, Steve 763-424-0805 251 B
syang@nhcc.edu
YANG, Steve 651-450-3330 249 F
syang@inverhills.edu
YANG, Xiaoyun 336-770-1457 358 E
yangx@uncsa.edu
YANG, Zhanjun 954-776-4476 103 J
zyang@keiseruniversity.edu
YANKE, Gaylyn 575-234-9216 301 B
gyanke@nmsu.edu
YANKELEWITZ, Yoel 718-846-1940 341 C
yyankelewitz@gmail.com
YANKELITIS, Wendy 570-348-6201 409 H
yankelitis@marywood.edu
YANKEY, Terry, L 606-474-3222 188 L
tly@kcu.edu
YANNI, Stephen 906-248-8478 231 N
syanni@bmcc.edu
YANNICK, Lisa 610-436-3075 416 C
lyannick@wcupa.edu
YANTA, Stacie 361-354-2207 454 G
yantas@coastalbend.edu
YAO, Chunmei 910-521-6295 358 C
chunmei.yao@uncp.edu
YAO, Min 562-985-5459 33 B
min.yao@csulb.edu
YAO, Richard 702-992-2632 284 J
richard.yao@nsc.edu
YAQUB, Samia 530-895-2484 29 F
yaqubsa@butte.edu
YARABECK, John 936-294-1785 471 D
slo_jxy@shsu.edu
YARBROUGH, David 707-546-4000 42 M
dyarbrough@empirecollege.com
YARBROUGH, David 337-482-1015 201 D
yarbrough@louisiana.edu
YARBROUGH, Denise 585-275-4321 338 K
dyarbrough@admin.rochester.edu
YARBROUGH, Erin, A 405-325-0206 389 B
eyarbrough@ou.edu
YARBROUGH, Ernest 216-687-2048 366 I
e.b.yarbrough@csuohio.edu
YARBROUGH, John 706-865-2134 128 D
jyarbrough@truett.edu
YARBROUGH, Kenny 615-230-3443 447 C
kenny.yarbrough@volstate.edu
YARBROUGH,
Kimberly Anne 650-493-4430 64 I
kimberly.christensen@sofia.edu
YARBROUGH, Laura 870-508-6122 19 B
YARBROUGH, Laura, L 336-249-8186 349 C
llyarbro@davidsoncc.edu
YARBROUGH, Mark, M 214-887-5011 457 C
myarbrough@dts.edu
YARBROUGH, Scott 843-863-7563 427 I
syarbrou@csuniv.edu

YORK-LEMELIN, Lisa .... 207-453-5128.. 203 K
lyork@kvcc.me.edu
YORKIN, Sheila .... 801-832-2685.. 483 D
syorkin@westminstercollege.edu
YORKOWITZ, Johnathan .. 325-670-1026.. 458 J
johnathan.yorkowitz@hsutx.edu
YORTSOS, Yannis, C .... 213-740-0617.... 72 D
yortsos@usc.edu
YOSHIDA, James, M .... 808-934-2508.. 131 J
jamesyos@hawaii.edu
YOSHIMI, Garret, T .... 808-956-3501.. 131 D
gyoshimi@hawaii.edu
YOSHIMORI-YAMAMOTO,
Denise .... 808-956-0864.. 131 H
dfyoshim@hawaii.edu
YOSHIMURA, Gregg .... 808-455-0607.. 132 C
greggy@hawaii.edu
YOSHIMURA, Nancy .... 949-480-4045.... 64 J
nyoshimura@soka.edu
YOSHIMURA, Takuya ...... 808-983-4105.. 130 I
yoshimura@tokai.edu
YOSHINA, Eileen .... 360-596-5383.. 508 A
eyoshina@spscc.edu
YOSHINO, Lori .... 909-621-8856.... 57 H
lori_yoshino@pitzer.edu
YOSHIOKA, Marianne ...... 413-585-7977.. 228 D
myoshioka@smith.edu
YOUATT, June, P .... 517-355-1524.. 237 I
youatt@msu.edu
YOUGH, Kelly .... 845-569-3184.. 322 B
kelly.yough@msmc.edu
YOUHOUSE, John .... 610-558-5518.. 411 E
youhousej@neumann.edu
YOUKEY, Jerry, R .... 864-455-7880.. 433 F
youkey@mailbox.sc.edu
YOUKEY, Jerry, R .... 864-455-7992.. 434 D
youkey@greenvillemed.sc.edu
YOUMANS, Karen .... 405-208-5680.. 385 E
kdyoumans@okcu.edu
YOUNG, Aaron .... 505-984-6140.. 301 I
aaron.young@sjc.edu
YOUNG, Alissa .... 270-707-3717.. 189 G
alissa.young@kctcs.edu
YOUNG, Allene .... 510-981-2908.... 57 B
ayoung@peralta.edu
YOUNG, Amber .... 256-824-6604...... 8 F
amber.young@uah.edu
YOUNG, Andrew .... 256-726-7000...... 6 B
ayoung@oakwood.edu
YOUNG, Andrew .... 812-888-4323.. 169 A
ayoung@vinu.edu
YOUNG, Ann, S .... 859-238-5480.. 187 H
ann.young@centre.edu
YOUNG, Barbara .... 626-966-4576.... 26 J
barbara@jamagency.com
YOUNG, Barbara .... 662-562-3202.. 260 C
ba_young@northwestms.edu
YOUNG, Beth .... 815-825-9448.. 144 F
beth.young@kishwaukeecollege.edu
YOUNG, Betty .... 478-553-2090.. 125 C
byoung@oftc.edu
YOUNG, Betty .... 740-753-3591.. 369 K
youngb@hocking.edu
YOUNG, Bradley, J .... 310-233-4066.... 49 I
youngbj@lahc.edu
YOUNG, Brandon .... 217-540-3512.. 145 D
byoung17159@lakeland.cc.il.us
YOUNG, Brandon, L .... 386-226-7245.... 99 A
youngbr@erau.edu
YOUNG, Brenda .... 907-277-1000.... 10 C
brenda.young@chartercollege.edu
YOUNG, Brian .... 719-389-6870.... 77 J
bay@coloradocollege.edu
YOUNG, C. Bryan .... 785-864-4225.. 185 D
cbyoung@ku.edu
YOUNG, Carole .... 651-638-6316.. 244 L
youcar@bethel.edu
YOUNG, Charles .... 203-596-4604.... 88 F
cyoung@post.edu
YOUNG, Charles .... 336-334-4822.. 350 B
hcyoung@gtcc.edu
YOUNG, Cheryl .... 409-933-8232.. 454 O
cyoung@com.edu
YOUNG, Cheryl, D .... 513-529-8600.. 372 K
youngcd@miamioh.edu
YOUNG, Christopher .... 219-980-6563.. 163 B
cjy@iun.edu
YOUNG, Colletta .... 541-956-7296.. 394 J
cyoung@roguecc.edu
YOUNG, Connie .... 217-709-0931.. 145 E
cyoung@lakeviewcol.edu
YOUNG, Corey, D .... 601-877-4063.. 256 F
cyoung1@alcorn.edu
YOUNG, Cynthia, V .... 724-653-2211.. 402 F
cyoung@dec.edu
YOUNG, Cynthia, Y .... 407-823-4376.. 111 E
cynthia.young@ucf.edu
YOUNG, Dale .... 478-445-6848.. 121 A
dale.young@gcsu.edu
YOUNG, Dana .... 541-881-5580.. 395 E
dyoung@tvcc.cc
YOUNG, Danielle .... 440-775-8692.. 374 C
danielle.young@oberlin.edu
YOUNG, Darlene, P .... 812-941-2306.. 163 F
dyoung01@ius.edu
YOUNG, David .... 405-974-2490.. 388 L
dyoung28@uco.edu
YOUNG, Denise .... 706-867-3281.. 128 F
denise.young@ung.edu
YOUNG, Derek, M .... 240-895-4207.. 210 E
dmyoung@smcm.edu
YOUNG, Djuana .... 832-842-9058.. 473 F
dyoun2@central.uh.edu
YOUNG, Donald, B .... 808-956-7703.. 131 F
young@hawaii.edu
YOUNG, Donna .... 480-423-6300.... 14 H
donna.young@scottsdalecc.edu
YOUNG, Eldon .... 714-484-7177.... 54 G
eyoung@cypresscollege.edu
YOUNG, Evelyn .... 661-654-2241.... 32 A
eyoung3@csub.edu
YOUNG, Frank .... 801-863-7202.. 482 C
frank.young@uvu.edu
YOUNG, Gail, B .... 773-298-3301.. 153 H
young@sxu.edu
YOUNG, Garland .... 423-461-8720.. 442 K
rgyoung@milligan.edu
YOUNG, Gerald .... 507-222-4057.. 245 C
gyoung@carleton.edu
YOUNG, Grace .... 978-556-3449.. 224 D
gyoung@necc.mass.edu
YOUNG, Greg .... 606-337-1072.. 187 I
gyoung@ccbbc.edu
YOUNG, Gretchen .... 508-286-8200.. 229 F
young_gretchen@wheatoncollege.edu
YOUNG, Gwyn .... 601-643-8318.. 257 D
gwyn.young@colin.edu
YOUNG, Heather, M .... 916-734-4745.... 69 A
heather.young@ucdmc.ucdavis.edu
YOUNG, Henry .... 401-739-5000.. 425 C
hyoung@neit.edu
YOUNG, Hester .... 843-863-8020.. 427 I
hyoung@csuniv.edu
YOUNG, J.R .... 412-536-1100.. 406 K
jr.young@laroche.edu
YOUNG, Jason .... 810-766-4109.. 231 D
YOUNG, Jeff .... 931-372-3311.. 445 B
jyoung@tntech.edu
YOUNG, Jill .... 570-389-4950.. 414 D
jyoung@bloomu.edu
YOUNG, Joanna .... 517-353-0722.. 237 I
jcyoung@msu.edu
YOUNG, John .... 315-781-3748.. 316 C
jyoung@hws.edu
YOUNG, John .... 973-328-5026.. 290 H
jyoung@ccm.edu
YOUNG, John .... 303-360-4707.... 79 E
john.young@ccaurora.edu
YOUNG, John .... 937-327-7800.. 381 F
jyoung@wittenberg.edu
YOUNG, John, O .... 248-370-2946.. 239 K
joyoung@oakland.edu
YOUNG, Johnny, W .... 757-683-3442.. 492 G
jwyoung@odu.edu
YOUNG, Jon .... 910-672-1460.. 356 E
jyoung@uncfsu.edu
YOUNG, Joseph .... 619-388-7672.... 60 H
jyoung@sdccd.edu
YOUNG, Julian, M .... 843-661-1228.. 430 B
jyoung@fmarion.edu
YOUNG, Kalbert, K .... 808-956-8903.. 131 D
kalbert@hawaii.edu
YOUNG, Karmalee .... 406-874-6305.. 276 H
youngk@milescc.edu
YOUNG, Kathryn .... 501-683-7302.... 23 B
kcyoung@ualr.edu
YOUNG, Kay .... 817-598-6303.. 479 E
kyoung@wc.edu
YOUNG, Kay, F .... 508-213-2114.. 227 A
kay.young@nichols.edu
YOUNG, Ken .... 516-323-4501.. 321 H
kyoung@molloy.edu
YOUNG, Kerry, A .... 315-786-2279.. 317 H
kyoung@sunyjefferson.edu
YOUNG, Kirk .... 716-338-1023.. 317 F
kirkyoung@mail.sunyjcc.edu
YOUNG, Kristen .... 702-895-0143.. 284 L
kristen.young@unlv.edu
YOUNG, Kristine .... 775-881-7509.. 285 G
kyoung@sierranevada.edu
YOUNG, Kristine, M .... 845-341-4700.. 325 H
president@sunyorange.edu
YOUNG, Lakisha .... 312-341-3530.. 152 H
lyoung@roosevelt.edu
YOUNG, Laura .... 501-450-3126.... 24 G
lyoung@uca.edu
YOUNG, Lavern .... 312-949-7430.. 142 A
lyoung@ico.edu
YOUNG, Lee .... 620-235-4109.. 184 C
lyoung@pittstate.edu
YOUNG, Lenna .... 864-250-8185.. 430 E
lenna.young@gvltec.edu
YOUNG, Lili .... 212-410-8032.. 323 C
lyoung@nycpm.edu
YOUNG, Lily, Y .... 848-932-7821.. 296 B
lily.young@rutgers.edu
YOUNG, Linda, C .... 334-556-2234...... 3 N
lyoung@wallace.edu
YOUNG, Linda, K .... 715-836-5287.. 520 A
younglk@uwec.edu
YOUNG, Linda, L .... 440-826-2127.. 363 M
lyoung@bw.edu
YOUNG, Lisa .... 580-559-5713.. 383 H
lyoung@ecok.edu
YOUNG, Lorraine .... 909-748-8108.... 71 K
lorraine_young@redlands.edu
YOUNG, Margaret, A .... 940-898-2015.. 472 G
myoung13@twu.edu
YOUNG, Marie .... 814-472-3022.. 418 F
myoung@francis.edu
YOUNG, Mark .... 406-994-4399.. 277 C
myoung@montana.edu
YOUNG, Mark, S .... 303-762-6902.... 79 I
president@denverseminary.edu
YOUNG, Mary, E .... 903-823-3369.. 467 C
maryellen.young@texarkanacollege.edu
YOUNG, MaryAnne .... 941-487-4801.. 111 D
myoung@ncf.edu
YOUNG, Meghan .... 301-369-2800.. 206 H
myoung@captechu.edu
YOUNG, Michael .... 508-531-1295.. 221 C
myoung@bridgew.edu
YOUNG, Michael, E .... 270-809-6831.. 192 A
myoung@murraystate.edu
YOUNG, Michael, K .... 979-845-2217.. 468 B
president@tamu.edu
YOUNG, Michael, W .... 212-327-8000.. 327 F
michael.young@rockefeller.edu
YOUNG, Michaela, J .... 315-386-7204.. 335 B
youngm@canton.edu
YOUNG, Michelle, L .... 315-268-4268.. 310 B
myoung@clarkson.edu
YOUNG, Misty .... 573-681-5580.. 266 I
youngm@lincolnu.edu
YOUNG, Monica .... 336-334-4822.. 350 B
mwyoung@gtcc.edu
YOUNG, Myriam .... 219-980-6548.. 163 B
myyoung@iun.edu
YOUNG, Nancy .... 410-455-2393.. 211 G
nyoung@umbc.edu
YOUNG, Nancy .... 816-960-2008.. 263 D
newstudents@cityvision.edu
YOUNG, Nate .... 602-331-7500.... 11 K
nlyoung@aii.edu
YOUNG, Nicole .... 731-989-6768.. 440 D
nyoung@fhu.edu
YOUNG, Nina .... 956-665-3670.. 476 E
nina.young@utrgv.edu
YOUNG, Norman .... 860-768-7819.... 89 G
young@hartford.edu
YOUNG, Patricia .... 707-864-7124.... 65 A
patricia.young@solano.edu
YOUNG, Patricia .... 925-969-4229.... 41 I
tyoung@dvc.edu
YOUNG, Patty, R .... 804-257-5605.. 500 B
pryoung@vuu.edu
YOUNG, Paul, R .... 307-674-6446.. 526 M
pyoung@sheridan.edu
YOUNG, Peter, C .... 240-684-5268.. 212 C
pete.young@umuc.edu
YOUNG, Randy .... 660-359-3948.. 269 I
ryoung@mail.ncmissouri.edu
YOUNG, Raymond .... 609-984-1141.. 297 F
ryoung@tesu.edu
YOUNG, Remmele .... 713-718-7742.. 459 B
remmele.young@hccs.edu
YOUNG, Rena .... 270-707-3732.. 189 G
rena.young@kctcs.edu
YOUNG, Rhett .... 740-283-6441.. 368 L
ryoung@franciscan.edu
YOUNG, Richard .... 207-581-1700.. 204 H
ryoung@maine.edu
YOUNG, Robert .... 410-386-8261.. 206 I
ryoung@carrollcc.edu
YOUNG, Robert .... 501-370-5365.... 21 G
ryoung@philander.edu
YOUNG, Robert .... 540-453-2500.. 496 F
youngb@brcc.edu
YOUNG, Robert .... 423-236-2805.. 444 B
ryoung@southern.edu
YOUNG, Sandra .... 610-989-1456.. 422 E
syoung@vfmac.edu
YOUNG, Sarah .... 309-457-2300.. 148 E
syoung@monmouthcollege.edu
YOUNG, Sarah, M .... 716-878-4631.. 332 F
youngsm@buffalostate.edu
YOUNG, Scott .... 816-235-1154.. 273 F
youngsc@umkc.edu
YOUNG, Scott .... 360-650-2593.. 509 E
scott.young@wwu.edu
YOUNG, Sean, B .... 262-243-5700.. 516 E
sean.young@cuw.edu
YOUNG, Shantreese .... 251-344-1203...... 3 J
syoung@fortiscollege.edu
YOUNG, Sherry .... 501-812-2724.... 21 H
sdyoung@pulaskitech.edu
YOUNG, Stacie, G .... 704-687-7203.. 358 A
sgyoung@uncc.edu
YOUNG, Stephen, W .... 513-732-5318.. 379 C
steve.young@uc.edu
YOUNG, Steve .... 850-718-2203.... 97 G
youngs@chipola.edu
YOUNG, Steve .... 828-694-1891.. 347 G
sd_young@blueridge.edu
YOUNG, Stuart .... 701-766-1321.. 360 A
stuart.young@littlehoop.edu
YOUNG, Sunya .... 706-821-8233.. 125 H
syoung@paine.edu
YOUNG, Sunya .... 903-730-4890.. 460 B
syoung@jarvis.edu
YOUNG, Susan .... 864-242-5100.. 427 E
YOUNG, Tammy .... 479-394-7622.... 22 B
tyoung@rmcc.edu
YOUNG, Tanya .... 215-567-7080.. 397 H
tyoung@aii.edu
YOUNG, Teresa .... 806-291-3472.. 479 D
teresa.young@wbu.edu
YOUNG, Terry .... 325-793-4683.. 461 F
tyoung@mcm.edu
YOUNG, Thomas, W .... 507-933-7551.. 246 J
tyoung3@gustavus.edu
YOUNG, Tim .... 714-556-3610.... 73 B
tyoung@vanguard.edu
YOUNG, Timothy .... 585-389-2840.. 322 D
tyoung6@naz.edu
YOUNG, Tommy .... 903-923-2137.. 457 G
tyoung@etbu.edu
YOUNG, Vickie .... 501-337-5000.... 19 K
vyoung@coto.edu
YOUNG, Wayne .... 402-280-2775.. 279 H
waynejr@creighton.edu
YOUNG ROSS, Bridgette . 404-727-6226.. 120 E
bridgette.ross@emory.edu
YOUNG WON, Duk .... 323-643-0301.... 26 H
YOUNGBLOOD, Amy .... 281-649-3413.. 458 L
ayoungblood@hbu.edu
YOUNGBLOOD, Beth .... 615-966-5072.. 441 F
beth.youngblood@lipscomb.edu
YOUNGBLOOD, Dan .... 317-278-7631.. 163 D
dyoungbl@iupui.edu
YOUNGBLOOD, Joseph ... 607-777-4351.. 297 F
jyoungblood@tesu.edu
YOUNGBLOOD, Kerry, L . 252-222-6140.. 348 B
youngbloodk@carteret.edu
YOUNGBLOOD, Merna ..... 618-842-3711.. 142 C
youngbloodm@iecc.edu
YOUNGBLOOD, Pamela .. 979-532-6542.. 479 J
pamy@wcjc.edu
YOUNGBLOOD, Randy .... 205-226-4700...... 2 C
ryoungbl@bsc.edu
YOUNGBLOOD, Rick .... 601-477-4014.. 258 E
rick.youngblood@jcjc.edu
YOUNGBULL, Natalie ...... 580-591-0203.. 383 D
YOUNGE, Jeffrey, W .... 507-344-7328.. 244 K
jeff.younge@blc.edu
YOUNGEN, Audra .... 330-823-6050.. 379 F
youngeau@mountunion.edu
YOUNGER, Allan .... 336-725-4746.. 349 G
ayounger@forsythtech.edu
YOUNGER, James .... 859-442-1719.. 189 D
james.younger@kctcs.edu
YOUNGER, Kyle .... 662-243-1975.. 257 G
kyounger@eastms.edu
YOUNGER, Toyia .... 651-201-1673.. 248 I
toyia.younger@so.mnscu.edu
YOUNGLOVE, Theodore ... 909-652-6402.... 37 D
ted.younglove@chaffey.edu
YOUNGREN, Malcolm .... 619-574-6909.... 55 G
myoungren@pacificcollege.edu
YOUNGREN, Malcolm .... 212-982-3456.... 55 G
myoungren@pacificcollege.edu
YOUNGS, Samuel, J .... 423-775-7514.. 439 B
syoungs2721@bryan.edu
YOUNGS, JR.,
Thomas, E .... 412-624-8785.. 421 G
tyoungs@cfo.pitt.edu
YOUNKIN, Michelle .... 402-486-2529.. 282 I
miyounki@ucollege.edu
YOUNT, Debra .... 828-726-2712.. 347 I
dyount@cccti.edu
YOUNT, Rebecca, H .... 401-333-7159.. 425 A
ryount@ccri.edu
YOUNT, Susan .... 520-222-3232.. 188 G
susan.yount@frontier.edu
YOUSE, Lauren .... 573-629-3122.. 265 G
lauren.youse@hlg.edu
YOUSNEY-ELSENER,
Kimberly .... 607-431-4408.. 315 E
yousey_elsek@hartwick.edu
YOVANOVICH, Michele ..... 239-590-7900.. 110 L
myovanov@fgcu.edu
YOVICH, Rudy .... 419-783-2380.. 368 A
ryovich@defiance.edu

YOW, Deborah .... 919-515-2109.. 357 B
d_yow@ncsu.edu
YOWELL, Lee, P .... 706-886-6831.. 128 C
lyowell@tfc.edu
YOXALL, Daniel .... 210-434-6711.. 463 C
dyoxall@lake.ollusa.edu
YRAGUEN, Jeremy .... 541-881-4863.. 395 E
jeremy.d.yraguen@doc.state.or.us
YSAIS, David .... 213-763-7063.... 50 C
ysaisdp@lattc.edu
YSEBAERT, Emily .... 920-498-5612.. 524 E
emily.ysebaert@nwtc.edu
YSURSA, JR., Bernie, J ... 618-235-2700.. 155 C
bernard.ysursa@swic.edu
YU, Alexander .... 330-471-8303.. 371 J
ayu@malone.edu
YU, Bin .... 401-456-8160.. 425 E
byu@ric.edu
YU, Fen .... 904-620-2015.. 112 B
fen.yu@unf.edu
YU, Jenny .... 323-469-3300.... 26 A
jyu@amda.edu
YU, Jerry .... 909-748-8353.... 71 K
jerry_yu@redlands.edu
YU, Lei .... 713-313-7282.. 470 D
yu_lx@tsu.edu
YU, Paul, K .... 858-534-1571.... 70 C
pyu@ucsd.edu
YU, Zhanjing (John) .... 510-464-3213.... 57 D
zyu@peralta.edu
YUAN, Qing .... 301-387-3043.. 207 G
qing.yuan@garrettcollege.edu
YUASA, Miyoko .... 808-946-3773.. 130 D
YUCELT, Baris .... 619-680-4430.... 30 A
baris.yucelt@cc-sd.edu
YUCHT, Nicole .... 352-846-3903.. 112 A
nyucht@ufl.edu
YUDIN, Lee, S .... 671-735-2002.. 530 B
lyudin@uguam.uog.edu
YUDT, Angela, L .... 312-413-3470.. 156 F
ayudt@uic.edu
YUEN, Dan .... 212-924-5900.. 336 I
dyuen@swedishinstitute.edu
YUEN, Karen .... 212-217-3650.. 314 B
karen_yuen@fitnyc.edu
YUHAS, Meredith .... 860-231-5366.... 90 B
myuhas@usj.edu
YULFO, Monserrate .... 787-891-0925.. 533 G
myulfo@aguadilla.inter.edu
YUNDEM, Mustafa .... 918-781-7312.. 382 D
yundemm@bacone.edu
YUNEK, Brent, W .... 949-824-6362.... 69 C
bwyunek@uci.edu
YUNG, Josephine .... 360-438-4375.. 506 G
jyung@stmartin.edu
YUNKAI, Chen .... 910-672-1957.. 356 E
ychen@uncfsu.edu
YUNKE, Laurie .... 215-955-1756.. 420 E
laurie.yunke@jefferson.edu
YUNKER, Julie .... 260-481-6827.. 163 C
yunkerja@ipfw.edu
YUNKER, Kristin, L .... 585-343-0055.. 315 C
klyunker@genesee.edu
YURA, Catherine, A .... 304-293-2547.. 514 C
cathy.yura@mail.wvu.edu
YURACHEK, Hunter .... 713-743-9370.. 473 F
hyurache@uh.edu
YURAN, Mark .... 832-813-6285.. 461 B
mark.a.yuran@lonestar.edu
YURECKO, Michele .... 973-290-4036.. 290 G
myurecko@cse.edu
YURMAN, David .... 718-261-5800.. 305 J
dyurman@bramsonort.edu
YUST, Becky .... 612-624-7461.. 255 H
byust@umn.edu
YUST, Rob .... 417-625-9395.. 268 H
yust-r@mssu.edu
YUSUF, Hamza .... 510-356-4760.... 76 E
YUSUFOV, Daniil .... 303-937-4572.... 77 K
dyusufov@chu.edu
YUTUC, Lloyd .... 301-891-4477.. 213 D
ylloyd@wau.edu
YVON, Karalee .... 413-265-2294.. 217 D
yvonk@elms.edu

Z

ZABALA, Juan .... 409-880-8419.. 471 A
juan.zabala@lamar.edu
ZABEL, Randy .... 405-491-6609.. 388 A
rzabel@snu.edu
ZABINSKI, John .... 856-256-4000.. 295 E
zabinski@rowan.edu
ZABOROWSKI, Barbara ... 814-262-6425.. 413 P
bzabor@pennhighlands.edu
ZABOROWSKI, Joseph, J 402-280-2100.. 279 H
josephzaborowski@creighton.edu
ZABOROWSKI, Shelley ... 402-472-2841.. 282 M
szaborowski3@unl.edu
ZABOROWSKI, Stephen .. 405-878-5481.. 387 J
fszaborowski@stgregorys.edu
ZABOSKI, Gerald, C .... 570-941-7900.. 422 B
gerald.zaboski@scranton.edu
ZABRISKIE, Mark .... 541-737-5774.. 393 H
mark.zabriskie@oregonstate.edu
ZACARIAS, Celina .... 805-437-8920.... 32 B
celina.zacarias@csuci.edu
ZACHARIAH, Sajit .... 216-687-4625.. 366 I
sajit.zachariah@csuohio.edu
ZACHARIAS, Holly .... 252-399-6366.. 341 P
hzacharias@barton.edu
ZACHARIAS, Larry .... 972-883-2232.. 476 C
larry.zacharias@utdallas.edu
ZACHARIAS, Paul .... 660-263-4100.. 269 D
paulz@macc.edu
ZACHARIASEN, Keith .... 785-320-4503.. 183 A
keithzachariasen@manhattantech.edu
ZACHARY, Bohdan .... 414-297-7661.. 524 A
zacharyb@matc.edu
ZACHEISS, Garry, P .... 617-253-1101.. 225 A
ZACHMEYER, Dru .... 805-756-6473.... 31 I
dzachmey@calpoly.edu
ZACK, Gary .... 314-719-8017.. 265 C
gzack@fontbonne.edu
ZACKER, John .... 301-314-8428.. 211 E
jzacker@umd.edu
ZACOVIC, Mark .... 415-241-2229.... 38 E
mzacovic@ccsf.edu
ZACZYK, John .... 814-838-7673.. 403 G
jzaczyk@fortisinstitute.edu
ZADNIK, Karla, S .... 614-292-6603.. 375 A
zadnik.4@osu.edu
ZAGALO-MELO, Paulo .... 406-243-0211.. 276 K
paulo.zagalo-melo@umontana.edu
ZAGNONI, Paul .... 602-212-0501.... 16 B
pzagnoni@theparalegalinstitute.edu
ZAGNONI, Paul .... 602-212-0501.... 11 N
ZAGNONI, Paul, L .... 480-314-2102.... 17 A
paul@sci.edu
ZAGORA, Marilyn, A .... 716-338-1049.. 317 F
marilynzagora@mail.sunyjcc.edu
ZAHED, Fereshtah .... 803-705-4771.. 427 D
zahedf@benedict.edu
ZAHEER, Srilata, A .... 612-624-7876.. 255 H
szaheer@umn.edu
ZAHLIS, Harry .... 559-442-4600.... 67 C
harry.zahlis@fresnocitycollege.edu
ZAHN, JoAnn .... 503-338-2422.. 390 G
jzahn@clatsopcc.edu
ZAHN, Julie .... 603-899-1159.. 287 A
zahnj@franklinpierce.edu
ZAHN, Karla .... 920-693-1247.. 523 E
karla.zahn@gotoltc.edu
ZAHN, Patricia .... 314-516-5267.. 274 A
zahnp@umsl.edu
ZAHOR, Audrey .... 212-472-1500.. 324 A
azahor@nysid.edu
ZAHORSKI-SCHMIDT,
Valerie, F .... 641-422-4435.. 175 E
zahorval@niacc.edu
ZAHZAM, Nancy, L .... 718-780-7915.. 305 L
nancy.zahzam@brooklaw.edu
ZAIDI, Syed .... 859-572-1907.. 192 B
zaidis1@nku.edu
ZAIDMAN, Ron .... 831-476-9424.. 43 M
president@fivebranches.edu
ZAIDMAN, Ron .... 408-260-0208.... 43 L
president@fivebranches.edu
ZAIS, Diana, P .... 781-239-4382.. 214 G
prescottzais@babson.edu
ZAISER, Greg .... 336-278-3566.. 344 D
zaiser@elon.edu
ZAJAC, Brendon .... 440-943-7600.. 377 A
bzajac@dioceseofcleveland.org
ZAJAC, SND, Brendon .... 440-943-7600.. 377 A
bzajac@dioceseofcleveland.org
ZAJACESKOWSKI, John ... 518-244-2253.. 327 H
zajacj@sage.edu
ZAJCHOWSKI, Ann .... 860-727-6757.... 87 H
azajchowski@goodwin.edu
ZAK, Melissa, A .... 303-492-6666.... 83 K
melissa.zak@colorado.edu
ZAK-MOSKAL, Agnes .... 716-896-0700.. 339 E
azakmoskal@villa.edu
ZAKAHI, Walter, R .... 309-677-3152.. 136 B
wzakahi@fsmail.bradley.edu
ZAKE, Ieva .... 609-771-3095.. 290 F
zakei@tcnj.edu
ZAKEL, Lori .... 937-512-3044.. 377 D
lori.zakel@sinclair.edu
ZAKERY, Fatemeh .... 314-340-5096.. 265 H
zakeryf@hssu.edu
ZAKOWSKI, Paul .... 630-942-2895.. 138 B
zakows@cod.edu
ZAKREWSKI, Christopher 773-298-3884.. 153 H
zakrewski@sxu.edu
ZAKRZEWSKI, Bruce .... 269-467-9945.. 234 B
bzakrzewski@glenoaks.edu
ZALACCA, James, A .... 315-267-2314.. 334 B
zalaccja@potsdam.edu
ZALAPI, Diane .... 248-476-1122.. 237 H
dzalapi@mispp.edu
ZALBA, Jeanette .... 734-487-1300.. 233 J
jzalba@emich.edu
ZALDIVAR, Edward .... 305-821-3333.. 101 B
ezaldivar@fnu.edu
ZALETEL, Cora .... 719-549-2576.... 79 B
cora.zaletel@csupueblo.edu
ZALIMAS, Robert .... 803-934-3181.. 431 E
rzalimas@morris.edu
ZAMAN, Malika .... 610-902-8502.. 399 D
maliha.s.zaman@cabrini.edu
ZAMAN, Naveed .... 304-766-3394.. 514 B
zamanna@wvstateu.edu
ZAMBARDI, Victor, A .... 248-370-3112.. 239 K
zambardi@oakland.edu
ZAMBELLA, BethAnn .... 740-587-6215.. 368 B
zambellab@denison.edu
ZAMBLE, Anthony .... 773-244-5568.. 149 I
azamble@northpark.edu
ZAMBON, Joseph .... 716-829-3940.. 331 C
jjzambon@buffalo.edu
ZAMBONINO, Maria .... 773-878-3813.. 153 E
mzambonino@staugustine.edu
ZAMBRANA, Maritza .... 787-279-1912.. 533 J
mzambrana@bayamon.inter.edu
ZAMBRANO, Thomas .... 732-987-2613.. 292 A
tzambrano@georgian.edu
ZAMOJSKI, Heather .... 219-989-2996.. 166 F
zamojski@pnw.edu
ZAMORA, Bradley .... 847-566-6401.. 157 G
bzamora@usml.edu
ZAMORA, David .... 909-794-1084.... 40 H
dzamora@communitychristiancollege.com
ZAMORA, Juan, M .... 305-628-6593.. 108 E
jzamora@stu.edu
ZAMORA, Sue .... 618-985-2828.. 143 F
suezamora@jalc.edu
ZAMORA, Teri .... 713-718-8464.. 459 B
teri.zamora@hccs.edu
ZAMPANO, Gary, S .... 570-941-4273.. 422 B
gary.zampano@scranton.edu
ZAMPARELLI, Jaime .... 609-497-7750.. 294 C
seminary relations@ptsem.edu
ZAMSKY, Robert .... 941-487-4225.. 111 D
rzamsky@ncf.edu
ZANCHELLI, Denise .... 845-451-1458.. 312 C
d_zanche@culinary.edu
ZANDBERGEN
Dianne, V .... 616-222-3000.. 236 F
dzandbergen@kuyper.edu
ZANDER, Kathleen .... 406-377-9403.. 276 D
kzander@dawson.edu
ZANDER, Kirk .... 406-756-3808.. 276 E
kzander@fvcc.edu
ZANDER, William, D .... 302-831-1209.... 91 F
dzander@udel.edu
ZANDERS, Ann .... 225-216-8723.. 195 H
zandersa@mybrcc.edu
ZANDERS, Joan, A .... 703-323-3014.. 497 H
jzanders@nvcc.edu
ZANDERS, Kimberly .... 225-216-8254.. 195 H
zanderskc@mybrcc.edu
ZANDI, Nader .... 205-853-1200...... 5 B
nzandi@jeffstateonline.com
ZANE, Cynthia, A .... 716-926-8923.. 316 B
czane@hilbert.edu
ZANE, Gary .... 207-509-7241.. 204 F
gzane@unity.edu
ZANELLA-LITKE, Joanne .. 508-999-8772.. 220 H
jlitke@umassd.edu
ZANG, Connie .... 740-366-9246.. 365 D
czang@cotc.edu
ZANG, Paul .... 810-766-4112.. 231 D
pzang01@baker.edu
ZANGER, Kate .... 563-588-6313.. 170 F
kate.zanger@clarke.edu
ZANGHI, Pamela .... 716-896-0700.. 339 E
zanghi@villa.edu
ZANGHI, Pamela, M .... 716-896-0700.. 339 E
zanghi@villa.edu
ZANIC, Van, E .... 724-847-6105.. 404 B
vgzanic@geneva.edu
ZANIE, Michael, R .... 540-458-8148.. 500 F
mzanie@wlu.edu
ZANK, Gary .... 256-824-6575........ 8 F
gary.zank@uah.edu
ZANNOTTI, Glenn .... 918-594-8438.. 386 B
gzannotti@osugiving.com
ZANSITIS, Richard, A .... 713-348-5237.. 464 E
zansitis@rice.edu
ZANT, Don .... 662-325-2231.. 259 D
dzant@bulldogetplan.msstate.edu
ZANTINGH, Ryan .... 708-239-4872.. 155 M
ryan.zantingh@trnty.edu
ZAPATA, Elizabeth .... 585-389-2461.. 322 D
ezapata5@naz.edu
ZAPATA, Fred .... 210-999-7401.. 473 A
fred.zapata@trinity.edu
ZAPATA, Grace .... 210-486-2269.. 450 E
zapata@alamo.edu
ZAPATA, Hector .... 225-578-8242.. 197 I
hozapat@lsu.edu
ZAPATA, Jesse, T .... 210-458-2700.. 477 A
jesse.zapata@utsa.edu
ZAPATA, Rafael, A .... 401-865-2878.. 425 D
rzapata@providence.edu
ZAPOLSKI, Mike .... 309-794-7223.. 135 D
mikezapolski@augustana.edu
ZAPPA, Carl, R .... 412-578-8861.. 400 C
crzappa@carlow.edu
ZAPPALORTI, Robert, E ... 203-287-3028.... 88 E
paier.admin@snet.net
ZAPPAS, Barbara .... 831-582-3908.... 33 E
bzappas@csumb.edu
ZAPPE, Christopher .... 717-337-6820.. 404 C
czappe@gettysburg.edu
ZAPPI, Mark, E .... 337-482-6685.. 201 D
zappi@louisiana.edu
ZAPPIA, Charles .... 619-388-2801.... 60 G
czappia@sdccd.edu
ZAPPIA, Gerard .... 585-389-2570.. 322 D
gzappia4@naz.edu
ZARAGOZA, Federico .... 210-485-0015.. 450 A
fzaragoza@alamo.edu
ZARATE, Alfonso .... 913-288-7489.. 182 C
azarate@kckcc.edu
ZARCHI, Shloime .... 718-434-0784.. 306 J
ZAREMBA, Terah .... 269-965-3931.. 236 A
zarembat@kellogg.edu
ZARET, David .... 812-855-5021.. 162 E
zaret@iu.edu
ZARET, David .... 812-855-8669.. 162 F
ovpia@iu.edu
ZARFAS, Ellen .... 503-375-7006.. 391 B
ezarfas@corban.edu
ZARGAR, Fataneh .... 562-622-3368.... 45 C
ZARGES, Bradford .... 617-745-3638.. 218 A
bradford.zarges@enc.edu
ZARKOWSKI, Pamela .... 313-993-1585.. 241 G
zarkowp1@udmercy.edu
ZARLING, Mark, G .... 507-354-8221.. 247 J
zarlinmg@mlc-wels.edu
ZAROBE, Michael .... 312-662-4033.. 134 I
mzarobe@adler.edu
ZARRILLO, Deirdre .... 518-292-1704.. 327 H
zarrid@sage.edu
ZARRINNAM, Ali, R .... 608-246-6446.. 523 F
azarrinnam@madisoncollege.edu
ZART, Leilani .... 319-352-8565.. 177 G
leilani.zart@wartburg.edu
ZARTNER, Ken .... 432-335-6606.. 463 B
kzartner@odessa.edu
ZASTOUPIL, Brenda .... 701-224-2541.. 360 B
brenda.zastoupil@ndus.edu
ZATAR, Wael .... 304-696-6043.. 513 D
zatar@marshall.edu
ZATZ, Marjorie .... 209-228-4723.... 70 A
mzatz@ucmerced.edu
ZAUFT, Richard .... 617-349-8001.. 220 B
richard.zauft@lesley.edu
ZAUHAR, Frances, M .... 570-348-6233.. 409 H
zauhar@marywood.edu
ZAUSCH, Jo .... 502-213-2200.. 190 A
jo.zausch@kctcs.edu
ZAVADA, Michael .... 432-552-2220.. 478 B
ZAVADA, Robert .... 570-674-8018.. 410 K
rzavada@misericordia.edu
ZAVADSKY, Cornelia .... 302-292-6100.... 93 F
ZAVADSKY, Cornelia .... 610-604-7700.... 93 F
ZAVALA, Joseph .... 858-642-8024.... 54 A
jzavala@nu.edu
ZAVALA-COLÓN,
Maria de los Angeles ... 787-993-8877.. 537 G
maria.zavala1@upr.edu
ZAVALA-PETHERBRIDGE,
Dina .... 701-788-4650.. 360 E
dina.petherbridge@mayvillestate.edu
ZAVALA-QUIÑONES,
Javier .... 787-993-8854.. 537 G
javier.zavala@upr.edu
ZAVARICH, Joyce .... 610-519-4080.. 422 G
joyce.zavarich@villanova.edu
ZAVATKAY, Debra .... 860-738-6309.... 87 A
dzavatkay@nwcc.edu
ZAVODNY, John .... 207-509-7122.. 204 F
jzavodny@unity.edu
ZAWADZKI, Kellen .... 513-244-8176.. 366 B
athletics@ccuniversity.edu
ZAWALICH, Barbara .... 508-849-3401.. 214 E
bzawalich@annamaria.edu
ZAWIA, Nasser, H .... 401-874-5909.. 426 D
nzawia@uri.edu
ZAWISTOWSKI, Lee .... 845-569-3229.. 322 B
lee.zawistowski@msmc.edu
ZAWODNY, Laurel, E .... 419-372-2211.. 364 E
lzawodn@bgsu.edu
ZAWOYSKY, Steve .... 360-676-2772.. 505 C
szawoysky@nwic.edu
ZAYAC, Lynn .... 413-572-8142.. 222 E
lzayac@westfield.ma.edu
ZAYAITZ, Anne .... 610-683-4155.. 415 C
zayaitz@kutztown.edu

ZAYAS, Brendaliz ... 787-258-1501.. 531 K
bzayas@columbiacentral.edu
ZAYAS, David ... 787-841-2000.. 535 I
dzayaz@pucpr.edu
ZAYAS, Luis, H ... 512-471-1937.. 476 B
lzayas@austin.utexas.edu
ZAYAS, Myriam ... 787-841-2000.. 535 I
mzayas@pucpr.edu
ZAYAS, Niza ... 787-786-3030.. 536 F
nzayas@ucb.edu.pr
ZAYAS, Ruth ... 201-216-9901.. 291 C
ruth.zayas@eicollege.edu
ZAYAS-HERNÁNDEZ,
Haydee, M ... 787-480-2370.. 531 J
hzayas@sanjuanciudadpatria.com
ZAZUETA, Fedro, S ... 352-392-0371.. 112 A
fsz@ufl.edu
ZAZZALI, Robert ... 856-256-4110.. 295 E
zazzali@rowan.edu
ZBIKOWSKI, Lawrence ... 773-702-8500.. 156 D
larry@uchicago.edu
ZDANCEWICZ, Heather ... 703-370-6600.. 492 I
ZDZIARSKI, Gene ... 312-362-8854.. 139 C
ezdziars@depaul.edu
ZEALAND, Matthew, J ... 434-582-2000.. 491 D
mjzealan@liberty.edu
ZEBALLOS, Jorge ... 269-965-3931.. 236 A
zeballosj@kellogg.edu
ZEBEDIS, Frank, J ... 803-323-3333.. 435 B
zebedisf@winthrop.edu
ZEBROWSKI, Michael, J . 414-288-7172.. 517 I
michael.zebrowski@marquette.edu
ZECH, Susan ... 212-686-9244.. 304 A
ZECKOVICH, Kim ... 906-932-4231.. 234 C
kimz@gogebic.edu
ZEEK, Raymond ... 203-285-2210.... 86 C
rzeek@gwcc.commnet.edu
ZEFF, Ira, A ... 402-465-2360.. 281 K
izeff@nebrwesleyan.edu
ZEFF, Jane ... 973-720-2379.. 298 G
zeffj@wpunj.edu
ZEGARSKI, Len ... 619-684-8788.... 54 C
lzegarski@newschoolarch.edu
ZEGER, Brian ... 212-799-5000.. 318 A
ZEGLEN, Marie ... 352-392-0456.. 112 A
zeglenm@ufl.edu
ZEH, David ... 775-784-1110.. 285 A
zehd@unr.edu
ZEHEL, Renee, G ... 570-961-4715.. 409 H
rzehel@marywood.edu
ZEHNDER, Sarah, B ... 785-227-3380.. 178 J
zehndersb@bethanylb.edu
ZEHR, David ... 603-535-2235.. 288 F
zehr@plymouth.edu
ZEHREN, Carolyn, F ... 218-477-2085.. 250 F
zehren@mnstate.edu
ZEICH, Heidi, E ... 202-319-5615.... 92 A
zeich@cua.edu
ZEICHNER, Veronica ... 201-360-4043.. 292 B
vzeichner@hccc.edu
ZEIDENSTEIN, Darrow ... 713-348-6090.. 464 E
darrowz@rice.edu
ZEIFANG, Kathleen ... 202-884-9705.... 94 A
zeifangk@trinitydc.edu
ZEIGER, Judy ... 507-389-7351.. 252 D
judy.zeiger@southcentral.edu
ZEIGLER, Helen, T ... 803-777-5432.. 433 F
helenz@mailbox.sc.edu
ZEIGLER, Michael ... 803-535-5340.. 428 B
mike.zeigler@claflin.edu
ZEIGLER, Michael, C ... 717-867-6060.. 408 F
zeigler@lvc.edu
ZEIGLER, Sara ... 859-622-2222.. 188 F
sara.zeigler@eku.edu
ZEILBERGER, Yeruchom .. 845-207-0330.. 305 D
ZEILE, Carol ... 989-463-7227.. 230 F
zeile@alma.edu
ZEILENGA, Jeffrey ... 573-882-5397.. 273 E
zeilingaj@missouri.edu
ZEIMANTZ, Erich ... 414-930-3527.. 518 F
zeimante@mtmary.edu
ZEIMET, Dan, L ... 563-333-6202.. 176 D
zeimetdaniell@sau.edu
ZEIND, Caroline ... 508-373-5825.. 225 C
caroline.zeind@mcphs.edu
ZEIRD, Susan ... 706-233-7466.. 127 A
szeird@shorter.edu
ZEISER, Richard, A ... 860-768-4181.... 89 G
zeiser@hartford.edu
ZEISS, P. Anthony ... 704-330-6566.. 348 E
tony.zeiss@cpcc.edu
ZEISS, Timothy ... 732-224-2887.. 289 I
tzeiss@brookdalecc.edu
ZEITHAML, Carl, P ... 434-924-3176.. 495 H
cpz6n@virginia.edu
ZELASKO, Sandra ... 360-538-4000.. 504 B
szelasko@ghc.edu
ZELDNER, Cynthia ... 860-512-3214.... 86 E
czeldner@manchestercc.edu
ZELENAK, Christine ... 609-896-5395.. 295 B
czelenak@rider.edu
ZELENSKI, Paul ... 517-371-5140.. 243 I
zelensp@cooley.edu
ZELENZ, Margot ... 715-682-1495.. 518 H
mzelenz@northland.edu
ZELESNIK, Kelly ... 440-365-5222.. 371 H
ZELEZNY, Lynnette ... 559-278-2636.... 32 F
lynnette@csufresno.edu
ZELINSKI, Bob ... 352-854-2322.... 97 R
zelinskb@cf.edu
ZELINSKI, Debbie ... 312-329-4231.. 148 F
debbie.zelinski@moody.edu
ZELL, Jennifer ... 845-687-5049.. 338 F
zellj@sunyulster.edu
ZELLAR, Nel ... 507-433-0832.. 251 H
nel.zellar@riverland.edu
ZELLER, John, H ... 215-898-5169.. 421 E
jzeller@upenn.edu
ZELLER, Lisa, L ... 303-963-3210.... 77 I
lzeller@ccu.edu
ZELLERS, Andrew ... 270-831-9627.. 189 F
andrew.zellers@kctcs.edu
ZELLERS, Jeff, W ... 740-826-8011.. 373 E
jzellers@muskingum.edu
ZELLERS, Victoria ... 215-751-8913.. 401 G
vzellers@ccp.edu
ZELLMER, Jill, A ... 617-627-3298.. 228 H
jill.zellmer@tufts.edu
ZELLNER, Wayne ... 719-632-8116.... 81 A
wzellner@intelliteccollege.edu
ZELNICK, Debra ... 215-503-9606.. 420 E
debra.zelnick@jefferson.edu
ZELTWANGER, Todd ... 574-936-8898.. 158 I
todd.zeltwanger@ancilla.edu
ZEMAN, Ellen ... 802-651-5912.. 483 F
zeman@champlain.edu
ZEMAN, Janet ... 845-569-3159.. 322 B
janet.zeman@msmc.edu
ZEMAN, Janice, L ... 757-221-3877.. 488 F
jlzema@wm.edu
ZEMAN, Mary Beth ... 973-720-2971.. 298 G
zemanm@wpunj.edu
ZEMAN, Scott ... 401-341-2222.. 426 C
scott.zeman@salve.edu
ZEMBAR, Mary Jo ... 937-327-7921.. 381 F
mzembar@wittenberg.edu
ZEMBRODT, Belle ... 859-572-5634.. 192 B
zembrodt@nku.edu
ZEMP, William ... 603-644-3179.. 287 I
w.zemp@snhu.edu
ZENCHECK, Jack ... 718-430-8889.. 341 G
zencheck@yu.edu
ZENDMAN, Ellen ... 914-606-6733.. 340 C
ellen.zendman@sunywcc.edu
ZENELIS, John, G ... 703-993-2491.. 490 B
jzenelis@gmu.edu
ZENG, Zheng ... 512-454-1188.. 451 E
info@aoma.edu
ZENGER, Sheahon ... 785-864-3143.. 185 D
kuathletics@ku.edu
ZENK, Leslie ... 704-687-5766.. 358 A
lzenk@uncc.edu
ZENO, Mark ... 419-448-2058.. 369 G
mzeno@heidelberg.edu
ZENTENO, Liz ... 432-685-4507.. 461 H
lzenteno@midland.edu
ZENTENO, Rene ... 210-458-4994.. 477 A
rene.zenteno@utsa.edu
ZENTMEYER, James, R ... 248-370-3570.. 239 K
zentmeye@oakland.edu
ZEONE, Alicia ... 507-280-3509.. 251 I
alicia.zeone@rctc.edu
ZEPEDA, Andrea ... 918-335-6833.. 386 F
azepeda@okwu.edu
ZEPEDA, Milani ... 408-855-5123.... 74 G
milani.zepeda@missioncollege.edu
ZEPEDA, Orlando, J ... 956-721-5102.. 460 F
orlando.zepeda@laredo.edu
ZEPHIER, Jessica ... 605-867-5856.. 436 G
jzephier@olc.edu
ZEPHIER-SWIFT,
Michelle ... 605-856-8186.. 436 I
michelle.zephier-swift@sintegleska.edu
ZEPPOS, Nicholas ... 615-322-1813.. 449 A
nick.zeppos@vanderbilt.edu
ZERAI, Assata ... 217-244-9157.. 157 A
azerai@illinois.edu
ZERANGUE, David ... 985-448-4090.. 201 A
david.zerangue@nicholls.edu
ZERBE, Bryan ... 415-565-4623.... 69 B
zerbeb@uchastings.edu
ZERBE, Linda ... 610-282-1100.. 402 B
linda.zerbe@desales.edu
ZERBONIA, Liza ... 563-355-3500.. 174 E
lzerbonia@kaplan.edu
ZERILLO, Barbara ... 617-236-8838.. 218 G
bzerillo@fisher.edu
ZERMENO, Christina ... 714-997-6517.... 37 F
curiel@chapman.edu
ZERNICK, Christine ... 814-262-6462.. 413 P
czernick@pennhighlands.edu
ZERNICKE, Ronald, F ... 734-764-5210.. 241 J
zernicke@umich.edu
ZEROSIMO, Veronica ... 201-360-4198.. 292 B
vzerosimo@hccc.edu
ZERTUCHE, Bernie ... 210-486-4879.. 450 C
zertuche@alamo.edu
ZERZAN, Phil ... 503-725-4782.. 394 G
pzerzan@pdx.edu
ZESWITZ, John ... 717-560-8278.. 407 E
jzeswitz@lbc.edu
ZETARSKI, Jennifer ... 802-225-3230.. 484 G
jennifer.zetarski@neci.edu
ZETTERGREN, David, G ... 901-678-2121.. 445 C
dzttrgrn@memphis.edu
ZETTLER, Chuck, H ... 561-868-3033.. 106 D
zettlerc@palmbeachstate.edu
ZEWE, Beth ... 814-732-1420.. 415 A
zewe@edinboro.edu
ZEYNEP LEUENBERGER,
Deniz ... 508-531-6125.. 221 C
dleuenberger@bridgew.edu
ZHAI, Lijuan ... 559-489-2224.... 67 C
lijuan.zhai@fresnocitycollege.edu
ZHAN, Lin ... 901-678-2020.. 445 C
lzhan@memphis.edu
ZHANG, Chunsheng ... 256-765-4898..... 9 C
czhang@una.edu
ZHANG, James ... 810-762-7949.. 236 C
jzhang@kettering.edu
ZHANG, Jane ... 510-763-7787.... 25 B
jane@acchs.edu
ZHANG, Jiajie, W ... 713-500-3922.. 477 C
jiajie.zhang@uth.tmc.edu
ZHANG, Li ... 530-754-8924.... 69 A
lizhang@ucdavis.edu
ZHANG, Ling ... 408-260-0208.... 43 M
sjadmin@fivebranches.edu
ZHANG, Lujia ... 732-548-6000.. 292 E
lzhang@middlesexcc.edu
ZHANG, Ming ... 360-650-4454.. 509 E
ming.zhang@wwu.edu
ZHANG, Minghua ... 631-632-8781.. 332 A
minghua.zhang@stonybrook.edu
ZHANG, Robert ... 412-365-1292.. 400 G
rzhang@chatham.edu
ZHANG, Sha Li ... 406-243-6800.. 276 K
shali.zhang@umontana.edu
ZHANG, Shouhong ... 605-688-6312.. 437 F
shouhong.zhang@sdstate.edu
ZHANG, Tong-Ai ... 361-570-4323.. 474 C
zhangt@uhv.edu
ZHANG, William, B ... 336-285-3048.. 356 F
wbzhang@ncat.edu
ZHANG, Xiao, Y ... 716-673-4806.. 331 D
xiao.zhang@fredonia.edu
ZHANG, Yang ... 808-956-5877.. 131 F
yz6@hawaii.edu
ZHAO, Jie (George) ... 626-873-2179.... 53 E
jzhao@mtsierra.edu
ZHAO, Joanna ... 408-260-0208.... 43 L
dean@fivebranches.edu
ZHAO, Joanna ... 831-476-9424.... 43 M
dean@fivebranches.edu
ZHAO, Lianna ... 949-451-5450.... 65 F
lzhao@ivc.edu
ZHAO, Yiping ... 516-739-1545.. 323 D
clinicmanager@nyctcm.edu
ZHENG, Henry, Y ... 610-758-3708.. 408 H
hyz216@lehigh.edu
ZHENG, Jilian ... 402-559-5656.. 283 A
jzheng@unmc.edu
ZHENG, John ... 662-254-3452.. 260 A
zheng@mvsu.edu
ZHONG, Baisong ... 713-780-9777.. 451 A
info@acaom.edu
ZHOU, Chenn ... 219-989-2665.. 166 F
czhou@pnw.edu
ZHOU, Claire ... 914-337-9300.. 311 F
claire.zhou@concordia-ny.edu
ZHOU, Kai ... 518-782-6888.. 330 E
kzhou@siena.edu
ZHOU, Lin ... 253-680-7105.. 501 E
lzhou@bates.ctc.edu
ZHOU, Sharon ... 408-481-9988.... 46 C
ZHOU, Wei ... 909-389-3200.... 60 B
wzhou@craftonhills.edu
ZHOU, Wei ... 301-985-7705.. 212 C
institutional-planning@umuc.edu
ZHOU, Wei ... 724-938-4074.. 414 E
zhou@calu.edu
ZHOU, Ying ... 252-737-1912.. 356 C
zhouy14@ecu.edu
ZHU, Jianping ... 216-687-3588.. 366 I
j.zhu94@csuohio.edu
ZHU, Jishan ... 516-876-3292.. 333 C
zhuj@oldwestbury.edu
ZHU, Lizhi (Frank) ... 718-522-9073.. 304 D
ZHUANG, Miao ... 361-593-4480.. 469 A
miao.zhuang@tamuk.edu
ZIADY, Nicola ... 513-556-3015.. 379 A
nicola.ziady@uc.edu
ZIAJKA, Alan, L ... 415-422-2846.... 72 C
ziajka@usfca.edu
ZIAVRAS, Sotirios, G ... 973-596-3462.. 293 D
sotirios.g.ziavras@njit.edu
ZIBBY-DAMRON,
Kathleen ... 618-437-5321.. 152 A
zibbyk@rlc.edu
ZIBELL, Tammy ... 509-533-8135.. 502 I
tammy.zibell@scc.spokane.edu
ZIBLUK, Patricia, M ... 203-392-6800.... 85 H
ziblukp1@southernct.edu
ZIC, Anthony ... 516-759-2040.. 339 G
azic@webb.edu
ZICCARDI, C. Anthony ... 973-313-6053.. 297 A
anthony.ziccardi@shu.edu
ZICHER, Marie-Ange ... 708-456-0300.. 156 C
marieangezicher@triton.edu
ZIEBARTH, Timothy, J ... 574-372-5100.. 161 B
ziebartj@grace.edu
ZIEGENGEIST, Roy, P ... 860-701-6509.. 529 A
roy.p.ziegengeist1@uscg.mil
ZIEGLER, Carol ... 216-373-6534.. 374 B
cziegler@ndc.edu
ZIEGLER, Chris ... 734-432-5662.. 237 D
cziegler@madonna.edu
ZIEGLER, Jennifer ... 219-464-5271.. 168 F
jennifer.ziegler@valpo.edu
ZIEGLER, John ... 724-738-9000.. 416 B
john.ziegler@sru.edu
ZIEGLER, Mark ... 510-780-4500.... 48 J
mzeigler@lifewest.edu
ZIEGLER, William ... 607-777-3583.. 331 B
ziegler@binghamton.edu
ZIELASKOWSKI, Cindy ... 518-743-2275.. 335 A
zielaskowskic@sunyacc.edu
ZIELINSKI, David ... 760-355-6470.... 46 J
david.zielinski@imperial.edu
ZIEMBA, Christine ... 661-255-1050.... 30 E
ZIEMBA, David ... 508-362-2131.. 223 C
dziemba@capecod.edu
ZIEMIAN, Joelle ... 434-381-6262.. 494 M
jziemian@sbc.edu
ZIEMIANSKI, Michael ... 812-357-6501.. 167 B
mziemianski@saintmeinrad.edu
ZIEMINSKI, Julie ... 763-424-0796.. 251 B
jzieminski@nhcc.edu
ZIEMNICK, Tom ... 540-338-1776.. 492 H
ZIENTARSKI, Nicholas, A 914-367-8216.. 329 C
nzientarski@dunwoodie.org
ZIER, Joni, I ... 423-236-2895.. 444 B
jzier@southern.edu
ZIERDT, Ginger ... 507-389-6214.. 250 E
ginger.zierdt@mns.edu
ZIEROLD, Norman ... 641-472-1313.. 175 A
nzierold@mum.edu
ZIESKE, Denise ... 518-595-1101.. 330 B
ziesked@sunysccc.edu
ZIESLER, Yasmine ... 802-224-3000.. 485 G
yasmine.ziesler@vsc.edu
ZIEZIULA, Amy ... 607-778-5307.. 332 D
zieziulaaj@sunybroome.edu
ZIKEL, Tara ... 724-925-4177.. 423 D
zikelt@wccc.edu
ZILBERMAN, Diana ... 410-462-7719.. 206 D
dzilberman@bccc.edu
ZILLGES, Virginia, K ... 757-822-1399.. 498 H
vzillges@tcc.edu
ZILLMAN, John ... 708-209-3011.. 138 G
john.zillman@cuchicago.edu
ZILLMER, Eric, A ... 215-895-1977.. 402 G
zillmer@drexel.edu
ZIMA DOWD, Bonnie ... 413-552-2253.. 223 E
bzimadowd@hcc.edu
ZIMBELMAN, Joel, A ... 530-898-4767.... 32 C
jzimbelman@csuchico.edu
ZIMLICH, Robert, L ... 502-272-8263.. 187 A
bzimlich@bellarmine.edu
ZIMMER, Brandi ... 785-738-9056.. 183 J
bzimmer@ncktc.edu
ZIMMER, Joseph ... 716-375-2121.. 328 B
jezimmer@sbu.edu
ZIMMER, Keri ... 712-388-6844.. 174 B
kzimmer@iwcc.edu
ZIMMER, Robert, J ... 773-702-8001.. 156 D
president@uchicago.edu
ZIMMER, Tim ... 618-262-8641.. 142 F
zimmert@iecc.edu
ZIMMER, Timothy, P ... 217-581-3520.. 139 H
tpzimmer@eiu.edu
ZIMMERMAN, Barri ... 410-543-6165.. 213 A
ebzimmerman@salisbury.edu
ZIMMERMAN, Brian ... 765-983-1256.. 160 G
zimmebr@earlham.edu
ZIMMERMAN, Christine .. 315-229-5394.. 329 D
christinezimmerman@stlawu.edu
ZIMMERMAN, Eileen, P .. 207-753-6970.. 202 D
ezimmerm@bates.edu
ZIMMERMAN, Gail ... 603-358-2842.. 288 E
gzimmerman@keene.edu
ZIMMERMAN, Heidi ... 615-898-2025.. 444 G
heidi.zimmerman@mtsu.edu

Accreditation Index of Institutions by Regional, National, Professional and Specialized Agencies

Degree levels are shown by the following symbols: (C) diploma/certificate; (A) associate; (B) baccalaureate; (M) master's; (S) beyond master's but less than doctorate; (FP) first professional; (D) doctorate.

AA: Commission on Accreditation of Allied Health Education Programs: anesthesiologist assistant (M)

AAB: Aviation Accreditation Board International: aviation (A,B,M)

AAFCS: American Association of Family and Consumer Sciences: family and consumer science (B)

ABHES: Accrediting Bureau of Health Education Schools: allied health (C,A,B)

ACAE: Accreditation Commission for Audiology Education: audiology (D)

ACBSP: Accreditation Council for Business Schools and Programs: business administration, management, accounting and related business fields (A,B,M,D)

ACCSC: Accrediting Commission of Career Schools and Colleges: occupational, trade, and technical education (C,A,B,M)

ACFEI: American Culinary Federation, Inc.: culinary arts and culinary management (C,A,B)

ACICS: Accrediting Council for Independent Colleges and Schools: business and business related programs (C,A,B,M)

Instituto de Banca y Comercio ... PR ... 533
Trinity College of Puerto Rico ... PR ... 536
Universal Technology College of Puerto Rico ... PR ... 536
Forrest College ... SC ... 430
Brightwood College ... TN ... 439
Daymar College ... TN ... 439
Miller-Motte Technical College ... TN ... 442
National College ... TN ... 443
SAE Institute Nashville ... TN ... 443
Brightwood College ... TX ... 453
Career Point College ... TX ... 453
Center for Advanced Legal Studies ... TX ... 453
Le Cordon Bleu College of Culinary Arts in Austin ... TX ... 460
North American University ... TX ... 462
Texas Health and Science University ... TX ... 470
Vet Tech Institute of Houston ... TX ... 478
Broadview University ... UT ... 480
Eagle Gate College ... UT ... 480
Neumont University ... UT ... 480
Provo College ... UT ... 481
American College of Commerce and Technology ... VA ... 486
American National University ... VA ... 486
Bon Secours Memorial College of Nursing ... VA ... 487
Columbia College ... VA ... 488
Everest College ... VA ... 489
Fortis College ... VA ... 489
Global Health College ... VA ... 490
iGlobal University ... VA ... 490
Miller-Motte Technical College ... VA ... 492
Sentara College of Health Sciences ... VA ... 494
Stratford University ... VA ... 494
University of North America ... VA ... 495
Virginia International University ... VA ... 499
Virginia University of Oriental Medicine ... VA ... 500
Pinchot University ... WA .. 506
Mountain State College ... WV .. 511
Valley College - Beckley Campus ... WV .. 511
Valley College - Martinsburg Campus ... WV .. 511
Valley College - Princeton Campus ... WV .. 511
West Virginia Business College ... WV .. 511
West Virginia Junior College ... WV .. 514
Madison Media Institute-College of Media Arts ... WI ... 517
Wright Graduate University for the Realization of Human Potential ... WI ... 526

ACUP: Accreditation Commission for Acupuncture and Oriental Medicine: acupuncture (C,M,D)

#Arizona School of Acupuncture and Oriental Medicine ... AZ ... 11
Han University of Traditional Medicine ... AZ ... 13
Phoenix Institute of Herbal Medicine and Acupuncture ... AZ ... 16
Academy of Chinese Culture and Health Sciences ... CA ... 25
Acupuncture and Integrative Medicine College-Berkeley ... CA ... 25
Alhambra Medical University ... CA ... 25
California Institute of Integral Studies ... CA ... 30
Dongguk University ... CA ... 42
Emperor's College of Traditional Oriental Medicine ... CA ... 42
Five Branches University, Graduate School of Traditional Chinese Medicine ... CA ... 43
@Golden State University ... CA ... 45
@Nine Star University of Health Sciences ... CA ... 54
Pacific College of Oriental Medicine ... CA ... 55
South Baylo University ... CA ... 65
Southern California University of Health Sciences ... CA ... 66
Southern California University School of Oriental Medicine & Acupuncture ... CA ... 66
University of East-West Medicine ... CA ... 71
Yo San University of Traditional Chinese Medicine ... CA ... 75
Colorado School of Traditional Chinese Medicine ... CO ... 78
Institute of Taoist Education and Acupuncture ... CO ... 80
University of Bridgeport ... CT ... 89
Academy for Five Element Acupuncture ... FL ... 94
Acupuncture & Massage College ... FL ... 95
Atlantic Institute of Oriental Medicine ... FL ... 95
Dragon Rises College of Oriental Medicine ... FL ... 98
East West College of Natural Medicine ... FL ... 98
Florida College of Integrative Medicine ... FL ... 100
Institute of Clinical Acupuncture and Oriental Medicine ... HI ... 131
World Medicine Institute ... HI ... 132
National University of Health Sciences ... IL ... 149
Maryland University of Integrative Health ... MD .. 209
New England School of Acupuncture ... MA .. 226
American Academy of Acupuncture and Oriental Medicine ... MN .. 244
Northwestern Health Sciences University ... MN .. 253
@Wongu University of Oriental Medicine ... NV .. 285
Southwest Acupuncture College ... NM .. 302
New York Chiropractic College ... NY .. 323
New York College of Health Professions ... NY .. 323
New York College of Traditional Chinese Medicine ... NY .. 323
Tri-State College of Acupuncture ... NY .. 338
Daoist Traditions College of Chinese Medical Arts ... NC .. 343
American Institute of Alternative Medicine ... OH .. 362
National University of Natural Medicine ... OR .. 392
Oregon College of Oriental Medicine ... OR .. 393
Won Institute of Graduate Studies ... PA ... 424
American College of Acupuncture and Oriental Medicine ... TX ... 451
AOMA Graduate School of Integrative Medicine ... TX ... 451
Texas Health and Science University ... TX ... 470
Kings Park University ... VA ... 491
Virginia University of Oriental Medicine ... VA ... 500
Bastyr University ... WA .. 501
Seattle Institute of Oriental Medicine ... WA .. 507
Midwest College of Oriental Medicine ... WI ... 518

ADNUR: Accreditation Commission for Education in Nursing: nursing (A)

Alabama Southern Community College ... AL ... 1
Bevill State Community College ... AL ... 2
Bishop State Community College ... AL ... 2
Calhoun Community College ... AL ... 2
Central Alabama Community College ... AL ... 2
Chattahoochee Valley Community College ... AL ... 2
Gadsden State Community College ... AL ... 3
George C. Wallace Community College - Dothan ... AL ... 3
George Corley Wallace State Community College - Selma ... AL ... 4
James H. Faulkner State Community College ... AL ... 4
Jefferson Davis Community College ... AL ... 5
Jefferson State Community College ... AL ... 5
Lawson State Community College ... AL ... 5
Lurleen B. Wallace Community College ... AL ... 5
Northeast Alabama Community College ... AL ... 5
Northwest - Shoals Community College ... AL ... 6
Shelton State Community College ... AL ... 6
Snead State Community College ... AL ... 6
Southern Union State Community College ... AL ... 7
Troy University ... AL ... 7
University of West Alabama, The ... AL ... 9
Wallace State Community College - Hanceville ... AL ... 9
Charter College ... AK ... 10
University of Alaska Anchorage ... AK ... 10
Arizona Western College ... AZ ... 11
Central Arizona College ... AZ ... 12
Chandler-Gilbert Community College ... AZ ... 13
Eastern Arizona College ... AZ ... 13
Estrella Mountain Community College ... AZ ... 14
Gateway Community College ... AZ ... 14
Glendale Community College ... AZ ... 14
Mesa Community College ... AZ ... 14
Mohave Community College ... AZ ... 15
Northland Pioneer College ... AZ ... 15
Paradise Valley Community College ... AZ ... 14
Phoenix College ... AZ ... 14
Pima Community College ... AZ ... 16
Scottsdale Community College ... AZ ... 14
Yavapai College ... AZ ... 18
Arkansas State University-Jonesboro ... AR ... 18
East Arkansas Community College ... AR ... 20
National Park College ... AR ... 21
North Arkansas College ... AR ... 21
Phillips Community College of the University of Arkansas ... AR ... 23
Southeast Arkansas College ... AR ... 22
University of Arkansas at Little Rock ... AR ... 23
University of Arkansas Community College at Batesville ... AR ... 23
Cerritos College ... CA ... 36
Chaffey College ... CA ... 37
College of the Canyons ... CA ... 40
Cypress College ... CA ... 54
Evergreen Valley College ... CA ... 62
Golden West College ... CA ... 39
Grossmont College ... CA ... 45
Long Beach City College ... CA ... 49
Los Angeles Harbor College ... CA ... 49
Los Angeles Valley College ... CA ... 50
Monterey Peninsula College ... CA ... 53
Moorpark College ... CA ... 73
Ohlone College ... CA ... 55
Pacific Union College ... CA ... 56
Palomar College ... CA ... 56
Riverside City College ... CA ... 59
Saddleback College ... CA ... 65
San Bernardino Valley College ... CA ... 60
San Diego City College ... CA ... 60
San Joaquin Delta College ... CA ... 61
Santa Ana College ... CA ... 58
Santa Barbara City College ... CA ... 63
Santa Monica College ... CA ... 63
Southwestern College ... CA ... 66
Ventura College ... CA ... 73
Aims Community College ... CO ... 76
Arapahoe Community College ... CO ... 76
Colorado Mesa University ... CO ... 77
Colorado Mountain College ... CO ... 78
Colorado Northwestern Community College ... CO ... 78
Denver School of Nursing ... CO ... 79
Front Range Community College ... CO ... 80
Lamar Community College ... CO ... 81
Morgan Community College ... CO ... 81
Northeastern Junior College ... CO ... 81
Otero Junior College ... CO ... 82
Pikes Peak Community College ... CO ... 82
Pueblo Community College ... CO ... 82
Trinidad State Junior College ... CO ... 83
Capital Community College ... CT ... 86
Gateway Community College ... CT ... 86
Goodwin College ... CT ... 87
Naugatuck Valley Community College ... CT ... 86
Northwestern Connecticut Community-Technical College ... CT ... 87
Norwalk Community College ... CT ... 87
St. Vincent's College ... CT ... 89
Three Rivers Community College ... CT ... 87
Delaware Technical Community College, Terry Campus ... DE ... 91
Broward College ... FL ... 96
Chipola College ... FL ... 97
College of Central Florida ... FL ... 97
Daytona State College ... FL ... 98
Florida Gateway College ... FL ... 100
Florida SouthWestern State College ... FL ... 101
Florida State College at Jacksonville ... FL ... 101
Gulf Coast State College ... FL ... 102
Hillsborough Community College ... FL ... 102
Indian River State College ... FL ... 103
Keiser University ... FL ... 103
Lake-Sumter State College ... FL ... 104
Mercy Hospital College of Nursing ... FL ... 105
Miami Dade College ... FL ... 105
Northwest Florida State College ... FL ... 105
Palm Beach State College ... FL ... 106
Pasco-Hernando State College ... FL ... 106
Pensacola State College ... FL ... 106
Polk State College ... FL ... 106
St. Johns River State College ... FL ... 108
St. Petersburg College ... FL ... 108
Santa Fe College ... FL ... 109
Seminole State College of Florida ... FL ... 109
South Florida State College ... FL ... 109
State College of Florida, Manatee-Sarasota ... FL ... 110
Tallahassee Community College ... FL ... 113
Valencia College ... FL ... 114
Abraham Baldwin Agricultural College ... GA .. 115
Athens Technical College ... GA .. 116
Bainbridge State College ... GA .. 117
Chattahoochee Technical College ... GA .. 118
College of Coastal Georgia ... GA .. 119
Columbus Technical College ... GA .. 119
Dalton State College ... GA .. 119
Darton State College ... GA .. 120
Georgia Highlands College ... GA .. 121
Georgia Northwestern Technical College ... GA .. 121
Gordon State College ... GA .. 122
Gwinnett Technical College ... GA .. 123
Middle Georgia State University ... GA .. 124
South Georgia State College ... GA .. 127
Southern Regional Technical College ... GA .. 127
West Georgia Technical College ... GA .. 129
Kapiolani Community College ... HI ... 131
University of Hawaii Hawaii Community College ... HI ... 131
University of Hawaii Kauai Community College ... HI ... 132
University of Hawaii Maui College ... HI ... 132
College of Southern Idaho ... ID ... 133
College of Western Idaho ... ID ... 133
Idaho State University ... ID ... 133
North Idaho College ... ID ... 134
Black Hawk College ... IL ... 135
Carl Sandburg College ... IL ... 136
City Colleges of Chicago Harry S Truman College ... IL ... 137
College of DuPage ... IL ... 138
College of Lake County ... IL ... 138
Danville Area Community College ... IL ... 139
Elgin Community College ... IL ... 140
Harper College ... IL ... 141
Heartland Community College ... IL ... 141
Illinois Central College ... IL ... 141
Illinois Eastern Community Colleges Frontier Community College ... IL ... 142
Illinois Eastern Community Colleges Lincoln Trail College ... IL ... 142
Illinois Eastern Community Colleges Olney Central College ... IL ... 142
Illinois Eastern Community Colleges Wabash Valley College ... IL ... 142
Illinois Valley Community College ... IL ... 143
Joliet Junior College ... IL ... 144
Kankakee Community College ... IL ... 144
Kaskaskia College ... IL ... 144
Lake Land College ... IL ... 145
Lewis and Clark Community College ... IL ... 145
Lincoln Land Community College ... IL ... 146
Malcolm X College, One of the City Colleges of Chicago ... IL ... 138
Moraine Valley Community College ... IL ... 148
Morton College ... IL ... 149
Oakton Community College ... IL ... 150
Parkland College ... IL ... 151
Prairie State College ... IL ... 151
Richland Community College ... IL ... 152
Southwestern Illinois College ... IL ... 155
Trinity College of Nursing & Health Sciences ... IL ... 156
Triton College ... IL ... 156
Waubonsee Community College ... IL ... 157
Bethel College ... IN ... 159
Ivy Tech Community College of Indiana-Central Indiana ... IN ... 164
University of Saint Francis ... IN ... 168
Vincennes University ... IN ... 169
Des Moines Area Community College ... IA ... 171
Mercy College of Health Sciences ... IA ... 175
North Iowa Area Community College ... IA ... 175
St. Luke's College ... IA ... 176
Barton County Community College ... KS ... 178
Butler Community College ... KS ... 179
Cloud County Community College ... KS ... 179
Colby Community College ... KS ... 180
Dodge City Community College ... KS ... 180
Fort Scott Community College ... KS ... 181
Garden City Community College ... KS ... 181
Hesston College ... KS ... 181
Hutchinson Community College ... KS ... 181
Johnson County Community College ... KS ... 182
Kansas City Kansas Community College ... KS ... 182
Labette Community College ... KS ... 182
Manhattan Area Technical College ... KS ... 183
Neosho County Community College ... KS ... 183
North Central Kansas Technical College ... KS ... 183
Seward County Community College ... KS ... 184
Ashland Community and Technical College ... KY ... 188
Bluegrass Community and Technical College ... KY ... 189
Eastern Kentucky University ... KY ... 188
Elizabethtown Community and Technical College ... KY ... 189
Galen College of Nursing ... KY ... 188
Henderson Community College ... KY ... 189
Hopkinsville Community College ... KY ... 189
Jefferson Community and Technical College ... KY ... 190
Kentucky State University ... KY ... 191
Madisonville Community College ... KY ... 190
Midway University ... KY ... 191
Morehead State University ... KY ... 191
Somerset Community College ... KY ... 190
Southeast Kentucky Community and Technical College ... KY ... 190
West Kentucky Community and Technical College ... KY ... 190
Western Kentucky University ... KY ... 194
Baton Rouge Community College ... LA ... 195
Bossier Parish Community College ... LA ... 195
Delgado Community College ... LA ... 196
L.E. Fletcher Technical Community College ... LA ... 196
Louisiana Delta Community College ... LA ... 196
Louisiana State University at Alexandria ... LA ... 197
Louisiana State University at Eunice ... LA ... 197
Louisiana Tech University ... LA ... 200
McNeese State University ... LA ... 200
Northwestern State University ... LA ... 201
Southern University at Shreveport-Louisiana ... LA ... 199
Central Maine Community College ... ME .. 203
Eastern Maine Community College ... ME .. 203
Kennebec Valley Community College ... ME .. 203
Maine College of Health Professions ... ME .. 203
Northern Maine Community College ... ME .. 203
Southern Maine Community College ... ME .. 203
University of Maine at Augusta ... ME .. 204
Allegany College of Maryland ... MD .. 205
Anne Arundel Community College ... MD .. 206
Baltimore City Community College ... MD .. 206
Cecil College ... MD .. 206
Chesapeake College ... MD .. 207
College of Southern Maryland ... MD .. 207

AIJS: Association of Institutions of Jewish Studies: Jewish studies (C, A,B)

ANEST: Council on Accreditation of Nurse Anesthesia Educational Programs: nurse anesthesia (C,M,D)

ARCPA: Accreditation Review Commission on Education for the Physician Assistant: physician assisting programs (C,A,B,M)

ART: National Association of Schools of Art and Design: art and design (C,A,B,M,D)

AUD: American Speech-Language-Hearing Association: audiology (D)

Gallaudet University .... DC 92
Nova Southeastern University .... FL ... 105
University of Florida .... FL ... 112
University of South Florida .... FL ... 112
Idaho State University .... ID ... 133
Illinois State University .... IL 143
Northern Illinois University .... IL 150
Northwestern University .... IL 150
Rush University .... IL 153
University of Illinois at Urbana-Champaign IL 157
Ball State University .... IN 159
Indiana University Bloomington .... IN 162
Purdue University Main Campus .... IN 166
University of Iowa .... IA 169
Wichita State University .... KS ... 185
#University of Louisville .... KY ... 194
Louisiana State University Health Sciences Center-New Orleans .... LA ... 198
Louisiana Tech University .... LA ... 200
Towson University .... MD .. 213
University of Maryland College Park .... MD .. 211
Northeastern University .... MA .. 227
University of Massachusetts .... MA .. 220
Central Michigan University .... MI 232
Wayne State University .... MI 243
Western Michigan University .... MI 243
University of Minnesota-Twin Cities .... MN .. 255
University of Southern Mississippi .... MS .. 261
Missouri State University .... MO .. 268
Washington University in St. Louis .... MO .. 274
University of Nebraska - Lincoln .... NE ... 282
Montclair State University .... NJ ... 293
City University of New York Brooklyn College .... NY ... 307
City University of New York Graduate Center .... NY ... 308
City University of New York Hunter College .... NY ... 308
Hofstra University .... NY ... 316
St. John's University .... NY ... 328
Syracuse University Main Campus .... NY ... 337
University at Buffalo-SUNY .... NY ... 331
East Carolina University .... NC .. 356
University of North Carolina at Chapel Hill NC .. 357
Ohio State University Main Campus, The . OH .. 375
Ohio University Main Campus .... OH .. 375
University of Cincinnati Main Campus .... OH .. 379
@Pacific University .... OR ... 394
Bloomsburg University of Pennsylvania .... PA ... 414
Salus University .... PA ... 419
University of Pittsburgh .... PA ... 421
University of Puerto Rico-Medical Sciences Campus .... PR ... 538
University of South Dakota, The .... SD ... 437
#East Tennessee State University .... TN ... 444
University of Memphis, The .... TN ... 445
University of Tennessee, Knoxville .... TN ... 448
Vanderbilt University .... TN ... 449
Lamar University .... TX ... 471
Texas Tech University Health Sciences Center .... TX ... 472
University of North Texas .... TX ... 475
University of Texas at Austin .... TX ... 476
University of Texas at Dallas, The .... TX ... 476
#University of Utah, The .... UT ... 481
Utah State University .... UT ... 482
James Madison University .... VA ... 490
University of Washington .... WA .. 508
West Virginia University .... WV .. 514
University of Wisconsin-Madison .... WI ... 519
University of Wisconsin-Stevens Point .... WI ... 521

BBT: Commission on Accreditation of Allied Health Education Programs: blood bank technology (C,M)

Rush University .... IL 153
Johns Hopkins University .... MD .. 208
University of Texas Medical Branch, The . TX ... 478

BI: Association for Biblical Higher Education: bible college education (C,A,B,M,FP,D)

Heritage Christian University .... AL 4
Huntsville Bible College .... AL 4
@Legacy Christian University .... AL 5
Selma University .... AL 6
Southeastern Bible College .... AL 7
Alaska Bible College .... AK 9
Ecclesia College .... AR 20
American Evangelical University .... CA 26
Bethesda University of California .... CA 28
Eternity Bible College .... CA 43
Grace Mission University .... CA 45
Hope International University .... CA 46
Horizon University .... CA 46
International Reformed University and Seminary .... CA 47
Life Pacific College .... CA 48
@Methodist Theological Seminary in America .... CA 52
Olivet University .... CA 55
Presbyterian Theological Seminary in America .... CA 58
SUM Bible College and Theological Seminary .... CA 67
William Jessup University .... CA 75
World Mission University .... CA 75
Nazarene Bible College .... CO 81
Hobe Sound Bible College .... FL ... 102
Robert E. Webber Institute for Worship Studies, The .... FL ... 107
South Florida Bible College .... FL ... 109
Trinity College of Florida .... FL ... 114
Beulah Heights University .... GA .. 117
#Carver College .... GA .. 118
Luther Rice College and Seminary .... GA .. 124
Pacific Rim Christian University .... HI 131
Boise Bible College .... ID 132
Lincoln Christian University .... IL 146
Moody Bible Institute .... IL 148
Crossroads Bible College .... IN 160
@Faith Bible Seminary .... IN 160
@Union Bible College .... IN 167
Emmaus Bible College .... IA 172
Faith Baptist Bible College and Seminary IA 172
Barclay College .... KS 178
@Kansas Christian College .... KS 182
Manhattan Christian College .... KS 183
Clear Creek Baptist Bible College .... KY 187
Kentucky Mountain Bible College .... KY 191
Simmons College of Kentucky .... KY 192
Northpoint Bible College .... MA .. 227
Grace Bible College .... MI 234
Kuyper College .... MI 236
Bethany Global University .... MN .. 244
Bethlehem College & Seminary .... MN .. 245
Oak Hills Christian College .... MN .. 254
Southeastern Baptist College .... MS .. 260
Baptist Bible College .... MO .. 262
@Brookes Bible College .... MO .. 262
Calvary University .... MO .. 262
Central Christian College of the Bible .... MO .. 263
Heartland Christian College .... MO .. 265
Midwest University .... MO .. 268
Ozark Christian College .... MO .. 269
Saint Louis Christian College .... MO .. 271
Montana Bible College .... MT .. 276
@Yellowstone Christian College .... MT .. 278
Grace University .... NE ... 280
@Summit Christian College .... NE ... 282
Pillar College .... NJ ... 294
Davis College .... NY ... 312
Carolina Christian College .... NC .. 342
Carolina College of Biblical Studies .... NC .. 342
Grace College of Divinity .... NC .. 344
John Wesley University .... NC .. 345
@Native American Bible College .... NC .. 347
Trinity Bible College & Graduate School .. ND .. 362
Allegheny Wesleyan College .... OH .. 362
Cincinnati Christian University .... OH .. 366
God's Bible School and College .... OH .. 369
Ohio Christian University .... OH .. 374
Rosedale Bible College .... OH .. 376
Tri-State Bible College .... OH .. 378
Valor Christian College .... OH .. 380
Family of Faith College .... OK .. 383
New Hope Christian College .... OR .. 393
@Pacific Bible College .... OR .. 394
Cairn University .... PA ... 399
Lancaster Bible College .... PA ... 407
Summit University of Pennsylvania .... PA ... 419
Universidad Pentecostal Mizpa .... PR ... 537
Universidad Teologica Del Caribe .... PR ... 537
Columbia International University .... SC ... 429
American Baptist College .... TN ... 438
Johnson University .... TN ... 440
Mid-South Christian College .... TN ... 442
Welch College .... TN ... 449
Williamson College .... TN ... 449
Arlington Baptist College .... TX ... 451
Baptist University of the Americas .... TX ... 452
B.H. Carroll Theological Institute .... TX ... 452
College of Biblical Studies-Houston .... TX ... 454
Dallas Christian College .... TX ... 455
King's University, The .... TX ... 460
Rio Grande Bible Institute .... TX ... 464
Bethel College .... VA ... 487
@Faith Bible College .... VA ... 489
Washington University of Virginia .... VA ... 500
@Wave Leadership College .... VA ... 500
Appalachian Bible College .... WV .. 510

BUS: AACSB-The Association to Advance Collegiate Schools of Business: business and management (B,M,D)

Auburn University .... AL 1
Auburn University at Montgomery .... AL 2
Jacksonville State University .... AL 4
Samford University .... AL 6
Tuskegee University .... AL 8
University of Alabama at Birmingham .... AL 8
University of Alabama in Huntsville .... AL 8
University of Alabama, The .... AL 8
University of Montevallo .... AL 9
University of North Alabama .... AL 9
University of South Alabama .... AL 9
University of Alaska Anchorage .... AK 10
University of Alaska Fairbanks .... AK 10
Arizona State University .... AZ 11
Northern Arizona University .... AZ 15
University of Arizona .... AZ 17
Arkansas State University-Jonesboro .... AR 18
Arkansas Tech University .... AR 19
Henderson State University .... AR 20
Ouachita Baptist University .... AR 21
Southern Arkansas University .... AR 22
University of Arkansas at Fort Smith .... AR 23
University of Arkansas at Little Rock .... AR 23
University of Arkansas Main Campus .... AR 22
University of Central Arkansas .... AR 24
California Polytechnic State University-San Luis Obispo .... CA 31
California State Polytechnic University-Pomona .... CA 31
California State University-Bakersfield .... CA 32
California State University-Chico .... CA 32
California State University-East Bay .... CA 32
California State University-Fresno .... CA 32
California State University-Fullerton .... CA 33
California State University-Long Beach .... CA 33
California State University-Los Angeles .... CA 33
California State University-Northridge .... CA 34
California State University-Sacramento .... CA 34
California State University-San Bernardino CA 34
California State University-Stanislaus .... CA 34
Chapman University .... CA 37
Claremont Graduate University .... CA 38
Loyola Marymount University .... CA 51
Menlo College .... CA 52
Naval Postgraduate School .... CA ... 528
Pepperdine University .... CA 56
Saint Mary's College of California .... CA 59
San Diego State University .... CA 35
San Francisco State University .... CA 35
San Jose State University .... CA 35
Santa Clara University .... CA 63
Sonoma State University .... CA 35
Stanford University .... CA 66
University of California-Berkeley .... CA 68
University of California-Davis .... CA 69
University of California-Irvine .... CA 69
University of California-Los Angeles .... CA 69
University of California-Riverside .... CA 70
University of California-San Diego .... CA 70
University of San Diego .... CA 72
University of San Francisco .... CA 72
University of Southern California .... CA 72
University of the Pacific .... CA 71
Woodbury University .... CA 75
Colorado State University .... CO 78
Colorado State University-Pueblo .... CO 79
Fort Lewis College .... CO 80
Metropolitan State University of Denver .... CO 81
United States Air Force Academy .... CO .. 528
University of Colorado Boulder .... CO 83
University of Colorado Colorado Springs .. CO 83
University of Colorado Denver|Anschutz Medical Campus .... CO 84
University of Denver .... CO 84
University of Northern Colorado .... CO 84
Central Connecticut State University .... CT 85
Fairfield University .... CT 87
Quinnipiac University .... CT 88
Sacred Heart University .... CT 88
United States Coast Guard Academy .... CT ... 529
University of Connecticut .... CT 89
University of Hartford .... CT 89
University of New Haven .... CT 90
Yale University .... CT 90
Delaware State University .... DE 90
University of Delaware .... DE 91
American University .... DC 91
George Washington University .... DC 92
Georgetown University .... DC 92
Howard University .... DC 93
Barry University .... FL 96
Florida Atlantic University .... FL ... 110
Florida Gulf Coast University .... FL ... 110
Florida International University .... FL ... 111
Florida Southern College .... FL ... 101
Florida State University .... FL ... 111
Jacksonville University .... FL ... 103
Rollins College .... FL ... 107
Stetson University .... FL ... 113
University of Central Florida .... FL ... 111
University of Florida .... FL ... 112
University of Miami .... FL ... 114
University of North Florida .... FL ... 112
University of South Florida .... FL ... 112
University of South Florida St. Petersburg FL ... 112
University of Tampa .... FL ... 114
University of West Florida .... FL ... 113
Augusta University .... GA .. 117
Berry College .... GA .. 117
Clark Atlanta University .... GA .. 118
Clayton State University .... GA .. 119
Columbus State University .... GA .. 119
Dalton State College .... GA .. 119
Emory University .... GA .. 120
Georgia College & State University .... GA .. 121
Georgia Institute of Technology .... GA .. 121
Georgia Southern University .... GA .. 122
Georgia Southwestern State University .... GA .. 122
Georgia State University .... GA .. 122
Kennesaw State University .... GA .. 123
Mercer University .... GA .. 124
Morehouse College .... GA .. 124
Savannah State University .... GA .. 126
University of Georgia .... GA .. 128
University of North Georgia .... GA .. 128
University of West Georgia .... GA .. 129
Valdosta State University .... GA .. 129
University of Hawaii at Hilo .... HI 131
University of Hawaii at Manoa .... HI 131
Boise State University .... ID 132
Idaho State University .... ID 133
University of Idaho .... ID 134
Bradley University .... IL 136
DePaul University .... IL 139
Dominican University .... IL 139
Eastern Illinois University .... IL 139
Illinois Institute of Technology .... IL 142
Illinois State University .... IL 143
Loyola University Chicago .... IL 146
Northeastern Illinois University .... IL 149
Northern Illinois University .... IL 150
Northwestern University .... IL 150
Saint Xavier University .... IL 153
Southern Illinois University Carbondale .... IL 154
Southern Illinois University Edwardsville ... IL 155
University of Chicago .... IL 156
University of Illinois at Chicago .... IL 156
University of Illinois at Springfield .... IL 156
University of Illinois at Urbana-Champaign IL 157
Western Illinois University .... IL 158
Ball State University .... IN 159
Butler University .... IN 159
Indiana State University .... IN 162
Indiana University Bloomington .... IN 162
Indiana University Kokomo .... IN 163
Indiana University Northwest .... IN 163
Indiana University-Purdue University Fort Wayne .... IN 163
Indiana University South Bend .... IN 163
Indiana University Southeast .... IN 163
Purdue University Main Campus .... IN 166
Purdue University Northwest .... IN 166
University of Evansville .... IN 167
University of Notre Dame .... IN 168
University of Southern Indiana .... IN 168
Valparaiso University .... IN 168
Iowa State University .... IA 169
University of Iowa .... IA 169
University of Northern Iowa .... IA 170
Emporia State University .... KS 180
Kansas State University .... KS 182
Pittsburg State University .... KS 184
University of Kansas Main Campus .... KS 185
Washburn University .... KS 185
Wichita State University .... KS 185
Bellarmine University .... KY 187
Eastern Kentucky University .... KY 188
Morehead State University .... KY 191
Murray State University .... KY 192
Northern Kentucky University .... KY 192
University of Kentucky .... KY 193
University of Louisville .... KY 194
Western Kentucky University .... KY 194
Grambling State University .... LA 200
Louisiana State University and Agricultural and Mechanical College .... LA 197
Louisiana State University in Shreveport .. LA 198
Louisiana Tech University .... LA 200
Loyola University New Orleans .... LA 198
McNeese State University .... LA 200
Nicholls State University .... LA 201
Northwestern State University .... LA 201
Southeastern Louisiana University .... LA 201

BUSA: AACSB-The Association to Advance Collegiate Schools of Business: accounting (B,M,D)

Iowa State University ... IA ... 169
University of Iowa ... IA ... 169
Kansas State University ... KS ... 182
University of Kansas Main Campus ... KS ... 185
Wichita State University ... KS ... 185
University of Kentucky ... KY ... 193
University of Louisville ... KY ... 194
Western Kentucky University ... KY ... 194
Louisiana Tech University ... LA ... 200
Nicholls State University ... LA ... 201
Southeastern Louisiana University ... LA ... 201
University of Louisiana at Lafayette ... LA ... 201
University of Louisiana at Monroe ... LA ... 201
University of New Orleans ... LA ... 198
Loyola University Maryland ... MD ... 208
Morgan State University ... MD ... 209
Salisbury University ... MD ... 213
Towson University ... MD ... 213
Bentley University ... MA ... 215
Suffolk University ... MA ... 228
University of Massachusetts ... MA ... 220
Central Michigan University ... MI ... 232
Grand Valley State University ... MI ... 234
Michigan State University ... MI ... 237
Oakland University ... MI ... 239
Western Michigan University ... MI ... 243
Mississippi State University ... MS ... 259
University of Mississippi ... MS ... 261
University of Southern Mississippi ... MS ... 261
Missouri State University ... MO ... 268
Saint Louis University ... MO ... 271
Truman State University ... MO ... 273
University of Central Missouri ... MO ... 273
University of Missouri - Columbia ... MO ... 273
University of Missouri - Saint Louis ... MO ... 274
University of Montana - Missoula ... MT ... 276
Creighton University ... NE ... 279
University of Nebraska at Omaha ... NE ... 283
University of Nebraska - Lincoln ... NE ... 282
University of Nevada, Las Vegas ... NV ... 284
University of Nevada, Reno ... NV ... 285
Rider University ... NJ ... 295
Seton Hall University ... NJ ... 297
New Mexico State University Main Campus ... NM ... 300
University of New Mexico Main Campus ... NM ... 302
Baruch College/City University of New York ... NY ... 307
Hofstra University ... NY ... 316
Pace University ... NY ... 325
St. John's University ... NY ... 328
University at Albany, SUNY ... NY ... 331
University at Buffalo-SUNY ... NY ... 331
North Carolina Agricultural and Technical State University ... NC ... 356
North Carolina State University ... NC ... 357
University of North Carolina at Charlotte ... NC ... 358
University of North Carolina at Greensboro ... NC ... 358
Wake Forest University ... NC ... 359
Bowling Green State University ... OH ... 364
Case Western Reserve University ... OH ... 365
Cleveland State University ... OH ... 366
John Carroll University ... OH ... 370
Kent State University Main Campus ... OH ... 370
Miami University ... OH ... 372
Ohio State University Main Campus, The ... OH ... 375
Ohio University Main Campus ... OH ... 375
University of Akron, Main Campus, The ... OH ... 378
University of Dayton ... OH ... 379
University of Toledo ... OH ... 380
Wright State University Main Campus ... OH ... 381
Oklahoma State University ... OK ... 385
University of Oklahoma Norman Campus ... OK ... 389
Oregon State University ... OR ... 393
Portland State University ... OR ... 394
University of Oregon ... OR ... 395
Lehigh University ... PA ... 408
Saint Joseph's University ... PA ... 418
Villanova University ... PA ... 422
University of Rhode Island ... RI ... 426
Clemson University ... SC ... 428
College of Charleston ... SC ... 428
University of South Carolina Columbia ... SC ... 433
Belmont University ... TN ... 438
East Tennessee State University ... TN ... 444
Middle Tennessee State University ... TN ... 444
Tennessee Technological University ... TN ... 445
University of Memphis, The ... TN ... 445
University of Tennessee at Chattanooga ... TN ... 448
University of Tennessee, Knoxville ... TN ... 448
Baylor University ... TX ... 452
Texas A & M University ... TX ... 468
Texas A & M University - Corpus Christi ... TX ... 468
Texas Christian University ... TX ... 469
Texas State University ... TX ... 471
Texas Tech University ... TX ... 472
University of Houston ... TX ... 473
University of Houston - Clear Lake ... TX ... 474
University of North Texas ... TX ... 475
University of Texas at Arlington, The ... TX ... 476
University of Texas at Austin ... TX ... 476
University of Texas at Dallas, The ... TX ... 476
University of Texas at El Paso ... TX ... 476
University of Texas at San Antonio ... TX ... 477
Brigham Young University ... UT ... 480
University of Utah, The ... UT ... 481
Utah State University ... UT ... 482
Weber State University ... UT ... 482
College of William & Mary ... VA ... 488
George Mason University ... VA ... 490
James Madison University ... VA ... 490
Old Dominion University ... VA ... 492
University of Richmond ... VA ... 495
University of Virginia ... VA ... 495
Virginia Commonwealth University ... VA ... 496
Virginia Polytechnic Institute and State University ... VA ... 499
Gonzaga University ... WA ... 504
University of Washington ... WA ... 508
Washington State University ... WA ... 508
Marshall University ... WV ... 513
West Virginia University ... WV ... 514
Marquette University ... WI ... 517
University of Wisconsin-Madison ... WI ... 519
University of Wisconsin-Milwaukee ... WI ... 520

CA: National Accrediting Agency for Clinical Laboratory Sciences: clinical assistant (C)

Indian Hills Community College ... IA ... 173
Northern Michigan University ... MI ... 239
Western Nebraska Community College ... NE ... 283
Clackamas Community College ... OR ... 390
Community College of Allegheny County ... PA ... 401
Edmonds Community College ... WA ... 503

CAATE: Commission on Accreditation of Athletic Training Education: athletic training (B,M)

#Samford University ... AL ... 6
Troy University ... AL ... 7
University of Alabama, The ... AL ... 8
#University of Mobile ... AL ... 9
#University of West Alabama, The ... AL ... 9
Grand Canyon University ... AZ ... 13
Northern Arizona University ... AZ ... 15
#Arkansas State University-Jonesboro ... AR ... 18
#Harding University Main Campus ... AR ... 20
#Henderson State University ... AR ... 20
#Southern Arkansas University ... AR ... 22
University of Arkansas Main Campus ... AR ... 22
University of Central Arkansas ... AR ... 24
Azusa Pacific University ... CA ... 28
California Baptist University ... CA ... 29
California State University-Fresno ... CA ... 32
California State University-Fullerton ... CA ... 33
California State University-Long Beach ... CA ... 33
California State University-Northridge ... CA ... 34
California State University-Sacramento ... CA ... 34
Chapman University ... CA ... 37
Concordia University ... CA ... 41
Point Loma Nazarene University ... CA ... 57
San Diego State University ... CA ... 35
San Jose State University ... CA ... 35
University of La Verne ... CA ... 71
University of the Pacific ... CA ... 71
Colorado Mesa University ... CO ... 77
Colorado State University-Pueblo ... CO ... 79
Fort Lewis College ... CO ... 80
Metropolitan State University of Denver ... CO ... 81
University of Northern Colorado ... CO ... 84
Central Connecticut State University ... CT ... 85
Quinnipiac University ... CT ... 88
Sacred Heart University ... CT ... 88
Southern Connecticut State University ... CT ... 85
University of Connecticut ... CT ... 89
University of Delaware ... DE ... 91
Barry University ... FL ... 96
Florida Gulf Coast University ... FL ... 110
Florida International University ... FL ... 111
#Florida Southern College ... FL ... 101
Florida State University ... FL ... 111
Nova Southeastern University ... FL ... 105
#Palm Beach Atlantic University ... FL ... 106
University of Central Florida ... FL ... 111
University of Florida ... FL ... 112
University of Miami ... FL ... 114
University of North Florida ... FL ... 112
University of South Florida ... FL ... 112
University of Tampa ... FL ... 114
University of West Florida ... FL ... 113
Georgia College & State University ... GA ... 121
Georgia Southern University ... GA ... 122
Life University ... GA ... 124
University of Georgia ... GA ... 128
University of North Georgia ... GA ... 128
Valdosta State University ... GA ... 129
University of Hawaii at Manoa ... HI ... 131
Boise State University ... ID ... 132
Idaho State University ... ID ... 133
University of Idaho ... ID ... 134
Aurora University ... IL ... 135
#Eastern Illinois University ... IL ... 139
Illinois State University ... IL ... 143
#Lewis University ... IL ... 145
#McKendree University ... IL ... 147
#Millikin University ... IL ... 148
North Central College ... IL ... 149
#North Park University ... IL ... 149
Northern Illinois University ... IL ... 150
#Olivet Nazarene University ... IL ... 150
Trinity International University ... IL ... 156
Western Illinois University ... IL ... 158
Anderson University ... IN ... 158
Ball State University ... IN ... 159
Franklin College of Indiana ... IN ... 160
Indiana State University ... IN ... 162
Indiana University Bloomington ... IN ... 162
#Indiana Wesleyan University ... IN ... 164
Manchester University ... IN ... 165
Purdue University Main Campus ... IN ... 166
University of Evansville ... IN ... 167
University of Indianapolis ... IN ... 168
#Buena Vista University ... IA ... 170
Central College ... IA ... 170
Clarke University ... IA ... 170
Coe College ... IA ... 170
#Graceland University ... IA ... 172
Iowa State University ... IA ... 169
#Loras College ... IA ... 174
Luther College ... IA ... 174
Northwestern College ... IA ... 176
Simpson College ... IA ... 176
University of Iowa ... IA ... 169
University of Northern Iowa ... IA ... 170
Upper Iowa University ... IA ... 177
#Benedictine College ... KS ... 178
Bethany College ... KS ... 178
Bethel College ... KS ... 179
Emporia State University ... KS ... 180
Fort Hays State University ... KS ... 180
Kansas State University ... KS ... 182
#MidAmerica Nazarene University ... KS ... 183
Southwestern College ... KS ... 184
Sterling College ... KS ... 185
#Tabor College ... KS ... 185
University of Kansas Main Campus ... KS ... 185
Washburn University ... KS ... 185
Wichita State University ... KS ... 185
Eastern Kentucky University ... KY ... 188
Georgetown College ... KY ... 188
#Murray State University ... KY ... 192
Northern Kentucky University ... KY ... 192
#Union College ... KY ... 193
University of Kentucky ... KY ... 193
#Louisiana College ... LA ... 195
Louisiana State University and Agricultural and Mechanical College ... LA ... 197
#McNeese State University ... LA ... 200
Nicholls State University ... LA ... 201
#Southeastern Louisiana University ... LA ... 201
#University of Louisiana at Lafayette ... LA ... 201
University of Maine ... ME ... 204
#University of Maine at Presque Isle ... ME ... 205
University of New England ... ME ... 205
University of Southern Maine ... ME ... 205
Frostburg State University ... MD ... 212
Salisbury University ... MD ... 213
Towson University ... MD ... 213
Boston University ... MA ... 216
#Bridgewater State University ... MA ... 221
Endicott College ... MA ... 218
Lasell College ... MA ... 219
#Massachusetts College of Liberal Arts ... MA ... 222
Merrimack College ... MA ... 225
Salem State University ... MA ... 222
Springfield College ... MA ... 228
#Westfield State University ... MA ... 222
Adrian College ... MI ... 230
Albion College ... MI ... 230
Alma College ... MI ... 230
Aquinas College ... MI ... 231
Central Michigan University ... MI ... 232
#Eastern Michigan University ... MI ... 233
Grand Valley State University ... MI ... 234
Hope College ... MI ... 235
Lake Superior State University ... MI ... 236
Michigan State University ... MI ... 237
Northern Michigan University ... MI ... 239
Saginaw Valley State University ... MI ... 240
University of Michigan-Ann Arbor ... MI ... 241
#Western Michigan University ... MI ... 243
Bethel University ... MN ... 244
College of Saint Scholastica, The ... MN ... 245
Gustavus Adolphus College ... MN ... 246
#Minnesota State University Moorhead ... MN ... 250
Minnesota State University, Mankato ... MN ... 250
St. Cloud State University ... MN ... 252
University of Minnesota Duluth ... MN ... 255
Winona State University ... MN ... 252
#Delta State University ... MS ... 257
University of Southern Mississippi ... MS ... 261
#Central Methodist University ... MO ... 263
#Culver-Stockton College ... MO ... 264
Evangel University ... MO ... 265
Lindenwood University ... MO ... 266
Missouri State University ... MO ... 268
#Missouri Valley College ... MO ... 269
#Park University ... MO ... 270
Saint Louis University ... MO ... 271
Southeast Missouri State University ... MO ... 272
#Southwest Baptist University ... MO ... 272
Truman State University ... MO ... 273
University of Central Missouri ... MO ... 273
University of Missouri - Columbia ... MO ... 273
#William Woods University ... MO ... 275
Montana State University - Billings ... MT ... 277
University of Montana - Missoula ... MT ... 276
Nebraska Wesleyan University ... NE ... 281
University of Nebraska at Kearney ... NE ... 282
#University of Nebraska at Omaha ... NE ... 283
University of Nebraska - Lincoln ... NE ... 282
University of Nevada, Las Vegas ... NV ... 284
#Colby-Sawyer College ... NH ... 285
#Keene State College ... NH ... 288
Plymouth State University ... NH ... 288
University of New Hampshire ... NH ... 288
#Kean University ... NJ ... 292
Montclair State University ... NJ ... 293
Rowan University ... NJ ... 295
Seton Hall University ... NJ ... 297
William Paterson University of New Jersey ... NJ ... 298
New Mexico State University Main Campus ... NM ... 300
University of New Mexico Main Campus ... NM ... 302
#Alfred University ... NY ... 303
#Canisius College ... NY ... 306
Daemen College ... NY ... 312
#Dominican College of Blauvelt ... NY ... 312
Hofstra University ... NY ... 316
Ithaca College ... NY ... 317
Marist College ... NY ... 320
State University of New York College at Cortland ... NY ... 333
State University of New York, The College at Brockport ... NY ... 332
Stony Brook University ... NY ... 332
Appalachian State University ... NC ... 356
Campbell University ... NC ... 342
Catawba College ... NC ... 343
East Carolina University ... NC ... 356
Gardner-Webb University ... NC ... 344
#Greensboro College ... NC ... 344
High Point University ... NC ... 345
#Lees-McRae College ... NC ... 345
Lenoir-Rhyne University ... NC ... 345
#Mars Hill University ... NC ... 346
Methodist University ... NC ... 346
#North Carolina Central University ... NC ... 357
#Shaw University ... NC ... 355
University of North Carolina at Chapel Hill ... NC ... 357
University of North Carolina at Charlotte ... NC ... 358
University of North Carolina at Greensboro ... NC ... 358
University of North Carolina at Pembroke ... NC ... 358
University of North Carolina Wilmington ... NC ... 358
Western Carolina University ... NC ... 359
#Wingate University ... NC ... 359
Minot State University ... ND ... 360
North Dakota State University Main Campus ... ND ... 361
University of Mary ... ND ... 362
University of North Dakota ... ND ... 360
Valley City State University ... ND ... 361
Ashland University ... OH ... 363
Baldwin Wallace University ... OH ... 363
#Bowling Green State University ... OH ... 364
Capital University ... OH ... 364
Cedarville University ... OH ... 365
#Defiance College, The ... OH ... 368
#Denison University ... OH ... 368
Heidelberg University ... OH ... 369
Kent State University Main Campus ... OH ... 370
Marietta College ... OH ... 372
#Miami University ... OH ... 372
Mount St. Joseph University ... OH ... 373
Ohio Northern University ... OH ... 374
Ohio State University Main Campus, The ... OH ... 375
Ohio University Main Campus ... OH ... 375
Otterbein University ... OH ... 376
#Shawnee State University ... OH ... 377
University of Akron, Main Campus, The ... OH ... 378
University of Cincinnati Main Campus ... OH ... 379

CACREP: Council for Accreditation of Counseling & Related Educational Programs: addiction counseling, career counseling, marriage, couple and family counseling, mental health counseling, school counseling, student affairs and college counseling (M) and counselor education and supervision (D)

Slippery Rock University of Pennsylvania ... PA ... 416
University of Pittsburgh ... PA ... 421
University of Scranton, The ... PA ... 422
Villanova University ... PA ... 422
Waynesburg University ... PA ... 423
West Chester University of Pennsylvania ... PA ... 416
Rhode Island College ... RI ... 425
Citadel, The Military College of South Carolina, The ... SC ... 428
Clemson University ... SC ... 428
Columbia International University ... SC ... 429
South Carolina State University ... SC ... 432
University of South Carolina Columbia ... SC ... 433
Winthrop University ... SC ... 435
Mount Marty College ... SD ... 436
University of South Dakota, The ... SD ... 437
Carson-Newman University ... TN ... 439
East Tennessee State University ... TN ... 444
Johnson University ... TN ... 440
Lincoln Memorial University ... TN ... 441
Lipscomb University ... TN ... 441
Middle Tennessee State University ... TN ... 444
Richmont Graduate University ... TN ... 443
Southern Adventist University ... TN ... 444
Tennessee Technological University ... TN ... 445
Trevecca Nazarene University ... TN ... 447
University of Memphis, The ... TN ... 445
University of Tennessee at Chattanooga ... TN ... 448
University of Tennessee, Knoxville ... TN ... 448
Vanderbilt University ... TN ... 449
Lamar University ... TX ... 471
St. Mary's University ... TX ... 464
Sam Houston State University ... TX ... 471
Stephen F. Austin State University ... TX ... 466
Texas A & M University - Commerce ... TX ... 468
Texas A & M University - Corpus Christi ... TX ... 468
Texas A & M University - Texarkana ... TX ... 469
Texas State University ... TX ... 471
Texas Tech University ... TX ... 472
Texas Woman's University ... TX ... 472
University of Houston - Victoria ... TX ... 474
University of Mary Hardin-Baylor ... TX ... 474
University of North Texas ... TX ... 475
University of Texas at San Antonio ... TX ... 477
University of Texas at Tyler ... TX ... 477
University of Vermont ... VT ... 485
College of William & Mary ... VA ... 488
Eastern Mennonite University ... VA ... 488
Hampton University ... VA ... 490
James Madison University ... VA ... 490
Liberty University ... VA ... 491
Lynchburg College ... VA ... 491
Marymount University ... VA ... 492
Old Dominion University ... VA ... 492
Radford University ... VA ... 493
Regent University ... VA ... 493
University of Virginia ... VA ... 495
Virginia Commonwealth University ... VA ... 496
Virginia Polytechnic Institute and State University ... VA ... 499
Central Washington University ... WA ... 501
City University of Seattle ... WA ... 502
Eastern Washington University ... WA ... 503
Gonzaga University ... WA ... 504
Seattle Pacific University ... WA ... 507
Seattle University ... WA ... 507
Western Washington University ... WA ... 509
West Virginia University ... WV ... 514
Marquette University ... WI ... 517
Mount Mary University ... WI ... 518
University of Wisconsin-Oshkosh ... WI ... 520
University of Wisconsin-River Falls ... WI ... 521
University of Wisconsin-Stout ... WI ... 521
University of Wisconsin-Whitewater ... WI ... 521
Viterbo University ... WI ... 522
University of Wyoming ... WY ... 527

CAEP: Council for the Accreditation of Educator Preparation: teacher education (B,M,D)

#University of Colorado Colorado Springs ... CO ... 83
Florida Atlantic University ... FL ... 110
Stetson University ... FL ... 113
Valdosta State University ... GA ... 129
#Southwestern College ... KS ... 184
College of Saint Scholastica, The ... MN ... 245
#Concordia College ... MN ... 246
Alcorn State University ... MS ... 256
Missouri Southern State University ... MO ... 268
Montana State University ... MT ... 277
University of Montana Western, The ... MT ... 277
University of New Hampshire ... NH ... 288
City University of New York Queens College ... NY ... 309
Mercy College ... NY ... 320
State University of New York at Fredonia ... NY ... 331
North Carolina State University ... NC ... 357
University of Cincinnati Main Campus ... OH ... 379
Ursuline College ... OH ... 380
Portland State University ... OR ... 394
Citadel, The Military College of South Carolina, The ... SC ... 428
Southern Utah University ... UT ... 481
Utah Valley University ... UT ... 482
Marymount University ... VA ... 492

CAHIIM: Commission on Accreditation for Health Informatics and Information Management Education: health information management and health informatics (A,B,M)

Alabama State University ... AL ... 1
Bishop State Community College ... AL ... 2
Wallace State Community College - Hanceville ... AL ... 9
University of Alaska Southeast ... AK ... 10
Central Arizona College ... AZ ... 12
Phoenix College ... AZ ... 14
Arkansas Tech University ... AR ... 19
National Park College ... AR ... 21
NorthWest Arkansas Community College ... AR ... 21
University of Arkansas for Medical Sciences ... AR ... 23
Brightwood College ... CA ... 29
City College of San Francisco ... CA ... 38
Cosumnes River College ... CA ... 51
Cypress College ... CA ... 54
East Los Angeles College ... CA ... 49
Fresno City College ... CA ... 67
Loma Linda University ... CA ... 49
Saddleback College ... CA ... 65
San Diego Mesa College ... CA ... 60
Santa Barbara City College ... CA ... 63
Arapahoe Community College ... CO ... 76
Front Range Community College ... CO ... 80
Regis University ... CO ... 82
Charter Oak State College ... CT ... 85
Lincoln College of New England ... CT ... 88
Broward College ... FL ... 96
College of Central Florida ... FL ... 97
Daytona State College ... FL ... 98
Florida Agricultural and Mechanical University ... FL ... 110
Florida SouthWestern State College ... FL ... 101
Florida State College at Jacksonville ... FL ... 101
Hodges University ... FL ... 102
Indian River State College ... FL ... 103
Keiser University ... FL ... 103
Lake-Sumter State College ... FL ... 104
Miami Dade College ... FL ... 105
Palm Beach State College ... FL ... 106
Pensacola State College ... FL ... 106
St. Johns River State College ... FL ... 108
St. Petersburg College ... FL ... 108
Santa Fe College ... FL ... 109
Seminole State College of Florida ... FL ... 109
Southern Technical College ... FL ... 109
University of Central Florida ... FL ... 111
Athens Technical College ... GA ... 116
Atlanta Technical College ... GA ... 117
Augusta University ... GA ... 117
Darton State College ... GA ... 120
Georgia Northwestern Technical College ... GA ... 121
Gwinnett Technical College ... GA ... 123
Ogeechee Technical College ... GA ... 125
Southern Crescent Technical College ... GA ... 127
West Georgia Technical College ... GA ... 129
Wiregrass Georgia Technical College ... GA ... 130
Idaho State University ... ID ... 133
Chicago State University ... IL ... 136
College of DuPage ... IL ... 138
College of Lake County ... IL ... 138
Danville Area Community College ... IL ... 139
DeVry University - Chicago Campus ... IL ... 139
Harper College ... IL ... 141
Illinois State University ... IL ... 143
John A. Logan College ... IL ... 143
Joliet Junior College ... IL ... 144
Midstate College ... IL ... 147
Moraine Valley Community College ... IL ... 148
Northwestern College ... IL ... 150
Oakton Community College ... IL ... 150
Rend Lake College ... IL ... 152
Resurrection University ... IL ... 152
Richland Community College ... IL ... 152
Shawnee Community College ... IL ... 154
Southwestern Illinois College ... IL ... 155
University of Illinois at Chicago ... IL ... 156
Waubonsee Community College ... IL ... 157
American National University ... IN ... 158
Indiana Tech ... IN ... 162
Indiana University Northwest ... IN ... 163
Indiana University-Purdue University Indianapolis ... IN ... 163
Ivy Tech Community College of Indiana-Central Indiana ... IN ... 164
Vincennes University ... IN ... 169
Indian Hills Community College ... IA ... 173
Kirkwood Community College ... IA ... 174
Northeast Iowa Community College ... IA ... 175
Northwest Iowa Community College ... IA ... 175
Scott Community College ... IA ... 172
Hutchinson Community College ... KS ... 181
Neosho County Community College ... KS ... 183
University of Saint Mary ... KS ... 185
Washburn University ... KS ... 185
Eastern Kentucky University ... KY ... 188
Gateway Community and Technical College ... KY ... 189
Hazard Community and Technical College ... KY ... 189
Jefferson Community and Technical College ... KY ... 190
Western Kentucky University ... KY ... 194
Delgado Community College ... LA ... 196
Louisiana Tech University ... LA ... 200
Southern University at New Orleans ... LA ... 199
Southern University at Shreveport-Louisiana ... LA ... 199
University of Louisiana at Lafayette ... LA ... 201
Beal College ... ME ... 202
Kennebec Valley Community College ... ME ... 203
Anne Arundel Community College ... MD ... 206
Community College of Baltimore County, The ... MD ... 207
Coppin State University ... MD ... 212
Montgomery College ... MD ... 209
Prince George's Community College ... MD ... 210
University of Maryland University College ... MD ... 212
Bristol Community College ... MA ... 223
Fisher College ... MA ... 218
Laboure College ... MA ... 219
Baker College of Flint ... MI ... 231
Davenport University ... MI ... 233
Ferris State University ... MI ... 233
Macomb Community College ... MI ... 237
St. Clair County Community College ... MI ... 240
Schoolcraft College ... MI ... 240
Southwestern Michigan College ... MI ... 241
Anoka Technical College ... MN ... 248
College of Saint Scholastica, The ... MN ... 245
Minnesota State Community and Technical College ... MN ... 250
Rasmussen College - St. Cloud ... MN ... 254
Ridgewater College ... MN ... 251
Rochester Community and Technical College ... MN ... 251
St. Catherine University ... MN ... 254
Saint Cloud Technical and Community College ... MN ... 252
Saint Paul College-A Community & Technical College ... MN ... 252
Hinds Community College ... MS ... 258
Itawamba Community College ... MS ... 258
Meridian Community College ... MS ... 258
Southwest Mississippi Community College ... MS ... 260
University of Mississippi Medical Center ... MS ... 261
Crowder College ... MO ... 264
East Central College ... MO ... 264
Jefferson College ... MO ... 266
Metropolitan Community College - Penn Valley ... MO ... 267
Missouri Western State University ... MO ... 269
Ozarks Technical Community College ... MO ... 270
St. Charles Community College ... MO ... 271
Saint Louis University ... MO ... 271
State Fair Community College ... MO ... 272
Stephens College ... MO ... 272
Great Falls College Montana State University ... MT ... 277
Central Community College ... NE ... 278
Clarkson College ... NE ... 279
Metropolitan Community College ... NE ... 280
Western Nebraska Community College ... NE ... 283
Brightwood College ... NV ... 283
College of Southern Nevada ... NV ... 284
Brookdale Community College ... NJ ... 289
Camden County College ... NJ ... 290
Passaic County Community College ... NJ ... 294
Raritan Valley Community College ... NJ ... 295
Rowan College at Burlington County ... NJ ... 295
Central New Mexico Community College ... NM ... 299
San Juan College ... NM ... 301
Alfred State College ... NY ... 334
City University of New York Borough of Manhattan Community College ... NY ... 307
City University of New York Graduate Center ... NY ... 308
Erie Community College ... NY ... 313
Medaille College ... NY ... 320
Mohawk Valley Community College ... NY ... 321
Monroe Community College ... NY ... 321
Onondaga Community College ... NY ... 325
SUNY Broome Community College ... NY ... 332
SUNY Polytechnic Institute ... NY ... 336
Trocaire College ... NY ... 338
Brunswick Community College ... NC ... 347
Catawba Valley Community College ... NC ... 348
Central Piedmont Community College ... NC ... 348
Craven Community College ... NC ... 349
Davidson County Community College ... NC ... 349
Durham Technical Community College ... NC ... 349
East Carolina University ... NC ... 356
Edgecombe Community College ... NC ... 349
McDowell Technical Community College ... NC ... 351
Pitt Community College ... NC ... 352
Southwestern Community College ... NC ... 353
North Dakota State College of Science ... ND ... 361
Cincinnati State Technical and Community College ... OH ... 366
Columbus State Community College ... OH ... 367
Cuyahoga Community College ... OH ... 367
Eastern Gateway Community College - Jefferson County Campus ... OH ... 368
Hocking College ... OH ... 369
Lakeland Community College ... OH ... 371
Marion Technical College ... OH ... 372
Mercy College of Ohio ... OH ... 372
Ohio State University Main Campus, The ... OH ... 375
Owens Community College ... OH ... 376
Sinclair Community College ... OH ... 377
Stark State College ... OH ... 377
Terra State Community College ... OH ... 377
University of Cincinnati-Clermont College ... OH ... 379
University of Cincinnati Main Campus ... OH ... 379
University of Northwestern Ohio ... OH ... 380
University of Toledo ... OH ... 380
Zane State College ... OH ... 382
Rose State College ... OK ... 387
Southwestern Oklahoma State University ... OK ... 388
Tulsa Community College ... OK ... 388
Central Oregon Community College ... OR ... 390
Oregon Health & Science University ... OR ... 393
Portland Community College ... OR ... 394
Community College of Allegheny County ... PA ... 401
Lehigh Carbon Community College ... PA ... 408
Peirce College ... PA ... 412
Pennsylvania College of Technology ... PA ... 413
South Hills School of Business and Technology ... PA ... 419
Temple University ... PA ... 420
University of Pittsburgh ... PA ... 421
Huertas College ... PR ... 532
University of Puerto Rico-Medical Sciences Campus ... PR ... 538
Florence - Darlington Technical College ... SC ... 429
Greenville Technical College ... SC ... 430
Midlands Technical College ... SC ... 431
University of South Carolina Upstate ... SC ... 434
Dakota State University ... SD ... 437
National American University ... SD ... 436
Chattanooga State Community College ... TN ... 445
Dyersburg State Community College ... TN ... 446
Roane State Community College ... TN ... 447
Tennessee State University ... TN ... 445
University of Tennessee Health Science Center ... TN ... 448
Volunteer State Community College ... TN ... 447
Walters State Community College ... TN ... 447
Austin Community College District ... TX ... 451
Brightwood College ... TX ... 453
College of the Mainland ... TX ... 454
Collin County Community College District ... TX ... 455
Del Mar College ... TX ... 457
El Paso Community College ... TX ... 457
Houston Community College ... TX ... 459
Lamar Institute of Technology ... TX ... 470
Lee College ... TX ... 460
Lone Star College System ... TX ... 461
McLennan Community College ... TX ... 461
Midland College ... TX ... 461
Panola College ... TX ... 463
St. Philip's College ... TX ... 450
San Jacinto College North ... TX ... 465
South Texas College ... TX ... 465
Tarrant County College District ... TX ... 467
Texas Southern University ... TX ... 470
Texas State Technical College Waco ... TX ... 470
Texas State University ... TX ... 471
Tyler Junior College ... TX ... 473
Vernon College ... TX ... 478
Wharton County Junior College ... TX ... 479
Weber State University ... UT ... 482
Western Governors University ... UT ... 483
Northern Virginia Community College ... VA ... 497
Tidewater Community College ... VA ... 498
Shoreline Community College ... WA ... 507
Spokane Community College ... WA ... 502
Tacoma Community College ... WA ... 508
University of Washington ... WA ... 508
Marshall University ... WV ... 513
Mountwest Community and Technical College ... WV ... 512
Pierpont Community & Technical College ... WV ... 512

- West Virginia Northern Community College ... WV .. 512
- Chippewa Valley Technical College ... WI ... 523
- Fox Valley Technical College ... WI ... 523
- Mid-State Technical College ... WI ... 523
- Moraine Park Technical College ... WI ... 524
- Northeast Wisconsin Technical College ... WI ... 524
- University of Wisconsin-Green Bay ... WI ... 520
- Waukesha County Technical College ... WI ... 524
- Western Technical College ... WI ... 524
- Wisconsin Indianhead Technical College . WI ... 525

CARTE: Commission on Accreditation of Recreational Therapy Education: recreational therapy (B,M)

- University of New Hampshire ... NH .. 288
- East Carolina University ... NC .. 356
- Western Carolina University ... NC .. 359
- Oklahoma State University ... OK .. 385
- Slippery Rock University of Pennsylvania . PA ... 416
- Temple University ... PA ... 420

CEA: Commission on English Language Program Accreditation: english language (C)

- University of Alabama at Birmingham ... AL ... 8
- University of Alabama, The ... AL ... 8
- University of Arizona ... AZ ... 17
- Arkansas State University-Jonesboro ... AR ... 18
- California State Polytechnic University-Pomona ... CA ... 31
- California State University-Long Beach ... CA ... 33
- Grossmont College ... CA ... 45
- Los Angeles Pacific College ... CA ... 50
- National Polytechnic College ... CA ... 53
- Orange Coast College ... CA ... 39
- San Jose State University ... CA ... 35
- University of California-Irvine ... CA ... 69
- University of California-San Diego ... CA ... 70
- University of San Diego ... CA ... 72
- Colorado State University ... CO ... 78
- University of Colorado Boulder ... CO ... 83
- University of Denver ... CO ... 84
- University of Northern Colorado ... CO ... 84
- Sacred Heart University ... CT ... 88
- University of Connecticut ... CT ... 89
- University of Delaware ... DE ... 91
- Gallaudet University ... DC ... 92
- Georgetown University ... DC ... 92
- Aviator College of Aeronautical Science & Technology ... FL ... 95
- Embry-Riddle Aeronautical University ... FL ... 99
- Saint Leo University ... FL ... 108
- St. Petersburg College ... FL ... 108
- University of Central Florida ... FL ... 111
- University of Florida ... FL ... 112
- University of Miami ... FL ... 114
- University of South Florida ... FL ... 112
- Valencia College ... FL ... 114
- Georgia Institute of Technology ... GA .. 121
- Georgia State University ... GA .. 122
- University of Hawaii at Hilo ... HI ... 131
- University of Hawaii at Manoa ... HI ... 131
- University of Idaho ... ID ... 134
- DePaul University ... IL ... 139
- Southern Illinois University Carbondale ... IL ... 154
- University of Illinois at Chicago ... IL ... 156
- University of Illinois at Urbana-Champaign IL ... 157
- Western Illinois University ... IL ... 158
- Ball State University ... IN ... 159
- Indiana University Bloomington ... IN ... 162
- Purdue University Northwest ... IN ... 166
- Taylor University ... IN ... 167
- University of Iowa ... IA ... 169
- University of Northern Iowa ... IA ... 170
- Emporia State University ... KS ... 180
- Kansas State University ... KS ... 182
- Pittsburg State University ... KS ... 184
- University of Kansas Main Campus ... KS ... 185
- Washburn University ... KS ... 185
- University of Maine ... ME .. 204
- University of Maryland College Park ... MD .. 211
- Boston University ... MA .. 216
- Eastern Michigan University ... MI ... 233
- Michigan State University ... MI ... 237
- Michigan Technological University ... MI ... 238
- Saginaw Valley State University ... MI ... 240
- University of Michigan-Dearborn ... MI ... 242
- University of Michigan-Flint ... MI ... 242
- Western Michigan University ... MI ... 243
- University of Minnesota-Twin Cities ... MN .. 255
- Missouri State University ... MO .. 268
- Missouri University of Science & Technology ... MO .. 274
- Southeast Missouri State University ... MO .. 272
- University of Central Missouri ... MO .. 273
- University of Missouri - Kansas City ... MO .. 273
- College of Southern Nevada ... NV ... 284
- University of Nevada, Reno ... NV ... 285
- Rutgers the State University of New Jersey New Brunswick Campus ... NJ ... 296
- Columbia University in the City of New York ... NY ... 311
- University at Buffalo-SUNY ... NY ... 331
- East Carolina University ... NC ... 356
- University of North Carolina Wilmington ... NC .. 358
- Ashland University ... OH .. 363
- Cleveland State University ... OH ... 366
- Ohio Northern University ... OH ... 374
- University of Dayton ... OH ... 379
- University of Findlay, The ... OH ... 379
- Wright State University Main Campus ... OH ... 381
- Xavier University ... OH ... 381
- University of Tulsa ... OK .. 389
- Oregon State University ... OR .. 393
- Portland State University ... OR .. 394
- University of Oregon ... OR ... 395
- Willamette University ... OR ... 396
- Drexel University ... PA ... 402
- Duquesne University ... PA ... 403
- Penn State University Park ... PA ... 412
- University of Pennsylvania ... PA ... 421
- University of Pittsburgh ... PA ... 421
- Wilkes University ... PA ... 423
- University of South Carolina Columbia ... SC ... 433
- University of Tennessee at Martin ... TN ... 448
- Dallas Baptist University ... TX ... 455
- Lone Star College System ... TX ... 461
- San Antonio College ... TX ... 450
- Stephen F. Austin State University ... TX ... 466
- Texas A & M University ... TX ... 468
- Texas State University ... TX ... 471
- University of Houston ... TX ... 473
- University of North Texas ... TX ... 475
- University of Texas at Arlington, The ... TX ... 476
- University of Texas at Austin ... TX ... 476
- University of Texas at San Antonio ... TX ... 477
- University of Utah, The ... UT ... 481
- Utah State University ... UT ... 482
- Utah Valley University ... UT ... 482
- Weber State University ... UT ... 482
- Saint Michael's College ... VT ... 484
- American National University ... VA ... 486
- George Mason University ... VA ... 490
- Stratford University ... VA ... 494
- Virginia Commonwealth University ... VA ... 496
- Virginia Polytechnic Institute and State University ... VA ... 499
- Gonzaga University ... WA .. 504
- University of Washington ... WA .. 508
- Washington State University ... WA .. 508
- University of Wisconsin-Milwaukee ... WI ... 520

CGTECH: National Accrediting Agency for Clinical Laboratory Sciences: cytogenetic technologist (B)

- University of Connecticut ... CT ... 89
- Kennesaw State University ... GA .. 123
- Northern Michigan University ... MI ... 239
- University of Texas MD Anderson Cancer Center, The ... TX ... 477

CHIRO: Council on Chiropractic Education: chiropractic education (FP,D)

- Life Chiropractic College West ... CA ... 48
- Southern California University of Health Sciences ... CA ... 66
- University of Bridgeport ... CT ... 89
- Life University ... GA .. 124
- National University of Health Sciences ... IL ... 149
- Palmer College of Chiropractic ... IA ... 176
- Cleveland University - Kansas City ... KS ... 179
- Northwestern Health Sciences University . MN .. 253
- Logan University ... MO .. 267
- D'Youville College ... NY ... 313
- New York Chiropractic College ... NY ... 323
- University of Western States ... OR .. 396
- Sherman College of Chiropractic ... SC ... 432
- Parker University ... TX ... 463
- Texas Chiropractic College ... TX ... 469

CIDA: Council for Interior Design Accreditation: interior design (B,M)

- Auburn University ... AL ... 1
- Samford University ... AL ... 6
- University of Alabama, The ... AL ... 8
- University of North Alabama ... AL ... 9
- Virginia College ... AL ... 3
- Arizona State University ... AZ ... 11
- Art Institute of Phoenix, The ... AZ ... 11
- Northern Arizona University ... AZ ... 15
- Southwest University of Visual Arts ... AZ ... 17
- Harding University Main Campus ... AR ... 20
- University of Arkansas Main Campus ... AR ... 22
- University of Central Arkansas ... AR ... 24
- #Academy of Art University ... CA ... 25
- #California College of the Arts ... CA ... 29
- California State Polytechnic University-Pomona ... CA ... 31
- California State University-Fresno ... CA ... 32
- California State University-Northridge ... CA ... 34
- California State University-Sacramento ... CA ... 34
- Design Institute of San Diego ... CA ... 42
- Interior Designers Institute ... CA ... 47
- #San Diego State University ... CA ... 35
- Woodbury University ... CA ... 75
- Art Institute of Colorado, The ... CO ... 76
- Colorado State University ... CO ... 78
- Rocky Mountain College of Art & Design . CO ... 83
- George Washington University ... DC ... 92
- Art Institute of Fort Lauderdale, The ... FL ... 95
- Florida International University ... FL ... 111
- Florida State University ... FL ... 111
- Miami International University of Art & Design ... FL ... 105
- Ringling College of Art and Design ... FL ... 107
- Sanford-Brown College Tampa ... FL ... 109
- University of Florida ... FL ... 112
- Art Institute of Atlanta, The ... GA ... 116
- Brenau University ... GA .. 118
- Georgia Southern University ... GA .. 122
- Savannah College of Art and Design ... GA .. 126
- University of Georgia ... GA .. 128
- Chaminade University of Honolulu ... HI ... 130
- University of Idaho ... ID ... 134
- Columbia College Chicago ... IL ... 138
- Illinois Institute of Art, The ... IL ... 142
- Illinois State University ... IL ... 143
- Southern Illinois University Carbondale ... IL ... 154
- Ball State University ... IN ... 159
- Indiana State University ... IN ... 162
- Indiana University Bloomington ... IN ... 162
- Indiana University-Purdue University Indianapolis ... IN ... 163
- Purdue University Main Campus ... IN ... 166
- Iowa State University ... IA ... 169
- University of Northern Iowa ... IA ... 170
- Kansas State University ... KS ... 182
- Sullivan College of Technology and Design ... KY ... 193
- University of Kentucky ... KY ... 193
- #University of Louisville ... KY ... 194
- Louisiana State University and Agricultural and Mechanical College ... LA ... 197
- Louisiana Tech University ... LA ... 200
- University of Louisiana at Lafayette ... LA ... 201
- Boston Architectural College ... MA .. 216
- Endicott College ... MA .. 218
- Mount Ida College ... MA .. 226
- Suffolk University ... MA .. 228
- Wentworth Institute of Technology ... MA .. 229
- Central Michigan University ... MI ... 232
- College for Creative Studies ... MI ... 232
- Eastern Michigan University ... MI ... 233
- Ferris State University ... MI ... 233
- Lawrence Technological University ... MI ... 237
- Michigan State University ... MI ... 237
- Western Michigan University ... MI ... 243
- Dunwoody College of Technology ... MN ... 246
- University of Minnesota-Twin Cities ... MN ... 255
- Mississippi College ... MS ... 259
- Mississippi State University ... MS ... 259
- University of Southern Mississippi ... MS ... 261
- Maryville University of Saint Louis ... MO ... 267
- University of Central Missouri ... MO ... 273
- University of Missouri - Columbia ... MO ... 273
- University of Nebraska at Kearney ... NE ... 282
- University of Nebraska - Lincoln ... NE ... 282
- University of Nevada Las Vegas ... NV ... 284
- Kean University ... NJ ... 292
- New Jersey Institute of Technology ... NJ ... 293
- Cornell University ... NY ... 312
- Fashion Institute of Technology ... NY ... 314
- New York Institute of Technology ... NY ... 323
- New York School of Interior Design ... NY ... 324
- Pratt Institute ... NY ... 326
- Rochester Institute of Technology ... NY ... 327
- School of Visual Arts ... NY ... 330
- State University of New York College at Buffalo ... NY ... 332
- Syracuse University Main Campus ... NY ... 337
- Villa Maria College of Buffalo ... NY ... 339
- Appalachian State University ... NC ... 356
- East Carolina University ... NC ... 356
- High Point University ... NC ... 345
- Meredith College ... NC ... 345
- University of North Carolina at Greensboro ... NC ... 358
- Western Carolina University ... NC ... 359
- North Dakota State University Main Campus ... ND .. 361
- Kent State University Main Campus ... OH ... 370
- Miami University ... OH ... 372
- Ohio State University Main Campus, The . OH ... 375
- Ohio University Main Campus ... OH ... 375
- University of Akron, Main Campus, The ... OH ... 378
- University of Cincinnati Main Campus ... OH ... 379
- Oklahoma Christian University ... OK ... 385
- Oklahoma State University ... OK ... 385
- University of Central Oklahoma ... OK ... 388
- University of Oklahoma Norman Campus . OK ... 389
- Art Institute of Portland, The ... OR ... 390
- Marylhurst University ... OR ... 392
- University of Oregon ... OR ... 395
- Art Institute of Philadelphia ... PA ... 397
- Art Institute of Pittsburgh ... PA ... 397
- Chatham University ... PA ... 400
- Drexel University ... PA ... 402
- La Roche College ... PA ... 406
- Moore College of Art and Design ... PA ... 411
- Philadelphia University ... PA ... 416
- Converse College ... SC ... 429
- Winthrop University ... SC ... 435
- South Dakota State University ... SD ... 437
- #Middle Tennessee State University ... TN ... 444
- O'More College of Design ... TN ... 443
- University of Memphis, The ... TN ... 445
- University of Tennessee at Chattanooga .. TN ... 448
- University of Tennessee, Knoxville ... TN ... 448
- Watkins College of Art, Design & Film ... TN ... 449
- Abilene Christian University ... TX ... 449
- Art Institute of Houston, The ... TX ... 451
- Baylor University ... TX ... 452
- Sam Houston State University ... TX ... 471
- Stephen F. Austin State University ... TX ... 466
- Texas Christian University ... TX ... 469
- Texas State University ... TX ... 471
- #Texas Tech University ... TX ... 472
- University of North Texas ... TX ... 475
- University of Texas at Arlington, The ... TX ... 476
- University of Texas at Austin ... TX ... 476
- University of Texas at San Antonio ... TX ... 477
- University of the Incarnate Word ... TX ... 474
- Utah State University ... UT ... 482
- Weber State University ... UT ... 482
- Marymount University ... VA ... 492
- Radford University ... VA ... 493
- Virginia Commonwealth University ... VA ... 496
- Virginia Polytechnic Institute and State University ... VA ... 499
- Art Institute of Seattle, The ... WA .. 501
- Bellevue College ... WA .. 501
- Washington State University ... WA .. 508
- University of Charleston ... WV .. 511
- #Mount Mary University ... WI ... 518
- University of Wisconsin-Madison ... WI ... 519
- University of Wisconsin-Stevens Point ... WI ... 521
- University of Wisconsin-Stout ... WI ... 521

CLPSY: American Psychological Association: clinical psychology (D)

- Auburn University ... AL ... 1
- University of Alabama at Birmingham ... AL ... 8
- University of Alabama, The ... AL ... 8
- University of Alaska Anchorage ... AK ... 10
- University of Alaska Fairbanks ... AK ... 10
- Arizona State University ... AZ ... 11
- University of Arizona ... AZ ... 17
- University of Arkansas Main Campus ... AR ... 22
- Alliant International University-San Diego . CA ... 25
- Argosy University, Orange County ... CA ... 27
- Azusa Pacific University ... CA ... 28
- Biola University ... CA ... 28
- California Lutheran University ... CA ... 31
- Fielding Graduate University ... CA ... 43
- Fuller Theological Seminary ... CA ... 44
- John F. Kennedy University ... CA ... 47
- Loma Linda University ... CA ... 49
- Palo Alto University ... CA ... 56
- Pepperdine University ... CA ... 56
- San Diego State University ... CA ... 35
- University of California-Berkeley ... CA ... 68
- University of California-Los Angeles ... CA ... 69
- University of California-San Diego ... CA ... 70
- University of La Verne ... CA ... 71
- University of Southern California ... CA ... 72
- Wright Institute, The ... CA ... 75
- University of Colorado Boulder ... CO ... 83
- University of Colorado Colorado Springs .. CO ... 83
- University of Colorado Denver|Anschutz Medical Campus ... CO ... 84
- University of Denver ... CO ... 84
- University of Connecticut ... CT ... 89
- University of Hartford ... CT ... 89
- Yale University ... CT ... 90
- University of Delaware ... DE ... 91
- American University ... DC ... 91
- Catholic University of America, The ... DC ... 92
- Gallaudet University ... DC ... 92
- George Washington University ... DC ... 92

Howard University ... DC ... 93
Florida Institute of Technology ... FL ... 100
Florida International University ... FL ... 111
Florida State University ... FL ... 111
Nova Southeastern University ... FL ... 105
University of Central Florida ... FL ... 111
University of Florida ... FL ... 112
University of Miami ... FL ... 114
University of South Florida ... FL ... 112
Emory University ... GA ... 120
Georgia Southern University ... GA ... 122
Georgia State University ... GA ... 122
University of Georgia ... GA ... 128
University of Hawaii at Manoa ... HI ... 131
Idaho State University ... ID ... 133
Adler University ... IL ... 134
DePaul University ... IL ... 139
Illinois Institute of Technology ... IL ... 142
Loyola University Chicago ... IL ... 146
Midwestern University ... IL ... 148
Northern Illinois University ... IL ... 150
Northwestern University ... IL ... 150
Roosevelt University ... IL ... 152
Rosalind Franklin University of Medicine & Science ... IL ... 153
Southern Illinois University Carbondale ... IL ... 154
University of Illinois at Chicago ... IL ... 156
University of Illinois at Urbana-Champaign ... IL ... 157
Wheaton College ... IL ... 158
Indiana State University ... IN ... 162
Indiana University Bloomington ... IN ... 162
Indiana University-Purdue University Indianapolis ... IN ... 163
Purdue University Main Campus ... IN ... 166
University of Indianapolis ... IN ... 168
University of Iowa ... IA ... 169
University of Kansas Main Campus ... KS ... 185
Wichita State University ... KS ... 185
Spalding University ... KY ... 192
University of Kentucky ... KY ... 193
University of Louisville ... KY ... 194
#Louisiana State University and Agricultural and Mechanical College ... LA ... 197
University of Maine ... ME ... 204
Loyola University Maryland ... MD ... 208
Uniformed Services University of the Health Sciences ... MD ... 528
University of Maryland Baltimore County ... MD ... 211
University of Maryland College Park ... MD ... 211
Boston University ... MA ... 216
Clark University ... MA ... 217
Harvard University ... MA ... 219
Suffolk University ... MA ... 228
University of Massachusetts ... MA ... 220
University of Massachusetts Boston ... MA ... 220
William James College ... MA ... 229
Central Michigan University ... MI ... 232
Eastern Michigan University ... MI ... 233
Michigan School of Professional Psychology ... MI ... 237
Michigan State University ... MI ... 237
University of Detroit Mercy ... MI ... 241
University of Michigan-Ann Arbor ... MI ... 241
Wayne State University ... MI ... 243
Western Michigan University ... MI ... 243
University of Minnesota-Twin Cities ... MN ... 255
Jackson State University ... MS ... 258
University of Mississippi ... MS ... 261
University of Southern Mississippi ... MS ... 261
Saint Louis University ... MO ... 271
University of Missouri - Columbia ... MO ... 273
University of Missouri - Kansas City ... MO ... 273
University of Missouri - Saint Louis ... MO ... 274
Washington University in St. Louis ... MO ... 274
University of Montana - Missoula ... MT ... 276
University of Nebraska - Lincoln ... NE ... 282
University of Nevada, Las Vegas ... NV ... 284
University of Nevada, Reno ... NV ... 285
Fairleigh Dickinson University ... NJ ... 291
Rutgers the State University of New Jersey New Brunswick Campus ... NJ ... 296
University of New Mexico Main Campus ... NM ... 302
Adelphi University ... NY ... 303
City University of New York John Jay College of Criminal Justice ... NY ... 308
City University of New York Queens College ... NY ... 309
City University of New York The City College ... NY ... 307
Fordham University ... NY ... 314
Hofstra University ... NY ... 316
New School, The ... NY ... 322
St. John's University ... NY ... 328
State University of New York at Binghamton ... NY ... 331
Stony Brook University ... NY ... 332
Syracuse University Main Campus ... NY ... 337
Teachers College, Columbia University ... NY ... 337
University at Albany, SUNY ... NY ... 331
University at Buffalo-SUNY ... NY ... 331
University of Rochester ... NY ... 338
Yeshiva University ... NY ... 341
Duke University ... NC ... 343
East Carolina University ... NC ... 356
University of North Carolina at Chapel Hill ... NC ... 357
University of North Carolina at Charlotte ... NC ... 358
University of North Carolina at Greensboro ... NC ... 358
University of North Dakota ... ND ... 360
Bowling Green State University ... OH ... 364
Case Western Reserve University ... OH ... 365
Kent State University Main Campus ... OH ... 370
Miami University ... OH ... 372
Ohio State University Main Campus, The ... OH ... 375
Ohio University Main Campus ... OH ... 375
University of Cincinnati Main Campus ... OH ... 379
University of Toledo ... OH ... 380
Wright State University Main Campus ... OH ... 381
Xavier University ... OH ... 381
Oklahoma State University ... OK ... 385
University of Tulsa ... OK ... 389
George Fox University ... OR ... 391
Pacific University ... OR ... 394
University of Oregon ... OR ... 395
Chestnut Hill College ... PA ... 400
Drexel University ... PA ... 402
Duquesne University ... PA ... 403
Immaculata University ... PA ... 406
Indiana University of Pennsylvania ... PA ... 415
La Salle University ... PA ... 407
Marywood University ... PA ... 409
Penn State University Park ... PA ... 412
Philadelphia College of Osteopathic Medicine ... PA ... 416
Temple University ... PA ... 420
University of Pennsylvania ... PA ... 421
University of Pittsburgh ... PA ... 421
Widener University ... PA ... 423
Carlos Albizu University ... PR ... 531
Ponce School of Medicine & Health Sciences ... PR ... 535
University of Rhode Island ... RI ... 426
University of South Carolina Columbia ... SC ... 433
University of South Dakota, The ... SD ... 437
East Tennessee State University ... TN ... 444
University of Memphis, The ... TN ... 445
University of Tennessee, Knoxville ... TN ... 448
Vanderbilt University ... TN ... 449
Baylor University ... TX ... 452
Sam Houston State University ... TX ... 471
Southern Methodist University ... TX ... 465
Texas A & M University ... TX ... 468
Texas Tech University ... TX ... 472
University of Houston ... TX ... 473
University of North Texas ... TX ... 475
University of Texas at Austin ... TX ... 476
University of Texas Southwestern Medical Center ... TX ... 478
Brigham Young University ... UT ... 480
University of Utah, The ... UT ... 481
University of Vermont ... VT ... 485
Eastern Virginia Medical School ... VA ... 489
George Mason University ... VA ... 490
Institute for the Psychological Sciences ... VA ... 490
Norfolk State University ... VA ... 492
Old Dominion University ... VA ... 492
Regent University ... VA ... 493
University of Virginia ... VA ... 495
Virginia Commonwealth University ... VA ... 496
Virginia Polytechnic Institute and State University ... VA ... 499
Seattle Pacific University ... WA ... 507
University of Washington ... WA ... 508
Washington State University ... WA ... 508
Marshall University ... WV ... 513
West Virginia University ... WV ... 514
Marquette University ... WI ... 517
University of Wisconsin-Madison ... WI ... 519
University of Wisconsin-Milwaukee ... WI ... 520
Wisconsin School of Professional Psychology ... WI ... 522
University of Wyoming ... WY ... 527

CNCE: Accrediting Council for Continuing Education and Training: continuing education (C,A)

Southwest Institute of Healing Arts ... AZ ... 17
Asher College ... CA ... 27
California Institute of Arts & Technology ... CA ... 30
Intercoast College ... CA ... 46
Los Angeles ORT College ... CA ... 50
United Education Institute ... CA ... 68
Hawaii Medical College ... HI ... 130
Chicago ORT Technical Institute ... IL ... 136
Elyon College ... NY ... 313
National Institute of Massotherapy ... OH ... 373
Mech-Tech College ... PR ... 534

COARC: Commission on Accreditation for Respiratory Care: respiratory care (A,B,M)

George C. Wallace Community College - Dothan ... AL ... 3
#Samford University ... AL ... 6
Shelton State Community College ... AL ... 6
University of South Alabama ... AL ... 9
Virginia College ... AL ... 3
Wallace State Community College - Hanceville ... AL ... 9
#Cochise College ... AZ ... 12
Gateway Community College ... AZ ... 14
Pima Community College ... AZ ... 16
Pima Medical Institute-Tucson ... AZ ... 16
#Arkansas State University-Mid-South ... AR ... 19
#Black River Technical College ... AR ... 19
#National Park College ... AR ... 21
NorthWest Arkansas Community College ... AR ... 21
Pulaski Technical College ... AR ... 21
South Arkansas Community College ... AR ... 22
Southeast Arkansas College ... AR ... 22
University of Arkansas for Medical Sciences ... AR ... 23
American Career College-Ontario ... CA ... 26
American River College ... CA ... 51
Antelope Valley College ... CA ... 27
Brightwood College ... CA ... 28
Butte College ... CA ... 29
California College San Diego ... CA ... 30
Concorde Career College ... CA ... 41
Crafton Hills College ... CA ... 60
East Los Angeles College ... CA ... 49
El Camino College ... CA ... 42
Foothill College ... CA ... 44
Fresno City College ... CA ... 67
Grossmont College ... CA ... 45
#Hartnell College ... CA ... 45
Loma Linda University ... CA ... 49
Los Angeles Valley College ... CA ... 50
Modesto Junior College ... CA ... 76
Mt. San Antonio College ... CA ... 53
Napa Valley College ... CA ... 53
Ohlone College ... CA ... 55
Orange Coast College ... CA ... 39
#Platt College ... CA ... 57
San Joaquin Valley College, Inc. - Visalia ... CA ... 61
Skyline College ... CA ... 62
Victor Valley College ... CA ... 73
Concorde Career College ... CO ... 79
Pueblo Community College ... CO ... 82
Goodwin College ... CT ... 87
Manchester Community College ... CT ... 86
Naugatuck Valley Community College ... CT ... 86
Norwalk Community College ... CT ... 87
University of Hartford ... CT ... 89
University of the District of Columbia ... DC ... 94
Broward College ... FL ... 96
Concorde Career Institute ... FL ... 97
Concorde Career Institute ... FL ... 98
Daytona State College ... FL ... 98
Eastern Florida State College ... FL ... 98
Florida Agricultural and Mechanical University ... FL ... 110
#Florida National University Hialeah Campus ... FL ... 101
Florida SouthWestern State College ... FL ... 101
Florida State College at Jacksonville ... FL ... 101
Gulf Coast State College ... FL ... 102
Hillsborough Community College ... FL ... 102
Indian River State College ... FL ... 103
Keiser University ... FL ... 103
Miami Dade College ... FL ... 105
#Nova Southeastern University ... FL ... 105
Palm Beach State College ... FL ... 106
Polk State College ... FL ... 106
St. Johns River State College ... FL ... 108
St. Petersburg College ... FL ... 108
Santa Fe College ... FL ... 109
Seminole State College of Florida ... FL ... 109
Tallahassee Community College ... FL ... 113
Armstrong State University ... GA ... 116
Augusta Technical College ... GA ... 117
Augusta University ... GA ... 117
Coastal Pines Technical College ... GA ... 119
Columbus Technical College ... GA ... 119
Dalton State College ... GA ... 119
Darton State College ... GA ... 120
Georgia Northwestern Technical College ... GA ... 121
Georgia State University ... GA ... 122
Gwinnett Technical College ... GA ... 123
Middle Georgia State University ... GA ... 124
Oconee Fall Line Technical College-South Campus ... GA ... 125
Southern Crescent Technical College ... GA ... 127
Kapiolani Community College ... HI ... 131
Boise State University ... ID ... 132
Idaho State University ... ID ... 133
#Blessing-Rieman College of Nursing ... IL ... 136
College of DuPage ... IL ... 138
Illinois Central College ... IL ... 141
Kankakee Community College ... IL ... 144
Kaskaskia College ... IL ... 144
Lincoln Land Community College ... IL ... 146
Malcolm X College, One of the City Colleges of Chicago ... IL ... 138
Moraine Valley Community College ... IL ... 148
Parkland College ... IL ... 151
Rock Valley College ... IL ... 152
Rush University ... IL ... 153
St. Augustine College ... IL ... 153
Southwestern Illinois College ... IL ... 155
Trinity College of Nursing & Health Sciences ... IL ... 156
Ball State University ... IN ... 159
Indiana University-Purdue University Indianapolis ... IN ... 163
Ivy Tech Community College of Indiana-Central Indiana ... IN ... 164
University of Indianapolis ... IN ... 168
University of Southern Indiana ... IN ... 168
Des Moines Area Community College ... IA ... 171
Hawkeye Community College ... IA ... 173
Kirkwood Community College ... IA ... 174
Northeast Iowa Community College ... IA ... 175
St. Luke's College ... IA ... 176
Southeastern Community College ... IA ... 176
#Hutchinson Community College ... KS ... 181
Johnson County Community College ... KS ... 182
Kansas City Kansas Community College ... KS ... 182
Labette Community College ... KS ... 182
Newman University ... KS ... 183
Northwest Kansas Technical College ... KS ... 183
Seward County Community College ... KS ... 184
Washburn University ... KS ... 185
Ashland Community and Technical College ... KY ... 188
Bellarmine University ... KY ... 187
Big Sandy Community and Technical College ... KY ... 189
Bluegrass Community and Technical College ... KY ... 189
Elizabethtown Community and Technical College ... KY ... 189
Jefferson Community and Technical College ... KY ... 190
Madisonville Community College ... KY ... 190
Maysville Community and Technical College ... KY ... 190
Morehead State University ... KY ... 191
Northern Kentucky University ... KY ... 192
Somerset Community College ... KY ... 190
Southcentral Kentucky Community and Technical College ... KY ... 190
Southeast Kentucky Community and Technical College ... KY ... 190
Spencerian College ... KY ... 192
Bossier Parish Community College ... LA ... 195
Delgado Community College ... LA ... 196
L.E. Fletcher Technical Community College ... LA ... 196
#Louisiana State University at Eunice ... LA ... 197
Louisiana State University Health Sciences Center at Shreveport ... LA ... 198
Louisiana State University Health Sciences Center-New Orleans ... LA ... 198
Our Lady of the Lake College ... LA ... 199
Southern University at Shreveport-Louisiana ... LA ... 199
Kennebec Valley Community College ... ME ... 203
Southern Maine Community College ... ME ... 203
Allegany College of Maryland ... MD ... 205
Baltimore City Community College ... MD ... 206
Community College of Baltimore County, The ... MD ... 207
Frederick Community College ... MD ... 207
Prince George's Community College ... MD ... 210
Salisbury University ... MD ... 213
Berkshire Community College ... MA ... 222
#Bunker Hill Community College ... MA ... 223
Massasoit Community College ... MA ... 223
North Shore Community College ... MA ... 224
Northern Essex Community College ... MA ... 224
Quinsigamond Community College ... MA ... 224
Springfield Technical Community College ... MA ... 224
Delta College ... MI ... 233
Ferris State University ... MI ... 233
Henry Ford College ... MI ... 235
Jackson College ... MI ... 235
Kalamazoo Valley Community College ... MI ... 235
Macomb Community College ... MI ... 237
Monroe County Community College ... MI ... 238
Mott Community College ... MI ... 238
Muskegon Community College ... MI ... 238
Oakland Community College ... MI ... 239
Lake Superior College ... MN ... 249

Northland Community and Technical College ... MN .. 251
St. Catherine University ... MN .. 254
Saint Paul College-A Community & Technical College ... MN .. 252
University of Minnesota-Twin Cities ... MN .. 255
#Coahoma Community College ... MS .. 257
Copiah-Lincoln Community College ... MS .. 257
Hinds Community College ... MS .. 258
Itawamba Community College ... MS .. 258
Meridian Community College ... MS .. 258
Northeast Mississippi Community College ... MS .. 260
Northwest Mississippi Community College ... MS .. 260
Pearl River Community College ... MS .. 260
Concorde Career College ... MO .. 263
Missouri Southern State University ... MO .. 268
#Missouri State University - West Plains ... MO .. 269
Ozarks Technical Community College ... MO .. 270
University of Missouri - Columbia ... MO .. 273
Great Falls College Montana State University ... MT .. 277
University of Montana - Missoula ... MT .. 276
Metropolitan Community College ... NE ... 280
Midland University ... NE ... 280
Nebraska Methodist College ... NE ... 281
Southeast Community College ... NE .. 282
College of Southern Nevada ... NV ... 284
River Valley Community College ... NH .. 286
Bergen Community College ... NJ .. 289
Brookdale Community College ... NJ .. 289
County College of Morris ... NJ ... 290
Central New Mexico Community College ... NM .. 299
Eastern New Mexico University-Roswell ... NM .. 299
New Mexico State University Dona Ana Community College ... NM .. 301
#San Juan College ... NM .. 301
Santa Fe Community College ... NM .. 301
City University of New York Borough of Manhattan Community College ... NY ... 307
Erie Community College ... NY ... 313
Genesee Community College ... NY ... 315
Hudson Valley Community College ... NY ... 315
#Mandl School - The College of Allied Health ... NY ... 319
Mohawk Valley Community College ... NY ... 321
Molloy College ... NY ... 321
Nassau Community College ... NY ... 322
State University of New York Upstate Medical University ... NY ... 332
Stony Brook University ... NY ... 332
#Sullivan County Community College ... NY ... 336
Westchester Community College ... NY ... 340
Carteret Community College ... NC .. 348
Catawba Valley Community College ... NC .. 348
Central Piedmont Community College ... NC .. 348
Durham Technical Community College ... NC .. 349
Edgecombe Community College ... NC .. 349
Fayetteville Technical Community College ... NC .. 349
Forsyth Technical Community College ... NC .. 349
Pitt Community College ... NC .. 352
Robeson Community College ... NC .. 352
Rockingham Community College ... NC .. 352
Sandhills Community College ... NC .. 353
Southwestern Community College ... NC .. 353
Stanly Community College ... NC .. 353
Wilkes Community College ... NC .. 354
North Dakota State University Main Campus ... ND .. 361
University of Mary ... ND .. 362
Cincinnati State Technical and Community College ... OH .. 366
Columbus State Community College ... OH .. 367
Cuyahoga Community College ... OH .. 367
Eastern Gateway Community College - Jefferson County Campus ... OH .. 368
James A. Rhodes State College ... OH .. 370
Kettering College ... OH .. 371
Lakeland Community College ... OH .. 371
North Central State College ... OH .. 373
Ohio State University Main Campus, The ... OH .. 375
Shawnee State University ... OH .. 377
Sinclair Community College ... OH .. 377
Stark State College ... OH .. 377
University of Akron, Main Campus, The ... OH .. 378
University of Cincinnati-Clermont College ... OH .. 379
University of Rio Grande ... OH .. 380
University of Toledo ... OH .. 380
Washington State Community College ... OH .. 381
Youngstown State University ... OH .. 382
Cameron University ... OK .. 382
Northern Oklahoma College ... OK .. 384
Oklahoma City Community College ... OK .. 385
Rose State College ... OK .. 387
Tulsa Community College ... OK .. 388
Concorde Career College ... OR .. 390
Lane Community College ... OR .. 391
Mt. Hood Community College ... OR .. 392
Oregon Institute of Technology ... OR .. 393
Brightwood Career Institute ... PA .. 398
#Carlow University ... PA ... 400
Community College of Allegheny County ... PA ... 401
Community College of Philadelphia ... PA ... 401
Delaware County Community College ... PA ... 401
Gannon University ... PA ... 404
Gwynedd Mercy University ... PA ... 404
Harrisburg Area Community College ... PA ... 405
Indiana University of Pennsylvania ... PA ... 415
Laurel Business Institute ... PA ... 408
Laurel Technical Institute ... PA ... 408
Luzerne County Community College ... PA ... 409
Mansfield University of Pennsylvania ... PA ... 415
Millersville University of Pennsylvania ... PA ... 415
Pennsylvania College of Health Sciences ... PA ... 413
Pittsburgh Career Institute ... PA ... 417
Reading Area Community College ... PA ... 417
West Chester University of Pennsylvania ... PA ... 416
York College of Pennsylvania ... PA ... 424
#YTI Career Institute ... PA ... 424
Community College of Rhode Island ... RI ... 425
#New England Institute of Technology ... RI ... 425
Florence - Darlington Technical College ... SC ... 429
Greenville Technical College ... SC ... 430
Midlands Technical College ... SC ... 431
Orangeburg-Calhoun Technical College ... SC ... 431
Piedmont Technical College ... SC ... 432
Spartanburg Community College ... SC ... 432
Trident Technical College ... SC ... 433
Dakota State University ... SD ... 437
Baptist College of Health Sciences ... TN ... 438
Chattanooga State Community College ... TN ... 445
Columbia State Community College ... TN ... 446
Concorde Career College ... TN ... 439
East Tennessee State University ... TN ... 444
#Miller-Motte Technical College ... TN ... 442
Roane State Community College ... TN ... 447
Tennessee State University ... TN ... 445
Volunteer State Community College ... TN ... 447
Walters State Community College ... TN ... 447
Alvin Community College ... TX ... 450
Amarillo College ... TX ... 450
Angelina College ... TX ... 451
Cisco College ... TX ... 454
Collin County Community College District ... TX ... 455
Del Mar College ... TX ... 457
El Centro College ... TX ... 456
El Paso Community College ... TX ... 457
Houston Community College ... TX ... 459
Howard College ... TX ... 459
Lamar Institute of Technology ... TX ... 470
Lone Star College System ... TX ... 461
McLennan Community College ... TX ... 461
Midland College ... TX ... 461
Midwestern State University ... TX ... 462
St. Philip's College ... TX ... 450
San Jacinto College Central ... TX ... 464
South Plains College ... TX ... 465
South Texas College ... TX ... 465
Tarrant County College District ... TX ... 467
Temple College ... TX ... 467
Texas Southern University ... TX ... 470
Texas State University ... TX ... 471
Tyler Junior College ... TX ... 473
University of Texas Health Science Center at San Antonio ... TX ... 477
University of Texas Medical Branch, The ... TX ... 478
#Victoria College ... TX ... 478
Weatherford College ... TX ... 479
Dixie State University ... UT ... 482
Independence University ... UT ... 480
Weber State University ... UT ... 482
Vermont Technical College ... VT ... 486
Central Virginia Community College ... VA ... 496
J. Sargeant Reynolds Community College ... VA ... 497
Jefferson College of Health Sciences ... VA ... 491
Mountain Empire Community College ... VA ... 497
Northern Virginia Community College ... VA ... 497
Shenandoah University ... VA ... 494
Tidewater Community College ... VA ... 498
Highline College ... WA ... 504
Seattle Central College ... WA ... 506
Spokane Community College ... WA ... 502
Tacoma Community College ... WA ... 508
BridgeValley Community & Technical College ... WV .. 511
Marshall University ... WV .. 513
Mountwest Community and Technical College ... WV .. 512
#Pierpont Community & Technical College ... WV .. 512
Southern West Virginia Community and Technical College ... WV .. 512
Wheeling Jesuit University ... WV ... 515
Chippewa Valley Technical College ... WI ... 523
Madison Area Technical College ... WI ... 523
Mid-State Technical College ... WI ... 523
Milwaukee Area Technical College ... WI ... 524
Moraine Park Technical College ... WI ... 524
Northeast Wisconsin Technical College ... WI ... 524
Western Technical College ... WI ... 524
Casper College ... WY .. 526

COARCP: Commission on Accreditation for Respiratory Care: polysomnography (C)

Valencia College ... FL ... 114
Southern Crescent Technical College ... GA ... 127
Stony Brook University ... NY ... 332
James A. Rhodes State College ... OH .. 370
Youngstown State University ... OH .. 382
Gannon University ... PA ... 404
Texas State University ... TX ... 471

COE: Council on Occupational Education: occupational, trade, and technical education (C,A)

J.F. Ingram State Technical College ... AL ... 4
Reid State Technical College ... AL ... 6
Advanced College ... CA ... 25
Advanced Computing Institute ... CA ... 25
Advanced Training Associates ... CA ... 25
East San Gabriel Valley Regional Occupational Program and Technical Center ... CA ... 42
Los Angeles Pacific College ... CA ... 50
Mayfield College ... CA ... 52
Spartan College of Aeronautics and Technology ... CA ... 66
Colorado Academy of Veterinary Technology ... CO ... 77
Academy for Nursing and Health Occupations ... FL ... 94
Praxis Institute, The ... FL ... 107
Professional Hands Institute ... FL ... 107
Saber College ... FL ... 107
Sullivan and Cogliano Training Centers ... FL ... 113
Taylor College ... FL ... 113
Brown College of Court Reporting ... GA ... 118
Gwinnett College-Marietta ... GA ... 123
#Interactive College of Technology ... GA ... 123
Oconee Fall Line Technical College-North Campus ... GA ... 125
Oconee Fall Line Technical College-South Campus ... GA ... 125
Midwestern Career College ... IL ... 148
Morrison Institute of Technology ... IL ... 148
Cameron College ... LA ... 194
Central Louisiana Technical & Community College-Huey P. Long Campus ... LA ... 196
Central Louisiana Technical College Avoyelles Campus ... LA ... 195
Central Louisiana Technical College Oakdale Campus ... LA ... 196
Central Louisiana Technical Community College ... LA ... 196
Louisiana Culinary Institute ... LA ... 197
Northshore Technical Community College ... LA ... 196
Northwest Louisiana Technical College Northwest Campus ... LA ... 196
South Central Louisiana Technical College Young Memorial Campus ... LA ... 196
Sowela Technical Community College ... LA ... 197
Career Quest Learning Center ... MI ... 232
Lancaster County Career and Technology Center ... PA ... 408
Concorde Career College ... TN ... 439
#Fortis Institute ... TN ... 440
North Central Institute ... TN ... 443
Center for Advanced Legal Studies ... TX ... 453
Fortis College ... TX ... 458
Interactive College of Technology ... TX ... 459
Quest College ... TX ... 463
#Vista College ... TX ... 478
Ogden-Weber Applied Technology College ... UT ... 481
Uintah Basin Applied Technology College ... UT ... 481
Chester Career College ... VA ... 488
Columbia College ... VA ... 488
Eastern Virginia Career College ... VA ... 489
Saint Michael College of Allied Health ... VA ... 493

COMTA: Commission on Massage Therapy Accreditation: massage therapy, bodywork, aesthetics/esthetics and skin care (C,A)

Gadsden State Community College ... AL ... 3
#International Professional School of Bodywork ... CA ... 47
Academy of Natural Therapy ... CO ... 76
Idaho State University ... ID ... 133
Elgin Community College ... IL ... 140
Moraine Valley Community College ... IL ... 148
National University of Health Sciences ... IL ... 149
SOLEX College ... IL ... 154
Spencerian College ... KY ... 192
Allegany College of Maryland ... MD .. 205
Community College of Baltimore County, The ... MD .. 207
Bristol Community College ... MA .. 223
Lansing Community College ... MI ... 237
Northwestern Health Sciences University ... MN .. 253
Central Oregon Community College ... OR ... 390
University of Western States ... OR ... 396
Community College of Rhode Island ... RI ... 425
Technical College of the Lowcountry ... SC ... 433
Roane State Community College ... TN ... 447
Parker University ... TX ... 463

CONST: American Council for Construction Education: construction education (A,B)

Auburn University ... AL ... 1
Jefferson State Community College ... AL ... 5
University of Alaska Anchorage ... AK ... 10
Arizona State University ... AZ ... 11
Northern Arizona University ... AZ ... 15
John Brown University ... AR ... 20
University of Arkansas at Little Rock ... AR ... 23
California Baptist University ... CA ... 29
California Polytechnic State University-San Luis Obispo ... CA ... 31
California State University-Chico ... CA ... 32
California State University-Fresno ... CA ... 32
California State University-Long Beach ... CA ... 33
California State University-Northridge ... CA ... 34
California State University-Sacramento ... CA ... 34
Colorado State University ... CO ... 78
Central Connecticut State University ... CT ... 85
Florida International University ... FL ... 111
Santa Fe College ... FL ... 109
University of Florida ... FL ... 112
University of North Florida ... FL ... 112
Georgia Institute of Technology ... GA ... 121
Georgia Southern University ... GA ... 122
Kennesaw State University ... GA ... 123
Boise State University ... ID ... 132
Bradley University ... IL ... 136
College of DuPage ... IL ... 138
Illinois State University ... IL ... 143
John A. Logan College ... IL ... 143
Southern Illinois University Edwardsville ... IL ... 155
Ball State University ... IN ... 159
Indiana State University ... IN ... 162
Purdue University Main Campus ... IN ... 166
Kansas State University ... KS ... 182
Eastern Kentucky University ... KY ... 188
Northern Kentucky University ... KY ... 192
Western Kentucky University ... KY ... 194
Louisiana State University and Agricultural and Mechanical College ... LA ... 197
University of Louisiana at Monroe ... LA ... 201
University of Maryland Eastern Shore ... MD ... 212
Wentworth Institute of Technology ... MA ... 229
Eastern Michigan University ... MI ... 233
Ferris State University ... MI ... 233
Michigan State University ... MI ... 237
Michigan Technological University ... MI ... 238
Minnesota State University Moorhead ... MN ... 250
Minnesota State University, Mankato ... MN ... 250
University of Minnesota-Twin Cities ... MN ... 255
University of Southern Mississippi ... MS ... 261
Missouri State University ... MO ... 268
State Fair Community College ... MO ... 272
University of Central Missouri ... MO ... 273
University of Nebraska - Lincoln ... NE ... 282
University of Nevada, Las Vegas ... NV ... 284
Central New Mexico Community College ... NM ... 299
University of New Mexico Main Campus ... NM ... 302
Alfred State College ... NY ... 334
State University of New York College of Technology at Delhi ... NY ... 335
Utica College ... NY ... 339
East Carolina University ... NC ... 356
North Carolina Agricultural and Technical State University ... NC ... 356
Western Carolina University ... NC ... 359
North Dakota State University Main Campus ... ND ... 361
Bowling Green State University ... OH ... 364
Cincinnati State Technical and Community College ... OH ... 366
Columbus State Community College ... OH ... 367
Ohio State University Main Campus, The ... OH ... 375
University of Cincinnati Main Campus ... OH ... 379
University of Oklahoma Norman Campus ... OK ... 389
Oregon State University ... OR ... 393
Drexel University ... PA ... 402
Pennsylvania College of Technology ... PA ... 413
Roger Williams University ... RI ... 426
Clemson University ... SC ... 428
South Dakota State University ... SD ... 437
Lamar University ... TX ... 471
North Lake College ... TX ... 456
Tarrant County College District ... TX ... 467
Texas A & M University ... TX ... 468

- Texas State University ... TX ... 471
- University of Houston ... TX ... 473
- University of Texas at San Antonio ... TX ... 477
- Brigham Young University ... UT ... 480
- Weber State University ... UT ... 482
- Virginia Polytechnic Institute and State University ... VA ... 499
- Central Washington University ... WA .. 501
- Edmonds Community College ... WA .. 503
- University of Washington ... WA .. 508
- Washington State University ... WA .. 508
- Milwaukee School of Engineering ... WI ... 518
- University of Wisconsin-Stout ... WI ... 521

COPSY: American Psychological Association: counseling psychology (D)

- Auburn University ... AL ... 1
- Arizona State University ... AZ ... 11
- University of Central Arkansas ... AR ... 24
- Colorado State University ... CO ... 78
- University of Denver ... CO ... 84
- University of Northern Colorado ... CO ... 84
- Howard University ... DC ... 93
- University of Florida ... FL ... 112
- University of Miami ... FL ... 114
- Georgia State University ... GA .. 122
- University of Georgia ... GA .. 128
- Loyola University Chicago ... IL ... 146
- Southern Illinois University Carbondale ... IL ... 154
- University of Illinois at Urbana-Champaign IL ... 157
- Ball State University ... IN ... 159
- Indiana State University ... IN ... 162
- Indiana University Bloomington ... IN ... 162
- Purdue University Main Campus ... IN ... 166
- Iowa State University ... IA ... 169
- University of Iowa ... IA ... 169
- University of Kansas Main Campus ... KS ... 185
- University of Kentucky ... KY ... 193
- University of Louisville ... KY ... 194
- Louisiana Tech University ... LA ... 200
- University of Maryland College Park ... MD .. 211
- Boston College ... MA .. 216
- Springfield College ... MA .. 228
- University of Massachusetts Boston ... MA .. 220
- Western Michigan University ... MI ... 243
- Saint Mary's University of Minnesota ... MN .. 254
- University of Minnesota-Twin Cities ... MN .. 255
- University of Saint Thomas ... MN .. 256
- University of Southern Mississippi ... MS .. 261
- University of Missouri - Columbia ... MO .. 273
- University of Missouri - Kansas City ... MO .. 273
- University of Nebraska - Lincoln ... NE ... 282
- Seton Hall University ... NJ ... 297
- New Mexico State University Main Campus ... NM .. 300
- Fordham University ... NY ... 314
- New York University ... NY ... 324
- Teachers College, Columbia University ... NY ... 337
- University at Albany, SUNY ... NY ... 331
- University of North Dakota ... ND ... 360
- Cleveland State University ... OH .. 366
- University of Akron, Main Campus, The ... OH .. 378
- Oklahoma State University ... OK ... 385
- University of Oklahoma Norman Campus . OK .. 389
- University of Oregon ... OR ... 395
- Carlow University ... PA ... 400
- Chatham University ... PA ... 400
- Lehigh University ... PA ... 408
- Penn State University Park ... PA ... 412
- Tennessee State University ... TN ... 445
- University of Memphis, The ... TN ... 445
- University of Tennessee, Knoxville ... TN ... 448
- Our Lady of the Lake University ... TX ... 463
- Texas A & M University ... TX ... 468
- Texas Tech University ... TX ... 472
- Texas Woman's University ... TX ... 472
- University of Houston ... TX ... 473
- University of North Texas ... TX ... 475
- University of Texas at Austin ... TX ... 476
- Brigham Young University ... UT ... 480
- University of Utah, The ... UT ... 481
- Radford University ... VA ... 493
- Virginia Commonwealth University ... VA ... 496
- Washington State University ... WA ... 508
- West Virginia University ... WV .. 514
- Marquette University ... WI ... 517
- University of Wisconsin-Madison ... WI ... 519
- University of Wisconsin-Milwaukee ... WI ... 520

CORE: Council of Rehabilitation Education: rehabilitation counseling and rehabilitation services (B,M)

- Alabama Agricultural and Mechanical University ... AL ... 1
- Alabama State University ... AL ... 1
- Auburn University ... AL ... 1
- Troy University ... AL ... 7
- University of Alabama, The ... AL ... 8
- University of Arizona ... AZ ... 17
- Arkansas State University-Jonesboro ... AR ... 18
- Arkansas Tech University ... AR ... 19
- University of Arkansas at Little Rock ... AR ... 23
- University of Arkansas Main Campus ... AR ... 22
- California State University-Fresno ... CA ... 32
- California State University-Los Angeles ... CA ... 33
- California State University-Sacramento ... CA ... 34
- California State University-San Bernardino CA ... 34
- San Diego State University ... CA ... 35
- San Francisco State University ... CA ... 35
- University of Northern Colorado ... CO ... 84
- Central Connecticut State University ... CT ... 85
- George Washington University ... DC ... 92
- Florida Atlantic University ... FL ... 110
- University of South Florida ... FL ... 112
- Fort Valley State University ... GA .. 120
- Georgia State University ... GA .. 122
- #Thomas University ... GA .. 128
- University of Hawaii at Manoa ... HI ... 131
- University of Idaho ... ID ... 134
- Adler University ... IL ... 134
- Illinois Institute of Technology ... IL ... 142
- Northeastern Illinois University ... IL ... 149
- Northern Illinois University ... IL ... 150
- Southern Illinois University Carbondale ... IL ... 154
- Ball State University ... IN ... 159
- Drake University ... IA ... 171
- University of Iowa ... IA ... 169
- Emporia State University ... KS ... 180
- University of Kentucky ... KY ... 193
- Louisiana State University Health Sciences Center-New Orleans ... LA ... 198
- Southern University and A&M College ... LA ... 199
- University of Southern Maine ... ME .. 205
- Coppin State University ... MD .. 212
- University of Maryland Eastern Shore ... MD .. 212
- Assumption College ... MA .. 214
- Springfield College ... MA .. 228
- University of Massachusetts Boston ... MA .. 220
- Michigan State University ... MI ... 237
- Wayne State University ... MI ... 243
- Western Michigan University ... MI ... 243
- Minnesota State University, Mankato ... MN .. 250
- St. Cloud State University ... MN .. 252
- Jackson State University ... MS .. 258
- Mississippi State University ... MS .. 259
- Maryville University of Saint Louis ... MO .. 267
- Montana State University - Billings ... MT .. 277
- New Mexico Highlands University ... NM .. 300
- City University of New York Hunter College ... NY ... 308
- Hofstra University ... NY ... 316
- University at Buffalo-SUNY ... NY ... 331
- East Carolina University ... NC ... 356
- North Carolina Agricultural and Technical State University ... NC ... 356
- University of North Carolina at Chapel Hill NC ... 357
- Winston-Salem State University ... NC ... 359
- Kent State University Main Campus ... OH .. 370
- Ohio University Main Campus ... OH .. 375
- Wilberforce University ... OH .. 381
- Wright State University Main Campus ... OH .. 381
- East Central University ... OK ... 383
- Langston University ... OK ... 383
- Portland State University ... OR ... 394
- Western Oregon University ... OR .. 396
- Clarion University of Pennsylvania ... PA ... 414
- Edinboro University ... PA ... 415
- Penn State University Park ... PA ... 412
- University of Pittsburgh ... PA ... 421
- University of Scranton, The ... PA ... 422
- Pontifical Catholic University of Puerto Rico, The ... PR ... 535
- Universidad Central de Bayamon ... PR ... 536
- University of Puerto Rico-Rio Piedras Campus ... PR ... 538
- Salve Regina University ... RI ... 426
- South Carolina State University ... SC ... 432
- University of South Carolina Columbia ... SC ... 433
- South Dakota State University ... SD ... 437
- University of Memphis, The ... TN ... 445
- University of Tennessee, Knoxville ... TN ... 448
- Stephen F. Austin State University ... TX ... 466
- Texas Tech University Health Sciences Center ... TX ... 472
- University of North Texas ... TX ... 475
- University of Texas at Austin ... TX ... 476
- University of Texas at El Paso ... TX ... 476
- University of Texas Rio Grande Valley, The ... TX ... 476
- University of Texas Southwestern Medical Center ... TX ... 478
- Utah State University ... UT ... 482
- Virginia Commonwealth University ... VA ... 496
- Western Washington University ... WA ... 509
- West Virginia University ... WV ... 514
- University of Wisconsin-Madison ... WI ... 519
- University of Wisconsin-Stout ... WI ... 521

CS: ABET, Inc.: computer science (B)

- Alabama Agricultural and Mechanical University ... AL ... 1
- Athens State University ... AL ... 1
- Auburn University ... AL ... 1
- Jacksonville State University ... AL ... 4
- Tuskegee University ... AL ... 8
- University of Alabama at Birmingham ... AL ... 8
- University of Alabama in Huntsville ... AL ... 8
- University of Alabama, The ... AL ... 8
- University of North Alabama ... AL ... 9
- University of South Alabama ... AL ... 9
- University of Alaska Anchorage ... AK ... 10
- University of Alaska Fairbanks ... AK ... 10
- Arizona State University ... AZ ... 11
- Northern Arizona University ... AZ ... 15
- University of Arizona ... AZ ... 17
- Arkansas Tech University ... AR ... 19
- University of Arkansas at Little Rock ... AR ... 23
- University of Arkansas Main Campus ... AR ... 22
- University of Central Arkansas ... AR ... 24
- California Polytechnic State University-San Luis Obispo ... CA ... 31
- California State Polytechnic University-Pomona ... CA ... 31
- California State University-Chico ... CA ... 32
- California State University-Dominguez Hills ... CA ... 32
- California State University-Fullerton ... CA ... 33
- California State University-Long Beach ... CA ... 33
- California State University-Los Angeles ... CA ... 33
- California State University-Northridge ... CA ... 34
- California State University-Sacramento ... CA ... 34
- California State University-San Bernardino CA ... 34
- National University ... CA ... 54
- San Diego State University ... CA ... 35
- San Jose State University ... CA ... 35
- Santa Clara University ... CA ... 63
- University of California-Berkeley ... CA ... 68
- University of California-Davis ... CA ... 69
- University of California-Irvine ... CA ... 69
- University of California-Los Angeles ... CA ... 69
- University of California-Riverside ... CA ... 70
- University of California-Santa Barbara ... CA ... 70
- University of Southern California ... CA ... 72
- University of the Pacific ... CA ... 71
- Metropolitan State University of Denver ... CO ... 81
- Regis University ... CO ... 82
- United States Air Force Academy ... CO .. 528
- University of Colorado Boulder ... CO ... 83
- University of Colorado Colorado Springs .. CO ... 83
- University of Colorado Denver|Anschutz Medical Campus ... CO ... 84
- Central Connecticut State University ... CT ... 85
- Quinnipiac University ... CT ... 88
- Southern Connecticut State University ... CT ... 85
- University of Connecticut ... CT ... 89
- University of New Haven ... CT ... 90
- Catholic University of America, The ... DC ... 92
- George Washington University ... DC ... 92
- Howard University ... DC ... 93
- University of the District of Columbia ... DC ... 94
- Embry-Riddle Aeronautical University ... FL ... 99
- Florida Agricultural and Mechanical University ... FL ... 110
- Florida Atlantic University ... FL ... 110
- Florida Institute of Technology ... FL ... 100
- Florida International University ... FL ... 111
- Florida Memorial University ... FL ... 101
- Florida State University ... FL ... 111
- University of Central Florida ... FL ... 111
- University of North Florida ... FL ... 112
- University of South Florida ... FL ... 112
- University of Tampa ... FL ... 114
- Armstrong State University ... GA .. 116
- Georgia College & State University ... GA .. 121
- Georgia Institute of Technology ... GA .. 121
- Georgia Southern University ... GA .. 122
- Kennesaw State University ... GA .. 123
- Mercer University ... GA .. 124
- Middle Georgia State University ... GA .. 124
- University of Georgia ... GA .. 128
- University of West Georgia ... GA .. 129
- Valdosta State University ... GA .. 129
- Boise State University ... ID ... 132
- University of Idaho ... ID ... 134
- Illinois Institute of Technology ... IL ... 142
- Illinois State University ... IL ... 143
- Southern Illinois University Carbondale ... IL ... 154
- Southern Illinois University Edwardsville ... IL ... 155
- University of Illinois at Chicago ... IL ... 156
- University of Illinois at Urbana-Champaign IL ... 157
- Indiana University-Purdue University Fort Wayne ... IN ... 163
- Indiana University-Purdue University Indianapolis ... IN ... 163
- Purdue University Main Campus ... IN ... 166
- Purdue University Northwest ... IN ... 166
- Rose-Hulman Institute of Technology ... IN ... 166
- University of Evansville ... IN ... 167
- University of Notre Dame ... IN ... 168
- Iowa State University ... IA ... 169
- Kansas State University ... KS ... 182
- University of Kansas Main Campus ... KS ... 185
- Wichita State University ... KS ... 185
- Eastern Kentucky University ... KY ... 188
- University of Kentucky ... KY ... 193
- University of Louisville ... KY ... 194
- Grambling State University ... LA ... 200
- Louisiana State University and Agricultural and Mechanical College ... LA ... 197
- Louisiana State University in Shreveport .. LA ... 198
- Louisiana Tech University ... LA ... 200
- McNeese State University ... LA ... 200
- Southeastern Louisiana University ... LA ... 201
- Southern University and A&M College ... LA ... 199
- University of Louisiana at Lafayette ... LA ... 201
- University of Louisiana at Monroe ... LA ... 201
- University of New Orleans ... LA ... 198
- University of Maine ... ME .. 204
- University of Southern Maine ... ME .. 205
- Bowie State University ... MD .. 212
- Hood College ... MD .. 208
- Johns Hopkins University ... MD .. 208
- Loyola University Maryland ... MD .. 208
- Towson University ... MD .. 213
- United States Naval Academy ... MD .. 529
- University of Maryland Baltimore County .. MD .. 211
- Bridgewater State University ... MA .. 221
- Fitchburg State University ... MA .. 221
- Massachusetts Institute of Technology ... MA .. 225
- Salem State University ... MA .. 222
- Tufts University ... MA .. 228
- University of Massachusetts Boston ... MA .. 220
- University of Massachusetts Dartmouth ... MA .. 220
- Wentworth Institute of Technology ... MA .. 229
- Westfield State University ... MA .. 222
- Andrews University ... MI ... 230
- Calvin College ... MI ... 232
- Grand Valley State University ... MI ... 234
- Kettering University ... MI ... 236
- Michigan State University ... MI ... 237
- Michigan Technological University ... MI ... 238
- Oakland University ... MI ... 239
- University of Michigan-Ann Arbor ... MI ... 241
- University of Michigan-Dearborn ... MI ... 242
- Western Michigan University ... MI ... 243
- Capella University ... MN .. 245
- St. Cloud State University ... MN .. 252
- University of Minnesota Duluth ... MN .. 255
- Walden University ... MN .. 256
- Jackson State University ... MS .. 258
- Mississippi State University ... MS .. 259
- Mississippi Valley State University ... MS .. 260
- University of Mississippi ... MS .. 261
- University of Southern Mississippi ... MS .. 261
- Missouri State University ... MO .. 268
- Missouri University of Science & Technology ... MO .. 274
- Southeast Missouri State University ... MO .. 272
- Southwest Baptist University ... MO .. 272
- University of Central Missouri ... MO .. 273
- University of Missouri - Columbia ... MO .. 273
- University of Missouri - Kansas City ... MO .. 273
- Montana State University ... MT .. 277
- Montana Tech of The University of Montana ... MT .. 277
- University of Montana - Missoula ... MT .. 276
- University of Nebraska at Omaha ... NE ... 283
- University of Nebraska - Lincoln ... NE ... 282
- University of Nevada, Las Vegas ... NV .. 284
- University of Nevada, Reno ... NV .. 285
- University of New Hampshire ... NH .. 288
- College of New Jersey, The ... NJ .. 290
- Fairleigh Dickinson University ... NJ .. 291
- Kean University ... NJ .. 292
- Monmouth University ... NJ .. 292
- Montclair State University ... NJ .. 293
- New Jersey Institute of Technology ... NJ .. 293
- Rowan University ... NJ .. 295
- Stevens Institute of Technology ... NJ .. 297
- William Paterson University of New Jersey ... NJ .. 298
- New Mexico Institute of Mining and Technology ... NM .. 300
- New Mexico State University Main Campus ... NM .. 300
- University of New Mexico Main Campus .. NM .. 302
- City University of New York The City College ... NY ... 307
- College of Staten Island CUNY ... NY ... 307
- Excelsior College ... NY ... 314
- Iona College ... NY ... 317
- Pace University ... NY ... 325
- Rochester Institute of Technology ... NY ... 327

CSHSE: Council for Standards in Human Services Education: human services (A,B,M)

CVT: Commission on Accreditation of Allied Health Education Programs: cardiovascular technology (C,A,B)

CYTO: Commission on Accreditation of Allied Health Education Programs: cytotechnology (C,B,M)

DA: American Dental Association: dental assisting (C,A)

DANCE: National Association of Schools of Dance: dance (C,A,B,M,D)

DEAC: Distance Education Accrediting Commission: home study schools (A,B,M,D)

DENT: American Dental Association: dentistry (FP,D)

DH: American Dental Association: dental hygiene (C,A,B,M)

DIETC: Academy of Nutrition and Dietetics: coordinated dietetics programs (B,M)

DIETD: Academy of Nutrition and Dietetics: didactic dietetics programs (B,M)

DIETI: Academy of Nutrition and Dietetics: dietetic post-baccalaureate internships

DIETT: Academy of Nutrition and Dietetics: dietetic technician (A)

Cincinnati State Technical and Community College .... OH .. 366
Columbus State Community College .... OH .. 367
Cuyahoga Community College .... OH .. 367
Owens Community College .... OH .. 376
Sinclair Community College .... OH .. 377
@Stark State College .... OH .. 377
Youngstown State University .... OH .. 382
Oklahoma State University - Oklahoma City .... OK .. 386
Community College of Allegheny County . PA ... 401
#Southwest Tennessee Community College .... TN ... 447
Tarrant County College District .... TX ... 467

DMOLS: National Accrediting Agency for Clinical Laboratory Sciences: diagnostic molecular scientist (C,B,M)

University of Connecticut .... CT 89
Northern Michigan University .... MI 239
State University of New York Upstate Medical University .... NY ... 332
University of North Carolina at Chapel Hill NC .. 357
Tarleton State University .... TX ... 467
Texas Tech University Health Sciences Center .... TX ... 472
University of Texas MD Anderson Cancer Center, The .... TX ... 477

DMS: Commission on Accreditation of Allied Health Education Programs: diagnostic medical sonography (C,A, B,M)

Lurleen B. Wallace Community College ... AL 5
Trenholm State Technical College .... AL 7
Virginia College .... AL 3
Wallace State Community College - Hanceville .... AL 9
Gateway Community College .... AZ 14
Arkansas State University-Jonesboro .... AR 13
University of Arkansas at Fort Smith .... AR 23
University of Arkansas for Medical Sciences .... AR 23
CBD College .... CA 35
Cypress College .... CA 54
Foothill College .... CA 44
Kaiser Permanente School of Allied Health Sciences .... CA 47
Loma Linda University .... CA 49
Merced College .... CA 52
Mt. San Jacinto College .... CA 53
Orange Coast College .... CA 39
Platt College .... CA 57
Santa Barbara City College .... CA 63
University of California-San Diego .... CA 70
University of Colorado Denver|Anschutz Medical Campus .... CO 84
Adventist University of Health Sciences ... FL 95
Broward College .... FL 96
Cambridge College .... FL 97
Hillsborough Community College .... FL ... 102
Keiser University .... FL ... 103
Miami Dade College .... FL ... 105
Nova Southeastern University .... FL ... 105
Palm Beach State College .... FL ... 106
Polk State College .... FL ... 106
Santa Fe College .... FL ... 109
Valencia College .... FL ... 114
Armstrong State University .... GA .. 116
Columbus Technical College .... GA .. 119
Georgia Northwestern Technical College . GA .. 121
Gwinnett Technical College .... GA .. 123
Ogeechee Technical College .... GA .. 125
Boise State University .... ID ... 132
College of DuPage .... IL 138
Harper College .... IL 141
John A. Logan College .... IL 143
Rush University .... IL 153
Southern Illinois University Carbondale ... IL 154
Triton College .... IL 156
St. Anthony School of Echocardiography . IN 166
University of Southern Indiana .... IN 168
Allen College .... IA 169
Mercy College of Health Sciences .... IA 175
University of Iowa .... IA 169
Labette Community College .... KS ... 182
Washburn University .... KS ... 185
Hazard Community and Technical College KY ... 189
Morehead State University .... KY ... 191
Southcentral Kentucky Community and Technical College .... KY ... 190
West Kentucky Community and Technical College .... KY ... 190
Baton Rouge Community College .... LA ... 195
Delgado Community College .... LA ... 196
Louisiana State University at Eunice .... LA ... 197

Howard Community College .... MD .. 208
Johns Hopkins University .... MD .. 208
Montgomery College .... MD .. 209
University of Maryland Baltimore County .. MD .. 211
Bunker Hill Community College .... MA .. 223
Middlesex Community College .... MA .. 224
Springfield Technical Community College MA .. 224
Delta College .... MI 233
Ferris State University .... MI 233
Grand Valley State University .... MI 234
Jackson College .... MI 235
Lake Michigan College .... MI 236
Lansing Community College .... MI 237
Madonna University .... MI 237
Oakland Community College .... MI 239
St. Catherine University .... MN .. 254
Saint Cloud Technical and Community College .... MN .. 252
Hinds Community College .... MS .. 258
Cox College .... MO .. 264
University of Missouri - Columbia .... MO .. 273
Bryan College of Health Sciences .... NE .. 278
Nebraska Methodist College .... NE .. 281
University of Nebraska Medical Center .... NE .. 283
College of Southern Nevada .... NV .. 284
NHTI-Concord's Community College .... NH .. 286
Bergen Community College .... NJ .. 289
Rowan College at Burlington County .... NJ .. 295
Rowan College at Gloucester County .... NJ .. 295
Central New Mexico Community College . NM .. 299
New Mexico State University Dona Ana Community College .... NM .. 301
Hudson Valley Community College .... NY ... 316
Rochester Institute of Technology .... NY ... 327
SUNY Downstate Medical Center .... NY ... 332
Asheville - Buncombe Technical Community College .... NC .. 347
Caldwell Community College and Technical Institute .... NC .. 347
Cape Fear Community College .... NC .. 348
Forsyth Technical Community College .... NC .. 349
Johnston Community College .... NC .. 350
Pitt Community College .... NC .. 352
South Piedmont Community College .... NC .. 353
Southwestern Community College .... NC .. 353
Central Ohio Technical College .... OH .. 365
Cincinnati State Technical and Community College .... OH .. 366
Cuyahoga Community College .... OH .. 367
Kettering College .... OH .. 371
Lorain County Community College .... OH .. 371
Marion Technical College .... OH .. 372
Ohio State University Main Campus, The . OH .. 375
Owens Community College .... OH .. 376
University of Findlay, The .... OH .. 379
University of Rio Grande .... OH .. 380
Oklahoma State University - Oklahoma City .... OK .. 386
Oregon Institute of Technology .... OR .. 393
Community College of Allegheny County . PA ... 401
Great Lakes Institute of Technology .... PA ... 404
Harrisburg Area Community College .... PA ... 405
Lackawanna College .... PA ... 407
Misericordia University .... PA ... 410
Mount Aloysius College .... PA ... 411
Northampton Community College .... PA ... 411
Pennsylvania College of Health Sciences PA ... 413
Pittsburgh Career Institute .... PA ... 417
South Hills School of Business and Technology .... PA ... 419
Thomas Jefferson University .... PA ... 420
Westmoreland County Community College .... PA ... 423
Community College of Rhode Island .... RI ... 425
Greenville Technical College .... SC ... 430
Horry-Georgetown Technical College .... SC ... 430
Southeast Technical Institute .... SD ... 437
Baptist College of Health Sciences .... TN ... 438
Chattanooga State Community College .... TN ... 445
South College .... TN ... 444
Vanderbilt University .... TN ... 449
Volunteer State Community College .... TN ... 447
Alvin Community College .... TX ... 450
Angelina College .... TX ... 451
Austin Community College District .... TX ... 451
Del Mar College .... TX ... 457
El Centro College .... TX ... 456
El Paso Community College .... TX ... 457
Houston Community College .... TX ... 459
Lamar Institute of Technology .... TX ... 470
Lone Star College System .... TX ... 461
Midland College .... TX ... 461
San Jacinto College Central .... TX ... 464
Southwest University at El Paso .... TX ... 466
Temple College .... TX ... 467
Tyler Junior College .... TX ... 473
Weatherford College .... TX ... 479
Northern Virginia Community College .... VA ... 497
Piedmont Virginia Community College .... VA ... 498

Southside Regional Medical Center Professional Schools .... VA .. 494
Tidewater Community College .... VA .. 498
Bellevue College .... WA .. 501
Seattle University .... WA .. 507
Spokane Community College .... WA .. 502
Tacoma Community College .... WA .. 508
University of Charleston .... WV .. 511
West Virginia University .... WV .. 514
Blackhawk Technical College .... WI .. 523
Chippewa Valley Technical College .... WI .. 523
Concordia University Wisconsin .... WI .. 518
Northeast Wisconsin Technical College .... WI .. 524
University of Wisconsin-Madison .... WI .. 519
University of Wisconsin-Milwaukee .... WI .. 520
Laramie County Community College .... WY .. 525

DNUR: Accreditation Commission for Education in Nursing: nursing (C)

Riverside College of Health Careers .... VA .. 493

DT: American Dental Association: dental laboratory technology (C,A)

Pima Community College .... AZ 16
Los Angeles City College .... CA 49
Pasadena City College .... CA 56
Indian River State College .... FL ... 103
Atlanta Technical College .... GA ... 117
Indiana University-Purdue University Fort Wayne .... IN ... 163
Kirkwood Community College .... IA ... 174
Louisiana State University Health Sciences Center-New Orleans .... LA ... 198
Middlesex Community College .... MA .. 224
Erie Community College .... NY ... 313
New York City College of Technology/City University of New York .... NY ... 309
Durham Technical Community College .... NC ... 349
Portland Community College .... OR ... 394
J. Sargeant Reynolds Community College VA ... 497
Bates Technical College .... WA ... 501

EH: New England Association of Schools and Colleges, Commission on Institutions of Higher Education

Albertus Magnus College .... CT 85
Asnuntuck Community College .... CT 86
Capital Community College .... CT 86
Central Connecticut State University .... CT 85
Charter Oak State College .... CT 85
Connecticut College .... CT 87
Eastern Connecticut State University .... CT 85
Fairfield University .... CT 87
Gateway Community College .... CT 86
Goodwin College .... CT 87
Hartford Seminary .... CT 88
Holy Apostles College and Seminary .... CT 88
Housatonic Community College .... CT 86
Lincoln College of New England .... CT 88
Manchester Community College .... CT 86
Middlesex Community College .... CT 86
Mitchell College .... CT 88
Naugatuck Valley Community College .... CT 86
Northwestern Connecticut Community-Technical College .... CT 87
Norwalk Community College .... CT 87
Post University .... CT 88
Quinebaug Valley Community College .... CT 87
Quinnipiac University .... CT 88
Sacred Heart University .... CT 88
St. Vincent's College .... CT 89
Southern Connecticut State University .... CT 85
Three Rivers Community College .... CT 87
Trinity College .... CT 89
Tunxis Community College .... CT 87
United States Coast Guard Academy .... CT ... 529
University of Bridgeport .... CT 89
University of Connecticut .... CT 89
University of Hartford .... CT 89
University of New Haven .... CT 90
University of Saint Joseph .... CT 90
Wesleyan University .... CT 90
Western Connecticut State University .... CT 85
Yale University .... CT 90
Bates College .... ME .. 202
Bowdoin College .... ME .. 202
Central Maine Community College .... ME .. 203
Colby College .... ME .. 202
College of the Atlantic .... ME .. 202
Eastern Maine Community College .... ME .. 203
Husson University .... ME .. 202
Institute for Doctoral Studies in the Visual Arts .... ME .. 203
Kennebec Valley Community College .... ME .. 203
Maine College of Art .... ME .. 203
Maine College of Health Professions .... ME .. 203
Maine Maritime Academy .... ME .. 204
Northern Maine Community College .... ME .. 203

Saint Joseph's College of Maine .... ME .. 204
Southern Maine Community College .... ME .. 203
Thomas College .... ME .. 204
Unity College .... ME .. 204
University of Maine .... ME .. 204
University of Maine at Augusta .... ME .. 204
University of Maine at Farmington .... ME .. 205
University of Maine at Fort Kent .... ME .. 205
University of Maine at Machias .... ME .. 205
University of Maine at Presque Isle .... ME .. 205
University of New England .... ME .. 205
University of Southern Maine .... ME .. 205
Washington County Community College .. ME .. 204
York County Community College .... ME .. 204
American International College .... MA .. 214
Amherst College .... MA .. 214
Andover Newton Theological School .... MA .. 214
Anna Maria College .... MA .. 214
Assumption College .... MA .. 214
Babson College .... MA .. 214
Bard College at Simon's Rock .... MA .. 214
Bay Path University .... MA .. 215
Bay State College .... MA .. 215
Becker College .... MA .. 215
Benjamin Franklin Institute of Technology MA .. 215
Bentley University .... MA .. 215
Berklee College of Music .... MA .. 215
Berkshire Community College .... MA .. 222
Boston Architectural College .... MA .. 216
Boston College .... MA .. 216
Boston Graduate School of Psychoanalysis .... MA .. 216
Boston University .... MA .. 216
Brandeis University .... MA .. 216
Bridgewater State University .... MA .. 221
Bristol Community College .... MA .. 223
Bunker Hill Community College .... MA .. 223
Cambridge College .... MA .. 217
Cape Cod Community College .... MA .. 223
Clark University .... MA .. 217
College of Our Lady of the Elms .... MA .. 217
College of the Holy Cross .... MA .. 217
Conway School of Landscape Design .... MA .. 217
Curry College .... MA .. 217
Dean College .... MA .. 217
Eastern Nazarene College .... MA .. 218
Emerson College .... MA .. 218
Emmanuel College .... MA .. 218
Endicott College .... MA .. 218
Fisher College .... MA .. 218
Fitchburg State University .... MA .. 221
Framingham State University .... MA .. 221
Franklin W. Olin College of Engineering ... MA .. 218
Gordon College .... MA .. 219
Gordon-Conwell Theological Seminary .... MA .. 219
Greenfield Community College .... MA .. 223
Hampshire College .... MA .. 219
Harvard University .... MA .. 219
Hebrew College .... MA .. 219
Hellenic College-Holy Cross Greek Orthodox School of Theology .... MA .. 219
Holyoke Community College .... MA .. 223
Hult International Business School .... MA .. 219
Laboure College .... MA .. 219
Lasell College .... MA .. 219
Lesley University .... MA .. 220
Massachusetts Bay Community College ... MA .. 223
Massachusetts College of Art and Design MA .. 222
Massachusetts College of Liberal Arts .... MA .. 222
Massachusetts Institute of Technology .... MA .. 225
Massachusetts Maritime Academy .... MA .. 222
Massachusetts School of Law at Andover MA .. 225
Massasoit Community College .... MA .. 223
MCPHS University .... MA .. 225
Merrimack College .... MA .. 225
MGH Institute of Health Professions .... MA .. 225
Middlesex Community College .... MA .. 224
Montserrat College of Art .... MA .. 225
Mount Holyoke College .... MA .. 226
Mount Ida College .... MA .. 226
Mount Wachusett Community College .... MA .. 224
National Graduate School of Quality Management, The .... MA .. 226
New England College of Business and Finance .... MA .. 226
New England College of Optometry .... MA .. 226
New England Conservatory of Music .... MA .. 226
New England Institute of Art, The .... MA .. 226
Newbury College .... MA .. 226
Nichols College .... MA .. 227
North Shore Community College .... MA .. 224
Northeastern University .... MA .. 227
Northern Essex Community College .... MA .. 224
#Pine Manor College .... MA .. 227
Quincy College .... MA .. 227
Quinsigamond Community College .... MA .. 224
Regis College .... MA .. 227
Roxbury Community College .... MA .. 224
Saint John's Seminary .... MA .. 227

EMT: Commission on Accreditation of Allied Health Education Programs: emergency medical technician-paramedic (C,A,B)

ENG: ABET, Inc.: engineering (B,M)

Oklahoma State University ... OK .. 385
Oral Roberts University ... OK .. 386
University of Central Oklahoma ... OK .. 388
University of Oklahoma Norman Campus . OK .. 389
University of Tulsa ... OK .. 389
George Fox University ... OR .. 391
Oregon Institute of Technology ... OR .. 393
Oregon State University ... OR .. 393
Portland State University ... OR .. 394
University of Portland ... OR .. 396
Bucknell University ... PA ... 398
Carnegie Mellon University ... PA ... 400
Drexel University ... PA ... 402
Elizabethtown College ... PA ... 403
Gannon University ... PA ... 404
Geneva College ... PA ... 404
Grove City College ... PA ... 404
Lafayette College ... PA ... 407
Lehigh University ... PA ... 408
Messiah College ... PA ... 410
Penn State University Park ... PA ... 412
Philadelphia University ... PA ... 416
Robert Morris University ... PA ... 418
Saint Francis University ... PA ... 418
Shippensburg University of Pennsylvania . PA ... 416
Swarthmore College ... PA ... 419
Temple University ... PA ... 420
University of Pennsylvania ... PA ... 421
University of Pittsburgh ... PA ... 421
University of Scranton, The ... PA ... 422
Villanova University ... PA ... 422
Widener University ... PA ... 423
Wilkes University ... PA ... 423
York College of Pennsylvania ... PA ... 424
Caribbean University ... PR ... 531
Inter American University of Puerto Rico Bayamon Campus ... PR ... 533
Universidad Del Turabo ... PR ... 536
Universidad Politecnica De Puerto Rico ... PR ... 537
University of Puerto Rico-Mayaguez Campus ... PR ... 538
Brown University ... RI ... 424
Roger Williams University ... RI ... 426
University of Rhode Island ... RI ... 426
Bob Jones University ... SC ... 427
Citadel, The Military College of South Carolina, The ... SC ... 428
Clemson University ... SC ... 428
South Carolina State University ... SC ... 432
University of South Carolina Columbia ... SC ... 433
South Dakota School of Mines and Technology ... SD ... 437
South Dakota State University ... SD ... 437
Christian Brothers University ... TN ... 439
Lipscomb University ... TN ... 441
Tennessee State University ... TN ... 445
Tennessee Technological University ... TN ... 445
Union University ... TN ... 448
University of Memphis, The ... TN ... 445
University of Tennessee at Chattanooga .. TN ... 448
University of Tennessee at Martin ... TN ... 448
University of Tennessee, Knoxville ... TN ... 448
Vanderbilt University ... TN ... 449
Baylor University ... TX ... 452
Lamar University ... TX ... 471
LeTourneau University ... TX ... 460
Midwestern State University ... TX ... 462
Prairie View A & M University ... TX ... 467
Rice University ... TX ... 464
St. Mary's University ... TX ... 464
Southern Methodist University ... TX ... 465
Tarleton State University ... TX ... 467
Texas A & M University ... TX ... 468
Texas A & M University - Commerce ... TX ... 468
Texas A & M University - Kingsville ... TX ... 469
Texas Christian University ... TX ... 469
Texas State University ... TX ... 471
Texas Tech University ... TX ... 472
Trinity University ... TX ... 473
University of Houston ... TX ... 473
University of Houston - Clear Lake ... TX ... 474
University of North Texas ... TX ... 475
University of Texas at Arlington, The ... TX ... 476
University of Texas at Austin ... TX ... 476
University of Texas at Dallas, The ... TX ... 476
University of Texas at El Paso ... TX ... 476
University of Texas at San Antonio ... TX ... 477
University of Texas at Tyler ... TX ... 477
University of Texas of the Permian Basin . TX ... 478
University of Texas Rio Grande Valley, The ... TX ... 476
West Texas A & M University ... TX ... 469
Brigham Young University ... UT ... 480
Southern Utah University ... UT ... 481
University of Utah, The ... UT ... 481
Utah State University ... UT ... 482
Utah Valley University ... UT ... 482
Weber State University ... UT ... 482
Norwich University ... VT ... 484
University of Vermont ... VT ... 485
Christopher Newport University ... VA ... 488
George Mason University ... VA ... 490
Hampton University ... VA ... 490
James Madison University ... VA ... 490
Liberty University ... VA ... 491
Norfolk State University ... VA ... 492
Old Dominion University ... VA ... 492
Sweet Briar College ... VA ... 494
University of Virginia ... VA ... 495
University of Virginia's College at Wise, The ... VA ... 495
Virginia Commonwealth University ... VA ... 496
Virginia Military Institute ... VA ... 499
Virginia Polytechnic Institute and State University ... VA ... 499
Virginia State University ... VA ... 499
DigiPen Institute of Technology ... WA .. 503
Eastern Washington University ... WA .. 503
Gonzaga University ... WA .. 504
Pacific Lutheran University ... WA .. 505
Saint Martin's University ... WA .. 506
Seattle Pacific University ... WA .. 507
Seattle University ... WA .. 507
University of Washington ... WA .. 508
Walla Walla University ... WA .. 508
Washington State University ... WA .. 508
Marshall University ... WV .. 513
West Virginia University ... WV .. 514
Marquette University ... WI ... 517
Milwaukee School of Engineering ... WI ... 518
University of Wisconsin-Madison ... WI ... 519
University of Wisconsin-Milwaukee ... WI ... 520
University of Wisconsin-Platteville ... WI ... 521
University of Wisconsin-Stevens Point ... WI ... 521
University of Wisconsin-Stout ... WI ... 521
University of Wyoming ... WY .. 527

ENGR: ABET, Inc.: applied science (A,B,M)

Troy University ... AL ... 7
University of North Alabama ... AL ... 9
University of Alaska Anchorage ... AK ... 10
University of Arizona ... AZ ... 17
University of California-Los Angeles ... CA ... 69
Colorado State University ... CO ... 78
Trinidad State Junior College ... CO ... 83
University of Florida ... FL ... 112
University of North Florida ... FL ... 112
University of South Florida ... FL ... 112
Kennesaw State University ... GA .. 123
Idaho State University ... ID ... 133
Illinois State University ... IL ... 143
University of Illinois at Chicago ... IL ... 156
Indiana State University ... IN ... 162
Purdue University Main Campus ... IN ... 166
Purdue University Northwest ... IN ... 166
University of Iowa ... IA ... 169
Pittsburg State University ... KS ... 184
Murray State University ... KY ... 192
Nicholls State University ... LA ... 201
Southeastern Louisiana University ... LA ... 201
Tulane University ... LA ... 200
Johns Hopkins University ... MD .. 208
Morgan State University ... MD .. 209
Uniformed Services University of the Health Sciences ... MD .. 528
University of Massachusetts Lowell ... MA .. 221
Kettering University ... MI ... 236
Oakland University ... MI ... 239
University of Michigan-Ann Arbor ... MI ... 241
St. Cloud State University ... MN .. 252
University of Minnesota-Twin Cities ... MN .. 255
University of Central Missouri ... MO .. 273
Montana Tech of The University of Montana ... MT .. 277
University of Nevada, Las Vegas ... NV ... 284
City University of New York Hunter College ... NY ... 308
East Carolina University ... NC ... 356
Air Force Institute of Technology ... OH .. 527
University of Akron, Main Campus, The ... OH .. 378
University of Cincinnati Main Campus ... OH .. 379
University of Findlay, The ... OH .. 379
University of Toledo ... OH .. 380
Oregon Institute of Technology ... OR .. 393
Oregon State University ... OR .. 393
Indiana University of Pennsylvania ... PA ... 415
Millersville University of Pennsylvania ... PA ... 415
Universidad Politecnica De Puerto Rico ... PR ... 537
Clemson University ... SC ... 428
Chattanooga State Community College ... TN ... 445
East Tennessee State University ... TN ... 444
Texas A & M University - Corpus Christi .. TX ... 468
University of Houston - Clear Lake ... TX ... 474
University of Texas Health Science Center at Houston (UTHealth), The ... TX ... 477
Brigham Young University ... UT ... 480
University of Utah, The ... UT ... 481
Utah State University ... UT ... 482
James Madison University ... VA ... 490
Virginia State University ... VA ... 499
Fairmont State University ... WV .. 513
Marshall University ... WV .. 513
West Virginia University ... WV .. 514
University of Wisconsin-Whitewater ... WI ... 521

ENGT: ABET, Inc.: engineering technology (A,B)

Alabama Agricultural and Mechanical University ... AL ... 1
Arizona State University ... AZ ... 11
University of Arkansas at Little Rock ... AR ... 23
California State Polytechnic University-Pomona ... CA ... 31
CSU Maritime Academy ... CA ... 33
Colorado State University-Pueblo ... CO ... 79
Metropolitan State University of Denver ... CO ... 81
Central Connecticut State University ... CT ... 85
Naugatuck Valley Community College ... CT ... 86
University of Hartford ... CT ... 89
Daytona State College ... FL ... 98
Florida Agricultural and Mechanical University ... FL ... 110
Augusta Technical College ... GA ... 117
Fort Valley State University ... GA ... 120
Georgia Piedmont Technical College ... GA ... 122
Georgia Southern University ... GA ... 122
Kennesaw State University ... GA ... 123
Savannah State University ... GA ... 126
Savannah Technical College ... GA ... 126
Idaho State University ... ID ... 133
Bradley University ... IL ... 136
DeVry University - Chicago Campus ... IL ... 139
Morrison Institute of Technology ... IL ... 148
Northern Illinois University ... IL ... 150
Southern Illinois University Carbondale ... IL ... 154
Indiana State University ... IN ... 162
Indiana University-Purdue University Fort Wayne ... IN ... 163
Indiana University-Purdue University Indianapolis ... IN ... 163
Ivy Tech Community College of Indiana-Central Indiana ... IN ... 164
Purdue University Main Campus ... IN ... 166
Purdue University Northwest ... IN ... 166
University of Northern Iowa ... IA ... 170
Butler Community College ... KS ... 179
Grantham University ... KS ... 181
Pittsburg State University ... KS ... 184
Wichita State University ... KS ... 185
Eastern Kentucky University ... KY ... 188
Murray State University ... KY ... 192
Northern Kentucky University ... KY ... 192
Delgado Community College ... LA ... 196
Grambling State University ... LA ... 200
Louisiana Tech University ... LA ... 200
Northwestern State University ... LA ... 201
Southeastern Louisiana University ... LA ... 201
Southern University and A&M College ... LA ... 199
Maine Maritime Academy ... ME .. 204
University of Maine ... ME .. 204
Capitol Technology University ... MD .. 206
Northeastern University ... MA .. 227
Springfield Technical Community College MA .. 224
University of Massachusetts Lowell ... MA .. 221
Wentworth Institute of Technology ... MA .. 229
Eastern Michigan University ... MI ... 233
Ferris State University ... MI ... 233
Lake Superior State University ... MI ... 236
Michigan Technological University ... MI ... 238
Northern Michigan University ... MI ... 239
Wayne State University ... MI ... 243
Western Michigan University ... MI ... 243
Dunwoody College of Technology ... MN .. 246
Minnesota State University, Mankato ... MN .. 250
University of Southern Mississippi ... MS .. 261
Missouri Southern State University ... MO .. 268
Missouri Western State University ... MO .. 269
Southeast Missouri State University ... MO .. 272
Montana State University ... MT .. 277
Montana State University - Northern ... MT .. 277
College of Southern Nevada ... NV .. 284
Nashua Community College ... NH .. 286
NHTI-Concord's Community College ... NH .. 286
University of New Hampshire ... NH .. 288
County College of Morris ... NJ .. 290
Essex County College ... NJ .. 291
Fairleigh Dickinson University ... NJ .. 291
Middlesex County College ... NJ .. 292
New Jersey Institute of Technology ... NJ .. 293
Passaic County Community College ... NJ .. 294
Rowan College at Burlington County ... NJ .. 295
Thomas Edison State University ... NJ .. 297
New Mexico State University Main Campus ... NM .. 300
Northern New Mexico College ... NM .. 301
Alfred State College ... NY ... 334
City University of New York Bronx Community College ... NY ... 307
City University of New York Queensborough Community College ... NY ... 309
College of Staten Island CUNY ... NY ... 307
Erie Community College ... NY ... 313
Excelsior College ... NY ... 314
Farmingdale State College ... NY ... 335
Hudson Valley Community College ... NY ... 316
Mohawk Valley Community College ... NY ... 321
Monroe Community College ... NY ... 321
Morrisville State College ... NY ... 336
Nassau Community College ... NY ... 322
New York City College of Technology/City University of New York ... NY ... 309
New York Institute of Technology ... NY ... 323
Paul Smith's College ... NY ... 326
Rochester Institute of Technology ... NY ... 327
State University of New York College at Buffalo ... NY ... 332
State University of New York College of Environmental Science and Forestry ... NY ... 334
SUNY Broome Community College ... NY ... 332
SUNY Canton-College of Technology ... NY ... 335
SUNY Polytechnic Institute ... NY ... 336
Technical Career Institutes ... NY ... 337
Vaughn College of Aeronautics and Technology ... NY ... 339
Central Piedmont Community College ... NC ... 348
Elizabeth City State University ... NC ... 356
Forsyth Technical Community College ... NC ... 349
Gaston College ... NC ... 350
University of North Carolina at Charlotte .. NC ... 358
Western Carolina University ... NC ... 359
Bismarck State College ... ND ... 361
Bowling Green State University ... OH ... 364
Central Ohio Technical College ... OH ... 365
Cincinnati State Technical and Community College ... OH ... 366
Cleveland State University ... OH ... 366
Columbus State Community College ... OH ... 367
Cuyahoga Community College ... OH ... 367
James A. Rhodes State College ... OH ... 370
Kent State University Main Campus ... OH ... 370
Lakeland Community College ... OH ... 371
Lorain County Community College ... OH ... 371
Miami University ... OH ... 372
Sinclair Community College ... OH ... 377
Stark State College ... OH ... 377
University of Akron, Main Campus, The ... OH ... 378
University of Cincinnati Main Campus ... OH ... 379
University of Dayton ... OH ... 379
University of Toledo ... OH ... 380
Youngstown State University ... OH ... 382
Zane State College ... OH ... 382
Oklahoma State University ... OK ... 385
Oklahoma State University Institute of Technology-Okmulgee ... OK ... 386
Southwestern Oklahoma State University . OK ... 388
Oregon Institute of Technology ... OR ... 393
Bloomsburg University of Pennsylvania ... PA ... 414
California University of Pennsylvania ... PA ... 414
Drexel University ... PA ... 402
Pennsylvania College of Technology ... PA ... 413
Point Park University ... PA ... 417
Temple University ... PA ... 420
University of Puerto Rico-Aguadilla ... PR ... 537
University of Puerto Rico at Arecibo ... PR ... 537
University of Puerto Rico at Bayamon ... PR ... 537
University of Puerto Rico at Ponce ... PR ... 538
University of Puerto Rico-Humacao ... PR ... 538
New England Institute of Technology ... RI ... 425
Denmark Technical College ... SC ... 429
Greenville Technical College ... SC ... 430
Midlands Technical College ... SC ... 431
Orangeburg-Calhoun Technical College ... SC ... 431
Piedmont Technical College ... SC ... 432
South Carolina State University ... SC ... 432
Spartanburg Community College ... SC ... 432
University of South Carolina Upstate ... SC ... 434
York Technical College ... SC ... 435
Austin Peay State University ... TN ... 444
Belmont University ... TN ... 438
Chattanooga State Community College ... TN ... 445
East Tennessee State University ... TN ... 444
Middle Tennessee State University ... TN ... 444
Southwest Tennessee Community College ... TN ... 447
Tennessee Technological University ... TN ... 445
University of Memphis, The ... TN ... 445
University of Tennessee at Chattanooga .. TN ... 448
Houston Community College ... TX ... 459
LeTourneau University ... TX ... 460
Prairie View A & M University ... TX ... 467
Texas A & M University ... TX ... 468
Texas A & M University - Corpus Christi .. TX ... 468
Texas Southern University ... TX ... 470
University of Houston ... TX ... 473
University of Houston - Downtown ... TX ... 474

University of North Texas ... TX ... 475
Brigham Young University ... UT ... 480
Southern Utah University ... UT ... 481
Weber State University ... UT ... 482
Vermont Technical College ... VT ... 486
Old Dominion University ... VA ... 492
Virginia State University ... VA ... 499
Central Washington University ... WA ... 501
Eastern Washington University ... WA ... 503
Western Washington University ... WA ... 509
Bluefield State College ... WV ... 512
BridgeValley Community & Technical College ... WV ... 511
Fairmont State University ... WV ... 513
Milwaukee School of Engineering ... WI ... 518
Northeast Wisconsin Technical College ... WI ... 524
University of Wisconsin-Stout ... WI ... 521
Waukesha County Technical College ... WI ... 524

EXSC: Commission on Accreditation of Allied Health Education Programs: exercise science (C,B,M)

Metropolitan State University of Denver ... CO ... 81
Central Connecticut State University ... CT ... 85
Southern Connecticut State University ... CT ... 85
University of North Florida ... FL ... 112
Georgia State University ... GA ... 122
Valdosta State University ... GA ... 129
Southern Illinois University Edwardsville ... IL ... 155
Indiana Wesleyan University ... IN ... 164
University of Indianapolis ... IN ... 168
Murray State University ... KY ... 192
University of Louisville ... KY ... 194
University of Louisiana at Monroe ... LA ... 201
University of Southern Maine ... ME ... 205
Salisbury University ... MD ... 213
Lasell College ... MA ... 219
Springfield College ... MA ... 228
Westfield State University ... MA ... 222
St. Catherine University ... MN ... 254
Missouri Baptist University ... MO ... 268
State University of New York, The College at Brockport ... NY ... 332
University of North Carolina at Charlotte ... NC ... 358
North Dakota State University Main Campus ... ND ... 361
University of Mary ... ND ... 362
Bowling Green State University ... OH ... 364
Kent State University Main Campus ... OH ... 370
Ohio Northern University ... OH ... 374
Wright State University Main Campus ... OH ... 381
University of Central Oklahoma ... OK ... 388
Bloomsburg University of Pennsylvania ... PA ... 414
East Stroudsburg University of Pennsylvania ... PA ... 414
Eastern University ... PA ... 403
Grove City College ... PA ... 404
Indiana University of Pennsylvania ... PA ... 415
Saint Francis University ... PA ... 418
Slippery Rock University of Pennsylvania ... PA ... 416
West Chester University of Pennsylvania ... PA ... 416
South Dakota State University ... SD ... 437
Lyndon State College ... VT ... 486
George Mason University ... VA ... 490
Liberty University ... VA ... 491
Longwood University ... VA ... 491
Lynchburg College ... VA ... 491
Old Dominion University ... VA ... 492
University of Wisconsin-Oshkosh ... WI ... 520

FEPAC: American Academy of Forensic Sciences: forensic science (B,M)

University of Alabama at Birmingham ... AL ... 8
University of New Haven ... CT ... 90
George Washington University ... DC ... 92
Florida International University ... FL ... 111
University of Tampa ... FL ... 114
Albany State University ... GA ... 115
#Loyola University Chicago ... IL ... 146
University of Illinois at Chicago ... IL ... 156
Indiana University-Purdue University Indianapolis ... IN ... 163
Eastern Kentucky University ... KY ... 188
Towson University ... MD ... 213
Boston University ... MA ... 216
Madonna University ... MI ... 237
Michigan State University ... MI ... 237
University of Mississippi ... MS ... 261
Alfred State College ... NY ... 334
City University of New York John Jay College of Criminal Justice ... NY ... 308
State University of New York College at Buffalo ... NY ... 332
Ohio University Main Campus ... OH ... 375
University of Central Oklahoma ... OK ... 388
Arcadia University ... PA ... 397
Cedar Crest College ... PA ... 400
Duquesne University ... PA ... 403
Penn State University Park ... PA ... 412
West Chester University of Pennsylvania ... PA ... 416
Sam Houston State University ... TX ... 471
Texas A & M University ... TX ... 468
University of North Texas ... TX ... 475
Virginia Commonwealth University ... VA ... 496
Marshall University ... WV ... 513
West Virginia University ... WV ... 514

FUSER: American Board of Funeral Service Education: funeral service education (C,A,B)

Bishop State Community College ... AL ... 2
Jefferson State Community College ... AL ... 5
Mesa Community College ... AZ ... 14
Arkansas State University-Mountain Home ... AR ... 19
University of Arkansas at Hope-Texarkana ... AR ... 24
American River College ... CA ... 51
Cypress College ... CA ... 54
Arapahoe Community College ... CO ... 76
Lincoln College of New England ... CT ... 88
University of the District of Columbia ... DC ... 94
Florida State College at Jacksonville ... FL ... 101
Miami Dade College ... FL ... 105
St. Petersburg College ... FL ... 108
Gupton Jones College of Funeral Service ... GA ... 122
Ogeechee Technical College ... GA ... 125
Carl Sandburg College ... IL ... 136
Malcolm X College, One of the City Colleges of Chicago ... IL ... 138
Southern Illinois University Carbondale ... IL ... 154
Worsham College of Mortuary Science ... IL ... 158
Ivy Tech Community College of Indiana-Central Indiana ... IN ... 164
Mid-America College of Funeral Service ... IN ... 165
Vincennes University ... IN ... 169
Des Moines Area Community College ... IA ... 171
Kansas City Kansas Community College ... KS ... 182
Southeast Kentucky Community and Technical College ... KY ... 190
Delgado Community College ... LA ... 196
Community College of Baltimore County, The ... MD ... 207
FINE Mortuary College ... MA ... 218
Mount Ida College ... MA ... 226
Wayne State University ... MI ... 243
University of Minnesota-Twin Cities ... MN ... 255
East Mississippi Community College ... MS ... 257
Holmes Community College ... MS ... 258
Mississippi Gulf Coast Community College ... MS ... 259
Northwest Mississippi Community College ... MS ... 260
Eastwick College ... NJ ... 291
Mercer County Community College ... NJ ... 292
American Academy McAllister Institute of Funeral Service ... NY ... 304
Hudson Valley Community College ... NY ... 316
Nassau Community College ... NY ... 322
SUNY Canton-College of Technology ... NY ... 335
Fayetteville Technical Community College ... NC ... 349
Cincinnati College of Mortuary Science ... OH ... 366
University of Central Oklahoma ... OK ... 388
Mt. Hood Community College ... OR ... 392
Northampton Community College ... PA ... 411
Pittsburgh Institute of Mortuary Science ... PA ... 417
Piedmont Technical College ... SC ... 432
John A. Gupton College ... TN ... 440
Amarillo College ... TX ... 450
Commonwealth Institute of Funeral Service ... TX ... 455
Dallas Institute of Funeral Service ... TX ... 457
San Antonio College ... TX ... 450
Salt Lake Community College ... UT ... 483
John Tyler Community College ... VA ... 497
Tidewater Community College ... VA ... 498
Lake Washington Institute of Technology ... WA ... 504
#Milwaukee Area Technical College ... WI ... 524

HSA: Commission on Accreditation of Healthcare Management Education: healthcare management (B,M)

University of Alabama at Birmingham ... AL ... 8
University of Arkansas for Medical Sciences ... AR ... 23
California State University-Long Beach ... CA ... 33
San Diego State University ... CA ... 35
University of California-Los Angeles ... CA ... 69
University of Southern California ... CA ... 72
University of Colorado Denver|Anschutz Medical Campus ... CO ... 84
George Washington University ... DC ... 92
Georgetown University ... DC ... 92
Florida International University ... FL ... 111
University of Central Florida ... FL ... 111
University of Florida ... FL ... 112
University of Miami ... FL ... 114
University of North Florida ... FL ... 112
University of South Florida ... FL ... 112
Armstrong State University ... GA ... 116
Georgia State University ... GA ... 122
Governors State University ... IL ... 140
Rush University ... IL ... 153
University of Illinois at Chicago ... IL ... 156
Indiana University-Purdue University Indianapolis ... IN ... 163
Des Moines University ... IA ... 171
University of Iowa ... IA ... 169
University of Kansas Main Campus ... KS ... 185
University of Kentucky ... KY ... 193
Tulane University ... LA ... 200
University of Southern Maine ... ME ... 205
Johns Hopkins University ... MD ... 208
Boston University ... MA ... 216
Simmons College ... MA ... 228
University of Michigan-Ann Arbor ... MI ... 241
University of Minnesota-Twin Cities ... MN ... 255
University of Saint Thomas ... MN ... 256
Saint Louis University ... MO ... 271
University of Missouri - Columbia ... MO ... 273
Seton Hall University ... NJ ... 297
Baruch College/City University of New York ... NY ... 307
Clarkson University ... NY ... 310
Columbia University in the City of New York ... NY ... 311
Cornell University ... NY ... 312
New York University ... NY ... 324
University of North Carolina at Chapel Hill ... NC ... 357
University of North Carolina at Charlotte ... NC ... 358
Ohio State University Main Campus, The ... OH ... 375
Xavier University ... OH ... 381
Portland State University ... OR ... 394
Penn State University Park ... PA ... 412
Temple University ... PA ... 420
University of Pittsburgh ... PA ... 421
University of Scranton, The ... PA ... 422
Widener University ... PA ... 423
University of Puerto Rico-Medical Sciences Campus ... PR ... 538
Medical University of South Carolina ... SC ... 431
University of South Carolina Columbia ... SC ... 433
University of Memphis, The ... TN ... 445
Baylor University ... TX ... 452
Texas A & M University ... TX ... 468
Texas State University ... TX ... 471
Texas Woman's University ... TX ... 472
Trinity University ... TX ... 473
University of North Texas Health Science Center at Fort Worth ... TX ... 475
University of the Incarnate Word ... TX ... 474
University of Utah, The ... UT ... 481
Weber State University ... UT ... 482
George Mason University ... VA ... 490
Marymount University ... VA ... 492
Virginia Commonwealth University ... VA ... 496
University of Washington ... WA ... 508
Washington State University ... WA ... 508

HT: National Accrediting Agency for Clinical Laboratory Sciences: histologic technology (C,A,B)

Phoenix College ... AZ ... 14
Mt. San Antonio College ... CA ... 53
Goodwin College ... CT ... 87
Barry University ... FL ... 96
Florida State College at Jacksonville ... FL ... 101
Miami Dade College ... FL ... 105
Darton State College ... GA ... 120
Elgin Community College ... IL ... 140
Indiana University-Purdue University Indianapolis ... IN ... 163
Harford Community College ... MD ... 208
North Hennepin Community College ... MN ... 251
State University of New York College of Agriculture and Technology at Cobleskill ... NY ... 334
Carolinas College of Health Sciences ... NC ... 343
University of North Dakota ... ND ... 360
Lakeland Community College ... OH ... 371
Drexel University ... PA ... 402
Harcum College ... PA ... 405
University of Pittsburgh ... PA ... 421
Community College of Rhode Island ... RI ... 425
Medical University of South Carolina ... SC ... 431
University of Tennessee Health Science Center ... TN ... 443
Houston Community College ... TX ... 459
St. Philip's College ... TX ... 450
Tarleton State University ... TX ... 467
University of Texas Health Science Center at San Antonio ... TX ... 477
University of Texas MD Anderson Cancer Center, The ... TX ... 477
Clover Park Technical College ... WA ... 502
West Virginia University ... WV ... 514

IACBE: International Assembly for Collegiate Business Education: business programs in institutions that grant bachelor/graduate degrees (A,B,M,D)

Stillman College ... AL ... 7
Alaska Pacific University ... AK ... 10
University of the Ozarks ... AR ... 24
Ashford University ... CA ... 27
Azusa Pacific University ... CA ... 28
Concordia University ... CA ... 41
CSU Maritime Academy ... CA ... 33
Humboldt State University ... CA ... 34
John F. Kennedy University ... CA ... 47
National University ... CA ... 54
Pacific Union College ... CA ... 56
Albertus Magnus College ... CT ... 85
Goldey-Beacom College ... DE ... 91
Wilmington University ... DE ... 91
Edward Waters College ... FL ... 98
Florida Institute of Technology ... FL ... 100
Hodges University ... FL ... 102
Lynn University ... FL ... 104
Nova Southeastern University ... FL ... 105
Palm Beach Atlantic University ... FL ... 106
Saint Leo University ... FL ... 108
Webber International University ... FL ... 115
Thomas University ... GA ... 128
University of Guam ... GU ... 530
Chaminade University of Honolulu ... HI ... 130
Lewis-Clark State College ... ID ... 134
Lincoln College ... IL ... 146
McKendree University ... IL ... 147
National-Louis University ... IL ... 149
North Park University ... IL ... 149
Robert Morris University - Illinois ... IL ... 152
Rockford University ... IL ... 152
Marian University ... IN ... 165
Oakland City University ... IN ... 166
Saint Joseph's College ... IN ... 166
Maharishi University of Management ... IA ... 175
Northwestern College ... IA ... 176
Grantham University ... KS ... 181
University of Saint Mary ... KS ... 185
Campbellsville University ... KY ... 187
Kentucky Wesleyan College ... KY ... 191
Lindsey Wilson College ... KY ... 191
Spalding University ... KY ... 192
University of Holy Cross ... LA ... 200
Husson University ... ME ... 202
University of Maine at Fort Kent ... ME ... 205
Capitol Technology University ... MD ... 206
Mount St. Mary's University ... MD ... 209
University of Maryland College Park ... MD ... 211
American International College ... MA ... 214
College of Our Lady of the Elms ... MA ... 217
Fitchburg State University ... MA ... 221
Massachusetts Maritime Academy ... MA ... 222
Nichols College ... MA ... 227
Springfield College ... MA ... 228
Wentworth Institute of Technology ... MA ... 229
Andrews University ... MI ... 230
Baker College of Flint ... MI ... 231
Davenport University ... MI ... 233
Lawrence Technological University ... MI ... 237
Bemidji State University ... MN ... 248
Saint Mary's University of Minnesota ... MN ... 254
Belhaven University ... MS ... 256
Avila University ... MO ... 262
Culver-Stockton College ... MO ... 264
Harris-Stowe State University ... MO ... 265
Carroll College ... MT ... 276
University of Montana Western, The ... MT ... 277
Bellevue University ... NE ... 278
Concordia University ... NE ... 279
Wayne State College ... NE ... 281
Roseman University of Health Sciences ... NV ... 285
Franklin Pierce University ... NH ... 287
Centenary College ... NJ ... 290
Felician University ... NJ ... 291
Saint Peter's University ... NJ ... 296
Cazenovia College ... NY ... 306
Concordia College ... NY ... 311
Daemen College ... NY ... 312
Dominican College of Blauvelt ... NY ... 312
D'Youville College ... NY ... 313
Excelsior College ... NY ... 314
Keuka College ... NY ... 318
Manhattanville College ... NY ... 319
Medaille College ... NY ... 320
Mount Saint Mary College ... NY ... 322
Nazareth College of Rochester ... NY ... 322
Roberts Wesleyan College ... NY ... 327
Sage Colleges, The ... NY ... 327
St. Thomas Aquinas College ... NY ... 329
State University of New York College at Potsdam ... NY ... 334

State University of New York Empire State College ... NY ... 335
Vaughn College of Aeronautics and Technology ... NY ... 339
Dickinson State University ... ND .. 360
Minot State University ... ND .. 360
University of Jamestown ... ND .. 362
University of Mary ... ND .. 362
Defiance College, The ... OH .. 368
Franklin University ... OH .. 369
Lake Erie College ... OH .. 371
Lourdes University ... OH .. 371
University of Rio Grande ... OH .. 380
Urbana University ... OH .. 380
Ursuline College ... OH .. 380
Bacone College ... OK .. 382
Oklahoma Wesleyan University ... OK .. 386
Southwestern Oklahoma State University . OK .. 388
Eastern Oregon University ... OR .. 391
Marylhurst University ... OR .. 392
Northwest Christian University ... OR .. 393
Oregon Institute of Technology ... OR .. 393
Cairn University ... PA ... 399
Chatham University ... PA ... 400
Gwynedd Mercy University ... PA ... 404
Keystone College ... PA ... 406
Mercyhurst University ... PA ... 410
Misericordia University ... PA ... 410
Point Park University ... PA ... 417
Saint Francis University ... PA ... 418
Seton Hill University ... PA ... 419
Waynesburg University ... PA ... 423
Inter American University of Puerto Rico San German Campus ... PR ... 534
Universidad Politecnica De Puerto Rico ... PR ... 537
Salve Regina University ... RI ... 426
Charleston Southern University ... SC ... 427
Dakota Wesleyan University ... SD ... 435
National American University ... SD ... 436
Presentation College ... SD ... 436
University of Sioux Falls ... SD ... 438
Bryan College ... TN ... 439
Southern Adventist University ... TN ... 444
Concordia University Texas ... TX ... 455
LeTourneau University ... TX ... 460
Southwestern Adventist University ... TX ... 466
Southwestern Assemblies of God University ... TX ... 466
Hampton University ... VA ... 490
#Davis & Elkins College ... WV .. 510
Ohio Valley University ... WV .. 511
Shepherd University ... WV .. 513
West Liberty University ... WV .. 513
Concordia University Wisconsin ... WI ... 516
Herzing University ... WI ... 516
Marian University ... WI ... 517

IFSAC: International Fire Service Accreditation Congress Degree Assembly: fire and emergency related degree (A,B)

Central Arizona College ... AZ 12
Yavapai College ... AZ 18
NorthWest Arkansas Community College . AR 21
Oxnard College ... CA 73
Aims Community College ... CO 76
Embry-Riddle Aeronautical University ... FL 99
Southern Illinois University Carbondale ... IL 154
Johnson County Community College ... KS ... 182
Ashland Community and Technical College ... KY ... 188
Bluegrass Community and Technical College ... KY ... 189
Eastern Kentucky University ... KY ... 188
Elizabethtown Community and Technical College ... KY ... 189
Gateway Community and Technical College ... KY ... 189
Hazard Community and Technical College KY ... 189
Jefferson Community and Technical College ... KY ... 190
Madisonville Community College ... KY ... 190
Maysville Community and Technical College ... KY ... 190
Owensboro Community and Technical College ... KY ... 190
Somerset Community College ... KY ... 190
Southcentral Kentucky Community and Technical College ... KY ... 190
West Kentucky Community and Technical College ... KY ... 190
Lake Superior State University ... MI ... 236
Lansing Community College ... MI ... 237
Macomb Community College ... MI ... 237
Hennepin Technical College ... MN .. 249
Ozarks Technical Community College ... MO .. 270
Helena College University of Montana ... MT .. 277
New Mexico State University Dona Ana Community College ... NM .. 301
Catawba Valley Community College ... NC .. 348
Gaston College ... NC .. 350
Cincinnati State Technical and Community College ... OH .. 366
Lakeland Community College ... OH .. 371
University of Akron, Main Campus, The ... OH .. 378
Oklahoma State University - Oklahoma City ... OK .. 386
Central Oregon Community College ... OR .. 390
Chemeketa Community College ... OR .. 390
Portland Community College ... OR .. 394
Holy Family University ... PA ... 405
Montgomery County Community College . PA ... 410
Blinn College ... TX ... 452
Utah Valley University ... UT ... 482
South Puget Sound Community College .. WA .. 508
University of Wisconsin-Oshkosh ... WI ... 520

IPSY: American Psychological Association: pre-doctoral internships in health service psychology

University of Alabama at Birmingham ... AL 8
Arizona State University ... AZ 11
University of Arizona ... AZ 17
University of Arkansas for Medical Sciences ... AR 23
Biola University ... CA 28
California State University-Fullerton ... CA 33
California State University-Long Beach ... CA 33
California State University-Northridge ... CA 34
Loma Linda University ... CA 49
San Jose State University ... CA 35
Stanford University ... CA 66
University of California-Berkeley ... CA 68
University of California-Davis ... CA 69
University of California-Irvine ... CA 69
University of California-Los Angeles ... CA 69
University of California-Riverside ... CA 70
University of California-San Diego ... CA 70
University of California-San Francisco ... CA 70
University of California-Santa Barbara ... CA 70
University of California-Santa Cruz ... CA 70
University of San Diego ... CA 72
University of San Francisco ... CA 72
University of Southern California ... CA 72
University of the Pacific ... CA 71
Colorado State University ... CO 78
University of Colorado Boulder ... CO 83
University of Colorado Denver|Anschutz Medical Campus ... CO 84
University of Denver ... CO 84
University of Northern Colorado ... CO 84
University of Connecticut ... CT 89
Yale University ... CT 90
University of Delaware ... DE 91
American University ... DC 91
Catholic University of America, The ... DC 92
George Washington University ... DC 92
Howard University ... DC 93
Florida Atlantic University ... FL ... 110
Florida International University ... FL ... 111
Florida State University ... FL ... 111
Nova Southeastern University ... FL ... 105
University of Central Florida ... FL ... 111
University of Florida ... FL ... 112
University of Miami ... FL ... 114
University of South Florida ... FL ... 112
Augusta University ... GA ... 117
Emory University ... GA .. 120
Georgia Institute of Technology ... GA .. 121
Georgia State University ... GA .. 122
University of Hawaii at Manoa ... HI 131
University of Idaho ... ID 134
Adler University ... IL 134
Illinois State University ... IL 143
Northern Illinois University ... IL 150
Northwestern University ... IL 150
Rush University ... IL 153
Southern Illinois University Carbondale ... IL 154
University of Chicago ... IL 156
University of Illinois at Chicago ... IL 156
University of Illinois at Urbana-Champaign IL 157
Ball State University ... IN 159
Butler University ... IN 159
Indiana University Bloomington ... IN 162
Indiana University-Purdue University Indianapolis ... IN 163
Purdue University Main Campus ... IN 166
University of Notre Dame ... IN 168
Iowa State University ... IA 169
University of Iowa ... IA 169
Kansas State University ... KS ... 182
University of Kansas Main Campus ... KS ... 185
Wichita State University ... KS ... 185
University of Kentucky ... KY ... 193
University of Louisville ... KY ... 194
Louisiana State University and Agricultural and Mechanical College ... LA ... 197
Louisiana State University Health Sciences Center-New Orleans ... LA ... 198
Tulane University ... LA ... 200
University of Maine ... ME .. 204
Johns Hopkins University ... MD .. 208
Towson University ... MD .. 213
University of Maryland Baltimore ... MD .. 211
University of Maryland Baltimore County .. MD .. 211
University of Maryland College Park ... MD .. 211
Boston University ... MA .. 216
Harvard University ... MA .. 219
Suffolk University ... MA .. 228
Tufts University ... MA .. 228
University of Massachusetts ... MA .. 220
University of Massachusetts Medical School ... MA .. 221
William James College ... MA .. 229
Grand Valley State University ... MI 234
Michigan State University ... MI 237
University of Michigan-Ann Arbor ... MI 241
Western Michigan University ... MI 243
University of Minnesota-Twin Cities ... MN .. 255
University of Saint Thomas ... MN .. 256
University of Mississippi Medical Center ... MS .. 261
University of Missouri - Columbia ... MO .. 273
University of Missouri - Kansas City ... MO .. 273
University of Missouri - Saint Louis ... MO .. 274
Montana State University ... MT .. 277
University of Nebraska - Lincoln ... NE .. 282
Dartmouth College ... NH .. 286
University of New Hampshire ... NH .. 288
New Mexico State University Main Campus ... NM .. 300
University of New Mexico Main Campus .. NM .. 302
Albany Medical College ... NY ... 303
Baruch College/City University of New York ... NY ... 307
Columbia University in the City of New York ... NY ... 311
Icahn School of Medicine at Mount Sinai . NY ... 317
New York University ... NY ... 324
Pace University ... NY ... 325
State University of New York Upstate Medical University ... NY ... 332
Stony Brook University ... NY ... 332
University at Albany, SUNY ... NY ... 331
University at Buffalo-SUNY ... NY ... 331
University of Rochester ... NY ... 338
Yeshiva University ... NY ... 341
Appalachian State University ... NC ... 356
Duke University ... NC ... 343
University of North Carolina at Chapel Hill NC ... 357
University of North Carolina at Charlotte .. NC ... 358
University of North Dakota ... ND ... 360
Bowling Green State University ... OH ... 364
Miami University ... OH ... 372
Ohio State University Main Campus, The . OH ... 375
University of Akron, Main Campus, The ... OH ... 378
Wright State University Main Campus ... OH ... 381
George Fox University ... OR .. 391
Oregon Health & Science University ... OR .. 393
Oregon State University ... OR .. 393
Pacific University ... OR .. 394
University of Oregon ... OR .. 395
Chestnut Hill College ... PA ... 400
Immaculata University ... PA ... 406
Lehigh University ... PA ... 408
Penn State University Park ... PA ... 412
Philadelphia College of Osteopathic Medicine ... PA ... 416
Temple University ... PA ... 420
University of Pennsylvania ... PA ... 421
University of Pittsburgh ... PA ... 421
Widener University ... PA ... 423
Ponce School of Medicine & Health Sciences ... PR ... 535
Brown University ... RI 424
Clemson University ... SC ... 428
Medical University of South Carolina ... SC ... 431
University of South Carolina Columbia ... SC ... 433
University of Memphis, The ... TN ... 445
University of Tennessee Health Science Center ... TN ... 448
University of Tennessee, Knoxville ... TN ... 448
Vanderbilt University ... TN ... 449
Baylor College of Medicine ... TX ... 452
Texas A & M University ... TX ... 468
Texas State University ... TX ... 471
Texas Tech University ... TX ... 472
Texas Woman's University ... TX ... 472
University of Houston ... TX ... 473
University of Texas at Austin ... TX ... 476
University of Texas at Dallas, The ... TX ... 476
University of Texas Health Science Center at San Antonio ... TX ... 477
University of Texas Southwestern Medical Center ... TX ... 478
Brigham Young University ... UT ... 480
University of Utah, The ... UT ... 481
Utah State University ... UT ... 482
University of Vermont ... VT ... 485
College of William & Mary ... VA ... 488
Eastern Virginia Medical School ... VA ... 489
George Mason University ... VA ... 490
James Madison University ... VA ... 490
University of Virginia ... VA ... 495
Virginia Commonwealth University ... VA ... 496
Virginia Polytechnic Institute and State University ... VA ... 499
Central Washington University ... WA ... 501
University of Puget Sound ... WA .. 508
University of Washington ... WA .. 508
Washington State University ... WA .. 508
West Virginia University ... WV .. 514
University of Wisconsin-Madison ... WI ... 519

JOUR: Accrediting Council on Education for Journalism and Mass Communications: journalism and mass communications (B,M)

Auburn University ... AL 1
Jacksonville State University ... AL 4
University of Alabama, The ... AL 8
University of North Alabama ... AL 9
University of Alaska Anchorage ... AK 10
Arizona State University ... AZ 11
University of Arizona ... AZ 17
Arkansas State University-Jonesboro ... AR 18
#University of Arkansas Main Campus ... AR 22
California State University-Chico ... CA 32
California State University-Fullerton ... CA 33
California State University-Long Beach ... CA 33
California State University-Northridge ... CA 34
San Diego State University ... CA 35
San Francisco State University ... CA 35
#San Jose State University ... CA 35
University of California-Berkeley ... CA 68
University of Southern California ... CA 72
Colorado State University ... CO 78
University of Colorado Boulder ... CO 83
University of Connecticut ... CT 89
American University ... DC 91
Howard University ... DC 93
Florida Agricultural and Mechanical University ... FL ... 110
Florida International University ... FL ... 111
University of Florida ... FL ... 112
University of South Florida St. Petersburg FL ... 112
Savannah State University ... GA ... 126
University of Georgia ... GA .. 128
University of Idaho ... ID 134
Eastern Illinois University ... IL 139
Northwestern University ... IL 150
Southern Illinois University Carbondale ... IL 154
Southern Illinois University Edwardsville ... IL 155
University of Illinois at Urbana-Champaign IL 157
Ball State University ... IN 159
Indiana University Bloomington ... IN 162
Drake University ... IA 171
Iowa State University ... IA 169
University of Iowa ... IA 169
Kansas State University ... KS ... 182
University of Kansas Main Campus ... KS ... 185
Murray State University ... KY ... 192
University of Kentucky ... KY ... 193
Western Kentucky University ... KY ... 194
Grambling State University ... LA ... 200
Louisiana State University and Agricultural and Mechanical College ... LA ... 197
Loyola University New Orleans ... LA ... 198
Nicholls State University ... LA ... 201
Southern University and A&M College ... LA ... 199
University of Louisiana at Lafayette ... LA ... 201
University of Maryland College Park ... MD .. 211
Central Michigan University ... MI 232
Michigan State University ... MI 237
St. Cloud State University ... MN .. 252
University of Minnesota-Twin Cities ... MN .. 255
University of Mississippi ... MS .. 261
University of Southern Mississippi ... MS .. 261
Southeast Missouri State University ... MO .. 272
University of Missouri - Columbia ... MO .. 273
University of Montana - Missoula ... MT .. 276
University of Nebraska - Lincoln ... NE .. 282
University of Nevada, Reno ... NV ... 285
University of New Mexico Main Campus .. NM .. 302
City University of New York Graduate Center ... NY ... 308
Columbia University in the City of New York ... NY ... 311
Hofstra University ... NY ... 316
Iona College ... NY ... 317
New York University ... NY ... 324
State University of New York College at Buffalo ... NY ... 332

Stony Brook University ... NY ... 332
Syracuse University Main Campus ... NY ... 337
Elon University ... NC .. 344
#North Carolina Agricultural and Technical State University ... NC .. 356
University of North Carolina at Chapel Hill NC .. 357
#Bowling Green State University ... OH .. 364
Kent State University Main Campus ... OH .. 370
Ohio University Main Campus ... OH .. 375
Oklahoma State University ... OK .. 385
University of Oklahoma Norman Campus . OK .. 389
University of Oregon ... OR .. 395
Penn State University Park ... PA ... 412
Shippensburg University of Pennsylvania . PA ... 416
Temple University ... PA ... 420
University of Puerto Rico at Arecibo ... PR ... 537
University of Puerto Rico-Rio Piedras Campus ... PR ... 538
University of South Carolina Columbia ... SC ... 433
Winthrop University ... SC ... 435
South Dakota State University ... SD ... 437
#University of South Dakota, The ... SD ... 437
Middle Tennessee State University ... TN ... 444
University of Memphis, The ... TN ... 445
University of Tennessee at Chattanooga .. TN ... 443
University of Tennessee at Martin ... TN ... 443
University of Tennessee, Knoxville ... TN ... 443
Abilene Christian University ... TX ... 449
Baylor University ... TX ... 452
#Texas Christian University ... TX ... 469
Texas State University ... TX ... 471
University of North Texas ... TX ... 475
University of Texas at Austin ... TX ... 473
Brigham Young University ... UT ... 480
Hampton University ... VA ... 490
Norfolk State University ... VA ... 492
Virginia Commonwealth University ... VA ... 495
Washington and Lee University ... VA ... 500
University of Washington ... WA .. 508
Marshall University ... WV .. 513
West Virginia University ... WV .. 514
#University of Wisconsin-Eau Claire ... WI ... 520
University of Wisconsin-Oshkosh ... WI ... 520

KIN: Commission on Accreditation of Allied Health Education Programs: kinesiotherapy (B)

University of Southern Mississippi ... MS .. 261
Shaw University ... NC .. 355
Norfolk State University ... VA ... 492

LAW: American Bar Association: law (FP,D)

Faulkner University ... AL ... 3
Samford University ... AL ... 6
University of Alabama, The ... AL ... 8
Arizona State University ... AZ ... 11
Arizona Summit Law School ... AZ ... 11
University of Arizona ... AZ ... 17
University of Arkansas at Little Rock ... AR ... 23
University of Arkansas Main Campus ... AR ... 22
California Western School of Law ... CA ... 36
Chapman University ... CA ... 37
Golden Gate University ... CA ... 45
Loyola Marymount University ... CA ... 51
Pepperdine University ... CA ... 56
Santa Clara University ... CA ... 63
Southwestern Law School ... CA ... 66
Stanford University ... CA ... 66
Thomas Jefferson School of Law ... CA ... 68
University of California-Berkeley ... CA ... 68
University of California-Davis ... CA ... 69
University of California-Hastings College of the Law ... CA ... 69
University of California-Irvine ... CA ... 69
University of California-Los Angeles ... CA ... 69
University of La Verne ... CA ... 71
University of San Diego ... CA ... 72
University of San Francisco ... CA ... 72
University of Southern California ... CA ... 72
University of the Pacific ... CA ... 71
Whittier College ... CA ... 75
University of Colorado Boulder ... CO ... 83
University of Denver ... CO ... 84
Quinnipiac University ... CT ... 88
University of Connecticut ... CT ... 89
Yale University ... CT ... 90
American University ... DC ... 91
Catholic University of America, The ... DC ... 92
George Washington University ... DC ... 92
Georgetown University ... DC ... 92
Howard University ... DC ... 93
University of the District of Columbia ... DC ... 94
Ave Maria School of Law ... FL ... 95
Barry University ... FL ... 96
Florida Agricultural and Mechanical University ... FL ... 110
Florida Coastal School of Law ... FL ... 100
Florida International University ... FL ... 111
Florida State University ... FL ... 111
Nova Southeastern University ... FL ... 105
St. Thomas University ... FL ... 108
Stetson University ... FL ... 113
University of Florida ... FL ... 112
University of Miami ... FL ... 114
Atlanta's John Marshall Law School ... GA ... 117
Emory University ... GA .. 120
Georgia State University ... GA .. 122
Mercer University ... GA .. 124
University of Georgia ... GA .. 128
University of Hawaii at Manoa ... HI ... 131
University of Idaho ... ID ... 134
DePaul University ... IL ... 139
John Marshall Law School ... IL ... 143
Loyola University Chicago ... IL ... 146
Northern Illinois University ... IL ... 150
Northwestern University ... IL ... 150
Southern Illinois University Carbondale ... IL ... 154
University of Chicago ... IL ... 156
University of Illinois at Urbana-Champaign IL ... 157
#Indiana Tech ... IN ... 162
Indiana University Bloomington ... IN ... 162
Indiana University-Purdue University Indianapolis ... IN ... 163
University of Notre Dame ... IN ... 168
Valparaiso University ... IN ... 168
Drake University ... IA ... 171
University of Iowa ... IA ... 169
University of Kansas Main Campus ... KS ... 185
Washburn University ... KS ... 185
Northern Kentucky University ... KY ... 192
University of Kentucky ... KY ... 193
University of Louisville ... KY ... 194
Louisiana State University and Agricultural and Mechanical College ... LA ... 197
Loyola University New Orleans ... LA ... 198
Southern University Law Center ... LA ... 200
Tulane University ... LA ... 200
University of Southern Maine ... ME .. 205
University of Baltimore ... MD .. 213
University of Maryland Baltimore ... MD .. 211
Boston College ... MA .. 216
Boston University ... MA .. 216
Harvard University ... MA .. 219
New England Law | Boston ... MA .. 226
Northeastern University ... MA .. 227
Suffolk University ... MA .. 228
#University of Massachusetts Dartmouth ... MA .. 220
Western New England University ... MA .. 229
Michigan State University ... MI ... 237
University of Michigan-Ann Arbor ... MI ... 241
Wayne State University ... MI ... 243
Western Michigan University Cooley Law School ... MI ... 243
Mitchell Hamline School of Law ... MN .. 253
University of Minnesota-Twin Cities ... MN .. 255
University of Saint Thomas ... MN .. 256
Mississippi College ... MS .. 259
University of Mississippi ... MS .. 261
Saint Louis University ... MO .. 271
University of Missouri - Columbia ... MO .. 273
University of Missouri - Kansas City ... MO .. 273
Washington University in St. Louis ... MO .. 274
University of Montana - Missoula ... MT .. 276
Creighton University ... NE .. 279
University of Nebraska - Lincoln ... NE .. 282
University of Nevada, Las Vegas ... NV .. 284
University of New Hampshire ... NH .. 288
Rutgers the State University of New Jersey Camden Campus ... NJ ... 296
Rutgers the State University of New Jersey Newark Campus ... NJ ... 296
Seton Hall University ... NJ ... 297
University of New Mexico Main Campus .. NM .. 302
Albany Law School ... NY ... 303
Brooklyn Law School ... NY ... 305
City University of New York Queens College ... NY ... 309
Columbia University in the City of New York ... NY ... 311
Cornell University ... NY ... 312
Fordham University ... NY ... 314
Hofstra University ... NY ... 316
New York Law School ... NY ... 323
New York University ... NY ... 324
Pace University ... NY ... 325
St. John's University ... NY ... 328
Syracuse University Main Campus ... NY ... 337
Touro College ... NY ... 337
University at Buffalo-SUNY ... NY ... 331
Yeshiva University ... NY ... 341
Campbell University ... NC ... 342
Charlotte School of Law ... NC ... 343
Duke University ... NC ... 343
Elon University ... NC ... 344
North Carolina Central University ... NC .. 357
University of North Carolina at Chapel Hill NC .. 357
Wake Forest University ... NC .. 359
University of North Dakota ... ND .. 360
Capital University ... OH .. 364
Case Western Reserve University ... OH .. 365
Cleveland State University ... OH .. 366
Ohio Northern University ... OH .. 374
Ohio State University Main Campus, The . OH .. 375
University of Akron, Main Campus, The ... OH .. 378
University of Cincinnati Main Campus ... OH .. 379
University of Dayton ... OH .. 379
University of Toledo ... OH .. 380
Oklahoma City University ... OK .. 385
University of Oklahoma Norman Campus . OK .. 389
University of Tulsa ... OK .. 389
#Concordia University ... OR .. 391
Lewis and Clark College ... OR .. 392
University of Oregon ... OR .. 395
Willamette University ... OR .. 396
Drexel University ... PA .. 402
Duquesne University ... PA .. 403
Penn State University Park ... PA .. 412
Temple University ... PA .. 420
University of Pennsylvania ... PA .. 421
University of Pittsburgh ... PA .. 421
Villanova University ... PA .. 422
Widener University ... PA .. 423
Inter American University of Puerto Rico School of Law ... PR .. 534
Pontifical Catholic University of Puerto Rico, The ... PR .. 535
University of Puerto Rico-Rio Piedras Campus ... PR .. 538
Roger Williams University ... RI .. 426
Charleston School of Law ... SC .. 427
University of South Carolina Columbia ... SC .. 433
University of South Dakota, The ... SD .. 437
Belmont University ... TN .. 438
#Lincoln Memorial University ... TN .. 441
University of Memphis, The ... TN .. 445
University of Tennessee, Knoxville ... TN .. 448
Vanderbilt University ... TN .. 449
Baylor University ... TX .. 452
Houston College of Law ... TX .. 459
St. Mary's University ... TX .. 464
Southern Methodist University ... TX .. 465
Texas A & M University ... TX .. 468
Texas Southern University ... TX .. 470
Texas Tech University ... TX .. 472
University of Houston ... TX .. 473
University of Texas at Austin ... TX .. 476
Brigham Young University ... UT .. 480
University of Utah, The ... UT .. 481
Vermont Law School ... VT .. 485
Appalachian School of Law ... VA .. 486
College of William & Mary ... VA .. 488
George Mason University ... VA .. 490
Judge Advocate General's Legal Center & School, The ... VA .. 527
Liberty University ... VA .. 491
Regent University ... VA .. 493
University of Richmond ... VA .. 495
University of Virginia ... VA .. 495
Washington and Lee University ... VA .. 500
Gonzaga University ... WA .. 504
Seattle University ... WA .. 507
University of Washington ... WA .. 508
West Virginia University ... WV .. 514
Marquette University ... WI .. 517
University of Wisconsin-Madison ... WI .. 519
University of Wyoming ... WY .. 527

LIB: American Library Association: librarianship (M)

University of Alabama, The ... AL ... 8
University of Arizona ... AZ ... 17
San Jose State University ... CA ... 35
University of California-Los Angeles ... CA ... 69
University of Denver ... CO ... 84
Catholic University of America, The ... DC ... 92
Florida State University ... FL ... 111
University of South Florida ... FL ... 112
Valdosta State University ... GA .. 129
University of Hawaii at Manoa ... HI .. 131
Dominican University ... IL ... 139
University of Illinois at Urbana-Champaign IL ... 157
Indiana University Bloomington ... IN ... 162
University of Iowa ... IA ... 169
Emporia State University ... KS ... 180
University of Kentucky ... KY ... 193
Louisiana State University and Agricultural and Mechanical College ... LA ... 197
University of Maryland College Park ... MD .. 211
Simmons College ... MA .. 228
University of Michigan-Ann Arbor ... MI ... 241
Wayne State University ... MI ... 243
St. Catherine University ... MN .. 254
University of Southern Mississippi ... MS .. 261
University of Missouri - Columbia ... MO .. 273
Rutgers the State University of New Jersey New Brunswick Campus ... NJ ... 296
City University of New York Queens College ... NY ... 309
#Pratt Institute ... NY ... 326
St. John's University ... NY ... 328
Syracuse University Main Campus ... NY ... 337
University at Albany, SUNY ... NY ... 331
University at Buffalo-SUNY ... NY ... 331
East Carolina University ... NC .. 356
North Carolina Central University ... NC .. 357
University of North Carolina at Chapel Hill NC .. 357
University of North Carolina at Greensboro ... NC .. 358
Kent State University Main Campus ... OH ... 370
University of Oklahoma Norman Campus . OK .. 389
Clarion University of Pennsylvania ... PA ... 414
Drexel University ... PA ... 402
University of Pittsburgh ... PA ... 421
University of Puerto Rico-Rio Piedras Campus ... PR ... 538
University of Rhode Island ... RI ... 426
University of South Carolina Columbia ... SC ... 433
University of Tennessee, Knoxville ... TN ... 448
Texas Woman's University ... TX ... 472
University of North Texas ... TX ... 475
University of Texas at Austin ... TX ... 476
University of Washington ... WA .. 508
University of Wisconsin-Madison ... WI .. 519
University of Wisconsin-Milwaukee ... WI .. 520

LSAR: American Society of Landscape Architects: landscape architecture (B,M)

Auburn University ... AL ... 1
Arizona State University ... AZ ... 11
University of Arizona ... AZ ... 17
University of Arkansas Main Campus ... AR ... 22
California Polytechnic State University-San Luis Obispo ... CA ... 31
California State Polytechnic University-Pomona ... CA ... 31
University of California-Berkeley ... CA ... 68
University of California-Davis ... CA ... 69
University of Southern California ... CA ... 72
Colorado State University ... CO ... 78
University of Colorado Denver|Anschutz Medical Campus ... CO ... 84
University of Connecticut ... CT ... 89
Florida International University ... FL ... 111
University of Florida ... FL ... 112
University of Georgia ... GA .. 128
University of Idaho ... ID ... 134
Illinois Institute of Technology ... IL ... 142
University of Illinois at Urbana-Champaign IL ... 157
Ball State University ... IN ... 159
Purdue University Main Campus ... IN ... 166
Iowa State University ... IA ... 169
Kansas State University ... KS ... 182
University of Kentucky ... KY ... 193
Louisiana State University and Agricultural and Mechanical College ... LA ... 197
Morgan State University ... MD .. 209
University of Maryland College Park ... MD .. 211
Boston Architectural College ... MA .. 216
Harvard University ... MA .. 219
University of Massachusetts ... MA .. 220
Michigan State University ... MI ... 237
University of Michigan-Ann Arbor ... MI ... 241
University of Minnesota-Twin Cities ... MN .. 255
Mississippi State University ... MS .. 259
Washington University in St. Louis ... MO .. 274
University of Nebraska - Lincoln ... NE ... 282
University of Nevada, Las Vegas ... NV ... 284
Rutgers the State University of New Jersey New Brunswick Campus ... NJ ... 296
University of New Mexico Main Campus .. NM .. 302
City University of New York The City College ... NY ... 307
Cornell University ... NY ... 312
State University of New York College of Environmental Science and Forestry ... NY ... 334
North Carolina Agricultural and Technical State University ... NC ... 356
North Carolina State University ... NC ... 357
North Dakota State University Main Campus ... ND .. 361
Ohio State University Main Campus, The . OH ... 375
Oklahoma State University ... OK ... 385
University of Oklahoma Norman Campus . OK .. 389
University of Oregon ... OR ... 395
Chatham University ... PA ... 400
Penn State University Park ... PA ... 412
Philadelphia University ... PA ... 416
Temple University ... PA ... 420
University of Pennsylvania ... PA ... 421
Universidad Politecnica De Puerto Rico ... PR ... 537
Rhode Island School of Design ... RI ... 426
University of Rhode Island ... RI ... 426

M: Middle States Commission on Higher Education

MAAB: Accrediting Bureau of Health Education Schools: medical assisting (C,A)

MAC: Commission on Accreditation of Allied Health Education Programs: medical assisting (C,A)

MACTE: Montessori Accreditation Council for Teacher Education: Montessori teacher education (C)

MEAC: Midwifery Education Accreditation Council: midwifery education (C,A,B,M,D)

MED: Liaison Committee on Medical Education: medicine (FP,D)

MFCD: American Association for Marriage and Family Therapy: marriage and family therapy (M,D)

MIDWF: Accreditation Commission for Midwifery Education: nurse midwifery (C,M,D)

MIL: Commission on Accreditation of Allied Health Education Programs: medical illustrator (M)

MLTAB: Accrediting Bureau of Health Education Schools: medical laboratory technician (C,A)

MLTAD: National Accrediting Agency for Clinical Laboratory Sciences: medical laboratory technician (C,A)

Casper College ... WY .. 526

MT: National Accrediting Agency for Clinical Laboratory Sciences: medical technology/laboratory scientist (C,B)

Auburn University at Montgomery ... AL ... 2
Tuskegee University ... AL ... 8
University of Alabama at Birmingham ... AL ... 8
University of Alaska Anchorage ... AK ... 10
Arizona State University ... AZ ... 11
Arkansas State University-Jonesboro ... AR ... 18
University of Arkansas for Medical Sciences ... AR ... 23
California State University-Dominguez Hills ... CA ... 32
Loma Linda University ... CA ... 49
San Francisco State University ... CA ... 35
San Jose State University ... CA ... 35
University of California-Davis ... CA ... 69
University of California-Irvine ... CA ... 69
University of California-San Diego ... CA ... 70
Metropolitan State University of Denver ... CO ... 81
University of Bridgeport ... CT ... 89
University of Connecticut ... CT ... 89
University of Delaware ... DE ... 91
George Washington University ... DC ... 92
Howard University ... DC ... 93
Barry University ... FL ... 96
Florida Gulf Coast University ... FL ... 110
Santa Fe College ... FL ... 109
University of Central Florida ... FL ... 111
University of North Florida ... FL ... 112
University of West Florida ... FL ... 113
Armstrong State University ... GA .. 116
Augusta University ... GA .. 117
Thomas University ... GA .. 128
University of Hawaii at Manoa ... HI ... 131
Idaho State University ... ID ... 133
Illinois State University ... IL ... 143
Northern Illinois University ... IL ... 150
Rush University ... IL ... 153
University of Illinois at Springfield ... IL ... 156
Indiana University-Purdue University Indianapolis ... IN ... 163
Allen College ... IA ... 169
Mercy College of Health Sciences ... IA ... 175
St. Luke's College ... IA ... 176
Wichita State University ... KS ... 185
Bellarmine University ... KY ... 187
Eastern Kentucky University ... KY ... 188
University of Kentucky ... KY ... 193
Louisiana State University Health Sciences Center at Shreveport ... LA ... 198
Louisiana State University Health Sciences Center-New Orleans ... LA ... 198
McNeese State University ... LA ... 200
Our Lady of the Lake College ... LA ... 199
University of Louisiana at Monroe ... LA ... 201
Morgan State University ... MD .. 209
Salisbury University ... MD .. 213
Stevenson University ... MD .. 211
University of Maryland Baltimore ... MD .. 211
University of Massachusetts Dartmouth ... MA .. 220
University of Massachusetts Lowell ... MA .. 221
Andrews University ... MI ... 230
Eastern Michigan University ... MI ... 233
Ferris State University ... MI ... 233
Grand Valley State University ... MI ... 234
Michigan State University ... MI ... 237
Northern Michigan University ... MI ... 239
Saginaw Valley State University ... MI ... 240
Wayne State University ... MI ... 243
St. Cloud State University ... MN .. 252
University of Minnesota-Twin Cities ... MN .. 255
Winona State University ... MN .. 252
University of Mississippi Medical Center ... MS .. 261
University of Southern Mississippi ... MS .. 261
Saint Louis University ... MO .. 271
Southeast Missouri Hospital College of Nursing and Health Sciences ... MO .. 272
Montana State University ... MT .. 277
University of Nebraska Medical Center ... NE .. 283
University of New Hampshire ... NH .. 288
University of New Mexico Main Campus .. NM .. 302
Albany College of Pharmacy and Health Sciences ... NY ... 303
City University of New York York College ... NY ... 310
College of Staten Island CUNY ... NY ... 307
Farmingdale State College ... NY ... 335
Marist College ... NY ... 320
St. John's University ... NY ... 328
State University of New York Upstate Medical University ... NY ... 332
Stony Brook University ... NY ... 332
University at Buffalo-SUNY ... NY ... 331
Carolinas College of Health Sciences ... NC .. 343
East Carolina University ... NC ... 356
University of North Carolina at Chapel Hill ... NC .. 357
Winston-Salem State University ... NC .. 359
University of North Dakota ... ND .. 360
Bowling Green State University ... OH .. 364
Ohio Northern University ... OH .. 374
Ohio State University Main Campus, The ... OH .. 375
University of Cincinnati Main Campus ... OH .. 379
University of Toledo ... OH .. 380
Wright State University Main Campus ... OH .. 381
Northeastern State University ... OK .. 384
Oregon Health & Science University ... OR .. 393
Oregon Institute of Technology ... OR .. 393
Neumann University ... PA ... 411
Pennsylvania College of Health Sciences ... PA ... 413
Thomas Jefferson University ... PA ... 420
Inter American University of Puerto Rico / Metropolitan Campus ... PR ... 534
Inter American University of Puerto Rico San German Campus ... PR ... 534
Pontifical Catholic University of Puerto Rico, The ... PR ... 535
University of Puerto Rico-Medical Sciences Campus ... PR ... 538
South Dakota State University ... SD ... 437
Austin Peay State University ... TN ... 444
Baptist College of Health Sciences ... TN ... 438
Lincoln Memorial University ... TN ... 441
University of Tennessee Health Science Center ... TN ... 448
University of Tennessee, Knoxville ... TN ... 448
Vanderbilt University ... TN ... 449
Tarleton State University ... TX ... 467
Texas A & M University - Corpus Christi .. TX ... 468
Texas Southern University ... TX ... 470
Texas State University ... TX ... 471
Texas Tech University Health Sciences Center ... TX ... 472
University of Texas at El Paso ... TX ... 476
University of Texas Health Science Center at San Antonio ... TX ... 477
University of Texas MD Anderson Cancer Center, The ... TX ... 477
University of Texas Medical Branch, The . TX ... 478
University of Texas Rio Grande Valley, The ... TX ... 476
Brigham Young University ... UT ... 480
Dixie State University ... UT ... 482
University of Utah, The ... UT ... 481
Weber State University ... UT ... 482
University of Vermont ... VT ... 485
Jefferson College of Health Sciences ... VA ... 491
Norfolk State University ... VA ... 492
Old Dominion University ... VA ... 492
Virginia Commonwealth University ... VA ... 496
Heritage University ... WA ... 504
University of Washington ... WA ... 508
Marshall University ... WV .. 513
West Liberty University ... WV .. 513
West Virginia University ... WV .. 514
Marquette University ... WI ... 517
University of Wisconsin-Milwaukee ... WI ... 520
University of Wisconsin-Stevens Point ... WI ... 521

MUS: National Association of Schools of Music: music (C,A,B,M,D)

Alabama State University ... AL ... 1
Auburn University ... AL ... 1
Birmingham-Southern College ... AL ... 2
Huntingdon College ... AL ... 4
Jacksonville State University ... AL ... 4
Judson College ... AL ... 5
Samford University ... AL ... 6
Stillman College ... AL ... 7
Troy University ... AL ... 7
University of Alabama at Birmingham ... AL ... 8
University of Alabama in Huntsville ... AL ... 8
University of Alabama, The ... AL ... 8
University of Mobile ... AL ... 9
University of Montevallo ... AL ... 9
University of North Alabama ... AL ... 9
University of South Alabama ... AL ... 9
University of Alaska Anchorage ... AK ... 10
University of Alaska Fairbanks ... AK ... 10
Arizona State University ... AZ ... 11
Northern Arizona University ... AZ ... 15
University of Arizona ... AZ ... 17
Arkansas State University-Jonesboro ... AR ... 18
Arkansas Tech University ... AR ... 19
Harding University Main Campus ... AR ... 20
Henderson State University ... AR ... 20
Hendrix College ... AR ... 20
Ouachita Baptist University ... AR ... 21
Southern Arkansas University ... AR ... 22
University of Arkansas at Fort Smith ... AR ... 23
University of Arkansas at Little Rock ... AR ... 23
University of Arkansas at Monticello ... AR ... 23
University of Arkansas at Pine Bluff ... AR ... 23
University of Arkansas Main Campus ... AR ... 22
University of Central Arkansas ... AR ... 24
Azusa Pacific University ... CA ... 28
Biola University ... CA ... 28
California Baptist University ... CA ... 29
California Jazz Conservatory ... CA ... 31
California Polytechnic State University-San Luis Obispo ... CA ... 31
California State Polytechnic University-Pomona ... CA ... 31
California State University-Chico ... CA ... 32
California State University-Dominguez Hills ... CA ... 32
California State University-East Bay ... CA ... 32
California State University-Fresno ... CA ... 32
California State University-Fullerton ... CA ... 33
California State University-Long Beach ... CA ... 33
California State University-Los Angeles ... CA ... 33
California State University-Northridge ... CA ... 34
California State University-Sacramento ... CA ... 34
California State University-San Bernardino CA ... 34
California State University-Stanislaus ... CA ... 34
Chapman University ... CA ... 37
Colburn School, The ... CA ... 39
Humboldt State University ... CA ... 34
La Sierra University ... CA ... 48
LACM, Los Angeles College of Music ... CA ... 48
Loyola Marymount University ... CA ... 51
Master's College and Seminary, The ... CA ... 52
Musicians Institute ... CA ... 53
Pacific Union College ... CA ... 56
Pepperdine University ... CA ... 56
Point Loma Nazarene University ... CA ... 57
San Francisco State University ... CA ... 35
San Jose State University ... CA ... 35
Sonoma State University ... CA ... 35
University of Redlands ... CA ... 71
University of the Pacific ... CA ... 71
Vanguard University of Southern California ... CA ... 73
Westmont College ... CA ... 75
Adams State University ... CO ... 76
Colorado Christian University ... CO ... 77
Colorado Mesa University ... CO ... 77
Colorado State University ... CO ... 78
Colorado State University-Pueblo ... CO ... 79
Fort Lewis College ... CO ... 80
Metropolitan State University of Denver ... CO ... 81
University of Colorado Boulder ... CO ... 83
University of Colorado Denver|Anschutz Medical Campus ... CO ... 84
University of Denver ... CO ... 84
University of Northern Colorado ... CO ... 84
Western State Colorado University ... CO ... 84
Central Connecticut State University ... CT ... 85
University of Connecticut ... CT ... 89
University of Hartford ... CT ... 89
Western Connecticut State University ... CT ... 85
University of Delaware ... DE ... 91
American University ... DC ... 91
Catholic University of America, The ... DC ... 92
Howard University ... DC ... 93
Baptist College of Florida, The ... FL ... 96
Bethune Cookman University ... FL ... 96
Broward College ... FL ... 96
Florida Atlantic University ... FL ... 110
Florida College ... FL ... 100
Florida Gulf Coast University ... FL ... 110
Florida International University ... FL ... 111
Florida Memorial University ... FL ... 101
Florida Southern College ... FL ... 101
Florida State University ... FL ... 111
Hillsborough Community College ... FL ... 102
Jacksonville University ... FL ... 103
Lynn University ... FL ... 104
Miami Dade College ... FL ... 105
Palm Beach Atlantic University ... FL ... 106
Rollins College ... FL ... 107
Stetson University ... FL ... 113
University of Central Florida ... FL ... 111
University of Florida ... FL ... 112
University of Miami ... FL ... 114
University of North Florida ... FL ... 112
University of South Florida ... FL ... 112
University of Tampa ... FL ... 114
University of West Florida ... FL ... 113
Armstrong State University ... GA .. 116
Augusta University ... GA .. 117
Berry College ... GA .. 117
Clayton State University ... GA .. 119
Columbus State University ... GA .. 119
Georgia College & State University ... GA .. 121
Georgia Southern University ... GA .. 122
Georgia State University ... GA .. 122
Kennesaw State University ... GA .. 123
Mercer University ... GA .. 124
Morehouse College ... GA .. 124
Reinhardt University ... GA .. 126
Shorter University ... GA .. 127
Spelman College ... GA .. 128
Toccoa Falls College ... GA .. 128
Truett McConnell College ... GA .. 128
University of Georgia ... GA .. 128
University of West Georgia ... GA .. 129
Valdosta State University ... GA .. 129
Wesleyan College ... GA .. 129
Young Harris College ... GA .. 130
University of Hawaii at Manoa ... HI ... 131
Boise State University ... ID ... 132
Brigham Young University-Idaho ... ID ... 132
Idaho State University ... ID ... 133
Northwest Nazarene University ... ID ... 134
University of Idaho ... ID ... 134
Augustana College ... IL ... 135
Bradley University ... IL ... 136
Chicago State University ... IL ... 136
Concordia University Chicago ... IL ... 138
DePaul University ... IL ... 139
Eastern Illinois University ... IL ... 139
Harper College ... IL ... 141
Illinois Central College ... IL ... 141
Illinois State University ... IL ... 143
Illinois Wesleyan University ... IL ... 143
Joliet Junior College ... IL ... 144
Millikin University ... IL ... 148
Moody Bible Institute ... IL ... 148
North Park University ... IL ... 149
Northeastern Illinois University ... IL ... 149
Northern Illinois University ... IL ... 150
Northwestern University ... IL ... 150
Olivet Nazarene University ... IL ... 150
Roosevelt University ... IL ... 152
Saint Xavier University ... IL ... 153
Southern Illinois University Carbondale ... IL ... 154
Southern Illinois University Edwardsville ... IL ... 155
University of Illinois at Urbana-Champaign IL ... 157
VanderCook College of Music ... IL ... 157
Western Illinois University ... IL ... 158
Wheaton College ... IL ... 158
Anderson University ... IN ... 158
Ball State University ... IN ... 159
Bethel College ... IN ... 159
Butler University ... IN ... 159
DePauw University ... IN ... 160
Indiana State University ... IN ... 162
Indiana University Bloomington ... IN ... 162
Indiana University-Purdue University Fort Wayne ... IN ... 163
Indiana University-Purdue University Indianapolis ... IN ... 163
Indiana University South Bend ... IN ... 163
Indiana Wesleyan University ... IN ... 164
Saint Mary-of-the-Woods College ... IN ... 166
Saint Mary's College ... IN ... 167
Taylor University ... IN ... 167
University of Evansville ... IN ... 167
University of Indianapolis ... IN ... 168
Valparaiso University ... IN ... 168
Central College ... IA ... 170
Clarke University ... IA ... 170
Coe College ... IA ... 170
Drake University ... IA ... 171
Iowa State University ... IA ... 169
Luther College ... IA ... 174
Morningside College ... IA ... 175
Simpson College ... IA ... 176
University of Iowa ... IA ... 169
University of Northern Iowa ... IA ... 170
Wartburg College ... IA ... 177
Baker University ... KS ... 178
Benedictine College ... KS ... 178
Bethany College ... KS ... 178
Emporia State University ... KS ... 180
Fort Hays State University ... KS ... 180
Friends University ... KS ... 181
Kansas State University ... KS ... 182
MidAmerica Nazarene University ... KS ... 183
Pittsburg State University ... KS ... 184
Southwestern College ... KS ... 184
Tabor College ... KS ... 185
University of Kansas Main Campus ... KS ... 185
Washburn University ... KS ... 185
Wichita State University ... KS ... 185
Asbury University ... KY ... 186
Campbellsville University ... KY ... 187
Eastern Kentucky University ... KY ... 188
Kentucky State University ... KY ... 191
Morehead State University ... KY ... 191
Murray State University ... KY ... 192
Northern Kentucky University ... KY ... 192
Southern Baptist Theological Seminary, The ... KY ... 192
University of Kentucky ... KY ... 193
University of Louisville ... KY ... 194
Western Kentucky University ... KY ... 194
Centenary College of Louisiana ... LA ... 194
Grambling State University ... LA ... 200
Louisiana College ... LA ... 195
Louisiana State University and Agricultural and Mechanical College ... LA ... 197

Eastern Washington University .... WA .. 503
Gonzaga University .... WA .. 504
Pacific Lutheran University .... WA .. 505
Seattle Pacific University .... WA .. 507
University of Puget Sound .... WA .. 508
Walla Walla University .... WA .. 508
Washington State University .... WA .. 508
Western Washington University .... WA .. 509
Whitworth University .... WA .. 509
Marshall University .... WV .. 513
Shepherd University .... WV .. 513
West Liberty University .... WV .. 513
West Virginia University .... WV .. 514
West Virginia Wesleyan College .... WV .. 515
Alverno College .... WI ... 515
Carthage College .... WI ... 516
Lawrence University .... WI ... 517
Silver Lake College of the Holy Family .... WI ... 519
University of Wisconsin-Eau Claire .... WI ... 520
University of Wisconsin-Green Bay .... WI ... 520
University of Wisconsin-La Crosse .... WI ... 520
University of Wisconsin-Madison .... WI ... 519
University of Wisconsin-Milwaukee .... WI ... 520
University of Wisconsin-Oshkosh .... WI ... 520
University of Wisconsin-Platteville .... WI ... 521
University of Wisconsin-River Falls .... WI ... 521
University of Wisconsin-Stevens Point .... WI ... 521
University of Wisconsin-Superior .... WI ... 521
University of Wisconsin-Whitewater .... WI ... 521
Viterbo University .... WI ... 522
Casper College .... WY .. 526
Northwest College .... WY .. 526
University of Wyoming .... WY .. 527

NAIT: The Association of Technology, Management, and Applied Engineering: technology, applied technology, engineering technology and technology-related programs (A,B,M)

Jacksonville State University .... AL 4
Arkansas State University-Beebe .... AR 18
University of Arkansas at Fort Smith .... AR 23
University of Arkansas at Pine Bluff .... AR 23
California Polytechnic State University-San Luis Obispo .... CA 31
California State University-Chico .... CA 32
California State University-Los Angeles .... CA 33
College of the Redwoods Community College District .... CA 40
San Jose State University .... CA 35
Central Connecticut State University .... CT 85
Idaho State University .... ID 133
University of Idaho .... ID 134
Eastern Illinois University .... IL 139
Illinois State University .... IL 143
Northern Illinois University .... IL 150
Southern Illinois University Carbondale .... IL 154
Western Illinois University .... IL 158
Indiana State University .... IN 162
Ivy Tech Community College of Indiana-Central Indiana .... IN 164
Purdue University Main Campus .... IN 166
Purdue University Northwest .... IN 166
Iowa State University .... IA 169
University of Northern Iowa .... IA 170
Eastern Kentucky University .... KY ... 188
Morehead State University .... KY ... 191
Western Kentucky University .... KY ... 194
Baton Rouge Community College .... LA ... 195
Bossier Parish Community College .... LA ... 195
Delgado Community College .... LA ... 196
L.E. Fletcher Technical Community College .... LA ... 196
Louisiana Delta Community College .... LA ... 196
Nicholls State University .... LA ... 201
Nunez Community College .... LA ... 196
River Parishes Community College .... LA ... 196
South Louisiana Community College .... LA ... 197
Southeastern Louisiana University .... LA ... 201
Sowela Technical Community College .... LA ... 197
University of Louisiana at Lafayette .... LA ... 201
University of Southern Maine .... ME ... 205
Central Michigan University .... MI ... 232
Bemidji State University .... MN ... 248
Minnesota State University Moorhead .... MN .. 250
St. Cloud State University .... MN .. 252
Alcorn State University .... MS .. 256
Jackson State University .... MS .. 258
East Central College .... MO .. 264
Southeast Missouri State University .... MO .. 272
State Technical College of Missouri .... MO .. 272
University of Central Missouri .... MO .. 273
University of Nebraska at Kearney .... NE ... 282
Farmingdale State College .... NY ... 335
State University of New York College at Buffalo .... NY ... 332
East Carolina University .... NC .. 356
North Carolina Agricultural and Technical State University .... NC .. 356
University of North Dakota .... ND .. 360
Bowling Green State University .... OH .. 364
Kent State University Main Campus .... OH .. 370
Ohio Northern University .... OH .. 374
Ohio University Main Campus .... OH .. 375
Owens Community College .... OH .. 376
Southwestern Oklahoma State University .... OK .. 388
California University of Pennsylvania .... PA ... 414
Millersville University of Pennsylvania .... PA ... 415
Pennsylvania College of Technology .... PA ... 413
Cleveland State Community College .... TN ... 445
Columbia State Community College .... TN ... 446
Jackson State Community College .... TN ... 446
Middle Tennessee State University .... TN ... 444
Motlow State Community College .... TN ... 446
Nashville State Community College .... TN ... 446
Northeast State Community College .... TN ... 446
Pellissippi State Community College .... TN ... 446
Tennessee State University .... TN ... 445
Tennessee Technological University .... TN ... 445
Walters State Community College .... TN ... 447
Texas A & M University - Kingsville .... TX ... 469
Texas Southern University .... TX ... 470
University of Houston .... TX ... 473
University of Texas at Tyler .... TX ... 477
Mountain Empire Community College .... VA ... 497
Norfolk State University .... VA ... 492
Virginia State University .... VA ... 499
Pierpont Community & Technical College .... WV .. 512
University of Wisconsin-Platteville .... WI ... 521

NATUR: Council on Naturopathic Medical Education: naturopathic medical education (FP,D)

Southwest College of Naturopathic Medicine & Health Sciences .... AZ 17
University of Bridgeport .... CT 89
National University of Health Sciences .... IL 149
National University of Natural Medicine .... OR .. 392
@Universidad Del Turabo .... PR ... 536
Bastyr University .... WA .. 501

NDT: Commission on Accreditation of Allied Health Education Programs: neurodiagnostic technology (C,A)

Gateway Community College .... AZ 14
Concorde Career College .... CA 41
Orange Coast College .... CA 39
Lincoln Land Community College .... IL 146
Kirkwood Community College .... IA 174
Scott Community College .... IA 172
Laboure College .... MA .. 219
Minneapolis Community and Technical College .... MN .. 250
Catawba Valley Community College .... NC .. 348
Pamlico Community College .... NC .. 351
Cuyahoga Community College .... OH .. 367
Southeast Technical Institute .... SD ... 437
Vanderbilt University .... TN ... 449
Alvin Community College .... TX ... 450
Concorde Career Institute .... TX ... 455
Bellevue College .... WA .. 501

NH: Higher Learning Commission, North Central Association

Arizona Christian University .... AZ 11
Arizona State University .... AZ 11
Arizona Western College .... AZ 11
Central Arizona College .... AZ 12
Chandler-Gilbert Community College .... AZ 13
Cochise College .... AZ 12
Coconino Community College .... AZ 12
Diné College .... AZ 12
Eastern Arizona College .... AZ 13
Estrella Mountain Community College .... AZ 14
Frank Lloyd Wright School of Architecture .... AZ 13
Gateway Community College .... AZ 14
Glendale Community College .... AZ 14
Grand Canyon University .... AZ 13
Mesa Community College .... AZ 14
Mohave Community College .... AZ 15
Northcentral University .... AZ 15
Northern Arizona University .... AZ 15
Northland Pioneer College .... AZ 15
Paradise Valley Community College .... AZ 14
Phoenix College .... AZ 14
Phoenix Seminary .... AZ 16
Pima Community College .... AZ 16
Prescott College .... AZ 16
Rio Salado College .... AZ 14
Scottsdale Community College .... AZ 14
South Mountain Community College .... AZ 14
Southwest College of Naturopathic Medicine & Health Sciences .... AZ 17
Southwest University of Visual Arts .... AZ 17
Tohono O'odham Community College .... AZ 17
University of Advancing Technology .... AZ 17
University of Arizona .... AZ 17
University of Phoenix .... AZ 17
Western International University .... AZ 18
Yavapai College .... AZ 18
Arkansas Baptist College .... AR 18
Arkansas Northeastern College .... AR 18
Arkansas State University-Beebe .... AR 18
Arkansas State University-Jonesboro .... AR 18
Arkansas State University-Mid-South .... AR 19
Arkansas State University-Mountain Home .... AR 19
Arkansas State University-Newport .... AR 19
Arkansas Tech University .... AR 19
Black River Technical College .... AR 19
Central Baptist College .... AR 19
College of the Ouachitas .... AR 19
Cossatot Community College of the University of Arkansas .... AR 23
Crowley's Ridge College .... AR 20
East Arkansas Community College .... AR 20
Harding University Main Campus .... AR 20
Henderson State University .... AR 20
Hendrix College .... AR 20
John Brown University .... AR 20
Lyon College .... AR 21
National Park College .... AR 21
North Arkansas College .... AR 21
NorthWest Arkansas Community College .... AR 21
Ouachita Baptist University .... AR 21
Ozarka College .... AR 21
Philander Smith College .... AR 21
Phillips Community College of the University of Arkansas .... AR 23
Pulaski Technical College .... AR 21
Rich Mountain Community College .... AR 22
South Arkansas Community College .... AR 22
Southeast Arkansas College .... AR 22
Southern Arkansas University .... AR 22
Southern Arkansas University Tech .... AR 22
University of Arkansas at Fort Smith .... AR 23
University of Arkansas at Hope-Texarkana .... AR 24
University of Arkansas at Little Rock .... AR 23
University of Arkansas at Monticello .... AR 23
University of Arkansas at Pine Bluff .... AR 23
University of Arkansas Community College at Batesville .... AR 23
University of Arkansas Community College at Morrilton .... AR 24
University of Arkansas for Medical Sciences .... AR 23
University of Arkansas Main Campus .... AR 22
University of Central Arkansas .... AR 24
University of the Ozarks .... AR 24
Williams Baptist College .... AR 24
#Adams State University .... CO 76
Aims Community College .... CO 76
@American Sentinel University .... CO 76
Arapahoe Community College .... CO 76
Art Institute of Colorado, The .... CO 76
College for Financial Planning .... CO 77
Colorado Christian University .... CO 77
Colorado College .... CO 77
Colorado Mesa University .... CO 77
Colorado Mountain College .... CO 78
Colorado Northwestern Community College .... CO 78
Colorado School of Mines .... CO 78
Colorado State University .... CO 78
Colorado State University-Global Campus .... CO 79
Colorado State University-Pueblo .... CO 79
Colorado Technical University .... CO 79
Community College of Aurora .... CO 79
Community College of Denver .... CO 79
Denver School of Nursing .... CO 79
Denver Seminary .... CO 79
Fort Lewis College .... CO 80
Front Range Community College .... CO 80
Iliff School of Theology .... CO 80
Lamar Community College .... CO 81
Metropolitan State University of Denver .... CO 81
Morgan Community College .... CO 81
Naropa University .... CO 81
Nazarene Bible College .... CO 81
Northeastern Junior College .... CO 81
Otero Junior College .... CO 82
Pikes Peak Community College .... CO 82
Pueblo Community College .... CO 82
Red Rocks Community College .... CO 82
Regis University .... CO 82
Rocky Mountain College of Art & Design .... CO 83
Rocky Vista University .... CO 83
Trinidad State Junior College .... CO 83
United States Air Force Academy .... CO .. 528
University of Colorado Boulder .... CO 83
University of Colorado Colorado Springs .... CO 83
University of Colorado Denver|Anschutz Medical Campus .... CO 84
University of Denver .... CO 84
University of Northern Colorado .... CO 84
University of the Rockies .... CO 84
Western State Colorado University .... CO 84
Adler University .... IL 134
American Academy of Art .... IL 134
American InterContinental University .... IL 135
Augustana College .... IL 135
Aurora University .... IL 135
Benedictine University .... IL 135
Black Hawk College .... IL 135
Blackburn College .... IL 135
Blessing-Rieman College of Nursing .... IL 136
Bradley University .... IL 136
Carl Sandburg College .... IL 136
Chamberlain College of Nursing-Addison .... IL 136
Chicago State University .... IL 136
Chicago Theological Seminary .... IL 137
City Colleges of Chicago Harold Washington College .... IL 137
City Colleges of Chicago Harry S Truman College .... IL 137
City Colleges of Chicago Kennedy-King College .... IL 137
City Colleges of Chicago Olive-Harvey College .... IL 137
City Colleges of Chicago Richard J. Daley College .... IL 137
City Colleges of Chicago Wilbur Wright College .... IL 137
#College of DuPage .... IL 138
College of Lake County .... IL 138
Columbia College Chicago .... IL 138
Concordia University Chicago .... IL 138
Danville Area Community College .... IL 139
DePaul University .... IL 139
DeVry University - Chicago Campus .... IL 139
Dominican University .... IL 139
#East-West University .... IL 139
Eastern Illinois University .... IL 139
Elgin Community College .... IL 140
Elmhurst College .... IL 140
Erikson Institute .... IL 140
Eureka College .... IL 140
Fox College .... IL 140
Garrett-Evangelical Theological Seminary .... IL 140
Governors State University .... IL 140
Greenville College .... IL 140
Harper College .... IL 141
Harrington College of Design .... IL 141
Heartland Community College .... IL 141
Hebrew Theological College .... IL 141
Highland Community College .... IL 141
Illinois Central College .... IL 141
Illinois College .... IL 141
Illinois College of Optometry .... IL 142
&Illinois Eastern Community Colleges Frontier Community College .... IL 142
&Illinois Eastern Community Colleges Lincoln Trail College .... IL 142
&Illinois Eastern Community Colleges Olney Central College .... IL 142
&Illinois Eastern Community Colleges Wabash Valley College .... IL 142
Illinois Institute of Art, The .... IL 142
Illinois Institute of Technology .... IL 142
Illinois State University .... IL 143
Illinois Valley Community College .... IL 143
Illinois Wesleyan University .... IL 143
Institute for Clinical Social Work .... IL 143
John A. Logan College .... IL 143
John Marshall Law School .... IL 143
John Wood Community College .... IL 143
Joliet Junior College .... IL 144
Judson University .... IL 144
Kankakee Community College .... IL 144
Kaskaskia College .... IL 144
Kendall College .... IL 144
Kishwaukee College .... IL 144
Knowledge Systems Institute .... IL 144
Knox College .... IL 145
Lake Forest College .... IL 145
Lake Forest Graduate School of Management .... IL 145
Lake Land College .... IL 145
Lakeview College of Nursing .... IL 145
Le Cordon Bleu College of Culinary Arts in Chicago .... IL 145
Lewis and Clark Community College .... IL 145
Lewis University .... IL 145
Lincoln Christian University .... IL 146
Lincoln College .... IL 146
Lincoln Land Community College .... IL 146
Loyola University Chicago .... IL 146
Lutheran School of Theology at Chicago .... IL 147
MacCormac College .... IL 147
#MacMurray College .... IL 147
Malcolm X College, One of the City Colleges of Chicago .... IL 138
McCormick Theological Seminary .... IL 147
McHenry County College .... IL 147

NMT: Joint Review Committee on Education Programs in Nuclear Medicine Technology: nuclear medicine technology (C,A,B)

NRPA: National Recreation and Park Association: recreation, park resources, and leisure studies (B)

NUR: Accreditation Commission for Education in Nursing: nursing (B, M,D)

NURSE: Commission on Collegiate Nursing Education: nursing (B,M,D)

Lynchburg College ... VA ... 491
Marymount University ... VA ... 492
Old Dominion University ... VA ... 492
Radford University ... VA ... 493
Sentara College of Health Sciences ... VA ... 494
Shenandoah University ... VA ... 494
Stratford University ... VA ... 494
University of Virginia ... VA ... 495
University of Virginia's College at Wise, The ... VA ... 495
Bellevue College ... WA .. 501
Gonzaga University ... WA .. 504
Northwest University ... WA .. 505
Olympic College ... WA .. 505
Pacific Lutheran University ... WA .. 505
Saint Martin's University ... WA .. 506
Seattle Pacific University ... WA .. 507
Seattle University ... WA .. 507
University of Washington ... WA .. 508
Walla Walla University ... WA .. 508
Washington State University ... WA .. 508
Western Washington University ... WA .. 509
Whitworth University ... WA .. 509
American Public University System ... WV .. 510
Bluefield State College ... WV .. 512
Fairmont State University ... WV .. 513
Shepherd University ... WV .. 513
West Liberty University ... WV .. 513
West Virginia University ... WV .. 514
Wheeling Jesuit University ... WV .. 515
Alverno College ... WI ... 515
Bellin College, Inc. ... WI ... 515
Cardinal Stritch University ... WI ... 515
Carroll University ... WI ... 515
Columbia College of Nursing ... WI ... 516
Concordia University Wisconsin ... WI ... 516
Edgewood College ... WI ... 516
Herzing University ... WI ... 516
Maranatha Baptist University ... WI ... 517
Marian University ... WI ... 517
Marquette University ... WI ... 517
Milwaukee School of Engineering ... WI ... 518
Silver Lake College of the Holy Family ... WI ... 519
University of Wisconsin-Eau Claire ... WI ... 520
University of Wisconsin-Green Bay ... WI ... 520
University of Wisconsin-Madison ... WI ... 519
University of Wisconsin-Milwaukee ... WI ... 520
University of Wisconsin-Oshkosh ... WI ... 520
University of Wisconsin-Stevens Point ... WI ... 521
Viterbo University ... WI ... 522
Wisconsin Lutheran College ... WI ... 522
University of Wyoming ... WY .. 527

NW: Northwest Commission on Colleges and Universities

Alaska Pacific University ... AK ... 10
Ilisagvik College ... AK ... 10
Prince William Sound Community College. AK ... 11
University of Alaska Anchorage ... AK ... 10
University of Alaska Fairbanks ... AK ... 10
University of Alaska Southeast ... AK ... 10
Boise State University ... ID ... 132
Brigham Young University-Idaho ... ID ... 132
College of Idaho, The ... ID ... 133
College of Southern Idaho ... ID ... 133
@College of Western Idaho ... ID ... 133
Eastern Idaho Technical College ... ID ... 133
Idaho State University ... ID ... 133
Lewis-Clark State College ... ID ... 134
North Idaho College ... ID ... 134
Northwest Nazarene University ... ID ... 134
University of Idaho ... ID ... 134
Aaniiih Nakoda College ... MT .. 275
Blackfeet Community College ... MT .. 276
Carroll College ... MT .. 276
Chief Dull Knife College ... MT .. 276
Dawson Community College ... MT .. 276
Flathead Valley Community College ... MT .. 276
Fort Peck Community College ... MT .. 276
Great Falls College Montana State University ... MT .. 277
Helena College University of Montana ... MT .. 277
Little Big Horn College ... MT .. 276
Miles Community College ... MT .. 276
Montana State University ... MT .. 277
Montana State University - Billings ... MT .. 277
Montana State University - Northern ... MT .. 277
Montana Tech of The University of Montana ... MT .. 277
Rocky Mountain College ... MT .. 278
Salish Kootenai College ... MT .. 278
Stone Child College ... MT .. 278
University of Great Falls ... MT .. 278
University of Montana - Missoula ... MT .. 276
University of Montana Western, The ... MT .. 277
College of Southern Nevada ... NV ... 284
Great Basin College ... NV ... 284
Nevada State College ... NV ... 284
Roseman University of Health Sciences ... NV ... 285
Sierra Nevada College ... NV ... 285
Truckee Meadows Community College ... NV ... 284
University of Nevada, Las Vegas ... NV ... 284
University of Nevada, Reno ... NV ... 285
Western Nevada College ... NV ... 285
Art Institute of Portland, The ... OR .. 390
Blue Mountain Community College ... OR .. 390
Central Oregon Community College ... OR .. 390
Chemeketa Community College ... OR .. 390
Clackamas Community College ... OR .. 390
Clatsop Community College ... OR .. 390
Columbia Gorge Community College ... OR .. 390
Concordia University ... OR .. 391
Corban University ... OR .. 391
Eastern Oregon University ... OR .. 391
George Fox University ... OR .. 391
Klamath Community College ... OR .. 391
Lane Community College ... OR .. 391
Lewis and Clark College ... OR .. 392
Linfield College ... OR .. 392
Linn-Benton Community College ... OR .. 392
Marylhurst University ... OR .. 392
Mount Angel Seminary ... OR .. 392
Mt. Hood Community College ... OR .. 392
Multnomah University ... OR .. 392
National University of Natural Medicine ... OR .. 392
Northwest Christian University ... OR .. 393
Oregon College of Art and Craft ... OR .. 393
Oregon Health & Science University ... OR .. 393
Oregon Institute of Technology ... OR .. 393
Oregon State University ... OR .. 393
Pacific Northwest College of Art ... OR .. 394
Pacific University ... OR .. 394
Portland Community College ... OR .. 394
Portland State University ... OR .. 394
Reed College ... OR .. 394
Rogue Community College ... OR .. 394
Southern Oregon University ... OR .. 395
Southwestern Oregon Community College OR .. 395
Tillamook Bay Community College ... OR .. 395
Treasure Valley Community College ... OR .. 395
Umpqua Community College ... OR .. 395
University of Oregon ... OR .. 395
University of Portland ... OR .. 396
University of Western States ... OR .. 396
Warner Pacific College ... OR .. 396
Western Oregon University ... OR .. 396
Western Seminary ... OR .. 396
Willamette University ... OR .. 396
Brigham Young University ... UT ... 480
Dixie State University ... UT ... 482
LDS Business College ... UT ... 480
Rocky Mountain University of Health Professions ... UT ... 481
Salt Lake Community College ... UT ... 483
Snow College ... UT ... 482
Southern Utah University ... UT ... 481
University of Utah, The ... UT ... 481
Utah State University ... UT ... 482
Utah Valley University ... UT ... 482
Weber State University ... UT ... 482
Western Governors University ... UT ... 483
Westminster College ... UT ... 483
Art Institute of Seattle, The ... WA .. 501
Bastyr University ... WA .. 501
Bates Technical College ... WA .. 501
Bellevue College ... WA .. 501
Bellingham Technical College ... WA .. 501
Big Bend Community College ... WA .. 501
Cascadia College ... WA .. 501
Central Washington University ... WA .. 501
Centralia College ... WA .. 502
City University of Seattle ... WA .. 502
Clark College ... WA .. 502
Clover Park Technical College ... WA .. 502
Columbia Basin College ... WA .. 502
Cornish College of the Arts ... WA .. 503
Eastern Washington University ... WA .. 503
Edmonds Community College ... WA .. 503
Everett Community College ... WA .. 503
Evergreen State College, The ... WA .. 503
Gonzaga University ... WA .. 504
#Grays Harbor College ... WA .. 504
Green River College ... WA .. 504
Heritage University ... WA .. 504
Highline College ... WA .. 504
Lake Washington Institute of Technology . WA .. 504
Lower Columbia College ... WA .. 504
North Seattle College ... WA .. 506
Northwest Indian College ... WA .. 505
Northwest University ... WA .. 505
Olympic College ... WA .. 505
Pacific Lutheran University ... WA .. 505
@Pacific Northwest University of Health Sciences ... WA .. 505
Peninsula College ... WA .. 505
Pierce College District ... WA .. 506
Renton Technical College ... WA .. 506
Saint Martin's University ... WA .. 506
Seattle Central College ... WA .. 506
Seattle Pacific University ... WA .. 507
Seattle University ... WA .. 507
Shoreline Community College ... WA .. 507
Skagit Valley College ... WA .. 507
South Puget Sound Community College .. WA .. 508
South Seattle Community College ... WA .. 507
Spokane Community College ... WA .. 502
Spokane Falls Community College ... WA .. 503
Tacoma Community College ... WA .. 508
University of Puget Sound ... WA .. 508
University of Washington ... WA .. 508
Walla Walla Community College ... WA .. 508
Walla Walla University ... WA .. 508
Washington State University ... WA .. 508
Wenatchee Valley College ... WA .. 509
Western Washington University ... WA .. 509
Whatcom Community College ... WA .. 509
Whitman College ... WA .. 509
Whitworth University ... WA .. 509
Yakima Valley College ... WA .. 510

NY: New York State Board of Regents

Bramson ORT College ... NY ... 305
Christie's Education, New York ... NY ... 306
City University of New York Stella and Charles Guttman Community College ... NY ... 309
Cold Spring Harbor Laboratory/Watson School of Biological Sciences ... NY ... 310
Elmezzi Graduate School of Molecular Medicine, The ... NY ... 313
Fei Tian College ... NY ... 314
Holy Trinity Orthodox Seminary ... NY ... 316
Louis V. Gerstner Jr. Graduate School of Biomedical Sciences, Memorial Sloa n Kettering Cancer Center ... NY ... 319
Memorial School of Nursing ... NY ... 320
New York Academy of Art ... NY ... 322
New York Career Institute ... NY ... 322
New York College of Health Professions .. NY ... 323
Phillips Beth Israel School of Nursing ... NY ... 326
Richard Gilder Graduate School at the American Museum of Natural History ... NY ... 327
Rockefeller University ... NY ... 327
Salvation Army College for Officer Training ... NY ... 329
Samaritan Hospital School of Nursing ... NY ... 329
Technical Career Institutes ... NY ... 337
USC The Business College ... NY ... 338
Wood Tobé-Coburn School ... NY ... 340

OPD: Commission on Opticianry Accreditation: opticianry (A)

Middlesex Community College ... CT ... 86
Broward College ... FL ... 96
Hillsborough Community College ... FL ... 102
Miami Dade College ... FL ... 105
Ogeechee Technical College ... GA .. 125
Benjamin Franklin Institute of Technology MA .. 215
College of Southern Nevada ... NV .. 284
Camden County College ... NJ .. 290
Essex County College ... NJ .. 291
Raritan Valley Community College ... NJ .. 295
Southwestern Indian Polytechnic Institute NM .. 302
Erie Community College ... NY ... 313
New York City College of Technology/City University of New York ... NY ... 309
Technical Career Institutes ... NY ... 337
Durham Technical Community College ... NC .. 349
Roane State Community College ... TN ... 447
J. Sargeant Reynolds Community College VA ... 497
Seattle Central College ... WA .. 506

OPE: Commission on Accreditation of Allied Health Education Programs: orthotics and prosthetics (C,B,M)

Alabama State University ... AL ... 1
California State University-Dominguez Hills ... CA ... 32
Loma Linda University ... CA ... 49
University of Hartford ... CT ... 89
St. Petersburg College ... FL ... 108
Georgia Institute of Technology ... GA ... 121
Northwestern University ... IL ... 150
Eastern Michigan University ... MI ... 233
Concordia University, St. Paul ... MN .. 246
University of Pittsburgh ... PA ... 421
Baylor College of Medicine ... TX ... 452
University of Texas Southwestern Medical Center ... TX ... 478
University of Washington ... WA .. 508

OPLT: Commission on Opticianry Accreditation: opthalmic laboratory technician (C)

Southwestern Indian Polytechnic Institute NM .. 302

OPT: American Optometric Association: optometry (FP,D)

University of Alabama at Birmingham ... AL ... 8
Marshall B. Ketchum University ... CA ... 51
University of California-Berkeley ... CA ... 68
Western University of Health Sciences ... CA ... 74
Nova Southeastern University ... FL ... 105
Illinois College of Optometry ... IL ... 142
@Midwestern University ... IL ... 148
Indiana University Bloomington ... IN ... 162
@University of Pikeville ... KY ... 194
MCPHS University ... MA .. 225
New England College of Optometry ... MA .. 226
Ferris State University ... MI ... 233
University of Missouri - Saint Louis ... MO .. 274
State University of New York College of Optometry ... NY ... 334
Ohio State University Main Campus, The . OH .. 375
Northeastern State University ... OK .. 384
Pacific University ... OR .. 394
Salus University ... PA ... 419
Inter American University of Puerto Rico School of Optometry ... PR ... 534
Southern College of Optometry ... TN ... 444
University of Houston ... TX ... 473
University of the Incarnate Word ... TX ... 474

OPTR: American Optometric Association: optometric residency programs

University of Alabama at Birmingham ... AL ... 8
Marshall B. Ketchum University ... CA ... 51
University of California-Berkeley ... CA ... 68
Nova Southeastern University ... FL ... 105
Illinois College of Optometry ... IL ... 142
Indiana University Bloomington ... IN ... 162
New England College of Optometry ... MA .. 226
Ferris State University ... MI ... 233
University of Missouri - Saint Louis ... MO .. 274
State University of New York College of Optometry ... NY ... 334
Ohio State University Main Campus, The . OH ... 375
Northeastern State University ... OK .. 384
Pacific University ... OR .. 394
Salus University ... PA ... 419
Inter American University of Puerto Rico Bayamon Campus ... PR ... 533
Southern College of Optometry ... TN ... 444
University of Houston ... TX ... 473
University of the Incarnate Word ... TX ... 474

OPTT: American Optometric Association: optometric technician (C,A)

Indiana University Bloomington ... IN ... 162
Madison Area Technical College ... WI ... 523

OSTEO: American Osteopathic Association, Office of Osteopathic Education: osteopathic medicine (FP,D)

@Alabama College of Osteopathic Medicine AL ... 1
Touro University California ... CA ... 68
Western University of Health Sciences ... CA ... 74
Rocky Vista University ... CO ... 83
Nova Southeastern University ... FL ... 105
Midwestern University ... IL ... 148
@Marian University ... IN ... 165
Des Moines University ... IA ... 171
University of Pikeville ... KY ... 194
University of New England ... ME .. 205
Michigan State University ... MI ... 237
William Carey University ... MS .. 261
A. T. Still University of Health Sciences ... MO .. 262
Kansas City University of Medicine & Biosciences ... MO .. 266
Rowan University ... NJ .. 295
@Burrell College of Osteopathic Medicine ... NM .. 299
New York Institute of Technology ... NY ... 323
Touro College ... NY ... 337
@Campbell University ... NC .. 342
Ohio University Main Campus ... OH .. 375
Lake Erie College of Osteopathic Medicine ... PA ... 407
Philadelphia College of Osteopathic Medicine ... PA ... 416
Lincoln Memorial University ... TN ... 441
University of North Texas Health Science Center at Fort Worth ... TX ... 475
@University of the Incarnate Word ... TX ... 474
Edward Via College of Osteopathic Medicine ... VA ... 489
@Liberty University ... VA ... 491
Pacific Northwest University of Health Sciences ... WA .. 505

OT: American Occupational Therapy Association: occupational therapy (M,D)

OTA: American Occupational Therapy Association: occupational therapy assistant (C,A)

PA: National Accrediting Agency for Clinical Laboratory Sciences: pathologist's assistant (C,M)

PAST: Association for Clinical Pastoral Education: clinical pastoral education

Indiana University-Purdue University Indianapolis ... IN ... 163
University of Iowa ... IA ... 169
University of Kentucky ... KY ... 193
University of Louisville ... KY ... 194
Dartmouth College ... NH .. 286
Albany Medical College ... NY ... 303
Jewish Theological Seminary of America . NY ... 317
New York Medical College ... NY ... 323
New York University ... NY ... 324
State University of New York Upstate Medical University ... NY ... 332
University of Rochester ... NY ... 338
Duke University ... NC .. 343
University of North Carolina at Chapel Hill NC .. 357
Kettering College ... OH .. 371
Thomas Jefferson University ... PA ... 420
University of Pennsylvania ... PA ... 421
University of Tennessee, Knoxville ... TN ... 448
Baylor University ... TX ... 452
Oblate School of Theology ... TX ... 463
University of Texas MD Anderson Cancer Center, The ... TX ... 477
University of Texas Southwestern Medical Center ... TX ... 478
Eastern Mennonite University ... VA ... 488
University of Virginia ... VA ... 495
Virginia Commonwealth University ... VA ... 496
University of Washington ... WA .. 508
West Virginia University ... WV .. 514

PCSAS: Psychological Clinical Science Accreditation System: psychological clinical science (D)

Arizona State University ... AZ ... 11
University of Arizona ... AZ ... 17
University of California-Berkeley ... CA ... 68
University of California-Los Angeles ... CA ... 69
University of Southern California ... CA ... 72
University of Delaware ... DE ... 91
University of South Florida ... FL ... 112
Emory University ... GA .. 120
University of Georgia ... GA .. 128
Northwestern University ... IL ... 150
University of Illinois at Urbana-Champaign IL ... 157
Indiana University Bloomington ... IN ... 162
University of Iowa ... IA ... 169
University of Kentucky ... KY ... 193
Harvard University ... MA .. 219
University of Minnesota-Twin Cities ... MN .. 255
University of Missouri - Columbia ... MO .. 273
Washington University in St. Louis ... MO .. 274
Rutgers the State University of New Jersey New Brunswick Campus ... NJ ... 296
Stony Brook University ... NY ... 332
Duke University ... NC .. 343
Ohio State University Main Campus, The . OH .. 375
University of Oregon ... OR .. 395
Temple University ... PA ... 420
University of Pennsylvania ... PA ... 421
University of Pittsburgh ... PA ... 421
University of Virginia ... VA ... 495
Virginia Polytechnic Institute and State University ... VA ... 499
University of Wisconsin-Madison ... WI ... 519

PDPSY: American Psychological Association: post-doctoral residency in health service psychology

Stanford University ... CA ... 66
University of California-San Diego ... CA ... 70
University of Southern California ... CA ... 72
Johns Hopkins University ... MD .. 208
University of Michigan-Ann Arbor ... MI ... 241
University of Rochester ... NY ... 338
Brown University ... RI ... 424
Virginia Commonwealth University ... VA ... 496
University of Washington ... WA .. 508
Medical College of Wisconsin ... WI ... 518

PERF: Commission on Accreditation of Allied Health Education Programs: perfusionist (C,B,M)

University of Arizona ... AZ ... 17
Quinnipiac University ... CT ... 88
Barry University ... FL ... 96
Rush University ... IL ... 153
University of Iowa ... IA ... 169
University of Nebraska Medical Center ... NE ... 283
State University of New York Upstate Medical University ... NY ... 332
University of Pittsburgh ... PA ... 421
Medical University of South Carolina ... SC ... 431
Vanderbilt University ... TN ... 449
University of Texas Health Science Center at Houston (UTHealth), The ... TX ... 477
Milwaukee School of Engineering ... WI ... 518

PH: Council on Education for Public Health: public health (B,M,D)

University of Alabama at Birmingham ... AL ... 8
University of Alaska Anchorage ... AK ... 10
University of Arizona ... AZ ... 17
University of Arkansas for Medical Sciences ... AR ... 23
California State University-Fresno ... CA ... 32
California State University-Fullerton ... CA ... 33
California State University-Long Beach ... CA ... 33
California State University-Northridge ... CA ... 34
Charles R. Drew University of Medicine & Science ... CA ... 37
Claremont Graduate University ... CA ... 38
Loma Linda University ... CA ... 49
National University ... CA ... 54
San Diego State University ... CA ... 35
San Francisco State University ... CA ... 35
San Jose State University ... CA ... 35
Touro University California ... CA ... 68
University of California-Berkeley ... CA ... 68
University of California-Davis ... CA ... 69
University of California-Irvine ... CA ... 69
University of California-Los Angeles ... CA ... 69
University of San Francisco ... CA ... 72
University of Southern California ... CA ... 72
Colorado State University ... CO ... 78
University of Colorado Denver|Anschutz Medical Campus ... CO ... 84
University of Northern Colorado ... CO ... 84
Southern Connecticut State University ... CT ... 85
Yale University ... CT ... 90
George Washington University ... DC ... 92
Florida Agricultural and Mechanical University ... FL ... 110
Florida International University ... FL ... 111
Florida State University ... FL ... 111
Nova Southeastern University ... FL ... 105
University of Florida ... FL ... 112
University of Miami ... FL ... 114
University of North Florida ... FL ... 112
University of South Florida ... FL ... 112
University of West Florida ... FL ... 113
Armstrong State University ... GA ... 116
Augusta University ... GA ... 117
Emory University ... GA .. 120
Georgia Southern University ... GA .. 122
Georgia State University ... GA .. 122
Mercer University ... GA .. 124
Morehouse School of Medicine ... GA .. 125
University of Georgia ... GA .. 128
University of Hawaii at Manoa ... HI ... 131
Idaho State University ... ID ... 133
Benedictine University ... IL ... 135
DePaul University ... IL ... 139
Loyola University Chicago ... IL ... 146
Northern Illinois University ... IL ... 150
Northwestern University ... IL ... 150
Southern Illinois University Carbondale ... IL ... 154
University of Illinois at Chicago ... IL ... 156
University of Illinois at Urbana-Champaign IL ... 157
Indiana University Bloomington ... IN ... 162
Indiana University-Purdue University Indianapolis ... IN ... 163
Des Moines University ... IA ... 171
University of Iowa ... IA ... 169
Kansas State University ... KS ... 182
University of Kansas Main Campus ... KS ... 185
Eastern Kentucky University ... KY ... 188
University of Kentucky ... KY ... 193
University of Louisville ... KY ... 194
Western Kentucky University ... KY ... 194
Louisiana State University Health Sciences Center at Shreveport ... LA ... 198
Louisiana State University Health Sciences Center-New Orleans ... LA ... 198
Louisiana State University in Shreveport .. LA ... 198
Tulane University ... LA ... 200
University of New England ... ME ... 205
Johns Hopkins University ... MD .. 208
Morgan State University ... MD .. 209
Uniformed Services University of the Health Sciences ... MD .. 528
University of Maryland Baltimore ... MD .. 211
University of Maryland College Park ... MD .. 211
Boston University ... MA .. 216
Harvard University ... MA .. 219
Northeastern University ... MA .. 227
Tufts University ... MA .. 228
University of Massachusetts ... MA .. 220
University of Michigan-Ann Arbor ... MI ... 241
Wayne State University ... MI ... 243
University of Minnesota-Twin Cities ... MN .. 255
Jackson State University ... MS .. 258
University of Southern Mississippi ... MS .. 261
A. T. Still University of Health Sciences ... MO .. 262
Missouri State University ... MO .. 268
Saint Louis University ... MO .. 271
University of Missouri - Columbia ... MO .. 273
Washington University in St. Louis ... MO .. 274
University of Montana - Missoula ... MT .. 276
University of Nebraska Medical Center ... NE .. 283
University of Nevada, Las Vegas ... NV .. 284
University of Nevada, Reno ... NV .. 285
Dartmouth College ... NH .. 286
University of New Hampshire ... NH .. 288
Montclair State University ... NJ .. 293
New Jersey Institute of Technology ... NJ .. 293
Rutgers the State University of New Jersey New Brunswick Campus ... NJ .. 296
New Mexico State University Main Campus ... NM .. 300
University of New Mexico Main Campus .. NM .. 302
City University of New York Brooklyn College ... NY ... 307
City University of New York Graduate Center ... NY ... 308
City University of New York Herbert H. Lehman College ... NY ... 308
City University of New York Hunter College ... NY ... 308
Columbia University in the City of New York ... NY ... 311
Icahn School of Medicine at Mount Sinai . NY ... 317
New York Medical College ... NY ... 323
New York University ... NY ... 324
State University of New York Upstate Medical University ... NY ... 332
Stony Brook University ... NY ... 332
SUNY Downstate Medical Center ... NY ... 332
Syracuse University Main Campus ... NY ... 337
University at Albany, SUNY ... NY ... 331
University at Buffalo-SUNY ... NY ... 331
University of Rochester ... NY ... 338
East Carolina University ... NC .. 356
University of North Carolina at Chapel Hill NC .. 357
University of North Carolina at Charlotte .. NC .. 358
University of North Carolina at Greensboro ... NC .. 358
University of North Carolina Wilmington ... NC .. 358
University of North Dakota ... ND .. 360
Bowling Green State University ... OH .. 364
Case Western Reserve University ... OH .. 365
Cleveland State University ... OH .. 366
Kent State University Main Campus ... OH .. 370
Northeast Ohio Medical University ... OH .. 373
Ohio State University Main Campus, The . OH .. 375
Ohio University Main Campus ... OH .. 375
University of Akron, Main Campus, The ... OH .. 378
University of Cincinnati Main Campus ... OH .. 379
University of Toledo ... OH .. 380
Wright State University Main Campus ... OH .. 381
Youngstown State University ... OH .. 382
Oregon Health & Science University ... OR .. 393
Oregon State University ... OR .. 393
Portland State University ... OR .. 394
Arcadia University ... PA ... 397
Drexel University ... PA ... 402
East Stroudsburg University of Pennsylvania ... PA ... 414
Temple University ... PA ... 420
Thomas Jefferson University ... PA ... 420
University of Pennsylvania ... PA ... 421
University of Pittsburgh ... PA ... 421
West Chester University of Pennsylvania . PA ... 416
Ponce School of Medicine & Health Sciences ... PR ... 535
University of Puerto Rico-Medical Sciences Campus ... PR ... 538
Brown University ... RI ... 424
University of South Carolina Columbia ... SC ... 433
East Tennessee State University ... TN ... 444
Meharry Medical College ... TN ... 442
Tennessee State University ... TN ... 445
University of Memphis, The ... TN ... 445
University of Tennessee, Knoxville ... TN ... 448
Vanderbilt University ... TN ... 449
Baylor University ... TX ... 452
Texas A & M University ... TX ... 468
University of North Texas Health Science Center at Fort Worth ... TX ... 475
University of Texas at El Paso ... TX ... 476
University of Texas Health Science Center at Houston (UTHealth), The ... TX ... 477
University of Texas Medical Branch, The . TX ... 478
Brigham Young University ... UT ... 480
University of Utah, The ... UT ... 481
Westminster College ... UT ... 483
Eastern Virginia Medical School ... VA ... 489
George Mason University ... VA ... 490
Old Dominion University ... VA ... 492
University of Virginia ... VA ... 495
Virginia Commonwealth University ... VA ... 496
Virginia Polytechnic Institute and State University ... VA ... 499
University of Washington ... WA .. 508
West Virginia University ... WV .. 514
Medical College of Wisconsin ... WI ... 518
University of Wisconsin-La Crosse ... WI ... 520
University of Wisconsin-Madison ... WI ... 519

PHAR: Accreditation Council for Pharmaceutical Education: pharmacy (FP,D)

Auburn University ... AL ... 1
Samford University ... AL ... 6
University of Arizona ... AZ ... 17
Harding University Main Campus ... AR ... 20
University of Arkansas for Medical Sciences ... AR ... 23
@California Health Sciences University ... CA ... 30
California Northstate University College of Pharmacy ... CA ... 31
@Chapman University ... CA ... 37
@Keck Graduate Institute ... CA ... 39
Loma Linda University ... CA ... 49
@Marshall B. Ketchum University ... CA ... 51
Touro University California ... CA ... 68
University of California-San Diego ... CA ... 70
University of California-San Francisco ... CA ... 70
University of Southern California ... CA ... 72
University of the Pacific ... CA ... 71
@West Coast University ... CA ... 74
Western University of Health Sciences ... CA ... 74
Regis University ... CO ... 82
University of Colorado Denver|Anschutz Medical Campus ... CO ... 84
University of Connecticut ... CT ... 89
University of Saint Joseph ... CT ... 90
Howard University ... DC ... 93
Florida Agricultural and Mechanical University ... FL ... 110
@Larkin Health Sciences Institute ... FL ... 104
Nova Southeastern University ... FL ... 105
Palm Beach Atlantic University ... FL ... 106
University of Florida ... FL ... 112
University of South Florida ... FL ... 112
Mercer University ... GA .. 124
South University ... GA .. 127
University of Georgia ... GA .. 128
University of Hawaii at Hilo ... HI ... 131
Idaho State University ... ID ... 133
Chicago State University ... IL ... 136
Midwestern University ... IL ... 148
Roosevelt University ... IL ... 152
Rosalind Franklin University of Medicine & Science ... IL ... 153
Southern Illinois University Edwardsville ... IL ... 155
University of Illinois at Chicago ... IL ... 156
Butler University ... IN ... 159
Manchester University ... IN ... 165
Purdue University Main Campus ... IN ... 166
Drake University ... IA ... 171
University of Iowa ... IA ... 169
University of Kansas Main Campus ... KS ... 185
Sullivan University ... KY ... 193
University of Kentucky ... KY ... 193
University of Louisiana at Monroe ... LA ... 201
Xavier University of Louisiana ... LA ... 202
Husson University ... ME ... 202
University of New England ... ME ... 205
Notre Dame of Maryland University ... MD .. 210
University of Maryland Baltimore ... MD .. 211
University of Maryland Eastern Shore ... MD .. 212
MCPHS University ... MA .. 225
Northeastern University ... MA .. 227
Western New England University ... MA .. 229
Ferris State University ... MI ... 233
University of Michigan-Ann Arbor ... MI ... 241
Wayne State University ... MI ... 243
University of Minnesota-Twin Cities ... MN .. 255
University of Mississippi ... MS .. 261
University of Mississippi Medical Center ... MS .. 261
St. Louis College of Pharmacy ... MO .. 271
University of Missouri - Columbia ... MO .. 273
University of Missouri - Kansas City ... MO .. 273
University of Montana - Missoula ... MT .. 276
Creighton University ... NE ... 279
University of Nebraska Medical Center ... NE ... 283
Roseman University of Health Sciences ... NV ... 285
Fairleigh Dickinson University ... NJ ... 291
Rutgers the State University of New Jersey New Brunswick Campus ... NJ ... 296
University of New Mexico Main Campus .. NM .. 302
Albany College of Pharmacy and Health Sciences ... NY ... 303
D'Youville College ... NY ... 313
St. John Fisher College ... NY ... 328
St. John's University ... NY ... 328
Touro College ... NY ... 337
University at Buffalo-SUNY ... NY ... 331
Campbell University ... NC ... 342
@High Point University ... NC ... 345
University of North Carolina at Chapel Hill NC ... 357
Wingate University ... NC ... 359

North Dakota State University Main Campus ... ND ... 361
Cedarville University ... OH ... 365
Northeast Ohio Medical University ... OH ... 373
Ohio Northern University ... OH ... 374
Ohio State University Main Campus, The ... OH ... 375
University of Cincinnati Main Campus ... OH ... 379
University of Findlay, The ... OH ... 379
University of Toledo ... OH ... 380
Southwestern Oklahoma State University ... OK ... 388
Oregon State University ... OR ... 393
Pacific University ... OR ... 394
Duquesne University ... PA ... 403
Lake Erie College of Osteopathic Medicine ... PA ... 407
Temple University ... PA ... 420
Thomas Jefferson University ... PA ... 420
University of Pittsburgh ... PA ... 421
University of the Sciences in Philadelphia ... PA ... 422
Wilkes University ... PA ... 423
University of Puerto Rico-Medical Sciences Campus ... PR ... 538
University of Rhode Island ... RI ... 426
Medical University of South Carolina ... SC ... 431
Presbyterian College ... SC ... 432
University of South Carolina Columbia ... SC ... 433
South Dakota State University ... SD ... 437
Belmont University ... TN ... 438
East Tennessee State University ... TN ... 444
Lipscomb University ... TN ... 441
South College ... TN ... 444
Union University ... TN ... 448
University of Tennessee Health Science Center ... TN ... 448
Texas A & M University - Kingsville ... TX ... 469
Texas Southern University ... TX ... 470
Texas Tech University Health Sciences Center ... TX ... 472
University of Houston ... TX ... 473
@University of North Texas Health Science Center at Fort Worth ... TX ... 475
University of Texas at Austin ... TX ... 476
@University of Texas at Tyler ... TX ... 477
University of the Incarnate Word ... TX ... 474
University of Utah, The ... UT ... 481
Appalachian College of Pharmacy ... VA ... 486
Hampton University ... VA ... 490
Shenandoah University ... VA ... 494
Virginia Commonwealth University ... VA ... 496
University of Washington ... WA ... 508
Washington State University ... WA ... 508
Marshall University ... WV ... 513
University of Charleston ... WV ... 511
West Virginia University ... WV ... 514
Concordia University Wisconsin ... WI ... 516
University of Wisconsin-Madison ... WI ... 519
University of Wyoming ... WY ... 527

PHLEB: National Accrediting Agency for Clinical Laboratory Sciences: phlebotomist (C)

Phillips Community College of the University of Arkansas ... AR ... 23
South Arkansas Community College ... AR ... 22
Southeast Arkansas College ... AR ... 22
Otero Junior College ... CO ... 82
Dalton State College ... GA ... 119
Kapiolani Community College ... HI ... 131
College of Lake County ... IL ... 138
Kankakee Community College ... IL ... 144
Moraine Valley Community College ... IL ... 148
South Suburban College of Cook County ... IL ... 154
Bossier Parish Community College ... LA ... 195
Delgado Community College ... LA ... 196
L.E. Fletcher Technical Community College ... LA ... 196
Southern University at Shreveport-Louisiana ... LA ... 199
Mid Michigan Community College ... MI ... 238
St. Catherine University ... MN ... 254
University of Southern Mississippi ... MS ... 261
Miles Community College ... MT ... 276
Western Nebraska Community College ... NE ... 283
Orange County Community College ... NY ... 325
Trocaire College ... NY ... 338
Asheville - Buncombe Technical Community College ... NC ... 347
Brunswick Community College ... NC ... 347
Cape Fear Community College ... NC ... 348
Carolinas College of Health Sciences ... NC ... 343
Halifax Community College ... NC ... 350
Nash Community College ... NC ... 351
Rockingham Community College ... NC ... 352
Southwestern Community College ... NC ... 353
Wake Technical Community College ... NC ... 353
Bismarck State College ... ND ... 361
Turtle Mountain Community College ... ND ... 362
Columbus State Community College ... OH ... 367
Edison State Community College ... OH ... 368
Lorain County Community College ... OH ... 371
Tulsa Community College ... OK ... 388
Community College of Beaver County ... PA ... 401
Community College of Philadelphia ... PA ... 401
Montgomery County Community College ... PA ... 410
Southwest Tennessee Community College ... TN ... 447
Austin Community College District ... TX ... 451
Weatherford College ... TX ... 479
Mid-State Technical College ... WI ... 523
Milwaukee Area Technical College ... WI ... 524
Northcentral Technical College ... WI ... 524

PLNG: Planning Accreditation Board: certified planning (B,M)

Alabama Agricultural and Mechanical University ... AL ... 1
Arizona State University ... AZ ... 11
University of Arizona ... AZ ... 17
California Polytechnic State University-San Luis Obispo ... CA ... 31
California State Polytechnic University-Pomona ... CA ... 31
San Jose State University ... CA ... 35
University of California-Berkeley ... CA ... 68
University of California-Irvine ... CA ... 69
University of California-Los Angeles ... CA ... 69
University of Southern California ... CA ... 72
University of Colorado Denver|Anschutz Medical Campus ... CO ... 84
Florida Atlantic University ... FL ... 110
Florida State University ... FL ... 111
University of Florida ... FL ... 112
Georgia Institute of Technology ... GA ... 121
University of Hawaii at Manoa ... HI ... 131
University of Illinois at Chicago ... IL ... 156
University of Illinois at Urbana-Champaign ... IL ... 157
Ball State University ... IN ... 159
Iowa State University ... IA ... 169
University of Iowa ... IA ... 169
Kansas State University ... KS ... 182
University of Kansas Main Campus ... KS ... 185
University of Louisville ... KY ... 194
University of New Orleans ... LA ... 198
Morgan State University ... MD ... 209
University of Maryland College Park ... MD ... 211
Harvard University ... MA ... 219
Massachusetts Institute of Technology ... MA ... 225
Tufts University ... MA ... 228
University of Massachusetts ... MA ... 220
Eastern Michigan University ... MI ... 233
Michigan State University ... MI ... 237
University of Michigan-Ann Arbor ... MI ... 241
Wayne State University ... MI ... 243
University of Minnesota-Twin Cities ... MN ... 255
Jackson State University ... MS ... 258
Missouri State University ... MO ... 268
University of Nebraska - Lincoln ... NE ... 282
Rutgers the State University of New Jersey New Brunswick Campus ... NJ ... 296
University of New Mexico Main Campus ... NM ... 302
City University of New York Hunter College ... NY ... 308
Columbia University in the City of New York ... NY ... 311
Cornell University ... NY ... 312
New York University ... NY ... 324
Pratt Institute ... NY ... 326
University at Albany, SUNY ... NY ... 331
University at Buffalo-SUNY ... NY ... 331
East Carolina University ... NC ... 356
University of North Carolina at Chapel Hill ... NC ... 357
Cleveland State University ... OH ... 366
Ohio State University Main Campus, The ... OH ... 375
University of Cincinnati Main Campus ... OH ... 379
University of Oklahoma Norman Campus ... OK ... 389
Portland State University ... OR ... 394
University of Oregon ... OR ... 395
Indiana University of Pennsylvania ... PA ... 415
Temple University ... PA ... 420
University of Pennsylvania ... PA ... 421
University of Puerto Rico-Rio Piedras Campus ... PR ... 538
Clemson University ... SC ... 428
University of Memphis, The ... TN ... 445
Texas A & M University ... TX ... 468
Texas Southern University ... TX ... 470
University of Texas at Arlington, The ... TX ... 476
University of Texas at Austin ... TX ... 476
University of Utah, The ... UT ... 481
University of Virginia ... VA ... 495
Virginia Commonwealth University ... VA ... 496
Virginia Polytechnic Institute and State University ... VA ... 499
Eastern Washington University ... WA ... 503
University of Washington ... WA ... 508
University of Wisconsin-Madison ... WI ... 519
University of Wisconsin-Milwaukee ... WI ... 520

PNUR: Accreditation Commission for Education in Nursing: practical nursing (C)

Bevill State Community College ... AL ... 2
Bishop State Community College ... AL ... 2
Calhoun Community College ... AL ... 2
Chattahoochee Valley Community College ... AL ... 2
Gadsden State Community College ... AL ... 3
George C. Wallace Community College - Dothan ... AL ... 3
George Corley Wallace State Community College - Selma ... AL ... 4
James H. Faulkner State Community College ... AL ... 4
Lawson State Community College ... AL ... 5
Northeast Alabama Community College ... AL ... 5
Shelton State Community College ... AL ... 6
Trenholm State Technical College ... AL ... 7
Wallace State Community College - Hanceville ... AL ... 9
Colorado Mesa University ... CO ... 77
Delaware Technical Community College, Terry Campus ... DE ... 91
Mercy Hospital College of Nursing ... FL ... 105
Pensacola State College ... FL ... 106
Augusta Technical College ... GA ... 117
Carl Sandburg College ... IL ... 136
Lake Land College ... IL ... 145
Lincoln Land Community College ... IL ... 146
Ivy Tech Community College of Indiana-Central Indiana ... IN ... 164
Vincennes University ... IN ... 169
Western Iowa Tech Community College ... IA ... 177
Hutchinson Community College ... KS ... 181
West Kentucky Community and Technical College ... KY ... 190
L.E. Fletcher Technical Community College ... LA ... 196
College of Southern Maryland ... MD ... 207
Hagerstown Community College ... MD ... 207
Howard Community College ... MD ... 208
Mount Wachusett Community College ... MA ... 224
North Shore Community College ... MA ... 224
Northern Essex Community College ... MA ... 224
Quincy College ... MA ... 227
Quinsigamond Community College ... MA ... 224
Davenport University ... MI ... 233
Grand Rapids Community College ... MI ... 234
Northwestern Michigan College ... MI ... 239
Schoolcraft College ... MI ... 240
Lake Superior College ... MN ... 249
Minneapolis Community and Technical College ... MN ... 250
Minnesota State College-Southeast Technical ... MN ... 250
Ridgewater College ... MN ... 251
Rochester Community and Technical College ... MN ... 251
Saint Cloud Technical and Community College ... MN ... 252
Saint Paul College-A Community & Technical College ... MN ... 252
Meridian Community College ... MS ... 258
Mississippi Gulf Coast Community College ... MS ... 259
Southeast Community College ... NE ... 282
Western Nebraska Community College ... NE ... 283
Brightwood College ... NV ... 283
College of Southern Nevada ... NV ... 284
Union County College ... NJ ... 298
Samaritan Hospital School of Nursing ... NY ... 329
Trocaire College ... NY ... 338
Durham Technical Community College ... NC ... 349
Edgecombe Community College ... NC ... 349
Gaston College ... NC ... 350
Rowan-Cabarrus Community College ... NC ... 352
Sampson Community College ... NC ... 352
Wayne Community College ... NC ... 354
Dickinson State University ... ND ... 360
North Dakota State College of Science ... ND ... 361
United Tribes Technical College ... ND ... 362
Hocking College ... OH ... 369
Lorain County Community College ... OH ... 371
Harrisburg Area Community College ... PA ... 405
Lehigh Carbon Community College ... PA ... 408
Northampton Community College ... PA ... 411
Pennsylvania College of Technology ... PA ... 413
Pittsburgh Technical Institute ... PA ... 417
Reading Area Community College ... PA ... 417
Community College of Rhode Island ... RI ... 425
Aiken Technical College ... SC ... 426
Central Carolina Technical College ... SC ... 427
Horry-Georgetown Technical College ... SC ... 430
Midlands Technical College ... SC ... 431
Orangeburg Calhoun Technical College ... SC ... 431
Technical College of the Lowcountry ... SC ... 433
Tri-County Technical College ... SC ... 433
Trident Technical College ... SC ... 433
York Technical College ... SC ... 435
Lake Area Technical Institute ... SD ... 436
Austin Community College District ... TX ... 451
El Centro College ... TX ... 456
Ogden-Weber Applied Technology College ... UT ... 481
Snow College ... UT ... 482
Uintah Basin Applied Technology College ... UT ... 481
Vermont Technical College ... VT ... 486
Centra College of Nursing ... VA ... 487
Global Health College ... VA ... 490
Riverside College of Health Careers ... VA ... 493
Milwaukee Area Technical College ... WI ... 524

POD: American Podiatric Medical Association: podiatry (FP,D)

Samuel Merritt University ... CA ... 59
Western University of Health Sciences ... CA ... 74
Barry University ... FL ... 96
Rosalind Franklin University of Medicine & Science ... IL ... 153
Des Moines University ... IA ... 171
New York College of Podiatric Medicine ... NY ... 323
Kent State University Main Campus ... OH ... 370
Temple University ... PA ... 420

POLYT: Commission on Accreditation of Allied Health Education Programs: polysomnographic technologist education (C,A)

Wallace State Community College - Hanceville ... AL ... 9
Gateway Community College ... AZ ... 14
Orange Coast College ... CA ... 39
Santa Fe College ... FL ... 109
Central Georgia Technical College ... GA ... 118
College of DuPage ... IL ... 138
Moraine Valley Community College ... IL ... 148
Delgado Community College ... LA ... 196
Community College of Baltimore County, The ... MD ... 207
Montgomery College ... MD ... 209
Northern Essex Community College ... MA ... 224
Baker College of Flint ... MI ... 231
Minneapolis Community and Technical College ... MN ... 250
Coahoma Community College ... MS ... 257
Southeast Community College ... NE ... 282
Thomas Edison State University ... NJ ... 297
Genesee Community College ... NY ... 315
Hudson Valley Community College ... NY ... 316
Stony Brook University ... NY ... 332
Catawba Valley Community College ... NC ... 348
Central Carolina Community College ... NC ... 348
Lenoir Community College ... NC ... 350
Pitt Community College ... NC ... 352
Sandhills Community College ... NC ... 353
University of North Carolina at Charlotte ... NC ... 358
Cuyahoga Community College ... OH ... 367
Mercy College of Ohio ... OH ... 372
Linn-Benton Community College ... OR ... 392
Oregon Institute of Technology ... OR ... 393
Concorde Career College ... TN ... 439
Miller-Motte Technical College ... TN ... 442
Roane State Community College ... TN ... 447
Volunteer State Community College ... TN ... 447
Alvin Community College ... TX ... 450
Collin County Community College District ... TX ... 455
Concorde Career Institute ... TX ... 455

PSPSY: American Psychological Association: combined professional-scientific psychology (D)

University of South Alabama ... AL ... 9
University of California-Santa Barbara ... CA ... 70
Florida State University ... FL ... 111
Northeastern University ... MA ... 227
Kean University ... NJ ... 292
Pace University ... NY ... 325
University at Buffalo-SUNY ... NY ... 331
Yeshiva University ... NY ... 341
Utah State University ... UT ... 482
James Madison University ... VA ... 490
University of Virginia ... VA ... 495

PTA: American Physical Therapy Association: physical therapy (M,D)

Alabama State University ... AL ... 1
@Samford University ... AL ... 6
University of Alabama at Birmingham ... AL ... 8
University of South Alabama ... AL ... 9
Northern Arizona University ... AZ ... 15
Arkansas State University-Jonesboro ... AR ... 18
Harding University Main Campus ... AR ... 20
@University of Arkansas for Medical Sciences ... AR ... 23

University of Central Arkansas ... AR ... 24
Azusa Pacific University ... CA ... 28
California State University-Fresno ... CA ... 32
California State University-Long Beach ... CA ... 33
California State University-Northridge ... CA ... 34
California State University-Sacramento ... CA ... 34
Chapman University ... CA ... 37
Loma Linda University ... CA ... 49
Mount Saint Mary's University ... CA ... 53
Samuel Merritt University ... CA ... 59
San Diego State University ... CA ... 35
San Francisco State University ... CA ... 35
University of California-San Francisco ... CA ... 70
University of St. Augustine for Health Sciences ... CA ... 72
University of Southern California ... CA ... 72
University of the Pacific ... CA ... 71
@West Coast University ... CA ... 74
Western University of Health Sciences ... CA ... 74
Regis University ... CO ... 82
University of Colorado Denver|Anschutz Medical Campus ... CO ... 84
Quinnipiac University ... CT ... 88
Sacred Heart University ... CT ... 88
University of Connecticut ... CT ... 89
University of Hartford ... CT ... 89
University of Delaware ... DE ... 91
George Washington University ... DC ... 92
#Howard University ... DC ... 93
@Adventist University of Health Sciences ... FL ... 95
Florida Agricultural and Mechanical University ... FL ... 110
Florida Gulf Coast University ... FL ... 110
Florida International University ... FL ... 111
Nova Southeastern University ... FL ... 105
University of Central Florida ... FL ... 111
University of Florida ... FL ... 112
University of Miami ... FL ... 114
University of North Florida ... FL ... 112
University of South Florida ... FL ... 112
Armstrong State University ... GA ... 116
Augusta University ... GA ... 117
@Brenau University ... GA ... 118
Emory University ... GA ... 120
Georgia State University ... GA ... 122
Mercer University ... GA ... 124
University of North Georgia ... GA ... 128
Idaho State University ... ID ... 133
Bradley University ... IL ... 136
Governors State University ... IL ... 140
Midwestern University ... IL ... 148
Northern Illinois University ... IL ... 150
Northwestern University ... IL ... 150
Rosalind Franklin University of Medicine & Science ... IL ... 153
University of Illinois at Chicago ... IL ... 156
@Indiana State University ... IN ... 162
Indiana University-Purdue University Indianapolis ... IN ... 163
@Trine University ... IN ... 167
University of Evansville ... IN ... 167
University of Indianapolis ... IN ... 168
@Briar Cliff University ... IA ... 170
Clarke University ... IA ... 170
Des Moines University ... IA ... 171
St. Ambrose University ... IA ... 176
University of Iowa ... IA ... 169
University of Saint Mary ... KS ... 185
Wichita State University ... KS ... 185
Bellarmine University ... KY ... 187
University of Kentucky ... KY ... 193
Western Kentucky University ... KY ... 194
Louisiana State University Health Sciences Center at Shreveport ... LA ... 198
Louisiana State University Health Sciences Center-New Orleans ... LA ... 198
Husson University ... ME ... 202
University of New England ... ME ... 205
University of Maryland Baltimore ... MD ... 211
University of Maryland Eastern Shore ... MD ... 212
American International College ... MA ... 214
Boston University ... MA ... 216
MCPHS University ... MA ... 225
MGH Institute of Health Professions ... MA ... 225
Northeastern University ... MA ... 227
Simmons College ... MA ... 228
Springfield College ... MA ... 228
University of Massachusetts Lowell ... MA ... 221
Andrews University ... MI ... 230
Central Michigan University ... MI ... 232
Grand Valley State University ... MI ... 234
Oakland University ... MI ... 239
University of Michigan-Flint ... MI ... 242
Wayne State University ... MI ... 243
College of Saint Scholastica, The ... MN ... 245
@Concordia University, St. Paul ... MN ... 246
St. Catherine University ... MN ... 254
University of Minnesota-Twin Cities ... MN ... 255
University of Mississippi Medical Center ... MS ... 261
@William Carey University ... MS ... 261
Maryville University of Saint Louis ... MO ... 267
Missouri State University ... MO ... 268
Rockhurst University ... MO ... 270
Saint Louis University ... MO ... 271
Southwest Baptist University ... MO ... 272
University of Missouri - Columbia ... MO ... 273
Washington University in St. Louis ... MO ... 274
University of Montana - Missoula ... MT ... 276
Creighton University ... NE ... 279
University of Nebraska Medical Center ... NE ... 283
University of Nevada, Las Vegas ... NV ... 284
Franklin Pierce University ... NH ... 287
@Kean University ... NJ ... 292
Rutgers the State University of New Jersey Camden Campus ... NJ ... 296
Seton Hall University ... NJ ... 297
Stockton University ... NJ ... 297
University of New Mexico Main Campus ... NM ... 302
City University of New York Hunter College ... NY ... 308
Clarkson University ... NY ... 310
College of Staten Island CUNY ... NY ... 307
Columbia University in the City of New York ... NY ... 311
Daemen College ... NY ... 312
Dominican College of Blauvelt ... NY ... 312
D'Youville College ... NY ... 313
Ithaca College ... NY ... 317
Mercy College ... NY ... 320
Nazareth College of Rochester ... NY ... 322
New York Institute of Technology ... NY ... 323
New York Medical College ... NY ... 323
New York University ... NY ... 324
Sage Colleges, The ... NY ... 327
State University of New York Upstate Medical University ... NY ... 332
Stony Brook University ... NY ... 332
SUNY Downstate Medical Center ... NY ... 332
Touro College ... NY ... 337
University at Buffalo-SUNY ... NY ... 331
Utica College ... NY ... 339
@Campbell University ... NC ... 342
Duke University ... NC ... 343
East Carolina University ... NC ... 356
Elon University ... NC ... 344
@High Point University ... NC ... 345
@Methodist University ... NC ... 346
University of North Carolina at Chapel Hill ... NC ... 357
Western Carolina University ... NC ... 359
@Wingate University ... NC ... 359
Winston-Salem State University ... NC ... 359
University of Jamestown ... ND ... 362
University of Mary ... ND ... 362
University of North Dakota ... ND ... 360
Cleveland State University ... OH ... 366
Mount St. Joseph University ... OH ... 373
Ohio State University Main Campus, The ... OH ... 375
Ohio University Main Campus ... OH ... 375
University of Cincinnati Main Campus ... OH ... 379
University of Dayton ... OH ... 379
University of Findlay, The ... OH ... 379
@University of Mount Union ... OH ... 379
University of Toledo ... OH ... 380
Walsh University ... OH ... 380
Youngstown State University ... OH ... 382
Langston University ... OK ... 383
George Fox University ... OR ... 391
Pacific University ... OR ... 394
@Alvernia University ... PA ... 397
Arcadia University ... PA ... 397
Chatham University ... PA ... 400
@DeSales University ... PA ... 402
Drexel University ... PA ... 402
Duquesne University ... PA ... 403
Gannon University ... PA ... 404
Lebanon Valley College ... PA ... 408
Misericordia University ... PA ... 410
Neumann University ... PA ... 411
Saint Francis University ... PA ... 418
Slippery Rock University of Pennsylvania ... PA ... 416
Temple University ... PA ... 420
Thomas Jefferson University ... PA ... 420
University of Pittsburgh ... PA ... 421
University of Scranton, The ... PA ... 422
University of the Sciences in Philadelphia ... PA ... 422
Widener University ... PA ... 423
University of Puerto Rico-Medical Sciences Campus ... PR ... 538
University of Rhode Island ... RI ... 426
Medical University of South Carolina ... SC ... 431
University of South Carolina Columbia ... SC ... 433
University of South Dakota, The ... SD ... 437
Belmont University ... TN ... 438
East Tennessee State University ... TN ... 444
@South College ... TN ... 444
Tennessee State University ... TN ... 445
University of Tennessee at Chattanooga ... TN ... 448
University of Tennessee Health Science Center ... TN ... 448
Angelo State University ... TX ... 472
Baylor University ... TX ... 452
Hardin-Simmons University ... TX ... 458
Texas State University ... TX ... 471
Texas Tech University Health Sciences Center ... TX ... 472
Texas Woman's University ... TX ... 472
@University of Mary Hardin-Baylor ... TX ... 474
University of North Texas Health Science Center at Fort Worth ... TX ... 475
University of Texas at El Paso ... TX ... 476
University of Texas Health Science Center at San Antonio ... TX ... 477
University of Texas Medical Branch, The ... TX ... 478
University of Texas Southwestern Medical Center ... TX ... 478
University of the Incarnate Word ... TX ... 474
Rocky Mountain University of Health Professions ... UT ... 481
University of Utah, The ... UT ... 481
University of Vermont ... VT ... 485
@Emory & Henry College ... VA ... 489
Hampton University ... VA ... 490
Lynchburg College ... VA ... 491
@Mary Baldwin College ... VA ... 491
Marymount University ... VA ... 492
Old Dominion University ... VA ... 492
Radford University ... VA ... 493
Shenandoah University ... VA ... 494
Virginia Commonwealth University ... VA ... 496
Eastern Washington University ... WA ... 503
University of Puget Sound ... WA ... 508
University of Washington ... WA ... 508
Marshall University ... WV ... 513
West Virginia University ... WV ... 514
Wheeling Jesuit University ... WV ... 515
Carroll University ... WI ... 515
Concordia University Wisconsin ... WI ... 516
Marquette University ... WI ... 517
University of Wisconsin-La Crosse ... WI ... 520
University of Wisconsin-Madison ... WI ... 519
University of Wisconsin-Milwaukee ... WI ... 520

PTAA: American Physical Therapy Association: physical therapy assistant (A)

Bishop State Community College ... AL ... 2
Calhoun Community College ... AL ... 2
George C. Wallace Community College - Dothan ... AL ... 3
Jefferson State Community College ... AL ... 5
Wallace State Community College - Hanceville ... AL ... 9
University of Alaska Anchorage ... AK ... 10
Brookline College ... AZ ... 11
Gateway Community College ... AZ ... 14
Mohave Community College ... AZ ... 15
Pima Medical Institute-Tucson ... AZ ... 16
Arkansas State University-Jonesboro ... AR ... 18
Arkansas Tech University ... AR ... 19
NorthWest Arkansas Community College ... AR ... 21
South Arkansas Community College ... AR ... 22
#Casa Loma College-Van Nuys ... CA ... 36
CBD College ... CA ... 36
Cerritos College ... CA ... 36
College of the Sequoias ... CA ... 40
Concorde Career College ... CA ... 41
Gurnick Academy of Medical Arts ... CA ... 45
Loma Linda University ... CA ... 49
Ohlone College ... CA ... 55
Sacramento City College ... CA ... 51
San Diego Mesa College ... CA ... 60
Stanbridge College ... CA ... 66
Arapahoe Community College ... CO ... 76
Concorde Career College ... CO ... 79
Pueblo Community College ... CO ... 82
Naugatuck Valley Community College ... CT ... 86
Norwalk Community College ... CT ... 87
Broward College ... FL ... 96
College of Central Florida ... FL ... 97
Concorde Career Institute ... FL ... 97
Concorde Career Institute ... FL ... 98
Daytona State College ... FL ... 98
@Eastern Florida State College ... FL ... 98
Florida Gateway College ... FL ... 100
Florida National University Hialeah Campus ... FL ... 101
Florida State College at Jacksonville ... FL ... 101
Gulf Coast State College ... FL ... 102
Hodges University ... FL ... 102
Indian River State College ... FL ... 103
Keiser University ... FL ... 103
Miami Dade College ... FL ... 105
Pensacola State College ... FL ... 106
Polk State College ... FL ... 106
Praxis Institute, The ... FL ... 107
@Saber College ... FL ... 107
St. Petersburg College ... FL ... 108
Seminole State College of Florida ... FL ... 109
State College of Florida, Manatee-Sarasota ... FL ... 110
Taylor College ... FL ... 113
Athens Technical College ... GA ... 116
#Atlanta Technical College ... GA ... 117
Chattahoochee Technical College ... GA ... 118
Darton State College ... GA ... 120
Lanier Technical College ... GA ... 123
South University ... GA ... 127
Kapiolani Community College ... HI ... 131
Brigham Young University-Idaho ... ID ... 132
College of Southern Idaho ... ID ... 133
#College of Western Idaho ... ID ... 133
Idaho State University ... ID ... 133
#Lewis-Clark State College ... ID ... 134
#North Idaho College ... ID ... 134
Black Hawk College ... IL ... 135
#College of DuPage ... IL ... 138
Elgin Community College ... IL ... 140
Fox College ... IL ... 140
@Heartland Community College ... IL ... 141
Illinois Central College ... IL ... 141
Kankakee Community College ... IL ... 144
Kaskaskia College ... IL ... 144
Lake Land College ... IL ... 145
Morton College ... IL ... 149
Oakton Community College ... IL ... 150
SOLEX College ... IL ... 154
Southern Illinois University Carbondale ... IL ... 154
Southwestern Illinois College ... IL ... 155
University of Evansville ... IN ... 167
University of Indianapolis ... IN ... 168
University of Saint Francis ... IN ... 168
Vincennes University ... IN ... 169
Hawkeye Community College ... IA ... 173
Indian Hills Community College ... IA ... 173
Iowa Western Community College ... IA ... 174
Kirkwood Community College ... IA ... 174
Mercy College of Health Sciences ... IA ... 175
North Iowa Area Community College ... IA ... 175
Western Iowa Tech Community College ... IA ... 177
Colby Community College ... KS ... 180
Hutchinson Community College ... KS ... 181
Kansas City Kansas Community College ... KS ... 182
Labette Community College ... KS ... 182
Washburn University ... KS ... 185
Hazard Community and Technical College ... KY ... 189
Jefferson Community and Technical College ... KY ... 190
Madisonville Community College ... KY ... 190
Somerset Community College ... KY ... 190
Southeast Kentucky Community and Technical College ... KY ... 190
West Kentucky Community and Technical College ... KY ... 190
Bossier Parish Community College ... LA ... 195
Delgado Community College ... LA ... 196
Louisiana College ... LA ... 195
Our Lady of the Lake College ... LA ... 199
Kennebec Valley Community College ... ME ... 203
University of Maine at Presque Isle ... ME ... 205
Allegany College of Maryland ... MD ... 205
Anne Arundel Community College ... MD ... 206
Baltimore City Community College ... MD ... 206
Carroll Community College ... MD ... 206
Cecil College ... MD ... 206
Chesapeake College ... MD ... 207
College of Southern Maryland ... MD ... 207
Howard Community College ... MD ... 208
Montgomery College ... MD ... 209
@Wor-Wic Community College ... MD ... 213
Bay State College ... MA ... 215
Berkshire Community College ... MA ... 222
Mount Wachusett Community College ... MA ... 224
North Shore Community College ... MA ... 224
@Quincy College ... MA ... 227
Springfield Technical Community College ... MA ... 224
Baker College of Flint ... MI ... 231
Delta College ... MI ... 233
Finlandia University ... MI ... 234
Henry Ford College ... MI ... 235
Kellogg Community College ... MI ... 236
Macomb Community College ... MI ... 237
Mid Michigan Community College ... MI ... 238
Mott Community College ... MI ... 238
Washtenaw Community College ... MI ... 242
Anoka-Ramsey Community College ... MN ... 248
Lake Superior College ... MN ... 249
Northland Community and Technical College ... MN ... 251
St. Catherine University ... MN ... 254
Hinds Community College ... MS ... 258
@Holmes Community College ... MS ... 258
Itawamba Community College ... MS ... 258
Meridian Community College ... MS ... 258
Pearl River Community College ... MS ... 260
@Central Methodist University ... MO ... 263

RABN: Association of Advanced Rabbinical and Talmudic Schools: rabbinical and Talmudic education (B,M,D)

RAD: Joint Review Committee on Education in Radiologic Technology: radiography (C,A,B)

RADDOS: Joint Review Committee on Education in Radiologic Technology: medical dosimetry (C, B,M)

RADMAG: Joint Review Committee on Education in Radiologic Technology: magnetic resonance (C,B)

RTT: Joint Review Committee on Education in Radiologic Technology: radiation therapist/technologist (C, A,B)

SC: Southern Association of Colleges and Schools, Commission on Colleges

SCPSY: American Psychological Association: school psychology (D)

SP: American Speech-Language-Hearing Association: speech-language pathology (M)

SPAA: Network of Schools of Public Policy, Affairs and Administration: public affairs and administration (M)

SURGA: Commission on Accreditation of Allied Health Education Programs: surgical assistant (C,A)

SURGT: Commission on Accreditation of Allied Health Education Programs: surgical technology (C,A)

SURTEC: Accrediting Bureau of Health Education Schools: surgical technologist (C,A)

SW: Council on Social Work Education: social work (B,M)

TEAC: Teacher Education Accreditation Council: teacher education (B,M,D)

TED: National Council for Accreditation of Teacher Education: teacher education (B,M,D)

THEA: National Association of Schools of Theatre: theatre (C,A,B, M,D)

THEOL: Association of Theological Schools: theology (M,FP,D)

Starr King School for the Ministry .... CA 66
Westminster Theological Seminary in California .... CA 74
World Mission University .... CA 75
Augustine Institute .... CO 77
Denver Seminary .... CO 79
Iliff School of Theology .... CO 80
St. John Vianney Theological Seminary ... CO 83
Hartford Seminary .... CT 88
Yale University .... CT 90
Catholic University of America, The .... DC 92
Howard University .... DC 93
Pontifical Faculty of the Immaculate Conception at the Dominican House of S tudies .... DC 93
Wesley Theological Seminary .... DC 94
Barry University .... FL 96
Knox Theological Seminary .... FL ... 104
St. Vincent De Paul Regional Seminary ... FL ... 108
Columbia Theological Seminary .... GA .. 119
Emory University .... GA .. 120
@Georgia Christian University .... GA .. 120
Interdenominational Theological Center .... GA .. 123
Mercer University .... GA .. 124
Bexley Seabury .... IL 135
Catholic Theological Union .... IL 136
Chicago Theological Seminary .... IL 137
Garrett-Evangelical Theological Seminary IL 140
Lincoln Christian University .... IL 146
Lutheran School of Theology at Chicago .. IL 147
McCormick Theological Seminary .... IL 147
Meadville Lombard Theological School .... IL 147
Moody Bible Institute .... IL 148
North Park University .... IL 149
Northern Seminary .... IL 150
Trinity International University .... IL 156
University of Chicago .... IL 156
University of Saint Mary of the Lake-Mundelein Seminary .... IL 157
Anabaptist Mennonite Biblical Seminary ... IN 158
Anderson University .... IN 158
Bethany Theological Seminary .... IN 159
Christian Theological Seminary .... IN 160
Concordia Theological Seminary .... IN 160
Earlham College and Earlham School of Religion .... IN 160
Grace College and Seminary .... IN 161
Indiana Wesleyan University .... IN 164
Mid-America Reformed Seminary .... IN 165
Oakland City University .... IN 166
Saint Meinrad School of Theology .... IN 167
University of Notre Dame .... IN 168
University of Dubuque .... IA 177
Wartburg Theological Seminary .... IA 177
Central Baptist Theological Seminary .... KS ... 179
Saint Paul School of Theology .... KS ... 184
Asbury Theological Seminary .... KY ... 186
Baptist Seminary of Kentucky .... KY ... 186
Lexington Theological Seminary .... KY ... 191
Louisville Presbyterian Theological Seminary .... KY ... 191
Southern Baptist Theological Seminary, The .... KY ... 192
New Orleans Baptist Theological Seminary .... LA ... 198
Notre Dame Seminary, Graduate School of Theology .... LA ... 199
Mount St. Mary's University .... MD .. 209
Saint Mary's Seminary and University ...... MD .. 210
Andover Newton Theological School .... MA .. 214
Boston College .... MA .. 216
Boston University .... MA .. 216
Episcopal Divinity School .... MA .. 218
Gordon-Conwell Theological Seminary ..... MA .. 219
Harvard University .... MA .. 219
Hellenic College-Holy Cross Greek Orthodox School of Theology .... MA .. 219
Pope St. John XXIII National Seminary .... MA .. 227
Saint John's Seminary .... MA .. 227
Andrews University .... MI ... 230
Calvin Theological Seminary .... MI ... 232
Cornerstone University .... MI ... 233
Ecumenical Theological Seminary .... MI ... 233
Puritan Reformed Theological Seminary .. MI ... 240
Sacred Heart Major Seminary .... MI ... 240
SS. Cyril and Methodius Seminary .... MI ... 241
Western Theological Seminary .... MI ... 244
Bethel University .... MN .. 244
Luther Seminary .... MN .. 247
Saint John's University .... MN .. 254
United Theological Seminary of the Twin Cities .... MN .. 255
University of Saint Thomas .... MN .. 256
Reformed Theological Seminary .... MS .. 260
Wesley Biblical Seminary .... MS .. 261
Aquinas Institute of Theology .... MO .. 262
Assemblies of God Theological Seminary MO .. 262
Concordia Seminary .... MO .. 263
Covenant Theological Seminary .... MO .. 264
Eden Theological Seminary .... MO .. 265
Kenrick-Glennon Seminary, Kenrick School of Theology .... MO .. 266
Midwestern Baptist Theological Seminary MO .. 268
Nazarene Theological Seminary .... MO .. 269
Urshan Graduate School of Theology .... MO .. 274
Drew University .... NJ ... 291
New Brunswick Theological Seminary ...... NJ ... 293
Princeton Theological Seminary .... NJ ... 294
Seton Hall University .... NJ ... 297
Christ the King Seminary .... NY ... 306
Colgate Rochester Crozer Divinity School NY ... 310
General Theological Seminary .... NY ... 315
New York Theological Seminary .... NY ... 324
Northeastern Seminary .... NY ... 325
Nyack College .... NY ... 325
Saint Bernard's School of Theology & Ministry .... NY ... 328
Saint Joseph's Seminary .... NY ... 329
Saint Vladimir's Orthodox Theological Seminary .... NY ... 329
Union Theological Seminary .... NY ... 338
Campbell University .... NC .. 342
Duke University .... NC .. 343
Gardner-Webb University .... NC .. 344
Hood Theological Seminary .... NC .. 345
Lenoir-Rhyne University .... NC .. 345
Shaw University .... NC .. 355
@Shepherds Theological Seminary .... NC .. 355
Southeastern Baptist Theological Seminary .... NC .. 355
Wake Forest University .... NC .. 359
Ashland University .... OH .. 363
Athenaeum of Ohio .... OH .. 363
Bexley Seabury .... OH .. 364
Cincinnati Christian University .... OH .. 366
Methodist Theological School in Ohio ...... OH .. 372
Payne Theological Seminary .... OH .. 376
Pontifical College Josephinum .... OH .. 376
Saint Mary Seminary and Graduate School of Theology .... OH .. 377
Trinity Lutheran Seminary .... OH .. 378
United Theological Seminary .... OH .. 378
Winebrenner Theological Seminary .... OH .. 381
Oral Roberts University .... OK .. 386
Phillips Theological Seminary .... OK .. 386
George Fox University .... OR .. 391
Mount Angel Seminary .... OR .. 392
Multnomah University .... OR .. 392
Western Seminary .... OR .. 396
Biblical Theological Seminary .... PA ... 398
Byzantine Catholic Seminary of Ss. Cyril and Methodius .... PA ... 399
Evangelical Theological Seminary .... PA ... 403
Lancaster Theological Seminary .... PA ... 408
Lutheran Theological Seminary at Gettysburg .... PA ... 409
Lutheran Theological Seminary at Philadelphia .... PA ... 409
Moravian College .... PA ... 411
Palmer Theological Seminary of Eastern University .... PA ... 412
Pittsburgh Theological Seminary .... PA ... 417
Reformed Episcopal Seminary .... PA ... 417
Reformed Presbyterian Theological Seminary .... PA ... 417
Saint Charles Borromeo Seminary .... PA ... 418
St. Tikhon's Orthodox Theological Seminary .... PA ... 418
Saint Vincent Seminary .... PA ... 419
Trinity Episcopal School for Ministry .... PA ... 421
Westminster Theological Seminary .... PA ... 423
Dominican Study Center of the Caribbean PR ... 532
Evangelical Seminary of Puerto Rico .... PR ... 532
Columbia International University .... SC ... 429
Erskine College .... SC ... 429
Sioux Falls Seminary .... SD ... 436
@Freed-Hardeman University .... TN ... 440
Lipscomb University .... TN ... 441
Memphis Theological Seminary .... TN ... 442
Milligan College .... TN ... 442
Pentecostal Theological Seminary .... TN ... 443
Sewanee: The University of the South ..... TN ... 443
Vanderbilt University .... TN ... 449
Abilene Christian University .... TX ... 449
Austin Presbyterian Theological Seminary. TX ... 452
Baptist Missionary Association Theological Seminary .... TX ... 452
Baylor University .... TX ... 452
@B.H. Carroll Theological Institute .... TX ... 452
Brite Divinity School .... TX ... 453
Dallas Theological Seminary .... TX ... 457
Hardin-Simmons University .... TX ... 458
Houston Graduate School of Theology ..... TX ... 459
@Lubbock Christian University .... TX ... 461
Oblate School of Theology .... TX ... 463
Redeemer Theological Seminary .... TX ... 463
Seminary of the Southwest .... TX ... 465
Southern Methodist University .... TX ... 465
Southwestern Baptist Theological Seminary .... TX ... 466
University of St. Thomas .... TX ... 475
Baptist Theological Seminary at Richmond .... VA ... 487
Eastern Mennonite University .... VA ... 488
John Leland Center for Theological Studies, The .... VA ... 491
Protestant Episcopal Theological Seminary in Virginia .... VA ... 492
Regent University .... VA ... 493
Union Presbyterian Seminary .... VA ... 494
Virginia Union University .... VA ... 500
@Washington University of Virginia .... VA ... 500
@Seattle Pacific University .... WA .. 507
Seattle School of Theology and Psychology, The .... WA .. 507
Seattle University .... WA .. 507
Nashotah House .... WI ... 518
Sacred Heart Seminary and School of Theology .... WI ... 519

TRACS: Transnational Association of Christian Colleges and Schools: christian studies education (C,A,B, M,D)

International Baptist College and Seminary .... AZ 13
Shorter College .... AR 22
Bethesda University of California .... CA 28
California Christian College .... CA 29
#Community Christian College .... CA 40
Epic Bible College & Graduate School ..... CA 43
Evangelia University .... CA 43
Grace Mission University .... CA 45
Oikos University .... CA 55
Shasta Bible College and Graduate School .... CA 64
Southern California Seminary .... CA 65
Veritas Evangelical Seminary .... CA 73
@West Coast Baptist College .... CA 73
World Mission University .... CA 75
Pensacola Christian College .... FL ... 106
Trinity Baptist College .... FL ... 113
University of Fort Lauderdale .... FL ... 114
Beulah Heights University .... GA ... 117
@Brewton-Parker College .... GA ... 118
Georgia Christian University .... GA ... 120
Luther Rice College and Seminary .... GA ... 124
@Reformed University .... GA ... 126
Pacific Islands University .... GU ... 530
New Saint Andrews College .... ID 134
Christian Life College .... IL 137
Morthland College .... IL 148
Mid-America Reformed Seminary .... IN 165
#Faith Theological Seminary .... MD ... 207
Maple Springs Baptist Bible College & Seminary .... MD ... 209
Boston Baptist College .... MA ... 216
@Association Free Lutheran Bible School and Seminary .... MN ... 244
Central Baptist Theological Seminary of Minneapolis .... MN ... 245
@Crossroads College .... MN ... 246
Lutheran Brethren Seminary .... MN ... 247
@Elim Bible Institute .... NY ... 313
Apex School of Theology .... NC ... 341
Charlotte Christian College and Theological Seminary .... NC ... 343
Heritage Bible College .... NC ... 344
Piedmont International University .... NC ... 354
Shepherds Theological Seminary .... NC ... 355
#Southern Evangelical Seminary .... NC ... 355
Randall University .... OK ... 387
Gutenberg College .... OR ... 391
Bob Jones University .... SC ... 427
Clinton College .... SC ... 428
@John Witherspoon College .... SD ... 436
@Crown College of the Bible, The .... TN ... 439
Hiwassee College .... TN ... 440
Oxford Graduate School .... TN ... 443
Visible Music College .... TN ... 449
Bakke Graduate University .... TX ... 452
Grace School of Theology .... TX ... 458
King's University, The .... TX ... 460
Messenger College .... TX ... 461
Paul Quinn College .... TX ... 463
Ivy Christian College .... VA ... 490
Patrick Henry College .... VA ... 492
Virginia Baptist College .... VA ... 496
Virginia Beach Theological Seminary .... VA ... 496
Virginia University of Lynchburg .... VA ... 500
Faith Evangelical College & Seminary ...... WA ... 503

VET: American Veterinary Medical Association: veterinary medicine (FP,D)

Auburn University .... AL 1
#Tuskegee University .... AL 8
University of California-Davis .... CA 69
Western University of Health Sciences ..... CA 74
Colorado State University .... CO 78
University of Florida .... FL ... 112
University of Georgia .... GA ... 128
University of Illinois at Urbana-Champaign IL 157
Purdue University Main Campus .... IN 166
Iowa State University .... IA 169
Kansas State University .... KS ... 182
Louisiana State University and Agricultural and Mechanical College .... LA ... 197
Tufts University .... MA ... 228
Michigan State University .... MI ... 237
University of Minnesota-Twin Cities .... MN .. 255
Mississippi State University .... MS .. 259
University of Missouri - Columbia .... MO .. 273
Cornell University .... NY ... 312
North Carolina State University .... NC ... 357
Ohio State University Main Campus, The . OH ... 375
Oklahoma State University .... OK ... 385
Oregon State University .... OR ... 393
University of Pennsylvania .... PA ... 421
@Lincoln Memorial University .... TN ... 441
University of Tennessee, Knoxville .... TN ... 448
Texas A & M University .... TX ... 468
Virginia Polytechnic Institute and State University .... VA ... 499
Washington State University .... WA .. 508
University of Wisconsin-Madison .... WI ... 519

WC: Western Association of Schools and Colleges, Accrediting Commission for Senior Colleges and Universities

Academy for Jewish Religion .... CA 24
Academy of Art University .... CA 25
Alliant International University-San Diego . CA 25
American Conservatory Theater .... CA 26
American Film Institute Conservatory .... CA 26
American Jewish University .... CA 26
American University of Armenia .... CA 26
Argosy University, Orange County .... CA 27
Art Center College of Design .... CA 27
Ashford University .... CA 27
Azusa Pacific University .... CA 28
Biola University .... CA 28
Brandman University .... CA 28
Broad Center for the Management of School Systems, The .... CA 29
California Baptist University .... CA 29
California College of the Arts .... CA 29
California Institute of Integral Studies ...... CA 30
California Institute of Technology .... CA 30
California Institute of the Arts .... CA 30
California Lutheran University .... CA 31
California Northstate University College of Pharmacy .... CA 31
California Polytechnic State University-San Luis Obispo .... CA 31
California Southern University .... CA 31
California State Polytechnic University-Pomona .... CA 31
California State University-Bakersfield ...... CA 32
California State University Channel Islands .... CA 32
California State University-Chico .... CA 32
California State University-Dominguez Hills .... CA 32
California State University-East Bay .... CA 32
California State University-Fresno .... CA 32
California State University-Fullerton .... CA 33
California State University-Long Beach .... CA 33
California State University-Los Angeles .... CA 33
California State University-Monterey Bay . CA 33
California State University-Northridge ...... CA 34
California State University-Sacramento .... CA 34
California State University-San Bernardino CA 34
California State University-San Marcos .... CA 34
California State University-Stanislaus ...... CA 34
Cedars-Sinai Medical Center Graduate Program in Biomedical Sciences and Tra nslational Medicine .... CA 36
Chapman University .... CA 37
Charles R. Drew University of Medicine & Science .... CA 37
Chicago School of Professional Psychology Los Angeles Campus .... CA 37
City of Hope .... CA 38
Claremont Graduate University .... CA 38
Claremont Lincoln University .... CA 38
Claremont McKenna College .... CA 38
Claremont School of Theology .... CA 39
Cogswell Polytechnical College .... CA 39
@Coleman University .... CA 39
Columbia College Hollywood .... CA 40
Concordia University .... CA 41
CSU Maritime Academy .... CA 33

WJ: Western Association of Schools and Colleges, Accrediting Commission for Community and Junior Colleges

Index of FICE Numbers

Code	Institution	State	Page
001355	Lamar Community College	CO	81
001358	Colorado Mesa University	CO	77
001359	Colorado Northwestern Cmty College	CO	78
001360	Metropolitan State Univ Denver	CO	81
001361	Northeastern Junior College	CO	81
001362	Otero Junior College	CO	82
001363	Regis University	CO	82
001365	Colorado State University-Pueblo	CO	79
001368	Trinidad State Junior College	CO	83
001369	United States Air Force Academy	CO	528
001370	University of Colorado Boulder	CO	83
001371	University of Denver	CO	84
001372	Western State Colorado University	CO	84
001374	Albertus Magnus College	CT	85
001378	Central Connecticut State Univ	CT	85
001379	Connecticut College	CT	87
001380	Western Connecticut State Univ	CT	85
001385	Fairfield University	CT	87
001387	Hartford Seminary	CT	88
001389	Holy Apostles College and Seminary	CT	88
001392	Manchester Community College	CT	86
001393	Mitchell College	CT	88
001397	University of New Haven	CT	90
001398	Northwestern CT Cmty-Tech College	CT	87
001399	Norwalk Community College	CT	87
001401	Post University	CT	88
001402	Quinnipiac University	CT	88
001403	Sacred Heart University	CT	88
001406	Southern Connecticut State Univ	CT	85
001409	University of Saint Joseph	CT	90
001414	Trinity College	CT	89
001415	United States Coast Guard Academy	CT	529
001416	University of Bridgeport	CT	89
001417	University of Connecticut	CT	89
001422	University of Hartford	CT	89
001424	Wesleyan University	CT	90
001425	Eastern Connecticut State Univ	CT	85
001426	Yale University	CT	90
001428	Delaware State University	DE	90
001429	Goldey-Beacom College	DE	91
001431	University of Delaware	DE	91
001433	Wesley College	DE	91
001434	American University	DC	91
001436	Capitol Technology University	MD	206
001437	The Catholic University of America	DC	92
001441	Univ of the District of Columbia	DC	94
001443	Gallaudet University	DC	92
001444	George Washington University	DC	92
001445	Georgetown University	DC	92
001448	Howard University	DC	93
001459	Strayer University	DC	93
001460	Trinity Washington University	DC	94
001464	Wesley Theological Seminary	DC	94
001466	Barry University	FL	96
001467	Bethune Cookman University	FL	96
001468	St. Thomas University	FL	108
001469	Florida Institute of Technology	FL	100
001470	Eastern Florida State College	FL	98
001471	College of Central Florida	FL	97
001472	Chipola College	FL	97
001475	Daytona State College	FL	98
001477	Florida SouthWestern State College	FL	101
001478	Edward Waters College	FL	98
001479	Embry-Riddle Aeronautical Univ	FL	99
001480	Florida A and M University	FL	110
001481	Florida Atlantic University	FL	110
001482	Florida College	FL	100
001484	Florida State College Jacksonville	FL	101
001485	Florida Keys Community College	FL	100
001486	Florida Memorial University	FL	101
001487	Eckerd College	FL	98
001488	Florida Southern College	FL	101
001489	Florida State University	FL	111
001490	Gulf Coast State College	FL	102
001493	Indian River State College	FL	103
001495	Jacksonville University	FL	103
001497	Jones College	FL	103
001500	Broward College	FL	96
001501	Florida Gateway College	FL	100
001502	Lake-Sumter State College	FL	104
001504	State Col of FL, Manatee-Sarasota	FL	110
001505	Lynn University	FL	104
001506	Miami Dade College	FL	105
001507	New College of Florida	FL	111
001508	North Florida Community College	FL	105
001509	Nova Southeastern University	FL	105
001510	Northwest Florida State College	FL	105
001512	Palm Beach State College	FL	106
001513	Pensacola State College	FL	106
001514	Polk State College	FL	106
001515	Rollins College	FL	107
001519	Santa Fe College	FL	109
001520	Seminole State College of Florida	FL	109
001521	Southeastern University	FL	109
001522	South Florida State College	FL	109
001523	St. Johns River State College	FL	108
001526	Saint Leo University	FL	108
001528	St. Petersburg College	FL	108
001531	Stetson University	FL	113
001533	Tallahassee Community College	FL	113
001535	University of Florida	FL	112
001536	University of Miami	FL	114
001537	University of South Florida	FL	112
001538	University of Tampa	FL	114
001540	Webber International University	FL	115
001541	Abraham Baldwin Agricultural Coll	GA	115
001542	Agnes Scott College	GA	115
001543	Darton State College	GA	120
001544	Albany State University	GA	115
001545	Andrew College	GA	116
001546	Armstrong State University	GA	116
001547	Point University	GA	126
001554	Berry College	GA	117
001555	Thomas University	GA	128
001556	Brenau University	GA	118
001557	Brewton-Parker College	GA	118
001558	College of Coastal Georgia	GA	119
001559	Clark Atlanta University	GA	118
001560	Columbia Theological Seminary	GA	119
001561	Columbus State University	GA	119
001563	Emmanuel College	GA	120
001564	Emory University	GA	120
001566	Fort Valley State University	GA	120
001568	Interdenominational Theol Center	GA	123
001569	Georgia Institute of Technology	GA	121
001571	Georgia Military College	GA	121
001572	Georgia Southern University	GA	122
001573	Georgia Southwestern State Univ	GA	122
001574	Georgia State University	GA	122
001575	Gordon State College	GA	122
001577	Kennesaw State University	GA	123
001578	LaGrange College	GA	123
001579	Augusta University	GA	117
001580	Mercer University	GA	124
001582	Morehouse College	GA	124
001585	University of North Georgia	GA	128
001586	Oglethorpe University	GA	125
001587	Paine College	GA	125
001588	Piedmont College	GA	125
001589	Reinhardt University	GA	126
001590	Savannah State University	GA	126
001591	Shorter University	GA	127
001592	South Georgia State College	GA	127
001594	Spelman College	GA	128
001596	Toccoa Falls College	GA	128
001597	Truett McConnell College	GA	128
001598	University of Georgia	GA	128
001599	Valdosta State University	GA	129
001600	Wesleyan College	GA	129
001601	University of West Georgia	GA	129
001602	Georgia College & State University	GA	121
001604	Young Harris College	GA	130
001605	Chaminade University of Honolulu	HI	130
001606	Brigham Young University Hawaii	HI	130
001610	University of Hawaii at Manoa	HI	131
001611	University of Hawaii at Hilo	HI	131
001612	Univ of Hawaii Honolulu Cmty Col	HI	132
001613	Kapiolani Community College	HI	131
001614	Univ of Hawaii Kauai Cmty College	HI	132
001615	Univ of Hawaii Maui College	HI	132
001616	Boise State University	ID	132
001617	The College of Idaho	ID	133
001619	College of Southern Idaho	ID	133
001620	Idaho State University	ID	133
001621	Lewis-Clark State College	ID	134
001623	North Idaho College	ID	134
001624	Northwest Nazarene University	ID	134
001625	Brigham Young University-Idaho	ID	132
001626	University of Idaho	ID	134
001628	American Academy of Art	IL	134
001632	Aquinas Institute of Theology	MO	262
001633	Augustana College	IL	135
001634	Aurora University	IL	135
001636	Southwestern Illinois College	IL	155
001637	Bethany Theological Seminary	IN	159
001638	Black Hawk College	IL	135
001639	Blackburn College	IL	135
001640	Prairie State College	IL	151
001641	Bradley University	IL	136
001643	Spoon River College	IL	155
001647	City Colleges of Chicago	IL	137
001648	City Cols of Chicago Harry Truman	IL	137
001649	City Cols of Chicago RJ Daley Col	IL	137
001650	Malcolm X College	IL	138
001652	City Cols of Chicago Washington Col	IL	137
001654	City Cols of Chicago Kennedy-King	IL	137
001655	City Cols of Chicago W Wright Col	IL	137
001657	Midwestern University	IL	148
001659	Rosalind Franklin U of Med/Science	IL	153
001661	Chicago Theological Seminary	IL	137
001663	Spertus Inst for Jewish Lrng & Ldrs	IL	155
001664	University of St. Francis	IL	157
001665	Columbia College Chicago	IL	138
001666	Concordia University Chicago	IL	138
001669	Danville Area Community College	IL	139
001671	DePaul University	IL	139
001672	DeVry University - Home Office	IL	139
001674	Eastern Illinois University	IL	139
001675	Elgin Community College	IL	140
001676	Elmhurst College	IL	140
001678	Eureka College	IL	140
001681	Highland Community College	IL	141
001682	Garrett-Evangelical Theol Seminary	IL	140
001684	Greenville College	IL	140
001685	Hebrew Theological College	IL	141
001688	Illinois College	IL	141
001689	Illinois College of Optometry	IL	142
001691	Illinois Institute of Technology	IL	142
001692	Illinois State University	IL	143
001693	Northeastern Illinois University	IL	149
001694	Chicago State University	IL	136
001696	Illinois Wesleyan University	IL	143
001698	John Marshall Law School	IL	143
001699	Joliet Junior College	IL	144
001700	Judson University	IL	144
001701	Kaskaskia College	IL	144
001703	Kendall College	IL	144
001704	Knox College	IL	145
001705	Illinois Valley Community College	IL	143
001706	Lake Forest College	IL	145
001707	Lewis University	IL	145
001708	Lincoln Christian University	IL	146
001709	Lincoln College	IL	146
001710	Loyola University Chicago	IL	146
001712	Lutheran School of Theology Chicago	IL	147
001716	MacCormac College	IL	147
001717	MacMurray College	IL	147
001721	McCormick Theological Seminary	IL	147
001722	McKendree University	IL	147
001723	Meadville Lombard Theol School	IL	147
001724	Millikin University	IL	148
001725	Monmouth College	IL	148
001727	Moody Bible Institute	IL	148
001728	Morton College	IL	149
001732	National Univ of Health Sciences	IL	149
001733	National-Louis University	IL	149
001734	North Central College	IL	149
001735	North Park University	IL	149
001736	Northern Seminary	IL	150
001737	Northern Illinois University	IL	150
001739	Northwestern University	IL	150
001741	Olivet Nazarene University	IL	150
001742	Illinois Eastern CC Olney Central	IL	142
001744	Principia College	IL	151
001745	Quincy University	IL	151
001746	Robert Morris University - Illinois	IL	152
001747	Rock Valley College	IL	152
001748	Rockford University	IL	152
001749	Roosevelt University	IL	152
001750	Dominican University	IL	139
001752	Sauk Valley Community College	IL	153
001753	School of the Art Institute Chicago	IL	154
001754	Bexley Seabury	IL	135
001756	Shimer College	IL	154
001757	Southeastern Illinois College	IL	154
001758	Southern Illinois Univ Carbondale	IL	154
001759	Southern Illinois Univ Edwardsville	IL	155
001765	Univ of Saint Mary Lake-Mundelein	IL	157
001767	Benedictine University	IL	135
001768	Saint Xavier University	IL	153
001769	South Suburban Col of Cook County	IL	154
001771	Trinity Christian College	IL	155
001772	Trinity International University	IL	156
001773	Triton College	IL	156
001774	University of Chicago	IL	156
001775	Univ of Illinois Urbana-Champaign	IL	157
001776	University of Illinois at Chicago	IL	156
001778	VanderCook College of Music	IL	157
001779	Illinois Eastern CC Wabash Valley	IL	142
001780	Western Illinois University	IL	158
001781	Wheaton College	IL	158
001783	Worsham College of Mortuary Science	IL	158
001784	Ancilla College	IN	158
001785	Anderson University	IN	158
001786	Ball State University	IN	159
001787	Bethel College	IN	159
001788	Butler University	IN	159
001789	Christian Theological Seminary	IN	160
001792	DePauw University	IN	160
001793	Earlham Col/Earlham Sch of Rel	IN	160
001795	University of Evansville	IN	167
001798	Franklin College of Indiana	IN	160
001799	Goshen College	IN	161
001800	Grace College and Seminary	IN	161
001801	Hanover College	IN	161
001803	Huntington University	IN	161
001804	University of Indianapolis	IN	168
001805	Indiana Tech	IN	162
001807	Indiana State University	IN	162
001808	University of Southern Indiana	IN	168
001809	Indiana University Bloomington	IN	162
001811	Indiana University East	IN	162
001813	Indiana Univ-Purdue Un Indianapolis	IN	163
001814	Indiana University Kokomo	IN	163
001815	Indiana University Northwest	IN	163
001816	Indiana University South Bend	IN	163
001817	Indiana University Southeast	IN	163
001820	Manchester University	IN	165
001821	Marian University	IN	165
001822	Indiana Wesleyan University	IN	164
001823	Anabaptist Mennonite Biblical Sem	IN	158
001824	Oakland City University	IN	166
001825	Purdue University Main Campus	IN	166
001827	Purdue University Northwest	IN	166
001828	Indiana Univ-Purdue Univ Fort Wayne	IN	163
001830	Rose-Hulman Institute of Technology	IN	166

Code	Institution	State	Page
002259	Eastern Michigan University	MI	233
002260	Ferris State University	MI	233
002261	Mott Community College	MI	238
002262	Kettering University	MI	236
002263	Glen Oaks Community College	MI	234
002264	Gogebic Community College	MI	234
002265	Grace Bible College	MI	234
002266	Cornerstone University	MI	233
002267	Grand Rapids Community College	MI	234
002268	Grand Valley State University	MI	234
002269	Great Lakes Christian College	MI	235
002270	Henry Ford College	MI	235
002272	Hillsdale College	MI	235
002273	Hope College	MI	235
002274	Jackson College	MI	235
002275	Kalamazoo College	MI	235
002276	Kellogg Community College	MI	236
002277	Lake Michigan College	MI	236
002278	Lansing Community College	MI	237
002279	Lawrence Technological University	MI	237
002282	Madonna University	MI	237
002284	Marygrove College	MI	237
002288	Rochester College	MI	240
002290	Michigan State University	MI	237
002292	Michigan Technological University	MI	238
002293	Lake Superior State University	MI	236
002294	Monroe County Community College	MI	238
002295	Montcalm Community College	MI	238
002297	Muskegon Community College	MI	238
002299	North Central Michigan College	MI	239
002301	Northern Michigan University	MI	239
002302	Northwestern Michigan College	MI	239
002303	Oakland Community College	MI	239
002307	Oakland University	MI	239
002308	Olivet College	MI	240
002310	St. Clair County Community College	MI	240
002311	Kuyper College	MI	236
002313	Sacred Heart Major Seminary	MI	240
002314	Saginaw Valley State University	MI	240
002315	Schoolcraft College	MI	240
002316	Siena Heights University	MI	241
002317	Southwestern Michigan College	MI	241
002318	Spring Arbor University	MI	241
002322	Finlandia University	MI	234
002323	University of Detroit Mercy	MI	241
002325	University of Michigan-Ann Arbor	MI	241
002326	University of Michigan-Dearborn	MI	242
002327	University of Michigan-Flint	MI	242
002328	Washtenaw Community College	MI	242
002329	Wayne State University	MI	243
002330	Western Michigan University	MI	243
002331	Western Theological Seminary	MI	244
002332	Anoka-Ramsey Community College	MN	248
002334	Augsburg College	MN	244
002335	Riverland Community College	MN	251
002336	Bemidji State University	MN	248
002337	Bethany Lutheran College	MN	244
002339	Central Lakes College	MN	248
002340	Carleton College	MN	245
002341	College of Saint Benedict	MN	245
002342	St. Catherine University	MN	254
002343	The College of Saint Scholastica	MN	245
002345	University of Saint Thomas	MN	256
002346	Concordia College	MN	246
002347	Concordia University, St. Paul	MN	246
002350	Vermilion Community College	MN	252
002353	Gustavus Adolphus College	MN	246
002354	Hamline University	MN	247
002355	Hibbing Community College	MN	249
002356	Itasca Community College	MN	249
002357	Luther Seminary	MN	247
002358	Macalester College	MN	247
002360	Minnesota State University, Mankato	MN	250
002361	Martin Luther College	MN	247
002362	Minneapolis Cmty & Tech College	MN	250
002365	Minneapolis College of Art & Design	MN	247
002366	Crossroads College	MN	246
002367	Minnesota State University Moorhead	MN	250
002369	North Central University	MN	253
002370	North Hennepin Community College	MN	251
002371	University of Northwestern St. Paul	MN	256
002373	Rochester Community & Tech College	MN	251
002375	Southwest Minnesota State Univ	MN	252
002377	St. Cloud State University	MN	252
002379	Saint John's University	MN	254
002380	St Mary's University of Minnesota	MN	254
002382	St. Olaf College	MN	254
002383	Crown College	MN	246
002385	Northland Community & Tech College	MN	251
002386	United Theol Seminary-Twin Cities	MN	255
002388	University of Minnesota Duluth	MN	255
002389	University of Minnesota-Morris	MN	255
002391	Mitchell Hamline School of Law	MN	253
002393	Minnesota State Col-Southeast Tech	MN	250
002394	Winona State University	MN	252
002396	Alcorn State University	MS	256
002397	Belhaven University	MS	256
002398	Blue Mountain College	MS	257
002401	Coahoma Community College	MS	257
002402	Copiah-Lincoln Community College	MS	257
002403	Delta State University	MS	257
002404	East Central Community College	MS	257
002405	East Mississippi Community College	MS	257
002407	Hinds Community College	MS	258
002408	Holmes Community College	MS	258
002409	Itawamba Community College	MS	258
002410	Jackson State University	MS	258
002411	Jones County Junior College	MS	258
002413	Meridian Community College	MS	258
002414	Millsaps College	MS	258
002415	Mississippi College	MS	259
002416	Mississippi Delta Community College	MS	259
002417	Mississippi Gulf Coast Cmty College	MS	259
002422	Mississippi University for Women	MS	259
002423	Mississippi State University	MS	259
002424	Mississippi Valley State University	MS	260
002426	Northeast Mississippi Cmty College	MS	260
002427	Northwest Mississippi Cmty College	MS	260
002430	Pearl River Community College	MS	260
002433	Rust College	MS	260
002435	Southeastern Baptist College	MS	260
002436	Southwest Mississippi Cmty College	MS	260
002439	Tougaloo College	MS	261
002440	University of Mississippi	MS	261
002441	University of Southern Mississippi	MS	261
002447	William Carey University	MS	261
002449	Avila University	MO	262
002450	Calvary University	MO	262
002453	Central Methodist University	MO	263
002454	University of Central Missouri	MO	273
002456	Columbia College	MO	263
002457	Concordia Seminary	MO	263
002458	Cottey College	MO	264
002459	Crowder College	MO	264
002460	Culver-Stockton College	MO	264
002461	Drury University	MO	264
002462	Eden Theological Seminary	MO	265
002463	Evangel University	MO	265
002464	Fontbonne University	MO	265
002466	Harris-Stowe State University	MO	265
002467	Conception Seminary College	MO	263
002468	Jefferson College	MO	266
002471	St Louis Cmty Col Center	MO	271
002473	Kansas City Art Institute	MO	266
002474	Kansas City Univ of Med & BioSci	MO	266
002476	Kenrick-Glennon Seminary	MO	266
002477	A. T. Still Univ of Health Sciences	MO	262
002479	Lincoln University	MO	266
002480	Lindenwood University	MO	266
002482	Maryville University of Saint Louis	MO	267
002484	Metropolitan Cmty Col-Penn Valley	MO	267
002485	Midwestern Baptist Theol Seminary	MO	268
002486	Mineral Area College	MO	268
002488	Missouri Southern State University	MO	268
002489	Missouri Valley College	MO	269
002490	Missouri Western State University	MO	269
002491	Moberly Area Community College	MO	269
002494	Nazarene Theological Seminary	MO	269
002495	Truman State University	MO	273
002496	Northwest Missouri State University	MO	269
002498	Park University	MO	270
002499	Rockhurst University	MO	270
002500	College of the Ozarks	MO	263
002501	Southeast Missouri State University	MO	272
002502	Southwest Baptist University	MO	272
002503	Missouri State University	MO	268
002504	St. Louis College of Pharmacy	MO	271
002506	Saint Louis University	MO	271
002509	Saint Paul School of Theology	KS	184
002512	Stephens College	MO	272
002514	North Central Missouri College	MO	269
002515	Univ of Missouri System Admin	MO	273
002516	University of Missouri - Columbia	MO	273
002517	Missouri Univ of Science Tech	MO	274
002518	Univ of Missouri - Kansas City	MO	273
002519	Univ of Missouri - Saint Louis	MO	274
002520	Washington University in St. Louis	MO	274
002521	Webster University	MO	275
002522	Wentworth Military Academy & Col	MO	275
002523	Westminster College	MO	275
002524	William Jewell College	MO	275
002525	William Woods University	MO	275
002526	Carroll College	MT	276
002527	University of Great Falls	MT	278
002528	Miles Community College	MT	276
002529	Dawson Community College	MT	276
002530	Montana State University - Billings	MT	277
002531	Montana Tech of the Univ of Montana	MT	277
002532	Montana State University	MT	277
002533	Montana State University - Northern	MT	277
002534	Rocky Mountain College	MT	278
002536	University of Montana - Missoula	MT	276
002537	The University of Montana Western	MT	277
002539	Chadron State College	NE	281
002540	College of Saint Mary	NE	279
002541	Concordia University	NE	279
002542	Creighton University	NE	279
002544	Doane University	NE	280
002547	Grace University	NE	280
002548	Hastings College	NE	280
002551	University of Nebraska at Kearney	NE	282
002553	Midland University	NE	280
002554	University of Nebraska at Omaha	NE	283
002555	Nebraska Wesleyan University	NE	281
002557	Mid-Plains Community College	NE	280
002559	Peru State College	NE	281
002560	Western Nebraska Community College	NE	283
002563	Union College	NE	282
002565	University of Nebraska - Lincoln	NE	282
002566	Wayne State College	NE	281
002567	York College	NE	283
002568	University of Nevada, Reno	NV	285
002569	University of Nevada, Las Vegas	NV	284
002572	Colby-Sawyer College	NH	285
002573	Dartmouth College	NH	286
002575	Franklin Pierce University	NH	287
002579	New England College	NH	287
002580	Southern New Hampshire University	NH	287
002581	NHTI-Concord's Community College	NH	286
002582	Manchester Community College	NH	286
002583	Great Bay Community College	NH	286
002586	Rivier University	NH	287
002587	Saint Anselm College	NH	287
002589	University of New Hampshire	NH	288
002590	Keene State College	NH	288
002591	Plymouth State University	NH	288
002595	Assumption College for Sisters	NJ	288
002596	Atlantic Cape Community College	NJ	288
002597	Bloomfield College	NJ	289
002598	Caldwell University	NJ	290
002599	Centenary College	NJ	290
002600	College of Saint Elizabeth	NJ	290
002601	Cumberland County College	NJ	290
002603	Drew University	NJ	291
002607	Fairleigh Dickinson University	NJ	291
002608	Georgian Court University	NJ	292
002609	Rowan University	NJ	295
002610	Felician University	NJ	291
002613	New Jersey City University	NJ	293
002615	Middlesex County College	NJ	292
002616	Monmouth University	NJ	292
002617	Montclair State University	NJ	293
002619	New Brunswick Theological Seminary	NJ	293
002621	New Jersey Institute of Technology	NJ	293
002622	Kean University	NJ	292
002624	Ocean County College	NJ	293
002625	William Paterson University of NJ	NJ	298
002626	Princeton Theological Seminary	NJ	294
002627	Princeton University	NJ	294
002628	Rider University	NJ	295
002629	Rutgers State Univ Central Office	NJ	295
002631	Rutgers State Univ - Newark	NJ	296
002632	Seton Hall University	NJ	297
002638	Saint Peter's University	NJ	296
002639	Stevens Institute of Technology	NJ	297
002642	The College of New Jersey	NJ	290
002643	Union County College	NJ	298
002649	Santa Fe Univ of Art and Design	NM	302
002650	University of the Southwest	NM	302
002651	Eastern New Mexico University	NM	299
002653	New Mexico Highlands University	NM	300
002654	New Mexico Inst of Mining & Tech	NM	300
002655	New Mexico Junior College	NM	300
002656	New Mexico Military Institute	NM	300
002657	NM State University-Main Campus	NM	300
002658	NM State University-Alamogordo	NM	301
002659	NM State University-Carlsbad	NM	301
002660	San Juan College	NM	301
002661	Eastern New Mexico Univ - Roswell	NM	299
002663	Univ of New Mexico Main Campus	NM	302
002664	Western New Mexico University	NM	303
002665	Vaughn Col of Aeronautics & Tech	NY	339
002666	Adelphi University	NY	303
002668	Alfred University	NY	303
002669	Bank Street College of Education	NY	304
002670	Summit University of Pennsylvania	PA	419
002671	Bard College	NY	304
002674	New York Theological Seminary	NY	324
002677	Brooklyn Law School	NY	305
002678	Bryant & Stratton College	NY	306
002681	Canisius College	NY	306
002685	Cazenovia College	NY	306
002687	CUNY Brooklyn College	NY	307
002688	CUNY City College	NY	307
002689	CUNY Hunter College	NY	308
002690	CUNY Queens College	NY	309
002691	CUNY Borough of Manhattan CC	NY	307
002692	CUNY Bronx Community College	NY	307
002693	CUNY John Jay Col Criminal Justice	NY	308
002694	CUNY Kingsborough Cmty College	NY	308
002696	NYC Col of Tech/City Univ of NY	NY	309
002697	CUNY Queensborough Cmty Col	NY	309
002698	College of Staten Island CUNY	NY	307
002699	Clarkson University	NY	310
002700	Colgate Roch Crozer Divinity School	NY	310
002701	Colgate University	NY	310
002703	College of Mount Saint Vincent	NY	310
002704	The College of New Rochelle	NY	311
002705	The College of Saint Rose	NY	311
002707	Columbia University in City of NY	NY	311
002708	Barnard College	NY	304
002709	Concordia College	NY	311
002710	Cooper Union	NY	311
002711	Cornell University	NY	312
002712	D'Youville College	NY	313
002713	Dominican College of Blauvelt	NY	312

Code	Institution	State	Page
003193	Eastern Oregon University	OR	391
003194	George Fox University	OR	391
003196	Lane Community College	OR	391
003197	Lewis and Clark College	OR	392
003198	Linfield College	OR	392
003199	Marylhurst University	OR	392
003203	Mount Angel Seminary	OR	392
003204	Mt. Hood Community College	OR	392
003206	Multnomah University	OR	392
003207	Pacific Northwest College of Art	OR	394
003208	Northwest Christian University	OR	393
003209	Western Oregon University	OR	396
003210	Oregon State University	OR	393
003211	Oregon Institute of Technology	OR	393
003212	Pacific University	OR	394
003213	Portland Community College	OR	394
003216	Portland State University	OR	394
003217	Reed College	OR	394
003218	Chemeketa Community College	OR	390
003219	Southern Oregon University	OR	395
003220	Southwestern Oregon Community Col	OR	395
003221	Treasure Valley Community College	OR	395
003222	Umpqua Community College	OR	395
003223	University of Oregon	OR	395
003224	University of Portland	OR	396
003225	Warner Pacific College	OR	396
003227	Willamette University	OR	396
003228	Bryn Athyn Col of the New Church	PA	398
003229	Albright College	PA	396
003230	Allegheny College	PA	397
003231	Community College of Allegheny Cty	PA	401
003233	Alvernia University	PA	397
003235	Arcadia University	PA	397
003237	Bryn Mawr College	PA	398
003238	Bucknell University	PA	398
003239	Bucks County Community College	PA	399
003240	Butler County Community College	PA	399
003241	Cabrini University	PA	399
003242	Carnegie Mellon University	PA	400
003243	Cedar Crest College	PA	400
003244	Chatham University	PA	400
003245	Chestnut Hill College	PA	400
003247	Misericordia University	PA	410
003249	Community College of Philadelphia	PA	401
003251	Curtis Institute of Music	PA	401
003252	Delaware Valley University	PA	402
003253	Dickinson College	PA	402
003256	Drexel University	PA	402
003258	Duquesne University	PA	403
003259	Eastern University	PA	403
003260	Palmer Theol Sem of Eastern Univ	PA	412
003262	Elizabethtown College	PA	403
003263	Evangelical Theological Seminary	PA	403
003265	Franklin & Marshall College	PA	403
003266	Gannon University	PA	404
003267	Geneva College	PA	404
003268	Gettysburg College	PA	404
003269	Grove City College	PA	404
003270	Gwynedd Mercy University	PA	404
003272	Harcum College	PA	405
003273	Harrisburg Area Community College	PA	405
003274	Haverford College	PA	405
003275	Holy Family University	PA	405
003276	Immaculata University	PA	406
003277	Indiana University of Pennsylvania	PA	415
003279	Juniata College	PA	406
003280	Keystone College	PA	406
003282	King's College	PA	406
003283	Lackawanna College	PA	407
003284	Lafayette College	PA	407
003285	Lancaster Bible College	PA	407
003286	Lancaster Theological Seminary	PA	408
003287	La Salle University	PA	407
003288	Lebanon Valley College	PA	408
003289	Lehigh University	PA	408
003290	Lincoln University	PA	409
003291	Lutheran Theol Seminary Gettysburg	PA	409
003292	Lutheran Theol Seminary at Phila	PA	409
003293	Lycoming College	PA	409
003294	Manor College	PA	409
003296	Marywood University	PA	409
003297	Mercyhurst University	PA	410
003298	Messiah College	PA	410
003300	Moore College of Art and Design	PA	411
003301	Moravian College	PA	411
003302	Mount Aloysius College	PA	411
003303	Carlow University	PA	400
003304	Muhlenberg College	PA	411
003306	University of Valley Forge	PA	422
003309	Peirce College	PA	412
003311	Salus University	PA	419
003313	Widener University	PA	423
003315	Bloomsburg Univ of Pennsylvania	PA	414
003316	California University of PA	PA	414
003317	Cheyney University of Pennsylvania	PA	414
003318	Clarion University of Pennsylvania	PA	414
003320	East Stroudsburg University of PA	PA	414
003321	Edinboro University	PA	415
003322	Kutztown University of Pennsylvania	PA	415
003323	Lock Haven University	PA	415
003324	Mansfield University of PA	PA	415
003325	Millersville University of PA	PA	415
003326	Shippensburg University of PA	PA	416
003327	Slippery Rock University of PA	PA	416
003328	West Chester University of PA	PA	416
003329	Penn State University Park	PA	412
003350	The University of the Arts	PA	421
003351	Cairn University	PA	399
003352	Philadelphia Col of Osteopathic Med	PA	416
003353	Univ of Sciences in Philadelphia	PA	422
003354	Philadelphia University	PA	416
003356	Pittsburgh Theological Seminary	PA	417
003357	Point Park University	PA	417
003358	Reformed Presbyterian Theo Seminary	PA	417
003359	Robert Morris University	PA	418
003360	Rosemont College	PA	418
003362	Seton Hill University	PA	419
003364	Saint Charles Borromeo Seminary	PA	418
003366	Saint Francis University	PA	418
003367	Saint Joseph's University	PA	418
003368	Saint Vincent College	PA	419
003369	Susquehanna University	PA	419
003370	Swarthmore College	PA	419
003371	Temple University	PA	420
003376	Thiel College	PA	420
003378	University of Pennsylvania	PA	421
003379	University of Pittsburgh	PA	421
003384	The University of Scranton	PA	422
003385	Ursinus College	PA	422
003386	Valley Forge Military College	PA	422
003388	Villanova University	PA	422
003389	Washington & Jefferson College	PA	422
003391	Waynesburg University	PA	423
003392	Westminster College	PA	423
003393	Westminster Theological Seminary	PA	423
003394	Wilkes University	PA	423
003395	Pennsylvania College of Technology	PA	413
003396	Wilson College	PA	424
003399	York College of Pennsylvania	PA	424
003401	Brown University	RI	424
003402	Bryant University	RI	424
003404	Johnson & Wales University	RI	425
003406	Providence College	RI	425
003407	Rhode Island College	RI	425
003408	Community College of Rhode Island	RI	425
003409	Rhode Island School of Design	RI	426
003410	Roger Williams University	RI	426
003411	Salve Regina University	RI	426
003413	Naval War College	RI	528
003414	University of Rhode Island	RI	426
003417	Allen University	SC	427
003418	Anderson University	SC	427
003419	Charleston Southern University	SC	427
003420	Benedict College	SC	427
003421	Bob Jones University	SC	427
003422	Southern Wesleyan University	SC	432
003423	The Citadel Military College of SC	SC	428
003424	Claflin University	SC	428
003425	Clemson University	SC	428
003426	University of South Carolina Sumter	SC	434
003427	Coker College	SC	428
003428	College of Charleston	SC	428
003429	Columbia International University	SC	429
003430	Columbia College	SC	429
003431	Converse College	SC	429
003432	Erskine College	SC	429
003434	Furman University	SC	430
003435	Lander University	SC	430
003436	Limestone College	SC	430
003438	Medical Univ of South Carolina	SC	431
003439	Morris College	SC	431
003440	Newberry College	SC	431
003441	North Greenville University	SC	431
003445	Presbyterian College	SC	432
003446	South Carolina State University	SC	432
003447	Spartanburg Methodist College	SC	433
003448	Univ of South Carolina-Columbia	SC	433
003449	University of South Carolina Aiken	SC	433
003450	Univ of South Carolina Beaufort	SC	434
003451	Coastal Carolina University	SC	428
003454	Univ of South Carolina Salkehatchie	SC	434
003455	Voorhees College	SC	434
003456	Winthrop University	SC	435
003457	Wofford College	SC	435
003458	Augustana University	SD	435
003459	Black Hills State University	SD	437
003461	Dakota Wesleyan University	SD	435
003463	Dakota State University	SD	437
003465	Mount Marty College	SD	436
003466	Northern State University	SD	437
003467	Presentation College	SD	436
003469	University of Sioux Falls	SD	438
003470	South Dakota Sch of Mines & Tech	SD	437
003471	South Dakota State University	SD	437
003474	The University of South Dakota	SD	437
003477	Aquinas College	TN	438
003478	Austin Peay State University	TN	444
003479	Belmont University	TN	438
003480	Bethel University	TN	438
003481	Carson-Newman University	TN	439
003482	Christian Brothers University	TN	439
003483	Columbia State Community College	TN	446
003484	Covenant College	GA	119
003485	Cumberland University	TN	439
003486	Lipscomb University	TN	441
003487	East Tennessee State University	TN	444
003490	Fisk University	TN	439
003492	Freed-Hardeman University	TN	440
003494	Hiwassee College	TN	440
003495	Johnson University	TN	440
003496	King University	TN	440
003499	Lane College	TN	440
003500	Lee University	TN	441
003501	LeMoyne-Owen College	TN	441
003502	Lincoln Memorial University	TN	441
003504	Martin Methodist College	TN	441
003505	Maryville College	TN	441
003506	Meharry Medical College	TN	442
003507	Memphis College of Art	TN	442
003509	The University of Memphis	TN	445
003510	Middle Tennessee State University	TN	444
003511	Milligan College	TN	442
003517	Southern College of Optometry	TN	444
003518	Southern Adventist University	TN	444
003519	Rhodes College	TN	443
003522	Tennessee State University	TN	445
003523	Tennessee Technological University	TN	445
003525	Tennessee Wesleyan College	TN	447
003526	Trevecca Nazarene University	TN	447
003527	Tusculum College	TN	447
003528	Union University	TN	448
003529	Univ of Tennessee Chattanooga	TN	448
003530	University of Tennessee, Knoxville	TN	448
003531	University of Tennessee at Martin	TN	448
003534	Sewanne: The University of the South	TN	443
003535	Vanderbilt University	TN	449
003536	Bryan College	TN	439
003537	Abilene Christian University	TX	449
003539	Alvin Community College	TX	450
003540	Amarillo College	TX	450
003541	Angelo State University	TX	472
003543	Austin College	TX	451
003544	Austin Presbyterian Theol Seminary	TX	452
003545	Baylor University	TX	452
003546	Coastal Bend College	TX	454
003549	Blinn College	TX	452
003553	Cisco College	TX	454
003554	Clarendon College	TX	454
003556	Commonwealth Inst Funeral Service	TX	455
003557	Concordia University Texas	TX	455
003558	North Central Texas College	TX	462
003560	Dallas Baptist University	TX	455
003561	Cedar Valley College	TX	456
003562	Dallas Theological Seminary	TX	457
003563	Del Mar College	TX	457
003564	East Texas Baptist University	TX	457
003565	Texas A & M University - Commerce	TX	468
003566	Seminary of the Southwest	TX	465
003568	Frank Phillips College	TX	458
003570	Grayson College	TX	458
003571	Hardin-Simmons University	TX	458
003572	Trinity Valley Community College	TX	473
003573	Hill College	TX	458
003574	Howard College	TX	459
003575	Howard Payne University	TX	459
003576	Houston Baptist University	TX	458
003577	Huston-Tillotson University	TX	459
003578	University of the Incarnate Word	TX	474
003579	Jacksonville College	TX	460
003580	Kilgore College	TX	460
003581	Lamar University	TX	471
003582	Laredo Community College	TX	460
003583	Lee College	TX	460
003584	LeTourneau University	TX	460
003586	Lubbock Christian University	TX	461
003588	University of Mary Hardin-Baylor	TX	474
003590	McLennan Community College	TX	461
003591	McMurry University	TX	461
003592	Midwestern State University	TX	462
003593	Navarro College	TX	462
003594	University of North Texas	TX	475
003595	Oblate School of Theology	TX	463
003596	Odessa College	TX	463
003598	Our Lady of the Lake University	TX	463
003599	Univ of Texas Rio Grande Valley	TX	476
003600	Panola College	TX	463
003601	Paris Junior College	TX	463
003602	Paul Quinn College	TX	463
003603	Ranger College	TX	463
003604	Rice University	TX	464
003606	Sam Houston State University	TX	471
003607	Alamo Cmty Coll Dist Central Office	TX	450
003608	St. Philip's College	TX	450
003609	San Jacinto College Central	TX	464
003610	Schreiner University	TX	465
003611	South Plains College	TX	465
003612	University of Houston - Downtown	TX	474
003613	Southern Methodist University	TX	465
003614	Southwest Texas Junior College	TX	466
003615	Texas State University	TX	471
003616	Southwestern Assemblies of God Univ	TX	466
003617	Southwestern Baptist Theol Seminary	TX	466
003618	Southwestern Christian College	TX	466
003619	Southwestern Adventist University	TX	466
003620	Southwestern University	TX	466
003621	St. Edward's University	TX	464

004707 .... Covenant Theological Seminary .... MO 264
004711 .... State Technical College of Missouri .... MO 272
004713 .... Three Rivers Community College .... MO 273
004731 .... Daniel Webster College .... NH 286
004736 .... Bergen Community College .... NJ 289
004740 .... Mercer County Community College .... NJ 292
004741 .... Rutgers State Univ - Camden .... NJ 296
004742 .... Central New Mexico Cmty College .... NM 299
004743 .... Clovis Community College .... NM 299
004759 .... CUNY York College .... NY 310
004765 .... CUNY Graduate Center .... NY 308
004776 .... Central Yeshiva Tomchei Tmimim .... NY 306
004788 .... Herkimer County Community College .... NY 316
004798 .... Mirrer Yeshiva Central Institute .... NY 321
004799 .... Monroe College .... NY 321
004804 .... New York Institute of Technology .... NY 323
004835 .... Caldwell Cmty College & Tech Inst .... NC 347
004838 .... Guilford Technical Community Col .... NC 350
004844 .... Wake Technical Community College .... NC 353
004845 .... Wilson Community College .... NC 354
004852 .... Clark State Community College .... OH 366
004853 .... Bradford School .... OH 364
004855 .... Davis College .... OH 367
004861 .... University of Northwestern Ohio .... OH 380
004866 .... Stautzenberger College .... OH 377
004868 .... Univ of Cincinnati Blue Ash College .... OH 379
004878 .... Clackamas Community College .... OR 390
004882 .... Oregon Health & Science University .... OR 393
004890 .... Central Penn College .... PA 400
004898 .... McCann School of Business & Tech .... PA 410
004902 .... Penn Commercial Business/Tech Sch .... PA 412
004910 .... Brightwood Career Institute .... PA 398
004920 .... Trident Technical College .... SC 433
004923 .... Clinton College .... SC 428
004924 .... Forrest College .... SC 430
004925 .... Horry-Georgetown Technical College .... SC 430
004926 .... Tri-County Technical College .... SC 433
004927 .... University of South Carolina Union .... SC 434
004934 .... Daymar College .... TN 439
004937 .... Jackson State Community College .... TN 446
004938 .... South College .... TN 444
004949 .... Baylor College of Medicine .... TX 452
004951 .... University of Texas HSC at Houston .... TX 477
004952 .... The Univ of Texas Medical Branch .... TX 478
004972 .... Galveston College .... TX 458
004977 .... Houston College of Law .... TX 459
004988 .... Central Virginia Community College .... VA 496
004992 .... Miller-Motte Technical College .... VA 492
004996 .... Dabney S. Lancaster Community Col .... VA 496
004999 .... Bellingham Technical College .... WA 501
005000 .... Pierce College District .... WA 506
005001 .... Edmonds Community College .... WA 503
005006 .... Walla Walla Community College .... WA 508
005007 .... West Virginia Junior College .... WV 514
005008 .... Mountain State College .... WV 511
005015 .... University of Wisconsin-Parkside .... WI 520
005019 .... Univ Adventista de las Antillas .... PR 536
005022 .... Universidad Central de Bayamon .... PR 536
005026 .... Inter Amer Univ of PR Arecibo .... PR 533
005027 .... Inter Amer Univ of PR Barranquitas .... PR 533
005028 .... Inter Amer Univ of PR Bayamon .... PR 533
005029 .... Inter Amer Univ of PR Ponce .... PR 534
005204 .... Beal College .... ME 202
005208 .... The College of Westchester .... NY 311
005220 .... Salt Lake Community College .... UT 483
005223 .... New River Community College .... VA 497
005245 .... Univ of Arkansas Cmty Col/Morrilton .... AR 24
005252 .... Ridgewater College .... MN 251
005254 .... Lanier Technical College .... GA 123
005256 .... Wiregrass Georgia Tech College .... GA 130
005257 .... GA Northwestern Technical College .... GA 121
005258 .... Univ of Hawaii Cmty College .... HI 131
005260 .... J.F. Drake State Cmty & Tech Col .... AL 4
005263 .... Minnesota West Cmty & Tech College .... MN 250
005264 .... Flint Hills Technical College .... KS 180
005265 .... North Central Kansas Tech College .... KS 183
005267 .... Northwest Kansas Technical College .... KS 183
005271 .... Southcentral KY Cmty & Tech Col .... KY 190
005273 .... Gateway Cmty & Technical College .... KY 189
005276 .... Central Maine Community College .... ME 203
005277 .... Eastern Maine Community College .... ME 203
005291 .... White Mountains Community College .... NH 286
005294 .... Waukesha County Technical College .... WI 524
005301 .... NE Wisconsin Technical College .... WI 524
005304 .... Chippewa Valley Technical College .... WI 523
005306 .... Bates Technical College .... WA 501
005309 .... Lake Area Technical Institute .... SD 436
005310 .... Pittsburgh Institute of Aeronautics .... PA 417
005313 .... North Central State College .... OH 373
005316 .... Coastal Carolina Community College .... NC 348
005317 .... Forsyth Technical Community College .... NC 349
005318 .... Catawba Valley Community College .... NC 348
005320 .... Cape Fear Community College .... NC 348
005363 .... Denmark Technical College .... SC 429
005372 .... South Puget Sound Community College ...... WA 508
005373 .... Lake Washington Inst of Technology .... WA 504
005378 .... Northeast State Community College .... TN 446
005380 .... Mid-State Technical College .... WI 523
005384 .... Nicolet Area Technical College .... WI 524
005387 .... Northcentral Technical College .... WI 524
005389 .... Gateway Technical College .... WI 523
005390 .... Blackhawk Technical College .... WI 523
005447 .... Randolph Community College .... NC 352
005448 .... Durham Technical Community College .... NC 349
005449 .... Central Carolina Community College .... NC 348
005461 .... Salem Community College .... NJ 296
005463 .... Alamance Community College .... NC 347
005464 .... Richmond Community College .... NC 352
005467 .... Sowela Technical Community College .... LA 197
005480 .... Central LA TCC Huey P Long Campus .... LA 196
005489 .... Central LA Tech Community College .... LA 196
005498 .... Wichita Area Technical College .... KS 185
005499 .... Salina Area Technical College .... KS 184
005500 .... Manhattan Area Technical College .... KS 183
005511 .... Coastal Pines Technical College .... GA 119
005525 .... Southern Maine Community College .... ME 203
005526 .... S Central LA Tech Col Young Mem Cam ...... LA 196
005533 .... St Paul Col A Cmty & Tech College .... MN 252
005534 .... Saint Cloud Technical & Cmty Coll .... MN 252
005535 .... Pine Tech & Cmty College .... MN 251
005537 .... South Central College .... MN 252
005541 .... Minnesota State Cmty & Tech College .... MN 250
005544 .... Alexandria Technical & Cmty Col .... MN 248
005599 .... Augusta Technical College .... GA 117
005600 .... Athens Technical College .... GA 116
005601 .... Albany Technical College .... GA 116
005615 .... Southern Regional Technical College .... GA 127
005617 .... South Georgia Technical College .... GA 127
005618 .... Savannah Technical College .... GA 126
005619 .... North Georgia Technical College .... GA 125
005621 .... Southern Crescent Technical College .... GA 127
005622 .... Georgia Piedmont Technical College .... GA 122
005624 .... Columbus Technical College .... GA 119
005691 .... Shelton State Community College .... AL 6
005692 .... Reid State Technical College .... AL 6
005697 .... Northwest-Shoals Community College .... AL 6
005699 .... George Wallace St Cmty Col-Selma .... AL 4
005707 .... Southeast Arkansas College .... AR 22
005732 .... Univ of Arkansas at Hope-Texarkana .... AR 24
005733 .... Bevill State Community College .... AL 2
005734 .... Trenholm State Technical College .... AL 7
005752 .... Clover Park Technical College .... WA 502
005753 .... Owens Community College .... OH 376
005754 .... Rowan-Cabarrus Community College .... NC 352
005757 .... Lake Superior College .... MN 249
005759 .... Northwest Technical College .... MN 251
005760 .... Northern Maine Community College .... ME 203
005761 .... L.E. Fletcher Technical Cmty Coll .... LA 196
005763 .... Central Georgia Technical College .... GA 118
006165 .... Los Angeles County Col of Nursing .... CA 50
006191 .... St. Vincent's College .... CT 89
006214 .... Blessing-Rieman College of Nursing .... IL 136
006225 .... Trinity Col Nursing/Hlth Sci .... IL 156
006228 .... Methodist College .... IL 147
006240 .... St Francis Med Ctr Col of Nursing .... IL 153
006250 .... Resurrection University .... IL 152
006273 .... Mercy College of Health Sciences .... IA 175
006305 .... Maine College of Health Professions .... ME 203
006324 .... Laboure College .... MA 219
006385 .... Chamberlain Col of Nursing-Addison .... IL 136
006389 .... Goldfarb School of Nursing .... MO 265
006392 .... Research College of Nursing .... MO 270
006399 .... Bryan College of Health Sciences .... NE 278
006404 .... Nebraska Methodist College .... NE 281
006438 .... Phillip Beth Israel Sch of Nursing .... NY 326
006443 .... Cochran School of Nursing .... NY 310
006445 .... Pomeroy Col of Nurs @ Crouse Hosp .... NY 305
006448 .... The Belanger School of Nursing .... NY 305
006461 .... St. Elizabeth College of Nursing .... NY 328
006467 .... St. Joseph's College of Nursing .... NY 329
006477 .... Cabarrus College of Health Sciences .... NC 342
006487 .... Aultman College Nursing/Health Sci .... OH 363
006489 .... Christ Col of Nursing & Health Sci .... OH 366
006494 .... Good Samaritan Col Nursing/Hlth Sci .... OH 369
006606 .... Baptist Hlth Sys Sch Hlth Profess .... TX 452
006622 .... Jefferson Col of Health Sciences .... VA 491
006639 .... Bellin College, Inc. .... WI 515
006640 .... Columbia College of Nursing .... WI 516
006656 .... College of DuPage .... IL 138
006661 .... Angelina College .... TX 451
006720 .... College of Alameda .... CA 57
006724 .... KY Community & Technical Col System .... KY 188
006725 .... Univ of Tennessee Health Sci Center .... TN 448
006731 .... Casa Loma College-Van Nuys .... CA 36
006750 .... Valencia College .... FL 114
006751 .... Univ of Hawaii Community Colleges .... HI 131
006753 .... Illinois Central College .... IL 141
006755 .... Brown Mackie College-Salina .... KS 179
006756 .... Northshore Technical Community Col .... LA 196
006760 .... University of Maine at Augusta .... ME 204
006768 .... Mid Michigan Community College .... MI 238
006771 .... College for Creative Studies .... MI 232
006775 .... Rainy River Community College .... MN 251
006777 .... Flathead Valley Community College .... MT 276
006782 .... Genesee Community College .... NY 315
006785 .... Schenectady County Cmty College .... NY 330
006787 .... Clinton Community College .... NY 310
006788 .... Tompkins Cortland Community College .... NY 337
006789 .... Columbia-Greene Community College .... NY 311
006791 .... Purchase College, SUNY .... NY 334
006799 .... Craven Community College .... NC 349
006804 .... Lakeland Community College .... OH 371
006807 .... Community College of Beaver County .... PA 401
006810 .... Lehigh Carbon Community College .... PA 408
006811 .... Luzerne County Community College .... PA 409
006815 .... Orangeburg-Calhoun Technical Col .... SC 431
006819 .... Blue Ridge Community College .... VA 496
006823 .... Evangelical Seminary of Puerto Rico .... PR 532
006835 .... Dyersburg State Community College .... TN 446
006836 .... Motlow State Community College .... TN 446
006858 .... Unity College .... ME 204
006863 .... Ventura County Cmty College Dist .... CA 73
006865 .... Camden County College .... NJ 290
006867 .... Columbus State Community College .... OH 367
006871 .... Thomas Nelson Community College .... VA 498
006895 .... University of Nebraska Medical Ctr .... NE 283
006901 .... Rowan College at Gloucester County .... NJ 295
006911 .... Montgomery College .... MD 209
006931 .... Waubonsee Community College .... IL 157
006938 .... Linn-Benton Community College .... OR 392
006941 .... Dallas Christian College .... TX 455
006942 .... Mid-America Christian University .... OK 384
006949 .... Kalamazoo Valley Community College .... MI 235
006951 .... Univ of South Carolina Upstate .... SC 434
006960 .... Maysville Cmty & Technical College .... KY 190
006961 .... Jefferson Cmty & Tech Col .... KY 190
006962 .... Hazard Community & Technical Coll .... KY 189
006964 .... Rutgers State Univ - New Brunswick .... NJ 296
006973 .... Canada College .... CA 62
006975 .... Lincoln University .... CA 49
006977 .... Great Basin College .... NV 284
006982 .... Naugatuck Valley Community College .... CT 86
006991 .... Rancho Santiago Cmty Col District .... CA 58
006994 .... Kern Community College District .... CA 47
007006 .... Grossmont-Cuyamaca C C District .... CA 45
007012 .... Samuel Merritt University .... CA 59
007022 .... CUNY Herbert H. Lehman College .... NY 308
007026 .... Icahn Sch of Medicine at Mt Sinai .... NY 317
007031 .... Pamlico Community College .... NC 351
007032 .... MidAmerica Nazarene University .... KS 183
007035 .... Kettering College .... OH 371
007047 .... Los Angeles Southwest College .... CA 50
007085 .... Mount Vernon Nazarene University .... OH 373
007096 .... College of the Mainland .... TX 454
007099 .... Virginia Highlands Community Col .... VA 499
007107 .... Essex County College .... NJ 291
007108 .... Univ of Puerto Rico-Rio Piedras .... PR 538
007109 .... SUNY College at Old Westbury .... NY 333
007110 .... Delaware County Community College .... PA 401
007111 .... North Country Community College .... NY 325
007113 .... Arizona Christian University .... AZ 11
007115 .... Moorpark College .... CA 73
007118 .... Parkland College .... IL 151
007119 .... Rend Lake College .... IL 152
007120 .... Des Moines Area Community College .... IA 171
007121 .... Faith Baptist Bible Col & Seminary .... IA 172
007164 .... Bryan University .... CA 29
007170 .... Lincoln Land Community College .... IL 146
007171 .... Kirtland Community College .... MI 236
007178 .... Western Seminary .... OR 396
007191 .... Northampton Community College .... PA 411
007206 .... University of Puerto Rico at Cayey .... PR 538
007228 .... Univ of Puerto Rico at Arecibo .... PR 537
007260 .... Southwest Virginia Community Col .... VA 498
007263 .... Holy Cross College .... IN 161
007264 .... Mesivta Torah Vodaath Seminary .... NY 321
007265 .... Carl Sandburg College .... IL 136
007266 .... Pima Community College .... AZ 16
007273 .... Baruch College/CUNY .... NY 307
007275 .... Eastern Gateway CC - Jefferson Co. .... OH 368
007276 .... Saint Meinrad School of Theology .... IN 167
007279 .... Hawaii Pacific University .... HI 130
007283 .... Central Arizona College .... AZ 12
007287 .... Brazosport College .... TX 453
007289 .... Central Wyoming College .... WY 526
007291 .... St. Luke's College .... IA 176
007296 .... Coleman University .... CA 39
007297 .... Redstone College .... CO 82
007304 .... The Culinary Institute of America .... NY 312
007316 .... Western Iowa Tech Community College .... IA 177
007350 .... Anoka Technical College .... MN 248
007351 .... Sanford-Brown Col-Mendota Heights .... MN 255
007358 .... Univ of NE-NE Col of Tech Agricult .... NE 283
007375 .... Island Drafting and Technical Inst .... NY 317
007394 .... Berkeley College .... NY 305
007401 .... Mandl School-The Col of Allied Hlth .... NY 319
007405 .... Wood Tobe-Coburn School .... NY 340
007430 .... Antonelli Institute .... PA 397
007436 .... Brightwood Career Institute .... PA 398
007437 .... Pittsburgh Technical Institute .... PA 417
007439 .... Fountainhead College of Technology .... TN 440
007440 .... Lincoln Col of Technology Nashville .... TN 441
007459 .... Paier College of Art .... CT 88
007465 .... American Academy of Dramatic Arts .... NY 304
007466 .... LIM College .... NY 318
007468 .... School of Visual Arts .... NY 330
007469 .... Hussian School of Art .... PA 406
007470 .... Art Institute of Pittsburgh .... PA 397
007484 .... Newbury College .... MA 226
007486 .... The New England Institute of Art .... MA 226
007491 .... Brightwood College .... MD 206
007502 .... Berkeley College .... NJ 289
007531 .... Academy of Art University .... CA 25
007532 .... Finger Lakes Community College .... NY 314
007536 .... Cosumnes River College .... CA 51
007540 .... Missouri Baptist University .... MO 268

Code	Institution	State	Page
030612	Midwest Col of Oriental Medicine	WI	518
030627	Platt College	CA	57
030633	NW Arkansas Community College	AR	21
030662	Bryan University	KS	179
030663	Bryan University	MO	262
030665	Southeastern Technical College	GA	127
030666	Bay Mills Community College	MI	231
030669	IntelliTec College	CO	81
030675	Institute of Technology	CA	46
030691	Allen College	IA	169
030695	Sage College	CA	59
030709	SE MO Hosp Coll Nurs & Health Sci	MO	272
030716	College of Business and Technology	FL	97
030719	Mount Carmel College of Nursing	OH	373
030722	Chandler-Gilbert Community College	AZ	13
030725	World Medicine Institute	HI	132
030737	Paralegal Inst at Brighton College	AZ	16
030761	Southwestern College	NM	302
030763	Beulah Heights University	GA	117
030775	Rabbi Jacob Joseph School	NJ	294
030790	ETI Technical College of Niles	OH	368
030791	North Central Institute	TN	443
030799	City College	FL	97
030819	YTI Career Institute	PA	424
030830	Ozarks Technical Community College	MO	270
030837	Galen College of Nursing	KY	188
030838	Heartland Community College	IL	141
030842	Valley College - Princeton Campus	WV	511
030844	Valley College - Beckley Campus	WV	511
030888	Watkins College of Art/Design/Film	TN	449
030893	Heritage Bible College	NC	344
030908	Lake Erie College of Osteo Medicine	PA	407
030913	Regent University	VA	493
030926	Messenger College	TX	461
030955	ASA College	NY	304
030964	Leech Lake Tribal College	MN	247
030970	Mercy College of Ohio	OH	372
030980	St. John's College	IL	153
030982	Yo San Univ of Trad Chinese Med	CA	75
031004	Coconino Community College	AZ	12
031007	Carroll Community College	MD	206
031009	Luther Rice College and Seminary	GA	124
031013	Granite State College	NH	288
031015	Bidwell Training Center	PA	398
031019	Trinity Baptist College	FL	113
031033	JNA Institute of Culinary Arts	PA	406
031034	South Texas College	TX	465
031042	Carolinas Col of Health Sciences	NC	343
031060	Missouri State Univ-West Plains	MO	269
031062	Our Lady of the Lake College	LA	199
031065	Sentara College of Health Sciences	VA	494
031070	SW Col of Naturopathic Med/Hlth Sci	AZ	17
031085	Everglades University	FL	99
031090	Living Arts Col @ Sch of Commun Art	NC	345
031091	Workforce Institute's City College	PA	424
031095	Dongguk University	CA	42
031108	Bakke Graduate University	TX	452
031121	Dewey University	PR	532
031136	Southern Calif Institute of Tech	CA	65
031147	The Praxis Institute	FL	107
031150	Arizona College	AZ	11
031151	Heritage College	OK	383
031155	Adventist University of Health Sci	FL	95
031158	Brightwood College	TX	453
031159	Trinity College of Puerto Rico	PR	536
031163	Ohio College of Massotherapy	OH	374
031166	E San Gabriel Vly Reg Occ Pgm Tech	CA	42
031169	Baptist Theol Seminary Richmond	VA	487
031203	CollegeAmerica-Flagstaff	AZ	12
031207	NY Conservatory for Dramatic Arts	NY	323
031226	Eastern International College	NJ	291
031229	York County Community College	ME	204
031239	Southeastern College	FL	109
031251	College of Menominee Nation	WI	516
031264	Centura College	VA	487
031268	Pacifica Graduate Institute	CA	56
031271	Yeshivas Novominsk	NY	341
031275	Advanced Technology Institute	VA	486
031281	The Col of Health Care Professions	TX	454
031287	Mt. Sierra College	CA	53
031291	Fond du Lac Tribal & Cmty College	MN	249
031292	Rabbinical College Ohr Shimon Yisr	NY	326
031305	Urban College of Boston	MA	229
031313	Five Brn Univ Grad Sch Trad Chn Med	CA	43
031473	Yeshiva D'Monsey Rabbinical College	NY	340
031533	Amer Col Acupuncture & Oriental Med	TX	451
031555	Oconee Fall Line Tech Col-North	GA	125
031563	Estrella Mountain Community College	AZ	14
031564	AOMA Grad Sch Integrative Medicine	TX	451
031576	Colegio de Cinema Artes y Televis	PR	531
031633	Pacific States University	CA	55
031643	Creative Center	NE	279
031703	Texas A & M University - Texarkana	TX	469
031713	Univ of St Augustine for Health Sci	CA	72
031733	Atlanta's John Marshall Law School	GA	117
031773	San Juan Bautista Sch of Medicine	PR	535
031795	Texas Health and Science University	TX	470
031804	Pennsylvania Highlands Cmty Col	PA	413
031823	New Hampshire Institute of Art	NH	287
031893	National Defense University	DC	528
031943	Boston Grad Sch of Psychoanalysis	MA	216
031983	Universidad Pentecostal Mizpa	PR	537
031993	Christian Life College	IL	137
032063	Mesalands Community College	NM	300
032103	Le Cordon Bleu Col of Culinary Arts	CA	48
032163	Unification Theological Seminary	NY	338
032183	University of the Potomac	DC	94
032253	American Univ of Health Sciences	CA	26
032353	MA School of Law at Andover	MA	225
032383	Florida College of Integrative Med	FL	100
032423	CNI College	CA	39
032483	Boston Baptist College	MA	216
032503	CBD College	CA	36
032553	Florida Gulf Coast University	FL	110
032563	Yeshiva Gedolah Rabbinical College	FL	115
032603	California State Univ-Monterey Bay	CA	33
032613	Metropolitan Cmty Col-Blue River	MO	267
032643	South Florida Bible College	FL	109
032663	Bethesda University of California	CA	28
032673	Capella University	MN	245
032723	Brightwood College	TX	453
032793	Myotherapy Institute	NE	281
032803	Seattle Inst of Oriental Medicine	WA	507
032883	Academy of Chinese Culture & Health	CA	25
032893	Colorado Heights University	CO	77
032943	Blue Cliff College	LA	194
032993	Pacific College	CA	55
033083	Bristol University	CA	29
033164	FINE Mortuary College	MA	218
033173	The American College Financial Svcs	PA	397
033213	The Scripps Research Institute	CA	64
033233	Little Priest Tribal College	NE	280
033274	Acupnct & Integrat Med Col-Berkeley	CA	25
033323	Southern California Seminary	CA	65
033394	Western Governors University	UT	483
033433	South Orange County Cmty Col Dist	CA	65
033434	North Dakota Univ System Office	ND	360
033436	Iowa Valley Cmty College District	IA	173
033437	Colorado State Univ System Office	CO	78
033438	SD State Board of Regents Sys Ofc	SD	436
033440	WV Higher Educ Policy Commission	WV	512
033441	Nebraska State College System	NE	281
033442	The Texas State University System	TX	470
033443	Board of Regents, State of Iowa	IA	169
033444	University of Louisiana System Ofc	LA	200
033445	NC Community College System	NC	347
033463	Acad for Nurs & Health Occupations	FL	94
033473	Intl Baptist College & Seminary	AZ	13
033554	Richmont Graduate University	TN	443
033673	Professional Golfers Career College	CA	58
033674	Community Care College	OK	383
033723	Northwest Vista College	TX	450
033733	Beacon College	FL	96
033743	Florida Coastal School of Law	FL	100
034003	Quest College	TX	463
034033	Epic Bible College & Graduate Sch	CA	43
034095	Chester Career College	VA	488
034143	Monteclaro Escuela de Hotel/Art Cul	PR	535
034145	Acupuncture & Massage College	FL	95
034165	Dallas Nursing Institute	TX	457
034183	Gwinnett College-Sandy Springs	GA	123
034194	Northeastern Seminary	NY	325
034224	College of Biblical Studies-Houston	TX	454
034244	Fortis College	TX	458
034253	Rosedale Bible College	OH	376
034263	The Col of Health Care Professions	TX	454
034275	University of Antelope Valley	CA	68
034283	Klamath Community College	OR	391
034296	Atlantic Inst of Oriental Medicine	FL	95
034297	East West College of Natural Med	FL	98
034343	Fortis College	FL	102
034383	Pacific Islands University	GU	530
034403	Baptist College of Health Sciences	TN	438
034433	New York Coll of Trad Chinese Med	NY	323
034563	Cld Sprg Hrbr Lab/Watson Sc Bio Sci	NY	310
034567	Crossroads Bible College	IN	160
034573	Allegheny Wesleyan College	OH	362
034613	Ilisagvik College	AK	10
034633	UT Col Dental Hygiene Careers Unltd	UT	481
034664	The Seattle Sch of Theology & Psych	WA	507
034684	National Institute of Massotherapy	OH	373
034754	Tri-State Bible College	OH	378
034784	Phoenix Seminary	AZ	16
034803	Fortis College	LA	195
034835	Cascadia College	WA	501
034963	Yeshiva Shaarei Torah of Rockland	NY	341
035043	National Grad Sch of Quality Mgmt	MA	226
035103	Erikson Institute	IL	140
035134	Apex School of Theology	NC	341
035135	Williamson College	TN	449
035163	The King's University	TX	460
035243	Academy Five Element Acupuncture	FL	94
035283	Midwest University	MO	268
035324	Advanced Training Associates	CA	25
035344	American Inst Alternative Medicine	OH	362
035393	American Public University System	WV	510
035423	Concorde Career Institute	TX	455
035424	Copper Mountain College	CA	41
035443	Atenas College	PR	530
035453	University of the Rockies	CO	84
035493	Ultimate Medical Acad-Clearwater	FL	114
035593	Appalachian School of Law	VA	486
035703	Carolina Christian College	NC	342
035705	Northpoint Bible College	MA	227
035793	Texas County Technical College	MO	272
035844	Colorado School of Healing Arts	CO	78
035924	City of Hope	CA	38
035933	Southwest Institute of Healing Arts	AZ	17
036115	Southern Evangelical Seminary	NC	355
036175	Phoenix Inst of Herbal Med/Acup	AZ	16
036273	Lamar Institute of Technology	TX	470
036353	Carver College	GA	118
036393	West Coast Ultrasound Institute	CA	73
036543	Eastern Virginia Career College	VA	489
036633	Hood Theological Seminary	NC	345
036653	Christendom College	VA	488
036654	Christie's Education, New York	NY	306
036663	Pillar College	NJ	294
036683	Birthingway College of Midwifery	OR	390
036763	Family of Faith College	OK	383
036863	Colorado Sch of Trad Chinese Med	CO	78
036894	Faith Evangelical Col & Seminary	WA	503
036914	Ave Maria School of Law	FL	95
036954	The Salvation Army Ofr Trng Crestmt	CA	59
036955	Arizona Sch of Acup/Oriental Med	AZ	11
036957	Santiago Canyon College	CA	58
036963	University of the West	CA	72
036964	Saber College	FL	107
036983	West Coast University	CA	74
037093	Edward Via Col of Osteo Med	VA	489
037133	Beis Medrash Heichal Dovid	NY	304
037233	Culinary Institute LeNotre	TX	455
037243	DigiPen Institute of Technology	WA	503
037303	Baton Rouge Community College	LA	195
037333	Baptist University of the Americas	TX	452
037353	Inst Clin Acupuncture/Oriental Med	HI	131
037384	SS. Cyril and Methodius Seminary	MI	241
037473	Bexley Seabury	OH	364
037524	SUM Bible Col & Theol Seminary	CA	67
037573	Advance Science Institute	FL	95
037603	Hawaii Tokai International College	HI	130
037723	Saginaw Chippewa Tribal College	MI	240
037844	Tohono O'odham Community College	AZ	17
037863	Advanced College	CA	25
037894	River Parishes Community College	LA	196
038023	U.T.A. Mesivta of Kiryas Joel	NY	339
038044	Gwinnett College-Marietta	GA	123
038103	Silicon Valley University	CA	64
038133	Northcentral University	AZ	15
038144	Soka University of America	CA	64
038214	Universal College of Healing Arts	NE	282
038224	Maple Springs Baptist Bible College	MD	209
038273	Charlotte Christian Col & Theol Sem	NC	343
038303	SAE Institute Nashville	TN	443
038333	American Acad Acupunct/Oriental Med	MN	244
038383	Nightingale College	UT	480
038385	Northwest Career College	NV	285
038403	Oxford Graduate School	TN	443
038425	Cambridge Inst Allied Health & Tech	FL	97
038513	Graduate Inst Applied Linguistics	TX	458
038533	Keck Graduate Institute	CA	39
038553	Ecclesia College	AR	20
038626	Virginia Baptist College	VA	496
038683	World Mission University	CA	75
038684	LACM, Los Angeles College of Music	CA	48
038713	Folsom Lake College	CA	51
038724	Institute Psychological Sciences	VA	490
038743	Cambridge Junior College	CA	36
038744	Community Christian College	CA	40
038883	Dragon Rises Col of Oriental Med	FL	98
038893	Stanbridge College	CA	66
038943	Huntsville Bible College	AL	4
039035	Southern Technical College	FL	110
039104	National Polytechnic College	CA	53
039153	Career Quest Learning Center	MI	232
039193	St Tikhon's Orthodox Theol Seminary	PA	418
039214	White Earth Tribal/Community Col	MN	256
039324	Gutenberg College	OR	391
039373	Yeshiva Col of the Nation's Capital	MD	214
039393	Wolford College	FL	115
039396	Daytona College	FL	98
039413	Ave Maria University	FL	95
039454	Logos Evangelical Seminary	CA	49
039463	Franklin W. Olin Col of Engineering	MA	218
039483	Harrisburg Univ Science/Technology	PA	405
039493	Won Institute of Graduate Studies	PA	424
039513	Patrick Henry College	VA	492
039563	South Louisiana Community College	LA	197
039573	Blue Ridge Cmty & Technical College	WV	511
039603	New River Community/Technical Col	WV	512
039653	New England Col Business & Finance	MA	226
039663	Virginia Beach Theol Seminary	VA	496
039704	WellSpring Sch Allied Health-KC	MO	275
039713	American Career College-Ontario	CA	26
039733	Ex'pression College	CA	43
039803	California State U-Channel Islands	CA	32
039823	Visible Music College	TN	449
039863	Aviator Col of Aeronaut Sci & Tech	FL	95
039893	Mid-America Reformed Seminary	IN	165
039923	Knox Theological Seminary	FL	104
039953	University of East-West Medicine	CA	71
040024	Ecumenical Theological Seminary	MI	233
040053	United States University	CA	68
040373	Los Angeles Film School	CA	50
040383	ATA College	KY	186
040385	Pierpont Community/Technical Col	WV	512

667143 .... Los Angeles Pacific College .... CA 50
667145 .... Rabbinical College Ohr Yisroel .... NY 326
667146 .... Bet Medrash Gadol Ateret Torah .... NY 305
667147 .... Yeshiva Sholom Shachna .... NY 341
667148 .... Virginia Tech Carilion Sch of Med .... VA 500
667149 .... Chamberlain Col of Nursing-Amin Ofc .... IL 136
667150 .... Presidio Graduate School .... CA 58
667151 .... Rockbridge Seminary .... MO 270
667152 .... KP Sch of Allied Health Sciences .... CA 47
667153 .... Bapt Hosp SE TX Sch of Rad Tech .... TX 452
667154 .... Finger Lakes Health Col of Nursing .... NY 314
667155 .... Unilatina International College .... FL 114
667156 .... Radiological Technologies Univ-VT .... IN 166
667157 .... Central Yeshiva Beth Joseph .... NY 306
667158 .... Kings Park University .... VA 491
667159 .... Univ of MD Ctr for Environment Sci .... MD 212
667160 .... University of the People .... CA 71
667203 .... Westcliff University .... CA 74
667204 .... Yeshivas Maharit Dsatmar .... NY 341
667205 .... Fei Tian College .... NY 314
667206 .... Univ of TX Hlth Sci Ctr at Tyler .... TX 477
667207 .... Nine Star University of Health Sci .... CA 54
667208 .... Virginia University of Oriental Med .... VA 500
667209 .... Summit Christian College .... NE 282
667210 .... Wave Leadership College .... VA 500
667211 .... Baptist Seminary of Kentucky .... KY 186
667212 .... Oikos University .... CA 55
667213 .... Ivy Christian College .... VA 490
667214 .... Antioch College .... OH 363
667215 .... Claremont Lincoln University .... CA 38
667217 .... California Jazz Conservatory .... CA 31
667218 .... California Health Sciences Univ .... CA 30
667219 .... Augustine Institute .... CO 77
667220 .... Med-Life Institute-Naples .... FL 104
667221 .... Med-Life Institute-Lauderdale Lakes .... FL 104
667222 .... Mercy Hospital College of Nursing .... FL 105
667223 .... Learnet Academy .... CA 48
667224 .... Wright Grad Univ-Realiz Human Poten .... WI 526
667226 .... Saint Michael Col of Allied Health .... VA 493
667227 .... Wyoming Catholic College .... WY 527
667228 .... Broad Ctr for the Mgmt of Sch Sys .... CA 29
667229 .... Santa Barbara & Ventura Col of Law .... CA 62
667230 .... Zaytuna College .... CA 76
667231 .... LA Academy of Figurative Art .... CA 49
667232 .... EC-Council University .... NM 299
667233 .... Southern University Law Center .... LA 200
667234 .... William Loveland College .... CO 85
667235 .... Assoc Free Lutheran Bible Sch/Sem .... MN 244
667236 .... Herguan University .... CA 46
667237 .... Kingston University .... CA 47
667238 .... Int'l College of Health Sciences .... FL 103
667239 .... Pacific Institute of Technology .... GA 125
667240 .... Northwest Suburban College .... IL 150
667241 .... University of North America .... VA 495
667242 .... Texas Tech University System .... TX 472
667245 .... Elim Bible Institute .... NY 313
667246 .... John Witherspoon College .... SD 436
667247 .... Reformed University .... GA 126
667248 .... Burrell Col of Osteopathic Medicine .... NM 299
667249 .... Bethlehem College & Seminary .... MN 245
667250 .... Faith Bible Seminary .... IN 160
667251 .... Legacy Christian University .... AL 5
667252 .... Pacific Bible College .... OR 394
667253 .... Union Bible College .... IN 167
667254 .... Yellowstone Christian College .... MT 278
667255 .... Christian Witness Theol Seminary .... CA 38
667256 .... China Evangelical Seminary N.A. .... CA 38
667257 .... NationsUniversity .... LA 198
667258 .... Bethesda College of Health Sciences .... FL 96
667259 .... Bais Medrash Zicron Meir .... NJ 289
667260 .... Yeshiva Gedolah Shaarei Schmuel .... NJ 298
667261 .... Golden State University .... CA 45
667262 .... Wongu Univ of Oriental Medicine .... NV 285
667263 .... Saint Katherine College .... CA 59
667264 .... Sacramento Ultrasound Institute .... CA 59
667265 .... Florida College of Health Science .... FL 100
667266 .... Medical Career Institute .... FL 104
667267 .... Medical Prep Institute .... FL 105
667268 .... West Coast Baptist College .... CA 73
667269 .... Union University of California .... CA 68
667270 .... Realtor University .... IL 151
667271 .... Women's Institute of Torah Seminary .... MD 213
667272 .... MJS College School of Nursing .... IN 165
667273 .... Amer Col of Commerce & Technology .... VA 486
667274 .... Nobel University .... CA 54
667275 .... Inter-American Defense College .... DC 93
667276 .... Express Training Services .... FL 99
667277 .... UAC School of Global Management .... FL 114
667278 .... Northeast Lakeview College .... TX 450
667279 .... Florida Polytechnic University .... FL 111
667280 .... Bais Medrash Mayan Hatorah .... NJ 289
667281 .... Yeshiva Chemdas Hatorah .... NJ 298
667282 .... Yeshiva Gedolah Keren Hatorah .... NJ 298
667283 .... Yeshiva Gedolah Tiferes Boruch .... NJ 298
667284 .... Yeshiva Ohr Naftoli .... NY 341
667285 .... Faith Bible College .... VA 489
667286 .... META Business School .... CA 52
667287 .... WMU Stryker MD School of Medicine .... MI 243
667288 .... Larkin Health Sciences Inst .... FL 104
667289 .... CA Inst of Arts & Technology .... CA 30
667290 .... Elyon College .... NY 313
667291 .... Yeshiva Bais Aharon .... NJ 298
667292 .... Universidad Ana G. Mendez .... PR 535
667293 .... Merit University .... CA 52
667294 .... San Diego Global Knowledge Univ .... CA 61
667295 .... Premiere International College .... FL 107
667296 .... Suncoast College of Health .... FL 113
667297 .... Process Work Institute .... OR 394
667298 .... Everest College .... VA 489
770617 .... Court Reporting Inst of St. Louis .... MO 264
770944 .... Touro College Los Angeles .... CA 68

Index of Universities, Colleges and Schools